SEVEN REASONS WHY THE EXPOSITOR'S STUDY BIBLE WILL HELP YOUR UNDERSTANDING OF THE WORD OF GOD

1. The King James Version is used, with the exception of Elizabethan words, such as "ye," "hast," "thy," etc., in some cases, changed to words presently used, making the Text much easier to understand.

2. Comments follow virtually every Scripture, giving an expanded meaning to each particular Passage.

3. The word "expository" presents a clinical meaning, which we have used in order to stay as close to the Text as possible.

4. We have availed ourselves of the scholarship of some of the very finest Hebrew and Greek Scholars.

5. Theological insights are taught.

6. The significance of particular individuals and events, as related to types and shadows of deeper spiritual truths, is shared.

7. Practical applications are presented, making *THE EXPOSITOR'S STUDY BIBLE Giant Print Edition* one of the most helpful tools on the market today, regarding the understanding of the Word of God.

THE BOOKS OF THE OLD AND NEW TESTAMENTS

in their proper order, with Book abbreviation, page number, and the number of Chapters

THE BOOKS OF THE OLD TESTAMENT

THE BOOKS OF THE NEW TESTAMENT

BIBLE STUDY HELPS

CONTRIBUTORS

E. LESLIE CARLSON, Th.D., Professor of Biblical Backgrounds and Archaeology, The
Southwestern Baptist Theological Seminary

LOWELL COOLIDGE, Ph.D., Chairman of the English Department, The College of Wooster

EARL L. CORE, Ph.D., Chairman of the Biology Department, The University of West Virginia

HUBER L. DRUMWRIGHT, Th.D., Professor of New Testament, The Southwestern Baptist
Theological Seminary

VIRTUS E. GIDEON, Th.D., Professor of New Testament, The Southwestern Baptist
Theological Seminary

THE FIRST BOOK OF MOSES, CALLED
GENESIS

CHAPTER 1
(4004 B.C.)
THE ORIGINAL CREATION

IN the beginning *(refers to the beginning of creation, or at least the creation as it refers to this universe; God, unformed, unmade, uncreated, had no beginning; He always was, always is, and always shall be)* God *(the phrase, "In the beginning God," explains the first cause of all things as it regards creation)* created the heaven and the Earth *(could be translated "the heavens and the Earth" because God created the entirety of the universe).*

CHAOS

2 And the Earth was without form, and void; and darkness was upon the face of the deep *(God did not originally create the Earth without form and void; it became this way after a cataclysmic happening; this happening was the revolt of Lucifer against God, which took place some time in the dateless past).* And the Spirit of God *(Holy Spirit)* moved upon the face of the waters *(the moving of the Holy Spirit signified and signifies the beginning of life).*

FIRST DAY

3 And God said *(presents the manner in which creation or re-creation was carried out; some ten times this phrase is used, and in the exact manner, with the exception of the last time, where it says, "And the LORD God said" [Gen. 2:18]),* Let there be light: and there was light *(God is the essence of light [Jn. 1:4-9]; God's Word is of such magnitude that light continues to expand in the universe at the rate of 186,000 miles a second).*

4 And God saw the light, that it was good *(it did what it was designed to do):* and God divided the light from the darkness *(simply refers to the fact that there were now periods of light and darkness; darkness is simply the absence of light).*

5 And God called the light Day *(a character description),* and the darkness He called Night *(has to do with the revolution of the Earth).*

And the evening and the morning were the first day *(literal 24-hour days).*

SECOND DAY

6 And God said, Let there be a firmament in the midst of the waters *(refers to an expanse between the waters, so to speak, called "the atmosphere"),* and let it divide the waters from the waters *(water in the rain clouds and water on the Earth).*

7 And God made the firmament *(there is a difference in "made" and "created"; "made" refers to something already created, but brought back to a useful existence),* and divided the waters which were under the firmament *(oceans, seas, rivers, etc.)* from the waters which were above the firmament *(water in the clouds, which comes down upon the Earth):* and it was so.

8 And God called the firmament heaven *(the word as used here pertains to the atmosphere around the Earth).* And the evening and the morning were the second day *(a 24-hour time frame).*

THIRD DAY

9 And God said, Let the waters under the heaven be gathered together unto one place *(refers to the places designed for the waters on the Earth, seas, oceans, rivers, etc.),* and let the dry land appear: and it was so *(refers to the continents being formed, which necessitated great convulsions on the Earth).*

10 And God called the dry land Earth *(refers to the Supreme Being naming what He had created);* and the gathering together of the waters called He Seas: and God saw that it was good *(Divine approval).*

11 And God said, Let the Earth bring forth grass *(a carpet),* the herb yielding seed *(vegetables),* and the fruit tree yielding fruit after his kind *(indicates that the different species of plants are already fixed),* whose seed is in itself, upon the Earth: and it was so *(the modern dogma of the origin of species by development is unbiblical).*

12 And the Earth brought forth grass *(at the Word of God),* and herb yielding seed after his

kind, and the tree yielding fruit, whose seed was in itself, after his kind *(the first creation of plant life did not come from seed, but that it came into being through the power of the Word):* and God saw that it was good *(pertains not only to the fact of creation, but as well the order of creation).*

13 And the evening and the morning were the third day *(on this day was the first creation of life, i.e., "the plants, etc.").*

FOURTH DAY

14 And God said, Let there be lights in the firmament of the heaven to divide the day from the night *(God is not here creating the sun, moon, and stars, that having already been done "in the beginning");* and let them be for signs, and for seasons, and for days, and years *(refers in essence to "time"):*

15 And let them be for lights in the firmament of the heaven to give light upon the Earth: and it was so *(proclaims the fact that God said it, and His glorious Word contained such power that these planetary bodies will ever carry out their prescribed function).*

16 And God made two great lights *(the sun and the moon);* the greater light to rule the day *(the sun),* and the lesser light to rule the night *(in fact, the moon has no light within itself; it is a reflection of the sun, hence much lesser, exactly as the Scripture says):* He made the stars also *(God "created" the sun, moon, and stars at some unknown period of time "in the beginning," and afterwards, when preparing the Earth for man, He "made," i.e., "pointed them in relation to the Earth [regulated them] as light-holders, as measurers of time, and as vehicles of revelation" [Ps. 19]).*

17 And God set them in the firmament of the heaven to give light upon the Earth *(refers to their function).*

18 And to rule over the day and over the night, and to divide the light from the darkness: and God saw that it was good *(everything is now set for animate life, i.e., "animal life as opposed to plant life").*

19 And the evening and the morning were the fourth day.

FIFTH DAY

20 And God said, Let the waters bring forth abundantly the moving creature that has life, and fowl that may fly above the Earth in the open firmament of heaven *(here the creatures of the sea are distinguished from all previous creations, and in particular from vegetation, as being possessed of a vital principle; this does not, of course, contradict the well-known Truth that plants are living organisms; only that the life principle of the animal kingdom is different from that of the vegetable kingdom).*

21 And God created great whales, and every living creature that moves, which the waters brought forth abundantly, after their kind, and every winged fowl after his kind: and God saw that it was good *(some ten times in the First Chapter of Genesis, the phrase, "after his kind," or similar is used; this completely shoots down the theory of evolution; Science has never been able to cross that barrier and, in fact, will never be able; in other words, there is no such thing as an animal that is half fish and half land animal; as well, there is no such thing as a fish that is half whale and half shark; the barrier regarding the different "kinds" remains, and ever shall remain).*

22 And God blessed them, saying, Be fruitful and multiply, and fill the waters in the seas, and let fowl multiply in the Earth *(it may be asked as why God did not bless the plant life? of them Moses simply says that God saw that it was good, but He did not bless them; but here, God begins a new way of propagation, namely, that from living bodies come forth other similar living bodies, which is not true of trees and plants; the pear tree, for example, does not bring forth another pear tree, but only a pear, while a bird produces a bird and a fish a fish, etc.; here, then, is a new creative work, for a living body propagates others out of itself; in fact, the Blessing of God means propagation; His Blessing is just as powerful to propagate as His curse is to cut off).*

23 And the evening and the morning were the fifth day.

THE SIXTH DAY

24 And God said, Let the Earth bring forth the living creature after his kind, cattle, and creeping thing, and beast of the Earth after his kind: and it was so *(proclaims the fact that God leaves nothing empty that He has made, but furnishes all with His store and riches).*

25 And God made the beast of the Earth after his kind, and cattle after their kind, and every thing that creeps upon the Earth after his kind: and God saw that it was good *(tells*

us unequivocally that God designed each species of the animal kingdom in such a way that it cannot be crossed).

26 And God said, Let Us make man in Our Image, after Our likeness *(the creation of man was preceded by a Divine consultation; as well, the pronouns "Us" and "Our" proclaim the consultation held by the Three Persons of the Divine Trinity, Who were One in the creative work; "image" and "likeness" enable us to have fellowship with God; however, it does not mean we are gods, or can become gods; "in Our Image after Our Likeness" actually refers to true Righteousness and Holiness [Eph. 4:24]):* and let them have dominion over the fish of the sea, and over the fowl of the air, and over the cattle, and over all the Earth, and over every creeping thing that creeps upon the Earth *(this dominion was given by God to man, and is always subject to God; the relationship of man to the balance of creation is now defined to be one of rule and supremacy; the sphere of His lordship is from the lowest to the highest of the subjects placed beneath his sway).*

27 So God created man in His Own Image *(the word "man" should have the definite article, and should read "the man," that is, Adam — the same man Adam spoken of in 2:7; these are not, therefore, two accounts of the creation of man, but one Divine statement),* in the Image of God created He him *(the Image of God was lost at the Fall; however, the restoration of the Image was carried out at the Cross, but the completion of that restoration will not take place until the First Resurrection);* male and female created He them *(represents, at least as far as we know, the first time that God has created the female gender, at least as it regards intelligent beings; there is no record of any female Angels).*

28 And God blessed them *(again, speaks of the ability to reproduce),* and God said unto them, Be fruitful, and multiply, and replenish the Earth *(the word "replenish" carries the idea of a former creation on the Earth before Adam and Eve; according to Isaiah 14 and Ezekiel 28, Lucifer ruled this world for an undetermined period of time, and did so in Righteousness and Holiness as a beautiful Angel created by God; if, in fact, he did rule the world at that time, it would stand to reason that there had to be some type of creation on the Earth for him to rule; the word "replenish" refers to that creation),* and subdue it *(and that man has done; however, he would have done it much sooner, but for the Fall):* and have dominion over the fish of the

sea, and over the fowl of the air, and over every living thing that moves upon the Earth.

29 And God said, Behold, I have given you every herb bearing seed, which is upon the face of all the Earth, and every tree, in the which is the fruit of a tree yielding seed; to you it shall be for meat *(refers to the fact that both animals and mankind were vegetarians before the Fall; incidentally, this was changed after the flood [Gen. 9:3]).*

30 And to every beast of the Earth, and to every fowl of the air, and to every thing that creeps upon the Earth, wherein there is life, I have given every green herb for meat: and it was so *(this tells us that animals were not originally created as predators; in other words, all animals were then vegetarian as well, which means that all, and not just some, were docile).*

31 And God saw every thing that He had made, and, behold, it was very good *(means that it was not simply good, but good exceedingly; it is not man alone whom God surveys, but the completed cosmos, with man as its crown and glory).* And the evening and the morning were the sixth day *(the word "evening" signified the fact that the new day began at sunset, instead of 12 midnight as it presently does in our reckoning of time).*

CHAPTER 2
(4004 B.C.)
SEVENTH DAY

THUS the heavens and the Earth were finished, and all the host of them *(proclaims the fact that when the heavens and the Earth were completed, they were a brilliant array).*

2 And on the seventh day God ended His work which He had made; and He rested on the seventh day from all His work which He had made *(it doesn't mean that God was tired, for He cannot be such [Isa. 40:28]; it simply means that He had finished the work).*

3 And God blessed the seventh day, and sanctified it: because that in it He had rested from all His work which God created and made *(the Sabbath, or seventh day, or Saturday, the last day of the week, is meant by God to be a Type of the Salvation Rest which one finds in Christ; that's the reason it was a part of the Ten Commandments).*

SUMMARY

4 These are the generations of the heavens

and of the Earth when they were created *("generations" here refer to "Divine divisions;" it refers to the manner in which all were created, as outlined in Chapter 1)*, **in the day that the LORD God made the Earth and the heavens** *(presents the new name of God as "Jehovah Elohim"; this Chapter reveals Christ as Jehovah Elohim, man's Redeemer; the First Chapter reveals Him as Elohim, man's Creator),*

5 **And every plant of the field before it was in the earth, and every herb of the field before it grew** *(the second day of creation is addressed here, which obviously preceded day three, when plant life was developed)*: **for the LORD God had not caused it to rain upon the Earth** *(it seems that rain came to the Earth on day three, which caused the Earth to "bring forth grass, the herb yielding seed, and the fruit tree yielding fruit after his kind")*, **and there was not a man to till the ground** *(all of this was before man was created, showing that he had nothing to do with the creation, that being altogether of God).*

6 **But there went up a mist from the Earth, and watered the whole face of the ground** *(this pertains to day two of Creation; at that time, day two, there went up a mist from the Earth, which prepared the Earth for the seed which God evidently planted on the beginning of day three, and which rain on day three then brought forth).*

7 **And the LORD God formed man of the dust of the ground** *(proclaims the physical body made of clay)*, **and breathed into his nostrils the breath of life** *(the "breath of life," which comes from God, pertains to the soul and spirit of man; this was done with the first man, Adam, God breathing the soul and the spirit into man, and thereafter it comes automatically at conception)*; **and man became a living soul** *(man is a soul, has a spirit, both which reside in the physical body; the soul addresses the body; the spirit addresses God; the physical body addresses the world).*

THE GARDEN OF EDEN

8 **And the LORD God planted a Garden eastward in Eden** *(it was actually planted before Adam was created; the area is believed by some Scholars to be the site where the city of Babylon would ultimately be built)*; **and there He put the man whom He had formed** *(the Garden of Eden was to be the home place of man).*

9 **And out of the ground made the LORD God to grow every tree that is pleasant to the sight** *(beautiful trees)*, **and good for food** *(every fruit tree imaginable, even those which bear nuts)*; **the tree of life also in the midst of the Garden** *(evidently contained a type of fruit; 3:22 says as much! the Tree of Life had the power of so renewing man's physical energies that his body, though formed of the dust of the ground and, therefore, naturally mortal, would, by its continual use, live on forever; Christ is now to us the "Tree of Life" [Rev. 2:7; 22:2]; and the "Bread of Life" [Jn. 6:48, 51])*, **and the tree of knowledge of good and evil** *(presents the tree of death).*

10 **And a river went out of Eden to water the Garden; and from thence it was parted, and became into four heads** *(four rivers).*

11 **The name of the first is Pison** *(is believed to be the "Ganges")*: **that is it which compasseth the whole land of Havilah, where there is gold** *(believed to be India)*;

12 **And the gold of that land is good: there is bdellium and the onyx stone** *(Verses 11 and 12 present the first mention in the Bible of the precious metal, gold; it is mentioned last in the Bible as it refers to the main thoroughfare of the New Jerusalem, in which we are told is "pure gold" [Rev. 21:21]).*

13 **And the name of the second river is Gihon** *(is believed to be the Nile)*: **the same is it that compasseth the whole land of Ethiopia.**

14 **And the name of third river is Hiddekel** *(is believed to be the Tigris)*: **that is it which goes toward the east of Assyria. And the fourth river is Euphrates.** *(These rivers at the present time have their sources far apart. The explanation, no doubt, lies in the flood, which altered the topography of the Earth. The headwaters of the first two were drastically changed, while the last two remain basically the same. In fact, it is believed that the Garden of Eden may have been located, as stated, at the joining of the Tigris and Euphrates, which is the site of ancient Babylon.)*

15 **And the LORD God took the man, and put him into the Garden of Eden to dress it and to keep it.**

16 **And the LORD God commanded the man, saying, Of every tree of the Garden you may freely eat** *(as stated, before the Fall, man was vegetarian)*:

17 **But of the tree of the Knowledge of Good and Evil, you shall not eat of it** *(as for the "evil," that was obvious; however, it is the "good" on this tree that deceives much of the world; the "good" speaks of religion; the definition of religion pertains to a system devised by men in order to bring about Salvation, to reach God, or*

to better oneself in some way; because it is devised by man, it is unacceptable to God; God's answer to the dilemma of the human race is "Jesus Christ and Him Crucified" [I Cor. 1:23]): **for in the day that you eat thereof you shall surely die** (speaks of spiritual death, which is separation from God; let it be understood that the tree of the knowledge of good and evil was not the cause of Adam's Fall; it was a failure to heed and obey the Word of God, which is the cause of every single failure; spiritual death ultimately brought on physical death, and has, in fact, filled the world with death, all because of the Fall).

GOD'S FORESIGHT FOR MAN

18 And the LORD God said, It is not good that the man should be alone (doesn't mean that the idea of a companion for Adam suddenly presented itself to the Lord; God never intended that man should be alone); **I will make him a help meet for him** (this is not meant to infer that the creation of woman was an afterthought; there is no Plan of God that is incomplete!).

ADAM AND THE ANIMAL WORLD

19 And out of the ground the LORD God formed every beast of the field, and every fowl of the air (the animals and the fowls were created out of dust, exactly as man); **and brought them unto Adam to see what he would call them: and whatsoever Adam called every living creature, that was the name thereof** (carried within the name that Adam gave to each one of these creatures are the characteristics of that particular animal or fowl; so we are speaking here of a man who had amazing intelligence; to do all of this, Adam had to have a distinct knowledge of speech, the meaning of all words, and the capacity of attaching words to ideas; why not? Adam had the greatest Teacher that man has ever had, "the LORD God").

20 And Adam gave names to all cattle, and to the fowl of the air, and to every beast of the field; but for Adam there was not found an help meet for him (we learn from this that the animal creation was of far greater magnitude and intelligence than at the present; it was the Fall which changed that creation [Rom. 8:19-23]).

THE CREATION OF WOMAN

21 And the LORD God caused a deep sleep

to fall upon Adam, and he slept (records the first anesthesia): **and he took one of his ribs** (the word "rib" here actually means "side"), **and closed up the flesh instead thereof** (the woman is not merely of a rib, but actually of one side of man);

22 And the rib (side), **which the LORD God had taken from man, made He a woman** (the Hebrew says, "built He a woman"; Horton says, "When God created the man, the word 'form' was used, which is the same word used of a potter forming a clay jar; but the word 'build' here seems to mean God paid even more attention to the creation of the woman"), **and brought her unto the man** (presents a formal presentation, with God, in essence, performing the first wedding; thus He instituted the bonds of the Marriage Covenant, which is actually called the Covenant of God [Prov. 2:17], indicating that God is the Author of this sacred institution; this is the marriage model, and was instituted by God; any other model, such as the homosexual marriages, so-called, can be constituted as none other than an abomination in the Eyes of God [Rom. 1:24-28]).

THE FIRST MARRIAGE UNION

23 And Adam said, This is now bone of my bones, and flesh of my flesh (that is, she is man's counterpart, not merely in feeling and sense — his flesh — but in his solid qualities): **she shall be called Woman, because she was taken out of Man** (God did not take the woman out of man's feet to be stepped on as an inferior; nor out of his head to be put on a pedestal as a superior; but from his side, close to his heart as an equal).

24 Therefore shall a man leave his father and his mother, and shall cleave unto his wife (this Passage must be viewed as an inspired declaration of the law of marriage): **and they shall be one flesh** (points to a unity of persons, not simply to a conjunction of bodies, or a community of interests, or even a reciprocity of affections).

THE STATE OF INNOCENCE

25 And they were both naked (refers to an absence of clothing, at least as we understand such; they were actually enswathed in ethereal and transfiguring light), **the man and his wife, and were not ashamed** (were not ashamed, because there was nothing of which to be ashamed).

CHAPTER 3
(4004 B.C.)
THE FALL OF MAN

NOW the serpent was more subtle than any beast of the field which the LORD God had made *(the word "subtle," as used here, is not negative, but rather positive; everything that God made before the Fall was positive; it describes qualities such as quickness of sight, swiftness of motion, activity of self-preservation, and seemingly intelligent adaptation to its surroundings)*. And he said unto the woman *(not a fable; the serpent before the Fall had the ability of limited speech; Eve did not seem surprised when he spoke to her!)*, Yes, has God said, You shall not eat of every tree of the Garden? *(The serpent evidently lent its faculties to Satan, even though the Evil One is not mentioned. That being the case, Satan spoke through the serpent, and questioned the Word of God.)*

2 And the woman said unto the serpent *(proclaims Satan leveling his attack against Eve, instead of Adam; his use of Eve was only a means to get to Adam)*, We may eat of the fruit of the trees of the Garden *(the trial of our first parents was ordained by God, because probation was essential to their spiritual development and self-determination; but as He did not desire that they should be tempted to their Fall, He would not suffer Satan to tempt them in a way that would surpass their human capacity; the tempted might, therefore, have resisted the tempter)*:

3 But of the fruit of the tree which is in the midst of the Garden, God has said, You shall not eat of it, neither shall you touch it, lest you die *(Eve quoted what the Lord had said about the prohibition, but then added, "neither shall you touch it")*.

4 And the serpent said unto the woman, You shall not surely die *(proclaims an outright denial of the Word of God; as God had preached to Adam, Satan now preaches to Eve; Jesus called Satan a liar, which probably refers to this very moment [Jn. 8:44])*:

5 For God does know that in the day you eat thereof, then your eyes shall be opened *(suggests the attainment of higher wisdom)*, and you shall be as gods, knowing good and evil. *(In effect says, "You shall be Elohim." It was a promise of Divinity. God is Omniscient, meaning that His knowledge of evil is thorough, but not by personal experience. By His very Nature, He is totally separate from all that is evil. The knowledge of evil that Adam and Eve would learn would be by moral degradation, which would bring wreckage. While it was proper to desire to be like God, it is proper only if done in the right way, and that is through Faith in Christ and what He has done for us at the Cross.)*

6 And when the woman saw that the tree was good for food *(presents the lust of the eyes)*, and that it was pleasant to the eyes *(the lust of the flesh)*, and a tree to be desired to make one wise *(the pride of life)*, she took of the fruit thereof, and did eat *(constitutes the Fall)*, and gave also unto her husband with her; and he did eat *(refers to the fact that evidently Adam was an observer to all these proceedings; some claim that he ate of the forbidden fruit which she offered him out of love for her; however, no one ever sins out of love; Eve submitted to the temptation out of deception, but "Adam was not deceived" [I Tim. 2:14]; he fell because of unbelief; he simply didn't believe what God had said about the situation; contrast Verse 6 with Luke 4:1-13; both present the three temptations, "the lust of the flesh," "the lust of the eyes," and "the pride of life"; the first man falls, the Second Man conquers)*.

7 And the eyes of them both were opened *(refers to the consciousness of guilt as a result of their sin)*, and they knew that they were naked *(refers to the fact that they had lost the enswathing light of purity, which previously had clothed their bodies)*; and they sewed fig leaves together, and made themselves aprons *(sinners clothe themselves with morality, sacraments, and religious ceremonies; they are as worthless as Adam's apron of fig leaves)*.

8 And they heard the Voice of the LORD God walking in the Garden in the cool of the day *(the "Voice" of the Lord had once been a welcome sound; it is now a dreaded sound, because of their sin; it is not that the Voice of the Lord had changed, for it hadn't; it was the same Voice that they had heard since creation; He hadn't changed, but they had)*: and Adam and his wife hid themselves from the presence of the LORD God amongst the trees of the Garden *(here is the dawn of a new era in the history of humanity; the eye of a guilt conscience is now opened for the first time, and God and the universe appear in new and terrible forms)*.

9 And the LORD God called unto Adam, and said unto him, Where are you? *(This is the first question in the Old Testament. "Where is he?" is the first question in the New Testament [Mat. 2:2]. The Old Testament, God seeking the sinner; the New Testament, the sinner seeking God.)*

FOREWORD

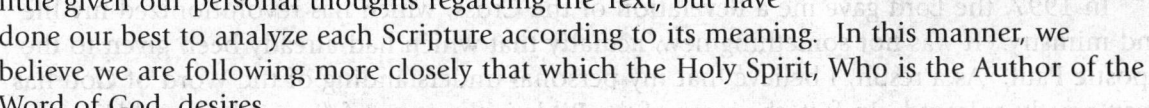

The Expositor's Study Bible is one of the most unique of its kind in the world today. It is designed with one thought in mind, and that is to help the Bible student to more properly understand the Word. In order to do this, we have utilized some of the finest Hebrew and Greek Scholars, coupled with our some sixty years of personal Bible study.

The two words, *"Expositor's"* and *"Commentary,"* are very similar in meaning; however, the word *"Expositor's"* refers to a more clinical approach, which refers to the fact that we have little given our personal thoughts regarding the Text, but have done our best to analyze each Scripture according to its meaning. In this manner, we believe we are following more closely that which the Holy Spirit, Who is the Author of the Word of God, desires.

Regrettably and sadly, the Bible is all too often an unread Book. That is tragic, inasmuch as the Word of God is the only revealed Truth in the world today, and, in fact, ever has been. Far too many Believers simply do not read the Bible, at least as they should, with the excuse being presented that they simply cannot understand what it says. Hopefully, *THE EXPOSITOR'S STUDY BIBLE* will help solve that problem by making the Text easier to understand.

Some time in the 1990's, the Lord began to deal with my heart about this effort, which is now the finished product. At the outset, the Lord gave me no instructions as to how this was to be done, and I speak of the format — just that it must be done! Some time in 2001, the Holy Spirit began to give me the format which we should follow, which, as far as I know, is unique.

I wrote the Expositor's notes for the New Testament first of all. When we released *THE EXPOSITOR'S NEW TESTAMENT* to the general public, I was elated at the favorable response. Scores of people have written or sent e-mails stating: *"Brother Swaggart, THE EXPOSITOR'S NEW TESTAMENT has helped me to understand the Word of God to a greater degree than ever before."* Of course, that is the goal toward which we ever strive, a greater understanding of the Word of God. And if our efforts bring that about, even to the smallest degree, then it has been worth all the work and labor.

After *THE EXPOSITOR'S NEW TESTAMENT* was released and received such favorable response, with constant requests that we also do the same with the Old Testament, and also knowing that this was what the Lord wanted, we set out immediately to bring it to pass.

The Word of God is under attack presently, possibly as never before, at least since the Reformation; however, the attack is subtle, little employing the frontal assault, but rather attacking the Bible by simply ignoring it, with interest being concentrated on religious books of sorts. In some small way, I would pray that our efforts concerning *THE EXPOSITOR'S STUDY BIBLE* will have a positive effect on changing this erroneous trend. Nothing can take the place of the Bible!

As the Reader will notice, we use exclusively the King James Version; however, in order that the Text might be a little easier to understand, in some cases, we have replaced the Elizabethan words such as *"ye," "hast," etc.,* with words more commonly used at the present time. We think this makes the Text much easier to understand, while it changes not at all the meaning. As well, the Scriptural Text is in black, with our expository notes in red. This makes the Scriptural Text stand out much more boldly, thereby being separate from the notes.

We think that *THE EXPOSITOR'S STUDY BIBLE* is very user-friendly. Scores of people have told us that the notes in many study Bibles, while helpful, are sometimes difficult to

find. As a result, many will not take the time to follow through. Our expository notes follow immediately after each Verse, which makes it overly easy to see, read, and understand.

I wish to express my deepest appreciation to my loving wife, Frances, who attends to so many duties at the Ministry, giving me the time to do the work and research needed for a Volume such as this. Our son, Donnie, falls into the same category.

As well, I wish to thank: my secretary, Nikki Tracy, who tries to keep my telephone from ringing more than 100 times a day; Barbara Eversberg, who typed, so expertly, every word, making our task a little easier; and Donna Simpson and Sharon Whitelaw, who organized and put everything together — a monumental task, to say the least.

However, all of this effort has been a labor of love, for there is nothing more rewarding than the study of the Word of God. Therefore, whatever good comes out of this effort, we give all the praise and glory to the Lord Jesus Christ.

In 1997, the Lord gave me a Revelation of the Cross, which has revolutionized my life and ministry. It was not something new, actually that which had already been given to the Apostle Paul. As a result, I believe that my personal understanding of the Word of God has been greatly enlarged. In fact, the story of the Bible is the story of *"Jesus Christ and Him Crucified."* One might also say that the story of *"Jesus Christ and Him Crucified"* is the story of the Bible. Truly, the Cross of Christ is the Foundation of every great Doctrine of the Word of God. Peter said:

"Forasmuch as you know that you were not redeemed with corruptible things, as silver and gold, from your vain conversation (lifestyle) *received by tradition from your fathers;*

"But with the Precious Blood of Christ, as of a Lamb without blemish and without spot:

"Who verily was foreordained before the foundation of the world, but was manifest in these last times for you" (I Pet. 1:18-20).

This means, as stated, that the Doctrine of the Cross was actually formulated in the mind of the Godhead even before the foundation of the world, making it the Foundation of every subject in the Word of God, that is, if each subject is interpreted correctly.

Being generous, one could probably say that about 10% of the Bible is given over to information regarding Salvation. About 90%, or more, is given over to instruction as it regards living for the Lord. And all of this instruction can be summed up in the extremely abbreviated form of just three phrases: 1. The Cross of Christ; 2. Your Faith; and, 3. The Holy Spirit. In overly simplistic form, these three phrases describe God's Prescribed Order of Victory.

We have done our very best to explain every Scripture in the entirety of the Bible according to this illumination.

JIMMY SWAGGART

For information on *THE EXPOSITOR'S STUDY BIBLE* or *THE EXPOSITOR'S NEW TESTAMENT*, please call 1-800-288-8350.

10 And he *(Adam)* said, I heard Your Voice in the Garden, and I was afraid *(fear is the first reaction of fallen man; Adam's consciousness of the effects of sin was keener than his sense of the sin itself)*, because I was naked; and I hid myself *(he was naked to the Judgment of God, because of sin, which must be judged; he tried to hide himself from God, even as untold millions have, but never with any success; God wanted Adam to know that he who hides himself from Him is never hidden from Him, and that he who runs away from Him can never escape Him).*

11 And He said, Who told you that you were naked *(carries Adam's mind from the effect to the sin that had caused it; as long as a man feels sorrow only for the results of his action, there is no Repentance, and no wish to return to the Divine Presence)*? Have you eaten of the tree, whereof I commanded you that you should not eat? *(The way the question is framed removes the pretext of ignorance, and also points to the fact that the sin had been carried out in direct violation of the Divine prohibition [Calvin].)*

12 And the man said, The woman whom You gave to be with me, she gave me of the tree, and I did eat *(Adam first of all blamed God, and then blamed Eve; he recapitulates the history, as if, in his view, it was a matter of course that he should act as he had done; man has been doing this ever since).*

13 And the LORD God said unto the woman, What is this that you have done? *(The two questions, "Where are you?" and "What is this that you have done?" comprise the human problem.)* And woman said, The serpent beguiled me, and I did eat *(presents Eve blaming the serpent; in a sense, she was blaming God as well, simply because God had made the serpent).*

THE ADAMIC COVENANT AND CURSES

14 And the LORD God said unto the serpent *(as we shall see, presents no question or interrogation being posed toward the serpent at all; God judges him, and it is in listening to this judgment that the guilty pair hear the first great Promise respecting Christ)*, Because you have done this, you are cursed above all cattle, and above every beast of the field *(refers to this animal being reduced from possibly the highest place and position in the animal kingdom to the lowest)*; upon your belly shall you go, and dust shall you eat all the days of your life *(if in fact the serpent was an unwitting tool in the*

hand of Satan, then I think that the Lord would not have placed a curse upon this animal):

15 And I will put enmity *(animosity)* between you and the woman *(presents the Lord now actually speaking to Satan, who had used the serpent; in effect, the Lord is saying to Satan, "You used the woman to bring down the human race, and I will use the woman as an instrument to bring the Redeemer into the world, Who will save the human race")*, and between your seed *(mankind which follows Satan)* and her Seed *(the Lord Jesus Christ)*; it *(Christ)* shall bruise your head *(the victory that Jesus won at the Cross [Col. 2;14-15])*, and you shall bruise His heel *(the sufferings of the Cross).*

16 Unto the woman He said, I will greatly multiply your sorrow and your conception *(the original Plan of God was that husband and wife would bring sons and daughters of God into the world; due to the Fall, they can only bring sons and daughters into the world in the "likeness of Adam" [Gen. 5:3])*; in sorrow you shall bring forth children *(as a result of the Fall, children would be born into a world of sorrow)*; and your desire shall be to your husband, and he shall rule over you *(her husband, instead of God, would now rule over her).*

17 And unto Adam He said, Because you have hearkened unto the voice of your wife *(Adam hearkened unto his wife instead of God)*, and have eaten of the tree, of which I commanded you, saying, You shall not eat of it *(the tree itself contained no evil properties in the fruit; the Fall, as stated, was caused rather by disobedience to the Word of God)*: cursed is the ground for your sake; in sorrow shall you eat of it all the days of your life *(Earth was originally intended to be a paradise, but now it will give up its largesse reluctantly; as well, the phrase, "all the days of your life," proclaims the death sentence, which means that life is now terminal, all as a result of "spiritual death," which was, and is, separation from God)*;

18 Thorns also and thistles shall it bring forth to you *(thorns and thistles were not originally in the creation of God, this being a result of the curse, which is a result of the sin of man)*; and you shall eat the herb of the field *(this would not now grow freely, as originally intended, but only now with great care and great labor)*;

19 In the sweat of your face shall you eat bread *(food will be obtained by hard labor)*, till you return unto the ground *(the life-source, which was formerly in God, is now in food, and which is woefully insufficient)*; for out of it

were you taken: for dust you are, and unto dust shall you return *(the Power of God alone could keep the dust alive; that being gone, to dust man returns)*.

20 And Adam called his wife's name Eve; because she was the mother of all living. *(God named the man, and called him Adam, which means "red earth." Adam named the woman, and called her Eve, which means "life." Adam bears the name of the dying body, Eve of the living soul.)*

21 Unto Adam also and to his wife did the LORD God make coats of skins, and clothed them *(in the making of coats of skins, God, in effect, was telling Adam and Eve that their fig leaves were insufficient; as well, He was teaching them that without the shedding of blood, which pertained to the animals that gave their lives, which were Types of Christ, is no remission of sin; in this first sacrifice was laid the foundation of the entirety of the Plan of God as it regards Redemption; also, it must be noticed that it is the "LORD God" Who furnished these coats, and not man himself; this tells us that Salvation is altogether of God and not at all of man; the Life of Christ given on the Cross, and given as our Substitute, provides the only covering for sin; everything else must be rejected)*.

EXPULSION FROM THE GARDEN

22 And the LORD God said, Behold, the man is become as one of Us, to know good and evil *(the Lord knew evil, not by personal experience, but rather through Omniscience; man now knows evil by becoming evil, which is the fountainhead of all sorrow in the world; the pronoun "Us" signifies the Godhead, "God the Father, God the Son, and God the Holy Spirit")*: and now, lest he put forth his hand, and take also of the tree of life, and eat, and live forever *(this would have been the worst thing of all, to have an Adolf Hitler to live forever, etc.)*:

23 Therefore the LORD God sent him forth from the Garden of Eden *(in effect this was an act of mercy; man is expelled from the Garden, lest by eating the Tree of Life he should perpetuate his misery; but God's Love for him, though fallen and guilty, is so strong that He accompanies him into exile; as well, through Jesus Christ, God's only Son, Who will be given in Sacrifice, the Lord will show Adam, and all who would follow him, how to come back into Paradise; regrettably, there is no record that Adam and Eve placed any faith in the Lord; unfortunately,*

untold billions have followed suit), to till the ground from whence he was taken *(refers to a place of toil, not to a place of torment)*.

24 So He *(God)* drove out the man *(implies the idea of force and displeasure)*; and He placed at the east of the Garden of Eden Cherubims *(these Cherubims signified the Holiness of God, which man had now forfeited)*, and a flaming sword which turned every way, to keep the way of the Tree of Life *(the "flaming sword" was emblematic of the Divine Glory in its attitude towards sin)*.

CHAPTER 4
(4003 B.C.)
CAIN AND ABEL

AND Adam knew Eve his wife *(is the Biblical connotation of the union of husband and wife in respect to the sex act)*; and she conceived, and bore Cain *(the first child born to this union, and would conclude exactly as the Lord said it would, with "sorrow")*, and said, I have gotten a man from the LORD *(by Eve using the title "LORD," which means "Covenant God," and which refers to the "Seed of the woman," [Gen. 3:15], she thought Cain was the Promised One; she evidently didn't realize that it was impossible for fallen man to bring forth the Promised Redeemer)*.

2 And she again bore his brother Abel *("Abel" means "vanity;" Cain being the oldest, this shows that Eve by now had become disillusioned with her firstborn, undoubtedly seeing traits in him which she knew could not be of the Promised Seed; she was losing faith in God)*. And Abel was a keeper of sheep, but Cain was a tiller of the ground *(both were honorable professions)*.

3 And in process of time it came to pass *(the phrase used here refers to a long indefinite period)*, that Cain brought of the fruit of the ground an offering unto the LORD. *(This was probably the first offering that he brought, even though the Lord had explained to the First Family the necessity of the Sacrificial System, that is, if they were to have any type of communion with God and forgiveness of sins. There is evidence that Adam, at least for a while, offered up sacrifices. Cain knew the type of Sacrifice that the Lord would accept, but he rebelled against that admonition, demanding that God accept the labor of his hands, which, in fact, God could not accept. So we have, in the persons of Cain and Abel, the first examples of a religious man of the world and a genuine man of Faith.)*

4 And Abel, he also brought of the firstlings of his flock and of the fat thereof *(this is what God demanded; it was a blood sacrifice of an innocent victim, a lamb, which proclaimed the fact that Abel recognized his need of a Redeemer, and that One was coming Who would redeem lost humanity; the Offering of Abel was a Type of Christ and the price that He would pay on the Cross of Calvary in order for man to be redeemed).* And the LORD had respect unto Abel and to his offering: *(As stated, this was a Type of Christ and the Cross, the only Offering which God will respect. Abel's Altar is beautiful to God's Eye and repulsive to man's. Cain's altar is beautiful to man's eye and repulsive to God's. These "altars" exist today; around the one that is Christ and His atoning work, few are gathered, around the other, many. God accepts the slain lamb and rejects the offered fruit; and the offering being rejected, so of necessity is the offerer.)*

5 But unto Cain and to his offering He had not respect *(let us say it again, God has no respect for any proposed way of Salvation, other than "Jesus Christ and Him Crucified" [I Cor. 1:23; 2:2]).* And Cain was very angry, and his countenance fell *(that which filled Abel with peace filled Cain with wrath; the carnal mind displays its enmity against all this Truth which so gladdens and satisfies the heart of the Believer).*

6 And the LORD said unto Cain *(God loves Cain, just as He did Abel, and wishes to bless him also),* Why are you angry *(Abel's Altar speaks of Repentance, of Faith, and of the Precious Blood of Christ, the Lamb of God without blemish; Cain's altar tells of pride, unbelief, and self-righteousness, which always elicits anger)?* and why is your countenance fallen *(anger, in one form or the other, accompanies self-righteousness, for that is what plagued Cain; God's Righteousness can only come by the Cross, while self-righteousness is by dependence on works)?*

7 If you do well, shall you not be accepted *(if you bring the correct sacrifice, and thereby place your faith)?* and if you do not well, sin *(a Sin-Offering)* lies at the door *(a lamb was at the door of the Tabernacle).* And unto you shall be his desire, and you shall rule over him *(the Lord promised Cain dominion over the Earth of that day, if he would only offer up, and place his trust in, the right sacrifice; He promises the same presently to all who trust Christ [Mat. 5:5]).*

CAIN MURDERS ABEL

8 And Cain talked with Abel his brother: and it came to pass, when they were in the field, that Cain rose up against Abel his brother, and killed him *(the first murder; Cain's religion was too refined to kill a lamb, but not too cultured to murder his brother; God's way of Salvation fills the heart with love; man's way of salvation enflames it with hatred; "Religion" has ever been the greatest cause of bloodshed).*

9 And the LORD said unto Cain, Where is Abel your brother? *(Adam sins against God and Cain sins against man. In their united conduct, we have sin in all its forms, and that on the first page of human history.)* And he said, I know not: Am I my brother's keeper *(He showed himself a "liar" in saying, "I know not"; "wicked and profane" in thinking he could hide his sin from God; "unjust" in denying himself to be his brother's keeper; "obstinate and desperate" in not confessing his sin)?*

10 And He *(God)* said, What have you done *(this concerns man's sins, the fruit of his sinful nature)?* The voice of your brother's blood cries unto Me from the ground. *(There is some Scriptural evidence that Cain cut his brother's throat. Thus, with the first shedding of human blood, that ominous thought sprang up, divinely bestowed, that the Earth will grant no peace to the one who has wantonly stained her fair face with the life-stream of man.)*

11 And now are you cursed from the Earth *(Cain repudiated the Cross, murdered his brother, and is now cursed by God; this is the first curse leveled by God against a human being),* which has opened her mouth to receive your brother's blood from your hand *(was the beginning of what has proven to be a saturation; from then until now, the Earth has been soaked with the blood of innocent victims);*

12 When you till the ground, it shall not henceforth yield unto you her strength *(presents the fact that Cain had polluted man's habitation, and now, when he tilled the soil, it would resist him as an enemy);* a fugitive and a vagabond shall you be in the Earth *(presents the search, not of a better lot, but under the compulsion of an evil conscience).*

13 And Cain said unto the LORD, My punishment is greater than I can bear *(Cain did not see the enormity of his sin, but the severity of his punishment; in other words, there was no repentance).*

14 Behold, You have driven me out this day from the face of the Earth *(Adam's sin brought expulsion from the inner circle, Cain's from the outer);* and from Your face shall I be hid *(to be*

hidden from the Face of God is to be not regarded by God, and not protected by His Guardian care); and I shall be a fugitive and a vagabond in the Earth *(a wanderer)*; and it shall come to pass, that every one who finds me shall *(seek to)* kill me. *(The reference by Cain to other individuals proves that in the some 100 plus years since Adam and Eve were created, the first parents had other children. By this time, there could very well have been several thousands of people on the Earth, and no doubt were.)*

15 And the LORD said unto him, Therefore whosoever kills Cain, vengeance shall be taken on him sevenfold *(Cain was allowed to live in order that he might be a perpetual warning to others that the blood of their fellowman must not be spilled; however, very few heeded, as few presently heed)*. And the LORD set a mark upon Cain, lest any finding him should kill him *(we aren't told what the mark was, but evidently, all knew)*.

THE FIRST CIVILIZATION

16 And Cain went out from the presence of the LORD *(those in rebellion against God do not at all desire His Presence, and for all the obvious reasons)*, and dwelt in the land of Nod, on the east of Eden *("Nod" means "wandering;" the majority of the human race "wander," because they don't know God and, therefore, have no peace)*.

17 And Cain knew his wife *(Biblical terminology for conception)*; and she conceived, and bore Enoch: and he built a city *(actually means "was building" or "began to build;" the idea is, it was not finished; and so it has been, and is, with the human race; nothing is ever quite finished with the unredeemed, simply because what is built doesn't satisfy)*, and called the name of the city, after the name of his son, Enoch *(carries the idea, due to the meaning of the name Enoch, that this city would be a place of education and learning — but it was education and learning without God)*.

18 And unto Enoch was born Irad: and Irad begat *(fathered)* Mehujael: and Mehujael begat Methusael: and Methusael begat Lamech *(all of this was three hundred or more years after the creation of Adam and Eve)*.

19 And Lamech took unto him two wives: the name of the one was Adah, and the name of the other Zillah *(the first instance of polygamy recorded in the Bible)*.

20 And Adah bore Jabal: he was the father of such as dwell in tents, and of such as have cattle.

21 And his brother's name was Jubal: he was the father of all such as handle the harp and organ *(it seems that Jubal was the originator of musical instruments; man's ear is now filled with other sounds than those which issue from Calvary, and his eye is filled with other objects than a Crucified Christ)*.

22 And Zillah, she also bore Tubal-cain, an instructor of every artificer in brass and iron: and the sister of Tubal-cain was Naamah *(Tubal-cain was the first one to begin to work with metals; the name of "Cain" was probably added to show that these were "Cainites;" "Naamah" means "beautiful")*.

23 And Lamech said unto his wives, Adah and Zillah, Hear my voice; you wives of Lamech, hearken unto my speech: for I have slain a man to my wounding, and a young man to my hurt.

24 If Cain shall be avenged sevenfold, truly Lamech seventy and sevenfold. *(This is the first recorded poem in human history. Like so much poetry ever since, it glorifies immorality and murder, and denies coming wrath. Man has attempted to deny judgment ever since; nevertheless, judgment one day is coming [Rev. 20:11-15].)*

THE SPIRITUAL SEED RENEWED

25 And Adam knew his wife again; and she bore a son, and called his name Seth *(after dealing with Cain's line in the beginnings of corruption of violence, Moses goes back some years to the birth of "Seth;" the Holy Spirit will single out "Seth," because he was in the lineage of Christ; the name "Seth" means "appointed substitute")*: For God, said she, has appointed me another seed instead of Abel, whom Cain killed. *(When "Cain" was born, Eve said, "I have gotten a man from the LORD," indicating that she believed in the Covenant of Genesis 3:15. Now she uses the term "God," in effect stating that she has lost faith in the Covenant. As stated, this "seed" would be the one through whom Christ would come, but because of faithlessness, Eve did not know or believe this.)*

26 And to Seth, to him also there was born a son; and he called his name Enos *(the name "Enos" means "sickly, mortal, decaying man;" the awful results of the Fall are now beginning to sink in)*: then began men to call upon the name of the LORD *(probably refers to contempt; quite possibly the family of Cain, knowing that Seth had now taken the place of Abel,*

as it regards the "firstborn" or "appointed one," contemptuously refers to them as the "God people," or the "Lord people").

CHAPTER 5
(4004 B.C.)
ADAM'S DESCENDANTS

THIS is the book of the generations of Adam *(corresponds with the phrase, "The Book of the Generation of Jesus Christ," Who was the Last Adam [Mat. 1:1]).* In the day that God created man, in the likeness of God made He him *(the "Likeness of God" is the "Glory of God" [II Cor. 4:6]. Through the Fall, man lost that glory; however, at the First Resurrection of Life, every Believer will regain that glory [Rom. 8:17]);*

2 Male and female created He them *(refers to the fact that homosexuality is a grievous sin before God);* and blessed them *(the blessing was lost as a result of the Fall, but has been regained in Christ),* and called their name Adam, in the day when they were created *(Adam, in the Hebrew, is the word for humankind in general beside the specific name for the first man).*

3 And Adam lived an hundred and thirty years, and begat *(fathered)* a son in his own likeness *(God originally intended for mankind to procreate "sons and daughters of God" into the world; due to the Fall, sons and daughters could be brought into the world only in the likeness of their original parent, Adam, a product of his fallen nature; it is called "original sin"),* and after his image *(means that Adam no longer had the Image of God; the "likeness" and "image" are now after Satan [Jn. 8:44]);* and called his name Seth *(even though Seth was not the Promised One, still, he represented a ray of hope; through him, rather his line, the Promised One would come):*

4 And the days of Adam after he had begotten Seth were eight hundred years: and he begat sons and daughters *(the intimation is, Adam was able to father children, and Eve to conceive, for some 800 years. Exactly how many children they brought into the world we aren't told. But it had to be many):*

5 And all the days that Adam lived were nine hundred and thirty years: and he died *(the family history of this, the Heavenly Race, is marked by death; no matter how long a member of the family lived, yet three words attend the name: "and he died").*

THE FAMILY OF SETH

6 And Seth lived an hundred and five years, and begat *(fathered)* Enos:

7 And Seth lived after he begat Enos eight hundred and seven years, and begat sons and daughters:

8 And all the days of Seth were nine hundred and twelve years: and he died.

THE FAMILY OF ENOS

9 And Enos lived ninety years, and begat Cainan:

10 And Enos lived after he begat Cainan eight hundred and fifteen years, and begat sons and daughters:

11 And all the days of Enos were nine hundred and five years: and he died.

THE FAMILY OF CAINAN

12 And Cainan lived seventy years, and begat Mahalaleel:

13 And Cainan lived after he begat Mahalaleel eight hundred and forty years, and begat sons and daughters:

14 And all the days of Cainan were nine hundred and ten years: and he died.

THE FAMILY OF MAHALALEEL

15 And Mahalaleel lived sixty and five years, and begat Jared:

16 And Mahalaleel lived after he begat Jared eight hundred and thirty years, and begat sons and daughters:

17 And all the days of Mahalaleel were eight hundred ninety and five years: and he died.

THE FAMILY OF JARED

18 And Jared lived an hundred sixty and two years, and he begat Enoch *(Enoch and Abel are the only two men from creation to the flood, with the exception of Noah, listed who lived for God. There may have been others, but the Bible doesn't say):*

19 And Jared lived after he begat Enoch eight hundred years, and begat sons and daughters:

20 And all the days of Jared were nine hundred sixty and two years: and he died.

THE FAMILY OF ENOCH

21 And Enoch lived sixty and five years, and

begat Methuselah (*apparently, Enoch was 65 years of age when he was converted and entered into this Divine fellowship; the name "Methuselah" means: "The Deluge (the flood) shall be sent when he is dead"; so, Methuselah was a living, walking testimony that judgment was coming upon the Earth because of its terrible wickedness; however, only Noah and his family believed; so the flood came a little less than a thousand years after Methuselah was born*):

22 And Enoch walked with God (*three statements are made in the Bible respecting Enoch: "he walked with God" [Gen. 5:22]; "he witnessed for God" [Jude, Vs. 14]; "he pleased God" [Heb. 11:5]*) after he begat Methuselah three hundred years, and begat sons and daughters (*Enoch did not live a life of isolation, but he did live a life of separation. Such is demanded of all Believers*):

23 And all the days of Enoch were three hundred sixty and five years (*converted at 65 years old, he faithfully lived for God some 300 years*):

24 And Enoch walked with God: and he was not; for God took him (*Enoch was one of the two men in history who did not die, Elijah being the other. He was translated, and as Paul said, "that he should not see death" [Heb. 11:5]*).

THE FAMILY OF METHUSELAH

25 And Methuselah lived an hundred eighty and seven years, and begat Lamech (*Noah will be born to Lamech*).

26 And Methuselah lived after he begat Lamech seven hundred eighty and two years, and begat sons and daughters:

27 And all the days of Methuselah were nine hundred sixty and nine years: and he died (*Methuselah lived longer than anyone has ever lived, 969 years; he apparently died just before Noah's flood; despite his Godly father, there is no record that he lived for God*).

THE FAMILY OF LAMECH

28 And Lamech lived an hundred eighty and two years, and begat a son:

29 And he called his name Noah (*we are now introduced to Noah, one of the central figures of the Bible, and of all time. His name means "rest"*), saying, This same shall comfort us concerning our work and toil of our hands, because of the ground which the LORD has cursed (*it seems that Lamech, the father of Noah, had been given a Revelation concerning this child.*

The comfort he brought, as it regards the curse, had to do with the Ark, and the One Who would ultimately come through his lineage, the Son of God, Who would remove the greater curse — the curse of the broken Law [Gal. 3:13]).

30 And Lamech lived after he begat Noah five hundred ninety and five years, and begat sons and daughters (*but none of the brothers and sisters of Noah believed the Word of the Lord, and thereby perished in the flood*):

31 And all the days of Lamech were seven hundred seventy and seven years: and he died.

THE FAMILY OF NOAH

32 And Noah was five hundred years old: and Noah begat Shem, Ham, and Japheth (*due to the fact that every human being on the face of the Earth died in the flood, with the exception of Noah and his family, this means that every person who has ever lived since then is a descendant of either Shem, Ham, or Japheth*).

CHAPTER 6
(2448 B.C.)
WICKEDNESS OF MANKIND

AND it came to pass, when men began to multiply on the face of the Earth, and daughters were born unto them (*the events of this Chapter probably begin at about the time of Enoch, which was about a thousand years before the flood. There were, no doubt, several millions of people on the face of the Earth at that time. Verse 1 is not meant to imply that the births of baby girls were more than that of baby boys, but is rather meant to set up the narrative for that which is about to be said*),

2 That the sons of God saw the daughters of men that they were fair; and they took them wives of all which they chose (*the "sons of God" portrayed here refer to fallen angels, which had thrown in their lot with Lucifer, who led a revolution against God some time in eternity past; in order to spoil the human lineage through which the Messiah would ultimately come, they would seek to corrupt that lineage, and to do so by marrying the "daughters of men," thereby producing a mongrel race, so to speak, of which at least some of these offspring turned out to be "giants"; at any rate, all who were the result of such a union were tainted; the term "sons of God" in the Old Testament, at least as it is used here, is never used of human beings, but always*

of angels, whether righteous or fallen [Job 1:6; 2:1]; in his short Epistle, Jude mentions these particular "angels." He said that they "kept not their first estate, but left their own habitation"; he then said what their sin was: "going after strange flesh." Concerning this, Jude also said that God "has reserved [them] in everlasting chains under darkness unto the judgment of the great day" [Jude, Vss. 6-7]).

THE WARNING OF GOD

3 And the LORD said, My Spirit *(Holy Spirit)* shall not always strive with man *(the Lord is speaking here of the man, Adam, and not mankind in general)*, for that he also is flesh *(refers to the fact that even though the first man was created personally by God, he still was flesh, and because of the Fall must ultimately die)*: yet his days shall be an hundred and twenty years *(from the time of this announcement, Adam was to be given 120 years to repent; there is no evidence that he did; many think that this 120 years refer to the time limit to repent before the flood; however, it has nothing to do with the flood, as we will later prove).*

4 There were giants in the Earth in those days *(as a result of the union of the fallen angels with the "daughters of men")*; and also after that *("those days" speak of the time before the flood, while "also after that" speaks of the time after the flood; in fact, Goliath, who was killed by David, was one of those specimens)*, when the sons of God came in unto the daughters of men, and they bore children to them, the same became mighty men which were of old, men of renown *(these terms, "mighty men, men of renown" shoot down the hypotheses of these terms referring merely to the lineage of Seth and the lineage of Cain).*

5 And God saw that the wickedness of man was great in the Earth *(these "men of renown," the giants, were developing more and more ways of wickedness)*, and that every imagination of the thoughts of his heart was only evil continually *(Due to this infestation, the evil began with the very thought processes, and incorporated every human being; this was a continuous action of evil which never let up, and constantly grew more degrading).*

6 And it repented the LORD that He had made man on the Earth *(God does not change as it regards His Nature; however, the fact that the Lord repents presents the truth that God, in consistency with His Immutability, assumes a changed position in respect to changed man)*, and it grieved Him at His Heart *(this is not merely an anthropomorphic statement, as some claim, but a true statement regarding the Nature of God; sin grieves the Lord!).*

7 And the LORD said, I will destroy man whom I have created from the face of the Earth *(the wickedness of man had become so great, if God had not done this, man would ultimately have destroyed himself, although it would have taken much longer. Sin has to be judged, and inevitably will be judged)*; both man, and beast, and the creeping thing, and the fowls of the air; for it repents Me that I have made them *(the animal kingdom was made for man, and if man is destroyed, there is no more purpose or reason for the animal kingdom; so it must be destroyed as well).*

NOAH AND THE ARK

8 But Noah found Grace in the sight of the LORD *(this is the first time that Grace is mentioned in the Bible. Grace refers to the Goodness of God extended to undeserving man).*

9 These are the generations of Noah *(the Holy Spirit brings this out, because Noah and his family were perfect in their lineage, in that it had not been corrupted by the union of fallen angels and women)*: Noah was a just man and perfect in his generations *(Noah was justified before God by Faith in the Promised Seed; for Paul later said that he was an heir of the Righteousness which is by Faith [Heb. 11:7])*, and Noah walked with God *(this was the only man on the face of the Earth at this time of which this could be said).*

10 And Noah begat three sons, Shem, Ham, and Japheth *(we learn from the last Verse of the previous Chapter that these sons were not born to Noah until he was some "500 years old").*

11 The Earth also was corrupt before God, and the earth was filled with violence *(meaning that all were corrupted respecting the lineage concerning the union of fallen angels and women).*

12 And God looked upon the Earth, and, behold, it was corrupt *("God looked" denotes a special observance, as though He had instituted an inquiry into its real condition [Ps. 14:2; 33:13-14]; for all flesh had corrupted his way upon the Earth *(the lineage of the entire race, due to the union of fallen angels and women, was marred. This was the plan of Satan to keep the Redeemer from coming into the world, Who*

could only function through an uncorrupted lineage. Other than Noah and his family, the entirety of the human race was polluted).

13 And God said unto Noah, The end of all flesh is come before Me *(the Lord had investigated the situation thoroughly);* for the Earth is filled with violence through them *(the Hebrew says, "For the Earth is filled with violence from their faces"; the idea is, they knew what they were doing, and thereby, in effect, dared God to stop them);* and, behold, I will destroy them with the Earth *(God had no choice! but for Noah, the human race would have been no more, and this world would have been turned back to a place "without form, and void, with darkness upon the face of the deep" [Gen. 1:2]).*

14 Make thee an Ark of gopher wood *(the Ark was a Type of Christ);* rooms shall you make in the Ark, and shall pitch it within and without with pitch.

15 And this is the fashion which you shall make it of: The length of the Ark shall be three hundred cubits, the width of it fifty cubits, and the height of it thirty cubits *(using 18 inches to the cubit, it was to be 450 feet long, 75 feet wide, and 45 feet high).*

16 A window shall you make to the Ark, and in a cubit shall you finish it above; and the door of the Ark shall you set in the side thereof; with lower, second, and third stories shall you make it *(the Hebrew words translated "window" and "door" carry a different meaning than appears on the surface; for instance, the word "window" was evidently a means, not merely of lighting the Ark, but also of ventilating it; it probably was an open space about 18 inches high, running all around the Ark, which would have given a sufficient supply of air, and would have been protected by the overhanging eaves of the roof; as well, it is believed that the "door" probably extended throughout the three floors or stories. The Ark would probably have displaced about 30,000 tons or more; consequently, it was a monstrous ship).*

17 And, behold, I, even I, do bring a flood of waters upon the Earth, to destroy all flesh, wherein is the breath of life, from under heaven; and every thing that is in the Earth shall die *(this referred to all things, with the exception of the fish in the sea [Vs. 20]).*

18 But with you will I establish My Covenant *(this is the first time that the word "Covenant" is used in the Bible. This pertains to the Covenant of the Promised Seed [Gen. 3;15]);* and you shall come into the Ark, you, and your

sons, and your wife, and your sons' wives with you *(presents the fact that his entire family was saved).*

19 And of every living thing of all flesh, two of every sort shall you bring into the Ark, to keep them alive with you; they shall be male and female *(Scientists declare the distinct species of four-footed animals to be about 250; if this number be doubled, and a certain proportion multiplied by 7 for the clean animals, and if an equal number of birds be added and 12 cubic feet allotted to each animal and to each bird, the total number of cubic feet so used would be about one million, leaving approximately two million cubic feet for provisions; so I think it should be obvious that there was an abundance of room in the Ark for its inhabitants).*

20 Of fowls after their kind, and of cattle after their kind, of every creeping thing of the Earth after his kind, two of every sort shall come unto you, to keep them alive *(I think it is obvious, from the phrase, "shall come unto you," that the Spirit of the Lord caused these animals and fowls to come to Noah).*

21 And take you unto you of all food that is eaten, and you shall gather it to you; and it shall be for food for you, and for them *(not knowing how long the flood waters would remain on the Earth, evidently Noah filled the vessel to the brim with provisions).*

22 Thus did Noah; according to all that God commanded him, so did he *(nothing greater could be said about any man!).*

CHAPTER 7
(2349 B.C.)
GOD'S COMMAND TO
ENTER THE ARK

AND the LORD said unto Noah, Come thou and all your house into the Ark *(the Epistle to the Hebrews states that Noah prepared this Ark because he believed the Divine warning; as well, the word "Come," as used by the Lord, presents the fact that God is the first One in the Ark; had He been outside, He would have said, "Go into the Ark!");* for you have I seen righteous before Me in this generation *(refers to Noah's Faith in the coming Redeemer, for that is the only Faith that God will recognize; Paul wrote of him: "And became heir of the Righteousness which is by Faith" [Heb. 11:7]; the Faith addressed here speaks of Christ and what He would do at the Cross; Noah only had a dim view of that coming time, but, as dim as it was, he placed*

his past, his present, and his future in the Promise of God to send the "Seed").

2 Of every clean beast you shall take to you by sevens, the male and his female: and of beasts that are not clean by two, the male and his female.

3 Of fowls also of the air by sevens, the male and the female; to keep seed alive upon the face of all the Earth (*this is not a reference to the Levitical Law, for that would not be given for another 900 years; probably the clean animals mentioned were such as from the days of Adam and Abel, as had been offered in sacrifice; thus, provision was made for Noah's sacrifice on his exit from the Ark, when the flood would subside*).

4 For yet seven days, and I will cause it to rain upon the Earth forty days and forty nights (*the command to enter the Ark was given a week before the rains would begin — and rain such as the world had never known*); and every living substance that I have made will I destroy from off the face of the Earth.

5 And Noah did according unto all that the LORD commanded him (*this is the second time that the Holy Spirit through Moses speaks of Noah's obedience*).

THE FLOOD BEGINS

6 And Noah was six hundred years old when the flood of waters was upon the Earth (*this Verse proves that the 120 years of Genesis 6:3 had nothing to do with the time limit until the flood; in fact, the Bible doesn't tell us how long it was that the warning was given to the people; the number six is generally a Scriptural symbol of suffering; in the Apocalypse, the sixth seal, the sixth trumpet, and the sixth vial introduce critical periods of affliction*).

7 And Noah went in, and his sons, and his wife, and his sons' wives with him, into the Ark, because of the waters of the flood (*concerning this time, Paul said in Hebrews 11:7 that they did this thing "being moved with fear and impelled by faith"*).

8 Of clean beasts, and of beasts that are not clean, and of fowls, and of every thing that creeps upon the Earth.

9 There went in two and two unto Noah into the Ark, the male and the female, as God had commanded Noah (*nothing short of Divine power could have effected such a timely and orderly entrance of the creatures into this huge vessel*).

10 And it came to pass after seven days, that the waters of the flood were upon the Earth (*that which Noah had preached for a number of years was now a reality*).

11 In the six hundredth year of Noah's life, in the second month, the seventeenth day of the month, the same day were all the fountains of the great deep broken up, and the windows of heaven were opened (*the water came from above and from below; as well, it is believed by some Scientists, and rightly so, that the waters came with such force from the Earth, that it would have taken only a few days to have cut the Grand Canyon and other such similarities*).

12 And the rain was upon the Earth forty days and forty nights (*the literal Hebrew translation is, "And there was violent rain . . ."*).

13 In the selfsame day entered Noah, and Shem, and Ham, and Japheth, the sons of Noah, and Noah's wife, and the three wives of his sons with them, into the Ark (*on the day the rains began, Noah and his family entered the Ark*);

14 They, and every beast after his kind, and all the cattle after their kind, and every creeping thing that creeps upon the Earth after his kind, and every fowl after his kind, every bird of every sort.

15 And they went in unto Noah into the Ark, two and two of all flesh, wherein is the breath of life (*the Lord gave these animals the instinct to do what they did*).

16 And they that went in, went in male and female of flesh, as God had commanded him: and the LORD shut him in (*the contrast between the two names of the Deity is most vividly presented here; in this one Verse, both "God" and "LORD" are used. It is "Elohim" Who commands Noah about the beasts; it is "Jehovah," the Covenant God, Who ensures his safety by closing the Ark behind him; nothing can more fully express the Believer's perfect security in Christ than those words, "the LORD shut him in"*).

17 And the flood was forty days upon the Earth; and the waters increased, and bore up the Ark, and it was lift up above the Earth (*wherever it was that Noah built the Ark, the flood waters reached it, and it began to float*).

18 And the waters prevailed, and were increased greatly upon the Earth; and the Ark went upon the face of the waters (*probably pertains to the fact that the scoffers flattered themselves that it would abate, and never come to extremity; but still it increased, and prevailed*).

19 And the waters prevailed exceedingly

upon the Earth; and all the high hills, that were under the whole heaven, were covered (*those who dwelt upon the tops of the loftiest mountains perished equally with those who lived in the deepest valleys; there was no difference; many who live upon the mountains of morality think themselves secure from the judgment of fire that is now coming, and pity the certain fate of those who live in the depths of vice; but without Christ, all will perish*).

20 Fifteen cubits upward (*above the highest mountains*) did the waters prevail; and the mountains were covered (*many Scholars believe that before the flood the tallest mountain in the world was approximately 10,000 feet or less; "the great deep being broken up" changed much of the topography of the world, making huge canyons and, at the same time, huge mountains*).

21 And all flesh died that moved upon the Earth, both of fowl, and of cattle, and of beast, and of every creeping thing that creeps upon the Earth, and every man (*the fish were not destroyed*):

22 All in whose nostrils was the breath of life, of all that was in the dry land, died (*not one wave of that judgment reached Noah; he was absolutely safe; Noah could not perish because the Ark could not perish; the Ark could not perish because Jehovah was in the Ark; in effect, the Ark was Christ; therefore, God was in Christ, reconciling man unto Himself*).

23 And every living substance was destroyed which was upon the face of the ground, both man, and cattle, and the creeping things, and the fowl of the heaven; and they were destroyed from the Earth: and Noah only remained alive, and they who were with him in the Ark (*only those who are "in Christ" are saved. There are no exceptions [Jn. 3:16]*).

24 And the waters prevailed upon the Earth an hundred and fifty days.

CHAPTER 8
(2348 B.C.)
THE WATERS RECEDE

AND God remembered Noah, and every living thing, and all the cattle that was with him in the Ark (*the idea of God remembering, as given here, does not mean that God had forgotten, or that He could forget; it simply means that He will now give His attention to whatever it is that is being addressed, whether of judgment or of blessing*): and God made a wind to pass over the Earth, and the waters asswaged

(*concerning this, Mackintosh says, "Now, it is thought that Enoch is a figure of the Church, which shall be taken away before human evil reaches its climax, and before the Divine Judgment falls thereon; Noah, on the other hand, is a figure of the remnant of Israel, who shall be brought through the deep waters of affliction, and through the fire of judgment, and led into the full enjoyment of Millennial bliss, in virtue of God's everlasting Covenant"*);

2 The fountains also of the deep and the windows of heaven were stopped, and the rain from heaven was restrained (*the two words in this Verse, "fountains" and "windows," proclaim to us the terrible ferocity of the flood; in fact, it was probably of such ferocity that it literally reshaped much of this world*);

3 And the waters returned from off the Earth continually: and after the end of the hundred and fifty days the waters were abated (*while it took the Lord only one day to handle the water which covered the Earth during the time of creation [Gen. 1:6-8], it took much longer as it regards the flood of Noah's time; while both of these floods were caused by sin, the first by the rebellion of Angels, and the second by the rebellion of men, we find that the rebellion caused by men requires a far greater extent of attention by the Lord; the reason? God gave far greater dominion to Adam, i.e., mankind, than He did the Angelic creation*).

4 And the Ark rested in the seventh month, on the seventeenth day of the month, upon the mountains of Ararat (*notice the following remarkable facts: "On the seventeenth day of Abib (April) the Ark rested on Mount Ararat; on the seventeenth day of Abib the Israelites passed over the Red Sea; on the seventeenth day of Abib, Christ, our Lord, rose again from the dead*).

5 And the waters decreased continually until the tenth month: in the tenth month, on the first day of the month, were the tops of the mountains seen (*from the time that the Ark found a resting place on Ararat until many mountains could be seen were three months*).

6 And it came to pass at the end of forty days, that Noah opened the window of the Ark which he had made (*Noah and God had dwelt together in the Ark for a full solar year, that is, from the seventeenth day of the second month until the twenty-seventh of the corresponding month in the following year — three hundred and sixty-five days*):

7 And he sent forth a raven, which went forth to and fro, until the waters were dried up

from off the Earth (the raven flew away, and did not return).

8 Also he sent forth a dove from him, to see if the waters were abated from off the face of the ground;

9 But the dove found no rest for the sole of her foot, and she returned unto him into the Ark, for the waters were on the face of the whole Earth: then he put forth his hand, and took her, and pulled her in unto him into the Ark (while the tops of some mountains were visible, still, these were a place of death instead of life; the dove could find no resting place in such an area, seeking that which was clean, so she comes back to the Ark).

10 And he stayed yet other seven days; and again he sent forth the dove out of the Ark;

11 And the dove came in to him in the evening; and, lo, in her mouth was an olive leaf plucked off: so Noah knew that the waters were abated from off the Earth.

12 And he stayed yet other seven days; and sent forth the dove; which returned not again unto him any more (the dove didn't return, because this time it no doubt found a suitable resting place, meaning that the waters were abating).

13 And it came to pass in the six hundredth and first year (Noah's age), in the first month, the first day of the month, the waters were dried up from off the Earth: and Noah removed the covering of the Ark, and looked, and, behold, the face of the ground was dry (this refers to its surface only. There would be about 57 or 58 more days, according to the next Verse, making a complete solar year of 365 days, from the time the flood began until it was sufficiently dry).

14 And in the second month, on the seven and twentieth day of the month, was the Earth dried.

LEAVING THE ARK

15 And God spoke unto Noah, saying (we find from this short Scripture that Noah waited on the Lord; he did nothing presumptuously),

16 Go forth of the Ark, you, and your wife, and your sons, and your sons' wives with you (the Lord, being in the Ark with Noah, would tell him "Go forth of the Ark").

17 Bring forth with you every living thing that is with you, of all flesh, both of fowl, and of cattle, and of every creeping thing that creeps upon the Earth; that they may breed

abundantly in the Earth, and be fruitful, and multiply upon the Earth (this proclaims the fact that the flood was universal).

18 And Noah went forth, and his sons, and his wife, and his sons' wives with him:

19 Every beast, every creeping thing, and every fowl, and whatsoever creeps upon the Earth, after their kinds, went forth out of the Ark (the idea is, the animals did not leave the Ark in confusion, or at random, but in orderly fashion, each one sorting to its own kind).

NOAH'S SACRIFICE

20 And Noah built an Altar unto the LORD; and took of every clean beast, and of every clean fowl, and offered Burnt Offerings on the Altar (Civilization, as it sprang from the sons of Noah, has its foundation in the Cross of Christ, i.e., "the Altar").

21 And the LORD smelled a sweet savor (the burning of the Sacrifice was sweet unto the Lord, because it spoke of the Coming Redeemer, Who would lift man out of this morass of evil); and the LORD said in His Heart, I will not again curse the ground any more for man's sake (the "curse" of which God speaks here refers to the fact that He will not again visit the Earth with a flood); for the imagination of man's heart is evil from his youth; neither will I again smite any more every thing living, as I have done (it means that God will take into consideration the results of the Fall, over which man at the time has no control; however, there is a remedy, which is the Altar, i.e., "the Cross").

22 While the Earth remained, seedtime and harvest, and cold and heat, and summer and winter, and day and night shall not cease (the Promise is given here that the seasons of the year will continue forever, because the Earth will remain forever).

CHAPTER 9
(2348 B.C.)
THE COVENANT

AND God blessed Noah and his sons, and said unto them, Be fruitful, and multiply, and replenish the Earth (the Blessing that God gave to Noah was in effect a Covenant; the Covenant concerned the subject matter of the Verse).

2 And the fear of you and the dread of you shall be upon every beast of the Earth, and upon every fowl of the air, upon all that moves

upon the Earth, and upon all the fish of the sea; into your hand are they delivered *(to be delivered into the hand of man refers to the fact that man would be able to tame and reduce certain animals to be of help to him)*.

3 Every moving thing that lives shall be meat for you; even as the green herb have I given you all things. *(All the animals, if so desired, could serve as food, as well as could vegetables; Genesis 1:29 implies that man was exclusively vegetarian before the flood.)*

4 But flesh with the life thereof, which is the blood thereof, shall you not eat *(man is prohibited from eating blood; there were several reasons; however, the main reason was because the shedding of blood in Sacrifices typified the Great Atonement which would be carried out by Christ, in the shedding of His Life's Blood)*.

5 And surely your blood of your lives will I require; at the hand of every beast will I require it, and at the hand of man; at the hand of every man's brother will I require the life of man *(this Verse condemns suicide, as well as homicide; this is a solemn proclamation of the sanctity of human life)*.

6 Whoso sheds man's blood, by man shall his blood be shed *(in this Covenant, we actually have the institution of Government; the Passage speaks of cold-blooded murder; that being the case, the State has the right to take the life of such a murderer)*: for in the Image of God made He man *(capital punishment is not meant by God to serve as a deterrent, but rather to portray the inherent worth of man)*.

7 And you, be ye fruitful, and multiply; bring forth abundantly in the Earth, and multiply therein *(were it not for demonic religion and man's rebellion against God, the Earth could easily care for 100 billion people)*.

8 And God spoke unto Noah, and to his sons with him, saying *(the problem with the world is that it ignores what God has said)*,

9 And I, behold, I establish My Covenant with you, and with your seed after you *(the Covenant that God established with Noah was to be extended to all thereafter; in fact, it still stands)*;

10 And with every living creature that is with you, of the fowl, of the cattle, and of every beast of the Earth with you; from all that go out of the Ark, to every beast of the Earth. *(This Covenant includes all of God's creation on Earth.)*

11 And I will establish My Covenant with you, neither shall all flesh be cut off any more by the waters of a flood; neither shall there any more be a flood to destroy the Earth. *(This Covenant guarantees that the world will never again be destroyed by water.)*

12 And God said, This is the token of the Covenant which I make between Me and you and every living creature that is with you, for perpetual generations *(means that generations of people will continue forever)*:

13 I do set My bow in the cloud, and it shall be for a token of a Covenant between Me and the Earth *(the whole creation rests, as to its exemption from a second deluge, on the eternal stability of God's Covenant, of which the bow is the token)*.

14 And it shall come to pass, when I bring a cloud over the Earth, that the bow shall be seen in the cloud *(the rainbow)*:

15 And I will remember My Covenant, which is between Me and you and every living creature of all flesh; and the waters shall no more become a flood to destroy all flesh *(it doesn't mean that there will not be local floods, but rather a flood to destroy the entirety of the Earth)*.

16 And the bow shall be in the cloud; and I will look upon it, that I may remember the Everlasting Covenant between God and every living creature of all flesh that is upon the Earth *(in this Passage, we are told that this Covenant is everlasting; in the Hebrew, it means "the Covenant of Eternity")*.

17 And God said unto Noah, This is the token of the Covenant, which I have established between Me and all flesh that is upon the Earth *(the Covenant being universal, the sign of the rainbow is also universal)*.

18 And the sons of Noah, who went forth of the Ark, were Shem, and Ham, and Japheth: and Ham is the father of Canaan. *(The entirety of the population of the Earth, and for all time since the flood, are descendants of Shem, Ham, and Japheth; "Canaan" is mentioned because his lineage will prove to be bitter enemies of Israel about 800 years into the future.)*

19 These are the three sons of Noah: and of them was the whole Earth overspread *(this means that every single person on the Earth died in the flood, with the exception of this family)*.

NOAH'S DRUNKENNESS

20 And Noah began to be an husbandman, and he planted a vineyard:

21 And he drank of the wine, and was drunken; and he was uncovered within his tent. *(This is the first mention of wine in the Bible,*

or any type of intoxicating beverage. Inasmuch as the first mention of intoxicating beverage in the Bible reveals such a shameful episode, we cannot help but garner from this illustration, as given by the Holy Spirit concerning Noah, the warning against alcohol taught here.)

22 And Ham, the father of Canaan, saw the nakedness of his father, and told his two brethren without *(sin is like leaven; it always spreads; Noah not only gets drunk, but now pulls off his clothes, and does so intentionally; there is a form of insanity about sin).*

23 And Shem and Japheth took a garment, and laid it upon both their shoulders, and went backward, and covered the nakedness of their father; and their faces were backward, and they saw not their father's nakedness *(a lack of love exposes sin, while the Love of God covers sin, but without condoning it).*

24 And Noah awoke from his wine, and knew what his younger son had done unto him *(there are some Scholars who believe that either Ham or Canaan, and more likely Canaan, committed an act of homosexuality on the Patriarch; while there is no concrete proof of such, there is definitely some indication in that direction).*

THE CURSE ON CANAAN

25 And he said, Cursed be Canaan; a servant of servants shall he be unto his brethren. *(What was this curse? It had absolutely nothing to do with the skin of some people being black. In fact, all the descendants of Ham and Canaan were not black; some were white, and we speak of those who occupied the land of Canaan. The evidence is, it was only upon those, and because they opposed Israel, hence the statement being "Cursed be Canaan." Even then, Canaanites who placed their faith in God could escape it. Rahab, a Canaanite and a harlot, is an excellent example. She placed her faith in God and after a period of purification, was brought into Israel's camp. She married an Israelite, and became an ancestress of David, and even the greater Son of David, the Lord Jesus Christ [Josh. 6:25; Mat. 1:5; Heb. 11:31].)*

26 And he said, Blessed be the LORD God of Shem *(through Shem would come the Jewish people, who would give the world the Word of God and, as well, would bring forth the Messiah, the Saviour of the world);* and Canaan shall be his servant *(the Canaanites in Israel were defeated by David, and became the servants of Israel).*

27 God shall enlarge Japheth, and he shall dwell in the tents of Shem *(Israel, the descendants of Shem, would reject Christ, while the descendants of Japheth would accept Him, which means that the Blessing intended for Shem, i.e., Israel, would instead go to the descendants of Japheth, i.e., the Gentiles);* and Canaan shall be his servant. *(The descendants of Canaan continue unto this hour [2003], in a sense, to be the servants of Japheth. For instance, the descendants of Canaan, wherever they might be, in a sense, answer to the United States, which part of the population are descendants of Japheth.)*

28 And Noah lived after the flood three hundred and fifty years.

29 And all the days of Noah were nine hundred and fifty years: and he died. *(This means that Noah lived almost to the birth of Abraham, and was thus, in all probability, a witness of the building of the Tower of Babel, and of the consequent dispersion of mankind.)*

CHAPTER 10
(2218 B.C.)
THE DESCENDANTS OF
THE SONS OF NOAH

NOW these are the generations of the sons of Noah, Shem, Ham, and Japheth: and unto them were sons born after the flood. *(The order was Shem, Ham, and Japheth; however, the order is now reversed, with Japheth, as we shall see, being first, because of his ascendancy.)*

THE SONS OF JAPHETH

2 The sons of Japheth; Gomer, and Magog, and Madai, and Javan, and Tubal, and Meshech, and Tiras.

3 And the sons of Gomer; Ashkenaz, and Riphath, and Togarmah.

4 And the sons of Javan; Elishah, and Tarshish, Kittim, and Dodanim.

5 By these were the Isles *(borders)* of the Gentiles divided in their lands; every one after his tongue, after their families, in their nations. *(This is the first mention of the word "Gentiles" in the Bible. Originally it was a general term for "nations," but gradually acquired a restricted sense by usage. It ultimately came to apply to all nations of the world, and all people, with the exception of the Jews. This Chapter explains the origin of nations.)*

THE SONS OF HAM

6 And the sons of Ham; Cush, and Mizraim,

and Phut, and Canaan.

7 And the sons of Cush; Seba and Havilah, and Sabtah, and Raamah, and Sabtechah: and the sons of Raamah; Sheba, and Dedan.

8 And Cush begat Nimrod: he began to be a mighty one in the Earth. *(The word "begat" speaks of the lineage. The great figure of this Chapter is Nimrod, and the great city of the Chapter is Babylon. He and his city foreshadow the coming Antichrist and his city. He may be assumed to have counseled and built the Tower of Babel of the next Chapter. He led the first organized rebellion against God.)*

9 He was a mighty hunter before the LORD *(has nothing to do with hunting animals, but rather refers to opposition to the Lord)*: wherefore it is said, Even as Nimrod the mighty hunter before the LORD. *(As stated, Nimrod instituted the first organized rebellion against the Lord, and thereby the ways of the Lord, and thereby those who followed the Lord. He "hunted" them down, possibly even killing those who worshipped Jehovah; consequently, Babylon has always stood for every false religion, every false doctrine, and every false way. That's why it is referred to as "the great whore . . . the mother of harlots and abominations of the Earth" [Rev. 17:1, 5].)*

10 And the beginning of his kingdom was Babel *(Babylon: Nimrod founded that city)*, and Erech, and Accad, and Calneh, in the land of Shinar.

11 Out of that land went forth Asshur, and built Nineveh, and the city Rehoboth, and Calah *(should be translated "out of that land went forth Nimrod in Assyria and built Nineveh," which means he founded both Babylon and Nineveh; Asshur was the son of Shem, and not Ham)*,

12 And Resen between Nineveh and Calah: the same is a great city.

13 And Mizraim begat Ludim, and Anamim, and Lehabim, and Naphtuhim,

14 And Pathrusim, and Casluhim, (out of whom came Philistim,) and Caphtorim.

15 And Canaan begat Sidon his firstborn, and Heth,

16 And the Jebusite, and the Amorite, and the Girgasite,

17 And the Hivite, and the Arkite, and Sinite,

18 And the Arvadite, and the Zemarite, and the Hamathite: and afterward were the families of the Canaanites spread abroad. *(The tribes listed in Verses 16 through 18 occupied the Land of Canaan, and were the greatest nemeses to Israel upon her attempts to conquer the land.*

These are the names read often in your Bible, as they refer to opposition against the people of God. This was planned by Satan, no doubt, from the time of Noah.)

19 And the border of the Canaanites was from Sidon, as you come to Gerar, unto Gaza; as you go, unto Sodom, and Gomorrah, and Admah, and Zeboim, even unto Lasha.

20 These are the sons of Ham, after their families, after their tongues, in their countries, and in their nations. *(Satan will do his best to place the enemies of your soul within your promised possession, just as he ultimately placed these enemies in the Land of Israel, who greatly opposed the people of God.)*

THE SONS OF SHEM

21 Unto Shem also, the father of all the children of Eber, the brother of Japheth the elder, even to him were children born.

22 The children of Shem; Elam, and Asshur, and Arphaxad, and Lud, and Aram.

23 And the children of Aram; Uz, and Hul, and Gether, and Mash.

24 And Arphaxad begat Salah; and Salah begat Eber.

25 And unto Eber were born two sons: the name of one was Peleg; for in his days was the Earth divided; and his brother's name was Joktan. *(Shem was in the lineage of the Promised Seed, so out of Shem ultimately sprang Jesus, the Plant of Renown [Ezek. 34:29; Lk. 3:36]. The Earth being divided in the days of Peleg refers to the time of the Tower of Babel, and the confusion of the languages by God. The name "Peleg" means "division." It refers here to language being divided, rather than land being divided.)*

26 And Joktan begat Almodad, and Sheleph, and Hazarmaveth, and Jerah,

27 And the Hadoram, and Uzal, and Diklah,

28 And Obal, and Abimael, and Sheba,

29 And Ophir, and Havilah, and Jobab: all these were the sons of Joktan.

30 And their dwelling was from Mesha, as you go unto Sephar a mount of the east.

31 These are the sons of Shem, after their families, after their tongues, in their lands, after their nations.

32 These are the families of the sons of Noah, after their generations, in their nations: and by these were the nations divided in the Earth after the flood. *(All the nations of the world sprang from the three sons of Noah, Japheth, Ham, and Shem. As stated, the "sons*

ISBN 0-9769530-3-X

08-401
WWP 1
COPYRIGHT © 2006
Published by, and the sole property of,
JIMMY SWAGGART MINISTRIES, BATON ROUGE, LA

HOLY BIBLE

Containing the Old and New Testaments
Authorized King James Version

—

1611 Elizabethan English is updated in some cases
to reflect present terminology, without changing
the true meaning of the word

THE EXPOSITOR'S STUDY BIBLE
GIANT PRINT EDITION

Translated out of the original tongues and with
previous translations diligently
compared and revised.

The exclusive comments following each Verse of the
sixty-six Books of the Bible were authored by
Evangelist Jimmy Swaggart.

Designed to help anyone who wants to understand
the Bible better and enjoy it more, the expositor's
notes are sure to be a benefit to the Bible study of
every person who has a hunger for God's Word.

JIMMY SWAGGART MINISTRIES
P.O. Box 262550
Baton Rouge, Louisiana 70826-2550
Website: www.jsm.org

of Shem" make up the Semitic people of the world, constituting mostly the Jews and the Arabs; however, the Jews do not recognize the Arabs in this capacity, concluding them to be Gentiles. As well, from this line, "the sons of Shem," would come the Messiah, the Saviour of the world, the Redeemer of mankind. It is ironic that even though the Redeemer came from this line, He is not now recognized as such by the far greater number of this lineage.)

CHAPTER 11
(2247 B.C.)
THE TOWER OF BABEL

AND the whole Earth was of one language, and of one speech *(before the flood and immediately after the flood, there was only one language on the face of the Earth; even though we have no way of knowing specifically, that language was probably Hebrew).*

2 And it came to pass, as they journeyed from the east *(doesn't refer to every single person, but rather that a great group went in that direction, more than likely led by Nimrod; the phrase, "from the east," should have been translated "in the east"),* that they found a plain in the land of Shinar; and they dwelt there. *(This prince, Nimrod, and his city, Babylon, and the plain on which it was erected, Shinar, all claim attention. They represent Satan's efforts, using man as his agent, to oppose and destroy God's Plans. God has His Prince and His City; so has Satan. And these opposing princes with their cities occupy most of the pages of the Bible — the closing pages of the Book revealing the triumph of Immanuel and Jerusalem over the Antichrist and Babylon.)*

3 And they said one to another, Go to, let us make brick, and burn them thoroughly. And they had brick for stone, and slime had they for morter *(considering the materials with which they were to use, they definitely did not plan for this city and tower to be temporary).*

4 And they said, Go to, let us build us a city and a tower, whose top may reach unto heaven *(probably signifies the worship of the Zodiac, i.e., "the planetary bodies");* and let us make us a name, lest we be scattered abroad upon the face of the whole Earth. *("They said" marks the undeniable evil of the human heart. They had no regard for what God wanted. In this one Verse, we find the seedbed of all rebellion against God, whether then or now! In fact, this was the very first organized rebellion against God. The*

Lord had told Noah and his sons to "be fruitful, multiply, and replenish the Earth" [9:1]. Now, the followers of Nimrod are doing the very opposite. The Lord wanted mankind to be scattered over the Earth, but these rebels were determined to defy what God desired.)

5 And the LORD came down to see the city and the tower, which the children of men built *(men rule, but God overrules).*

6 And the LORD said, Behold, the people is one, and they have all one language *(which was actually the Will of God);* and this they begin to do *(to rebel against God)*: and now nothing will be restrained from them, which they have imagined to do *(in other words, their rebellion will only intensify).*

7 Go to, let Us go down, and there confound their language, that they may not understand one another's speech. *(The pronoun "Us", as it regards the Lord, proclaims the Trinity; there is one God, but manifest in three Persons, "God the Father, God the Son, and God the Holy Spirit." At least a hundred or more languages were here introduced, which made it impossible for these rebels to function together with any type of cohesion.)*

8 So the LORD scattered them abroad from thence upon the face of all the Earth *(those who spoke the same language banded together and went elsewhere)*: and they left off to build the city *(there is some evidence that they finished the tower, but not the city).*

9 Therefore is the name of it called Babel *(means "confusion;" "Babel" is also the Hebrew name for "Babylon;" the tower of Babel and the city itself, for that matter, had their origin in deliberate, determined, enthusiastic, exalting hostility to the Divine purpose, that they should spread themselves abroad upon the face of the whole Earth; and herein lies the essence of all rebellion: whatever thought, counsel, or word derives its inspiration, be it only in an infinitesimal degree, from antagonism to the Mind of God, that is sin);* because the LORD did there confound the language of all the Earth: and from thence did the LORD scatter them abroad upon the face of all the Earth. *(As stated, men rule, but God overrules!)*

THE GENERATIONS OF SHEM

10 These are the generations of Shem: Shem was an hundred years old, and begat Arphaxad two years after the flood:

11 And Shem lived after he begat Arphaxad

five hundred years, and begat sons and daughters.

12 And Arphaxad lived five and thirty years, and begat Salah:

13 And Arphaxad lived after he begat Salah four hundred and three years, and begat sons and daughters.

14 And Salah lived thirty years, and begat Eber:

15 And Salah lived after he begat Eber four hundred and three years, and begat sons and daughters.

16 And Eber lived four and thirty years, and begat Peleg:

17 And Eber lived after he begat Peleg four hundred and thirty years, and begat sons and daughters.

18 And Peleg lived thirty years, and begat Reu:

19 And Peleg lived after he begat Reu two hundred and nine years, and begat sons and daughters.

20 And Reu lived two and thirty years, and begat Serug:

21 And Reu lived after he begat Serug two hundred and seven years, and begat sons and daughters.

22 And Serug lived thirty years, and begat Nahor:

23 And Serug lived after he begat Nahor two hundred years, and begat sons and daughters.

24 And Nahor lived nine and twenty years, and begat Terah:

25 And Nahor lived after he begat Terah an hundred and nineteen years, and begat sons and daughters.

26 And Terah lived seventy years, and begat Abram, Nahor, and Haran. *(The generations now pick up again with Shem, because through his lineage the Son of God would be born into the world; however, it stops here with Abraham, and for a specific reason. It was to this man that the Lord gave the meaning of Justification by Faith. Regarding spiritual things, this was a great step forward.)*

THE DESCENDANTS OF TERAH

27 Now these are the generations of Terah: Terah begat Abram, Nahor, and Haran; and Haran begat Lot.

28 And Haran died before his father Terah in the land of his nativity, in Ur of the Chaldees.

29 And Abram *(Abraham)* and Nahor took them wives: the name of Abram's wife was Sarai; and the name of Nahor's wife, Milcah, the daughter of Haran, the father of Milcah, and the father of Iscah.

30 But Sarai was barren; she had no child. *(Abraham now comes into view, and will prove to be one of the greatest men of God who ever lived. Even though Sarah was barren, the Lord, years later, even when she was 90 years of age, would rectify that problem. In fact, from the loins of Abraham and the womb of Sarah would come the Jewish people, raised up for the express purpose of giving the world the Word of God and, as well, serving, one might say, as the womb of the Messiah.)*

TERAH MOVES FROM UR TO HARAN

31 And Terah took Abram his son, and Lot the son of Haran his son's son, and Sarai his daughter in law, his son Abram's wife; and they went forth with them from Ur of the Chaldees, to go into the land of Canaan; and they came unto Haran, and dwelt there.

32 And the days of Terah were two hundred and five years: and Terah died in Haran. *(With the entire family leaving Ur of the Chaldees, and journeying toward Canaan, we know that by now Abraham has had the great Revelation from God. How this Revelation came to him, we aren't told! The entire family goes with Abraham, which seems to not have been the Will of God.)*

CHAPTER 12
(1921 B.C.)
THE ABRAHAMIC COVENANT

NOW the LORD had said unto Abram *(referring to the Revelation which had been given to the Patriarch a short time before; this Chapter is very important, for it records the first steps of this great Believer in the path of Faith)*, Get thee out of your country *(separation)*, and from your kindred *(separation)*, and from your father's house *(separation)*, unto a land that I will show you *(refers to the fact that Abraham had no choice in the matter; he was to receive his orders from the Lord, and go where those orders led him)*:

2 And I will make of you a great nation *(the nation which God made of Abraham has changed the world, and exists even unto this hour; in fact, this nation "Israel" still has a great part to play, which will take place in the coming Kingdom*

Age), **and I will bless you, and make your name great** *(according to Scripture, "to bless" means "to increase;" the builders of the Tower of Babel sought to "make us a name," whereas God took this man, who forsook all, and "made his name great")*; **and you shall be a blessing:** *(Concerns itself with the greatest blessing of all. It is the glory of Abraham's Faith. God would give this man the meaning of Salvation, which is "Justification by Faith," which would come about through the Lord Jesus Christ, and what Christ would do on the Cross. Concerning this, Jesus said of Abraham, "Your father Abraham rejoiced to see My day: and he saw it, and was glad" [Jn. 8:56].)*

3 And I will bless them who bless you *(to bless Israel, or any Believer, for that matter, guarantees the Blessings of God)*, **and curse him who curses you** *(to curse Israel, or any Believer, guarantees that one will be cursed by God)*: **and in you shall all families of the Earth be blessed.** *(It speaks of Israel, which sprang from the loins of Abraham and the womb of Sarah, giving the world the Word of God and, more particularly, bringing the Messiah into the world. Through Christ, every family in the world who desires blessing from God can have that Blessing, i.e., "Justification by Faith.")*

4 So Abram departed, as the LORD had spoken unto him; *(this was his first surrender; there were seven in all: 1. He surrenders here his native land; 2. He surrenders his family; 3. He then surrenders the vale of the Jordan; 4. He then surrenders the riches of Sodom; 5. He surrenders self; 6. He then surrenders Ishmael; and lastly, 7. He surrenders Isaac; each painful surrender was followed by increased spiritual wealth)*; **and Lot went with him: and Abram was seventy and five years old when he departed out of Haran** *(the Holy Spirit notes Abraham's age upon his departure, signifying that the revelation may have come several years earlier)*.

5 And Abram took Sarai his wife, and Lot his brother's son, and all their substance that they had gathered, and the souls that they had gotten in Haran; and they went forth to go into the land of Canaan; and into the land of Canaan they came. *(From Haran to Canaan was approximately 350 miles. Abraham had 318 trained men with him [14:14], meaning that they were trained to fight as soldiers. In fact, there may have been as many as a thousand people in this entourage.)*

6 And Abram passed through the land unto the place of Sichem, unto the plain of Moreh. And the Canaanite was then in the land. *(Abraham finds the hateful, impure, and hostile Canaanite in God's land. That being an example, the young Believer expects after conversion to find nothing in his nature hostile to Christ, but is distressed and perplexed very soon to painfully learn that, alas, the Canaanite is in the land, and that he is now commencing a lifelong battle with what the New Testament calls "the flesh." — Williams)*

7 And the LORD appeared unto Abram *(though the hostile Canaanite was in the land, the Lord was there as well)*, **and said, Unto your seed will I give this land** *(the "seed" through Isaac, and not Ishmael; Satan has contested this Promise from the very beginning, with the struggle continuing even unto this hour, as it regards Israel and the Palestinians)*: **and there built he an Altar unto the LORD, Who appeared unto him.** *(The "Altar" and its Sacrifice represented the Lord Jesus Christ, and the price He would pay on the Cross in order to redeem humanity. The Promises of God to Abraham, as are all the Promises of God, are built upon the foundation of the "Altar," i.e., "the Cross.")*

8 And he removed from thence unto a mountain on the east of Beth-el, and pitched his tent, having Beth-el on the west, and Hai on the east *("Beth-el" means "House of God," while "Hai" means "the heap of ruins")*: **and there he built an Altar unto the LORD, and called upon the Name of the LORD.** *(The "Altar" and the "tent" give us the two great features of Abraham's character. He was a worshipper of God, hence the Cross, and a stranger in the world, hence the tent. Our prayers are based upon our Faith in Christ and what Christ has done for us at the Cross, of which the Altar was a Type.)*

9 And Abram journeyed, going on still toward the south *("south" was toward Egypt, which direction Abraham should not have gone)*.

ABRAM'S SOJOURN IN EGYPT

10 And there was a famine in the land *(a famine in God's land? it was allowed by the Lord as a test of Faith, as everything for the Believer is a test of Faith)*: **and Abram went down into Egypt to sojourn there** *(the Lord didn't call Abram to Egypt, but rather to Canaan; better to starve in Canaan, than to live in luxury in Egypt)*; **for the famine was grievous in the land.**

11 And it came to pass, when he was come

near to enter into Egypt (*it is not possible to go into Egypt, spiritually speaking, without partaking of Egypt*), that he said unto Sarai his wife, Behold now, I know that you are a fair woman to look upon (*now begins the repulsive picture of contemptible and abject cowardice*):

12 Therefore it shall come to pass, when the Egyptians shall see you, that they shall say, This is his wife: and they will kill me, but they will save you alive.

13 Say, I pray you, you are my sister: that it may be well with me for your sake; and my soul shall live because of you. (*God had a Plan: that Plan was for Abraham and Sarah to bring a son into the world, through whom ultimately the Messiah, the Redeemer of the world, would come. Satan had a plan: that plan was to foil the Plan of God, and to do so through the weakness of Abraham. Abraham had a plan: but Abraham's plan is not now the Plan of God, but is rather a plan of deception, which God can never honor.*)

ABRAM DECEIVES PHARAOH

14 And it came to pass, that, when Abram was come into Egypt, the Egyptians beheld the woman that she was very fair.

15 The princes also of Pharaoh saw her, and commended her before Pharaoh: and the woman was taken into Pharaoh's house. (*"Pharaoh" was the official title of the kings of Egypt. The particular Monarch who occupied the Egyptian throne at the time of Abraham's arrival is believed to have been "Necao;" with some thinking he may have been "Ramessemenes." Sarah is taken into Pharaoh's house in order that she might become the mother of a child by the Egyptian king, thus defeating the Messianic Promise made to Abraham. This was Satan's plan.*)

16 And he (*Pharaoh*) entreated Abram well for her sake: and he had sheep, and oxen, and he asses, and menservants, and maidservants, and she asses, and camels (*all of these Pharaoh gave to Abraham; the riches he acquired in Egypt were nothing by comparison to the riches he stood to lose*).

17 And the LORD plagued Pharaoh and his house with great plagues because of Sarai Abram's wife. (*In Canaan, Abraham was a blessing; in the land of Egypt, he is a curse. In the path of faith, the Christian is likewise a blessing to the world, but in the path of self-will, a curse.*)

18 And Pharaoh called Abram and said (*in what manner Pharaoh came to know that the plagues falling on his house were because of Sarah, we aren't told; Sarah was blameless in this, the fault being that of Abraham*), What is this that you have done unto me? why did you not tell me that she was your wife? (*Abraham had told those who were representing Pharaoh that Sarah was his sister. In fact, this was a half-truth. She was the daughter of his father, but not the daughter of his mother [20:12]. But because he intended to deceive, God looked at this episode as a "lie."*)

19 Why did you say, She is my sister? so I might have taken her to me to wife: now therefore behold your wife, take her, and go your way (*because of Abraham's deception, this heathen prince hurries this man of God out of his land as he would chase away a pestilence; it was not Abraham's finest hour*).

20 And Pharaoh commanded his men concerning him (*Abraham*): and they sent him away, and his wife, and all that he had (*the mighty Pharaoh saw the Power of God, even though it was in a negative way; what effect it had on him, other than this which we see in the Scripture, we aren't told*).

CHAPTER 13
(1918 B.C.)
RETURN TO CANAAN

AND Abram went up out of Egypt, he, and his wife, and all that he had, and Lot with him, into (*from*) the south (*if Abraham went "down" into Egypt in 12:10, Grace brings him "up" out of Egypt, as recorded in this Verse; they left the south to go north, back to Canaan*).

2 And Abram was very rich in cattle, in silver, and in gold (*these were the blessings of God, but it did not make up for his lapse of Faith*).

3 And he went on his journeys from the south even to Beth-el, unto the place where his tent had been at the beginning, between Beth-el and Hai;

4 Unto the place of the Altar, which he had made there at the first: and there Abram called on the Name of the LORD. (*He went back to the mountaintop where his tent had been at the beginning, and there, doubtless with tears and shame, he called by Sacrifice on the Name of the Lord. His backslidings were forgiven, his soul was restored, and he resumes his true life as a pilgrim and a worshipper with his tent and his Altar, neither of which he had in Egypt. Until the Believer comes back to the Cross, of which the Altar is a Type, true Restoration cannot be found.*)

ABRAM AND LOT

5 And Lot also, which went with Abram, had flocks, and herds, and tents *(Lot didn't seem to realize that his blessings were strictly because of Abraham)*.

6 And the land was not able to bear them, that they might dwell together: for their substance was great, so that they could not dwell together. *(Worldly substance generally causes problems, even as it did here. There was strife in the Church. In fact, the "Church" of that day consisted of the families of Abraham and Lot, at least as far as we know.)*

7 And there was a strife between the herdmen of Abram's cattle and the herdmen of Lot's cattle: and the Canaanite and the Perizzite dwelled then in the land. *(The strife no more produced the worldliness in Lot than it produced the faith in Abraham; it only manifested, in the case of each, what was really there. The Canaanite and the Perizzite observed this "strife," as they always observe such. What did they see?)*

8 And Abram said unto Lot, Let there be no strife, I pray you, between me and you, and between my herdmen and your herdmen; for we be Brethren. *(The bent toward Sodom is now beginning to exert itself in the heart of Lot. This "bent" demands its "rights," which demands to be able to choose for itself, which, at the same time, means that it does not trust God to make the choice.)*

9 Is not the whole land before you? separate yourself, I pray you, from me: if you will take the left hand, then I will go to the right; or if you depart to the right hand, then I will go to the left. *(This was a test for both Abraham and Lot.)*

10 And Lot lifted up his eyes, and beheld all the plain of Jordan, that it was well watered everywhere, before the LORD destroyed Sodom and Gomorrah, even as the Garden of the LORD, like the land of Egypt, as you come unto Zoar *("the lust of the eyes")*.

11 Then Lot chose him all the plain of Jordan; and Lot journeyed east: and they separated themselves the one from the other. *(Lot didn't seem to realize, as most don't realize, that he was blessed by God because of Abraham. He should have said to Abraham, that whatever the Patriarch desired, that's what he desired. But instead, he chose for himself, and as the future will prove, chose very unwisely. When he separated himself from Abraham, he separated himself from the Blessing.)*

12 Abram dwelt in the land of Canaan, and Lot dwelt in the cities of the plain, and pitched his tent toward Sodom. *(Slowly but surely, the self-will of Lot takes him toward destruction, even as self-will always does.)*

13 But the men of Sodom were wicked and sinners before the LORD exceedingly *(the Holy Spirit through Moses, as he wrote the text, is very quick to characterize Sodom and its inhabitants)*.

THE COVENANT

14 And the LORD said unto Abram, after that Lot was separated from him *(directly Lot departs, God draws near to Abraham)*, Lift up now your eyes, and look from the place where you are northward, and southward, and eastward, and westward *(the Lord tells Abraham that the Promises are given to him, and not to Lot)*:

15 For all the land which you see, to you will I give it, and to your seed for ever. *(The modern Palestinians should look at the statement, "And to your seed forever.")*

16 And I will make your seed as the dust of the earth *(Sarah is barren, and yet God promises a number beyond comprehension)*: so that if a man can number the dust of the Earth, then shall your seed also be numbered. *(This includes not only the Jews who serve the Lord, but also every Gentile Believer who has ever lived.)*

17 Arise, walk through the land in the length of it and in the breadth of it; for I will give it unto you *(this is a walk of Faith)*.

18 Then Abram removed his tent, and came and dwelt in the plain of Mamre, which is in Hebron, and built there an Altar unto the LORD. *(There was no Altar in Sodom, which Lot chose. All who travel in that direction are in quest of something quite different from that. It is never the worship of God, but the love of the world that leads them thither. Abraham builds an Altar unto the Lord, which means that his Faith is reestablished in Christ, and what Christ will do to redeem humanity by dying on the Cross. Hebron was about 22 miles south of Jerusalem, on the way to Beer-sheba.)*

CHAPTER 14
(1913 B.C.)
ABRAM RESCUES LOT

AND it came to pass in the days of Amraphel king of Shinar, Arioch king of Ellasar, Chedorlaomer king of Elam, and Tidal king of

nations; *(If it is to be noticed, the Spirit of God occupies Himself with the movements of "kings and their armies" only when such movements are in any wise connected with the people of God; otherwise, they are of little significance!)*

2 That these made war with Bera king of Sodom, and with Birsha king of Gomorrah, Shinab king of Admah, and Shemeber king of Zeboiim, and the king of Bela, which is Zoar.

3 All these were joined together in the vale of Siddim, which is the salt sea.

4 Twelve years they served Chedorlaomer, and in the thirteenth year they rebelled. *(These five kings had been ruled by Chedorlaomer for some twelve years, and now they rebel.)*

5 And in the fourteenth year came Chedorlaomer, and the kings who were with him, and smote the Rephaims in Ashteroth Karnaim, and the Zuzims in Ham, and the Emims in Shaveh Kiriathaim,

6 And the Horites in their mount Seir, unto El-paran, which is by the wilderness. *(In the names "Rephaims," "Zuzims," and "Emims," and possibly even the "Horites," we have, once again, the entrance of the giants, which were a product of the union of fallen angels and women [6:4]. Irrespective of their size, "Chedorlaomer" defeated them.)*

7 And they returned, and came to En-mishpat, which is Kadesh, and smote all the country of the Amalekites, and also the Amorites, who dwelt in Hazezon-tamar.

8 And there went out the king of Sodom, and the king of Gomorrah, and the king of Admah, and the king of Zeboiim, and the king of Bela (the same is Zoar;) and they joined battle with them in the vale of Siddim;

9 With Chedorlaomer the king of Elam, and with Tidal king of nations, and Amraphel king of Shinar, and Arioch king of Ellasar; four kings with five. *(We have in Verse 8 the mention of Sodom, where Lot dwelt, and which causes the interest of Jehovah, and points to the reason for all this being included in these Passages. It is obvious from the Text that Lot was not at all in proper relationship with the Lord; however, the Lord, despite that fact, continued to monitor his every move and, in effect, to exercise a form of security and protection for him, despite his having moved in with the Sodomites. Every Believer should understand the significance of all of this. You are bought with a price; that price is the shed Blood of the Lord Jesus Christ.)*

10 And the vale of Siddim was full of slimepits; and the kings of Sodom and Gomorrah fled, and fell there; and they who remained fled to the mountain.

11 And they took all the goods of Sodom and Gomorrah, and all their victuals, and went their way.

12 And they took Lot, Abram's brother's son, who dwelt in Sodom, and his goods, and departed. *(Lot, in his compromised position, could neither deliver Sodom nor himself. The only way to help and bless the world is to live apart from it, in fellowship with God.)*

13 And there came one who had escaped, and told Abram the Hebrew; for he dwelt in the plain of Mamre the Amorite, brother of Eshcol, and brother of Aner: and these were confederate with Abram.

14 And when Abram heard that his brother was taken captive, he armed his trained servants, born in his own house, three hundred and eighteen, and pursued them unto Dan.

15 And he divided himself against them, he and his servants, by night, and smote them, and pursued them unto Hobah, which is on the left hand of Damascus.

16 And he brought back all the goods, and also brought again his brother Lot, and his goods, and the women also, and the people. *(Abraham had little interest in the happenings, had it not been for Lot. He hears that Lot has been taken captive, and sets about to rescue him. Concerning this, Mackintosh says: "The claims of a brother's trouble are answered by the affections of a brother's heart. This is Divine. Genuine Faith, while it always renders us independent, never renders us indifferent. It will never wrap itself up in its fleece while a brother shivers in the cold.")*

MELCHIZEDEK

17 And the king of Sodom went out to meet him *(Abraham)* after his return from the slaughter of Chedorlaomer, and of the kings who were with him, at the valley of Shaveh, which is the king's dale. *(As we shall see here, there is no time so dangerous to the Christian as the morrow after a great spiritual victory.)*

18 And Melchizedek *(this man appears on the scene, who is a King and a Priest and, above all, who is a Type of Christ [Ps. 110:4; Heb. 5:5-6]; some Scholars believe that Melchizedek could actually have been Shem, the son of Noah; Shem was alive at this time, and actually lived for about 60 years more; in fact, some think he died when Abraham was about 150 years of age; his*

name means, "King of Righteousness" and "King of Peace" [Heb. 7:2]) **king of Salem** (Jerusalem) **brought forth bread and wine** (the "bread and wine" symbolize the broken Body and shed Blood of our Lord, which was necessary for the Salvation of mankind [Mat. 26:29; Mk., Chpt. 14; Lk. 22:15; Rom. 8:21]): **and he was the Priest of the Most High God.** (Melchizedek, as a Priest, symbolized the coming Christ, Who is our Great High Priest [Heb. 7:15-17]. David prophesied, about a thousand years after Abraham, "The Lord has sworn, and will not repent, You [Christ] are a Priest forever after the order of Melchizedek" [Ps. 110:4]. Abraham is here introduced to God by a different name than he had previously known, "El Elyon," meaning "Most High God.")

19 **And he** (Melchizedek) **blessed him** (Abraham), **and said, Blessed be Abram of the Most High God, Possessor of heaven and Earth:** (Melchizedek blessing Abraham means that the standing of Melchizedek was greater than that of Abraham. The reason? Melchizedek was a Type of Christ [Heb. 7:4, 7].)

20 **And blessed be the Most High God, Who has delivered your enemies into your hand.** (We find here that Melchizedek did not come forth when Abraham was in pursuit of Chedorlaomer, but when the king of Sodom was in pursuit of Abraham. This makes a great moral difference. Mackintosh says: "A deeper character of communion was needed to meet the deeper character of conflict.") **And he gave him tithes of all.** (This is the first time that "tithes" are mentioned in Scripture. It refers to a tenth part. Abraham paid tithe to Melchizedek, who was a Type of Christ; consequently, Abraham's children, which make up the Church presently, are to continue to pay tithe to those carrying out the Work of God.)

THE TEMPTATION

21 **And the king of Sodom said unto Abram, Give me the persons, and take the goods to yourself.** (Satan will now use the king of Sodom, endeavoring to draw Abraham into his web. He will use money to do so.)

22 **And Abram said to the king of Sodom, I have lift up my hand unto the LORD, the Most High God, the Possessor of Heaven and Earth** (the king of Sodom may have proposed an amalgamation of sorts with Abraham; but the Patriarch proclaims to all concerned that his allegiance is totally and completely to "the LORD,

the Most High God, the Possessor of Heaven and Earth"; in this, he proclaims the fact that he is beholden to no man, but yet gracious to all men),

23 **That I will not take from a thread even to a shoelatchet, and that I will not take any thing that is yours, lest you should say, I have made Abram rich** (the temptation is strong, and in more ways than one; however, the Patriarch passes the test with flying colors):

24 **Save only that which the young men have eaten, and the portion of the men which went with me, Aner, Eshcol, and Mamre; let them take their portion.** (Abraham was held to a much higher standard than those with him. While it was no problem for them to take some of the goods, he could not take even as much as a "shoelatchet." The man of God presently should understand the lesson taught here, that while we are in the world, we are never to be of the world.)

CHAPTER 15
(1913 B.C.)
THE ABRAHAMIC COVENANT

AFTER these things the Word of the LORD came unto Abram in a Vision (this presents one of the four ways which God spoke to individuals in Old Testament times [Num. 12:6-8]: 1. He spoke in Visions [Amos 7:1]; 2. He spoke in dreams [Gen. 41:1; Dan. 2:1]; 3. He revealed Himself by speaking directly to the Prophets "mouth to mouth" [Dan. 12:8]; and, 4. He spoke through His Word [Mat. 4:4]; [the time of the Gospels was still under Old Testament authority]), **saying, Fear not, Abram** (shows that fear had been present; he was afraid he would be killed by enemies before the great Promise of God could come to pass in his life, regarding a son being brought into the world, which was necessary as it regards the coming Incarnation of Christ): **I am your shield** (protection), **and your exceeding great reward** (the Lord was telling the Patriarch that he had his eyes too much on the Promise, instead of the Giver of the Promise; the Lord is to always be looked at as the reward, and then the Promise is sure to come; but too often we get our eyes on the gift instead of the Giver).

2 **And Abram said, LORD God, what will you give me, seeing I go childless, and the steward of my house is this Eliezer of Damascus?** (Seeing I have no child, how can the promise be brought to pass? Can Eliezer be my heir? Even looking toward Eliezer portrays telltale signs of

the flesh, which will come to sad fruition regarding the episode with Hagar.)

3 And Abram said, Behold, to me You have given no seed *(no son)*: and, lo, one born in my house is my heir *(translation: as it stands at the present, "the son of my house," not born of me, is of now my heir; Eliezer is his name).*

4 And, behold, the Word of the LORD came unto him, saying *(the Lord rejects this thinking)*, This shall not be your heir *(not Eliezer)*; but he who shall come forth out of your own bowels shall be your heir *(the Lord can only accept that which He brings forth).*

5 And He *(the Lord)* brought him *(Abraham)* forth abroad, and said, Look now toward Heaven *(the answer is from Heaven, and not otherwise)*, and tell the stars *(count the stars)*, if you be able to number them: and He *(the Lord)* said unto him *(Abraham)*, So shall your seed be. *(While Abraham was worrying about having one son, in fact, the Lord tells him, his seed shall be as the stars of the heavens for multitude. And so it is!)*

6 And he *(Abraham)* believed in the LORD *(exercised Faith, believing what the Lord told him)*; and He *(the Lord)* counted it to him *(Abraham)* for Righteousness. *(This is one of the single most important Scriptures in the entirety of the Word of God. In this simple term, "Abraham believed the Lord," we find the meaning of Justification by Faith. Abraham was saved by Grace through Faith, not by his good works. There is no other way of Salvation anywhere in the Bible. God demands Righteousness; however, it is the Righteousness afforded strictly by Christ and Christ Alone. Anything else is self-righteousness, and totally unacceptable to God. Directly the sinner believes God's testimony about His Beloved Son, he is not only declared righteous, but he is made a son and an heir.)*

THE SACRIFICE

7 And He *(the Lord)* said unto him *(Abraham)*, I am the LORD who brought you out Ur of the Chaldees, to give you this land to inherit it. *(The Lord now reaffirms and, greater yet, expands the Revelation. We find from the examples of the Bible Greats, and our own experiences as well, that the Lord has to constantly reaffirm His Promises to us and, as well, to strengthen our Faith. It doesn't take much to weaken our Faith, despite our claims to the contrary.)*

8 And he said, LORD God, whereby shall I know that I shall inherit it? *(Abraham asks two questions, "What will You give me?" [15:2], and "Whereby shall I know?" Christ is the answer to the first question; the Covenant to the second.)*

9 And He *(the Lord)* said unto him *(to Abraham)*, Take Me an heifer of three years old, and a she goat of three years old, and a ram of three years old, and a turtledove, and a young pigeon. *(The Covenant is founded on Grace, for five living creatures are sacrificed to establish it. Five in the Scripture is the number of Grace; and these five sacrifices set out the fullness of the great Sacrifice of Calvary. – Williams.*

The "heifer" symbolized the Priestly Office of Christ. The "she goat" symbolized His Prophetic Office. The "ram" symbolized His Kingly Office. Jesus was Priest, Prophet, and King. The "turtledove" symbolized Him being led and guided strictly by the Holy Spirit, while the "young pigeon" symbolized Him obeying the Spirit in every capacity.)

10 And he *(Abraham)* took unto him all these, and divided them in the midst, and laid each piece one against another: but the birds divided he not *(the dividing of the three larger animals in Sacrifice, which means their bodies were literally cut in two pieces, with one piece on one side and the other piece on the other, signified the terrible depth of sin which the Cross alone could answer).*

11 And when the fowls came down upon the carcases *(the fowls represent the opposition to the Cross by demon spirits)*, Abram drove them away *(in the Name of Jesus, we have power over demon spirits and, as Abraham, we must "drive them away").*

12 And when the sun was going down, a deep sleep fell upon Abram; and, lo, an horror of great darkness fell upon him *(represents the sufferings which would come to God's people Israel and, as well, to Saints presently).*

13 And He *(the Lord)* said unto Abram, Know of a surety that your seed shall be a stranger in a land that is not theirs, and shall serve them; and they shall afflict them four hundred years *(the four hundred years pertain to the time from the weaning of Isaac to the deliverance of the Children of Israel from Egyptian bondage; the time frame covered the time spent both in Canaan, before it belonged to them, and Egypt, as well)*;

14 And also that nation, whom they shall serve, will I judge *(Egypt)*: and afterward shall they come out with great substance *(much gold and silver, etc., given to them by the Egyptians*

when they left [Ex. 11:1-3]).

15 And you shall go to your fathers in peace *(while Abraham would not see that coming time, nevertheless, it would come; the word "peace" proclaims the fact that what God had called him to do, he will have done);* **you shall be buried in a good old age** *(he was 175 years old when he died).*

16 But in the fourth generation they shall come hither again *(the count began when the sons of Jacob were born; the first generation began with Levi, the second with Kohath, the third being Amram, and "the fourth generation" being Moses; Moses would lead them out of Egyptian bondage):* **for the iniquity of the Amorites is not yet full.** *(As the Book of Job teaches, Job's friends were wrong when they thought that God immediately brings judgment on sinners. In fact, He is patient and long-suffering; however, He is also just, and the judgment will eventually come, if there is no repentance, even as it did on the Amorites.)*

17 And it came to pass, that, when the sun went down, and it was dark *(represents the state of this world, now filled with sin),* **behold a smoking furnace** *(proclaims the furnace of affliction that Israel will have to pass through, and, in fact, every Believer),* **and a burning lamp that passed between those pieces** *(the "burning lamp" passed between the pieces of the Sacrifice, and proclaims the "Word of God"; this presents the Biblical authority of the Cross, which the Sacrifices represented).*

THE COVENANT CONCERNING
THE BOUNDARIES

18 In the same day the LORD made a Covenant with Abram, saying, Unto your seed have I given this land *(Promises based on the Precious Blood of Christ are so absolutely sure that faith can claim them as already possessed; hence, the Believer in the Lord Jesus Christ is neither ashamed nor afraid to say, "I am saved"),* **from the river of Egypt unto the great river, the river Euphrates** *(the actual area promised by God to Abraham goes all the way to the Nile River in Egypt, which includes the Sinai, the Arab Peninsula, much of modern Iraq, most of Syria, and all of Lebanon):*

19 The Kenites, and the Kenizzites, and the Kadmonites,

20 And the Hittites, and the Perizzites, and the Rephaims,

21 And the Amorites, and the Canaanites, and the Girgashites, and the Jebusites. *(Ten nations are listed here, nations which occupied the land of Canaan. Ten is the number of completeness in the Bible, and indicates that the entirety of this land, which would also include other tribes, would be given to Abraham's descendants.)*

CHAPTER 16
(1913 B.C.)
SARAH AND HAGAR

NOW Sarai Abram's wife bore him no children: and she had an handmaid, an Egyptian, whose name was Hagar *(the previous Chapter sets out the faithfulness of God, this Chapter, the faithlessness of Abraham).*

2 And Sarai said unto Abram *(meaning that it wasn't the Lord who spoke to Abraham),* **Behold now, the LORD has restrained me from bearing** *(proclaims the impatience of unbelief; the "flesh" quickly tires of waiting for the Divine promise):* **I pray you, go in unto my maid** *(the path of Faith is full of dignity, the path of unbelief full of degradation);* **it may be that I may obtain children by her** *(tired of waiting, they no longer set their hopes upon God, but rather upon the Egyptian slave girl).* **And Abram hearkened to the voice of Sarai** *(which means that the Patriarch was not hearkening to the Voice of the Lord).*

3 And Sarai Abram's wife took Hagar her maid the Egyptian *(the Epistle to the Galatians declares that Sarah and Hagar represent the two principles of Law and Grace; Hagar represents salvation by works; Sarah Salvation by Faith; these principles are opposed to one another; Ishmael is born as the result of man's planning and energy; Isaac is born as the result of God's planning and energy; in the birth of Ishmael, God had nothing to do with it and, as regards the birth of Isaac, man was dead; so it is today, salvation by works entirely depends on man's capacity to produce them; Salvation by Faith upon God's ability to perform them; under a covenant of works, God stands still in order to see what man can do; under the Covenant of Grace, man stands still to see what God has done; the two covenants are opposed; it must be either Hagar or Sarah; if Hagar, God has nothing to do with it; if Sarah, man has nothing to do with it — Williams),* **after Abram had dwelt ten years in the land of Canaan, and gave her to her husband Abram to be his wife.** *(As stated, ten being the number of completion, is it possible*

that, at this time, God had planned to bring forth Isaac? Or better yet, how much do our failures of faith hinder in our lives that which God desires to do? Or worse still, how much does it delay us with what He desires to do?)

4 And he *(Abraham)* went in unto Hagar, and she conceived: and when she saw that she had conceived, her mistress was despised in her eyes *(she began to act unkindly toward Sarah, actually with contempt!).*

5 And Sarai said unto Abram, My wrong be upon you *(Abraham and Sarah think that, by their clever plan, they can hasten and bring to pass the Divine Promise; the result is misery; he succeeds in his plan, Ishmael is born; but better were it for Abraham and the world had he never been born! It is disastrous when the self-will plans of the Christian succeed)*: I have given my maid into your bosom; and when she saw that she had conceived, I was despised in her eyes: the LORD judge between me and you. *(Sarah now sees her wrong, but too late! Works of the flesh, and this definitely was a work of the flesh, always bring on dissension.)*

6 But Abram said unto Sarai, Behold, your maid is in your hand; do to her as it pleases you. And when Sarai dealt hardly with her, she fled from her face *(the Scripture doesn't tell us what Sarah did).*

THE ANGEL

7 And the Angel of the LORD found her by a fountain of water in the wilderness, by the fountain in the way to Shur *(every evidence is, this "Angel of the Lord" is none other than a pre-incarnate appearance of the Lord Jesus Christ).*

8 And He said, Hagar, Sarai's maid, from where did you come? and where will you go? And she said, I flee from the face of my mistress Sarai.

9 And the Angel of the LORD said unto her, Return to your mistress, and submit yourself under her hands *(had she not obeyed, she would no doubt have died in the wilderness).*

10 And the Angel of the LORD said unto her, I will multiply your seed exceedingly, that it shall not be numbered for multitude. *(However, the Lord said nothing about Faith, because there was no faith in the heart of Hagar, and neither would there be any in the heart of her son, Ishmael.)*

11 And the Angel of the LORD said unto her, Behold, you are with child, and you shall bear a son, and shall call his name Ishmael; because the LORD has heard your affliction. *(The fault of her situation did not belong with Hagar, but rather with Abraham and Sarah; however, she ultimately forfeited what the Lord could have done for her by opposing His Plan, which was Isaac. "Ishmael" means "God hears;" however, it has nothing to do with Ishmael, but rather the plight of Hagar.)*

12 And he will be a wild man; his hand will be against every man, and every man's hand against him; and he shall dwell in the presence of all his brethren. *(These predictions describe the Arab people perfectly. They cannot get along with anyone in the world, and they cannot even get along among themselves. The descendants of Ishmael dwell in the presence of all his brethren [Israel], but do not subdue them and, in fact, never will subdue them!)*

13 And she called the name of the LORD Who spoke unto her *(Hagar recognized that the Angel was, in fact, the Lord, actually the God of Abraham)*, your God sees me: for she said, Have I also here looked after Him Who sees me? *(Hagar gave the name to the Lord of "El Roi," which means, "You are a God Who permits Himself to be seen." As is obvious, she truly had a wonderful Revelation, but, sadly and regrettably, her self-will overrode her faith. She wanted her son, Ishmael, to be the heir of Promise, but that was not to be. She would even go so far, even as we will see, to try to kill Isaac. And so do all who reject the Cross follow in her footsteps.)*

14 Wherefore the well was called Beer-lahai-roi; behold, it is between Kadesh and Bered. *("Beer-lahai-roi" means "Well of the Living-Seeing God.")*

15 And Hagar bore Abram a son: and Abram called his son's name, which Hagar bore, Ishmael. *(Hagar, without doubt, related to Abraham all that had happened, placed herself under the authority of Sarah, and Abraham was then careful to name the boy what the Lord had said — "Ishmael.")*

ISHMAEL IS BORN

16 And Abram was fourscore and six years old *(86)*, when Hagar bore Ishmael to Abram. *(Abraham would yet have to wait some 14 years before the Promise would be fulfilled. As previously asked, I have to wonder if this lapse of faith did not prolong the waiting period for the Promise to be realized!)*

CHAPTER 17
(1898 B.C.)
THE REVELATION

AND when Abram was ninety years old and nine, the LORD appeared to Abram (*some thirteen years have passed since his last Revelation*), and said unto him, I am the Almighty God (*in the Hebrew is "El Shaddai," which means "Strong so as to overpower;" the Lord is telling the Patriarch that He is able to bring to pass what He has promised*); walk before Me, and be thou perfect (*the Patriarch must be perfect in his Faith; it must not waver as it had done regarding the situation with Hagar, but must rest in Almighty God, Who is able to perform what He has promised*).

2 And I will make My Covenant between Me and you, and will multiply you exceedingly (*the Lord now renews the Covenant with Abraham, which greatly enlarges upon the Promises previously made*).

3 And Abram fell on his face: and God talked with him, saying (*either the Power of God was so great that the Patriarch "fell," or else, he did so out of reverence, which is probably the case*),

ABRAHAM

4 As for Me, behold, My Covenant is with you, and you shall be a father of many nations (*and so he was!*).

5 Neither shall your name any more be called Abram (*which means "exalted father"*), but your name shall be Abraham ("*father of the multitudes*"); for a father of many nations have I made you.

THE COVENANT ENLARGED

6 And I will make you exceeding fruitful, and I will make nations of you, and kings shall come out of you (*He was saying to the Patriarch, and as stated, that He was able, whatever the need*).

7 And I will establish My Covenant between Me and you and your seed after you in their generations for an Everlasting Covenant (*that means this Covenant is valid even to this moment and, in fact, ever will be; the Palestinians should learn that*), to be a God unto you, and to your seed after you (*this Covenant is linked to "Justification by Faith," which means that it is now a part of the New Covenant,* which is also referred to as "The Everlasting Covenant" [Heb. 13:20]*).

8 And I will give unto you, and to your seed after you, the land wherein you are a stranger, all the land of Canaan, for an everlasting possession; and I will be their God (*the Jews, having forfeited their possession through rebellion against God, and especially their rejection of Jesus Christ, have caused a rupture; however, the Covenant still stands, and will come to full bloom in the coming Kingdom Age, which is not long off*).

CIRCUMCISION

9 And God said unto Abraham, you shall keep My Covenant therefore, you, and your seed after you in their generations (*this could well be called a "Covenant of Grace," and as such is everlasting; it is "from" everlasting in the counsels of it, and "to" everlasting in the consequences of it*).

10 This is My Covenant, which you shall keep, between Me and you and your seed after you; Every man child among you shall be circumcised (*this Covenant had only one outward ordinance, and that was Circumcision; the balance was entirely of Faith*).

11 And you shall circumcise the flesh of your foreskin; and it shall be a token of the Covenant between Me and you (*Circumcision, in a sense, is a Type of the Cross; blood is shed and separation is made*).

12 And he who is eight days old shall be circumcised among you, every man child in your generations, he who is born in the house, or, bought with money of any stranger, which is not of your seed (*the little boy baby was not to be circumcised until he was eight days old, because at that time the blood would coagulate; before then, he could bleed to death; as well, every male in the family of Abraham must be circumcised, and later that would include the entirety of the nation of Israel*).

13 He who is born in your house, and he who is bought with your money, must needs be circumcised: and My Covenant shall be in your flesh for an Everlasting Covenant (*this Covenant is everlasting, but only in Christ; under the New Covenant, Paul stated that we are to experience the circumcision of the heart, which is a spiritual work [Phil. 3:3]; under the New Covenant, everything being fulfilled in Christ, of which circumcision was a Type of His Sacrifice, the rite is no longer necessary;*

in fact, it carries no spiritual meaning now whatsoever).

14 And the uncircumcised man child whose flesh of his foreskin is not circumcised, that soul shall be cut off from his people; he has broken My Covenant *(in effect, Israelite men who refused to be circumcised, or mothers who refused to circumcise their baby boys, had broken the Covenant and, if continuing that direction of rebellion, would be eternally lost; it was, and is, the same as disavowing the Cross).*

SARAH

15 And God said unto Abraham, As for Sarai your wife, you shall not call her name Sarai *("my princess," referring to the fact that she was Abraham's princess alone)*, but Sarah shall her name be *(simply means "princess;" the idea is, whereas she was formerly Abraham's princess only, she will now be recognized as a princess generally and, in fact, in a sense, could be referred to as the "mother of the Church").*

16 And I will bless her, and give you a son also of her *(this is the first time in all of God's dealings with Abraham that He had mentioned the fact that the promised son would be of Sarah)*: yes, I will bless her, and she shall be a mother of nations; kings of people shall be of her *(her "blessing" spoke of increase, which includes even the Church and, in a sense, the Lord Jesus Christ).*

17 Then Abraham fell upon his face, and laughed, and said in his heart, Shall a child be born unto him who is an hundred years old *(Abraham's laughter was that of joy [Jn. 8:56]?* and shall Sarah, who is ninety years old, bear *(Paul said of him: "He considered not the deadness of Sarah's womb" [Rom. 4:19])?*

18 And Abraham said unto God, O that Ishmael might live before You! *(Abraham asked the Lord that Ishmael might have some place, and not be completely left out.)*

19 And God said, Sarah your wife shall bear you a son indeed; and you shall call his name Isaac *(the name Isaac means "laughter")*: and I will establish My Covenant with him for an Everlasting Covenant, and with his seed after him. *(The Covenant is to be established with Isaac and not Ishmael. This completely shoots down the contention of the Muslims that Ishmael was the chosen one, unless you don't believe the Bible. Through Isaac the Lord Jesus Christ, the Saviour of mankind, would ultimately come.)*

ISHMAEL

20 And as for Ishmael, I have heard you: Behold, I have blessed him, and will make him fruitful, and will multiply him exceedingly *(the Lord would bless Ishmael, but not as it regards the Covenant)*; twelve princes shall he beget, and I will make him a great nation *(the blessing here pronounced was not because of Ishmael, but because of Abraham, and Abraham alone).*

21 But My Covenant will I establish with Isaac, which Sarah shall bear unto you at this set time in the next year *(so now they know when the child will be born).*

22 And He *(the Lord)* left off talking with him, and God went up from Abraham *(Communion with the Lord is the most profitable exercise there is).*

THE SEALED COVENANT

23 And Abraham took Ishmael his son, and all who were born in his house, and all who were bought with his money *(servants)*, every male among the men of Abraham's house; and circumcised the flesh of their foreskin in the self-same day, as God had said unto him *(the obedience of Abraham in circumcising the entirety of his house, servants and all, should be a lesson to us).*

24 And Abraham was ninety years old and nine, when he was circumcised in the flesh of his foreskin.

25 And Ishmael his son was thirteen years old, when he was circumcised in the flesh of his foreskin *(even though Ishmael was circumcised, he who was born after the flesh was by his natural birth a rebel, even though he may enter in an outward covenant).*

26 In the selfsame day was Abraham circumcised, and Ishmael his son *(two men were circumcised; by that rite both men entered the Covenant; however, only one of the men, Abraham, was saved).*

27 And all the men of his house, born in the house, and bought with money of the stranger, were circumcised with him. *(This one Passage tells us that every single man in the house of Abraham was saved, whether servants, slaves, or family, that is, if they believed. The Epistles to the Romans, to the Galatians, and to the Colossians teach that Christians are circumcised in the Cross of Christ, baptized into the Death of Christ, and raised in the Resurrection of Christ, all of which circumcision was a Type.)*

CHAPTER 18
(1898 B.C.)
HEAVENLY VISITORS

AND the LORD appeared unto him *(Abraham)* in the plains of Mamre: and he sat in the tent door in the heat of the day *(the First Verse of this Chapter confirms the experience of the Christian that a fresh Revelation of the Lord to the soul follows upon obedience to a Divine command — Williams)*;

2 And he lift up his eyes and looked, and, lo, three men stood by Him *(stood by the Lord; these were Angels)*: and when he saw them, he ran to meet them from the tent door, and bowed himself toward the ground *(implies worship, for he knew this was the Lord)*,

3 And said, My LORD, if now I have found favor in Your sight, pass not away, I pray You, from Your servant *(Abraham had found favor in God's sight, but only by and through the Faith which he exhibited)*:

4 Let a little water, I pray You, be fetched, and wash Your feet, and rest yourselves under the tree *(the Lord and the angels did not need such; however, the "washing of the feet" and the "rest" symbolized a spiritual truth; it spoke of the humility which is required on the part of Believers and, as well, the "rest" which the Lord alone can provide)*:

5 And I will fetch a morsel of bread, which will comfort Your hearts *(bread is a Type of the Word of God and, as well, of the Lord Jesus Christ [Jn. 6:35]; Abraham giving the Lord bread, along with His Angelic associates, proclaims what the Lord will do for the whole of humanity and, above all, that He would actually be that bread; this is the "bread" which satisfies all spiritual hunger)*; after that You shall pass on *(but not before I have shown You the dignity and respect You deserve)*: for therefore are You come to Your servant. And they said, So do, as you have said *(the Lord favorably received guarantees the favorable blessing)*.

6 And Abraham hastened into the tent unto Sarah, and said, Make ready quickly three measures of fine meal, knead it, and make cakes upon the hearth *(spiritual activity in the heart of one servant of Christ's stirs up activity in the hearts of other servants)*.

7 And Abraham ran unto the herd, and fetched a calf tender and good, and gave it unto a young man; and he hastened to dress it *(as the calf would be killed, likewise would the Son of God, all of which served as a Type)*.

8 And he took butter, and milk, and the calf which he had dressed, and set it before Them; and he stood by Them under the tree, and They did eat *(Jesus told us that we must eat as well; I speak of the "eating of Christ," which, in effect, speaks of evidencing Faith in Him and what He has done for us at the Cross [Jn. 6:53-58, 63])*.

SARAH

9 And They *(the Lord and the Angels)* said unto him *(Abraham)*, Where is Sarah your wife? And he said, Behold, in the tent *(one of the greatest announcements ever made in human history is now forthcoming)*.

10 And He *(the Lord)* said, I will certainly return unto you according to the time of life *(according to this time next year)*; and, lo, Sarah your wife shall have a son. And Sarah heard it in the tent door, which was behind Him.

11 Now Abraham and Sarah were old and well stricken in age *(Abraham was 100 and Sarah was 90)*; and it ceased to be with Sarah after the manner of women.

12 Therefore Sarah laughed within herself, saying, After I am waxed old shall I have pleasure, my lord *(Abraham)* being old also? *(Unbelief makes men cowards and liars. Sarah laughs with unbelief, and then, through fear, denies the fact. Despite, however, her incredulity, and despite Satan's seeming success in having retarded the birth of a child till it was impossible to nature — despite it all, the mighty words of Grace and Promise are spoken — "Sarah shall have a son!")*

13 And the LORD said unto Abraham, Wherefore did Sarah laugh, saying, Shall I of a surety bear a child, which am old? *(There is in the Scripture the laughter of faith and the laughter of unbelief. Psalm 126:2 fulfills the former, and Matthew 9:24 the latter. Sarah's laughter was that of unbelief.)*

14 Is any thing too hard for the LORD? *(the actual Hebrew says: "Is anything too wonderful for Jehovah?")* At the time appointed I will return unto you, according to the time of life, and Sarah shall have a son.

15 Then Sarah denied, saying, I laughed not *(she lied)*; for she was afraid *(unbelief tenders fear)*. And He said, No; but you did laugh *(the Lord gently rebukes her)*.

SODOM AND GOMORRAH

16 And the men *(the Lord and the Angels)*

rose up from thence, and looked toward Sodom *(it was not a look of Grace, and because of their great sin)*: and Abraham went with them to bring them on the way *(walked a little distance with Them)*.

17 And the LORD said, Shall I hide from Abraham that thing which I do *(the secret of the Lord is with them who fear Him)*;

18 Seeing that Abraham shall surely become a great and mighty nation, and all the nations of the Earth shall be blessed in him? *(Both predictions came through exactly as spoken by the Lord.)*

19 For I know him, that he will command his children and his household after him *(the actual Hebrew says, "For I have known him in order that he may command his sons . . ."),* and they shall keep the way of the LORD, to do justice and judgment *(this is the responsibility of the modern Church as well, a responsibility, incidentally, which by and large has been abrogated)*; that the LORD may bring upon Abraham that which He has spoken of him *(looking back from this present time to the time of Abraham, all have come to pass exactly as the Lord promised)*.

20 And the LORD said, Because the cry of Sodom and Gomorrah is great, and because their sin is very grievous *(the sin of these twin cities had become so great that it threatened contamination of the entirety of that part of the world; consequently, they had to be destroyed; in other words, the Lord had to perform major surgery, just as a surgeon does presently in order to save the patient)*;

21 I will go down now, and see whether they have done altogether according to the cry of it, which is come unto Me; and if not, I will know *(all sin is inherently offensive in the Eyes of the Almighty; but some forms of wickedness are more presumptuously daring or more intrinsically loathsome than others, and of such sort were the sins of Sodom; the phrase, "I will know," doesn't mean that God didn't already know, for He knows all things, past, present, and future; the statement has reference to the Perfect Justice of God; at the Judgment, no one will be able to claim insensitivity or unfairness on the part of God [Rev. 20:11-15])*.

22 And the men *(the two Angels)* turned their faces from thence *(from Abraham)*, and went toward Sodom: but Abraham stood yet before the LORD *(after the Lord explained to Abraham what He was about to do, Abraham would now intercede for Lot)*.

LOT

23 And Abraham drew near, and said, Will You also destroy the righteous with the wicked *(he was thinking of Lot)*?

24 Peradventure there be fifty righteous within the city: will You also destroy and not spare the place for the fifty righteous who are therein *(we find from this narrative how important the righteous are, as it involves the overall scheme of things)*?

25 That be far from You to do after this manner, to slay the righteous with the wicked: and that the righteous should be as the wicked, that be far from You: Shall not the Judge of all the Earth do right? *(We can be confident that the Judge of the Earth shall do right. That Judge is the Lord!)*

26 And the LORD said, If I find in Sodom fifty righteous within the city, then I will spare all the place for their sakes.

27 And Abraham answered and said, Behold now, I have taken upon me to speak unto the LORD, which am but dust and ashes *(we find here the humility of the great Patriarch)*:

28 Peradventure there shall lack five of the fifty righteous: will You destroy all the city for lack of five? And He said, If I find there forty and five, I will not destroy it.

29 And he *(Abraham)* spoke unto Him *(the Lord)* yet again, and said, Peradventure there shall be forty found there. And He said, I will not do it for forty's sake.

30 And he said unto Him, Oh let not the LORD be angry, and I will speak *(I think it can easily be said that the Lord delights in the Believer pressing, as it regards petitions and desires)*: Peradventure there shall thirty be found there. And He said, I will not do it, if I find thirty there.

31 And he said, Behold now, I have taken upon me to speak unto the LORD: Peradventure there shall be twenty found there. And He said, I will not destroy it for twenty's sake.

32 And he said, Oh let not the LORD be angry, and I will speak yet but this once: Peradventure ten shall be found there. And He said, I will not destroy it for ten's sake. *(We are here witnessing true Intercession.)*

33 And the LORD went His way, as soon as He had left communing with Abraham: and Abraham returned unto his place. *(While the Lord now goes His way, He doesn't do so until Abraham ceases his petitioning. Abraham ceased asking before God ceased giving.)*

CHAPTER 19
(1898 B.C.)
TWO ANGELS

AND there came two Angels *(referred to previously as two men)* to Sodom at evening; and Lot sat in the gate of Sodom *(Lot sitting at the gate probably denoted position and authority; he may have even been the mayor of Sodom)*: and Lot seeing them rose up to meet them; and he bowed himself with his face toward the ground *(from this action, it is possible that the two Angels revealed themselves and their mission to Lot at this time)*;

2 And he said, Behold now, my lords, turn in, I pray you, into your servant's house, and tarry all night, and wash your feet, and you shall rise up early, and go on your ways *(as it regards Abraham and Lot, the Lord remained to commune with the Patriarch, while he merely sent His two Angels to Sodom as it regards Lot)*. And they said, No; but we will abide in the street all night *(in fact, the Angels, as we see here, didn't even desire to enter into the house of Lot; what a rebuke!)*.

3 And he *(Lot)* pressed upon them greatly; and they turned in unto him, and entered into his house *(the Angels, on their part, had to be pressed to accept hospitality from the nephew which they at once accepted from the uncle; fellowship with the world hinders and limits communion and makes the soul lethargic)*; and he made them a feast, and did bake unleavened bread, and they did eat *(the "unleavened Bread" speaks of Christ)*.

THE MOB

4 But before they lay down *(retired for the night)*, the men of the city, even the men of Sodom *(homosexuals)*, compassed the house round, both old and young, all the people from every quarter: *(The principle of evil, which the Bible calls "sin," and which has wrought such ruin in human nature, painfully appears in this Chapter. Sodom is the end result of the reprobate mind [Rom. 1:24-28].)*

5 And they called unto Lot, and said unto him, Where are the men which came in to you this night? *(the sin of homosexuality was the primary sin which occasioned the destruction of Sodom and Gomorrah [Jude, Vss. 6-7])* bring them out unto us, that we may know them *(the words "know them" pertained to the loathsomeness of the homosexual act)*.

6 And Lot went out at the door unto them, and shut the door after him *(locked the door to his house, so these depraved men could not enter)*,

7 And said, I pray you, brethren, do not so wickedly *(the Text marks this sin as unspeakably vile, by telling us that they commanded Lot to bring out his guests so that they could seduce them publicly and in the sight of the whole population; they had lost all sense of shame and decency, for they make no attempt at perpetrating this shameful vice in secret)*.

8 Behold now, I have two daughters which have not known man; let me, I pray you, bring them out unto you, and do you to them as is good in your eyes *(wisdom from the lukewarm Believer is always flawed, as is evidenced here)*: only unto these men do nothing; for therefore came they under the shadow of my roof *(we cannot profit by the world and, at the same time, bear effectual testimony against its wickedness)*.

9 And they said, Stand back. And they said again, This one fellow came in to sojourn, and he will needs be a judge *(it seems that Lot, however, had spoken out against these things so often that the men of Sodom accused him of wanting to play the judge)*: now will we deal worse with you, than with them. And they pressed sore upon the man, even Lot, and came near to break the door. *(Due to Abraham having rescued many Sodomites from Chedorlaomer, evidently these homosexuals had declared Lot, the nephew of Abraham, off limits. But now, due to Lot's protection of the two Angels, they are breaking their commitment to him.)*

THE ANGELS

10 But the men *(the two Angels)* put forth their hand *(opened the door and grabbed Lot)*, and pulled Lot into the house to them, and shut to the door *(little did these perverts know as to who these men actually were)*.

11 And they smote the men who were at the door of the house with blindness, both small and great: so that they wearied themselves to find the door *(the word in the Hebrew actually means that they were not totally blind, but that they would not see properly)*.

LOT

12 And the men *(the Angels)* said unto Lot, Have you here any besides? son in law, and your sons, and your daughters, and whatsoever

you have in the city, bring them out of this place *(to attempt to reprove the world's ways, while we profit by association with it, is vanity; thus it was too with Lot's testimony to his sons-in-law)*:

13 For we will destroy this place *(has happened no doubt many times in many places in history past)*, because the cry of them is waxen great before the face of the LORD *(all sin is in God's Face, which will ultimately, if not repented of, end in judgment)*; and the LORD has sent us to destroy it.

THE SONS-IN-LAW

14 And Lot went out, and spoke unto his sons in law, which married his daughters *(which were to marry)*, and said, Up, get you out of this place; for the LORD will destroy this city. But he seemed as one who mocked unto his sons in law *(the nearer the world approaches the end, the more it laughs at the Divine threats pronounced upon the wicked)*.

LOT DELIVERED

15 And when the morning arose, then the Angels hastened Lot, saying, Arise, take your wife, and your two daughters, which are here; lest you be consumed in the iniquity of the city *(as the Angels hastened Lot, likewise the Holy Spirit is hastening the modern Church, as it regards the Rapture)*.

16 And while he *(Lot)* lingered, the men *(the two Angels)* laid hold upon his hand, and upon the hand of his wife, and upon the hand of his two daughters; the LORD being merciful unto him: and they brought him forth, and set him without the city *(the loving patience of the Angels with this unhappy procrastinator was most touching; its cause is revealed in the words, "the LORD being merciful unto him")*.

17 And it came to pass, when they *(the two Angels)* had brought them forth abroad, that he *(one of the Angels)* said, Escape for your life; look not behind you, neither stay you in all the plain; escape to the mountain, lest you be consumed *(God demanded of them a total abandonment in heart and will of the condemned cities)*.

18 And Lot said unto them, Oh, not so, my LORD *(it seems that now Jehovah Himself, though not mentioned, has now appeared upon the scene)*:

19 Behold now, your servant has found grace in Your sight, and You have magnified Your mercy, which You have showed unto me in saving my life; and I cannot escape to the mountain, lest some evil take me, and I die *(the folly of Lot in lingering, and further in preferring his own place of safety to that proposed by the Angels, illustrate the deep unbelief of the heart)*:

20 Behold now, this city is near to flee unto, and it is a little one: Oh, let me escape thither, (is it not a little one?) and my soul shall live *(people do not do stupid things when they are in the Will of God; it's when they are attempting to function in the realm of disobedience that they become foolish in their direction)*.

21 And He *(the Lord)* said unto him, See, I have accepted you concerning this thing also *(his request to go into this little city instead of the mountain)*, that I will not overthrow this city, for the which you have spoken *(it was a prayer that Lot would have wished had never been answered in a positive way; the Believer must always be careful to ask in the Will of God)*.

22 Make haste, escape quickly; for I cannot do any thing till you come out of Sodom. *(The Lord had promised Abraham that Lot would be spared; therefore, destruction could not come to Sodom and Gomorrah until Lot was safely removed; in a sense, this typifies the coming Rapture of the Church; the Judgment of God, which is coming on this world, in fact, cannot come, until the Believers are removed [I Thess. 5:9].)* Therefore the name of the city was called Zoar *(the city which the Lord allowed Lot to enter into)*.

DESTRUCTION

23 The sun was risen upon the Earth when Lot entered into Zoar.

24 Then the LORD rained upon Sodom and upon Gomorrah brimstone and fire from the LORD out of heaven *(the Lord, Whom we now know as God the Son, called judgment from the Lord out of heaven, Whom we now know as God the Father; considering that the Holy Spirit inspired the writing of this, we have here the Trinity)*;

25 And He overthrew those cities, and all the plain, and all the inhabitants of the cities, and that which grew upon the ground *(all the cities of the plain were destroyed, except Zoar; the cause was supernatural, not natural; therefore, this wasn't an earthquake, as some have claimed)*.

LOT'S WIFE

26 But his wife looked back from behind him *(disobeying the Word of the Lord [Vs. 17]; the Hebrew means that "she kept looking back steadily, wistfully, and with desire;" her heart was in Sodom, so her soul was in Sodom, as well; regrettably and sadly, it is now in Hell),* **and she became a pillar of salt** *(Jesus reminded the world of this episode by pointedly saying, "Remember Lot's wife" [Lk. 17:32]).*

ABRAHAM

27 And Abraham got up early in the morning to the place where he stood before the LORD *(indicates that he was in prayer):*

28 And he looked toward Sodom and Gomorrah, and toward all the land of the plain, and beheld, and, lo, the smoke of the country went up as the smoke of a furnace *(these cities were situated at the southern extremity of the Dead Sea; the word "furnace" indicates that this was no ordinary fire, but that the heat was so intense that everything melted, which means there was nothing left).*

29 And it came to pass, when God destroyed the cities of the plain, that God remembered Abraham, and sent Lot out of the midst of the overthrow, when he overthrew the cities in the which Lot dwelt *(the words, "God remembered Abraham," proclaim the fact that Abraham's intercessory petition did not go unanswered; in this case, Abraham was a Type of Christ, serving as a mediator between God and Lot).*

MOAB AND BEN-AMMI

30 And Lot went up out of Zoar, and dwelt in the mountain, and his two daughters with him; for he feared to dwell in Zoar *(having disobeyed the Lord, Lot now lives in fear; he is fearful that God will destroy Zoar as well, so he moves to a nearby mountain):* and he dwelt in a cave, he and his two daughters *(his wealth had once been so great that he and Abraham could not dwell together because of the size of their herds; but now he is living in a cave, with this being his miserable home; wealth or no wealth, there is no profit in going in the direction of Satan).*

31 And the firstborn said unto the younger, Our father is old, and there is not a man in the Earth to come in unto us after the manner of all the Earth *(the preservation of the family line was important in ancient times; since Lot was*

old, and now poor, with all his belongings destroyed along with Sodom, his daughters saw no prospect for marriage; so now, they will commit a monstrous sin):

32 Come, let us make our father drink wine *(the second occasion in the Bible that the word "wine" is used indicating intoxicating beverage, the first occasion being that of Noah [9:20-22]; the only course for the Child of God is total abstinence as it regards any and all intoxicating beverage),* and we will lie with him, that we may preserve seed of our father. *(His own daughters make him drunk, and in his drunkenness, he becomes the instrument of bringing into existence the Ammonites and the Moabites — the determined enemies of the people of God. What a volume of solemn instruction is here!)*

33 And they made their father drink wine that night: and the firstborn went in, and lay with her father; and he perceived not when she lay down, nor when she arose *(this was no drunken orgy, but still, it was a revolting sin; the cause was a lack of faith, as the cause of all sin is a lack of faith).*

34 And it came to pass on the morrow, that the firstborn said unto the younger, Behold, I lay yesternight with my father: let us make him drink wine this night also; and you go in, and lie with him, that we may preserve seed of our father *(the details of this account clearly show that Lot, when he went to the mountain cave, endeavored to escape from his problems, not by carrying them to the Throne of God, where all Believers should carry them, but by drowning them in dissipation).*

35 And they made their father drink wine that night also: and the younger arose, and lay with him; and he perceived not when she lay down, nor when she arose *(considering that these girls had been raised in Sodom, at least for a good part of their lives, it is not strange that the older daughter suggested incest as the only way they could preserve the family line; they had been greatly influenced by the low moral standards of their environment).*

36 Thus were both the daughters of Lot with child by their father *(after this, Lot disappears from sacred history, not even his death being recorded; even though there is no Biblical record, it is believed that Abraham took Lot and his daughters into his home and supported them).*

37 And the firstborn bore a son, and called his name Moab *(means "from my father"):* the same is the father of the Moabites unto this day.

38 And the younger, she also bore a son, and called his name Ben-ammi *(means "son of my people")*: the same is the father of the children of Ammon unto this day *(despite their ignoble beginnings, the Lord showed a concern for them as descendants of Lot [Deut. 2:9, 19], but regrettably, they later became enemies of Israel [I Sam. 14:47; II Ki. 3:5; II Chron. 20:1, 22]).*

CHAPTER 20
(1898 B.C.)
ABRAHAM AND ABIMELECH

AND Abraham journeyed from thence toward the south country, and dwelled between Kadesh and Shur, and sojourned in Gerar. *(The sin and misery that resulted years before from journeying "toward the south country" should have taught him never again to move in that direction. But man, as such, never learns nor can learn spiritual lessons. We will find here that sin is just as hateful in a man of God as in a man of the world, and its guilt is greater. Abraham must have been deeply shocked at the power of unbelief in his nephew Lot, but was he equally shocked at the power of evil in himself, as this Chapter records?)*

2 And Abraham said of Sarah his wife, She is my sister *(Abraham once more forsakes the path of Faith; and, in denying his wife, sinks to a depth of moral degradation that is contemptible in the extreme; we find here that an old sin is an easy sin)*: and Abimelech king of Gerar sent, and took Sarah. *(His fall on this occasion was deeper than the prior one; for he now had the Divine Promise that, within that very year, Sarah should become the mother of a miraculous child. So long as the Christian walks in the path of Faith, he is clothed with dignity and ennobled with courage. But, when directly he leaves that path, he falls lower than even the children of the Evil One.)*

3 But God came to Abimelech in a dream by night, and said to him, Behold, you are but a dead man, for the woman which you have taken; for she is a man's wife. *(If God had not intervened, Abraham's sin would have been disastrous. If it is to be noticed, Sarah is again referred to by the Holy Spirit as Abraham's wife. The "sister" thing was mentioned only by Abraham, and not by the Lord. While she was Abraham's half-sister, still, Abraham's claim to Abimelech was a half-truth, therefore, looked at by God as a lie.)*

4 But Abimelech had not come near her: and he said, LORD, will You slay also a righteous nation? *(The Philistine Prince, already knowing of the destruction of Sodom and Gomorrah, fears that he and his people are in the same destruction, unless the Lord is pacified quickly.)*

5 Said he not unto me, She is my sister? and she, even she herself said, He is my brother: in the integrity of my heart and innocency of my hands have I done this *(in fact, the man was innocent; it was Abraham and Sarah who had done wrong).*

6 And God said unto him in a dream, Yes, I know that you did this in the integrity of your heart; for I also withheld you from sinning against Me: therefore suffered I you not to touch her.

7 Now therefore restore the man his wife; for he is a Prophet, and he shall pray for you, and you shall live: and if you restore her not, know you that you shall surely die, you, and all who are yours. *(All of these facts reveal the unsparing truth, and make it plain, that Abraham, by natural disposition and character, was cowardly and false. He was only noble when energized by faith.)*

8 Therefore Abimelech rose early in the morning, and called all his servants, and told all these things in their ears: and the men were sore afraid *(it is emphasized in this Chapter that natural goodness and integrity, as in the case of Abimelech, do not necessarily make a man a Child of God and, on the other hand, a temporary moral lapse through fear does not unmake the Believer a member of the household of faith).*

9 Then Abimelech called Abraham, and said unto him, What have you done unto us? and what have I offended you, that you have brought on me and on my kingdom a great sin? you have done deeds unto me that ought not to be done. *(It is interesting that this heathen king understood the word "sin," which means that he had some knowledge of God, which was greatly increased after the dream which he had. On the path of Faith, God's people are a blessing to the world; on the path of unbelief, they are a curse.)*

10 And Abimelech said unto Abraham, What did you see, that caused you to do this thing? *(How guilty all of us are in this respect. We as Believers are recipients and projectors of His Light. But how so often what we in fact project is not entirely that which we have received.)*

11 And Abraham said, Because I thought, Surely the fear of God is not in this place; and

they will kill me for my wife's sake *(once the path of faith is abandoned, the judgment of the Child of God becomes faulty)*.

12 And yet indeed she is my sister; she is the daughter of my father, but not the daughter of my mother; and she became my wife *(as stated, Abraham dwells on the fact that Sarah is indeed his half-sister, while the Holy Spirit emphasizes the fact of the lady being his wife [Vss. 2-3, 7])*.

13 And it came to pass, when God caused me to wander from my father's house, that I said unto her, This is your kindness which you shall show unto me; at every place where we shall come, say of me, He is my brother *(this scheme, formulated by Abraham at the very beginning, was not of God, but rather out of his own mind and, therefore, a work of the flesh, which direction always brings trouble, extreme trouble)*.

14 And Abimelech took sheep, and oxen, and menservants, and womenservants, and gave them unto Abraham, and restored him Sarah his wife *(despite the wrongdoing on the part of Abraham, the Lord blessed the Patriarch; he does the same with us oftentimes)*.

15 And Abimelech said, Behold, my land is before you: dwell where it pleases you *(Abimelech had sense enough to realize that the Blessings of God were upon Abraham; consequently, he offers him a place in "his land;" he no doubt experienced great blessings from God because of this act, and so will anyone else who blesses God's children)*.

16 And unto Sarah he said, Behold, I have given your brother a thousand pieces of silver *(by referring to Abraham as her "brother," in effect, this heathen prince is telling her, "Don't do that again; it doesn't become you")*: behold, he is to you a covering of the eyes, unto all who are with you, and with all other: thus she was reproved. *(Abimelech, in effect, is saying, "If you openly claim Abraham as your husband, this, to be sure, will be protection enough for you and, in fact, for the entirety of your clan. It is sad when we, as Believers, have to take reproof from the world. A Divine principle, however, shines forth in this sad Chapter. And that is that God, in His Amazing Grace, is not ashamed to be called the God of a poor, feeble, imperfect, and stumbling man, if there is, despite all the weakness, faith and love in the heart. The Patriarch, by his own faithlessness, has deeply degraded himself so as to be justly rebuked by the heathen prince, yet God, in His faithfulness, clothes him with dignity, and honors him in the presence of Abimelech.)*

17 So Abraham prayed unto God: and God healed Abimelech, and his wife, and his maidservants; and they bore children.

18 For the LORD had fast closed up all the wombs of the house of Abimelech, because of Sarah Abraham's wife. *(The closing Verses of this Chapter contain a solemn lesson for all Believers. Because of Abraham's abandonment of the path of Faith, and for as long as he failed to walk in that path, there were no children born to Abimelech and to his household. This physical fact illustrates a spiritual reality in Christian experience. It is not unreasonable to learn from all this that the birth of spiritual children in the Gospel is hindered or delayed by the inconsistent conduct of Believers — Williams.)*

CHAPTER 21
(1892 B.C.)
THE BIRTH OF ISAAC

AND the LORD visited Sarah as He had said, and the LORD did unto Sarah as He had spoken *(despite all of Satan's hindrances, Isaac, the progenitor and Type of the Messiah, is born)*.

2 For Sarah conceived, and bore Abraham a son in his old age, at the set time of which God had spoken to him. *(Referring back to the past Chapter, if it be objected that this whole occurrence is incredible, because no heathen prince would desire to marry a woman upwards of ninety years of age, or to conceive such a passion for her that to secure her he would murder her husband — the very fate which Abraham feared for himself — it may be replied that God must have miraculously renewed her youth, so that she became sufficiently youthful in appearance to suitably be desirable. Three times in these first two verses, the clause points to the supernatural character of Isaac's birth.)*

3 And Abraham called the name of his son that was born unto him, whom Sarah bore to him, Isaac. *(The name means "laughter." It speaks of blessing, increase, healing, life, and well-being [Jn. 10:10]. As Isaac was a Type of Christ, it would not be wrong to say that one of the names of Christ is "laughter.")*

4 And Abraham circumcised his son Isaac being eight days old, as God had commanded him *(this was a sign of the Covenant that God would ultimately send a Redeemer into this world)*.

5 And Abraham was an hundred years old, when his son Isaac was born unto him *(this*

verse is placed in the Text so that all may know that Isaac's birth was indeed miraculous).

6 And Sarah said, God has made me to laugh, so that all who hear will laugh with me. (The mention of Sarah's name some five times thus far in this Chapter is done for purpose and reason; the Holy Spirit is impressing the fact that Sarah was in truth the very mother of this miraculous child. Sarah had once laughed in unbelief; she now laughs in Faith, a laughter incidentally expressing joy which will never end. It all pointed to Christ. Because of Christ, untold millions have laughed for joy.)

7 And she said, Who would have said unto Abraham, that Sarah should have given children suck? for I have born him a son in his old age (this is a poem, and could very well have been a song, and probably was).

8 And the child grew, and was weaned (the custom in those days was to nurse children for two to three years before they were weaned; however, there is some indication that Isaac was approximately five years old when he was weaned): and Abraham made a great feast the same day that Isaac was weaned (at this time, the boy was turned over to his father for training, at which time his education began).

THE BONDWOMAN AND HER SON

9 And Sarah saw the son of Hagar the Egyptian, which she had born unto Abraham, mocking. (The effect of the birth of Isaac, a work of the Spirit, was to make manifest the character of Ishmael, a work of the flesh. The end result of the "mocking" was that Ishmael actually desired to murder Isaac [Gal. 4:29]. Ishmael was probably eighteen to twenty years old at this time.)

10 Wherefore she said unto Abraham, Cast out this bondwoman and her son: (Isaac and Ishmael symbolize the new and the old natures in the Believer. Hagar and Sarah typify the two Covenants of works and Grace, of bondage and liberty [Gal., Chpt. 4]. The birth of the new nature demands the expulsion of the old. It is impossible to improve the old nature. How foolish, therefore, appears the doctrine of moral evolution!) for the son of this bondwoman shall not be heir with my son, even with Isaac. (Allowed to remain, Ishmael would murder Isaac; allowed to remain, the flesh will murder the Spirit. The Divine way of holiness is to "put off the old man," just as Abraham "put off" Ishmael.

Man's way of holiness is to improve the "old man," that is, to improve Ishmael. The effort is both foolish and hopeless.)

11 And the thing was very grievous in Abraham's sight because of his son. (It is always a struggle to cast out this element of bondage, that is, salvation by works, of which this is a type. For legalism is dear to the heart. Ishmael was the fruit, and, to Abraham, the fair fruit of his own energy and planning, which God can never accept.)

12 And God said unto Abraham, Let it not be grievous in your sight because of the lad, and because of your bondwoman; in all that Sarah has said unto you, hearken unto her voice; for in Isaac shall your seed be called. (It is labor lost to seek to make a crooked thing straight. Hence, all efforts after the improvement of nature are utterly futile, so far as God is concerned. The "flesh" must go, which typifies the personal ability, strength, and efforts of the Believer. The Faith of the Believer must be entirely in Christ and what Christ has done at the Cross. Then, and then alone, can the Holy Spirit have latitude to work in our lives, bringing forth perpetual victory [Rom. 6:14]. It must ever be understood, "in Isaac [in Christ] shall your seed be called.")

13 And also of the son of the bondwoman will I make a nation, because he is your seed (out of this "work of the flesh" ultimately came the religion of Islam, which claims that Ishmael is the promised seed, and not Isaac).

14 And Abraham rose up early in the morning, and took bread, and a bottle of water, and gave it unto Hagar, putting it on her shoulder, and the child, and sent her away: and she departed, and wandered in the wilderness of Beer-sheba. (This moment marks a distinct advance in the spiritual experience of Abraham. From this moment onwards all is strength and victory. He casts out the bondwoman and her son; he no longer fears the prince of this world [Abimelech], but reproves him; and now that the heir is come, Christ in Type, he knows himself to be the possessor of Heavenly as well as earthly promises.)

15 And the water was spent in the bottle, and she cast the child under one of the shrubs (she told Ishmael to sit down, with a shrub providing a little shade; "child," in the Hebrew, can refer to a "young man," which applies to Ishmael).

16 And she went, and sat her down over against him a good way off, as it were a bow

The
Expositor's
STUDY BIBLE
JIMMY SWAGGART

Presented to

_____

From

_____

_____

Occasion

_____

Date

_____

shot: for she said, Let me not see the death of the child. And she sat over against him, and lift up her voice, and wept *(without water, both of them would die very soon)*.

THE COVENANT

17 And God heard the voice of the lad; and the Angel of God called to Hagar out of heaven, and said unto her, What ails you, Hagar? fear not; for God has heard the voice of the lad where he is. *(It is not said that either Ishmael or his mother prayed to God in their distress. Hence the Divine interposition on their behalf was due solely to Mercy and to God's love for Abraham.)*

18 Arise, lift up the lad, and hold him in your hand; for I will make him a great nation. *(Ishmael, being between 18 and 20 years old at this time, the phrase actually means, "place your hand on his shoulder and steady him." True to God's Promise, the Arabs sprang from Ishmael.)*

19 And God opened her eyes, and she saw a well of water; and she went, and filled the bottle with water, and gave the lad drink *(evidently, the Lord had purposely blinded her to the well, until certain things could be made known to her, and that she would acknowledge them, which required a modicum of Faith)*.

20 And God was with the lad *(which means that the Lord, despite Ishmael's murderous attitude toward Isaac, did all for the sake of Abraham)*; and he grew, and dwelt in the wilderness, and became an archer.

21 And he dwelt in the wilderness of Paran: and his mother took him a wife out of the land of Egypt *(we have here the beginning of the Arab people)*.

ABRAHAM

22 And it came to pass at that time, that Abimelech and Phichol the chief captain of his host spoke unto Abraham, saying, God is with you in all that you do *(It is evident that Abimelech was a smart man; he had sense enough to know that if God was with Abraham, He would be with all who befriended Abraham; modern Christians could take a lesson from this man)*:

23 Now therefore swear unto me here by God that you will not deal falsely with me, nor with my son, nor with my son's son: but according to the kindness that I have done unto you, you shall do unto me, and to the land wherein you have sojourned *(Abimelech wants the covenant to extend even to his grandson)*.

24 And Abraham said, I will swear *(Abimelech recognized that Abraham had power with God; he wanted to be on the positive side of that power, and not the negative)*.

25 And Abraham reproved Abimelech because of a well of water, which Abimelech's servants had violently taken away *(the ownership of wells in that part of the world was a jealously guarded possession)*.

26 And Abimelech said, I do not know who has done this thing; neither did you tell me, neither yet heard I of it, but today *(this shows that Abimelech was not dealing falsely with Abraham; he did not know of the situation)*.

27 And Abraham took sheep and oxen, and gave them unto Abimelech; and both of them made a covenant *(these animals evidently were for sacrifice)*.

28 And Abraham set seven ewe lambs of the flock by themselves *(this was a symbol of a covenant, with which Abimelech was not familiar)*.

29 And Abimelech said unto Abraham, What do these seven ewe lambs mean which you have set by themselves? *(Seven ewe lambs are picked out and placed by themselves, and by accepting these, Abimelech bound himself to acknowledge and respect Abraham's title to the well. Apparently this manner of ratifying an oath was unknown to the Philistines.)*

30 And he *(Abraham)* said, For these seven ewe lambs shall you take of my hand, that they may be a witness unto me, that I have dug this well. *(If Abimelech takes the seven lambs, which he obviously did, this shows that he agrees with Abraham's contention concerning the fact that the well had originally belonged to him, and had been fraudulently taken.)*

31 Wherefore he called that place Beer-sheba; because there they did swear both of them. *(The word in Hebrew for "swearing" is a passive verb, literally signifying "to be sevened," that is, done or confirmed by seven.)*

32 Thus they made a covenant at Beer-sheba: then Abimelech rose up, and Phichol the chief captain of his host, and they returned into the land of the Philistines. *(This area ruled by Abimelech is called here "the land of the Philistines" for the first time; however, the main body of the Philistines who established their cities in the south coastal plain of Canaan did not arrive until later.)*

33 And Abraham planted a grove *(tree)* in Beer-sheba *(accordingly he takes possession of*

the land, thereby planting a tree; in the Hebrew the word is "tree" and not "grove"), and called there on the Name of the LORD, the everlasting God. *(The Patriarch now refers to Jehovah as "El'olam." In 14:22, Abraham claimed for Jehovah that He was "El Elyon," the supreme God; in 17:1, Jehovah reveals Himself as "El Shaddai," the Almighty God; and now Abraham claims for him the attribute of eternity. As he advanced in holiness, Abraham also grew in knowledge of the manifold nature of the Deity of God.)*

34 And Abraham sojourned in the Philistines' land many days *(the Patriarch would actually live here until he died).*

CHAPTER 22
(1872 B.C.)
ISAAC

AND it came to pass after these things, that God did tempt Abraham *(the word "tempt" should have been translated "test" or "prove," for that's what it means in the Hebrew; it is a high honor to be tested by God)*, and said unto him, Abraham: and he said, Behold, here I am.

2 And He said, Take now your son, your only son Isaac, whom you love *(the first mention of love in the Bible)*, and go into the land of Moriah *(the name "Moriah" means "Jehovah is Provider")*; and offer him there for a Burnt Offering upon one of the mountains which I will tell you of *(human sacrifice was abhorrent to the nature of Jehovah, so the Patriarch must now prove to himself that what he is hearing is definitely from God; this object lesson, perhaps the greatest in human history, would portray to Abraham the means by which God would redeem humanity — by death, the death of His only Son, of which Isaac, as the only son of Abraham, was a Type).*

3 And Abraham rose up early in the morning *(prompt obedience)*, and saddled his ass, and took two of his young men with him, and Isaac his son, and clave the wood for the Burnt Offering, and rose up, and went unto the place of which God had told him. *(For the salvation of humanity, human sacrifice was demanded, because the blood of bulls and goats could not take away sins [Heb. 10:4]; however, it would have to be the sacrifice of One Who is Perfect, hence, the necessity of the Incarnation [Isa. 7:14].)*

4 Then on the third day Abraham lifted up his eyes, and saw the place afar off *(this was no doubt the longest three days of Abraham's life).*

5 And Abraham said unto his young men, Abide you here with the ass; and I and the lad will go yonder and worship *(praise is what we do, while worship is what we are; every part and particle of our life and living should be worship of the Lord; while all worship is not praise, all praise definitely is worship; this is the first time that the word "worship" is used in the Bible)*, and come again to you *(he believed that God would raise the boy from the dead).*

6 And Abraham took the wood of the Burnt Offering, and laid it upon Isaac his son *(symbolic of Christ carrying the Cross [Jn. 19:17])*; and he took the fire in his hand *(typical of the judgment of God which would fall upon Christ instead of upon sinful man)*, and a knife *(symbolic of the death that Christ would die)*; and they went both of them together *(God was in Christ, reconciling the world unto Himself [II Cor. 5:19]).*

7 And Isaac spoke unto Abraham his father, and said, My father *(Isaac, as the unresisting Burnt Offering, is a striking Type of Him Who said, "I delight to do Your Will, O My God")*: and he said, Here am I, my son. And he said, Behold the fire and the wood: but where is the lamb for a Burnt Offering? *(John the Baptist would answer that question by saying, "Behold the Lamb of God, Which takes away the sin of the world" [Jn. 1:29].)*

8 And Abraham said, My son, God will provide Himself a lamb for a Burnt Offering: so they went both of them together. *(Isaac was to be a Type of the Son of God, provided by the Lord, Who would redeem mankind by the giving of Himself in Sacrifice on the Cross.)*

A RAM

9 And they came to the place which God had told him of *(this would be the place of the threshingfloor which David bought, and where Solomon's Temple would be built)*; and Abraham built an Altar there *(it is believed that the Holy of Holies, which contained the Ark of the Covenant in the Temple, was built over this exact spot)*, and laid the wood in order *(signifying the Cross)*, and bound Isaac his son *(typical of Jesus being nailed to the Cross)*, and laid him on the Altar upon the wood *(typical of Jesus stretched on the Cross).*

10 And Abraham stretched forth his hand, and took the knife to slay his son *(perhaps the Lord asked more of Abraham than He has ever asked of any man; when Abraham took the knife,*

his surrender was complete).

11 And the Angel of the LORD *(this was the Lord Himself)* called unto him out of heaven, and said, Abraham, Abraham *(He Who said, "Abraham, Abraham," was the same One Who said, "Martha, Martha," "Simon, Simon," and "Saul, Saul"; the repetition denotes urgency)*: and he said, Here am I. *(It was the trial that God intended, not the act.)*

12 And He said, Lay not your hand upon the lad, neither do you any thing unto him *(Abraham didn't have to kill the boy to prove himself to God, but he had to fully intend to do so, and that he did!)*: for now I know that you fear God, seeing you have not withheld your son, your only son from Me *(should have been translated, "for I the knowing One knew that you feared God, and that you would not withhold your son, your only son, from Me")*.

13 And Abraham lifted up his eyes, and looked, and behold behind him a ram caught in a thicket by his horns *(this is the doctrine of Substitution plainly laid out; the ram was offered up in Sacrifice instead of his son; likewise, Jesus was offered up as our Substitute)*: and Abraham went and took the ram, and offered him up for a Burnt Offering in the stead of his son *(even though the Doctrine of Substitution is clearly set forth here, its corresponding Doctrine of Identification is not so clearly stated, that awaiting Moses [Num. 21:9]; but still, we are seeing here the very heart of the Salvation Plan)*.

14 And Abraham called the name of that place Jehovah-jireh *(meaning "the Lord will provide")*: as it is said to this day, In the mount of the LORD it shall be seen *(should read "in this mount Jehovah shall be seen"; this was fulfilled in II Samuel 24:25; I Chronicles 21:26; II Chronicles 7:1-3)*.

THE COVENANT CONFIRMED

15 And the Angel of the LORD called unto Abraham out of heaven the second time *(this will involve Revelation; however, let the Reader understand that the "Revelation" is entirely dependent upon the Substitution; in other words, "No Cross, no Revelation!")*,

16 And said, By Myself have I sworn, saith the LORD, for because you have done this thing, and have not withheld your son, your only son *(while Isaac wasn't sacrificed, actually in a figure he was and, as well, in a figure raised from the dead [Heb. 11:18-19]; in essence, he was a figure of Christ)*:

17 That in blessing I will bless you *(blessing always refers to increase)*, and in multiplying I will multiply your seed as the stars of the heaven, and as the sand which is upon the sea shore *(this includes the Church as well, and for all time)*; and your seed shall possess the gate of his enemies *(this speaks of Jesus Christ defeating Satan, and doing so by removing Satan's legal right to hold man in bondage, which legal right is sin; Jesus did it at the Cross; there the gates of Hell were torn down [Mat. 16:18])*;

18 And in your seed shall all the nations of the Earth be blessed *(the "Seed" is the Lord Jesus Christ [Gal. 3:16])*; because you have obeyed My voice *(obedience to the Word of God is the requirement)*.

19 So Abraham returned unto his young men, and they rose up and went together to Beer-sheba; and Abraham dwelt at Beer-sheba. *(The return of Abraham to Beer-sheba with Isaac had to be the happiest journey that Abraham ever took. It was truly a journey of victory.)*

20 And it came to pass after these things, that it was told Abraham, saying, Behold, Milcah, she has also born children unto your brother Nahor *(this Chapter concludes with an account of Nahor's family, who settle at Haran [Gen. 12:1-5]; none of this would have been given, but for the connection which it had with the Work of God on Earth; from these people mentioned here both Isaac and Jacob took wives, which had to do with the formation of the nation of Israel, and ultimately the birth of Christ)*;

21 Huz his firstborn, and Buz his brother, and Kemuel the father of Aram,

22 And Chesed, and Hazo, and Pildash, and Jidlaph, and Bethuel.

23 And Bethuel begat Rebekah: these eight Milcah did bear to Nahor, Abraham's brother.

24 And his concubine, whose name was Reumah, she bore also Tebah, and Gaham, and Thahash, and Maachah.

CHAPTER 23
(1860 B.C.)
SARAH

AND Sarah was an hundred and twenty-seven years old: these were the years of the life of Sarah *(Sarah is the only woman in the Bible whose age, death, and burial are recorded)*.

2 And Sarah died in Kirjath-arba; the same is Hebron in the land of Canaan: and Abraham came to mourn for Sarah, and to weep for her. *(The phrase, "in the land of Canaan," is given*

regarding the place of Sarah's death, in order that we might know that she did not die in the country of the Philistines, but rather in the "Promised Land." She had fought this good fight of Faith with Abraham every step of the way; consequently, in a sense, as he was the "father of us all" [Rom. 4:16], Sarah was the "mother of us all" [I Pet. 3:6].)

3 And Abraham stood up from before his dead, and spoke unto the sons of Heth, saying,

4 I am a stranger and a sojourner with you *(this was a confession of his real inheritance, a better country, even an Heavenly [Heb. 11:13]):* give me a possession of a buryingplace with you, that I may bury my dead out of my sight *(this request of the sons of Heth was a sign to Abraham of his right and title to the land of Canaan, which the sons of Heth would not have understood).*

5 And the children of Heth answered Abraham, saying unto him,

6 Hear us, my lord: you are a mighty prince among us: in the choice of our sepulchres bury your dead; none of us shall withhold from you his sepulchre, but that you may bury your dead.

7 And Abraham stood up, and bowed himself to the people of the land, even to the children of Heth.

8 And he communed with them, saying, If it be your mind that I should bury my dead out of my sight; hear me, and intreat for me to Ephron the son of Zohar *(they had no idea that Abraham was looking forward to the possession of the whole land; and because he did so look forward, the possession of a grave was by no means a small matter to him),*

9 That he may give me the cave of Machpelah, which he has, which is in the end of his field; for as much money as it is worth he shall give it me for a possession of a buryingplace among you. *(In the purchasing of Machpelah for a buryingplace, Abraham gave expression to his Faith as it regards Resurrection. "He stood up from before his dead." Faith cannot long keep death in view; it has a higher object. Resurrection is that which ever fills the vision of Faith and, in the power thereof, it can rise up from before the dead.).*

10 And Ephron dwelt among the children of Heth: and Ephron the Hittite answered Abraham in the audience of the children of Heth, even of all who went in at the gate of his city, saying,

11 No, my lord, hear me: the field give I to you, and the cave that is therein, I give it to you; in the presence of the sons of my people I give it to you: bury your dead *(the Canaanites had no idea of the expectations which were giving character to Abraham's actions on this occasion).*

12 And Abraham bowed down himself before the people of the land. *(His purchase of this tomb was not only a proof of his love for Sarah, but a testimony to his belief that she would rise again and with him possess the whole land, which, to be sure, he will see in totality in the coming Kingdom Age.)*

13 And he spoke unto Ephron in the audience of the people of the land, saying, But if you will give it, I pray you, hear me: I will give you money for the field; take it of me, and I will bury my dead there *(this is the first time that money is mentioned in the Bible as a medium of exchange).*

14 And Ephron answered Abraham, saying unto him,

15 My lord, hearken unto me: the land is worth four hundred shekels of silver; what is that between me and you? bury therefore your dead *(the reason so much attention is given to this by the Holy Spirit is because it proclaims the hope of Resurrection and the inheritance founded thereon).*

16 And Abraham hearkened unto Ephron; and Abraham weighed to Ephron the silver, which he had named in the audience of the sons of Heth, four hundred shekels of silver, current money with the merchant *(while Abraham would pay the Canaanites for Machpelah, he would look to the Lord for the entirety of the land of Canaan, which most certainly one day will be his).*

17 And the field of Ephron which was in Machpelah, which was before Mamre, the field, and the cave which was therein, and all the trees that were in the field, that were in all the borders round about, were made sure *(in the cave of Machpelah, his own remains, and those of Isaac, Rebekah, Jacob, and Leah were deposited; Rachel alone of the great Patriarchal family was not buried here)*

18 Unto Abraham for a possession in the presence of the children of Heth, before all who went in at the gate of his city *(the bargain was sealed).*

19 And after this, Abraham buried Sarah his wife in the cave of the field of Machpelah before Mamre: the same is Hebron in the land of Canaan.

20 And the field, and the cave that is therein,

were made sure unto Abraham for a possession of a buryingplace by the sons of Heth. *(Abraham's love for Sarah demanded an honored tomb for her precious dust, and faith in respect of her furnishes a testimony as to her resurrection. Love bent down over her sleeping face, and faith "stood up" from before its dead, proclaiming the Resurrection that is most surely to come.)*

CHAPTER 24
(1857 B.C.)
ELIEZER

AND Abraham was old, and well stricken in age: and the LORD had blessed Abraham in all things. *(Abraham was now about 140 years old, and would actually live to the age of 175 [25:7]. He lived some 35 years after Isaac was married, and lived to see Esau and Jacob nearly grown up.*

Chapters 22 through 24 present a startling picture. In Chapter 22, the son is offered up; in Chapter 23, Sarah is laid aside, which represents Israel being laid aside; and in Chapter 24, the servant is sent forth to procure a bride for him who had been, as it were, received from the dead in a figure.

When we turn to the New Testament, we see a remarkable similarity: 1. The rejection and death of Christ, corresponding to the offering up of Isaac; 2. The setting aside of Israel after the flesh, corresponding with the death of Sarah; and, 3. The calling out of the Church to occupy the high position of the Bride of the Lamb, typified by a bride for Isaac.)

2 And Abraham said unto his oldest servant of his house *(Eliezer)*, who ruled over all that he had, Put, I pray you, your hand under my thigh *(Eliezer, in a sense, is a Type of the Holy Spirit; the putting the hand under the thigh of the Patriarch, which was the source of posterity, points to Abraham's future descendants, and in particular to Christ, the Promised Seed; so the oath was equivalent to a swearing by Him Who was to come, namely Christ)*:

3 And I will make you swear by the LORD, the God of heaven, and the God of the Earth, that you shall not take a wife unto my son of the daughters of the Canaanites, among whom I dwell *(these were descendants of Ham, and not Shem, with the latter being the lineage through which Christ would come, and only through that lineage [9:26])*:

4 But you shall go unto my country, and to my kindred *(descendants of Shem)*, and take a wife unto my son Isaac *(typical of the Holy Spirit calling out Believers as a bride for Christ, of Whom Isaac was a Type)*.

5 And the servant *(Eliezer)* said unto him *(Abraham)*, Peradventure the woman will not be willing to follow me unto this land: must I needs bring your son again unto the land from where you came?

6 And Abraham said unto him, You beware that you bring not my son thither again *(by no means was Isaac to be taken to the particular land where his wife was to be found; the Promised Land was his home, and opportunity for temptation must not be put in his way)*.

7 The LORD God of heaven, which took me from my father's house, and from the land of my kindred, and Who spoke unto me, and Who swore unto me, saying, Unto your seed will I give this land; He shall send His Angel before you, and you shall take a wife unto my son from thence *(the Lord would send an Angel who would precede Eliezer, and thereby prepare the way)*.

8 And if the woman will not be willing to follow you, then you shall be clear from this my oath: only bring not my son thither again *(the instructions were specific: Isaac was to remain in Canaan, and the woman was to come to Canaan to be with him)*.

9 And the servant put his hand under the thigh of Abraham his master *(as Abraham had demanded)*, and swore to him concerning that matter.

PRAYER

10 And the servant took ten camels of his master, and departed *(the number "ten" portrays completeness; the Salvation of our Lord is a complete Salvation)*; for all the goods of his master were in his hand *(all the goods of our Heavenly Father are in the Hand of the Holy Spirit, of Whom Eliezer was a Type)*: and he arose, and went to Mesopotamia, unto the city of Nahor *(the Holy Spirit came to this Earth on the Day of Pentecost in a new dimension, of which Mesopotamia was a Type)*.

11 And he made his camels to kneel down without the city by a well of water at the time of the evening, even the time that women go out to draw water *(the "well of water" is a Type of the "Living Water")*.

12 And he said O LORD God of my master Abraham, I pray you, send me good speed this

day, and show kindness unto my master Abraham *(Eliezer does not trust his own instincts or personal wisdom; he rather seeks leading from the Lord, ever conscious of the significance of his journey).*

13 Behold, I stand here by the well of water; and the daughters of the men of the city come out to draw water:

14 And let it come to pass, that the damsel to whom I shall say, Let down your pitcher, I pray you, that I may drink; and she shall say, Drink, and I will give your camels drink also: let the same be she that You have appointed for Your servant Isaac; and thereby shall I know that You have showed kindness unto my master *(the "fleece," so to speak, was not simple or easy; camels drink an awful lot of water, and for a young lady to draw enough water to slake the thirst of ten camels, and for her to volunteer to do so, even without being asked, would have to be the Lord).*

REBEKAH

15 And it came to pass, before he had done speaking, that, behold, Rebekah came out, who was born to Bethuel, son of Milcah, the wife of Nahor, Abraham's brother, with her pitcher upon her shoulder *(we have the first mention here of Rebekah, who will be the wife of Isaac, and who will figure so prominently in the great Plan of God).*

16 And the damsel was very fair to look upon, a virgin, neither had any man known her: and she went down to the well, and filled her pitcher, and came up *(a Type of the Church partaking of the Water of Life).*

17 And the servant *(Eliezer)* ran to meet her, and said, Let me, I pray you, drink a little water of your pitcher.

18 And she said, Drink, my lord: and she hasted, and let down her pitcher upon her hand, and gave him drink.

19 And when she had done giving him drink, she said, I will draw water for your camels also, until they have done drinking. *(Most of the wells in those days were fed by a spring, with a series of steps that led down to the water; consequently, to walk up those steps carrying one or two goatskins full of water was no easy task, especially to slake the thirst of ten camels.)*

20 And she hasted, and emptied her pitcher into the trough, and ran again unto the well to draw water, and drew for all his camels *(a Type of the Church giving the "Water of Life" to a lost world).*

21 And the man wondering at her held his peace, to witness whether the LORD had made his journey prosperous or not *("wondering at her" means that he "eagerly or carefully watched her").*

22 And it came to pass, as the camels had done drinking, that the man took a golden earring *(a jewel for her forehead)* of half a shekel weight, and two bracelets for her hands of ten shekels weight of gold *(worth about $5,000 in 2003 money; a Type of the "gifts" given by the Holy Spirit to the Church);*

23 And said, Whose daughter are you? tell me, I pray you: is there room in your father's house for us to lodge in? *(presents the question that the Holy Spirit asks of every believing sinner).*

24 And she said unto him, I am the daughter of Bethuel the son of Milcah, which she bore unto Nahor *(Rebekah mentions her father's mother to show that she was descended from a high born wife, and not from a concubine).*

25 She said moreover unto him, We have both straw and provender enough, and room to lodge in *(Rebekah said, "There is room;" the Holy Spirit awaits the same answer from us).*

26 And the man bowed down his head, and worshipped the LORD.

27 And he said, Blessed be the LORD God of my master Abraham, who has not left destitute my master of his mercy and his truth: I being in the way, the LORD led me to the house of my master's brethren *(the prayer of Eliezer shows that he understood the significance of all of this).*

28 And the damsel ran, and told them of her mother's house these things.

29 And Rebekah had a brother, and his name was Laban: and Laban ran out unto the man, unto the well *(Rebekah was a witness of what she had experienced, which brought others to Eliezer; we must be a witness as well).*

30 And it came to pass, when he saw the earring and the bracelets upon his sister's hands *(does the world see in us Righteousness and Holiness, of which these gifts were a Type?),* and when he heard the words of Rebekah his sister, saying, Thus spoke the man unto me; that he came unto the man; and, behold, he stood by the camels at the well *(the Bible said that Laban "saw" and "heard;" the world must "see" and they must "hear"!).*

31 And he said, Come in, you blessed of the LORD; why do you stand without? for I have

prepared the house, and room for the camels *(many people want the "gifts" of the Spirit, but they don't want to make room for the camels, i.e., that which they consider to be an imposition; but if we are to have the "gifts," we must make room for the camels).*

32 And the man *(Eliezer)* came into the house: and he *(Laban)* ungirded his camels, and gave straw and provender for the camels, and water to wash his feet, and the men's feet who were with him *(with Eliezer).*

ELIEZER

33 And there was set meat before him *(before Eliezer)* to eat: but he said, I will not eat, until I have told my errand. And he *(Laban)* said, Speak on *(the "Marriage Supper of the Lamb" cannot commence until the errand of the Holy Spirit has been completed, which is to secure the Bride for Christ).*

34 And he said, I am Abraham's servant *(he is careful to say exactly what Abraham has said; we as well must be very careful that we faithfully deliver the Word of the Lord, and not err in that delivery).*

35 And the LORD has blessed my master greatly; and he is become great: and He has given him flocks, and herds, and silver, and gold, and menservants, and maidservants, and camels, and asses *(after Eliezer identifies himself, he promotes Abraham, which the Holy Spirit always does, of Whom Eliezer was a Type, as it regards God the Father and God the Son).*

36 And Sarah my master's wife bore a son to my master when she was old: and unto him has he given all that he has *(the Heavenly Father has given all things unto the "Son").*

37 And my master made me swear, saying, You shall not take a wife to my son of the daughters of the Canaanites, in whose land I dwell:

38 But you shall go unto my father's house, and to my kindred, and take a wife unto my son *(Israel was to be that wife, but having forfeited the position, the Church now takes Israel's place, at least during the Dispensation of Grace).*

39 And I said unto my master, Peradventure the woman will not follow me.

40 And he said unto me, The LORD, before Whom I walk *(order my behavior)*, will send His Angel with you, and prosper your way; and you shall take a wife for my son of my kindred, and of my father's house *(under the New Covenant, we now have the constant help of the Holy Spirit [Jn. 14:16], which is even greater than the help of Angels):*

41 Then shall you be clear from this my oath, when you come to my kindred; and if they give not you one *(will not allow the girl to go)*, you shall be clear from my oath.

42 And I came this day unto the well, and said, O LORD God of my master Abraham, if now You do prosper my way which I go:

43 Behold, I stand by the well of water; and it shall come to pass, that when the virgin comes forth to draw water, and I say to her, Give me, I pray you, a little water of your pitcher to drink;

44 And she said to me, Both *(Eliezer and those with him)* you drink, and I will also draw water for your camels: let the same be the woman whom the LORD has appointed out for my master's son.

45 And before I had done speaking in my heart, behold, Rebekah came forth with her pitcher on her shoulder; and she went down unto the well, and drew water: and I said unto her, Let me drink, I pray you.

46 And she made haste, and let down her pitcher from her shoulder, and said, Drink, and I will give your camels drink also: so I drank, and she made the camels drink also.

47 And I asked her, and said, Whose daughter are you? And she said, The daughter of Bethuel, Nahor's son, whom Milcah bore unto him: and I put the earring upon her face *(on her forehead)*, and the bracelets upon her hands.

48 And I bowed down my head, and worshipped the LORD, and blessed the LORD God of my master Abraham, which had led me in the right way to take my master's brother's daughter unto his son.

49 And now if you will deal kindly and truly with my master, tell me: and if not, tell me; that I may turn to the right hand, or to the left.

REBEKAH'S JOURNEY

50 Then Laban and Bethuel answered and said, The thing proceeds from the LORD: we cannot speak unto you bad or good. *(They obviously recognized the Hand of the Lord in all of these things, and conducted themselves accordingly.)*

51 Behold, Rebekah is before you, take her, and go, and let her be your master's son's wife, as the LORD has spoken. *(The journey she would travel would be about 700 miles distant. It was very long in those days, and they would*

probably never see Rebekah again.)

52 And it came to pass, that, when Abraham's servant heard their words, he worshipped the LORD, bowing himself to the earth. *(If it is to be noticed, Eliezer frequently worships the Lord, being careful to give Him thanks.)*

53 And the servant brought forth jewels of silver, and jewels of gold, and raiment, and gave them to Rebekah: he gave also to her brother and to her mother precious things. *(Considering how rich Abraham was, and how important this event, the worth of all of this was undoubtedly staggering. Thus are the spiritual gifts to the Church, made possible by Christ and what He did at the Cross, and given to us by the Holy Spirit. He has given to us "precious things.")*

54 And they did eat and drink, he and the men who were with him, and tarried all night; and they rose up in the morning, and he *(Eliezer)* said, Send me away unto my master *(give me permission to leave!).*

55 And her brother and her mother said, Let the damsel abide with us a few days, at the least ten; after that she shall go.

56 And he said unto them, Hinder me not, seeing the LORD has prospered my way; send me away that I may go to my master *(knowing the urgency of his mission, Eliezer is anxious to get underway).*

57 And they said, We will call the damsel, and enquire at her mouth.

58 And they called Rebekah, and said unto her, Will you go with this man *(this is the question that the Holy Spirit is asking everyone who would be a part of the Bride of Christ)?* And she said, I will go. *(She was leaving her family and, as stated, possibly to never see them again. Whenever we come to Christ, we, in effect, as well, must give up our families, our friends, and everything, for that matter. Our answer must be as quick as was the answer of Rebekah, "I will go"!)*

59 And they sent away Rebekah their sister, and her nurse, and Abraham's servant, and his men.

60 And they blessed Rebekah, and said unto her, You are our sister, be thou the mother of thousands of millions, and let your seed possess the gate of those which hate them. *(Little did they realize the staggering numbers they presented would in fact come to pass. Every single person who has ever come to Christ is a part of these "thousands of millions." As well, her "Seed," the Lord Jesus Christ, has "possessed the gate" of all enemies, signifying total victory in every capacity.)*

61 And Rebekah arose, and her damsels, and they rode upon the camels, and followed the man *(as well, we are to follow the Holy Spirit in all of His leading, and always without exception, He will lead us to Christ):* and the servant *(Eliezer)* took Rebekah, and went his way.

ISAAC AND REBEKAH

62 And Isaac came from the way of the well Lahai-roi; for he dwelt in the south country.

63 And Isaac went out to meditate in the field at the eventide *(evening):* and he lifted up his eyes, and saw, and, behold, the camels were coming *(while in prayer, he happened to look up and, behold, he saw the camel train coming).*

64 And Rebekah lifted up her eyes, and when she saw Isaac, she lighted off the camel *(Rebekah would meet Isaac at his place of prayer).*

65 For she had said unto the servant *(Eliezer),* What man is this who walks in the field to meet us? And the servant had said, It is my master: therefore she took a vail, and covered herself *(the Lord had arranged this marriage, and all marriages which He arranges are as they should be; Rebekah was beautiful, a virgin and, above all, she was the Will of the Lord for Isaac).*

66 And the servant told Isaac all things that he had done *(it was quite a story!).*

67 And Isaac brought her into his mother Sarah's tent, and took Rebekah, and she became his wife; and he loved her: and Isaac was comforted after his mother's death. *(In those days, the primitive marriage ceremony consisted solely of the taking of a bride before witnesses. The word "death" is added here by the translators. It was not in the original Text. It is as if the Holy Spirit would not conclude this beautiful and joyful narrative with a note of sorrow.)*

CHAPTER 25
(1800 B.C.)
KETURAH

THEN again Abraham took a wife, and her name was Keturah *(Sarah having waxed old and vanished away [Heb. 9:13], that is, the Jewish Covenant of works, Keturah, the Gentile, now appears with her sons; thus is the future pictured).*

2 And she bore him Zimran, and Jokshan, and Medan, and Midian, and Ishbak, and Shuah.

3 And Jokshan begat Sheba and Dedan. And the sons of Dedan were Asshurim, and Letushim, and Leummim.

4 And the sons of Midian; Ephah, and Epher, and Hanoch, and Abidah, and Eldaah. All these were the children of Keturah. *(Abraham was probably between 140 and 150 years old when these sons were born. So, we must conclude that the rejuvenation given to Abraham by the Lord, as it regards the birth of Isaac, carried over for many more years, which it no doubt did. With God all things are possible! This having been accomplished, the nations of the Earth [represented by Keturah and her sons] will be raised up as children of Abraham and receive their inheritance, which of course speaks of the Church.)*

5 And Abraham gave all that he had unto Isaac *(only the Child of the Spirit can be heir to the Promises).*

6 But unto the sons of the concubines, which Abraham had, Abraham gave gifts, and sent them away from Isaac his son, while he yet lived, eastward, unto the east country *(there is a vast difference in mere "gifts" than the entirety of the inheritance; in the natural or literal sense the same holds true; those who follow the way of the Cross can have no fellowship with those who follow the way of the flesh).*

ABRAHAM'S DEATH AND BURIAL

7 And these are the days of the years of Abraham's life which he lived, an hundred threescore and fifteen years *(175 years).*

8 Then Abraham gave up the ghost, and died in a good old age, an old man, and full of years; and was gathered to his people. *(Abraham was born about two years after the death of Noah, and was contemporary with Shem, Noah's son, for many years. Few men in history, if any, have affected the world as did Abraham. That which characterized his person and his life was that of Faith, and we speak of Faith in Christ and what Christ would do to redeem the fallen sons of Adam's lost race. It could be said of him as it was said of Paul, "He fought a good fight, finished the course, and kept the faith" [II Tim. 4:7-8].)*

9 And his sons Isaac and Ishmael buried him in the cave of Machpelah, in the field of Ephron the son of Zohar the Hittite, which is before Mamre; *(It is pleasant to read that Isaac and Ishmael stood side by side at their father's grave, which speaks to us of prophetic overtones. This will literally happen in the coming Kingdom Age.)*

10 The field which Abraham purchased of the sons of Heth: there was Abraham buried, and Sarah his wife. *(This burial plot alone belonged to Abraham and Sarah when they died; however, that burial place proclaimed to all that one day the entirety of the land, which would ultimately be called "Israel," would belong to him; and it yet shall, in the coming Kingdom Age.)*

11 And it came to pass after the death of Abraham, that God blessed his son Isaac; and Isaac dwelt by the well Lahai-roi *("well of the living one;" God blessed Isaac, but it doesn't mention anything about God blessing the other sons of Abraham).*

DESCENDANTS OF ISHMAEL

12 Now these are the generations of Ishmael, Abraham's son, whom Hagar the Egyptian, Sarah's handmaid, bore unto Abraham *(Ishmael had every opportunity to serve God, but, regrettably, he chose another path):*

13 And these are the names of the sons of Ishmael, by their names, according to their generations: the firstborn of Ishmael, Nebajoth; and Kedar, and Adbeel, and Mibsam,

14 And Mishma, and Dumah, and Massa,

15 Hadar, and Tema, Jetur, Naphish, and Kedemah:

16 These are the sons of Ishmael, and these are their names, by their towns, and by their castles; twelve princes according to their nations.

17 And these are the years of the life of Ishmael, an hundred and thirty and seven years: and he gave up the ghost and died; and was gathered unto his people.

18 And they dwelt from Havilah unto Shur, that is before Egypt, as you go toward Assyria: and he died in the presence of all his brethren. *(Ishmael was the head of the Arab people, who regrettably, at least for the most part, chose also a path of faithlessness. Christ being rejected, as always is the case, a false deity filled the void. That false deity was Muhammad, who has enslaved the Arab people from then until now. For there is no freedom outside of Christ.)*

ESAU AND JACOB

19 And these are the generations of Isaac, Abraham's son: Abraham begat Isaac *(Isaac was born of the Spirit):*

20 And Isaac was forty years old when he took Rebekah to wife, the daughter of Bethuel the Syrian of Padan-aram, the sister to Laban the Syrian *("Laban the Syrian" is mentioned here simply because he will figure very prominently*

as it regards Jacob, Rebekah's son).

21 And Isaac intreated the LORD for his wife, because she was barren *(Satan hindered the birth of Jacob for twenty years)*: and the LORD was intreated of him, and Rebekah his wife conceived *(God overruled the malice of Satan to emphasize once more the great truth that He displays the riches of His Grace and Glory where nature is dead; this is a principle in the spiritual life which nature is unwilling to learn).*

22 And the children struggled together within her *(they were twins in her womb; two energies struggled within her, the one believing and the other unbelieving, and were present even before they were born; it is like the two natures, sin nature and Divine Nature, within the Believer)*; and she said, If it be so, why am I thus *(could be paraphrased, "If, in answer to prayer, God is about to give me the joy of being a mother, why am I so physically oppressed that I am in danger of death?"; it must indeed have appeared perplexing to her that such an answer to prayer should be accompanied by such mysterious suffering)*? And she went to enquire of the LORD.

23 And the LORD said unto her, Two nations are in your womb, and two manner of people shall be separated from your bowels *(those two nations were Edomites and Israelites; from the time of their birth, Esau and Jacob would be separated, divided, even hostile, for they would have nothing in common)*; and the one people shall be stronger than the other people *(Jacob, who was younger, would be the stronger, but only through the Lord)*; and the elder shall serve the younger *(every person is born with a sin nature, which makes that the "elder;" the Divine Nature comes into the Believer at conversion, and is the younger; however, if we follow God's pattern of victorious living, which is Jesus Christ and Him Crucified, "the elder shall serve the younger," meaning that the Divine nature will be victorious over the sin nature).*

24 And when her days to be delivered were fulfilled, behold, there were twins in her womb.

25 And the first came out red, all over like an hairy garment; and they called his name Esau *(his name means "the hairy one," which speaks of sensuality).*

26 And after that came his brother out, and his hand took hold on Esau's heel *(Jacob taking hold of Esau's heel at birth portrays the Believer trying to gain spiritual supremacy by means of the flesh and not the Spirit, which*

characterized Jacob for many years); and his name was called Jacob *(meaning "heel-catcher" or "supplanter")*: and Isaac was threescore years old *(60)* when she bore them.

THE BIRTHRIGHT

27 And the boys grew: and Esau was a cunning hunter, a man of the field; and Jacob was a plain man, dwelling in tents *(the original Hebrew proclaims Esau as a wild, undisciplined man, and Jacob as a quiet, mature individual; he was sensible, diligent, dutiful, and peaceful).*

28 And Isaac loved Esau *(preferred Esau above Jacob, which proclaims a character flaw in Isaac, which was to bring him grief; the Holy Spirit in the Epistle to the Hebrews calls Esau a "profane person," and this because he sold his birthright)*, because he did eat of his venison: but Rebekah loved Jacob *(she remembered the prediction of Verse 23).*

29 And Jacob sod pottage *(a stew)*: and Esau came from the field, and he was faint:

30 And Esau said to Jacob, Feed me, I pray you, with that same red pottage; for I am faint: therefore was his name called Edom *(the father of the Edomites).*

31 And Jacob said, Sell me this day your birthright. *(The birthright then dealt primarily with spiritual things, of which Esau had no regard or concern. It had to do with the earthly inheritance of Canaan, but would take place hundreds of years in the future. It referred to the possession of the Covenant Blessing, which included his seed being as the stars of the sky and all the families of the Earth being blessed in him. As well, it was the progenitorship of the Promised Seed, which was the greatest Blessing of all, and spoke of Christ. The firstborn was to receive the birthright, and Esau was the firstborn.)*

32 And Esau said, Behold, I am at the point to die: and what profit shall this birthright do to me? *(Esau bartered future and eternal wealth for present and temporary need. He had no concern for spiritual things, so the birthright meant nothing to him.)*

33 And Jacob said, Swear to me this day; and he swore unto him: and he sold his birthright unto Jacob. *(Jacob, deplorable as was his character, valued Divine and eternal blessing; and, had he placed himself in God's Hands, the prophecy made to his mother before he was born would have been fulfilled to him, and without the degradation and suffering which his own scheming brought upon him.)*

34 Then Jacob gave Esau bread and pottage of lentiles; and he did eat and drink, and rose up, and went his way: thus Esau despised his birthright. *(The natural heart places no value on the things of God, as we see evidenced in the choices made by Esau. To the natural heart, God's Promises are a vague, valueless, powerless thing, simply because God is not known. Upon that which the unredeemed cannot see, they place no value. Thus it was with Esau.)*

CHAPTER 26
(1804 B.C.)
ISAAC

AND there was a famine in the land, beside the first famine that was in the days of Abraham *(it is not so difficult for Satan to break down the faith of a Believer; so small a matter as a famine is sufficient)*. And Isaac went unto Abimelech king of the Philistines unto Gerar *("Abimelech" is a title, somewhat like "President" or "Pharaoh;" so this was not the same man who dealt with Abraham, a time of some 80 or more years having now passed)*.

2 And the LORD appeared unto him, and said, Go not down into Egypt; dwell in the land which I shall tell you of *(if it is disastrous to the Spiritual Life for the Christian to go down into "Egypt," it is dangerous to go down unto "Gerar," for it is a halfway house to Egypt)*:

3 Sojourn in this land *(the Land of Promise)*, and I will be with you, and will bless you *(the Blessing was conditional on staying in the "Promised Land," as the same Blessing is conditional presently in the spiritual sense)*; for unto you, and unto your seed, I will give all these countries, and I will perform the oath which I swore unto Abraham your father; *(Horton says: "The reason Isaac could inherit the Promise and enjoy God's Presence and Blessing was because Abraham obeyed God, fulfilled the obligations of God put on him, kept the requirements, commandments, rules, and instructions God gave him." Many times, our blessings are predicated on the obedience of someone else. We should not forget that, thinking that it's our great faith.)*

4 And I will make your seed to multiply as the stars of heaven, and will give unto your seed all these countries; and in your seed shall all the nations of the Earth be blessed *(basically, the Lord reaffirms the Promise He had already made to Abraham, and which He now makes to Isaac)*;

5 Because that Abraham obeyed My voice, and kept My charge, My commandments, My statutes, and My laws. *(In essence, the Lord is telling Isaac that if he wants to continue to enjoy God's blessings, he must continue in the same sort of faith and obedience as did his father Abraham. Regrettably, much of the modern Church is trying to change the "charge.")*

ABIMELECH

6 And Isaac dwelt in Gerar: *(There is no indication that the Lord told Isaac to go to Gerar. The indication is that he went there according to his own leading and direction. Events prove that.)*

7 And the men of the place asked him of his wife; and he said, She is my sister: *(The Patriarch practices deception here exactly as did his father Abraham. It is positive that Isaac knew in detail of his father's episode in Egypt, and the wrongness of the act. So why did he follow the same course?)* for he feared to say, She is my wife; lest, said he, the men of the place should kill me for Rebekah; because she was fair to look upon. *(The Child of God must never act out of "fear," but always from the position of "faith.")*

8 And it came to pass, when he had been there a long time, that Abimelech king of the Philistines looked out at a window, and saw, and, behold, Isaac was sporting with Rebekah his wife. *(His deception is found out. The Lord always leaves a "window.")*

9 And Abimelech called Isaac, and said, Behold, of a surety she is your wife; and how did you say, She is my sister? And Isaac said unto him, Because I said, Lest I die for her. *(Once again, God's primary emissary on Earth is humiliated. In fact, sin always humiliates.)*

10 And Abimelech said, What is this you have done unto us? one of the people might lightly have lain with your wife, and you should have brought guiltiness upon us. *(Matthew Henry said: "There is nothing in Isaac's denial of his wife to be imitated, or even excused. The impartiality of the sacred historian records it for our warning, and to show that Righteousness comes not by the Law, but by Faith in Christ.")*

11 And Abimelech charged all his people, saying, He who touches this man or his wife shall surely be put to death. *(The sin of Isaac was greater than the sin of his father Abraham. While no sin is to be excused, Isaac had this unsavory example before him, so there was no excuse for what he did.)*

12 Then Isaac sowed in that land, and received in the same year an hundredfold: and the LORD blessed him. *(We find here that God blessed Isaac materially, but we also find that there is a vast difference between material blessings and Spiritual Blessings.)*

13 And the man waxed great, and went forward, and grew until he became very great *(we can never judge that a person's condition with the Lord is right because of prosperous circumstances)*:

14 For he had possession of flocks, and possession of herds, and great store of servants: and the Philistines envied him. *(A man may, like Isaac, become rich in "Gerar," but it is not recorded that Jehovah appeared to Isaac in Gerar. He appeared to him before he went there [in Lahai-roi] and, in fact, the very night of the day that he left.)*

15 For all the wells which his father's servants had dug in the days of Abraham his father, the Philistines had stopped them, and filled them with earth *(did so after Isaac arrived)*.

16 And Abimelech said unto Isaac, Go from us; for you are much mightier than we.

ISAAC, THE WELL-DIGGER

17 And Isaac departed thence, and pitched his tent in the valley of Gerar, and dwelt there. *(We find that Isaac still wasn't in the place where the Lord wanted him, as far as him dwelling in the Land was concerned. He is still in Gerar, which is Philistine country. How many do we see surrounded by God's Blessings, but do not have God's Presence?)*

18 And Isaac dug again the wells of water, which they had dug in the days of Abraham his father; for the Philistines had stopped them after the death of Abraham *(these wells had been stopped for some time)*: and he called their names after the names by which his father had called them *(wells in that part of the world, then and now, are extremely important)*.

19 And Isaac's servants dug in the valley, and found there a well of springing water.

20 And the herdmen of Gerar *(Philistines)* did strive with Isaac's herdmen, saying, The water is ours: and he called the name of the well Esek *(contention)*; because they did strive with him *(many times the opposition we receive, while definitely wrong on the part of the one who is doing the opposing, still, the Lord uses these things, at times, to further His Cause in our lives)*.

21 And they dug another well, and did strive for that also: and he called the name of it Sitnah *(hatred)*.

22 And he removed from thence, and dug another well; and for that they did not strive: and he called the name of it Rehoboth *(there is room)*; and he said, For now the LORD has made room for us, and we shall be fruitful in the land. *(Despite the fact that there is no contention for this particular well, Isaac seems to now understand that he still isn't exactly where God wants him to be.)*

23 And he went up from thence to Beer-sheba. *(Several years of strife and contention could have been avoided had Isaac earnestly sought the Lord in the beginning as it regarded his dwelling place. The Lord wanted the Patriarch in Beer-sheba.)*

24 And the LORD appeared unto him the same night *(immediately when Isaac left Gerar and went to Beer-sheba, which was where the Lord wanted him, "The Lord appeared unto him the same night")*, and said, I am the God of Abraham your father: fear not, for I am with you, and will bless you, and multiply your seed for my servant Abraham's sake. *(The Lord intends for Isaac to emulate his father, hence Him holding up Abraham as an example. As well, Abraham is spoken of, although dead, but not as one who has ceased to be. In fact, Abraham right then was in Paradise, along with Abel, Enoch, Noah, and probably many others.)*

25 And he built an Altar there *(this typified Christ and the price He would pay; in fact, "Jesus Christ and Him Crucified" was what it was all about, and is what it's all about; Isaac built no Altar in Gerar, because the Cross and disobedience do not go together)*, and called upon the Name of the LORD *(there is a difference in calling on the Name of the Lord when one is outside the Will of God than when one is in the center of God's Will; this "calling" is anchored in faith and victory, and will be rewarded accordingly)*, and pitched his tent there *(because the Lord was there)*: and there Isaac's servants dug a well *(the Hebrew word used here means that they opened the well, which had been stopped or closed by violence or neglect)*.

THE COVENANT

26 Then Abimelech went to him from Gerar, and Ahuzzath one of his friends, and Phichol the chief captain of his army *(Abimelech now seeks peace with Isaac, because the fear of the*

Lord is on Isaac).

27 And Isaac said unto them, Why do you come to me, seeing you hate me, and have sent me away from you? *(Williams says, "It is when Isaac definitely separates himself from the men of Gerar that they come to him seeking blessing through him from God. All the time that he dwelt among them, it is not recorded that they approached him in this way. This is one of the many lessons in the Bible which teach the Christian that he best helps the world when living in separation from it.")*

28 And they said, We saw certainly that the LORD was with you *(the Hand of the Lord is now on Isaac for power and protection, which had not previously been; it was obvious even to the enemies of the Patriarch)*: and we said, Let there be now an oath between us, even between us and you, and let us make a covenant with you *(a covenant to settle the strife)*;

29 That you will do us no hurt, as we have not touched you, and as we have done unto you nothing but good, and have sent you away in peace: you are now the blessed of the LORD. *(Abimelech had enough sense to recognize that Isaac was now "blessed of the Lord," and that he must act accordingly. Regrettably, many in the modern Church do not seemingly have even as much spiritual discernment as that heathen prince of long ago.)*

30 And he made them a feast, and they did eat and drink *(the covenant was made)*.

31 And they rose up at a certain time in the morning, and swore one to another: and Isaac sent them away, and they departed from him in peace.

32 And it came to pass the same day, that Isaac's servants came, and told him concerning the well which they had dug, and said unto him, We have found water. *(The water here is symbolic of the water of life which would be afforded by the Lord Jesus Christ, the "Seed" of Abraham, Isaac and Jacob.)*

33 And he called it Shebah *(which means "the well of the oath;" it was symbolic of the Covenant made by the Lord with Abraham concerning Redemption)*: therefore the name of the city is Beer-sheba unto this day.

ESAU'S WIVES

34 And Esau was forty years old when he took to wife Judith the daughter of Beeri the Hittite, and Bashemath the daughter of Elon the Hittite *(these girls were in the line of Ham*

and Canaan, which was cursed [9:25-26]; at this time the Lord recognized only the line of Shem, because through Shem the Messiah would come):

35 Which were a grief of mind unto Isaac and to Rebekah.

CHAPTER 27
(1760 B.C.)
THE STOLEN BLESSING

AND it came to pass, that when Isaac was old, and his eyes were dim, so that he could not see *(as the physical dimness, there was spiritual dimness as well)*, he called Esau his oldest son *(older than Jacob by just a few minutes; in fact, they were twins, but totally dissimilar in both appearance and character)*, and said unto him, My son: and he said unto him, Behold, here am I.

2 And he said, Behold now, I am old, I know not the day of my death *(in fact, it would be many years before Isaac would die)*:

3 Now therefore take, I pray you, your weapons, your quiver and your bow, and go out to the field, and take me some venison *(Esau sold his birthright for a mess of pottage; his father was prepared to sell if for a dish of venison! Williams says: "Humbling picture of a man of God under the power of his lower sensual nature!")*;

4 And make me savoury meat, such as I love, and bring it to me, that I may eat; that my soul may bless you before I die. *(This was to be the blessing of the birthright; Isaac had been told by God at the time of Jacob's birth that Jacob was to possess the birthright. But yet he ignores this Word from the Lord, and proceeds in his determination to give the birthright to Esau, despite the fact that Esau knew the Lord not at all!)*

5 And Rebekah heard when Isaac spoke to Esau his son. And Esau went to the field to hunt for venison, and to bring it. *(Rebekah, overhearing the intentions of Isaac, proceeds now to manage the affairs herself; therefore, she steps outside the path of Faith.)*

6 And Rebekah spoke unto Jacob her son, saying, Behold, I heard your father speak unto Esau your brother, saying *(the history of Jacob is a treasure house of spiritual instruction for the people of God; Jacob as no other man symbolizes the Sanctification process; Jacob symbolizes it so well, because he is a sad illustration of the destructive power of fallen human nature)*,

7 Bring me venison, and make me savoury

meat, that I may eat, and bless you before the LORD before my death.

8 Now therefore, my son, obey my voice according to that which I command you *(Rebekah schemes in order to get Jacob the birthright, exactly as Sarah schemed to give Abraham a son; both were on the path of self-will).*

9 Go now to the flock, and fetch me from thence two good kids of the goats; and I will make them savoury meat for your father, such as he loves *(Jacob's history, as we shall see, teaches the lesson which the natural will is so unwilling to learn, that planning for self instead of resting in the Hand of God brings sorrow):*

10 And you shall bring it to your father, that he may eat, and that he may bless you before his death *(to obtain the birthright by subterfuge).*

11 And Jacob said to Rebekah his mother, Behold, Esau my brother is a hairy man, and I am a smooth man *(now the deception begins in earnest):*

12 My father peradventure will feel me, and I shall seem to him as a deceiver; and I shall bring a curse upon me, and not a blessing. *(Jacob's history, as we shall see, teaches the lesson, which the natural will is so unwilling to learn, that planning for self instead of resting in the Hand of God brings sorrow.)*

13 And his mother said unto him, Upon me be your curse, my son: only obey my voice, and go fetch me them. *(Abraham and Sarah attempted to deceive Pharaoh; Isaac and Rebekah attempted to deceive Abimelech; Jacob and Rebekah attempted to deceive Isaac. Such is the path of self-will.)*

14 And he went, and fetched, and brought them *(two kids of the goats)* to his mother: and his mother made savoury meat, such as his father loved.

15 And Rebekah took goodly raiment of her eldest son Esau, which were with her in the house, and put them upon Jacob her younger son:

16 And she put the skins of the kids of the goats upon his hands, and upon the smooth of his neck:

17 And she gave the savoury meat and the bread, which she had prepared, into the hand of her son Jacob *(all of this which we observe is a perfect description of resorting to the flesh; such never pleases God [Rom. 8:8]).*

18 And he came unto his father, and said, My father: and he said, Here am I; who are you, my son?

19 And Jacob said unto his father, I am Esau your firstborn; I have done according as you bade me: arise, I pray thee, sit and eat of my venison, that your soul may bless me *(Jacob lies to his father, which God can never condone).*

20 And Isaac said unto his son, How is it that you have found it so quickly, my son? And he said, Because the LORD your God brought it to me *(a Believer's sin is worse than the sin of an unbeliever, simply because it makes the Lord, in essence, a part of the sin; thus, blasphemy is added to disobedience).*

21 And Isaac said unto Jacob, Come near, I pray you, that I may feel you, my son, whether you be my very son Esau or not. *(Henry says, "It was one of those crooked measures which have too often been adopted to accomplish the Divine Promises; as if the end would justify, or at least excuse, the means.")*

22 And Jacob went near unto Isaac his father; and he *(Isaac)* felt him *(Jacob)*, and said, The voice is Jacob's voice, but the hands are the hands of Esau *(the entirety of this transaction speaks of fraud).*

23 And he discerned him not, because his hands were hairy, as his brother Esau's hands: so he blessed him. *(Isaac was wrong; Rebekah was wrong; and Jacob was wrong.)*

24 And he said, Are you my very son Esau? And he said, I am.

25 And he said, Bring it near to me, and I will eat of my son's venison, that my soul may bless you. And he brought it near to him, and he did eat: and he brought him wine, and he drank.

26 And his father Isaac said unto him, Come near now, and kiss me, my son.

27 And he came near, and kissed him: and he smelled the smell of his raiment, and blessed him, and said, See, the smell of my son is as the smell of a field which the LORD has blessed:

28 Therefore God give you of the dew of heaven, and the fatness of the Earth, and plenty of corn and wine: *(There are two grand points brought out in Jacob's history — God's purpose of Grace, on the one hand; and on the other, self-will plotting and scheming to reach what that purpose would have infallibly brought about without any plot or scheme at all.)*

29 Let people serve you, and nations bow down to you: be lord over your brethren, and let your mother's sons bow down to you: cursed be every one who curses you, and blessed be he who blesses you. *(This part of*

the Blessing points to Christ, Who would be in the lineage of Jacob. God did not need the aid of such elements as Rebekah's cunning and Jacob's gross deceit in order to accomplish His Purpose. He had said, "The elder shall serve the younger." This was enough — enough for Faith, but not enough for self-will, which must ever adopt its own ways and, as stated, know nothing of what it is to wait on God.)

DECEPTION DISCOVERED

30 And it came to pass, as soon as Isaac had made an end of blessing Jacob, and Jacob was yet scarce gone out from the presence of Isaac his father, that Esau his brother came in from his hunting.

31 And he also had made savoury meat, and brought it unto his father, and said unto his father, Let my father arise, and eat of his son's venison, that your soul may bless me *(even though Jacob had tried to obtain the birthright by having Esau sell it to him, it is obvious here that Esau did not recognize what had transpired [25:27-34]).*

32 And Isaac his father said unto him, Who are you? And he said, I am your son, your firstborn Esau. *(Esau represents those in the Church who would walk the path of self-will. Jacob represents those who know the path of Faith, but would leave that path and suffer greatly. Isaac represents those who are in positions of leadership, and know so little of the Mind of God that they would give the birthright to the Devil instead of to Christ.)*

33 And Isaac trembled very exceedingly *(he trembled exceedingly at what he had almost done in giving the birthright to Esau, considering that he had been told by God at the time of Jacob's birth that he [Jacob] was to possess the birthright; he trembles exceedingly under a just fear; this fear brings him back into the path of Faith, and directly he returns to that path, he steps from self-will to dignity)*, and said, Who? where is he who has taken venison, and brought it to me, and I have eaten of all before you came, and have blessed him? yes, and he shall be blessed *("the will of the flesh" made Isaac wish to bless Esau, but Faith in the end conquered [Heb. 11:20], and he cries respecting Jacob: "I have blessed him, and he shall be blessed").*

ESAU'S REMORSE

34 And when Esau heard the words of his father, he cried with a great and exceeding bitter cry, and said unto his father, Bless me, even me also, O my father *(Esau wanted the material part of the blessing, but had no regard whatsoever for the spiritual part; unfortunately, far too many in the modern Church follow the same path of material possessions; Jesus said so [Rev. 3:17]).*

35 And he *(Isaac)* said, Your brother came with subtilty, and has taken away your blessing *(the birthright normally belonged to the firstborn, which Esau here claims; however, it had been promised to Jacob by the Lord [25:23]; however, this gave Jacob no right whatsoever to practice deceit).*

36 And he *(Esau)* said, Is not he rightly named Jacob? for he has supplanted me these two times: he took away my birthright; and, behold, now he has taken away my blessing. And he said, Have you not reserved a blessing for me? *(First of all, the "blessing" went with the "birthright." As well, only one son could inherit the spiritual prerogatives of the birthright, and the temporal lordship which accompanied it.)*

37 And Isaac answered and said unto Esau, Behold, I have made him your lord, and all his brethren have I given to him for servants; and with corn and wine have I sustained him: and what shall I do now unto you, my son? *(In other words, there is no more blessing, and rightly so! All Blessing comes in and through Christ and what He did at the Cross, and Esau had no regard for that. Millions want the blessing, but not Christ! Such cannot be.)*

38 And Esau said unto his father, Have you but one blessing, my father? bless me, even me also, O my father. And Esau lifted up his voice, and wept *(however, once again we reiterate, his remorse was not for the true blessing, but only for the material benefits).*

39 And Isaac his father answered and said unto him, Behold, your dwelling shall be the fatness of the Earth, and of the dew of heaven from above *(most Expositors consider that the preposition "of" should be translated "from;" thus, it would read, "Behold, your dwelling shall be away from the fat places of the Earth, and away from the dew of heaven from above, and by your sword you shall live");*

40 And by your sword shall you live *(they have been, and are, a violent people)*, and you shall serve your brother *(the Edomites were the descendants of Esau, and they served Israel for nearly 900 years)*; and it shall come to pass

when you shall have the dominion, that you shall break his yoke from off your neck *(in the first days of Joram, and then of Ahaz, Edom revolted, and recovered its freedom, exactly as Isaac had prophesied; so, in reality, there was no blessing for Esau, as there can be no blessing for those who demean Christ and the price that He has paid for man's redemption).*

JACOB FLEES FROM ESAU

41 And Esau hated Jacob because of the blessing wherewith his father blessed him *(despite the deception, Esau had no cause to hate Jacob; he knew that the prophecy had given the birthright to Jacob; as well, he knew that his profligate lifestyle did not warrant such; he had no desire to be the Priest of the family, in fact, no desire for the things of God whatsoever; so his hatred was fueled by ungodliness, not by any imagined wrong):* and Esau said in his heart, The days of mourning for my father are at hand; then will I kill my brother Jacob *(the flesh always tries to kill that which is of the Spirit).*

42 And these words of Esau her elder son were told to Rebekah: and she sent and called Jacob her younger son, and said unto him, Behold, your brother Esau, as touching you, does comfort himself, purposing to kill you. *(Jacob himself was a sad illustration of the destructive power of fallen human nature. But yet, he truly loved the Lord, and truly wanted the things of the Lord. He just tried to obtain them in the wrong way.)*

43 Now therefore, my son, obey my voice; and arise, flee thou to Laban my brother to Haran *(now, the bitter fruits of sin rise to the surface);*

44 And tarry with him a few days, until your brother's fury turn away *(that "few days" would turn into twenty years; in fact, Jacob would never see his mother again);*

45 Until your brother's anger turn away from you, and he forget that which you have done to him: then I will send, and fetch you from thence: why should I be deprived also of you both in one day?

46 And Rebekah said to Isaac, I am weary of my life because of the daughters of Heth: if Jacob take a wife of the daughters of Heth, such as these which are of the daughters of the land, what good shall my life do me? *(There is no doubt that Rebekah was concerned about "the daughters of the land," and none of them being a suitable wife for Jacob; however, her real reason* at this time for sending Jacob away was not that which she told Isaac, but rather because she feared for his life as it regards the anger of Esau.

From this Chapter, we learn what a profane person actually is, even as the Holy Spirit describes Esau [Heb. 12:16]. It is one who would like to hold both worlds, one who would like to enjoy the present without forfeiting his title to the future. It is the person who attempts to use God, instead of God using him.)

CHAPTER 28
(1760 B.C.)
JACOB

AND Isaac called Jacob, and blessed him, and charged him, and said unto him, You shall not take a wife of the daughters of Canaan *(it was not the Will of God for Esau or Jacob to marry "the daughters of the land," but now that Jacob was the recipient of the Blessing, thereby the chosen one as it regards the birthright, which had to do with the coming of the Redeemer into the world, it was imperative that he not marry one of the Canaanite girls, as had his brother Esau; their lineage was of the cursed line of Canaan; he was rather to take a wife of one of the daughters of Laban, his mother's brother).*

2 Arise, go to Padan-aram, to the house of Bethuel your mother's father; and take you a wife from thence of the daughters of Laban your mother's brother *(now we have the commencing of God's special dealings with Jacob; now begins the "making of a man").*

3 And God Almighty bless you, and make you fruitful, and multiply you, that you may be a multitude of people *(the appellative "God Almighty" means "El-Shaddai," and promises guardianship and companionship");*

4 And give you the Blessing of Abraham, to you, and to your seed with you; that you may inherit the land wherein you are a stranger, which God gave unto Abraham *(Paul addressed the "Blessing of Abraham" [Gal. 3:14]; it means "Justification by Faith;" it refers to a believing sinner who is justified before God by simply having Faith in Christ and what Christ has done for us at the Cross).*

5 And Isaac sent away Jacob: and he went to Padan-aram unto Laban, son of Bethuel the Syrian, the brother of Rebekah, Jacob's and Esau's mother *(Isaac now fully seems to have returned to the path of Faith; there is now no attempt to substitute Esau for Jacob, or to lessen the privileges of the latter, but, with hearty*

cheerfulness, he blesses the younger son, and confirms him in the possession of the whole Abrahamic Blessing).

6 When Esau saw that Isaac had blessed Jacob, and sent him away to Padan-aram, to take him a wife from thence; and that as he blessed him he gave him a charge, saying, You shall not take a wife of the daughters of Canaan *(Esau, knowing nothing of the path of Faith, concludes erroneously that the reason that Isaac gave Jacob the Blessing is because he [Esau] had married Canaanite women);*

7 And that Jacob obeyed his father and his mother, and was gone to Padan-aram *(the "obedience" mentioned here of Jacob was the opposite of that concerning Esau);*

8 And Esau seeing that the daughters of Canaan pleased not Isaac his father;

9 Then went Esau unto Ishmael, and took unto the wives which he had Mahalath the daughter of Ishmael Abraham's son, the sister of Nebajoth, to be his wife. *(In fact, Ishmael had been dead now for some years, so it refers to Esau going to the family of Ishmael. The truth is, Ishmael was no closer to acceptance than the daughters of Canaan. He had long before been rejected by the Holy Spirit, and had been thrust out of the family of Abraham. This portrays any Believer who doesn't understand the true path of Faith and tries to build his case on a work of the flesh. And, if the Believer doesn't understand the Cross, he will, without fail, resort to the flesh.)*

JACOB'S VISION

10 And Jacob went out from Beer-sheba, and went toward Haran *(Jacob is alone, but yet God and all the Holy Angels are with him, as we shall see).*

11 And he stopped at a certain place, and tarried there all night, because the sun was set; and he took of the stones of that place, and put them for his pillows, and lay down in that place to sleep *(the "sleep" represents him ceasing from his personal activity and God beginning His Personal activity; Jacob has much to learn, and it will begin here).*

12 And he dreamed, and behold a ladder set up on the Earth, and the top of it reached to Heaven: and behold the Angels of God ascending and descending on it *(in a sense, the "ladder" represents Christ; He Alone is the Way to Heaven; He would refer to this at the beginning of His Ministry [Jn. 1:51]).*

13 And, behold, the LORD stood above it, and said, I am the LORD God of Abraham your father, and the God of Isaac: the land whereon you lie, to you will I give it, and to your seed *(the words "above it" in the original Hebrew actually should read "beside him"; not only did the Angels descend by it to him, but God Himself descended this stairway of glory and stood by him; the Patriarch, destitute and with a stone for a pillow, literally having to leave this land, is now told by the Lord, "To you will I give it, and to your seed;" only Faith could accept such a Promise);*

14 And your seed shall be as the dust of the Earth, and you shall spread abroad to the west, and to the east, and to the north, and to the south: and in you and in your seed shall all the families of the Earth be blessed *(all of this speaks of Christ, Who Alone is the Blessing; His Gospel, through the Cross, would go and, in fact, has gone, to the entirety of the world).*

15 And, behold, I am with you, and will keep you in all places where you go, and will bring you again into this land; for I will not leave you, until I have done that which I have spoken to you of *(the Lord said to Jacob: 1. I am with you; 2. I will keep you; 3. I will bring you again into this land; and, 4. I won't leave you, until I have done all that of which I have spoken to you; these same Promises are to us as well!).*

JACOB'S VOW

16 And Jacob awaked out of his sleep, and he said, Surely the LORD is in this place; and I knew it not *(for the first time, the Lord reveals Himself to Jacob; this is the night that Jacob was "born from above"; all of this tells us that all hopes of the flesh must die before the Spirit can properly be revealed to us).*

17 And he was afraid, and said, How dreadful is this place! this is none other but the House of God, and this is the Gate of Heaven *(could be translated, "How all-inspiring is this place!"; the "Gate of Heaven" is Jesus Christ).*

18 And Jacob rose up early in the morning, and took the stone that he had put for his pillows, and set it up for a pillar, and poured oil upon the top of it *(the "stone" is a Type of Christ, with the "oil" serving as a symbol of the Holy Spirit; no doubt, he was inspired by the Lord to do this).*

19 And he called the name of that place Bethel: but the name of that city was called Luz at the first *("Beth-el" means "House of God"; "Luz"*

means "separation"; the Lord can turn "Luz" into the "House of God," only as the Believer is separated from the world).

20 And Jacob vowed a vow *(the first recorded vow in the Bible),* saying, If God be with me *(should read, "Since God be with me"),* and will keep me in this way that I go, and will give me bread to eat, and raiment to put on,

21 So that I come again to my father's house in peace *(free from Esau's avenging threats);* then shall the LORD be my God:

22 And this stone *(representing Christ),* which I have set for a pillar, shall be God's House *(all of this sets the stage for the Holy Spirit making the Believer His Sanctuary; it was all made possible by the Cross [Jn. 14:16-20]):* and of all that You shall give me I will surely give the tenth unto you. *(This obviously means that Jacob gave a tenth of his vast herds of sheep and cattle to the Lord as a Sacrifice. If that, in fact, was the case, we now find Jacob offering up Sacrifices to a degree as no one else. If the tithe which we propose to give to the Lord doesn't advance the grand Message of "Jesus Christ and Him Crucified" [I Cor. 1:23; 2:2], then we actually aren't really paying tithe. The first occasion of tithing mentioned in the Bible was when Abraham paid tithes to Melchizedek, who was a Type of Christ as our Great High Priest. Jesus would become this by dying on the Cross as a Sacrifice [14:18-20]. So both occasions of paying tithes speak to the Cross.)*

CHAPTER 29
(1760 B.C.)
JACOB MEETS RACHEL

THEN Jacob went on his journey, and came into the land of the people of the east *(this "journey" would last for some twenty years).*

2 And he looked, and behold a well in the field, and, lo, there were three flocks of sheep lying by it; for out of that well they watered the flocks: and a great stone was upon the well's mouth.

3 And there were all the flocks gathered: and they rolled the stone from the well's mouth, and watered the sheep, and put the stone again upon the well's mouth in his place.

4 And Jacob said unto them, My brethren, from where are you? And they said, Of Haran are we.

5 And he said unto them, Do you know Laban the son of Nahor? And they said, We know him *(Laban is Jacob's mother's brother).*

6 And he said unto them, Is he well? And they said, He is well: and, behold, Rachel his daughter comes with the sheep *(this is the first mention of Rachel in the Bible; she will figure very prominently in the great Plan of God, being the mother of both Joseph and Benjamin; she was the ancestress of three of the great Tribes of Israel, Benjamin, Ephraim, and Manasseh, the latter two being the sons of Joseph).*

7 And he said, Lo, it is yet high day, neither is it time that the cattle should be gathered together: water ye the sheep, and go and feed them.

8 And they said, We cannot, until all the flocks be gathered together, and till they roll the stone from the well's mouth; then we water the sheep *(the reason probably was that Laban owned the well, and the other flocks could not be watered until Rachel first of all had watered her flock).*

9 And while he *(Jacob)* yet spoke with them, Rachel came with her father's sheep: for she kept them *(we readily see the Hand of the Lord working in this situation regarding the meeting of Jacob with Rachel).*

10 And it came to pass, when Jacob saw Rachel the daughter of Laban his mother's brother, and the sheep of Laban his mother's brother, that Jacob went near, and rolled the stone from the well's mouth, and watered the flock of Laban his mother's brother *(three times the Holy Spirit has Moses, when writing this account, to repeat the term, "his mother's brother"; it is not done unintentionally; the idea is, Jacob has met with his own relations, with "his bone and his flesh").*

11 And Jacob kissed Rachel, and lifted up his voice, and wept *(the Patriarch is overcome with emotion, and I think mostly at the joy of seeing the Hand of God working in his life).*

12 And Jacob told Rachel that he was her father's brother, and that he was Rebekah's son: and she ran and told her father *(Jacob was actually the nephew of Laban).*

13 And it came to pass, when Laban heard the tidings of Jacob his sister's son, that he ran to meet him, and embraced him, and kissed him, and brought him to his house. And he *(Jacob)* told Laban all these things *(Laban would no doubt have been well over 100 years of age at this time, possibly even as much as 120; Laban did now almost exactly what he had done those many years before, when he was told by Rebekah his sister of Eliezer [24:29]).*

14 And Laban said to him, Surely you are

my bone and my flesh. And he abode with him the space of a month (*after this, he went out and obtained his own place*).

LABAN

15 And Laban said unto Jacob, Because you are my brother, should you therefore serve me for nought? tell me, what shall your wages be? (*Jacob the dealer meets now with Laban the dealer, and they are both seen, as it were, straining every nerve to outwit each other.*)

16 And Laban had two daughters: the name of the elder was Leah, and the name of the younger was Rachel.

17 Leah was tender eyed; but Rachel was beautiful and well favored.

18 And Jacob loved Rachel; and said, I will serve you seven years for Rachel your younger daughter (*Jacob is now about to begin to reap the bitter fruit of his sin*).

19 And Laban said, It is better that I give her to you, than that I should give her to another man: abide with me.

20 And Jacob served seven years for Rachel; and they seemed unto him but a few days, for the love he had to her (*it is a popular mistake to suppose that Jacob did not marry Rachel till the end of the seven years, or even the second seven years; every evidence is that he took her immediately for his wife, and then served the time allotted*).

JACOB AND LEAH

21 And Jacob said unto Laban, Give me my wife, for my days are fulfilled, that I may go in unto her (*his "days" being fulfilled simply means that the contract had been agreed upon, that he was to serve Laban seven years for Rachel; this is proven by Verse 30*).

22 And Laban gathered together all the men of the place, and made a feast.

23 And it came to pass in the evening, that he took Leah his daughter, and brought her to him; and he went in unto her (*when Leah went in to Jacob, she no doubt was wearing a veil and, as well, the room was probably dark; Jacob thought it was Rachel*).

24 And Laban gave unto his daughter Leah Zilpah his maid for an handmaid.

25 And it came to pass, that in the morning, behold, it was Leah: and he said to Laban, What is this you have done unto me? did I not serve (*agree*) with you for Rachel? wherefore then have you beguiled me? (*The deception that Jacob practiced upon Isaac cost him at least 14 years of servitude.*)

26 And Laban said, It must not be so done in our country, to give the younger before the firstborn (*this was a custom that Laban had concocted on his own; there is no evidence of such in that part of the world*).

27 Fulfill her week (*serve me seven years for Leah*), and we will give you this also for the service (*give him Rachel*) which you shall serve with me yet seven other years.

RACHEL

28 And Jacob did so, and fulfilled her week (*he agreed to the transaction of seven more years, making a total of fourteen*): and he gave him Rachel his daughter to wife also.

29 And Laban gave to Rachel his daughter Bilhah his handmaid to be her maid.

30 And he went in also unto Rachel, and he loved also Rachel more than Leah, and served with him yet seven other years (*in all of this we find that the Lord is chastising Jacob; the Lord doesn't actually punish his children, but He definitely does chastise his children; chastisement is designed to teach us something, while punishment contains no instruction, only hurt; Jacob is being chastised; he seems to recognize this, and accept it*).

LEAH'S CHILDREN

31 And when the LORD saw that Leah was hated (*the word "hated" here means "loved less"*), he opened her womb: but Rachel was barren (*there is no indication that Jacob mistreated Leah, but there is indication that Rachel did; the Lord saw all of this and, as a result, He made Leah fruitful and, at the same time, He made Rachel barren; in fact, Leah was the ancestress of both David and our Lord; and there could have been no greater honor than that! We should allow this to be a lesson to us, in that the Lord sees everything, and acts accordingly*).

32 And Leah conceived, and bore a son, and she called his name Reuben (*the name actually means, "See, a son"*): for she said, Surely the LORD has looked upon my affliction; now therefore my husband will love me (*Leah was not to blame in all of this situation, so Rachel, her sister, shouldn't have taken the situation out on her; as noted, the Lord didn't take kindly to what was happening*).

33 And she conceived again, and bore a son; and said, Because the LORD has heard I was hated, He has therefore given me this son also: and she called his name Simeon *(his name means "hearing"; she is functioning from the position that the Lord has heard her petition).*

34 And she conceived again, and bore a son; and said, Now this time will my husband be joined unto me, because I have born him three sons: therefore was his name called Levi *(his name means "joined").*

35 And she conceived again, and bore a son: and she said, Now will I praise the LORD: therefore she called his name Judah; and left bearing. *(Judah means "praise." So, in these four sons we have a symbol of the entirety of the Plan of Redemption. The "son" is born, it "hears" the Gospel, it is "joined" to the Lord, and it "praises" the Lord. But, as we shall see in the next Chapter, it doesn't end here.)*

CHAPTER 30
(1745 B.C.)
BILHAH

AND when Rachel saw that she bore Jacob no children, Rachel envied her sister; and said unto Jacob, Give me children, or else I die *(Rachel pictures Israel; Leah, the Church; Rachel is first loved, but not possessed – sorrowful and childless; Leah, blessed with children and triumphant; Paul, in a sense, addressed this in Galatians 4:27; Rachel blames Jacob, but the fault is not that of Jacob, but rather hers; instead of seeking Jacob, she should have sought the Lord).*

2 And Jacob's anger was kindled against Rachel: and he said, Am I in God's stead, Who has withheld from you the fruit of the womb? *(Jacob directs Rachel to the Lord.)*

3 And she said, Behold my maid Bilhah, go in unto her; and she shall bear upon my knees, that I may also have children by her *(all of this shows precious little Faith in God; while it seems that both Rachel and Leah understood somewhat the significance of them having children, their understanding was only partial, because they seemed to walk more by sight than by Faith).*

4 And she gave him Bilhah her handmaid to wife: and Jacob went in unto her *(this was the custom in those days; the child that Bilhah would have would be looked at as that of Rachel, but only in a sense; the Holy Spirit plainly proclaims the actual mother).*

JACOB'S CHILDREN

5 And Bilhah conceived, and bore Jacob a son. *(Concerning this, Calvin says, "So, God often strives to overcome men's wickedness through kindness, and pursues the unworthy with His Grace.")*

6 And Rachel said, God has judged me, and has also heard my voice, and has given me a son: therefore called she his name Dan. *(The name means "judging." Whether Jacob understood such or not is open to question; however, he must have 13 sons in order to found the nation of Israel. Twelve would be for the regular tribes, while one would be for the Priestly Tribe. But, as usual, even as here, the flesh is mixed with faith.)*

7 And Bilhah Rachel's maid conceived again, and bore Jacob a second son.

8 And Rachel said, With great wrestlings have I wrestled with my sister, and I have prevailed: and she called his name Naphtali *(his name means "wrestling").*

9 When Leah saw that she had left bearing, she took Zilpah her maid, and gave her Jacob to wife *(resorts to the flesh).*

10 And Zilpah Leah's maid bore Jacob a son.

11 And Leah said, A troop comes: and she called his name Gad *(Gad means, "good fortune").*

12 And Zilpah Leah's maid bore Jacob a second son.

13 And Leah said, Happy am I, for the daughters will call me blessed: and she called his name Asher *(means "happy").*

14 And Reuben went in the days of wheat harvest, and found mandrakes in the field, and brought them unto his mother Leah. Then Rachel said to Leah, Give me, I pray you, of your son's mandrakes. *(These Passages present a perfect picture of prayer mixed with superstition. According to Oriental superstition, the mandrake possessed the virtue of promoting fruitfulness and fertility. It was an apple-like fruit.)*

15 And she said unto her, Is it a small matter that you should take my husband? and would you take away my son's mandrakes also? And Rachel said, Therefore he shall lie with you tonight for your son's mandrakes *(Rachel makes a bargain with Leah).*

16 And Jacob came out of the field in the evening, and Leah went out to meet him, and said, You must come in unto me; for surely I have hired you with my son's mandrakes. And he lay with her that night.

17 And God hearkened unto Leah, and she

conceived, and bore Jacob the fifth son. *(From this Verse, we know that Leah sought the Lord as it regards her conceiving another son, which she did. The Lord heard and answered her prayer, and this despite the fact that superstition had been involved regarding the mandrakes. How so much the Lord overlooks in answering prayer for all of us.)*

18 And Leah said, God has given me my hire, because I have given my maiden to my husband: and she called his name Issachar *(means, "reward")*.

19 And Leah conceived again, and bore Jacob the sixth son.

20 And Leah said, God has endued me with a good dowry; now will my husband dwell with me, because I have born him six sons: and she called his name Zebulun. *(Means "dwelling." So, in the six sons of Leah, we have the totality of the Plan of God. A "son" is born; he "hears" the Gospel; he is "joined" to Christ; he "praises" the Lord; he is "rewarded"; and he will "dwell" with the Lord forever.)*

21 And afterwards she bore a daughter, and called her name Dinah.

JOSEPH

22 And God remembered Rachel *(that the mandrakes could not remove sterility, the Lord demonstrated by allowing Rachel's barrenness to continue at least two years longer, though she had made use of this supposed remedy, and by opening Leah's womb without them; we should learn from all of this how the Lord rules in all things; but, once again, it's so easy for any of us to resort to the flesh)*, and God hearkened to her, and opened her womb *(it seems that Rachel finally resorted strictly to the Lord)*.

23 And she conceived, and bore a son; and said, God has taken away my reproach *(God Alone can take away the reproach)*:

24 And she called his name Joseph; and said, The LORD shall add to me another son. *(Joseph's name means "adding." So, Rachel prophesies that the Lord will give her another son. As well, all of these sons are Types of Christ. Reuben: Jesus is the "Son" of God. Simeon: through Jesus we "hear" God. Levi: through Jesus we are "joined" to the Father. Judah: through Jesus, God had accepted our "praises." Dan: Jesus has taken the "judgment" due us. Naphtali: Jesus has "wrestled" the power of darkness, all on our behalf, and has defeated the foe. Gad: Jesus is the "troop" Who has fought on*

our behalf, and has brought us "good fortune." Asher: Jesus has made us "happy." Issachar: Jesus is our "reward." Zebulun: Jesus has made it possible for Believers to "dwell" in the House of the Lord forever. Joseph: Jesus has "added" all Believers to the Kingdom. Benjamin: Jesus is the Father's "strong right hand," and sits with Him in Heavenly Places. And as He does, so do we [Eph. 2:6]. Manasseh and Ephraim will be born to Joseph. There will be no tribe named Joseph, his two sons taking his place, making the total of the necessary 13 tribes.)

WAGES

25 And it came to pass, when Rachel had born Joseph, that Jacob said unto Laban, Send me away, that I may go unto my own place, and to my country. *(The phrase, "For whom I have served you, and let me go," proves that both Leah and Rachel became his wives immediately and then he served the fourteen years for them.)*

26 Give me my wives and my children, for whom I have served you, and let me go: for you know my service which I have done you.

27 And Laban said unto him, I pray you, if I have found favor in your eyes, tarry: for I have learned by experience that the LORD has blessed me for your sake. *(Laban did not really serve the Lord; however, he did know that Jehovah was real, and that the Blessings of God were definitely upon Jacob. So, for material benefits alone, he desires that the Patriarch remain with him as long as possible. We should learn a lesson from all of this. The Blessings of the Lord upon any individual will fall out as well on those around such a person.)*

28 And he *(Laban)* said, Appoint me your wages, and I will give it.

29 And he *(Jacob)* said unto him *(unto Laban)*, You know how I have served you, and how your cattle was with me.

30 For it was little which you had before I came, and it is now increased unto a multitude; and the LORD has blessed you since my coming: and now when shall I provide for my own house also?

31 And he *(Laban)* said, What shall I give you? And Jacob said, You shall not give me any thing: if you will do this thing for me, I will again feed and keep your flock:

32 I will pass through all your flock today, removing from thence all the speckled and spotted cattle, and all the brown cattle among

the sheep, and the spotted and speckled among the goats: and of such shall be my hire.

33 So shall my righteousness answer for me in time to come *(God will bless me)*, when it shall come for my hire before your face: every one that is not speckled and spotted among the goats, and brown among the sheep, that shall be counted stolen with me *(all that are speckled, spotted, or brown shall be mine)*.

34 And Laban said, Behold, I would it might be according to your word. *(Some have criticized Jacob, as it regards this particular agreement. They have attributed such to devious ways, trickery, and even dishonesty; however, it would appear that he acted honestly. The Lord will never bless sin and dishonesty, or even the slightest hint of evil. So, if the Lord is involved, and He definitely was, we must conclude that the acts, whatever they may have been, were righteous.)*

35 And he removed that day the he goats that were ringstraked and spotted, and all the she goats that were speckled and spotted, and every one that had some white in it, and all the brown among the sheep, and gave them into the hand of his *(Jacob's)* sons.

36 And he *(Laban)* set three days' journey between himself and Jacob: and Jacob fed the rest of Laban's flocks. *(Laban required that there should be an interval of between 30 and 40 miles between "himself," that is, his flocks, and those of Jacob. His wealth in sheep and goats must have been enormous to require so large a separate feeding ground. All of this, we learn from Verse 30, had been the result of Jacob's care.)*

PROSPERITY

37 And Jacob took him rods of green poplar, and of the hazel and chestnut tree; and pilled white strakes in them, and made the white appear which was in the rods. *(Whenever Jacob proposed his plan, which would give him all of the spotted and mingled sheep and goats, Laban reasoned, and rightly so under normal circumstances, that the number of animals falling into this category would be small indeed. The Lord told Jacob what to do in this situation. It is said to have been frequently observed that, particularly in the case of sheep, whatever fixes their attention in copulation is marked upon the young; however, it will be safer to ascribe this to Divine Blessing than to human craft.)*

38 And he set the rods which he had pilled before the flocks in the gutters in the watering troughs when the flocks came to drink, that they should conceive when they came to drink.

39 And the flocks conceived before the rods, and brought forth cattle ringstraked, speckled, and spotted.

40 And Jacob did separate the lambs, and set the faces of the flocks toward the ringstraked, and all the brown in the flock of Laban; and he put his own flocks by themselves, and put them not unto Laban's cattle. *(Incidentally, the term "cattle," as used in the Old Testament, can refer to all domestic animals, such as lambs, goats, oxen, or heifers. In the Passages of our study, it seems to refer to all types.)*

41 And it came to pass, whensoever the stronger cattle did conceive, that Jacob laid the rods before the eyes of the cattle in the gutters, that they might conceive among the rods.

42 But when the cattle were feeble, he put them not in: so the feebler were Laban's, and the stronger Jacob's.

43 And the man *(Jacob)* increased exceedingly, and had much cattle, and maidservants, and menservants, and camels, and asses. *(We must conclude that the proposal of such a singular condition on the part of Jacob was an act, not of folly, but of faith, being tantamount to a committal of his cause to God instead of Laban. The acceptance of the agreement on the part of Laban was a display of greed, and a proof that the bygone years of prosperity had only increased that greed. Increase in the best sense is God's Promise. It will be sent as He wills, and when He wills, but will be found the true answer to prayer and the true manifestation of love. On all that belongs to us, the blessing rests.)*

CHAPTER 31

(1739 B.C.)

JEALOUSY

AND he *(Jacob)* heard the words of Laban's sons, saying, Jacob has taken away all that was our father's; and of that which was our father's has he gotten all this glory. *(As long as Jacob was increasing the wealth of Laban, and he [Jacob] remained poor, Laban had no problem with that. But once Jacob begins to prosper, and begins to do so in a grand way, this creates jealousy in Laban.)*

2 And Jacob beheld the countenance of Laban, and, behold, it was not toward him as before *(jealousy)*.

3 And the LORD said unto Jacob, Return unto the land of your fathers, and to your

kindred; and I will be with you *(it is so pleasing to the heart to note the minute leading of the Lord in the life of the Patriarch; it is now time for him to return to Canaan; he has been away for some twenty years)*.

4 And Jacob sent and called Rachel and Leah to the field unto his flock,

5 And said unto them, I see your father's countenance, that it is not toward me as before; but the God of my father has been with me *(he gives the praise to the Lord for his prosperity)*.

6 And you know that with all my power I have served your father.

7 And your father has deceived me, and changed my wages ten times; but God suffered him not to hurt me. *(When Laban saw that Jacob's flocks were increasing according to the bargain originally made, he then changed the rules. Whatever it was that he did we aren't told; however, we do note that God overruled whatever it is that Laban did, and continued to bless Jacob.)*

8 If he said thus, The speckled shall be your wages; then all the cattle bore speckled: and if he said thus, The ringstraked shall be your hire; then bore all the cattle ringstraked *(men rule, but God overrules!)*.

9 Thus God has taken away the cattle of your father, and given them to me *(from all of this, we learn that Jacob had not done anything wrong, or else God would not have prospered him)*.

10 And it came to pass at the time that the cattle conceived, that I lifted up my eyes, and saw in a dream, and, behold, the rams which leaped upon the cattle were ringstraked, speckled, and grisled *(specifying to Jacob that it was the Lord Who had given the increase)*.

CANAAN

11 And the Angel of God spoke unto me in a dream, saying, Jacob: And I said, Here am I *(this is actually Jehovah!)*.

12 And He *(the Lord)* said, Lift up now your eyes, and see, all the rams which leap upon the cattle are ringstraked, speckled, and grisled: for I have seen all that Laban has done unto you *(we should take a lesson from this, understanding that the Lord sees and notes all)*.

13 I am the God of Beth-el *(He reaffirms that He is the God of Beth-el, which proclaims the fact that every promise given there to Jacob still held true)*, where you anointed the pillar *(which spoke of Christ and the Holy Spirit)*, and

where you vowed a vow unto Me *(this was the "tenth" that was to be given to the Lord; all of these animals had been offered up in sacrifice, seeming that Jacob had been faithful to the vow [28:20])*: now arise, you get out from this land, and return unto the land of your kindred *(as stated, twenty years had passed since he had seen his kindred)*.

JACOB

14 And Rachel and Leah answered and said unto him, Is there yet any portion or inheritance for us in our father's house? *(Both Rachel and Leah understood completely the duplicity of their father. He not only had done Jacob wrong, but he had wronged them as well.)*

15 Are we not counted of him strangers? for he has sold us, and has quite devoured also our money *(it's a shame that Laban figures so prominently in the Gospel Message, but yet never came to know the Lord)*.

16 For all the riches which God has taken from our father, that is ours, and our children's: now then, whatsoever God has said unto you, do *(they recognized the Hand of God in all of this, and readily acquiesced to Jacob's proposal to leave)*.

17 Then Jacob rose up, and set his sons and his wives upon camels;

18 And he carried away all his cattle, and all his goods which he had gotten, the cattle of his getting, which he had gotten in Padan-aram, for to go to Isaac his father in the land of Canaan *(these twenty years that Jacob has been gone are silent regarding Isaac)*.

19 And Laban went to shear his sheep: and Rachel had stolen the images that were her father's *(the images had to do with her inheritance, of which we will momentarily address)*.

20 And Jacob stole away unawares to Laban the Syrian, in that he told him not that he fled.

21 So he fled with all that he had; and he rose up, and passed over the river, and set his face toward the mount Gilead *(for Jacob to leave in this manner shows that the situation had become intolerable)*.

THE PURSUIT

22 And it was told Laban on the third day that Jacob was fled.

23 And he took his brethren *(his sons and others)* with him, and pursued after him *(after Jacob)* seven days' journey; and they overtook

him in the mount Gilead.

24 And God came to Laban the Syrian in a dream by night, and said unto him, Take heed that you speak not to Jacob either good or bad *(the Lord warning Laban in a dream indicates that the man intended to do Jacob harm).*

25 Then Laban overtook Jacob. Now Jacob had pitched his tent in the mount: and Laban with his brethren pitched in the mount of Gilead.

26 And Laban said to Jacob, What have you done, that you have stolen away unawares to me, and carried away my daughters, as captives taken with the sword? *(This was totally untrue. Rachel and Leah had voluntarily accompanied their husband in his departure.)*

27 Wherefore did you flee away secretly, and steal away from me; and did not tell me, that I might have sent you away with mirth, and with songs, with tabret, and with harp?

28 And have not suffered me to kiss my sons and my daughters? you have now done foolishly in so doing. *(Laban's words are hypocritical. More than likely, the Lord told Jacob to depart as he did because of Laban's hostile intentions.)*

29 It is in the power of my hand to do you hurt: but the God of your father spoke unto me yesternight, saying, You take heed that you speak not to Jacob either good or bad.

30 And now, though you would need be gone, because you sore longed after your father's house, yet wherefore have you stolen my gods? *(Jacob had no idea that Rachel had taken these things.)*

31 And Jacob answered and said to Laban, Because I was afraid: for I said, Peradventure you would take by force your daughters from me.

32 With whomsoever you find your gods, let him not live: before our brethren discern for you what is yours with me, and take it to you. For Jacob knew not that Rachel had stolen them. *(When there was any question about the inheritance, the person who had the teraphim [gods] was considered to have the right to the double portion of the primary heir. When Jacob first came, he was welcomed into the family and adopted as the heir, since Laban had no sons at the time. But Laban had sons born shortly after, and that normally would invalidate Jacob's claim unless he possessed the teraphim. Rachel felt Jacob deserved more than he was getting, so she stole them for his benefit, and for the benefit of Jacob's family. There is no evidence she wanted*

to worship these images — Horton.)

33 And Laban went into Jacob's tent, and into Leah's tent, and into the two maidservants' tents; but he found them not. Then went he out of Leah's tent, and entered into Rachel's tent. *(How foolish for Laban to call those things his gods which could be stolen! Could he expect protection from things that could neither resist nor discover their invaders?)*

34 Now Rachel had taken the images, and put them in the camel's furniture, and sat upon them. And Laban searched all the tent, but found them not.

35 And she said to her father, Let it not displease my lord that I cannot rise up before you; for the custom of women is upon me. And he searched but found not the images. *(She apologized for not standing, claiming that she was having her "period." Whether this was correct or not, we have no way of knowing; but there is a good possibility that it was.)*

36 And Jacob was angry, and did chide with Laban: and Jacob answered and said to Laban, What is my trespass? what is my sin, that you have so hotly pursued after me? *(Jacob was now very angry. Instead of Laban being sad regarding his two daughters and all of his grandchildren leaving, and knowing that he would possibly never see them again, he was more interested in material things than anything else.)*

37 Whereas you have searched all my stuff *(it is interesting that Jacob referred to these images as "stuff"),* what have you found of all your household stuff? set it here before my brethren and your brethren, that they may judge between us both.

38 This twenty years have I been with you; your ewes and your she goats have not cast their young, and the rams of your flock have I not eaten.

39 That which was torn of beasts I brought not unto you; I bore the loss of it; of my hand did you require it, whether stolen by day, or stolen by night.

40 Thus I was; in the day the drought consumed me, and the frost by night; and my sleep departed from my eyes.

41 Thus have I been twenty years in your house; I served you fourteen years for your two daughters, and six years for your cattle: and you have changed my wages ten times. *(Jacob rehearses his twenty years with Laban and, in effect, is saying that Laban has absolutely no reason to be angry with him.)*

42 Except the God of my father, the God of

Abraham *(Whom Laban did not serve)*, and the fear of Isaac, had been with me, surely you had sent me away now empty. God has seen my affliction and the labor of my hands, and rebuked you yesternight. *(The dream that the Lord gave to Laban. What a spectacle of infinite humor, if it were not so sad — a man seeking for his lost gods! The Gospel presents us with the opposite picture — the ever present God seeking for His lost children.)*

THE COVENANT

43 And Laban answered and said unto Jacob, These daughters are my daughters, and these children are my children, and these cattle are my cattle, and all that you see is mine: and what can I do this day unto these my daughters, or unto their children which they have born? *(At Beth-el, Jacob learned what God was; at Haran, what man was. And what a difference! At Beth-el, God enriched him: at Haran, man robbed him! Laban wrongly claims everything that Jacob has, but recognizes, due to the Power of God, that there is nothing he can do regarding the taking of them.)*

44 Now therefore you come, let us make a Covenant, I and you; and let it be for a witness between me and you. *(Laban wanted this Covenant because he was afraid, relative to what the Lord had told him in the dream.)*

45 And Jacob took a stone *(a Type of Christ)*, and set it up for a pillar.

46 And Jacob said unto his brethren, Gather stones; and they took stones, and made an heap: and they did eat there upon the heap *(for both to eat signified an agreement)*.

47 And Laban called it Jegar-sahadutha *(the heap of witness)*: but Jacob called it Galeed *(in Hebrew, it means the same thing, "the heap of witness")*.

48 And Laban said, This heap is a witness between me and you this day. Therefore was the name of it called Galeed;

49 And Mizpah *(a "beacon or watchtower")*; for he *(Laban)* said, The LORD watch between me and you, when we are absent one from another *(Laban uses the Name of the "Lord," but really does not know Him)*.

50 If you shall afflict my daughters, or if you shall take other wives beside my daughters, no man is with us; see, God is witness between me and you *(at this stage, Laban makes a show of piety as it regards his daughters, but his actions have spoken much louder than his words)*.

51 And Laban said to Jacob, Behold this heap, and behold this pillar, which I have cast between me and you:

52 This heap be witness, and this pillar be witness, that I will not pass over this heap to you, and that you shall not pass over this heap and this pillar unto me, for harm.

53 The God of Abraham, and the god of Nahor, the god of their father, judge between us *(Laban now adds an oath to the covenant, calling on the God of Abraham, and the gods of Nahor, to judge between Jacob and Laban; all of this proves that Laban worshipped many so-called gods; he really doesn't know the God of Abraham, but only puts Him into the mix, and on the same level as the gods of Nahor)*. And Jacob swore by the fear of his father Isaac. *(Jacob ignored the gods of Nahor, and took his oath only in the name of the only True God, Who was the "fear" of, or "the One Reverenced by, Isaac.")*

54 Then Jacob offered sacrifice upon the mount, and called his brethren to eat bread: and they did eat bread, and tarried all night in the mount. *(The Sacrifice meant nothing to Laban, even though he was well acquainted with this practice, but everything to Jacob. In essence, Jacob was saying that he was placing his faith and confidence in what the Sacrifice represented, namely the coming of the Lord Jesus Christ, and the price that He would pay to redeem the lost sons of Adam's fallen race.)*

55 And early in the morning Laban rose up, and kissed his sons and his daughters, and blessed them: and Laban departed, and returned unto his place. *(So, Laban passes from the scene, not to be mentioned again, except in passing [46:18, 25]. He had seen the Hand of God greatly so in the life of Jacob, with the Lord, as stated, even speaking to him in a dream; however, he has no heart for God, and thereby the opportunity of Heaven was eternally lost to him.)*

CHAPTER 32
(1739 B.C.)
ESAU

AND Jacob went on his way, and the Angels of God met him *(obeying the Lord, the Patriarch has the assurance of the protection of Angels)*.

2 And when Jacob saw them *(the Lord pulls back the cover of the spirit world, and allows Jacob to see the Angelic Host which will accompany him)*, he said, This is God's host: and he called the name of that place Mahanaim *(at

Beth-el, some twenty years before, his possessions consisted of a staff; but now he has become a host; "Mahanaim" means "two camps — his feeble camp and the encircling camp of God's mighty Angels").

3 And Jacob sent messengers before him to Esau his brother unto the land of Seir, the country of Edom *(some believe that Esau was the founder of the ancient city of Petra, and may have been there when Jacob sent for him).*

4 And he commanded them, saying, Thus shall you speak unto my lord Esau; Your servant Jacob says thus, I have sojourned with Laban, and stayed there until now:

5 And I have oxen, and asses, flocks, and menservants, and women-servants: and I have sent to tell my lord, that I may find grace in your sight.

6 And the messengers returned to Jacob, saying, We came to your brother Esau, and also he comes to meet you, and four hundred men with him. *(One doesn't bring that many men, as it regards a mere greeting. It is almost positive that Esau had other things in mind, and they were not exactly meant to be pleasant.)*

7 Then Jacob was greatly afraid and distressed *(did he not remember the host of Angels around him? But before we criticize Jacob, we must, as well, look at ourselves)*: and he divided the people who were with him, and the flocks, and herds, and the camels, into two bands;

8 And said, If Esau come to the one company, and smite it, then the other company which is left shall escape.

9 And Jacob said, O God of my father Abraham, and God of my father Isaac, the LORD which said unto me, Return unto your country, and to your kindred, and I will deal well with you: *(Like many today, Jacob first makes his plans and then prays! He should have reversed the action. But the sense of having acted wrongly those years ago regarding his brother, Esau, fills the heart with a thousand fears, and robs the Christian of confidence toward God and dignity before man.)*

10 I am not worthy of the least of all the mercies *(Jacob's prayer is the first recorded in the Bible)*, and of all the truth, which you have showed unto your servant; for with my staff I passed over this Jordan; and now I am become two bands. *(His prayer was correct, but his faith, as of yet, wasn't!)*

11 Deliver me, I pray you, from the hand of my brother, from the hand of Esau: for I fear him, lest he will come and smite me, and the mother with the children. *(Jacob asked the Lord to deliver him, but then turns around and tries to appease Esau with a present. Was he placing more confidence in a few lambs than he did Jehovah, to Whom he had just been committing himself? But, as stated, before we criticize him, we had best look into the glass of our own hearts.)*

12 And You said, I will surely do you good, and make your seed as the sand of the sea, which cannot be numbered for multitude.

13 And he lodged there that same night; and took of that which came to his hand a present for Esau his brother *(concerning this, Mackintosh says: "Now, praying and planning will never go together. If I plan, I am leaning more or less on my plan; but when I pray, I should lean exclusively upon God. Hence, the two things are perfectly incompatible, they virtually cancel out each other. When my eyes fill with my own management of things, I am not prepared to see God acting for me; and, in that case, prayer is not the utterance of my need, but the mere superstitious performance of something which I think ought to be done, or it may be asking God to sanctify my plans. This will never do. The life of Faith is not asking God to sanctify and bless my means, but it is asking Him to do it all Himself");*

14 Two hundred she goats, and twenty he goats, two hundred ewes, and twenty rams,

15 Thirty milk camels with their colts, forty cattle, and ten bulls, twenty she asses, and ten foals.

16 And he delivered them into the hand of his servants, every drove by themselves; and said unto his servants, Pass over before me, and put a space between drove and drove.

17 And he commanded the foremost *(the men in the lead)*, saying, When Esau my brother meets you, and asks you, saying, For Whom do you work? and where are you going? and whose are these before you?

18 Then you shall say, They be your servant Jacob's; it is a present sent unto my lord Esau: and, behold, also he *(Jacob)* is behind us.

19 And so commanded he the second, and the third, and all that followed the droves, saying, On this manner shall you speak unto Esau, when you find him.

20 And say ye moreover, Behold, your servant Jacob is behind us. For he said, I will appease him with the present that goes before me, and afterward I will see his face; peradventure he will accept of me. *(In 2003 currency,*

these gifts would have amounted to well over $100,000. Jacob's idea was that the gifts to Esau would be given drove by drove. If he accepted them, this would mean that he came to Jacob in peace. No sooner had the Patriarch quit praying, that he started planning, which means that he wasn't really trusting the Lord as he should have been.)

21 So went the present over before him: and himself lodged that night in the company *(with his family).*

22 And he rose up that night, and took his two wives, and his two womenservants, and his eleven sons, and passed over the ford Jabbok.

23 And he took them *(his family),* and sent them over the brook, and sent over that he had. *(The brook Jabbok crosses the Jordan about 30 miles north of the Dead Sea.)*

ISRAEL

24 And Jacob was left alone; and there wrestled a Man with him until the breaking of the day. *(In this Chapter, and in Hosea [Chpt. 12], this Man is called God, the Angel, Elohim Sabaoth, and Jehovah. In this scenario, we find that it was not with Esau, his brother, with whom he had to contend, but with Jehovah Himself. This is always the case with every Believer.)*

25 And when He saw *(the Lord saw)* that He prevailed not against him *(against Jacob),* He touched the hollow of his thigh *(Jacob's thigh);* and the hollow of Jacob's thigh was out of joint, as He wrestled with him. *(The great principle that God cannot give victory to "the flesh" appears in this night scene. It is the broken heart that begins to experience what Divine Power means. Better for the sun to rise upon a limping Israel than to set upon a lying Jacob. Jacob, for his misconduct, was exiled from the Promised Land, having nothing but his staff. He returns a wealthy prince, but lamed. So, Israel, cast out of Jehovah's Land because of her sin, will return with abundance, but broken and contrite in spirit.)*

26 And He said *(the Lord said),* Let Me go, for the day breaks. And he said *(Jacob said),* I will not let You go, except You bless me. *(Williams says, "When sore broken by that mighty Hand, he ceased to wrestle and clung with weeping and supplication to the very God Who wounded him, then it was that he got the victory and the glorious name of Israel.")*

27 And He *(the Lord)* said unto him, What is

your name? And he said, Jacob. *(Of course, the Lord already knew Jacob's name. So, why did He insist on Jacob pronouncing his name? He wanted Jacob to admit who and what he actually was, which the name Jacob adequately portrayed. True Faith requires that we admit what we are, before we can receive what He is!)*

28 And He *(the Lord)* said, Your name shall be called no more Jacob *(meaning deceiver or supplanter),* but Israel *(a Prince of God):* for as a Prince have you power with God and with men, and have prevailed *(as we shall see, Jacob's change was instant, but yet gradual).*

29 And Jacob asked Him, and said, Tell me, I pray You, Your Name. And He said, Wherefore is it that you do ask after My name? *(The Lord's answer is revealing. He responds with another question: the idea is, Jacob, by now, ought to know Who the One is with Whom he has been struggling. And the next statements prove that he did.)* and He *(the Lord)* blessed him *(Jacob)* there *(He gave him power with God and with men).*

30 And Jacob called the name of the place Peniel *(means "the Face of God"):* for I have seen God face to face, and my life is preserved *(Jacob will never be the same again).*

31 And as he passed over Penuel the sun rose upon him, and he halted upon his thigh. *(The sun is now rising, but upon a crippled Jacob. If the Lord is to reveal Himself to an individual, the flesh must be crippled. That is an absolute necessity!)*

32 Therefore the children of Israel eat not of the sinew which shrank, which is upon the hollow of the thigh, unto this day: because He *(the Lord)* touched the hollow of Jacob's thigh in the sinew that shrank. *(This particular sinew is the proper name for the large tendon which takes its origin from the spinal chord and extends down the thigh unto the ankle. It was called by the Greeks the "tendo Achillis," because it reaches the heel. So, the "heel-catcher" became a "Prince with God.")*

CHAPTER 33
(1739 B.C.)
RECONCILIATION

AND Jacob lifted up his eyes, and looked, and, behold, Esau came, and with him four hundred men. And he divided the children unto Leah *(those who belonged to Leah),* and unto Rachel *(those who belonged to Rachel),* and unto the two handmaids *(etc.).*

2 And he put the handmaids and their children foremost, and Leah and her children after, and Rachel and Joseph hindermost *(those he considered his greatest love were at the rear)*.

3 And he passed over before them, and bowed himself to the ground seven times, until he came near to his brother.

4 And Esau ran to meet him, and embraced him, and fell on his neck, and kissed him: and they wept *(the action of Esau shows how groundless were Jacob's fears, and how needless his plans)*.

5 And he lifted up his eyes, and saw the women and the children; and said, Who are those with you? And he said, The children which God has graciously given your servant. *(It is obvious that Esau is a powerful Chieftain. How so sad that this man did not see the great spiritual truths. In that case, it would have been "the God of Abraham, Isaac, and Esau." But such was not to be!)*

6 Then the handmaidens came near, they and their children, and they bowed themselves.

7 And Leah also with her children came near, and bowed themselves: and after came Joseph near and Rachel, and they bowed themselves.

8 And he said, What is the meaning of all these droves which I met? And he said *(Jacob said)*, These are to find grace in the sight of my lord.

9 And Esau said, I have enough, my brother; keep that you have unto yourself.

10 And Jacob said, No, I pray you, if now I have found grace in your sight, then receive my present at my hand: for therefore I have seen your face, as though I had seen the face of God, and you were pleased with me.

11 Take, I pray you, my blessing that is brought to you; because God has dealt graciously with me, and because I have enough. And he urged him, and he took it. *(Esau accepting the gift, as well, stated that he had accepted Jacob, and there were no hard feelings.)*

12 And he said *(Esau said)*, Let us take our journey, and let us go, and I will go before you.

13 And he *(Jacob)* said unto him, My lord knows that the children are tender, and the flocks and herds with young are with me: and if men should overdrive them one day, all the flock will die.

14 Let my lord, I pray you, pass over before his servant: and I will lead on softly, according as the cattle that goes before me and the children be able to endure, until I come unto my lord unto Seir *(Jacob never did get to Seir)*.

15 And Esau said, Let me now leave with you some of the folk who are with me. And he said, There is no need! let me find grace in the sight of my lord.

16 So Esau returned that day on his way unto Seir.

CANAAN

17 And Jacob journeyed to Succoth, and built him an house *(this is the first mention of a "house" as it regards the Patriarchs)*, and made booths for his cattle: therefore the name of the place is called Succoth. *(Jacob went to Succoth. But the Lord had not said, "I am the God of Succoth," but rather, "I am the God of Beth-el." Events will prove that Jacob was not in the Will of God.)*

18 And Jacob came to Shalem, a city of Shechem, which is in the land of Canaan, when he came from Padan-aram; and pitched his tent before the city *(referred to the fact that he was claiming this area as his domicile)*.

19 And he bought a parcel of a field, where he had spread his tent, at the hand of the children of Hamor, Shechem's father, for an hundred pieces of money.

20 And he erected there an Altar, and called it El-elohe-Israel. *(Jacob erects an Altar at Shechem, for the conscience is uneasy without religious forms, but the Divinely chosen place for the Altar was Beth-el.)*

CHAPTER 34
(1739 B.C.)
DINAH

AND Dinah the daughter of Leah, which she bore unto Jacob, went out to see the daughters of the land *(this seems very innocent; however, these daughters led to a companionship with shame; the Christian has to be very careful concerning the world and its ways)*.

2 And when Shechem the son of Hamor the Hivite, prince of the country, saw her, he took her, and lay with her, and defiled her *(Pulpit says, "Dinah paid the full penalty of her carelessness; she suffered the fate which Satan had planned for Sarah and Rebekah in the land of Pharaoh and Abimelech; she was seen and taken by the son of the prince, forcibly, it seems, against her will, but yet with the claims of affection by her lover)*.

3 And his soul clave unto Dinah the daughter of Jacob, and he loved the damsel,

and spoke kindly unto the damsel (*probably refers to marriage*).

4 And Shechem spoke unto his father Hamor, saying, Get me this damsel to wife (*marriages were arranged in those days, so Shechem asked his father Hamor to work out the arrangements*).

5 And Jacob heard that he had defiled Dinah his daughter: now his sons were with his cattle in the field: and Jacob held his peace until they were come.

6 And Hamor the father of Shechem went out unto Jacob to commune with him (*supposedly to make arrangements for the marriage*).

7 And the sons of Jacob came out of the field when they heard it: and the men were grieved, and they were very angry, because he (*Shechem*) had wrought folly in Israel in lying with Jacob's daughter: which thing ought not to be done (*in this Verse, the word "Israel" is used for the first time to designate Jacob's descendants, which actually became the great nation of Israel; the phrase, "folly in Israel," became a standing expression for acts done against the sacred character which belonged to Israel as a separated and covenanted community, as the people of God*).

8 And Hamor communed with them, saying, The soul of my son Shechem longs for your daughter: I pray you give her him to wife (*the special wickedness of Shechem consisted in dishonoring a daughter of one who was the head of the theocratic line and, therefore, under peculiar obligations to lead a holy life*).

9 And you make marriages with us, and give your daughters unto us, and take our daughters unto you (*by the act of intermarriage, Satan will compromise and corrupt the sacred lineage*).

10 And you shall dwell with us: and the land shall be before you; dwell and trade you therein, and get you possessions therein (*the end result of this plan, as fomented by Satan, was to ultimately stop the Incarnation; the lineage must be kept pure*).

11 And Shechem said unto her father and unto her brethren, Let me find grace in your eyes, and what you shall say unto me I will give (*in essence, Shechem was saying that whatever they asked, as far as monetary value was concerned, he would pay it*).

12 Ask me never so much dowry and gift, and I will give according as you shall say unto me: but give me the damsel to wife.

13 And the sons of Jacob answered Shechem and Hamor his father deceitfully, and said, because he had defiled Dinah their sister (*the sons of Jacob practice deceit in this situation, in which Jacob had no part therein; however, God no more overlooks deceit in His Own than He does in those outside the Covenant*):

14 And they (*the brothers of Dinah*) said unto them (*Shechem and those with him*), We cannot do this thing, to give our sister to one who is uncircumcised; for that were a reproach unto us:

15 But in this will we consent unto you: If you will be as we be, that every male of you be circumcised;

16 Then will we give our daughters unto you, and we will take your daughters to us, and we will dwell with you, and we will become one people (*the sons of Jacob are now beginning to show the traits which will ultimately lead to their desire to murder Joseph*).

17 But if you will not hearken unto us, to be circumcised; then will we take our daughter, and we will be gone.

REVENGE

18 And their words pleased Hamor, and Shechem Hamor's son.

19 And the young man deferred not to do the thing (*did not want to put it off*), because he had delight in Jacob's daughter: and he was more honorable than all the house of his father (*in other words, Shechem was sincere*).

20 And Hamor and Shechem his son came unto the gate of their city, and communed with the men of their city, saying (*presented the proposal to them*),

21 These men are peaceable with us; therefore let them dwell in the land, and trade therein; for the land, behold, it is large enough for them; let us take their daughters to us for wives, and let us give them our daughters (*Jacob's sons were of the Semitic stock and, therefore, possessed of high physical and mental endowments; and, as they were rich in cattle and other wealth, their incorporation with the people of Shechem, or so they reasoned, would raise it to a high rank; so they agreed to Hamor's proposal*).

22 Only herein will the men (*Jacob's clan*) consent unto us for to dwell with us, to be one people, if every male among us be circumcised, as they are circumcised.

23 Shall not their cattle and their substance and every beast of theirs be ours? only let us

consent unto them, and they will dwell with us *(we find here that Hamor is practicing deceit as well; this was not the idea of Shechem, he being more honorable than his father, but it was the idea of his father and the other men of the city).*

24 And unto Hamor and unto Shechem his son hearkened all who went out of the gate of his city; and every male was circumcised, all who went out of the gate of his city *(in that Hamor agreed so readily, we must come to the conclusion that circumcision was something not unknown to them and, as well, something that they regarded as a small price to pay for what they believed they would receive).*

25 And it came to pass on the third day, when they were sore, that two of the sons of Jacob, Simeon and Levi, Dinah's brothers, took each man his sword, and came upon the city boldly, and killed all the men *(there is nothing that would justify what these men did).*

26 And they killed Hamor and Shechem his son with the edge of the sword, and took Dinah out of Shechem's house, and went out.

27 The sons of Jacob came upon the slain, and spoiled the city, because they had defiled their sister *(in fact, the annals of uncivilized warfare scarcely record a more atrocious crime).*

28 They took their sheep, and their oxen, and their asses, and that which was in the city, and that which was in the field,

29 And all their wealth, and all their little ones, and their wives took they captive, and spoiled even all that was in the house *(and we must understand, this was the Church of that day!).*

30 And Jacob said to Simeon and Levi, You have troubled me to make me to stink among the inhabitants of the land, among the Canaanites and the Perizzites: and I being few in number, they shall gather themselves together against me, and kill me; and I shall be destroyed, I and my house *(Jacob readily sees the hand of Satan in all of this and, but for the protection of the Lord, he was right).*

31 And they said, Should he deal with our sister as with an harlot?

CHAPTER 35
(1732 B.C.)
BETHEL

AND God said unto Jacob, Arise, go up to Beth-el, and dwell there *(in essence, this is what the Lord had told Jacob to do when he first came back to Canaan; to be out of the Will of God, as was Jacob, always invites disaster!):* and make there an Altar unto God, Who appeared unto you when you fled from the face of Esau your brother. *(Nearly ten years had passed since Jacob had come back to the Land of Promise. At that time, those ten years ago, the Lord had said to Jacob, "Return unto your Land, I am the God of Bethel." The Lord did not say, "I am the God of Succoth." But how slow was he to obey this command! And it cost him dearly.)*

2 Then Jacob said unto his household, and to all who were with him, Put away the strange gods that are among you, and be clean, and change your garments *(when Jacob learns that he is to meet God publicly at Bethel, he at once feels that idols cannot be brought into fellowship with that House and, accordingly, he commands the surrender of all the strange gods that were in their hands and in their ears, and he buried them beneath the oak at Shechem; these were either brought by Jacob's servants from Mesopotamia, or adopted in Canaan, or perhaps possessed by the women taken captive during the problem of the recent past):*

3 And let us arise, and go up to Beth-el *(now at last he goes "up unto Bethel"; physically, and morally, it was indeed a going-up; but how slow he had been the last ten years to obey this command! Had he gone swiftly to Bethel, when he left Syria, and had he "dwelt" there, as commanded, what sin and sorrow would have been avoided!);* and I will make there an Altar unto God, Who answered me in the day of my distress, and was with me in the way which I went. *(The "Altar" was a Type of Christ and the death He would die on the Cross in order to redeem fallen humanity. It was the centerpiece of man's relationship with God in Old Testament times, and it continues to be such presently in the form of the Cross. If the Cross is removed, or ignored, or set aside in any way, then it ceases to be Faith that God will recognize. The Faith that God recognizes is that which is anchored squarely in the Cross [Rom. 6:3-14; 8:1-2, 11; I Cor. 1:17-18, 21, 23; 2:2; Col. 2:14-15].)*

4 And they gave unto Jacob all the strange gods which were in their hand, and all their earrings which were in their ears; and Jacob hid them under the oak which was by Shechem. *(At Shechem Jacob kept his Saviour and his Salvation to himself, and permitted his family and household to retain their idols. But this cannot be suffered if God is to be recognized and publicly confessed as the God of Bethel. The "strange*

gods" must go!)

5 And they journeyed: and the terror of God was upon the cities that were round about them, and they did not pursue after the sons of Jacob *(the Lord protected them, or else they would have been slaughtered by surrounding enemies).*

6 So Jacob came to Luz, which is in the land of Canaan, that is, Beth-el, he and all the people who were with him.

7 And he built there an Altar, and called the place El-beth-el *(the "God of the House of God"):* because there God appeared unto him, when he fled from the face of his brother *(some thirty years before).*

8 But Deborah Rebekah's nurse died, and she was buried beneath Beth-el under an oak: and the name of it was called Allon-bachuth *("the oak of weeping"; Rebekah was Jacob's mother; no doubt, he was attached to Deborah, who had been a servant of his mother for many years; he would miss her greatly).*

9 And God appeared unto Jacob again, when he came out of Padan-aram, and blessed him *(which was done some ten years before, when Jacob wrestled with the Lord; it should be noted that the Lord did not appear to Jacob while he was at Succoth, except to speak to him and tell him to leave the place; the Revelation of the Lord, as it regards blessing, cannot come to us unless we are in the center of God's Will).*

10 And God said unto him, Your name is Jacob: your name shall not be called any more Jacob, but Israel shall be your name: and He *(God)* called his name Israel *(the renewal of the name given to Jacob some ten years earlier at Peniel was most possibly done because the Patriarch feared that he had forfeited the Blessing; but the calling of the gifts is without repentance).*

11 And God said unto him, I am God Almighty *(El-Shaddai, the all sufficient One):* be fruitful and multiply *(which can only be done with the Blessings of the Lord)*; a nation and a company of nations shall be of you, and kings shall come out of your loins *(and so they did)*;

12 And the land which I gave Abraham and Isaac, to you I will give it, and to your seed after you will I give the Land. *(Satan has fought this from then until now. The latest in the long line of opposers are the Palestinians; however, let it be known, that what God says will happen, will happen. In the coming Kingdom Age, Israel will then possess all that God has promised, and in totality.)*

13 And God went up from him in the place where He talked with him.

14 And Jacob set up a pillar in the place where he talked with him, even a pillar of stone *(a Type of Christ):* and he poured a Drink Offering thereon *(the first mention of a "Drink Offering" in Scripture),* and he poured oil thereon. *(This Stone figures Christ the Rock of Ages, anointed with the Holy Spirit, typified by the oil, and filled with the joy of God, typified by the "Drink Offering.")*

15 And Jacob called the name of the place where God spoke with him, Beth-el *(House of God).*

BENJAMIN

16 And they journeyed from Beth-el; and there was but a little way to come to Ephrath: and Rachel travailed, and she had hard labour.

17 And it came to pass, when she was in hard labour, that the midwife said unto her, Fear not; you shall have this son also *(the midwife is speaking of the prophecy given to Rachel when Joseph was born, that "the Lord shall add to me another son" [30:22-24]).*

18 And it came to pass, as her soul was in departing, (for she died) that she called his name Ben-oni: but his father called him Benjamin. *(Sorrowing nature calls him "Ben-oni," i.e., "child of my sorrow." Faith calls him "Benjamin," i.e., "son of the right hand." Prophetic picture of Him Who was to be at first the "Man of Sorrows," and then the "Man at God's Right Hand.")*

19 And Rachel died, and was buried in the way to Ephrath, which is Beth-lehem *(she was buried where the Son of God, some 1,700 years later, would be born).*

20 And Jacob set a pillar upon her grave: that is the pillar of Rachel's grave unto this day.

21 And Israel journeyed *(throughout the Chapter, the Patriarch is called Jacob, except in Verses 21-22, where three times the Holy Spirit names him Israel; how strange this contradiction appears to human wisdom! Jacob is his name of weakness, Israel, of strength; and yet is he only named Israel in connection with wandering and dishonor? when we are weak, He is strong [II Cor. 12:10]),* and spread his tent beyond the tower of Edar.

22 And it came to pass, when Israel dwelt in that land, that Reuben went and lay with Bilhah his father's concubine: and Israel heard it. Now the sons of Jacob were twelve *(with this sin, Reuben, the firstborn, forfeited the birthright; Jesus would not be born through that line, but*

rather through the Tribe of Judah):

23 The sons of Leah; Reuben, Jacob's first-born, and Simeon, and Levi, and Judah, and Issachar, and Zebulun:

24 The sons of Rachel; Joseph, and Benjamin:

25 And the sons of Bilhah, Rachel's handmaid; Dan, and Naphtali:

26 And the sons of Zilpah, Leah's handmaid: Gad, and Asher: these are the sons of Jacob, which were born to him in Padan-aram. *(The twelve sons of Jacob are listed here, who would head up the Tribes of Israel, with Manasseh and Ephraim taking the place of Joseph, making the total thirteen. There would actually be thirteen Tribes, counting Levi, which was the Priestly Tribe.)*

THE DEATH OF ISAAC

27 And Jacob came unto Isaac his father unto Mamre, unto the city of Arbah, which is Hebron, where Abraham and Isaac sojourned.

28 And the days of Isaac were an hundred and fourscore years *(180 years).*

29 And Isaac gave up the ghost, and died, and was gathered unto his people, being old and full of days: and his sons Esau and Jacob buried him. *(They laid Isaac beside his ancestral greats in the family burying-place of Machpelah, where already slept the lifeless bodies of Abraham and Sarah, awaiting the Resurrection, while his spirit went to company with theirs in the better country, even an Heavenly. Jacob was with Isaac when he died, and Esau came to the grave.)*

CHAPTER 36
(1715 B.C.)
ESAU

NOW these are the generations of Esau, who is Edom. *(This is important only in the sense of showing us the portion of Esau, who had his place in this life, and not the life to come [Ps. 17:14]. It shows his sons establishing themselves in the world, with their riches and their possessions, while the heirs of Promise, that is, Jacob and his sons, are still pilgrims and strangers. This furnishes a prophetic picture.)*

2 Esau took his wives of the daughters of Canaan *(from the cursed line of Canaan [9:23-27]);* Adah the daughter of Elon the Hittite, and Aholibamah the daughter of Anah the daughter of Zibeon the Hivite;

3 And Bashemath Ishmael's daughter, sister of Nebajoth.

4 And Adah bore to Esau Eliphaz; and Bashemath bore Reuel;

5 And Aholibamah bore Jeush, and Jaalam, and Korah: these are the sons of Esau, which were born unto him in the land of Canaan.

6 And Esau took his wives, and his sons, and his daughters, and all the persons of his house, and his cattle, and all his beasts, and all his substance, which he had got in the land of Canaan; and went into the country from the face of his brother Jacob.

7 For their riches were more than that they might dwell together; and the land wherein they were strangers could not bear them because of their cattle.

8 Thus dwelt Esau in mount Seir: Esau is Edom. *(In all of this, we find that Esau is repeatedly called Edom. This is the name which perpetuated the remembrance of his selling his birthright for a mess of pottage. We find that Esau continued the same profane despiser of heavenly things, despite being a member of the sacred family.)*

9 And these are the generations of Esau the father of the Edomites in mount Seir *(Petra):*

10 These are the names of Esau's sons; Eliphaz the son of Adah the wife of Esau, Reuel the son of Bashemath the wife of Esau.

11 And the sons of Eliphaz were Teman, Omar, Zepho, and Gatam, and Kenaz.

12 And Timna was concubine to Eliphaz Esau's son; and she bore to Eliphaz Amalek: these were the sons of Adah Esau's wife. *(The "Amalek" mentioned here is probably the Amalekite nation which attacked Israel at Horeb. In Biblical typology, Amalek is looked at as a type of the flesh. When Israel experienced the miracle of the water coming from the Rock, which was a Type of Christ and the Holy Spirit, the Scripture says, "Then came Amalek, and fought with Israel in Rephidim" [Ex. 17:6-8].)*

13 And these are the sons of Reuel; Nahath, and Zerah, Shammah, and Mizzah: these were the sons of Bashemath Esau's wife.

14 And these were the sons of Aholibamah, the daughter of Anah the daughter of Zibeon, Esau's wife: and she bore to Esau Jeush, and Jaalam, and Korah.

15 These were dukes of the sons of Esau: the sons of Eliphaz the firstborn son of Esau; duke Teman, duke Omar, duke Zepho, duke Kenaz,

16 Duke Korah, duke Gatam, and duke Amalek: these are the dukes who came of Eliphaz in the land of Edom; these were the sons of Adah.

17 And these are the sons of Reuel Esau's son; duke Nahath, duke Zerah, duke Shammah, duke Mizzah: these are the dukes who came of Reuel in the land of Edom; these are the sons of Bashemath Esau's wife.

18 And these are the sons of Aholibamah Esau's wife; duke Jeush, duke Jaalam, duke Korah: these were the dukes who came of Aholibamah the daughter of Anah, Esau's wife.

19 These are the sons of Esau, who is Edom, and these are their dukes.

20 These are the sons of Seir the Horite, who inhabited the land; Lotan, and Shobal, and Zibeon, and Anah,

21 And Dishon, and Ezer, and Dishan: these are the dukes of the Horites, the children of Seir in the land of Edom.

22 And the children of Lotan were Hori and Hemam; and Lotan's sister was Timna.

23 And the children of Shobal were these; Alvan, and Manahath, and Ebal, Shepho, and Onam.

24 And these are the children of Zibeon; both Ajah, and Anah: this was that Anah who found the mules in the wilderness, as he fed the asses of Zibeon his father.

25 And the children of Anah were these; Dishon, and Aholibamah the daughter of Anah.

26 And these are the children of Dishon; Hemdan, and Eshban, and Ithran, and Cheran.

27 The children of Ezer are these; Bilhan, and Zaavan, and Akan.

28 The children of Dishan are these; Uz, and Aran.

29 These are the dukes who came of the Horites; duke Lotan, duke Shobal, duke Zibeon, duke Anah,

30 Duke Dishon, duke Ezer, duke Dishan: these are the dukes who came of Hori, among their dukes in the land of Seir.

THE KINGS OF EDOM

31 And these are the kings who reigned in the land of Edom, before there reigned any king over the children of Israel. *(Concerning this Chapter, Matthew Henry says, "In external prosperity and honor, the children of the Covenant are often cast behind, and those who are out of the Covenant, such as Esau, seemingly get ahead. We may suppose it is a trial to the Faith of God's Israel to hear of the pomp and power of the kings of Edom, while they were bond slaves in Egypt; but those who look for great things from God must be content to wait for them; God's time is the best time.*

"Observe, Mount Seir is called the land of their possession. While the Israelites dwelt in the house of bondage, and their Canaan was only the Land of Promise, the Edomites dwelt in their own habitations, and Seir was in their possession. The children of this world have their all in hand, and nothing in hope [Lk. 16:25]; while the children of God have their all in hope, and little in hand. But all things considered, it is better to have Canaan in Promise than Mount Seir in possession.")

32 And Bela the son of Beor reigned in Edom: and the name of his city was Dinhabah.

33 And Bela died, and Jobab the son of Zerah of Bozrah reigned in his stead.

34 And Jobab died, and Husham of the land of Temani reigned in his stead.

35 And Husham died, and Hadad the son of Bedad, who smote Midian in the field of Moab, reigned in his stead: and the name of his city was Avith.

36 And Hadad died, and Samlah of Masrekah reigned in his stead.

37 And Samlah died, and Saul of Rehoboth by the river reigned in his stead.

38 And Saul died, and Baal-hanan the son of Achbor reigned in his stead.

39 And Baal-hanan the son of Achbor died, and Hadar reigned in his stead: and the name of his city was Pau; and his wife's name was Mehetabel, the daughter of Matred, the daughter of Mezahab.

40 And these are the names of the dukes who came of Esau, according to their families, after their places, by their names; duke Timnah, duke Alvah, duke Jetheth,

41 Duke Aholibamah, duke Elah, duke Pinon,

42 Duke Kenaz, duke Teman, duke Mibzar,

43 Duke Magdiel, duke Iram: these be the dukes of Edom, according to their habitations in the land of their possession: he is Esau the father of the Edomites.

CHAPTER 37
(1729 B.C.)
JOSEPH'S DREAMS

AND Jacob dwelt in the land wherein his father was a stranger, in the land of Canaan *(having dispensed with Esau in the previous Chapter, and having mentioned him at all simply because he was a son of Isaac, we now pick up the narrative of Jacob, which includes the story of Joseph).*

2 These are the generations of Jacob. Joseph, being seventeen years old, was feeding the flock with his brethren (*Joseph is one of the most, if not the most, remarkable Types of Christ found in the entirety of the Old Testament*); and the lad was with the sons of Bilhah (*Dan and Naphtali*), and with the sons of Zilpah (*Gad and Asher*), his father's wives: and Joseph brought unto his father their evil report (*these men were in the Covenant, but not of the Covenant*).

3 Now Israel (*Jacob*) loved Joseph more than all his children (*the name "Israel" is used here of Jacob by the Holy Spirit, signifying that what Jacob had done, as it regards loving Joseph, was not wrong, but rather right; some claim that Jacob caused the problem among his sons by favoring Joseph; not true!*), because he was the son of his old age (*actually means that Joseph possessed the wisdom of an old man though so young*): and he made him a coat of many colors. (*Such a coat was given to the son for whom the birthright was designed. The Holy Spirit proclaimed that it should go to Joseph, and not Reuben, who was actually the firstborn. Whoever had this position was to be the high priest of the family, which, in essence, Joseph was after Jacob died. The future, as we shall see, bears this out.*)

4 And when his brethren saw that their father loved him more than all his brethren, they hated him, and could not speak peaceably unto him. (*This perfectly epitomizes Christ; of Whom Joseph was one of the most remarkable Types found in the Word of God. God loved His Son, and showed it greatly by lavishing upon Him all the Power of the Holy Spirit. As a result, the Jews, who were His brethren, so to speak, hated Him. Such follows to the present, in that those who are of the Spirit [the Cross] are hated by those who are of the flesh.*)

5 And Joseph dreamed a dream, and he told it his brethren: and they hated him yet the more. (*The Lord revealed the future to Joseph in a dream. While the dream definitely referred to him, it more so referred to Christ and Israel, with these men who hated Joseph being a type of Israel. He told his brothers the truth, and they hated him even more. Thus was it with Joseph's great antitype. Christ bore witness to the Truth, and His testimony to the Truth was answered, on man's part, by the Cross.*)

6 And he said unto them, Hear, I pray you, this dream which I have dreamed:

7 For, behold, we were binding sheaves in the field, and, lo, my sheaf arose, and also stood upright; and, behold, your sheaves stood round about, and made obeisance (*bowed*) to my sheaf. (*It was the Will of the Lord to relate this dream, which these brothers would remember, and would see come to pass exactly as the dream proclaimed. Pulpit Commentary says, regarding this, "He related this dream, in the simplicity of his heart, and in doing so he was also guided, unconsciously it may be, but still really, by an overruling providence, Who made use of this very telling of the dream as a step toward its fulfillment."*)

REJECTION

8 And his brethren said to him, Shall you indeed reign over us? or shall you indeed have dominion over us? And they hated him yet the more for his dreams, and for his words. (*The hatred that Joseph's brethren exhibited toward him represents the Jews in Christ's day. "He came to His Own, and His Own received Him not." He had "no form nor comeliness" in their eyes. They would not own Him as the Son of God, or as the King of Israel. They hated Him!*)

9 And he dreamed yet another dream, and told it his brethren, and said, Behold, I have dreamed a dream more; and behold, the sun and the moon and the eleven stars made obeisance to me. (*This prophetically portrays the Second Coming, when all the Tribes of Israel will, at the time, bow at the feet of Christ [Zech. 12:10; 13:1, 6; 14:9].*)

10 And he told it to his father, and to his brethren: and his father rebuked him, and said unto him, What is this dream that you have dreamed? Shall I and your mother and your brethren indeed come to bow down ourselves to you to the earth? (*This is exactly what they did after Joseph became Viceroy of Egypt. It is exactly what Israel, as well, will do, in a coming glad day.*)

11 And his brethren envied him; but his father observed the saying (*even though Jacob had rebuked Joseph, still, the Patriarch realized that there was more to this than a mere dream*),

12 And his brethren went to feed their father's flock in Shechem (*about 50 miles distance*).

13 And Israel (*Jacob*) said unto Joseph, Do not your brethren feed the flock in Shechem? come, and I will send you unto them. And he said to him, Here am I. (*The short phrase, "Here am I," foreshadows the statement of Christ, "Then said I, Lo, I come: in the volume of the Book it*

is written of Me, I delight to do Your Will, O My God: yes, Your Law is within My Heart" [Ps. 40:7-8].)

14 And he *(Jacob)* said to him *(to Joseph)*, Go, I pray you, see whether it is well with your brethren, and well with the flocks; and bring me word again. So he sent him out of the vale of Hebron, and he came to Shechem. *(All of this portrays the fact that Jacob little understood the degree of hatred the brothers had against Joseph.)*

15 And a certain man found him, and, behold, he was wandering in the field: and the man asked him, saying, What do you seek?

16 And he said, I seek my brethren: tell me, I pray you, where they feed their flocks.

17 And the man said, They are departed hence; for I heard them say, Let us go to Dothan *(about 12 miles north of Shechem, making the total distance that Joseph had come approximately 62 miles).* And Joseph went after his brethren, and found them in Dothan.

THE PLOT

18 And when they saw him afar off, even before he came near unto them, they conspired against him to kill him. *(It was thus with Christ as well. When He was born, Herod sought to kill Him [Mat., Chpt. 2].)*

19 And they said one to another, Behold, this dreamer comes *(little did they realize that these dreams would come to pass exactly according to their portrayal).*

20 Come now therefore, and let us kill him, and cast him into some pit, and we will say, Some evil beast has devoured him: and we shall see what will become of his dreams *(we see here the ruling of the sin nature).*

21 And Reuben heard it, and he delivered him out of their hands; and said, Let us not kill him. *(Reuben was the firstborn. This meant that when Jacob died, he would receive a double portion of the inheritance; however, the birthright had been given to Joseph. So Reuben would have had more to gain from Joseph's death than anyone, but he seemed to have a heart that wasn't totally hardened.)*

22 And Reuben said unto them, Shed no blood, but cast him into this pit that is in the wilderness, and lay no hand upon him; that he might rid him out of their hands, to deliver him to his father again. *(He thought later to come back and rescue Joseph, as evidently he had to go somewhere, but he would come back too late. They would have sold Joseph as a slave.)*

23 And it came to pass, when Joseph was come unto his brethren, that they stripped Joseph out of his coat, his coat of many colors that was on him *(the flesh hates the Spirit, the latter of which the coat was a Type; however, when they took the coat, they did not take the anointing, for the coat was only a symbol of such);*

24 And they took him, and cast him into a pit: and the pit was empty, there was no water in it. *(When we look at Joseph in the pit and in the prison, and look at him afterwards as ruler over all the land of Egypt, we see the difference between the thoughts of God and the thoughts of men; and so when we look at the Cross, and then "the Throne of the Majesty in the Heavens," we see the same thing.)*

25 And they sat down to eat bread *(evidently, their idea was, when they put him in the pit, to let him starve to death; but now a change of events comes about):* and they lifted up their eyes and looked, and, behold, a company of Ishmeelites came from Gilead with their camels bearing spicery and balm and myrrh, going to carry it down to Egypt.

26 And Judah said unto his brethren, What profit is it if we kill our brother, and conceal his blood?

27 Come, and let us sell him to the Ishmeelites, and let not our hand be upon him; for he is our brother and our flesh. And his brethren were content. *(Along with Reuben, Judah is the one who saved the life of Joseph, suggesting that they sell him as a slave; however, this was little an act of mercy on the part of Judah, inasmuch as under normal circumstances, they were consigning him to a life worse than death.)*

EGYPT

28 Then there passed by Midianites merchantmen *(they were along with the Ishmeelites)*; and they drew and lifted up Joseph out of the pit, and sold Joseph to the Ishmeelites for twenty pieces of silver: and they brought Joseph into Egypt. *(Joseph being a Type of Christ, the Saviour was sold for thirty pieces of silver. As Joseph was taken into Egypt, likewise, the Gentiles accepted Christ.)*

DECEPTION

29 And Reuben returned unto the pit; and, behold, Joseph was not in the pit; and he rent his clothes. *(When Reuben returned, it seems*

that he was genuinely sorry about the turn of events; however, his brothers explained to him what they had done, and the record proclaims the fact that he did nothing further.)

30 And he returned unto his brethren, and said, The child is not; and I, whither shall I go? *(What shall I do?)*

31 And they took Joseph's coat, and killed a kid of the goats, and dipped the coat in the blood *(as Rebekah and Jacob had used a "kid of the goats" to deceive Isaac [27:9], likewise, Jacob is deceived by a "kid of the goats");*

32 And they sent the coat of many colors, and they brought it to their father; and said, This have we found: know now whether it be your son's coat or no *(they evidently got a servant or a slave to take the bloody coat to Jacob, and to give him the story they had concocted).*

33 And he knew it, and said, It is my son's coat; an evil beast has devoured him; Joseph is without doubt rent in pieces *(it seems that they who brought the news to Jacob had suggested this, and Jacob believed it).*

34 And Jacob rent his clothes, and put sackcloth upon his loins, and mourned for his son many days *(this terrible heartache, this terrible sorrow, would last for twenty years, meaning that it was one of the greatest tests that God ever called upon a man to undergo).*

35 And all his sons and all his daughters rose up to comfort him; but he refused to be comforted; and he said, For I will go down into the grave unto my son mourning. Thus his father wept for him. *(Jacob knew that the Lord had told him to give Joseph the birthright. That being the case, why would the Lord then allow his life to be taken by a wild animal, or so Jacob thought?)*

36 And the Midianites sold him into Egypt unto Potiphar, an officer of Pharaoh's, and captain of the guard. *(The Hand of the Lord, although having no part whatsoever in the evil being carried out, still, guided events, even as we shall see.)*

CHAPTER 38
(1729 B.C.)
JUDAH

AND it came to pass at that time, that Judah went down from his brethren, and turned in to a certain Adullamite, whose name was Hirah. *(This Chapter is a parenthesis introduced here as an actual picture of the sin, darkness, corruption, and self-will of Joseph's brethren*

during the whole period of his absence from them and as the certain fruit of their rejection of him. It is, as well, a fore-picture of the moral condition of the Jews today, as the result of their rejection of the Messiah.)

2 And Judah saw there a daughter of a certain Canaanite, whose name was Shuah; and he took her, and went in unto her *(Judah marrying a Canaanite sinned with his eyes open, for he must have known the Will of God in that matter [Gen. 24:3; 26:35; 27:36; 28:1]).*

3 And she conceived, and bore a son; and he called his name Er.

4 And she conceived again, and bore a son; and she called his name Onan.

5 And she yet again conceived, and bore a son; and called his name Shelah: and he was at Chezib, when she bore him. *(Chronologically, it is believed by some that Chapter 38 should follow Chapter 33.)*

6 And Judah took a wife for Er his firstborn, whose name was Tamar. *(This Chapter is also placed here in order to show the connection between Christ and His predecessor, Judah. Chapter 1 of Matthew shows how truly Christ made Himself of no reputation and, by being born a member of the Tribe of Judah, humbled Himself. For in that genealogy the names Tamar and Bathsheba appear. But He in no wise inherited from these any taint of sin, for He was conceived of the Holy Spirit, and, though born of a woman, was wholly free from moral corruption.)*

7 And Er, Judah's firstborn, was wicked in the sight of the LORD, and the LORD killed him *(exactly as to how this happened, we aren't told; it probably means that he became grossly involved in Canaanite idolatry).*

8 And Judah said unto Onan, Go in unto your brother's wife, and marry her, and raise up seed to your brother.

9 And Onan knew that the seed should not be his *(he didn't want it to be his)*; and it came to pass, when he went in unto his brother's wife, that he spilled it on the ground, lest that he should give seed to his brother *(Judah demanded this in order that the lineage would continue; however, Onan, in essence, was saying by his actions that he cared nothing about a Redeemer coming into the world; he didn't want Tamar for a wife, so he refused the command of his father, Judah).*

10 And the thing which he did displeased the LORD: wherefore He killed him also. *(Again, in what manner the Lord did this, we aren't told. The major reason all of this was so*

grievous in the sight of the Lord was because it had to do with the lineage of the coming Redeemer, which was the single most important thing in the world.)

11 Then said Judah to Tamar his daughter in law, Remain a widow at your father's house, till Shelah my son be grown: for he said, Lest peradventure he die also, as his brethren did. And Tamar went and dwelt in her father's house.

12 And in process of time the daughter of Shuah Judah's wife died; and Judah was comforted, and went up unto his sheepshearers to Timnath, he and his friend Hirah the Adullamite.

TAMAR

13 And it was told Tamar, saying, Behold your father in law goes up to Timnath to shear his sheep.

14 And she put her widow's garments off from her, and covered her face with a vail, and wrapped herself, and sat in an open place, which is by the way to Timnath; for she saw that Shelah was grown, and she was not given unto him to wife. *(It does not follow that Judah blamed Tamar for the deaths of his two sons; however, the loss of these two in succession must have frightened him, for he made no move to give his third son, Shelah, to her for marriage.)*

15 When Judah saw her, he thought her to be an harlot; because she had covered her face.

16 And he turned unto her by the way, and said, Go to, I pray you, let me come in unto you; (for he knew not that she was his daughter in law.) And she said, What will you give me, that you may come in unto me? *(The conduct of Tamar, though in every way reprehensible, is not to be attributed to mere lust, or inordinate desire for children, but was most probably to assert her right to a place among the ancestresses of the Patriarchal family. We find from all of this, and as should be obvious, that God will show that His choice is of Grace, and not of merit, and that Christ came into the world to save sinners, even the chiefest of sinners, and is not ashamed, upon their repentance, to be allied to them.)*

17 And he said, I will send you a kid from the flock *(a baby lamb).* And she said, Will you give me a pledge, till you send it? *(something she could hold that was personally his, until she received the animal).*

18 And he said, What pledge shall I give you?

And she said, Your signet, and your bracelets, and your staff that is in your hand. And he gave it to her, and came in unto her, and she conceived by him. *(This is what she had planned; the pledge she demanded would incriminate Judah. His problem was lust, while hers was commitment.)*

19 And she arose, and went away, and laid by her vail from her, and put on the garments of her widowhood.

20 And Judah sent the kid *(baby lamb)* by the hand of his friend the Adullamite, to receive his pledge from the woman's hand: but he found her not.

21 Then he asked the men of that place, saying, Where is the harlot, who was openly by the way side? And they said, There was no harlot in this place.

22 And he returned to Judah, and said, I cannot find her; and also the men of the place said, that there was no harlot in this place.

23 And Judah said, Let her take it to her, lest we be shamed *(she had the items of his pledge with her):* behold, I sent this kid *(baby lamb),* and you have not found her.

24 And it came to pass about three months after, that it was told Judah, saying, Tamar your daughter in law has played the harlot; and also, behold, she is with child by whoredom *(while she was with child, it was not by whoredom; how so quick we are to judge).* And Judah said, Bring her forth, and let her be burned *(Judah was quick to condemn her, when, in reality, he was just as guilty, even much more so).*

25 When she was brought forth, she sent to her father in law, saying, By the man, whose these are, am I with child: and she said, Discern, I pray you, whose are these, the signet, and bracelets, and staff.

26 And Judah acknowledged them, and said, She has been more righteous than I; because that I gave her not to Shelah my son. And he knew her again no more. *(But still, the sons were his, and Tamar was now an ancestress of the Patriarchal family.)*

TWINS

27 And it came to pass in the time of her travail, that, behold, twins were in her womb.

28 And it came to pass, when she travailed, that the one put out his hand: and the midwife took and bound upon his hand a scarlet thread, saying, This came out first. *(All of this had to do with the coming Redeemer.)*

29 And it came to pass, as he drew back his hand, that, behold, his brother came out: and she said, How have you broken forth? this breach be upon you: therefore his name was called Pharez (*this one was in the lineage of Christ, because he was the firstborn*).

30 And afterward came out his brother, that had the scarlet thread upon his hand: and his name was called Zarah. (*Luther asks why such things were placed in Scripture. He answers: 1. That no one should be self-righteous; 2. That no one should despair. There is forgiveness for all who will humbly come to the Lord; and, 3. To remind us that Gentiles, by natural right, are brothers, mothers, and sisters to our Lord; the Word of Salvation is a Word for the whole world.*)

CHAPTER 39
(1727 B.C.)
JOSEPH

AND Joseph was brought down to Egypt; and Potiphar, an officer of Pharaoh, captain of the guard, and Egyptian, bought him of the hands of the Ishmeelites, which had brought him down thither. (*An Eastern race then governed Egypt, hence the reason that Potiphar is three times declared to be an "Egyptian." In the story of Joseph, we will perceive a remarkable chain of events, all tending to one grand point, namely, the exaltation of the man who had been in the pit — once again, a Type of Christ.*)

2 And the LORD was with Joseph, and he was a prosperous man; and he was in the house of his master the Egyptian. (*Some eight times in this Chapter, in one way or the other, it is said that the Lord was with Joseph. Eight speaks of Resurrection, so it tells us that whatever happened to Joseph, no matter how adverse it seemed at the moment, a Resurrection was coming.*)

BLESSINGS

3 And his master saw that the LORD was with him, and that the LORD made all that he did to prosper in his hand. (*Potiphar had more sense than most modern Christians. He saw that the Hand of the Lord was on Joseph, and took advantage of that, even as he should have done. Many times the Church will regrettably respond with jealousy; consequently, the Work of God is greatly hindered by such action and attitudes.*)

4 And Joseph found grace in his sight, and he served him: and he made him overseer over his house, and all that he had he put into his hand. (*This does not imply that Potiphar was acquainted with Jehovah, but simply that he concluded Joseph to be under the Divine protection. So he made him the business manager of all his holdings, which, no doubt, were considerable.*)

5 And it came to pass from the time that he had made him overseer in his house, and over all that he had, that the LORD blessed the Egyptian's house for Joseph's sake (*we are blessed for Jesus' sake*); and the Blessing of the LORD was upon all that he had in the house, and in the field. (*How do we correlate all of this, with the Lord being with Joseph, and yet he is a slave? Even though not for a moment is the wrongdoing of his brothers condoned by the Lord, still, the Lord was in all of this; even though Joseph did not know what the future held, he maintained his Faith in the Lord, thereby walking by Faith instead of by sight. Had he done otherwise, the Lord could not have blessed him. Many Christians forfeit blessing, simply because they refuse to humble themselves before the Lord. Joseph could easily have grown bitter, until the bitterness overtook him. But he put it all in the Hands of his Lord, even as we must do.*)

6 And he left all that he had in Joseph's hand; and he knew not ought he had, save the bread which he did eat. And Joseph was a goodly person, and well favored (*he was impeccably honest and, as well, very handsome*).

7 And it came to pass after these things, that his master's wife cast her eyes upon Joseph, and she said, Lie with me. (*Tradition says that Zuleikah was her name; she was at first the most virtuous of women, but when she saw Joseph, she was so affected, that she lost all self-control, and became a slave to her passions. It is said that she made a dinner inviting 40 of the most beautiful women in Egypt, who, when they saw Joseph, were so moved with admiration that they exclaimed with one accord that he must be an Angel.*)

8 But he refused, and said unto his master's wife, Behold, my master trusts me with all that is in the house, and he has committed all that he has to my hand (*the action of Joseph in resisting this temptation pressed upon him showed him to be the true firstborn*);

9 There is none greater in this house than I; neither has he kept back any thing from me but you, because you are his wife: how then can I do this great wickedness, and sin against God? (*Williams says that Joseph urged three

reasons against this wrongdoing: "1. Gratitude to his master, who had put everything into his hand; 2. Respect for the woman, seeing that she was Potiphar's wife; and, 3. Fear of God.")

10 And it came to pass, as she spoke to Joseph day by day, that he hearkened not unto her, to lie by her, or to be with her (it was a continuing temptation, pressed upon day-by-day, with him continuing to resist).

11 And it came to pass about this time, that Joseph went into the house to do his business; and there was none of the men of the house there within. (Evaluating Joseph, some would claim that after advances had been made, he should not have gone back into the house; however, of this he had no choice. His business demanded that he frequent the place. It is certain that he would have done anything to have avoided contact with this woman, but the situation actually presented itself as a trap. And so the trap is ultimately sprung.)

12 And she caught him by his garment, saying, Lie with me: and he left his garment in her hand, and fled, and got him out. (This is the second occasion that the Sacred History speaks of Joseph's garment. His brothers took the one; Potiphar's wife the other. They tried to hide their sin with that garment; she tried to hide hers in the same manner.)

13 And it came to pass, when she saw that he had left his garment in her hand, and was fled forth,

WRONGLY ACCUSED

14 That she called unto the men of her house, and spoke unto them, saying, See, he (Potiphar) has brought in an Hebrew unto us to mock us; he came in unto me to lie with me, and I cried with a loud voice:

15 And it came to pass, when he heard that I lifted up my voice and cried, that he left his garment with me, and fled, and got him out. (Matthew Henry says: "Chaste and holy love will continue, though slighted; but sinful love is easily changed into sinful hatred. Those who have broken the bonds of modesty will never be held by the bonds of Truth.")

16 And she laid up his garment by her, until his lord (Potiphar) came home. (The Devil would surmise that if he cannot get Joseph to do that which is wrong, he will have him locked up in prison for years. Of course, the Lord could have stopped all of this; however, the remainder of the Chapter tells us why not!)

17 And she spoke unto him (Potiphar) according to these words, saying, The Hebrew servant, which you have brought unto us, came in unto me to mock me:

18 And it came to pass, as I lifted up my voice and cried, that he left his garment with me, and fled out.

PRISON

19 And it came to pass, when his master heard the words of his wife, which she spoke unto him, saying, After this manner did your servant to me; that his anger was kindled (Satan's trap is now sprung).

20 And Joseph's master took him, and put him into the prison, a place where the king's prisoners were bound: and he was there in the prison. (In one moment, Joseph exchanged a palace for a prison. Psalms 105:17-20 states that he was laid in iron and his feet hurt with fetters.)

21 But the LORD was with Joseph, and showed him mercy, and gave him favor in the sight of the keeper of the prison. (The Lord was with Joseph as much in the prison as he had been in the palace. We should take a lesson from this.)

22 And the keeper of the prison committed to Joseph's hand all the prisoners who were in the prison; and whatsoever they did there, he was the doer of it. (This was Joseph's training ground. Would he pass the test? In fact, he passed it with flying colors.)

23 The keeper of the prison looked not to any thing that was under his hand; because the LORD was with him, and that which he did, the LORD made it to prosper. (However, this would not have been the case had Joseph grown bitter. He accepted this position, without saying a word or attempting to justify or defend himself. In other words, he left everything up to the Lord.)

CHAPTER 40
(1718 B.C.)
THE DREAMS

AND it came to pass after these things, that the butler of the king of Egypt and his baker had offended their lord the king of Egypt.

2 And Pharaoh was angry against two of his officers, against the chief of the butlers, and against the chief of the bakers.

3 And he put them in ward in the house of the captain of the guard, into the prison, the place where Joseph was bound.

4 And the captain of the guard charged Joseph with them, and he served them: and they continued a season in ward. *(In Chapter 39, Satan uses Potiphar's wife; and in Chapter 40, he uses Pharaoh's chief butler. The former he used to put Joseph into the dungeon; and the latter he used to keep him there, through his ungrateful negligence; but all in vain. God was behind the scenes. His finger was guiding all things.)*

5 And they dreamed a dream both of them, each man his dream in one night, each man according to the interpretation of his dream, the butler and the baker of the king of Egypt, which were bound in the prison. *(In studying the Word of God, it becomes obvious that the Lord quite often uses dreams to carry forth His Work in some way.)*

6 And Joseph came in unto them in the morning, and looked upon them, and, behold, they were sad.

7 And he asked Pharaoh's officers who were with him in the ward of his lord's house, saying, Wherefore look you so sadly to day? *(They sensed that the dreams were important.)*

8 And they said unto him, We have dreamed a dream, and there is no interpreter of it *(it seems they had sought the help of others to interpret the dreams, but to no avail)*. And Joseph said unto them, Do not interpretations belong to God? tell me them, I pray you. *(Joseph "served" the prisoners, and, no doubt, with gentle sympathy; he pleased his master; and he preached faithfully the Word of the Lord, whether it announced Grace or wrath — Williams.)*

THE BUTLER'S DREAM

9 And the chief butler told his dream to Joseph, and said to him, In my dream, behold, a vine was before me;

10 And in the vine were three branches: and it was as though it budded, and her blossoms shot forth; and the clusters thereof brought forth ripe grapes:

11 And Pharaoh's cup was in my hand: and I took the grapes, and pressed them into Pharaoh's cup, and I gave the cup into Pharaoh's hand.

12 And Joseph said unto him, This is the interpretation of it: The three branches are three days:

13 Yet within three days shall Pharaoh lift up your head, and restore you unto your place: and you shall deliver Pharaoh's cup into his hand, after the former manner when you were his butler.

JOSEPH'S REQUEST

14 But think on me when it shall be well with you, and show kindness, I pray you, unto me, and make mention of me unto Pharaoh, and bring me out of this house:

15 For indeed I was stolen away out of the land of the Hebrews: and here also have I done nothing that they should put me into the dungeon. *(Verses 14 and 15 record the fact that Joseph never accused his brethren. He merely referred to him being stolen away. Likewise, Jesus did not come to condemn, but to save.)*

THE BAKER'S DREAM

16 When the chief baker saw that the interpretation was good, he said unto Joseph, I also was in my dream, and, behold, I had three white baskets on my head:

17 And in the uppermost basket there was of all manner of bakemeats for Pharaoh; and the birds did eat them out of the basket upon my head.

18 And Joseph answered and said, This is the interpretation thereof: The three baskets are three days:

19 Yet within three days shall Pharaoh lift up your head from off you, and shall hang you on a tree; and the birds shall eat your flesh from off you. *(God Alone knows the future, and He is able to reveal it to men, should He so desire. The manner in which the Holy Spirit used Joseph in this instance would come under the heading of three New Testament Gifts of the Spirit: "discerning of spirits," "the Word of Knowledge," and "the Word of Wisdom" [I Cor. 12:8-10].)*

DREAMS FULFILLED

20 And it came to pass the third day, which was Pharaoh's birthday, that he made a feast unto all his servants: and he lifted up the head of the chief butler and of the chief baker among his servants.

21 And he restored the chief butler unto his butlership again; and he gave the cup into Pharaoh's hand *(exactly as Joseph had stated*

would happen):

22 But he hanged the chief baker: as Joseph had interpreted to them *(once again, exactly as Joseph had stated).*

23 Yet did not the chief butler remember Joseph, but forgot him. *(Divine discipline permitted that Joseph should be tempted in all points, and so the chief cupbearer forgot him, although he knew his innocence, and that he possessed a mysterious relationship to God. All these facts helped to build up Joseph as a very striking Type of Israel's Saviour and the world's Redeemer.)*

CHAPTER 41
(1715 B.C.)
PHARAOH'S DREAM

AND it came to pass at the end of two full years, that Pharaoh dreamed: and, behold, he stood by the river *(as to exactly how long that Joseph spent in prison, we aren't told; however, we do know that he stayed there two more years after the interpretation of the dream for the chief butler).*

2 And, behold, there came up out of the river seven well favored cattle and fatfleshed; and they fed in a meadow.

3 And, behold, seven other cattle came up after them out of the river, ill favored and leanfleshed; and stood by the other cattle upon the brink of the river.

4 And the ill favored and leanfleshed cattle did eat up the seven well favored and fat cattle. So Pharaoh awoke.

5 And he slept and dreamed the second time: and, behold, seven ears of corn *(either barley or wheat, for there was no corn in that part of the world at that time, as we know of such presently)* came up upon one stalk, rank and good.

6 And, behold, seven thin ears and blasted with the east wind sprung up after them.

7 And the seven thin ears devoured the seven rank and full ears. And Pharaoh awoke, and, behold, it was a dream.

INTERPRETATION SOUGHT

8 And it came to pass in the morning that his spirit was troubled; and he sent and called for all the magicians of Egypt, and all the wise men thereof: and Pharaoh told them his dream; but there was none who could interpret them unto Pharaoh. *(The Egyptian "Book of the Dead," now in the British Museum in London, with its sacred cows and mystic number "seven" — a book beyond doubt well known to Pharaoh — must have helped to convince the king that this double dream was supernatural.)*

9 Then spoke the chief butler unto Pharaoh, saying, I do remember my faults this day *(with none of the magicians able to interpret the dream, or at least to Pharaoh's satisfaction, it began to be known in the Palace as to the dilemma, until it reached the chief butler):*

10 Pharaoh was angry with his servants, and put me in ward in the captain of the guard's house, both me and the chief baker:

11 And we dreamed a dream in one night, I and he; we dreamed each man according to the interpretation of his dream.

12 And there was there with us a young man, an Hebrew, servant to the captain of the guard; and we told him, and he interpreted to us our dreams; to each man according to his dream he did interpret.

13 And it came to pass, as he interpreted to us, so it was; me he *(you)* restored unto mine office, and him he *(you)* hanged.

THE INTERPRETATION

14 Then Pharaoh sent and called Joseph, and they brought him hastily out of the dungeon: and he shaved himself and changed his raiment, and came in unto Pharaoh. *(Events now transpire which no human hand could manipulate. Only God could do such a thing. This should teach us that we should allow the Lord to plan for us. Men forgot Joseph, but it is double certain that God didn't forget Joseph. And neither will He forget you. This is at least one of the reasons that we must look to God instead of men.)*

15 And Pharaoh said unto Joseph, I have dreamed a dream and there is none who can interpret it: and I have heard say of you, that you can understand a dream to interpret it. *(The Lord, once again, uses dreams to reveal His Will.)*

16 And Joseph answered Pharaoh, saying, It is not in me: God shall give Pharaoh an answer of peace. *(Joseph could have claimed great things, but instead he gave all the glory to God for giving him the interpretation of these dreams.)*

17 And Pharaoh said unto Joseph, In my dream, behold, I stood upon the bank of the river *(the Nile River):*

18 And, behold, there came up out of the river seven cattle, fatfleshed and well favored;

and they fed in a meadow.

19 And, behold, seven other cattle came up after them, poor and very ill favored and leanfleshed, such as I never saw in all the land of Egypt for badness:

20 And the lean and the ill favored cattle did eat up the first seven fat cattle:

21 And when they had eaten them up, it could not be known that they had eaten them; but they were still ill favored, as at the beginning. So I awoke.

22 And I saw in my dream, and, behold, seven ears came up in one stalk, full and good:

23 And, behold, seven ears, withered, thin, and blasted with the east wind, sprung up after them:

24 And the thin ears devoured the seven good ears: and I told this unto the magicians; but there was none that could declare it to me.

25 And Joseph said unto Pharaoh, The dream of Pharaoh is one: God has showed Pharaoh what He is about to do. *(The dream was doubled, in order, as Joseph says in Verse 32, to denote its Divine certainty and, as well, to portray its immediate happening, as well as its futuristic happening.)*

26 The seven good cattle are seven years; and the seven good ears are seven years: the dream is one.

27 And the seven thin and ill favored cattle that came up after them are seven years; and the seven empty ears blasted with the east wind shall be seven years of famine. *(Discoveries many years ago at the First Cataract, and at El-Kab, record the fact of this seven years famine. The date is given as 1700 B.C. This date accords with accepted Bible chronology.)*

28 This is the thing which I have spoken unto Pharaoh: What God is about to do He shows unto Pharaoh.

29 Behold, there come seven years of great plenty throughout all the land of Egypt:

30 And there shall arise after them seven years of famine; and all the plenty shall be forgotten in the land of Egypt; and the famine shall consume the land;

31 And the plenty shall not be known in the land by reason of that famine following; for it shall be very grievous.

32 And for that the dream was doubled unto Pharaoh twice; it is because the thing is established by God, and God will shortly bring it to pass. *(The interpretation, as given by Joseph, and which greatly concerned Pharaoh, was to take place in the immediate future. But due to*

the fact of the dream being doubled, it has an End-time meaning, as well, and which will be of far greater magnitude than that which would take place in Joseph's day. It is as follows:

We know that this terrible famine which would follow the seven years of plenty would bring Joseph's brothers to him, ultimately along with his father, Jacob. This represents Israel coming to Christ, for Joseph is a Type of Christ, which they shall do at the conclusion of the seven-year Great Tribulation Period. So, the seven years of famine point to the coming seven-year Great Tribulation Period prophesied by Daniel and foretold by our Lord [Dan. 9:27; Mat. 24:21].

As well, the "east wind" mentioned in Verse 27 localizes the Great Tribulation Period that is coming, which will affect the entire Earth, but will have its beginning in the Middle East.

As it regards the seven years of plenty which immediately preceded the seven years of famine, looking at it in the prophetic sense, we can take the number "seven" in two different ways.

The number "seven," which is God's number of perfection, could pertain to the Church, and it being completed, and then taken out of the world immediately before the seven years of Tribulation. Or, even as the seven years of famine correspond exactly to the coming seven years of Great Tribulation, the seven years of plenty could refer to a tremendous harvest of souls immediately preceding the Rapture, which will be followed by the Great Tribulation. Quite possibly, both particulars will come into play. There will be a great harvest of souls, fulfilling the Prophecy of Joel about the Lord pouring out His Spirit upon all flesh, which Peter infers will be in the last days in a greater way than ever, which will conclude the Church Age [Acts. 2:16-21].)

33 Now therefore let Pharaoh look out a man discreet and wise, and set him over the land of Egypt.

34 Let Pharaoh do this, and let him appoint officers over the land, and take up the fifth part of the land of Egypt in the seven plentiful years.

35 And let them gather all the food of those good years that come, and lay up corn *(grain)* under the hand of Pharaoh, and let them keep food in the cities.

36 And that food shall be for store to the land against the seven years of famine, which shall be in the land of Egypt; that the land perish not through the famine. *(This famine was designed by God, not only to bless and instruct Egypt, but mainly to be the means of*

bringing Joseph's brothers in repentance to his feet. It is all, as well, and as stated, a picture of present and future facts.)

JOSEPH

37 And the thing was good in the eyes of Pharaoh, and in the eyes of all his servants *(Pharaoh recognized the wisdom of what he was hearing from the young man, Joseph).*

38 And Pharaoh said unto his servants, Can we find such a one as this is, a man in whom the Spirit of God is? *(The term "Spirit of God," as used by Pharaoh, in the Hebrew is "Ruach Elohim," and would have been understood by Pharaoh as referring to the sagacity and intelligence of a Deity. Other than that, he would have had no knowledge as to What or Who the Spirit of God actually was.)*

39 And Pharaoh said unto Joseph, Forasmuch as God has showed you all this, there is none so discreet and wise as you are *(Joseph, while yet in humiliation, becomes the interpreter of the thoughts and counsels of God; and in his elevation executes with power those counsels, and subjects all Egypt to Him Who sat upon the throne.*

In all this was Joseph a wonderfully full Type of Christ, Who, in the humiliation of His First Advent, revealed the counsels and affections of God's Heart, and Who will, in the glory of His Second Advent, establish the Kingdom of God in power over the whole Earth.):

40 You shall be over my house, and according unto your word shall all my people be ruled: only in the throne will I be greater than you. *(So, in a moment's time, Joseph is promoted to the august position of the Prime Minister of Egypt, and is thus one of the most powerful men in the world.)*

41 And Pharaoh said unto Joseph, See, I have set you over all the land of Egypt.

42 And Pharaoh took off his ring from his hand, and put it upon Joseph's hand, and arrayed him in vestures of fine linen, and put a gold chain about his neck *(giving Joseph his ring proclaimed the fact that Joseph's position was real and not merely honorary; Joseph's authority was to be absolute and universal, which it was; there was no part of Egypt over which he didn't have control)*;

43 And he made him to ride in the second chariot which he had; and they cried before him, Bow the knee: and he made him ruler over all the land of Egypt.

44 And Pharaoh said unto Joseph, I am Pharaoh, and without you shall no man lift up his hand or foot in all the land of Egypt.

45 And Pharaoh called Joseph's name Zaphnath-paaneah *(the very name that Pharaoh gave Joseph was prophetic; his Hebrew name, Joseph, means "Jehovah shall add"; his Egyptian name means "life more abundant"; so, in essence, both of his names meant "Jehovah shall add life more abundant," which portrays Christ, as well [Jn. 10:10])*; and he gave him to wife Asenath the daughter of Poti-pherah priest of On. And Joseph went out over all the land of Egypt.

46 And Joseph was thirty years old when he stood before Pharaoh king of Egypt. And Joseph went out from the presence of Pharaoh, and went throughout all the land of Egypt. *(Our Lord, as well, began His public ministry at 30 years old.)*

47 And in the seven plenteous years the earth brought forth by handfuls.

48 And he *(Joseph)* gathered up all the food of the seven years, which were in the land of Egypt, and laid up the food in the cities: the food of the field, which was round about every city, laid he up in the same.

49 And Joseph gathered corn *(grain)* as the sand of the sea, very much, until he left numbering; for it was without number.

50 And unto Joseph were born two sons before the years of famine came, which Asenath the daughter of Poti-pherah priest of On bore unto him.

51 And Joseph called the name of the firstborn Manasseh: For God, said he, has made me forget all my toil, and all my father's house.

52 And the name of the second called he Ephraim: For God has caused me to be fruitful in the land of my affliction. *(Joseph was given a Gentile wife, which was a type of the Gentile wife given to Christ, for the Church is mostly Gentile. Manasseh means "forgetfulness," while Ephraim means "fruitfulness." This is indicative of his spiritual condition. He forgot the injustice done to him, and the Lord made him fruitful. It should be a lesson to us.)*

53 And the seven years of plenteousness, that was in the land of Egypt, were ended.

FAMINE

54 And the seven years of famine began to come, according as Joseph had said: and the famine was in all lands *(refers to all lands of*

the Middle East); **but in all the land of Egypt there was bread.** *(It was Egypt only which had food, and because of Pharaoh heeding what the Lord had said, and appointing Joseph to head up the program.)*

55 **And when all the land of Egypt was famished, the people cried to Pharaoh for bread: and Pharaoh said unto all the Egyptians, Go unto Joseph; what he says to you, do.** *(No nation has ever had a more honest man to guide its affairs than did Egypt with Joseph.)*

56 **And the famine was over all the face of the Earth** *(that part of the world)*: **and Joseph opened all the storehouses, and sold unto the Egyptians; and the famine waxed sore in the land of Egypt.** *(Just as the Lord said it would!)*

57 **And all countries** *(in the Middle East)* **came into Egypt to Joseph for to buy corn** *(grain)*; **because that the famine was so sore in all lands.** *(While there were, no doubt, many reasons for the famine, at least one of the primary reasons was to bring Jacob and his family into Egypt, just as the coming Great Tribulation will bring Israel to Christ.)*

CHAPTER 42
(1707 B.C.)
JOSEPH'S BRETHREN

NOW **when Jacob saw that there was corn** *(grain)* **in Egypt, Jacob said unto his sons, Why do you look one upon another?** *(in other words, go down into Egypt and buy grain!)*

2 **And he said, Behold, I have heard that there is corn** *(grain)* **in Egypt: get you down thither, and buy for us from thence; that we may live, and not die** *(evidently, the famine was severe in Canaan).*

3 **And Joseph's ten brethren went down to buy corn** *(grain)* **in Egypt** *(a group of this nature was much safer than one or two making the trip).*

4 **But Benjamin, Joseph's brother, Jacob sent not with his brethren; for he said, Lest peradventure mischief befall him** *(not only did Jacob love this boy, and because he was the son of Rachel, but, as well, he no doubt felt, Joseph now being lost, that the Lord would place the mantel on Benjamin).*

5 **And the sons of Israel came to buy corn** *(grain)* **among those who came** *(many others from Canaan and other parts of the Middle East were in Egypt, as well, in order to buy grain)*: **for the famine was in the land of Canaan.**

6 **And Joseph was the governor over the land, and he it was who sold to all the people** of the land: **and Joseph's brethren came, and bowed down themselves before him with their faces to the earth** *(Joseph's dream concerning the sheaves bowing down to him [37:7] is now fulfilled).*

7 **And Joseph saw his brethren, and he knew them, but made himself strange unto them, and spoke roughly unto them; and he said unto them, From where do you come? And they said, From the land of Canaan to buy food.** *(Had Joseph thought of his own dignity and of his own affection, he would have revealed himself at once to his brothers. Such a revelation, however, would have produced only confusion, but not repentance. He loved them and, therefore, sought their spiritual welfare; consequently, he acted so as to bring their sin to remembrance, to make them confess it with their own lips, and not just to him and in his presence, for he still concealed himself from them, but to God and in His Presence — Williams.)*

8 **And Joseph knew his brethren, but they knew not him.**

9 **and Joseph remembered the dreams which he dreamed of them, and said unto them, You are spies; to see the nakedness of the land you are come** *(this accusation was morally true; for the men who were guilty of the treachery, cruelty, and stupidity of 34:25-29 would have acted similarly in Egypt, if they had had the power; however, as events will prove, they were not the same men they had been those many years before).*

10 **And they said unto him, No, my lord, but to buy food are your servants come.**

11 **We are all one man's sons; we are true men, your servants are no spies.**

12 **And he said unto them, No, but to see the nakedness of the land you are come.**

13 **And they said, Your servants are twelve brethren, the sons of one man in the land of Canaan; and, behold, the youngest is this day with our father, and one is not.**

14 **And Joseph said unto them, That is it that I spoke unto you, saying, You are spies:**

15 **Hereby you shall be proved: By the life of Pharaoh you shall not go forth hence, except your youngest brother come hither.** *(Reasoning that Jacob had probably transferred the birthright to Benjamin, he wanted to know the attitude of these men toward Benjamin. So he "proves them.")*

THE BROTHERS

16 **Send one of you, and let him fetch your**

brother, and you shall be kept in prison, that your words may be proved, whether there be any truth in you: or else by the life of Pharaoh surely you are spies.

17 And he put them all together into ward three days. *(Likewise, Israel will be under tremendous pressure by the Antichrist for a little over three years.)*

18 And Joseph said unto them the third day, This do, and live; for I fear God *(what must these men have thought when Joseph mentions "Elohim," the God of the Hebrews? All of this had to be extremely strange to them, because they knew that Elohim was little known, if at all, outside of their respective family)*:

19 If you be true men, let one of your brethren be bound in the house of your prison: go you, carry corn *(grain)* for the famine of your houses *(Joseph now softens his demands, in that he at first stated that nine of the brothers would remain in Egypt, while one was sent to fetch Benjamin; but now he limits that to just one remaining in Egypt, while the nine go back home)*:

20 But bring your youngest brother unto me; so shall your words be verified, and you shall not die. And they did so *(when they return, Benjamin must come with them)*.

21 And they said one to another, We are verily guilty concerning our brother, in that we saw the anguish of his soul, when he besought us, and we would not hear; therefore is this distress come upon us *(as Israel in a coming sad day, of which they are a type, the brothers of Joseph are called to pass through deep and searching trial, through intensely painful exercises of conscience)*.

22 And Reuben answered them, saying, Did I not speak unto you, saying, Do not sin against the child; and you would not hear? therefore, behold, also his blood is required *(after all of these years, their consciences still bother them, and rightly so! Sin can only be forgotten when it is properly forgiven by the Lord. And it cannot be properly forgiven until one properly confesses such to the Lord)*.

23 And they knew not that Joseph understood them; for he spoke unto them by an interpreter *(but he did understand them)*.

SIMEON

24 And he turned himself about from them, and wept; and returned to them again, and communed with them, and took from them Simeon, and bound him before their eyes *(why* Simeon was chosen, we aren't told; he could have been the ringleader in the terrible sin that had been committed against Joseph those long years earlier)*.

25 Then Joseph commanded to fill their sacks with corn *(grain)*, and to restore every man's money into his sack, and to give them provision for the way: and thus did he unto them *(this coincides with the sustenance that the Lord will give Israel during the Great Tribulation [Rev. 12:6])*.

26 And they loaded their asses with the corn *(grain)*, and departed thence.

27 And as one of them opened his sack to give his ass provender in the inn, he espied *(found)* his money; for, behold, it was in his sack's mouth *(easily found)*.

28 And he said unto his brethren, My money is restored; and, lo, it is even in my sack: and their heart failed them, and they were afraid, saying one to another, What is this that God has done unto us? *(Actually, they were right! It was God Who was guiding these events, giving Joseph instructions all along the way as to how he could handle the situation; however, because of their sin, a sin committed about 20 years before, they were thinking of God in a very negative way. It is no different presently.)*

JACOB

29 And they came unto Jacob their father unto the land of Canaan, and told him all that befell unto them, saying,

30 The man, who is the lord of the land, spoke roughly to us, and took us for spies of the country.

31 And we said unto him, We are true men; we are no spies:

32 We be twelve brethren, sons of our father; one is not, and the youngest is this day with our father in the land of Canaan.

33 And the man, the lord of the country, said unto us, Hereby shall I know that you are true men; leave one of your brethren here with me, and take food for the famine of your households, and be gone:

34 And bring your youngest brother unto me: then shall I know that you are no spies, but that you are true men: so will I deliver you your brother, and you shall traffick in the land.

35 And it came to pass as they emptied their sacks, that, behold, every man's bundle of money was in his sack: and when both they and their father saw the bundles of money,

they were afraid. *(From the terminology used by these men at this present time, it is obvious that a change has taken place in their lives; however, it is a change that is not quite yet complete.)*

SORROW

36 And Jacob their father said unto them, Me have you bereaved of my children: Joseph is not, and Simeon is not, and you will take Benjamin away: all these things are against me. *(Jacob thinks that Joseph is dead; and likewise, Israel thinks that Jesus is dead, denying that He rose from the dead.)*

37 And Reuben spoke unto his father, saying, Kill my two sons, if I bring him *(Benjamin)* not to you: deliver him into my hand, and I will bring him to you again.

38 And he said, My son shall not go down with you; for his brother is dead, and he is left alone: if mischief befall him by the way in the which you go, then shall you bring down my gray hairs with sorrow to the grave. *(This Verse speaks of Jacob's great sorrow. The Great Tribulation Period is called "the time of Jacob's trouble." But then it says, "but he shall be saved out of it" [Jer. 30:7]. Likewise, Jacob will be saved out of this "sorrow.")*

CHAPTER 43
(1707 B.C.)
EGYPT

AND the famine was sore in the land *(likewise, the Great Tribulation, which is yet to come, and of which this Verse is a type, will be "sore in the land of Israel").*

2 And it came to pass, when they had eaten up the corn which they had brought out of Egypt, their father said unto them, Go again, buy us a little food *(it seems that the grain which they obtained in Egypt was used solely as their own personal food, with the flocks and herds evidently eating other things).*

3 And Judah spoke unto him, saying, The man did solemnly protest unto us, saying, You shall not see my face, except your brother be with you *(Reuben is the firstborn, and should have taken the lead in all these matters, but it is Judah who in fact stands in the position of leadership; Jesus will come from the Tribe of Judah).*

4 It you will send our brother with us, we will go down and buy you food:

5 But if you will not send him, we will not go down: for the man said unto us, You shall not see my face, except your brother be with you *(Joseph's skill — that skill which only love can give — in leading his brothers step by step to a confession of their sin against him, and to a sense of its blackness in the sight of God, is a picture of the future action of the Lord Jesus Christ in bringing Israel to recognize her sin in rejecting Him, and the consequent enormity of that sin against God — Williams).*

6 And Israel said, Wherefore dealt you so ill with me, as to tell the man whether you had yet a brother? *(The Holy Spirit now refers to Jacob as "Israel." This refers to the fact of Jacob's obedience in sending Benjamin, even though he did not desire to do so. Whenever the Holy Spirit uses the name "Israel" as it refers to Jacob, always and without exception, it is referring to Faith and, in a sense, a milestone in his faith walk.)*

7 And they said, The man asked us straitly of our state, and of our kindred, saying, Is your father yet alive? have you another brother? and we told him according to the tenor of these words: could we certainly know that he would say, Bring your brother down?

8 And Judah said unto Israel his father, Send the lad with me, and we will arise and go; that we may live, and not die, both we, and you, and also our little ones.

9 I will be surety for him; of my hand shall you require him: if I bring him not unto you, and set him before you, then let me bear the blame for ever:

10 For except we had lingered, surely now we had returned this second time *(had it not been for this critical issue, the taking of Benjamin, due to the lack of food, they would have already returned).*

11 And their father Israel said unto them, If it must be so now, do this; take of the best fruits in the land in your vessels, and carry down the man a present, a little balm, and a little honey, spices, and myrrh, nuts, and almonds:

12 And take double money in your hand; and the money that was brought again in the mouth of your sacks, carry it again in your hand; peradventure it was an oversight *(all of this was to prove that they were honest men; little did they realize what Joseph's intentions actually were):*

13 Take also your brother, and arise, go again unto the man *(under no consideration would Jacob have allowed Benjamin to have gone to Egypt, but that he had reached the place to where there was no choice; this was God's Will, and sometimes the Lord has to box us into a corner,*

before we will obey that Will):

14 And God Almighty give you mercy before the man, that he may send away your other brother, and Benjamin. If I be bereaved of my children, I am bereaved. *(By using the title, "God Almighty," which means "El Shaddai," the Patriarch is referring to the Covenant God of Abraham [17:1]. El Shaddai means "the All-Sufficient One.")*

15 And the men took that present, and they took double money in their hand, and Benjamin; and rose up, and went down to Egypt, and stood before Joseph. *(He was their brother and their saviour, but yet they did not know him. Likewise, Israel will stand before Christ at the Second Coming, and will not know Him [Zech. 13:6].)*

16 And when Joseph saw Benjamin with them, he said to the ruler of his house, Bring these men home, and kill *(slaughter a lamb for a meal)*, and make ready; for these men shall dine with me at noon. *(The union of Benjamin with Joseph points forward to the day when Christ, as Benjamin, will be the Son of the Right Hand to Israel and, as Joseph, King over all the Earth.)*

17 And the man did as Joseph bade; and the man brought the men into Joseph's house. *(Israel will one day be brought to the Heavenly Joseph's house. Paul said so [Rom. 11:26-27].)*

FEAR

18 And the men were afraid, because they were brought into Joseph's house; and they said, Because of the money that was returned in our sacks at the first time are we brought in; that he may seek occasion against us, and fall upon us, and take us for bondmen, and our asses *(the special attention they were being given, they erroneously read as negative).*

19 And they came near to the steward of Joseph's house, and they communed with him at the door of the house,

20 And said, O sir, we came indeed down at the first time to buy food:

21 And it came to pass, when we came to the inn, that we opened our sacks, and, behold, every man's money was in the mouth of his sack, our money in full weight: and we have brought it again in our hand.

22 And other money have we brought down in our hands to buy food: we cannot tell who put our money in our sacks.

23 And he said *(the steward said)*, Peace be to you, fear not: your God, and the God of your father, has given you treasure in your sacks: I had your money. And he brought Simeon out unto them. *(Strangely, the steward speaks of Elohim, Whom the Egyptians did not know. The conduct of Joseph cannot be explained except on the ground of his inspiration. He is not acting. He is not trifling with human feelings. He is not merely following the dictate of his own personal affections. He is, under Divine direction, planning for the removal of his father's house to Egypt, that the people of God may pass through their season of trial in the house of bondage — Spence.)*

24 And the man brought the men into Joseph's house, and gave them water, and they washed their feet; and he gave their asses provender *(food)*.

25 And they made ready the present against Joseph came at noon: for they heard that they should eat bread there *(the further it goes, the stranger it becomes; surely, the lord of Egypt didn't invite rank strangers from other nations of the Earth into his house to eat with him, and especially lowly shepherds! But yet here they were).*

JOSEPH

26 And when Joseph came home, they brought him the present which was in their hand into the house, and bowed themselves to him to the earth *(again, they fulfilled his dream [37:7, 9]).*

27 And he asked them of their welfare, and said, Is your father well, the old man of whom you spoke? Is he yet alive? *(It must have seemed strange to the sons of Jacob to hear the lord of Egypt asking personal questions about their father and his health, etc.)*

28 And they answered, Your servant our father is in good health, he is yet alive. And they bowed down their heads, and made obeisance *(it had been approximately 20 years since Joseph had seen his father, Jacob).*

29 And he lifted up his eyes, and saw his brother Benjamin, his mother's son, and said, Is this your younger brother, of whom you spoke unto me? And he said, God be gracious unto you, my son. *(This is the first time that Joseph had seen Benjamin. He had not yet been born when Joseph was sold into Egypt.)*

WEEPING

30 And Joseph made haste; for his bowels

did yearn upon his brother: and he sought where to weep; and he entered into his chamber, and wept there. *(The scene was poignant, not only as it expressed the feelings of the moment, but it presents itself in a much larger way, even as it typifies that coming day when Christ will stand before Israel. At long last, the sons of Jacob will have come home. In fact, in all of history, there has never been anything so drastic as the fall of Jacob, and I speak of the nation of Israel and their rejection of Christ. It eclipses every other happening [Rom. 11:15].)*

31 And he washed his face, and went out, and refrained himself, and said, Set on bread *(serve the meal)*.

THE BANQUET

32 And they set on for him by himself, and for them by themselves, and for the Egyptians, which did eat with him, by themselves: because the Egyptians might not eat bread with the Hebrews; for that is an abomination unto the Egyptians. *(The meal presented here is indicative of that which will take place at the Second Coming, when both Jews and Gentiles will fellowship with Christ, of Whom Joseph was a Type.)*

33 And they sat before him, the firstborn according to his birthright, and the youngest according to his youth: and the men marvelled one at another *(they were seated according to their ages, beginning with Reuben, who was the firstborn, unto Benjamin, who was the youngest. How did the lord of Egypt know these things, Joseph's brothers must have pondered?)*.

34 And he took and sent messes *(the food)* unto them from before him: but Benjamin's mess was five times so much as any of theirs. And they drank, and were merry with him. *(The number "five" is the number of the Grace of God. The name "Benjamin" means "My strong right hand," typifying Christ. In a coming day, when Israel comes back to Christ, even though Christ has "a strong right hand," He will deal with Israel in "Grace," signified by the food given to Benjamin, which was five times more than his brothers.)*

CHAPTER 44
(1707 B.C.)
THE FINAL TEST

AND he commanded the steward of his house, saying, Fill the men's sacks with food, as much as they can carry, and put every man's money in his sack's mouth.

2 And put my cup, the silver cup, in the sack's mouth of the youngest, and his corn *(grain)* money. And he did according to the word that Joseph had spoken.

3 As soon as the morning was light, the men were sent away, they and their asses.

4 And when they were gone out of the city, and not yet far off, Joseph said unto his steward, Up, follow after the men; and when you do overtake them, say unto them, Wherefore have you rewarded evil for good? *(The casual reader may think that Joseph is being somewhat harsh respecting this particular episode; however, due to enormity of the sin of these brothers, with the exception of Benjamin, Joseph must make certain that there has indeed been true Repentance in their hearts.)*

5 Is not this it in which my lord drinks, and whereby indeed he divines? you have done evil in so doing.

6 And he overtook them, and he spoke unto them these same words *(no doubt, Joseph had told the man exactly what to say to his brothers)*.

7 And they said unto him, Wherefore says my lord these words? God forbid that your servants should do according to this thing:

8 Behold, the money, which we found in our sacks' mouths, we brought again unto you out of the land of Canaan: how then should we steal out of your lord's house silver or gold?

9 With whomsoever of your servants it be found, both let him die, and we also will be my lord's bondmen. *(They are right, and they are wrong! They are right in that they didn't steal the cup, but they are wrong in that it's not in one of the sacks.)*

10 And he said, Now also let it be according unto your words: he with whom it is found shall be my servant *(slave)*: and you shall be blameless. *(The same steward who has greeted them previously now stands before them, as it regards the cup that is supposedly missing. He is the one who had placed the cup in Benjamin's sack, so he knew exactly where is was.)*

11 Then they speedily took down every man his sack to the ground, and opened every man his sack.

12 And he searched, and began at the eldest, and left at the youngest: and the cup was found in Benjamin's sack.

13 Then they rent their clothes, and loaded every man his ass, and returned to the city.

JUDAH

14 And Judah and his brethren came to Joseph's house; for he was yet there: and they fell before him on the ground. *(Joseph's detention of Simeon, and afterwards of Benjamin, was skillfully designed so as to find out if they still were indifferent to the cries of a captive brother and the tears of a bereaved father.)*

15 And Joseph said unto them, What deed is this that you have done? do you not know that a man as I can certainly divine?

16 And Judah said, What shall we say unto my lord? what shall we speak? or how shall we clear ourselves? God has found out the iniquity of your servants: behold, we are my lord's servants, both we, and he also with whom the cup is found. *(The distress of Judah and the others shows that they were no longer, in heart, the men of some twenty years back. None can teach like God. He Alone can produce in the conscience the true sense of sin, and bring the soul down into the profound depths of its own condition in His Presence. The "iniquity" of which Judah spoke was that of the selling of their brother so many long years before. They can only think of this one great commanding sin, the rejection of their brother Joseph.)*

17 And he *(Joseph)* said, God forbid that I should do so *(he is saying that he has no desire to keep all the brothers, only the one in whose sack the cup was found, namely Benjamin)*: but the man in whose hand the cup is found, he shall be my servant *(slave)*; and as for you, get you up in peace unto your father.

18 Then Judah came near unto him, and said, Oh my lord, let your servant, I pray you, speak a word in my lord's ears, and let not your anger burn against your servant: for you are even as Pharaoh. *(This Chapter contains one of the most impassioned pleas ever made by one man to another. Judah makes this plea unto Joseph.)*

19 My lord asked his servants, saying, Have you a father, or a brother?

20 And we said unto my lord, we have a father, an old man, and a child of his old age, a little one; and his brother is dead, and he alone is left of his mother, and his father loves him.

21 And you said unto your servants, Bring him down unto me, that I may set my eyes upon him.

22 And we said unto my lord, The lad cannot leave his father: for if he should leave his father, his father would die.

23 And you said unto your servants, Except your youngest brother come down with you, you shall see my face no more.

24 And it came to pass when we came up unto your servant my father, we told him the words of my lord.

25 And our father said, Go again, and buy us a little food.

26 And we said, We cannot go down: if our youngest brother be with us, then will we go down: for we may not see the man's face, except our youngest brother be with us.

27 And your servant my father said unto us, You know that my wife bore me two sons:

28 And the one went out from me, and I said, Surely he is torn in pieces; and I saw him not since:

29 And if you take this also from me, and mischief befall him, you shall bring down my gray hairs with sorrow to the grave.

30 Now therefore when I come to your servant my father, and the lad be not with us; seeing that his life is bound up in the lad's life;

31 It shall come to pass, when he sees that the lad is not with us, that he will die: and your servants shall bring down the gray hairs of your servant our father with sorrow to the grave.

32 For your servant became surety for the lad unto my father, saying, If I bring him not unto you, then I shall bear the blame to my father for ever.

33 Now therefore, I pray you, let your servant abide instead of the lad a bondman *(a slave)* to my lord; and let the lad go up with his brethren.

34 For how shall I go up to my father, and the lad be not with me? lest peradventure I see the evil that shall come on my father.

CHAPTER 45

(1707 B.C.)

JOSEPH

THEN Joseph could not refrain himself before all them who stood by him; and he cried, Cause every man to go out from me. And there stood no man with him, while Joseph made himself known unto his brothers *(Zechariah the Prophet said, and speaking of a coming day: "And they shall look upon Me Whom they have pierced," of which this scene of Joseph and his brothers is a type [Zech. 12:10]).*

2 And he wept aloud: and the Egyptians and the house of Pharaoh heard *(the Egyptians, who had just left the room, could not help but*

overhear his loud sobbing; they reported these happenings to Pharaoh).

3 And Joseph said unto his brothers, I am Joseph *(the effect of this announcement can be better imagined than described; hitherto he had been known to his brothers as Zaphnath-paaneah; he evidently now speaks to them in Hebrew);* does my father yet live? And his brothers could not answer him; for they were troubled at his presence. *(What will Israel's reaction be when Christ says to them at the Second Coming, "I am Jesus"?)*

4 And Joseph said unto his brothers, Come near to me, I pray you. And they came near. And he said, I am Joseph your brother, whom you sold into Egypt. *(The Text indicates that they don't know what to do. Quite possibly, he wondered if they understood when he first said, "I am Joseph." So now he identifies himself in such a way that there can be no misunderstanding. He is the brother whom they sold as a slave.)*

5 Now therefore be not grieved, nor angry with yourselves, that you sold me hither: for God did send me before you to preserve life. *(Joseph's heart beat true to God and to his brothers. He kept pressing upon them that it was God Who had taken him out of the pit and placed him upon the Throne. The way he says all of this leads them to feel that it was against God that they had sinned, rather than against himself, which actually was true, and made the sin even worse.)*

6 For these two years has the famine been in the land: and yet there are five years, in the which there shall neither be earing nor harvest.

7 And God sent me before you to preserve you a posterity in the Earth, and to save your lives by a great deliverance. *(Joseph attempts to lessen their grief and sorrow by showing them that whatever it was they intended, God overruled it, and turned it around for good. Only God can take that which is wrong and make it right.)*

8 So now it was not you who sent me hither, but God: and he has made me a father to Pharaoh, and lord of all his house, and a ruler throughout all the land of Egypt. *(In fact, only God could have done this. Men rule, but God overrules!)*

JACOB

9 Make haste, and go up to my father, and say unto him, Thus saith your son Joseph, God

has made me lord of all Egypt: come down unto me, tarry not *(now Joseph gives instructions as to his father Jacob; but with that, the brothers now have another problem; they're going to have to confess to Jacob as to what happened with Joseph those long years before):*

10 And you shall dwell in the land of Goshen *(the richest part of Egypt),* and you shall be near unto me, you, and your children, and your children's children, and your flocks, and your herds, and all that you have:

11 And there will I nourish you; for yet there are five years of famine; lest you, and your household, and all that you have, come to poverty *(this is typical of Israel in the coming Great Tribulation, when God will sustain them [Rev. 12:6]).*

12 And, behold, your eyes see, and the eyes of my brother Benjamin, that it is my mouth that speaks unto you *(Joseph is telling his brothers to inspect him closely, and they will see, even beyond the shadow of a doubt, that it is truly Joseph who is speaking to them).*

13 And you shall tell my father of all my glory in Egypt and of all that you have seen; and you shall haste and bring down my father hither *(this is a type of Israel, when, at a coming glad day, "they [Israel] shall declare My Glory [of Christ] among the Gentiles" [Isa. 66:19]).*

14 And he fell upon his brother Benjamin's neck, and wept; and Benjamin wept upon his neck.

15 Moreover he kissed all his brothers, and wept upon them: and after that his brothers talked with him. *(This scene is typical of the coming day when Israel will recognize Christ, which will be at the Second Coming [Zech. 12:10]. Joseph kissing all of his brothers portrays the seal of recognition, of reconciliation, and of Salvation.)*

PHARAOH'S INVITATION

16 And the fame thereof was heard in Pharaoh's house, saying, Joseph's brothers are come: and it pleased Pharaoh well, and his servants.

17 And Pharaoh said unto Joseph, Say unto your brothers, This do you; load your beasts, and go, get you unto the land of Canaan;

18 And take your father and your households, and come unto me: and I will give you the good of the land of Egypt, and you shall eat the fat of the land. *(Joseph's Grace in covering up their sin directly they confessed it, in hiding*

it from Pharaoh, and in hasting to acknowledge them before Pharaoh as his brothers, illustrate the richer Grace of Him Who says, "Your sins and iniquities will I remember no more" [Heb. 10:17].)

19 Now you are commanded, this do you; take you wagons out of the land of Egypt for your little ones, and for your wives, and bring your father, and come.

20 Also regard not your stuff; for the good of all the land of Egypt is yours. *(And so will it be that of Israel in a coming glad day, when they finally accept the Lord Jesus Christ as their Saviour and Messiah.)*

JOSEPH

21 And the Children of Israel did so *(the Holy Spirit referring here to Jacob as "Israel" signifies the fact that it is the Will of God for Jacob to come into Egypt)*: and Joseph gave them wagons, according to the commandment of Pharaoh, and gave them provision for the way.

22 To all of them he gave each man changes of raiment *(spiritually speaking, Israel, in a coming glad day, will have a "change of raiment," i.e., "the robe of Righteousness")*; but to Benjamin he gave three hundred pieces of silver, and five changes of raiment. *("Silver" speaks of Redemption and what will transpire with Israel. "Five" speaks of Grace, and speaks of the fact that the Grace of God will award Israel a robe of Righteousness, which, in effect, is the Righteousness of Christ, and which can only be given by Grace [Eph. 2:8-9].)*

23 And to his father he sent after this manner; ten asses loaded with the good things of Egypt, and ten she asses loaded with corn *(grain)* and bread and meat for his father by the way *(the famine will touch them no longer [Jer. 30:7]).*

24 So he sent his brothers away, and they departed: and he said unto them, See that you fall not out by the way *(don't be delayed).*

25 And they went up out of Egypt, and came into the land of Canaan unto Jacob their father *(the implication is, they will not only give him this most wonderful news, the most wonderful that Jacob will have ever heard, but, as well, they will have to tell him the truth concerning what they did to Joseph so many years before)*,

26 And told him *(meaning that they told him everything)*, saying, Joseph is yet alive *(for some 20 years, Jacob has suffered; the suffering is now over; Joseph is yet alive; Christ is alive! What more can we say!)*, and he is governor over all the land of Egypt. And Jacob's heart fainted, for he believed them not. *(The scene with Joseph revealing himself to his brothers was, in fact, one of the most, if not the most, poignant in history; then the scene with the brothers before their father Jacob had to be a close second.)*

27 And they told him all the words of Joseph, which he had said unto them: and when he saw the wagons which Joseph had sent to carry him, the spirit of Jacob their father revived *(the Patriarch knew that his sons personally had no way to obtain such wagons; he now knows that they are telling him the truth)*:

28 And Israel said, It is enough; Joseph my son is yet alive: I will go and see him before I die *(it is noteworthy that Jacob is again referred to in this Verse as "Israel"; it refers to his Faith, as feeble as it was, being rewarded, and rewarded grandly, "Joseph is yet alive"!).*

CHAPTER 46
(1706 B.C.)
EGYPT

AND Israel took his journey with all that he had *(by the Holy Spirit using here the name "Israel," this tells us that Jacob moves forward with a renewed confidence and Faith in God, Who had originally changed his name; in other words, he is now in the direct center of the Perfect Will of God, which alone God can bless)*, and came to Beer-sheba, and offered Sacrifices *(these Sacrifices epitomized God, Who would become flesh and dwell with men, and thereby go to the Cross, offering Himself up as a Sacrifice, which alone could atone for the sin of man)* unto the God of his father Isaac *(this stipulates that what God had given to Abraham had been passed down to Isaac, and now is passed down to Jacob; in other words, the Vision is the same).*

2 And God spoke unto Israel in the visions of the night *(once again, by the use of the name "Israel," such signifies Faith on the part of Jacob)*, and said, Jacob, Jacob *(why the use of both names by the Lord of "Israel" and "Jacob"? When we look at this Verse, we are looking at Sanctification in both its positional and conditional form. The "spiritual position" of Jacob was that of perfect Sanctification, as it is with all Believers; however, our "spiritual condition" is not necessarily up to our spiritual position. In fact, it is the Work of the Holy Spirit, Who strives throughout our lives to bring our "condition" up to our "position." He can only do such as our Faith is anchored firmly in Christ and*

the Cross, which then gives Him latitude to work). And he said, Here am I (Jacob's Faith was now such that he could hear the Word of the Lord).

3 And He said, I am God (in the Hebrew, "I am the El, the Mighty One"), the God of your father (the same Message that God gave to Isaac, He also gives to Jacob; in brief, it refers to God becoming flesh, dwelling with man, and dying on a Cross, in order that man might be redeemed; Angels could not redeem man because they were of another creation; so God would have to redeem man, and would have to do so by becoming man, with Redemption being carried out by the God-Man, the Lord Jesus Christ, going to the Cross, where there, and there alone, Redemption could be effected [Gen. 3:15; Rom. 5:1; 6:3-14; I Cor. 1:17-18, 21, 23; 2:2; Eph. 2:13-18; Col. 2:14-15]): fear not to go down into Egypt (Jacob did fear to go down into Egypt, simply because his father Isaac had been forbidden by God to go there); for I will there make of you a great nation (the Lord's plans are far bigger than we can even dare to think; He will now use Egypt to further His purposes):

4 I will go down with you into Egypt (this is not the idea of a local deity following them when they changed their abodes, and thereby confined to the district in which they happen, for the time being, to reside, but a metaphorical expression for the efficiency and completeness of the Divine protection — Kalisch); and I will also surely bring you up again (this has a twofold meaning, in that Jacob would be brought back to Canaan for burial and, as well, that the nation which would come from his loins would, as well, be brought back): and Joseph shall put his hand upon your eyes (he had never thought to see Joseph; however, the Lord here assures him that he will not only see his son, but that Joseph will be with him when he dies).

5 And Jacob rose up from Beer-sheba (Jacob was 130 years old at the time, and this event was 215 years after the call of Abraham; Jacob now truly "rises up" in Faith, and because he has heard from Heaven): and the sons of Israel carried Jacob their father, and their little ones, and their wives, in the wagons which Pharaoh had sent to carry him (the name "Israel" is again used by the Holy Spirit, signifying Jacob's Faith; the principle of Faith was the only commodity, so to speak, which would propel Jacob nearer to the Lord).

6 And they took their cattle, and their goods, which they had gotten in the land of Canaan, and came into Egypt, Jacob, and all

his seed with him (a spiritual threshold is now being crossed; even though it will be some 255 years before Israel will actually possess the Promise, as it regards the land of Canaan, great strides are now being made):

7 His sons, and his sons' sons with him, his daughters, and his sons' daughters, and all his seed brought he with him into Egypt.

JACOB'S FAMILY

8 And these are the names of the Children of Israel (the Holy Spirit once again uses the Faith name of Jacob, "Israel"), which came into Egypt, Jacob and his sons: Reuben, Jacob's firstborn.

9 And the sons of Reuben; Hanoch, and Phallu, and Hezron, and Carmi.

10 And the sons of Simeon; Jemuel, and Jamin, and Ohad, and Jachin, and Zohar, Shaul the son of a Canaanitish woman.

11 And the sons of Levi; Gershon, Kohath, and Merari.

12 And the sons of Judah (the Tribe from which our Lord would come [49:10]); Er, and Onan, and Shelah, and Pharez, and Zarah: But Er and Onan died in the land of Canaan. And the sons of Pharez were Hezron and Hamul.

13 And the sons of Issachar; Tola, and Phuvah, and Job (this is the same Job of the Book which bears his name), and Shimron.

14 And the sons of Zebulun; Sered, and Elon, and Jahleel.

15 These be the sons of Leah, which she bore unto Jacob in Padan-aram, with his daughter Dinah: all the souls of his sons and his daughters were thirty-three.

16 And the sons of Gad; Ziphion, and Haggi, Shuni, and Ezbon, Eri, and Arodi, and Areli.

17 And the sons of Asher; Jimnah, and Ishuah, and Isui, and Beriah, and Serah their sister: and the sons of Beriah; Heber, and Malchiel.

18 These are the sons of Zilpah, whom Laban gave to Leah his daughter, and these she bore unto Jacob, even sixteen souls.

19 The sons of Rachel, Jacob's wife; Joseph, and Benjamin.

20 And unto Joseph in the land of Egypt were born Manasseh and Ephraim, which Asenath the daughter of Poti-pherah priest of On bore unto him.

21 And the sons of Benjamin were Belah, and Becher, and Ashbel, Gera, and Naaman, Ehi, and Rosh, Muppim, and Huppim, and Ard.

22 These are the sons of Rachel, which were born to Jacob: all the souls were fourteen.

23 And the sons of Dan; Hushim.

24 And the sons of Naphtali; Jahzeel, and Guni, and Jezer, and Shillem.

25 These are the sons of Bilhah, which Laban gave unto Rachel his daughter, and she bore these unto Jacob: all the souls were seven.

26 All the souls who came with Jacob into Egypt, which came out of his loins, besides Jacob's sons' wives, all the souls were sixty-six;

27 And the sons of Joseph, which were born him in Egypt *(but nevertheless were Israelites)*, were two souls: all the souls of the house of Jacob, which came into Egypt, were seventy.

28 And he sent Judah before him unto Joseph, to direct his face unto Goshen; and they came into the land of Goshen *(we see here that the Tribe of Judah is taking the lead, the Tribe, as stated, from which our Lord would come)*.

JOSEPH AND JACOB

29 And Joseph made ready his chariot, and went up to meet Israel his father, to Goshen, and presented himself unto him *(the translation here tells us little; however, in the Hebrew such terminology is commonly used of the appearance of God or His Angels; it is employed here in this manner to indicate the glory in which Joseph came to meet Jacob; this meeting is symbolic of the great meeting which will take place in the near future of the Second Coming, when our Heavenly Joseph will present Himself to Israel [Zech. 13:6])*; and he fell on his neck, and wept on his neck a good while *(however, they were tears of joy, just as it will be at the Second Coming, when Jesus and Jacob will meet in Grace)*.

30 And Israel *(Faith)* said unto Joseph, Now let me die, since I have seen your face, because you are yet alive *(national Israel doesn't yet know it or believe it, but Jesus is yet alive)*.

31 And Joseph said unto his brethren, and unto his father's house, I will go up, and show Pharaoh, and say unto him, My brethren, and my father's house, which were in the land of Canaan, are come unto me *(one of the greatest moments in human history will be when Israel finally comes to Christ)*;

32 And the men are shepherds, for their trade has been to feed cattle; and they have brought their flocks, and their herds, and all that they have.

33 And it shall come to pass, when Pharaoh shall call you, and shall say, What is your occupation?

34 That you shall say, Your servants' trade has been about cattle from our youth even until now *(the word "cattle" stood for heifers, oxen, sheep, goats, etc.)*, both we, and also our fathers: that you may dwell in the land of Goshen *(the most fertile part of Egypt, at least as it referred to the grazing of cattle and sheep)*; for every shepherd is an abomination unto the Egyptians *(the word "abomination," as used here, refers to the fact that there was some type of religious connotation to the attitude of Egyptians towards shepherds; at any rate, Joseph does not attempt to conceal from Pharaoh the low caste of shepherds, his brothers, but he trusts in God that what was an abomination to the Egyptians will be made, by the Grace of God, acceptable; and so it was)*.

CHAPTER 47
(1706 B.C.)

JACOB MEETS PHARAOH

THEN Joseph came and told Pharaoh, and said, My father and my brethren, and their flocks, and their herds, and all that they have, are come out of the land of Canaan; and, behold, they are in the land of Goshen.

2 And he took some of his brethren, even five men, and presented them unto Pharaoh *(as far as we know, no one in Egypt ever knew anything about the wickedness of the past deeds of Joseph's brothers; such is true forgiveness; it not only forgives sin, but it forgets, as well)*.

3 And Pharaoh said unto his brethren, What is your occupation? And they said unto Pharaoh, Your servants are shepherds, both we, and also our fathers *(that the brothers were shepherds, which Joseph had been, as well, served as a Type of the Good Shepherd, Who would give His Life for the sheep [Jn. 10:11])*.

4 They said moreover unto Pharaoh, For to sojourn in the land are we come; for your servants have no pasture for their flocks; for the famine is sore in the land of Canaan: now therefore, we pray you, let your servants dwell in the land of Goshen.

5 And Pharaoh spoke unto Joseph, saying, Your father and your brethren are come unto you:

6 The land of Egypt is before you; in the best of the land make your father and brethren to dwell; in the land of Goshen let them dwell: and if you know any men of activity

among them, then make them rulers over my cattle. *(Joseph, raised from the pit to the throne, another Type of Christ, enriches his brothers with all the Promises which they, by their rejection of him, had forfeited, but which are now, upon the ground of Grace, restored to them. At the same time, they are given the richest province in Egypt. The Egyptians, themselves representative of all the nations of the Earth, are saved from death by Joseph. All of this is a striking picture of what is yet to come to pass. This is the subject of Romans, Chapters 9, 10, and 11, in which Chapters it is pointed out that Israel and the Gentiles will inherit the Promises, in fellowship, solely upon the ground of pure Grace.)*

7 And Joseph brought in Jacob his father, and set him before Pharaoh: and Jacob blessed Pharaoh. *(And without contradiction, the less is blessed of the greater. The least and most faltering of God's children is superior to the mightiest Monarch, and is conscious of such superiority. — Williams)*

8 And Pharaoh said unto Jacob, How old are you?

9 And Jacob said unto Pharaoh, The days of the years of my pilgrimage are an hundred and thirty years: few and evil have the days of the years of my life been, and have not attained unto the days of the years of the life of my fathers in the days of their pilgrimage *(more than likely, there was no one in Egypt who was as old as Jacob; as well, he will not die until he is 147 years of age, some 17 years after coming into Egypt).*

10 And Jacob blessed Pharaoh, and went out from before Pharaoh *(for the second time, the Holy Spirit proclaims the Patriarch blessing Pharaoh, again signifying that while Pharaoh may be the greatest in the eyes of men, Jacob is the greatest in the Eyes of God, Whose Eyes Alone matter).*

JOSEPH

11 And Joseph placed his father and his brothers, and gave them a possession in the land of Egypt, in the best of the land, in the land of Rameses, as Pharaoh had commanded.

12 And Joseph nourished his father, and his brothers, and all his father's household, with bread, according to their families.

13 And there was no bread in all the land; for the famine was very sore, so that the land of Egypt and all the land of Canaan fainted by reason of the famine. *(We now learn just how severe this famine actually was. Had it not been for Joseph, Egypt would have seen the starvation of tens of thousands of its people. So, Joseph was the great benefactor of this land and its people, exactly as Jesus will be the Great Benefactor of the Gentiles at the Second Coming, when the world, at that time, will be in a critical state.)*

THE PLAN

14 And Joseph gathered up all the money that was found in the land of Egypt, and in the land of Canaan, for the corn *(grain)* which they bought: and Joseph brought the money into Pharaoh's house.

15 And when money failed in the land of Egypt, and in the land of Canaan *(meaning that the people had no more money to buy grain)*, all the Egyptians came unto Joseph, and said, Give us bread: for why should we die in your presence? for the money fails *(we have no more money)*.

16 And Joseph said, Give your cattle; and I will give you for your cattle *(give you grain)*, if money fail.

17 And they brought their cattle unto Joseph *(whether sheep, goats, cattle, horses, etc.)*: and Joseph gave them bread in exchange for horses, and for the flocks, and for the cattle of the herds, and for the asses, and he fed them with bread for all their cattle for that year.

18 When that year was ended, they came unto him the second year, and said unto him, We will not hide it from my lord, how that our money is spent; my lord also has our herds of cattle; there is not ought left in the sight of my lord, but our bodies, and our lands:

19 Wherefore shall we die before your eyes, both we and our land? buy us and our land for bread, and we and our land will be servants unto Pharaoh: and give us seed, that we may live, and not die, that the land be not desolate.

20 And Joseph bought all the land of Egypt for Pharaoh; for the Egyptians sold every man his field, because the famine prevailed over them: so the land became Pharaoh's.

21 And as for the people, he removed them to cities from one end of the borders of Egypt even to the other end thereof.

THE PRIESTS

22 Only the land of the priests bought he not; for the priests had a portion assigned them

of Pharaoh, and did eat their portion which Pharaoh gave them: wherefore they sold not their lands. *(Some have claimed that Joseph robbed the Egyptians of their liberties, and converted a free people into a horde of abject slaves. Nothing could be further from the truth. In fact, had it not been for Joseph, and the Divine Wisdom which he was given during this extremely trying time, as stated, hundreds of thousands of people would literally have starved to death. As it was, the people were looked after, and there is no record that anyone starved.)*

TENANT LAWS

23 Then Joseph said unto the people, Behold, I have bought you this day and your land for Pharaoh: lo, here is seed for you, and you shall sow the land.

24 And it shall come to pass in the increase, that you shall give the fifth part unto Pharaoh, and four parts shall be your own, for seed of the field, and for your food, and for them of your households, and for food for your little ones. *(When Joseph levied the 20% tax, this was one of the fairest arrangements that any people had ever known. No doubt, this wisdom was given to him by the Lord. For instance, at this particular time [2003], counting state, local, and federal income taxes, the rate is approximately 50%.)*

25 And they said, You have saved our lives: let us find grace in the sight of my lord, and we will be Pharaoh's servants.

26 And Joseph made it a law over the land of Egypt unto this day, that Pharaoh should have the fifth part; except the land of the priests only, which became not Pharaoh's.

JACOB

27 And Israel dwelt in the land of Egypt, in the country of Goshen; and they had possessions therein, and grew, and multiplied exceedingly *(they came in 70 strong, and would leave out, about 215 years later, upwards of over 2 million people).*

28 And Jacob lived in the land of Egypt seventeen years: so the whole age of Jacob was an hundred forty and seven years.

29 And the time drew near that Israel must die *(by the use of the name "Israel," the Holy Spirit tells us that Jacob would die in Faith, and great Faith at that)*: and he called his son Joseph, and said unto him, If now I have found grace in your sight, put, I pray you, your hand under my thigh, and deal kindly and truly with me; bury me not, I pray you, in Egypt *(feeble as was his body, and imperfect as was his faith, as all faith regrettably is imperfect, yet did Jacob esteem God's land, the land of Canaan, and the Promises connected therewith, as unspeakably superior to Egypt, with all its prosperity and glory)*:

30 But I will lie with my fathers, and you shall carry me out of Egypt, and bury me in their buryingplace. And he said, I will do as you have said.

31 And he said, Swear unto me. And he swore unto him. And Israel bowed himself upon the bed's head. *(He makes Joseph swear that when he dies, he will put his bones where his heart was, in the land of Canaan. As a Believer, where is your heart?)*

CHAPTER 48
(1689 B.C.)
THE SONS OF JOSEPH

AND it came to pass after these things *(Hebrews 11:21 throws much light on the beautiful Forty-eighth Chapter of Genesis; in fact, in Chapters 48 and 49, Jacob shines as never before; if it is to be noticed, the Holy Spirit refers to him again and again as "Israel"; this is the great Faith action of his life; feeble and dying, and having nothing except the staff on which he leaned and worshipped, he yet bestowed vast and unseen possessions on his grandsons — Williams)*, that one told Joseph, Behold, your father is sick: and he took with him his two sons, Manasseh and Ephraim *(these boys must have been about 18 or 20 years old at the time).*

2 And one told Jacob, and said, Behold, your son Joseph comes unto you: and Israel strengthened himself, and sat upon the bed. *(Joseph wants his two grandsons to know and realize that even though they have been born in Egypt, and all they have ever known is Egypt, still, they aren't Egyptians, but rather of the house of Jacob, i.e., Israelites. Such is a portrayal of Believers born in this present world, but nevertheless not of this world, but rather of the world to come. And finally, the significance of the change of name from "Jacob" to "Israel" is not to be overlooked. By faith [it is always Faith], the great Patriarch, moved upon by the Lord, will claim the Promises, and chart the course of Israel. Though the eyes of the Patriarch are, in the natural, very dim, even as we*

shall see, his Faith burns brightly, actually brighter than ever; hence he is called "Israel.")

3 And Jacob said unto Joseph, God Almighty *(Jacob refers to God as "El Shaddai," using the same name which God had used of Himself, when He appeared to the Patriarch at Bethel, which was after the sad experience of Shechem [35:7-15])* **appeared unto me at Luz in the land of Canaan, and blessed me,**

4 And said unto me, Behold, I will make you fruitful, and multiply you, and I will make of you a multitude of people; and will give this land to your seed after you for an everlasting possession. *(The Palestinians should read these words very carefully.)*

5 And now your two sons, Ephraim and Manasseh, which were born unto you in the land of Egypt before I came unto you into Egypt are mine; as Reuben and Simeon, they shall be mine. *(By this, Jacob indicated he was bypassing the older sons and was making sure that Joseph would get the double portion of the birthright. This would apply to Ephraim and Manasseh, hence Jacob, by the Holy Spirit, claiming them as his own.)*

6 And your issue, which you beget after them, shall be yours, and shall be called after the name of their brethren in their inheritance. *(Even though he may have, there is no Scriptural record that Joseph had children other than Ephraim and Manasseh. But if he did, they could not be reckoned, as it regards the "blessing," as it pertained to Ephraim and Manasseh. In other words, their blessing would have to be in the blessing of the two. All of this was of extreme significance, and because it pertained to the raising up of the nation of Israel, through which the Messiah would come, and the Word of God would be given. In fact, nothing in the world was more important than this, hence the Holy Spirit instructing Jacob accordingly.)*

7 And as for me, when I came from Padan, Rachel died by me in the land of Canaan in the way, when yet there was but a little way to come unto Ephrath: and I buried her there in the way of Ephrath; the same is Beth-lehem *(where Rachel died is where Jesus would be born; "except a grain of wheat fall into the ground and die, it abides alone: but if it die, it brings forth much fruit" [Jn. 12:24]).*

THE BLESSING

8 And Israel beheld Joseph's sons, and said, Who are these? *(That Jacob did not at first*

discern the presence of the sons of Joseph shows that his adoption of them into the number of the theocratic family was prompted, not by the accidental impulse of a natural affection excited through beholding these young men, but by the inward prompting of the Spirit of God.)

9 And Joseph said unto his father, They are my sons, whom God has given me in this place. And he said, Bring them, I pray you, unto me, and I will bless them. *(The "blessing" consisted of Joseph's double portion, with a portion being given to each of these sons, which, as stated, contained a significance all out of proportion to natural thinking.)*

10 Now the eyes of Israel were dim for age, so that he could not see. And he brought them near unto him; and he kissed them, and embraced them. *(Even though the Patriarch was blind, or nearly so, the Holy Spirit refers to him as "Israel," because he could "see" by Faith.)*

11 And Israel said unto Joseph, I had not thought to see your face: and, lo, God has shown me also your seed. *(Satan had told the Patriarch that he would never see Joseph again. But now the Holy Spirit says, "You have not only seen Joseph, but his sons, as well." True Faith in God is never disappointed.)*

12 And Joseph brought them out from between his knees, and he bowed himself with his face to the earth *(proclaims the fact that Joseph understood the tremendous import of what was here being said and done).*

13 And Joseph took them both, Ephraim in his right hand toward Israel's left hand *(because Ephraim was the younger)*, **and Manasseh in his left hand toward Israel's right hand** *(because he was the older)*, **and brought them near unto him.**

14 And Israel stretched out his right hand, and laid it upon Ephraim's head, who was the younger *(signifying by his right hand that the greater part of the blessing would go to Ephraim, even though he was the younger)*, **and his left hand upon Manasseh's head, guiding his hands wittingly** *(guided by the Holy Spirit)*; **for Manasseh was the firstborn** *(but for the Spirit of God would have received the greater portion).*

15 And he blessed Joseph *(the double portion would go to Joseph's sons; just before Jacob blesses these young men, the aged Patriarch takes his staff and, leaning upon it so as not to fall, bows in grateful worship before God; Paul mentioned this [Heb. 11:21])*, **and said, God, before whom my fathers Abraham and Isaac did walk, the God which fed me all my life long unto**

this day *(he specifies that the blessing about to be pronounced was from God and God Alone)*,

16 The Angel which redeemed me from all evil *(the Lord is referred to here as an Angel, but is not to be confused with that particular creation)*, bless the lads; and let my name be named on them, and the name of my fathers Abraham and Isaac; and let them grow into a multitude in the midst of the Earth. *(The "name" spoke of Promise, while the "multitude" spoke of Blessing. The Promise had to do with the coming Redeemer, Who definitely did come. The blessing concerns the multitude, and has only partially been fulfilled, but definitely will be fulfilled in the coming Millennium, when Israel will be the leading nation on Earth.)*

17 And when Joseph saw that his father laid his right hand upon the head of Ephraim, it displeased him *(because Ephraim was the younger, and thereby normally should not receive the greater portion)*: and he held up his father's hand, to remove it from Ephraim's head unto Manasseh's head.

18 And Joseph said unto his father, Not so, my father: for this is the firstborn *(Manasseh is the first born)*; put your right hand upon his head.

19 And his father refused, and said, I know it, my son, I know it: he also shall become a people, and he also shall be great: but truly his younger brother shall be greater than he, and his seed shall become a multitude of nations. *(The northern kingdom of Israel, about 800 years into the future, would also be called "Ephraim"; however, the greater fulfillment concerning "a multitude of nations" awaits the coming Kingdom Age.)*

20 And he blessed them that day, saying, In you shall Israel bless, saying, God make you as Ephraim and as Manasseh: and he set Ephraim before Manasseh.

21 And Israel said unto Joseph, Behold, I die: but God shall be with you, and bring you again unto the land of your fathers *(which would happen about 240 years into the future)*.

22 Moreover I have given to you one portion above your brethren, which I took out of the hand of the Amorite with my sword and with my bow. *(We aren't told exactly what Jacob meant by his statement. This could very well have been a conflict with the Amorites, of which we are given no information; however, it could speak of the coming day when Israel will vanquish all who contest their right to the Promised Land, which will take place at the Second Coming.)*

CHAPTER 49
(1689 B.C.)
THE PROPHECY

AND Jacob called unto his sons, and said, Gather yourselves together, that I may tell you that which shall befall you in the last days. *(This Chapter forms one of the great dispensational prophecies of the Word of God. It concerns the "latter days," and the "last days." This is the first occurrence of this expression: "the last days."*

The Prophecy may be thus divided: Reuben, Simeon, and Levi, the moral history of Israel up to the First Advent; Judah, the apparition of the Messiah and His rejection; Zebulun and Issachar, the dispersion and subjugation of the Jews among the Gentiles; Dan, the appearing and kingdom of the Antichrist. Gad, Asher, and Naphtali present the cry of anguish of the elect sons of Israel for the Second Coming of Christ. Joseph and Benjamin together predict the Second Coming, in glory, of Israel's Messiah — Williams.)

2 Gather yourselves together and hear, you sons of Jacob; and hearken unto Israel your father. *(In Verses 1 and 2, the Holy Spirit impresses the use of both names, "Jacob" and "Israel." As the twelve sons gather in his presence, he is referred to as "Jacob"; however, when it refers to the prophecies that will be given, he is referred to by his princely name, "Israel.")*

3 Reuben, you are my firstborn, my might, and the beginning of my strength, the excellency of dignity, and the excellency of power *(this is what Reuben should have been)*:

4 Unstable as water, you shall not excel *(no Prophet, Ruler, or great man sprang out of Reuben)*; because you went up to your father's bed; then you defiled it: he went up to my couch *(35:22)*.

5 Simeon and Levi are brothers *(guilty of the same sin)*; instruments of cruelty are in their habitations *(34:25-29)*.

6 O my soul, do not come into their secret *(secret plottings to murder the Shechemites)*; unto their assembly *(preparation for the slaughter)*, my honor, with them do not be united *(Jacob had no part in the slaughter of the Shechemites)*: for in their anger they killed a man, and in their selfwill they dug down a wall *(in their taking matters into their own hands, instead of following the Lord, they greatly hindered the protective wall of the Lord around Jacob)*.

7 Cursed be their anger, for it was fierce; and their wrath, for it was cruel: I will divide

them in Jacob, and scatter them in Israel. *(The Tribe of Simeon, when coming into the Land of Israel several centuries into the future, would have no inheritance, but, in fact, would have their part in the inheritance of Judah. As well, Levi would have no inheritance at all, but would have their curse turned into a blessing as they became the Priestly Tribe of Israel, but yet scattered over the nation, fulfilling the prophecy.)*

8 Judah, you are he whom your brethren shall praise *(the name Judah means "praise," and it is from this Tribe that the Messiah would come)*: Your hand shall be in the neck of Your enemies *(speaks of the great victory that Christ would win over Satan and all the powers of darkness at the Cross [Col. 2:14-15])*; your father's children shall bow down before You *(Israel will do this at the Second Coming)*.

9 Judah is a lion's whelp *(refers to a young lion, in the power of its youth, absolutely invincible; this represented Christ in the flower of His manhood, full of the Holy Spirit, healing the sick, casting out demons, raising the dead, and doing great and mighty things, with every demon spirit trembling at His Feet)*: from the prey *(the lion is always seeking the prey, never the prey seeking the lion)*, my son *(Jesus is the Son of God)*, You are gone up *(meaning that Christ is always on the offensive)*: He stooped down, He couched as a lion *(a rampant lion, standing on his hind feet, ready to pounce, which, in fact, was the emblem of the Tribe of Judah)*, and as an old lion *(referring to one ripening into its full strength and ferocity)*; who shall rouse Him up? *(Who would be so foolish as to contest the absolute invincibility of Christ?)*

10 The sceptre shall not depart from Judah *(the "Sceptre" is defined as "a staff of office and authority," which pertains to Christ)*, nor a Lawgiver from between His feet *(refers to the fact that Judah was meant to be a guardian of the Law, which they were; the Temple was in Jerusalem, which was a part of the Tribe of Judah, and which had to do with the Law)*, until Shiloh come *(when Jesus came, typified by the name "Shiloh," Who, in fact, was, and is, the True Lawgiver, He fulfilled the Law in totality by His life and His death, thereby satisfying all of its just demands)*; and unto Him shall the gathering of the people be *(the only way to God the Father is through Christ the Son; the only way to Christ the Son is through the Cross; the only way to the Cross is through an abnegation of self [Lk. 9:23-24])*.

11 Binding his foal unto the vine *(the "Vine" speaks of fruit, and, in fact, "the blood of grapes,"* which speaks of what He did on the Cross in the shedding of His Life's Blood, in order to bring forth this fruit [Jn. 15:1])*, and his animal's colt unto the choice vine; He washed his garments in wine, and His clothes in the blood of grapes *(all of this speaks of the Cross, and Him washing His garments in wine, i.e., "in blood")*:

12 His eyes shall be red with wine *(His eyes ever toward the Cross)*, and His teeth white with milk *(speaks of the Righteousness of Christ; it is Righteousness which He has always had, but now is made possible to us, due to what He did in His sufferings, i.e., "the blood of grapes")*.

13 Zebulun shall dwell at the haven of the sea; and he shall be for an haven of ships *(this portrayal of Zebulun is not so much geographical as it is occupational; the closest that this Tribe came to the Mediterranean was about 10 miles; however, the great trade routes from north to south, etc., went through Zebulun, with them being very active in commerce)*; and his border shall be unto Zidon *(should have been translated, "And his borders shall be towards Zidon")*.

14 Issachar is a strong ass couching down between two burdens:

15 And he saw *(Issachar saw)* that rest was good, and the land that it was pleasant, and bowed his shoulder to bear *(the Tribe of Issachar bordered the Jordan River and, as a result, favored some of the best agricultural areas in all of Israel)*, and became a servant unto tribute *(has to do with agricultural pursuits, and not subjugation by another nation)*.

16 Dan shall judge his people, as one of the tribes of Israel.

17 Dan shall be a serpent by the way, an adder in the path, that bites the horse heels, so that his rider shall fall backward. *(Dan had the ability to bear rule, yet became a treacherous serpent. It is certainly observable that the first introduction of idolatry in Israel is ascribed to the Tribe of Dan [Judg., Chpt. 18] and, in the numbering of the Tribes of Revelation, Chapter 7, the name Dan is omitted.*

As well, it is believed that the Antichrist, who will be Jewish, will spring from the Tribe of Dan, once again likened to "an adder in the path," a most venomous serpent.)

18 I have waited for Your salvation, O LORD *(speaks of the Second Coming)*.

19 Gad, a troop shall overcome him: but he shall overcome at the last *("Gad" will be overcome by the Antichrist during the Great Tribulation, but "shall overcome at the last," which speaks of the Second Coming)*.

20 Out of Asher his bread shall be fat, and he shall yield royal dainties. *("Asher" could well be the first of the Tribes to welcome Christ upon His Second Coming. The phrase, "yield royal dainties," pertains to an excellent presentation for the King. That King is the Lord Jesus Christ.)*

21 Naphtali is a hind *(a female deer)* let loose: he gives goodly words. *("Naphtali" will have wonderful words for Christ upon His return. They will be words of repentance [Zech. 13:1].)*

22 Joseph is a fruitful bough, even a fruitful bough by a well; whose branches run over the wall *(Joseph, as Judah, is a Type of Christ, hence the flowing and glowing superlatives. Judah is portrayed as Christ in His sufferings; while Joseph is portrayed as Christ in His Millennial Blessings):*

23 The archers have sorely grieved Him, and shot at Him, and hated Him *(all speaks of what Israel did to Christ):*

24 But His bow abode in strength, and the arms of His hands were made strong by the hands of the mighty God of Jacob *(Christ did, despite the opposition, what He came to do, which refers to the Cross);* (from thence is the Shepherd, the Stone of Israel:) *(Christ is referred to here by two names, "Shepherd" and "Stone of Israel.")*

25 Even by the God of Your Father, Who shall help You *(it is Christ Alone Who enjoys the Blessings of the Father; and those Blessings come upon Him in every manner);* and by the Almighty, Who shall bless you with blessings of heaven above, blessings of the deep that lie under, blessings of the breasts, and of the womb *(we must understand that God does not bless man, per se, but rather He blesses Christ; if one is in Christ, then one is blessed):*

26 The blessings of Your Father have prevailed above the blessings of my progenitors *(ancestors)* unto the utmost bound of the everlasting hills *(as long as the hills last, the Blessings of God will last; inasmuch as the hills are "everlasting," this means that the Blessings of God, through Christ, are everlasting, as well):* they shall be on the head of Joseph *(the Blessings will be upon Christ, of Whom Joseph was a Type),* and on the crown of the head of Him Who was separate from His brethren *(even though Christ was a man, still, He was separate from all other men, and because, as well, He was the Son of God).*

27 Benjamin shall ravin *(something seized as prey)* as a wolf *(the Tribe of Benjamin may very well be the leading Tribe to oppose the Antichrist; it is plain by this that Jacob was guided in what he said by the Spirit of Prophecy, and not by natural affection; else he would have spoken with more tenderness of his beloved son Benjamin):* in the morning he shall devour the prey, and at night he shall divide the spoil *(could well take place during the coming Great Tribulation, as the Tribe of Benjamin fully opposes the Antichrist).*

28 All these are the twelve tribes of Israel: and this is it that their father spoke unto them, and blessed them; every one according to his blessing he blessed them *(even though Reuben, Simeon, and Levi were under the marks of their father's displeasure, yet he is said to bless them, every one according to his blessing; for none of them were rejected as Esau).*

29 And he charged them, and said unto them, I am to be gathered unto my people: bury me with my fathers in the cave that is in the field of Ephron the Hittite *(the heart of the Patriarch was not set upon the wealth of his luxurious bedchamber, but was far away in God's chosen land; we, as well, must ever remember that while we are in the world, we must not be of the world; our treasure is elsewhere),*

30 In the cave that is in the field of Machpelah, which is before Mamre, in the land of Canaan, which Abraham bought with the field of Ephron the Hittite for a possession of a buryingplace *(the great Patriarch never allowed all of the splendor of Egypt and its ease to turn his Faith from its correct object; it was ever in Christ and the Cross).*

31 There they buried Abraham and Sarah his wife; there they buried Isaac and Rebekah his wife; and there I buried Leah. *(His demand that he be buried where Abraham and Isaac were buried proclaimed, within itself, and made a statement, that all of these were staking a claim to the entirety of the land. God had promised it to them, and ultimately that Promise would be realized.)*

32 The purchase of the field and of the cave that is therein was from the children of Heth.

THE DEATH OF JACOB

33 And when Jacob had made an end of commanding his sons, he gathered up his feet into the bed, and yielded up the ghost, and was gathered unto his people. *(The last hours of the great Patriarch were filled with prophecies and predictions concerning the twelve Tribes of Israel, which would ultimately bring the Redeemer*

into the world. He died when that prophecy was uttered, but he did not die until it was uttered. It must be said of Jacob that he kept the Faith that was once delivered unto Abraham and his father Isaac. He had not allowed that torch to fall to the ground, or even be dimmed. At his death, it burned brightly and, in fact, brighter than ever.)

CHAPTER 50
(1689 B.C.)
BURIAL OF JACOB

AND Joseph fell upon his father's face, and wept upon him, and kissed him. *(Joseph closed his father's eyes, as predicted by the Lord to Jacob [46:4]. Verse 1 is a picture of Christ weeping over Israel. Jacob was dead physically, and alive spiritually. Israel was alive physically, and dead spiritually.)*

2 And Joseph commanded his servants the physicians to embalm his father: and the physicians embalmed Israel *(Jacob's body was embalmed, but his soul and spirit went into Paradise, there to be with his grandfather Abraham and his father Isaac, and every other Believer who had lived up until this time).*

3 And forty days were fulfilled for him; for so are fulfilled the days of those which are embalmed *(it took that long for the process)*: and the Egyptians mourned for him seventy days *(death is an enemy; it is the last enemy which will be defeated [I Cor. 15:26]; Jesus took the sting out of death at the Cross but, at the end of the Kingdom Age, death will then be totally defeated, and forever [Rev., Chpt. 20]).*

4 And when the days of his mourning were past, Joseph spoke unto the house of Pharaoh, saying, If now I have found grace in your eyes, speak, I pray you, in the ears of Pharaoh, saying *(the fact that Joseph did not speak personally to Pharaoh accords with discoveries which show that mourners at that time did not shave and, therefore, could not enter into the royal presence)*,

5 My father made me swear, saying, Lo, I die: in my grave which I have dug for me in the land of Canaan, there shall you bury me. Now therefore let me go up, I pray you, and bury my father, and I will come again *(as stated, Joseph was speaking to Pharaoh through members of the royal court)*.

6 And Pharaoh said, Go up, and bury your father, according as he made you swear.

7 And Joseph went up to bury his father:

and with him went up all the servants of Pharaoh, the elders of his house, and all the elders of the land of Egypt *(the grandeur of Jacob's funeral procession must have been a wonder to behold; it is amazing to think of this great Patriarch, a pilgrim all his life, being carried to his final resting place by the grandeur of mighty Egypt; it is one of the few times in history that the world recognized the greatness that was among them)*,

8 And all the house of Joseph, and his brethren, and his father's house: only their little ones, and their flocks, and their herds, they left in the land of Goshen.

9 And there went up with him both chariots and horsemen: and it was a very great company.

10 And they came to the threshingfloor of Atad, which is beyond Jordan, and there they mourned with a great and very sore lamentation: and he made a mourning for his father seven days *(they were now in the land of Canaan; "seven" is God's perfect number; as such, it speaks of a perfect Salvation, which will ultimately lead to the Resurrection).*

11 And when the inhabitants of the land, the Canaanites, saw the mourning in the floor of Atad, they said, This is a grievous mourning to the Egyptians: wherefore the name of it was called Abel-mizraim, which is beyond Jordan. *(The Canaanites had no understanding of what Joseph was doing, thinking this was some type of ritual concerning the Egyptians.)*

12 And his sons *(Jacob's sons)* did unto him according as he commanded them:

13 For his sons carried him into the land of Canaan, and buried him in the cave of the field of Machpelah, which Abraham bought with the field for a possession of a buryingplace of Ephron the Hittite, before Mamre *(Abraham, Isaac, and Jacob were very wealthy in flocks, gold, and silver; however, when they died, as all, the only thing they took with them was their Faith).*

JOSEPH

14 And Joseph returned into Egypt, he, and his brothers, and all who went up with him to bury his father, after he had buried his father.

15 And when Joseph's brothers saw that their father was dead, they said, Joseph will peradventure hate us, and will certainly requite us all the evil which we did unto him. *(Joseph's brothers never did quite understand who their*

brother was, or what he was. *Now that Jacob was dead, they expected evil of Joseph. They did not, and even perhaps could not, understand that Joseph, being a Type of Christ, would deal with them, not with judgment, but with Mercy and Grace.)*

16 And they sent a messenger unto Joseph, saying, Your father did command before he died, saying *(they claimed that Jacob had said before he died that they should ask Joseph to forgive them of their great sin against him),*

17 So shall you say unto Joseph, Forgive, I pray you now, the trespass of your brothers, and their sin; for they did unto you evil: and now, we pray you, forgive the trespass of the servants of the God of your father *(they are quoting the words to Joseph which Jacob had told them to say).* And Joseph wept when they spoke unto him. *(Concerning this, Williams says, "The incurable unbelief of the heart is illustrated by the cruel thoughts of Joseph's brothers as to his affection for them. This unbelief moved Joseph to tears; and in his action and language he once more stands forth as, perhaps, the most remarkable Type of Christ in the entirety of the Bible.")*

18 And his brothers also went and fell down before his face; and they said, Behold, we be your servants. *(This Verse records the last of five times the brothers bowed before Joseph, fulfilling the dreams [37:5-11]. One day, in its greater fulfillment, which will be in the latter days, Israel will fall down at the Feet of the Lord Jesus Christ, of Whom Joseph was a Type.)*

19 And Joseph said unto them, Fear not: for am I in the place of God? *(The question of Joseph, in effect, says, "I am not the Judge and, therefore, I do not punish. If any punishment is meted out, it will be God Who does it, and not me. You have nothing to fear from me.")*

20 But as for you, you thought evil against me; but God meant it unto good, to bring to pass, as it is this day, to save much people alive. *(This Verse holds one of the greatest Promises found in the entirety of the Word of God. God can take the evil which is planned against the Believer, that is, if the Believer will fully trust, and turn it to good, until there is nothing left but good.)*

21 Now therefore do not fear: I will nourish you, and your little ones. And he comforted them, and spoke kindly unto them *(a perfect Type of Christ).*

JOSEPH'S DEATH

22 And Joseph dwelt in Egypt, he, and his father's house: and Joseph lived an hundred and ten years.

23 And Joseph saw Ephraim's children of the third generation: the children also of Machir the son of Manasseh were brought up upon Joseph's knees. *(Joseph was 110 years old when he died. He lived in Egypt 93 years, and his father's descendants lived there 215 years. This man who was sold as a slave into Egypt became a viceroy of the most powerful and richest nation on the face of the Earth. He was without a doubt one of the most beautiful Types of Christ who ever lived.)*

24 And Joseph said unto his brothers, I die: and God will surely visit you, and bring you out of this land unto the land which He swore to Abraham, to Isaac, and to Jacob. *(Joseph using the names of his great-grandfather, his grandfather, and his father portrays the fact that when the torch of Faith was passed to him, he did not allow it to dim.)*

25 And Joseph took an oath of the Children of Israel, saying, God will surely visit you, and you shall carry up my bones from hence. *(When the Children of Israel left out of Egypt, some 3 million strong, which they would do approximately 122 years later, Moses was careful to "take the bones of Joseph with him" [Ex. 13:19]. Wandering some 40 years in the wilderness, making a total of approximately 162 years from when Joseph died, Joshua, no doubt, attended the burial of those sacred bones — sacred because of Faith.)*

26 So Joseph died, being an hundred and ten years old: and they embalmed him, and he was put in a coffin in Egypt. *(The Book of Genesis begins with life and ends with death. It starts with creation and ends with a coffin. It begins with a living God and ends with a dead man, and all because of the Fall.)*

THE SECOND BOOK OF MOSES, CALLED
EXODUS

CHAPTER 1
(1706 B.C.)
ISRAEL IN EGYPT

NOW these are the names of the Children of Israel, which came into Egypt; every man and his household came with Jacob. *(We look at the 70 souls, Jacob's family, which, by the Hand of Lord, were brought from Canaan to Egypt, and brought there for safe-keeping, one might say. They were insignificant in the eyes of the world, but, if God be in it, we must never despise the day of small things.)*

2 Reuben, Simeon, Levi, and Judah,

3 Issachar, Zebulun, and Benjamin,

4 Dan, and Naphtali, Gad, and Asher.

5 And all the souls who came out of the loins of Jacob were seventy souls: for Joseph was in Egypt already. *(The Book of Genesis is the story of the Fall of man. The Book of Exodus is the story of the Redemption of man. Hence, the work of Redemption by Christ is called His "Exodus" [decease, going out of the world, Lk. 9:31].)*

6 And Joseph died, and all his brothers, and all that generation. *(If we are to notice, this Book begins with names, hence, Salvation is a personal matter. Joseph died about 80 years before Moses was born.)*

7 And the Children of Israel were fruitful, and increased abundantly, and multiplied, and waxed exceeding mighty; and the land was filled with them *(the Blessings of the Lord were upon Israel).*

OPPRESSION

8 Now there arose up a new king over Egypt, which knew not Joseph *(who had no regard for Joseph; this "new king" was probably either Rameses I, or his son, Seti I).*

9 And he said unto his people, Behold, the people of the Children of Israel are more and mightier than we *(it is believed they numbered approximately 2 1/2 million; it has been stated by some that in the Egyptian records there is no mention of the Hebrews, as the Bible claims; however, it is known that at about the time of the Hebrew sojourn, there was in Egypt a subject race, often employed in forced labors, called* "Aperu" or "Aperiu," *and it seems impossible to deny that this word is a very fair Egyptian equivalent for the Biblical "Hebrews"; we are forced, therefore, either to suppose there were in Egypt, at one and the same time, two subject races with names almost identical, or to admit the identification of the "Aperu" with the descendants of Jacob):*

10 Come on, let us deal wisely with them; lest they multiply, and it come to pass, that, when there falls out any war, they join also unto our enemies, and fight against us, and so get them up out of the land. *(Pharaoh sets out to destroy God's people. To be sure, his plans to do so were keen and far-reaching, at least as long as God was left out; but the entrance of God into these plans turned their wisdom to folly. All schemes which ignore God illustrate the same.)*

11 Therefore they did set over them taskmasters to afflict them with their burdens. And they built for Pharaoh treasure cities, Pithom and Raamses. *(The ruins of these two cities exist presently and, in fact, the latter was the residence of the Court. There is a good possibility that the miracles of Moses recorded in Exodus, Chapter 7 took place in this Court [Ps. 78:12, 43]. So, the great palaces built by the Children of God, who were used as slaves, would see the mighty Power of God made evident in them.)*

12 But the more they afflicted them, the more multiplied and grew. And they were grieved because of the Children of Israel. *(Concerning this, Mackintosh says, "In reference to the king of Egypt, it may assuredly be said, he did 'greatly err' not knowing God or His changeless counsels. He knew not that, hundreds of years back, before even he had breathed the breath of mortal life, God's Word and Oath — 'two immutable things' — had infallibly secured the full and glorious deliverance of that very people, in fact, a people which, at that time, the time of the Oath of God, didn't even exist, whom Pharaoh was going, in his earthly wisdom, to crush. All this was unknown to him and, therefore, all his thoughts and plans were founded upon ignorance of that great foundation — truth of all truths, namely that 'God is.' Pharaoh vainly imagined that he, by his management, could*

prevent the increase of those concerning whom God had said, 'They shall be as the stars of Heaven, and as the sand which is upon the seashore.' His wise dealings, therefore, were simply madness and folly.")

13 And the Egyptians made the children of Israel to serve with rigour *("rigour" is derived from a root which means "to break in pieces, to crush")*:

14 And they made their lives bitter with hard bondage, in morter, and in brick, and in all manner of service in the field: all their service, wherein they made them serve, was with rigour.

15 And the king of Egypt spoke to the Hebrew midwives, of which the name of the one was Shiphrah, and the name of the other Puah *(it is ironic that the names of the mighty Pharaohs of that day are all but lost to history, whereas the names of these two women who obeyed God are recognized by multiple millions in every generation; the two named here were evidently in charge of many, if not all, of the midwives among the people of Israel)*:

16 And he said, When you do the office of a midwife to the Hebrew women, and see them upon the stools *(when the child is about to be born)*; if it be a son, then you shall kill him: but if it be a daughter, then she shall live. *(This murderous scheme hatched up by Pharaoh, or someone in his court, was supposed to weaken Israel by denying further growth. Some may ask as to why the Lord allowed such to happen? The answer is quite simple! Had Israel not suffered greatly, they would not have wanted to leave Egypt.)*

17 But the midwives feared God, and did not as the king of Egypt commanded them, but saved the men children alive. *(The midwives, as well, concocted a scheme, no doubt inspired by the Lord, that would bring about the desired results.)*

18 And the king of Egypt called for the midwives *(Shiphrah and Puah)*, and said unto them, Why have you done this thing, and have saved the men children alive?

19 And the midwives said unto Pharaoh, Because the Hebrew women are not as the Egyptian women; for they are lively, and are delivered ere the midwives come in unto them. *(This scheme called for the midwives to be late, which brought about the desired results.)*

20 Therefore God dealt well with the midwives *(meaning that this is what the Lord told them to do, and He blessed them for their obedience)*: **and**

the people multiplied, and waxed very mighty *(Pharaoh's scheme was foiled)*.

21 And it came to pass, because the midwives feared God *(they feared God above Pharaoh)*, that He *(God)* made them houses *(gave them large families)*.

THE CRUEL COMMAND

22 And Pharaoh charged all his people, saying, Every son who is born you shall cast into the river, and every daughter you shall save alive. *(While Pharaoh desired to weaken the Israelites by demanding that the boy babies be killed at birth, Satan's plan was far more sinister. This is the serpent's enmity against the Seed of the woman. If this could have been carried out concerning the male children being destroyed, there would have been no David, just to name one instance, and, if no David, no David's Son. There is no record that the Israelites obeyed this injunction concerning the river. In fact, God used the river, even as we shall see, to bring about His Divine Will.)*

CHAPTER 2
(1571 B.C.)
THE BIRTH OF MOSES

AND there went a man of the house of Levi, and took to wife a daughter of Levi. *(This means that Moses was a member of the Tribe of Levi, which was to be the Priestly Tribe. He was a Type of Christ, our Great High Priest.)*

2 And the woman conceived, and bore a son: and when she saw him that he was a goodly child, she hid him three months. *(Miriam and Aaron, Moses' sister and brother, were already born when Moses was born. Jochebed was his mother, with Amram being his father.*

Concerning Moses, Pink says, "From Adam to Christ there is none greater than Moses. He is one of the few characters of Scripture whose course is sketched from his infancy to his death. The fierce light of criticism has been turned upon him for generations, but he is still the most commanding figure of the ancient world.

"In character, and faith, in the unique position assigned him as the mediator of the Old Covenant, and in achievements, he stands first among the heroes of the Old Testament.

"All of God's early dealings with Israel were transacted through Moses. He was a Prophet, Priest, and King in one person, and so united all the great and important functions which later

were distributed among a plurality of persons. The history of such an one is worthy of the strictest attention, and his remarkable life deserves the closest study.")

3 And when she *(the mother of Moses)* could not longer hide him *(Pharaoh had given the orders that all boy babies were to be instantly killed)*, she took for him an ark of bulrushes, and daubed it with slime and with pitch, and put the child therein; and she laid it in the flags by the river's brink. *(That which stands out so vividly in this account is the faith of Jochebed, the mother of Moses. She no doubt was led by the Lord in doing this.)*

4 And his sister stood afar off, to witness what would be done to him.

MOSES' EARLY YEARS

5 And the daughter of Pharaoh came down to wash herself at the river *(the Lord had something in mind that Jochebed could not have possibly dreamed)*; and her maidens walked along by the river's side *(the Nile River)*; and when she saw the ark among the flags, she sent her maid to fetch it *(the Holy Spirit had everything timed just right — the place, the person, and the progress)*.

6 And when she *(the daughter of Pharaoh)* had opened it, she saw the child: and, behold, the babe wept. And she had compassion on him, and said, This is one of the Hebrews' children. *(Someone has well said, "On that memorable day, God floated His navy on the tears of a baby's cheeks.")*

7 Then said his sister *(Moses' sister, Miriam)* to Pharaoh's daughter, Shall I go and call to you a nurse of the Hebrew women, that she may nurse the child for you? *(Miriam was led by the Lord in doing this.)*

8 And Pharaoh's daughter said to her, Go. And the maid went and called the child's mother *(however, Pharaoh's daughter did not, at least at this time, know that this was Moses' mother)*.

9 And Pharaoh's daughter said unto her, Take this child away, and nurse it for me, and I will give you your wages. And the woman took the child, and nursed it. *(So Jochebed would take care of baby Moses, and be paid by the State for doing so. I wonder what Satan thought of this?)*

10 And the child grew, and she brought him unto Pharaoh's daughter, and he became her son. *(At a given time, the daughter of Pharaoh*

wanted Moses to come live with her in the Palace. Him becoming her son proclaims the fact that else her mother was dead or could not have children, so Moses was being raised to be the Pharaoh of Egypt.) And she called his name Moses: and she said, Because I drew him out of the water. *(To show how little the Holy Spirit thought of the palace of Pharaoh, He, in effect, devotes only one Verse to these years of Moses' life.)*

THE EGYPTIAN

11 And it came to pass in those days, when Moses was grown, that he went out unto his brethren, and looked on their burdens *(from the language of Hebrews 11:24, it is clear that a time came when Moses had the choice of accepting or refusing the throne of Egypt; he refused, and cast in his lot with the hated and oppressed Hebrews)*: and he spied an Egyptian smiting an Hebrew, one of his brethren.

12 And he looked this way and that way, and when he saw that there was no man, he killed the Egyptian, and hid him in the sand. *(This was a "work of the flesh" on the part of Moses and, as all works of the flesh, it could have nothing but disastrous consequences.)*

13 And when he went out the second day, behold, two men of the Hebrews strove together: and he said to him who did the wrong, Why do you smite your fellow?

14 And he said, Who made you a prince and a judge over us? do you intend to kill me, as you killed the Egyptian? And Moses feared, and said, Surely this thing is known.

15 Now when Pharaoh heard this thing, he sought to kill Moses. *(Josephus said that the Egyptians, from the throne down, were envious of Moses, and partly afraid of him. They thought, due to his great success in defeating the Ethiopians [the Jewish Targums say that Moses was a General in the Egyptian army], that he might take advantage of his good fortune and try to subvert their government. So, when Moses, in defending the Hebrew, killed an Egyptian, this was the proverbial straw that broke the camel's back.)* But Moses fled from the face of Pharaoh, and dwelt in the land of Midian: and he sat down by a well. *(Haldeman says of Moses: "The life of Moses presents a series of striking antitheses. For instance, he was the child of a slave, and the son of a queen. He was born in a hut, and lived in a palace. He inherited poverty, and enjoyed unlimited wealth. He was the*

leader of armies, and the keeper of flocks. He was the mightiest of warriors, and the meekest of men. He was educated in the court of Egypt, and yet dwelt in the desert. He had the wisdom of Egypt, and the faith of a child. He was fitted for the city, and wandered in the wilderness. He was tempted with the pleasures of sin, and endured the hardships of virtue. He was backward in speech, and yet talked with God. He had the rod of a shepherd, and the power of the Infinite. He was a fugitive from Pharaoh, and an ambassador from Heaven. He was the giver of the Law, and the forerunner of Grace.")

16 Now the priest of Midian had seven daughters *(this man had three names, "Reuel," "Jethro," and "Raguel"; the last name means "a friend of God"; he was a descendant of Abraham by Keturah; he was a worshipper of the True God)*: and they came and drew water, and filled the troughs to water their father's flock.

17 And the shepherds came and drove them away: but Moses stood up and helped them, and watered their flock.

18 And when they came to Reuel their father, he said, How is it that you are come so soon to day? *(Meaning that they had finished watering the flock early.)*

19 And they said, An Egyptian delivered us out of the hand of the shepherds, and also drew water enough for us, and watered the flock. *(Moses was really not an Egyptian, but evidently the young ladies thought he was.)*

20 And he said unto his daughters, And where is he? why is it that you have left the man? call him, that he may eat bread.

21 And Moses was content to dwell with the man: and he gave Moses Zipporah his daughter. *(We must assume that the Lord led Moses to Jethro [Reuel], and that Zipporah was destined to be his wife. But yet, Zipporah didn't prove to be as close to Moses as she should have been.)*

22 And she bore him a son, and he called his name Gershom: for he said, I have been a stranger in a strange land. *(Moses is about to begin his true education of 40 years duration. Some have said that it took about 40 hours to get Moses out of Egypt, but about 40 years to get Egypt out of Moses.)*

23 And it came to pass in process of time, that the king of Egypt died *(this refers to the Pharaoh who desired to kill Moses)*: and the children of Israel sighed by reason of the bondage, and they cried, and their cry came up unto God by reason of the bondage. *(The pressure from Egypt is now becoming so hard and so difficult on the Israelites that they are now ready to leave. To be frank, they would in no way have left Egypt had the blessings continued, as it was during the time of Joseph. At times, the Lord has to allow difficulties, in order for us to become willing to do His Will.)*

24 And God heard their groaning, and God remembered His Covenant with Abraham, with Isaac, and with Jacob. *(It is not clear here how much the Israelites were conscious of God, or whether they had almost forgotten Him. We do know that it was God Who took the initiative in their deliverance in view of His Covenants and Promises to their fathers. God always keeps His Word!)*

25 And God looked upon the children of Israel, and God had respect unto them. *(The glorious Name "Elohim" occurs five times in Verses 23-25. As yet, He was not now known to Israel as "Jehovah." That would come a little later. Five is the number of Grace. No moral excellence in the Children of Israel attracted God's love; it was their misery that drew out His Heart to them: A. He "heard" their groaning; B. He "remembered" His Covenant; C. He "looked" upon them; and, D. He "had respect" unto them.)*

CHAPTER 3
(1491 B.C.)
THE BURNING BUSH

NOW Moses kept the flock of Jethro his father in law, the priest of Midian: and he led the flock to the backside of the desert, and came to the mountain of God, even to Horeb. *(What God would do with Moses was not learned in the palaces of Egypt, but was learned at "the backside of the desert.")*

2 And the Angel of the Lord *(actually, the Lord Himself)* appeared unto him in a flame of fire out of the midst of a bush *(40 years in the desert was needed to humble the strength of the "flesh" and destroy its hope; the possible king of Egypt was now an obscure shepherd)*: and he looked, and, behold, the bush burned with fire, and the bush was not consumed. *(The flame of fire in the lowly desert bush — the emblem of Deity and Humanity of Christ — and the great name "I AM" proceeding out from the fire revealed this Almighty Power to Moses. If it's done in the flesh, it will consume the person, i.e., "the bush"; however, if it's done by the Power of the Holy Spirit, the bush will burn and not be consumed.)*

3 And Moses said, I will now turn aside, and see this great sight, why the bush is not burnt.

4 And when the LORD saw that he *(Moses)* turned aside to see, God called unto him out of the midst of the bush, and said, Moses, Moses. And he said, Here am I. *(The Voice that called, "Moses, Moses," was the very same Voice that said, "Martha, Martha." Nothing can be more interesting or instructive than the mode in which Jehovah was pleased to reveal Himself to Moses.)*

5 And He *(God)* said, Draw not near hither: put off your shoes from off your feet, for the place whereon you stand is Holy ground. *(Wherever God is, that place is Holy. And it is Holy only as long as God is there.)*

6 Moreover He said, I am the God of your father, the God of Abraham, the God of Isaac, and the God of Jacob *(the God of the Covenants given unto these men)*. And Moses hid his face; for he was afraid to look upon God. *(As far as we know, this appearance by God to Moses was the first appearance since Jacob's going down into Egypt about 215 years before. As well, if it is to be noticed, the Lord didn't say, "I 'was' the God of Abraham . . ." etc., but "I 'am' . . .," proving that these Patriarchs were still alive, even though they had died physically a long time before.)*

7 And the LORD said, I have surely seen the affliction of My people which are in Egypt, and have heard their cry by reason of their taskmasters; for I know their sorrows *(the Lord has "seen," He has "heard," and He "knows")*;

8 And I am come down to deliver them out of the hand of the Egyptians *(Egypt was a type of the world; "the Lord delivers us from this present evil world"; he does so by the means of the Cross [Gal. 1:4])*, and to bring them up out of that land unto a good land and a large, unto a land flowing with milk and honey *(the Lord delivers us from something [sin], and thereby to something [Salvation], typified by Canaanland)*; unto the place of the Canaanites, and the Hittites, and the Amorites, and the Perizzites, and the Hivites, and the Jebusites. *(While Egypt represents the world, these various tribes which then occupied the Promised Land typify "flesh" which endeavors to hinder the Believer. All victory is won by and through Christ and the Cross.)*

THE COMMISSION

9 Now therefore, behold, the cry of the Children of Israel is come unto Me: and I have also seen the oppression wherewith the Egyptians oppress them. *(Henry says concerning this: "As the poorest of the oppressed are not below God's cognizance, so the highest and greatest of their oppressors are not above His check, but He will surely visit for these things.")*

10 Come now therefore, and I will send you unto Pharaoh, that you may bring forth My people the Children of Israel out of Egypt. *(With one man, the Lord would deliver nearly 3 million of His people out of the mightiest nation on Earth, determined to hold them captive. It is the same presently! All the Lord needs is one man, or woman, who will be willing to preach His Word, and deliverance will be effected, even for the hardest cases. God is able!)*

11 And Moses said unto God, Who am I, that I should go unto Pharaoh, and that I should bring forth the children of Israel out of Egypt? *(The carnal mind is not subject to the Law of God, neither indeed can be. The very Moses, who in 2:11-13 stepped forward with energy to champion his people, is the very same Moses, who in 3:11-13 steps back and declares himself unequal to the task. Faith neither steps forward nor backward, but holds the Hand which says: "Certainly I will be with you.")*

12 And he said, Certainly I will be with you; and this shall be a token unto you, that I have sent you: When you have brought forth the people out of Egypt, you shall serve God upon this mountain *(Mount Sinai, where the Law was given, and which happened exactly as the Lord said it would)*.

13 And Moses said unto God, Behold, when I come unto the Children of Israel, and shall say unto them, The God of your fathers has sent me unto you; and they shall say to me, What is His Name? what shall I say unto them? *(The human heart is full of questions; consequently, it reasons and questions when unhesitating obedience is that which is due to God; and still more marvelous is the Grace that bears with all the reasonings and answers all the questions. To the Israelites, God had been known by titles, such as "El" or "Elohim," which mean "The Lofty One"; or "Shaddai," which means "The Powerful"; or "Jahveh" or "Jehovah," "The Existent One." However, these Names were more descriptions than anything else.)*

14 And God said unto Moses, I AM THAT I AM: and He said, Thus shall you say unto the Children of Israel, I AM has sent me unto you. *(Dr. Pentecost translated the Name, "I was, I*

am, and I shall always continue to be." I am whatever you need!)

15 And God said moreover unto Moses, Thus shall you say unto the Children of Israel, The LORD God of your fathers, the God of Abraham, the God of Isaac, and the God of Jacob, has sent me unto you: this is My Name for ever, and this is My memorial unto all generations. *(The Lord reminds Moses to tell Israel that He is the same One Who spoke to the Patriarchs and, as well, that this Name, "I AM THAT I AM," will be His Name forever. He changes not; He is the same yesterday, and today, and forever. His Name is Jesus; and that is God's greatest Name!)*

16 Go, and gather the Elders of Israel together, and say unto them, The LORD God of your fathers, the God of Abraham, of Isaac, and of Jacob, appeared unto me, saying, I have surely visited you, and seen that which is done to you in Egypt *(God sees everything that is done to His children, be it negative or positive)*:

17 And I have said, I will bring you up out of the affliction of Egypt unto the land of the Canaanites, and the Hittites, and the Amorites, and the Perizzites, and the Hivites, and the Jebusites, unto a land flowing with milk and honey. *(Before, Moses had made the plans [when he killed the Egyptian], and they could not succeed. Now, God makes the plans, and they are guaranteed of success.)*

18 And they shall hearken to your voice *(this was the Message; and Moses' faith in delivering it was strengthened beforehand by the Divine assurance that it would be believed)*: and you shall come, you and the Elders of Israel, unto the king of Egypt, and you shall say unto him, the LORD God of the Hebrews has met with us: and now let us go, we beseech you, three days' journey into the wilderness, that we may sacrifice to the LORD our God. *(The three days' journey was not deceitfully proposed by God, but furnished as a test for Pharaoh.)*

19 And I am sure that the king of Egypt will not let you go, no, not by a mighty hand. *(Through foreknowledge, God knew that Pharaoh would not allow the Children of Israel to leave.)*

20 And I will stretch out My hand, and smite Egypt with all My wonders which I will do in the midst thereof: and after that he will let you go. *(The Lord would use Pharaoh's obstinate heart to serve as a warning of the Power and Glory of God to all the surrounding nations.)*

21 And I will give this people favor in the sight of the Egyptians: and it shall come to pass, that, when you go, you shall not go empty *(God planned that His people should receive proper wages for all their hard labor before leaving Egypt, and so they did!)*:

22 But every woman shall borrow *(ask)* of her neighbor, and of her who sojourns in her house, jewels of silver, and jewels of gold, and raiment: and you shall put them upon your sons, and upon your daughters; and you shall spoil the Egyptians. *(Upon hearing this, I'm sure the Elders of Israel must have been somewhat surprised! They couldn't imagine Pharaoh letting them go, much less loading them down with jewels and raiment, etc. However, whatever God says that He will do, irrespective as to how preposterous it might seem at the beginning, how unlikely, how virtually impossible, to be sure will come to pass. God cannot lie!)*

CHAPTER 4
(1491 B.C.)
THE ROD

AND Moses answered and said, But, behold, they will not believe me, nor hearken unto my voice: for they will say, The LORD has not appeared unto you. *(The hesitating and timid Moses of Mount Horeb was the same courageous and self-reliant Moses who smote the Egyptian dead! His strength then unfitted him as a Divine instrument, and now his weakness unfits him — Williams.)*

2 And the LORD said unto him, What is that in your hand? And he said, A rod. *(The "rod," within itself, was nothing!)*

3 And He *(God)* said, Cast it on the ground. And he cast it on the ground, and it became a serpent; and Moses fled from before it. *(By the rod turning to a serpent, a venomous one at that, Moses, in essence, was being told that he was going to come up against the powers of darkness. Egypt was actually ruled by demon spirits, which worked through Pharaoh and the magicians, etc. It was a nation wholly taken over by demon spirits, and ruled thereby.)*

4 And the LORD said unto Moses, Put forth your hand, and take it by the tail. And he put forth his hand, and caught it, and it became a rod in his hand *(this told Moses that he had power over Satan)*:

5 That they may believe that the LORD God of their fathers, the God of Abraham, the God of Isaac, and the God of Jacob, has appeared

unto you. *(The Lord would help Moses, thereby letting the people know that he was functioning within the boundaries of the same Promises which God had given to the Patriarchs.)*

6 And the LORD said furthermore unto him, Put now your hand into your bosom. And he put his hand into his bosom: and when he took it out, behold, his hand was leprous as snow. *(Putting his hand into his bosom showed him what man is, a sinner, hence symbolized by leprosy.)*

7 And he said, Put your hand into your bosom again. And he put his hand into his bosom again, and plucked it out of his bosom, and, behold, it was turned again as his other flesh. *(Thus we see here, in this particular "sign," that which Jesus Christ can perform, as it regards the Salvation of the soul. He can cleanse from all sin, and He Alone can cleanse from all sin. While Christ is always the Source, the Cross is always the Means.)*

8 And it shall come to pass, if they will not believe you, neither hearken to the voice of the first sign, that they will believe the voice of the latter sign. *(The only answer to the serpent, i.e., "Satan," and the sin which he causes, which is so hideous it can only be symbolized by the dread disease of "leprosy," is the Blood, the Precious Blood, of the Lord Jesus Christ, epitomized in the next Verse.)*

9 And it shall come to pass, if they will not believe also these two signs, neither hearken unto your voice, that you shall take of the water of the river, and pour it upon the dry land: and the water which you take out of the river shall become blood upon the dry land. *(The only answer to sin is the shed blood of the Lord Jesus Christ. The pronoun "they" refers to the Elders of the Israelites.)*

10 And Moses said unto the LORD, O my Lord, I am not eloquent, neither heretofore, nor since You have spoken unto Your servant: but I am slow of speech, and of a slow tongue. *(Verses 10 through 12 portray the Call of God upon man. "I am not eloquent." And even if we were, it would not save anyone.)*

11 And the LORD said unto him, Who has made man's mouth? or who makes the dumb, or deaf, or the seeing, or the blind? have not I the LORD? *(God could and would have cured the defect in Moses' speech, whatever it was; could and would have added eloquence to his other gifts, if he had even at this point yielded himself unreservedly to the Lord's guidance and heartily accepted his mission. Nothing is too hard for*

the Lord.)

12 Now therefore go, and I will be with your mouth, and teach you what you shall say.

13 And he said, O my Lord, send, I pray you, by the hand of him whom you will send. *(Moses would feel safer leaning on the arm of Aaron than leaning on the arm of Jehovah! And yet Aaron was no real help to him, but the contrary; Aaron made the golden calf.)*

AARON

14 And the anger of the LORD was kindled against Moses, and he said, Is not Aaron the Levite your brother? I know that he can speak well. And also, behold, he comes forth to meet you: and when he sees you, he will be glad in his heart. *(Nothing is more dishonoring to God, or more dangerous for us, than a mock humility. When we refuse to occupy a position which the Grace of God assigns us because of our not possessing certain virtues and qualifications, this is not humility, but rather unbelief!)*

15 And you shall speak unto him, and put words in his mouth: and I will be with your mouth, and with his mouth, and will teach you what you shall do. *(The Lord would give Moses the words to say, and it would be the duty of Aaron to accept what Moses said as Divine.)*

16 And he shall be your spokesman unto the people: and he shall be, even he shall be to you instead of a mouth, and you shall be to him instead of God. *(In other words, Moses speaking to Aaron was the same as God speaking to him.)*

17 And you shall take this rod in your hand, wherewith you shall do signs. *(In effect, the Lord is telling Moses that He could use anything, even a wooden stick. This should have made Moses very ashamed!)*

18 And Moses went and returned to Jethro his father in law, and said unto him, Let me go, I pray you, and return unto my brethren which are in Egypt, and see whether they be yet alive. And Jethro said to Moses, Go in peace. *(Had Moses left for Egypt without first notifying his father-in-law, it would have been grossly discourteous, and even the height of ingratitude. This act of Moses manifested his thoughtfulness of others and his appreciation of favors received.)*

EGYPT

19 And the LORD said unto Moses in Midian, Go, return into Egypt: for all the men are dead

which sought your life. *(From the way the Lord commands Moses here, it would seem that he was still reluctant to go. The Lord would reassure him by telling him that "all" the men in Egypt who sought to kill him from 40 years back were now dead. So, there need be no fear from this source; however, before we criticize the reluctance of Moses, we should look at ourselves first of all.)*

20 And Moses took his wife and his sons, and set them upon an ass, and he returned to the land of Egypt: and Moses took the rod of God in his hand. *(His sons were Gershom [2:22], and Eliezer [18:4], the latter probably an infant. This "rod" is the same one of Verse 2, which had now become "the Rod of God," and because of the miracles of Verses 3 and 4. The Lord commands him to take this Rod to Egypt.)*

21 And the LORD said unto Moses, When you go to return into Egypt, see that you do all those wonders before Pharaoh, which I have put in your hand: but I will harden his heart, that he shall not let the people go. *(The hardening of Pharaoh's heart doesn't mean that God tampered with Pharaoh's will, but rather, by foreknowledge, that he looked at the heart of the Monarch, and thereby knew what Pharaoh would do. God would simply supply the opportunity.)*

22 And you shall say unto Pharaoh, Thus saith the LORD, Israel is My son, even My firstborn *(Pharaoh would understand this terminology fully, for he, himself, was called "Son of Ra"):*

23 And I say unto you, Let My son go, that he may serve Me: and if you refuse to let him go, behold, I will kill your son, even your firstborn. *(So, at the outset, Moses was to tell Pharaoh that if he didn't let the Children of Israel go, his firstborn would die. So, the Monarch was not without warning. At any point he could have repented, and his firstborn would have been spared, as well as the destruction of Egypt.)*

24 And it came to pass by the way in the inn, that the LORD met him *(met Moses)*, and sought to kill him *(threatened to kill the child; this was Eliezer, the infant; concerning this, Williams says: "Moses was commanded to announce to Pharaoh that Jehovah, the God of Israel, was about to slay his [Pharaoh's] son; but Moses had to learn that disobedience and rebellion in him was just as hateful as in Pharaoh; and that God, because of His nature, must judge with death sin wherever found").*

25 Then Zipporah *(the wife of Moses)* took a sharp stone, and cut off the foreskin of her son, and cast it at his feet, and said, Surely a

bloody husband are you to me. *(We find here that the wife of Moses was not too very much in sympathy with the things of God. So, Moses, not desiring to create a family problem, had evidently acquiesced to his wife, and had neglected to circumcise the baby boy.)*

26 So He *(God)* let him *(the child)* go: then she said, A bloody husband you are, because of the circumcision. *(Even though Zipporah circumcised the child, she, with anger and passion, declared that her husband's religion was a religion of blood, i.e., "of blood-stained rites." Thus, Moses had to learn that God would judge him before He judged Pharaoh, and that rebellion in the one was the same as rebellion in the other; and this lesson must have enabled Moses to proclaim this dreadful truth with the force of a personal experience — Williams.)*

MOSES AND AARON

27 And the LORD said to Aaron, Go into the wilderness to meet Moses. And he went, and met him in the mount of God, and kissed him. *(Aaron met Moses at Mount Sinai, perhaps very shortly after he received the revelation of the burning bush, etc. The brothers had been separated for some 40 years.)*

28 And Moses told Aaron all the words of the LORD Who had sent him, and all the signs which He had commanded him. *(And now Aaron is to find out that he is to be the spokesman for Moses as it regards the tremendous confrontation, which would take place quite a number of times, between Moses and the Monarch of Egypt.)*

29 And Moses and Aaron went and gathered together all the Elders of the children of Israel *(the Scripture is silent regarding the trip to Egypt; the Scripture seems to indicate that Moses sent his wife and children back to Jethro [18:2]):*

30 And Aaron spoke all the words which the LORD had spoken unto Moses, and did the signs in the sight of the people *(the serpent, the leprous hand, and the blood, all observed by the Elders).*

31 And the people believed: and when they heard that the LORD had visited the Children of Israel, and that He had looked upon their affliction, then they bowed their heads and worshipped. *(Moses had said, "The people will not believe me." But the question was not as to whether they would believe him, but whether they would believe God. Their faith reached out at this time and, in fact, they did believe.)*

CHAPTER 5
(1491 B.C.)
PHARAOH

AND afterward Moses and Aaron went in, and told the Pharaoh *(according to many authorities, the Pharaoh at that time was "Menephthap," the son and successor of "Rameses II"; history records that he was a weak individual, but, because of certain events, had an exalted opinion of himself; the close of Chapter 4 presents the people worshipping in believing joy; the close of Chapter 5 sets before the reader the same people filled with unbelieving bitterness; the glad tidings of Salvation is one thing; the struggle against the power that tries to keep the soul in bondage is quite another),* Thus saith the LORD God of Israel, Let My people go, that they may hold a feast unto Me in the wilderness. *(If it is to be noticed, the Holy Spirit, in giving Moses direction regarding the Sacred Text, in no way recognizes the splendor of Egypt. The character of the Message that Moses was to deliver to Pharaoh was not calculated to compromise or pacify.)*

2 And Pharaoh said, Who is the LORD, that I should obey His voice to let Israel go? I know not the LORD, neither will I let Israel go. *(Satan will not easily allow his captives to go free; and God permits the bitter experience of Satan's power in order to exercise and strengthen Faith. Mackintosh says: "When we contemplate Israel amid the brick kilns of Egypt, we behold a graphic figure of the condition of every child of Adam's fallen race by nature. There they were, crushed beneath the enemy's galling yoke, and having no power to deliver themselves. The mere mention of the word 'liberty' only caused the oppressor to bind his captives with a stronger fetter, and to lade them with a still more grievous burden. Consequently, it was absolutely necessary that deliverance should come from without." Nevertheless, Pharaoh will soon find out exactly "Who is the Lord!")*

3 And they *(Moses and Aaron)* said, The God of the Hebrews has met with us: let us go, we pray you, three days' journey into the desert, and sacrifice unto the LORD our God; lest He fall upon us with pestilence, or with the sword. *(This simple statement tells us, even as given to Moses by the Lord, that it is the Cross only which holds back the Judgment of God. In other words, the only thing standing between man and Hell is the Cross of Christ.)*

HARDENED HEART

4 And the king of Egypt said unto them, Why do you, Moses and Aaron, let the people from their works? get you unto your burdens. *(They will now find that the burdens are increased. As the Children of Israel, it seems that many do not too very much mind being slaves to Satan, until the burdens become so heavy that they cannot be borne. Invariably, that will happen!)*

5 And Pharaoh said, Behold, the people of the land now are many *(the Israelites)*, and you make them rest from their burdens.

6 And Pharaoh commanded the same day the taskmasters of the people, and their officers, saying,

7 You shall no more give the people straw to make brick, as heretofore: let them go and gather straw for themselves. *(Oftentimes, the setting to carry out the Will of God will result in Satan's anger, with opposition being increased.)*

8 And the tale *(number)* of the bricks, which they did make heretofore, you shall lay upon them; you shall not diminish ought thereof: for they be idle; therefore they cry, saying, Let us go and sacrifice to our God. *(At the mention of Sacrifice, Pharaoh increased the pressure and the workload, almost to a killing pace. When the Believer first begins to hear the Message of the Cross, he will find the opposition of Satan greatly increasing. This will be confusing at first, but the Believer should take heart. The enemy does this because he knows the Believer has now found the source of victory; therefore, he seeks to move the Believer's faith from the Cross to other things, by discouragement, etc.)*

9 Let there more work be laid upon the men, that they may labor therein, and let them not regard vain words. *(Pharaoh regarded the offering of "Sacrifices" as "vain words." Regrettably, much of the modern Church does the same, as it regards the Cross.)*

10 And the taskmasters of the people went out, and their officers, and they spoke to the people, saying, Thus saith Pharaoh, I will not give you straw.

11 Go ye, get you straw where you can find it: yet not ought of your work shall be diminished. *(Even though you have to get the straw yourselves, you must turn out just as much work as previously.)*

12 So the people were scattered abroad throughout all the land of Egypt to gather stubble instead of straw. *(It is good for a man*

to learn painfully the nature of sin's dominion, and his absolute helplessness in the grip of that monarch.)

13 And the taskmasters hasted them, saying, Fulfill your works, your daily tasks, as when there was straw. *(The first move of Israel toward deliverance plunged her into deeper misery so that the people would have preferred being left quiet in their slavery. This is oftentimes the spiritual experience of awakened sinners, or even awakened Christians to the Message of the Cross.)*

14 And the officers of the Children of Israel, which Pharaoh's taskmasters had set over them, were beaten, and demanded, Wherefore have you not fulfilled your task in making brick both yesterday and today, as heretofore? *(Satan wanted them to be willing to remain as slaves in Egypt. He almost succeeded!)*

15 Then the officers of the Children of Israel came and cried unto Pharaoh, saying, Why do you deal thus with your servants? *(Instead of crying unto the Lord, these leaders of the Israelites turned unto Pharaoh for relief. So often we as modern Believers follow suit. We appeal to man instead of God.)*

16 There is no straw given unto your servants, and they say to us, Make brick: and, behold, your servants are beaten; but the fault is in your own people. *(The natural man ever prefers to lean upon an arm of flesh than be supported by Him Who is invisible.)*

17 But he *(Pharaoh)* said, You are idle, you are idle: therefore you say, Let us go and do Sacrifice to the LORD. *(It is the "Sacrifice" which rankled Pharaoh, even though he would not have been aware as to what exactly it all meant. The Cross always rankles Satan.)*

18 Go therefore now, and work; for there shall no straw be given you, yet shall you deliver the tale *(number)* of bricks. *(We should learn that it's not Scriptural for us to make plans and then ask God to bless those plans. If God makes the plans, they are assured of blessing. So, leave Pharaoh alone, and depend exclusively on the Lord for all that is to be done.)*

MOSES

19 And the officers of the Children of Israel did see that they were in evil case, after it was said, You shall not minish *(reduce)* ought from your bricks of your daily task.

20 And they met Moses and Aaron, who stood in the way, as they came forth from Pharaoh:

21 And they said unto them, The LORD look upon you, and judge; because you have made our savour to be abhorred in the eyes of Pharaoh, and in the eyes of his servants, to put a sword in their hand to kill us. *(Moses was no doubt prepared for the rebuff which he had himself received from Pharaoh, for the Lord had plainly said that He would harden the king's heart. But, so far as the inspired record informs us, nothing has been told him that he would meet with discouragement and opposition from his own brethren. A real testing was this for God's servant, for it is far more trying to be criticized by our own Brethren, by those whom we are anxious to help, than it is to be persecuted by the world.)*

22 And Moses returned unto the LORD, and said, LORD, wherefore have You so evil entreated this people? why is it that You have sent me? *(The second sentence of this Verse should read: "Lord, wherefore have you suffered Your people to be so evil entreated?")*

23 For since I came to Pharaoh to speak in Your Name, he has done evil to this people; neither have You delivered Your people at all. *(The opposition of Pharaoh, and the unbelief and anger of Israel, were a double discouragement for Moses.)*

CHAPTER 6
(1619 B.C.)
THE COVENANT

THEN the LORD said unto Moses, Now shall you see what I will do to Pharaoh: for with a strong hand shall He *(the Lord)* let them go, and with a strong hand shall He *(the Lord)* drive them out of his *(Pharaoh's)* land. *(As stated here, the "Strong Hand" is not Pharaoh's, but God's. In essence, the Lord is saying, "By means of My Strong Hand [or "overpowering might"] laid upon him shall he be induced to let them go.)*

2 And God spoke unto Moses, and said unto him, I am the LORD *(concerning all of this, Pink says: "There is much for us to learn in this; we defeat ourselves by being occupied with the difficulties of the way; God has made known to us the triumphant outcome of good over evil and, instead of being harassed by the fiery darts which the Evil One now hurls against us, we ought to rest on the assuring Promise that 'The God of Peace shall bruise Satan under your feet shortly'" [Rom. 16:20]):*

3 And I appeared unto Abraham, unto

Isaac, and unto Jacob, by the name of God Almighty *("All-Sufficient One")*, but by My Name JEHOVAH was I not known to them. *(In fact, the Name "Jehovah" was used from the very beginning; however, the full meaning of it was not made known unto Israel until it was time to fulfill the Promises and Covenants with them as a nation.)*

4 And I have also established My Covenant with them *(instead of turning away from so unbelieving and petulant a people, God, in His love, pity, and Grace, encourages them and Moses by telling them Who He was, What He was, and What He would do)* to give them the land of Canaan, the land of their pilgrimage, wherein they were strangers. *(As we have stated, they must not look at the difficulties, and neither must we. We must instead look at the Promise.)*

5 And I have also heard the groaning of the Children of Israel, whom the Egyptians keep in bondage; and I have remembered My Covenant. *(Five times He declares that He is "Jehovah" [Vss. 2-3, 6-8]; and seven times He utters the great words, "I will," [Vss. 6-8]; and three times He declares, "I have," [Vss. 4-5].)*

6 Wherefore say unto the Children of Israel, I am the LORD, and I will bring you out from under the burdens of the Egyptians, and I will rid you out of their bondage, and I will redeem you with a stretched out arm, and with great judgments *(this is a perfect example of the Believer held in bondage; the Believer is being held captive by an intelligent force, namely Satan and his demon spirits; consequently, these evil powers do not yield to the Band-Aids of man; they will only yield to a superior force, and the only superior force in the universe is the Lord Jesus Christ; the Source of deliverance is always Christ, while the Means of deliverance is always the Cross [Col. 2:14-15]):*

7 And I will take you to Me for a people, and I will be to you a God: and you shall know that I am the LORD your God, which brings you out from under the burdens of the Egyptians. *(This was all done, in essence, by the Cross, of which the slain lamb and the blood applied to the doorposts were symbols [12:3, 7, 13].)*

8 And I will bring you in unto the land, concerning the which I did swear to give it to Abraham, to Isaac, and to Jacob; and I will give it you for an heritage: I am the LORD. *(If we can believe it, He can do it.)*

9 And Moses spoke so unto the Children of Israel: but they hearkened not unto Moses for anguish of spirit, and for cruel bondage. *(Hope deferred makes the heart sick. The Israelites, who had expected a speedy deliverance, and found themselves the more downtrodden for Moses' interference, were too much dispirited to be cheered even by the gracious Promises and Assurances which Moses was commissioned to give. The Samaritan version of this account says: "And they said to Moses, Let us alone, let us serve the Egyptians; for it is better for us to serve the Egyptians than die in a wilderness."*

Lest we think of the Israelites too harshly, we should look at ourselves. As evidenced here, the Promises of God do not mean a problem-free environment. The Lord allows the problems to teach us trust and obedience. But all too often we allow the problems to stop us from receiving God's best.)

10 And the LORD spoke unto Moses, saying,

11 Go in, speak unto Pharaoh king of Egypt, that he let the Children of Israel go out of his land. *(Moses is to continue to demand of Pharaoh that he let Israel go. And that's the same thing that we must do as Believers. Because the demon forces of darkness do not yield at the beginning does not mean they aren't going to yield. We are to stand our ground, keep believing that what Jesus did at the Cross is sufficient, which it most certainly is, and keep commanding the Evil One to go.)*

12 And Moses spoke before the LORD, saying, Behold, the Children of Israel have not hearkened unto me; how then shall Pharaoh hear me, who is of uncircumcised lips? *(Moses is speaking of his inability to speak properly. Concerning this, Matthew Henry says: "Though our infirmities ought to humble us, yet they ought not to discourage us from doing our very best in any service we have to do for God. His strength is made perfect in our weakness.")*

13 And the LORD spoke unto Moses and unto Aaron, and gave them a charge unto the Children of Israel, and unto Pharaoh king of Egypt, to bring the Children of Israel out of the land of Egypt. *(The Lord seemingly ignored the complaint of Moses, rather giving a "charge" to both Moses and Aaron. That "charge" is incumbent upon us presently, as well! We are to stand upon the Promises of God, and command Satan to leave that which God has promised to us. All of this is a perfect example to us.)*

GENEALOGIES

14 These be the heads of their fathers' houses: The sons of Reuben the firstborn of

Israel; Hanoch, and Pallu, Hezron, and Carmi: these be the families of Reuben.

15 And the sons of Simeon; Jemuel, and Jamin, and Ohad, and Jachin, and Zohar, and Shaul the son of a Canaanitish woman: these are the families of Simeon.

16 And these are the names of the sons of Levi according to their generations; Gershon, and Kohath, and Merari: and the years of the life of Levi were an hundred thirty and seven years.

17 The sons of Gershon; Libni, and Shimi, according to their families.

18 And the sons of Kohath; Amram, and Izhar, and Hebron, and Uzziel: and the years of the life of Kohath were an hundred thirty and three years.

19 And the sons of Merari; Mahali and Mushi: these are the families of Levi according to their generations.

20 And Amram took him Jochebed his father's sister to wife; and she bore him Aaron and Moses: and the years of the life of Amram were an hundred and thirty and seven years.

21 And the sons of Izhar; Korah, and Nepheg, and Zichri.

22 And the sons of Uzziel; Mishael, and Elzaphan, and Zithri.

23 And Aaron took him Elisheba, daughter of Amminadab, sister of Naashon, to wife; and she bore him Nadab, and Abihu, Eleazar, and Ithamar.

24 And the sons of Korah; Assir, and Elkanah, and Abiasaph: these are the families of the Korhites.

25 And Eleazar Aaron's son took him one of the daughters of Putiel to wife; and she bore him Phinehas: these are the heads of the fathers of the Levites according to their families. *(The Grace that gave the Promises of the First Chapter records the names of those whom Pharaoh declared to be his slaves.)*

26 These are that Aaron and Moses, to whom the LORD said, Bring out the Children of Israel from the land of Egypt according to their armies. *(God numbers those who belong to Himself, and He calls them "My people," though they still were in the power of the enemy [5:1].)*

27 These are they which spoke to Pharaoh king of Egypt, to bring out the Children of Israel from Egypt: these are that Moses and Aaron. *(To make this Grace more amazing, the three Tribes of Reuben, Simeon, and Levi are chosen as representing the whole nation.)*

28 And it came to pass on the day when the LORD spoke unto Moses in the land of Egypt,

29 That the LORD spoke unto Moses, saying, I am the LORD: speak thou unto Pharaoh king of Egypt all that I say unto you. *(Moses was not to add to, or subtract from, that which the Lord had said; and neither are we!)*

30 And Moses said before the LORD, Behold, I am of uncircumcised lips, and how shall Pharaoh hearken unto me? *(To these two, God would give the charge, and to these two would come the victory, despite the fact that Moses was a man of "uncircumcised lips.")*

CHAPTER 7
(1491 B.C.)
PHARAOH

AND the LORD said unto Moses, See, I have made you a god to Pharaoh: and Aaron your brother shall be your prophet. *(Moses having declared that he was of "uncircumcised lips," that is, that he was wanting in eloquence, Grace once more pitied his fears, and Aaron is appointed to be his prophet, i.e., "his spokesman.")*

2 You shall speak all that I command you *(the Word of God Alone holds the answer)*: and Aaron your brother shall speak unto Pharaoh, that he send the Children of Israel out of his land. *(The weakness of the instrument was fully manifested that it might the better be seen that the power was in Jehovah Alone, and of Jehovah acting not so much in response to Faith, as in Covenant faithfulness and in sovereign Grace.)*

3 And I will harden Pharaoh's heart *(the Lord hardened Pharaoh's heart, by providing the means for the monarch to do so; in fact, He does the same with all; some accept the Lord, while some rebel, even as did Pharaoh)*, and multiply My signs and My wonders in the land of Egypt. *(It is God's purpose that Israel shall be preeminent in the Earth; and, therefore, everyone who presumes to stand in the way of that preeminence must be set aside. Divine Grace must find its object; and everyone who would act as a barrier in the way of that Grace must be taken out of the way, whether it be Egypt, Babylon, or "the beast that was, is not, and yet is"; it matters not. Divine Power will clear the channel for Divine Grace to flow and eternal woe be to all who stand in the way. The Palestinians should read these words very carefully.)*

4 But Pharaoh shall not hearken unto you *(through foreknowledge, the Lord knew this)*, that I may lay My hand upon Egypt, and bring forth My armies, and My people the Children

of Israel, out of the land of Egypt by great judgments. *(The idea is, Pharaoh would not yield, would not give in, would not heed the voice of God, as given him through Moses and Aaron, so the Lord turns the tables on him, using his obstinacy to further the Glory of God.)*

5 And the Egyptians shall know that I am the LORD, when I stretch forth My hand upon Egypt, and bring out the Children of Israel from among them. *(He will allow Egypt to do her worst, to put forth her best, to use all the power that she possessed, to keep the Children of Israel as slaves, but, despite this power, the Lord will prevail.)*

6 And Moses and Aaron did as the LORD commanded them, so did they. *(That's all the Lord requires of us, as well!)*

7 And Moses was fourscore years old *(80 years old)*, and Aaron fourscore and three years old *(83 years old)*, when they spoke unto Pharaoh.

THE SERPENT

8 And the LORD spoke unto Moses and unto Aaron, saying *(Verses 8 and 9 portray the beginning of miracles, at least as it regards Egypt; each miracle was designed by God to embarrass and show the utter helplessness of Egypt's gods against the God of Israel),*

9 When Pharaoh shall speak unto you, saying, show a miracle for you: then you shall say unto Aaron, Take your rod, and cast it before Pharaoh, and it shall become a serpent. *(This is the first miracle, but yet it is not counted among the ten which would affect Egypt. The first miracle that would affect Egypt, which would be the first of the ten, would be the turning of all water to blood, including the mighty Nile River. The serpent is a type of Satan. The Lord was saying by this rod turning to a serpent that the kingdom of Egypt was Satanic.)*

10 And Moses and Aaron went in unto Pharaoh, and they did so as the LORD had commanded: and Aaron cast down his rod before Pharaoh, and before his servants, and it became a serpent. *(Let the Reader understand that this happened exactly as the Word of God said it happened. To deny that is to deny God!)*

11 Then Pharaoh also called the wise men and the sorcerers: now the magicians of Egypt, they also did in like manner with their enchantments. *(This proclaims the fact that these magicians did actually bring about this miracle, in which Satan himself helped them.)*

12 For they cast down every man his rod, and they became serpents: but Aaron's rod swallowed up their rods. *(The only power on Earth that is greater than the power of Satan is the Power of God, evidenced here by "Aaron's rod swallowing up their rod," i.e., "the serpent.")*

13 And He *(God)* hardened Pharaoh's heart, that he hearkened not unto them; as the LORD had said *(7:3-4)*.

14 And the LORD said unto Moses, Pharaoh's heart is hardened, he refuses to let the people go. *(Satan does not give in easily, as should be obvious.)*

15 Get thee unto Pharaoh in the morning; lo, he goes out unto the water; and you shall stand by the river's brink against he come; and the rod which was turned to a serpent shall you take in your hand. *(This would be the scene of the first miracle designed to affect Egypt.)*

16 And you shall say unto him, the LORD God of the Hebrews has sent me unto you, saying, Let My people go, that they may serve Me in the wilderness: and, behold, hitherto you would not hear.

17 Thus saith the LORD, In this you shall know that I am the LORD *(will see His miracle-working power)*: behold, I will smite with the rod that is in My hand upon the waters which are in the river, and they shall be turned to blood. *(The Nile is a large river, so this must have seemed totally preposterous to Pharaoh. The necessity of the shed blood of Christ seems preposterous to the world; nevertheless, it is true.)*

18 And the fish that is in the river shall die *(at least three species of the Nile fish were sacred — the "oxyrhineus," the "lepidotus," and the "phagrus"; in fact, the River Nile was worshipped by the Egyptians under various names and symbols; it was called the "father of life," and the "father of the gods"; thus, this miracle was a blow to the gods of Egypt)*, and the river shall stink; and the Egyptians shall loathe to drink of the water of the river.

BLOOD

19 And the LORD spoke unto Moses, Say unto Aaron, Take your rod, and stretch out your hand upon the waters of Egypt, upon their streams, upon their rivers, and upon their ponds, and upon all their pools of water, that they may become blood; and that there may be blood throughout all the land of Egypt, both in vessels of wood, and in vessels of stone. *(The Egyptians abhorred blood, and their horror*

must have been extreme when they saw that their sacred river, and all other water in their country, turned to blood. Again, let it be emphasized that this literally happened.)

20 And Moses and Aaron did so, as the LORD commanded; and he lifted up the rod, and smote the waters that were in the river, in the sight of Pharaoh, and in the sight of his servants; and all the waters that were in the river were turned to blood.

21 And the fish that was in the river died; and the river stank, and the Egyptians could not drink of the water of the river; and there was blood throughout all the land of Egypt.

22 And the magicians of Egypt did so with their enchantments: and Pharaoh's heart was hardened, neither did he hearken unto them; as the LORD had said. *(We find that the effect on Pharaoh's heart was to harden it. Such is the incurable hatred of the natural heart that Divine judgments harden instead of subdue it.)*

23 And Pharaoh turned and went into his house, neither did he set his heart to this also. *(He refused to yield!)*

24 And all the Egyptians dug round about the river for water to drink; for they could not drink of the water of the river.

25 And seven days were fulfilled *(the blood remained for that long)*, after that the LORD had smitten the river *(the number "seven" indicates that God will be fully able to accomplish what He has declared).*

CHAPTER 8
(1491 B.C.)
FROGS

A ND the LORD spoke unto Moses, Go unto Pharaoh, and say unto him, Thus saith the LORD, Let My people go, that they may serve Me. *(This Verse, as others, portrays the demand by God to Satan, "Let My people go, that they may serve Me." This is the only power that Satan recognizes. The Church flounders helplessly when it uses the "ways of Egypt" to attempt to deliver men from Egypt. It simply cannot be done. Only God can deliver.)*

2 And if you refuse to let them go, behold, I will smite all your borders with frogs *(this plague was directed against the frog-god that was an object of worship in Egypt; it was worshipped as a symbol of fertility):*

3 And the river shall bring forth frogs abundantly, which shall go up and come into your house, and into your bedchamber, and upon your bed, and into the house of your servants, and upon your people, and into your ovens, and into your kneadingtroughs *(due to the fact that the frog was a god to the Egyptians, they could not kill them, but yet the frogs drove them to the point of insanity; their animal-worship was thus proved absurd and ridiculous; the type of frog that invaded Egypt at that time has the scientific name of "Rana Mosaica," and resembles our toad, and is a disgusting object, which crawls rather than leaps, and croaks perpetually):*

4 And the frogs shall come up both on you, and upon your people, and upon all your servants *(the frogs coming up on Pharaoh proved the helplessness of his claim as a "god").*

5 And the LORD spoke unto Moses, Say unto Aaron, Stretch forth your hand with your rod over the streams, over the rivers, and over the ponds, and cause frogs to come up upon the land of Egypt.

6 And Aaron stretched out his hand over the waters of Egypt; and the frogs came up, and covered the land of Egypt *(over the entirety of the land, with the exception of Goshen, where the Children of Israel resided [Vs. 22]).*

7 And the magicians did so with their enchantments, and brought up frogs upon the land of Egypt *(considering that the land was literally inundated with frogs, I'm sure the people really appreciated the Egyptian magicians bringing even more frogs on the scene).*

8 Then Pharaoh called for Moses and Aaron, and said, Intreat the LORD, that He may take away the frogs from me, and from my people; and I will let the people go, that they may do sacrifice unto the LORD *(this request by Pharaoh was an admission that the Lord was greater than all the gods of Egypt; this is the first time that he had sent for Moses and Aaron).*

9 And Moses said unto Pharaoh, Glory over me *(of what do I have this honor?)*: when shall I intreat for you, and for your servants, and for your people, to destroy the frogs from you and your houses, that they may remain in the river only? *(Even though the Scripture is silent regarding this, it is more than likely possible that Pharaoh's magicians tried to take away the frogs, but could not succeed in doing so.)*

10 And he said, Tomorrow. *(What a stupid answer! They could have been taken away immediately. One more night with the frogs.)* And he said, Be it according to your word: that you may know that there is none like unto the LORD our God *(and Pharaoh was helpless to contest this claim).*

11 And the frogs shall depart from you, and from your houses, and from your servants, and from your people; they shall remain in the river only.

12 And Moses and Aaron went out from Pharaoh: and Moses cried unto the LORD because of the frogs which he had brought against Pharaoh.

13 And the LORD did according to the word of Moses; and the frogs died out of the houses, out of the villages, and out of the fields.

14 And they gathered them together upon heaps: and the land stank *(hundreds of millions of frogs died at once, and one can well imagine the stench that filled the land)*.

15 But when Pharaoh saw that there was respite, he hardened his heart, and hearkened not unto them; as the LORD had said. *(With the plague of frogs lifted, Pharaoh reneges on his promise to let the people go, which is indicative of most of humanity. God is quickly forgotten when the judgment lifts.)*

LICE

16 And the LORD said unto Moses, Say unto Aaron, Stretch out your rod, and smite the dust of the land, that it may become lice throughout all the land of Egypt *(the hardened heart of the Monarch was answered by a plague of lice)*.

17 And they did so; for Aaron stretched out his hand with his rod, and smote the dust of the earth, and it became lice in man, and in beast; all the dust of the land became lice throughout all the land of Egypt. *(When Aaron smote the ground, and its "dust" became lice, and the lice came upon the Egyptians, it was a graphic showing-forth of the awful fact that man by nature is under the curse of a thrice-Holy God.)*

18 And the magicians did so with their enchantments to bring forth lice, but they could not: so there were lice upon man, and upon beast. *(By slight of hand, it was possible, it seems, for Jannes and Jambres, the lead magicians of Egypt, to turn rods into serpents, water into blood, and to bring up frogs out of the river; however, it was impossible for them to turn dust into lice. The only other living creature that the Bible says is made out of dust is man. Thus, they were helpless.)*

19 Then the magicians said unto Pharaoh, This is the finger of God *(the term actually reads "of a God"; all that they meant to say was, "This is beyond the power of man — it is supernatural — some god must be helping the Israelites")*:

and Pharaoh's heart was hardened, and he hearkened not unto them; as the LORD had said. *(As we shall see, the stubbornness of Pharaoh only falls out to a portrayal of the Power of God. Either way, some way, God is glorified!)*

FLIES

20 And the LORD said unto Moses, Rise up early in the morning, and stand before Pharaoh; lo, he comes forth to the water; and say unto him, Thus saith the LORD, Let My people go, that they may serve Me.

21 Else, if you will not let My people go, behold, I will send swarms of flies upon you, and upon your servants, and upon your people, and into your houses: and the houses of the Egyptians shall be full of swarms of flies, and also the ground whereon they are. *(This miracle was designed to manifest the helplessness of Beelzebub, the god of flies, who was supposed to have power to prevent flies. The type of fly mentioned here is said to have been the "Blatta Orientalis." It was a kind of beetle, which inflicts very painful bites with their jaws. They also gnaw and destroy clothes, household furniture, leather, and articles of every kind, and either consume or render worthless all eatables. It is said they can even drive people out of their houses and, at the same time, devastate the fields.)*

22 And I will sever in that day the land of Goshen, in which My people dwell, that no swarms of flies shall be there; to the end you may know that I am the LORD in the midst of the Earth. *(The indication is that none of the plagues affected the Children of Israel, and neither were they meant to affect the Children of Israel.)*

23 And I will put a division between My people and your people: tomorrow shall this sign be. *(That "division" is still maintained by the Lord as it regards the world and His people. While the Lord may chastise His people, He never sends judgment, because such judgment was tendered at Calvary.)*

24 And the LORD did so; and there came a grievous swarm of flies into the house of Pharaoh, and into his servants' houses, and into all the land of Egypt: the land was corrupted by reason of the swarm of flies. *(This means all the crops were lost, plus all the grass eaten. In other words, Egypt was left denuded, with the exception of Goshen.)*

25 And Pharaoh called for Moses and for

Aaron, and said, Go ye, sacrifice to your God in the land. *(This is the first compromise made by Pharaoh: "Sacrifice to your God in the land." It is Satan's trick that the Believer be not only in the world, but, as well, of the world.)*

26 And Moses said, It is not meet *(possible)* to do so; for we shall sacrifice the abomination of the Egyptians to the LORD our God: lo, shall we sacrifice the abomination of the Egyptians before their eyes, and will they not stone us? *(Pharaoh knew this, as well!)*

27 We will go three days' journey into the wilderness, and sacrifice to the LORD our God, as He shall command us. *(Moses did not take the bait.)*

28 And Pharaoh said, I will let you go, that you may sacrifice to the LORD your God in the wilderness; only you shall not go very far away: intreat for me. *(This was the second compromise! Go, but not very far away. As Believers, we must never forget that one of the great themes of the Bible is "separation.")*

29 And Moses said, Behold, I go out from you, and I will intreat the LORD that the swarms of flies may depart from Pharaoh, from his servants, and from his people, tomorrow: but let not Pharaoh deal deceitfully any more in not letting the people go to sacrifice to the LORD.

30 And Moses went out from Pharaoh, and intreated the LORD *(asked the Lord to remove the flies).*

31 And the LORD did according to the word of Moses; and He removed the swarms of flies from Pharaoh, from his servants, and from his people; there remained not one. *(In fact, everything the Lord did in this situation, in one way or the other, constituted a miracle. There were billions of flies, buzzing, gnawing, and eating; and then the next moment there wasn't even "one.")*

32 And Pharaoh hardened his heart at this time also, neither would he let the people go.

CHAPTER 9
(1491 B.C.)
THE CATTLE

THEN the LORD said unto Moses, Go in unto Pharaoh, and tell him, Thus saith the LORD God of the Hebrews, Let My people go, that they may serve Me. *(This Chapter portrays the plagues of God deepening in their intensity. When they are concluded, mighty Egypt will be seriously affected. The Lord God of Heaven was*

not ashamed to call Himself "the Lord God of the Hebrews," individuals who were slaves. He calls them "My people.")

2 For if you refuse to let them go, and will hold them still *(a people still amid the defilements and abominations of Egypt could not have been a witness for the Holy One; nor can anyone now, while mixed up with the defilements of a corrupt, worldly religion, possibly be a bright and steady witness for a crucified and risen Christ),*

3 Behold, the hand of the LORD is upon your cattle which is in the field *(did not include those in stalls, etc.),* upon the horses, upon the asses, upon the camels, upon the oxen, and upon the sheep: there shall be a very grievous murrain *(their three popular gods were the bull, the cow, and the ram; "murrain" means a plague that kills).*

4 And the LORD shall sever between the cattle of Israel and the cattle of Egypt *(the word "cattle" stood for all type of domestic animals):* and there shall nothing die of all that is the Children's of Israel. *(All of this affords a striking demonstration of the absolute rulership of God. He completely controls every creature He has made. The herds of the Egyptians might be dying all around them, but the cattle of Israel were as secure as though there had been no epidemic at all.*

There is a spiritual meaning and application to all of this. And it is that meaning that we here, as Believers under the New Covenant, must derive.

This world and all its works will be destroyed — as completely as were the beasts of Egypt. By contrast, the sparing of the cattle of the Israelites intimates that the works of the new nature in the Believer will "abide" [I Cor. 3:14].)

5 And the LORD appointed a set time, saying, Tomorrow the LORD shall do this thing in the land. *(If it is to be noticed, the Lord gave time to Pharaoh to repent, in other words, to obey in allowing Israel to leave before He brought this other plague on the land. But all were to no avail.)*

6 And the LORD did that thing on the morrow, and all the cattle of Egypt died *(all domestic animals):* but of the cattle of the Children of Israel died not one.

7 And Pharaoh sent, and, behold, there was not one of the cattle of the Israelites dead. And the heart of Pharaoh was hardened, and he did not let the people go. *(The Cross of Christ has not only put away the Believer's sins, but also*

dissolved forever our connection with the world; and, on the ground of this, we are privileged to regard the world as a crucified thing, and to be regarded by it as a crucified one [Gal. 2:20]. Thus, it stands with the Believer and the world — it is crucified to him and he to it. This is the real, dignified position of every true Believer. And, to be sure, this position will ultimately guarantee release from all of Satan's bondages.)

BOILS

8 And the LORD said unto Moses and unto Aaron, Take to you handfuls of ashes of the furnace, and let Moses sprinkle it toward the Heaven in the sight of Pharaoh. (The "furnace" mentioned here was probably the furnace where human victims to the god Typhon were offered in sacrifice. These victims were offered in order to avert plagues.)

9 And it shall become small dust in all the land of Egypt, and shall be a boil breaking forth with blains upon man, and upon beast, throughout all the land of Egypt. (If the sacrifices of human victims among the Egyptians were offered to avert plagues, the ashes which Moses was ordered by the Lord to scatter instead of doing so brought a fresh plague, which proclaims the helplessness of these demon gods.)

10 And they took ashes of the furnace, and stood before Pharaoh; and Moses sprinkled it up toward Heaven; and it became a boil breaking forth with blains upon man, and upon beast. (This was the sixth plague, and was brought about without any notice. It was also, like the third, a plague which inflicted direct injury upon the person. As well, this plague proclaims the fact that the Lord can send sickness upon individuals, if He so desires. While all sickness and death are the result of the Fall, still, the Lord has total control of these things, as should be obvious.)

11 And the magicians could not stand before Moses because of the boils; for the boil was upon the magicians, and upon all the Egyptians. (The magicians made no attempt to exert their so-called magical powers, and for all the obvious reasons. The boils were upon Pharaoh as well. But, instead of it causing him to humble himself before God, it seemed to have the very opposite effect.)

12 And the Lord hardened the heart of Pharaoh, and he hearkened not unto them; as the LORD had spoken unto Moses. (Once again, the Lord provided the means for Pharaoh to harden his own heart. The Lord did not tamper with the will of the Monarch in all of this. In other words, Pharaoh was not forced by the Lord to take the position which he took. All of this was of his own volition.)

HAIL

13 And the LORD said unto Moses, Rise up early in the morning, and stand before Pharaoh, and say unto him, Thus saith the LORD God of the Hebrews, Let My people go, that they may serve Me. (In all of this, we learn that Satan does not let God's people go easily. In other words, when the Believer first begins to hear the Message of the Cross, and this great truth is made real to his heart, and he realizes through the Cross that he can be free from the dominion of sin, Satan always puts up quite a fight in order to discourage such a Believer from continuing on this course of victory. All of this concerning the Children of Israel and Pharaoh's obstinacy portray the example. But, as the example continues, if the Believer will persevere, total and complete victory will be his [Rom. 6:14; 8:1-2, 11].)

14 For I will at this time send all My plagues upon your heart, and upon your servants, and upon your people; that you may know that there is none like Me in all the Earth. (With Pharaoh failing to respond to Mercy and Grace, the Lord resorts to judgment, i.e., "plagues," and first of all for the purpose that Egypt, and all the other surrounding nations, might know that their gods, whatever they were, were nothing but fanciful objects and, in reality, there was only one God, i.e., "Jehovah.")

15 For now I will stretch out My hand, that I may smite you and your people with pestilence; and you shall be cut off from the Earth. (God will further show Pharaoh that He is the Supreme One over the elements, and that they, under His Will and Command, can be either instruments of blessing or destruction. Actually, this Verse proclaims Grace, for it gave Pharaoh warning.)

16 And in very deed for this cause have I raised you up, for to show in you My power; and that My name may be declared throughout all the Earth. (Up until now, Jehovah was known only to the descendants of Abraham. But now, and because of the obstinacy of Pharaoh, all the nations in that vicinity would learn Who Jehovah was, and eventually the entirety of the Earth, which is now the case.)

17 As yet you exalt yourself against My

people, that you will not let them go? (As stated, Satan does not give up easily; however, if the Believer will keep his Faith in Christ and the Cross, to be sure, ultimately victory will be his [I Jn. 5:4].)

18 Behold, tomorrow about this time I will cause it to rain a very grievous hail, such as has not been in Egypt since the foundation thereof even until now. (The Lord gives warning as to when the next plague was going to come — tomorrow. Once again, this is Grace.)

19 Send therefore now, and gather your cattle, and all that you have in the field; for upon every man and beast which shall be found in the field, and shall not be brought home, the hail shall come down upon them, and they shall die.

20 He who feared the Word of the LORD among the servants of Pharaoh made his servants and his cattle flee into the houses (those who believed the Word of the Lord, and feared it, would get under shelter; he who did not regard the Word of the Lord would ignore the shelter — but to their peril; it is the same presently; they who believe the Word give their hearts to Christ; they who do not, ignore that Word, and to their peril):

21 And he who regarded not the Word of the LORD left his servants and his cattle in the field. (It would seem strange, and considering the miracles of the recent past, that anyone in Egypt would still be in a state of unbelief; however, this Passage plainly tells us that such persons existed. It is the same presently!)

22 And the LORD said unto Moses, Stretch forth your hand toward Heaven, that there may be hail in all the land of Egypt, upon man, and upon beast, and upon every herb of the field, throughout the land of Egypt. (Whatever crops there were in Egypt at that time were totally and completely destroyed, along with all cattle and sheep which were left unattended.)

23 And Moses stretched forth his rod toward Heaven: and the LORD sent thunder and hail, and the fire ran along upon the ground; and the LORD rained hail upon the land of Egypt. (This "hail" was mingled with fire, such as Egypt, and no doubt the world, had never seen.)

24 So there was hail, and fire mingled with the hail, very grievous, such as there was none like it in all the land of Egypt since it became a nation. (As the "boils" were physical portrayals of the spiritual morality of unredeemed man, likewise, this judgment was expressive of the wrath of a Holy and sin-hating God.)

25 And the hail smote throughout all the land of Egypt all that was in the field, both man and beast; and the hail smote every herb of the field, and broke every tree of the field. (This plague of "thunder, hail, and fire" was directed against "Isis" and "Osiris," the gods of light, health, fertility, arts, and agriculture. Water, fire, earth, and air were all objects of Egyptian idolatry. God showed Pharaoh and his people that He was the Supreme One over these elements, and that, instead of helping the Egyptians, they, under God's Will and Command, were instruments of destruction.)

26 Only in the land of Goshen, where the Children of Israel were, was there no hail. (The only thing that stands between man and Hell-fire is the Cross of Christ.)

27 And Pharaoh sent, and called for Moses and Aaron, and said unto them, I have sinned this time: the LORD is righteous, and I and my people are wicked. (While the right words were said, it was an insincere repentance. He was only admitting what was obviously the truth. He didn't intend to change his ways. True Repentance is a turning from the wrong direction to the right direction. And Repentance cannot be true unless Faith is anchored in Christ and the Cross, of which the Sacrifices which Moses demanded were a symbol.)

28 Intreat the LORD (for it is enough) that there be no more mighty thunderings and hail; and I will let you go, and you shall stay no longer. (His words were hollow, and because his repentance was insincere.)

29 And Moses said unto him, As soon as I am gone out of the city, I will spread abroad my hands unto the LORD; and the thunder shall cease, neither shall there be any more hail; that you may know how that the Earth is the LORD's. (As Pharaoh would not admit that the Earth is the Lord's, neither will modern man.)

30 But as for you and your servants, I know that you will not yet fear the LORD God. (Moses knew that the repentance of Pharaoh was surface only.)

31 And the flax and the barley was smitten: for the barley was in the ear, and the flax was bolled (the "flax" and the "barley" harvests were lost, which no doubt caused great hardship in Egypt).

32 But the wheat and the rie were not smitten: for they were not grown up (were not yet planted; the previous two Verses tell us that the entirety of the time frame of the ten plagues probably was about three to four months in duration).

33 And Moses went out of the city from Pharaoh, and spread abroad his hands unto the LORD: and the thunders and hail ceased, and the rain was not poured upon the Earth. *(Moses and Aaron evidently had some type of shelter over their heads to protect them as they left the palace, or else the Lord withheld the hail and rain from them wherever they went, which very well could have been the case.)*

34 And when Pharaoh saw that the rain and the hail and the thunders were ceased, he sinned yet more, and hardened his heart, he and his servants. *(Such is the state of many. They repent at the threat of judgment or its actual advent, but when it is lifted, they renege on their promise.)*

35 And the heart of the Pharaoh was hardened, neither would he let the Children of Israel go; as the LORD had spoken by Moses. *(A few days ago, I was praying for particular individuals, asking the Lord to warn them. He spoke to my heart, telling me, "I am warning them constantly, and in many and varied ways, but they will not see or listen.")*

CHAPTER 10
(1491 B.C.)
LOCUSTS

AND the LORD said unto Moses, Go in unto Pharaoh: for I have hardened his heart, and the heart of his servants, that I might show these My signs before him *(God used the stubbornness of the Monarch to reveal His Power; as shown here in Pharaoh, if a person wills resistance to God, the Lord Wills the ability to resist even more; if they will Righteousness, God Wills more Righteousness [Mat. 5:6])*:

2 And that you may tell in the ears of your son, and of your son's son, what things I have wrought in Egypt, and My signs which I have done among them; that you may know how that I am the LORD. *(God would do such great things in this situation that even the Holy Spirit would constantly speak of this particular time in the centuries that followed. The Psalms proclaimed this fact [Ps. 78; 105; 106; 68:6-7; 77:14-20; 81:5-6; 124:1-3; 135:8-9; 136:10-15].)*

3 And Moses and Aaron came in unto Pharaoh, and said unto him, Thus saith the LORD God of the Hebrews, How long will you refuse to humble yourself before Me? let My people go, that they may serve Me. *(This was the seventh and final time that God would make this demand. This Verse also presents the great question that God ever asks the human family, "How long will you refuse to humble yourself before Me?")*

4 Else, if you refuse to let My people go, behold, tomorrow will I bring the locusts into your coast *(the god Serapis was believed by the Egyptians to protect them from the locusts; this eighth plague struck at that belief)*:

5 And they shall cover the face of the Earth, that one cannot be able to see the Earth: and they shall eat the residue of that which is escaped, which remains unto you from the hail, and shall eat every tree which grows for you out of the field *(in other words, Egypt, for all practical purposes, would be completely destroyed)*:

6 And they shall fill your houses, and the houses of all your servants, and the houses of all the Egyptians; which neither your fathers, nor your fathers' fathers have seen, since the day that they were upon the Earth unto this day. And he *(Moses)* turned himself, and went out from Pharaoh *(in other words, Moses didn't even wait for a response from Pharaoh)*.

7 And Pharaoh's servants said unto him, How long shall this man be a snare unto us? let the men go, that they may serve the LORD their God: do you not know that Egypt is destroyed? *(This Verse proclaims, for the first time, that Pharaoh's officers intervened and requested Pharaoh to yield.)*

8 And Moses and Aaron were brought again unto Pharaoh: and he said unto them, Go, serve the LORD your God: but who are they who shall go? *(There was no reason for this question, considering that the demand had been very clear in the past; everyone who pertained to Israel would go.)*

9 And Moses said, We will go with our young and with our old, with our sons and with our daughters, with our flocks and with our herds will we go; for we must hold a feast unto the LORD. *(Every Believer should ask for, and claim, the Salvation of the entirety of his family, excluding none.)*

10 And he *(Pharaoh)* said unto the them, Let the LORD be so with you, as I will let you go, and your little ones: look to it; for evil is before you. *(In essence, Pharaoh, who concludes himself to be a god, pits himself against Jehovah. What a foolish move it would prove to be! The "evil" was not before Moses and Aaron, but before Pharaoh.)*

11 Not so: go now you who are men, and serve the LORD *(the third compromise is proposed by Pharaoh; he will let the men go to offer Sacrifice unto the Lord, but not the wives and

children); for that you did desire. And they were driven out from Pharaoh's presence *(dismissed with hostility).*

12 And the LORD said unto Moses, Stretch out your hand over the land of Egypt for the locusts, that they may come up upon the land of Egypt, and eat every herb of the land, even all that the hail has left *(Mercy rejected, always and without exception, brings Judgment).*

13 And Moses stretched forth his rod over the land of Egypt, and the LORD brought an east wind upon the land all that day, and all that night; and when it was morning, the east wind brought the locusts *(the wind blowing from the east all that day and all that night should have been a warning to Pharaoh; however, and as stated, he who wills resistance to God has resistance willed to him by God).*

14 And the locusts went up over all the land of Egypt, and rested in all the coasts of Egypt: very grievous were they; before them there were no such locusts as they, neither after them shall be such. *(When the locusts had finished, there would not be a green thing left in Egypt. Such portrays the terrible devastation of sin.)*

15 For they covered the face of the whole Earth, so that the land was darkened; and they did eat every herb of the land, and all the fruit of the trees which the hail had left: and there remained not any green thing in the trees, or in the herbs of the field, through all the land of Egypt. *(If the officers of Pharaoh thought that Egypt was destroyed [Vs. 7], they now know that it is completely destroyed.)*

16 Then Pharaoh called for Moses and Aaron in haste; and he said, I have sinned against the LORD your God, and against you. *(How many hours or days the locusts plagued Egypt before Pharaoh sent for Moses and Aaron, we aren't told; however, it was probably only a few hours when Moses and Aaron were hastily called back. All sin, either directly or indirectly, is directed against God. It is an affront to His Holiness, His Righteousness, and to His very Being. It is the ruination of all that is good!)*

17 Now therefore forgive, I pray you, my sin only this once, and intreat the LORD your God, that He may take away from me this death only. *(The Monarch said the right words; however, once again, his confession was "a shallow-mouthed confession." The only answer for sin is the Cross of Christ.)*

18 And he *(Moses)* went out from Pharaoh, and intreated *(requested of)* the LORD.

19 And the LORD turned a mighty strong west wind, which took away the locusts, and cast them into the Red Sea; there remained not one locust in all the coasts of Egypt. *(As the Lord removed all the locusts, which were destroying Egypt, likewise, He can remove all sin and its effects. The requirement is that we fully trust Christ and what He has done for us at the Cross [Heb. 10:12].)*

20 But the LORD hardened Pharaoh's heart, so that he would not let the Children of Israel go. *(Again we state, he who wills resistance against the Lord is willed more resistance by the Lord.)*

DARKNESS

21 And the LORD said unto Moses, Stretch out your hand toward Heaven, that there may be darkness over the land of Egypt, even darkness which may be felt. *(This is the ninth plague, and it robs the Egyptians of their supreme god, the Sun, and proved Jehovah Alone to be God. The Sun was worshipped by the Egyptians under the title of "Ra." In fact, the name "Ra" came conspicuously forward in the title of the kings, Pharaoh, or rather "Phra," meaning "the Sun," which meant that Pharaoh was god. What a pitiful god he was!)*

22 And Moses stretched forth his hand toward Heaven, and there was a thick darkness in all the land of Egypt three days *(Moses stretching his hands toward Heaven signified that God was in complete and full charge, and not man; whatever man may say or do, Heaven will always have the final word):*

23 They saw not one another, neither rose any from his place for three days: but all the Children of Israel had light in their dwellings. *(In Goshen, there was light. This was literal; however, it was, as well, meant by the Holy Spirit to symbolize the spiritual light which the Children of Israel did have, and which the Egyptians did not have.)*

24 And Pharaoh called unto Moses, and said, Go ye, serve the LORD; only let your flocks and your herds be stayed: let your little ones also go with you. *(This was the fourth proposal by Pharaoh of compromise: A. "Go ye, sacrifice to your God in the land" — 8:25; B. "Sacrifice to the Lord your God in the wilderness; only you shall not go very far away" — 8:28; C. "Go now you who are men [men only], and serve the Lord" — 10:11; and, D. "Go ye, serve the Lord; only let your flocks and your herds be stayed" — 10:24.)*

25 And Moses said, You must give us also sacrifices and burnt offerings, that we may sacrifice unto the LORD our God. *(Moses turns down flat this offer by Pharaoh, and further demands that Pharaoh provide them with sheep for the Burnt Offerings.)*

26 Our cattle also shall go with us; there shall not an hoof be left behind *(the Believer should not allow Satan to have any part of one's possessions)*; for thereof must we take to serve the LORD our God; and we know not with what we must serve the LORD, until we come thither. *(The statement of this Verse points to a lesson true at all times. The second step in the spiritual life is not revealed until the first is taken [Jn. 7:17]. "Egypt" must be left, that is the first step, before the nature of spiritual worship, which is the second step, can be learned.)*

27 But the LORD hardened Pharaoh's heart, and he would not let them go.

28 And Pharaoh said unto him, Get you from me, take heed to yourself, see my face no more; for in that day you see my face you shall die. *(The reply of Pharaoh indicates violent anger.)*

29 And Moses said, You have spoken well, I will see your face again no more. *(It is generally believed that Moses did not leave out of the presence of Pharaoh with these particular words, but continued to address the Monarch for some little time, actually his parting words being those which are given in Verses 4 through 8 of the next Chapter.)*

CHAPTER 11
(1491 B.C.)
VALUABLES

AND the LORD said unto Moses, Yet will I bring one plague more upon Pharaoh, and upon Egypt *(this tenth and last plague would touch the dearest of all in Egypt, the firstborn, and that from Pharaoh down; sin touches all!)*; afterwards he will let you go hence: when he shall let you go, he shall surely thrust you out hence altogether. *(Egypt, by now, was wreckage. What had formerly been the most powerful nation on the face of the Earth was now virtually destroyed. Anyone or anything who and which sets themselves against God, no matter how strong, rich, or powerful, will face certain doom. As well, regarding the Believer who totally places his Faith and trust in Christ and what Christ has done at the Cross, to be sure, Satan will let them go. He has no choice [Rom. 6:14].)*

2 Speak now in the ears of the people, and let every man borrow *(ask)* of his neighbour, and every woman of her neighbour, jewels of silver and jewels of gold. *(The Hebrew word "Shaal," translated "borrow," actually should have been translated "ask." "Borrow" carries the connotation that the object obtained will be returned; however, Israel wasn't coming back into Egypt, so there was no thought of returning these items, and the Egyptians understood that as well! By the silver and gold being given to the Israelites in copious amounts, the Lord was paying Israel for their years of servitude; therefore, they left out of Egypt rich.)*

3 And the LORD gave the people favour in the sight of the Egyptians. Moreover the man Moses was very great in the land of Egypt, in the sight of Pharaoh's servants, and in the sight of the people. *(At the beginning, Moses was disdained; however, by the Power of God, the situation has radically changed. In the coming Kingdom Age, the world will look at all Believers in the same light that Egypt then looked at Moses.)*

DEATH

4 And Moses said, Thus saith the LORD *(believed to have been spoken at the conclusion of the plague of darkness)*, About midnight will I go out into the midst of Egypt *(Moses gives Pharaoh the final word from the Lord and, to be sure, it is a chilling assessment; truly it was "midnight" for Egypt; the day of Grace was over, and the final judgment is about to begin)*:

5 And all the firstborn in the land of Egypt shall die, from the firstborn of Pharaoh who sits upon his throne, even unto the firstborn of the maidservant who is behind the mill: and all the firstborn of beasts. *(The death of all the "firstborn" in Egypt constituted a severe blow. The monarchy was hereditary, and the oldest son was known as the "hereditary Crowned Prince." Estates descended to the oldest son and, in many cases, high dignities also. As well, it was believed by the Egyptians that their "afterlife" [life after death] continued through the firstborn. In other words, if the firstborn was lost, there was no afterlife. So, this "plague" was the greatest of all and, as well, the most far-reaching.)*

6 And there shall be a great cry throughout all the land of Egypt, such as there was none like it, nor shall be like it any more. *(The "cry" that was registered in Egypt must not be blamed*

on a loving and compassionate God, but on the stubbornness of Pharaoh and, as well, of a hard-hearted people. Men tend to blame God; however, if this situation is studied carefully, we find that God dealt with Egypt through Grace upon Grace, but they would not yield. In such cases, even the "judgment of God" must be concluded as Grace.)

7 But against any of the Children of Israel shall not a dog move his tongue, against man or beast: that you may know how that the LORD does put a difference between the Egyptians and Israel. *(As is obvious here, there is a great "difference" between the Redeemed and the unredeemed. The former are protected by the Lord, while the latter enjoy no such protection.)*

8 And all these your servants *(Pharaoh's servants)* shall come down unto me *(to Moses)*, and bow down themselves unto me, saying. Get thee out, and all the people who follow you *(get out of Egypt)*: and after that I will go out. And he *(Moses)* went out from Pharaoh in a great anger. *(This Passage portrays Moses delivering the last message to Pharaoh. It is straight and to the point. Moses went out from the presence of Pharaoh with great anger, because he knew that all of this was so unnecessary. Hundreds of thousands would die, and the truth is, not one single person needed to die. Moses was angry at the stubbornness of the Monarch, who had watched Egypt, little by little, as it was destroyed, but who still refused to acquiesce to the demands of Almighty God.)*

9 And the LORD said unto Moses. Pharaoh shall not hearken unto you: that My wonders may be multiplied in the land of Egypt. *(The Lord would use the stubbornness of the Monarch to glorify the Power of God.)*

10 And Moses and Aaron did all these wonders before Pharaoh: and the LORD hardened Pharaoh's heart, so that he would not let the Children of Israel go out of his land. *(But the hour would shortly come when Pharaoh would have no choice; as well, Satan has no choice but to let go of the Believer who has placed his Faith exclusively in Christ and the Cross [Rom. 6:3-14].)*

CHAPTER 12
(1491 B.C.)
THE PASSOVER

AND the LORD spoke unto Moses and Aaron in the land of Egypt saying *(this Chapter is a perfect picture of Christ, the True Pascal Lamb)*,

2 This month shall be unto you the beginning of months: it shall be the first month of the year to you. *(The person doesn't really begin to live until he comes to Christ; as well, the Believer doesn't really begin to enjoy the "more abundant life" afforded him by Christ until he learns God's Prescribed Order of Victory, which is Faith in Christ and the Cross exclusively, which then gives the Holy Spirit latitude to work, thereby bringing about the graces of the Fruit of the Spirit [Rom. 8:1-2, 11; Gal. 5:16-25]. All Believers have "more abundant life" [Jn. 10:10], but all Believers are not enjoying more abundant life and, in fact, cannot until they learn God's Prescribed Order of Victory, which is the Cross [I Cor. 1:17-18, 21, 23; 2:2; Gal. 6:14; Col. 2:14-15].)*

3 Speak ye unto all the congregation of Israel, saying *(Another great lesson learned here is the fact that neither Moses nor Aaron introduced any legislation of their own, either at this time or later. The whole system, spiritual, political, and ecclesiastical, was received by Divine Revelation, commanded by God, and merely established by the agency of the two brothers. This proclaims the fact that Salvation is all of God and none of man. This problem presents itself when man attempts to insert his means and ways into that which God has devised, which, in fact, the modern Church is now doing)*, In the tenth day of this month they shall take to them every man a lamb, according to the house of their fathers, a lamb for an house: *(In the Fourth Chapter of Genesis, it is a lamb for each person. Now it is a lamb for each house. Upon the giving of the Law, it would be a lamb for the entirety of the nation. But when Jesus came, He would be the Lamb for the entirety of the world [Jn. 1:29]. The offering up of the Lamb in Sacrifice was a Type of Christ, and what He would do at the Cross, all on our behalf. The lamb represented innocence and gentleness. The Prophets represented the tender compassion of God for His people under the figure of the Shepherd and the Lamb [Isa. 40:11], and ultimately the intention of God for His people used the lamb as an important symbol; therefore, the Lamb was a worthy symbol of our Saviour, Who, in innocence, patiently endured suffering as our Substitute [I Pet. 1:19].)*

4 And if the household be too little for the lamb, let him and his neighbour next unto his house take it according to the number of the souls: every man according to his eating shall make your count for the lamb. *(Every person*

had to partake of the Passover. This was mandatory. Even though the lamb represented the entire
house, it had to be partaken by each and every
individual in that house. It is the same as it
regards Salvation, which is always very personal.)

5 Your lamb shall be without blemish
(Christ was without blemish, Who the lamb represented, "holy, harmless, undefiled" — a "lamb
without spot" [I Pet. 1:19]), a male of the first
year (meant to portray the virile manhood of
Christ; in other words, He didn't die in the throes
of old age, but rather in the prime of manhood): you shall take it out from the sheep, or
from the goats (the "goats" then represented
were different from our goats presently; then
they were very similar to the sheep, actually, with
their long flowing mane, even more beautiful
than the sheep):

6 And you shall keep it up until the fourteenth day of the same month (they were to
select the animal on the tenth day, and then kill
it on the fourteenth day [Vs. 3]; it was to be
minutely inspected during these four days, that
no trace of illness would be observed; representing Christ, it had to be perfect): and the whole
assembly of the congregation of Israel shall
kill it in the evening. (The actual Hebrew says,
"between the two evenings," which was about 3
p.m. This was the exact time that Jesus died on
the Cross of Calvary [Mat. 27:46].)

7 And they shall take of the blood (which
represented the shed Blood of the Lord Jesus
Christ), and strike it on the two side posts and
on the upper door post of the houses, wherein
they shall eat it (eat the Passover; in I Corinthians
5:7-8, we have the Divine Authority for our regarding the contents of Exodus, Chapter 12, as
typical of what our Blessed Saviour did on the
Cross; at the deliverance of the Children of Israel from Egypt, the blood, which represented
the shed Blood of Christ, was to be put on the
side posts and the upper posts of the house; later,
it would be applied to the Mercy Seat on the
Great Day of Atonement; now, by Faith, it is
applied to our hearts [Jn. 3:16; Eph. 2:13-18]).

8 And they shall eat the flesh in that night
(in essence, Jesus was referring to this in John
6:53-55; of course, He wasn't speaking of His
flesh literally being eaten, but was speaking
rather of our Faith in Him and what He would
do for us at the Cross; our Faith must be in the
entirety of His Finished Work), roast with fire
(this spoke of the Judgment of God that would
come upon Him as the Sin-Bearer, which was
death, instead of us), and unleavened bread

(this typified the Perfection of Christ; He was
Holy, harmless, and undefiled [Heb. 7:26], of
which the lack of leaven was a Type); and with
bitter herbs they shall eat it (the "bitter herbs"
were to remind the Children of Israel of the slavery which they had experienced in Egypt [Ex.
1:14]; as well, the Cross ever reminds us presently of that from which we were redeemed, abject slavery to Satan).

9 Eat not of it raw, nor sodden at all with
water (this speaks of accepting Christ, but without the Cross, which God cannot condone), but
roast with fire (speaks of the Cross and the price
paid there): his head with his legs, and with
the purtenance thereof. (The purtenance pertained to the intestines, which were removed and
washed, and then placed back in the animal and,
as obvious here, to be eaten when the lamb was
consumed. This speaks of partaking of all of the
Cross. Sin goes to the very vitals; therefore, for
sin to be properly addressed, and in every capacity, everything that Christ did at the Cross must
be accepted, and without fail.)

10 And you shall let nothing of it remain
until the morning (all of it must be consumed,
referring to the fact that we must accept all of
Christ, or else we will not have any of Christ;
untold millions attempt to accept Christ as a
good man, a great example, even a miracle worker,
but they care not for the Cross; if Christ is to be
had at all, He can only be had by and through
the Cross; otherwise, we have "another Jesus"
[II Cor. 11:4]); and that which remains of it
until the morning you shall burn with fire.
(This tells us that Christ cannot be received in
stages. He can only be received in totality. Burning the remainder "with fire" once again points
to the Cross. We must always remember, Christ
is the Source, while the Cross is the Means.)

11 And thus shall you eat it: with your loins
girded, your shoes on your feet, and your staff
in your hand (proclaims the fact that they were
leaving Egypt; after the Law was given, and Israel was safely ensconced in the Promised Land,
they were to eat the Passover resting, and for all
the obvious reasons): and you shall eat it in
haste (the same admonition, however, should
hold true for the modern Believer, in that we
should be eagerly awaiting the moment when
the Trump of God shall sound and, thereby, we
will be raptured away [I Thess. 4:13-18]): it is
the LORD's Passover. (Concerning this, Pink
says: "The Death of Christ glorified God if never
a single sinner had been saved by the virtue of
it. The more we study the teaching of Scripture

on this subject, and the more we lay hold by simple Faith of what the Cross meant to God, the more stable will be our peace, and the deeper our joy and praise." The Passover was ever a Type of the Cross. In I Corinthians 5:7, we read: "Christ our Passover." He is now "our" Passover, because He was first the "LORD's Passover.")

12 For I will pass through the land of Egypt this night, and will smite all the firstborn in the land of Egypt, both man and beast: and against all the gods of Egypt I will execute judgment: I am the LORD. *(The words "pass through" could be translated "go through," since the word used is entirely unconnected with the "Passover." According to Exodus 12:23, the Lord did not personally go through the land of Egypt that particular night, but rather that He used an Angel. The "beasts" were included, because animal worship was an important part of the religion of the Egyptians. So, the Lord directed His judgment against every facet of Egyptian life and living.)*

13 And the blood shall be to you for a token upon the houses where you are *(the blood applied to the door posts meant that their Faith and trust were in the Pascal Lamb; the blood then applied was only a "token," meaning that it was then but a symbol of One Who was to come, Who would redeem mankind by the shedding of His Life's Blood)*: and when I see the blood, I will pass over you *(this is, without a doubt, one of the single most important Scriptures in the entirety of the Word of God; the lamb had taken the fatal blow; and because it had taken the blow, those in the house would be spared; it was not a question of personal worthiness, self had nothing whatever to do in the matter; it was a matter of faith; all under the cover of the blood were safe, just as all presently under the cover of the Blood are safe; this means that they were not merely in a savable state, but rather that they were "saved"; as well, they were not partly saved and partly exposed to judgment, they were wholly saved, and because there is no such thing as partial Justification; the Lord didn't say, "When I see you," or, "When I see your good works," etc., but, "When I see the blood"; this speaks of Christ and what He would do at the Cross in order that we might be saved, which pertained to Him giving Himself in Sacrifice, which necessitated the shedding of His Precious Blood [I Pet. 1:18-19])*, and the plague shall not be upon you to destroy you, when I smite the land of Egypt. *(Salvation from the "plague" of Judgment is afforded only by the shed Blood of the Lamb, and Faith in that shed Blood.)*

14 And this day shall be unto you for a memorial; and you shall keep it a feast to the LORD throughout your generations: you shall keep it a feast by an ordinance for ever. *(The Passover is continued in the Lord's Supper [I Cor. 5:7-8]. In this way, the Passover may be regarded as still continuing unto Christianity, and is intended to continue, at least throughout the Kingdom Age, which is yet to come. The Passover per se is not continued, simply because it represented the Type, which was carried out through the offering of clean animals. Now that Christ has come and fulfilled the Type, it would not be proper to eat the Passover as it once was celebrated, and because all that it symbolized or represented was fulfilled in Christ.)*

15 Seven days shall you eat unleavened bread *(the Feast of "Unleavened Bread" was to be kept in conjunction with the Passover Feast; the "Unleavened Bread" symbolized the Perfection of Christ; the number "seven" symbolized His Perfection in totality; in other words, He was not Perfect just some of the time, but was Perfect all of the time)*: even the first day you shall put away leaven out of your houses: for whosoever eats leavened bread from the first day until the seventh day, that soul shall be cut off from Israel *(would be eternally lost; sin destroys and destroys completely! the entire idea of the Cross was to atone for all sin and, as well, to make it possible for the Believer to live a life free from the domination of sin, which can only be done by one ever making the Cross the object of one's Faith, which then gives the Holy Spirit latitude to work in one's life; otherwise, it cannot be done [Rom. 6:3-14; 8:1-2, 11; Gal. 6:14])*.

16 And in the first day there shall be an holy convocation *(all of this was "holy" unto the Lord, and what it typified, which speaks of what Christ did at the Cross, had better be holy to us, as well)*, and in the seventh day there shall be an holy convocation to you *(the "first day" and the "seventh day" indicated that the entirety of this convocation was "holy")*: no manner of work shall be done in them *(signifying that it is "not of works, lest any man should boast" [Eph. 2:8-9])*, save that which every man must eat, that only may be done of you *(the only "works" that God will recognize is the Work of Christ at the Cross, and our Faith in that Finished Work)*.

17 And you shall observe the Feast of Unleavened Bread; for in this selfsame day have I brought your armies out of the land of Egypt:

therefore shall you observe this day in your generations by an ordinance for ever. *(The Cross is referred to as "The Everlasting Covenant" [Heb. 13:20].)*

18 In the first month, on the fourteenth day of the month at evening, you shall eat unleavened bread, until the one and twentieth day of the month at evening. *(The phrase "in the first month," as it regards this Verse, refers to the fact that Christ and His Cross are to be first and foremost. In fact, the Cross is not within itself a Doctrine, but rather the Foundation of all Doctrine [I Pet. 1:18-19].)*

19 Seven days shall there be no leaven found in your houses: for whosoever eats that which is leavened, even that soul shall be cut off from the congregation of Israel, whether he be a stranger, or born in the land. *(The absence of leaven proclaims the fact that what Jesus would do would make it possible for us to live free of the domination of sin. As well, "Jesus Christ and Him Crucified" is the answer for the entirety of the world, and the only answer!)*

20 You shall eat nothing leavened *(meaning that we are to have victory over all sin)*; in all your habitations shall you eat unleavened bread *(while the Bible doesn't teach sinless perfection, it definitely does teach that sin is not to have dominion over us [Rom. 6:14])*.

21 Then Moses called for all the Elders of Israel, and said unto them, Draw out and take you a lamb according to your families, and kill the Passover. *(The "Elders" of Israel were to take the lead, and the people were to follow. If Preachers will presently "preach the Cross," most of the people will follow. Concerning the Passover, Pink says: "The institution and ritual of the Passover supply us with one of the most striking and blessed foreshadowments of the Crosswork of Christ to be found anywhere in the Old Testament. Its importance may be gathered from the frequency which the title of 'Lamb' is afterwards applied to the Saviour, a title which looks back to what is before us in Exodus 12" [Jn. 1:29; I Pet. 1:19].)*

22 And you shall take a bunch of hyssop *(the "hyssop" was not connected with the "Lamb," but with the application of its blood; it speaks, then, not of Christ, but of the sinner's appropriation of the Sacrifice of Christ; "hyssop" was a type of grass which grew in crevices between the rocks)*, and dip it in the blood that is in the bason, and strike the lintel and the two side posts with the blood that is in the bason *(in fact, the blood applied to the header [lintel] and*

two side posts formed a perfect cross; we are to never regard the Cross of Christ as a mere circumstance in the Life of Christ referring to His sin-bearing; it was the grand and only scene of sin-bearing; He did not bear our sins anywhere else; He did not bear them in the manger, nor in the wilderness, nor in the Garden, but "only on the Tree" [I Pet. 2:24]); and none of you shall go out at the door of his house until the morning. *(The death Angel was to come through at night and, beyond the protection of the Blood of the Lamb, there was no assurance of safety. In fact, there was no safety outside of this application, just as there is no safety presently outside of this application.)*

23 For the LORD will pass through to smite the Egyptians; and when He sees the blood upon the lintel, and on the two side posts, the LORD will pass over the door, and will not suffer the destroyer to come in unto your houses to smite you. *(The word "destroyer" implies the fact that the Lord sent an Angel to carry out this task. The only protection from judgment is the Cross of Christ.)*

24 And you shall observe this thing for an ordinance to you and to your sons for ever. *(Some three times the Lord ordered Israel to "keep the Feast of the Passover forever" [Ex. 12:14, 17, 24], and implied it in Exodus 13:10. In essence, this tells us that the Work of Christ on the Cross was, and is, a Finished Work, which means that it will never have to be repeated, and there will never have to be anything added.)*

25 And it shall come to pass, when you be come to the land which the LORD will give you, according as He has promised, that you shall keep this service. *(Every "Promise" of God is based, without exception, on the great Sacrifice of Christ.)*

26 And it shall come to pass, when your children shall say unto you, What mean you by this service? *(In this Passage, we are plainly told that it is our responsibility to properly relate and explain the great Sacrifice of Christ to our children. This we must not fail to do.)*

27 That you shall say, It is the sacrifice of the LORD's Passover, who passed over the houses of the Children of Israel in Egypt, when He smote the Egyptians, and delivered our houses. *(The application of the Blood spelled Salvation for the Children of Israel, but destruction for the Egyptians. Spiritually speaking, it is no less presently!)* And the people bowed the head and worshipped. *(Without a proper understanding of the Cross, true Worship of God cannot be*

properly enjoined.)

28 And the Children of Israel went away, and did as the LORD had commanded Moses and Aaron, so did they. *(They went to prepare the Passover, and no doubt paid careful attention to that preparation. Their very lives and eternal souls depended on it.)*

DEATH OF THE FIRSTBORN

29 And it came to pass, that at midnight the LORD smote all the firstborn in the land of Egypt, from the firstborn of Pharaoh who sat on his throne unto the firstborn of the captive that was in the dungeon; and all the firstborn of cattle. *(The blame for all the deaths of the firstborn in Egypt had to be laid at the feet of Pharaoh, and not God.)*

30 And Pharaoh rose up in the night, he, and all his servants, and all the Egyptians; and there was a great cry in Egypt; for there was not a house where there was not one dead. *(Believing that the afterlife consisted of the prosperity of the firstborn, what had happened to them was tantamount to a Christian being consigned to eternal darkness, the loss of the soul. The "great cry" was not only for their dead, but, as well, that Pharaoh would let Israel go.)*

31 And he called for Moses and Aaron by night, and said, Rise up, and get you forth from among my people, both you and the Children of Israel; and go, serve the LORD, as you have said. *(At the beginning, the Monarch had asked the question, "Who is the Lord, that I should obey His Voice to let Israel go?" [5:2]. He now knows as to exactly Who is the Lord!)*

32 Also take your flocks and your herds, as you have said, and be gone; and bless me also. *(Trembling with fear, the Monarch requests of Moses and Aaron that they should "bless him also." To be sure, the less will be blessed of the better.)*

33 And the Egyptians were urgent upon the people, that they might send them out of the land in haste; for they said, We be all dead men. *(The Lord knew this would happen; consequently, He told Israel, as it regards the Passover, "You shall eat it in haste" [Vs. 11]. In other words, "Be ready to go!")*

34 And the people took their dough before it was leavened, their kneadingtroughs being bound up in their clothes upon their shoulders. *(They were ready to go!)*

35 And the Children of Israel did according to the word of Moses: and they borrowed (asked) of the Egyptians jewels of silver, and jewels of gold, and raiment:

36 And the LORD gave the people favour in the sight of the Egyptians, so that they lent *(gave, with no thought of it being returned)* unto them such things as they required. And they spoiled the Egyptians *(meaning that much gold and silver, etc., were given to the Israelites)*.

THE EXODUS

37 And the Children of Israel journeyed from Rameses to Succoth *(a distance of about 15 miles)*, about six hundred thousand on foot who were men, beside children *(refers to men of war, between 20 and 50 years of age; counting all the women and children, and men over 50, the total number was approximately 3 million)*.

38 And a mixed multitude went up also with them *(Egyptian sympathizers, of which the number was considerable)*; and flocks, and herds, even very much cattle *(as Moses said, "Not one hoof shall be left behind" [10:26])*.

39 And they baked unleavened cakes of the dough which they brought forth out of Egypt, for it was not leavened; because they were thrust out of Egypt, and could not tarry, neither had they prepared for themselves any victual. *(They were ordered to leave immediately, and did so.)*

40 Now the sojourning of the Children of Israel, who dwelt in Egypt, was four hundred and thirty years. *(This doesn't mean that they dwelt in Egypt for 430 years, but it is rather from the time of Abraham, when he was 75 years old, and called of God to leave Ur of Chaldees, that the 430 years are reckoned. They actually spent some 215 years in Egypt proper.)*

41 And it came to pass at the end of the four hundred and thirty years, even the selfsame day it came to pass, that all the hosts of the LORD went out from the land of Egypt. *(The phrase, "the hosts of the Lord," refers to the fact that they belonged to Him.)*

42 It is a night to be much observed unto the LORD for bringing them out from the land of Egypt: this is that night of the LORD to be observed of all the Children of Israel in their generations. *(This first Passover-night was a night of the Lord, much to be observed; but the last Passover-night, in which Christ was betrayed, and in which the first Passover, with the rest of the ceremonial institutions, was superseded and abolished, was a night of the Lord much more to be observed; when a yoke, heavier than that of*

Egypt, was broken from off our necks, and a land better than that of Canaan, set before us. That first Passover was a temporal deliverance to be celebrated in their generation; this an eternal Redemption to be celebrated in the praises of glorious Saints, world without end — Matthew Henry.)

THE PASSOVER

43 And the LORD said unto Moses and Aaron, This is the Ordinance of the Passover: There shall no stranger eat thereof *(the idea is, they were the Lord's by purchase — bought with a price; the unredeemed have no understanding of Christ and what He has done for us at the Cross; consequently, they cannot partake of Him without accepting Him as Saviour and Lord):*

44 But every man's servant who is bought for money, when you have circumcised him, then shall he eat thereof. *(Circumcision has its antitype in the Cross. The male alone was circumcised; the female was represented in the male. So, in the Cross, Christ represents His Church, and hence the Church is crucified with Christ; nevertheless the Church lives by the Life of Christ known and exhibited on Earth, through the Power of the Holy Spirit [Rom. 8:1-2, 11; Gal. 2:20].)*

45 A foreigner and an hired servant shall not eat thereof. *(The ordinance of circumcision formed the grand boundary line between the Israel of God and all the nations that were upon the face of the Earth; the Cross of our Lord Jesus Christ forms the boundary between the Church and the world.)*

46 In one house shall it be eaten; you shall not carry forth ought of the flesh abroad out of the house; neither shall you break a bone thereof. *(The flesh of the Lamb was not to be taken out of the house, but rather eaten in the house, typifying the fact that none are saved outside of the Family of God. The "house" is Christ. And let it be known, there is no Salvation out of this "house." As well, not a bone of Christ was broken in the Crucifixion, signifying that the True Body of Christ is one.)*

47 All the congregation of Israel shall keep it. *(As all of Israel were to keep the Passover, likewise, all Believers must look to the Cross. There is no exception.)*

48 And when a stranger shall sojourn with you, and will keep the passover to the LORD, let all his males be circumcised, and then let him come near and keep it; and he shall be as one who is born in the land: for no uncircumcised person shall eat thereof. *(The word "stranger" refers to Gentiles. They could come into the Covenant, but only if they came God's Way. It is the same presently. To be saved, irrespective as to who the person might be, they must exhibit Faith in Christ and what He has done for us at the Cross.)*

49 One law shall be to him who is homeborn, and unto the stranger who sojourns among you. *(The Lord doesn't have two ways of Salvation, only "one." That is Christ, even as it has always been Christ.)*

50 Thus did all the Children of Israel; as the LORD commanded Moses and Aaron, so did they. *(It was the Word of the Lord, and to disobey meant death.)*

51 And it came to pass the selfsame day, that the LORD did bring the Children of Israel out of the land of Egypt by their armies. *(The word "armies" refers to the fact that the people were organized as they came out of Egypt, which means they did not come out as a rabble. The Lord was their Captain and, through Him, they possessed great power.)*

CHAPTER 13
(1491 B.C.)
THE FIRSTBORN

AND the LORD spoke unto Moses, saying,

2 Sanctify unto Me all the firstborn, whatsoever opens the womb among the Children of Israel, both of man and of beast: It is mine. *(The "firstborn," who were to be sanctified to the Lord, which means set apart unto the Lord, were to typify Christ. Jesus is the Son of God, in essence, regarding His humanity, the "firstborn.")*

3 And Moses said unto the people, Remember this day, in which you came out from Egypt, out of the house of bondage; for by strength of hand the LORD brought you out from this place *(Israel was to understand that they had been delivered out of this "house of bondage," not by their own ingenuity, strength, ability, or talent, but by the "Power of God." It takes Almighty Power to overcome sin. That Power is registered in the Holy Spirit. He works exclusively within the parameters of the Finished Work of Christ, and demands that we have Faith in that Finished Work [Rom. 6:3-14]):* there shall no leavened bread be eaten. *(Once again, the "Unleavened Bread" symbolizes the Perfection of Christ, which was absolutely necessary, if He was to serve as the Perfect Sacrifice. The Cross*

alone deals with sin.)

4 This day came ye out in the month Abib. *(This was a certain day, on a certain month, in which the Children of Israel were brought out of Egyptian bondage. This tells us, and in no uncertain terms, that Salvation is not merely a philosophical quest, but rather a genuine, "know-so" Salvation.)*

5 And it shall be when the LORD shall bring you into the land of the Canaanites, and the Hittites, and the Amorites, and the Hivites, and the Jebusites, which He swore unto your fathers to give you, a land flowing with milk and honey, that you shall keep this service in this month. *(The Land which the Lord would give them would be grand and great, but would be filled with enemies; however, if they faithfully followed the Lord, every enemy would be defeated, and so it is presently. The Christian can walk in perpetual victory only as he understands the Cross, which is the secret of all victory. The Cross must ever be the object of our Faith, by and through which the Holy Spirit works, thereby making His Power available to us [Rom. 8:1-2, 11].)*

6 Seven days you shall eat unleavened bread, and in the seventh day shall be a feast to the LORD. *(In fact, this Feast lasted throughout the entirety of the seven days, but the first day and the last were to be kept especially holy [Lev. 23:6-8]. The seventh day of the seven days, deemed a special day, refers to the Finished Work of Christ, in that His Mission would be a completed Mission.)*

7 Unleavened bread shall be eaten seven days *(the number "seven" specifies and symbolizes a perfect victory afforded the Child of God, all made possible by Christ, and what He would do at the Cross)***; and there shall no leavened bread be seen with you, neither shall there be leaven seen with you in all your quarters.** *(Leaven was a type of sin. The Christian is to be free from all sin, as it regards domination [Rom. 6:14].)*

8 And you shall show your son in that day, saying, This is done because of that which the LORD did unto me when I came forth out of Egypt. *(We as Believers must "boast" of the Cross, and do so constantly [Gal. 6:14].)*

9 And it shall be for a sign unto you upon your hand, and for a memorial between your eyes, that the LORD's Law may be in your mouth: for with a strong hand has the LORD brought you out of Egypt. *(There can be little doubt that the Jewish system of "phylacteries"*

grew mainly out of this Passage, and was intended as a fulfillment of the commands contained in it. "Phylacteries" were strips of parchment with Passages of Scripture written upon them and deposited in small boxes, which were fastened by a strap, either to the left arm, or across the forehead.)

10 You shall therefore keep this Ordinance in his season from year to year. *(Immediately that Israel was redeemed out of Egypt, instructions were given respecting the annual observance of the Passover. That is to say, Israel was to perpetually confess to the world that her salvation out of Egypt, and her settlement in Canaan, was wholly due to the preciousness of the Blood of the Pascal Lamb. The people of God presently are to give a like testimony.)*

11 And it shall be when the LORD shall bring you into the land of Canaanites, as He swore unto you and to your fathers, and shall give it you,

12 That you shall set apart unto the LORD all that opens the matrix *(the womb)***, and every firstling that comes of a beast which you have; the males shall be the LORD's.**

13 And every firstling of an ass you shall redeem with a lamb; and if you will not redeem it, then you shall break his neck: and all the firstborn of man among your children shall you redeem. *(This Verse legislated the Redemption of man and of an ass by the death of a lamb. This is humbling to human pride. The ass was an unclean animal; and, with its broken neck, fitly pictured the true moral condition of the most cultivated man. But the death of the lamb obtained redemption. Only thus can sinners by saved. If the ass wasn't redeemed, it was to be killed. It is the same with unbelievers; failure to accept Christ, of which the lamb was a Type, means the loss of the soul.)*

14 And it shall be when your son asks you in time to come, saying, What is this? that you shall say unto him, By strength of hand the LORD brought us out from Egypt, from the house of bondage *(all of this concerning the "firstborn" were symbolisms of Christ, as God's Son, Who would redeem humanity by going to the Cross; Israel was delivered on that basis)***:**

15 And it came to pass, when Pharaoh would hardly let us go, that the LORD slew all the firstborn in the land of Egypt, both the firstborn of man, and the firstborn of beast: therefore I sacrifice to the LORD all that opens the matrix, being males; but all the firstborn of my children I redeem. *(Man's firstborn is a*

Type of the firstborn of God, in His Authority and Priestly function among His brethren, and as the object of the Father's love and trust. The death of Egypt's firstborn did burst the bonds of Israel; the death of God's firstborn, the bonds of His people. So, the Cross has a double effect: it condemns the Christ-rejecter, and it brings to Salvation the Christ-acceptor.)

16 And it shall be for a token upon your hand, and for frontlets between your eyes: for by strength of hand the LORD brought us forth out of Egypt. *(Once again, this refers to "phylacteries," the same as in Verse 9.)*

THE CLOUD AND THE FIRE

17 And it came to pass, when Pharaoh had let the people go, that God led them not through the way of the land of the Philistines, although that was near; for God said, Lest peradventure the people repent when they see war, and they return to Egypt *(we should ever seek the Lord as it regards direction and leading; if we let Him make the plans, the plans will succeed; if we make the plans ourselves, and expect Him to bless those plans, that He will not do)*:

18 But God led the people about, through the way of the wilderness of the Red Sea *(He would lead them into and through the wilderness, in order to teach them trust, faith, and obedience)*: and the Children of Israel went up harnessed out of the land of Egypt *(could be translated, "The Children of Israel went up by five in a rank out of the land of Egypt"; "five" in Scripture ever speaks of Grace or favor; this probably refers to five large groups)*.

19 And Moses took the bones of Joseph with him: for he *(Joseph)* had straitly sworn the Children of Israel, saying, God will surely visit you; and you shall carry up my bones away hence with you *(even though Joseph had the glory of Egypt given to him by God, still, his heart was never in Egypt, but in Canaanland, for that was the land promised to Abraham by God, where a mighty nation would rise up, a nation totally different than any other nation in the world, a people who belonged exclusively to Jehovah; as well, there is some small evidence in the Text that not only were the bones of Joseph brought out, but also the bones of all the sons of Jacob)*.

20 And they took their journey from Succoth *(means "booths" or "tents"; this spoke plainly of the "pilgrim" character which lay before them)*, and encamped in Etham, in the edge of the wilderness.

21 And the LORD went before them by day in a pillar of a cloud, to lead them the way; and by night in a pillar of fire, to give them light; to go by day and night *(concerning this, Mackintosh says: "The Lord not only conducted them safely outside the bounds of Egypt, but He also came down, as it were, in His traveling chariot, to be their Companion through all the vicissitudes of their wilderness journey; this was Divine Grace; they were not merely delivered out of the furnace of Egypt and then allowed to make the best of their way to Canaan — such was not God's manner toward them; He went before them; He was 'a guide, a glory, a defense, to save them from every fear'")*:

22 He took not away the pillar of the cloud by day, nor the pillar of fire by night, from before the people. *(As Israel was led both day and night by this particular "cloud," likewise, the Holy Spirit is to the Believer, "The Spirit of Wisdom and Understanding, the Spirit of Counsel and Might, the Spirit of Knowledge and of the Fear of the Lord" [Isa. 11:2].)*

CHAPTER 14
(1491 B.C.)
INSTRUCTIONS

AND the LORD spoke unto Moses, saying,

2 Speak unto the Children of Israel, that they turn and encamp before Pi-hahiroth, between Migdol and the sea, over against Baal-zephon: before it shall you encamp by the sea. *(The Lord continues to direct Israel as to exactly where they should go. From the military point of view, Israel had blundered badly, or so Pharaoh thought! In effect, they were hemmed in. But God was leading them and, as well, had a Plan and Purpose for taking them on this particular route, as we shall see. If we as Believers make the plans, they are guaranteed of failure. If God makes them, they are guaranteed of success.)*

3 For Pharaoh will say of the Children of Israel, They are entangled in the land, the wilderness has shut them in. *(Through foreknowledge, the Lord knew what Pharaoh would reckon in his evil heart, when he saw the Children of Israel seemingly hemmed in.)*

4 And I will harden Pharaoh's heart, that he shall follow after them *(the idea is, God would provide the means by which Pharaoh would harden his own heart; God is said to do many things, when, in fact, He does not personally do*

such, *but does set the stage)*; and I will be honoured upon Pharaoh, and upon all his host; that the Egyptians may know that I am the LORD. And they did so. *(Pharaoh's continued rebellion will fall out instead to the Glory of God. If God's people truly follow the Lord, whatever Satan does will always fall out to the Glory of God, but only if God's people fully trust and obey.)*

5 And it was told the king of Egypt that the people fled: and the heart of Pharaoh and of his servants was turned against the people, and they said, Why have we done this, that we have let Israel go from serving us? *(Satan doesn't easily give up his attempts to hold Believers in bondage. But, if the Believer doesn't flag in his faith, and I speak of Faith in Christ and the Cross, total and complete victory is guaranteed [Rom. 6:14].)*

6 And he *(Pharaoh)* made ready his chariot, and took his people with him:

7 And he took six hundred chosen chariots, and all the chariots of Egypt, and captains over every one of them. *(Josephus records that Pharaoh had 50,000 horsemen and 200,000 footmen, as well as all the chariots.)*

8 And the LORD hardened the heart of Pharaoh king of Egypt, and he pursued after the Children of Israel: and the Children of Israel went out with an high hand. *(The "high hand" refers to a certain degree of pride and confidence. Regrettably, the "high hand" would change when they faced the Red Sea.)*

9 But the Egyptians pursued after them, all the horses and chariots of Pharaoh, and his horsemen, and his army, and overtook them encamping by the sea, beside Pi-hahiroth, before Baal-zephon. *(As stated, Pharaoh thought he had them hemmed in. So, in his mind, his victory was assured.)*

10 And when Pharaoh drew near, the Children of Israel lifted up their eyes, and, behold, the Egyptians marched after them; and they were sore afraid: and the Children of Israel cried out unto the LORD. *(Verses 10 through 12 record the complaints of Israel. The fear, unbelief, and anger of the very people who had witnessed God's wonders in the land of Egypt would appear incredible, but that each Bible student finds these evils in his own heart, and learns by sad experience that great depression of mind usually follows exceptional spiritual triumphs — Williams.)*

11 And they said unto Moses, Because there were no graves in Egypt, have you taken us away to die in the wilderness? wherefore have you dealt thus with us, to carry us forth out of Egypt? *(Unbelief cried out: "The wilderness will become our grave"; but the result was that the sea became Pharaoh's grave.)*

12 Is not this the word that we did tell you in Egypt, saying, Let us alone, that we may serve the Egyptians? *(All Israel could see at this time was either slavery to the Egyptians, or to die in the wilderness. So most Christians compromise with the world and stay in slavery. They do not understand deliverance, because they're looking for it in the wrong place. There is an alternative to Egypt, and to dying in the wilderness. It is the Cross [Gal. 6:14].)* For it had been better for us to serve the Egyptians, than that we should die in the wilderness.

13 And Moses said unto the people *(from this statement, we learn what the Preacher is supposed to preach),* Fear ye not *(that has always been the Word of the Lord; with God on our side, and us looking wholly to Him, we have nothing to fear [II Tim. 1:7]),* stand still *(all attempts at self-help must end; all activities of the flesh must cease; the workings of nature must be subdued; our Faith must rest completely in Christ and the Cross, and nothing else),* and see the Salvation of the LORD *(please notice, it is the "Salvation of the Lord," and not at all of us; it is all by virtue of His Sacrificial, Atoning Work at the Cross),* which He will show to you today *(victory is yours "today," if you will only believe and, by that, I mean believe correctly, which refers to the fact that the Cross is ever the object of our Faith [Rom. 6:3-14]):* for the Egyptians whom you have seen today, you shall see them again no more forever. *(This didn't mean that they would never again see Egyptians, but it meant that they would never see them in this posture of what looked like victory for the Egyptians. The Believer may see the vices in the world, but they will no longer control him or, in fact, have any part in him. And this victory is "forever" [Jn. 14:16-17].)*

14 The LORD shall fight for you, and you shall hold your peace. *(The Lord could fight for Israel only as long as they "stood still." Had they turned and tried to fight the Egyptians themselves, and in any capacity, this would have hindered the Lord fighting for them, and they no doubt would have been defeated. Someone has well said, "In Justification, the Lord fights 'for' us, and in Sanctification, He fights 'in' us.")*

15 And the LORD said unto Moses, Wherefore do you cry unto Me? *(The Children of*

Israel were crying unto the Lord, but their cry was not of Faith, but rather of defeat. They complained, and accused Moses, which was the same as accusing God.) **speak unto the Children of Israel, that they go forward** *(Faith is ever "forward")*:

16 But you lift up your rod, and stretch out your hand over the sea, and divide it *(with the command to go forward came the provision of Grace; this was to be the greatest miracle yet since creation; but the Lord has now performed even a greater miracle in delivering His people, and I refer to the Cross and the Resurrection)*: **and the Children of Israel shall go on dry ground through the midst of the sea.** *(From this it is very clear that the waters of the Red Sea did not begin to divide until the feet of the Israelites came to their very brink, otherwise they would have crossed by sight, and not "by Faith.")*

17 And I, behold, I will harden the hearts of the Egyptians, and they shall follow them: and I will get Me honour upon Pharaoh, and upon all his host, upon his chariots, and upon his horsemen. *(Men do not have the final word, that belongs to God. We must never forget, God's honor is always at stake. Proper Faith in Him will always vindicate His honor, despite the decision of men.)*

18 And the Egyptians shall know that I am the LORD, when I have gotten me honour upon Pharaoh, upon his chariots, and upon his horsemen.

19 And the Angel of God, which went before the camp of Israel, removed and went behind them *(the "Angel of God" spoken of in this Verse is actually a preincarnate appearance of the Lord Jesus Christ; the Lord Jesus is Jehovah and, one might say, the Jehovah of the Old Testament; He placed Himself between Israel and the enemy; in the same manner, the Believer may look for his difficulties, and not find them, because God is between him and them)*; **and the pillar of the cloud went from before their face, and stood behind them** *(this is the Holy Spirit)*:

20 And it came between the camp of the Egyptians and the camp of Israel; and it was a cloud and darkness to them *(to the Egyptians)*, **but it gave light by night to these** *(to Israel)*: **so that the one came not near the other all the night.** *(Concerning this, Mackintosh says: "How like the Cross of our Lord Jesus Christ!*

"Truly, that Cross has a double aspect likewise. It forms the foundation of the Believer's peace and, at the same time, seals the condemnation of a guilty world. The self-same blood

which purges the Believer's conscience, and gives him perfect peace, stains this Earth and consummates its guilt. The very mission of the Son of God which strips the world of its cloak, and leaves it wholly without excuse, clothes Believers with a fair mantle of Righteousness, and fills her mouth with ceaseless praise.

"The very same Lamb Who will terrify, by His unmitigated wrath, all tribes and classes of Earth, will lead, by His gentle Hand, His Blood-bought flock through the green pastures and beside the still waters forever!" [Rev. 6:15-17; 7:13-17].)

THE RED SEA

21 And Moses stretched out his hand over the Sea; and the LORD caused the Sea to go back by a strong east wind all that night, and made the Sea dry land, and the waters were divided. *(The "strong east wind" that God used to push back a path through the Sea was a Divine miracle, not something accomplished by the mere uncontrolled forces of nature itself. The indication is, the Children of Israel began to walk out into the Sea, with God opening it before them. The Sea opened at about the pace that they could slowly walk.)*

22 And the Children of Israel went into the midst of the Sea upon the dry ground *(this puts to rest the fallacy of the skeptics, that the Sea was only about two inches deep at this juncture; they didn't walk across through shallow water, but rather on "dry ground")*: **and the waters were a wall unto them on their right hand, and on their left.** *(It is believed that the path through the Sea was from ten to twelve miles wide. Its depth was somewhere between 20 and 40 feet. The location was probably in the vicinity of the modern Suez, between the Bitter Lakes. The Lakes were then a part of the Gulf. The Psalmist said, "He made the waters to stand as an heap" [Ps. 78:13]. This must have been quite a sight with that wall of water standing up on either side!)*

23 And the Egyptians pursued, and went in after them to the midst of the Sea, even all Pharaoh's horses, his chariots, and his horsemen. *(Whether Pharaoh actually went in himself, the Scripture doesn't say; however, I choose to believe that the pride of Pharaoh demanded that he lead this charge and this attack.)*

24 And it came to pass, that in the morning watch the LORD looked unto the host of the Egyptians through the pillar of fire and of the cloud, and troubled the host of the Egyptians *(Josephus says concerning this: "Showers of rain*

came down from the sky, and dreadful thunders and lightning, with flashes of fire; thunderbolts also were darted upon them; nor was there anything which could be sent by God upon man as indications of His wrath, which did not happen upon this occasion." The words, "troubled the host," in the Hebrew, actually mean "threw it into confusion"),

25 And took off their chariot wheels, that they drove them heavily *(they found that their mighty chariot army did them no good)*: so that the Egyptians said, Let us flee from the face of Israel; for the LORD fights for them against the Egyptians. *(They saw that the Lord was not only fighting for the Children of Israel, but was, at the same time, fighting against the Egyptians. They had been led into a trap, caused by their own rebellion against God. So, they had no one but themselves to blame.)*

26 And the LORD said unto Moses, Stretch out your hand over the Sea, that the waters may come again upon the Egyptians, upon their chariots, and upon their horsemen. *(The Lord not only delivered Israel, but, as well, defeated the Egyptians. At Calvary, the Lord not only delivered us, but He also defeated Satan [Col. 2:14-15].)*

27 And Moses stretched forth his hand over the Sea, and the Sea returned to his strength when the morning appeared *(at about daybreak)*; and the Egyptians fled against it; and the LORD overthrew the Egyptians in the midst of the Sea. *(Exactly as the Lord had said, Israel would see these Egyptians no more.)*

28 And the waters returned, and covered the chariots, and the horsemen, and all the host of Pharaoh that came into the Sea after them; there remained not so much as one of them. *(As every Egyptian was totally and completely defeated, Satan was totally and completely defeated, as well, at the Cross. Not one single bondage of darkness was excluded, but rather Jesus addressed them all.)*

29 But the Children of Israel walked upon dry land in the midst of the Sea; and the waters were a wall unto them on their right hand, and on their left. *(It doesn't matter what type of deliverance is needed, God is able!)*

30 Thus the LORD saved Israel that day out of the hand of the Egyptians; and Israel saw the Egyptians dead upon the sea shore. *(Thus concluded the stubbornness of Pharaoh! Faith in Christ and the Cross renders death to the forces of evil.)*

31 And Israel saw that great work which the

LORD did upon the Egyptians *(God always performs a "great work"; He is still performing great works, and He shall ever continue to perform great works)*: and the people feared the LORD, and believed the LORD, and His servant Moses. *(But regrettably, we will soon find that their faith was a shallow faith.)*

CHAPTER 15
(1491 B.C.)
THE SONG OF MOSES

THEN sang Moses and the Children of Israel this song unto the LORD, and spoke, saying *(there was no singing in Egypt; there was groaning; singing only follows Redemption; Moses began and ended his wilderness life with a song; that of Deuteronomy, Chapter 32 is the one referred to in Revelation 15:3; this song portrayed in this Chapter is the oldest song of praise in existence; its theme is Jehovah Jesus; it begins with Redemption, and ends with Glory)*, I will sing unto the LORD, for He has triumphed gloriously: the horse and his rider has He thrown into the sea. *(The Lord is given the praise here. This song, accompanied by musical instruments [Vs. 20], proclaims at least one of the greatest, if not the greatest, means of praise and worship found in the Bible. We know this, simply because the Book of Psalms, which contains 150 songs, is the longest Book in the Bible. By devoting this much space to music and singing, the Holy Spirit is telling us here of its value, as it regards the worship of the Lord.)*

2 The LORD is my strength and song *(the phrase actually says in the Hebrew, "My strength and song is JAH"; in fact, the name "JAH" had not previously been used; it is an abbreviated form of Jehovah)*, and He is become my Salvation: He is my God, and I will prepare Him an habitation *(means, in the Hebrew, "I will glorify Him")*; my father's God, and I will exalt Him. *(The pronouns, as it refers to the Lord, "He," "Him," "Thy," "Thou," and "Thee," are found 33 times in this Psalm! How significant and how searching is this!)*

3 The LORD is a man of war *(not we ourselves; when we try to place ourselves in that position, we get defeated every time; in fact, the only fight that we are called upon to fight is "the good fight of Faith" [I Tim. 6:12])*: the LORD is His Name *(could be translated, "Jehovah, the Alone-Existing One"; before Him, all other existence fades and falls into nothingness)*.

4 Pharaoh's chariots and his host has He

cast into the Sea: his chosen captains also are drowned in the Red Sea. *(It would be some time before Egypt would recover. One thing is certain, they didn't try to follow Israel into the wilderness.)*

5 The depths have covered them: they sank into the bottom as a stone *(covered with armor, it served only as a weight to drown them, which it did).*

6 Your right hand, O LORD, is become glorious in power: Your right hand, O LORD, has dashed in pieces the enemy. *(The "right hand," as it refers to the Lord, is used as a figure of speech. It signifies power.)*

7 And in the greatness of Your excellency You have overthrown them who rose up against You: You sent forth Your wrath, which consumed them as stubble. *(The verbs in this Verse are future. Consequently, it should read, "You will overthrow them who rise up against You." And then, "You will send forth your wrath." The last phrase, "which consumed them as stubble," is present tense, and concerns the victory over the Egyptians. So, in this Verse, we have an account not only of what the Lord has done regarding the Egyptians, but the Promise that He will fight thusly for us as well!)*

8 And with the blast of Your nostrils the waters were gathered together, the floods stood upright as an heap, and the depths were congealed in the heart of the Sea. *(Concerning the word "congealed," some have taken it to mean that the waters froze; however, considering the climate of Egypt, that is unlikely; and yet, it definitely could have happened. Still others have asked the question, "Are we justified in taking literally the strong expressions of a highly wrought poetical description?"*

We definitely are justified. It is the Holy Spirit Who gave Moses these very words, and, to be sure, the description in no way stretches the truth as it regards what God has done, and, above all, what He can do.)

9 The enemy said, I will pursue, I will overtake, I will divide the spoil; my lust shall be satisfied upon them; I will draw my sword, my hand shall destroy them. *(If the Devil could do all the things that he claims that he will do, he would have done them a long time ago. He hasn't done them, because he can't do them. "He is a liar, and the father of it" [Jn. 8:44].)*

10 You did blow with Your wind, the Sea covered them: they sank as lead in the mighty waters. *(Here we have another fact that is not mentioned in the account, but yet which is implied. The immediate cause of the return of the waters was a wind. As a "strong east wind" had caused the water to part, now this new wind, and that which had been devised by the Lord, must have arisen contrary to the former wind, blowing from the northwest or the north, and thus produced the effect described.)*

11 Who is like unto You, O LORD, among the gods? *(gods mentioned in this Verse pertain to the gods worshipped by the Egyptians)* Who is like You, glorious in holiness, fearful in praises, doing wonders? *(How few today "glory" in God's Holiness! How few "praise" Him for His "Faithfulness"! How few are acquainted with His "wonders"!)*

12 You stretch out Your right hand, the Earth swallowed them. *(His Hand Alone defeated one of the mightiest armies in the world, and did so by the use of the elements.)*

13 You in Your mercy have led forth the people which You have redeemed *(to purchase the slave out of the marketplace)*: You have guided them in Your strength unto Your holy habitation. *(The ultimate conclusion of this "holy habitation" is the Holy Spirit dwelling in the Believer, which has been made possible by the Cross [I Cor. 3:16].)*

14 The people shall hear, and be afraid *(what is the world presently hearing as it regards the Church?)*: sorrow shall take hold on the inhabitants of Palestina *(and this is exactly what happened!).*

15 Then the dukes of Edom shall be amazed; the mighty men of Moab, trembling shall take hold upon them; all the inhabitants of Canaan shall melt away.

16 Fear and dread shall fall upon them; by the greatness of Your arm they shall be as still as a stone; till Your people pass over, O LORD, till the people pass over, which You have purchased. *(All of this portrays in Type what Christ accomplished at the Cross [Col. 2:14-15]. As these enemy nations feared Israel, likewise, all fallen angels and demon spirits, even Satan himself, greatly fear the Child of God who understands and knows that he has "passed over" into the inheritance, purchased for us by the Lord Jesus Christ.)*

17 You shall bring them in, and plant them in the mountain of Your inheritance, in the place, O LORD, which You have made for You to dwell in, in the Sanctuary, O LORD, which Your hands have established. *(While this pointed to Canaan, Jerusalem, and the future building of the Temple, more than all, its total meaning has to do with the Believer's position in Christ,*

for Biblical history has always strained toward this conclusion.)

18 The LORD shall reign forever and ever. *(This closes this great and beautiful Song. It ends as it began — with "the Lord." Faith views the eternal future without fear.)*

THE SONG OF MIRIAM

19 For the horse of Pharaoh went in with his chariots and with his horsemen into the Sea, and the LORD brought again the waters of the sea upon them; but the Children of Israel went on dry land in the midst of the Sea. *(This is the song of Miriam, which will be explained more fully in Verse 21.)*

20 And Miriam the Prophetess, the sister of Aaron, took a timbrel in her hand; and all the women went out after her with timbrels and with dances. *(Miriam was the sister of both Moses and Aaron. She is the first woman whom the Bible honors with the title of "Prophetess." Pulpit says of her: "Miriam is regarded by the Prophet Micah [Mic. 6:4] as having had a share in the deliverance of Israel, with her claiming the prophetic gift in Numbers 12:2. Her claim appears to be allowed both in the present Passage, and in Numbers 12:6-8, where the degree of her inspiration, however, is placed below that of Moses.")*

21 And Miriam answered them, Sing ye to the LORD, for He has triumphed gloriously; the horse and his rider has He thrown into the Sea. *(The idea seems to be, that the men would sing a Verse of the song, with Miriam, and tens of thousands of women, answering them with the words of Verse 19. This would have been quite a moment, with all of these women, led by Miriam, answering each Verse. Thus, we see how the Lord uses the women here in praise and worship, with Miriam also being used as a Prophetess.)*

THE BITTER WATERS

22 So Moses brought Israel from the Red Sea, and they went out into the wilderness of Shur; and they went three days in the wilderness, and found no water. *(God tests Faith in order to strengthen and enrich it.)*

23 And when they came to Marah, they could not drink of the waters of Marah, for they were bitter: therefore the name of it was called Marah. *(Marah means "bitter." Pink says: "While the wilderness may and will make*

manifest the weakness of God's Saints and, as well, our failures, this is only to magnify the Power and Mercy of Him Who brought us into the place of testing. Further, and we must understand, God always has in view our ultimate good." The bitter waters of Marah typify life and its disappointments.)

24 And the people murmured against Moses, saying, What shall we drink? *(Three days before, the Children of Israel were rejoicing on the shores of the Red Sea. Now, some 72 hours later, they are "murmuring against Moses." Such presents a lack of Faith. "Tests" brought upon us by the Lord portray what is in us. Regrettably, it doesn't take much to bring out the unbelief.)*

25 And he cried unto the LORD *(Moses set the example; there is no help outside of the Lord, but man, even the Church, seem to find difficulty in believing this)*: and the LORD showed him a Tree *(the "tree" is a Type of the Cross [Acts 5:30; 10:39; 13:29; Gal. 3:13; I Pet. 2:24])*, which when he had cast into the waters, the waters were made sweet *(we must put the Cross into every difficulty and problem of life, which alone holds the answer; only by this means can the bitter waters be made "sweet")*: there He *(God)* made for them a Statute and an Ordinance, and there He proved them *(tested them! We must understand that God doesn't give victory to men, only to Christ; His victory becomes ours, as we are properly in Him [Jn. 14:20; Rom. 6:3-5]).*

26 And said, If you will diligently hearken to the voice of the LORD your God, and will do that which is right in His sight, and will give ear to His Commandments, and keep all His Statutes, I will put none of these diseases upon you, which I have brought upon the Egyptians: for I am the LORD Who heals you. *(It is demanded that all these "Statutes" and "Ordinances" be perfectly kept; however, no man can boast of such; Christ has perfectly kept all the Commandments and, as our Substitute, kept them perpetually. Looking to Him, we can claim this blessing. As well, the "healing" Promised here has to do not only with physical diseases but, as well, of emotional and spiritual diseases. The Cross is to be put into the bitter waters of these problems, whatever they might be. They can then be made sweet. The name "Lord," in the Hebrew, as used here, is "Jehovah-Ropheka," which means "Jehovah, the Healer." Jehovah has proven Himself as the Deliverer of Israel, and now He proclaims Himself as their "Healer.")*

27 And they came to Elim, where were

twelve wells of water *(the number "twelve" is the number of God's Government; but we must remember, this is God's Government, and not particular governments devised by man; it symbolized the Twelve Tribes of Israel and, futuristically, the Twelve Apostles, on which, in a sense, the New Covenant would be built, because they were eyewitnesses of Christ, regarding His Life, Ministry, Crucifixion, Resurrection, Ascension and, by faith, His Exaltation)*, and threescore and ten palm trees *(the 70 Palm Trees are symbolic of Ministry, which must be built on the foundation of the Apostles and Prophets, Jesus Christ Himself being the Chief Cornerstone [Lk. 10:1, 17])*: and they encamped there by the waters *(signals the place in which the Believer is to rest [Mat. 11:28]; as long as the Doctrine is "Jesus Christ and Him Crucified," which speaks of the foundation, Typed by the "twelve wells of water," and the Ministry, Typed by the "threescore and ten Palm Trees," Christ will be found in all His Glory, and will be to the Believer what He desires to be)*.

CHAPTER 16
(1491 B.C.)
THE WILDERNESS OF SIN

A ND they took their journey from Elim, and all the congregation of the Children of Israel came unto the wilderness of Sin, which is between Elim and Sinai, on the fifteenth day of the second month after their departing out of the land of Egypt. *(This First Verse tells us that the Children of Israel had been on the road exactly one month, having left Egypt the fifteenth of the first month. It must be remembered that "the Pillar of the Cloud" led them in this direction; and yet, it was a direction that seemed to be most inhospitable. But the Lord had a purpose for this direction.)*

2 And the whole congregation of the Children of Israel murmured against Moses and Aaron in the wilderness: *(If we murmur against God's man or woman, we have, in effect, murmured against God. Pink says: "Here was the selfsame people who had been Divinely spared from the ten plagues on Egypt, who had been brought forth from the land of bondage, miraculously delivered at the Red Sea, Divinely guided by a Pillar of Cloud and Fire, day and night — now 'murmuring,' complaining, rebelling!")*

3 And the Children of Israel said unto them, Would to God we had died by the hand of the LORD in the land of Egypt *(as we read these words, we are reading an "oath"; this means that their sin was aggravated by an oath; they took the Divine Name "in vain"; the future proves the fact that they got exactly that for which they asked; they didn't die in Egypt, but they did die in the wilderness; as Believers, we must be very careful as to what we say)*, when we sat by the flesh pots, and when we did eat bread to the full *(they lied! as slaves of the merciless Egyptians, there is no ground whatsoever for us to suppose that they "sat by the flesh pots" or "ate bread to the full"; unbelief is always based on a lie)*; for you have brought us forth into this wilderness, to kill this whole assembly with hunger. *(God had promised that they should worship Him at Sinai [3:12]; consequently, it was not possible, then, for them to die with hunger in the wilderness. In the face of difficulties, we tend to forget the Promises of God.)*

4 Then said the LORD unto Moses, Behold, I will rain bread from Heaven for you *(the Manna prefigured the descent of the True Bread, of which if a man eat he shall live forever [Jn. 6:51])*; and the people shall go out and gather a certain rate every day *(this proclaims the fact that we are to partake of Christ every day)*, that I may prove them, whether they will walk in My law, or no. *(Everything the Lord does with us is to "prove us." How will we act? How will we react?)*

5 And it shall come to pass, that on the sixth day they shall prepare that which they bring in; and it shall be twice as much as they gather daily. *(They were to gather twice as much on the sixth day as they had on the previous days, but which the Lord would miraculously multiply, in order that they may have sustenance the next day, on which they would not be allowed to do any work. Very shortly, the Lord would institute the Sabbath.)*

6 And Moses and Aaron said unto all the Children of Israel, At evening, then you shall know that the LORD has brought you out from the land of Egypt *(even though Moses didn't record it here, Verse 13 proclaims the fact that quails were sent in the evening)*:

7 And in the morning, then you shall see the Glory of the LORD; for that He hears your murmurings against the LORD: and what are we, that you murmur against us? *(The next morning, the Manna was sent. The murmurings of Verses 6 through 8 proclaim that God hears and sees all the acts of man and will hold each person responsible as to "right" and "wrong" in every detail [I Cor. 3:11-15].)*

8 And Moses said, This shall be, when the LORD shall give you in the evening flesh to eat, and in the morning bread to the full; for that the LORD hears your murmurings which you murmur against Him: and what are we? your murmurings are not against us, but against the LORD. *(Verse 8 is basically a repetition of Verse 7; but it emphasizes the statements of that Verse, and prepares the way for what follows. When looking back toward Egypt, Israel murmured; when looking forward toward the wilderness, they saw the Glory of the Lord. Discontent magnifies what is past, and vilifies what is present, without regard to truth or reason. The absurd then murmurs!)*

9 And Moses spoke unto Aaron, Say unto all the congregation of the Children of Israel, Come near before the LORD: for He has heard your murmurings. *(Those in positions of Godly leadership do not hear all the murmurs of those whom they are attempting to lead. It is well that we do not, perhaps because we could not bear it: but God hears, and yet bears.)*

10 And it came to pass, as Aaron spoke unto the whole congregation of the Children of Israel, that they looked toward the wilderness, and, behold, the Glory of the LORD appeared in the Cloud. *(This Verse seems to indicate that the entirety of the Children of Israel should present themselves as a "whole congregation" to the Lord. Concerning the "Glory of the Lord" appearing in the Cloud, it is not known whether something was visible or not, but, more than likely, the Cloud took on a new appearance of greater glory.)*

11 And the LORD spoke unto Moses, saying,

12 I have heard the murmurings of the Children of Israel: speak unto them, saying, At evening you shall eat flesh *(the quail)*, and in the morning you shall be filled with bread *(the Manna)*; and you shall know that I am the LORD your God. *(Past miracles are convincing. But unless there are fresh evidences of God, the natural man will soon forget and lapse into unbelief again. "Murmuring" was the first sin committed by Israel after being delivered from Egyptian bondage. We must understand how displeased the Lord is at such action.)*

QUAIL AND MANNA

13 And it came to pass, that at evening the quails came up, and covered the camp: and in the morning the dew lay round about the host. *(It seems that the quails, as appears by the subsequent narrative, were supplied, not regularly, but only on rare occasions; in fact [so far as appears] only here in the wilderness of Sin, and at Kibroth-hattavah in the wilderness of Paran [Num. 11:31-34]. The mention of the "dew" in this manner implies that, that which looked like dew was, in part, dew, but not wholly so. The next Verse explains it to a greater degree.)*

14 And when the dew that lay was gone up, behold, upon the face of the wilderness there lay a small round thing, as small as the hoar frost on the ground.

15 And when the Children of Israel saw it, they said one to another, It is Manna: for they wist not what it was. And Moses said unto them, This is the Bread which the LORD has given you to eat. *(The Manna was so precious that it could not bear contact with the Earth. It fell upon the dew and had to be gathered before the Sun came up. This teaches us that yesterday's blessing will not do for today, nor today's for tomorrow. Thus must the Christian feed upon Christ daily as He reveals Himself in the Scriptures.)*

16 This is the thing which the LORD has commanded, Gather of it every man according to his eating, an omer for every man, according to the number of your persons; take ye every man for them which are in his tents. *(In Egypt, Israel had slave food; in the desert, Angel's food. The test quickly revealed that the natural man had little appetite for Heavenly things, for the people soon called it "light food.")*

17 And the Children of Israel did so, and gathered, some more, some less. *(Israel in the desert presented a striking picture! Egypt was behind them, Canaan was before them, the wilderness was around them, and the Manna was above them.)*

18 And when they did mete it with an omer *(an "omer" is the equivalent of six pints; considering there were approximately 3 million people, this would play out to some 18 million pints, or about 13.5 million pounds gathered daily; to help us understand it even more, it would take a train pulling 45 cars, each car having in it 15 tons, to take care of one day's supply; this means that approximately 1.5 million tons of Manna were gathered annually by Israel; and let it be remembered that this continued for nearly 40 years! Great is our God!)*, he who gathered much had nothing over, and he who gathered little had no lack *(Christians who hoard money will find that it will not grow as*

they think; Christians who give generously to the Work of God will find that personally, and for their family, they will "have no lack"; God blesses us, in order that we may bless His Work); they gathered every man according to his eating. *(That which the Lord gives to us as Believers should be used according to our need, and the balance be given to the Work of God; however, we must make certain that what we are supporting is truly the Work of God.)*

19 And Moses said, Let no man leave of it till the morning. *(What they gathered, they were to eat. None was to be left over for the next day. This means that we must partake of Christ every day. As well, what we receive today from the Lord will not suffice for tomorrow. Tomorrow must, and will, bring a fresh enduement of power from on high.)*

20 Notwithstanding they hearkened not unto Moses; but some of them left of it until the morning, and it bred worms, and stank: and Moses was angry with them. *(That which some Christians are trying to present to the world "stinks," at least in the nostrils of God, because it is someone else's vision, or yesterday's blessing.)*

21 And they gathered it every morning, every man according to his eating: and when the sun waxed hot, it melted. *(Thus must the Christian feed upon Christ every day.)*

22 And it came to pass, that on the sixth day they gathered twice as much bread, two omers for one man: and all the rulers of the congregation came and told Moses. *(They were allowed to gather twice as much on the sixth day, because the Manna would not fall on the seventh day.)*

THE SABBATH REST

23 And he said unto them, This is that which the LORD has said, Tomorrow is the rest of the Holy Sabbath unto the LORD: bake that which you will bake today, and seethe that you will seethe; and that which remains over lay up for you to be kept until the morning. *(The day of rest here suddenly reappears after a silence of more than 2,000 years. Redemption being accomplished, typified by deliverance from Egypt, the Sabbath is gifted to Israel. The Jewish Sabbath was meant to serve as a portrayal of the "rest" that one receives when coming to Christ. In other words, Christ is the fulfillment of the Sabbath, hence that particular day not being kept, in the old manner, under the New Covenant.)*

24 And they laid it up *(the Manna)* till the morning, as Moses bade: and it did not stink, neither was there any worm therein *(the double amount gathered on Friday, with the leftover to be used on Saturday).*

25 And Moses said, Eat that today; for today is a sabbath unto the LORD: today you shall not find it *(the Manna)* in the field.

26 Six days you shall gather it; but on the seventh day, which is the sabbath, in it there shall be none.

27 And it came to pass, that there went out some of the people on the seventh day for to gather, and they found none. *(Man has little heart for God's rest. His nature is bad. He can neither rest with, nor work for, God. If God makes a rest for him, he will not keep it; and if God tells him to work, he will not do it. In this Chapter, Israel, at least to a certain degree, refused the Sabbath as a gift, and in Numbers 15 disobeyed it as a Law.)*

28 And the LORD said unto Moses, How long refuse you to keep My commandments and My laws?

29 See, for that the LORD has given you the Sabbath, therefore He gives you on the sixth day the bread of two days; abide ye every man in his place, let no man go out of his place on the seventh day.

30 So the people rested on the seventh day. *(As stated, this particular day, the Sabbath, commanded by God for Israel to keep, was meant to serve as a Type of Christ, and the "rest" He would give, on acceptance of Him [Mat. 11:28-30].)*

31 And the House of Israel called the name thereof Manna: and it was like coriander seed, white; and the taste of it was like wafers made with honey. *(Manna was a provision made for God's people. It was not a question of Redemption, that having been obtained by the Blood at the Cross, and there alone. Manna was meant to proclaim Christ, and His sustenance for the Saints, and that on a daily basis. The wilderness afforded little. In Jehovah Alone was their portion.)*

A TESTIMONY

32 And Moses said, This is the thing which the LORD commands, Fill an omer of it to be kept for your generations; that they may see the bread wherewith I have fed you in the wilderness, when I brought you forth from the land of Egypt. *(A container of Manna was to be kept as a most precious memorial of the faithfulness of God. Whereas the Manna held over*

would normally breed worms and stink, the Manna addressed here in this Verse would be sustained by the Power of God for many, many centuries. The miracles of the past are to never be forgotten, but related over and over.)

33 And Moses said unto Aaron, Take a pot, and put an omer full of Manna therein, and lay it up before the LORD, to be kept for your generations.

34 As the LORD commanded Moses, so Aaron laid it up before the Testimony, to be kept. (The "Testimony" was the Ten Commandments, kept on two tablets of stone, and preserved in the Ark of the Covenant.)

35 And the Children of Israel did eat Manna forty years, until they came to a land inhabited; they did eat Manna, until they came unto the borders of the land of Canaan.

36 Now an omer is the tenth part of an ephah.

CHAPTER 17
(1491 B.C.)
WATER

AND all the congregation of the Children of Israel journeyed from the wilderness of Sin, after their journeys, according to the Commandment of the Lord, and pitched in Rephidim: and there was no water for the people to drink. (It might seem strange that God, Who professed to love Israel, should lead them into a desert, both foodless and waterless. But love led them there that they might learn the desperate unbelief of their own hearts, and the unfailing faithfulness of God's heart.)

2 Wherefore the people did chide with Moses, and said, Give us water that we may drink. And Moses said unto them, Why chide you with me? wherefore do ye tempt the Lord? (Only in a desert could God reveal what He can be to those who trust Him; for only there was Israel dependent upon Him for everything. Without God — nothing; with God — everything. When we criticize God's man, we are in essence criticizing God. The questions of the wilderness are: "What?" "Where?" "How?" Faith has a brief but comprehensive answer to all three, namely, "God!")

3 And the people thirsted there for water; and the people murmured against Moses, and said, Wherefore is this that you have brought us up out of Egypt, to kill us and our children and our cattle with thirst? (First of all, they tempted the Lord, which is a want of Faith, and now they "murmur," which proved to be one of their greatest sins, because murmuring always exhibits unbelief.)

4 And Moses cried unto the LORD saying, What shall I do unto this people? they be almost ready to stone me. (One of the most prominent traits of the character of Moses is that, at the occurrence of a difficulty, he always carried it straight to God [Ex. 15:25; 24:15; 32:30; 33:8; Num. 11:2, 11; 12:11; 14:13-19].)

5 And the LORD said unto Moses, Go on before the people, and take with you of the Elders of Israel; and your rod, wherewith you smote the river, take in your hand, and go.

6 Behold, I will stand before you there upon the Rock in Horeb; and you shall smite the Rock, and there shall come water out of it, that the people may drink. And Moses did so in the sight of the Elders of Israel. (This is one of the most beautiful Types found in the entirety of Scripture. The "Rock" was a Type of Christ [I Cor. 10:1-4]. The Rock being "smitten" typified the Cross [Isa. 53:4]. The "water" coming out of the Rock was a Type of the Holy Spirit [Jn. 7:37-39]. However, the water, i.e., "the Holy Spirit," was not available until the Rock [Christ] was smitten [crucified — Jn. 14:16-20]. In fact, Christ, the Cross, our Faith, and the Holy Spirit constitute the basis of Christianity [Gal., Chpt. 5].)

7 And he called the name of the place Massah (contention), and Meribah (strife), because of the chiding of the Children of Israel, and because they tempted the LORD, saying, Is the LORD among us, or not? (This proclaims the fact that the smitten Rock, which gushed forth with a river of water, was not brought about because of the Righteousness and Holiness of the people, but strictly because of the Grace of God; however, for the Believer to stay on a wrong path of unbelief will ultimately bring total destruction [Rom. 8:12].)

AMALEK

8 Then came Amalek, and fought with Israel in Rephidim. (The reception of the Holy Spirit, of which the water was a Type, immediately causes war. It's the war between the "flesh" and the "Holy Spirit" [Gal. 5:17].)

9 And Moses said unto Joshua, Choose us out men, and go out, fight with Amalek: tomorrow I will stand on the top of the hill with the Rod of God in my hand. (Up to this point God had fought for them. Then, Israel was to stand still and see His Salvation [14:13-14]; but

the command now is to go out and fight. There is an immense difference between Justification and Sanctification. The one is Christ fighting "for" us; the other, the Holy Spirit fighting "in" us. The entrance of the new nature is the beginning of warfare with the old.)

10 So Joshua did as Moses had said to him, and fought with Amalek: and Moses, Aaron, and Hur went up to the top of the hill. (Amalek pictures the old carnal nature. He was the grandson of Esau, who before and after birth tried to murder Jacob, and who preferred the mess of pottage to the birthright. This carnal nature wars against the Spirit; "it is not subject to the Law of God, neither indeed can be" [Rom. 8:7]. "Hur" means "light" — the emblem of Divine Holiness, and so points to the Holy Spirit. "Joshua" was a Type of Christ.)

11 And it came to pass, when Moses held up his hand, that Israel prevailed: and when he let down his hand, Amalek prevailed. (The hands "upheld" signified total dependence on the Lord. When the Believer is totally depending on the Lord, and what He did for us at the Cross, the victory of Christ belongs to us; otherwise, it doesn't!)

12 But Moses' hands were heavy; and they took a stone, and put it under him, and he sat thereon; and Aaron and Hur stayed up his hands, the one on the one side, and the other on the other side; and his hands were steady until the going down of the sun. (The "Stone," as well, is symbolic of Christ. Moses' exhaustion portrays the fact that our own efforts soon result in spiritual burn-out. But once we are in God's glorious way [sitting on the Stone], the victory is ours. "Aaron" was a Type of Christ as our Great High Priest, and "Hur," whose name means "light," speaks to us of the Holy Spirit. This is the help afforded the Child of God. But unfortunately, most Christians are trying to hold up their hands [trusting in God] by their own personal strength, which is doomed to failure.)

13 And Joshua discomfited Amalek and his people with the edge of the sword. (The "sword" here is a Type of the Word of God [Eph. 6:17]. The Word of God holds the answer to every single problem which pertains to "Life and Godliness" [II. Pet. 1:3-4].)

14 And the LORD said unto Moses, Write this for a memorial in the Book (this Verse presents the birth of the Bible as a written Book; the command was "Write this in 'the' Book," not in 'a' book), and rehearse it in the ears of Joshua: for I will utterly put out the remembrance of

Amalek from under Heaven. (It is remarkable that the first mention of the Bible should be in connection with the hostility of the natural man [Amalek] to the spiritual man [Israel].)

15 And Moses built an Altar, and called the name of it Jehovah-nissi (the Lord my Banner; the "Altar," of course, is a Type of Calvary; Christ is our Banner only through the Cross):

16 For he said, Because the LORD has sworn that the LORD will have war with Amalek from generation to generation. (Amalek was to dwell in the land, but not to reign in it. Romans 6:12 says, "Let not sin therefore reign in your mortal bodies." The command would be unmeaning if the sin nature were not existing in the Christian. The sin nature dwells in a Believer, but dwells and reigns in an unbeliever.)

CHAPTER 18
(1491 B.C.)
JETHRO

WHEN Jethro, the priest of Midian, Moses' father in law, heard of all that God had done for Moses, and for Israel His people, and that the LORD had brought Israel out of Egypt (in the Hebrew, "father-in-law" and "brother-in-law" present the same word; Reuel, Moses' father-in-law was dead, and had been succeeded by Jethro, probably his son and, therefore, the brother-in-law, and not the father-in-law, of Moses);

2 Then Jethro, Moses' father-in-law, took Zipporah, Moses' wife, after he had sent her back (it is obvious from the account given in Chapter 4 that Moses sent his wife, Zipporah, along with their two sons, Eliezer and Gershom, back to her own kin folk, the Midianites, before he went to Egypt),

3 And her two sons; of which the name of the one was Gershom; for he said, I have been an alien in a strange land:

4 And the name of the other was Eliezer; for the God of my father, said he, was my help, and delivered me from the sword of Pharaoh:

5 And Jethro, Moses' father-in-law, came with his sons and his wife (Moses' sons and wife) unto Moses into the wilderness, where he encamped at the Mount of God (concerning the time factor of this visit by Jethro, Pink says that Exodus, Chapter 18 is a parenthesis, interrupting the chronological order of the Book, which the Holy Spirit intended to do; he went on to say that Exodus, Chapter 17 portrays Israel at Rephidim, and then, in Chapter 19, they are

viewed at Sinai; so the incident recorded in Chapter 18 occurred just as Israel was about to leave Sinai and enter into the wilderness of Paran; it was in the third month after leaving Egypt that Israel reached the Mount of the Law; it was eleven months later that Jethro came to bring Moses' wife and children):

6 And he said unto Moses, I your father-in-law Jethro am come unto you, and your wife, and her two sons with her.

7 And Moses went out to meet his father-in-law, and did obeisance, and kissed him; and they asked each other of their welfare; and they came into the tent.

8 And Moses told his father-in-law all that the LORD had done unto Pharaoh and to the Egyptians for Israel's sake, and all the travail that had come upon them by the way, and how the LORD delivered them.

9 And Jethro rejoiced for all the goodness which the LORD had done to Israel, whom He had delivered out of the hand of the Egyptians.

10 And Jethro said, Blessed be the LORD, Who has delivered you out of the hand of the Egyptians, and out of the hand of Pharaoh, Who has the people from under the hand of the Egyptians.

11 Now I know that the LORD is greater than all gods: for in the thing wherein they dealt proudly He was above them *(from this statement, it seems that Jethro, like most heathen, believed in a plurality of gods and, therefore, had regarded the God of Israel as merely one among many equals; now he renounces this creed, and emphatically declares his belief that Jehovah is above all other gods; however, even though he has now confessed Jehovah as greater, still, it seems that he clings to the belief that other gods existed)*.

12 And Jethro, Moses' father-in-law, took a Burnt Offering and Sacrifices for God: and Aaron came, and all the Elders of Israel, to eat bread with Moses' father-in-law before God *(this Verse proclaims the fact that Moses knew and understood, as well as all the Elders of Israel, which he now relates to Jethro, that Israel's might and power were all in the Blood of the Lamb)*.

MAN'S ADVICE

13 And it came to pass on the morrow, that Moses sat to judge the people: and the people stood by Moses from the morning unto the evening.

14 And when Moses' father-in-law saw all that he did to the people, he said, What is this thing that you do to the people? why do you sit alone, and all the people stand by you from morning unto evening? *(Moses, for this particular time, succumbed to the temptation of the flesh, to rely on the weak arm of flesh. He listened to man instead of God. That problem persists with us even unto this hour.)*

15 And Moses said unto his father-in-law, Because the people come unto me to enquire of God *(while the responsibility of Moses was immense, he was not asked to bear these people alone, for God was with him)*:

16 When they have a matter, they come unto me; and I judge between one and another, and I do make them know the Statutes of God, and His laws *(it was God Who actually was bearing them; Moses was but the instrument; he might just as well have spoken of his rod as bearing the people; he was merely an instrument in God's Hand, as the rod was in his)*.

17 And Moses' father-in-law said unto him, The thing that you do is not good *(it is here the servants of Christ constantly fail; and the failure is all the more dangerous because it wears the appearance of humility)*.

18 You will surely wear away, both you, and this people who is with you: for this thing is too heavy for you; you are not able to perform it yourself alone *(if God has imposed the responsibility, He will surely do with the person what is necessary to sustain it)*.

19 Hearken now unto my voice, I will give you counsel, and God shall be with you: Be the representative of the people to God, that you may bring the causes unto God *(it is never the fruit of humility to depart from a Divinely-appointed post; on the contrary, the deepest humility will express itself by remaining there, which is simple dependence upon God)*:

20 And you shall teach them ordinances and laws, and shall show them the way wherein they must walk, and the work that they must do *(it is a sure evidence of being occupied with self when we shrink from Service on the ground of inability; God does not call us unto Service on the ground of our ability, but of His Own; the truth is, the advice given by Jethro was not of God)*.

21 Moreover you shall provide out of all the people able men, such as fear God, men of truth, hating covetousness; and place such over them, to be rulers of thousands, and rulers of hundreds, rulers of fifties, and rulers of tens

(the question is not of the advice offered by Jethro, whether good or bad, but rather that it came from the heart of man, and not from God; that's where the problem was; Moses was to look to the Lord for everything, which the Lord demands that we do presently; while I value the advice and counsel of my brother and sister in the Lord, it is the Holy Spirit Who guides me into all truth [Jn. 16:13-15]):

22 And let them judge the people at all seasons: and it shall be, that every great matter they shall bring unto you, but every small matter they shall judge: so shall it be easier for yourself, and they shall bear the burden with you. *(Some may ask, "Could not God use one such as Jethro to give advice and counsel?" God can use anything; however, had He been using Jethro, He would first of all have related this to Moses.)*

23 If you shall do this thing, and God command you so, then you shall be able to endure, and all this people shall also go to their place in peace.

24 So Moses hearkened to the voice of his father-in-law, and did all that he had said *(in essence, Moses complained of the burden, and the burden was speedily removed; but with it the high honor of being allowed to carry it).*

25 And Moses chose able men out of all Israel, and made them heads over the people, rulers of thousands, rulers of hundreds, rulers of fifties, and rulers of tens *(there was no fresh power introduced; it was the same Spirit, whether in one or in many; there was no more value or virtue in the flesh of many men than in the flesh of one man).*

26 And they judged the people at all seasons: the hard causes they brought unto Moses, but every small matter they judged themselves.

27 And Moses let his father-in-law depart; and he went his way into his own land. *(There was nothing in this wrong way of power gained, but a great deal in the way of dignity lost, by this movement on the part of Moses, as he listened to Jethro, instead of the Lord. There is a distinct possibility that the rebellion of Korah came out of these man-devised plans [Num., Chpt. 16].)*

CHAPTER 19
(1491 B.C.)
SINAI

IN the third month, when the Children of Israel were gone forth out of the land of Egypt, the same day came they into the wilderness of Sinai.

2 For they were departed from Rephidim, and were come to the desert of Sinai *(this desert, immediately before Mount Sinai, is approximately two miles long and a half mile wide; it is nearly flat, and could easily accommodate the nearly 3 million Israelites who would gather here)*, and had pitched in the wilderness; and there Israel camped before the Mount *(the Feast of the Passover witnessed Israel's departure from Egypt, and now they are soon to come to the Feast of Pentecost, which would occasion the giving of the Law, 50 days after Passover).*

THE COVENANT

3 And Moses went up unto God, and the LORD called unto him out of the mountain, saying, Thus shall you say to the house of Jacob, and tell the Children of Israel *(this is Mount Sinai, where the Law was given);*

4 You have seen what I did unto the Egyptians, and how I bore you on eagles' wings, and brought you unto Myself *(this speaks of a Salvation wholly of God).*

5 Now therefore, if you will obey My voice indeed, and keep My Covenant, then you shall be a peculiar treasure unto Me above all people: for all the Earth is Mine *(now, in Christ, spiritual Israel, which is the Church, is a part of this "peculiar treasure"):*

6 And you shall be unto Me a kingdom of priests, and an holy nation. These are the words which you shall speak unto the Children of Israel *(these were God's people, in fact, the only people on the face of the Earth who fell into this category; even though all the Earth was His, still, these were the only people who knew Him).*

7 And Moses came and called for the Elders of the people, and laid before their faces all these words which the LORD commanded him.

8 And all the people answered together, and said, All that the LORD has spoken we will do. And Moses returned the words of the people unto the LORD. *(Man has ever proclaimed his ability to obey God, and has ever portrayed his constant failure. Had they known their own hearts, they would have replied that such a condition was impossible to them; and they would have cast themselves upon God that He would give them new hearts capable of such an obedience. This would have been granted, and the*

Feast promised in Chapter 5 enjoyed. Instead of the Feast, there was fear and judgment.)

THE PEOPLE

9 And the LORD said unto Moses, Lo, I come unto you in a thick cloud, that the people may hear when I speak with you, and believe you for ever. And Moses told the words of the people unto the LORD. *(God is "thrice-Holy." As such, He has to veil Himself when He speaks to sinful man.)*

10 And the LORD said unto Moses, Go unto the people, and sanctify them today and tomorrow, and let them wash their clothes *(the word "sanctify" actually means "set apart" and, in this case, "set apart exclusively to the Lord"),*

11 And be ready against the third day: for the third day the LORD will come down in the sight of all the people upon Mount Sinai *(three days were to be spent in preparation of the people).*

12 And you shall set bounds unto the people round about, saying, Take heed to yourselves, that you go not up into the Mount, or touch the border of it: whosoever touches the Mount shall be surely put to death *(as is obvious, before the Cross, man was very limited as to how he could approach God; since the Cross, "whosoever will may come" [Rev. 22:17]):*

13 There shall not an hand touch it, but he shall surely be stoned, or shot through; whether it be beast or man, it shall not live: when the trumpet sounds long, they shall come up to the Mount.

14 And Moses went down from the Mount unto the people, and sanctified the people; and they washed their clothes *(sanctification then was mostly external, meaning symbolic; however, since the Cross, Sanctification is a spiritual work).*

15 And he said unto the people, Be ready against the third day: come not at your wives *(once again, this had to do with the sanctification process).*

16 And it came to pass on the third day in the morning, that there were thunders and lightnings, and a thick cloud upon the Mount, and the voice of the trumpet exceeding loud; so that all the people that was in the camp trembled. *(And rightly so! The Cross alone has opened up the way.)*

17 And Moses brought forth the people out of the camp to meet with God; and they stood at the nether part of the Mount. *(It is not that*

God is unapproachable. In fact, He wanted man to approach, but, due to the sinfulness of man, this, at the time, was the best that could be done.)

18 And Mount Sinai was altogether on a smoke, because the LORD descended upon it in fire: and the smoke there ascended as the smoke of a furnace, and the whole Mount quaked greatly. *(All of this proclaims the awful Holiness of God Almighty. What a mighty God we serve!)*

MOSES

19 And when the voice of the trumpet sounded long, and waxed louder and louder, Moses spoke, and God answered him by a voice *(may be translated, "And God kept answering him by a voice"; this explains how the following Chapters were given to Moses).*

20 And the LORD came down upon Mount Sinai, on the top of the Mount: and the LORD called Moses up to the top of the Mount; and Moses went up *(it is believed that Aaron at this time may have been with Moses).*

21 And the LORD said unto Moses, Go down, charge the people, lest they break through unto the LORD to gaze, and many of them perish *(no sooner had Moses arrived at the appointed place that the Lord told him to go back down; once again, the people must be warned).*

22 And let the priests also, which come near to the LORD, sanctify themselves, lest the LORD break forth upon them *(none were excluded, concerning the warning).*

23 And Moses said unto the LORD, The people cannot come up to Mount Sinai: for you charged us, saying, Set bounds about the Mount, and sanctify it *(if men presently attempt to come into the Presence of God by any means other than the Cross, spiritual death is the result, and sometimes physical death [Eph. 2:13-18]).*

24 And the LORD said unto him, Away, get thee down, and you shall come up, you, and Aaron with you: but let not the priests and the people break through to come up unto the LORD, lest He *(the Lord)* break forth upon them.

25 So Moses went down unto the people, and spoke unto them.

CHAPTER 20
(1491 B.C.)
THE TEN COMMANDMENTS

AND God spoke all these words, saying *(the Ten Commandments given by God to Moses*

on Mount Sinai are the foundation of all law, at least law that is righteous, for the entire world; it is the moral Law of God and, as such, cannot change),

2 I am the LORD your God, which have brought you out of the land of Egypt, out of the house of bondage (the Lord doesn't appeal to the Israelites as Creator, even though He definitely was that; He appealed to them as their Deliverer; as a result, He was to be obeyed by His people from a sentiment of love, not by fear).

3 You shall have no other gods before Me (the manner in which this First Commandment is given indicates that each individual of the nation is addressed severally, and is required personally to obey the Law, a mere general national obedience being insufficient; this Commandment requires the worship of one God Alone, Jehovah; it implies, in point of fact, that there is no other God).

4 You shall not make unto yourself any graven image, or any likeness of any thing that is in Heaven above, or that is in the Earth beneath, or that is in the water under the Earth.

5 You shall not bow down yourself to them, nor serve them: for I the LORD your God am a jealous God, visiting the iniquity of the fathers upon the children unto the third and fourth generation of them who hate Me;

6 And showing mercy unto thousands of them who love Me, and keep My Commandments. (The prohibition intended here does not forbid the arts of sculptor, painting, photography, etc., or even to condemn the use of them, but to disallow the worship of God under material forms. Those who ignore this Commandment are guilty of the sin of idolatry. Also, many have tried to derive from Verse 5 that which they refer to as the "family curse"; however, let it be known and understood, every curse was addressed at the Cross of Calvary [Gal. 3:13-14]. As well, Jesus has perfectly kept all the Commandments, and all who trust Him, and what He did for us at the Cross, are participants of God's gracious Mercy.)

7 You shall not take the name of the Lord your God in vain; for the LORD will not hold him guiltless who takes His name in vain (taking the name of the Lord in vain pertains to all blasphemy, all swearing, all perjury and, in fact, all irreverent use of God's Name in ordinary life).

8 Remember the sabbath day, to keep it holy.

9 Six days you shall labour, and do all your work:

10 But the seventh day is the sabbath of the LORD your God: in it you shall not do any work, you, nor your son, nor your daughter, your manservant, nor your maidservant, nor your cattle, nor your stranger that is within your gates:

11 For in six days the LORD made Heaven and Earth, the sea, and all that in them is, and rested the seventh day: wherefore the LORD blessed the sabbath day, and hallowed it. (The seventh day was not so much to be a day of worship, as we think of such now, but rather a day of "rest." Even the very beasts, pressed into man's service since the Fall, shall rest. All were to observe this day. Everything pertaining to the Law of Moses, in some way, spoke of Christ. The "Sabbath" was no exception. It was meant to portray the fact that there is "rest" in Christ and, in fact, that there is rest "only in Christ" [Mat. 11:28-30]. So, when a person presently accepts Christ, they are in effect keeping the Sabbath, which speaks of the "rest" that we have in Christ — rest from self-effort to attain unto Righteousness. Even though there was no written command by the Holy Spirit to do so, gradually we find Believers, during the time of the Early Church, as recorded in the Book of Acts, making Sunday, the first day of the week, the day of our Lord's Resurrection, their day of worship, etc., which is different than the Sabbath of old, because Christ has fulfilled in totality the old Jewish Sabbath.)

12 Honour your father and your mother: that your days may be long upon the land which the LORD your God gives you (honoring the father and the mother sets the stage for the honoring of God; the first five Commandments have to do with man's obligation toward God, while the last five have to do with his obligation toward his fellowman).

13 You shall not kill (should have been translated, "Thou shalt do no murder"; God, in His Holy Word, commands magistrates to put evil men to death [Rom. 13:4]; that is not murder; to "kill" and to "commit murder" are two different verbs in the Hebrew Text).

14 You shall not commit adultery (regarding this sin, both man and woman are placed in the same category; our duty toward our neighbor is to respect the bond on which the family is based, and that conjugal honor which to the true man is dearer than life; marriage, according to the original institution, makes the husband and wife "one flesh" [Gen. 2:24]; and to break in upon this sacramental union was at once a crime

and a profanity; it is a sin against man and against God).

15 You shall not steal (as it regards our neighbor, we are to respect his property; we simply don't take that which doesn't belong to us).

16 You shall not bear false witness against your neighbour (false witness is of two kinds, public and private; we may either seek to damage our neighbor by giving false evidence against him in a court of justice, or simply culminate him to others in our social intercourse with them).

17 You shall not covet your neighbour's house, you shall not covet your neighbour's wife, nor his manservant, nor his maidservant, nor his ox, nor his ass, nor any thing that is your neighbour's (covetousness addresses what causes the evil deed; this Commandment teaches men that there is One Who sees the heart; to Whose Eyes "all things are naked and open"; and Who cares far less for the outward act than the inward thought or motive from which the act proceeds).

FEAR

18 And all the people saw the thunderings, and the lightnings, and the noise of the trumpet, and the mountain smoking: and when the people saw it, they removed, and stood afar off (the word "saw" in this Verse is a particular type of Hebrew verb which means "perceive, witness"; in other words, no one of the hundreds of thousands of the Children of Israel had any doubt as to what they had witnessed and experienced).

19 And they said unto Moses, You speak with us, and we will hear: but let not God speak with us, lest we die (as powerful as was this manifestation, one far more powerful was yet to be manifested, and we speak of the coming of Christ, Who manifested the Father as He had not been manifested before).

20 And Moses said unto the people, Fear not: for God is come to prove you, and that His fear may be before your faces, that you sin not (the Lord manifesting Himself in this fashion was not meant to strike fear in the people, even though it definitely did that, but rather that the people would want to obey the Lord, because of His Almighty Power).

21 And the people stood afar off, and Moses drew near unto the thick darkness where God was (the Cross made it possible for all who "stand afar off" to now "come near" [Rev. 22:17]).

WORSHIP

22 And the LORD said unto Moses, Thus you shall say unto the Children of Israel, You have seen that I have talked with you from Heaven (the greatest Revelation yet!).

23 You shall not make with Me gods of silver, neither shall you make unto you gods of gold (no image was to be made of what they thought God looked like; even if made of silver or gold it would be grossly wrong).

24 An Altar of earth you shall make unto Me, and shall sacrifice thereon your Burnt Offerings, and your Peace Offerings, your sheep, and your oxen: in all places where I record My name I will come unto you, and I will bless you. (The Altar pictures Christ and what He would do for us at the Cross. The earth pictured His humanity; the stone, His Deity; the shed blood of the animal sacrificed, His priceless Life sacrificed to put away sin and bring the sinner back to God [I Pet. 3:18]. All blessings come exclusively through the Cross, and no blessings come other than through the Cross, at least not from God.)

25 And if you will make Me an Altar of stone, you shall not build it of hewn stone: for if you lift up your tool upon it, you have polluted it. (No tool was to embellish the Altar; it was perfect in its beauty to the eye of God. And such was, and is, Jesus. As well, one might seek to paint the lily or adorn the rose, as for man to attempt to add to the beauty of Him Who is altogether lovely. As well, man must not seek to add to Calvary, or take from Calvary, which the "tool" would do, and which it is doing in countless places at present.)

26 Neither shall you go up by steps unto My Altar, that your nakedness be not discovered thereon. (When man exalts himself above God, he only exposes his own moral nakedness. The Cross, of which the Altar was a Type, must not be changed in any way. If so, meaning if men try to picture or present Christ in another fashion rather than "Jesus Christ and Him Crucified" [I Cor. 1:23], they then find themselves with "another Jesus" [II Cor. 11:4]. Lifting up the tool upon the stone, desiring to make it into their own likes or dislikes, thereby pollutes the Message. This is the great sin of the modern Church.)

CHAPTER 21
(1491 B.C.)
SERVANTS

NOW these are the judgments which you shall set before them (the legislation

involving this Chapter, and the following two, points to a loving God charting a moral course for a corrupt people).

2 If you buy an Hebrew servant, six years he shall serve: and in the seventh he shall go out free for nothing *(the servants in the economy of Israel, as designed by God, had no kindred spirit whatsoever with that which we think of today as slavery; it was the same as an individual hiring himself to a particular master or family to serve for a period of time, which payment would include certain things; the time for this particular servitude was six years).*

3 If he came in by himself, he shall go out by himself: if he were married, then his wife shall go out with him *(if the man was married when he indentured himself, when he had served the agreed upon time, his wife would be free with him).*

4 If his master have given him a wife, and she have born him sons or daughters; the wife and her children shall be her master's, and he shall go out by himself *(in this case, he would have to make arrangements as it regards his wife and children).*

5 And if the servant shall plainly say, I love my master, my wife, and my children; I will not go out free *(all of this proclaims the Servanthood of Christ and, thereby, the manner in which we are to serve the Lord):*

6 Then his master shall bring him unto the judges; he shall also bring him to the door, or unto the door post; and his master shall bore his ear through with an aul; and he shall serve him for ever. *(This perfectly Types our Lord Jesus Christ. He indentured Himself to the human race, and served perfectly. During this time, He gained a wife, i.e., "the Church" [Rom. 7:4]. The union of Himself with this corporate body has brought forth "children" [Eph. 2:13-18]. Furthermore, He was "pierced" on the Cross for you and me, thereby guaranteeing His position as "Intercessor" on our behalf, and forever. He did this because He loves the Father, and He loves us.)*

7 And if a man sell his daughter to be a maidservant, she shall not go out as the menservants do.

8 If she please not her master, who has betrothed her to himself, then shall he let her be redeemed: to sell her unto a strange nation he shall have no power, seeing he has dealt deceitfully with her.

9 And if he have betrothed her unto his son, he shall deal with her after the manner of daughters.

10 If he take him another wife; her food, her raiment, and her duty of marriage, shall he not diminish.

11 And if he do not these three unto her, then shall she go out free without money. *(How does all of this picture Christ? It does so in the fact that He has bought us [I Cor. 6:20; 7:23]. The "maidservant" refers to Israel. Israel desired to remain under the Law; therefore, she chose a secondary position. "Another wife" refers to the Church. But yet, Israel is to continue to be supported, which the Lord has done with this people in a distant way. Not desiring to remain at all, she has been allowed to go her own way. But that way has proven to be most unsatisfactory. But even as Hosea predicted, and showed by his own personal experiences, Israel will return.*

While all of this had to do with everyday life and living as it regards Israel of long ago, still, it had a prophetic meaning, as well, to which we have briefly alluded. We must never forget that Jesus is the True Israel, just as He is the True Church and the True Man.)

MURDER

12 He who smites a man, so that he die, shall be surely put to death *(this speaks of that which we now refer to as "cold-blooded murder").*

13 And if a man lie not in wait, but God deliver him into his hand; then I will appoint you a place where he shall flee. *(These statements involve aggravated assault, or even second-degree murder. Six cities of refuge were to be designated, where the shedder of blood might flee, and where he might be safe from relatives of the deceased, until his cause was tried before the men of his own city, or else the High Priest dies [Num. 35:22-25]. When the High Priest died, the accused could then go free. Of course, this had to do with Christ, our Great High Priest, Who died on the Cross of Calvary that we might go free.)*

14 But if a man come presumptuously upon his neighbour, to kill him with guile; you shall take him from My Altar, that he may die. *(Joab is a perfect example of this [I Ki. 2:28-34]. The idea is, in some cases, the condemned could grab hold of the horns of the Altar and be spared; however, this was only in cases where his action had seemed justified. Bringing it up to the present time, the Holy Spirit is telling us here that one cannot claim to trust Christ and what Christ did at the Cross and, at the same time, continue*

presumptuously in sin. *Many have the erroneous idea that if they claim to have Faith in Christ, this covers their wayward direction. It doesn't! Jesus saves us from sin, not in sin!*)

PARENTS

15 And he who smites his father, or his mother, shall be surely put to death.

KIDNAPPING

16 And he who steals *(kidnaps)* a man, and sells him *(as a slave)* , or if he be found in his hand, he shall surely be put to death.

PARENTAL DISHONOR

17 And he who curses his father, or his mother, shall surely be put to death. *(Pulpit Commentary says concerning this: "The unsystematic character of the arrangement in this Chapter is remarkably shown by this interruption of the consideration of different sorts of homicide, in order to introduce offenses of quite a different character, and those not very closely allied to each other." Three capital crimes requiring capital punishment are noted here: 1. The dishonoring of parents, whether striking the parent by the child, or 2. Cursing the mother or the father, both were punishable by death; and, 3. Kidnapping is as well punishable by death.*

The severity of the sentence indicates that in God's sight such sins are of the deepest dye.)

OFFENSES

18 And if men strive together, and one smite another with a stone, or with his fist, and he die not, but keeps his bed:

19 If he rise again, and walk abroad upon his staff, then shall he who smote him be quit *(acquitted)*: only he shall pay for the loss of his time, and shall cause him to be thoroughly healed.

20 And if a man smite his servant, or his maid, with a rod, and he die under his hand; he shall be surely punished.

21 Notwithstanding, if he continue a day or two, he shall not be punished: for he is his money *(meaning that he has paid for the services of the servant and, providing the cause was just, he must not be punished, even though he did hit him).*

22 If men strive, and hurt a woman with child, so that her fruit depart from her *(the pregnancy is terminated)*, and yet no mischief follow: he shall be surely punished, according as the woman's husband will lay upon him; and he shall pay as the judges determine.

23 And if any mischief follow, then you shall give life for life,

24 Eye for eye, tooth for tooth, hand for hand, foot for foot,

25 Burning for burning, wound for wound, stripe for stripe. *(The order of retaliation, as it referred to here, was seldom carried out under Jewish Law, but was rather settled by the giving of money or labor, etc.; however, let it ever be understood, the Scripture also says: "Vengeance is Mine; I will repay, saith the Lord" [Lev. 19:18; Deut. 32:35]. Jesus said, "With what measure you mete, it shall be measured to you again" [Mat. 7:1]. The Word of God, in one way or the other, will always be carried out.)*

26 And if a man smite the eye of his servant, or the eye of his maid, that it perish; he shall let him go free for his eye's sake.

27 And if he smite out his manservant's tooth, or his maidservant's tooth; he shall let him go free for his tooth's sake.

28 If an ox gore a man or a woman, that they die: then the ox shall be surely stoned, and his flesh shall not be eaten; but the owner of the ox shall be quit *(won't be responsible).*

29 But if the ox were wont to push with his horn in time past, and it had been testified to his owner, and he has not kept him in, but that he has killed a man or a woman; the ox shall be stoned, and his owner also shall be put to death.

30 If there be laid on him a sum of money, then he shall give for the ransom of his life whatsoever is laid upon him *(pay money instead of forfeiting his life, which was what was normally done).*

31 Whether he have gored a son, or have gored a daughter, according to this judgment shall it be done unto him.

32 If the ox shall push a manservant or a maidservant; he shall give unto their master thirty shekels of silver, and the ox shall be stoned.

33 And if a man shall open a pit, or if a man shall dig a pit, and not cover it, and an ox or an ass fall therein;

34 The owner of the pit shall make it good, and give money unto the owner of them; and the dead beast shall be his.

35 And if one man's ox hurt another's, that

he die; then they shall sell the live ox, and divide the money of it, and the dead ox also they shall divide.

36 Or if it be known that the ox has used to push in time past, and his owner has not kept him in; he shall surely pay ox for ox; and the dead shall be his own. *(He will be responsible. We also see in all of this that God is no respecter of persons. What was applicable to the poorest of the poor was just as applicable to the rich and the powerful.*

All of this shows us the amazing love of God, and the shocking depravity of man. It is humiliating to learn that such laws had to be made to protect men from the appalling evil which prompted them to oppress one another. On the other hand, the tender Love of God shines forth like the Sun in this legislation. That mighty love even thought upon the tooth of a little slave girl, and enacted that she should be set free if so slightly injured [Vs. 27].)

CHAPTER 22

(1491 B.C.)

RESTITUTION

IF a man shall steal an ox, or a sheep, and kill it, or sell it; he shall restore five oxen for an ox, and four sheep for a sheep.

2 If a thief be found breaking up *(breaking into a house)*, and be smitten that he die, there shall no blood be shed for him *(justifiable homicide)*.

3 If the sun be risen upon him, there shall be blood shed for him *(the thief has no intention of harming anyone; therefore, if he is maliciously killed, the man who kills him may very well suffer the same fate from the man's relatives)*; for he should make full restitution *(the thief should replace what he has stolen)*; if he have nothing, then he shall be sold for this theft *(sold as a slave, in order that the debt be paid)*.

4 If the theft be certainly found in his hand alive, whether it be ox, or ass, or sheep; he shall restore double.

5 If a man shall cause a field or vineyard to be eaten, and shall put in his beast, and shall feed in another man's field; of the best of his own field, and of the best of his own vineyard, shall he make restitution *(as I'm certain is obvious by now, property rights were held sacred)*.

6 If fire break out, and catch in thorns, so that the stacks of corn, or the standing corn, or the field, be consumed therewith; he who kindled the fire shall surely make restitution.

7 If a man shall deliver unto his neighbour money or stuff to keep, and it be stolen out of the man's house; if the thief be found, let him pay double.

8 If the thief be not found, then the master of the house shall be brought unto the judges, to see whether he have put his hand unto his neighbour's goods. *(The Law of Moses, which in reality is the Law of God, taught Israel many things. It taught them how they should conduct themselves toward God, and also went into minute detail as to how they should conduct themselves toward their fellowman. Nothing was left out, with every single thing covered; Israel was expected to abide by this legislation.)*

9 For all manner of trespass, whether it be for ox, for ass, for sheep, for raiment, or for any manner of lost thing which another challenges to be his, the cause of both parties shall come before the judges *(a trial)*; and whom the judges shall condemn, he shall pay double unto his neighbour.

10 If a man deliver unto his neighbour an ass, or an ox, or a sheep, or any beast, to keep; and it die, or be hurt, or driven away, no man seeing it:

11 Then shall an oath of the LORD be between them both, that he has not put his hand unto his neighbour's goods; and the owner of it shall accept thereof, and he shall not make it good.

12 And if it be stolen from him, he shall make restitution unto the owner thereof.

13 If it be torn in pieces, then let him bring it for witness, and he shall not make good that which was torn.

14 And if a man borrow ought of his neighbour, and it be hurt, or die, the owner thereof being not with it, he shall surely make it good.

15 But if the owner thereof be with it, he shall not make it good: if it be an hired thing, it came for his hire. *(While the Law was totally fulfilled in Christ, which means that it is not now incumbent upon Believers, still, the principle of Law will always, and without exception, be carried out in Christ, that is, if Christ is properly addressed.)*

ENTICEMENT

16 And if a man entice a maid that is not betrothed, and lie with her, he shall surely endow her to be his wife *(if this law was followed now, this sin would be greatly decreased)*.

17 If her father utterly refuse to give her unto him, he *(the one who committed the sin)* shall pay money according to the dowry of virgins.

CAPITAL CRIMES

18 You shall not suffer a witch to live *(this applied to Israel only, and is not incumbent on modern Believers; however, it must be readily understood that God is unalterably opposed to all type of witchcraft).*

19 Whosoever lies with a beast *(engage in intercourse)* shall surely be put to death *(this sin is grossly unnatural, in that it insults God, as it regards His role as Creator; any such act pulls one down to the level of an animal, thereby insulting God's highest form of creation, which is man).*

20 He who sacrifices unto any god, save unto the LORD only, he shall be utterly destroyed. *(Pulpit says: "Sacrifice was the chief act of worship; and to sacrifice to a false god was to renounce the True God. Under a theocracy, which Israel was, this was rebellion, and rightly punished with death. In states which were not a theocracy [God-ruled], and none were with the exception of Israel, such would not be a civil offense, and would be left to the final judgment of the Almighty.")*

VARIOUS DUTIES

21 You shall neither vex a stranger *(a Gentile)* nor oppress him: for you were strangers in the land of Egypt.

22 You shall not afflict any widow, or fatherless child.

23 If you afflict them in any wise, and they cry at all unto Me, I will surely hear their cry;

24 And My wrath shall wax hot, and I will kill you with the sword; and your wives shall be widows, and your children fatherless. *(The Gentile, referred to as a "stranger," was placed with the widow and the orphan, and made the special object of God's care. In fact, it was on account of the neglect of this precept that the capture of Jerusalem by Nebuchadnezzar, and the destruction of its inhabitants, was allowed to take place [Jer. 22:3-5].)*

25 If you lend money to any of My people that is poor by you, you shall not be to him as an usurer, neither shall you lay upon him usury. *(In the lending of money, Jews were not to charge other Jews interest on that money. On the other hand, it was distinctly declared that interest might be taken from strangers [Deut. 23:20].)*

26 If you at all take your neighbour's raiment to pledge *(as collateral),* you shall deliver it unto him by that the sun goes down:

27 For that is his covering only, it is his raiment for his skin: wherein shall he sleep? and it shall come to pass, when he cries unto Me, that I will hear; for I am gracious.

28 You shall not revile the gods *(Judges or Magistrates),* nor curse the ruler of your people *(the office must be respected).*

29 You shall not delay to offer the first of your ripe fruits, and of your liquors *(Tithes):* the firstborn of your sons shall you give unto Me *(dedicate to the Lord).*

30 Likewise shall you do with your oxen, and with your sheep: seven days it shall be with his dam *(the mother);* on the eighth day you shall give it Me *(due to the Fall, birth was viewed as an unclean process, which it was, and is, and, therefore, nothing was fit for presentation to God except after a particular interval, here, seven days).*

31 And you shall be holy men unto Me *("to be set apart exclusively unto God"):* neither shall you eat any flesh that is torn of beasts in the field; you shall cast it to the dogs. *(It was because the blood of such an animal would not be properly drained from it. Some would remain in the tissues, and thence the animal would be unclean.)*

CHAPTER 23
(1491 B.C.)
ETHICAL MATTERS

YOU shall not raise a false report: put not your hand with the wicked to be an unrighteous witness. *(This deals with the Ninth Commandment, in that we must not bear false witness.)*

2 You shall not follow a multitude to do evil; neither shall you speak in a cause to decline after many to wrest judgment *(just because a multitude of people may champion a particular cause doesn't necessarily mean that it's right):*

3 Neither shall you countenance a poor man in his cause *(in courts of justice, strict justice is to be rendered without any leaning either towards the rich or towards the poor; to lean either way is to pervert judgment).*

4 If you meet your enemy's ox or his ass going astray, you shall surely bring it back to him again *(it is remarkable as to how close*

this particular law comes to New Testament Christianity).

5 If you see the ass of him who hates you lying under his burden, and would forbear to help him, you shall surely help with him *(do unto others as you would have them do unto you).*

6 You shall not wrest the judgment of your poor in his cause *(while Verse 3 warned that the poor were not to be favored simply because they were poor, this Verse goes a step further, in effect, stating that the poor must not be maltreated simply because they are poor).*

7 You must keep far from a false matter; and the innocent and righteous slay you not: for I will not justify the wicked *(in effect, the Holy Spirit through Moses is saying here that the innocent and the righteous can be seriously hurt by the spreading of "false matters").*

8 And you shall take no gift: for the gift blinds the wise, and perverts the words of the righteous *(this Verse condemns all bribery).*

9 Also you shall not oppress a stranger *(Gentile)*: for you know the heart of a stranger, seeing you were strangers in the land of Egypt.

10 And six years you shall sow your land, and shall gather in the fruits thereof:

11 But the seventh year you shall let it rest and lie still; that the poor of your people may eat: and what they leave the beasts of the field shall eat. In like manner you shall deal with your vineyard, and with your oliveyard. *(The seventh year was to be a sabbatical year, when no crops were to be planted, and the land was to lie fallow. It is believed that the "seventy years" of captivity by the Babylonians were intended to make up for the failure of this observance of the sabbatical year. This being the case, we must understand that God says what He means, and means what He says!)*

12 Six days you shall do your work, and on the seventh day you shall rest: that your ox and your ass may rest, and the son of your handmaid, and the stranger, may be refreshed *(as well, Israel was to remember the Sabbath, which speaks of the seventh day; as stated, this was a symbol of the "rest" which one would find in Christ).*

13 And in all things that I have said unto you be circumspect *(be careful to obey these laws)*: and make no mention of the name of other gods, neither let it be heard out of your mouth *(Israelites were not to mention the names of heathen gods; they were rather to praise the Lord, and do so constantly).*

THREE NATIONAL FEASTS

14 Three times you shall keep a Feast unto Me in the year. *(Man's corrupt doctrine is never to be added to the fact of Atonement; hence the importance and sweetness of the expressions "My Sacrifice" and "Feast unto Me" — Williams.)*

15 You shall keep the feast of Unleavened Bread: (you shall eat unleavened bread seven days, as I commanded you, in the time appointed of the month Abib; for in it you came out from Egypt: and none shall appear before Me empty:) *(This Feast took place during the time of the barley harvest, which would correspond with our April. During the seven day period, three Feasts were observed: "Passover," "Unleavened Bread," and "Firstfruits." All typified Christ: "Crucifixion," "Perfect Life," "Resurrection." As well, none were to come before the Lord without the proper Sacrifice.)*

16 And the Feast of Harvest, the firstfruits of your labours, which you have sown in the field *(this was the Feast of Pentecost, which took place 50 days after Passover, corresponding with our May; it typified Christ as the Baptizer with the Holy Spirit)*: and the Feast of Ingathering, which is in the end of the year, when you have gathered in your labours out of the field. *(This was the Feast of Tabernacles, which took place at the time of the fruit harvest, corresponding with our October; it incorporated three Feasts: "Trumpets," "Atonement," and "Tabernacles." The entire time was approximately 15 days.)*

17 Three times in the year all your males *(from each family)* shall appear before the LORD God *(at these seven Feasts conducted three times a year, April, May, and October).*

18 You shall not offer the blood of My Sacrifice with leavened bread; neither shall the fat of My Sacrifice remain until the morning. *(It shall be burned immediately on the Altar. Nothing must be added to the Cross, or taken from the Cross. The Cross of Christ is the revealed truth of God's judgment on sin. Never associate the idea of martyrdom with the Cross of Christ. It was the supreme triumph, and it shook the very foundations of Hell. There is nothing in time or eternity more certain and irrefutable than what Jesus Christ accomplished on the Cross — He made it possible for the entire human race to be brought back into a right-standing relationship with God.)*

19 The first of the firstfruits of your land you shall bring into the house of the LORD your God. You shall not seethe *(boil)* a kid

(baby lamb) in his mother's milk. *(This is repeated three times in the Law of Moses [Ex. 23:19; 34:16; Deut. 14:21]. This prohibition had to do with the lamb being a symbol, or even a Type, of the coming Son of God, Who would give Himself for our sins on the Cross of Calvary. Christ did not die in the womb and, as well, even though Satan tried his hardest, He obviously was not killed as a baby. So, it was prohibited that a baby lamb would be used in this fashion.)*

INSTRUCTIONS

20 Behold, I send an Angel before you, to keep you in the way, and to bring you into the place which I have prepared. *(The "Angel" mentioned here is the "Son of God.")*

21 Beware of Him, and obey His voice, provoke Him not; for He will not pardon your transgressions: for My Name is in Him. *(Jewish Commentators claim the Angel to be Moses; however, the expressions, "pardon" and "My Name is in Him," are too high for Moses, or any man, for that matter.)*

22 But if you shall indeed obey His voice, and do all that I speak; then I will be an enemy unto your enemies, and an adversary unto your adversaries. *(This holds true at present, as well!)*

23 For My Angel shall go before you, and bring you in unto the Amorites, and the Hittites, and the Perizzites, and the Canaanites, the Hivites, and the Jebusites: and I will cut them off. *(While the enemies would be present in the Promised Land, Israel didn't have to worry; the Lord would go before them and handle the situation. He does the same for us presently.)*

24 You shall not bow down to their gods, nor serve them, nor do after their works: but you shall utterly overthrow them, and quite break down their images. *(Israel was to rid the land of all heathen gods.)*

25 And you shall serve the LORD your God, and He shall bless your bread, and your water; and I will take sickness away from the midst of you. *(What a Promise!)*

26 There shall nothing cast their young, nor be barren, in your land *(Israel would be fruitful as it regards large families)*: the number of your days I will fulfill *(long life)*.

27 I will send My fear before you, and will destroy all the people to whom you shall come, and I will make all your enemies turn their backs unto you. *(The Lord promises to destroy all the enemies of Israel. Can modern Believers claim the same Promises? We can claim these Promises,*

and even greater, because we now have a better Covenant, based on better Promises [Heb. 8:6].)

28 And I will send hornets before you, which shall drive out the Hivite, the Canaanite, and the Hittite, from before you. *(The Lord has the entirety of creation at His disposal to use as He sees fit. So, He can take something as small as a "hornet" and use it as His army, which He did.)*

29 I will not drive them out from before you in one year; lest the land become desolate, and the beast of the field multiply against you.

30 By little and little I will drive them out from before you, until you be increased, and inherit the land. *(Had their obedience been more complete, the power of the Canaanitish nations would have been more thoroughly broken, and the sufferings and servitude related in the Book of Judges would not have had to be endured.)*

31 And I will set your bounds from the Red Sea *(takes in all of Sinai, the exact area occupied by Israel some years back, when they defeated the Egyptians, but given back to Egypt in the Camp David Accords)* even unto the Sea of the Philistines *(the Mediterranean)*, and from the desert *(marks the eastern boundary, which probably included some of modern-day Saudi Arabia)* unto the river *(the "river" in the Pentateuch is always the "Euphrates," which marked the northern boundary; so we can see from all of this that Israel was promised much more than what they actually attained, except under David)*: for I will deliver the inhabitants of the land into your hand; and you shall drive them out before you. *(We are living as Believers in a fallen world. It is ruled by the prince of darkness; consequently, the Lord sets boundaries, as it regards His Children, with guaranteed victories within those boundaries, that is, if we properly follow the Lord.)*

32 You shall make no covenant with them, nor with their gods. *(Every enemy must be rooted out of the land, just as every enemy must be rooted out of our own lives. Total trust in the Lord, and what He accomplished at Calvary, which gives the Holy Spirit the latitude to work in our lives, is the only way this can be done [Rom. 6:3-14; 8:1-2, 11; Gal. 6:14].)*

33 They shall not dwell in your land, lest they make you sin against Me: for if you serve their gods, it will surely be a snare unto you. *(Anything we leave in our lives that is a reproach to the Lord will ultimately be a "snare unto us." Everything that is un-Christlike must be rooted out!)*

CHAPTER 24
(1491 B.C.)
THE BLOOD

AND He *(the Lord)* said unto Moses, Come up unto the LORD, you, and Aaron, and Nadab, and Abihu *(Aaron's sons)*, and seventy of the elders of Israel; and you shall worship afar off. *(The short phrase "afar off" proclaims the best the Law can do. One can search out the Law, and not be able to find the two words, "Draw nigh." The Blood of Jesus Alone makes it possible for believing sinners to "draw nigh," and that alone [Eph. 2:13-18].)*

2 And Moses alone shall come near the LORD: but they *(all the others)* shall not come near: neither shall the people go up with him.

3 And Moses came and told the people all the words of the LORD, and all the judgments: and all the people answered with one voice, and said, All the words which the LORD has said will we do. *(That which Moses told the people as he came down from the mountain pertained to the legislation given us in Chapters 21-23.)*

4 And Moses wrote all the words of the LORD, and rose up early in the morning, and built an Altar under the hill, and twelve pillars, according to the twelve tribes of Israel. *(The "Altar" represents Christ and what He would do at the Cross. The "twelve pillars" represent the Government of God, with the number "twelve" in the Bible always standing for that principle. So, we see here that the Government of God is built on the Foundation of the Cross, which, in effect, was in the Mind of God from before the foundation of the world [I Pet. 1:18-20]. If we attempt to build a government outside of the Cross, or to tamper in any way with the Cross, as it regards the changing of its meaning, we have just instituted a government devised by man, which God can never accept. And that's exactly what the modern Church is doing.)*

5 And he sent young men of the Children of Israel which offered Burnt Offerings, and sacrificed Peace Offerings of oxen unto the LORD. *(The "Burnt Offerings" signified that God would give His all as it refers to the Redemption of man, and the "Peace Offerings" signified that the "Whole Burnt Offering" was accepted by God, and peace is now restored. The "Peace Offering" could also be offered after the "Sin" and "Trespass Offerings.")*

6 And Moses took half of the blood, and put it in basons: and half of the blood he sprinkled on the Altar. *(The blood, which symbolized the life of the victim, was the essential part of every Sacrifice, and was usually poured over the Altar, or, at any rate, sprinkled upon it, as the very crowning act of Offering [Lev. 1:5; 3:8].)*

7 And he took the Book of the Covenant, and read in the audience of the people *(the first mention of the Bible, at least in its beginning form, is given in Exodus 17:14; it is interesting that the first mention would be in connection with the hostility of the natural man, symbolized by Amalek, to the spiritual man, symbolized by Israel; and now the Bible is mentioned again in connection with the giving of the Law)*: and they said, All that the LORD has said will we do, and be obedient. *(While they possibly desired to be obedient, there was no way they could be, because the obedience that God demands is a perfect obedience, which man is incapable of rendering. Their only recourse was the "Altar," i.e., "the Cross.")*

8 And Moses took the blood, and sprinkled it on the people, and said, Behold the Blood of the Covenant, which the LORD has made with you concerning all these words. *(The blood being sprinkled on the people probably pertained to their leaders and representatives. It could hardly have referred to being sprinkled on nearly 3 million people. Half of the blood was sprinkled on the Altar, thus pledging God to His engagement; the other half was sprinkled upon the people, so pledging them.)*

9 Then went up Moses, and Aaron, Nadab, and Abihu, and seventy of the Elders of Israel *(before the invitation of Verse 1 could be accepted, the Blood of the Burnt and Peace Offerings must be shed; men, even though they may be as distinguished as these Princes, cannot approach God in their own person; they can only draw near through the Blood of Jesus)*:

10 And they saw the God of Israel *(John 1:18 says: "No man has seen God at any time"; this statement given by Moses does not contradict that statement; for the word "seen" in John 1:18 refers to "comprehend," or to "fully comprehend"; in other words, "No man has fully comprehended God at any time.")*: and there was under His feet as it were a paved work of a Sapphire Stone *(the Sapphire Stone expressed the purity of God)*, and as it were the body of Heaven in His clearness *(means that they saw Him clearly)*.

11 And upon the nobles of the Children of Israel he laid not His hand: also they saw God, and did eat and drink. *(Previously, they couldn't even approach the mountain. So, how do we explain here the difference? We must assume that it was the "Altar" which made the difference. Blood had been shed, a Covenant had been made.)*

FORTY

12 And the LORD said unto Moses, Come up to Me into the Mount, and be there: and I will give you Tables of Stone, and a Law, and Commandments which I have written: that you may teach them. *(It's our business as Preachers of the Gospel to teach the Word of God to the people.)*

13 And Moses rose up, and his minister Joshua: and Moses went up into the Mount of God. *(Evidently, Moses was instructed by the Lord to take Joshua with him. It is doubtful that Joshua was able to go into the very Presence of God as did Moses; nevertheless, he at least went part way, and evidently stayed the entirety of the time, because we find him coming down with Moses, when, some forty days later, Moses descended from the mountain [32:17].)*

14 And he *(Moses)* said unto the Elders *(70 men)*, Tarry ye here for us, until we come again unto you: and, behold, Aaron and Hur are with you: if any man have any matters to do, let him come unto them *(the latter two were left in charge)*.

15 And Moses went up into the Mount, and a Cloud covered the Mount. *(Evidently, Moses stopped when he arrived at the Cloud.)*

16 And the Glory of the LORD abode upon Mount Sinai, and the Cloud covered it six days: and the seventh day He called unto Moses out of the midst of the Cloud. *(Moses evidently waited until the Lord called him.)*

17 And the sight of the Glory of the LORD was like devouring fire on the top of the Mount in the eyes of the Children of Israel. *(It looked like the entirety of the top of the Mountain was on fire, with this being seen by all of the Children of Israel.)*

18 And Moses went into the midst of the Cloud *(Joshua stayed at the edge of the Cloud, and did not go further)*, and got him up into the Mount: and Moses was in the Mount forty days and forty nights *(without food or water; so the Lord had to miraculously sustain him)*.

CHAPTER 25
(1491 B.C.)
THE TABERNACLE

AND the LORD spoke unto Moses, saying,

2 Speak unto the Children of Israel, that they bring Me an Offering: of every man who gives it willingly with his heart you shall take

My Offering. *(Pink says: "We have now arrived at the longest, and most blessed, but least read and understood section of this precious Book of Exodus. From the beginning of Chapter 25 to the end of Chapter 40 — except the important parenthesis in 32 to 34 — the Holy Spirit has given us a detailed description of the Tabernacle, its structure, furniture, and Priesthood. When we consider, and understand, that more space is devoted to the account of the Tabernacle than to any other single object or subject treated in the Bible, we then begin to understand its vast significance. It took but two Chapters to portray the record of God's Work in creating this Earth, and fitting it for human habitation. By comparison, some 12 Chapters are needed to tell us about the Tabernacle.*

The reason? Everything about the Tabernacle pointed to Christ, and was a Type of Christ in some way.")

3 And this is the Offering which you shall take of them; gold, and silver, and brass,

4 And blue, and purple, and scarlet, and fine linen, and goats' hair,

5 And rams' skins dyed red, and badgers' skins, and shittim wood,

6 Oil for the light, spices for anointing oil, and for sweet incense,

7 Onyx stones, and stones to be set in the Ephod, and in the Breastplate. *(The Lord could have brought about these "Offerings" in any number of ways; however, His method is that we give to His Work, and then He blesses us. You can't out-give God!)*

8 And let them make Me a Sanctuary: that I may dwell among them. *(As far as is known, the Ark of Noah, the Tabernacle of Moses, and the Temple of Solomon, with the plans for the last one actually given to David, are the only buildings ever erected from plans furnished by direct Revelation from God [Gen. 6:14-16; I Chron. 28:11-12, 19]. Since the Fall of man in the Garden of Eden, the Lord has been working steadily to bring man back to Himself. He longs to dwell with us, and that He now does, all made possible by the Cross.)*

9 According to all that I show you, after the pattern of the Tabernacle, and the pattern of all the instruments thereof, even so shall you make it. *(The "Pattern" was all of God, and not at all of man. Salvation is the same! We must not deviate from the blueprint, of which both are identical — Jesus.)*

ARK OF THE COVENANT

10 And they shall make an Ark *(the Ark of*

the Covenant, a Type of the Throne of God) of shittim wood (referred to as "indestructible wood," and a Type of the Perfect, unsullied, physical Body of our Lord): two cubits and a half shall be the length thereof (3 and 3/4 feet), and a cubit and a half the breadth thereof (2 and 1/4 feet), and a cubit and a half the height thereof (2 and 1/4 feet).

11 And you shall overlay it with pure gold, within and without shall you overlay it (a type of the Deity of Christ), and shall make upon it a crown of gold round about (represents the status of our Lord as King).

12 And you shall cast four rings of gold for it (staves were to be inserted in the rings for the Ark to be moved, which it was occasionally, at least until the Temple was built about 500 years later; it signifies Christ Who desires to be with us at all times), and put them in the four corners thereof (wherever we are led to go, north, south, east, or west, He will be with us); and two rings shall be in the one side of it, and two rings in the other side of it. (If we are in His Will, He will be with us, just as much one place as the other.)

13 And you shall make staves of shittim wood (once again, portraying the Perfect Humanity of Christ), and overlay them with gold (portraying His Deity; while Jesus is Very Man, He is also Very-God; He is with us as God, by virtue of the fact that He came to be with us as Man, and for the purpose of going to the Cross, which makes His perpetual Presence possible).

14 And you shall put the staves into the rings by the sides of the Ark, that the Ark may be borne with them (the assurance of the perpetual Presence of Christ).

15 The staves shall be in the rings of the Ark: they shall not be taken from it. (This would be the case until Solomon's Temple, when the Priests would bring the Ark of the Covenant into the House of the Lord, place it under the giant Cherubim, and then would "draw out the staves" [I Ki. 8:6-8].)

16 And you shall put into the Ark the Testimony which I shall give you (the two tables of stone, containing the Ten Commandments).

17 And you shall make a Mercy Seat of pure gold (the Mercy Seat formed the covering for the Ark; on it was sprinkled the Atoning Blood, which the High Priest did once a year, on the Great Day of Atonement; it was of this Blood-sprinkled Mercy Seat that God spoke when He said: "There will I meet with you"; here, in Type, was the only meeting place between God and the sinner;

here, Righteousness and Peace kissed each other; it was all gold, signifying the Deity of Christ, signifying also that His Deity was not marred by Him becoming Man; Christ is the Mercy Seat): two cubits and a half shall be the length thereof (3 and 3/4 feet), and a cubit and a half the breadth thereof (2 and 1/4 feet).

18 And you shall make two Cherubims of gold (they pertained to God's Judicial authority; they seemed to be the highest among the Angelic order, or at least in the capacity in which they function), of beaten work shall you make them, in the two ends of the Mercy Seat. (They were not attached to the ends of the Mercy Seat, but were actually a part of the Mercy Seat. In other words, the Mercy Seat and the two Cherubims were all one piece of gold. The two Cherubims looked down on the Mercy Seat.)

19 And make one Cherub on the one end, and the other Cherub on the other end: even of the Mercy Seat shall you make the Cherubims on the two ends thereof.

20 And the Cherubims shall stretch forth their wings on high, covering the Mercy Seat with their wings (stretched above their heads, and pointing forward, with the four wings meeting each other in the middle), and their faces shall look one to another; toward the Mercy Seat shall the faces of the Cherubims be. (They looked down upon the blood which was applied to the Mercy Seat once a year, on the Great Day of Atonement.)

21 And you shall put the Mercy Seat above upon the Ark; and in the Ark you shall put the Testimony (Ten Commandments) that I shall give you.

22 And there I will meet with you, and I will commune with you from above the Mercy Seat, from between the two Cherubims which are upon the Ark of the Testimony, of all things which I will give you in Commandment unto the Children of Israel. (It is only above the Blood-stained Mercy Seat that God will meet with sinful human beings, because that's the only place that He can meet with sinful human beings, and not malign His Righteousness and Holiness. Concerning this, Mackintosh says: "Thus it is that the soul of the believing sinner finds peace. He sees that God's Righteousness and His Justification rest upon precisely the same basis, namely Christ's accomplished Work. When man, under the powerful action of the Truth of God, takes his place as a sinner, God can, in the exercise of Grace, take His place as a Saviour, and then every question is settled, for the Cross having

answered all the claims of Divine Justice, Mercy's copious streams can flow unhindered. When a Righteous God and a ruined sinner meet on a Blood-sprinkled platform, all is settled forever — settled in such a way as perfectly glorifies God, and eternally saves the sinner.")

TABLE OF SHEWBREAD

23 You shall also make a table of shittim wood (once again, this indestructible wood, a perfect Type of the Perfection of the Humanity of Christ): two cubits shall be the length thereof (3 feet), and a cubit the breadth thereof (1 and 1/2 feet), and a cubit and a half the height thereof (2 and 1/4 feet).

24 And you shall overlay it with pure gold (typical of the Deity of Christ), and make thereto a crown of gold round about (Christ is King).

25 And you shall make unto it a border of an hand breadth round about (it is interesting that the width of the crown is described as a "hand breadth," which is approximately three to four inches high; this corresponds with the Words of Christ: "Neither shall any pluck them out of My hand" [Jn. 10:28]), and you shall make a golden crown to the border thereof round about. (The table was to hold bread, which, again, was a Type of Christ. The crown would tend to keep the bread in place, so that it would not slip off the table, especially during times when Israel was instructed by the Lord to move. This speaks of the security of the Believer, all in Christ.)

26 And you shall make for it four rings of gold, and put the rings in the four corners that are on the four feet thereof.

27 Over against the border shall the rings be for places of the staves to bear the table.

28 And you shall make the staves of shittim wood, and overlay them with gold, that the table may be borne with them. (Wherever the Lord led Israel, even though it was in the wilderness, His Table accompanied them! So, wherever the Christian's lot may be cast, even though it may be in a prison, such as Paul, the Believer can continue to feed on Christ, for Christ is ever with him.)

29 And you shall make the dishes thereof, and spoons thereof, and covers thereof, and bowls thereof, to cover withal: of pure gold shall you make them. (The "dishes" were no doubt used by the Priests when they ate the Bread on the seventh day. The "spoons" and the "cover" were more than likely used in connection with the Frankincense, which was to be poured over the Bread, symbolizing the Fragrance and Purity of Christ. The "bowls" were probably cups, and were used in connection with the "Drink Offerings," which were poured out before the Lord "in the Holy Place" [Num. 28:7].)

30 And you shall set upon the Table Shewbread before Me always. (This was a Type of Christ, as the "Bread of Life" [Jn. 6:58]. Christ is always before the Father, making Intercession for us [Heb. 7:25].)

GOLDEN CANDLESTICK

31 And you shall make a candlestick of pure gold (should have been translated "Lampstand"): of beaten work shall the candlestick be made: his shaft, and his branches, his bowls, his knops, and his flowers, shall be of the same. (The idea is, the entirety of the Lampstand was made out of one piece of gold. The Lampstand was the only source of light in the entirety of the Holy Place. It is a Type of Christ as the Light of the world.

The "bowls" or "cups" formed the first ornament on each branch, and are likened to almonds, which signify the Resurrection [Num. 17:1-8]. The "knops" could have been translated "pomegranates," which speak of fruit. The "flowers" could have been translated "lilies," and speak of purity. The lily-blossoms supported the lamps, which were separate.)

32 And six branches shall come out of the sides of it: three branches of the Lampstand out of the one side, and three branches of the Lampstand out of the other side (six is the number of man, and which is the Body of Christ, whether Israel or the Church; Verse 36 tells us that the entirety of the Lampstand was "one beaten work of pure gold," meaning that these branches were not welded or fastened to the side of the main stem, but were rather a part of the main stem; this speaks of our being "in Christ"):

33 Three bowls made like unto almonds, with a knop and a flower in one branch: and three bowls made like almonds in the other branch, with a knop and a flower: so in the six branches that come out of the Lampstand. (We might ask the question as to why there were three bowls [almond-blossoms] on each stem, and only one pomegranate and only one lily? This tells us that the almond-blossom, which represents Resurrection, which speaks of the Cross, is the foundation on which everything is based. This is where the emphasis must always be [I Cor. 1:17].)

34 And in the Lampstand shall be four bowls made like unto almonds, with their knops and their flowers. *(The main middle stem had "four bowls," along with "four knops," and "four flowers." This made twelve ornaments, which speaks of the Government of Christ.)*

35 And there shall be a knop under two branches of the same, and a knop under two branches of the same, and a knop under two branches of the same, according to the six branches that proceed out of the Lampstand.

36 Their knops and their branches shall be of the same: all it shall be one beaten work of pure gold. *(Even though the branches came out even at the top, even with the main shaft, as would be obvious, the outward branch would be the longest of all, with the middle branch next to the longest, with the branch closest to the stem being the shortest. But yet, all of them had the same number of ornamentation.*

This tells us that all Believers can enjoy Resurrection Life, bear fruit, and develop purity. All done by the Holy Spirit, because of the Cross [I Cor. 1:23].)

37 And you shall make the seven lamps thereof *("seven" is God's number of perfection, and here speaks of perfect illumination, which only the Holy Spirit can do)*: and they shall light the lamps thereof *(the Lamps were cleaned and lit twice a day, at the time of the morning and evening Sacrifices [9 a.m. and 3 p.m.])*, that they may give light over against it *(over against the Table of Shewbread and the Altar of Incense)*.

38 And the tongs thereof, and the snuffdishes thereof, shall be of pure gold *(had to do with the cleaning of the wick, or replacing the wick, in order that the light might burn clean and bright)*.

39 Of a talent of pure gold shall he make it, with all these vessels *(weighed about 120 pounds; at January 2004 prices, it would have been worth about $750,000)*.

40 And look that you make them after their pattern, which was shewed you in the Mount. *(Moses was instructed to follow the Pattern exactly, which means it was not to be deviated from in any capacity. This tells us that the Work of the Spirit in our hearts and lives must be carried out strictly on God's Terms, and His Terms alone.)*

CHAPTER 26
(1491 B.C.)
CURTAIN OF LINEN

MOREOVER you shall make the Tabernacle with ten curtains of fine twined linen, and blue, and purple, and scarlet: with Cherubims of cunning work shall you make them *(the Tabernacle was one, as it regarded its purpose; it pictured, in its every facet, the Person and Work of Christ; these "ten curtains" had to do with the inner covering of the Tabernacle; they were elaborately embroidered, and joined together; the "linen" was a Type of the Righteousness of Christ; the color "blue" represents the Heavenly Place of Christ; the "purple" His Royalty as King; the "scarlet" speaks of His shed Blood; the "Cherubims" denote His Holiness)*.

2 The length of one curtain shall be eight and twenty cubits *(42 feet)*, and the breadth of one curtain four cubits *(6 feet)*: and every one of the curtains shall have one measure *(probably the curtains formed the ceiling of the Tabernacle; this suggests that the curtains set before us the One Who humbled Himself, and became obedient unto death, but Who is now exalted and glorified on high)*.

3 The five curtains shall be coupled together one to another *(Grace is the keynote of all this, and so expressed by the number "five" and its multiples)*; and other five curtains shall be coupled one to another.

4 And you shall make loops of blue upon the edge of the one curtain from the selvedge in the coupling; and likewise shall you make in the uttermost edge of another curtain, in the coupling of the second *(these "couplings" fasten the whole of the ten curtains together so that they were "one Tabernacle"; thus, they pointed to the blessed unity and uniformity of the Character and Life of Christ)*.

5 Fifty loops shall you make in the one curtain, and fifty loops shall you make in the edge of the curtain that is in the coupling of the second; that the loops may take hold one of another.

6 And you shall make fifty taches of gold, and couple the curtains together with the taches: and it shall be one Tabernacle *(the gold, as always, represents the Deity of Christ)*.

GOATS' HAIR

7 And you shall make curtains of goats' hair to be a covering upon the Tabernacle: eleven curtains shall you make. *(There were four coverings to the top of the Tabernacle. The second covering immediately above the linen, which was the part that could not be seen, was a covering of "goats' hair." This symbolized the Prophetic*

Office of Christ.)

8 The length of one curtain shall be thirty cubits *(45 feet)*, and the breadth of one curtain four cubits *(6 feet)*: and the eleven curtains shall be all of one measure.

9 And you shall couple five curtains by themselves, and six curtains by themselves, and shall double the sixth curtain in the fore-front of the Tabernacle *("five" is the number of Grace, while "six" is the number of man; so we have here the Grace of God shown to man, Who is Christ).*

10 And you shall make fifty loops on the edge of the one curtain that is outmost in the coupling, and fifty loops in the edge of the curtain which couples the second.

11 And you shall make fifty taches of brass *(copper)*, and put the taches into the loops, and couple the tent together, that it may be one.

12 And the remnant that remains of the curtains of the tent, the half curtain that remains, shall hang over the backside of the Tabernacle.

13 And a cubit on the one side, and a cubit on the other side of that which remains in the length of the curtains of the tent, it shall hang over the sides of the tabernacle on this side and on that side, to cover it.

RAMS' AND BADGERS' SKINS

14 And you shall make a covering for the tent of rams' skins *(typified Christ as King)* dyed red *(the King Who died on the Cross)*, and a covering above of badgers' skins. *(These denote the Office of Christ as High Priest. There were four coverings which made up the top of the Tabernacle: Fine twined linen, Goats' hair, Rams' skins, and Badgers' skins. The Badgers' skins were the top covering, and the only covering seen from the outside. As well, this last covering was the least attractive of all. "There is no beauty that we should desire Him" [Isa. 53:2].)*

BOARDS AND SILVER SOCKETS

15 And you shall make boards for the Tabernacle of shittim wood standing up. *(These boards for the inside walls of the Tabernacle typified the Redemptive Work of Christ, even as we shall see. From the outside, they could not be seen, because the top of the Tabernacle covered by the various skins reached down to the ground on either side.)*

16 Ten cubits *(15 feet)* shall be the length of a board, and a cubit and a half *(2 and 1/4 feet)*

shall be the breadth *(width)* of one board.

17 Two tenons *(an open hand)* shall there be in one board, set in order one against another: thus shall you make for all the boards of the Tabernacle. *(Two "tenons" were under each board, making a total of 100 tenons.)*

18 And you shall make the boards for the Tabernacle, twenty boards on the south side southward.

19 And you shall make forty sockets of silver under the twenty boards *(silver denotes Redemption)*; two sockets under one board for his two tenons, and two sockets under another board for his two tenons. *(It is believed that each socket of silver weighed about a talent, which is about 120 pounds; consequently, this would have provided a tremendous foundation, which was intended.)*

20 And for the second side of the Tabernacle on the north side there shall be twenty boards:

21 And their forty sockets of silver; two sockets under one board, and two sockets under another board.

22 And for the sides of the Tabernacle westward you shall make six boards.

23 And two boards shall you make for the corners of the Tabernacle in the two sides.

24 And they shall be coupled together beneath, and they shall be coupled together above the head of it unto one ring: thus shall it be for them both; they shall be for the two corners.

25 And they shall be eight boards, and their sockets of silver, sixteen sockets; two sockets under one board, and two sockets under another board.

OUTSIDE BARS

26 And you shall make bars of shittim wood *(once again, this indestructible wood proclaims the Perfect Humanity of Christ)*; five for the boards of the one side of the Tabernacle,

27 And five bars for the boards of the other side of the Tabernacle, and five bars for the boards of the side of the Tabernacle, for the two sides westward. *(The Tabernacle was to always face the east; therefore, there were no boards on this side, but rather five pillars. This was the entrance, as well.)*

THE MIDDLE BAR

28 And the middle bar in the midst of the boards shall reach from end to end.

THE GOLD OVERLAY

29 And you shall overlay the boards with gold *(typical of the Deity of Christ)*, **and make their rings of gold for places for the bars: and you shall overlay the bars with gold.** *(These "rings of gold" were evidently attached to the boards, through which the bars passed. They pertained to the Work of the Spirit in connecting all the Ministries of Christ. Even though our Saviour had different Ministries, all ultimately played out to Christ as Saviour.)*

30 And you shall rear up the Tabernacle according to the fashion thereof which was shewed you in the Mount. *(In other words, Moses must not add anything to the design nor take something from the design. It was all of God and none of man.)*

THE INNER VEIL

31 And you shall make a veil of blue, and purple, and scarlet, and fine twined linen of cunning work: with Cherubims shall it be made *(this was the inner Veil, which separated the Holy Place from the Holy of Holies; once again, the colors represented Christ from above, hence the "blue," with the "purple" representing His Royalty, and the "scarlet," His shed Blood, while the "linen" represented His Righteousness, and the Cherubims, His Holiness)*:

32 And you shall hang it upon four pillars of shittim wood overlaid with gold *(portrays both the Humanity and the Deity of Christ)*: **their hooks shall be of gold, upon the four sockets of silver** *(speaks of Redemption, which was the purpose of the Cross; the object of a "veil" is to hide; "Come not" [Lev. 16:2] was the warning which it consistently gave forth; thus, the Veil foreshadowed the moral glories of the Saviour, but, at the same time, showed, by the very display of such Heavenliness of Character, how far fallen man was away from God — Pink).*

TABERNACLE FURNITURE

33 And you shall hang up the Veil under the taches, that you may bring in thither within the Veil the Ark of the Testimony *(Ark of the Covenant)*: **and the Veil shall divide unto you between the Holy Place** *(first compartment)* **and the Most Holy** *(the Holy of Holies, where resided the Ark of the Covenant).*

34 And you shall put the Mercy Seat upon the Ark of the Testimony in the Most Holy Place.

35 And you shall set the table without the Veil, and the Lampstand over against the Table on the side of the Tabernacle toward the south: and you shall put the Table on the north side. *(These Sacred Vessels were placed in the Holy Place, the first compartment.)*

THE OUTER VEIL

36 And you shall make an hanging for the door of the tent *(the front)*, of blue, and purple, and scarlet, and fine twined linen, wrought with needlework. *(The "Veil" had "Cherubims" embroidered upon it, while the Door described here had none. The Veil was suspended from four pillars, while the Door was suspended from five. The outstanding difference between them was this: The Veil was to shut out, whereas the Door was to give admittance. The Veil barred the way into the Holiest, the "Door" was for the constant entrance of the Priests into the Holy Place. Incidentally, the colors given here never vary, because the Work of Christ never varies.)*

37 And you shall make for the hanging five pillars of Shittim Wood *(the Humanity of Christ, with "five" being the number of Grace)*, **and overlay them with gold, and their hooks shall be of gold** *(portraying the Deity of Christ)*: **and you shall cast five sockets of brass** *(copper)* **for them.** *(Copper, symbolically, prefigures Judgment, which Jesus would endure at the Cross, all in our stead.)*

CHAPTER 27
(1491 B.C.)
THE BRAZEN ALTAR

AND you shall make an Altar *(typified the Cross)* of Shittim Wood *(the Humanity of Christ)*, **five cubits long** *(7 and 1/2 feet long)*, **and five cubits broad; the Altar shall be foursquare** *(it is the same Gospel for all of mankind, whether north, south, east, or west)*: **and the height thereof shall be three cubits** *(4 and 1/2 feet).*

2 And you shall make the horns *(speaks of total dominion over sin, which would be purchased at the Cross)* of it upon the four corners thereof *(signifying that Salvation is the same for all)*: **his horns shall be of the same: and you shall overlay it with brass.** *(This Altar of indestructible wood was to be "overlaid with copper." Until the metallurgy of the not-too-distant past, copper had a greater resistance to fire, even than gold or silver. It would consequently protect the*

wood, that it would not catch fire and be con-sumed. Pink says: "The copper plates on the Altar protected it from the fervent heat and pre-vented it from being burned up; so Christ passed through the fires of God's wrath without being consumed. He is mighty to save, because He was mighty to endure.")

3 And you shall make his pans to receive his ashes *(ashes from the sacrifices which were burned)*, and his shovels, and his basons, and his fleshhooks, and his firepans: all the ves-sels thereof you shall make of brass. *(Ashes testified to the thoroughness of the fire's work in having wholly consumed the Offering. They also witnessed to the acceptance of the Sacrifice on behalf of the offerer, and so they were to him a token that his sins were gone. The Words of Christ from the Cross expressed the fulfillment of this detail of our Type: "It is finished" an-nounced that the Sacrifice had been offered, ac-cepted, and gone up to God as a sweet savour — Pink.)*

4 And you shall make for it a grate of net-work of brass; and upon the net shall you make four brazen rings in the four corners thereof *(the "rings" were for the moving of the Altar from place to place)*.

5 And you shall put it under the compass of the Altar beneath, that the net may be even to the midst of the Altar *(somewhere along-side the middle of the Altar, there seemed to be a protrusion all the way around, on which the Priests could stand, in order to properly attend the Sacrifices)*.

6 And you shall make staves for the Altar, staves of shittim wood, and overlay them with brass. *(These "staves" were for moving the Al-tar. When Israel moved, everything had to be moved. This teaches us that there never comes a period in the Christian life where the Atoning Blood of Christ, of which this Altar was a Type, can be dispensed with.)*

7 And the staves shall be put into the rings, and the staves shall be upon the two sides of the Altar, to bear it.

8 Hollow with boards shall you make it: as it was shewed you in the Mount, so shall they make it. *(Once again, the Pattern must be followed minutely.)*

THE OUTER COURT

9 And you shall make the Court of the Tab-ernacle *(this was at the front of the Tabernacle, facing the east)*: for the south side southward

there shall be hangings for the court of fine twined linen of an hundred cubits long for one side *(using 18 inches to the cubit, it was 150 feet long and 75 feet wide; the "linen" typi-fied the Perfect Righteousness of Christ)*:

10 And the twenty pillars thereof and their twenty sockets shall be of brass *(copper)*; the hooks of the pillars and their fillets shall be of silver *(the "copper" spoke of Judgment, which Jesus took on our behalf, while the "silver" spoke of Redemption, which came forth from the Judgment)*.

11 And likewise for the north side in length there shall be hangings of an hundred cubits longs, and his twenty pillars and their twenty sockets of brass: the hooks of the pillars and their fillets of silver.

12 And for the breadth *(width)* of the Court on the west side shall be hangings of fifty cu-bits *(75 feet)*: their pillars ten, and their sock-ets ten. *(There were 60 pillars placed at inter-vals of five cubits all around the Court. This, as well, speaks of the Grace of God. Verse 10 seems to indicate that the Pillars were made of copper; however, in the original Hebrew, in which this was written, there is indication that the modify-ing clause "of copper" refers only to the "sock-ets" and not to the Pillars. Possibly the Pillars were made of "Shittim Wood," the same as the Pillars for the Door and for the support of the Veil. Once again, this all speaks of the Perfect Humanity of Christ.)*

13 And the breadth of the Court on the east side eastward shall be fifty cubits.

14 The hangings of one side of the gate shall be fifteen cubits: their pillars three, and their sockets three.

15 And on the other side shall be hangings fifteen cubits: their pillars three, and their sockets three.

THE GATE

16 And for the gate of the Court shall be an hanging of twenty cubits *(the Gate which led into the Outer Court was 30 feet wide)*, of blue, and purple, and scarlet, and fine twined linen, wrought with needlework: and their pillars shall be four, and their sockets four. *(This is the "gate" at the front of the Outer Court, fac-ing the east, through which all Israelites came, in order to offer Sacrifices.)*

17 All the pillars round about the Court shall be filleted with silver: their hooks shall be of silver, and their sockets of brass. *(The Court was as far as the Israelites, other than the Priests,*

could come, at least as it regards the Tabernacle, and then only so far as the Brazen Altar. But everything about the Outer Court, as well as the Tabernacle, spoke of Christ in either His Atoning, Mediatorial, or Intercessory Work, even down to the small pins, which were of brass. As always, the latter spoke of the Judgment that He would undergo on our behalf.)

18 The length of the Court shall be an hundred cubits (150 feet), and the breadth (width) fifty every where (75 feet), and the height five cubits (7 and 1/2 feet high) of fine twined linen, and their sockets of brass.

19 All the Vessels of the Tabernacle in all the service thereof, and all the pins thereof, and all the pins of the court, shall be of brass (copper).

THE OIL

20 And you shall command the Children of Israel, that they bring you pure oil olive (there was no source of light in the Tabernacle, with the exception of the Golden Lampstand; this portrays Christ as the Light of the world, but, as well, portrays the Work of the Holy Spirit within His Heart and Life, which was to a degree not known by anyone else) beaten for the light (the word "beaten" emphasizes the fact that this particular oil did not come easily; the crushing of the olives was typical of the price paid by Christ for our Redemption), to cause the lamp to burn always. (This light was to never go out, inasmuch as the Light of Christ is never extinguished.)

21 In the Tabernacle of the congregation without the Veil, which is before the Testimony (Ark of the Covenant), Aaron and his sons shall order it from evening to morning before the LORD (twice a day Aaron and his sons, and those who would follow him in that order, would replenish the oil in the Golden Lampstand, and trim the wicks; it was commanded by God that this be done into infinity): it shall be a Statute for ever unto their generations on the behalf of the Children of Israel. (The sadness is, the Lamp is going out presently in many Churches.)

CHAPTER 28
(1491 B.C.)
THE PRIESTHOOD

AND take thou unto thee Aaron your brother, and his sons with him, from among the Children of Israel, that he may minister unto Me in the Priest's office, even Aaron, Nadab

and Abihu, Eleazar and Ithamar, Aaron's sons. (Five Priests were chosen from among the Tribe of Levi, headed up by Aaron as the High Priest. In fact, all High Priests were to succeed from Aaron. "Five" being the beginning, "Grace" is the foundation and energy of the Priesthood.)

2 And you shall make holy garments for Aaron your brother for glory and for beauty. (These garments were designed solely by the Lord, and were designed to portray Christ in His High Priestly Ministry.)

3 And you shall speak unto all who are wise hearted, whom I have filled with the Spirit of wisdom (the Holy Spirit), that they may make Aaron's garments to consecrate him, that he may minister unto Me in the Priest's office.

GARMENTS

4 And these are the garments which they shall make: a Breastplate, and an Ephod, and a Robe, and a broidered Coat, a Mitre, and a Girdle: and they shall make holy garments for Aaron your brother, and his sons, that he may minister unto Me in the Priest's office.

THE MATERIALS

5 And they shall take gold, and blue, and purple, and scarlet, and fine linen (as stated, these colors do not vary).

THE EPHOD

6 And they shall make the Ephod of gold, of blue, and of purple, of scarlet, and fine twined linen, with cunning work. (This was the outer Robe worn by the High Priest. It was made of two parts, one covering the back, and the other covering the front, these being joined together at the shoulders by golden clasps, which formed the setting for the onyx stones.)

7 It shall have the two shoulder-pieces thereof joined at the two edges thereof: and so it shall be joined together.

8 And the Curious Girdle of the Ephod, which is upon it, shall be of the same, according to the work thereof: even of gold, of blue, and purple, and scarlet, and fine twined linen. (The "Curious Girdle" was a sash of sorts, tied around the waist. It speaks of preparation for service. "He took a towel and girded Himself" [Jn. 13:4].)

9 And you shall take two onyx stones, and grave on them the names of the Children of

Israel *(these two onyx stones were a part of the Ephod, and were actually designed to join the back and the front of the Ephod together at the shoulders)*:

10 Six of their names on one stone, and the other six names of the rest on the other stone, according to their birth. *(These were worn on the shoulders of the High Priest, portraying strength, typifying Christ, Who protected Israel at all times. Pink says: "The shoulder which sustains the universe [Heb. 1:3] upholds the feeblest and most obscure member of the Bloodbought congregation.")*

11 With the work of an engraver in stone, like the engravings of a signet, shall you engrave the two stones with the names of the Children of Israel: you shall make them to be set in ouches of gold. *(The "gold" declares the Deity of Christ, hence, the power of Almighty God was available to all of Israel.)*

12 And you shall put the two stones upon the shoulders of the Ephod for stones of memorial unto the Children of Israel: and Aaron shall bear their names before the LORD upon his two shoulders for a memorial. *(God doesn't forget, and that "memorial" will come to fruition at the Second Coming, when Jacob will come home.)*

13 And you shall make ouches of gold;

14 And two chains of pure gold at the ends; of wreathen work shall you make them, and fasten the wreathen chains to the ouches. *(These "chains" tie us to Christ!)*

THE BREASTPLATE

15 And you shall make the Breastplate of Judgment with cunning work *(the "Breastplate" was attached to the front of the Ephod)*: after the work of the Ephod you shall make it: of gold, of blue, and of purple, and of scarlet, and of fine twined linen, shall you make it. *(Incidentally, the word "curious" simply means "cunning," signifying that its design was extraordinary.)*

16 Foursquare it shall be being doubled: a span shall be the length thereof, and a span shall be the breadth thereof *(a span equaled about 8 inches)*.

17 And you shall set in it settings of stones, even four rows of stones: the first two shall be a sardius, a topaz, and a carbuncle: this shall be the first row.

18 And the second row shall be an emerald, a sapphire, and a diamond.

19 And the third row a ligure, an agate, and an amethyst.

20 And the fourth row a beryl, and an onyx, and a jasper: they shall be set in gold in their inclosings. *(There were twelve jewels in number, one for each Tribe, set in four rows of three each.)*

21 And the stones shall be with the names of the Children of Israel, twelve, according to their names, like the engravings of a signet: every one with his name shall they be according to the twelve tribes. *(As the names of the Tribes of the Children of Israel were inscribed on the onyx stones on the shoulders of the High Priest, signifying strength, likewise, the same names were to be inscribed on the twelve stones worn over the heart of the High Priest, signifying the Love of God. So, this means that every single Believer, for we are spiritual Israel, is secured by both "strength" and "love," all anchored in the Cross [Jn. 3:16].)*

22 And you shall make upon the Breastplate chains at the ends of wreathen work of pure gold.

23 And you shall make upon the Breastplate two rings of gold, and shall put the two rings on the two ends of the Breastplate.

24 And you shall put the two wreathen chains of gold in the two rings which are on the ends of the Breastplate.

25 And the other two ends of the two wreathen chains you shall fasten in the two ouches, and put them on the shoulderpieces of the Ephod before it.

26 And you shall make two rings of gold, and you shall put them upon the two ends of the Breastplate in the border thereof, which is in the side of the Ephod inward.

27 And two other rings of gold you shall make, and shall put them on the two sides of the Ephod underneath, toward the forepart thereof, over against the other coupling thereof, above the Curious Girdle of the Ephod.

28 And they shall bind the Breastplate by the rings thereof unto the rings of the Ephod with a lace of blue, that it may be above the Curious Girdle of the Ephod, and that the Breastplate be not loosed from the Ephod.

29 And Aaron shall bear the names of the Children of Israel in the Breastplate of Judgment upon his heart, when he goes in unto the Holy Place, for a memorial before the LORD continually. *(Thus, the people of God, as represented by our names, are chained to our Great High Priest.)*

URIM AND THUMMIN

30 And you shall put in the Breastplate of Judgment the Urim and the Thummin *(there was a pocket of sorts in the back of the Breastplate, next to Aaron's heart, where was kept the "Urim" and the "Thummin"; the first word means "Lights," while the second means "Perfections"; so we must conclude that the judgment rendered would be "perfect"; the Bible doesn't say exactly what these things were, but some believe they must have been material objects of some kind, possibly one stone with the word "yes" inscribed on it, and the second stone with the word "no" inscribed on it)*; and they shall be upon Aaron's heart, when he goes in before the LORD: and Aaron shall bear the judgment of the Children of Israel upon his heart before the LORD continually. *(As wonderful as that was, due to the Cross, we today have much more. The Holy Spirit Himself abides continually within our hearts and lives, and is ready at all times to give us His Leading and Guidance [Jn. 14:16-17; 16:13-15].)*

THE ROBE

31 And you shall make the Robe of the Ephod all of blue. *(This symbolizes Christ as our Great High Priest in Heaven [Heb. 8:4]. It was all of "blue," signifying that Intercession would be, and, in fact, is, carried forth in Heaven [Heb. 7:25].)*

32 And there shall be an hole in the top of it, in the midst thereof: it shall have a binding of woven work round about the hole of it, as it were the hole of an habergeon, that it be not rent. *(This Robe was worn beneath the "Ephod" and the "Breastplate.")*

33 And beneath upon the hem of it you shall make pomegranates of blue, and of purple, and of scarlet, round about the hem thereof *(the pomegranates were made like tassels, and signified the "Fruit of the Spirit" [Gal. 5:22-23])*; and bells of gold between them round about *(these represented the "Gifts of the Spirit" [I Cor. 12:7-10])*:

34 A golden bell and a pomegranate, a golden bell and a pomegranate, upon the hem of the robe round about.

35 And it shall be upon Aaron to minister: and his sound shall be heard when he goes in unto the Holy Place before the LORD *(on the Great Day of Atonement, the High Priest would wear this beautiful garment into the Holy Place, and then remove it, leaving only the linen undergarments, signifying that Christ redeemed us, not with "glory and beauty," but rather with His spotless Righteousness, signified by His shed Blood, symbolized by the white linen; He would then offer up blood on the Mercy Seat, and come back into the Holy Place, where he would then put on the blue Robe once again)*, and when he comes out, that he die not. *(When he put on the Robe, the bells would begin to ring, and the people then knew that the sacrificial blood had been accepted, because they could hear the ringing of the bells.)*

THE HOLY CROWN

36 And you shall make a plate of pure gold, and grave upon it, like the engravings of a signet, HOLINESS TO THE LORD. *(This Golden Plate was the symbol of the essential Holiness of the Lord Jesus. The Saints are represented by Him and accepted in Him. Because of our legal and vital union with Him, His Holiness is ours. So, what am I saying? I'm saying that you as a Believer must look away from yourself, with your ten thousand failures, and put your eye on that Golden Plate. You can behold in the perfections of your Great High Priest the measure of your eternal acceptance with God. Christ is our Sanctification as well as our Righteousness.)*

37 And you shall put it on a blue lace *(signifies Heaven)*, that it may be upon the Mitre *(a Turban)*: upon the forefront of the Mitre it shall be.

38 And it shall be upon Aaron's forehead, that Aaron may bear the iniquity of the holy things, which the Children of Israel shall hallow in all their holy gifts: and it shall be always upon his forehead, that they may be accepted before the LORD. *(Imperfection attaches to everything that man does; and even the Sacrifices that the people offered to God required to be atoned for and purified. It was granted to the High Priest in his official capacity to make the necessary Atonement, and so render the people's gifts acceptable.)*

THE GARMENTS

39 And you shall embroider the Coat of fine linen, and you shall make the Mitre of fine linen, and you shall make the Girdle of needlework. *(The very fact of embroidery speaks of a Finished Work. The fact that the garments of Aaron's sons contain no embroidery tells us that their work was never finished, which, in fact, it*

wasn't. They were continually offering up Sacrifices, simply because the blood of bulls and goats could not really take away sins. But Aaron being the more particular Type of Christ specified what the Work of Christ would be, which would be one Sacrifice, once and for all, the Sacrifice of Himself, which would suffice forever. The "embroidery" specified this [Heb. 10:12].)

40 And for Aaron's sons you shall make coats, and you shall make for them girdles, and bonnets shall you make for them, for glory and for beauty. *(This seems to imply that the attire of the Priests, other than the High Priest, was a dress of pure white, without anything ornamental, such as the colors on Aaron's garments. Still, these snow-white garments, signifying the Righteousness of Christ, were still looked at as garments "for glory and for beauty" [Lev. 16:4; Mk. 9:3; Jn. 20:12; Acts 1:10; Rev. 4:4; 6:11; 7:9, 14].)*

41 And you shall put them upon Aaron your brother, and his sons with him: and shall anoint them, and consecrate them, and sanctify them, that they may minister unto Me in the Priest's office. *(All of this which was done was only a representation in symbolic form of what Christ would do in reality [Heb. 8:6-7.])*

42 And you shall make them linen breeches to cover their nakedness; from the loins even unto the thighs they shall reach *(the clothing covering the "nakedness" had as much, or more, to do with covering the Judgment of God than it did modesty)*:

43 And they shall be upon Aaron, and upon his sons, when they come in unto the Tabernacle of the congregation, or when they come near unto the Altar to minister in the Holy Place; that they bear not iniquity, and die: it shall be a Statute for ever unto him and his seed after him. *(This was to be taken so seriously that the Priests were warned, if they ignored any part of their garments, even those which were covered, such as the undergarments, they could be stricken that they die.)*

CHAPTER 29
(1491 B.C.)
CONSECRATION

AND this is the thing that you shall do unto them to hallow them, to minister unto Me in the Priest's office: Take one young bullock, and two rams without blemish. *(This Chapter pertains to the consecration of the Priests. It began with Sacrifice, i.e., "the Cross."*

All consecration must begin with the Cross, or else it isn't consecration. The "young bullock" symbolized the Manhood of Christ, while the two rams symbolized His Kingly Nature.)*

2 And unleavened bread, and cakes unleavened tempered with oil, and wafers unleavened anointed with oil: of wheaten flour shall you make them. *(The "unleavened bread" signifies the Perfect Life of Christ, and the "oil" typified the Holy Spirit, which was upon Him without measure [Jn. 3:34]. The "flour" symbolized the purity and glory of Christ.)*

3 And you shall put them into one basket, and bring them in the basket, with the bullock and the two rams. *(The unleavened bread and the wafers were put into one basket, because all pertained to Christ.)*

CLEANSING

4 And Aaron and his sons you shall bring unto the door of the Tabernacle of the congregation, and shall wash them with water. *(Even though it does not mention it here, this was probably before the great Laver. The washing with water speaks of the Word of God [I Cor. 6:11].)*

THE HIGH PRIEST

5 And you shall take the garments, and put upon Aaron the Coat, and the Robe of the Ephod, and the Ephod, and the Breastplate, and gird him with the Curious Girdle of the Ephod:

6 And you shall put the Mitre upon his head, and put the Holy Crown upon the Mitre. *(All of these things were Types of Christ, in His Atoning, Intercessory, and Mediatorial Work. It was topped off by the placing of the "Holy Crown" upon his head. It marked the royal character of the High Priest, who, as the main Type of Christ in the Mosaic Law, was bound to be "Prophet, Priest, and King." But yet, all of these things were but types, and carry no reality, except by Faith. Everything looked forward to the One Who was to come, Who would redeem humanity, and do so by going to the Cross.)*

7 Then you shall take the anointing oil, and pour it upon his head, and anoint him. *(This signified, as would be obvious, the Holy Spirit [Lk. 4:18-19].)*

THE ORDER

8 And you shall bring his sons, and put

Coats upon them.

9 And you shall gird them with Girdles, Aaron and his sons, and put the Bonnets on them: and the Priest's office shall be theirs for a perpetual Statute: and you shall consecrate Aaron and his sons. *(If it is to be noticed, Aaron was anointed before the blood was shed, as it respects the Sacrifices being offered. This was done in this manner, because he stands before us as the Type of Christ, Who, in virtue of what He was in His Own Person, was anointed with the Holy Spirit long before the work of the Cross was accomplished. The sons of Aaron, even as we shall see, on the other hand, who in a sense represent Believers, were not anointed until after the blood was shed, presenting the fact that the Holy Spirit could not come until after the Cross.)*

THE SIN OFFERING

10 And you shall cause a bullock to be brought before the Tabernacle of the congregation: and Aaron and his sons shall put their hands upon the head of the bullock *(in effect, transferring their sins to this innocent victim; this portrays Christ taking our sins upon Himself, and then paying the penalty for those sins, which we will see momentarily).*

11 And you shall kill the bullock before the LORD, by the door of the Tabernacle of the congregation. *(This was commanded by the Lord. This tells us that Jesus had to die. In fact, His Crucifixion was not an execution, or an assassination, it was a Sacrifice. It had been planned by God from before the foundation of the world. It was the very purpose for why Christ came [I Pet. 1:18-20].)*

12 And you shall take of the blood of the bullock, and put it upon the horns of the Altar with your finger *("horns" specify power; as well, these horns were on all four corners of the Altar, pointing toward the north, south, east, and west; this signified the power of the Cross in delivering man from sin [I Cor. 1:18], and that this great Salvation would be for all of humanity, hence, the horns pointing in all directions),* and pour all the blood beside the bottom of the Altar. *(This signified the Blood that would be shed by Christ at the Crucifixion, in the pouring out of His Life, which would redeem humanity, at least for those who will believe [Eph. 2:13-18].)*

13 And you shall take all the fat that covers the inwards, and the caul that is above the liver, and the two kidneys, and the fat that is upon them, and burn them upon the Altar. *(The "fat" signified the health and prosperity of the animal, symbolizing that God would give His best for our Redemption and, as well, it signified blessing upon the one who receives Redemption [Gal. 2:20-21].)*

14 But the flesh of the bullock, and his skin, and his dung, shall you burn with fire without the camp: it is a Sin Offering. *(The curse of sin, which was on them, made them unfit for food, and even unworthy of burial within the camp. So the remains were to be taken outside the camp, and burned with fire. Jesus was the Sin-Offering. He suffered "without the camp," i.e., "without the gate" [Heb. 13:12].)*

THE BURNT OFFERING

15 You shall also take one ram; and Aaron and his sons shall put their hands upon the head of the ram.

16 And you shall slay the ram, and you shall take his blood, and sprinkle it round about upon the Altar. *(The portrayal in the Levitical Offerings of Substitution and Identification is the very heart of the Gospel. Jesus Christ became our Substitute, and we identify with Him, and are, thereby, saved [Rom. 5:1]. As the "young bullock" of Verse 10 represented Christ at the height of His Manhood giving Himself for the sin of the world, the "ram" represented Christ in His position as King. The "ram" signified that the death of Christ was not merely the death of just anyone, it was the death of the Son of God, the "King of kings and Lord of lords" [Jn. 3:16].)*

17 And you shall cut the ram in pieces *(signifying that sin is more than a surface problem; it goes to the very vitals of the individual),* and wash the inwards of him *(this portrays the purity of Christ),* and his legs *(signifying that the "walk" of Christ was perfect),* and put them unto his pieces, and unto his head *(portrays the fact that Christ was perfectly lucid at all times during the Crucifixion).*

18 And you shall burn the whole ram upon the Altar: it is a Burnt Offering unto the LORD *(the "Burnt Offering" signifies consecration; the Lord would give Heaven's best for our Redemption):* it is a sweet savour *(it was such because it represented what Christ would do in order to redeem fallen humanity),* an offering made by fire unto the LORD. *(The "fire" signified the Judgment of God which came upon Christ, instead of upon us. Once again, it's the Doctrine of Substitution and Identification.)*

CONSECRATION

19 And you shall take the other ram; and Aaron and his sons shall put their hands upon the head of the ram *(do so before it was killed)*.

20 Then shall you kill the ram, and take of his blood, and put it upon the tip of the right ear of Aaron *(presenting the fact that Christ heard only the Father [Jn. 14:24]),* and upon the tip of the right ear of his sons, and upon the thumb of their right hand *(proclaims the fact that Christ always did right),* and upon the great toe of their right foot *(Christ always walked right regarding character),* and sprinkle the blood upon the Altar round about. *(This proclaimed the fact that they could not live as they ought to live, do as they ought to do, be as they ought to be, without Faith in Christ and what He would do for us at the Cross [Rom. 6:3-5].)*

21 And you shall take of the blood that is upon the Altar, and of the anointing oil, and sprinkle it upon Aaron, and upon his garments, and upon his sons, and upon the garments of his sons with him *(it seems that the "blood" and the "anointing oil" were mixed together, and then sprinkled upon Aaron, upon his garments, as well as upon his sons, etc.; this proclaims the way in which the Holy Spirit works; He works entirely within the parameters of the great Sacrifice of Christ, typified by the "blood" [Rom. 8:2-3]):* and he shall be hallowed *(consecrated),* and his garments, and his sons, and his sons' garments with him.

22 Also you shall take of the ram the fat and the rump, and the fat that covers the inwards, and the caul above the liver, and the two kidneys, and the fat that is upon them, and the right shoulder; for it is a ram of consecration:

23 And one loaf of bread, and one cake of oiled bread, and one wafer out of the basket of the unleavened bread that is before the LORD:

24 And you shall put all in the hands of Aaron, and in the hands of his sons; and shall wave them for a Wave Offering before the LORD. *(All of this specifies thankfulness for material blessings, but, above all, for what Christ would do in order to redeem humanity. "Wave Offerings" now are carried out by Believers lifting their hands and praising the Lord.)*

25 And you shall receive them of their hands, and burn them upon the Altar for a Burnt Offering, for a Sweet Savour before the LORD: it is an Offering made by fire unto the LORD. *(This signifies that our praises to the Lord are done strictly because of what Christ has done at*
the Cross, and such are accepted by the Lord solely because of our Faith in Christ and His Atoning Work at the Cross [Eph. 2:13-18].)*

THE PEACE OFFERINGS

26 And you shall take the breast of the ram of Aaron's consecration, and wave it for a Wave Offering before the LORD: and it shall be your part. *(In other words, they could take this part for themselves for food, symbolizing the eating of Christ [Jn. 6:53].)*

27 And you shall sanctify the breast of the Wave Offering, and the shoulder of the Heave Offering, which is waved, and which is heaved up of the ram of the consecration, even of that which is for Aaron, and of that which is for his sons *(the shoulder was to be "heaved," while the breast was to be "waved"; the former typified Christ taking our sins upon Himself, while the latter typified thankfulness that He had done so):*

28 And it shall be Aaron's and his sons' by a Statute for ever from the Children of Israel: for it is an Heave Offering: and it shall be an Heave Offering from the Children of Israel of the Sacrifice of their Peace Offerings, even their Heave Offering unto the LORD. *(When a Burnt, Sin, or Trespass Offering was presented to the Lord by the Priests, and on behalf of the people, then a "Peace Offering" was to be presented to the Lord. It signified that God had accepted the Offerings, and Peace with God was restored. A part of the flesh of the Peace Offering was to be given to the Priests and, as well, to the individuals who offered up the Sacrifice. They were then to have a feast, celebrating the restored Peace. Under the New Covenant, we do the same thing now, by simply praising the Lord; however, all of this tells us that our praises must ever be based on the fact of what Christ did for us at the Cross [Col. 2:14-15].)*

29 And the holy garments of Aaron shall be his sons' after him, to be anointed therein, and to be consecrated in them.

30 And that son that is Priest in his stead shall put them on seven days, when he comes into the Tabernacle of the congregation to minister in the Holy Place. *(The High Priesthood was to ever remain in the family of Aaron, which it did down through the centuries, with the exception of the last years when Jesus came. Then it was dictated by Rome. The consecration which lasted for "seven days," "seven" being God's number of perfection, all typified the Perfection*

of Christ [Heb. 7:26-27].)

31 And you shall take the ram of the consecration, and seethe *(roast)* his flesh in the Holy Place.

32 And Aaron and his sons shall eat the flesh of the ram, and the bread that is in the basket *(which Jesus addressed in John 6:53-63; this is symbolic of one accepting all that Christ did at the Cross),* by the door of the Tabernacle of the congregation *(Jesus is the "Door" [Jn. 10:1, 9]).*

33 And they shall eat those things wherewith the Atonement was made, to consecrate and to sanctify them: but a stranger shall not eat thereof, because they are holy *(a stranger could not partake of this repast, referring to the fact that the person who doesn't know Christ surely cannot partake of His Blessings [Jn. 3:3]).*

34 And if ought of the flesh of the consecrations, or of the bread, remain unto the morning, then you shall burn the remainder with fire: it shall not be eaten, because it is holy. *(This pertains to the fact that one must partake of all of Christ, in other words, the entirety of the Cross, which all of this typifies.)*

35 And thus shall you do unto Aaron, and to his sons, according to all things which I have commanded you: seven days shall you consecrate them.

36 And you shall offer every day a bullock for a Sin Offering for Atonement: and you shall cleanse the Altar, when you have made an Atonement for it, and you shall anoint it, to sanctify it. *(This proclaims the fact that Christ sanctified the Cross, but the Cross didn't sanctify Him, because He didn't need such. This completely abrogates the erroneous doctrine, as taught by some, that "Jesus died spiritually" while on the Cross. This meant He died as a sinner and went to the burning side of Hell, which is not taught in the Bible. The Bible doesn't teach that Redemption was afforded in Hell, but rather on the Cross [Eph. 2:13-18; Col. 2:14-15]. Despite the fact that the Cross was a place where sin was atoned, still, Christ, by His Perfection, sanctified it in totality.)*

37 Seven days you shall make an Atonement for the Altar, and sanctify it; and it shall be an Altar most holy: whatsoever touches the Altar shall be holy. *(Jesus sanctified the Cross; consequently, everything done there is "most holy." As well, everyone who places their faith and trust in Christ, and what He did at the Cross, is "holy"; however, it is all of Him, and none of us [I Cor. 1:17-18]. All of this tells us that there is no holiness for Believers outside of the "Cross.")*

THE DAILY OFFERINGS

38 Now this is that which you shall offer upon the Altar: two lambs of the first year day by day continually. *(The word "continually" stresses the fact that the Believer must place his faith and trust in Christ and the Cross, doing so daily, and everlastingly [Lk. 9:23-24].)*

39 The one lamb you shall offer in the morning *(9 a.m.)*; and the other lamb you shall offer at evening *(3 p.m.; Jesus was placed on the Cross at 9 a.m., the time of the morning sacrifice, and died at 3 p.m., the time of the evening sacrifice [Lk. 23:44-46]):*

40 And with the one lamb a tenth deal of the flour *(typifying the Perfect Manhood and Perfect Life of Christ)* mingled with the fourth part of an hin of beaten oil *(typifying the Holy Spirit, which was on Him and in Him, as in no other, and brought to fruition after the wilderness experience, hence, the word "beaten," which speaks of the crushing of the olives [Mat. 3:16; 4:1-11]);* and the fourth part of an hin *(about a quart)* of wine for a Drink Offering *(which speaks of "joy," which all will have who follow Christ [I Pet. 1:8]).*

41 And the other lamb you shall offer at evening, and shall do thereto according to the Meat Offering *(Thanksgiving Offering)* of the morning, and according to the Drink Offering thereof, for a Sweet Savour, an Offering made by fire unto the LORD *(all of this represents what Christ would do at the Cross and, as such, is a "Sweet Savour" to God the Father [Mat. 3:17]).*

42 This shall be a continual Burnt Offering throughout your generations at the door of the Tabernacle of the congregation before the LORD *(a continual trust in Christ and the Cross; hence Paul referred to the Cross as "The Everlasting Covenant" [Heb. 13:20]):* where I will meet you, to speak there unto you. *(Christ is the Source, but the Cross is the Means by which God meets with us, and the only Means!)*

43 And there I will meet with the Children of Israel, and the Tabernacle shall be sanctified by My Glory *(His Glory is only upon that which is of Christ, and is extended to man by and through what Christ did at the Cross [Heb. 10:10]).*

44 And I will sanctify the Tabernacle of the congregation, and the Altar: I will sanctify also both Aaron and his sons, to minister to Me in the Priest's office *(the Lord sanctified the Tabernacle, because it was a Type of Christ; the Altar, as well, was sanctified, because it represented*

Christ and what He would do at the Cross; all the Priests were sanctified, because they were Types of Christ; it must be noted that it is all in Christ and what He did at the Cross).

THE PROMISE

45 And I will dwell among the Children of Israel, and will be their God. *(Due to the Cross, the Lord now dwells within the heart and life of the Believer [I Cor. 3:16].)*

46 And they shall know that I am the LORD their God, Who brought them forth out of the land of Egypt, that I may dwell among them: I am the LORD their God. *(All of this tells us that the Lord will meet with us and dwell with us, only as we go by the way of the slain Lamb [Jn. 1:29].)*

CHAPTER 30
(1491 B.C.)
ALTAR OF INCENSE

AND you shall make an Altar to burn Incense upon *(this was the Altar of Incense, which portrays Christ making Intercession for us constantly [Heb. 7:25-26])*: of shittim wood shall you make it *(indestructible wood, portraying the perfect manhood of Christ [I Cor. 15:45-47]).*

2 A cubit shall be the length thereof, and a cubit the breadth *(width)* thereof *(1 and 1/2 feet)*; foursquare shall it be: and two cubits *(3 feet)* shall be the height thereof: the horns thereof shall be of the same *(as the four horns of the Brazen Altar signified that the power of Redemption was for all, likewise, the four horns of the Altar of Incense stipulate the fact that the Believer can have total and complete victory in Christ, with sin having no dominion over us [Rom. 6:14]; however, it can only be done by the Believer placing his faith exclusively in Christ and the Cross, which then gives the Holy Spirit latitude to perform the work within our lives [Rom. 6:3-14; 8:1-2, 11]).*

3 And you shall overlay it with pure gold *(while the wood typified the Humanity of Christ, the "gold" typified His Deity)*, the top thereof, and the sides thereof round about, and the horns thereof; and you shall make unto it a crown of gold round about *(signifying the Kingly character of Christ [Jn. 19:19]).*

4 And two golden rings shall you make to it under the crown of it, by the two corners thereof, upon the two sides of it shall you make it *("two" is the number of "witness," and speaks of the Holy Spirit, Who is here to testify of Christ [Jn. 15:26])*; and they shall be for places for the staves to bear it withal *(the "staves" of wood overlaid with gold intimate that it is the God-Man Whom the Spirit is here to glorify; at times it had to be moved, so it was to be a day and night companion of a pilgrim people [Mat. 28:20]).*

5 And you shall make the staves of shittim wood, and overlay them with gold.

6 And you shall put it before the Veil that is by the Ark of the Testimony *(Ark of the Covenant)*, before the Mercy Seat that is over the Testimony *(the Ten Commandments inside the Ark of the Covenant)*, where I will meet with you. *(The "Altar of Incense" was to sit immediately in front of the Veil, which separated the Holy Place from the Holy of Holies. So, in point of fact, it was situated immediately in front of the Ark of the Covenant. Even though the "Veil" separated these two Sacred Vessels, the very fact that they were this close tells us that the separation was only temporary. When Christ came, the "Veil" would be removed [Mat. 27:51; Rev. 22:17].)*

7 And Aaron shall burn thereon sweet incense every morning: when he dresses the lamps *(the Golden Lampstand)*, he shall burn incense upon it.

8 And when Aaron lights the lamps at evening, he shall burn Incense upon it, a perpetual Incense before the LORD throughout your generations. *(One or more coals of fire were to be taken from the Brazen Altar, which typified the Cross, and placed on the Altar of Incense, with Incense poured over the coals, which filled the Holy Place with a sweet fragrance, all typifying the Intercession of Christ on our behalf; however, it must be understood that the Intercession of Christ does not really pertain to Him doing anything in Heaven on our behalf, but that the fact of His Presence at the Throne of God guarantees that Intercession [Heb. 7:25-26]. If something other than His mere Presence was required, that would mean that the work which He did at the Cross was not a Finished Work. But it was a Finished Work, and requires nothing else added [Jn. 19:30; Heb. 10:12-14].)*

9 You shall offer no strange incense thereon *(the Incense poured on the burning coals had to be that which the Lord had designed, and no other kind; anything else would be called "strange incense," and would be unacceptable! As we will later study, the Incense was made of ingredients which pictured and portrayed Christ in*

His Atoning Work; that and that alone is what God will recognize), **nor burnt sacrifice** *(the Lord will recognize no Sacrifice but that of the Cross, of which the Brazen Altar was a Type; the Altar of Incense was for worship and intercession only, all made possible by the Cross; "works religion" typifies a sacrifice offered on the Altar of Incense, which God can never accept)*, **nor Meat Offering** *(concerning this, Pink says: "This, in figure, tells us that our Great High Priest expects no blessings which His Blood has not purchased, and expects pardon from Divine Justice for no sins for which Faith has not been evidenced. And incidentally, the measure of the Blessings which are given is God's estimate of the life which He gave")*; **neither shall you pour Drink Offering thereon.** *(Anytime the Believer places his faith and trust in anything other than the Cross, he violates the Cross of Christ, and wrongly uses the Altar of Incense, which, if continued, will bring on great chastisement from the Lord [Heb. 12:5-11].)*

10 **And Aaron shall make an Atonement upon the horns of it once in a year with the Blood of the Sin Offering of Atonements: once in the year shall he make Atonement upon it throughout your generations: it is most holy unto the LORD.** *(This speaks of the Great Day of Atonement, which took place once a year. The "Blood" applied to the "horns" typifies the fact that the Believer can have total dominion over sin, but can only do so by faith and trust in Christ and the shedding of His Blood on the Cross of Calvary. Victory comes by that route alone! [Rom. 6:3-5].)*

ATONEMENT MONEY

11 **And the LORD spoke unto Moses, saying,**

12 **When you take the sum** *(census)* **of the Children of Israel after their number, then shall they give every man a ransom for his soul unto the LORD, when you number them; that there be no plague among them, when you number them.** *(Verses 11 through 16 portray the ransom or Redemption money. The money was a special tax of registration in Israel, as a memorial or reminder of God's provision of Redemption, and of their obligation under the terms of the Mosaic Covenant. Christ died on the Cross; "He gave Himself a ransom for all" [I Tim. 2:6].)*

13 **This they shall give, every one who passes among them that are numbered, half a shekel after the shekel of the sanctuary: (a shekel is twenty gerahs:) an half shekel shall be the Offering of the LORD** *(equal to about $40 in 2004 money)*.

14 **Every one who passes among them who are numbered, from twenty years old and above, shall give an Offering unto the LORD.**

15 **The rich shall not give more, and the poor shall not give less that half a shekel, when they give an Offering unto the LORD, to make an Atonement for your souls.** *(All gave the same whether "rich" or "poor," placing every man on an equal footing in relation to God and obligation to the Law. It should be noted that the money did not actually redeem the soul. Not even the blood of bulls and other animals did this [Heb. 10:4; I Pet. 1:18-23], but rather Faith in the Blood of the coming Redeemer, of which the blood of sacrifices was a Type. It was strictly for a "memorial," even as the next Verse proclaims. Incidentally, this shekel was of silver, hence, silver is a type of Redemption.)*

16 **And you shall take the Atonement money of the Children of Israel, and shall appoint it for the service of the Tabernacle of the congregation; that it may be a memorial unto the Children of Israel before the LORD, to make an Atonement for your souls.** *(A "census" taken of the Children of Israel was important, because they belonged to God, and they belonged to Him by virtue of the slain lamb, and their faith in that Sacrifice [Gen. 15:6; Rom. 4:3].)*

THE BRAZEN LAVER

17 **And the LORD spoke unto Moses, saying,**

18 **You shall also make a Laver of brass** *(copper)*, **and his foot also of brass** *(a pedestal on which it sat)*, **to wash withal: and you shall put it between the Tabernacle of the congregation and the Altar** *(Brazen Altar)*, **and you shall put water therein.** *(The "water" was a Type of the Word of God. One might say that the Brazen Altar was for the sinner; the Brazen Laver for the Saint. The former testified of the Blood of Christ; the latter, of the Word of God; the former cleansed the conscience; the latter, the conduct [Eph. 5:26].)*

19 **For Aaron and his sons shall wash their hands and their feet thereat:**

20 **When they go into the Tabernacle of the congregation, they shall wash with water, that they die not; or when they come near to the Altar to minister, to burn Offerings made by fire unto the LORD:**

21 **So they shall wash their hands and their feet, that they die not: and it shall be a Statute**

for ever to them, even to him and to his seed throughout their generations. *(The "hands" spoke of their "doing," while the "feet" spoke of their "walk," referring to lifestyle. Before attending to the duties of the Lord, they needed cleansing from constant defilement, hence the command for the "hands" and "feet" continually to be washed. The Word of God, of which the Brazen Laver was a Type, works on the same principle for us presently. The Word of God directs us to the Cross, which alone makes right our conduct. As they needed constant washing, we, as well, need constant washing.)*

HOLY ANOINTING OIL

22 Moreover the LORD spoke unto Moses, saying,

23 Take thou also unto you principal spices, of pure myrrh *(a gum which exudes from a particular tree through incisions made for the purpose; this typifies Christ Who was pierced for us, and from Whose wounds there flowed a sweet smelling savour to God [Isa. 53:5])* five hundred shekels *(the shekel at that time was actually a "weight" instead of a coin; it was about one third of a modern ounce; representing silver, the five hundred shekels were worth, in 2004 money, about $500)*, and of sweet cinnamon half so much, even two hundred and fifty shekels *(Cinnamon was very rare at that time; it came from the inner bark or rind of a tree allied to the laurel)*, and of sweet calamus two hundred and fifty shekels *(came from aromatic reeds)*,

24 And of cassia five hundred shekels *(came from the inner bark distinct from the Cinnamon tree)*, after the shekel of the sanctuary, and of oil olive an hin *(about a gallon; all of these spices were extracted by either cutting or crushing or both; such proclaimed the fact that the great Work carried out by Christ on the Cross of Calvary presents, in a sense, a "cutting" and a "crushing" [Isa. 53:5])*:

25 And you shall make it an oil of holy ointment, an ointment compound after the art of the apothecary *(maker of perfumes)*: it shall be an holy anointing oil. *(The "oil" was a Type of the Holy Spirit, with the perfumes being a Type of Christ. The minutest emotions of Christ's Nature as a Man were perfect; and all were "of like weight" in His sinless Nature.)*

26 And you shall anoint the Tabernacle of the congregation therewith, and the Ark of the Testimony *(signifying that it was all dedicated to the Lord)*,

27 And the Table *(Table of Shewbread)* and all his vessels, and the Candlestick *(Lampstand)* and his vessels, and the Altar of Incense,

28 And the Altar of Burnt Offering with all his vessels *(the Brazen Altar)*, and the laver and his foot *(Brazen Laver)*.

29 And you shall sanctify them, that they may be most holy: whatsoever touches them shall be holy *(because it symbolized Christ)*.

30 And you shall anoint Aaron and his sons, and consecrate them, that they may minister unto Me in the Priest's office *(they were Types of Christ, as well)*.

31 And you shall speak unto the Children of Israel, saying, This shall be an holy anointing oil unto Me throughout your generations *(or at least until the Cross was a fact, and the Holy Spirit could then come in a new dimension; then, these things would no longer be needed)*.

32 Upon man's flesh shall it not be poured, neither shall you make any other like it, after the composition of it: it is holy, and it shall be holy unto you. *(This ointment was not to be imitated, nor poured upon man's flesh. Spiritual graces cannot be imitated, nor can they be given to men "in the flesh.")*

33 Whosoever compounds any like it, or whosoever puts any of it upon a stranger *(Gentile)*, shall even be cut off from his people *(meaning that this particular Israelite would lose his soul; the Holy Spirit, Who glorifies Christ, must not be trifled with [Mat. 12:31-32].*

THE INCENSE

34 And the LORD said unto Moses, Take unto you sweet spices, stacte, and onycha, and galbanum: these sweet spices with pure frankincense *(these four typified the Intercessory Work of Christ, all on our behalf)*: of each shall there be a like weight *(as stated, Christ was Perfect in every respect)*:

35 And you shall make it a perfume, a confection after the art of the apothecary, tempered together, pure and holy *(prepared by one who was skilled in this art)*:

36 And you shall beat some of it very small *(refers to the fact that Intercession by Christ on our behalf is needed in all things, even in the very small things)*, and put of it before the Testimony in the Tabernacle of the congregation, where I will meet with you: it shall be unto you most holy. *(These spices mentioned are those which made up the Incense that was poured*

upon the coals of fire, which were brought from the Brazen Altar, and placed on the Altar of Incense.)

37 And as for the perfume which you shall make, you shall not make to yourselves according to the composition thereof: it shall be unto you holy for the LORD *(to be used only as directed by the Word of God; God's Government is exact in His Word; it must not be changed, diluted, added to, or taken from).*

38 Whosoever shall make like unto that, to smell thereto, shall even be cut off from his people *(will lose his soul; all of this, in one way or the other, points to Christ and the Cross; if the Cross is rejected, then Salvation is rejected, as well!).*

CHAPTER 31
(1491 B.C.)
THE WORKMEN

AND the LORD spoke unto Moses, saying,

2 See, I have called by name Bezaleel the son of Uri, the son of Hur, of the Tribe of Judah *(it is believed that "Bezaleel" was the grandson of Hur, who it is believed was the brother-in-law of Moses, having married his sister Miriam; the choice of these principal workmen was that of God, and not Moses):*

3 And I have filled him with the Spirit of God, in wisdom, and in understanding, and in knowledge, and in all manner of workmanship *(before the Cross, the Holy Spirit only came upon individuals who had been called of God for a certain task, even as Bezaleel; now, since the Cross, the Holy Spirit resides in the hearts and lives of all Believers [I Cor. 3:16]),*

4 To devise cunning works, to work in gold, and in silver, and in brass,

5 And in cutting of stones, to set them, and in carving of timber, to work in all manner of workmanship. *(All of this shows us that the Holy Spirit can, and will, help us in every aspect of our life and living, providing what we do is right.)*

6 And I, behold, I have given with him Aholiab, the son of Ahisamach, of the tribe of Dan: and in the hearts of all who are wise hearted I have put wisdom, that they may make all that I have commanded you *(if it is to be noticed, the Lord said here "wise hearted," instead of "wise headed"; this means that the Holy Spirit functioned in the hearts of these individuals, leading them and helping them as to what*

they should do);

7 The Tabernacle of the congregation, and the Ark of the Testimony, and the Mercy Seat that is thereupon, and all the furniture of the Tabernacle,

8 And the Table and his furniture, and the pure candlestick with all his furniture, and the Altar of Incense,

9 And the Altar of Burnt Offering with all his furniture, and the Laver and his foot,

10 And the cloths of service, and the holy garments for Aaron the Priest, and the garments of his sons, to minister in the Priest's office,

11 And the anointing oil, and sweet incense for the holy place: according to all that I have commanded you shall they do. *(We must remember, the Holy Spirit worked with these individuals to prepare that which pointed to Christ, and what He would do, which speaks of the Cross. Now, the Holy Spirit points back to a Finished Work [Rom. 8:2].)*

THE SABBATH

12 And the LORD spoke unto Moses, saying,

13 Speak thou also unto the Children of Israel, saying, Verily my Sabbaths you shall keep: for it is a sign between Me and you throughout your generations; that you may know that I am the LORD Who does sanctify you. *(The Sabbath, as stated, represented the "rest," which one now finds in Christ. This "sign" was to be between the Lord and Israel. It was never meant to be a sign between the Lord and the Church.)*

14 You shall keep the Sabbath therefore; for it is holy unto you: every one who defiles it shall surely be put to death: for whosoever does any work therein, that soul shall be cut off from among his people *(will lose his soul).*

15 Six days may work be done; but in the seventh is the Sabbath of rest, holy to the LORD *(because it represented Christ and what Christ would do in order to bring "rest" to the soul):* whosoever does any work in the Sabbath day, he shall surely be put to death.

16 Wherefore the Children of Israel shall keep the Sabbath, to observe the Sabbath throughout their generations, for a perpetual Covenant.

17 It is a sign between Me and the Children of Israel for ever: for in six days the LORD made Heaven and Earth, and on the seventh day He rested, and was refreshed.

TWO STONE TABLES

18 And He gave unto Moses, when He had made an end of communing with him upon Mount Sinai, two Tables of Testimony, tables of stone, written with the Finger of God *(these were the Ten Commandments, five on one stone, and five on the other).*

CHAPTER 32

(1491 B.C.)

THE GOLDEN CALF

AND when the people saw that Moses delayed to come down out of the Mount, the people gathered themselves together unto Aaron, and said unto him, Up, make us gods, which shall go before us; for as for this Moses, the man who brought us up out of the land of Egypt, we wot not what is become of him. *(Israel, as we shall see, could not go very long without strong spiritual leadership; neither can the modern Church. Without Moses being present, the people would cry, "Make us gods." It has little changed! Aaron will acquiesce to the demands of the people, as too much of the spiritual leadership does presently.)*

2 And Aaron said unto them, Break off the golden earrings, which are in the ears of your wives, of your sons, and of your daughters, and bring them unto me.

3 And all the people broke off the golden earrings which were in their ears, and brought them unto Aaron. *(Unless we hover close to Christ, none of us are very far from the "golden calf." For instance, most Churches give people what they want, instead of what they need. The "seeker-sensitive" Churches and, in fact, most all, are perfect examples of this [Acts 5:29].)*

4 And he received them at their hand, and fashioned it with a graving tool, after he had made it a molten calf: and they said, These be your gods, O Israel, which brought you up out of the land of Egypt. *(The calf was the great god of the Egyptians. It was carried in the vanguard of their processions. Sacrifices were offered to it, and lascivious dances executed in its honor. It was worshipped as the generator of life, with, no doubt, the Israelites being very familiar with this practice. Golden calves, regrettably, at the present time, abound plentifully.)*

5 And when Aaron saw it, he built an Altar before it *(all golden calves are religious)*; and Aaron made proclamation, and said, Tomorrow is a feast to the LORD. *(Williams says:*

"One of the great ploys of Satan is not to abolish God, but to represent Him by something visible. Also, Satan can, through a religious teacher like Aaron, associate idolatry with Christ, recognize the good in all religions, and provide a worship that appeals to man's natural heart. In fact, everything was done by Aaron under the cover of 'religion.'")

6 And they rose up early on the morrow, and offered burnt offerings, and brought peace offerings; and the people sat down to eat and to drink, and rose up to play. *(Their "play" referred to licentiousness and vulgarity of the worst order. Cain had the right Altar, but the wrong sacrifice [Gen., Chpt. 4]. Israel here had the right sacrifices, but the wrong altar. The Lord could not accept either one, because both were man-devised — and that is the great problem of the modern Church [II Cor. 11:4].)*

7 And the LORD said unto Moses, Go, get thee down; for your people, which you brought out of the land of Egypt, have corrupted themselves *(by the use of the pronouns "thy" and "thou," we learn that God had disowned Israel here; in Verse 11, Moses disowns them himself; in a sense, the entirety of the nation of Israel, at least as a whole, had made spiritual orphans of themselves)*:

8 They have turned aside quickly out of the way which I commanded them: they have made them a molten calf, and have worshipped it, and have sacrificed thereunto, and said, These be your gods, O Israel, which have brought you up out of the land of Egypt. *(These were a people "in whom was no Faith" [Deut. 32:20; Heb. 4:1-2].)*

9 And the LORD said unto Moses, I have seen this people, and, behold, it is a stiffnecked people *(hardened heart)*:

10 Now therefore let Me alone, that My wrath may wax hot against them, and that I may consume them: and I will make of you a great nation. *(The only thing that stands between man and eternal Hell is the Cross of Christ. That being abandoned, as it was by Israel, judgment must follow — and it always does!)*

INTERCESSION

11 And Moses besought the LORD his God, and said, LORD, why does Your wrath wax hot against Your people, which You have brought forth out of the land of Egypt with great power, and with a mighty hand? *(All of these things, as wonderful as they were and, in a sense, is the*

same presently with every Believer, still, cannot condone sin. As should be obvious, this refutes the unscriptural doctrine of unconditional eternal security.)

12 Wherefore should the Egyptians speak, and say, For mischief did He bring them out, to kill them in the mountains, and to consume them from the face of the Earth? Turn from Your fierce wrath, and repent of this evil against Your people.

13 Remember Abraham, Isaac, and Israel, Your servants, to whom You swore by Your Own Self, and said unto them, I will multiply your seed as the stars of Heaven, and all this land that I have spoken of will I give unto your seed, and they shall inherit it for ever. *(As much as anything, this was a test for Moses. I think most Bible Scholars, in addressing this scenario, make God too little and Moses too big.)*

14 And the LORD repented of the evil which He thought to do unto His people. *(This doesn't mean that the Lord did something wrong, but rather that He simply turned aside from the proposed direction. Oftentimes, even as here, what God does is predicated on what we do. In fact, the entirety of this generation did die in the wilderness, and did so because of unbelief.)*

MOSES

15 And Moses turned, and went down from the Mount, and the two Tables of the Testimony were in his hand: the tables were written on both their sides; on the one side and on the other were they written *(the Ten Commandments, written by the "Finger of God" [31:18]).*

16 And the tables were the work of God, and the writing was the writing of God, graven upon the tables. *(The Law began with the Judgment of God, even as all Law must begin with the Judgment of God.)*

17 And when Joshua heard the noise of the people as they shouted, he said unto Moses, There is a noise of war in the camp. *(It seems that Joshua has waited for Moses for the entirety of the 40 days and 40 nights. He did so about halfway down the mountain. He will now accompany Moses to the base of the Mountain.)*

18 And he said, It is not the voice of them who shout for mastery, neither is it the voice of them who cry for being overcome: but the noise of them that sing do I hear. *(This was a far cry from the song of Moses, which celebrated the deliverance of the Children of Israel from Egyptian bondage [Ex., Chpt. 15.)*

19 And it came to pass, as soon as he came near into the camp, that he saw the calf, and the dancing: and Moses' anger waxed hot, and he cast the tables out of his hands, and broke them beneath the Mount. *(The anger of Moses was righteous indignation, and rightly so. He broke the Tables as a symbol of the anger of God, and not by him losing his temper.)*

20 And he took the calf which they had made, and burnt it in the fire, and ground it to powder, and strawed it upon the water, and made the Children of Israel drink of it. *(The Lord wanted Moses to do what he did, in order to show the people the utter, absolute worthlessness of this idol they had made.)*

21 And Moses said unto Aaron, What did this people unto you, that you have brought so great a sin upon them? *(Verses 21-24 record Aaron's excuse. He blames his actions on the people. Bible Repentance demands that God be justified, and we be condemned. This means that God demands that we accept the blame for our failure. This is the only kind of Repentance that He will honor.)*

22 And Aaron said, Let not the anger of my lord wax hot: you know the people, that they are set on mischief. *(Most Preachers presently, like Aaron, are little concerned about sin. This means they do not properly understand sin or the Cross!)*

23 For they said unto me, Make us gods, which shall go before us: for as for this Moses, the man who brought us up out of the land of Egypt, we wot not what is become of him. *(In a fashion, he is now blaming the situation on Moses!)*

24 And I said unto them, Whosoever has any gold, let them break it off. So they gave it me: then I cast it into the fire, and there came out this calf *(at least one of the most lame excuses that's ever been offered; and yet, as far as we know, the Lord did not direct Moses to punish Aaron in any way; it was not because he was the brother of Moses, because God is no respecter of persons; quite possibly, the magnitude of what he had done, which directly caused the deaths of some 3,000 men, creating a terrible amount of suffering, was punishment enough; as the High Priest, he was to stand as a mediator between God and the people, thereby saving their lives; and for him to be the cause of their deaths had to weigh heavily upon him).*

IDOLATERS SLAIN

25 And when Moses saw that the people

were naked; (for Aaron had made them naked unto their shame among their enemies [this refers not only to licentiousness, but, as well, to them being naked to the Judgment of God]:)

26 Then Moses stood in the gate of the camp, and said, Who is on the LORD's side? (The Hebrew actually says, "Who for Jehovah?" It formed an excellent rallying cry. Those who were engaging in this licentiousness, and those who saw no fault in it, obviously were not on the Lord's side. Neither are those which are in that camp presently!) let him come unto me. And all the sons of Levi gathered themselves together unto him. (That day, the sons of Levi won the Priesthood. The curse was broken [Gen. 49:5-7].)

27 And he said unto them, Thus saith the LORD God of Israel, Put every man his sword by his side, and go in and out from gate to gate throughout the camp, and kill every man his brother, and every man his companion, and every man his neighbour. (This which was to be done, first of all, was instruction from the Lord. Concerning this, Pink says: "So in preaching to idolaters today it is the 'wrath' of a Holy God, and not His Love [which is a Truth for His Own people only], which needs pressing upon them" [Rom. 1:18].)

28 And the Children of Levi did according to the word of Moses: and there fell of the people that day about three thousand men. (These were the ones who had mocked the call of Moses, and had continued on in their wicked ways. They were determined to continue to worship the golden calf. This tells us that at the giving of the Law, three thousand men lost their lives, and their souls. On the Day of Pentecost, the beginning of Grace, three thousand men were saved [Acts 2:41].)

29 For Moses had said, Consecrate yourselves to day to the LORD, even every man upon his son, and upon his brother; that he may bestow upon you a blessing this day. (This concerned the Tribe of Levi, and that they would be installed as Priests of the Lord on this particular day.)

30 And it came to pass on the morrow, that Moses said unto the people, You have sinned a great sin: and now I will go up unto the LORD; peradventure I shall make an Atonement for your sin. (The people had sinned, and the only thing that could make Atonement for sin was the Cross of Christ, which was portrayed in symbolic form respecting the Sacrifices. Moses could not atone for sin; the following terminology proves

the point. For all practical purposes, it seems that the Lord ignored his statements.)

31 And Moses returned unto the LORD, and said, Oh, this people have sinned a great sin, and have made them gods of gold. (Some sins are worse than others, and idolatry, which comes in many forms, is one of the worst of all [Jn. 19:11].)

32 Yet now, if You will forgive their sin—; and if not, blot me, I pray You, out of Your Book which You have written. (This is the first mention of the "Book of Life" found in the Bible. God could only forgive the sins of those who asked for such forgiveness [I Jn. 1:9].)

33 And the LORD said unto Moses, Whosoever has sinned against Me, him will I blot out of My Book. (Concerning this, Williams says: "Moses descended from on high with the Law. Confronted with man's sin, he broke both Tables, then returned with a cheerless 'peradventure' on his lips to seek an uncertain forgiveness. He failed!

"Christ descended from on high, fulfilled the Law, and having, on behalf of sinners, suffered its full penalty, returned to Heaven having shed His Precious Blood, the sign of His accomplished Atonement, to obtain an absolutely certain forgiveness.")

34 Therefore now go, lead the people unto the place of which I have spoken unto you: behold, My Angel shall go before you: nevertheless in the day when I visit I will visit their sin upon them. (It has been argued, and even conjectured, that this "Angel" is different from the "Angel" of Exodus 23:20. It is my thought that this is the same Angel. It seems as though the Lord had threatened to remove this Angel, Who, in essence, was a pre-incarnate appearance of Christ, but now consents that He may remain with Israel, thereby continuing to lead and to watch over them.)

35 And the LORD plagued the people, because they made the calf, which Aaron made. (The word "plagued" here means "to push, defeat, inflict disease, kill, smite, put to the worst." Exactly what the Lord did, we aren't told. It seems to have been in the form of chastisement, and seems somewhat, as the next Chapter proclaims, to have had a positive effect.)

CHAPTER 33
(1491 B.C.)
THE JOURNEY

AND the LORD said unto Moses, Depart, and go up hence, you and the people

which you have brought up out of the land of Egypt, unto the land which I swore unto Abraham, to Isaac, and to Jacob, saying, Unto your seed will I give it *(the host, according to the command of the Lord, will now start toward the Promised Land; however, the unbelief which brought about the golden calf would also shut the door to entrance into the Promised Land; that generation would die in the wilderness, and take 38 years to do so; so their sin delayed the Plan of God, as all sin delays the Plan of God)*:

2 And I will send an Angel before you; and I will drive out the Canaanite, the Amorite, and the Hittite, and the Perizzite, the Hivite, and the Jebusite *(the Lord never said that the Promised Land would be free of enemies, but He does promise victory over those enemies; regrettably, Israel, as we will later see, did not believe Him)*:

3 Unto a land flowing with milk and honey: for I will not go up in the midst of you; for you are a stiffnecked people: lest I consume you in the way *(to have the Presence of the Lord is the greatest thing in the world, unless the Believer decides on a wrong direction; that being the case, that "Presence," which is meant to bless, will instead destroy)*.

CONSECRATION

4 And when the people heard these evil tidings, they mourned: and no man did put on him his ornaments. *(Due to their great sin, the Lord wanted them to know that this was no time for festivities, levity, or decorations. In other words, they must take the matter very seriously.)*

5 For the LORD had said unto Moses, Say unto the Children of Israel, You are a stiffnecked people: I will come up into the midst of you in a moment, and consume you: therefore now put off your ornaments from yourself, that I may know what to do unto you. *(In essence, the Lord was telling the Children of Israel that what Pharaoh could not do, He could do in a moment.)*

6 And the Children of Israel stripped themselves of their ornaments by the mount Horeb.

THE TENT

7 And Moses took the Tabernacle, and pitched it without the camp, afar off from the camp, and called it the Tabernacle of the Congregation. And it came to pass, that every one which sought the Lord went out unto the Tabernacle of the Congregation, which was without the camp. *(The Hebrew word used here is "ohel," which means "tent," and should have been translated accordingly. The Hebrew word for "Tabernacle" is "mishkan," which was not used here. Moses moved his own tent outside the camp, because the main Tabernacle had not yet been built.)*

8 And it came to pass, when Moses went out unto the Tabernacle *(tent)*, that all the people rose up, and stood every man at his tent door, and looked after Moses, until he was gone into the Tabernacle. *(The Lord telling Moses to take his tent outside of the Camp was really an act of Grace. Had it remained in the Camp, judgment may very well have fallen on the people.)*

9 And it came to pass, as Moses entered into the Tabernacle, the cloudy pillar descended, and stood at the door of the Tabernacle, and the LORD talked with Moses *(the "cloudy pillar" denoted the Presence of God)*.

10 And all the people saw the cloudy pillar stand at the Tabernacle door: and all the people rose up and worshipped, every man in his tent door. *(But yet, the worship will prove to be somewhat shallow, more out of fear than anything else.)*

11 And the LORD spoke unto Moses face to face, as a man speaks unto his friend. And he *(Moses)* turned again into the camp: but his servant Joshua, the son of Nun, a young man, departed not out of the Tabernacle. *(Joshua would one day take the place of Moses, even though it would be many years into the future. But the Holy Spirit had already begun his training, showing the preparation time that was needed.)*

THE GLORY

12 And Moses said unto the LORD, See, You say unto me, Bring up this people: and you have not let me know whom You will send with me. Yet You have said, I know you by name, and you have also found grace in My sight. *(Moses reminds the Lord of the Promises the Lord has made to him. We are encouraged to do the same [Isa. 43:26].)*

13 Now therefore, I pray Thee, if I have found grace in Your sight, show me now Your way, that I may know You, that I may find grace in Your sight: and consider that this nation is Your people. *(Moses makes "Grace" the foundation of his petition, which foundation alone God will honor. If we come to Him on the basis*

of supposed merit, we will not be received. And we must always remember, Grace comes to the Believer strictly on the premise of the Finished Work of Christ. In fact, it can come no other way! [Gal. 2:20-21; 5:4].)

14 And He *(the Lord)* said, My Presence shall go with you, and I will give you rest.

15 And he *(Moses)* said unto Him *(the Lord),* If Your presence go not with me, carry us not up hence. *(Moses, in essence, demands that the Presence of God accompany him, and that the enterprise was impossible without the companionship of the Lord.)*

16 For wherein shall it be known here that I and Your people have found grace in Your sight? Is it not in that You go with us? so shall we be separated, I and Your people, from all the people who are upon the face of the Earth. *(It was that companionship, and nothing else, that separated Israel from the surrounding nations.)*

17 And the LORD said unto Moses, I will do this thing also that you have spoken: for you have found grace in My sight, and I know you by name. *(This speaks of relationship far more than the mere knowledge of Moses' name. In fact, the Lord knows the name of every person on the Earth.)*

18 And he said, I beseech You, show me Your glory. *(Grace comes first, then glory.)*

19 And He *(the Lord)* said, I will make all My goodness pass before you, and I will proclaim the Name of the LORD before you; and will be gracious to whom I will be gracious, and will show mercy on whom I will show mercy. *(The Lord shows "Grace" and "Mercy" to those who meet His conditions. Those conditions are simple: Faith in Christ and what Christ has done for us at the Cross, and that exclusively.)*

20 And He *(the Lord)* said, You can not see My face: for there shall no man see Me, and live. *(We must remember that Moses was asking to see God in all His Glory, which, we learn here, is impossible, and for any number of reasons.)*

21 And the LORD said, Behold, there is a place by Me, and you shall stand upon a rock *(Henry says concerning this: "The 'Rock' in Horeb was typical of Christ the Rock; the Rock of Israel, and the Rock of Ages, the Rock of refuge, Salvation, and strength; comparable to one for shelter, solidity, firmness, strength, and duration; happy are they who stand upon this Rock; they are safe and secure, they stand on high, and have noble prospects of the perfections of God, and of the riches of His Grace and Goodness" [Ps. 40:2; Isa. 33:16; Mat. 7:24]):*

22 And it shall come to pass, while My glory passes by, that I will put you in a clift of the rock, and will cover you with My hand while I pass by *(the "clift of the Rock" could be likened to the precious shed Blood of Jesus Christ, which covers the individual whose Faith is placed therein; it is believed that this particular "clift" is the same cave where Elijah would go, while in a very depressed state, some 800 years into the future [I Ki. 19:9]):*

23 And I will take away My hand, and you shall see My back parts: but My face shall not be seen. *(Some have claimed that these statements are merely anthropomorphisms; however, I think not! From the descriptions given in the Word of God, I personally believe that the Lord has a Spirit Body that, if seen, would be very similar to a human body, at least as far as shape is concerned.)*

CHAPTER 34
(1491 B.C.)
THE SECOND TABLES

AND the LORD said unto Moses, Hew thee two tables of stone like unto the first: and I will write upon these tables the words that were in the first tables, which you broke. *(The Ten Commandments were given again, but they were to be committed to the Ark of the Covenant — the symbol of Him Who said, "Thy Word have I hid in My heart" — Williams.)*

2 And be ready in the morning, and come up in the morning unto Mount Sinai, and present yourself there to Me in the top of the Mount. *("Grace" is the keynote of this Chapter.)*

3 And no man shall come up with you, neither let any man be seen throughout all the Mount; neither let the flocks nor herds feed before that Mount. *(While the Lord told Moses to hew the tables of stone all over again, because Moses had broken the first two, there is no record that God reprimanded him. Perhaps we could say that the repetition of the giving of the Ten Commandments the second time underlines God's Love and Patience with us. Many times He has to do the work all over again within our lives.)*

4 And he hewed two tables of stone like unto the first; and Moses rose up early in the morning, and went up unto Mount Sinai, as the LORD had commanded him, and took in his hand the two tables of stone. *(The Law is written on stone, while Grace is written on the heart.)*

REVELATION

5 And the LORD descended in the cloud, and stood with him there, and proclaimed the Name of the LORD. *(The Lord revealed His Character and Nature, which His Name proclaims.)*

6 And the LORD passed by before him, and proclaimed, The LORD, the LORD God, merciful and gracious, longsuffering, and abundant in goodness and truth *(all of this was epitomized in the Lord Jesus Christ)*.

7 Keeping mercy for thousands, forgiving iniquity and transgression and sin, and that will by no means clear the guilty *(the unrepentant cannot experience forgiveness from the Lord)*; visiting the iniquity of the fathers upon the children, and upon the children's children, unto the third and to the fourth generation. *(However, once any member of a family comes to Christ, this curse is broken [II Cor. 5:17].)*

8 And Moses made haste, and bowed his head toward the earth, and worshipped.

9 And he said, If now I have found Grace in Your sight, O Lord, let my Lord, I pray You, go among us: for it is a stiffnecked people; and pardon our iniquity and our sin, and take us for Your inheritance. *(The wondrous Revelation of God in this Chapter is declared in II Corinthians to have been the ministration of death; for as the people were still under Law, the more gracious God was, the more guilty they were [II Cor. 3:6-9].)*

THE COVENANT

10 And He *(the Lord)* said, Behold, I make a Covenant: before all your people I will do marvels, such as have not been done in all the Earth, nor in any nation: and all the people among which you are shall see the work of the LORD: for it is a terrible thing that I will do with you. *(For all this, Israel still had problems believing, which cost that generation the Promised Land.)*

11 Observe thou that which I command you this day: behold, I drive out before you the Amorite, and the Canaanite, and the Hittite, and the Perizzite, and the Hivite, and the Jebusite. *(The Lord driving out these enemies, at least when Israel came to the Promised Land, was contingent upon them rendering proper obedience, even as it is presently.)*

12 Take heed to yourself, lest you make a covenant with the inhabitants of the land where you go, lest it be for a snare in the midst of you *(to make a covenant with the world is to invite disaster)*:

13 But you shall destroy their altars, break their images, and cut down their groves *(in this Verse is found the first mention of Phallic worship in the Bible; such was the object of worship described here as a "grove" or "Ashera"; in blunt language, this is the male member [II Cor. 6:14-18; 7:1])*:

14 For you shall worship no other god: for the LORD, Whose Name is Jealous, is a jealous God *(in this sense, the jealousy of God is of the essence of His Moral Character, a major cause for worship and confidence on the part of His people, and a ground for fear on the part of His enemies; the Lord will not share His people with Satan; as well, the jealousy evidenced by the Lord is in no way selfish, as it is with mankind)*:

15 Lest you make a covenant with the inhabitants of the land, and they go a whoring after their gods, and do sacrifice unto their gods, and one call you, and you eat of his sacrifice;

16 And you take of their daughters unto your sons, and their daughters go a whoring after their gods, and make your sons go a whoring after their gods.

17 You shall make yourself no molten gods. *(The Word of God is emphatic, that it teaches separation from the world; however, it doesn't teach isolation. There is a great difference in the two.)*

INSTRUCTIONS

18 The feast of unleavened bread shall you keep. Seven days you shall eat unleavened bread, as I commanded you, in the time of the month Abib: for in the month Abib you came out from Egypt. *(It is touching to recognize the love which repeated the Ten Commandments and the Sacrifices and Feasts connected therewith. This was not mere repetition; it was loving instruction.)*

19 All that open the matrix *(womb)* is Mine; and every firstling among your cattle, whether ox or sheep, that is male. *(The "firstborn," not only of man, but even the male animals, were to be given to the Lord. This was typical of Christ, Who was God's Son. Regarding the Incarnation, He was the "firstborn" [Jn. 3:16].)*

20 But the firstling of an ass you shall redeem with a lamb *(by offering up a lamb in sacrifice, which was typical of Christ being offered up for unclean humanity, of which the*

"ass" was a type): and if you redeem him not, then shall you break his neck. All the first-born of your sons you shall redeem. And none shall appear before Me empty. (The firstborn could not be redeemed, unless sacrifice was of-fered; likewise, there is no Redemption for hu-manity without Faith in the Sacrifice of Christ, of which all of this was a Type.)

21 Six days you shall work, but on the sev-enth day you shall rest: in earing time (plow-ing time) and in harvest you shall rest. (Christ is God's rest [Heb., Chpt. 4]. The honor, or dishonor, done to the Sabbath was a test under Law; the honor, or dishonor, done to Christ, the test under Grace. Death was the penalty of dis-honoring the Sabbath; a similar penalty attaches to dishonoring Christ [Rom. 6:23].)

22 And you shall observe the feast of weeks, of the firstfruits of wheat harvest (the feast of Pentecost, which took place in our May or June), and the feast of ingathering at the year's end (of Tabernacles, which took place in October).

23 Thrice in the year shall all your menchil-dren appear before the Lord GOD, the God of Israel (April, June, and October).

24 For I will cast out the nations before you, and enlarge your borders: neither shall any man desire your land, when you shall go up to appear before the LORD your God thrice in the year (with all the men gathered in Jerusa-lem, enemies might think this would be the time to attack Israel; however, the Lord promises His Protection).

25 You shall not offer the blood of My sacri-fice with leaven (many, if not most, Jewish Schol-ars, I believe, limit this prohibition to the Pass-over Lamb; in fact, concerning the Feast of Pen-tecost, leaven is required [Lev. 23:17]); neither shall the sacrifice of the feast of the Passover be left unto the morning (this represents the fact that one must partake totally of Christ, and not partially).

26 The first of the firstfruits of your land you shall bring unto the House of the LORD your God ("Firstfruits" speak of Tithes). You shall not seethe a kid in his mother's milk (the little baby lamb was not to be boiled in his mother's milk; killing the little animal at its birth, and cooking it in this manner, showed a disrespect for the coming Redeemer, represented by the lamb).

MOSES

27 And the LORD said unto Moses, You write these words: for after the tenor of these words I have made a Covenant with you and with Israel. (The words which Moses wrote are those found in Verses 10 through 26.)

28 And he was there with the LORD forty days and forty nights; he did neither eat bread, nor drink water. And He (the Lord) wrote upon the tables the words of the Covenant, the Ten Commandments. (The latter portion of this Verse seems to imply that Moses wrote the Ten Commandments on the two Tables of stone; how-ever, it was the Lord Who wrote these Words [34:1; Deut. 10:2].)

29 And it came to pass, when Moses came down from Mount Sinai with the two tables of Testimony in Moses' hand, when he came down from the Mount, that Moses wist not that the skin of his face shone while he talked with him (with Aaron — this was the Presence of God on Moses).

30 And when Aaron and all the Children of Israel saw Moses, behold, the skin of his face shone; and they were afraid to come near him (this shining indicated that the Glory of God on Moses' face was like rays or darts of lightning shooting forth).

31 And Moses called unto them; and Aaron and all the rulers of the congregation returned unto him: and Moses talked with them.

32 And afterward all the Children of Israel came near: and he gave them in command-ment all that the LORD had spoken with him in Mount Sinai.

33 And till Moses had done speaking with them, he put a veil on his face. (Paul addressed this incident in II Corinthians, Chapter 3. In a context that stresses the transforming Power of God in the life of the Believer, Paul first ex-plores Moses' motive in using the veil. It was so that the Israelites might not gaze at his face "while the radiance was fading away" [II Cor. 3:13].)

34 But when Moses went in before the LORD to speak with Him, he took the veil off, until he came out. And he came out, and spoke unto the Children of Israel that which he was commanded.

35 And the Children of Israel saw the face of Moses, that the skin of Moses' face shone: and Moses put the veil upon his face again, until he went in to speak with Him (with the Lord — Richards says concerning this: "The veil sym-bolizes hiding our real selves from one another and must be removed in our relationships with other Believers; because Jesus is within Believ-ers, effecting our inner transformation, we see

His Face in one another's lives, for we 'are being transformed into His likeness' by the Work of the Holy Spirit; this attitude of openness is in contrast to the position Moses took, but it is necessary within the Church").

CHAPTER 35
(1491 B.C.)
THE SABBATH

AND Moses gathered all the congregation of the Children of Israel together, and said unto them, These are the words which the LORD has commanded, that you should do them *(God's rest [the Sabbath] opens this section, and His resting place [the Tabernacle] closes it)*.

2 Six days shall work be done, but on the seventh day there shall be to you an holy day, a Sabbath of rest to the LORD: whosoever does work therein shall be put to death.

3 You shall kindle no fire throughout your habitations upon the Sabbath day. *(Concerning this, Williams says: "What distinguishes God's people is participation in God's rest. Christ is God's rest [Heb., Chpt. 4]. The honor, or dishonor, done to the Sabbath was the test under Law. The honor, or dishonor, done to Christ, the test under Grace. Death was the penalty of dishonoring the Sabbath; a similar penalty attaches to dishonoring Christ.")*

THE TABERNACLE

4 And Moses spoke unto all the congregation of the Children of Israel, saying, This is the thing which the LORD commanded, saying *(these commands were for the entirety of the people of Israel; none were to be excluded)*,

5 Take ye from among you an offering unto the LORD; whosoever is of a willing heart, let him bring it, an offering of the LORD; gold, and silver, and brass,

6 And blue, and purple, and scarlet, and fine linen, and goats' hair,

7 And rams' skins dyed red, and badgers' skins, and shittim wood,

8 And oil for the light, and spices for anointing oil, and for the sweet incense,

9 And onyx stones, and stones to be set for the Ephod, and for the Breastplate. *(As Verse 5 states, this Offering is to be of a "willing heart," which means that it is not a tax. In fact, all Offerings to the Lord, whether back under Law, or presently under Grace, must be of a "willing*

heart," or else it is not recognized by the Lord.)

10 And every wise hearted among you shall come and make all that the LORD has commanded *(all were to participate, giving of their valuables, and for those who had talent in certain areas, as well, of their time and labor)*;

11 The Tabernacle, his tent, and his covering, his taches, and his boards, his bars, his pillars, and his sockets *(all, in one way or the other, were Types of Christ, in either His Mediatorial, Intercessory, or Atoning Work)*,

12 The Ark, and the staves thereof, with the Mercy Seat, and the Veil of the covering,

13 The table *(Table of Shewbread)*, and his staves, and all his vessels, and the shewbread,

14 The Candlestick *(Lampstand)* also for the light, and his furniture, and his lamps, with the oil for the light,

15 And the Incense Altar, and his staves, and the anointing oil, and the sweet incense, and the hanging for the door at the entering in of the Tabernacle,

16 The Altar of Burnt Offering, with his brasen grate, his staves, and all his vessels, the Laver and his foot,

17 The hangings of the court, his pillars, and their sockets, and the hanging for the door of the court,

18 The pins of the Tabernacle, and the pins of the court, and their cords,

19 The cloths of service, to do service in the Holy Place, the holy garments for Aaron the Priest, and the garments of his sons, to minister in the Priest's office. *(Although the world at that time would have understood this not at all, the truth is, the Tabernacle was the single most important thing happening on the face of the Earth. As well, at the present time, the activities of the Holy Spirit in the Body of Christ fall into the same category.)*

20 And all the congregation of the Children of Israel departed from the presence of Moses.

21 And they came, every one whose heart stirred him up, and every one whom his spirit made willing, and they brought the LORD's Offering to the work of the Tabernacle of the congregation, and for all his service and for the holy garments *(the "willing hearted" and the "wise hearted" and the "stirred hearted" offered themselves and their gifts to the Lord; thus "willingness" and "obedience" characterized the people)*.

22 And they came, both men and women, as many as were willing hearted, and brought bracelets, and earrings, and rings, and tablets,

all jewels of gold: and every man who offered offered an offering of gold unto the LORD.

23 And every man, with whom was found blue, and purple, and scarlet, and fine linen, and goats' hair, and red skins of rams, and badgers' skins, brought them.

24 Every one who did offer an offering of silver and brass brought the LORD's Offering: and every man, with whom was found shittim wood for any work of the service, brought it.

25 And all the women who were wise hearted did spin with their hands, and brought that which they had spun, both of blue, and of purple, and of scarlet, and of fine linen.

26 And all the women whose heart stirred them up in wisdom spun goats' hair. *(However, all of this work was done exactly according to the pattern which the Lord had given to Moses. They must not deviate from that pattern one iota; likewise, as all of this was a pattern of Redemption, this tells us that we must not depart whatsoever from the Word of God, and in any capacity.)*

27 And the rulers brought onyx stones, and stones to be set, for the Ephod, and for the Breastplate;

28 And spice, and oil for the light, and for the anointing oil, and for the sweet incense.

29 The Children of Israel brought a willing offering unto the LORD, every man and woman, whose heart made them willing to bring for all manner of work, which the LORD had commanded to be made by the hand of Moses. *(At Calvary, Christ was a "Willing Offering.")*

ANOINTED WORKERS

30 And Moses said unto the Children of Israel, See, the LORD has called by name Bezaleel the son of Uri, the son of Hur, of the Tribe of Judah *(Christ was from the Tribe of Judah; so, in a sense, Bezaleel was a Type of Christ)*;

31 And He *(the Lord)* has filled him with the Spirit of God, in wisdom, in understanding, and in knowledge, and in all manner of workmanship *(Christ was filled and anointed by the Holy Spirit for all manner of service [Lk. 4:18-19])*;

32 And to devise curious works *(beautifully crafted)*, to work in gold, and in silver, and in brass,

33 And in the cutting of stones, to set them, and in the carving of wood, to make any manner of cunning work. *(The work then was in items; the Work of the Holy Spirit now is in hearts and lives, which the Spirit does by the Authority of Christ [Jn. 16:14].)*

34 And He *(the Lord)* has put in his heart *(Bezaleel's)* that he may teach, both he, and Aholiab, the son of Ahisamach, of the Tribe of Dan.

35 Them has He filled with wisdom of heart, to work all manner of work, of the engraver, and of the cunning workman, and of the embroiderer, in blue, and in purple, in scarlet, and in fine linen, and of the weaver, even of them who do any work, and of those who devise cunning work. *(A part of the Work of the Holy Spirit was to give to Bezaleel the gift of being able to teach others, and so enabled him to form a body of skilled workmen to carry out his conceptions.)*

CHAPTER 36
(1491 B.C.)
ABUNDANCE

THEN wrought Bezaleel and Aholiab, and every wise hearted man, in whom the LORD put wisdom and understanding to know how to work all manner of work for the service of the Sanctuary, according to all that the LORD had commanded. *(There is a volume of instruction in all of this. We are too prone to regard the Word of God as insufficient for the minute details connected with His worship and service. This is a great mistake — a mistake which has proved the fruitful source of evils and errors in the professing Church.)*

2 And Moses called Bezaleel and Aholiab, and every wise hearted man, in whose heart the LORD had put wisdom, even everyone whose heart stirred him up to come unto the work to do it *(if the Word of God furnishes a man thoroughly unto "all good works" [II Tim. 3:16-17], it follows, as a necessary consequence, that whatever I find not in its pages cannot possibly be a good work)*:

3 And they received of Moses all the offering, which the Children of Israel had brought for the work of the service of the Sanctuary, to make it withal. And they brought yet unto him free offerings every morning *(such giving will always bring about great blessing)*.

4 And all the wise men, who wrought all the work of the Sanctuary, came every man from his work which they made;

5 And they spoke unto Moses, saying, The people bring much more than enough for the service of the work, which the LORD commanded to make. *(Concerning all of this, Williams says,*

"The minute repetition in these Chapters of the materials used in the construction of the Tabernacle, and of the vessels and furniture of that place of worship, is tiresome to a secular reader, but precious to a spiritual eye. Why this minute repetition? Because the Tabernacle, its curtains, its boards, its hooks, its sockets, its pins, its spoons — everything connected with it, displayed to God's heart the infinite perfections and glories of His Dearly Beloved Son.")

6 And Moses gave commandment, and they caused it to be proclaimed throughout the camp, saying, Let neither man nor woman make any more work for the offering of the Sanctuary. So the people were restrained from bringing.

7 For the stuff they had was sufficient for all the work to make it, and too much. *(We find in these Passages a beautiful picture of the devotion that the people gave to the Work of the Lord, as it involved the Sanctuary. It needed no effort to move the hearts of the people to give, no earnest appeals, no impressive arguments. The Scripture says that their "hearts stirred them up." This was the true way, and it is still the true way; consequently, the streams of voluntary devotion flowed from within. They all felt it was their sweet privilege to give to the Lord, not with a narrow heart, but after a princely fashion, until they had given "enough, and too much.")*

THE LINEN CURTAINS

8 And every wise hearted man among them who wrought the work of the Tabernacle made ten curtains of fine twined linen *(portraying the Righteousness of Christ)*, and blue *(signifying Christ came from Heaven)*, and purple *(signifying His Royalty as a King)*, and scarlet *(signifying His shed Blood on the Cross of Calvary)*: with Cherubims of cunning work *(beautiful, exact work)* made he them *(signifying the Holiness of Christ)*.

9 The length of one curtain was twenty and eight cubits *(42 feet)*, and the breadth of one curtain four cubits *(6 feet)*: the curtains were all of one size. *(This was the covering that was seen on the inside of the Tabernacle at the ceiling. The curtains symbolized the Righteousness of Christ.)*

10 And he coupled the five curtains one unto another *(five signifies Grace)*: and the other five curtains he coupled one unto another.

11 And he made loops of blue on the edge of one curtain from the selvedge in the coupling:

likewise he made in the uttermost side of another curtain, in the coupling of the second.

12 Fifty loops made he in one curtain, and fifty loops made he in the edge of the curtain which was in the coupling of the second: the loops held one curtain to another.

13 And he made fifty taches *(knobs)* of gold, and coupled the curtains one unto another with the taches: so it became one Tabernacle. *(All of this signifies that the Body of Christ is "one," made that way by Christ and what He has done for us at the Cross.)*

GOATS' HAIR

14 And he made curtains of goats' hair for the tent over the Tabernacle: eleven curtains he made them. *(This was placed on the backside of the curtain of linen, which means it could not be seen. It signified the Prophetic Office of Christ.)*

15 The length of one curtain was thirty cubits *(45 feet)*, and four cubits *(6 feet)* was the breadth *(width)* of one curtain: the eleven curtains were of one size.

16 And he coupled five curtains by themselves, and six curtains by themselves.

17 And he made fifty loops upon the uttermost edge of the curtain in the coupling, and fifty loops made he upon the edge of the curtain which couples the second.

18 And he made fifty taches of brass to couple the tent together, that it might be one. *(We are one in Christ.)*

RAMS' AND BADGERS' SKINS

19 And he made a covering for the tent of rams' skins *(signified Christ as King)* dyed red *(signifying that a King would Die on the Cross, thereby shedding His Life's Blood)*, and a covering of badgers' skins above that *(this was the last and final covering, actually the covering seen by all the people; this signified Christ as the High Priest of His people)*.

BOARDS AND SOCKETS

20 And he made boards for the Tabernacle of shittim wood, standing up *(these were for the sides of the Tabernacle; the "shittim wood" was also referred to as "indestructible wood," which means that it was a Type of the Humanity of Christ)*.

21 The length of a board was ten cubits *(15*

feet), and the breadth (width) of a board one cubit and a half (2 and 1/4 feet).

22 One board had two tenons (hands), equally distant one from another: thus did he make for all the boards of the Tabernacle.

23 And he made boards for the Tabernacle; twenty boards for the south side southward:

24 And forty sockets of silver (Redemption is symbolized in the Old Testament by silver) he made under the twenty boards; two sockets under one board for his two tenons, and two sockets under another board for his two tenons.

25 And for the other side of the Tabernacle, which is toward the north corner, he made twenty boards,

26 And their forty sockets of silver; two sockets under one board, and two sockets under another board.

27 And for the sides of the Tabernacle westward (the rear) he made six boards.

28 And two boards made he for the corners of the Tabernacle in the two sides.

29 And they were coupled beneath, and coupled together at the head thereof, to one ring: thus he did to both of them in both the corners. (All Believers are coupled to Christ, Who is "Head.")

30 And there were eight boards, and their sockets were sixteen sockets of silver, under every board two sockets.

THE BARS

31 And he made bars of shittim wood; five for the boards of the one side of the Tabernacle,

32 And five bars for the boards of the other side of the Tabernacle, and five bars for the boards of the Tabernacle for the sides westward.

33 And he made the middle bar to shoot through the boards from the one end to the other. (As should by now be overly obvious, the Lord gave to Moses minute instructions concerning the design of the Tabernacle. Everything was planned by God, down to the minutest detail, which means that it was not to be changed in any capacity.)

GOLD

34 And he overlaid the boards with gold (signifying the Deity of Christ), and made their rings of gold to be places for the bars, and overlaid the bars with gold. (The "bars" held the boards in place and, as well, signified the one purpose of Christ, to which He was confined, which was the Cross [Isa. 50:7].)

THE INNER VEIL

35 And he made a Veil of blue, and purple, and scarlet, and fine twined linen (if it is to be noticed, these colors did not vary): with Cherubims (signifying the Holiness of Christ) made he it of cunning work.

36 And he made thereunto four pillars of shittim wood (the Humanity of Christ), and overlaid them with gold (the Deity of Christ): their hooks were of gold; and he cast for them four sockets of silver (the latter represented Redemption; however, due to the fact that Jesus was God, hence the "gold," He would have to become a man, The Man Christ Jesus, in order to die on a Cross, thereby effecting this Redemption; the "four pillars" represent the fourfold Gospel, typified by the Gospel of John, Jesus Saves; the Gospel of Mark, Jesus heals; the Gospel of Luke, Jesus Baptizes with the Holy Spirit; and the Gospel of Matthew, Jesus is coming again).

THE OUTER VEIL

37 And he made an hanging for the Tabernacle door of blue, and purple, and scarlet, and fine twined linen, of needlework;

38 And the five pillars of it with their hooks: and he overlaid their chapiters and their fillets with gold: but their five sockets were of brass. ("Five" in Biblical numerology specifies "Grace." Jesus had five names [Isa. 9:6]. As well, the Ministry is made up of five callings, "Apostles, Prophets, Evangelists, Pastors, and Teachers" [Eph. 4:11]. The "chapiters" represent the "Finished Work of Christ" [I Ki. 7:15-20]. These "five pillars" were set in "sockets of copper," whereas the others were in sockets of silver. "Copper" represents the Judgment of God, which Jesus suffered on our behalf. It would result in Redemption, hence, the "silver sockets" under the four Pillars. Once again, we see only Christ, but we see, as well, the Cross.)

CHAPTER 37
(1491 B.C.)
ARK OF THE COVENANT

AND Bezaleel made the Ark of shittim wood: two cubits and a half (3 and 3/4 feet) was the length of it, and a cubit and a half (2 and 1/4 feet) the breadth (width) of it, and a cubit

and a half the height of it (in a sense, this was God's dwelling place on Earth, as it regards His association with man):

2 And he overlaid it with pure gold within and without (signifying the Deity of Christ), and made a crown of gold to it round about (signifying that Jesus was a King).

3 And he cast for it four rings of gold, to be set by the four corners of it; even two rings upon the one side of it, and two rings upon the other side of it.

4 And he made staves of shittim wood (the wood signified the humanity of Christ), and overlaid them with gold.

5 And he put the staves into the rings by the sides of the Ark to bear the Ark. (When the people were told by the Lord to move, the Ark, plus all the other Sacred Vessels of the Tabernacle, were to move as well. Due to the Cross, the Holy Spirit now lives within our hearts and lives, at least all who are born again and, consequently, is with us at all times. As should be obvious, the abiding Presence of the Holy Spirit is far better than the old method, hence Paul saying that we now have a "Better Covenant" [Heb. 8:6].)

MERCY SEAT

6 And he made the Mercy Seat of pure gold (which sat on top of the Ark of the Covenant): two cubits and a half (3 and 3/4 feet) was the length thereof, and one cubit and a half (2 and 1/4 feet) the breadth (width) thereof.

7 And he made two Cherubims of gold, beaten out of one piece made he them, on the two ends of the Mercy Seat (meaning that the two Cherubims and the Mercy Seat were all of one piece of gold);

8 One Cherub on the end on this side, and another cherub on the other end on that side: out of the Mercy Seat made he the Cherubims on the two ends thereof. (The Mercy of God, based on the Holiness of God, tells us that only Christ can come near. He Alone is Holy!)

9 And the Cherubims spread out their wings on high, and covered with their wings over the Mercy Seat (the four wings touched each other in the middle), with their faces one to another; even to the Mercy Seatward were the faces of the Cherubims (the faces looked down toward the Mercy Seat; inside the Ark were the Ten Commandments on two tablets of stone; man had broken them repeatedly; so they saw the broken Law; however, with the blood applied

to the Mercy Seat, which it was once a year by the High Priest, instead of seeing the broken law, they saw the blood [Ex. 12:13]).

TABLE OF SHEWBREAD

10 And he made the Table (holding twelve loaves) of shittim wood: two cubits (3 feet) was the length thereof, and a cubit (1 and 1/2 feet) the breadth (width) thereof, and a cubit and a half (2 and 1/4 feet) the height thereof:

11 And he overlaid it with pure gold (as the "wood" signified the Humanity of Christ, which was necessary in order that He might go to the Cross, the "gold" typified His Deity; while He laid aside the expression of His Deity, He never laid aside the possession of His Deity), and made thereunto a crown of gold round about (signifying the Kingship of Christ).

12 Also he made thereunto a border of an handbreadth round about; and made a crown of gold for the border thereof round about. (In essence, there were two crowns around the Table of Shewbread. They spoke of His two comings. He came the first time as a King, but was not recognized as such. When He comes back the second time, He definitely will be recognized as King, "King of kings, and Lord of lords.")

13 And he cast for it four rings of gold, and put the rings upon the four corners that were in the four feet thereof.

14 Over against the border were the rings, the places for the staves to bear the table (when it was moved).

15 And he made the staves of shittim wood, and overlaid them with gold, to bear the Table.

16 And he made the vessels which were upon the Table, his dishes, and his spoons, and his bowls, and his covers to cover withal, of pure gold. (The above Verses portray the Table of Shewbread, a Type of Christ as the Bread of Life.)

THE GOLDEN CANDLESTICK

17 And he made the Candlestick of pure gold (the Lampstand is a Type of Christ as the Light of the world; incidentally, the Hebrew word should have been translated Lampstand, because it's not a candlestick; in fact, no candles were involved): of beaten work made he the Candlestick (beaten and shaped by the craftsman's hand, this portrays Christ in His sufferings); his shaft (the middle stem, which portrayed Christ as the

Source of all Blessings), and his branch, his bowls, his knops, and his flowers, were of the same:

18 And six branches going out of the sides thereof; three branches of the Candlestick out of the one side thereof, and three branches of the Candlestick out of the other side thereof *(the three on each side, totaling "six," which is the number of man, represent the Church, the Body of Christ; the middle prong, representing Christ, added with the six totaled "seven," which is God's perfect number; the idea is, the people of God cannot be complete, not at all, without Christ)*:

19 Three bowls made after the fashion of almonds in one branch *(represents the Resurrection of Christ)*, a knop *(represents pomegranates, i.e., "fruit")* and a flower *(was no doubt the lily, denoting "purity")*; and three bowls made like almonds in another branch, a knop and a flower: so throughout the six branches going out of the Candlestick.

20 And in the Candlestick were four bowls made like almonds, his knops, and his flowers *(the "four bowls" represent the fourfold Gospel, "Salvation, Holy Spirit Baptism, Divine Healing, and the Second Coming")*:

21 And a knop under two branches of the same, and a knop under two branches of the same, and a knop under two branches of the same, according to the six branches going out of it *(the repetition of the branches proclaims the fact that all in the Church are treated the same by the Holy Spirit and, abiding by the Word, will receive the same blessings from the Lord)*.

22 Their knops and their branches were of the same: all of it was one beaten work of pure gold *(all being one piece signifies that the Mercy of God is based entirely upon the Holiness of God)*.

23 And he made his seven lamps *("seven," being God's perfect number, proclaims perfect illumination)*, and his snuffers *(for the trimming of the wicks)*, and his snuffdishes, of pure gold *(signifying that God Alone can make the Believer what the Believer ought to be)*.

24 Of a talent of pure gold made he it, and all the vessels thereof *(worth about $500,000 in 2004 money)*.

INCENSE ALTAR

25 And he made the Incense Altar of shittim wood: the length of it was a cubit *(1 and 1/2 feet)*, and the breadth *(width)* of it a cubit *(the Incense Altar, which sat immediately in front of the Veil which separated the Holy Place from the Holy of Holies, was a Type of the Intercessory Work of our Lord, as our Great High Priest [Heb. 7:26-28])*; it was foursquare *(stipulating the fact that the Intercession is the same for all men everywhere, at least for those who believe)*; and two cubits *(3 feet)* was the height of it; the horns thereof were of the same *(four horns protruded out from the Altar, one at each corner)*.

26 And he overlaid it with pure gold, both the top of it, and the sides thereof round about, and the horns of it: also he made unto it a crown of gold round about *(once again, stipulating Christ as King)*.

27 And he made two rings of gold for it under the crown thereof, by the two corners of it, upon the two sides thereof, to be places for the staves to bear it withal.

28 And he made the staves of shittim wood, and overlaid them with gold *(the staves inserted in the rings, by which the Altar of Incense could be handled when it was moved, speaks to us of the constant need of Intercession, irrespective as to where we might be)*.

ANOINTING OIL

29 And he made the Holy Anointing Oil, and the pure incense of sweet spices, according to the work of the apothecary. *(For the composition of the oil, see Exodus 30:23-25. The composition of the Incense is given in Exodus 30:34-35.)*

CHAPTER 38
(1491 B.C.)
THE BRASEN ALTAR

AND he made the Altar of Burnt Offering of shittim wood: five cubits was the length thereof *(7 and 1/2 feet)*, and five cubits the breadth *(width)* thereof; it was foursquare; and three cubits *(4 and 1/2 feet)* the height thereof. *(This was the Altar where the Burnt Offerings were offered. The vessel sat outside immediately in front of the Tabernacle.)*

2 And he made the horns thereof on the four corners of it *(horns stand for power and dominion; the idea is that the Sacrifice of Christ would be a total and complete Sacrifice, answering every problem of the entirety of the human race, consequently, the "four corners")*; the horns thereof were of the same: and he overlaid it with brass.

3 And he made all the vessels of the Altar, the pots, and the shovels, and the basons, and the fleshhooks, and the firepans: all the vessels thereof made he of brass. *(The "copper," which characterizes this particular Vessel, speaks of Judgment, and Judgment which came upon Christ instead of upon us.)*

4 And he made for the Altar a brasen grate of network under the compass thereof beneath unto the midst of it. *(Evidently, this was an extension on the Altar, which protruded out, and encircled the Altar. It was there, evidently, to catch parts of the Sacrifice which might fall off, so that they not fall to the ground. No part of the Sacrifice of Christ must be lost.)*

5 And he cast four rings for the four ends of the grate of brass, to be places for the staves.

6 And he made the staves of shittim wood, and overlaid them with brass *(copper)*.

7 And he put the staves into the rings on the sides of the Altar, to bear it withal; he made the Altar hollow with boards. *(As all the other Sacred Vessels had to be transported when the Camp of Israel moved, so did the great Brazen Altar. This tells us, among other things, that there is never a time, place, or situation in which we no longer need the Cross of Christ, of which the Altar was a Type.)*

THE LAVER

8 And he made the laver of brass *(the copper Laver, filled with water, symbolized the Word of God, with Jesus as the Living Word [Jn. 1:1])*, and the foot of it of brass *(the pedestal on which it sat)*, of the lookingglasses of the women assembling, which assembled at the door of the Tabernacle of the congregation. *(The women who assembled here portrayed their zeal for the things of God, and contributed their bronze plates, which emitted a high polish and were used as mirrors, from which the Brazen Laver was made. As it was easy to see one's reflection in the high polish of the Laver, likewise, one can see one's self in the Word of God, of which the Laver was a type.)*

THE COURT

9 And he made the court *(which surrounded the Tabernacle)*: on the south side southward the hangings of the court were of fine twined linen *(symbolizing the Righteousness of Christ)*, an hundred cubits *(150 feet)*:

10 Their pillars were twenty *(were probably made of shittim wood)*, and their brasen sockets twenty *(the "sockets" in which the pillars sat)*; the hooks of the pillars and their fillets were of silver. *(The silver symbolizes Redemption. The spotless white walls that surrounded the Tabernacle on every side were a standing witness to the Holiness of Him Whose dwelling it was.)*

11 And for the north side the hangings were an hundred cubits *(150 feet)*, their pillars were twenty, and their sockets of brass twenty; the hooks of the pillars and their fillets of silver.

12 And for the west side were hangings of fifty cubits *(75 feet)*, their pillars ten, and their sockets ten; the hooks of the pillars and their fillets of silver.

13 And for the east side eastward fifty cubits.

14 The hangings of the one side of the gate were fifteen cubits *(22 and 1/2 feet)*; their pillars three, and their sockets three.

15 And for the other side of the court gate, on this hand and that hand, were hangings of fifteen cubits; their pillars three, and their sockets three. *(The "gate," or entrance, into the Court was 20 cubits, or 30 feet, wide [Ex. 27:16], which left 15 cubits, or 22 and 1/2 feet, on each side, making up the total of 50 cubits, or 75 feet, for each end. As one can see, the "gate," or entrance, to the Court was wide. The entrance was a Type of Christ, Who said, "I am the Door: by Me if any man enter in, he shall be saved, and shall go in and out, and find pasture" [Jn. 10:9].)*

16 All the hangings of the court round about were of fine twined linen *(snow-white, typifying the Righteousness of Christ)*.

17 And the sockets for the pillars were of brass; the hooks of the pillars and their fillets of silver; and the overlaying of their chapiters of silver; and all the pillars of the court were filleted with silver *(once again, expressing Redemption, all in Christ)*.

THE GATE

18 And the hanging for the gate of the court was needlework, of blue *(typifying the Heavenly origin of Christ)*, and purple *(typifying His Position as King)*, and scarlet *(typifying His shed Blood on the Cross of Calvary)*, and fine twined linen *(typifying His Righteousness)*: and twenty cubits *(30 feet)* was the length, and the height in the breadth was five cubits *(7 and 1/2 feet; the merely curious could not see over this fence)*, answerable to the hangings of the court.

19 And their pillars were four, and their sockets of brass four; their hooks of silver, and the overlaying of their chapiters and their fillets of silver.

20 And all the pins of the Tabernacle, and of the court round about, were of brass.

THE OFFERINGS

21 This is the sum of the Tabernacle, even of the Tabernacle of Testimony, as it was counted, according to the Commandment of Moses, for the service of the Levites, by the hand of Ithamar, son of Aaron the Priest. *(Ithamar was placed in charge. Aaron had four sons, and Ithamar was the youngest. Two of the sons, Nadab and Abihu, would be slain by the Lord for using "strange fire" [Lev. 10:1-2].)*

22 And Bezaleel the son of Uri, the son of Hur, of the Tribe of Judah, made all that the LORD commanded Moses *(was in charge)*.

23 And with him was Aholiab, son of Ahisamach, of the Tribe of Dan, an engraver, and a cunning workman, and an embroiderer in blue, and in purple, and in scarlet, and fine linen. *(Everything was designed by the Lord, even down to the minute details. These designs were to be followed minutely and without fail.)*

24 All the gold that was occupied for the work in all the work of the Holy Place, even the gold of the offering, was twenty and nine talents, and seven hundred and thirty shekels, after the shekel of the sanctuary *(about $14,000,000, in 2004 currency)*.

25 And the silver of them that were numbered of the congregation was an hundred talents, and a thousand seven hundred and threescore and fifteen shekels , after the shekel of the sanctuary *(about $750,000, in 2004 currency)*:

26 A bekah for every man, that is, half a shekel, after the shekel of the sanctuary, for every one who went to be numbered, from twenty years old and upward *(these were men of war and, if a census was taken, each man was responsible to pay a half shekel of silver, worth about $3; as silver signified Redemption, this tells us that Israel's power and strength did not rest upon force of arms, but rather on the Power of God and, more particularly, the shed Blood of the Lamb, which Redemption portrayed)*, for six hundred thousand and three thousand and five hundred and fifty men *(603,550 at the time of this census, and, as stated, all men of war; these were counted from 20 years old upward to 50 years old; counting those younger*

and older, as well as all the women and girls, the population would then have been approximately 3 million).

27 And of the hundred talents of silver were cast the sockets of the sanctuary, and the sockets of the Veil; an hundred sockets of the hundred talents, a talent for a socket *(about 75 pounds)*.

28 And of the thousand seven hundred seventy and five shekels he made hooks for the pillars, and overlaid their chapiters, and filleted them.

29 And the brass *(copper)* of the offering was seventy talents, and two thousand and four hundred shekels.

30 And therewith he made the sockets to the door of the Tabernacle of the congregation, and the Brasen Altar, and the brasen grate for it, and all the vessels of the Altar *(copper signified judgment)*.

31 And the sockets of the court round about, and the sockets of the court gate, and all the pins of the Tabernacle, and all the pins of the court round about.

CHAPTER 39
(1491 B.C.)
THE PRIESTLY GARMENTS

AND of the blue, and purple, and scarlet, they made cloths of service, to do service in the Holy Place *(the first compartment of the Tabernacle)*, and made the holy garments for Aaron; as the LORD commanded Moses. *(The reason the study of the Tabernacle is of such spiritual profit is simply because every part and parcel of this structure, plus all of its Sacred Vessels, symbolized Christ in some manner; therefore, to learn the Tabernacle is to learn Christ.)*

2 And he made the Ephod *(the outer Robe worn by the High Priest)* of gold, blue, and purple, and scarlet, and fine twined linen *(this contained all the colors used by the other material, but with one addition, "gold"; actually, this was more than a mere color, but rather gold wires, as portrayed in the next Verse, and probably woven into the hem)*.

3 And they did beat the gold into thin plates, and cut it into wires, to work it in the blue, and in the purple, and in the scarlet, and in the fine linen, with cunning work. *(This garment must have been strikingly beautiful! In fact, as far as we know, these are the only garments in the history of man that were designed by the Lord of Glory.)*

4 They made shoulderpieces for it, to couple it together: by the two edges was it coupled together (*the back and the front were coupled together at the shoulders*).

5 And the curious girdle (*a sash, tied around the waist*) of his Ephod, that was upon it, was of the same, according to the work thereof; of gold, blue, and purple, and scarlet, and fine twined linen; as the Lord commanded Moses (*this girdle presents Christ as it regards His preparation for service*).

6 And they wrought onyx stones inclosed in ouches of gold, graven, as signets are graven, with the names of the Children of Israel. (*These were shoulderboards, one might say, one to each shoulder, with the names of the Children of Israel inscribed on these stones, six to the side.*)

7 And he put them on the shoulders of the Ephod, that they should be stones for a memorial to the Children of Israel; as the LORD commanded Moses (*inasmuch as these were worn on the shoulders of the High Priest, it tells us that these twelve Tribes were, in effect, worn on the shoulders of Christ, with the shoulders denoting strength, of which all of this was a type*).

8 And he made the Breastplate of cunning work (*the Breastplate also carried the names of the twelve Tribes of Israel inscribed on precious stones; thus, Israel was carried not only on the shoulders of Christ, but, as well, over His heart*), like the work of the Ephod; of gold, blue, and purple, and scarlet, and fine twined linen.

9 It was foursquare; they made the breastplate double: a span was the length thereof (*about 9 inches*), and a span the breadth thereof, being doubled (*the "Breastplate" being doubled probably pertained to the pouch which contained the Urim and the Thummin, which was somewhat of a pocket on the inside of the front of the Breastplate*).

10 And they set in it four rows of stones: the first row was a sardius, a topaz, and a carbuncle: this was the first row.

11 And the second row, an emerald, a sapphire, and a diamond.

12 And the third row, a ligure, an agate, and an amethyst.

13 And the fourth row, a beryl, an onyx, and a jasper: they were inclosed in ouches of gold in their inclosings (*settings*).

14 And the stones were according to the names of the Children of Israel, twelve, according to their names (*"twelve" is God's number for His Government*), like the engravings of a signet, every one with his name, according to the Twelve Tribes. (*All of these were precious stones, signifying the worth and value which God placed upon His people.*)

15 And they made upon the Breastplate chains at the ends, of wreathen work of pure gold (*the chains fastened the Breastplate to the shoulderpieces of the Ephod*).

16 And they made two ouches of gold, and two gold rings; and put the two rings in the two ends of the Breastplate.

17 And they put the two wreathen chains of gold in the two rings on the ends of the Breastplate.

18 And the two ends of the two wreathen chains they fastened in the two ouches, and put them on the shoulderpieces of the Ephod, before it (*the chains signified the binding of Christ to the Believer, and the Believer to Christ*).

19 And they made two rings of gold, and put them on the two ends of the Breastplate, upon the border of it, which was on the side of the Ephod inward. (*All of these tedious explanations, as it regards this garment worn by the High Priest, might seem somewhat excessive to the unspiritual eye. However, the Holy Spirit has a reason for including all of this information.*

Inasmuch as the High Priest was a Type of Christ, this helps us to learn more about the Person of Christ, as it regards His Atoning, Mediatorial, and High Priestly Work. As well, it shows our relationship with Him, inasmuch as we are tied to Him, even as portrayed by the "chains," and forever fastened to Him, as portrayed by the "rings.")

20 And they made two other golden rings, and put them on the two sides of the Ephod underneath, toward the forepart of it, over against the other coupling thereof, above the curious girdle of the Ephod.

21 And they did bind the Breastplate by his rings unto the rings of the Ephod with a lace of blue, that it might be above the curious girdle of the Ephod, and that the Breastplate might not be loosed from the Ephod; as the LORD commanded Moses. (*Of all the garments, the "Breastplate" was the chief and most costly of the vestments, the other garments being, as it were, a foundation and background for it — this central article pointing to the very "heart" of Christ Himself.*)

22 And he made the robe of the Ephod of woven work, all of blue. (*This Robe embodied the color of the Heavens; it was all of blue, stipulating the Heavenly Character of our Great*

High Priest.)

23 And there was an hole in the midst of the Robe, as the hole of an habergeon, with a band round about the hole, that it should not rend.

24 And they made upon the hems of the Robe pomegranates *(fruit)* of blue, and purple, and scarlet, and twined linen. *(This portrays the fact that the Ministry of Christ brings forth much "fruit" and, as well, we are to do the same [Jn., Chpt. 15].)*

25 And they made bells of pure gold *(whereas the "pomegranate" was merely a form, actually a tassel, the "golden bell" was actually a real article, which rang every time the High Priest walked or moved)*, and put the bells between the pomegranates upon the hem of the robe, round about between the pomegranates;

26 A bell and a pomegranate, a bell and a pomegranate, round about the hem of the robe to minister in; as the LORD commanded Moses. *(It was at His Ascension that our Great High Priest passed into the Heavenly Sanctuary, and consequent upon this, on the Day of Pentecost, His "sound" was heard in the outpouring of the Spirit, which was carried by the Apostles, ultimately to the ends of the Earth. The "fruit" is seen in the multitudes who have been saved. Even more glorious will be His Sound and Fruit when "He comes out" again, and returns to this Earth, and redeems His people, Israel, and sets up His Kingdom.*

Even though this Robe was worn by the High Priest of Israel, the very embodiment of the Levitical Law, still, this is most important, for it defines the essential nature of Christianity as contra-distinguished from Judaism. The whole system takes its character from the Priest. Because Christ is the Heavenly Priest, His people are partakers of a Heavenly Calling [Heb. 3:1], and our inheritance is also there [I Pet., Chpt. 1].)

27 And they made coats of fine linen of woven work for Aaron, and for his sons *(the word "coats" in this Verse is an unfortunate translation; actually these were underclothes, which consisted of a long white linen tunic or shirt, having tight-fitting sleeves, and reaching nearly to the feet)*,

28 And a mitre of fine linen *(a turban worn by the High Priest)*, and goodly bonnets of fine linen *(worn by all the other Priests)*, and linen breeches of fine twined linen *(as always, the snow-white linen portrayed the Righteousness of Christ)*,

29 And a girdle of fine twined linen, and blue, and purple, and scarlet, of needlework; as the LORD commanded Moses *(the "Curious Girdle")*.

30 And they made the plate of the holy crown of pure gold *(the symbol of the essential Holiness of our Lord)*, and wrote upon it a writing, like to the engravings of a signet, HOLINESS TO THE LORD *(the assignment of a crown to the High Priest gave him a great dignity, which marked him as a Type of our Lord in His Threefold Office of Prophet, Priest, and King)*.

31 And they tied unto it a lace of blue, to fasten it on high upon the mitre; as the LORD commanded Moses. *(Pink says, "Because of our legal and vital union with Christ, His Holiness is ours." Pink goes on to say, "O Christian Reader, look away from yourself, with your ten thousand failures, and fix your eyes on that Golden Plate. Behold in the perfections of your Great High Priest the measure of your eternal acceptance with God. Christ is our Sanctification as well as our Righteousness!")*

SUMMARY

32 Thus was all the work of the Tabernacle of the tent of the congregation finished: and the Children of Israel did according to all that the LORD commanded Moses, so did they. *(The frequent repetition of the words, "as the Lord commanded Moses," should be noted. Nothing was left to man's ingenuity or taste.)*

33 And they brought the Tabernacle unto Moses, the tent, and all his furniture, his taches, his boards, his bars, and his pillars, and his sockets,

34 And the covering of rams' skins dyed red, and the covering of badgers' skins, and the veil of the covering,

35 The Ark of the Testimony, and the staves thereof, and the Mercy Seat,

36 The Table, and all the vessels thereof, and the shewbread,

37 The pure Candlestick *(Lampstand)*, with the lamps thereof, even with the lamps to be set in order, and all the vessels thereof, and the oil for light,

38 And the Golden Altar, and the anointing oil, and the sweet incense, and the hanging for the Tabernacle door,

39 The Brasen Altar, and his grate of brass, his staves, and all his vessels, the Laver and his foot,

40 The hangings of the court, his pillars, and his sockets, and the hanging for the court gate, his cords, and his pins, and all the vessels of

the service of the Tabernacle, for the tent of the congregation,

41 The cloths of service to do service in the holy place, and the holy garments for Aaron the Priest, and his sons' garments, to minister in the Priest's office.

42 According to all that the LORD commanded Moses, so the Children of Israel made all the work.

43 And Moses did look upon all the work, and, behold, they had done it as the LORD had commanded, even so had they done it: and Moses blessed them. *(In all of this, and as we have repeatedly stated, nothing is left to chance, no place allowed for scheming. All is God.*

Those Israelites skilled in all the wisdom of the Egyptians, the greatest builders in the world of that day, were not allowed to build this structure. Instead, Moses was bidden to make all things after the pattern shown him in the Mount.

And, as well, after the "Pattern" had been completely set before Moses, the Lord makes known to him who were to be the principal workmen. The choice of them was His, not Moses'; and this means that their equipment for the work was Divine and not human.

All of this pertains to the fact that Salvation is all of the Lord, and not at all of human participation. In fact, the moment we seek to add to, or take from, God's Plan, the Plan is of no more use. The Plan of Redemption is of Heavenly Origin, and it must not be sullied by Earthly intervention.)

CHAPTER 40
(1491 B.C.)
THE TABERNACLE

AND the LORD spoke unto Moses, saying,

2 On the first day of the first month shall you set up the Tabernacle of the tent of the congregation. *(The setting up of the Tabernacle, with the Sacred Vessels placed in proper order so that the proper worship of the Lord may begin, was the single most important thing on Earth at that particular time. One year had passed since they had left Egypt.)*

3 And you shall put therein the Ark of the Testimony *(Ark of the Covenant)*, and cover the Ark with the Veil *(hang the "Veil" between the Holy Place and the Holy of Holies, with the Ark situated in the latter; the "Veil" thereby hid it from view).*

4 And you shall bring in the Table, and set in order the things that are to be set in order upon it *(put the twelve loaves of bread on the Table)*; and you shall bring in the Candlestick *(Lampstand)*, and light the lamps thereof *(the Lampstand sat on the north side of the Tabernacle, with the Table of Shewbread situated on the south side).*

5 And you shall set the Altar of gold for the incense before the Ark of the Testimony, and put the hanging of the door to the Tabernacle *(this was at the front of the Tabernacle, which led into the Holy Place).*

6 And you shall set the Altar of the Burnt Offering before the door of the Tabernacle of the tent of the congregation *(this Brazen Altar was a Type of the Cross).*

7 And you shall set the Laver between the tent of the congregation and the Altar, and shall put water therein *(the Priests, upon entering the Holy Place, which they did constantly, had to wash their hands and feet in this water each time they went in, signifying the cleansing by the Word, which is needed by all Believers, and constantly).*

8 And you shall set up the court round about *(the fence)*, and hang up the hanging at the court gate *(the one entrance into the Court).*

9 And you shall take the anointing oil *(a Type of the Holy Spirit, which would anoint Christ [Lk. 4:18-19])*, and anoint the Tabernacle *(a Type of Christ)*, and all that is therein, and shall hallow it *(consecrate it totally to the Lord)*, and all the vessels thereof: and it shall be holy.

10 And you shall anoint the Altar of the Burnt Offering, and all his vessels, and sanctify the Altar: and it shall be an Altar most holy. *(Christ sanctified the Altar, i.e., "the Cross," meaning that the Cross didn't sanctify Christ. This completely refutes the unscriptural doctrine that Jesus died spiritually on the Cross. That statement means that some believe and teach that Jesus became a sinner on the Cross, died and went to Hell, as all sinners do, and was born-again in Hell, etc. None of that happened! The Cross, and the Cross alone, was the place of victory, and total victory at that. When He said, "It is finished," the Scripture tells us that "the Veil of the Temple was rent in twain from the top to the bottom" [Mat. 27:51]. This tells us that the Cross opened up the way for all of mankind, by exhibiting Faith in Christ, to enter the very Holy of Holies.)*

11 And you shall anoint the laver and his foot, and sanctify it.

CONSECRATION

12 And you shall bring Aaron and his sons unto the door of the Tabernacle of the congregation, and wash them with water. *(The "water" is typical of the Word of God [Eph. 5:26].)*

13 And you shall put upon Aaron the holy garments, and anoint him, and sanctify him; that he may minister unto Me in the Priest's office. *(There is no more Priesthood in the New Covenant, because Christ has satisfied all the demands of Mediation, with Himself becoming the Mediator. It was all done through the Cross [I Tim. 2:5].)*

14 And you shall bring his sons, and clothe them with coats:

15 And you shall anoint them, as you did anoint their father, that they may minister unto Me in the Priest's office: for their anointing shall surely be an everlasting priesthood throughout their generations *(as long as the Old Covenant lasted, which it did unto Christ).*

16 Thus did Moses: according to all that the LORD commanded him, so did he *(he never deviated from the pattern, not whatsoever).*

17 And it came to pass in the first month in the second year, on the first day of the month, that the Tabernacle was reared up. *(The first day of the first month of the second year, in a sense, tells Israel that they now have a new beginning. They should be careful that they make the most of it.)*

18 And Moses reared up the Tabernacle, and fastened his sockets, and set up the boards thereof, and put in the bars thereof, and reared up his pillars.

19 And he spread abroad the tent over the Tabernacle, and put the covering of the tent above upon it; as the LORD commanded Moses. *(Today, these things are but a memory, having all been satisfied by what Christ did at the Cross, which made them unnecessary. But until Christ came, the Tabernacle and the Temple were necessary, for God sought to dwell among His people.)*

20 And he took and put the Testimony *(Ten Commandments, written on two stone tablets)* into the Ark, and set the staves on the Ark, and put the Mercy Seat above upon the Ark:

21 And he brought the Ark into the Tabernacle *(into the Holy of Holies)*, and set up the Veil of the covering *(separating the Holy of Holies from the Holy Place)*, and covered the Ark of the Testimony; as the LORD commanded Moses.

22 And he put the Table *(Table of Shewbread)* in the tent of the congregation, upon the side of the Tabernacle northward, without the Veil.

23 And he set the bread in order upon it before the LORD *(twelve loaves)*; as the LORD had commanded Moses.

24 And he put the Candlestick *(Lampstand)* in the tent of the congregation, over against the Table, on the side of the Tabernacle southward.

25 And he lighted the lamps before the LORD; as the LORD commanded Moses. *(Moses lit the lamps "before the Lord," which referred to the fact that the Lord was minutely inspecting everything that was done.)*

26 And he put the Golden Altar *(Altar of Incense)* in the tent of the congregation before the Veil *(it was situated in the Holy Place, in fact, sitting immediately in front of the Ark of the Covenant, but separated by the "Veil"):*

27 And he burnt sweet incense thereon; as the LORD commanded Moses *(it was burned twice a day, at the time of the morning and evening Sacrifices — 9 a.m. and 3 p.m.).*

28 And he set up the hanging at the door of the Tabernacle *(the front door, covered by a curtain containing the same colors as the Veil immediately in front of the Holy of Holies).*

29 And he put the Altar of Burnt Offering *(a Type of the Cross)* by the door of the Tabernacle of the tent of the congregation, and offered upon it the Burnt Offering and the Meat Offering; as the LORD commanded Moses. *(The Tabernacle, having been made according to the Divine Pattern, even as we shall see, was filled with the Divine Glory, but not until precious blood had been shed by the Sacrifices on the Brazen Altar, and with all anointed with holy oil. Only in a Crucified and Anointed Saviour can God dwell with man.)*

30 And he set the Laver between the tent of the congregation and the Altar, and put water there, to wash withal.

31 And Moses and Aaron and his sons washed their hands and their feet thereat:

32 When they went into the tent of the congregation, and when they came near unto the Altar, they washed; as the LORD commanded Moses. *(The "water" typified the Word, with the "washing" typifying its application. Without the Word being applied to our lives, it serves no purpose.)*

33 And he reared up the court round about the Tabernacle and the Altar *(the fence)*, and set up the hanging of the court gate *(the entrance to the Court)*. So Moses finished the

work *(and exactly as the Lord had instructed him)*.

THE GLORY

34 Then a cloud covered the tent of the congregation, and the Glory of the LORD filled the Tabernacle. *(The glory that filled the Tabernacle fills our hearts and lives presently in the Person of the Holy Spirit.)*

35 And Moses was not able to enter into the tent of the congregation, because the cloud abode thereon, and the Glory of the LORD filled the Tabernacle. *(The idea seems to be that Moses attempted to enter the Tabernacle, but the Glory of the Lord occupied the Tabernacle, at least at this time, in such a powerful way that the Lawgiver was unable to do so. There is even a possibility that it knocked him off his feet.)*

36 And when the cloud was taken up from over the Tabernacle, the Children of Israel went onward in all their journeys. *(Israel did not determine or decide where they would go, or how long they would stay where they were. Not even Moses decided this. It was all decided by the moving of the Cloud. The great question is, "Where is the Cloud?")*

37 But if the cloud were not taken up, then they journeyed not till the day that it was taken up. *(They didn't move until the Cloud moved.)*

38 For the cloud of the LORD was upon the Tabernacle by day, and fire was on it by night, in the sight of all the House of Israel, throughout all their journeys. *(So, the great Book of Exodus closes out with the "Glory of the Lord." It began with the people of God serving as slaves in Egypt. It ends with them free from Egyptian bondage and, furthermore, the Glory of the Lord residing in their midst.)*

THE THIRD BOOK OF MOSES, CALLED
LEVITICUS

CHAPTER 1
(1490 B.C.)
LAW OF BURNT OFFERINGS

AND the LORD called unto Moses, and spoke unto him out of the Tabernacle of the congregation, saying *(the Holy Spirit has now taken up abode in the Tabernacle, actually in the Holy of Holies, where He dwelt between the Mercy Seat and the Cherubim [I Cor. 3:16])*,

2 Speak unto the Children of Israel, and say unto them, If any man of you bring an Offering unto the LORD, you shall bring your Offering of the cattle, even of the herd, and of the flock. *(There is no mention of any woman bringing an Offering to the Lord, as it regards the Sacrifice of an animal. This was always done by a man. Why?*

Even though Eve sinned first, it was Adam, the fountainhead of the human race, who dragged down mankind through the Fall. Whatever happened to him would pass on to the entirety of mankind. This is the reason that the "Last Adam" was necessary [I Cor. 15:45]. As well, the Sacrificial System had been instituted immediately after the Fall [Gen., Chpt. 4]. However, it didn't come into full bloom until the Law was given, as here noted.)

3 If his offering be a Burnt Sacrifice of the herd *(a whole Burnt Offering, typifying Christ giving His all)*, let him offer a male without blemish *(symbolic of the perfection of Christ)*: he shall offer it of his own voluntary will *(would probably be better translated, "he shall offer it for the Lord's acceptance"; if the Offering was accepted, so was the offerer; if the Offering was rejected, the offerer was rejected as well!)* at the door of the Tabernacle of the congregation before the LORD. *(The man had sinned before the Lord, so the Sacrifice must be presented before the Lord.)*

4 And he shall put his hand upon the head of the Burnt Offering *(in effect, transferring his sin and guilt to the innocent victim, all typifying Christ taking our sins upon Himself)*; and it shall be accepted for him to make Atonement for him *(refers to the animal being accepted as a Substitute on behalf of the sinner; at the Cross, Christ became our Substitute,* and our identification with Him guarantees us Atonement)*.

5 And he shall kill the bullock before the LORD *(typifying the death of Christ on the Cross)*: and the Priests, Aaron's sons, shall bring the blood, and sprinkle the blood round about upon the Altar that is by the door of the Tabernacle of the congregation *(the assisting Priest would catch in a basin the blood that poured from the slain animal's throat; he would then take the blood to the Brazen Altar, and throw it around the bottom of the Altar; in some respects, this was the most essential part of the ceremony, the blood representing the life [Lev. 17:11], which was symbolically received at the hands of the offerer, and presented by the Priests to God; in the antitype, our Lord exercised the function of the sacrificing Priest, when He presented His Own Life to the Father, as He hung upon the Altar of the Cross)*.

6 And he shall flay the Burnt Offering, and cut it into his pieces *(this signified how terrible and how deep a thing that sin actually is; sin is not merely exterior; it is interior; it is a disease of the vitals, affecting every single part of the human being)*.

7 And the sons of Aaron the Priest shall put fire upon the Altar *(typical of the Judgment of God, which Christ took upon Himself, all on our behalf)*, and lay the wood in order upon the fire *(the "wood" was typical of the Cross)*:

8 And the Priests, Aaron's sons, shall lay the parts, the head, and the fat, in order upon the wood that is on the fire which is upon the Altar *(the parts, as designated here, signify that the Cross dealt with every aspect of the sinner and sin)*:

9 But his inwards and his legs shall he wash in water: and the Priest shall burn all on the Altar, to be a Burnt Sacrifice *(a Whole Burnt Offering)*, an Offering made by fire, of a sweet savour unto the LORD. *(The "Burnt Offering," the "Meat Offering," and the "Peace Offering" are sacrifices of a "sweet savour." The expression is never used with regard to the "Sin Offering" and "Trespass Offering." The "washing" signified the purity of Christ.*

We should have a very defective apprehension of the mystery of the Cross were we only to see in

it that which meets man's need as a sinner. There were depths in that mystery which only the Mind of God could fathom. It is, therefore, important to see that when the Holy Spirit would furnish us with foreshadowings of the Cross, He gives us, in the very first place, one which sets it forth in its aspect Godward. This alone would be sufficient to teach us that there are heights and depths in the Doctrine of the Cross which man never could reach. There is in the Cross that which only God could know and appreciate. Hence, it is that the Burnt Offering gets the first place. It typifies Christ's death as viewed and valued by God Alone.)

10 And if his Offering be of the flocks, namely, of the sheep, or of the goats, for a Burnt Sacrifice; he shall bring it a male without blemish. *(The ritual of the Burnt Offering was the same, whether the victim was a bullock, sheep, or goat.)*

11 And he shall kill it on the side of the Altar northward before the LORD *(Heaven is to the north [Ps. 48:2; Isa. 14:13])*: and the Priests, Aaron's sons, shall sprinkle his blood round about upon the Altar.

12 And he shall cut it into his pieces, with his head and his fat: and the Priest shall lay them in order on the wood that is on the fire which is upon the Altar:

13 But he shall wash the inwards and the legs with water: and the Priest shall bring it all, and burn it upon the Altar: it is a Burnt Sacrifice, an Offering made by fire, of a sweet savour unto the LORD. *(Even though the instructions are basically the same for the lamb as they had been for the bullock, they are meticulously given again. The significance lies in Who the Offering represented.)*

14 And if the Burnt Sacrifice for his Offering to the LORD be of fowls, then he shall bring his Offering of turtledoves, or of young pigeons. *(The fowls were for the poorest of the poor, stating the fact that the shedding of the blood of an innocent victim was absolutely necessary, and that was the case, whether rich or poor.)*

15 And the Priest shall bring it unto the Altar, and wring off his head, and burn it on the Altar; and the blood thereof shall be wrung out at the side of the Altar *(the Jews say that the sacrifice of birds was one of the most difficult services the Priests had to do; they would need to take as much care in offering this sacrifice as in any of the others)*:

16 And he shall pluck away his crop with his feathers, and cast it beside the Altar on the east part, by the place of the ashes *(the "ashes" signified that all sin was atoned)*:

17 And he shall cleave it with the wings thereof, but shall not divide it asunder: and the Priest shall burn it upon the Altar, upon the wood that is upon the fire: it is a Burnt Sacrifice, an offering made by fire, of a sweet savour unto the LORD. *(These little turtledoves, or young pigeons, were accepted by the Lord as much as that of an ox or bullock, or even a lamb.)*

CHAPTER 2
(1490 B.C.)
LAW OF MEAT OFFERINGS

AND when any will offer a Meat Offering unto the LORD *(presently, "meat" refers to flesh; however, in Bible times, it just simply referred to food; the Hebrew for "Meat Offering" is "Minchah," and means "a gift made by an inferior to a superior"; it actually was a "Gratitude or Thanksgiving Offering"; this is the only Sacrifice where blood was not shed; as the "Burnt Offering" typified Christ in "death," the "Meat Offering" typified Him in "life")*, his offering shall be of fine flour *(presents the Perfect Manhood of Christ, typified by the "fine flour")*; and he shall pour oil upon it *(typical of the Holy Spirit upon Christ)*, and put frankincense thereon *(frankincense is "white," which speaks of the "purity of Christ"; as well, frankincense is bitter, which speaks of the bitterness that Christ had to undergo, not only in His Life and living, but, as well, in His Death on the Cross [Isa 53:3])*:

2 And he shall bring it to Aaron's sons the Priests *(so close was the union of the Burnt Offering and the Meat Offering, that the Burnt Offering was never offered without the accompaniment of the Meat Offering [Num. 15:4])*: and he shall take thereout his handful of the flour thereof, and of the oil thereof, with all the frankincense thereof; and the Priest shall burn the memorial of it upon the Altar, to be an Offering made by fire, of a sweet savour unto the LORD *(the "memorial" pertained to the Israelite not failing to remember what the Lord had done for him; as well, it pertains to the fact that God will not forget His Promises [Ps. 20:4])*:

3 And the remnant of the Meat Offering shall be Aaron's and his sons' *(when the Meat Offering was brought to the Priests, and I speak of it being brought by Israelites who were offering up Sacrifices, only about a handful was*

burned on the Altar along with the Burnt Offering, with the Priests taking the remainder for themselves, for this is what was ordered by the Lord): it is a thing most holy of the Offerings of the LORD made by fire *(they had to eat it within the precincts of the Tabernacle, as was the case with all food that was "most holy"; this included the "Shewbread" and the flesh of the "Sin Offering" and of the "Trespass Offering" [Lev. 10:12]).*

4 And if you bring an oblation *(a sacrificial present)* of a Meat Offering baked in the oven *(prepared before it was brought to the Tabernacle)*, it shall be unleavened cakes *(a Type of the sinlessness of Christ)* of fine flour *(Perfect Life of Christ)* mingled with oil, or unleavened wafers anointed with oil *(Type of the Holy Spirit on Christ)*.

5 And if your oblation be a Meat Offering baked in a pan, it shall be of fine flour unleavened, mingled with oil.

6 You shall part it in pieces, and pour oil thereon: it is a Meat Offering. *(The Reader lacking in spirituality may grow weary at the tedious instructions given, wondering why all of this was necessary. All of this represents Christ and the Perfect Life that He lived, which alone could serve as a Perfect Sacrifice; consequently, we should understand that anything that portrays Christ is of the utmost significance.)*

7 And if your oblation be a Meat Offering baked in the fryingpan, it shall be made of fine flour with oil.

8 And you shall bring the Meat Offering that is made of these things unto the LORD: and when it is presented unto the Priest, he shall bring it unto the Altar *(the "Altar" always represents the Cross; as this "Offering" was prepared for the Altar, likewise, Christ was prepared for the Altar)*.

9 And the Priest shall take from the Meat Offering a memorial thereof, and shall burn it upon the Altar: it is an Offering made by fire, of a sweet savour unto the LORD *(it was a "sweet savour," simply because it represented the Perfection of Christ)*.

10 And that which is left of the Meat Offering shall be Aaron's and his sons': it is a thing most holy of the Offerings of the LORD made by fire.

11 No Meat Offering, which you shall bring unto the LORD, shall be made with leaven: for you shall burn no leaven, nor any honey, in any Offering of the LORD made by fire. *(Leaven represents decay and corruption, which,*

of course, was, and is, the opposite of Christ, Who had no sin. So, the more we understand about these instructions given, the more we understand Christ. "Honey," as well, causes fermentation, so it could not be used. There was neither error nor corruption in Jesus.)*

12 As for the oblation of the firstfruits, you shall offer them unto the LORD: but they shall not be burnt on the Altar for a sweet savour *(the Altar represents the Crucifixion of Christ, and the price that He would pay there; consequently, this is a price that we couldn't pay, so our goodness, etc., is not to be added to the Finished Work of Christ)*.

13 And every oblation of your Meat Offering shall you season with salt *(salt is a preservative and, therefore, serves as a Type in the Old Testament of the Word of God)*; neither shall you suffer the salt of the Covenant of your God to be lacking from your Meat Offering: with all your Offerings you shall offer salt. *(It is called "the salt of the Covenant," referring to the enduring character of the Covenant. God Himself has so ordained it in all things, which means that nothing can alter it and no influence can ever corrupt it, because it is the unalterable, unchangeable, indescribable, eternal Word of Almighty God.*

The "salt" proclaims, "Thus saith the Lord" and, as such, runs at cross purposes with men's desires. Every true Preacher of the Gospel will have his Message "seasoned with salt" [Mat. 5:13; Col. 4:6].)

14 And if you offer a Meat Offering of your firstfruits unto the LORD, you shall offer for the Meat Offering of your firstfruits green ears of corn *(grain)* dried by the fire, even corn *(grain)* beaten out of full ears. *(The Meat Offering was not a Sin Offering, but rather a "sweet savour" Offering. Thus, its meaning is definitely fixed; and, moreover, the intelligent interpretation of it must ever guard, with holy jealousy, the precious truth of Christ's spotless Humanity, and the true nature of His associations, which the Meat Offering represents.)*

15 And you shall put oil upon it, and lay frankincense thereon: it is a Meat Offering.

16 And the Priest shall burn the memorial of it, part of the beaten corn *(grain)* thereof, and part of the oil thereof, with all the frankincense thereof: it is an Offering made by fire unto the LORD. *(Inasmuch as part of the Meat Offering was burned in the fire, and part eaten by the Priests, we should understand that this symbolized Christ in His Perfect Life, but yet a*

life that would be given on the Cross, hence the burning of the Meat Offering on the Altar. This signifies, as well, that Christ came to this world but for one purpose, and that was to go to the Cross. His Life was Perfect, His Demeanor Perfect, His Way Perfect, His Manner Perfect, all for the purpose of being a Perfect Sacrifice.)

CHAPTER 3
(1490 B.C.)
PEACE OFFERINGS

AND if his oblation *(a sacrificial present or gift)* be a Sacrifice of Peace Offering, if he offer it of the herd; whether it be a male or female, he shall offer it without blemish before the LORD. *(The Burnt Offering pictured Christ dying; the Meat Offering, Christ living. The Peace Offering presents Him as making peace by the Blood of His Cross, and so establishing for man communion with God. In both the "Peace Offering" and the "Trespass Offering," we learn of the presence of the Sin Nature in the heart and life of the Believer. But we find out, even more fully in the Peace Offering, that even though the Sin Nature dwells in us, it is not to rule in us [Rom. 6:12].)*

2 And he shall lay his hand upon the head of his Offering *(this portrays the beautiful doctrine of Substitution and Identification; the animal became the substitute in the sinner's place, and by the laying of his hand or hands on the head of his Offering, he identified with that substitute; that, in effect, is the heart of the Gospel; Christ became our Substitute, and we identify with Him in all He did, but, more particularly, what He did for us at the Cross)*, and kill it at the door of the Tabernacle of the congregation *(the person who brought the Sacrifice had to personally kill it)*: and Aaron's sons the Priests shall sprinkle the blood upon the Altar round about. *(The sinner trusted in what the Sacrifice represented, and its blood was sprinkled on the Altar round about; for fellowship is encircled by Atonement, and only exists within it. Thus, God and the worshipper were brought into fellowship. Peace was established. Its eternal and unshakeable foundation was not the worthfulness of the worshipper, but the preciousness of the sprinkled blood.)*

3 And he shall offer of the Sacrifice of the Peace Offering an Offering made by fire unto the LORD; the fat that covers the inwards, and all the fat that is upon the inwards *(the "fat" and the "blood" symbolized the priceless*

life and the precious inward affections of the Lamb of God),

4 And the two kidneys, and the fat that is on them, which is by the flanks, and the caul above the liver, with the kidneys, it shall he take away.

5 And Aaron's sons shall burn it on the Altar upon the Burnt Sacrifice, which is upon the wood that is on the fire: it is an Offering made by fire, of a sweet savour unto the LORD.

6 And if his Offering for a Sacrifice of Peace Offering unto the LORD be of the flock; male or female, he shall offer it without blemish *(the "male or female" of the animals being allowed stipulates that all, both man and woman, can have fellowship and peace with God)*.

7 If he offer a lamb for his Offering, then shall he offer it before the LORD *(whether the poor man's lamb or goat were offered, or the rich man's heifer, all were precious in God's sight, and received the same ceremony)*.

8 And he shall lay his hand upon the head of his Offering, and kill it before the Tabernacle of the congregation: and Aaron's sons shall sprinkle the blood thereof round about upon the Altar.

9 And he shall offer of the Sacrifice of the Peace Offering an Offering made by fire unto the LORD; the fat thereof, and the whole rump, it shall he take off hard by the backbone; and the fat that covers the inwards, and all the fat that is upon the inwards *(the fire does not represent Hell, as some teach; it represents the Judgment of God poured out upon Christ instead of us, and speaks of the death that Christ would die; His Death totally and completely finished the work of Redemption [Lk. 23:46; Jn. 19:30; Mat. 27:50-51])*,

10 And the two kidneys, and the fat that is upon them, which is by the flanks, and the caul above the liver, with the kidneys, it shall he take away.

11 And the Priest shall burn it upon the Altar: it is the food of the Offering made by fire unto the LORD *(all of this specifies that God gave His Best, as it regards the giving of His Only Son)*.

12 And if his Offering be a goat, then he shall offer it before the LORD.

13 And he shall lay his hand upon the head of it, and kill it before the Tabernacle of the congregation: and the sons of Aaron shall sprinkle the blood thereof upon the Altar round about.

14 And he shall offer thereof his Offering,

even an Offering made by fire unto the LORD; the fat that covers the inwards, and all the fat that is upon the inwards,

15 And the two kidneys, and the fat that is upon them, which is by the flanks, and the caul above the liver, with the kidneys, it shall he take away.

16 And the Priest shall burn them upon the Altar: it is the food of the Offering made by fire for a sweet savour: all the fat is the LORD's.

17 It shall be a perpetual Statute for your generations throughout all your dwellings, that you eat neither fat nor blood. *(As the "fat" represented the prosperity of Christ given to us, likewise, the "blood" represented His Life freely given for us. The Peace Offering represented the blessedness and joyousness of communion between God and man. Like the Passover, the Peace Offering at once commemorated a historical event, and prefigured a blessing to come. The Passover, for instance, always looked backwards to the deliverance from Egypt, but yet forward to "Christ our Passover sacrificed for us" [I Cor. 5:7]. In like manner, the Peace Offering commemorated the making of the Covenant, and prefigured the blessed state of communion to be brought about by the Sacrifice of the Cross.)*

CHAPTER 4
(1490 B.C.)
SIN OFFERINGS

AND the LORD spoke unto Moses, saying,

2 Speak unto the Children of Israel, saying, If a soul shall sin through ignorance against any of the Commandments of the LORD concerning things which ought not to be done, and shall do against any of them *(Chapter 4 represents the "Sin Offering"; Christ became a Sin Offering on the Cross [Isa. 53:10]; the words in this Verse, "through ignorance," signified that a person, irrespective of his knowledge of the Word of God, cannot really know what sin actually is; this is humbling and comforting; it reveals that the efficacy of Christ's Atonement for sin is not to be measured by man's consciousness of sin, but by God's measurement of it; to believe this fact fills the heart with a Divine peace)*:

3 If the Priest that is anointed do sin according to the sin of the people; then let him bring for his sin, which he has sinned, a young bullock without blemish unto the LORD for a Sin Offering. *(In the "Burnt Offering," the*

sinlessness of the victim was transferred to the worshipper. In the "Sin Offering," the sinfulness of the sinner was transferred to the victim.)

4 And he shall bring the bullock unto the door of the Tabernacle of the congregation before the LORD; and shall lay his hand upon the bullock's head, and kill the bullock before the LORD. *(The "sin of ignorance" is committed constantly at the present time, by both Preacher and people. Not understanding the Cross, millions make other things the object of their faith, which, in effect, puts them in the position of committing the sin of "spiritual adultery" [Rom. 7:1-4]. Even though this sin, at least most of the time, is committed in ignorance, it is still sin before God, and gross sin at that!)*

5 And the Priest that is anointed shall take of the bullock's blood, and bring it to the Tabernacle of the congregation:

6 And the Priest shall dip his finger in the blood, and sprinkle of the blood seven times before the LORD, before the Veil of the Sanctuary *(this blood was sprinkled on the Altar of Incense; it was sprinkled "seven times," denoting a complete and full cleansing afforded by Christ; "seven" is God's number of completion and perfection)*.

7 And the Priest shall put some of the blood upon the horns of the Altar of sweet incense before the LORD, which is in the Tabernacle of the congregation *(the blood applied to the four horns of the Altar of Incense speaks to the fact that even though forgiveness for Believers is available at all times, which the golden Altar of Incense represents, the horns, which speak of dominion, testify to us that we in fact should have dominion over all sin; but it also testifies to the fact that such dominion cannot come about except by the Cross of Christ and our Faith in that Finished Work, typified by the "blood" applied to the "horns" [Rom. 6:3-14])*; and shall pour all the blood of the bullock at the bottom of the Altar of the Burnt Offering, which is at the door of the Tabernacle of the congregation. *(The effectiveness of the blood applied to the horns of the Altar of Incense is all based upon the fact that a Whole Burnt Offering has been originally offered on the Brazen Altar, which means that everything is predicated on that.*

In the Redemption of the transgressor, the Priest did everything; the man, nothing. He stood, he looked, he listened, he believed! Like action today in relation to Christ on the Cross ensures conscious Salvation.)

8 And he shall take off from it all the fat of

the bullock for the Sin Offering; the fat that covers the inwards, and all the fat that is upon the inwards,

9 And the two kidneys, and the fat that is upon them, which is by the flanks, and the caul above the liver, with the kidneys, it shall he take away,

10 As it was taken off from the bullock of the Sacrifice of Peace Offerings: and the Priest shall burn them upon the Altar of the Burnt Offering.

11 And the skin of the bullock, and all his flesh, with his head, and with his legs, and his inwards, and his dung,

12 Even the whole bullock shall he carry forth without the camp unto a clean place, where the ashes are poured out, and burn him on the wood with fire: where the ashes are poured out shall he be burnt. *(The carcass of the slain animal was not to be burned upon the Brazen Altar, at least as it regards the Sin Offering, but rather taken to a place "without the camp," and burned there. Why?*

This means that when the Christian sins, as bad as it is, the Christian doesn't have to get saved all over again. In the "Sin Offering," we see the means and the manner by which relationship is restored. "Ashes" signify that what was there has been consumed, typifying our sin being consumed by Christ in His Sacrificial, Atoning Work. Properly confessed, there is nothing left of those sins.)

LAWS

13 And if the whole congregation of Israel sin through ignorance, and the thing be hid from the eyes of the assembly, and they have done somewhat against any of the Commandments of the LORD concerning things which should not be done, and are guilty *(as we have stated, "sins of ignorance" are not confined only to Old Testament times; in fact, more Believers presently are committing such sins than ever before in history; if the Believer doesn't understand the Cross as it regards our Sanctification [Rom., Chpt. 6], such a Believer will attempt to live this life by means of the flesh; God labels such as "spiritual adultery" [Rom. 7:1-4]; such constitutes trust placed in anything other than Christ and the Cross, and is sin [Rom. 8:8]);*

14 When the sin, which they have sinned against it, is known, then the congregation shall offer a young bullock for the sin, and bring him before the Tabernacle of the congregation *(this Passage proclaims the fact that the only solution for sin of any nature is the Cross; then and now the Believer is directed to the Cross).*

15 And the Elders of the congregation shall lay their hands upon the head of the bullock before the LORD *(transferring the guilt to the innocent victim, typifying Christ on the Cross suffering for our sins)*: and the bullock shall be killed before the LORD *(signifying Christ Who died for our sins).*

16 And the Priest Who is anointed shall bring of the bullock's blood to the Tabernacle of the congregation *(the Blood of Jesus Christ alone cleanses from all sin, of which this is a Type [I Jn. 1:7]):*

17 And the Priest shall dip his finger in some of the blood, and sprinkle it seven times before the LORD, even before the Veil *(sprinkle it on the Altar of Incense; "seven times" signifies the Perfect Redemption afforded by Christ).*

18 And he shall put some of the blood upon the horns of the Altar which is before the LORD, that is in the Tabernacle of the congregation *(these four horns on the Altar of Incense signified the dominion that the Believer is to have over all sin [Rom. 6:14]; the blood being applied to all four of the horns tells us that the Believer can have total and complete victory within his life; if the Believer properly places his faith exclusively in Christ and the Cross, understanding that all that he receives from the Lord comes to him directly through the Cross, this will give the Holy Spirit latitude to work in one's life, thereby bringing about victory over the world, the flesh, and the Devil; in fact, this is God's Prescribed Order, and His only prescribed order; anything else will bring defeat [Gal. 5:4-5]),* and shall pour out all the blood at the bottom of the Altar of the Burnt Offering *(the Brazen Altar),* which is at the door of the Tabernacle of the congregation *(forgiveness and victory are all made possible by the Cross, and the Cross alone, typified by the Brazen Altar, and the blood being poured out at its base).*

19 And he shall take all his fat from him, and burn it upon the Altar *(the "fat" typifies Blessing and prosperity, which can only come through Christ, and what He has done for us at the Cross).*

20 And he shall do with the bullock as he did with the bullock for a Sin Offering, so shall he do with this: and the Priest shall make an Atonement for them, and it shall be forgiven them *(God, being just, passes over sin until it is made known by the conscience, the Word, and*

the Holy Spirit; then He holds Believers respon-sible and will judge and severely chastise them, if the sin is allowed to continue [Jn. 16:7-11; Rom. 2:12-16]).

21 And he shall carry forth the bullock with-out the camp, and burn him as he burned the first bullock: it is a Sin Offering for the con-gregation. *(While the "fat" was to be burned on the Altar, with the blood poured out at its base, the carcass of the animal, constituting the "Sin Offering," must be taken outside the camp and burned. The blood signifies that the sin is atoned, and the carcass being burned outside the camp signifies that all sin is now gone.)*

22 When a ruler has sinned, and done some-what through ignorance against any of the Commandments of the LORD his God con-cerning things which should not be done, and is guilty;

23 Or if his sin, wherein he has sinned, come to his knowledge; he shall bring his Offering, a kid of the goats, a male without blemish *(if it is to be noticed, even though the ritual varied a little bit according to who it was that sinned, in effect, the remedy was the same, the shed blood of the innocent victim, typifying Christ):*

24 And he shall lay his hand upon the head of the goat, and kill it in the place where they kill the Burnt Offering before the LORD: it is a Sin Offering. *(As with all, even if it is a Priest or a ruler, the guilt of sin must be transferred to the innocent victim, and is done so by the laying on of hands on the head of the victim, all typifying Christ. As stated, in the Whole Burnt Offering, the perfection of the victim is passed to the sinner. In the Sin Offering, the sin of the individual is passed to the innocent victim, all typifying Christ [Heb. 7:27].)*

25 And the Priest shall take of the blood of the Sin Offering with his finger, and put it upon the horns of the Altar of Burnt Offering, and shall pour out his blood at the bottom of the Altar of Burnt Offering *(the blood being ap-plied to the four horns at the four corners of the Brazen Altar typify that Christ and Him Cruci-fied is the only answer for the sin of humanity, and that refers to all of humanity [Jn. 3:16]).*

26 And he shall burn all his fat upon the Altar, as the fat of the sacrifice of Peace Offer-ings: and the Priest shall make an Atonement for him as concerning his sin, and it shall be forgiven him.

27 And if any one of the common people sin through ignorance, while he does somewhat against any of the Commandments of the LORD concerning things which ought not to be done, and be guilty;

28 Or if his sin, which he has sinned, come to his knowledge: then he shall bring his Of-fering, a kid of the goats, a female without blemish, for his sin which he has sinned. *(As is obvious here, in the eyes of God, sin is sin, irre-spective as to who commits it. It must be ad-dressed and, in essence, addressed the same way, even if it's a "common person," or a "ruler," or a "Priest," or even the entirety of the nation of Israel. The only answer is the Cross.)*

29 And he shall lay his hand upon the head of the Sin Offering, and slay the Sin Offering in the place of the Burnt Offering *(Jesus be-came a Sin Offering on the Cross [Isa. 53:10]).*

30 And the Priest shall take of the blood thereof with his finger and put it upon the horns of the Altar of Burnt Offering, and shall pour out all the blood thereof at the bot-tom of the Altar. *(If it is to be noticed, the solution for all, with some minor variations, is the same. So, why the constant repetition? It is that we might know the seriousness of the mat-ter, as it regards the horror of sin, and its only solution, which is the shed Blood of Jesus Christ [Eph. 2:13-18].)*

31 And he shall take away all the fat thereof, as the fat is taken away from off the Sacrifice of Peace Offerings; and the Priest shall burn it upon the Altar for a sweet savour unto the LORD; and the Priest shall make an Atone-ment for him, and it shall be forgiven him. *(Under the Old Covenant, how could a person know for sure that he was forgiven? First of all, he had to place his faith in the trustworthiness of the Word spoken to him. Second, he had to understand the value of the Blood shed for him, at least in a sense, knowing that it pointed to One Who was to come.)*

32 And if he bring a lamb for a Sin Offering, he shall bring it a female without blemish. *(In this case, a female lamb was required, in effect stating that it was through Eve that the first temptation came, and that it would be through a woman that Redemption would come [Isa. 7:14].)*

33 And he shall lay his hand upon the head of the Sin Offering, and slay it for a Sin Of-fering in the place where they kill the Burnt Offering.

34 And the Priest shall take of the blood of the Sin Offering with his finger, and put it upon the horns of the Altar of Burnt Offering, and shall pour out all the blood thereof at the

bottom of the Altar:

35 And he shall take away all the fat thereof, as the fat of the lamb is taken away from the Sacrifice of the Peace Offerings; and the Priest shall burn them upon the Altar, according to the Offerings made by fire unto the LORD: and the Priest shall make an Atonement for his sin that he has committed, and it shall be forgiven him. *(In order to obtain forgiveness for his sin, the man said nothing, and did nothing, except to lay his hand upon the head of the spotless substitute, thus transferring his guilt and its doom to the substitute. The Law claimed the man's life as the just penalty for his sin. The sin being transferred, the Law then claimed the life of the substitute; and directly that life was surrendered, the full claim of the Law was satisfied and the man thereby saved, all typifying Christ.)*

CHAPTER 5
(1490 B.C.)
THE TRESPASS OFFERING

AND if a soul sin, and hear the voice of swearing, and is a witness, whether he has seen or known of it; if he do not utter it, then he shall bear his iniquity *(the Trespass Offering was provided to atone for trespass against God, and trespass against man; in trespass against God, Sacrifice came first and restitution afterwards; in trespass against man, this order was reversed).*

2 Or if a soul touch any unclean thing, whether it be a carcase of an unclean beast, or a carcase of unclean cattle, or the carcase of unclean creeping things, and if it be hidden from him; he also shall be unclean, and guilty *(the carcass insinuates death; death is caused by original sin; so, if a dead animal or dead human being was touched, the person doing so was rendered unclean, and had to go through a particular ceremony to once again be clean; these are constant reminders in the old Law of sin and its effect).*

3 Or if he touch the uncleanness of man, whatsoever uncleanness it be that a man shall be defiled withal, and it be hid from him; when he knows of it, then he shall be guilty *(pertains to touching a leper or a dead body).*

4 Or if a soul swear, pronouncing with his lips to do evil, or to do good, whatsoever it be that a man shall pronounce with an oath, and it be hid from him; when he knows of it, then he shall be guilty in one of these *(we should learn from all this that there are no little sins in the eyes of God; there is not a Christian on Earth, however eminent, who does not, every day he lives, accumulate guilt enough to ruin him forever, were it not that he has "An Advocate with the Father, Jesus Christ the Righteous" [I Jn. 2:1-2]).*

5 And it shall be, when he shall be guilty in one of these things, that he shall confess that he has sinned in that thing *(Seiss says: "With all his efforts, prayers, joys, and consecration, the best Christian is still very faulty." He goes on to say: "Christ has taught us to pray daily, 'Forgive us our trespasses'; but why continue praying for forgiveness, if we have not continual trespasses to be forgiven? I know and preach that 'the Blood of Jesus Christ cleanses from all sin.' That is a precious Truth to me. But did He not continue a Priest forever, daily presenting His Atoning Blood anew on our behalf, we should most certainly come into condemnation. It is only because 'He continues ever,' that He is 'able to save them to the uttermost who come unto God by Him, seeing He ever lives to make intercession for them.' If He did not ever live to make intercession for us, we could not stand for a single day" [Heb. 7:25]):*

6 And he shall bring his Trespass Offering unto the LORD for his sin which he has sinned, a female from the flock, a lamb or a kid of the goats, for a Sin Offering; and the Priest shall make an Atonement for him concerning his sin *(once again, the only answer for sin is the Cross).*

7 And if he be not able to bring a lamb, then he shall bring for his trespass, which he has committed, two turtledoves, or two young pigeons, unto the LORD; one for a Sin Offering, and the other for a Burnt Offering *(as is obvious here, provision was made for the poorest of the poor; "turtledoves" and "pigeons" were very inexpensive; and yet, if sin was committed, sacrifice had to be offered, irrespective as to who the person might be; the first pigeon or turtledove was a "Sin Offering," which required the shedding of blood, and the second was a "Burnt Offering," symbolizing satisfaction to God by perfect obedience to Him in making Atonement; both symbolized the Perfect Obedience of Christ as man's Substitute).*

8 And he shall bring them unto the Priest, who shall offer that which is for the Sin Offering first, and wring off his head from his neck, but shall not divide it asunder *(if it was divided, considering the smallness of the turtledove*

or pigeon, blood might be spilled, and there would not be enough to apply to the Altar; this tells us of the effectiveness and necessity of the Blood):

9 And he shall sprinkle of the blood of the Sin Offering upon the side of the Altar; and the rest of the blood shall be wrung out at the bottom of the Altar: it is a Sin Offering. *(As the Christian advances in this Divine life, he becomes conscious that those sins that he has committed are but branches from a root, streams from a fountain; and, moreover, that sin in his nature is that fountain — that root. This leads to a far deeper exercise which can only be met by a deeper insight into the Work of the Cross. In a word, the Cross will need to be apprehended as that in which God Himself has "condemned sin in the flesh" [Rom. 8:3].)*

10 And he shall offer the second *(second Offering)* for a Burnt Offering, according to the manner: and the Priest shall make an Atonement for him for his sin which he has sinned, and it shall be forgiven him. *(In the "Burnt Offering," we are conducted to a point beyond which it is impossible to go, and that is the Work of the Cross, as accomplished under the immediate Eye of God, and as the expression of the unswerving devotion of the heart to Christ. In all cases, we begin with the Cross, and end with the Cross.)*

11 But if he be not able to bring two turtledoves, or two young pigeons, then he who sinned shall bring for his Offering the tenth part of an ephah of fine flour *(about two double handfuls)* for a Sin Offering; he shall put no oil upon it *(this is for the poorest of the poor; but yet sin has to be dealt with; no "oil" could be applied to this Offering, simply because there was no shedding of blood; the Holy Spirit, of which the oil was a Type, works only within the parameters of the Finished Work of Christ; this means if the Cross is not preached, the Holy Spirit will not work)*, neither shall he put any frankincense thereon: for it is a Sin Offering *(frankincense was not to be added either, because it represented the bitter Life of Christ, which would be given on the Cross in Sacrifice; while the "fine flour" represented that Perfect Life, due to the fact that no blood was shed, it could not represent the Cross)*.

12 Then shall he bring it to the Priest, and the Priest shall take his handful of it, even a memorial thereof, and burn it on the Altar, according to the Offerings made by fire unto the LORD: it is a Sin Offering. *(Let it be understood, the non-bloody substitute, namely the flour, being permitted was only an exception for the benefit of the very poor, and only in the cases specified, which does not invalidate the general rule that without the shedding of blood there is no remission of sin; the "flour" was burned on the Altar, and the Altar typified the Cross, which, in this case, sufficed.)*

13 And the Priest shall make an Atonement for him as touching his sin that he has sinned in one of these, and it shall be forgiven him: and the remnant shall be the Priest's, as a Meat Offering *(about a handful of flour was given to the Priest, with him using it as a "Meat Offering"; the "Meat Offering" was not an offering for sin; it was a Thank Offering, in that sin had now been atoned)*.

14 And the LORD spoke unto Moses, saying,

15 If a soul commit a trespass, and sin through ignorance, in the holy things of the LORD *(anything pertaining to the Work or the Word of God is considered "holy"; to be sure, it is very easy to sin in these matters; the "flesh" so often intrudes [Rom. 8:8])*; then he shall bring for his trespass unto the LORD a ram without blemish out of the flocks, with your estimation by shekels of silver, after the shekel of the Sanctuary, for a Trespass Offering *(whatever was the worth of the ram, a fifth part of that value was also to be given to the Priest in shekels of silver; the silver represented Redemption)*.

16 And he shall make amends for the harm that he has done in the holy thing, and shall add the fifth part thereto, and give it unto the Priest: and the Priest shall make an Atonement for him with the ram of the Trespass Offering, and it shall be forgiven him. *(We find in the Trespass Offering, by the fifth part being added, that through the Cross, God has not merely received back what was lost, but has actually become a gainer. He has gained more by Redemption than ever He lost by the Fall. He reaps a richer harvest of glory, honor, and praise from the Cross of Redemption than ever He could have reaped from that of Creation.*

As it regards the Believer, Faith evidenced in the Cross will give back all that was lost, and more besides [Mk. 9:23]. Concerning this, Mackintosh says: "Who could have conceived this? When we behold man, and the creation of which he was lord, laid in ruins at the feet of the enemy, how could we conceive that, from amid those ruins, God should gather richer and nobler spoils than any which our unfallen world could have yielded? Blessed be the Name of Jesus in all of this! It is to Him we owe it all. It is by

His precious Cross that ever a truth so amazing, so Divine, could be enunciated. Assuredly, the Cross involved a mysterious wisdom 'which none of the princes of this world knew: for had they known it, they would not have crucified the Lord of Glory'" [I Cor. 2:8].)

17 And if a soul sin, and commit any of these things which are forbidden to be done by the Commandments of the LORD; though he wist it not, yet is he guilty, and shall bear his iniquity. *(Sins committed in ignorance will have the same negative results as sins committed knowingly. Presently, to the greater extent, this refers to Believers who do not understand the Cross as it refers to Sanctification, and, thereby, attempt to live for God in all the wrong ways. This constitutes sin, because "whatsoever is not of faith [Faith in Christ and the Cross] is sin" [Rom. 14:23]. This is very confusing to the Believer, especially if he is sincere before the Lord; however, the Lord cannot overlook sin in any fashion. And tragically, the great sin of the modern Church is its ignorance of the Cross, whether knowing or otherwise. The results are catastrophic.)*

18 And he shall bring a ram without blemish out of the flock, with your estimation, for a Trespass Offering, unto the Priest: and the Priest shall make an Atonement for him concerning his ignorance wherein he erred and wist it not, and it shall be forgiven him.

19 It is a Trespass Offering: he has certainly trespassed against the LORD. *(The expressions, "through ignorance" and "wist it not," or "knew it not," dispose of the popular fallacy that sincerity secures Salvation.)*

CHAPTER 6
(1490 B.C.)
RESTITUTION

AND the LORD spoke unto Moses, saying,

2 If a soul sin, and commit a trespass against the LORD, and lie unto his neighbour in that which was delivered him to keep, or in fellowship, or in a thing taken away by violence, or has deceived his neighbour;

3 Or have found that which was lost, and lies concerning it, and swears falsely; in any of all these that a man does, sinning therein:

4 Then it shall be, because he has sinned, and is guilty, that he shall restore that which he took violently away, or the thing which he has deceitfully gotten, or that which was delivered him to keep, or the lost thing which he found, *(Concerning this, Mackintosh says: "There is a fine principle involved in the expression in Verse 2, 'against the Lord.' Although the matter in question was a wrong done to one's neighbor, yet the Lord looked upon it as a trespass against Himself. Everything must be viewed in reference to the Lord. It matters not who may be affected; Jehovah must get first place. Thus, when David's conscience was pierced by the arrow of conviction, in reference to his treatment of Uriah, he exclaims, 'I have sinned against the Lord' [II Sam. 12:13]. This principle does not in the least, however, interfere with the injured man's claim.")*

5 Or all that about which he has sworn falsely; he shall even restore it in the principal *(restore its full value)*, and shall add the fifth part more thereto, and give it unto him to whom it appertains, in the day of his Trespass Offering.

6 And he shall bring his Trespass Offering unto the LORD, a ram without blemish out of the flock, with your estimation, for a Trespass Offering, unto the Priest *(not only must the guilty party restore what he has taken from his neighbor, and do so fully, with even adding twenty percent; as well, he must take a ram to the Priest to be offered in Sacrifice, and also it seems that twenty percent in silver must be added; the idea of all of this is to show that sin is a costly business!)*:

7 And the Priest shall make an Atonement for him before the LORD: and it shall be forgiven him for any thing of all that he has done in trespassing therein. *(So, when a person has trespassed against his neighbor, restitution must be made first before the sacrifice can be offered. Jesus addressed this very thing, when He said, "Therefore if you bring your gift to the Altar, and there remember that your brother has ought against you; leave there your gift before the Altar, and go your way; first be reconciled to your brother, and then come and offer your gift" [Mat. 5:23-24].)*

THE BURNT OFFERING

8 And the LORD spoke unto Moses, saying,

9 Command Aaron and his sons, saying, This is the Law of the Burnt Offering: It is the Burnt Offering, because of the burning upon the Altar all night unto the morning, and the fire of the Altar shall be burning in it. *(Beginning with Verse 8 through the Seventh Chapter,*

we have the "Law of the Burnt Offering," the "Meat Offering," the "Sin Offering," the "Trespass Offering," and the "Peace Offering." We also have the Law of the High Priest's "Consecration Offering.")

10 And the Priest shall put on his linen garment, and his linen breeches shall he put upon his flesh (the "linen" symbolized the Righteousness of Christ [Rev. 19:8]), and take up the ashes which the fire has consumed with the Burnt Offering on the Altar, and he shall put them beside the Altar (this points to the fact that the Cross has reduced our sins to nothing, typified by the ashes).

11 And he shall put off his garments, and put on other garments (garments of glory and beauty), and carry forth the ashes without the camp unto a clean place. (Only the Blood of Christ can make the sinner "clean." As well, as the Burnt Offering was to burn all night, this represents the night of mystery of the fragrance of Christ's offering up of Himself to God, which ascends continually. "In the morning" He will appear to His people Israel in His double glory as the White-robed Priest and the Glory-crowned Mediator; and it will then be demonstrated to the world, as foreshadowed here by the honourable treatment of the ashes, that His Person and His Work have been accepted of God.)

12 And the fire upon the Altar shall be burning in it; it shall not be put out: and the Priest shall burn wood on it every morning, and lay the Burnt Offering in order upon it; and he shall burn thereon the fat of the Peace Offerings. (The fire that burned, and was to never go out, testified on the one hand to the unceasing delight of God in the Sacrifice of Christ and, on the other hand, to His unceasing hatred of sin. False teachers today put this fire out by denying the doctrines of the Atonement and of the wrath to come. The "fire" addresses both, "Atonement" and "wrath.")

13 The fire shall ever be burning upon the Altar; it shall never go out (the fire that consumed the Burnt Offering, and was to never go out, originally came from Heaven [9:24]).

MEAT OFFERING

14 And this is the Law of the Meat Offering: the sons of Aaron shall offer it before the LORD; before the Altar. (As we shall see, the Meat Offering, as the other Offerings, was first for God and His glory, and then for man and his need. It being offered before the Altar signifies that God can only receive our thanksgiving which is based upon the Cross, for the Meat Offering was, in essence, a "Thank Offering.")

15 And he shall take of it his handful, of the flour of the Meat Offering (the "flour" typified the Perfection of Christ), and of the oil thereof (typifying the Holy Spirit upon Christ), and all the frankincense which is upon the Meat Offering (typifying the bitterness that Christ would suffer, all on our behalf), and shall burn it upon the Altar (typifying the Cross) for a sweet savour (sweet to God, because it represented our Redemption, and our thankfulness for that Redemption), even the memorial of it, unto the LORD. (As the "Meat Offering" was to ever be a memorial of what God would do to redeem humanity, likewise, the Lord's Supper serves the same purpose [I Cor. 11:24-25]. As the "Meat Offering" was then to be a memorial of what He would do, now it is a memorial of what He has done.)

16 And the remainder thereof shall Aaron and his sons eat (symbolic of what Christ said concerning His Flesh and His Blood, symbolic of the Cross [Jn. 6:53-54, 63]): with unleavened bread shall it be eaten in the Holy Place (the unleavened bread typifies the Perfection of Christ); in the court of the Tabernacle of the congregation they shall eat it (proclaiming the fact that it must be eaten near the "Altar," i.e., the "Cross").

17 It shall not be baked with leaven. I have given it unto them for their portion of My Offerings made by fire; it is most holy, as is the Sin Offering, and as the Trespass Offering (as the Sin Offering and the Trespass Offering, so was the "Meat Offering" "most Holy"; thus, the Holy Spirit testifies to the sinlessness of Christ as a man, and at the moment in which He was "made to be a Sin Offering" upon the Cross).

18 All the males among the Children of Aaron shall eat of it (pertained only to the Priests; today, due to the Cross, every Believer can partake of Christ, because all Believers are "kings and priests unto God" [Rev. 1:6]). It shall be a Statute for ever in your generations concerning the Offerings of the LORD made by fire: every one who touches them shall be holy (because it represents Christ, Who is altogether Holy).

THE PRIESTS

19 And the LORD spoke unto Moses, saying,

20 This is the Offering of Aaron and of his sons, which they shall offer unto the LORD in the day when he is anointed (which would take

place very shortly — Chapter 8); the tenth part of an ephah of fine flour for a Meat Offering perpetual, half of it in the morning, and half thereof at night (this proclaims the special relationship of the High Priest to the Meat Offering; his Meat Offering was to be offered morning and evening; it was to be wholly burnt, not eaten [Heb. 7:27]; Aaron, though High Priest, was a sinner, and twice every day had to shelter himself, in type, behind a sinless Saviour).

21 In a pan it shall be made with oil (typical of the Holy Spirit upon Christ); and when it is baked, you shall bring it in: and the baked pieces of the Meat Offering shall you offer for a sweet savour unto the LORD.

22 And the Priest of his sons that is anointed in his stead shall offer it: it is a Statute for ever unto the LORD; it shall be wholly burnt.

23 For every Meat Offering for the Priest shall be wholly burnt: it shall not be eaten (part of it, in fact, was to be eaten [Vss. 16-18], but this particular part was not to be eaten, but rather burned on the Altar; this signified that one cannot partake of Christ, unless he does so through and by the Cross).

SIN OFFERING

24 And the LORD spoke unto Moses, saying,

25 Speak unto Aaron and to his sons, saying, This is the Law of the Sin Offering (the Personal Holiness of Christ is more strikingly presented in the Sin Offering, than in any of the other Sacrifices): In the place where the Burnt Offering is killed shall the Sin Offering be killed before the LORD: it is most holy. (Concerning this, Mackintosh says: "This is most marked and striking. The Holy Spirit did not need to guard with such jealousy the Personal Holiness of Christ in the Burnt Offering; but lest the soul should, by any means, lose sight of that Holiness while contemplating the place which the Blessed One became the Sin Offering, we are again and again reminded of it by the words 'it is most holy.'

"The same point is observable 'in the Law of the Trespass Offering' [Lev. 7:1-6]. Never was the Lord Jesus more fully seen to be 'the Holy One of God' than when He was 'made sin' upon the cursed tree. The vileness and blackness of that with which He stood identified on the Cross only served to show out more clearly that He was 'most holy.' Though a sin-bearer, He was sinless; though enduring the Wrath of God, He was the Father's delight; though deprived of the Light of God's countenance, He dwelt in the Father's bosom."

As should be obvious, this completely destroys the erroneous doctrine that Jesus died spiritually while on the Cross, thus becoming a sinner, etc.)

26 The Priest who offers it for sin shall eat it: in the Holy Place shall it be eaten, in the court of the Tabernacle of the congregation. (God gave the Sin Offering as food for the Priests to bear the iniquity of the congregation, and to make Atonement for them [Lev. 10:17]. Once again, we go back to John, Chapter 6, in the eating of the flesh and the drinking of the blood regarding Christ.

The flesh provided by the Sin Offering constituted a part of the livelihood of the Priests, as it constitutes our spiritual livelihood presently [Ezek. 44:28-29]. It was to be eaten in the Holy Place of the Sanctuary. In fact, eight of the Offerings [there were others besides the blood Sacrifices] had to be eaten in the precincts of the Sanctuary.)

27 Whatsoever shall touch the flesh (flesh of the Sin Offering) thereof shall be holy (in a sense, making this the holiest Offering of them all): and when there is sprinkled of the blood thereof upon any garment, you shall wash that whereon it was sprinkled in the Holy Place (this proclaims to us the preciousness of the Blood).

28 But the earthen vessel wherein it (the Sin Offering) is sodden shall be broken: and if it be sodden in a brasen pot, it shall be both scoured, and rinsed in water (so desperate a malady is sin, that anything that came in contact with the Sin Offering had to be washed, broken, or scoured).

29 All the males among the Priests shall eat thereof: it is most holy.

30 And no Sin Offering, whereof any of the blood is brought into the Tabernacle of the congregation to reconcile withal in the Holy Place, shall be eaten: it shall be burnt in the fire. (Concerning this, Williams says: "The Sin Offering whose blood was brought into the Sanctuary symbolizes Christ bearing before God the sin of the whole world. The Sin Offering whose blood was not so brought in, but whose flesh was eaten by the Priest, presents Christ as making His Own the sins of the individual sinner who believes upon Him.)

CHAPTER 7
(1490 B.C.)
TRESPASS OFFERINGS

LIKEWISE this is the Law of the Trespass Offering: it is most holy (the "Meat Offering," the "Sin Offering," and the "Trespass

Offering" were labeled as "most holy"; the "Whole Burnt Offering" and the "Peace Offering" were "holy").

2 In the place where they kill the Burnt Offering shall they kill the Trespass Offering: and the blood thereof shall he sprinkle round about upon the Altar *(the Burnt Offering and the Sin and Trespass Offerings being slain upon the one spot sets out the unity of the death of Christ in its two aspects; at Golgotha He was, at one and the same moment, accursed of God as the Sin and Trespass Offerings, and Beloved of the Father as the Burnt Offering).*

3 And he shall offer of it all the fat thereof; the rump, and the fat that covers the inwards,

4 And the two kidneys, and the fat that is on them, which is by the flanks, and the caul that is above the liver, with the kidneys, it shall he take away:

5 And the Priest shall burn them upon the Altar for an Offering made by fire unto the LORD: it is a Trespass Offering *(the "fat" and inwards of the animal were to be burned on the Altar, symbolizing the vitals of the human being, ruined by sin, which only the Cross of Christ could assuage, symbolized by the Altar).*

6 Every male among the Priests shall eat thereof: it shall be eaten in the Holy Place: it is most holy *(understanding this proclaims to us, in no uncertain terms, the absolute Holiness, the "most Holiness," of the Cross of Calvary).*

7 As the Sin Offering is, so is the Trespass Offering: there is one law for them: the Priest who makes Atonement therewith shall have it *(the same rule, as stated in Leviticus 6:27-28, applies to both Offerings; hence, what is omitted in the regulation of the one must be supplied from the directions given in the other).*

8 And the Priest who offers any man's Burnt Offering, even the Priest shall have to himself the skin of the Burnt Offering which he has offered *(the animal stripped of its skin proclaims the fact that sin is more than mere surface; it goes to the very vitals of the human being).*

9 And all the Meat Offering that is baked in the oven, and all that is dressed in the fryingpan, and in the pan, shall be the Priest's who offers it.

10 And every Meat Offering, mingled with oil, and dry, shall all the sons of Aaron have, one as much as another *(the Priests were Types of Christ; their receiving these portions typified the giving of Himself).*

THE PEACE OFFERING

11 And this is the Law of the Sacrifice of Peace Offerings, which he shall offer unto the LORD *(pertains to the individual bringing the sacrifice; a part was to be eaten by him, and a part by the Priests [Vss. 28-34]).*

12 If he *(the one who brings the sacrifice)* offer it for a thanksgiving *(thanksgiving that peace has been restored between himself and God, due to the Sin or Trespass Offerings being presented to the Lord, and accepted),* then he shall offer with the Sacrifice of thanksgiving unleavened cakes mingled with oil, and unleavened wafers anointed with oil, and cakes mingled with oil, of fine flour, fried *(all symbolize Christ, His Perfection, and Anointing by the Holy Spirit).*

13 Besides the cakes, he shall offer for his Offering leavened bread with the Sacrifice of thanksgiving of his Peace Offerings *(the Law of the Peace Offering commanded unleavened cakes and leavened bread; the former symbolize the sinless Humanity of Christ; the latter, the sinful humanity of the worshipper; Christ had sin on Him as the sin-bearer, but not in Him; the worshipper, on the other hand, had sin in him, but not on him, meaning that he could not atone for his own sin).*

14 And of it he shall offer one out of the whole oblation for an Heave Offering unto the LORD *(the right shoulder),* and it shall be the Priest's who sprinkles the blood of the Peace Offerings.

15 And the flesh of the sacrifice of his Peace Offerings for thanksgiving shall be eaten the same day that it is offered; he shall not leave any of it until the morning *(this typifies that we must partake of all of Christ, and not merely a part of Christ; many desire Him as a good man, but not as a Sacrifice; some as Saviour, but not as Baptizer with the Holy Spirit, etc.).*

16 But if the Sacrifice of his Offering be a vow, or a voluntary offering, it shall be eaten the same day that he offers his Sacrifice: and on the morrow also the remainder of it shall be eaten:

17 But the remainder of the flesh of the Sacrifice on the third day shall be burnt with fire.

18 And if any of the flesh of the Sacrifice of his Peace Offerings be eaten at all on the third day, it shall not be accepted, neither shall it be imputed unto him who offers it: it shall be an abomination, and the soul who eats of it shall bear his iniquity. *(Concerning this, Williams says: "This Law taught the offerer to closely*

associate the death and sufferings of the slain lamb with the blessing for which he gave thanks. It teaches men today the same lesson. To disassociate worship and thanksgiving from the anguish and blood-shedding of the Lord Jesus, in other words, to separate all of this from the Cross, is to offer to God an abomination, and to bring death into the soul and into the Church.")

19 And the flesh *(of the Sacrifice)* that touches any unclean thing shall not be eaten; it shall be burnt with fire: and as for the flesh, all that be clean shall eat thereof.

20 But the soul that eats of the flesh of the Sacrifice of Peace Offerings, that pertain unto the LORD, having his uncleanness upon him, even that soul shall be cut off from his people.

21 Moreover the soul that shall touch any unclean thing, as the uncleanness of man, or any unclean beast *(dead bodies or lepers)*, or any abominable unclean thing, and eat of the flesh of the Sacrifice of Peace Offerings, which pertain unto the LORD, even that soul shall be cut off from his people. *(Ceremonial cleanliness was obligatory before eating the Peace Offering. Disobedience in this matter entailed death. To profess faith in the Person and Atonement of Christ, and claim fellowship with Him, and be secretly unclean ensures the wrath of God. In other words, while there is definitely liberty in the Cross, there is not license in the Cross.)*

FAT AND BLOOD

22 And the LORD spoke unto Moses, saying,

23 Speak unto the Children of Israel, saying, You shall eat no manner of fat, of ox, or of sheep, or of goat.

24 And the fat of the beast that dies of itself, and the fat of that which is torn with beasts, may be used in any other use: but you shall in no wise eat of it.

25 For whosoever eats the fat of the beast, of which men offer an Offering made by fire unto the LORD, even the soul that eats it shall be cut off from his people. *(The fat of the animal signified its health and prosperity; consequently, it served as a Type of God giving His very Best, as it regards the Lord Jesus Christ, from Whom we receive all good things. As well, the fat being burned on the Altar symbolizes the means by which all of these good things come to us, and that is through the Cross.)*

26 Moreover you shall eat no manner of blood, whether it be of fowl or of beast, in any of your dwellings.

27 Whatsoever soul it be that eats any manner of blood, even that soul shall be cut off from his people. *(The prohibition against the eating of blood was brought over, as well, into the New Covenant [Acts 15:19-20]. The life of the flesh is in the blood, and the "blood" symbolizes the Life of Christ poured out, all on our behalf, which alone could cleanse from all sin [Eph. 2:13-18].)*

THE PRIESTS

28 And the LORD spoke unto Moses, saying,

29 Speak unto the Children of Israel, saying, He who offers the Sacrifice of his Peace Offerings unto the LORD shall bring his oblation unto the LORD of the Sacrifice of his Peace Offerings *(the Peace Offering being offered to God signified that peace had been interrupted by sin, and now had been restored)*.

30 His own hands shall bring the Offerings of the LORD made by fire *(the one who had sinned must personally bring the Peace Offering)*, the fat with the breast, it shall he bring, that the breast may be waved for a Wave Offering before the LORD *(the "Wave Offering" derived its name from the fact that whatever was offered was waved first of all toward the Brazen Altar, symbolizing the price that Christ would pay, and thanking Him for paying it, and then the Priest would turn, continuing to lift the Offering high, and wave the breast toward the four corners of the universe, in effect saying that what Christ would do at the Cross would suffice for all)*.

31 And the Priest shall burn the fat upon the Altar: but the breast shall be Aaron's and his sons'.

32 And the right shoulder shall you give unto the Priest for an Heave Offering of the Sacrifices of your Peace Offerings.

33 He among the sons of Aaron, who offers the blood of the Peace Offerings, and the fat, shall have the right shoulder for his part.

34 For the wave breast and the heave shoulder have I taken of the Children of Israel from off the Sacrifices of their Peace Offerings, and have given them unto Aaron the Priest and unto his sons by a Statute for ever from among the Children of Israel. *(Christ's shoulder "upholds," and His breast "consoles," all those who trust in Him. The "Heave Offering" was lifted up and down several times, up as a symbol of offering it to God, Who is above, and down again as a symbol of God coming to this Earth and*

becoming man in the form of the Lord Jesus Christ.)

35 This is the portion of the anointing of Aaron, and of the anointing of his sons, out of the Offerings of the LORD made by fire, in the day when he presented them to minister unto the LORD in the Priest's office;

36 Which the LORD commanded to be given them of the Children of Israel, in the day that He anointed them, by a Statute for ever throughout their generations. *(The "Statute" that these two parts of the Peace Offering are to be given to Aaron and his descendants, who may officiate at the Sacrifice, is binding upon the Israelites as long as the Priesthood lasts.)*

37 This is the Law of the Burnt Offering, of the Meat Offering, and of the Sin Offering, and of the Trespass Offering, and of the consecrations, and of the Sacrifice of the Peace Offerings *(five Offerings: "five" is God's number of Grace; Jesus would satisfy all of these Offerings by the one Sacrifice of Himself on the Cross of Calvary)*;

38 Which the LORD commanded Moses in Mount Sinai, in the day that he commanded the Children of Israel to offer their oblations unto the LORD, in the wilderness of Sinai.

CHAPTER 8
(1490 B.C.)
CONSECRATION OF THE PRIESTS

A ND the LORD spoke unto Moses, saying,

2 Take Aaron and his sons with him, and the garments, and the anointing oil, and a bullock for the Sin Offering, and two rams, and a basket of unleavened bread; *(As we study this Book of Leviticus, we will find that its major subject is "a Sacrifice, a Priest, and a Place of Worship." Chapters 8 through 10 pertain to Priesthood, but Sacrifice is the foundation of it all. This speaks of the Cross of Christ. The sinner needs a Sacrifice, the worshipper needs a Priest. Christ is both. All of these things mentioned in the Second Verse point to Christ and Christ alone.)*

3 And you gather all the congregation together unto the door of the Tabernacle of the congregation *(even though only the representatives of the people could actually observe the ritual, considering there were approximately 3 million, still, the answer for "all" then was Christ and the Cross, and the answer now for "all" is Christ and the Cross).*

4 And Moses did as the LORD commanded him; and the assembly was gathered together unto the door of the Tabernacle of the congregation.

5 And Moses said unto the congregation, This is the thing which the LORD commanded to be done. *(Concerning this, Mackintosh says: "Had the Word been disregarded, the glory would not have appeared [9:23-24]. The two things were intimately connected. The slightest deviation from 'Thus saith Jehovah' would have prevented beams of the Divine Glory from appearing to the congregation of Israel. Had there been the introduction of a single rite or ceremony not enjoined by the Word, or had there been the omission of ought which that Word commanded, the Lord would not have manifested His Glory. He could not sanction, by the Glory of His Presence, the neglect or rejection of His Word. He can bear with ignorance and infirmity [spiritual weakness], but He cannot sanction neglect or disobedience.")*

6 And Moses brought Aaron and his sons, and washed them with water *(as these Priests were Types of Christ, this "washing" was meant to portray the sublime purity of Jesus, Who "was Holy, harmless, undefiled, separate from sinners" [Heb. 7:26]).*

THE CLOTHING

7 And he put upon him the coat *(speaks of the Deity of Christ)*, and girded him with the girdle *(speaks of the service of Christ to humanity)*, and clothed him with the robe *(speaks of the Righteousness of Christ)*, and put the Ephod upon him *(presents the strength of Christ)*, and he girded him with the Curious Girdle of the Ephod, and bound it unto him therewith *(typifies the Work of the Spirit within the Life of Christ [Lk. 4:18-19]).*

8 And he put the breastplate upon him *(inasmuch as this was worn over the heart of the Priest, it pertained to the Love of Christ, in that He would give Himself for humanity)*: also he put in the Breastplate the Urim and the Thummim *(the two words mean "lights and perfection"; they concern the leading of the Holy Spirit).*

9 And he put the Mitre upon his head *(speaks of authority; Jesus is the "Head" of the Church [Col. 1:18-19])*; also upon the Mitre, even upon his forefront, did he put the Golden Plate, and Holy Crown *(on this appeared the solemn inscription, "Holiness to the Lord"; this,*

of course, represented the absolute Holiness of Christ); as the LORD commanded Moses.

ANOINTING

10 And Moses took the anointing oil, and anointed the Tabernacle and all that was therein, and sanctified them (the "oil" was a Type of the Holy Spirit, Who can now function literally, and not merely in a symbolic sense, all because of the Cross of Christ [Rom. 8:2]).

11 And he sprinkled thereof upon the Altar seven times (the number "seven" speaks of the total dominion over sin which the Holy Spirit can give us, all made possible by the Cross [Rom. 6:14; Rev. 5:6]), and anointed the Altar (Type of the Cross) and all his vessels, both the Laver and his foot (Type of the Word of God), to sanctify them (this Passage tells us that Sanctification can only be brought about by the Holy Spirit; no man, by his own strength, no matter how sincere, can sanctify himself [Rom. 8:1-2, 11]).

12 And he poured of the anointing oil upon Aaron's head, and anointed him, to sanctify him (the anointing oil was "poured" upon Aaron, who typified Christ, "Who was anointed with the oil of gladness above His fellows" [Ps. 45:7; Heb. 1:9]).

13 And Moses brought Aaron's sons, and put coats upon them, and girded them with girdles, and put bonnets upon them; as the LORD commanded Moses. (Aaron and his sons together represent Christ and His Priestly house [Rev. 1:6]; Aaron alone represents Christ in His Sacrificial and Intercessory function; Moses and Aaron together represent Christ as King and Priest.)

THE OFFERINGS

14 And he brought the bullock for the Sin Offering (in fact, Aaron and his sons stood as penitent sinners by the side of the Sin Offering, which was now offered for the first time; the "Sin Offering" was called "most holy," because it cleansed the sinner from all sin; in the "Whole Burnt Offering," Christ took His Perfection and gave it to the sinner; in the "Sin Offering," Christ took the sinner's sin and made it His Own, thereby justifying the sinner, because Christ has paid the price for that sin and, in fact, all sin [I Jn. 2:2]): and Aaron and his sons laid their hands upon the head of the bullock for the Sin Offering (this represented their sins being transferred to the innocent victim, typifying Christ taking our sins upon Himself [Heb. 7:27]).

15 And he slew it (the guilty party had to personally kill the innocent animal, symbolizing the fact that it was our sins which put Christ on the Cross); and Moses took the blood (signified Christ shedding His Life's Blood on the Cross of Calvary), and put it upon the horns of the Altar round about with his finger (signified that God's Plan of Redemption was for the entirety of the universe), and purified the Altar (Christ sanctified the Cross, the Cross didn't sanctify Christ; this puts to rest the erroneous idea that Jesus died spiritually on the Cross), and poured the blood at the bottom of the Altar, and sanctified it, to make reconciliation upon it (this signified the purpose of the Altar, and its purpose alone! The "Altar" is the place of death, and, more specifically, the place of the Death of Christ, which alone atoned for the sin of the world [Jn. 1:29]).

16 And he took all the fat that was upon the inwards, and the caul above the liver, and the two kidneys, and their fat, and Moses burned it upon the Altar (signified that sin is more than merely surface; it goes to the very vitals of man, which the Cross alone addresses; it took the best, symbolized by the "fat," that God had, His only Son, to redeem mankind [Jn. 3:16]).

17 But the bullock, and his hide, his flesh, and his dung, he burnt with fire without the camp; as the LORD commanded Moses. (The bullock was a "Sin Offering"; consequently, it could not be burned on the Altar. Of the four bloody Offerings, it was only the Whole Burnt Offering which could be burned totally upon the Altar, because it represented the Perfection of Christ, and not sin. All of these things being taken outside the camp and burned typified our sins being taken away, and all because of the Cross.)

BURNT OFFERING

18 And he brought the ram for the Burnt Offering (this represented the Perfection of Christ, so it could be wholly burned on the Altar): and Aaron and his sons laid their hands upon the head of the ram (transferring their sins to this innocent victim, typifying Christ).

19 And he killed it: and Moses sprinkled the blood upon the Altar round about.

20 And he cut the ram into pieces (signifying that Christ gave His all); and Moses burnt the head, and the pieces, and the fat (signifying Christ taking our judgment).

21 And he washed the inwards and the legs

in water (*portrayed the purity of Christ*); and Moses burnt the whole ram upon the Altar: it was a Burnt Sacrifice for a sweet savour, and an Offering made by fire unto the LORD; as the LORD commanded Moses.

CONSECRATION RAM

22 And he brought the other ram, the ram of consecration (*we find from the sacrifice of the ram that true consecration can only come about through the Cross, and our Faith in that Finished Work [Rom. 6:3-14]*): and Aaron and his sons laid their hands upon the head of the ram (*even though Aaron had been chosen by the Lord as the Great High Priest, he and his sons, who were Priests as well, had to undergo the same Sacrificial Offerings as the worst sinner in Israel*).

23 And he slew it; and Moses took of the blood of it (*whether we contemplate the Doctrine of Sacrifice, or the Doctrine of Consecration, we find the shedding of blood gets the same important place; this portrays the fact that the Cross is not only for Salvation but, as well, is for Sanctification [Rom. 8:1-2, 11]*), and put it upon the tip of Aaron's right ear (*a blood-stained ear was needed to hearken to the Divine communications*), and upon the thumb of his right hand (*a blood-stained hand was needed to execute the services of the Sanctuary*), and upon the great toe of his right foot (*a blood-stained foot was needed to tread the courts of the Lord's House*).

24 And he brought Aaron's sons, and Moses put of the blood upon the tip of their right ear, and upon the thumbs of their right hands, and upon the great toes of their right feet: and Moses sprinkled the blood upon the Altar round about. (*The shedding of blood was the foundation of all sacrifice for sin, and it stood connected with all the vessels of the Ministry, and with all the functions of the Priesthood. The reason for so much false doctrine in the modern Church is because most presently little understand the typology of the Old Testament, as it presents Christ in the entirety of His Work.*)

25 And he took the fat, and the rump, and all the fat that was upon the inwards, and the caul above the liver, and the two kidneys, and their fat, and the right shoulder:

26 And out of the basket of unleavened bread, that was before the LORD, he took one unleavened cake (*there was only "One" Who was Perfect, and that was Christ*), and a cake of oiled bread (*the Holy Spirit upon Christ [Lk. 4:18-19]*), and one wafer, and put them on the fat, and upon the right shoulder (*all signifies Christ, Who Alone could satisfy the righteous demands of a thrice-Holy God*):

WAVE OFFERING

27 And he put all upon Aaron's hands, and upon his sons' hands, and waved them for a Wave Offering before the LORD (*the "Wave Offering" signified thanksgiving unto the Lord, and that He Alone was the Author of Salvation*).

28 And Moses took them from off their hands, and burnt them on the Altar upon the Burnt Offering (*once again, we are taken back to the Cross, typified by the Burnt Offering*): they were consecrations for a sweet savour (*all of this tells us that the Lord is pleased only with Christ and the Cross, which means that if we are to please God, our Faith must rest entirely in the Cross of Christ; that alone is a "sweet savour" to the Lord*): it is an Offering made by fire unto the LORD.

29 And Moses took the breast, and waved it for a Wave Offering before the LORD: for of the ram of consecration it was Moses' part; as the LORD commanded Moses (*this signified that even Moses had to partake of Christ, as do all*).

THE ANOINTING

30 And Moses took of the anointing oil, and of the blood which was upon the Altar, and sprinkled it upon Aaron (*Aaron and his sons had already been anointed with oil and had the blood applied; it is now done again, which were fitting conclusions to their consecration; it was meant to show that the Sanctification process is an ongoing process, thereby the necessity of continued trust in the Blood and need of continued anointing with the Holy Spirit*), and upon his garments, and upon his sons, and upon his sons' garments with him; and sanctified Aaron, and his garments, and his sons, and his sons' garments with him. (*Beautiful and costly as was the raiment of Aaron, yet the oil and the blood were applied. This simply means that the beauty and glory of Salvation, typified by the garments of Aaron, are all made possible by what Jesus did at the Cross.*)

THE FOOD

31 And Moses said unto Aaron and to his

sons, Boil the flesh at the door of the Tabernacle of the congregation: and there eat it with the bread that is in the basket of consecrations, as I commanded, saying, Aaron and his sons shall eat it *(this furnishes a fine Type of Christ and His people feeding together upon the results of the accomplished Atonement).*

32 And that which remains of the flesh and of the bread shall you burn with fire *(this signifies that all of Christ must be consumed; in other words, it is all of Christ, or it's none of Christ! He cannot be accepted in part).*

CONSECRATION

33 And you shall not go out of the door of the Tabernacle of the congregation in seven days, until the days of your consecration be at an end: for seven days shall he consecrate you *(the number "seven" typifies perfection; only by Faith in Christ and the Cross can a perfect consecration be entertained, all brought about by the Holy Spirit [Rom. 8:1-2, 11]).*

34 As he has done this day, so the LORD has commanded to do, to make an Atonement for you *(by the Sacrificial Offerings).*

35 Therefore shall you abide at the door of the Tabernacle of the congregation day and night seven days, and keep the charge of the LORD, that you die not: for so I am commanded *(it has not changed! If we fail to abide by the Word of God, we will spiritually die).*

36 So Aaron and his sons did all things which the LORD commanded by the hand of Moses *(they were not to deviate at all from the ritual, because it all represented Christ).*

CHAPTER 9
(1490 B.C.)
OFFERINGS OF AARON

AND it came to pass on the eighth day, that Moses called Aaron and his sons, and the Elders of Israel *(this Chapter describes Aaron in his role of mediation as the High Priest; it symbolizes Christ in this intercessory role, which He now occupies [Heb. 7:25]; the "eighth day" corresponds with Jesus being raised from the dead, which He was, in essence, on the eighth day; He was raised on the first day of the week, which was eight days after a full Sabbath week; according to ancient tradition, the eighth day of Aaron was the first day of March);*

2 And he said unto Aaron, You take a young calf for a Sin Offering, and a ram for a Burnt Offering, without blemish, and offer them before the LORD. *(Concerning this, Seiss says: "Everywhere, even in our holiest moods and most sacred doings, there still flashes out the stern and humiliating accusation — 'O man, you are a sinner! All your goodness is but abomination apart from Christ! Your only hope is in Him Whose body was broken and Whose Blood was shed for the remission of sins!'"*

All of this means that our hand must be ever kept on the brow of the Atoning Lamb. We must never cease to rest upon Jesus and His offering of Himself for us. We must ever look to the Cross.)

3 And unto the Children of Israel you shall speak, saying, You take a kid of the goats for a Sin Offering, and a calf and a lamb, both of the first year, without blemish, for a Burnt Offering;

4 Also a bullock and a ram for Peace Offerings, to sacrifice before the LORD; and a Meat Offering mingled with oil: for today the LORD will appear unto you.

PREPARATIONS

5 And they brought that which Moses commanded before the Tabernacle of the congregation: and all the congregation drew near and stood before the LORD *(all of Israel was commanded to bring forth the specified Sacrifices, which, no doubt, the Elders of Verse 1 did, on behalf of all the people).*

6 And Moses said, This is the thing which the LORD commanded that you should do: and the Glory of the LORD shall appear unto you *(if it is to be noticed, everything depended on the Sacrifices; this means everything presently depends on the Cross, of which the Sacrifices were a Type; if the true "Glory of God" is to appear, it can only be done through and by the Cross of Christ).*

7 And Moses said unto Aaron, Go unto the Altar, and offer your Sin Offering, and your Burnt Offering, and make an Atonement for yourself, and for the people: and offer the offering of the people, and make an Atonement for them; as the LORD commanded. *(Atonement means reconciliation. Its ultimate conclusion is the reconciliation of God and man through the Sacrificial Death of Jesus Christ, of which all of this was a Type.)*

OFFERINGS FOR THE PRIESTS

8 Aaron therefore went unto the Altar, and

killed the calf of the Sin Offering, which was for himself (Aaron, although the Great High Priest, still, was a sinner who needed the saving Grace of Christ).

9 And the sons of Aaron brought the blood unto him: and he dipped his finger in the blood, and put it upon the horns of the Altar, and poured out the blood at the bottom of the Altar (without the shedding of blood, and only a particular blood at that, the Blood of Christ, there is no remission of sins [Heb. 10:4]):

10 But the fat, and the kidneys, and the caul above the liver of the Sin Offering, he burnt upon the Altar; as the LORD commanded Moses.

11 And the flesh and the hide he burnt with fire without the camp. (Proclaims the fact that all sin would be completely expiated in the Death of Christ, which means "to do away with the guilt incurred." The whole curse fell upon the Substitute. The Atonement was not completed until the whole sacrifice was consumed.)

12 And he slew the Burnt Offering; and Aaron's sons presented unto him the blood, which he sprinkled round about upon the Altar.

13 And they presented the Burnt Offering unto him, with the pieces thereof, and the head: and he burnt them upon the Altar (the "Burnt Offering" symbolized the Perfection of Christ, and Him giving that Perfection to the sinner).

14 And he did wash the inwards and the legs (portraying the purity of Christ), and burnt them upon the Burnt Offering on the Altar.

OFFERINGS FOR THE PEOPLE

15 And he brought the people's Offering, and took the goat, which was the Sin Offering for the people, and killed it, and offered it for sin, as the first (sin has to be dealt with first of all!).

16 And he brought the Burnt Offering, and offered it according to the manner (with sin handled, then the Perfection of Christ can be given to the cleansed sinner, typified by the Burnt Offering).

17 And he brought the Meat Offering, and took an handful thereof, and burnt it upon the Altar, beside the Burnt Sacrifice of the morning (this was a handful of flour, which was to render thanks for God accepting the Offerings that had been presented).

18 He slew also the bullock and the ram for a sacrifice of Peace Offerings, which was for the people: and Aaron's sons presented unto him the blood, which he sprinkled upon the Altar round about (with the sin question settled,

and thanksgiving offered, and the Perfection of Christ rendered to the seeking one, the Peace of God, which had been interrupted, is now restored, typified by the "Peace Offering"),

19 And the fat of the bullock and of the ram, the rump, and that which covered the inwards, and the kidneys, and the caul above the liver:

20 And they put the fat upon the breasts, and he burnt the fat upon the Altar:

21 And the breasts and the right shoulder Aaron waved for a Wave Offering before the LORD; as Moses commanded. (The "Wave Offering" signified that all the Blessings came from above, which means that Redemption would come from above, and would do so in the form of the Lord Jesus Christ, of which these sacrifices were Types.)

22 And Aaron lifted up his hand toward the people, and blessed them, and came down from offering of the Sin Offering, and the Burnt Offering, and Peace Offerings. (The lifting up of the hands of the Priests became a custom in blessing the people when completing their duties for them in the rituals; however, the "blessing" could be pronounced only on the basis of the completed sacrifice, i.e., "the Cross.")

23 And Moses and Aaron went into the Tabernacle of the congregation, and came out, and blessed the people: and the Glory of the LORD appeared unto all the people. (There is no "Glory" other than through the Cross.)

24 And there came a fire out from before the LORD (it came from the Holy of Holies, actually from the Ark of the Covenant, and passed through the Veil and, as well, the hanging curtain at the front, without burning it), and consumed upon the Altar the Burnt Offering and the fat: which when all the people saw, they shouted, and fell on their faces. (This was a visible manifestation of the Judgment of God upon the Sacrifice. It was a type of the Judgment that Jesus would take while on the Cross, all on our behalf. But remember the following:

That judgment is assuaged only by Christ and the Cross; otherwise, it comes upon the individual, irrespective as to whoever that individual might be.)

CHAPTER 10

(1490 B.C.)

STRANGE FIRE

AND Nadab and Abihu, the sons of Aaron (they were Priests), took either of them

his censer, and put fire therein, and put incense thereon, and offered strange fire before the LORD, which He commanded them not. *(This was "fire" which came from something other than the Brazen Altar. As such, it was not a type of Christ and Him Crucified and, therefore, could not be recognized by God. It was the sin of Cain. They attempted to put the "strange fire" on the Altar of Incense, situated immediately in front of the Veil. All false doctrine falls into this same category and, thereby, presents a fearful spectacle.)*

2 And there went out fire from the LORD *(from the Ark of the Covenant, which passed through the Veil without burning it)*, and devoured them, and they died before the LORD. *(A short time earlier, fire had come out from this same place and consumed the Sacrifice on the Altar [9:24]. Inasmuch as the Cross of Christ was ignored here, that same fire came upon the sinner instead of the Sacrifice.)*

3 Then Moses said unto Aaron, This is it that the LORD spoke, saying, I will be sanctified in them who come near Me, and before all the people I will be glorified. And Aaron held his peace. *(The Lord is saying by this statement that if men place on His Altar the workings of their own corrupt will, what must be the result? Judgment!)*

4 And Moses called Mishael and Elzaphan, the sons of Uzziel the uncle of Aaron, and said unto them, Come near, carry your brethren from before the Sanctuary out of the camp.

5 So they went near, and carried them in their coats out of the camp; as Moses had said. *(It seems that the bolt of lightning which killed the both of them didn't even burn their coats. That they were the sons of Aaron did not stop the judgment, meaning that all must understand that it is the Cross or death.)*

6 And Moses said unto Aaron, and unto Eleazar and unto Ithamar, his sons *(the only two left to Aaron)*, Uncover not your heads, neither rend your clothes; lest you die, and lest wrath come upon all the people: but let your brethren, the whole house of Israel, bewail the burning which the LORD has kindled. *(While normally it would have been proper for the people of Israel to have mourned the deaths of these Priests, the High Priest and his remaining sons must prove their submission to the Divine chastisement by crushing their individual feeling of sorrow. In fact, a murmur on their part would have brought God's Wrath on themselves, and possibly even on Israel as a whole,*

whom they represented.)

7 And you shall not go out from the door of the Tabernacle of the congregation, lest you die: for the anointing oil of the LORD is upon you. And they did according to the word of Moses. *(For the remaining Priests to have mourned would, in essence, have been saying that the Cross was of little significance; regrettably, that's what many modern Preachers are now saying.)*

REGULATIONS

8 And the LORD spoke unto Aaron, saying,

9 Do not drink wine nor strong drink, you, nor your sons with you, when you go into the Tabernacle of the congregation, lest you die: it shall be a Statute for ever throughout your generations *(the Law given here by the Lord has led to the thought that Nadab and Abihu had acted under the excitement of intoxicating drink; in other words, they were drunk; so we have here in this Verse a prohibition "forever" against any type of strong drink)*:

10 And that you may put difference between holy and unholy, and between unclean and clean *(without a proper understanding of the Cross, it is very difficult to properly discern the difference as demanded here [Gal. 2:20-21])*;

11 And that you may teach the Children of Israel all the Statutes which the LORD has spoken unto them by the hand of Moses. *(The Priests, which number would grow extensively very shortly, were to teach the people the Law of Moses. It is the same now with God-called Preachers [Eph. 4:11-12].)*

12 And Moses spoke unto Aaron, and unto Eleazar and unto Ithamar, his sons who were left, Take the Meat Offering that remains of the Offerings of the LORD made by fire, and eat it without leaven beside the Altar: for it is most holy *(the "Meat Offering" was the only Offering of the five Sacrifices which was an unbloody Sacrifice; in other words, even though it was referred to as a "Meat Offering," in fact, it had no meat, as we think of such, but rather grain, which was ground into a fine flour; this Offering signified Christ in His Perfection and, as well, it signified thanksgiving to God for giving humanity such a Gift [Jn. 3:16]; it was to be eaten beside the Altar, typifying the Cross, which tells us that everything comes to us through the Cross)*:

13 And you shall eat it in the Holy Place, because it is your due, and your sons' due, of

the Sacrifices of the LORD made by fire: for so I am commanded *(this was a part of their duties, because it symbolized the partaking of Christ).*

14 And the wave breast and heave shoulder shall you eat in a clean place; you, and your sons, and your daughters with you: for they be your due, and your sons' due, which are given out of the Sacrifices of Peace Offerings of the Children of Israel *(the "Peace Offerings" were to be eaten by the family, thereby celebrating "Peace" which had been restored).*

15 The heave shoulder and the wave breast shall they bring with the Offerings made by fire of the fat, to wave it for a Wave Offering before the LORD; and it shall be yours, and your sons' with you, by a Statute for ever; as the LORD has commanded *(the "heave-up" signified that this God-man would come from Heaven; the "heave-down" signified that He would come down to this Earth; the "Wave Offering" signified Thanksgiving).*

16 And Moses diligently sought the goat of the Sin Offering, and, behold, it was burnt: and he was angry with Eleazar and Ithamar, the sons of Aaron which were left alive, saying *(Aaron and his two remaining sons should have eaten the goat of the Sin Offering, so making the sins of the people their own; but his personal grief unfitted him for bearing their sorrows; how different the True Aaron in John 16:22; He laid His Own immeasurable griefs aside and His loving Heart engaged itself with those of His Disciples).*

17 Wherefore have you not eaten the Sin Offering in the Holy Place, seeing it is most holy, and God has given it you to bear the iniquity of the congregation, to make Atonement for them before the LORD? *(Priests in the Sanctuary were not to bewail, but to worship — they were not to weep, as in the presence of death, but to bow their anointed heads in the Presence of the Divine visitation.)*

18 Behold, the blood of it was not brought in within the Holy Place: you should indeed have eaten it in the Holy Place, as I commanded. *(When Moses began to inquire into this particular "rite," he found that no blood had been brought into the Holy Place, and that the carcass of the Sin Offering had been mistakenly burned, when it should have been eaten. Moses was angry! He was concerned that if any part of the ritual was mishandled, misinterpreted, or ignored, the Judgment of God might now fall on the remaining Priests.)*

19 And Aaron said unto Moses, Behold, this day have they offered their Sin Offering and their Burnt Offering before the LORD; and such things have befallen me; and if I had eaten the Sin Offering today, should it have been accepted in the sight of the LORD? *(Concerning this, Ellicott says, "But while he, Eleazar, and Ithamar were thus duly performing the Sacrificial rites, Nadab and Abihu, the other two sons, transgressed, and were suddenly struck down dead, thus overwhelming the survivors with sorrow, and rendering them unfit to partake of the Sacrifices. Unfitted as they thus were by mourning and the sense of their own sinfulness, that if they had partaken of this solemn meal it would not have been acceptable to the Lord." They were right!)*

20 And when Moses heard that, he was content. *(Moses acknowledged Aaron's plea to be just, and that he had himself spoken hastily. Hence, Jewish tradition ascribed the mistake to Moses, not to Aaron. Jewish tradition further says, when Moses heard it, he approved of the explanation. Whereupon he sent a herald through the whole camp of Israel, saying, "It is I from whom the Law had been hid, and my brother Aaron brought it to my remembrance.")*

CHAPTER 11
(1490 B.C.)
ANIMALS

AND the LORD spoke unto Moses and to Aaron, saying unto them,

2 Speak unto the Children of Israel, saying, These are the beasts which you shall eat among all the beasts that are on the Earth *(Priesthood having been established, to it was now committed the judgment of that which was defiled).*

3 Whatsoever parts the hoof, and is clovenfooted, and chews the cud, among the beasts, that shall you eat *(the Laws of this Chapter and following for several Chapters were not only a test of obedience, and a loving provision for the health and happiness of the people, but they also give a humbling picture of the weakness and corruption of fallen human nature).*

4 Nevertheless these shall you not eat of them that chew the cud, or of them that divide the hoof: as the camel, because he chews the cud, but divides not the hoof; he is unclean unto you *(it should be noted that the Word of the Lord was the one and only judge in all of these matters).*

5 And the coney, because he chews the cud, but divides not the hoof; he is unclean unto you.

6 And the hare *(rabbit)*, because he chews the cud, but divides not the hoof; he is unclean unto you.

7 And the swine, though he divide the hoof, and be clovenfooted, yet he chews not the cud; he is unclean to you.

8 Of their flesh shall you not eat, and their carcase shall you not touch; they are unclean to you. *(Why would the Lord give specific instructions of this nature, as it regarded the eating of certain animals and fowls, etc.? In Acts, Chapter 10, as it regards the vision given to Simon Peter, all of these rulings were rescinded. In fact, as it regards Christianity, which is the outgrowth of true Judaism, there are no prohibitions whatsoever of this nature. The reason for these particular laws, and the understanding of them, such knowledge was not totally necessary, but rather obedience, because Israel was a set-apart people, actually raised up for the very purpose of bringing Christ the Redeemer into the world. As they were to be the womb of the Messiah, so to speak, things which the Lord specified as being "unclean" were forbidden. As stated, they didn't have to understand it all, but they definitely must obey. Once Christ came, all of these prohibitions ended.)*

9 These shall you eat of all that are in the waters: whatsoever has fins and scales in the waters, in the seas, and in the rivers, them shall you eat.

10 And all that have not fins and scales in the seas, and in the rivers, of all that move in the waters, and of any living thing which is in the waters, they shall be an abomination unto you:

11 They shall be even an abomination unto you; you shall not eat of their flesh, but you shall have their carcases in abomination.

12 Whatsoever has no fins nor scales in the waters, that shall be an abomination unto you.

13 And these are they which you shall have in abomination among the fowls; they shall not be eaten, they are an abomination: the eagle, and the ossifrage, and the ospray,

14 And the vulture, and the kite after his kind;

15 Every raven after his kind;

16 And the owl, and the night hawk, and the cuckow, and the hawk after his kind,

17 And the little owl, and the cormorant, and the great owl,

18 And the swan, and the pelican, and the gier eagle,

19 And the stork, the heron after her kind, and the lapwing, and the bat.

20 All fowls that creep, going upon all four, shall be an abomination unto you.

21 Yet these may you eat of every flying creeping thing that goes upon all four, which have legs above their feet, to leap withal upon the Earth;

22 Even these of them you may eat; the locust after his kind, and the bald locust after his kind, and the beetle after his kind, and the grasshopper after his kind.

23 But all other flying creeping things, which have four feet, shall be an abomination unto you.

24 And for these you shall be unclean: whosoever touches the carcase of them shall be unclean until the evening *(an unclean animal, fish, bird, or reptile, when dead, defiled whatsoever it touched).*

25 And whosoever bears ought of the carcase of them shall wash his clothes, and be unclean until the evening *(which means that in the meantime, the person could not offer Sacrifices).*

26 The carcases of every beast which divides the hoof, and is not clovenfooted, nor chews the cud, are unclean unto you: every one who touches them shall be unclean.

27 And whatsoever goes upon his paws, among all manner of beasts that go on all four, those are unclean unto you: whoso touches their carcase shall be unclean until the evening *(approximately 6 p.m.).*

28 And he who bears the carcase of them shall wash his clothes, and be unclean until the evening; they are unclean unto you.

29 These also shall be unclean unto you among the creeping things that creep upon the Earth; the weasel, and the mouse, and the tortoise after his kind,

30 And the ferret, and the chameleon, and the lizard, and the snail, and the mole.

31 These are unclean to you among all that creep: whosoever does touch them, when they be dead, shall be unclean until the evening.

32 And upon whatsoever any of them, when they are dead, does fall, it shall be unclean; whether it be any vessel of wood, or raiment, or skin, or sack, whatsoever vessel it be, wherein any work is done, it must be put into water, and it shall be unclean until the evening; so it shall be cleansed. *(All of this may seem to*

be tedious to the unspiritual eye and mind; however, we must understand that God desired to keep His people free from the defilement consequent upon touching, tasting, or handling that which was unclean. They were not their own and, hence, they were not to do as they pleased. They belonged to Jehovah; His Name was called upon them; they were identified with Him. As a result, His Word was to be their grand regulating standard in every case. Other nations might eat what they pleased, but Israel enjoyed the high privilege of eating that only which was pleasing to Jehovah.)

33 And every earthen vessel, whereinto any of them falls, whatsoever is in it shall be unclean; and you shall break it *(not only were Israelites forbidden to touch that which was unclean, if their property came into contact with such, such was to be destroyed)*.

34 Of all meat which may be eaten, that on which such water comes shall be unclean: and all drink that may be drunk in every such vessel shall be unclean.

35 And every thing whereupon any part of their carcase falls shall be unclean; whether it be oven, or ranges for pots, they shall be broken down: for they are unclean, and shall be unclean unto you.

CLEAN AND UNCLEAN

36 Nevertheless a fountain or pit, wherein there is plenty of water, shall be clean: but that which touches their carcase shall be unclean.

37 And if any part of their carcase fall upon any sowing seed which is to be sown, it shall be clean.

38 But if any water be put upon the seed, and any part of their carcase fall thereon, it shall be unclean unto you.

39 And if any beast, of which you may eat, die; he who touches the carcase thereof shall be unclean until the evening.

40 And he who eats of the carcase of it shall wash his clothes, and be unclean until the evening; he also who bears the carcase of it shall wash his clothes, and be unclean until the evening.

41 And every creeping thing that creeps upon the Earth shall be an abomination; it shall not be eaten.

42 Whatsoever goes upon the belly, and whatsoever goes upon all four, or whatsoever has more feet among all creeping things that creep upon the Earth, them you shall not eat; for they are an abomination.

43 You shall not make yourselves abominable with any creeping thing that creeps, neither shall you make yourselves unclean with them, that you should be defiled thereby.

HOLY

44 For I am the LORD your God: you shall therefore sanctify yourselves, and you shall be holy; for I am holy: neither shall you defile yourselves with any manner of creeping thing that creeps upon the Earth. *(We would ask ourselves the question as to whether the keeping of all these rules and regulations actually made one holy? The truth is, the keeping of these rules and regulations did not make one holy, even as the Sacrifices did not save one. But what it all represented definitely did have a bearing and effect upon these individuals. In some way, all of these things, and whatever they might have been, pointed to Christ. It is from Him Alone that all Holiness and Righteousness come to us. So, faith in the One to Whom all these rules, regulations, and Sacrifices pointed would make one holy.)*

45 For I am the LORD Who brought you up out of the land of Egypt, to be your God: you shall therefore be holy, for I am holy. *(Concerning personal holiness in its present posture, there can be no progress in the condition of Holiness into which the Believer is introduced, but there is, and ought to be, progress in the apprehension, experience, and practical exhibition of that Holiness. These things should never be confounded. All true Believers are in the same condition of Holiness and Sanctification, but their practical measure may vary to any conceivable degree.*

Actually, this should be easy to understand. The condition arises out of our being brought near to God by the Blood of the Cross; the practical measure will depend upon our keeping near by the power of the Spirit [Rom. 8:1-2, 11].)

46 This is the law of the beasts, and of the fowl, and of every living creature that moves in the waters, and of every creature that creeps upon the Earth:

47 To make a difference between the unclean and the clean, and between the beast that may be eaten and the beast that may not be eaten. *(To be sure, the Holy Spirit continues to "make a difference between the unclean and the clean." True Holiness is to "walk after the Spirit" [Rom. 8:1]. This can be done only according to God's*

prescribed order of victory, which is for the Believer to understand that everything we receive from the Lord comes to us exclusively by the means of the Cross. Christ is the Source, but the Cross is the Means; consequently, the Cross must ever be the object of our faith. That done and maintained, the Holy Spirit will then perform His Work of Christlikeness within our hearts and lives, but only after that manner [Gal. 2:20-21; Rom. 6:3-14; 8:1-11].)

CHAPTER 12
(1490 B.C.)
PURIFICATION OF WOMEN

AND the LORD spoke unto Moses saying,

2 Speak unto the Children of Israel, saying, If a woman have conceived seed, and has given birth to a man child: then she shall be unclean seven days; according to the days of the separation for her infirmity shall she be unclean *(the birth of a child recalled the sin and disobedience of Eden, and that the woman was the instrument of that rebellion).*

3 And in the eighth day the flesh of his foreskin *(all baby boys)* shall be circumcised. *(Circumcision was the physical sign of the Old Covenant; it symbolized separation from this world unto God. Concerning this, Mackintosh says, "The effect of all Scripture, when properly interpreted to one's own soul, which is done directly by the Power of the Holy Spirit, is to lead us out of self to Christ. Wherever we see our fallen nature, at whatever stage of its history we contemplate it — whether in its conception, at its birth, or at any point along its whole career from the womb to the coffin — it wears the double stamp of infirmity and defilement.)*

4 And she shall then continue in the blood of her purifying three and thirty days *(adding the seven days of Verse 2, upon the birth of a little boy the woman was to be unclean 40 days);* she shall touch no hallowed thing, nor come into the Sanctuary, until the days of her purifying be fulfilled. *(All of this proclaims original sin, and its terrible ruin. While man may try to deny the fact of sin, he cannot deny the results of sin.)*

5 But if she bear a maid child *(a little girl),* then she shall be unclean two weeks, as in her separation: and she shall continue in the blood of her purifying threescore and six days *(totals 80 days; the doubling of the time of defilement, as it regarded the birth of a little girl, was meant to portray the fact that it was Eve who had first sinned).*

THE OFFERING

6 And when the days of her purifying are fulfilled, for a son, or for a daughter, she shall bring a lamb of the first year for a Burnt Offering, and a young pigeon, or a turtledove, for a Sin Offering, unto the door of the Tabernacle of the congregation, unto the Priest *(the shadow of the Cross passes before us in a double way in this Chapter. First, it is in the circumcision of the "manchild" and, second, it is in the Burnt Offering and the Sin Offering, whereby the mother was restored from every defiling influence.*

As an aside, the extreme poverty of our Lord's Earthly parents was evidenced by their bringing two pigeons, the one for a Sin Offering, and the other for a Burnt Offering [Lk. 2:24]):

7 Who shall offer it before the LORD, and make an Atonement for her; and she shall be cleansed from the issue of her blood. This is the law for her who has born a male or a female. *(In both of these Offerings, the "Burnt Offering" and the "Sin Offering," the two grand aspects of the Death of Christ are introduced here as the only thing which could possibly meet and perfectly remove the defilement connected with man's natural birth. The "Burnt Offering" signified the Perfection of Christ offered up in Sacrifice, which God demanded, that is, if the sin debt was to be forever settled. The "Sin Offering" presents the Death of Christ as bearing upon the sinner's need. In other words, the Sin Offering proclaimed the sinner's sin placed on Christ, while the Burnt Offering portrayed the Perfection of Christ given to the sinner.*

All of this tells us that nothing but bloodshedding could impart cleanness. The Cross is the only remedy for man's infirmity and man's defilement. Wherever that glorious work is apprehended by Faith, and we speak of the Sacrifice of Christ, there is perfect cleanness in joy.)

8 And if she be not able to bring a lamb, then she shall bring two turtles, or two young pigeons; the one for the Burnt Offering, and the other for a Sin Offering: and the Priest shall make an Atonement for her, and she shall be clean. *(The Priest alone could make atonement for her, that is, if she brought the proper sacrifices; the Priest was a Type of Christ.)*

CHAPTER 13
(1490 B.C.)
THE SIGNS OF LEPROSY

A ND the LORD spoke unto Moses and Aaron, saying,

2 When a man shall have in the skin of his flesh a rising, a scab, or bright spot, and it be in the skin of his flesh like the plague of leprosy; then he shall be brought unto Aaron the Priest, or unto one of his sons the Priests (considering all the minute attention given to this disease, we know that God intended for leprosy to be a type of sin. From this Chapter, we will learn how absolutely horrible, putrefying, deadly, evil and destructive that sin actually is, which the Holy Spirit strongly desires that we learn.

If it is to be noticed, if it was thought that the person possibly had contracted leprosy, he was to be brought to the Priests for inspection, and not to a physician. This further shows that God intended for this dread malady to be a portrayal, a type, of sin. The Priest was a Type of Christ; so the sinner is to be brought to Christ):

3 And the Priest shall look on the plague in the skin of the flesh: and when the hair in the plague is turned white, and the plague in sight be deeper than the skin of his flesh, it is a plague of leprosy: and the Priest shall look on him, and pronounce him unclean. (The Priest alone could diagnose the plague of leprosy. It really didn't matter what others said, only what the Priest said; likewise, it is what Christ, i.e., "the Word," says that provides the true course. It doesn't matter what man says about sin; it's what the Lord says about sin.)

4 If the bright spot be white in the skin of his flesh, and in sight be not deeper than the skin, and the hair thereof be not turned white; then the Priest shall shut up him who has the plague seven days (the Priest was not guided by his own thoughts, his own feelings, or his own wisdom; he was to be guided strictly by the Word of the Lord, which had been given to him by Moses):

5 And the Priest shall look on him the seventh day: and, behold, if the plague in his sight be at a stay, and the plague spread not in the skin; then the Priest shall shut him up seven days more:

6 And the priest shall look on him again the seventh day: and, behold, if the plague be somewhat dark, and the plague spread not in the skin, the Priest shall pronounce him clean: it is but a scab: and he shall wash his clothes, and be clean. (We learn from this that Holiness cannot permit anyone to remain in who ought to be out; and, on the other hand, Grace will not have anyone out who ought to be in.)

7 But if the scab spread much abroad in the skin, after that he has been seen of the Priest for his cleansing, he shall be seen of the Priest again.

8 And if the Priest see that, behold, the scab spreads in the skin, then the Priest shall pronounce him unclean: it is a leprosy. (If the Word is not the infallible guide, then terrible injustices will be done, people will be hurt, and souls could even be lost. It is incumbent upon Preachers and, in fact, all Believers, that the Word of God be the deciding factor in everything.)

9 When the plague of leprosy is in a man, then he shall be brought unto the Priest (leprosy was, for the most part, hereditary; after afflicting the parent, it was very apt to break out in the child; this is a perfect description of the terrible malady of sin; sin began in Adam, our first parent, and has passed on to the entirety of the human race):

10 And the Priest shall see him: and, behold, if the rising be white in the skin, and it have turned the hair white, and there be quick raw flesh in the rising:

11 It is an old leprosy in the skin of his flesh, and the Priest shall pronounce him unclean, and shall not shut him up: for he is unclean (in other words, there is no doubt that this individual has leprosy).

12 And if a leprosy break out abroad in the skin, and the leprosy cover all the skin of him who has the plague from his head even to his foot, wheresoever the Priest looks;

13 Then the Priest shall consider: and, behold, if the leprosy have covered all his flesh, he shall pronounce him clean who has the plague: it is all turned white: he is clean. (A leper, white all over, was clean. He was a leper, but the disease was not active in him; it was, in a sense, dead. Thus, "sin" should be "dead" in the Christian [Rom., Chpt. 6].)

14 But when raw flesh appears in him, he shall be unclean.

15 And the Priest shall see the raw flesh, and pronounce him to be unclean: for the raw flesh is unclean: it is a leprosy. (As the signs of leprosy were obvious here, likewise, ultimately, the signs of sin will become obvious.)

16 Or if the raw flesh turn again, and be changed unto white, he shall come unto the Priest;

17 And the Priest shall see him: and, behold, if the plague be turned into white; then the Priest shall pronounce him clean who has the plague: he is clean. *(Everyone who trusts Christ and what He has done for us at the Cross can be pronounced as "clean.")*

18 The flesh also, in which, even in the skin thereof, was a boil, and is healed,

19 And in the place of the boil there be a white rising, or a bright spot, white, and somewhat reddish, and it be shewed to the Priest;

20 And if, when the Priest sees it, behold, it be in sight lower than the skin, and the hair thereof be turned white; the Priest shall pronounce him unclean: it is a plague of leprosy broken out of the boil.

21 But if the Priest look on it, and, behold, there be no white hairs therein, and if it be not lower than the skin, but be somewhat dark; then the Priest shall shut him up seven days:

22 And if it spread much abroad in the skin, then the Priest shall pronounce him unclean: it is a plague. *(It is the responsibility of the Preacher of the Gospel to pronounce sin as sin; unfortunately, the modern Church has, by and large, attempted to redefine sin by referring to it by other names. For instance, drunkenness is referred to as a disease.)*

23 But if the bright spot stay in his place, and spread not, it is a burning boil: and the Priest shall pronounce him clean.

24 Of if there be any flesh, in the skin whereof there is a hot burning, and the quick flesh that burns have a white bright spot, somewhat reddish, or white;

25 Then the Priest shall look upon it: and, behold, if the hair in the bright spot be turned white, and it be in sight deeper than the skin; it is a leprosy broken out of the burning: wherefore the Priest shall pronounce him unclean: it is the plague of leprosy. *(As is painfully obvious, the very smallest speck of leprosy was intolerable; likewise, the smallest amount of sin is intolerable with God.)*

26 But if the Priest look on it, and, behold, there be no white hair in the bright spot, and it be no lower than the other skin, but be somewhat dark; then the Priest shall shut him up seven days *(for inspection)*:

27 And the Priest shall look upon him the seventh day: and if it be spread much abroad in the skin, then the Priest shall pronounce him unclean: it is the plague of leprosy.

28 And if the bright spot stay in his place, and spread not in the skin, but it be somewhat dark; it is a rising of the burning, and the Priest shall pronounce him clean: for it is an inflammation of the burning.

29 If a man or woman have a plague upon the head or the beard;

30 Then the Priest shall see the plague: and, behold, if it be in sight deeper than the skin; and there be in it a yellow thin hair; then the Priest shall pronounce him unclean: it is a dry scall, even a leprosy upon the head or beard.

31 And if the Priest look on the plague of the scall, and, behold, it be not in sight deeper than the skin, and that there is no black hair in it; then the Priest shall shut up him who has the plague of the scall seven days:

32 And in the seventh day the Priest shall look on the plague: and, behold, if the scall spread not, and there be in it no yellow hair, and the scall be not in sight deeper than the skin;

33 He shall be shaven, but the scall shall he not shave; and the Priest shall shut up him who has the scall seven days more:

34 And in the seventh day the Priest shall look on the scall: and, behold, if the scall be not spread in the skin, nor be in sight deeper than the skin; then the Priest shall pronounce him clean: and he shall wash his clothes, and be clean.

35 But if the scall spread much in the skin after his cleansing;

36 Then the Priest shall look on him: and, behold, if the scall be spread in the skin, the Priest shall not seek for yellow hair; he is unclean.

37 But if the scall *(a scab-like sore which was surface only)* be in his sight at a stay, and that there is black hair grown up therein; the scall is healed, he is clean: and the Priest shall pronounce him clean.

38 If a man also or a woman have in the skin of their flesh bright spots, even white bright spots;

39 Then the Priest shall look: and, behold, if the bright spots in the skin of their flesh be darkish white: it is a freckled spot that grows in the skin; he is clean.

40 And the man whose hair is fallen off his head, he is bald; yet is he clean.

41 And he who has his hair fallen off from the part of his head toward his face, he is forehead bald: yet is he clean. *(The minute directions given in this Chapter, and the care and patience enjoined by the Priests, show how God distinguishes between sin and infirmity.)*

42 And if there be in the bald head, or bald forehead, a white reddish sore; it is a leprosy sprung up in his bald head, or his bald forehead.

43 Then the Priest shall look upon it: and, behold, if the rising of the sore be white reddish in his bald head, or in his bald forehead, as the leprosy appears in the skin of the flesh;

44 He is a leprous man, he is unclean: the Priest shall pronounce him utterly unclean: his plague is in his head. *(As the Priest pronounced the leprosy, likewise, the true Preacher of the Gospel, as previously stated, is to correctly identify sin.)*

45 And the leper in whom the plague is, his clothes shall be rent *(carries the spiritual meaning that man's personal righteousness is insufficient for acceptance by God; the leper's torn garment says, "I am undone, useless, and I am separated from God")*, and his head bare *(this signifies that the sinner had, and has, no protection against the anger and wrath of God; in other words, he is naked to the Judgment of God)*, and he shall put a covering upon his upper lip, and shall cry, Unclean, unclean. *(When any person professes Salvation by any means other than Christ and the Cross, whether they realize it or not, they are saying, "Unclean, unclean.")*

46 All the days wherein the plague shall be in him he shall be defiled *(sin defiles, and in every capacity)*; he is unclean: he shall dwell alone *(despite the noise and the crowds, there is a terrible loneliness about sin)*; without the camp shall his habitation be *(sin separates people from God)*.

47 The garment also that the plague of leprosy is in, whether it be a woolen garment, or a linen garment;

48 Whether it be in the warp, or woof; of linen, or of woolen; whether in a skin, or in any thing made of skin;

49 And if the plague be greenish or reddish in the garment, or in the skin, either in the warp, or in the woof, or in any thing of skin; it is a plague of leprosy, and shall be shewed unto the Priest:

50 And the Priest shall look upon the plague, and shut up it that has the plague seven days:

51 And he shall look on the plague on the seventh day: if the plague be spread in the garment, either in the warp, or in the woof, or in a skin, or in any work that is made of skin; the plague is a fretting leprosy; it is unclean.

52 He shall therefore burn that garment, whether warp or woof, in woolen or in linen, or any thing of skin, wherein the plague is: for it is a fretting leprosy; it shall be burnt in the fire.

53 And if the Priest shall look, and, behold the plague be not spread in the garment, either in the warp, or in the woof, or in any thing of skin;

54 Then the Priest shall command that they wash the thing wherein the plague is, and he shall shut it up seven days more:

55 And the Priest shall look on the plague, after that it is washed: and, behold, if the plague have not changed his color, and the plague be not spread; it is unclean; you shall burn it in the fire; it is fret inward, whether it be bare within or without.

56 And if the Priest look, and, behold, the plague be somewhat dark after the washing of it; then he shall rend it out of the garment, or out of the skin, or out of the warp, or out of the woof:

57 And if it appear still in the garment, either in the warp, or in the woof, or in any thing of skin; it is a spreading plague: you shall burn that wherein the plague is with fire.

58 And the garment, either warp, or woof, or whatsoever thing of skin it be, which you shall wash, if the plague be departed from them, then it shall be washed the second time, and shall be clean.

59 This is the law of the plague of leprosy in a garment of wool or linen, either in the warp, or woof, or any thing of skins, to pronounce it clean, or to pronounce it unclean. *(Leprosy in a garment is a type of sin in a man's circumstances, or habits. The Priest was commanded to show the same patience and care in judging a garment as in judging a man.*

Sometimes a Christian must abandon part of his business because of evil attaching to it, and sometimes he must abandon it all together. This is a principle which affects the whole Christian life.

The carnal mind finds this Chapter tiresome, uninteresting, and unpleasant; however, to the spiritual mind, it is humbling and comforting. Love untiring and infinite wisdom are the foundation of these Statutes. The Reader finds himself as a moral leper in the tender, patient, wise, and loving hands of the Heavenly Priest; and, accordingly, he studies every word with humiliation and adoration — Williams.)

CHAPTER 14
(1490 B.C.)
CLEANSING LAWS

AND the LORD spoke unto Moses, saying,

2 This shall be the law of the leper in the day of his cleansing: He shall be brought unto the Priest *(as the Priest was a Type of Christ, there is cleansing for sin only in Christ and the Cross; so the sinner must be brought to Christ, and not the Church, or good works, etc.)*:

3 And the Priest shall go forth out of the camp *(Christ came from Heaven for the sole purpose of seeking out sinners)*; and the Priest shall look *(Christ Alone can diagnose and cleanse)*, and, behold, if the plague of leprosy be healed in the leper;

4 Then shall the Priest command to take for him who is to be cleansed two birds alive and clean *(one was to be killed, typifying the Cross, and the other was to be let loose into the Heavens, typifying the Resurrection)*, and cedar wood *(a Type of the Cross)*, and scarlet *(speaks of a piece of cloth that was the color of scarlet, which typified the shed Blood of Christ)*, and hyssop *(typifies the humanity of Christ, i.e., "Incarnation," God becoming man; the "hyssop" sprinkled the blood, typifying the blood being sprinkled from the wounds of Christ on the Cross)*:

5 And the Priest shall command that one of the birds be killed in an earthen vessel over running water *(the "earthen vessel" speaks of the humanity of Christ, just as the hyssop; the "running water" symbolizes the Word of God, in which Jesus was, and is, the Living Word)*:

6 As for the living bird, he shall take it, and the cedar wood, and the scarlet, and the hyssop, and shall dip them and the living bird in the blood of the bird that was killed over the running water *(all were based upon the preciousness and efficacy of the shed blood; apart from the Blood of Jesus, moral reformation and spiritual power are impossible)*:

7 And he shall sprinkle upon him who is to be cleansed from the leprosy seven times *("seven" is God's number, which proclaims a total and complete cleansing)*, and shall pronounce him clean *(if one fully trusts Christ and what He has done for us at the Cross, he can be "pronounced clean")*, and shall let the living bird loose into the open field *(typifying Resurrection, "raised with Him in newness of life" [Rom. 6:3-5])*.

8 And he who is to be cleansed shall wash his clothes, and shave off all his hair, and wash himself in water, that he may be clean *(excepting the washing of himself in water, the leper did nothing for his cleansing; the Priest did everything)*: and after that he shall come into the camp, and shall tarry abroad out of his tent seven days.

9 But it shall be on the seventh day, that he shall shave all his hair off his head and his beard and his eyebrows, even all his hair he shall shave off: and he shall wash his clothes, also he shall wash his flesh in water, and he shall be clean. *(Directly the repentant sinner is cleansed by the Precious Blood of Christ, he is called upon to "cleanse himself" from all defilement of the flesh and spirit [II Cor. 7:1]. This cleansing is effected by the washing of water by the Word [Eph. 5:26]. That is, he judges himself and his habits [his clothes] by the infallible standard of the Holy Scriptures, and he resolutely turns away from everything condemned by the Word. Thus, he cleanses himself.)*

THE SACRIFICES

10 And on the eighth day he shall take two he lambs without blemish, and one ewe lamb of the first year without blemish, and three tenth deals of fine flour for a Meat Offering, mingled with oil, and one log of oil. *(The leper was cleansed by blood, by water, and by oil. These symbolized the Blood of Christ, the Word of God, and the Holy Spirit.)*

11 And the Priest who makes him clean shall present the man that is to be made clean, and those things, before the LORD, at the door of the Tabernacle of the congregation *(this triple cleansing restored him to the camp, to his family, and to the Tabernacle)*:

12 And the Priest shall take one he lamb, and offer him for a Trespass Offering, and the log of oil, and wave them for a Wave Offering before the LORD *(as the Trespass Offering was presented by the Priest, it was done differently than normally done for other Trespass Offerings; in the case before us, not only did oil accompany it, but both the Trespass Offering and the oil were waved by the Priest, which did not take place on any other occasion in connection with the Trespass Offering and Sin Offering; actually, in no other case was the entire victim waved before the Lord)*:

13 And he shall slay the lamb in the place where he shall kill the Sin Offering and the Burnt Offering, in the Holy Place: for as the

Sin Offering is the Priest's, so is the Trespass Offering: it is most holy *(these two Offerings, plus the Meat Offering, were labeled as "most holy" [Lev. 2:3]; the Whole Burnt Offering and the Peace Offering were labeled as "holy." Why the difference? The overriding thrust of all that Christ did was deliverance from sin, of which leprosy was a type, hence these particular Offerings being labeled "most holy")*:

14 And the Priest shall take some of the blood of the Trespass Offering, and the Priest shall put it upon the tip of the right ear of him who is to be cleansed *(typifying that all "hearing" had now been cleansed by the blood and, henceforth, he would hear only that which is of the Lord)*, and upon the thumb of his right hand *(now he would "do" right)*, and upon the great toe of his right foot *(now he would "walk" right [Rom. 8:1])*:

15 And the Priest shall take some of the log of oil, and pour it into the palm of his own left hand *(the "oil" typifies the Holy Spirit; the blood having been applied, the Holy Spirit can now effect His Work in the heart and life of the former leper, i.e., "sinner")*:

16 And the Priest shall dip his right finger in the oil that is in his left hand, and shall sprinkle of the oil with his finger seven times before the LORD *(the oil being sprinkled before the Lord seven times proclaimed a perfect cleansing; this means that the Holy Spirit has put His seal of approval on the Finished Work of Christ)*:

17 And of the rest of the oil that is in his hand shall the Priest put upon the tip of the right ear of him who is to be cleansed, and upon the thumb of his right hand, and upon the great toe of his right foot, upon the blood of the Trespass Offering *(the "oil," a Type of the Holy Spirit, could not be applied until the "blood," a Type of the Sacrifice of Christ, was first applied)*:

18 And the remnant of the oil that is in the Priest's hand he shall pour upon the head of him who is to be cleansed: and the Priest shall make an Atonement for him before the LORD *(again we state, and unequivocally, that it's all based on the Blood; the Holy Spirit works entirely within the parameters of the Finished Work of Christ, and no other way [Rom. 8:2])*.

19 And the Priest shall offer the Sin Offering, and make an Atonement for him who is to be cleansed from his uncleanness; and afterward he shall kill the Burnt Offering *(the other ewe lamb mentioned in Verse 10 is now offered as a Sin Offering; symbolically, this pictures Christ taking the sinner's guilt; after the Sin Offering was presented, the Priest was now to kill the "Burnt Offering"; as the Sin Offering took the sinner's guilt and placed it on Christ, the Burnt Offering would now take the Perfection of Christ and give it to the believing sinner)*:

20 And the Priest shall offer the Burnt Offering and the Meat Offering upon the Altar: and the Priest shall make an Atonement for him, and he shall be clean *(a small part of the "Meat Offering" was burned on the Altar, and the balance eaten by the Priest)*.

21 And if he be poor, and cannot get so much; then he shall take one lamb for a Trespass Offering to be waved, to make an Atonement for him, and one tenth deal of fine flour mingled with oil for a Meat Offering, and a log of oil;

22 And two turtledoves, or two young pigeons, such as he is able to get; and the one shall be a Sin Offering, and the other a Burnt Offering. *(Even though the Sacrifices may be altered somewhat, the ritual was identical for the poor man's sacrifices as it was for the rich. The solemnity and imposing nature of the service is not diminished, as both rich and poor are alike in the Presence of the Lord.)*

23 And he shall bring them on the eighth day for his cleansing unto the Priest, unto the door of the Tabernacle of the congregation, before the LORD *(the "eighth day" is Resurrection Day, Jesus having been raised on that day)*.

24 And the Priest shall take the lamb of the Trespass Offering, and the log of oil, and the Priest shall wave them for a Wave Offering before the LORD:

25 And he shall kill the lamb of the Trespass Offering, and the Priest shall take some of the blood of the Trespass Offering, and put it upon the tip of the right ear of him who is to be cleansed, and upon the thumb of his right hand, and upon the great toe of his right foot:

26 And the Priest shall pour of the oil into the palm of his own left hand:

27 And the Priest shall sprinkle with his right finger some of the oil that is in his left hand seven times before the LORD:

28 And the Priest shall put of the oil that is in his hand upon the tip of the right ear of him who is to be cleansed, and upon the thumb of his right hand, and upon the great toe of his right foot, upon the place of the blood of the Trespass Offering:

29 And the rest of the oil that is in the Priest's

hand he shall put upon the head of him who is to be cleansed, to make an Atonement for him before the LORD. *(Two great facts shine here with exceptional luster; and both were of Grace. First, the uniting together of God's House with the leper's house; and, second, the placing side by side of the High Priest and the leper; for these two were sprinkled with blood and anointed with oil. Only Aaron's sons were similarly consecrated; and thus, ceremonially, was the leper "put among the sons.")*

30 And he shall offer the one of the turtle-doves, or of the young pigeons, such as he can get *(the Priest represented our Great High Priest passed into the Heavens; his double cleansing of the leper illustrated Justification and Sanctification)*;

31 Even such as he is able to get, the one for a Sin Offering, and the other for a Burnt Offering, with the Meat Offering: and the Priest shall make an Atonement for him who is to be cleansed before the LORD. *(The first cleansing, one might say, pictured Christ's Atoning Work for the sinner; the second cleansing, the Holy Spirit's Work in the Believer, giving him assurance of Salvation, deliverance from his sins, and power to live a holy life and to enter into the Presence of God. The blood was his title, and the Spirit [oil], his capacity.)*

32 This is the law of him in whom is the plague of leprosy, whose hand is not able to get that which pertains to his cleansing. *(Verses 21 through 32 legislated, in Grace, for those who were too poor to provide the more costly Sacrifices; but, in such cases, it still was absolute that the Sacrifice must be a Sacrifice of blood [Heb., Chpts. 9-10.)*

LEPROSY IN HOUSES

33 And the LORD spoke unto Moses and unto Aaron, saying,

34 When you be come into the land of Canaan, which I give to you for a possession, and I put the plague of leprosy in a house of the land of your possession;

35 And he who owns the house shall come and tell the Priest, saying, It seems to me there is as it were a plague in the house *(in all of this, even as we have seen, and shall see, there is but one cure for sin, whether in an individual, or a community, or in nature, and that one cure is the cleansing Blood of Christ)*:

36 Then the Priest shall command that they empty the house, before the Priest go into it to see the plague, that all that is in the house be not made unclean: and afterward the Priest shall go in to see the house:

37 And he shall look on the plague, and, behold, if the plague be in the walls of the house with hollow strakes, greenish or reddish, which in sight are lower than the wall *(bringing this up to the time of the Cross, we will attempt to apply it to our modern circumstances; the Church at Corinth is an excellent example; it was a spiritual house, composed of spiritual stones; in that particular house at Corinth, there was found the plague of leprosy, i.e., "a man who had taken up with his father's wife," evidently while the father was still alive [I Cor., Chpt. 5]; Paul informed the Church that this man had to repent, which means dissolving the relationship, as should be obvious, or else he had to be excommunicated; he used "leaven" as an example; if it's not removed, it will ultimately infect the whole)*;

38 Then the Priest shall go out of the house to the door of the house, and shut up the house seven days:

39 And the Priest shall come again the seventh day, and shall look: and, behold, if the plague be spread in the walls of the house;

40 Then the Priest shall command that they take away the stones in which the plague is, and they shall cast them into an unclean place without the city:

41 And he shall cause the house to be scraped within round about, and they shall pour out the dust that they scrape off without the city into an unclean place:

42 And they shall take other stones, and put them in the place of those stones; and he shall take other morter, and shall plaister the house.

43 And if the plague come again, and break out in the house, after that he has taken away the stones, and after he has scraped the house, and after it is plaistered;

44 Then the priest shall come and look, and, behold, if the plague be spread in the house, it is a fretting leprosy in the house; it is unclean.

45 And he shall break down the house, the stones of it, and the timber thereof, and all the morter of the house; and he shall carry them forth out of the city into an unclean place. *(Bringing the type unto the present, and actually into the entirety of the Church Age, we must conclude that if a Fellowship or Denomination has left the ways of the Lord and is going in another direction, there must be a clean break from that particular "house." While the house may continue to exist, and even thrive according*

to the standards of the world, as far as God is concerned, it is "no more." The leprosy, i.e., "sin," began small; however, it was not properly addressed and ultimately, and eventually, it overtook the entirety of the house, with it then, at least spiritually speaking, slated for destruction.)

46 Moreover he who goes into the house all the while that it is shut up shall be unclean until the evening. (Continuing to bring the situation into the present, the Believer cannot remain in an unscriptural environment, as it regards false doctrine. Association brings spiritual uncleanliness. If there's anything this "type" shows us, it is this Truth.)

47 And he who lies in the house shall wash his clothes; and he who eats in the house shall wash his clothes.

48 And if the Priest shall come in, and look upon it, and, behold, the plague has not spread in the house, after the house was plaistered: then the Priest shall pronounce the house clean, because the plague is healed.

49 And he shall take to cleanse the house two birds, and cedar wood, and scarlet, and hyssop:

50 And he shall kill the one of the birds in an earthen vessel over running water:

51 And he shall take the cedar wood, and the hyssop, and the scarlet, and the living bird, and dip them in the blood of the slain bird, and in the running water, and sprinkle the house seven times:

52 And he shall cleanse the house with the blood of the bird, and with the running water, and with the living bird, and with the cedar wood, and with the hyssop, and with the scarlet:

53 But he shall let go the living bird out of the city into the open fields, and make an Atonement for the house: and it shall be clean. (For all practical purposes, the cleansing of the house, which, as is obvious, presents a material structure, as it regards the plague of leprosy, was the same as the cleansing of the leper himself. In all cases, even material objects, the blood had to be applied.)

54 This is the law for all manner of plague of leprosy, and scall,

55 And for the leprosy of a garment, and of a house,

56 And for a rising, and for a scab, and for a bright spot:

57 To teach when it is unclean, and when it is clean: this is the law of leprosy. (Regarding this, Mackintosh says: "I do not doubt in the least that this whole subject of leprosy has a great dispensational bearing, not only upon the house of Israel, but also upon the professing Church."

As an example, the Divine Priest stands in a judicial attitude with respect to His house at Pergamos [Rev. 2:12-16]. He could not be indifferent to symptoms so alarming, but He patiently and graciously gives time to repent. If reproof, warning, and discipline prove unavailing, judgment must take its course.

While we preach Christ Crucified, and that Salvation comes by Faith alone, simply because the Word proclaims that [Eph. 2:8-9], still, true Salvation will always point to a surrender of self to the obedience of Christ. In other words, there must be a total change in the whole manner of life.

We must come to the conclusion that if what we profess is not powerful enough to work a complete revolution in our lives, leading us to obey and follow Christ, it will avail us nothing before God.)

CHAPTER 15
(1490 B.C.)
DEFILEMENT

AND the LORD spoke unto Moses and to Aaron, saying,

2 Speak unto the Children of Israel, and say unto them, When any man has a running issue out of his flesh, because of his issue he is unclean (the Hebrew word for "issue" is "zuwb," and means "to have a sexual flux"; it probably refers to "gonorrhea" or "blenorrhea").

3 And this shall be his uncleanness in his issue: whether his flesh run with his issue, or his flesh be stopped from his issue, it is his uncleanness.

4 Every bed, whereon he lies that has the issue, is unclean: and every thing, whereon he sits, shall be unclean. (We note here the corruption of fallen nature; it is defiled. Walking or sleeping, sitting, standing, or lying, its very touch conveyed pollution — a painful lesson for proud humanity — Williams.)

5 And whosoever touches his bed shall wash his clothes, and bathe himself in water, and be unclean until the evening.

6 And he who sits on any thing whereon he sat who has the issue shall wash his clothes, and bathe himself in water, and be unclean until the evening.

7 And he who touches the flesh of him who

has the issue shall wash his clothes, and bathe himself in water, and be unclean until the evening.

8 And if he who has the issue spit upon him who is clean; then he shall wash his clothes, and bathe himself in water, and be unclean until the evening.

9 And what saddle soever he rides upon who has the issue shall be unclean.

10 And whosoever touches any thing that was under him shall be unclean until the evening: and he who bears any of those things shall wash his clothes, and bathe himself in water, and be unclean until the evening.

11 And whomsoever he touches who has the issue, and has not rinsed his hands in water, he shall wash his clothes, and bathe himself in water, and be unclean until the evening.

12 And the vessel of earth, that he touches which has the issue, shall be broken: and every vessel of wood shall be rinsed in water.

13 And when he who has an issue is cleansed of his issue; then he shall number to himself seven days for his cleansing, and wash his clothes, and bathe his flesh in running water, and shall be clean. *(The giving of these ceremonial rituals, for they within themselves cleansed nothing, were given in order that we may understand not only the terrible power of sin, but, as well, the totality of the Fall and, above all, the cure for these terrible things, which alone is the Cross of Christ. When we read these Passages, these are the truths that the Holy Spirit means for us to comprehend and understand.)*

SACRIFICES

14 And on the eighth day he shall take to him two turtledoves, or two young pigeons, and come before the LORD unto the door of the Tabernacle of the congregation, and give them unto the Priest:

15 And the Priest shall offer them, the one for a Sin Offering, and the other for a Burnt Offering; and the Priest shall make an atonement for him before the LORD for his issue. *(It is amazing how deep-seated the contaminations of sin are. Even the Godliest Believer, who loves the Lord supremely, and is attempting to live for God to the best of his ability, who trusts in Christ and what Christ has done for us at the Cross, still, due to the contamination, will find sin unintentionally escaping from him, contaminating himself and those who come in contact with him, or touching what he has touched,*

spiritually speaking. In fact, even though we don't like to admit it, the whole nature of the Believer is yet so full of remaining corruption, that the least agitation causes it to trickle over [Rom. 7:21]. That's the reason that glorification is an absolute necessity.)

16 And if any man's seed of copulation go out from him, then he shall wash all his flesh in water, and be unclean until the evening.

17 And every garment, and every skin, whereon is the seed of copulation, shall be washed with water, and be unclean until the evening.

18 The woman also with whom man shall lie with seed of copulation, they shall both bathe themselves in water, and be unclean until the evening. *(We find in this section that the cleansing power of the shed Blood, and the sanctifying virtue of the Word of God, is the only way of cleansing and Holiness.)*

PURIFICATION OF WOMEN

19 And if a woman have an issue, and her issue in her flesh be blood, she shall be put apart seven days: and whosoever touches her shall be unclean until the evening *(this pertains to the monthly period of women; it denotes impurity, which is a result of the Fall; this doesn't mean that the woman is sinning because of such action, but it does mean that she was defiled; the Cross of Christ, thankfully, took away that impurity).*

20 And every thing that she lies upon in her separation shall be unclean: every thing also that she sits upon shall be unclean.

21 And whosoever touches her bed shall wash his clothes, and bathe himself in water, and be unclean until the evening.

22 And whosoever touches any thing that she sat upon shall wash his clothes, and bathe himself in water, and be unclean until the evening.

23 And if it be on her bed, or on any thing whereon she sits, when he touches it, he shall be unclean until the evening.

24 And if any man lie with her at all, and her flowers *(discharge)* be upon him, he shall be unclean seven days; and all the bed whereon he lies shall be unclean. *(Superficial views of sin would lead men to imagine that a sin done in ignorance is not a guilty thing. God says differently, because He looks into the heart and discerns the deep-seated source.)*

25 And if a woman have an issue of her

blood many days out of the time of her separation, or if it run beyond the time of her separation; all the days of the issue of her uncleanness shall be as the days of her separation: she shall be unclean *(Mk. 5:25-29)*.

26 Every bed whereon she lies all the days of her issue shall be unto her as the bed of her separation: and whatsoever she sits upon shall be unclean, as the uncleanness of her separation.

27 And whosoever touches those things shall be unclean, and shall wash his clothes, and bathe himself in water, and be unclean until the evening.

28 But if she be cleansed of her issue, then she shall number to herself seven days, and after that she shall be clean.

SACRIFICES

29 And on the eighth day she shall take unto her two turtles *(turtledoves)*, or two young pigeons, and bring them unto the Priest, to the door of the Tabernacle of the congregation.

30 And the Priest shall offer the one for a Sin Offering, and the other for a Burnt Offering; and the Priest shall make an Atonement for her before the LORD for the issue of her uncleanness.

31 Thus shall you separate the Children of Israel from their uncleanness; that they die not in their uncleanness, when they defile My Tabernacle that is among them. *(In truth, as we study this, we are encouraged to come into a knowledge that sin is a much larger matter than we are conscious of; that, in fact, it goes beyond all our conceptions but, at the same time, it is within the reach and grasp of our Lord's Atoning Power. If He thus sets our sins, and even our secret sins, in the light of His countenance, it is that He may have them entirely removed.)*

32 This is the law of him who has an issue, and of him whose seed goes from him, and is defiled therewith;

33 And of her who is sick of her flowers *(discharge)*, and of him who has an issue, of the man, and of the woman, and of him who lies with her who is unclean.

CHAPTER 16
(1490 B.C.)
THE DAY OF ATONEMENT

AND the LORD spoke unto Moses after the death of the two sons of Aaron, when they offered before the LORD, and died *(mention is made here again of the two sons of Aaron who were stricken dead by the Lord because of their offering up of "strange fire," and done so in order that Aaron might understand the total and complete seriousness of these rituals. If it is to be noticed, there is a voluminous amount of repetition in all of these instructions given to Moses by the Lord. Regarding this, Seiss says: "The success of the pulpit, and the benefit of our weekly attentions upon the Sanctuary, depend much more upon the continuous reiteration of the same great Truths of the Gospel, than upon any power of invention in the Preacher. It is not so much the presentation of new thoughts and brilliant originalities that converts men and builds them up in Holiness, as the clear and constant exhibition of the plain doctrines of Grace");*

2 And the LORD said unto Moses, Speak unto Aaron your brother, that he come not at all times into the Holy Place within the Veil before the Mercy Seat, which is upon the Ark; that he die not: for I will appear in the cloud upon the Mercy Seat. *(This is one of the most important Chapters in the Bible. It deals with the Great Day of Atonement. The Lord is saying here to Aaron that even though he is the Great High Priest, still, he is not to come into the Holy of Holies any other time, except on the one day each year of Atonement. To do so meant that he would die. All of this foreshadows the Lamb of God taking away the sin of the world [Jn. 1:29].)*

3 Thus shall Aaron come into the Holy Place *(the Holy of Holies where the Ark of the Covenant was)*: with a young bullock for a Sin Offering, and a ram for a Burnt Offering. *(The phrase, "Come into the Holy Place," would have been better translated, "within the Veil." These two Offerings were not for Israel, but rather for Aaron himself. He was ever reminded that even though he was the Great High Priest chosen of God, and chosen to stand between God and Israel, still, he was but a sinner and, thereby, had to offer up Sacrifice the same as the most ungodly in Israel.)*

4 He shall put on the holy linen coat *(representing the Righteousness of Christ; he was to divest himself of his garments of glory and beauty, meaning that Jesus did not redeem us by His Glory, but rather by His Righteousness; he was the Perfect, Righteous Sacrifice; therefore, He was accepted by God)*, and he shall have the linen breeches upon his flesh, and shall be

girded with a linen girdle, and with the linen mitre shall he be attired: these are holy garments *("linen" in the Old Testament represented Righteousness [Rev. 19:14])*; therefore shall he wash his flesh in water, and so put them on *(he must be "personally" and "characteristically" pure and spotless).*

5 And he shall take of the congregation of the Children of Israel two kids of the goats for a Sin Offering, and one ram for a Burnt Offering *(these Offerings were for Israel).*

6 And Aaron shall offer his bullock of the Sin Offering, which is for himself, and make an Atonement for himself, and for his house *(he had to offer these Sacrifices for himself, before he could offer Sacrifices for Israel).*

7 And he shall take the two goats, and present them before the LORD at the door of the Tabernacle of the congregation *(according to tradition, the two goats were to be the same in size, color, and value, and as nearly alike as possible).*

8 And Aaron shall cast lots upon the two goats; one lot for the LORD, and the other lot for the scapegoat *(one goat would be offered in Sacrifice, and the other would be sent alive into the wilderness, and called the "goat of departure").*

9 And Aaron shall bring the goat upon which the LORD's lot fell, and offer him for a Sin Offering *(the two goats represented and completed one Atonement for sin; the goat that died typified the Death of Christ, which addressed the root cause of sin; the scapegoat represented all acts of sin removed and taken away).*

10 But the goat, on which the lot fell to be the scapegoat, shall be presented alive before the LORD, to make an Atonement with him, and to let him go for a scapegoat into the wilderness *(when the goat was led into the wilderness, Atonement was complete; the sins transferred figuratively on the goat were already atoned for, and blood was sprinkled before the Lord; both animals represented one Sin Offering).*

THE SIN OFFERING FOR THE
HIGH PRIEST AND HIS FAMILY

11 And Aaron shall bring the bullock of the Sin Offering, which is for himself, and shall make an Atonement for himself, and for his house, and shall kill the bullock of the Sin Offering which is for himself:

12 And he shall take a censer full of burning coals of fire from off the Altar *(the Brazen*

Altar) before the LORD, and his hands full of sweet incense beaten small, and bring it within the Veil *(fire from the Brazen Altar, typifying Christ and the Cross, was the only fire acceptable; any other fire was "strange fire," and would bring death):*

13 And he shall put the incense upon the fire before the LORD, that the cloud of the incense may cover the Mercy Seat that is upon the Testimony, that he die not *(the incense was made of the particular spices of "Stacte," "Onycha," "Galbanum," with "pure Frankincense" [Ex. 30:34]. Holding the censer containing the coals of fire from the Brazen Altar in one hand, and the container with the Incense in the other hand, the High Priest went through the Veil that separated the Holy Place from the Holy of Holies, and advanced to the Ark of the Covenant, where he deposited the censer between its two staves.*

The High Priest now poured the crushed spices upon the coals in the censer, and stayed there until the whole place was filled with a cloud of smoke, taking special care that the Mercy Seat and the Cherubim should be enveloped in the cloud. If this wasn't done properly, he could be stricken dead. The "Incense" typified the Intercession of Christ, which He has offered on behalf of all Saints, from the time of the Cross):

14 And he shall take of the blood of the bullock, and sprinkle it with his finger upon the Mercy Seat eastward *(the solemn ritual of the Great Day of Atonement declared that entrance into the Presence of God was barred to the sinner, and that the blood of bulls and goats could not rend the Veil that shut men out from God.*

It further declared that atoning blood was the basis for entrance to God's Throne; hence, the nearer the worshipper approached to that Throne, the greater was the value attached to the Blood shed at the Brazen Altar. In fact, the entire way from the Brazen Altar by the Brazen Laver, the Golden Altar, and the Veil, and up to the Throne, represented by the Ark of the Covenant, was a blood-sprinkled way.

Standing before the Ark of the Covenant, in the midst of the cloud furnished by the Incense upon the coals of fire, he would dip his finger in the blood of the slain bullock, and sprinkle it upon the Mercy Seat); and before the Mercy Seat shall he sprinkle of the Blood with his finger seven times *(sprinkled "seven times" on the Mercy Seat signified that the Redemption afforded by Christ would be a perfect Redemption).*

THE SIN OFFERING FOR THE PEOPLE

15 Then shall he kill the goat of the Sin Offering, that is for the people, and bring his blood within the Veil, and do with that blood as he did with the blood of the bullock, and sprinkle it upon the Mercy Seat, and before the Mercy Seat *(Aaron will now enter the Holy of Holies for the third time; the first time he offered Incense, and the second time he offered the blood of the bullock for himself and his family; this time he will enter in regard to Israel as a whole; we learn from this, by the entrance of the High Priest into the Holy of Holies, that Atonement could only be effected before the Throne of Jehovah; as well, only the Blood of Christ, typified by these particular Sacrifices, could make that Atonement)*:

16 And he shall make an Atonement for the Holy Place, because of the uncleanness of the Children of Israel, and because of their transgressions in all their sins: and so shall he do for the Tabernacle of the congregation, that remains among them in the midst of their uncleanness *(even though these were God's chosen people, they still needed Atonement; as well, only the Blood of Christ, typified by these particular Sacrifices, could make that Atonement; so this means, as ought to be obvious, that any other proposed way of Salvation, any other proposed means of Salvation, in fact, anything instituted by man, will instantly be unacceptable to God; only the Blood of Jesus Christ, God's Son, can "cleanse from all sin" [I Jn. 1:7])*.

17 And there shall be no man in the Tabernacle of the congregation when he goes in to make an Atonement in the Holy Place, until he come out, and have made an Atonement for himself, and for his household, and for all the congregation of Israel. *(When the High Priest atoned for the Holy Place, no man was to be present other than himself. This nullifies all the arguments and practices of pretentious Priesthoods that make claims of direct representation as mediators between God and the people, while Christ is in the Heavenly Tabernacle, as now, carrying on His Priestly Work [Heb. 4:14-16; 5:1-14]. Christ is the only Mediator between God and men [I Tim. 2:4-6; Heb. 9:24].)*

18 And he shall go out unto the Altar that is before the LORD *(the Altar of Incense, which sat immediately in front of the Veil in the Holy Place)*, and make an Atonement for it; and shall take of the blood of the bullock, and of the blood of the goat, and put it upon the horns of the Altar round about *(horns in the Bible signify dominion or rulership; the idea is, by the blood being applied to these horns, which spoke of what Christ would do for us at the Cross, the fact that the horns pointed in all four directions of the compass signifies that we can have, and, in fact, are meant to have, total and complete dominion over all works of the flesh; we are told how to do this in the Sixth Chapter of Romans)*.

19 And he shall sprinkle of the blood upon it with his finger seven times, and cleanse it, and hallow it from the uncleanness of the Children of Israel *(the blood sprinkled "seven times" signifies a total dominion; in other words, what Christ did for us at the Cross, if we follow God's Prescribed Order, no sin will have dominion over us, but only if we follow His Order [Rom. 6:14])*.

THE SCAPEGOAT

20 And when he has made an end of reconciling the Holy Place, and the Tabernacle of the congregation, and the Altar, he shall bring the live goat:

21 And Aaron shall lay both his hands upon the head of the live goat, and confess over him all the iniquities of the Children of Israel, and all their transgressions in all their sins, putting them upon the head of the goat *(inasmuch as the blood of bulls and goats could not take away sins [Heb. 10:4], the conscience of the people of Israel was not eased; there was still a nagging knowledge, so to speak, that the sins remained [Heb. 9:9]; this being the case, something else was needed, something visible, which could portray their sins being removed; that which filled this void was the scapegoat)*, and shall send him away by the hand of a fit man into the wilderness *(this "fit man" was one who had been appointed for the occasion)*:

22 And the goat shall bear upon him all their iniquities unto a land not inhabited: and he shall let go the goat in the wilderness. *(As stated, this goat was actually labeled "the goat of departure," which referred to the sins of the people departing from them, which, in a sense, gave them a visible sign that their sins were now atoned. Concerning this, Keil says: "The reason for making use of two animals is to be found purely in the physical impossibility of combining all features that had to be set forth in the Sin Offering in one animal.")*

23 And Aaron shall come into the Tabernacle of the congregation, and shall put off the linen garments, which he put on when he went

into the Holy Place, and shall leave them there *(the work of Atonement now finished, Aaron could once again put on his garments of glory and beauty)*:

24 And he shall wash his flesh with water in the holy place, and put on his garments, and come forth, and offer his Burnt Offering, and the Burnt Offering of the people, and make an Atonement for himself, and for the people. *(The "Sin Offerings" now presented, which means that sin is atoned, the "Burnt Offerings" can now be offered, which will be two rams, one for himself, and one for the people. The "Sin Offering" proclaimed the sins of Israel being taken by Christ, so now the "Burnt Offerings" can be engaged, which means that the Perfection of Christ can be given to Aaron and the people.)*

25 And the fat of the Sin Offering shall he burn upon the Altar *(the "fat" was always burned on the Altar, regardless of the type of Offering, typifying the prosperity of Christ given to those who would accept Him as Lord and Redeemer; a sickly animal had very little, if any, fat, while a healthy animal, as would be obvious, would have fat surrounding the various internal organs)*.

26 And he who let go the goat for the scapegoat shall wash his clothes, and bathe his flesh in water, and afterward come into the camp *(we derive from this the fact of the defilement of sin; any contact with the scapegoat, because it was bearing the sins of Israel, defiled the one making the contact)*.

27 And the bullock for the Sin Offering, and the goat for the Sin Offering, whose blood was brought in to make Atonement in the Holy Place, shall one carry forth without the camp; and they shall burn in the fire their skins, and their flesh, and their dung *(the majority of the Sin Offering was eaten by the Priests [10:17-18], signifying the taking of Christ in totality, which is done by expressing faith in Him and what He did at the Cross [Jn. 6:53-56]; while the "fat" was burned on the Altar, the residue, such as the "skin," etc., was taken outside the camp and burned, signifying that Christ, as the Sin Offering, died outside the camp [Heb. 13:11-12]; as well, the residue reduced to ashes signified that our sins are no more)*.

28 And he who burns them shall wash his clothes, and bathe his flesh in water, and afterward he shall come into the camp *(the one who burned the skins of the animals, etc.)*.

THE DAY OF ATONEMENT

29 And this shall be a Statute for ever unto you: that in the seventh month, on the tenth day of the month, you shall afflict your souls, and do no work at all, whether it be one of your own country, or a stranger who sojourns among you *(the Great Day of Atonement was the only "fast" day a year for Israel; the purpose of the abstinence from food and labor was to bring the soul of each individual into harmony with the solemn rites of purification publicly performed, not by themselves, but by the High Priest)*:

30 For on that day shall the Priest make an Atonement for you, to cleanse you, that you may be clean from all your sins before the LORD.

31 It shall be a Sabbath day of rest unto you, and you shall afflict your souls, by a Statute for ever *(the Great Day of Atonement was observed more or less until the Babylonian captivity, and afterward in their restoration until the destruction of Jerusalem in A.D. 70)*.

32 And the Priest, whom he shall anoint, and whom he shall consecrate to minister in the Priest's office in his father's stead, shall make the Atonement, and shall put on the linen clothes, even the holy garments *(the idea of this Verse pertains to the succession of High Priests who would follow down through the centuries)*:

33 And he shall make an Atonement for the Holy Sanctuary, and he shall make an Atonement for the Tabernacle of the congregation, and for the Altar, and he shall make an Atonement for the Priests, and for all the people of the congregation. *(All the High Priests who would follow Aaron were to perform the service of expiation of sin, as detailed in this Chapter.)*

34 And this shall be an everlasting Statute unto you, to make an Atonement for the Children of Israel for all their sins once a year. And he *(Aaron)* did as the LORD commanded Moses. *(The "Everlasting Statute" lasted as long as the Earthly Jerusalem lasted, and until the Heavenly Jerusalem, so to speak, was instituted, when it had a spiritual fulfillment once for all. In other words, Jesus Christ, by His Life and living, and, above all, by the Sacrificial, Atoning Sacrifice of Himself, fulfilled all of the Law of Moses. In fact, Christ was, one might say, "The Great Day of Atonement," referring to an enlightened day that will never end, and a darkness which has been dispelled forever.)*

CHAPTER 17
(1490 B.C.)
ONE PLACE OF SACRIFICE

AND the LORD spoke unto Moses, saying *(if it is to be noticed, over and over again this phrase is used, signifying that all was of God and nothing at all of man; in other words, Moses must not deviate from what the Lord had told him; this is a lesson that religious man finds very difficult to obey)*,

2 Speak unto Aaron, and unto his sons, and unto all the Children of Israel, and say unto them; This is the thing which the LORD has commanded, saying,

3 What man soever there be of the house of Israel, who kills an ox, or lamb, or goat, in the camp, or who kills it out of the camp *(should have been translated "sacrifices," in the place of "kills")*,

4 And brings it not unto the door of the Tabernacle of the congregation, to offer an Offering unto the LORD before the Tabernacle of the LORD; blood shall be imputed unto that man; he has shed blood; and that man shall be cut off from among his people *(Mackintosh says: "A man might say, Can I not offer a Sacrifice in one place as well as another? The answer is, Life belongs to God, and His claim thereto must be recognized in the place where He has appointed — before the Tabernacle of the Lord. That was the only meeting-place between God and man. To offer elsewhere proved that the heart did not want God.*

"The moral of this is plain. There is one place where God has appointed to meet the sinner, and that is the Cross — the antitype of the Brazen Altar. There and there alone has God's claims upon the life been duly recognized. To reject this meeting-place is to bring down judgment upon one's self — it is to trample underfoot the just claims of God, and to arrogate to one's self a right to life which all have forfeited"):

5 To the end that the Children of Israel may bring their Sacrifices, which they offer in the open field *(which they have been offering in the open field)*, even that they may bring them unto the LORD, unto the door of the Tabernacle of the congregation, unto the Priest, and offer them for Peace Offerings unto the LORD *(in essence, some three times the warning is given concerning the offering up of Sacrifices in places except the Tabernacle, or Temple, that is, when the Temple would be built [Vss. 4, 7, 10])*.

6 And the Priest shall sprinkle the blood upon the Altar of the LORD at the door of the Tabernacle of the congregation, and burn the fat for a sweet savour unto the LORD. *(Expositors say: "The Blood of Christ is the foundation of everything. It is the ground of God's Righteousness in justifying an ungodly sinner who believes on the Name of the Son of God; and it is the ground of the sinner's confidence in drawing near to a Holy God, Who is of purer eyes than to behold evil. God would be just in the condemnation of the sinner; but through the Death of Christ, He can be just and the Justifier of him who believes — a just God and a Saviour.*

"The Righteousness of God is His consistency with Himself — His acting in harmony with His revealed character. Hence, were it not for the Cross, His consistency with Himself would, of necessity, demand the death and judgment of the sinner; but in the Cross, that death and judgment were borne by the sinner's surety, so that the same Divine consistency is perfectly maintained, while a Holy God justifies an ungodly sinner through Faith. It is all through the Blood of Jesus — nothing less, nothing more, and nothing different.")

7 And they shall no more offer their sacrifices unto devils, after whom they have gone a whoring, This shall be Statute for ever unto them throughout their generations *(by the use of the words "no more," we know that the Children of Israel, or at least some of them, did sacrifice unto devils while in Egypt; the short phrase "Statute forever" means exactly what it says; the Cross is the Way of Salvation, and it will never change; Paul referred to it as "The Everlasting Covenant" [Heb. 13:20])*.

8 And you shall say unto them, Whatsoever man there be of the house of Israel, or of the strangers which sojourn among you, who offers a Burnt Offering or sacrifice,

9 And brings it not unto the door of the Tabernacle of the congregation, to offer it unto the LORD; even that man shall be cut off from among his people *(once again the warning is given about offering sacrifices in places other than at "the door of the Tabernacle"; this typifies one Sacrifice, the Lord Jesus Christ; and one place of Sacrifice, the Cross of Calvary)*.

THE EATING OF BLOOD FORBIDDEN

10 And whatsoever man there be of the house of Israel, or of the strangers who sojourn among you, who eats any manner of blood; I will even set my face against that soul

who eats blood, and will cut him off from among his people *(the blood represents life, and, above all, the Life of Christ poured out on behalf of lost sinners; this prohibition was as well carried over into the New Covenant [Acts 15:19-20]).*

11 For the life of the flesh is in the blood *(it should be translated "for the soul of the flesh is in the blood"; the Hebrew word here rendered "life" occurs twice more in this very Verse, and is properly translated "soul"):* and I have given it to you upon the Altar to make an Atonement for your souls: for it is the blood *(the Blood of Christ)* that makes an Atonement for the soul. *(This latter phrase plainly and purely tells us that the Death of Christ on the Cross, which was brought about by the shedding of His Precious Blood, which means that in the shedding of His Blood, His Life poured out, is not only the means of Salvation, but, in fact, is the only means of Salvation.*

The expositor says: "When man duly takes his place as one possessing no title whatsoever to life — when he fully recognizes God's claims upon him, then the Divine record is, 'I have given you the life to make an Atonement for your soul.' Yes, Atonement is God's gift to man; and be it carefully noted that this Atonement is in the Blood, and only in the Blood, and we speak of the Blood of Christ. It is not the Blood and something else. The Word is most explicit. It attributes Atonement exclusively to the Blood" [Heb. 9:22; Eph. 1:7; Col. 1:14; I Jn. 1:6; Rev., Chpt. 12].)

12 Therefore I said unto the Children of Israel, No soul of you shall eat blood, neither shall any stranger who sojourns among you eat blood.

13 And whatsoever man there be of the Children of Israel, or of the strangers *(Gentiles)* who sojourn among you, which hunts and catches any beast or fowl that may be eaten; he shall even pour out the blood thereof, and cover it with dust.

14 For it is the life of all flesh; the blood of it is for the life thereof: therefore I said unto the Children of Israel, You shall eat the blood of no manner of flesh: for the life of all flesh is the blood thereof: whosoever eats it shall be cut off *(considering the sternness of the warnings given, and considering that this prohibition, as stated, was carried over as well into the New Covenant, we should realize how significant these words are, and how so very much the Lord means exactly what He says; for Him to say*

something one time is of extreme significance, for Him to say it two times, and even three or more, the point should be well taken).*

15 And every soul who eats that which died of itself, or that which was torn with beasts, whether it be one of your own country, or a stranger *(Gentile)*, he shall both wash his clothes, and bathe himself in water, and be unclean until the evening: then shall he be clean.

16 But if he wash them not, nor bathe his flesh; then he shall bear his iniquity *(the problem of the human race is that it does not take the Word of God very seriously, or does not consider it at all; but let all understand, there are consequences, severe consequences, to ignoring the Word of God).*

CHAPTER 18
(1490 B.C.)
INCEST FORBIDDEN

A ND the LORD spoke unto Moses, saying,

2 Speak unto the Children of Israel, and say unto them, I am the LORD your God. *(In this Chapter, we will have revealed to us the Character of God, and the character of man. We will see that the character of man is desperately evil. This is the condition of man without God, and, as is painfully obvious, none are excluded.)*

3 After the doings of the land of Egypt, wherein you dwelt, shall you not do: and after the doings of the land of Canaan, where I will bring you, shall you not do: neither shall you walk in their ordinances. *(The expositors say, "It was not, by any means, the judgment of an Israelite in opposition to the judgment of an Egyptian or of a Canaanite; but it was the Judgment of God above all. Egypt might have her practices and her opinions, and so might Canaan; but Israel was to have the opinions and practices laid down in the Word of God, even as we shall see in the next two Verses.")*

4 You shall do My Judgments, and keep My Ordinances, to walk therein: I am the LORD your God *(the Word of the Lord must always be the criteria for all things).*

5 You shall therefore keep My Statutes, and My Judgments: which if a man do, he shall live in them: I am the LORD. *(Our life and living must always be based strictly upon the Word. And as we learn the Word, we will find that the short phrase, "Jesus Christ and Him Crucified," is the story of the Word, meaning that the Cross*

is the provision for all, and the only provision for all.)

6 None of you shall approach to any who is near of kin to him, to uncover their nakedness: I am the LORD *(incest is forbidden)*.

7 The nakedness of your father, or the nakedness of your mother, shall you not uncover: she is your mother; you shall not uncover her nakedness.

8 The nakedness of your father's wife shall you not uncover: it is your father's nakedness.

9 The nakedness of your sister, the daughter of your father, or daughter of your mother, whether she be born at home, or born abroad, even their nakedness you shall not uncover.

10 The nakedness of your son's daughter, or of your daughter's daughter, even their nakedness you shall not uncover: for their's is your own nakedness.

11 The nakedness of your father's wife's daughter, begotten of your father, she is your sister, you shall not uncover her nakedness.

12 You shall not uncover the nakedness of your father's sister: she is your father's near kinswoman.

13 You shall not uncover the nakedness of your mother's sister: for she is your mother's near kinswoman.

14 You shall not uncover the nakedness of your father's brother, you shall not approach to his wife: she is your aunt.

15 You shall not uncover the nakedness of your daughter-in-law: she is your son's wife; you shall not uncover her nakedness.

16 You shall not uncover the nakedness of your brother's wife: it is your brother's nakedness.

17 You shall not uncover the nakedness of a woman and her daughter, neither shall you take her son's daughter, or her daughter's daughter, to uncover her nakedness; for they are her near kinswomen: it is wickedness.

18 Neither shall you take a wife to her sister, to vex her, to uncover her nakedness, beside the other in her life time. *(The word "nakedness" refers to sexual intercourse, whether in the bonds of incestuous marriage, which marriage would be sinful, or outside of the bonds of marriage, which would be fornication. Concerning these things, Pulpit says, "Verses 6 through 19 contain the law of incest, or the prohibited degrees of marriage. The positive law of marriage, as implanted in the human heart, would be simply that any man of full age might marry any woman of full age, provided that both*

parties were willing. But this liberty is at once controlled by a number of restrictions, the main purpose of which is to prevent incest, which, however much one nation may come to be indifferent to one form of it, and other to another, is yet abhorrent to the feelings and principles of mankind. The Hebrew restrictive law is contained in one Verse, 'None of you shall approach to any who is near of kin to him, to uncover their nakedness: I am the LORD.'
"In fact, all these Verses are simply an amplification and an explanation of the words, 'near of kin to him.'")

IMMORALITY

19 Also you shall not approach unto a woman to uncover her nakedness, as long as she is put apart for her uncleanness *(refers to a woman's monthly period)*.

20 Moreover you shall not lie carnally with your neighbour's wife, to defile yourself with her *(the prohibition against adultery)*.

21 And you shall not let any of your seed pass through the fire to Molech *(this was the so-called deity associated with Ammon, which was a neighbor of Israel [I Ki. 11:7]; this idol was called "the abomination of the Ammonites," and was associated with the sacrifice of children in the fire [Lev. 20:2-5; II Ki. 17:31; 23:10; Jer. 32:35]; "Molech" is also sometimes called "Milcom")*, neither shall you profane the Name of your God: I am the LORD. *(The idea is that under no circumstances were children to be offered up to Idols in sacrifice, which was the abominable habit of the heathen, and actually world-wide in scope.)*

22 You shall not lie with mankind, as with womankind: it is abomination *(proclaims the terrible sin of the abomination of homosexuality; whatever man says, God says it is an abomination; God help America to see the awfulness of homosexual marriages)*.

23 Neither shall you lie with any beast to defile yourself therewith: neither shall any woman stand before a beast to lie down thereto: it is confusion. *(Concerning this sin, Ellicott says: "The necessity for the prohibition of this shocking crime, for which the Mosaic Law enacts the penalty of death [Lev. 20:15-16; Ex. 22:18], will appear all the more important when it is borne in mind that this degrading practice actually formed a part of the religious worship of the Egyptians in connection with the goat deities. In other words, the Israelites were very*

familiar with this perversion, having lived in Egypt for so long."

It is said that the disease of syphilis originated with men cohabiting with sheep.)

WARNINGS

24 Defile not ye yourselves in any of these things: for in all these the nations are defiled which I cast out before you:

25 And the land is defiled: therefore I do visit the iniquity thereof upon it, and the land itself vomits out her inhabitants. *(From the creation, the Earth itself shared in the punishment of man's guilt [Gen. 3:17], and, at the restitution of all things, she is to participate in man's restoration [Rom. 8:19-22]. The physical condition of the land, therefore, at least after a measure, depends on the moral conduct of man. That's the reason that most nations cannot feed themselves. And what little true Christianity there is in America is the reason for the abundant harvests; however, we are fastly losing what little Christianity we presently have, and that points to a dire future.)*

26 You shall therefore keep My Statutes and My judgments, and shall not commit any of these abominations *(obey the Word of the Lord)*; neither any of your own nation, nor any stranger who sojourns among you *(don't allow the heathen to practice their abominations in the land of Israel; God help America in the opening of her arms to the abominable religion of Islam)*:

27 (For all these abominations have the men of the land done, which were before you, and the land is defiled;) *(in other words, that's the reason I'm going to dispel the Canaanites who presently occupy the land of Canaan, and give it to you).*

28 That the land spue not you out also, when you defile it, as it spued out the nations that were before you *(in other words, if you ignore My Word, I will vomit you out, even though you are My chosen people, just as I vomited out the heathen; and that's exactly what happened).*

29 For whosoever shall commit any of these abominations, even the souls who commit them shall be cut off from among their people *(the warning is given).*

30 Therefore shall you keep My Ordinance, that you commit not any one of these abominable customs, which were committed before you, and that you defile not yourselves therein: I am the LORD your God. *(The last phrase*

lends a weight to these Commandments that is beyond compare. His Word better be heeded, now as well as then.)*

CHAPTER 19
(1490 B.C.)
HOLINESS

AND the LORD spoke unto Moses, saying,

2 Speak unto all the congregation of the Children of Israel, and say unto them, You shall be holy: for I the LORD your God am holy. *(Before the Cross, Israelites were severely limited in their ability to keep the Word of God. It was because animal blood was insufficient to take away the sin of man; consequently, the Holy Spirit, without Whose help Holiness cannot be perfected, was severely limited. After the Cross, which addressed in totality the sin debt, taking it all away, the Holy Spirit can now abide permanently within the hearts and lives of Believers, and will help us to live holy, providing our faith is ever placed in Christ and the Cross [Jn. 14:16-17; 16:7-14; Rom. 8:1-2, 11].)*

HONOR PARENTS; KEEP THE SABBATH

3 You shall fear every man his mother, and his father *(render due honor to parents)*, and keep My Sabbaths: I am the LORD your God *(the Sabbath in the Old Testament was a type of the "rest" which would be had in Christ when He came; trusting Christ and what He has done for us at the Cross constitutes, presently, the keeping of Sabbaths; since the Cross, the word "Sabbath" has nothing to do with a day or time, but rather Christ).*

IDOLATRY

4 Turn ye not unto idols, nor make to yourselves molten gods: I am the LORD your God. *(Anything presently which adds to "Christ and Him Crucified," or ignores it altogether, is idolatry. In fact, religion is the greatest idol of all.)*

THE PEACE OFFERING

5 And if you offer a Sacrifice of Peace Offerings unto the LORD, you shall offer it at your own will *(could include a lamb, a goat, or a bullock [Lev., Chpt. 3]. It signified that peace had been restored between this particular individual who had brought the Offering and God.*

The phrase, "You shall offer it at your own will," would have been better translated, "You shall offer it for your acceptance." If the Offering was accepted, the offerer was accepted as well, because the Offering was a Type of Christ).

6 It shall be eaten the same day you offer it, and on the morrow: and if ought remain until the third day, it shall be burnt in the fire. *(All the Offering was to be consumed in the allotted time, which typified Christ being totally accepted. Some of the Offering being left over for the third day, or even later, in essence, said that Christ was not being accepted totally in that which He did for us, which, in fact, pertains to the Cross.)*

7 And if it be eaten at all on the third day, it is abominable; it shall not be accepted *(as stated, if the Offering was rejected by God, then the offerer was rejected, as well; Cain is a perfect example of this [Gen., Chpt. 4]).*

8 Therefore every one who eats it *(eats it after the second day)* shall bear his iniquity *(shall be held responsible by God for sinning),* because he has profaned the hallowed thing of the LORD *(because it pointed strictly to Christ):* and that soul shall be cut off from among his people *(if he does not repent).*

LAW OF GLEANINGS

9 And when you reap the harvest of your land, you shall not wholly reap the corners of your field, neither shall you gather the gleanings of your harvest.

10 And you shall not glean your vineyard, neither shall you gather every grape of your vineyard; you shall leave them for the poor and stranger: I am the LORD your God *(the object of this Law is to inculcate a general spirit of mercy, which is willing to give up its own exact rights in kindness to others suffering from want; it is to be done in the spirit of Christ, Who has given us everything, in fact, the greatest gift of all, Salvation purchased at great price; this means that presently our spirit, attitude, and personality must always be in the capacity of the spirit of the Cross).*

PROHIBITIONS

11 You shall not steal, neither deal falsely *(the Eighth Commandment),* neither lie one to another *(the Ninth Commandment [Ex., Chpt. 20]).*

12 And you shall not swear by My Name falsely, neither shall you profane the Name of your God: I am the LORD *(the Third Commandment).*

OPPRESSION

13 You shall not defraud your neighbour, neither rob him: the wages of him who is hired shall not abide with you all night until the morning *(in other words, common laborers were to be paid each day at the end of the day, because their needs were great).*

14 You shall not curse the deaf, nor put a stumblingblock before the blind, but shall fear your God: I am the LORD *(all who were handicapped were to be treated with the deepest compassion).*

15 You shall do no unrighteousness in judgment: you shall not respect the person of the poor, nor honour the person of the mighty: but in righteousness shall you judge your neighbour *(the poor must not be allowed to break the Law because they are poor, and the rich must not be allowed to break the Law because they are rich; all are to be treated, as it regards the Law, equally).*

FALSE WITNESS

16 You shall not go up and down as a talebearer among your people *(would have been better translated, "You shall not go about slandering"):* neither shall you stand against the blood of your neighbour; I am the LORD *(refers to the fact of lying against a fellowman, which could cause his death; the short phrase, "I am the LORD," in effect says if this be done, the Lord will have vengeance on the perpetrator [Rom. 12:18-19]).*

LOVE

17 You shall not hate your brother in your heart: you shall in any wise rebuke your neighbour, and not suffer sin upon him *(Jesus addressed this in Matthew 18:15-17).*

18 You shall not avenge, nor bear any grudge against the children of your people, but you shall love your neighbour as yourself: I am the LORD *(fulfills the second half of the entirety of the Ten Commandments).*

SEPARATION

19 You shall keep My Statutes. You shall not

let your cattle gender with a diverse kind: you shall not sow your field with mingled seed: neither shall a garment mingled of linen and wool come upon you. *(The spiritual application of this Passage presently has to do with the mixing of false doctrine with the True. Paul said: "You cannot drink the cup of the Lord, and the cup of devils" [I Cor. 10:21]. Hooker says: "He cannot love the Lord Jesus with all his heart who lends one ear to His Apostles and another to false teachers.")*

SEXUAL ACTIVITY

20 And whosoever lies carnally with a woman *(sexual intercourse)*, who is a bondmaid *(a slave, or else a woman who was working in a certain household for a period of time in order to pay off a debt)*, betrothed to an husband *(engaged to be married to someone else)*, and not at all redeemed, nor freedom given her; she shall be scourged *(for committing this act)*; they shall not be put to death *(the man and the woman)*, because she was not free *(the death penalty was not demanded because she was not free to make a choice; but yet, she was still guilty, so scourging was required)*.

21 And he shall bring his Trespass Offering unto the LORD *(the man has sinned against the woman)*, unto the door of the Tabernacle of the congregation, even a ram for a Trespass Offering *(thereby suffering the expense of doing such, which was the punishment for the man committing this sin)*.

22 And the Priest shall make an Atonement for him with the ram of the Trespass Offering before the LORD for his sin which he has done: and the sin which he has done shall be forgiven him *(the basic idea of this prohibition concerns itself not so much with the sin of adultery as it does cohabiting with someone who is engaged to be married to another; adultery is forbidden in any case, but the sin compounds itself, if committed with one who is engaged to be married to someone else)*.

FRUIT

23 And when you shall come into the land, and shall have planted all manner of trees for food, then you shall count the fruit thereof as uncircumcised: three years shall it be as uncircumcised unto you: it shall not be eaten of. *(It is said that fruit trees yield better fruit afterwards if the blossoms be nipped off ["circumcised"]*

during the earliest years. It is even said that the fruit of the first year is unwholesome.)

24 But in the fourth year all the fruit thereof shall be holy to praise the LORD withal. *(In the fourth year, the fruit was to be dedicated to the Lord. It was offered up to Him with songs of praise; perhaps with festival songs, as in that seen in the vineyards of Shiloh [Judg. 21:19-21].)*

25 And in the fifth year shall you eat of the fruit thereof, that it may yield unto you the increase thereof: I am the LORD your God. *(This entire precept was in some way a memorial of the "forbidden tree of paradise." Every fruit tree was to stand unused for three years, as a test of obedience. Every stranger saw, in Israel's orchards and vineyards, proof of their obedience to their supreme Lord — a witness for Him. And what a solemn shadow they cast over the fallen sons of Adam there, reminding them of the first father's sin. As well, "five" is God's number of Grace. As fruit was allowed to develop, likewise, Believers are to develop in the Lord, and can do so only by the Grace of God [Jn. 15:1-8].)*

PAGAN PRACTICES

26 You shall not eat any thing with the blood *(blood was not to be eaten, and, in fact, was, in a sense, to be held sacred)*: neither shall you use enchantment, nor observe times *(any type of superstition was to be avoided)*.

27 You shall not round the corners of your heads, neither shall you mar the corners of your beard *(all had to do with superstition, and must not be engaged by God's people)*.

28 You shall not make any cuttings in your flesh for the dead, nor print any marks upon you: I am the LORD. *(Pagans were accustomed to making small incisions in their physical bodies, or to putting marks upon their flesh as a sign of mourning for their loved ones who had recently died. But the Lord forbade anything of this nature among His people.*

The incision represented a separation and, in fact, an eternal separation, in the minds of the pagans. In essence, by the Lord commanding His people to not engage in such activities, He, in effect, was telling them that death, that is if they would faithfully serve Him, did not end it all. In other words, if their loved ones had been in the Covenant, and had Faith in the Covenant, and the ones living continued to have Faith in the Covenant, they would see each other again.)

PROSTITUTION

29 Do not prostitute your daughter, to cause her to be a whore; lest the land fall to whoredom, and the land become full of wickedness. *(This refers to the worship of heathen gods, which demanded temple prostitutes, and which was common among the heathen. Israel must not engage in such.*

As well, all adultery and fornication were a violation of the Second and the Seventh Commandments [Ex. 20:4, 14]. In fact, there must be no form of sexual immorality among God's people. The people of the Lord must be clean physically and morally.)

THE SABBATH AND THE SANCTUARY

30 You shall keep My Sabbaths *(the Sabbath was not actually a day of worship, but rather a day of "rest"; it was so important, because it pictured in type the "rest" which would be afforded by Christ when He would come; so when a Christian presently serves the Lord, he has entered into His "rest" and, by doing this, is, at the same time, keeping the Sabbath — a Spiritual Sabbath [Mat. 11:28-30]),* and reverence My Sanctuary: I am the LORD *(then it referred to a Tabernacle or Temple; now it refers to the physical body and mind [I Cor. 3:16; Rom. 12:1-2]).*

THE OCCULT

31 Regard not them who have familiar spirits *(a "familiar spirit" is a demon spirit that is invisible, which possesses the individual, and helps that person relate certain things to those who seek counsel and advice),* neither seek after wizards, to be defiled by them *(functions in the occult, pretending to tell the people answers to their questions):* I am the LORD your God *(we as Believers are to have no association with such works of darkness; we are to be led strictly by the Holy Spirit [Jn. 16:13-15]).*

HONOR

32 You shall rise up before the hoary head, and honour the face of the old man, and fear your God: I am the LORD *(respect is to be shown to the aged; however, it goes deeper here than that; it refers to one who, by experience and age, has great knowledge of the Lord and God's Word; they are to be deeply respected for that knowledge).*

OPPRESSION

33 And if a stranger sojourn with you in your land, you shall not vex him *(pertains to a Gentile who had willingly come under the Covenant of Abraham).*

34 But the stranger who dwells with you shall be unto you as one born among you, and you shall love him as yourself; for you were strangers in the land of Egypt: I am the LORD your God *(a proselyte was to be treated exactly as another Jew).*

INJUSTICE

35 You shall do no unrighteousness in judgment, in meteyard, in weight, or in measure *(portrays honesty in all things).*

36 Just balances, just weights, a just ephah, and a just hin, shall you have: I am the LORD your God, which brought you out of the land of Egypt *(as well, as modern Believers we are to look at these commands as presently being incumbent upon us, just as they were upon Israel).*

37 Therefore shall you observe all My Statues, and all My Judgments, and do them: I am the LORD *(the Lord didn't say that Israel was to observe some of His Statutes and Commandments, but rather all of them).*

CHAPTER 20
(1490 B.C.)
SEVERE PENALTIES

AND the LORD spoke unto Moses, saying *(the constant use of this statement proclaims that all of this is the Word of the Lord and, therefore, must not be changed in any manner, and must be adhered to strictly),*

2 Again, you shall say to the Children of Israel, Whosoever he be of the Children of Israel, or of the strangers *(Gentiles)* who sojourn in Israel, who gives any of his seed *(his children)* unto Molech *(as stated, the Ammonite god);* he shall surely be put to death: the people of the land shall stone him with stones *(this particular sin was looked at as a capital crime, which, if continued, would destroy Israel, which sadly it ultimately did; its penalty was death by stoning).*

3 And I will set My face against that man, and will cut him off from among his people *(if he does not repent, he will be eternally lost);* because he has given of his seed unto Molech, to defile My Sanctuary, and to profane My Holy

Name *(under the New Covenant, the Sanctuary of the Lord is the physical body and mind of the Believer; idolatry, which this is, and which presently stands for anything in which one places one's faith other than Christ and the Cross, will ultimately bring destruction on the individual, if Repentance is not forthcoming [I Cor. 3:16-17]).*

4 And if the people of the land do any ways hide their eyes from the man, when he gives of his seed unto Molech, and kill him not:

5 Then I will set My face against that man, and against his family, and will cut him off, and all that go a whoring after him, to commit whoredom with Molech, from among their people *(the present meaning is that if a true Preacher of the Gospel does not stand up against false doctrine, God will ultimately visit such a Preacher with judgment, with the possibility being that he could definitely lose his soul [Ezek. 3:17-21]).*

THE OCCULT

6 And the soul who turns after such as have familiar spirits, and after wizards, to go whoring after them, I will even set My face against that soul, and will cut him off from among his people *(presently, any direction that's not "Christ and Him Crucified" falls, in one way or the other, into occultism, irrespective of the religious face it carries [I Cor. 1:17-18, 23; 2:2]).*

HOLINESS

7 Sanctify yourselves therefore, and be ye holy: for I am the LORD your God.

8 And you shall keep My statutes, and do them: I am the LORD which sanctify you *(Israel could "sanctify themselves" only by trying to obey the Lord; if their hearts were in the Word, and their Faith was anchored in what the Sacrifices represented, namely the coming Redeemer, on that basis the Lord would sanctify them, but only on that basis [Lev. 9:22-24]).*

PARENTAL DISRESPECT

9 For every one who curses his father or his mother shall be surely put to death: he has cursed his father or his mother; his blood shall be upon him *(death for cursing one's parents may seem harsh; however, Israel was being prepared to bring the Messiah into the world; consequently, great restrictions were placed upon them, for the obvious reasons; Godly parents were*

to be looked at as a symbol of God; in other words, if children would curse their parents, they would as well curse God, for the former symbolized the latter).*

DEATH FOR ADULTERY

10 And the man who commits adultery with another man's wife, even he who commits adultery with his neighbour's wife, the adulterer and the adulteress shall surely be put to death *(these penalties are not carried over into the New Covenant; but let the Reader understand that while adultery may not bring on physical death under the New Covenant, it definitely will bring on spiritual death, that is, if one continues such a course, thereby refusing to repent).*

DEATH FOR INCEST

11 And the man who lies with his father's wife has uncovered his father's nakedness: both of them shall surely be put to death; their blood shall be upon them.

12 And if a man lie with his daughter-in-law, both of them shall surely be put to death: they have wrought confusion; their blood shall be upon them *(the idea of the statement, "their blood shall be upon them," pertains to the fact that the penalty for the crime is the fault of the perpetrator).*

DEATH FOR HOMOSEXUALITY

13 If a man also lie with mankind, as he lies with a woman, both of them have committed an abomination: they shall surely be put to death; their blood shall be upon them *(the Lord speaks here of homosexuality as "an abomination"; the word "Abomination," in the Hebrew, is "towebah," and means "something disgusting, an abhorrence").*

DEATH FOR INCEST

14 And if a man take a wife and her mother, it is wickedness: they shall be burnt with fire, both he and they; that there be no wickedness among you *(the necessity of the Lord having to give these Commands and Warnings portrays to us the glaring fact of man's total depravity).*

DEATH FOR BESTIALITY

15 And if a man lie *(engage in intercourse)*

with a beast, he shall surely be put to death: and you shall kill the beast.

16 And if a woman approach unto any beast, and lie down thereto, you shall kill the woman, and the beast: they shall surely be put to death; their blood shall be upon them.

DEATH FOR OTHER SEXUAL SINS

17 And if a man shall take his sister, his father's daughter, or his mother's daughter, and see her nakedness, and she see his nakedness; it is a wicked thing; and they shall be cut off in the sight of their people: he has uncovered his sister's nakedness; he shall bear his iniquity.

18 And if a man shall lie with a woman having her sickness *(monthly period)*, and shall uncover her nakedness; he has discovered her fountain, and she has uncovered the fountain of her blood: and both of them shall be cut off from among their people *(the monthly discharge of the feminine gender speaks of impurity, and harks back to the original sin of Eve; to engage in intercourse at such a time, in essence, was a denial of the Fall and its cause; due to Christ and what He did at the Cross, this particular prohibition no longer applies, at least in the sense that it did before the Cross; nevertheless, it still should be held to in principle, and for all the obvious reasons).*

19 And you shall not uncover the nakedness of your mother's sister, nor of your father's sister: for he uncovers his near kin: they shall bear their iniquity *(all of this, as is obvious, pertains to incest, which was common among the surrounding nations).*

20 And if a man shall lie with his uncle's wife, he has uncovered his uncle's nakedness: they shall bear their sin; they shall die childless *(which was a great reproach).*

21 And if a man shall take his brother's wife, it is an unclean thing: he has uncovered his brother's nakedness; they shall be childless.

COMMANDS

22 You shall therefore keep all My Statutes, and all My Judgments, and do them: that the land, where I bring you to dwell therein, spue you not out *(the Commands of the Lord were to be the guiding structure of Israel, and not the ways of the heathen nations which surrounded them; it is the same presently under the New Covenant).*

23 And you shall not walk in the manners of

the nation, which I cast out before you: for they committed all these things, and therefore I abhorred them *(God hates sin, wherever it is found).*

24 But I have said unto you, You shall inherit their land, and I will give it unto you to possess it, a land that flows with milk and honey: I am the LORD your God, which have separated you from other people *(this is carried over into the New Covenant, as well, with the Holy Spirit, through Paul, stating basically the same thing [II Cor. 6:14-18]; the Lord here plainly says that one cannot at the same time have "milk and honey" and "sin").*

25 You shall therefore put difference between clean beasts and unclean, and between unclean fowls and clean: and you shall not make your souls abominable by beast, or by fowl, or by any manner of living thing that creeps on the ground, which I have separated from you as unclean *(certain prohibitions were leveled against Israel that are not carried over into the New Covenant, because Israel was to be the womb of the Messiah, so to speak).*

26 And you shall be holy unto Me: for I the LORD am holy, and have severed you from other people, that you should be Mine *(Israel was to belong to the Lord, and to belong to the Lord exclusively; it is the same with Believers presently).*

MEDIUMS AND WIZARDS

27 A man also or woman who has a familiar spirit, or who is a wizard, shall surely be put to death: they shall stone them with stones: their blood shall be upon them *(the greater gist of this Verse is that Israel look exclusively to the Lord for leading and guidance, and not to other means, especially the means of the powers of darkness).*

CHAPTER 21
(1490 B.C.)
HOLINESS

A ND the LORD said unto Moses, Speak unto the Priests the sons of Aaron, and say unto them, There shall none be defiled for the dead among his people:

2 But for his kin, that is near unto him, that is, for his mother, and for his father, and for his son, and for his daughter, and for his brother,

3 And for his sister a virgin, who is near

unto him, which has had no husband; for her may he be defiled *(it meant that the Priests were not to touch a dead body, with the exception of their close relatives; both physical and spiritual death are the result of sin, hence this prohibition)*.

4 But he shall not defile himself, being a chief man among his people, to profane himself *(Chapters 21 and 22, with great detail, portray the Divine requirements in reference to those who are Priests unto God)*.

5 They shall not make baldness upon their head, neither shall they shave off the corner of their beard, nor make any cuttings in their flesh *(the heathen did this whenever a loved one died, etc.)*.

6 They shall be holy unto their God, and not profane the Name of their God: for the Offerings of the LORD made by fire, and the bread of their God, they do offer: therefore they shall be holy *(in effect, they portrayed Christ and the Cross)*.

7 They shall not take a wife who is a whore, or profane; neither shall they take a woman put away from her husband *(divorced)*: for he is holy unto his God.

8 You shall sanctify him therefore; for he offers the bread of your God: he shall be holy unto you: for I the LORD, which sanctify you, am holy.

9 And the daughter of any Priest, if she profane herself by playing the whore, she profanes her father: she shall be burnt with fire.

THE HIGH PRIEST

10 And he who is the High Priest among his brethren, upon whose head the anointing oil was poured, and who is consecrated to put on the garments, shall not uncover his head, nor rend his clothes *(the instructions now shift from what we might refer to as ordinary Priests to the High Priest; even if a loved one died, he was not to alter his appearance at all)*;

11 Neither shall he go in to any dead body, nor defile himself for his father, or for his mother;

12 Neither shall he go out of the Sanctuary, nor profane the Sanctuary of his God *(even if he hears of the death of a near relative, whatever duties he is performing in the Sanctuary must not be stopped)*; for the crown of the anointing oil of his God is upon him: I am the LORD.

13 And he shall take a wife in her virginity.

14 A widow, or a divorced woman, or profane, or an harlot, these shall he not take: but he shall take a virgin of his own people to wife *(whereas it seems that an ordinary Priest could marry a widow, the High Priest could only marry a virgin)*.

15 Neither shall he profane his seed among his people: for I the LORD do sanctify him *(when the father who was High Priest died, his oldest son was to be the next High Priest; so they were to prepare from the time they were children; they were to live a sanctified life)*.

NO BLEMISH

16 And the LORD spoke unto Moses, saying,

17 Speak unto Aaron, saying, Whosoever he be of your seed in their generations who has any blemish, let him not approach to offer the bread of his God *(that Holiness becomes God's House forever is true in all periods of time; God demanded an unblemished Priest and an unblemished Sacrifice; such was Christ as Priest and Sacrifice)*.

18 For whatsoever man he be who has a blemish, he shall not approach: a blind man, or a lame, or he who has a flat nose, or any thing superfluous *(exceeding what is sufficient or necessary)*,

19 Or a man who is brokenfooted, or brokenhanded,

20 Or crookbackt, or a dwarf, or who has a blemish in his eye, or be scurvy, or scabbed, or has his stones *(testicles)* broken;

21 No man who has a blemish of the seed of Aaron the Priest shall come near to offer the Offerings of the LORD made by fire: he has a blemish; he shall not come near to offer the bread of his God.

22 He shall eat the bread of his God, both of the most holy *(Sin Offering, Trespass Offering, and Meat Offering)*, and of the holy *(Whole Burnt Offering and Peace Offering; the Law forbade a Priest who was physically imperfect to exercise his office; however, Grace furnished him his daily bread; in other words, if he was blemished in some way, he could still serve as a Priest, but could only attend certain duties)*.

23 Only he shall not go in unto the Veil, nor come near unto the Altar *(he could not offer Sacrifices)*, because he has a blemish; that he profane not My Sanctuaries: for I the LORD do sanctify them.

24 And Moses told it unto Aaron, and to his sons, and unto all the Children of Israel.

CHAPTER 22
(1490 B.C.)
THE HOLINESS OF OFFERINGS

AND the LORD spoke unto Moses, saying,

2 Speak unto Aaron and to his sons, that they separate themselves from the holy things of the Children of Israel, and that they profane not My Holy Name in those things which they hallow unto Me: I am the LORD *(as the last Chapter concluded with the command to disqualify certain Priests to offer Sacrifices, this Chapter opens with conditions under which even the legally qualified Priests must not partake of the Offerings).*

3 Say unto them, Whosoever he be of all your seed among your generations, who goes unto the holy things, which the Children of Israel hallow unto the LORD *(pertains to the Priests eating certain of the Sacrifices, which they were required to do),* having his uncleanness upon him *(meaning that he had defiled himself in some way, or was defiled through no fault of his own),* that soul shall be cut off from My Presence: I am the LORD *(in the case of defilement, for whatever reason, the Priest was to undergo purification before he could once again partake of the Sacrifices; to fail to do so could cause the loss of his soul).*

4 What man soever of the seed of Aaron *(a Priest)* is a leper, or has a running issue; he shall not eat of the holy things *(the Sacrifices),* until he be clean *(has been purified).* And whoso touches any thing that is unclean by the dead, or a man whose seed goes from him *(masturbation);*

5 Or whosoever touches any creeping thing, whereby he may be made unclean, or a man of whom he may take uncleanness, whatsoever uncleanness he has;

6 The soul which has touched any such shall be unclean until evening *(continues to speak of Priests),* and shall not eat of the holy things *(the Sacrifices),* unless he wash his flesh with water *(the purification process).*

7 And when the sun is down, he shall be clean, and shall afterward eat of the holy things; because it is his food.

8 That which dies of itself, or is torn with beasts, he shall not eat to defile himself therewith; I am the LORD.

9 They shall therefore keep My Ordinance, lest they bear sin for it, and die therefore, if they profane it: I the LORD do sanctify them.

(Mackintosh says: "Had they to be warned against unholy contact? So have we. Had they to be warned against unholy alliance? So have we. Had they to be warned against all manner of ceremonial uncleanliness? So have we to be warned against 'all filthiness of the flesh and spirit' [I Cor. 7:1]. Were they shorn of many of their loftiest Priestly privileges by bodily blemish and imperfect natural growth? So are we by moral blemish and imperfect spiritual growth.")

MORE INSTRUCTIONS

10 There shall no stranger *(Gentile)* eat of the holy thing: a sojourner of the Priest, or an hired servant, shall not eat of the holy thing *(cannot partake of the Sacrifices).*

11 But if the Priest buy any soul with his money *(servant),* he shall eat of it, and he who is born in his house: they shall eat of his meat *(meaning that these members of his family can partake of the Sacrifices, as well).*

12 If the Priest's daughter also be married unto a stranger *(Gentile),* she may not eat of an Offering of the holy things.

13 But if the Priest's daughter be a widow, or divorced, and have no child, and is returned unto her father's house, as in her youth, she shall eat of her father's meat: but there shall be no stranger *(Gentile)* eat thereof.

14 And if a man *(someone in the house of the Priest)* eat of the holy thing *(Sacrifices)* unwittingly *(not knowing that it is a part of a Sacrifice),* then he shall put the fifth part thereof unto it *(20 percent of what it's worth in money),* and shall give it unto the Priest with the holy thing *(with the remainder of the Sacrifice).*

15 And they shall not profane the holy things of the Children of Israel, which they offer unto the LORD;

16 Or suffer them to bear the iniquity of trespass, when they eat their holy things: for I the LORD do sanctify them.

LAWS

17 And the LORD spoke unto Moses, saying,

18 Speak unto Aaron, and to his sons, and unto all the Children of Israel, and say unto them, Whatsoever he be of the house of Israel, or of the strangers in Israel *(Gentile proselytes),* who will offer his oblation for all his vows, and for all his freewill Offerings, which they will offer unto the LORD for a Burnt Offering;

19 You shall offer at your own will a male

without blemish, of the beeves, of the sheep, or of the goats (*speaks of people offering Sacrifices*).

20 But whatsoever has a blemish, that shall you not offer: for it shall not be acceptable for you.

21 And whosoever offers a Sacrifice of Peace Offerings unto the LORD to accomplish his vow, or a freewill offering in beeves or sheep, it shall be perfect to be accepted; there shall be no blemish therein (*these Sacrifices represented Christ; therefore, they must be perfect; the temptation was always there to offer a sickly animal, because it wasn't worth much anyway*).

22 Blind, or broken, or maimed, or having a wen, or scurvy, or scabbed, you shall not offer these unto the LORD, nor make an Offering by fire of them upon the Altar unto the LORD.

23 Either a bullock or a lamb that has any thing superfluous or lacking in his parts, that may you offer for a freewill offering; but for a vow it shall not be accepted.

24 You shall not offer unto the LORD that which is bruised, or crushed, or broken, or cut; neither shall you make any offering thereof in your land.

25 Neither from a stranger's (*Gentile's*) hand shall you offer the bread of your God of any of these; because their corruption is in them, and blemishes be in them: they shall not be accepted for you.

INSTRUCTIONS

26 And the LORD spoke unto Moses, saying,

27 When a bullock, or a sheep, or a goat, is brought forth, then it shall be seven days under the dam (*its mother*); and from the eighth day (*eight days old*) and thenceforth it shall be accepted for an Offering made by fire unto the LORD.

28 And whether it be cow, or ewe, you shall not kill it and her young both in one day.

29 And when you will offer a Sacrifice of Thanksgiving unto the LORD, offer it at your own will.

30 On the same day it shall be eaten up (*a Thanksgiving Offering, consisting of bread*); you shall leave none of it until the morrow (*represents the fact that Christ must be accepted totally*): I am the LORD.

31 Therefore shall you keep My Commandments, and do them: I am the LORD.

32 Neither shall you profane My Holy Name; but I will be hallowed among the Children of Israel: I am the LORD which hallow you,

33 That brought you out of the land of Egypt, to be your God: I am the LORD. (*All of this typifies Christ and what He would do at the Cross, as it regards the Redemption of lost humanity. That's the reason the instructions were so minute, so delicate, so detailed.*)

CHAPTER 23
(1490 B.C.)
THE FEASTS

AND the LORD spoke unto Moses, saying,

2 Speak unto the Children of Israel, and say unto them, Concerning the Feasts of the LORD, which you shall proclaim to be holy convocations, even these are My Feasts. (*Israel's sacred year contained one weekly and seven annual Feasts, but the annual Feasts were related to the weekly Feast. The weekly Feast was the Sabbath; the seven annual Feasts were: Passover, Unleavened Bread, Firstfruits, Pentecost, Trumpets, Atonement, and Tabernacles. All proclaimed the Work of Christ in the Plan of Redemption, in some fashion.*)

3 Six days shall work be done: but the seventh day is the Sabbath of rest, an holy convocation; you shall do no work therein: it is the Sabbath of the LORD in all your dwellings (*the Feast of the Sabbath stood apart as being God's rest; it was a Prophecy and a Promise of the rest in Christ that remained to the people of God, which we presently enjoy; in other words, whereas the Sabbath then was a day, now it is a Person, the Lord Jesus Christ; acceptance of Him and resting in Him presently constitute the keeping of the Sabbath*).

PASSOVER

4 These are the Feasts of the LORD, even holy convocations, which you shall proclaim in their seasons.

5 In the fourteenth day of the first month at evening is the LORD's Passover (*the words "at evening" should read "between the evenings," i.e., at any time from sunset of one day to sunset of the next; "Passover" figures Redemption, as carried out by our Lord*).

UNLEAVENED BREAD

6 And on the fifteenth day of the same month is the Feast of Unleavened Bread unto

the LORD: seven days you must eat Unleavened Bread.

7 In the first day you shall have an holy convocation: you shall do no servile work therein.

8 But you shall offer an Offering made by fire unto the LORD seven days: in the seventh day is an holy convocation: you shall do no servile work therein. *(Unleavened Bread figured the perfect, unspotted, unsullied life of Christ, which was offered up in Sacrifice. On the first and seventh day no work was to be done, signifying that Salvation is not by works [Eph. 2:8-9]. Let all understand that we can know nothing of "rest," nothing of "holiness," and nothing of "fellowship," save on the ground of the death of Christ. It is peculiarly striking, significant, and beautiful to observe that directly God's rest is spoken of, and we speak of the Sabbath in Verse 3, the next thing introduced is the blood of the paschal lamb, symbolizing the Crucifixion of Christ.)*

FIRSTFRUITS

9 And the LORD spoke unto Moses, saying,

10 Speak unto the Children of Israel, and say unto them, When you be come into the land which I give unto you, and shall reap the harvest thereof, then you shall bring a sheaf of the firstfruits of your harvest unto the Priest:

11 And he shall wave the sheaf before the LORD, to be accepted for you: on the morrow after the Sabbath the Priest shall wave it *(the sheaf of Firstfruits was to be waved on the day after the Sabbath; that was the day that Christ rose from the grave; no Sin Offering accompanied the sheaf, for Jesus was sinless).*

12 And you shall offer that day when you wave the sheaf an he lamb without blemish of the first year for a Burnt Offering unto the LORD *(signifying the perfection of Christ given to believing man).*

13 And the Meat Offering thereof shall be two tenth deals of fine flour *(signified the Perfect Life of Christ)* mingled with oil *(the Holy Spirit on and within Christ [Lk. 4:18-19]),* an Offering made by fire unto the LORD for a sweet savour *(the cakes were to be burned on the Altar, signifying the death of Christ, and that such was pleasing to God):* and the Drink Offering thereof shall be of wine, the fourth part of an hin *(symbolizing the joy that comes of Salvation, all afforded by Christ).*

14 And you shall eat neither bread, nor parched corn, nor green ears, until the selfsame day that you have brought an Offering unto your God: it shall be a Statute for ever throughout your generations in all your dwellings *(part of this Offering was to be eaten by the Priests, and part burned on the Altar; "Firstfruits" symbolized the Resurrection of Christ).*

PENTECOST

15 And you shall count unto you from the morrow after the Sabbath, from the day that you brought the sheaf of the Wave Offering; seven Sabbaths shall be complete *(the day after seven complete weeks was the fiftieth day, hence the name "Pentecost," which actually meant, in the Hebrew, "fifty" or "fiftieth"):*

16 Even unto the morrow after the seventh Sabbath shall you number fifty days; and you shall offer a new Meat Offering unto the LORD *(a Thanksgiving Offering, which contained no flesh, but rather grain).*

17 You shall bring out of your habitations two wave loaves of two tenth deals; they shall be of fine flour; they shall be baked with leaven; they are the Firstfruits unto the LORD *(the "leaven" is intended to foreshadow those who, though filled with the Holy Spirit, and adorned with His gifts and graces, have, nevertheless, "evil" dwelling is us; in other words, the sin nature is still in the Child of God [Rom., Chpt. 6]; although the sin nature dwells there, it is not to rule and reign [Rom. 6:12]).*

18 And you shall offer with the bread seven lambs without blemish of the first year, and one young bullock, and two rams: they shall be for a Burnt Offering unto the LORD, with their Meat Offering, and their Drink Offerings, even an Offering made by fire, of sweet savour unto the LORD.

19 Then you shall sacrifice one kid of the goats for a Sin Offering, and two lambs of the first year for a sacrifice of Peace Offerings. *(Concerning this, Mackintosh says: "The assembly, on the Day of Pentecost, for this was the day that the Holy Spirit was outpoured, stood in the full value of the Blood of Christ, and was crowned with the Gifts of the Holy Spirit; but there was leaven there also. No power of the Spirit could do away with the fact there was evil dwelling in the people of God. It might be suppressed and kept out of view, but it was there. This fact is foreshadowed in the 'type' by the leaven in the two loaves, and it is set forth in the actual history of the Church; for albeit God the Holy Spirit*

was present in the assembly, the flesh was there likewise. Flesh is flesh, nor can it ever be made ought else than flesh.

"The Holy Spirit did not come down on the Day of Pentecost to improve nature or to do away with the fact of its incurable evil, but to baptize Believers into one body, and connect them with their Living Head in Heaven.")

20 And the Priest shall wave them with the bread of the firstfruits for a Wave Offering before the LORD, with the two lambs: they shall be holy to the LORD for the Priest.

21 And you shall proclaim on the selfsame day, that it may be an holy convocation unto you: you shall do no servile work therein: it shall be a Statute for ever in all your dwellings throughout your generations. *(The command to do no servile work is repeated ten times in connection with these Feasts. Man's activities were forbidden to intrude themselves into a Salvation which was Divine and perfect. God desired happy redeemed children in his family, not slaves. Pentecost proclaimed Christ as the Baptizer with the Holy Spirit, all made possible by the Cross.)*

22 And when you reap the harvest of your land, you shall not make clean riddance of the corners of your field when you reap, neither shall you gather any gleaning of your harvest: you shall leave them unto the poor, and to the stranger *(Gentiles)*: I am the LORD your God *(this Verse proclaims God's welfare program; for those who did not own land, and found themselves on hard times, they, according to the Law, could reap the corners of the fields, and thereby obtain grain that they could use for food).*

TRUMPETS

23 And the LORD spoke unto Moses, saying,

24 Speak unto the Children of Israel, saying, In the seventh month, in the first day of the month, shall you have a Sabbath, a memorial of blowing of trumpets, an holy convocation *(the Feast of Trumpets pertains both to the Church and to Israel; it speaks, first of all, to the Church, which will signal the Rapture, and thereby the close of the Church Age; but the same trumpets which signal the end of the Church will, at the same time, signal the beginning of the restoration of Israel).*

25 You shall do no servile work therein: but you shall offer an Offering made by fire unto the LORD.

ATONEMENT

26 And the LORD spoke unto Moses, saying,

27 Also on the tenth day of this seventh month there shall be a day of Atonement: it shall be an holy convocation unto you; and you shall afflict your souls, and offer an Offering made by fire unto the LORD *(this was the only day in the Jewish year where Israel was ordered to fast; however, it was followed by a great Feast).*

28 And you shall do no work in that same day: for it is a day of Atonement, to make an Atonement for you before the LORD your God *(this was the one day of the year that the High Priest went into the Holy of Holies to offer up Incense, and blood on the Mercy Seat, all for himself and the entirety of Israel).*

29 For whatsoever soul it be that shall not be afflicted in that same day, he shall be cut off from among his people *(anyone who refused to "fast," and remained in that frame of mind, could lose their soul).*

30 And whatsoever soul it be that does any work in that same day, the same soul will I destroy from among his people *(the demand that no work be done on this particular day was meant to portray Salvation by Faith, and not by works [Eph. 2:8-9]).*

31 You shall do no manner of work: it shall be a Statute for ever throughout your generations in all your dwellings *(until Christ would come, Who, in effect, was the Atonement, which would be brought about on the Cross of Calvary).*

32 It shall be unto you a Sabbath of rest, and you shall afflict your souls: in the ninth day of the month at evening, from evening unto evening, shall you celebrate your Sabbath *(Israel was to "rest" on this day, typifying the rest that Christ would bring, and which would come to the seeking soul; whereas then it was only one day of rest, typified every week by the Sabbath, now it is a perpetual rest, because all is in Christ [Mat. 11:28-30]).*

TABERNACLES

33 And the LORD spoke unto Moses, saying,

34 Speak unto the Children of Israel, saying, The fifteenth day of this seventh month shall be the Feast of Tabernacles for seven days unto the LORD *(this Feast pictures Israel safe in Christ, and enjoying the coming Millennial reign, when she will finally gain her place and position ordained by the Lord so long, long ago, as chief of the nations).*

35 On the first day shall be an holy convocation: you shall do no servile work therein *(the Feast of Tabernacles took place in the month of October, the time of the fruit harvest; it began some five days after the Great Day of Atonement).*

36 Seven days you shall offer an Offering made by fire unto the LORD: on the eighth day shall be an holy convocation unto you; and you shall offer an Offering made by fire unto the LORD: it is a solemn assembly; and you shall do no servile work therein.

37 These are the Feasts of the LORD, which you shall proclaim to be holy convocations, to offer an Offering made by fire unto the LORD, a Burnt Offering, and a Meat Offering, a Sacrifice, and Drink Offerings, every thing upon his day *(daily Sacrifices)*:

38 Beside the Sabbaths of the LORD, and beside your gifts, and beside all your vows, and beside all your freewill Offerings, which you give unto the LORD *(the Feast of Tabernacle Offerings were to be over and above the regular Offerings, whatever they may have been).*

39 Also in the fifteenth day of the seventh month, when you have gathered in the fruit of the land, you shall keep a Feast unto the LORD seven days: on the first day shall be a Sabbath, and on the eighth day shall be a Sabbath.

40 And you shall take you on the first day the boughs of goodly trees, branches of palm trees, and the boughs of thick trees, and willows of the brook; and you shall rejoice before the LORD your God seven days *(somewhat like a Campmeeting).*

41 And you shall keep it a Feast unto the LORD seven days in the year. It shall be a Statute for ever in your generations: you shall celebrate it in the seventh month *(as stated, our October).*

42 You shall dwell in booths seven days; all who are Israelites born shall dwell in booths:

43 That your generations may know that I made the Children of Israel to dwell in booths, when I brought them out of the land of Egypt. I am the LORD your God *(in a sense, this would remind them of their wilderness wanderings).*

44 And Moses declared unto the Children of Israel the Feasts of the LORD.

CHAPTER 24
(1490 B.C.)
THE LAMPS

AND the LORD spoke unto Moses, saying,

2 Command the Children of Israel, that they bring unto you pure oil olive beaten for the light *(the "pure oil" represents the Grace of the Holy Spirit, founded upon the Work of Christ, as exhibited by the Lampstand of "beaten gold"),* to cause the Lamps to burn continually *(the "olive" was pressed to yield "oil," and the gold was "beaten" to form the Lampstand; in other words, the Grace and Light of the Spirit are founded upon the Death of Christ and maintained in clearness and power by the Priesthood of Christ; the lamp burning "continually" refers to the fact that Christ was led perfectly by the Holy Spirit at all times).*

3 Without the Veil of the Testimony, in the Tabernacle of the congregation *(in the Holy Place, the first room of the Tabernacle),* shall Aaron order it from the evening unto the morning before the LORD continually *(the "Lamps" were to be attended by the Priests every morning at 9 a.m., the time of the morning Sacrifice, and every evening at 3 p.m., the time of the evening Sacrifice; at that time, the wicks were to be trimmed, or replaced, and the oil replenished):* it shall be a Statute for ever in your generations *(its fulfillment under the New Covenant pertains to the Holy Spirit abiding in the heart and life of the Believer forever [Jn. 14:16-17]).*

4 He shall order the Lamps upon the pure candlestick *(Lampstand)* before the LORD continually *(this was a continuous process that demanded attention every morning and every evening, and must not be neglected; it was "before the Lord").*

SHEWBREAD

5 And you shall take fine flour *(Type of the Perfect Life of Christ),* and bake twelve cakes thereof *("twelve" is God's number for Government; however, we must always remember that it's the Government of God, as outlined in God's Word, and not the government of man; this has always been the greatest hindrance to the Work of God; men attempt to change the Government of God by instituting man-devised government, and claiming it to be of God):* two tenth deals shall be in one cake *(the "cake" represents Christ, and refers to the fact that Government is strictly of Him [Rev. 1:12-16]).*

6 And you shall set them in two rows, six on a row *(all of this "bread" representing Christ),* upon the pure table before the LORD *(this "pure table" was covered with "pure gold" that stood before the Lord; "pure frankincense" was*

to be burned upon the "pure table"; this signifies that all things connected with Jehovah and
His worship were to be pure, thus typifying the
purity of life and conduct of the worshippers
who come before Him).

7 And you shall put pure frankincense (a
bitter substance) upon each row (there were two
stacks of cakes, six to the stack, with a container
of frankincense on top of each stack, continually
burning), that it may be on the bread for a memorial (the memory of Christ must be kept alive
constantly, which, by and large, pertains to what
He did for us at the Cross), even an Offering
made by fire unto the LORD (the burning of the
frankincense at the top of the stacks made the
Shewbread an Offering made by fire unto Jehovah; actually, the loaves were not burned in the
fire, for they were to be eaten by the Priests in the
Holy Place as the most holy of the Offerings; the
"fire" represented judgment, whether the burning out of dross in the lives of Believers [Mat.
3:11], or judgment for sin [Lev. 10:1-2]).

8 Every Sabbath he shall set it in order before the LORD continually (every Sabbath, all
twelve loaves of the bread were to be eaten by the
Priests, with new loaves taking their place; it
was a Type of our partaking of Christ as the
Bread of Life [Jn. 6:58]), being taken from the
Children of Israel by an Everlasting Covenant
(pertains to the fact that every Israelite had to
give a half shekel of silver each year, which contributed annually toward the maintenance of
the service in the Sanctuary, the securing of ingredients, etc.; "silver" represented Redemption,
which is what Christ would bring about as a
result of His death on the Cross).

9 And it shall be Aaron's and his sons' (refers to the entirety of the Priesthood, which were
to be in the lineage of Aaron); and they shall
eat it (each Sabbath) in the Holy Place (the first
room of the Tabernacle): for it is most holy
(because it typified Christ in His Perfection, with
that perfection given to Believers, typified by the
bread being eaten by the Priests) unto him of
the Offerings of the LORD made by fire by a
perpetual Statute (all of this was fulfilled in
Christ, but it continues to be perpetual in that
Believers are to partake of Christ constantly; He
is our "rest," typified by the Sabbath).

BLASPHEMY

10 And the son of an Israelitish woman,
whose father was an Egyptian, went out among
the Children of Israel: and this son of the
Israelitish woman and a man of Israel strove
together in the camp (this is a picture, in type,
of the nation of Israel itself, represented by the
son of the Israelitish woman, who would seek to
kill the true man of Israel, the Lord Jesus Christ);

11 And the Israelitish woman's son blasphemed the Name of the Lord and cursed (the
idea is, he cursed God and God's Law). And they
brought him unto Moses: (and his mother's
name was Shelomith, the daughter of Dibri,
of the tribe of Dan [the fact that both her personal and tribal names are so distinctly specified
here indicates that the record of this incident is
designed to point out the ungodly issue of so unholy an alliance, and to guard the Hebrew
women against intermarriage with heathen]:)

12 And they put him in ward (a jail cell),
that the mind of the LORD might be shown
them (the subjection of mind that appears in
this Verse, and the anxiety to do what God wished,
and not to act in the heat of their own judgment, is very gracious — Williams).

THE VERDICT

13 And the LORD spoke unto Moses, saying,

14 Bring forth him who has cursed without
the camp; and let all who heard him lay their
hands upon his head, and let all the congregation stone him (physical death under the New
Covenant is not now demanded, because Jesus
fulfilled the Law in every respect, in effect dying
for all; but still, to be sure, spiritual death follows for anyone who takes the Word of God
lightly).

15 And you shall speak unto the Children
of Israel, saying, Whosoever curses his God
shall bear his sin (shall suffer the consequences).

16 And he who blasphemes the Name of the
Lord, he shall surely be put to death, and all
the congregation shall certainly stone him: as
well the stranger (Gentile), as he who is born
in the land, when he blasphemes the Name of
the Lord, shall be put to death.

17 And he who kills (murders) any man shall
surely be put to death.

18 And he who kills a beast shall make it good;
beast for beast (these Laws had already been
given and recorded in Exodus, Chapter 21; at
least one of the reasons they are repeated is that it
must be known that they are applicable alike to
the proselyte, the Gentile, and the Israelite).

19 And if a man cause a blemish in his
neighbour; as he has done, so shall it be done
to him;

20 Breach for breach, eye for eye, tooth for tooth: as he has caused a blemish in a man, so shall it be done to him again (*actually, these Laws were seldom carried out; most of the time, a value in money was placed upon the infraction, with it being paid to the victim, that is, if wrong had actually been done*).

21 And he who kills a beast, he shall restore it: and he who kills a man, he shall be put to death.

22 You shall have one manner of Law, as well for the stranger, as for one of your own country: for I am the LORD your God (*as previously stated, there must be "one manner of Law," applicable in the same manner for all*).

23 And Moses spoke to the Children of Israel, that they should bring forth him who had cursed out of the camp, and stone him with stones. And the Children of Israel did as the LORD commanded Moses.

CHAPTER 25
(1491 B.C.)
THE SEVENTH YEAR

AND the LORD spoke unto Moses in Mount Sinai, saying,

2 Speak unto the Children of Israel, and say unto them, When you come into the land which I give you, then shall the land keep a Sabbath unto the LORD.

3 Six years you shall sow your field, and six years you shall prune your vineyard, and gather in the fruit thereof;

4 But in the seventh year shall be a Sabbath of rest unto the land, a Sabbath for the LORD: you shall neither sow your field, nor prune your vineyard. (*The doctrine of this Chapter is that the people of Israel and the land of Israel belong to Jehovah, and that He, as the Divine Redeemer, has redeemed them both at the expense of His Own Precious Blood — Williams.*)

5 That which grows of its own accord of your harvest you shall not reap, neither gather the grapes of your vine undressed: for it is a year of rest unto the land (*once again, this Sabbatical year, coming about every seventh year, symbolized the "rest" found only in Christ [Mat. 11:28-30]*).

6 And the Sabbath of the land shall be meat for you; for you, and for your servant, and for your maid, and for your hired servant, and for your stranger that sojourns with you,

7 And for your cattle, and for the beast that are in your land, shall all the increase thereof be meat. (*Incidentally, in later years, Israel went about 490 years ignoring this Sabbath year, which would total 70 Sabbath years that they ignored the Command of the Lord. In respect to this, the land lay fallow for 70 years, while Israel languished in Babylon. We must understand that God says what He means, and means what He says [26:43].*)

YEAR OF JUBILEE

8 And you shall number seven Sabbaths of years unto you, seven times seven years; and the space of the seven Sabbaths of years shall be unto you forty and nine years. (*So there was a weekly Sabbath, a seventh year Sabbath, and a fiftieth year Sabbath. The fiftieth year Sabbath would actually entail two years of Sabbatical years in succession. The first one would be the seventh year of the seven year cycle, and the next one would be the fiftieth year, which was the Year of Jubilee.*)

9 Then shall you cause the trumpet of the Jubilee to sound on the tenth day of the seventh month (*this is the Year of Jubilee, which came every fiftieth year*), in the Day of Atonement shall you make the trumpet sound throughout all your land (*the trumpet blowing throughout the land was done on the Great Day of Atonement, which was the first day of the Year of Jubilee*).

10 And you shall hallow the fiftieth year (*every fiftieth year was the Year of Jubilee*), and proclaim liberty throughout all the land unto all the inhabitants thereof (*at the beginning of this particular year, every prisoner went free, every debt was cancelled, and all property went back to the original owner; in fact, the Jubilee voided all contracts and released all slaves; it was symbolic of the new beginning which a person experiences when they come to Christ*): it shall be a Jubilee (*joy*) unto you; and you shall return every man unto his possession, and you shall return every man unto his family.

11 A jubilee shall that fiftieth year be unto you: you shall not sow, neither reap that which grows of itself in it, nor gather the grapes in it of your vine undressed.

12 For it is the jubilee; it shall be holy unto you (*because it represented Christ, Who would set men free by virtue of the Cross*): you shall eat the increase thereof out of the field (*what grew of its own accord in the Year of Jubilee*).

13 In the year of this Jubilee you shall return every man unto his possession (*all real

property, such as land and houses, was to return to the original owner; so when something was purchased, it was actually only leased until the Year of Jubilee).

14 And if you sell ought unto your neighbour, or buy ought of your neighbour's hand, you shall not oppress one another (if somebody lost their property through foreclosure, it was to come back to them on the Year of Jubilee; this practice stopped much oppression):

15 According to the number of years after the Jubilee you shall buy of your neighbour, and according unto the number of years of the fruits he shall sell unto you (all transactions were judged according to the number of years left before the Year of Jubilee):

16 According to the multitude of years you shall increase the price thereof, and according to the fewness of years you shall diminish the price of it: for according to the number of the years of the fruits does he sell unto you.

17 You shall not therefore oppress one another; but you shall fear your God: for I am the LORD your God (meaning that the Lord made these Laws, not man!).

18 Wherefore you shall do My Statutes, and keep My Judgments, and do them; and you shall dwell in the land in safety (in other words, the safety of Israel depended on her abiding by the Word of the Lord).

19 And the land shall yield her fruit, and you shall eat your fill, and dwell therein in safety (all prosperity depended on obedience to the Word of God).

20 And if you shall say, What shall we eat the seventh year? behold, we shall not sow, nor gather in our increase:

21 Then I will command My blessing upon you in the sixth year, and it shall bring forth fruit for three years (for the sixth year; for the seventh year, which is to be a Sabbath; and then the following year, which is the fiftieth year; among other things, the "Year of Jubilee" taught faith and trust in the Lord).

22 And you shall sow the eighth year (the year after the Year of Jubilee), and eat yet of old fruit until the ninth year; until her fruits come in you shall eat of the old store (eat of the increase that the Lord gave on the sixth year [Vs. 21]).

23 The land shall not be sold for ever: for the land is Mine; for you are strangers and sojourners with Me. (The Land of Israel still belongs to God, just as much as it did those thousands of years ago. The Palestinians should

learn and understand that.)

REDEMPTION OF PROPERTY

24 And in all the land of your possession you shall grant a redemption for the land (the land could be redeemed by a near relative).

25 If your brother be waxed poor, and has sold away some of his possession, and if any of his kin come to redeem it, then shall he redeem that which his brother sold.

26 And if the man have none to redeem it (the original owner who lost the property), and himself be able to redeem it (the near of kin who desires to redeem it);

27 Then let him count the years of the sale thereof, and restore the overplus unto the man to whom he sold it; that he may return unto his possession (the redemption price would be according to the number of years left before the Year of Jubilee).

28 But if he be not able to restore it to him, then that which is sold shall remain in the hand of him who has bought it until the Year of Jubilee: and in the Jubilee it shall go out, and he shall return unto his possession (it will go back to the original owner).

29 And if a man sell a dwelling house in a walled city, then he may redeem it within a whole year after it is sold; within a full year may he redeem it (he can buy it back within a year at the price for which he sold it, if he so desires).

30 And if it be not redeemed within the space of a full year, then the house that is in the walled city shall be established for ever to him who bought it throughout his generations: it shall not go out in the Jubilee (houses in cities were looked at differently; they were not to go back to the original owner on the Year of Jubilee, that is, if they were not redeemed during the first year after the sale).

31 But the houses of the villages which have no wall round about them shall be counted as the fields of the country: they may be redeemed, and they shall go out in the Jubilee (go back to the original owner on the Year of Jubilee).

32 Notwithstanding the cities of the Levites, and the houses of the cities of their possession, may the Levites redeem at any time (the Levites were not bound by the Year of Jubilee).

33 And if a man purchase of the Levites, then the house that was sold, and the city of his possession, shall go out in the Year of Jubilee:

for the houses of the cities of the Levites are their possession among the Children of Israel (*at any rate, exactly as most others, all property purchased from Levites would go back to them on the Year of Jubilee*).

34 But the field of the suburbs of their cities may not be sold; for it is their perpetual possession (*land which belonged to the Levites could not be sold, but must remain in their possession; so, if they incurred debts, that debt had to be settled another way other than confiscating their property*).

REDEEMING THE POOR

35 And if your brother be waxed poor, and fallen in decay with you (*to your knowledge*); then you shall relieve him (*help him*): yes, though he be a stranger (*Gentile*), or a sojourner; that he may live with you (*Gentile proselytes to the Covenant of Abraham must be treated exactly as Israelites*).

36 Take thou no usury of him, or increase (*regarding loans, no Israelite was to charge interest of another Israelite or proselyte*): but fear your God; that your brother may live with you (*on an equal status*).

37 You shall not give him your money upon usury, nor lend him your victuals for increase (*don't try to make money regarding one in need, but rather help him by loaning him money at no interest, etc.*).

38 I am the LORD your God, which brought you forth out of the land of Egypt, to give you the land of Canaan, and to be your God.

39 And if your brother who dwells by you be waxed poor, and be sold unto you; you shall not compel him to serve as a bondservant (*you must not treat him as a slave*):

40 But as an hired servant, and as a sojourner, he shall be with you, and shall serve you unto the Year of Jubilee (*ever how long that might be*).

41 And then shall he depart from you, both he and his children with him, and shall return unto his own family, and unto the possession of his fathers shall he return (*completely free of all obligations, whatever they may have been*).

42 For they are My servants, which I brought forth out of the land of Egypt: they shall not be sold as bondmen (*the Lord had redeemed all Israelites out of Egypt; therefore, no Israelite must make a slave of a fellow Israelite*).

43 You shall not rule over him with rigour; but shall fear your God (*in today's terminology, we must remember that every other Believer belongs to the Lord, and treat him accordingly, whether we like him or not*).

44 Both your bondmen, and your bondmaids, which you shall have, shall be of the heathen who are round about you; of them shall you buy bondmen and bondmaids (*of the Gentiles*).

45 Moreover of the Children of the strangers (*Gentiles*) who do sojourn among you, of them shall you buy, and of their families who are with you, which they begat in your land: and they shall be your possession (*but fellow Israelites must not be bought and sold as bondmen and bondmaids*).

46 And you shall take them as an inheritance for your children after you, to inherit them for a possession (*if the father bought the bondman or bondmaid, when he died, they were then to be the property of the children*); they shall be your bondmen for ever: but over your brethren the Children of Israel, you shall not rule one over another with rigour (*while these were slaves, they were not so in the sense that we think of such presently; they were to be treated with all kindness, not like the Israelites had been treated in Egypt [Deut. 15:15]*).

SERVANTS REDEEMED

47 And if a sojourner or stranger (*Gentile*) wax rich by you, and your brother who dwells by him wax poor, and sell himself unto the stranger or sojourner by you, or to the stock of the stranger's family:

48 After that he is sold he may be redeemed again; one of his brethren may redeem him (*where a Gentile slave couldn't be redeemed and set free, an Israelite slave, who had been bought by a Gentile, could*):

49 Either his uncle, or his uncle's son, may redeem him or any who is near of kin unto him of his family may redeem him; or if he be able, he may redeem himself.

50 And he shall reckon with him who bought him from the year that he was sold to him unto the Year of Jubilee: and the price of his sale shall be according unto the number of years, according to the time of an hired servant shall it be with him. (*The new start in business at the end of Jubilee was based upon another year of release fifty years in the future, and, thereby, increased or diminished the value of a sale or mortgage. Likewise, as the Christian*

realizes the nearness or remoteness of the Coming of the Lord, so he places a low or a high value on earthly things.)

51 If there be yet many years behind, according unto them he shall give again the price of his redemption out of the money that he was bought for.

52 And if there remain but few years unto the Year of Jubilee, then he shall count with him, and according unto his years shall he give him again the price of his redemption *(the price would be according to the number of years served, and the number of years left, before the Year of Jubilee).*

53 And as a yearly hired servant shall he be with him: and the other shall not rule with rigour over him in your sight *(a fellow Israelite, as stated, was not to be treated as a slave, but rather as a hired servant, in other words, an employee).*

54 And if he be not redeemed in these years, then he shall go out in the Year of Jubilee, both he, and his children with him *(set free).*

55 For unto Me the Children of Israel are servants; they are My servants whom I brought forth out of the land of Egypt: I am the LORD your God. *(In order to save fallen man, our Saviour had to become man, in effect becoming our "kinsman." He did this in order to possess the right to offer the price of Redemption [Heb. 2:14].)*

CHAPTER 26
(1491 B.C.)
NO IDOLATRY

YOU shall make you no idols nor graven image, neither rear you up a standing image, neither shall you set up any image of stone in your land, to bow down unto it: for I am the LORD your God *(of this terrible sin, which embraced all types of immorality, every other nation in the world was guilty).*

2 You shall keep My Sabbaths, and reverence My Sanctuary: I am the LORD. *(If any other "god" is worshipped, there can be no Sabbatical "rest." The "rest" we now have in Christ is based solely upon His Finished Work, and our Faith anchored in that Sacrifice.*

If the Preacher is not preaching the Cross, thereby his hearers placing their faith in something else, whether they realize it or not, they are serving "another Jesus," which, pure and simple, is idol worship of some sort. That is the great sin of the modern Church [II Cor. 11:4].)

BLESSINGS OF OBEDIENCE

3 If you walk in My Statues, and keep My Commandments, and do them *(following this condition, "if," we find some of the most glorious Promises found anywhere in the Word of God. In truth, fallen man simply could not keep the Statutes and Commandments. Not even Israel, in the very best of circumstances, or the very best among them, could accomplish this task. But they were to try! The Sacrificial System, the very core of Mosaic Law, was the answer, and the only answer to failure);*

4 Then I will give you rain in due season, and the land shall yield her increase, and the trees of the field shall yield their fruit *(failure to obey the Word of the Lord, with most cases it being totally ignored, with other gods worshipped, presents the reason that most nations in the world cannot feed themselves).*

5 And your threshing shall reach unto the vintage, and the vintage shall reach unto the sowing time: and you shall eat your bread to the full, and dwell in your land safely *(Divine abundance, and Divine protection).*

6 And I will give peace in the land, and you shall lie down, and none shall make you afraid: and I will rid evil beasts out of the land, neither shall the sword go through your land *(freedom from war).*

7 And you shall chase your enemies, and they shall fall before you by the sword *(promised victory).*

8 And five of you shall chase an hundred, and an hundred of you shall put ten thousand to flight: and your enemies shall fall before you by the sword *(the Lord promised to give the best in Israel a 100-to-1 superiority in power, and the least among them 20-to-1).*

9 For I will have respect unto you, and make you fruitful, and multiply you, and establish My Covenant with you *(promised fruitfulness).*

10 And you shall eat old store, and bring forth the old because of the new *(will not have eaten all of the old before the new is ready, because of abundance).*

11 And I will set My Tabernacle among you: and My soul shall not abhor you *(the secret of Israel's prosperity was that the Lord was among them).*

12 And I will walk among you, and will be your God, and you shall be My people *(under the New Covenant, it is even better, far better; the Holy Spirit now lives constantly in our hearts and lives [Jn. 14:17]).*

13 I am the LORD your God, which brought you forth out of the land of Egypt, that you should not be their bondmen; and I have broken the bands of your yoke, and made you go upright. *(The Lord delivered Israel from Egyptian bondage by virtue of the slain Lamb, with the blood applied to the doorposts. Victory presently is found in the same manner, only in the Cross! Only in the Cross! [Rom. 6:3-14].)*

PENALTIES FOR DISOBEDIENCE

14 But if you will not hearken unto Me, and will not do all these Commandments;

15 And if you shall despise My Statutes, or if your soul abhor My Judgments, so that you will not do all My Commandments, but that you break My Covenant *(the glowing Promises of Blessings for obedience are now followed by a catalogue of calamities of the most appalling nature, which will overtake the Israelites if they disobey the Divine Commandments)*:

16 I also will do this unto you: I will even appoint over you terror, consumption, and the burning ague *(fever)*, that shall consume the eyes, and cause sorrow of heart: and you shall sow your seed in vain, for your enemies shall eat it *(if the Lord be for us, who can be against us? [Rom. 8:31]; and if the Lord be against us, who can be for us?)*.

17 And I will set My face against you, and you shall be slain before your enemies: they who hate you shall reign over you; and you shall flee when none pursues you *(instead of being victorious, their enemies would be victorious over them; fear would rule them, even as it rules all Believers who try to live for God outside of the Cross [Rom. 8:15; II Tim. 1:7])*.

18 And if you will not yet for all this hearken unto Me, then I will punish you seven times more for your sins *(if all of these things do not have the desired effect, which is to bring Israel back to God, then the Judgment will be multiplied seven times)*.

19 And I will break the pride of your power *(the Lord promised to break the pride of their power, which means that their trust would ultimately come to rest in their own army, instead of God; their enemies would waste these armies that looked mighty in their sight; with God, no nation or group of nations in the world could even think of overrunning Israel; without God, the weakest nation could overcome them)*; and I will make your Heaven as iron, and your Earth as brass *(instead of Heaven being opened to their prayers, it would be closed, "as iron"; instead of the Earth yielding its increase, it would be "as brass")*:

20 And your strength shall be spent in vain *(wasted effort)*: for your land shall not yield her increase, neither shall the trees of the land yield their fruits *(all blessings were dependent upon obedience to God; it is the same presently!)*.

PLAGUES

21 And if you walk contrary unto Me, and will not hearken unto me; I will bring seven times more plagues upon you according to your sins *(Judgment will at times bring people back to God; but, if it doesn't, God has promised to increase the pressure, even seven times more than had previously been rendered; all Believers should read these words very carefully)*.

22 I will also send wild beasts among you, which shall rob you of your children, and destroy your cattle, and make you few in number; and your high ways shall be desolate *(because of the fear of bandits)*.

23 And if you will not be reformed by Me by these things, but will walk contrary unto Me;

24 Then will I also walk contrary unto you, and will punish you yet seven times for your sins *(to have the Lord contrary to us, which sin does, is the single worst thing that can ever happen to any individual)*.

25 And I will bring a sword upon you, that shall avenge the quarrel of My Covenant: and when you are gathered together within your cities, I will send the pestilence among you; and you shall be delivered into the hand of the enemy *(those who persist in rebellion are here told that they cannot escape the Lord; wherever they go, they will be found, and the results will not be pleasant)*.

26 And when I have broken the staff of your bread, ten women shall bake your bread in one oven, and they shall deliver you your bread again by weight: and you shall eat, and not be satisfied *(food would be in such short supply that ten families, represented by "ten women," would have to exist or subsist on the amount that would normally be consumed by one family)*.

27 And if you will not for all this hearken unto Me, but walk contrary unto Me;

28 Then I will walk contrary unto you also in fury; and I, even I, will chastise you seven times for your sins *("seven" is God's number for perfection, totality, and universality; it is*

that in blessing, and it will be the same in chastisement; in other words, the chastisement will be total).

29 And you shall eat the flesh of your sons, and the flesh of your daughters shall you eat *(famine because of sin).*

30 And I will destroy your high places, and cut down your images, and cast your carcases upon the carcases of your idols, and My soul shall abhor you. *(As the Lord would use His Power for blessing upon obedience, He will use His Power here for judgment because of disobedience. The judgment declared here shows the helplessness of the gods worshipped. To prove the point, the enemies of Israel would slaughter tens of thousands of Israelites, even in the very presence of their idols, showing again their helplessness.)*

31 And I will make your cities waste, and bring your Sanctuaries unto desolation, and I will not smell the savour of your sweet odours. *(The great Temple in Jerusalem, which had once been the House of God, was destroyed by the Babylonian Monarch, Nebuchadnezzar. This meant the Sacrifices would now be stopped, which would signal the total doom of Israel, because these Sacrifices represented the Cross. That repudiated and taken away, there was nothing left! Let the modern Church read these words very carefully.)*

32 And I will bring the land into desolation: and your enemies which dwell therein shall be astonished at it *(what had once been such a verdant garden will now become a cesspool, even to the extent that Israel's enemies would be astonished at it).*

33 And I will scatter you among the heathen *(which is exactly what happened),* and will draw out a sword after you: and your land shall be desolate, and your cities waste.

34 Then shall the land enjoy her Sabbaths, as long as it lies desolate, and you be in your enemies' land; even then shall the land rest, and enjoy her Sabbaths. *(The "Sabbaths" of both days and years were so very important, because of what they symbolized. In their totality, whether on the seventh day of the week, or the seventh year, or the fiftieth year, they all, and without exception, symbolized the "rest" which would come with Christ, and one's acceptance of Him. If we try to make less of the Sabbaths than this, we greatly misinterpret Scripture. If we try to make more, it is an impossible task, for there could be nothing greater than Christ, and what Christ would do at the Cross for Adam's fallen race.)*

35 As long as it lies desolate it shall rest; because it did not rest in your Sabbaths, when you dwelt upon it. *(For about 490 years, Israel ignored the seventh year Sabbaths. This meant that 70 years of Sabbaths were owed to God. He collected those Sabbaths by forcing Israel into Babylonian bondage, where they stayed exactly 70 years.)*

36 And upon them who are left alive of you I will send a faintness into their hearts in the lands of their enemies; and the sound of a shaken leaf shall chase them; and they shall flee, as fleeing from a sword; and they shall fall when none pursues *(constant fear!).*

37 And they shall fall one upon another, as it were before a sword, when none pursues: and you shall have no power to stand before your enemies *(the Cross alone provides such power [I Cor. 1:18]; all other efforts are fruitless).*

38 And you shall perish among the heathen, and the land of your enemies shall eat you up.

39 And they who are left of you shall pine away in their iniquity in your enemies' lands; and also in the iniquities of their fathers shall they pine away with them. *(Verses 36 through 39 predict the destruction of Israel by the Babylonians, and then by the Romans. They also predict these ancient people in great sorrow, scattered all over the world, which is exactly what has happened, because of their forsaking the Lord their God.)*

40 If they shall confess their iniquity, and the iniquity of their fathers, with their trespass which they trespassed against Me, and that also they have walked contrary unto Me *("if they shall confess their iniquity"; this is the one condition for personal and national restoration);*

41 And that I also have walked contrary unto them, and have brought them into the land of their enemies; if then their uncircumcised hearts be humbled, and they then accept of the punishment of their iniquity *(this is basically the same as I John 1:9)*:

42 Then will I remember My Covenant with Jacob, and also My Covenant with Isaac, and also My Covenant with Abraham will I remember; and I will remember the land *(the moment the people, through confession of their sins, attempt to come back into the Covenant, they will be readily accepted).*

43 The land also shall be left of them *(should be translated, "But the land shall be deserted by them"),* and shall enjoy her Sabbaths, while she lies desolate without them: and they shall accept of the punishment of their iniquity:

because, even because they despised My Judgments, and because their soul abhorred My Statutes *(in essence, the Lord plainly predicted here that Israel would, in fact, ignore His Word)*.

44 And yet for all that, when they be in the land of their enemies, I will not cast them away, neither will I abhor them, to destroy them utterly, and to break My Covenant with them: for I am the LORD their God. *(God's Covenants, at least on His part, cannot be broken. While men may break the Covenant, which Israel definitely did, and which many do as it regards the New Covenant, the Covenant stands. But, to be sure, those, whoever they might be, who register unbelief toward the Covenant will definitely be lost.)*

45 But I will for their sakes remember the Covenant of their ancestors, whom I brought forth out of the land of Egypt in the sight of the heathen, that I might be their God: I am the LORD. *(In these Passages, plus many others given in the Word of God [Rom., Chpts. 9-11], we find the Lord promising that the Covenant He made with the Patriarchs will ultimately and in totality be fulfilled. This completely abrogates the foolish notion held by some in the modern Church, who claim that Israel is no longer of any spiritual significance. I find that as difficult to believe as I do the denial of the Cross.)*

46 These are the Statutes and Judgments and Laws, which the LORD made between Him and the Children of Israel in Mount Sinai by the hand of Moses. *(Every one of these Laws was instituted by God, which means that man had no part in their formation at all. Inasmuch as these were the Laws of God, they were perfect in every respect.)*

CHAPTER 27
(1491 B.C.)
VOWS

AND the LORD spoke unto Moses, saying,

2 Speak unto the Children of Israel, and say unto them, When a man shall make a singular vow, the persons shall be for the LORD by your estimation *(as a people, Israel was birthed by the Lord, and done so for a particular principle and purpose; as such, they had to be taught the significance of all their doings, and especially vows made to God; they had to understand that these were not just idle words made in the heat of necessity, but that the Lord looked at these vows as serious things indeed)*.

3 And your estimation shall be of the male from twenty years old even unto sixty years old, even your estimation shall be fifty shekels of silver, after the shekel of the Sanctuary *(the amounts stipulated were in silver, which figured Redemption; for the "vow," whatever it may have been, to have been binding, the amount of money stipulated, and for the different people, must be given to the Sanctuary)*.

4 And if it be a female, then your estimation shall be thirty shekels.

5 And if it be from five years old even unto twenty years old, then your estimation shall be of the male twenty shekels, and for the female ten shekels.

6 And if it be from a month old even unto five years old, then your estimation shall be of the male five shekels of silver, and for the female your estimation shall be three shekels of silver.

7 And if it be from sixty years old and above: if it be a male, then your estimation shall be fifteen shekels, and for the female ten shekels.

8 But if he be poorer than your estimation, then he shall present himself before the Priest, and the Priest shall value him: according to his ability who vowed shall the Priest value him. *(The Priest, in this case, becomes the exponent of Grace. Israel at Mount Horeb made a "singular vow," which, when tested by the standard of Righteousness, failed. But the True Aaron, the Great High Priest, the Lord Jesus Christ, will estimate her in Grace, and will fulfill for her all the righteous requirements of a vow.)*

VOWS INVOLVING ANIMALS

9 And if it be a beast, whereof men bring an Offering unto the LORD, all that any man gives of such unto the LORD shall be holy *(makes a vow concerning a Sacrifice)*.

10 He shall not alter it, nor change it, a good for a bad, or a bad for a good: and if he shall at all change beast for beast, then it and the exchange thereof shall be holy.

11 And if it be any unclean beast, of which they do not offer a Sacrifice unto the LORD, then he shall present the beast before the Priest *(it is said that no vow mentally made or conceived was deemed binding; it had to be distinctly pronounced in words before the Lord and before the Priest)*:

12 And the Priest shall value it, whether it be good or bad: as you value it, you who are

the Priest, so shall it be *(a value was put on the animal which could not be sacrificed because it was unclean, and that amount of money was to be paid to the Sanctuary to satisfy the vow)*

13 But if he will at all redeem it, then he shall add a fifth part thereof unto your estimation *(whatever the Priest valued the animal, 20 percent was to be added, at least in this case, simply because it was an animal which was unclean, and could not be offered in Sacrifice to begin with)*.

VOWS CONCERNING A HOUSE

14 And when a man shall sanctify his house to be holy unto the LORD *(make a vow concerning his house)*, then the Priest shall estimate it, whether it be good or bad: as the Priest shall estimate it, so shall it stand.

15 And if he who sanctified it will redeem his house *(pay money to the Sanctuary instead)*, then he shall add the fifth part of the money of your estimation unto it, and it shall be his *(the vow will be satisfied)*.

VOWS CONCERNING THE FIELDS

16 And if a man shall sanctify unto the LORD some part of a field of his possession, then your estimation shall be according to the seed thereof: an homer of barley seed shall be valued at fifty shekels of silver *(the value would be judged according to the amount of grain grown on the land)*.

17 If he sanctify his field from the Year of Jubilee, according to your estimation it shall stand.

18 But if he sanctify his field after the Jubilee, then the Priest shall reckon unto him the money according to the years that remain, even unto the Year of the Jubilee, and it shall be abated from your estimation *(in this case, all were valued according to the number of years left before the Year of Jubilee)*.

19 And if he who sanctified the field *(vowed the field)* will in any wise redeem it, then he shall add the fifth part of the money of your estimation unto it, and it shall be assured to him *(if anyone else redeemed it, they would do so at the estimation; however, if the man who made the vow redeemed it, he was to add 20 percent to the estimation of the Priest)*.

20 And if he will not redeem the field, or if he have sold the field to another man, it shall not be redeemed any more.

21 But the field, when it goes out in the Jubilee *(the time runs out)*, shall be holy unto the LORD, as a field devoted; the possession thereof shall be the Priest's *(the field now belongs to the Sanctuary, and is to be used for its upkeep)*.

22 And if a man sanctify unto the LORD a field which he has bought, which is not of the fields of his possession:

23 Then the priest shall reckon unto him the worth of your estimation, even unto the Year of the Jubilee: and he shall give your estimation in that day, as a holy thing unto the LORD *(if a man vowed a vow concerning a field he did not really own, when the Year of Jubilee came around, the Priest was to estimate the worth, with the man giving that much money to the Sanctuary, which would then satisfy the vow)*.

24 In the Year of the Jubilee the field shall return unto him of whom it was bought, even to him to whom the possession of the land did belong *(in other words, when the Year of Jubilee came about, the land would not revert to the man who made the vow, who really did not own the field, but would revert to its rightful owner, whoever that may have been)*.

25 And all your estimations shall be according to the shekel of the Sanctuary: twenty gerahs shall be the shekel *(the "shekel" was not actually a coin, at least at that time, but a particular weight of silver, approximately one ounce)*.

FIRSTBORN OF ANIMALS

26 Only the firstling of the beasts, which should be the LORD's firstling, no man shall sanctify it: whether it be ox, or sheep: it is the LORD's *(two classes of objects were forbidden to be vowed: 1. The firstborn of beasts; and, 2. Devoted things)*.

27 And if it be of an unclean beast, then he shall redeem it according to your estimation *(the estimation of the Priest)*, and shall add a fifth part of it thereto: or if it be not redeemed, then it shall be sold according to your estimation *(a vow could be made of the firstborn of unclean animals, and then the amount of money paid to the Sanctuary according to the estimation of the Priest, which would satisfy the vow; however, if it was the firstborn of a clean animal, such as a lamb, goat, heifer, etc., it could not be vowed)*.

ANY DEDICATED THING

28 Notwithstanding no devoted thing, that

a man shall devote unto the LORD of all that he has, both of man and beast, and of the field of his possession, shall be sold or redeemed: every devoted thing is most holy unto the LORD *(all gifts devoted to the Lord in this manner became the property of the Sanctuary [Num. 18:14]).*

29 None devoted, which shall be devoted of men, shall be redeemed; but shall surely be put to death. *(This speaks of clean animals devoted to God from birth. They could not be redeemed, but had to be offered in Sacrifice. Christ was totally devoted to the Lord by His parents when He was a child, and rightly so, and was not redeemed, and was put to death. But He was put to death, not for His Own sins, for He had no sins, but for the sins of others; consequently, He made it possible for all of mankind to be redeemed, at least those who will believe [Jn. 3:16].)*

TITHES

30 And all the tithe *(10 percent)* of the land, whether of the seed of the land, or of the fruit of the tree, is the LORD's: it is holy unto the LORD. *(Tithing did not begin with Moses or the Law. The first mention of tithing refers to Abraham giving tithes to Melchizedek [Gen. 14:26; Heb. 7:4]. As well, Jacob vowed the tenth to the Lord [Gen. 28:22]. Although included in the Mosaic institution, the fact is, tithing preceded the Law, and continues unto this hour. Tithing is the tenth, for that's what the word means, and fell into the same category as the "firstborn."*

In other words, as the firstborn of both man and beast belonged to the Lord, likewise, tithes belong to the Lord presently.

As stated, Abraham paid tithe to Melchizedek. This man, even as Paul reiterates in Hebrews, Chapter 7, was a Type of Christ. Abraham is a type of all Believers. Inasmuch as Abraham paid tithe to this man, we, as Believers, the children of Abraham, continue to pay tithe to Christ, by supporting His Work, of whom Melchizedek was a Type [Heb. 7:1-5].)

31 And if a man will at all redeem ought of his tithes, he shall add thereto the fifth part thereof *(meaning that he fails to pay his tithes when they are owed, and when they are actually paid, he has to add 20 percent).*

32 And concerning the tithe of the herd, or of the flock, even of whatsoever passes under the rod, the tenth shall be holy unto the LORD *(it is still holy unto the Lord, and ever shall be; this is the Lord's way of financing His Work, and I speak of both Tithes and Offerings; I cannot conceive of a Believer, at least a true Believer, considering what the Lord has done for him, not wanting to support the Work of God by paying his Tithe, and even more).*

33 He shall not search whether it be good or bad, neither shall he change it: and if he change it at all, then both it and the change thereof shall be holy: it shall not be redeemed *(we must not figure God out of our giving by trying to make changes).*

34 These are the Commandments, which the LORD commanded Moses for the Children of Israel in Mount Sinai.

THE FOURTH BOOK OF MOSES, CALLED
NUMBERS

CHAPTER 1
(1490 B.C.)
THE CENSUS

AND the LORD spoke unto Moses in the wilderness of Sinai, in the Tabernacle of the congregation, on the first day of the second month, in the second year after they were come out of the land of Egypt, saying *(unfortunately, the wilderness experience seems to be absolutely necessary, at least in some manner, for every Christian)*,

2 Take ye the sum of all the congregation of the Children of Israel, after their families, by the house of their fathers, with the number of their names, every male by their polls *(every person in Israel was numbered, and done so at the command of the Lord, even as every Believer presently is numbered by the Lord)*;

3 From twenty years old and upward, all who are able to go forth to war in Israel: you and Aaron shall number them by their armies. *(While the theme of Leviticus is worship, that of Numbers is warfare. This means that spiritual Israelites are to be warriors as well as worshippers. Paul said, "War a good warfare" [I Tim. 1:18]. In Exodus 30:11, it was commanded that whenever a census was taken of the men of Israel, a half shekel of silver [about half an ounce] had to be given to the Sanctuary for every man. Silver, in the Old Testament, was a type of Redemption, thereby stating that Israel's power was not in her standing army, whatever that might have been, but rather the fact that she was bought by the blood of the Lamb.)*

THE CENSUS TAKERS

4 And with you there shall be a man of every tribe; every one head of the house of his fathers *(the head of each Tribe would be responsible for the census of that Tribe)*.

5 And these are the names of the men who shall stand with you: of the tribe of Reuben; Elizur the son of Shedeur.

6 Of Simeon; Shelumiel the son of Zurishaddai.

7 Of Judah; Nahshon the son of Amminadab.

8 Of Issachar; Nethaneel the son of Zuar.

9 Of Zebulun; Eliab the son of Helon.

10 Of the children of Joseph: of Ephraim; Elishama the son of Ammihud: of Manasseh; Gamaliel the son of Pedahzur.

11 Of Benjamin; Abidan the son of Gideoni.

12 Of Dan; Ahiezer the son of Ammishaddai.

13 Of Asher; Pagiel the son of Ocran.

14 Of Gad; Eliasaph the son of Deuel.

15 Of Naphtali; Ahira the son of Enan.

16 These were the renowned of the congregation, princes of the tribes of their fathers, heads of thousands in Israel.

17 And Moses and Aaron took these men which are expressed by their names *(all of these men were chosen by God, and none by Moses or Aaron)*:

THE ASSEMBLY

18 And they assembled all the congregation together on the first day of the second month, and they declared their pedigrees after their families, by the house of their fathers, according to the number of the names, from twenty years old and upward, by their polls *(this was 13 months after they had left Egypt)*.

19 As the LORD commanded Moses, so he numbered them in the wilderness of Sinai *(they had been in the wilderness for 13 months)*.

REUBEN: 46,500

20 And the Children of Reuben, Israel's oldest son, by their generations, after their families, by the house of their fathers, according to the number of the names, by their polls, every male from twenty years old and upward, all who were able to go forth to war *(Fellowship with God means warfare with the world; hence 14 times in this Chapter occur the words, "all who were able to go forth to war")*;

21 Those who were numbered of them, even of the tribe of Reuben, were forty and six thousand and five hundred.

SIMEON: 59,300

22 Of the Children of Simeon, by their

generations, after their families, by the house of their fathers, those who were numbered of them, according to the number of the names, by their polls, every male from twenty years old and upward, all who were able to go forth to war;

23 Those who were numbered of them, even of the tribe of Simeon, were fifty and nine thousand and three hundred.

GAD: 45,650

24 Of the Children of Gad, by their generations, after their families, by the house of their fathers, according to the number of the names, from twenty years old and upward, all who were able to go forth to war;

25 Those who were numbered of them, even of the tribe of Gad, were forty and five thousand six hundred and fifty.

JUDAH: 74,600

26 Of the Children of Judah, by their generations, after their families, by the house of their fathers, according to the number of the names, from twenty years old and upward, all who were able to go forth to war;

27 Those who were numbered of them, even of the Tribe of Judah, were threescore and fourteen thousand and six hundred (*Judah was the largest Tribe, and was the Tribe from which Jesus came [Gen. 49:10]*).

ISSACHAR: 54,400

28 Of the Children of Issachar, by their generations, after their families, by the house of their fathers, according to the number of the names, from twenty years old and upward, all who were able to go forth to war;

29 Those who were numbered of them, even of the tribe of Issachar, were fifty and four thousand and four hundred.

ZEBULUN: 57,400

30 Of the Children of Zebulun, by their generations, after their families, by the house of their fathers, according to the number of the names, from twenty years old and upward, all who were able to go forth to war;

31 Those who were numbered of them, even of the Tribe of Zebulun, were fifty and seven thousand and four hundred.

EPHRAIM: 40,500

32 Of the Children of Joseph, namely, of the Children of Ephraim, by their generations, after their families, by the house of their fathers, according to the number of the names, from twenty years old and upward, all who were able to go forth to war;

33 Those who were numbered of them, even of the Tribe of Ephraim, were forty thousand and five hundred.

MANASSEH: 32,200

34 Of the Children of Manasseh, by their generations, after their families, by the house of their fathers, according to the number of the names, from twenty years old and upward, all who were able to go forth to war;

35 Those who were numbered of them, even of the Tribe of Manasseh, were thirty and two thousand and two hundred.

BENJAMIN: 35,400

36 Of the Children of Benjamin, by their generations, after their families, by the house of their fathers, according to the number of the names, from twenty years old and upward, all who were able to go forth to war;

37 Those who were numbered of them, even of the Tribe of Benjamin, were thirty and five thousand and four hundred. (*Christian conflict is not a warfare with personal doubts and fears as to one's Salvation, but it is a succession of battles with enemies of God within and without, i.e., "sin and self" — Williams.*)

DAN: 62,700

38 Of the Children of Dan, by their generations, after their families, by the house of their fathers, according to the number of the names, from twenty years old and upward, all who were able to go forth to war;

39 Those who were numbered of them, even of the Tribe of Dan, were threescore and two thousand and seven hundred.

ASHER: 41,500

40 Of the Children of Asher, by their generations, after their families, by the house of their fathers, according to the number of the names, from twenty years old and upward, all

who were able to go forth to war;

41 Those who were numbered of them, even of the Tribe of Asher, were forty and one thousand and five hundred.

NAPHTALI: 53,400

42 Of the Children of Naphtali, throughout their generations, after their families, by the house of their fathers, according to the number of the names, from twenty years old and upward, all who were able to go forth to war;

43 Those that were numbered of them, even of the tribe of Naphtali, were fifty and three thousand and four hundred.

GRAND TOTAL: 603,550

44 These are those who were numbered, which Moses and Aaron numbered, and the princes of Israel, being twelve men: each one was for the house of his fathers.

45 So were all those who were numbered of the Children of Israel, by the house of their fathers, from twenty years old and upward, all who were able to go forth to war in Israel;

46 Even all they who were numbered were six hundred thousand and three thousand and five hundred and fifty. *(Of this first census, all perished because of unbelief, except two, Joshua and Caleb. The Holy Spirit, in I Cor., Chpt. 10, says that these facts are recorded to admonish those who think they stand to take heed lest they fall.)*

LEVITES NOT NUMBERED

47 But the Levites after the Tribe of their fathers were not numbered among them *(this was the Priestly Tribe)*.

48 For the LORD had spoken unto Moses, saying,

49 Only you shall not number the Tribe of Levi, neither take the sum of them among the Children of Israel:

APPOINTMENT

50 But you shall appoint the Levites over the Tabernacle of Testimony, and over all the vessels thereof, and over all things that belong to it: they shall bear the Tabernacle, and all the vessels thereof; and they shall minister unto it, and shall encamp round about the Tabernacle.

51 And when the Tabernacle sets forward, the Levites shall take it down: and when the Tabernacle is to be pitched, the Levites shall set it up: and the stranger *(Gentile)* who comes near shall be put to death.

52 And the Children of Israel shall pitch their tents, every man by his own camp, and every man by his own standard, throughout their hosts. *(In the Tribes, Ephraim took the place of Joseph, and Manasseh took the place of Levi in the Twelve-Tribe arrangement of Israel. The Tribe of Levi was not counted, being chosen as the Ministers of the other Tribes, and without any definite allotment of land among the other Twelve Tribes.)*

53 But the Levites shall pitch round about the Tabernacle of Testimony, that there be no wrath upon the congregation of the Children of Israel: and the Levites shall keep the charge of the Tabernacle of Testimony. *(The Levites were not included in the numbering, which means they were exempted by Divine direction. Their function was the Tabernacle, and in every capacity. When Israel camped, the Tribe of Levi pitched their tents around the Tabernacle, and were responsible for its protection. No one else of the other Tribes was to penetrate this cordon of protection, except to bring Sacrifices. All the Priesthood was of the Tribe of Levi; however, all Levites were not Priests, the latter group coming solely from the family of Aaron.)*

54 And the Children of Israel did according to all that the LORD commanded Moses, so did they.

CHAPTER 2
(1490 B.C.)
CAMP ASSIGNMENTS

AND the LORD spoke unto Moses and unto Aaron, saying,

2 Every man of the Children of Israel shall pitch by his own standard, with the ensign of their father's house: far off about the Tabernacle of the congregation shall they pitch *(the position of the standard was determined by the position of the Tabernacle; the Tabernacle was the center of everything, even as Christ must be the center of everything presently, of Whom the Tabernacle was a Type)*.

THE EAST SIDE

3 And on the east side toward the rising of the sun shall they of the standard of the camp

of Judah pitch throughout their armies: and Nahshon the son of Amminadab shall be captain of the Children of Judah.

4 And his host, and those who were numbered of them, were threescore and fourteen thousand and six hundred.

5 And those who do pitch next unto him shall be the Tribe of Issachar: and Nethaneel the son of Zuar shall be captain of the Children of Issachar.

6 And his host, and those who were numbered thereof were fifty and four thousand and four hundred.

7 Then the Tribe of Zebulun: and Eliab the son of Helon shall be captain of the Children of Zebulun.

8 And his host, and those who numbered thereof, were fifty and seven thousand and four hundred. (The three Tribes of Judah, Issachar, and Zebulun were to camp on the east side of the Tabernacle. These were their assigned places, and they were not to deviate from those places. As well, the Lord assigns a particular Ministry for each and every Believer. Regrettably, most never know what that Ministry is, because of a lack of consecration. As well, many, if not most, try to fill a position designed by men, or themselves, and not the Lord. It is the same as one of the Tribes of Israel camping in a spot not designated for them.)

9 All who were numbered in the camp of Judah were an hundred thousand and fourscore thousand and six thousand and four hundred, throughout their armies (these three Tribes, numbering 186,400, were said to be in the "Camp of Judah"). These shall first set forth. (Judah means "praise." So, when the camp moved, Judah was to go first, which meant that Israel was to be led by "praise.")

THE SOUTH SIDE

10 On the south side shall be the standard of the camp of Reuben according to their armies: and the captain of the children of Reuben shall be Elizur the son of Shedeur.

11 And his host, and those who were numbered thereof, were forty and six thousand and five hundred.

12 And those which pitch by him shall be the Tribe of Simeon: and the captain of the Children of Simeon shall be Shelumiel the son of Zurishaddai. (Even though "Simeon" had a place here in the wilderness, when Israel went into the Promised Land, because of the curse

[Gen. 49:5-7], they had no place. Levi was under this curse, as well, but became the Priestly Tribe, because of standing with Moses, as it regarded the Golden Calf [Ex. 32:25-28]. Simeon ultimately had his inheritance within the inheritance of Judah [Josh. 19:1]. Likewise, the entirety of the human race has been cursed because of the Fall; however, our Heavenly Judah, the Lord Jesus Christ, has made provision for us to have an inheritance within His vast Inheritance [Rom. 8:17].)

13 And his host, and those who were numbered of them, were fifty and nine thousand and three hundred.

14 Then the Tribe of Gad: and the captain of the sons of Gad shall be Eliasaph the son of Reuel.

15 And his host, and those who were numbered of them, were forty and five thousand and six hundred and fifty.

16 All who were numbered in the camp of Reuben were an hundred thousand and fifty and one thousand and four hundred and fifty, throughout their armies. And they shall set forth in the second rank (the three Tribes of Reuben, Simeon, and Gad were to encamp on the south side of the Tabernacle. All three Tribes numbered 151,450).

LEVITES: 22,000

17 Then the Tabernacle of the congregation shall set forward with the camp of the Levites in the midst of the camp: as they encamp, so shall they set forward, every man in his place by their standards. (As the camp moved, Judah led the way with "praise." The rear was brought up by Dan, whose name means "judgment," meaning that anyone who attacked Israel would be judged by God. At the center were the Levites, whose name means "joined," or "communion.")

THE WEST SIDE

18 On the west side shall be the standard of the camp of Ephraim according to their armies: and the captain of the sons of Ephraim shall be Elishama the son of Ammihud.

19 And his host, and those who were numbered of them, were forty thousand and five hundred.

20 And by him shall be the tribe of Manasseh: and the captain of the children of Manasseh shall be Gamaliel the son of Pedahzur.

21 And his host, and those who were numbered of them, were thirty and two thousand and two hundred.

22 Then the Tribe of Benjamin: and the captain of the sons of Benjamin shall be Abidan the son of Gideoni.

23 And his host, and those who were numbered of them, were thirty and five thousand and four hundred.

24 All who were numbered of the camp of Ephraim were an hundred thousand and eight thousand and an hundred, throughout their armies. And they shall go forward in the third rank. (When encamped or on the march, Ephraim, Benjamin, and Manasseh were nearest to the Mercy Seat. Hence their being named in Psalms 80:1-2. There were 108,100 in the three Tribes of Ephraim, Manasseh, and Benjamin.)

THE NORTH SIDE

25 The standard of the camp of Dan shall be on the north side by their armies: and the captain of the Children of Dan shall be Ahiezer the son of Ammishaddai.

26 And his host, and those who were numbered of them, were threescore and two thousand the seven hundred.

27 And those who encamp by him shall be the Tribe of Asher: and the captain of the Children of Asher shall be Pagiel the son of Ocran.

28 And his host, and those who were numbered of them, were forty and one thousand and five hundred.

29 Then the Tribe of Naphtali: and the captain of the Children of Naphtali shall be Ahira the son of Enan.

30 And his host, and those who were numbered of them, were fifty and three thousand and four hundred.

31 All they who were numbered in the camp of Dan were an hundred thousand and fifty and seven thousand and six hundred. They shall go hindmost with their standards. (The three Tribes of Dan, Asher, and Naphtali were encamped on the north side, with their total population of 157,600.)

GRAND TOTAL: 603,550 MEN
BESIDES THE LEVITES

32 These are those which were numbered of the Children of Israel by the house of their fathers: all those who were numbered of the camps throughout their hosts were six hundred thousand and three thousand and five hundred and fifty.

33 But the Levites were not numbered among the Children of Israel; as the LORD commanded Moses.

34 And the Children of Israel did according to all that the LORD commanded Moses: so they pitched by their standards, and so they set forward, every one after their families, according to the house of their fathers. (As we have surveyed this Chapter, we have learned about God's order. We have learned, as stated, that "praise" must lead the way. And if "praise" rightly leads the way, drawing sustenance from the "communion" that is in the center, which comes from the Tabernacle, i.e., "Christ," and nourishes all, then Divine Judgment will protect the rear guard against all the powers of darkness that would seek to hinder the Church of the Living God.)

CHAPTER 3
(1490 B.C.)
THE SONS OF AARON

THESE also are the generations of Aaron and Moses in the day that the LORD spoke with Moses in Mount Sinai.

2 And these are the names of the sons of Aaron; Nadab the firstborn, and Abihu, Eleazar, and Ithamar.

3 These are the names of the sons of Aaron, the Priests which were anointed, whom he consecrated to minister in the Priest's office.

4 And Nadab and Abihu died before the LORD, when they offered strange fire before the LORD, in the wilderness of Sinai, and they had no children: and Eleazar and Ithamar ministered in the Priest's office in the sight of Aaron their father. (God cannot abide sin in any form, and when it's sin against the Cross, as was the sin of Nadab and Abihu, it is most grievous indeed. The tragedy is, this sin, the sin of "strange fire," is being committed today as never before; and the results are the same, "death" [Gal. 5:2-4].)

THE LEVITES

5 And the LORD spoke unto Moses, saying,

6 Bring the Tribe of Levi near, and present them before Aaron the Priest, that they may minister unto him. (As we will find out in this Chapter, Grace entrusted the Levites with the Tabernacle and its vessels when on the march,

and Love apportioned to each the load suited to his strength.)

7 And they shall keep his charge, and the charge of the whole congregation before the Tabernacle of the congregation, to do the service of the Tabernacle. *(The Holy Spirit had originally said of the Tribe of Levi, through the Patriarch Jacob, "O my soul, come not thou into their secret," which spoke of the evil of their hearts in all its unrighteousness; yet the Lord could bring Levi into His Secret, and unite him to His Assembly. He could take him out of his habitation, wherein were instruments of cruelty, and bring him into the Tabernacle to be occupied with the holy instruments and vessels that were there. Only the Grace of God could do such a thing!)*

8 And they shall keep all the instruments of the Tabernacle of the congregation, and the charge of the Children of Israel, to do the service of the Tabernacle *(this same "charge" is given to all Believers presently).*

9 And you shall give the Levites unto Aaron and to his sons: they are wholly given unto him out of the Children of Israel.

10 And you shall appoint Aaron and his sons, and they shall wait on their Priest's office: and the stranger *(Gentile)* who comes near shall be put to death *(because they were not under the Abrahamic Covenant).*

THE SUBSTITUTE

11 And the LORD spoke unto Moses, saying,

12 And I, behold, I have taken the Levites from among the Children of Israel instead of all the firstborn that opens the matrix among the Children of Israel: therefore the Levites shall be mine *(it seems that the Lord had originally planned to use the firstborn of every family as the Priestly Tribe; but, due to a series of events, the Grace of God would give the Tribe of Levi that high and holy honor.*

Concerning this, Mackintosh says: "In Faith's arithmetic, God is the only significant figure; and having Him, you may add as many ciphers as you please. If all your Faith is in the Living God, it ceases to be a question of your need, and resolves itself into a question of His Sufficiency");

13 Because all the firstborn are Mine; for on the day that I smote all the firstborn in the land of Egypt I hallowed unto Me all the firstborn in Israel, both man and beast: Mine shall they be: I am the LORD.

DUTIES ASSIGNED TO THE LEVITES

14 And the LORD spoke unto Moses in the wilderness of Sinai, saying,

15 Number the Children of Levi after the house of their fathers, by their families: every male from a month old and upward shall you number them. *(Whereas the numbering of all the other Tribes began at 20, it began at one month old regarding the boy babies of the Levites.)*

16 And Moses numbered them according to the Word of the LORD, as he was commanded.

17 And these were the sons of Levi by their names; Gershon, and Kohath, and Merari.

18 And these are the names of the sons of Gershon by their families; Libni, and Shimei.

19 And the sons of Kohath by their families; Amram, and Izehar, Hebron, and Uzziel.

20 And the sons of Merari by their families; Mahli, and Mushi. These are the families of the Levites according to the house of their fathers.

21 Of Gershon was the family of the Libnites, and the family of the Shimites: these are the families of the Gershonites:

22 Those who were numbered of them, according to the number of all the males, from a month old and upward, even those who were numbered of them were seven thousand and five hundred.

23 The families of the Gershonites shall pitch behind the Tabernacle westward.

24 And the chief of the house of the father of the Gershonites shall be Eliasaph the son of Lael.

THE CHARGE

25 And the charge of the sons of Gershon in the Tabernacle of the congregation shall be the Tabernacle, and the tent, the covering thereof, and the hanging for the door of the Tabernacle of the congregation,

26 And the hangings of the court, and the curtain for the door of the court, which is by the Tabernacle, and by the Altar round about, and the cords of it for all the service thereof. *(The Gershonites were in charge of the things listed, as it regards the Tabernacle. It was their responsibility for taking down this part of the Tabernacle, whenever the Holy Spirit desired that the Camp of Israel be moved. They were responsible, as well, for re-erecting it. Also, it was their duty to protect it and maintain it when it was erected.)*

THE KOHATHITES

27 And of Kohath was the family of the Amramites, and the family of the Izeharites, and the family of the Hebronites, and the family of the Uzzielites: these are the families of the Kohathites.

28 In the number of all the males, from a month old and upward, were eight thousand and six hundred, keeping the charge of the Sanctuary.

29 The families of the sons of Kohath shall pitch on the side of the Tabernacle southward.

30 And the chief of the house of the father of the families of the Kohathites shall be Elizaphan the son of Uzziel.

31 And their charge shall be the Ark, and the Table, and the Candlestick, and the Altars, and the vessels of the Sanctuary wherewith they minister, and the hanging, and all the service thereof.

32 And Eleazar the son of Aaron the Priest shall be chief over the chief of the Levites, and have the oversight of them who keep the charge of the Sanctuary. *(As the Tabernacle proper was the charge of the Gershonites, the sacred vessels which went inside of the Tabernacle were the charge of the Kohathites.)*

THE MERARITES

33 Of Merari was the family of the Mahlites, and the family of the Mushites: these are the families of Merari.

34 And those who were numbered of them, according to the number of all the males, from a month old and upward, were six thousand and two hundred.

35 And the chief of the house of the father of the families of Merari was Zuriel the son of Abihail: these shall pitch on the side of the Tabernacle northward.

36 And under the custody and charge of the sons of Merari shall be the boards of the Tabernacle, and the bars thereof, and the pillars thereof, and the sockets thereof, and all the vessels thereof, and all that serves thereto,

37 And the pillars of the court round about, and their sockets, and their pins, and their cords.

38 But those who encamp before the Tabernacle toward the east, even before the Tabernacle of the congregation eastward, shall be Moses, and Aaron and his sons, keeping the charge of the Sanctuary for the charge of the Children of Israel; and the stranger *(Gentile)* who comes near shall be put to death.

39 All who were numbered of the Levites, which Moses and Aaron numbered at the Commandment of the LORD, throughout their families, all the males from a month old and upward, were twenty and two thousand. *(The charge of the Merarites consisted of everything not included in that of the Gershonites and the Kohathites. It must be understood that there was a greater dignity in carrying a lowly "pin" of the Tabernacle than in wielding the mighty scepter of Egypt.)*

REDEMPTION

40 And the LORD said unto Moses, Number all the firstborn of the males of the Children of Israel from a month old and upward, and take the number of their names. *(One should be careful to note the Divine order of all things, and that neither Moses nor the Levites were to deviate one iota from that which had been instructed.)*

41 And you shall take the Levites for me (I am the LORD) instead of all the firstborn among the Children of Israel; and the cattle of the Levites instead of all the firstlings among the cattle of the Children of Israel.

42 And Moses numbered, as the LORD commanded him, all the firstborn among the Children of Israel.

43 And all the firstborn males by the number of names, from a month old and upward, of those who were numbered of them, were twenty and two thousand two hundred and threescore and thirteen *(the number was 22,273; this does not refer to all the firstborn of the Children of Israel, which would have numbered much higher, but rather to those baby boys which had been born since coming out of Egypt, a time frame of about 13 months)*.

THE LEVITES

44 And the LORD spoke unto Moses, saying,

45 Take the Levites instead of all the firstborn among the Children of Israel, and the cattle of the Levites instead of their cattle; and the Levites shall be Mine: I am the LORD.

46 And for those who are to be redeemed of the two hundred and threescore and thirteen of the firstborn of the Children of Israel, which are more than the Levites;

47 You shall even take five shekels apiece

by the poll, after the shekel of the Sanctuary shall you take them: (the shekel is twenty gerahs:)

48 And you shall give the money (about $30 in 2004 currency), wherewith the odd number of them is to be redeemed, unto Aaron and to his sons.

49 And Moses took the redemption money of them who were over and above them who were redeemed by the Levites:

50 Of the firstborn of the Children of Israel took he the money; a thousand three hundred and threescore and five shekels, after the shekel of the Sanctuary (a little over $8,000 in 2004 currency):

51 And Moses gave the money of them who were redeemed unto Aaron and to his sons, according to the Word of the LORD, as the LORD commanded Moses. (It must have been perfectly beautiful to mark God's workers in the wilderness. Each one was at his post, and each moved in his Divinely appointed sphere. Hence, the moment the cloud was lifted up, and the order issued to strike, every man knew what he had to do, and he addressed himself to that and to nothing else. No man had any right to think for himself in these capacities: Jehovah thought for all. Unfortunately, far too many in the modern Church are attempting to push the Lord aside, and to serve in the place of the Lord, in effect, doing the thinking for the people. This the Lord can never accept, because He Alone is the "Head" of the Church. He will never abrogate that position [Col. 1:17-19].)

CHAPTER 4

(1490 B.C.)

THE DUTIES OF THE KOHATHITES

AND the LORD spoke unto Moses and unto Aaron, saying,

2 Take the sum of the sons of Kohath from among the sons of Levi, after their families, by the house of their fathers,

3 From thirty years old and upward even until fifty years old, all who enter into the host, to do the work in the Tabernacle of the congregation. (Those who would be Priests, who were of the family of Aaron, and those who would serve in the various appointments of the Levites, as given here, were to be 30 years of age before they began this work, and were to cease their activity at 50 years of age. Jesus was 30 years old, fulfilling this type, when He began His Ministry [Lk. 3:23].)

4 This shall be the service of the sons of Kohath in the Tabernacle of the congregation, about the most holy things:

5 And when the camp sets forward, Aaron shall come, and his sons, and they shall take down the covering Veil (the Veil that hung between the Holy Place and the Holy of Holies), and cover the Ark of Testimony with it (the Ark of the Covenant, when it was to be moved):

6 And shall put thereon the covering of badgers' skins (which was to lay over the Veil), and shall spread over it a cloth wholly of blue (the last covering, typifying that this was of Heaven), and shall put in the staves thereof (so it could be carried on the shoulders of the Priests).

7 And upon the Table of Shewbread they shall spread a cloth of blue, and put thereon the dishes, and the spoons, and the bowls, and covers to cover withal: and the continual bread shall be thereon (this Fourth Chapter portrays the work of the Priests, along with the Levites, who served in the tearing down, moving, and setting up again of the Tabernacle, plus all of its holy Vessels; God gave explicit instructions concerning the same; they were to be followed to the letter):

8 And they shall spread upon them a cloth of scarlet, and cover the same with a covering of badgers' skins, and shall put in the staves thereof (the disposition of the coverings that hid the Ark, the Table, the Lampstand, the Altar of Incense, the Vessels of Ministry, and the Brazen Altar set forth the sufferings of Christ and the glories that should follow).

9 And they shall take a cloth of blue, and cover the Candlestick (Lampstand) of the light, and his lamps, and his tongs, and his snuffdishes, and all the oil vessels thereof, wherewith they minister unto it:

10 And they shall put it and all the Vessels thereof within a covering of badgers' skins, and shall put it upon a bar (the outward covering in each case was badger-skin, except the Ark of the Covenant, which was a type of the Throne of Jehovah; its outermost covering was a cloth of blue, to illustrate possibly the Heavenly character of the kingdom which was proposed then to be set up upon Earth, and which will be introduced at the Second Coming).

11 And upon the Golden Altar (the Altar of Incense) they shall spread a cloth of blue, and cover it with a covering of badgers' skins, and shall put to the staves thereof:

12 And they shall take all the instruments of Ministry, wherewith they minister in the Sanctuary, and put them in a cloth of blue, and cover them with a covering of badgers' skins, and shall put them on a bar *(an apparatus used for their transportation)*:

13 And they shall take away the ashes from the Altar, and spread a purple cloth thereon *(the "ashes" symbolized all sin atoned and, in fact, no sin left, made possible by virtue of Christ and the Cross)*:

14 And they shall put upon it all the Vessels thereof, wherewith they minister about it, even the censers, the fleshhooks, and the shovels, and the basons, all the Vessels of the Altar *(the Brazen Altar)*; and they shall spread upon it a covering of badgers' skins, and put to the staves of it *("badgers' skins" were a type of the High Priestly Ministry of Christ)*.

15 And when Aaron and his sons have made an end of covering the Sanctuary, and all the Vessels of the Sanctuary, as the camp is to set forward; after that, the sons of Kohath shall come to bear it: but they shall not touch any holy thing, lest they die. These things are the burden of the sons of Kohath in the Tabernacle of the congregation. *(After the Priests had prepared all the Sacred Vessels for transportation, then, and then only, could the Kohathites come in to take them away. They were not for a moment to go in and look upon the holy things, lest they die [II Sam. 6:7]. Concerning this, Williams says: "When God dwells in power in the camp, it is as when a wire is charged with electricity. Hence, when He withdrew, men could look on, and handle, these holy things with impunity. The carnal curiosity which would analyze Christ's Human Nature brings death unto the soul.")*

16 And to the office of Eleazar the son of Aaron the Priest pertains the oil for the light, and the sweet incense, and the daily Meat Offering, and the anointing oil, and the oversight of all the Tabernacle, and of all that therein is, in the Sanctuary, and in the Vessels thereof *(Eleazar, the son of Aaron, was in charge of the Kohathites)*.

THE KOHATHITES

17 And the LORD spoke unto Moses and unto Aaron saying,

18 Cut ye not off the tribe of the families of the Kohathites from among the Levites:

19 But thus do unto them, that they may live, and not die, when they approach unto the most holy things: Aaron and his sons shall go in, and appoint them every one to his service and to his burden *(Kohathites had to be especially careful in the handling of the Sacred Vessels, that they not die; that's how critical the situation was, and that's how critical the situation still is; spiritual death is the end result of mishandling the Word of God)*:

20 But they shall not go in to see when the holy things are covered, lest they die *(they could only go in to carry these things out after they had been properly covered and attended to by the Priests)*.

THE DUTIES OF THE GERSHONITES

21 And the LORD spoke unto Moses, saying,

22 Take also the sum of the sons of Gershon, throughout the houses of their fathers, by their families;

23 From thirty years old and upward until fifty years old shall you number them; all who enter in to perform the service, to do the work in the Tabernacle of the congregation.

24 This is the service of the families of the Gershonites, to serve, and for burdens:

25 And they shall bear the curtains of the Tabernacle, and the Tabernacle of the congregation, his covering, and the covering of the badgers' skins that is above upon it *(the roof)*, and the hanging for the door of the Tabernacle of the congregation,

26 And the hangings of the Court, and the hanging for the door of the gate of the Court *(the entrance into the Court)*, which is by the Tabernacle and by the Altar round about, and their cords, and all the instruments of their service, and all that is made for them: so shall they serve.

27 At the appointment of Aaron and his sons shall be all the service of the sons of the Gershonites, in all their burdens, and in all their service: and you shall appoint unto them in charge all their burdens.

28 This is the service of the families of the sons of Gershon in the Tabernacle of the congregation: and their charge shall be under the hand of Ithamar the son of Aaron the Priest *(the Gershonites carried all the hangings belonging to the Tabernacle and to the Outer Court, with the single exception of the "Veil," which was wrapped around the Ark of the Covenant; as well, Ithamar, the son of Aaron, was in charge of the Gershonites)*.

THE DUTIES OF THE MERARITES

29 As for the sons of Merari, you shall number them after their families, by the house of their fathers;

30 From thirty years old and upward even unto fifty years old shall you number them, every one who enters into the service, to do the work of the Tabernacle of the congregation.

31 And this is the charge of their burden, according to all their service in the Tabernacle of the congregation; the boards of the Tabernacle, and the bars thereof, and the pillars thereof, and sockets thereof,

32 And the pillars of the court round about, and their sockets, and their pins, and their cords, with all their instruments, and with all their service: and by name you shall reckon the instruments of the charge of their burden.

33 This is the service of the families of the sons of Merari, according to all their service, in the Tabernacle of the congregation, under the hand of Ithamar the son of Aaron the Priest. *(The "charge" they were given was very important, even down to the "pins," which seemed to be the least of the items. If it's of the Lord, irrespective as to how small it might seem to be, it is important. Ithamar was in charge of this group as well, which means they were under Christ, for the Priesthood was a Type of Christ.)*

KOHATH NUMBERED: 2,750

34 And Moses and Aaron and the chief of the congregation numbered the sons of the Kohathites after their families, and after the house of their fathers,

35 From thirty years old and upward even unto fifty years old, every one who entered into the service, for the work in the Tabernacle of the congregation:

36 And those who were numbered of them by their families were two thousand seven hundred and fifty.

37 These were they who were numbered of the families of the Kohathites, all who might do service in the Tabernacle of the congregation, which Moses and Aaron did number according to the Commandment of the LORD by the hand of Moses. *(We find the word "numbered" used over and over in these Verses. This tells us that each person is very special in the Eyes of God.)*

GERSHON NUMBERED: 2,630

38 And those who were numbered of the sons of Gershon, throughout their families, and by the house of their fathers,

39 From thirty years old and upward even unto fifty years old, every one who enters into the service, for the work in the Tabernacle of the congregation,

40 Even those who were numbered of them, throughout their families, by the house of their fathers, were two thousand and six hundred and thirty.

41 These are they who were numbered of the families of the sons of Gershon, of all who might do service in the Tabernacle of the congregation, whom Moses and Aaron did number according to the Commandment of the LORD.

MERARI NUMBERED: 3,200

42 And those who were numbered of the families of the sons of Merari, throughout their families, by the house of their fathers,

43 From thirty years old and upward even unto fifty years old, every one who entered into the service, for the work in the Tabernacle of the congregation,

44 Even those who were numbered of them after their families, were three thousand and two hundred.

45 These be those who were numbered of the families of the sons of Merari, whom Moses and Aaron numbered according to the Word of the Lord by the hand of Moses.

THREE GROUPS: 8,580

46 All those who were numbered of the Levites, whom Moses and Aaron and the chief of Israel numbered, after their families, and after the house of their fathers,

47 From thirty years old and upward even unto fifty years old, every one who came to do the service of the Ministry, and the service of the burden in the Tabernacle of the congregation.

48 Even those who were numbered of them, were eight thousand and five hundred and fourscore,

49 According to the Commandment of the LORD they were numbered by the hand of Moses, every one according to his service, and according to his burden: thus were they numbered of him, as the LORD commanded Moses.

(Everything we are now studying is tied to Christ and the Cross. In fact, every single thing about the Tabernacle, all of its Vessels, the Sacrificial System, the Priesthood, their duties, and the duties of the Levites, all pictured Christ and His Redemptive Work, which, of course, is the Cross [I Cor. 1:17-18, 21, 23; 2:2; Gal. 6:14].)

CHAPTER 5
(1490 B.C.)
CAMP REGULATIONS

A ND the LORD spoke unto Moses, saying,

2 Command the Children of Israel that they put out of the camp every leper, and every one who has an issue, and whosoever is defiled by the dead *(where God dwells, evil must be put out; where evil was committed, provision was made for restitution and forgiveness; but it had to be done God's Way; "leprosy" was a type of sin, and "death" was the result of sin [Rom. 6:23])*:

3 Both male and female shall you put out, without the camp shall you put them; that they defile not their camps, in the midst whereof I dwell *(sin unconfessed and lacking Repentance separates one from God; the two, God and sin, cannot dwell together)*.

4 And the Children of Israel did so, and put them out without the camp: as the LORD spoke unto Moses, so did the Children of Israel.

LAW OF RESTITUTION

5 And the LORD spoke unto Moses, saying,

6 Speak unto the Children of Israel, When a man or woman shall commit any sin that men commit, to do a trespass against the LORD, and that person be guilty *(Verses 5 through 10 concern trespasses against the Lord and against one's fellowman; while all sin is against the Lord, the weight of this Commandment is toward one Believer trespassing against another)*;

7 Then they shall confess their sin which they have done: and he shall recompense his trespass with the principal thereof, and add unto it the fifth part thereof, and give it unto him against whom he has trespassed.

8 But if the man have no kinsman to recompense the trespass unto, let the trespass be recompensed unto the LORD, even to the Priest; beside the ram of the Atonement, whereby an Atonement shall be made for him. *(In the case of private wrongs, restitution was to be made to the full amount of the injury done, with the addition of one-fifth to that amount. In case of the death of the person who suffered the injury, restitution should be made to his near kinsman. But also, in the event of there being no near kinsman, restitution should be made to the Lord, by giving the stipulated amount to the Priests, in order that it be used for the service of the Sanctuary.)*

9 And every Offering of all the holy things of the Children of Israel, which they bring unto the Priest, shall be his *(shall belong to the Priest)*.

10 And every man's hallowed things shall be his: whatsoever any man gives the Priest, it shall be his.

JEALOUSY

11 And the LORD spoke unto Moses, saying,

12 Speak unto the Children of Israel, and say unto them, If any man's wife go aside, and commit a trespass against him *(the sin of adultery)*,

13 And a man lie with her carnally, and it be hid from the eyes of her husband, and be kept close, and she be defiled, and there be no witness against her, neither she be taken with the manner;

14 And the spirit of jealousy come upon him, and he be jealous of his wife, and she be defiled *(he suspects that adultery has been committed, but has no proof)*: or if the spirit of jealousy come upon him, and he be jealous of his wife, and she be not defiled *(his suspicion is wrong)*:

15 Then shall the man bring his wife unto the Priest, and he shall bring her Offering for her, the tenth part of an ephah of barley meal; he shall pour no oil upon it, nor put frankincense thereon; for it is an Offering of jealousy, an Offering of memorial, bringing iniquity to remembrance *(designed, if there in fact be iniquity, that it be exposed)*.

16 And the Priest shall bring her near, and set her before the LORD:

17 And the Priest shall take holy water in an earthen vessel; and of the dust that is in the floor of the Tabernacle the Priest shall take, and put it into the water *(the water of jealousy was a loving provision made by God for the protection of helpless women; however, it had a greater spiritual meaning; the "earthen vessel" was a Type of the Humanity of Christ; the "dust" from the floor of the Tabernacle symbolized the misery, hurt, and depravity of the human race; it symbolizes fallen man)*:

18 And the Priest shall set the woman before the LORD, and uncover the woman's head, and put the Offering of memorial in her hands, which is the jealousy Offering: and the Priest shall have in his hand the bitter water that causes the curse:

19 And the Priest shall charge her by an oath, and say unto the woman, If no man has laid with you, and if you have not gone aside to uncleanness with another instead of your husband, be thou free from this bitter water that causes the curse:

20 But if you have gone aside to another instead of your husband, and if you be defiled, and some man has laid with you beside your husband:

21 Then the Priest shall charge the woman with an oath of cursing, and the Priest shall say unto the woman, The LORD make you a curse and an oath among your people, when the LORD does make your thigh to rot, and your belly to swell *(the bitter water, if the woman were guilty, would cause tremendous physical infirmities, meaning that she could not have children; if not guilty, there would be no ill effect; no doubt, the Holy Spirit superintended this)*;

22 And this water that causes the curse shall go into your bowels, to make your belly to swell, and your thigh to rot *(providing the woman is guilty)*: And the woman shall say, Amen, amen. *(The truth is, all of humanity was guilty. Jesus drank the bitter water on our behalf, and died on the Cross, even though He was not guilty at all. He took our place, and "redeemed us from the curse of the Law, being made a curse for us" [Gal. 3:13].)*

23 And the Priest shall write these curses in a book, and he shall blot them out with the bitter water:

24 And he shall cause the woman to drink the bitter water that causes the curse: and the water that causes the curse shall enter into her, and become bitter.

25 Then the Priest shall take the jealousy Offering out of the woman's hand, and shall wave the Offering before the Lord, and offer it upon the Altar *(this signified thankfulness to the Lord, that He would ascertain the right or the wrong in this situation; in other words, the Lord would be the Judge)*:

26 And the Priest shall take an handful of the Offering, even the memorial thereof, and burn it upon the Altar, and afterward shall cause the woman to drink the water *(as always,* the Altar and the burning typified what Christ would do on the Cross)*.

27 And when he has made her to drink the water, then it shall come to pass, that, if she be defiled, and have done trespass against her husband, that the water that causes the curse shall enter into her, and become bitter, and her belly shall swell, and her thigh shall rot: and the woman shall be a curse among her people *(in a broader interpretation of this "law of jealousies," such portrays the record of Israel's shame and sin in departing from the Living God and crucifying her Saviour, which was all blotted out in the bitter waters of Calvary [Col 2:14; Isa. 43:25])*.

28 And if the woman be not defiled, but be clean; then she shall be free, and shall conceive seed *(will be able to bear children, meaning that she wouldn't be able to bear children were she guilty)*.

29 This is the law of jealousies, when a wife goes aside to another instead of her husband, and is defiled;

30 Or when the spirit of jealousy comes upon him, and he be jealous over his wife, and shall set the woman before the LORD, and the Priest shall execute upon her all this law.

31 Then shall the man be guiltless from iniquity, and this woman shall bear her iniquity. *(While this was true under the Law, as it could only be true under the Law, it is no longer true presently. Christ has taken our place. "He was wounded for our transgressions, He was bruised for our iniquities" [Isa. 53:5].)*

CHAPTER 6
(1490 B.C.)
THE NAZARITE

AND the LORD spoke unto Moses, saying,

2 Speak unto the Children of Israel and say unto them, When either man or woman shall separate themselves to vow a vow of a Nazarite, to separate themselves unto the LORD *(from the Nazarite idea came the Rachabites, the Essenes, Anchorites, Hermits, Monks, and other monastic orders; to say that Christ was a Nazarite is unscriptural, for He drank of the fruit of the vine and touched the dead, which Nazarites were forbidden to do [Mat. 9:25; 11:19; 26:29; Mk. 14:25])*:

3 He shall separate himself from wine and strong drink, and shall drink no vinegar of wine, or vinegar of strong drink, neither shall

he drink any liquor of grapes, nor eat moist grapes, or dried (*the Nazarite must not touch any type of alcoholic beverage, or even anything that pertained to a vineyard, such as grapes or grape juice*).

4 All the days of his separation shall he eat nothing that is made of the vine tree, from the kernels even to the husk (*while the life of the Nazarite was one of separation, it was not to be one of isolation; in fact, his life was to be one of action, one of uninterrupted devotion to the Divine Service*).

5 All the days of the vow of his separation there shall no razor come upon his head: until the days be fulfilled, in the which he separates himself unto the LORD, he shall be holy, and shall let the locks of the hair of his head grow (*in those days, long hair on a man signified weakness, and the evidence is, most of those who entertained a Nazarite vow were men; so, by demanding this, the Holy Spirit was showing the weakness of man, irrespective as to who the person might be*).

6 All the days that he separates himself unto the LORD he shall come at no dead body (*death in all of its forms is a product originally of sin [Rom. 6:23]*).

7 He shall not make himself unclean for his father, or for his mother, for his brother, or for his sister, when they die: because the consecration of his God is upon his head (*even if a close loved one died, he was not to touch them*).

8 All the days of his separation he is holy unto the LORD.

9 And if any man die very suddenly by him, and he has defiled the head of his consecration (*has touched a dead body*); then he shall shave his head in the day of his cleansing, on the seventh day shall he shave it.

10 And on the eighth day (*Resurrection day*) he shall bring two turtles (*turtledoves*), or two young pigeons, to the Priest, to the door of the Tabernacle of the congregation:

11 And the Priest shall offer the one for a Sin Offering, and the other for a Burnt Offering, and make an Atonement for him, for that he sinned by the dead, and shall hallow his head that same day (*all sin, and all defilement, and to any degree, can only be addressed at the Cross*).

12 And he shall consecrate unto the LORD the days of his separation, and shall bring a lamb of the first year for a Trespass Offering: but the days that were before shall be lost, because his separation was defiled.

13 And this is the law of the Nazarite, when the days of his separation are fulfilled: he shall be brought unto the door of the Tabernacle of the congregation:

14 And he shall offer his Offering unto the LORD, one he lamb of the first year without blemish for a Burnt Offering, and one ewe lamb of the first year without blemish for a Sin Offering, and one ram without blemish for Peace Offerings (*even though Christ never took the Nazarite vow, the truth is, He was the One True and Perfect Nazarite in the world. He maintained from the first to the last the most complete separation from all mere earthly joy. Concerning this, Mackintosh says, "From the moment He entered upon His Public Work, He kept Himself apart from all that was of this world, His Heart was fixed upon God and His Work, with a devotion that nothing could shake. No claims of Earth or nature were ever allowed, for a single moment, to come in-between His Heart and that Work which He came to do. His Eye was single and His heart undivided. This is apparent from the first to the last. He could say to His Disciples, 'I have meat to eat that you know not of'; and when they, not knowing the deep significance of His Words, said 'Has any man brought Him ought to eat?' He replied, 'My meat is to do the Will of Him Who sent Me, and to finish His Work'" [Jn. 4:34]*),

15 And a basket of unleavened bread, cakes of fine flour mingled with oil, and wafers of unleavened bread anointed with oil, and their Meat Offering, and their Drink Offerings (*everything said here typified Christ in some fashion, regarding His Mediatorial, Intercessory, and Atoning Work*).

16 And the Priest shall bring them before the LORD, and shall offer his Sin Offering, and his Burnt Offering:

17 And he shall offer the ram for a Sacrifice of Peace Offerings unto the LORD (*with the Sin Offering and Burnt Offering now offered, the "Peace Offerings" can now be offered, simply because peace with God has now been reestablished*), with the basket of unleavened bread (*typifying the Perfection of Christ as a Man*): the Priest shall offer also his Meat Offering (*a Thanksgiving Offering*), and his Drink Offering (*typifying a life poured out solely for the Lord*).

18 And the Nazarite shall shave the head of his separation at the door of the Tabernacle of the congregation, and shall take the hair of the head of his separation, and put it in the fire

which is under the Sacrifice of the Peace Offerings (*the long hair, which the Nazarite might be tempted to keep as a proud memorial of his consecration, he had to place into the fire to be burnt; and so will the Holy Spirit do to our pride, if we allow Him proper latitude*).

19 And the Priest shall take the sodden shoulder of the ram, and one unleavened cake out of the basket, and one unleavened wafer, and shall put them upon the hands of the Nazarite, after the hair of his separation is shaven:

20 And the Priest shall wave them for a Wave Offering before the LORD: this is holy for the Priest, with the wave breast (*thanksgiving to the Lord*) and heave shoulder (*symbolizes Christ coming from Heaven to this Earth, in order to give His Life that humanity might be redeemed*): and after that the Nazarite may drink wine.

21 This is the law of the Nazarite who has vowed, and of his Offering unto the LORD for his separation, beside that that his hand shall get: according to the vow which he vowed, so he must do after the law of his separation. (*Even though all the separation was done by the Nazarite, he must ever understand that the separation itself contained no Blessing. The Blessing came from the Lord and, more particularly, from Christ, and what He would do at the Cross, typified by the many Sacrifices offered.*)

PRIESTLY BENEDICTION

22 And the LORD spoke unto Moses, saying,

23 Speak unto Aaron and unto his sons, saying, On this wise you shall bless the Children of Israel, saying unto them (*how very many times we think that the Blessings come upon us because of our separation, consecration, or dedication; however, it must forever be understood that God cannot bless sinful man, irrespective of his dedication or consecration, but rather He blesses Christ within us, and Christ Alone*),

24 The LORD bless you, and keep you:

25 The LORD make His face shine upon you, and be gracious unto you (*Christ is the Source of all blessings, with the Cross being the Means; Grace is made possible solely by the Cross [Gal. 2:21; 5:2-4]*):

26 The LORD lift up His countenance upon you, and give you peace.

27 And they shall put My Name upon the Children of Israel; and I will bless them. (*Above all, God is a God of blessing. He desires to do such for His children. All blessings come*

exclusively, as stated, through Christ and the Cross; consequently, the Cross must ever be the object of our Faith, which then gives the Holy Spirit latitude to work within our lives [Rom. 6:3-14; 8:1-2, 11].)

CHAPTER 7
(1490 B.C.)
THE ALTAR

AND it came to pass on the day that Moses had fully set up the Tabernacle, and had anointed it, and sanctified it, and all the instruments thereof, both the Altar and all the Vessels thereof, and had anointed them, and sanctified them;

2 That the princes of Israel, heads of the house of their fathers, who were the princes of the Tribes, and were over them who were numbered, offered (*Chapter 7 concerns itself with the dedication of the Brazen Altar and the gifts of the twelve Tribes of Israel*):

3 And they brought their Offering before the LORD, six covered wagons, and twelve oxen; a wagon for two of the princes, and for each one an ox: and they brought them before the Tabernacle (*all Offerings must be to the Lord, and we must make doubly certain that they are never for self-aggrandizement*).

SERVICE

4 And the LORD spoke unto Moses, saying,

5 Take it of them, that they may be to do the service of the Tabernacle of the congregation; and you shall give them unto the Levites, to every man according to his service (*it seems that the Lord had laid it on the hearts of the Princes of the Tribes to bring covered wagons, which were to be used for the transportation of the Tabernacle, when it was disassembled and, according to the Holy Spirit, moved to another place*).

6 And Moses took the wagons and the oxen, and gave them unto the Levites.

7 Two wagons and four oxen he gave unto the sons of Gershon, according to their service:

8 And four wagons and eight oxen he gave unto the sons of Merari, according unto their service, under the hand of Ithamar the son of Aaron the Priest.

9 But unto the sons of Kohath he gave none: because the service of the Sanctuary belonging unto them was that they should bear upon their shoulders (*this included the*

Ark of the Covenant, the Golden Lampstand, the Altar of Worship, and the Table of Shewbread, along with the Brazen Altar and the Brazen Laver; however, the balance of the Tabernacle and the fence could be carried in the wagons, etc.).

10 And the princes offered for dedicating of the Altar in the day that it was anointed, even the princes offered their Offering before the Altar *(Brazen Altar)*.

11 And the LORD said unto Moses, They shall offer their Offering, each prince on his day, for the dedicating of the Altar *(this means that the "Altar" was the centerpiece of the whole of Israel, typifying the Cross, which is the centerpiece of Christianity)*.

12 And he who offered his Offering the first day was Nahshon the son of Amminadab, of the Tribe of Judah *("Judah" means "praise"; so the dedication of the Altar began with Praise)*:

13 And his Offering was one silver charger, the weight thereof was an hundred and thirty shekels *(worth about $780 in 2004 currency)*, one silver bowl of seventy shekels *(worth about $420)*, after the shekel of the Sanctuary; both of them were full of fine flour *(typical of the Perfection of the Manhood of Christ)* mingled with oil *(typical of the Holy Spirit on Christ)* for a Meat Offering *(a Thanksgiving Offering to God for giving us Christ)*:

14 One spoon of ten shekels of gold, full of incense:

15 One young bullock, one ram, one lamb of the first year, for a Burnt Offering:

16 One kid of the goats for a Sin Offering:

17 And for a Sacrifice of Peace Offerings, two oxen, five rams, five he goats, five lambs of the first year: this was the Offering of Nahshon the son of Amminadab. *(Concerning this, Williams says: "The human historian would compress the Offerings of these Princes into one Verse — for they were all identical; but to God they were so precious that they are minutely detailed and repeated.")*

18 On the second day Nethaneel the son of Zuar, prince of Issachar, did offer:

19 He offered for his Offering one silver charger, the weight whereof was an hundred and thirty shekels, one silver bowl of seventy shekels, after the shekel of the Sanctuary; both of them full of fine flour mingled with oil for a Meat Offering:

20 One spoon of gold of ten shekels, full of incense:

21 One young bullock, one ram, one lamb of the first year, for a Burnt Offering:

22 One kid of the goats for a Sin Offering:

23 And for a Sacrifice of Peace Offerings, two oxen, five rams, five he goats, five lambs of the first year: this was the Offering of Nethaneel the son of Zuar.

24 On the third day Eliab the son of Helon, prince of the Children of Zebulun, did offer:

25 His offering was one silver charger, the weight whereof was an hundred and thirty shekels, one silver bowl of seventy shekels, after the shekel of the Sanctuary; both of them full of fine flour mingled with oil for a Meat Offering:

26 One golden spoon of ten shekels, full of incense:

27 One young bullock, one ram, one lamb of the first year, for a Burnt Offering:

28 One kid of the goats for a Sin Offering:

29 And for a Sacrifice of Peace Offerings, two oxen, five rams, five he goats, five lambs of the first year: this was the Offering of Eliab the son of Helon.

30 On the fourth day Elizur the son of Shedeur, prince of the Children of Reuben, did offer:

31 His offering was one silver charger of the weight of an hundred and thirty shekels, one silver bowl of seventy shekels, after the shekel of the Sanctuary; both of them full of fine flour mingled with oil for a Meat Offering:

32 One golden spoon of ten shekels, full of incense:

33 One young bullock, one ram, one lamb of the first year, for a Burnt Offering:

34 One kid of the goats for a Sin Offering:

35 And for a Sacrifice of Peace Offerings, two oxen, five rams, five he goats, five lambs of the first year: this was the Offering of Elizur the son of Shedeur.

36 On the fifth day Shelumiel the son of Zurishaddai, prince of the Children of Simeon, did offer:

37 His offering was one silver charger, the weight whereof was an hundred and thirty shekels, one silver bowl of seventy shekels, after the shekel of the Sanctuary; both of them full of fine flour mingled with oil for a Meat Offering:

38 One golden spoon of ten shekels, full of incense:

39 One young bullock, one ram, one lamb of the first year, for a Burnt Offering:

40 One kid of the goats for a Sin Offering:

41 And for a Sacrifice of Peace Offerings, two oxen, five rams, five he goats, five lambs

of the first year: this was the Offering of Shelumiel the son of Zurishaddai.

42 On the sixth day Eliasaph the son of Deuel, prince of the Children of Gad, offered:

43 His offering was one silver charger of the weight of an hundred and thirty shekels, a silver bowl of seventy shekels, after the shekel of the Sanctuary; both of them full of fine flour mingled with oil for a Meat Offering:

44 One golden spoon of ten shekels, full of incense:

45 One young bullock, one ram, one lamb of the first year, for a Burnt Offering:

46 One kid of the goats for a Sin Offering:

47 And for a Sacrifice of Peace Offerings, two oxen, five rams, five he goats, five lambs of the first year: this was the Offering of Eliasaph the son of Deuel.

48 On the seventh day Elishama the son of Ammihud, prince of the Children of Ephraim, offered:

49 His offering was one silver charger, the weight whereof was an hundred and thirty shekels, one silver bowl of seventy shekels, after the shekels of the Sanctuary; both of them full of fine flour mingled with oil for a Meat Offering:

50 One golden spoon of ten shekels, full of incense:

51 One young bullock, one ram, one lamb of the first year, for a Burnt Offering:

52 One kid of the goats for a Sin Offering:

53 And for a Sacrifice of Peace Offerings, two oxen, five rams, five he goats, five lambs of the first year: this was the offering of Elishama the son of Ammihud.

54 On the eighth day offered Gamaliel the son of Pedahzur, prince of the Children of Manasseh:

55 His offering was one silver charger of the weight of an hundred and thirty shekels, one silver bowl of seventy shekels, after the shekel of the Sanctuary; both of them full of fine flour mingled with oil for a Meat Offering:

56 One golden spoon of ten shekels, full of incense:

57 One young bullock, one ram, one lamb of the first year, for a Burnt Offering:

58 One kid of the goats for a Sin Offering:

59 And for a Sacrifice of Peace Offerings, two oxen, five rams, five he goats, five lambs of the first year: this was the Offering of Gamaliel the son of Pedahzur.

60 On the ninth day Abidan the son of Gideoni, prince of the Children of Benjamin, offered:

61 His offering was one silver charger, the weight whereof was an hundred and thirty shekels, one silver bowl of seventy shekels, after the shekel of the Sanctuary; both of them full of fine flour mingled with oil for a Meat Offering:

62 One golden spoon of ten shekels, full of incense:

63 One young bullock, one ram, one lamb of the first year, for a Burnt Offering:

64 One kid of the goats for a Sin Offering:

65 And for a Sacrifice of Peace Offerings, two oxen, five rams, five he goats, five lambs of the first year: this was the Offering of Abidan the son of Gideoni. *(The Tribe of Benjamin was one of the smallest; thus we find that the Offering of the smallest Tribe was given as much importance in the Eyes of God as the Offering of the greatest Tribe.)*

66 On the tenth day Ahiezer the son of Ammishaddai, prince of the Children of Dan, offered:

67 His offering was one silver charger, the weight whereof was an hundred and thirty shekels, one silver bowl of seventy shekels, after the shekel of the Sanctuary; both of them full of fine flour mingled with oil for a Meat Offering:

68 One golden spoon of ten shekels, full of incense:

69 One young bullock, one ram, one lamb of the first year, for a Burnt Offering:

70 One kid of the goats for a Sin Offering:

71 And for a Sacrifice of Peace Offerings, two oxen, five rams, five he goats, five lambs of the first year: this was the Offering of Ahiezer the son of Ammishaddai.

72 On the eleventh day Pagiel the son of Ocran, prince of the Children of Asher, offered:

73 His offering was one silver charger, the weight whereof was an hundred and thirty shekels, one silver bowl of seventy shekels, after the shekel of the Sanctuary; both of them full of fine flour mingled with oil for a Meat Offering:

74 One golden spoon of ten shekels, full of incense:

75 One young bullock, one ram, one lamb of the first year, for a Burnt Offering:

76 One kid of the goats for a Sin Offering:

77 And for a Sacrifice of Peace Offerings, two oxen, five rams, five he goats, five lambs of the first year: this was the offering of Pagiel the son of Ocran.

78 On the twelfth day Ahira the son of Enan, prince of the Children of Naphtali, offered:

79 His offering was one silver charger, the weight whereof was an hundred and thirty shekels, one silver bowl of seventy shekels, after the shekel of the Sanctuary; both of them full of fine flour mingled with oil for a Meat Offering.

80 One golden spoon of ten shekels, full of incense:

81 One young bullock, one ram, one lamb of the first year, for a Burnt Offering:

82 One kid of the goats for a Sin Offering:

83 And for a Sacrifice of Peace Offerings, two oxen, five rams, five he goats, five lambs of the first year: this was the offering of Ahira the son of Enan.

84 This was the dedication of the Altar, in the day when it was anointed, by the princes of Israel: twelve chargers of silver, twelve silver bowls, twelve spoons of gold:

85 Each charger of silver weighing an hundred and thirty shekels, each bowl seventy: all the silver vessels weighed two thousand and four hundred shekels, after the shekel of the Sanctuary:

86 The golden spoons were twelve, full of incense, weighing ten shekels apiece, after the shekel of the Sanctuary: all the gold of the spoons was an hundred and twenty shekels.

87 All the oxen for the Burnt Offering were twelve bullocks, the rams twelve, the lambs of the first year twelve, with their Meat Offering: and the kids of the goats for Sin Offering twelve.

88 And all the oxen for the Sacrifice of the Peace Offerings were twenty and four bullocks, the rams sixty, the he goats sixty, the lambs of the first year sixty. This was the dedication of the Altar, after that it was anointed. *(As stated, the "Brazen Altar" was the single most important Vessel. Some may argue that the Ark of the Covenant was the most important; in the true sense of the word that would be true. But yet, there was no way that the Ark of the Covenant could be reached, unless one first went by the Brazen Altar, of which the latter was typical of Christ and the Cross.)*

MOSES

89 And when Moses was gone into the Tabernacle of the congregation to speak with Him, then he heard the Voice of one speaking unto him from off the Mercy Seat that was upon the Ark of Testimony, from between the two Cherubims: and He *(God)* spoke unto him.

(The Voice that spoke to Moses from the flame of the Mercy Seat was also the same Voice that spoke from the flame of the burning bush, and from the Glory of Revelation 1:12. It was also the Voice that said, "Learn of Me" [Mat. 11:29].)

CHAPTER 8
(1490 B.C.)
THE LAMPS

AND the LORD spoke unto Moses, saying,

2 Speak unto Aaron, and say unto him, When you light the lamps, the seven lamps shall give light over against the Candlestick. *(These "Lamps" were a Type of Christ, Who is the "Light of the world" [Jn. 8:12]. Christ is the Source of that light, the Cross is the Means of that light, and the Holy Spirit is the Instrument by and through which the light comes to fallen humanity, typified by the oil. So, in the Golden Lampstand, we have Christ, the Cross, and the Holy Spirit. The Reader must understand that all the things which the Lord is, and He is everything, cannot be given to the lost sons of Adam's fallen race, except by the means of the Cross [I Cor. 1:23].)*

3 And Aaron did so; he lit the lamps thereof over against the Candlestick *(Lampstand)*, as the LORD commanded Moses.

4 And this work of the Candlestick was of beaten gold *(typifying Christ, Who is God, but Who would become Man, hence the word "beaten")*, unto the shaft thereof *(the central shaft of the Golden Lampstand typifies Christ)*, unto the flowers thereof, was beaten work *(the "flowers" come about in the life of the Believer, which the six stems on the two sides of the shaft represent, only as those stems are properly in Christ, i.e., the main shaft)*: according unto the pattern which the LORD had showed Moses, so he made the Candlestick *(the "Pattern" is the Word of God; we must not deviate from that Word)*.

THE LEVITES

5 And the LORD spoke unto Moses, saying,

6 Take the Levites from among the Children of Israel, and cleanse them. *(The "Levites" were representatives of the congregation, whereas the Priests were representatives of Christ. The Priests had already been consecrated, and now the Levites were, as well, to be consecrated for service, i.e., "cleansed," which could only be done by the "blood of the lamb.")*

7 And thus shall you do unto them, to cleanse them: Sprinkle water of purifying upon them *(a Type of the Word of God, water taken from the Brazen Laver)*, and let them shave all their flesh, and let them wash their clothes, and so make themselves clean *(the "shaving" and "washing" were symbolic of Sanctification, which could only truly come about upon the advent of the Holy Spirit in a new Dispensation, after the Cross [Jn. 14:16-17])*.

8 Then let them take a young bullock *(Sin Offering)* with his Meat Offering *(a Thanksgiving Offering consisting of bread, and no flesh)*, even fine flour *(Perfection of Christ)* mingled with oil *(Holy Spirit upon Christ)*, and another young bullock shall you take for a Sin Offering.

9 And you shall bring the Levites before the Tabernacle of the congregation: and you shall gather the whole assembly of the Children of Israel together:

10 And you shall bring the Levites before the LORD *(near the Brazen Altar)*: and the Children of Israel shall put their hands upon the Levites *(probably the tribal Princes; the laying on of hands signified that the obligation to assist personally in the service of the Sanctuary was transferred from the whole congregation to the Levites)*:

11 And Aaron shall offer the Levites before the LORD for an Offering *(Wave Offering)* of the Children of Israel, that they may execute the service of the LORD. *(There numbered more than 8,000 Levites, so, most probably, leaders among them marched up and down beside the Altar, symbolic of the Wave Offering. They now belonged to the Lord, and were to do His service only.)*

12 And the Levites shall lay their hands upon the heads of the bullocks *(transferring their sins to the bullocks in type, symbolic of Christ, Who would take our sins on the Cross)*: and you shall offer the one *(bullock)* for a Sin Offering, and the other for a Burnt Offering, unto the LORD, to make an Atonement for the Levites *(there was no Peace Offering; for the subject here was not worship and fellowship, as in Leviticus, but the service and warfare of the Wilderness)*.

13 And you shall set the Levites before Aaron, and before his sons, and offer them for an Offering unto the LORD.

14 Thus shall you separate the Levites from among the Children of Israel: and the Levites shall be Mine *(for the Lord's service only)*.

15 And after that shall the Levites go in to do the service of the Tabernacle of the congregation: and you shall cleanse them, and offer them for an Offering.

16 For they are wholly given unto Me from among the Children of Israel: instead of such as open every womb, even instead of the firstborn of all the Children of Israel, have I taken them unto Me. *(Previously, it seems that the Lord had designated that the firstborn of the males would serve in this capacity, but changed it to the sons of Levi, i.e., "the Levites.")*

17 For all the first born of the Children of Israel are Mine, both man and beast: on the day that I smote every firstborn in the land of Egypt I sanctified them for Myself *(the "firstborn," in a sense, were types of Christ, Who would be the "Firstborn among many brethren," signifying Christ as the originator of Salvation [Rom. 8:29])*.

18 And I have taken the Levites for all the firstborn of the Children of Israel *(the Levites took the place of the firstborn, as it regards service to the Sanctuary)*.

19 And I have given the Levites as a gift to Aaron and to his sons from among the Children of Israel, to do the service of the Children of Israel in the Tabernacle of the congregation, and to make an Atonement for the Children of Israel: that there be no plague among the Children of Israel, when the Children of Israel come near unto the Sanctuary. *(The idea of the Levites "making an Atonement" has to do with the fact that they functioned in the realm of the Sanctuary, with its chief purpose being the Brazen Altar and the Sacrifices. Believers helping to take the Message of the Cross to a dying world fall into the same category. Paul said so [Phil. 4:17-19]. The only thing that stands between the people and the "plague" is the Cross of Christ.)*

20 And Moses, and Aaron, and all the congregation of the Children of Israel, did to the Levites according unto all that the LORD commanded Moses concerning the Levites, so did the Children of Israel unto them.

21 And the Levites were purified, and they washed their clothes: and Aaron offered them as an Offering before the LORD; and Aaron made an Atonement for them to cleanse them.

22 And after that went the Levites in to do their service in the Tabernacle of the congregation before Aaron, and before his sons: as the LORD had commanded Moses concerning the Levites, so did they unto them. *(This refers only to the time that the Tabernacle was to be*

moved. *If anybody but the Priests went in any other time, they could be stricken dead.)*

LEVITICAL SERVICE

23 And the LORD spoke unto Moses, saying,

24 This is it that belongs unto the Levites: from twenty and five years old and upward they shall go in to wait upon the service of the Tabernacle of the congregation *(it was changed here from 30 to 25 and during the time of David it was changed to 20 [I Chron. 23:24-27]):*

25 And from the age of fifty years they shall cease waiting upon the service thereof, and shall serve no more:

26 But shall minister with their brethren in the Tabernacle of the congregation, to keep the charge, and shall do no service. Thus shall you do unto the Levites touching their charge. *(Those over 50 were given some honorary duties, that they might have some place and post in the House of God.)*

CHAPTER 9
(1490 B.C.)
THE PASSOVER

AND the LORD spoke unto Moses, in the wilderness of Sinai, in the first month of the second year after they were come out of the land of Egypt, saying,

2 Let the Children of Israel also keep the Passover at his appointed season *(which would have been in our April; they had kept the Passover one year earlier in Egypt).*

3 In the fourteenth day of this month, at evening, you shall keep it in his appointed season: according to all the rites of it, and according to all the ceremonies thereof, shall you keep it. *(Redemption by blood was their foundation and, as well, is the foundation also of all Christian experience. It cleanses the conscience, restores the soul, and inspires the songs and feasts of Canaan. Never in this world, nor in that which is to come, will redeemed men reach a degree of holiness that will permit them to dispense with the Precious Blood of Christ. The indication is, this was the last time they kept the Passover in the wilderness, which was a time frame of approximately 40 years. Considering that there were approximately 3 million people, it is not known exactly how they accomplished this Passover, considering the river of blood that would have to be poured out at the Altar. It is believed it would have taken well*

over 100,000 lambs. All of this tells us that our Salvation didn't come cheaply.)

4 And Moses spoke unto the Children of Israel, that they should keep the Passover.

5 And they kept the Passover on the fourteenth day of the first month at evening in the wilderness of Sinai: according to all that the LORD commanded Moses, so did the Children of Israel.

6 And there were certain men, who were defiled by the dead body of a man, that they could not keep the Passover on that day: and they came before Moses and before Aaron on that day:

7 And those men said unto him, We are defiled by the dead body of a man: wherefore are we kept back, that we may not offer an Offering of the LORD in His appointed season among the Children of Israel?

8 And Moses said unto them, Stand still, and I will hear what the LORD will command concerning you. *(Let all Believers understand that we must have the Mind of the Lord in all things.)*

UNCLEAN

9 And the LORD spoke unto Moses, saying,

10 Speak unto the Children of Israel, saying, If any man of you or of your posterity shall be unclean by reason of a dead body, or be in a journey afar off, yet he shall keep the Passover unto the LORD.

11 The fourteenth day of the second month at evening they shall keep it, and eat it with unleavened bread and bitter herbs. *(This meant they could eat it a month late. If they were unclean, they would have time now to be purified. If they were on a journey, and could be back before the appointed time, they could then eat it.)*

12 They shall leave none of it unto the morning, nor break any bone of it: according to all the ordinances of the Passover they shall keep it *(even though they were doing so of themselves at a later time; but all the Ordinances must be kept).*

13 But the man who is clean, and is not in a journey, and forbears to keep the Passover *(does not keep the Passover),* even the same soul shall be cut off from among his people: because he brought not the Offering of the LORD in his appointed season, that man shall bear his sin *(one would lose one's soul if the Passover was ignored; likewise, one will lose one's soul*

presently, if the Cross is ignored).

14 And if a stranger shall sojourn among you, and will keep the Passover unto the LORD; according to the ordinance of the Passover, and according to the manner thereof, so shall he do: you shall have one ordinance, both for the stranger *(Gentile)*, and for him who was born in the land *(in essence, Faith in Christ and the Cross is identical for all).*

THE CLOUD

15 And on the day that the Tabernacle was reared up the cloud *(Glory of the Lord)* covered the Tabernacle, namely, the tent of the Testimony: and at evening there was upon the Tabernacle as it were the appearance of fire, until the morning *(the Testimony was the Decalogue written on the two tables of stone, and enshrined within the Ark of the Covenant, the moral law which lay at the heart of Judaism; the tent of the Testimony was the Holy of Holies, in which the Ark dwelt).*

16 So it was always: the cloud covered it by day, and the appearance of fire by night *(this supernatural phenomenon was not transitory, but rather permanent, at least as long as the Israelites were in the wilderness).*

17 And when the cloud was taken up from the Tabernacle, then after that the Children of Israel journeyed: and in the place where the cloud abode, there the Children of Israel pitched their tents. *(Williams says, "God protected them by day and by night. He planned for them. He chose their camping ground. He decided when they were to march and when they were to rest. According to the Word of the Lord, they journeyed and, according to the Word of the Lord, they abode in their tents — whether by day or by night, or whether it were two days, or a month, or a year. Thus, Israel's Shepherd led His flock by the hand of Moses and Aaron.")*

18 At the Commandment of the LORD the Children of Israel journeyed, and at the Commandment of the LORD they pitched: as long as the cloud abode upon the Tabernacle they rested in their tents.

19 And when the cloud tarried long upon the Tabernacle many days, then the Children of Israel kept the charge of the LORD, and journeyed not *(everything was according to the disposition of the cloud).*

20 And so it was, when the cloud was a few days upon the Tabernacle; according to the Commandment of the LORD they abode in their tents, and according to the Commandment of the LORD they journeyed.

21 And so it was, when the cloud abode from evening unto the morning, and that the cloud was taken up in the morning, then they journeyed: whether it was by day or by night that the cloud was taken up, they journeyed.

22 Or whether it were two days or a month, or a year, that the cloud tarried upon the Tabernacle, remaining thereon, the Children of Israel abode in their tents, and journeyed not: but when it was taken up, they journeyed.

23 At the Commandment of the LORD they rested in the tents, and at the Commandment of the LORD they journeyed: they kept the charge of the LORD, at the commandment of the LORD by the hand of Moses.

CHAPTER 10
(1490 B.C.)
TWO TRUMPETS

A ND the LORD spoke unto Moses, saying,

2 Make thee two trumpets of silver *(in the Old Testament, "silver" portrays Redemption);* of a whole piece shall you make them: that you may use them for the calling of the Assembly, and for the journeying of the camps *(the two silver trumpets illustrate the Old and the New Testaments; they were made of one piece; and their testimony to the host of Israel, however varied the Message, was one; their ministry was: first, to gather the people together around the Tabernacle; and, second, to set them in motion for Canaan).*

3 And when they shall blow with them, all the Assembly shall assemble themselves to you at the door of the Tabernacle of the congregation.

4 And if they blow but with one trumpet, then the princes, which are heads of the thousands of Israel, shall gather themselves unto you.

5 When you blow an alarm, then the camps that lie on the east parts shall go forward *(the trumpets were used to sound an alarm for war and, as well, a joyful sound for Festival).*

6 When you blow an alarm the second time, then the camps that lie on the south side shall take their journey: they shall blow an alarm for their journeys *(the trumpets, as well, were a Type of the Word of God being rightly divided and presented to the people).*

7 But when the congregation is to be

gathered together, you shall blow, but you shall not sound an alarm *(this particular blast did not signal war, but rather a Festival gathering)*.

8 And the sons of Aaron, the Priests, shall blow with the trumpets; and they shall be to you for an Ordinance for ever throughout your generations *(as stated, the sound of these trumpets continue in the presentation of the Word of God, and shall do so forever)*.

9 And if you go to war in your land against the enemy that oppresses you, then you shall blow an alarm with the trumpets; and you shall be remembered before the LORD your God, and you shall be saved from your enemies *(in the Word of the Lord alone do we find victory over our enemies, and that particular word is the Cross [Rom. 6:3-14; I Cor. 1:17-18, 21, 23; 2:2; Gal. 6:14])*.

10 Also in the day of your gladness, and in your solemn days, and in the beginnings of your months, you shall blow with the trumpets over your Burnt Offerings, and over the Sacrifices of your Peace Offerings; that they may be to you for a memorial before your God: I am the LORD your God *(whether in war or in worship, the purpose was not to convoke the people, nor to give signals to the host, but to put God in mind of His Promises, and to invoke His Covenanted Grace; if systematically the Priests were to blow the trumpets the first of each month over their Sacrifices, which signified the Cross, this means that unless we preach the Cross, we aren't blowing the correct sound [I Cor. 1:18])*.

LEAVING SINAI

11 And it came to pass on the twentieth day of the second month, in the second year, that the cloud was taken up from off the Tabernacle of the testimony *(Israel had rested an entire year at Mount Sinai; the tender love which planned such rest after the excitement of the coming out of Egypt, and the march to Horeb, showed how real was the care and affection that God had for His people; the "cloud" moved, so they were to move)*.

12 And the Children of Israel took their journeys out of the wilderness of Sinai; and the cloud rested in the wilderness of Paran *(even though it was a wilderness, the "cloud" was there; the Presence of the Lord can turn a wilderness into a Paradise, that is, if we will only believe Him)*.

13 And they first took their journey according to the Commandment of the LORD by the hand of Moses.

ORDER OF THE MARCH

14 In the first place went the standard of the camp of the Children of Judah according to their armies: and over his host was Nahshon the son of Amminadab *(Judah means "praise," so Israel was led by praise when they marched; this is our example, so it should be followed presently, as well; everything should begin by Praise to the Lord [I Cor. 10:6-7])*.

15 And over the host of the Tribe of the Children of Issachar was Nethaneel the son of Zuar.

16 And over the host of the Tribe of the Children of Zebulun was Eliab the son of Helon.

17 And the Tabernacle was taken down; and the sons of Gershon and the sons of Merari set forward, bearing the Tabernacle *(the general structure of the apparatus was packed upon the six wagons provided for this purpose [7:5-9])*.

18 And the standard of the camp of Reuben set forward according to their armies: and over his host was Elizur the son of Shedeur.

19 And over the host of the Tribe of the Children of Simeon was Shelumiel the son of Zurishaddai.

20 And over the host of the Tribe of the Children of Gad was Eliasaph the son of Deuel.

21 And the Kohathites set forward, bearing the Sanctuary: and the other did set up the Tabernacle against they came *(the Kohathites could not set up the sacred Vessels of which they were in charge, until the Tabernacle was erected, of which the Gershonites and Merarites were in charge)*.

22 And the standard of the camp of the Children of Ephraim set forward according to their armies: and over his host was Elishama the son of Ammihud.

23 And over the host of the tribe of the Children of Manasseh was Gamaliel the son of Pedahzur.

24 And over the host of the Tribe of the Children of Benjamin was Abidan the son of Gideoni.

25 And the standard of the camp of the Children of Dan set forward, which was the rereward of all the camps throughout their hosts: and over his host was Ahiezer the son of Ammishaddai *(the Tribe of Dan brought up the rear, whose name means "judgment"; this meant that any enemy who attempted to strike Israel from the rear would be judged by the Lord)*.

26 And over the host of the Tribe of the Children of Asher was Pagiel the son of Ocran.

27 And over the host of the Tribe of the

Children of Naphtali was Ahira the son of Enan (*it is sad when we read here these names, and realize that they all perished in the wilderness because of a lack of Faith [Heb. 4:1-6]*).

28 Thus were the journeyings of the Children of Israel according to their armies, when they set forward.

29 And Moses said unto Hobab, the son of Raguel the Midianite, Moses' father in law, We are journeying unto the place of which the LORD said, I will give it you: come thou with us, and we will do you good: for the LORD has spoken good concerning Israel (*it is not exactly certain as to who was Hobab; some think this could have been another name for Jethro; there is no Hebrew name for father-in-law; the Hebrew word simply means "a marriage relation"; so this man probably was Jethro or a brother of Jethro*).

30 And he said unto him, I will not go; but I will depart to my own land, and to my kindred (*Hobab foolishly refused to join the people of God; as a result, his descendants [I Sam. 15:6] nearly perished as the result of their ancestor's folly; wherever the Lord is, that is where we should desire to be*).

31 And he said, Leave us not, I pray you; forasmuch as you know how we are to encamp in the wilderness, and you may be to us instead of eyes (*this had nothing to do with direction, that being provided entirely by the Lord; it rather pertained to the peculiarities of the wilderness, of which Hobab evidently was greatly familiar*).

32 And it shall be, if you go with us, yes, it shall be, that what goodness the LORD shall do unto us, the same will we do unto you (*the same invitation is now given to all! [Mat. 11:28-30]*).

33 And they departed from the Mount of the LORD three days' journey: and the Ark of the Covenant of the LORD went before them in the three days' journey, to search out a resting place for them (*this was their first move after leaving Sinai, but, regrettably, because of unbelief, the future would not bode well*).

34 And the cloud of the LORD was upon them by day, when they went out of the camp (*they journeyed, the entire near 3 million of them, under the shadow of the cloud; today we have more and better, in that the Holy Spirit abides permanently within us [I Cor. 3:16]*).

35 And it came to pass, when the Ark set forward, that Moses said, Rise up, LORD, and let Your enemies be scattered; and let them who hate You flee before You (*the 68th Psalm seems to have been written as a result of this prayer of Moses; let it ever be known, if our Faith is firmly anchored in the Cross of Christ, giving the Holy Spirit latitude to work within our lives, the "enemies" will most definitely be scattered [Rom. 8:1-2, 11]*).

36 And when it rested, he said, Return, O LORD, unto the many thousands of Israel. (*When the Ark and the Cloud set forward, it was the Almighty God going on before to victory; when the Ark and the Cloud rested, it was the all-merciful God returning to protect and cherish His Own.*)

CHAPTER 11
(1490 B.C.)
COMPLAINT

AND when the people complained, it displeased the LORD: and the LORD heard it (*complaining means unbelief, and unbelief always leads to spiritual death; before they came to Sinai, the Lord had passed over similar murmurings without any chastisement [Ex. 15:24; 16:2]; but He will not let this pass; by now, they should know better; we must never take God's Mercy and Grace as a condoning of sin; if sin continues, as it did here with Israel, chastisement will ultimately come*); and His anger was kindled; and the fire of the LORD burnt among them, and consumed them who were in the uttermost parts of the camp (*most probably, this fire came from the Holy of Holies, striking down the complainers, exactly as it did Nadab and Abihu [Lev. 10:1-2]*).

2 And the people cried unto Moses; and when Moses prayed unto the LORD, the fire was quenched (*Moses served as a Type of Christ, our Intercessor*).

3 And he called the name of the place Taberah (*a burning*): because the fire of the LORD burnt among them (*because of unbelief*).

ISRAEL'S DEMAND

4 And the mixt multitude who was among them fell a lusting (*this "mixt multitude" were Egyptians, who had come out of Egypt with Israel; this proves the fact that although they were "in" Israel, they were not "of" Israel; they "lusted" for flesh to eat, registering dissatisfaction with what the Lord had provided; complaints, as here, generally draw sympathy from the disgruntled*): and the Children of Israel also wept again, and said, Who shall give us flesh to eat? (*They had

flocks and herds, but the increase of them would little more than suffice for sacrifice; so, they could not slaughter them for ordinary eating.)

5 We remember the fish, which we did eat in Egypt freely; the cucumbers, and the melons, and the leeks, and the onions, and the garlick *(unbelief forgot the slavery, as unbelief always forgets that which it should not forget, and remembers that which it should not remember)*:

6 But now our soul is dried away: there is nothing at all, besides this manna, before our eyes *(it only needed the test of the Wilderness to make visible the incurable unbelief and ignorance of their hearts; forgetting the lash of the taskmaster, they recalled the perishing bread of Egypt and turned away with loathing from the Manna! To a heart not in communion with God, Christ, the True Manna, becomes distasteful, and nourishment is sought in "the world," which holds in bondage those who go down to it).*

7 And the Manna was as coriander seed *(a flavoring type of seed, which probably had the capacity to flavor the Manna to whatever was desired)*, and the colour thereof as the colour of bdellium *(white [Ex. 16:31]).*

8 And the people went about, and gathered it, and ground it in mills, or beat it in a mortar, and baked it in pans, and made cakes of it: and the taste of it was as the taste of fresh oil *(in Exodus 16:31, it is said to have tasted like wafers made with honey).*

9 And when the dew fell upon the camp in the night, the Manna fell upon it *(there seems to be little or no connection between the dew and the Manna; when the dew evaporated in the morning, it left a deposit of Manna upon the ground).*

MOSES COMPLAINS

10 Then Moses heard the people weep throughout their families, every man in the door of his tent *(such was the contagion of evil, that every family was infected; they seemed to be acting as a petulant child, who, throwing a tantrum, thinks thereby to get his way)*: and the anger of the LORD was kindled greatly; Moses also was displeased *(the complaining was directed against God, and against Moses as His Minister).*

11 And Moses said unto the LORD, Wherefore have you afflicted your servant? *(These passionate complaints were clearly wrong, because exaggerated)* and wherefore have I not found favor in Your sight, that You lay the burden of all this people upon me? *(In a word, Moses forgot himself and his duty as mediator, and, in his indignation at the sin of the people, committed the same sin himself.)*

12 Have I conceived all this people? have I begotten them, that You should say unto me, Carry them in your bosom, as a nursing father bears the sucking child, unto the land which You swear unto their fathers?

13 Whence should I have flesh *(meat)* to give unto all this people? for they weep unto me, saying, Give us flesh, that we may eat.

14 I am not able to bear all this people alone, because it is too heavy for me *(evidently, Jethro's advice seemed ultimately to be of no consequence; in fact, it was of no consequence [Ex., Chpt. 18]).*

15 And if you deal thus with me, kill me, I pray you, out of hand, if I have found favour in Your sight; and let me not see my wretchedness *(like Elijah, Moses petulantly calls upon God to kill him out of hand; and yet, these two men appeared with the God of Glory upon the Mount of Transfiguration!).*

SEVENTY MEN

16 And the LORD said unto Moses, Gather unto Me seventy men of the Elders of Israel, whom you know to be the Elders of the people, and officers over them *(these were chosen by God, and not by Jethro; it is believed that the Sanhedrin, the ruling body of Israel, originated with the Seventy Elders)*; and bring them unto the Tabernacle of the congregation, that they may stand there with you.

17 And I will come down and talk with you there: and I will take of the Spirit *(Holy Spirit)* which is upon you, and will put it upon them; and they shall bear the burden of the people with you, that you bear it not yourself alone *(a pitying Grace relieved him of the weight of his charge while upbraiding him; however, Moses was, in truth, no whit less burdened, for the spiritual power granted to the Seventy Elders was taken from him).*

18 And say thou unto the people, Sanctify yourselves against to morrow, and you shall eat flesh: for you have wept in the ears of the LORD, saying, Who shall give us flesh to eat? for it was well with us in Egypt *(this is what they said, and what came up into the ears of the Lord. What a travesty! It wasn't well with them in Egypt. They were slaves, and, thereby, begging God to deliver them [Ex. 3:9])*: therefore the LORD will give you flesh, and you shall eat.

19 You shall not eat one day, nor two days, nor five days, neither ten days, nor twenty days;

20 But even a whole month, until it come out at your nostrils, and it be loathsome unto you: because that you have despised the LORD which is among you, and have wept before him, saying, Why came we forth out of Egypt? *(We as Believers had better be careful for what we pray. It might be answered!)*

21 And Moses said, The people, among whom I am are six hundred thousand footmen *(men of war, beside those younger and older, and the women and children)*; and you have said, I will give them flesh, that they may eat a whole month *(unbelief is registered in Moses' statement)*.

22 Shall the flocks and the herds be slain for them, to suffice them? or shall all the fish of the sea be gathered together for them, to suffice them? *(Moses had complained, so it hindered his faith. Complaining always hinders faith. If Moses' faith, in the world of that day, could be hindered, what about us presently?)*

23 And the LORD said unto Moses, Is the LORD's hand waxed short? you shall see now whether My Word shall come to pass unto you or not *(there is no situation which the Lord cannot handle, if His people will only believe Him)*.

24 And Moses went out, and told the people the words of the LORD, and gathered the seventy men of the Elders of the people, and set them round about the Tabernacle *(evidently, the Lord told Moses to place these "Elders" in a certain place and position)*.

25 And the LORD came down in a cloud, and spoke unto him, and took of the Spirit *(Holy Spirit)* that was upon him, and gave it unto the seventy Elders: and it came to pass, that, when the Spirit rested upon them, they prophesied, and did not cease. *(The "cloud" was the perpetual Presence with them. When the Spirit of the Lord came upon the Elders, they could then function in the service of the Lord. Without that Presence, they could do nothing. The crying need of the Church at this hour is a fresh enduement of "power from on high."*

Concerning Moses and this situation, Theodoret says, "Just as a man who kindles a thousand flames from one flame does not lessen the first in communicating light to others, so God did not diminish the Grace imparted to Moses by the fact that he communicated of it to the seventy." The prophesying of these men, no doubt, was a

declaration of God's wonderful Works.)

26 But there remained two of the men in the camp, the name of the one was Eldad, and the name of the other Medad: and the Spirit rested upon them; and they were of them who were written, but went not out unto the Tabernacle: and they prophesied in the camp. *(These two were of the seventy. However, because of other duties, more than likely, that demanded their attention, they could not accompany the others to the Tabernacle. Nevertheless, the Spirit of the Lord came upon them as well, even where they were, wherever that may have been.*

This is a symbol of the outpouring of the Holy Spirit, which would begin at the Tabernacle, i.e., Temple in Jerusalem, but would quickly spread all over the world. Peter said so [Acts 2:39].)

27 And there ran a young man, and told Moses, and said, Eldad and Medad do prophesy in the camp.

28 And Joshua the son of Nun, the servant of Moses, one of his young men, answered and said, My lord Moses, forbid them *(whereas Joshua, although wrong, was not wrong from a malicious spirit; regrettably, untold numbers of modern Church leaders are now trying to do what Moses would not do, "forbid them")*.

29 And Moses said unto him, Do you envy for my sake? would God that all the LORD's people were Prophets, and that the LORD would put His Spirit upon them! *(This is the correct spirit of all true men and women of God.)*

30 And Moses got him into the camp *(left the Tabernacle, and went into the camp)*, he and the Elders of Israel.

GOD SENDS QUAIL

31 And there went forth a wind from the LORD *(a wind Divinely sent for this purpose [Ps. 78:26])*, and brought quails from the sea, and let them fall by the camp, as it were a day's journey on this side, and as it were a day's journey on the other side, round about the camp, and as it were two cubits *(3 feet)* high upon the face of the Earth *(this doesn't mean that the quails were piled upon the ground to a height of 3 feet, but that they flew at that height, and so were easily captured)*.

32 And the people stood up all that day, and all that night, and all the next day, and they gathered the quails: he who gathered least gathered ten homers *(about 60 bushels)*: and they spread them all abroad for themselves round about the camp.

THE PLAGUE

33 And while the flesh was yet between their teeth, ere it was chewed, the wrath of the LORD was kindled against the people, and the LORD smote the people with a very great plague. *(What the "plague" was, we aren't told. As well, as to how many were stricken, we aren't told. Israel desired God's gifts, but had no heart for the Giver. To accept the gifts of that bountiful Hand, and to seek to enjoy them independently of it, brings death into the soul. There is indication that some of them gave credit to one of the gods of the Egyptians for the quail instead of Jehovah, hence the judgment.)*

34 And he *(Moses)* called the name of that place Kibroth-hattaavah: because there they buried the people who lusted *(whatever the plague was, it killed some of the people).*

35 And the people journeyed from Kibroth-hattaavah unto Hazeroth; and abode at Hazeroth. *("Kibroth-hattaavah" means "graves of greediness.")*

CHAPTER 12
(1490 B.C.)
MIRIAM AND AARON

AND Miriam *(Moses' sister)* and Aaron spoke against Moses because of the Ethiopian woman whom he had married: for he had married an Ethiopian woman. *(Some claim that this was actually Zipporah, and others claim that it was not, but rather that Zipporah had died, and Moses had taken this woman as his wife; or else Zipporah had not died, and Moses had taken to himself a second wife. The latter is doubtful!*

At any rate, this woman was of dark skin, and greatly envied by Miriam, who evidently felt she was not worthy of such a place and position. Also, Miriam being first mentioned shows that she was the leader of this complaint. As we shall see, the Lord did not at all take kindly to the accusations of these two. It is obvious that Satan was attempting to use this to diminish Moses in the eyes of the people, and attempted to do so by Moses' closest relatives.)

2 And they said, Has the LORD indeed spoken only by Moses? has he not spoken also by us? And the LORD heard it. *(Miriam and Aaron claimed here that the Lord had told them to do what they were doing. It's bad enough to do wrong, but worse yet when we pull God into our wrong, by attempting to make Him the*

Author of such. God heard that then, and He hears such now; as well, the end result will be the same now as then — severe chastisement for the guilty party.)*

3 *(Now the man Moses was very meek, above all the men which were upon the face of the Earth [inasmuch as this is a parenthetical statement, the probability is strong that Moses didn't actually write it, but that it was written by someone else later, and inserted into the Sacred Text and, as well, sanctioned by the Holy Spirit; it is highly unlikely that Moses would have said such of himself].)*

GOD DEFENDS MOSES

4 And the LORD spoke suddenly unto Moses, and unto Aaron, and unto Miriam *(how the Lord did this, we aren't told; however, the word "suddenly" points to something unexpected and unusual)*, Come out you three *(from the camp)* unto the Tabernacle of the congregation. And they three came out.

5 And the LORD came down in the pillar of the cloud, and stood in the door of the Tabernacle, and called Aaron and Miriam: and they both came forth.

6 And He said, Hear now My words: If there be a Prophet among you, I the LORD will make Myself known unto him in a vision, and will speak unto him in a dream *(the way that Prophecies are generally given by the Lord).*

7 My servant Moses is not so *(the Lord here puts Moses above all the Prophets of the Old Testament, other than John the Baptist, who introduced Christ [Lk. 7:28])*, who is faithful in all My house. *(Miriam and Aaron were saying that Moses wasn't faithful, and we speak of the marriage, but the Lord said the opposite. We had better be certain that we say exactly what the Lord is saying.)*

8 With him will I speak mouth to mouth, even apparently, and not in dark speeches; and the similitude of the LORD shall he behold *(the idea is that Moses, at times, literally saw the Spirit Body of the Lord; it is not possible, I think, to derive anything else from this Text; as well, the Lord in this manner spoke to Moses, and, one might say, "face to face")*: wherefore then were you not afraid to speak against My servant Moses? *(The words "speak against" refer to finding fault, but fault that didn't exist. As we shall see, the Lord did not look upon their sin sympathetically, even as He can never look upon sin sympathetically.)*

9 And the anger of the LORD was kindled against them; and He *(the Lord)* departed. *(It's one thing to have man angry with us; it is something else altogether to have the Lord angry at us. The cause of this anger was the cruel criticism of Moses' sister and brother. The Holy Spirit through James addressed this as well, as it regards modern Believers [James, Chpt. 3].)*

LEPROSY

10 And the cloud departed from off the Tabernacle; and, behold, Miriam became leprous, white as snow: and Aaron looked upon Miriam, and, behold, she was leprous. *(This plainly tells us that Miriam was the leader in this rebellion. Even though Aaron sinned by going along with her, he was not the instigator. The Hebrew Text points to the fact that the leprosy put on Miriam by the Lord was its worst and final stage. The word "looked" means that the High Priest gazed with astonishment.)*

11 And Aaron said unto Moses, Alas, my lord, I beseech you, lay not the sin upon us, wherein we have done foolishly, and wherein we have sinned. *(The manner in which Aaron now addresses Moses tells us that he rightly acknowledges Moses' superior position, thereby abandoning all pretension to equality. As well, he frankly confesses his sin, which he should have done.)*

12 Let her *(Miriam)* not be as one dead, of whom the flesh is half consumed when he comes out of his mother's womb *(as well, Aaron also conducts himself as a High Priest, which he was, thereby interceding on behalf of his sister; he was horrified at the condition of Miriam, as all leprosy of this type affects the victim in its final stages; in other words, Miriam would have died shortly had not the Lord healed her).*

INTERCESSION

13 And Moses cried unto the LORD, saying, Heal her now, O God, I beseech you *(he pleads for her, who had done so wrong, which is true Christlikeness; Jesus addressed this when He said, "Pray for them which despitefully use you, and persecute you" [Mat. 5:44]).*

14 And the LORD said unto Moses, If her father had but spit in her face, should she not be ashamed seven days? *(The Lord proclaims at to how serious this sin was; Miriam had attempted to embarrass Moses publicly; in turn, the Lord embarrassed her publicly; once again, Jesus addressed this by saying, "With what measure you mete, it shall be measured to you again" [Mat. 7:2].)* let her be shut out from the camp seven days, and after that let her be received in again.

15 And Miriam was shut out from the camp seven days: and the people journeyed not till Miriam was brought in again. *(Miriam's sin stopped the entirety of the Work of God, numbering nearly 3 million people, for an entire week. From this we should understand just how serious that sin actually is.)*

16 And afterward the people removed from Hazeroth, and pitched in the wilderness of Paran. *(They were not far from the Promised Land, and the Lord intended for them to now go in; however, as we shall see, unbelief caused them to languish over 38 more years in that wilderness.)*

CHAPTER 13
(1490 B.C.)
TWELVE SPIES

AND the LORD spoke unto Moses, saying,

2 Send thou men, that they may search the land of Canaan, which I give unto the Children of Israel: of every tribe of their fathers shall you send a man, every one a ruler among them. *(Deuteronomy 1:25 proclaims the fact that these rulers had demanded this, and the Lord had agreed to allow them to do such. Why did they need to search the land when the Lord had already told them what it was? As well, they were committing the terrible sin of unbelief by questioning the Lord. It would cost them dearly.)*

3 And Moses by the Commandment of the LORD sent them from the wilderness of Paran: all those men were heads of the Children of Israel.

4 And these were their names: of the Tribe of Reuben, Shammua the son of Zaccur.

5 Of the Tribe of Simeon, Shaphat the son of Hori.

6 Of the Tribe of Judah, Caleb the son of Jephunneh.

7 Of the Tribe of Issachar, Igal the son of Joseph.

8 Of the Tribe of Ephraim, Oshea *(Joshua)* the son of Nun.

9 Of the Tribe of Benjamin, Palti the son of Raphu.

10 Of the Tribe of Zebulun, Gaddiel the son

of Sodi.

11 Of the Tribe of Joseph, namely, of the Tribe of Manasseh, Gaddi the son of Susi.

12 Of the Tribe of Dan, Ammiel the son of Gemalli.

13 Of the Tribe of Asher, Sethur the son of Michael.

14 Of the Tribe of Naphtali, Nahbi the son of Vophsi.

15 Of the Tribe of Gad, Geuel the son of Machi.

16 These are the names of the men which Moses sent to spy out the land. And Moses called Oshea the son of Nun Jehoshua *(means help or Salvation; it was changed to Joshua, which means "Saviour" [Neh. 8:17]. The fact that our Saviour received the same name, because He was our Saviour, throws a halo of glory about it, which we cannot ignore. In the Divine providence Hoshea became Joshua, because he was destined to be the temporal saviour of his people, and to lead them into their promised rest — Pulpit. All of these men listed above, with the exception of Caleb and Joshua, registered unbelief, and thereby delayed the Plan of God for over 38 years. More than likely they, as well, lost their souls).*

THE SPIES

17 And Moses sent them to spy out the land of Canaan, and said unto them, Get you up this way southward, and go up into the mountain:

18 And see the land, what it is, and the people who dwell therein, whether they be strong or weak, few or many *(it would seem that Moses was guilty here of at least some indiscretion in the giving of these directions; irrespective as to the condition of the people, whether weak or strong, it was God Who was to give them the land; they had only to take possession boldly);*

19 And what the land is that they dwell in, whether it be good or bad; and what cities they be that they dwell in, whether in tents, or in strong holds;

20 And what the land is, whether it be fat or lean, whether there be wood therein, or not. And be ye of good courage, and bring of the fruit of the land. Now the time was the time of the firstripe grapes.

21 So they went up, and searched the land from the wilderness of Zin *(the extreme southern boundary of the Promised Land [Josh. 15:1-3])* unto Rehob, as men come to Hamath.

22 And they ascended by the south, and came unto Hebron; where Ahiman, Sheshai, and Talmai, the children of Anak, were. *(These very well could have been giants, the result of co-habitation between fallen angels and women [Gen. 6:4]. This was Satan's plan to pollute the human race, through which Jesus would have to come, that is, if man was to be delivered.)* (Now Hebron was built seven years before Zoan in Egypt *[one of the oldest cities in the world].*)

23 And they came unto the Brook of Eshcol, and cut down from thence a branch with one cluster of grapes, and they bore it between two upon a staff *(quite a large cluster)*; and they brought of the pomegranates, and of the figs.

24 The place was called the brook Eshcol, because of the cluster of grapes which the Children of Israel cut down from thence.

25 And they returned from searching of the land after forty days. *("Forty" is God's probationary number in the Bible. Regrettably, as Adam and Eve, they failed that probation. Although not stated in the Bible, most probably Adam and Eve walked with the Lord some forty days before the Fall.)*

THE EVIL REPORT

26 And they went and came to Moses, and to Aaron, and to all the congregation of the Children of Israel, unto the wilderness of Paran, to Kadesh; and brought back word unto them, and unto all the congregation, and shewed them the fruit of the land.

27 And they told him, and said, We came unto the land where you sent us, and surely it flows with milk and honey; and this is the fruit of it *(in other words, it was exactly as the Lord said it would be).*

28 Nevertheless the people be strong who dwell in the land, and the cities are walled, and very great: and moreover we saw the children of Anak there *(giants).*

29 The Amalekites dwell in the land of the south: and the Hittites, and the Jebusites, and the Amorites, dwell in the mountains: and the Canaanites dwell by the sea, and by the coast of Jordan.

30 And Caleb stilled the people before Moses *(the evil report of faithlessness given by ten of the spies had greatly unsettled the people; little did they realize it would cost them their lives)*, and said, Let us go up at once, and possess it; for we are well able to overcome it *(this was the language of faith; but Faith and Truth are never popular [14:10]; had they only believed and acted upon their faith, they were, in fact,*

well able to overcome it, because the Lord was with them).

31 But the men who went up with him said, We be not able to go up against the people; for they are stronger than we *(but they were not stronger than God; however, doubt and unbelief always look to self, and say, "We cannot," while faith looks to the Lord, and says, "We can!").*

32 And they brought up an evil report of the land which they had searched unto the Children of Israel *(to doubt and deny the Word of God is always constituted "an evil report"),* saying, The land, through which we have gone to search it, is a land that eats up the inhabitants thereof; and all the people that we saw in it are the men of a great stature *(doubt and unbelief see the difficulties, while faith sees the victory).*

33 And there we saw the giants, the sons of Anak, which come of the giants: and we were in our own sight as grasshoppers, and so we were in their sight. *(As a Believer, what do you see? Giants or God? Grasshoppers or God's greatness?)*

CHAPTER 14
(1490 B.C.)
REBELLION

AND all the congregation lifted up their voice, and cried; and the people wept that night *(it was the weeping of unbelief).*

2 And all the Children of Israel murmured against Moses and against Aaron: and the whole congregation said unto them, Would God that we had died in the land of Egypt! or would God we had died in this wilderness! *(They were to get exactly what they said. That entire generation died in the wilderness.)*

3 And wherefore has the LORD brought us unto this land, to fall by the sword, that our wives and our children should be a prey? were it not better for us to return into Egypt? *(God is now blamed, whereas before they had only blamed Moses and Aaron.)*

4 And they said one to another, Let us make a captain, and let us return into Egypt. *(Pulpit says, "Nothing less than an entire and deliberate revolt was involved in the wish to elect a captain for themselves, for the Lord was the Captain of this host [Josh. 5:14-15]. The proposal to depose Him, and to choose another in His place, marked the extremity of the unbelief, and the ingratitude of the people.")*

5 Then Moses and Aaron fell on their faces before all the Assembly of the congregation of the Children of Israel *(this was not so much to make intercession for them, but mostly because of the enormity of the sin, and what Moses and Aaron knew would follow).*

JOSHUA AND CALEB

6 And Joshua the son of Nun, and Caleb the son of Jephunneh, which were of them who searched the land, rent their clothes *(the "tearing of their clothes" was meant to serve as a symbol unto the people of the extremity of the situation, hoping to turn them around):*

7 And they spoke unto all the company of the Children of Israel, saying, The land, which we passed through to search it, is an exceeding good land.

8 If the LORD delight in us, then He will bring us into this land, and give it us; a land which flows with milk and honey.

9 Only rebel not ye against the LORD, neither fear ye the people of the land; for they are bread for us: their defense is departed from them, and the LORD is with us: fear them not. *("If the Lord be with us, who can be against us?")*

GOD'S ANGER

10 But all the congregation bade stone them with stones *(that was the answer to the Faith of Joshua and Caleb).* And the glory of the LORD appeared in the Tabernacle of the congregation before all the Children of Israel *(whatever type of demonstration there was, the Children of Israel observed it all).*

11 And the LORD said unto Moses, How long will this people provoke Me? and how long will it be ere they believe Me, for all the signs which I have shown among them? *(Signs and wonders, even those which are real, will little turn the head of doubt. It is simple faith in God's Word which one must have [Rom. 5:1; Eph. 2:8-9].)*

12 I will smite them with the pestilence, and disinherit them, and will make of you a greater nation and mightier than they. *(I personally feel that this was a test for Moses, as it regarded personal ambition. If that, in fact, is correct, he passed it with flying colors.)*

INTERCESSION

13 And Moses said unto the LORD, then the Egyptians shall hear it, (for You brought up

this people in Your might from among them;)

14 And they will tell it to the inhabitants of this land: for they have heard that You LORD are among this people, that You LORD are seen face to face, and that Your cloud stands over them, and that You go before them, by day time in a pillar of a cloud, and in a pillar of fire by night.

15 Now if You shall kill all this people as one man, then the nations which have heard the fame of You will speak, saying,

16 Because the LORD was not able to bring this people into the land which He swore unto them, therefore He has slain them in the wilderness. *(Pulpit says, "Moral or religious difficulties could not be comprehended by the heathen nations as standing in the way of God's purposes. Physical hindrances were the only ones they could understand; so if the Lord killed all the Israelites in the wilderness, it could only be in order, or so they would think, to cover His Own defeat and failure before the rival deities of the surrounding nations.")*

17 And now, I beseech You, let the power of my LORD be great, according as You have spoken, saying *(Moses brings before the Lord His Own argument, which, as would be obvious, was a telling force)*,

18 The LORD is longsuffering, and of great mercy, forgiving iniquity and transgression *(if proper Repentance is engaged)*, and by no means clearing the guilty *(if Repentance is not forthcoming, judgment will definitely come)*, visiting the iniquity of the fathers upon the children unto the third and fourth generation *(that is, if there is no Repentance)*.

19 Pardon, I beseech You, the iniquity of this people according unto the greatness of Your mercy, and as You have forgiven this people, from Egypt even until now. *(The Lord pardoned the iniquity of the Israelites only so far as stopping the judgment of total destruction. Unfortunately, they really did not ask for forgiveness, and engaged in no true Repentance.)*

PUNISHMENT

20 And the LORD said, I have pardoned according to your word *("The effectual fervent prayer of a righteous man availeth much" [James 5:16])*:

21 But as truly as I live, all the Earth shall be filled with the Glory of the LORD *(this will come about to a great extent during the coming Millennial Reign, and totally in the coming*

Perfect Age, which will last forever [Rev., Chpts. 21-22]).

22 Because all those men which have seen My Glory, and My miracles, which I did in Egypt and in the wilderness, and have tempted Me now these ten times, and have not hearkened to My Voice *(the ten temptations were: Red Sea, Ex., Chpt. 14; Marah, Ex., Chpt. 15; Sin, Ex., Chpt. 16; Manna, Ex. 16:20; Manna, Ex. 16:27; Rephidim, Ex., Chpt. 17; Horeb, Ex., Chpt. 32; Taberah, Num., Chpt. 11; Kibroth, Num., Chpt. 11; Kadesh, Num., Chpt. 14)*;

23 Surely they shall not see the land which I swore unto their fathers, neither shall any of them who provoked Me see it *(all who were twenty years old or older would die in the wilderness; it seems that the Levites were exempted from this curse, inasmuch as they had no representative among the spies)*:

24 But My servant Caleb, because he had another spirit with him, and has followed Me fully, him will I bring into the land whereinto he went; and his seed shall possess it *(God honors Faith wherever it is found)*.

25 (Now the Amalekites and the Canaanites dwelt in the valley.) To morrow turn you, and get you into the wilderness by the way of the Red Sea. *(It seems this statement was made in reference to Caleb. When, some forty years later, his inheritance was given to him, the "Vale of Hebron" was occupied by two hostile peoples; nevertheless he, and again because of his Faith, would definitely prevail.)*

26 And the LORD spoke unto Moses and unto Aaron, saying,

27 How long shall I bear with this evil congregation, which murmur against Me? I have heard the murmurings of the Children of Israel, which they murmur against Me *(as should be obvious, the Lord hears all; we as Believers should remember that, and speak accordingly; the Lord honors Faith words, but delights not at all in doubt words)*.

28 Say unto them, As truly as I live, saith the LORD, as you have spoken in My ears, so will I do to you *(they had wished to die in the wilderness, and in the wilderness they would die! [14:2])*:

29 Your carcases shall fall in this wilderness; and all that were numbered of you, according to your whole number, from twenty years old and upward which have murmured against Me *(this included all who had been enrolled as soldiers of the Lord, but had refused, and had incurred the guilt of mutiny;*

that offense is punishable by death [Chpts. 1-2]).

30 Doubtless you shall not come into the land, concerning which I swore to make you dwell therein, save Caleb the son of Jephunneh, and Joshua the son of Nun *(as stated, God honored the Faith of these two men).*

31 But your little ones, which you said should be a prey *(to the enemy),* them will I bring in, and they shall know the land which you have despised *(how so much this should be a lesson to all modern Believers; God cannot abide doubt and unbelief).*

32 But as for you *(said with contempt),* your carcases, they shall fall in this wilderness.

33 And your children shall wander in the wilderness forty years, and bear your whoredoms, until your carcases be wasted in the wilderness *(until this generation died off, the younger ones could not go into the Promised Land).*

34 After the number of the days in which you searched the land, even forty days, each day for a year, shall you bear your iniquities, even forty years, and you shall know My breach of promise *(they were to know and understand that the quantity and quality of their punishment was entirely due to themselves; and it needed no other justification; if God assigns reasons at all, He assigns such as can be understood by those to whom He speaks).*

35 I the LORD have said, I will surely do it unto all this evil congregation, who are gathered together against Me: in this wilderness they shall be consumed, and there they shall die *(faithlessness is always "against God").*

DEATH OF THE TEN SPIES

36 And the men, which Moses sent to search the land, who returned, and made all the congregation to murmur against Him by bringing up a slander upon the land *(when we slander God's gift, we slander God; wherever God places the Believer, even in a wilderness, the Believer must thank the Lord constantly, and never allow a word of doubt to come out of his mouth),*

37 Even those men who did bring up the evil report upon the land, died by the plague before the LORD *(it seems they all died at one time, by what method we aren't told, but which was visible to the entire congregation).*

38 But Joshua the son of Nun, and Caleb the son of Jephunneh, which were of the men who went to search the land, lived still *(in one way or the other, that plague continues to operate; it*

is only Faith which spares mankind, and, we might quickly add, Faith in Christ and the Cross [I Cor. 1:17]).

39 And Moses told these sayings unto all the Children of Israel: and the people mourned greatly. *(However, it seems that their "mourning" did not lead them to true Repentance.)*

ISRAEL DEFEATED

40 And they rose up early in the morning, and got them up into the top of the mountain, saying, Lo, we be here, and will go up unto the place which the LORD has promised: for we have sinned *(theirs was not a true Repentance, but merely consisted of a frantic effort to avoid the punishment which their sin had incurred).*

41 And Moses said, Wherefore now do you transgress the Commandment of the LORD? but it shall not prosper. *(Concerning this, Williams says, "Verses 39 through 45 illustrate the presumption of the natural heart, just as the closing Verses of Chpt. 13 illustrate the cowardice. The carnal mind [Rom., Chpt. 8] cannot serve God; it is timid when it should be bold, and bold when it should be timid. It advances when it should stand still; and it stands still when it should advance.")*

42 Go not up, for the LORD is not among you; that you be not smitten before your enemies.

43 For the Amalekites and the Canaanites are there before you, and you shall fall by the sword: because you are turned away from the LORD, therefore the LORD will not be with you.

44 But they presumed to go up unto the hill top *(they operated on presumption):* nevertheless the Ark of the Covenant of the LORD, and Moses, departed not out of the camp *(this attitude shows that their repentance was not true; they are still disobeying the Lord).*

45 Then the Amalekites came down, and the Canaanites which dwelt in that hill, and smote them, and discomfited them, even unto Hormah. *(God with them, they could not be defeated; without the Lord, they were already defeated.)*

CHAPTER 15
(1490 B.C.)
OFFERINGS

AND the LORD spoke unto Moses, saying,

2 Speak unto the Children of Israel, and say unto them, When you be come into the

land of your habitations, which I give unto you *(meaning that these things would not be carried out until they reached the Promised Land; we have no way of knowing as to exactly when the Lord gave this information to Moses)*,

3 And will make an Offering by fire unto the LORD, a Burnt Offering, or a Sacrifice in performing a vow, or in a freewill offering, or in your solemn feasts, to make a sweet savour unto the LORD, of the herd or of the flock *(these Offerings were somewhat different than the ordinary Offerings)*:

4 Then shall he who offers his Offering unto the LORD bring a Meat Offering of a tenth deal of flour mingled with the fourth part of an hin of oil.

5 And the fourth part of an hin of wine for a Drink Offering shall you prepare with the Burnt Offering or Sacrifice, for one lamb *(the "Drink Offering" portrayed the Life of Christ, which would be poured out)*.

6 Or for a ram, you shall prepare for a Meat Offering two tenth deals of flour mingled with the third part of an hin of oil.

7 And for a Drink Offering you shall offer the third part of an hin of wine, for a sweet savour unto the LORD.

8 And when you prepare a bullock for a Burnt Offering, or for a Sacrifice in performing a vow, or Peace Offerings unto the LORD:

9 Then shall he bring with a bullock a Meat Offering of three tenth deals of flour mingled with half an hin of oil *(the "Meat Offerings" actually had no flesh, but were altogether grain, made into loaves of bread)*.

10 And you shall bring for a Drink Offering half an hin of wine, for an Offering made by fire *(the Burnt Offerings or the Peace Offerings)*, of a sweet savour unto the LORD.

11 Thus shall it be done for one bullock, or for one ram, or for a lamb, or a kid *(a baby lamb)*.

12 According to the number that you shall prepare, so shall you do to every one according to their number *(the strict proportion of the Meat and Drink Offering was to be carried out with respect to the number of animals offered, as well as the individual value of the Sacrifices)*.

13 All who are born of the country shall do these things after this manner, in offering an Offering made by fire, of a sweet savour unto the LORD.

14 And if a stranger *(Gentile)* sojourn with you, or whosoever be among you in your generations, and will offer an Offering made by fire, of a sweet savour unto the LORD; as you do, so he shall do.

15 One ordinance shall be both for you of the congregation, and also for the stranger who sojourns with you, an ordinance for ever in your generations: as you are, so shall the stranger *(Gentile)* be before the LORD *(one Sacrifice was to be for the congregation, and also for the stranger; and so Christ offered up Himself, not only to redeem Israel, but also to save the world [Jn. 3:16])*.

16 One law and one manner shall be for you, and for the stranger who sojourns with you.

MORE INSTRUCTIONS

17 And the LORD spoke unto Moses, saying,

18 Speak unto the Children of Israel, and say unto them, When you come into the land where I bring you,

19 Then it shall be, that, when you eat of the bread of the land, you shall offer up an Heave Offering unto the LORD *(was to be "heaved" up and down, signifying that Christ would come from Heaven to this Earth, in order to redeem fallen humanity)*.

20 You shall offer up a cake of the first of your dough for an Heave Offering: as you do the Heave Offering of the threshingfloor, so shall you heave it.

21 Of the first of your dough you shall give unto the LORD an Heave Offering in your generations. *(Verses 17 through 21 taught the people that the bread that came up out of the ground for their nutriment was as great a miracle as the bread that came down from Heaven. Hence, the perpetual Heave Offering of Verse 21 acknowledged that Jehovah not only gave them the land, but also was the Creator of the "bread of the land.")*

22 And if you have erred, and not observed all these Commandments, which the LORD has spoken unto Moses *(these were sins of ignorance; provision is made here for the forgiveness of such sins — a provision which was sorely needed, considering the great complexity of the Law, and the inadequate training they had had for the accurate observance of it)*,

23 Even all that the LORD has commanded you by the hand of Moses, from the day that the LORD commanded Moses, and henceforward among your generations *(future generations must know and understand the Law, and in every respect)*;

24 Then it shall be, if ought be committed by ignorance without the knowledge of the congregation, that all the congregation shall offer one young bullock for a Burnt Offering, for a sweet savour unto the LORD, with his Meat Offering, and his Drink Offering, according to the manner, and one kid of the goats for a Sin Offering. *(Verses 22 through 28 provided the sweet-savour offering for the sin of omission, i.e., "ignorance," whether committed by all the people, or by an individual. The Burnt Offering, the Sin Offering, the Meat Offering, and the Drink Offering typified the infinite Sacrifice of the Lamb of God as being necessary to cover even so small a sin as the sin of omission. This means that the Cross of Christ is absolutely needed in every aspect of life and living, and we speak of present times.)*

25 And the Priest shall make an Atonement for all the congregation of the Children of Israel, and it shall be forgiven them; for it is ignorance: and they shall bring their Offering, a Sacrifice made by fire unto the LORD, and their Sin Offering before the LORD, for their ignorance:

26 And it shall be forgiven all the congregation of the Children of Israel, and the stranger *(Gentile)* who sojourns among them; seeing all the people were in ignorance.

27 And if any soul sin through ignorance, then he shall bring a she goat of the first year for a Sin Offering.

28 And the Priest shall make an Atonement for the soul that sins ignorantly, when he sins by ignorance before the LORD, to make an Atonement for him; and it shall be forgiven him.

29 You shall have one law for him who sins though ignorance, both for him who is born among the Children of Israel, and for the stranger *(Gentile)* who sojourns among them.

30 But the soul that does ought presumptuously *(defiantly)*, whether he be born in the land, or a stranger, the same reproaches the LORD; and that soul shall be cut off from among his people.

31 Because he has despised the Word of the LORD, and has broken His Commandment, that soul shall utterly be cut off; his iniquity shall be upon him *(this refers to viciously, with purpose, and openly flouting the Law of God; such a person would be "cut off," would face the ultimate penalty — death, and the loss of his soul).*

THE SABBATH-BREAKER

32 And while the Children of Israel were in the wilderness, they found a man who gathered sticks upon the Sabbath day.

33 And they who found him gathering sticks brought him unto Moses and Aaron, and unto all the congregation.

34 And they put him in ward *(in a holding cell)*, because it was not declared what should be done to him *(Moses would seek the Lord)*.

35 And the LORD said unto Moses, The man shall be surely put to death: all the congregation shall stone him with stones without the camp.

36 And all the congregation brought him without the camp, and stoned him with stones, and he died; as the LORD commanded Moses. *(Provision was made for the sin of ignorance in connection with obedience to the Word of the Lord, but there was no Offering commanded for the sin of indifference. Regrettably, that sin is very visible today in modern Christendom. Human opinion is set above Divine injunction.)*

FRINGES ON GARMENTS

37 And the LORD spoke unto Moses, saying,

38 Speak unto the Children of Israel, and bid them that they make them fringes in the borders of their garments throughout their generations, and that they put upon the fringe of the borders a ribband of blue *(this was to make it visible to all of Israel that they were a Heavenly people, and that this great fact should especially be present to their hearts when necessarily coming in closest touch with the Earth; it was to be worn on the outer garment, and on each of the four corners as a tassel of blue)*:

39 And it shall be unto you for a fringe, that you may look upon it, and remember all the Commandments of the LORD, and do them; and that you seek not after your own heart and your own eyes, after which you use to go a whoring *(the tasseled Hebrew was a marked man in other eyes, and in his own; he could not pass himself off as one of the heathen; he was perpetually reminded of the special relation in which he stood to the Lord; in other words, he wore the colors of the Lord; that color was blue, reminding him that his help came from above)*:

40 That you may remember, and do all My Commandments, and be holy unto your God.

41 I am the LORD your God, which brought you out of the land of Egypt, to be your God; I

am the LORD your God. *(Concerning this, Pulpit says, "This intensely solemn formula twice repeated here may serve to show how intimately the smallest observances of the Law were connected with the most profound and most comforting of spiritual truths, if only observed in faith and true obedience. The whole of their experience with the Lord, both theoretical and practical, lay in those words, and was symbolized in the tassel.")*

CHAPTER 16
(1454 B.C.)
KORAH'S REBELLION

NOW Korah, the son of Izhar, the son of Kohath, the son of Levi, and Dathan and Abiram, the sons of Eliab, and On, the son of Peleth, sons of Reuben, took men: *(This Chapter reveals the incurable evil of the human heart. It is naturally opposed to God, and all that pertains to God, as evidenced by the rebellion of Korah. Korah was first cousin, it seems, to Moses and Aaron. He was camped close to the Tribe of Reuben, hence their association in this rebellion.*

The phrase "took men" emphasizes the fact that he persuaded them as to his cause. And what was that cause?)

2 And they rose up before Moses, with certain of the Children of Israel, two hundred and fifty princes of the assembly, famous in the congregation, men of renown: *(Is it possible that Jethro's unspiritual and unscriptural advice to Moses had a part in this? [Ex. Chpts. 18, 21-22]. God chose Aaron to be High Priest. Korah "gainsayed" that, which means that he disputed God's choice of Aaron as High Priest [Jude, Vs. 11]. As well, the Princes of Reuben attacked the kingship given to Moses by God. The spirit, therefore, of this rebellion was to cast down the Blessed One — Christ — Whom God has appointed both King and Priest.)*

3 And they gathered themselves together against Moses and against Aaron, and said unto them, You take too much upon you, seeing all the congregation are holy, every one of them, and the LORD is among them: wherefore then lift you up yourselves above the congregation of the LORD? *(Korah and those who followed him attempted to change the Government of God, which has always been the crowning sin of the Church, whether the Church before the Cross, or the Church after the Cross. God's Word is His Government. To stray from that Word at all, which Korah did, is to instigate rebellion against the Lord, which God cannot countenance in any form.)*

4 And when Moses heard it, he fell upon his face *(that is, he stepped aside so the rebels should stand face-to-face with God; he did not attempt to defend himself and Aaron; he left all to the judgment of God and, to be sure, that judgment was terrible)*:

5 And he spoke unto Korah and unto all his company, saying, Even tomorrow the LORD will shew who are his, and who is holy; and will cause him to come near unto Him: even him whom He has chosen will He cause to come near unto Him. *(Their sin was not only rebellion against God in the normal sense of the word, but, in actuality, they were opposing the Headship of Christ. They were, in a sense, saying that there were many men in Israel who could fill the shoes of Moses, and many who could fill the shoes of Aaron as the High Priest. So, in a sense, they were not only denying the Headship of Christ, but, as well, His High Priestly Ministry. We should read these words carefully, because, in essence, we are reading here the sin of the modern Church.)*

6 This do; Take you censers, Korah, and all his company *(the "censers" were used by the Priests, and especially the High Priest, as it regarded the Holy Place, where the Table, the Lampstand, and the Altar of Incense were; they spoke of the Intercession of Christ, all on behalf of Believers; so, in effect, these individuals were claiming they could serve in this capacity the same as Aaron)*;

7 And put fire therein *(this fire was supposed to come from the Brazen Altar)*, and put incense in them before the LORD tomorrow: and it shall be that the man whom the LORD does choose, he shall be holy: you take too much upon you, you sons of Levi. *(They should have remembered what happened to Nadab and Abihu [Lev. 10:1-2]. To be sure, their sin was even worse than that of these two Priests, who had been stricken dead by the Lord. Rebellious man, however, always seeks to put a religious face on his erroneous direction.)*

8 And Moses said unto Korah, Hear, I pray you, you sons of Levi *(evidently, others in the Tribe of Levi, the Priestly Tribe, had sided with Korah)*:

9 Seems it but a small thing unto you, that the God of Israel has separated you from the congregation of Israel, to bring you near to Himself to do the service of the Tabernacle of the LORD, and to stand before the

congregation to minister unto them? *(Moses is addressing this to the Tribe of Levi, in effect telling them that they were usurping that which God had called them to do. They were rebelling against God's order.)*

10 And He has brought you near to Him, and all your brethren the sons of Levi with you: and seek ye the Priesthood also? *(The "Priesthood" of Israel of old was a Type of Christ. Everything they did symbolized Christ in either His Mediatorial, Intercessory, or Atoning Work. The Lord had given specific instructions as to how the entirety of the Sacrificial System was to be carried out, and who was to carry it out. So, in effect, these rebels were pushing Christ aside. That is the sin of the modern Church. While the unredeemed world attempts to create another god, the Church, sadly, attempts to create another Sacrifice. Only the Sacrifice of Christ is acceptable. Anyone or anything else, no matter how religious it might be, can never be accepted by God.)*

11 For which cause both you and all your company are gathered together against the LORD *(Let it ever be known, when we pervert the Word of the Lord, this puts us "against the Lord")*: and what is Aaron, that you murmur against him? *(Moses is saying that Aaron is just a poor, weak human being, attempting to carry out the Work of the Lord. While they thought they were opposed to Aaron, in truth, they were opposed to the Lord. When we oppose that which is of God, we have, in essence, opposed God.)*

12 And Moses sent to call Dathan and Abiram, the sons of Eliab: which said, We will not come up *(meaning that they would not obey what Moses said; evidently they were in league with Korah)*:

13 Is it a small thing that you have brought us up out of a land that flows with milk and honey *(they were referring to Egypt)*, to kill us in the wilderness, except you make yourself altogether a prince over us? *(In the first place, Moses didn't put himself in this position, God did!)*

14 Moreover you have not brought us into a land that flows with milk and honey, or given us inheritance of fields and vineyards: will you put out the eyes of these men? we will not come up. *(They refused to recognize that they were still in the wilderness because of their unbelief. Being condemned to 38 years of wandering in that wilderness was their fault, and not the fault of Moses and Aaron. Men forever attempt to blame their circumstances on others, instead of where it rightfully belongs — themselves.)*

JUDGMENT

15 And Moses was very wroth, and said unto the LORD, Respect not thou their offering: I have not taken one ass from them, neither have I hurt one of them *(he had not enriched himself one iota as a result of his position; as well, he is asking the Lord that their sacrifices not be accepted, which means that unless the situation was rectified, they would be eternally lost).*

16 And Moses said unto Korah, Be thou and all your company before the LORD, thou, and they, and Aaron, to morrow:

17 And take every man his censer, and put incense in them, and bring ye before the LORD every man his censer, two hundred and fifty censers; you also, and Aaron, each of you his censer *(they were demanding that they serve in some capacity in the Priesthood, so their claims would now be put to the test).*

18 And they took every man his censer, and put fire in them *(whether it was fire from the Brazen Altar or not, we aren't told)*, and laid incense thereon, and stood in the door of the Tabernacle of the congregation with Moses and Aaron *(the "door of the Tabernacle" probably referred here to the opening, or gate, that led into the Court; so, they stood in that opening, or else immediately outside, where they could be observed by all the people).*

19 And Korah gathered all the congregation against them unto the door of the Tabernacle of the congregation: and the Glory of the LORD appeared unto all the congregation. *(There seemed to have been quite a number who sided with Korah against Moses and Aaron. In answer to this, the Lord appeared. What exactly that means, we aren't told. At any rate, the entirety of the congregation of Israel knew that it was the Lord.)*

SEPARATION

20 And the LORD spoke unto Moses and unto Aaron, saying,

21 Separate yourselves from among this congregation, that I may consume them in a moment. *(The situation was different before the Cross, and for many reasons; however, to be sure, although in a different way, the Lord is still consuming those who rebel against Christ and the Cross. While it may take a different form,*

the end result is the same [Rom. 1:18].)

22 And they *(Moses and Aaron)* fell upon their faces, and said, O God, the God of the spirits of all flesh *(Who made man)*, shall one man sin *(Korah)*, and will You be wroth with all the congregation? *(Moses intercedes for Israel that they not be judged for Korah's sin. It was this man who had misled all the rest. Deceiving spirits were at work then, even as now.)*

JUDGMENT

23 And the LORD spoke unto Moses, saying,

24 Speak unto the congregation, saying, Get you up from about the Tabernacle of Korah, Dathan, and Abiram.

25 And Moses rose up and went unto Dathan and Abiram; and the Elders of Israel followed him.

26 And he spoke unto the congregation, saying, Depart, I pray you, from the tents of these wicked men, and touch nothing of theirs, lest you be consumed in all their sins. *(Evidently, Moses and the Elders of Israel were standing near the tents of these individuals. The Lord has already told him that judgment was soon to come.)*

27 So they got up from the Tabernacle of Korah, Dathan, and Abiram, on every side: And Dathan and Abiram came out, and stood in the door of their tents, and their wives, and their sons, and their little children *(regrettably, the judgment would include the entirety of the families).*

28 And Moses said, Hereby you shall know that the LORD has sent me to do all these works; for I have not done them of my own mind.

29 If these men die the common death of all men, or if they be visited after the visitation of all men; then the LORD has not sent me *(the die is now cast!).*

30 But if the LORD make a new thing, and the Earth open her mouth, and swallow them up, with all that appertain unto them, and they go down quick into the pit; then you shall understand that these men have provoked the LORD. *(Knowing of all the miracles that Moses had seen, and that the Lord had worked through the hand of this man to do mighty things, one would think that these men would have repented; however, deception is a powerful force. Even though proof is offered, deception cannot see the reality, because deception doesn't want to see the reality; therefore, it believes a lie, which is the condition of most of the world, and even most*

of the Church.)

31 And it came to pass, as he had made an end of speaking all these words, that the ground clave asunder that was under them *(this must have been a very fearful sight and, to be sure, many observed it).*

32 And the Earth opened her mouth, and swallowed them up, and their houses, and all the men that appertained unto Korah, and all their goods *(this speaks of the entirety of these three families of Korah, Dathan, and Abiram).*

33 They, and all that appertained to them, went down alive into the pit *(into Hell itself)*, and the Earth closed upon them: and they perished from among the congregation.

34 And all Israel that were round about them fled at the cry of them: for they said, Lest the Earth swallow us up also.

35 And there came out a fire from the LORD *(from the Ark of the Covenant in the Holy of Holies)*, and consumed the two hundred and fifty men who offered incense *(exactly as it did Nadab and Abihu [Lev. 10:1-2]).*

THE ALTAR

36 And the LORD spoke unto Moses, saying,

37 Speak unto Eleazar the son of Aaron the Priest, that he take up the censers out of the burning *(from among the charred and smouldering corpses)*, and scatter thou the fire yonder; for they are hallowed *(the censers had been made holy by their proposed use, even though sacrilegiously; they pointed to Christ in His Intercessory Work).*

38 The censers of these sinners against their own souls *(the people attempting to use them were woefully wrong, and their use in this manner was wrong; however, the censers were still "hallowed," because of what they represented)*, let them make them broad plates for a covering of the Altar *(the Brazen Altar: everything used in the rituals and ceremonies of the Tabernacle was, in some way, attached to the Altar, as everything presently, as it pertains to the Lord, is attached to the Cross, of which the Altar was a Type)*: for they offered them before the LORD, therefore they are hallowed: and they shall be a sign unto the Children of Israel. *(In other words, every time they brought their Sacrifices to be offered, they would see the Altar, and the plates of the censers that covered the Altar, in effect stating, "Don't blaspheme this Altar.")*

39 And Eleazar the Priest took the brasen censers, wherewith they that were burnt had

offered; and they were made broad plates for a covering of the Altar:

40 To be a memorial unto the Children of Israel, that no stranger, which is not of the seed of Aaron, come near to offer incense before the LORD; that he be not as Korah, and as his company: as the LORD said to him by the hand of Moses. *(Unfortunately, under the New Covenant, many are presently committing the sin of Korah. They are substituting a government of their own making; however, they must remember, as the Cross is the means of all blessings, at the same time, it is also the means of all judgment.)*

MURMURINGS

41 But on the morrow all the congregation of the Children of Israel murmured against Moses and against Aaron, saying, You have killed the people of the LORD. *(They had, in truth, forfeited their own lives, and Moses and Aaron had no more part in their deaths than Peter had in the deaths of Ananias and Sapphira. They didn't seem to realize that their own immunity from judgment was due to the intercession of those whom they were now falsely charging. An evil heart that refuses to change cannot change.)*

42 And it came to pass, when the congregation was gathered against Moses and against Aaron, that they looked toward the Tabernacle of the congregation: and, behold, the cloud covered it, and the glory of the LORD appeared *(once again, they were angering the Lord, and greatly so!).*

43 And Moses and Aaron came before the Tabernacle of the congregation.

ANOTHER PLAGUE

44 And the LORD spoke unto Moses, saying,

45 Get you up from among this congregation, that I may consume them as in a moment. And they fell upon their faces *(once again, Moses intercedes on behalf of the people, even though they are murmuring constantly against him; we should learn here as to what the Lord thinks of such).*

46 And Moses said unto Aaron, Take a censer *(typical of the Intercession of Christ)*, and put fire therein from off the Altar *(typical of the Cross)*, and put on incense, and go quickly unto the congregation, and make an Atonement for them: for there is wrath gone out

from the LORD; the plague is begun. *(There is no intimation in Scripture that this had ever been done before, and I speak of going among the people with Incense. As it had no precedent, so it never seems to have been repeated. No Sacrifice was offered; however, there could well have been a Sacrifice on the Altar at that time, with the blood poured out at the base. At any rate, the fire came from the Altar, where Sacrifices were offered repeatedly, with the blood poured out at the base of the Altar. So, in a sense, as should be obvious, there had been shedding of blood.)*

47 And Aaron took as Moses commanded, and ran into the midst of the congregation; and, behold, the plague was begun among the people: and he put on incense, and made an Atonement for the people *(this is a portrayal, in Type, of the Gospel being taken to dying humanity; against the plague of sin there is no other hope).*

48 And he stood between the dead and the living; and the plague was stayed *(the only thing that stands between dying, lost humanity and eternal judgment is the Cross of Christ [I Cor. 1:23; 2:2; Eph. 2:13-18; Col. 2:14-15]).*

49 Now they who died in the plague were fourteen thousand and seven hundred, beside them who died about the matter of Korah *(exactly what the plague was, we aren't told; evidently, those who "murmured against Moses and Aaron" were stricken).*

50 And Aaron returned unto Moses unto the door of the Tabernacle of the congregation: and the plague was stayed. *(As stated, there is only one thing that will stop the plague of sin and all of its effects, and that is the Cross. When the modern Church proposes humanistic psychology, or any other supposed solution, it is tantamount to blasphemy against the Lord. The answer is the Cross, and the Cross alone!)*

CHAPTER 17
(1454 B.C.)
AARON'S ROD THAT BUDDED

AND the LORD spoke unto Moses, saying,

2 Speak unto the Children of Israel, and take of every one of them a rod according to the house of their fathers, of all their princes according to the house of their fathers twelve rods: you write every man's name upon his rod. *(Each rod of the twelve bore a mighty name. Through the night in which they lay hidden*

within the Tabernacle, the sons of Israel might have expressed confidence in such-and-such a name, as today many in the modern Church do the same. But, in the morning, all the rods were found to be dead sticks, notwithstanding the names they bore, except the rod of Aaron. It, alone, was living, beautiful, and accepted. — Williams.)

3 And you shall write Aaron's name upon the rod of Levi: for one rod shall be for the head of the house of their fathers (concerning Aaron's rod, the total would have been thirteen).

4 And you shall lay them up in the Tabernacle of the congregation before the testimony, where I will meet with you (evidently the rods were placed in the Holy Place before the Veil which hid the Ark of the Covenant).

5 And it shall come to pass, that the man's rod, whom I shall choose, shall blossom: and I will make to cease from Me the murmurings of the Children of Israel, whereby they murmur against you (the problem was, they didn't want God's choice, but rather a choice of their own).

6 And Moses spoke unto the Children of Israel, and every one of their princes gave him a rod apiece, for each prince one, according to their fathers' houses, even twelve rods: and the rod of Aaron was among their rods.

7 And Moses laid up the rods before the LORD in the Tabernacle of witness (verification would be made).

8 And it came to pass, that on the morrow Moses went into the Tabernacle of witness; and, behold, the rod of Aaron for the house of Levi was budded, and brought forth buds, and bloomed blossoms, and yielded almonds (this did not signify the greatness of Aaron, but the One of Whom Aaron was a Type, the Lord Jesus Christ; it signified His Death, hence, the dead stick to begin with, and Resurrection, signified by the buds, blossoms, and almonds).

9 And Moses brought out all the rods from before the LORD unto all the Children of Israel: and they looked, and took every man his rod.

10 And the LORD said unto Moses, Bring Aaron's rod again before the testimony, to be kept for a token against the rebels; and you shall quite take away their murmurings from Me, that they die not (because of Christ, which the rod represented, Mercy was granted, even though the people did not at all deserve such).

11 And Moses did so: as the LORD commanded him, so did he.

12 And the Children of Israel spoke unto Moses, saying, Behold, we die, we perish, we all perish (as someone has said, "They were fearful to offend, yet not loving to obey").

13 Whosoever comes any thing near unto the Tabernacle of the LORD shall die: shall we be consumed with dying? (But yet, the dying was their fault, and theirs alone, even though they tried to blame Moses and Aaron, which, in essence, was blaming the Lord. It is man's age-old problem of refusing to accept responsibility.)

CHAPTER 18
(1454 B.C.)
PRIESTLY FUNCTIONS

AND the LORD said unto Aaron, You and your sons and your father's house with you shall bear the iniquity of the Sanctuary: and you and your sons with you shall bear the iniquity of your Priesthood. (Thus the Children of Israel found security in that very Priest Whom they despised and rejected. It is the same with Christ! The Lord of Glory, despised and rejected by the world, at the same time, is their only hope.)

2 And your brethren also of the Tribe of Levi, the Tribe of your father, bring thou with you, that they may be joined unto you, and minister unto you: but you and your sons with you shall minister before the Tabernacle of witness (the Levites were to help in certain ways; much work was to be done, and done constantly, which required the hands of a good number of people; and yet, even as we shall see, the duties of the Levites were limited).

3 And they shall keep your charge, and the charge of all the Tabernacle (do exactly what Aaron told them to do): only they shall not come near the vessels of the Sanctuary and the Altar, that neither they, nor you also, die (if Aaron did not properly assign their duties to them, and warn of the danger, not only would they die, but he would die as well; it is the same presently! All of this represented the Cross and, if the Cross today is improperly attended, to be sure, spiritual death is the result).

4 And they shall be joined unto you, and keep the charge of the Tabernacle of the congregation, for all the service of the Tabernacle: and a stranger (in this case, one not a Levite) shall not come near unto you.

5 And you shall keep the charge of the Sanctuary, and the charge of the Altar (the "Altar" was the single most important vessel of

the entire installation): **that there be no wrath any more upon the Children of Israel** (the "Altar" alone stood between the people and death, and is the same presently!).

6 And I, behold, I have taken your brethren the Levites from among the Children of Israel: to you they are given as a gift for the LORD, to do the service of the Tabernacle of the congregation.

7 Therefore you and your sons with you shall keep your Priest's office for every thing of the Altar (the Brazen Altar, typifying the Cross), **and within the Veil** (the Ark of the Covenant, into which presence the High Priest could come only once a year, on the Great Day of Atonement; however, the way to the Ark of the Covenant, in a sense a symbol of the Throne of God, could only be reached by the way of the "Altar"); **and you shall serve: I have given your Priest's office unto you as a service of gift: and the stranger** (one not a Levite) **who comes near shall be put to death.**

OFFERINGS

8 And the LORD spoke unto Aaron, Behold, I also have given you the charge of My Heave Offerings of all the hallowed things of the Children of Israel; unto you have I given them by reason of the anointing, and to your sons, by an Ordinance for ever (all of this information concerning the Priesthood comes immediately after the rebellion of Korah to intrude into that high and Holy Office).

9 This shall be yours of the most holy things, reserved from the fire: every oblation of theirs, every Meat Offering of theirs (the people), **and every Sin Offering of theirs, and every Trespass Offering of theirs, which they shall render unto Me, shall be most holy for you and for your sons** (these three particular Offerings were "most holy," simply because they represented Christ, and what He would do on the Cross to address the terrible problem of Sin; the Burnt Offering and the Peace Offering were designated as "holy").

10 In the most holy place shall you eat it; every male shall eat it: it shall be holy unto you. (Concerning this, Williams says, "Aaron and his sons were to make the sins of the people so truly their own that they were to eat the Sin Offerings, as already commanded in Leviticus.")

11 And this is yours; the Heave Offering of their gift (heaved up and down by the Priests, signifying that Christ would come from above, down to this Earth), **with all the Wave Offerings** (signifying that all Blessings come from the Lord) **of the Children of Israel: I have given them unto you, and to your sons and to your daughters with you, by a Statute for ever: every one who is clean in your house shall eat of it.**

12 All the best of the oil, and all the best of the wine, and of the wheat, the firstfruits of them which they shall offer unto the LORD, them have I given you (the love that appointed this Ministry provided for its maintenance, by granting to it all the best of the oil, and all the best of the wine, and of the wheat; along with particular Offerings, which could be eaten by the Priests and their families, this provided most of their sustenance; when the people drifted from the Lord, as they, at times did, thereby omitting most of the Sacrifices, the Priests went hungry).

13 And whatsoever is first ripe in the land, which they shall bring unto the LORD, shall be yours; every one who is clean in your house shall eat of it (meaning they were not ceremonially defiled in some way).

14 Every thing devoted in Israel shall be yours (the thing devoted, whatever it was, was to be brought to the Sanctuary).

15 Every thing that opens the matrix in all flesh, which they bring unto the LORD, whether it be of men or beasts, shall be yours: nevertheless the firstborn of man shall you surely redeem, and the firstling of unclean beasts shall you redeem (with the appropriate amount of money).

16 And those that are to be redeemed from a month old shall you redeem, according to your estimation, for the money of five shekels, after the shekel of the Sanctuary, which is twenty gerahs.

17 But the firstling of a cow, or the firstling of a sheep, or the firstling of a goat, you shall not redeem; they are holy: you shall sprinkle their blood upon the Altar, and shall burn their fat for an Offering made by fire, for a sweet savour unto the LORD.

18 And the flesh of them shall be yours, as the wave breast and as the right shoulder are yours.

19 All the Heave Offerings of the holy things, which the Children of Israel offer unto the LORD, have I given you, and your sons and your daughters with you, by a Statute for ever: it is a covenant of salt for ever before the LORD unto you and to your seed with you (salt was the natural emblem of that which

is incorruptible; therefore, a Type of the Word of God).

20 And the LORD spoke unto Aaron, You shall have no inheritance in their land, neither shall you have any part among them: I am your part and your inheritance among the Children of Israel *(in essence, the portion given to the Priests was more desirable than any other portion; the Lord faithfully blesses those who faithfully serve Him).*

TITHES

21 And behold, I have given the Children of Levi all the tenth *(Tithe)* in Israel for an inheritance, for their service which they serve, even the service of the Tabernacle of the congregation. *(The record of the first Tithe being paid was that of Abraham paying Tithe to Melchizedek [Gen. 14:17-20]. Now the Tithes were assigned to the Levites and their maintenance. There were thousands of them; however, if all of Israel were faithful in this respect, the needs of each one would be met. Regrettably, they were not always faithful.*

It is the same presently regarding Tithing. As it went then to support the Work of God, it continues to do the same.)

22 Neither must the Children of Israel henceforth come near the Tabernacle of the congregation, lest they bear sin, and die *(the Priests and the Levites alone could attend to the duties of the Tabernacle).*

23 But the Levites shall do the service of the Tabernacle of the congregation, and they shall bear their iniquity: it shall be Statute for ever throughout your generations, that among the Children of Israel they have no inheritance.

24 But the Tithes of the Children of Israel, which they offer as an Heave Offering unto the LORD, I have given to the Levites to inherit: therefore I have said unto them, Among the Children of Israel they shall have no inheritance.

THE LEVITES

25 And the LORD spoke unto Moses, saying,

26 Thus speak unto the Levites, and say unto them, When you take of the Children of Israel the tithes which I have given you from them for your inheritance, then you shall offer up an Heave Offering of it for the LORD, even a tenth part of the tithe. *(Thus, the principle of giving a tenth part of all to God was carried out consistently throughout the whole of God's people.)*

27 And this your Heave Offering shall be reckoned unto you, as though it were the corn of the threshingfloor, and as the fullness of the winepress.

28 Thus you also shall offer an Heave Offering unto the LORD of all your tithes, which you receive of the Children of Israel; and you shall give thereof the LORD's Heave Offering to Aaron the Priest *(the Levites tithed the people, the Priests tithed the Levites).*

29 Out of all your gifts you shall offer every Heave Offering of the LORD, of all the best thereof, even the hallowed part thereof out of it *(the best was to always go to the Lord).*

30 Therefore you shall say unto them, When you have heaved the best thereof from it, then it shall be counted unto the Levites as the increase of the threshingfloor, and as the increase of the winepress *(the "increase" pertained to the tithe, a tenth).*

31 And you shall eat it in every place, you and your households: for it is your reward for your service in the Tabernacle of the congregation.

32 And you shall bear no sin by reason of it, when you have heaved from it the best of it *(they would not incur any guilty responsibility by enjoying it, as and where they pleased)*: neither shall you pollute the holy things of the Children of Israel, lest you die *(the Levites must not intrude into the office of the Priests).*

CHAPTER 19
(1454 B.C.)
THE RED HEIFER

AND the LORD spoke unto Moses and unto Aaron, saying,

2 This is the Ordinance of the Law which the LORD has commanded *(Williams says, "This Chapter being found in Numbers and not in Leviticus shows inspiration. Had the sacrifice of the red heifer been invented by Jewish Priests, as some affirm, they would have placed it in the Book of Leviticus),* saying, Speak unto the Children of Israel, that they bring you a red heifer without spot, wherein is no blemish, and upon which never came yoke *(the heifer symbolizes Christ; it was spotless externally and without blemish internally; "without yoke" means it was free from any bondage whatever; as well, the color "red" refers to the fact that Christ robed Himself with the red earth of manhood):*

3 And you shall give her unto Eleazar the Priest, that he may bring her forth without the camp, and one shall slay her before his face *(Christ was led of the Spirit to Calvary, where He offered up Himself)*:

4 And Eleazar the Priest shall take of her blood with his finger, and sprinkle of her blood directly before the Tabernacle of the congregation seven times *(the sprinkling of the blood seven times speaks of a perfect Redemption, all made possible by the death of Christ on the Cross, necessitating the shedding of His Blood [Eph. 2:13-18])*:

5 And one shall burn the heifer in his sight; her skin, and her flesh, and her blood, with her dung, shall he burn *(the fire had a double meaning: 1. It spoke first of all of the Judgment of God upon Christ, instead of upon us to whom it rightfully belonged — all of humanity; and, 2. The Judgment poured out upon Christ signified that all sin was atoned; Justification means that one is declared by God as "not guilty," but it goes further and means that one is also "innocent"; it also refers to the fact that every sin is forgiven, and taken away; and last of all, the justified person is placed in a position before God as if he had never sinned; that is Justification [Rom. 5:1-2])*:

6 And the Priest shall take cedar wood *(typical of the Cross)*, and hyssop *(typical of the Humanity of Christ)*, and scarlet *(typical of the shed Blood)*, and cast it into the midst of the burning of the heifer *(meaning that the heifer is a Type of Christ dying on the Cross of Calvary, atoning for the sin of mankind)*.

7 Then the Priest shall wash his clothes, and he shall bathe his flesh in water, and afterward he shall come into the camp, and the Priest shall be unclean until the evening. *(Even though the Priests were Types of Christ, still they were only types; consequently, when dealing with sin, which this ritual did, they became unclean, and had to go through a cleansing process. The difference in the Type and Christ is that Christ dealt with sin on the Cross, but dealt with it in regard to its penalty. His Perfection was never marred or sullied by sin. In other words, He sanctified the Cross with His Perfection and, above all, His shed Blood.)*

8 And he who burns her *(the heifer)* shall wash his clothes in water, and bathe his flesh in water, and shall be unclean until the evening.

9 And a man who is clean shall gather up the ashes of the heifer, and lay them up without the camp in a clean place *(signifying that the price that Christ would pay would be total, and would leave nothing of sin; the nothingness was symbolized by the ashes)*, and it shall be kept for the congregation of the Children of Israel for a water of separation: it is a purification for sin *(of course, this was only a symbolism of the real purification that would come with the death of Christ on the Cross; in the symbol, the ashes would be mixed with water, and then applied to that which was polluted)*.

10 And he who gathers the ashes of the heifer shall wash his clothes, and be unclean until the evening: and it shall be unto the Children of Israel, and unto the stranger who sojourns among them, for a Statute for ever *(the word "forever" pertained to the entirety of the time of the Law; when Jesus came, this was fulfilled, and was no longer needed, because His Blood cleanses from all sin [I Jn. 1:7])*.

WATER OF PURIFICATION

11 He who touches the dead body of any man shall be unclean seven days *(death in all its forms is the ultimate conclusion of sin, and is a result of the Fall)*.

12 He shall purify himself with it on the third day, and on the seventh day he shall be clean: but if he purify not himself the third day, then the seventh day he shall not be clean. *(Williams says, "Restoration was only possible after an application of the ashes of the heifer on the third day and on the seventh day. The three days prior to the first purging fastened on the conscience the hatefulness of sin to God; the four days prior to the second and final application of the ashes and running water instructed the conscience as to the perfection of the purge and the wonders of the grace that provided it."*

He goes on to say, "Possibly the third day pointed to the Resurrection of Christ; the seventh day to His return in glory. During the first period only an imperfect sense of the fullness of His sacrifice is possible; but in the coming glorious seventh day there will be a perfected consciousness of this fullness.")

13 Whosoever touches the dead body of any man who is dead, and purifies not himself, defiles the Tabernacle of the LORD *(the uncleanness of death was not simply a personal matter; it involved, if not duly purged, the whole congregation, and reached even to God Himself, for its defilement spread to the Sanctuary)*; and that soul shall be cut off from Israel: because the water of separation was not sprinkled

upon him, he shall be unclean; his uncleanness is yet upon him (*the ashes were to be mixed with the water, and then applied to that which was polluted; it was called "the water of separation"*).

14 This is the Law, when a man dies in a tent: all who come into the tent, and all who are in the tent, shall be unclean seven days.

15 And every open vessel, which has no covering bound upon it, is unclean. (*Pulpit says, "If the vessel was open, its contents were polluted by the odour of death."*)

16 And whosoever touches one who is slain with a sword in the open fields, or a dead body, or a bone of a man, or a grave, shall be unclean seven days (*this means that if a bone is touched, even though a thousand years old, it will defile the individual who does the touching, and will bring about exclusion from the camp, at least for seven days; even then, the purification process must be engaged*).

17 And for an unclean person they shall take the ashes of the burnt heifer of purification for sin, and running water shall be put thereto in a vessel:

18 And a clean person shall take hyssop, and dip it in the water, and sprinkle it upon the tent, and upon all the vessels, and upon the persons who were there, and upon him who touched a bone, or one slain, or one dead, or a grave (*this is what Jesus was referring to in Matthew 23:27*):

19 And the clean person shall sprinkle upon the unclean on the third day, and on the seventh day: and on the seventh day he shall purify himself, and wash his clothes, and bathe himself in water, and shall be clean at evening (*the words "at evening" refer to the defiled person pronounced clean; this speaks of the preciousness of Christ's atoning Blood, and its sufficiency to cleanse from all sin; at the evening of life, this is the greatest assurance of all*).

20 But the man who shall be unclean, and shall not purify himself, that soul shall be cut off from among the congregation, because he has defiled the Sanctuary of the LORD: the water of separation has not been sprinkled upon him; he is unclean (*in New Covenant terminology, this speaks of the individual who ignores the only remedy for sin, which is the shed Blood of Jesus Christ, thereby placing his faith in something else; he will be eternally lost*).

21 And it shall be a perpetual Statute unto them, that he who sprinkles the water of separation shall wash his clothes; and he who touches the water of separation shall be unclean until evening.

22 And whatsoever the unclean person touches shall be unclean; and the soul that touches it shall be unclean until evening. (*All of this is meant to portray the awfulness of sin. The whole design of this ritual is meant to impress upon mankind this truth. The defilement of sin reached even to the very means Divinely appointed as a remedy. This is what Paul meant when he said, "Who shall deliver me from the body of this death?" [Rom. 7:24]. When he used the pronoun "Who" instead of "what," the Apostle was on his way to truth.*)

CHAPTER 20
(1453 B.C.)
MIRIAM

THEN came the Children of Israel, even the whole congregation, into the desert of Zin in the first month (*this is the first month of the fortieth year after they had come out of Egypt; from the time of the spies until the occurrences of this Chapter was 38 years, of which nothing is recorded; this tells us that "unbelief," for this is what caused the delay, does nothing for God; how many days, weeks, months, or even years of our lives are wasted, all because we were outside of the Will of God?*): and the people abode in Kadesh; and Miriam died there, and was buried there. (*Is it possible that Miriam never allowed her heart to be properly cleansed from her rebellion against Moses, which, if so, could have contributed unto her untimely death?*)

2 And there was no water for the congregation: and they gathered themselves together against Moses and against Aaron. (*This is a new generation, and yet they too murmur against the great Lawgiver and the High Priest, both which mean they are murmuring against the Lord.*)

LACK OF WATER

3 And the people chode with Moses, and spoke, saying, Would God that we had died when our brethren died before the LORD!

4 And why have you brought up the congregation of the LORD into this wilderness, that we and our cattle should die there? (*The Lord had brought them there, not Moses.*)

5 And wherefore have you made us to come up out of Egypt, to bring us in unto this evil place? it is no place of seed, or of figs, or of

vines, or of pomegranates; neither is there any water to drink. *(In fact, it was a difficult place! However, the Lord led them here because He loved them. He desired to reveal to them His inexhaustible resources, that is, if they would only believe. It is the same with us presently! Everything is a test. How will we respond?)*

6 And Moses and Aaron went from the presence of the Assembly unto the door of the Tabernacle of the congregation, and they fell upon their faces: and the glory of the LORD appeared unto them *(they took the situation to the Lord).*

WATER FROM THE ROCK

7 And the LORD spoke unto Moses, saying,

8 Take the rod *(the same rod with which Moses had smitten the Rock in Rephidim [Ex. 17:6]),* and you gather the assembly together, you, and Aaron your brother, and you speak unto the Rock before their eyes *(the "Rock" represents Christ, and what He would do at Calvary to redeem fallen humanity; it had already been smitten, typifying the once-for-all Sacrifice of Christ [Heb. 10:12]; to call forth the blessings was all that was now needed)*; and it shall give forth his water, and you shall bring forth to them water out of the Rock *(typifying the Work of the Holy Spirit that would be made possible by Christ and what He did at the Cross; Christ is the Source, while the Cross is the Means)*: so you shall give the congregation and their beasts drink.

9 And Moses took the rod from before the LORD, as He commanded him.

10 And Moses and Aaron gathered the congregation together before the Rock, and he said unto them, Hear now, you rebels; must we fetch you water out of this Rock? *(In his irritation, Moses placed himself and Aaron in the position of supplying the water, when the Lord Alone could do such a thing.)*

11 And Moses lifted up his hand, and with his rod he smote the Rock twice *(the Lord told him to speak to the Rock, not smite the Rock; to smite the Rock, in essence, greatly abrogated the Type; the Rock smitten in Rephidim was a Type of the Sacrifice of Christ on the Cross; to smite the Rock again, in essence, stated that the first Sacrifice was insufficient, and would have to be repeated; such a sin was great! Regrettably, much of the modern Church world continues to smite the Rock, committing the same sin as Moses; in fact, the sin is much worse presently, because the*

Rock is now history instead of prophetic): and the water came out abundantly, and the congregation drank, and their beasts also *(we should not mistake the Blessings of the Lord for the approval of the Lord; that is always a mistake).*

THE PENALTY

12 And the LORD spoke unto Moses and Aaron, Because you believed Me not, to sanctify Me in the eyes of the Children of Israel, therefore you shall not bring this congregation into the land which I have given them. *(The penalty, i.e., "chastisement," was severe, because the sin was severe. Is the Lord saying to the modern Church Leaders, "Because you believe Me not, to sanctify Me in the eyes of Believers?" Anything that denigrates the Cross is sin, gross sin!)*

13 This is the water of Meribah *(strife)*; because the Children of Israel strove with the LORD, and He was sanctified in them *(in that He brought water out of the Rock, despite the sin of Moses; Paul said, "And that Rock was Christ" [I Cor. 10:4]).*

THE EDOMITES

14 And Moses sent messengers from Kadesh unto the king of Edom, Thus saith your brother Israel *(this phrase recalled the history of Esau and Jacob, and of the brotherly kindness which the former had shown to the latter, at a time when he had him in his power [Gen., Chpt. 33]),* You know all the travail that has befallen us:

15 How our fathers went down into Egypt, and we have dwelt in Egypt a long time *(215 years)*; and the Egyptians vexed us, and our fathers *(made slaves of the Israelites)*:

16 And when we cried unto the LORD, He heard our voice, and sent an Angel, and has brought us forth out of Egypt: and, behold, we are in Kadesh, a city in the uttermost of your border *(close to your border)*:

17 Let us pass, I pray you, through your country: we will not pass through the fields, or through the vineyards, neither will we drink of the water of the wells: we will go by the king's high way, we will not turn to the right hand nor to the left, until we have passed your borders.

18 And Edom said unto him, You shalt not pass by me, lest I come out against you with the sword. *(This exchange between Israel and Edom portrayed the gentleness of the one and*

the hatred of the other; however, just as God would not let Esau injure Jacob, so now He forbade Jacob to injure Esau [Deut. 2:4-5].)

19 And the Children of Israel said unto him, We will go by the high way: and if I and my cattle drink of your water, then I will pay for it: I will only, without doing any thing else, go through on my feet.

20 And he said, You shall not go through. And Edom came out against him with much people, and with a strong hand.

21 Thus Edom refused to give Israel passage through his border: wherefore Israel turned away from him. *(Pulpit says, "This was the first of a series of hostile acts, prompted by vindictive jealousy, which ultimately brought down the wrath of God upon Edom.")*

22 And the Children of Israel, even the whole congregation, journeyed from Kadesh, and came unto Mount Hor.

AARON'S DEATH

23 And the LORD spoke unto Moses and Aaron in Mount Hor, by the coast of the land of Edom, saying,

24 Aaron shall be gathered unto his people: for he shall not enter into the land which I have given unto the Children of Israel, because you rebelled against My word at the water of Meribah *(Aaron was held guilty, exactly as Moses).*

25 Take Aaron and Eleazar his son, and bring them up unto mount Hor.

26 And strip Aaron of his garments, and put them upon Eleazar his son: and Aaron shall be gathered unto his people, and shall die there. *(I know this hurt Moses greatly, to be told these words by the Lord.)*

27 And Moses did as the LORD commanded: and they went up into Mount Hor in the sight of all the congregation. *(No doubt, the announcement had been made to Israel that their High Priest, the very first one, was going to die. But the pain must have been felt more keenly by Moses.)*

28 And Moses stripped Aaron of his garments, and put them upon Eleazar his son *(it affects the heart greatly to picture the farewell of Moses and Aaron upon Mount Hor; both were representatives of the Law, and the Law could never inherit the Promised Land; so both must die without going into the Promised Land);* and Aaron died there in the top of the Mount: and Moses and Eleazar came down from the Mount.

29 And when all the congregation saw that Aaron was dead, they mourned for Aaron thirty days, even all the house of Israel.

CHAPTER 21
(1453 B.C.)
THE CANAANITES

AND when king Arad the Canaanite, which dwelt in the south, heard tell that Israel came by the way of the spies; then he fought against Israel, and took some of them prisoners.

2 And Israel vowed a vow unto the LORD, and said, If You will indeed deliver this people into my hand then I will utterly destroy their cities *(the Lord had instructed Israel to do this, even though it had not yet been recorded; such commands were given by the Lord in this fashion because of the gross iniquity of the people — iniquity so bad, such as incest, bestiality, homosexuality, etc., which means they were totally taken over by demon spirits; consequently, their execution was like the removal of a cancer).*

3 And the LORD hearkened to the voice of Israel, and delivered up the Canaanites; and they utterly destroyed them and their cities: and He called the name of the place Hormah *(close to the southern tip of the Dead Sea).*

THE FIERY SERPENTS

4 And they journeyed from Mount Hor by the way of the Red Sea, to compass the land of Edom: and the soul of the people was much discouraged because of the way *(the "way" is not always easy, but this difficult way was their own doing; if their fathers had believed the Lord, they would have been in the Promised Land approximately 38 years before).*

5 And the people spoke against God, and against Moses, Wherefore have you brought us up out of Egypt to die in the wilderness? for there is no bread, neither is there any water; and our soul loathes this light bread *(hates the Manna. They had the same heart of rebellion as their fathers. Wherever the Believer finds himself, and no matter how difficult may seem the way at present, he must not complain. To do so presents a gross insult to the Lord, and for many and varied reasons. We should thank the Lord, and do so daily, irrespective of the circumstances. If the "way" is hard, we should try to learn the lesson which the Lord is trying to teach us, and ask Him to deliver us. He will!)*

6 And the LORD sent fiery serpents among the people, and they bit the people; and much people of Israel died. *(It says that the "LORD" sent these fiery serpents. Let all understand, everything which happens to a Believer, be it negative or positive, is either "caused" by the Lord, or "allowed" by the Lord. Believers belong to the Lord. As such, Satan can do nothing against us, unless the Lord allows it.)*

7 Therefore the people came to Moses, and said, We have sinned, for we have spoken against the LORD, and against you; pray unto the LORD, that He take away the serpents from us. And Moses prayed for the people. *(This is the first and only recorded occasion on which the people directly asked for the intercession of Moses — Pulpit.)*

SERPENT OF BRASS

8 And the LORD said unto Moses, Make thee a fiery serpent, and set it upon a pole *(the "serpent," i.e., "sin and Satan," was the reason for the Cross, and the pole was a Type of the Cross)*: and it shall come to pass, that every one who is bitten, when he looks upon it, shall live *(everyone who looks to Christ and the Cross has the sentence of death abated and, therefore, shall "live")*.

9 And Moses made a serpent of brass *(copper)*, and put it upon a pole and it came to pass, that if a serpent had bitten any man, when he beheld the serpent of brass, he lived *(approximately 400 years earlier, the Lord had shown Abraham the manner of Salvation; it would be through the death of an innocent victim, namely the Son of God [Jn. 8:36]; it was to Moses, however, as recorded here, that the Lord proclaimed the way that the Son of God would die; it would be by the Cross, symbolized by the serpent on the pole)*.

THE MARCH TOWARD MOAB

10 And the Children of Israel set forward, and pitched in Oboth.

11 And they journeyed from Oboth, and pitched at Ije-abarim, in the wilderness which is before Moab, toward the sunrising.

12 From thence they removed, and pitched in the valley of Zared.

13 From thence they removed, and pitched on the other side of Arnon, which is in the wilderness that comes out of the coasts of the Amorites: for Arnon is the border of Moab, between Moab and the Amorites.

14 Wherefore it is said in the book of the wars of the LORD *(such a book did not survive antiquity)*, What He did in the Red Sea, and in the brooks of Arnon,

15 And at the stream of the brooks that goes down to the dwelling of Ar, and lies upon the border of Moab.

16 And from thence they went to Beer: that is the well whereof the LORD spoke unto Moses, Gather the people together, and I will give them water. *(Pulpit says, "That they were told to dig for water instead of receiving it from the Rock showed the end of the wilderness journey to be at hand, and the transition shortly to be made from the miraculous to natural supplies.")*

17 Then Israel sang this song, Spring up, O well; sing ye unto it *(a great Truth is here given us. Problems? Sing to them, and I speak of songs of Faith. The longest Book in the Bible, Psalms, is given over totally to music and singing, showing us the high value that the Lord places on this type of worship, "Sing ye unto it")*:

18 The princes dug the well, the nobles of the people dug it, by the direction of the Lawgiver, with their staves *(the Lord gave this direction to Moses, and Moses gave it to the people)*. And from the wilderness they went to Mattanah:

19 And from Mattanah to Nahaliel: and from Nahaliel to Bamoth:

20 And from Bamoth in the valley, that is in the country of Moab, to the top of Pisgah, which looks toward Jeshimon.

VICTORY

21 And Israel sent messengers unto Sihon king of the Amorites, saying,

22 Let me pass through your land: we will not turn into the fields, or into the vineyards; we will not drink of the waters of the well: but we will go along by the king's high way, until we be past your borders.

23 And Sihon would not suffer Israel to pass through his border: but Sihon gathered all his people together, and went out against Israel into the wilderness: and he came to Jahaz, and fought against Israel.

24 And Israel smote him with the edge of the sword, and possessed his land from Arnon unto Jabbok, even unto the Children of Ammon: for the border of the Children of Ammon was strong.

25 And Israel took all these cities: and Israel dwelt in all the cities of the Amorites, in Heshbon, and in all the villages thereof.

26 For Heshbon was the city of Sihon the king of the Amorites, who had fought against the former king of Moab, and taken all his land out of his hand, even unto Arnon. *(Strengthened by the waters of the hidden well, Israel entered upon a life of continuous victory. Sihon fell before the celestial pilgrims. Then the Amorites were driven out. And, finally, Og, the king of Bashan, and his people were destroyed until there were none left alive. The Amorites had been given 400 years in which to repent [Gen. 15:16], but in vain. And God, in His love to the human family, ordained the total destruction of these unspeakably depraved people.)*

27 Wherefore they who speak in proverbs, say, Come into Heshbon, let the city of Sihon be built and prepared:

28 For there is a fire gone out of Heshbon, a flame from the city of Sihon: it has consumed Ar of Moab, and the lords of the high places of Arnon. *(As the next Verses proclaim, the boasts of these heathen would turn to bitterness.)*

29 Woe to you, Moab! you are undone, O people of Chemosh *(Chemosh was the national god of the Moabites [I Ki. 11:7; Jer. 48:7])*: he has given his sons who escaped, and his daughters, into captivity unto Sihon king of the Amorites.

30 We *(Israel)* have shot at them; Heshbon is perished even unto Dibon, and we have laid them waste even unto Nophah, which reaches unto Medeba.

31 Thus Israel dwelt in the land of Amorites. *(With God on their side, Israel couldn't lose. The Amorites were given up to be the most powerful people of that region; however, they were totally defeated by Israel.)*

32 And Moses sent to spy out Jaazer, and they took the villages thereof, and drove out the Amorites who were there.

VICTORY OVER OG

33 And they turned and went up by the way of Bashan: and Og the king of Bashan went out against them, he, and all his people, to the battle at Edrei. *(Og was of the race of the giants, made that way by the ungodly union of fallen angels and women [Gen. 6:4]. This was Satan's great attempt to pollute the region from which the Messiah would ultimately come. This also was one of the reasons that God gave for all*

these people to be destroyed. These were polluted, contaminated races, and for the reasons mentioned.)

34 And the LORD said unto Moses, Fear him not: for I have delivered him into your hand, and all his people, and his land; and you shall do to him as you did unto Sihon king of the Amorites, which dwelt at Heshbon.

35 So they smote him, and his sons, and all his people, until there was none left him alive: and they *(Israel)* possessed his land. *(If obedience and Faith are rendered, the word from the Lord always is, "Fear not"!)*

CHAPTER 22
(1452 B.C.)

BALAAM

AND the Children of Israel set forward, and pitched in the plains of Moab on this side Jordan by Jericho.

2 And Balak the son of Zippor saw all that Israel had done to the Amorites.

3 And Moab was sore afraid of the people, because they were many: and Moab was distressed because of the Children of Israel *(the Lord will make our enemies to be fearful of us, that is, if our path is a path of obedience).*

4 And Moab said unto the Elders of Midian, Now shall this company lick up all that are round about us, as the ox licks up the grass of the field. And Balak the son of Zippor was king of the Moabites at that time.

5 He sent messengers therefore unto Balaam the son of Beor to Pethor *(an out-of-Covenant Prophet)*, which is by the river of the land of the children of his people, to call him, saying, Behold, there is a people come out from Egypt: behold, they cover the face of the Earth, and they abide over against me *(even though the miracle of their deliverance had taken place nearly 40 years before, still, it was very well known by all the surrounding countries what God had done there).*

6 Come now therefore, I pray thee, curse me this people *(Balak requests of Balaam)*; for they are too mighty for me: peradventure I shall prevail, that we may smite them, and that I may drive them out of the land: for I know that he whom you bless is blessed, and he whom you curse is cursed *(evidently, Balaam had some type of reputation).*

7 And the Elders of Moab and the Elders of Midian departed with the rewards of divination in their hand *(which Peter calls "the*

wages of unrighteousness"); and they came unto Balaam, and spoke unto him the words of Balak.

8 And he said unto them, Lodge here this night, and I will bring you word again, as the LORD shall speak unto me: and the princes of Moab abode with Balaam *(had he been where he should have been with the Lord, he would not have had to seek the Lord as it regards cursing or blessing Israel; he would have already known they were God's people)*.

GOD FORBIDS BALAAM

9 And God came unto Balaam, and said, What men are these with you?

10 And Balaam said unto God, Balak the son of Zippor, king of Moab, has sent unto me, saying,

11 Behold, there is a people come out of Egypt, which covers the face of the Earth: come now, curse me them; peradventure I shall be able to overcome them, and drive them out.

12 And God said unto Balaam, You shall not go with them; you shall not curse the people: for they are blessed *(what God has blessed, nothing can curse)*.

13 And Balaam rose up in the morning, and said unto the princes of Balak, Get you into your land: for the LORD refuses to give me leave to go with you.

14 And the princes of Moab rose up, and they went unto Balak, and said, Balaam refuses to come with us.

GOD PERMITS BALAAM

15 And Balak sent yet again princes, more, and more honourable than they.

16 And they came to Balaam, and said to him, Thus saith Balak the son of Zippor, Let nothing, I pray you, hinder you from coming unto me:

17 For I will promote you unto very great honour, and I will do whatsoever you say unto me: come therefore, I pray you, curse me this people *(the world still gives such allurements; stupid are the people and, above all, the Preachers, who heed such a call; they will find themselves, every time, fighting God, a battle they cannot win)*.

18 And Balaam answered and said unto the servants of Balak, If Balak would give me his house full of silver and gold, I cannot go beyond the word of the LORD my God, to do less or more.

19 Now therefore, I pray you, tarry you also here this night, that I may know what the LORD will say unto me more *(the Lord had already spoken to Balaam; but we know that, in his heart, Balaam doesn't want to obey the Lord; the truth is, the Lord isn't saying what Balaam wants to hear)*.

20 And God came unto Balaam at night, and said unto him, If the men come to call you, rise up, and go with them; but yet the word which I shall say unto you, that shall you do. *(Many have argued that Balaam was not a true worshipper of the Lord and, therefore, not a true Prophet, but merely a soothsayer, etc. But, every Scriptural indication is that whatever Balaam may be at this time, he once was a true Prophet. If Balaam will not obey the Lord, the Lord will use him anyway, to deliver a Message, a series of Prophecies, some of the most astounding in history.)*

THE ANGEL

21 And Balaam rose up in the morning, and saddled his ass, and went with the princes of Moab.

22 And God's anger was kindled because he went *(as it regards Believers, even those of Balaam's stripe, everything is a test. How will we act? How will we react? Even though Balaam had received permission from the Lord to go, the truth is, he was going anyway, hence the anger of the Lord)*: and the Angel of the LORD stood in the way for an adversary against him. Now he was riding upon his ass, and his two servants were with him *(he was determined to curse the people of God, and for money; let it ever be said, God is "against" all who follow such a course)*.

23 And the ass saw the Angel of the LORD standing in the way, and his sword drawn in his hand: and the ass turned aside out of the way, and went into the field: and Balaam smote the ass, to turn her into the way *(events are caused by the Lord, but far too often men fail to see that)*.

24 But the Angel of the LORD stood in a path of the vineyards, a wall being on this side, and a wall on that side.

25 And when the ass saw the Angel of the LORD, she thrust herself unto the wall, and crushed Balaam's foot against the wall: and he smote her again.

26 And the Angel of the LORD went further, and stood in a narrow place, where was no

way to turn either to the right hand or to the left *(today, as on that day, disobeying God degrades man below the brute beast).*

27 And when the ass saw the Angel of the LORD, she fell down under Balaam: and Balaam's anger was kindled, and he smote the ass with a staff.

28 And the LORD opened the mouth of the ass, and she said unto Balaam, What have I done unto you, that you have smitten me these three times? *(Self-will refused to be instructed by circumstances, but a will yielded to God is careful to observe them. Three times Balaam refused to learn from the animal on which he rode; and so blinded was he by the love of money that the dumb beast, speaking with man's voice, failed to make him hesitate — Williams. No, this is not a fable! The Lord actually caused the animal to speak. If we deny such, then we deny God and His Word.)*

29 And Balaam said unto the ass, Because you have mocked me: I would there were a sword in my hand, for now would I kill you.

30 And the ass said unto Balaam, Am not I your ass, upon which you have ridden ever since I was yours unto this day? was I ever wont to do so unto you? And he said, No. *(The astounding thing about this is that Balaam was so full of covetousness that the speaking of the animal didn't seem to faze him. And now he answers the animal, once again brushing aside the phenomenon of what has taken place. Sin can have such a hold upon a person that they take all leave of their senses, in order to carry out their devious design.)*

31 Then the LORD opened the eyes of Balaam, and he saw the Angel of the LORD standing in the way, and his sword drawn in his hand: and he bowed down his head, and fell flat on his face *(he now knows that if he says the wrong thing, he's a dead man).*

32 And the Angel of the LORD said unto him, Wherefore have you smitten your ass these three times? behold, I went out to withstand you, because your way is perverse before me *("perverse" means "leading headlong to destruction"):*

33 And the ass saw me, and turned from me these three times: unless she had turned from me, surely now also I had killed you, and saved her alive.

34 And Balaam said unto the Angel of the LORD, I have sinned; for I knew not that you stood in the way against me: now therefore, if it displease you, I will get me back again.

(Pharaoh, Balaam, Achan, Saul, David, and Judas said respectively, "I have sinned"; but only David said this sincerely.)

35 And the Angel of the LORD said unto Balaam, Go with the men: but only the word that I shall speak unto you, that you shall speak. So Balaam went with the princes of Balak *(still blinded by greed, the man doesn't realize that he has just signed his death warrant).*

BALAK

36 And when Balak heard that Balaam was come, he went out to meet him unto a city of Moab, which is in the border of Arnon, which is in the utmost coast.

37 And Balak said unto Balaam, Did I not earnestly send unto you to call you? wherefore did you not come unto me? am I not able indeed to promote you to honour?

38 And Balaam said unto Balak, Lo, I am come unto you: have I now any power at all to say any thing? the Word that God puts in my mouth, that shall I speak. *(He did speak the Word of the Lord, even as we shall see; however, he also spoke other words, which the Lord did not give him, and which brought about his own death, even as we shall see.)*

39 And Balaam went with Balak *(he could go with the Lord or with Balak; he couldn't go with both),* and they came unto Kirjath-huzoth.

40 And Balak offered oxen and sheep, and sent to Balaam, and to the princes who were with him *(there is even a possibility that Balak offered these sacrifices to Jehovah; nevertheless, such, if it be the case, could never be accepted by the Lord).*

41 And it came to pass on the morrow, that Balak took Balaam, and brought him up into the high places of Baal, that thence he might see the utmost part of the people.

CHAPTER 23
(1452 B.C.)
SACRIFICES

AND Balaam said unto Balak, Build me here seven altars, and prepare me here seven oxen and seven rams. *(There is only one "Altar," i.e., "Cross," not seven. Man always tends to change what God has originally ordained. Why? It is easier to "walk after the flesh," than it is to "walk after the Spirit" [Rom. 8:1].)*

2 And Balak did as Balaam had spoken; and Balak and Balaam offered on every altar a

bullock and a ram *(God will never sanction a corruption of His Word)*.

3 And Balaam said unto Balak, Stand by your burnt offering, and I will go: peradventure the LORD will come to meet me: and whatsoever he shows me I will tell you. And he went to an high place *(where exactly that was, we are not told)*.

4 And God met Balaam *(as to how, again we aren't told)*: and he *(Balaam)* said unto Him *(God)*, I have prepared seven altars, and I have offered upon every altar a bullock and a ram.

5 And the LORD put a word in Balaam's mouth, and said, Return unto Balak and thus you shall speak *(the Lord ignored the so-called sacrifices, exactly as He ignores every sacrifice presently which is not the Cross)*.

FIRST PROPHECY

6 And he *(Balaam)* returned unto him *(Balak)*, and, lo, he stood by his burnt sacrifice, he, and all the princes of Moab.

7 And he took up his parable, and said, Balak the king of Moab has brought me from Aram, out of the mountains of the east, saying, Come, curse me Jacob, and come, defy Israel *(Satan has not stopped this type of attack from then until now)*.

8 How shall I curse, whom God has not cursed? or how shall I defy, whom the LORD has not defied? *(The doctrine of Balaam's first Prophecy is that of Rom., Chpt. 9-11. It is that God has chosen, numbered, separated, and blessed the Children of Israel.)*

9 For from the top of the rocks I see him, and from the hills I behold him: lo, the people shall dwell alone, and shall not be reckoned among the nations. *(And so it has been from then until now. Israel is different than any nation in the world, and it is because they are the chosen of God. Admittedly, they've been away from the Lord for a long, long time; however, that is soon to change, which will take place at the Second Coming.)*

10 Who can count the dust of Jacob, and the number of the fourth part of Israel? *(From his vantage point, Balaam, more than likely, could only see one of the four great camps into which the host was divided, so say the Jewish Targums.)* Let me die the death of the righteous, and let my last end be like his! *(The "Righteousness" of which Balaam speaks is a spotless, Divine Righteousness. It can only be obtained by Faith in Christ, and what Christ has done at the Cross*

[Rom. 6:3-14]. By saying this, Balaam meant that God would be to blame if he did not so die. Sadly, he did not die the death of the righteous.)

11 And Balak said unto Balaam, What have you done unto me? I took you to curse my enemies, and, behold, you have blessed them altogether.

12 And he answered and said, Must I not take heed to speak that which the LORD has put in my mouth?

13 And Balak said unto him, Come, I pray you, with me unto another place, from where you may see them: you shall see but the utmost part of them, and shall not see them all: and curse me them from there. *(The people of God cannot be cursed. Jesus answered the curse of the broken law at the Cross of Calvary, which, as well, handled every other curse, and of every description [Gal. 3:13].)*

14 And he brought him into the field of Zophim, to the top of Pisgah, and built seven altars, and offered a bullock and a ram on every Altar. *(The first seven evidently not being enough, he builds seven more altars. While law is open-ended, Grace is complete within itself.)*

15 And he said unto Balak, Stand here by your burnt offering, while I meet the LORD yonder.

16 And the LORD met Balaam, and put a word in his mouth, and said, Go again unto Balak, and say thus.

SECOND PROPHECY

17 And when he came to him, behold, he stood by his burnt offering, and the princes of Moab with him. And Balak said unto him, What has the LORD spoken? *(This heathen recognized Jehovah as God, but only among many other gods.)*

18 And he took up his parable, and said, Rise up, Balak, and hear; hearken unto Me, you son of Zippor:

19 God is not a man, that He should lie; neither the son of man that He should repent *(God does not change; through the loins of Abraham and the womb of Sarah, the Lord had raised up the Jewish people; even though they have strayed, as stated, they will be brought back, because God has said it, and He doesn't lie)*: has He said, and shall He not do it? or has He spoken, and shall He not make it good?

20 Behold, I have received Commandment to bless: and He has blessed; and I cannot reverse it *(Satan and all his power cannot reverse*

the Blessings of God upon the one who follows a path of obedience [Lk. 9:23-24]).

21 He has not beheld iniquity in Jacob, neither has He seen perverseness in Israel *(this speaks of Justification by faith)*: the LORD his God is with him, and the shout of a king is among them *(Christ is that King).*

22 God brought them out of Egypt; he *(Israel)* has as it were the strength of an unicorn *(probably refers to the African Rhino).*

23 Surely there is no enchantment against Jacob, neither is there any divination against Israel *(no witchcraft against the people of God will ever prosper)*: according to this time it shall be said of Jacob and of Israel, What has God wrought!

24 Behold, the people shall rise up as a great lion, and lift up himself as a young lion *(the Lion of the Tribe of Judah [Rev. 5:5])*: he shall not lie down until he eat of the prey, and drink the blood of the slain *(predicts the fate of the Antichrist [Ezek. 39:3-5]).*

25 And Balak said unto Balaam, Neither curse them at all, nor bless them at all.

26 But Balaam answered and said unto Balak, Told I not you, saying, All that the LORD speaks, that I must do?

27 And Balak said unto Balaam, Come, I pray you, I will bring you unto another place; peradventure it will please God that you may curse me them from there.

28 And Balak brought Balaam unto the top of Peor, that looks toward Jeshimon.

29 And Balaam said unto Balak, Build me here seven altars, and prepare me here seven bullocks and seven rams *(the third group of seven, but to no avail).*

30 And Balak did as Balaam had said, and offered a bullock and a ram on every altar.

CHAPTER 24
(1452 B.C.)
THIRD PROPHECY

AND when Balaam saw that it pleased the LORD to bless Israel, he went not, as at other times, to seek for enchantments, but he set his face toward the wilderness. *(Concerning this, Williams says, "This Chapter shows that the Prophet in his 'madness' was willing to listen to the voice of the Devil, though unwilling to listen to the voice of the Lord. The corruption, depravity, and rebellion of man's will is fearfully and mysteriously illustrated in Balaam. Even at the time of being consciously subject to the Moving of the Holy Spirit, in his thirst for money he sought by enchantments to become inspired of an Unclean Spirit. So, knowledge of spiritual things is not spiritual knowledge.")*

2 And Balaam lifted up his eyes, and he saw Israel abiding in his tents according to their Tribes; and the Spirit of God came upon him *(but it doesn't mean that he had the Spirit of God, for he definitely didn't!).*

3 And he took up his parable, and said, Balaam the son of Beor has said, and the man whose eyes are open has said *(meaning that he saw a vision)*:

4 He has said, which heard the Words of God, which saw the Vision of the Almighty, falling into a trance, but having his eyes open:

5 How goodly are your tents, O Jacob, and your tabernacles, O Israel! *(The Lord looked at Israel in that manner, and He presently looks at the Church, the true Church, that is, in the same manner.)*

6 As the valleys are they spread forth, as gardens by the river's side, as the trees of lign aloes which the LORD has planted, and as cedar trees beside the waters. *(Israel is meant to be a blessing to the entirety of the world, and definitely will fulfill that role in the coming Kingdom Age.)*

7 He shall pour the water out of his buckets, and his seed shall be in many waters *(in the Kingdom Age, Israel will enrich all nations)*, and his king *(the Lord Jesus Christ)* shall be higher than Agag, and his kingdom shall be exalted *(Israel will be the leading nation in the world in the Kingdom Age).*

8 God brought him forth out of Egypt; he has as it were the strength of an unicorn *(once again, the strength of an African Rhino)*: he shall eat up the nations his enemies, and shall break their bones, and pierce them through with his arrows *(even though this covers a wide spectrum of time, the major fulfillment will be during the Battle of Armageddon; Israel will then do all of these things, but with the help of the Messiah [Zech. 14:3]).*

9 He couched, he lay down as a lion, and as a great lion: who shall stir him up? Blessed is he who blesses you, and cursed is he who curses you *(the first promise that God gave concerning Israel, when they were yet in the loins of Abraham [Gen. 12:1-3]).*

10 And Balak's anger was kindled against Balaam, and he smote his hands together: and Balak said unto Balaam, I called you to curse my enemies, and, behold, you have altogether

blessed them these three times.

11 Therefore now flee thou to your place: I thought to promote you unto great honour; but, lo, the LORD has kept you back from honour.

12 And Balaam said unto Balak, Spake I not also to your messengers which you sent unto me, saying,

13 If Balak would give me his house full of silver and gold, I cannot go beyond the Commandment of the LORD, to do either good or bad of my own mind; but what the LORD says, that will I speak?

FOURTH PROPHECY

14 And now, behold, I go unto my people: come therefore, and I will advertise you what this people shall do to your people in the latter days *(speaks of the coming Kingdom Age)*.

15 And he took up his parable, and said, Balaam the son of Beor has said, and the man whose eyes are open has said:

16 He has said, which heard the Words of God, and knew the knowledge of the Most High, which saw the vision of the Almighty, falling into a trance, but having his eyes open:

17 I shall see Him, but not now *(the Messiah would come, but not then)*: I shall behold Him, but not nigh *(not at this time, the time of Balaam)*: there shall come a Star out of Jacob, and a Sceptre shall rise out of Israel *(the Messiah, the Lord Jesus Christ)*, and shall smite the corners of Moab, and destroy all the children of Sheth.

18 And Edom shall be a possession, Seir also shall be a possession for His enemies; and Israel shall do valiantly *(in the coming Kingdom Age, Israel will occupy most of the area of the Middle East)*.

19 Out of Jacob shall come He Who shall have dominion *(the Lord Jesus Christ)*, and shall destroy him who remains of the city *(the Battle of Armageddon, when the Antichrist and his armies shall be destroyed)*.

FIFTH PROPHECY

20 And when he looked on Amalek, he took up his parable, and said, Amalek was the first of the nations *(to attack Israel, and did so when they came out of Egypt [Ex. 17:8-16])*; but his latter end shall be that he perish for ever *(in typology, Amalek is a type of the flesh; this prediction tells us that the way*

of the flesh will ultimately be totally defeated; it will take place at the coming Resurrection of Life [I Cor. 15:51-54]).

21 And he looked on the Kenites, and took up his parable, and said, Strong is your dwellingplace, and you put your nest in a rock.

22 Nevertheless the Kenite shall be wasted, until Asshur shall carry you away captive *(speaks of the Antichrist making his debut of world domination, which will fail)*.

23 And he took up his parable, and said Alas, who shall live when God does this!

24 And ships shall come from the coast of Chittim, and shall afflict Asshur, and shall afflict Eber, and he also shall perish for ever *(pertains to the last days, and speaks of the Antichrist, who will perish in the Battle of Armageddon)*.

25 And Balaam rose up, and went and returned to his place: and Balak also went his way.

CHAPTER 25
(1452 B.C.)
BAAL

AND Israel abode in Shittim, and the people began to commit whoredom with the daughters of Moab *(Balaam could not get the Lord to curse Israel, so he concocted another scheme; through this counsel, Israel would be seduced [31:16])*.

2 And they called the people unto the sacrifices of their gods *(and Israel was invited, under the guise of peace)*: and the people did eat, and bowed down to their gods.

3 And Israel joined himself unto Baal-peor *(seduced by the daughters of Moab)*: and the anger of the LORD was kindled against Israel *(while nothing could cause the Lord to be angry at Israel as His people, He definitely was angered at their sin, as He is all sin)*.

JUDGMENT

4 And the LORD said unto Moses, Take all the heads of the people, and hang them up before the LORD against the sun *(in other words, execute those who are guilty)*, that the fierce anger of the LORD may be turned away from Israel *(if they continued on this course, the entirety of the nation could be destroyed)*.

5 And Moses said unto the judges of Israel *(the first place where judges are mentioned by this name)*, Slay ye every one his men who were joined unto Baal-peor *(the worship of*

this heathen god entailed every type of sexual immorality, which was used to seduce Israel).

6 And, behold, one of the Children of Israel came and brought unto his brethren a Midianitish woman in the sight of Moses, and in the sight of all the congregation of the Children of Israel *(flaunting their wickedness before all)*, who were weeping before the door of the Tabernacle of the congregation *(realizing the depths of this depravity, and the judgment that it would bring upon Israel, a great foreboding filled the hearts of many, and rightly so!).*

7 And when Phinehas, the son of Eleazar, the son of Aaron the Priest, saw it, he rose up from among the congregation, and took a javelin in his hand *(he seems to have been the only son of Eleazar, then the High Priest, and his natural successor in the office of High Priest).*

8 And he went after the man of Israel into the tent, and thrust both of them through, the man of Israel, and the woman through her belly. So the plague was stayed from the Children of Israel. *(God cannot abide sin in any form. If Christ is accepted, judgment is stopped, because He has borne the judgment for all, at least all who will accept Him. If Christ is rejected, then ultimately judgment must come upon the sinner. There is no alternative.)*

9 And those who died in the plague were twenty and four thousand. *(In I Corinthians 10:8, Paul said "twenty-three thousand." There is no contradiction. The ones addressed by Paul took place in one day. Evidently, a thousand died the following day.)*

THE PRIESTHOOD

10 And the LORD spoke unto Moses, saying,

11 Phinehas, the son of Eleazar, the son of Aaron the Priest, has turned My wrath away from the Children of Israel, while he was zealous for My sake among them, that I consumed not the Children of Israel in My jealousy. *(We are to be as zealous today against sin as was Phinehas so long ago; however, the type of zealousness presently commanded is that the Believer be determined to rid himself of all sin, which can only be done by making the Cross of Christ the object of one's Faith, which then gives the Holy Spirit latitude to perform the Work, Who Alone can do such [Rom. 8:1-2, 11].)*

12 Wherefore say, Behold, I give unto him My Covenant of peace:

13 And he shall have it, and his seed after him, even the Covenant of an everlasting Priesthood; because he was zealous for his God, and made an Atonement for the Children of Israel. *(Phinehas, by his act, became a Type of Christ, Who would defeat Satan at the Cross. The "Everlasting Priesthood" belongs to Christ, and will belong to Him forever [Heb. 7:21-24].)*

14 Now the name of the Israelite who was slain, even who was slain with the Midianitish woman, was Zimri, the son of Salu, a prince of a chief house among the Simeonites.

15 And the name of the Midianitish woman who was slain was Cozbi, the daughter of Zur; he was head over a people, and of a chief house in Midian.

WILES OF SATAN

16 And the LORD spoke unto Moses, saying,

17 Vex the Midianites, and smite them:

18 For they vex you with their wiles, wherewith they have beguiled you in the matter of Peor, and in the matter of Cozbi, the daughter of a prince of Midian, their sister, which was slain in the day of the plague for Peor's sake. *(All of this tells us that the women of Midian were employed by their rulers, on the advice of Balaam, in a deliberate plot to entangle the Israelites in heathen rites and heathen sins, which would alienate them from the favor of God. While the Lord would greatly punish Israel for her sin, as stated here, He also took vengeance on those who enticed them into that sin. Some seven years later, Balaam was also killed by the Children of Israel [Josh. 13:22]. Due to his rebellion against God, he did not die the death of the righteous. His love of money closed that door, and did so forever.)*

CHAPTER 26
(1452 B.C.)
NUMBERING ISRAEL

AND it came to pass after the plague, that the LORD spoke unto Moses and unto Eleazar the son of Aaron the Priest, saying,

2 Take the sum of all the congregation of the Children of Israel, from twenty years old and upward, throughout their fathers' house, all who are able to go to war in Israel. *(Concerning this, Williams says, "Their pilgrimage ended. Israel was now about to enter the Promised Land. The remaining Chapters of this Book are occupied, therefore, with matters proper to that great event: and accordingly in this Chapter*

God numbers afresh His people, and counts them by name as heirs ready to take possession of the inheritance.")

3 And Moses and Eleazar the Priest *(High Priest)* spoke with them in the plains of Moab by Jordan near Jericho, saying,

4 Take the sum of the people, from twenty years old and upward; as the LORD commanded Moses and the Children of Israel, which went forth out of the land of Egypt. *(Concerning the last census that Moses took, nearly forty years earlier at Sinai, concerning those who were twenty years old and older, not a single one of those individuals were left, with the exception of Caleb and Joshua. The Holy Spirit in Hebrews, Chpts. 3-4, states that these perished because the Word preached did not profit them, because they had no faith.*

Victorious Christian living results from believing the Word of God, and acting upon it. Merely listening to the Gospel avails precious little. Power to realize Salvation, to overcome sin, and to grow in Grace comes as the Word of God is grasped by Faith. Faith alone takes possession of all that God offers.)

TRIBE OF REUBEN: 43,730

5 Reuben, the oldest son of Israel *(Jacob)*: the Children of Reuben; Hanoch, of whom comes the family of the Hanochites: of Pallu, the family of the Palluites:

6 Of Hezron, the family of the Hezronites: of Carmi, the family of the Carmites.

7 These are the families of the Reubenites: and they who were numbered of them were forty and three thousand and seven hundred and thirty. *(Reuben, as predicted in Genesis 49:4, shows a decrease of 2,730. This is one of the many undesigned evidences in the Bible of inspiration.)*

8 And the sons of Pallu; Eliab.

9 And the sons of Eliab; Nemuel, and Dathan, and Abiram. This is that Dathan and Abiram, which were famous in the congregation, who strove against Moses and against Aaron in the company of Korah, when they strove against the LORD *(even though they were "famous" among the people, they were not famous at all with the Lord; in fact, they tried to usurp authority over the Lord, and lost their souls in the process)*:

10 And the Earth opened her mouth, and swallowed them up together with Korah, when that company died, what time the fire devoured two hundred and fifty men: and they became

a sign.

11 Notwithstanding the Children of Korah died not. *(In fact, the descendants of Korah were prominent in Solomon's Temple. Samuel and Heman were of them; as well, two groups of Psalms are associated with them: 42 through 49 and 84 through 88.)*

TRIBE OF SIMEON: 22,200

12 The sons of Simeon after their families: of Nemuel, the family of the Nemuelites: of Jamin, the family of the Jaminites: of Jachin, the family of the Jachinites:

13 Of Zerah, the family of the Zarhites: of Shaul, the family of the Shaulites.

14 These are the families of the Simeonites, twenty and two thousand and two hundred.

TRIBE OF GAD: 40,500

15 The Children of Gad after their families: of Zephon, the family of the Zephonites: of Haggi, the family of the Haggites: of Shuni, the family of the Shunites:

16 Of Ozni, the family of the Oznites: of Eri, the family of the Erites:

17 Of Arod, the family of the Arodites: of Areli, the family of the Arelites.

18 These are the families of the Children of Gad according to those who were numbered of them, forty thousand and five hundred.

TRIBE OF JUDAH: 76,500

19 The sons of Judah were Er and Onan: and Er and Onan died in the land of Canaan.

20 And the sons of Judah after their families were; of Shelah, the family of the Shelanites: of Pharez, the family of the Pharzites: of Zerah, the family of the Zarhites.

21 And the sons of Pharez were; of Hezron, the family of the Hezronites: of Hamul, the family of the Hamulites.

22 These are the families of Judah according to those who were numbered of them, threescore and sixteen thousand and five hundred.

TRIBE OF ISSACHAR: 64,300

23 Of the sons of Issachar after their families: of Tola, the family of the Tolaites: of Pua, the family of the Punites:

24 Of Jashub, the family of the Jashubites: of Shimron, the family of the Shimronites.

25 These are the families of Issachar according to those who were numbered of them, threescore and four thousand and three hundred.

TRIBE OF ZEBULUN: 60,500

26 Of the sons of Zebulun after their families: of Sered, the family of the Sardites: of Elon, the family of the Elonites: of Jahleel, the family of the Jahleelites.

27 These are the families of the Zebulunites according to those who were numbered of them, threescore thousand and five hundred.

TRIBE OF MANASSEH: 52,700

28 The sons of Joseph after their families were Manasseh and Ephraim.

29 Of the sons of Manasseh: of Machir, the family of the Machirites: and Machir begat Gilead: of Gilead come the family of the Gileadites.

30 These are the sons of Gilead: of Jeezer, the family of the Jeezerites: of Helek, the family of the Helekites:

31 And of Asriel, the family of the Asrielites: and of Shechem, the family of the Shechemites:

32 And of Shemida, the family of the Shemidaites: and of Hepher, the family of the Hepherites.

33 And Zelophehad the son of Hepher had no sons, but daughters: and the names of the daughters of Zelophehad were Mahlah, and Noah, Hoglah, Milcah, and Tirzah.

34 These are the families of Manasseh, and those who were numbered of them, fifty and two thousand and seven hundred.

TRIBE OF EPHRAIM: 32,500

35 These are the sons of Ephraim after their families: of Shuthelah, the family of the Shuthalhites: of Becher, the family of the Bachrites: of Tahan, the family of the Tahanites.

36 And these are the sons of Shuthelah: of Eran, the family of the Eranites.

37 These are the families of the sons of Ephraim according to those that were numbered of them, thirty and two thousand and five hundred. These are the sons of Joseph after their families.

TRIBE OF BENJAMIN: 45,600

38 The sons of Benjamin after their families: of Bela, the family of the Belaites: of Ashbel, the family of the Ashbelites: of Ahiram, the family of the Ahiramites:

39 Of Shupham, the family of the Shuphamites: of Hupham, the family of the Huphamites.

40 And the sons of Bela were Ard and Naaman: of Ard, the family of the Ardites: and of Naaman, the family of the Naamites.

41 These are the sons of Benjamin after their families: and they that were numbered of them were forty and five thousand and six hundred.

TRIBE OF DAN: 64,400

42 These are the sons of Dan after their families: of Shuham, the family of the Shuhamites. These are the families of Dan after their families.

43 All the families of the Shuhamites, according to those who were numbered of them, were threescore and four thousand and four hundred.

TRIBE OF ASHER: 53,400

44 Of the Children of Asher after their families: of Jimna, the family of the Jimnites: of Jesui, the family of the Jesuites: of Beriah, the family of the Beriites.

45 Of the sons of Beriah: of Heber, the family of the Heberites: of Malchiel, the family of the Malchielites.

46 And the name of the daughter of Asher was Sarah.

47 These are the families of the sons of Asher according to those who were numbered of them; who were fifty and three thousand and four hundred.

TRIBE OF NAPHTALI: 45,400

48 Of the sons of Naphtali after their families: of Jahzeel, the family of the Jahzeelites: of Guni, the family of the Gunites:

49 Of Jezer, the family of the Jezerites: of Shillem, the family of the Shillemites.

50 These are the families of Naphtali according to their families: and they who were numbered of them were forty and five thousand and four hundred.

GRAND TOTAL: 601,730

51 These were the numbered of the Children

of Israel, six hundred thousand and a thousand seven hundred and thirty.

DIVISION OF THE LAND

52 And the LORD spoke unto Moses, saying,

53 Unto these the land shall be divided for an inheritance according to the number of names.

54 To many you shall give the more inheritance, and to few you shall give the less inheritance: to every one shall his inheritance be given according to those who were numbered of him *(in other words, the larger portions will be given to the larger Tribes, and the smaller portions to the smaller Tribes).*

55 Notwithstanding the land shall be divided by lot *(according to the Urim and the Thummim; these items were carried in the Breastplate of the High Priest; so this means that the Holy Spirit would actually be the One Who would divide up the land among the Tribes):* according to the names of the Tribes of their fathers they shall inherit.

56 According to the lot shall the possession thereof be divided between many and few.

LEVITES NUMBERED: 23,000

57 And these are they who were numbered of the Levites after their families: of Gershon, the family of the Gershonites: of Kohath, the family of the Kohathites: of Merari, the family of the Merarites.

58 These are the families of the Levites: the family of the Libnites, the family of the Hebronites, the family of the Mahlites, the family of the Mushites, the family of the Korathites. And Kohath begat Amram.

59 And the name of Amram's wife was Jochebed, the daughter of Levi, whom her mother bore to Levi in Egypt: and she bore unto Amram Aaron and Moses, and Miriam their sister.

60 And unto Aaron was born Nadab, and Abihu, Eleazar, and Ithamar.

61 And Nadab, and Abihu died, when they offered strange fire before the LORD.

62 And those who were numbered of them were twenty and three thousand, all males from a month old and upward: for they were not numbered among the Children of Israel, because there was no inheritance given them among the Children of Israel.

A NEW GENERATION

63 These are they who were numbered by Moses and Eleazar the Priest, who numbered the Children of Israel in the plains of Moab by Jordan near Jericho.

64 But among these there was not a man of them whom Moses and Aaron the Priest numbered, when they numbered the Children of Israel in the wilderness of Sinai.

65 For the LORD had said of them, They shall surely die in the wilderness. And there was not left a man of them, save Caleb the son of Jephunneh, and Joshua the son of Nun. *(Thirty-eight years were wasted, plus an entire generation of people, simply because of unbelief.)*

CHAPTER 27
(1452 B.C.)
THE LAW OF INHERITANCE

THEN came the daughters of Zelophehad, the son of Hepher, the son of Gilead, the son of Machir, the son of Manasseh, of the families of Manasseh the son of Joseph: and these are the names of his daughters; Mahlah, Noah, and Hoglah, and Milcah, and Tirzah.

2 And they stood before Moses, and before Eleazar the Priest, and before the Princes and all the congregation, by the door of the Tabernacle of the congregation, saying,

3 Our father died in the wilderness, and he was not in the company of them who gathered themselves together against the LORD in the company of Korah; but died in his own sin, and had no sons.

4 Why should the name of our father be done away from among his family, because he has no son? Give unto us therefore a possession among the brethren of our father.

5 And Moses brought their cause before the LORD. *(The faith of the daughters of Zelophehad presents a striking contrast to the unbelief of those who fell in the desert. While yet in the Wilderness, they claim by faith the unseen fields of Canaan; and, further, their faith leaped a barrier which both nature and Law set before them.*

This was precious and refreshing to the heart of God; and, accordingly, special legislation was given to meet their faith — Williams.)

THE VICTORY OF FAITH

6 And the LORD spoke unto Moses, saying,

7 The daughters of Zelophehad speak right: you shall surely give them a possession of an inheritance among their father's brethren; and you shall cause the inheritance of their father to pass unto them.

8 And you shall speak unto the Children of Israel, saying, If a man die, and have no son, then you shall cause his inheritance to pass unto his daughter.

9 And if he have no daughter, then you shall give his inheritance unto his brethren.

10 And if he have no brethren, then you shall give his inheritance unto his father's brethren.

11 And if his father have no brethren, then you shall give his inheritance unto his kinsman who is next to him of his family, and he shall possess it: and it shall be unto the Children of Israel a Statute of judgment, as the LORD commanded Moses *(a Statute determining a legal right)*.

MOSES AND JOSHUA

12 And the LORD said unto Moses, Get thee up into this mount Abarim, and see the land which I have given unto the Children of Israel. *(Moses had already been told that he should not enter the Promised Land [20:12], yet he is allowed the consolation of seeing it with his eyes before his death. It would seem from Deut. 3:25-27 that this favor was accorded him in answer to his prayer — Pulpit.)*

13 And when you have seen it, you also shall be gathered unto your people, as Aaron your brother was gathered.

14 For you rebelled against My Commandment in the desert of Zin, in the strife of the congregation, to sanctify Me at the water before their eyes: that is the water of Meribah in Kadesh in the wilderness of Zin.

15 And Moses spoke unto the LORD, saying,

16 Let the LORD, the God of the spirits of all flesh, set a man over the congregation,

17 Which may go out before them, and which may go in before them, and which may lead them out, and which may bring them in; that the congregation of the LORD be not as sheep which have no shepherd. *(The Expositors say, "For himself not even a word of complaint at his punishment, which must have seemed, thus close at hand, more inexplicably severe than ever; all his thoughts and his prayers for the people — that one might take his place, and reap for himself and Israel the reward of all his toil and patience.")*

18 And the LORD said unto Moses, Take thee Joshua the son of Nun, a man in whom is the Spirit, and lay your hand upon him *(it seems that the hand of Moses was laid upon him in view of all of Israel, at least of its representatives; but let it be noted that the Lord chose Joshua, and not Moses; as well, the Lord had told Moses long before that Joshua would take his place, and Moses, no doubt, did his best to prepare him)*;

19 And set him before Eleazar the Priest, and before all the congregation; and give him a charge in their sight *(give him instructions regarding his duties)*.

20 And you shall put some of your honour upon him, that all the congregation of the Children of Israel may be obedient *(the blessing of Moses would go a long way toward Joshua being accepted by the people of Israel)*.

21 And he shall stand before Eleazar the Priest, who shall ask counsel for him after the judgment of Urim before the LORD *(this is the Urim and Thummim of Exodus 28:30 and Leviticus 8:8; what they actually were, and how they were actually used in consulting God, it is not told us in Scripture; it does not appear that Moses ever sought the judgment of the Urim, for he possessed more direct means of ascertaining the direct Will of God; nor does it seem ever to have been resorted to after the time of David, for the "more sure Word of Prophecy" seemed to have superseded it)*: at his word *(the word of Joshua)* shall they go out, and at his word they shall come in, both he, and all the Children of Israel with him, even all the congregation.

22 And Moses did as the LORD commanded him: and he took Joshua, and set him before Eleazar the Priest, and before all the congregation:

23 And he laid his hands upon him, and gave him a charge, as the LORD commanded by the hand of Moses.

CHAPTER 28
(1452 B.C.)
THE DAILY OFFERINGS

AND the LORD spoke unto Moses, saying,

2 Command the Children of Israel, and say unto them, My Offering, and My Bread for My Sacrifices made by fire, for a sweet savour unto Me, shall you observe to offer unto Me in their due season. *(All of this, in some way, represented Christ, in either His Atoning, Mediatorial,*

or Intercessory Work. When He came, and went to the Cross, it was all fulfilled, for Christ is the end of the Law [Rom. 10:4].)

3 And you shall say unto them, This is the Offering made by fire which you shall offer unto the LORD; two lambs of the first year without spot day-by-day, for a continual Burnt Offering.

4 The one lamb you shall offer in the morning *(9 a.m.)*, and the other lamb shall you offer at evening *(3 p.m.)*;

5 And a tenth part of an ephah of flour for a Meat Offering *(a Thanksgiving Offering)*, mingled with the fourth part of an hin of beaten oil *(oil derived from olives being crushed typified the Holy Spirit, Who was within and upon Christ)*.

6 It is a continual Burnt Offering, which was ordained in Mount Sinai for a sweet savour, a Sacrifice made by fire unto the LORD.

7 And the Drink Offering *(symbolic of the Life of Christ poured out)* thereof shall be the fourth part of an hin for the one lamb: in the Holy Place shall you cause the strong wine to be poured unto the LORD for a Drink Offering.

8 And the other lamb shall you offer at evening: as the Meat Offering of the morning, and as the Drink Offering thereof, you shall offer it, a Sacrifice made by fire, of a sweet savour unto the LORD *(sweet to the Lord, simply because it represented Christ, Who was to come, and Who would redeem fallen humanity)*.

WEEKLY SACRIFICES

9 And on the Sabbath day two lambs of the first year without spot, and two tenth deals of flour for a Meat Offering, mingled with oil, and the Drink Offering thereof *(on the Sabbath, the Sacrifices were to be doubled regarding the lambs, two in the morning, and two in the evening)*:

10 This is the Burnt Offering of every Sabbath, beside the continual Burnt Offering, and his Drink Offering.

MONTHLY SACRIFICES

11 And in the beginnings of your months you shall offer a Burnt Offering unto the LORD; two young bullocks, and one ram, seven lambs of the first year without spot *(these were to be offered on the first day of each month, which would be the time of the full moon)*;

12 And three tenth deals of flour for a Meat Offering, mingled with oil, for one bullock; and two tenth deals of flour for a Meat Offering, mingled with oil, for one ram;

13 And a several tenth deal of flour mingled with oil for a Meat Offering unto one lamb; for a Burnt Offering of a sweet savour, a Sacrifice made by fire unto the LORD.

14 And their Drink Offerings shall be half an hin of wine unto a bullock, and the third part of an hin unto a ram, and a fourth part of an him unto a lamb: this is the Burnt Offering of every month throughout the months of the year.

15 And one kid of the goats for a Sin Offering unto the LORD shall be offered, beside the continual Burnt Offering, and his Drink Offering. *(The doctrine of these Offerings and those of Leviticus is the same, i.e., life and righteousness through an atoning Saviour: and that doctrine was as fresh and as precious to Moses at the close as at the beginning of his Ministry.*

The Sacrifices in Leviticus mainly provided for the life of the Wilderness; these in Numbers for that of the Promised Land.

The Levitical Sacrifices rather set out, in type, the results of Christ's Atonement and the blessing of sinners; the Offerings of these two Chapters direct attention to the glory and perfection of Him Who accomplished the Atonement.

But, it will be noted throughout these Chapters that no matter what the day or feast, when in Canaan, the Sin Offering was never to be omitted; for no spiritual attainment negates the need of the Atoning Death of Christ. — Williams.)

THE PASSOVER

16 And in the fourteenth day of the first month is the Passover of the LORD *(this was conducted once a year, even as all the Feasts; the "first month" corresponded with our April; it was a Type of the Death of Christ on the Cross).*

UNLEAVENED BREAD

17 And in the fifteenth day of this month is the feast: seven days shall unleavened bread be eaten *(this Feast began a day after the Passover; it pictured the Perfect life of Christ).*

18 In the first day shall be an holy convocation; you shall do no manner of servile work therein *(Salvation is by faith, and not of works [Eph. 2:8-9]; ironically enough, the Law was*

made up entirely of works; however, it pointed toward the One Who was to come, Who would do away with all works, because of His great Work at the Cross of Calvary):

19 But you shall offer a Sacrifice made by fire for a Burnt Offering unto the LORD; two young bullocks, and one ram, and seven lambs of the first year: they shall be unto you without blemish *(the Offerings are outlined here as to what will be done when they came into the Promised Land; thus, the great lesson is taught that Salvation from Egypt, maintenance in the Desert, and rest in the Promised Land are all based upon the Precious Blood of Christ):*

20 And their Meat Offering *(Thanksgiving Offering)* shall be of flour *(typifying the Perfect Life of Christ)* mingled with oil *(typifying the Holy Spirit upon and within Christ [Lk. 4:18-19])*: three tenth deals shall you offer for a bullock, and two tenth deals for a ram *(the Thanksgiving Offering was to be presented along with the Burnt Offering; in one way or the other, all typified Christ in His Mediatorial, Intercessory, and Atoning Work);*

21 A several tenth deal shall you offer for every lamb *(Thanksgiving Offering)*, throughout the seven lambs:

22 And one goat for a Sin Offering, to make an Atonement for you. *(As we have stated, it must be noted that no matter what the day or the Feast, when in Canaan, the Sin Offering was never to be omitted; for no spiritual work can be accomplished without there first being the atoning Death of Christ, as typified by the Sin Offering. This means that presently we are to understand that our Salvation, and our victorious daily living, are predicated solely on the Cross of Christ. The moment we cease to make the Cross of Christ the total object of our faith, at that moment, we are in the flesh, and cannot please God [Rom. 8:8].)*

23 You shall offer these beside the Burnt Offering in the morning, which is for a continual Burnt Offering *(the Burnt Offering typified Christ giving His all, for this was the only Offering which was wholly burned on the Altar; it proclaimed the Perfection of Christ, the "all" of Christ, given to the believing sinner).*

24 After this manner you shall offer daily, throughout the seven days *(of Unleavened Bread)*, the meat of the sacrifice made by fire, of a sweet savour unto the LORD: it shall be offered beside the continual Burnt Offering, and his Drink Offering *(this was the Offering made of flour and oil, in other words, a cereal or bread Offering, which was the Thanksgiving Offering, but referred to as the "Meat Offering").*

25 And on the seventh day you shall have an holy convocation; you shall do no servile work *(regarding the people, no work was to be done on the first and seventh day of Unleavened Bread, which immediately followed the Passover; as stated, this portrayed the fact that Salvation is entirely of Grace through Faith, and not of Works [Eph. 2:8-9]).*

FEAST OF PENTECOST

26 Also in the day of the firstfruits, when you bring a new Meat Offering unto the LORD, after your weeks be out *(seven weeks after the Passover)*, you shall have an holy convocation; you shall do no servile work *(this is the Feast of Pentecost, held the last of May; it typified Christ as the Baptizer with the Holy Spirit [Mat. 3:11]):*

27 But you shall offer the Burnt Offering for a sweet savour unto the LORD; two young bullocks, one ram, seven lambs of the first year;

28 And their Meat Offering of flour mingled with oil, three tenth deals unto one bullock, two tenth deals unto one ram,

29 A several tenth deal unto one lamb, throughout the seven lambs;

30 And one kid of the goats, to make an atonement for you *(a Sin Offering).*

31 You shall offer them beside the continual Burnt Offering, and his Meat Offering, (they shall be unto you without blemish) and their Drink Offerings *(the last Offering typified the Life of Christ poured out on the Cross of Christ).*

CHAPTER 29
(1452 B.C.)
FEAST OF TRUMPETS

AND in the seventh month, on the first day of the month *(our October)*, you shall have an holy convocation; you shall do no servile work: it is a day of blowing the trumpets unto you *(proclaims Christ as the First Resurrection of Life, i.e., "the Rapture of the Church" [I Thess. 4:13-18]).*

2 And you shall offer a Burnt Offering for a sweet savour unto the LORD; one young bullock, one ram, and seven lambs of the first year without blemish:

3 And their Meat Offering shall be of flour mingled with oil, three tenth deals for

a bullock, and two tenth deals for a ram,

4 And one tenth deal for one lamb, throughout the seven lambs:

5 And one kid of the goats for a Sin Offering, to make an Atonement for you *(thus, day-by-day, week-by-week, month-by-month, and year-by-year, there was to be a national and unbroken testimony to the Preciousness of Christ as God's Beloved Son, in Whom His Soul delighted; and a confession that their possession of that land, and its milk and honey, was wholly due to the Preciousness of the Blood shed by that Saviour for the remission of their sins)*:

6 Beside the Burnt Offering of the month, and his Meat Offering, and the daily Burnt Offering, and his Meat Offering, and their Drink Offerings, according unto their manner, for a sweet savour, a Sacrifice made by fire unto the LORD.

GREAT DAY OF ATONEMENT

7 And you shall have on the tenth day of this seventh month an holy convocation; and you shall afflict your souls: you shall not do any work therein *(this is the Great Day of Atonement, when the High Priest went into the Holy of Holies, offering up blood on the Mercy Seat, the only day of the year he, and he alone, could enter the Holiest; on this day, the entirety of Israel was to fast, actually the only fast day of the year; they were to do no work, signifying Salvation by Grace)*:

8 But you shall offer a Burnt Offering unto the LORD for a sweet savour; one young bullock, one ram, and seven lambs of the first year; they shall be unto you without blemish *(typifying the Perfection of Christ)*:

9 And their Meat Offering shall be of flour mingled with oil, three tenth deals to a bullock, and two tenth deals to one ram,

10 A several tenth deal for one lamb, throughout the seven lambs:

11 One kid of the goats for a Sin Offering *(the Sin Offering is never absent)*; beside the Sin Offering of Atonement, and the continual Burnt Offering, and the Meat Offering of it, and their Drink Offerings.

FEAST OF TABERNACLES

12 And on the fifteenth day of the seventh month you shall have an holy convocation; you shall do no servile work, and you shall keep a feast unto the LORD seven days *(the entirety of this time, which incorporated the three Feasts of Trumpets, Atonement, and Tabernacles, lasted approximately 22 days; a representative man from every family was required to attend)*:

13 And you shall offer a Burnt Offering, a Sacrifice made by fire, of a sweet savour unto the LORD; thirteen young bullocks, two rams, and fourteen lambs of the first year; they shall be without blemish:

14 And their Meat Offering shall be of flour mingled with oil, three tenth deals unto every bullock of the thirteen bullocks, two tenth deals to each ram of the two rams,

15 And a several tenth deal to each lamb of the fourteen lambs:

16 And one kid of the goats for a Sin Offering; beside the continual Burnt Offering, his Meat Offering, and his Drink Offering.

17 And on the second day you shall offer twelve young bullocks, two rams, fourteen lambs of the first year without spot:

18 And their Meat Offering and their Drink Offerings for the bullocks, for the rams, and for the lambs, shall be according to their number, after the manner:

19 And one kid of the goats for a Sin Offering; beside the continual Burnt Offering, and the Meat Offering thereof, and their Drink Offerings.

20 And on the third day eleven bullocks, two rams, fourteen lambs of the first year without blemish;

21 And their Meat Offering and their Drink Offerings for the bullocks, for the rams, and for the lambs, shall be according to their number, after the manner:

22 And one goat for a Sin Offering; beside the continual Burnt Offering, and his Meat Offering, and his Drink Offering.

23 And on the fourth day ten bullocks, two rams, and fourteen lambs of the first year without blemish:

24 Their Meat Offering and their Drink Offerings for the bullocks, for the rams, and for the lambs, shall be according to their number, after the manner:

25 And one kid of the goats for a Sin Offering; beside the continual Burnt Offering, his Meat Offering, and his Drink Offering.

26 And on the fifth day nine bullocks, two rams, and fourteen lambs of the first year without spot:

27 And their Meat Offering and their Drink Offerings for the bullocks, for the rams, and for the lambs, shall be according to their

number, after the manner:

28 And one goat for a Sin Offering; beside the continual Burnt Offering, and his Meat Offering, and his Drink Offering.

29 And on the sixth day eight bullocks, two rams, and fourteen lambs of the first year without blemish:

30 And their Meat Offering and their Drink Offerings for the bullocks, for the rams, and for the lambs, shall be according to their number, after the manner:

31 And one goat for a Sin Offering; beside the continual Burnt Offering, his Meat Offering, and his Drink Offering.

32 And on the seventh day seven bullocks, two rams, and fourteen lambs of the first year without blemish:

33 And their Meat Offering and their Drink Offerings for the bullocks, for the rams, and for the lambs, shall be according to their number, after the manner:

34 And one goat for a Sin Offering; beside the continual Burnt Offering, his Meat Offering, and his Drink Offering.

35 On the eighth day you shall have a solemn assembly: you shall do no servile work therein:

36 But you shall offer a Burnt Offering, a sacrifice made by fire, of a sweet savour unto the LORD: one bullock, one ram, seven lambs of the first year without blemish:

37 Their Meat Offering and their Drink Offerings for the bullock, for the ram, and for the lambs, shall be according to their number, after the manner:

38 And one goat for a Sin Offering; beside the continual Burnt Offering, and His Meat Offering, and his Drink Offering.

39 These things you shall do unto the LORD in your set feasts, beside your vows, and your freewill offerings, for your Burnt Offering, and for your Meat Offerings, and for your Drink Offerings, and for your Peace Offerings.

40 And Moses told the Children of Israel according to all that the LORD commanded Moses.

CHAPTER 30
(1452 B.C.)
VOWS

AND Moses spoke unto the heads of the Tribes concerning the Children of Israel, saying, This is the thing which the LORD has commanded.

2 If a man vow a vow unto the LORD, or swear an oath to bind his soul with a bond; he shall not break his word, he shall do according to all that proceeds out of his mouth *(in that these were God's people, their word was to be as the Word of the Lord; hence, when the Man Christ Jesus said, "I will pay my vows unto Jehovah," and "I delight to do Your Will, O My God," there was no release for Him; the bitter cup of Gethsemane had to be drained [Ps. 50:14; 40:8]).*

SINGLE WOMEN

3 If a woman also vow a vow unto the LORD, and bind herself by a bond, being in her father's house in her youth;

4 And her father hear her vow, and her bond wherewith she has bound her soul, and her father shall hold his peace at her; then all her vows shall stand, and every bond wherewith she has bound her soul shall stand.

5 But if her father disallow her in the day that he hears; not any of her vows, or of her bonds wherewith she has bound her soul, shall stand: and the LORD shall forgive her, because her father disallowed her. *(If the vow had been made before witnesses, no doubt the father's veto must be pronounced before witnesses also, that is, if he desired to do such, which he had the right to do under the Law.)*

MARRIED WOMEN

6 And if she had at all an husband, when she vowed, or uttered ought out of her lips, wherewith she bound her soul;

7 And her husband heard it, and held his peace at her in the day that he heard it: then her vows shall stand, and her bonds wherewith she bound her soul shall stand.

8 But if her husband disallowed her on the day that he heard it; then he shall make her vow which she vowed, and that which she uttered with her lips, wherewith she bound her soul, of none effect: and the LORD shall forgive her *(as far as the legal status of the woman was concerned, there was little difference under Jewish Law whether she was married or only betrothed; in either case, she was accounted as belonging to her husband, with all that she had [Deut. 22:23-24; Mat. 1:19-20]).*

WIDOWS AND DIVORCEES

9 But every vow of a widow, and of her who is divorced, wherewith they have bound

their souls, shall stand against her.

10 And if she vowed in her husband's house, or bound her soul by a bond with an oath;

11 And her husband heard it, and held his peace at her, and disallowed her not: then all her vows shall stand, and every bond wherewith she bound her soul shall stand.

12 But if her husband has utterly made them void on the day he heard them (meaning that vows must be spoken audibly, meaning that mental vows were not recognized); then whatsoever proceeds out of her lips concerning her vows, or concerning the bond of her soul, shall not stand: her husband has made them void; and the LORD shall forgive her.

13 Every vow, and every binding oath to afflict the soul, her husband may establish it, or her husband may make it void.

14 But if her husband altogether hold his peace at her from day to day; then he establishes all her vows, or all her bonds, which are upon her: he confirms them, because he held his peace at her in the day that he heard them (did not disallow the vows).

15 But if he shall any ways make them void after that he has heard them; then he shall bear her iniquity. (Williams says, "There was release for a woman, but she could not effect it herself; only one who was related to her, and who loved her, could do so. Such was Israel. She vowed at Sinai to perform all that Jehovah commanded. Her Divine Bridegroom and Husband permitted the vow; but she, having failed to keep it, came, therefore, under the sentence of death. To redeem her from this doom, her Husband, in grace, took it upon Himself, and so delivered her from her vow. She could not deliver herself.")

16 These are the Statutes, which the LORD commanded Moses, between a man and his wife, between the father and his daughter, being yet in her youth in her father's house. (One may wonder why vows were so important and, thereby, such space in the Bible given to them? As stated, the word of all Believers, whether Israel of old, or Believers presently, is to be as the Word of the Lord. Jesus said, "Let your communication be, Yes, yes; No, no: for whatsoever is more that these comes of evil [Mat. 5:37].)

CHAPTER 31
(1452 B.C.)
MIDIANITES

A ND the LORD spoke unto Moses saying,

2 Avenge the Children of Israel of the Midianites: afterward shall you be gathered unto your people. (In effect, the Lord is telling Moses here that his work on Earth was not done so long as the Midianites remained unpunished. The sin of Chapter 25 occasioned this war. Christians make wars for themselves by forming fellowships with the world. The warfare to which we are actually called to accomplish is that of Ephesians 6, and our wisdom and our obedience is to pass through this world as strangers and pilgrims, having no relations whatsoever, except those of Gospel testimony and natural sympathy, with those whom we must necessarily meet as we journey.

However, if, because of that forbidden union, war results, God gives a complete victory; provided that which did the seducing be utterly destroyed — Williams.)

3 And Moses spoke unto the people, saying, Arm some of yourselves unto the war, and let them go against the Midianites, and avenge the LORD of Midian. (In seducing the people of the Lord, the Midianites had insulted and injured the majesty of God Himself.)

4 Of every Tribe a thousand, throughout all the Tribes of Israel, shall you send to the war (the Lord selected the number).

5 So there were delivered out of the thousands of Israel, a thousand of every Tribe, twelve thousand armed for war.

6 And Moses sent them to the war, a thousand of every Tribe, them and Phinehas the son of Eleazar the Priest, to the war, with the holy instruments, and the trumpets to blow in his hand. (If it is to be noted, Joshua, who normally would have been sent to fight this battle, has, in his place, Phinehas, the son of the High Priest, Eleazar. This tells us that this was a war that Israel would not have had to wage if she had not forsaken the road of obedience to the Word of God, as outlined in Chapter 25.)

7 And they warred against the Midianites, as the LORD commanded Moses; and they killed all the males.

8 And they killed the kings of Midian, beside the rest of them who were slain; namely, Evi, and Rekem, and Zur, and Hur, and Reba, five kings of Midian: Balaam also the son of Beor they slew with the sword. (Balaam did not die the death of the righteous, but perished fighting against the people of God. Money was his downfall.)

9 And the Children of Israel took all the women of Midian captives, and their little

ones, and took the spoil of all their cattle, and all their flocks, and all their goods.

10 And they burnt all their cities wherein they dwelt, and all their goodly castles, with fire.

11 And they took all the spoil, and all the prey, both of men and of beasts.

12 And they brought the captives, and the prey, and the spoil, unto Moses, and Eleazar the Priest, and unto the congregation of the Children of Israel, unto the camp at the plains of Moab, which are by Jordan near Jericho.

13 And Moses, and Eleazar the Priest, and all the princes of the congregation, went forth to meet them without the camp.

14 And Moses was angry with the officers of the host, with the captains over thousands, and captains over hundreds, which came from the battle.

15 And Moses said unto them, Have you saved all the women alive? *(Evidently, orders had been given by Moses that all were to be killed, men, women, and children. Many may object to this, thinking it exceedingly cruel; however, it must be remembered that it is God Who gave these instructions, and not Moses. This tells us two things: 1. Those who oppress God's people will ultimately be destroyed. But we must always remember that vengeance belongs to the Lord, and not man. In other words, we are to let the Lord do the doing [Rom. 12:19]; and, 2. As well, these people had become so depraved that their continued existence could have greatly hindered civilization. The Lord giving such instructions was the same as a cancer being removed from a patient in order that the patient might live.)*

16 Behold, these caused the Children of Israel, through the counsel of Balaam, to commit trespass against the LORD in the matter of Peor, and there was a plague among the congregation of the LORD *(back when that sin was committed some months before).*

17 Now therefore kill every male among the little ones, and kill every woman who has known man by lying with him.

18 But all the women children, who have not known a man by lying with him, keep alive for yourselves *(not for immoral purposes, as some have claimed, but for domestic service; in fact, upon reaching the age of accountability, she could become a member of the Family of Israel, and claim her freedom, after one to seven years, if she so desired).*

19 And you must abide without the camp seven days: whosoever has killed any person, and whosoever has touched any slain, purify both yourselves and your captives on the third day, and on the seventh day *(death has always been the ultimate result of original sin).*

20 And purify all your raiment, and all that is made of skins, and all work of goats' hair, and all things made of wood.

21 And Eleazar the Priest said unto the men of war which went to the battle, This is the Ordinance of the Law which the LORD commanded Moses;

22 Only the gold, and the silver, the brass *(copper)*, the iron, the tin, and the lead.

23 Every thing that may abide the fire, you shall make it go through the fire, and it shall be clean *(clothing, of course, would be burned in the fire, and so could not be kept)*, nevertheless it shall be purified with the water of separation *(from the red heifer, Chapter 19)*: and all who abide not the fire you shall make go through the water *(the soldiers themselves, having killed or having touched the dead, must go through a purification process, which pertained to the "water of separation").*

24 And you shall wash your clothes on the seventh day, and you shall be clean, and afterward you shall come into the camp *(speaking to the soldiers who had participated in this conflict).*

DIVIDING THE SPOILS

25 And the LORD spoke unto Moses, saying,

26 Take the sum of the prey that was taken, both of man and of beast, you, and Eleazar the Priest, and the chief fathers of the congregation:

27 And divide the prey into two parts; between them who took the war upon them, who went out to battle, and between all the congregation:

28 And levy a tribute unto the LORD of the men of war which went out to battle: one soul of five hundred, both of the persons, and of the beeves, and of the asses, and of the sheep:

29 Take it of their half, and give it unto Eleazar the Priest, for an Heave Offering of the LORD *(part was to be given to the Priests).*

30 And of the Children of Israel's half, you shall take one portion of fifty, of the person, of the beeves, of the asses, and of the flocks, of all manner of beasts, and give them unto the Levites, which keep the charge of the Tabernacle of the LORD. *(As the soldiers were to give a tithe, so to speak, to the Priests, they were, as well, to give a tithe unto the Levites, although the amounts were different.)*

31 And Moses and Eleazar the Priest did as the LORD commanded Moses.

32 And the booty, being the rest of the prey which the men of war had caught, was six hundred thousand and seventy thousand and five thousand sheep (675,000).

33 And threescore and twelve thousand beeves (72,000 cattle),

34 And threescore and one thousand asses (61,000),

35 And thirty and two thousand persons in all, of women who had not known man by lying with him.

36 And the half, which was the portion of them who went out to war, was in number three hundred thousand and seven and thirty thousand and five hundred sheep (337,500):

37 And the LORD's tribute of the sheep was six hundred and threescore and fifteen (675).

38 And the beeves were thirty and six thousand; of which the LORD's tribute was threescore and twelve (72).

39 And the asses were thirty thousand and five hundred; of which the LORD's tribute was threescore and one (61).

40 And the persons were sixteen thousand; of which the LORD's tribute was thirty and two persons.

41 And Moses gave the tribute, which was the LORD's Heave Offering, unto Eleazar the Priest, as the LORD commanded Moses.

42 And of the Children of Israel's half, which Moses divided from the men who warred,

43 (Now the half that pertained unto the congregation was three hundred thousand and thirty thousand and seven thousand and five hundred sheep,

44 And thirty and six thousand beeves,

45 And thirty thousand asses and five hundred,

46 And sixteen thousand persons;)

47 Even of the Children of Israel's half, Moses took one portion of fifty, both of man and of beast, and gave them unto the Levites, which kept the charge of the Tabernacle of the LORD; as the Lord commanded Moses (thus the Priests and the Levites were maintained as well).

48 And the officers which were over thousands of the host, the captains of thousands, and captains of hundreds, came near unto Moses:

49 And they said unto Moses, Your servants have taken the sum of the men of war which are under our charge, and there lacks not one man of us. (Williams says, "Through this great conflict the twelve thousand came through without the loss of one man, and through the greater conflict of Rev., Chpts. 7 through 14, the 144,000 [12,000 times 12] will also triumphantly come, and stand, not one missing, with the Lamb upon Mount Zion.")

50 We have therefore brought an oblation for the LORD what every man has gotten, of jewels of gold, chains, and bracelets, rings, earrings, and tablets, to make an atonement for our souls before the LORD (it seems they kept nothing of these precious metals, etc.).

51 And Moses and Eleazar the Priest took the gold of them, even all wrought jewels.

52 And all the gold of the Offering that they offered up to the LORD, of the captains of thousands, and of the captains of hundreds, was sixteen thousand seven hundred and fifty shekels (worth approximately $1.5 million in 2004 currency).

53 (For the men of war had taken spoil, every man for himself.)

54 And Moses and Eleazar the Priest took the gold of the captains of thousands and of hundreds, and brought it into the Tabernacle of the congregation, for a memorial for the Children of Israel before the LORD.

CHAPTER 32
(1452 B.C.)
REUBEN AND GAD

NOW the Children of Reuben and the Children of Gad had a very great multitude of cattle: and when they saw the land of Jazer, and the land of Gilead, that, behold, the place was a place for cattle;

2 The Children of Gad and the Children of Reuben came and spoke unto Moses, and to Eleazar the Priest, and unto the princes of the congregation, saying,

3 Ataroth, and Dibon, and Jazer, and Nimrah, and Heshbon, and Elealeh, and Shebam, and Nebo, and Beon,

4 Even the country which the LORD smote before the congregation of Israel, is a land for cattle, and your servants have cattle:

5 Wherefore, said they, if we have found grace in your sight, let this land be given unto your servants for a possession, and bring us not over Jordan. (God's Plan for Israel was, first, to conquer Canaan, and second, the vast region between the Jordan and the Euphrates. Reuben and his allies elected to reverse this; the

result was present suffering and future loss. Self-will always, and without exception, leads to loss.)

6 And Moses said unto the Children of Gad and to the Children of Reuben, Shall your brethren go to war, and shall you sit here?

7 And wherefore discourage you the heart of the Children of Israel from going over into the land which the LORD has given them? *(There is always a tendency in the heart to find a resting place in the blessings on the Wilderness side of Jordan rather than to desire eagerly the richer inheritance beyond Jordan. If the Believer would enjoy the highest possible life, there must be a passing out of the Wilderness of a stunted Christian life into the Canaan of a life of joy and of power in the Holy Spirit. In other words, the Believer must cease all self-will, thereby placing our Faith exclusively in Christ and His Cross, which then gives the Holy Spirit latitude to work within our lives, and thereby to bring about the desired results, which He Alone can do [Rom. 8:1-2, 11].)*

8 Thus did your fathers, when I sent them from Kadesh-barnea to see the land.

9 For when they went up unto the valley of Eshcol, and saw the land, they discouraged the heart of the Children of Israel, that they should not go into the land which the LORD had given them.

10 And the LORD's anger was kindled the same time, and He swore, saying,

11 Surely none of the men who came up out of Egypt, from twenty years old and upward, shall see the land which I swore unto Abraham, unto Isaac, and unto Jacob; because they have not wholly followed me:

12 Save Caleb the son of Jephunneh the Kenezite, and Joshua the son of Nun: for they have wholly followed the LORD *(the Lord never forgets unbelief on the part of His people, and neither does He ever forget Faith).*

13 And the LORD's anger was kindled against Israel, and he made them wander in the wilderness forty years, until all the generation, who had done evil in the sight of the LORD, was consumed *(unbelief can never inherit the land [Heb. 3:11; 4:6]).*

14 And, behold, you are risen up in your father's stead, an increase of sinful men, to augment yet the fierce anger of the LORD toward Israel *(in other words, Moses told Israel that they were little better than their fathers, if at all).*

15 For if you turn away from after Him, He will yet again leave them in the wilderness;

and you shall destroy all this people *(to leave the Perfect Will of God, even to the slightest degree, always has its negative results).*

COMPROMISE

16 And they came near unto him, and said, We will build sheepfolds here for our cattle, and cities for our little ones:

17 But we ourselves will go ready armed before the Children of Israel, until we have brought them unto their place: and our little ones shall dwell in the fenced cities because of the inhabitants of the land.

18 We will not return unto our houses, until the Children of Israel have inherited every man his inheritance. *(This meant that they were to immediately bid farewell to their wives and children and march away to a seven-year war, in which many of them would probably lose their lives. If we plan for ourselves, there is always trouble; if the Lord plans for us, everything falls into place, a good place.)*

19 For we will not inherit with them on yonder side Jordan, or forward; because our inheritance is fallen to us on this side Jordan eastward *(in a spiritual sense, the Promised Land side of Jordan symbolizes a death to self).*

20 And Moses said unto them, If you will do this thing, if you will go armed before the LORD to war *(it doesn't too much seem that Moses sought the Lord about this decision, which, if correct, is always a mistake),*

21 And will go all of you armed over Jordan before the LORD, until He has driven out His enemies from before Him,

22 And the land be subdued before the LORD: then afterward you shall return, and be guiltless before the LORD and before Israel; and this land shall be your possession before the LORD.

23 But if you will not do so, behold, you have sinned against the LORD: and be sure your sin will find you out *(in essence, they had made a vow).*

24 Build you cities for your little ones, and folds for your sheep; and do that which has proceeded out of your mouth.

25 And the Children of Gad and the Children of Reuben spoke unto Moses, saying, Your servants will do as my lord commands.

26 Our little ones, our wives, our flocks, and all our cattle, shall be there in the cities of Gilead:

27 But your servants will pass over, every

man armed for war, before the LORD to battle, as my lord says.

28 So concerning them Moses commanded Eleazar the Priest, and Joshua the son of Nun, and the chief fathers of the Tribes of the Children of Israel:

29 And Moses said unto them, If the Children of Gad and the Children of Reuben will pass with you over Jordan, every man armed to battle, before the LORD, and the land shall be subdued before you; then you shall give them the land of Gilead for a possession:

30 But if they will not pass over with you armed, they shall have possessions among you in the land of Canaan.

31 And the Children of Gad and the Children of Reuben answered, saying, As the LORD has said unto your servants, so will we do.

32 We will pass over armed before the LORD into the land of Canaan, that the possession of our inheritance on this side Jordan may be ours.

33 And Moses gave unto them, even to the Children of Gad, and to the Children of Reuben, and unto half the Tribe of Manasseh the son of Joseph, the kingdom of Sihon king of the Amorites, and the kingdom of Og king of Bashan, the land, with the cities thereof in the coasts, even the cities of the country round about.

34 And the Children of Gad built Dibon, and Ataroth, and Aroer,

35 And Atroth, Shophan, and Jaazer, and Jogbehah,

36 And Beth-nimrah, and Beth-haran, fenced cities: and folds for sheep.

37 And the Children of Reuben built Heshbon, and Elealeh, and Kirjathaim,

38 And Nebo, and Baal-meon, (their names being changed,) and Shibmah: and gave other names unto the cities which they built.

MANASSEH

39 And the Children of Machir the son of Manasseh went to Gilead, and took it, and dispossessed the Amorite which was in it.

40 And Moses gave Gilead unto Machir the son of Manasseh; and he dwelt therein.

41 And Jair the son of Manasseh went and took the small towns thereof, and called them Havoth-jair.

42 And Nobah went and took Kenath, and the villages thereof, and called it Nobah, after his own name.

CHAPTER 33
(1490 B.C.)
A SUMMARY

THESE are the journeys of the Children of Israel, which went forth out of the land of Egypt with their armies under the hand of Moses and Aaron.

2 And Moses wrote their goings out according to their journeys by the Commandment of the LORD and these are their journeys according to their goings out. *(Williams says, "The love that led Israel through the great and terrible Wilderness for forty years, so that they lacked nothing, commanded Moses to minutely record their wanderings. This command, and this record, reveal the most tender love, and prove that their Divine Shepherd accompanied them every step of the way from Egypt to Canaan. In all their afflictions, He was afflicted; He cherished them as a nurse her children; He suffered not their garments to wax old, nor their feet to swell [Neh., Chpt. 9]. This Chapter shows that He never lost sight of them for a single day.")*

3 And they departed from Rameses in the first month, on the fifteenth day of the first month; on the morrow after the Passover the Children of Israel went out with an high hand in the sight of all the Egyptians.

4 For the Egyptians buried all their first born, which the LORD had smitten among them: upon their gods also the LORD executed judgments *(Egypt was left a waste).*

5 And the Children of Israel removed from Rameses, and pitched in Succoth *(the Lord commanded this historical narrative be written, not only for historical interest, but to show us that the Lord watches over us continually, in fact, never takes an eye off our doings, recording all things; we should remember this, thereby making every day, even every minute, count for the Lord).*

6 And they departed from Succoth, and pitched in Etham, which is in the edge of the wilderness.

7 And they removed from Etham, and turned again unto Pi-hahiroth, which is before Baal-zephon: and they pitched before Migdol.

8 And they departed from before Pi-hahiroth, and passed through the midst of the sea into the wilderness *(the great miracle of the Red Sea opening),* and went three days' journey in the wilderness of Etham, and pitched in Marah.

9 And they removed from Marah *(where the*

Lord had made the bitter waters sweet — Ex., Chpt. 15), and came unto Elim: and in Elim were twelve fountains of water, and threescore and ten palm trees; and they pitched there.

10 And they removed from Elim, and encamped by the Red Sea.

11 And they removed from the Red Sea, and encamped in the wilderness of Sin.

12 And they took their journey out of the wilderness of Sin, and encamped in Dophkah.

13 And they departed from Dophkah, and encamped in Alush.

14 And they removed from Alush, and encamped at Rephidim, where was no water for the people to drink *(the Rock was there smitten, with a veritable river of water pouring out — Ex., Chpt. 17)*.

15 And they departed from Rephidim, and pitched in the wilderness of Sinai.

16 And they removed from the desert of Sinai, and pitched at Kibroth-hattaavah.

17 And they departed from Kibroth-hattaavah, and encamped at Hazeroth.

18 And they departed from Hazeroth, and pitched in Rithmah.

19 And they departed from Rithmah, and pitched at Rimmon-parez.

20 And they departed from Rimmon-parez, and pitched in Libnah.

21 And they removed from Libnah, and pitched at Rissah.

22 And they journeyed from Rissah, and pitched in Kehelathah.

23 And they went from Kehelathah, and pitched in mount Shapher.

24 And they removed from mount Shapher, and encamped in Haradah.

25 And they removed from Haradah, and pitched in Makheloth.

26 And they removed from Makheloth, and encamped at Tahath.

27 And they departed from Tahath, and pitched at Tarah.

28 And they removed from Tarah, and pitched in Mithcah.

29 And they went from Mithcah, and pitched in Hashmonah.

30 And they departed from Hashmonah, and encamped at Moseroth.

31 And they departed from Moseroth, and pitched in Bene-jaakan.

32 And they removed from Bene-jaakan, and encamped at Hor-hagidgad.

33 And they went from Hor-hagidgad, and pitched in Jotbathah.

34 And they removed from Jotbathah, and encamped at Ebronah.

35 And they departed from Ebronah, and encamped at Ezion-gaber.

36 And they removed from Ezion-gaber, and pitched in the wilderness of Zin, which is Kadesh.

37 And they removed from Kadesh, and pitched in mount Hor, in the edge of the land of Edom.

38 And Aaron the Priest went up into mount Hor at the Commandment of the LORD, and died there, in the fortieth year after the Children of Israel were come out of the land of Egypt, in the first day of the fifth month *(this is the only place where the date of Aaron's death is given)*.

39 And Aaron was an hundred and twenty and three years old when he died in mount Hor.

40 And king Arad the Canaanite, which dwelt in the south in the land of Canaan, heard of the coming of the Children of Israel.

41 And they departed from Mount Hor, and pitched in Zalmonah.

42 And they departed from Zalmonah, and pitched in Punon.

43 And they departed from Punon, and pitched in Oboth.

44 And they departed from Oboth, and pitched in Ije-abarim, in the border of Moab.

45 And they departed from Iim, and pitched in Dibon-gad.

46 And they removed from Dibon-gad, and encamped in Almon-diblathaim.

47 And they removed from Almon-diblathaim, and pitched in the mountains of Abarim, before Nebo.

48 And they departed from the mountains of Abarim, and pitched in the plains of Moab by Jordan near Jericho.

49 And they pitched by Jordan, from Beth-jesimoth even unto Abel-shittim in the plains of Moab.

PREPARATIONS

50 And the LORD spoke unto Moses in the plains of Moab by Jordan near Jericho, saying,

51 Speak unto the Children of Israel, and say unto them, When you are passed over Jordan into the land of Canaan;

52 Then you shall drive out all the inhabitants of the land from before you, and destroy all their pictures, and destroy all their molten images, and quite pluck down all their high

places (in the spiritual sense, every Believer must "lay aside every weight, and the sin which does so easily beset us" [Heb. 12:1], which can be done only as our Faith is anchored firmly in Christ and the Cross, which then gives the Holy Spirit latitude to work in our lives, bringing about the desired results; any other way is futile [Rom. 6:3-14; 8:1-2, 11; Gal. 6:14]):

53 And you shall dispossess the inhabitants of the land, and dwell therein: for I have given you the land to possess it (but yet, the enemies must be dispossessed; as repeatedly stated, this can only come about by Faith in Christ and the Cross).

54 And you shall divide the land by lot (the Urim and the Thummim) for an inheritance among your families: and to the more you shall give the more inheritance, and to the fewer you shall give the less inheritance: every man's inheritance shall be in the place where his lot falls (meaning that the Holy Spirit through the Urim and the Thummim would draw the boundaries); according to the Tribes of your fathers you shall inherit.

55 But if you will not drive out the inhabitants of the land from before you; then it shall come to pass, that those which you let remain of them shall be pricks in your eyes, and thorns in your sides, and shall vex you in the land wherein you dwell (the works of the flesh must go, or else we will find that they will cause us tremendous problems [II Cor. 6:14-18; 7:1]).

56 Moreover it shall come to pass, that I shall do unto you, as I thought to do unto them (sin in the Believer, if left unaddressed, can be condoned by the Lord no more than sin in the unbeliever — even less)

CHAPTER 34
(1452 B.C.)
BORDERS OF CANAAN

AND the LORD spoke unto Moses, saying,

2 Command the Children of Israel, and say unto them, When you come into the land of Canaan; (this is the land that shall fall unto you for an inheritance, even the land of Canaan with the coasts (borders) thereof:) (The hand of love that guided the sons of Israel through the desert, in this Chapter, fixed the bounds of their habitation. It was only a very real and tender love that could occupy itself with such details. But the people were Jehovah's people — the land, Emmanuel's land — and to love, nothing is small

or unimportant — Williams.)

3 Then your south quarter shall be from the wilderness of Zin along by the coast of Edom, and your south border shall be the outmost coast of the salt sea (Dead Sea) eastward:

4 And your border shall turn from the south to the ascent of Akrabbim, and pass on to Zin: and the going forth thereof shall be from the south to Kadesh-barnea, and shall go on to Hazar-addar, and pass on to Azmon:

5 And the border shall fetch a compass from Azmon unto the river of Egypt (some conclude this "River" to be about halfway of Sinai, with others believing that it is the Suez), and the goings out of it shall be at the sea (Mediterranean).

6 And as for the western border, you shall even have the great sea (Mediterranean) for a border: this shall be your west border.

7 And this shall be your north border: from the great sea you shall point out for you Mount Hor:

8 From Mount Hor you shall point out your border unto the entrance of Hamath; and the goings forth of the border shall be to Zedad:

9 And the border shall go on to Ziphron, and the goings out of it shall be at Hazar-enan: this shall be your north border. (This took in most of modern Syria, actually going about 75 miles north of Damascus. It was occupied during the time of David, but was not held by the following kings. In the coming Kingdom Age, the borders of Israel will include all of this and much more.)

10 And you shall point out your east border from Hazar-enan to Shepham:

11 And the coast shall go down from Shepham to Riblah, on the east side of Ain; and the border shall descend, and shall reach unto the side of the sea of Chinnereth eastward:

12 And the border shall go down to Jordan, and the goings out of it shall be at the salt sea (Dead Sea): this shall be your land with the coasts thereof round about (the eastern border would have included most of modern Jordan, but, again, David alone conquered this particular territory; the kings which followed, by and large, lost it to heathen tribes).

13 And Moses commanded the Children of Israel, saying, This is the land which you shall inherit by lot, which the LORD commanded to give unto the nine tribes, and to the half tribe (as with Israel of old, presently, we fail to obtain all of our inheritance; we, regrettably, settle for half measures, or even less; such should not be! All that the Lord has promised us, even

though it may not be easy to obtain, it most definitely can be obtained, because He has promised it to us; in other words, everything for which He paid such a price at the Cross, and I speak of the "firstfruits" which we can now have, we should make certain, in Christ, that we obtain it all [Rom. 8:23]):

14 For the Tribe of the Children of Reuben according to the house of their fathers, and the Tribe of the Children of Gad according to the house of their fathers, have received their inheritance; and half the Tribe of Manasseh have received their inheritance:

15 The two Tribes and the half Tribe have received their inheritance on this side Jordan near Jericho eastward, toward the sunrising. *(The two Tribes of Reuben and Gad received their inheritance on the eastern side of the Jordan River, in what is now modern day Jordan. As well, half of the Tribe of Manasseh also was on the eastern side of Jordan, with the other part on the western side. In fact, Manasseh had the largest portion, with the exception of Judah.)*

THE LEADERS

16 And the LORD spoke unto Moses, saying,

17 These are the names of the men which shall divide the land unto you: Eleazar the Priest, and Joshua the son of Nun.

18 And you shall take one prince of every tribe, to divide the land by inheritance.

19 And the names of the men are these: Of the tribe of Judah, Caleb the son of Jephunneh.

20 And of the tribe of the Children of Simeon, Shemuel the son of Ammihud.

21 Of the tribe of Benjamin, Elidad the son of Chislon.

22 And the prince of the Tribe of the Children of Dan, Bukki the son of Jogli.

23 The prince of the Children of Joseph, for the Tribe of the Children of Manasseh, Hanniel the son of Ephod.

24 And the prince of the Tribe of the Children of Ephraim, Kemuel the son of Shiphtan.

25 And the prince of the Tribe of the Children of Zebulun, Elizaphan the son of Parnach.

26 And the prince of the Tribe of the Children of Issachar, Paltiel the son of Azzan.

27 And the prince of the Tribe of the Children of Asher, Ahihud the son of Shelomi.

28 And the prince of the Tribe of the Children of Naphtali, Pedahel the son of Ammihud.

29 These are they whom the Lord commanded to divide the inheritance unto the Children of Israel in the land of Canaan. *(If it is to be noticed, the Lord selected the men who were to head up the Tribes, a man from each Tribe, with Eleazar, the High Priest, and Joshua being in charge, thus, satisfying the ecclesiastical and military heads respectively of the theocracy.)*

CHAPTER 35
(1451 B.C.)
CITIES OF THE LEVITES

AND the LORD spoke unto Moses in the plains of Moab by Jordan near Jericho, saying,

2 Command the Children of Israel, that they give unto the Levites of the inheritance of their possession cities to dwell in; and you shall give also unto the Levites suburbs for the cities round about them. *(Concerning the Levites, Williams says, "The tender love that portioned out a goodly heritage to each Tribe — to the weakest as well as to the strongest — did not fail to provide a fitting maintenance for Levi. Forty-eight cities were given to him in all Israel. Thus, the prediction of Gen. 49:7 was fulfilled and, at the same time, turned into honor and blessing because of the faithfulness expressed in Ex. 32:26.*

"Jehovah became Levi's inheritance, they were His personal servants and, therefore, wholly cast upon Him for their daily bread. They were to concern themselves about His Service, He having undertaken to concern Himself about their maintenance.")

3 And the cities *(48)* shall they have to dwell in; and the suburbs *(surrounding land)* of them shall be for their cattle, and for their goods, and for all their beasts.

4 And the suburbs of the cities, which you shall give unto the Levites, shall reach from the wall of the city and outward a thousand cubits *(1,500 feet)* round about *(a little over a quarter of a mile around the city was portioned off for the Levites, that they might graze their stock on this particular land).*

5 And you shall measure from without the city on the east side two thousand cubits *(3,000 feet)*, and on the south side two thousand cubits, and on the west side two thousand cubits, and on the north side two thousand cubits; and the city shall be in the midst: this shall be to them the suburbs of the cities. *(Along with the 1,500 feet surrounding these cities, a further measure of 3,000 feet was granted beside that. Buildings on the inner grant might be sold by the Levites, but none of the land outside of that.)*

6 And among the cities which you shall give unto the Levites there shall be six cities for refuge, which you shall appoint for the manslayer, that he may flee thither: and to them you shall add forty and two cities. *(This refers to an individual who kills someone by accident. These cities were not for murderers. If the "manslayer" could reach one of these cities, the relatives of the victim could not touch him. He was to stay in this City of Refuge until the death of the High Priest. When the High Priest died, the man was free and, by Law, the victim's relatives must not bother him.*

The Avenger of Blood symbolized the Law. It demanded the death of the manslayer. The death of the High Priest satisfied this claim and liberated the manslayer. Christ's Death, not His Life, rent the Veil, and frees the sinner from the curse of the broken Law. Similarly, the death of the Lamb, not its spotlessness, redeemed the Lawbreaker of Lev., Chpt. 4. The manslayer was then at liberty to return to his possession.

When Israel shall look upon Him Whom they have pierced, it will be then revealed to them that His Death restores them to the land and Family of God.)

7 So all the cities which you shall give to the Levites shall be forty and eight cities: them shall you give with their suburbs.

8 And the cities which you shall give shall be of the possession of the Children of Israel: from them who have many you shall give many; but from them who have few you shall give few: every one shall give of his cities unto the Levites according to his inheritance which he inherits.

CITIES OF REFUGE

9 And the Lord spoke unto Moses, saying,

10 Speak unto the Children of Israel, and say unto them, When you be come over Jordan into the land of Canaan;

11 Then you shall appoint you cities to be cities of refuge for you; that the slayer may flee thither, which kills any person at unawares *(accidentally)*.

12 And they shall be unto you cities for refuge from the avenger; that the manslayer die not, until he stand before the congregation in judgment *(after the High Priest died, if it was felt by the authorities that a trial was necessary, one could then be conducted)*.

13 And of these cities which you shall give six cities shall you have for refuge.

14 You shall give three cities on this side Jordan, and three cities shall you give in the land of Canaan, which shall be cities of refuge *(three cities were to be on the east side of the Jordan River, and three cities on the west side)*.

15 These six cities shall be a refuge, both for the Children of Israel, and for the stranger *(Gentile)*, and for the sojourner among them: that every one who kills any person unawares *(accidentally)* may flee thither. *(Those six cities were: "Kadesh, Golan, Shechem, Ramoth, Hebron, and Bezer.")*

WILLFUL MURDER

16 And if he smite him with an instrument of iron, so that he die, he is a murderer: the murderer shall surely be put to death *(in other words, there were no cities of refuge for murderers)*.

17 And it he smite him with throwing a stone, wherewith he may die, and he die, he is a murderer: the murderer shall surely be put to death.

18 Or if he smite him with an hand weapon of wood, wherewith he may die, and he die, he is a murderer: the murderer shall surely be put to death.

19 The revenger of blood himself shall slay the murderer: when he meets him, he shall slay him *(the relatives or friends of the one murdered)*.

20 But if he thrust him of hatred, or hurl at him by laying of wait, that he die;

21 Or in enmity smite him with his hand, that he die: he who smote him shall surely be put to death; for he is a murderer: the revenger of blood shall slay the murderer, when he meets him.

INVOLUNTARY KILLING

22 But if he thrust him suddenly without enmity, or have cast upon him any thing without laying of wait,

23 Or with any stone, wherewith a man may die, seeing him not, and cast it upon him, that he die, and was not his enemy, neither sought his harm *(was done accidentally)*.

24 Then the congregation shall judge between the slayer and the revenger of blood according to these judgments *(a trial was to be conducted)*:

25 And the congregation shall deliver the slayer out of the hand of the revenger of blood, and the congregation shall restore him to the

city of his refuge, whither he was fled: and he shall abide in it unto the death of the High Priest, which was anointed with the holy oil *(Jesus was our High Priest; His death satisfied all claims against us, and gave us our freedom).*

26 But if the slayer shall at any time come without the border of the city of his refuge, whither he was fled;

27 And the revenger of blood find him without the borders of the city of his refuge, and the revenger of blood kill the slayer; he shall not be guilty of blood *(if the individual leaves the city of refuge before the death of the High Priest, and is killed by friends or relatives of the victim, they will not be charged with any crime):*

28 Because he should have remained in the city of his refuge until the death of the High Priest: but after the death of the High Priest the slayer shall return into the land of his possession *(and there be protected by the Law).*

29 So these things shall be for a Statute of judgment unto you throughout your generations in all your dwellings. *(Rather until Christ would come, Who, as our High Priest, would fulfill all obligations, thereby making moot and invalid these particular Laws. Christ satisfied all the requirements of the Law in every respect, and did so by His Perfect Life. As well, He satisfied the demands of the broken Law, of which all were guilty, except Christ, and did so by dying on the Cross [Gal. 3:13-14]. So when a person accepts and receives Christ as one's personal Saviour, all the claims of the Law are satisfied in that acceptance.)*

MURDERERS

30 Whoso kills any person, the murderer shall be put to death by the mouth of witnesses: but one witness shall not testify against any person to cause him to die *(under the Law of Moses, there had to be two or more eye witnesses to the crime before the person could be put to death; one eye witness was not enough; such shows the high value that God placed upon life).*

31 Moreover you shall take no satisfaction for the life of a murderer, which is guilty of death: but he shall be surely put to death *(if there are two or more personal witnesses to the crime, the guilty person is to be put to death).*

32 And you shall take no satisfaction for him who is fled to the city of his refuge *(he cannot claim safety and protection in one of the cities of refuge, as could one who had accidentally killed another),* that he should come again to dwell in the land, until the death of the Priest *(the Cities of Refuge were to never be a haven for murderers).*

33 So you shall not pollute the land wherein you are: for blood it defiles the land: and the land cannot be cleansed of the blood that is shed therein, but by the blood of him who shed it *(if a person commits cold-blooded murder, and there are two or more eye witnesses, such a person must be executed; to not take proper steps in such situations pollutes the land; so that means, regarding the untold thousands of abortions performed each year in the United States, that the land is polluted with blood; one day God will demand payment).*

34 Defile not therefore the land which you shall inhabit, wherein I dwell: for I the LORD dwell among the Children of Israel. *(This was under the old Law; however, it applies presently to the nations of the world which consider themselves to be predominantly Christian. God does not change, even as God cannot change.)*

CHAPTER 36
(1451 B.C.)
FEMALE INHERITANCE

AND the chief fathers of the families of the Children of Gilead, the son of Machir, the son of Manasseh, of the families of the sons of Joseph, came near, and spoke before Moses, and before the princes, the chief fathers of the Children of Israel *(as necessities arose in the Wilderness journey, or in the conquest of Canaan, there were additions made to the Civil Law, as for instance in this Chapter, but never any change in the legislation respecting Atonement and Worship):*

2 And they said, The LORD commanded my lord *(Moses)* to give the land for an inheritance by lot *(the Urim and the Thummim)* to the Children of Israel: and my lord was commanded by the LORD to give the inheritance of Zelophehad our brother unto his daughters.

3 And if they be married to any of the sons of the other tribes of the Children of Israel, then shall their inheritance be taken from the inheritance of our fathers, and shall be put to the inheritance of the Tribe whereunto they are received: so shall it be taken from the lot of our inheritance.

4 And when the Jubilee *(Year of Jubilee)* of the Children of Israel shall be, then shall their inheritance be put unto the inheritance of the Tribe whereunto they are received: so shall

their inheritance be taken away from the inheritance of the Tribe of our fathers. *(In practice, no property would be considered to have finally changed hands until the Year of Jubilee, when an extensive re-settlement took place, and when all titles not successfully challenged would be considered as confirmed.)*

MARRIAGE

5 And Moses commanded the Children of Israel according to the Word of the LORD, saying, The Tribe of the sons of Joseph has said well.

6 This is the thing which the LORD does command concerning the daughters of Zelophehad, saying, Let them marry to whom they think best; only to the family of the Tribe of their father shall they marry *(to gain the inheritance of their father, these young women must marry a man from their own Tribe).*

7 So shall not the inheritance of the Children of Israel remove from Tribe to Tribe *(the boundaries of each Tribe must not be moved):* for every one of the Children of Israel shall keep himself to the inheritance of the Tribe of his fathers.

8 And every daughter, who possesses an inheritance in any Tribe of the Children of Israel, shall be wife unto one of the family of the Tribe of her father, that the Children of Israel may enjoy every man the inheritance of his fathers.

9 Neither shall the inheritance remove from one Tribe to another Tribe; but every one of the Tribes of the Children of Israel shall keep himself to his own inheritance.

10 Even as the LORD commanded Moses, so did the daughters of Zelophehad:

11 For Mahlah, Tirzah, and Hoglah, and Milcah, and Noah, the daughters of Zelophehad, were married unto their father's brothers' sons:

12 And they were married into the families of the sons of Manasseh the son of Joseph, and their inheritance remained in the Tribe of the family of their father.

13 These are the Commandments and the Judgments, which the LORD commanded by the hand of Moses unto the Children of Israel in the plains of Moab by Jordan near Jericho.

THE FIFTH BOOK OF MOSES, CALLED
DEUTERONOMY

CHAPTER 1
(1451 B.C.)
THE PROMISE OF GOD

THESE be the words which Moses spoke unto all Israel on this side Jordan in the wilderness, in the plain over against the Red Sea, between Paran, and Tophel, and Laban, and Hazeroth, and Dizahab. *(This Message was given by Moses to Israel shortly before the great Law-giver died, and thereby shortly before Israel went into the Promised Land.)*

2 (There are eleven days' journey from Horeb by the way of mount Seir unto Kadesh-barnea *[Eleven days' journey from Mount Sinai, where the Law was given].)*

3 And it came to pass in the fortieth year, in the eleventh month, on the first day of the month, that Moses spoke unto the Children of Israel, according unto all that the LORD had given him in Commandment unto them *(this will be his last word to Israel; the time of these "Words" will be approximately a month previous to his death; the theme of his Message is that possession of Canaan was dependent upon the keeping of the Law given at Sinai; Sinai was one of the peaks of a mountain mass named Horeb)*;

4 After he had slain Sihon the king of the Amorites, which dwelt in Heshbon, and Og the king of Bashan, which dwelt at Astaroth in Edrei *(by the destruction of these kings, who sought to bar the access of the Israelites to the Promised Land, God had given proof that He would indeed fulfill His Promise to His people)*:

5 On this side Jordan, in the land of Moab, began Moses to declare this Law, saying *(nothing but prosperity was promised upon fidelity to that Law, and nothing but misery if unfaithful thereto; a lesson of the Book is the impossibility of the natural man taking hold upon and keeping Divine privileges)*,

6 The LORD our God spoke unto us in Horeb, saying, You have dwelt long enough in this Mount *(the phrase, "Lord our God," implies the Covenant union of Israel with Jehovah, and presupposes the existence of that Covenant, which was entered into at Sinai)*:

7 Turn you, and take your journey, and go to the Mount of the Amorites, and unto all the places near thereunto, in the plain, in the hills, and in the vale, and in the south, and by the sea side, to the land of the Canaanites, and unto Lebanon, unto the great river, the river Euphrates. *(This description encompasses the whole of the Promised Land. It included all of modern Jordan, Syria, and even Iraq, at least as far as the Euphrates River. It was considerably larger than the small portion claimed by Israel presently. To be sure, in the coming Kingdom Age, Israel will occupy all of this, and possibly even more.)*

8 Behold, I have set the land before you: go in and possess the land which the LORD swore unto your fathers, Abraham, Isaac, and Jacob, to give unto them and to their seed after them *(God keeps His Promises! As well, Israel could have occupied the land 38 years earlier had they evidenced faith)*.

JUDGES

9 And I spoke unto you at that time, saying, I am not able to bear you myself alone:

10 The LORD your God has multiplied you, and, behold, you are this day as the stars of Heaven for multitude *(exactly as the Lord told Abraham it would be [Gen. 15:5-6])*.

11 (The LORD God of your fathers make you a thousand times so many more as you are, and bless you, as He has promised you! *[God desires to bless His people. The only qualification is obedience.]*)

12 How can I myself alone bear your cumbrance *(entanglements)*, and your burden, and your strife?

13 Take you wise men, and understanding, and known among your Tribes, and I will make them rulers over you *(you select the ones you desire)*.

14 And you answered me, and said, The thing which you have spoken is good for us to do.

15 So I took the chief of your Tribes, wise men, and known, and made them heads over you, captains over thousands, and captains over hundreds, and captains over fifties, and captains over tens, and officers among your Tribes.

16 And I charged your Judges at that time, saying, Hear the causes between your brethren,

and judge righteously between every man and his brother, and the stranger who is with him.

17 You shall not respect persons in judgment; but you shall hear the small as well as the great; you shall not be afraid of the face of man: for the Judgment is God's: and the cause that is too hard for you, bring it unto me, and I will hear it.

18 And I commanded you at that time all the things which you should do. (It appears from the following Passages that this arrangement of the people selecting leaders over them did not turn out too very well. These leaders, even as the following Passages proclaim, registered unbelief, and doomed that generation of Israel in the wilderness.)

REBELLION

19 And when we departed from Horeb, we went through all that great and terrible wilderness, which you saw by the way of the mountain of the Amorites, as the LORD our God commanded us: and we came to Kadesh-barnea.

20 And I said unto you, You are come unto the mountain of the Amorites, which the LORD our God does give unto us.

21 Behold, the LORD your God has set the land before you: go up and possess it, as the LORD God of your fathers has said unto you; fear not, neither be discouraged.

22 And you came near unto me every one of you, and said, We will send men before us, and they shall search us out the land, and bring us word again by what way we must go up, and into what cities we shall come. (If we plan for ourselves, in some way, the plans are always wrong. If we allow God to plan for us, His plans are guaranteed of success. Israel did not allow the Lord, at least at this juncture, to plan for them. The knowledge they sought portrayed a lack of faith.)

23 And the saying pleased me well: and I took twelve men of you, one of a Tribe (Moses was guilty somewhat in this situation, as well; he should have taken the matter to the Lord, but the evidence is that he didn't):

24 And they turned and went up into the mountain, and came unto the valley of Eshcol, and searched it out.

25 And they took of the fruit of the land in their hands, and brought it down unto us, and brought us word again, and said, It is a good land which the LORD our God does give us.

26 Notwithstanding you would not go up,

but rebelled against the Commandment of the LORD your God:

27 And you murmured in your tents, and said, Because the LORD hated us, He has brought us forth out of the land of Egypt, to deliver us into the hand of the Amorites, to destroy us (they lied on God; to be sure, that is one of the biggest sins in the modern Church, as well!).

28 Whither shall we go up? Our brethren have discouraged our heart, saying, The people is greater and taller than we; the cities are great and walled up to Heaven: and moreover we have seen the sons of the Anakims there (they saw the walled cities and the giants; what is it that you see?).

29 Then I said unto you, Dread not, neither be afraid of them (we are to "see" the Promises of God alone, for we walk by Faith and not by sight).

30 The LORD your God which goes before you, He shall fight for you, according to all that He did for you in Egypt before your eyes (they had seen the great miracles of the Lord, so they should have known better);

31 And in the wilderness, where you have seen how that the LORD your God bore you, as a man does bear his son, in all the way that you went, until you came into this place (the miracles which began in Egypt continued in the wilderness, and were obvious to all).

32 Yet in this thing you did not believe the LORD your God (they registered a continuing unbelief),

33 Who went in the way before you, to search you out a place to pitch your tents in, in fire by night, to show you by what way you should go, and in a cloud by day (the visible Presence of God was obvious, both day and night, and for all to see; as well, that visible Presence led them, and supplied their every need; so, again and again, due to the constant miracles, they had no cause for unbelief — and neither do we).

PUNISHMENT

34 And the LORD heard the voice of your words, and was angry, and swore, saying,

35 Surely there shall not one of these men of this evil generation see that good land, which I swore to give unto your fathers (all Promises of God to us are dependent upon our obedience, and that speaks of continuing Faith in Him).

36 Save Caleb the son of Jephunneh; he shall

see it, and to him will I give the land that he has trodden upon, and to his children, because he has wholly followed the LORD (*God is no respecter of persons; what He did for Caleb and Joshua, He will do for any and all who believe Him*).

37 Also the LORD was angry with me for your sakes, saying, You also shall not go in thither (*speaks of his own failure in striking the Rock, when he was told to speak to It [Num. 20:7-12]*).

38 But Joshua the son of Nun, which stands before you, he shall go in thither: encourage him: for he shall cause Israel to inherit it (*as Joshua, even the greatest among us need encouragement*).

39 Moreover your little ones, which you said should be a prey, and your children, which in that day had no knowledge between good and evil, they shall go in thither, and unto them will I give it, and they shall possess it (*they had accused God of bringing their children into the wilderness in order to kill them, and He, in answer to that accusation, told them that their children would survive the wilderness and inherit the Promised Land, but they would not [Num., Chpt. 14]*).

40 But as for you, turn you, and take your journey into the wilderness by the way of the Red Sea.

DEFEAT

41 Then you answered and said unto me, We have sinned against the LORD, we will go up and fight, according to all that the LORD our God commanded us. And when you had girded on every man his weapons of war, you were ready to go up into the hill. (*However, what they were doing now was in the flesh; the only result could be defeat. Many in the modern Church are fighting, but they are fighting a battle which the Lord never designed. Presently, we are told to fight only one fight, "the good fight of faith," which refers to Faith in Christ, and what He has done for us at the Cross [I Tim. 6:12].*)

42 And the LORD said unto me, Say unto them, Go not up, neither fight: for I am not among you: lest you be smitten before your enemies (*they were warned!*).

43 So I spoke unto you: and you would not hear, but rebelled against the Commandment of the LORD, and went presumptuously up into the hill (*presumption is one of the great*

sins of the modern Church).

44 And the Amorites, which dwelt in that mountain, came out against you, and chased you, as bees do, and destroyed you in Seir, even unto Hormah.

45 And you returned and wept before the LORD; but the LORD would not hearken to your voice, nor give ear unto you (*the weeping was for their dilemma, and not the weeping of the soul for their sin of unbelief*).

46 So you abode in Kadesh many days, according unto the days that you abode there (*out of the Will of God, the days are long!*).

CHAPTER 2
(1453 B.C.)
FORTY YEARS

THEN we turned, and took our journey into the wilderness by the way of the Red Sea, as the LORD spoke unto me: and we compassed Mount Seir many days. (*These "many days" are the thirty-eight years, during which the people wandered in the wilderness before they camped the second time at Kadesh. Out of the Will of God, men tend to run in circles.*)

2 And the LORD spoke unto me, saying,

3 You have compassed this mountain long enough: turn you northward (*after 38 years, they are now turning toward Canaan; this means that the generation of unbelief had now died*).

4 And command you the people, saying, You are to pass through the coast of your brethren the children of Esau, which dwell in Seir; and they shall be afraid of you; take you good heed unto yourselves therefore:

5 Meddle not with them: for I will not give you of their land, no, not so much as a foot breadth; because I have given Mount Seir unto Esau for a possession (*Gen. 36:8*).

6 You shall buy meat of them for money, that you may eat: and you shall also buy water of them for money, that you may drink (*the Lord told them exactly what to do*).

7 For the LORD your God has blessed you in all the works of your hand: he knows your walking through this great wilderness: these forty years the LORD your God has been with you: you have lacked nothing (*the Lord proved to Israel that even though they were in a wilderness, still, He could "set a table for them," which He did [Ps. 78:19-29]*).

8 And when we passed by from our brethren the children of Esau, which dwelt in Seir, through the way of the plain from Elath, and

from Ezion-gaber, we turned and passed by the way of the wilderness of Moab.

MOAB

9 And the LORD said unto me, Distress not the Moabites, neither contend with them in battle: for I will not give you of their land for a possession; because I have given Ar unto the children of Lot for a possession *(Gen. 19:36-38)*.

10 The Emims dwelt therein in times past, a people great, and many, and tall, as the Anakims;

11 Which also were accounted giants, as the Anakims; but the Moabites called them Emims *(these were a race of giants, the result of the ungodly union of fallen angels and women [Gen. 6:4])*.

12 The Horims also dwelt in Seir before time: but the children of Esau succeeded them, when they had destroyed them from before them, and dwelt in their stead; as Israel did unto the land of his possession, which the LORD gave unto them.

13 Now rise up, said I, and get you over the brook Zered. And we went over the brook Zered.

14 And the space in which we came from Kadesh-barnea, until we were come over the brook Zered, was thirty and eight years: until all the generation of the men of war were wasted out from among the host, as the LORD swore unto them.

15 For indeed the hand of the LORD was against them, to destroy them from among the host, until they were consumed *(Heb. 4:1-6)*.

16 So it came to pass, when all the men of war were consumed and dead from among the people *(Israel lay for 38 years in the wilderness, paralyzed by unbelief, like the man at the Pool of Bethesda [Jn. 5:5]; he pictured the nation; Jesus, the true Joshua, brought him over the unseen Jordan into the goodly land; but the Pharisees and Scribes of that day were as blind to such wonders as are the Pharisees and Scribes of the present time)*,

17 That the LORD spoke unto me, saying,

18 You are to pass over through Ar, the coast of Moab, this day:

THROUGH AMMON

19 And when you come near over against the Children of Ammon, distress them not, nor meddle with them: for I will not give you of the land of the children of Ammon any possession; because I have given it unto the children of Lot for a possession *(Gen. 19:38)*.

20 (That also was accounted a land of giants: giants dwelt therein in old time; and the Ammonites call them Zamzummims;

21 A people great, and many, and tall, as the Anakims; but the LORD destroyed them before them; and they succeeded them, and dwelt in their stead:

22 As He did to the children of Esau, which dwelt in Seir, when He destroyed the Horims, from before them; and they succeeded them, and dwelt in their stead even unto this day:

23 And the Avims which dwelt in Hazerim, even unto Azzah, the Caphtorims, which came forth out of Caphtor, destroyed them, and dwelt in their stead.) *(The "giants" spoken of in these Verses, who were nine-feet-plus tall, were the offspring of the union of fallen angels and women [Gen. 6:4]. Satan tried this tactic before the flood, and after the flood. In fact, this was one of the great reasons for the flood. After the flood, Satan would seek to populate the area of the Promised Land, in order to hinder the Children of Israel, polluting them, so as to stop the coming of the Messiah. If it is to be noticed, the Verses of our study proclaim the fact that the Lord helped various people to defeat these giants, without them, of course, knowing it was the Lord Who had done such.)*

THE AMORITE

24 Rise ye up, take your journey, and pass over the river Arnon: behold, I have given into your hand Sihon the Amorite, king of Heshbon, and his land: begin to possess it, and contend with him in battle *(as should be overly obvious, the Lord is the One Who gives the victory; the river Arnon was on the east side of the Dead Sea, about half way of that body of water)*.

25 This day will I begin to put the dread of you and the fear of you upon the nations who are under the whole Heaven, who shall hear report of you, and shall tremble, and be in anguish because of you *(speaking of the nations near the Promised Land; they would have had this 38 years before, but for unbelief)*.

26 And I sent messengers out of the wilderness of Kedemoth unto Sihon king of Heshbon with words of peace, saying,

27 Let me pass through your land: I will go

along by the high way, I will neither turn unto the right hand nor to the left.

28 You shall sell me meat for money, that I may eat; and give me water for money, that I may drink: only I will pass through on my feet *(meaning they would not stop for any length of time)*;

29 (As the children of Esau which dwell in Seir, and the Moabites which dwell in Ar, did unto me;) until I shall pass over Jordan into the land which the LORD our God gives us.

30 But Sihon king of Heshbon would not let us pass by him: for the LORD your God hardened his spirit, and made his heart obstinate, that he might deliver him into your hand, as appears this day *(in these statements, as given by Moses, we are given a behind-the-scenes view of the manner in which the Lord works; when His Children are in His Will, thereby walking obediently, He pulls all the strings, so to speak; He will do such now, exactly as He did then, if the Believer will walk in obedience)*.

31 And the LORD said unto me, Behold, I have begun to give Sihon and his land before you: begin to possess, that you may inherit his land.

32 Then Sihon came out against us, he and all his people, to fight at Jahaz.

33 And the LORD our God delivered him before us; and we smote him, and his sons, and all his people.

34 And we took all his cities at that time, and utterly destroyed the men, and the women, and the little ones of every city, we left none to remain:

35 Only the cattle we took for a prey unto ourselves, and the spoil of the cities which we took.

36 From Aroer, which is by the brink of the river of Arnon, and from the city that is by the river, even unto Gilead, there was not one city too strong for us: the LORD our God delivered all unto us *(as these enemies were defeated, under the New Covenant, every enemy in our lives can be defeated, but only if we do it God's Way; that Way is for us to fully trust Christ and what He has done for us at the Cross; in other words, the Cross of Christ must ever be the object of our Faith; that being the case, the Holy Spirit, Who works exclusively within the parameters of the Finished Work of Christ, will then mightily help us, as only He can do; this is God's Prescribed Order of Victory [Rom. 6:3-14; 8:1-2, 11; I Cor. 1:17-18, 21, 23; 2:2; Eph. 2:13-18; Col. 2:14-15])*:

37 Only unto the land of the children of Ammon you came not, nor unto any place of the river Jabbok, nor unto the cities in the mountains, nor unto whatsoever the LORD our God forbad us.

CHAPTER 3
(1452 B.C.)
VICTORY

THEN we turned, and went up the way to Bashan: and Og the king of Bashan came out against us, he and all his people, to battle at Edrei.

2 And the LORD said unto me, Fear him not: for I will deliver him, and all his people, and his land, into your hand; and you shall do unto him as you did unto Sihon king of the Amorites, which dwelt at Heshbon.

3 So the LORD our God delivered into our hands Og also, the king of Bashan, and all his people: and we smote him until none was left to him remaining.

4 And we took all his cities at that time, there was not a city which we took not from them, threescore cities *(60)*, all the region of Argob, the kingdom of Og in Bashan.

5 All these cities were fenced with high walls, gates, and bars; beside unwalled towns a great many.

6 And we utterly destroyed them, as we did unto Sihon king of Heshbon, utterly destroying the men, women, and children, of every city *(again, with the Lord leading the charge, victory is certain in all capacities)*.

7 But all the cattle, and the spoil of the cities, we took for a prey to ourselves.

8 And we took at that time out of the hand of the two kings of the Amorites the land that was on this side Jordan, from the river of Arnon unto Mount Hermon;

9 (Which Hermon the Sidonians call Sirion; and the Amorites call it Shenir;)

10 All the cities of the plain, and all Gilead, and all Bashan, unto Salchah and Edrei, cities of the kingdom of Og in Bashan.

11 For only Og king of Bashan remained of the remnant of giants; behold his bedstead was a bedstead of iron; is it not in Rabbath of the children of Ammon? nine cubits *(13 1/2 feet)* was the length thereof, and four cubits *(6 feet)* the breadth of it, after the cubit of a man. *(Once again, a part of the population was made up of the "giants," which were easily defeated by God's people. To have the help of the Lord is to have*

everything. To not have that help is to have nothing.)

EAST OF THE JORDAN

12 And this land, which we possessed at that time, from Aroer, which is by the river Arnon, and half Mount Gilead, and the cities thereof, gave I unto the Reubenites and to the Gadites.

13 And the rest of Gilead, and all Bashan, being the kingdom of Og, gave I unto the half tribe of Manasseh; all the region of Argob, with all Bashan, which was called the land of giants.

14 Jair the son of Manasseh took all the country of Argob unto the coasts of Geshuri and Maachathi; and called them after his own name, Bashan-havoth-jair, unto this day.

15 And I gave Gilead unto Machir.

16 And unto the Reubenites and unto the Gadites I gave from Gilead even unto the river Arnon half the valley, and the border even unto the river Jabbok, which is the border of the children of Ammon;

17 The plain also, and Jordan, and the coast thereof, from Chinnereth *(Sea of Galilee)* even unto the sea of the plain, even the salt sea *(Dead Sea)*, under Ashdoth-pisgah eastward.

18 And I commanded you at that time, saying, The LORD your God has given you this land to possess it: you shall pass over armed before your brethren the Children of Israel, all who are meet for the war.

19 But your wives, and your little ones, and your cattle, (for I know that you have much cattle,) shall abide in your cities which I have given you;

20 Until the LORD have given rest unto your brethren, as well as unto you, and until they also possess the land which the LORD your God has given them beyond Jordan: and then shall you return every man unto his possession, which I have given you.

CHARGE TO JOSHUA

21 And I commanded Joshua at that time, saying, Your eyes have seen all that the LORD your God has done unto these two kings: so shall the LORD do unto all the kingdoms where you passed.

22 You shall not fear them: for the LORD your God He shall fight for you. *(When the Lord fights for us, victory is guaranteed. He will do so presently, that is if our Faith has the*

correct object, which must always be the Cross [Gal. 6:14].)

THE PROMISED LAND

23 And I besought the LORD at that time, saying,

24 O LORD God, You have begun to show Your servant Your greatness, and Your mighty hand: for what God is there in Heaven or in Earth, Who can do according to Your works, and according to Your might?

25 I pray You, let me go over, and see the good land that is beyond Jordan, that goodly mountain, and Lebanon.

26 But the LORD was wroth with me for your sakes, and would not hear me: and the LORD said unto me, Let it suffice you; speak no more unto Me of this matter. *(As much as wrongly striking the Rock the second time, which, in effect, denied the veracity of Calvary, which was a grievous sin, Moses being the great Law-giver, and due to the fact that the Law can never inherit the Promises, this, I feel, was at least a part of the reason that Moses could not go in [Gal. 3:18].)*

27 Get thee up into the top of Pisgah, and lift up your eyes westward, and northward, and southward, and eastward, and behold it with your eyes: for you shall not go over this Jordan.

28 But charge Joshua, and encourage him, and strengthen him: for he shall go over before this people, and he shall cause them to inherit the land which you shall see *(the Law could "see" Salvation, but it took Faith to obtain it [Eph. 2:8-9]).*

29 So we abode in the valley over against Beth-peor.

CHAPTER 4
(1451 B.C.)
GOD'S LAW

NOW therefore hearken, O Israel, unto the Statutes and unto the Judgments, which I teach you, for to do them, that you may live, and go in and possess the land which the LORD God of your fathers gives you. *(The Law of God was divided into three parts, the Civil, the Ceremonial, and the Moral. The truth is, due to man's fallen condition, keeping the Law of God was beyond his ability. So, the Sacrificial System served as a means to atone for sin; however, every Israelite was definitely to try to keep*

the Law. The only One Who kept the Law perfectly, and in every respect, was the Lord Jesus Christ, Who did it all on our behalf [Gal. 4:4].)

2 You shall not add unto the Word which I command you, neither shall you diminish ought from it, that you may keep the Commandments of the LORD your God which I command you *(regrettably, Israel decimated this Command; by the time of Christ, they had added over 600 oral laws to the original Law of Moses, even claiming that the oral laws were more important; diminishing the Word of God, or adding to the Word of God, or ignoring it altogether is the sin of the modern Church).*

3 Your eyes have seen what the LORD did because of Baal-peor: for all the men who followed Baal-peor, the LORD your God has destroyed them from among you *(this should have been a lesson!).*

4 But you who did cleave unto the LORD your God are alive every one of you this day.

5 Behold, I have taught you Statutes and Judgments, even as the LORD my God commanded me, that you should do so in the land where you go to possess it.

6 Keep therefore and do them; for this is your wisdom and your understanding in the sight of the nations, which shall hear all these Statutes, and say, Surely this great nation is a wise and understanding people. *(The Law of God, devised totally by the Lord, placed Israel light-years ahead of all the surrounding nations, and in every capacity.)*

7 For what nation is there so great, who has God so near unto them, as the LORD our God is in all things that we call upon Him for? *(In fact, no other nation throughout the entirety of the world was so blessed as Israel. The Lord belonged to Israel exclusively.)*

8 And what nation is there so great, that has Statutes and Judgments so righteous as all this Law, which I set before you this day? *(None!)*

9 Only take heed to yourself, and keep your soul diligently, lest you forget the things which your eyes have seen, and lest they depart from your heart all the days of your life: but teach them to your sons, and your sons' sons *(this was the key to all continued blessings);*

10 Specially the day that you stood before the LORD your God in Horeb, when the LORD said unto me, Gather Me the people together, and I will make them hear My words, that they may learn to fear Me all the days that they shall live upon the Earth, and that they may teach their children.

11 And you came near and stood under the mountain; and the mountain burned with fire unto the midst of Heaven, with darkness, clouds, and thick darkness *(Moses takes Israel back, at least in their remembrance, to Mount Sinai, where the Law was originally given).*

12 And the LORD spoke unto you out of the midst of the fire: you heard the voice of the words, but saw no similitude; only you heard a voice *(they did not see the shape of God).*

13 And He declared unto you His Covenant, which He commanded you to perform, even Ten Commandments; and He wrote them upon two tables of stone. *(This was the Moral Law, and it is still in force, because Moral Law cannot change. Believers keep the Law by simply trusting Christ and what Christ did at the Cross, which gives the Holy Spirit the latitude to develop Righteousness and Holiness in one's life. The Moral Law is then kept, and kept fully, without the Believer even having to address the subject [Rom. 8:2].)*

14 And the LORD commanded me at that time to teach you Statutes and Judgments, that you might do them in the land where you go over to possess it *(it was required of every Israelite that they understand the Law).*

WARNING AGAINST IDOLATRY

15 Take ye therefore good heed unto yourselves; for you saw no manner of similitude on the day that the LORD spoke unto you in Horeb out of the midst of the fire:

16 Lest you corrupt yourselves, and make you a graven image, the similitude of any figure, the likeness of male or female *(in other words, had they seen a similitude of God, they would have fashioned an idol as to what they had seen; the implication here is that God has a Spirit Body),*

17 The likeness of any beast that is on the Earth, the likeness of any winged fowl that flies in the air *(no image is to be made of anything of this nature),*

18 The likeness of any thing that creeps on the ground, the likeness of any fish that is in the waters beneath the Earth:

19 And lest you lift up your eyes unto Heaven, and when you see the sun, and the moon, and the stars, even all the host of Heaven, should be driven to worship them, and serve them, which the LORD your God has divided unto all nations under the whole

Heaven *(most of the nations of the world worshipped these things mentioned here by the Lord)*.

20 But the LORD has taken you, and brought you forth out of the iron furnace, even out of Egypt, to be unto Him a people of inheritance, as you are this day.

21 Furthermore the LORD was angry with me for your sakes, and swore that I should not go over Jordan, and that I should not go in unto that good land, which the LORD your God gives you for an inheritance:

22 But I must die in this land, I must not go over Jordan: but you shall go over, and possess that good land *(how these words must have hurt Moses)*.

A WARNING

23 Take heed unto yourselves, lest you forget the Covenant of the LORD your God, which He made with you, and make you a graven image, or the likeness of any thing, which the LORD your God has forbidden you.

24 For the LORD your God is a consuming fire, even a jealous God *(He is jealous over His People, because He loves us, and will not endure any rivalry in our affection and devotion)*.

25 When you shall beget children, and children's children, and you shall have remained long in the land, and shall corrupt yourselves, and make a graven image, or the likeness of any thing, and shall do evil in the sight of the LORD your God, to provoke Him to anger *(while those in the modern Church do not make graven images of sorts, still, idolatry, sadly, is alive and well; anything that we place before Christ and Him Crucified becomes an idol; to be sure, such provokes the Lord to anger)*:

26 I call Heaven and Earth to witness against you this day, that you shall soon utterly perish from off the land whereunto you go over Jordan to possess it; you shall not prolong your days upon it, but shall utterly be destroyed *(the warning is clear!)*.

27 And the LORD shall scatter you among the nations *(and that's exactly what happened)*, and you shall be left few in number among the heathen, whither the LORD shall lead you *(whatever nation that the Israelites found themselves in, they would always be in the minority, and treated accordingly)*.

28 And there you shall serve gods, the work of men's hands, wood and stone, which neither see, nor hear, nor eat, nor smell.

29 But if from thence you shall seek the LORD your God, you shall find Him, if you seek Him with all your heart and with all your soul. *(What a beautiful Promise! If honesty and sincerity find lodging in the heart of any person, irrespective as to what they have done, if the Lord is sought, He will be found.)*

30 When you are in tribulation, and all these things are come upon you, even in the latter days *(actually refers to the coming Great Tribulation [Mat. 24:21])*, if you turn to the LORD your God, and shall be obedient unto His Voice;

31 (For the LORD your God is a merciful God;) He will not forsake you, neither destroy you, nor forget the Covenant of your fathers which He swore unto them *(ultimately, the Lord will bring the Jews back to their rightful place, with every Promise being kept, which will take place at the Second Coming [Zech. 13:6])*.

ISRAEL CHOSEN BY GOD

32 For ask now of the days that are past, which were before you, since the day that God created man upon the Earth, and ask from the one side of Heaven unto the other, whether there has been any such thing as this great thing is, or has been heard like it? *(The Lord delivered Israel out of Egyptian bondage and, as well, was with Israel through the entirety of the past forty years, performing miracles on a daily basis; no, there had never been anything like it.)*

33 Did ever people hear the voice of God speaking out of the midst of the fire, as you have heard, and live?

34 Or has God assayed to go and take him a nation from the midst of another nation, by temptations, by signs, and by wonders, and by war, and by a mighty hand, and by a stretched out arm, and by great terrors, according to all that the LORD your God did for you in Egypt before your eyes?

35 Unto you it was shown, that you might know that the LORD He is God; there is none else beside Him *(there is no other God)*.

36 Out of Heaven He made you to hear His Voice, that He might instruct you: and upon Earth He showed you His great fire; and you heard His words out of the midst of the fire.

37 And because He loved your fathers *(Abraham, Isaac, Jacob, etc.)*, therefore he chose their seed after them, and brought you out in His sight with His mighty power out of Egypt;

38 To drive out nations from before you

greater and mightier than you are, to bring you in, to give you their land for an inheritance, as it is this day.

39 Know therefore this day, and consider it in your heart, that the LORD He is God in Heaven above, and upon the Earth beneath: there is none else.

40 You shall keep therefore His Statutes, and His Commandments, which I command you this day, that it may go well with you, and with your children after you, and that you may prolong your days upon the Earth, which the LORD your God gives you, for ever. *(The Expositors say, "The sum of this whole exhortation is, first of all, to acknowledge and lay to heart that God is the alone God of the universe, in Heaven and on Earth; hence, as well, to be obedient to His Laws; and so, to have, as a recompense, a happy continuance in the beloved land.")*

CITIES OF REFUGE

41 Then Moses severed three cities on this side Jordan toward the sunrising *(as cities of refuge)*;

42 That the slayer might flee thither, which should kill his neighbour unawares, and hated him not in times past; and that fleeing unto one of these cities he might live *(not for murderers, but for those who would kill accidentally)*:

43 Namely, Bezer in the wilderness, in the plain country, of the Reubenites; and Ramoth in Gilead, of the Gadites; and Golan in Bashan, of the Manassites.

THE MOSAIC LAW

44 And this is the Law which Moses set before the Children of Israel:

45 These are the Testimonies, and the Statutes, and the Judgments, which Moses spoke unto the Children of Israel, after they came forth out of Egypt,

46 On this side Jordan, in the valley over against Beth-peor, in the land of Sihon king of the Amorites, who dwelt at Heshbon, whom Moses and the Children of Israel smote, after they were come forth out of Egypt:

47 And they possessed his land, and the land of Og king of Bashan, two kings of the Amorites, which were on this side Jordan toward the sunrising;

48 From Aroer, which is by the bank of the river Arnon, even unto Mount Sion, which is Hermon,

49 And all the plain on this side Jordan eastward, even unto the sea of the plain, under the springs of Pisgah.

CHAPTER 5
(1451 B.C.)
ISRAEL AND GOD'S COVENANT

AND Moses called all Israel, and said unto them, Hear O Israel, the Statutes and Judgments which I speak in your ears this day, that you may learn them, and keep, and do them *(the necessity of all of Israel learning the Law; likewise, modern Believers must learn the Bible, and do so for themselves)*.

2 The LORD our God made a Covenant with us in Horeb.

3 The LORD made not this Covenant with our fathers, but with us, even us, who are all of us here alive this day *(the Covenant made at Sinai, with Israel as a people)*.

4 The LORD talked with you face to face in the Mount of the midst of the fire,

5 (I stood between the LORD and you at that time, to show you the Word of the LORD: for you were afraid by reason of the fire, and went not up into the Mount;) saying,

THE TEN COMMANDMENTS

6 I am the LORD your God, which brought you out of the land of Egypt, from the house of bondage.

7 You shall have none other gods before Me. *(Expositors say, "In this, the First Commandment, the great principle and basis of all true spirituality is asserted — monotheism [one God], as opposed to polytheism [many gods]. There is but one God, and that God is Jehovah, the self-existent and eternal, Who yet has personal relations with men.")*

8 You shall not make you any graven image, or any likeness of any thing that is in Heaven above, or that is in the Earth beneath, or that is in the waters beneath the Earth:

9 You shall not bow down yourself unto them, nor serve them: for I the LORD your God am a jealous God, visiting the iniquity of the fathers upon the children unto the third and fourth generation of them who hate Me *(this Passage is often used to buttress the false doctrine of the family curse, so-called; it is true that there is a curse upon succeeding generations, but only those who hate the Lord; the Salvation of one person in such a family breaks*

such a curse, not only for the person, but greatly ameliorates the effect on the unsaved members of the family also [II Cor. 5:17]),

10 And showing mercy unto thousands of them who love Me and keep My Commandments (this Commandment no doubt accounts for the fact that Israel alone of the civilized nations of antiquity has left no monuments of art for the instruction or admiration of posterity).

11 You shall not take the Name of the LORD your God in vain: for the LORD will not hold him guiltless that takes His Name in vain (this Commandment addresses all profanity, and false swearing by the Name of God and, as well, all irreverent use of the Name [Lev. 19:12]).

12 Keep the Sabbath day to sanctify it, as the LORD your God has commanded you.

13 Six days you shall labor, and do all your work:

14 But the seventh day is the Sabbath of the LORD your God: in it you shall not do any work, you, nor your son, nor your daughter, nor your manservant, nor your maidservant, nor your ox, nor your ass, nor any of your cattle, nor your stranger that is within your gates; that your manservant and your maidservant may rest as well as you.

15 And remember that you were a servant in the land of Egypt, and that the LORD your God brought you out thence through a mighty hand and by a stretched out arm: therefore the LORD your God commanded you to keep the Sabbath day. (Williams says, "The observance of the Sabbath, which in Exodus 20 is urged because of God's creation rest, is commanded here in the interest of slaves as well. This shows God's tender pity for the defenseless. Israel is enjoined here to remember that she herself was a slave in the land of Egypt." Presently, all who accept Christ, Who in effect is the Sabbath, in essence keep the Sabbath. The Sabbath in its entirety speaks of "rest," which is a type of the rest which is found only in Christ [Mat. 11:28-30].)

16 Honour your father and your mother, as the LORD your God has commanded you; that your days may be prolonged, and that it may go well with you, in the land which the LORD your God gives you. (Pulpit says, "Where parents are not honored, a flaw lies at the basis, and the stability of the entire social fabric is endangered; as well, those who will not honor their parents will not honor God.")

17 You shall not kill (shall not murder).

18 Neither shall you commit adultery (extends to all forms of immorality).

19 Neither shall you steal (the property of another must not be taken by fraud or outright theft).

20 Neither shall you bear false witness against your neighbour (speaks of gossip, outright lying, and slander of every nature).

21 Neither shall you desire your neighbour's wife, neither shall you covet your neighbour's house, his field, or his manservant, or his maidservant, his ox, or his ass, or any thing that is your neighbour's (covetousness means that a person must not even desire, at least in a fraudulent manner, that which belongs to another).

GOD'S PRESENCE

22 These words the LORD spoke unto all your assembly in the mount out of the midst of the fire, of the cloud, and of the thick darkness, with a great voice: and He added no more. And He wrote them in two tables of stone, and delivered them unto me (the Lord spoke the Ten Commandments audibly to Israel, and then wrote them on two tables of stone, and gave them to Moses).

23 And it came to pass, when you heard the voice out of the midst of the darkness, (for the mountain did burn with fire,) that you came near unto Me, even all the heads of your Tribes, and your Elders;

24 And you said, Behold, the LORD our God has showed us His glory and His greatness, and we have heard His voice out of the midst of the fire: we have seen this day that God does talk with man, and he lives (they did not die upon hearing the Voice of God).

25 Now therefore why should we die? for this great fire will consume us: if we hear the voice of the LORD our God any more, then we shall die (they were afraid if God continued to talk with them with an audible voice, that ultimately they would die as a result).

26 For who is there of all flesh, who has heard the voice of the Living God speaking out of the midst of the fire, as we have, and lived?

27 Go thou near, and hear all that the LORD our God shall say: and speak thou unto us all that the LORD our God shall speak unto you; and we will hear it, and do it (they asked that the Lord speak solely with Moses, and He could convey the message to them).

28 And the LORD heard the voice of your words, when you spoke unto me; and the LORD said unto me, I have heard the voice of the words of this people, which they have spoken

unto you: they have well said all that they have spoken *(the Lord approved of what Israel had requested, because they expressed a proper reverence and a due sense on their part of the unworthiness of sinful men to come into the presence of the Great and Holy God).*

29 O that there were such an heart in them, that they would fear Me, and keep all My Commandments always, that it might be well with them, and with their children for ever! *(God looks upon the heart, and will accept no service or worship that is not rendered from the heart.)*

30 Go say to them, Get you into your tents again *(this was at the time of the giving of the Law at Mount Sinai).*

31 But as for you *(Moses)*, you stand here by Me, and I will speak unto you all the Commandments, and the Statutes, and the Judgments, which you shall teach them, that they may do them in the land which I give them to possess it.

32 You shall observe to do therefore as the LORD your God has commanded you: you shall not turn aside to the right hand or to the left.

33 You shall walk in all the ways which the LORD your God has commanded you, that you may live, and that it may be well with you, and that you may prolong your days in the land which you shall possess. *(All of this is of extreme significance, in that these people were raised up for the purpose of serving, one might say, as the womb of the Messiah, and to whom the Word of God would be given; consequently, all of this pertains to our Salvation. When we read these Old Testament accounts, we should understand that each happening brings us a few steps closer to the Redemption we now possess in Christ. Understanding it in that fashion makes it much more important — actually, the single most important thing in the world.)*

CHAPTER 6
(1451 B.C.)
THE GREAT COMMANDMENT

NOW these are the Commandments, the Statutes, and the Judgments, which the LORD your God commanded to teach you, that you might do them in the land where you go to possess it *(the prosperity of Israel, and the Blessings of the Lord upon the "land," and in every capacity, had to do with Israel understanding and obeying the Law; it is the same with us presently as it regards obeying the Word of God):*

2 That you might fear the LORD your God, to keep all his Statutes and his Commandments, which I command you, you, and your son, and your son's son, all the days of your life; and that your days may be prolonged *(the "fear" mentioned here is not a slavish fear, but rather a fear of the Lord in respect to disobeying Him, and of that to which such disobedience would lead).*

3 Hear therefore, O Israel, and observe to do it; that it may be well with you, and that you may increase mightily, as the LORD God of your fathers has promised you, in the land that flows with milk and honey *(to do the best they could to obey the Law; the Lord promised that it would go well with them, and that they would be greatly blessed; the word "blessing" actually refers to "increase"; so Israel's increase depended upon her obedience to the Lord).*

4 Hear, O Israel: the LORD our God is one LORD *(there are two Hebrew words for the English word "one"; the first means a single or only one; the second, a compound unity; it is the second that is used in this Verse; so this Verse implies the Trinity):*

5 And you shall love the LORD your God with all your heart, and with all your soul, and with all your might *(Jesus quoted this Verse in Matthew 22:37).*

DUTIES OF PARENTS

6 And these words, which I command you this day, shall be in your heart *(Alexander says, "Where true love to God exists in the heart, it will manifest itself in a regard to His Will, and in the diligent keeping of His Commandments"; the Believer can keep the Commandments of the Lord only by understanding that Christ is the Source, while the Cross is the Means; when our Faith is anchored exclusively in Christ and His Cross, the Holy Spirit will keep the Commandments through us):*

7 And you shall teach them diligently unto your children, and shall talk of them when you sit in your house, and when you walk by the way, and when you lie down, and when you rise up *(the Word of God must be the criteria for all things; the command given then has not changed, it is the same presently).*

8 And you shall bind them for a sign upon your hand, and they shall be as frontlets between your eyes *(the Israelites took this literally, and made phylacteries, putting them on their foreheads and their wrists; it was a small*

boxlike affair, containing a thin piece of leather on which were inscribed one or more Passages of Scripture; unfortunately, the Jews made a ritual of such, doing it more for show than anything else [Mat. 23:5]).

9 And you shall write them upon the posts of your house, and on your gates *(the Word of God was to ever be before Israel, and in every capacity).*

DISOBEDIENCE

10 And it shall be, when the LORD your God shall have brought you into the land which He swore unto your fathers, to Abraham, to Isaac, and to Jacob, to give you great and goodly cities, which you built not,

11 And houses full of all good things, which you filled not, and wells digged, which you dug not, vineyards and olive trees, which you planted not; when you shall have eaten and be full;

12 Then beware lest you forget the LORD, which brought you forth out of the land of Egypt, from the house of bondage *(prosperity often occasions forgetfulness of God).*

13 You shall fear the LORD your God, and serve Him, and shall swear by His Name *(refers to worship).*

14 You shall not go after other gods, of the gods of the people which are round about you *(the command still holds for modern Believers [II Cor. 6:14-18]);*

15 (For the LORD your God is a jealous God among you) lest the anger of the LORD your God be kindled against you, and destroy you from off the face of the Earth *(God cannot abide sin in His Own, any more than in the world; in fact, He can abide it, much less in His Own; He is "jealous" of anything in the life of any Believer which is not wholly according to the Word of God).*

16 You shall not tempt the LORD your God, as you tempted Him in Massah *(the Lord quoted this Verse to Satan in the temptation in the Wilderness).*

17 You shall diligently keep the Commandments of the LORD your God, and His Testimonies, and his Statutes, which He has commanded you *(Jesus said the same thing in John 14:15; as stated, this can only be done by Christ living this life through us, which He does according to our Faith anchored in Himself and the Cross, which then gives the Holy Spirit latitude to work in our lives; then, and only then,* will the Commandments be kept [Gal. 2:20-21; Rom. 8:1-2, 11]).

18 And you shall do that which is right and good in the sight of the LORD: that it may be well with you, and that you may go in and possess the good land which the LORD swore unto your fathers,

19 To cast out all your enemies from before you, as the LORD has spoken. *(The Lord working thusly for Israel was predicated solely upon them keeping the Law. Being unable to do so, they were at least to try, and then fall back on the Sacrificial System, which pointed to the One Who was to come. Unfortunately, Israel tried to obtain Righteousness by keeping the Law, with a dependence on self instead of the Lord [Rom. 10:3-4].)*

THE CHILDREN

20 And when your son asks you in time to come, saying, What mean the Testimonies, and the Statutes, and the Judgments, which the LORD our God has commanded you?

21 Then you shall say unto your son, We were Pharaoh's bondmen in Egypt; and the LORD brought us out of Egypt with a mighty hand:

22 And the LORD showed signs and wonders, great and sore, upon Egypt, upon Pharaoh, and upon all his household, before our eyes:

23 And He brought us out from thence, that He might bring us in, to give us the land which He swore unto our fathers. *(This was to be told repeatedly and, as well, so is our conversion to be told repeatedly.)*

24 And the LORD commanded us to do all these Statutes, to fear the LORD our God, for our good always, that He might preserve us alive, as it is at this day.

25 And it shall be our Righteousness, if we observe to do all these Commandments before the LORD our God, as He has commanded us. *(As stated, Israel had to try; however, no man except Christ was fully able to keep the Law; consequently, they were to fall back on the Sacrificial System, and what it represented, namely Christ and the Cross. Righteousness has never come to anyone except by Faith, and that refers to Faith in Christ [Gen. 15:6]. Unfortunately, Israel attempted to attain to Righteousness by the simple fact of their effort to keep the Commandments, which meant that their faith was in themselves instead of the Lord. The modern Church has the same problem.)*

CHAPTER 7
(1451 B.C.)
SEPARATION

WHEN the LORD your God shall bring you into the land where you go to possess it, and has cast out many nations before you, the Hittites, and the Girgashites, and the Amorites, and the Canaanites, and the Perizzites, and the Hivites, and the Jebusites, seven nations greater and mightier than you *(the Lord could easily have destroyed these nations, exactly as He did Sodom and Gomorrah, etc., but He deemed it desirable that Israel dispel them in order that Israel might learn trust and faith; faith comes by hearing the Word; however, faith put to practice can only come about by experience; it is the same with us presently; the Holy Spirit "helps us," which means that we have a part to play ourselves; that part is Faith in Christ and the Cross [Rom. 8:26])*;

2 And when the LORD your God shall deliver them before you; you shall smite them, and utterly destroy them; you shall make no covenant with them, nor show mercy unto them *(the wickedness of these tribes had reached such a state that there was nothing left but extermination; but God made that decision, not man, even though man was the instrument in carrying it out; likewise, anything and everything in our lives which isn't Christlike must be "smitten" and "destroyed")*:

3 Neither shall you make marriages with them; your daughter you shall not give unto his son, nor his daughter shall you take unto your son.

4 For they will turn away your son from following Me, that they may serve other gods: so will the anger of the LORD be kindled against you, and destroy you suddenly. *(When we join the world, thinking to win the world, the world instead wins us. The unredeemed are brought to the Lord God's Way. Any other way has the opposite effect. God's Way is the Word being preached and anointed by the Spirit, with conviction seizing the heart of the unredeemed [Jn. 16:7-14; I Cor. 2:2.])*

5 But thus shall you deal with them; you shall destroy their altars, and break down their images, and cut down their groves, and burn their graven images with fire *(there can be no compromise with sin)*

6 For you are an holy people unto the LORD your God: the LORD your God has chosen you to be a special people unto Himself, above all people who are upon the face of the Earth *(Israel, God's chosen people!)*.

ISRAEL

7 The LORD did not set His love upon you, nor choose you because you were more in number than any people; for you were the fewest of all people *(in fact, the entirety of the line had begun with Abraham and Sarah)*:

8 But because the LORD loved you, and because He would keep the oath which He had sworn unto your fathers *(Abraham, Isaac, and Jacob)*, has the LORD brought you out with a mighty hand, and redeemed you out of the house of bondmen, from the hand of Pharaoh king of Egypt *(God loved Israel, and all He asked in return was that they love Him; it is the same presently with Believers!)*.

9 Know therefore that the LORD your God, He is God, the faithful God, which keeps covenant and mercy with them who love Him and keep His Commandments to a thousand generations *(God has never broken His Covenants, and never will break His Covenants; it is man who breaks the Covenants)*;

10 And repays them who hate Him to their face, to destroy them: He will not be slack to him who hates Him, He will repay him to his face *(Israel is warned again against disobedience; if they come to the place that they "hate" the Lord, destruction is sure; and that's exactly what happened!)*.

OBEDIENCE

11 You shall therefore keep the Commandments, and the Statutes, and the judgments, which I command you this day, to do them. *(The Law of Moses, which was really the Law of God, was hands-down the fairest legislation the world had ever known. In fact, it was the only legislation that had come strictly from God, and not at all from man. As a result, the fact of having this Law put Israel far ahead of the surrounding nations or, in fact, any nation in the world.)*

12 Wherefore it shall come to pass, if you hearken to these Judgments, and keep, and do them, that the LORD your God shall keep unto you the Covenant and the Mercy which He swore unto your fathers:

13 And He will love you, and bless you, and multiply you: He will also bless the fruit of your womb, and the fruit of your land, your

corn, and your wine, and your oil, the increase of your cattle, and the flocks of your sheep, in the land which He swore unto your fathers to give you.

14 You shall be blessed above all people: there shall not be male or female barren among you, or among your cattle.

15 And the LORD will take away from you all sickness, and will put none of the evil diseases of Egypt, which you know, upon you; but will lay them upon all them who hate you. *(However, we must remember that all of these blessings are conditional, even as blessings now are conditional. The condition is obedience.)*

16 And you shall consume all the people which the LORD your God shall deliver you; your eye shall have no pity upon them: neither shall you serve their gods; for that will be a snare unto you *(the world is a snare to many Christians presently).*

17 If you shall say in your heart, These nations are more than I, how can I dispossess them?

18 You shall not be afraid of them: but shall well remember what the LORD your God did unto Pharaoh, and unto all Egypt *(we should remember and recount the great Blessings of the Lord concerning the past, which will give us faith for the present and for the future);*

19 The great temptations which your eyes saw, and the sign, and the wonders, and the mighty hand, and the stretched out arm, whereby the LORD your God brought you out: so shall the LORD your God do unto all the people of whom you are afraid *(in other words, you don't have to be afraid; the Lord is with you!).*

20 Moreover the LORD your God will send the hornet among them, until they who are left, and hide themselves from you, be destroyed *(God has all of creation at His disposal, which He may use at any time, even something as lowly as a "hornet").*

21 You shall not be affrighted at them: for the LORD your God is among you, a mighty God and terrible *(whatever the enemy has or is, God is greater!).*

22 And the LORD your God will put out those nations before you by little and little: you may not consume them at once, lest the beasts of the field increase upon you *(likewise, Sanctification is of the same process; little by little, the works of the flesh fall by the wayside, or at least that's the way it ought to be).*

23 But the LORD your God shall deliver them unto you, and shall destroy them with a mighty destruction, until they be destroyed *(faith exercised on the part of God's people guarantees the mighty Power of God evidenced on our behalf).*

24 And He shall deliver their kings into your hand, and you shall destroy their name from under Heaven: there shall no man be able to stand before you, until you have destroyed them *(but, once again, there were conditions).*

25 The graven images of their gods shall you burn with fire: you shall not desire the silver or gold that is on them, nor take it unto you, lest you be snared therein: for it is an abomination to the LORD your God *(unfortunately, idolatry is still alive and well, and comes in many forms; in fact, religion is the worst idolatry of all!).*

26 Neither shall you bring an abomination into your house, lest you be a cursed thing like it: but you shall utterly detest it, and you shall utterly abhor it; for it is a cursed thing *(idols or parts of idols; all such were cursed by God, which means they were devoted to destruction).*

CHAPTER 8
(1451 B.C.)
MERCY

ALL the Commandments which I command you this day shall you observe to do, that you may live, and multiply, and go in and possess the land which the LORD swore unto your fathers.

2 And you shall remember all the way which the LORD your God led you these forty years in the wilderness, to humble you, and to prove you, to know what was in your heart, whether you would keep His Commandments, or no. *(With the Believer, everything is a test. How will we act? How will we react?)*

3 And He humbled you, and suffered you to hunger, and fed you with Manna, which you knew not, neither did your fathers know; that He might make you know that man does not live by bread only, but by every word that proceeds out of the mouth of the LORD does man live. *(These very words were uttered by Christ to Satan regarding the temptation in the wilderness [Mat. 4:4]. Every "Word" in the Bible is important. We must as well understand that the Bible is the Word of God, which means that it doesn't merely contain the Word of God.)*

4 Your raiment waxed not old upon you, neither did your foot swell, these forty years

(this means that God supernaturally caused their clothing to last for forty years, as well as their shoes; what a miracle!).

5 You shall also consider in your heart, that, as a man chastens his son, so the LORD your God chastens you *(in fact, if the Lord doesn't chasten us, this means we aren't His Child [Heb. 12:8]).*

6 Therefore you shall keep the Commandments of the LORD your God, to walk in His ways, and to fear Him *(we are to walk in His Ways, and not our ways).*

CANAAN

7 For the LORD your God brings you into a good land, a land of brooks of water, of fountains and depths that spring out of valleys and hills;

8 A land of wheat, and barley, and vines, and fig trees, and pomegranates; a land of oil olive, and honey;

9 A land wherein you shall eat bread without scarceness, you shall not lack any thing in it; a land whose stones are iron, and out of whose hills you may dig brass *(copper).*

WARNINGS

10 When you have eaten and are full, then you shall bless the LORD your God for the good land which He has given you.

11 Beware that you forget not the LORD your God, in not keeping His Commandments, and His Judgments, and His Statutes, which I command you this day:

12 Lest when you have eaten and are full, and have built goodly houses, and dwelt therein;

13 And when your herds and your flocks multiply, and your silver and your gold is multiplied, and all that you have is multiplied;

14 Then your heart be lifted up, and you forget the LORD your God, which brought you forth out of the land of Egypt, from the house of bondage;

15 Who led you through that great and terrible wilderness, wherein were fiery serpents, and scorpions, and drought, where there was no water; Who brought you forth water out of the Rock of flint;

16 Who fed you in the wilderness with Manna, which your fathers knew not, that He might humble you, and that He might prove you, to do you good at your latter end;

17 And you say in your heart, My power and the might of my hand have gotten me this wealth.

18 But you shall remember the LORD your God: for it is He Who gives you power to get wealth, that He may establish His covenant which He swore unto your fathers, as it is this day. *(Williams says, "They were to be watchful lest prosperity caused them to forget the Redeemer Who delivered them from the bondage of Egypt; and they were to guard against thinking that their prosperity was due to their own intelligence and power.")*

19 And it shall be, if you do at all forget the LORD your God, and walk after other gods, and serve them, and worship them, I testify against you this day that you shall surely perish.

20 As the nations which the LORD destroyed before your face, so shall you perish; because you would not be obedient unto the voice of the LORD your God. *(In effect, and clearly so, the Lord is saying, as He destroyed the heathen nations and gave their land to the Children of Israel, if Israel turned her back upon Him, He would destroy them as well; and that's exactly what happened!)*

CHAPTER 9
(1451 B.C.)
THE LAND PROMISED TO ISRAEL

HEAR, O Israel: You are to pass over Jordan this day, to go in to possess nations greater and mightier than yourself, cities great and fenced up to Heaven,

2 A people great and tall, the children of the Anakims, whom you know, and of whom you have heard say, Who can stand before the children of Anak! *(Without the Lord, there was no way that Israel could have taken the land of Canaan. But with the Lord, they could do all things.)*

3 Understand therefore this day, that the LORD your God is He which goes over before you; as a consuming fire He shall destroy them, and He shall bring them down before your face: so shall you drive them out, and destroy them quickly, as the LORD has said unto you.

4 Speak not thou in your heart, after that the LORD your God has cast them out from before you, saying, For my righteousness the LORD has brought me in to possess this land: but for the wickedness of these nations the LORD does drive them out from before you *(it wasn't because Israel was so good that these*

nations were driven out, but simply because the pagans were so wicked).

5 Not for your righteousness, or for the uprightness of your heart, do you go to possess their land: but for the wickedness of these nations the LORD your God does drive them out from before you, and that He may perform the word which the LORD swore unto your fathers, Abraham, Isaac, and Jacob *(Gen. 15:16).*

ISRAEL'S FAILURE AND REBELLION

6 Understand therefore, that the LORD your God gives you not this good land to possess it for your righteousness; for you are a stiffnecked people.

7 Remember, and forget not, how you provoked the LORD your God to wrath in the wilderness: from the day that you did depart out of the land of Egypt, until you came unto this place, you have been rebellious against the LORD. *(Many blessings are promised here, but promised not at all because of the righteousness of Israel. The truth was, they were stiffnecked and rebellious. But God loved them just the same, and sought, again and again, to bless them.)*

8 Also in Horeb you provoked the LORD to wrath, so that the LORD was angry with you to have destroyed you *(Ex. 32:9-10).*

9 When I was gone up into the Mount to receive the tables of stone, even the tables of the Covenant which the LORD made with you, then I abode in the Mount forty days and forty nights, I neither did eat bread nor drink water.

10 And the LORD delivered unto me two tables of stone written with the Finger of God; and on them was written according to all the words, which the LORD spoke with you in the Mount out of the midst of the fire in the day of the assembly *(the Ten Commandments [Ex., Chpt. 20]).*

11 And it came to pass at the end of forty days and forty nights, that the LORD gave me the two tables of stone, even the tables of the Covenant.

12 And the LORD said unto me, Arise, get thee down quickly from hence; for your people which you have brought forth out of Egypt have corrupted themselves; they are quickly turned aside out of the way which I commanded them; they have made them a molten image *(the golden calf [Ex., Chpt. 32]).*

13 Furthermore the LORD spoke unto me, saying, I have seen this people, and, behold, it is a stiffnecked people:

14 Let Me alone, that I may destroy them, and blot out their name from under Heaven: and I will make of you a nation mightier and greater than they.

15 So I turned and came down from the Mount, and the Mount burned with fire: and the two tables of the Covenant were in my two hands.

16 And I looked, and, behold, you had sinned against the LORD your God, and had made you a molten calf: you had turned aside quickly out of the way which the LORD had commanded you.

17 And I took the two tables, and cast them out of my two hands, and broke them before your eyes *(there is no record that the Lord reprimanded Moses for this act).*

18 And I fell down before the LORD, as at the first, forty days and forty nights: I did neither eat bread, nor drink water, because of all your sins which you sinned, in doing wickedly in the sight of the LORD, to provoke Him to anger.

19 For I was afraid of the anger and hot displeasure, wherewith the LORD was angry against you to destroy you. But the LORD hearkened unto me at that time also *(Moses pleaded for the Lord to spare Israel [Ex. 32:31-35]).*

20 And the LORD was very angry with Aaron to have destroyed him: and I prayed for Aaron also the same time *(the evidence here is that the Lord would have killed Aaron had not Moses interceded for him).*

21 And I took your sin, the calf which you had made, and burnt it with fire, and stamped it, and ground it very small, even until it was small as dust: and I cast the dust thereof into the brook that descends out of the Mount.

22 And at Taberah, and at Massah, and at Kibroth-hattaavah, you provoked the LORD to wrath *(Num. 11:1-3).*

23 Likewise when the LORD sent you from Kadesh-barnea, saying, Go up and possess the land which I have given you; then you rebelled against the Commandment of the LORD your God, and you believed Him not, nor hearkened to His voice *(Num. 13:17-33; 14:1-45]).*

24 You have been rebellious against the LORD from the day that I knew you.

INTERCESSION

25 Thus I fell down before the LORD forty days and forty nights, as I fell down at the

first; because the LORD had said he would destroy you.

26 I prayed therefore unto the LORD, and said, O LORD God, destroy not Your people and Your inheritance, which You have redeemed through Your greatness, which You have brought forth out of Egypt with a mighty hand.

27 Remember Your servants, Abraham, Isaac, and Jacob; look not unto the stubbornness of this people, nor to their wickedness, nor to their sin (*Moses served as a mediator between God and Israel*):

28 Lest the land whence you brought us out say, Because the LORD was not able to bring them into the land which He promised them, and because He hated them, He has brought them out to slay them in the wilderness.

29 Yet they are Your people and Your inheritance, which You brought out by Your mighty power and by Your stretched out arm.

CHAPTER 10
(1491 B.C.)
THE TABLES OF STONE

AT that time the LORD said unto me, Hew thee two tables of stone like unto the first, and come up unto Me into the Mount, and make thee an Ark of wood (*the Ark of the Covenant*).

2 And I will write on the tables the words that were in the first tables which you broke, and you shall put them in the Ark.

3 And I made an Ark of shittim wood, and hewed two tables of stone like unto the first, and went up into the Mount, having the two tables in my hand.

4 And He wrote on the tables, according to the first writing, the Ten Commandments, which the LORD spoke unto you in the Mount out of the midst of the fire in the day of the Assembly: and the LORD gave them unto me. (*The Ten Commandments, when investigated thoroughly, are found to be the foundation of all sensible law in the world and, in fact, ever have been. When a nation strays from its concepts, sooner or later, that nation begins to pay the price.*)

5 And I turned myself and came down from the Mount, and put the tables in the Ark which I had made: and there they be, as the LORD commanded me.

6 And the Children of Israel took their journey from Beeroth of the children of Jaakan to Mosera: there Aaron died, and there he was buried: and Eleazar his son ministered in the Priest's office in his stead (*the office of the High Priest*).

7 From thence they journeyed unto Gudgodah: and from Gudgodah to Jotbath, a land of rivers of waters.

8 At that time the LORD separated the Tribe of Levi, to bear the Ark of the Covenant of the LORD, to stand before the LORD to minister unto Him, and to bless in His name, unto this day (*the appointment of the Tribe of Levi for service took place in connection with that of Aaron and his sons to the Priesthood [Num. 3:4]*).

9 Wherefore Levi has no part nor inheritance with his brethren: the LORD is his inheritance, according as the LORD your God promised him.

10 And I stayed in the Mount, according to the first time, forty days and forty nights; and the LORD hearkened unto me at that time also, and the LORD would not destroy you.

11 And the LORD said unto me, Arise, take your journey before the people, that they may go in and possess the land, which I swore unto their fathers to give unto them.

THE EXHORTATION

12 And now, Israel, what does the LORD your God require of you, but to fear the LORD your God, to walk in all His ways, and to love Him, and to serve the LORD your God with all your heart and with all your soul,

13 To keep the Commandments of the LORD, and His Statutes, which I command you this day for your good? (*God had shown great favor to Israel. What return did He require? Only that they would fear Him, love Him, and obey Him.*)

14 Behold, the Heaven and the Heaven of Heavens is the LORD's your God, the Earth also, with all that therein is (*the Lord is the Creator of all things*).

15 Only the LORD had a delight in your fathers to love them, and He chose their seed after them, even you above all people, as it is this day (*meaning that Israel was honored more than any other people on the face of the Earth*).

16 Circumcise therefore the foreskin of your heart, and be no more stiffnecked (*they were to humble their heart before God*).

17 For the LORD your God is God of gods, and LORD of lords, a great God, a mighty, and a terrible, which regards not persons, nor takes

reward *(the Lord is the complex and sum of all that is Divine)*:

18 He does execute the judgment of the fatherless and widow, and loves the stranger, in giving him food and raiment *(the Lord vindicates the right of the defenseless, if they will only look to Him [Ps. 68:6; 146:9])*.

19 Love ye therefore the stranger: for you were strangers in the land of Egypt *(Israel knew what it was to be a stranger in a strange land; so they were to reciprocate with strangers, and even at the command of the Lord)*.

20 You shall fear the LORD your God; Him shall you serve, and to Him shall you cleave, and swear by His Name *(the last phrase refers to praising the Lord)*.

21 He is your praise, and He is your God, Who has done for you these great and terrible things, which your eyes have seen.

22 Your fathers went down into Egypt with threescore and ten persons *(70 people)*; and now the LORD your God has made you as the stars of Heaven for multitude *(Gen. 15:5)*.

CHAPTER 11
(1491 B.C.)
GREATNESS OF THE LORD

THEREFORE you shall love the LORD your God, and keep His charge, and His Statutes, and His Judgments, and His Commandments, always.

2 And know ye this day: for I speak not with your children which have not known, and which have not seen the chastisement of the LORD your God, His greatness, His mighty hand, and His stretched out arm,

3 And His miracles, and His acts, which He did in the midst of Egypt unto Pharaoh the king of Egypt, and unto all His land;

4 And what He did unto the army of Egypt, unto their horses, and to their chariots; how He made the water of the Red Sea to overflow them as they pursued after you, and how the LORD has destroyed them unto this day *(the Red Sea opening, and the defeat of the Egyptian army, which was in hot pursuit after Israel, with the water closing over them, was one of the greatest miracles the world has ever known; forty years later, the Holy Spirit through Moses declares that Egypt still had not yet recovered)*;

5 And what He did unto you in the wilderness, until you came into this place;

6 And what He did unto Dathan and Abiram, the sons of Eliab, the son of Reuben: how the Earth opened her mouth, and swallowed them up, and their households, and their tents, and all the substance that was in their possession, in the midst of all Israel:

7 But your eyes have seen all the great acts of the LORD which He did *(so they knew the Power of God, and had witnessed it firsthand)*.

8 Therefore shall you keep all the Commandments which I command you this day, that you may be strong, and go in and possess the land, where you go to possess it;

9 And that you may prolong your days in the land, which the LORD swore unto your fathers to give unto them and to their seed, a land that flows with milk and honey.

DESCRIPTION

10 For the land, where you go in to possess it, is not as the land of Egypt, from whence you came out, where you sowed your seed, and watered it with your foot, as a garden of herbs *(countries in those days, and in that part of the world, irrigated their crops by pumping an apparatus with the foot, which pumped the water; to say the least, it was a difficult task)*:

11 But the land, where you go to possess it, is a land of hills and valleys, and drinks water of the rain of Heaven:

12 A land which the LORD your God cares for: the eyes of the LORD your God are always upon it, from the beginning of the year even unto the end of the year *(a land on which Jehovah's regard was continually fixed, over which He watched with unceasing care, and which was sustained by His bounty; a land, therefore, wholly dependent on Him, and so a fitting place for a people also wholly dependent on Him, who owed to His Grace all that they were and had)*.

CONDITIONS

13 And it shall come to pass, if you shall hearken diligently unto My Commandments which I command you this day, to love the LORD your God, and to serve Him with all your heart and with all your soul.

14 That I will give you the rain of your land in his due season, the first rain and the latter rain, that you may gather in your corn, and your wine, and your oil.

15 And I will send grass in your fields for your cattle, that you may eat and be full *(the Lord was the Author of all Blessings, as He is*

still the Author of all Blessings).

16 Take heed to yourselves, that your heart be not deceived, and you turn aside, and serve other gods, and worship them *(regrettably, this is exactly what Israel ultimately did);*

17 And the Lord's wrath be kindled against you, and He shut up the Heaven, that there be no rain, and that the land yield not her fruit; and lest you perish quickly from off the good land which the LORD gives you *(as is overly obvious, the Lord could turn it on, and He could turn it off; the blessing depended on obedience).*

18 Therefore shall you lay up these My words in your heart and in your soul, and bind them for a sign upon your hand, that they may be as frontlets between your eyes *(phylacteries).*

19 And you shall teach them your children, speaking of them when you sit in your house, and when you walk by the way, when you lie down, and when you rise up *(the Word of the Lord was to be on the lips of all of God's people all of the time; it should be the same presently as well).*

20 And you shall write them upon the door posts of your house, and upon your gates *(this signified that their blessings were due to the Word of God):*

21 That your days may be multiplied, and the days of your children, in the land which the LORD swore unto your fathers to give them, as the days of Heaven upon the Earth *(the world has tried repeatedly to duplicate this, but all to no avail; only the Lord can make it "Heaven on Earth").*

22 For if you shall diligently keep all these Commandments which I command you, to do them, to love the LORD your God, to walk in all His ways, and to cleave unto Him:

23 Then will the LORD drive out all these nations from before you, and you shall possess greater nations and mightier than yourselves *(all because of the help of the Lord).*

24 Every place whereon the soles of your feet shall tread shall be yours *(respecting the area of which the Lord had promised them):* from the wilderness and Lebanon, from the river, the river Euphrates, even unto the uttermost sea *(the Mediterranean)* shall your coast be.

25 There shall no man be able to stand before you: for the LORD your God shall lay the fear of you and the dread of you upon all the land that you shall tread upon, as He has said unto you.

A BLESSING AND A CURSE

26 Behold, I set before you this day a Blessing and a curse *(Jesus took the penalty of the curse upon Himself, all on our behalf [Gal. 3:13]);*

27 A blessing, if you obey the Commandments of the LORD your God, which I command you this day:

28 And a curse, if you will not obey the Commandments of the LORD your God, but turn aside out of the way which I command you this day, to go after other gods, which you have not known *(regrettably, this is exactly what Israel did; but, as stated, Jesus, on the Cross, took the penalty of the broken law upon Himself, at least for all who will believe [Jn. 3:16]).*

29 And it shall come to pass, when the LORD your God has brought you in unto the land whither you go to possess it, that you shall put the blessing upon Mount Gerizim *(called the Mount of Blessing),* and the curse upon Mount Ebal *(called the Mount of evil. The two mountains named stand opposite to each other, with a valley between, about two hundred yards broad at the widest part, in which stood the town of Shechem. They were selected for the purpose mentioned, doubtless, because of their relative position, and probably also because they stand in the center of the land, both from north to south, and from east to west. Incidentally, Gerizim, the Mount of Blessing, was, and is, fertile and smooth. Ebal is the opposite, barren and rugged. As stated, they make excellent object lessons, which the Lord intended).*

30 Are they not on the other side Jordan, by the way where the sun goes down, in the land of the Canaanites, which dwell in the champaign over against Gilgal, beside the plains of Moreh?

31 For you shall pass over Jordan to go in to possess the land which the LORD your God gives you, and you shall possess it, and dwell therein.

32 And you shall observe to do all the Statutes and Judgments which I set before you this day.

CHAPTER 12
(1451 B.C.)
DESTROY IDOL WORSHIP

THESE are the Statutes and Judgments, which you shall observe to do in the land, which the LORD God of your fathers gives you

to possess it, all the days that you live upon the Earth.

2 You shall utterly destroy all the places, wherein the nations which you shall possess served their gods, upon the high mountains, and upon the hills, and under every green tree *(all places of idol worship, wherever they were found, were to be totally and completely destroyed, when Israel entered the land)*:

3 And you shall overthrow their altars, and break their pillars, and burn their groves with fire; and you shall hew down the graven images of their gods, and destroy the names of them out of that place *(they were to utterly destroy everything having even a remote connection with idolatry)*.

4 You shall not do so unto the LORD your God *(Israel was not to build altars, as did the heathen, but was to have one designated place)*.

ONE PLACE OF SACRIFICE

5 But unto the place which the LORD your God shall choose out of all your Tribes to put His Name there, even unto His habitation shall you seek, and there you shall come *(the one center for national worship foreshadowed Calvary, to which, in spirit, all must go in order to meet God, and worship Him; one center for worship secured purity of doctrine and national unity)*:

6 And there you shall bring your Burnt Offerings, and your Sacrifices, and your Tithes, and Heave Offerings of your hand, and your Vows, and your freewill Offerings, and the firstlings of your herds and of your flocks:

7 And there you shall eat before the LORD your God, and you shall rejoice in all that you put your hand unto, you and your households, wherein the LORD your God has blessed you *(if it is to be noticed, the Lord, at this time, did not tell Israel as to where that place would be)*.

8 You shall not do after all the things that we do here this day, every man whatsoever is right in his own eyes.

9 For you are not as yet come to the rest and to the inheritance, which the LORD your God gives you *(upon entering Canaan, the Lord would bring about a more structured government, all based on the Law)*.

10 But when you go over Jordan, and dwell in the land which the LORD your God gives you to inherit, and when He gives you rest from all your enemies round about, so that you dwell in safety;

11 Then there shall be a place which the LORD your God shall choose to cause His Name to dwell there; there shall you bring all that I command you; your Burnt Offerings, and your Sacrifices, your Tithes, and the Heave Offering of your hand, and all your choice Vows which you vow unto the LORD:

12 And you shall rejoice before the LORD your God, you, and your sons, and your daughters, and your menservants, and your maidservants, and the Levite that is within your gates; forasmuch as he has no part nor inheritance with you *(all of this is repeatedly presented as a scene of rejoicing; even slaves were to have their share in the joy)*.

13 Take heed to yourself that you offer not your Burnt Offerings in every place that you see:

14 But in the place which the LORD shall choose in one of your Tribes, there you shall offer your Burnt Offerings, and there you shall do all that I command you *(while there were definitely set places in Israel where the Tabernacle was pitched, still, it was not until the Temple was built by Solomon that a permanent place was established, which was about 500 years from the time of Moses)*.

15 Notwithstanding you may kill and eat flesh in all your gates, whatsoever your soul does lust after, according to the blessing of the LORD your God which He has given you: the unclean and the clean may eat thereof, as of the roebuck, and as of the hart *(they could feel free to kill and eat that which they desired, but it must not be a Sacrifice)*.

16 Only you shall not eat the blood; you shall pour it upon the earth as water *(the life of the flesh is in the blood; Jesus would shed His Blood in order to obtain Salvation for Adam's fallen race; consequently, the blood is never to be eaten, and is to be handled in a certain way, as proclaimed here)*.

HOLY THINGS

17 You may not eat within your gates the tithe of your corn, or of your wine, or of your oil, or the firstlings of your herds or of your flock, nor any of your vows which you vowed, nor your freewill offerings, or Heave Offering of your hand *(these had to do with the Peace Offerings and such, or anything dedicated to the Lord)*:

18 But you must eat them before the LORD your God in the place which the LORD your God shall choose, you, and your son, and your

daughter, and your manservant, and your maid-servant, and the Levite that is within your gates: and you shall rejoice before the LORD your God in all that you put your hands unto. *(The Lord would appoint a place, which would be where the Tabernacle was located, and then, later on, the Temple, which would be situated in Jerusalem. If the Offering entailed a feast, which all Peace Offerings did, then it must be eaten at the designated place. That place was where the Altar was, typifying Calvary. This tells us that all restoration, all fellowship, all rejoicing, in fact, all things which come from the Lord, are made possible by Christ, of which the Sacrifices typified, and the means is the Cross, typified by the Altar.)*

19 Take heed to yourself that you forsake not the Levite as long as you live upon the Earth *(the "Levites" tended the things of the Lord, without which the people could not approach God; in a sense, the fivefold Ministry presently serves in that capacity [Eph. 4:11-13])*.

20 When the LORD your God shall enlarge your border, as He has promised you, and you shall say, I will eat flesh, because your soul longs to eat flesh; you may eat flesh, whatsoever your soul lusteth after *(desires)*.

21 If the place which the LORD your God has chosen to put His Name there be too far from you, then you shall kill of your herd and of your flock, which the LORD has given you *(all prosperity for the Believer is made possible solely by the Lord)*, as I have commanded you, and you shall eat in your gates whatsoever your soul lusts *(seeks)* after.

22 Even as the roebuck and the hart is eaten, so you shall eat them: the unclean and the clean shall eat of them alike *(pertains to animals not offered in Sacrifice)*.

23 Only be sure that you eat not the blood: for the blood is the life; and you may not eat the life with the flesh. *(Concerning this, Expositors say, "The Hebrew word used is 'nephesh.' By this word, the Hebrews designated the animal life-principle in men and in beasts; and as without this the body was a mere inert mass, the word came to be used for 'life' generally. Of this life the blood was believed to be the seat, and was regarded as the symbol, so that to shed blood was tantamount to the taking away of life. As the blood, moreover, was the life, in it was supposed to lie the propitiatory [satisfying] power — the power, when shed, of atoning for sin, as the giving of life for life.*

"The prohibition of eating it doubtless had

respect to this. It was not merely to prevent ferocity in men towards the lower animals that the eating of blood was interdicted, but specially because there was in this a sort of profanation, a putting to a common use of what appertained to a sacred rite.")

24 You shall not eat it; you shall pour it upon the Earth as water.

25 You shall not eat it; that it may go well with you, and with your children after you, when you shall do that which is right in the sight of the LORD.

26 Only your holy things which you have, and your vows, you shall take, and go unto the place which the LORD shall choose:

27 And you shall offer your Burnt Offerings, the flesh and the blood, upon the Altar of the LORD your God: and the blood of your sacrifices shall be poured out upon the Altar of the LORD your God, and you shall eat the flesh. *(This Scripture points to the fact as to why the blood is so sacred. The "Altar" represented the Cross, and the "blood" typified the poured out Life of the Son of God, Who would give Himself for the Redemption of humanity. Original sin passes down to man through the blood, which is the life of the flesh; consequently, the entirety of the human race is polluted and sick with sin. The only remedy, and thank God there is a remedy, is the shed Blood of Jesus Christ, Whose Blood was Perfect, because He was not born of natural procreation, but was conceived in the womb of Mary by the decree of the Holy Spirit; as well, He lived a Perfect, unsullied, unspotted Life, totally without sin. Therefore, He could go to the Cross as a Perfect Sacrifice, and when His Blood was shed, it atoned for all sin, past, present, and future, at least for all who will believe [Eph. 2:13-18].)*

28 Observe and hear all these words which I command you, that it may go well with you, and with your children after you for ever, when you do that which is good and right in the sight of the LORD your God *(the Lord required obedience)*.

29 When the LORD your God shall cut off the nations from before you, where you go to possess them, and you succeed them, and dwell in their land;

30 Take heed to yourself that you be not snared by following them, after that they be destroyed from before you; and that you enquire not after their gods, saying, How did these nations serve their gods? even so will I do likewise *(don't emulate the heathen and, as*

well, we presently are not to emulate the world).

31 You shall not do so unto the LORD your God: for every abomination to the LORD, which He hates, have they done unto their gods; for even their sons and their daughters they have burnt in the fire to their gods (human sacrifices).

32 What thing soever I command you, observe to do it: you shall not add thereto, nor diminish from it (don't add to My Word, or take from My Word).

CHAPTER 13
(1451 B.C.)
FALSE PROPHETS

IF there arise among you a prophet, or a dreamer of dreams, and gives you a sign or a wonder,

2 And the sign or the wonder come to pass, whereof he spoke unto you, saying, Let us go after other gods, which you have not known, and let us serve them (no matter the signs or the wonders, if what is being said is not Scriptural, it must not be heeded);

3 You shall not hearken unto the words of that Prophet, or that dreamer of dreams: for the LORD your God proves you, to know whether you love the LORD your God with all your heart and with all your soul. (The Lord allows false preachers and false teachers to succeed for a while, in order to test His people. To be sure, He already knows what His people will do, or won't do. The test is for our benefit.)

4 You shall walk after the LORD your God, and fear him, and keep His Commandments, and obey His voice, and you shall serve Him, and cleave unto Him (the Lord and His Word alone are to be the objects of our Faith, and not other things).

5 And that Prophet, or that dreamer of dreams shall be put to death; because he has spoken to turn you away from the LORD your God, which brought you out of the land of Egypt, and redeemed you out of the house of bondage, to thrust you out of the way which the LORD your God commanded you to walk in. So shall you put the evil away from the midst of you. (Presently, if God's people refuse to support such, the Ministry of false prophets would simply die. But unfortunately, most modern Christians so little know their Bible that they little know anymore what is right or wrong, true or false; therefore, most of the modern Church supports that which is not of God, which

means it's of the Devil, thinking all the time they are supporting the Lord's Work.)

6 If your brother, the son of your mother, or your son, or your daughter, or the wife of your bosom, or your friend, which is as your own soul, entice you secretly, saying, Let us go and serve other gods, which you have not known, you, nor your fathers;

7 Namely, of the gods of the people which are round about you, near unto you, or far off from you, from the one end of the Earth even unto the other end of the Earth;

8 You shall not consent unto him, nor hearken unto him; neither shall your eye pity him, neither shall you spare, neither shall you conceal him:

9 But you shall surely kill him; your hand shall be first upon him to put him to death, and afterwards the hand of all the people.

10 And you shall stone him with stones, that he die; because he has sought to thrust you away from the LORD your God, which brought you out of the land of Egypt, from the house of bondage.

11 And all Israel shall hear, and fear, and shall do no more any such wickedness as this is among you. (Stern measures were demanded, simply because the nation was at stake. To be sure, Satan would use the tactic of false prophets graphically so to try to turn Israel away from God. Ultimately, he would succeed. He is doing the same presently and, regrettably, succeeding admirably so! Satan is a master at making people believe that what is actually of God, isn't, and what isn't of God, is!)

IDOLATROUS CITIES

12 If you shall hear say in one of your cities, which the LORD your God has given you to dwell there, saying,

13 Certain men, the Children of Belial, are gone out from among you, and have withdrawn the inhabitants of their city, saying, Let us go and serve other gods, which you have not known;

14 Then shall you enquire, and make search, and ask diligently; and, behold, if it be truth, and the thing certain, that such abomination is wrought among you;

15 You shall surely smite the inhabitants of that city with the edge of the sword, destroying it utterly, and all that is therein, and the cattle thereof, with the edge of the sword.

16 And you shall gather all the spoil of it

into the midst of the street thereof, and shall burn with fire the city, and all the spoil thereof every whit, for the LORD your God: and it shall be an heap for ever; it shall not be built again *(everything that false doctrine touches is soiled and polluted, spiritually speaking)*.

17 And there shall cleave nought of the cursed thing to your hand: that the LORD may turn from the fierceness of His anger, and show you mercy, and have compassion upon you, and multiply you, as He has sworn unto your fathers;

18 When you shall hearken to the voice of the LORD your God, to keep all His commandments which I command you this day, to do that which is right in the eyes of the LORD your God. *(Every trace of idol worship was to be utterly destroyed; for what men do not see does not tempt them so powerfully as what they do see.)*

CHAPTER 14
(1451 B.C.)
CLEAN AND UNCLEAN FOOD

YOU are the children of the LORD your God: you shall not cut yourselves, nor make any baldness between your eyes for the dead *(the heathen did this)*.

2 For you are an holy people unto the LORD your God, and the LORD has chosen you to be a peculiar people unto Himself, above all the nations that are upon the Earth *(Israel was to receive the Word of the Lord from Jehovah and give it to the world; as well, they were to be the womb of the Messiah, hence all the restrictions — and all the restrictions were done for purpose and reason, which, if violated, would hinder Israel's very purpose)*.

3 You shall not eat any abominable thing.

4 These are the beasts which you shall eat: the ox, the sheep, and the goat,

5 The hart, and the roebuck, and the fallow deer, and the wild goat, and the pygarg *(antelope)*, and the wild ox, and the chamois *(wild sheep)*.

6 And every beast that parts the hoof, and cleaves the cleft into two claws, and chews the cud among the beasts, that you shall eat.

7 Nevertheless these you shall not eat of them that chew the cud, or of them that divide the cloven hoof; as the camel, and the hare, and the coney: for they chew the cud, but divide not the hoof; therefore they are unclean unto you.

8 And the swine *(hogs)*, because it divides the hoof, yet chews not the cud, it is unclean unto you: you shall not eat of their flesh, nor touch their dead carcase.

9 These you shall eat of all that are in the waters: all that have fins and scales shall you eat:

10 And whatsoever has not fins and scales you may not eat; it is unclean unto you.

11 Of all clean birds you shall eat.

12 But these are they of which you shall not eat: the eagle, and the ossifrage, and the ospray,

13 And the glede, and the kite, and the vulture after his kind,

14 And every raven after his kind,

15 And the owl, and the night hawk, and the cuckow, and the hawk after his kind,

16 The little owl, and the great owl, and the swan,

17 And the pelican, and the gier eagle, and the cormorant,

18 And the stork, and the heron after her kind, and the lapwing, and the bat.

19 And every creeping thing that flies is unclean unto you: they shall not be eaten.

20 But of all clean fowls you may eat.

21 You shall not eat of anything that dies of itself: you shall give it unto the stranger that is in your gates, that he may eat it; or you may sell it unto an alien *(Gentile)*: for you are an holy people unto the LORD your God. You shall not seethe a kid *(a baby lamb)* in his mother's milk *(for the reason that the "lamb" was more typical of Christ than any other of the animal kingdom [Jn. 1:29]; when Jesus went to the Cross, all of these particular rules regarding eating were concluded; this is proven in Acts, Chpt. 10, regarding the Vision given to Simon Peter)*.

TITHES

22 You shall truly tithe all the increase of your seed, that the field brings forth year by year. *(Tithing means to give a tenth. The foundation for tithing was not given in the Law, but rather some 400 years earlier with Abraham. He paid tithe to Melchizedek, who was a Type of Christ [Gen. 14:19-20; Heb. 5:6]. All of us are children of Abraham [Gal. 3:7], so that means that tithing continues, even unto this hour. Inasmuch as Abraham paid tithe to Melchizedek, who was a Type of Christ, tithing continues even under the New Covenant. We are to pay tithe to help finance the Work of God, which is the same as paying them to Christ.)*

23 And you shall eat before the LORD your God, in the place which He shall choose to place His Name there, the tithe of your corn, of your wine, and of your oil, and the firstlings of your herds and of your flocks; that you may learn to fear the LORD your God always.

24 And if the way be too long for you, so that you are not able to carry it; or if the place be too far from you, which the LORD your God shall choose to set His Name there, when the LORD your God has blessed you:

25 Then shall you turn it into money, and bind up the money in your hand, and shall go unto the place which the LORD your God shall choose *(if the Israelite lived a long distance from the Tabernacle or Temple, which means that he could not drive animals that distance, or take great amounts of wheat, etc., he was to sell the tenth, and then take the money to the Tabernacle, and purchase the animals there that were needed for sacrifice, etc.)*:

26 And you shall bestow that money for whatsoever your soul lusts after *(desires)*, for oxen, or for sheep, or for wine, or for strong drink, or for whatsoever your soul desires: and you shall eat there before the LORD your God, and you shall rejoice, you, and your household,

27 And the Levite that is within your gates; you shall not forsake him; for he has no part nor inheritance with you.

28 At the end of three years you shall bring forth all the tithe of your increase the same year, and shall lay it up within your gates:

29 And the Levite, (because he has no part nor inheritance with you,) and the stranger, and the fatherless, and the widow, which are within your gates, shall come, and shall eat and be satisfied; that the LORD your God may bless you in all the work of your hand which you do. *(The meaning of the third year is as follows: the tithe of the first and second years was to be eaten before the Lord at the Sanctuary. What was not used, and they only used a small part, the balance was given to the Sanctuary; the tithe of the third year was for the poor and needy, including the Levites.)*

CHAPTER 15
(1451 B.C.)
SABBATICAL YEAR

AT the end of every seven years you shall make a release.

2 And this is the manner of the release: Every creditor that lends ought unto his neighbour shall release it; he shall not exact it of his neighbour, or of his brother; because it is called the LORD's release. *(This didn't mean that the debt was no longer owed, but only that the debtor on the seventh year was not to be pressed for payment. As during the Sabbatical year the land lay uncultivated, and the debtor consequently would earn nothing, it was reasonable that he should not then be pressed for payment. So, every loan took this seventh year into account.)*

3 Of a foreigner you may exact it again *(meaning that this law did not apply to the foreigner)*: but that which is yours with your brother your hand shall release;

4 Save when there shall be no poor among you; for the LORD shall greatly bless you in the land which the LORD your God gives you for an inheritance to possess it *(the Lord wants to bless His people, that all poverty be erased; and if God's People will wholly follow Him, rendering obedience, it will be erased, because this is the Will of the Lord; this Fourth Verse says so!)*:

5 Only if you carefully hearken unto the Voice of the LORD your God, to observe to do all these Commandments which I command you this day.

6 For the LORD your God blesses you, as He promised you: and you shall lend unto many nations, but you shall not borrow; and you shall reign over many nations, but they shall not reign over you *(in other words, if the Lord's People would carefully hearken unto the Lord, they would be the most blessed nation on Earth; that was God's intention, but, regrettably, Israel did the very opposite)*.

RELIEF FOR THE POOR

7 If there be among you a poor man of one of your brethren within any of your gates in your land which the LORD your God gives you, you shall not harden your heart, nor shut your hand from your poor brother *(despite the Promise of great Blessing, regrettably, many simply would not hearken unto the Voice of the Lord, but would rather hearken unto their own voice, or the voice of others; in one way or the other, poverty will always be the result)*:

8 But you shall open your hand wide unto him, and shall surely lend him sufficient for his need, in that which he wants *(faith-filled Believers are to be generous)*.

9 Beware that there be not a thought in

your wicked heart, saying, The seventh year, the year of release, is at hand; and your eye be evil against your poor brother, and you give him nought; and he cry unto the LORD against you, and it be sin unto you (*in other words, don't take advantage of the seventh year to refuse to lend money to one in need, just because it's the sixth year; to conduct oneself in a greedy manner constitutes sin*).

10 You shall surely give him, and your heart shall not be grieved when you give unto him: because that for this thing the LORD your God shall bless you in all your works, and in all that you put your hand unto (*if those in Israel wanted the blessings of the Lord, they must obey the Lord, seeking diligently to carry out His Word*).

11 For the poor shall never cease out of the land (*despite the Promises of God, regrettably, some will not properly heed*): therefore I command you, saying, You shall open your hand wide unto your brother, to your poor, and to your needy, in your land. (*Israel's welfare program was the third year of tithing the produce of the entirety of the land, to be given to the poor and needy, along with the Levites. Not failing this and, as well, lending to those who were truly in need, one can readily see that the welfare program was generous.*)

RELEASE OF SERVANTS

12 And if your brother, an Hebrew man, or an Hebrew woman, be sold unto you, and serve you six years; then in the seventh year you shall let him go free from you.

13 And when you send him out free from you, you shall not let him go away empty:

14 You shall furnish him liberally out of your flock, and out of your floor, and out of your winepress: of that wherewith the LORD your God has blessed you you shall give unto him.

15 And you shall remember that you were a bondman in the land of Egypt, and the LORD your God redeemed you: therefore I command you this thing to day. (*The unchanging motive, perpetually repeated, why Israel should be compassionate to the needy and to strangers was the remembrance of their own bondage in Egypt and the Grace that delivered them from it. They were not to receive the Grace of God in vain; they were to show that Grace to others in order that no discredit should attach to their Redeemer's Name.*)

16 And it shall be, if he say unto you, I will not go away from you; because he loves you and your house, because he is well with you (*in other words, the servant doesn't want to be set free, because he is being treated right, and desires to remain where he is*);

17 Then you shall take an aul, and thrust it through his ear unto the door (*the doorframe*), and he shall be your servant for ever (*but he does so voluntarily, and proven by the mark left by the aul*). And also unto your maidservant you shall do likewise.

18 It shall not seem hard unto you, when you send him away free from you; for he has been worth a double hired servant to you, in serving you six years: and the LORD your God shall bless you in all that you do.

CONSECRATION OF THE FIRSTLINGS

19 All the firstling males that come of your herd and of your flock you shall sanctify unto the LORD your God: you shall do no work with the firstling of your bullock, nor shear the firstling of your sheep.

20 You shall eat it before the LORD your God year by year in the place which the LORD shall choose, you and your household. (*The firstborn of the flock, whatever it might be, that is, if it is healthy, must not be used for commerce of any nature. It must be taken to the Sanctuary, and offered in Sacrifice, with that which wasn't needed given to the service of the Sanctuary.*)

21 And if there be any blemish therein, as if it be lame, or blind, or have any ill blemish, you shall not sacrifice it unto the LORD your God.

22 You shall eat it within your gates: the unclean and the clean person shall eat it alike, as the roebuck, and as the hart (*it can be used as common food*).

23 Only you shall not eat the blood thereof; you shall pour it upon the ground as water (*this law was given concerning the firstborn of animals as a portrayal of Christ, Who would be the "firstborn among many brethren," which referred to Him being the Author of all Salvation [Rom. 8:29]*).

CHAPTER 16
(1451 B.C.)
THE PASSOVER

OBSERVE the month of Abib (*our April*), and keep the Passover unto the LORD your God: for in the month of Abib the LORD your God brought you forth out of Egypt by

night *(the Passover was to remind Israel and future generations of the great deliverance from Egypt, and that they were to never forget it).*

2 You shall therefore sacrifice the Passover unto the LORD your God, of the flock and the herd, in the place which the LORD shall choose to place His Name there *(the greatest reason for the Passover was that it would serve as a Type of the coming Redeemer, Who would die on a Cross on this very day; in effect, Jesus was the Passover).*

UNLEAVENED BREAD

3 You shall eat no leavened bread with it; seven days shall you eat unleavened bread therewith, even the bread of affliction; for you came forth out of the land of Egypt in haste: that you may remember the day when you came forth out of the land of Egypt all the days of your life. *(The Feast of Unleavened Bread began the day after Passover, and lasted seven days. Whatever it meant to the Jews then, its total meaning had reference to Christ and His Perfection, symbolized by the bread that was unleavened. "Leaven" is a type of fermentation.)*

4 And there shall be no leavened bread seen with you in all your coast seven days; neither shall there any thing of the flesh, which you sacrificed the first day at evening, remain all night until the morning.

5 You may not sacrifice the Passover within any of your gates, which the LORD your God gives you:

6 But at the place which the LORD your God shall choose to place His Name in, there you shall sacrifice the Passover at evening, at the going down of the sun, at the season that you came forth out of Egypt.

7 And you shall roast and eat it in the place which the LORD your God shall choose: and you shall turn in the morning, and go unto your tents.

8 Six days you shall eat unleavened bread: and on the seventh day shall be a solemn assembly to the LORD your God: you shall do no work therein *(symbolizing the fact that Salvation is by Grace through Faith, and not of works [Eph. 2:8-9]).*

FEAST OF PENTECOST

9 Seven weeks shall you number unto you: begin to number the seven weeks from such time as you begin to put the sickle to the corn *(wheat; there was no corn there as we think of such now; the Feast of Pentecost took place exactly 50 days after the Passover).*

10 And you shall keep the feast of weeks unto the LORD your God with a tribute of a freewill offering of your hand, which you shall give unto the LORD your God, according as the LORD your God has blessed you *(nothing is specifically prescribed; each was to give of his own freewill, as the Lord had prospered him):*

11 And you shall rejoice before the LORD your God, you, and your son, and your daughter, and your manservant, and your maidservant, and the Levite who is within your gates, and the stranger, and the fatherless, and the widow, who are among you, in the place which the LORD your God has chosen to place His Name there. *(As to the Feasts, Williams says, "God surrounded Himself with joy, He invited His people to share that joy, and He urged them to bring the stranger and the needy into that joy. Christ and His fullness were pictured in these gladsome Feasts.*

"But there was an interesting distinction between the joy of Pentecost and the joy of Tabernacles. The one was associated with redemption from Egypt, and its joy was to be joined with watchfulness. But the joy of Tabernacles was to be without care, for it foreshadowed the kingdom.")

12 And you shall remember that you were a bondman in Egypt: and you shall observe and do these Statutes.

FEAST OF TABERNACLES

13 You shall observe the Feast of Tabernacles seven days, after that you have gathered in your corn and your wine *(this is a type of the coming Kingdom Age, when Christ will reign supreme over the entirety of the world):*

14 And you shall rejoice in your feast, you, and your son, and your daughter, and your manservant, and your maidservant, and the Levite, the stranger, and the fatherless, and the widow, who are within your gates.

15 Seven days shall you keep a solemn Feast unto the LORD your God in the place which the LORD shall choose: because the LORD your God shall bless you in all your increase, and in all the works of your hands, therefore you shall surely rejoice.

16 Three times in a year shall all your males appear before the LORD your God in the place which He shall choose; in the Feast

of Unleavened Bread *(April)*, and in the Feast of Weeks *(the first days of June)*, and in the Feast of Tabernacles *(October)*: and they shall not appear before the LORD empty *(must bring Sacrifices)*:

17 Every man shall give as he is able, according to the blessing of the LORD your God which He has given you.

LAWS OF JUSTICE

18 Judges and Officers shall you make you in all your gates, which the LORD your God gives you, throughout your Tribes: and they shall judge the people with just judgment *(no instruction is given as to the number of Judges and Officers, or as to the mode of appointing them)*.

19 You shall not wrest judgment *(do not render dishonest judgment)*; you shall not respect persons *(whether rich or poor)*, neither take a gift *(no bribery)*: for a gift does blind the eyes of the wise, and pervert the words of the righteous.

20 That which is altogether just shall you follow, that you may live, and inherit the land which the LORD your God gives you.

21 Thou shall not plant thee a grove of any trees near unto the Altar of the LORD your God, which you shall make thee. *(This was not the planting of trees, as we think of such, but rather the erecting of the "asherah." This was an idol of wood in the form of a pillar, usually placed by the side of the altars of Baal. It was the symbol of Astarte, the great Canaanitish goddess, the companion and revealer of Baal. Unspeakable orgies were also conducted at these sites.)*

22 Neither shall you set up any image; which the LORD your God hates *(there must be nothing that lends toward idolatry)*.

CHAPTER 17

(1451 B.C.)

IMPERFECT SACRIFICES

YOU shall not sacrifice unto the LORD your God any bullock, or sheep, wherein is blemish, or any evilfavouredness: for that is an abomination unto the LORD your God *(the Sacrifices were meant to be types of Christ; as such, they had to be perfect; otherwise, they were an insult to God, as would be obvious)*.

DEATH PENALTY

2 If there be found among you, within any of your gates which the LORD your God gives you, man or woman, who has wrought wickedness in the sight of the LORD your God, in transgressing His Covenant,

3 And has gone and served other gods, and worshipped them, either the sun, or moon, or any of the host of Heaven, which I have not commanded;

4 And it be told you, and you have heard of it, and enquired diligently, and, behold, it be true, and the thing certain, that such abomination is wrought in Israel:

5 Then shall you bring forth that man or that woman, which have committed that wicked thing, unto your gates, even that man or that woman, and shall stone them with stones, till they die *(the land must be kept free from all idolatry; regrettably, Israel ultimately succumbed to this travesty)*.

6 At the mouth of two witnesses, or three witnesses, shall he who is worthy of death be put to death; but at the mouth of one witness he shall not be put to death *(one eyewitness was not enough evidence, at least regarding the Law of Moses, to condemn a person to death; there must be two or three witnesses; an extremely high value was placed by the Lord on life)*.

7 The hands of the witnesses shall be first upon him to put him to death *(the two or three witnesses were to throw the first stones)*, and afterward the hands of all the people. So you shall put the evil away from among you.

SUPREME COURT

8 If there arise a matter too hard for you in judgment, between blood and blood, between plea and plea, and between stroke and stroke, being matters of controversy within your gates: then shall you arise, and get you up into the place which the LORD your God shall choose;

9 And you shall come unto the Priests the Levites, and unto the judge who shall be in those days, and enquire; and they shall show you the sentence of judgment *(a declaration of what was legally right)*:

10 And you shall do according to the sentence, which they of that place which the LORD shall choose shall show you; and you shall observe to do according to all that they inform you *(matters of controversy were not to be decided independently of God, but, on the contrary, in direct connection with Him)*:

11 According to the sentence of the law which they shall teach you, and according to

the judgment which they shall tell you, you shall do: you shall not decline from the sentence which they shall show you, to the right hand, nor to the left *(the law is to be observed)*.

DEATH FOR IRREVERENCE

12 And the man who will do presumptuously, and will not hearken unto the Priest who stands to minister there before the LORD your God, or unto the judge, even that man shall die: and you shall put away the evil from Israel *(no one must take the law into their own hands)*.

13 And all the people shall hear, and fear, and do no more presumptuously.

CHOICE OF A KING

14 When you are come unto the land which the LORD your God gives you, and shall possess it, and shall dwell therein, and shall say, I will set a king over me, like as all the nations that are about me;

15 You shall in any wise set him king over you, whom the LORD your God shall choose *(the Lord must choose the king, not the people)*: one from among your brethren shall you set king over you: you may not set a stranger over you, which is not your brother *(no one but a Jew could be king over Israel)*.

16 But he shall not multiply horses to himself *(in other words, the strength of the army of Israel was to be the Lord and not horses and chariots)*, nor cause the people to return to Egypt, to the end that he should multiply horses *(don't look to Egypt, but look to the Lord)*: forasmuch as the LORD has said unto you, You shall henceforth return no more that way *(this was at least one of the great sins of Israel, which occasioned their defeat at the hands of the Babylonians; they trusted in Egypt instead of the Lord [Jer. 37:5-10])*.

17 Neither shall he multiply wives to himself, that his heart turn not away *(evidently, Solomon did not heed these words)*: neither shall he greatly multiply to himself silver and gold *(men who have great sums of money, or even nations, tend to trust in the money instead of God)*.

18 And it shall be, when he sits upon the throne of his kingdom, that he shall write him a copy of this Law in a book out of that which is before the Priests the Levites *(should Israel desire a king, he was to obey the instructions of Verses 14-20; he was, with his own hand, to write*

a copy of the Bible; he was to read it every day; he was to obey it; he was not to deviate from it in any particular):

19 And it shall be with him, and he shall read therein all the days of his life: that he may learn to fear the LORD his God, to keep all the words of this Law and these Statutes, to do them *(the modern Christian should heed these words, as well, making the Bible a part of his everyday life and study)*:

20 That his heart be not lifted up above his brethren, and that he turn not aside from the Commandment, to the right hand, or to the left: to the end that he may prolong his days in his kingdom, he, and his children, in the midst of Israel.

CHAPTER 18
(1451 B.C.)
PRIESTS AND LEVITES

THE Priests the Levites, and all the Tribe of Levi, shall have no part nor inheritance with Israel: they shall eat the Offerings of the LORD made by fire, and his inheritance. *(Only one of the five Levitical Offerings was consumed wholly, which was the Burnt Offering. The other four Offerings were to be given to the Priests, with the exception of the fat and certain other things of the animal, which were to be burned on the Altar. If the people did what they should do, which means they should offer Sacrifices as they needed to, which was often, the Levites would then have sufficient maintenance; otherwise, not so!)*

2 Therefore shall they have no inheritance among their brethren: the LORD is their inheritance, as He has said unto them.

3 And this shall be the Priest's due from the people, from them who offer a Sacrifice, whether it be ox or sheep; and they shall give unto the Priest the shoulder, and the two cheeks, and the maw *(parts of the animal)*.

4 The firstfruit also of your corn, of your wine, and of your oil, and the first of the fleece of your sheep, shall you give him *(a tenth of their crops were to go to the Priests and the Sanctuary, i.e., "firstfruit")*.

5 For the LORD your God has chosen him out of all your Tribes, to stand to minister in the Name of the LORD, him and his sons for ever *(continually until the Messiah would come, Who, by His Death on the Cross of Calvary, would bring to an end the necessity of Priests, and Sacrifices, etc.)*.

6 And if a Levite come from any of your

gates out of all Israel, where he sojourned, and come with all the desire of his mind unto the place which the LORD shall choose *(only some of the Levites were engaged in the service of the Sanctuary; the rest lived in their towns throughout the country; if they should feel led of the Lord to go and serve at the Tabernacle or Temple, they should be accepted)*;

7 Then he shall minister in the Name of the LORD his God, as all his brethren the Levites do, which stand there before the LORD.

8 They shall have like portions to eat, beside that which comes of the sale of his patrimony *(having sold his home; he should not be expected to use those funds, whatever they may have been, but should share in the Offerings brought, the same as the other Priests, or Levites)*.

PAGAN PRACTICES FORBIDDEN

9 When you are come into the land which the LORD your God gives you, you shall not learn to do after the abominations of those nations *(again and again, Israel was warned concerning this)*.

10 There shall not be found among you any one who makes his son or his daughter to pass through the fire *(human sacrifice)*, or who uses divination, or an observer of times, or an enchanter, or a witch,

11 Or a charmer, or a consulter with familiar spirits, or a wizard, or a necromancer. *(The last is one who professed to call up the dead, and from them to learn the secrets of the future. All of these things had to do with witchcraft, and were not at all to be a part of Israel, and for all the obvious reasons. Israel was to look to God, and never to these abominations.)*

12 For all who do these things are an abomination unto the LORD: and because of these abominations the LORD your God does drive them out from before you *(in other words, this is at least part of the reason that these heathen tribes were driven from Canaan)*.

13 You shall be perfect with the LORD your God *(the word "perfect" means single-hearted, that is, pure from idolatry)*.

14 For these nations, which you shall possess, hearkened unto observers of times, and unto diviners: but as for you, the LORD your God has not suffered you so to do.

THE PROPHET MESSIAH

15 The LORD your God will raise up unto you a Prophet from the midst of you, of your brethren, like unto me; unto Him you shall hearken *(that Prophet would be the Lord Jesus Christ)*;

16 According to all that you desired of the LORD your God in Horeb in the day of the Assembly, saying, Let me not hear again the voice of the LORD my God, neither let me see this great fire any more, that I die not *(the Holiness of God was more than Israel could stand)*.

17 And the LORD said unto me, They have well spoken that which they have spoken.

18 I will raise them up a Prophet from among their brethren, like unto you, and will put My words in His mouth; and He shall speak unto them all that I shall command Him. *(All that Christ taught and the very words He used in His teaching were from God. There was no misgiving in the Divine Mind as to that certitude. Seven times He asserted that all His Words and Statements were given to Him by God.)*

19 And it shall come to pass, that whosoever will not hearken unto My words which He shall speak in My name, I will require it of him. *(Israel had to answer for their rejection of Christ. They would not heed His Words. They lost that generation, plus all the generations since, and they lost their nation. Likewise, every person now who hears the Gospel and turns Christ aside will one day answer for what he has heard. It is called the Great White Throne Judgment [Rev. 20:11-15].)*

FALSE PROPHETS

20 But the Prophet, which shall presume to speak a word in My Name, which I have not commanded him to speak, or that shall speak in the name of other gods, even that Prophet shall die *(that was the sentence in Israel, and for all the obvious reasons; it is the same presently, spiritually speaking)*.

21 And if you say in your heart, How shall we know the word which the LORD has not spoken?

22 When a Prophet speaks in the Name of the LORD, if the thing follow not, nor come to pass, that is the thing which the LORD has not spoken, but the Prophet has spoken it presumptuously: you shall not be afraid of him *(how many self-anointed Prophets presently are constantly giving forth prophecies, even with names and dates, which do not come to pass; and the modern Church is so jaded, they do not*

seem to realize that they have been hearing a false prophet).

CHAPTER 19
(1451 B.C.)
CITIES OF REFUGE

WHEN the LORD your God has cut off the nations, whose land the LORD your God gives you, and you succeed them, and dwell in their cities, and in their houses;

2 You shall separate three cities for you in the midst of your land, which the LORD your God gives you to possess it *(the cities of refuge are addressed in Numbers 35:11).*

3 You shall prepare you a way, and divide the coasts of your land, which the LORD your God gives you to inherit, into three parts, that every slayer may flee thither.

4 And this is the case of the slayer, which shall flee thither, that he may live: Whoso kills his neighbour ignorantly, whom he hated not in time past *(the cities of refuge were for individuals who killed someone accidentally; they could flee to one of these cities, and the relatives of the victim could not touch there the one who had become embroiled in the situation; however, these cities were not for murderers);*

5 As when a man goes into the wood with his neighbour to hew wood, and his hand fetched a stroke with the axe to cut down the tree, and the head slips from the helve, and lights upon his neighbour, that he die; he shall flee unto one of those cities, and live *(accidental death):*

6 Lest the avenger of the blood *(a relative or friend of the victim)* pursue the slayer, while his heart is hot, and overtake him, because the way is long, and kill him; whereas he was not worthy of death, inasmuch as he hated him not in time past *(as stated, the man's death was an unfortunate accident).*

7 Wherefore I command you, saying, You shall separate three cities for you *(for this purpose).*

8 And if the LORD your God enlarge your coast, as He has sworn unto your fathers, and give you all the land which He promised to give unto your fathers;

9 If you shall keep all these Commandments to do them, which I command you this day, to love the LORD your God, and to walk ever in His ways; then shall you add three cities more for you, beside these three *(these latter three would be on the east side of the Jordan River):*

10 That innocent blood be not shed in your land, which the LORD your God gives you for an inheritance, and so blood be upon you *(the design of appointing these cities was to prevent the shedding of innocent blood, which would be the case if the unintentional manslayer was killed by one of the relatives of the man he had accidentally killed).*

11 But if any man hate his neighbour, and lie in wait for him, and rise up against him, and smite him mortally that he die, and flees into one of these cities:

12 Then the elders of his city shall send and fetch him thence, and deliver him into the hand of the avenger of blood, that he may die *(as stated, the cities of refuge were not for murderers, but for those who killed someone accidentally).*

13 Your eye shall not pity him, but you shall put away the guilt of innocent blood from Israel, that it may go well with you. *(Capital punishment for capital crimes is one of the Commandments of the Lord; while execution of the guilty does not serve as a deterrent, it does serve to show the worth that God places on human life. If a man or a woman in cold blood takes the life of another, his or her life is to be forfeited, as well [Rom. 13:1-7].)*

LANDMARKS

14 You shall not remove your neighbour's landmark, which they of old time have set in your inheritance, which you shall inherit in the land that the LORD your God gives you to possess it *(this pertains to landmarks which have been placed to mark the boundaries of possessions; they were not to be surreptitiously altered).*

WITNESSES

15 One witness shall not rise up against a man for any iniquity, or for any sin, in any sin that he sins: at the mouth of two witnesses, or at the mouth of three witnesses, shall the matter be established *(as in courts of law presently, even an eyewitness account is often faulty; that's the reason that two or more are demanded here, in order that the rights of individuals be protected).*

PERJURY

16 If a false witness rise up against any man to testify against him that which is wrong;

17 Then both the men, between whom the

controversy is, shall stand before the LORD, before the Priests and the Judges, which shall be in those days;

18 And the Judges shall make diligent inquisition: and, behold, if the witness be a false witness, and has testified falsely against his brother;

19 Then shall you do unto him, as he had thought to have done unto his brother: so shall you put the evil away from among you.

20 And those which remain shall hear, and fear, and shall henceforth commit no more any such evil among you (such directions were given in order that individuals would be fearful of lying on someone else).

21 And your eye shall not pity; but life shall go for life, eye for eye, tooth for tooth, hand for hand, foot for foot (most of the time, this was never carried out, but, instead, certain amounts of money were given to satisfy the situation).

CHAPTER 20
(1451 B.C.)
WAR

WHEN you go out to battle against your enemies, and see horses, and chariots, and a people more than you, be not afraid of them: for the LORD your God is with you, which brought you up out of the land of Egypt. (The Lord promised to be with Israel in time of war, that is, if the cause of Israel was right.

Even though this Promise was addressed to a nation, it holds true for modern Believers, as well, as it regards spiritual warfare; however, the warfare in which every Christian must engage, and it is incumbent upon all, can be engaged successfully only if we function according to God's prescribed order. That order is: Christ is always the "Source" of all things which come from God. The Cross is the "Means" by which it is given to us. This means that we must ever make the Cross the object of our Faith, and not allow it to be moved anywhere else. This done, the Holy Spirit, Who works conclusively within the Finished Work of Christ, will work on our behalf, guaranteeing victory within our lives. In this way, and this way only, can victory be won and maintained [Rom. 6:3-14; 8:1-2, 11; Eph. 2:13-18; Col. 2:14-15; Gal., Chpt. 5; 6:14].)

2 And it shall be, when you are come near unto the battle, that the Priest shall approach and speak unto the people (by the "Priest" being used instead of a military commander, this shows that the battle was more spiritual than anything else; with the Child of God, in one way or the other, everything is spiritual),

3 And shall say unto them, Hear, O Israel, you approach this day unto battle against your enemies: let not your hearts faint, fear not, and do not tremble, neither be you terrified because of them;

4 For the LORD your God (as by now is obvious, the phrase, "LORD your God," so often used, refers to Covenant) is He Who goes with you, to fight for you against your enemies, to save you (with the Lord, Israel was invincible! Without the Lord, Israel was easily defeated; it is the same presently in our own personal hearts and lives).

MILITARY SERVICE

5 And the officers shall speak unto the people, saying, What man is there who has built a new house, and has not dedicated it? let him go and return to his house, lest he die in the battle, and another man dedicate it.

6 And what man is he who has planted a vineyard, and has not yet eaten of it? let him also go and return unto his house, lest he die in the battle, and another man eat of it.

7 And what man is there who has betrothed a wife, and has not taken her? let him go and return unto his house, lest he die in the battle, and another man take her (according to Josephus, this exemption was for a year).

8 And the officers shall speak further unto the people, and they shall say, What man is there who is fearful and fainthearted? let him go and return unto his house, lest his brethren's heart faint as well as his heart. (Fear and doubt are contagious; so the Holy Spirit says, "Those who are plagued with such, get them out of the army." He is saying the same thing presently. More than anything else, the Church needs people who truly believe God.)

9 And it shall be, when the officers have made an end of speaking unto the people, that they shall make captains of the armies to lead the people (evidently, these individuals were to be chosen more for their Faith in the Lord, and we do not mean reckless presumption, than for their military expertise).

FOREIGN CITIES

10 When you come near unto a city to fight against it, then proclaim peace unto it (invite it peaceably to surrender).

11 And it shall be, if it make you answer of peace, and open unto you, then it shall be, that all the people who are found therein shall be tributaries unto you, and they shall serve you (service rendered as tribute, whether for a season or in perpetuity).

12 And if it will make no peace with you, but will make war against you, then you shall besiege it:

13 And when the LORD your God has delivered it into your hands, you shall smite every male thereof with the edge of the sword:

14 But the women, and the little ones, and the cattle, and all that is in the city, even all the spoil thereof, shall you take unto yourself; and you shall eat the spoil of your enemies, which the LORD your God has given you.

15 Thus shall you do unto all the cities which are very far off from you, which are not of the cities of these nations. (The information given in these Passages has to do with foreign cities, and not the heathenistic tribes which occupied the land of Canaan. At times, invaders from afar would come against Israel. If that happened, Israel would not only defeat their army, but sometimes would have to attack their homeland, wherever that was. If they did, certain rules were laid down by the Lord, which they were to follow.)

LOCAL BATTLES

16 But of the cities of these people, which the LORD your God does give you for an inheritance (those who were occupying the land of Canaan), you shall save alive nothing that breathes:

17 But you shall utterly destroy them; namely, the Hittites, and the Amorites, the Canaanites, and the Perizzites, the Hivites, and the Jebusites; as the LORD your God has commanded you (to these particular people, no offer of peaceful submission was to be made, and when the city was taken, all the inhabitants without reserve were to be destroyed. Why? The next Verse tells us why):

18 That they teach you not to do after all their abominations, which they have done unto their gods; so should you sin against the LORD your God (if the abominations of these heathen tribes, who served all types of gods, were taken up by the Israelites, they would lose their way and be destroyed exactly as the heathen; and that's exactly what ultimately happened!).

19 When you shall besiege a city a long time, in making war against it to take it, you shall not destroy the trees thereof by forcing an axe against them: for you may eat of them, and you shall not cut them down (for the tree of the field is man's life) to employ them in the siege (fruit bearing trees):

20 Only the trees which you know that they be not trees for meat, you shall destroy and cut them down; and you shall build bulwarks against the city that makes war with you, until it be subdued.

CHAPTER 21
(1451 B.C.)
UNSOLVED MURDER

IF one be found slain in the land which the LORD your God gives you to possess it, lying in the field, and it be not known who has killed him:

2 Then your elders and your judges shall come forth, and they shall measure unto the cities which are round about who is killed:

3 And it shall be, that the city which is next unto the slain man, even the elders of that city shall take an heifer, which has not been wrought with, and which has not drawn in the yoke (the Lord was to be brought into all of this, thus showing His tender Solicitude for individuals as well as for nations, and the regard He had for family life — Williams);

4 And the elders of that city shall bring down the heifer unto a rough valley, which is neither eared nor sown, and shall strike off the heifer's neck there in the valley (break the heifer's neck; this was not a sacrifice, but simply a symbolical representation of the infliction of death on the undiscovered murderer):

5 And the Priests the sons of Levi shall come near; for them the LORD your God has chosen to minister unto Him, and to bless in the Name of the LORD; and by their word shall every controversy and every stroke be tried (the Priests were to be heavily involved, because everything as it pertained to Israel was spiritual):

6 And all the elders of that city, who are next unto the slain man, shall wash their hands over the heifer that is beheaded in the valley:

7 And they shall answer and say, Our hands have not shed this blood, neither have our eyes seen it (again, all of this shows the sacredness of human life).

8 Be merciful, O LORD, unto Your people Israel, whom You have redeemed, and lay not innocent blood unto Your people of Israel's

charge. And the blood shall be forgiven them.

9 So shall you put away the guilt of innocent blood from among you, when you shall do that which is right in the sight of the LORD *(expiation was made by the killing of the transgressor, when he could be found [19:13]; when he was not known, by the process described here; of course, if afterwards he was apprehended, he would suffer the penalty he had incurred).*

MARRIAGE

10 When you go forth to war against your enemies, and the LORD your God has delivered them into your hands, and you have taken them captive,

11 And you see among the captives a beautiful woman, and have a desire unto her, that you would have her to your wife;

12 Then you shall bring her home to your house, and she shall shave her head, and pare her nails;

13 And she shall put the raiment of her captivity from off her, and shall remain in your house, and bewail her father and her mother a full month: and after that you shall go in unto her, and be her husband, and she shall be your wife *(all of these things demanded were signs of purification, of separation from former heathenism, preparatory to reception among the covenant people of Jehovah).*

14 And it shall be, if you have no delight in her, then you shall let her go where she will; but you shall not sell her at all for money, you shall not make merchandise of her, because you have humbled her *(the Law of God, as given to Moses, which took into account even the feelings of a slave girl, so to speak, which as well guaranteed her rights; at that time, there was no law in the world that was even remotely as fair and equitable as the Law of God).*

THE FIRSTBORN

15 If a man have two wives, one beloved, and another hated, and they have born him children, both the beloved and the hated; and if the firstborn son be hers that was hated:

16 Then it shall be, when he makes his sons to inherit that which he has, that he may not make the son of the beloved firstborn before the son of the hated, which is indeed the firstborn:

17 But he shall acknowledge the son of the hated for the firstborn, by giving him a double portion of all that he has: for he is the beginning of his strength; the right of the firstborn is his *(the firstborn inherited twice as much as any of the other sons).*

DEATH

18 If a man have a stubborn and rebellious son, which will not obey the voice of his father, or the voice of his mother, and that, when they have chastened him, will not hearken unto them:

19 Then shall his father and his mother lay hold on him, and bring him out unto the elders of his city, and unto the gate of his place;

20 And they shall say unto the elders of his city, This our son is stubborn and rebellious, he will not obey our voice; he is a glutton, and a drunkard.

21 And all the men of his city shall stone him with stones, that he die: so shall you put evil away from among you; and all Israel shall hear, and fear *(gluttony and drunkenness were regarded by the Hebrews as highly criminal; the word rendered by "glutton" includes other kinds of excess besides eating; it designates one who is prodigal, who wastes his means or wastes his person by indulgence).*

CRIMINALS

22 And if a man have committed a sin worthy of death, and he be to be put to death, and you hang him on a tree:

23 His body shall not remain all night upon the tree, but you shall in any wise bury him that day; (for he who is hanged is accursed of God;) that your land be not defiled, which the LORD your God gives you for an inheritance. *(This is the reason that the religious leaders of Israel demanded that Jesus be put on the Cross [Mat. 27:23]. They knew that one put on the tree was accursed of God, and so they reasoned that the people would then think, were He really the Messiah, God would never allow Him to be put on a Cross. They did not realize that the Lord had foretold the event of the Cross some 1,500 years earlier, as it concerned the brazen serpent on the pole [Num. 21:8-9]. It was necessary that Jesus go to the Cross, in order that He might atone for all the sins of mankind, at least for all who will believe]Jn. 3:16]. So, Jesus was made a curse on the Cross, not because of His sins, for He had none, but for the sin of the whole world, and for all time [Jn. 1:29; Gal. 3:13].)*

CHAPTER 22

(1451 B.C.)

LAWS

YOU shall not see your brother's ox or his sheep go astray, and hide yourself from them: you shall in any case bring them again unto your brother.

2 And if your brother be not near unto you, or if you know him not, then you shall bring it unto your own house, and it shall be with you until your brother seek after it, and you shall restore it to him again.

3 In like manner shall you do with his ass; and so shall you do with his raiment; and with all lost thing of your brother's, which he has lost, and you have found, shall you do likewise: you may not hide yourself. *(This law had been given in Exodus 23:4-5. Honesty is demanded here in all things.)*

VARIOUS REGULATIONS

4 You shall not see your brother's ass or his ox fall down by the way, and hide yourself from them: you shall surely help him to lift them up again *(provide help for those who need such).*

5 The woman shall not wear that which pertains unto a man, neither shall a man put on a woman's garment: for all who do so are abomination unto the LORD your God. *(Pulpit says, "The Divinely instituted distinction between the sexes was to be sacredly observed and, in order to do this, the dress and other things appropriate to the one were not to be used by the other. Whatever tended to obliterate the distinction between the sexes tends to licentiousness."*

So as not to misunderstand this, both men and women in those days wore robes; however, the robes for the men were different than the robes for the women, as would be obvious. At times, presently, women wear slacks, i.e., "trousers." However, as is also obvious, the trousers worn by a woman are different than those worn by a man. So, that means it's not wrong for a woman to wear slacks, i.e., "trousers," etc.)

6 If a bird's nest chance to be before you in the way in any tree, or on the ground, whether they be young ones, or eggs, and the dam *(mother)* sitting upon the young, or upon the eggs, you shall not take the dam with the young:

7 But you shall in any wise let the dam go, and take the young to you; that it may be well with you, and that you may prolong your days. *(The Expositors say, "These precepts are designed to foster humane feelings toward the lower animals, not less to preserve regard to that affectionate relation between parents and their young, which God has also established as a law in the animal world.")*

8 When you build a new house, then you shall make a battlement for your roof, that you bring not blood upon your house, if any man fall from thence *(the roof of houses in that part of the world is mostly flat; as well, during the summer, oftentimes, members of the family, or others, will sleep on the roof, in order to catch the night breeze; a banister was to be erected around the roof to serve as protection).*

9 You shall not sow your vineyard with divers seeds: lest the fruit of your seed which you have sown, and the fruit of your vineyard, be defiled.

10 You shall not plow with an ox and an ass together.

11 You shall not wear a garment of divers sorts, as of woollen and linen together. *(Concerning this, Williams says, "Mixed teaching, like mixed seeds, produces sterility. At creation [Gen. 1], there was no mixture; and, hence, fertility. Every seed was 'after his kind,' and was pronounced by God to be 'good.' The seed that Christian workers and Ministers are to sow must be the unmixed Word of God. His Word is not to be mixed with man's philosophy. Christ, the True Minister, said, 'I have given them Your Word,' 'I have not spoken from Myself.'*

"The ox was 'clean,' the ass 'unclean.' Together they formed an unequal yoke. When Christian people join with the unconverted in Christian work, or marriage, or business, it is an unequal yoke, and can never have Divine approval.")

12 You shall make yourself fringes upon the four quarters of your vesture, wherewith you cover yourself *(tassels with blue thread, signifying that their help came from Heaven).*

CHASTITY

13 If any man take a wife, and go in unto her, and hate her,

14 And give occasions of speech against her, and bring up an evil name upon her, and say, I took this woman, and when I came to her, I found her not a maid *(claiming that she wasn't a virgin):*

15 Then shall the father of the damsel, and her mother, take and bring forth the tokens of the damsel's virginity unto the elders of the city in the gate:

16 And the damsel's father shall say unto the elders, I gave my daughter unto this man to wife, and he hates her;

17 And, lo, he has given occasions of speech against her, saying, I found not your a daughter a maid; and yet these are the tokens of my daughter's virginity. And they shall spread the cloth before the elders of the city.

18 And the elders of that city shall take that man and chastise him (*meaning that he lied about the girl, because he didn't want her for other reasons, whatever they might have been*);

19 And they shall amerce him in an hundred shekels of silver, and give them unto the father of the damsel, because he has brought up an evil name upon a virgin of Israel: and she shall be his wife; he may not put her away all his days (*if he did so, he was adding sin to sin*).

20 But if this thing be true, and the tokens of virginity be not found for the damsel:

21 Then they shall bring out the damsel to the door of her father's house, and the men of her city shall stone her with stones that she die: because she has wrought folly in Israel, to play the whore in her father's house: so shall you put evil away from among you. (*The nation had to be kept pure, at least as far as possible, because, as stated, it was to serve as the womb of the Messiah. As such, immorality must be put away and, if not, severe penalties attached.*)

22 If a man be found lying with a woman married to an husband, then they shall both of them die, both the man that lay with the woman, and the woman: so shall you put away evil from Israel.

23 If a damsel who is a virgin be betrothed unto an husband, and a man find her in the city, and lie with her;

24 Then you shall bring them both out unto the gate of that city, and you shall stone them with stones that they die; the damsel, because she cried not, being in the city; and the man, because he has humbled his neighbour's wife: so you shall put away evil from among you. (*This was the case with the young woman who was brought to Jesus by the Pharisees, described in John 8:1-11. The difference is, they brought the young woman to Jesus, but didn't bring the man. They were quite ready to stone her, which they used to entrap Christ. Of course, their scheme didn't work; however, the Law had to be kept by Christ. So, how could He say to her, knowing that without a doubt she was guilty of adultery, "Neither do I condemn you: Go, and sin no more"? [Jn. 8:11].*

He kept the Law perfectly by dying in her place, exactly as He did for all of us; therefore, the Law was kept perfectly.)

25 But if a man find a betrothed damsel in the field, and the man force her, and lie with her: then the man only who lay with her shall die.

26 But unto the damsel you shall do nothing; there is in the damsel no sin worthy of death: for as when a man rises against his neighbour, and kills him, even so is this matter:

27 For he found her in the field, and the betrothed damsel cried, and there was none to save her.

28 If a man find a damsel who is a virgin, which is not betrothed, and lay hold on her, and lie with her, and they be found;

29 Then the man who lay with her shall give unto the damsel's father fifty shekels of silver, and she shall be his wife; because he has humbled her, he may not put her away all his days.

30 A man shall not take his father's wife, nor discover his father's skirt (*this is a prohibition against all types of incestuous connections*).

CHAPTER 23
(1451 B.C.)
EXCLUDED FROM THE CONGREGATION

HE who is wounded in the stones (*testicles*), or has his privy member cut off, shall not enter into the congregation of the LORD. (*This did not pertain to accidents, etc. It rather pertained to prohibitions concerning idolatry. Parents in the heathen tribes surrounding Israel often mutilated in various ways their children, either in honor of their gods, or else to get higher wages for them as servants. Israel was not to conduct herself at all in this manner. Of course, children who would be treated thusly, who had no choice in the matter, could certainly be forgiven by the Lord; however, if such children were in the Tribe of Levi, they couldn't function as Priests, although they could definitely be saved.*)

2 A bastard shall not enter into the congregation of the LORD; even to his tenth generation shall he not enter into the congregation of the LORD. (*As well, this pertains to idolatry. Many children in heathen tribes were born, not in wedlock, but as a result of idolatrous, licentious ceremonies. As well, it pertained to one born out of wedlock in any case. Again, to be*

sure, the child would have no responsibility in the matter. But, still, while it could certainly be saved and live for God, such a child could not be a Priest, even if a Levite.)

3 An Ammonite or Moabite shall not enter into the congregation of the LORD; even to their tenth generation shall they not enter into the congregation of the LORD for ever (the number "ten," at least used in this fashion, was a number of indefiniteness; in other words, it meant forever; Ammon and Moab had met the Israelites with hostility, and had brought Balaam to curse them, which curse God turned upon these heathen tribes; however, those who evidenced Faith in God, even as it was with Ruth, who was a Moabitess, could definitely enter into the congregation of the Lord; in fact, Ruth, due to her Faith, was an ancestress of our Saviour [Mat. 1:5]):

4 Because they (the Ammonites and Moabites) met you not with bread and with water in the way, when you came forth out of Egypt; and because they hired against you Balaam the son of Beor of Pethor of Mesopotamia, to curse you.

5 Nevertheless the LORD your God would not hearken unto Balaam; but the LORD your God turned the curse into a blessing unto you, because the LORD your God loved you (the entirety of the human race, because of the Fall, is plagued with a curse; but Jesus turned the curse into a Blessing, and did so at the Cross [Gal. 3:13-14]).

6 You shall not seek their peace nor their prosperity all your days for ever (God blesses those who bless His People, and places a curse upon those who do the opposite; in other words, the harm that the world would seek to do to the people of God is ultimately turned by God against the world).

7 You shall not abhor an Edomite for he is your brother: you shall not abhor (hate) an Egyptian; because you were a stranger in his land (the Edomites were descendants of Esau, therefore, the brother of Jacob; even though the Egyptians harmed Israel greatly at the last, Egypt, in fact, gave solace and help to Jacob at the beginning; God does not forget that done to His Children, good or bad).

8 The children who are begotten of them shall enter into the congregation of the LORD in their third generation (providing they desired to become a proselyte Jew).

RULES FOR SANITATION

9 When the host goes forth against your enemies, then you must keep yourself from every wicked thing (when the people went forth to war, all impurity and defilement were to be kept out of their camp, because their victory depended on the Blessings of the Lord; and God cannot bless that which is wicked).

10 If there be among you any man, who is not clean by reason of uncleanness that chances him by night, then shall he go abroad out of the camp, he shall not come within the camp:

11 But it shall be, when evening comes on, he shall wash himself with water: and when the sun is down, he shall come into the camp again (as is obvious here, purity was demanded at all times).

12 You shall have a place also without the camp, where you shall go forth abroad:

13 And you shall have a paddle upon your weapon; and it shall be, when you will ease yourself abroad, you shall dig therewith, and shall turn back and cover that which comes from you (sanitary conditions were demanded, because these people were God's People):

14 For the LORD your God walks in the midst of your camp, to deliver you, and to give up your enemies before you; therefore shall your camp be holy: that He see no unclean thing in you, and turn away from you (while the Lord walked up and down among them at that time, the Holy Spirit now lives within the hearts and lives of Believers [I Cor. 3:16]; consequently, the same demands, as would be obvious, and even more, are upon the modern Child of God; every single thing we do, we are to keep in mind that the Holy Spirit is with us at all times and, thereby, conduct ourselves accordingly).

VARIOUS REGULATIONS

15 You shall not deliver unto his master the servant which is escaped from his master unto you (the reference is to a foreign slave who had fled from the harsh treatment of his heathen master, and desired to seek refuge in Israel; he was to be given that refuge and not returned to his heathen master):

16 He shall dwell with you, even among you, in that place which he shall choose in one of your gates, where it likes him best: you shall not oppress him (all of this was a type of the lost coming to Christ, and entering into the Family of God).

17 There shall be no whore of the daughters of Israel, nor a sodomite of the sons of Israel (whoredom in every capacity is banned, as well

as homosexuality).

18 You shall not bring the hire of a whore, or the price of a dog *(the latter has nothing to do with the canine variety, but rather likens homosexuals to dogs)*, into the house of the LORD your God for any vow: for even both these are abomination unto the LORD your God *(but yet, Rahab the harlot was allowed to come into the Family of God, and even to become an ancestress of Christ; she did so by Faith, which always overrides all law [Mat. 1:5]; none of this means that such people cannot be saved, but only that Israel must oppose these sins greatly).*

19 You shall not lend upon usury to your brother; usury of money, usury of victuals, usury of any thing that is lent upon usury *(an Israelite was to not charge interest on a loan given to a fellow Israelite):*

20 Unto a stranger *(Gentile)* you may lend upon usury *(can charge interest)*; but unto your brother you shall not lend upon usury: that the LORD your God may bless you in all that you set your hand to in the land where you go to possess it *(the Blessings of the Lord then, and the Blessings of the Lord now, depend upon obedience to Him; then it was obedience to the Law, now it is obedience to Grace).*

21 When you shall vow a vow unto the LORD your God, you shall not slack to pay it: for the LORD your God will surely require it of you; and it would be sin in you *(don't vow if you don't intend to pay it, because God is going to collect the vow in one way or the other; it is the same thing presently with Tithes; every Christian pays Tithes, whether willingly or not; God, in one way or the other, will collect).*

22 But if you shall forbear to vow, it shall be no sin in you *(no one is under any obligation to vow, this is to be a purely voluntary act).*

23 That which is gone out of your lips you shall keep and perform; even a freewill offering, according as you have vowed unto the LORD your God, which you have promised with your mouth *(our word is to be the same as the Word of the Lord, at least as it regards integrity and veracity).*

24 When you come into your neighbour's vineyard, then you may eat grapes your fill at your own pleasure; but you shall not put any in your vessel *(eat all you want, but don't take any with you, because the grapes belong to someone else).*

25 When you come into the standing corn *(grain)* of your neighbour, then you may pluck the ears with your hand; but you shall not move a sickle unto your neighbour's standing corn *(complete honesty is demanded at all times).*

CHAPTER 24
(1451 B.C.)
LAW OF DIVORCE

WHEN a man has taken a wife, and married her, and it come to pass that she find no favour in his eyes, because he has found some uncleanness in her: then let him write her a bill of divorcement, and give it in her hand, and send her out of his house.

2 And when she is departed out of his house, she may go and be another man's wife.

3 And if the latter husband hate her, and write her a bill of divorcement, and gives it in her hand, and sends her out of his house; or if the latter husband die, which took her to be his wife;

4 Her former husband, which sent her away, may not take her again to be his wife, after that she is defiled; for that is abomination before the LORD: and you shall not cause the land to sin, which the LORD your God gives you for an inheritance. *(Concerning this, Pulpit says, "This is not a law sanctioning or regulating divorce; this is simply assumed as what might occur; and what is regulated here is the treatment by the first husband of a woman who has been divorced a second time." The minute regulations of these Chapters show how God came into the most intimate concerns of His People. To those who loved Him, this was a deep joy, but to those who did not love Him, an intolerable and irritating intrusion — Williams.)*

LAWS FOR NEWLYWEDS

5 When a man has taken a new wife, he shall not go out to war, neither shall he be charged with any business: but he shall be free at home one year, and shall cheer up his wife which he has taken *(this proclaims the fact that family life in Israel was very important, hence this regulation).*

PLEDGES

6 No man shall take the nether or the upper millstone to pledge: for he takes a man's life to pledge *(if a man were deprived of that by which food for the sustaining of life could be prepared, his life itself would be imperiled; so such an item could not used as a pledge or mortgage).*

KIDNAPPING

7 If a man be found stealing any of his brethren of the children of Israel *(kidnapping)*, and makes merchandise of him, or sells him; then that thief shall die; and you shall put evil away from among you *(the penalty for kidnapping was death)*.

LEPROSY

8 Take heed in the plague of leprosy, that you observe diligently, and do according to all that the Priests the Levites shall teach you: as I commanded them, so you shall observe to do.

9 Remember what the LORD your God did unto Miriam by the way, after that you were come forth out of Egypt *(Lev., Chpts. 13-14])*.

SACREDNESS OF THE HOME

10 When you do lend your brother any thing, you shall not go into his house to fetch his pledge.

11 You shall stand abroad, and the man to whom you do lend shall bring out the pledge abroad unto you. *(This concerns someone who had borrowed a sum of money on something in his house, such as furniture, etc. If he could not pay the money, the one to whom the mortgage was given could not come into his house and collect. The man must bring it out.)*

12 And if the man be poor, you shall not sleep with his pledge *(concerning one who had pledged his garment)*:

13 In any case you shall deliver him the pledge again when the sun goes down, that he may sleep in his own raiment, and bless you: and it shall be righteousness unto you before the LORD your God. *(Williams says, "The spirit of all these ordinances is very touching as showing the goodness and pity of God, Who deigns to take knowledge of all these things, and to teach His People delicacy, propriety, consideration for others, sensitiveness — in a word, Christlikeness.")*

OPPRESSION

14 You shall not oppress an hired servant who is poor and needy, whether he be of your brethren, or of your strangers *(Gentiles)* who are in your land within your gates:

15 At his day you shall give him his hire, neither shall the sun go down upon it *(at the end of each day's work, the wages for the day were to be paid to day laborers)*; for he is poor, and sets his heart upon it: lest he cry against you unto the LORD, and it be sin unto you.

INDIVIDUAL RESPONSIBILITY

16 The fathers shall not be put to death for the children, neither shall the children be put to death for the fathers: every man shall be put to death for his own sin *(this Passage completely obliterates the modern false teaching of the family curse)*.

INJUSTICE

17 You shall not pervert the judgment of the stranger, nor of the fatherless; nor take a widow's raiment to pledge:

18 But you shall remember that you were a bondman in Egypt, and the LORD your God redeemed you thence: therefore I command you to do this thing *(to enforce this, the people are reminded that they themselves as a nation had been in the condition of strangers and bondmen in Egypt)*.

GLEANING

19 When you cut down your harvest in your field, and have forgotten a sheaf in the field, you shall not go again to fetch it: it shall be for the stranger, for the fatherless, and for the widow: that the LORD your God may bless you in all the work of your hands *(in a sense, this was at least a part of God's welfare program)*.

20 When you beat your olive tree, you shall not go over the boughs again: it shall be for the stranger, for the fatherless, and for the widow *(leave something for the poor)*.

21 When you gather the grapes of your vineyard, you shall not glean it afterward: it shall be for the stranger, for the fatherless, and for the widow.

22 And you shall remember that you were a bondman in the land of Egypt: therefore I command you to do this thing.

CHAPTER 25
(1451 B.C.)
SCOURGING

IF there be a controversy between men, and they come unto judgment, that the judges may judge them; then they shall justify the

righteous, and condemn the wicked (wickedness must not be condoned).

2 And it shall be, if the wicked man be worthy to be beaten, that the judge shall cause him to lie down, and be beaten before his face, according to his fault, by a certain number.

3 Forty stripes he may give him, and not exceed: lest, if he should exceed, and beat him above these with many stripes, then your brother should seem vile unto you ("forty" is God's probationary number; however, such punishment was to be rendered by the judge, and not at all by individuals taking the law into their own hands).

CARE OF BEASTS

4 You shall not muzzle the ox when he treads out the corn. (The Expositors say, "The leaving of the ox unmuzzled when treading out the grain was in order that the animal might be free to eat of the grain which its labor severed from the husk. This prohibition, therefore, was dictated by a regard for the rights and claims of animals employed in labor; but there is involved in it the general principle that all labor is to be duly requited, whether by animal or man; hence, Paul used this very Verse to proclaim the necessity of supporting the Work of God" [I Cor. 9:9].)

FAMILIES

5 If brethren dwell together, and one of them die, and have no child, the wife of the dead shall not marry without unto a stranger: her husband's brother shall go in unto her, and take her to him to wife, and perform the duty of an husband's brother unto her (that is, if he was not already married, or if the woman had no children).

6 And it shall be, that the firstborn which she bears shall succeed in the name of his brother which is dead, that his name be not put out of Israel (shall be enrolled in the family register as heir of the deceased, and shall perpetuate his name; this had to do with the fact that the Messiah would come from a certain family in Israel, hence each family was to be kept intact as far as possible).

7 And if the man like not to take his brother's wife, then let his brother's wife go up to the gate unto the elders, and say, My husband's brother refuses to raise up unto his brother a name in Israel, he will not perform the duty of my husband's brother.

8 Then the elders of his city shall call him, and speak unto him: and if he stand to it, and say, I like not to take her;

9 Then shall his brother's wife come unto him in the presence of the elders, and loose his shoe from off his foot, and spit in his face, and shall answer and say, So shall it be done unto that man who will not build up his brother's house.

10 And his name shall be called in Israel, The house of him who has his shoe loosed (an example of this is found in Gen., Chpt. 38, even long before the Law was given).

ASSAULT AND BATTERY

11 When men strive together one with another, and the wife of the one draws near for to deliver her husband out of the hand of him who smites him, and puts forth her hand, and takes him by the secrets (shall not induce such pain by bruising the testicles, which could make the man impotent):

12 Then you shall cut off her hand, your eye shall not pity her.

JUST WEIGHTS AND MEASURES

13 You shall not have in your bag divers weights, a great and a small.

14 You shall not have in your house divers measures, a great and a small.

15 But you shall have a perfect and just weight, a perfect and just measure shall you have: that your days may be lengthened in the land which the LORD your God gives you.

16 For all who do such things and all who do unrighteously, are an abomination unto the LORD your God (honesty in all things).

AMALEK

17 Remember what Amalek did unto you by the way, when you were come forth out of Egypt;

18 How he met you by the way, and smote the hindmost of you, even all who were feeble behind you, when you were faint and weary; and he feared not God.

19 Therefore it shall be, when the LORD your God has given you rest from all your enemies round about, in the land which the LORD your God gives you for an inheritance to possess it, that you shall blot out the remembrance of Amalek from under Heaven;

you shall not forget it. *(Amalek was to be utterly destroyed; not so the Egyptian. The Egyptian pictures man, as such; the Amalekite, man as the willing agent of evil. This means that the attitude of the Christian toward ordinary men of the world is necessarily different from that towards the willing and determined enemies of goodness and justice.*

God Who condemned Amalek to utter extinction was the very same God Who tenderly sheltered the little bird of Verse 22:6. The same God appeared in flesh, and in Luke 12:5-6 taught that the hand that upholds the little sparrow also thrusts wicked men into Hell. As well, Amalek, in Biblical typology, is a type of the flesh, which must be eradicated in the hearts and lives of Believers. This can be done only by the Believer placing his Faith exclusively in Christ and the Cross, which then gives the Holy Spirit latitude to work in our lives, Who Alone can perform this task [Rom. 6:3-14; Gal., Chpt. 5].)

CHAPTER 26
(1451 B.C.)
FIRSTFRUITS

AND it shall be, when you are come in unto the land which the LORD your God gives you for an inheritance, and possess it, and dwell therein;

2 That you shall take of the first of all the fruit of the Earth, which you shall bring of your land that the LORD your God gives you, and shall put it in a basket, and shall go unto the place which the LORD your God shall choose to place His Name there *(the best of the first of the harvest; there is no specification as to the amount to be offered; it was to be brought to the Tabernacle, and later on to the Temple).*

3 And you shall go unto the Priest who shall be in those days, and say unto him, I profess this day unto the LORD your God, that I am come unto the country which the LORD swore unto our fathers for to give us *(as well, this produce was to now belong to the Priest, who was a Type of Christ; all of this means that the Place, the Priest, the Worshipper, and the character of his worship all foreshadowed Calvary, the Great High Priest, the Lord Jesus Christ, Salvation by Grace, and the thankfulness and holiness which are the fruits of Grace).*

4 And the Priest shall take the basket out of your hand, and set it down before the Altar of the LORD your God *(the "Altar" was the Brazen Altar, which was a Type of Calvary; this tells us that all worship must have as its foundation the Cross of Christ, hence Paul saying, "We preach Christ Crucified" [I Cor. 1:23]).*

5 And you shall speak and say before the LORD your God, A Syrian ready to perish was my father, and he went down into Egypt, and sojourned there with a few, and became there a nation, great, mighty, and populous *(the reference is to Jacob, the father of the Twelve Tribes):*

6 And the Egyptians evil entreated us, and afflicted us, and laid upon us hard bondage:

7 And when we cried unto the LORD God of our fathers, the LORD heard our voice, and looked on our affliction, and our labour, and our oppression:

8 And the LORD brought us forth out of Egypt with a mighty hand, and with an outstretched arm, and with great terribleness, and with signs, and with wonders:

9 And He has brought us into this place, and has given us this land, even a land that flows with milk and honey.

10 And now, behold, I have brought the firstfruits of the land, which You, O LORD, have given me. And you shall set it before the LORD your God, and worship before the LORD your God *(the worshipper is confessing here that Grace has brought him into this good land promised to the fathers; and that the same Grace has filled his cup to overflowing, the bounty of which the basket of firstfruits was the evidence):*

11 And you shall rejoice in every good thing which the LORD your God has given unto you, and unto your house, you, and the Levite, and the stranger who is among you *(the worshipper as described here was to come with joy bearing his basket of firstfruits to the place of the Burnt and Sin Offerings chosen by God; the basket testified that God was the Author of all the worshipper's happiness; it was a joying before God in the enjoyment of what He had given; but due to the fact that it was to be brought to the "Altar," such proclaims to us that all Blessings flow to the Believer as a result of what Jesus did at the Cross, and that alone).*

TITHES

12 When you have made an end of tithing all the tithes of your increase the third year *(the year that all tithes were to go to the Priests and the Sanctuary [Num. 18:24]),* which is the year of tithing, and have given it unto the Levite, the stranger, the fatherless, and the widow, that they may eat within your gates,

and be filled;

13 Then you shall say before the LORD your God, I have brought away the hallowed things out of my house, and also have given them unto the Levite, and unto the stranger, to the fatherless, and to the widow, according to all Your Commandments which You have commanded me: I have not transgressed Your Commandments, neither have I forgotten them:

14 I have not eaten thereof in my mourning, neither have I taken away ought thereof for any unclean use, nor given ought thereof for the dead: but I have hearkened to the voice of the LORD my God, and have done according to all that You have commanded me. *(This is not a self-righteous boast; it is rather a solemn profession of attention to duties which might have been neglected, and refers, not to the keeping of every Commandment, but to the having faithfully done all that the Law required in respect of Tithes.)*

15 Look down from Your holy habitation, from Heaven, and bless Your people Israel, and the land which You have given us, as You swore unto our fathers, a land that flows with milk and honey *(blessing is here requested, and, to be sure, blessing will be abundantly given).*

OBEDIENCE

16 This day the LORD your God has commanded you to do these Statutes and Judgments: you shall therefore keep and do them with all your heart, and with all your soul.

17 You have avouched the LORD this day to be your God, and to walk in His ways, and to keep His Statutes, and His Commandments, and His Judgments, and to hearken unto His voice:

18 And the LORD has avouched you this day to be His peculiar people, as He has promised you, and that you should keep all His Commandments;

19 And to make you high above all nations which He has made, in praise, and in name, and in honour; and that you may be an holy people unto the LORD your God, as He has spoken. *(Moses concludes his address by a solemn admonition to the people to keep and observe the Laws and Commandments, which the Lord by him had laid upon them, reminding them that they had entered into covenant with God, and had thereby pledged themselves to obedience to all that He had enjoined; as He on His part had pledged Himself to be their Benefactor,*

Who would fulfill to them all His gracious Promises, and would exalt them above all the nations of the Earth — Pulpit.

In truth, it was not possible for Israel to properly keep these Laws and Commandments; however, they were to try, and to do so with all of their hearts. For their failures, the Sacrificial System was provided as Atonement for sin, which was a Type of the Cross. On that basis, God would greatly bless them; however, if they ignored His Laws and Commandments, which they sadly did, judgment would come upon them, which regrettably did happen.)

CHAPTER 27
(1451 B.C.)
THE ALTAR

AND Moses with the elders of Israel commanded the people, saying, Keep all the Commandments which I command you this day *(possession of the land depended on obedience to the Law).*

2 And it shall be on the day when you shall pass over Jordan unto the land which the LORD your God gives you, that you shall set up great stones, and plaister them with plaister:

3 And you shall write upon them all the words of this Law, when you are passed over, that you may go in unto the land which the LORD your God gives you, a land that flows with milk and honey; as the LORD God of your fathers has promised you *(it is not actually known as to whether each and all of the legislative enactments of the Torah were to be recorded, or rather the substance and essence of the Law; but even if the whole was to be inscribed, there would be no serious difficulty in the way of carrying this into effect, seeing there is no limitation as to the number of the stones to be set up; at any rate, this Law was to be plain and clear for all to see).*

4 Therefore it shall be when you be gone over Jordan, that you shall set up these stones, which I command you this day, in Mount Ebal, and you shall plaister them with plaister *(Mount Ebal, which was right beside Mount Gerizim, and located in the very center of Israel, was referred to as the "Mount of cursing," which pertained to the Judgment of God; the stones were to be set up upon this Mount, stipulating that if the Laws were broken, the curse of the broken Law would come upon the perpetrators, even as we shall see in the latter part of this Chapter).*

5 And there shall you build an Altar unto

the LORD your God, an Altar of stones: you shall not lift up any iron tool upon them.

6 You shall build the Altar of the LORD your God of whole stones: and you shall offer Burnt Offerings thereon unto the LORD your God (*the stones which made up the Altar, which was a Type of Christ and the Cross, were to be whole stones, and not stones which had been made to fit by man; this tells us that the Cross of Christ must not be altered in any way; the fact that this "Altar" was to be set up on Mount Ebal, the place of cursing, tells us that man's problem is sin; it was not to be set up on Mount Gerizim, which was the Mount of Blessing; but regrettably, this is where the modern Church has set her Altar, which refuses to admit that man's problem is sin; as well, the Law was kept only by Christ, hence, the Altar on Mount Ebal; and we as Believers can keep the Moral Law, which is still incumbent upon all, only by fully trusting Christ and what He has done for us at the Cross*):

7 And you shall offer Peace Offerings, and shall eat there, and rejoice before the LORD your God (*Burnt Offerings and Peace Offerings were commanded, but no Sin Offering; for the action of that day presupposes a redeemed people, but placed under the curse if they should break the Law; the Apostle Paul based his argument in Galatians 3 upon this Chapter — Williams*).

8 And you shall write upon the stones all the words of this Law very plainly. (*The blessings of Gerizim are entirely omitted here, for the subject was the judgment that would surely follow upon failure in a full obedience to the Commandments engraved upon the stones.*

As stated, the Altar was erected on Ebal, not on Gerizim; and, as pointed out, Sin Offerings are not mentioned. The Burnt Offerings and Peace Offerings were to be presented by those who had fulfilled the righteousness of the Law. Only one Man accomplished that; and He on the Mount of cursing erected an Altar upon which He offered up Himself as a Sin Offering for all those who by disobedience had brought upon themselves the doom of the Law, that is, death. At the same time, in thus offering up Himself, He became, on behalf of these guilty Law-breakers, the Burnt Offering and the Peace Offering, which our sin and failure made it impossible to bring to God — Williams.)

9 And Moses and the Priests the Levites spoke unto all Israel, saying, Take heed, and hearken, O Israel; this day you are become the people of the LORD your God (*much responsibility was upon them*).

10 You shall therefore obey the voice of the LORD your God, and do His Commandments and His Statutes, which I command you this day.

11 And Moses charged the people the same day, saying,

12 These shall stand upon Mount Gerizim to bless the people, when you are come over Jordan; Simeon, and Levi, and Judah, and Issachar, and Joseph, and Benjamin (*these particular Tribes were to stand upon Mount Gerizim, which was very close to Mount Ebal, and pronounce blessings upon Israel, which account of Blessings is given in the next Chapter*):

13 And these shall stand upon Mount Ebal to curse; Reuben, Gad, and Asher, and Zebulun, Dan, and Naphtali (*they were to stand for the curse; it does not say they were to curse the people; all who broke the Law were cursed*).

CURSES

14 And the Levites shall speak, and say unto all the men of Israel with a loud voice (*they were probably situated between the two mountains, with a Levite standing a voice distance away from another, and shouting loudly the Message of the Lord, in order that all of Israel might hear*),

15 Cursed be the man who makes any graven or molten image, an abomination unto the LORD, the work of the hands of the craftsman, and puts it in a secret place. And all the people shall answer and say, Amen (*each of the first eleven curses is directed against some particular sin already denounced in the Law*).

16 Cursed be he who sets light by his father or his mother. And all the people shall say, Amen (*the failure to honor the father and the mother*).

17 Cursed be he who removes his neighbour's landmark. And all the people shall say, Amen (*by fraud, attempts to steal another's property by secretly moving the boundary*).

18 Cursed be he who makes the blind to wander out of the way. And all the people shall say, Amen (*cruel to the handicapped*).

19 Cursed be he who perverts the judgment of the stranger (*Gentile*), fatherless, and widow. And all the people shall say, Amen (*failure to show kindness to all, even the least among them*).

20 Cursed be he who lies with his father's wife; because he uncovers his father's skirt. And all the people shall say, Amen (*incest*).

21 Cursed be he who lies with any manner of beast. And all the people shall say, Amen (*bestiality, which was prominent among the*

heathen).

22 Cursed be he who lies with his sister, the daughter of his father, or the daughter of his mother. And all the people shall say, Amen *(again, incest is mentioned).*

23 Cursed be he who lies with his mother in law. And all the people shall say, Amen *(the sin of incest was prominent among the heathen, therefore, the triple admonition).*

24 Cursed be he who smites his neighbour secretly. And all the people shall say, Amen *(tries to harm him behind his back).*

25 Cursed be he who takes reward to slay an innocent person. And all the people shall say, Amen *(contract killings).*

26 Cursed be he who confirms not all the words of this Law to do them. And all the people shall say, Amen *(the Law, as given by God, was to govern Israel in all that she did; in fact, Israel constituted the only people in the world who had the Law of God, which made them superior in every respect).*

CHAPTER 28
(1451 B.C.)
THE BLESSINGS

AND it shall come to pass, if you shall hearken diligently unto the voice of the LORD your God, to observe and to do all His Commandments which I command you this day, that the LORD your God will set you on high above all nations of the Earth *(the condition for all the Blessings which will be pronounced is obedience)*:

2 And all these Blessings shall come on you, and overtake you, if you shall hearken unto the voice of the LORD your God *(the Blessings will be so abundant that they will literally chase down the people of God).*

3 Blessed shall you be in the city, and blessed shall you be in the field *(the location doesn't matter, the Blessings will come).*

4 Blessed shall be the fruit of your body *(the children)*, and the fruit of your ground *(crops)*, and the fruit of your cattle, the increase of your kine, and the flocks of your sheep *(herds).*

5 Blessed shall be your basket and your store *(the storehouses will be full).*

6 Blessed shall you be when you come in, and blessed shall you be when you go out *(no time limit on the Blessings).*

7 The LORD shall cause your enemies who rise up against you to be smitten before your face: they shall come out against you one way,

and flee before you seven ways *(because the Lord will fight for Israel).*

8 The LORD shall command the Blessing upon you in your storehouses, and in all that you set your hand unto; and He shall bless you in the land which the LORD your God gives you *(when the Command from the Lord is given, nothing can stop that Command).*

9 The LORD shall establish you an holy people unto himself, as He has sworn unto you, if you shall keep the Commandments of the LORD your God, and walk in His ways *(once again, the condition of obedience is put before the people).*

10 And all people of the Earth shall see that you are called by the Name of the LORD; and they shall be afraid of you *(the fame of Israel, and her Blessings given by the Lord, will be spread abroad, with all heathen nations afraid of attacking her, because of her God).*

11 And the LORD shall make you plentiful in goods, in the fruit of your body, and in the fruit of your cattle, and in the fruit of your ground, in the land which the LORD swore unto your fathers to give you *(everything will be bountiful).*

12 The LORD shall open unto you His good treasure, the Heaven to give the rain unto your land in his season, and to bless all the work of your hand: and you shall lend unto many nations, and you shall not borrow *(the treasure-house of Heaven would be open to Israel).*

13 And the LORD shall make you the head, and not the tail; and you shall be above only, and you shall not be beneath; if that you hearken unto the Commandments of the LORD your God, which I command you this day, to observe and to do them *(again, obedience is set before Israel):*

14 And you shall not go aside from any of the words which I command you this day, to the right hand, or to the left, to go after other gods to serve them *(Israel was to faithfully obey the Law; as well, Believers under the New Covenant can claim the same Promises, in fact, much more easily than Israel of old, because of Christ and the Cross; as wonderful as this is which the Lord promises Israel, He now promises even more under the New Covenant, which Paul referred to as a "Better Covenant" [Heb. 8:6]).*

DISOBEDIENCE

15 But it shall come to pass, if you will not hearken unto the voice of the LORD your God,

to observe to do all His Commandments and His Statutes which I command you this day; that all these curses shall come upon you, and overtake you *(the curse thus appears as the exact counterpart of the blessing, and because of disobedience)*:

16 Cursed shall you be in the city, and cursed shall you be in the field *(as the blessings were nationwide, the curse likewise shall be)*.

17 Cursed shall be your basket and your store *(the storehouses will be empty)*.

18 Cursed shall be the fruit of your body, and the fruit of your land, the increase of your kine, and the flocks of your sheep *(the children will be sickly, and the herds will be few and thin)*.

19 Cursed shall you be when you come in, and cursed shall you be when you go out *(nothing that is done will stop the curse)*.

20 The LORD shall send upon you cursing, vexation, and rebuke, in all that you set your hand unto for to do, until you be destroyed, and until you perish quickly; because of the wickedness of your doings, whereby you have forsaken Me *(Blessings for obedience, destruction for disobedience; it is the same presently)*.

21 The LORD shall make the pestilence cleave unto you, until He has consumed you from off the land, where you go to possess it *(sickness will be the lot of Israel)*.

22 The LORD shall smite you with a consumption, and with a fever, and with an inflammation, and with an extreme burning, and with the sword, and with blasting, and with mildew; and they shall pursue you until you perish *(if the Lord be against us, who can be for us?)*.

23 And your Heaven that is over your head shall be brass *(prayers will not be answered)*, and the Earth that is under you shall be iron *(will not yield crops)*.

24 The LORD shall make the rain of your land powder and dust *(there will be no rain)*: from Heaven shall it come down upon you, until you be destroyed *(the curses shall come from Heaven, because of disobedience)*.

25 The LORD shall cause you to be smitten before your enemies: you shall go out one way against them, and flee seven ways before them: and shall be removed into all the kingdoms of the Earth *(this happened totally in A.D. 70, when Titus, the Roman General, laid Jerusalem waste, with hundreds of thousands of Jews sold all over the world as slaves, and they remained scattered for nearly 2,000 years)*.

26 And your carcase shall be meat unto all fowls of the air, and unto the beasts of the Earth, and no man shall fray them away *(utter defeat in battle)*.

27 The LORD will smite you with the botch of Egypt, and with the emerods, and with the scab, and with the itch, whereof you can not be healed *(the Lord controls diseases and sickness, as is obvious here)*.

28 The LORD shall smite you with madness, and blindness, and astonishment of heart *(fear and insanity)*:

29 And you shall grope at noonday, as the blind gropes in darkness, and you shall not prosper in your ways: and you shall be only oppressed and spoiled evermore, and no man shall save you *(once again, if God be against us, who can be for us?)*.

30 You shall betroth a wife, and another man shall lie with her: you shall build an house, and you shall not dwell therein: you shall plant a vineyard, and shall not gather the grapes thereof *(plans and labor will be in vain)*.

31 Your ox shall be slain before your eyes, and you shall not eat thereof: your ass shall be violently taken away from before your face, and shall not be restored to you: your sheep shall be given unto your enemies, and you shall have none to rescue them *(without God, Israel will be helpless before her enemies)*.

32 Your sons and your daughters shall be given unto another people, and your eyes shall look, and fail with longing for them all the day long; and there shall be no might in your hand *(Israel will be powerless)*.

33 The fruit of your land, and all your labours, shall a nation which you know not eat up; and you shall be only oppressed and crushed always *(labor will be wasted)*:

34 So that you shall be mad for the sight of your eyes which you shall see *(all that is seen is destruction)*.

35 The LORD shall smite you in the knees, and in the legs, with a sore botch that cannot be healed, from the sole of your foot unto the top of your head *(the Lord can heal, and the Lord can bring about disease)*.

36 The LORD shall bring you and your king which you shall set over you, unto a nation which neither you nor your fathers have known; and there shall you serve others gods, wood and stone *(and this is exactly what happened!)*.

37 And you shall become an astonishment, a proverb, and a byword, among all nations where the LORD shall lead you *(this has been*

fulfilled to the letter, as well!).

38 You shall carry much seed out into the field, and shall gather but little in; for the locust shall consume it *(efforts will be wasted)*.

39 You shall plant vineyards, and dress them, but shall neither drink of the wine, nor gather the grapes; for the worms shall eat them.

40 You shall have olive trees throughout all your coasts, but you shall not anoint yourself with the oil; for your olive shall cast his fruit *(will not bring forth fruit)*.

41 You shall beget sons and daughters, but you shall not enjoy them; for they shall go into captivity *(will be stolen as slaves by heathen tribes)*.

42 All your trees and fruit of your land shall the locust consume.

43 The stranger that is within you shall get up above you very high; and you shall come down very low *(Gentiles in Israel will prosper, but Israelites won't)*.

44 He shall lend to you, and you shall not lend to him: he shall be the head, and you shall be the tail.

45 Moreover all these curses shall come upon you, and shall pursue you, and overtake you, till you be destroyed; because you hearkened not unto the voice of the LORD your God, to keep His Commandments and His Statutes which He commanded you *(disobedience)*:

46 And they shall be upon you for a sign and for a wonder, and upon your seed for ever *(this, though it may imply the final and utter rejection of Israel as a nation, does not, however, preclude the hope of restoration; in fact, Israel will be restored, and fully [Rom. 11:25-27])*.

47 Because you served not the LORD your GOD with joyfulness, and with gladness of heart, for the abundance of all things *(all of these curses would come upon them, because they would not serve God)*;

48 Therefore shall you serve your enemies which the LORD shall send against you, in hunger, and in thirst, and in nakedness, and in want of all things: and he shall put a yoke of iron upon your neck, until he have destroyed you *(if Israel would not serve God, they would have to serve their enemies)*.

49 The LORD shall bring a nation against you from far, from the end of the Earth, as swift as the eagle flies; a nation whose tongue you shall not understand *(and that happened, again and again)*;

50 A nation of fierce countenance, which shall not regard the person of the old, nor show favour to the young *(and so are all nations which don't know God)*:

51 And he shall eat the fruit of your cattle, and the fruit of your land, until you be destroyed: which also shall not leave you either corn, wine, or oil, or the increase of your kine, or flocks of your sheep, until he have destroyed you *(complete destruction)*.

52 And he shall besiege you in all your gates, until your high and fenced walls come down, wherein you trusted, throughout all your land: and he shall besiege you in all your gates throughout all your land, which the LORD your God has given you *(these cities will be destroyed, which they were by the Babylonians)*.

53 And you shall eat the fruit of your own body, the flesh of your sons and of your daughters, which the LORD your God has given you, in the siege, and in the straitness, wherewith your enemies shall distress you *(exactly as predicted here, Israel ultimately resorted to cannibalism [II Ki. 6:28-29; Jer. 19:9; Lam. 2:20; 4:10])*:

54 So that the man who is tender among you, and very delicate, his eye shall be evil toward his brother, and toward the wife of his bosom, and toward the remnant of his children which he shall leave *(there will be no love in the family, but only hatred)*:

55 So that he will not give to any of them of the flesh of his children whom he shall eat: because he has nothing left him in the siege, and in the straitness, wherewith your enemies shall distress you in all your gates *(that Israel could be reduced to such is beyond comprehension, but they were; however, they couldn't say that they were not warned)*.

56 The tender and delicate woman among you, which would not adventure to set the sole of her foot upon the ground for delicateness and tenderness, her eye shall be evil toward the husband of her bosom, and toward her son, and toward her daughter,

57 And toward her young one who comes out from between her feet, and toward her children which she shall bear: for she shall eat them for want of all things secretly in the siege and straitness, wherewith your enemy shall distress you in your gates. *(How could the greatest people on the face of the Earth, so favored by God, fall so low? The answer is simple. When we forsake God, and continue to do so despite continued warnings to return, God will ultimately forsake us. These terrible situations predicted here are the result of such disobedience.)*

58 If you will not observe to do all the words of this law that are written in this Book, that you may fear this glorious and fearful name, THE LORD YOUR GOD *(this speaks of the entirety of the Book of the Law)*;

59 Then the LORD will make your plagues wonderful, and the plagues of your seed, even great plagues, and of long continuance, and sore sicknesses, and of long continuance.

60 Moreover He will bring upon you all the diseases of Egypt, which you were afraid of; and they shall cleave unto you.

61 Also every sickness, and every plague, which is not written in the Book of this Law, them will the LORD bring upon you, until you be destroyed *(we learn from this, as should be obvious, that God controls all sickness and disease; he may use Satan as His instrument to bring about such, but, still, it is the Lord Who is always in control)*.

62 And you shall be left few in number, whereas you were as the stars of Heaven for multitude; because you would not obey the voice of the LORD your God *(once again, disobedience of the Word of the Lord is the cause)*.

63 And it shall come to pass, that as the LORD rejoiced over you to do you good, and to multiply you; so the LORD will rejoice over you to destroy you, and to bring you to nought; and you shall be plucked from off the land where you go to possess it *(the Lord rejoices in doing good for those who obey Him, and continues to rejoice over bringing evil on those who disobey Him; the idea is, the Lord rejoices in stamping out evil, even if such evil is found in His chosen People)*.

64 And the LORD shall scatter you among all people, from the one end of the Earth even unto the other; and there you shall serve other gods, which neither you nor your fathers have known, even wood and stone *(in other words, if they wouldn't serve God, then they would have to serve idols)*.

65 And among these nations shall you find no ease, neither shall the sole of your foot have rest: but the LORD shall give you there a trembling heart, and failing of eyes, and sorrow of mind:

66 And your life shall hang in doubt before you; and you shall fear day and night, and shall have none assurance of your life *(a continued vexation of spirit)*:

67 In the morning you shall say, Would God it were evening! and at evening you shall say, Would God it were morning! for the fear of your heart wherewith you shall fear, and for the sight of your eyes which you shall see *(the person of disobedience is plagued by fear constantly)*.

68 And the LORD shall bring you into Egypt again with ships, by the way whereof I spoke unto you, You shall see it no more again: and there you shall be sold unto your enemies for bondmen and bondwomen, and no man shall buy you *(after the capture of Jerusalem by Titus, the Jews were in large numbers carried into Egypt, and there subjected to the most ignominious bondage, exactly as the Scripture foretold)*.

CHAPTER 29
(1451 B.C.)
THE COVENANT

THESE are the words of the Covenant, which the LORD commanded Moses to make with the Children of Israel in the land of Moab, beside the Covenant which He made with them in Horeb *(this was not a new Covenant in addition to that made at Sinai, but simply a renewal and reaffirmation of that Covenant)*.

2 And Moses called unto all Israel, and said unto them, You have seen all that the LORD did before your eyes in the land of Egypt unto Pharaoh, and unto all his servants, and unto all his land *(in other words, what the Lord had just said he will render for disobedience, He is able to do; remember Egypt!)*;

3 The great temptations which your eyes have seen, the signs, and those great miracles *(so they knew what God could do)*:

4 Yet the LORD has not given you an heart to perceive, and eyes to see, and ears to hear, unto this day *(the Lord gave you a heart in order that you might perceive, and eyes that you might see, and ears that you might hear, so that you are without excuse)*.

5 And I have led you forty years in the wilderness: your clothes are not waxed old upon you, and your shoe is not waxed old upon your foot *(even the very clothing they wore constituted a miracle, in that it did not wear out in all of the forty years of wandering in that awful wilderness)*.

6 You have not eaten bread, neither have you drunk wine or strong drink: that you might know that I am the LORD your God *(whatever they had in the wilderness, God gave it to them, in order that they might know)*.

7 And when you came unto this place, Sihon the king of Heshbon, and Og the king of

Bashan, came out against us unto battle, and we smote them:

8 And we took their land, and gave it for an inheritance unto the Reubenites, and to the Gadites, and to the half tribe of Manasseh (the Lord helped us to do this).

A COMMAND

9 Keep therefore the words of this Covenant, and do them, that you may prosper in all that you do (prosperity has always followed a true obedience of the Word of the Lord).

10 You stand this day all of you before the LORD your God; your captains of your Tribes, your elders, and your officers, with all the men of Israel,

11 Your little ones, your wives, and the stranger who is in your camp, from the hewer of your wood unto the drawer of your water:

12 That you should enter into Covenant with the LORD your God, and into His oath, which the LORD your God makes with you this day (the Covenant was to include all, then and in the future):

13 That He may establish you to day for a people unto Himself, and that He may be unto you a God, as He has said unto you, and as He has sworn unto your fathers, to Abraham, to Isaac, and to Jacob (all the Promises the Lord made to the Patriarchs, He will carry out, that is, if the people will only serve Him with an obedient heart).

14 Neither with you only do I make this Covenant and this oath;

15 But with him who stands here with us this day before the LORD our God, and also with him who is not here with us this day (the Covenant was not only with Abraham, Isaac, and Jacob, but all who were present that day, and all Israelites who would be born thereafter, at least until the Messiah came, Who would bring about the New Covenant [Gal. 4:4-5]):

DISOBEDIENCE

16 (For you know how we have dwelt in the land of Egypt; and how we came through the nations which you passed by;

17 And you have seen their abominations, and their idols, wood and stone, silver and gold, which were among them [in the Hebrew language, these terms concerning heathen gods are given in contempt]:)

18 Lest there should be among you man, or woman, or family, or Tribe, whose heart turns away this day from the LORD our God, to go and serve the gods of these nations; lest there should be among you a root that bears gall and wormwood (a striking image of the destructive fruit borne by idolatry; and let the Reader understand, idolatry, even in Christendom, isn't dead; any worship that is centered up in anything except Jesus Christ and Him Crucified can be construed as nothing more than idolatry [I Jn. 5:21]);

19 And it come to pass, when he hears the words of this curse, that he bless himself in his heart, saying, I shall have peace, though I walk in the imagination of my heart, to add drunkenness to thirst (the idea is, for the individual who functions in disobedience, let him not think that because he seems to be doing well at the moment, that judgment is not forthcoming; it will come!):

20 The LORD will not spare him, but then the anger of the LORD and His jealousy shall smoke against that man, and all the curses that are written in this Book shall lie upon him, and the LORD shall blot out his name from under Heaven (will remove his name out of the Book of Life, which means he will be eternally lost, that is, if no true Repentance is forthcoming).

21 And the LORD shall separate him unto evil out of all the Tribes of Israel, according to all the curses of the Covenant that are written in this Book of the Law (if the entirety of the Tribe is living for God except one man, the righteousness of the entirety of the Tribe will not cover the one man; the Lord will seek him out, and he will answer for his own sin; let no one think they can escape the awful Eye of God):

22 So that the generation to come of your children who shall rise up after you, and the stranger who shall come from a far land, shall say, when they see the plagues of that land, and the sicknesses which the LORD has laid upon it;

23 And that the whole land thereof is brimstone, and salt, and burning, that it is not sown, nor bears, nor any grass grows therein, like the overthrow of Sodom, and Gomorrah, Admah, and Zeboim, which the LORD overthrew in His anger, and in His wrath:

24 Even all nations shall say, Wherefore has the LORD done thus unto this land? what means the heat of this great anger?

25 Then men shall say, Because they have forsaken the Covenant of the LORD God of

their fathers, which He made with them when He brought them forth out of the land of Egypt:

26 For they went and served other gods, and worshipped them, gods whom they knew not, and whom He had not given unto them:

27 And the anger of the LORD was kindled against this land, to bring upon it all the curses that are written in this Book:

28 And the LORD rooted them out of their land in anger, and in wrath, and in great indignation, and cast them into another land, as it is this day (the whole world will know why they were dispelled, and so it is!).

29 The secret things belong unto the LORD our God: but those things which are revealed belong unto us and to our children for ever, that we may do all the words of this Law. (Williams says, "This Verse is much misunderstood. It does not mean that the secret things belong to God, and the revealed things to His People; but it does mean that God's Purposes, whether secret or revealed, all belong to Israel." So there was no excuse for Israel, as there is no excuse for modern day Believers. As they had the Law before them, we have the Word of God, as well, before us!)

CHAPTER 30
(1451 B.C.)
TRUE REPENTANCE REWARDED

AND it shall come to pass, when all these things are come upon you, the blessing and the curse, which I have set before you, and you shall call them to mind among all the nations, where the LORD your God has driven you (in effect, the Lord through Moses tells Israel that they will fail Him, thereby bringing the curses upon themselves),

2 And shall return unto the LORD your God, and shall obey His voice according to all that I command you this day, you and your children, with all your heart, and with all your soul (true Repentance);

3 That then the LORD your God will turn your captivity, and have compassion upon you, and will return and gather you from all the nations, whither the LORD your God has scattered you (this will take place at the Second Coming [Zech. 12:1]).

4 If any of yours be driven out unto the outmost parts of Heaven, from thence will the LORD your God gather you, and from thence will He fetch you (at the Second Coming, the Lord will gather every Jew from all the nations of the world, and bring them to Israel

[Jer. 32:37-41]):

5 And the LORD your God will bring you into the land which your fathers possessed, and you shall possess it; and He will do you good, and multiply you above your fathers (all the Blessings promised will now be possessed, because of obedience, which includes, above all, the acceptance of the Lord Jesus Christ as their Messiah and Saviour [Zech. 13:6]).

6 And the LORD your God will circumcise your heart, and the heart of your seed, to love the LORD your God with all your heart, and with all your soul, that you may live (this speaks of the New Covenant accepted by Israel, which refers to the Lord Jesus Christ, and which Paul mentioned [Rom. 2:28-29]).

7 And the LORD your God will put all these curses upon your enemies, and on them who hate you, which persecuted you.

8 And you shall return and obey the voice of the LORD, and do all His Commandments which I command you this day.

9 And the LORD your God will make you plenteous in every work of your hand, in the fruit of your body, and in the fruit of your cattle, and in the fruit of your land, for good: for the LORD will again rejoice over you for good, as He rejoiced over your fathers (a complete restoration, which the Holy Spirit through Paul also predicted [Rom. 11:26]):

10 If you shall hearken unto the voice of the LORD your God, to keep His Commandments and His Statutes which are written in this Book of the Law, and if you turn unto the LORD your God with all your heart, and with all your soul (in other words, if Israel would only try to obey, Blessings would be theirs; but if they forsook the Lord, as they ultimately did, the Blessings would be replaced with judgment, which they were).

GOD'S WORD

11 For this Commandment which I command you this day, it is not hidden from you, neither is it far off (if any were ignorant, it was because they desired to be; the way had been made plain to them).

12 It is not in Heaven, that you should say, Who shall go up for us to Heaven, and bring it unto us, that we may hear it, and do it? (While the law originated in Heaven, the Lord had sent it down to Earth.)

13 Neither is it beyond the sea, that you should say, Who shall go over the sea for us, and bring it unto us, that we may hear it, and

do it? (The Law was not in another place, hard to find.)

14 But the word is very near unto you, in your mouth, and in your heart, that you may do it (in other words, if Israel was ignorant, or anyone among them, it was a willful ignorance; it is the same presently with modern Christians; anyone who wants to know the Word of God can know the Word of God).

OBEDIENCE

15 See, I have set before you this day life and good, and death and evil (Israel had a choice, even as modern Christians have a choice);

16 In that I command you this day to love the LORD your God, to walk in His ways, and to keep His Commandments and His Statutes and His Judgments, that you may live and multiply: and the LORD your God shall bless you in the land where you go to possess it (the ingredients for blessings, so to speak, were as near to them as the Bible; and so it is presently!).

17 But if your heart turn away, so that you will not hear, but shall be drawn away, and worship other gods, and serve them;

18 I denounce unto you this day, that you shall surely perish, and that you shall not prolong your days upon the land, where you pass over Jordan to go to possess it (the warning is amply given).

19 I call Heaven and Earth to record this day against you, that I have set before you life and death, blessing and cursing: therefore choose life, that both you and your seed may live (once again, the choice was theirs; the way had been made crystal clear to them; therefore, they could not claim ignorance):

20 That you may love the LORD your God, and that you may obey His voice, and that you may cleave unto Him: for He is your life, and the length of your days: that you may dwell in the land which the LORD swore unto your fathers, to Abraham, to Isaac, and to Jacob, to give them (Israel is told here to cleave unto the Lord, for He is everything they need; once again, it is the same presently! Jesus is all that we need [Lk. 4:18-19]).

CHAPTER 31
(1451 B.C.)
MOSES

AND Moses went and spoke these words unto all Israel.

2 And he said unto them, I am an hundred and twenty years old this day (this day, whatever it might have been, was his birthday); I can no more go out and come in (not because of a lack of physical strength, but because his Ministry was now finished): also the LORD has said unto me, You shall not go over this Jordan (Moses was a type of the Law, and the Law can never possess the land, because of the feebleness of man's moral nature, all brought about by the Fall; only Grace can inherit the Promise [Gal. 3:18]).

3 The LORD your God, He will go over before you, and He will destroy these nations from before you, and you shall possess them: and Joshua, He shall go over before you, as the LORD has said. (Joshua was chosen by the Lord to lead Israel into the Promised Land. He is a Type of Christ. Actually, the Jewish name of Jesus was "Joshua." It means "Saviour." Jesus has done for us what we could not do for ourselves. In other words, He became our Substitute, and our identification with Him guarantees us His Victory [Jn. 14:20].)

4 And the LORD shall do unto them as He did to Sihon and to Og, kings of the Amorites, and unto the land of them, whom He destroyed (while Israel was the instrument, it was the Lord Who actually destroyed these enemies, as He Alone can do such!).

5 And the LORD shall give them up before your face, that you may do unto them according unto all the Commandments which I have commanded you (with the Lord, Israel could not be defeated).

6 Be strong and of a good courage, fear not, nor be afraid of them: for the LORD your God, He it is Who does go with you; He will not fail you, nor forsake you (What a Promise! And to be sure, this Promise holds true even unto this moment, and even greater [Heb. 8:6]).

JOSHUA

7 And Moses called unto Joshua, and said unto him in the sight of all Israel, Be strong and of a good courage: for you must go with this people unto the land which the LORD has sworn unto their fathers to give them: and you shall cause them to inherit it (our Heavenly Joshua Alone has already done for us everything that is needed; for us to possess the Heavenly Promise, we must but place our Faith exclusively in Christ and the Cross; the Holy Spirit will then see to it that every Promise is possessed

[Rom. 8:1-2, 11]).

8 And the LORD, He it is Who does go before you: He will be with you, He will not fail you, neither forsake you: fear not, neither be dismayed (let the Reader understand that this Promise given to Israel so long ago is just as valid now, and even more so, because of Christ and what He has done for us at the Cross [Rom. 6:3-14]).

THE PRIESTS

9 And Moses wrote this Law, and delivered it unto the Priests the sons of Levi, which bore the Ark of the Covenant of the LORD, and unto all the elders of Israel.

10 And Moses commanded them, saying, At the end of every seven years, in the solemnity of the year of release, in the Feast of Tabernacles,

11 When all Israel is come to appear before the LORD your God in the place which He shall choose, you shall read this law before all Israel in their hearing (the entirety of the Law was to be read every seven years, and all of Israel was required to hear it).

12 Gather the people together, men and women, and children, and your stranger that is within your gates, that they may hear, and that they may learn, and fear the LORD your God, and observe to do all the words of this Law (none were to be excluded, all were to be included):

13 And that their children, which have not known any thing, may hear, and learn to fear the LORD your God, as long as you live in the land where you go over Jordan to possess it (future generations were commanded by the Lord to know the Law, exactly as these here this day).

GOD'S MESSAGE TO MOSES

14 And the LORD said unto Moses, Behold, the days approach that you must die: call Joshua, and present yourselves in the Tabernacle of the congregation, that I may give him a charge. And Moses and Joshua went, and presented themselves in the Tabernacle of the congregation (Moses and Joshua were instructed by the Lord to go into the Sanctuary).

15 And the LORD appeared in the Tabernacle in a pillar of a cloud: and the pillar of the cloud stood over the door of the Tabernacle (the Presence of the Lord).

16 And the LORD said unto Moses, Behold, you shall sleep with your fathers; and this people will rise up, and go a whoring after the gods of the strangers (Gentiles) of the land, where they go to be among them, and will forsake Me, and break My Covenant which I have made with them (the Lord predicts that Israel will fail, which they did!).

17 Then My anger shall be kindled against them in that day, and I will forsake them, and I will hide My face from them, and they shall be devoured, and many evils and trouble shall befall them; so that they will say in that day, Are not these evils come upon us, because our God is not among us? (This was not very pleasant for Moses to hear, but it was the truth.)

18 And I will surely hide My face in that day for all the evils which they shall have wrought, in that they are turned unto other gods (idolatry was the basic cause of the downfall of Israel, at least when the Lord allowed them to be taken over by the Babylonians, which would be approximately 800-plus years into the future).

19 Now therefore write ye this song for you, and teach it the Children of Israel: put it in their mouths, that this song may be a witness for Me against the Children of Israel (this refers to the song which follows in the next Chapter; this shows the value that the Holy Spirit places on songs which glorify the Lord).

20 For when I shall have brought them into the land which I swore unto their fathers, that flows with milk and honey; and they shall have eaten and filled themselves, and waxed fat: then will they turn unto other gods, and serve them, and provoke Me, and break My Covenant (prosperity oftentimes causes people to forsake the Lord).

21 And it shall come to pass, when many evils and troubles are befallen them, that this song shall testify against them as a witness; for it shall not be forgotten out of the mouths of their seed: for I know their imagination which they go about, even now, before I have brought them into the land which I swore (were this a history of human imagination, the inventor would never dream of closing the service of one great Chieftain, and beginning the exploits of another, in such a cloud of gloom and depression)

THE CHARGE

22 Moses therefore wrote this song the same day, and taught it the Children of Israel.

23 And he gave Joshua the son of Nun a charge, and said, Be strong and of a good courage: for you shall bring the Children of Israel

into the land which I swore unto them: and I will be with you.

24 And it came to pass, when Moses had made an end of writing the words of this Law in a Book, until they were finished,

THE LEVITES

25 That Moses commanded the Levites, which bore the Ark of the Covenant of the LORD, saying,

26 Take this Book of the Law, and put it in the side of the Ark of the Covenant of the LORD your God, that it may be there for a witness against you *(there was to be no excuse!)*.

27 For I know your rebellion, and your stiff neck: behold, while I am yet alive with you this day, you have been rebellious against the LORD; and how much more after my death?

28 Gather unto me all the Elders of your Tribes, and your officers, that I may speak these words in their ears, and call Heaven and Earth to record against them.

29 For I know that after my death you will utterly corrupt yourselves, and turn aside from the way which I have commanded you: and evil will befall you in the latter days *(has double meaning: the destruction of Israel in A.D. 70, and the acceptance of the Antichrist by Israel, which is yet future, which will bring about the Great Tribulation [Mat. 24:21])*; because you will do evil in the sight of the LORD, to provoke Him to anger through the work of your hands.

30 And Moses spoke in the ears of all the congregation of Israel the words of this song, until they were ended.

CHAPTER 32
(1451 B.C.)
THE SONG OF MOSES

GIVE ear, O ye Heavens, and I will speak: and hear, O Earth, the words of My mouth *(both Heaven and Earth are called to account, because this song affects both)*.

2 My doctrine shall drop as the rain, My speech shall distil as the dew, as the small rain upon the tender herb, and as the showers upon the grass *(the Word of the Lord always brings prosperity)*:

3 Because I will publish the Name of the LORD: ascribe ye greatness unto our God *(it is the Greatness of God as the Almighty that is celebrated here)*.

4 He is the Rock, His work is perfect: for all His ways are judgment: a God of truth and without iniquity, just and right is He. *(Five times in this Song Jehovah is praised as the Rock [Vss. 4, 15, 18, 30-31]. The occurrences in Verses 31 and 37 ironically refer to the false rocks of the nations. Five is the number of Grace.)*

5 They have corrupted themselves, their spot is not the spot of His children: they are a perverse and crooked generation. *(Israel claimed to be the Children of God, but they were not; they were rather a stain and a reproach [Isa. 1:4]. How much does this pertain to the modern Church?)*

6 Do ye thus requite the LORD *(repay Him for His Blessings by corrupting yourselves)*, O foolish people and unwise? Is not He your father Who has bought you? Has He not made you, and established you?

7 Remember the days of old, consider the years of many generations: ask your father, and he will show you: your elders, and they will tell you.

8 When the Most High divided to the nations their inheritance, when He separated the sons of Adam, He set the bounds of the people according to the number of the Children of Israel *(long before there was an Israel, the Lord was planning for them)*.

9 For the LORD's portion is His people: Jacob is the lot of His inheritance *(the Lord measured out the inheritance of Israel, and did it Personally)*.

10 He found him in a desert land, and in the waste howling wilderness; He led him about, He instructed him, He kept him as the apple of His eye *(this must be taken as indicating that Israel is ever in the Eye of the Lord, the object of His constant and tenderest care)*.

11 As a eagle stirs up her nest, flutters over her young, spreads abroad her wings, takes them, bears them on her wings:

12 So the LORD Alone did lead him, and there was no strange god with him *(Israel must admit that none of the strange gods worshipped by the heathen had anything to do with what the Lord Alone had done for them)*.

13 He made him ride on the high places of the Earth, that he might eat the increase of the fields: and He made him to suck honey out of the rock, and oil out of the flinty rock *(blessings)*;

14 Butter of kine *(cattle)*, and milk of sheep, with fat of lambs, and rams of the breed of Bashan, and goats, with the fat of kidneys of wheat; and you did drink the pure blood of

the grape. *(This does not speak of fermented wine, as some claim. What they esteemed as a luxury was the pure unadulterated juice of the grape, freshly pressed out and drunk with the foam on it. Verses 7-14 celebrate His Goodness and Bounty during the period of the Pentateuch.)*

15 But Jeshurun waxed fat *("Jeshurun" means "righteous"; He predicts that Israel will fall into a state, the opposite of that to which it was destined),* and kicked: you are waxed fat, you are grown thick, you are covered with fatness; then he forsook God which made him, and lightly esteemed the Rock of his Salvation. *(Verses 15-19 record Israel's evil response to that goodness during the period of their kings. They foolishly esteemed the "Rock.")*

16 They provoked Him to jealousy with strange gods, with abominations provoked they Him to anger *(sinners in the hands of an angry God).*

17 They sacrificed unto devils *(demons),* not to God; to gods whom they knew not, to new gods that came newly up, whom your fathers feared not *(gods recently invented or discovered).*

18 Of the Rock Who begat you you are unmindful, and have forgotten God Who formed you *(rebelled against their Maker).*

19 And when the LORD saw it *(saw the idols),* He abhorred them, because of the provoking of His sons, and of His daughters.

20 And He said, I will hide My face from them, I will see what their end shall be: for they are a very froward generation, children in whom is no faith. *(This Verse contemplates the period between the Captivity in Babylon and the Advent of the Messiah. They had faith all right, but it was in the wrong thing, their own religion. It is the same problem presently!)*

21 They have moved Me to jealousy with that which is not God: they have provoked Me to anger with their vanities: and I will move them to jealousy with those which are not a people: I will provoke them to anger with a foolish nation. *(This Verse relates to the period of the Acts of the Apostles [Rom. 10:11]. It pertains to the Lord turning to the Gentiles.)*

22 For a fire is kindled in My anger, and shall burn unto the lowest Hell, and shall consume the Earth with her increase, and set on fire the foundations of the mountains. *(Verses 22-33 relate to Israel's dispersion among the nations of the world, after A.D. 70.)*

23 I will heap mischiefs upon them: I will spend My arrows upon them *(as Righteousness brings blessings, wickedness brings judgment).*

24 They shall be burnt with hunger, and devoured with burning heat, and with bitter destruction: I will also send the teeth of beasts upon them, with the poison of serpents of the dust.

25 The sword without, and terror within, shall destroy both the young man and the virgin, the suckling also with the man of gray hairs *(has happened to Israel countless times in the last nearly 2,000 years, but more particularly during the Holocaust of World War II).*

26 I said, I would scatter them into corners, I would make the remembrance of them to cease from among men *(at least what they once had been):*

27 Were it not that I feared the wrath of the enemy *(could be translated, "That I should be provoked to wrath by the enemy ascribing the destruction of Israel to their own prowess"),* lest their adversaries *(Israel's adversaries)* should behave themselves strangely, and lest they should say, Our hand is high, and the LORD has not done all this *(the enemies of Israel should realize that they can only do to Israel what God allows them to do; and to be sure, one day He will turn on the enemies of Israel, and will do so with a fury [Ezek., Chpts. 38-39]).*

28 For they are a nation void of counsel, neither is there any understanding in them.

29 O that they were wise, that they understood this, that they would consider their latter end! *(The end result of forsaking God.)*

30 How should one chase a thousand, and two put ten thousand to flight, except their Rock had sold them, and the LORD had shut them up?

31 For their rock is not as our Rock, even our enemies themselves being judges *(that "Rock" was Christ [I Cor. 10:4]).*

32 For their vine is of the vine of Sodom, and of the fields of Gomorrah: their grapes are grapes of gall, their clusters are bitter *(by using Sodom and Gomorrah as comparisons, the Lord is saying that Israel is good for nothing but destruction):*

33 Their wine is the poison of dragons, and the cruel venom of asps *(and this is said of Israel by the Lord; so we know now why they crucified the Saviour).*

34 Is not this laid up in store with Me, and sealed up among My treasures? *(Verses 34-43 pertain to Israel's sufferings under the future Antichrist, and their final restoration.)*

35 To Me belongs vengeance and recompence: their foot shall slide in due time: for the day

of their calamity is at hand, and the things that shall come upon them make haste *(the coming Great Tribulation [Mat. 24:21])*.

36 For the LORD shall judge His people, and repent himself for His servants, when He sees that their power is gone, and there is none shut up, or left *(Israel is at the place of extermination, which they will be under the Antichrist; then the Lord will in effect say, "It's enough!")*.

37 And He shall say, Where are their gods, their rock in whom they trusted,

38 Which did eat the fat of their sacrifices, and drank the wine of their Drink Offerings? let them rise up and help you, and be your protection *(of course, there will be none to help; this speaks of the coming Battle of Armageddon)*.

39 See now that I, even I, am He, and there is no god with Me: I kill, and I make alive; I wound, and I heal: neither is there any who can deliver out of My hand *(there is no God but Jehovah)*.

40 For I lift up My hand to Heaven, and say, I live for ever.

41 If I whet My glittering sword, and My hand take hold on judgment; I will render vengeance to My enemies, and will reward them who hate Me.

42 I will make My arrows drunk with blood, and My sword shall devour flesh: and that with the blood of the slain and of the captives, from the beginning of revenges upon the enemy *(this is the Battle of Armageddon, described in Ezekiel, Chapters 38-39)*.

43 Rejoice, O ye nations, with His people: for He will avenge the blood of His servants, and will render vengeance to His adversaries, and will be merciful unto His land, and to His people *(this pertains to the Second Coming, when the Lord will then "avenge the blood of His servants" [Zech. 14:1-4])*.

MOSES CHARGES ISRAEL

44 And Moses came and spoke all the words of this song in the ears of the people, he, and Hoshea *(Joshua)* the son of Nun.

45 And Moses made an end of speaking all these words to all Israel:

46 And he said unto them, Set your hearts unto all the words which I testify among you this day, which you shall command your children to observe to do, all the words of this Law.

47 For it is not a vain thing for you: because it is your life: and through this thing you shall prolong your days in the land, where you go

over Jordan to possess it *(Moses tells Israel that the entirety of their lives and living were bound up in obedience to the Law; it is the same presently with the Word of the Lord; but, sadly, the modern Church is leaving the Word of the Lord)*.

CANAAN

48 And the LORD spoke unto Moses that selfsame day, saying,

49 Get thee up into this mountain Abarim, unto Mount Nebo, which is in the land of Moab, that is over against Jericho; and behold the land of Canaan, which I give unto the Children of Israel for a possession:

50 And die in the mount where you go up, and be gathered unto your people: as Aaron your brother died in Mount Hor, and was gathered unto his people:

51 Because you trespassed against Me among the Children of Israel at the waters of Meribah-Kadesh, in the wilderness of Zin; because you sanctified Me not in the midst of the children of Israel. *(The sin of striking the Rock the second time instead of speaking to it, as the Lord commanded, was actually a grievous sin. The Rock typified Christ, Who would be smitten at Calvary and, from what He would do at the Cross, a life-giving stream would pour forth for thirsting humanity. To turn and strike the Rock again at a later time, in essence, spoiled the Type, which in effect said that the Cross of Christ, regarding its Sacrifice, was insufficient. In other words, it was a repudiation of the Cross, which, no doubt, Moses did not intend to do. But, nevertheless, it was done [Num. 20:11-13]. Let all know and understand, if works of the law, and we refer to law that's made up by any individual or religious Denomination, are resorted to, pure and simple, "Christ shall profit you nothing" [Gal. 5:2]. Everything we receive from the Lord, Christ is the Source and the Cross is the Means [Rom. 6:3-14].)*

52 Yet you shall see the land before you; but you shall not go thither unto the land which I give the Children of Israel. *(As previously stated, the Law can never inherit the Promise. It is not that the Law is unfavorable, but rather that man is unable to render perfect Law-keeping [Gal. 3:18].)*

CHAPTER 33
(1451 B.C.)
MOSES BLESSED ISRAEL

AND this is the Blessing, wherewith Moses the man of God blessed the Children of

Israel before his death.

2 And he said, The LORD came from Sinai, and rose up from Seir unto them; He shined forth from Mount Paran, and He came with ten thousands of Saints: from His right hand went a fiery law for them *(from His celestial seat, where myriads of Angels surround His Throne).*

3 Yea, He loved the people; all His Saints are in Your hand: and they sat down at Your feet; every one shall receive of Your words *(everyone shall be blessed who receives Your Words).*

4 Moses commanded us a Law, even the inheritance of the congregation of Jacob *(Israel inherited the Law, which placed them in a category all to themselves, far ahead of all the other nations of the world, at least as long as they obeyed that Law).*

5 And He was king in Jeshurun *(meaning the upright ones, which was God's tender name for His people),* when the heads of the people and the Tribes of Israel were gathered together.

REUBEN

6 Let Reuben live, and not die; and let not his men be few *(Reuben was prophesied by Jacob to be "unstable as water" [Gen. 49:4]; but the Lord through Moses gives Reuben a promise, in effect saying that the Tribe would not die, despite the sin that had been committed [Gen. 35:22]).*

JUDAH

7 And this is the Blessing of Judah: and he said, Hear, LORD, the voice of Judah, and bring him unto his people: let his hands be sufficient for him; and You be an help to him from his enemies *(the Blessing of Judah is in the form of a prayer to the Lord; the prayer was answered in that Judah's hands were sufficient in that this Tribe brought forth the Messiah).*

LEVI

8 And of Levi he said, Let your Thummim and your Urim be with your Holy One, Whom you did prove at Massah, and with Whom you did strive at the waters of Meribah;

9 Who said unto his father and to his mother, I have not seen him; neither did he acknowledge his brethren, nor knew his own children: for they have observed Your word, and kept Your covenant.

10 They shall teach Jacob Your judgments, and Israel Your Law: they shall put incense before You, and Whole Burnt Sacrifice upon Your Altar.

11 Bless, LORD, his substance, and accept the work of his hands; smite through the loins of them who rise against him, and of them who hate him, that they rise not again. *(Even though Levi was cursed by God, as recorded in Genesis 49:5-7, that curse was wiped away because "they have observed Your Word, and kept Your Covenant" [Num. 25:1-13]. Moses passes over Simeon, possibly because, as Jacob foretold, he was to be scattered among his brethren [Gen. 49:7]. In fact, his inheritance was within the territory of Judah [Josh. 19:2-9]. So the blessing on Judah would have been the blessing on Simeon.)*

BENJAMIN

12 And of Benjamin he said, The beloved of the LORD shall dwell in safety by him; and the LORD shall cover him all the day long, and he shall dwell between His shoulders *("to be between the shoulders" is to be carried on the back [I Sam. 17:6]; as a father might thus bear his child, so should Benjamin be borne of the Lord).*

JOSEPH

13 And of Joseph he said, Blessed of the LORD be his land, for the precious things of Heaven, for the dew, and for the deep that couches beneath,

14 And for the precious fruits brought forth by the sun, and for the precious things put forth by the moon,

15 And for the chief things of the ancient mountains, and for the precious things of the lasting hills,

16 And for the precious things of the Earth and the fullness thereof, and for the good will of him who dwelt in the bush: let the Blessing come upon the head of Joseph, and upon the top of the head of him who was separated from his brethren.

17 His glory is like the firstling of his bullock, and his horns are like the horns of unicorns: with them he shall push the people together to the ends of the Earth: and they are the ten thousands of Ephraim, and they are the thousands of Manasseh *(Ephraim and Manasseh were the sons of Joseph, and it is actually two Tribes which Moses here blesses; all the blessings of all the Tribes will come to fulfillment in the*

Kingdom Age, and not before; if it is to be noticed, there is no reprimanding of the Tribes here whatsoever).

ZEBULUN AND ISSACHAR

18 And of Zebulun he said, Rejoice, Zebulun, in your going out; and, Issachar, in your tents.

19 They shall call the people unto the mountain; there they shall offer sacrifices of righteousness: for they shall suck of the abundance of the seas, and of treasures hid in the sand.

GAD

20 And of Gad he said, Blessed be he who enlarges Gad: he dwells as a lion, and tears the arm with the crown of the head.

21 And he provided the first part for himself, because there, in a portion of the Lawgiver, was he seated; and he came with the heads of the people, he executed the justice of the LORD, and his judgments with Israel.

DAN

22 And of Dan he said, Dan is a lion's whelp: he shall leap from Bashan.

NAPHTALI

23 And of Naphtali he said, O Naphtali, satisfied with favour, and full with the blessing of the LORD: possess thou the west and the south.

ASHER

24 And of Asher he said, Let Asher be blessed with children; let him be acceptable to his brethren, and let him dip his foot in oil *(some have endeavored to claim that this pointed to crude oil, which was in the vicinity of the boundaries of the Tribe of Asher; however, it doesn't refer to that at all; it refers to the Moving and Operation of the Holy Spirit, Who is symbolized by "oil").*

25 Your shoes shall be iron and brass *(refers to the fact that the dwelling of Asher shall be strong and impregnable)*; and as your days, so shall your strength be.

26 There is none like unto the God of Jeshurun *(means "the upright one")*, Who rides upon the Heaven in your help, and in His excellency on the sky *(the Lord is far above the ridiculous idol gods of the heathen nations).*

27 The eternal God is your refuge, and underneath are the everlasting arms: and He shall thrust out the enemy from before you; and shall say, Destroy them *(God is the Refuge or Dwelling-place of His People; over us is His sheltering protection, and underneath us is the support of His everlasting Arms).*

28 Israel then shall dwell in safety alone: the fountain of Jacob shall be upon a land of corn and wine; also his Heavens shall drop down dew.

29 Happy are you, O Israel: who is like unto you, O people saved by the LORD, the Shield of your help, and Who is the Sword of your excellency! And your enemies shall be found liars unto you; and you shall tread upon their high places. *(As stated, all of these great predictions given by the Holy Spirit through Moses looked beyond the present time, and even the distant future, to the coming glad day when Israel will, at long last, fully accept the Lord Jesus Christ as her Saviour, her Messiah, and her Lord. This will be at the Second Coming, commencing the Kingdom Age. Then Israel will fulfill all of these predictions.)*

CHAPTER 34
(1451 B.C.)
THE DEATH OF MOSES

AND Moses went up from the plains of Moab unto the mountain of Nebo, to the top of Pisgah, that is over against Jericho. And the LORD showed him all the land of Gilead, unto Dan *(this was no doubt done by Revelation).*

2 And all Naphtali, and the land of Ephraim, and Manasseh, and all the land of Judah, unto the utmost sea.

3 And the south, and the plain of the valley of Jericho, the city of palm trees, unto Zoar.

4 And the LORD said unto him, This is the land which I swore unto Abraham, unto Isaac, and unto Jacob, saying, I will give it unto your seed: I have caused you to see it with your eyes, but you shall not go over thither. *(Moses, as the servant of Jehovah, and the Mediator of the First Covenant, could not bring Israel into the Resurrection Life beyond Jordan. Was Moses disappointed? I don't think so! I cannot conceive of the Lord allowing disappointment to cloud the home-going of the great Law-giver. He saw the land, but he could not obtain it, because, as stated, the Law can never inherit the*

Promise. But, in Christ, he did obtain it, and shall, because of the Cross [Lk. 9:28-31].)

5 So Moses the servant of the LORD died there in the land of Moab, according to the Word of the LORD. *(The phrase is actually, "at the mouth of the Lord." It is interpreted by some Jewish scholars as, "by a kiss of the Lord." Perhaps Maimonides explained it best. He said, "Moses died in a moment of holiest joy in the knowledge and love of God.")*

6 And He *(the Lord)* buried him in a valley in the land of Moab, over against Beth-peor: but no man knows of his sepulcher unto this day. *(Man is so insensate and idolatrous that Israel would, without doubt, have given Divine honors to the Great Leader when dead, who, while living, they treated with ingratitude, and more than once set about to murder! Such is man, and such is his nature!)*

7 And Moses was an hundred and twenty years old when he died: his eye was not dim, nor his natural force abated *(his natural strength was not weakened by old age)*.

8 And the Children of Israel wept for Moses in the plains of Moab thirty days: so the days of weeping and mourning for Moses were ended.

JOSHUA

9 And Joshua the son of Nun was full of the spirit of wisdom *(the Holy Spirit)*; for Moses had laid his hands upon him: and the Children of Israel hearkened unto him, and did as the LORD commanded Moses *(Joshua had been selected by the Lord, and there was no doubt about his place and position).*

10 And there arose not a Prophet since in Israel like unto Moses, whom the LORD knew face to face *(as long as this First Covenant was to last, no Prophet could arise in Israel like unto Moses; there is but One Who is worthy of greater honor than Moses, namely, the Apostle and High Priest of our profession, Who is placed as a Son over all the House of God, in which Moses was found faithful as a servant, Jesus Christ, the Founder and Mediator of the New and Everlasting Covenant [Heb. 3:2-6; 13:20]),*

11 In all the signs and the wonders, which the LORD sent him to do in the land of Egypt to Pharaoh, and to all his servants, and to all his land,

12 And in all that mighty hand, and in all the great terror which Moses showed in the sight of all Israel. *(Moses died, but God did not die!)*

THE BOOK OF
JOSHUA

CHAPTER 1
(1451 B.C.)
GOD COMMISSIONS JOSHUA

NOW after the death of Moses the servant of the LORD it came to pass, that the LORD spoke unto Joshua the son of Nun, Moses' minister, saying *(as to how the Lord spoke to Joshua, we aren't told; however, the greater weight seems to point toward inward Revelation)*,

2 Moses My servant is dead, now therefore arise, go over this Jordan, you, and all this people, unto the land which I do give to them, even to the Children of Israel *(Joshua begins his Ministry at the banks of Jordan, where Christ was baptized, and enters upon the public exercise of his Prophetic Office; I'm sure the Reader knows that the name Joshua is the Hebrew derivative of the Greek "Jesus," the Name of our Blessed Lord Himself; Israel had dwelt in the wilderness for some forty years; it was now time for them to go into the Promised Land)*.

3 Every place that the sole of your foot shall tread upon, that have I given unto you, as I said unto Moses *(it was not God's Will that one foot breadth was to rest in the hands of its former owners; likewise, the Holy Spirit intends presently for everything in our lives to be removed which hinders our progress with the Lord; it is God's Will that we possess the entirety of the Promise, which pertains to total victory over the world, the flesh, and the devil [James 4:5])*.

4 From the wilderness and this Lebanon even unto the great river, the river Euphrates, all the land of the Hittites, and unto the great sea toward the going down of the sun, shall be your coast *(this includes modern Syria, Jordan, and part of Arabia; all of this was never actually in the hand of the Israelites, save during the reigns of David and Solomon; however, during the coming Kingdom Age, Israel will possess all of that, and more)*.

5 There shall not any man be able to stand before you *(before Joshua)* all the days of your life: as I was with Moses, so I will be with you: I will not fail you, nor forsake you. *(Concerning this, Williams says, "Moses, as representing the Law, could not bring Israel into the Promised Land; he must die, for he had made one*

failure under that Law, and possession of Canaan by Law could only be by a perfect obedience to it. Man, being a sinner, cannot give this perfect obedience. Joshua, Type of the risen Saviour, brought Israel into the goodly Land. Grace, operating in the Power of the Holy Spirit, which it always does, can bring men into the enjoyment of that which the Law, because of man's moral weakness, on which it acts, can never do.")*

6 Be strong and of a good courage: for unto this people shall you divide for an inheritance the land, which I swore unto their fathers to give them. *(Moses was a servant in the Wilderness, Joshua, a son in the Land. The subject of Deuteronomy is the Wilderness; that of Joshua is the Land. Most Christian people are satisfied to be servants in the Wilderness; few ambition to be sons in the Land.*

Joshua's success depended upon his obedience to his two companions — the Eternal Word, manifested in this Verse, and the Written Word, manifested in Verse 8; that is, Jesus and the Bible. Obedience to such companionship alone gives a victorious Christian experience — Williams.)

7 Only be thou strong and very courageous, that you may observe to do according to all the Law, which Moses My servant commanded you: turn not from it to the right hand or to the left, that you may prosper whithersoever you go. *(Prosperity depended upon a strict adherence to the Law of God. Whereas Israel, at that time, only had a partial Revelation, the Law, now, we have the entirety of the Revelation of God, given in the entirety of His Word. It, and it alone, portrays the Way. To deviate from the Word of God is to deviate from prosperity. To adhere to the Word of God is to prosper, and to prosper in all things.)*

8 This Book of the Law shall not depart out of your mouth *(Israel was to talk the Word constantly)*; but you shall meditate therein day and night *(think upon the Word constantly)*, that you may observe to do according to all that is written therein *(as stated, we must not deviate)*: for then you shall make your way prosperous, and then you shall have good success. *(What a Promise!)*

9 Have not I commanded you? Be strong and of a good courage *(go forward, and don't be discouraged)*; be not afraid *(Satan will blow and bluster, but there is nothing he can do,*

providing we will continue to trust the Lord, and continue forward), **neither be thou dismayed** *(there will be hindrances, but don't let them deter you or even slow you down):* **for the LORD your God is with you wheresoever you go** *(and if the Lord be with us, and He most definitely will, if we adhere strictly to the Word, Satan is then defeated, and prosperity of every stripe is guaranteed).*

JOSHUA ASSUMES COMMAND

10 Then Joshua commanded the officers of the people, saying,

11 Pass through the host, and command the people, saying, Prepare you victuals; for within three days you shall pass over this Jordan, to go in to possess the land, which the LORD your God gives you to possess it. *(They could have possessed it some 38 years earlier, had they only evidenced faith. But unbelief caused them to languish in the wilderness for some 38 extra years; likewise, far too many modern Christians languish in a spiritual wilderness because of misplaced faith. To inherit the Promised Land, we must, without fail, evidence Faith in Christ and the Cross, which will give the Holy Spirit latitude to work in our lives, Who Alone can help us to possess all that God has promised [I Cor. 1:17-18, 21, 23; 2:2].)*

12 And to the Reubenites, and to the Gadites, and to half the Tribe of Manasseh, spoke Joshua, saying,

13 Remember the word which Moses the servant of the LORD commanded you, saying, The LORD your God has given you rest, and has given you this land.

14 Your wives, your little ones, and your cattle, shall remain in the land which Moses gave you on this side Jordan; but you shall pass before your brethren armed, all the mighty men of valour, and help them;

15 Until the LORD have given your brethren rest, as He has given you, and they also have possessed the land which the LORD your God gives them: then you shall return unto the land of your possession, and enjoy it, which Moses the LORD's servant gave you on this side Jordan toward the sunrising. *(Had the two Tribes and the half Tribe permitted God to choose for them, how much happier and safer they would have been! But they chose for themselves land on the wrong side of Jordan, and brought upon themselves many sorrows and early captivity [I Ki. 22:3]. Such is the sad experience*

of Christian people who plan for themselves and do not have fellowship with the thoughts of God. God's Plan was, first, to conquer Canaan, and then the land stretching from the Jordan to the Euphrates. The two Tribes and the half Tribe thought the reverse would be the better plan. It wasn't! Even as man's plans are never the better plan.)

JOSHUA'S LEADERSHIP

16 And they answered Joshua, saying, All that you command us we will do, and wheresoever you send us, we will go *(obedience is easy when all goes well with us, and when it makes little demand upon our faith).*

17 According as we hearkened unto Moses in all things *(this was not at all absolutely correct)*, so will we hearken unto you: only the LORD your God be with you, as He was with Moses.

18 Whosoever he be who does rebel against your commandment, and will not hearken unto your words in all that you command him, he shall be put to death: only be strong and of a good courage. *(The worthlessness of man's promises of fidelity at the close of this Chapter contrasts with the worthfulness of God's Promises of faithfulness at the opening of the Chapter.)*

CHAPTER 2
(1451 B.C.)
TWO SPIES

AND Joshua the son of Nun sent out of Shittim two men to spy secretly, saying, Go view the land, even Jericho. And they went, and came into an harlot's house, named Rahab, and lodged there. *(This was an Inn of sorts. The two spies did not know that Rahab was a harlot. As well, some have attempted to claim that Rahab had been forced into temple prostitution; however, the Greek Text of Hebrews 11:31 proves that she was a common harlot.*

The "two spies" served no military purpose whatsoever. So why did Joshua send them?

The Lord told him to do such, because of Rahab, even though Joshua did not know or understand such at the time. The Lord knew that Faith lodged in the heart of this harlot, and God will go to any lengths to honor Faith [Heb., Chpt. 11].)

RAHAB

2 And it was told the king of Jericho, saying,

Behold, there came men in hither to night of the Children of Israel to search out the country *(how the king found this out, we aren't told)*.

3 And the king of Jericho sent unto Rahab, saying, Bring forth the men who are come to you, which are entered into your house: for they be come to search out all the country.

4 And the woman took the two men, and hid them, and said thus, There came men unto me, but I did not know from where they came:

5 And it came to pass about the time of shutting of the gate, when it was dark, that the men went out: where the men went I do not know: pursue after them quickly; for you shall overtake them.

6 But she had brought them up to the roof of the house, and hid them with the stalks of flax, which she had laid in order upon the roof.

7 And the men pursued after them the way to Jordan unto the fords: and as soon as they which pursued after them were gone out, they shut the gate. *(We know from this that Rahab lied. The sacred historian simply narrates the fact, and makes no comment whatever upon it.*

The roofs of houses, then as now, were flat in those regions. She hid the men on the roof under stalks of flax. The germ of Faith was already stirring in her heart, and it was Faith that would be amply rewarded. We must not judge Rahab, for all of this was shortly before her conversion. To be sure, we must not judge Rahab at all.)

THE PLEDGE

8 And before they *(the two spies)* were laid down *(to go to sleep)*, she came up unto them upon the roof;

9 And she said unto the men, I know that the LORD has given you the land, and that your terror is fallen upon us, and that all the inhabitants of the land faint because of you *(Rahab's Faith is shown by the expression, "has given"; what God wills, she regarded as already done)*.

10 For we have heard how the LORD dried up the water of the Red Sea for you, when you came out of Egypt *(despite the fact that this took place about forty years earlier)*; and what you did unto the two kings of the Amorites, who were on the other side Jordan, Sihon and Og, whom you utterly destroyed.

11 And as soon as we had heard these things, our hearts did melt, neither did there remain any more courage in any man, because of you: for the LORD your God, He is God in Heaven above, and in Earth beneath. *(This declaration, bearing in mind the circumstances of the person who uttered it, is as remarkable as Peter's, "You are the Christ, the Son of the Living God" [Mat. 16:16-17]. Upon the utterance of this statement of Faith, Rahab was saved.)*

12 Now therefore, I pray you, swear unto me by the LORD, since I have showed you kindness, that you will also show kindness unto my father's house, and give me a true token *(Williams says, "Rahab was a debauched member of a doomed race. Yet Grace saved her. She based her plea for Salvation upon the fact that she was justly ordained by God to destruction. Many people refuse to bestir themselves in the matter of personal Salvation because of the belief that if they are ordained to be saved, they will be saved, and if ordained to be lost, they will be lost; however, all sinners are justly ordained to be lost [Rom. 5:12] and, therefore, all sinners may be saved.*

"Rahab prefaced her plea for Salvation by declaring that she knew all were doomed to destruction, and because of this Divine Judgment, she asked for a true token that would assure her of her safety in the Day of Wrath that was coming"):

13 And that you will save alive my father, and my mother, and my brethren, and my sisters, and all that they have, and deliver our lives from death *(a Faith that is born of God always evidences itself by seeking the Salvation of others; her petition was answered favorably)*.

14 And the men answered her, Our life for yours, if you utter not this our business. And it shall be, when the LORD has given us the land, that we will deal kindly and truly with you.

15 Then she let them down by a cord through the window: for her house was upon the town wall, and she dwelt upon the wall.

16 And she said unto them, Get you to the mountain, lest the pursuers meet you; and hide yourselves there three days, until the pursuers be returned: and afterward may you go your way.

THE SCARLET THREAD

17 And the men said unto her, We will be blameless of this your oath which you have made us swear *(if you do not obey what we are about to tell you to do)*.

18 Behold, when we come into the land, you shall bind this line of scarlet thread in the window which you did let us down by:

and you shall bring your father, and your mother, and your brethren, and all your father's household, home unto you *(upon her request, the way of Salvation was immediately made clear and plain to her; it was a very simple way; all she had to do was to hang a piece of scarlet cloth [thread] in the window; a child could do that; as well, Salvation presently from the Wrath to come is equally simple; trusting in the Lord Jesus Christ, and in His Precious Blood, secures eternal Salvation).*

19 And it shall be, that whosoever shall go out of the doors of your house into the street, his blood shall be upon his head, and we will be guiltless: and whosoever shall be with you in the house, his blood shall be on our head, if any hand be upon him.

20 And if you utter this our business, then we will not honor your oath which you have made us to swear. *(The assurance of Salvation to Rahab was not built upon an inward experience, but rather upon an outward evidence — that is, the scarlet line. In it was perfection; in herself imperfection. Looking upon that "true token" and believing the testimony respecting it, she was assured of deliverance in the Day of Doom that was coming. Thus, the outward token gave an inward peace. The Believer in Jesus enjoys a similar peace. The preciousness of Christ's Blood, and the Testimony of the Holy Scriptures concerning it, is the outward token which brings assurance of Salvation to the heart that trusts Christ. It was vain for Rahab to seek for Salvation upon the ground of personal worthiness; for she was vile indeed. It is equally vain for the most moral to claim Salvation today, for all have sinned, none are righteous, and all are under sentence of death [Rom. 5:12].*

The condition was that the red cord would hang from the window, and that all must stay in the house where the window was. To leave the house would leave its protection. Safety was guaranteed for all who remained in the house, destruction for all who left the house. It is the same with the Blood of Christ, which the scarlet thread represented.

As long as we remain in the house of safety provided by the Blood, we are safe. To leave this house of safety, which is Faith in Christ and Him Crucified, guarantees destruction.)

THE REPORT

21 And she said, According unto your words, so be it. And she sent them away, and they departed: and she bound the scarlet line in the window. *(Rahab lost not a moment in making her calling and election sure. She bound the scarlet thread in the window; and as directly she did so, she was saved — that is, she was in safety, and assured of safety. Prior to binding the scarlet line in the window, she was ordained to destruction, but, from the moment she trusted that "true token," she was ordained to Salvation, as well as all her family, provided they stayed in the house, which means that they placed their trust in the scarlet thread as well.)*

22 And they went, and came unto the mountain, and abode there three days, until the pursuers were returned: and the pursuers sought them throughout all the way, but found them not.

23 So the two men returned, and descended from the mountain, and passed over, and came to Joshua the son of Nun, and told him all things that befell them:

24 And they said unto Joshua, Truly the LORD has delivered into our hands all the land; for even all the inhabitants of the country do faint because of us. *(Their report was one of faith, totally unlike the report that had been given some 38 years earlier, which doomed a generation to die in the wilderness [Num., Chpt. 13].)*

CHAPTER 3
(1451 B.C.)
THE JORDAN RIVER

AND Joshua rose early in the morning; and they removed from Shittim, and came to Jordan, he and all the Children of Israel, and lodged there before they passed over *(they were not told how they would pass over, only that it would be done).*

INSTRUCTIONS

2 And it came to pass after three days, that the officers went through the host *(they had evidently been told by Joshua what to tell the people);*

3 And they commanded the people, saying, When you see the Ark of the Covenant of the LORD your God, and the Priests the Levites bearing it, then you shall remove from your place, and go after it. *(The "Priests" who carried the Ark on their shoulders, and the staves on each side of the Ark were for that very purpose, were types of Christ, Who Alone has the Glory of God,*

represented by the Ark. Jesus said to the prospective Disciples, "Follow Me." He is still saying the same thing to millions of people. Regrettably, far too many are following other things.)

4 Yet there shall be a space between you and it, about two thousand cubits *(about 3,000 feet)* by measure: come not near unto it, that you may know the way by which you must go: for you have not passed this way heretofore. *(Before the Cross, men could not approach God, at least not directly, because the blood of bulls and goats could not take away sin [Heb. 10:4]. Since the Cross, we are invited to come boldly to the Throne of Grace, and to do so as often as we like [Heb. 4:16].)*

5 And Joshua said unto the people, Sanctify yourselves: for to morrow the LORD will do wonders among you *(they were to make certain they were ceremonially clean, for that was the best they could do at that time).*

6 And Joshua spoke unto the Priests, saying, Take up the Ark of the Covenant, and pass over before the people. And they took up the Ark of the Covenant, and went before the people *(as is here obvious, all the plans were God's Plans, and not at all of man; a perfect blueprint is laid out here for us; we should not fail to use it).*

THE PROMISE

7 And the LORD said unto Joshua, This day will I begin to magnify you in the sight of all Israel, that they may know that, as I was with Moses, so I will be with you.

8 And you shall command the Priests who bear the Ark of the Covenant, saying, When you are come to the brink of the water of Jordan, you shall stand still in Jordan. *(Deliverance from Egypt was not necessarily a type of Salvation, as many think. In fact, while in Egypt, the Lord referred to the Israelites as "My people" [Ex. 3:7]. They were saved, not by being delivered out of Egypt, but by trusting in the Abrahamic Covenant [Gen. 15:6]. The deliverance from Egypt typified deliverance from domination of the sin nature [Rom. 6:14]. That deliverance was effected, even as it is effected presently, by faith in the slain lamb [Ex. 12:13].*

In the wilderness, Israel ceased to have faith in the slain lamb, and thereby wandered aimlessly for some 38 years, and with an entire generation dying in that wasteland. Regrettably and sadly, millions of modern Christians follow suit. They take their faith away from the slain

lamb and place it in something else. Such a direction always guarantees death.

Crossing the Jordan is a Type of the Baptism with the Holy Spirit, for it is impossible to claim the Promises of God without the Leading, Guidance, and Power of the Spirit, Who, however, always works within the framework of Christ and the Cross [Rom. 8:2].)

PROPHECY

9 And Joshua said unto the Children of Israel, Come hither and hear the Words of the LORD your God.

10 And Joshua said, Hereby you shall know that the Living God is among you, and that He will without fail drive out from before you the Canaanites, and the Hittites, and the Hivites, and the Perizzites, and the Girgashites, and the Amorites, and the Jebusites *(these heathen tribes typify enemies of the flesh which seek to hinder our progress with the Lord; victory can come to the Believer only as the Believer maintains his Faith in Christ and the Cross, which gives the Holy Spirit latitude to work within our lives [Rom. 6:3-14; 8:1-2, 11]).*

11 Behold, the Ark of the Covenant of the LORD of all the Earth passes over before you into Jordan *(Christ, of which the Ark of the Covenant was a Type, has gone before us and secured the victory; Faith and trust in Him guarantees us His Victory; to be sure, it is a victory which He has won solely for us).*

12 Now therefore take you twelve men out of the Tribes of Israel, out of every Tribe a man *(the number "twelve" is God's number of Government; however, it is His Government, and not that of man; this means that man must not dilute it in any way).*

13 And it shall come to pass, as soon as the soles of the feet of the Priests who bear the Ark of the LORD, the LORD of all the Earth, shall rest in the waters of Jordan, that the waters of Jordan shall be cut off from the waters that come down from above; and they shall stand upon an heap. *(The Priests being a Type of Christ as well, the moment their feet touched the waters, the waters fled! Such is the Power of Christ over the enemies of our soul. But, understand, Jordan will flee only before Christ, and not at all before us.)*

WATERS DIVIDED

14 And it came to pass, when the people

removed from their tents, to pass over Jordan, and the Priests bearing the Ark of the Covenant before the people;

15 And as they who bore the Ark were come unto Jordan, and the feet of the Priests who bore the Ark were dipped in the brim of the water, (for Jordan overflowed all his banks all the time of harvest *[flooded every spring. Normally the Jordan River is about 30 to 40 feet wide. It is said, however, when it flooded during those times, which it did every spring, that its depth would increase to about 40 feet, and its width to nearly two miles. No doubt, Jericho felt somewhat safe, thinking that Israel could not cross the swollen river. They reckoned without the Power of God]*,)

16 That the waters which came down from above stood and rose up upon an heap very far from the city Adam, that is beside Zaretan: and those that came down toward the sea of the plain, even the salt sea *(Dead Sea)*, failed, and were cut off: and the people passed over right against Jericho. *(This can be construed as none other than one of the greatest miracles ever performed by the Lord. Furthermore, the Lord had them to cross opposite Jericho, with the inhabitants of that city, no doubt, observing this spectacle.)*

17 And the Priests who bore the Ark of the Covenant of the LORD stood firm on dry ground in the midst of Jordan, and all the Israelites passed over on dry ground, until all the people were passed clean over Jordan. *(Many people think of Jordan, as described here, as a type of death, with Canaan as a Type of Heaven; however, while Jordan is a type of death, it is rather a type of the death of the flesh, with Canaan a Type of our possession of the Promises of God by the Power of the Holy Spirit.)*

CHAPTER 4
(1451 B.C.)
TWELVE STONES

AND it came to pass, when all the people were clean passed over Jordan, that the LORD spoke unto Joshua, saying,

2 Take you twelve men out of the people, out of every Tribe a man,

3 And command you them, saying, Take you hence out of the midst of Jordan, out of the place where the Priests' feet stood firm, twelve stones, and you shall carry them over with you, and leave them in the lodging place, where you shall lodge this night. *(We will find*

in this Chapter that there are two distinct memorials set up, both consisting of twelve stones.)

4 Then Joshua called the twelve men, whom he had prepared of the Children of Israel, out of every Tribe a man:

5 And Joshua said unto them, Pass over before the Ark of the LORD your God into the midst of Jordan, and take you up every man of you a stone upon his shoulder, according unto the number of the Tribes of the Children of Israel:

6 That this may be a sign among you, that when your children ask their fathers in time to come, saying, What mean you by these stones?

7 Then you shall answer them, That the waters of Jordan were cut off before the Ark of the Covenant of the LORD; when it passed over Jordan, the waters of Jordan were cut off: and these stones shall be for a memorial unto the Children of Israel for ever. *(Four facts are stated about these stones. They were "taken," they were "carried," they were "laid down," and they were "set up." The origin of the stones was the deep bed of Jordan; their purpose was to testify that Israel owed her entrance into the goodly land only and wholly to Divine Grace and Power. In the Baptism of Christ, the Believer dies to his old life and rises into a new life; and we are reminded that, as to our moral origin, we were buried beneath the waters of the Wrath of God; that, as to our present position, we are now set up upon Resurrection ground; and it is our duty to testify daily to the Glory of Christ, the one and only Saviour. The Lord Jesus Christ said to the Pharisees that if the children were silent, the very stones would cry out! These stones set up at Gilgal cried out day and night!)*

8 And the Children of Israel did so as Joshua commanded, and took up twelve stones out of the midst of Jordan, as the LORD spoke unto Joshua, according to the number of the Tribes of the Children of Israel, and carried them over with them unto the place where they lodged, and laid them down there.

9 And Joshua set up twelve stones in the midst of Jordan, in the place where the feet of the Priests which bore the Ark of the Covenant stood: and they are there unto this day. *(The first memorial could no doubt be referred to as Jordan stones, but these spoken of in this 9th Verse must be referred to as Wilderness stones. These twelve stones buried on the bottom of the Jordan River, where the feet of the Priests had stood, signify the death and burial of Israel's*

forty years of unbelief and sinning in the Wilderness. The Lord is saying to Israel that that time is over, buried, out of sight, and forgotten, typical of all our sins of the past, that is, if we have properly trusted Christ [I Jn. 1:9]. Unfortunately, far too many modern Christians seem to take delight in diving down to the bottom of Jordan, spiritually speaking, and retrieving those stones and bringing them to the surface, thereby constantly reminding people of such-and-such sin. I would hope we could see the terrible insult to Christ that such a thing is, and, in fact, that such action is sinful and wicked. Sins forgiven are to never be held over someone's head.)

10 For the Priests which bore the Ark stood in the midst of Jordan, until every thing was finished that the LORD commanded Joshua to speak unto the people, according to all that Moses commanded Joshua: and the people hasted and passed over. *(What a scene this must have been! The majestic Ark of the Covenant held on the shoulders of the Priests, all in the midst of Jordan, with the waters held up by the mighty Power of God, that the people could walk across on dry ground, flood or not!)*

11 And it came to pass, when all the people were clean passed over, that the Ark of the LORD passed over, and the Priests, in the presence of the people.

12 And the Children of Reuben, and the Children of Gad, and half the Tribe of Manasseh, passed over armed before the Children of Israel, as Moses spoke unto them:

13 About forty thousand prepared for war passed over before the LORD unto battle, to the plains of Jericho.

14 On that day the LORD magnified Joshua in the sight of all Israel; and they feared him, as they feared Moses, all the days of his life. *(Joshua was a Type of Christ, Who actually carried the name, "Joshua," which means "Saviour." The Greek derivative is "Jesus.")*

THE JORDAN

15 And the LORD spoke unto Joshua, saying *(this is the way of the Lord; He calls men and women, and then He speaks to them, giving leading and guidance; unfortunately, most of the Church have long since ceased to hear from the Lord, that is, if they ever heard from Him, and are thereby led by men; the results are obvious),*

16 Command the Priests that bear the Ark of the Testimony, that they come up out of Jordan.

17 Joshua therefore commanded the Priests, saying, Come ye up out of Jordan.

18 And it came to pass, when the Priests who bore the Ark of the Covenant of the LORD were come up out of the midst of Jordan, and the soles of the Priests' feet were lifted up unto the dry land, that the waters of Jordan returned unto their place, and flowed over all his banks, as they did before. *(Williams says, "There was but one way into Canaan and that the Divine way made by the Ark of the Covenant. There is but one way into Heaven. Jesus says, "I am the way." The Ark typified Him — its precious wood, His Humanity; its gold, His Deity; its blood-sprinkled cover, His Atonement. As the Ark descended into the depth of Jordan and rolled back its waters, so Christ descended into the deep waters of the Wrath of God and opened the one way into everlasting life.")*

GILGAL

19 And the people came up out of Jordan on the tenth day of the first month, and encamped in Gilgal, in the east border of Jericho *(the name "Gilgal" means "rolled away"; their encampment in this place typified that the sins, doubt, and unbelief of the Wilderness had rolled away).*

20 And those twelve stones, which they took out of Jordan, did Joshua pitch in Gilgal *(this was an appropriate place for these twelve memorial stones to be set up; in a sense, it was a new beginning for Israel; with Faith in Christ, any individual can have a new beginning).*

21 And he *(Joshua)* spoke unto the Children of Israel, saying, When your children shall ask their fathers in time to come, saying, What mean these stones?

22 Then you shall let your children know, saying, Israel came over this Jordan on dry land. *(The miracles of the past which the Lord has given us are to be related again and again, in essence, lived again and again. While we cannot live off past miracles, they do give us faith for the present times and the future, which they are meant to do.)*

23 For the LORD your God dried up the waters of Jordan from before you, until you were passed over, as the LORD your God did to the Red Sea, which He dried up from before us, until we were gone over *(of the nearly three million people who left Egypt, some forty years before, only two of them would actually go into the Promised Land, Joshua and Caleb; doubt and*

unbelief killed the others, while Faith brought Joshua and Caleb through):

24 That all the people of the Earth might know the hand of the LORD, that it is mighty: that you might fear the LORD your God for ever *(the "hand of the Lord" is mighty to save!).*

CHAPTER 5
(1451 B.C.)
CIRCUMCISION

AND it came to pass, when all the kings of the Amorites, which were on the side of Jordan westward, and all the kings of the Canaanites, which were by the sea, heard that the LORD had dried up the waters of Jordan from before the Children of Israel, until we were passed over, that their heart melted, neither was there spirit in them any more, because of the Children of Israel. *(Even though the hearts of the kings of the Amorites melted with fear before Israel, still, as Chapter 10 proclaims, they would oppose Israel. No matter what, Satan will oppose the Child of God, but victory is assured if God's Way is followed, even as did Joshua.)*

2 At that time the LORD said unto Joshua, Make thee sharp knives, and circumcise again the Children of Israel the second time.

3 And Joshua made him sharp knives, and circumcised the Children of Israel at the hill of the foreskins.

4 And this is the cause why Joshua did circumcise: All the people who came out of Egypt who were males, even all the men of war, died in the wilderness by the way, after they came out of Egypt.

5 Now all the people who came out were circumcised: but all the people who were born in the wilderness by the way as they came forth out of Egypt, them they had not circumcised. *(Israel was about to smite the Seven Nations of Canaan with the Sword of the Lord. But before they were fitted to use that Sword on others, they must themselves feel its sharpness and "die beneath its stroke." This was illustrated in Circumcision, which in essence is a Type of the Cross. Separation was made and blood was shed. We as Believers are to be separated from the world, and this can only be done by looking to Christ and the Cross, which latter the blood symbolizes.*

Only those are fitted to use the Sword of the Spirit, which is the Word of God, who have themselves experienced the death-stroke which it gives to "Nature" — that is, to the natural man, his

wisdom and his goodness. It is most bitter to a man to learn that all his goodness must be slain with the Sword of the Lord just as much as all his badness. But to the true Believer, this is most sweet; for it brings him into a Resurrection life, and the power of that life takes all strength from Satan. Man, as man, let him be ever so religious, has no strength against Satan. Jericho's walls never fall before him!

So, circumcision was a symbol of Christ and the Cross, and the price that He would there pay in order to deliver fallen humanity.)

6 For the Children of Israel walked forty years in the wilderness, till all the people who were men of war, which came out of Egypt, were consumed, because they obeyed not the voice of the LORD: unto whom the LORD swore that He would not show them the land, which the LORD swore unto their fathers that He would give us, a land that flows with milk and honey. *(An entire generation died because of unbelief. As stated, the only two, of the nearly three million who left Egypt, who finally reached the Promised Land were Joshua and Caleb. Unbelief was the downfall, while Faith was the victory [I Jn. 5:4].)*

7 And their children, whom He *(the Lord)* raised up in their stead, them Joshua circumcised: for they were uncircumcised, because they had not circumcised them by the way *(while in the wilderness).*

8 And it came to pass, when they had done circumcising all the people, that they abode in their places in the camp, till they were whole *(in the face of the enemy, Joshua rendered the entirety of the male population helpless; but their weakness would be their strength [II Cor. 12:9-10]).*

9 And the LORD said unto Joshua, This day have I rolled away the reproach of Egypt from off you. Wherefore the name of the place is called Gilgal unto this day. *(The reproach of Egypt was dual. So long as Israel wandered in the Wilderness, Egypt reproached them with the taunt that Jehovah could not bring them into the Promised Land; and, further, all of Egypt that attaches to a servant of God is a reproach to him. That double reproach was "rolled away" at Gilgal.)*

THE PASSOVER

10 And the Children of Israel encamped in Gilgal, and kept the Passover on the fourteenth day of the month at evening in the plains of

Jericho. *(This is the first Passover in the Promised Land. Israel eating the Passover proclaims that her Redemption out of Egypt, and her position in the Land of Promise, were alike due to the preciousness of the Blood of the Lamb. True spiritual victories can only be won where there is this Testimony to the Person and Work of the Lord Jesus Christ. Circumcision symbolized "the death of self." The Passover symbolized "testimony to the Blood of the Lamb.")*

MANNA CEASES

11 And they did eat of the old corn of the land on the morrow after the Passover, unleavened cakes, and parched corn in the selfsame day.

12 And the Manna ceased on the morrow after they had eaten of the old corn of the land; neither had the Children of Israel Manna any more; but they did eat of the fruit of the land of Canaan that year. *(Manna was Angel's food — it was sufficient for the Wilderness and its defective spiritual life; however, the "old corn of the land" symbolized the Word of God, and is a necessity of the strength needed for spiritual conquests. Everything must be by the Word.)*

THE MAN WITH A DRAWN SWORD

13 And it came to pass, when Joshua was by Jericho, that he lifted up his eyes and looked, and, behold, there stood a man over against him with his sword drawn in his hand: and Joshua went unto him, and said unto him, Are you for us, or for our adversaries? *(This was a pre-incarnate appearance of Christ, Whom Joshua didn't recognize.)*

14 And He *(the Lord)* said, No; but as Captain of the Host of the LORD am I now come. And Joshua fell on his face to the earth, and did worship, and said unto Him, What saith my Lord unto His servant? *(Joshua then recognized Him as the Lord. Concerning this, Williams says, "An absolute condition of victory is full surrender to Christ as Lord. He must be accepted as Captain, be permitted to plan, and be fully obeyed.)*

15 And the Captain of the LORD's Host said unto Joshua, Loose your shoe from off your foot; for the place whereon you stand is holy. And Joshua did so. *(The demand that the shoes be removed from Joshua's feet, and the removal of those shoes, guaranteed that He Who now spoke to Joshua was a Divine Person, actually,* as stated, a pre-incarnate appearance of Christ.

The removal of the shoes in essence indicated that Joshua was giving up all ownership and leadership, thereby giving Christ total control.

We have four steps to victory here: 1. The death of self — circumcision; 2. Testimony to the Blood of the Lamb — Passover; 3. Feeding on the Word of God — old corn of the land; and, 4. Subjection to Christ as Lord — pulling off the shoes.)

CHAPTER 6
(1451 B.C.)
JERICHO

NOW Jericho was straitly shut up because of the Children of Israel: none went out, and none came in *(the strong fortress barred Israel's entrance to the land; Satan will always have such a fortress to hinder our spiritual progress; it was impregnable, therefore, its conquest was impossible to Israel, but not impossible to God!).*

2 And the LORD said unto Joshua, See, I have given into your hand Jericho, and the king thereof, and the mighty men of valour *(evidently, the Lord told Joshua these things when He appeared to him, as recorded in the previous Chapter).*

3 And you shall compass the city, all you men of war, and go round about the city once. Thus shall you do six days *(probably the strangest plan of battle ever formed).*

4 And seven Priests shall bear before the Ark seven trumpets of rams' horns: and the seventh day you shall compass the city seven times, and the Priests shall blow with the trumpets *(the number "seven" as used here is not without purpose and design; Biblically the number symbolizes perfection, totality, and universality; these are God's Plans, and they always succeed; we should cease to make plans for ourselves, and let God plan for us; as stated, His Plans always succeed).*

5 And it shall come to pass, that when they make a long blast with the ram's horn, and when you hear the sound of the trumpet, all the people shall shout with a great shout; and the wall of the city shall fall down flat, and the people shall ascend up every man straight before him. *(This was a shout of obedience and a shout of victory. Spiritually, the "shout" had everything to do with the wall falling down flat, but, physically and materially, it had no effect at all, as would be obvious. The wall falling*

down flat was strictly a Miracle of God.)

6 And Joshua the son of Nun called the Priests, and said unto them, Take up the Ark of the Covenant, and let seven Priests bear seven trumpets of rams' horns before the Ark of the LORD.

7 And he said unto the people, Pass on, and compass the city, and let him who is armed pass on before the Ark of the LORD. *(The Lord didn't need Israel to march around Jericho seven days, or even one day, for the walls to fall down. So why did He have them do this? It was to teach them trust, dependence on Him, and obedience, even though they did not at all understand the directions, as neither would anyone; however, understanding what the Lord is doing is not necessarily the criteria, obedience is!)*

8 And it came to pass, when Joshua had spoken unto the people, that the seven Priests bearing the seven trumpets of rams' horns passed on before the LORD, and blew with the trumpets: and the Ark of the Covenant of the LORD followed them.

9 And the armed men went before the Priests who blew with the trumpets, and the rereward came after the Ark, the Priests going on, and blowing with the trumpets. *(There is another problem that arises out of this illustration. Many have marched around particular obstacles, when the Lord had not said to do so, and when the ingredient was presumption instead of faith. Let the Reader understand that presumption is just as bad as disobedience. Presumption brings reproach on the Work of the Lord, just as bad as disobedience!)*

10 And Joshua had commanded the people, saying, You shall not shout, nor make any noise with your voice, neither shall any word proceed out of your mouth, until the day I bid you shout; then shall you shout. *(As a military maneuver, all of this was worse than useless. But it was not a military maneuver, but rather that which was spiritual.)*

11 So the Ark of the LORD compassed the city, going about it once: and they came into the camp, and lodged in the camp *(they only marched around the city one time, ever how long that took, after which they went back to their camp, along with the Ark of the Lord).*

12 And Joshua rose early in the morning, and the Priests took up the Ark of the LORD.

13 And seven Priests bearing seven trumpets of rams' horns before the Ark of the LORD went on continually, and blew with the trumpets: and the armed men went before them;

but the rereward came after the Ark of the LORD, the Priests going on, and blowing with the trumpets.

14 And the second day they compassed the city once, and returned into the camp: so they did six days.

15 And it came to pass on the seventh day, that they rose early about the dawning of the day, and compassed the city after the same manner seven times: only on that day they compassed the city seven times *(according to the directions of the Lord).*

16 And it came to pass at the seventh time, when the Priests blew with the trumpets, Joshua said unto the people, Shout; for the LORD has given you the city.

17 And the city shall be accursed, even it, and all who are therein, to the LORD: only Rahab the harlot shall live, she and all who are with her in the house, because she hid the messengers that we sent *(Faith will take the city, and Faith will save Rahab).*

18 And you, in any wise keep yourselves from the accursed thing, lest you make yourselves accursed, when you take of the accursed thing, and make the camp of Israel a curse, and trouble it. *(Unfortunately, there was one man who didn't obey, which caused Israel great trouble. Everything about the city was cursed by God, because it was wholly given over to idol worship. The modern Christian, likewise, must be very careful about his entanglement with the world. While we are "in" the world, we are not to be "of" the world. In fact, if the world gets into the Believer, it is the same as water getting into the ship. Ruin is the result!)*

19 But all the silver, and gold, and vessels of brass and iron, are consecrated unto the LORD: they shall come into the treasury of the LORD *(an expression used of anything specially devoted to God).*

THE FALL OF JERICHO

20 So the people shouted when the Priests blew with the trumpets: and it came to pass, when the people heard the sound of the trumpet, and the people shouted with a great shout, that the wall fell down flat, so that the people went up into the city, every man straight before him, and they took the city. *(Had they attempted to do so without the leading of the Lord, casualties would have been great; however, following the Lord, there is no record that there were any casualties among the army of*

Israel at all.)

21 And they utterly destroyed all that was in the city, both man and woman, young and old, and ox, and sheep, and ass, with the edge of the sword *(this they were commanded to do!).*

RAHAB AND HER FAMILY

22 But Joshua had said unto the two men who had spied out the country, Go into the harlot's house, and bring out thence the woman, and all that she has, as you swore unto her. *(Salvation by the scarlet line was not only simple, it was also sure. When the Day of Wrath came, it gave the safety it promised. Thus will it be in the Day of the Wrath to come. That Day will prove how sure is the Salvation which follows upon simply trusting Jesus — Williams.)*

23 And the young men who were spies went in, and brought out Rahab, and her father, and her mother, and her brethren, and all that she had; and they brought out all her kindred, and left them without the camp of Israel *(and so Rahab and the entirety of her family were saved).*

24 And they burnt the city with fire, and all that was therein: only the silver, and the gold, and the vessels of brass and of iron, they put into the treasury of the House of the LORD.

25 And Joshua saved Rahab the harlot alive, and her father's household, and all that she had; and she dwells in Israel even unto this day *(proving that this account was written during her lifetime)*; because she hid the messengers, which Joshua sent to spy out Jericho. *(Although slated for destruction, her Faith saved her. Rahab married Salmon, one of the princes of Israel. She is included in our Lord's genealogy [Mat. 1:5]. To what heights of glory her Faith took her, and so may it be for all who will dare to believe God. The Lord took her harlotry and turned it into Holiness. He took the curse that was upon her and turned it into a Blessing. What He did for her, He will do for you.)*

CURSE ON JERICHO

26 And Joshua adjured them at that time, saying, Cursed be the man before the LORD, who rises up and builds this city Jericho: he shall lay the foundation thereof in his firstborn, and in his youngest son shall he set up the gates of it. *(The object of this solid pronouncement was to preserve Jericho as a spot devoted to God forever. And for this reason a curse was pronounced upon anyone who should attempt to build a city upon the devoted spot. It does not seem that it was forbidden to build habitations on the spot, for Jericho is frequently mentioned in the New Testament. What seems to have been forbidden was the erection of a fortified city. This curse pronounced by Joshua actually fell on the reckless Hiel [I Ki. 16:34]; he saw the laying of its foundation marked by the death of his eldest son, while the death of his youngest followed its completion.)*

27 So the LORD was with Joshua; and his fame was noised throughout all the country *(what an honor for the Holy Spirit to say that the Lord is with anyone).*

CHAPTER 7
(1451 B.C.)
AI

BUT the Children of Israel committed a trespass in the accursed thing: for Achan, the son of Carmi, the son of Zabdi, the son of Zerah, of the Tribe of Judah, took of the accursed thing: and the anger of the LORD was kindled against the Children of Israel. *(Sin, as we shall see, was the cause. If one single member of the community of Israel violated the specific laws laid down by God imposed on them, the whole body was liable for his sin, until it had purged itself by a public act of restitution. So, Paul regards the Corinthian Church as polluted by the presence of one single offender, until he was publicly expelled, or he repented. There is some evidence that he repented [I Cor. 5:2, 6-7; II Cor. 2:4-11].)*

2 And Joshua sent men from Jericho to Ai, which is beside Beth-aven, on the east of Bethel, and spoke unto them, saying, Go up and view the country. And the men went up and viewed Ai. *(Had Joshua prayed about Ai, and it doesn't seem that he did, the sin would have been immediately discovered and defeat avoided. The danger after a victory is evident, because of overconfidence. In such an atmosphere, it is easy to forget to pray.)*

3 And they returned to Joshua, and said unto him, Let not all the people go up; but let about two or three thousand men go up and smite Ai; and make not all the people to labour there; for they *(the people of Ai)* are but few.

4 So there went up there of the people about three thousand men: and they fled before the men of Ai.

5 And the men of Ai smote of them about thirty and six men: for they chased them from before the gate even unto Shebarim, and smote them in the going down: wherefore the hearts of the people melted, and became as water. *(Hidden sin was the cause of this failure. In the life of victory, God is the one and only strength of the Believer; he has no other strength. But God cannot give that strength if sin be indulged. If He did, He would deny His Own Nature, which is Holiness. When He acts in Power, in the midst of His people, He must act in harmony with His Own Nature; and hence, He must judge sin in the camp of Israel with the same "fierce anger" with which He judged it in the city of Jericho. That judgment in both cases was death.*

Sin can be overcome in the life of the Believer only by the Believer looking exclusively to Christ and the Cross. It is at the Cross where sin was addressed, and only at the Cross. When the Believer places his Faith exclusively in Christ and the Cross, and it must be in both, the Holy Spirit will then work mightily in the heart and life of such a Believer, giving total and complete victory [Rom. 8:1-2, 11; I Cor. 1:17-18, 21, 23; 2:2; Gal. 6:14; Col. 2:14-15].)

6 And Joshua rent his clothes, and fell to the earth upon his face before the Ark of the LORD until the eventide, he and the elders of Israel, and put dust upon their heads. *(They knew something was wrong, bad wrong, but didn't know what it was. As stated, they evidently had not prayed about the situation at Ai before now. Had they done so, the lives of 36 men would have been spared.)*

7 And Joshua said, Alas, O LORD God, wherefore have You at all brought this people over Jordan, to deliver us into the hand of the Amorites, to destroy us? would to God we had been content, and dwelt on the other side Jordan!

8 O LORD, what shall I say, when Israel turns their backs before their enemies!

9 For the Canaanites and all the inhabitants of the land shall hear of it, and shall environ us round, and cut off our name from the Earth: and what will You do unto Your great name? *(It doesn't take very much for the faith of even the strongest Saint, such as Joshua, to be weakened. He had just seen one of the greatest moves of God in the history of man, the opening of the Jordan River, and the destruction of the city of Jericho without the loss of a single Israelite. So why will he now question the Lord? If there is a problem, then it's not the Lord's fault, but rather ours!)*

SIN UNCOVERED

10 And the LORD said unto Joshua, Get thee up; wherefore liest thou thus upon your face?

11 Israel has sinned, and they have also transgressed My Covenant which I commanded them: for they have even taken of the accursed thing, and have also stolen, and dissembled also, and they have put it even among their own stuff *(however, the Lord did not tell Joshua who it was).*

12 Therefore the Children of Israel could not stand before their enemies, but turned their backs before their enemies, because they were accursed: neither will I be with you any more, except you destroy the accursed from among you *(to the point and simple! God cannot bless sin, and this is one of the greatest examples that one could ever know. If God would not bless Israel then because of sin, He will not bless us now, if we are guilty of the same thing).*

13 Up, sanctify the people, and say, Sanctify yourselves against tomorrow: for thus saith the LORD God of Israel, There is an accursed thing in the midst of you, O Israel: you can not stand before your enemies, until you take away the accursed thing from among you. *(Regrettably, millions of modern Christians fall into this category. The "accursed thing" could fall into many categories. The only way that it can be defeated is for the Believer to express his Faith exclusively in Christ and what Christ has done at the Cross. Then, and only then, can and will the Holy Spirit work within one's life, Who Alone can remove the "accursed thing" [Rom. 6:3-14; I Cor. 1:17-18, 23; Gal. 6:14].)*

14 In the morning therefore you shall be brought according to your Tribes: and it shall be, that the Tribe which the LORD takes shall come according to the families thereof; and the family which the LORD shall take shall come by households; and the household which the LORD shall take shall come man by man.

15 And it shall be, that he who is taken with the accursed thing shall be burnt with fire *(stoned to death, and then burned with fire, which was then the system),* he and all who he has: because he has transgressed the Covenant of the LORD, and because he has wrought folly in Israel. *(The enemies of the Lord would claim that such is barbaric; however, the truth is, it is the sin that is barbaric, because it allows Satan*

to "steal, kill, and destroy" [Jn. 10:10]. Instructions had been plainly and clearly given to the entirety of the army of Israel that no spoil was to be taken in Jericho by the soldiers, or anyone else of the Tribes of Israel. So, to disobey this was to do so in the face of God, with defiance and arrogance, which, if allowed to continue, would wreck Israel.

If someone has a contagious disease, it is not cruel to quarantine that person where they cannot infect others. In fact, it would be cruel not to do so. No, the Lord was not cruel in what He demanded; He would have been cruel not to have done so.)

ACHAN

16 So Joshua rose up early in the morning, and brought Israel by their Tribes; and the Tribe of Judah was taken *(how the Lord informed Joshua of this, we aren't told)*:

17 And he brought the family of Judah; and he took the family of the Zarhites: and he brought the family of the Zarhites man by man; and Zabdi was taken *(again, in some manner, the Holy Spirit said, "This is the one")*:

18 And he brought his household man by man; and Achan, the son of Carmi, the son of Zabdi, the son of Zerah, of the Tribe of Judah, was taken.

19 And Joshua said unto Achan, My son, give, I pray you, glory to the LORD God of Israel, and make confession unto Him; and tell me now what you have done; hide it not from me.

20 And Achan answered Joshua, and said, Indeed I have sinned against the LORD God of Israel, and thus and thus have I done:

21 When I saw among the spoils a goodly Babylonish garment, and two hundred shekels of silver, and a wedge of gold, of fifty shekels weight, then I coveted them, and took them; and, behold, they are hid in the earth in the midst of my tent, and the silver under it.

JUDGMENT

22 So Joshua sent messengers, and they ran unto the tent; and, behold, it was hid in his tent, and the silver under it.

23 And they took them out of the midst of the tent, and brought them unto Joshua, and unto all the Children of Israel, and laid them out before the LORD.

24 And Joshua, and all Israel with him, took Achan the son of Zerah, and the silver, and the garment, and the wedge of gold, and his sons, and his daughters, and his oxen, and his asses, and his sheep, and his tent, and all that he had: and they brought them unto the valley of Achor.

25 And Joshua said, Why have you troubled us? the LORD shall trouble you this day. And all Israel stoned him with stones, and burned them with fire, after they had stoned them with stones. *(Babylon and money have a hateful attraction for the Christian. He finds these things among the unconverted around him, as Achan found them in Jericho, and his heart covets them. This explains the weakness of the modern Church. These sins are indulged instead of being confessed and forsaken. God has, therefore, withdrawn His Power, and there is universal weakness and defeat. Fellowship with God can only be enjoyed if resolute separation from all evil be observed.*

Achan involved his family in the like ruin with himself. The use of the plural in the Hebrew Text suggests that they, like Sapphira, were privy to the theft [Acts 5:1-2].)

26 And they raised over him a great heap of stones unto this day. So the LORD turned from the fierceness of His anger. Wherefore the name of that place was called, The valley of Achor, unto this day. *(If the discovery and judgment of sin be painful, and if there be faithfulness in dealing with it, then Grace gives both blessing and victory, and the valley of Achor becomes a Door of Hope [Hos. 2:5]. Sin should be greatly feared, but neither its bitterness nor its punishment should be dreaded, that is, if it is properly confessed [I Jn. 1:9]; for it is at this point that God resumes His victory, thereby restoring fellowship to His errant child.*

Let the Reader understand that Israel was under Law, whereas presently we are under Grace. Observing what Law is, and how it must be enforced, should cause every Believer to shrink back from engaging in Law. If the Christian tries to live by Law, which, regrettably, the far greater majority of the modern Church is attempting to do, Law, incidentally, devised by man, but still Law nevertheless, they are then brought under its curse [Gal. 3:10]. And, to be sure, that's not the way that any Believer wants to live.

This is the age of Grace, and Grace comes to the Child of God in an uninterrupted flow, which is the only way we can successfully live for God, providing the Believer places his Faith exclusively in Christ and the Cross. This is imperative [Gal., Chpt. 5].)

CHAPTER 8
(1451 B.C.)
AI

AND the LORD said unto Joshua, Fear not, neither be thou dismayed: take all the people of war with you, and arise, go up to Ai: see, I have given into your hand the king of Ai, and his people, and his city, and his land *(if God gives something, then the obtaining of such treasure must be done in God's Way; the problem with the modern Church is that it has abrogated God's Government, instituted government of its own devisings, papered it with a Scripture or two, and then labeled it as "God's Government"; that which man conceives is never of God, irrespective as to how religious it may be)*:

2 And you shall do to Ai and her king as you did unto Jericho and her king: only the spoil thereof, and the cattle thereof, shall you take for a prey unto yourselves: you must lay an ambush for the city behind it *(when God gives directions, victory is the guaranteed result; if proper relationship with Him through prayer, the study of the Word, and, above all, constant Faith in Christ and the Cross, such will then guarantee proper leading)*.

3 So Joshua arose, and all the people of war, to go up against Ai: and Joshua chose out thirty thousand mighty men of valour, and sent them away by night.

4 And he commanded them, saying, Behold, you shall lie in wait against the city, even behind the city: go not very far from the city, but all of you be ready *(they were ready, simply because they were following directions given directly by the Lord)*:

5 And I, and all the people who are with me, will approach unto the city: and it shall come to pass, when they come out against us, as at the first, that we will flee before them,

6 (For they will come out after us) till we have drawn them from the city; for they will say, They flee before us, as at the first: therefore we will flee before them.

7 Then you shall rise up from the ambush, and seize upon the city: for the LORD your God will deliver it into your hand.

8 And it shall be, when you have taken the city, that you shall set the city on fire: according to the Commandment of the LORD shall you do. See, I have commanded you *(the taking of these cities, and the destruction of them, were symbolic of the victory that is to be won within our present-day lives and living; the Promised Land was God's land; consequently, all enemies must be put to the sword; likewise, we as Believers now belong to the Lord; everything in our lives that is not proper must be subjected to the sword of the Spirit, with the fire of the Spirit burning out the dross [Mat. 3:11; Eph. 6:17])*.

CAPTURE OF THE CITY

9 Joshua therefore sent them forth: and they went to lie in ambush, and abode between Beth-el and Ai, on the west side of Ai: but Joshua lodged that night among the people *(among the army)*.

10 And Joshua rose up early in the morning, and numbered the people, and went up, he and the Elders of Israel, before the people to Ai. *(God numbers exactly those who would do battle in His service. It was then physical, as well as spiritual; it is now altogether spiritual. The fight at present is "the good fight of faith" [I Tim. 6:12-13]. This "fight" in which we are called upon to engage pertains to our faith. This refers to one exclusively placing his Faith in Christ and the Cross. The Cross must never be separated from Christ, and we speak of its benefits [Eph. 2:13-18; Gal. 6:14].)*

11 And all the people, even the people of war who were with him, went up, and drew near, and came before the city, and pitched on the north side of Ai: now there was a valley between them and Ai.

12 And he took about five thousand men, and set them to lie in ambush between Beth-el and Ai, on the west side of the city.

13 And when they had set the people, even all the host that was on the north of the city, and their liers in wait on the west of the city, Joshua went that night into the midst of the valley.

14 And it came to pass, when the king of Ai saw it, that they hasted and rose up early, and the men of the city went out against Israel to battle, he and all his people, at a time appointed, before the plain; but he did not know that there were liers in ambush against him behind the city.

15 And Joshua and all Israel made as if they were beaten before them, and fled by the way of the wilderness.

16 And all the people who were in Ai were called together to pursue after them: and they pursued after Joshua, and were drawn away from the city.

17 And there was not a man left in Ai or Beth-el, who went not out after Israel: and they left the city open, and pursued after Israel *(which the Lord knew they would do!)*.

18 And the LORD said unto Joshua, Stretch out the spear that is in your hand toward Ai; for I will give it into your hand. And Joshua stretched out the spear that he had in his hand toward the city *(the Lord told Joshua to stretch out the spear toward the city, which was a symbol of Faith)*.

19 And the ambush arose quickly out of their place, and they ran as soon as he had stretched out his hand: and they entered into the city, and took it, and hasted and set the city on fire.

20 And when the men of Ai looked behind them, they saw, and, behold, the smoke of the city ascended up to Heaven, and they had no power to flee this way or that way: and the people who fled to the wilderness turned back upon the pursuers *(the army of Israel ceased their fleeing, and then turned to fight the men of Ai)*.

21 And when Joshua and all Israel saw that the ambush had taken the city, and that the smoke of the city ascended, then they turned again, and slew the men of Ai *(everything in our lives not proper with the Lord must be slain, and can be slain, but only by the Believer placing his Faith exclusively in Christ and the Cross [Rom. 6:3-14])*.

22 And the other issued out of the city against them *(the soldiers of Israel came out of the city against the soldiers of Ai)*; so they were in the midst of Israel, some on this side, and some on that side *(Israel had the army of Ai between two forces, soldiers of Israel on one side, and soldiers of Israel on the other side)*: and they smote them, so that they let none of them remain or escape.

23 And the king of Ai they took alive, and brought him to Joshua.

VICTORY

24 And it came to pass, when Israel had made an end of slaying all the inhabitants of Ai in the field, in the wilderness wherein they chased them, and when they were all fallen on the edge of the sword, until they were consumed, that all the Israelites returned unto Ai, and smote it with the edge of the sword.

25 And so it was, that all who fell that day, both of men and women, were twelve thousand, even all the men of Ai.

26 For Joshua drew not his hand back, wherewith he stretched out the spear, until he had utterly destroyed all the inhabitants of Ai. *(These individuals were so steeped in sin and idolatry that one Archaeologist stated, "The God of Israel, Who gave instructions that all of these heathen tribes in the land of Canaan be exterminated, did future generations an untold service." Second, had they been allowed to remain, knowing the human heart, Israel would have been corrupted. Regrettably, after the death of Joshua, some were allowed to remain, and the corruption of Israel is exactly what took place. If weights and sins in our lives aren't exterminated, which can only be exterminated by the Cross, they will ultimately wreck us [Heb. 12:1-2].)*

27 Only the cattle and the spoil of that city Israel took for a prey unto themselves, according unto the Word of the LORD which He commanded Joshua.

28 And Joshua burnt Ai, and made it an heap for ever, even a desolation unto this day *(I have personally been to this site, and there is nothing left, not even ruins)*.

29 And the king of Ai he hanged on a tree until eventide: and as soon as the sun was down, Joshua commanded that they should take his carcase down from the tree, and cast it at the entering of the gate of the city, and raise thereon a great heap of stones, that remains unto this day *(the day that the Book of Joshua was written; it was probably written by Joshua, with the exception of the last five Verses, which record his death)*.

VICTORY CELEBRATED

30 Then Joshua built an Altar unto the LORD God of Israel in Mount Ebal *(according to the Word of the Lord, the Altar was built on Mount Ebal, the Mount of Cursing, which relates to the curse of sin, and not Mount Gerizim, the Mount of Blessing. Christ, Who Alone perfectly obeyed the Law, had, therefore, enjoyed, as a Man, its blessing, yet, voluntarily, in love for those who, by sinning, had incurred its curse, ascended the hill of malediction, and, in His Own Person, suffered the judgment, and thus brought out from under the curse those who were sentenced to death [Gal. 3:13-14]. Regrettably, the modern Church is attempting to build the Altar, i.e., "the Cross," that is, if the Cross is considered at all, on Mount Gerizim, the Mount of Blessing, which is a denial of the real problem of man, which is sin)*,

31 As Moses the servant of the LORD commanded the Children of Israel, as it is written in the Book of the Law of Moses, an Altar of whole stones, over which no man has lift up any iron *(the Altar, a Type of the Cross, built of stones unshaped, symbolizes the fact that we must not add to the Cross nor take from the Cross):* and they offered thereon Burnt Offerings unto the LORD, and sacrificed Peace Offerings *(all of this typified the fact that sin is man's problem, and that the Cross is the only remedy).*

32 And he *(Joshua)* wrote there upon the stones a copy of the Law of Moses *(exactly as he had been commanded by Moses to do [Deut. 27:2, 8]),* which he wrote in the presence of the Children of Israel.

33 And all Israel, and their Elders, and Officers, and their Judges, stood on this side the Ark and on that side before the Priests the Levites, which bore the Ark of the Covenant of the LORD, as well the stranger, as he who was born among them; half of them over against Mount Gerizim, and half of them over against Mount Ebal; as Moses the servant of the LORD had commanded before, that they should bless the people of Israel *(all of these stood at the foot of Mount Gerizim, the Mount of Blessing, where the Ark of the Covenant was then located, and pronounced Blessings upon Israel; but let it be understood, all of these Blessings were predicated on a proper understanding of the "Altar" and its use).*

34 And afterward he read all the words of the Law, the blessings and cursings, according to all that is written in the Book of the Law.

35 There was not a word of all that Moses commanded, which Joshua read not before all the congregation of Israel, with the women, and the little ones, and the strangers who were conversant among them. *(It is incumbent upon us presently, as Preachers of the Gospel, to announce to the entirety of the Church the Word of the Lord, taking nothing from it, nor adding anything to it.)*

CHAPTER 9
(1451 B.C.)
ALLIANCE

AND it came to pass, when all the kings which were on this side Jordan, in the hills, and in the valleys, and in all the coasts of the great sea over against Lebanon, the Hittite, and the Amorite, the Canaanite, the Perizzite, the Hivite, and the Jebusite, heard thereof;

2 That they gathered themselves together, to fight with Joshua and with Israel, with one accord *(this is but an example of the enemy coming against the modern Child of God with reinforcements; however, as Joshua and Israel of old, if directions from the Lord are sought and received, victory will be sure)*

THE GIBEONITES

3 And when the inhabitants of Gibeon heard what Joshua had done unto Jericho and to Ai,

4 They did work wilily, and went and made as if they had been ambassadors, and took old sacks upon their asses, and wine bottles *(wine skins),* old, and rent, and bound up;

5 And old shoes and clouted upon their feet, and old garments upon them; and all the bread of their provision was dry and mouldy.

6 And they went to Joshua unto the camp at Gilgal *(Gilgal was about three miles east of Jericho),* and said unto him, and to the men of Israel, We be come from a far country *(Gibeon was actually only about fifteen miles west of Jericho):* now therefore make you a league with us *(this was strictly forbidden in Exodus 23:32; 34:12)*

7 And the men of Israel said unto the Hivites *(its chief city was Gibeon, but the people were Hivites),* Peradventure you dwell among us; and how shall we make a league with you?

8 And they said unto Joshua, We are your servants. And Joshua said unto them, Who are you? and from where do you come?

9 And they said unto him, From a very far country your servants are come because of the Name of the LORD your God: for we have heard the fame of Him, and all that He did in Egypt,

10 And all that He did to the two kings of the Amorites, who were beyond Jordan, to Sihon king of Heshbon, and to Og king of Bashan, which was at Ashtaroth *(to buttress their deceit, they carefully neglected to mention Jericho and Ai, which were recent victories).*

11 Wherefore our elders and all the inhabitants of our country spoke to us, saying, Take victuals with you for the journey, and go to meet them, and say unto them, We are your servants: therefore now make you a league with us.

12 This our bread we took hot for our provision out of our houses on the day we came forth to go unto you; but now, behold, it is dry,

and it is mouldy:

13 And these bottles *(skins)* of wine, which we filled, were new; and, behold, they be rent: and these our garments and our shoes are become old by reason of the very long journey *(as stated, it was actually only about fifteen miles, which could be easily traversed in one day).*

14 And the men took of their victuals, and asked not counsel at the Mouth of the LORD. *(The Holy Spirit is careful to delineate this failure on the part of Israel. At Ai, Israel trusted her own strength, and did not pray, and was defeated. At Gibeon, she trusted her own wisdom, and did not pray, and was defeated! The sharp lesson taught at Ai was quickly forgotten. Such is the natural heart!)*

15 And Joshua made peace with them, and made a league with them, to let them live: and the princes of the congregation swore unto them. *(Satan is more to be dreaded as a humble supplicant than as a roaring lion. To make him flee, he only needs to be resisted; but to stand against his wiles, the whole armor of God must be employed. Had Joshua asked counsel at the Mouth of the Lord instead of putting the moldy bread of the Gibeonites into his own mouth, so to speak, he would not have fallen into this snare. Satan, through the mouth of the Gibeonite, abundantly quoted the Bible to Joshua [Vss. 6, 9-10, 24], just as afterwards he did to the greater than Joshua, but the Lord defeated him with three Verses out of the Law.*

Had Joshua so acted, he would have gotten the victory as well.

Satan can only deceive the Christian when we take the management into our own hands, instead of consulting the Lord.)

DECEPTION DISCOVERED

16 And it came to pass at the end of three days after they had made a league with them, that they heard that they were their neighbours, and that they dwelt among them *(only about fifteen miles due west).*

17 And the Children of Israel journeyed, and came unto their cities on the third day. Now their cities were Gibeon, and Chephirah, and Beeroth, and Kirjath-jearim.

18 And the Children of Israel smote them not, because the princes of the congregation had sworn unto them by the LORD God of Israel. And all the congregation murmured against the princes.

19 But all the princes said unto all the congregation, We have sworn unto them by the LORD God of Israel: now therefore we may not touch them *(the word of the Child of God is to be as the Word of the Lord).*

PUNISHMENT

20 This we will do to them; we will even let them live, lest wrath be upon us, because of the oath which we swore unto them.

21 And the princes said unto them, Let them live; but let them be hewers of wood and drawers of water unto all the congregation; as the princes had promised them. *(The Gibeonites became the Nethinim. The word means "given," i.e., devoted to the Sanctuary of Jehovah. Their lives were spared because the princes of Israel had taken an oath to them in the Name of Jehovah; but, because of their deceit, they were condemned to be drawers of water to the House of the Lord. They were not condemned to domestic slavery to the Israelites, but rather to "the congregation," which refers to the Tabernacle, and later the Temple. Grace, therefore, brought them into the glory and joy of Psalms 84:10, and instructed David to appoint them to high position in the Temple [Ezra 8:20]. In fact, they were the first to return with Ezra and Nehemiah from Babylonian captivity, pledging themselves to keep the Statutes given by God to Moses [Ezra 2:43-58; Neh. 7:60]. They are last read of in Nehemiah 3:26; 10:28; and 11:21, as making their homes outside the water-gate of Jerusalem. Why the water-gate? Because being near the water supply, they could more readily discharge the honorable bondage to which Joshua had condemned them, of being drawers of water to the Temple of Jehovah. Thus, a curse justly pronounced by Law becomes, by Grace, a Blessing.)*

22 And Joshua called for them, and he spoke unto them, saying, Wherefore have you beguiled us, saying, We are very far from you; when *(in fact)* you dwell among us?

23 Now therefore you are cursed, and there shall none of you be freed from being bondmen, and hewers of wood and drawers of water for the House of my God.

24 And they answered Joshua, and said, Because it was certainly told your servants, how that the LORD your God commanded his servant Moses to give you all the land, and to destroy all the inhabitants of the land from before you, therefore we were sore afraid of our lives because of you, and have done this thing.

25 And now, behold, we are in your hand: as it seems good and right unto you to do unto us, do.

26 And so did he *(Joshua)* unto them, and delivered them out of the hand of the Children of Israel, that they slew them not *(as stated, the curse of the Law was turned to a Blessing)*.

27 And Joshua made them that day hewers of wood and drawers of water for the congregation, and for the Altar of the LORD, even unto this day, in the place which he should choose *(to their credit, as stated, they ever remained faithful)*

CHAPTER 10
(1451 B.C.)
THE AMORITE CONFEDERATION

NOW it came to pass, when Adoni-zedec king of Jerusalem had heard how Joshua had taken Ai, and had utterly destroyed it *(this is the first mention of Jerusalem in the Bible, as a proper name; it was mentioned first, about 500 years earlier, as "Salem")*; as he had done to Jericho and her king, so he had done to Ai and her king; and how the inhabitants of Gibeon had made peace with Israel, and were among them;

2 That they feared greatly, because Gibeon was a great city, as one of the royal cities, and because it was greater than Ai, and all the men thereof were mighty.

3 Wherefore Adoni-zedec king of Jerusalem, sent unto Hoham king of Hebron, and unto Piram king of Jarmuth, and unto Japhia king of Lachish, and unto Debir king of Eglon, saying,

4 Come up unto me, and help me, that we may smite Gibeon: for it has made peace with Joshua and with the Children of Israel. *(When anyone makes peace with the Divine Joshua, he brings upon himself the anger of his companions. Thus it was with Gibeon; however, Joshua was able to protect and deliver the Gibeonites. Our Lord is able to deliver from our enemies those who know Him as their Peace.)*

5 Therefore the five kings of the Amorites, the king of Jerusalem, the king of Hebron, the king of Jarmuth, the king of Lachish, the king of Eglon, gathered themselves together, and went up, they and all their hosts, and encamped before Gibeon, and made war against it.

THE APPEAL TO JOSHUA

6 And the men of Gibeon sent unto Joshua to the camp to Gilgal, saying, Slack not your hand from your servants; come up to us quickly, and save us, and help us: for all the kings of the Amorites who dwell in the mountains are gathered together against us. *(Let the Believer understand that it is our Heavenly Joshua Alone Who can help us. No one else can. He does so by us evidencing Faith in Him and what He has done for us at the Cross. Then, and then alone, the Holy Spirit can work mightily on behalf of us against the powers of darkness. To be sure, He has never lost a battle [Rom. 6:3-14; 8:1-2, 11; Gal. 6:14].)*

7 So Joshua ascended from Gilgal, he, and all the people of war with him, and all the mighty men of valour.

8 And the LORD said unto Joshua, Fear them not *(the keynote of Joshua's life and ministry, as of the keynote of every soldier of God)*: for I have delivered them into your hand; there shall not a man of them stand before you.

9 Joshua therefore came unto them suddenly, and went up from Gilgal all night.

HAILSTONES

10 And the LORD discomfited them before Israel, and slew them with a great slaughter at Gibeon, and chased them along the way that goes up to Beth-horon, and smote them to Azekah, and unto Makkedah *(a distance of about 25 miles)*.

11 And it came to pass, as they fled from before Israel, and were in the going down to Beth-horon, that the LORD cast down great stones from Heaven upon them unto Azekah, and they died: they were more which died with hailstones than they whom the Children of Israel slew with the sword *(the Power of the Lord is not limited respecting those who have Faith in Him; however, such Power is available only if we go according to His Direction, and not from the position of presumption)*.

THE SUN

12 Then spoke Joshua to the LORD in the day when the LORD delivered up the Amorites before the Children of Israel, and he *(Joshua)* said in the sight of Israel, Sun, stand thou still upon Gibeon; and thou, Moon, in the valley of Ajalon.

13 And the Sun stood still, and the Moon stayed, until the people had avenged themselves upon their enemies. Is not this written

in the Book of Jasher? *(A book no longer in existence, nor any of its copies.)* So the Sun stood still in the midst of Heaven, and hasted not to go down about a whole day. *(It is said that this is confirmed by State documents of Egypt, China, and Mexico, which record this double-day. It is said that Herodotus, and Lord Kingsborough, in his history of the Mexicans, and the Chinese philosopher Huai-nan-Tzu quoted these records. The hill of Gibeon, at the moment when Joshua spoke, was behind him to the east, and the sun was setting in front of him to the west. It was evening, and a continuance of the daylight was needed in order to complete the victory.)*

14 And there was no day like that before it or after it, that the LORD hearkened unto the voice of a man: for the LORD fought for Israel. *(God is a miracle-working God. The Bible opens with miracles, continues with miracles, and concludes with miracles, i.e., "proclaims them into the eternal future.")*

VICTORY OVER THE ENEMY

15 And Joshua returned, and all Israel with him, unto the camp to Gilgal *(returned in victory)*.

16 But these five kings fled, and hid themselves in a cave at Makkedah.

17 And it was told Joshua, saying, The five kings are found hid in a cave at Makkedah.

18 And Joshua said, Roll great stones upon the mouth of the cave, and set men by it for to keep them:

19 And stay ye not, but pursue after your enemies, and smite the hindmost of them; suffer them not to enter into their cities: for the LORD your God has delivered them into your hand *(they were not to be diverted from the purpose of annihilating the enemy by the important news that the heads of the confederacy were in their hands)*.

20 And it came to pass, when Joshua and the Children of Israel had made an end of slaying them with a very great slaughter, till they were consumed, that the rest which remained of them entered into fenced cities *(under guard)*.

21 And all the people returned to the camp to Joshua at Makkedah in peace: none moved his tongue against any of the Children of Israel. *(Who would be so foolish as to speak negative things against ones being used so mightily by God? Regrettably, the modern Church seems to have little learned this lesson.)*

22 Then said Joshua, Open the mouth of the cave, and bring out those five kings unto me out of the cave.

23 And they did so, and brought forth those five kings unto him out of the cave, the king of Jerusalem, the king of Hebron, the king of Jarmuth, the king of Lachish, and the king of Eglon.

24 And it came to pass, when they brought out those kings unto Joshua, that Joshua called for all the men of Israel, and said unto the captains of the men of war which went with him, Come near, put your feet upon the necks of these kings. And they came near, and put their feet upon the necks of them. *(There is but one way to deal with sin, and that is to place the triumphant foot of faith upon its neck, and put it to death. It is impossible to improve sin, just as, in the Judgment of God, it was impossible for Israel to improve these five kings. Man, in his folly, tries to improve what is opposed to God; but the failure of his efforts ever reveals its foolishness. There is no such thing as moral evolution. The Cross of Christ is the only answer for sin, and, to be sure, sin is the problem.)*

25 And Joshua said unto them, Fear not, nor be dismayed, be strong and of good courage: for thus shall the LORD do to all your enemies against whom you fight. *(This great Promise, and even greater, is to us as well. Paul said, "Sin [the sin nature] shall not have dominion over you" [Rom. 6:14]; however, there is only one way that such victory can be assured. The Believer must understand that all things come to us from God by the Person of Christ, with the Means being the Cross [Rom. 6:3-14]. The Holy Spirit, Who Alone can bring about these victories, and Who works exclusively within the parameters of the Finished Work of Christ, will then do great and mighty things for us [Rom. 8:1-2, 11].)*

26 And afterward Joshua smote them, and slew them, and hanged them on five trees: and they were hanging upon the trees until the evening. *(As stated, victory over sin, of which all of this is a type, can only come about by it being utterly destroyed within our lives. This was all made possible at the Cross, and only at the Cross. There sin was dealt with, as it regards its cause and its cure [Jn. 1:29].)*

27 And it came to pass at the time of the going down of the Sun, that Joshua commanded, and they took them down off the trees, and cast them into the cave wherein they had been hid, and laid great stones in the cave's mouth, which remain until this very day.

COMPLETION OF THE CONQUEST

28 And that day Joshua took Makkedah, and smote it with the edge of the sword, and the king thereof he utterly destroyed, them, and all the souls who were therein; he let none remain: and he did to the king of Makkedah as he did unto the king of Jericho *(this king was not with the five listed in Verse 23)*.

29 Then Joshua passed from Makkedah, and all Israel with him; unto Libnah, and fought against Libnah *(due west of Gilgal, about 40 miles)*:

30 And the LORD delivered it also, and the king thereof, into the hand of Israel; and he smote it with the edge of the sword, and all the souls who were therein; he let none remain in it; but did unto the king thereof as he did unto the king of Jericho.

31 And Joshua passed from Libnah, and all Israel with him, unto Lachish, and encamped against it, and fought against it *(about 40 miles southwest of Gilgal)*:

32 And the LORD delivered Lachish into the hand of Israel, which took it on the second day, and smote it with the edge of the sword, and all the souls who were therein, according to all that He *(the Lord)* had done to Libnah. *(If it is to be noticed, it was not the stratagem of Israel that won these victories, but rather the Lord, Who told Joshua what to do. If we seek the Face of the Lord as we should, as well, He will give us guidance and direction. Jesus said so [Jn. 16:13-15].)*

33 Then Horam king of Gezer came up to help Lachish; and Joshua smote him and his people, until he had left him none remaining. *(No sin of any nature is to be left remaining in our lives. But let us say it again, because it is so very, very important. Victory for the Child of God can be obtained only by looking exclusively to Christ, understanding that everything He gives us is by the means of the Cross; consequently, the Cross must ever be the object of our Faith. Then the Holy Spirit will gloriously work on our behalf [Rom. 8:1-2, 11; Col. 2:14-15].)*

34 And from Lachish Joshua passed unto Eglon, and all Israel with him; and they encamped against it, and fought against it *(about 45 miles southwest of Gilgal)*:

35 And they took it on that day, and smote it with the edge of the sword, and all the souls who were therein he utterly destroyed that day, according to all that he had done to Lachish.

36 And Joshua went up from Eglon, and all Israel with him, unto Hebron; and they fought against it *(about 35 miles south of Gilgal)*:

37 And they took it, and smote it with the edge of the sword, and the king thereof, and all the cities thereof, and all the souls who were therein; he left none remaining, according to all that he had done to Eglon; but destroyed it utterly, and all the souls who were therein.

38 And Joshua returned, and all Israel with him, to Debir; and fought against it *(about 45 miles southwest of Gilgal)*:

39 And he took it, and the king thereof, and all the cities thereof; and they smote them with the edge of the sword, and utterly destroyed all the souls who were therein; he left none remaining: as he had done to Hebron, so he did to Debir, and to the king thereof; as he had done also to Libnah, and to her king.

40 So Joshua smote all the country of the hills, and of the south, and of the vale, and of the springs, and all their kings: he left none remaining, but utterly destroyed all who breathed, as the LORD God of Israel commanded. *(To get every enemy out of our lives with the exception of one is not sufficient. The one that remains can cause us tremendous problems and difficulties; so all, as it pertains to sin of any nature, must be destroyed, as these victories of Joshua symbolize.)*

41 And Joshua smote them from Kadesh-barnea even unto Gaza, and all the country of Goshen, even unto Gibeon.

42 And all these kings and their land did Joshua take at one time, because the LORD God of Israel fought for Israel.

43 And Joshua returned, and all Israel with him, unto the camp to Gilgal. *(True strength is always to be had at Gilgal; there self is judged and mortified, and God and His Power realized and enjoyed. The repeated mention, therefore, of Gilgal in this Chapter expresses an important principle which must be true in the experience of the Christian, if he is to win victories over sin. "Gilgal" was the place of circumcision, which, in a sense, is a Type of the Cross. Separation is made, and blood is shed. This is the only manner in which "self" can be properly addressed — at the Cross [Jn. 5:1-9].)*

CHAPTER 11

(1450 B.C.)

DAY OF VICTORY

AND it came to pass, when Jabin king of Hazor had heard those things, that he sent

to Jobab king of Madon, and to the king of Shimron, and to the king of Achshaph *(Hazor was about 90 miles due north of Gilgal; it was about 10 miles north of the Sea of Galilee)*,

2 And to the kings who were on the north of the mountains, and of the plains south of Chinneroth *(Sea of Galilee)*, and in the valley, and in the borders of Dor on the west *(located on the Mediterranean Sea)*,

3 And to the Canaanite on the east and on the west, and to the Amorite, and the Hittite, and the Perizzite, and the Jebusite in the mountains, and to the Hivite under Hermon in the land of Mizpeh.

4 And they went out, they and all their host with them, much people, even as the sand that is upon the sea shore in multitude, with horses and chariots very many *(all the heathen kings)*.

5 And when all these kings were met together, they came and pitched together at the waters of Merom, to fight against Israel *(about 10 miles northwest of the Sea of Galilee)*.

6 And the LORD said unto Joshua, Be not afraid because of them: for to morrow about this time will I deliver them up all slain before Israel: you shall hough their horses, and burn their chariots with fire *(hamstring their horses, which made them unfit for war, but not for agriculture)*.

7 So Joshua came, and all the people of war with him, against them by the waters of Merom suddenly; and they fell upon them.

8 And the LORD delivered them into the hand of Israel, who smote them, and chased them unto great Zidon, and unto Misrephoth-maim, and unto the valley of Mizpeh eastward; and they smote them, until they left them none remaining.

9 And Joshua did unto them as the LORD bade him: he houghed their horses, and burnt their chariots with fire *(Israel had no horses or chariots, but yet they defeated these enemies, who were far superior to them, regarding military warfare; Israel defeated them, because the Lord was with Israel)*.

10 And Joshua at that time turned back, and took Hazor, and smote the king thereof with the sword: for Hazor beforetime was the head of all those kingdoms. *(Williams says, "The frequent mention of Hazor [Vss. 1, 10-11, 13] introduces a great principle. Hazor was the center of power of that part of the world. Natural wisdom would propose to make it the seat of government, so that it should be that for God which before it had been for the world. But God*

will in no wise allow the world's seat of power to become that of His People. His People were to depend exclusively on Him, and to dwell with Him at Gilgal. Accordingly, Hazor is totally destroyed. Not a vestige of its former power must remain to compete with Gilgal. The center and source of power must be all Divine.")

11 And they smote all the souls that were therein with the edge of the sword, utterly destroying them: there was not any left to breathe: and he burnt Hazor with fire *(the fire of the Spirit will destroy every vestige of the world within our lives, if we will only look to Christ and the Cross [Mat. 3:11])*.

SUMMARY

12 And all the cities of those kings, and all the kings of them, did Joshua take, and smote them with the edge of the sword, and he utterly destroyed them, as Moses the servant of the LORD commanded.

13 But as for the cities that stood still in their strength, Israel burned none of them, save Hazor only; that did Joshua burn *(should have been translated, "But, as for the cities that still stood, in their strength, Israel burned none of them, save Hazor only")*.

14 And all the spoil of these cities *(the cities that were not burned)*, and the cattle, the Children of Israel took for a prey unto themselves; but every man they smote with the edge of the sword, until they had destroyed them, neither left they any to breathe.

15 As the LORD commanded Moses His servant, so did Moses command Joshua, and so did Joshua; he left nothing undone of all that the LORD commanded Moses *(the Holy Spirit says this often concerning Joshua, meaning that "obedience to the Lord" was the secret of his strength)*.

16 So Joshua took all that land, the hills, and all the south country, and all the land of Goshen, and the valley, and the plain, and the mountain of Israel, and the valley of the same;

17 Even from the mount Halak, that goes up to Seir, even unto Baal-gad in the valley of Lebanon under Mount Hermon: and all their kings he took, and smote them, and slew them.

18 Joshua made war a long time with all those kings.

19 There was not a city that made peace with the Children of Israel, save the Hivites the inhabitants of Gibeon: all other they took in battle.

20 For it was of the LORD to harden their hearts, that they should come against Israel in battle, that he *(Joshua)* might destroy them utterly, and that they might have no favour, but that he might destroy them, as the LORD commanded Moses. *(All of this is symbolic of the victories we must win in our Christian experience. But let the Reader understand, God does not give victory to sinful men, but only to His Son, the Lord Jesus Christ, which was paid for at the Cross. The Believer, properly in Christ, can have this victory, but only as we are properly in Christ [Jn. 14:20].)*

21 And at that time came Joshua, and cut off the Anakims from the mountains, from Hebron, from Debir, from Anab, and from all the mountains of Judah, and from all the mountains of Israel: Joshua destroyed them utterly with their cities.

22 There was none of the Anakims left in the land of the Children of Israel: only in Gaza, in Gath, and in Ashdod, there remained. *(These were the giants, a product of the union of fallen angels and women [Gen. 6:4]. The offspring of those who remained in Gaza, etc., which would later be the country of the Philistines, would be destroyed by David. Goliath was one of them [I Sam., Chpt. 17]. Why the Lord didn't have Joshua to defeat these as well, we aren't told; however, we do know that everything the Lord does is for purpose and reason. In other words, everything that pertains to His Children is a test. How will we act? How will we react?)*

23 So Joshua took the whole land, according to all that the LORD said unto Moses; and Joshua gave it for an inheritance unto Israel according to their divisions by their Tribes. And the land rested from war *(it is believed that this conquest took possibly from five to seven years).*

CHAPTER 12
(1450 B.C.)
EASTERN CANAAN

NOW these are the kings of the land, which the Children of Israel smote, and possessed their land on the other side Jordan toward the rising of the sun, from the river Arnon unto Mount Hermon, and all the plain on the east *(as we study this Chapter, we will find that where there was faithfulness, there was rest; but where Israel was disobedient, thereby not destroying all which they were commanded to destroy, there was compromise and defeat; this is an ever-present principle in the experience of the Believer; to a mind which is governed by the spirit of this world, Chapters in the Bible which contain lists of names are uninteresting, but not so to those who sit where Mary sat, when she hungrily listened to Christ [Lk. 10:38-42]; we hang with appetite over every word that the Holy Spirit has written; consequently, to such Believers the list of victories in this Chapter is full of interest)*:

2 Sihon king of the Amorites, who dwelt in Heshbon, and ruled from Aroer, which is upon the bank of the river Arnon, and from the middle of the river, and from half Gilead, even unto the river Jabbok, which is the border of the children of Ammon;

3 And from the plain to the Sea of Chinneroth *(Sea of Galilee)* on the east, and unto the Sea of the plain, even the Salt Sea *(Dead Sea)* on the east, the way to Beth-jeshimoth; and from the south, under Ashdoth-pisgah:

4 And the coast of Og king of Bashan, which was of the remnant of the giants, who dwelt at Ashtaroth and at Edrei,

5 And reigned in mount Hermon, and in Salcah, and in all Bashan, unto the border of the Geshurites and the Maachathites, and half Gilead, the border of Sihon king of Heshbon.

6 Them did Moses the servant of the LORD and the Children of Israel smite: and Moses the servant of the LORD gave it for a possession unto the Reubenites, and the Gadites, and the half Tribe of Manasseh.

THE WEST SIDE OF JORDAN

7 And these are the kings of the country which Joshua and the Children of Israel smote on this side Jordan on the west, from Baal-gad in the valley of Lebanon even unto the Mount Halak, that goes up to Seir; which Joshua gave unto the Tribes of Israel for a possession according to their divisions;

8 In the mountains, and in the valleys, and in the plains, and in the springs, and in the wilderness, and in the south country; the Hittites, the Amorites, and the Canaanites, the Perizzites, the Hivites, and the Jebusites:

9 The king of Jericho, one; the king of Ai, which is beside Beth-el, one;

10 The king of Jerusalem, one; the king of Hebron, one;

11 The king of Jarmuth, one; the king of Lachish, one;

12 The king of Eglon, one; the king of Gezer, one;

13 The king of Debir, one; the king of Geder, one;

14 The king of Hormah, one; the king of Arad, one;

15 The king of Libnah, one; the king of Adullam, one;

16 The king of Makkedah, one; the king of Beth-el, one;

17 The king of Tappuah, one; the king of Hepher, one;

18 The king of Aphek, one; the king of Lasharon, one;

19 the king of Madon, one; the king of Hazor, one;

20 The king of Shimron-meron, one; the king of Achshaph, one;

21 The king of Taanach, one; the king of Megiddo, one;

22 The king of Kedesh, one; the king of Jokneam of Carmel, one;

23 The king of Dor in the coast of Dor, one; the king of the nations of Gilgal, one;

24 The king of Tirzah, one: all the kings thirty and one. *(Concerning this, Williams says, "On the Wilderness side of Jordan Israel conquered only two kings, on the Canaan side thirty-one. So it is in the Christian life.*

"Those who are satisfied to stop short of claiming and enjoying all the exceeding great and precious Promises of the New Covenant win but few victories over sin and self and the world, but those who go on unto perfection [Heb. 6:1] win many victories.

"It is encouraging and touching to read of these thirty-one victories so definitely and individually recorded. There were not just thirty victories, but thirty-one. Each several victory was important in the Eye of God and precious to the heart of God, however uninteresting and small they might appear to man. No victory over the enemy is small to God's mind.")

CHAPTER 13
(1445 B.C.)
LANDS YET UNCONQUERED

NOW Joshua was old and stricken in years; and the LORD said unto him, You are old and stricken in years *(Joshua, at this time, was 101 years of age)*, and there remains yet very much land to be possessed. *(The account in this Chapter given to us concerning the possession of the land, or the lack thereof, points to every Believer that which the Lord has prepared for us; however, there are enemies between the*

Promise and the Possession. God has a Perfect Plan for us, but, regrettably, so few of us press through to that Perfect Plan. We all too often stop short! The words, "there remains yet very much land to be possessed," should strike long, hard, and true to the heart of every Believer.)

2 This is the land that yet remains: all the borders of the Philistines, and all Geshuri *(and we must remember, it is the Holy Spirit Who is delineating these things)*,

3 From Sihor, which is before Egypt, even unto the borders of Ekron northward, which is counted to the Canaanite: five lords of the Philistines; the Gazathites, and the Ashdothites, the Eshkalonites, the Gittites, and the Ekronites; also the Avites:

4 From the south, all the land of the Canaanites, and the Mearah that is beside the Sidonians, unto Aphek, to the borders of the Amorites:

5 And the land of the Giblites, and all Lebanon, toward the sunrising, from Baal-gad under mount Hermon unto the entering into Hamath.

6 All the inhabitants of the hill country from Lebanon unto Misrephoth-maim, and all the Sidonians, them will I drive out from before the Children of Israel: only divide you it by lot unto the Israelites for an inheritance, as I have commanded you.

7 Now therefore divide this land for an inheritance unto the nine tribes, and the half tribe of Manasseh,

8 With whom the Reubenites and the Gadites have received their inheritance, which Moses gave them, beyond Jordan eastward, even as Moses the servant of the LORD gave them;

9 From Aroer, that is upon the bank of the river Arnon, and the city that is in the midst of the river, and all the plain of Medeba unto Dibon;

10 And all the cities of Sihon king of the Amorites, which reigned in Heshbon, unto the border of the Children of Ammon;

11 And Gilead, and the border of the Geshurites and Maachathites, and all mount Hermon, and all Bashan unto Salcah;

12 All the kingdom of Og in Bashan, which reigned in Ashtaroth and in Edrei, who remained of the remnant of the giants: for these did Moses smite, and cast them out.

13 Nevertheless the Children of Israel expelled not the Geshurites, nor the Maachathites: but the Geshurites and the Maachathites dwell

among the Israelites until this day. *(The word "nevertheless" proclaims failure among the people of God to possess all that was promised. Such is the sad condition of far too many Believers. While some victories are won, "nevertheless" some things remain — things which steal, kill, and destroy. How many enemies remain unsubdued in the hearts of Believers?*

There is only one way that victory can be attained in the life of the Christian. Not ten ways, not five ways, not even two ways, only one way.

All victory over sin, and in every capacity, and, to be sure, sin is the problem, was purchased and thereby attained at the Cross of Calvary [Eph. 2:13-18; Col. 2:14-15; Gal., Chpt. 5; 6:14]. As a result, the Believer's Faith, and this is so very, very important, must ever have the Cross of Christ as its object [Rom. 6:3-14]. If the Believer is faithful in anchoring his Faith in the Cross of Christ, and maintaining his Faith in the Cross of Christ, the Holy Spirit, Who works exclusively within the parameters of the Finished Work of Christ, will, without fail, subdue every enemy within our hearts and lives [Rom. 8:1-2, 11]. That, and that alone, is God's Prescribed Order Of Victory; otherwise, instead of the Believer subduing the enemies of his soul, the enemies of his soul will subdue him.)

14 Only unto the Tribes of Levi He gave none inheritance; the Sacrifices of the LORD God of Israel made by fire are their inheritance, as He said unto them *(they were to be Ministers of the Sanctuary exclusively).*

REUBEN'S INHERITANCE

15 And Moses gave unto the Tribe of the Children of Reuben inheritance according to their families.

16 And their coast was from Aroer, that is on the bank of the river Arnon, and the city that is in the midst of the river, and all the plain by Medeba;

17 Heshbon, and all her cities that are in the plain; Dibon, and Bamoth-baal, and Beth-baal-meon,

18 And Jahaza, and Kedemoth, and Mephaath,

19 And Kirjathaim, and Sibmah, and Zareth-shahar in the mount of the valley,

20 And Beth-peor, and Ashdoth-pisgah, and Beth-jeshimoth,

21 And all the cities of the plain, and all the kingdom of Sihon king of the Amorites, which reigned in Heshbon, whom Moses smote with the princes of Midian, Evi, and Rekem, and Zur, and Hur, and Reba, which were dukes of Sihon, dwelling in the country. *(All of these places named represent victories by God's people over their enemies. Considering that the Holy Spirit inspired all of this, even down to naming the places, portrays to us a tremendous truth.*

In Heaven, the Lord enumerates our victories, which are all precious in His sight, and, as well, mentions the failures, and does so by using the word "nevertheless" in Verse 13.

To be sure, Satan will do his best to hinder in every capacity. As should be obvious, he doesn't want us to win any victories; however, we definitely can have all that the Lord has promised us, and we must not stop short of total victory. In Christ and the Cross, coupled with our Faith, which gives the Holy Spirit latitude to work, we can, spiritually speaking, possess the entirety of the land [Rom. 8:2, 11].)

BALAAM SLAIN

22 Balaam also the son of Beor, the soothsayer, did the Children of Israel slay with the sword among them who were slain by them. *(If Balaam originally was a true Prophet of God, the tragedy is that he sold his gift to the highest bidder, and was reduced in the mind of God to nothing more than a "soothsayer." How many modern Prophets fall into the same category?*

It seems, instead of returning to his own land, he went to visit the Midianites, whose elders had joined in the invitation given by Moab [Num. 22:7], and persuaded them to entice the Israelites into idolatry and licentiousness [Num., Chpt. 25]. For this crime, he met with the punishment he had deserved, and was involved in the destruction which fell on the Midianites by God's express command, in consequence of their treachery [Num. 25:16-18] — Blunt.)

REUBEN'S INHERITANCE

23 And the border of the Children of Reuben was Jordan, and the border thereof. This was the inheritance of the Children of Reuben after their families, the cities and the villages thereof *(the borders of Reuben's inheritance seem to go from the river Arnon, which was about half way the length of the Dead Sea, and went a little ways north past the Dead Sea, with the Jordan River as its western boundary).*

GAD'S INHERITANCE

24 And Moses gave inheritance unto the Tribe of Gad, even unto the Children of Gad, even unto the Children of Gad according to their families.

25 And their coast was Jazer, and all the cities of Gilead, and half the land of the children of Ammon, unto Aroer that is before Rabbah;

26 And from Heshbon unto Ramath-mizpeh, and Betonim; and from Mahanaim unto the border of Debir;

27 And in the valley, Beth-aram, and Beth-nimrah, and Succoth, and Zaphon, the rest of the kingdom of Sihon king of Heshbon, Jordan and his border, even unto the edge of the sea of Chinnereth on the other side Jordan eastward.

28 This is the inheritance of the Children of Gad after their families, the cities, and their villages.

MANASSEH'S INHERITANCE

29 And Moses gave inheritance unto the half tribe of Manasseh: and this was the possession of the half tribe of the Children of Manasseh by their families.

30 And their coast was from Mahanaim, all Bashan, all the kingdom of Og king of Bashan, and all the towns of Jair, which are in Bashan, threescore cities:

31 And half Gilead, and Ashtaroth, and Edrei, cities of the kingdom of Og in Bashan, were pertaining unto the Children of Machir the son of Manasseh, even to the one half of the Children of Machir by their families.

32 These are the countries which Moses did distribute for inheritance in the plains of Moab, on the other side Jordan, by Jericho, eastward.

33 But unto the Tribe of Levi Moses gave not any inheritance: the LORD God of Israel was their inheritance, as he said unto them.

CHAPTER 14
(1444 B.C.)
CANAAN DIVIDED BY LOT

AND these are the countries which the Children of Israel inherited in the land of Canaan, which Eleazar the Priest, and Joshua the son of Nun, and the heads of the fathers of the Tribes of the Children of Israel, distributed for inheritance to them.

2 By lot was their inheritance, as the LORD commanded by the hand of Moses, for the nine Tribes, and for the half Tribe. *(The words "by lot" had to do with the Urim and the Thummim; whatever these things were, they were kept in a pouch on the back of the Breastplate of the High Priest; some think they were two stones, with the word "yes" on one, and the word "no" on the other; however, that description is only speculation. Irrespective, it was the Holy Spirit Who parceled off the land and its boundaries, and did so through the means of the Urim and the Thummim.)*

3 For Moses had given the inheritance of two Tribes and an half Tribe on the other side Jordan *(the east side of Jordan)*: but unto the Levites he gave none inheritance among them.

4 For the Children of Joseph were two Tribes, Manasseh and Ephraim: therefore they gave no part unto the Levites in the land, save cities to dwell in, with their suburbs for their cattle and for their substance.

5 As the LORD commanded Moses, so the Children of Israel did, and they divided the land.

CALEB

6 Then the Children of Judah came unto Joshua in Gilgal: and Caleb the son of Jephunneh the Kenezite said unto him, You know the thing that the LORD said unto Moses the man of God concerning me and you in Kadesh-barnea.

7 Forty years old was I when Moses the servant of the LORD sent me from Kadesh-barnea to espy out the land; and I brought him word again as it was in mine heart.

8 Nevertheless my brethren that went up with me made the heart of the people melt: but I wholly followed the LORD my God.

9 And Moses swore on that day, saying, Surely the land whereon your feet have trodden shall be your inheritance, and your children's for ever, because you have wholly followed the LORD my god.

10 And now, behold, the LORD has kept me alive, as he said, these forty and five years, even since the LORD spoke this word unto Moses, while the Children of Israel wandered in the wilderness: and now, lo, I am this day fourscore and five years old *(85 years old)*

11 As yet I am as strong this day as I was in the day that Moses sent me: as my strength was then, even so is my strength now, for war,

both to go out, and to come in. *(Out of all of this, Caleb's Faith shines like the Sun. His was a Divine Faith. Such Faith overcomes the world.)*

12 Now therefore give me this mountain, whereof the LORD spoke in that day; for you heard in that day how the Anakims were there, and that the cities were great and fenced: if so be the LORD will be with me, then I shall be able to drive them out, as the LORD said. *(Williams says, "Giant sins entrenched on strong mountains are helpless before a Faith that is born of God. This fact may be experienced by any and all Believers, if they will but wholly follow the Lord as did Caleb.")*

13 And Joshua blessed him, and gave unto Caleb the son of Jephunneh Hebron for an inheritance.

14 Hebron therefore became the inheritance of Caleb the son of Jephunneh the Kenezite unto this day, because that he wholly followed the LORD God of Israel.

15 And the name of Hebron before was Kirjath-arba; which Arba was a great man among the Anakims. And the land had rest from war. *(The record proclaims that Caleb, because of his Faith in God, took possession of this mountain, and expelled the greatest of the giants, whose name was Arba. The result was that Kirjath-arba — that is, the city of Arba — became Hebron — that is, "fellowship," for that's what Hebron means! As well, where there is true faith, there is "rest from war.")*

CHAPTER 15
(1444 B.C.)
THE BOUNDARIES OF JUDAH

THIS then was the lot of the Tribe of the Children of Judah by their families *(the Tribe from which Jesus would come)*: even to the border of Edom the wilderness of Zin southward was the uttermost part of the south coast. *(By far, Judah had the largest portion. In fact, her portion was so large that Simeon had her portion within the portion of Judah, but which only took up a small part of that vast area. The portion of Simeon included the city of Beersheba. Judah's portion extended all the way from Jerusalem in the north to the brook of Egypt due south, a distance of well over a hundred miles.)*

2 And their south border was from the shore of the salt sea, from the bay that looks southward:

3 And it went out to the south side to Maaleh-acrabbim, and passed along to Zin, and ascended up on the south side unto Kadesh-barnea, and passed along to Hezron, and went up to Adar, and fetched a compass to Karkaa:

4 From thence it passed toward Azmon, and went out unto the river of Egypt; and the going out of that coast were at the sea: this shall be your south coast.

5 And the east border was the salt sea, even unto the end of Jordan. And their border in the north quarter was from the bay of the sea at the uttermost part of Jordan:

6 And the border went up to Beth-hogla, and passed along by the north of Beth-arabah; and the border went up to the stone of Bohan the son of Reuben:

7 And the border went up toward Debir from the valley of Achor, and so northward, looking toward Gilgal, that is before the going up to Adummim, which is on the south side of the river: and the border passed toward the waters of En-shemesh, and the goings out thereof were at En-rogel:

8 And the border went up by the valley of the son of Hinnom unto the south side of the Jebusite; the same is Jerusalem: and the border went up to the top of the mountain that lies before the valley of Hinnom westward, which is at the end of the valley of the giants northward:

9 And the border was drawn from the top of the hill unto the fountain of the water of Nephtoah, and went out of the cities of mount Ephron; and the border was drawn to Baalah, which is Kirjath-jearim:

10 And the border compassed from Baalah westward unto mount Seir, and passed along unto the side of mount Jearim, which is Chesalon, on the north side, and went down to Beth-shemesh, and passed on to Timnah:

11 And the border went out unto the side of Ekron northward: and the border was drawn to Shicron, and passed along to mount Baalah, and went out unto Jabneel; and the going out of the border were at the Sea.

12 And the west border was to the great sea, and the coast thereof. This is the coast of the children of Judah round about according to their families.

CALEB'S PORTION

13 And unto Caleb the son of Jephunneh he gave a part among the Children of Judah, according to the Commandment of the LORD to

Joshua, even the city of Arba the father of Anak, which city is Hebron.

14 And Caleb drove thence the three sons of Anak, Sheshai, and Ahiman, and Talmai, the children of Anak.

15 And he went up thence to the inhabitants of Debir: and the name of Debir before was Kirjath-sepher.

16 And Caleb said, He who smites Kirjath-sepher, and takes it, to him will I give Achsah my daughter to wife.

17 And Othniel the son of Kenaz, the brother of Caleb, took it: and he gave him Achsah his daughter to wife. *(The Holy Spirit is quick to record the victory of Othniel. When God enriches His people, everything is real, substantial, and definite. He gives largely; and His Blessings may, without fear of disappointment, be counted just as this Chapter records the 116 cities given to Judah.*

However, a life of blessing with God has definite borders, just as the lot of Judah had its Divinely marked boundaries. It is important that God should choose a lot in life for each one of His People, and that we not choose such a lot ourselves, and that we be satisfied with what God gives us. But, one of the problems is that far too many Believers, not satisfied with what God has given them, seek to enlarge their borders of their own volition, which God will never honor. And yet, the Lord, at times, does stretch our faith, even as He did that of Othniel, which can claim added blessings; however, the Holy Spirit, in such a case, will always inform the Believer, which means that such a Believer must never function from the position of presumption.)

18 And it came to pass, as she came unto him, that she moved him to ask of her father a field: and she lighted off her ass; and Caleb said unto her, What would you?

19 Who answered, Give me a blessing; for you have given me a south land; give me also springs of water. And he gave her the upper springs, and the nether springs. *(Achsah's Faith is to be commended. She asked for a "blessing," and, to be sure, the Lord will always honor such a request. Her father gave her the springs of water, which would water the land, making it very fertile. This is a Type of the Holy Spirit, given to those who ask [Lk. 11:13]. Without the springs of water, the land was basically worthless. With the springs, it was extremely valuable.*

Likewise, without the Holy Spirit, of which these springs, in a sense, were a Type, the life of the Believer is unproductive. With the Christ and the Cross as the object of the Believer's Faith, such a life will be extremely fertile and productive.)*

THE CITIES OF JUDAH

20 This is the inheritance of the Tribe of the children of Judah according to their families.

21 And the uttermost cities of the Tribe of the Children of Judah toward the coast of Edom southward were Kabzeel, and Eder, and Jagur,

22 And Kinah, and Dimonah, and Adadah,

23 And Kedesh, and Hazor, and Ithnan,

24 Ziph, and Telem, and Bealoth,

25 And Hazor, Hadattah, and Kerioth, and Hezron, which is Hazor,

26 Amam, and Shema, and Moladah,

27 And Hazar-gaddah, and Heshmon, and Beth-palet,

28 And Hazar-shual, and Beer-sheba, and Bizjothjah,

29 Baalah, and Iim, and Azem,

30 And Eltolad, and Chesil, and Hormah,

31 And Ziklag, and Madmannah, and Sansannah,

32 And Lebaoth, and Shilhim, and Ain, and Rimmon: all the cities are twenty and nine, with their villages:

33 And in the valley, Eshtaol, and Zoreah, and Ashnah,

34 And Zanoah, and En-gannim, Tappuah, and Enam,

35 Jarmuth, and Adullam, Socoh, and Azekah,

36 And Sharaim, and Adithaim, and Gederah, and Gederothaim; fourteen cities with their villages:

37 Zenan, and Hadashah, and Migdal-gad,

38 And Dilean, and Mizpeh, and Joktheel,

39 Lachish, and Bozkath, and Eglon,

40 And Cabbon, and Lahmam, and Kithlish,

41 And Gederoth, Beth-dagon, and Naamah, and Makkedah; sixteen cities with their villages:

42 Libnah, and Ether, and Ashan,

43 And Jiphtah, and Ashnah, and Nezib,

44 And Keilah, and Achzib, and Mareshah; nine cities with their villages:

45 Ekron, with her towns and her villages:

46 From Ekron even unto the sea, all that lay near Ashdod, with their villages:

47 Ashdod with her towns and her villages, Gaza with her towns and her villages, unto the river of Egypt, and the great sea, and the border thereof:

48 And in the mountains, Shamir, and Jattir, and Socoh,

49 And Dannah, and Kirjath-sannah, which is Debir,

50 And Anab, and Eshtemoh, and Anim,

51 And Goshen, and Holon, and Giloh; eleven cities with their villages:

52 Arab, and Dumah, and Eshean,

53 And Janum, and Beth-tappuah, and Aphekah,

54 And Humtah, and Kirjath-arba, which is Hebron, and Zior; nine cities with their villages:

55 Maon, Carmel, and Ziph, and Juttah,

56 And Jezreel, and Jokdeam, and Zanoah,

57 Cain, Gibeah, and Timnah; ten cities with their villages:

58 Halhul, Beth-zur, and Gedor,

59 And Maarath, and Beth-anoth, and Eltekon; six cities with their villages:

60 Kirjath-baal, which is Kirjath-jearim, and Rabbah; two cities with their villages:

61 In the wilderness, Beth-arabah, Middin, and Secacah,

62 And Nibshan, and the city of Salt, and En-gedi; six cities with their villages.

THE JEBUSITES

63 As for the Jebusites the inhabitants of Jerusalem, the Children of Judah could not drive them out: but the Jebusites dwell with the Children of Judah at Jerusalem unto this day. *(Jerusalem remained in the power of the Jebusite until David, a type of Israel's mighty King, captured it. In how many lives is found a fortress opposed to the Government of the Lord, which ought to have been conquered at the beginning.*

Satan knew that Jerusalem would ultimately become the Capital of Israel; therefore, he would seek to make it his stronghold, which he did for many, many years.

This tells us that the very area in the Believer's life which is ungodly, and which the Believer has the greatest difficulty in conquering, is the very area which the Holy Spirit desires to make our strong suit, in essence, His Capital. This is why the battle is so intense in such a capacity. Spiritually speaking, the Jebusite must be driven out of the land, with nothing left of that former enemy.)

CHAPTER 16
(1444 B.C.)
THE SONS OF JOSEPH

AND the lot of the Children of Joseph fell from Jordan by Jericho, unto the water of Jericho on the east, to the wilderness that goes up from Jericho throughout Mount Beth-el,

2 And goes out from Beth-el to Luz, and passes along unto the borders of Archi to Ataroth,

3 And goes down westward to the coast of Japhleti, unto the coast of Beth-horon the nether, and to Gezer: and the going out thereof are at the sea.

4 So the Children of Joseph, Manasseh and Ephraim, took their inheritance.

BORDERS OF EPHRAIM

5 And the border of the Children of Ephraim according to their families was thus: even the border of their inheritance on the east side was Ataroth-addar, unto Beth-horon the upper;

6 And the border went out toward the sea to Michmethah on the north side; and the border went about eastward unto Taanath-shiloh, and passed by it on the east of Janohah;

7 And it went down from Janohah to Ataroth, and to Naarath, and came to Jericho, and went out at Jordan.

8 The border went out from Tappuah westward unto the river Kanah; and the goings out thereof were at the sea. This is the inheritance of the Tribe of the children of Ephraim by their families.

9 And the separate cities for the Children of Ephraim were among the inheritance of the Children of Manasseh, all the cities with their villages.

10 And they drove not out the Canaanites who dwelt in Gezer: but the Canaanites dwell among the Ephraimites unto this day, and serve under tribute. *(This was wrong for Ephraim to have done. They were to destroy these nations, whatever they may have been, and not put them to tribute [Deut. 31:3]. The Holy Spirit is never satisfied with half measures. Every vestige of evil must be destroyed in our lives. It is not enough that we merely have victory over the weakness, whatever it might be. The weakness itself, and in every capacity, must be removed. This can be done only by the Believer understanding that everything comes to us through Christ and the Cross, which demands that the Cross ever be the object of our Faith. And, as we've said over and over again, the Holy Spirit will then help us grandly, thereby performing the work as it needs to be performed, and which only He can do [Rom. 8:1-2, 11].)*

CHAPTER 17
(1444 B.C.)
BORDERS OF MANASSEH

THERE was also a lot for the Tribe of Manasseh; for he was the firstborn of Joseph; to wit, for Machir the firstborn of Manasseh, the father of Gilead: because he was a man of war, therefore he had Gilead and Bashan. *(The whole land was, in effect, first given to Judah and Joseph, the other Tribes receiving their portions according as they stood in relationship to the Royal and firstborn sons of Jacob. These sons, united, typify Christ, to Whom the whole land is promised [Ps. 2; 110].*

All was according to the Word of the Lord. The casting of lots, the men who were to cast them, the divisions by families, by Tribes, and by names — all was Divine — nothing was left either to the will or wisdom of man.

The portions were allotted "according to their families." This expressed the measure of their need; and it was richly supplied. In Ephesians, the Believer's "lot" is given, not necessarily in proportion to either faith or need, "but according to His riches" [Eph., Chpt. 1].

Williams says, "The meanings of the Hebrew names of the towns and mountains, etc., which, on the one side, separated a Tribe from the world, and, on the other side, from a brother-Tribe, are full of valuable teaching for the Believer. They plainly show how fellowship with evil, on the one hand, or a lack of fellowship with truth, on the other hand, sap faith and rob the servant of God of power to drive out the inhabitants of the Land.")

2 There was also a lot for the rest of the Children of Manasseh by their families; for the Children of Abiezer, and for the Children of Abiezer, and for the Children of Helek, and for the Children of Asriel, and for the Children of Shechem, and for the Children of Hepher, and for the Children of Shemida: these were the male Children of Manasseh the son of Joseph by their families.

3 But Zelophehad, the son of Hepher, the son of Gilead, the son of Machir, the son of Manasseh, had no sons, but daughters: and these are the names of his daughters, Mahlah, and Noah, Hoglah, Milcah, and Tirzah.

4 And they came near before Eleazar the Priest, and before Joshua the son of Nun, and before the princes, saying, The LORD commanded Moses to give us an inheritance among our brethren. Therefore according to the Commandment of the LORD he gave them an inheritance among the brethren of their father. *(Some four times the Holy Spirit records the faith of the five daughters of Zelophehad [Num. 26:33; 27:1; 36:11; Josh. 17:4]. Even though they were women, and no provision had been made for them in the Law, as it regards inheritance, their faith claimed such just the same as their male counterparts. As well, through faith, they forged a path, not only for themselves, but for all other families in Israel where all the offspring were females.)*

5 And there fell ten portions to Manasseh, beside the land of Gilead and Bashan, which were on the other side Jordan;

6 Because the daughters of Manasseh had an inheritance among his sons: and the rest of Manasseh's sons had the land of Gilead. *(We are told here where the "daughters of Manasseh" had their inheritance. It was on the west side of the Jordan River. [Manasseh had a portion on both sides of the Jordan River.])*

7 And the coast of Manasseh was from Asher to Michmethah, that lies before Shechem; and the border went along on the right hand unto the inhabitants of En-tappuah.

8 Now Manasseh had the land of Tappuah: but Tappuah on the border of Manasseh belonged to the Children of Ephraim:

9 And the coast descended unto the river Kanah, southward of the river: these cities of Ephraim are among the cities of Manasseh: the coast of Manasseh also was on the north side of the river, and the outgoings of it were at the sea:

10 Southward it was Ephraim's, and northward it was Manasseh's, and the sea is his border; and they met together in Asher on the north, and in Issachar on the east.

11 And Manasseh had in Issachar and in Asher Beth-shean and her towns, and Ibleam and her towns, and the inhabitants of Dor and her towns, and the inhabitants of En-dor and her towns, and the inhabitants of Taanach and her towns, and the inhabitants of Megiddo and her towns, even three countries.

12 Yet the Children of Manasseh could not drive out the inhabitants of those cities: but the Canaanites would dwell in that land.

13 Yet it came to pass, when the Children of Israel were waxed strong, that they put the Canaanites to tribute; but did not utterly drive them out. *(Once again, we have the Word of God being compromised, which would fall out to tremendous problems and trouble later on for Israel.)*

COMPLAINTS

14 And the Children of Joseph spoke unto Joshua, saying, Why have you given me but one lot and one portion to inherit, seeing I am a great people, forasmuch as the LORD has blessed me hitherto?

15 And Joshua answered them, If you be a great people, then get thee up to the wood country, and cut down for yourself there in the land of the Perizzites and of the giants, if Mount Ephraim be too narrow for you.

16 And the Children of Joseph said, The hill is not enough for us: and all the Canaanites who dwell in the land of the valley have chariots of iron, both they who are of Beth-shean and her towns, and they who are of the valley of Jezreel.

17 And Joshua spoke unto the house of Joseph, even to Ephraim and to Manasseh, saying, You are a great people, and have great power: you shall not have one lot only:

18 But the mountain shall be yours: for it is a wood, and you shall cut it down: and the outgoings of it shall be yours: for you shall drive out the Canaanites, though they have iron chariots, and though they be strong. *(The boasting, discontent, unbelief, selfishness, and cowardice of the Children of Joseph was, with fine scorn, rebuked by Joshua, who was himself of the Tribe of Joseph. Despite the encouragement given by Joshua, the Children of Joseph did not drive the Canaanites out, as Verses 11-13 show. The reason for this was that they did not trust in God, but preferred an unworthy compromise with neighbors, who, however rich in warlike material, were sunk in sensuality and sloth — Pulpit.)*

CHAPTER 18
(1444 B.C.)
THE TABERNACLE

AND the whole congregation of the Children of Israel assembled together at Shiloh, and set up the Tabernacle of the congregation there. And the land was subdued before them. *(Shiloh was about 25 miles north of Jerusalem. It was pretty much in the center of the land. The Tabernacle remained at Shiloh and Gibeon for 300 years, and ceased to be used when replaced by Solomon's Temple.)*

UNPOSSESSED LAND

2 And there remained among the Children of Israel seven Tribes, which had not yet received their inheritance.

3 And Joshua said unto the Children of Israel, How long are you slack to go to possess the land, which the LORD God of your fathers has given you? *(Seven of the Tribes, as we see here, had been very slow to proceed forward. That is symbolic of far too many Christians. Is it possible that our Heavenly Joshua is asking the same question of modern Christians, as Joshua asked of Israel of old?)*

4 Give out from among you three men for each Tribe: and I will send them, and they shall rise, and go through the land, and describe it according to the inheritance of them; and they shall come again to me.

5 And they shall divide it into seven parts: Judah shall abide in their coast on the south, and the house of Joseph shall abide in their coasts on the north.

6 You shall therefore describe the land into seven parts, and bring the description hither to me, that I may cast lots for you here before the LORD our God *(determine exactly what the Lord would desire)*.

7 But the Levites have no part among you; for the Priesthood of the LORD is their inheritance: and Gad, and Reuben, and half the tribe of Manasseh, have received their inheritance beyond Jordan on the east, which Moses the servant of the LORD gave them.

8 And the men arose, and went away: and Joshua charged them who went to describe the land, saying, Go and walk through the land, and describe it, and come again to me, that I may here cast lots for you before the LORD in Shiloh. *(Evidently, they were to describe what they desired regarding the partitioning of the land, with the Lord, of course, having the final say. This tells us that it is perfectly proper for Believers to describe to the Lord what they want, but always with the idea that our primary objective is the Will of God, which means that it's what He wants.)*

9 And the men went and passed through the land, and described it by cities into seven parts in a book, and came again to Joshua to the host at Shiloh.

10 And Joshua cast lots for them in Shiloh before the LORD *(the Urim and the Thummim)*: and there Joshua divided the land unto the Children of Israel according to their divisions.

BENJAMIN'S TERRITORY

11 And the lot of the Tribe of the Children

of Benjamin came up according to their families (this means that the Lord provided for Benjamin a plot sufficiently large to amply take care of each family; no one family, therefore, needed to be apprehensive as to the supply of its necessities): and the coast of their lot came forth between the Children of Judah and the Children of Joseph.

12 And their border on the north side was from Jordan; and the border went up to the side of Jericho on the north side, and went up through the mountains westward; and the goings out thereof were at the wilderness of Beth-aven.

13 And the border went over from thence toward Luz, to the side of Luz, which is Beth-el, southward; and the border descended to Ataroth-adar, near the hill that lies on the south side of the nether Beth-horon.

14 And the border was drawn thence, and compassed the corner of the sea southward, from the hill that lies before Beth-horon southward; and the goings out thereof were at Kirjath-baal, which is Kirjath-jearim, a city of the Children of Judah: this was the west quarter.

15 And the south quarter was from the end of Kirjath-jearim, and the border went out on the west, and went out to the well of waters of Nephtoah:

16 And the border came down to the end of the mountain that lies before the valley of the son of Hinnom, and which is in the valley of the giants on the north, and descended to the valley of Hinnom, to the side of Jebusi on the south, and descended to En-rogel,

17 And was drawn from the north, and went forth to En-shemesh, and went forth toward Geliloth, which is over against the going up of Adummim, and descended to the stone of Bohan the son of Reuben,

18 And passed along toward the side over against Arabah northward, and went down unto Arabah:

19 And the border passed along to the side of Beth-hoglah northward: and the outgoings of the border were at the north bay of the salt sea at the south end of Jordan: this was the south coast.

20 And Jordan was the border of it on the east side. This was the inheritance of the Children of Benjamin, by the coasts thereof round about, according to their families.

21 Now the cities of the Tribe of the Children of Benjamin according to their families were Jericho, and Beth-hoglah, and the valley of Keziz,

22 And Beth-arabah, and Zemaraim, and Beth-el,

23 And Avim, and Parah, and Ophrah,

24 And Chephar-haammonai, and Ophni, and Gaba; twelve cities with their villages:

25 Gibeon, and Ramah, and Beeroth,

26 And Mizpeh, and Chephirah, and Mozah,

27 And Rekem, and Irpeel, and Taralah,

28 And Zelah, Eleph, and Jebusi, which is Jerusalem, Gibeah, and Kirjath; fourteen cities with their villages. This is the inheritance of the Children of Benjamin according to their families.

CHAPTER 19
(1444 B.C.)
THE INHERITANCE OF SIMEON

AND the second lot came forth to Simeon, even for the Tribe of the Children of Simeon according to their families: and their inheritance was within the inheritance of the Children of Judah. (Simeon, because of his misconduct [Gen. 49:7], was under a curse. As a result, he was really to have no inheritance in the Promised Land. And so he didn't, and again, so he did!

Judah shared her inheritance with the outcast brother, and thus doubled her joy. Dividing Divine blessing with others doubles it. This is a great principle, and should motivate our actions at all times.

Thus it was that Simeon, justly doomed to wrath, was taken up in Grace — the curse being turned into a blessing — and given a seat among the sons at the King's table; for the Lord sprang out of Judah [Heb. 7:14].

Simeon was saved by Grace, not by works; the name means "hearing." The Holy Spirit in Galatians 3:2 contrasts salvation by doing and salvation by hearing, and teaches that only upon the latter principle can sinners be given a portion in the Heavenly Canaan — Williams.

In truth, Simeon and Judah proclaim a type of the human race, and our Lord in His Grace. The whole of the human race is cursed. But our Heavenly Judah, by His Grace, and certainly not through any good thing that we have done, has made room for us in His inheritance. And, to be sure, a place in Judah's inheritance is the greatest position of all.)

2 And they had in their inheritance Beersheba, and Sheba, and Moladah,

3 And Hazar-shual, and Balah, and Azem,

4 And Eltolad, and Bethul, and Hormah,

5 And Ziklag, and Beth-marcaboth, and Hazar-susah,

6 And Beth-lebaoth, and Sharuhen; thirteen cities and their villages;

7 Ain, Remmon, and Ether, and Ashan; four cities and their villages:

8 And all the villages that were round about these cities to Baalath-beer, Ramath of the south. This is the inheritance of the Tribe of the Children of Simeon according to their families.

9 Out of the portion of the Children of Judah was the inheritance of the Children of Simeon: for the part of the Children of Judah was too much for them: therefore the Children of Simeon had their inheritance within the inheritance of them.

THE INHERITANCE OF ZEBULUN

10 And the third lot came up for the Children of Zebulun according to their families: and the border of their inheritance was unto Sarid:

11 And their border went up toward the sea, and Maralah, and reached to Dabbasheth, and reached to the river that is before Jokneam;

12 And turned from Sarid eastward toward the sunrising unto the border of Chisloth-tabor, and then goes out to Daberath, and goes up to Japhia,

13 And from thence passes on along on the east to Gittah-hepher, to Ittah-kazin, and goes out of Remmon-methoar to Neah;

14 And the border compasses it on the north side to Hannathon: and the outgoings thereof are in the valley of Jiphthah-el:

15 And Kattath, and Nahallal, and Shimron, and Idalah, and Beth-lehem: twelve cities with their villages.

16 This is the inheritance of the Children of Zebulun according to their families, these cities with their villages.

THE INHERITANCE OF ISSACHAR

17 And the fourth lot came out to Issachar, for the Children of Issachar according to their families.

18 And their border was toward Jezreel, and Chesulloth, and Shunem,

19 And Haphraim, and Shihon, and Anaharath,

20 And Rabbith, and Kishion, and Abez,

21 And Remeth, and En-gannim, and En-haddah, and Beth-pazzez;

22 And the coast reaches to Tabor, and Shahazimah, and Beth-shemesh; and the outgoings of their border were at Jordan: sixteen cities with their villages.

23 This is the inheritance of the Tribe of the Children of Issachar according to their families, the cities and their villages.

THE INHERITANCE OF ASHER

24 And the fifth lot came out for the Tribe of the Children of Asher according to their families.

25 And their border was Helkath, and Hali, and Beten, and Achshaph,

26 And Alammelech, and Amad, and Misheal; and reaches to Carmel westward, and to Shihor-libnath;

27 And turns toward the sunrising to Beth-dagon, and reaches to Zebulun, and to the valley of Jiphthah-el toward the north side of Beth-emek, and Neiel, and goes out of Cabul on the left hand,

28 And Hebron, and Rehob, and Hammon, and Kanah, even unto great Zidon;

29 And then the coast turns to Ramah, and to the strong city Tyre; and the coast turns to Hosah; and the outgoings thereof are at the sea from the coast to Achzib:

30 Ummah also, and Aphek, and Rehob: twenty and two cities with their villages.

31 This is the inheritance of the Tribe of the Children of Asher according to their families, these cities with their villages.

THE INHERITANCE OF NAPHTALI

32 The sixth lot came out to the Children of Naphtali, even for the Children of Naphtali according to their families.

33 And their coast was from Heleph, from Allon to Zaanannim, and Adami, Nekeb, and Jabneel, unto Lakum; and the outgoings thereof were at Jordan:

34 And then the coast turns westward to Aznoth-tabor, and goes out from thence to Hukkok, and reaches to Zebulun on the south side, and reaches to Asher on the west side, and to Judah upon Jordan toward the sunrising.

35 And the fenced cities are Ziddim, Zer, and Hammath, Rakkath, and Chinnereth,

36 And Adamah, and Ramah, and Hazor,

37 And Kedesh, and Edrei, and En-hazor,

38 And Iron, and Migdal-el, Horem, and Beth-anath, and Beth-shemesh; nineteen cities with their villages.

39 This is the inheritance of the Tribe of the Children of Naphtali according to their families, the cities and their villages.

THE INHERITANCE OF DAN

40 And the seventh lot came out for the Tribe of the Children of Dan according to their families.

41 And the coast of their inheritance was Zorah, and Eshtaol, and Ir-shemesh,

42 And Shaalabbin, and Ajalon, and Jethlah,

43 And Elon, and Thimnathah, and Ekron,

44 And Eltekeh, and Gibbethon, and Baalath,

45 And Jehud, and Bene-berak, and Gath-rimmon,

46 And Me-jarkon, and Rakkon, with the border before Japho.

47 And the coast of the Children of Dan went out too little for them: therefore the Children of Dan went up to fight against Leshem, and took it, and smote it with the edge of the sword, and possessed it, and dwelt therein, and called Leshem, Dan, after the name of Dan their father.

48 This is the inheritance of the Tribe of the Children of Dan according to their families, these cities with their villages.

JOSHUA'S INHERITANCE

49 When they had made an end of dividing the land for inheritance by their coasts (borders), the Children of Israel gave an inheritance to Joshua the son of Nun among them:

50 According to the Word of the LORD they gave him the city which he asked, even Timnath-serah in Mount Ephraim: and he built the city, and dwelt therein. (First of all, Joshua did not ask for anything for himself until all the others had received their portions. He asked for a particular city, and the Lord said that he could have it. "Timnath" means "the portion that remains," while "Serah" means "city of the Sun." This could well be symbolic of the Baptism with the Holy Spirit, i.e., "the portion that remains." As well, "Serah" could typify the life that flows from the Spirit, as it flows from the Sun.)

51 These are the inheritances, which Eleazar the Priest, and Joshua the son of Nun, and the heads of the fathers of the Tribes of the Children of Israel, divided for an inheritance by lot in Shiloh before the LORD, at the door of the Tabernacle of the congregation. So they made an end of dividing the country. (Here the fact is emphasized that God distributed the land to Israel; He employed others to do such; however, it was all done with the decorum of proper proceedings. The fact that God decided the portion for each Tribe effectually prevented any challenge as to the justness of the distribution. From this, the lesson may be learned that the right way is to allow the Lord to choose for us, instead of us choosing for ourselves.)

CHAPTER 20
(1444 B.C.)
SIX CITIES OF REFUGE

THE LORD also spoke unto Joshua, saying,

2 Speak to the Children of Israel, saying, Appoint out for you cities of refuge, whereof I spoke unto you by the hand of Moses:

3 That the slayer who kills any person unawares and unwittingly may flee there: and they shall be your refuge from the avenger of blood. (The cities of refuge were not for murderers, but rather to protect those who had killed someone accidentally; protect them from members of the family of the victim who sought revenge, and for whatever reason.)

4 And when he who does flee unto one of those cities shall stand at the entering of the gate of the city, and shall declare his cause in the ears of the elders of that city, they shall take him into the city unto them, and give him a place, that he may dwell among them.

5 And if the avenger of blood pursue after him, then they shall not deliver the slayer up into his hand; because he smote his neighbour unwittingly, and hated him not beforetime (there was no bad blood between them, so to speak).

6 And he shall dwell in that city, until he stand before the congregation for judgment, and until the death of the High Priest who shall be in those days: then shall the slayer return, and come unto his own city, and unto his own house, unto the city from where he fled. (The High Priest is a Type of Christ. When the High Priest died, the man was free to return to his home, and would be protected by law. When Jesus died on the Cross, this made it possible for men to be free, at least those who would accept Him, of which all of this was a type [Rom. 8:2].)

7 And they appointed Kedesh in Galilee in Mount Naphtali, and Shechem in Mount Ephraim, and Kirjath-arba, which is Hebron, in the mountain of Judah.

8 And on the other side Jordan by Jericho eastward, they assigned Bezer in the wilderness upon the plain out of the Tribe of Reuben, and Ramoth in Gilead out of the Tribe of Gad, and Golan in Bashan out of the Tribe of Manasseh. *(Hebrews 6:18 sets forth Christ as the City of Refuge for sinners guilty of His Blood; and the six cities appointed by Joshua display, by the meaning of their names, something of the sufficiency of that Saviour; for in Him is found: "Holiness" [Kadesh]; "Strength" [Shechem]; "Fellowship" [Hebron]; "Safety" [Bezer]; "Uplifting" [Ramoth]; and, "Happiness" [Golan]. God puts Holiness first and Happiness last. Man reverses this — Williams.)*

9 These were the cities appointed for all the Children of Israel, and for the stranger who sojourns among them, that whosoever kills any person at unawares might flee there, and not die by the hand of the avenger of blood, until he stood before the congregation.

CHAPTER 21
(1444 B.C.)
THE LEVITES

THEN came near the heads of the fathers of the Levites unto Eleazar the Priest *(the High Priest)*, and unto Joshua the son of Nun, and unto the heads of the fathers of the Tribes of the Children of Israel;

2 And they spoke unto them at Shiloh in the land of Canaan, saying, The LORD commanded by the hand of Moses to give us cities to dwell in, with the suburbs thereof for our cattle.

3 And the Children of Israel gave unto the Levites out of their inheritance, at the Commandment of the LORD, these cities and their suburbs.

4 And the lot came out for the families of the Kohathites: and the Children of Aaron the Priest, which were of the Levites, had by lot out of the Tribe of Judah, and out of the Tribe of Simeon, and out of the Tribe of Benjamin, thirteen cities *(the Kohathites were in charge of the Vessels of the Sanctuary [Num. 3:31]).*

5 And the rest of the Children of Kohath had by lot out of the families of the Tribe of Ephraim, and out of the Tribe of Dan, and out of the half Tribe of Manasseh, ten cities.

6 And the Children of Gershon had by lot out of the families of the Tribe of Issachar, and out of the Tribe of Asher, and out of the Tribe of Naphtali, and out of the half Tribe of Manasseh in Bashan, thirteen cities *(the Gershonites were in charge of the Tabernacle proper [Num. 3:25]).*

7 The Children of Merari by their families had out of the Tribe of Reuben, and out of the Tribe of Gad, and out of the Tribe of Zebulun, twelve cities *(the Merarites were in charge of the structure of the Tabernacle [Num. 3:36]).*

COMMAND OF THE LORD

8 And the Children of Israel gave by lot unto the Levites these cities with their suburbs, as the LORD commanded by the hand of Moses. *(The Lord did not at all fail to provide for the Tribe of Levi, even though they had brought upon themselves a curse due to their slaughter of the Shechemites [Gen., Chpt. 34]. As a result, judgment scattered them in Israel, but Grace made them a Kingdom of Priests and gave them 48 cities with their pasture-lands. Some three times this was declared to have been the Commandment of the Lord [Vss. 2-3, 8].)*

9 And they gave out of the Tribe of the Children of Judah, and out of the Tribe of the Children of Simeon, these cities which are here mentioned by name,

10 Which the Children of Aaron, being of the families of the Kohathites, who were of the Children of Levi, had: for theirs was the first lot.

11 And they gave them the city of Arba the father of Anak, which city is Hebron, in the hill country of Judah, with the suburbs thereof round about it.

12 But the fields of the city, and the villages thereof, gave they to Caleb the son of Jephunneh for his possession.

13 Thus they gave to the Children of Aaron the Priest Hebron with her suburbs, to be a city of refuge for the slayer; and Libnah with her suburbs,

14 And Jattir with her suburbs, and Eshtemoa with her suburbs,

15 And Holon with her suburbs, and Debir with her suburbs,

16 And Ain with her suburbs, and Juttah with her suburbs, and Beth-shemesh with her suburbs; nine cities out of those two tribes.

17 And out of the Tribe of Benjamin, Gibeon with her suburbs, Geba with her suburbs,

18 Anathoth with her suburbs, and Almon with her suburbs; four cities.

19 All the cities of the Children of Aaron, the Priests, were thirteen cities with their suburbs.

20 And the families of the Children of Kohath, the Levites which remained of the Children of Kohath, even they had the cities of their lot out of the Tribe of Ephraim.

21 For they gave them Shechem with her suburbs in Mount Ephraim, to be a city of refuge for the slayer; and Gezer with her suburbs,

22 And Kibzaim with her suburbs, and Beth-horon with her suburbs; four cities.

23 And out of the Tribe of Dan, Eltekeh with her suburbs, Gibbethon with her suburbs,

24 Aijalon with her suburbs, Gath-rimmon with her suburbs; four cities.

25 And out of the half Tribe of Manasseh, Tanach with her suburbs, and Gath-rimmon with her suburbs; two cities.

26 All the cities were ten with their suburbs for the families of the children of Kohath that remained.

27 And unto the children of Gershon, of the families of the Levites, out of the other half Tribe of Manasseh they gave Golan in Bashan with her suburbs, to be a city of refuge for the slayer; and Beesh-terah with her suburbs; two cities.

28 And out of the Tribe of Issachar, Kishon with her suburbs, Dabareh with her suburbs,

29 Jarmuth with her suburbs, En-gannim with her suburbs; four cities.

30 And out of the Tribe of Asher, Mishal with her suburbs, Abdon with her suburbs,

31 Helkath with her suburbs, and Rehob with her suburbs; four cities.

32 And out of the Tribe of Naphtali, Kedesh in Galilee with her suburbs, to be a city of refuge for the slayer; and Hammoth-dor with her suburbs, and Kartan with her suburbs; three cities.

33 All the cities of the Gershonites according to their families were thirteen cities with their suburbs.

34 And unto the families of the children of Merari, the rest of the Levites, out of the Tribe of Zebulun, Jokneam with her suburbs, and Kartah with her suburbs,

35 Dimnah with her suburbs, Nahalal with her suburbs; four cities.

36 And out of the Tribe of Reuben, Bezer with her suburbs, and Jahazah with her suburbs,

37 Kedemoth with her suburbs, and Mephaath with her suburbs; four cities.

38 And out of the Tribe of Gad, Ramoth in Gilead with her suburbs, to be a city of refuge for the slayer; and Mahanaim with her suburbs,

39 Heshbon with her suburbs, Jazer with her suburbs; four cities in all.

40 So all the cities for the children of Merari by their families, which were remaining of the families of the Levites, were by their lot twelve cities. *(Six cities were appointed as cities of refuge [20:7-8]; however, Chapter 21 only mentions five of these cities: Verse 13, Hebron; Verse 21, Shechem; Verse 27, Bashan; Verse 32, Kadesh; and, Verse 38, Ramoth. "Bezer" is not mentioned. Why? 22:10-34 may provide the answer.*

An altar, which was the product of man's imagination, rebellious imagination we might quickly add, was set up close to Bezer. This neutralized it as a city of refuge. Why? God has but one center of Atonement and Blessing in Type, and that is Calvary. Any other center, even an exact pattern, denies that Divine Center. Bezer's sufficiency as a refuge was based upon the atoning sacrifices at Shiloh, as was everything else in Israel. The erection of the Reubenite altar destroyed that sufficiency, because it destroyed that base.

In this present modern age, man is putting forth all types of solutions as imitations of Christ's atoning work; consequently, the Cross has been set aside. But let it ever be known, there is no other refuge for sinners, only the Cross! Only the Cross! Only the Cross!)

THE PORTION OF THE LEVITES

41 All the cities of the Levites within the possession of the Children of Israel were forty and eight cities with their suburbs.

42 These cities were every one with their suburbs round about them: thus were all these cities *(scattered all over Israel)*.

THE POSSESSION

43 And the LORD gave unto Israel all the land which He swore to give unto their fathers; and they possessed it, and dwelt therein. *(The Book of Joshua is the story of the Promised Land, and its possession. Even though the Lord gave it to Israel, they had to take it, which must be a lesson for us presently.*

The Promise and the Possession are two different things. The Lord has designed it that we have to use our Faith and Trust in Him in order to possess the land. If we follow His Word

exactly, we will see nothing but victory. If we veer from the designed course, a course incidentally laid out by the Lord, we will suffer defeat. So, as a Believer, we should study this Book of Joshua intently, for it is, in type, God's blueprint for victory.)

44 And the LORD gave them rest round about, according to all that He swore unto their fathers: and there stood not a man of all their enemies before them; the LORD delivered all their enemies into their hand. *(While the Lord definitely did deliver these enemies into their hand, at times, Israel failed to do their part regarding Faith [16:10; 17:12-13].)*

45 There failed not ought of any good thing which the LORD had spoken unto the House of Israel; all came to pass *(all definitely will come to pass, if we will only believe the Lord).*

CHAPTER 22
(1444 B.C.)
THE BLESSING AND THE WARNING

THEN Joshua called the Reubenites, and the Gadites, and the half Tribe of Manasseh,

2 And said unto them, You have kept all that Moses the servant of the LORD commanded you, and have obeyed my voice in all that I commanded you:

3 You have not left your brethren these many days unto this day, but have kept the charge of the Commandment of the LORD your God.

4 And now the LORD your God has given rest unto your brethren, as He promised them: therefore now return ye, and get you unto your tents, and unto the land of your possession, which Moses the servant of the LORD gave you on the other side Jordan *(on the eastern side).*

5 But take diligent heed to do the Commandment and the Law which Moses the servant of the LORD charged you, to love the LORD your God, and to walk in all His ways, and to keep His Commandments, and to cleave unto Him, and to serve Him with all your heart and with all your soul.

6 So Joshua blessed them, and sent them away: and they went unto their tents.

7 Now to the one half of the Tribe of Manasseh Moses had given possession in Bashan: but unto the other half thereof gave Joshua among their brethren on this side Jordan westward. And when Joshua sent them away also unto their tents, then he blessed them,

8 And he spoke unto them, saying, Return with much riches unto your tents, and with very much cattle, with silver, and with gold, and with brass, and with iron, and with very much raiment: divide the spoil of your enemies with your brethren.

9 And the Children of Reuben and the Children of Gad and the half Tribe of Manasseh returned, and departed from the Children of Israel out of Shiloh, which is in the land of Canaan, to go unto the country of Gilead, to the land of their possession, whereof they were possessed, according to the Word of the LORD by the hand of Moses.

THE ALTAR

10 And when they came unto the borders of Jordan, that are in the land of Canaan, the Children of Reuben and the Children of Gad and the half Tribe of Manasseh built there an altar by Jordan, a great altar to see to. *(Such an altar was sternly forbidden by God; for it opened the door to idolatry. There was to be only one place for the Altar, the place which God appointed, which now was Shiloh [Deut. 12:5-8].*

Jesus Christ and Him Crucified is the answer [I Cor. 1:23]. Anything else proposed, even that which looks right but is not actually the Cross, must be rejected out of hand, because God has rejected all such things. He accepts the Cross of Christ, and nothing else!)

THE DISPUTE

11 And the Children of Israel heard say, Behold, the Children of Reuben and the Children of Gad and the half Tribe of Manasseh have built an altar over against the land of Canaan, in the borders of Jordan, at the passage of the Children of Israel *(close by where the Jordan River was miraculously opened).*

12 And when the Children of Israel heard of it, the whole congregation of the Children of Israel gathered themselves together at Shiloh, to go up to war against them.

13 And the Children of Israel sent unto the Children of Reuben, and to the Children of Gad, and to the half Tribe of Manasseh, into the land of Gilead, Phinehas the son of Eleazar the Priest,

14 And with him ten princes, of each chief house a prince throughout all the Tribes of Israel; and each one was an head of the house of their fathers among the thousands of Israel.

15 And they came unto the Children of

Reuben, and to the Children of Gad, and to the half Tribe of Manasseh, unto the land of Gilead, and they spoke with them, saying,

16 Thus saith the whole congregation of the LORD, What trespass is this that you have committed against the God of Israel, to turn away this day from following the LORD, in that you have built you an altar, that you might rebel this day against the LORD?

17 Is the iniquity of Peor too little for us, from which we are not cleansed until this day, although there was a plague in the congregation of the LORD.

18 But that you must turn away this day from following the LORD? and it will be, seeing you rebel today against the LORD, that to morrow He will be wroth with the whole congregation of Israel.

19 Notwithstanding, if the land of your possession be unclean, then pass ye over unto the land of the possession of the LORD, wherein the LORD's Tabernacle dwells, and take possession among us: but rebel not against the LORD, nor rebel against us, in building you an altar beside the Altar of the LORD our God.

20 Did not Achan the son of Zerah commit a trespass in the accursed thing, and wrath fell on all the congregation of Israel? and that man perished not alone in his iniquity.

THE EXPLANATION

21 Then the Children of Reuben and the Children of Gad and the half Tribe of Manasseh answered, and said unto the heads of the thousands of Israel,

22 The LORD God of gods, the LORD God of gods, He knows, and Israel he shall know; if it be in rebellion, or if in transgression against the LORD, (save us not this day,)

23 That we have built us an altar to turn from following the LORD, or if to offer thereon Burnt Offering or Meat Offering, or if to offer Peace Offerings thereon, let the LORD himself require it;

24 And if we have not rather done it for fear of this thing, saying, In time to come your children might speak unto our children, saying, What have you to do with the LORD God of Israel?

25 For the LORD has made Jordan a border between us and you, you Children of Reuben and Children of Gad; you have no part in the LORD: so shall your children make our children cease from fearing the LORD.

26 Therefore we said, Let us now prepare to build us an altar, not for Burnt Offering, nor for Sacrifice:

27 But that it may be a witness between us, and you, and our generations after us, that we might do the service of the LORD before Him with our Burnt Offerings, and with our Sacrifices, and with our Peace Offerings; that your children may not say to our children in time to come, You have no part in the LORD.

28 Therefore said we, that it shall be, when they should so say to us or to our generations in time to come, that we may say again, Behold the pattern of the altar of the LORD, which our fathers made, not for Burnt Offerings, nor for Sacrifices; but it is a witness between us and you.

29 God forbid that we should rebel against the LORD, and turn this day from following the LORD, to build an altar for Burnt Offerings, for Meat Offerings, or for Sacrifices, beside the Altar of the LORD our God that is before His Tabernacle.

PHINEHAS

30 And when Phinehas the Priest, and the princes of the congregation and heads of the thousands of Israel which were with him, heard the words that the Children of Reuben and the Children of Gad and the Children of Manasseh spoke, it pleased them.

31 And Phinehas the son of Eleazar the Priest said unto the Children of Reuben, and to the Children of Gad, and to the Children of Manasseh, This day we perceive that the LORD is among us, because you have not committed this trespass against the LORD: now you have delivered the Children of Israel out of the hand of the LORD.

32 And Phinehas the son of Eleazar the Priest, and the princes, returned from the Children of Reuben, and from the Children of Gad, out of the land of Gilead, unto the land of Canaan, to the Children of Israel, and brought them word again.

33 And the thing pleased the Children of Israel; and the Children of Israel blessed God, and did not intend to go up against them in battle, to destroy the land wherein the Children of Reuben and Gad dwelt.

34 And the Children of Reuben and the Children of Gad called the altar Ed: for it shall be

a witness between us that the LORD is God. *(This should have been translated, "And the sons of Reuben and the sons of Gad gave a name to the altar, 'For it is a witness between us.'" The account does not say that God was well-pleased; nor does it say that Joshua asked counsel of God in the matter. The truth is, it was not well-pleasing to the Lord, and Eleazar the High Priest should have demanded that it be torn down.)*

CHAPTER 23
(1427 B.C.)
THE EXHORTATION

AND it came to pass a long time after that the LORD had given rest unto Israel from all their enemies round about, that Joshua waxed old and stricken in age *(the "long time" was approximately 8 years).*

2 And Joshua called for all Israel, and for their elders, and for their heads, and for their judges, and for their officers, and said unto them, I am old and stricken in age:

3 And you have seen all that the LORD your God has done unto all these nations because of you; for the LORD your God is He Who has fought for you.

4 Behold, I have divided unto you by lot these nations that remain, to be an inheritance for your Tribes, from Jordan, with all the nations that I have cut off, even unto the Great Sea *(the Mediterranean)* westward.

5 And the LORD your God, He shall expel them from before you, and drive them from out of your sight; and you shall possess their land, as the LORD your God has promised unto you. *(All the enemies were not yet driven out, but the Promise is given here that if the people will obey the Lord, to be sure, total victory will be the result, with no enemies left. Thus far, no enemies stood before them, at least for those who truly followed the Lord. Continued victory is promised here!)*

6 Be ye therefore very courageous to keep and to do all that is written in the Book of the Law of Moses, that you turn not aside therefrom to the right hand or to the left *(Israel is told here that prosperity depends upon their fidelity to the Bible; it is the same presently! We must not add to the Word of God, nor take from the Word of God);*

7 That you come not among these nations, these who remain among you; neither make mention of the name of their gods, nor cause to swear by them, neither serve them, nor bow yourselves unto them *(presently, any form of worship that is not anchored squarely in "Jesus Christ and Him Crucified" can only be construed as idolatry [I Cor. 1:17-18, 21, 23; 2:2]):*

8 But cleave unto the LORD your God, as you have done unto this day *(give fidelity to His Book, and love to Him Personally).*

9 For the LORD has driven out from before you great nations and strong: but as for you, no man has been able to stand before you unto this day.

10 One man of you shall chase a thousand: for the LORD your God, He it is Who fights for you, as He has promised you. *(What a Promise!)*

11 Take good heed therefore unto yourselves, that you love the LORD your God.

12 Else if you do in any wise go back, and cleave unto the remnant of these nations, even these who remain among you, and shall make marriages with them, and go in unto them, and they to you:

13 Know for a certainty that the LORD your God will no more drive out any of these nations from before you; but they shall be snares and traps unto you, and scourges in your sides, and thorns in your eyes, until you perish from off this good land which the LORD your God has given you *(regrettably, that's exactly what happened!).*

14 And, behold, this day I am going the way of all the Earth: and you know in all your hearts and in all your souls, that not one thing has failed of all the good things which the LORD your God spoke concerning you; all are come to pass unto you, and not one thing has failed thereof *(from that time until now, about 3,500 years, the same thing can still be said; not one Word of the Lord has ever failed, and, in fact, cannot fail).*

15 Therefore it shall come to pass, that as all good things are come upon you, which the LORD your God promised you; so shall the LORD bring upon you all evil things, until He has destroyed you from off this good land which the LORD your God has given you *(as the Lord blesses for obedience, at the same time, He will send judgment for disobedience; this must not be forgotten).*

16 When you have transgressed the Covenant of the LORD your God, which He commanded you, and have gone and served other gods, and bowed yourselves to them; then shall the anger of the LORD be kindled against you, and you shall perish quickly from off the good land which He has given unto you.

CHAPTER 24
(1427 B.C.)
JOSHUA'S FAREWELL ADDRESS

AND Joshua gathered all the Tribes of Israel to Shechem, and called for the elders of Israel, and for their heads, and for their judges, and for their officers; and they presented themselves before God *(at the Tabernacle, where the Altar and the Ark of the Covenant were)*.

2 And Joshua said unto all the people. Thus saith the LORD God of Israel, Your fathers dwelt on the other side of the flood in old time, even Terah, the father of Abraham, and the father of Nachor: and they served other gods. *(When Grace found Abraham, he was an idolater. In fact, in one way or the other, all who do not know the Lord are guilty of the sin of idolatry. With many it is the worship of "self." Even in Christendom, idols are plentiful, although in a different form than during the time of Joshua. Many worship their Churches, their Denominations, etc.)*

3 And I took your father Abraham from the other side of the flood *(the Euphrates River)*, and led him throughout all the land of Canaan, and multiplied his seed, and gave him Isaac *(the Lord was the Author of all of these things, as it pertained to Abraham)*.

4 And I gave unto Isaac Jacob and Esau: and I gave unto Esau Mount Seir, to possess it; but Jacob and his children went down into Egypt.

5 I sent Moses also and Aaron, and I plagued Egypt, according to that which I did among them: and afterward I brought you out. *(From this Chapter, we learn that Joshua stood in the Office of the Prophet. We find the proof of this in Verses 2 and 27. In fact, everything between these two Verses, and including those Verses, is prophetic.)*

6 And I brought your fathers out of Egypt: and you came unto the Sea; and the Egyptians pursued after your fathers with chariots and horsemen unto the Red Sea.

7 And when they cried unto the LORD, He put darkness between you and the Egyptians, and brought the Sea upon them, and covered them; and your eyes have seen what I have done in Egypt: and you dwelt in the wilderness a long season. *(It was the Will of the Lord that Israel would spend a short period of time in the wilderness, in order that they might learn faith and trust in Him. That time frame would have been approximately 2 years; however, they instead would spend approximately 40 years in the wilderness because of unbelief. It was truly "a long season.")*

8 And I brought you into the land of the Amorites, which dwelt on the other side Jordan; and they fought with you: and I gave them into your hand, that you might possess their land; and I destroyed them from before you *(as long as Israel served the Lord, the Lord fought for them)*.

9 Then Balak the son of Zippor, king of Moab, arose and warred against Israel, and sent and called Balaam the son of Beor to curse you:

10 But I would not hearken unto Balaam; therefore he blessed you still: so I delivered you out of his hand.

11 And you went over Jordan, and came unto Jericho: and the men of Jericho fought against you, the Amorites, and the Perizzites, and the Canaanites, and the Hittites, and the Girgashites, the Hivites, and the Jebusites; and I delivered them into your hand *(seven nations strong, which were defeated by the Lord)*.

12 And I sent the hornet before you, which drove them out from before you, even the two kings of the Amorites; but not with your sword, nor with your bow *(the Lord used the lowly hornet to effect victory)*.

13 And I have given you a land for which you did not labour, and cities which you built not, and you dwell in them; of the vineyards and oliveyards which you planted not do you eat.

14 Now therefore fear the LORD, and serve Him in sincerity and in truth: and put away the gods which your fathers served on the other side of the flood, and in Egypt; and serve ye the LORD.

15 And if it seem evil unto you to serve the LORD, choose you this day whom you will serve; whether the gods which your fathers served who were on the other side of the flood, or the gods of the Amorites, in whose land you dwell: but as for me and my house, we will serve the LORD *(the warrior cannot answer for others, but he does answer for himself; and his answer should be the answer of every human being on Earth)*.

16 And the people answered and said, God forbid that we should forsake the LORD, to serve other gods;

17 For the LORD our God, He it is Who brought us up and our fathers out of the land of Egypt, from the house of bondage, and which did those great signs in our sight, and preserved us in all the way wherein we went, and among all the people through whom we passed:

18 And the LORD drove out from before us all the people, even the Amorites which dwell

in the land: therefore will we also serve the LORD; for He is our God. *(The people answered correctly; however, as the near future would prove, their hearts were not exactly according to their words.)*

19 And Joshua said unto the people, You cannot serve the LORD: for He is an Holy God; He is a jealous God; He will not forgive your transgressions nor your sins. *(The idea is, the word "forgive," as used here, "signifies to remove or to bear the burden of guilt." In other words, God could not do such, if proper Atonement is not made, which is the proper Sacrifice, which is a Type of the Cross, and Faith in that Sacrifice. "Transgressions" signifies "a breach of covenant." One can have Forgiveness, Mercy, and Grace only on the basis of the Crucified Christ, and Faith in that atoning Work [Jn. 3:16; Eph. 2:8-9].)*

20 If you forsake the LORD, and serve strange gods, then He will turn and do you hurt, and consume you, after that He has done you good *(in all of this, God doesn't change; He rewards obedience, and brings judgment on disobedience).*

THE COVENANT

21 And the people said unto Joshua, No; but we will serve the LORD.

22 And Joshua said unto the people, You are witnesses against yourselves that you have chosen you the LORD, to serve Him. And they said, We are witnesses.

23 Now therefore put away, said he, the strange gods which are among you, and incline your heart unto the LORD God of Israel. *(This Passage proves that there was still idolatry among the Israelites, despite the great things done for them by the Lord. This is why John the Beloved said, "Little children, keep yourselves from idols" [I Jn. 5:21].)*

24 And the people said unto Joshua, The LORD our God will we serve, and His voice will we obey.

25 So Joshua made a Covenant with the people that day, and set them a Statute and an Ordinance in Shechem.

THE MONUMENT

26 And Joshua wrote these words in the Book of the Law of God, and took a great stone, and set it up there under an oak, that was by the Sanctuary of the LORD.

27 And Joshua said unto all the people, Behold, this stone shall be a witness unto us; for it has heard all the words of the LORD which He spoke unto us: it shall be therefore a witness unto you, lest you deny your God *(the Lord told the Pharisees that the very stones were prepared to give their testimony to His Person and Mission [Lk. 19:40]).*

28 So Joshua let the people depart, every man unto his inheritance. *(This would be the last time that many of them would see Joshua, one of the greatest men of God who ever lived.)*

JOSHUA'S DEATH

29 And it came to pass after these things, that Joshua the son of Nun, the servant of the LORD, died, being an hundred and ten years old. *(No higher accolade could be given to any man or woman than to refer to them as "the servant of the Lord." Joshua closed his life with the full consciousness that he had discharged the duties God had imposed upon him, and had done so without failure of Faith.)*

30 And they buried him in the border of his inheritance in Timnath-serah, which is in Mount Ephraim, on the north side of the hill of Gaash. *(Tradition says that they carved the rising Sun on the stone placed over the entrance to the tomb. This commemorated the tremendous miracle wrought by the Lord, when Joshua asked for the day to be lengthened that the victory may be complete. God honored his request.)*

31 And Israel served the LORD all the days of Joshua, and all the days of the elders that overlived Joshua, and which had known all the works of the LORD, that He had done for Israel. *(We see here the value of personal influence. All the days of Joshua's government were only 14 years, and all the days of the Elders who outlived him only 3 years; and then came Israel's swift lapse into the abominations of idolatry — Williams.)*

32 And the bones of Joseph, which the Children of Israel brought up out of Egypt, buried they in Shechem, in a parcel of ground which Jacob bought of the sons of Hamor the father of Shechem for an hundred pieces of silver: and it became the inheritance of the Children of Joseph. *(Incidentally, both Joseph and Joshua each lived to be 110 years old [Gen. 50:24-26].)*

33 And Eleazar the son of Aaron died; and they buried him in a hill that pertained to Phinehas his son, which was given him in Mount Ephraim. *(A glorious Chapter closes, with now a darker Chapter concerning Israel about to begin.)*

THE BOOK OF
JUDGES

CHAPTER 1
(1425 B.C.)
JUDAH AND SIMEON

NOW after the death of Joshua it came to pass, that the Children of Israel asked the LORD, saying, Who shall go up for us against the Canaanites first, to fight against them? *(Joshua died, but God didn't die! They "asked the Lord" as to what they should do, which is what they should have done. In fact, we as Believers should ask the Lord about everything.)*

2 And the LORD said, Judah shall go up: behold, I have delivered the land into his hand. *(Christ came from the Tribe of Judah; so, in essence, the Lord is saying that if we follow our Heavenly Judah, victory will be ours.)*

3 And Judah said unto Simeon his brother, Come up with me into my lot, that we may fight against the Canaanites; and I likewise will go with you into your lot. So Simeon went with him. *(Simeon had been cursed because of the slaughter of the Shechemites, which, of course, had taken place many years before. The curse meant that they would have no inheritance in Israel, when, in fact, Israel possessed the land; however, the Tribe of Judah, which had the largest inheritance of all, gave Simeon an inheritance within their inheritance [Josh. 19:1; Gen. 49:5-7]. Likewise, the whole of humanity was cursed, because of the Fall; consequently, we had no inheritance. But our Heavenly Judah made a way for us, by giving us a part in His inheritance. If we go with Judah, i.e., "our Heavenly Judah," we are guaranteed the victory.)*

4 And Judah went up: and the LORD delivered the Canaanites and the Perizzites into their hand: and they slew of them in Bezek ten thousand men.

5 And they found Adoni-bezek in Bezek: and they fought against him, and they slew the Canaanites and the Perizzites.

6 But Adoni-bezek fled; and they pursued after him, and caught him, and cut off his thumbs and his great toes.

7 And Adoni-bezek said, Threescore and ten kings, having their thumbs and their great toes cut off, gathered their meat under my table: as I have done, so God has requited me. And they brought him to Jerusalem, and there he died. *(Evidently, he had committed the same atrocity on some 70 lesser kings, which rendered them helpless to hold a sword, or to properly run. Apparently, the leaders of the Tribe of Judah had heard about his atrocities, and treated him accordingly.)*

VICTORIES

8 Now the Children of Judah had fought against Jerusalem, and had taken it, and smitten it with the edge of the sword, and set the city on fire *(but evidently they didn't hold it)*.

9 And afterward the Children of Judah went down to fight against the Canaanites, who dwelt in the mountain, and in the south, and in the valley.

10 And Judah went against the Canaanites who dwelt in Hebron: (now the name of Hebron before was Kirjath-arba:) and they slew Sheshai, and Ahiman, and Talmai *(this was evidently done by Caleb [Josh. 15:14]; these were most likely giants)*.

11 And from thence he went against the inhabitants of the Debir: and the name of Debir before was Kirjath-sepher:

12 And Caleb said, He who smites Kirjath-sepher, and takes it, to him will I give Achsah my daughter to wife.

13 And Othniel the son of Kenaz, Caleb's younger brother, took it: and he gave him Achsah his daughter to wife.

14 And it came to pass, when she came to him, that she moved him to ask of her father a field: and she lighted from off her ass; and Caleb said unto her, What will you?

15 And she said unto him, Give me a blessing: for you have given me a south land; give me also springs of water. And Caleb gave her the upper springs and the nether springs. *(If the field was to be given to her, then she felt she also had the right to ask for the springs of water to make the field fertile, which she did, and which she received. In a sense, the springs are a Type of the Holy Spirit, without which there would be no spiritual fertility in our lives.)*

CONQUESTS AND FAILURES

16 And the children of the Kenite, Moses' father in law *(or rather "brother-in-law")*, went up out of the city of the palm trees *(Jericho)* with the Children of Judah into the wilderness of Judah, which lies in the south of Arad; and they went and dwelt among the people. *(Evidently, Hobab, who declined to go when invited some time earlier, eventually accepted Moses' offer [Num. 10:29-30].)*

17 And Judah went with Simeon his brother, and they slew the Canaanites who inhabited Zephath, and utterly destroyed it. And the name of the city was called Hormah. *(In Verse 3, it says, "Simeon went with Judah," because the places which follow were all in Judah's portion; but now we read, "Judah went with Simeon," because the two places named were in Simeon's portion [Josh. 19:4].)*

18 Also Judah took Gaza with the coast thereof, and Askelon with the coast thereof, and Ekron with the coast thereof.

19 And the LORD was with Judah; and he drove out the inhabitants of the mountain: but could not drive out the inhabitants of the valley, because they had chariots of iron. *(The first phrase, "The LORD was with Judah," means that they could definitely have driven out those with the chariots of iron had they only exercised proper Faith. Evidently, they didn't! The truth is, without God, it was all impossible for Israel, but, with the Lord, all things are possible.)*

20 And they gave Hebron unto Caleb, as Moses said: and he expelled thence the three sons of Anak *(Vs. 10)*.

21 And the Children of Benjamin did not drive out the Jebusites who inhabited Jerusalem; but the Jebusites dwell with the Children of Benjamin in Jerusalem unto this day. *(The same held true for Benjamin as it did for Judah; they evidently did not exercise proper Faith. The "Jebusites," one of the most fierce and warlike tribes, continued to inhabit Jerusalem until the time of David, when he expelled them, some 500 years later. That's a long time to have an enemy in one's very midst; however, it is typical of Satan endeavoring to build strongholds in our lives. Only proper Faith in Christ and the Cross, which gives the Holy Spirit latitude to work in our lives, can bring about victory over the world, the flesh, and the Devil. Far too many Believers have "Jebusites" in their lives!)*

FAILURE

22 And the house of Joseph, they also went up against Beth-el: and the LORD was with them. *(By this phrase, we are shown what God can do, regarding the heart which trusts Him. But the ground won by Faith can only be held by Faith; and very soon, therefore, the Canaanite and the Philistine recovered possession of what they had lost.)*

23 And the house of Joseph sent to descry Beth-el. (Now the name of the city before was Luz.)

24 And the spies saw a man come forth out of the city, and they said unto him, Show us, we pray thee, the entrance into the city, and we will show you mercy.

25 And when he showed them the entrance into the city, they smote the city with the edge of the sword; but they let go the man and all his family.

26 And the man went into the land of the Hittites, and built a city, and called the name thereof Luz: which is the name thereof unto this day. *(The man was determined to build what God had determined to destroy. He had an opportunity to know the God of Israel, but rebelled against that opportunity.*

Rahab's action was the reverse. She and her family were the only ones saved out of the doom of Jericho. But Grace changed her heart, and she joined the people of God.)

27 Neither did Manasseh drive out the inhabitants of Beth-shean and her towns, nor Taanach and her towns, nor the inhabitants of Dor and her towns, nor the inhabitants of Ibleam and her towns, nor the inhabitants of Megiddo and her towns: but the Canaanites would dwell in that land.

28 And it came to pass, when Israel was strong, that they put the Canaanites to tribute, and did not utterly drive them out. *(As failure after failure is recorded, it doesn't mean that Israel didn't have the power to drive out the heathen, but rather that they just simply disobeyed God, and let them remain, which proved to be exactly what the Lord said would happen. Instead of Israel winning the heathen to Jehovah, the heathen won the people of God to their heathen idols. It is the same with the modern Church.*

While the Bible does not teach isolation from the world, it definitely does teach separation. We are "in" the world, but never to be "of" the world. The ship is in the water, but trouble

comes, and greatly so, when the water gets in the ship [II Cor. 6:14-18; 7:1].)

29 Neither did Ephraim drive out the Canaanites that dwelt in Gezer: but the Canaanites dwelt in Gezer among them.

30 Neither did Zebulun drive out the inhabitants of Kitron, nor the inhabitants of Nahalol; but the Canaanites dwelt among them, and became tributaries.

31 Neither did Asher drive out the inhabitants of Accho, nor the inhabitants of Zidon, nor of Ahlab, nor of Achzib, nor of Helbah, nor of Aphik, nor of Rehob:

32 But the Asherites dwelt among the Canaanites, the inhabitants of the land: for they did not drive them out.

33 Neither did Naphtali drive out the inhabitants of Beth-shemesh, nor the inhabitants of Beth-anath; but he dwelt among the Canaanites, the inhabitants of the land: nevertheless the inhabitants of Beth-shemesh and of Beth-anath became tributaries unto them.

34 And the Amorites forced the Children of Dan into the mountain: for they would not suffer them to come down to the valley *(as stated, if the enemy is allowed to remain, he will ultimately make a slave out of the Believer. The situation had become so bad in Israel that the Tribe of Dan could not even live in the valley, or plant crops therein; they were virtual prisoners in their own land; and so it is):*

35 But the Amorites would dwell in Mount Heres in Aijalon, and in Shaalbim: yet the hand of the house of Joseph prevailed, so that they became tributaries *(they should have driven them out).*

36 And the coast of the Amorites was from the going up to Akrabbim, from the rock, and upward.

CHAPTER 2
(1425 B.C.)
THE LORD

A ND an Angel of the LORD *(actually, a preincarnate appearance of Christ)* came up from Gilgal to Bochim, and said, I made you to go up out of Egypt, and have brought you unto the land which I swore unto your fathers; and I said, I will never break My Covenant with you *(the Lord has never broken a Covenant, but, most definitely, man breaks it repeatedly).*

2 And you shall make no league with the inhabitants of this land; you shall throw down their altars: but you have not obeyed My voice: why have you done this? *(This is the question the Lord continues to ask of many Believers! As stated, if we make a league with the world, the world doesn't become more Christian, but rather we become more worldly.)*

3 Wherefore I also said, I will not drive them out from before you; but they shall be as thorns in your sides, and their gods shall be a snare unto you *(in other words, if Israel disobeyed the Lord, He would withhold His help; in that case, Israel could but fail!).*

4 And it came to pass, when the Angel of the LORD spoke these words unto all the Children of Israel, that the people lifted up their voice, and wept *(as to exactly how the Lord delivered this Word unto Israel, we aren't told here; perhaps He used the High Priest; however, any guess is but speculation).*

5 And they called the name of that place Bochim *(means "weeping")*: and they sacrificed there unto the LORD. *(Exactly where "Bochim" was, we aren't told, but many think that it was near Shiloh. In fact, the Sacrifices were probably carried out at Shiloh. It seems that the people repented; however, it is also obvious that their repentance was shallow.)*

JOSHUA

6 And when Joshua had let the people go, the Children of Israel went every man unto his inheritance to possess the land *(this was after Joshua's farewell address, given to us in Chapter 24 of his Book).*

7 And the people served the LORD all the days of Joshua, and all the days of the elders who outlived Joshua, who had seen all the great works of the LORD, that He did for Israel.

8 And Joshua the son of Nun, the servant of the LORD, died, being an hundred and ten years old. *(This happened before the events of Verses 1-5.)*

9 And they buried him in the border of his inheritance in Timnath-heres, in the Mount of Ephraim, on the north side of the hill Gaash.

10 And also all that generation were gathered unto their fathers: and there arose another generation after them, which knew not the LORD, nor yet the works which He had done for Israel. *(The statement about Joshua and the elders is repeated here designedly by the Holy Spirit, in order to justify the righteous indignation and words of the Angel of Jehovah — Williams.)*

APOSTASY

11 And the Children of Israel did evil in the sight of the LORD, and served Baalim *(some six times this phrase is used in this Book of Judges; in all of these six Passages, the definite article, "the evil", should be used; it means "idolatry" [2:11; 3:7, 12; 4:1; 6:1; 10:6; 13:1])*:

12 And they forsook the LORD God of their fathers, which brought them out of the land of Egypt, and followed other gods, of the gods of the people who were round about them, and bowed themselves unto them, and provoked the LORD to anger. *(The doctrine of this Chapter is that the Lord cannot give victories to the flesh [Rom. 8:8]. These people had seen God move mightily at the crossing of the Jordan, the fall of Jericho, and a hundred other similar victories; however, miracles, as wonderful as they are, seldom, if ever, hold people to the tried and true. It is Faith alone which can accomplish that, and, above all, Faith in the correct object, which is Christ and the Cross, i.e., the Word of God [I Cor. 1:17-18, 21, 23; 2:2].)*

13 And they forsook the LORD, and served Baal and Ashtaroth *(Baal and Ashtaroth are frequently coupled together; this was the god of the Zidonians; their worship was accompanied by the most vile immoralities).*

14 And the anger of the LORD was hot against Israel, and He delivered them into the hands of spoilers who spoiled them, and He sold them into the hands of their enemies round about, so that they could not any longer stand before their enemies.

15 Whithersoever they went out, the hand of the LORD was against them for evil, as the LORD had said, and as the LORD had sworn unto them: and they were greatly distressed *(gods invented by men are served faithfully; however, the fact that Israel was at perpetual war with Jehovah proclaims the fact that the Lord was not an invention of man; as the Lord had worked for Israel, He now works against Israel; God hasn't changed; what He did then, He does now!).*

JUDGES

16 Nevertheless the LORD raised up Judges, which delivered them out of the hand of those who spoiled them. *(The Hebrew word for "judge" means "one who sets right what has been put wrong." We will find that all of these Judges were all distinguished by some disability, as will* appear when each one's history is studied, and they will be found to illustrate the principle that God uses weak things to confound the mighty [I Cor. 1:27].)*

17 And yet they would not hearken unto their Judges, but they went a whoring after other gods, and bowed themselves unto them: they turned quickly out of the way which their fathers walked in, obeying the Commandments of the LORD; but they did not so.

18 And when the LORD raised them up Judges, then the LORD was with the Judge, and delivered them out of the hand of their enemies all the days of the Judge: for it repented the LORD because of their groanings by reason of them who oppressed them and vexed them. *(With these Judges, God gave gracious revivals; but, after each revival, the nation fell into deeper sin and bondage.)*

19 And it came to pass, when the Judge was dead, that they returned, and corrupted themselves more than their fathers, in following other gods to serve them, and to bow down unto them; they ceased not from their own doings, nor from their stubborn way. *(Without proper spiritual leadership, basically every time the Church will go into apostasy. That is the problem with the modern Church. Its leadership, for all practical purposes, is man-appointed, which God can never recognize.)*

20 And the anger of the LORD was hot against Israel; and He said, Because that this people has transgressed My Covenant which I commanded their fathers, and have not hearkened unto My voice;

21 I also will not henceforth drive out any from before them of the nations which Joshua left when he died:

22 That through them I may prove Israel, whether they will keep the way of the LORD to walk therein, as their fathers did keep it, or not.

23 Therefore the LORD left those nations, without driving them out hastily; neither delivered He them into the hand of Joshua. *(Everything, as it regards the Child of God, is a test. How will we act? How will we react?)*

CHAPTER 3
(1406 B.C.)
PROVING ISRAEL

NOW these are the nations which the LORD left, to prove Israel by them, even as many of Israel as had not known all the wars of

Canaan *(the younger generation had not witnessed the miracles of the recent past; they would now need to be proven, as to whether they would follow the Lord or heathen idols; every Believer, in one way or the other, is "proven"; this is not that the Lord might know, for He already knows, but, rather, that we might know);*

2 Only that the generations of the Children of Israel might know, to teach them war, at the least such as before knew nothing thereof *(a considerable period of "rest" had followed Joshua's conquests, during which the younger Israelites had no experience of war; but, if they were to keep their hold of Canaan, it was needful that they understand war and victory; every generation of Believers must be "proven"; will they lean on the arm of flesh, or will they look to Christ and the Cross? Unfortunately, the sword held by most in the modern Church is not "of the Spirit," which is actually the Word of God, but rather something else altogether [Eph. 6:17]);*

3 Namely, five lords of the Philistines, and all the Canaanites, and the Sidonians, and the Hivites who dwelt in Mount Lebanon, from Mount Baal-hermon unto the entering in of Hamath.

4 And they were to prove Israel by them, to know whether they would hearken unto the Commandments of the LORD, which He commanded their fathers by the hand of Moses.

5 And the Children of Israel dwelt among the Canaanites, Hittites, and Amorites, and Perizzites, and Hivites, and Jebusites:

6 And they took their daughters to be their wives, and gave their daughters to their sons, and served their gods.

7 And the Children of Israel did evil in the sight of the LORD, and forgot the LORD their God, and served Baalim and the groves. *(As we have stated, friendship with the world doesn't make the world more Godly, but rather the Christian more worldly.)*

OTHNIEL

8 Therefore the anger of the LORD was hot against Israel, and He sold them into the hand of Chushan-rishathaim king of Mesopotamia: and the Children of Israel served Chushan-rishathaim eight years. *(Idolatry always leads to slavery in some way. For Israel, it was to a heathen power; presently, it is to Satan himself. And we must remember, any worship that's not anchored in Christ and the Cross is unscriptural, and, in fact, in one way or the other, is idolatry!)*

9 And when the Children of Israel cried unto the LORD, the LORD raised up a deliverer to the Children of Israel, who delivered them, even Othniel the son of Kenaz, Caleb's younger brother. *(Any time that Israel cried to the Lord, irrespective as to how wrong they had previously been, He always heard their cry, and answered with deliverance. It is the same presently! No matter the problem, if you will sincerely cry to the Lord, He will hear and answer, irrespective as to what you may have done in the past that is wrong.)*

10 And the Spirit of the LORD came upon him, and he judged Israel, and went out to war: and the LORD delivered Chushan-rishathaim king of Mesopotamia into his hand; and his hand prevailed against Chushan-rishathaim. *(Othniel was the first Judge of Israel. He was able to perform this mighty feat of valor, because the "Spirit of the Lord" was upon him. The secret then was the Spirit of the Lord, and the secret now is the Spirit of the Lord. There are all type of things greater than we are, but there is nothing greater than the Spirit of the Lord, for He is God [Jn. 14:17-20].)*

11 And the land had rest forty years. And Othniel the son of Kenaz died. *(After the death of Othniel, Israel will, once again, be without proper leadership, and apostasy was the result, as apostasy is always the result in such case.)*

APOSTASY

12 And the Children of Israel did evil again in the sight of the LORD: and the LORD strengthened Eglon the king of Moab against Israel, because they had done evil in the sight of the LORD. *(If it is to be noticed, it was the Lord Who strengthened Eglon, the king of Moab, even though this heathen had no personal knowledge of the reason for his military strength. As well, the Lord directed the mind of this man toward Israel. Why? Unless they were in dire straits, Israel simply would not function properly. So the Lord brought upon them great misery through this heathen king.*

All of this tells us that the Lord presently does the same thing with Believers who are going in the wrong direction. Paul called it, "chastisement" [Heb. 12:5-14]. Sometimes the Lord uses sickness, sometimes He uses the unredeemed, etc.; however, everything He does, irrespective as to what it might be, is all done for our good. So, even though the person who wrongs us, that is, if the Lord uses such, is wrong himself or herself

in what is being done, to be sure, such an individual will answer to the Lord. Still, we must understand that the Lord has allowed such, and not allow bitterness to get in our heart toward such a person. Even though the Lord may use such, it doesn't mean that He condones their action. To be sure, as Eglon, they will ultimately answer.)

13 And he *(Eglon)* gathered unto him the Children of Ammon and Amalek, and went and smote Israel, and possessed the city of palm trees *(Jericho)*.

14 So the Children of Israel served Eglon the king of Moab eighteen years *(eighteen years of bondage that wasn't necessary at all; it was because they had done evil in the sight of the Lord)*.

EHUD

15 But when the Children of Israel cried unto the LORD, the LORD raised them up a deliverer, Ehud the son of Gera, a Benjamite, a man lefthanded: and by him the Children of Israel sent a present unto Eglon the king of Moab. *(In some way, each one of these Judges expressed some form of weakness; Othniel was the son of a younger brother; Ehud was left-handed; Shamgar had but an ox goad; Deborah was a woman; Gideon was the least in the poorest family in Manasseh; Jephthah was the son of a harlot; and Samson was a Nazarite.)*

16 But Ehud made him a dagger which had two edges, of a cubit length; and he did gird it under his raiment upon his right thigh.

17 And he brought the present unto Eglon king of Moab: and Eglon was a very fat man.

18 And when he had made an end to offer the present, he sent away the people who bore the present *(that he and Eglon might be alone)*.

19 But he himself turned again from the quarries *(should have been translated, "graven images")* that were by Gilgal *(we learn from this that idols had been set up at Gilgal — an outrage upon the hallowed associations of that sacred spot; it was the dwelling-place of the Angel of Jehovah, or had been [2:1]. Gilgal pictures the broken and contrite heart in which God dwells. If He be grieved away from such an heart, very quickly it becomes the home of graven images — Williams)*, and said, I have a secret errand unto you, O king: who said, Keep silence. And all who stood by him went out from him.

20 And Ehud came unto him; and he was sitting in a summer parlour, which he had for himself alone. And Ehud said, I have a message from God unto you. And he arose out of his seat. *(The "Message from God" is always that every enemy in our life be put to the sword, i.e., "the sword of the Spirit," which is the Word of God, which means that the enemy not merely be defeated, but be slain [Eph. 6:17].)*

21 And Ehud put forth his left hand, and took the dagger from his right thigh, and thrust it into his belly:

22 And the haft also went in after the blade; and the fat closed upon the blade, so that he could not draw the dagger out of his belly; and the dirt came out *(spiritually speaking, this is the only way to get the "dirt" out of our lives)*.

23 Then Ehud went forth through the porch, and shut the doors of the parlour upon him, and locked them.

24 When he was gone out, his servants came; and when they saw that, behold, the doors of the parlour were locked, they said, Surely he covers his feet in his summer chamber *(is asleep)*.

25 And they tarried till they were ashamed *(could have been several hours, or even as much as a whole day)*: and, behold, he *(Eglon)* opened not the doors of the parlour; therefore they took a key, and opened them: and, behold, their lord was fallen down dead on the earth.

VICTORY OVER MOAB

26 And Ehud escaped while they tarried, and passed beyond the quarries *(graven images)*, and escaped unto Seirath.

27 And it came to pass, when he was come, that he blew a trumpet in the mountain of Ephraim, and the Children of Israel went down with him from the Mount, and he before them *(Ehud, the second Judge of Israel, blew the trumpet of war, because the Lord through him would deliver Israel; if there was ever a time in the modern Church to "blow the trumpet," it is now!)*.

28 And he said unto them, Follow after me: for the LORD has delivered your enemies the Moabites into your hand. And they went down after him, and took the fords of Jordan toward Moab, and suffered not a man to pass over *(Moab was on the eastern side of the Dead Sea; it was the area occupied, as well, by the Tribe of Reuben)*.

29 And they slew of Moab at that time about ten thousand men, all lusty, and all men of

valour; and there escaped not a man (*no casualties of Israel are listed; therefore, the indication is that there were none; when Israel had the Lord with them, nothing could defeat them, and when they didn't have the Lord, they were already defeated*).

30 So Moab was subdued that day under the hand of Israel. And the land had rest fourscore years (*80 years*).

SHAMGAR

31 And after him was Shamgar the son of Anath, which slew of the Philistines six hundred men with an ox goad: and he also delivered Israel. (*Nothing more is known of Shamgar, except the mention of him in Deborah's song [5:6]. The Text indicates that this one man, armed with nothing but an ox goad, which was something like a spear, killed 600 Philistines single-handedly. Obviously, the Spirit of God helped him mightily. But, despite the help of the Lord, which was obvious to all, still, again and again, Israel would go into apostasy. Such is the heart of the natural man!*)

CHAPTER 4
(1316 B.C.)
CANAAN OPPRESSES ISRAEL

AND the Children of Israel again did evil in the sight of the LORD, when Ehud was dead (*again, we state, without proper spiritual leadership, the Church is like a ship without a rudder*).

2 And the LORD sold them into the hand of Jabin king of Canaan, who reigned in Hazor; the captain of whose host was Sisera, which dwelt in Harosheth of the Gentiles.

3 And the Children of Israel cried unto the LORD: for he (*Sisera*) had nine hundred chariots of iron; and twenty years he mightily oppressed the Children of Israel (*having 900 chariots of iron tells us that Sisera was a mighty warlord; as well, the words, "mightily oppressed," proclaim the fact that Israel had virtually become slaves in their own land — slaves to Sisera; sin will take a person further than they want to go, at a price higher than they can afford to pay*).

DEBORAH

4 And Deborah, a prophetess, the wife of Lapidoth, she judged Israel at that time. (*This Chapter and the following could be cited as the women's Chapters. We find that Deborah's Faith brought about a great victory, and Jael's fidelity destroyed a great tyrant. Both of these women were raised up by God for their respective Ministries. So, this puts to rest the idea that God does not call women to preach, etc. Paul said that in Christ "there is neither male nor female: for you are all one in Christ Jesus" [Gal. 3:28].*)

5 And she dwelt under the palm tree of Deborah between Ramah and Beth-el in Mount Ephraim: and the Children of Israel came up to her for judgment. (*Williams says of her, "There was one heart that did not tremble before Sisera and his 900 chariots of iron. She 'sat as Judge' under a palm tree near Beth-el. Her namesake, Rebecca's nurse, was buried there, about 400 years back."*)

6 And she sent and called Barak the son of Abinoam out of Kedesh-naphtali, and said unto him, Has not the LORD God of Israel commanded, saying, Go and draw toward Mount Tabor, and take with you ten thousand men of the Children of Naphtali and of the Children of Zebulun? (*Deborah speaks here as a Prophetess, announcing God's commands, not her own opinions; declaring God's Promises, not merely her own hopes or wishes — Pulpit.*)

7 And I will draw unto you to the river Kishon Sisera, the captain of Jabin's army, with his chariots and his multitude; and I will deliver him into your hand (*this is the Promise*).

8 And Barak said unto her, If you will go with me, then I will go: but if you will not go with me, then I will not go (*we have little history on Barak; we do know that his faith seemed to be weak; he wanted someone near and visible upon whom he could lean; to such a feeble faith, the arm, even of a woman, gives more confidence than the Arm of God; consequently, God did not honor him, because he did not honor God; God is best honored by being trusted*).

9 And she said, I will surely go with you: notwithstanding the journey that you take shall not be for your honour; for the LORD shall sell Sisera into the hand of a woman. And Deborah arose, and went with Barak to Kedesh. (*Jael would be the woman. What a rebuke to Barak!*)

VICTORY

10 And Barak called Zebulun and Naphtali to Kedesh; and he went up with ten thousand men at his feet: and Deborah went up with him (*10,000 men went with him*).

11 Now Heber the Kenite, which was of the children of Hobab the father in law of Moses, had severed himself from the Kenites, and pitched his tent unto the plain of Zaanaim, which is by Kedesh.

12 And they showed Sisera that Barak the son of Abinoam was gone up to Mount Tabor.

13 And Sisera gathered together all his chariots, even nine hundred chariots of iron, and all the people who were with him, from Harosheth of the Gentiles unto the river of Kishon *(a formidable army)*.

14 And Deborah said unto Barak, Up; for this is the day in which the LORD has delivered Sisera into your hand: is not the LORD gone out before you? So Barak went down from Mount Tabor, and ten thousand men after him. *(In the natural, what could they do against all of these iron chariots? However, they were not functioning in the natural, but rather by the Power of God.)*

15 And the LORD discomfited Sisera, and all his chariots, and all his host, with the edge of the sword before Barak; so that Sisera lighted down off his chariot, and fled away on his feet *(the Hebrew word for "discomfited" implies supernatural discomfiture)*.

16 But Barak pursued after the chariots, and after the host, unto Harosheth of the Gentiles: and all the host of Sisera fell upon the edge of the sword; and there was not a man left. *(It was a defeat that was total, and there is no indication that the army of Israel lost even a single man. Without the Lord, some minor victories may be won, but at a fearful price. With Him, it is total victory, at no loss whatsoever.)*

SISERA SLAIN

17 Howbeit Sisera fled away on his feet to the tent of Jael the wife of Heber the Kenite: for there was peace between Jabin the king of Hazor and the house of Heber the Kenite *(Jabin was the king of Canaan)*.

18 And Jael went out to meet Sisera, and said unto him, Turn in, my lord, turn in to me; fear not. And when he had turned in unto her into the tent, she covered him with a mantle.

19 And he said unto her, Give me, I pray you, a little water to drink; for I am thirsty. And she opened a bottle of milk, and gave him drink, and covered him.

20 Again he said unto her, Stand in the door of the tent, and it shall be, when any man does come and enquire of you, and say, Is there any man here? that you shall say, No. *(The mighty military commander of the Canaanites is reduced here to depending on a woman. Such are the ways of the Lord, concerning those who oppose Him.)*

21 Then Jael Heber's wife took a nail of the tent, and took an hammer in her hand, and went softly unto him, and smote the nail into his temples, and fastened it into the ground: for he was fast asleep and weary. So he died. *(Williams says, "God, Who energized Shamgar to destroy the Philistine with an ox goad, strengthened Jael to slay the Syrian with a tent-peg.")*

22 And, behold, as Barak pursued Sisera, Jael came out to meet him, and said unto him, Come, and I will show you the man whom you seek. And when he came into her tent, behold, Sisera lay dead, and the nail was in his temples. *(The Holy Spirit labels only two women as preeminently "blessed among women"; the one was Jael [5:24], and the other the Virgin Mary [Lk. 1:28]. Mary, of course, is associated with the advent of Israel's, and the world's, Redeemer; Jael, with the judgment of Israel's oppressor.)*

JABIN

23 So God subdued on that day Jabin the king of Canaan before the Children of Israel.

24 And the hand of the Children of Israel prospered, and prevailed against Jabin the king of Canaan, until they had destroyed Jabin king of Canaan *(a tremendous victory!)*.

CHAPTER 5
(1316 B.C.)
SONG OF TRIUMPH

THEN sang Deborah and Barak the son of Abinoam on that day, saying *(victory precedes singing, while defeat precedes weeping)*,

2 Praise ye the LORD for the avenging of Israel, when the people willingly offered themselves *(the people willingly offered themselves to be used of the Lord, and the Lord willingly avenged Israel)*.

3 Hear, O you kings; give ear, O ye princes; I, even I, will sing unto the LORD; I will sing praise to the LORD God of Israel *(the "kings" and "princes" were those of the enemy; they found out as to Who exactly was the God of Israel)*.

4 LORD, when You went out of Seir, when You marched out of the field of Edom, the Earth trembled, and the Heavens dropped, the clouds also dropped water.

5 The mountains melted from before the LORD, even that Sinai from before the LORD God of Israel *(the mighty Power of God formerly manifested toward Israel is now recalled)*.

6 In the days of Shamgar the son of Anath, in the days of Jael, the highways were unoccupied, and the travellers walked through byways *(Israel was so beaten down by the enemy that they were afraid to even walk on the roads; because of sin, the people of God had been reduced to this low state)*.

7 The inhabitants of the villages ceased, they ceased in Israel, until that I Deborah arose, that I arose a mother in Israel *(until the Lord at this time raised up Deborah, Israel was leaderless)*.

8 They chose new gods; then was war in the gates: was there a shield or spear seen among forty thousand in Israel? *(Israel was guilty of idolatry, which had reduced the people to being defenseless; the only defense against Satan is the Cross of Christ; anything else leaves the Believer defenseless [I Cor. 1:17-18].)*

9 My heart is toward the governors of Israel, who offered themselves willingly among the people. Bless ye the LORD *(the leaders in Israel were to "bless the Lord," because of the great victory that had been won)*.

10 Speak, you who ride on white asses, you who sit in judgment, and walk by the way *(they were not only to bless the Lord, they were also to speak the Blessings; and what they were to speak is set out in the next Verse)*.

11 They who are delivered from the noise of archers in the places of drawing water, there shall they rehearse the righteous acts of the LORD, even the righteous acts toward the inhabitants of his villages in Israel: then shall the people of the LORD go down to the gates *(the idea is this: the water wells were where gossip was exchanged and news proclaimed; instead of the Syrians talking at these wells about their great victory over Israel, which would have been the case had they won, instead, Israel would boast; however, they were to boast about the "righteous acts of the Lord," and not the achievements of individuals)*.

12 Awake, awake, Deborah: awake, awake, utter a song: arise, Barak, and lead your captivity captive, thou son of Abinoam *(Deborah seems to go back to the time the Lord moved upon her with the Divine Call)*.

13 Then He *(the Lord)* made him who remains have dominion over the nobles among the people: the LORD made me have dominion over the mighty *(the Lord gave her victory over Sisera and the king of Canaan)*.

14 Out of Ephraim was there a root of them against Amalek; after you, Benjamin, among your people; out of Machir came down governors, and out of Zebulun they who handle the pen of the writer. *(The Holy Spirit through Deborah delineates those who helped in the battle, and those who didn't. The Tribes of Ephraim, Benjamin, Zebulun, and Issachar helped bring about the victory.)*

15 And the princes of Issachar were with Deborah; even Issachar, and also Barak: he was sent on foot into the valley. For the divisions of Reuben there were great thoughts of heart *(Reuben was divided, and division always stops the "great thoughts of heart")*.

16 Why abode thou among the sheepfolds, to hear the bleatings of the flocks? For the divisions of Reuben there were great searchings of heart *(God gives the "Vision," and brings about "provision"; however, Satan then comes in, attempting to bring about "division"; this is what happened to Reuben, and the Holy Spirit is quick to say so)*.

17 Gilead abode beyond Jordan *(probably pertains to the Tribe of Dan, which portion was on the east side of Jordan; they seemed to think that the conflict did not include them, simply because of their location)*: and why did Dan remain in ships? *(The celebrated harbor of Joppa was in the Tribe of Dan; they did not want to interrupt their business, so the Tribe of Dan neglected to help.)* Asher continued on the sea shore, and abode in his breaches *(the Tribe of Asher bordered the Mediterranean Sea; with them it was business as usual, as well!)*.

18 Zebulun and Naphtali were a people who jeoparded their lives unto the death in the high places of the field *(the Holy Spirit speaks very highly of these two Tribes, as is obvious here)*.

19 The *(heathen)* kings came and fought, then fought the kings of Canaan in Taanach by the waters of Megiddo; they took no gain of money *(these "kings" had thought to plunder Israel; instead they would all die)*.

20 They fought from Heaven *(according to Josephus, a great storm arose in the face of the Canaanites, which led to their utter defeat)*; the stars in their courses fought against Sisera *(whatever the phrase means, the Lord used the elements against the enemies of Israel)*.

21 The river of Kishon swept them away, that ancient river, the river Kishon. O my soul, you have trodden down strength *(this*

river is normally a very narrow stream; however, the storm evidently caused the river to flood, which played havoc with the chariots, etc.).

22 Then were the horsehoofs broken by the means of the pransings, the pransings of their mighty ones *(the flooding river caused this).*

23 Curse ye Meroz, said the Angel of the LORD, curse ye bitterly the inhabitants thereof; because they came not to the help of the LORD, to the help of the LORD against the mighty. *(The inhabitants of the city of Meroz could easily have been of great help and great service in this battle, but evidently refused to do so. The Holy Spirit tells us here that a curse was placed on them by the "Angel of the Lord," in other words, the Lord Almighty!*

When the Holy Spirit begins to do a certain thing, and Believers take a neutral position, they lose the manifestation and the experience of the Power of God. But if, like these people of Meroz, they are so placed that they can help, but refuse to do so, then they bring death upon their souls.)

24 Blessed above women shall Jael the wife of Heber the Kenite be, blessed shall she be above women in the tent *(as stated, the only other woman spoken of in this fashion by the Holy Spirit was Mary the Mother of our Lord).*

25 He *(Sisera)* asked water, and she gave him milk; she brought forth butter in a lordly dish *(this made him feel that she was overwhelmed by his supposed greatness).*

26 She put her hand to the nail, and her right hand to the workmen's hammer; and with the hammer she smote Sisera, she smote off his head, when she had pierced and stricken through his temples.

27 At her feet he bowed, he fell, he lay down: at her feet he bowed, he fell: where he bowed, there he fell down dead *(to be killed in battle by a woman presented, at that time, the height of disgrace).*

28 The mother of Sisera looked out at a window, and cried through the lattice, Why is his chariot so long in coming? why tarry the wheels of his chariots? *(Meaning that he wasn't coming home!)*

29 Her wise ladies answered her, yes, she returned answer to herself *(their answer could not have been more wrong),*

30 Have they not sped? have they not divided the prey; to every man a damsel or two; to Sisera a prey of divers colours, a prey of divers colours of needlework, of divers colours of needlework on both sides, meet for the necks of them who take the spoil? *(The comfort these ladies tried to give to the mother of Sisera would turn to ashes in their mouths.)*

31 So let all your enemies perish, O LORD: but let them who love Him be as the Sun when he goes forth in his might. And the land had rest forty years. *(Each such victory was a foretaste of the final victory over sin and death, which took place at the Cross, and of the glory of the redeemed Church.)*

CHAPTER 6
(1249 B.C.)
APOSTASY

A ND the Children of Israel did evil in the sight of the LORD: and the LORD delivered them into the hand of Midian seven years *(despite what Israel had seen regarding the great victory over Sisera, they once again lapsed into apostasy).*

2 And the hand of Midian prevailed against Israel *(because the Lord allowed such)*: and because of the Midianites the Children of Israel made them the dens which are in the mountains, and caves, and strong holds *(the people of God, who were to be the strongest on the face of the Earth, are now reduced to living in dens and caves, because of fear).*

3 And so it was, when Israel had sown *(sowed the seed for crops)*, that the Midianites came up, and the Amalekites, and the children of the east, even they came up against them;

4 And they encamped against them, and destroyed the increase of the earth, till thou come unto Gaza, and left no sustenance for Israel, neither sheep, nor ox, nor ass *(Israel is reduced to starvation; such are the wages of iniquity!).*

5 For they *(the enemy)* came up with their cattle and their tents, and they came as grasshoppers for multitude; for both they and their camels were without number: and they entered into the land to destroy it *(the Lord allowed all of this, because of Israel's idolatry; let not the Believer think that because this is the day of Grace, God operates any differently; He doesn't!).*

6 And Israel was greatly impoverished because of the Midianites; and the Children of Israel cried unto the LORD *(as stated, irrespective as to what they had done, when Israel cried unto the Lord, without fail, He always heard and answered them; He will do the same presently [I Jn. 1:9]).*

THE PROPHET

7 And it came to pass, when the Children of Israel cried unto the LORD because of the Midianites, *(Why is it that so many Believers will have to come to a place of utter defeat and humiliation, before they will properly cry to the Lord? If we would cry to the Lord at all times, there would be no impoverishment, as addressed in the previous Verse.)*

8 That the LORD sent a prophet unto the Children of Israel, which said unto them, Thus saith the LORD God of Israel, I brought you up from Egypt, and brought you forth out of the house of bondage;

9 And I delivered you out of the hand of the Egyptians, and out of the hand of all who oppressed you, and drove them out from before you, and gave you their land;

10 And I said unto you, I am the LORD your God; fear not the gods of the Amorites, in whose land you dwell: but you have not obeyed My voice. *(To their cry of distress, a Prophet is sent by the Lord; however, his call to Repentance is unheeded. This appears, as we shall see, from the fact that the men of Gideon's village wished to kill him, because he destroyed their idols.)*

GIDEON

11 And there came an Angel of the LORD, and sat under an oak which was in Ophrah, that pertained unto Joash the Abiezrite: and his son Gideon threshed wheat by the winepress, to hide it from the Midianites. *(The Israelites, God's chosen people, because of their sin, were hard put to even feed themselves, much less enjoy prosperity, because the enemy took everything they had. Let's say it again: sin will take you further than you want to go, and cost you more than you can afford to pay.)*

12 And the Angel of the LORD *(in fact, this was a preincarnate appearance of the Lord Jesus Christ)* appeared unto him, and said unto him, The LORD is with you, you mighty man of valour. *(If the Lord appeared to you at this moment, what would He say about you?)*

13 And Gideon said unto Him, Oh my Lord, if the LORD be with us, why then is all this befallen us? and where be all His miracles which our fathers told us of, saying, Did not the LORD bring us up from Egypt? but now the LORD has forsaken us, and delivered us into the hands of the Midianites. *(Oppression breathed in every word spoken by Gideon. The truth was, the Lord had not forsaken Israel, but, instead, Israel had forsaken the Lord. This was the reason for all of their problems.)*

14 And the LORD *(proving that this Angel was, in fact, the Lord of Glory)* looked upon him, and said, Go in this your might, and you shall save Israel from the hand of the Midianites: have not I sent you? *(The Lord commissions Gideon at this moment, and it is a commission of astounding proportions. Why Gideon?)*

15 And he said unto Him, Oh my Lord, wherewith shall I save Israel? *(A note of sarcasm!)* behold, my family is poor in Manasseh, and I am the least in my father's house. *(This was at least one of the reasons that the Lord chose Gideon. He had an exalted opinion of the Lord, but none at all of himself. "Meekness and lowliness" are absolute necessities if one is to be truly used of God [Mat. 11:28-30].)*

16 And the LORD said unto him, Surely I will be with you, and you shall smite the Midianites as one man *(the Lord being with Gideon is the key, and alone the key).*

17 And he said unto Him, If now I have found grace in Your sight, then show me a sign that You talk with me. *(Considering what the Lord has told him that he must do, Gideon wants to make certain that it is the Lord to Whom he is speaking, and not something else. So he asks for a sign.)*

18 Depart not hence, I pray You, until I come unto You, and bring forth my present *(a Sacrificial Offering)*, and set it before You. And He *(the Lord)* said, I will tarry until you come again *(until you come with the Sacrifice).*

19 And Gideon went in, and made ready a kid *(a young lamb for Sacrifice)*, and unleavened cakes of an ephah of flour *(the Thanksgiving Offering)*: the flesh he put in a basket, and he put the broth in a pot, and brought it out unto Him under the oak, and presented it *("presented," as used here, is a Hebrew word especially used of Sacrifices and Offerings [Amos 5:25]).*

20 And the Angel of God said unto him, Take the flesh and the unleavened cakes, and lay them upon this rock, and pour out the broth. And he did so *(the "Rock" became an Altar).*

21 Then the Angel of the LORD put forth the end of the staff that was in His hand, and touched the flesh and the unleavened cakes; and there rose up fire out of the rock, and consumed the flesh and the unleavened cakes. Then the Angel of the LORD departed out of his sight. *(The consuming of the Sacrifice by fire from Heaven was the token of its being*

accepted. It was a type of the Judgment of God, which would fall on the Lord Jesus Christ, necessitating His Death, in the giving of Himself as a Perfect Sacrifice, which will atone for the sins of man. Gideon's action proclaims the fact that he based everything on the atoning Sacrifice. Faith in that Sacrifice, and what it represented, is the primary reason that the Lord chose Gideon. Faith in the atoning work of Christ is the only Faith that God will recognize. Regrettably, as it regards the Church as a whole, this type of Faith seems to be in short supply.)

22 And when Gideon perceived that He was an Angel of the LORD, Gideon said, Alas, O LORD God! for because I have seen an Angel of the LORD face to face.

23 And the LORD said unto him, Peace be unto you, fear not: you shall not die *(this was said to Gideon before the Lord departed out of his sight)*.

24 Then Gideon built an Altar there unto the LORD, and called it Jehovah-shalom *(the Lord is peace)*: unto this day it is yet in Ophrah of the Abiezrites.

GIDEON OBEYS THE LORD

25 And it came to pass the same night, that the LORD said unto him, Take your father's young bullock, even the second bullock of seven years old, and throw down the altar of Baal that your father has, and cut down the grove that is by it *(it seems that Gideon was basically the only one in his family who truly lived for God; his father worshipped "Baal," one of the most vulgar and hideous idol gods)*:

26 And build an Altar unto the LORD your God upon the top of this rock *(where the altar of Baal had been; this is the crying need of the modern Church; it needs to turn from altars of its own making, and place its Faith exclusively in Christ and His Cross)*, in the ordered place, and take the second bullock, and offer a Burnt Sacrifice with the wood of the grove which you shall cut down *(the "grove" was really idols of the "Asherah," several of which evidently had been made out of wood; this was one of the most despicable of idols, actually a portrayal of the male member; this is how far that Gideon's family had sunk down spiritually)*.

27 Then Gideon took ten men of his servants, and did as the LORD had said unto him: and so it was, because he feared his father's household, and the men of the city, that he could not do it by day, that he did it by night *(men grow angry when their idols are touched, and religious men most of all)*.

28 And when the men of the city arose early in the morning, behold, the altar of Baal was cast down, and the grove was cut down that was by it, and the second bullock was offered upon the Altar that was built *(the Altar to the Lord)*.

29 And they said one to another, Who has done this thing? And when they enquired and asked, they said, Gideon the son of Joash has done this thing.

30 Then the men of the city said unto Joash, Bring out your son, that he may die: because he has cast down the altar of Baal, and because he has cut down the grove that was by it. *(Those who follow idolatry, even in modern-day religion, and to be sure, and sadly, the modern Church is full of it, respond to the Cross exactly as these men did to Gideon, wanting to kill him.)*

31 And Joash said unto all who stood against him, Will you plead for Baal? will you save him? he who will plead for him, let him be put to death while it is yet morning: if he be a god, let him plead for himself, because one has cast down his altar. *(It seems as if the courage of Joash, Gideon's father, was rising under the influence of his son's brave deed. In essence, he says that instead of Gideon being killed, that he, Joash, would kill anyone who would plead for Baal. His answer was, "Let Baal plead for himself"; however, these heathen gods were nothing, only figments of man's imagination.)*

32 Therefore on that day he called him *(called Gideon)* Jerub-baal *("is an idol anything?")*, saying, Let Baal plead against him *(against Gideon)*, because he has thrown down his altar *(Gideon was given a nickname, so to speak, which showed his contempt for these heathen gods)*.

33 Then all the Midianites, and the Amalekites and the children of the east were gathered together, and went over, and pitched in the valley of Jezreel *(this seemed to be their periodic foray into Israel, at which time they would plunder the land; they would find that their reception now would not be as before)*.

34 But the Spirit of the LORD came upon Gideon, and he blew a trumpet; and Abiezer was gathered after him *(the whole family of Abiezer, numbering probably thousands, sprang to his side; the Spirit of the Lord was upon him, and the blowing of the trumpet, in essence, said it was time to strike)*.

35 And he sent messengers throughout all

Manasseh; who also was gathered after him: and he sent messengers unto Asher, and unto Zebulun, and unto Naphtali *(various Tribes)*; and they came up to meet them.

THE FLEECE

36 And Gideon said unto God, If you will save Israel by my hand, as You have said,

37 Behold, I will put a fleece of wool in the floor; and if the dew be on the fleece only, and it be dry upon all the earth beside, then shall I know that you will save Israel by my hand, as You have said.

38 And it was so: for he rose up early on the morrow, and thrust the fleece together, and wringed the dew out of the fleece, a bowl full of water.

39 And Gideon said unto God, Let not Your anger be hot against me, and I will speak but this once: let me prove, I pray You, but this once with the fleece; let it now be dry only upon the fleece, and upon all the ground let there be dew.

40 And God did so that night: for it was dry upon the fleece only, and there was dew on all the ground. *(Concerning this, Williams says, "The double test with the fleece made plain to Gideon that God could withhold and grant blessing. He could bless Gideon, and no one else; and, on the other hand, He could bless everybody else, and not Gideon. Rahab and Jericho illustrate the one action and Nineveh and Jonah the other.")*

CHAPTER 7
(1249 B.C.)
THREE HUNDRED MEN

THEN Jerub-baal, who is Gideon, and all the people who were with him, rose up early, and pitched beside the well of Harod: so that the host of the Midianites were on the north side of them, by the hill of Moreh, in the valley *(the nickname "Jerub-baal" is used here by the Holy Spirit in order to proclaim the fact that Gideon is opposed to all idols, and of every description)*.

2 And the LORD said unto Gideon, The people who are with you are too many for Me to give the Midianites into their hands, lest Israel vaunt themselves against Me, saying, My own hand has saved me *(man, it seems, always wants to have a hand in his own Salvation and*

victory in the Lord; this is the bane of the Church!).

3 Now therefore go to, proclaim in the ears of the people, saying, Whosoever is fearful and afraid, let him return and depart early from Mount Gilead. And there returned of the people twenty and two thousand; and there remained ten thousand *(the cowardly were given the option of returning home, and 22,000 did so; there is no place for "fear" in the Work of God; the Lord cannot use such, as is so very much evidenced here)*.

4 And the LORD said unto Gideon, The people are yet too many; bring them down unto the water, and I will try them for you there: and it shall be, that of whom I say unto you, This shall go with you, the same shall go with you; and of whomsoever I say unto you, This shall not go with you, the same shall not go.

5 So he brought down the people unto the water: and the LORD said unto Gideon, Every one who laps of the water with his tongue, as a dog laps, him shall you set by himself; likewise every one who bows down upon his knees to drink.

6 And the number of them who lapped, putting their hand to their mouth, were three hundred men: but all the rest of the people bowed down upon their knees to drink water.

7 And the LORD said unto Gideon, By the three hundred men who lapped will I save you, and deliver the Midianites into your hand: and let all the other people go every man unto his place.

8 So the people took victuals in their hand, and their trumpets: and he sent all the rest of Israel every man unto his tent, and retained those three hundred men: and the host of Midian was beneath him in the valley. *(Jonathan, Saul's son, would later say, "There is no restraint to the Lord to save by many or by few" [I Sam. 14:6]. Those who lapped water had their hands free in order to fight, if necessary, and thereby showed their diligence. There were three hundred of these, and the Lord used those particular people. In fact, He did not really need anyone, as ought to be obvious, but He allows us to participate in His Work, in order to build us up in the Faith.)*

THE SIGN OF VICTORY

9 And it came to pass the same night, that the LORD said unto him, Arise, get thee down unto the host; for I have delivered it into your hand *(the Lord has a way, and He has a time)*.

10 But if you fear to go down, go thou with

Phurah your servant down to the host *(the "host" consisted of approximately 135,000 men [8:10]; Gideon was to face this "host" with just 300 men; despite what the Lord had told him, one can well understand his consternation)*:

11 And you shall hear what they say; and afterward shall your hands be strengthened to go down unto the host. Then went he down with Phurah his servant unto the outside of the armed men who were in the host.

12 And the Midianites and the Amalekites and all the children of the east lay along in the valley like grasshoppers for multitude; and their camels were without number, as the sand by the sea side for multitude *(Satan, it seems, always brings formidable odds against the Believer)*.

13 And when Gideon was come, behold, there was a man who told a dream unto his fellow, and said, Behold, I dreamed a dream, and, lo, a cake of barley bread tumbled into the host of Midian, and came unto a tent, and smote it that it fell, and overturned it, that the tent lay along *(Gideon and his servant, standing outside the tent in the dark, overheard this conversation; bread made from barley was the poorest of all bread; so the Lord is showing Gideon that one cake of barley bread, with God behind it, could overturn the greatest tent in the camp of Midian, symbolizing the leadership of the army of the enemy)*.

14 And his fellow answered and said, This is nothing else save the sword of Gideon the son of Joash, a man of Israel: for into his hand has God delivered Midian, and all the host *(the dream and the interpretation are striking evidences of the terror which Gideon's name had already inspired among the Midianites; the Lord had placed the fear of Gideon into the hearts of the enemy)*.

TRUMPETS, LAMPS, AND PITCHERS

15 And it was so, when Gideon heard the telling of the dream, and the interpretation thereof, that he worshipped, and returned into the host of Israel, and said, Arise; for the LORD has delivered into your hand the host of Midian *(the fear is gone, and faith remains)*.

16 And he divided the three hundred men into three companies, and he put a trumpet in every man's hand, with empty pitchers, and lamps within the pitchers *(clay pitchers)*.

17 And he said unto them, Look on me, and do likewise: and, behold, when I come to the outside of the camp, it shall be that, as I do, so shall you do *(the 300 were to watch Gideon, and do exactly what he was doing; the Lord, no doubt, had given him instructions as to exactly what he should do)*.

18 When I blow with a trumpet, I and all who are with me, then blow ye the trumpets also on every side of all the camp, and say, The Sword of the LORD, and of Gideon *(all were to blow the trumpets at a given signal, and all were to shout, "The Sword of the Lord, and of Gideon")*.

19 So Gideon, and the hundred men who were with him, came unto the outside of the camp in the beginning of the middle watch; and they had but newly set the watch *(close to 11 p.m.)*: and they blew the trumpets, and broke the pitchers that were in their hands *(which they had been told to do)*.

20 And the three companies blew the trumpets, and broke the pitchers, and held the lamps in their left hands, and the trumpets in their right hands to blow withal: and they cried, The Sword of the LORD, and of Gideon.

21 And they stood every man in his place round about the camp; and all the host ran, and cried, and fled *(fear already gripped the enemy, and, with the shouting, the glowing lights from the broken pitchers, along with the blowing of the trumpets, they imagined all sorts of things, which is exactly what the Lord intended)*.

22 And the three hundred blew the trumpets, and the LORD set every man's sword against his fellow, even throughout all the host *(the Midianites, thinking the enemy was upon them, not being able, in the dark, to distinguish friend from foe, mistook their own people who were running from pursuing Israelites, and fell upon and slew one another)*: and the host fled to Beth-shittah in Zererath, and to the border of Abel-meholah, unto Tabbath.

VICTORY

23 And the men of Israel gathered themselves together out of Naphtali, and out of Asher, and out of all Manasseh, and pursued after the Midianites.

24 And Gideon sent messengers throughout all Mount Ephraim, saying, Come down against the Midianites, and take before them the waters unto Beth-barah and Jordan. Then all the men of Ephraim gathered themselves together, and took the waters unto Beth-barah and Jordan *(to cut off the potential escape of*

the Midianites).

25 And they took two princes of the Midianites, Oreb and Zeeb; and they slew Oreb upon the rock Oreb, and Zeeb they slew at the winepress of Zeeb, and pursued Midian, and brought the heads of Oreb and Zeeb to Gideon on the other side Jordan. *(The capture of Oreb and Zeeb is celebrated in Psalms 83:11 and Isaiah 10:26. So, we learn from this just how important was this victory which the Lord gave to Gideon.)*

CHAPTER 8
(1249 B.C.)
THE KINGS OF MIDIAN

AND the men of Ephraim said unto him, Why have you served us thus, that you called us not, when you went to fight with the Midianites? And they did chide with him sharply *(Gideon had not consulted them, nor asked their aid; now that the war had been so successful, the men of Ephraim were much displeased at not having been consulted).*

2 And he said unto them, What have I done now in comparison of you? Is not the gleaning of the grapes of Ephraim better than the vintage of Abiezer? *(Gideon seems to have known the answer of Solomon, even some 500 years before the birth of that King, "The soft answer turns away wrath" [Prov. 15:1].)*

3 God has delivered into your hands the princes of Midian, Oreb and Zeeb: and what was I able to do in comparison of you? Then their anger was abated toward him, when he had said that *(the men of Ephraim had captured the two mightiest princes of the Midianites).*

4 And Gideon came to Jordan, and passed over, he, and the three hundred men who were with him, faint, yet pursuing them *(pursuing the enemy).*

5 And he said unto the men of Succoth, Give, I pray you, loaves of bread unto the people who follow me; for they be faint, and I am pursuing after Zebah and Zalmunna, kings of Midian.

6 And the princes of Succoth said, Are the hands of Zebah and Zalmunna now in your hand, that we should give bread unto your army? *(For fear that Gideon should fail, and thereby that the Midianites would rise back up, they refused even food to his weary followers.*

It is sad when petulance is shown because of a seeming slight in connection with the Lord's Work, as it was with Ephraim, but it is very much sadder when sympathy is shown to the enemy, and help refused to the servants of God, who, though faint, are yet pursuing. The problem witnessed here is all too often the problem in the modern Church. Many Christians, instead of helping to win victories for the Lord, try to hinder those who are winning victories.)

7 And Gideon said, Therefore when the LORD has delivered Zebah and Zalmunna into my hand, then I will tear your flesh with the thorns of the wilderness and with briers *(it is not clear as to exactly what is meant by these statements concerning punishment; the lack of faith among the people of Succoth is what seems to have irritated Gideon the most, and rightly so!).*

8 And he went up thence to Penuel, and spoke unto them likewise: and the men of Penuel answered him as the men of Succoth had answered him *(from all of this, we see that Israel had become very fragmented, with each Tribe somewhat standing on its own, in other words, close to the place of being twelve distinct nations).*

9 And he spoke also unto the men of Penuel, saying, When I come again in peace, I will break down this tower *(what tower it was, we aren't told).*

10 Now Zebah and Zalmunna were in Karkor, and their hosts with them, about fifteen thousand men, all who were left of all the hosts of the children of the east: for there fell an hundred and twenty thousand men who drew sword *(as is obvious here, Israel had won a tremendous victory).*

11 And Gideon went up by the way of them who dwelt in tents on the east of Nobah and Jogbehah, and smote the host; for the host was secure *(or thought they were).*

12 And when Zebah and Zalmunna fled, he pursued after them, and took the two kings of Midian, Zebah and Zalmunna, and discomfited all the host *(Gideon's attention was directed at these two kings, so some of the 15,000 may have escaped; however, to be sure, they would no more harm Israel).*

13 And Gideon the son of Joash returned from battle before the sun was up,

14 And caught a young man of the men of Succoth, and enquired of him: and he described unto him the princes of Succoth, and the elders thereof, even threescore and seventeen (77) men.

15 And he came unto the men of Succoth, and said, Behold Zebah and Zalmunna, with

whom you did upbraid me, saying, Are the hands of Zebah and Zalmunna now in your hand, that we should give bread unto your men who are weary?

16 And he took the elders of the city, and thorns of the wilderness and briers, and with them he taught the men of Succoth *(it seems they were put to death).*

17 And he beat down the tower of Penuel, and slew the men of the city *(if he killed these, then he killed those of Succoth, as well!).*

18 Then said he unto Zebah and Zalmunna. What manner of men were they whom you slew at Tabor? And they answered, As you are, so were they; each one resembled the children of a king *(at this stage, these two heathen kings seemed not to have known that these men whom they killed were brothers of Gideon).*

19 And he said, They were my brethren, even the sons of my mother: as the LORD lives, if you had saved them alive, I would not kill you *(as to exactly when his brothers had lost their lives, we aren't told).*

20 And he said unto Jether his firstborn, Up, and kill them. But the youth drew not his sword: for he feared, because he was yet a youth.

21 Then Zebah and Zalmunna said, Rise thou, and fall upon us: for as the man is, so is his strength. And Gideon arose, and slew Zebah and Zalmunna, and took away the ornaments that were on their camels' necks *(crescent-shaped ornaments of gold and silver, which, as well as "chains," were hung as ornaments on their camels' necks).*

22 Then the men of Israel said unto Gideon, Rule thou over us, both you, and your son, and your son's son also: for you have delivered us from the hand of Midian *(in essence, they wanted Gideon to be a king over Israel; however, the time predicted by Moses that a king would, in fact, rule over Israel was not yet come [Deut. 17:14-15]).*

23 And Gideon said unto them, I will not rule over you, neither shall my son rule over you: the LORD shall rule over you *(Gideon answered correctly).*

24 And Gideon said unto them, I would desire a request of you, that you would give me every man the earrings of his prey. (For they had golden earrings, because they were Ishmaelites.)

25 And they answered, We will willingly give them. And they spread a garment, and did cast therein every man the earrings of his prey.

26 And the weight of the golden earrings that he requested was a thousand and seven hundred shekels of gold *(worth about $340,000 in 2004 currency);* beside ornaments, and collars, and purple raiment that was on the kings of Midian, and beside the chains that were about their camels' necks.

27 And Gideon made an ephod thereof, and put it in his city, even in Ophrah: and all Israel went thither a whoring after it: which thing became a snare unto Gideon, and to his house. *(The people of Israel began to worship this thing, which was very displeasing to the Lord. Why did Gideon do what he did, and why did Israel worship this thing?*

What more commendable and pleasing to the religious mind than to use the wealth of the enemy in making an ephod? Was not an ephod a Bible garment? Was it not of Divine ordination? And Gideon put his foot in the snare; and the very man who had destroyed a gross form of idolatry in his home and his city set up a refined form of the same evil in his kingdom.)

28 Thus was Midian subdued before the Children of Israel, so that they lifted up their heads no more. And the country was in quietness forty years in the days of Gideon.

GIDEON'S CHILDREN

29 And Jerub-baal *(Gideon)* the son of Joash went and dwelt in his own house.

30 And Gideon had threescore and ten sons *(70 sons)* of his body begotten: for he had many wives.

31 And his concubine who was in Shechem, she also bore him a son, whose name he called Abimelech.

32 And Gideon the son of Joash died in a good old age, and was buried in the sepulchre of Joash his father, in Ophrah of the Abiezrites. *(Gideon remains to us as one of the most remarkable characters of the Old Testament, not indeed without faults and blemishes, and not wholly unspoiled by prosperity, but still a great man, and an eminent servant of God — Pulpit.)*

APOSTASY

33 And it came to pass, as soon as Gideon was dead, that the Children of Israel turned again, and went a whoring after Baalim, and made Baal-berith their god.

34 And the Children of Israel remembered not the LORD their God, Who had delivered

them out of the hands of all their enemies on every side:

35 Neither showed they kindness to the house of Jerub-baal, namely, Gideon, according to all the goodness which he had showed unto Israel. (*Hervey says, "Forgetfulness of God is often the parent of ingratitude to men. The heart of stone which is not touched by the love of Christ is also insensible to the kindness of man."*)

CHAPTER 9
(1209 B.C.)
ABIMELECH

A ND Abimelech the son of Jerub-baal went to Shechem unto his mother's brethren, and communed with them, and with all the family of the house of his mother's father, saying,

2 Speak, I pray you, in the ears of all the men of Shechem, Whether is better for you, either that all the sons of Jerub-baal, which are threescore and ten *(70)* persons, reign over you, or that one reign over you? remember also that I am your bone and your flesh.

3 And his mother's brethren spoke of him in the ears of all the men of Shechem all these words: and their hearts inclined to follow Abimelech; for they said, He is our brother.

4 And they gave him threescore and ten *(70)* pieces of silver out of the house of Baal-berith, wherewith Abimelech hired vain and light persons, which followed him.

5 And he went unto his father's house at Ophrah, and killed his brethren the sons of Jerub-baal, being threescore and ten persons, upon one stone: notwithstanding yet Jotham the youngest son of Jerub-baal was left; for he hid himself.

6 And all the men of Shechem gathered together, and all the house of Millo, and went, and made Abimelech king, by the plain of the pillar that was in Shechem. (*Abimelech was a son of Gideon. It is amply illustrated, in this Chapter, that he who sows to the flesh shall of the flesh reap corruption. Abimelech, born of the will of the flesh, became a channel and an instrument of evil to Israel. Israel would have fared much better, and the family of Gideon as well, had he never been born! When Gideon looked at this baby when he was born, little did he realize that he had given conception to a monster. A wrong action, which, at the time, seems harmless, bears bitter fruit in after-years. To become king of sorts, he would murder all of his brothers, some 69 total.*)

JOTHAM

7 And when they told it to Jotham, he went and stood in the top of Mount Gerizim, and lifted up his voice, and cried, and said unto them, Hearken unto me, you men of Shechem, that God may hearken unto you (*as stated in Verse 5, Jotham was the youngest son of Gideon, and the only one left alive of the slaughter of his 69 brothers — all murdered by Abimelech*).

8 The trees went forth on a time to anoint a king over them; and they said unto the olive tree, Reign thou over us.

9 But the olive tree said unto them, Should I leave my fatness, wherewith by me they honour God and man, and go to be promoted over the trees?

10 And the trees said to the fig tree, Come thou, and reign over us.

11 But the fig tree said unto them, Should I forsake my sweetness, and my good fruit, and go to be promoted over the trees?

12 Then said the trees unto the vine, Come thou, and reign over us.

13 And the vine said unto them, Should I leave my wine, which cheers God and man, and go to be promoted over the trees?

14 Then said all the trees unto the bramble, Come thou, and reign over us.

15 And the bramble said unto the trees, If in truth you anoint me king over you, then come and put your trust in my shadow: and if not, let fire come out of the bramble, and devour the cedars of Lebanon. (*Jotham's allegory was both a parable and a prophecy. It had an immediate fulfillment; for the men of Shechem elected the bramble to rule over them, and mutual destruction was the result.*

But the allegory had a wider significance. In the Scriptures, Israel is figured as a fig tree, an olive tree, and a vine. These symbolize national blessing, covenant blessing, and spiritual blessing. The bramble is a fore-picture of the coming Antichrist. In the future dark day of Israel's rebellion, she will turn aside from all Divine fullness, and put her trust in the rule of the Antichrist; and mutual destruction will be the result — Williams.)

16 Now therefore, if you have done truly and sincerely, in that you have made Abimelech king, and if you have dealt well with Jerub-baal and his house, and have done unto him according to the deserving of his hands;

17 (For my father fought for you, and adventured his life far, and delivered you out of the hand of Midian:

18 And you are risen up against my father's house this day, and have slain his sons, threescore and ten persons, upon one stone, and have made Abimelech, the son of his maidservant, king over the men of Shechem, because he is your brother;)

19 If you then have dealt truly and sincerely with Jerub-baal and with his house this day, then rejoice ye in Abimelech, and let him also rejoice in you:

20 But if not, let fire come out from Abimelech, and devour the men of Shechem, and from the house of Millo, and devour Abimelech.

21 And Jotham ran away, and fled, and went to Beer, and dwelt there, for fear of Abimelech his brother.

THE REVOLT

22 When Abimelech had reigned three years over Israel,

23 Then God sent an evil spirit between Abimelech and the men of Shechem; and the men of Shechem dealt treacherously with Abimelech (*if men desire evil, as did Abimelech, God will see to it that they get evil*):

24 That the cruelty done to the threescore and ten sons of Jerub-baal might come, and their blood be laid upon Abimelech their brother, which slew them; and upon the men of Shechem, which aided him in the killing of his brethren.

25 And the men of Shechem set liers in wait for him in the top of the mountains, and they robbed all who came along that way by them: and it was told Abimelech.

26 And Gaal the son of Ebed came with his brethren, and went over to Shechem: and the men of Shechem put their confidence in him.

27 And they went out into the fields, and gathered their vineyards, and trode the grapes, and made merry, and went into the house of their god, and did eat and drink, and cursed Abimelech (*the evil spirit is at work here, doing what God sent him to do*).

28 And Gaal the son of Ebed said, Who is Abimelech, and who is Shechem, that we should serve him? is not he the son of Jerubbaal? and Zebul his officer? serve the men of Hamor the father of Shechem: for why should we serve him?

29 And would to God this people were under my hand! then would I remove Abimelech. And he said to Abimelech, Increase your army, and come out (*Gaal sends a challenge to Abimelech to come out and fight him*).

THE PLOT

30 And when Zebul the ruler of the city heard the words of Gaal the son of Ebed, his anger was kindled (*Zebul, it appears, was governor of the city under Abimelech*).

31 And he sent messengers unto Abimelech privily, saying, Behold, Gaal the son of Ebed and his brethren be come to Shechem; and, behold, they fortify the city against you.

32 Now therefore up by night, you and the people that is with you, and lie in wait in the field:

33 And it shall be, that in the morning, as soon as the sun is up, you shall rise early, and set upon the city: and, behold, when he and the people that is with him come out against you, then may you do to them as you shall find occasion.

34 And Abimelech rose up, and all the people who were with him, by night, and they laid wait against Shechem in four companies.

35 And Gaal the son of Ebed went out, and stood in the entering of the gate of the city: and Abimelech rose up, and the people that were with him, from lying in wait.

ABIMELECH

36 And when Gaal saw the people, he said to Zebul, Behold, there come people down from the top of the mountains. And Zebul said unto him, You see the shadow of the mountains as if they were men.

37 And Gaal spoke again, and said, See there come people down by the middle of the land, and another company come along by the plain of Meonenim.

38 Then said Zebul unto him, Where is now your mouth, wherewith you said, Who is Abimelech, that we should serve him? is not this the people that you have despised? go out, I pray now, and fight with them.

39 And Gaal went out before the men of Shechem, and fought with Abimelech.

40 And Abimelech chased him, and he fled before him, and many were overthrown and wounded, even unto the entering of the gate.

41 And Abimelech dwelt at Arumah: and Zebul thrust out Gaal and his brethren, that

they should not dwell in Shechem.

SHECHEM

42 And it came to pass on the morrow, that the people went out into the field; and they told Abimelech.

43 And he took the people, and divided them into three companies, and laid wait in the field, and looked, and, behold, the people were come forth out of the city; and he rose up against them, and smote them.

44 And Abimelech, and the company that was with him, rushed forward, and stood in the entering of the gate of the city: and the two other companies ran upon all the people who were in the fields, and slew them.

45 And Abimelech fought against the city all that day; and he took the city, and slew the people that was therein, and beat down the city, and sowed it with salt.

46 And when all the men of the tower of Shechem heard that, they entered into an hold of the house of the god Berith.

47 And it was told Abimelech, that all the men of the tower of Shechem were gathered together.

48 And Abimelech gat him up to Mount Zalmon, he and all the people that were with him; and Abimelech took an axe in his hand, and cut down a bough from the trees, and took it, and laid it on his shoulder, and said unto the people who were with him, What you have seen me do, make haste, and do as I have done.

49 And all the people likewise cut down every man his bough, and followed Abimelech, and put them to the hold, and set the hold on fire upon them; so that all the men of the tower of Shechem died also, about a thousand men and women.

DEATH OF ABIMELECH

50 Then went Abimelech to Thebez, and encamped against Thebez, and took it.

51 But there was a strong tower within the city, and thither fled all the men and women, and all they of the city, and shut it to them, and gat them up to the top of the tower.

52 And Abimelech came unto the tower, and fought against it, and went hard unto the door of the tower to burn it with fire.

53 And a certain woman cast a piece of a millstone upon Abimelech's head, and all to brake his skull.

54 Then he called hastily unto the young man his armourbearer, and said unto him, Draw your sword, and slay me, that men say not of me, A women slew him. And his young man thrust him through, and he died.

55 And when the men of Israel saw that Abimelech was dead, they departed every man unto his place.

56 Thus God rendered the wickedness of Abimelech, which he did unto his father, in slaying his seventy brethren:

57 And all the evil of the men of Shechem did God render upon their heads: and upon them came the curse of Jotham the son of Jerubbaal. *(Thus we see the low state to which Israel had fallen, and all because of sin.)*

CHAPTER 10
(1206 B.C.)
TOLA AND JAIR

AND after Abimelech there arose to defend Israel Tola the son of Puah, the son of Dodo, a man of Issachar; and he dwelt in Shamir in Mount Ephraim.

2 And he judged Israel twenty and three years, and died, and was buried in Shamir *(this is the only information we are given as it regards Tola)*.

3 And after him arose Jair, a Gileadite, and judged Israel twenty and two years.

4 And he had thirty sons who rode on thirty ass colts, and they had thirty cities, which are called Havoth-jair unto this day, which are in the land of Gilead.

5 And Jair died, and was buried in Camon *(this is the totality of information we have about this man, as well)*.

APOSTASY

6 And the Children of Israel did evil again in the sight of the LORD, and served Baalim, and Ashtaroth, and the gods of Syria, and the gods of Zidon, and the gods of Moab, and the gods of the children of Ammon, and the gods of the Philistines, and forsook the LORD, and served not Him. *(As is obvious, Israel had now sunk to an all time low. This appears to be the lowest point of debasement that they touched at this period of their history.)*

7 And the anger of the LORD was hot against Israel, and He sold them into the hands of the Philistines, and into the hands of the

children of Ammon. *(They seemed to forget, or else they didn't know, that the Lord, Whom they were supposed to serve, could bring about any situation He so desired. It is still the same presently. Everything that happens to a Child of God is either caused or allowed by the Lord. This we must never forget.)*

8 And that year they vexed and oppressed the Children of Israel: eighteen years, all the Children of Israel who were on the other side Jordan in the land of the Amorites, which is in Gilead.

9 Moreover the children of Ammon passed over Jordan to fight also against Judah, and against Benjamin, and against the house of Ephraim; so that Israel was sore distressed. *(The words of Verse 8 may be translated "broke and crushed them." In earlier days, when serving one false god, they were oppressed but on one side, but now, serving a multitude of idols, they are oppressed on both sides. This fact is as true for men and nations presently as it was then.)*

ISRAEL CRIES TO GOD

10 And the Children of Israel cried unto the LORD, saying, We have sinned against You, both because we have forsaken our God, and also served Baalim. *(Williams says, "But there was sufficient energy of life in Israel to bring out the cry of confession. To be conscious of misery is a sign of life. Because of the deceitfulness of the heart, and because of the deceitfulness of sin, bondage is accepted after a slight struggle, and then, after a time, the slave becomes unconscious of the slavery.*

"The confession 'we have sinned against You' showed true Repentance, for it showed a sense of injury done to God, and not merely sorrow because of the miseries that lay upon themselves. Remorse is not repentance — mental distress because of the painful results of sin is not repentance; but a sense of the grief and dishonor occasioned to God, and sorrow because He has been sinned against, that is Repentance. David and Simon Magus illustrate true and false repentance. The one cried out, 'I have sinned against the Lord.' His first thought was God and His Glory. The other said, 'Pray for me that none of these things come upon me.' His first thought was himself and to secure exemption from punishment.")

11 And the LORD said unto the Children of Israel, Did not I deliver you from the Egyptians, and from the Amorites, from the children of Ammon, and from the Philistines?

12 The Zidonians also, and the Amalekites, and the Maonites, did oppress you; and you cried to Me, and I delivered you out of their hand. *(All of this was a matter of record, and many alive at that time knew at least some of these deliverances.)*

13 Yet you have forsaken Me, and served other gods: wherefore I will deliver you no more.

14 Go and cry unto the gods which you have chosen; let them deliver you in the time of your tribulation. *(Well, of course, these so-called gods were merely figments of men's imaginations. They didn't even exist! So why did Israel, who had the privilege of having relationship with Jehovah, the only True God, desire to submit themselves to such evil?*

The problem was, and is, the sin nature. This is the nature of man that bends itself toward sin, and all because of the Fall. While they had no excuse, still, before the Cross, they did not have the Holy Spirit abiding within their lives on a permanent basis; therefore, they were, for all practical purposes, denied much of the help the Holy Spirit now gives.

And even presently, if the Believer doesn't understand that all victory is received and maintained by our Faith in Christ and the Cross, the sin nature will once again begin to dominate the person [Rom. 8:32; 6:12-13].)

GENUINE REPENTANCE

15 And the Children of Israel said unto the LORD, We have sinned: do Thou unto us whatsoever seems good unto You; deliver us only, we pray Thee, this day.

16 And they put away the strange gods from among them, and served the LORD: and His soul was grieved for the misery of Israel. *(The soul of the Lord being "grieved" means that He literally could not bear their suffering any longer. He would answer their prayer and deliver them.)*

17 Then the children of Ammon were gathered together, and encamped in Gilead. And the Children of Israel assembled themselves together, and encamped in Mizpeh.

18 And the people and princes of Gilead said one to another, What man is he who will begin to fight against the Children of Ammon? he shall be head over all the inhabitants of Gilead.

CHAPTER 11
(1161 B.C.)
JEPHTHAH

NOW Jephthah the Gileadite was a mighty man of valour, and he was the son of an harlot: and Gilead begat Jephthah. *(Perhaps because he was the son of a harlot, he was despised, rejected, and hated; however, God used him greatly, even as we shall see. If a person's heart is toward God, irrespective of the past, God can use such a person, and often does so in order to rebuke His People, and to confound man's wisdom and power.)*

2 And Gilead's wife bore him sons; and his wife's sons grew up, and they thrust out Jephthah, and said unto him, You shall not inherit in our father's house; for you are the son of a strange woman *(in a word, Jephthah was disinherited)*.

3 Then Jephthah fled from his brethren, and dwelt in the land of Tob: and there were gathered vain men to Jephthah, and went out with him *(these were broken or bankrupt men, who gravitated toward Jephthah, as, at a later time, similar individuals joined David in the Cave of Adullam)*.

4 And it came to pass in process of time, that the children of Ammon made war against Israel.

5 And it was so, that when the children of Ammon made war against Israel, the elders of Gilead went to fetch Jephthah out of the land of Tob *(evidently, Jephthah had made a name for himself in some way, as it regards military expertise)*:

6 And they said unto Jephthah, Come, and be our captain, that we may fight with the children of Ammon.

7 And Jephthah said unto the elders of Gilead, Did not you hate me, and expel me out of my father's house? And why are you come unto me now when you are in distress? *(This proclaims the fact that his expulsion was not the private act of his own brothers turning him out of the house they lived in, but rather a tribal act in which the elders of Gilead had taken a part.)*

8 And the elders of Gilead said unto Jephthah, Therefore we turn again to you now, that you may go with us, and fight against the children of Ammon, and be our head over all the inhabitants of Gilead.

9 And Jephthah said unto the elders of Gilead, If you bring me home again to fight against the children of Ammon, and the LORD deliver them before me, shall I be your head?

10 And the elders of Gilead said unto Jephthah. The LORD be witness between us, if we do not so according to your words.

11 Then Jephthah went with the elders of Gilead, and the people made him head and captain over them: and Jephthah uttered all his words before the LORD in Mizpeh. *(As is obvious here, Jephthah was a man of Faith, and, thereby, desired the Will of God in these matters.)*

12 And Jephthah sent messengers unto the king of the children of Ammon, saying, What have you to do with me, that you are come against me to fight in my land?

13 And the king of the children of Ammon answered unto the messengers of Jephthah, Because Israel took away my land, when they came up out of Egypt, from Arnon even unto Jabbok, and unto Jordan: now therefore restore those lands again peaceably *(this king demanded the surrender of a certain area of land as the only condition of peace)*.

14 And Jephthah sent messengers again unto the king of the children of Ammon.

15 And said unto him, Thus saith Jephthah, Israel took not away the land of Moab, nor the land of the children of Ammon:

16 But when Israel came up from Egypt, and walked through the wilderness unto the Red Sea, and came to Kadesh;

17 Then Israel sent messengers unto the king of Edom, saying, Let me, I pray you, pass through your land: but the king of Edom would not hearken thereto. And in like manner they sent unto the king of Moab: but he would not consent: and Israel abode in Kadesh. *(All of this of which this king relates took place over 300 years before.)*

18 Then they went along through the wilderness, and compassed the land of Edom, and the land of Moab, and came by the east side of the land of Moab, and pitched on the other side of Arnon, but came not within the border of Moab: for Arnon was the border of Moab.

19 And Israel sent messengers unto Sihon king of the Amorites, the king of Heshbon; and Israel said unto him, Let us pass, we pray you, through your land into my place.

20 But Sihon trusted not Israel to pass through his coast *(borders)*: but Sihon gathered all his people together, and pitched in Jahaz, and fought against Israel.

21 And the LORD God of Israel delivered Sihon and all his people into the hand of Israel,

and they smote them: so Israel possessed all the land of the Amorites, the inhabitants of that country.

22 And they possessed all the coasts of the Amorites, from Arnon even unto Jabbok, and from the wilderness even unto Jordan.

23 So now the LORD God of Israel has dispossessed the Amorites from before His people Israel, and should you possess it? *(In other words, Israel had come by these lands legitimately.)*

24 Will not you possess that which Chemosh your god gives you to possess? So whomsoever the LORD our God shall drive out from before us, them will we possess. *(In effect, Jephthah is pitting the Lord God against the idols of the Ammonites.)*

25 And now are you any thing better than Balak the son of Zippor, king of Moab? did he ever strive against Israel, or did he ever fight against them *(Jephthah now advances another argument to prove the justice of his cause and the unreasonableness of the Ammonite claim. If the territory in question was Moabite property, how came it that Balak laid no claim to it? So, if Balak, those long years before, had laid no claim to this area, neither should the Ammonites)*,

26 While Israel dwelt in Heshbon and her towns, and in Aroer and her towns, and in all the cities that be along by the coasts of Arnon, three hundred years? Why therefore did you not recover them within that time? *(Good question!)*

27 Wherefore I have not sinned against you, but you do me wrong to war against me: the LORD the Judge be judge this day between the Children of Israel and the children of Ammon.

28 Howbeit the king of the children of Ammon hearkened not unto the words of Jephthah which he sent him.

JEPHTHAH'S RASH VOW

29 Then the Spirit of the LORD came upon Jephthah, and he passed over Gilead, and Manasseh, and passed over Mizpeh of Gilead, and from Mizpeh of Gilead he passed over unto the children of Ammon. *(The Spirit of the Lord is what is guiding Jephthah, and he makes his move according to the Lord's command.)*

30 And Jephthah vowed a vow unto the LORD, and said, If you shall without fail deliver the children of Ammon into my hands,

31 Then it shall be, that whatsoever comes forth of the doors of my house to meet me,

when I return in peace from the children of Ammon, shall surely be the LORD's, and I will offer it up for a Burnt Offering *(the word "and" in the Hebrew is frequently translated "or" in the Scriptures; so, it would then read, "shall surely be the Lord's, or I will offer it up for a Burnt Offering")*.

VICTORY

32 So Jephthah passed over unto the children of Ammon to fight against them; and the LORD delivered them into his hands.

33 And he smote them from Aroer, even till you come to Minnith, even twenty cities, and unto the plain of the vineyards, with a very great slaughter. Thus the children of Ammon were subdued before the Children of Israel.

JEPHTHAH'S VOW FULFILLED

34 And Jephthah came to Mizpeh unto his house, and, behold, his daughter came out to meet him with timbrels and with dances: and she was his only child; beside her he had neither son nor daughter.

35 And it came to pass, when he saw her, that he rent his clothes, and said, Alas, my daughter! You have brought me very low, and you are one of them that trouble me: for I have opened my mouth unto the LORD, and I cannot go back.

36 And she said unto him, My father, if you have opened your mouth unto the LORD, do to me according to that which has proceeded out of your mouth; forasmuch as the LORD has taken vengeance for you of your enemies, even of the children of Ammon.

37 And she said unto her father, Let this thing be done for me: let me alone two months, that I may go up and down upon the mountains, and bewail my virginity, I and my fellows.

38 And he said, Go. And he sent her away for two months: and she went with her companions, and bewailed her virginity upon the mountains.

39 And it came to pass at the end of two months, that she returned unto her father, who did with her according to his vow which he had vowed: and she knew no man. And it was a custom in Israel,

40 That the daughters of Israel went yearly to lament the daughter of Jephthah the Gileadite four days in a year. *(Jephthah did not put his daughter to death and offer up her body*

as a Burnt Sacrifice to Jehovah, for such sacrifices were sternly forbidden in the Law [Lev. 18:21; 20:2-5]. What he did was the following:

He dedicated his daughter to Jehovah by a perpetual virginity. This is conclusive from the statement in Verse 39 that after her father had performed his vow, "she knew no man," that is, she never was married.

Considering that no children would be born into this family, this meant that the line of Jephthah would end with his death and her death; however, Jephthah is mentioned in Hebrews 11:32 as one of the great giants of Faith. And so he was!)

CHAPTER 12
(1143 B.C.)
THE EPHRAIMITES

AND the men of Ephraim gathered themselves together, and went northward, and said unto Jephthah, Wherefore passed you over to fight against the children of Ammon, and did not call us to go with you? We will burn your house upon you with fire. (Carnal men with carnal ideas, as were the Ephraimites, tread where Angels fear to tread. In the first place, they had no right whatsoever to speak to Jephthah in this fashion; second, did they not realize that they were insulting the man who had just defeated the Ammonites, and, above all, that God was with him?)

2 And Jephthah said unto them, I and my people were at great strife with the children of Ammon; and when I called you, you delivered me not out of their hands. (It seems that Jephthah asked the help of Ephraim when he was first made chief of the Gileadites, and they refused, partly because they thought the attempt desperate, and partly because it seems they were offended at his leadership.)

3 And when I saw that you delivered me not, I put my life in my hands, and passed over against the children of Ammon, and the LORD delivered them into my hand: wherefore then are you come up unto me this day, to fight against me?

4 Then Jephthah gathered together all the men of Gilead, and fought with Ephraim: and the men of Gilead smote Ephraim, because they said, You Gileadites are fugitives of Ephraim among the Ephraimites, and among the Manassites.

5 And the Gileadites took the passages of Jordan before the Ephraimites: and it was so,

that when those Ephraimites which were escaped said, Let me go over; that the men of Gilead said unto him, Are you an Ephraimite? If he said, No;

6 Then said they unto him, Say now Shibboleth (which means, in the Hebrew, "a stream"): and he said Sibboleth (means "a burden"): for he could not frame to pronounce it right. Then they took him, and slew him at the passages of Jordan: and there fell at that time of the Ephraimites forty and two thousand (it's probably not translated correctly; it probably should be "forty plus two thousand," i.e., 2,040).

JEPHTHAH'S DEATH

7 And Jephthah judged Israel six years. Then died Jephthah the Gileadite, and was buried in one of the cities of Gilead.

IBZAN, ELON, AND ABDON

8 And after him Ibzan of Beth-lehem judged Israel.

9 And he had thirty sons, and thirty daughters, whom he sent abroad, and took in thirty daughters from abroad for his sons. And he judged Israel seven years.

10 Then died Ibzan, and was buried at Bethlehem (from no record of Ibzan's Judgeship being preserved, we may infer that no important events took place in his time).

11 And after him Elon, a Zebulonite, judged Israel; and he judged Israel ten years.

12 And Elon the Zebulonite died, and was buried in Aijalon in the country of Zebulun.

13 And after him Abdon the son of Hillel, a Pirathonite, judged Israel.

14 And he had forty sons and thirty nephews, who rode on threescore and ten (70) ass colts: and he judged Israel eight years.

15 And Abdon the son of Hillel the Pirathonite died, and was buried in Pirathon in the land of Ephraim, in the mount of the Amalekites. (Jephthah and Abdon present a contrast. The one risked his life, won a great victory, delivered Israel, and after a childless life was buried in an unknown grave. Such is the gratitude of man!

The other risked nothing that is recorded. He had forty sons and thirty grandsons, and his grave is described with great minuteness. But the Holy Spirit, as stated, in Hebrews 11:32, places Jephthah's valorous name among the golden tablets of the eternal records, and ignores Abdon. God

never forgets those who trust and serve Him, however much they may be forgotten by man — Williams.)

CHAPTER 13
(1161 B.C.)
THE ANGEL

AND the Children of Israel did evil again in the sight of the LORD; and the LORD delivered them into the hand of the Philistines forty years. *(Over and over again, we see this terrible disposition of Israel. They go into deep sin; and to bring them to their senses, the Lord allows them to be taken over by the heathen. After they suffer immeasurably for a period of time, they begin to call on the Name of the Lord, begging for help; and, always, the Lord would hear and answer, even as He will always hear and answer such a plea. But what a sad commentary on the plight of the human heart.*

The Philistines now become prominent, and continue to be so up to the time of David, when they were finally subdued.

The Philistine represents a fact: Samson, whom we will study in the next four Chapters, represents a principle.

The fact is, there are enemies within the Christian's heart, for the Philistine was an inward, and not an outward, foe. The principle is that this inward enemy can only be defeated by the Believer understanding that his victory comes exclusively through Christ and what Christ has done at the Cross, demanding our ever constant Faith in Christ and the Cross. Then, and then only, can the Holy Spirit function and work within our lives, bringing about the desired consecration [I Cor. 1:17-18, 21, 23; 2:2; Gal. 6:14].)

2 And there was a certain man of Zorah, of the family of the Danites, whose name was Manoah; and his wife was barren, and bore not,

3 And the Angel of the LORD appeared unto the woman, and said unto her, Behold now, you are barren, and bearest not: but you shall conceive, and bear a son. *(This is very similar to Abraham and Sarah [Gen. 17:19; 18:10, 14], to Hannah [I Sam. 1:17], to Elizabeth [Lk. 1:13], and to the Blessed Virgin [Lk. 1:31]. The Angel of Jehovah, incidentally, was the same Angel Who appeared to Gideon, actually, the Lord Jesus Christ in angelic form.)*

4 Now therefore beware, I pray you, and drink not wine nor strong drink, and eat not any unclean thing *(until Samson would be born, his mother was to consecrate herself as a Nazarite)*:

5 For, lo, you shall conceive, and bear a son; and no razor shall come on his head: for the child shall be a Nazarite unto God from the womb: and he shall begin to deliver Israel out of the hand of the Philistines. *(Samson was to be a Nazarite from his mother's womb. That meant that he was not to drink any type of intoxicating drink, or even grape juice. He was not to cut his hair, nor was he to go near a dead body, even that of his nearest relation. If the last rule was inadvertently broken, the Nazarite had to undergo closely-detailed purification rites. If it is to be noticed, Samson would not actually deliver Israel from the Philistines, but most definitely would begin the process.)*

6 Then the woman came and told her husband, saying, A Man of God came unto me, and His countenance was like the countenance of an Angel of God, very terrible: but I asked him not whence He was, neither told He me His name:

7 But He said unto me, Behold, you shall conceive, and bear a son; and now drink no wine nor strong drink, neither eat any unclean thing: for the child shall be a Nazarite to God from the womb to the day of his death.

ANOTHER APPEARANCE

8 Then Manoah intreated the LORD, and said, O my Lord, let the Man of God which You did send come again unto us, and teach us what we shall do unto the child that shall be born *(no matter how evil that Israel became, there were always a few who still looked to God, even as evidently did Manoah and his wife)*.

9 And God hearkened to the voice of Manoah; and the Angel of God came again unto the woman as she sat in the field: but Manoah her husband was not with her.

10 And the woman made haste, and ran, and showed her husband, and said unto him, Behold, the Man has appeared unto me, Who came unto me the other day.

11 And Manoah arose, and went after his wife, and came to the Man, and said unto Him, Are you the Man Who spoke unto the woman? And He said, I am.

12 And Manoah said, Now let Your words come to pass. How shall we order the child, and how shall we do unto him? *(He knew this would be a special child.)*

13 And the Angel of the LORD said unto Manoah, Of all that I said to the woman let her beware.

14 She may not eat of any thing that comes of the vine, neither let her drink wine or strong drink, nor eat any unclean thing: all that I commanded her let her observe.

15 And Manoah said unto the Angel of the LORD, I pray You, let us detain You, until we shall have made ready a kid for You *(a young lamb for sacrifice)*.

16 And the Angel of the LORD said unto Manoah, Though you detain Me, I will not eat of your bread: and if you will offer a Burnt Offering, you must offer it unto the LORD. For Manoah knew not that He was an Angel of the LORD.

17 And Manoah said unto the Angel of the LORD, What is Your name, that when Your sayings come to pass we may do You honour? *(The faith of Manoah was very admirable, and his ignorance very deplorable; for if not rebuked, he would have given Divine honor to a person whom he believed to be a creature and not the Creator; however, this was, in fact, a pre-incarnate appearance of the Lord Jesus Christ.)*

18 And the Angel of the LORD said unto him, Why ask you thus after My name, seeing it is secret?

19 So Manoah took a kid *(small lamb)* with a Meat Offering, and offered it upon a rock unto the LORD: and the Angel did wonderously; and Manoah and his wife looked on.

20 For it came to pass, when the flame went up toward Heaven from off the Altar, that the Angel of the LORD ascended in the flame of the Altar. And Manoah and his wife looked on it, and fell on their faces to the ground. *(In essence, when asked what was His name, the Angel replied, "Wonderful." This, in the Hebrew Text, is the same word as in Isaiah 9:6. His doing wondrously in ascending up to Heaven in the flame of fire proved Him to be entitled to this Great Name.*

Christ is a Wonderful Saviour. He is Wonderful for what He is to sinners, and Wonderful because of what He does for Saints.)

21 But the Angel of the LORD did no more appear to Manoah and to his wife. Then Manoah knew that He was an Angel of the LORD.

22 And Manoah said unto his wife, We shall surely die, because we have seen God *(Manoah now knows that this Angel is actually the Lord)*.

23 But his wife said unto him, If the LORD were pleased to kill us, He would not have received a Burnt Offering and a Meat Offering at our hands, neither would He have showed us all these things, nor would as at this time have told us such things as these. *(It seems that Manoah's wife had a deeper insight into the things of the Lord than did her husband. The Divine directions respecting the child having been given to the Mother is a striking instance of the fact that the boy's future, as with all boys, largely depends upon a mother's proper training.*

Her reasoning was right; the fact that the Angel accepted the Sacrifice was an evidence of Salvation and Life, and not of condemnation and death. The truth is, Jesus is All in All!

Sinners are saved, not so much by their acceptance of Christ, but by God's acceptance of Christ on our behalf; but sinners must accept this Saviour in order to profit by the Divine acceptance of His Person and Work [Jn. 1:12].)

THE BIRTH OF SAMSON

24 And the woman bore a son, and called his name Samson: and the child grew, and the LORD blessed him.

25 And the Spirit of the LORD began to move him at times in the camp of Dan between Zorah and Eshtaol. *(Israel had at this time fallen so completely into the power of the enemy that only a Nazarite could be used by God to deliver them. But, as always, so in this case, man failed. Christ was the true Nazarite. The source of His Strength was a secret unknown to the world. At that time, Israel was in a worse bondage than that of the Philistines, who didn't even know the Lord; and He, the Lord Jesus Christ, in the power of full consecration, walked among sinners separate from them — separate from evil — yet He was in the midst of them as their Light and their Salvation. So, as Samson, He began to save His people from the Philistine in His First Advent, and, as David, He will complete His saving Work in His Second Advent — Williams.)*

CHAPTER 14
(1141 B.C.)
SAMSON

AND Samson went down to Timnath, and saw a woman in Timnath of the daughters of the Philistines.

2 And he came up, and told his father and his mother, and said, I have seen a woman in Timnath of the daughters of the Philistines: now therefore get her for me to wife. *(Samson's history illustrates the tendency of the Christian to fall at any moment from the position of whole-hearted*

separation unto God into all that in which the world finds its joy and strength. We find here that while God made use of Samson's marriage to a Philistine in order to punish that people, still, that did not excuse Samson's folly and disobedience. The Law of God said that there was to be no marriage with the heathen; therefore, had he yielded himself unto God, and his members as instruments of righteousness [Rom. 6:13], how much greater and more glorious would have been the victories granted to him!)

3 Then his father and his mother said unto him, Is there never a woman among the daughters of your brethren, or among all my people, that you go to take a wife of the uncircumcised Philistines? And Samson said unto his father, Get her for me; for she pleases me well.

4 But his father and his mother knew not that it was of the LORD, that He sought an occasion against the Philistines: for at that time the Philistines had dominion over Israel. *(Concerning this, Williams says, "The depths of Satan may be recognized in his action toward Israel in connection with the Philistines. The other nations 'mightily oppressed' Israel, but it is not stated that the Philistines did so. They simply 'ruled' Israel; and so insensible had Israel become to slavery that they accepted this yoke. This is the sad history of many a Christian life. Bondage to some inward form of evil is submitted to, its rule accepted, and spiritual insensibility results.*

"Satan, therefore, introduced this new form of rule and bondage as distinct from the former violence and cruelty; and Samson's countrymen were satisfied with it. He, therefore, could not get them to join him in a general revolt, as was the case with former Judges; and, therefore, it was necessary that a private cause of quarrel should arise. Samson's proposed marriage furnished such an occasion, and God used it to that end.")

SAMSON AND THE LION

5 Then went Samson down, and his father and his mother, to Timnath, and came to the vineyards of Timnath *(in a sense, the vineyards typify the Fruit of the Spirit)*: and, behold, a young lion roared against him *(Satan, as a roaring lion, seeks to stop the spiritual progress of the Child of God [I Pet. 5:8]).*

6 And the Spirit of the LORD came mightily upon him, and he *(Samson)* rent him as he would have rent a kid *(small lamb)*, and he had nothing in his hand: but he told not his father or his mother what he had done *(the Spirit of the Lord enabled him to kill this lion with his bare hands).*

7 And he went down, and talked with the woman; and she pleased Samson well.

8 And after a time he returned to take her *(possibly several weeks)*, and he turned aside to see the carcase of the lion: and, behold, there was a swarm of bees and honey in the carcase of the lion *(the "honey" represents here the Blessings of the Lord, which come to us in respect to the defeat of Satan, which we accomplish by our Faith; however, it must be Faith in Christ and the Cross; so, if the Believer "walks after the Spirit" [Rom. 8:1-2], Satan will be defeated, and his attack turned into blessing).*

9 And he took thereof *(the honey)* in his hands, and went on eating, and came to his father and mother, and he gave them, and they did eat: but he told not them that he had taken the honey out of the carcase of the lion *(in other words, the Spirit of the Lord had begun His glorious work in the life of Samson, and did so by strengthening him to such an extent that he could kill a lion with his bare hands, which typified Christ overcoming the powers of darkness, and bringing about the sweet results of victory; victory, incidentally, which is ours, because we are in Him [Jn. 14:20]).*

THE FEAST AND THE RIDDLE

10 So his father went down unto the woman: and Samson made there a feast; for so used the young men to do *(to celebrate the wedding).*

11 And it came to pass, when they *(the Philistines)* saw him, that they brought thirty companions to be with him *(indicating that Samson's family was one of wealth and position).*

12 And Samson said unto them, I will now put forth a riddle unto you: if you can certainly declare it me within the seven days of the feast, and find it out, then I will give you thirty sheets *(shirts)* and thirty change of garments:

13 But if you cannot declare it me, then shall you give me thirty sheets *(shirts)* and thirty change of garments. And they said unto him, Put forth your riddle, that we may hear it *(riddles and their interpretation were a favorite form of entertainment at that particular time).*

14 And he said unto them, Out of the eater came forth meat, and out of the strong came forth sweetness. And they could not in three days expound the riddle *(in effect, he was telling the Philistines that the Spirit of the Lord had*

already begun to come upon him, which began with the killing of the lion, which was a type of Satan and the Philistines; the resultant honey was the sweetness that would come forth from this great deliverance; however, the Philistines, of course, had no idea as to what he meant).

SAMSON'S WIFE

15 And it came to pass on the seventh day, that they said unto Samson's wife, Entice your husband, that he may declare unto us the riddle, lest we burn you and your father's house with fire: have you called us to take that we have? is it not so? *(In other words, we're not giving this Israelite anything.)*

16 And Samson's wife wept before him, and said, You do but hate me, and love me not: you have put forth a riddle unto the children of my people, and have not told it me. And he said unto her, Behold, I have not told it my father nor my mother, and shall I tell it thee?

17 And she wept before him the seven days, while their feast lasted *(trying to get him to relate to her the answer to the riddle)*: and it came to pass on the seventh day, that he told her, because she lay sore upon him: and she told the riddle to the children of her people.

18 And the men of the city said unto him on the seventh day before the sun went down, What is sweeter than honey? and what is stronger than a lion? and he said unto them, If you had not plowed with my heifer, you had not found out my riddle *(Samson knew that his wife had told them the answer)*.

SAMSON'S VENGEANCE

19 And the Spirit of the LORD came upon him, and he went down to Ashkelon, and slew thirty men of them, and took their spoil, and gave change of garments unto them which expounded the riddle. And his anger was kindled, and he went up to his father's house. *(The Philistines would find the answer to the riddle, but they as of yet had no idea as to who exactly Samson was, nor the damage he would do to them.)*

20 But Samson's wife was given to his companion, whom he had used as his friend. *(So he was betrayed on all counts: by the Philistines, typifying the world; by his wife, typifying companionship with the world; and by his friend, typifying an unholy alliance.)*

CHAPTER 15
(1141 B.C.)
REVENGE

BUT it came to pass within a while after, in the time of wheat harvest *(late May or early June)*, that Samson visited his wife with a kid *(a small lamb)*; and he said, I will go in to my wife into the chamber. But her father would not suffer him to go in.

2 And her father said, I verily thought that you had utterly hated her; therefore I gave her to your companion: is not her younger sister fairer than she? take her, I pray you, instead of her. *(Life is usually marked by folly, when self-will is the spring of action. On the contrary, when God's Will governs the life, prudence and prosperity result. Accordingly, Samson foolishly returned to the woman who so basely betrayed him.)*

3 And Samson said concerning them, Now shall I be more blameless than the Philistines, though I do them a displeasure *(my revenge will be a just one)*.

4 And Samson went and caught three hundred foxes *(should have been translated "jackals")*, and took firebrands, and turned tail to tail, and put a firebrand in the midst between two tails.

5 And when he had set the brands on fire, he let them go into the standing corn *(wheat)* of the Philistines, and burnt up both the shocks, and also the standing corn, with the vineyards and olives *(considerable damage!)*.

THE PHILISTINES

6 Then the Philistines said, Who has done this? And they answered, Samson, the son in law of the Timnite, because he had taken his wife, and given her to his companion. And the Philistines came up, and burnt her and her father with fire *(as stated, they little knew, so to speak, as to exactly whom they were fooling with)*.

A GREAT SLAUGHTER

7 And Samson said unto them, Though you have done this *(killed his wife and her father)*, yet will I be avenged of you, and after that I will cease *(in essence, "If this is the way you treat me, be sure that I will not cease until I have had my full revenge")*.

8 And he smote them hip and thigh with a great slaughter: and he went down and dwelt

in the top of the rock Etam. *(The Believer may wonder how the Lord could be in all of these things? However, it must be understood that Israel was at an extremely low state at this particular time. In fact, I think it can be said that Samson, for all of his weaknesses, was the best of the lot.*

In a sense, Samson was a Type of Christ, at least as it regards his victories. These victories represent the Lord overcoming every enemy, all on our behalf.)

9 Then the Philistines went up, and pitched in Judah, and spread themselves in Lehi *(they prepared for war against Israel).*

10 And the men of Judah said, Why are you come up against us? And they answered, To bind Samson are we come up, to do to him as he has done to us.

THE SLAUGHTER OF A THOUSAND PHILISTINES

11 Then three thousand men of Judah went to the top of the rock Etam, and said to Samson, Knowest thou not that the Philistines are rulers over us? what is this that you have done unto us? And he said unto them, As they did unto me, so have I done unto them. *(The language of these cowardly men portrays the fact as to how completely the Philistine yoke was fastened upon the necks of Judah. The opposition of the world is bitter to the Nazarite Christian, but the opposition of the Church is more bitter. The Philistines ruled over Israel, and Israel was content to have it so. They did not wish to have a Nazarite in their midst who would disturb their peace and excite the world against them. They were quite ready to hand Samson over to a cruel death in order to maintain their so-called peace. This condition of spiritual degradation marks, and has marked, the history of the Christian Church. Instead of hailing Samson as a deliverer, the Israelites treated him as an enemy.*

Believers are very quick to talk about the foibles of Samson, but very seldom mention the leaders of Israel, who were in far worse spiritual condition.)

12 And they said unto him, We are come down to bind you, that we may deliver you into the hand of the Philistines. And Samson said unto them, Swear unto me, that you will not fall upon me yourselves *(evidently, they had agreed with the Philistines that if they could deliver Samson to them, the Philistines would not start the war; the truth is, they didn't care* about Samson, and neither did they care about the Will of the Lord; they sought only to appease the world, which is the attitude of most of the modern Church).*

13 And they spoke unto him, saying, No; but we will bind you fast, and deliver you into their hand: but surely we will not kill you. And they bound him with two new cords, and brought him up from the rock *(they thought they had their problem solved).*

14 And when he came unto Lehi, the Philistines shouted against him: and the Spirit of the LORD came mightily upon him, and the cords that were upon his arms became as flax that was burnt with fire, and his bands loosed from off his hands.

15 And he found a new jawbone of an ass *(the skeleton)*, and put forth his hand, and took it, and slew a thousand men therewith. *(By far, this was his mightiest achievement to date. As stated, Israel should have helped him, and, in fact, had they done so, they would have been delivered from the Philistine yoke at that moment. But they were so far away from God that they were quite satisfied with that yoke. They reasoned that their situation was not nearly so bad as it had been under other conquerors. So, they would live with this problem, and they didn't want Samson rocking the boat.*

How so like far too many modern Believers. They are quite satisfied to live under the dominion of Satan, providing it doesn't get too bad. So, when they hear the Message of the Cross, which is the only means of deliverance, they by and large shrug it off, thinking that such is not necessary for them. They know of others who desperately need the Message of the Cross, but they never put themselves in the same category. At best, such Christians are of no use to the Kingdom of God, and, at worst, they lose their souls.)

16 And Samson said, With the jawbone of an ass, heaps upon heaps, with the jaw of an ass have I slain a thousand men *(a song of sorts).*

17 And it came to pass, when he had made an end of speaking, that he cast away the jawbone out of his hand, and called that place Ramath-lehi *(meaning "the casting away of the jawbone," referring to the fact that the jawbone had no special qualities at all, but rather that this was carried out by the Spirit of God; had he not thrown away this item, Israel would have probably worshipped the thing; such is the human heart).*

18 And he was sore athirst, and called on the LORD, and said, You have given this great deliverance into the hand of Your servant: and now shall I die for thirst, and fall into the hand of the uncircumcised? *(We may note from this that the more God gives, the more He encourages us to ask.)*

19 But God clave an hollow place *(possibly even in a rock)* that was in the jaw *(where he had thrown the jawbone)*, and there came water thereout; and when he had drunk, his spirit came again, and he revived: wherefore he called the name thereof En-hakkore, which is in Lehi unto this day *(means "the well of him who called," or, "cried" [Ps. 34:6]).*

20 And he judged Israel in the days of the Philistines twenty years.

CHAPTER 16
(1120 B.C.)
SAMSON AT GAZA

THEN went Samson to Gaza, and saw there an harlot, and went in unto her. *(The word "then" tells us that this incident occurred after the slaughter of the thousand Philistines, but it doesn't tell us how long after. Samson could rend lions and conquer Philistines, but he could not rend his lust nor conquer his appetites.*

There is only one way that victory over these things can be accomplished, not five ways, or two ways, just one way. The Believer must understand that Christ is the Source of all things which we need, and the Cross is the Means. This means that the Believer should anchor his Faith squarely in Christ and the Cross, ever making such the object of his Faith. This occasions the Holy Spirit, Who works entirely within the parameters of the Finished Work of Christ, greatly helping us. In fact, He will help us only on these terms [Rom. 6:3-14; 8:1-2, 11].)

2 And it was told the Gazites *(the inhabitants of Gaza)*, saying, Samson is come hither. And they compassed him in, and laid wait for him all night in the gate of the city, and were quiet all the night, saying, In the morning, when it is day, we shall kill him.

3 And Samson lay till midnight, and arose at midnight, and took the doors of the gate of the city, and the two posts, and went away with them, bar and all, and put them upon his shoulders, and carried them up to the top of an hill that is before Hebron. *(All of this could well have weighed a thousand pounds or more. Within himself, he could not even remotely have*

done such a thing. But, with the help of the Holy Spirit, it could be done, and, in fact, was done.

In a sense, but without the unholy union, this was a Type of Christ, Who descended to Earth, not to have guilty union with its fallen inhabitants, but to redeem them. And, at the dawning of the day, He burst the bars of the tomb, and ascended to the Heavenly Hebron, thereby securing eternal life for the degraded sons of men [Jn. 3:16].)

SAMSON AND DELILAH

4 And it came to pass afterward, that he loved a woman in the valley of Sorek, whose name was Delilah. *(A Believer, when governed by self-will, can fall deeper into folly and sin than even a man of the world. This explains Samson's incredible conduct with Delilah.)*

5 And the lords of the Philistines came up unto her, and said unto her, Entice him, and see wherein his great strength lies, and by what means we may prevail against him, that we may bind him to afflict him; and we will give you every one of us eleven hundred pieces of silver *(by now, the Philistines were extremely wary of Samson; in fact, they could not see any way to defeat him; but yet, they knew there must be some secret to his strength; in fact, there was!).*

6 And Delilah said to Samson, Tell me, I pray you, wherein your great strength lies, and wherewith you might be bound to afflict you.

7 And Samson said unto her, If they bind me with seven green withs *(probably refers to "catgut")* that were never dried, then shall I be weak, and be as another man.

8 Then the lords of the Philistines brought up to her seven green withs which had not been dried, and she bound him with them.

9 Now there were men lying in wait, abiding with her in the chamber. And she said unto him, The Philistines be upon you, Samson. And he broke the withs, as a thread of tow is broken when it touches the fire. So his strength was not known *(the secret of his strength).*

NEW ROPES

10 And Delilah said unto Samson, Behold, you have mocked me, and told me lies: now tell me, I pray you, wherewith you might be bound.

11 And he said unto her, If they bind me fast with new ropes that never were occupied, then

shall I be weak, and be as another man.

12 Delilah therefore took new ropes, and bound him therewith, and said unto him, The Philistines be upon you, Samson. And there were liers in wait abiding in the chamber. And he broke them from off his arms like a thread.

THE HAIR

13 And Delilah said unto Samson, Hitherto you have mocked me, and told me lies: tell me wherewith you might be bound. And he said unto her, If you weave the seven locks of my head with the web. *(For the first time, he mentions his hair, which is a symbol of his strength. It is not possible to have close communion with the world without at last becoming a part of the world. And that which happened to Samson will happen to anyone. As God doesn't change, neither do the allurements of the world, nor its dangers, change.)*

14 And she fastened it with the pin, and said unto him, The Philistines be upon you, Samson. And he awaked out of his sleep, and went away with the pin of the beam, and with the web.

THE SECRET

15 And she said unto him, How can you say, I love you, when your heart is not with me? you have mocked me these three times, and have not told me wherein your great strength lies.

16 And it came to pass, when she pressed him daily with her words, and urged him, so that his soul was vexed unto death *(he should have never been in this place; it is not possible, I think, for any Believer to submit himself to such a situation but that the end result will be exactly as that of Samson; fellowship with the world is at least one the greatest dangers, if not the greatest danger, to the Child of God [I Jn. 2:15-17]);*

17 That he told her all his heart, and said unto her, There has not come a razor upon my head; for I have been a Nazarite unto God *(separated unto God)* from my mother's womb: if I be shaved, then my strength will go from me, and I shall become weak, and be like any other man.

18 And when Delilah saw that he had told her all his heart, she sent and called for the lords of the Philistines, saying, Come up this once, for he has showed me all his heart. Then the lords of the Philistines came up unto her, and brought money in their hand *(the love of money is the root of all evil).*

19 And she made him sleep upon her knees; and she called for a man, and she caused him to shave off the seven locks of his head; and she began to afflict him, and his strength went from him.

THE DEPARTURE OF THE LORD

20 And she said, The Philistines be upon you, Samson. And he awoke out of his sleep, and said, I will go out as at other times before, and shake myself *(shake off the Philistines).* And he wist not that the LORD was departed from him *(there is nothing worse that can be said of a person than that the Spirit of the Lord has departed).*

21 But the Philistines took him, and put out his eyes, and brought him down to Gaza, and bound him with fetters of brass; and he did grind in the prison house. *(The Philistines put his eyes out and degraded him to the abject position of grinding meal and making sport of him. Such is ever the moral result of association with the world — it obtains the mastery, the Christian loses his eyesight and liberty, and becomes a mere purveyor of entertainments to the Church — and that is basically the far lower level to which the modern Church has succumbed. It is no more than a social center, which provides good entertainment. God help us!)*

SAMSON'S RESTORATION

22 Howbeit the hair of his head began to grow again after he was shaved *(the fallen Believer can come back; the hair, spiritually speaking, can begin to grow again).*

23 Then the lords of the Philistines gathered them together for to offer a great sacrifice unto Dagon their god, and to rejoice: for they said, Our god has delivered Samson our enemy into our hand. *(They equated Samson's loss of strength as their god, Dagon, defeating Jehovah, the God of the Israelites. Dagon had the head, breast, and hands of a human, and the balance of the body shaped like a fish.)*

24 And when the people saw him, they praised their god: for they said, Our god has delivered into our hands our enemy, and the destroyer of our country, which slew many of us.

25 And it came to pass, when their hearts were merry, that they said, Call for Samson, that he may make us sport *(they didn't seem to*

realize that his hair had grown back). And they called for Samson out of the prison house; and he made them sport: and they set him between the pillars (the two pillars which held up this house of Dagon worship).

26 And Samson said unto the lad who held him by the hand, Suffer me that I may feel the pillars whereupon the house stands, that I may lean upon them.

27 Now the house was full of men and women; and all the lords of the Philistines were there; and there were upon the roof about three thousand men and women (no doubt, the elite of the Philistines), who beheld while Samson made sport (made sport of him, which, in his blindness, he had no recourse).

28 And Samson called unto the LORD (the type of prayer prayed by Samson will always be heard by the Lord), and said, O Lord God (the term "Lord God" refers to the "God of Covenants," which, in itself, speaks volumes), remember me, I pray You (a petition of humility), and strengthen me, I pray Thee, only this once, O God, that I may be at once avenged of the Philistines for my two eyes.

29 And Samson took hold of the two middle pillars upon which the house stood, and on which it was borne up, of the one with his right hand, and of the other with his left. (I wonder what these thousands of Philistines were thinking, when they saw him put his arms around these two pillars? The jesting and the mocking could probably be heard for quite a distance.)

30 And Samson said, Let me die with the Philistines (he did not commit suicide, but rather gave his life). And he bowed himself with all his might; and the house fell upon the lords, and upon all the people who were therein. So the dead which he slew at his death were more than they which he slew in his life.

31 Then his brethren and all the house of his father came down, and took him, and brought him up, and buried him between Zorah and Eshtaol in the buryingplace of Manoah his father. And he judged Israel twenty years. (Had they come to him when he was alive, instead of only when he was dead, the situation might have been different.)

CHAPTER 17
(1120 B.C.)
MICAH'S IDOLS

AND there was a man of Mount Ephraim, whose name was Micah. (The balance of this Book no longer concerns itself with Judges raised up by the Lord, but rather the internal affairs of Israel. It is done, of course, for purpose, which is to show the inward moral condition of the nation, which was despicable, to say the least. It is a sad picture of confusion, idolatry, sin, and violence; it all resulted from neglect of the Bible. Four times in this section of the Book it states, "Every man did that which was right in his own eyes.")

2 And he said unto his mother, The eleven hundred shekels of silver that were taken from you, about which you cursed, and spoke of also in my ears, behold, the silver is with me; I took it, And his mother said, Blessed be you of the LORD, my son. (Evidently, Micah had stolen this amount of silver from his mother. As we shall see, it is connected with idolatry.)

3 And when he had restored the eleven hundred shekels of silver to his mother (worth about $6,000 in 2004 currency), his mother said, I had wholly dedicated the silver unto the LORD from my hand for my son, to make a graven image and a molten image: now therefore I will restore it unto you. (As we see here, the greater part of Israel, of which the Holy Spirit desires that this household serve as a type, equated the Lord and idols as one and the same.

Presently, any doctrine in the modern Church which is not based squarely on the Foundation of "Christ and Him Crucified" [I Cor. 1:23], pure and simple, is idolatry. Such false worship is "another Jesus, brought about by another spirit, which gives us another gospel" [II Cor. 11:4]. If that, in fact, is correct, and it definitely is, due to the paucity of the preaching of the Cross [I Cor. 1:21], almost the entirety of the modern Church world is corrupted by idolatry [I Jn. 5:21].)

4 Yet he restored the money unto his mother; and his mother took two hundred shekels of silver, and gave them to the founder, who made thereof a graven image and a molten image: and they were in the house of Micah (far too many modern Churches are actually founders of graven and molten images, but in a different form now than then; it is now in the form of Denominationalism, methodology, false doctrine, etc.).

5 And the man Micah had an house of gods, and made an ephod, and teraphim, and consecrated one of his sons, who became his priest. (These images, together with the ephod, teraphim, and priests, suggest that this domestic chapel was a corrupt imitation of the Tabernacle. All was contrary to the Word of God.

The Word commanded one place of worship only; it forbade images. And it permitted none to be Priests but the sons of Aaron. No description is given in the Bible of the "teraphim"; however, it is believed they were a particular object shaped in the form of an idol, which was consulted.)

6 In those days there was no king in Israel, but every man did that which was right in his own eyes. *(Due to improper leadership in the modern Church, which, in the Eyes of God, is no leadership at all, most of the people are being led wrong. Yesterday it was "Promise Keepers," and presently it is "The Government of Twelve," or "Seeker Sensitive Churches," or "The Word of Faith doctrine," etc., all falling into the unscriptural column. The difference between now and then is that the people are not so much presently doing that which is right in their own eyes, but rather in the eyes of someone else, who is rather a wolf in sheep's clothing [Mat. 7:14-20].)*

THE PRIESTS

7 And there was a young man out of Beth-lehem-judah of the family of Judah, who was a Levite, and he sojourned there *(the statement in this Verse doesn't mean that this Levite was from the Tribe of Judah, but rather that he had made his home in Bethlehem, which was in the realm of the Tribe of Judah).*

8 And the man departed out of the city from Beth-lehem-judah to sojourn where he could find a place: and he came to Mount Ephraim to the house of Micah, as he journeyed *(if Phinehas, the High Priest, and the nation had obeyed the Scriptures, this Levite would not have had to travel about looking for a place to serve).*

9 And Micah said unto him, From where do you come? And he said unto him, I am a Levite of Beth-lehem-judah, and I go to sojourn where I may find a place.

10 And Micah said unto him, Dwell with me, and be unto me a father and a priest, and I will give you ten shekels of silver by the year, and a suit of apparel, and your victuals. So the Levite went in. *(Micah called his chapel a "House of God," which it actually is in the original Hebrew, but the Holy Spirit called it a house of idols [Vs. 5]. The true House of God was neglected and as hard to find then as it is today; and too often when found, amusements rather than worship characterize it [21:21-23]. It seems that Preachers are for sale now, just as they were then.]*

11 And the Levite was content to dwell with the man; and the young man was unto him as one of his sons.

12 And Micah consecrated the Levite; and the young man became his priest, and was in the house of Micah.

13 Then said Micah, Now know I that the LORD will do me good, seeing I have a Levite to my priest. *(It didn't exactly turn out this way, for he was afterwards robbed of both his idols and his priest. He had, like some people at the present time, a little knowledge of Scriptural Worship, but only sufficient to make him idolatrous and superstitious.)*

CHAPTER 18
(1406 B.C.)
MICAH AND THE DANITES

IN those days there was no king in Israel: and in those days the Tribe of the Danites sought them an inheritance to dwell in; for unto that day all their inheritance had not fallen unto them among the Tribes of Israel. *(The time frame of this Chapter probably occurred when Othniel was the Judge in Israel. The portion assigned to the Tribe of Dan was in the area of the Philistines [Josh. 19:40]. However, it seems they did not have enough faith to overcome the Philistines; so, instead, and out of the Will of God, they undertook an expedition against a small and defenseless people in the extreme north of the land, built a city there, which they called "Dan" — thus originating the expression "from Dan even to Beersheba" — and publicly established idolatry. This is probably the reason for the omission of their name in Rev., Chpt. 7.)*

2 And the Children of Dan sent of their family five men from their coasts *(borders)*, men of valour, from Zorah, and from Eshtaol, to spy out the land, and to search it; and they said unto them, Go, search the land: who when they came to Mount Ephraim, to the house of Micah, they lodged there.

3 When they were by the house of Micah, they knew the voice of the young man the Levite: and they turned in thither, and said unto him, Who brought you here? and what are you doing in this place? and what have you here?

4 And he said unto them, Thus and thus dealt Micah with me, and has hired me, and I am his priest.

5 And they said unto him, Ask counsel, we pray you, of God, that we may know whether our way which we go shall be prosperous. *(They should have themselves prayed before they*

left, and they would have then known the Will of God, instead of depending on someone else.)

6 And the priest said unto them, Go in peace: before the LORD is your way wherein you go. *(The action of the Danites in asking this Levite to divine for them — no doubt by means of the teraphim or the ephod — shows how far at this early date the Word of God was departed from. They ought to have been shocked and grieved at a Levite assuming Priestly functions; and they should have been indignant at the existence of a house of idols in rivalry with the Tabernacle of Jehovah.)*

7 Then the five men departed, and came to Laish *(about 30 miles north of the Sea of Galilee)*, and saw the people who were therein, how they dwelt careless, after the manner of the Zidonians, quiet and secure; and there was no magistrate in the land, that might put them to shame in any thing; and they were far from the Zidonians, and had no business with any man.

8 And they came unto their brethren to Zorah and Eshtaol: and their brethren said unto them, What do you say?

9 And they said, Arise, that we may go up against them: for we have seen the land, and, behold, it is very good: and are you still? *(still desirous to take the land?)* be not slothful to go, and to enter to possess the land *(in other words, do it now!).*

10 When you go, you shall come unto a people secure, and to a large land: for God has given it into your hands; a place where there is no want of any thing that is in the Earth. *(Even though they used the name of "God," there is no record that the Holy Spirit had allotted to the Tribe of Dan this territory up north. This was their own doings, and, accordingly, would not turn out well.)*

STOLEN IMAGES

11 And there went from thence of the family of the Danites, out of Zorah and out of Eshtaol, six hundred men appointed with weapons of war.

12 And they went up, and pitched in Kirjath-jearim, in Judah: wherefore they called that place Mahaneh-dan unto this day: behold, it is behind Kirjath-jearim.

13 And they passed thence unto Mount Ephraim, and came unto the house of Micah.

14 Then answered the five men who went to spy out the country of Laish, and said unto their brethren, Do you know that there is in these houses an ephod, and teraphim, and a graven image, and a molten image? now therefore consider what you have to do *(in other words, take the images).*

15 And they turned thitherward, and came to the house of the young man the Levite, even unto the house of Micah, and saluted him.

16 And the six hundred men appointed with their weapons of war, which were of the Children of Dan, stood by the entering of the gate.

17 And the five men who went to spy out the land went up, and came in thither, and took the graven image, and the ephod, and the teraphim, and the molten image: and the Priest stood in the entering of the gate with the six hundred men who were appointed with weapons of war.

18 And these went into Micah's house, and fetched the carved image, the ephod, and the teraphim, and the molten image. Then said the Priest unto them, What are you doing?

19 And they said unto him, Hold your peace, lay your hand upon your mouth, and go with us, and be to us a father and a priest: is it better for you to be a Priest unto the house of one man, or that you be a Priest unto a tribe and a family in Israel?

20 And the Priest's heart was glad, and he took the ephod, and the teraphim, and the graven image, and went in the midst of the people *(the priest was for sale, and the Tribe of Dan paid more, so he went with them).*

21 So they turned and departed and put the little ones and the cattle and the carriage before them.

MICAH

22 And when they were a good way from the house of Micah, the men who were in the houses near to Micah's house were gathered together, and overtook the Children of Dan *(a goodly number of men who were neighbors to Micah joined him to try to retrieve the stolen items from the Children of Dan).*

23 And they cried unto the Children of Dan. And they turned their faces, and said unto Micah, What ails you, that you come with such a company?

24 And he said, You have taken away my gods which I made, and the priest, and you are gone away: and what have I more? and what is this that you say unto me, What ails you? *(It is strange, but Micah worships gods which he made,*

and which can be taken by others, proving they are of no value; and, yet, almost all the modern world functions presently in the same manner. It worships gods that it has made, and the god of religion is the biggest god of all.)

25 And the Children of Dan said unto him, Let not your voice be heard among us, lest angry fellows run upon you, and you lose your life, with the lives of your household.

26 And the Children of Dan went their way: and when Micah saw that they were too strong for him, he turned and went back unto his house.

THE CITY OF DAN

27 And they took the things which Micah had made, and the priest which he had, and came unto Laish, unto a people who were at quiet and secure: and they smote them with the edge of the sword, and burnt the city with fire.

28 And there was no deliverer (no deliverer for those of Laish), because it was far from Zidon, and they had no business with any man; and it was in the valley that lies by Beth-rehob. And they built a city, and dwelt therein.

29 And they called the name of the city Dan, after the name of Dan their father, who was born unto Israel: howbeit the name of the city was Laish at the first. (The Holy Spirit using the name of "Israel" in this Verse emphasizes the depth of Dan's guilt in setting up idolatry.)

IDOLATRY

30 And the Children of Dan set up the graven image: and Jonathan, the son of Gershom, the son of Manasseh, he and his sons were priests to the Tribe of Dan until the day of the captivity of the land. (Jonathan was the grandson of Moses. So ashamed were the Jews of what this man had done, and so unwilling to dishonor Moses by publicly reading aloud his name in this Verse, they instead used the name "Manasseh" in the place of Moses.)

31 And they set them up Micah's graven image, which he made, all the time that the house of God was in Shiloh. (All of this was especially forbidden by the Lord, and, therefore, constituted idolatry. And, worse still, Moses' grandson headed up this terrible form of idolatry.)

CHAPTER 19
(1406 B.C.)
THE CONCUBINE

AND it came to pass in those days, when there was no king in Israel, that there was a certain Levite sojourning on the side of Mount Ephraim, who took to him a concubine out of Beth-lehem-judah. (As to exactly when this was, we aren't told; however, it was definitely before the time of Saul.

The Lord said that Moses, because of the hardness of their hearts, suffered them to have more than one wife, but that in the beginning it was not so. The Levite, therefore, in having a secondary wife — they were called concubines — did not stand in a dishonorable relation to her.)

2 And his concubine played the whore against him, and went away from him unto her father's house to Beth-lehem-judah, and was there four whole months. (This woman, in sinning against her husband, little dreamed of the dreadful doom that would result from her action. The Devil pays hard wages. Concerning this, Williams says, "The terrible story pictures the misery, shame, and ruin that comes upon the heart that, unfaithful to the True Husband, lives in guilty union with the world. The night in such a heart is dark indeed; and all the world gives is abuse and not honor [Vs. 25].)

3 And her husband arose, and went after her, to speak friendly unto her, and to bring her again, having his servant with him, and a couple of asses: and she brought him into her father's house: and when the father of the damsel saw him, he rejoiced to meet him.

4 And his father in law, the damsel's father, retained him; and he abode with him three days: so they did eat and drink, and lodged there.

5 And it came to pass on the fourth day, when they arose early in the morning, that he rose up to depart: and the damsel's father said unto his son in law, Comfort your heart with a morsel of bread, and afterward go your way (in other words, have breakfast before you go).

6 And they sat down, and did eat and drink both of them together: for the damsel's father had said unto the man, Be content, I pray you, and tarry all night, and let your heart be merry (he wanted him to stay another night).

7 And when the man rose up to depart, his father in law urged him: therefore he lodged there again (stayed the extra night).

8 And he arose early in the morning on the

fifth day to depart *(had stayed there five days)*; and the damsel's father said, Comfort your heart, I pray you. And they tarried until afternoon, and they did eat both of them.

9 And when the man rose up to depart, he, and his concubine, and his servant, his father in law, the damsel's father, said unto him, Behold, now the day draws toward evening, I pray you tarry all night: behold, the day grows to an end, lodge here, that your heart may be merry; and to morrow get you early on your way, that you may go home *(tries yet to get him to stay even another night)*.

GIBEAH

10 But the man would not tarry that night, but he rose up and departed, and came over against Jebus, which is Jerusalem; and there were with him two asses saddled, his concubine also was with him.

11 And when they were by Jebus, the day was far spent; and the servant said unto his master, Come I pray you, and let us turn in into this city of the Jebusites, and lodge in it.

12 And his master said unto him, We will not turn aside hither into the city of a stranger *(Gentile)*, that is not of the Children of Israel; we will pass over to Gibeah *(actually, a suburb of Jerusalem)*.

13 And he said unto his servant, Come, and let us draw near to one of these places to lodge all night, in Gibeah, or in Ramah.

14 And they passed on and went their way; and the sun went down upon them when they were by Gibeah, which belongs to Benjamin *(the Tribe of Benjamin)*.

15 And they turned aside thither, to go in and to lodge in Gibeah: and when he went in, he sat him down in a street of the city: for there was no man who took them into his house to lodging. *(Pulpit says, "The absence of the common rites of hospitality toward strangers was a sign of the degraded character of the men of Gibeah. In those days, there were very few inns; consequently, travelers stayed, normally, in people's homes [Lk. 11:5-13].)*

16 And, behold, there came an old man from his work out of the field at evening, which was also of Mount Ephraim; and he sojourned in Gibeah: but the men of the place were Benjamites.

17 And when he had lifted up his eyes, he saw a wayfaring man in the street of the city: and the old man said, Where are you going? and from where have you come?

18 And he said unto him, We are passing from Beth-lehem-judah toward the side of Mount Ephraim; from thence am I: and I went to Beth-lehem-judah, but I am now going to the house of the LORD; and there is no man who receives me to house *(no man who gives me lodging; the "House of the Lord" probably refers to the Tabernacle at Shiloh)*.

19 Yet there is both straw and provender for our asses; and there is bread and wine also for me, and for your handmaid, and for the young man which is with your servants: there is no want of any thing *(in other words, I will not be a burden to anyone, because I have my own food, etc.)*.

20 And the old man said, Peace be with you; howsoever let all your wants lie upon me; only lodge not in the street.

21 So he brought him into his house, and gave provender unto the asses: and they washed their feet, and did eat and drink.

THE SODOMITES

22 Now as they were making their hearts merry, behold, the men of the city, certain sons of Belial *(worthless individuals)*, beset the house round about, and beat at the door, and spoke to the master of the house, the old man, saying, Bring forth the man who came into your house, that we may know him. *(These were homosexuals; it would have been better for the Levite to have spent the night with the heathen Jebusites than with the professed children of God; for the latter had already become viler than the former, although Joshua was not long dead! The singular resemblance of the whole narrative to that in Gen., Chpt. 19 suggests that the Israelites, by their contact with the accursed Canaanites, had reduced themselves to the level of Sodom and Gomorrah. The illustration given in this Chapter proclaims the wisdom of the command to destroy utterly these workers of abomination. Some sins are worse than others, and the sin of homosexuality is one of the most vile. It is the only sin that has occasioned the destruction of entire cities, and we speak of Sodom and Gomorrah, and done so instantly, and done so by God. The United States, and especially this country, because of the great Gospel Light it has been given, will ultimately face the Judgment of God in its sanctioning of homosexual marriages, so-called. The sin itself is bad enough; however, to legitimize it, which this nation is doing, will ultimately*

bring upon our heads the Wrath of God, and rightly so!)

23 And the man, the master of the house, went out unto them, and said unto them, No, my brethren, no, I pray you, do not so wickedly; seeing that this man is come into my house, do not this folly.

24 Behold, here is my daughter a maiden, and his concubine; them I will bring out now, and humble ye them, and do with them what seems good unto you: but unto this man do not so vile a thing. *(Lot's last night in Sodom gives a similar illustration of the loathsome depths to which men sink when they cease to retain God in their knowledge [Rom. 1:18-32].)*

25 But the men would not hearken to him: so the man took his concubine, and brought her forth unto them; and they knew her, and abused her all the night until the morning: and when the day began to spring, they let her go. *(How despicable was her husband, who allowed such a thing!)*

26 Then came the woman in the dawning of the day, and fell down at the door of the man's house where her lord was, till it was light.

27 And her lord rose up in the morning, and opened the doors of the house, and went out to go his way: and, behold, the woman his concubine was fallen down at the door of the house, and her hands were upon the threshold.

28 And he said unto her, Up, and let us be going. But none answered. Then the man took her up upon an ass, and the man rose up, and gat him unto his place. *(The woman died from the abuse she had taken that night. God help us!)*

VENGEANCE

29 And when he was come into his house, he took a knife, and laid hold on his concubine, and divided her, together with her bones, into twelve pieces, and sent her into all the coasts of Israel.

30 And it was so, that all who saw it said, There was no such deed done nor seen from the day that the Children of Israel came up out of the land of Egypt unto this day: consider of it, take advice, and speak your minds. *(The closing Chapters of the Book of Judges picture the moral darkness that settles down upon a nation, or a Church, when the Bible is disregarded, and men follow the religious and social teachings of their own minds and hearts. The general sense of the whole nation was to call a national council to decide what to do. At least,*

and despite his cowardice, the Levite had succeeded in arousing the indignation of the Twelve Tribes to avenge this terrible wrong.)

CHAPTER 20
(1406 B.C.)
THE ACCOUNT

THEN all the Children of Israel went out, and the congregation was gathered together as one man, from Dan even to Beersheba, with the land of Gilead, unto the LORD in Mizpeh. *(Mizpeh seemed to have been a national meeting place. As well, the phrase, "unto the Lord," could mean that the Tabernacle was brought here from Shiloh [Vs. 26].)*

2 And the chief of all the people, even of all the Tribes of Israel, presented themselves in the assembly of the people of God, four hundred thousand footmen who drew sword *(it was a mighty gathering).*

3 (Now the Children of Benjamin heard that the Children of Israel were gone up to Mizpeh.) Then said the Children of Israel, Tell us, how was this wickedness? *(The inquiry regarding details is now made.)*

4 And the Levite, the husband of the woman who was slain, answered and said, I came into Gibeah that belongs to Benjamin, I and my concubine, to lodge.

5 And the men of Gibeah rose against me, and beset the house round about upon me by night, and thought to have slain me: and my concubine have they forced, that she is dead.

6 And I took my concubine, and cut her in pieces, and sent her throughout all the country of the inheritance of Israel: for they have committed lewdness and folly in Israel. *(How painful it must have been to the Spirit of God to have to record such vileness!)*

WAR

7 Behold, you are all Children of Israel; give here your advice and counsel. *(However, there is no record that they sought the Lord, at least at this time, which would prove to be disastrous. The men of Israel were shocked at the fruits of the "flesh" in Gibeah, but they were blind to the activities and power of that same principle of evil in themselves. They were filled with anger because of the conduct of these men against a Levite and his wife; but there is no record of their sense of the terribleness of this sin against God, and of the evil of idolatry, which,*

at the time, existed in their midst. So it is presently. A sin against God is lightly regarded, but a sin against society is mercilessly judged.)

8 And all the people arose as one man, saying, We will not any of us go to his tent, neither will we any of us turn into his house *(no one would go home until due punishment had been afflicted upon Gibeah of Benjamin).*

9 But now this shall be the thing which we will do to Gibeah; we will go up by lot against it *(the word "lot" could refer to the Urim and the Thummim; however, if this, in fact, is the case, it doesn't mean they asked the Will of the Lord in the matter regarding whether to go or not, but rather who would go);*

10 And we will take ten men of an hundred throughout all the Tribes of Israel, and an hundred of a thousand, and a thousand out of ten thousand, to fetch victual for the people, that they may do, when they come to Gibeah of Benjamin, according to all the folly that they have wrought in Israel.

11 So all the men of Israel were gathered against the city, knit together as one man.

12 And the Tribes of Israel sent men through all the Tribe of Benjamin, saying, What wickedness is this that is done among you?

13 Now therefore deliver us the men, the children of Belial, which are in Gibeah, that we may put them to death, and put away evil from Israel. But the Children of Benjamin would not hearken to the voice of their brethren the Children of Israel *(it is believed that they did not ask properly; irrespective, Benjamin's response was totally wrong, and they would suffer dearly, along with the balance of Israel):*

THE BENJAMITES

14 But the Children of Benjamin gathered themselves together out of the cities unto Gibeah, to go out to battle against the Children of Israel *(Satan loves it, when God's people are fighting each other).*

15 And the Children of Benjamin were numbered at that time out of the cities twenty and six thousand men who drew sword, beside the inhabitants of Gibeah, which were numbered seven hundred chosen men.

16 Among all this people there were seven hundred chosen men lefthanded; every one could sling stones at an hair breadth, and not miss.

17 And the men of Israel, beside Benjamin, were numbered four hundred thousand men who drew sword: all these were men of war *(meaning they were proficient in battle).*

ISRAEL BEATEN

18 And the Children of Israel arose, and went up to the house of God, and asked counsel of God, and said, Which of us shall go up first to the battle against the Children of Benjamin? And the LORD said, Judah shall go up first *(once again, Israel did not ask the Lord as to whether they should go or not, but as to who were to go).*

19 And the Children of Israel rose up in the morning, and encamped against Gibeah.

20 And the men of Israel went out to battle against Benjamin; and the men of Israel put themselves in array to fight against them at Gibeah.

21 And the Children of Benjamin came forth out of Gibeah, and destroyed down to the ground of the Israelites that day twenty and two thousand men. *(Why would the Lord tell Judah to go forth to the battle, and then they would lose this great number? Had the Children of Israel acted at the beginning as they did later on, in Verse 26, they would not have suffered the two defeats of Verses 21 and 25. Their planning without God was one of the fruits of that fallen nature which they shared in common with the men of Gibeah. It is true that, after they had made their plans, they prayed, but only after the plans were made.*

Williams says, concerning this, "There is instruction in this for Believers for all times. Before the Tribes were fitted to judge evil in others they needed a sharp discipline to teach them to judge evil in themselves. So dead in their souls had the people become that they never thought of asking God how the matter was to be dealt with; nor were they conscious that they themselves were guilty of sins which cried out for Divine wrath.

"It was necessary, therefore, that they should learn a deep moral lesson; for God cannot give victories to man's natural will.")

ISRAEL BEATEN AGAIN

22 And the people the men of Israel encouraged themselves, and set their battle again in array in the place where they put themselves in array the first day.

23 (And the Children of Israel went up and wept before the LORD until evening, and asked counsel of the LORD, saying, Shall I go

up again to battle against the Children of Benjamin my brother? And the LORD said, Go up against him.)

24 And the Children of Israel came near against the Children of Benjamin the second day.

25 And Benjamin went forth against them out of Gibeah the second day, and destroyed down to the ground of the Children of Israel again eighteen thousand men; all these drew the sword (in other words, strong men of war, and yet they were beaten; in fact, in the two battles they had lost some 40,000 men, which, as is obvious, is a catastrophe).

TRUE REPENTANCE

26 Then all the Children of Israel, and all the people, went up, and came unto the House of God, and wept, and sat there before the LORD, and fasted that day until evening, and offered Burnt Offerings and Peace Offerings before the LORD. (The offering up of "Burnt Offerings" and "Peace Offerings" proclaims the fact that Israel is now engaging in true Repentance, because their Faith is once again in the shed Blood of the Lamb. The nation at last draws near to God in Repentance and sorrow, confessing themselves to be sinners. As interpreted by the New Testament, they confessed their own guilt, they declared themselves worthy of the Wrath of God, and they pleaded the Person and Work of Christ, the Lamb of God, for pardon and acceptance; their souls now humbled and taught, they were in a fit moral state to go up against Gibeah. It indeed deserved wrath, and will receive that wrath, but Israel merited wrath herself, and had, in a figure, to suffer it in and with Christ before drawing the sword against Benjamin.

God recognizes nothing with the exception of Christ and what He has done for us at the Cross. This means that man is recognized only so long as his Faith is in Christ, and, more than all, what Christ has done for us at the Cross. This shows that man understands as to who exactly he is, a sinner in need of a Saviour, and exactly as to Who Christ is, the only Redeemer.)

27 And the Children of Israel enquired of the LORD, (for the Ark of the Covenant of God was there in those days,

28 And Phinehas, the son of Eleazar, the son of Aaron, stood before it in those days,) saying, Shall I yet again go out to battle against the Children of Benjamin my brother, or shall I cease? And the LORD said, Go up for to

morrow I will deliver them into your hand (but only on the basis of the slain lamb; we must never forget that, because it hasn't changed unto this moment and, in fact, will never change; that's why Paul referred to it as "The Everlasting Covenant" [Heb. 13:20]).

BENJAMIN NEARLY DESTROYED

29 And Israel set liers in wait round about Gibeah.

30 And the Children of Israel went up against the Children of Benjamin on the third day, and put themselves in array against Gibeah, as at other times.

31 And the Children of Benjamin went out against the people, and were drawn away from the city; and they began to smite of the people, and kill, as at other times, in the highways, of which one goes up to the House of God, and the other to Gibeah in the field, about thirty men of Israel (about 30 were killed).

32 And the Children of Benjamin said, They are smitten down before us, as at the first. But the Children of Israel said, Let us flee, and draw them from the city unto the highways.

33 And all the men of Israel rose up out of their place, and put themselves in array at Baal-tamar: and the liers in wait of Israel came forth out of their places, even out of the meadows of Gibeah (they did so to spring the trap).

34 And there came against Gibeah ten thousand chosen men out of all Israel, and the battle was sore: but they knew not that evil was near them (the army of Benjamin didn't know).

35 And the LORD smote Benjamin before Israel (now the Lord will take a hand in the battle, because Israel has finally repented before Him); and the Children of Israel destroyed of the Benjamites that day twenty and five thousand and an hundred men: all these drew the sword (proficient men of war, who were killed).

36 So the Children of Benjamin saw that they were smitten: for the men of Israel gave place to the Benjamites, because they trusted unto the liers in wait (in ambush) which they had set beside Gibeah.

37 And the liers in wait hasted, and rushed upon Gibeah; and the liers in wait drew themselves along, and smote all the city with the edge of the sword.

38 Now there was an appointed sign between the men of Israel and the liers in wait,

that they should make a great flame with smoke rise up out of the city.

39 And when the men of Israel retired in the battle, Benjamin began to smite and kill of the men of Israel about thirty persons: for they said, Surely they are smitten down before us, as in the first battle.

40 But when the flame began to arise up out of the city with a pillar of smoke, the Benjamites looked behind them, and, behold, the flame of the city ascended up to Heaven.

41 And when the men of Israel turned again, the men of Benjamin were amazed: for they saw that evil was come upon them.

42 Therefore they turned their backs before the men of Israel unto the way of the wilderness; but the battle overtook them; and them *(the Benjamites)* which came out of the cities they *(the men of Israel)* destroyed in the midst of them.

43 Thus they inclosed the Benjamites round about, and chased them, and trode them down with ease over against Gibeah toward the sunrising.

44 And there fell of Benjamin eighteen thousand men; all these were men of valour.

45 And they turned and fled toward the wilderness unto the rock of Rimmon: and they gleaned of them in the highways five thousand men; and pursued hard after them unto Gidom, and slew two thousand men of them.

46 So that all which fell that day of Benjamin were twenty and five thousand men who drew the sword; all these were men of valour.

47 But six hundred men turned and fled to the wilderness unto the rock Rimmon, and abode in the rock Rimmon four months.

48 And the men of Israel turned again upon the Children of Benjamin, and smote them with the edge of the sword, as well the men of every city, as the beast, and all who came to hand: also they set on fire all the cities that they came to. *(Counting both men of Israel and those of Benjamin, the total loss was a little over 65,000 men; all because of sin in the realm of vice, which plagued Benjamin, and self-righteousness, which plagued the men of Israel. It is ironic that more were lost to self-righteousness than to vice. Just think about the sorrow and heartache that this brought to untold thousands of families in Israel, husbands, fathers, brothers, and sons! As stated, sin will take one further than one desires to go, and cost more than one can afford to pay.)*

CHAPTER 21
(1406 B.C.)
SORROW

NOW the men of Israel had sworn in Mizpeh, saying, There shall not any of us give his daughter unto Benjamin to wife. *(A circumstance not mentioned before was now brought forward, as is another in Verse 5.)*

2 And the people came to the house of God, and abode there till evening before God, and lifted up their voices, and wept sore;

3 And said, O LORD God of Israel, why is this come to pass in Israel, that there should be to day one Tribe lacking in Israel? *(When people are governed by excitement, and not by the Word of God, they bind themselves by oaths which lead to difficulty, and even to bloodshed.*

It is true that the Benjamites merited punishment, because their refusal to judge the evil at Gibeah showed that they thought little of it, or that they sympathized with it. And again, had Israel followed the Word of the Lord from the beginning, and had they waited upon God for direction, how different would be the history of this Chapter!)

4 And it came to pass on the morrow, that the people rose early, and built there an Altar, and offering Burnt Offerings and Peace Offerings *(the men of Israel are now functioning correctly; they are depending on the slain lamb)*.

5 And the Children of Israel said, Who is there among all the Tribes of Israel who came not up with the congregation unto the LORD? For they had made a great oath concerning him who came not up to the LORD to Mizpeh, saying, He shall surely be put to death *(referring to those who refused to fight the Benjamites)*.

6 And the Children of Israel repented them for Benjamin their brother, and said, There is one tribe cut off from Israel this day.

WIVES FOR THE BENJAMITES

7 How shall we do for wives for them who remain, seeing we have sworn by the LORD that we will not give them of our daughters to wives? *(Evidently, all the women of Benjamin had been killed, causing the death toll to rise to astronomical proportions. What a horror!)*

8 And they said, What one is there of the Tribes of Israel that came not up to Mizpeh to the LORD? And, behold, there came none to the camp from Jabesh-gilead to the assembly.

9 For the people were numbered, and,

behold, there were none of the inhabitants of Jabesh-gilead there.

10 And the congregation sent thither twelve thousand men of the valiantest, and commanded them, saying, Go and smite the inhabitants of Jabesh-gilead with the edge of the sword, with the women and the children.

11 And this is the thing that you shall do, You shall utterly destroy every male, and every woman who has lain by man. *(Again, several thousand people are killed. And the truth is, none of this was necessary. The Lord did not tell them to do this thing. If they made a rash vow, which they evidently did [Vs. 5], they should have asked the Lord to forgive them, which He most definitely would have done, and let the matter rest; however, the men of Israel were no doubt very angry, considering their losses, that the men of Jabesh-gilead did not participate. So, they would kill them, and so they did!)*

12 And they found among the inhabitants of Jabesh-gilead four hundred young virgins, who had known no man by lying with any male: and they brought them unto the camp to Shiloh, which is in the land of Canaan *(evidently they had taken the Tabernacle back to Shiloh).*

13 And the whole congregation sent some to speak to the Children of Benjamin who were in the rock Rimmon, and to call peaceably unto them *(20:47).*

14 And Benjamin came again at that time; and they gave them wives which they had saved alive of the women of Jabesh-gilead: and yet so they sufficed them not *(there were not enough women to go around).*

15 And the people repented them for Benjamin, because that the LORD had made a breach in the Tribes of Israel *(it is true, but it was the fault of all the Tribes of Israel, and not of God).*

SHILOH

16 Then the elders of the congregation said, How shall we do for wives for them who remain, seeing the women are destroyed out of Benjamin?

17 And they said, There must be an inheritance for them who be escaped of Benjamin, that a Tribe be not destroyed out of Israel *(the word "inheritance" should have been translated "succession," thereby reading, "there must be heirs to succeed, and therefore we must find wives*

for them").

18 Howbeit we may not give them wives of our daughters: for the Children of Israel have sworn, saying, Cursed be he who gives a wife to Benjamin.

19 Then they said, Behold, there is a feast of the LORD in Shiloh yearly in a place which is on the north side of Beth-el, on the east side of the highway that goes up from Beth-el to Shechem, and on the south of Lebonah. *(Williams says, "It gives a sad picture of the condition of the nation at this time that, although the Benjamites lived within a short distance of Shiloh where the Tabernacle was pitched, yet so complete was their neglect of it that the minute directions of Verse 19 had to be given them to enable them to find it; and, further, the mention of only one yearly Feast — God having commanded three — was an added proof of departure from His Word.")*

20 Therefore they commanded the Children of Benjamin, saying, Go and lie in wait in the vineyards;

21 And see, and, behold, if the daughters of Shiloh come out to dance in dances, then come ye out of the vineyards, and catch you every man his wife of the daughters of Shiloh, and go to the land of Benjamin *(these "dances" showed how heathen customs had invaded the House of God; for no such dancing was ordained in the Book of Leviticus; it is all a mournful illustration of that today which professes to be the House of God; all too often, amusement displaces worship).*

22 And it shall be, when their fathers or their brethren come unto us to complain, that we will say unto them, Be favourable unto them for our sakes: because we reserved not to each man his wife in the war: for you did not give unto them at this time, that you should be guilty *(could be translated, "You need not fear the guilt of the broken oath, because you did not give your daughters, so as to violate the oath, but they were taken from you by force").*

23 And the Children of Benjamin did so, and took them wives, according to their number, of them who danced, whom they caught: and they went and returned unto their inheritance, and repaired the cities, and dwelt in them.

24 And the Children of Israel departed thence at that time, every man to his Tribe and to his family, and they went out from thence every man to his inheritance.

ANARCHY

25 In those days there was no king in Israel: every man did that which was right in his own eyes. *(As should be obvious, the lessons of this Book are painful, but yet necessary. These lessons teach us that our Faith must ever be registered in Christ and what He has done for us at the Cross. That being done, the Holy Spirit will have latitude within our lives. To be sure, prayer and the study of the Word will then become prominent within our experience. Let it ever be understood that no height of Christian experience, nor miraculous manifestations, as glorious as they might be, can keep the soul from falling. Only daily fellowship with God, meditation upon and obedience to His Holy Word, and the ever-present power of the indwelling Holy Spirit, which can only come about, as stated, by Faith in Christ and the Cross, can preserve the Christian from spiritual declension.*

It is a solemn truth that experiences of the past, as wonderful as they may have then been, are useless to the heart that is out of fellowship with God. Israel's history abundantly illustrates this fact. God help us to learn from the myriad of illustrations given in this Book, as painful as they are!)

THE BOOK OF
RUTH

CHAPTER 1
(1322 B.C.)
ELIMELECH AND NAOMI

NOW it came to pass in the days when the judges ruled *(as to exactly when this was, we aren't told)*, that there was a famine in the land *(famines were sent by the Lord upon Israel as a Judgment because of spiritual declension).* And a certain man of Beth-lehem-judah *(Bethlehem means "house of bread")* went to sojourn in the country of Moab, he, and his wife, and his two sons *(going to a country outside of Israel to live was forbidden by the Lord; and yet, we will see how the Lord would take this wrong and turn it into right, but with great loss, as accompanies all failure).*

2 And the name of the man was Elimelech, and the name of his wife Naomi, and the name of his two sons Mahlon and Chilion, Ephrathites of Beth-lehem-judah. And they came into the country of Moab, and continued there *(because of the famine; however, better to be in a famine in that which belongs to the Lord, as did Israel, than to be in a place of prosperity, and it be filled with idolatry, as was Moab).*

SUFFERING

3 And Elimelech Naomi's husband died; and she was left, and her two sons *(to be out of the Will of God always brings suffering).*

4 And they took them wives of the women of Moab *(it was not forbidden in the Law for a Hebrew to marry a Moabite woman, but a Moabite, because of being cursed by God, was forbidden to enter the congregation of the Lord [Deut. 23:3]; however, Faith could overcome that, which it did with Ruth)*; the name of the one was Orpah, and the name of the other Ruth *(two Books in the Bible are named after women — Ruth and Esther; in the one, a Gentile woman marries a Hebrew, and, in the other, a Hebrew woman marries a Gentile; both marriages predict, as foretold [Gen. 12:3; 18:18; 22:18; 26:4; Ps. 72:17; Acts 3:25], that the Gentiles, as such, are to be brought into the Kingdom of God in connection with Israel)*: and they dwelled there about ten years *(it's very*

easy, spiritually speaking, to go into wrong directions; however, very hard to leave that wrong direction in order to come back to the right way).*

5 And Mahlon and Chilion died also both of them; and the woman was left of her two sons and her husband *(more suffering!).*

NAOMI

6 Then she arose with her daughters in law, that she might return from the country of Moab: for she had heard in the country of Moab how that the LORD had visited His people in giving them bread *(the Jewish Targums say that an Angel spoke to her and gave this information; in other words, the famine was over; it evidently lasted a number of years).*

7 Wherefore she went forth out of the place where she was, and her two daughters in law with her; and they went on the way to return unto the land of Judah.

8 And Naomi said unto her two daughters in law, Go, return each to her mother's house: the LORD deal kindly with you, as you have dealt with the dead, and with me. *(It seems that Naomi, at least at this stage, had so little faith in the Promises of God, and such a poor experience as the result of her own disobedience, that she discouraged her daughters-in-law from returning with her. This she should not have done; however, the same faithlessness that caused her and her family to leave Israel plagues her still. But, as we shall see, when she does return to Israel, her faith will begin to come back. Moab was not the place of faith, as the world system is never the place of faith. Israel was the place of faith, and so it is presently, spiritually speaking.)*

9 The LORD grant you that you may find rest, each of you in the house of her husband *(Naomi knew that there was no "rest" in the land of Moab, because it was a place of idolatry).* Then she kissed them; and they lifted up their voice, and wept.

10 And they said unto her, Surely we will return with you unto your people *(by the statement, "your people," they were speaking, as well, of Israel's God).*

11 And Naomi said, Turn again, my daughters: why will you go with me? are there yet

any more sons in my womb, that they may be your husbands? *(Once again, doubt and unbelief rule. Naomi was walking by sight, instead of by faith. Such a direction always limits God.)*

12 Turn again, my daughters, go your way; for I am too old to have an husband. If I should say, I have hope, if I should have an husband also to night, and should also bear sons;

13 Would you tarry for them till they were grown? would you stay for them from having husbands? *(In other words, wait until they were grown, thereby not marrying anyone else.)* no, my daughters; for it grieves me much for your sakes that the hand of the LORD is gone out against me. *(Naomi felt that she had suffered the tragic loss of her husband and two sons because of being out of the Will of God, by leaving Israel to come to Moab. There was, no doubt, some truth in that; however, we must always remember, God doesn't work from what might have been, but rather from "what is.")*

RUTH

14 And they lifted up their voice, and wept again: and Orpah kissed her mother in law; but Ruth clave unto her *(Orpah left, and we never hear from her again; how sad!).*

15 And she *(Naomi)* said, Behold, your sister in law is gone back unto her people, and unto her gods: return thou after your sister in law. *(From the statement, "unto her gods," it is obvious that the great contending factor here was the gods of Moab versus the God of Israel. Orpah chose "her gods," and missed the greatest thing that could ever happen to any individual — eternal life. In essence, Naomi asked Ruth if that is what she is going to do as well! Exactly as to what Naomi had in mind, we can only guess. It seems that she didn't want to promise them things that she could not fulfill. This seems to have been her intention. But yet, in all of this her faith, it seems, was very, very low.)*

16 And Ruth said, Intreat me not to leave you, or to return from following after you: for where you go, I will go: and where you lodge, I will lodge: your people shall be my people, and your God my God:

17 Where you die, will I die, and there will I be buried; the LORD do so to me, and more also, if ought but death part you and me. *(This has to be one of the greatest statements, one of the greatest affirmations of Salvation, found in the entirety of the Word of God. In essence, it is that which must characterize all who come*

to Christ.

In this consecration, there is no looking back. The die is cast. She will forever turn her back on the world of idolatry and rebellion against God. She will forever throw in her lot with those who worship the Lord of Glory. Even when she dies, she does not want to be sent back to Moab, but rather buried in the land of Israel, which she was. She cut all ties with the past, even her family, and everything else. This is exactly the consecration that is demanded by God of all who come to Him. Anything less constitutes no Salvation at all!)

18 When she *(Naomi)* saw that she *(Ruth)* was stedfastly minded to go with her, then she left speaking unto her *("steadfastly minded" must be the character of every Believer).*

19 So they two went until they came to Bethlehem. And it came to pass, when they were come to Beth-lehem, that all the city was moved about them, and they said, Is this Naomi? *(The words, "they said," proclaim a wealth of information. They carry the idea that the poverty which enveloped Naomi was obvious to all. Beside that, her husband and two sons were absent, meaning they were dead. As well, and above all, she is accompanied by a Moabitess, which was a reproach within itself. Little did the people of Bethlehem realize that this Moabitess would be the ancestress of the Messiah!)*

20 And she said unto them, Call me not Naomi, call me Mara *(bitter)*: for the Almighty has dealt very bitterly with me. *(This was not correct! The Lord had not dealt bitterly with Naomi. While problems may be allowed by the Lord, they are because of our wrongdoing, and certainly not His.)*

21 I went out full and the LORD has brought me home again empty *(in her thinking, "empty" described her situation; however, she was far more full than she could even begin to think; Ruth would prove to be the greatest blessing of all; unbelief sees "empty," while faith sees "full")*: why then call ye me Naomi, seeing the LORD has testified against me, and the Almighty has afflicted me?

22 So Naomi returned, and Ruth the Moabitess, her daughter in law, with her, which returned out of the country of Moab *(the Holy Spirit wants us to know who Ruth is, that we may know what Ruth becomes; He is, at the same time, telling us that, as He changed Ruth's life, He can change our lives, as well)*: and they came to Beth-lehem in the beginning of barley harvest. *(This was April, Passover time. In*

effect, the Holy Spirit is saying, "When I see the Blood, I will pass over you." There is no sin the Blood cannot cover. There is no life the cleansing of the Blood cannot change. It will change Ruth; it can change us.)

CHAPTER 2
(1312 B.C.)
THE FIELD OF BOAZ

AND Naomi had a kinsman of her husband's, a mighty man of wealth, of the family of Elimelech; and his name was Boaz. *(In a sense, Boaz is a Type of Christ; Ruth, a Gentile, is a Type of the Church. The terrible losses in the land of Moab portray the dispersion and, thereby, judgment of Israel.*

Boaz will prove to be the kinsman redeemer of Ruth. There is one Hebrew word for "kinsman" and "redeemer," for he only had "the right to redeem" who was a kinsman. Hence, it was necessary that the Lord Jesus Christ should become Man in order to redeem man. Ruth's marriage, and the wealthy home into which she was brought, picture the satisfying joy and fullness of blessing which union with Christ secures for the heart that trusts Him — Williams.)

2 And Ruth the Moabitess said unto Naomi, Let me now go to the field, and glean ears of corn *(grain)* after him in whose sight I shall find grace. And she said unto her, Go, my daughter. *(This portrays the fact that Naomi was poverty stricken. The welfare system of Israel in that day, which was given by God in the Law of Moses, stated that the poor, during the harvest, could go into the fields and glean the leavings. In this law, the reapers were instructed to not glean the corners of the fields, and to leave a little something along the way.)*

3 And she went, and came, and gleaned in the field after the reapers *(we find that Ruth, although a beautiful young lady, was not adverse to hard work; those who are, are seldom, if ever, used by the Lord)*: and her hap was to light on a part of the field belonging unto Boaz, who was of the kindred of Elimelech. *(Of course, the Holy Spirit was guiding her all the way. She did not know Boaz, but the Lord did. When the Lord plans for us, beautiful things result; when we plan for ourselves, there are no positive results!)*

FAVOR

4 And, behold, Boaz came from Beth-lehem,

and said unto the reapers, The LORD be with you. And they answered him, The LORD bless you. *(Boaz was extremely wealthy. He was of the Tribe of Judah, and in the direct line of the Messiah.)*

5 Then said Boaz unto his servant who was set over the reapers, Whose damsel is this? *(This question, even though asked casually by Boaz, would be answered by the Holy Spirit. Ruth would be the great-grandmother of David, and, thereby, of the Son of David.)*

6 And the servant who was set over the reapers answered and said, It is the Moabitish damsel who came back with Naomi out of the country of Moab *(to those around her, Ruth was reduced to the level of gleaning, as she was poverty stricken; also, she was a Moabitess, with all its resultant connotations; however, Heaven would answer the question in a much different way)*:

7 And she *(Ruth)* said, I pray you *(speaking to the servant)*, let me glean and gather after the reapers among the sheaves: so she came, and has continued even from the morning until now, that she tarried a little in the house *(she has reaped constantly, only resting a short time in the house)*.

8 Then said Boaz unto Ruth, Hearest thou not, my daughter? Go not to glean in another field, neither go from hence, but abide here fast by my maidens *(Boaz, after being made aware of Ruth, and being introduced to her, now shows her favor)*:

9 Let your eyes be on the field that they do reap, and go thou after them *(after the maidens)*: have I not charged the young men that they shall not touch you? and when you are athirst, go unto the vessels, and drink of that which the young men have drawn.

10 Then she fell on her face, and bowed herself to the ground, and said unto him, Why have I found grace in your eyes, that you should take knowledge of me, seeing I am a stranger? *(A Gentile! Boaz had done far more than merely take notice of her. Her action toward him denotes humility, a trait, incidentally, enjoyed by precious few.)*

11 And Boaz answered and said unto her, It has fully been showed me, all that you have done unto your mother in law since the death of your husband: and how you have left your father and your mother, and the land of your nativity, and are come unto a people which you knew not heretofore. *(Boaz makes it clear that he had already been informed of her consecration as a proselyte to the Hebrew faith, and*

of her decision to leave her own people, her native land, and its gods, to live with a people who were strangers to her. He then pronounced a blessing from the God of Israel upon her. The Hebrew Targum adds to this answer of Boaz: "It has been certainly told me by the word of the wise, that what the Lord has decreed [Deut. 23:3]. And it has surely said to me by prophecy, that kings and prophets shall proceed from you because of the good which you have done")

12 The LORD recompense your work, and a full reward be given you of the LORD God of Israel, under Whose wings you are come to trust *(in his own way, Boaz welcomes Ruth into the family of God).*

13 Then she said, Let me find favour in your sight, my Lord; for that you have comforted me, and for that you have spoken friendly unto your handmaid, though I be not like unto one of your handmaidens *(she places herself socially beneath the other Jewish girls who were gleaning, with the idea in mind that she is a Gentile).*

14 And Boaz said unto her, At mealtime come thou hither, and eat of the bread, and dip your morsel in the vinegar. And she sat beside the reapers: and he reached her parched corn *(grain)*, and she did eat, and was sufficed, and left *(still, Ruth doesn't actually know who Boaz really is).*

15 And when she was risen up to glean, Boaz commanded his young men, saying, Let her glean even among the sheaves, and reproach her not:

16 And let fall also some of the handfuls of purpose for her, and leave them, that she may glean them, and rebuke her not. *(Boaz, in his instructions to the reapers, directed them to give Ruth greater liberty than that commanded by the Law. The "handfuls of purpose," in effect, state that handfuls of grain were to be dropped just for her. As stated, she was truly favored.)*

17 So she gleaned in the field until evening, and beat out that she had gleaned: and it was about an ephah of barley *(about a bushel).*

18 And she took it up, and went into the city: and her mother in law saw what she had gleaned: and she brought forth, and gave to her that she had reserved after she was sufficed *(she had gleaned far more than Naomi had thought she would be able to do).*

NAOMI'S ADVICE

19 And her mother in law said unto her, Where have you gleaned to day? and where have you worked? blessed be he who did take knowledge of you. And she showed her mother in law with whom she had wrought *(worked)*, and said, The man's name with whom I wrought *(worked)* to day is Boaz. *(The way that Ruth answered proclaims more than a mere identification. She sensed something more, but Naomi would have to fill in the blanks, which she instantly did.)*

20 And Naomi said unto her daughter in law, Blessed be he of the LORD, Who has not left off His kindness to the living and to the dead *(her husband and her two sons).* And Naomi said unto her, The man is near of kin unto us, one of our next kinsmen. *(Naomi was speaking of the law of the kinsman redeemer. It referred to buying back a relative's property and to marrying his widow. When a Hebrew was forced to sell his inheritance because of poverty, the nearest relative was to redeem it for him [Lev. 25:25]. If one acted as a kinsman redeemer for one who had died without a son, he was obliged to marry the widow. Should he refuse to take possession of the property, he was not under obligation to marry the widow. Boaz had no right to redeem the property until the nearest kinsman refused, which he did.)*

21 And Ruth the Moabitess said, He said unto me also, You shall keep fast by my young men, until they have ended all my harvest *(in other words, Boaz told Ruth to not go glean in any other field except his).*

22 And Naomi said unto Ruth her daughter in law, It is good, my daughter, that you go out with his maidens, that they meet you not in any other field *(the implication is, Boaz wanted to see more of Ruth).*

23 So she kept fast by the maidens of Boaz to glean unto the end of barley harvest and of wheat harvest; and dwelt with her mother in law. *(During the time of barley harvest, which was in April, three Feasts were to be kept: Passover, Unleavened Bread, and First Fruits. During the time of the wheat harvest, which came in the latter part of May or early June, was to be the Feast of Pentecost. It was fifty days after Passover.)*

CHAPTER 3
(1312 B.C.)
INSTRUCTIONS

THEN Naomi her mother in law said unto her, My daughter, shall I not seek rest for you, that it may be well with you? *(In this*

instance, Naomi is a Type of the Holy Spirit, Who seeks our good. His business is to ever lead us to Christ.)

2 And now is not Boaz of our kindred, with whose maidens thou were? Behold, he winnows barley to night in the threshingfloor *(separates the husk from the grain; this is a type of what the Holy Spirit does for us by separating us from the "flesh," i.e., "the frail strength of man" [Mat. 3:11]).*

3 Wash yourself therefore *(this is a type of Redemption [I Cor. 6:11]),* and anoint thee *(this speaks of the Baptism with the Holy Spirit, hence the anointing, which follows the Salvation experience [Acts 2:4]),* and put your raiment upon you *(the garment of praise; it is not only an inward change, but it is an outward change, as well; it is the change effected by the Power of the Holy Spirit working within our hearts and lives; it speaks of an inward change that produces itself outwardly [Isa. 61:3]),* and get thee down to the floor *(this speaks of humility; the literal meaning of the word "humility" is "a river that runs low" [I Pet. 5:5]):* but make not yourself known unto the man, until he shall have done eating and drinking.

4 And it shall be, when he lies down, that you shall mark the place where he shall lie, and you shall go in, and uncover his feet, and lay thee down; and he will tell you what you shall do. *(There was nothing unseemly about this. It was a part of Hebrew Law. She was making a move, as instructed her by Naomi, which would bring Boaz to a place of decision. It is the same as the believing sinner coming to the feet of Christ, after which he will inherit everything that belongs to Christ, exactly as did Ruth regarding Boaz.)*

OBEDIENCE

5 And she *(Ruth)* said unto her *(Naomi),* All that you say unto me I will do. *(Naomi, being a type of the Holy Spirit, gives instructions, and Ruth promptly obeys.)*

6 And she went down unto the floor, and did according to all that her mother in law bade her *(which pertains to the next evening, after the day's work had been finished).*

7 And when Boaz had eaten and drunk, and his heart was merry, he went to lie down at the end of the heap of corn *(grain):* and she came softly, and uncovered his feet, and laid her down *(she did what Naomi told her to do).*

KINSMAN

8 And it came to pass at midnight, that the man was afraid, and turned himself: and, behold, a woman lay at his feet. *(Again, let the Reader understand that there was nothing unseemly or untoward going on here. This was a custom in those days, regarding a kinsman redeemer who had not stepped up to carry out the law.)*

9 And he said, Who are you? And she answered, I am Ruth your handmaid: spread therefore your skirt over your handmaid; for you are a near kinsman *(this is what Naomi had told her to say, which was correct).*

10 And he said, Blessed be thou of the LORD, my daughter: for you have showed more kindness in the latter end than at the beginning, inasmuch as you followed not young men, whether poor or rich *("the kindness which you are showing to your husband now that he is gone is still greater than what you did show him while he lived," hence the words, "more kindness in the latter end than at the beginning").*

11 And now, my daughter, fear not; I will do to you all that you require: for all the city of my people does know that you are a virtuous woman *(for months, the small town had observed Ruth, and the conclusion was one of virtue, as it regarded her).*

12 And now it is true that I am your near kinsman: howbeit there is a kinsman nearer than I. *(The kinsman nearer to Ruth is the one referred to in 4:1 as "Ho, such a one." We might say that this individual represented the Law. In effect, it had first claim on the Lord Jesus Christ; however, it refused its right of redemption. It refused because the Law could never save. Only Boaz, our Heavenly Redeemer, could save.)*

KINSMAN REDEMPTION

13 Tarry this night, and it shall be in the morning, that if he will perform unto you the part of a kinsman, well; let him do the kinsman's part *(this particular one was nearer kinsman to Naomi than Boaz):* but if he will not do the part of a kinsman to you, then will I do the part of a kinsman to you, as the LORD lives: lie down until the morning *(Ruth knew very little about these procedures, but Boaz knew them minutely).*

14 And she lay at his feet until the morning: and she rose up before one could know another *(before daylight).* And he said, Let it not

be known that a woman came into the floor. *(In other words, don't relate to anyone what happened last night. There was no impropriety in Ruth's action. It was the Law and custom of the time. To draw a portion of a kinsman's mantle over one was the legal way of claiming protection and Redemption. Ruth effected this with great delicacy and skill. She chose a public place, such as the threshingfloor, where many persons were present: but not to embarrass Boaz, but to give him liberty to act as he wished, she made her claim under the cover of darkness. Boaz, whose character commands admiration, immediately responded to her Faith and love.)*

15 Also he said, Bring the vail that you had upon you, and hold it. And when she held it, he measured six measures of barley, and laid it on her: and she went into the city *(back to Naomi!)*.

16 And when she came to her mother in law, she *(Naomi)* said, Who are you, my daughter? *(The question actually was, "Are you Boaz's betrothed?")* And she told her all that the man had done to her *(had said to her)*.

17 And she said, These six measures of barley gave he me; for he said to me, Go not empty unto your mother in law. *(Christ, symbolized by Boaz, will give us all that we need, and even more, according to what the Holy Spirit, symbolized by Naomi, has told us to do. When we follow the leading of the Spirit, we will not return empty.)*

18 Then said she, Sit still, my daughter *(herein lies the principle of Salvation by Faith; the second Chapter of Galatians contrasts two principles for the obtaining of life and righteousness: the first is "works of law," which pertained to religious ceremonies, personal moral efforts, and works of the flesh; it can never save; the second is "Salvation by Faith," which depends on no works, but totally upon Christ and what He has done for us at the Cross; the Holy Spirit teaches us that nothing can be had upon the first principle, but everything upon the second; so, Ruth would "sit still," wholly trusting Boaz, and, as a result, obtain her heart's desire)*, until you know how the matter will fall: for the man will not be in rest, until he have finished the thing this day.

CHAPTER 4
(1312 B.C.)
THE INHERITANCE

THEN went Boaz up to the gate, and sat him down there *(this is where business was conducted in cities of that day)*: and, behold, the kinsman of whom Boaz spoke came by *(the one who was nearer kin to Naomi than was Boaz)*; unto whom he said, Ho, such a one! turn aside, sit down here. And he turned aside, and sat down *(desirous of knowing what business that Boaz wanted to discuss)*.

2 And he took ten men of the elders of the city, and said, Sit ye down here. And they sat down *(they were to serve as witnesses)*.

3 And he said unto the kinsman, Naomi, who is come again out of the country of Moab, sells a parcel of land *(has determined to sell this parcel of land)*, which was our brother Elimelech's:

4 And I thought to advertise you, saying, Buy it before the inhabitants, and before the elders of my people. If you will redeem it, redeem it: but if you will not redeem it, then tell me, that I may know: for there is none *(before you)* to redeem it beside you; and I am after you. And he said, I will redeem it *(but found he couldn't!)*.

5 Then said Boaz, What day you buy the field of the hand of Naomi, you must buy it also of Ruth the Moabitess, the wife of the dead, to raise up the name of the dead upon his inheritance. *(This means that the man must marry Ruth, as well as redeem the land. If a child was born to such a union, that child would inherit the land when the parents died, even though the father may even have other children who were older. In this manner, the inheritance would not be lost, which was the intention.)*

6 And the kinsman said, I cannot redeem it for myself, lest I mar my own inheritance *(he was probably already married)*: redeem thou my right to yourself; for I cannot redeem it. *(Boaz had to purchase Ruth from a kinsman who had a prior claim, but who declared that he could not redeem her. The Law has a prior claim to sinners, but it cannot redeem them. Christ, the Divine Kinsman, became Man in order to redeem. It cost Boaz nothing to redeem Ruth, beyond the setting aside of himself and his own interests, but it cost Christ everything to redeem sinners.*

Thus, Ruth, a "wild olive tree," was grafted into, and became a partaker of, "the root and fatness of the olive tree," i.e., Israel; but she could not boast that this was due to any commanding personal claim; all she could say was, "Why have I found grace in your eyes, seeing I am a Gentile?" [2:10] — Williams.)

7 Now this was the manner in former time

in Israel concerning redeeming and concerning changing, for to confirm all things; a man plucked off his shoe, and gave it to his neighbour: and this was a testimony in Israel (when land was sold, the one previously owning the land would give his shoe to the one who had bought it, signifying that he freely gave up his right to walk upon the soil in favor of the person who had acquired the possession).

8 Therefore the kinsman said unto Boaz, Buy it for you. So he drew off his shoe (in other words, Boaz bought the land).

9 And Boaz said unto the elders, and unto all the people, You are witnesses this day, that I have bought all that was Elimelech's, and all that was Chilion's and Mahlon's, of the hand of Naomi (by all the names being mentioned here, even though there was only one estate, there was a succession in the proprietorship).

10 Moreover Ruth the Moabitess, the wife of Mahlon, have I purchased to be my wife, to raise up the name of the dead upon his inheritance, that the name of the dead be not cut off from among his brethren, and from the gate of his place: you are witnesses this day.

BOAZ MARRIES RUTH

11 And all the people who were in the gate, and the elders, said, We are witnesses. The LORD make the woman who is come into your house like Rachel and like Leah, which two did build the House of Israel: and do you worthily in Ephratah, and be famous in Bethlehem (the latter phrase is more a prophecy than a statement; Bethlehem will ever be famous; the reason is that the Son of David, the great descendant of Ruth, would be born in Bethlehem some 1,200 years later; how beautifully and wondrously this prophecy has come to pass):

12 And let your house be like the house of Pharez, whom Tamar bore unto Judah, of the seed which the LORD shall give you of this young woman (to be sure, this "House" was blessed far more than the house of Pharez could ever be blessed, and, in fact, every other house, for it would be the House of the Lord Jesus Christ).

13 So Boaz took Ruth, and she was his wife: and when he went in unto her, the LORD gave her conception, and she bore a son. (When she looked at her newborn baby, I wonder what the thoughts were in her mind. Little did she realize the consequences of it all, and neither do we!)

14 And the women said unto Naomi, Blessed be the LORD, which hath not left you this day without a kinsman, that his name may be famous in Israel. (It is Ruth's little son who is the kinsman referred to, the nearest kinsman, still nearer than Boaz. To be sure, the child, who was the ancestor of David, and, ultimately, the Son of David, is linked to fame in a greater way than even these women could think.)

15 And he (the child) shall be unto you (Naomi) a restorer of your life, and a nourisher of your old age: for your daughter in law, which loves you, which is better to you than seven sons, has born him (given birth to him).

16 And Naomi took the child, and laid it in her bosom, and became nurse unto it.

17 And the women her neighbours gave it a name, saying, There is a son born to Naomi (meaning that he was born to Naomi through Boaz and Ruth, who were fulfilling the Law by raising up seed for the dead [Ruth's dead husband], and keeping his name alive; their seed was reckoned, or counted, to carry on his place in Israel [Deut. 25:5-10]; this "Son," Who would be born of Israel [Naomi], will one day rule the world; His Name ultimately would be "the Lord Jesus Christ," the Son of David, the Son of Abraham [Mat. 1:1]); and they called his name Obed: he is the father of Jesse, the father of David.

RUTH, BOAZ, AND DAVID

18 Now these are the generations of Pharez: Pharez begat Hezron (Esrom).

19 And Hezron begat Ram (Aram), and Ram, begat Amminadab,

20 And Amminadab begat Nahshon (Naason), and Nahshon begat Salmon.

21 And Salmon begat Boaz (Booz), and Boaz begat Obed,

22 And Obed begat Jesse, and Jesse begat David. (Most of the time, the genealogies given in the Bible, exactly as here, are not complete, and neither are they meant to be complete. They are merely meant to link certain individuals with others, although several times removed.

We know that Jesse was the father of David; however, we don't know if Obed was the immediate father of Jesse, or several times removed. In the Hebrew, there is no word for grandfather, or great-grandfather, etc. They are all looked at as the father.

We also know that Rahab married Salmon [Mat. 1:5]; however, we also know that Salmon

was not the immediate father of Boaz, simply because Rahab and Salmon lived several hundreds of years before Boaz; however, we do know that Salmon was the father of Boaz several times removed.

All of this is very important, because it is an *integral part of the genealogy of King David's great descendant, his "Lord," and ours. In other words, it pertains to the Incarnation of Christ, God becoming Man, in order to redeem humanity by dying on a Cross. Nothing is more important than that!)*

THE FIRST BOOK OF
SAMUEL

CHAPTER 1
(1171 B.C.)
SAMUEL'S PARENTS

NOW there was a certain man of Rama-thaim-zophim, of Mount Ephraim, and his name was Elkanah, the son of Jeroham, the son of Elihu, the son of Tohu, the son of Zuph, an Ephrathite *(Elkanah, the father of Samuel, was a Levite, and of the order of the Kohathites, who were responsible for the Vessels of the Sanctuary [Num. 3:27-31]):*

2 And he had two wives; the name of the one was Hannah, and the name of the other Peninnah: and Peninnah had children, but Hannah had no children. *(We find that Elkanah was not untouched by the corruption of his day, for he had two wives. Domestic misery was the result. Hannah had no children, and, in those days, to be barren was a disgrace.)*

3 And this man *(Elkanah)* went up out of his city yearly to worship and to sacrifice unto the LORD of Hosts in Shiloh. *(The Tabernacle was then at Shiloh.)* And the two sons of Eli *(the High Priest)*, Hophni and Phinehas, the Priests of the LORD, were there. *(The latter two were evil men, and yet occupied, officially, a certain relationship to God. Under the Covenant of Law, and its Divinely appointed Priesthood, such a position was possible; but under the Covenant of Grace, where there is no Earthly Priesthood, it is impossible. But men, not recognizing the distinction between the two Covenants, have invented an order of priests and clothed them with the sacramental powers of the sons of Aaron!)*

4 And when the time was that Elkanah offered *(offered Sacrifices)*, he gave to Peninnah his wife, and to all her sons and her daughters, portions:

5 But unto Hannah he gave a worthy portion; for he loved Hannah: but the LORD had shut up her womb. *(The Lord did this for a particular purpose, as He does everything for a particular purpose. It was a test of Hannah's faith, as everything is a test of our faith, all meant to do us good.)*

6 And her adversary *(Peninnah, the other wife of Elkanah)* also provoked her sore, for to make her fret, because the LORD had shut up her womb *(made fun of her!)*.

7 And as he *(Elkanah)* did so year by year, when she *(Hannah)* went up to the House of the LORD, so she *(Peninnah)* provoked her; therefore she *(Hannah)* wept, and did not eat. *(This "test" went on for several years. Evidently, Peninnah was provoking Hannah by telling her that she was cursed by God, hence, the failure to bear children. This hurt her much, as would be obvious, and the Lord allowed it to happen. So, this test was not only for Hannah, but Peninnah, as well, with the latter failing miserably!)*

8 Then said Elkanah her husband to her, Hannah, why do you weep? and why do you not eat? and why is your heart grieved? am I not better to you than ten sons?

HANNAH'S PRAYER AND VOW

9 So Hannah rose up after they had eaten in Shiloh, and after they had drunk *(the Peace Offering).* Now Eli the Priest *(High Priest)* sat upon a seat by a post of the Temple of the LORD *(the first time the Tabernacle is referred to as a "Temple").*

10 And she *(Hannah)* was in bitterness of soul, and prayed unto the LORD, and wept sore *(this is the type of praying that the Lord always hears and answers, that is, if such is in His Perfect Will).*

11 And she vowed a vow, and said, O LORD of hosts *("Jehovah Sabaioth"; could be translated "Lord of armies")*, if You will indeed look on the affliction of Your handmaid *(the word "handmaid" denotes "humility")*, and remember me, and not forget Your handmaid, but will give unto Your handmaid a man child *(she wanted a little boy)*, then I will give him unto the LORD all the days of his life, and there shall no razor come upon his head *(in other words, she would dedicate him as a Nazarite, even from birth, which he would be all of his life; this was her "vow").*

12 And it came to pass, as she continued praying before the LORD, that Eli marked her mouth *(evidently, where she was praying, she could be seen by Eli).*

13 Now Hannah, she spoke in her heart; only

her lips moved, but her voice was not heard *(she was praying silently)*: therefore Eli thought she had been drunk. *(Two things are said here: 1. Eli thinking that Hannah was drunk portrays that such must have been common at the time; and, 2. The spirituality of the High Priest evidently was not what it should have been, or he would have detected the Godly spirit of this woman.)*

14 And Eli said unto her, How long will you be drunk? put away your wine from you *(this must have stung Hannah)*.

15 And Hannah answered and said, No, my lord, I am a woman of a sorrowful spirit: I have drunk neither wine nor strong drink, but have poured out my soul before the LORD *(evidently, Eli had not seen very much of such a prayerful attitude around the Tabernacle; regrettably, much of the modern Church falls into the same category)*.

16 Count not your handmaid for a daughter of Belial *(worthless)*: for out of the abundance of my complaint and grief have I spoken hitherto.

17 Then Eli answered and said, Go in peace: and the God of Israel grant you your petition that you have asked of Him. *(Whatever spiritual condition which characterized Eli, still, God used him to give Hannah this great word of prophecy. Her prayer had been heard after all these years.)*

18 And she said, Let your handmaid find grace in your sight. So the woman went her way, and did eat, and her countenance was no more sad. *(She knew the Lord had heard, and she knew the answer was on the way. It's a wonderful thing when one knows that the Lord has heard our petition, and the answer is positive.)*

19 And they rose up in the morning early, and worshipped before the LORD, and returned, and came to their house to Ramah: and Elkanah knew Hannah his wife *(Biblical terminology for sexual relations)*; and the LORD remembered her *(she became pregnant)*.

THE BIRTH OF SAMUEL

20 Wherefore it came to pass, when the time was come about after Hannah had conceived, that she bore a son, and called his name Samuel, saying, Because I have asked him of the LORD. *(Samuel would be the last Judge of Israel, and the first man to stand in the office of the Prophet [Acts 3:24]. In fact, he was one of the greatest men of God who ever lived. He will anoint*

David to be king, through whose family the Messiah would ultimately come [I Sam. 16:1, 11-13; II Sam. 7:11-13].)*

21 And the man Elkanah, and all his house, went up to offer unto the LORD the yearly sacrifice, and his vow *(his vow shows that Elkanah had ratified Hannah's words by adding thereto a Thank Offering from himself)*.

22 But Hannah went not up; for she said unto her husband, I will not go up until the child be weaned *(probably 3-5 years old; weaning was delayed much longer in that culture than with us presently)*, and then I will bring him, that he may appear before the LORD, and there abide for ever.

23 And Elkanah her husband said unto her, Do what seems thee good; tarry until you have weaned him; only the LORD establish His Word. So the woman abode *(stayed home)*, and gave her son suck until she weaned him.

THE VOW

24 And when she had weaned him, she took him up with her *(to the Tabernacle)*, with three bullocks *(for Sacrifice)*, and one ephah of flour *(a Thank Offering)*, and a bottle of wine *(a Drink Offering)*, and brought him unto the House of the LORD in Shiloh *(where the Tabernacle was located)*: and the child was young *(probably close to 5 years old)*.

25 And they slew a bullock, and brought the child to Eli.

26 And she said, Oh my lord, as your soul lives, my lord, I am the woman that stood by you here, praying unto the LORD.

27 For this child I prayed; and the LORD has given me my petition which I asked of Him:

28 Therefore also I have lent him to the LORD *(the word "lent" is not the best translation; actually, Hannah is saying, "I have given him to the Lord")*; as long as he lives he shall be lent *(given)* to the LORD *(and he was)*. And he *(should have been translated "they")* worshipped the LORD there.

CHAPTER 2

(1165 B.C.)

THE SONG OF HANNAH

AND Hannah prayed *(the Chaldee reads, "And Hannah prayed in the Spirit of Prophecy")*, and said, My heart rejoices in the LORD, my horn *(a part of a woman's headdress, at least in that culture, at that time)* is exalted in

the LORD: my mouth is enlarged over my enemies; because I rejoice in Your Salvation *(that Salvation is Christ, which Hannah will acknowledge in Verse 10).*

2 There is none holy as the LORD *(the reason for her holy joy is first God's absolute Holiness)*: for there is none beside You *(the second reason is His absolute existence, in which she finds the proof of His Holiness)*: neither is there any rock like our God *(in referring to the Lord as a "Rock," she assigns to Him strength, calm, immovable, enduring, but a strength which avails for the safety of His People).*

3 Talk no more so exceeding proudly; let not arrogancy come out of your mouth: for the LORD is a God of knowledge, and by Him actions are weighed. *(God judges all things in the light of His Omniscience, which signifies every type of knowledge, past, present, and future. Knowing this, man had best be careful as to what he says.)*

4 The bows of the mighty men are broken, and they who stumbled are girded with strength *(the working of this attribute of Deity tells us that human events are not the result of chance, but of God's direction).*

5 They who were full have hired out themselves for bread; and they who were hungry ceased: so that the barren has born seven; and she who has many children is waxed feeble *(this Verse typifies the Gentile Church, which is now abundant, by contrast with Israel, who is now barren, even though Hannah would not have understood this [Gal. 4:27]).*

6 The LORD kills, and makes alive: He brings down to the grave, and brings up *(oftentimes, the Lord brings a man to the very brink of the grave, and then, when all hope seems past, raises him up again).*

7 The LORD makes poor, and makes rich: he brings low, and lifts up *(therefore, "promotion comes from the Lord" [Ps. 75:6-7]).*

8 He raises up the poor out of the dust, and lifts up the beggar from the dunghill, to set them among princes, and to make them inherit the Throne of Glory: for the pillars of the Earth are the LORD's, and He has set the world upon them. *(This speaks of Salvation, when man is raised out of dust to the Glory of God. The "pillars" refer to everything hanging upon God and God Alone. This is a fact of Divine Government, which is distasteful to man.)*

9 He will keep the feet of His Saints *(the Lord does such by the Believer placing his Faith and trust exclusively in Christ and the Cross,* which then gives the Holy Spirit latitude to work in one's life, Who Alone can bring about the needed change and strength [Rom. 6:3-14; 8:1-2, 11])*, and the wicked shall be silent in darkness; for by strength shall no man prevail *("the flesh," one's own personal strength [Rom. 8:1, 8]).*

10 The adversaries of the LORD shall be broken to pieces *(whoever it be who contends with Him)*; out of Heaven shall He thunder upon them *(the Lord is the supreme Judge)*: the LORD shall judge the ends of the Earth *(the whole Earth up to its remotest quarters)*; and He shall give strength unto His King *(is a distinct prophecy of David's kingdom)*, and exalt the horn of His Anointed. *(Looks onward to the Messiah, David's greater Son. This is the first time that the term "His Anointed" is used, as it refers to the Messiah. It is even more special in that Hannah used it. From this point on, others take up the theme of God's Anointed One — the Messiah [Ps. 2:2; 45:7; Isa. 61:1; Dan. 9:25-26]. And so the song of Hannah ends here, but actually continues on in the hearts and lives of untold millions.)*

11 And Elkanah went to Ramah to his house. And the child *(Samuel)* did minister unto the LORD before Eli the Priest *(certain duties, which he, as a child, could perform, were assigned to him).*

ELI'S SONS

12 Now the sons of Eli were sons of Belial *(worthless, even though they were Priests)*; they knew not the LORD *(how many modern Preachers fall into the same category?).*

13 And the Priest's custom with the people was, that, when any man offered Sacrifice, the Priest's servant came, while the flesh was in seething, with a fleshhook of three teeth in his hand;

14 And he struck it into the pan, or kettle, or caldron, or pot; all that the fleshhook brought up the Priest took for himself. So they did in Shiloh unto all the Israelites who came thither.

15 Also before they burnt the fat, the Priest's servant came, and said to the man who sacrificed, Give flesh to roast for the Priest; for he will not have sodden flesh of you, but raw.

16 And if any man said unto him, Let them not fail to burn the fat presently, and then take as much as your soul desires; then he would answer him, No; but you shall give it me now: and if not, I will take it by force.

17 Wherefore the sin of the young men was

very great before the LORD: for men abhorred the Offering of the LORD. *(The legal due of the Priests was for the right shoulder and the wave breast; but, before he took them, they were to be consecrated to God by the burning of the fat upon the Altar [Lev. 3:5; 7:31, 34]. But, beside the due and legal portion, which, nevertheless, they took in an illegal way, they demanded a part of the flesh reserved for the feast of the offerer, and to which they had absolutely no right [Lev. 8:31; II Chron. 35:13]. Considering the situation, the people of Israel were loathe to bring Sacrifices to the Lord, because of these evil Priests.)*

SAMUEL

18 But Samuel ministered before the LORD, being a child *(in his early teens)*, girded with a linen Ephod *(a linen robe; there seemed to have been many irregularities in the Tabernacle program at that time; first of all, no child was supposed to minister to the Lord in the Tabernacle; even though the Lord would not hold this against Samuel, He would hold it against Eli, who was responsible)*.

19 Moreover his mother made him a little coat, and brought it to him from year to year, when she came up with her husband to offer the yearly sacrifice *(this was the garment worn under the Ephod)*.

HANNAH

20 And Eli blessed Elkanah and his wife, and said, The LORD give you seed of this woman for the loan which is lent *(given)* to the LORD. And they went unto their own home *(Hannah had not asked simply for a son, but for a son whom she might dedicate to God; and now Eli prays that Jehovah will give her children to be her own)*.

21 And the LORD visited Hannah, so that she conceived, and bore three sons and two daughters. And the child Samuel grew before the LORD *(the prayer of Eli was answered)*.

JUDGMENT

22 Now Eli was very old, and heard all that his sons did unto all Israel; and how they lay with the women who assembled at the door of the Tabernacle of the congregation *(their sin was the greater because the women whom they corrupted were those dedicated to Tabernacle service [Ex. 38:8])*.

23 And he said unto them, Why do ye such things? for I hear of your evil dealings by all this people. *(The two sons of Eli who were Priests were Hophni and Phinehas. We may ask as to why the Lord didn't kill these two Priests as He killed Nadab and Abihu? [Lev. 10:1-2]. The answer is: the Lord, at that time, was dwelling in power in the camp; but during Eli's time, He had withdrawn Himself because of Israel's apostasy. There is a great difference in an electric wire when charged and not charged.)*

24 Nay, my sons; for it is no good report that I hear: you make the LORD's people to transgress *(you make Jehovah's people cease to worship Him)*.

25 If one man sin against another, the judge shall judge him: but if a man sin against the LORD, who shall intreat for him? Notwithstanding they hearkened not unto the voice of their father, because the LORD would slay them. *(They had passed the point of no return, and judgment would soon come. I wonder how many modern Preachers fall into the same category?)*

26 And the child Samuel grew on, and was in favour both with the LORD, and also with men. *(The Holy Spirit keeps mentioning this, signifying its importance [Vs. 21].)*

27 And there came a man of God unto Eli *(the Holy Spirit did not tell us who he was)*, and said unto him, Thus saith the LORD, Did I plainly appear unto the house of your father, when they were in Egypt in Pharaoh's house?

28 And did I choose him *(Aaron)* out of all the Tribes of Israel to be My Priest, to offer upon My Altar, to burn incense, to wear an Ephod before Me? and did I give unto the house of your father all the Offerings made by fire of the Children of Israel?

29 Wherefore kick ye at My Sacrifice and at My Offering, which I have commanded in My habitation; and honourest your sons above Me, to make yourselves fat with the chiefest of all the Offerings of Israel My people? *(Eli's sons treated the Ordinances, which had raised them to rank, and given them wealth and power, as if they were mundane and insignificant things. And Eli, instead of removing them from the office which they disgraced, preferred the ties of relationship to his duty to God and the moral welfare of the people.)*

30 Wherefore the LORD God of Israel said, I said indeed that your house, and the house of your father, should walk before Me for ever: but now the LORD says, Be it far from Me; for them who honour Me I will honour, and they

who despise Me shall be lightly esteemed. *(Smith says, "By thus acting, Eli became an accomplice in the abomination of his sons, and God, therefore, revoked his grant of a perpetual Priesthood." The promise had been made to Aaron's family as a whole [Ex. 29:9], and had then been renewed to the house of Eleazar [Num. 25:13]. Under Eli, the line of Ithamar, another son of Aaron, had ascended, but now it will diminish. This means that God's Promises are conditional. He honors those who honor Him, etc.)*

31 Behold, the days come, that I will cut off your arm, and the arm of your father's house *(the arm is the usual metaphor for strength)*, that there shall not be an old man in your house *(the prophecy was amply fulfilled in the slaughter of Eli's house, which took place a little later)*.

32 And you shall see an enemy in My habitation, in all the wealth which God shall give Israel: and there shall not be an old man in your house for ever *(while Israel will be blessed, his house will diminish)*.

33 And the man of yours, whom I shall not cut off from My Altar, shall be to consume your eyes, and to grieve your heart: and all the increase of your house shall die in the flower of their age *(cut down as young men, which they were)*.

34 And this shall be a sign unto you, that shall come upon your two sons, on Hophni and Phinehas; in one day they shall die both of them *(they died in battle, as the following account will proclaim)*.

35 And I will raise Me up a faithful Priest, who shall do according to that which is in My heart and in My mind: and I will build Him a sure house; and He shall walk before My anointed for ever *(this speaks of the Lord Jesus Christ, our Great High Priest, Who will rule in the Millennial Reign; the Priests who will serve under Him will also be "anointed," and will be so forever)*.

36 And it shall come to pass, that every one who is left in your house shall come and crouch to him for a piece of silver and a morsel of bread, and shall say, Put me, I pray you, into one of the Priests' offices, that I may eat a piece of bread. *(In the near future, this did happen to the descendants of Eli. After a period of time, it seems that Samuel did much to raise from their misery the descendants of Eli, and there is no reason for imagining that the family ever again fell into distress, nor do the terms of the prophecy warrant such a supposition.)*

CHAPTER 3
(1165 B.C.)
SAMUEL

AND the child Samuel ministered unto the LORD before Eli *(served in the Tabernacle)*. And the Word of the LORD was precious *(rare)* in those days; there was no open vision. *(Although prophetic utterances had been given, even as we witnessed in the last Chapter, still, the Office of the Prophet had not yet been established. In fact, Samuel would be the first one to occupy that office. Considering that the Priesthood was corrupt, the nation, for all practical purposes, was then without spiritual leadership.)*

2 And it came to pass at that time, when Eli was laid down in his place, and his eyes began to wax dim, that he could not see *(it was night, and, as well, Eli was almost blind)*;

3 And ere the Lamp of God went out in the Temple of the LORD *(meaning that the Golden Lampstand, which was to be resupplied with oil morning and evening [9 a.m. and 3 p.m.], had obviously been neglected)*, where the Ark of God was *(the Ark of God was in the Holy of Holies, while the Lampstand was in the Holy Place, which was immediately in front of the Holy of Holies, separated by a Veil)*, and Samuel was laid down to sleep *(as stated, it was night)*;

4 That the LORD called Samuel: and he answered, Here am I *(it is believed that Samuel possibly was about 14 or 15 years old at this time)*.

5 And he ran unto Eli, and said, Here am I; for you called me. And he *(Eli)* said, I called not; lie down again. And he went and lay down.

6 And the LORD called yet again, Samuel. And Samuel arose and went to Eli, and said, Here am I; for you did call me. And he answered, I called not, my son; lie down again.

7 Now Samuel did not yet know the LORD, neither was the Word of the LORD yet revealed unto him *(it didn't mean that the boy did not know the Lord regarding Salvation, but that he did not yet know Him regarding the prophetic voice; that is soon to change)*.

8 And the LORD called Samuel again the third time. And he arose and went to Eli, and said, Here am I; for you did call me. And Eli perceived that the LORD had called the child *(the Lord now reveals Himself to Israel, but to a boy!)*.

9 Therefore Eli said unto Samuel, Go, lie down: and it shall be, if He call you, that you shall say, Speak, LORD; for Your servant hears.

So Samuel went and lay down in his place (*from all this, we know that Eli knew the Ways of the Lord, but he had not walked in those ways*).

THE MESSAGE

10 And the LORD came, and stood, and called as at other times (*the last three times*), Samuel, Samuel (*this is another proof that the Jehovah of the Old Testament and the Jesus of the New Testament are One and The Same; He Who said, "Samuel, Samuel," was the very same One Who said, "Martha, Martha," and "Simon, Simon"; the style reveals the Author*). Then Samuel answered, Speak; for Your servant hears.

11 And the LORD said to Samuel, Behold, I will do a thing in Israel, at which both the ears of every one who hears it shall tingle. (*Even though the Word of the Lord may be delayed a few years, ultimately, it will be fulfilled. It happened exactly as the Lord said, with the defeat of Israel in battle, the capture of the Ark of the Covenant by the Philistines, and, as well, the destruction of the Sanctuary at Shiloh.*)

12 In that day I will perform against Eli all things which I have spoken concerning his house: when I begin, I will also make an end. (*With proper Repentance, could Eli have changed the course of events? True Repentance always changes things. Some judgment may have fallen, but it would have been lessened greatly.*)

13 For I have told him that I will judge his house for ever for the iniquity which he knows; because his sons made themselves vile, and he restrained them not. (*These Messages were warnings, but, despite the warnings, there is no record that Eli changed anything. Why? Probably the greatest reason is unbelief.*)

14 And therefore I have sworn unto the house of Eli, that the iniquity of Eli's house shall not be purged with Sacrifice nor Offering for ever. (*Sacrifices, as Biblical as they were, had no effect if there was no Repentance. It is the same presently. Calvary is a fact; however, its benefits are effective only for those who will truly repent, thereby making the Lord their Saviour.*)

THE MESSAGE RELAYED

15 And Samuel lay until the morning, and opened the doors of the House of the LORD (*which was obviously one of his duties*). And Samuel feared to show Eli the Vision.

16 Then Eli called Samuel, and said, Samuel, my son. And he answered, Here am I.

17 And he said, What is the thing that the LORD has said unto you? I pray you hide it not from me: God do so to you, and more also, if you hide any thing from me of all the things that He said unto you.

18 And Samuel told him every whit, and hid nothing from him. And he said, It is the LORD: let Him do what seems Him good. (*Despite Eli hearing these words, there is still no record that the old man repented. True Repentance would have demanded that he move his sons out of the Priesthood, and denounce their activities, and do so publicly. For whatever reasons, there is no record that he did such!*)

THE PROPHET

19 And Samuel grew (*Samuel is now a young man*), and the LORD was with him, and did let none of his words fall to the ground (*in other words, his Prophecies were all of the Lord*).

20 And all Israel from Dan even to Beersheba knew that Samuel was established to be a Prophet of the LORD. (*As stated, even though there had previously been Prophets in Israel, Samuel was the first one to stand in this established office. Throughout the balance of Israel's history, the Lord led the nation through the Ministry of the Prophet. While some of the announcements of the Prophets were predictions, their Ministry was mostly a Ministry of Righteousness. They were ever called to whip the nation into shape. In fact, John the Baptist, the greatest Prophet of them all, made precious few predictions, but served almost altogether as a Preacher of Righteousness. God is still calling Prophets presently [Eph. 4:11]; however, the Church is presently led by the Ministry of the Apostle, which credentials are a special Message from the Lord as it regards the Church, but which will always coincide with the Word of the Lord [Rom. 1:1-5].*)

21 And the LORD appeared again in Shiloh: for the LORD revealed Himself to Samuel in Shiloh by the Word of the LORD (*the Lord now begins to speak to Samuel on a regular basis*).

CHAPTER 4
(1141 B.C.)
THE PHILISTINES

AND the word of Samuel came to all Israel (*this phrase, according to the manuscripts, belongs at the conclusion of the last Verse of the*

last Chapter; it makes it seem here as if the Lord through Samuel is calling Israel to battle, which is not the case). **Now Israel went out against the Philistines to battle, and pitched beside Eben-ezer: and the Philistines pitched in Aphek** (it seems that Israel had enjoyed comparative freedom and peace for a period of time, up to now).

2 And the Philistines put themselves in array against Israel: and when they joined battle, Israel was smitten before the Philistines: and they slew of the army in the field about four thousand men.

3 And when the people were come into the camp, the elders of Israel said, Wherefore has the LORD smitten us to day before the Philistines? Let us fetch the Ark of the Covenant of the LORD out of Shiloh unto us, that, when it comes among us, it may save us out of the hand of our enemies. (They didn't ask the Lord if they could take the Ark of the Covenant, neither did the Lord tell them to do so. If Israel had fallen on their faces before God in weeping and contrition, repenting of their sins before the door of the Tabernacle, the future could have been different. Instead, they would try to use the Ark as a magic symbol, thinking, somehow, it would atone for their evil and guarantee the Presence and Blessings of God. How so much today does the modern Church follow suit!)

4 So the people sent to Shiloh, that they might bring from thence the Ark of the Covenant of the LORD of hosts, which dwells between the Cherubims: and the two sons of Eli, Hophni and Phinehas, were there with the Ark of the Covenant of God (two evil men accompanied the Ark, which should tell us something about the spiritual condition of Israel).

5 And when the Ark of the Covenant of the LORD came into the camp, all Israel shouted with a great shout, so that the Earth rang again. (As the heart gets further and further from God, symbols and ceremonies become very important. As Israel, many try to cover up the barrenness of their possession by the loudness of their profession. Israel had nothing to shout about. They needed to repent.)

6 And when the Philistines heard the noise of the shout, they said, What means the noise of this great shout in the camp of the Hebrews? And they understood that the Ark of the LORD was come into the camp.

7 And the Philistines were afraid, for they said, God is come into the camp. And they said, Woe unto us! for there has not been such a thing heretofore. (How wonderful it would have been if God had actually come into the camp!)

8 Woe unto us! who shall deliver us out of the hand of these mighty Gods? these are the Gods that smote the Egyptians with all the plagues in the wilderness. (The Ark was but a symbol of the Divine Presence. Now, when confronted by the enemy, the symbol was made to displace the Substance; however, such was not to be, even as such could not be. Had God overthrown the Philistines at Aphek, He would thereby have associated Himself with the evil of His people. God can make no compromise with evil; for the Lord to have granted victory that day would have shown that God thought lightly of sin; and that He was willing to identify Himself with the moral condition of a people living in willing bondage to the most gross of evils — Williams.)

9 Be strong, and quit yourselves like men, O ye Philistines, that you be not servants unto the Hebrews, as they have been to you: quit yourselves like men, and fight. (The Philistine was a domestic, not a foreign, enemy. He illustrates the power of the enemy inside the professing Christian Church, and is more to be dreaded than any enemy who stands outside.)

10 And the Philistines fought, and Israel was smitten, and they fled every man into his tent: and there was a very great slaughter; for there fell of Israel thirty thousand footmen (a terrible slaughter! They are called "footmen" because the Israelites had neither cavalry nor chariots).

THE ARK CAPTURED

11 And the Ark of God was taken; and the two sons of Eli, Hophni and Phinehas, were slain (exactly as the Lord had said [2:34]; the greater tragedy was that the "Ark of God" was taken by the enemy).

THE DEATH OF ELI

12 And there ran a man of Benjamin out of the army, and came to Shiloh (where the Tabernacle was located) **the same day with his clothes rent, and with earth upon his head** (a sign of tragedy).

13 And when he came, lo, Eli sat upon a seat by the wayside watching: for his heart trembled for the Ark of God. And when the man came into the city, and told it, all the city cried out.

14 And when Eli heard the noise of the crying, he said, What means the noise of this tumult? And the man came in hastily, and told Eli.

15 Now Eli was ninety and eight years old; and his eyes were dim, that he could not see *(couldn't see well)*.

16 And the man said unto Eli, I am he who came out of the army, and I fled to day out of the army. And he said, What is there done, my son?

17 And the messenger answered and said, Israel is fled before the Philistines, and there has been also a great slaughter among the people, and your two sons also, Hophni and Phinehas, are dead, and the Ark of God is taken.

18 And it came to pass, when he made mention of the Ark of God, that he fell from off the seat backward by the side of the gate, and his neck broke, and he died: for he was an old man, and heavy. And he had judged Israel forty years. *(Had he judged in fellowship with God, and in obedience to the Scriptures, the disasters that took place on this day of his death would never have happened; and yet, in his death, he showed that the interests of God's Kingdom had a true place in his heart. Three messages were given to Eli: 1. The battle is lost, and thirty thousand Israelites are dead; 2. Your two sons, Hophni and Phinehas, are dead; and, 3. The Ark of God is taken. While each message was tragic, the loss of the Ark of God was the most tragic of all!)*

ICHABOD

19 And his daughter in law, Phinehas' wife, was with child, near to be delivered: and when she heard the tidings that the Ark of God was taken, and that her father in law and her husband were dead, she bowed herself and travailed; for her pains came upon her.

20 And about the time of her death the women who stood by her said unto her, Fear not; for you have born a son. But she answered not, neither did she regard it.

21 And she named the child Ichabod, saying, The glory is departed from Israel: because the Ark of the God was taken, and because of her father in law and her husband.

22 And she said, The glory is departed from Israel: for the Ark of God is taken. *(Concerning this, Williams says, "The last four Verses of this Chapter throw a shaft of light across the darkness; and the detail into which the Holy Spirit enters in the narrative shows how precious to Him was the measure of Divine life in the soul of this true-hearted woman. She is placed here upon the face of the Divine record with great vividness. The Holy Spirit recalls her affection for her aged father-in-law, and for her godless and faithless husband, but points with emphasis to the fact that grief for God's Kingdom swallowed up the joy of motherhood" [Jn. 16:21].)*

CHAPTER 5
(1141 B.C.)
THE ARK OF GOD

AND the Philistines took the Ark of God, and brought it from Eben-ezer unto Ashdod. *(The Ark of God would not be a blessing to unrepentant Israel, but it would be a curse to the mocking Philistines. We will learn from this Chapter that God rules all.)*

2 When the Philistines took the Ark of God, they brought it into the house of Dagon, and set it by Dagon. *(The Philistines, knowing nothing about the ways of God, would automatically think that Israel was defeated because their god Dagon was more powerful than Israel's God, Who was represented by the Ark. Unfortunately, unregenerate men always make ridiculous judgments regarding God [I Cor. 2:14]. This so-called god, Dagon, was portrayed as a man to the waist and with the tail of a fish. The Philistines putting the Ark of the Covenant by this fish-god Dagon was intended as a public demonstration that the God of the Israelites was inferior to, and had been vanquished by, the national deity of the Philistines.)*

3 And when they of Ashdod arose early on the morrow, behold, Dagon was fallen upon his face to the earth before the Ark of the LORD. And they *(the priests of Dagon)* took Dagon, and set him in his place again. *(At Ashdod, one of the five main cities of Philistia, there was a temple of Dagon, the national god. Their god falling over was a way of God telling the Philistines that "every knee shall bow, and every tongue shall confess" [Rom. 14:11]. There is only one God, and all others that call themselves god, in effect, are no gods at all. They were actually representatives of demon spirits, exactly as false religions fall into the same category presently.)*

4 And when they arose early on the morrow morning, behold, Dagon was fallen upon his face to the ground before the Ark of the

LORD; and the head of Dagon and both the palms of his hands were cut off upon the threshold; only the stump of Dagon was left to him *(by severing the head and the hands, the Lord was telling the Philistines that their god had no power against Him).*

5 Therefore neither the priests of Dagon, nor any who come into Dagon's house, tread on the threshold of Dagon in Ashdod unto this day *(apparently, the Books of Samuel were written some time after the events recorded in them took place).*

6 But the hand of the LORD was heavy upon them of Ashdod, and He destroyed them, and smote them with emerods *(skin tumors),* even Ashdod and the coasts thereof.

JUDGMENT

7 And when the men of Ashdod saw that it was so, they said, The Ark of the God of Israel shall not abide with us: for his hand is sore upon us, and upon Dagon our god. *(Williams says, "It is not at all a pleasant thing for the people of this world to have God in their midst. He keeps up a perpetual controversy with their sins and their idolatries; and as the Philistines were not willing to become His People, they determined that the best thing they could do was to get rid of Him. In fact, that attitude has not changed, being the spirit of society presently.")*

8 They sent therefore and gathered all the lords of the Philistines unto them, and said, What shall we do with the Ark of the God of Israel? And they answered, Let the Ark of the God of Israel be carried about unto Gath. And they carried the Ark of the God of Israel about thither *(in their superstition, they evidently thought that possibly a change of cities in Philistia would solve their problems; they were to find out differently).*

9 And it was so, that, after they had carried it about, the hand of the LORD was against the city with a very great destruction: and he smote the men of the city, both small and great, and they had emerods in their secret parts *(the idea seems to be that the tumors buried themselves deep in the flesh and, becoming thus incurable, ended in causing the death of the sufferers).*

EKRON

10 Therefore they sent the Ark of God to Ekron *(another Philistine city).* And it came to pass, as the Ark of God came to Ekron, that the Ekronites cried out, saying, They have brought about the Ark of the God of Israel to us, to slay us and our people. *(It is strange that they saw the great Power of God, but still would not yield to Him. The only thought was, "Get rid of the Ark.")*

11 So they sent and gathered together all the lords of the Philistines, and said, Send away the Ark of the God of Israel, and let it go again to His Own place, that it slay us not, and our people: for there was a deadly destruction throughout all the city; the Hand of God was very heavy there *("deadly destruction," in the Hebrew, refers to many who were dying, and many who had died).*

12 And the men who died not were smitten with the emerods: and the cry of the city went up to Heaven.

CHAPTER 6
(1140 B.C.)
COUNSEL

AND the Ark of the LORD was in the country of the Philistines seven months *(it could have been seven months of Heaven, had the Philistines only accepted the Lord; otherwise, it was seven months of Hell!).*

2 And the Philistines called for the priests and the diviners, saying, What shall we do to the Ark of the LORD? tell us wherewith we shall send it to his place. *(Amazing is the ability of man to resist and reject God. The deep ignorance and incurable rebellion of man's heart appear throughout this episode. When God evidenced His mighty Power before the Philistines, they were convinced, but not converted. Men, presently, proudly declare that they will become Christians if convinced by evidence. They deceive themselves. They are by nature Philistines, and Philistines they will remain, in spite of the most overwhelming proof of God's Being and Power.)*

3 And they said, If you send away the Ark of the God of Israel, send it not empty; but in any wise return Him a trespass offering: then you shall be healed, and it shall be known to you why His hand is not removed from you *(they were still trying to convince themselves that quite possibly their problems were not due to the Ark of God).*

4 Then said they, What shall be the trespass offering which we shall return to Him? They answered, Five golden emerods, and five

golden mice, according to the number of the lords of the Philistines: for one plague was on you all, and on your lords. *(Is it any different presently? We try to give God our talent, education, ability, etc. He will accept none of it. He will only accept His Son, the Lord Jesus Christ, and the Blood that was shed at Calvary's Cross [Mat. 3:17].)*

5 Wherefore you shall make images of your emerods, and images of your mice that mar the land; and you shall give glory unto the God of Israel: peradventure He will lighten His hand from off you, and from off your gods, and from off your land. *(Thinking that the giving of these images to the Lord would give Him glory presents the normal idea of the unredeemed. They do not know God, nor anything about God. It is called "total depravity." How can one know the Lord, when one is dead [dead to God] in trespasses and sins [Eph. 2:1].)*

6 Wherefore then do you harden your hearts, as the Egyptians and Pharaoh hardened their hearts? when He had wrought wonderfully among them, did they not let the people go, and they departed? *(On this reference to Egypt, it is remarkable that Dagon's priests so correctly point out that it was the stubbornness of the Egyptians which made their punishment so severe. They knew all of this, but they still wouldn't accept the Lord.)*

7 Now therefore make a new cart, and take two milch kine *(two cows)*, on which there hath come no yoke, and tie the kine to the cart, and bring their calves home from them *(the separation of the cows from their calves was for the purpose of demonstrating whether the plague was supernatural after all; if, however, the cows acted in a manner contrary to nature, their last doubt would be removed, and that's exactly what happened!)*:

8 And take the Ark of the LORD, and lay it upon the cart; and put the jewels of gold, which you return Him for a trespass offering, in a coffer by the side thereof; and send it away, that it may go *(on this cart they would place the Ark of the Covenant. This was contrary to the Law of God, because the Ark was to be borne by Priests who were consecrated and otherwise qualified to do so. Being ignorant of the Word of God, the Philistines would escape the judgment of this act; however, David's "new cart" would produce sad results [II Sam. 6:1-11]).*

9 And see, if it goes up by the way of His own coast to Beth-shemesh, then He has done us this great evil: but if not, then we shall know that it is not His hand that smote us: it was a chance that happened to us *(if the cows, unaccustomed to the yoke, left their calves behind, and drew the cart by the most direct route unto the land of Judah, this would give the required proof that the Philistines were smitten by the hand of Jehovah, and that it was no mere chance that had happened unto them).*

THE RETURN OF THE ARK

10 And the men did so; and took two milch cows, and tied them to the cart, and shut up their calves at home:

11 And they laid the Ark of the LORD upon the cart, and the coffer with the mice of gold and the images of their emerods.

12 And the cows took the straight way to the way of Beth-shemesh, and went along the highway, lowing as they went, and turned not aside to the right hand or to the left; and the lords of the Philistines went after them unto the border of Beth-shemesh *(this action, the cows leaving their calves, and especially going straight toward Beth-shemesh, proved to the Philistines, beyond the shadow of a doubt, that all of this was of the Lord).*

13 And they of Beth-shemesh were reaping their wheat harvest in the valley: and they lifted up their eyes, and saw the Ark, and rejoiced to see it.

14 And the cart came into the field of Joshua, a Beth-shemite, and stood there, where there was a great stone: and they did cleave the wood of the cart, and offered the cows *(as)* a Burnt Offering unto the LORD.

15 And the Levites took down the Ark of the LORD, and the coffer that was with it, wherein the jewels of gold were, and put them on the great stone: and the men of Beth-shemesh offered Burnt Offerings and sacrificed Sacrifices the same day unto the LORD. *(As we see here, the Israelites had an inquisitive irreverence in respect to the Ark. God had commanded that it should be veiled by the curtains of the Tabernacle, and only approached through a Divinely appointed High Priest, with confession of sin, and the presentation of atoning blood. These people, like many today, pushed all of the Word of the Lord aside and, assisted by the Levites, exposed the Ark, and, one might even say, the Throne of God, to public view.*

The Ark was not only the Throne of God on Earth, but was also, as revealed in the Books of Exodus and Leviticus, a beautiful symbol of Christ

in His essential Deity and sinless Humanity. Concerning this, Williams said, "Ever since He rose from the dead, many who profess to be His disciples not only deny Him in His Office as the Atoning Mediator between God and men, but, with bold impiety, try to subject His mysterious nature to the demonstrations of human wisdom, impelled by the same spirit which urged the men at Beth-shemesh to look into the Ark.")

16 And when the five lords of the Philistines had seen it, they returned to Ekron the same day.

17 And these are the golden emerods which the Philistines returned for a trespass offering unto the LORD; for Ashdod one, for Gaza one, for Askelon one, for Gath one, for Ekron one;

18 And the golden mice, according to the number of all the cities of the Philistines belonging to the five lords, both of fenced cities, and of country villages, even unto the great stone of Abel, whereon they set down the Ark of the LORD: which stone remains unto this day in the field of Joshua, the Beth-shemite.

19 And He *(the Lord)* smote the men of Beth-shemesh, because they had looked into the Ark of the LORD, even He smote of the people fifty thousand and threescore and ten men: and the people lamented, because the LORD had smitten many of the people with a great slaughter. *(First of all, the people of Israel, except for the soldiers in the previous battle lost, had never seen the Ark of God. As well, they evidently had not been taught the proper respect and reverence for this which was the holiest of God. In fact, their curiosity was little different than the Philistines'.*

There is some question here regarding the number given of the people slain, simply because of the smallness of the population in this area and the similarity of the Hebrew letters, which could have caused a copyist mistake. In fact, the Septuagint reads, "He smote among them seventy men, including fifty of the men's thousand." Even seventy killed in such a small place would constitute a great loss. At any rate, whatever the actual number, men died because of their casual curiosity.)

20 And the men of Beth-shemesh said, Who is able to stand before this holy LORD God? and to whom shall He go up from us? *(Seeing what had happened, the men of this area, as well, wanted to rid themselves of the Ark. Presently, far too many desire a semblance of God, but only a semblance. There is no danger in the semblance, and great danger in the reality, that is, if* the Lord is treated with contempt; therefore, many presently are satisfied with the mere echo!)*

21 And they sent messengers to the inhabitants of Kirjath-jearim, saying, The Philistines have brought again the Ark of the LORD; come ye down, and fetch it up to you. *(When the cover is pulled off and we are put to the test, the modern Church, as Beth-shemesh, little wants the Lord. If God is there, the spectacle of His Blessing and Judgment are side by side. The Church has repeatedly through the ages tried to have only one aspect of God, namely the Blessing. That is not possible! We must never forget that there is Redemption, and there is Judgment; consequently, there is Heaven, and there is Hell. Moses said, "I set before you the way of life and the way of death" [Deut. 30:19].)*

CHAPTER 7
(1112 B.C.)
THE HOUSE OF ABINADAB

AND the men of Kirjath-jearim came, and fetched up the Ark of the LORD, and brought it into the house of Abinadab in the hill, and sanctified Eleazar his son to keep the Ark of the LORD. *(There is much evidence that the Ark was neglected and not at all respected. Kirjath-jearim was about eight miles northeast of Beth-shemesh. It would remain in this location for approximately twenty years, in which time Israel was more or less under the yoke of the Philistines. It seems, as well, that it would remain there during the forty-year reign of Saul. David would reign approximately ten years [seven years in Judah and three years over the whole of Israel] before the Ark would be brought to Jerusalem. This is a total of approximately seventy years.*

Furthermore, when the Ark was finally found by David, it seems that it had been discarded and was standing alone out in a field next to the woods. The Psalm of David says, "Lo, we heard of it at Ephratah: we found it in the fields of the wood" [Ps. 132:6]. Whether that can be taken literally or not, we cannot say; yet, I wonder if the Glory of God has not been abandoned in the modern Church even more so than it was with Israel?)

2 And it came to pass, while the Ark abode in Kirjath-jearim, that the time was long; for it was twenty years: and all the House of Israel lamented after the LORD. *(The time is always long, when one is out of the Will of God. One possibly could as well say, "The Lord lamented after Israel.")*

REPENTANCE

3 And Samuel spoke unto all the House of Israel, saying, If you do return unto the LORD with all your hearts (*this was a Message of Repentance; God's true servants always preach as Samuel preached; they arouse people to a consciousness of their sinful condition before God; they set forth the Lamb of God evidently crucified among them [Gal. 3:1; 5:9, 17] as the Divine Way of pardon and Righteousness; and they denounce all compromise with evil*), then put away the strange gods and Ashtaroth from among you (*everything that's not "Jesus Christ and Him Crucified" is idolatry, i.e., "strange gods"*), and prepare your hearts unto the LORD (*people are not won to the Lord by the route of intellectualism, but rather by appealing to their hearts*), and serve Him only (*the bane of Israel was serving the Lord as well as idols; it is the same presently! Paul refers to such worship as "another Jesus, another spirit, and another gospel" [II Cor. 11:4]*): and He will deliver you out of the hand of the Philistines. (*The die is cast! The Lord will deliver, but only on His terms, and those terms are spelled out in Samuel's Message. God hasn't changed; if deliverance is to be obtained presently, He demands the same now as He did of Israel of old.*)

4 Then the Children of Israel did put away Baalim and Ashtaroth, and served the LORD only.

5 And Samuel said, Gather all Israel to Mizpeh, and I will pray for you unto the LORD. (*Israel is about to see a Move of God, the first one seen in a long, long time. It is time, as well, for the Church!*)

6 And they gathered together to Mizpeh, and drew water, and poured it out before the LORD (*this was a Type of Christ pouring out His all on the Cross, which He did without reservation*), and fasted on that day, and said there, We have sinned against the LORD (*and sin is the cause of all problems*). And Samuel judged the Children of Israel in Mizpeh (*and did so according to the Word of the Lord*).

VICTORY

7 And when the Philistines heard that the Children of Israel were gathered together to Mizpeh, the lords of the Philistines went up against Israel. And when the Children of Israel heard it, they were afraid of the Philistines. (*It would seem that what the Philistines had seen,* as it regards the Ark of God, would have caused them to have the exact opposite reaction; however, miracles seldom draw people to God! As well, Israel, now that Repentance was the order of the day, had no reason to be afraid.*)

8 And the Children of Israel said to Samuel, Cease not to cry unto the LORD our God for us, that He will save us out of the hand of the Philistines (*if there is not a strong spiritual leader, the people perish [Eph. 4:11]*).

9 And Samuel took a sucking lamb, and offered it for a Burnt Offering wholly unto the LORD (*the whole Burnt Offering was a Type of Christ giving His Perfection to imperfect people, at least to those who will believe; Samuel was a Levite and, accordingly [I Chron. 23:27-32], he could offer a Burnt Offering; he could not enter the Tabernacle, though, not being a son of Aaron; in fact, the Tabernacle, at this time, was useless as a center of worship; for the Throne of God, that is, the Ark, had been removed from it*): and Samuel cried unto the LORD for Israel; and the LORD heard him. (*Every generation must have a Samuel, or else the Church is set back immeasurably, oftentimes taking a century or more to recover.*)

10 And as Samuel was offering up the Burnt Offering, the Philistines drew near to the battle against Israel (*however, Israel's strength now is based upon the shed blood of the slain lamb*): but the LORD thundered with a great thunder on that day upon the Philistines, and discomfited them, and they were smitten before Israel. (*As is obvious here, the Lord cannot give victory to sinful man. He can give victory only to His Son, and our Saviour, the Lord Jesus Christ; however, if we are properly in Christ, which we can only be by virtue of what He has done for us at the Cross, His victory will be ours, and that's the way it's meant to be [Jn. 14:20].*)

11 And the men of Israel went out of Mizpeh, and pursued the Philistines, and smote them, until they came under Beth-car. (*It is the Will of God for us to pursue the Devil, in the sense of discomfiting him, instead of him pursuing us. But let us not forget, we can do such a thing only in the power of the slain lamb, i.e., "the Cross".*)

12 Then Samuel took a stone (*"and that Rock was Christ" [I Cor. 10:4]*), and set it between Mizpeh and Shen, and called the name of it Eben-ezer, saying, Hitherto has the LORD helped us (*and again I say, the Lord will always help us, providing Christ is looked at as the Source, with the Cross as the Means*).

13 So the Philistines were subdued, and they came no more into the coast of Israel: and the Hand of the LORD was against the Philistines all the days of Samuel. *(Every enemy of our soul can be subdued, and "come again no more," as long as our Faith is in Christ and Him Crucified [I Cor. 1:23].)*

14 And the cities which the Philistines had taken from Israel were restored to Israel, from Ekron even unto Gath; and the coasts *(borders)* thereof did Israel deliver out of the hands of the Philistines. And there was peace between Israel and the Amorites *("were restored to Israel"; the Lord wants to give back all that Satan has stolen and, in the Cross, it can be done, and only in the Cross can it be done).*

SAMUEL JUDGES ISRAEL

15 And Samuel judged Israel all the days of his life. *(In fact, Samuel was the last Judge, with the order of events now being changed, but not by God, but rather by the people. Ideas and schemes which are born by man can never be blessed by God.)*

16 And he went from year to year in circuit to Beth-el, and Gilgal, and Mizpeh, and judged Israel in all those places.

17 And his return was to Ramah; for there was his house; and there he judged Israel; and there he built an Altar unto the LORD. *(From this, we see that the Aaronic Priesthood was now in abeyance, meaning that Samuel was not only a Prophet and a Judge, but also a Priest. Thus, he was a Type of Christ! Under David the Priesthood would be restored, with the Ark brought back to its rightful place, but that would be some years yet.)*

CHAPTER 8
(1112 B.C.)
SAMUEL'S SONS

AND it came to pass, when Samuel was old, that he made his sons judges over Israel. *(Samuel was probably about 60 years old at this time. As Godly as Samuel was, the Text reveals the fact that he wasn't perfect. There is no hint that he asked the Lord for guidance as it regards putting his sons in places of authority. Simply put, they were not spiritually qualified.)*

2 Now the name of his firstborn was Joel; and the name of his second, Abiah: they were judges in Beer-sheba.

3 And his sons walked not in his ways, but turned aside after lucre *(money)*, and took bribes, and perverted judgment. *(This sin was expressly forbidden by the Law [Ex. 23:6, 8; Deut. 16:19], and it marks the high spirit of the nation that it was so indignant at justice being thus perverted.)*

4 Then all the elders of Israel gathered themselves together, and came to Samuel unto Ramah *(because of the corruption of Samuel's sons),*

5 And said unto him, Behold, you are old, and your sons walk not in your ways: now make us a king to judge us like all the nations. *(Israel's sin was twofold: 1. They wanted their own ways instead of God's Ways and 2. Their desire for a king to be like other nations was a work of the flesh and not of the Spirit. It would, thereby, bring untold sorrow.*

A king whom they could see, although he would be only a feeble, foolish, and dying man, was preferred to an unseen, Almighty King, Wise and Eternal.

The nation wished to be like the surrounding nations, forgetting that their glory and happiness consisted in being unlike these nations.

It was God's Will for them to have a King, but not at this present time. To be sure, there was no way they would correct the wrong that was then being done in Israel by committing another wrong. In other words, by not looking exclusively to the Lord, proverbially speaking, they were jumping out of the frying pan into the fire.)

A KING

6 But the thing displeased Samuel, when they said, Give us a king to judge us. And Samuel prayed unto the LORD *(Samuel's displeasure had nothing to do with them rejecting his sons, but rather because of the rebellion and impatience of the people in not waiting for the king whom God had promised [Gen. 17:7, 16; Num. 24:17; Deut. 17:14-20]).*

7 And the LORD said unto Samuel, Hearken unto the voice of the people in all that they say unto you: for they have not rejected you, but they have rejected Me, that I should not reign over them. *(Oftentimes, when it is thought that a particular man is rejected, and for reasons which some think are valid, in reality, it is God Who has been rejected. This is a sobering thought that we should deeply contemplate. To reject God is simply the most serious thing that a person can do, and for a Believer to*

reject Him presents something even far worse.)

8 According to all the works which they have done since the day that I brought them up out of Egypt even unto this day, where with they have forsaken Me, and served other gods, so do they also unto you *(to reject God's man is to reject God!).*

9 Now therefore hearken unto their voice: howbeit yet protest solemnly unto them, and show them the manner of the king that shall reign over them. *(God, in His tender love, would plainly tell them the treatment they would receive from the king of their own choice. Six times the fact is repeated: "he will take," and referring to this particular king. Oftentimes, through a work of the flesh, we can bring things into existence which are contrary to God's Will. No matter the face that we put upon it, it will only bring troubles and difficulties.)*

10 And Samuel told all the words of the LORD unto the people who asked of him a king *(so they had no excuse!).*

THE WARNING

11 And he said, This will be the manner of the king who shall reign over you: He will take your sons, and appoint them for himself, for his chariots, and to be his horsemen; and some shall run before his chariots.

12 And he will appoint him captains over thousands, and captains over fifties; and will set them to ear his ground *(plant the crops)*, and to reap his harvest, and to make his instruments of war, and instruments of his chariots.

13 And he will take your daughters to be confectionaries *(makers of ointments and scents, i.e., "perfume")*, and to be cooks, and to be bakers.

14 And he will take your fields, and your vineyards, and your oliveyards, even the best of them, and give them to his servants.

15 And he will take the tenth of your seed *(a tenth of the harvest as a tax)*, and of your vineyards, and give to his officers, and to his servants.

16 And he will take your menservants, and your maidservants, and your goodliest young men, and your asses, and put them to his work.

17 He will take the tenth of your sheep: and you shall be his servants.

18 And you shall cry out in that day because of your king which you shall have chosen you; and the LORD will not hear you in that day.

(As with Israel, so in many cases, God permits self-will to have its own way. But how much happier would it have been for Israel to have placed themselves and their difficulties in God's Hands and asked Him to plan for them! As stated, it was God's Will for them to have a king, but in His due time. In fact, that first king was to be David, but Israel wasn't prepared to wait.)

THE DEMAND

19 Nevertheless the people refused to obey the voice of Samuel; and they said, No; but we will have a king over us *(Williams says, "Just as impoverishment and servitude resulted as predicted by Samuel from Israel's self-willed establishment of a human government, so spiritual poverty and loss of liberty follow in the Christian life when there is subjection to the commandments and doctrines of men, instead of to the authority of the Word of God");*

20 That we also may be like all the nations; and that our king may judge us, and go out before us, and fight our battles *(it is true, because of the corrupt judgment of Samuel's sons, that Israel had problems; however, taking matters into their own hands, instead of being led by the Lord, did not make the matter better, but rather worse).*

21 And Samuel heard all the words of the people, and he rehearsed them in the ears of the LORD *(prayed about what was being said and done).*

22 And the LORD said to Samuel, Hearken unto their voice, and make them a king. And Samuel said unto the men of Israel, Go ye every man unto his city. *(We find from this example, and scores of others in the Bible, while the Lord will speak to us, deal with us, move upon us, all with the effort of bending us to His Will, He will never force the issue. If we are determined to go in a wrong direction, He will let us go, but the end results will never be good.)*

CHAPTER 9
(1095 B.C.)
THE GENEALOGY OF SAUL

NOW there was a man of Benjamin, whose name was Kish, the son of Abiel, the son of Zeror, the son of Bechorath, the son of Aphiah, a Benjamite, and mighty man of power *(of wealth).*

2 And he had a son, whose name was Saul,

a choice young man, and a goodly: and there was not among the Children of Israel a goodlier person than he: from his shoulders and upward he was higher than any of the people. *(It is believed that Saul was about 7 feet tall. For a moment, let us look at the contrast to the Apostle Paul. Both men had the same name; both were members of the same Tribe, Benjamin; but the one exhibits the power of the "flesh," the other of the "Spirit." As to physical strength and personal attractive appearance, Saul of Tarsus was wholly unlike King Saul, for Paul's "bodily presence" was weak [II Cor. 10:10]; King Saul "was a work of the flesh," and would bring only destruction. Paul of the New Testament was "a work of the Spirit," and would bring only life. Beauty and height of stature distinguish the son of Kish, but his life illustrated the fruitless effort of the "old man" to live as the "new man" [Rom., Chpt. 7].)*

THE LOST ANIMALS

3 And the asses of Kish Saul's father were lost. And Kish said to Saul his son, Take now one of the servants with you, and arise, go seek the asses. *(The entire Passage from Verses 3-27 illustrates the Gospel Message. It pictures a wanderer vainly seeking a lost possession. So man vainly seeks lost innocence.)*

4 And he passed through Mount Ephraim, and passed through the land of Shalisha, but they found them not: then they passed through the land of Shalim, and there they were not: and he passed through the land of the Benjamites, but they found them not.

5 And when they were come to the land of Zuph, Saul said to his servant who was with him, Come, and let us return; lest my father leave caring for the asses, and take thought for us *(be concerned that we met with trouble).*

6 And he said unto him, Behold now, there is in this city a man of God, and he is an honourable man; all that he says comes surely to pass: now let us go thither; peradventure he can show us our way that we should go. *(It is amazing! Saul seemed to have little knowledge of Samuel, if any at all. He was totally ignorant of the man of God. The servant had to tell Saul as to who exactly Samuel was, "a man of God." Likewise, we must be Christ's servants and tell the lost about Jesus.)*

7 Then said Saul to his servant, But, behold, if we go, what shall we bring the man? for the bread is spent in our vessels, and there is not a present to bring to the man of God: what have we? *(As Saul, man tries to purchase Redemption, when he does hear of it. Saul would try to purchase Samuel's favor. Sinners conceive that it is possible to purchase Salvation by religious efforts and emotions — which are absolutely valueless.)*

8 And the servant answered Saul again, and said, Behold, I have here at hand the fourth part of a shekel of silver: that will I give to the man of God, to tell us our way.

9 (Beforetime in Israel, when a man went to enquire of God, thus he spoke, Come, and let us go to the Seer: for he who is now called a Prophet was beforetime called a Seer *[one who sees into the future].*)

10 Then said Saul to his servant, Well said; come, let us go. So they went unto the city where the man of God was.

11 And as they went up the hill to the city, they found young maidens going out to draw water, and said unto them, Is the Seer here?

12 And they answered them, and said, He is; behold, he is before you: make haste now, for he came to day to the city; for there is a sacrifice of the people to day in the high place *(these young ladies pointed the way; the Lord can use any Believer to point the way; we are "way-showers," while Jesus is the "Way" [Jn. 14:6]):*

13 As soon as you be come into the city, you shall straightway find him before he go up to the high place to eat: for the people will not eat until he come, because he does bless the Sacrifice; and afterwards they eat that be bidden. Now therefore get you up; for about this time you shall find him.

14 And they went up into the city: and when they were come into the city, behold, Samuel came out against them, for to go up to the high place *(the Tabernacle had been destroyed by the Philistines, so, as of now, this place at Ramah was where Sacrifices were offered and, at this time, sanctioned by the Lord).*

ANOINT SAUL

15 Now the LORD had told Samuel in his ear a day before Saul came, saying *(simply refers to the fact that the Lord told Samuel as to what would transpire the next day regarding Saul),*

16 To morrow about this time I will send you a man out of the land of Benjamin, and you shall anoint him to be captain over My people Israel, that he may save My people out

of the hand of the Philistines: for I have looked upon My people, because their cry is come unto Me. *(Though Samuel had lightened the yoke of the Philistines by his victory at Mizpeh, yet he had by no means altogether broken their power. Saul, as a Benjamite, belonged to the bravest and most warlike Tribe of Israel, and one whose country was the seat of perpetual combat with the Philistines; therefore, whatever victory that Samuel had won in the recent past, still, Israel was again suffering from Philistine domination. The Lord desires that His People be free; and freedom can only come by the Believer placing his Faith exclusively in Christ and the Cross, through which the Holy Spirit works. The victory we need and, in fact, everything we receive from the Lord, has to be accomplished in our lives by the Power of the Holy Spirit, and the Cross is the means by which this is done, which ever requires the Cross as the object of our Faith, and the only object of our Faith.)*

17 And when Samuel saw Saul, the LORD said unto him, Behold the man whom I spoke to you of! this same shall reign over My people.

18 Then Saul drew near to Samuel in the gate, and said, Tell me, I pray you, where the Seer's house is *(as stated, Saul had little or no knowledge at all of Samuel, which, within itself, tells us volumes)*.

19 And Samuel answered Saul, and said, I am the Seer: go up before me unto the high place; for you shall eat with me to day, and to morrow I will let you go, and will tell you all that is in your heart. *(Of course, the Lord knew exactly what the future held; still, as the record will show, He will do everything to try to make it work, but, as we shall see, all to no avail!)*

20 And as for your asses that were lost three days ago, set not your mind on them; for they are found. And on whom is all the desire of Israel? Is it not on you, and on all your father's house. *(Saul evidently looked great to Samuel, considering that he was imposing, actually, about 7 feet tall. So, the Lord would also teach Samuel a lesson in all of this. It is so easy for even the best of us, whoever that might be, to look at the outward appearance of something, and be fooled thereby!)*

21 And Saul answered and said, Am not I a Benjamite, of the smallest of the Tribes of Israel? and my family the least of all the families of the Tribe of Benjamin? wherefore then speak you so to me? *(Saul was right about the Tribe of Benjamin, it almost having been destroyed some years earlier [Judg. 21:6].)*

22 And Samuel took Saul and his servant, and brought them into the parlour, and made them sit in the chiefest place among them who were bidden, which were about thirty persons. *(Saul being seated in the chief place and, as well, given a portion of the Sacrifice, i.e., "the Peace Offering," stated, within itself, that Saul was the chosen one, with all present understanding that.)*

23 And Samuel said unto the cook, Bring the portion which I gave you, of which I said unto you, Set it by you.

24 And the cook took up the shoulder, and that which was upon it, and set it before Saul. And Samuel said, Behold that which is left! set it before you, and eat: for unto this time has it been kept for you since I said, I have invited the people. So Saul did eat with Samuel that day. *(When, on the previous day, the Revelation was made to Samuel that Israel's future king would present himself the next day, the Prophet at once made preparations to receive him with due solemnity, and for this purpose arranged a Sacrifice, and invited thirty of the chief citizens of Ramah to assemble at the high place, and to sit at the banquet with him.)*

25 And when they were come down from the high place into the city, Samuel communed with Saul upon the top of the house *(houses in that part of the world are normally flat on top; oftentimes, especially during the summer, people slept on top of the house to catch the cool breezes)*.

26 And they arose early: and it came to pass about the spring of the day, that Samuel called Saul to the top of the house, saying, Up, that I may send you away. And Saul arose, and they went out both of them, he and Samuel, abroad. *(Evidently, Saul and his servant had slept on the top of the house that night.)*

27 And as they were going down to the end of the city, Samuel said to Saul, Bid the servant pass on before us, (and he passed on), but stand you still a while, that I may show you the Word of God. *(Samuel will now tell Saul that he is to be king.)*

CHAPTER 10
(1095 B.C.)
SAMUEL ANOINTS SAUL

THEN Samuel took a vial of oil, and poured it upon his head, and kissed him *(the kissing was the mode in that day of expressing homage to a Sovereign)*, and said, Is it not because

the LORD has anointed you to be captain over His inheritance? *(We find that all the outward trappings of God's help is here; however, that which was outward could not change that which was inward — an evil heart of unbelief. That which is not God's Will can easily be outwardly anointed by men, and often is; still, such is not God's choice, and will bear no good fruit.)*

2 When you are departed from me to day, then you shall find two men by Rachel's sepulchre in the border of Benjamin at Zelzah; and they will say unto you, The asses which you went to seek are found: and, lo, your father has left the care of the asses, and sorrows for you, saying, What shall I do for my son? *(Meeting two men by Rachel's sepulchre was meant to be a sign to Saul; however, Saul would little understand that. Jacob loved Rachel greatly, as God loved Saul. But, still, Rachel was barren, as Saul was barren. Part of her problem was her hatred of Leah [Gen. 29:31]. Then Rachel would resort to superstition [mandrakes — Gen. 30:14]. Saul will ultimately resort to witchcraft, as well. Thankfully, Rachel would find her way with God. Saul would not!)*

3 Then shall you go on forward from thence, and you shall come to the plain of Tabor, and there shall meet you three men going up to God to Beth-el, one carrying three kids *(baby lambs)*, and another carrying three loaves of bread, and another carrying a bottle of wine:

4 And they will salute you, and give you two loaves of bread; which you shall receive of their hands. *(These signs were for many things; however, mainly they were designed to confirm in Saul's mind the conviction that Samuel was indeed the Prophet of the Lord; for it must not be forgotten that although but a few miles separated their homes, yet 9:6 makes it clear that Saul was such a stranger to God and His Kingdom that he did not know even of the existence of this mighty Prophet. So, why would the Lord choose such a man to be the king of Israel? In reality, the Lord did not choose him; he was rather chosen by the people.)*

5 After that you shall come to the hill of God, where is the garrison of the Philistines *(this shows that most of the Tribe of Benjamin was subject to that nation and, as well, disarmed; but, probably, as long as the tribute was paid, its internal administration was not interfered with)*: and it shall come to pass, when you are come thither to the city, that you shall meet a company of Prophets coming down from the high place with a psaltery, and a tabret, and a pipe, and a harp, before them; and they shall prophesy *(we find here that music dedicated to the Glory of God is a great aid in the worship of God, and in the exercise of the gifts; years afterwards David was thus educated, and learned at one of Samuel's schools that skill in metre and psalmody which, added to his natural gifts, made him "the sweet singer of Israel")*:

6 And the Spirit of the LORD will come upon you, and you shall prophesy with them, and shall be turned into another man *(the Lord would do all that He could to help Saul be the man that he should be)*.

7 And let it be, when these signs are come unto you, that you do as occasion serve you; for God is with you *(press onward, and the kingdom is your own, and success is sure)*.

8 And you shall go down before me to Gilgal; and, behold, I will come down unto you, to offer Burnt Offerings, and to sacrifice Sacrifices of Peace Offerings: seven days shall you tarry, till I come to you, and show you what you shall do. *(In this, Samuel was telling Israel's future king that success depended upon Faith in the "Burnt Offerings" and "Peace Offerings," which were symbolic of Christ and Him Crucified. Regrettably, Saul would never see this, as most modern Christians never see it; unfortunately, the end result of these modern Christians will be the same as that of Saul!)*

THE CHANGED HEART

9 And it was so, that when he had turned his back to go from Samuel, God gave him another heart: and all those signs came to pass that day. *(Smith says, "The Hebrew is remarkable here: 'When he turned his shoulder to go from Samuel, God also turned for him another heart,' i.e., God turned him around by giving him a changed heart. He grew internally up to the level of his changed circumstances.")*

10 And when they came thither to the hill, behold, a company of Prophets met him *(exactly as Samuel said would happen)*; and the Spirit of God came upon him, and he prophesied among them. *(Saul should have learned from all of this to lean heavily upon Samuel. But, regrettably, he didn't!)*

11 And it came to pass, when all who knew him beforetime saw that, behold, he prophesied among the Prophets, then the people said one to another, What is this that is come unto the son of Kish? Is Saul also among the Prophets? *(As stated, the Lord would do all with this*

man that was humanly possibly, but it would all be to no avail!)

12 And one of the same place answered and said. But who is their father? Therefore it became a Proverb. Is Saul also among the Prophets? *(The idea of all of this, gifts from the Lord aren't inherited. They come from God [I Cor. 12:28-31].)*

13 And when he had made an end of prophesying, he came to the high place.

14 And Saul's uncle said unto him and to his servant, Where did you go? And he said, To seek the asses: and when we saw that they were no where, we came to Samuel *(this would be Abner [14:50-51; I Chron. 8:33]).*

15 And Saul's uncle said, Tell me, I pray you, what Samuel said unto you.

16 And Saul said unto his uncle, He told us plainly that the asses were found. But of the matter of the Kingdom, whereof Samuel spoke, he told him not.

SAUL INSTALLED AS KING

17 And Samuel called the people together unto the LORD to Mizpeh;

18 And said unto the Children of Israel, Thus saith the LORD God of Israel, I brought up Israel out of Egypt, and delivered you out of the hand of the Egyptians, and out of the hand of all kingdoms, and of them who oppressed you *(Samuel points out in his address to the assembled people that Jehovah always had done for them the very thing for which they desired a king; they wish for deliverance from the Philistines, but their deliverance by Jehovah had been made dependent upon their own conduct; they were required to repent of their sins, and to purge the land from idolatry, before victory could be theirs; what they actually wanted was national independence freed from this condition of Repentance, etc., and secured by an organization of their military resources):*

19 And you have this day rejected your God, Who Himself saved you out of all your adversities and your tribulations; and you have said unto Him, No, but set a king over us. Now therefore present yourselves before the LORD by your tribes, and by your thousands. *(Even though what they desired and, in fact, demanded, was so wrong, but yet God would grant their request, it being a law of His Providence to leave men free to choose.)*

20 And when Samuel had caused all the Tribes of Israel to come near, the Tribe of Benjamin was taken *(the Lord pointed out that Tribe to Samuel, which Samuel already knew, but which was done for the sake of the people).*

21 When he had caused the Tribe of Benjamin to come near by their families, the family of Matri was taken, and Saul the son of Kish was taken: and when they sought him, he could not be found. *(In all of this, we will find that Saul was the greatest work of the flesh that could be found, and yet, even as we shall see, that was woefully insufficient, as it is always woefully insufficient.)*

22 Therefore they enquired of the LORD further, if the man should yet come thither. And the LORD answered, Behold, he has hid himself among the stuff. *(At the beginning, Saul's humility is commendable; regrettably, it would not remain this way.)*

23 And they ran and fetched him thence *(because the Lord had revealed where he was)*: and when he stood among the people, he was higher than any of the people from his shoulders and upward. *(As stated, he looked every bit a king. But still, it was but a work of the flesh, because this was not God's Way, but rather the way of man. It would fail, as all such ways fail. But regrettably, most of the Church world base their judgment on what can be seen outwardly.)*

24 And Samuel said to all the people, See ye him whom the LORD has chosen, that there is none like him among all the people? And all the people shouted, and said, God save the king. *(The lesson of the "flesh" is not easily learned. Even the great Prophet Samuel would have to learn this lesson. He too was enamored with Saul, but would find, to his dismay, that no matter the effort made, "they who are in the flesh cannot please God" [Rom. 8:8].)*

25 Then Samuel told the people the manner of the Kingdom, and wrote it in a book, and laid it up before the LORD. And Samuel sent all the people away, every man to his house.

26 And Saul also went home to Gibeah; and there went with him a band of men, whose hearts God had touched. *(The Lord not only gave Saul a new heart, but those around him a "touched heart," as well! As stated, every effort was being made to make this thing work.)*

27 But the children of Belial *(worthless ones)* said, How shall this man save us? And they despised him, and brought him no presents. But he held his peace. *(Even though it was not the Will of God for Israel at this time to have a king, still, what these men did was very wrong, and the Holy Spirit noted it by referring to them*

as "worthless," for that's what the word "Belial" means.)

CHAPTER 11
(1095 B.C.)
THE AMMONITES

THEN Nahash the Ammonite came up, and encamped against Jabesh-gilead: and all the men of Jabesh said unto Nahash, Make a covenant with us, and we will serve you. *(The Ammonites were old enemies of the Israelites, alleging that Israel had taken possession of territory east of the Jordan which rightfully belonged to them [Judg. 11:13]. But after their defeat by Jephthah, their power was so broken that they allowed a century to elapse before they ventured again to assert their claim. Jabesh-gilead was a city on the eastern side of Jordan, in the Tribe of Manasseh.*

The name "Nahash" means "bright shining serpent." "Jabesh-gilead" means "hill of witnessing." Satan will encamp against us to destroy our "witness." If we make a "covenant" with him, even as "the men of Jabesh" tried to do, our "witness" will be destroyed. No covenant of any fashion can be made with Satan.)

2 And Nahash the Ammonite answered them. On this condition will I make a covenant with you, that I may thrust out all your right eyes, and lay it for a reproach upon all Israel. *(Men in those days fought behind a shield, with the top covering their face with the exception of their right eye. That being put out, they could not see to fight; consequently, they would be a reproach.*

Regrettably, most of the modern Church little sees how to fight, because their right eye has been blinded. They have made a covenant with Satan, which means they are preaching everything except "Jesus Christ and Him Crucified" [I Cor. 1:23].)

3 And the elders of Jabesh said unto him *(unto Nahash)*, Give us seven days' respite, that we may send messengers unto all the coasts of Israel: and then, if there be no man to save us, we will come out to you *(Nahash would hold them in such contempt that he would accede to their request).*

4 Then came the messengers to Gibeah of Saul, and told the tidings in the ears of the people: and all the people lifted up their voices, and wept.

5 And, behold, Saul came after the herd out of the field *(Saul had been plowing)*: and Saul said, What ails the people that they weep? And they told him the tidings of the men of Jabesh.

6 And the Spirit of God came upon Saul when he heard those tidings, and his anger was kindled greatly *(the only answer to Satan is the "Spirit of God," Who works exclusively within the framework of the Finished Work of Christ [Jn. 14:16-17]; Saul was angry, and Believers today should likewise be angry at the threats of Satan).*

7 And he took a yoke of oxen, and hewed them in pieces, and sent them throughout all the coasts *(borders)* of Israel by the hands of messengers, saying, Whosoever comes not forth after Saul and after Samuel, so shall it be done unto his oxen *(in other words, the enemy would take everything they had).* And the fear of the LORD fell on the people, and they came out with one consent *(if the modern Church cannot agree on anything else, surely it can agree on the fact that Satan is making havoc of God's People; the only answer to that is the Cross [11:15; Gal. 6:14]).*

8 And when he *(Saul)* numbered them in Bezek, the Children of Israel were three hundred thousand, and the men of Judah thirty thousand *(the Lord "numbers" all who will fight the good fight of Faith [I Tim. 6:12-13]).*

9 And they said unto the messengers who came, Thus shall you say unto the men of Jabesh-gilead. To morrow, by that time the sun be hot *(about 8 a.m.)*, you shall have help. And the messengers came and showed it to the men of Jabesh; and they were glad *(the Holy Spirit now is our Helper [Jn. 14:16]).*

10 Therefore the men of Jabesh said *(to the Ammonites)*, To morrow we will come out unto you, and you shall do with us all that seems good unto you *(Israel was playing for time, in order to get the army together).*

11 And it was so on the morrow, that Saul put the people in three companies *(those three companies are "the Name of Jesus," "the Blood of the Lamb," and "the Word of God")*; and they came into the midst of the host in the morning watch *(between 6 and 9 a.m.)*, and slew the Ammonites until the heat of the day *(until noon)*: and it came to pass, that they *(the Ammonites)* which remained were scattered, so that two of them were not left together.

SAUL CONFIRMED KING

12 And the people said unto Samuel, Who is

he who said, Shall Saul reign over us? bring the men, that we may put them to death (the people now were drawn to Saul, and bitterly opposed to those who were not).

13 And Saul said, There shall not a man be put to death this day: for to day the LORD has wrought Salvation in Israel (one of the few times that Saul acted in Righteousness).

14 Then said Samuel to the people, Come, and let us go to Gilgal, and renew the kingdom there ("Gilgal" means "the reproach has rolled away"; it was appropriate for the Kingdom of Israel to be started and accepted at Gilgal, for this was their first place of entrance into Canaan [Josh. 5:2-10]).

15 And all the people went to Gilgal (about 35 miles south of Jabesh-gilead); and there they made Saul king before the LORD in Gilgal (his confirmation): and there they sacrificed Sacrifices of Peace Offerings before the LORD; and there Saul and all the men of Israel rejoiced greatly. (The "Peace Offerings" signified the Cross of Jesus, thereby the putting to death of self-will. As well, it was the secret of power for war — as illustrated by Joshua's starting from and returning to that center many years before — a war in which the weapons are spiritual and not carnal. Saul could physically accompany Samuel there, and also "rejoice greatly," and yet remain a stranger, as we shall see, to the real and inward significance of the place.)

CHAPTER 12
(1095 B.C.)

SAMUEL RETIRES AS JUDGE

AND Samuel said unto all Israel, Behold, I have hearkened unto your voice in all that you said unto me, and have made a king over you. (However, it was their voice, and not the Voice of God. The Voice of God had said the opposite [8:5-7].)

2 And now, behold, the king walks before you: and I am old and grayheaded; and, behold, my sons are with you: and I have walked before you from my childhood unto this day (in effect, Samuel is retiring as the governmental leader of the people and, as well, his sons will have no more place and position).

3 Behold, here I am: witness against me before the LORD, and before His anointed (before Saul): whose ox have I taken? Or whose ass have I taken? Or whom have I defrauded? Whom have I oppressed? or of whose hand have I received any bribe to blind my eyes

therewith? And I will restore it you (other than his sons, his life was spotless).

4 And they said, You have not defrauded us, nor oppressed us, neither have you taken ought of any man's hand.

5 And he said unto them, The LORD is witness against you, and His anointed is witness this day, that you have not found ought in my hand. And they answered, He is witness (we are told here unequivocally that the Lord witnesses all things).

SAMUEL'S MESSAGE

6 And Samuel said unto the people, It is the LORD Who advanced Moses and Aaron, and Who brought your fathers up out of the land of Egypt. (If the Lord does not advance the subject, there is, in reality, no advancement. As well, we should only desire the advancement that God gives. It is seldom that religious leaders advance anyone except to make that person beholden to them.)

7 Now therefore stand still, that I may reason with you before the LORD of all the righteous acts of the LORD, which He did to you and to your fathers.

8 When Jacob was come into Egypt, and your fathers cried unto the LORD, then the LORD sent Moses and Aaron, which brought forth your fathers out of Egypt, and made them dwell in this place (in other words, neither this king nor any other king did such, only the Lord).

9 And when they forgot the LORD their God, He sold them into the hand of Sisera, captain of the host of Hazor, and into the hand of the Philistines, and into the hand of the king of Moab, and they (the Moabites) fought against them (against Israel; if the Believer rebels against the Lord, ultimately, the Lord will "sell" that Believer into the hand of the enemy; the only cure for this is the Cross [I Cor. 1:18]).

10 And they cried unto the LORD, and said, We have sinned, because we have forsaken the LORD, and have served Baalim and Ashtaroth: but now deliver us out of the hand of our enemies, and we will serve You (the Lord Alone can deliver!).

11 And the LORD sent Jerub-baal, and Bedan (Barak), and Jephthah, and Samuel, and delivered you out of the hand of your enemies on every side, and you dwelled safe (while the Lord uses human instrumentation, but is not confined to such, still, it is the Lord Alone Who delivers).

12 And when you saw that Nahash the king of the children of Ammon came against you, you said unto me, No; but a king shall reign over us: when the LORD your God was your king *(they didn't want the Almighty Arm of God to lean on, but rather the frail arm of a human being; how so like the modern Church!).*

13 Now therefore behold the king whom you have chosen *(their choice, and not God's),* and whom you have desired! And, behold, the LORD has set a king over you *(He has given you what you demanded, even though He knows that it will ultimately bring you great harm).*

14 If you will fear the LORD, and serve Him, and obey His voice, and not rebel against the Commandment of the LORD, then shall both you and also the king who reigns over you continue following the LORD your God *(however, even though the Blessings of God are promised here, without proper leadership, and in Saul they would not have that proper leadership, such Blessings were impossible):*

15 But if you will not obey the voice of the LORD, but rebel against the Commandment of the LORD *(against His Law),* then shall the hand of the LORD be against you, as it was against your fathers. *(As portrayed here, the Hand of the Lord for us is conditional. We must obey His Commandments, and this can be done only by the Believer trusting solely in Christ, and what Christ has done for us at the Cross. Jesus has obeyed the Law in every capacity, and has satisfied its just demands by what He has done at the Cross, and did it all for us. Trusting in Him exclusively gives us His victory [Rom. 8:15-17].)*

16 Now therefore stand and see this great thing, which the LORD will do before your eyes *(take your places in solemn order).*

17 Is it not wheat harvest to day? *(first part of June.)* I will call unto the LORD, and He shall send thunder and rain *(which almost never happened at that time of the year);* that you may perceive and see that your wickedness is great, which you have done in the sight of the LORD, in asking you a king *(it was the Will of the Lord for Israel to ultimately have a king, but not now; the first king that was meant to be was David).*

18 So Samuel called unto the LORD; and the LORD sent thunder and rain that day: and all the people greatly feared the LORD and Samuel *(the thunderstorm being sent at this time of the year was Divine evidence of the just anger of God because of their rejection of Him).*

19 And all the people said unto Samuel. Pray for your servants unto the LORD your God, that we die not: for we have added unto all our sins this evil, to ask us a king.

SAMUEL'S EXHORTATION

20 And Samuel said unto the people, Fear not: you have done all this wickedness: yet turn not aside from following the LORD, but serve the LORD with all your heart *(the answer to sin is not discontinuing our serving the Lord, but rather in throwing ourselves at His Feet, asking forgiveness, and continuing to serve Him "with all our hearts");*

21 And turn ye not aside: for then should you go after vain things, which cannot profit nor deliver; for they are vain *(whether we succeed or fail, God is the answer; whether there is victory or defeat, God is still the answer; everything else is "vain"; it has no answer).*

22 For the LORD will not forsake His people for His great name's sake: because it has pleased the LORD to make you His people. *(The Lord does not work from the position of "what might have been," but rather from the position of "what is.")*

23 Moreover as for me, God forbid that I should sin against the LORD in ceasing to pray for you: but I will teach you the good and the right way *(even though Samuel had abdicated the position of governmental leader, he definitely had not abdicated the position of spiritual leader):*

24 Only fear the LORD, and serve Him in truth with all your heart *(Truth is "Jesus Christ and Him Crucified" [I Cor. 1:23]):* for consider how great things He has done for you *(and that He has!).*

25 But if you shall still do wickedly, you shall be consumed, both you and your king *(God cannot abide unrepentant wickedness, even in His chosen people).*

CHAPTER 13
(1093 B.C.)

WAR AGAINST THE PHILISTINES

SAUL reigned one year; and when he had reigned two years over Israel *(this statement of Verse 1 is the sad record given by the Holy Spirit that Saul only "reigned" two years in fellowship with God; his entire reign was forty years [Acts 13:21], which means that for thirty-eight years he was not in fellowship with God;*

the length of time between Verse 1 and Verse 2 was approximately twenty years; they are passed over in silence by the Spirit of God),

2 Saul chose him three thousand men of Israel; whereof two thousand were with Saul in Michmash and in Mount Beth-el, and a thousand were with Jonathan (his son) in Gibeah of Benjamin: and the rest of the people he sent every man to his tent.

3 And Jonathan smote the garrison of the Philistines that was in Geba, and the Philistines heard of it (Jonathan is a fine illustration of the possibilities and energies of a Divinely-given Faith in the face of hostile circumstances both of parentage and environment). And Saul blew the trumpet throughout all the land, saying, Let the Hebrews hear (Jonathan acted in the energy of Faith, Saul in the energy of nature; Jonathan would call his people "Israelites," as God called them; Saul called them "Hebrews," as the Philistines called them).

4 And all Israel heard say that Saul had smitten a garrison of the Philistines (Saul, as a natural man, and as God's officially-appointed king, could follow the impulse of faith in the heart of Jonathan, but he did not personally possess it; that which seeks its strength in the wisdom and energy of man can never go beyond the source from which it springs), and that Israel also was had in abomination with the Philistines. And the people were called together after Saul to Gilgal (Israel held in abomination by the Philistines presented a far cry from that which God had intended!).

5 And the Philistines gathered themselves together to fight with Israel, thirty thousand chariots, and six thousand horsemen, and people as the sand which is on the sea shore in multitude: and they came up, and pitched in Michmash, eastward from Beth-aven (whenever Faith acts, Satan opposes; and, hence, the Philistines are found quickly encamped against Israel; Satan, who knows and dreads the power of Faith, brought up his agents in multitude as the sand which is on the seashore).

6 When the men of Israel saw that they were in a strait, (for the people were distressed,) then the people did hide themselves in caves, and in thickets, and in rocks, and in high places, and in pits (this is a sad commentary as it regards the people of God; they were to be the head of all nations, but instead they are hiding in "pits"; regrettably, spiritually speaking, this is the condition of the modern Church!).

7 And some of the Hebrews (used here contemptuously) went over Jordan to the land of Gad and Gilead (ran away in a cowardly manner). As for Saul, he was yet in Gilgal, and all the people followed him trembling (trembling for fear).

SELF-WILL

8 And he tarried seven days, according to the set time that Samuel had appointed: but Samuel came not to Gilgal; and the people were scattered from him (scattered from Saul; Williams says, "It is plain from Verses 8 and 13 that Samuel, from the mouth of the Lord, had commanded Saul to summon the people to Gilgal, and there to wait seven days for him; and this was purposely designed by God as a test as to whether Saul would subject himself to God's Will or act in the energy of his own." As we shall see, he didn't pass the test).

9 And Saul said, Bring hither a Burnt Offering to me, and Peace Offerings. And he offered the Burnt Offering. (He did not offer it himself, but rather by the hand of the attendant Priest, Ahiah, who was, we know, with him [14:3]. Saul, who was in charge, and who gave instructions for such to be done, is said to have done it himself. By Saul doing this, it showed that he had no confidence in what the Sacrifices represented; they were to him a mere ceremony. Millions presently treat the Cross in the same manner. It is just a ceremony!)

10 And it came to pass, that as soon as he had made an end of offering the Burnt Offering, behold, Samuel came; and Saul went out to meet him, that he might salute him.

11 And Samuel said, What have you done? And Saul said, Because I saw that the people were scattered from me, and that you came not within the days appointed (but he did!), and that the Philistines gathered themselves together at Michmash;

12 Therefore said I, The Philistines will come down now upon me to Gilgal, and I have not made supplication unto the LORD: I forced myself therefore, and offered a Burnt Offering. (Saul had, as men have today, a religious argument in favor of his disobedience. He had his eyes upon the people, as recorded in Verse 11, and not upon God and His Commandments.)

SAMUEL ANNOUNCES JUDGMENT

13 And Samuel said to Saul, You have done foolishly: you have not kept the Commandment

of the LORD your God, which He commanded you: for now would the LORD have established your kingdom upon Israel for ever.

14 But now your kingdom shall not continue *(Saul's line would not continue as king; he did not lose the throne because of the power of the Philistines, but rather because of the fault that was between his heart and God)*: the LORD has sought him a man after His own heart *(that man would be David)*, and the LORD has commanded him to be captain over His people, because you have not kept that which the LORD commanded you. *(Had Saul truly repented, he might have been forgiven; for God's threatenings, like His Promises, are conditional. There is no fatalism in the Bible, but a loving discipline for man's recovery. But behind it stands the Divine foreknowledge and omnipotence; and so, to the prophetic view, Saul's refusal to repent, his repeated disobedience, and the succession of David were all revealed as accomplished facts — Smith.)*

SAUL'S ARMY

15 And Samuel arose, and got him up from Gilgal unto Gibeah of Benjamin. And Saul numbered the people who were present with him, about six hundred men *(this small number was to face the 30,000 chariots and 6,000 horsemen, plus foot-soldiers as the sand which is on the seashore [Vs. 5]).*

16 And Saul, and Jonathan his son, and the people who were present with them, abode in Gibeah of Benjamin: but the Philistines encamped in Michmash *(Saul represents modern Christendom as officially the visible Kingdom of God upon Earth, but corrupted and enslaved; yet within this broken kingdom it is still possible for faith to win her victories, as Jonathan won his, even as we shall see).*

17 And the spoilers came out of the camp of the Philistines in three companies: one company turned unto the way that leads to Ophrah, unto the land of Shual:

18 And another company turned the way to Beth-horon: and another company turned to the way of the border that looks to the valley of Zeboim toward the wilderness *(the conduct of the Philistines is that of men overconfident in their strength).*

19 Now there was no smith *(blacksmith)* found throughout all the land of Israel: for the Philistines said, Lest the Hebrews make them swords or spears *(this accounts for the contemptuous disregard of Saul by the Philistines; the people were disarmed, and resistance impossible; the picture here is truly sad! Those who professed to be the people of God and heirs of the Promises are found unarmed in the presence of enemies who despoil them; but faith in God may be exercised no matter what the condition of the people of God may be; and God will ever honor it)*:

20 But all the Israelites went down to the Philistines, to sharpen every man his share, and his coulter, and his axe, and his mattock.

21 Yet they had a file for the mattocks, and for the coulters, and for the forks, and for the axes, and to sharpen the goads.

22 So it came to pass in the day of battle, that there was neither sword nor spear found in the hand of any of the people who were with Saul and Jonathan: but with Saul and with Jonathan his son was there found. *(Only Saul and Jonathan had a spear. So, not only were there but 600 Israelites who were to face this horde of Philistines, but even the 600 had no weapons of war. This is a perfect picture of the modern Church, which has no spiritual weapons in order to engage in spiritual warfare, because it doesn't understand the Cross respecting Sanctification [Rom. 6:3-14].)*

23 And the garrison of the Philistines went out to the passage of Michmash.

CHAPTER 14
(1087 B.C.)
JONATHAN'S EXPLOIT

NOW it came to pass upon a day, that Jonathan the son of Saul said unto the young man who bore his armour, Come, and let us go over to the Philistines' garrison, that is on the other side. But he told not his father. *(Without a doubt, the Lord told Jonathan to do this. Williams says, "If the last Chapter shows the folly and effects of unbelief, this Chapter shows the wisdom and results of Faith; for wherever Faith is found, God displays His strength. Thus, the ugliness of unbelief in Saul is contrasted with the beauty of Faith in Jonathan.")*

2 And Saul tarried in the uttermost part of Gibeah under a pomegranate tree which is in Migron: and the people who were with him were about six hundred men *(and, as we have said, without weapons)*;

3 And Ahiah, the son of Ahitub, Ichabod's brother, the son of Phinehas, the son of Eli, the LORD's priest in Shiloh, wearing an Ephod.

And the people knew not that Jonathan was gone *(the Hebrew word here used for "Ephod" refers as well to the Breastplate, which contained the Urim and the Thummim, by which the Will of God was sought [Lev. 8:7-8]).*

4 And between the passages, by which Jonathan sought to go over unto the Philistines' garrison, there was a sharp rock on the one side, and a sharp rock on the other side: and the name of the one was Bozez, and the name of the other Seneh. *(Faith never lessens nor creates difficulties. Her path is open, very narrow, and made difficult by sharp rocks on either hand.)*

5 The forefront of the one was situate northward over against Michmash, and the other southward over against Gibeah.

6 And Jonathan said to the young man who bore his armour, Come, and let us go over unto the garrison of these uncircumcised: it may be that the LORD will work for us: for there is no restraint to the LORD to save by many or by few. *(Williams says, "Jonathan did not think of himself; and his words to his armorbearer do not express doubt as to God's ability to overcome them, but assurance. Faith's fair flower looks never so fair as when blooming in such a rocky and savaged defile, beset with enemies, such as is pictured here.")*

7 And his armourbearer said unto him, Do all that is in your heart: turn thee; behold, I am with you according to your heart. *(The greatest asset a man or a woman of God can have is for individuals to follow them in their Faith. As well, it must be said, "Woe be unto the individual who follows a man in his unbelief.")*

8 Then said Jonathan, Behold, we will pass over unto these men, and we will discover ourselves unto them *(reveal themselves to the Philistines, which, no doubt, the Lord told him to do; it was quite true that Israel, at this time, was no more than a moral ruin; but Faith overcomes all of this, and reaches out toward God, expecting great and mighty things — and God never fails).*

9 If they say thus unto us, Tarry until we come to you; then we will stand still in our place, and will not go up unto them.

10 But if they say thus, Come up unto us; then we will go up: for the LORD has delivered them into our hand: and this shall be a sign unto us. *(Faith is not presumption, and, in fact, is never presumptuous. Most of that today which is called "faith" is, in fact, presumption.*

It presumes upon that which God has not said and does not intend. True Faith never creates difficulties, nor leaps from the pinnacle of the Temple expecting God to bear the consequences. Thus, there was no boasting in Jonathan, as there is in presumption. There is only expectation from God.)

11 And both of them discovered themselves unto the garrison of the Philistines: and the Philistines said, Behold, the Hebrews come forth out of the holes where they had hid themselves *(only two men!; but there is a third with them, yet unseen; it is the Lord).*

12 And the men of the garrison answered Jonathan and his armourbearer, and said, Come up to us, and we will show you a thing. And Jonathan said unto his armourbearer, Come up after me: for the LORD has delivered them into the hand of Israel *(Faith always lifts men up, hence Jonathan saying, "Come up after me").*

13 And Jonathan climbed up upon his hands and upon his feet, and his armourbearer after him: and they fell before Jonathan; and his armourbearer slew after him *(evidently, the Lord turned the attention of the Philistines elsewhere in order that they not see the ascent of Jonathan and his armor-bearer).*

14 And that first slaughter, which Jonathan and his armourbearer made, was about twenty men, within as it were an half acre of land, which a yoke of oxen might plow *(God will not begin to move until Faith begins to act).*

THE MIRACULOUS VICTORY

15 And there was trembling in the host, in the field, and among all the people: the garrison, and the spoilers, they also trembled, and the Earth quaked: so it was a very great trembling *(Faith's great passion is always that God should manifest Himself; a supernatural terror seized the Philistines, for it was manifest that God and not Jonathan was the Author of these manifestations).*

16 And the watchmen of Saul in Gibeah of Benjamin looked; and, behold, the multitude melted away, and they went on beating down one another *(the words "melted away" do not exactly give the meaning; the Philistines were not dispersing, but rather were "reeling," moving to and fro purposeless, and in confusion; they also carry the idea of "terror").*

17 Then said Saul unto the people who were with him, Number now, and see who is gone

from us. And when they had numbered, behold, Jonathan and his armourbearer were not there *(at the very moment that God is giving a tremendous victory to Israel with the Philistines being defeated, the flesh in the person of Saul is trying to find out what's going on; the "flesh" refers to the frail ability of man, which God can never bless [Rom. 8:8]).*

18 And Saul said unto Ahiah, Bring hither the Ark of God. For the Ark of God was at that time with the Children of Israel. *(In Jonathan is seen the quietness and confidence of the "new man," but in Saul the fussiness, excitement, folly, and impotence of the "old man." Unbelief never knows what to do, but it can furnish itself with accessories of religious ceremony. It can build an Altar [Vs. 35], call for the Ark [Vs. 18], and lean upon the priestly member of a condemned house [Vs. 19], but it never knows what to do. It is all excitement, activity, and emotion, but no Faith.)*

19 And it came to pass, while Saul talked unto the Priest, that the noise that was in the host of the Philistines went on and increased: and Saul said unto the Priest, Withdraw your hand *(Saul, impatient of delay, cannot wait till the Will of God is made known to him).*

20 And Saul and all the people who were with him assembled themselves, and they came to the battle: and, behold, every man's sword was against his fellow *(the Philistines were killing each other)*, and there was a very great discomfiture.

21 Moreover the Hebrews who were with the Philistines before that time, which went up with them into the camp from the country round about, even they also turned to be with the Israelites who were with Saul and Jonathan *(in this great Revival, one might say, the Children of God who had lost their way completely, going out into the world, now come back to the Lord as a result of Jonathan's Faith).*

22 Likewise all the men of Israel which had hid themselves in Mount Ephraim, when they heard that the Philistines fled, even they also followed hard after them in the battle *(a move of God evidenced by Faith, which results in victory, brings out even the cowardly and the timid; but that's what Faith is supposed to do!).*

23 So the LORD saved Israel that day: and the battle passed over unto Beth-aven *(if the Lord can get someone to believe Him, He can do great things; to be sure, God, Who is Almighty, doesn't need the help of anyone; however, He has purposely allowed Believers to have a part in His great Work, and that great part is Faith [Rom. 10:17]).*

SAUL'S FOOLISH OATH

24 And the men of Israel were distressed that day: for Saul had adjured the people, saying, Cursed be the man who eats any food until evening, that I may be avenged on my enemies. So none of the people tasted any food. *(Now the "flesh" continues to hinder the Spirit of God. The flesh must do something, so Saul will forbid the people to eat any food. Carnal zeal hinders or limits victory, and when man intrudes himself into the Work of God — bringing his own strength into it — he stops it. His foolish command to put to death those who failed to obey his laws only made more visible the disobedience of his own heart to obey God's Laws. Men love to make laws, and religious men most of all! And they love to force people to obey them, which has been the cause of so much heartache and even bloodshed down through the ages.)*

25 And all they of the land came to a wood; and there was honey upon the ground. *(In the path of Faith, there is honey; and in the path of unbelief, there is hunger. God furnishes ample refreshment upon the Heavenly Way, so that there was a "stream of honey" upon the very battlefield. But that which is an invitation of faith made it a duty, under sentence of death, to partake of it. The corrupt Christian Church is a sad illustration today of the same intrusion of man's will into God's Kingdom.)*

26 And when the people were come into the wood, behold, the honey dropped; but no man put his hand to his mouth: for the people feared the oath *(man-made laws keep God's people from accepting and, thereby, benefiting from that which God has provided; God help us!).*

JONATHAN

27 But Jonathan heard not when his father charged the people with the oath: wherefore he put forth the end of the rod that was in his hand, and dipped it in an honeycomb, and put his hand to his mouth; and his eyes were enlightened *(there are those today who, like happy Jonathan, live and fight with God, and whose Faith in Him leads them so far ahead on the celestial road that they neither hear nor heed the senseless laws which poor men, holding official office in Christendom, make).*

28 Then answered one of the people, and said, Your father straitly charged the people with an oath, saying, Cursed be the man who eats any food this day. And the people were faint *(unscriptural laws made by religious men only tend to make the people "faint").*

29 Then said Jonathan, My father has troubled the land: see, I pray you how my eyes have been enlightened, because I tasted a little of this honey *(has brought disaster to the land; this disaster was the incompleteness of the victory, owing to the people being too exhausted to continue the pursuit; once again, senseless religious laws, which have no Scriptural foundation, only tend to hinder the victory).*

30 How much more, if haply the people had eaten freely to day of the spoil of their enemies which they found? for had there not been now a much greater slaughter among the Philistines? *(Unscriptural religious laws only hinder Faith; they never help!)*

31 And they smote the Philistines that day from Michmash to Aijalon: and the people were very faint *(insinuating that a much greater victory could have been brought about, were it not for Saul; as a Believer, you can be a hindrance or you can be a help).*

THE SIN OF ISRAEL

32 And the people flew upon the spoil, and took sheep, and oxen, and calves, and slew them on the ground: and the people did eat them with the blood *(without properly draining the blood from the carcasses, which was unlawful!).*

33 Then they told Saul, saying, Behold, the people sin against the LORD, in that they eat with the blood. And he said, You have transgressed: roll a great stone unto me this day *(the purpose of this stone was to raise up the carcasses of the slaughtered animals from the ground, so that the blood might drain away from them).*

34 And Saul said, Disperse yourselves among the people, and say unto them, Bring me hither every man his ox, and every man his sheep, and slay them here, and eat; and sin not against the LORD in eating with the blood. And all the people brought every man his ox with him that night, and slew them there.

35 And Saul built an Altar unto the LORD: the same was the first Altar that he built unto the LORD *(the Altar was a Type of the Cross on which Christ would die; however, it is not a magic talisman to be used at one's convenience).*

36 And Saul said, Let us go down after the Philistines by night, and spoil them until the morning light, and let us not leave a man of them. And they said, Do whatsoever seems good unto you. Then said the Priest, Let us draw near hither unto God *(to consult the Lord; Ahiah may have done this because he disapproved of Saul's project, or because generally God ought to be consulted before undertaking anything of importance; already this neglect on the part of Saul had led to no good results).*

37 And Saul asked counsel of God, Shall I go down after the Philistines? will You deliver them into the hand of Israel? But He answered him not that day.

38 And Saul said, Draw ye near hither, all the chief of the people: and know and see wherein this sin has been this day. *(The fault is in him and him alone, and not the people!)*

39 For, as the LORD lives, which saves Israel, though it be in Jonathan my son, he shall surely die. But there was not a man among all the people who answered him *(thus, twice in the same day he is guilty of the sin of rash swearing; the people condemn him by their silence).*

40 Then said he unto all Israel, Be ye on one side, and I and Jonathan my son will be on the other side. And the people said unto Saul, Do what seems good unto you.

41 Therefore Saul said unto the LORD God of Israel, Give a perfect lot *(give us the answer).* And Saul and Jonathan were taken: but the people escaped *(it seems that the Urim and the Thummim were being used by the Priests to divine an answer; Saul is claiming that someone has sinned, and that's the reason the Lord will not answer him; so now, the answer is towards both Saul and Jonathan, but not in the way one would think).*

42 And Saul said, Cast lots between me and Jonathan my son. And Jonathan was taken *(while the Holy Spirit points out Jonathan, in no way does this imply that Jonathan has sinned; it is rather meant to portray the fact that it is Saul who has disobeyed the Lord, with his foolish rules, and just how foolish they have been).*

THE PEOPLE SAVE JONATHAN FROM DEATH

43 Then Saul said to Jonathan, Tell me what you have done. And Jonathan told him, and said, I did but taste a little honey with the end of the rod that was in my hand, and, lo, I must die *(the statement made by Jonathan could*

be in the form of a question, or even sarcastic resignation).

44 And Saul answered, God do so and more also: for you shall surely die, Jonathan (the "flesh" will always try to kill the "Spirit"!).

45 And the people said unto Saul, Shall Jonathan die, who has wrought this great salvation in Israel? God forbid: as the LORD lives, there shall not one hair of his head fall to the ground; for he has wrought with God this day. So the people rescued Jonathan, that he died not (the answer of the Lord through the people is, "God forbid"!).

SAUL'S VICTORIES

46 The Saul went up from following the Philistines: and the Philistines went to their own place (so long as Jonathan by Faith took the lead, everything prospered, but when Saul, that is, unbelief, put himself at the head, the effect was to lose the full fruit of the victory).

47 So Saul took the kingdom over Israel, and fought against all his enemies on every side, against Moab, and against the children of Ammon, and against Edom, and against the kings of Zobah, and against the Philistines: and whithersoever he turned himself, he vexed them.

48 And he gathered an host, and smote the Amalekites, and delivered Israel out of the hands of them that spoiled them. (These Verses account for his victories. Even now, God would accept Saul and bless him greatly, if only he would turn with his "whole heart" to the Lord. But that was not to be!)

SAUL'S FAMILY

49 Now the sons of Saul were Jonathan, and Ishui, and Melchi-shua: and the names of his two daughters were these; the name of the first born Merab, and the name of the younger Michal:

50 And the name of Saul's wife was Ahinoam, the daughter of Ahimaaz: and the name of the captain of his host was Abner, the son of Ner, Saul's uncle.

51 And Kish was the father of Saul; and Ner the father of Abner was the son of Abiel.

52 And there was sore war against the Philistines all the days of Saul: and when Saul saw any strong man, or any valiant man, he took him unto him. (If the Philistines plague us "all our days," it must tell us that flesh is attempting to thwart the Philistine instead of

the Holy Spirit. If we walk after the flesh, we die. If we follow after the Spirit, we live [Rom. 8:1-2]. Ultimately, Saul would die at the hands of the Philistines. Ultimately, David would live at the hands of the Holy Spirit.

The principle is the same presently. To live a victorious life, the Believer must anchor his Faith exclusively in Christ and the Cross, which constitutes "walking after the Spirit." That being done, the help of the Holy Spirit will be forthcoming, with great victories brought about in such a life [Rom. 8:1-2, 11; Gal. 6:14].)

CHAPTER 15
(1079 B.C.)
AMALEK

SAMUEL also said unto Saul, The LORD sent me to anoint you to be king over his people, over Israel: now therefore hearken thou unto the voice of the Words of the LORD. (We find that Saul was tested twice and failed under each test. The Philistine was God's instrument in the first test; the Amalekite, in the second. The first test proved him to be carnal, for he waited on God, but not for God. The second test showed him to be disobedient, for he set his own will above God's Will. In the first test, he failed to trust God; in the second test, to obey God. These two words, "trust" and "obey," are keynotes in the Christian life, and are impossible to those outside that life — Williams.)

2 Thus saith the LORD of hosts, I remember that which Amalek did to Israel, how he laid wait for him in the way, when he came up from Egypt (the Lord forgets neither wrongs nor rights, unless the wrongs are washed by His Blood, and then they are forgotten).

3 Now go and smite Amalek, and utterly destroy all that they have, and spare them not; but slay both man and woman, infant and suckling, ox and sheep, camel and ass. (The key word is "utterly destroy." Amalek, in Old Testament typology, is a "type of the flesh." The flesh pertains to the "Adamic nature" or the "sin nature." It characterizes man's own efforts to save himself, whether by good works, money, education, or religion. It is the bane of the Child of God. It is the source of the Christian's greatest conflict. Paul said, "For if you live after the flesh, you shall die" [Rom. 8:13].)

SAUL'S INCOMPLETE OBEDIENCE

4 And Saul gathered the people together,

and numbered them in Telaim, two hundred thousand footmen, and ten thousand men of Judah.

5 And Saul came to a city of Amalek, and laid wait in the valley.

6 And Saul said unto the Kenites, Go, depart, get you down from among the Amalekites, lest I destroy you with them: for you showed kindness to all the Children of Israel, when they came up out of Egypt. So the Kenites departed from among the Amalekites.

7 And Saul smote the Amalekites from Havilah until you come to Shur, that is over against Egypt. (*The Amalekites were the determined and cruel enemies of the people of God. They were the first to attack them in the desert [Ex., Chpt. 17]. When Israel was faint and weary, they attacked the feeble among them [Deut. 25:18]. Because of this hatred, God commanded their extinction, and urged His people not to forget that duty so soon as they were settled in Canaan [Deut. 25:19]. They did forget; but God did not forget.*

In fact, God gave Amalek five hundred years respite for Repentance, but in vain. That nation, like the seven nations of Canaan, resisted every Divine impulse, and finally became so corrupt that, in the interests of humanity, love decreed its absolute extinction.)

8 And he took Agag the king of the Amalekites alive, and utterly destroyed all the people with the edge of the sword. (*This has always been the problem of Christians. We desire to destroy "everything that is vile and refuse"; however, it is very difficult for us to destroy "the best."*

What do we mean by "the best"? It pertains to anything and everything which we trust, other than Christ and what Christ has done for us at the Cross. Anything that becomes the object of our faith, other than the Cross, no matter how good it might be in its own right, must be eliminated. Faith in everything else must be "utterly destroyed.").

9 But Saul and the people spared Agag, and the best of the sheep, and of the oxen, and of the fatlings, and the lambs, and all that was good, and would not utterly destroy them: but every thing that was vile and refuse, that they destroyed utterly. (*And so we have here a perfect picture, not only of that time, but, as well, of modern Christendom. The only thing that God will accept is "Jesus Christ and Him Crucified" [I Cor. 1:23]. The Message of the Cross is easy to understand, but not easy to believe. Religious man still likes to hold on to his own particular efforts and works, whatever they might be, which God can never accept.*)

JUDGMENT

10 Then came the Word of the LORD unto Samuel, saying,

11 It repents Me that I have set up Saul to be king: for he is turned back from following Me, and has not performed My Commandments. And it grieved Samuel; and he cried unto the LORD all night. (*These words, as given by the Lord, simply mean that God had changed His Purpose or Plan concerning Saul. Had he been obedient, then his kingdom would have been established [13:13], but because he had been disobedient, and it seemed he was continuing to function in this capacity, his kingdom would not continue with him.*)

12 And when Samuel rose early to meet Saul in the morning, it was told Samuel, saying, Saul came to Carmel, and, behold, he set him up a place, and is gone about, and passed on, and gone down to Gilgal.

13 And Samuel came to Saul (*it probably took several days to reach Saul, because of the distance*): and Saul said unto him, Blessed be thou of the LORD: I have performed the Commandment of the LORD (*and so he had performed the Commandment of the Lord, halfway, as men generally keep God's Commandments, doing that part which is agreeable to themselves, and leaving that part undone which gives them neither pleasure nor profit — Smith*).

14 And Samuel said, What means then this bleating of the sheep in my ears, and the lowing of the oxen which I hear? (*Unfortunately, in the modern Church, the "bleating of the sheep" and the "lowing of the oxen" are so constant that anymore they are hardly noticed.*)

15 And Saul said, They have brought them from the Amalekites: for the people spared the best of the sheep and of the oxen, to sacrifice unto the LORD your God; and the rest we have utterly destroyed. (*The Holy Spirit says that "Saul and the people" spared Agag and the best of the spoil [Vs. 9], but Saul said that it was "the people who spared them," trying to absolve himself of blame!*)

16 Then Samuel said unto Saul, Stay, and I will tell you what the LORD has said to me this night. And he said unto him, Say on (*the Message would not be too pleasant!*).

17 And Samuel said, When you were little

in your own sight, were you not made the head of the Tribes of Israel, and the LORD anointed you king over Israel?

18 And the LORD sent you on a journey, and said, Go and utterly destroy the sinners the Amalekites, and fight against them until they be consumed.

19 Wherefore then did you not obey the voice of the LORD, but did fly upon the spoil, and did evil in the sight of the LORD?

20 And Saul said unto Samuel, Yea, I have obeyed the voice of the LORD, and have gone the way which the LORD sent me, and have brought Agag the king of Amalek, and have utterly destroyed the Amalekites.

21 But the people took of the spoil, sheep and oxen, the chief of the things which should have been utterly destroyed, to sacrifice unto the LORD your God in Gilgal.

22 And Samuel said, Has the LORD as great delight in Burnt Offerings and Sacrifices, as in obeying the voice of the LORD? Behold, to obey is better than sacrifice, and to hearken than the fat of rams. *(It is much better to obey the Lord in the first place than to disobey and then to have to ask for forgiveness, trusting in the Sacrifice of Calvary. While forgiveness is always available [I Jn. 1:9], it is better to not need forgiveness!)*

23 For rebellion is as the sin of witchcraft *(the taproot of all sin is "rebellion"; witchcraft is the effort to manipulate the spirit world through demon spirits; how is that like rebellion? To rebel against God's order, which is "Christ and Him Crucified," is to take matters into one's own hands, which is the same as witchcraft)*, and stubbornness is as iniquity and idolatry *("stubbornness" is an intractable spirit that refuses to believe God's Word)*. Because you have rejected the Word of the LORD, He has also rejected you from being king.

SAUL'S HUMILIATION

24 And Saul said unto Samuel, I have sinned: for I have transgressed the Commandment of the LORD, and your words: because I feared the people, and obeyed their voice.

25 Now therefore, I pray thee, pardon my sin, and turn again with me, that I may worship the LORD. *(All these statements were falsehoods. Saul's professions of Repentance were false, for he thought only of the threatened punishment and his own honor. True Repentance is toward God — and hence David said, "I have*

sinned against Jehovah," while Saul said only, "I have sinned.")

THE REJECTION OF SAUL

26 And Samuel said unto Saul, I will not return with you: for you have rejected the Word of the LORD, and the LORD has rejected you from being king over Israel *(to reject the Word of the Lord is to be rejected by the Lord)*.

27 And as Samuel turned about to go away, he *(Saul)* laid hold upon the skirt of his mantle, and it rent.

28 And Samuel said unto him, The LORD has rent the kingdom of Israel from you this day, and has given it to a neighbour of yours, that is better than you. *(Even though David is not mentioned here, David is the one of whom the Holy Spirit speaks. Even though Saul would continue to serve for a period of time as king of Israel, in God's mind the change had begun in the spirit realm at that moment.)*

29 And also the Strength of Israel will not lie nor repent: for He is not a man, that He should repent. *(This was quoted by Samuel from the account of Balaam, as given in Numbers 23:19. The Divine title, "the Strength of Israel," refers to the Lord, and is used here for the very first time in Scripture.)*

30 Then he said, I have sinned: yet honour me now, I pray you, before the elders of my people, and before Israel, and turn again with me, that I may worship the LORD your God. *(It seems that Saul was more concerned about how he looked in regards to the people than with God. So it is with the majority of that which is presently called "the Church.")*

31 So Samuel turned again after Saul; and Saul worshipped the LORD *(although Samuel turned again after Saul, it does not say that he joined him in his act of official worship, for as soon as possible he left him forever).*

SAMUEL SLAYS AGAG

32 Then said Samuel, Bring ye hither to me Agag the king of the Amalekites. And Agag came unto him delicately *(the Hebrew word rendered "delicately" should have been translated "in bonds")*. And Agag said, Surely the bitterness of death is past *(Agag came trembling for his life).*

33 And Samuel said, As your sword has made women childless, so shall your mother be childless among women. And Samuel hewed

Agag in pieces before the LORD in Gilgal. *(The Passage means that Samuel commanded the execution to be carried out; he did not do it personally. In the spiritual sense, we love our "Agags." The idea of hewing them in pieces is very distasteful; nevertheless, all "works of the flesh," of which Agag was a type, must be "hewed in pieces.")*

34 Then Samuel went to Ramah; and Saul went up to his house to Gibeah of Saul.

35 And Samuel came no more to see Saul until the day of his death: nevertheless Samuel mourned for Saul: and the LORD repented that He had made Saul king over Israel. *(Saul, due to rebellion against God, was no longer the representative of Jehovah and, consequently, Samuel no more came to him, bearing messages and commands, and giving him counsel and guidance from God. The Lord had cut him off.)*

CHAPTER 16
(1063 B.C.)
JESSE THE BETHLEHEMITE

A ND the LORD said unto Samuel *(interrupts the great Prophet's negative thoughts)*, How long will you mourn for Saul *(Samuel was mourning and, at the same time, God was planning the greatest moment in Israel's history; the truth is, we have nothing to mourn, for, at this moment, God is planning great things for us; we must remember that!)*, seeing I have rejected him from reigning over Israel? *(The Lord rejects all who will not obey His Word.)* fill your horn with oil *(a Type of the Holy Spirit)*, and go *(if the Holy Spirit is present, it is always in order that a mission be accomplished)*, I will send you to Jesse the Beth-lehemite: for I have provided Me a king among his sons *(of course, that was David, but, above all, the provision was the Greater Son of David)*.

2 And Samuel said, How can I go? if Saul hear it, he will kill me *(the "flesh" always tries to kill the Spirit; the two cannot abide; this work of the flesh demanded by Israel will hinder and, quite possibly, delay the work of the Spirit; how so much the Church deprives itself because it follows the ways of man and not of the Lord; it is said that the very work of the flesh which causes us so much difficulty and problem is, in fact, created by our own design)*. And the LORD said, Take an heifer with you, and say, I am come to Sacrifice to the LORD *(the selection of David centered up in the Sacrifice of Calvary, and this was the real mission of the Prophet)*.

3 And call Jesse to the Sacrifice, and I will show you what you shall do: and you shall anoint unto Me him whom I name unto you *(if it is to be noticed, the Lord did not divulge to Samuel as to which of Jesse's sons He would choose)*.

4 And Samuel did that which the LORD spoke, and came to Beth-lehem. And the elders of the town trembled at his coming, and said, Do you come peaceably? *(They feared the Prophet, because they knew that whatever he said always came to pass. But this time, they had nothing to fear.)*

5 And he said, Peaceably: I am come to sacrifice unto the LORD: sanctify yourselves, and come with me to the Sacrifice. And he sanctified Jesse and his sons, and called them to the Sacrifice *(the Lord is calling the entirety of mankind to "Come to the Sacrifice," which refers to coming to the Cross; there is no Salvation or Victory outside of the Cross of Christ)*.

DAVID CHOSEN

6 And it came to pass, when they were come *(Jesse and his sons)*, that he *(Samuel)* looked on Eliab, and said, Surely the LORD's anointed is before him. *(This was David's brother, and he looked the part of the king. This shows us that even a great Prophet like Samuel cannot trust his own intuition. To have done so would have been to have grossly violated the Will of God. We must ardently seek God concerning His Will, as it regards all things, both small and large.)*

7 But the LORD said unto Samuel, Look not on his countenance, or on the height of his stature; because I have refused him: for the Lord sees not as man sees; for man looks on the outward appearance, but the LORD looks on the heart *(and only God knows the heart of man)*.

8 Then Jesse called Abinadab, and made him pass before Samuel. And he said, Neither has the LORD chosen this.

9 Then Jesse made Shammah to pass by. And he said, Neither has the LORD chosen this.

10 Again, Jesse made seven of his sons to pass before Samuel. And Samuel said unto Jesse, The LORD has not chosen these.

11 And Samuel said unto Jesse, Are here all your children? And he said, There remains yet the youngest, and, behold, he keeps the sheep *(a Type of Christ as the good Shepherd)*. And

Samuel said unto Jesse, Send and fetch him: for we will not sit down till he comes hither. *(David was the youngest, and apparently his father Jesse thought it would be useless to bring him into the house. Generally, those who are totally rejected by men are the very ones whom God chooses.)*

12 And he sent, and brought him in. Now he was ruddy *(red-haired)*, and withal of a beautiful countenance *(the Hebrew says, "with beautiful eyes")*, and goodly to look to *(to look at, handsome)*. And the LORD said, Arise, anoint him: for this is he. *(It is believed that David was probably about 15 years of age at this time. It would be years before he would take the Throne, but this is the beginning of the glory days of Israel.)*

13 Then Samuel took the horn of oil, and anointed him in the midst of his brethren *(this was Samuel's last and crowning work; he would train the man who more nearly than any other approached unto the ideal of the theocratic king, and was to Israel the type of their coming Messiah; it was Samuel's wisdom in teaching his young men music which gave David the skill to be the sweet singer of the Sanctuary; and we may feel sure also that when David arranged the service of the House of God, and gave Priests and Levites their appointed duties [I Chron. 23:26], the model which he set before him was that in which he had so often taken part with Samuel at Ramah, with, of course, the Lord guiding it all — Smith)*: and the Spirit of the LORD came upon David from that day forward *(which would be the means by which all things good were accomplished in David's life; David's name would be the very first human name in the New Testament and the very last human name in the New Testament; in fact, the Messiah would be referred to as "the Son of David," because He would come through the lineage of David's family [II Sam., Chpt. 7])*. So Samuel rose up, and went to Ramah.

THE SPIRIT OF THE LORD DEPARTS FROM SAUL

14 But the Spirit of the LORD departed from Saul, and an evil spirit from the LORD troubled him. *(The Spirit of the Lord did not arbitrarily depart from Saul, but did so because Saul no longer wanted God. Because the Holy Spirit was not wanted, an evil spirit was allowed to go to Saul and trouble him, but only because of Saul's rebellion.)*

15 And Saul's servants said unto him, Behold now, an evil spirit from God troubles you.

16 Let our lord now command your servants, which are before you, to seek out a man, who is a cunning player on an harp: and it shall come to pass, when the evil spirit from God is upon you, that he shall play with his hand, and you shall be well. *(Verses 14-23 do not follow the previous part of the Chapter in chronological order. Actually, this latter Passage comes between 19:9 and 19:10, to show the contrast between the two spirits of Saul and David and the success of one and the failure of the other. Quite possibly, the attendants of Saul had learned the value of consecrated music from Samuel.)*

17 And Saul said unto his servants, Provide me now a man who can play well, and bring him to me.

18 Then answered one of the servants, and said, Behold, I have seen a son of Jesse the Beth-lehemite, who is cunning *(skillful)* in playing, and a mighty valiant man, and a man of war, and prudent in matters, and a comely person, and the LORD is with him. *(Williams says, "God did not at once set David upon the throne as He had done in the case of Saul. He had first to be tested, and humbled, and made to feel his dependence on God, and the sufficiency of God to uphold him and maintain him. Hence, at the outset of his career, he is brought face-to-face with Satan. So was it with the Blessed One, of Whom David was a Type. His public life began with an encounter with the Devil. It was thus, and by his subsequent sufferings, that David was molded and trained to be the channel through which the Psalms were given to the world.")*

SAUL SENDS FOR DAVID

19 Wherefore Saul sent messengers unto Jesse, and said, Send me David your son, which is with the sheep.

20 And Jesse took an ass laden with bread, and a bottle of wine, and a kid *(baby lamb)*, and sent them by David his son unto Saul.

21 And David came to Saul, and stood before him: and he loved him greatly; and he became his armourbearer *(it was apparently after the combat with Goliath that Saul sent to Jesse, and asked that David might be always with him, at least until his jealousy intervened)*.

22 And Saul sent to Jesse, saying, Let David, I pray you, stand before me; for he has found

favour in my sight.

23 And it came to pass, when the evil spirit from God was upon Saul, that David took an harp, and played with his hand: so Saul was refreshed, and was well, and the evil spirit departed from him. *(When we read this Verse, we are actually reading the very first mention of God's use of music for worship, for refreshing, and for healing. In fact, music is one of the greatest healing agents on the face of the Earth, and it is derived from the 23rd Verse, "So Saul was refreshed, and was well"; however, for such to be, it has to be music that is ordained by the Lord and, thereby, sanctified by the Spirit.)*

CHAPTER 17
(1063 B.C.)
GOLIATH

NOW the Philistines gathered together their armies to battle, and were gathered together at Shochoh, which belongs to Judah, and pitched between Shochoh and Azekah, in Ephes-dammim. *(We are told, "There was sore war against the Philistines all the days of Saul" [14:52]. The Philistines were an inward foe, which is much worse than an outward foe. Because Saul never did quite defeat this inward foe, at least conclusively, that inward foe would ultimately defeat him.*

Spiritually, it is the same presently. We must defeat all inward foes. This can be done only by the Believer placing his Faith exclusively in Christ and the Cross. The Cross must not be eliminated or pushed aside. If this is done, the Holy Spirit will not help us, and that leaves such a person with no course but that of defeat [Rom. 7:15].)

2 And Saul and the men of Israel were gathered together, and pitched by the valley of Elah, and set the battle in array against the Philistines.

3 And the Philistines stood on a mountain on the one side, and Israel stood on a mountain on the other side: and there was a valley between them.

4 And there went out a champion out of the camp of the Philistines, named Goliath, of Gath, whose height was six cubits and a span. *(This means that he was over 9 feet tall. In a spiritual sense, this is exactly what every Believer faces; and, to be sure, it is not possible for us to defeat such opposition within our own power and strength. There is only one way it can be done, and that is by looking to the Cross. When the Holy Spirit through Paul told Believers how*

to live for God, He took us, first of all, to the Cross. It is found in Romans 6:3-5. If the Believer doesn't understand the Cross as it regards Sanctification, then it's impossible for such a Believer to defeat the Goliaths which come against him [Rom., Chpt. 7; Gal., Chpt. 5].)

5 And he had an helmet of brass upon his head, and he was armed with a coat of mail; and the weight of the coast was five thousand shekels of brass *(about 125 pounds)*.

6 And he had greaves of brass upon his legs, and a target of brass between his shoulders.

7 And the staff of his spear was like a weaver's beam; and his spear's head weighed six hundred shekels of iron *(about 15 pounds)*: and one bearing a shield went before him. *(The number "six" is stamped upon Goliath. He was six cubits high, and he had six pieces of armor, counting the weapons. The number "six" was stamped upon Nebuchadnezzar's golden image. And it will identify the future Antichrist, the number of whose name will be 666 [Rev. 13:18].)*

8 And he stood and cried unto the armies of Israel, and said unto them, Why are you come out to set your battle in array? am not I a Philistine, and you servants to Saul? choose you a man for you, and let him come down to me. *(Goliath was one of the last giants which were a product between fallen angels and women [Gen. 6:4]. This effort of Satan was meant to corrupt the bloodline, which would stop the coming of the Messiah, which occasioned Noah's flood, with this last insurgence meant to take over the Promised Land, which would deny God's people a place, and thereby, as well, stop the coming of the Messiah.)*

9 If he be able to fight with me, and to kill me, then will we be your servants: but if I prevail against him, and kill him, then shall you be our servants, and serve us. *(Regrettably, most Christians are now serving the Philistines, i.e., "bondages," because they do not understand the Cross [Rom. 6:3-14.)*

10 And the Philistine said, I defy the armies of Israel this day; give me a man, that we may fight together. *(The only "fight" we are called upon as Believers to engage is the "good fight of Faith" [I Tim. 6:12].)*

11 When Saul and all Israel heard those words of the Philistine, they were dismayed, and greatly afraid. *(If they were going to attempt to fight him by natural means, they had every right to be afraid; once again, in reading these words, the Believer should understand that in the spiritual realm you are facing Goliaths.*

There is no way you can defeat these terrible powers of darkness, unless you do it according to God's prescribed order [Rom. 6:14].)

DAVID

12 Now David was the son of that Ephrathite of Beth-lehem-judah, whose name was Jesse; and he had eight sons: and the man went among men for an old man in the days of Saul.

13 And the three eldest sons of Jesse went and followed Saul to the battle: and the names of his three sons who went to the battle were Eliab the first born, and next unto him Abinadab, and the third Shammah.

14 And David was the youngest: and the three eldest followed Saul.

15 But David went and returned from Saul to feed his father's sheep at Beth-lehem. *(This seems to be after the occasion of David playing the harp for Saul, which probably happened about two years earlier. Two years for a teenager brings about great changes, which is probably the reason that Saul did not recognize David, as we shall see.)*

16 And the Philistine drew near morning and evening, and presented himself forty days. *(The probationary number in the Bible is 40. Through David, who, in this instance, was a Type of Christ, Israel would pass this test.)*

17 And Jesse said unto David his son, Take now for your brethren an ephah of this parched corn, and these ten loaves, and run to the camp to your brethren;

18 And carry these ten cheeses unto the captain of their thousand, and look how your brethren fare, and take their pledge *(meaning they would give some token to David to take back to them, signifying that they were well and healthy)*.

19 Now Saul, and they, and all the men of Israel, were in the valley of Elah, fighting with the Philistines *(actually, there had not been any heavy fighting as of yet, but such fighting was the intention)*.

20 And David rose up early in the morning, and left the sheep with a keeper, and took, and went, as Jesse had commanded him; and he came to the trench, as the host was going forth to the fight, and shouted for the battle.

21 For Israel and the Philistines had put the battle in array, army against army.

22 And David left his carriage *(stuff)* in the hand of the keeper of the carriage, and ran into the army, and came and saluted his brethren.

THE TAUNT OF THE GIANT

23 And as he *(David)* talked with them *(his brothers)*, behold, there came up the champion, the Philistine of Gath, Goliath by name, out of the armies of the Philistines, and spoke according to the same words: and David heard them *(the challenge of Verses 8-10)*.

24 And all the men of Israel, when they saw the man, fled from him, and were sore afraid.

25 And the men of Israel said, Have you seen this man that is come up? surely to defy Israel is he come up: and it shall be, that the man who kills him, the king will enrich him with great riches, and will give him his daughter, and make his father's house free in Israel *(probably meant that the family was free from taxes, and maybe even personal service in the army)*.

26 And David spoke to the men who stood by him, Saying, What shall be done to the man who kills this Philistine, and takes away the reproach from Israel? for who is this uncircumcised Philistine, that he should defy the armies of the living God?

27 And the people answered him after this manner, saying, So shall it be done to the man who kills him.

28 And Eliab his eldest brother heard when he spoke unto the men; and Eliab's anger was kindled against David, and he said, Why did you come here? and with whom have you left those few sheep in the wilderness? *(Meant sarcastically.)* I know your pride, and the naughtiness of your heart; for you are come down that you might see the battle *(said with contempt!)*.

29 And David said, What have I now done? is there not a cause? *(In effect, David said, "I was only talking about this challenge, and was doing no wrong.")*

30 And he *(David)* turned from him *(Eliab)* toward another, and spoke after the same manner: and the people answered him again after the former manner *(they told him that Saul would enrich anyone who killed the giant)*.

31 And when the words were heard which David spoke, they rehearsed them before Saul: and he sent for him *(evidently, David had been stating that he would fight the giant, which seems to have infuriated his brother)*.

DAVID KILLS GOLIATH

32 And David said to Saul *(after he was taken to the king)*, Let no man's heart fail because of

him; your servant will go and fight with this Philistine (*undoubtedly, at this point, the Lord had already told David what to do; consequently, his statements are now made on the basis of the principle of faith*).

33 And Saul said to David, You are not able to go against this Philistine to fight with him: for you are but a youth, and he a man of war from his youth (*in the natural, all of this was correct!*).

34 And David said unto Saul, Your servant kept his father's sheep, and there came a lion, and a bear, and took a lamb out of the flock:

35 And I went out after him, and smote him, and delivered it out of his mouth: and when he arose against me, I caught him by his beard, and smote him, and slew him (*all of this because the Spirit of the Lord was upon David from the time of his anointing [16:13]*).

36 Your servant slew both the lion and the bear: and this uncircumcised Philistine shall be as one of them, seeing he has defied the armies of the Living God (*to boast accordingly in the natural would have been foolish indeed; however, and as stated, the Lord had no doubt already told David what to do*).

37 David said moreover, The LORD Who delivered me out of the paw of the lion, and out of the paw of the bear, he will deliver me out of the hand of this Philistine. And Saul said unto David, Go, and the LORD be with you.

38 And Saul armed David with his armour, and he put an helmet of brass upon his head; also he armed him with a coat of mail.

39 And David girded his sword upon his armour, and he assayed to go; for he had not proved it. And David said unto Saul, I cannot go with these; for I have not proved them. And David put them off him. (*The "flesh" will ever try to hinder faith by clothing it with unbelief. Saul's armor will defeat no Philistines. It will destroy no Goliath and, yet, the Church keeps trying to wear it. Take it off and put on the whole armor of God.*

David would be detained a moment by unbelief, but would soon gather his spiritual perspective and allow faith to proceed. The "armor" of Saul is the bane of the Church!)

40 And he took his staff in his hand (*a Type of the Word of God; in fact, the history of these families was carved upon the staffs and, in David's case, would have included the Lord's dealings with him*), and chose him five smooth stones (*five is the number of Grace; with an uninterrupted flow of Grace, which is the Goodness of God freely given to us, anything can be done*) out of the brook (*a Type of the Holy Spirit*), and put them in a shepherd's bag which he had (*represents the Gifts of the Spirit*), even in a scrip; and his sling was in his hand: and he drew near to the Philistine.

41 And the Philistine came on and drew near unto David; and the man that bore the shield went before him (*before Goliath*).

42 And when the Philistine looked about, and saw David, he disdained him: for he was but a youth, and ruddy, and of a fair countenance (*the Giant made fun of David and, more than likely, the Philistine army was laughing, as well*).

THE RESPONSE OF THE GIANT

43 And the Philistine said unto David, Am I a dog, that you come to me with staves? And the Philistine cursed David by his gods (*he probably claimed the help of Dagon, the Philistine god*).

44 And the Philistine said to David, Come to me, and I will give your flesh unto the fowls of the air, and to the beasts of the field (*or so he thought!*).

THE RESPONSE OF DAVID

45 Then said David to the Philistine, You come to me with a sword, and with a spear, and with a shield: but I come to you in the name of the LORD of Hosts, the God of the armies of Israel, whom you have defied (*as Goliath cursed David by his gods, David now invokes the "Name of the Lord of Hosts"; so, in effect, it is Jehovah against "Dagon"*).

46 This day will the LORD deliver you into my hand (*as stated, the Lord had already told him what to do*); and I will smite you, and take your head from you; and I will give the carcases of the host of the Philistines this day unto the fowls of the air, and to the wild beasts of the Earth; that all the Earth may know that there is a God in Israel. (*David wasn't dealing from presumption, but rather from a sure Word of the Lord; hence, he could boast!*)

47 And all this assembly shall know that the LORD saves not with sword and spear: for the battle is the LORD's, and He will give you into our hands. (*To be sure, the "battle is the Lord's"; however, we have to function against the giants which come against us according to God's prescribed order, or else we will lose the conflict.*

That "order" is Christ and what He did for us at the Cross, which must ever be the object of our Faith. That being the case, the Holy Spirit will then take our part, exactly as He did for David, and we are assured of victory [Rom. 8:1-2, 11].)

48 And it came to pass, when the Philistine arose, and came, and drew near to meet David, that David hasted, and ran toward the army to meet the Philistine *(Faith does not retreat, but rather runs toward its foe).*

49 And David put his hand in his bag, and took thence a stone, and slang it, and smote the Philistine in his forehead, that the stone sunk into his forehead; and he fell upon his face to the earth. *(This was a type of what Jesus would ultimately do to Satan. It had been predicted by the Lord immediately after the Fall, when He said to Satan through the serpent, "And I will put enmity between you and the woman, and between your seed and her Seed; it [He] shall bruise your head, and you shall bruise His heel" [Gen. 3:15].)*

50 So David prevailed over the Philistine with a sling and with a stone, and smote the Philistine, and slew him; but there was no sword in the hand of David. *(God is not limited as to what He can use to bring about victory. In this case, He would use "a sling and a stone," but possessed by a boy who had faith.)*

51 Therefore David ran, and stood upon the Philistine *(the Christian is meant to stand upon his Goliaths, and not them standing upon him),* and took his sword *(the Sword of the Spirit),* and drew it out of the sheath thereof, and slew him, and cut off his head therewith. And when the Philistines saw their champion was dead, they fled.

52 And the men of Israel and of Judah arose, and shouted, and pursued the Philistines, until you come to the valley, and to the gates of Ekron. And the wounded of the Philistines fell down by the way to Shaaraim, even unto Gath, and unto Ekron.

53 And the Children of Israel returned from chasing after the Philistines, and they spoiled their tents *(took all the spoils which had been left).*

54 And David took the head of the Philistine, and brought it to Jerusalem; but he put his armour in his tent *(about a thousand years later, our Heavenly David would walk out of the tomb with the head of Satan, so to speak, in His Hand; and, because He lives, we shall live also).*

55 And when Saul saw David go forth against the Philistine, he said unto Abner, the captain of the host, Abner, whose son is this youth? And Abner said, As your soul lives, O king, I cannot tell.

56 And the king said, Enquire thou whose son the stripling is.

57 And as David returned from the slaughter of the Philistine, Abner took him, and brought him before Saul with the head of the Philistine in his hand.

58 And Saul said to him, Whose son are you, you young man? And David answered, I am the son of your servant Jesse the Beth-lehemite *(as stated, possibly some two years or more had passed since David had played the harp for Saul, so he didn't recognize the young man as the same one who had calmed him with music).*

CHAPTER 18
(1063 B.C.)
JONATHAN AND DAVID

AND it came to pass, when he had made an end of speaking unto Saul, that the soul of Jonathan *(the son of Saul)* was knit with the soul of David, and Jonathan loved him as his own soul *(Jonathan was to David as an older brother).*

2 And Saul took him that day, and would let him go no more home to his father's house *(brought David into the court).*

3 Then Jonathan and David made a covenant, because he loved him as his own soul.

4 And Jonathan stripped himself of the robe that was upon him, and gave it to David, and his garments, even to his sword, and to his bow, and to his girdle. *(The covenant basically meant that whatever belonged to Jonathan now belonged to David. [In effect, he was giving David the kingdom, because he knew that God had called him for such.] Whatever belonged to David now belonged to Jonathan, as well! They would go so far as to lay down their lives for each other, if necessary. It would also extend to their children; hence, this is the reason that David would bring Mephibosheth into the palace and give him place and position [II Sam., Chpt. 9].*

The covenant that is spoken of is basically a type of the New Covenant made by Christ on the Cross. We enter into that Covenant by the virtue of Faith in Christ and what He has done for us [Jn. 3:16].)

SAUL BECOMES JEALOUS OF DAVID

5 And David went out whithersoever Saul

sent him, and behaved himself wisely (*the Holy Spirit will bear this out concerning David several times; he did this by the help of the Spirit*): and Saul set him over the men of war (*a special group*), and he was accepted in the sight of all the people, and also in the sight of Saul's servants.

6 And it came to pass as they came, when David was returned from the slaughter of the Philistine, that the women came out of all cities of Israel, singing and dancing, to meet king Saul, with tabrets, with joy, and with instruments of musick (*because of their victories*).

7 And the women answered one another as they played, and said, Saul has slain his thousands, and David his ten thousands.

8 And Saul was very angry, and the saying displeased him; and he said, They have ascribed unto David ten thousands, and to me they have ascribed but thousands: and what can he have more but the kingdom? (*When Saul had stood powerless before the enemy, a shepherd boy had stepped forth and given him the victory. This stripling, taken to be his companion in arms, had shown so great qualities that the people reckoned him at ten times Saul's worth. Due to a total lack of spirituality, Saul could not handle this.*)

9 And Saul eyed David from that day and forward (*with intent to harm him*).

10 And it came to pass on the morrow, that the evil spirit from God came upon Saul, and he prophesied in the midst of the house (*however, he wasn't prophesying by the Spirit of God, but rather by the power of demon spirits*): and David played with his hand, as at other times (*played the harp*): and there was a javelin in Saul's hand.

11 And Saul cast the javelin; for he said, I will smite David even to the wall with it. And David avoided out of his presence twice (*instead of allowing David to draw him to the Lord, he took the opposite road, and tried to kill David*).

12 And Saul was afraid of David, because the LORD was with him, and was departed from Saul (*in effect, he sees the handwriting on the wall!*).

13 Therefore Saul removed him from him, and made him his captain over a thousand; and he went out and came in before the people. (*Evidently the administrative affairs of the kingdom had been neglected, with David now functioning somewhat in this capacity. In a sense, Saul promoted David, giving him the charge of*

a thousand men; but David was no longer in the presence of Saul. *Evidently, Saul didn't know what to do with him, because he was so popular with the people.*)

14 And David behaved himself wisely in all his ways; and the LORD was with him (*that was the reason for the blessings*).

15 Wherefore when Saul saw that he behaved himself very wisely, he was afraid of him.

16 But all Israel and Judah loved David, because he went out and came in before them (*he was totally trustworthy, and, as stated, "behaved himself wisely"!*).

DAVID MARRIES SAUL'S DAUGHTER

17 And Saul said to David, Behold my elder daughter Merab, her will I give you to wife: only be thou valiant for me, and fight the LORD's battles. For Saul said, Let not my hand be upon him, but let the hand of the Philistines be upon him (*constantly sending David out to battle, Saul believed that he would ultimately be killed, which he desired*).

18 And David said unto Saul, Who am I? and what is my life, or my father's family in Israel, that I should be son in law to the king?

19 But it came to pass at the time when Merab Saul's daughter should have been given to David, that she was given unto Adriel the Meholathite to wife. (*The king's promise to give his daughter to the victor was not kept; but, on the contrary, a snare was set for David's foot. Merab was indeed proposed, but upon the added condition that David should venture his life and slay more of the Philistines, and thereby, as Saul hoped, lose his life. But this plan having failed, the king laid another snare for him. He grossly insulted him by giving the bride, a day or two before the marriage, to another man. By this, no doubt, he hoped to sting David into some disloyal language or conduct that would justify his being put to death. But this also failed.*)

20 And Michal Saul's daughter loved David: and they told Saul, and the thing pleased him.

21 And Saul said, I will give him her, that she may be a snare to him, and that the hand of the Philistines may be against him. Wherefore Saul said to David, You shall this day be my son in law in the one of the twain (*David will marry the other daughter*).

22 And Saul commanded his servants, saying, Commune with David secretly, and say, Behold, the king has delight in you, and all his

servants love you: now therefore be the king's son in law.

23 And Saul's servants spoke those words in the ears of David. And David said, Seem it to you a light thing to be a king's son in law, seeing that I am poor man, and lightly esteemed?

24 And the servants of Saul told him, saying, On this manner spoke David *(they told Saul what David said, which means that David said nothing as it regards what Saul had done to him, by giving his first daughter to another man, instead of to David, as promised).*

25 And Saul said, Thus shall you say to David, The king desires not any dowry, but an hundred foreskins of the Philistines, to be avenged of the kings' enemies. But Saul thought to make David fall by the hand of the Philistines *(this was the snare which he planned).*

26 And when his servants told David these words, it pleased David well to be the king's son in law: and the days were not expired *(David was given a certain period of time for this to be done).*

27 Wherefore David arose and went, he and his men and slew of the Philistines two hundred men; and David brought their foreskins, and they gave them in full tale to the king, that he might be the king's son in law. And Saul gave him Michal his daughter to wife. *(All of this was so known among so many people that Saul couldn't go back on this. Some may blanch at David killing so many Philistines; however, they were God's enemies and, in slaying them, David acted as God's servant, and not as Saul's instrument.)*

28 And Saul saw and knew that the LORD was with David, and that Michal Saul's daughter loved him.

29 And Saul was yet the more afraid of David; and Saul became David's enemy continually.

30 Then the princes of the Philistines went forth: and it came to pass, after they went forth, that David behaved himself more wisely than all the servants of Saul; so that his name was much set by *(we learn from all of this that what God has blessed, nothing can curse!).*

CHAPTER 19
(1062 B.C.)
JONATHAN'S FRIENDSHIP WITH DAVID

AND Saul spoke to Jonathan his son, and to all his servants, that they should kill David. *(As we have repeatedly said, the "flesh" must always persecute the "Spirit." This is a* spiritual war that began at the very outset [Cain and Abel], and will not cease until the Trump of God sounds. The biggest enemy to the Work of God is religion, which is a product of the flesh. That's where Satan does his best or most destructive work. [Religion is a concoction of man, designed to reach God, or to better one's self in someway. In any form it is unacceptable to God.])*

2 But Jonathan Saul's son delighted much in David: and Jonathan told David, saying, Saul my father seeks to kill you: now therefore, I pray you, take heed to yourself until the morning, and abide in a secret place, and hide yourself:

3 And I will go out and stand beside my father in the field where you are, and I will commune with my father of you; and what I see, that I will tell you.

4 And Jonathan spoke good of David unto Saul his father, and said unto him, Let not the king sin against his servant, against David; because he has not sinned against you, and because his works have been to you-ward very good:

5 For he did put his life in his hand, and slew the Philistine, and the LORD wrought a great Salvation for all Israel: you saw it, and did rejoice: wherefore then will you sin against innocent blood, to kill David without a cause?

6 And Saul hearkened unto the voice of Jonathan: and Saul swore, As the LORD lives, he shall not be killed.

7 And Jonathan called David, and Jonathan showed him all those things. And Jonathan brought David to Saul, and he was in his presence, as in times past.

SAUL AGAIN TRIES TO KILL DAVID

8 And there was war again: and David went out, and fought with the Philistines, and slew them with a great slaughter; and they fled from him.

9 And the evil spirit from the LORD was upon Saul, as he sat in his house with his javelin in his hand: and David played *(the harp)* with his hand.

10 And Saul sought to smite David even to the wall with the javelin: but he slipped away out of Saul's presence, and he smote the javelin into the wall: and David fled, and escaped that night.

11 Saul also sent messengers unto David's house, to watch him, and to kill him in the

morning: and Michal David's wife told him, saying, If you save not your life to night, to morrow you shall be slain. *(Williams says, "Saul presents here a sad and terrible picture! One moment generous and kind; the next, murderous and cruel! One moment controlled by the Spirit of God; the next, by the spirit of the Demon! A useless ruined vessel, his life was wrecked because he hated David. Apart from that hatred, little is recorded to lead to the belief that his public or private conduct was unworthy of a man and a king; and men would have little known that there were such depths of malignity in his character had David never appeared. David's person and victories made manifest Saul's true character.*

"So was it with man when the Greater than David appeared. His apparition immediately made manifest fallen man's true nature; just as light makes manifest Darkness.")

12 So Michal let David down through a window: and he went, and fled, and escaped.

13 And Michal took an image, and laid it in the bed, and put a pillow of goats' hair for his bolster, and covered it with a cloth.

14 And when Saul sent messengers to take David, she said, He is sick.

15 And Saul sent the messengers again to see David, saying, Bring him up to me in the bed, that I may kill him.

16 And when the messengers were come in, behold, there was an image in the bed, with a pillow of goats' hair for his bolster.

17 And Saul said unto Michal, Why have you deceived me so, and sent away my enemy, that he is escaped? And Michal answered Saul, He said unto me, Let me go; why should I kill you? *(Michal pretends that David had told her not to force him to kill her by refusing to give aid in his escape.)*

SAMUEL

18 So David fled, and escaped, and came to Samuel to Ramah, and told him all that Saul had done to him. And he and Samuel went and dwelt in Naioth.

19 And it was told Saul, saying, Behold, David is at Naioth in Ramah *(a school for Prophets).*

20 And Saul sent messengers to take David: and when they saw the company of the Prophets prophesying, and Samuel standing as appointed over them, the Spirit of God was upon the messengers of Saul, and they also prophesied *(which turned them away from their murderous mission).*

21 And when it was told Saul, he sent other messengers, and they prophesied likewise. And Saul sent messengers again the third time, and they prophesied also.

22 Then went he also to Ramah, and came to a great well that is in Sechu: and he asked and said, Where are Samuel and David? And one said, Behold, they be at Naioth in Ramah.

23 And he went thither to Naioth in Ramah: and the Spirit of God was upon him also, and he went on, and prophesied, until he came to Naioth in Ramah *(this records the last attempt by God to salvage Saul; as would be obvious, this prophesy was from the "Spirit of God" and not evil spirits).*

24 And he stripped off his clothes also, and prophesied before Samuel in like manner, and lay down naked all that day and all that night. Wherefore they say, Is Saul also among the prophets? *(It does not mean that Saul stripped off his clothing. It means that he stripped off his armor and kingly robes. In other words, he was "naked" of these items, but not naked as we think of nakedness.*

As stated, this was God's last attempt to bring Saul back to the right way. After this, Saul would go even deeper into spiritual oblivion.)

CHAPTER 20
(1062 B.C.)

A NEW COVENANT BETWEEN JONATHAN AND DAVID

AND David fled from Naioth in Ramah, and came and said before Jonathan, What have I done? what is my iniquity? and what is my sin before your father, that he seeks my life? *(As Saul, who represented the leadership of Israel, rejected David, with a part of that leadership, who is Jonathan, accepting him, this portrays the highest of Israel rejecting the Lord Jesus Christ, with part of its leadership accepting Him; however, as Jonathan, the small part of the leadership which did accept Christ [Joseph of Arimathaea and Nicodemus] had very little influence on the decision of the hierarchy. In this instance, David was, and is, a Type of the true King of Israel, now rejected and hated by the world. But just as the Kingdom came ultimately to David, and just as he gave high positions in that Kingdom to those who had loved him when an outcast, so will Christ the Lord ultimately receive the dominion of the Earth, and He will*

appoint to great honor those who now love and follow Him.)

2 And he *(Jonathan)* said unto him *(David)*, God forbid; you shall not die: behold, my father will do nothing either great or small, but that he will show it me: and why should my father hide this thing from me? it is not so. *(Jonathan, who still had hopes that his father would come to his senses, is a picture of those in the institutionalized Church who are torn between David, God's anointed, and Saul, man's anointed. As Jonathan was dearly beloved by the Lord, so are these individuals, whoever they may be. Still, as Jonathan died trying to defend Saul, likewise, they will die trying to defend man's anointed.)*

3 And David swore moreover, and said, Your father certainly knows that I have found grace in your eyes; and he says, Let not Jonathan know this, lest he be grieved: but truly as the LORD lives, and as your soul lives, there is but a step between me and death *(David was right!)*.

4 Then said Jonathan unto David, Whatsoever your soul desires, I will even do it for you.

5 And David said unto Jonathan, Behold, to morrow is the new moon, and I should not fail to sit with the king at meat: but let me go, that I may hide myself in the field unto the third day at evening.

6 If your father at all miss me, then say, David earnestly asked leave of me that he might run to Beth-lehem his city: for there is a yearly sacrifice there for all the family.

7 If he say thus, It is well; your servant shall have peace: but if he be very wroth, then be sure that evil is determined by him.

8 Therefore you shall deal kindly with your servant; for you have brought your servant into a covenant of the LORD with you: notwithstanding, if there be in me iniquity, kill me yourself; for why should you bring me to your father?

9 And Jonathan said, Far be it from you: for if I knew certainly that evil were determined by my father to come upon you, then would not I tell it to you?

10 Then said David to Jonathan, Who shall tell me? or what if your father answer you roughly?

11 And Jonathan said unto David, Come, and let us go out into the field. And they went out both of them into the field. *(David's question had shown Jonathan that there were grave difficulties in the situation, and so Jonathan proposes that they should take a walk into the country, to be able to talk with one another more freely, and to try to make plans for the future.)*

12 And Jonathan said unto David, O LORD God of Israel, when I have sounded my father about to morrow any time, or the third day, and, behold, if there be good toward David, and I then send not unto you, and show it to you;

13 The LORD do so and much more to Jonathan: but if it please my father to do you evil, then I will show it to you, and send you away, that you may go in peace: and the LORD be with you, as He has been with my father.

14 And you shall not only while yet I live show me the kindness of the LORD, that I die not:

15 But also you shall not cut off your kindness from my house for ever: no, not when the LORD has cut off the enemies of David every one from the face of the Earth. *(From these Passages, we learn that Jonathan knew that David would one day be king of Israel. In that event, he is asking David to show mercy to his family. As we will later see, that's exactly what David did!)*

16 So Jonathan made a covenant with the house of David, saying, Let the LORD even require it at the hand of David's enemies. *(Because David had made the covenant with Jonathan, even David's enemies would have to recognize it, or else deal with David. In a sense, this is the same Covenant that we now have as Believers with the Lord Jesus Christ, of Whom David is a Type. Even the Lord's enemies, and we speak of the powers of darkness, have to recognize this Covenant, and, above all, recognize this Covenant!)*

17 And Jonathan caused David to swear again, because he loved him: for he loved him as he loved his own soul.

18 Then Jonathan said to David, To morrow is the new moon: and you shall be missed, because your seat will be empty.

19 And when you have stayed three days, then you shall go down quickly, and come to the place where you did hide yourself when the business was in hand, and shall remain by the stone Ezel.

20 And I will shoot three arrows on the side thereof, as though I shot at a mark.

21 And, behold, I will send a lad, saying, Go, find out the arrows. If I expressly say unto the lad, Behold, the arrows are on this side of you,

take them; then you can come: for there is peace to you, and no hurt; as the LORD lives.

22 But if I say thus unto the young man, Behold, the arrows are beyond you; go your way: for the LORD has sent you away.

23 And as touching the matter which you and I have spoken of, behold, the LORD be between you and me for ever *(all of this would tell David of Saul's true disposition toward him)*.

JONATHAN AND SAUL

24 So David hid himself in the field: and when the new moon was come, the king sat him down to eat meat.

25 And the king sat upon his seat, as at other times, even upon a seat by the wall: and Jonathan arose, and Abner sat by Saul's side, and David's place was empty.

26 Nevertheless Saul spoke not any thing that day: for he thought, Something has befallen him, he is not clean; surely he is not clean *(supposing some ceremonial defilement [Lev. 15:2-16])*.

27 And it came to pass on the morrow, which was the second day of the month, that David's place was empty: and Saul said unto Jonathan his son, Wherefore comes not the son of Jesse to meat *(to the meal)*, neither yesterday, nor to day?

28 And Jonathan answered Saul, David earnestly asked leave of me to go to Beth-lehem:

29 And he said, Let me go, I pray you; for our family has a sacrifice in the city; and my brother, he has commanded me to be there: and now, if I have found favour in your eyes, let me get away, I pray you, and see my brethren. Therefore he comes not unto the king's table.

30 Then Saul's anger was kindled against Jonathan, and he said unto him, You son of the perverse rebellious woman, do not I know that you have chosen the son of Jesse to your own confusion, and unto the confusion of your mother's nakedness? *(In that culture, the greatest possible insult to a man is to call his mother vile names. The latter phrase refers to a mother feeling ashamed and disgraced at having born such a son.)*

31 For as long as the son of Jesse lives upon the ground, you shall not be established, nor your kingdom. Wherefore now send and fetch him unto me, for he shall surely die.

32 And Jonathan answered Saul his father, and said unto him, Wherefore shall he be slain? what has he done?

33 And Saul cast a javelin at him *(at Jonathan)*

to smite him: whereby Jonathan knew that it was determined of his father to kill David.

34 So Jonathan arose from the table in fierce anger, and did eat no meat the second day of the month: for he was grieved for David, because his father had done him shame *(had done David shame!)*.

THE PARTING OF JONATHAN AND DAVID

35 And it came to pass in the morning, that Jonathan went out into the field at the time appointed with David, and a little lad with him.

36 And he said unto his lad, Run, find out now the arrows which I shoot. And as the lad ran, he shot an arrow beyond him.

37 And when the lad was come to the place of the arrow which Jonathan had shot, Jonathan cried after the lad, and said, Is not the arrow beyond you? *(This was the prearranged sign that David was in acute danger [Vs. 22].)*

38 And Jonathan cried after the lad, Make speed, haste, stay not. And Jonathan's lad gathered up the arrows, and came to his master.

39 But the lad knew not any thing: only Jonathan and David knew the matter *(the child had no knowledge what was taking place, at least as it regards the matter between David and Jonathan)*.

40 And Jonathan gave his artillery unto his lad, and said unto him, Go, carry them to the city.

41 And as soon as the lad was gone, David arose out of a place toward the south, and fell on his face to the ground, and bowed himself three times: and they kissed one another, and wept one with another, until David exceeded *(broke down, and was completely mastered by his grief)*.

42 And Jonathan said to David, Go in peace, forasmuch as we have sworn both of us in the Name of the LORD, saying, The LORD be between me and you, and between my seed and your seed for ever *(the covenant would stand [18:3-4])*. And he *(David)* arose and departed: and Jonathan went into the city.

CHAPTER 21
(1062 B.C.)

DAVID FLEES FROM SAUL

THEN came David to Nob to Ahimelech the Priest *(High Priest)*: and Ahimelech was

afraid at the meeting of David, and said unto him, Why are you alone, and no man with you? *(It seemed strange to Ahimelech that David was traveling in this manner, considering that he was the king's son-in-law.)*

THE SHEWBREAD

2 And David said unto Ahimelech the Priest, The king has commanded me a business *(which was a lie)*, and has said unto me, Let no man know any thing of the business whereabout I send you, and what I have commanded you: and I have appointed my servants to such and such a place. *(All of this teaches the bitter lesson that departure from the path of faith not only means loss of all personal dignity, but it involves injury to others as well! Thus, as Abraham, when he left the path of faith, became the occasion of sickness and disease to the Egyptians [Gen. 12:17], so David's conduct caused the death of the High Priest and 85 of his fellow Priests, together with their wives and children [22:18-19].)*

3 Now therefore what is under your hand? give me five loaves of bread in my hand, or what there is present.

4 And the Priest answered David, and said, There is no common bread under my hand, but there is hallowed bread *(these were the twelve loaves of the Shewbread, which were baked fresh every week and placed on the Table of Shewbread; at the end of the week, they were then eaten by the Priests in the Holy Place [Lev. 24:8-9], with fresh loaves then replacing that which had been eaten)*; if the young men have kept themselves at least from women. *(As Ahimelech could not venture to refuse David's request, he asked if his attendants are at least ceremonially clean, as in that case the urgency of the king's business might excuse the breach of the letter of the Commandment. Our Lord in Matthew 12:3 cites this a case in which the inward spirit of the Law was kept, and the violation of its literal precept thereby justified — Smith.)*

5 And David answered the Priest, and said unto him, Of a truth women have been kept from us about these three days, since I came out, and the vessels of the young men are holy, and the bread is in a manner common, yes, though it were sanctified this day in the vessel *(the whole Chapter sets David before us in a very humiliating light)*.

6 So the Priest gave him hallowed bread: for there was no bread there but the shewbread, that was taken from before the LORD, to put hot bread in the day when it was taken away.

7 Now a certain man of the servants of Saul was there that day, detained before the LORD *(shut up in close seclusion within the precincts of the Tabernacle, either for some vow, or for purification)*; and his name was Doeg, an Edomite, the chiefest of the herdmen that belonged to Saul.

DAVID TAKES GOLIATH'S SWORD

8 And David said unto Ahimelech, And is there not here under your hand spear or sword? for I have neither brought my sword nor my weapons with me, because the king's business required haste.

9 And the Priest said, The sword of Goliath the Philistine, whom you slew in the valley of Elah, behold, it is here wrapped in a cloth behind the Ephod: if you will take that, take it: for there is no other save that here. And David said, There is none like that; give it me *(the sword of Goliath did not save the giant; neither could it save David)*.

DAVID FLEES TO GATH

10 And David arose and fled that day for fear of Saul, and went to Achish the king of Gath *(in effect, David was going over to the enemies of God; so much of the wrongdoing that comes by the Child of God is caused by fear)*.

11 And the servants of Achish said unto him, Is not this David the king of the land? did they not sing one to another of him in dances, saying, Saul has slain his thousands, and David his ten thousands? *(To be sure, they were nonplussed at David appearing among them.)*

12 And David laid up these words in his heart, and was sore afraid of Achish the king of Gath.

13 And he changed his behaviour before them, and feigned himself mad in their hands, and scrabbled on the doors of the gate, and let his spittle fall down upon his beard *(as is obvious, this is an extremely low point in David's life; however, it portrays what even the greatest will do, even as David, when we depart from the path of faith)*.

14 Then said Achish unto his servants, Lo, you see the man is mad: wherefore then have you brought him to me?

15 Have I need of mad men, that you have brought this fellow to play the mad man in my

presence? shall this fellow come into my house? *(Evidently, David's ploy worked, with the Philistines thinking that he was crazy and, thereby, letting him go his way. He should never have been there to begin with.)*

CHAPTER 22
(1062 B.C.)
DAVID FLEES TO ADULLAM

DAVID therefore departed thence, and escaped to the cave Adullam: and when his brethren and all his father's house heard it, they went down thither to him. *(This cave was a large one near the city of Adullam in Judah, which was about 12 miles southwest of Bethlehem. This would be David's headquarters for a period of time. He would compose Psalm 57 on this occasion. Actually, many of the Psalms which were composed by David and, we might add, inspired by the Holy Spirit, were written during times of great distress. As well, he composed Psalm 56 when he was in the land of the Philistines.)*

2 And every one who was in distress, and every one who was in debt, and every one who was discontented, gathered themselves unto him; and he became a captain over them: and there were with him about four hundred men. *(David's position in the "cave Adullam" is a type of the small remnant who truly are called of God and live for God. This is the position today in Christendom. The outward form of a testimony for God exists, but its living reality is only found among those who know, love, and serve their rejected Lord. Such persons are despised by the great and proud and, as well, by much of the religious hierarchy; however, the Lord calls them "the excellent in the Earth," and He says that in them is all His delight [Ps. 16:3].)*

3 And David went thence to Mizpeh of Moab: and he said unto the king of Moab, Let my father and my mother, I pray you, come forth, and be with you, till I know what God will do for me. *(Faith is an unworldly virtue. It very seldom explains more than a step at a time. To fully realize its benefits and to gather all its guarantees, one must learn trust and dependence. These David would learn the hard way!)*

4 And he brought them *(his parents)* before the king of Moab: and they dwelt with him all the while that David was in the hold. *(As Saul had waged war on Moab [14:47], the king was probably glad to help one who would keep Saul employed at home. As well, some*

think that the phrase "the hold" refers to Masada; however, that is only speculation.)

5 And the Prophet Gad said unto David, Abide not in the hold; depart, and get thee into the land of Judah. Then David departed, and came into the forest of Hareth. *(Thus, we are now introduced to Gad the Prophet. Gad, probably by Samuel's command, came to be David's counselor. In fact, the advice he now gives is most important. David was to leave Moab and go back to Judah, which he did. "Hareth" was about 3 miles from the cave of Adullam.)*

6 When Saul heard that David was discovered *(back in Judah)*, and the men who were with him, (now Saul abode in Gibeah under a tree in Ramah, having his spear in his hand, and all his servants were standing about him *[Saul evidently was holding a formal court to decide what steps should be taken now that David had openly revolted from him]*;)

7 Then Saul said unto his servants who stood about him, Hear now, you Benjamites; will the son of Jesse give every one of you fields and vineyards, and make you all captains of thousands, and captains of hundreds;

8 That all of you have conspired against me, and there is none who shows me that my son has made a league with the son of Jesse, and there is none of you that is sorry for me, or shows unto me that my son has stirred up my servant against me, to lie in wait, as at this day? *(These statements proclaim the fact that Saul knew that there was a covenant between Jonathan and David. Saul has lied so much about David that he now has come to believe his own lies.)*

DOEG THE EDOMITE

9 Then answered Doeg the Edomite, which was set over the servants of Saul, and said, I saw the son of Jesse coming to Nob, to Ahimelech the son of Ahitub *(it should have been translated, "Doeg the Edomite, who stood there with the servants of Saul"; these Benjamites would not have endured to have an Edomite set over them)*.

10 And he enquired of the LORD for him, and gave him victuals, and gave him the sword of Goliath the Philistine.

THE PRIESTS

11 Then the king sent to call Ahimelech the

Priest, the son of Ahitub, and all his father's house, the Priests who were in Nob: and they came all of them to the king *(they little realized what was in store for them!)*.

12 And Saul said, Hear now, you son of Ahitub. And he answered, Here I am, my lord.

13 And Saul said unto him, Why have you conspired against me, you and the son of Jesse, in that you have given him bread, and a sword, and have enquired of God for him, that he should rise against me, to lie in wait, as at this day?

14 Then Ahimelech answered the king, and said, And who is so faithful among all your servants as David, which is the king's son in law, and goes at your bidding, and is honourable in your house?

15 Did I then begin to enquire of God for him? be it far from me: let not the king impute any thing unto his servant, nor to all the house of my father: for your servant knew nothing of all this, less or more *(Ahimelech's answers are those of an innocent man who had supposed that what he did was a matter of course)*.

16 And the king said, You shall surely die, Ahimelech, You, and all your father's house *(Saul imagines conspiracies on every hand; the wicked flee when no man pursues)*.

17 And the king said unto the footmen who stood about him, Turn, and slay the Priests of the LORD: because their hand also is with David, and because they knew when he fled, and did not show it to me. But the servants of the king would not put forth their hand to fall upon the Priests of the LORD.

18 And the king said to Doeg, Turn thou, and fall upon the Priests. And Doeg the Edomite turned, and he fell upon the Priests, and slew on that day fourscore and five *(85)* persons who did wear a linen Ephod. *(The fact that they were thus clad in their official dress added not to the wickedness, but to the impiety of this revolting act — Smith. That day, Saul would kill all the Priests with the exception of "Abiathar," who escaped and fled after David, even as we shall see. Saul would kill some 85 men of God, as well as women and children. Incidentally, Abiathar was of the line of the Priests of Eli. He had a son who was also joint Priest with Zadok for a while [I Chron. 18:16; 24:6]. Solomon, many years later, deposed Abimelech because he espoused his brother's cause to become king, and Zadok became sole High Priest [I Ki. 1:7-42]. Thus, the prophecy to Eli of the cutting off of his house as Priests was*

finally fulfilled [I Sam. 2:31], for Abiathar was the last of his line to be High Priest. Eli and Abiathar were of the house of Ithamar, and Zadok was of the house of Eleazar. By this act of Saul, he caused the transfer of the Urim and Thummim to David and, as stated, the prophecy to Eli of the cutting off of his house was fulfilled.).

19 And Nob, the city of the Priests, smote he with the edge of the sword, both men and women, children and sucklings, and oxen, and asses, and sheep, with the edge of the sword. *(This act perpetrated by Saul, in the killing of the Priests and the massacre of all in the city of Nob, was an act unparalleled in Jewish history for its barbarity. Nor was it an act of barbarity only, but also of insane and wanton stupidity. This is the end result of rebellion against God!)*

ABIATHAR

20 And one of the sons of Ahimelech the son of Ahitub, named Abiathar, escaped, and fled after David.

21 And Abiathar showed David that Saul had slain the LORD's Priests.

22 And David said unto Abiathar, I knew it that day, when Doeg the Edomite was there, that he would surely tell Saul: I have occasioned the death of all the persons of your father's house.

23 Abide thou with me, fear not: for he who seeks my life seeks your life: but with me you shall be in safeguard.

CHAPTER 23
(1061 B.C.)
DAVID DEFEATS THE PHILISTINES

THEN they told David, saying, Behold, the Philistines fight against Keilah, and they rob the threshingfloors *(by leaving Moab, and coming back to Judah, and thus protecting the people from the Philistines, which Saul could no longer do, David grew in reputation and power and, from the list of those who joined him at Ziklag [I Chron. 12:1-22], it is evident not only that such was the case, but that there was a strong enthusiasm for him at this time, throughout not merely Judah, but all Israel)*.

2 Therefore David enquired of the LORD, saying, Shall I go and smite these Philistines? And the LORD said unto David, Go, and smite the Philistines, and save Keilah. *(More than likely, David's means of communicating with the Lord was by the "Urim and Thummim." As*

we have stated elsewhere, what the "Urim and Thummim" were, no one exactly knows. It is known that whatever they were, they were kept in some type of pocket or container in the back of the "Ephod." This was a vest-like garment worn by the Great High Priest. The word "Urim" means "lights," with the word "Thummim" meaning "perfection." It seems that questions were asked, and, when the lot was drawn from the "Ephod," it would give a "Yes" or "No" answer.)

3 And David's men said unto him, Behold, we be afraid here in Judah: how much more then if we come to Keilah against the armies of the Philistines? (Though David had heard from the Lord, still, the men with him were not eager at all to fight the Philistines; but yet, David did not proudly and scornfully scold them for their want of faith, as many would do presently, but he sympathized with their fears, and said he would again ask God for guidance.)

4 Then David enquired of the LORD yet again. And the LORD answered him and said, Arise, go down to Keilah; for I will deliver the Philistines into your hand.

5 So David and his men went to Keilah (they evidently now acquiesced to David), and fought with the Philistines, and brought away their cattle, and smote them with a great slaughter. So David saved the inhabitants of Keilah.

SAUL ATTEMPTS TO KILL DAVID

6 And it came to pass, when Abiathar the son of Ahimelech fled to David to Keilah, that he came down with an Ephod in his hand.

7 And it was told Saul that David was come to Keilah. And Saul said, God has delivered him into my hand; for he is shut in, by entering into a town that has gates and bars. (It is interesting! Saul had become so demented that he thought that God was actually helping him; however, most who walk paths of evil claim God as their partner!)

8 And Saul called all the people together to war, to go down to Keilah, to besiege David and his men.

9 And David knew that Saul secretly practised mischief against him; and he said to Abiathar the Priest, Bring hither the Ephod.

10 Then said David, O LORD God of Israel, your servant has certainly heard that Saul seeks to come to Keilah, to destroy the city for my sake.

11 Will the men of Keilah deliver me up into his hand? will Saul come down, as your servant has heard? O LORD God of Israel, I beseech you, tell Your servant. And the LORD said, He will come down.

12 Then said David, Will the men of Keilah deliver me and my men into the hand of Saul? And the LORD said, They will deliver you up. (David had saved them from the Philistines, and yet they would deliver him to Saul! To tell the truth, the modern Church, like Keilah of old, cannot abide David, even though he has delivered them. Again, as Keilah, it opts for Saul. What a travesty!)

DAVID ESCAPES TO THE WILDERNESS

13 Then David and his men, which were about six hundred, arose and departed out of Keilah, and went whithersoever they could go. And it was told Saul that David was escaped from Keilah; and he forbare to go forth (Saul ceased his pursuit of David).

14 And David abode in the wilderness in strong holds, and remained in a mountain in the wilderness of Ziph. And Saul sought him every day, but God delivered him not into his hand. (David's way may have seemed precarious and, to the natural eye, it was; however, Saul's way was impossible. What God has placed His anointing upon, men, despite their eagerness and effort, cannot overcome.)

15 And David saw that Saul was come out to seek his life: and David was in the wilderness of Ziph in a wood.

JONATHAN AND DAVID

16 And Jonathan Saul's son arose, and went to David into the wood, and strengthened his hand in God. (Evidently, there was a strong conviction in Jonathan's mind that the Lord was transferring the kingdom from Saul to David, and that consequently David's final success was inevitable! Jonathan, no doubt, relayed his feelings to David, which probably greatly encouraged the Psalmist.)

17 And he said unto him, Fear not: for the hand of Saul my father shall not find you; and you shall be king over Israel, and I shall be next unto you; and that also Saul my father knows.

18 And they two made a covenant before the LORD: and David abode in the wood, and Jonathan went to his house. (Jonathan would in no way have helped his father Saul in his attempts to kill David, but, at the same time, he

never fully threw in his lot with David either. If he had broken with Saul completely, joining David in his test of Faith and not returning to his house, quite possibly that which he said, "And I shall be next unto you," would have been realized. He did not do that, and he was never heard from again in the Holy Scriptures until he appears slain by the Philistines on Mount Gilboa.)

THE ZIPHITES

19 Then came up the Ziphites to Saul to Gibeah, saying, Does not David hide himself with us in strong holds in the wood, in the hill of Hachilah, which is on the south of Jeshimon? *(The Ziphites would seek to betray David to Saul.)*

20 Now therefore, O king, come down according to all the desire of your soul to come down; and our part shall be to deliver him into the king's hand.

21 And Saul said, Blessed be ye of the LORD; for you have compassion on me. *(How many presently, as Saul, use Scriptural terminology, but their hearts, as Saul's, are black with sin!)*

22 Go, I pray you, prepare yet, and know and see his place where his haunt is, and who has seen him there: for it is told me that he deals very subtilly.

23 See therefore, and take knowledge of all the lurking places where he hides himself, and come ye again to me with the certainty, and I will go with you: and it shall come to pass, if he be in the land, that I will search him out throughout all the thousands of Judah.

24 And they arose, and went to Ziph before Saul: but David and his men were in the wilderness of Maon, in the plain on the south of Jeshimon.

25 Saul also and his men went to seek him. And they told David: wherefore he came down into a rock, and abode in the wilderness of Maon. And when Saul heard that, he pursued after David in the wilderness of Maon.

26 And Saul went on this side of the mountain, and David and his men on that side of the mountain: and David made haste to get away for fear of Saul; for Saul and his men compassed David and his men round about to take them. *(Sometimes God, in His wisdom, does not deliver His servant until all appears lost, and faith seems a deception. David was apparently overcome, with escape impossible. But, at the very last moment, he was delivered.)*

DAVID ESCAPES SAUL

27 But there came a messenger unto Saul, saying, Haste thee, and come; for the Philistines have invaded the land. *(This was Divine intervention to protect David when Saul was about to overtake him. Faith may bring its results at the last minute, but it is never late. All faith must be tested, and great Faith must be tested greatly.)*

28 Wherefore Saul returned from pursuing after David, and went against the Philistines: therefore they called that place Selahammahle-koth.

29 And David went up from thence, and dwelt in strong holds at En-gedi *(this is very near the shore of the Dead Sea).*

CHAPTER 24
(1061 B.C.)
DAVID SPARES SAUL'S LIFE

AND it came to pass, when Saul was returned from following the Philistines, that it was told him, saying, Behold, David is in the wilderness of En-gedi. *(We learn at least two great truths in this Chapter: 1. The great lengths that Saul will go to in order to kill David. Saul is a type of apostate religion that must kill, or at least attempt to kill, that which is of God, of which David is a Type; and, 2. The great reluctance that David will have to harm Saul. This portrays the true Child of God, who will not take matters into his own hands, but will place all in the Hands of the Lord.)*

2 Then Saul took three thousand chosen men out of all Israel, and went to seek David and his men upon the rocks of the wild goats. *(Saul's enemy was not David; it was the Philistines. But yet, most of his energy is spent trying to kill God's anointed. Once again, this is a picture of apostate Christianity at work.)*

3 And he came to the sheepcotes by the way, where was a cave; and Saul went in to cover his feet: and David and his men remained in the sides of the cave *(of course, Saul didn't know they were there).*

4 And the men of David said unto him, Behold the day of which the LORD said unto you, Behold, I will deliver your enemy into your hand, that you may do to him as it shall seem good unto you. Then David arose, and cut off the skirt of Saul's robe privily. *(Evidently, Saul had laid down to rest, and had gone to sleep. The supposed promise of this Verse had*

actually never been given by God. Such is man! Promises that are given, he lightly esteems, and Promises that are not given, he invents and believes. The Child of God must be careful that he does not read into the Word of God what is not there. As well, he should not fail to claim all the Promises of God.)

5 And it came to pass afterward, that David's heart smote him, because he had cut off Saul's skirt. *(The carnal mind immediately takes advantage of such an opportunity; however, the spiritual mind knows that this is not God's Way. The Lord had evidently told David that he was not to touch Saul; that's the reason for his consternation at this time.)*

6 And he said unto his men, The LORD forbid that I should do this thing unto my master, the LORD's anointed, to stretch forth my hand against him, seeing he is the anointed of the LORD. *(This does not mean that Saul was anointed by the Holy Spirit, for he was not. It means that he had been "anointed" to be king of Israel. Even though Saul was man's choice, still, God had played a part in allowing this man to be king of Israel. So, if it was wrong to stretch forth one's hand regarding harm against one like Saul, who was, in fact, demon-possessed, how much more is it wrong to touch one who is truly God's anointed!)*

7 So David stayed his servants with these words, and suffered them not to rise against Saul. But Saul rose up out of the cave, and went on his way.

DAVID SPEAKS TO SAUL

8 David also arose afterward, and went out of the cave, and cried after Saul, saying, My lord the king. And when Saul looked behind him, David stooped with his face to the earth and bowed himself.

9 And David said to Saul *(evidently, David was on the side of a hill, with Saul on another hill, with a ravine running between),* Wherefore hearest thou men's words, saying, Behold, David seeks your hurt?

10 Behold, this day your eyes have seen how that the LORD had delivered you to day into my hand in the cave: and some bade me kill you: but my eye spared you; and I said, I will not put forth my hand against my lord; for he is the LORD's anointed.

11 Moreover, my father, see, yea, see the skirt of your robe in my hand: for in that I cut off the skirt of your robe, and killed you not,

know thou and see that there is neither evil nor transgression in my hand, and I have not sinned against you; yet you hunt my soul to take it.

12 The LORD judge between me and you, and the LORD avenge me of you: but my hand shall not be upon you.

13 As saith the proverb of the ancients, Wickedness proceeds from the wicked: but my hand shall not be upon you.

14 After whom is the king of Israel come out? after whom do you pursue? after a dead dog, after a flea.

15 The LORD therefore be judge, and judge between me and you, and see, and plead my cause, and deliver me out of your hand.

SAUL ACKNOWLEDGES HIS WRONG

16 And it came to pass, when David had made an end of speaking these words unto Saul, that Saul said, Is this your voice, my son David? And Saul lifted up his voice, and wept. *(Evidently, the Spirit of the Lord was dealing with Saul and, for a moment, he seemed to have turned toward the right way; regrettably, it wouldn't last long.)*

17 And he said to David, You are more righteous than I: for you have rewarded me good, whereas I have rewarded you evil.

18 And you have showed this day how that you have dealt well with me: forasmuch as when the LORD had delivered me into your hand, you killed me not.

19 For if a man find his enemy, will he let him go well away? wherefore the LORD reward you good for that you have done unto me this day.

20 And now, behold, I know well that you shall surely be king, and that the kingdom of Israel shall be established in your hand. *(Obviously, Saul knew the prophecy concerning David, as had been given by Samuel the Prophet. In fact, this is the very reason he had been trying to kill David. His repentance wouldn't last long. Saul is a perfect picture of the apostate Church, which will go to any length to preserve its power. As well, it should be a perfect picture of the true Church of Jesus Christ, which will go to any length not to intrude into the sole domain of the Lord; however, this in no way prevents the true Child of God from "contending for the faith once delivered unto the Saints.")*

21 Swear now therefore unto me by the LORD, that you will not cut off my seed after

me, and that you will not destroy my name out of my father's house.

22 And David swore unto Saul. And Saul went home; but David and his men got them up unto the hold. *(When David became king, the only one left of the house of Saul was Mephibosheth. David showed great kindness to this grandson of Saul, exactly as he had promised [II Sam., Chpt. 9].)*

CHAPTER 25
(1060 B.C.)
THE DEATH OF SAMUEL

AND Samuel died; and all the Israelites were gathered together, and lamented him, and buried him in his house at Ramah. And David arose, and went down to the wilderness of Paran. *(It is supposed that Samuel died when he was about 98 years of age. He probably died about 2 years before Saul was killed. Whether David went to the funeral of Samuel is not known, but to him it was clear that with Samuel's death came the removal of the last restraining power in Saul's life; so David went down into the wilderness of Paran, which was south of Judea.)*

NABAL

2 And there was a man in Maon whose possessions were in Carmel; and the man was very great, and he had three thousand sheep, and a thousand goats: and he was shearing his sheep in Carmel.

3 Now the name of the man was Nabal; and the name of his wife Abigail: and she was a woman of good understanding, and of a beautiful countenance: but the man was churlish and evil in his doings; and he was of the house of Caleb. *(The name "Nabal" means "fool," and, to be sure, the man lived up to his namesake. He was "of the house of Caleb," but not of the spirit and faith of Caleb.)*

4 And David heard in the wilderness that Nabal did shear his sheep.

5 And David sent out ten young men, and David said unto the young men, Get you up to Carmel, and go to Nabal, and greet him in my name:

6 And thus shall you say to him who lives in prosperity, Peace be both to you, and peace be to your house, and peace be unto all that you have.

7 And now I have heard that you have shearers: now your shepherds which were with us, we hurt them not, neither was there ought missing unto them, all the while they were in Carmel.

8 Ask your young men, and they will show you. Wherefore let the young men find favour in your eyes: for we come in a good day: give, I pray you, whatsoever comes to your hand unto your servants, and to your son David.

9 And when David's young men came, they spoke to Nabal according to all those words in the name of David, and ceased. *(David had a right to ask this favor, considering that he and his men had, in a sense, been a protector to the great flocks of Nabal, keeping bandits away, etc.)*

NABAL REFUSES TO HELP

10 And Nabal answered David's servants, and said, Who is David? and who is the son of Jesse? there be many servants now a days who break away every man from his master. *(The man insults David, insinuating that David is a mere slave who has run away from his master, who is Saul.)*

11 Shall I then take my bread, and my water, and my flesh that I have killed for my shearers, and give it unto men, whom I know not whence they be?

12 So David's young men turned their way, and went again, and came and told him all those sayings *(in other words, he gave them nothing!)*.

13 And David said unto his men, Gird ye on every man his sword. And they girded on every man his sword; and David also girded on his sword: and there went up after David about four hundred men; and two hundred abode by the stuff *(stayed in the camp; no man is perfect, even though he be a Type of Christ; and David, like the Apostle Paul [Acts 23:3], stung with the injustice of Nabal's language, started out to punish him; but the Lord delivered him from the snare; Abigail, as we shall see, was the instrument of that deliverance).*

ABIGAIL

14 But one of the young men told Abigail, Nabal's wife, saying, Behold, David sent messengers out of the wilderness to salute our master; and he railed on them.

15 But the men were very good unto us, and we were not hurt, neither missed we any thing, as long as we were conversant with them, when

we were in the fields:

16 There were a wall unto us both by night and day, all the while we were with them keeping the sheep. *(David's men, encamped close by Nabal's possessions, were a blessing instead of a hindrance. As Nabal did not know, understand, or even care for these things, likewise, the world in general does not realize or recognize the "salt of the Earth" that is in its midst.)*

17 Now therefore know and consider what you will do; for evil is determined against our master, and against all his household: for he is such a son of Belial, that a man cannot speak to him *("Belial" means "worthless"; so coarse and violent was Nabal that it was hopeless to expostulate with him)*.

18 Then Abigail made haste, and took two hundred loaves *(very large loaves of bread)*, and two bottles of wine *(two large wineskins, with each holding many gallons)*, and five sheep ready dressed, and five measures of parched corn *(either barley or wheat, for there was no such thing as "corn," as we know such, in the Middle East of that day; corn was first introduced by Indians to the early settlers of the North American continent)*, and an hundred clusters of raisins, and two hundred cakes of figs, and laid them on asses.

19 And she said unto her servants, Go on before me; behold, I come after you. But she told not her husband Nabal.

20 And it was so, as she rode on the ass, that she came down by the covert of the hill, and, behold, David and his men came down against her; and she met them. *(Not only is Abigail beautiful in person, but she is even more beautiful in character. Her faith and her intelligence are admirable. She judges both Nabal and Saul as God judged them. She recognizes in David his title as king, despite his personal imperfection. She also recognizes his valor in fighting God's battles and, where others only see a rebel, she sees a redeemer. All of this is not merely just the intelligence of the head; it is accompanied by the affection of the heart as well!)*

21 Now David had said, Surely in vain have I kept all that this fellow has in the wilderness, so that nothing was missed of all that pertained unto him: and he has requited me evil for good.

22 So and more also do God unto the enemies of David, if I leave of all who pertain to him by the morning light any who urinates against the wall *(David fully intended to kill Nabal, and any who resisted with him)*.

ABIGAIL MEETS DAVID

23 And when Abigail saw David, she hasted, and lighted off the ass, and fell before David on her face, and bowed herself to the ground,

24 And fell at his feet, and said, Upon me, my lord, upon me let this iniquity be: and let your handmaid, I pray you, speak in your audience, and hear the words of your handmaid.

25 Let not my lord, I pray you, regard this man of Belial, even Nabal: for as his name is, so is he; Nabal is his name, and folly is with him: but I your handmaid saw not the young men of my lord, whom you did send *(from the Text, it seems that Nabal's great wealth had been brought about by the wisdom of his wife)*.

26 Now therefore, my lord, as the LORD lives, and as your soul lives, seeing the LORD has withheld you from coming to shed blood, and from avenging yourself with your own hand, now let your enemies, and they who seek evil to my lord, be as Nabal *(the lady begins her appeal by affirming that it was Jehovah Who thus made her come to prevent bloodshed)*.

27 And now this blessing which your handmaid has brought unto my lord, let it even be given unto the young men that follow my lord *(the "blessing" pertained to the foodstuff)*.

28 I pray you, forgive the trespass of your handmaid: for the LORD will certainly make my lord a sure house; because my lord fights the battles of the LORD, and evil has not been found in you all your days. *(From these statements, we learn that Abigail knew all about David and, most definitely, her husband, Nabal, did as well. So his response to the appeal for help was not on the basis of ignorance, but rather from the basis of stupidity.)*

29 Yet a man is risen to pursue you, and to seek your soul *(she speaks of Saul)*: but the soul of my lord shall be bound in the bundle of life with the LORD your God *(meaning that God is determining David's destiny)*; and the souls of your enemies, them shall He sling out, as out of the middle of a sling *(and that's exactly what ultimately happened!)*.

30 And it shall come to pass, when the LORD shall have done to my lord according to all the good that He has spoken concerning you, and shall have appointed you ruler over Israel *(she knows, as did most of Israel, that David had been anointed by Samuel to be king)*;

31 That this shall be no grief unto you, nor offence of heart unto my lord, either that you have shed blood causeless, or that my lord has

avenged himself: but when the LORD shall have dealt well with my lord, then remember your handmaid *(in other words, Abigail tells David not to do something that may cause him problems later on, which, of course, was excellent advice).*

DAVID SPARES NABAL

32 And David said to Abigail, Blessed be the LORD God of Israel, which sent you this day to meet me *(David sees the Hand of God in the remonstrance of this woman)*:

33 And blessed be your advice, and blessed be you, which has kept me this day from coming to shed blood, and from avenging myself with my own hand.

34 For in very deed, as the LORD God of Israel lives, which has kept me back from hurting you, except you had hasted and come to meet me, surely there had not been left unto Nabal by the morning light any who urinates against the wall *(all the men who were with Nabal would have been killed).*

35 So David received of her hand that which she had brought him, and said unto her, Go up in peace to your house; see, I have hearkened to your voice, and have accepted your person.

NABAL'S DEATH

36 And Abigail came to Nabal; and, behold, he held a feast in his house, like the feast of a king *(he had food for all of this, but none for David)*; and Nabal's heart was merry within him, for he was very drunk: wherefore she told him nothing, less or more, until the morning light.

37 But it came to pass in the morning, when the wine was gone out of Nabal, and his wife had told him these things, that his heart died within him, and he became as a stone.

38 And it came to pass about ten days after, that the LORD smote Nabal, that he died. *(By his actions toward David, this man's life was cut short by a number of years; however, it was the Lord Who did this, and not David. How so often we hurt ourselves by not leaving things in the Hand of the Lord.)*

DAVID MARRIES ABIGAIL

39 And when David heard that Nabal was dead, he said, Blessed be the LORD, Who has pleaded the cause of my reproach from the hand of Nabal, and has kept His servant from evil *(the Lord used Abigail to do this)*: for the LORD has returned the wickedness of Nabal upon his own head. And David sent and communed with Abigail, to take her to him to wife.

40 And when the servants of David were come to Abigail to Carmel, they spoke unto her, saying, David sent us unto you, to take you to him to wife.

41 And she arose, and bowed herself on her face to the earth, and said, Behold, let your handmaid be a servant to wash the feet of the servants of my lord.

42 And Abigail hasted, and arose and rode upon an ass, with five damsels of hers who went after her; and she went after the messengers of David, and became his wife.

43 David also took Ahinoam of Jezreel; and they were also both of them his wives.

44 But Saul had given Michal his daughter, David's wife, to Phalti the son of Laish, which was of Gallim. *(Williams says, "Had David kept closely to the teaching of the Bible, he would have had but one wife; for so it was ordained 'from the beginning'" [Mat. 19:8]. By this action, David set a poor example for his son Solomon, who took many wives, some of them of heathen nations, which turned his heart away from God.)*

CHAPTER 26
(1060 B.C.)
DAVID SPARES SAUL'S LIFE AGAIN

AND the Ziphites came unto Saul to Gibeah, saying, Does not David hide himself in the hill of Hachilah, which is before Jeshimon? *(This is the third time that David would be betrayed by his own countrymen — actually twice by the Ziphites. These individuals sought to curry favor with Saul by betraying David.)*

2 Then Saul arose, and went down to the wilderness of Ziph, having three thousand chosen men of Israel with him, to seek David in the wilderness of Ziph. *(In this Chapter, we see a portrayal of the unregenerate religious man, totally controlled by the Adamic or sin nature. We also witness the regenerate God-called man, even though still retaining the sin nature, nevertheless, not being controlled by it.)*

3 And Saul pitched in the hill of Hachilah, which is before Jeshimon, by the way. But David abode in the wilderness, and he saw that Saul came after him into the wilderness. *(It would seem from the 24th Chapter, and according to*

the great display of love that David showed toward Saul, that this man would have ceased his relentless quest to kill "God's anointed." However, we see that "the natural man," totally controlled by the "sin nature," is the helpless but willing tool of evil. We also see that the "spiritual man" never accustoms himself to evil, even though at times failing. Saul illustrates the first example; David, the second.)

4 David therefore sent out spies, and understood that Saul was come in very deed. (Saul knew that David was God's chosen king, and that he would certainly reign and, yet, he again and again sought to destroy him. Such is the power of evil! Satan is also the helpless but willing agent of sin; this fact respecting man's fallen nature proves the absolute necessity of a new moral creation.)

5 And David arose, and came to the place where Saul had pitched: and David beheld the place where Saul lay, and Abner the son of Ner, the captain of his host: and Saul lay in the trench, and the people pitched round about him. (David illustrates the truth that the "spiritual nature" can never accustom itself to evil. Man's sinful, unregenerate, wicked nature accustoms itself to evil after a little time, even ceasing to be shocked by its manifestations.)

6 Then answered David and said to Ahimelech the Hittite, and to Abishai the son of Zeruiah, brother to Joab, saying, Who will go down with me to Saul to the camp? And Abishai said, I will go down with you. (As Ahimelech is mentioned before Abishai, he must have held an honorable place with David, as did subsequently another Hittite, Uriah [II Sam. 11:3].)

7 So David and Abishai came to the people by night: and, behold, Saul lay sleeping within the trench, and his spear stuck in the ground at his bolster (pillow): but Abner and the people lay round about him.

8 Then said Abishai to David, God has delivered your enemy into your hand this day: now therefore let me smite him, I pray you, with the spear even to the earth at once, and I will not smite him the second time (in other words, Abishai would kill Saul with the first thrust).

9 And David said to Abishai, Destroy him not: for who can stretch forth his hand against the LORD's anointed, and be guiltless? (David forbids the deed, not because of Saul's character, but because of Saul's office; consequently, he leaves him in Jehovah's hand, even as he should have done.)

10 David said furthermore, As the LORD lives, the LORD shall smite him; or his day shall come to die; or he shall descend into battle, and perish. (Whenever religious man usurps Christ's position as "Head of the Church," he eagerly will kill God's anointed, thinking he is doing God a service. However, when the Spirit of Christ reigns, the Headship of Christ is never abrogated.)

11 The LORD forbid that I should stretch forth my hand against the LORD's anointed: but I pray you, take thou now the spear that is at his bolster, and the cruse of water, and let us go. (It would seem so natural to the carnal mind, even though a follower of God's anointed, for one to take advantage of this opportunity; however, God's Ways are not man's ways. In retrospect, if David had killed Saul, it would have been a black stain on David's life that would have sullied the title, "A man after God's Own Heart." In David's actions regarding Saul, we see "God's Own Heart." God is ever seeking the sinner; He is ever showing Mercy; He is ever extending Grace. God's Hand ever calls, "Come unto Me." So, as we view David's actions regarding Saul, we are viewing the actions of Christ toward even the vilest of sinners who seek to destroy God's Work.)

12 So David took the spear and the cruse of water from Saul's bolster; and they got them away, and no man saw it, nor knew it, neither awaked: for they were all asleep; because a deep sleep from the LORD was fallen upon them. (The Lord would supernaturally protect David; however, had David taken matters into his own hands, as was suggested by his associate, quite possibly this protection by the Lord would not have been forthcoming. We can only expect God's best, if we go entirely God's Way.)

DAVID REPROACHES ABNER

13 Then David went over to the other side, and stood on the top of an hill afar off; a great space being between them (in this world, there is "a great space" between the "spiritual" and the "natural" natures, just as is described in this Verse; these "two natures" are eternally separated; it is impossible to cultivate the one so that it will develop into the other; many have believed this to be possible; it is known as the doctrine of "moral evolution"; even though man has tried to bridge this gap with education, culture, religious activity, etc., still, there is a great gulf fixed between these two natures, which makes a transition from the one to the

other impossible; hence, the necessity of being "created anew in Christ Jesus" [Eph. 2:10]):

14 And David cried to the people, and to Abner the son of Ner, saying Answerest thou not, Abner? Then Abner answered and said, Who are you who cries to the king?

15 And David said to Abner, Are you not a valiant man? and who is like to you in Israel? wherefore then have you not kept your lord the king? for there came one of the people in to destroy the king your lord.

16 This thing is not good that you have done. As the LORD lives, you are worthy to die, because you have not kept your master, the LORD's anointed. And now see where the king's spear is, and the cruse of water that was at his bolster.

DAVID PLEADS WITH SAUL

17 And Saul knew David's voice, and said, Is this your voice, my son David? And David said, It is my voice, my lord, O king.

18 And he said, Wherefore does my lord thus pursue after his servant? for what have I done? or what evil is in my hand?

19 Now therefore, I pray you, let my lord the king hear the words of his servant. If the LORD has stirred you up against me, let Him accept an Offering: but if they be the children of men, cursed be they before the LORD; for they have driven me out this day from abiding in the inheritance of the LORD, saying, Go, serve other gods. (In effect, Saul, and those with him, had told David to go serve heathen gods, for there was no room for him in Israel. As the situation then, modern religion follows suit. It will not serve God, and tries to hinder all who would serve the Lord.)

20 Now therefore, let not my blood fall to the earth before the face of the LORD: for the king of Israel is come out to seek a flea, as when one does hunt a partridge in the mountains. (The point of David's appeal is not that his life may be spared, but that he may not thus be driven far away from the land where Jehovah manifests Himself. As well, David is telling Saul that instead of trying to cause David problems, he should be opposing those who are truly enemies of the Lord; however, like Saul, the institutionalized Church follows suit.)

SAUL ACKNOWLEDGES HIS SIN

21 Then said Saul, I have sinned: return, my son David: for I will no more do you harm, because my soul was precious in your eyes this day: behold, I have played the fool, and have erred exceedingly. (While Saul's words are correct, and possibly sincere for the moment, still, self-will would shortly gain the upper hand, as it always did. For the modern Christian, "self" can only be handled at the Cross. Self-ability must be denied, with Faith placed totally in Christ and what Christ has done for us at the Cross. Only then can the Holy Spirit develop within us His Fruit [Gal. 5:22-23; Lk. 9:23-24].)

22 And David answered and said, Behold the king's spear! and let one of the young men come over and fetch it.

23 The LORD render to every man his righteousness and his faithfulness: for the LORD delivered you into my hand to day, but I would not stretch forth my hand against the LORD's anointed. (This was the second time that such a situation had been brought about. Much of this was a test originated by the Lord, as it regards David. In fact, every single thing that happens to a Believer is a test. How will we act? How will we react?)

24 And, behold, as your life was much set by this day in my eyes, so let my life be much set by in the eyes of the LORD, and let Him deliver me out of all tribulation. (These words proclaim the fact that it is the Lord Who Alone can truly deliver. We must never forget that!)

25 Then Saul said to David, Blessed be thou, my son David: you shall both do great things, and also shall still prevail (should have been translated, "You shall both do mightily, and you shall surely prevail"). So David went on his way, and Saul returned to his place.

CHAPTER 27
(1060 B.C.)
DAVID GOES TO GATH

AND David said in his heart, I shall now perish one day by the hand of Saul (David now resorts to fear instead of faith; a short time before he had remonstrated that the Lord would deliver him; as the pressure intensifies, it becomes increasingly more difficult to keep one's eye on nothing but the Promises of God; fear crowds from every side, so he says, "I shall now perish"): there is nothing better for me than that I should speedily escape into the land of the Philistines; and Saul shall despair of me, to seek me any more in any coast (border) of Israel: so shall I escape out of his hand

(David seems to forget the sure promises made to him — promises that even Saul acknowledged [24:20]; there is no place for the Believer among the Philistines!).

2 And David arose, and he passed over with the six hundred men who were with him unto Achish, the son of Maoch, king of Gath. *(There is no half way house between fellowship with God and fellowship with the Philistine. If the Philistine is made a refuge, then must David dwell in the midst of them, and declare himself ready to fight with them against the people of God. In this position, no Believer delights to find himself. Faith never leads one on this path, only fear.)*

3 And David dwelt with Achish at Gath, he and his men, every man with his household, even David with his two wives, Ahinoam the Jezreelitess, and Abigail the Carmelitess, Nabal's wife *(David knows that Saul will not follow him here, knowing that such would provoke a war, for which he was not now prepared).*

4 And it was told Saul that David was fled to Gath: and he sought no more again for him.

DAVID AT ZIKLAG

5 And David said unto Achish, If I have now found grace in your eyes, let them give me a place in some town in the country, that I may dwell there: for why should your servant dwell in the royal city with you?

6 Then Achish gave him Ziklag that day: wherefore Ziklag pertains unto the kings of Judah unto this day. *(This phrase proves that the Book of Samuel must have been compiled at a date subsequent to the revolt of Jeroboam, while the concluding words, "unto this day," equally plainly indicate a date prior to the Babylonian exile.)*

7 And the time that David dwelt in the country of the Philistines was a full year and four months *(16 months out of the Will of God).*

DAVID DECEIVES ACHISH

8 And David and his men went up, and invaded the Geshurites, and the Gezrites, and the Amalekites: for those nations were of old the inhabitants of the land, as you go to Shur, even unto the land of Egypt.

9 And David smote the land, and left neither man nor woman alive, and took away the sheep, and the oxen, and the asses, and the camels, and the apparel, and returned, and came to Achish. *(Here was a man who would not harm Saul when given the opportunity, yet would ruthlessly kill hundreds or even thousands of men and women among the heathen, and probably even the children. While it is true that God had given directions that these tribes [Geshurites, Gezrites, and Amalekites] were to be destroyed, He did not thus intend in this fashion. No doubt, David justified his actions, as we justify our actions in wrongdoing; still, this did not make it right.)*

10 And Achish said, Where have you made a road to day? and David said, Against the south of Judah, and against the south of the Jerahmeelites, and against the south of the Kenites.

11 And David saved neither man nor woman alive, to bring tidings to Gath, saying, Lest they should tell on us, saying, So did David, and so will be his manner all the while he dwells in the country of the Philistines *(David wanted the Philistine king to think that he was invading villages in Judah, which, of course, he wasn't!).*

12 And Achish believed David *(believed David's lie),* saying, He has made his people Israel utterly to abhor him; therefore he shall be my servant for ever *(David's action in joining Achish, and then carrying out the deeds which he did, which were evil, no doubt delayed his possession of the Kingdom).*

CHAPTER 28
(1056 B.C.)
WAR

AND it came to pass in those days, that the Philistines gathered their armies together for warfare, to fight with Israel. And Achish said unto David, Know thou assuredly, that you shall go out with me to battle, you and your men *(it was probably the rapid decline of Saul's power which encouraged the Philistines to attempt once again to place their yoke upon the neck of Israel).*

2 And David said to Achish, Surely you shall know what your servant can do. And Achish said to David, Therefore will I make you keeper of my head for ever. *(When a Christian seeks the protection and patronage of a man of the world, he must place himself and his spiritual gifts at the disposition of his protector. This is a sad and degrading bondage. This was David's unworthy and God-dishonoring relation with Achish. In such circumstances, Satan does not fail to provide Earthly*

honors and, accordingly, Achish makes David captain of his bodyguard.)

3 Now Samuel was dead, and all Israel had lamented him, and buried him in Ramah, even in his own city *(immediately in this Verse, the Holy Spirit records, "Now Samuel was dead"; the spiritual tide of Israel had never been worse; David was God's only light, and now it dims low).* And Saul had put away those who had familiar spirits, and the wizards, out of the land *(which he should have done!).*

4 And the Philistines gathered themselves together, and came and pitched in Shunem: and Saul gathered all Israel together, and they pitched in Gilboa.

SAUL CONSULTS THE MEDIUM

5 And when Saul saw the host of the Philistines, he was afraid, and his heart greatly trembled *(Mercy and the Grace of God had been extended to Saul for some 40 years; he had spurned each Gospel call).*

6 And when Saul enquired of the LORD, the LORD answered him not, neither by dreams, nor by Urim, nor by Prophets *(it must be quickly added that Saul did not inquire of the Lord in humble Contrition and Repentance; to have truly repented, he would have to have made things right with David; that he did not do; we can only expect an answer from the Lord when we ask on God's terms; regrettably, most do not desire to do that).*

7 Then said Saul unto his servants, Seek me a woman who has a familiar spirit, that I may go to her, and enquire of her. And his servants said to him, Behold, there is a woman who has a familiar spirit at En-dor. *(Sadly, the majority of the world, through horoscopes, psychic readings, fortune-telling, and psychologists, endeavor to receive instruction, guidance, counsel, or leading. All of these, and many more that we have not named, have demon spirits as the underlying factors. Demon spirits are always the underlying agents in all false doctrine, error, or direction that leads one astray from the Word of God. The Bible forbids any trafficking with demon spirits, whether directly or indirectly.)*

8 And Saul disguised himself, and put on other raiment, and he went, and two men with him, and they came to the woman by night: and he said, I pray you, divine unto me by the familiar spirit, and bring me him up, whom I shall name unto you.

9 And the woman said unto him, Behold, you know what Saul has done, how he has cut off those who have familiar spirits, and the wizards, out of the land: wherefore then lay you up a snare for my life, to cause me to die? *(Evidently, she didn't know that she was speaking directly to Saul.)*

10 And Saul swore to her by the LORD, saying, As the LORD lives, there shall no punishment happen to you for this thing. *(Not only had Saul in the earlier part of his reign been earnest in his zeal for the Mosaic Law, but even now it seems as if a witch was in danger of death; for he has to take an oath before she will acknowledge that she practices any illicit art. All of this portrays the fact that the Law, no matter how zealously kept, cannot change a person's heart.)*

11 Then said the woman, Whom shall I bring up unto you? and he said, Bring me up Samuel.

12 And when the woman saw Samuel, she cried with a loud voice: and the woman spoke to Saul, saying, Why have you deceived me? for you are Saul *(now she recognizes the king).*

13 And the king said unto her, Be not afraid: for what sawest thou? And the woman said unto Saul, I saw gods ascending out of the Earth.

14 And he said unto her, What form is he of? And she said, An old man comes up; and he is covered with a mantle. And Saul perceived that it was Samuel, and he stooped with his face to the ground, and bowed himself. *(The Scripture doesn't say that Saul actually saw Samuel, but that, from her description, he perceived that it was Samuel.)*

SAUL IS GREATLY DISTRESSED

15 And Samuel said to Saul, Why have you disquieted me, to bring me up? And Saul answered, I am sore distressed; for the Philistines make war against me, and God is departed from me, and answers me no more, neither by Prophets, nor by dreams: therefore I have called you, that you may make known unto me what I shall do.

16 Then said Samuel, Wherefore then do you ask of me, seeing the LORD is departed from you, and is become your enemy?

17 And the LORD has done to him, as he spoke by me: for the LORD has rent the kingdom out of your hand, and given it to your neighbour, even to David:

18 Because you obeyed not the voice of the

LORD, nor executed His fierce wrath upon Amalek, therefore has the LORD done this thing unto you this day.

19 Moreover the LORD will also deliver Israel with you into the hand of the Philistines: and to morrow shall you and your sons be with me *(shall be dead)*: the LORD also shall deliver the host of Israel into the hand of the Philistines. *(There is much controversy by Bible Scholars as to whether Samuel actually came up, or whether it was a demon spirit impersonating Samuel. Either could have been possible; however, this truth should be made known:*

Saul received absolutely no help whatsoever from trying to communicate with the dead; likewise, all others seeking such will receive the same — nothing.)

THE REACTION OF SAUL

20 Then Saul fell straightway all along on the earth, and was sore afraid, because of the words of Samuel: and there was no strength in him; for he had eaten no bread all the day, nor all the night.

21 And the woman came unto Saul, and saw that he was sore troubled, and said unto him, Behold, your handmaid has obeyed your voice, and I have put my life in my hand, and have hearkened unto your words which you spoke unto me.

22 Now therefore, I pray you, hearken thou also unto the voice of your handmaid, and let me set a morsel of bread before you; and eat, that you may have strength, when you go on your way.

23 But he refused, and said, I will not eat. But his servants, together with the woman, compelled him; and he hearkened unto their voice. So he arose from the earth, and sat upon the bed.

24 And the woman had a fat calf in the house; and she hasted, and killed it, and took flour, and kneaded it, and did bake unleavened bread thereof:

25 And she brought it before Saul, and before his servants; and they did eat. Then they rose up, and went away that night. *(Saul's namesake, Saul of Tarsus, also "fell to the Earth" [Acts 9:4]. But how great was the contrast! The one rose and went away "that night," with a deeper night in his soul, to his doom; the other rose and went his way, with a great Light in his heart, to receive the Crown of Righteousness that was laid up for him — Williams.)*

CHAPTER 29
(1056 B.C.)
THE PHILISTINES MISTRUST DAVID

NOW the Philistines gathered together all their armies to Aphek: and the Israelites pitched by a fountain which is in Jezreel. *(This Chapter records the story of failure, both on the part of David and Saul. David will climb out, ever depending on the Lord, while Saul will not. The Holy Spirit will graphically record the happenings.)*

2 And the lords of the Philistines passed on by hundreds, and by thousands: but David and his men passed on in the rereward with Achish *(as stated, David and his men were bodyguards for Achish, the Philistine leader)*.

3 Then said the princes of the Philistines, What do these Hebrews here? And Achish said unto the princes of the Philistines, Is not this David, the servant of Saul the king of Israel, which has been with me these days, or these years, and I have found no fault in him since he fell unto me unto this day? *(The term, "Hebrews," was a Philistine term of contempt.)*

4 And the princes of the Philistines were wroth *(angry)* with him *(with Achish)*; and the princes of the Philistines said unto him, Make this fellow return, that he may go again to his place which you have appointed him, and let him not go down with us to battle, lest in the battle he be an adversary to us: for wherewith should he reconcile himself unto his master? should it not be with the heads of these men?

5 Is not this David, of whom they sang one to another in dances, saying, Saul slew his thousands, and David his ten thousands? *(Bible Scholars have long since argued what David's intentions were regarding the events of this Chapter. We can only form conclusions according to that which the Holy Spirit gives us. This was not a high point of David's life to date. Actually, it would be the lowest and most wretched to this moment. It would seem that he would profess himself ready and eager to fight against God's beloved people, and to help Satan destroy them! He told many lies to Achish, the king of the Philistines, but the lie of this Chapter was the crowning lie to date. He professed devotion to the Philistine Monarch, while, no doubt, rejoicing secretly at escaping from so dreadful a position. All of this shows how deeply a Child of God can fall when he leans upon the hand of man, and not upon the Hand of God.)*

ACHISH DISMISSES DAVID

6 Then Achish called David, and said unto him, Surely, as the LORD lives, you have been upright *(Achish using the name of Jehovah seems strange)*, and your going out and your coming in with me in the host is good in my sight: for I have not found evil in you since the day of your coming unto me unto this day: nevertheless the lords favour you not. *(Concerning this, Williams says, "The path of faith is wearying to nature; and there is an ever-present temptation to seek ease from the thorns through which that path sometimes leads. The persecution by professors of religion has oftentimes the effect of throwing the servant of God into the arms of the enemies of God; just as Saul's hatred drove David to the Philistines. But this only happens when the Christian follows his own will, and thinks, by doing so, to avoid the very difficulties which, had he walked with God, would have become channels of teaching and refreshment to his soul. The more glorious a work there is for faith, the more sure is nature to weary if faith grows feeble.")*

7 Wherefore now return, and go in peace, that you displease not the lords of the Philistines.

8 And David said unto Achish, But what have I done? and what have you found in your servant so long as I have been with you unto this day, that I may not go fight against the enemies of my lord the king? *(It should always be remembered that failure, despite the Grace of God, always, and without exception, carries with it its own punishment — even more in the life of the one who has been grandly touched by the Holy Spirit. Too often Christendom reads only perfection into the life of God's champions; however, they do so by ignoring the Word of God. The individual is never called by God because he meets God's requirements. Actually, he never does. Always, he is woefully unprepared, immature, and lacking in proper faith. It is the Work of the Holy Spirit, among other things, to bring David, and others like him, to the place of maturity that God desires. It does not come easily. A great call always demands a great test.*

Sooner or later, there will be failure; it is inevitable. It may not be known all the time to the general Christian public, but God knows. It is a part of the growing process. Regrettably, oftentimes one learns more from the failures than one does from the victories. The reason should be obvious. At times, faith shines brighter during failure than during victory, the reason being the pressure applied. Faith will either rise to the occasion, or else quit. True men of God may fail, but they do not quit.)

9 And Achish answered and said to David, I know that you are good in my sight, as an Angel of God: notwithstanding the princes of the Philistines have said, He shall not go up with us to the battle.

10 Wherefore now rise up early in the morning with your master's servants who are come with you: and as soon as you be up early in the morning, and have light, depart.

11 So David and his men rose up early to depart in the morning, to return into the land of the Philistines. And the Philistines went up to Jezreel. *(Despite David's failure of faith, and all failure is, in some way, a failure of faith, the Lord will keep David from sinning even greater. God uses failures to teach. Regrettably, fellow Christians oftentimes use failures to destroy.)*

CHAPTER 30
(1056 B.C.)
ZIKLAG BURNED

AND it came to pass, when David and his men were come to Ziklag on the third day *(the third day after they had left the Philistines)*, that the Amalekites had invaded the south, and Ziklag, and smitten Ziklag, and burned it with fire;

2 And had taken the women captives, who were therein: they slew not any, either great or small, but carried them away, and went on their way. *(This bitter Trial brings David back to the Lord and effects a true Restoration of his soul. Suffering and loss accompany departure from the Lord and His Ways, and there must be chastisement in order for communion to be restored. While chastisement is grievous, still, it yields the peaceable fruit of righteousness [Heb. 12:11].)*

3 So David and his men came to the city, and, behold, it was burned with fire; and their wives, and their sons, and their daughters, were taken captives. *(The Amalekites spared their lives, not because they were merciful, but because women and children were valuable as slaves. They probably intended to send the best to Egypt for sale.)*

4 Then David and the people who were with him lifted up their voice and wept, until they had no more power to weep *(they knew what was in store for their loved ones)*.

5 And David's two wives were taken captives, Ahinoam the Jezreelitess, and Abigail

the wife of Nabal the Carmelite.

DAVID'S GREAT DISTRESS

6 And David was greatly distressed *(this, no doubt, was the low-watermark in David's life, as he stood looking at the ashes of Ziklag, knowing that his family, as well as the families of all of his men, had been taken captive; many people have to be brought to a "burnt Ziklag" before finally making things right with the Lord; even though it would look grievous, still, all of this was allowed by the Lord because He loved David)*; for the people spoke of stoning him, because the soul of all the people was grieved, every man for his sons and for his daughters *(Williams says, "The first resource of nature was seen in David's men — they murmured and grew angry. The first resource of Faith appeared in David — he cast his burden upon the Lord")*: but David encouraged himself in the LORD his God *(the Hebrew says literally, "He strengthened himself in Jehovah"; he turned to the Lord, because the Lord was the only One Who could help; it is the same presently; however, the modern Church seems to turn to everything except the Lord)*.

THE ANSWER FROM THE LORD

7 And David said to Abiathar the Priest, Ahimelech's son, I pray you, bring me hither the Ephod. And Abiathar brought thither the Ephod to David. *(The Ephod contained the Urim and the Thummim, which was designed by the Holy Spirit that direction might be received from the Lord. In the Twenty-seventh Chapter, when David went over to the Philistines, there is no record that he "enquired of the Lord." But now victory has been restored. David is once again seeking counsel from the One Who can really help him.)*

8 And David enquired at the LORD, saying, Shall I pursue after this troop? shall I overtake them? And He answered him, Pursue: for you shall surely overtake them, and without fail recover all. *(When it says that the Lord answered David, that is one of the most beautiful statements that could ever be made. Spiritual victory must be ours before material, financial, or physical victory can come. David now proceeds with the assurance that the Lord is with him and, that being the case, he will "recover all." It is the Will of the Lord that you recover all that Satan has stolen from you.)*

DAVID PURSUES

9 So David went, he and the six hundred men who were with him, and came to the brook Besor, where those who were left behind stayed *(David pursued hurriedly; just because the Lord has promised success, doesn't mean that we aren't to do our part)*.

10 But David pursued, he and four hundred men: for two hundred abode behind, which were so faint that they could not go over the brook Besor.

11 And they found an Egyptian in the field, and brought him to David, and gave him bread, and he did eat; and they made him drink water;

12 And they gave him a piece of a cake of figs, and two clusters of raisins: and when he had eaten, his spirit came again to him: for he had eaten no bread, nor drunk any water, three days and three nights.

13 And David said unto him, To whom do you belong? and from where did you come? And he said, I am a young man of Egypt, servant to an Amalekite; and my master left me, because three days agone I fell sick.

14 We made an invasion upon the south of the Cherethites, and upon the coast which belongs to Judah, and upon the south of Caleb; and we burned Ziklag with fire.

15 And David said to him, Can you bring me down to this company? and he said, Swear unto me by God, that you will neither kill me, nor deliver me into the hands of my master, and I will bring you down to this company.

16 And when he *(the Egyptian)* had brought him *(David)* down, behold, they were spread abroad upon all the earth, eating and drinking, and dancing, because of all the great spoil that they had taken out of the land of the Philistines, and out of the land of Judah.

VICTORY

17 And David smote them from the twilight even unto the evening of the next day: and there escaped not a man of them, save four hundred young men, which rode upon camels, and fled.

18 And David recovered all that the Amalekites had carried away: and David rescued his two wives.

19 And there was nothing lacking to them, neither small nor great, neither sons nor daughters, neither spoil, nor any thing that they had

taken to them: David recovered all *(exactly as the Lord had said he would do).*

20 And David took all the flocks and the herds, which they drove before those other cattle, and said, This is David's spoil. *(They recovered all they had personally lost and, as well, they gained much more besides, probably five or ten times what they had lost. So, when the Lord helps us to recover what has been lost, He always gives us much more besides.)*

DIVISION OF THE SPOILS

21 And David came to the two hundred men, which were so faint that they could not follow David, whom they had made also to abide at the brook Besor: and they went forth to meet David, and to meet the people who were with him: and when David came near to the people, he saluted them *(in victory!).*

22 Then answered all the wicked men and men of Belial *(worthless individuals),* of those who went with David, and said, Because they went not with us, we will not give them ought of the spoil that we have recovered, save to every man his wife and his children, that they may lead them away, and depart.

23 Then said David, You shall not do so, my brethren, with that which the LORD has given us, Who has preserved us, and delivered the company that came against us into our hand.

24 For who will hearken unto you in this matter? but as his part is who goes down to the battle, so shall his part be who tarries by the stuff: they shall part alike. *(Paul, in Romans, Chapter 10, basically says the same thing, "The sender is just as important as the one sent.")*

25 And it was so from that day forward, that he made it a Statute and an Ordinance for Israel unto this day.

26 And when David came to Ziklag, he sent of the spoil unto the elders of Judah, even to his friends, saying, Behold a present for you of the spoil of the enemies of the LORD *(there is no blessing that comes from man's choice, which had been Saul; there is great blessing that comes from God's choice, which is David; the leadership of Israel demanded that no help be given unto David, so those who helped David during these years of crisis did so at their own risk; now, there would begin a blessing to these individuals that would never stop);*

27 To them which were in Beth-el, and to them which were in south Ramoth, and to them which were in Jattir,

28 And to them which were in Aroer, and to them which were in Siphmoth, and to them which were in Eshtemoa,

29 And to them which were in Rachal, and to them which were in the cities of the Jerahmeelites, and to them which were in the cities of the Kenites,

30 And to them which were in Hormah, and to them which were in Chor-ashan, and to them which were in Athach,

31 And to them which were in Hebron, and to all the places where David himself and his men were wont to haunt.

CHAPTER 31
(1056 B.C.)

THE DEATH OF SAUL AND HIS SONS

NOW the Philistines fought against Israel: and the men of Israel fled from before the Philistines, and fell down slain in mount Gilboa. *(If Saul had yielded totally to the Lord, the Philistines would have long since been defeated, and this battle would have never taken place.)*

2 And the Philistines followed hard upon Saul and upon his sons; and the Philistines slew Jonathan, and Abinadab, and Melchi-shua, Saul's sons. *(How much we lose when we go the wrong way! How many Philistines are left fighting us when, if our consecration had been complete, they would long since have ceased to be?)*

3 And the battle went sore against Saul, and the archers hit him; and he was sore wounded of the archers. *(There was no other way it could go. Samuel was dead and David had been spurned by Saul, who had attempted many times to kill him. As well, Saul had now resorted to demon spirits.)*

4 Then said Saul unto his armourbearer, Draw your sword, and thrust me through therewith; lest these uncircumcised come and thrust me through, and abuse me. But his armourbearer would not; for he was sore afraid. Therefore Saul took a sword, and fell upon it. *(The horror of total despair records every moment of this scene. How different it could have been! There was a time that the Spirit of God came upon Saul, but now the Philistines come upon him instead. Israel's first king commits suicide.)*

5 And when his armourbearer saw that Saul was dead, he fell likewise upon his sword, and died with him.

6 So Saul died, and his three sons, and his armourbearer, and all his men, that same day

together. *(Self-will wrecked Saul's life [I Chron. 10:13-14]. Only a Spirit-born man can serve and please God. Saul was raised up, as a king after the people's heart, to deliver them from the Philistines; and if it were possible for "the natural man" to do God's Will, then Saul would have succeeded; but he perished at the hands of the very enemies whom he set out to conquer! Such must ever be the result when "the flesh" attempts to do battle for God.)*

7 And when the men of Israel who were on the other side of the valley, and they who were on the other side Jordan, saw that the men of Israel fled, and that Saul and his sons were dead, they forsook the cities, and fled; and the Philistines came and dwelt in them. *(As stated, the flesh can win no victories. The Spirit of the Lord Alone can do such! The way to "walk after the Spirit," and the only way, is for the Believer to place his Faith exclusively in Christ and the Cross, which then gives the Holy Spirit latitude to work [Rom. 8:1-2, 11]. To "walk after the flesh" is simply to trust in anything except Christ and the Cross; such will always bring about defeat [Rom. 8:8].)*

8 And it came to pass on the morrow, when the Philistines came to strip the slain, that they found Saul and his three sons fallen in Mount Gilboa. *(As the spoiling was deferred to the next day, the struggle must have been obstinately contested, and decided only just before nightfall. But no matter how intense the struggle,* the flesh simply cannot win. It is impossible!)*

9 And they cut off his head *(this was probably done not simply in retaliation for what had happened to their champion, Goliath, but in accordance with the customs of ancient warfare),* **and stripped off his armour, and sent into the land of the Philistines round about, to publish it in the house of their idols, and among the people.** *(The fierce joy of the Philistines over the fallen Saul proves how great had been their fear of him, and how successful he had been in breaking their yoke off Israel's neck, at least up to a point. They gave the credit to their god, Dagon [I Chron. 10:10].)*

10 And they put his armour in the house of Ashtaroth: and they fastened his body to the wall of Beth-shan *(as also the bodies of his sons).*

11 And when the inhabitants of Jabesh-gilead heard of that which the Philistines had done to Saul;

12 All the valiant men arose, and went all night, and took the body of Saul and the bodies of his sons from the wall of Beth-shan, and came to Jabesh, and burnt them there.

13 And they took their bones, and buried them under a tree at Jabesh, and fasted seven days. *(Cremation, though highly practiced among certain nations, is mentioned here for the first time in Holy Scripture, and was probably resorted to on this occasion, rather than burying them, to ensure the bodies of Saul and his sons against further maltreatment.)*

THE SECOND BOOK OF
SAMUEL

CHAPTER 1
(1056 B.C.)

DAVID LEARNS OF SAUL'S DEATH

NOW it came to pass after the death of Saul, when David was returned from the slaughter of the Amalekites, and David had abode two days in Ziklag *(using the phrase, "when David was returned," the Holy Spirit has far more in mind than the return to Ziklag; David had, as well, returned from some 16 months of disobedience to God; what a glorious moment when the Child of God realizes his fault and his failure, and then "returns to total dependence on God")*;

2 It came even to pass on the third day, that, behold, a man came out of the camp from Saul with his clothes rent, and earth upon his head: and so it was, when he came to David, that he fell to the earth, and did obeisance.

3 And David said unto him, From where do you come? And he said unto him, Out of the camp of Israel am I escaped.

4 And David said unto him, How went the matter? I pray you, tell me. And he answered, That the people are fled from the battle, and many of the people also are fallen and dead; and Saul and Jonathan his son are dead also.

5 And David said unto the young man who told him, How do you know that Saul and Jonathan his son are dead?

6 And the young man who told him said, As I happened by chance upon Mount Gilboa, behold, Saul leaned upon his spear; and, lo, the chariots and horsemen followed hard after him.

7 And when he looked behind him, he saw me, and called unto me. And I answered him, Here am I.

8 And he said unto me, Who are you? And I answered him, I am an Amalekite.

9 He said unto me again, Stand, I pray you, upon me, and kill me: for anguish is come upon me, because my life is yet whole in me.

10 So I stood upon him, and killed him, because I was sure that he could not live after that he was fallen: and I took the crown that was upon his head, and the bracelet that was on his arm, and have brought them hither unto my lord. *(The story of the Amalekite is a most improbable fiction, and utterly untrue. He knew nothing as to the manner of Saul's death, but found the body, probably some time after the king had fallen. He then took these particular items from the corpse.)*

11 Then David took hold on his clothes, and rent them; and likewise all the men who were with him:

12 And they mourned, and wept, and fasted until evening, for Saul, and for Jonathan his son, and for the people of the LORD, and for the House of Israel; because they were fallen by the sword.

13 And David said unto the young man who told him, Who are you? And he answered, I am the son of a stranger, an Amalekite.

14 And David said unto him, How was it that you were not afraid to stretch forth your hand to destroy the LORD's anointed?

15 And David called one of the young men, and said, Go near, and fall upon him. And he smote him that he died.

16 And David said unto him, Your blood be upon your head; for your mouth has testified against you, saying, I have slain the LORD's anointed. *("Amalek" is a type of the flesh. We will either kill it, or it will kill us. As well, it must ever be remembered that we cannot kill the "Amalekite" in our own strength. Flesh cannot overcome flesh. The Holy Spirit through us must slay "Amalek," which He does upon our Faith being placed consistently in Christ and the Cross [Rom. 8:1-2, 11].)*

THE LAMENTATION OF DAVID

17 And David lamented with this lamentation over Saul and over Jonathan his son *(this is really a martial ode, and one of the first and finest odes in the Old Testament; David's own sufferings are forgotten while his fervent love and deep grief for his king and his best friend, Jonathan, are expressed; there is no bitter or revengeful word or exultation over the death of his greatest enemy, Saul)*:

18 (Also he bade them teach the Children of Judah the use of the bow: behold, it is written

in the book of Jasher [the title of the ode in Hebrew is "Kesheth, the bow." The Book of Jasher would be equivalent to "Hero-book." The Hebrews always looked to the moral rather than the physical prowess of their great men].)

19 The beauty of Israel is slain upon your high places: how are the mighty fallen! (Only a Divine love could cause David to speak thusly about the man who had made many attempts to kill him.)

20 Tell it not in Gath, publish it not in the streets of Askelon; lest the daughters of the Philistines rejoice, lest the daughters of the uncircumcised triumph (in the course of time, "Tell it not in Gath" became a proverb [Mic. 1:10]).

21 You mountains of Gilboa, let there be no dew, neither let there be rain, upon you, nor fields of offerings: for there the shield of the mighty is vilely cast away, the shield of Saul, as though he had not been anointed with oil (it should have been translated, "For there the shield of heroes, yea, the shield of Saul, was defiled," stained, that is, with blood).

22 From the blood of the slain, from the fat of the mighty, the bow of Jonathan turned not back, and the sword of Saul returned not empty.

23 Saul and Jonathan were lovely and pleasant in their lives, and in their death they were not divided: they were swifter than eagles, they were stronger than lions. (Jonathan had ever been his father's faithful friend and companion; moreover, his affection for David never made him untrue to the ties of natural affection. And David generously commends his friend for thus acting.)

24 You daughters of Israel, weep over Saul, who clothed you in scarlet, with other delights, who put on ornaments of gold upon your apparel.

25 How are the mighty fallen in the midst of the battle! O Jonathan, you were slain in your high places.

26 I am distressed for you, my brother Jonathan: very pleasant have you been unto me: your love to me was wonderful, passing the love of women (never was there a purer friendship than that of Jonathan for David).

27 How are the mighty fallen, and the weapons of war perished! (Saul won many great victories for Israel, but never conquered the demons within himself; consequently, he was ultimately killed by that from without, because he never conquered that from within. It is a lesson we should studiously learn.)

CHAPTER 2
(1056 B.C.)
DAVID BECOMES KING OF JUDAH

AND it came to pass after this, that David enquired of the LORD, saying, Shall I go up into any of the cities of Judah? and the LORD said unto him, Go up. And David said, Where shall I go up? And He said, Unto Hebron. (There is a marked spiritual turn in David's life from Ziklag on. The Ziklags are terrible to the flesh and invigorating to the spirit. David is now seeking the Lord, and receiving directions from the Lord.)

2 So David went up thither, and his two wives also, Ahinoam the Jezreelitess, and Abigail Nabal's wife the Carmelite.

3 And his men who were with him did David bring up, every man with his household: and they dwelt in the cities of Hebron.

4 And the men of Judah came, and there they anointed David king over the House of Judah. And they told David, saying, That the men of Jabesh-gilead were they who buried Saul. (So begins the golden age of Israel, and yet for seven and a half years only a small part of the Church of that day will accept God's anointed.)

5 And David sent messengers unto the men of Jabesh-gilead, and said unto them, Blessed are you of the LORD, that you have showed this kindness unto your lord, even unto Saul, and have buried him.

6 And now the LORD show kindness and truth unto you: and I also will requite you this kindness, because you have done this thing.

7 Therefore now let your hands be strengthened, and be ye valiant: for your master Saul is dead, and also the house of Judah have anointed me king over them. (As we shall see, active opposition to Christ and His Kingdom quickly follows upon the establishment of a rival kingdom in the heart. Abner, having set up his own king, very quickly took the further step of attacking God's King and Kingdom.)

ABNER

8 But Abner the son of Ner, captain of Saul's host, took Ish-bosheth the son of Saul, and brought him over to Mahanaim;

9 And made him king over Gilead, and over the Ashurites, and over Jezreel, and over Ephraim, and over Benjamin, and over all Israel. (More than likely, David's consorting for

the past 16 months with the Philistines now causes him great problems. Many of Israel distrust him, giving Abner room to do what he did; irrespective, it was not God's Will for someone else to be king of Israel.)

10 Ish-bosheth Saul's son was forty years old when he began to reign over Israel, and reigned two years, But the house of Judah followed David.

11 And the time that David was king in Hebron over the house of Judah was seven years and six months.

CIVIL STRIFE

12 And Abner the son of Ner, and the servants of Ish-bosheth the son of Saul, went out from Mahanaim to Gibeon. *(David had taken no steps to obtain for himself the kingdom "over all Israel." Therefore, this opened the door for Abner to win Judah as well.)*

13 And Joab the son of Zeruiah, and the servants of David, went out, and met together by the pool of Gibeon: and they sat down, the one on the one side of the pool, and the other on the other side of the pool. *(All of this pictures "the house of Saul" and "the house of David." They stand in opposition one to the other. The one pictures the life as governed by self; the other, the life as governed by God. The latter life alone secures victory.)*

14 And Abner said to Joab, Let the young men now arise, and play before us. And Joab said, Let them arise *(the statement is grim enough, though intended to gloss over the cruel reality).*

15 Then there arose and went over by number twelve of Benjamin, which pertained to Ish-bosheth the son of Saul, and twelve of the servants of David. *(On each side twelve of the most skillful champions were to be selected, who were to fight in stern earnest with one another, while the rest gazed upon the fierce spectacle. It is by no means certain that Abner meant that this single combat should decide the war, but the conclusion was to give indication.)*

16 And they *(the men of Joab)* caught every one his fellow by the head *(the men of Abner)*, and thrust his sword in his fellow's side; so they fell down together: wherefore that place was called Helkath-hazzurim, which is in Gibeon.

17 And there was a very sore battle that day; and Abner was beaten, and the men of Israel, before the servants of David. *(The battle followed the contest, with only 19 of David's warriors falling, while Abner lost 360, and was forced to flee.)*

ABNER KILLS ASAHEL

18 And there were three sons of Zeruiah there, Joab, and Abishai, and Asahel: and Asahel was as light of foot as a wild roe *(deer)*.

19 And Asahel pursued after Abner; and in going he turned not to the right hand nor to the left from following Abner *(the sharp swords which mutually destroyed the young men should have been used against the Philistines, not against one another; the destructive energy which rival groups within the Church employ against each other would accomplish great things if used otherwise).*

20 Then Abner looked behind him, and said, Are you Asahel? And he answered, I am.

21 And Abner said to him, Turn thee aside to your right hand or to your left, and lay thee hold on one of the young men, and take thee his armour. But Asahel would not turn aside from following of him.

22 And Abner said again to Asahel, Turn thee aside from following me: wherefore should I smite you to the ground? how then should I hold up my face to Joab your brother?

23 Howbeit he refused to turn aside: wherefore Abner with the hinder end of the spear smote him under the fifth rib, that the spear came out behind him; and he fell down there, and died in the same place: and it came to pass, that as many as came to the place where Asahel fell down and died stood still *(so violent was the blow, that Asahel dropped down dead without a struggle).*

24 Joab also and Abishai pursued after Abner: and the sun went down when they were come to the hill of Ammah, that lieth before Giah by the way of the wilderness of Gibeon *(the sight of their slaughtered brother made them only the more determined in the pursuit).*

FURTHER STRIFE AVERTED

25 And the Children of Benjamin gathered themselves together after Abner, and became one troop, and stood on the top of an hill.

26 Then Abner called to Joab, and said, Shall the sword devour for ever? knowest thou not that it will be bitterness in the latter end? how long shall it be then, ere you bid the people return from following their brethren?

27 And Joab said, As God lives, unless you had spoken, surely then in the morning the people had gone up every one from following his brother *(Joab throws the whole blame, and rightly so, on Abner).*

28 So Joab blew a trumpet, and all the people stood still, and pursued after Israel no more, neither fought they any more *(Joab was not a man of a tender heart, but he was wise and sensible, and fully aware that the slaughter of Abner and his men, even if he could have destroyed them all, would only have rankled in the minds of all Israel, and set them against David and his rule).*

29 And Abner and his men walked all that night through the plain, and passed over Jordan, and went through all Bithron, and they came to Mahanaim.

30 And Joab returned from following Abner: and when he had gathered all the people together, there lacked of David's servants nineteen men and Asahel.

31 But the servants of David had smitten of Benjamin, and of Abner's men, so that three hundred and threescore *(360)* men died.

32 And they took up Asahel, and buried him in the sepulchre of his father, which was in Beth-lehem. And Joab and his men went all night, and they came to Hebron at break of day. *(This last Verse of this Chapter closes with the words, "And they came to Hebron at break of day." The sun was now beginning to rise for Israel. The long night of spiritual declension was over. There would be other hardships and difficulties; however, the sun was not setting; it was rising.)*

CHAPTER 3
(1048 B.C.)
DAVID'S FAMILY IN HEBRON

NOW there was long war between the house of Saul and the house of David: but David waxed stronger and stronger, and the house of Saul waxed weaker and weaker. *(Williams says, "The House of Saul was opposed to, and persecuted, the House of David. Fellowship was impossible. As then, he who was born after the flesh persecuted him who was born after the Spirit, so is it now [Gal. 4:29]. A carnal nature is the enemy of the spiritual; but victory is assured to the latter," that is, if the Believer follows God's prescribed order.)*

2 And unto David were sons born in Hebron: and his firstborn was Amnon, of Ahinoam the Jezreelitess;

3 And his second, Chileab, of Abigail the wife of Nabal the Carmelite; and the third, Absalom the son of Maacah the daughter of Talmai king of Geshur;

4 And the fourth, Adonijah the son of Haggith; and the fifth, Shephatiah the son of Abital;

5 And the sixth, Ithream, by Eglah David's wife. These were born to David in Hebron. *(Without once inquiring of the Lord for direction in any of these matters, David follows a crooked, tortuous path, in effect, the dark ways of man. Neglecting the teaching of the Book of Genesis, he became a polygamist — marriages which bore bitter fruit in Amnon, Absalom, and Adonijah. Other mistakes, as we shall see, were made as well.*

Had David fully consulted the Lord in all these matters, his "house" would have grown stronger much faster.)

ABNER DESERTS TO DAVID

6 And it came to pass, while there was war between the house of Saul and the house of David, that Abner made himself strong for the house of Saul.

7 And Saul had a concubine, whose name was Rizpah, the daughter of Aiah: and Ish-bosheth said to Abner, Wherefore have you gone in unto my father's concubine? *(The harem of a deceased king was looked upon as the special inheritance of his successor. So, in a sense, Abner had greatly overstepped his bounds.)*

8 Then was Abner very wroth for the words of Ish-bosheth *(this extreme indignation on Abner's part is not easy to understand; for he could scarcely have expected Ish-bosheth to endure quietly what at least was a great insult),* and said, Am I a dog's head, which against Judah do show kindness this day unto the house of Saul your father, to his brethren, and to his friends, and have not delivered you into the hand of David, that you charge me to day with a fault concerning this woman?

9 So do God to Abner, and more also, except, as the LORD has sworn to David, even so I do to him;

10 To translate the kingdom from the house of Saul, and to set up the throne of David over Israel and over Judah, from Dan even to Beer-sheba.

11 And he *(Ish-bosheth)* could not answer Abner a word again, because he feared him.

12 And Abner sent messengers to David on his behalf, saying, Whose is the land? saying also, Make your league with me, and, behold, my hand shall be with you, to bring about all Israel unto you.

13 And he said, Well; I will make a league with you: but one thing I require of you, that is, You shall not see my face, except you first bring Michal Saul's daughter, when you come to see my face. *(There is no record that David sought the Lord about this matter. How long does it take us to learn that no "league" can ever be made between the flesh and the Spirit? One is carnal and of the world and, thereby, of Satan. The other is spiritual and of Heaven and, thereby, of God.)*

14 And David sent messengers to Ish-bosheth Saul's son, saying, Deliver me my wife Michal, which I espoused to me for an hundred foreskins of the Philistines *(David did not pray about this matter either!).*

15 And Ish-bosheth sent, and took her from her husband even from Phaltiel the son of Laish. *(Besides David's affection for Michal, there were political reasons for demanding her restoration. Saul's despotic act in giving her in marriage to another man, when she had already been engaged to David [I Sam. 25:44], had been a public disavowal of David as the son-in-law of the royal house. In effect, David's rights were all declared null by such an act. Now, Ish-bosheth must with equal publicity reverse his father's deed, and restore to David his lost position. As well, for David to demand such, and Ish-bosheth not being able to do anything about the situation, portrayed his great weakness.)*

16 And her husband went with her along weeping behind her to Bahurim. Then said Abner unto him, Go, return. And he returned. *(Phaltiel had been Michal's husband for eight or nine years, and, as well, he had no part, as far as we know, as it regards the situation between David and Saul; thereby, his sorrow at losing her excites sympathy for them both.*

Should David have done what he did? Inasmuch as his reasons were political, which we have already addressed, I think, had he spoken to the Lord about the matter, the Lord would not have allowed such to happen.)

17 And Abner had communication with the elders of Israel, saying, You sought for David in times past to be king over you:

18 Now then do it: for the LORD has spoken of David, saying, By the hand of My servant David I will save My people Israel out of the hand of the Philistines, and out of the hand of all their enemies. *(If Abner knew all of this, and he definitely did, why did he wait this long? Regrettably, most Believers will not do right, until it is in their best interest to do so. In other words, if it costs them something, they will not step up to the plate, so to speak!)*

19 And Abner also spoke in the ears of Benjamin: and Abner went also to speak in the ears of David in Hebron all that seemed good to Israel, and that seemed good to the whole house of Benjamin.

20 So Abner came to David to Hebron, and twenty men with him. And David made Abner and the men who were with him a feast.

21 And Abner said unto David, I will arise and go, and will gather all Israel unto my lord the king, that they may make a league with you, and that you may reign over all that your heart desires. And David sent Abner away; and he went in peace. *(There is no record that David sought the Lord concerning this, as well! The Christian is in danger in the time of war and in the time of peace; however, he is probably in greater danger in the time of peace. During war, he has a greater tendency to seek the help of the Lord, because he knows that it is the Lord Alone Who can deliver. In peace, the temptation is to coast.)*

JOAB KILLS ABNER

22 And, behold, the servants of David and Joab came from pursuing a troop, and brought in a great spoil with them: but Abner was not with David in Hebron; for he had sent him away, and he was gone in peace.

23 When Joab and all the host who were with him were come, they told Joab, saying, Abner the son of Ner came to the king, and he has sent him away, and he is gone in peace.

24 Then Joab came to the king, and said, What have you done? behold, Abner came unto you; why is it that you have sent him away, and he is quite gone?

25 You know Abner the son of Ner, that he came to deceive you, and to know your going out and your coming in, and to know all that you do.

26 And when Joab was come out from David, he sent messengers after Abner, which brought him again from the well of Sirah: but David knew it not.

27 And when Abner was returned to Hebron, Joab took him aside in the gate to speak with

him quietly, and smote him there under the fifth rib, that he died, for the blood of Asahel his brother.

28 And afterward when David heard it, he said, I and my kingdom are guiltless before the LORD for ever from the blood of Abner the son of Ner:

29 Let it rest on the head of Joab, and on all his father's house; and let there not fail from the house of Joab one who has an issue, or who is a leper, or who leans on a staff, or who falls on the sword, or who lacks bread.

30 So Joab, and Abishai his brother slew Abner, because he had slain their brother Asahel at Gibeon in the battle *(what Joab did was wrong and probably delayed the Plan of God in some way for several years).*

DAVID MOURNS FOR ABNER

31 And David said to Joab, and to all the people who were with him, Rend your clothes, and gird you with sackcloth, and mourn before Abner. And king David himself followed the bier.

32 And they buried Abner in Hebron: and the king lifted up his voice, and wept at the grave of Abner; and all the people wept.

33 And the king lamented over Abner, and said, Died Abner as a fool dies?

34 Your hands were not bound, nor your feet put into fetters: as a man falls before wicked men, so fell you. And all the people wept again over him.

35 And when all the people came to cause David to eat meat while it was yet day, David swore, saying, So do God to me, and more also, if I taste bread, or ought else, till the sun be down.

36 And all the people took notice of it, and it pleased them: as whatsoever the king did pleased all the people.

37 For all the people and all Israel understood that day that it was not of the king to kill Abner the son of Ner.

38 And the king said unto his servants, Know ye not that there is a prince and a great man fallen this day in Israel?

39 And I am this day weak, though anointed king: and these men the sons of Zeruiah be too hard for me: the LORD shall reward the doer of evil according to his wickedness. *(Abner was related to Ish-bosheth as Joab was to David. Joab was clever, ambitious, bloodthirsty, and heartless. He was an ungodly man who*

deemed it politically correct to effect a zeal for God [24:3]. In fact, Abner was morally superior to Joab; but yet Abner was a traitor to his master and a rebel to his God. He had no real heart for David as God's king, but was moved to help him by wounded pride. He reaped as he sowed; however, and as stated, his reaping did not absolve Joab of blame.)

CHAPTER 4
(1048 B.C.)
ISH-BOSHETH MURDERED

AND when Saul's son heard that Abner was dead in Hebron, his hands were feeble, and all the Israelites were troubled. *(Ish-bosheth knew that the Lord had called David to be the king of Israel; however, as with so many, he wasn't that interested in the Will of God, but rather his own self-will. It would cost him dearly!)*

2 And Saul's son had two men who were captains of bands: the name of the one was Baanah, and the name of the other Rechab, the sons of Rimmon a Beerothite, of the Children of Benjamin: (for Beeroth also was reckoned to Benjamin.

3 And the Beerothites fled to Gittaim, and were sojourners there until this day.)

4 And Jonathan, Saul's son, had a son that was lame of his feet. He was five years old when the tidings came of Saul and Jonathan out of Jezreel, and his nurse took him up, and fled: and it came to pass, as she made haste to flee, that he fell, and became lame. And his name was Mephibosheth. *(This is mentioned to show that Saul's lineage virtually became extinct on Ish-bosheth's death. Mephibosheth, the heir, was a cripple, and physically incapable of reigning, for that was the custom of those days.)*

5 And the sons of Rimmon the Beerothite, Rechab and Baanah, went, and came about the heat of the day to the house of Ish-bosheth, who lay on a bed at noon.

6 And they came thither into the midst of the house, as though they would have fetched wheat; and they smote him under the fifth rib: and Rechab and Baanah his brother escaped.

7 For when they came into the house, he lay on his bed in his bedchamber, and they smote him, and slew him, and beheaded him, and took his head, and got them away through the plain all night.

8 And they brought the head of Ish-bosheth unto David to Hebron, and said to the king,

Behold the head of Ish-bosheth the son of Saul your enemy, which sought your life; and the LORD has avenged my lord the king this day of Saul, and of his seed. *(While Saul had sought David's life, there is no record that Ish-bosheth was a party to such attempts. Still, had he been victorious, David, as his rival, would certainly have been put to death.)*

DAVID EXECUTES THE MURDERERS

9 And David answered Rechab and Baanah his brother, the sons of Rimmon the Beerothite, and said unto them, As the LORD lives, who has redeemed my soul out of all adversity,

10 When one told me, saying, Behold, Saul is dead, thinking to have brought good tidings, I took hold of him, and slew him in Ziklag, who thought that I would have given him a reward for his tidings:

11 How much more, when wicked men have slain a righteous person in his own house upon his bed? shall I not therefore now require his blood of your hand, and take you away from the Earth?

12 And David commanded his young men, and they slew them, and cut off their hands and their feet, and hanged them up over the pool in Hebron. But they took the head of Ish-bosheth, and buried it in the sepulchre of Abner in Hebron. *(The cutting off of their hands and feet was not intended for the purpose of mutilation, but to carry out an eastern idea of retaliation. The hands were cut off because they had committed the murder; the feet, because they had brought the head to Hebron. Still, David was violating the spirit of the Mosaic Law. It ordered that the body of a man who had been put to death should be buried the same day [Deut. 21:23].*

However, the previous Chapter tells us that David took no action whatsoever regarding the murder of Abner by Joab. Why?

God's men do not always do everything right, but we can be assured that God's men always pay the penalty for doing wrong. Joab would be a thorn, so to speak, in David's side for the entirety of his reign.)

CHAPTER 5
(1048 B.C.)
DAVID MADE KING OVER ALL ISRAEL

THEN came all the Tribes of Israel to David unto Hebron, and spoke, saying, Behold,

we are your bone and your flesh. *(Finally, after so much bloodshed, the Will of God begins to be carried out in Israel. It was easy to get Saul, man's choice, on the throne; however, it was difficult to get David, God's choice, on the throne.)*

2 Also in time past, when Saul was king over us, you were he who led out and brought in Israel: and the LORD said to you, You shall feed My people Israel, and you shall be a Captain over Israel *(the Elders of Israel knew this all the time, and yet waited seven and a half years to carry out the Will of God).*

3 So all the Elders of Israel came to the king to Hebron; and king David made a league with them in Hebron before the LORD: and they anointed David king over Israel. *(Actually, this was the third anointing; first, by Samuel, when David was but a boy; second, when he was anointed to be king over Judah; and now, over the entirety of Israel. Why did it take Israel so long to do this?*

Believers, regrettably, are not prone to do right, until it's in their best interest to do so. So, the Elders of Israel will now anoint David to be king over all of Israel, because they think it's in their best interest.)

4 David was thirty years old when he began to reign, and he reigned forty years. *(David was a Type of Christ; therefore, Christ began His public ministry when He was 30 years old. He reigned over the powers of darkness, albeit not over Israel. One day soon He will reign, not only over the powers of darkness, but over Israel as well and, in fact, over the entirety of the world.)*

5 In Hebron he reigned over Judah seven years and six months: and in Jerusalem he reigned thirty and three years over all Israel and Judah.

DAVID CAPTURES JERUSALEM

6 And the king and his men went to Jerusalem unto the Jebusites, the inhabitants of the land *(though the Jebusites had been conquered by Joshua [Josh. 11:3], and Jerusalem captured [Judg. 1:8], yet, as the Children of Judah did not occupy it, but "set the city on fire," it seems to have been soon repopulated by its old inhabitants; through the entirety of his forty-year reign, Saul never captured it either; so we had the enemy situated right in the middle of the Promised Land; the taking of this city was the first thing that David did; if we do not destroy the enemy within, we will be ultimately defeated by the*

enemy without, as was Saul!): which spoke unto David, saying, Except you take away the blind and the lame, you shall not come in hither: thinking, David cannot come in hither *(to paraphrase, the Jebusites taunted David by saying, "We are so strong, and you are so weak, our blind and lame can keep you out of the city"; to be sure, Satan will taunt the Believer, telling him that there is no way that he can be victorious).*

7 Nevertheless David took the strong hold of Zion: the same is the city of David. *(It seems that the Seventy-sixth Psalm may have been written to glorify God and to commemorate this great victory. The Lord intends for that which has been the stronghold of Satan in our lives to become the "stronghold of Zion." This can be, but only if our Faith is exclusively in Christ and the Cross, which then gives the Holy Spirit latitude to work within our lives [Rom. 8:1-2, 11, 13].)*

8 And David said on that day, Whosoever gets up to the gutter, and smites the Jebusites, and the lame and the blind, that are hated of David's soul, he shall be chief and captain *(in essence, David is saying, in the spiritual sense, that he "hated" anything that would cause Israel to be spiritually "lame" or "blind")*. Wherefore they said, The blind and the lame shall not come into the house. *(This is not meant to be a sarcastic statement regarding the handicapped, but rather it is said in the spiritual sense. No Believer needs to be spiritually blind or lame. But regrettably, due to not understanding the Cross, most presently are!)*

9 So David dwelt in the fort, and called it the city of David. And David built round about from Millo and inward. *(The "gutter" mentioned in Verse 8 had to do with an underground water tunnel, through which Joab's men found their way into the city, which was otherwise impregnable. This is a Type of the "water of life" afforded only by Christ, and what He did at the Cross, which then affords the help of the Holy Spirit [Rom. 8:1-2, 11; Jn. 7:37-39].)*

10 And David went on, and grew great, and the LORD God of hosts was with him. *(Had he not dislodged this cancer right in the midst of Israel, he would not have "gone on and grown great." If you as a Believer allow strongholds of Satan to remain in your life, they will destroy you. They must be removed, and they can be removed, by Faith in Christ and the Cross.)*

HIRAM BUILDS DAVID A HOUSE

11 And Hiram king of Tyre sent messengers to David, and cedar trees, and carpenters, and masons: and they built David an house. *(When David, the Type of Christ, became king, Hiram, the Gentile, brought gifts to David; likewise, the Gentile world will bring gifts to Christ when He begins to rule in the Kingdom Age.)*

12 And David perceived that the LORD had established him king over Israel, and that he had exalted His kingdom for His people Israel's sake. *(It was the Will of the Lord for David to be the first king of Israel, and not Saul; however, the people jumped the gun, so to speak, demanding a king before it was time, and Saul was the result. It didn't turn out well. Now, with Israel in the center of God's Will, the nation will prosper greatly.)*

DAVID'S FAMILY AT JERUSALEM

13 And David took him more concubines and wives out of Jerusalem, after he was come from Hebron: and there were yet sons and daughters born to David.

14 And these be the names of those who were born unto him in Jerusalem; Shammuah, and Shobab, and Nathan, and Solomon,

15 Ibhar also, and Elishua, and Nepheg, and Japhia,

16 And Elishama, and Eliada, and Eliphalet. *(Verses 13-16 refer to David's polygamy, which was not the Will of God; however, Grace in the midst of failure will shine. In the Fourteenth Verse, the two names "Nathan" and "Solomon" are given unto us. The Davidic line all the way to Christ will follow through Solomon. As well, the kingly line through Mary will come through Nathan.)*

DAVID DEFEATS THE PHILISTINES

17 But when the Philistines heard that they had anointed David king over Israel *(Satan has little concern until he hears of the "anointing"; nothing will break his yoke except the "anointing")*, all the Philistines came up to seek David; and David heard of it, and went down to the hold. *(The moment the person makes Jesus King in his life, the Philistines will appear. Many are discouraged and surprised on meeting strong opposition directly upon the establishment of Christ's Kingdom in their hearts; but it must ever be so till He comes in glory.)*

18 The Philistines also came and spread themselves in the valley of Rephaim *("Rephaim" means "giants"; so Satan throws his biggest and*

his best at us).

19 And David enquired of the LORD, saying, Shall I go up to the Philistines? will You deliver them into my hand? And the LORD said unto David, Go up: for I will doubtless deliver the Philistines into your hand *(as Believers, we must seek the counsel of the Lord in everything; having that, we cannot lose; and, to be sure, if we ask, He will hear and answer [Lk. 11:5-13]).*

20 And David came to Baal-perazim, and David smote them there, and said, the LORD has broken forth upon my enemies before me, as the breach of waters. Therefore he called the name of that place Baal-perazim *("Baal-perazim" means "the plain of breaches"; David made a breach in the lines of the Philistines).*

21 And there they left their images, and David and his men burned them *(should have been translated, "took them away"; they took them as trophies, showing that these "gods" were helpless!).*

22 And the Philistines came up yet again, and spread themselves in the valley of Rephaim *(Satan will always be back; the battle is unceasing, this "fighting the good fight of Faith" [I Tim. 6:12]).*

23 And when David enquired of the LORD, He said, You shall not go up *(previously, the Lord had said, "Go up"; now, He says, "You shall not go up"; we must never take the Will of God for granted; what may have been His Will previously, may not be His Will presently!);* but fetch a compass behind them, and come upon them over against the mulberry trees *(the Philistines, no doubt, would have been expecting the army of Israel to come the same way as they did before).*

24 And let it be, when you hear the sound of a going in the tops of the mulberry trees, that then you shall bestir yourself: for then shall the LORD go out before you, to smite the host of the Philistines. *(The sound of a "going" meant the sound of a mighty army on the march, which struck terror to the Philistines, and caused them to be confused and panic-stricken. It is said that the sound was the noise of horses' hoofs. The Philistines would have reasoned that some other mighty army was appearing suddenly behind them to help David. This was God's Way of bringing the victory. How easy are His Ways; how difficult are our ways!)*

25 And David did so, as the LORD had commanded him; and smote the Philistines from Geba until you come to Gazer.

CHAPTER 6
(1042 B.C.)

DAVID BRINGS THE ARK TO JERUSALEM

AGAIN, David gathered together all the chosen men of Israel, thirty thousand *(I Chronicles 13:1 says, "David consulted with every leader." Before fighting the Philistines, David "enquired of the Lord." Before performing the Work of God, David will not enquire of the Lord, but rather men. Why? His not doing so would cause tremendous problems.).*

2 And David arose, and went with all the people who were with him from Baale of Judah, to bring up from thence the Ark of God, Whose name is called by the Name of the LORD of hosts Who dwells between the Cherubims. *(For approximately 70 years, the Ark of God had been without a home. Actually, it had been at the "house of Abinadab." There is some indication, according to the Psalms, that it was little attended to, possibly even sitting out in a field [Ps. 132:6]. Regrettably, the modern Church treats the Presence of God, of which the Ark was a Type, in pretty much the same fashion. To be frank, in most Churches, His Presence simply isn't wanted or desired.)*

3 And they set the Ark of God upon a new cart, and brought it out of the house of Abinadab that was in Gibeah *(the Law of Moses said that the Priests must carry the Ark upon their shoulders; the Priests were types of Christ; but Israel borrowed the way of the Philistines, and set the Ark, contrary to the Word of God, on a "new cart"; unfortunately, "new carts" abound presently!):* and Uzzah and Ahio, the sons of Abinadab, drove the new cart *(how many spiritual leaders, so-called, presently are driving the "new carts," thinking all the time they are doing great things for God?).*

4 And they brought it out of the house of Abinadab which was at Gibeah, accompanying the Ark of God: and Ahio went before the Ark *(that which seemed to begin so greatly would end so poorly).*

5 And David and all the house of Israel played before the LORD on all manner of instruments made of fir wood, even on harps, and on psalteries, and on timbrels, and on cornets, and on cymbals. *("New carts" are always accompanied by great religious activity; however, all of this is a work of the flesh.*

Had David enquired of the Lord and consulted the Bible [Num. 4:15], success and not

disaster would have resulted. But he consulted man [I Chron., Chpt. 13], imitated the Philistine, and organized a great public function in which David and his plans largely obscured God and His Glory; consequently, the day ended in anger and fear. All of this was the planning of the "flesh.")

UZZAH DIES

6 And when they came to Nachon's threshingfloor, Uzzah put forth his hand to the Ark of God, and took hold of it; for the oxen shook it. (What man has set up, he feels himself bound to sustain. But the God of Israel needed not, as the gods of the nations, a human hand to uphold Him. It must be learned that God will judge the "flesh" even more in an Israelite than in a Philistine. The Living God is a consuming fire to the actions of the carnal nature, whether inside or outside the Family of God.)

7 And the anger of the LORD was kindled against Uzzah; and God smote him there for his error; and there he died by the Ark of God (of all people, Uzzah, who was supposed to have attended the Ark of God for all of his adult life, should have known better than to touch the Sacred Vessel).

8 And David was displeased, because the LORD had made a breach upon Uzzah: and he called the name of the place Perez-uzzah to this day (displeased or not, God would not change His Word, even for one who was "after His Own Heart").

9 And David was afraid of the LORD that day, and said, How shall the Ark of the LORD come to me? (Had David consulted the Bible, he would have known how the Ark of the Lord should come to him!)

10 So David would not remove the Ark of the LORD unto him into the city of David: but David carried it aside into the house of Obed-edom the Gittite. (What had been a curse to Uzzah, now would be a blessing to Obed-edom. We say, "We need revival!" However, if true revival actually comes, it will bring both death and life. So, most Christians are very much willing to just leave the Ark in the "field of the wood.")

11 And the Ark of the LORD continued in the house of Obed-edom the Gittite three months: and the LORD blessed Obed-edom, and all his household. (Evidently, Obed-edom consulted the Word of God, and attended to the Ark in the correct manner. Such brought tremendous blessing.)

THE ARK IS BROUGHT TO JERUSALEM

12 And it was told king David, saying, The LORD has blessed the house of Obed-edom, and all that pertains unto him, because of the Ark of God. So David went and brought up the Ark of God from the house of Obed-edom into the city of David with gladness. (Now David knew that God was not angry with him without cause. So, according to the Word of the Lord, he corrects the situation, and brings up the Ark of God "with gladness.")

13 And it was so, that when they who bore the Ark of the LORD had gone six paces, he sacrificed oxen and fatlings (about every 18 feet; to the carnal mind, this would seem extravagant; however, when we speak of Calvary, of which the Sacrifices were representative, there can be no extravagance).

14 And David danced before the LORD with all his might; and David was girded with a linen ephod. (Now it is not mere religious ceremony, but rather "in the Spirit," because it says "before the LORD." Religious ceremony producing religious activity has no spiritual merit whatsoever; however, activity produced by the "Spirit" is the blessing of the Church. The "linen ephod" was probably a garment like that worn by little children. It is doubtful that David would have donned a Priestly garment, which he had no right to wear.)

15 So David and all the house of Israel brought up the Ark of the LORD with shouting, and with the sound of the trumpet. (We are looking here at Holy Spirit Revival. This is the strength of Israel, not its mighty army, not its wealth, but "the Ark of the LORD," which represented the Presence of God.)

16 And as the Ark of the LORD came into the city of David, Michal Saul's daughter looked through a window, and saw king David leaping and dancing before the LORD; and she despised him in her heart. (This Verse tells us that the "flesh" can never approve of the things of the "Spirit." Speaking of David's wife, Michal, she is referred to here by the Holy Spirit as "Saul's daughter." David did not do himself well by demanding that she come again to be his wife [3:14-16].)

17 And they brought in the Ark of the LORD, and set it in his place, in the midst of the Tabernacle that David had pitched for it: and David offered Burnt Offerings and Peace Offerings before the LORD.

18 And as soon as David had made an end of offering Burnt Offerings and Peace Offerings, he blessed the people in the name of the LORD of hosts.

19 And he dealt among all the people, even among the whole multitude of Israel, as well to the women as men, to every one a cake of bread, and a good piece of flesh, and a flagon of wine. So all the people departed every one to his house. *(This speaks of Jesus as the Bread of Life, giving His Perfect Body on Calvary's Cross for our Salvation, and through which comes the joy of the Lord.)*

DAVID REPROVES MICHAL

20 Then David returned to bless his household. And Michal the daughter of Saul came out to meet David, and said, How glorious was the king of Israel to day, who uncovered himself to day in the eyes of the handmaids of his servants, as one of the vain fellows shamelessly uncovers himself! *(All that happened in the realm of the Holy Spirit was repulsive to "the daughter of Saul." Likewise, the Moving of the Holy Spirit is always repulsive to those in the Church, in which there seems to be an abundance of "the flesh.")*

21 And David said unto Michal, It was before the LORD, which chose me before your father, and before all his house, to appoint me ruler over the people of the LORD, over Israel: therefore will I play before the LORD.

22 And I will yet be more vile than thus, and will be base in my own sight: and of the maidservants which you have spoken of, of them shall I be had in honour. *(And to be sure, he was! David was honored more than any other human being by him being the namesake of the Messiah, "the Son of David.")*

23 Therefore Michal the daughter of Saul had no child unto the day of her death *(for the "flesh" — let it be ever so dignified — cannot bring forth fruit unto God; such was the pride of the "flesh").*

CHAPTER 7
(1042 B.C.)
THE TEMPLE

AND it came to pass, when the king sat in his house, and the LORD had given him rest round about from all his enemies *(this pictures the Lord Jesus Christ in a posture of absolute Lordship; the great Plan of Redemption* has been won at Calvary, and He today is "sat down at the right hand of the Father" [Heb. 1:3]; every enemy has been defeated, and He did it all for us; consequently, it is the Will of God for us as Believers to have victory over every enemy of our soul; this can be done only by and through what Christ did at the Cross, and our Faith in that Finished Work);*

2 That the king said unto Nathan the Prophet *(here Nathan the Prophet first appears; he will figure prominently in David's life)*, See now, I dwell in an house of cedar, but the Ark of God dwells within curtains *(it was in a tent).*

3 And Nathan said to the king, Go, do all that is in your heart; for the LORD is with you *(at the moment, Nathan did not seek the Lord; consequently, his answer was rash and, thereby, wrong!).*

GOD'S COVENANT WITH DAVID

4 And it came to pass that night, that the word of the LORD came unto Nathan, saying,

5 Go and tell My servant David, Thus saith the LORD, Shall you build Me an house for Me to dwell in? *(There is no disapproval of David's purpose as such; but only the deferring of its full execution unto the days of his son, Solomon. But there is more than this. The idea which runs through the Divine Message is that the dwelling of Jehovah in a tent was a fitting symbol of Israel's unsure possession of the land. In fact, they had conquered the land a long time before, but had never been able to maintain their liberty unimpaired. David would rectify that.)*

6 Whereas I have not dwelt in any house since the time that I brought up the Children of Israel out of Egypt, even to this day, but have walked in a tent and in a Tabernacle.

7 In all the places wherein I have walked with all the Children of Israel spoke I a word with any of the Tribes *(Judges)* of Israel, whom I commanded to feed My people Israel, saying, Why build ye not Me an house of cedar? *(For a proper House for the Lord to be built, proper leadership must first be established — leadership that would properly feed the people. To properly feed is to properly govern. David was the first one to fit this bill, so to speak; therefore, the plans would be given to him, but not the right to actually build. That would go to Solomon.)*

8 Now therefore so shall you say unto My servant David, Thus saith the LORD of Hosts, I took you from the sheepcote, from following

the sheep, to be ruler over My people, over Israel (now the Lord tells David that admittance into this House will be by the way of humility and the shed blood, hence "the sheep"):

9 And I was with you wheresoever you went, and have cut off all your enemies out of your sight, and have made you a great name, like unto the name of the great men who are in the Earth. (The widespread conquests of David, and his great empire, were not for the sake of mere Earthly dominion. It was, first of all, a Type of Messiah's reign, to Whom God has promised the heathen for His Inheritance, and that His Gospel shall be carried to the ends of the Earth [Mk. 16:15].)

10 Moreover I will appoint a place for My people Israel, and will plant them, that they may dwell in a place of their own, and move no more; neither shall the children of wickedness afflict them any more, as beforetime (in Genesis, Chapter 15, God promised the land to Abraham's Seed. In this Chapter, He promises the Throne to David's Seed. The Seed is Christ; and, therefore, in each instance the Covenant is unconditional, for there can be no failure on Christ's part),

11 And as since the time that I commanded judges to be over My people Israel, and have caused you to rest from all your enemies. Also the LORD tells you that He will make you an house. (In Genesis 49:10, through Jacob, the Lord promised that the Messiah would come from the Tribe of Judah. And now, He selects the family in Judah which will bring forth the Messiah, and David is clearly chosen. David had thought to build the Lord a house, but, instead, the Lord tells him that He [the Lord] will build David a house.)

12 And when your days be fulfilled, and you shall sleep with your fathers, I will set up your seed after you, which shall proceed out of your bowels, and I will establish His Kingdom (this speaks of the Lord Jesus Christ).

13 He shall build an house for My Name, and I will stablish the Throne of His Kingdom for ever (as stated, this is an unconditional Promise; it will most definitely come to pass).

THE THRONE ESTABLISHED FOREVER

14 I will be his father, and he shall be my son. If he commit iniquity, I will chasten him with the rod of men, and with the stripes of the children of men (this pertains to Solomon and those who would follow after him in the lineage of David, through whom the Messiah would come, which pertains to the first phrase of the Verse):

15 But My mercy shall not depart away from him, as I took it from Saul, whom I put away before you (this means that whatever happened, the Messiah would come through the lineage of David).

16 And your house and your kingdom shall be established for ever before you: your throne shall be established for ever (and so shall it be in Christ, and will be established at the Second Coming).

17 According to all these words, and according to all this Vision, so did Nathan speak unto David (no doubt, we only have a small portion here of what Nathan actually said, but yet the full ingredients).

DAVID'S THANKSGIVING TO GOD

18 Then went king David in, and sat before the LORD, and he said, Who am I, O LORD God? and what is my house, that You have brought me hitherto? (The magnitude of all this overwhelms David, as well it should! God's thoughts are always so much bigger than our thoughts.)

19 And this was yet a small thing in Your sight, O LORD God; but You have spoken also of Your servant's house for a great while to come. And is this the manner of man, O LORD God? (While there is no direct reference here to the Messiah in David's words, yet the Psalms indicate that he did connect the duration of his house with the Messiah's advent [Ps. 2:8; 89:27]. In effect, he was saying, "So this is the manner in which You will redeem man. You will do so by God becoming Man, fulfilling Genesis 3:15.")

20 And what can David say more unto You? for You, LORD God, know Your servant ("LORD God," in the Hebrew, is "LORD Jehovah," signifying Covenant relationship).

21 For Your Word's sake, and according to Your Own heart, have You done all these great things, to make Your servant know them (from this statement we know that David knew that the Lord had chosen him for this great honor, not because He saw something good in David, but because of the good within Himself).

22 Wherefore You are great, O LORD God: for there is none like You, neither is there any God beside you, according to all that we have heard with our ears (until we see God as David did, in His Mercy and Grace, we really do not

know Him).

23 And what one nation in the Earth is like Your people, even like Israel, whom God went to redeem for a people to Himself, and to make Him a name, and to do for You great things and terrible, for Your land, before Your people, which You redeemed to Yourself from Egypt, from the nations and their gods? *(Israel both was and remains to this day a nation unique in its history, both in those early dealings of God with it, and also in its later history, and even its marvelous preservation unto this day.)*

24 For You have confirmed to Yourself Your people Israel to be a people unto You for ever: and You, LORD, are become their God. *(Until Jesus came, the people of Israel, with the exception of a few proselytes, were the only people on Earth who truly knew God. Even though Israel rejected her Messiah, and has suffered terribly, the prediction by the Prophets, and especially by the Apostle Paul, is that Israel will be restored, which is yet future, and will take place at the Second Coming [Rom. 11:25-27].)*

25 And now, O LORD God, the Word that You have spoken concerning Your servant, and concerning his house, establish it for ever, and do as You have said.

26 And let Your Name be magnified for ever, saying, The LORD of Hosts is the God over Israel: and let the house of Your servant David be established before You *(the special relation of Jehovah to Israel is throughout constantly in view; for Jehovah is the Name of Deity in Covenant with His People).*

27 For You, O LORD of Hosts, God of Israel, have revealed to Your servant, saying, I will build you an house; therefore has Your servant found in his heart to pray this prayer unto You *(could be translated, "Therefore has Your Servant been bold to pray this prayer").*

28 And now, O LORD God, You are that God, and Your Words be true, and You have promised this goodness unto Your servant *(could be translated, "You are the One True God; consequently, Your Words are True"):*

29 Therefore now let it please You to bless the house of Your servant, that it may continue for ever before You: for You, O LORD God, have spoken it: and with Your blessing let the house of Your servant be blessed for ever *(David prays that the blessing may now at once begin to take effect; it is the language of firm faith, and should be rendered, "And now begin of Your Own good will, and bless the house of Your servant").*

CHAPTER 8
(1040 B.C.)

DAVID EXTENDS HIS KINGDOM

AND after this it came to pass that David smote the Philistines, and subdued them: and David took Metheg-ammah out of the hand of the Philistines. *(We have in this Chapter a brief summary of the wars which raised Israel from the position of a struggling and oppressed race to the possession of widest empire, in effect, what the Lord had promised Abraham. "Metheg-ammah" refers to the reigning mother city, Gath, and all her towns, the head city of the Philistines from which they held sway over Israel. While it is true that in our spiritual lives we have defeated many of the lesser demons, still, we must also defeat the "spiritual wickedness in high places" [Eph. 6:12].)*

2 And he smote Moab, and measured them with a line, casting them down to the ground; even with two lines measured he to put to death, and with one full line to keep alive *(what a refreshing thought that the Holy Spirit is measuring our enemies for defeat instead of the enemy measuring us for defeat).* And so the Moabites became David's servants, and brought gifts *(they paid an annual tribute).*

3 David smote also Hadadezer, the son of Rehob, king of Zobah, as he went to recover his border at the river Euphrates. *(Thus, for the first time, Israel extends her possessions to the River Euphrates, the eastern border of the Promised Land. It was promised in Gen. 15:18-21 and I Chron. 18:3. The Word of God has promised us complete victory. Have we taken all the land, or is there some that is still occupied by the enemy?)*

4 And David took from him a thousand chariots, and seven hundred horsemen, and twenty thousand footmen: and David houghed all the chariot horses, but reserved of them for an hundred chariots *(the word "houghed," as used here, refers to the fact that they were made useless for war but not for agriculture).*

5 And when the Syrians of Damascus came to succour Hadadezer king of Zobah, David slew of the Syrians two and twenty thousand men. *(David is here a Type of the conquering Christ. So when we read these accounts, spiritually we should understand that Christ Alone can defeat the enemies in our lives. In fact, He has already defeated these enemies, and did so at Calvary [Col. 2:14-15].)*

6 Then David put garrisons in Syria of

Damascus: and the Syrians became servants to David, and brought gifts. And the LORD preserved David whithersoever he went (*these great victories were all as a result of the Hand of the Lord, as all such victories must be of the Hand of the Lord*).

7 And David took the shields of gold that were on the servants of Hadadezer, and brought them to Jerusalem (*before David, what little that Israel had was taken by the enemy; now, with David, because he was God's choice, the spoil of the enemy is brought to Israel*).

8 And from Betah, and from Berothai, cities of Hadadezer, king David took exceeding much brass (*all of this would ultimately be used in the construction of the Temple*).

9 When Toi king of Hamath heard that David had smitten all the host of Hadadezer,

10 Then Toi sent Joram his son unto king David, to salute him, and to bless him, because he had fought against Hadadezer, and smitten him: for Hadadezer had wars with Toi. And Joram brought with him vessels of silver, and vessels of gold, and vessels of brass (*the material value of the gifts is left in the background; their worth lies in their being the acknowledgment of the Divine favor resting upon David; in Psalms 18:43-44, we have proof of the great pleasure which this embassy from so great a nation gave to David*):

11 Which also king David did dedicate unto the LORD, with the silver and gold that he had dedicated of all nations which he subdued (*dedicated to the Lord in regard to the future construction of the Temple, which would be carried out by Solomon*);

12 Of Syria, and of Moab, and of the children of Ammon, and of the Philistines, and of Amalek, and of the spoil of Hadadezer, son of Rehob, king of Zobah. (*All of these heathen were worshippers of idol gods, but now saw how useless their gods were beside David. Is the Holy Spirit at this moment cataloging the victories we have won, which can only be won in Christ?*)

13 And David got him a name when he returned from smiting of the Syrians in the valley of salt, being eighteen thousand men (*should have been translated "the Edomites"; the Edomites, believing that David was engaged in a struggle beyond his powers with the Syrians, took the opportunity to invade Israel; it was a bad mistake on their part; David defeated both the Syrians and the Edomites [I Chron. 18:12]*).

14 And he put garrisons in Edom; throughout all Edom put he garrisons, and all they of Edom became David's servants. And the LORD preserved David whithersoever he went (*once again, the Holy Spirit proclaims to us the secret of David's great victories*).

15 And David reigned over all Israel; and David executed judgment and justice unto all his people (*this is the type of government, whether it be civil or spiritual, that God demands*).

DAVID'S OFFICERS

16 And Joab the son of Zeruiah was over the host (*the commanding general of the army*); and Jehoshaphat the son of Ahilud was recorder (*it was his office to reduce the king's decrees to writing, and also to see that they were carried into execution*);

17 And Zadok the son of Ahitub, and Ahimelech the son of Abiathar, were the Priests (*in effect, at least at this time, there were two High Priests*); and Seraiah was the Scribe (*similar to the Secretary of State*);

18 And Benaiah the son of Jehoiada was over both the Cherethites and the Pelethites (*these were either the bodyguards of David, or else they served in some similar type of position*); and David's sons were chief rulers (*the term "chief rulers" refers more to a spiritual capacity than anything else*).

CHAPTER 9
(1040 B.C.)
MEPHIBOSHETH

AND David said, Is there yet any that is left of the house of Saul, that I may show him kindness for Jonathan's sake? (*This Verse proclaims the great truth that God pardons and blesses sinners "for Christ's sake" [Eph. 4:3]. There is no merit in any of us that would warrant the "kindness" of God, but all is done for us because of Christ. David is actually referring back to the happenings of I Sam., Chpt. 18, where he made a covenant with Jonathan. The Covenant pertains to the great price that Jesus paid at Calvary. Verse 1 shows David seeking Mephibosheth. Ever is the Lord seeking the sinner [Jn. 3:16].*)

2 And there was of the house of Saul a servant whose name was Ziba. And when they had called him unto David, the king said unto him, Are you Ziba? and he said, Your servant is he.

3 And the king said, Is there not yet any of the house of Saul, that I may show the kindness

of God unto him? And Ziba said unto the king, Jonathan has yet a son, which is lame on his feet. *(Jesus desires to show the kindness of God to sinners. In fact, that's what He came to do, and did so by dying on the Cross. "Lame on his feet," presents an apt description of the lost soul which doesn't know the Lord Jesus Christ. Spiritually speaking, they cannot walk properly.)*

4 And the king said unto him, Where is he? and Ziba said unto the king, Behold, he is in the house of Machir, the son of Ammiel, in Lodebar *("Lodebar" means "the desert place"; that's where all unsaved people live, irrespective of their financial or social position; they live in a "desert place," which refers to the fact that they are bereft of all things of God).*

5 Then king David sent, and fetched him out of the house of Machir, the son of Ammiel, from Lo-debar *(we talk about finding the Lord, but, in reality, He found us; and, when He found us, He sent the Holy Spirit to "fetch us").*

6 Now when Mephibosheth *(his name means "the shameful thing," which portrays all who don't know the Lord)*, the son of Jonathan, the son of Saul *(meaning that he was the lost son of a doomed race)*, was come unto David, he fell on his face, and did reverence *(to be accepted, there must be a brokenness before the Lord; the Lord gives Grace to the humble, but He resists the proud).* And David said, Mephibosheth. And he answered, Behold your servant!

7 And David said unto him, Fear not *(in those days, potential heirs to the throne, as Mephibosheth, were instantly killed by those in power; many think of the Lord in the same fashion; however, the Word of the Lord has always been "fear not"):* for I will surely show you kindness for Jonathan your father's sake *(God shows us kindness for Jesus' sake)*, and will restore you all the land of Saul your father *("Restoration" is the great truth of the Gospel; coming to Christ, we regain what was lost by Adam);* and you shall eat bread at my table continually *(the greater part of Salvation is the fellowship we can now have with the Lord).*

8 And he bowed himself, and said, What is your servant, that you should look upon such a dead dog as I am? *(Mephibosheth did what is so hard for most people to do. He admitted that he was a spiritual cripple, deformed, and unable to save himself.)*

9 Then the king called to Ziba, Saul's servant, and said unto him, I have given unto your master's son all that pertained to Saul and to all his house *(what has been lost can be regained, but only in Christ).*

10 Thou therefore, and your sons, and your servants, shall till the land for him *(Ziba was to do this for Mephibosheth)*, and you shall bring in the fruits, that your master's son may have food to eat: but Mephibosheth your master's son shall eat bread alway at my table. Now Ziba had fifteen sons and twenty servants.

11 Then said Ziba unto the king, According to all that my lord the king has commanded his servant, so shall your servant do. As for Mephibosheth, said the king, he shall eat at my table, as one of the king's sons. *(All of this portrays "Restoration," then "productivity" [fruit-bearing], and "fellowship.")*

12 And Mephibosheth had a young son, whose name was Micha. And all who dwelt in the house of Ziba were servants unto Mephibosheth *(this son of Mephibosheth became the representative of the house of Saul, and had numerous offspring, who were leading men in the Tribe of Benjamin until the captivity [I Chron. 8:35-40; 9:40-44]).*

13 So Mephibosheth dwelt in Jerusalem: for he did eat continually at the king's table; and was lame on both his feet. *(This grand blessing was all because of the covenant made between David and Jonathan; likewise, there is a Covenant presently called "the New Covenant," and all are free to enter, and the blessings will be of untold degree.)*

CHAPTER 10
(1037 B.C.)
DAVID'S VICTORIES

AND it came to pass after this, that the king of the children of Ammon died, and Hanun his son reigned in his stead.

2 Then said David, I will show kindness unto Hanun the son of Nahash *(means "shining serpent")*, as his father showed kindness unto me. And David sent to comfort him by the hand of his servants for his father. And David's servants came into the land of the children of Ammon. *(Remarkably enough, Verse 1 of Chapter 9 starts out with the words, "that I may show him kindness." So, there is a vast similarity in David's dealings, both with Mephibosheth and also the heathen king, "Hanun." However, the responses were totally different.)*

3 And the princes of the children of Ammon said unto Hanun their lord, Do you think that David does honour your father, that he has sent comforters unto you? has not

David rather sent his servants unto you, to search the city, and to spy it out, and to overthrow it? *(Most foolish advice which they gave the young king.)*

4 Wherefore Hanun took David's servants, and shaved off the one half of their beards, and cut off their garments in the middle, even to their buttocks, and sent them away. *(In that culture, the beard was the mark of a man being free. To cut it off on one side was not merely an insult to David's ambassadors, but was treating them like slaves. The entire episode was the height of insult.)*

5 When they told it unto David, he sent to meet them, because the men were greatly ashamed: and the king said, Tarry at Jericho until your beards be grown, and then return.

6 And when the children of Ammon saw that they stank before David, the children of Ammon sent and hired the Syrians of Bethrehob and the Syrians of Zoba, twenty thousand footmen, and of king Maacah a thousand men, and of Ish-tob twelve thousand men.

7 And when David heard of it, he sent Joab, and all the host of the mighty men *(the idea is, the Israelites had now become practised in war and, thereby, veterans).*

8 And the children of Ammon came out, and put the battle in array at the entering in of the gate: and the Syrians of Zoba, and of Rehob, and Ish-tob, and Maacah, were by themselves in the field.

9 When Joab saw that the front of the battle was against him before and behind, he chose of all the choice men of Israel, and put them in array against the Syrians *(the object of Joab was to prevent at all hazards the junction of the Syrians with the Ammonites, and he was only just in time to throw himself between them):*

10 And the rest of the people he delivered into the hand of Abishai his brother, that he might put them in array against the children of Ammon *(of the two, the Syrians were the stronger).*

11 And he said, If the Syrians be too strong for me, then you shall help me: but if the children of Ammon be too strong for you, then I will come and help you.

12 Be of good courage, and let us play the men for our people, and for the cities of our God: and the LORD do that which seems Him good. *(The honor of Israel's God was in jeopardy. Come good or bad, he and Abishai would do their utmost.)*

13 And Joab drew near, and the people who were with him, unto the battle against the Syrians: and they fled before him.

14 And when the children of Ammon saw that the Syrians were fled, then fled they also before Abishai, and entered into the city. So Joab returned from the children of Ammon, and came to Jerusalem.

15 And when the Syrians saw that they were smitten before Israel, they gathered themselves together.

16 And Hadarezer sent, and brought out the Syrians who were beyond the river: and they came to Helam; and Shobach the captain of the host of Hadarezer went before them *(Hadarezer summoned troops from all the surrounding states in order to attack Israel).*

17 And when it was told David, he gathered all Israel together, and passed over Jordan, and came to Helam. And the Syrians set themselves in array against David, and fought with him *(the presence of David guaranteed victory).*

18 And the Syrians fled before Israel; and David slew the men of seven hundred chariots of the Syrians, and forty thousand horsemen, and smote Shobach the captain of their host, who died there *(the Hebrew word for "chariots" refers to any vehicle or animal for riding).*

19 And when all the kings who were servants to Hadarezer saw that they were smitten before Israel, they made peace with Israel, and served them. So the Syrians feared to help the children of Ammon any more *(in other words, the kings which had been subject to Hadarezer now place themselves under the supremacy of David, and pay to him the tribute which they had previously paid to Zobah).*

CHAPTER 11
(1035 B.C.)
DAVID'S SIN WITH BATH-SHEBA

AND it came to pass, after the year was expired, at the time when kings go forth to battle, that David sent Joab, and his servants with him, and all Israel; and they destroyed the children of Ammon, and besieged Rabbah. But David tarried still at Jerusalem. *(This Chapter portrays one of the saddest accounts concerning failure found in the entirety of the Word of God. The sin could not have been blacker or the crime more heinous. David, the man after God's Own heart, would murder one of his choice servants in cold blood and then take his wife; however, out of this horror will come the great attributes of God that will be a*

signal portrayal of the Grace of God.

This Chapter testifies to the inspiration of the Bible, for only the Holy Spirit would record so faithfully such infamy and horror. It gives us a true insight into man's nature as sinful and fallen, and it teaches the Reader the humbling lesson that such is the nature he possesses.

Also, if Divine restraints are withheld and temptation sufficiently attractive and skillfully proffered, there is no depth of evil, shame, and falsehood to which man will not fall.)

2 And it came to pass in an eveningtide, that David arose from off his bed, and walked upon the roof of the king's house: and from the roof he saw a woman washing herself; and the woman was very beautiful to look upon. *(No blame, at this juncture, must be attached to Bath-sheba. The place where she was bathing was regarded as perfectly secluded, and probably neither she nor her husband Uriah had ever suspected that what went on there could be observed from the roof of the king's palace.)*

3 And David sent and enquired after the woman. And one said, Is not this Bath-sheba, the daughter of Eliam, the wife of Uriah the Hittite? *(Uriah was one of David's mighty men, which means that he was an elite warrior [23:39].)*

4 And David sent messengers, and took her; and she came in unto him, and he lay with her; for she was purified from her uncleanness *(even though she committed an act of gross immorality, she nevertheless carefully observed the ceremonial enactment commanded in Leviticus 15:18)*: and she returned unto her house.

5 And the woman conceived, and sent and told David, and said, I am with child. *(In fact, her crime was one that made her liable to the penalty of death [Lev. 20:10]. Had David immediately repented of his sin, a sin incidentally against God, against Uriah, against Bath-sheba, and against the people of Israel, and then cast himself with anguish of heart upon God, the Lord would have made a way of escape and forgiveness consistent with Himself and morally instructive to David. Instead, David attempts to cover-up his sin.*

It should be ever understood that there is no covering of sin except for the precious Blood of Jesus Christ. As well, that cannot be obtained unless one humbly and truly repents before God.)

DAVID'S PLAN TO COVER HIS SIN

6 And David sent to Joab, saying, Send me Uriah the Hittite. And Joab sent Uriah to David

(Joab, at this stage, had absolutely no idea as to why David sent for Uriah).

7 And when Uriah was come unto him, David demanded of him how Joab did, and how the people did, and how the war prospered *(as well, Uriah had no idea as to why David sent for him).*

8 And David said to Uriah, Go down to your house, and wash your feet *(in other words, take a little time off).* And Uriah departed out of the king's house, and there followed him a mess of meat from the king.

9 But Uriah slept at the door of the king's house with all the servants of his lord, and went not down to his house *(no doubt, the Lord had a hand in what Uriah did).*

10 And when they had told David, saying, Uriah went not down unto his house, David said unto Uriah, Camest thou not from your journey? why then did you not go down unto your house?

11 And Uriah said unto David, The Ark, and Israel, and Judah, abide in tents; and my lord Joab, and the servants of my lord, are encamped in the open fields; shall I then go into my house, to eat and to drink, and to lie with my wife? as you live, and as your soul lives, I will not do this thing. *(David had felt sure that Uriah would go to his house and be with his wife, and then the pregnancy would be covered. Everyone would think that the child was Uriah's. But Uriah didn't go along with David's plans.)*

12 And David said to Uriah, Tarry here to day also, and to morrow I will let you depart. So Uriah abode in Jerusalem that day, and the morrow.

13 And when David had called him, he did eat and drink before him; and he made him drunk *(David thus adds sin to sin; but, even when intoxicated, Uriah kept to his determination)*: and at evening he went out to lie on his bed with the servants of his lord, but went not down to his house *(so, everything that David does to cover-up his sin fails, as fail it must!).*

DAVID ARRANGES THE DEATH OF URIAH

14 And it came to pass in the morning, that David wrote a letter to Joab, and sent it by the hand of Uriah. *(The warrior didn't know it, but David had written Uriah's death warrant. It will amount to murder in cold blood, and of one of his loyal subjects.)*

15 And he wrote in the letter, saying, Set ye

Uriah in the forefront of the hottest battle, and retire ye from him, that he may be smitten, and die. *(How could the man who wrote the 23rd Psalm do this? Sin never betters itself. The slide is always downward. Irrespective of how holy man has been or how educated he might be, sin is a force and power that can only be dealt with by the precious Blood of Jesus Christ. Sin is so powerful that even though God could speak worlds into existence, still, due to His Nature, He could not speak sin out of existence. He would have to die on a cruel Cross, offering up Himself as a Perfect Sacrifice in order to pay in full sin's demands.*

The Holy Spirit intends for us here to see not only David's terrible sins, but also our sins as well!)

16 And it came to pass, when Joab observed the city, that he assigned Uriah unto a place where he knew that valiant men were *(the most dangerous and hottest part of the battle).*

17 And the men of the city went out, and fought with Joab: and there fell some of the people of the servants of David; and Uriah the Hittite died also.

18 Then Joab sent and told David all the things concerning the war;

19 And charged the messenger, saying, When you have made an end of telling the matters of the war unto the king,

20 And if so be that the king's wrath arise, and he say unto you, Wherefore approached ye so near unto the city when you did fight? did you not know that they would shoot from the wall?

21 Who smote Abimelech the son of Jerubbesheth *(Gideon)*? did not a woman cast a piece of a millstone upon him from the wall, that he died in Thebez? why went you near the wall? then you say, Your servant Uriah the Hittite is dead also *(the wording of the Text tells us that Joab now knew at least something about the situation, if not its entirety).*

22 So the messenger went, and came and showed David all that Joab had sent him for.

23 And the messenger said unto David, Surely the men prevailed against us, and came out unto us into the field, and we were upon them even unto the entering of the gate *(chased after them).*

24 And the shooters shot from off the wall upon your servants; and some of the king's servants be dead, and your servant Uriah the Hittite is dead also.

25 Then David said unto the messenger, Thus shall you say unto Joab, Let not this thing displease you, for the sword devours one as well as another: make your battle more strong against the city, and overthrow it: and encourage thou him *(give Joab a message of encouragement from me).*

DAVID MARRIES BATH-SHEBA

26 And when the wife of Uriah heard that Uriah her husband was dead, she mourned for her husband *(Uriah died serving his king, never knowing that his king had made his wife pregnant, and had, in fact, ordered his own death, but God knew!).*

27 And when the mourning was past, David sent and fetched her to his house, and she became his wife, and bore him a son. But the thing that David had done displeased the LORD *(the record reveals that God will show no more favor to "His anointed" than He will to the most ungodly!).*

CHAPTER 12
(1035 B.C.)
NATHAN THE PROPHET

AND the LORD sent Nathan unto David. *(On Nathan's last visit to David, as recorded in Chapter 7, the Prophet had brought the greatest message that could ever be brought to a mere mortal. He said to David that through his lineage would come the Messiah, the King of kings [II Sam. 7:18-19]. Now God, by the same Prophet, sends the worst message that a man could ever hear. Beautifully and strangely enough, because of the Grace of God, the second message of doom because of David's great sin does not nullify the great Message of honor and Redemption that had been given at the beginning.)* And he came unto him, and said unto him, There were two men in one city; the one rich, and the other poor.

2 The rich man had exceeding many flocks and herds:

3 But the poor man had nothing, save one little ewe lamb, which he had bought and nourished up: and it grew up together with him, and with his children; it did eat of his own meat, and drank of his own cup, and lay in his bosom, and was unto him as a daughter.

4 And there came a traveler unto the rich man, and he spared to take of his own flock and of his own herd, to dress for the wayfaring man who was come unto him; but took the

poor man's lamb, and dressed it for the man who was come to him.

5 And David's anger was greatly kindled against the man; and he said to Nathan, As the LORD lives, the man who has done this thing shall surely die (the correct translation should be, "A man who would do such a thing is a wretch who deserves to die"):

6 And he shall restore the lamb fourfold, because he did this thing, and because he had no pity (the sentence that he passed, of fourfold restitution, is exactly in accordance with the Mosaic Law [Ex. 22:1]).

DAVID IS THE GUILTY ONE

7 And Nathan said to David, You are the man. (Abruptly, and with sudden vehemence, comes the application to David himself. So skillfully had the parable been contrived, that up to this point David had no suspicion that he was the rich man who had acted so meanly by his poorer neighbor Uriah. And now he stood self-condemned! When we pass judgment, we had better be careful, as David, that we aren't passing judgment on ourselves.) Thus saith the LORD God of Israel, I anointed you king over Israel, and I delivered you out of the hand of Saul (consequently, his sin was worse);

8 And I gave you your master's house, and your master's wives into your bosom, and gave you the house of Israel and of Judah; and if that had been too little, I would moreover have given unto you such and such things.

9 Wherefore have you despised the Commandment of the LORD, to do evil in His sight? (All sin is against God. It is an insult to God, a slap in His Face, a denial of His Rulership, a threat against His Kingdom. It is the ruination of all that is good.) you have killed Uriah the Hittite with the sword, and have taken his wife to be your wife, and have slain him with the sword of the children of Ammon (what David had covered, the Lord openly and fully revealed).

THE PENALTIES

10 Now therefore the sword shall never depart from your house; because you have despised Me, and have taken the wife of Uriah the Hittite to be your wife. (And so it was! This sentence was fulfilled in the murder of Amnon [13:28], who had been encouraged in his crime by his father's example. Upon this

followed Absalom's rebellion and death [18:14]. And finally, when, in his last hours, David made Solomon his successor, he knew that he was virtually passing the sentence of death upon Adonijah, the eldest of his surviving sons. But what a fearful choice! For had he not done so, then Bath-sheba and her four sons would doubtless have been killed.)

11 Thus saith the LORD, Behold, I will raise up evil against you out of your own house (this was fulfilled for political purposes by Absalom, under the advice of Bath-sheba's grandfather [16:22]), and I will take your wives before your eyes, and give them unto your neighbour, and he shall lie with your wives in the sight of this sun (Absalom, in his evil, fulfilled this prediction [16:20-22]).

12 For you did it secretly: but I will do this thing before all Israel, and before the sun.

13 And David said unto Nathan, I have sinned against the LORD (David had a true knowledge of God and, therefore, when charged with his sin, his first thought was not the punishment that would surely follow, but the injury done to God). And Nathan said unto David, The LORD also has put away your sin; you shall not die (God's response to true Repentance was the same as it always has been; however, that does not abrogate the penalty for sin, which, incidentally, must be left up to the Lord and not man).

14 Howbeit, because by this deed you have given great occasion to the enemies of the LORD to blaspheme, the child also that is born unto you shall surely die (considering the stigma it would have carried, the Lord did the child a favor).

THE BABY DIES

15 And Nathan departed unto his house. And the LORD struck the child that Uriah's wife bore unto David, and it was very sick. (If it is to be noticed, over and over again, the Holy Spirit refers to Bath-sheba as "Uriah's wife.")

16 David therefore besought God for the child; and David fasted, and went in, and lay all night upon the earth (he hoped that the Lord would have pity and change the direction).

17 And the elders of his house arose, and went to him, to raise him up from the earth: but he would not, neither did he eat bread with them (grieved as he was at the child's sickness, and at the mother's sorrow, yet his grief was mainly for his sin; and he was willing that

all should know how intense was his shame and self-reproach).

18 And it came to pass on the seventh day, that the child died. And the servants of David feared to tell him that the child was dead: for they said, Behold, while the child was yet alive, we spoke unto him, and he would not hearken unto our voice: how will he then vex himself, if we tell him that the child is dead?

19 But when David saw that his servants whispered, David perceived that the child was dead: therefore David said unto his servants, Is the child dead? And they said, He is dead.

20 Then David arose from the earth, and washed, and anointed himself, and changed his apparel, and came into the House of the LORD, and worshipped *(the sweet Psalmist of Israel knew the Ways of the Lord, and the Lord accepted his worship):* then he came to his own house; and when he required, they set bread before him, and he did eat.

21 Then said his servants unto him, What thing is this that you have done? you did fast and weep for the child, while it was alive; but when the child was dead, you did rise and eat bread.

22 And he said, While the child was yet alive, I fasted and wept: for I said, Who can tell whether God will be gracious to me, that the child may live?

23 But now he is dead, wherefore should I fast? can I bring him back again? I shall go to him, but he shall not return to me. *(Every single parent who has trusted Jesus Christ as his Saviour, upon the death of a tiny loved one, can say the same identical thing, because of the price paid at Calvary and the Resurrection.)*

THE BIRTH OF SOLOMON

24 And David comforted Bath-sheba his wife, and went in unto her, and lay with her: and she bore a son, and he called his name Solomon: and the LORD loved him. *(Sadly, I suppose that the majority of the Church world would curse the fruit of this union called "Solomon." But the Scripture says, "The LORD loved him.")*

25 And he sent by the hand of Nathan the Prophet; and he called his name Jedidiah, because of the LORD. *("Jedidiah" means "beloved of the Lord." This child, of all of David's sons, would ultimately rule Israel, and oversee its greatest prosperity, while, at the same time, being a Type of Christ.)*

VICTORY OVER THE AMMONITES

26 And Joab fought against Rabbah of the children of Ammon, and took the royal city.

27 And Joab sent messengers to David, and said, I have fought against Rabbah, and have taken the city of waters.

28 Now therefore gather the rest of the people together, and encamp against the city, and take it: lest I take the city, and it be called after my name.

29 And David gathered all the people together, and went to Rabbah, and fought against it, and took it.

30 And he took their king's crown from off his head, the weight whereof was a talent of gold with the precious stones: and it was set on David's head. And he brought forth the spoil of the city in great abundance. *(As David came to take the surrender of the king of Rabbah, his eyes, no doubt, looked at the place by the wall where Uriah had died. Quite possibly, in David's heart, he said of Uriah, as he had said of the child who died, "I shall go to him, but he shall not return to me.")*

31 And he brought forth the people who were therein, and put them under saws, and under harrows of iron, and under axes of iron, and made them pass through the brickkiln: and thus did he unto all the cities of the children of Ammon. So David and all the people returned unto Jerusalem. *(It is not known exactly as to what the "brickkiln" actually was; however, some think it may have been where the Ammonites sacrificed their children to the god Moloch. Perhaps David put some of the people to death in this way.)*

CHAPTER 13
(1032 B.C.)
AMNON'S SIN AGAINST TAMAR

A ND it came to pass after this, that Absalom the son of David had a fair sister, whose name was Tamar; and Amnon the son of David loved her. *(Tamar was the half-sister of Amnon. She was the daughter of Maacah, a princess of Geshur, one of David's wives. Amnon was David's first-born, the son of Ahinoam of Jezreel. Absalom was also the son of Maacah. At this time, Amnon was about 22 years old; Absalom, 20; Tamar, 15; and Solomon, 2. David was 53 years old. This Chapter begins with "Absalom," as if the Holy Spirit is warning us that the coming rebellion led by Absalom begins here.)*

2 And Amnon was so vexed, that he fell sick for his sister Tamar; for she was a virgin (*his problem was lust, with the end result being incest; it was all inspired by Satan*); and Amnon thought it hard for him to do any thing to her (*the wives of David had each their own dwelling, and the daughters were kept in strict seclusion*).

3 But Amnon had a friend, whose name was Jonadab, the son of Shimeah David's brother: and Jonadab was a very subtil man (*the word "subtil," as here used, is not used in a bad sense, but means "clever, ready in devising means"*).

4 And he (*Jonadab*) said unto him (*Amnon*), Why are you, being the king's son, lean from day to day? will you not tell me? And Amnon said unto him, I love Tamar, my brother Absalom's sister.

5 And Jonadab said unto him, Lay thee down on your bed, and make yourself sick: and when your father comes to see you, say unto him, I pray you, let my sister Tamar come, and give me meat, and dress the meat in my sight, that I may see it, and eat it at her hand (*Jonadab was unscrupulous enough to suggest a plan that would make Tamar her brother's victim*).

6 So Amnon lay down, and made himself sick (*made as if he was sick*): and when the king was come to see him, Amnon said unto the king, I pray you, let Tamar my sister come, and make me a couple of cakes in my sight, that I may eat at her hand.

7 Then David (*suspecting nothing*) sent home to Tamar, saying, Go now to your brother Amnon's house, and dress him meat. (*It would seem that David should have suspected something, but evidently he didn't, not dreaming at all at the evil that was being plotted. Sadly, this evil actually began with David.*)

8 So Tamar went to her brother Amnon's house; and he was laid down. And she took flour, and kneaded it, and made cakes in his sight, and did bake the cakes.

9 And she took a pan, and poured them out before him; but he refused to eat. And Amnon said, Have out all men from me. And they went out every man from him.

10 And Amnon said unto Tamar, Bring the meat into the chamber, that I may eat of your hand. And Tamar took the cakes which she had made, and brought them into the chamber to Amnon her brother.

11 And when she had brought them unto him to eat, he took hold of her, and said unto her, Come lie with me, my sister (*as stated, this definitely was not love, but rather lust*).

12 And she answered him, No, my brother, do not force me; for no such thing ought to be done in Israel: do not thou this folly (*literally, "do not humble me"; all of this bears testimony to the nobleness of the Hebrew women, who regarded their chastity as their crown of honor*).

13 And I, whither shall I cause my shame to go? And as for you, you shall be as one of the fools in Israel (*to call a man "a fool" in Israel was to attribute to him every possible kind of wickedness [Mat. 5:22]*). Now therefore, I pray you, speak unto the king; for he will not withhold me from you. (*Marriages between half-brothers and half-sisters were strictly forbidden according to Levitical Law [Lev. 18:9; Deut. 27:22]. It is certain that Tamar knew this, but possibly she was trying anything to stop the ungodly advances of her half-brother.*)

14 Howbeit he would not hearken unto her voice: but, being stronger than she, forced her, and lay with her (*in other words, he raped her*).

15 Then Amnon hated her exceedingly (*he blamed her for what he had done*); so that the hatred wherewith he hated her was greater than the love wherewith he had loved her (*it doesn't mean that he really loved her, but is given in this manner to express the degree of his present hatred; as stated, he falsely blamed her*). And Amnon said unto her, Arise, be gone.

16 And she said unto him, There is no cause: this evil in sending me away is greater than the other that you did unto me. But he would not hearken unto her.

17 Then he called his servant who ministered unto him, and said, Put now this woman out from me, and bolt the door after her. (*How ever much we may disapprove of Absalom's conduct in avenging his sister, Amnon richly deserved the punishment which he ultimately got.*)

18 And she had a garment of divers colours upon her: for with such robes were the king's daughters who were virgins apparelled. Then his servant brought her out, and bolted the door after her.

19 And Tamar put ashes on her head, and rent her garment of divers colours that was on her, and laid her hand on her head, and went on crying (*this particular garment denoted her as the king's daughter, and her virginity*).

20 And Absalom her brother said unto her, Has Amnon your brother been with you? but hold now your peace, my sister: he is your

brother; regard not this thing. So Tamar remained desolate in her brother Absalom's house *(Absalom now plotted revenge, although every evidence is that he did not relate such to Tamar)*.

21 But when king David heard of all these things, he was very wroth *(angry)*.

ABSALOM'S PLOT

22 And Absalom spoke unto his brother Amnon neither good nor bad *(Absalom's outward demeanor was one of utter indifference, concealing a cruel determination)*: for Absalom hated Amnon, because he had forced his sister Tamar *(had raped her)*.

23 And it came to pass after two full years *(Absalom did bide his time)*, that Absalom had sheepshearers in Baal-hazor, which is beside Ephraim: and Absalom invited all the king's sons.

24 And Absalom came to the king, and said, Behold now, your servant has sheepshearers, let the king, I beseech you, and his servants go with your servant *(Absalom was inviting David, plus all his half-brothers, to the feast)*.

25 And the king said to Absalom, No, my son, let us not all now go, lest we be chargeable unto you. And he pressed him: howbeit he would not go, but blessed him *(David would not himself go)*.

26 Then said Absalom, If not, I pray you, let my brother Amnon go with us. And the king said unto him, Why should he go with you? *(It seems that David should have suspected something here, but inasmuch as approximately two years had passed, with Absalom saying nothing about the rape of his sister Tamar, perhaps David thought that the incident had been forgotten.)*

27 But Absalom pressed him, that he let Amnon and all the king's sons go with him *(Absalom got what he wanted; he really didn't want David to be there in the first place)*.

THE MURDER OF AMNON

28 Now Absalom had commanded his servants, saying, Mark ye now when Amnon's heart is merry with wine, and when I say unto you, Smite Amnon; then kill him, fear not: have not I commanded you? be courageous, and be valiant *(though Tamar's wrong was the mainspring of Absalom's conduct, yet, Absalom being the second in line to the throne, neither he nor his men could forget that Amnon, the first-born, stood between him and the crown)*.

THE CRIME COMMITTED

29 And the servants of Absalom did unto Amnon as Absalom had commanded. Then all the king's sons arose, and every man got him up upon his mule, and fled.

30 And it came to pass, while they were in the way, that tidings came to David, saying, Absalom has killed all the king's sons, and there is not one of them left *(evidently, some of the servants who fled immediately upon Amnon's death thought that Absalom was intending to kill all the king's sons, which was not the case; but this is the message that David then received)*.

31 Then the king arose, and tore his garments, and lay on the earth; and all his servants stood by with their clothes rent *(the bitter payments of sin are now coming due)*.

32 And Jonadab, the son of Shimeah David's brother, answered and said, Let not my lord suppose that they have slain all the young men the king's sons; for Amnon only is dead: for by the appointment of Absalom this has been determined from the day that he forced his sister Tamar *(evidently, at the time, Jonadab did not reveal his complicity in helping Amnon in the first place, in getting his sister into his evil clutches)*.

33 Now therefore let not my lord the king take the thing to his heart, to think that all the king's sons are dead: for Amnon only is dead.

34 But Absalom fled. And the young man who kept the watch lifted up his eyes, and looked, and, behold, there came much people by the way of the hill side behind him *(David's other sons were returning)*.

35 And Jonadab said unto the king, Behold, the king's sons come: as your servant said, so it is.

36 And it came to pass, as soon as he had made an end of speaking, that, behold, the king's sons came, and lifted up their voice and wept: and the king also and all his servants wept very sore *(no doubt, at this time, the terrible thought came to David's mind, which had been told him by the Lord concerning his sin with Bath-sheba, that "the sword should never depart from his house")*.

ABSALOM FLEES

37 But Absalom fled, and went to Talmai, the son of Ammihud, king of Geshur. And David mourned for his son every day *(mourned for Amnon, his first-born)*.

38 So Absalom fled, and went to Geshur, and was there three years.

39 And the soul of king David longed to go forth unto Absalom *(longed to have him return)*: for he was comforted concerning Amnon, seeing he was dead.

CHAPTER 14
(1027 B.C.)
JOAB'S PLOT

NOW Joab the son of Zeruiah perceived that the king's heart was toward Absalom. *(The Hebrew word rendered "toward" should have been rendered "against," for that is its actual meaning. "The king's heart was against Absalom," because of the crime he had committed, even though David loved him dearly.)*

2 And Joab sent to Tekoah and fetched thence a wise woman, and said unto her, I pray you, feign yourself to be a mourner, and put on now mourning apparel, and anoint not yourself with oil, but be as a woman who had a long time mourned for the dead:

3 And come to the king, and speak on this manner unto him. So Joab put the words in her mouth *(told her what to say and do)*.

THE WOMAN OF TEKOAH

4 And when the woman of Tekoah spoke to the king, she fell on her face to the ground, and did obeisance, and said, Help, O king.

5 And the king said unto her, What ails you? And she answered, I am indeed a widow woman, and my husband is dead.

6 And your handmaid had two sons, and they two did strive together in the field, and there was none to part them, but the one smote the other, and killed him.

7 And, behold, the whole family is risen against your handmaid, and they said, Deliver him who smote his brother, that we may kill him, for the life of his brother whom he slew; and we will destroy the heir also: and so they shall quench my coal which is left, and shall not leave to my husband neither name nor remainder upon the earth *(there is a great force and beauty also in the description of her son as the last live coal left to keep the family hearth burning, hence her using such terminology)*.

8 And the king said unto the woman, Go to your house, and I will give charge concerning you.

9 And the woman of Tekoah said unto the king, My lord, O king, the iniquity be on me, and on my father's house: and the king and his throne be guiltless.

10 And the king said, Whosoever saith ought unto you, bring him to me, and he shall not touch you any more.

11 Then said she, I pray you, let the king remember the LORD your God, that you would not suffer the revengers of blood to destroy any more, lest they destroy my son. And he said, As the LORD lives, there shall not one hair of your son fall to the earth. *(Williams says concerning this, "The argument of the woman was very clever. It dealt with the secret wish of the king to pardon his son, and with the hindrance thereto which public opinion and the Divine Law presented. She skillfully persuaded him that exceptional provocation justified a setting aside of the Law, and a defiance of the people; and she got the king to pledge himself to this in the interests of her supposed son.")*

12 Then the woman said, Let your handmaid, I pray you, speak one word unto my lord the king. And he said, Say on.

13 And the woman said, Wherefore then have you thought such a thing against the people of God? for the king does speak this thing as one which is faulty, in that the king does not fetch home again his banished *(of course, she is speaking of Absalom, saying all the things that Joab has told her to say)*.

14 For we must needs die, and are as water spilt on the ground, which cannot be gathered up again; neither does God respect any person: yet does He devise means, that His banished be not expelled from Him. *(The woman's argument is as follows: she says, "Death is not a penalty exacted as a punishment, but, on the contrary, God is merciful, and, when a man has sinned, instead of putting him to death, the Lord is ready to forgive and welcome back one rejected because of his wickedness."*

The application is plain. The king cannot restore Amnon to life, and neither must he kill the guilty Absalom, but must recall his banished son.

The argument is full of poetry, and touching to the feelings, but it is not spiritually or Scripturally sound. For God requires Repentance and change of heart; and there was no sign of contrition on Absalom's part. At any rate, David fell for the ploy.)

15 Now therefore that I am come to speak of this thing unto my lord the king, it is because the people have made me afraid: and

your handmaid said, I will now speak unto the king; it may be that the king will perform the request of his handmaid.

16 For the king will hear, to deliver his handmaid out of the hand of the man who would destroy me and my son together out of the inheritance of God.

17 Then your handmaid said, The word of my lord the king shall now be comfortable: for as an Angel of God, so is my lord the king to discern good and bad: therefore the LORD your God will be with you *(in other words, her story about her son was fiction; it had all been a ploy regarding Absalom).*

JOAB

18 Then the king answered and said unto the woman, Hide not from me, I pray you, the thing that I shall ask you. And the woman said, Let my lord the king now speak.

19 And the king said, Is not the hand of Joab with you in all this? And the woman answered and said, As your soul lives, my lord the king, none can turn to the right hand or to the left from ought that my lord the king has spoken: for your servant Joab, he bade me, and he put all these words in the mouth of your handmaid:

20 To fetch about this form of speech has your servant Joab done this thing: and my lord is wise, according to the wisdom of an Angel of God, to know all things that are in the Earth.

ABSALOM IS BROUGHT BACK

21 And the king said unto Joab, Behold now, I have done this thing: go therefore, bring the young man Absalom again. *(When dependence upon God and subjection to His Word cease to govern the life, then is it easy for the wisdom of this world to entangle the heart. Therefore, it was that the wise woman of Tekoah easily entrapped David to indulge his affection as a father rather than performing his duty as a ruler. The Law of God commanded the death of Absalom. The king should have obeyed the Law. Had he done so, many lives would have been saved, and much sin and suffering escaped. Had he obeyed the Word of the Lord and put Amnon to death, still greater evil would have been thereby prevented. All this teaches the lesson, which man is so slow to learn, that a Christian embitters his days by acting independently of God. Amid*

all the movements of this Chapter was the Will of God sought? No, the Lord does not once appear — Williams.)*

22 And Joab fell to the ground on his face, and bowed himself, and thanked the king: and Joab said, To day your servant knows that I have found grace in your sight, my lord, O king, in that the king has fulfilled the request of his servant. *(Joab's design in this matter was to make Absalom indebted to him, and thus to get both the present and future king, for Absalom was in line for the throne, into his power, or so he thought!)*

23 So Joab arose and went to Geshur, and brought Absalom to Jerusalem.

24 And the king said, Let him turn to his own house, and let him not see my face. So Absalom returned to his own house, and saw not the king's face *(allowing him to return home, still, David would have no fellowship with him).*

25 But in all Israel there was none to be so much praised as Absalom for his beauty: from the sole of his foot even to the crown of his head there was no blemish in him *(once again, a work of the flesh, which looked beautiful outwardly, but inwardly was a ravening wolf; but yet, as usual, the people would fall for this outward expression, because the flesh appeals to the flesh).*

26 And when he polled his head, (for it was at every year's end that he polled it: because the hair was heavy on him, therefore he polled it [cut it]:) he weighed the hair of his head at two hundred shekels after the king's weight *(about six pounds when wet).*

27 And unto Absalom there were born three sons, and one daughter, whose name was Tamar: she was a woman of a fair countenance. *(She was named after her aunt, the girl who had been raped, and, like her, possessed great beauty. The Septuagint states that she became the wife of Rehoboam, the king who succeeded Solomon, and the mother of Abijah, who succeeded Rehoboam.)*

ABSALOM DEMANDS TO SEE DAVID

28 So Absalom dwelt two full years in Jerusalem, and saw not the king's face *(in other words, David would not see him).*

29 Therefore Absalom sent for Joab, to have sent him to the king; but he would not come to him: and when he sent again the second time, he would not come.

30 Therefore he said unto his servants, See,

Joab's field is near mine, and he has barley there; go and set it on fire. And Absalom's servants set the field on fire (*which Absalom felt would guarantee Joab coming to see him, which it did!*).

31 Then Joab arose, and came to Absalom unto his house, and said unto him, Wherefore have your servants set my field on fire?

32 And Absalom answered Joab, Behold, I sent unto you, saying, Come hither that I may send you to the king, to say, Wherefore am I come from Geshur? it had been good for me to have been there still: now therefore let me see the king's face; and if there be any iniquity in me, let him kill me.

33 So Joab came to the king, and told him: and when he had called for Absalom, he came to the king, and bowed himself on his face to the ground before the king: and the king kissed Absalom (*David's kiss was, as in the case of the prodigal son, the sign of reconciliation, and of the restoration of Absalom to his place as a son, with all its privileges*).

CHAPTER 15
(1024 B.C.)
ABSALOM REVOLTS AGAINST DAVID

AND it came to pass after this, that Absalom prepared him chariots and horses, and fifty men to run before him. (*This was the accompaniment of royalty. In other words, Absalom was preparing the way for his revolt.*)

2 And Absalom rose up early, and stood beside the way of the gate (*most business dealings and judicial renderings were normally done at the gate of the city, with buildings constructed there for just such a purpose*): and it was so, that when any man who had a controversy came to the king for judgment, then Absalom called unto him, and said, Of what city are you? And he said, Your servant is of one of the Tribes of Israel.

3 And Absalom said unto him, See, your matters are good and right, but there is no man deputed of the king to hear you (*in other words, the king may not decide in your favor, but I definitely would, if I had the power*).

4 Absalom said moreover, Oh that I were made judge in the land, that every man which has any suit or cause might come unto me, and I would do him justice!

5 And it was so, that when any man came near to him to do him obeisance, he put forth his hand, and took him, and kissed him.

6 And on this manner did Absalom to all Israel who came to the king for judgment: so Absalom stole the hearts of the men of Israel. (*Absalom easily deceived people by a profession of devotion to them, and as easily deceived his father by a profession of devotion to God. Because man has fallen from God's moral image, therefore, he can readily deceive and be deceived [II Tim. 3:13]. He deceived the people of Israel by flattery, which was altogether insincere! All too often, the Absalom spirit still prevails in the modern Church. A deceitful heart projects such, and a deceitful mind accepts such.*)

7 And it came to pass after forty years (*some have said that this is a copyist mistake, and it should have been rendered "four years"; however, others say that this was speaking of David, and not Absalom; David was about 16 years old when he was anointed king by Samuel [I Sam., Chpt. 16]; considering that he was now about 56 years old, this means that it was forty years since his anointing; either one could be true*), that Absalom said unto the king, I pray you, let me go and pay my vow, which I have vowed unto the LORD, in Hebron (*the Lord was the furthest thing from the mind of Absalom*).

8 For your servant vowed a vow while I abode at Geshur in Syria, saying, If the LORD shall bring me again indeed to Jerusalem, then I will serve the LORD.

9 And the king said unto him, Go in peace. So he arose, and went to Hebron.

10 But Absalom sent spies throughout all the Tribes of Israel, saying, As soon as you hear the sound of the trumpet, then you shall say, Absalom reigns in Hebron. (*Absalom would now attempt to take the throne away from his father. But God had not called Absalom to the throne, but rather David.*)

11 And with Absalom went two hundred men out of Jerusalem, who were called; and they went in their simplicity, and they knew not any thing (*were not aware of Absalom's plot to take the throne*):

12 And Absalom sent for Ahithophel the Gilonite, David's counsellor, from his city, even from Giloh, while he offered sacrifices. And the conspiracy was strong; for the people increased continually with Absalom. (*Ahithophel was Bath-sheba's grandfather. He was one of the wisest men in Israel, but evidently showed little wisdom here. He should have known that if Absalom had truly been successful in becoming king, that Bath-sheba and all her sons would be*

killed; however, most probably, Absalom had guaranteed their safety.

Israel was, at the present time, the most prosperous nation on the face of the Earth, and that prosperity was due to David; however, Israel evidently didn't see that, and would now seek to throw David over. How so much like the modern Church! It seeks to destroy that which is its Salvation, and accepts that which is its ruin. Why?

The reason is the same now as then. "Flesh responds to flesh," which means that most of the Church is "walking after the flesh," which refers to walking after their own wisdom, and not that of God [Rom. 8:1, 8].)

DAVID FLEES FROM JERUSALEM

13 And there came a messenger to David, saying, The hearts of the men of Israel are after Absalom.

14 And David said unto all his servants who were with him at Jerusalem, Arise, and let us flee; for we shall not else escape from Absalom: make speed to depart, lest he overtake us suddenly, and bring evil upon us, and smite the city with the edge of the sword.

15 And the king's servants said unto the king, Behold, your servants are ready to do whatsoever my lord the king shall appoint.

16 And the king went forth, and all his household after him. And the king left ten women, which were concubines, to keep the house. (At this time, David wrote several Psalms [Ps. 3-4, 40-41, 63]. All of this, the writing of the Psalms as given to him by the Holy Spirit, despite his past problems, show just how close to God that David now was.)

17 And the king went forth, and all the people after him, and tarried in a place that was far off.

18 And all his servants passed on beside him; and all the Cherethites, and all the Pelethites, and all the Gittites, six hundred men which came after him from Gath, passed on before the king (these were powerful warriors).

DAVID'S ADVICE TO ITTAI

19 Then said the king to Ittai the Gittite, Why do you go also with us? return to your place, and abide with the king: for you are a stranger, and also an exile (this man was evidently a Gentile, but now a proselyte to the Jewish Faith).

20 Whereas you came but yesterday, should I this day make you go up and down with us? seeing I go where I may, return thou, and take back your brethren: mercy and truth be with you.

21 And Ittai answered the king, and said, As the LORD lives, and as my lord the king lives, surely in what place my lord the king shall be, whether in death or life, even there also will your servant be (a consecration very similar to that of Ruth the Moabitess).

22 And David said to Ittai, Go and pass over. And Ittai the Gittite passed over, and all his men, and all the little ones who were with him. (The presence of all his family with him shows that this man had broken entirely with the Philistines, and left his country for good, vowing to go with David, wherever David went. In other words, David's fortunes would be his fortunes, whatever that may have meant. This converted Gentile showed more spiritual sense than most of Israel.)

23 And all the country wept with a loud voice, and all the people passed over: the king also himself passed over the brook Kidron, and all the people passed over, toward the way of the wilderness.

DAVID'S ADVICE TO ZADOK

24 And lo Zadok also, and all the Levites were with him, bearing the Ark of the Covenant of God: and they set down the Ark of God; and Abiathar went up (both men, Zadok and Abiathar, served as High Priests at that time), until all the people had done passing out of the city.

25 And the king said unto Zadok, Carry back the Ark of God into the city: if I shall find favour in the eyes of the LORD, He will bring me again, and show me both it, and His habitation:

26 But if He thus say, I have no delight in you; behold, here am I, let Him do to me as seems good unto Him (David places himself entirely now within the Hands of the Lord).

27 The king said also unto Zadok the Priest, Are you not a seer? return into the city in peace, and your two sons with you, Ahimaaz your son, and Jonathan the son of Abiathar (and take the Ark of the Covenant with you).

28 See, I will tarry in the plain of the wilderness, until there come word from you to certify me.

29 Zadok therefore and Abiathar carried the

Ark of God again to Jerusalem: and they tarried there *(they obeyed David)*.

DAVID WEEPS AND PRAYS

30 And David went up by the ascent of Mount Olivet, and wept as he went up, and had his head covered, and he went barefoot: and all the people who were with him covered every man his head, and they went up, weeping as they went up *(the Grace of God is the basis of all blessing; David was conscious that he merited only wrath; and this he publicly confessed with bared foot, covered head, and tear-dimmed eye)*.

31 And one told David, saying, Ahithophel is among the conspirators with Absalom. And David said, O LORD, I pray You, turn the counsel of Ahithophel into foolishness *(David prayed, but his faith seemed to be weak)*.

DAVID'S ADVICE TO HUSHAI

32 And it came to pass, that when David was come to the top of the Mount, where he worshipped God, behold, Hushai the Archite came to meet him with his coat rent, and earth upon his head *(signifying his grief at what was happening)*:

33 Unto whom David said, If you pass on with me, then you shall be a burden unto me *(most likely because Hushai was old and infirm)*:

34 But if you return to the city, and say unto Absalom, I will be your servant, O king; as I have been your father's servant hitherto, so will I now also be your servant: then may you for me defeat the counsel of Ahithophel. *(David had prayed for the help of the Lord, but what he now proposes was not really such help. David was meeting treachery by treachery, which the Lord could not condone. Jehovah can never be a party to sin or wrongdoing of any nature! Hushai was evidently also one of the wise men of Israel.)*

35 And have you not there with you Zadok and Abiathar the Priests? therefore it shall be, that what thing soever you shall hear out of the king's house, you shall tell it to Zadok and Abiathar the Priests.

36 Behold, they have there with them their two sons, Ahimaaz Zadok's son, and Jonathan Abiathar's son; and by them you shall send unto me every thing that you can hear.

37 So Hushai David's friend came into the city, and Absalom came into Jerusalem *(came to take the Throne)*.

CHAPTER 16
(1023 B.C.)

ZIBA LIES ABOUT MEPHIBOSHETH

AND when David was a little past the top of the hill, behold, Ziba the servant of Mephibosheth met him, with a couple of asses saddled, and upon them two hundred loaves of bread, and an hundred bunches of raisins, and an hundred of summer fruits, and a bottle of wine.

2 And the king said unto Ziba, What do you mean by these? And Ziba said, The asses be for the king's household to ride on; and the bread and summer fruit for the young men to eat; and the wine, that such as be faint in the wilderness may drink.

3 And the king said, And where is your master's son *(speaking of Mephibosheth)*? And Ziba said unto the king, Behold, he abides at Jerusalem: for he said, To day shall the house of Israel restore me the kingdom of my father *(Ziba lied about Mephibosheth)*.

4 Then said the king to Ziba, Behold, you are all that pertains unto Mephibosheth. And Ziba said, I humbly beseech you that I may find grace in your sight, my lord, O king. *(This man Ziba lies and schemes to effect a gain of property. At this time of all times, every man in Israel should have been crying to God for help; however, some would take advantage of the crisis as opportunity for personal gain. I'm afraid that "Ziba" is too much akin to so many in the modern Church.)*

SHIMEI CURSES DAVID

5 And when king David came to Bahurim *(the Holy Spirit uses the word "king," as it refers to David, to portray the fact that, even though many of the people were claiming that Absalom was now king, the Holy Spirit said otherwise)*, behold, thence came out a man of the family of the house of Saul, whose name was Shimei, the son of Gera: he came forth, and cursed still as he came *(cursed David! The words given in this Verse do not mean that this man was a near relative of Saul, but that he was a member of the Tribe of Benjamin)*.

6 And he cast stones at David, and at all the servants of king David: and all the people and all the mighty men were on his right hand and on his left.

7 And thus said Shimei when he cursed, Come out, come out, you bloody man, and

you man of Belial *(he refers to David as one worthless)*:

8 The LORD has returned upon you all the blood of the house of Saul *(the man was lying! David had not shed any of the blood of this particular house)*, in whose stead you have reigned; and the LORD has delivered the kingdom into the hand of Absalom your son: and, behold, you are taken in your mischief, because you are a bloody man *(in effect, Shimei was accusing David of being the murderer of Saul; that was wholly untrue! However, David could not resent it, because he was the murderer of Uriah)*.

9 Then said Abishai the son of Zeruiah unto the king, Why should this dead dog curse my lord the king? let me go over, I pray you, and take off his head.

10 And the king said, What have I to do with you, you sons of Zeruiah? so let him curse, because the LORD has said unto him, Curse David. Who shall then say, Wherefore have you done so? *(David evidently suffered this as a part of the chastening of God for his sin with Bath-sheba. His answer to Abishai expressed a deep and humble resignation to the course of providence. Insults such as this are very difficult to endure, but not for David, as he fully recognized himself as under the Divine Hand of chastening for his sin. For the balance of his life, he was mindful of this cursing by Shimei, but he was determined never to avenge it in his lifetime. He left the matter to the wisdom of Solomon, with it being one of the last things he mentioned in his dying hour [I Ki. 2:8-11].)*

11 And David said to Abishai, and to all his servants, Behold, my son, which came forth of my bowels, seeks my life: how much more now may this Benjamite do it? let him alone, and let him curse; for the LORD has bidden him *(evidently, the Lord spoke this to David's heart)*.

12 It may be that the LORD will look on my affliction, and that the LORD will require me good for his cursing this day *(so I should accept it without recourse)*.

13 And as David and his men went by the way, Shimei went along on the hill's side over against him, and cursed as he went, and threw stones at him, and cast dust *(in front of all the people, as would be overly obvious, this was a great insult to the king of Israel and, in fact, one worthy of death)*.

14 And the king, and all the people who were with him, came weary, and refreshed themselves there.

ABSALOM ENTERS JERUSALEM

15 And Absalom, and all the people the men of Israel, came to Jerusalem, and Ahithophel with him *(advising Absalom as to what he should do)*.

16 And it came to pass, when Hushai the Archite, David's friend, was come unto Absalom, that Hushai said unto Absalom, God save the king, God save the king.

17 And Absalom said to Hushai, Is this your kindness to your friend? why went you not with your friend? *(Absalom knew that Hushai was a very close friend of his father, David.)*

18 And Hushai said unto Absalom, No; but whom the LORD, and this people, and all the men of Israel, choose, his will I be, and with him will I abide *(while there had been general lamentation at David's departure [15:23], yet the citizens had admitted Absalom without a struggle, and submitted to him)*.

19 And again, whom should I serve? should I not serve in the presence of his son? as I have served in your father's presence, so will I be in your presence. *(Hushai was not telling the truth! While the cause was right, the method was wrong. God cannot sanction lying. But yet, the Grace of God, as it has with all of us at one time or the other, overrode the wrong direction, and brought it all out to a successful conclusion; however, He could have done so in a much better way, had David looked to the Lord exclusively, instead of praying, and then trying to answer his own prayers [15:31-37].)*

AHITHOPHEL

20 Then said Absalom to Ahithophel, Give counsel among you what we shall do.

21 And Ahithophel said unto Absalom, Go in unto your father's concubines, which he has left to keep the house; and all Israel shall hear that you are abhorred of your father: then shall the hands of all who are with you be strong. *(This fulfilled what the Lord said would happen [12:11]. Ahithophel's counsel was abominable, even though the deed would not be regarded by any of the Israelites as incestuous. A king inherited his predecessor's harem, and Absalom's act was a coarse and rude assertion that David's rights were at an end, and that crown and lands and property, even unto his wives, now all belonged to the usurper. So, Ahithophel, for his own selfish purposes, led Absalom on to a crime which rendered a reconciliation with David impossible,*

and which pledged all the conspirators to carry out the matter to the bitter end.)

22 So they spread Absalom a tent upon the top of the house; and Absalom went in unto his father's concubines in the sight of all Israel (it was when walking on this very roof that David had given way to guilty passion, and now it is the scene of his dishonor).

23 And the counsel of Ahithophel, which he counselled in those days, was as if a man had enquired at the oracle of God: so was all the counsel of Ahithophel both with David and with Absalom. (As stated, Ahithophel was Bathsheba's grandfather. Why in the world did he do what he was doing? Why did he have such a hatred for David, who, in fact, had given him everything that he presently had? Considering that this man was perhaps the wisest man in Israel, he should have known better.

To every great gift there is a drawback. Ahithophel obviously trusted his own wisdom instead of looking to the Lord for guidance. As wise as he was, he simply wasn't wise enough, and neither is any other man.)

CHAPTER 17
(1023 B.C.)
AHITHOPHEL AND HUSHAI

MOREOVER Ahithophel said unto Absalom, Let me now choose out twelve thousand men, and I will arise and pursue after David this night (this Chapter symbolizes the rejection of the Son of David by Judas; it is exactly as the Israel of Jesus' day; most of the people loved David, but much of its leadership seemingly didn't; most of the people of Israel loved Jesus, but its leadership, at least for the most part, didn't; Ahithophel, like Judas, betrayed David, and then hung himself; so we are seeing here a forepicture of what would happen approximately a thousand years later):

2 And I will come upon him while he is weary and weak handed, and will make him afraid: and all the people who are with him shall flee; and I will smite the king only (the proposal to single out David and murder him "pleased Absalom well, and all the Elders of Israel" [Vs. 4]; and yet Absalom was David's son; as well, all the Elders of Israel had received nothing from him but good! How true is it that the heart is desperately wicked [Jer. 17:9]):

3 And I will bring back all the people unto you: the man whom you seek is as if all returned: so all the people shall be in peace

(Ahithophel tells Absalom that his plan will guarantee the Throne).

4 And the saying pleased Absalom well, and all the Elders of Israel. (As we have stated, the prosperity of Israel, which was then the greatest in the world, was all due to the blessings of the Lord upon David. And yet the Elders of Israel did not seem to know this. How so like most modern religious leaders!)

5 Then said Absalom, Call now Hushai the Archite also, and let us hear likewise what he says (the Lord, no doubt, engineered this).

6 And when Hushai was come to Absalom, Absalom spoke unto him, saying, Ahithophel has spoken after this manner: shall we do after his saying? if not; speak thou.

7 And Hushai said unto Absalom, The counsel that Ahithophel has given is not good at this time.

8 For, said Hushai, you know your father and his men, that they be mighty men, and they be chafed in their minds, as a bear robbed of her whelps in the field: and your father is a man of war, and will not lodge with the people.

9 Behold, he is hid now in some pit, or in some other place: and it will come to pass, when some of them be overthrown at the first, that whosoever hears it will say, There is a slaughter among the people who follow Absalom.

10 And he also who is valiant, whose heart is as the heart of a lion, shall utterly melt: for all Israel knows that your father is a mighty man, and they which be with him are valiant men.

11 Therefore I counsel that all Israel be generally gathered unto you, from Dan even to Beer-sheba, as the sand that is by the sea for multitude, and that you go to battle in your own person.

12 So shall we come upon him in some place where he shall be found, and we will light upon him as the dew falls on the ground: and of him and of all the men who are with him there shall not be left so much as one.

13 Moreover, if he be gotten into a city, then shall all Israel bring ropes to that city, and we will draw it into the river, until there be not one small stone found there.

14 And Absalom and all the men of Israel said, The counsel of Hushai the Archite is better than the counsel of Ahithophel. For the LORD had appointed to defeat the good counsel of Ahithophel, to the intent that the LORD might bring evil upon Absalom. (The Lord

used Hushai to appeal to the pride of Absalom. This upstart could see himself marching at the head of thousands of troops, with all of Israel at his feet. Truly, Ahithophel's counsel had been perfect. David did not yet have time to marshal his forces and, at this stage, was not ready to fight. Ahithophel knew this, but his advice was not taken, which was ordered by the Lord.)

HUSHAI'S COUNSEL TO DAVID

15 Then said Hushai unto Zadok and to Abiathar the Priests *(High Priests)*, Thus and thus did Ahithophel counsel Absalom and the Elders of Israel; and thus and thus have I counselled.

16 Now therefore send quickly, and tell David, saying, Lodge not this night in the plains of the wilderness, but speedily pass over *(pass over the Jordan River)*; lest the king be swallowed up, and all the people who are with him *(Absalom may change his mind, and adopt Ahithophel's advice after all; so David must hurry!)*.

17 Now Jonathan and Ahimaaz stayed by Enrogel; for they might not be seen to come into the city *(Jonathan was the son of Abiathar, while Ahimaaz was the son of Zadok, all who were confederate with David, even though Absalom was not aware of such; the two young men were sent by Hushai to give David the message as to what he ought to do)*: and a wench went and told them; and they went and told king David *(the word "wench" should have been translated "maidservant"; in this Verse, we see this "handmaid" named along with the mighty king of Israel, "king David," and all by the Holy Spirit; this is an encouraging instance of how useful the most insignificant person can be to the Lord of Glory in the interests of His Kingdom)*.

18 Nevertheless a lad saw them, and told Absalom: but they went both of them away quickly, and came to a man's house in Bahurim, which had a well in his court; whither they went down *(the two young men hid in the well for a short period of time)*.

19 And the woman took and spread a covering over the well's mouth, and spread ground corn thereon; and the thing was not known *(the two young men were not discovered)*.

20 And when Absalom's servants came to the woman to the house, they said, Where is Ahimaaz and Jonathan? And the woman said unto them, They be gone over the brook of water. And when they had sought and could not find them, they returned to Jerusalem *(of course, she had hidden them in the well)*.

21 And it came to pass, after they were departed, that they came up out of the well, and went and told king David, and said unto David, Arise, and pass quickly over the water *(over the Jordan River)*: for thus has Ahithophel counselled against you *(they told David all the plans of Ahithophel, and then how Hushai had gotten Absalom to listen to him instead, which would give David time, which he desperately needed)*.

22 Then David arose, and all the people who were with him, and they passed over Jordan: by the morning light there lacked not one of them who was not gone over Jordan.

AHITHOPHEL'S SUICIDE

23 And when Ahithophel saw that his counsel was not followed, he saddled his ass, and arose, and got him home to his house, to his city, and put his household in order, and hanged himself, and died, and was buried in the sepulchre of his father. *(So died the man who would not forgive David and had fomented a rebellion to dethrone "God's anointed." The Child of God must ever understand that he is obligated to forgive those whom God forgives. To do less is to set oneself on the road to disaster.)*

ABSALOM PURSUES DAVID

24 Then David came to Mahanaim. *(The word means "two camps." It was on the east side of Jordan. It was named by Jacob of old, when he came out of Syria at the behest of the Lord on the way back to the Promised Land. He was met by two camps of Angels, hence the name [Gen. 32:1-2]. One must wonder if David came here intentionally. As well, did he have Jacob in mind at this time of great distress, when he "came to Mahanaim"? This we do know, it was at this time that he wrote the Forty-second and Forty-third Psalms.)* And Absalom passed over Jordan, he and all the men of Israel with him.

25 And Absalom made Amasa captain of the host instead of Joab: which Amasa was a man's son, whose name was Ithra an Israelite, who went in to Abigail the daughter of Nahash, sister to Zeruiah Joab's mother. *(It is ironic that both Joab and Amasa were David's nephews. Joab, at this time, remained loyal; Amasa joined the rebellion.)*

26 So Israel and Absalom pitched in the land of Gilead. *(All who joined the rebellion would*

rue this day. If men could only understand that they must follow "God's anointed," rather than the "Absalom spirit." Admittedly, sometimes it takes great faith to do so, especially when we realize that God rests His Spirit in "earthen vessels." Regrettably, not all men have faith.)

BARZILLAI'S KINDNESS TO DAVID

27 And it came to pass, when David was come to Mahanaim, that Shobi the son of Nahash of Rabbah of the children of Ammon, and Machir the son of Ammiel of Lo-debar and Barzillai the Gileadite of Rogelim,

28 Brought beds, and basons, and earthen vessels, and wheat, and barley, and flour, and parched corn, and beans, and lentiles, and parched pulse,

29 And honey, and butter, and sheep, and cheese of kine *(cattle)*, for David, and for the people who were with him, to eat: for they said, The people is hungry, and weary, and thirsty, in the wilderness. *(Three men brought these gifts, "Shobi," "Machir," and "Barzillai." At a time like this, for anyone to say, "I love you," is a blessing that can only be understood if one has walked where David walked. The Holy Spirit was so gracious as to record the kindness of these men. He will likewise record for eternity the kindness of all those who will stand by "God's anointed.")*

CHAPTER 18
(1023 B.C.)
ABSALOM DEFEATED

AND David numbered the people who were with him, and set captains of thousands, and captains of hundreds over them.

2 And David sent forth a third part of the people under the hand of Joab, and a third part under the hand of Abishai the son of Zeruiah, Joab's brother, and a third part under the hand of Ittai the Gittite *(this man was a Philistine, who had become a proselyte to the God of Israel)*. And the king said unto the people, I will surely go forth with you myself also.

3 But the people answered, You shall not go forth: for if we flee away, they will not care for us; neither if half of us die, will they care for us: but now you are worth ten thousand of us: therefore now it is better that you succour us out of the city *(the chief argument of the people is that David would be of more use if, posted with a body of troops at this city, he could*

help any division that might be in danger).

4 And the king said unto them, What seems you best I will do. And the king stood by the gate side, and all the people came out by hundreds and by thousands.

5 And the king commanded Joab and Abishai and Ittai, saying, Deal gently for my sake with the young man, even with Absalom. And all the people heard when the king gave all the captains charge concerning Absalom.

6 So the people went out into the field against Israel: and the battle was in the wood of Ephraim;

7 Where the people of Israel were slain before the servants of David, and there was there a great slaughter that day of twenty thousand men. *(This is speaking of the army of rebellious Israel. It doesn't say how many men David's army lost, if any.)*

8 For the battle was there scattered over the face of all the country: and the wood devoured more people that day than the sword devoured. *(Because of this rebellion, 20,000 men would lose their lives, bringing untold sorrow and heartache to Israel, and all because they followed the "Absalom spirit." Rebellion against that which belongs to God is rebellion against God!)*

ABSALOM SLAIN BY JOAB

9 And Absalom met the servants of David. And Absalom rode upon a mule, and the mule went under the thick boughs of a great oak, and his head caught hold of the oak, and he was taken up between the Heaven and the Earth; and the mule that was under him went away *(Josephus writes that Absalom was entangled by his long hair in the boughs of the tree; his death must, therefore, have been one of prolonged agony, until terminated by the lances of his former friend Joab and those men with him)*.

10 And a certain man saw it, and told Joab, and said, Behold, I saw Absalom hanged in an oak.

11 And Joab said unto the man who told him, And, behold, you saw him, and why did you not smite him there to the ground? and I would have given you ten shekels of silver, and a girdle.

12 And the man said unto Joab, Though I should receive a thousand shekels of silver in my hand, yet would I not put forth my hand against the king's son: for in our hearing the king charged you and Abishai and Ittai, saying, Beware that none touch the

young man Absalom.

13 Otherwise I should have wrought falsehood against my own life: for there is no matter hid from the king, and you yourself would have set yourself against me.

14 Then said Joab, I may not tarry thus with you. And he took three darts in his hand, and thrust them through the heart of Absalom, while he was yet alive in the midst of the oak.

15 And ten young men who bore Joab's armour compassed about and smote Absalom, and slew him.

16 And Joab blew the trumpet, and the people returned from pursuing after Israel: for Joab held back the people *(stopped the slaughter)*.

17 And they took Absalom, and cast him into a great pit in the wood, and laid a very great heap of stones upon him: and all Israel fled every one to his tent. *(This "heap of stones" marked the aim and the end of ambition. Such must ever be the inglorious end of all who rebel against God's elect King, the Lord Jesus Christ — for He is exactly the One Whom Absalom rebelled against.)*

18 Now Absalom in his lifetime had taken and reared up for himself a pillar, which is in the king's dale: for he said, I have no son to keep my name in remembrance: and he called the pillar after his own name: and it is called unto this day, Absalom's place. *(What was the difference in David's sin and Absalom's sin? Of course, all sin is heinous in the eyes of God, and is actually directed against Him. The difference is the following: David's sin was a sin of passion, with the murder of Uriah an effort to cover-up the sin. Absalom's sin had as its fountain the sin of Satan himself in his rebellion against God. In other words, Absalom entered into Satan's rebellion. It was a far more heinous sin than his father David's; however, most of the Church world does not see it that way, but actually would join Absalom, because outwardly it looks so right.*

David's sin was not joined by anyone else, whereas Absalom's sin was joined by the majority of Israel. In other words, they became associates with his sin, which, in fact, threatened the very foundation of Israel's existence.

David repented immediately when his sin was found out, because he was a man of God. There is no record that Absalom ever really knew God and, therefore, there was no Repentance.)

NEWS OF THE VICTORY

19 Then said Ahimaaz the son of Zadok, Let me now run, and bear the king tidings, how that the LORD has avenged him of his enemies.

20 And Joab said unto him, You shall not bear tidings this day, but you shall bear tidings another day: but this day you shall bear no tidings, because the king's son is dead *(in other words, the king will not receive your message as you think)*.

21 Then said Joab to Cushi, Go tell the king what you have seen. And Cushi bowed himself unto Joab, and ran *(Joab was unwilling to expose Ahimaaz to the king's displeasure, and we gather from Verse 27 that the sending of a person of low rank, which Cushi was, would be understood to signify evil tidings)*.

22 Then said Ahimaaz the son of Zadok yet again to Joab, But howsoever, let me, I pray you, also run after Cushi. And Joab said, Wherefore will you run, my son, seeing that you have no tidings ready? *(Should have been translated, "Seeing that you have no message that will find for you the king's favor and reward.")*

23 But howsoever, said he, let me run. And he said unto him, Run. Then Ahimaaz ran by the way of the plain, and overran Cushi *(Ahimaaz would not be denied, so Joab allowed him to go)*.

24 And David sat between the two gates: and the watchman went up to the roof over the gate unto the wall, and lifted up his eyes, and looked, and behold a man running alone.

25 And the watchman cried, and told the king. And the king said, If he be alone, there is tidings in his mouth. And he came apace, and drew near *(if David's army had been defeated, then there would be many stragglers hurrying back; but, since there was only one man coming, and then a second one a short time later, this bade good tidings)*.

26 And the watchman saw another man running: and the watchman called unto the porter, and said, Behold another man running alone. And the king said, He also brings tidings *(this second one was Cushi)*.

27 And the watchman said, Me think the running of the foremost is like the running of Ahimaaz the son of Zadok. And the king said, He is a good man, and comes with good tidings.

28 And Ahimaaz called, and said unto the king, All is well. And he fell down to the earth upon his face before the king, and said, Blessed be the LORD your God, which has delivered up the men who lifted up their hand against my lord the king.

DAVID INQUIRES ABOUT ABSALOM

29 And the king said, Is the young man Absalom safe? and Ahimaaz answered, When Joab sent the king's servant, and me your servant, I saw a great tumult, but I knew not what it was. *(Ahimaaz did know what had happened to Absalom, but, seeing the king's face, now knew why Joab was reluctant for him to come bearing this particular message. So, he is evasive in his answer.)*

30 And the king said unto him, Turn aside, and stand here. And he turned aside, and stood still.

31 And, behold, Cushi came; and Cushi said, Tidings, my lord the king: for the LORD has avenged you this day of all them who rose against you.

32 And the king said unto Cushi, Is the young man Absalom safe? And Cushi answered, The enemies of my lord the king, and all who rise against you to do you hurt, be as that young man is.

33 And the king was much moved, and went up to the chamber over the gate, and wept: and as he went, thus he said, O my son Absalom, my son, my son Absalom! would God I had died for you, O Absalom, my son, my son! *(David's bitter grief was, no doubt, deepened by the consciousness that his own sin had perhaps contributed in some way toward Absalom's rebellion and death. As well, the pain and the hurt were deepened by the realization that there was no hope in such a death. He knew that Absalom died lost.)*

CHAPTER 19
(1023 B.C.)
JOAB REPROVES DAVID

AND it was told Joab, Behold, the king weeps and mourns for Absalom.

2 And the victory that day was turned into mourning unto all the people: for the people heard say that day how the king was grieved for his son. *(The "mourning" was justified, but not for Absalom. Israel was in a terrible state, considering that the majority of the nation had joined in the rebellion with Absalom, thereby rebelling against David, who was God's anointed. As well, Verse 9 says, "And all the people were at strife throughout all the Tribes of Israel.")*

3 And the people got them by stealth that day into the city, as people being ashamed steal away when they flee in battle *(the soldiers returned from victory, but yet were met with what seemed like defeat)·*

4 But the king covered his face, and the king cried with a loud voice, O my son Absalom, O Absalom, my son, my son! *(Absalom died lost, and this was the reason for David's great grief and, of course, he blamed himself!)*

5 And Joab came into the house to the king, and said, You have shamed this day the faces of all your servants, which this day have saved your life, and the lives of your sons and of your daughters, and the lives of your wives, and the lives of your concubines;

6 In that you love your enemies, and hate your friends. For you have declared this day, that you regard neither princes nor servants: for this day I perceive, that if Absalom had lived, and all we had died this day, then it had pleased you well. *(Amid the incessant movement of this Chapter, it is not once mentioned that David "enquired of the Lord." The result was that he allowed his selfish and excessive affection for his rebellious son to smother the affection which he should have shown for his brave and faithful soldiers.)*

7 Now therefore arise, go forth, and speak comfortably unto your servants: for I swear by the LORD, if you go not forth, there will not tarry one with you this night: and that will be worse unto you than all the evil that befell you from your youth until now.

8 Then the king arose, and sat in the gate. And they told unto all the people, saying, Behold, the king does sit in the gate. And all the people came before the king: for Israel had fled every man to his tent *(by thus acting in accordance with Joab's wise counsel, David probably saved the nation from years of anarchy, and a fresh civil war)·*

DAVID IS ACCEPTED AGAIN AS KING

9 And all the people were at strife throughout all the Tribes of Israel, saying, The king saved us out of the hand of our enemies, and he delivered us out of the hand of the Philistines; and now he is fled out of the land for Absalom. *(Due to David's great sin, the people had lost confidence in the king. If they had faced the situation according to the Word of God, and understood and accepted David's Repentance, the confidence would not have been lost; nevertheless, like so many, everything is consulted but the Word of God. It must ever be stated that the Word of God is the criteria for any and all situations.*

What man says or thinks is of little import, if it does not agree with the Word of God. The state of Israel, as presented here, is a perfect picture of the Church in most times of crisis. Man's opinions and viewpoints are adhered to, with the Word of God little consulted.)

10 And Absalom, whom we anointed over us, is dead in battle. Now therefore why speak ye not a word of bringing the king back? *(With this anointing, there must also have been a formal renunciation of David's rule and, being thus dethroned, he does not attempt to return until the nation summons him back.)*

11 And king David sent to Zadok and to Abiathar the Priests, saying, Speak unto the Elders of Judah, saying, Why are you the last to bring the king back to his house? seeing the speech of all Israel is come to the king, even to his house.

12 You are my brethren *(the Tribe of Judah)*, you are my bones and my flesh: wherefore then are you the last to bring back the king? *(The rebellion had begun at Hebron, which was a large city in Judah, and probably many of the leading chiefs were deeply implicated in Absalom's proceedings. Probably they now regretted it, but hung back through fear of punishment. They wanted to first of all be sure of David's kindly feelings toward them!)*

13 And say ye to Amasa, Are you not of my bone, and of my flesh? God do so to me, and more also, if you be not captain of the host before me continually in the room of Joab. *(This was a most unwise move on the part of David. Not one time in this Chapter does it say that David inquired of the Lord; consequently, he was making decisions which were faulty!)*

14 And he *(David)* bowed the heart of all the men of Judah, even as the heart of one man; so that they sent this word unto the king, Return thou, and all your servants.

DAVID RETURNS TO JERUSALEM

15 So the king returned, and came to Jordan. And Judah came to Gilgal, to go to meet the king, to conduct the king over Jordan.

16 And Shimei the son of Gera, a Benjamite, which was of Bahurim, hasted and came down with the men of Judah to meet king David.

17 And there were a thousand men of Benjamin with him, and Ziba the servant of the house of Saul, and his fifteen sons and his twenty servants with him; and they went over Jordan before the king *(Shimei evidently desired*

to impress David with his greatness, hoping that he now would not kill him).

18 And there went over a ferry boat to carry over the king's household, and to do what he thought good. And Shimei the son of Gera fell down before the king, as he was come over Jordan;

19 And said unto the king, Let not my lord impute iniquity unto me, neither do thou remember that which your servant did perversely the day that my lord the king went out of Jerusalem, that the king should take it to his heart.

20 For your servant does know that I have sinned: therefore, behold, I am come the first this day of all the house of Joseph to go down to meet my lord the king.

21 But Abishai the son of Zeruiah answered and said, Shall not Shimei be put to death for this, because he cursed the LORD's anointed?

22 And David said, What have I to do with you, you sons of Zeruiah, that you should this day be adversaries unto me? shall there any man be put to death this day in Israel? for do not I know that I am this day king over Israel?

23 Therefore the king said unto Shimei, You shall not die. And the king swore unto him. *(David pardoned this man, swearing unto him by Jehovah — an oath which he should not have taken [I Ki. 2:8-9] — when he ought to have judged him. But yet, he probably felt that, due to his own sin against Uriah, he could little execute judgment upon Shimei. Nevertheless, one of the last requests that David made when dying was to ask Solomon to deal with this man as he saw fit when he turned the kingdom over to him [I Ki. 2:8-9, 36-46].*

Even though Verse 20 records him claiming that he had sinned, he in no way truly repented from the heart. Shimei's statement was a matter of expediency. This proved to be so when he rebelled against Solomon, and paid with his life.)

MEPHIBOSHETH'S FAITHFULNESS

24 And Mephibosheth the son of Saul came down to meet the king, and had neither dressed his feet, nor trimmed his beard, nor washed his clothes, from the day the king departed until the day he came again in peace *(not only did Mephibosheth love David, but, as well, he knew that if Absalom had succeeded in his rebellion, he would have been one of the many who would have been killed).*

25 And it came to pass, when he was come

to Jerusalem to meet the king, that the king said unto him, Wherefore went not you with me, Mephibosheth?

26 And he answered, My lord, O king, my servant deceived me: for your servant said, I will saddle me an ass, that I may ride thereon, and go to the king; because your servant is lame.

27 And he has slandered your servant unto my lord the king; but my lord the king is as an Angel of God: do therefore what is good in your eyes. *(Ziba did what Mephibosheth commanded; however, he left Mephibosheth in the lurch, went to David, and lied about his Master [16:1-4].)*

28 For all of my father's house were but dead men before my lord the king: yet did you set your servant among them who did eat at your own table. What right therefore have I yet to cry any more unto the king?

29 And the king said unto him, Why speak thou any more of your matters? I have said, You and Ziba divide the land.

30 And Mephibosheth said unto the king, Yea, let him take all, forasmuch as my lord the king is come again in peace unto his own house. *(David condemned Mephibosheth when he should have done him justice; he rewarded Ziba when he should have punished him. Once again, he never consulted the Lord about this matter!)*

BARZILLAI REWARDED

31 And Barzillai the Gileadite came down from Rogelim, and went over Jordan with the king, to conduct him over Jordan.

32 Now Barzillai was a very aged man, even fourscore years old *(80 years old)*: and he had provided the king of sustenance while he lay at Mahanaim; for he was a very great man.

33 And the king said unto Barzillai, Come thou over with me, and I will feed you with me in Jerusalem.

34 And Barzillai said unto the king, How long have I to live, that I should go up with the king unto Jerusalem?

35 I am this day fourscore years old: and can I discern between good and evil? can your servant taste what I eat or what I drink? can I hear any more the voice of singing men and singing women? wherefore then should your servant be yet a burden unto my lord the king?

36 Your servant will go a little way over Jordan with the king: and why should the king recompense it me with such a reward?

37 Let your servant, I pray you, turn back again, that I may die in my own city, and be buried by the grave of my father and of my mother. But behold your servant Chimham; let him go over with my lord the king; and do to him what shall seem good unto you.

38 And the king answered, Chimham shall go over with me, and I will do to him that which shall seem good unto you: and whatsoever you shall require of me, that will I do for you.

39 And all the people went over Jordan. And when the king was come over, the king kissed Barzillai; and blessed him; and he returned unto his own place. *(In the eveningtide of his life, the Holy Spirit portrays Barzillai standing by the side of God's anointed, irrespective of the conduct of the majority of Israel. This man knew the Word of God. He did not deter from the righteous path. What a glorious way to live, and what a glorious way to go out!)*

40 Then the king went on to Gilgal, and Chimham went on with him: and all the people of Judah conducted the king, and also half the people of Israel *(David remembered Barzillai's kindness to the last and, on his dying bed, especially commended Chimham and his brothers to the care of Solomon).*

ISRAEL'S JEALOUSY OF JUDAH

41 And, behold, all the men of Israel came to the king, and said unto the king, Why have our brethren the men of Judah stolen you away, and have brought the king, and his household, and all David's men with him, over Jordan?

42 And all the men of Judah answered the men of Israel, Because the king is near of kin to us: wherefore then be ye angry for this matter? have we eaten at all of the king's cost? or has he given us any gift?

43 And the men of Israel answered the men of Judah, and said, We have ten parts in the king, and we have also more right in David than you: why then did you despise us, that our advice should not be first had in bringing back our king? And the words of the men of Judah were fiercer than the words of the men of Israel. *(Verses 41-43 record the division between Judah and Benjamin, on the one side, and the ten Tribes on the other. Little by little, it crystallized and became even wider with each new crisis. About 50 years from this time, they were definitely divided into two kingdoms [I Ki., Chpt. 12].)*

CHAPTER 20
(1022 B.C.)
SHEBA REVOLTS AGAINST DAVID

AND there happened to be there a man of Belial *(worthless)*, whose name was Sheba, the son of Bichri, a Benjamite: and he blew a trumpet, and said, We have no part in David, neither have we inheritance in the son of Jesse: every man to his tents, O Israel.

2 So every man of Israel went up from after David, and followed Sheba the son of Bichri: but the men of Judah clave unto their king, from Jordan even to Jerusalem. *(The ten Tribes had come down to the Jordan to bring the king back in triumph, but, on finding that the men of Judah had forestalled them, they had a quarrel. It ended in open revolt, and they transferred their allegiance to the worthless Sheba. So David now has a great problem on his hands!)*

3 And David came to his house at Jerusalem; and the king took the ten women his concubines, whom he had left to keep the house, and put them in ward, and fed them, but went not in unto them *(these whom Absalom had desecrated)*. So they were shut up unto the day of their death, living in widowhood *(it actually meant until the day of David's death)*.

JOAB MURDERS AMASA

4 Then said the king to Amasa, Assemble me the men of Judah within three days, and be thou here present.

5 So Amasa went to assemble the men of Judah: but he tarried longer than the set time which he *(David)* had appointed him. *(These Verses proclaim David's intention of replacing Joab with Amasa as the military leader of Israel; however, Amasa's lack of energy showed incapacity or disloyalty, for the Scripture says, "He tarried longer than the set time.")*

6 And David said to Abishai, Now shall Sheba the son of Bichri do us more harm than did Absalom: take thou your lord's servants, and pursue after him, lest he get him fenced cities, and escape us.

7 And there went out after him Joab's men, and the Cherethites, and the Pelethites, and all the mighty men: and they went out of Jerusalem, to pursue after Sheba the son of Bichri.

8 When they were at the great stone which is in Gibeon, Amasa went before them. And Joab's garment that he had put on was girded unto him, and upon it a girdle with a sword fastened upon his loins in the sheath thereof; and as he went forth it fell out.

9 And Joab said to Amasa, Are you in health, my brother? And Joab took Amasa by the beard with the right hand to kiss him.

10 But Amasa took no heed to the sword that was in Joab's hand: so he smote him therewith in the fifth rib, and shed out his bowels to the ground, and struck him not again; and he died. So Joab and Abishai his brother pursued after Sheba the son of Bichri.

JOAB PURSUES SHEBA

11 And one of Joab's men stood by him, and said, He who favours Joab, and he who is for David, let him go after Joab. *(It must be understood that Joab's occupation of this position is not because of fidelity to the Lord or His anointed, but because of place and position. How many today are in the Church, fulfilling particular duties, not because of love for God, but because of position, money, popularity, or self-will?)*

12 And Amasa wallowed in blood in the midst of the highway. And when the man saw that all the people stood still, he removed Amasa out of the highway into the field, and cast a cloth upon him, when he saw that every one who came by him stood still.

13 When he was removed out of the highway, all the people went on after Joab, to pursue after Sheba the son of Bichri *(those who had been following Amasa now follow Joab, showing the hold that Joab had over the army of Israel)*.

THE DEATH OF SHEBA

14 And he went through all the Tribes of Israel unto Abel, and to Beth-maachah, and all the Berites: and they were gathered together, and went also after him.

15 And they came and besieged him *(besieged Sheba)* in Abel of Beth-maachah, and they cast up a bank against the city, and it stood in the trench: and all the people who were with Joab battered the wall, to throw it down.

16 Then cried a wise woman out of the city, Hear, hear; say, I pray you, unto Joab, Come near hither, that I may speak with you.

17 And when he was come near unto her, the woman said, Are you Joab? And he answered, I am he. Then she said unto him, Hear the words of your handmaid. And he answered, I do hear.

18 Then she spoke, saying, They were wont to speak in old time, saying, They shall surely ask counsel at Abel: and so they ended the matter *(in other words, the judgment rendered in Abel was given up to be very wise)*.

19 I am one of them who is peaceable and faithful in Israel: you seek to destroy a city and a mother in Israel: why will you swallow up the inheritance of the LORD?

20 And Joab answered and said, Far be it, far be it from me, that I should swallow up or destroy.

21 The matter is not so: but a man of Mount Ephraim, Sheba the son of Bichri by name, has lifted up his hand against the king, even against David: deliver him only, and I will depart from the city. And the woman said unto Joab, Behold, his head shall be thrown to you over the wall.

22 Then the woman went unto all the people in her wisdom. And they cut off the head of Sheba the son of Bichri, and cast it out to Joab. And he blew a trumpet, and they retired from the city, every man to his tent. And Joab returned to Jerusalem unto the king *(the revolt of Sheba had been quelled)*.

THE OFFICERS OF DAVID

23 Now Joab was over all the host of Israel: and Benaiah the son of Jehoiada was over the Cherethites and over the Pelethites:

24 And Adoram was over the tribute: and Jehoshaphat the son of Ahilud was recorder:

25 And Sheva was Scribe: and Zadok and Abiathar were the Priests *(both were High Priests)*:

26 And Ira also the Jairite was a chief ruler about David. *(Verses 23-26 record by the Holy Spirit the restoration of David's kingdom, but at great cost. All that had gone on before was the effort of Satan. The ordered structure under David was now recorded, despite the ungodliness of some of its participants, such as Joab, as God's Will. How so much better off Israel would have been had they adhered to that in the beginning.*

This Verse says, "about David." Israel would have inserted "Absalom," or even "Sheba." Man, and even the Church, so seldom desire God's Ways.)

CHAPTER 21
(1021 B.C.)

A THREE-YEAR FAMINE

THEN there was a famine in the days of David three years, year after year; and David enquired of the LORD. And the LORD answered, It is for Saul, and for his bloody house, because he slew the Gibeonites. *(Famines were generally a sign from God of His disapproval concerning Israel's spiritual declension. David finally asked the Lord as to the cause of the famine. The Lord said it was because Saul "slew the Gibeonites." Nearly 500 years before, Joshua had made a Covenant with the Gibeonites, promising to protect them [Josh., Chpt. 9]. Saul had broken that Covenant, and killed some of the Gibeonites. This Chapter will portray to us the fact that God keeps His Promises. Joshua had make a Covenant with these people, and God expected that Covenant to be kept.)*

2 And the king called the Gibeonites, and said unto them; (now the Gibeonites were not of the Children of Israel, but of the remnant of the Amorites; and the Children of Israel had sworn unto them: and Saul sought to kill them in his zeal to the Children of Israel and Judah *[the Scripture is silent as to when this happened]*.)

3 Wherefore David said unto the Gibeonites, What shall I do for you? and wherewith shall I make the atonement, that you may bless the inheritance of the LORD? *(The Lord had told David the reason for the famine, but there is no record that He had told David what to do about it. David should not have asked the Gibeonites; he should have asked the Lord as to how the anger of God could be appeased.)*

4 And the Gibeonites said unto him, We will have no silver nor gold of Saul, nor of his house; neither for us shall you kill any man in Israel. And he said, What you shall say, that will I do for you.

5 And they answered the king, The man who consumed us, and who devised against us that we should be destroyed from remaining in any of the coasts of Israel,

6 Let seven men of his sons be delivered unto us, and we will hang them up unto the LORD in Gibeah of Saul, whom the LORD did choose. And the king said, I will give them.

SEVEN SONS OF SAUL HANGED

7 But the king spared Mephibosheth, the son of Jonathan the son of Saul, because of the LORD's oath that was between them, between David and Jonathan the son of Saul.

8 But the king took the two sons of Rizpah the daughter of Aiah, whom she bore unto Saul, Armoni and Mephibosheth *(not the son of Jonathan, but another Mephibosheth)*; and the

five sons of Michal the daughter of Saul, whom she brought up for Adriel the son of Barzillai the Meholathite:

9 And he delivered them into the hands of the Gibeonites, and they hanged them in the hill before the LORD: and they fell all seven together, and were put to death in the days of harvest, in the first days, in the beginning of barley harvest. (Once again, David did not inquire of the Word of the Lord. For the Law of Moses plainly said, "Neither shall the children be put to death for the father's: every man shall be put to death for his own sin" [Deut. 24:16]. So, David taking these relatives of Saul and executing them for Saul's sin was ungodly and unscriptural. When we deviate from the Word of God, terrible injustice is always done.)

THE BURIAL

10 And Rizpah the daughter of Aiah took sackcloth, and spread it for her upon the rock, from the beginning of harvest until water dropped upon them out of Heaven, and suffered neither the birds of the air to rest on them by day, nor the beasts of the field by night (the two sons of Rizpah were hanged with the other five).

11 And it was told David what Rizpah the daughter of Aiah, the concubine of Saul, had done (she maintained a vigil in the open field on that shadeless rock, exposed to heat by day and cold by night, for about 5 months).

12 And David went and took the bones of Saul and the bones of Jonathan his son from the men of Jabesh-gilead, which had stolen them from the street of Beth-shan, where the Philistines had hanged them, when the Philistines had slain Saul in Gilboa:

13 And he brought up from thence the bones of Saul and the bones of Jonathan his son; and they gathered the bones of them who were hanged.

14 And the bones of Saul and Jonathan his son buried they in the country of Benjamin in Zelah, in the sepulcher of Kish his father: and they performed all that the king commanded. And after that God was intreated for the land (even though this was not done God's Way, still, the Lord ended the famine).

ABISHAI RESCUES DAVID
FROM THE GIANT

15 Moreover the Philistines had yet war again with Israel; and David went down, and his servants with him, and fought against the Philistines: and David waxed faint. (However, it should be quickly added that David "waxed faint" because he was fighting the battles of the Lord. The only ones who never wax faint are those who never fight. Regrettably, the Church is full of them.

Unfortunately, the Church doesn't look too favorably upon those who "wax faint." Regrettably, the Church as a whole does not fight many Philistines either. The reason?

The modern Church is not only "in" the world, but basically it is also "of" the world.)

16 And Ishbi-benob (his name means "a man who dwells on the mountain"), which was of the sons of the giant (some think he was the son of Goliath, whom David had killed over 40 years before), the weight of whose spear weighed three hundred shekels of brass (copper) in weight (nearly 20 pounds), he being girded with a new sword, thought to have slain David. (These were the product of fallen angels and the daughters of men, actually the last uprising [Gen. 6:4].)

17 But Abishai the son of Zeruiah succoured him, and smote the Philistine, and killed him. (Abishai had to have been helped by the Lord in the doing of this. Presently, it seems that Ishbi-benob has joined the Church. So the question must be asked, "Which are you, an Ishbi-benob or an Abishai?" One would try to kill David; the other would "succour" him.) Then the men of David swore unto him, saying, You shall go no more out with us to battle, that you quench not the light of Israel. (How could they call David the light of Israel, especially after the episode with Bath-sheba and Uriah? They called him "the light of Israel" because he was "the light of Israel." It shows that God not only forgives sin, but He forgets sin. The Child of God should do the same.)

18 And it came to pass after this, that there was again a battle with the Philistines at Gob: then Sibbechai the Hushathite slew Saph, which was of the sons of the giant (could have been another son of Goliath).

19 And there was again a battle in Gob with the Philistines, where Elhanan the son of Jaare-oregim, a Beth-lehemite, slew the brother of Goliath the Gittite, the staff of whose spear was like a weaver's beam.

20 And there was yet a battle in Gath, where was a man of great stature, who had on every hand six fingers, and on every foot six toes,

four and twenty in number; and he also was born to the giant.

21 And when he defied Israel, Jonathan the son of Shimeah the brother of David killed him.

22 These four were born to the giant in Gath, and fell by the hand of David, and by the hand of his servants. *(And yet, the great feats of courage evidenced by David's servants were only because of David's anointing. David was a giant-killer, and those who came under him followed suit.)*

CHAPTER 22
(1018 B.C.)
DAVID'S LAST SONG

AND David spoke unto the LORD the words of this song *(this Song, or Psalm, is virtually identical to the Eighteenth Psalm, but with some minor exceptions)* in the day that the LORD had delivered him out of the hand of all his enemies, and out of the hand of Saul *(only the Lord can truly deliver; as well, this probably refers to the close of his life)*.

2 And he said, The LORD is my rock, and my fortress, and my deliverer *(the words used here portray the fact of the power arrayed against us as Believers; we are delivered by Faith in Christ and the Cross, which then gives the Holy Spirit latitude to work in our lives; He can overcome anything, for He is God [Rom. 8:1-2,11])*;

3 The God of my rock; in Him will I trust: He is my shield, and the horn of my salvation, my high tower, and my refuge, my saviour; Thou savest me from violence *("Rock" suggests an immovable might; it is often used for God's Glory as being the Strength and Protection of His People; the "shield," of course, is for defense, while the "horn" is for attack; the "high tower" signifies a place of refuge, which saves the blessed one from the violence of his enemies)*.

4 I will call on the LORD *(actually says, in the Hebrew, "Whenever I call, I am saved")*, Who is worthy to be praised: so shall I be saved from my enemies *(in all times of difficulties, praise brings immediate deliverance)*.

5 When the waves of death compassed me, the floods of ungodly men made me afraid *(Satan, time and time again, attempted to kill David, as he does many Believers)*;

6 The sorrows of Hell compassed me about; the snares of death prevented me *(the attacks originated in Hell)*;

7 In my distress I called upon the LORD, and cried to my God: and He did hear my voice out of His temple, and my cry did enter into His ears *(the Lord is the only One Who can actually help; the implication is, if we truly call on Him, He will always hear; the "temple" should have been translated "Heavenly temple")*.

8 Then the Earth shook and trembled; the foundations of Heaven moved and shook, because He was wroth *(this is intended to magnify to us the spiritual conception of God's justice coming forth to visit the Earth and to do right with equal justice)*.

9 There went up a smoke out of His nostrils, and fire out of His mouth devoured: coals were kindled by it *(this has to do with when the Lord descended on Mount Sinai, with the manifestations resembling this which David says; out of this came the Law, in effect, the Righteousness of God)*.

10 He bowed the Heavens also, and came down; and darkness was under His feet *(all of this portrays the Glory of God)*.

11 And He rode upon a Cherub *(His traveling Throne)*, and did fly: and He was seen upon the wings of the wind *(once again, portrays Mount Sinai, and the various manifestations of His Appearance, with some who actually observed Him [Ex. 24:9-11])*.

12 And He made darkness pavilions round about Him, dark waters, and thick clouds of the skies *(the dark storm-clouds are gathered round the Almighty, to veil His awful Form from sight as He goes forth for judgment)*.

13 Through the brightness before Him were coals of fire kindled *(this brightness is the "Shechinah," to which Paul also refers, where he says that God's dwelling is in "the unapproachable light")*.

14 The LORD thundered from Heaven, and the most High uttered His voice. *(This happened at Sinai, and it also happened for Israel when the Lord thundered against the Philistines [I Sam. 7:10]. It also happened on the Day of Pentecost [Acts 2:2].)*

15 And He sent out arrows, and scattered them; lightning, and discomfited them *(once again, the Lord is speaking of various happenings of this nature, when He helped Israel against her enemies [I Sam. 14:15])*.

16 And the channels of the sea appeared, the foundations of the world were discovered, at the rebuking of the LORD, at the blast of the breath of His nostrils *(the word "discovered" should have been translated "laid bare")*.

17 He sent from above, He took me; He drew

me out of many waters *(the Lord will do the same, and we speak of Deliverance, of anyone and everyone who will call on Him out of a repentant heart)*;

18 He delivered me from my strong enemy, and from them who hated me: for they were too strong for me *(to be sure, Satan will always attack with overwhelming force; within ourselves, we are no match; Believers presently, at least since the Cross, are meant to place their Faith exclusively in Christ and His Cross, which will then give the Holy Spirit the latitude to work within our lives, bringing about the desired victory [Rom., Chpt. 6; 8:1-2, 11])*.

19 They prevented me in the day of my calamity: but the LORD was my stay *(David faced death many times, but the Lord always delivered him)*.

20 He brought me forth also into a large place: He delivered me, because He delighted in me *(the Lord "delights" in us, only according to our Faith in Christ and His Cross; basically it was the same before the Cross, but centered up in the Sacrifices, which were a Type of the Cross)*.

21 The LORD rewarded me according to my righteousness: according to the cleanness of my hands has He recompensed me *(the "cleanness" of any hands can only be claimed by Faith in Christ and His shed Blood, which cleanses from all sin; otherwise, it is a farce [I Jn. 1:7; Eph. 2:13-18])*.

22 For I have kept the ways of the LORD, and have not wickedly departed from my God *(David is not claiming here sinless perfection, but rather that he did not try to address his sins other than by Faith in the Lord, and that alone; to do otherwise is to sin wickedly)*.

23 For all His judgments were before me: and as for His Statutes, I did not depart from them *(once again, David went to the Word of God for help, whether in time of affliction, or respecting forgiveness for sin; he did not depart from the Word of God)*.

24 I was also upright before Him, and have kept myself from my iniquity *(he took the iniquity to the Lord, and left it there [Ps. 51])*.

25 Therefore the LORD has recompensed me according to my righteousness; according to my cleanness in his eye sight *(this Psalm has two persons as its intended subjects, David and the Messiah, the Lord Jesus Christ; however, the greater meaning is, by far, referring to our Lord; it points prophetically to the Messiah, Who, in His sufferings and the glories which are to follow, will fulfill and satisfy the language of these utterances)*.

26 With the merciful you will show Yourself merciful, and with the upright man You will show yourself upright *(the Holy Spirit placed this Psalm at the conclusion of the historical narrative of David to portray the difference of fallibility, which was David, and infallibility, which was the Holy Spirit upon David; self-righteousness can never understand the Grace of God; it can only see David's terrible sins and faults; it can never see the repentant heart, or the Blood of Jesus Christ that cleanses from all sin)*.

27 With the pure You will show Yourself pure; and with the froward You will show Yourself unsavoury *(it is not by luck or good fortune that prosperity attends the righteous, nor is it by chance that things go awry with the fraudulent, but it is by the Law of God's providence)*.

28 And the afflicted people You will save: but Your eyes are upon the haughty, that You may bring them down *("God resists the proud, but gives Grace to the humble" [James 4:6])*.

29 For You are my Lamp, O LORD: and the LORD will lighten my darkness *("the Lord is a Lamp unto our feet, and a Light unto our path" [Ps. 119:105])*.

30 For by You I have run through a troop: by my God have I leaped over a wall *(the Lord gives strength to those who trust Him)*.

31 As for God, His way is perfect; the Word of the LORD is tried: He is a buckler to all them who trust in Him *(this does not mean only that it is proved by experience and found true, but that it is absolutely good and perfect like refined gold)*.

32 For Who is God, save the LORD? and Who is a Rock, save our God? *(Jehovah Alone is God, and He Alone is a Rock of safety for His people.)*

33 God is my strength and power: and He makes my way perfect *(it signifies that God will direct the upright man in his good way)*.

34 He makes my feet like hinds' feet *(as fast as the feet of deer)*: and sets me upon my high places *(master over everything)*.

35 He teaches my hands to war; so that a bow of steel is broken by my arms *(as the Lord gave Israel great victory over her enemies, likewise, He gives the present Believer victory over the powers of darkness [Col. 2:14-15])*.

36 You have also given me the shield of Your salvation: and Your gentleness has made me great *("gentleness" is a fruit of the Spirit [Gal. 5:22-23])*.

37 You have enlarged my steps under me; so

that my feet did not slip *(we "walk after the Spirit," because we keep our eyes on Christ and the Cross [Rom. 8:1]).*

38 I have pursued my enemies, and destroyed them; and turned not again until I had consumed them *(this can be done only by one trusting in Christ, which refers to what He did for us at the Cross [I Cor. 1:17-18], and doing so exclusively).*

39 And I have consumed them, and wounded them, that they could not arise: yea, they are fallen under my feet *(all victory comes through the Cross of Christ [Col. 2:14-15]).*

40 For You have girded me with strength to battle: them who rose up against me have You subdued under me *(as David overcame his enemies in the physical sense, likewise, we do so in the spiritual sense [Rom. 6:14]).*

41 You have also given me the necks of my enemies, that I might destroy them who hate me *(every Believer is intended to be completely victorious over the world, the flesh, and the Devil, and can do so through the Cross, and only through the Cross [Rom. 6:3-14]).*

42 They looked, but there was none to save; even unto the LORD, but He answered them not *(the Lord will not help or answer those who trust in self, or anything else other than the Cross [I Cor. 1:21, 23; 2:2]).*

43 Then did I beat them as small as the dust of the earth, I did stamp them as the mire of the street, and did spread them abroad *(this is what we are to do with every "sin which doth so easily beset us" [Heb. 12:1]; we are to overcome all, and nothing must overcome us; it can be done only in Christ).*

44 You also have delivered me from the strivings of my people, You have kept me to be head of the heathen: a people which I knew not shall serve me *(while this happened with David, its greater fulfillment awaits the greater Son of David, which will take place upon His Second Advent; the entire world will then serve Him).*

45 Strangers shall submit themselves unto me: as soon as they hear, they shall be obedient unto me *(once again, refers to the Second Coming, with the whole world bowing at the Feet of Christ; it will happen!).*

46 Strangers shall fade away, and they shall be afraid out of their close places *(Christ shall rule with great Power; strangers to His Grace and Ways will soon be no more).*

47 The LORD lives; and blessed be my rock; and exalted be the God of the Rock of my Salvation *(after the Cross, He was most definitely "exalted" [Phil. 2:9]).*

48 It is God Who avenges me, and Who brings down the people under me *(the Believer must not take vengeance into his own hands, but leave all such to the Lord [Rom. 12:19-21]).*

49 And Who brings me forth from my enemies: You also have lifted me up on high above them Who rose up against me: You have delivered me from the violent man *(as David was delivered from Saul, we are delivered from the powers of darkness, but only as our Faith is placed in Christ and the Cross [Gal., Chpt. 5]).*

50 Therefore I will give thanks unto You, O LORD, among the heathen, and I will sing praises unto Your name *(because He has done so much for us!).*

51 He is the tower of Salvation for His King: and shows mercy to His anointed, unto David, and to his seed for evermore *(speaks of David, but more particularly to the Son of David).*

CHAPTER 23
(1018 B.C.)
THE LAST WORDS OF DAVID

NOW these be the last words of David *(we know what the heart of David was by these "last words").* David the son of Jesse said, and the man who was raised up on high, the anointed of the God of Jacob *(this refers to God, Who met Jacob when he had nothing, and deserved nothing, and Who promised him all things — the God of all Grace; in effect, David puts himself in the same category as this poor, scheming Jacob, who was ultimately changed by God),* and the sweet Psalmist of Israel *(refers to the fact that God had given David many of the Psalms; actually, he wrote over half of these great songs),* said,

2 The Spirit of the LORD spoke by me, and His Word was in my tongue *(this means that the mouth belonged to David, but the Words were those of the Lord; this statement claims and guarantees Inspiration).*

3 The God of Israel said, the Rock of Israel spoke to me, He Who rules over men must be just, ruling in the fear of God *(both Verses 3 and 4 speak of the Advent of Christ, and compare His Rule with that of man).*

4 And He shall be as the light of the morning, when the sun rises, even a morning without clouds; as the tender grass springing out of the earth by clear shining after rain. *(Verses 3 and 4 foretell the Advent of One Who should rule*

men righteously, in the fear of God; and that His Rule, contrasted with man's, would be comparable to the cloudless sunshine of a beautiful morning following the black shadows of a dark night, and to the rich herbage produced by refreshing rain, which alone can clothe barren land. In fact, these two Verses leap ahead to the coming Millennial Reign, when Christ will rule supreme.)

5 Although my house be not so with God (meaning that neither he nor any member of his family fulfilled, or, in fact, could fulfill, the promises of this Prophecy); yet He has made with me an Everlasting Covenant, ordered in all things, and sure: for this is all my Salvation, and all my desire, although He make it not to grow. (The last phrase should be translated, "Shall He not make it to grow?" In the statement of this Fifth Verse, the Holy Spirit through David says that even though David had failed in realizing the better purposes of his heart, still, it was God's good pleasure that the Covenant, despite personal failure, will remain firm and secure. There would be born into his family the great King described in these Verses. That King would be Christ, and so it was!)

6 But the sons of Belial shall be all of them as thorns thrust away, because they cannot be taken with hands ("Belial" means "worthless," and, in this case, "vicious worthlessness"; it is from this worthlessness that opposition arises; it cannot be defeated by man's ability, but only by the Lord):

7 But the man who shall touch them must be fenced with iron and the staff of a spear; and they shall be utterly burned with fire in the same place (in other words, there is no way that man, with his limited power, can overcome the powers of darkness; he can only win the victory by being "fenced with iron," which speaks of the Power of the Holy Spirit, which will burn out the dross in our lives with unquenchable fire [Mat. 3:11]; God's Prescribed Order of Victory is Christ and the Cross, with the Cross ever being the object of our Faith, which then gives the Holy Spirit latitude to work within our lives, bringing about the desired results [I Cor. 1:17-18, 21, 23; 2:2; Gal. 6:14; Col. 2:14-15]).

DAVID'S MIGHTY MEN

8 These be the names of the mighty men whom David had (it must be understood that they were "mighty" because of being with David): The Tachmonite who sat in the seat, chief among the captains; the same was Adino the Eznite: he lift up his spear against eight hundred, whom he slew at one time. (Humanly possible? No! But with God, all things are possible. The Holy Spirit gave this man amazing power, in order for him to accomplish this feat against God's enemies. The enemies of our soul must be killed. No compromise can be entertained.)

9 And after him was Eleazar the son of Dodo the Ahohite, one of the three mighty men with David, when they defied the Philistines who were there gathered together to battle, and the men of Israel were gone away (Israel was being defeated, and its soldiers were fleeing):

10 He arose, and smote the Philistines until his hand was weary, and his hand clave unto the sword: and the LORD wrought a great victory that day; and the people returned after him only to spoil. (One man stemmed the tide, one man who had Faith. Eleazar refused to run, but rather "arose and began to smite the Philistines," and did so to such an extent that, when it was all over and with the battle won, others had to pry his fingers loose from the sword. God give us men and women who will be as tenacious for the Lord presently as was Eleazar then!)

11 And after him was Shammah the son of Agee the Hararite. And the Philistines were gathered together into a troop, where was a piece of ground full of lentiles (a pea patch): and the people fled from the Philistines. (Israel would plant her crops, and then, as here, when they were ready to be harvested, the Philistines would swoop down and take it all. This is so indicative of so many modern Christians. We work and labor, and then allow Satan to take the harvest.)

12 But he stood in the midst of the ground, and defended it, and slew the Philistines: and the LORD wrought a great victory. (In effect, Shammah said, "Even though all of the other Israelites have fled, I will stand my ground and defend what is rightly mine." The Lord gave him special strength and, thereby, a great victory was won. We must learn two things from this: 1. Faith does not go into action until we put it into action; and, 2. You've got to tell the Devil, "I've left this pea patch my last time!")

13 And three of the thirty chief went down, and came to David in the harvest time unto the cave of Adullam: and the troop of the Philistines pitched in the valley of Rephaim.

14 And David was then in an hold, and the garrison of the Philistines was then in

Beth-lehem *(this was before David became king).*

15 And David longed, and said, Oh that one would give me drink of the water of the well of Beth-lehem, which is by the gate! *(David was a Type of Christ. God help us to be so close to the Heart of Christ that we can hear His Sigh regarding the great needs of those in other parts of the world, who desperately need to be touched with the "water of life.")*

16 And the three mighty men broke through the host of the Philistines, and drew water out of the well of Beth-lehem, that was by the gate, and took it, and brought it to David: nevertheless he would not drink thereof, but poured it out unto the LORD *(all Drink Offerings poured out before the Lord in Old Testament times pictured Christ pouring out Himself for the sin of mankind, which He did at Calvary's Cross).*

17 And he said, Be it far from me, O LORD, that I should do this: is not this the blood of the men that went in jeopardy of their lives? therefore he would not drink it. These things did these three mighty men *(the Holy Spirit called them "mighty"; how many is He referring to as such presently?).*

18 And Abishai, the brother of Joab, the son of Zeruiah, was chief among three. And he lifted up his spear against three hundred, and slew them, and had the name among three *(in this Verse, Joab is only mentioned as "the brother of Abishai," not as one of David's mighty men).*

19 Was he not most honourable of three? therefore he was their captain: howbeit he attained not unto the first three *(the first three were Adino, Eleazar, and Shammah).*

20 And Benaiah the son of Jehoiada, the son of a valiant man, of Kabzeel, who had done many acts, he slew two lionlike men of Moab: he went down also and slew a lion in the midst of a pit in time of snow *(he was a very important person throughout David's reign, being commander of the bodyguard [8:18], and General of the third brigade of 24,000 men [I Chron. 27:5]):*

21 And he slew an Egyptian, a goodly man: and the Egyptian had a spear in his hand; but he went down to him with a staff, and plucked the spear out of the Egyptian's hand, and slew him with his own spear.

22 These things did Benaiah the son of Jehoiada, and had the name among three mighty men *(they were "mighty" because the Lord was with them).*

23 He was more honourable than the thirty, but he attained not to the first three. And David set him over his guard *(as stated, he was the head of the bodyguard of David).*

24 Asahel the brother of Joab was one of the thirty; Elhanan the son of Dodo of Beth-lehem *(this man was killed by Abner [2:18-23]),*

25 Shammah the Harodite, Elika the Harodite,

26 Helez the Paltite, Ira the son of Ikkesh the Tekoite,

27 Abiezer the Anethothite, Mebunnai the Hushathite,

28 Zalmon the Ahohite, Maharai the Netophathite,

29 Heleb the son of Baanah, a Netophathite, Ittai the son of Ribai out of Gibeah of the Children of Benjamin,

30 Benaiah the Pirathonite, Hiddai of the brooks of Gaash,

31 Abi-albon the Arbathite, Azmaveth the Barhumite,

32 Eliahba the Shaalbonite, of the sons of Jashen, Jonathan,

33 Shammah the Hararite, Ahiam the son of Sharar the Hararite,

34 Eliphelet the son of Ahasbai, the son of the Maachathite, Eliam the son of Ahithophel the Gilonite,

35 Hezrai the Carmelite, Paarai the Arbite,

36 Igal the son of Nathan of Zobah, Bani the Gadite,

37 Zelek the Ammonite, Nahari the Beerothite, armourbearer to Joab the son of Zeruiah,

38 Ira an Ithrite, Gareb an Ithrite,

39 Uriah the Hittite: thirty and seven in all. *(Verses 24-39 record other mighty men. All of these typify that records are kept in the portals of Glory concerning the acts of Faith of every Child of God. What does the record show concerning you and me?)*

CHAPTER 24
(1017 B.C.)
DAVID'S SIN IN TAKING A NATIONAL CENSUS IN AN UNSCRIPTURAL WAY

AND again the anger of the LORD was kindled against Israel, and he moved David against them to say, Go, number Israel and Judah. *(The word "again" signals the fact that the Lord had been angry with Israel many times before. I Chron., Chpt. 21 says, "And Satan . . . provoked David to number Israel." There is no contradiction. While Satan did this,*

it was the Lord Who allowed it to be done. Why? The evidence seems to be that both David and Israel had grown prideful in the power of the nation, seemingly forgetting that it was the Lord Who gave all of this.)

2 For the king said to Joab the captain of the host, which was with him, Go now through all the Tribes of Israel, from Dan even to Beer-sheba, and number ye the people, that I may know the number of the people. *(The taking of the census was not unlawful or displeasing to God; however, the reason it was taken, and the neglect of the Word of God, is what made it so sinful. When a census was taken, a half-shekel of silver, with silver being a token of Redemption, was to be paid for each man numbered [Ex. 30:11-16]. This portrayed the fact that Israel's blessing and prosperity were anchored solely in the shed blood of the lamb. This is the reason that all were to pay the same amount alike. In the matter of Atonement, all worshippers stood on one common ground — the slain lamb. David ignored this extremely important command of the Lord.)*

3 And Joab said unto the king, Now the LORD your God add unto the people, how many soever they be, an hundredfold, and that the eyes of my lord the king may see it: but why does my lord the king delight in this thing? *(It is easy to detect the "flesh" in another, and so Joab, a man of the world, readily recognized the folly of David. David's action ministered only to his self-importance, for he said in Verse 2, "that I may know.")*

4 Notwithstanding the king's word prevailed against Joab, and against the captains of the host. And Joab and the captains of the host went out from the presence of the king, to number the people of Israel. *(Other than Joab, the chief officers also attempted to dissuade David, but to no avail. David had made up his mind, and would take no advice.)*

5 And they passed over Jordan, and pitched in Aroer, on the right side of the city that lies in the midst of the river of Gad, and toward Jazer:

6 Then they came to Gilead, and to the land of Tahtim-hodshi; and they came to Dan-jaan, and about to Zidon,

7 And came to the strong hold of Tyre, and to all the cities of the Hivites, and of the Canaanites: and they went out to the south of Judah, even to Beer-sheba.

8 So when they had gone through all the land, they came to Jerusalem at the end of nine months and twenty days.

9 And Joab gave up the sum of the number of the people unto the king: and there were in Israel eight hundred thousand valiant men who drew the sword; and the men of Judah were five hundred thousand men *(portrays the fact as to how strong the Tribe of Judah actually was)*.

DAVID'S REPENTANCE

10 And David's heart smote him after that he had numbered the people *(one of the chief Operations of the Holy Spirit is to smite with conviction when sin has been committed; the modern Church is trying to eliminate this capacity of the Holy Spirit; however, to eliminate any part of His Work is to eliminate Him altogether; He will not function with half measures)*. And David said unto the LORD, I have sinned greatly in that I have done *(to be forgiven of sin, one has to admit that one has sinned, and do so to the Lord [I Jn. 1:9])*: and now, I beseech you, O LORD, take away the iniquity of your servant *(the Lord Alone can take away our iniquity; and He does such by virtue of Christ and what He has done at the Cross; the Cross is the only answer for sin, which was typified by the Altar of the Tabernacle [Heb. 10:12-14])*; for I have done very foolishly *(sin makes fools, even out of the wisest and most brilliant of men)*.

11 For when David was up in the morning the word of the LORD came unto the prophet Gad, David's Seer, saying *(the Ministry of the Prophet is to call the nation and, in this case, the king, to Righteousness; while the Prophet at times foretells, the greater part of his or her Ministry is to call the nation and the Church to Repentance; most of all, the Prophet is a Preacher of Righteousness [Mat. 3:1-12])*,

DAVID CHOOSES HIS PUNISHMENT

12 Go and say unto David, Thus saith the LORD, I offer you three things; choose you one of them, that I may do it unto you *(there is always a penalty to sin; even though the Lord forgives and cleanses, there is still a penalty; however, it is the Lord Alone Who stipulates and carries out the penalty, and not man)*.

13 So Gad came to David, and told him, and said unto him, Shall seven years of famine come unto you in your land? or will you flee three months before your enemies, while they pursue you? or that there be three days' pestilence in your land? now advise, and see what answer I shall return to Him Who sent me.

14 And David said unto Gad, I am in a great strait *(sin always puts an individual in a great strait)*: let us fall now into the hand of the LORD; for His mercies are great: and let me not fall into the hand of man *(man shows little mercy, and religious man none at all)*.

THE PLAGUE

15 So the LORD sent a pestilence upon Israel from the morning even to the time appointed *(three days and nights)*: and there died of the people from Dan even to Beer-sheba seventy thousand men. *(This is a staggering number of men to have died in so short a time. This tells us of the awfulness of sin! It might be shocking to realize that wars, pestilence, earthquakes, famine, etc., which presently plague parts of the Earth, follow in the same train of that which happened to Israel of so long ago.)*

DAVID PRAYS FOR MERCY

16 And when the Angel stretched out his hand upon Jerusalem to destroy it *(who instigated the plague as well)*, the LORD repented Him of the evil *(the Repentance of the Lord is not the same as that of man; man repents of sin; God merely changes His Direction, because of certain actions on Earth)*, and said to the Angel that destroyed the people, It is enough: stay now your hand. And the Angel of the LORD was by the threshingplace of Araunah the Jebusite *(actually, this would be the very spot where the great Temple would be built by Solomon)*.

17 And David spoke unto the LORD when he saw the Angel who smote the people, and said, Lo, I have sinned, and I have done wickedly: but these sheep *(speaking of Israel)*, what have they done? let Your hand, I pray You, be against me, and against my father's house *(this was true intercession on the part of David)*.

THE PLAGUE IS STAYED

18 And Gad came that day to David, and said unto him, Go up, rear an Altar unto the LORD in the threshingfloor of Araunah the Jebusite *(the only answer for sin, and I mean the only answer, is the "Altar," i.e., "the Cross," of which the Altar was a Type)*.

19 And David, according to the saying of Gad, went up as the LORD commanded.

20 And Araunah looked, and saw the king and his servants coming on toward him: and Araunah went out, and bowed himself before the king on his face upon the ground *(Araunah was a Jebusite and, in fact, condemned to death; his life was spared by the mercy of David)*.

21 And Araunah said, Wherefore is my lord the king come to his servant? And David said, To buy the threshingfloor of you, to build an Altar unto the LORD, that the plague may be stayed from the people.

22 And Araunah said unto David, Let my lord the king take and offer up what seems good unto him: behold, here be oxen for burnt sacrifice, and threshing instruments and other instruments of the oxen for wood *(evidently, Araunah knew some things about the Sacrificial System of Israel, even though he was a heathen)*.

23 All these things did Araunah, as a king, give unto the king. And Araunah said unto the king, The LORD your God accept you *(in his own words, he was praying that the Lord would accept the Sacrifice)*.

24 And the king said unto Araunah, No; but I will surely buy it of you at a price: neither will I offer Burnt Offerings unto the LORD my God of that which does cost me nothing. So David bought the threshingfloor and the oxen for fifty shekels of silver *(all of this tells us that everything we offer to the Lord must be offered on the basis of the Lord Jesus Christ, and what He did for us at the Cross; otherwise, we are attempting to offer to God that which costs nothing, and which God will never accept)*.

25 And David built there an Altar unto the LORD, and offered Burnt Offerings and Peace Offerings. So the LORD was intreated for the land, and the plague was stayed from Israel. *(There is a "plague" called "sin" that is destroying this world, and causing multiple hundreds of millions to be eternally lost. There is only one cure for that plague, and that is the precious, atoning, Vicarious Offering of the Blood of the Lord Jesus Christ, which was done at the Cross, and our acceptance of Him. All the Churches in the world will never stay the "plague." All the good works, good intentions, money, religion, prestige, or education will not stop this plague of sin. Only the precious Blood of Jesus Christ can, here symbolized by the "Altar.")*

THE FIRST BOOK OF
THE KINGS

CHAPTER 1
(1015 B.C.)
DAVID'S LAST DAYS

NOW king David was old and stricken in years *(at this time, David was either 69 or 70 years old)*; and they covered him with clothes, but he got no heat *(the first king of Israel, Saul, is not once mentioned in I Kings or II Kings; it is as if he never existed, because Saul was the people's choice, while David was God's choice).*

2 Wherefore his servants said unto him, Let there be sought for my lord the king a young virgin: and let her stand before the king, and let her cherish him, and let her lie in your bosom, that my lord the king may get heat *(a common experience of the aged; David's early hardships and later sorrows and anxieties appear to have aged him prematurely; as well, what was suggested was somewhat common in those days; nothing sexual is intimated).*

3 So they sought for a fair damsel throughout all the coasts of Israel, and found Abishag a Shunammite, and brought her to the king.

4 And the damsel was very fair, and cherished the king, and ministered to him: but the king knew her not *(had no intimate relations with her).*

ADONIJAH PLOTS TO BE KING

5 Then Adonijah the son of Haggith exalted himself, saying, I will be king: and he prepared him chariots and horsemen, and fifty men to run before him. *(This is the fourth son of David, and now apparently the oldest surviving son. Adonijah, Joab the military leader, and Abiathar the High Priest would set up their kingdom in opposition to God's elect king. God had no place in their hearts, and so Solomon did not suit them either. In fact, God's choice never does suit man. This unholy triumvirate is a type of that which controls so much of the Church world presently.)*

6 And his father had not displeased him at any time in saying, Why have you done so? and he also was a very goodly man; and his mother bore him after Absalom *(as well, he had the Absalom spirit).*

7 And he conferred with Joab the son of Zeruiah, and with Abiathar the Priest; and they following Adonijah helped him. *(Abiathar had been very close to David; so, he must have chafed at sharing the Priesthood with Zadok, and now makes his move to gain the number one spot all to himself. Such an attitude has no regard for the Will of God or the Call of God. Unfortunately, the modern Church is full of these "religious leaders.")*

8 But Zadok the Priest, and Benaiah the son of Jehoiada, and Nathan the Prophet, and Shimei, and Rei, and the mighty men which belonged to David, were not with Adonijah *(the Holy Spirit is quick to point out these individuals who placed no stock in Adonijah, even though he was the eldest son, but rather waited on the Lord).*

9 And Adonijah slew sheep and oxen and fat cattle by the stone of Zoheleth, which is by En-rogel, and called all his brethren the king's sons, and all the men of Judah the king's servants *(even though sacrifices were offered, which gave it a religious leaning, still, for Adonijah to be king was not the Will of God; in fact, had he gained the Throne, it would have destroyed Israel, as all such usurpation "steals, kills, and destroys," because it is of Satan [Jn. 10:10]):*

NATHAN WARNS BATH-SHEBA
ABOUT ADONIJAH

10 But Nathan the Prophet, and Benaiah, and the mighty men, and Solomon his brother, he called not *(it is clear from this Verse that Adonijah perfectly understood that he had in Solomon a rival; the word had no doubt gotten around that it was the Will of God that Solomon succeed David).*

11 Wherefore Nathan spoke unto Bathsheba, the mother of Solomon, saying, Have you not heard that Adonijah the son of Haggith does reign, and David our lord knows it not? *(In other words, David has had nothing to do with the aspirations of Adonijah, proving that they were not of the Lord.)*

12 Now therefore come, let me, I pray you, give you counsel, that you may save your own life, and the life of your son Solomon. *(The*

idea is, these men would go to any lengths to secure their positions, even to killing Bath-sheba and Solomon, and anyone else, for that matter, who would seem to stand in their way. Such is the way and world of religion.)

13 Go and get thee in unto king David, and say unto him, Did not you, my lord, O king, swear unto your handmaid, saying, Assuredly Solomon your son shall reign after me, and he shall sit upon my throne? why then does Adonijah reign? *(This oath of David to Bath-sheba is not elsewhere recorded, but it was evidently well known to Nathan, and, no doubt, to others as well.)*

14 Behold, while you yet talked there with the king, I also will come in after you, and confirm your words *(the meaning is not to amplify, but rather to corroborate).*

BATH-SHEBA ASKS DAVID TO CROWN SOLOMON KING

15 And Bath-sheba went in unto the king into the chamber: and the king was very old *(here the word refers to feebleness rather than age)*; and Abishag the Shunammite ministered unto the king *(introduced to show the king's helplessness).*

16 And Bath-sheba bowed, and did obeisance unto the king. And the king said, What would you? *(It rather means, "What do you want?" or "What is your business?")*

17 And she said unto him, My lord, you swore by the LORD your God unto your handmaid, saying, Assuredly Solomon your son shall reign after me, and he shall sit upon my throne.

18 And now, behold, Adonijah reigns; and now, my lord the king, you know it not *(I know that you didn't have anything to do with this concerning Adonijah):*

19 And he has killed oxen and fat cattle and sheep in abundance, and has called all the sons of the king, and Abiathar the Priest, and Joab the captain of the host: but Solomon your servant has he not called. *(She says it in this manner to prove there was a plot. Spence says, "It showed the cloven foot.")*

20 And you, my lord, O king, the eyes of all Israel are upon you, that you should tell them who shall sit on the throne of my lord the king after him *(it is certain that all of Israel was indeed abuzz about this).*

21 Otherwise it shall come to pass, when my lord the king shall sleep with his fathers, that I and my son Solomon shall be counted offenders *(in other words, we will be killed).*

NATHAN SUPPORTS THE PLEA OF BATH-SHEBA

22 And, lo, while she yet talked with the king, Nathan the Prophet also came in.

23 And they told the king, saying, Behold Nathan the Prophet. And when he was come in before the king, he bowed himself before the king with his face to the ground.

24 And Nathan said, My lord, O king, have you said, Adonijah shall reign after me, and he shall sit upon my throne? *(Nathan puts it thus forcibly, in order to draw from the king a disclaimer.)*

25 For he is gone down this day, and has slain oxen and fat cattle and sheep in abundance, and has called all the king's sons, and the captains of the host, and Abiathar the Priest; and, behold, they eat and drink before him, and say, God save king Adonijah *(put to him in this manner, David will now have to take action).*

26 But me, even me your servant, and Zadok the Priest, and Benaiah the son of Jehoiada, and your servant Solomon, has he not called *(this speaks volumes!).*

27 Is this thing done by my lord the king, and you have not showed it unto your servant, who should sit on the throne of my lord the king after him? *(The repetition is well calculated to impress upon the king the importance of nominating a successor at once.)*

DAVID'S OATH TO BATH-SHEBA

28 Then king David answered and said, Call me Bath-sheba. And she came into the king's presence, and stood before the king *(Bath-sheba had evidently left the chamber when Nathan came in; she now joins Nathan before David).*

29 And the king swore, and said, As the LORD lives, Who has redeemed my soul out of all distress *(in essence, David uses the term, "by the life of Jehovah," which gives his statement about to uttered great force),*

30 Even as I swore unto you *(Bath-sheba)* by the LORD God of Israel, saying, Assuredly Solomon your son shall reign after me, and he shall sit upon my throne in my stead; even so will I certainly do this day.

31 Then Bath-sheba bowed with her face to the earth, and did reverence to the king, and

said, Let my lord king David live for ever.

DAVID INSTRUCTS ZADOK
AND NATHAN

32 And king David said, Call me Zadok the Priest, and Nathan the Prophet, and Benaiah the son of Jehoiada. And they came before the king (*the order of the names marks the position of the persons with respect to the matter at hand*).

33 The king also said unto them, Take with you the servants of your lord (*these were the Cherethites and Pelethites, about 600 men, a formidable force, to say the least*), and cause Solomon my son to ride upon my own mule, and bring him down to Gihon (*the riding of David's mule was not merely a mark of honor, but a public and very significant indication of David's will respecting his successor; the populace would perceive at once who was destined to sit in David's seat; actually, it was death to ride on the king's mule without his permission*):

34 And let Zadok the Priest and Nathan the Prophet anoint him there king over Israel (*the "anointing," and especially considering that it was done by Zadok the High Priest and Nathan the Prophet, signified the spiritual aspect of the office of King over Israel; in fact, this was the single most important position on the face of the Earth; through this family would come the Messiah, the King of kings and Lord of lords, the Lord Jesus Christ*): and blow ye with the trumpet (*signifying the proclamation of a new king*), and say, God save king Solomon (*which chant was expected to be picked up by all the people of Israel*).

35 Then you shall come up after him, that he may come and sit upon my throne (*in every possible way, his accession was to be proclaimed and confirmed*); for he shall be king in my stead: and I have appointed him to be ruler over Israel and over Judah (*"he" and "him" are emphasized in the original Hebrew Text*).

36 And Benaiah the son of Jehoiada answered the king, and said, Amen: the LORD God of my lord the king say so too (*Benaiah is saying, in effect, "This is of the Lord"*).

37 As the LORD has been with my lord the king, even so be He with Solomon, and make his throne greater than the throne of my lord king David (*this was said from a full and honest heart, not to flatter David's vanity; it is thoroughly characteristic of Benaiah, so far as we know him; and the prayer was fulfilled*).

SOLOMON ANOINTED KING

38 So Zadok the Priest (*High Priest*), and Nathan the Prophet, and Benaiah the son of Jehoiada, and the Cherethites, and the Pelethites (*these latter two groups had the military might to back up whatever was done; they were David's royal bodyguard, consisting of sizable forces*), went down, and caused Solomon to ride upon king David's mule, and brought him to Gihon (*considering this crack special guard accompanying Solomon, this must have been quite a procession*).

39 And Zadok the Priest took an horn of oil out of the Tabernacle, and anointed Solomon. And they blew the trumpet; and all the people said, God save king Solomon (*this was the "holy anointing oil" [Ex. 30:25, 31]; they fulfilled exactly what David had told them to do; Solomon was confirmed in his office and, as well, by the approval of the people*).

40 And all the people came up after him, and the people piped with pipes, and rejoiced with great joy, so that the Earth rent with the sound of them (*there was great joy in Jerusalem*).

ADONIJAH'S SUBMISSION
TO SOLOMON

41 And Adonijah and all the guests who were with him heard it as they had made an end of eating (*celebrating, they thought, their new position*). And when Joab heard the sound of the trumpet, he said, Wherefore is this noise of the city being in an uproar? (*Joab seems at once to have suspected the significance of the blowing of the trumpet.*)

42 And while he yet spoke, behold, Jonathan the son of Abiathar the Priest came: and Adonijah said unto him, Come in; for you are a valiant man, and bring good tidings (*Adonijah's misgivings reveal themselves in these words; he fears the worst, but strives to put on a cheerful face, and to encourage his guests — Spence*).

43 And Jonathan answered and said to Adonijah, Verily our lord king David has made Solomon king.

44 And the king has sent with him Zadok the Priest, and Nathan the Prophet, and Benaiah the son of Jehoiada, and the Cherethites, and the Pelethites, and they have caused him to ride upon the king's mule:

45 And Zadok the Priest and Nathan the Prophet have anointed him king in Gihon: and they are come up from thence rejoicing, so

that the city rang again. This is the noise that you have heard.

46 And also Solomon sits on the throne of the kingdom.

47 And moreover the king's servants came to bless our lord king David, saying, God make the name of Solomon better than your name, and make his throne greater than your throne. And the king bowed himself upon the bed *(bowed himself in worship of the Lord, because he knows that he has just carried out the Will of God).*

48 And also thus said the king, Blessed be the LORD God of Israel, which has given one to sit on my throne this day, my eyes even seeing it *(this is exceptional, because most kings die before they are succeeded by others).*

49 And all the guests who were with Adonijah were afraid, and rose up, and went every man his way *(this fear and flight betray a consciousness of guilt).*

50 And Adonijah feared because of Solomon, and arose, and went, and caught hold on the horns of the Altar *(by "laying hold of the horns," the offender, thereby, placed himself under the protection of the saving and helping Grace of God, at least if it was agreed to by the authorities).*

51 And it was told Solomon, saying, Behold, Adonijah fears king Solomon: for, lo, he has caught hold on the horns of the Altar, saying, Let king Solomon swear unto me to day that he will not slay his servant with the sword *(by Adonijah referring to Solomon as the king, it is a virtual abdication of his claim to the throne, and a direct acknowledgment of the new Monarch; in this statement, Adonijah indirectly confesses that he has merited death).*

52 And Solomon said, If he will show himself a worthy man, there shall not an hair of him fall to the earth: but if wickedness shall be found in him, he shall die.

53 So king Solomon sent, and they brought him down from the Altar. And he came and bowed himself to king Solomon: and Solomon said unto him, Go to your house *(this was not a sentence of banishment from the Court, but merely a dismissal to a private life, involving a tacit admonition to live quietly and be thankful that his life was spared him — Spence).*

CHAPTER 2

(1014 B.C.)

DAVID'S CHARGE TO SOLOMON

NOW the days of David drew near that he should die; and he charged Solomon his son, saying *(how long David lived after making Solomon king is not stated, but it was probably only a few months),*

2 I go the way of all the Earth: be thou strong therefore, and show yourself a man *(David's charge was not that of a revengeful private person, but rather the judicial act of a Chief Magistrate conscious of his responsibility when handing over his office to his successor);*

3 And keep the charge of the LORD your God, to walk in His Ways, to keep His Statutes, and His Commandments, and His Judgments, and His Testimonies, as it is written in the Law of Moses, that you may prosper in all that you do, and whithersoever you turn yourself *(David points out to Solomon that success lay only in close adherence and full subjection to the written Word of God; it has not changed from then until now):*

4 That the LORD may continue His Word which He spoke concerning me, saying, If your children take heed to their way, to walk before me in truth with all their heart and with all their soul, there shall not fail thee (said He) a man on the throne of Israel *(in effect, David is saying that whoever sits on the Throne of Israel must adhere strictly to the Word of God, hence him giving this great charge in the previous Verse).*

5 Moreover you know also what Joab the son of Zeruiah did to me, and what he did to the two captains of the hosts of Israel, unto Abner the son of Ner, and unto Amasa the son of Jether, whom he slew, and shed the blood of war in peace, and put the blood of war upon his girdle that was about his loins, and in his shoes that were on his feet *(David is proclaiming the fact that Joab is a murderer, meaning that he was stained with innocent blood, blood which cried to Heaven for vengeance [Gen. 4:10]).*

6 Do therefore according to your wisdom, and let not his hoar head go down to the grave in peace *(the Lord had no doubt told David what was to be done, as it regards Joab).*

7 But show kindness unto the sons of Barzillai the Gileadite, and let them be of those who eat at your table: for so they came to me when I fled because of Absalom your brother *(as the Holy Spirit gave directions of judgment concerning Joab, as well, He gives directions of blessing concerning the sons of Barzillai; the old man had helped David when David was in dire straits; David never forgot it, telling us that the Holy Spirit never forgets anything, good or bad, with the exception of sins that are washed*

by the Blood of the Lamb).

8 And, behold, you have with you Shimei the son of Gera, a Benjamite of Bahurim, which cursed me with a grievous curse in the day when I went to Mahanaim: but he came down to meet me at Jordan, and I swore to him by the LORD, saying, I will not put you to death with the sword.

9 Now therefore hold him not guiltless: for you are a wise man, and know what you ought to do unto him; but his hoar head you bring down to the grave with blood *(David's words were not inspired by malice or cruelty, but rather for the sake of the Kingdom of God; these men so named in judgment had no regard for God, or the ways of the Lord; so they had to be dealt with, or they would cause grievous problems shortly!).*

THE DEATH OF DAVID

10 So David slept with his fathers, and was buried in the city of David. *(And so died one of the greatest men of God who ever lived. David wrote over half of the Psalms. In some ways, he filled the Offices of Prophet, Priest, and King. He was a Type of Christ, and his successor would ultimately be called "The Son of David," and then "King of kings and Lord of lords." Despite the sins, faults, and failures, his heart was ever after God.*

His name is the first human name in the New Testament [Mat. 1:1] and the last human name in the New Testament [Rev. 22:16]. During the great Kingdom Age to come under the Lord Jesus Christ, David will once again rule Israel in all her glory, fulfilling the great prophecies that were given to him by Nathan the Prophet.)

11 And the days that David reigned over Israel were forty years: seven years reigned he in Hebron, and thirty and three years reigned he in Jerusalem *(in the coming Kingdom Age, under Christ, he will reign in Jerusalem for a thousand years).*

12 Then sat Solomon upon the throne of David his father; and his kingdom was established greatly. *(As David was a Type of Christ Who brought Salvation to Israel and the world, likewise, Solomon is a Type of Christ Who will reign over an established kingdom, with all enemies defeated, in what is known as the "Kingdom Age," or the "Millennial Reign." However, it must ever be remembered that David and Solomon were but types, and poor, frail, human types at that, who ultimately always fail;*

nevertheless, the One to Whom they pointed, the Lord Jesus Christ, has never failed and, in fact, will never fail.

Solomon was perhaps about 20 years of age when he took the Throne.)

ADONIJAH IS EXECUTED

13 And Adonijah the son of Haggith came to Bath-sheba the mother of Solomon. And she said, Do you come peaceably? And he said, Peaceably *(foiled in his purpose to mount the Throne by direct means, Adonijah and his advisors had recourse to intrigue and subtlety; by the aid of Abishag, he hopes to accomplish what his chariots and horsemen had failed to effect).*

14 He said moreover, I have somewhat to say unto you. And she said, Say on.

15 And he said, You know that the kingdom was mine, and that all Israel set their faces on me, that I should reign: howbeit the kingdom is turned about, and is become my brother's: for it was his from the LORD *(the "me" is emphatic by its position; so is the "mine" used just before; in fact, these statements were not correct; anyway, this Verse shows that Adonijah had not renounced his pretensions to the Throne; if he couldn't get it one way, he will try another; his stating that the Throne was Solomon's, "from the LORD," was stated only to placate Bath-sheba; in fact, he believed no such thing).*

16 And now I ask one petition of you, deny me not. And she said unto him, Say on.

17 And he said, Speak, I pray you, unto Solomon the king, (for he will not say you nay,) that he give me Abishag the Shunammite to wife *(as husband of the late Monarch's widow, Abishag, and as the older brother, Adonijah could dispute the Throne with Solomon; his asking for Abishag revealed his purpose and manifested his treason; it is amazing that Bath-sheba did not seem to be aware of these implications!).*

18 And Bath-sheba said, Well; I will speak for you unto the king.

19 Bath-sheba therefore went unto king Solomon, to speak unto him for Adonijah, And the king rose up to meet her, and bowed himself unto her, and sat down on his throne, and caused a seat to be set for the king's mother; and she sat on his right hand.

20 Then she said, I desire one small petition of you; I pray you, say me not nay. And the king said unto her, Ask on, my mother: for I will not say no to you.

21 And she said, Let Abishag the Shunammite

be given to Adonijah your brother to wife (*possibly she thought that she held the threads of a love story in her hands, that it would be a small thing for Solomon to make these handsome lovers happy; she seemed to be ignorant of Adonijah's real motives*).

22 And king Solomon answered and said unto his mother, And why do you ask Abishag the Shunammite for Adonijah? ask for him the kingdom also; for he is my elder brother; even for him, and for Abiathar the Priest, and for Joab the son of Zeruiah. (*Immediately, Solomon saw through the scheme, and that Abiathar and Joab were complices in this high treason — for that's what it was! For one to marry the wife of a former king gave such a person a claim to the Throne, and this is exactly what Adonijah was attempting to do.*)

23 Then king Solomon swore by the LORD, saying, God do so to me, and more also, if Adonijah have not spoken this word against his own life.

24 Now therefore, as the LORD lives, which has established me, and set me on the throne of David my father, and Who has made me an house, as He promised, Adonijah shall be put to death this day.

25 And king Solomon sent by the hand of Benaiah the son of Jehoiada; and he fell upon him that he died (*this was right and just in the Eyes of God; had Adonijah had his way, which incidentally was inspired by Satan, he would have taken over the Throne, killed Solomon, who was God's choice and, as well, would have killed Bath-sheba and all others around the Throne; Israel would have quickly become a Hell*).

ABIATHAR IS REMOVED FROM THE PRIESTHOOD

26 And unto Abiathar the Priest said the king, You get to Anathoth, unto your own fields; for you are worthy of death: but I will not at this time put you to death, because you did bear the Ark of the LORD God before David my father, and because you have been afflicted in all wherein my father was afflicted.

27 So Solomon thrust out Abiathar from being Priest unto the LORD; that he might fulfill the Word of the LORD, which he spoke concerning the house of Eli in Shiloh (*this removal of Abiathar from the Priesthood was a definite fulfillment of the cutting off of the house of Eli; here we have the fulfillment of God's rejection of the house of Ithamar [I Chron.*

24:3], *to which Eli belonged, and the reestablishment of the High Priesthood in the line of Eleazar, which had long before been predicted [I Sam. 2:31-35]*).

JOAB IS EXECUTED

28 Then tidings came to Joab: for Joab had turned after Adonijah, though he turned not after Absalom. And Joab fled unto the Tabernacle of the LORD, and caught hold on the horns of the Altar (*his action is almost certain evidence of his guilt; it is thought that Joab had suggested to Adonijah the plan of marriage with Abishag*).

29 And it was told king Solomon that Joab was fled unto the Tabernacle of the LORD; and, behold, he is by the Altar. Then Solomon sent Benaiah the son of Jehoiada, saying, Go, fall upon him.

30 And Benaiah came to the Tabernacle of the LORD, and said unto him, Thus saith the king, Come forth. And he said, No; but I will die here. And Benaiah brought the king word again, saying, Thus said Joab, and thus he answered me. (*Joab had had the privilege of being associated, and very closely, with the greatest man of God in the world of that day, David. In a sense, he was "in" the Church, but not "of" the Church, exactly as are millions presently. He knew of David's God, but he did not really know David's God. He knew the way, but he didn't want to walk in the way. So, at the last moment, he seems to have put his hope in the Altar, i.e., the Cross. Whether it was superstition or sincerity, the Judgment Day alone will tell. I pray that it was sincerity.*)

31 And the king said unto him, Do as he has said, and fall upon him, and bury him, that you may take away the innocent blood, which Joab shed, from me, and from the house of my father (*Solomon evidently believed that the guilt of blood regarding Joab was upon him and his house so long as Abner's and Amasa's blood remained unavenged; the truth is, Jewish law imperatively demanded the death of Joab, and to spare him was to violate all law and to imperil the Throne and the people*).

32 And the LORD shall return his blood upon his own head, who fell upon two men more righteous and better than he, and slew them with the sword, my father David not knowing thereof, to wit, Abner the son of Ner, captain of the host of Israel, and Amasa the son of Jether, captain of the host of Judah

(Solomon thinks of the unjust suspicions which these crimes cast upon his father).

33 Their blood shall therefore return upon the head of Joab, and upon the head of his seed for ever: but upon David, and upon his seed, and upon his house, and upon his Throne, shall there be peace for ever from the LORD *(had there been true Repentance on the part of Joab those years earlier, Mercy would have been shown to him, exactly as it had been shown to David regarding his murder of Uriah; however, there was no Repentance on the part of Joab, so the Law must take its course).*

34 So Benaiah the son of Jehoiada went up, and fell upon him, and killed him: and he was buried in his own house in the wilderness *(and so died Joab, not in battle fighting the enemies of the Lord, but as a traitor to his king and his Lord).*

35 And the king put Benaiah the son of Jehoiada in his room over the host: and Zadok the Priest did the king put in the room of Abiathar.

SHIMEI IS EXECUTED

36 And the king sent and called for Shimei, and said unto him, Build thee an house in Jerusalem, and dwell there, and go not forth thence any whither *(where he could be under surveillance and where his sinister influence with the men of Benjamin would be neutralized).*

37 For it shall be, that on the day you go out, and pass over the brook Kidron, you shall know for certain that you shall surely die: your blood shall be upon your own head *(Shimei could not say that he had not been sufficiently warned).*

38 And Shimei said unto the king, The saying is good: as my lord the king has said, so will your servant do. And Shimei dwelt in Jerusalem many days.

39 And it came to pass at the end of three years, that two of the servants of Shimei ran away unto Achish son of Maachah king of Gath. And they told Shimei, saying, Behold, your servants be in Gath.

40 And Shimei arose, and saddled his ass, and went to Gath to Achish to seek his servants: and Shimei went, and brought his servants from Gath *(he went to Gath with his eyes open, and nothing but a great provocation, such as mockery and defiance, will account for his going).*

41 And it was told Solomon that Shimei had gone from Jerusalem to Gath, and was come again *(evidently, Solomon had Shimei under surveillance).*

42 And the king sent and called for Shimei, and said unto him, Did I not make you to swear by the LORD, and protested unto you, saying, Know for a certain on the day you go out, and walk abroad any whither, that you shall surely die? and you said unto me, The word that I have heard is good.

43 Why then have you not kept the oath of the LORD, and the commandment that I have charged you with? *(It would seem, concerning what had happened to Adonijah and Joab, that Shimei should have reckoned that Solomon meant what he said; but evidently his arrogance caused him to think otherwise.)*

44 The king said moreover to Shimei, You knew all the wickedness which your heart is privy to, that you did to David my father: therefore the LORD shall return your wickedness upon your own head *(according to these words, Solomon is carrying out the Word of the Lord in pronouncing death upon Shimei);*

45 And king Solomon shall be blessed, and the Throne of David shall be established before the LORD for ever *(it is inconceivable that Solomon could have spoken thus if he had been conscious either of sharp practice, spite, or cruelty; the words are those of one who is sure that he is doing God service — Spence).*

46 So the king commanded Benaiah the son of Jehoiada; which went out, and fell upon him, that he died. And the kingdom was established in the hand of Solomon. *(This Verse proclaims the approval by the Holy Spirit of Solomon's actions regarding "Joab, Abiathar, and Shimei," for it says, "And the kingdom was established in the hand of Solomon.")*

CHAPTER 3
(1014 B.C.)

SOLOMON MARRIES PHARAOH'S DAUGHTER

AND Solomon made affinity with Pharaoh king of Egypt *(even though this was not an "alliance," but rather a relationship, still, Solomon broke the Law of God, which forbade making alliances and intermarrying with foreign nations, lest they should lead the hearts of Israel away from Jehovah to other gods [Ex. 34:16; Deut. 7:3-4]; we do not find the Lord rebuking him in this Chapter, even though the Holy Spirit did record the event; nevertheless, it was unlawful;*

we find it referred to elsewhere as his folly [11:1-9]), **and took Pharaoh's daughter, and brought her into the city of David** (even though Solomon was not reprimanded now by the Lord, still, what he did was wrong; the worst thing that can happen to a Believer is for the Believer to succeed in his wrongdoing, even as Solomon did here; in such a case, success is taken for approval; but disobedience of the Word of God is never right, and will always ultimately lead to great trouble), **until he had made an end of building his own house, and the House of the LORD, and the wall of Jerusalem round about** (despite the great Work of God being done here, the Holy Spirit is, as well, showing us the seed of destruction that is being planted in its very midst, which was because of self-will on the part of Solomon; it is a warning to us not to do the same).

2 Only the people sacrificed in high places, because there was no house built unto the name of the LORD, until those days. (This seems to be more a statement of regret rather than censure. It introduces a contrast by the writer, seeming to say that this was a blight on the flourishing condition of the nation. The Law of God did not necessarily condemn a high place, but the wrong use of one for idolatry. All high places used for idolatry were to be destroyed [Deut. 12:2]. In effect, these high places, mentioned here by the Holy Spirit, although now used for the worship of God, would later lead to idolatry.)

SOLOMON ASKS FOR WISDOM

3 And Solomon loved the LORD, walking in the Statutes of David his father: only he sacrificed and burnt Incense in high places (the "high places" seemed to be an ignorance that God winked at, at least at this time).

4 And the king went to Gibeon to sacrifice there; for that was the great high place: a thousand Burnt Offerings did Solomon offer upon that Altar. (Gibeon was about 4 miles from Jerusalem. The Tabernacle Moses made was located here [II Chron. 1:3-4]. There was, as well, another Tabernacle in Jerusalem [3:15], which housed the Ark of the Covenant. So, Verses 2 and 4 suggest that there were, contrary to the Law, divided places of worship in Israel.

In all of this, we learn of the frailty of the human family and the glory of the Grace of God. The Holy Spirit is ever seeking to lead the individual into that which is totally God's Way. God starts with imperfect people and concludes with imperfect people. He looks for a yielding,

obedient heart.

To offer a thousand animals in sacrifice portrayed, at that time, that Solomon understood that the prosperity, strength, and veracity of Israel were all based on the shed Blood of the Lamb.)

5 In Gibeon the LORD appeared to Solomon in a dream by night: and God said, Ask what I shall give you. (The offering up of the sacrifices probably took several days and, at the end of their being offered, the Lord appeared to Solomon. So we might say that this which followed was based strictly upon the Cross of Christ.)

6 And Solomon said, You have showed unto Your servant David my father great mercy, according as he walked before You in Truth, and in righteousness, and in uprightness of heart with You; and You have kept for him this great kindness, that You have given him a son to sit on his Throne, as it is this day.

7 And now, O LORD my God, You have made Your servant king instead of David my father: and I am but a little child: I know not how to go out or come in (Solomon was about 20 years old at the time).

8 And Your servant is in the midst of Your people which You have chosen, a great people, who cannot be numbered nor counted for multitude.

9 Give therefore Your servant an understanding heart to judge Your people, that I may discern between good and bad: for who is able to judge this Your so great a people? (In effect, Solomon asks for wisdom!)

SOLOMON GETS WISDOM AND RICHES

10 And the speech pleased the LORD, that Solomon had asked this thing (some claim that he should have asked for this or that, etc., but the Scripture says that this for which Solomon asked "pleased the Lord"; if it pleased the Lord, it certainly should please us).

11 And God said unto him, Because you have asked this thing, and have not asked for yourself long life; neither have asked riches for yourself, nor have asked the life of your enemies (destruction of enemies in battle); **but have asked for yourself understanding to discern judgment;**

12 Behold, I have done according to your words: lo, I have given you a wise and an understanding heart; so that there was none like

you before you, neither after you shall any arise like unto you *(referring to the degree of wisdom given to Solomon by the Lord).*

13 And I have also given you that which you have not asked, both riches, and honour: so that there shall not be any among the kings like unto you all your days *(during the time of Solomon, Israel was the most powerful nation on the face of the Earth, and was that because of the Blessings of the Lord upon Solomon).*

14 And if you will walk in My ways, to keep My Statutes and My Commandments, as your father David did walk, then I will lengthen your days *(regrettably and sadly, Solomon did not do this, and died at 60 years old).*

15 And Solomon awoke; and, behold, it was a dream. And he came to Jerusalem, and stood before the Ark of the Covenant of the LORD, and offered up Burnt Offerings, and offered Peace Offerings, and made a feast to all his servants. *(This means there must have been another Brazen Altar at the Tabernacle in Jerusalem, as there was at Gibeon. If this was so, then it was not according to the Commandment of the Lord. It would not be rectified until some years later, when the Temple would be completed.)*

WISDOM

16 Then came there two women, who were harlots, unto the king, and stood before him *(I think the reason the Holy Spirit placed the account of two women who were harlots into the Sacred Text is to portray the fact that justice was equal for all in the reign of Solomon, typifying that that's the way it ought to be).*

17 And the one woman said, O my lord, I and this woman dwell in one house; and I was delivered of a child with her in the house.

18 And it came to pass the third day after that I was delivered, that this woman was delivered also: and we were together; there was no stranger with us in the house, save we two in the house.

19 And this woman's child died in the night; because she overlaid it.

20 And she arose at midnight, and took my son from beside me, while your handmaid slept, and laid it in her bosom, and laid her dead child in my bosom.

21 And when I rose in the morning to give my child suck, behold, it was dead: but when I had considered it in the morning, behold, it was not my son, which I did bear.

22 And the other woman said, No; but the living is my son, and the dead is your son. And this said, No; but the dead is your son, and the living is my son. Thus they spoke before the king.

23 Then said the king, The one says, This is my son who lives, and your son is the dead: and the other says, No; but your son is the dead, and my son is the living.

24 And the king said, Bring me a sword. And they brought a sword before the king *(I wonder what the thoughts were of the many who, no doubt, were present that day, when the king asked for a sword?).*

25 And the king said, Divide the living child in two, and give half to the one, and half to the other.

26 Then spoke the woman whose the living child was unto the king, for her bowels yearned upon her son, and she said, O my lord, give her the living child, and in no wise kill it. But the other said, Let it be neither mine nor thine, but divide it.

27 Then the king answered and said, Give her the living child, and in no wise slay it: she is the mother thereof.

28 And all Israel heard of the judgment which the king had judged; and they feared the king: for they saw that the Wisdom of God was in him, to do judgment.

CHAPTER 4
(1014 B.C.)
SOLOMON'S OFFICERS

SO king Solomon was king over all Israel. *(Verses 2-19 give his principal officers. It seems their appointment was made according to Solomon's great wisdom, which, in effect, was an appointment by the Holy Spirit. Had the "work of the flesh" of Chapter 2 prevailed concerning "Adonijah" and "Joab," with "Abiathar," tyrants would now have ruled Israel, making life utterly miserable for the whole kingdom.)*

2 And these were the princes which he had; Azariah the son of Zadok the Priest *(Zadok was the High Priest, with many other Priests under him),*

3 Elihoreph and Ahiah, the sons of Shisha, scribes; Jehoshaphat the son of Ahilud, the recorder *(Jehoshaphat held the same office under David, and is mentioned in all three lists [II Sam. 8:17; 20:25; I Chron. 18:15]).*

4 And Benaiah the son of Jehoiada was over the host: and Zadok and Abiathar were the Priests *(Abiathar is probably mentioned here*

simply because he had been High Priest along with Zadok for a short period of time when Solomon first came to power; there is no record that he was restored):

5 And Azariah the son of Nathan was over the officers: and Zabud the son of Nathan was principal officer, and the king's friend *(the "Nathan" mentioned here was probably David's son and, thereby, Solomon's half-brother; if, in fact, this is the same Nathan, then Mary, the Mother of our Lord, had her lineage to David through this Nathan):*

6 And Ahishar was over the household: and Adoniram the son of Abda was over the tribute.

7 And Solomon had twelve officers over all Israel, which provided victuals for the king and his household: each man his month in a year made provision.

8 And these are their names: The son of Hur, in Mount Ephraim:

9 The son of Dekar, in Makaz, and in Shaalbim, and Beth-shemesh, and Elon-beth-hanan.

10 The son of Hesed, in Aruboth; to him pertained Sochoh, and all the land of Hepher:

11 The son of Abinadab, in all the region of Dor; which had Taphath the daughter of Solomon to wife:

12 Baana the son of Ahilud; to him pertained Taanach and Megiddo, and all Beth-shean, which is by Zartanah beneath Jezreel, from Beth-shean to Abel-meholah, even unto the place that is beyond Jokneam:

13 The son of Geber, in Ramoth-gilead; to him pertained the towns of Jair the son of Manasseh, which are in Gilead; to him also pertained the region of Argob, which is in Bashan, threescore great cities with walls and brasen bars:

14 Ahinadab the son of Iddo had Mahanaim:

15 Ahimaaz was in Naphtali; he also took Basmath the daughter of Solomon to wife:

16 Baanah the son of Hushai was in Asher and in Aloth:

17 Jehoshaphat the son of Paruah, in Issachar:

18 Shimei the son of Elah, in Benjamin:

19 Geber the son of Uri was in the country of Gilead, in the country of Sihon king of the Amorites, and of Og king of Bashan; and he was the only officer which was in the land.

SOLOMON'S DAILY PROVISION

20 Judah and Israel were many, as the sand which is by the sea in multitude, eating and drinking, and making merry. *(All of this resulted from the one fact that Solomon, God's choice, was king.*

The destruction of the rebels and the enthronement of God's elect prince originated this universal contentment and prosperity. It is a forepicture of the happy day that awaits the Earth, when the rebels who now govern it and fill it with misery will be overthrown, and the Prince of Peace, the greater than Solomon [Mat 12:42], will take unto Himself His great Power and reign gloriously before His ancient People, Israel.

The present miseries that oppress the nations, which they vainly try to remove by repeated efforts, will have an end whenever the Messiah returns and takes the government of this world into His Mighty Hands — Williams.)

21 And Solomon reigned over all kingdoms from the river *(the Euphrates, which would have taken in about half of present day Iraq)* unto the land of the Philistines *(the Mediterranean shore was the western border of his realm)*, and unto the border of Egypt *(this was probably all the way to the Gulf of Suez, which included the entirety of the Sinai Peninsula; actually, David had conquered all of these territories, which included that promised by the Lord to Abraham [Gen. 15:18])*: they brought presents, and served Solomon all the days of his life *(likewise, the nations of the world will serve Christ during the coming Millennial Reign, of Whom Solomon was a Type).*

22 And Solomon's provision for one day was thirty measures of fine flour *(about 6 bushels)*, and threescore measures of meal *(about 12 bushels)*,

23 Ten fat oxen, and twenty oxen out of the pastures, and an hundred sheep, beside harts *(deer)*, and roebucks, and fallowdeer, and fatted fowl.

SOLOMON'S GREATNESS AND WISDOM

24 For he had dominion over all the region on this side the river, from Tiphsah even to Azzah, over all the kings on this side the river: and he had peace on all sides round about him. *(As Solomon then had dominion, Christ will have "dominion" over the entirety of the Earth during the coming Kingdom Age. Tyrants, rebels, and despots will have no place in this coming grand and glorious Kingdom; consequently, there will be peace. In fact, there can*

only be peace when the Prince of Peace returns!)

25 And Judah and Israel dwelt safely, every man under his vine and under his fig tree, from Dan even to Beer-sheba, all the days of Solomon. *(Once again, this pictures the peace and prosperity which will prevail in the Earth during the reign of the Messiah. Just as surely as it was with Solomon, who was a Type of Christ, as surely it will be under Christ, and even far, far greater. For a greater than Solomon is here.)*

26 And Solomon had forty thousand stalls of horses for his chariots, and twelve thousand horsemen. *(In the parallel Passage in Chronicles, the number is stated as four thousand. Four thousand agrees, and forty thousand does not, with the other numbers given here. Consequently, this must have been a mistake by a Scribe. The Hebrew language does not contain numbers, but rather uses letters for its numbers; and some of the letters are very nearly identical, making it easy to miscopy. At any rate, Solomon was a very rich man, in fact, the richest man on the face of the Earth of his day.)*

27 And those officers provided victual for king Solomon, and for all who came unto king Solomon's table, every man in his month: they lacked nothing *(unfortunately, at the present time, millions go to bed hungry; however, let it ever be said that according to the Word of God, when Jesus Christ returns, of every nation and every person on the face of the Earth, it will be said, "They lacked nothing.")*

28 Barley also and straw for the horses and dromedaries *(mules)* brought they unto the place where the officers were, every man according to his charge.

29 And God gave Solomon wisdom and understanding exceeding much, and largeness of heart, even as the sand that is on the sea shore *(these different words indicate the variety and scope of his talents, which were beyond compare; in fact, and as stated, there has never been one before or after like Solomon).*

30 And Solomon's wisdom excelled the wisdom of all the children of the east country, and all the wisdom of Egypt *(the learning of Egypt was of great repute in the Old World; Solomon exceeded that!).*

31 For he was wiser than all men; than Ethan the Ezrahite, and Heman, and Chalcol, and Darda, the sons of Mahol: and his fame was in all nations round about *(typical of the fame of Christ, which will spread over the entirety of the Earth, in the coming Kingdom Age [Isa. 66:19]).*

32 And he spoke three thousand proverbs:

and his songs were a thousand and five *(of his Proverbs, less than one-third are preserved in the Book of Proverbs; the rest are lost to us; of his songs, the only two remaining are Psalms 72 and 127; some think he may have also written Psalm 128).*

33 And he spoke of trees, from the cedar tree that is in Lebanon even unto the hyssop that springs out of the wall: he spoke also of beasts, and of fowl, and of creeping things, and of fishes *(this means that his knowledge was not only speculative, but scientific; in his acquaintance with natural history, he outshone the Egyptians; he dealt with the least productions of nature, as well the greatest).*

34 And there came of all people to hear the wisdom of Solomon, from all kings of the Earth, which had heard of his wisdom. *(Not only was Israel greatly blessed, but every nation that took advantage of Solomon's wisdom was blessed as well. The great questions were brought to Solomon, and the answers were forthcoming, resulting in tremendous prosperity for all.*

In the days of the coming Kingdom Age, when Jesus Christ rules and reigns in Jerusalem, "All kings of the Earth" will come to Him as well.)

CHAPTER 5
(1014 B.C.)
SOLOMON'S AGREEMENT
WITH HIRAM

AND Hiram king of Tyre sent his servants unto Solomon; for he had heard that they had anointed him king in the room of his father: for Hiram was ever a lover of David. *(The Hiram during the time of Solomon was the son of Hiram who reigned during the time of David. There was never a record of any type of conflict between Lebanon and Israel during the time of David or Solomon. The Hebrews were always at peace with the Phoenicians. They would now share in the great Blessing of God that would come upon Israel. "Hiram" is a type of the Gentile kings, presidents, and world leaders during the time of the Kingdom Age, who will ever be "lovers of the Lord Jesus Christ.")*

2 And Solomon sent to Hiram, saying *(according to Josephus, he wrote a letter, which, together with Hiram's reply, was preserved among the public archives of Tyre),*

3 You know how that David my father could not build an house unto the name of the LORD his God for the wars which were about him on every side, until the LORD put them

under the soles of his feet *(Hiram could not fail to know this, as his relations with David had been close and intimate — Spence)*.

4 But now the LORD my God has given me rest on every side, so that there is neither adversary nor evil occurrent. *(Since the Garden of Eden, planet Earth has suffered and labored under the curse of sin. Satan has ruled as a "prince of the powers of the air." The results have been chaos, murder, hatred, pain, starvation, and war. When Jesus comes back, there will be "rest on every side." As well, there will be "neither adversary nor evil occurrent." Sickness, suffering, starvation, and want will no longer be.)*

5 And, behold, I purpose to build an house unto the name of the LORD my God, as the LORD spoke unto David my father, saying, Your son, whom I will set upon your throne in your room, he shall build an house unto My name. *(Spence says, "He thus gives Hiram to understand that he is carrying out his father's plans, and plans which had the Divine sanction, and that this is no fanciful project of a young prince.")*

6 Now therefore command thou that they hew me cedar trees out of Lebanon; and my servants shall be with your servants: and unto you will I give hire for your servants according to all that you shall appoint *(whatever their wages should be)*: for you know that there is not among us any who can skill to hew timber like unto the Sidonians *(the Zidonians constructed their houses of wood, and were celebrated from the earliest times as skillful builders)*.

HIRAM REJOICES GREATLY

7 And it came to pass, when Hiram heard the words of Solomon, that he rejoiced greatly, and said, Blessed be the LORD this day, which has given unto David a wise son over this great people *(from the historic accounts, there seems to be no record that Hiram had accepted Jehovah, but that he did believe that Jehovah existed, and used language here that he knew would be acceptable to Solomon; it is a shame, as so many others, he came close, but not close enough!)*.

8 And Hiram sent to Solomon, saying, I have considered the things which you sent to me for: and I will do all your desire concerning timber of cedar, and concerning timber of fir *(it is said that the art of writing was communicated to the Greeks by the Phoenicians)*.

9 My servants shall bring them down from Lebanon unto the sea: and I will convey them by sea in floats unto the place that you shall appoint me, and will cause them to be discharged there, and you shall receive them: and you shall accomplish my desire, in giving food for my household *(this was no small task, conveying these huge timbers from Lebanon to Israel; this was at least one of the reasons that this Temple, which would be built by Solomon, would be the most expensive building ever constructed)*.

10 So Hiram gave Solomon cedar trees and fir trees according to all his desire.

11 And Solomon gave Hiram twenty thousand measures of wheat for food to his household *(about 4,000 bushels)*, and twenty measures of pure oil *(about 60 gallons)*: thus gave Solomon to Hiram year by year *(so long as the construction lasted, and it's possible that the agreement may have been for a still longer period)*.

12 And the LORD gave Solomon wisdom, as he promised him: and there was peace between Hiram and Solomon; and they two made a league together *(cut a covenant; Hiram did not have nearly the wisdom that Solomon had, but he had enough sense to look to the one who had wisdom)*.

13 And king Solomon raised a levy out of all Israel; and the levy was thirty thousand men.

14 And he sent them to Lebanon, ten thousand a month by courses: a month they were in Lebanon, and two months at home: and Adoniram was over the levy *(not a great hardship at all!)*.

15 And Solomon had three score and ten thousand *(70,000)* who bore burdens, and fourscore thousand *(80,000)* hewers in the mountains *(these 150,000 were not Israelites, but Canaanites; we learn from II Chron. 2:17-18 that "all the strangers who were in the land of Israel" were subjected to forced labor by Solomon; these occupied a very different position from that of the 30,000 Hebrews)*;

16 Beside the chief of Solomon's officers which were over the work, three thousand and three hundred, which ruled over the people who wrought in the work.

17 And the king commanded, and they brought great stones, costly stones, and hewed stones, to lay the foundation of the house *(it is said that the largest stone that has been found in modern Jerusalem, which may have come from the Temple of Solomon, is 38 feet, 9 inches long, and weighs a little bit over 100 tons; no doubt, there were many stones like this)*.

18 And Solomon's builders and Hiram's builders did hew them, and the stonesquarers: so they prepared timber and stones to build the house. (*Understanding that there were at least 183,300 laborers and overseers who worked on the Temple, and considering the length of time it took to build the Temple [7 years], along with the costly materials, one can understand the reason for the price tag in 2004 inflated dollars. To duplicate the Temple now, and to build it in the same manner as it was then built, using the same type of equipment, etc., the price tag would be over $1 trillion [$1,000,000,000,000].*)

CHAPTER 6
(1012 B.C.)
SOLOMON BUILDS THE TEMPLE

AND it came to pass in the four hundred and eightieth year after the Children of Israel were come out of the land of Egypt, in the fourth year of Solomon's reign over Israel, in the month Zif, which is the second month, that he began to build the House of the LORD. (*The 480 year number given in the Text has been debated for many centuries. It is virtually impossible to tally up the years of the Judges, considering that the possibility exists that some of these times overlapped. I personally feel that the number "480 years" is correct as stated, but with the following variations:*

This Verse illustrates the Promise that God not only forgives sin, but also forgets sin. Thus, the years of Israel's bondage to the nations are omitted. The lesson, at the same time, is taught that years or days spent in bondage to the world are forever lost. Thus, what appears to be a chronological error in the Sacred Text is found to be a designed Message of comfort and warning.

It is doubtful that the 480 years stated in the Text include the whole period of time between the Exodus and the fourth year of Solomon's reign. It really refers to the 480th year of the security of Israel as a nation. It does not include the 40 years of Sinai and the wandering in the wilderness, the period of the conquest of Canaan and division of the land [about 10 years], or the three years of confusion under Abimelech and the 111 years of servitude during the Judges.

It is believed that the entire period from the Exodus to the fourth year of Solomon was approximately 645 years. However, as stated, there is a possibility that some of the periods of the Judges overlapped with other periods, which could shorten the entirety of the time by a number of years.

But this we do know:
The beginning of the construction of the "House of the Lord," as designated here by the Holy Spirit, was extremely significant in the great Plan of God.)

2 And the house which king Solomon built for the LORD, the length thereof was three-score cubits (*counting 18 inches to the cubit, this would mean it was 90 feet long*), and the breadth thereof twenty cubits (*30 feet wide*), and the height thereof thirty cubits (*45 feet high*).

3 And the porch before the temple of the house, twenty cubits (*30 feet*) was the length thereof, according to the breadth of the house; and ten cubits (*15 feet*) was the breadth thereof before the house (*according to the chronology of Usshher, Solomon began building the Temple in 3000 B.C., in our month of May*).

4 And for the house he made windows of narrow lights.

5 And against the wall of the house he built chambers round about, against the walls of the house round about, both of the temple and of the oracle (*Holy of Holies*): and he made chambers round about (*the floors were divided by partitions into distinct compartments*):

6 The nethermost chamber was five cubits broad (*7 1/2 feet*), and the middle was six cubits broad (*9 feet*), and the third was seven cubits broad (*10 1/2 feet*): for without in the wall of the house he made narrowed rests round about, that the beams should not be fastened in the walls of the house (*these measurements are those of the interior; the remarkable way in which this thing was built should be of note; the stories were shaped and prepared beforehand in the quarry, so that there was nothing to do on their arrival in the Temple area but to fit the stones to their place in the building*).

7 And the house, when it was in building, was built of stone made ready before it was brought thither: so that there was neither hammer nor axe nor any tool of iron heard in the house, while it was in building. (*The plans for this Building were totally of the Lord, and none of man. In fact, they were given to David, but he was not allowed to construct the edifice, that being the task of his son who succeeded him. As the Tabernacle, the Temple, in all of its Grace, symbolized Christ in His Atoning, Mediatorial, and Intercessory Work. Inasmuch as the Holy Spirit would be the One Who would occupy the Holy of Holies in this Building, it was to be constructed in absolute silence. For a structure*

of this nature, especially considering the huge stones, etc., this presents an astounding feat. This is one of the many reasons that the structure cost so much to build.)

8 The door for the middle chamber was in the right side of the house: and they went up with winding stairs into the middle chamber, and out of the middle into the third *(the third story)*.

9 So he built the house, and finished it; and covered the house with beams and boards of cedar.

10 And then he built chambers against all the house, five cubits *(7 1/2 feet)* high: and they rested on the house with timber of cedar.

11 And the word of the LORD came to Solomon, saying *(probably through the Prophet Nathan)*,

12 Concerning this house which you are in building, if you will walk in My Statutes, and execute My Judgments, and keep all My Commandments to walk in them; then will I perform My Word with you, which I spoke unto David your father *(while no man was able to keep the Law perfectly, and for any number of reasons, still, the idea was that every effort be made to do so. If the heart was after God, a desire to carry out His Will, and to do so at all cost, even though at times the Law was broken, a repentant heart would always automatically see an instant Restoration, with all the great Promises of God guaranteed to such an individual. David was that kind of man, and was ever held up as the example. He sinned at times, and did so grievously; however, he was always quick to repent. Sadly, we will find that Solomon drifted, and did so in a terrible way)*:

13 And I will dwell among the Children of Israel, and will not forsake My people Israel. *(God had previously pledged His Presence to the Tabernacle [Ex. 25:8; 29:45; Lev. 26:11]. The Temple, as well, was reared to be His dwelling-place [II Chron. 6:2]. He now assures the royal builder that He will occupy it.)*

14 So Solomon built the house, and finished it.

15 And he built the walls of the house within with boards of cedar, both the floor of the house, and the walls of the ceiling: and he covered them on the inside with wood, and covered the floor of the house with planks of fir.

16 And he built twenty cubits *(30 feet)* on the sides of the house, both the floor and the walls with boards of cedar: he even built them

for it within, even for the Oracle, even for the Most Holy Place *(this was the Holy of Holies, where the Ark of the Covenant was kept, and which was actually the dwelling-place of the Lord, Who dwelt between the Mercy Seat and the Cherubim)*.

17 And the house, that is, the Temple before it, was forty cubits long *(60 feet)*.

18 And the cedar of the house within was carved with knops and open flowers: all was cedar; there was no stone seen *(actually, the cedar wasn't seen either, because all of it was covered with gold)*.

19 And the Oracle he prepared in the house within, to set there the Ark of the Covenant of the LORD.

20 And the Oracle in the forepart was twenty cubits in length *(30 feet)*, and twenty cubits in breadth, and twenty cubits in the height thereof: and he overlaid it with pure gold; and so covered the Altar which was of cedar. *(This tells us that the "Holy of Holies" was 30 feet square and 30 feet high. This was the same width as the House. In II Chron., Chpt. 4, we also see that the great Brazen Altar was also 20 cubits square [30 feet]. The reason was that Atonement and Glory are one. Atonement is the theology of Heaven, and the entrance to God's Home is as wide as the Home itself. What a thrilling Revelation! In other words, Calvary is just as large as the House of God.)*

21 So Solomon overlaid the house within with pure gold: and he made a partition by the chains of gold before the oracle; and he overlaid it with gold. *(Gold typified Deity, meaning that the One Who occupied this House was God. As well, the One Whom the House symbolized, namely the Lord Jesus Christ, is also God!)*

22 And the whole house he overlaid with gold, until he had finished all the house: also the whole Altar that was by the Oracle he overlaid with gold.

23 And within the Oracle he made two Cherubims of olive tree, each ten cubits high *(15 feet high)*.

24 And five cubits *(7 1/2 feet)* was the one wing of the Cherub, and five cubits the other wing of the Cherub: from the uttermost part of the one wing unto the uttermost part of the other were ten cubits *(15 feet)*.

25 And the other Cherub was ten cubits *(15 feet)*: both the Cherubims were of one measure and one size *(these were in the Holy of Holies)*.

26 The height of the one Cherub was ten cubits *(15 feet)*, and so was it of the other Cherub.

27 And he set the Cherubims within the inner house *(the Holy of Holies)*: and they stretched forth the wings of the Cherubims, so that the wing of the one touched the one wall, and the wing of the other Cherub touched the other wall; and their wings touched one another in the midst of the house. *(Each Cherub had four wings, two stretching out behind which touched the back wall, and two stretching out in front which touched the wings of the other Cherub. So the wings of both Cherubs spanned the entirety of the Holy of Holies. Actually, this particular room, it is said, sat immediately above the rock where Abraham was to offer Isaac, and where presently the Dome of the Rock of the Muslims is built.)*

28 And he overlaid the Cherubims with gold.

29 And he carved all the walls of the house round about with carved figures of Cherubims and palm trees and open flowers, within and without. *(The "Cherubims" speak of the Holiness of God and, thereby, that all about Him must be Holy. The "palm trees" speak of a perfect climate, meaning that the elements will no longer be in revolt after the Second Coming of Christ. The "open flowers" speak of beauty, which will characterize the Kingdom Age, of which the Temple is a Type.*

Due to the fact that the Cherubims symbolize the Holiness of God, they likewise must symbolize Judgment. Their wings met over the blood-sprinkled Mercy Seat and reached, as stated, to either extremity of the Most Holy Place. God's Judgments have Calvary for their center, and are as wide as His Home.)

30 And the floors of the house he overlaid with gold, within and without.

31 And for the entering of the Oracle he made doors of olive tree: the lintel and side posts were a fifth part of the wall. *(Beneath the huge Cherubims, whose wings stretched from wall to wall, was placed the Ark of the Covenant with the Mercy Seat. The smaller Cherubim that Moses had made were attached to the Mercy Seat and made of the same mass of gold. The smaller Cherubims looked downward upon the sprinkled blood; the huge Cherubims, made of olive wood and covered with gold, looked outward. Whereas Moses' Tabernacle in the wilderness, before the erection of the Temple, was a Type of Calvary and Redemption, Solomon's Temple was a type*

of the Kingdom Age and of Righteousness.

God's Perfect Judgments will, in the Millennium, be enabled to look out from Calvary upon a Kingdom wherein shall dwell Righteousness. This is not now possible, for Righteousness retreated to Heaven when Christ went to the Father [Jn. 16:10].)

32 The two doors also were of olive tree; and he carved upon them carvings of Cherubims and palm trees and open flowers, and overlaid them with gold, and spread gold upon the Cherubims, and upon the palm trees.

33 So also made he for the door of the temple posts of olive tree, a fourth part of the wall.

34 And the two doors were of fir tree: the two leaves of the one door were folding, and the two leaves of the other door were folding.

35 And he carved thereon Cherubims and palm trees and open flowers: and covered them with gold fitted upon the carved work.

36 And he built the inner court with three rows of hewed stone, and a row of cedar beams.

37 In the fourth year was the foundation of the house of the LORD laid, in the month Zif *(our May)*:

38 And in the eleventh year, in the month Bul, which is the eighth month, was the house finished throughout all the parts thereof, and according to all the fashion of it. So was he seven years in building it. *(As stated, Solomon's Temple was a type of the coming Kingdom Age, when and where Righteousness will fill the Earth, because Christ is then present, with Satan and all of his minions of darkness locked away [Rev. 20:1-3].)*

CHAPTER 7
(1005-992 B.C.)
SOLOMON'S PALACE

BUT Solomon was building his own house thirteen years, and he finished all his house. *(As the Temple was built first, likewise, it will be built first in the coming Kingdom Age, and then the government buildings will be constructed. The Temple must be first, because the Worship of God, of which the Temple is a type, is the singular most important thing there is [Ezek., Chpts. 40-48].)*

2 He built also the house of the forest of Lebanon; the length thereof was an hundred cubits *(150 feet)*, and the breadth thereof fifty cubits *(75 feet)*, and the height thereof thirty cubits *(45 feet)*, upon four rows of cedar pillars,

with cedar beams upon the pillars.

3 And it was covered with cedar above upon the beams, that lay on forty five pillars, fifteen in a row.

4 And there were windows in three rows, and light was against light in three ranks.

5 And all the doors and posts were square, with the windows: and light was against light in three ranks.

6 And he made a porch of pillars; the length thereof was fifty cubits (*75 feet*), and the breadth thereof thirty cubits (*45 feet*): and the porch was before them: and the other pillars and the thick beam were before them (*this was, no doubt, a covered colonnade; it had a roof but no sides; in fact, the pillars were its only walls*).

7 Then he made a porch for the throne where he might judge, even the porch of judgment: and it was covered with cedar from one side of the floor to the other.

8 And his house where he dwelt had another court within the porch, which was of the like work. Solomon made also an house for Pharaoh's daughter, whom he had taken to wife, like unto this porch (*this would seem to have been the private residence of the queen, not the harem where all the wives and concubines were gathered*).

9 All these were of costly stones, according to the measures of hewed stones, sawed with saws, within and without, even from the foundation unto the coping, and so on the outside toward the great court.

10 And the foundation was of costly stones, even great stones, stones of ten cubits (*15 feet*), and stones of eight cubits (*12 feet; the foundations of the palaces, consequently, were much less than those of the Temple platform, with some of those stones measuring some 24 feet*).

11 And above were costly stones, after the measures of hewed stones, and cedars.

12 And the great court round about was with three rows of hewed stones, and a row of cedar beams, both for the inner court of the House of the LORD, and for the porch of the house.

HIRAM OF TYRE

13 And king Solomon sent and fetched Hiram out of Tyre (*even though this man bore the same name, this Hiram was not the king of Tyre; he was a metalworker, and had charge of all the castings of pillars, the Brazen Sea, and many other things used in the Temple furnishings*).

14 He was a widow's son of the Tribe of Naphtali, and his father was a man of Tyre, a worker in brass (*in a sense, Hiram, as addressed here, is a Type of the Holy Spirit; as well, the brass [copper] is a type of humanity; it can be shined to a high gloss, but, at the same time, it can tarnish very easily*): and he was filled with wisdom, and understanding, and cunning to work all works in brass (*typical of the Holy Spirit*). And he came to king Solomon, and wrought all his work (*the Holy Spirit is attempting to make the Child of God what the Lord Jesus wants, not necessarily what we want*).

15 For he cast two pillars of brass, of eighteen cubits high apiece (*27 feet*): and a line of twelve cubits (*18 feet*) did compass either of them about (*in a sense, these pillars are types of the Child of God; Jesus said, "Him who overcomes will I make a pillar in the Temple of My God" [Rev. 3:12]; as the Temple was a Type of Christ, and the pillars a type of the Child of God, Jesus no doubt had these pillars in mind when He made the statement concerning the overcoming Christian*).

16 And he made two chapiters of molten brass, to set upon the tops of the pillars: the height of the one chapiter was five cubits (*7 1/2 feet*), and the height of the other chapiter was five cubits:

17 And nets of checker work, and wreaths of chain work, for the chapiters which were upon the top of the pillars; seven for the one chapiter, and seven for the other chapiter (*the "chain work" represents the umbilical cord, so to speak, between Christ and the Believer*).

18 And he made the pillars, and two rows round about upon the one network, to cover the chapiters that were upon the top, with pomegranates (*a type of the Fruit of the Spirit*): and so did he for the other chapiter.

19 And the chapiters that were upon the top of the pillars were of lily work (*typifies purity*) in the porch, four cubits (*6 feet*).

20 And the chapiters upon the two pillars had pomegranates also above, over against the belly which was by the network: and the pomegranates were two hundred in rows round about upon the other chapiter.

21 And he set up the pillars in the porch of the Temple: and he set up the right pillar, and called the name thereof Jachin (*the name means "he shall establish"*): and he set up the left pillar, and called the name thereof Boaz (*means "in it is strength"*).

22 And upon the top of the pillars was lily

work: so was the work of the pillars finished. *(The reason this much description is given of the pillars is because, and as stated, they typify the Child of God in relationship to Christ. The pillars sat in front of the Temple, but actually they did not hold up anything. They stood alone facing the east. When the sun would come up each morning over Mount Olivet, its first rays would strike the highly polished pillars, which was a sight to behold.*

Pillars normally serve as a support; however, these are for ornamentation only. The idea is this:

The Lord really doesn't need us. In a sense, we are ornamentation; however, through His Love and Grace, He gives us the most prominent position in His Kingdom. But we must remember, the reflection of our glory, of which these pillars were types, is strictly from Christ. It is none of us and all of Him.)

SACRED VESSELS

23 And he made a molten sea *(the Brazen Laver)*, ten cubits *(15 feet)* from the one brim to the other: it was found all about, and his height was five cubits *(7 1/2 feet)*: and a line of thirty cubits *(45 feet)* did compass it round about.

24 And under the brim of it round about there were knops compassing it, ten in a cubit, compassing the sea round about: the knops were cast in two rows, when it was cast.

25 It stood upon twelve oxen, three looking toward the north, and three looking toward the west, and three looking toward the south, and three looking toward the east: and the sea was set above upon them, and all their hinder parts were inward *(the "twelve oxen" symbolized the Government of God, which will encompass the Earth during the time of the Kingdom Age; that Government will be the strongest the world has ever known, hence typified by the "oxen"; as well, it will be the same all over the world, hence all four points of the compass being named)*.

26 And it was an hand breadth thick, and the brim thereof was wrought like the brim of a cup, with flowers of lilies *(symbolizing the fact that this Government of God will be pure, the only pure Government that has ever existed)*: it contained two thousand baths.

27 And he made ten bases of brass; four cubits *(6 feet)* was the length of one base, and four cubits the breadth thereof, and three cubits *(4 1/2 feet)* the height of it.

28 And the work of the bases was on this manner: they had borders, and the borders were between the ledges:

29 And on the borders that were between the ledges were lions, oxen, and Cherubims: and upon the ledges there was a base above: and beneath the lions and oxen were certain additions made of thin work.

30 And every base had four brasen wheels, and plates of brass: and the four corners thereof had undersetters: under the laver were undersetters molten, at the side of every addition.

31 And the mouth of it within the chapiter and above was a cubit: but the mouth thereof was round after the work of the base, a cubit and an half: and also upon the mouth of it were gravings with their borders, four square, not round.

32 And under the borders were four wheels; and the axletrees of the wheels were joined to the base: and the height of a wheel was a cubit and half a cubit *(it must be remembered, the Lord designed all of this in totality; none of it, not even the tiniest amount, was the work of a human being; it was all of God)*.

33 And the work of the wheels was like the work of a chariot wheel: their axletrees, and their naves, and their felloes, and their spokes, were all molten.

34 And there were four undersetters to the four corners of one base: and the undersetters were of the very base itself.

35 And in the top of the base was there a round compass of half a cubit high: and on the top of the base the ledges thereof and the borders thereof were of the same.

36 For on the plates of the ledges thereof, and on the borders thereof, he graved Cherubims, lions, and palm trees, according to the proportion of every one, and additions round about.

37 After this manner he made the ten bases: all of them had one casting, one measure, and one size.

38 Then made he ten lavers of brass: one laver contained forty baths: and every laver was four cubits: and upon every one of the ten bases one laver.

39 And he put five bases on the right side of the house, and five on the left side of the house: and he set the sea on the right side of the house eastward over against the south. *(The entirety of this huge apparatus weighed 25 to 30 tons. It would have held well over 15,000 gallons of water,*

and, with the water, would have weighed over 100 tons. There were ten small lavers that were supposed to contain roughly 300 gallons of water each, with these lavers weighing about 2 tons each. Jewish writers say that the water was changed daily, so as to always be pure for use in the ceremonial worship.

At the front of the Tabernacle in the wilderness there was but one laver; in the Temple of Solomon there were eleven. These magnificent vessels of polished brass, highly ornamented, foreshadowed the purity, the glory, the grace, the sufficiency, the perfection, and the power of the government which Immanuel will establish in the future Millennial Earth.

In this Chapter, the Holy Spirit designedly omits any mention of the great Brazen Altar, for here attention is drawn to the King Himself, and not to the subject of access to Him!)

HIRAM

40 And Hiram made the lavers, and the shovels, and the basons. So Hiram made an end of doing all the work that he made king Solomon for the house of the LORD:

41 The two pillars, and the two bowls of the chapiters that were on the top of the two pillars; and the two networks, to cover the two bowls of the chapiters which were upon the top of the pillars;

42 And four hundred pomegranates for the two networks, even two rows of pomegranates for one network, to cover the two bowls of the chapiters that were upon the pillars;

43 And the ten bases, and ten lavers on the bases;

44 And one sea, and twelve oxen under the sea;

45 And the pots, and the shovels, and the basons: and all these vessels, which Hiram made to king Solomon for the house of the LORD, were of bright brass (copper).

THE CASTING OF THE VESSELS

46 In the plain of Jordan did the king cast them, in the clay ground between Succoth and Zarthan. (All of these brass fixtures had consisted of ornamentation in heathen temples, etc., which David had taken as spoils after particular battles. They are types of you and me being taken out of the world by our Heavenly David. All of these vessels were then cast into a furnace and melted, typifying the fact that all the old identity of the new Believer which he had when he was in the world must be totally lost. It can only be melted down in the furnace of affliction. It is then cast into a mold and made into vessels in the service of the Lord, all typifying the consecration and making of the Believer by the Holy Spirit.).

47 And Solomon left all the vessels unweighed, because they were exceeding many: neither was the weight of the brass found out. (The spiritual meaning has to do with what we were before conversion. Ever how so great we thought we were, the Holy Spirit tells us here that, in the Eyes of God, all we were didn't matter. It is rather what He will make of us.)

FURNISHINGS OF GOLD IN THE TEMPLE

48 And Solomon made all the vessels that pertained unto the House of the LORD: the Altar of gold (the Altar of Incense), and the table of gold, whereupon the shewbread was,

49 And the candlesticks (Lampstands) of pure gold, five on the right side, and five on the left, before the Oracle (Holy of Holies), with the flowers, and the lamps, and the tongs of gold (there was only one golden Lampstand in the Tabernacle, but here there are ten, five on each side; as well, there were ten tables of shewbread, five on each side [II Chron. 4:8]; all of these, including the Altar of Incense, were in the Holy Place, which was immediately in front of the Holy of Holies; in fact, as it regards the main structure of the Temple, there were only two rooms, the Holy Place and the Holy of Holies),

50 And the bowls, and the snuffers, and the basons, and the spoons, and the censers of pure gold; and the hinges of gold, both for the doors of the inner house, the Most Holy Place, and for the doors of the house, to wit, of the Temple.

51 So was ended all the work that king Solomon made for the House of the LORD. And Solomon brought in the things which David his father had dedicated; even the silver, and the gold, and the vessels, did he put among the treasures of the House of the LORD. (It seems that all the precious metal that David had prepared was not absorbed in the construction of the Temple. There would seem to have been a considerable overplus, which was stored in the Temple treasury.)

CHAPTER 8
(1004 B.C.)
BRINGING THE ARK
INTO THE TEMPLE

THEN Solomon assembled the Elders of Israel, and all the heads of the Tribes, the chief of the fathers of the Children of Israel, unto king Solomon in Jerusalem, that they might bring up the Ark of the Covenant of the LORD out of the city of David, which is Zion. *(The Eighth Chapter portrays the dedication of the Temple, and also prefigures the origination of worship in the coming Kingdom Age. Approximately a year would lapse between the completion of the Temple and its dedication. This great event would occur in the Year of Jubilee, during the Feast of Tabernacles, and in connection with the Great Day of Atonement. The Feast of Trumpets, which was a type in Jewish history of the Rapture of the Church, would be extended to last for some seven days. This would be followed by the Great Day of Atonement, which prefigures the cleansing of Israel at the beginning of the Kingdom Age. Then following the Great Day of Atonement was the Feast of Tabernacles, which, within itself, symbolizes the Kingdom Age. These three great Jewish Feast days have not yet been fulfilled in type. They will be fulfilled when the great Millennial Temple is built, as is recorded in Ezekiel, Chapters 40-48, of which Solomon's Temple was a type. All of this took place in the month of October.*

For many years [over 100], the Ark of the Covenant and the Tabernacle had been separated. The Tabernacle was now at Gibeon with the other of its holy vessels, while the Ark of the Covenant was elsewhere in Jerusalem.)

2 And all the men of Israel assembled themselves unto king Solomon at the feast in the month Ethanim, which is the seventh month *(October).*

3 And all the Elders of Israel came, and the Priests took up the Ark *(the Priests alone were set apart to carry the Ark [Deut. 10:8]; Solomon, therefore, did not make the mistake David had made by seeking to bring it to Jerusalem on a cart).*

4 And they brought up the Ark of the LORD, and the Tabernacle of the congregation, and all the holy vessels that were in the Tabernacle, even those did the Priests and the Levites bring up *(as far as we know, none of these vessels, with the exception of the Ark of the Covenant, were used; they were simply preserved as treasures of the past, and placed in the treasury of side-chambers).*

5 And king Solomon, and all the congregation of Israel, that were assembled unto him, were with him before the Ark, sacrificing sheep and oxen, that could not be told nor numbered for multitude *(the sacrifice of all of these animals proclaims the fact that, despite the gold and glamour of the great Temple, the most expensive structure ever built, still, Calvary was the foundation for everything, of which all of these sacrifices were Types; the Cross has always been the Foundation for everything).*

6 And the Priests brought in the Ark of the Covenant of the LORD unto his place, into the Oracle of the house, to the Most Holy Place, even under the wings of the Cherubims *(these were the two huge Cherubims that were made of olive wood and overlaid with gold; their wingspan spread from one wall to the other wall; the two wings covering the Ark were the inner wings of the Cherubim that touched each other in the center of the room; each Cherubim had two sets of wings, with the outside wings reaching to the back wall, and the front set of wings reaching forward, touching the wings of the opposite Cherubim; the wingspread of each was about 15 feet; the Ark rested under all of this).*

7 For the Cherubims spread forth their two wings over the place of the Ark, and the Cherubims covered the Ark and the staves thereof above *(the Ark of the Covenant rested in complete darkness, under the outstretched wings of the Cherubims; God dwelt here between the Cherubims and the Mercy Seat, which, in effect, was the lid of the Ark).*

8 And they drew out the staves, that the ends of the staves were seen out in the Holy Place before the Oracle, and they were not seen without: and there they are unto this day *(the two staves, which went into the rings on either side of the Ark, were partially taken out, so that the ends could be seen from the Holy Place, which was the room immediately in front of the Holy of Holies, but not from the porch outside the Holy Place; this way, the Ark never needed to be handled, as the staves could easily be put back into the rings without even touching the Ark; it seems that it was unlawful to take them wholly out of the rings; pulling the staves out so the ends could be seen indicated the Ark had found its resting place in the Temple, and was not to be carried anymore; it had a permanent house, not a tent, as before).*

9 There was nothing in the Ark save the

two tables of stone *(the Ten Commandments)*, which Moses put there at Horeb *(over 500 years before)*, when the LORD made a Covenant with the Children of Israel, when they came out of the land of Egypt. *(In Hebrews 9:4, Paul mentioned the golden pot of Manna and Aaron's rod being in the Ark. He was speaking of the Ark while in the Tabernacle instead of the Temple. It is not known when these two things were removed; it was either by the Philistines when they had the Ark, or when the events of I Sam., Chpts. 5 and 6, took place. At any rate, whatever did happen, God did not allow the "two tables of stone" containing the Ten Commandments to be taken. There was a reason for this.*

"Aaron's rod" and the "pot of Manna" were Types of Christ, which in type would not be necessary with the advent of Christ Himself; however, the "Ten Commandments" were a Type of the Word of God, which endures forever. For the Law of God was hidden in the Messiah's Heart [Ps. 119:11], as it was hidden in the Ark. The Law will be the basis and rule of Righteousness which will govern the Millennium in the coming Kingdom Age.)

10 And it came to pass, when the Priests were come out of the Holy Place, that the cloud filled the House of the LORD *(the "cloud" represented the Glory of God and, thereby, signified the Presence of God)*,

11 So that the Priests could not stand to minister because of the cloud: for the Glory of the LORD had filled the House of the LORD. *(It simply means that the Power of God was so strong that the knees of the Priests buckled. The "Glory" is the secret of the Church, without which the Church is nothing more than a human institution; however, with this, "the cloud," the Church is a living organism, different than anything on the face of the Earth. Regrettably, the modern Church knows precious little about the Glory of God.)*

SOLOMON'S MESSAGE

12 Then spoke Solomon, The LORD said that He would dwell in the thick darkness *(is probably referring to Ex. 19:9 and 20:21)*.

13 I have surely built You an house to dwell in, a settled place for You to abide in for ever *(the Temple was more than anything a shrine for the Ark, between the Cherubims of the Mercy Seat [where God dwelt]; due to the Cross, He now abides within the heart and life of the Believer [I Cor. 3:16])*.

14 And the king turned his face about, and blessed all the congregation of Israel: (and all the congregation of Israel stood;)

15 And he said, Blessed be the LORD God of Israel, which spoke with His mouth unto David my father, and has with His hand fulfilled it, saying,

16 Since the day that I brought forth My people Israel out of Egypt, I chose no city out of all the Tribes of Israel to build an house, that My name might be therein; but I chose David to be over My people Israel *(Satan would fight this choice, as he ever fights all of God's choices)*.

17 And it was in the heart of David my father to build an house for the Name of the LORD God of Israel.

18 And the LORD said unto David my father, Whereas it was in your heart to build an house unto My name, you did well that it was in your heart.

19 Nevertheless you shall not build the house; but your son who shall come forth out of your loins, he shall build the house unto My Name *(Solomon did not mention here the reason for this [II Sam. 7:11-12])*.

20 And the LORD has performed His Word that He spoke, and I am risen up in the room of David my father, and sit on the Throne of Israel, as the LORD promised, and have built an house for the Name of the LORD God of Israel.

21 And I have set there a place for the Ark, wherein is the Covenant of the LORD, which He made with our fathers, when He brought them out of the land of Egypt.

SOLOMON'S PRAYER

22 And Solomon stood before the Altar of the LORD in the presence of all the congregation of Israel, and spread forth his hands toward Heaven *(actually Solomon was close by the Brazen Altar of Sacrifice, on a platform about 4 1/2 feet high; all these rites took place in the open air)*:

23 And he said, LORD God of Israel, there is no God like you, in Heaven above, or on Earth beneath, Who keeps Covenant and mercy with Your servants who walk before You with all their heart *(the meaning is: the God of Israel stands Alone, and Alone is God)*:

24 Who has kept with Your servant David my father that You promised him: You spoke also with Your mouth, and have fulfilled it

with Your hand, as it is this day *(Solomon sees in this a special pledge of God's Faithfulness and Truth)*.

25 Therefore now, LORD God of Israel, keep with Your servant David my father that You promised him, saying, There shall not fail you a man in My sight to sit on the Throne of Israel; so that your children take heed to their way, that they walk before Me as you have walked before Me *(God keeping His Promise was contingent on their keeping His Commandments)*.

26 And now, O God of Israel, let Your Word, I pray You, be verified, which You spoke unto Your servant David my father.

27 But will God indeed dwell on the Earth? behold, the Heaven and Heaven of heavens cannot contain You; how much less this house that I have built? *(Solomon never denies for a moment that the Temple was a real habitation of Jehovah, or that a real Presence was manifested there. He only denies that the Deity can be contained in earthly Temples. He had no unworthy ideas, such as were prevalent in that age, of God as a local deity, limited to space. His words clearly prove his grasp of the Omnipresence and Infinity of God.)*

28 Yet have You respect unto the prayer of Your servant, and to his supplication, O LORD my God, to hearken unto the cry and to the prayer, which Your servant prays before You to day:

29 That Your eyes may be open toward this house night and day, even toward the place of which You have said, My name shall be there: that You may hearken unto the prayer which Your servant shall make toward this place *(now that God has revealed His Presence in the Temple, the Jew, wherever he might be, would and, as a matter of fact, did, pray toward it [Dan. 6:10; Ps. 5:7; Jonah 2:4])*.

30 And hearken Thou to the supplication of Your servant, and of Your people Israel, when they shall pray toward this place: and hear Thou in Heaven Your dwelling place: and when You hear, forgive.

31 If any man trespass against his neighbour, and an oath be laid upon him to cause him to swear, and the oath come before Your Altar in this house *(the Altar of Sacrifice is meant; in fact, every prayer to the Lord must come via Calvary; all of our worship must go through Calvary; all of our position in Christ must be at Calvary)*:

32 Then hear Thou in Heaven, and do, and judge Your servants, condemning the wicked, to bring his way upon his head; and justifying the righteous, to give him according to his righteousness.

33 When Your people Israel be smitten down before the enemy, because they have sinned against You, and shall turn again to You, and confess Your Name, and pray, and make supplication unto You in this house:

34 Then hear Thou in Heaven, and forgive the sin of Your people Israel, and bring them again unto the land which You gave unto their fathers.

35 When Heaven is shut up, and there is no rain, because they have sinned against You; if they pray toward this place, and confess Your Name, and turn from their sin, when You afflict them:

36 Then hear Thou in Heaven and forgive the sin of Your servants, and of Your people Israel, that You teach them the good way wherein they should walk, and give rain upon Your land, which You have given to Your people for an inheritance *(forgive, because they have learned the lesson Your discipline of drought was meant to teach; the chastisement has fulfilled its purpose)*.

37 If there be in the land famine, if there be pestilence, blasting, mildew, locust, or if there be caterpiller; if their enemy besiege them in the land of their cities; whatsoever plague, whatsoever sickness there be;

38 What prayer and supplication soever be made by any man, or by all Your people Israel, which shall know every man the plague of his own heart, and spread forth his hands toward this house:

39 Then hear Thou in Heaven Your dwelling place, and forgive, and do, and give to every man according to his ways, whose heart You know; (for You, even You only, know the hearts of all the children of men;)

40 That they may fear You all the days that they live in the land which You gave unto our fathers *(Solomon anticipates that a Godly fear will be the result of Forgiveness and Restoration)*.

41 Moreover concerning a stranger *(Gentile)*, who is not of Your people Israel, but comes out of a far country for Your Name's sake;

42 (For they shall hear of Your great Name, and of Your strong hand, and of Your stretched out arm;) when he shall come and pray toward this house *(Solomon is continuing to speak of Gentiles)*;

43 Hear Thou in Heaven Your dwelling place,

and do according to all that the stranger calls to You for: that all people of the Earth may know Your Name, to fear You, as do Your people Israel: and that they may know that this house, which I have built, is called by Your Name.

44 If Your people go out to battle against their enemy, whithersoever You shall send them, and shall pray unto the LORD toward the city which You have chosen *(Jerusalem)*, and toward the house *(the Temple)* that I have built for Your Name *(these words clearly imply that the war, whether defensive or offensive [for the chastisement of other nations], is one which had God's sanction and, indeed, was waged by His appointment; they have gone God's Way, they may, therefore, look the way of God's House for help; executing God's commission, they might justly expect His Blessing)*:

45 Then hear Thou in Heaven their prayer and their supplication, and maintain their cause.

46 If they sin against You, (for there is no man who sins not *[the question is not "if man sins"; the question is "when man sins"; even for the best of us, whoever that might be, were it not for the constant intercession of Christ, we wouldn't last a day]*,) and you be angry with them, and deliver them to the enemy *(because they have sinned)*, so that they carry them away captives unto the land of the enemy, far or near;

47 Yet if they shall bethink themselves in the land where they were carried captives, and repent, and make supplication unto You in the land of them who carried them captives, saying, We have sinned, and have done perversely, we have committed wickedness *(that which the Lord demands [I Jn. 1:9])*;

48 And so return unto You with all their heart, and with all their soul, in the land of their enemies, which led them away captive, and pray unto You toward their land, which You gave unto their fathers, the city which You have chosen, and the house which I have built for Your Name *(under the New Covenant, we do not pray toward Jerusalem, because the Lord no longer dwells in a building made by hands, but rather within the heart and life of each respective Believer [Jn. 14:16-17]; we now pray directly to the Father in Heaven [Mat. 6:9-13])*:

49 Then hear Thou their prayer and their supplication in Heaven Your dwelling place, and maintain their cause *(even though God is everywhere, still, His "dwelling-place" is Heaven;*

in fact, God the Father is in Heaven, while God the Holy Spirit would occupy the Temple, residing between the Mercy Seat and the Cherubim, functioning on the premise of what God the Son would do at Calvary, typified by the Sacrifices; and yet there is only One God, but manifested in Three Persons),

50 And forgive Your people who have sinned against You, and all their transgressions wherein they have transgressed against You, and give them compassion before them who carried them captive, that they may have compassion on them *(this Verse shouts "forgiveness" and "compassion," which are the hallmarks of the great Grace of God)*:

51 For they be Your people, and Your inheritance, which You brought forth out of Egypt, from the midst of the furnace of iron *(only the Lord can deliver; so to have His Deliverance, we must function according to His Directions, which, in reality, is Faith in Christ and what He did for us at the Cross, which then gives us the help of the Holy Spirit [Ex. 12:13; Rom. 6:3-14; 8:1-2, 11])*:

52 That Your eyes may be open unto the supplication of Your servant, and unto the supplication of Your people Israel, to hearken unto them in all that they call for unto You.

53 For You did separate them from among all the people of the Earth, to be Your inheritance, as You spoke by the hand of Moses Your servant, when You brought our fathers out of Egypt, O LORD God *(there is a constant recurrence throughout the Old Testament to Israel's great deliverance from Egypt; and with good reason, for it was the real birthday of the nation, and was also a pledge of future health and favor)*.

SOLOMON BLESSED GOD

54 And it was so, that when Solomon had made an end of praying all this prayer and supplication unto the LORD, he arose from before the Altar of the LORD *(the huge Brazen Altar situated immediately in front of the Temple)*, from kneeling on his knees with his hands spread up to Heaven.

55 And he stood, and blessed all the congregation of Israel with a loud voice, saying *(the words of blessing given here prove that Solomon did not assume Priestly functions in putting a blessing upon the people, which only the Priests, who were Types of Christ, could do [Num. 6:27]; he rather blessed the Lord, which all of us should*

do, and constantly),

56 Blessed be the LORD, Who has given rest unto His people Israel, according to all that He promised: there has not failed one word of all His good promise, which He promised by the hand of Moses His servant *(Lev. 26:3-13; Deut. 28:1-14; Josh. 21:44).*

57 The LORD our God be with us, as He was with our fathers: let Him not leave us, nor forsake us:

58 That He may incline our hearts unto Him, to walk in all His ways, and to keep His Commandments, and His Statutes, and His Judgments, which He commanded our fathers *(these were the conditions on which God's Blessings were guaranteed).*

59 And let these my words, wherewith I have made supplication before the LORD, be near unto the LORD our God day and night, that He maintain the cause of His servant, and the cause of His people Israel at all times, as the matter shall require:

60 That all the people of the Earth may know that the LORD is God, and that there is none else *(the thoughts of Solomon now go not only to Israel, but to the entirety of the world; the House now dedicated, he prays that the Gentiles will come to its Light [Isa. 2:2-3]).*

61 Let your heart *(the hearts of the people of Israel)* therefore be perfect with the LORD our God, to walk in His Statutes, and to keep His Commandments, as at this day.

SOLOMON OFFERS UP SACRIFICES

62 And the king, and all Israel with him, offered Sacrifice before the LORD *(proclaiming the fact that Israel's safety, protection, blessing, and prosperity depended solely upon the shed Blood of the Lamb).*

63 And Solomon offered a Sacrifice of Peace Offerings, which he offered unto the LORD, two and twenty thousand oxen, and an hundred and twenty thousand sheep. So the king and all the Children of Israel dedicated the House of the LORD. *(The tremendous number of Sacrifices offered typified the great Sacrifice of Christ. But yet, even though all these sheep and oxen were offered, they still were insufficient to take away sin. They only covered sin until Christ would come [Heb. 10:4], Who would take sin away [Jn. 1:29].)*

64 The same day did the king hallow the middle of the Court that was before the House of the LORD: for there he offered Burnt Offerings, and Meat Offerings, and the fat of the Peace Offerings: because the Brasen Altar that was before the LORD was too little to receive the Burnt Offerings, and Meat Offerings, and the fat of the Peace Offerings. *(In fact, the great Altar was thirty feet wide and thirty feet long, actually the same size as the Holy of Holies, signifying that His Answer to sin, which is the Cross, is as great as His Throne, signified by the Holy of Holies. But yet, even the great Altar was too small to receive all the Offerings, so the entirety of the Court was used, at least for the slaughter. No doubt, this lasted for several days.)*

65 And at that time Solomon held a feast, and all Israel with him, a great congregation, from the entering in of Hamath unto the river of Egypt, before the LORD our God, seven days and seven days, even fourteen days. *(All the people were required to eat their portion of the "Peace Offerings," which signified that "Peace with God" had been restored, now that the proper Burnt Offerings had been sacrificed. The Burnt Offerings signified that the Lord would give His all, His Perfection, to the people. The Sin and Trespass Offerings signified that the people would give their sin and trespasses to the Lord.)*

66 On the eighth day he sent the people away *(on the eighth day of the second feast, which, together with the first feast, totaled fourteen days)*: and they blessed the king, and went unto their tents joyful and glad of heart for all the goodness that the LORD had done for David His servant, and for Israel His people. *(This typifies the coming Kingdom Age, when Christ will personally reign supreme from Jerusalem, and do so over the entirety of the world. Then there will be "joy and gladness of heart" for all people [Jer., Chpts. 30-31; Zech. 12:4-14; Chpts. 13-14].)*

CHAPTER 9

(992 B.C.)

GOD'S COVENANT WITH SOLOMON

AND it came to pass, when Solomon had finished the building of the House of the LORD, and the king's house, and all Solomon's desire which he was pleased to do,

2 That the LORD appeared to Solomon the second time *(approximately 20 years after the first appearance [Vs. 10])*, as He had appeared unto him at Gibeon *(appeared in a dream [3:5]).*

3 And the LORD said unto him, I have heard your prayer and your supplication, that

you have made before Me: I have hallowed this house, which you have built, to put My Name there for ever; and My eyes and My heart shall be there perpetually. *(In II Chron. 7:12, we read, "And have chosen this place to Myself for a house of sacrifice," proclaiming the fact that the Cross, so to speak, was the foundation of Israel's blessings and prosperity.)*

4 And if you will walk before Me, as David your father walked *(David was ever used as the example; self-righteousness would have great difficulty in accepting David as such, especially considering his great failures; however, only Pharisees or self-righteousness would have such difficulty; those who truly know themselves and truly know God and His Grace have no difficulty whatsoever)*, in integrity of heart, and in uprightness, to do according to all that I have commanded you, and will keep My Statutes and My Judgments:

5 Then I will establish the throne of your kingdom upon Israel for ever, as I promised to David your father, saying, There shall not fail you a man upon the Throne of Israel. *(The committal to Solomon and Israel was conditional upon obedience. This means that the path of safety pointed out by God to Solomon was obedience and attachment to the Bible.)*

6 But if you shall at all turn from following Me, you or your children, and will not keep My Commandments and My Statutes which I have set before you, but go and serve other gods, and worship them:

7 Then will I cut off Israel out of the land which I have given them; and this house, which I have hallowed for My Name, will I cast out of My sight; and Israel shall be a proverb and a byword among all people *(tragically and sadly, that's exactly what happened)*:

8 And at this house, which is high, every one who passes by it shall be astonished, and shall hiss; and they shall say, Why has the LORD done thus unto this land, and to this house? *(In effect, the Lord is telling Solomon that it doesn't matter how "big" or how "high" this house is, it will be pulled down. And when the world asks "Why?" the next Verse records the answer!*

9 And they shall answer, Because they forsook the LORD their God, Who brought forth their fathers out of the land of Egypt, and have taken hold upon other gods, and have worshipped them, and served them: therefore has the LORD brought upon them all this evil. *(The Lord delivered Israel out of Egypt by virtue*

of the slain lamb. And if Israel forsakes that way, they will be lost, which they were. Regrettably, the modern Church seems to be quickly following suit.)*

10 And it came to pass at the end of twenty years, when Solomon had built the two houses, the house of the LORD, and the king's house. *(In a sense, both houses are regarded as one house. If the house of Sacrifice, i.e., "the Cross," maintains its way, the other house, which symbolizes Government, the Government of God, will be correct, as well. When the Cross is ignored, or rejected, the government also goes awry.)*

11 (Now Hiram the king of Tyre had furnished Solomon with cedar trees and fir trees, and with gold, according to all his desire,) that then king Solomon gave Hiram twenty cities in the land of Galilee. *(Even though this area bordered the kingdom of Tyre, Solomon should not have done this. No part of Immanuel's land must be conveyed to a foreigner, that they may have dominion over the people of the Lord [Lev. 25:23; Deut. 17:15].)*

12 And Hiram came out from Tyre to see the cities which Solomon had given him; and they pleased him not.

13 And he said, What cities are these which you have given me, my brother? And he called them the land of Cabul unto this day. *("Cabul," in a sense, means "worthless." They were not at all worthless to the Lord, because Galilee would be the area where the Messiah, the Lord Jesus Christ, would make His Headquarters. This shows that Solomon did not realize their significance either. Not one part of our life or living as a Believer must be given over to Satan.)*

14 And Hiram sent to the king sixscore talents of gold *(equal to approximately $30 million in 2004 calculations)*.

15 And this is the reason of the levy which king Solomon raised; for to build the House of the LORD, and his own house, and Millo, and the wall of Jerusalem, and Hazor, and Megiddo, and Gezer.

16 For Pharaoh king of Egypt had gone up, and taken Gezer, and burnt it with fire, and slain the Canaanites who dwelt in the city, and given it for a present unto his daughter, Solomon's wife *(Gezer, nearly 600 years before, had been allotted to Ephraim [Josh. 16:3], and was designated as a Levitical city [Josh. 21:21]; but apparently, the Canaanite inhabitants had never been dispossessed, until Pharaoh dispossessed them)*.

17 And Solomon built Gezer, and Beth-horon the nether *(nearby Gezer)*,

18 And Baalath, and Tadmor in the wilderness, in the land,

19 And all the cities of store that Solomon had, and cities for his chariots, and cities for his horsemen, and that which Solomon desired to build in Jerusalem, and in Lebanon, and in all the land of his dominion.

20 And all the people who were left of the Amorites, Hittites, Perizzites, Hivites, and Jebusites, which were not of the Children of Israel,

21 Their children who were left after them in the land, whom the Children of Israel also were not able utterly to destroy, upon those did Solomon levy a tribute of bondservice unto this day.

22 But of the Children of Israel did Solomon make no bondmen: but they were men of war, and his servants, and his princes, and his captains, and rulers of his chariots, and his horsemen.

23 These were the chief of the officers who were over Solomon's work, five hundred and fifty, which bore rule over the people who wrought in the work.

24 But Pharaoh's daughter came up out of the city of David unto her house which Solomon had built for her: then did he build Millo. *(The daughter of Pharaoh had dwelt in David's palace on Mount Zion, but Solomon was constrained to relieve her, because he looked upon all the precincts now as consecrated [II Chron. 8:11].)*

25 And three times in a year did Solomon offer Burnt Offerings and Peace Offerings upon the Altar *(the great Brazen Altar, which sat in front of the Temple)* which he built unto the LORD, and he burnt Incense upon the Altar that was before the LORD *(situated in the Holy Place, immediately before the Ark of the Covenant; in reality, Solomon did not do these things, but saw to it that the Priests, who alone could do such, officiated accordingly)*. So he finished the house *(the "three times in a year" were Passover, in April; Pentecost, in June; and Tabernacles, in October; a representative male from each household was required to be there at these three respective times)*.

26 And king Solomon made a navy of ships in Ezion-geber, which is beside Eloth, on the shore of the Red Sea, in the land of Edom *(this subjugation of Edom is mentioned in II Sam. 8:14)*.

27 And Hiram sent in the navy his servants, shipmen who had knowledge of the sea, with the servants of Solomon *(the Tyrians helped Solomon form his fleet)*.

28 And they came to Ophir, and fetched from thence gold, four hundred and twenty talents, and brought it to king Solomon *(it is not known exactly where Ophir was)*.

CHAPTER 10
(992 B.C.)
THE QUEEN OF SHEBA

AND when the queen of Sheba heard of the fame of Solomon concerning the Name of the LORD, she came to prove him with hard questions. *(Sheba, a grandson of Cush, settled in Abyssinia. Even though many Gentile kings and potentates came to Solomon, none of these Monarchs are mentioned particularly, except the Queen of Sheba, the Holy Spirit reserving that dignity for a woman. She is further honored by the Lord Himself in Mat. 12:42, where He predicts her reappearance in the Resurrection.*

Evidently, the Queen of Sheba heard many wonderful things about Solomon, but it seems that at first she did not believe the reports. But after a little, moved by its repetition, she determines to put the matter to the test. She undertakes a long and expensive journey, and her quest was not disappointed.

How many today, as this African Queen of old, hear of the fame of the "greater than Solomon" and, like her, they do not believe the report, but, unlike her, they do not bestir themselves to test what they have heard — Williams.

In the coming Kingdom Age, great men and women will come from all over the world to sit at the feet of Jesus, and will do so to have their "hard questions" answered, as it regards agriculture, industry, science, medicine, and other things. As Solomon of old, our Saviour will give these ambassadors the answer to their hardest questions.)

2 And she came to Jerusalem with a very great train, with camels that bore spices, and very much gold, and precious stones: and when she was come to Solomon, she communed with him of all that was in her heart. *(Our Lord lays great stress on this long journey [Mat. 12:42; Lk. 11:31]. "That which was in her heart" pertained to spiritual questions, which were answered readily by Solomon. All the other, the gold, the precious stones, etc., were mere window dressing by comparison to the great questions of Deity and eternity.)*

3 And Solomon told her all her questions: there was not any thing hid from the king, which he told her not. *(Whatever these questions were, the greater question, as the Text indicates, was spiritual. She now knew that it was God Who had given Solomon these great gifts.)*

4 And when the queen of Sheba had seen all Solomon's wisdom, and the house that he had built,

5 And the meat of his table, and the sitting of his servants, and the attendance of his ministers, and their apparel, and his cupbearers, and his ascent by which he went up unto the House of the LORD; there was no more spirit in her. *(This is indicative of what will take place in the coming Kingdom Age, when ambassadors from all over the world come to Christ and, for the first time in human history, man will see what this planet can be like with Satan locked away, and the Lord Jesus Christ reigning as King of kings and Lord of lords.)*

6 And she said to the king, It was a true report that I heard in my own land of your acts and of your wisdom *(even though it is a "true report," many today, even most, will not believe the Lord, but, in the coming Kingdom Age, they will, and unreservedly!)*.

7 Howbeit, I believed not the words, until I came, and my eyes had seen it: and, behold, the half was not told me: your wisdom and prosperity exceed the fame which I heard *(whatever can be said about Christ, of Whom Solomon was a Type, the "half has not been told" [I Cor. 2:9-10])*.

8 Happy are your men, happy are these your servants, which stand continually before you, and that hear your wisdom *(happy are all those who follow Christ and what He has done for us at the Cross)*.

9 Blessed be the LORD your God, which delighted in you, to set you on the throne of Israel: because the LORD loved Israel for ever, therefore made He thee king, to do judgment and justice *(proclaiming the fact that this Queen now knows the Lord, having thereby accepted Him as the Lord of her life)*.

10 And she gave the king an hundred and twenty talents of gold *(about $60 million in 2004 currency)*, and of spices very great store, and precious stones: there came no more such abundance of spices as these which the queen of Sheba gave to king Solomon *(in the coming Kingdom Age, of which all of this is a type, such gifts will be given to Christ, but always, and without exception, what He gives back will be*

far, far greater!)*.

11 And the navy also of Hiram, that brought gold from Ophir, brought in from Ophir great plenty of almug trees, and precious stones.

12 And the king made of the almug trees pillars for the House of the LORD, and for the king's house, harps also and psalteries for singers: there came no such almug trees, nor were seen unto this day *(it is said that the wood of these almug trees was most sought after for the making of musical instruments)*.

13 And king Solomon gave unto the queen of Sheba all her desire, whatsoever she asked, beside that which Solomon gave her of his royal bounty. So she turned and went to her own country, she and her servants. *(She left with far more than she came. According to the custom of that time, tradition says that she bore Solomon a son, Melimelek by name, from whom the past sovereigns of Abyssina [Ethiopia] claimed to derive their descent.)*

SOLOMON'S GREAT WEALTH AND FAME

14 Now the weight of gold that came to Solomon in one year was six hundred threescore and six talents of gold *(about $350 million in 2004 currency; however, it is not possible presently to know the true worth, simply because we do not know the purchasing power of gold during the time of Solomon; more than likely, it would have been worth much, much more than the amount we have given, possibly even several billions of dollars)*,

15 Beside that he had of the merchantmen, and of the traffic of the spice merchants, and of all the kings of Arabia, and of the governors of the country.

16 And king Solomon made two hundred targets of beaten gold: six hundred shekels of gold went to one target *(nearly a quarter of a million dollars per target; a "target" was an exceedingly large shield)*.

17 And he made three hundred shields of beaten gold; three pounds of gold went to one shield *(about $20,000 each)*: and the king put them in the house of the forest of Lebanon *(the governmental house built in Jerusalem of timber from the forest of Lebanon)*.

18 Moreover the king made a great throne of ivory, and overlaid it with the best gold *(the ivory was solid, and then overlaid with gold)*.

19 The throne had six steps, and the top of the throne was round behind: and there were stays on either side on the place of the seat,

and two lions stood beside the stays. *(Even though Solomon was a Type of Christ, he was only a type. The number "six" is stamped upon his government. The weight of gold paid each year to Solomon was 666 talents. He had six steps up to his throne, which stamps imperfection upon all his glory. "Six" is the number of man, who, incidentally, was created on the sixth day, and comes short of "seven," which is God's number of perfection. So, this tells us that, as glorious as was Solomon's reign, it was still stamped with imperfection, hence the number "six." The reign of Christ will be perfect. It will not fall short in anything.)*

20 And twelve lions stood there on the one side and on the other upon the six steps: there was not the like made in any kingdom. *(It is most probable that the Lord gave Solomon the design for all of this, with the number "twelve" signifying God's Government. It is that Government which made Israel so prosperous at this time, far above any other kingdom at that time in the world.)*

21 And all king Solomon's drinking vessels were of gold, and all the vessels of the house of the forest of Lebanon were of pure gold; none were of silver: it was nothing accounted of in the days of Solomon *(there was so much gold that they did not even bother to count the silver, even though in abundance)*.

22 For the king had at sea a navy of Tharshish with the navy of Hiram: once in three years came the navy of Tharshish, bringing gold, and silver, ivory, and apes, and peacocks.

23 So king Solomon exceeded all the kings of the Earth for riches and for wisdom.

24 And all the Earth sought to Solomon, to hear his wisdom, which God had put in his heart *(this is indicative of Christ, of Whom Solomon was a Type, which will be made evident to the entirety of the world, in the coming Kingdom Age [Zech. 14:8-10, 16-21])*.

25 And they brought every man his present, vessels of silver, and vessels of gold, and garments, and armour, and spices, horses, and mules, a rate year by year *(paying tribute to Solomon and to Israel, in order to partake of his wisdom)*.

26 And Solomon gathered together chariots and horsemen: and he had a thousand and four hundred chariots, and twelve thousand horsemen, whom he bestowed in the cities for chariots, and with the king at Jerusalem *(all of this was maintained strictly for the sake of pomp and display)*.

27 And the king made silver to be in Jerusalem as stones, and cedars made he to be as the sycomore trees that are in the vale, for abundance *(the sycamore trees of that time were of extreme value, equal to the cedars)*.

28 And Solomon had horses brought out of Egypt, and linen yarn: the king's merchants received the linen yarn at a price.

29 And a chariot came up and went out of Egypt for six hundred shekels of silver, and an horse for an hundred and fifty: and so for all the kings of the Hittites, and for the kings of Syria, did they bring them out by their means. *(For many years, it was claimed by critics that Hittite kings did not exist at that time; however, excavations in Asia Minor proved that assumption to be false. Hittite kings did exist at that time. As a result of such incidents, most archaeologists presently refrain from making announcements if they excavate something that seems to contradict the Bible. Just a little later, as it has proved time and time again, future excavations will prove the Bible to be true.*

For instance, except for the Bible, it was claimed that no historical proof was found that David ever existed; however, in 2002, if I remember the year correctly, archaeological excavations proved that king David actually existed. But, of course, Believers of the Word of God do not need archaeological excavations to prove its veracity, even though that particular proof is always forthcoming.)

CHAPTER 11
(984 B.C.)
SOLOMON'S WIVES AND IDOLATRY

BUT king Solomon loved many strange women, together with the daughter of Pharaoh, women of the Moabites, Ammonites, Edomites, Zidonians, and Hittites *(we have already heard of the multiplication of silver and gold [10:14-25], in defiance of Deuteronomy 17:17, and of the multiplication of horses [10:27-29], in disregard of Deuteronomy 17:16; we now read how the ruin of this great prince was completed by the multiplication of wives, and heathen wives at that)*:

2 Of the nations concerning which the LORD said unto the Children of Israel, You shall not go in to them, neither shall they come in unto you: for surely they will turn away your heart after their gods: Solomon clave unto these in love *(to disobey the Word of God is to invite disaster)*.

3 And he had seven hundred wives, princesses, and three hundred concubines: and his wives turned away his heart. *(Why? Past Blessings from God, even though of tremendous import at the time, will not suffice for today's journey. There must ever be fresh revelations. Due to Solomon's backsliding, there were no fresh revelations.*

The great gift of wisdom did not deter Solomon's transgression. Such cannot take the place of a constant day-by-day walk of holiness and humility before the Lord.

As well, pride played its part, and probably the biggest part.

All of this shows us that Believers do not fare too very well in a life of blessings only. These tend to take their eyes off of God, and onto themselves.)

4 For it came to pass, when Solomon was old, that his wives turned away his heart after other gods: and his heart was not perfect with the LORD his God, as was the heart of David his father. *(Self-righteousness could never understand this statement, especially due to the fact of the horrid sin of David with Bath-sheba and then the murder of her husband, Uriah. David failed in many other areas, as well; however, his heart was perfect toward God, because he always took these terrible sins to God [Ps. 51]; moreover, David suffered terribly for these sins, which is always the case with sin.)*

5 For Solomon went after Ashtoreth the goddess of the Zidonians, and after Milcom the abomination of the Ammonites. *(The words "and served them" should be added. There is no sadder picture in the Bible than that of Solomon's fall. His extraordinary gift of wisdom did not save him from disobedience to the Law of God. His neglect of that Law, and his loss of the fellowship of God which gives power to it, opened the door wide to the entrance of every form of evil. Had he clung to the Sacred Scriptures, how bright would have been his life! He was probably about 50 years of age when he apostatized.)*

6 And Solomon did evil in the sight of the LORD, and went not fully after the LORD, as did David his father. *(David was always held up as the example, because, as stated, he always turned to the Lord. The ironical thing was, Solomon continued to worship the Lord, at least after a fashion, while at the same time worshiping idols. How so indicative of the modern Church!)*

7 Then did Solomon build an high place for Chemosh, the abomination of Moab, in the hill that is before Jerusalem *(the Mount of Olivet)*, and for Molech, the abomination of the children of Ammon *(with some of these, human sacrifice was offered up, most of the time that of little children; however, we have no record of Jewish children being sacrificed to idols before the time of Ahaz, which was a little over 200 years after Solomon).*

8 And likewise did he for all his strange wives, which burnt incense and sacrificed unto their gods.

GOD'S JUDGMENT ON SOLOMON

9 And the LORD was angry with Solomon, because his heart was turned from the LORD God of Israel, which had appeared unto him twice. *(There is a special Hebrew verb used in the Bible for "to be angry." It is only used of Divine anger. It occurs fourteen times. Here, and in five other passages, a form of the verb is used expressing the forcing of oneself to be angry with a person who is loved. In other words, the Lord, because of His Nature, and despite Solomon's spiritual declension, had to force Himself to be angry with Solomon. He loved him that much!)*

10 And had commanded him concerning this thing, that he should not go after other gods: but he kept not that which the LORD commanded *(the idea is: the Lord dealt with him over and over again about this matter).*

11 Wherefore the LORD said unto Solomon, Forasmuch as this is done of you, and you have not kept My Covenant and My Statutes, which I have commanded you, I will surely rend the kingdom from you, and will give it to your servant. *(This message was probably delivered by the Prophet Ahijah. Even though the Lord appeared in a dream to Solomon twice, there is no record that there was a third appearance.)*

12 Notwithstanding in your days I will not do it for David your father's sake: but I will rend it out of the hand of your son. *(The threatening had two gracious and merciful limitations: 1. The blow would not fall until after his death [21:29]; and, 2. The disruption should be but partial.)*

13 Howbeit I will not rend away all the kingdom: but will give one Tribe to your son for David My servant's sake, and for Jerusalem's sake which I have chosen. *(This was probably one Tribe other than Judah, which was Benjamin. As well, the Tribe of Simeon, which was within*

*the boundaries of the Tribe of Judah, also would
be in this small group. It could be said that the
Tribe of Levi was a part of the group, as well,
although they had no certain boundaries, but
was rather scattered over Israel. This would take
place under Rehoboam, Solomon's son.)*

SOLOMON'S ADVERSARIES

14 And the LORD stirred up an adversary
unto Solomon, Hadad the Edomite, he was of
the king's seed in Edom *(functioning outside
of the Will of God pulls down the hedge that is
around every Believer; in some rare cases, as
with Job, it can be pulled down by the Lord
through no fault of the individual; however, that
is rare [Job, Chpts. 1-2])*.

15 For it came to pass, when David was in
Edom, and Joab the captain of the host was
gone up to bury the slain, after he had smitten
every male in Edom;

16 (For six months did Joab remain there
with all Israel, until he had cut off every male
in Edom *[possibly the cruelties of the Edomites
had provoked this act of retribution (Ps. 137:7;
Obad., Vss. 10-14)]*:)

17 That Hadad fled, he and certain Edomites
of his father's servants with him, to go into
Egypt; Hadad being yet a little child.

18 And they arose out of Midian, and came
to Paran: and they took men with them out of
Paran, and they came to Egypt, unto Pharaoh
king of Egypt; which gave him an house, and
appointed him victuals, and gave him land *(his
relations with the royal family of Egypt were so
extremely intimate, it is believed, that he may
have been fed from the royal table)*.

19 And Hadad found great favour in the
sight of Pharaoh, so that he gave him to wife
the sister of his own wife, and sister of Tahpenes
the queen *(this was probably during the time
of David)*.

20 And the sister of Tahpenes bore him
Genubath his son, whom Tahpenes weaned in
Pharaoh's house: and Genubath was in Pharaoh's
household among the sons of Pharaoh.

21 And when Hadad heard in Egypt that
David slept with his fathers, and that Joab the
captain of the host was dead, Hadad said to
Pharaoh, Let me depart, that I may go to my
own country.

22 Then Pharaoh said unto him, But what
have you lacked with me, that, behold, you seek
to go to your own country? And he answered,
Nothing: howbeit let me go in any wise.

ANOTHER ADVERSARY

23 And God stirred him up another adversary, Rezon the son of Eliadah, which fled from
his lord Hadadezer king of Zobah:

24 And he gathered men unto him, and became captain over a band, when David slew
them of Zobah: and they went to Damascus,
and dwelt therein, and reigned in Damascus.

25 And he was an adversary to Israel all the
days of Solomon, beside the mischief that
Hadad did: and he abhorred Israel, and reigned
over Syria. *(David subdued Syria [II Sam.,
Chpt. 8]. Solomon, weakened by sin, lost it.*

*It is to be understood that Hadad joined Rezon,
and, on the death or disappearance of that chieftain, became king of Syria and founder of the
Dynasty afterward known as Ben-hadad, and
which brought such suffering upon Israel. The
sin of today ensures the suffering of tomorrow,
for Solomon's conduct originated Ben-hadad.)*

JEROBOAM

26 And Jeroboam the son of Nebat, an
Ephrathite of Zereda, Solomon's servant,
whose mother's name was Zeruah, a widow
woman, even he lifted up his hand against
the king. *(All of this was permitted by the
Lord, because of Solomon's sin. Had the Word
of God been obeyed, all of this would have been
avoided.)*

27 And this was the cause that he lifted up
his hand against the king: Solomon built
Millo, and repaired the breaches of the city of
David his father.

28 And the man Jeroboam was a mighty man
of valour: and Solomon seeing the young man
that he was industrious, he made him ruler
over all the charge of the house of Joseph.
*(Spence says concerning this, "The Tribe of
Ephraim, with its constant envy of Judah, must
have been mortified to find themselves employed
— though it was but in the modified service of
Israelites — on the fortifications of Jerusalem.
Their murmurings revealed to Jeroboam the un-
popularity of Solomon, and perhaps suggested
thoughts of overt rebellion to his mind.")*

29 And it came to pass at that time when
Jeroboam went out of Jerusalem, that the
prophet Ahijah the Shilonite found him in the
way; and he had clad himself with a new garment; and they two were alone in the field
*(Ahijah the Prophet; the Prophet Nathan was no
doubt by now dead)*:

30 And Ahijah caught the new garment that was on him, and rent it in twelve pieces:

31 And he said to Jeroboam, Take thee ten pieces: for thus saith the LORD, the God of Israel, Behold, I will rend the kingdom out of the hand of Solomon, and will give ten Tribes to you:

32 (But he shall have one Tribe for my servant David's sake *[one Tribe other than Judah, which would be Benjamin]*, and for Jerusalem's sake, the city which I have chosen out of all the Tribes of Israel *[the Tribe of Benjamin incorporated Jerusalem on the northern side, while the Tribe of Judah incorporated Jerusalem on the southern side]*:)

33 Because that they have forsaken Me, and have worshipped Ashtoreth the goddess of the Zidonians, Chemosh the god of the Moabites, and Milcom the god of the children of Ammon, and have not walked in My Ways, to do that which is right in My eyes, to keep My Statutes and My Judgments, as did David his father. *(More than likely, this same Prophet had delivered this same message to Solomon some time earlier, but evidently to no avail!)*

34 Howbeit I will not take the whole kingdom out of his hand: but I will make him prince all the days of his life for David My servant's sake, whom I chose, because he kept My Commandments and My Statutes *(this doesn't mean that David was perfect in his life, for, as is overly obvious, he wasn't; it does mean that whatever the problem, sin or otherwise, David ultimately took it to the Lord; as well, David was untouched by idolatry)*:

35 But I will take the kingdom out of his son's hand, and will give it unto you, even ten tribes.

36 And unto his son will I give one Tribe *(one Tribe other than Judah, which was Benjamin)*, that David My servant may have a light alway before Me in Jerusalem, the city which I have chosen Me to put My Name there *(the idea is not so much that of a home, but rather a family issue — David's family, through whom the Messiah would come)*.

37 And I will take you, and you shall reign according to all that your soul desires, and shall be king over Israel.

38 And it shall be, if you will hearken unto all that I command you, and will walk in My Ways, and do that is right in My sight, to keep My Statutes and My Commandments, as David My servant did; that I will be with you, and build you a sure house, as I built for David, and will give Israel unto you. *(Observe, however, there was no promise to Jeroboam, as there was to David, of an enduring kingdom. It was not God's design to take away the kingdom from David in perpetuity.)*

39 And I will for this afflict the seed of David, but not for ever *(it will be brought back in the coming Kingdom Age [Acts 15:16]).*

40 Solomon sought therefore to kill Jeroboam. And Jeroboam arose, and fled into Egypt, unto Shishak king of Egypt, and was in Egypt until the death of Solomon. *(It has been assumed that Solomon did this because of this Prophecy; however, there is no record that Solomon ever heard of the Prophecy. It is believed that Jeroboam, not willing to wait for the Lord to work out the situation, sought to bring about an insurrection almost immediately; consequently, he incurred the wrath of Solomon. His rebellion is the more inexcusable because Ahijah had expressly stated that Solomon was to retain the kingdom during his lifetime.)*

THE DEATH OF SOLOMON

41 And the rest of the acts of Solomon, and all that he did, and his wisdom, are they not written in the book of the acts of Solomon? *(The sources of this history are mentioned more specifically in II Chronicles 9:29 — Pulpit.)*

42 And the time that Solomon reigned in Jerusalem over all Israel was forty years. *(The first three kings of Israel, Saul, David, and now Solomon, each reigned forty years.)*

43 And Solomon slept with his fathers, and was buried in the city of David his father: and Rehoboam his son reigned in his stead. *(So far as appears, his only son. Verse 42 presents the last statement made by the Holy Spirit about Solomon personally. The next fact records his death. Did he repent at the end? The Scripture doesn't say. We can only hope that the writer of Proverbs, Ecclesiastes, and Song of Solomon definitely did make his way back to God. There is some small evidence that he did, which we will address in II Chronicles.)*

CHAPTER 12
(975 B.C.)
REHOBOAM MADE KING

AND Rehoboam went to Shechem: for all Israel were come to Shechem to make him king. *(The first step taken by Rehoboam was a judicious one. He, no doubt, sought to cement*

the dissatisfied Ephraimites to himself by being crowned in their chief city. This should have caused them to submit to the Tribe of Judah, as this was a great honor given them.

Shechem lay on the flank of Mount Gerazim, directly opposite Mount Ebal, the Mounts of curses and blessings [Deut. 11:29; 27:1-8]. It was a national sanctuary [Josh. 24:1], and the site of Abraham's first Altar [Gen. 12:6]. Isaac and Jacob had both lived here. Joseph was buried here; Jacob's well was also located here [Jn. 4:5].

Because of the unrest, Rehoboam's motives, no doubt, were political. Sadly, the majority of the motives of the modern Church are too often political. Jerusalem was the city where God had chosen to place His Name. It was where the Temple was constructed, and that by the command of the Lord. Jerusalem was the spiritual center of Israel. This should have been the place to crown Rehoboam king; however, Rehoboam, as many, if not most, chose the political way instead of the spiritual.)

2 And it came to pass, when Jeroboam the son of Nebat, who was yet in Egypt, heard of it, (for he was fled from the presence of king Solomon, and Jeroboam dwelt in Egypt;)

3 That they sent and called him. And Jeroboam and all the congregation of Israel came, and spoke unto Rehoboam, saying *(while Rehoboam was trying to appease the northern kingdom of Israel, they were sending to Egypt to bring in Jeroboam)*,

4 Your father made our yoke grievous: now therefore you make the grievous service of your father, and his heavy yoke which he put upon us, lighter, and we will serve you.

5 And he said unto them, Depart yet for three days, then come again to me. And the people departed.

6 And king Rehoboam consulted with the old men, who stood before Solomon his father while he yet lived, and said, How do you advise that I may answer this people?

7 And they spoke unto him, saying, If you will be a servant unto this people this day, and will serve them, and answer them, and speak good words to them, then they will be your servants for ever *(their words were wise and right)*.

8 But he forsook the counsel of the old men, which they had given him, and consulted with the young men who were grown up with him, and which stood before him:

9 And he said unto them, What counsel give you that we may answer this people, who have spoken to me, saying, Make the yoke which your father did put upon us lighter?

10 And the young men who were grown up with him spoke unto him, saying, Thus shall you speak unto this people who spoke unto you, saying, Your father made our yoke heavy, but you make it lighter unto us; thus shall you say unto them, My little finger shall be thicker than my father's loins.

11 And now whereas my father did lade you with a heavy yoke, I will add to your yoke: my father has chastised you with whips, but I will chastise you with scorpions. *(This was a scourge, and more painful than a whip. In the action of Rehoboam and of the people is exhibited the folly of the natural heart and its incurable hostility to God. In the difficulty in which they find themselves, the king consults "man" instead of God; and the people trust themselves into the cruel hands of Jeroboam, instead of the gracious hands of Emmanuel.)*

12 So Jeroboam and all the people came to Rehoboam the third day, as the king had appointed, saying, Come to me again the third day.

13 And the king answered the people roughly, and forsook the old men's counsel that they gave him;

14 And spoke to them after the counsel of the young men, saying, My father made your yoke heavy, and I will add to your yoke: my father also chastised you with whips, but I will chastise you with scorpions.

15 Wherefore the king hearkened not unto the people; for the cause was from the LORD, that He might perform His saying, which the LORD spoke by Ahijah the Shilonite unto Jeroboam the son of Nebat. *(Through foreknowledge, the Lord knew what Rehoboam would ultimately do, and, thereby, pressured him to listen to the wrong advice, which his heart was prone to do at any rate. The Lord didn't force his will, and neither did He interfere to stop the wrong decision.)*

THE TEN TRIBES REVOLT

16 So when all Israel saw that the king hearkened not unto them, the people answered the king, saying, What portion have we in David? neither have we inheritance in the son of Jesse: to your tents, O Israel: now see to your own house, David. So Israel departed unto their tents. *(This was the beginning of over 250 years of division and strife between the two nations of Judah and Israel. While Rehoboam was foolish,*

the northern kingdom of Israel, sometimes referred to as Ephraim or Samaria, didn't better themselves by their action.)

17 But as for the Children of Israel which dwelt in the cities of Judah, Rehoboam reigned over them.

18 Then king Rehoboam sent Adoram, who was over the tribute; and all Israel stoned him with stones, that he died. Therefore king Rehoboam made speed to get him up to his chariot, to flee to Jerusalem. *(Such a man as Adoram, guided by such counselors, and inflated by the sense of his own power and importance, would naturally think of force rather than of conciliation or concessions. The situation turned out very badly.)*

19 So Israel rebelled against the house of David unto this day.

20 And it came to pass, when all Israel heard that Jeroboam was come again, that they sent and called him unto the congregation, and made him king over all Israel: there was none who followed the house of David, but the Tribe of Judah only *(as the following Verses proclaim, the Tribe of Benjamin was included with Judah, as well).*

21 And when Rehoboam was come to Jerusalem, he assembled all the house of Judah, with the Tribe of Benjamin, an hundred and fourscore thousand *(180,000)* chosen men, which were warriors, to fight against the house of Israel, to bring the kingdom again to Rehoboam the son of Solomon.

22 But the Word of God came unto Shemaiah the man of God, saying,

23 Speak unto Rehoboam, the son of Solomon, king of Judah, and unto all the house of Judah and Benjamin, and to the remnant of the people, saying,

24 Thus saith the LORD, You shall not go up, nor fight against your brethren the Children of Israel: return every man to his house; for this thing is from Me. They hearkened therefore to the Word of the Lord, and returned to depart, according to the Word of the Lord. *(Three times in this one sentence the "Word of the Lord" is referred to, showing its great significance. The Holy Spirit is telling us that if the "Word of the Lord" had been adhered to all along, Israel would not have come to this sad state.)*

JEROBOAM LEADS ISRAEL
INTO IDOLATRY

25 Then Jeroboam built Shechem in Mount Ephraim, and dwelt therein; and went out from thence, and built Penuel *(Jeroboam made Shechem the capital of the northern kingdom).*

26 And Jeroboam said in his heart, Now shall the kingdom return to the house of David *(Jeroboam saw that fortresses and armies would be of no avail for the defense of his realm, so long as Jerusalem remained the one Sanctuary of the land; so he would do something about this):*

27 If this people go up to do sacrifice in the House of the LORD at Jerusalem, then shall the heart of this people turn again unto their lord, even unto Rehoboam king of Judah, and they shall kill me, and go again to Rehoboam king of Judah.

28 Whereupon the king took counsel *(but not from God)*, and made two calves of gold, and said unto them, It is too much for you to go up to Jerusalem: behold your gods, O Israel, which brought you up out of the land of Egypt.

29 And he set the one in Beth-el, and the other put he in Dan. *(The great Redemption given to Israel by God concerning their deliverance from Egypt was now attributed to a "golden calf." I wonder if we are doing any differently today in the modern Church, when we attribute the help that God gives us to humanistic psychology?)*

30 And this thing became a sin: for the people went to worship before the one, even unto Dan. *(The expression concerning Jeroboam, "made Israel to sin," is used twenty-three times. This "sin" was idolatry, which led to all other types of sin.)*

31 And he made an house of high places, and made Priests of the lowest of the people, which were not of the sons of Levi *(the Levites had all migrated to Jerusalem; so, Jeroboam selected the base and the vile to be his priests; to be sure, this would suffice for the worship of golden calves).*

32 And Jeroboam ordained a feast in the eighth month, on the fifteenth day of the month, like unto the feast that is in Judah, and he offered upon the Altar. So did he in Beth-el, sacrificing unto the calves that he had made: and he placed in Beth-el the priests of the high places which he had made *(he conducted his feasts at the same time that Judah conducted the Feasts of the Lord).*

33 So he offered upon the Altar which he had made in Beth-el the fifteenth day of the eighth month, even in the month which he had devised of his own heart; and ordained a

feast unto the Children of Israel: and he offered upon the Altar, and burnt incense. *(We may perhaps see in Jeroboam's ministering and person not only the design to invest the new ordinance with exceptional interest and splendor, but also the idea of encouraging his new priests to enter on their unauthorized functions without fear. The history, or even the traditions, of Nadab and Abihu [Lev., Chpt. 10] and of Korah and his company [Num. 16:40] may very well have made them hesitate. And that their fears of a Divine interposition were not groundless, the sequel shows — Spence.)*

CHAPTER 13
(975 B.C.)
A PROPHET FROM JUDAH
WARNS JEROBOAM

AND, behold, there came a man of God out of Judah by the Word of the LORD unto Beth-el: and Jeroboam stood by the Altar to burn incense. *(Israel, the northern kingdom, is very comfortable with her new religion — "the two calves of gold." Jeroboam, arrayed as king and priest, stands by his altar offering incense to his "god." The entire court assists, together with a vast multitude of worshippers, so-called. In fact, nothing is lacking to win the admiration of the religious world. But then, the spectacle is interrupted by a "man of God out of Judah," who has a "Word from the Lord.")*

2 And he cried against the altar in the Word of the LORD, and said, O altar, altar, thus saith the LORD; Behold, a child shall be born unto the house of David, Josiah by name; and upon you shall he offer the priests of the high places who burn incense upon you, and men's bones shall be burnt upon you. *(This altar, one might say, was a "bastard" altar, designed by man, which referred to golden calves as god. There was only one Altar in all of Israel that God would recognize, and that was in Jerusalem. The Altar that was in Jerusalem at the Temple was designed by the Holy Spirit, and it portrayed Calvary, yet to come. This "altar" of Jeroboam would deliver no one. It is representative of the multitudinous altars of this world, devised by the hand of man, with many of them in Christendom.*

"Josiah," nearly 350 years later, exactly as the prophecy predicted, would destroy this altar; likewise, all false religion in Israel, and elsewhere in the world, will ultimately be destroyed by "a child that shall be born unto the house of David" with the Name of the Lord Jesus Christ [Zech. 13:2].)

3 And he gave a sign the same day, saying, This is the sign which the LORD has spoken; Behold, the Altar shall be rent, and the ashes that are upon it shall be poured out *(which was to happen almost immediately!)*.

4 And it came to pass, when king Jeroboam heard the saying of the man of God, which had cried against the Altar in Beth-el, that he put forth his hand from the Altar, saying, Lay hold on him. And his hand, which he put forth against him, dried up, so that he could not pull it in again to him. *(Man has ever tried to stop the Word of God. He will listen to every false message that is given, by every heathen priest, with no reaction, but the moment the "Word of the Lord" is pronounced, he will resort even to violence to stop it.*

The extended "dried up" hand of Jeroboam is a picture of that which will happen to the Antichrist during the Battle of Armageddon. The "man of sin" will put forth his hand against the Lord Jesus Christ, and he will see it "dry up" before his very eyes.)

5 The altar also was rent, and the ashes poured out from the Altar, according to the sign which the man of God had given by the Word of the LORD.

6 And the king answered and said unto the man of God, Intreat now the face of the LORD your God, and pray for me, that my hand may be restored me again. And the man of God besought the LORD, and the king's hand was restored him again, and became as it was before. *(Despite the fact that one of the most striking displays of power is recorded, still, Jeroboam did not repent. It is amazing at man's ability to see and sense the Power of God in operation and still rebel. Miracles, as wonderful as they are, do not bring people to Jesus. It is the convicting Power of the Holy Spirit upon a weeping heart that does so.)*

7 And the king said unto the man of God, Come home with me, and refresh yourself, and I will give you a reward. *(This is the greatest danger that the Church presently faces. It is very difficult to turn down the "reward." The modern Church all too often seeks after the accommodations of the world, its plaudits, approval, and reward, and, to receive such, it will compromise its message, substitute its altar, and seek "unity" at any price.)*

8 And the man of God said unto the king, If you will give me half your house, I will not go in with you, neither will I eat bread nor drink water in this place:

9 For so was it charged me by the Word of the LORD, saying, Eat no bread, nor drink water, nor turn again by the same way that you came. *(The Prophet's refusal to participate was consequently a practical and forcible disclaimer of all fellowship, a virtual excommunication, a public repudiation of the calf-worshippers.)*

10 So he went another way, and returned not by the way that he came to Beth-el.

THE PROPHET'S DISOBEDIENCE AND DEATH

11 Now there dwelt an old Prophet in Beth-el; and his sons came and told him all the works that the man of God had done that day in Beth-el: the words which he had spoken unto the king, them they told also to their father. *(This "old Prophet" had long since turned his back on God. Why didn't God use the "old Prophet" to speak to Jeroboam? He, no doubt, lived within walking distance of the "altar." The word "old" signifies that the man had once known the Lord, but now had compromised his ministry and his message.)*

12 And their father said unto them, What way went he? For his sons had seen what way the man of God went, which came from Judah.

13 And he said unto his sons, Saddle me the ass. So they saddled him the ass: and he rode thereon,

14 And went after the man of God, and found him sitting under an oak: and he said unto him, Are you the man of God who came from Judah? And he said, I am.

15 Then he said unto him, Come home with me, and eat bread.

16 And he said, I may not return with you, nor go in with you: neither will I eat bread nor drink water with you in this place:

17 For it was said to me by the Word of the LORD, You shall eat no bread nor drink water there, nor turn again to go by the way that you came.

18 He said unto him, I am a Prophet also as you are; and an Angel spoke unto me by the Word of the LORD, saying, Bring him back with you into your house, that he may eat bread and drink water. But he lied unto him *(even if an Angel did speak, which he really didn't, still, nothing must take precedence over the Word of God [Gal. 1:8]).*

19 So he went back with him; and did eat bread in his house, and drank water. *(This was in direct disobedience to the Word of God. It would cost him his life. As well, it will cost the life of the Church. The two greatest dangers of the Church are the "Jeroboams," who represent the world and its ways, and, second, "the old Prophets," who represent the apostate Church.*

The old Prophet, whose duty it was to have testified against the evil around him, bore with it, and, by his silence, sanctioned it; therefore, he was very anxious that the "man of God" should approve his unfaithfulness by association with it; consequently, the "man of God" was ensnared.)

20 And it came to pass, as they sat at the table, that the Word of the LORD came unto the Prophet who brought him back:

21 And he cried unto the man of God who came from Judah, saying, Thus saith the LORD, Forasmuch as you have disobeyed the mouth of the LORD, and have not kept the Commandment which the LORD your God commanded you,

22 But came back, and have eaten bread and drunk water in the place, of the which the LORD did say to you, Eat no bread, and drink no water; your carcase shall not come unto the sepulchre of your fathers. *(Strangely enough, the Lord will use the "old Prophet" to cry out "against the man of God," and to deliver a message of judgment against him. He would disobey God by originally listening to this man, and, in turn, God would have this man pronounce his doom. Many blanch at the fierceness of the Lord in bringing about the demise of the man of God. However, the sin of compromising the Word is far worse than sins of passion. God's pronouncement of judgment upon a wayward Israel was now compromised by the "man of God" associating with its backslidden "old Prophet." In God's eyes, the compromise of the "old Prophet" was as bad as Jeroboam's two golden calves. The true Prophet of God entered into that compromise when he disobeyed the Lord by going to this man's house.)*

23 And it came to pass, after he had eaten bread, and after he had drunk, that he saddled for him the ass, to wit, for the Prophet whom he had brought back.

24 And when he was gone, a lion met him by the way, and slew him: and his carcase was cast in the way, and the ass stood by it, the lion also stood by the carcase *(the lion was sent and instructed by God).*

25 And, behold, men passed by, and saw the carcase cast in the way, and the lion standing by the carcase: and they came and told it in the city where the old prophet dwelt.

26 And when the prophet who brought him back from the way heard thereof, he said, It is the man of God, who was disobedient unto the Word of the LORD: therefore the LORD has delivered him unto the lion, which has torn him, and slain him, according to the Word of the LORD, which he spoke unto him.

27 And he spoke to his sons, saying, Saddle me the ass. And they saddled him.

28 And he went and found his carcase cast in the way, and the ass and the lion standing by the carcase: the lion had not eaten the carcase, nor torn the ass (which was completely contrary to the nature of such an animal).

29 And the prophet took up the carcase of the man of God, and laid it upon the ass, and brought it back: and the old prophet came to the city, to mourn and to bury him.

30 And he laid his carcase in his own grave; and they mourned over him, saying, Alas, my brother!

31 And it came to pass, after he had buried him, that he spoke to his sons, saying, When I am dead, then bury me in the sepulchre wherein the man of God is buried; lay my bones beside his bones (he had no problem being with him in death, but he would not stand with him in life):

32 For the saying which he cried by the Word of the LORD against the altar in Beth-el, and against all the houses of the high places which are in the cities of Samaria, shall surely come to pass.

JEROBOAM PERSISTS IN HIS EVIL

33 After this thing Jeroboam returned not from his evil way, but made again of the lowest of the people priests of the high places: whosoever would, he consecrated him, and he became one of the priests of the high places. (According to Josephus, the old Prophet now explained away the miracles of the Prophet of Judah, alleging that the altar had fallen because it was new, and the king's hand had become powerless from fatigue.)

34 And this thing became sin unto the house of Jeroboam, even to cut it off, and to destroy it from off the face of the Earth. (The just anger of God in destroying his idolatrous altar and the amazing Grace of God in restoring his withered hand are alike resisted by him. The word "sin" in this Verse should read "the sin," because it contains the definite article. It spoke of idolatry, but more than anything of the repudiation of the True Cross, and the substituting of another. In fact, that has always been the sin. The Message is, "Jesus Christ and Him Crucified" [I Cor. 1:23]. Man has ever attempted to change that, and, regrettably, the Church most of all.)

CHAPTER 14
(956 B.C.)

JEROBOAM SENDS HIS WIFE
TO AHIJAH THE PROPHET

AT that time Abijah the son of Jeroboam fell sick. (Through this sickness, which will result in death, the Lord makes a final appeal to Jeroboam, just as He has made such to untold millions.)

2 And Jeroboam said to his wife, Arise, I pray you, and disguise yourself, that you be not known to be the wife of Jeroboam; and get thee to Shiloh: behold, there is Ahijah the Prophet, which told me that I should be king over this people. (Concerning this, Williams says, "The darkness of Jeroboam's heart is further seen in his asking the Queen to disguise herself lest the people should know her to be the Queen. To openly seek help from God on behalf of his son would show the people that he himself had no faith in the idol he had set up, and would affect the stability of his kingdom. His folly is further to be seen in that his wife was to try to deceive the God of Israel, although she sought unto Him for Truth!)

3 And take with you ten loaves, and cracknels, and a cruse of honey, and go to him: he shall tell you what shall become of the child (his idol gods surely couldn't tell him, and, in his heart, he knew that the True God of Israel held the answer, and that He Alone held the answer).

4 And Jeroboam's wife did so, and arose, and went to Shiloh, and came to the house of Ahijah. But Ahijah could not see; for his eyes were set by reason of his age. (In Verses 1-4, one can see the depths of sin to which Jeroboam had taken Israel. He had no confidence in these "golden calves," which had taken the northern kingdom of Israel to the depths. The "calves" were merely political expediency to keep Israel from going to Jerusalem to worship God. He knew that Jehovah controlled all. Still, he would not serve Him.)

5 And the LORD said unto Ahijah, Behold, the wife of Jeroboam comes to ask a thing of you for her son; for he is sick: thus and thus shall you say unto her: for it shall be, when

she comes in, that she shall feign herself to be another woman. *(Few men have been dealt with by the Lord such as Jeroboam. It almost seems as if the Lord is pleading with him to repent.)*

6 And it was so, when Ahijah heard the sound of her feet, as she came in at the door, that he said, Come in, thou wife of Jeroboam; why do you feign yourself to be another? for I am sent to you with heavy tidings. *(Even the "heavy tidings" was the Hand of God. He would try to bring Jeroboam to his senses, as He has tried to bring multiple hundreds of millions to their senses, but, tragically, to no avail!)*

THE PROPHECY AGAINST JEROBOAM

7 Go, tell Jeroboam, Thus saith the LORD God of Israel, Forasmuch as I exalted you from among the people, and made you prince over My people Israel *(even though the Lord gave him this position, he executed the position totally contrary to the Will of the Lord; every Preacher should read these words very carefully)*,

8 And rent the kingdom away from the house of David, and gave it you: and yet you have not been as My servant David, who kept My Commandments, and who followed Me with all his heart, to do that only which was right in My eyes *(a self-righteous Church world can never understand this, especially considering Bath-sheba and Uriah; nevertheless, the answer is simple; David repented! All sin repented of, and, consequently, washed by the Blood of Jesus Christ, is not only forgiven by God, but forgotten; it is called "Justification"; it then stands in the Eyes of God as though it never happened)*;

9 But have done evil above all that were before you: for you have gone and made you other gods, and molten images, to provoke Me to anger, and have cast Me behind your back *(it would seem from this statement that Jeroboam had once known the Lord in a very real way; he had received Prophecies, and then was promised a sure house and a kingdom if he would obey; this one Passage alone, along with all the many others in the Word of God, dispute the fallacious doctrine of "unconditional eternal security" [Heb. 6:1-6; 10:26-31])*:

10 Therefore, behold, I will bring evil upon the house of Jeroboam, and will cut off from Jeroboam him who urinates against the wall *(all the men of the family)*, and him who is shut up and left in Israel, and will take away the remnant of the house of Jeroboam, as a man takes away dung, till it be all gone *(the Lord set up Jeroboam, and the Lord will take down Jeroboam)*.

11 Him who dies of Jeroboam in the city shall the dogs eat; and him who dies in the field shall the fowls of the air eat: for the LORD has spoken it. *(There could be no greater disgrace to a Jew than this. As well, we see that the Prophet Ahijah did not mince words, even though he was talking with the Queen. How many Prophets presently will deliver the Word of the Lord without addition or deletion? I'm afraid not many!)*

12 Arise thou therefore, get thee to your own house: and when your feet enter into the city, the child shall die. *(The word "child" in the Hebrew, as used here, has reference to one who could be in his late teens, or even early twenties. There are few men whom God dealt with as He dealt with Jeroboam. If the death of a son [or daughter] has no effect on a parent regarding their relationship with God, then there is very little else that God can do.)*

13 And all Israel shall mourn for him, and bury him: for he only of Jeroboam shall come to the grave, because in him there is found some good thing toward the LORD God of Israel in the house of Jeroboam. *(Evidently, Abijah had some qualities in him toward God that endeared him to the whole of Israel. So, God would take the young man, as a flower would be plucked from a garbage dump.)*

14 Moreover the LORD shall raise Him up a king over Israel, who shall cut off the house of Jeroboam that day: but what? even now. *(Even though it began at that moment, it would be some twenty years before Baasha would destroy all of Jeroboam's seed. This Prophecy in no way meant that Baasha would be Godly; in fact, he was evil. It does show that God rules in the affairs of men, setting up one and pulling down another.)*

15 For the LORD shall smite Israel, as a reed is shaken in the water, and he shall root up Israel out of this good land, which he gave to their fathers, and shall scatter them beyond the river, because they have made their groves, provoking the LORD to anger. *(This refers to the River Euphrates, when Israel would be taken captive by the Assyrians. It happened about 250 years after the Prophecy was given.)*

16 And He shall give Israel up because of the sins of Jeroboam, who did sin, and who made Israel to sin. *(The very fact that Jeroboam sent his wife to the Prophet Ahijah shows that the*

Lord was dealing with him. So why did he not repent then? As we shall see, the Prophecy given to him by his wife, as it had been given to her by the Prophet, even with the death of his son, had no effect. He continued on in his evil ways, and would not repent. It is remarkable as to the stubbornness of the human heart when it comes to God. Men do not repent quickly or easily!)

THE DEATH OF JEROBOAM'S SON

17 And Jeroboam's wife arose, and departed, and came to Tirzah: and when she came to the threshold of the door, the child died (exactly as the Prophet said would happen [Vs. 12]);

18 And they buried him; and all Israel mourned for him, according to the Word of the LORD, which He spoke by the hand of His servant Ahijah the Prophet. (If the Word of the Lord is ignored, the end result will not be happy!)

THE DEATH OF JEROBOAM

19 And the rest of the acts of Jeroboam, how he warred, and how he reigned, behold, they are written in the book of the Chronicles of the Kings of Israel.

20 And the days which Jeroboam reigned were two and twenty years: and he slept with his fathers, and Nadab his son reigned in his stead. (The exploits of this long reign find no mention in Scripture; the historian dwells exclusively on the sin, the consequences of which were of so much greater moment.)

THE REIGN OF REHOBOAM; THE SINS OF JUDAH

21 And Rehoboam the son of Solomon reigned in Judah. Rehoboam was forty and one years old when he began to reign, and he reigned seventeen years in Jerusalem, the city which the LORD did choose out of all the Tribes of Israel, to put His name there. And his mother's name was Naamah an Ammonitess. (The writer of I Kings reminds us that Jerusalem was by God's appointment the spiritual center of the land; that Bethel and Dan were no sanctuaries of His choosing; and that, however much the realm of Rehoboam was restricted, he still reigned in the capital of God's choice — Spence.)

22 And Judah did evil in the sight of the LORD, and they provoked Him to jealousy with their sins which they had committed, above all that their fathers had done. (For the first three years the nation remained steadfast in the faith [II Chron. 12:1]. The defection commenced when Rehoboam began to feel himself secure [II Chron. 11:17; 12:1]. Idolatry was unfaithfulness to God, and provoked the Lord to jealousy.)

23 For they also built them high places, and images, and groves, on every high hill, and under every green tree. (The word "images" actually refers to pillars or statues. This was probably the Asherah, which was the male reproductive member. Its system of worship incorporated all types of immoral rites. In other words, it was the most abominable of the abominable.)

24 And there were also sodomites in the land: and they did according to all the abominations of the nations which the LORD cast out before the Children of Israel. (Sodomites are homosexuals [Gen., Chpt. 17]. Here it refers to male prostitutes dedicated to idolatry involving this sin [II Ki. 23:7]. Such was forbidden by the Law of God [Deut. 23:17-18]. The Lord refers to this sin as an "abomination." A nation begins to lose its way when three sins become prominent, "pedophilia," "homosexuality," and "murder.")

SHISHAK OF EGYPT SPOILS JERUSALEM

25 And it came to pass in the fifth year of king Rehoboam, that Shishak king of Egypt came up against Jerusalem (Shishak was founder of the 22nd Egyptian Dynasty):

26 And he took away the treasures of the House of the LORD, and the treasures of the king's house; he even took away all: and he took away all the shields of gold which Solomon had made.

27 And king Rehoboam made in their stead brasen (copper) shields, and committed them unto the hands of the chief of the guard, which kept the door of the king's house.

28 And it was so, when the king went into the House of the LORD, that the guard bore them, and brought them back into the guard chamber. (The "shields of gold," in some way, represented God's Blessings upon Israel. The "shields of copper," in some way, represented the sorry state in which Israel now found herself. Just a short time before, she was the most powerful nation on the face of the Earth. And now, because of her transgression against God, the

Lord allows the "king of Egypt" to do damage to Israel. The "gold" was a Type of Deity, referring to the fact that God ruled in Judah. Brass, or copper, was a type of humanity, which states that men are now guiding Judah instead of God, hence the disruption and declension.)

REHOBOAM DIES

29 Now the rest of the acts of Rehoboam, and all that he did, are they not written in the book of the Chronicles of the Kings of Judah?

30 And there was war between Rehoboam and Jeroboam all their days.

31 And Rehoboam slept with his fathers, and was buried with his fathers in the city of David *(Jerusalem)*. And his mother's name was Naamah an Ammonitess. And Abijam his son reigned in his stead. *(Twice the Holy Spirit refers to the mother of Rehoboam as "the Ammonitess." It can hardly be doubted that she was one of the "Ammonitesses" who turned away Solomon's heart. In fact, she was the one who brought the worship of Moloch to Jerusalem, and was, as well, influential, no doubt, in the spiritual declension of her son, and, thereby, the wreckage of Judah.)*

CHAPTER 15
(951 B.C.)
THE SHORT, WICKED
REIGN OF ABIJAM

NOW in the eighteenth year of king Jeroboam the son of Nebat reigned Abijam over Judah.

2 Three years reigned he in Jerusalem. And his mother's name was Maachah, the daughter of Abishalom. *(In II Chron., Chpt. 11, it is stated that she was the daughter of Absalom; II Chron., Chpt. 13, states that she was the daughter of Uriel. In the Old Testament, there were no terms for granddaughter, etc. In fact, the terms for both "daughter" and "granddaughter" are identical. The Bible does not distinguish between the two. It seems that his mother was the daughter of the son-in-law of Absalom.)*

3 And he walked in all the sins of his father, which he had done before him: and his heart was not perfect with the LORD his God, as the heart of David his father *(his "heart not being right" proclaims the fact that the "Absalom spirit" had its deadly effect on all whom it touched; once again, David is held up as the example of Righteousness).*

4 Nevertheless for David's sake did the LORD his God give him a lamp in Jerusalem, to set up his son after him, and to establish Jerusalem *("for David's sake," the Blessings of the Lord would be given to Judah and Jerusalem; likewise, "for Jesus' sake," we, who deserve nothing, are given everything):*

5 Because David did that which was right in the eyes of the LORD *(it is not important regarding the "eyes of man," but very important regarding the "eyes of the Lord"; if all men smile and God frowns, the smile of man will serve little; if all men frown and God smiles, then all the frowns will not hinder),* and turned not aside from any thing that He *(the Lord)* commanded him all the days of his life, save only in the matter of Uriah the Hittite. *(This statement about Uriah proclaims the Grace of God and, at the same time, the anger of God against sin, which He cannot condone in any case. The only place for sin is at the foot of the Cross; nothing else will have any measurable impact.)*

6 And there was war between Rehoboam and Jeroboam all the days of his life. *(Israelites fighting each other is exactly what Satan desired. Regrettably, too much of the modern Church seems to follow suit.)*

7 Now the rest of the acts of Abijam, and all that he did, are they not written in the book of the Chronicles of the Kings of Judah? And there was war between Abijam and Jeroboam *(Abijam evidently took up where his father Jeroboam left off).*

8 And Abijam slept with his fathers; and they buried him in the city of David: and Asa his son reigned in his stead. *(In II Chron. 12:16, the king's name is recorded as Abijah; but the sacred affix "Jah" was very quickly changed by the Holy Spirit into the word "jam." Such is the case in many a life; there is a fair start, but a foul ending! The first title means "Jehovah is my Father"; the second, "the Sea is my Father." The Heavenly contrasted with an earthly birth — the restless sea with the peace-filled Heaven.)*

ASA'S LONG REIGN

9 And in the twentieth year of Jeroboam king of Israel reigned Asa over Judah.

10 And forty and one years reigned he in Jerusalem. And his mother's name was Maachah, the daughter of Abishalom. *(This is the same as Verse 2. Probably the best explanation is that she was the same one of Verse 2, and was actually the grandmother of Asa. There is*

no word for "grandmother" in the Hebrew language. She could have retained her position, maybe by force of character, or because Asa's mother was dead.)

11 And Asa did that which was right in the eyes of the LORD, as did David his father. *(How refreshing it is to see a king over Judah spoken of by the Holy Spirit in this fashion!)*

12 And he took away the sodomites out of the land *(what he did with them, we aren't told)*, and removed all the idols that his fathers had made.

13 And also Maachah his mother *(grandmother)*, even her he removed from being queen, because she had made an idol in a grove; and Asa destroyed her idol, and burnt it by the brook Kidron.

14 But the high places were not removed: nevertheless Asa's heart was perfect with the LORD all his days *(the failure to remove the "high places" was brought out by the Holy Spirit for a reason; they were generally locations where altars to Jehovah were built and proper sacrifices offered; however, most of them were soon turned into idolatry, where every immoral act imaginable was practiced; we are given very little information, and it seems that the Holy Spirit absolved Asa of responsibility, considering what He says about him).*

15 And he brought in the things which his father had dedicated, and the things which himself had dedicated, into the house of the LORD, silver, and gold, and vessels *(these were probably the spoils of the war with the Ethiopians [II Chron. 14:15; 15:11]).*

WAR BETWEEN ASA AND BAASHA

16 And there was war between Asa and Baasha king of Israel all their days *(probably refers to hostility).*

17 And Baasha king of Israel went up against Judah, and built Ramah, that he might not suffer any to go out or come in to Asa king of Judah.

18 Then Asa took all the silver and the gold that were left in the treasures of the House of the LORD, and the treasures of the king's house, and delivered them into the hand of his servants: and king Asa sent them to Ben-hadad, the son of Tabrimon, the son of Hezion, king of Syria, who dwelt at Damascus, saying *(Asa's calling Ben-hadad to his aid was condemned by the Prophet, Hanani [II Chron. 17:7]),*

19 There is a league between me and you, and between my father and your father: behold, I have sent unto you a present of silver and gold; come and break your league with Baasha king of Israel, that he may depart from me.

20 So Ben-hadad hearkened unto king Asa, and sent the captains of the hosts which he had against the cities of Israel, and smote Ijon, and Dan, and Abel-beth-maachah, and all Cinneroth, with all the land of Naphtali.

21 And it came to pass, when Baasha heard thereof, that he left off building of Ramah, and dwelt in Tirzah.

22 Then king Asa made a proclamation throughout all Judah; none was exempted: and they took away the stones of Ramah, and the timber thereof, wherewith Baasha had built; and king Asa built with them Geba of Benjamin, and Mizpah.

ASA'S DEATH

23 The rest of all the acts of Asa, and all his might, and all that he did, and the cities which he built, are they not written in the book of the Chronicles of the Kings of Judah? Nevertheless in the time of his old age he was diseased in his feet. *("Old age" refers to the time of his death. The Holy Spirit also signifies that his resorting to the physicians of that day was displeasing to the Lord [II Chron. 16:12]. Most "physicians" then functioned in the realm of demon spirits, hence the objection by the Holy Spirit. He didn't lose his soul by this act, but the implication is that he shortened his life.)*

24 And Asa slept with his fathers, and was buried with his fathers in the city of David his father: and Jehoshaphat his son reigned in his stead.

THE EVIL REIGN OF NADAB, KING OF ISRAEL

25 And Nadab the son of Jeroboam began to reign over Israel in the second year of Asa king of Judah, and reigned over Israel two years.

26 And he did evil in the sight of the LORD, and walked in the way of his father, and in his sin *(idolatry)* wherewith he *(Jeroboam)* made Israel to sin.

THE REIGN OF BAASHA, THIRD KING OF ISRAEL

27 And Baasha the son of Ahijah, of the house

of Issachar, conspired against him; and Baasha smote him at Gibbethon, which belonged to the Philistines; for Nadab and all Israel laid siege to Gibbethon. *(Had Nadab attacked idolatry instead of attacking the Philistines, how different would have been his conclusion!)*

28 Even in the third year of Asa king of Judah did Baasha slay him, and reigned in his stead.

29 And it came to pass, when he reigned, that he smote all the house of Jeroboam; he left not to Jeroboam any who breathed, until he had destroyed him, according unto the saying of the LORD, which He spoke by His servant Ahijah the Shilonite *(14:10-14)*:

30 Because of the sins of Jeroboam which he sinned, and which he made Israel sin, by his provocation wherewith he provoked the LORD God of Israel to anger.

31 Now the rest of the acts of Nadab, and all that he did, are they not written in the book of the Chronicles of the Kings of Israel?

32 And there was war between Asa and Baasha king of Israel all their days.

33 In the third year of Asa king of Judah began Baasha the son of Ahijah to reign over all Israel in Tirzah, twenty and four years.

34 And he did evil in the sight of the LORD, and walked in the way of Jeroboam, and in his sin *(idolatry)* wherewith he *(Jeroboam)* made Israel to sin. *(As the account, whether righteous or unrighteous, is inscribed by the Holy Spirit, and for all eternity, so it is with every person [Rev. 20:12-13].)*

CHAPTER 16
(930 B.C.)
JEHU'S PROPHECY AGAINST BAASHA

THEN the Word of the LORD came to Jehu the son of Hanani against Baasha, saying *(the reigns of these five kings of Israel are related with great brevity; the Holy Spirit is concerned only with the events of their reigns insofar as they relate to the Kingdom of God)*,

2 Forasmuch as I exalted you out of the dust, and made you prince over My people Israel; and you have walked in the way of Jeroboam, and have made My people Israel to sin, to provoke Me to anger with their sins *(according to Verse 1, the message was not "to him," but rather "against him")*;

3 Behold, I will take away the posterity of Baasha, and the posterity of his house; and will make your house like the house of Jeroboam the son of Nebat *("take away" means*

"exterminate").

4 Him who dies of Baasha in the city shall the dogs eat; and him who dies of his in the fields shall the fowls of the air eat *(all the Prophets in succession have the same Message from God for the same sins)*.

5 Now the rest of the acts of Baasha, and what he did, and his might, are they not written in the book of the chronicles of the kings of Israel? *(Their wars and their acts are stated to be recorded in the Chronicles of the Kings of Israel. Where is this book? It is lost. Why? Because there is no profit to be had from the doings of the workers of iniquity.)*

6 So Baasha slept with his fathers, and was buried in Tirzah: and Elah his son reigned in his stead.

7 And also by the hand of the Prophet Jehu the son of Hanani came the Word of the LORD against Baasha, and against his house, even for all the evil that he did in the sight of the LORD, in provoking Him to anger with the work of his hands, in being like the house of Jeroboam; and because he *(Baasha)* killed him *(killed Jeroboam; it seems like Baasha executed the judgment with personal and cruel delight, therefore, God smote his family; later on in the Bible, this same principle reappears; the Babylonians were judged by God because they also mercilessly executed His Wrath upon Israel; Believers should never indulge in personal satisfaction on witnessing or hearing of Divine chastisement upon others)*.

ELAH'S TWO-YEAR REIGN OVER ISRAEL

8 In the twenty and sixth year of Asa king of Judah began Elah the son of Baasha to reign over Israel in Tirzah, two years.

ZIMRI'S SEVEN-DAY REIGN

9 And his servant Zimri, captain of half his chariots, conspired against him, as he was in Tirzah, drinking himself drunk in the house of Arza steward of his house in Tirzah.

10 And Zimri went in and smote him, and killed him, in the twenty and seventh year of Asa king of Judah, and reigned in his stead.

11 And it came to pass, when he began to reign, as soon as he sat on his throne, that he slew all the house of Baasha: he left him not one who urinates against a wall, neither of his kinsfolks, nor of his friends *(he was not content with exterminating the royal family; he, as*

well, put to death all who were connected with Baasha in any way).

12 Thus did Zimri destroy all the house of Baasha, according to the Word of the LORD, which He spoke against Baasha by Jehu the Prophet,

13 For all the sins of Baasha, and the sins of Elah his son, by which they sinned, and by which they made Israel to sin, in provoking the LORD God of Israel to anger with their vanities (*these kings leave one sad record upon the page of sacred history — that they did evil*).

14 Now the rest of the acts of Elah, and all that he did, are they not written in the book of the chronicles of the kings of Israel?

THE WICKEDNESS OF OMRI

15 In the twenty and seventh year of Asa king of Judah did Zimri reign seven days in Tirzah. And the people were encamped against Gibbethon, which belonged to the Philistines.

16 And the people who were encamped heard say, Zimri has conspired, and has also slain the king: wherefore all Israel made Omri, the captain of the host, king over Israel that day in the camp.

17 And Omri went up from Gibbethon, and all Israel with him, and they besieged Tirzah.

18 And it came to pass, when Zimri saw that the city was taken, that he went into the palace of the king's house, and burnt the king's house over him with fire, and died,

19 For his sins which he sinned in doing evil in the sight of the LORD, in walking in the way of Jeroboam, and in his sin which he did, to make Israel to sin (*all of this tells us that the Lord cut short the lives of these kings because of their evil*).

20 Now the rest of the acts of Zimri, and his treason that he wrought, are they not written in the book of the chronicles of the kings of Israel? (*The casual reader may wonder why all of this is important? It is important because these people were raised up by God to carry His Name in the Earth. In fact, Israel and Judah were the only two nations in the world which knew Jehovah. Sadly and regrettably, they were poor examples, and were such until they were finally destroyed; however, the promises and predictions of the Prophets are clear that Israel will be restored, and that restoration has already begun. It will come to its successful conclusion at the Second Coming, when Israel then accepts Christ as her Saviour and her Lord.*)

21 Then were the people of Israel divided into two parts: half of the people followed Tibni the son of Ginath, to make him king; and half followed Omri.

22 But the people who followed Omri prevailed against the people who followed Tibni the son of Ginath: so Tibni died, and Omri reigned.

23 In the thirty and first year of Asa king of Judah began Omri to reign over Israel, twelve years: six years reigned he in Tirzah.

24 And he bought the hill Samaria of Shemer for two talents of silver, and built on the hill, and called the name of the city which he built, after the name of Shemer, owner of the hill, Samaria (*because of this, the northern kingdom at times was referred to as "Samaria"*).

25 But Omri wrought evil in the eyes of the LORD, and did worse than all who were before him (*this seems to point to the organization of the calf-worship into a regular formal system*).

26 For he walked in all the way of Jeroboam the son of Nebat, and in his sin wherewith he made Israel to sin, to provoke the LORD God of Israel to anger with their vanities. (*It seems this man Jeroboam was the epitome of evil, because all evil was judged against his evil. His wickedness was not merely a wickedness of passion, but rather of design; therefore, it was more evil.*)

27 Now the rest of the acts of Omri which he did, and his might that he showed, are they not written in the book of the chronicles of the kings of Israel?

WICKED AHAB REIGNS OVER ISRAEL

28 So Omri slept with his fathers, and was buried in Samaria: and Ahab his son reigned in his stead.

29 And in the thirty and eighth year of Asa king of Judah began Ahab the son of Omri to reign over Israel: and Ahab the son of Omri reigned over Israel in Samaria twenty and two years.

30 And Ahab the son of Omri did evil in the sight of the LORD above all who were before him (*under Ahab, positive idolatry was established and fostered — the worship of foreign and shameful deities*).

AHAB MARRIES JEZEBEL

31 And it came to pass, as if it had been a

light thing for him to walk in the sins of Jeroboam the son of Nebat, that he took to wife Jezebel the daughter of Ethbaal king of the Zidonians, and went and served Baal, and worshipped him. *(Baal was the supreme male god of the Canaanitish races, as Ashtoreth was their great female divinity. Jezebel would introduce Baal worship in Israel in a manner that it had not known previously — a sin that God hated supremely.)*

32 And he reared up an Altar for Baal in the house of Baal, which he had built in Samaria *(the house and its contents alike were ultimately destroyed by Jehu [II Ki. 10:27]).*

33 And Ahab made a grove; and Ahab did more to provoke the LORD God of Israel to anger than all the kings of Israel who were before him *(without sincere Repentance, evil can only get worse and worse!).*

34 In his days did Hiel the Beth-elite build Jericho: he laid the foundation thereof in Abiram his firstborn, and set up the gates thereof in his youngest son Segub, according to the Word of the LORD, which He spoke by Joshua the son of Nun. *(The Holy Spirit takes the occasion in this Verse to introduce the fulfilling of the Prophecy given to "Joshua, the son of Nun." Ignoring or despising the Bible, Hiel moves against the prediction of Joshua given some 500 years before and rebuilds the walls which the judgment of God had thrown down. Upon laying the foundations, his oldest son is smitten with death. It also seems that his youngest son died whenever the wall was finished. Ahab should have learned from this how vain and how deadly are the results of opposing God.)*

CHAPTER 17
(910 B.C.)
THE ENTRANCE OF THE
PROPHET ELIJAH

AND Elijah the Tishbite, who was of the inhabitants of Gilead *(his name means "God is Jehovah"; he is considered one of the greatest of the Prophets; he is brought on the scene by the Holy Spirit without fanfare, and even without introduction)*, said unto Ahab, As the LORD God of Israel lives, before Whom I stand, there shall not be dew nor rain these years, but according to my word. *(The idolatrous priests no doubt claimed for Baal dominion over nature and absolute control over the clouds and rain; however, Elijah would portray the fact that it was Jehovah Who ordered the elements, and not Baal. The impotency of Baal to remove the ban would prove the impotency of their god and their claims.)*

THE RAVENS FEED ELIJAH

2 And the Word of the LORD came unto him, saying *(in all this which he did, Elijah was guided by the Word of the Lord, which cannot fail),*

3 Get thee hence, and turn thee eastward, and hide yourself by the brook Cherith, that is before Jordan *("Cherith" means "separation"; even though Elijah was in Israel, which at the time was notoriously wicked, he was separate from its impurity, which the Lord intended; as Believers, we are to be "in" the world, but not "of" the world).*

4 And it shall be, that you shall drink of the brook; and I have commanded the ravens to feed you there *(as the Lord had total control over the elements, as well, He had total control over the fowls of the Heavens, which He had created and, in fact, He has control over everything; when we tap into His Resources, we are tapping into an unlimited supply).*

5 So he went and did according unto the Word of the LORD: for he went and dwelt by the brook Cherith, that is before Jordan.

6 And the ravens brought him bread and flesh in the morning, and bread and flesh in the evening; and he drank of the brook *(to deny this is to deny the fact that God has total control over His Creation).*

7 And it came to pass after a while, that the brook dried up, because there had been no rain in the land *(as to exactly how long this was, we aren't told; it is almost positive, however, that it was more than two years that the Prophet dwelt there).*

ELIJAH RAISES THE WIDOW'S SON

8 And the Word of the LORD came unto him, saying,

9 Arise, get thee to Zarephath, which belongs to Zidon, and dwell there: behold, I have commanded a widow woman there to sustain you *(this woman was a Gentile, and, as we shall see, she was also poverty stricken; Jesus mentioned this incident [Lk. 4:25-26]).*

10 So he arose and went to Zarephath. And when he came to the gate of the city, behold, the widow woman was there gathering of sticks: and he called to her, and said, Fetch me,

I pray you, a little water in a vessel, that I may drink *(even though this woman was a Gentile and, therefore, not a part of the Covenant of Abraham, it must have been that she had turned her back on the heathen gods which she had previously worshipped, and had now called on Jehovah, the God of Israel; irrespective as to where it is, or from whom it comes, God will always honor Faith).*

11 And as she was going to fetch it, he called to her, and said, Bring me, I pray you, a morsel of bread in your hand *(what Elijah knew at this point, we aren't told; however, the Lord was about to test her, just as He tests all of us).*

12 And she said, As the LORD your God lives *(notice, she subscribed Jehovah to Elijah, and not to herself; she had not been serving Jehovah, but rather heathen idols; but things are about to change),* I have not a cake *(a piece of bread),* but an handful of meal in a barrel, and a little oil in a cruse: and, behold, I am gathering two sticks, that I may go in and dress it for me and my son, that we may eat it, and die *(as is obvious, her situation was desperate!).*

13 And Elijah said unto her, Fear not; go and do as you have said: but make me thereof a little cake first, and bring it unto me, and after make for you and for your son. *(This was her test. What would she do? A great lesson is taught here. The economy of the Lord was about to be introduced to this woman. The world says, "Give to me first, and then maybe I'll give something back to you." However, the Lord says, "Give to Me first, whatever it is you have, however meager it might be, at least if it represents your best, and then I will give back to you.")*

14 For thus saith the LORD God of Israel, The barrel of meal shall not waste, neither shall the cruse of oil fail, until the day that the LORD sends rain upon the Earth. *(The woman now had the Promise before her. Would she believe it and act upon it? Or would she reject it? Thank God, she believed the Promise, and acted accordingly.*

To be sure, that Promise given by the Holy Spirit through Elijah so long, long ago is just as apropos today as it was then. If we "seek first the Kingdom of God, and His Righteousness; then all of these things shall be added unto us" [Mat. 6:33].)

15 And she went and did according to the saying of Elijah: and she, and he, and her house, did eat many days *("her house" refers to her relatives, and possibly even her friends; no matter how much meal she took out of the* barrel, or how much oil was taken from the cruse, as much or more remained; once again, please allow me to state that this is a Law of God, which applies even now, at least for those who will dare to believe Him).*

16 And the barrel of meal wasted not, neither did the cruse of oil fail, according to the Word of the LORD, which He spoke by Elijah *(having received a Prophet in the name of a Prophet, she received a Prophet's reward [Mat. 10:41-42]).*

17 And it came to pass after these things, that the son of the woman, the mistress of the house, fell sick; and his sickness was so sore, that there was no breath left in him *(he was dead!).*

18 And she said unto Elijah, What have I to do with you, O thou man of God? are you come unto me to call my sin to remembrance, and to slay my son? *(Whenever the Lord moves mightily, as He did here, Satan will then attack. This means that the second trial of Faith is oftentimes harder than the first trial. But please remember: all of it, irrespective of the course it might take, is a test of our Faith.)*

19 And he said unto her, Give me your son. And he took him out of her bosom, and carried him up into a loft, where he abode, and laid him upon his own bed. *(Elijah laid the corpse upon his own bed. Why did the Prophet take the boy to his own personal room, afforded him by the widow? It was done as a token to show that his presence in her house was definitely a blessing and not a curse.)*

20 And he cried unto the LORD, and said, O LORD my God, have You also brought evil upon the widow with whom I sojourn, by slaying her son? *(Elijah proclaims the fact that God controls all things, and especially life and death.)*

21 And he stretched himself upon the child three times, and cried unto the LORD, and said, O LORD my God, I pray you, let this child's soul come into him again. *(Again, this shows that the boy was dead. Why "three times"? The Lord evidently told him to do this. It actually had nothing to do with the miracle which transpired, but was rather to symbolically portray the Triune God — "God the Father," "God the Son," and "God the Holy Spirit.")*

22 And the LORD heard the voice of Elijah; and the soul of the child came into him again, and he revived *(recovered, and did so instantly!).*

23 And Elijah took the child, and brought him down out of the chamber into the house,

and delivered him unto his mother: and Elijah said, See, your son lives. *(Death had been suspended by and through the barrel of meal and the cruse of oil not failing, and now, again, it had been suspended by being miraculously dismissed [Jn. 10:10].)*

24 And the woman said to Elijah, Now by this I know that you are a man of God, and that the Word of the LORD in your mouth is truth *(presents a statement of Faith far greater than the present miracle; this Gentile woman is exclaiming the fact that Israel's God is now her God).*

CHAPTER 18
(906 B.C.)
ELIJAH GOES TO MEET AHAB

AND it came to pass after many days, that the Word of the LORD came to Elijah in the third year *(the third year of the drought)*, saying, Go, show yourself unto Ahab; and I will send rain upon the Earth. *(The New Testament distinctly states that the drought lasted "three years and six months" [Lk. 4:25; James 5:17]. So, there must have been several months from the time that the Lord spoke to Elijah until he actually did see Ahab, which would total the three and a half years which the drought lasted.)*

2 And Elijah went to show himself unto Ahab. And there was a sore famine in Samaria. *(The famine that was in the land of Samaria due to the drought was also indicative of the spiritual condition. Presently, despite the innumerable Churches in America, I'm afraid the true picture is actually far different than appears on the surface. There is presently a famine in the land, as it refers to the Word of God.)*

3 And Ahab called Obadiah *(this is not the same Prophet who wrote the Book which bears that name)*, which was the governor of his house. (Now Obadiah feared the LORD greatly *(the Lord placed this man in this high office in Samaria that He might use him to protect true Prophets of the Lord, among other things)*:

4 For it was so, when Jezebel cut off the Prophets of the LORD, that Obadiah took an hundred Prophets, and hid them by fifty in a cave, and fed them with bread and water.)

5 And Ahab said unto Obadiah, Go into the land, unto all fountains of water, and unto all brooks: peradventure we may find grass to save the horses and mules alive, that we lose not all the beasts *(as is obvious, the situation had become desperate).*

6 So they divided the land between them to pass throughout it: Ahab went one way by himself, and Obadiah went another way by himself.

7 And as Obadiah was in the way, behold, Elijah met him: and he knew him, and fell on his face, and said, Are you that my lord Elijah?

8 And he answered him, I am: go, tell your lord, Behold, Elijah is here.

9 And he said, What have I sinned, that you would deliver your servant into the hand of Ahab, to kill me?

10 As the LORD your God lives, there is no nation or kingdom, whither my lord has not sent to seek you: and when they said, He is not there; he took an oath of the kingdom and nation, that they found you not. *(Why was Ahab this desperate to find Elijah? The answer is simple; it was Elijah who had stopped the rain, and it was Elijah alone who could bring back the rain [James 5:17-18].)*

11 And now you say, Go, tell your lord, Behold, Elijah is here.

12 And it shall come to pass, as soon as I am gone from you, that the Spirit of the LORD shall carry you whither I know not; and so when I come and tell Ahab, and he cannot find you, he shall kill me: but I your servant fear the LORD from my youth.

13 Was it not told my lord what I did when Jezebel slew the Prophets of the LORD, how I hid an hundred men of the LORD's Prophets by fifty in a cave, and fed them with bread and water? *(Considering the drought and the famine, this was a considerable undertaking.)*

14 And now you say, Go, tell your lord, Behold, Elijah is here: and he shall kill me.

15 And Elijah said, As the LORD of Hosts lives, before Whom I stand, I will surely show myself unto him to day *(because the Lord had told him to do so [Vs. 1]).*

16 So Obadiah went to meet Ahab, and told him: and Ahab went to meet Elijah.

17 And it came to pass, when Ahab saw Elijah, that Ahab said unto him, Are you he who troubles Israel?

18 And he answered, I have not troubled Israel; but you, and your father's house, in that you have forsaken the Commandments of the LORD, and you have followed Baalim *(in other words, this was the cause of all of Israel's problems).*

19 Now therefore send, and gather to me all Israel unto Mount Carmel, and the prophets of Baal four hundred and fifty, and the

Prophets of the groves four hundred, which eat at Jezebel's table *(these were two different sets of false prophets, totaling 850; 400 were supported by Jezebel).*

THE CONTEST ON MOUNT CARMEL

20 So Ahab sent unto all the Children of Israel, and gathered the prophets together unto Mount Carmel *(this took some days, and possibly several weeks).*

21 And Elijah came unto all the people *(when they all had gathered at Mount Carmel)*, and said, How long halt you between two opinions? if the LORD be God, follow Him: but if Baal, then follow him. And the people answered him not a word *(the objective of Elijah was to prove that Jehovah, and not Baal, was God).*

22 Then said Elijah unto the people, I, even I only, remain a Prophet of the LORD *(not the only Prophet of the Lord in Israel, but the only one present that day on Mount Carmel)*; but Baal's prophets are four hundred and fifty men *(one man against 450).*

23 Let them therefore give us two bullocks; and let them choose one bullock for themselves, and cut it in pieces, and lay it on wood, and put no fire under: and I will dress the other bullock, and lay it on wood, and put no fire under *(the Lord had no doubt told him to do this):*

24 And call ye on the name of your gods, and I will call on the Name of the LORD: and the God Who answers by fire, let Him be God. And all the people answered and said, It is well spoken *(Baal claimed to be the Sun-god and lord of the elements and forces of nature; while Jehovah, as well, identified Himself with this token [Lev. 9:24; I Chron. 21:26; II Chron. 7:1]).*

THE FUTILE EFFORTS OF
BAAL'S PROPHETS

25 And Elijah said unto the prophets of Baal, Choose you one bullock for yourselves, and dress it first; for you are many; and call on the name of your gods, but put no fire under.

26 And they took the bullock which was given them, and they dressed it, and called on the name of Baal from morning even until noon, saying, O Baal, hear us. But there was no voice, nor any who answered. And they leaped upon the altar which was made. *(Let the words, "there was no answer," be amply heard!*

Of all the religious superstition in the world presently, there is no answer from that source. As then, so now!)

27 And it came to pass at noon, that Elijah mocked them, and said, Cry aloud: for he is a god; either he is talking, or he is pursuing, or he is in a journey, or perhaps he sleeps, and must be awakened *(in other words, Elijah is mocking them!).*

28 And they cried aloud, and cut themselves after their manner with knives and lancets, till the blood gushed out upon them *(they were becoming desperate!).*

29 And it came to pass, when midday was past, and they prophesied until the time of the offering of the evening sacrifice *(about 3 p.m.)*, that there was neither voice, nor any to answer, nor any who regarded *(their petitions went unanswered).*

THE FIRE FROM HEAVEN CONSUMES
ELIJAH'S SACRIFICE

30 And Elijah said unto all the people, Come near unto me. And all the people came near unto him. And he repaired the Altar of the LORD that was broken down. *(The "Altar" was a type of the coming Cross, and what Jesus would do there. As is obvious, Israel no longer believed in the Altar of Jehovah and, above all, what it represented, namely the Cross. Elijah repaired the Altar, which had once been used, but had fallen into disrepair. The Church presently desperately needs to "repair the Altar of the Lord that is broken down." In other words, it desperately needs to re-establish its faith in Christ and the Cross.)*

31 And Elijah took twelve stones, according to the number of the tribes of the sons of Jacob, unto whom the Word of the LORD came, saying, Israel shall be your name:

32 And with the stones he built an Altar *(repaired the Altar)* in the Name of the LORD *("twelve" is God's number of Government; all of this plainly tells us that God's Government must have the Cross as its foundation, or else it's not God's Government [I Pet. 1:18-20]):* and he made a trench about the Altar *(the "trench" speaks of separation from the world, which the Cross will always bring about)*, as great as would contain two measures of seed.

33 And he put the wood in order *(typifying the Cross)*, and cut the bullock in pieces *(typifying the death of Christ)*, and laid him on the wood, and said, Fill four barrels with water

(typical of the Word of God, with the number "four" typifying all four corners of the compass, referring to the fact that Jesus died for the whole world [Jn. 3:16]), and pour it on the Burnt Sacrifice, and on the wood *(signifying that the Word of God, symbolized by the water, covered everything that Jesus would do).*

34 And he said, Do it the second time. And they did it the second time. And he said, Do it the third time. And they did it the third time *(once again, signifying the Triune God!).*

35 And the water ran round about the Altar; and he filled the trench also with water *(typifying that all were saturated in the Word of God, of which the water was a type).*

36 And it came to pass at the time of the offering of the evening Sacrifice, that Elijah the Prophet came near, and said, LORD God of Abraham, Isaac, and of Israel, let it be known this day that You are God in Israel, and that I am Your servant, and that I have done all these things at Your Word *(in other words, the Lord told him exactly what to do in all of this situation).*

37 Hear me, O LORD, hear me, that this people may know that You are the LORD God, and that You have turned their heart back again *(all of this would be done to turn the hearts of Israel back to God).*

38 Then the fire of the LORD fell, and consumed the Burnt Sacrifice, and the wood, and the stones, and the dust, and licked up the water that was in the trench *(the "fire" was a type of the Judgment of God that would fall on Christ when He hung on the Cross, with Him suffering death, and all on our behalf).*

39 And when all the people saw it, they fell on their faces: and they said, The LORD, He is the God; the LORD; He is the God *(not Baal, but Jehovah).*

40 And Elijah said unto them, Take the Prophets of Baal; let not one of them escape. And they took them: and Elijah brought them down to the brook Kishon, and slew them there *(there is no record that Elijah carried out this task himself, but rather that the people of Israel did).*

RAIN IS COMING

41 And Elijah said unto Ahab, Get thee up, eat and drink; for there is a sound of abundance of rain *(the people had been directed back to the Cross, of which the Altar was a type, and now the rain of the Spirit could fall; before the Holy Spirit can work, the Church must come back to the Cross; there is no other way!).*

42 So Ahab went up to eat and to drink. And Elijah went up to the top of Carmel; and he cast himself down upon the Earth, and put his face between his knees *(the posture witnessed to the intensity of his supplication),*

43 And said to his servant, Go up now, look toward the sea. And he went up, and looked, and said, There is nothing. And he said, Go again seven times *("seven" is God's number of perfection; in other words, the rain that was coming would be in proportion to God Who was sending it; even though the Lord had promised this, we find that Elijah had to persevere; this should be a lesson to us; if we ask and we do not receive, we ought to keep asking [Lk. 11:6-13]).*

44 And it came to pass at the seventh time, that he said, Behold, there arises a little cloud out of the sea, like a man's hand. And he said, Go up, say unto Ahab, Prepare your chariot, and get thee down that the rain stop you not.

45 And it came to pass in the mean while, that the heaven was black with clouds and wind, and there was a great rain. And Ahab rode, and went to Jezreel.

46 And the Hand of the LORD was on Elijah; and he girded up his loins, and ran before Ahab to the entrance of Jezreel *(for Elijah to have been able to physically do this would once again demand the Power of God; it was done in order to show Ahab that the supernatural Power of God was on Elijah the Prophet, as if what had just happened concerning the falling of the fire was not enough!).*

CHAPTER 19
(906 B.C.)

ELIJAH FLEES FROM JEZEBEL

AND Ahab told Jezebel all that Elijah had done, and withal how he had slain all the prophets *(of Baal)* with the sword.

2 Then Jezebel sent a messenger unto Elijah, saying, So let the gods do to me, and more also, if I make not your life as the life of one of them by to morrow about this time. *(She claimed she would kill Elijah. It should have been obvious to the Prophet that her threats were empty. Almost immediately after a great victory in the Lord, Satan often attacks with great success. In this, we must remember that the faith of yesterday does not suffice for the need of today. The Child of God must ever have a continued deposit of the touch of God, even on a*

daily basis. If Jezebel was so sure of her position, why did she not send soldiers to kill Elijah, instead of a messenger with the threat? She did not do so, because she feared for the life of the soldiers, and even herself. As the fear of Elijah was totally unfounded, so is the fear of every other Child of God unfounded.)

3 And when he saw that, he arose, and went for his life, and came to Beer-sheba, which belongs to Judah, and left his servant there. *(The mighty Prophet is now operating from a position of fear. Fear always leads one away from the Will of God. Faith always leads one toward the Will of God. But fear is now in control.*

As well, fear always seeks isolation, so he left his servant in Beer-sheba.)

4 But he himself went a day's journey into the wilderness *(the "wilderness" is somewhat of a type of his own spiritual position)*, and came and sat down under a juniper tree; and he requested for himself that he might die; and said, It is enough; now, O LORD, take away my life; for I am not better than my fathers. *(Elijah, by Faith, has just overcome 450 prophets of Baal and, now, he is fearful of one woman. Satan's threats come in every direction. Too often we believe his lies instead of the truth of the Word of God.)*

5 And as he lay and slept under a juniper tree, behold, then an Angel touched him, and said unto him. Arise and eat *(did he know this was an Angel?)*.

6 And he looked, and, behold, there was a cake baken on the coals, and a cruse of water at his head. And he did eat and drink, and laid him down again *(in fact, the Angel of the Lord had followed him all the way from Mount Carmel)*.

7 And the Angel of the LORD came again the second time, and touched him, and said, Arise and eat; because the journey is too great for you. *(This was a journey not ordained of God. In fact, it would be a round-trip of approximately 500 miles, all of it out of the Will of God. And yet, in this wayward journey, the Lord would never leave Elijah's side. How many wayward trips have all of us taken? And yet the Lord never leaves us nor forsakes us.*

The fact is: every journey of fear is too great for us. The reason is: our energy is from the flesh and not the Spirit.)

ELIJAH GOES TO HOREB

8 And he arose, and did eat and drink, and

went in the strength of that meat forty days and forty nights unto Horeb the Mount of God. *(Horeb was about 180 miles from where he had sat under a "juniper tree." Evidently, the food prepared for him by the Angel was supernatural, and provided a supernatural strength.)*

9 And he came thither unto a cave, and lodged there; and, behold, the Word of the LORD came to him, and He said unto him, What doest thou here, Elijah? *(Even though it cannot be proven, there is a possibility that the cave that Elijah arrived at was the "clift of the rock" in which Moses had stood while the Lord passed by [Ex. 33:22]. He had come all this distance, and now the Lord asks him as to why he is here?)*

10 And he said, I have been very jealous for the LORD God of Hosts: for the Children of Israel have forsaken Your Covenant, thrown down Your altars, and slain Your Prophets with the sword; and I, even I only, am left; and they seek my life, to take it away. *(The angry Prophet, crouching with embittered heart in the cavern, pictured the nation. The "flesh" in him was just as hateful as the "flesh" in them. He is invited to come forth and meet God. As Israel refused, Elijah likewise refuses. He must, therefore, be compelled to come forth.)*

11 And He said, Go forth, and stand upon the mount before the LORD. And, behold, the LORD passed by, and a great and strong wind rent the mountains, and broke in pieces the rocks before the LORD; but the LORD was not in the wind: and after the wind an earthquake; but the LORD was not in the earthquake:

12 And after the earthquake a fire; but the LORD was not in the fire: and after the fire a still small voice. *(While the Lord was the cause of all of these things, this was not the manner in which He would speak to the Prophet. Unfortunately, far too many in the modern Church have traded the "still small voice" for the fire, wind, earthquake, etc. And then they wonder why they get into trouble!)*

13 And it was so, when Elijah heard it, that he wrapped his face in his mantle, and went out, and stood in the entering in of the cave. And, behold, there came a voice unto him, and said, What doest thou here, Elijah? *(Why does the Lord keep asking the Prophet this question? He does so for all the various reasons. The Lord didn't bring him here, so why has he come? If it's not the Lord, it should not be done! I personally think the Lord is asking this same question of many, even at this present time. What*

are you doing here?)

14 And he said, I have been very jealous for the LORD God of Hosts: because the Children of Israel have forsaken Your Covenant, thrown down Your Altars, and slain Your Prophets with the sword; and I, even I only, am left; and they seek my life, to take it away. *(As is obvious here, Elijah's emphasis is strictly on himself and not the Lord. When self is not properly hidden in Christ [Jn. 14:20], self always becomes king, and brings about many problems. That's the reason that Jesus told us that we must "deny ourselves" [Lk. 9:23].)*

15 And the LORD said unto him, Go, return on your way to the wilderness of Damascus: and when you come, anoint Hazael to be king over Syria:

16 And Jehu the son of Nimshi shall you anoint to be king over Israel: and Elisha the son of Shaphat of Abel-meholah shall you anoint to be Prophet in your room. *(There is no record that Elijah physically anointed anyone. It may very well have happened, but no more information is given.*

In the first place, Syria was by and large the enemy of Israel. So, it's hard to imagine that any Syrian would have allowed Elijah to do such, considering that, in some way, it would have been a recognition of Jehovah, which, of course, Syria would not do.

All of this is probably the Lord telling Elijah what is going to happen in the near future.)

17 And it shall come to pass, that him who escapes the sword of Hazael shall Jehu slay: and him who escapes from the sword of Jehu shall Elisha slay. *(Some of this was literal, but, concerning the Prophet Elisha, who would take the place of Elijah, the term was used strictly in the spiritual sense, for Elisha was a man of peace.)*

18 Yet I have left Me seven thousand in Israel, all the knees which have not bowed unto Baal, and every mouth which has not kissed him. *(We gather from Job 31:26-27 that it was customary to kiss the hand of the idol, or object of worship — Pulpit. Whether the number "seven thousand" is to be taken literally or not, we have no way of knowing. It could very well have been symbolic and, again, it could very well have been literal.)*

THE CALL OF ELISHA

19 So he departed thence, and found Elisha the son of Shaphat, who was plowing with twelve yoke of oxen before him, and he with the twelfth: and Elijah passed by him, and cast his mantle upon him. *(Nearby was a school of the Prophets, but upon none of these did Elijah cast his mantle; but, guided by the Holy Spirit, he cast it upon a plowboy. How different are God's thoughts from man's! He chose "Amos," who was a gatherer of sycamore fruit, and "Paul," who was not one of the twelve, and "Moody," who was uneducated. Through men like these, He rebukes and refreshes the "official Ministry.")*

20 And he left the oxen, and ran after Elijah, and said, Let me, I pray you, kiss my father and my mother, and then I will follow you. And he said unto him, Go back again: for what have I done to you? *(A greater readiness to obey the prophetic summons Elisha could not well have shown. He only asked that he be allowed to go bid his parents farewell, which was the right thing for him to do, and to which Elijah readily acquiesced.)*

21 And he returned back from him, and took a yoke of oxen, and slew them, and boiled their flesh with the instruments of the oxen, and gave unto the people, and they did eat. Then he arose, and went after Elijah, and ministered unto him. *(This was a symbolic act, expressive of Elisha's entire renunciation of his secular calling. This was a farewell, not a religious feast. He was in essence saying that he would not be back. He was obeying the call to the full, even as he should have done.)*

CHAPTER 20
(901 B.C.)
BEN-HADAD BESIEGES SAMARIA

AND Ben-hadad the king of Syria gathered all his host together: and there were thirty and two kings with him, and horses, and chariots; and he went up and besieged Samaria, and warred against it *(evidently, these 32 kings were vassals, not allied powers; at any rate, it was a formidable force).*

2 And he sent messengers to Ahab king of Israel into the city, and said unto him, Thus saith Ben-hadad *(as he laid siege to the city),*

3 Your silver and your gold is mine; your wives also and your children, even the goodliest, are mine. *(Even though Israel was far, far from God, still, whatever it is they had belonged to God. So, Ben-hadad's threat was actually against the Lord, even though he would not have realized such.)*

4 And the king of Israel answered and said,

My lord, O king, according to your saying, I am yours, and all that I have *(as we shall see, Ben-hadad didn't exactly believe Ahab)*.

5 And the messengers came again, and said, Thus speaks Ben-hadad, saying, Although I have sent unto you, saying, You shall deliver me your silver, and your gold, and your wives, and your children;

6 Yet I will send my servants unto you to morrow about this time, and they shall search your house, and the houses of your servants; and it shall be, that whatsoever is pleasant in your eyes, they shall put it in their hand, and take it away *(the object of Ben-hadad was to couch his message in the most offensive and humiliating terms)*.

7 Then the king of Israel called all the elders of the land, and said, Mark, I pray you, and see how this man seeks mischief: for he sent unto me for my wives, and for my children, and for my silver, and for my gold; and I denied him not.

8 And all the elders and all the people said unto him, Hearken not unto him, nor consent.

9 Wherefore he said unto the messengers of Ben-hadad, Tell my lord the king, All that you did send for to your servant at the first I will do: but this thing I may not do. And the messengers departed, and brought him *(Ben-hadad)* word again.

10 And Ben-hadad sent unto him *(Ahab)*, and said, The gods do so unto me, and more also, if the dust of Samaria shall suffice for handfuls for all the people who follow me *(my army is big enough to reduce Samaria to a pile of dust)*.

11 And the king of Israel answered and said, Tell him, Let not him who girds on his harness boast himself as he who puts it off *(this was the message sent by Ahab to Ben-hadad)*.

12 And it came to pass, when Ben-hadad heard this message, as he was drinking, he and the kings in the pavilions, that he said unto his servants, Set yourselves in array. And they set themselves in array against the city *(against Samaria)*.

GOD PROMISES VICTORY FOR AHAB

13 And, behold, there came a Prophet unto Ahab king of Israel, saying, Thus saith the LORD, Have you seen all this great multitude? behold, I will deliver it into your hand this day; and you shall know that I am the LORD. *(Despite the great evil being committed*

by Israel, the Lord, at this time, would deem it desirable to deliver His people. Israel belonged to Him, even though most were far from God.

We learn from this that all had best be careful in laying their hands on that which belongs to the Lord. In fact, God gives no man the right to chastise another brother or sister in the Lord [James 4:12]. While the Lord, at times, may use human instrumentation to carry out chastisement, it is always unwitting on the part of the subjects. In other words, the individuals being used are not conscious of such a fact.)

14 And Ahab said, By whom? And he said, Thus saith the LORD, Even by the young men of the princes of the provinces. Then he said, Who shall order the battle? And he answered, You.

VICTORY OVER THE SYRIANS

15 Then he numbered the young men of the princes of the provinces, and they were two hundred and thirty two: and after them he numbered all the people, even all the Children of Israel, being seven thousand *(a miserably small group of men to meet the powerful Syrian army)*.

16 And they went out at noon. But Ben-hadad was drinking himself drunk in the pavilions, he and the kings, the thirty and two kings who helped him.

17 And the young men of the princes of the provinces went out first; and Ben-hadad sent out, and they told him, saying, There are men come out of Samaria.

18 And he said, Whether they be come out for peace, take them alive; or whether they be come out for war, take them alive.

19 So these young men of the princes of the provinces *(from Israel)* came out of the city, and the army which followed them *(such as it was!)*.

20 And they slew every one his man: and the Syrians fled; and Israel pursued them: and Ben-hadad the king of Syria escaped on an horse with the horsemen.

21 And the king of Israel went out, and smote the horses and chariots, and slew the Syrians with a great slaughter *(of course, all of this was done by the Lord!)*.

THE PROPHET WARNS AHAB

22 And the Prophet *(the same one who came at the first, whom the Word of God does not*

identify) came to the king of Israel, and said unto him, Go, strengthen yourself, and mark, and see what you do: for at the return of the year the king of Syria will come up against you.

23 And the servants of the king of Syria said unto him, Their gods are gods of the hills; therefore they were stronger than we; but let us fight against them in the plain, and surely we shall be stronger than they. *(The Syrians recognized that it was God Who had defeated them, but they looked at Jehovah as a local deity, and, in this case, a God of the hills. So, if they fight in the valley, the God of Israel will be helpless, or so they think. Unredeemed man has no idea of Who God is, or What God is!)*

24 And do this thing, Take the kings away, every man out of his place, and put captains in their rooms *(put veteran military men at the head of each unit):*

25 And number thee an army, like the army that you have lost, horse for horse, and chariot for chariot: and we will fight against them in the plain, and surely we shall be stronger than they. And he hearkened unto their voice, and did so.

26 And it came to pass at the return of the year, that Ben-hadad numbered the Syrians, and went up to Aphek, to fight against Israel *(exactly as the Prophet had said would happen).*

27 And the Children of Israel were numbered, and were all present, and went against them: and the Children of Israel pitched before them like two little flocks of kids *(a tiny army)*; but the Syrians filled the country *(outnumbered Israel, probably 100 to 1, or even more).*

28 And there came a man of God, and spoke unto the king of Israel, and said, Thus saith the LORD, Because the Syrians have said, The LORD is God of the hills, but He is not God of the valleys, therefore will I deliver all this great multitude into your hand, and you shall know that I am the LORD. *(Whether this "man of God" was the same person as the "Prophet" of Verses 13 and 22 is not quite clear. This was being done for Israel by the Lord for their benefit, but also that neighboring nations might learn His Power, and that His Name might be magnified among them.)*

29 And they pitched one over against the other seven days. And so it was, that in the seventh day the battle was joined: and the Children of Israel slew of the Syrians an hundred thousand footmen in one day *(did so by the Power of God, for that was the only way it could be done).*

30 But the rest fled to Aphek, into the city; and there a wall fell upon twenty and seven thousand of the men who were left. And Ben-hadad fled, and came into the city, into an inner chamber *(evidently, the 27,000 men had gotten on the wall, or else were sitting against the wall, when the Lord caused it to fall; whatever happened, it was caused totally by the Lord).*

AHAB SINS IN SPARING THE LIFE OF BEN-HADAD

31 And his servants said unto him, Behold now, we have heard that the kings of the house of Israel are merciful kings: let us, I pray you, put sackcloth on our loins, and ropes upon our heads, and go out to the king of Israel: peradventure he will save your life.

32 So they girded sackcloth on their loins, and put ropes on their heads, and came to the king of Israel, and said, Your servant Ben-hadad says, I pray you, let me live *(compare this abject petition for life with the arrogant insolence of Verses 6 and 10).* And he *(Ahab)* said, Is he *(Ben-hadad)* yet alive? he is my brother *(a most ridiculous position for Ahab to take).*

33 Now the men did diligently observe whether any thing would come from him, and did hastily catch it: and they said, Your brother Ben-hadad. Then he said, Go ye, bring him. Then Ben-hadad came forth to him; and he caused him to come up into the chariot.

34 And Ben-hadad said unto him, The cities, which my father took from your father, I will restore; and you shall make streets for you in Damascus, as my father made in Samaria. Then said Ahab, I will send you away with this covenant. So he made a covenant with him, and sent him away *(which was greatly displeasing to the Lord!).*

THE PROPHET REBUKES AHAB

35 And a certain man of the sons of the Prophets said unto his neighbour in the Word of the LORD, Smite me, I pray you. And the man refused to smite him. *(The "neighbor" was a companion Prophet, hence the seriousness of his ignoring the Word of the Lord. In fact, this was a school of the Prophets, which owed its existence, more than likely, to Samuel, who began it about 200 years before.)*

36 Then said he unto him, Because you have not obeyed the voice of the LORD, behold, as

soon as you are departed from me, a lion shall kill you. And as soon as he was departed from him, a lion found him, and killed him *(at first glance, it may seem as if the punishment was severe; however, again we emphasize: to ignore the plain, clear, and simple Word of God is a most serious thing)*.

37 Then he found another man, and said, Smite me, I pray you. And the man smote him, so that in smiting he wounded him.

38 So the Prophet departed, and waited for the king by the way, and disguised himself with ashes upon his face.

39 And as the king passed by, he cried unto the king: and he said, Your servant went out into the midst of the battle; and, behold, a man turned aside, and brought a man unto me, and said, Keep this man: if by any means he be missing, then shall your life be for his life, or else you shall pay a talent of silver *(through the Prophet, the Lord presents an object lesson to Ahab)*.

40 And as your servant was busy here and there, he was gone *(escaped)*. And the king of Israel said unto him, So shall your judgment be; yourself have decided it *(Ahab himself now pronounces that the judgment is just)*.

41 And he hasted, and took the ashes away from his face; and the king of Israel discerned him that he was of the Prophets.

42 And he said unto him, Thus saith the LORD, Because you have let go out of your hand a man whom I appointed to utter destruction *(whom the Lord appointed)*, therefore your life shall go for his life, and your people for his people *(Ahab has seriously displeased the Lord in letting Ben-hadad go free; he will now pay the price, even though it will be a couple of years in coming)*.

43 And the king of Israel went to his house heavy and displeased, and came to Samaria.

CHAPTER 21
(899 B.C.)
NABOTH REFUSES TO SELL
HIS VINEYARD TO AHAB

AND it came to pass after these things, that Naboth the Jezreelite had a Vineyard, which was in Jezreel, hard by the palace of Ahab king of Samaria. *(The entirety of this Chapter concerns this Vineyard. Naboth's Vineyard is a type of the spiritual inheritance that every Child of God has. As his Vineyard bordered Ahab's palace, so our spiritual inheritance*

[Vineyard] borders the world.)

2 And Ahab spoke unto Naboth, saying, Give me your Vineyard, that I may have it for a garden of herbs, because it is near unto my house: and I will give you for it a better vineyard than it; or, if it seem good to you, I will give you the worth of it in money. *(The same pressure that was applied by Ahab against Naboth to sell his Vineyard will be applied to us by the forces of darkness to compromise our convictions. As this battle was to the death, so will the battle that we fight be unto the death. We have but one of two choices: 1. We can refuse Satan any part in that which God has given us; or, 2. We can sell out to Ahab — the world.*

The first one will bring physical death but spiritual life. The second one will bring physical life but spiritual death.

Satan professes to have better Vineyards. He lies. If he has better Vineyards, why does he want yours?)

3 And Naboth said to Ahab, The LORD forbid it me, that I should give the inheritance of my fathers unto you. *(As Naboth's Vineyard was given unto him by the Lord of Glory, likewise, our Vineyard of Salvation is given to us by the Lord of Glory.*

Actually, the Law of Moses forbade the sale of ancestral rights, except in extreme destitution and, even then, the property would always return to the original owners in the Year of Jubilee [Lev. 25:23-25; Num. 36:7].)

4 And Ahab came into his house heavy and displeased because of the word which Naboth the Jezreelite had spoken to him: for he had said, I will not give you the inheritance of my fathers. And he laid him down upon his bed, and turned away his face, and would eat no bread *(pouting)*.

JEZEBEL HAS NABOTH KILLED

5 But Jezebel his wife came to him, and said unto him, Why is your spirit so sad, that you eat no bread?

6 And he said unto her, Because I spoke unto Naboth the Jezreelite, and said unto him, Give me your Vineyard for money, or else, if it please you, I will give you another Vineyard for it: and he answered, I will not give you my Vineyard.

7 And Jezebel his wife said unto him, Do you now govern the kingdom of Israel? arise, and eat bread, and let your heart be merry: I will give you the Vineyard of Naboth the

Jezreelite *(I will give it to you; you don't need to buy it)*.

8 So she wrote letters in Ahab's name, and sealed them with his seal, and sent the letters unto the elders and to the nobles who were in his city, dwelling with Naboth.

9 And she wrote in the letters, saying, Proclaim a fast, and set Naboth on high among the people *(a place of honor)*:

10 And set two men, sons of Belial *(worthless)*, before him, to bear witness against him, saying, You did blaspheme God and the king. And then carry him out, and stone, him, that he may die. *(They first pretended to honor him, and now they claim to have found this great fault in him; so he must be stoned to death.)*

11 And the men of his city, even the elders and the nobles who were the inhabitants in his city, did as Jezebel had sent unto them, and as it was written in the letters which she had sent unto them.

12 They proclaimed a fast, and set Naboth on high among the people.

13 And there came in two men, children of Belial, and sat before him: and the men of Belial witnessed against him, even against Naboth, in the presence of the people, saying, Naboth did blaspheme God and the king. Then they carried him forth out of the city, and stoned him with stones, that he died *(it was all a planned farce from the very beginning)*.

14 Then they sent to Jezebel, saying, Naboth is stoned, and is dead.

15 And it came to pass, when Jezebel heard that Naboth was stoned, and was dead, that Jezebel said to Ahab, Arise, take possession of the Vineyard of Naboth the Jezreelite, which he refused to give you for money: for Naboth is not alive, but dead.

16 And it came to pass, when Ahab heard that Naboth was dead, that Ahab rose up to go down to the Vineyard of Naboth the Jezreelite, to take possession of it *(this was the day after the murder)*.

ELIJAH PRONOUNCES JUDGMENT ON AHAB AND JEZEBEL

17 And the Word of the LORD came to Elijah the Tishbite, saying,

18 Arise, go down to meet Ahab king of Israel, which is in Samaria: behold, he is in the Vineyard of Naboth, where he is gone down to possess it.

19 And you shall speak unto him, saying,

Thus saith the LORD, Have you killed, and also taken possession? and you shall speak unto him, saying, Thus saith the LORD, In the place where dogs licked the blood of Naboth shall dogs lick your blood, even yours *(Jesus said, "With what measure you mete, it shall be measured to you again" [Mat. 7:2])*.

20 And Ahab said to Elijah, Have you found me, O my enemy? and he answered, I have found you: because you have sold yourself to work evil in the sight of the LORD. *(This Chapter opens with Ahab refusing to listen to God's loving voice, which is spoken to him so plainly in the remarkable victory given to him over the Syrians, but willingly listening to Jezebel's cruel voice prompting him to commit perhaps the blackest of his black crimes.)*

21 Behold, I will bring evil upon you, and will take away your posterity, and will cut off from Ahab him who urinates against the wall, and him who is shut up and left in Israel,

22 And will make your house like the house of Jeroboam the son of Nebat, and like the house of Baasha the son of Ahijah, for the provocation wherewith you have provoked me to anger, and made Israel to sin *(Ahab and Jezebel led Israel ever deeper into sin)*.

23 And of Jezebel also spoke the LORD, saying, The dogs shall eat Jezebel by the wall of Jezreel *(retribution should overtake her near the scene of her latest crime [II Ki. 9:36]; by this, the just judgment of God would be made the more conspicuous)*.

24 Him who dies of Ahab in the city the dogs shall eat; and him who dies in the field shall the fowls of the air eat.

25 But there was none like unto Ahab, which did sell himself to work wickedness in the sight of the LORD, whom Jezebel his wife stirred up *(Ahab was the most wicked king of Israel thus far; and, in fact, this program of ever-increasing wickedness continued until the whole nation had to be destroyed)*.

26 And he did very abominably in following idols, according to all things as did the Amorites, whom the LORD cast out before the Children of Israel.

AHAB'S REPENTANCE

27 And it came to pass, when Ahab heard those words, that he rent his clothes, and put sackcloth upon his flesh, and fasted, and lay in sack cloth, and went softly. *(It seems that this man's Repentance was sincere — at least for a*

time. God would not have spoken to a half-hearted repentance.)

28 And the Word of the LORD came to Elijah the Tishbite, saying,

29 Do you see how Ahab humbles himself before Me? because he humbles himself before Me, I will not bring the evil in his days: but in his son's days will I bring the evil upon his house. *(There is no threat of punishment against the innocent instead of the guilty, as might at first sight appear. For, in the first place, God knew well what the son would be, and, in the second place, if the son had departed from his father's sins, he would have been spared, as well [Ezek. 18:14]; judgment was deferred to give the house of Ahab another chance, but, regrettably, to no avail!)*

CHAPTER 22
(897 B.C.)

JEHOSHAPHAT AGREES TO HELP AHAB

AND they continued three years without war between Syria and Israel. *(This was because of the two great defeats that Syria had suffered at the hands of Israel, and because of Ahab's Repentance. But now, Ahab resorts to his old ways.)*

2 And it came to pass in the third year, that Jehoshaphat the king of Judah came down to the king of Israel *(he not only came down topographically, but spiritually as well)*.

3 And the king of Israel said unto his servants, Know ye that Ramoth in Gilead is ours, and we be still, and take it not out of the hand of the king of Syria? *(This great frontier fortress was, in the hands of Syria, even after many reverses, a constant menace against Israel.)*

4 And he said unto Jehoshaphat, Will you go with me to battle to Ramoth-gilead? And Jehoshaphat said to the king of Israel, I am as you are, my people as your people, my horses as your horses *(in reality, Jehoshaphat was totally unlike Ahab)*.

AHAB LISTENS TO FALSE PROPHETS

5 And Jehoshaphat said unto the king of Israel, Enquire, I pray you, at the Word of the LORD to day *(remembering how Ahab's late victories had been foretold by a Prophet, and had been won by the help of Jehovah, Jehoshaphat might well suppose that his new ally would be eager to know the Word of the Lord)*.

6 Then the king of Israel gathered the prophets together, about four hundred men, and said unto them, Shall I go against Ramoth-gilead to battle, or shall I forbear? And they said, Go up; for the LORD shall deliver it into the hand of the king. *(These prophets claimed to be of the Lord, but were not. They characterize the myriad of those who call themselves Prophets in Christendom today. In fact, there were precious few true Prophets of God then; there are precious few true Prophets of God now.)*

7 And Jehoshaphat said, Is there not here a Prophet of the LORD besides, that we might enquire of him? *(The falsity of these prophets was evident to Jehoshaphat. The tragedy is: the Church presently hardly knows the difference in the prophets who prophesy out of their own minds, and those who speak, "Thus saith the Lord.")*

8 And the king of Israel said unto Jehoshaphat, There is yet one man, Micaiah the son of Imlah, by whom we may enquire of the LORD; but I hate him; for he does not prophesy good concerning me, but evil. And Jehoshaphat said, Let not the king say so. *(Elijah was also alive at this time, and had already given several messages to Ahab, but was now ignored, or perhaps he was elsewhere in the kingdom.*

The truth is, the true Prophet's task is a thankless task. He is seldom sent to bring good news, but mostly bad. By and large, he is hated, not only by the world, but by a carnal Church as well!)

9 Then the king of Israel called an officer, and said, Hasten hither Micaiah the son of Imlah.

10 And the king of Israel and Jehoshaphat the king of Judah sat each on his throne, having put on their robes, in a void place in the entrance of the gate of Samaria; and all the prophets prophesied before them.

11 And Zedekiah the son of Chenaanah made him horns of iron: and he said, Thus saith the LORD, With these shall you push the Syrians, until you have consumed them.

12 And all the prophets prophesied so, saying, Go up to Ramoth-gilead, and prosper: for the LORD shall deliver it into the king's hand. *(The major words in modern Christendom today are, as then, "prosperity" and "success." These messages, as delivered then by false prophets, are delivered today by false prophets. The word should be "Repentance" and "Repentance.")*

MICAIAH'S TRUE PROPHESY

13 And the messenger that was gone to call

Micaiah spoke unto him, saying, Behold now, the words of the prophets declare good unto the king with one mouth: let your word, I pray you, be like the word of one of them, and speak that which is good *(true Prophets seldom speak that which is good, at least about the present time!).*

14 And Micaiah said, As the LORD lives, what the LORD says unto me, that will I speak *(God give us men, as Micaiah, that money cannot buy, who will not compromise their message, who will hear only what "thus saith the Lord," and who will not be fearful of delivering that Word to a lost and dying world!).*

15 So he came to the king. And the king said unto him, Micaiah, shall we go against Ramoth-gilead to battle, or shall we forbear? And he answered him, Go, and prosper: for the LORD shall deliver it into the hand of the king. *(No doubt Micaiah's mocking tone showed that his words were ironical; but Ahab's hollow tone had already proved to Micaiah that he was insincere, that he did not care to know the Will of the Lord, and that he wanted prophets who would speak to him smooth things and prophesy deceits [Isa. 30:10].)*

16 And the king said unto him, How many times shall I adjure thee that you tell me nothing but that which is true in the Name of the LORD? *(Ahab's feigned desire to hear the truth is spoken for the benefit of Jehoshaphat. In reality, he has no desire to hear the truth.)*

17 And he *(Micaiah)* said, I saw all Israel scattered upon the hills, as sheep that have not a shepherd: and the LORD said, These have no master: let them return every man to his house in peace *(Ahab was a false shepherd and, whether he believes it or not, he is about to die).*

18 And the king of Israel said unto Jehoshaphat, Did I not tell you that he would prophesy no good concerning me, but evil? *(It is clear that Ahab had understood perfectly the purport of Micaiah's words — Pulpit.)*

19 And he *(Micaiah)* said, Hear thou therefore the Word of the LORD: I saw the LORD sitting on His throne, and all the host of Heaven standing by Him on His right hand and on His left *(Micaiah is given a vision of the Throne of God and its happenings there, which he now relates to both Ahab and Jehoshaphat).*

20 And the LORD said, Who shall persuade Ahab, that he may go up and fall at Ramoth-gilead? And one said on this manner, and another said on that manner *(the meaning is that Ahab's death in battle had been decreed in the counsels of God, and that the Divine Wisdom had devised means for accomplishing God's purpose — Spence).*

21 And there came forth a spirit *(an evil spirit),* and stood before the LORD, and said, I will persuade him. *(We learn from this, as well as from Job, Chpt. 1, that spirits of darkness, as well as Satan, at times have access to the Throne of God. During the coming Great Tribulation, Satan and all such will be cast out of Heaven, allowed no more access [Rev. 12:7-9].)*

22 And the LORD said unto him, Wherewith? And he said, I will go forth, and I will be a lying spirit in the mouth of all his prophets. And He said, You shall persuade him, and prevail also: go forth, and do so. *(This "lying spirit" would inspire these false prophets to prophesy the evil that was desired. All of this reveals that God and His Heavenly hosts, including demons on certain occasions, have conferences concerning the affairs of men on Earth.*

The idea is that God permitted such deception to take the place of the rejected truth. If men will not have the truth, they will automatically have a substitute that will be more in harmony with their wicked ways for the time being. Ahab would not have the truth, and would not listen to Jehovah, despite all the attempts made by the Lord to reach this man, but he would believe lies and listen to his false prophets.

This Passage simply gives an insight into the spirit realm, showing that behind all human acts there are good and bad spirits seeking to carry out the respective wills of their masters. The Lord protects as long as He can and, when there is nothing else He can do to turn men from their wicked ways, error, and harm, at least by righteous means, He then permits demon spirits to deceive. This causes the individual in question to go further astray — and, in this case with Ahab, even unto death.)

23 Now therefore, behold, the LORD has put a lying spirit in the mouth of all these your prophets, and the LORD has spoken evil concerning you *(true enough, it was not what Ahab wanted to hear).*

24 But Zedekiah the son of Chenaanah went near, and smote Micaiah on the cheek, and said, Which way went the Spirit of the LORD from me to speak unto you? *(The prophesy of Zedekiah and the prophecy of Micaiah were totally different. The first spoke of blessing, while the latter spoke of doom. Both could not be right. In essence, it is the same presently.*

Thousands of false prophets are prophesying

blessings and victory upon an apostate Church, while the few true Prophets are attempting to call the Church to Repentance. As with Ahab, both cannot be right.)

25 And Micaiah said, Behold, you shall see in that day, when you shall go into an inner chamber to hide yourself (which no doubt happened when news came of Ahab's death).

26 And the king of Israel said, Take Micaiah, and carry him back unto Amon the governor of the city, and to Joash the king's son;

27 And say, Thus saith the king, Put this fellow in the prison, and feed him with bread of affliction and with water of affliction, until I come in peace.

28 And Micaiah said, If you return at all in peace, the LORD has not spoken by me. And he said, Hearken, O people, every one of you. (The bravery of Micaiah condemns the cowardice of Jehoshaphat. Jehoshaphat should have stepped down from his throne, thrown his mantel around the courageous Prophet, and valiantly taken his stand at his side.

There is no one more cowardly and contemptible than a Christian who walks with the religious world. Micaiah is led away to prison and to torture, and Jehoshaphat raises neither a hand nor a voice on his behalf.)

THE DEATH OF AHAB

29 So the king of Israel and Jehoshaphat the king of Judah went up to Ramoth-gilead.

30 And the king of Israel said unto Jehoshaphat, I will disguise myself, and enter into the battle; but you put on your robes. And the king of Israel disguised himself, and went into the battle. (Two royal fools at once meet in these Verses. Jehoshaphat was a fool to go into battle, at Ahab's suggestion, in his royal robes, or at all, for that matter. Ahab was a greater fool to propose to escape the Divine doom pronounced upon him by going into battle without his royal robes.)

31 But the king of Syria commanded his thirty and two captains that had rule over his chariots, saying, Fight neither with small nor great, save only with the king of Israel (the Syrians intended to kill Ahab!).

32 And it came to pass, when the captains of the chariots saw Jehoshaphat, that they said, Surely it is the king of Israel. And they turned aside to fight against him; and Jehoshaphat cried out (it was a cry for Divine help, and the Lord heard and answered).

33 And it came to pass, when the captains of the chariots perceived that it was not the king of Israel, that they turned back from pursuing him (they wanted Ahab, not Jehoshaphat).

34 And a certain man drew a bow at a venture, and smote the king of Israel between the joints of the harness: wherefore he said unto the driver of his chariot, Turn your hand, and carry me out of the host; for I am wounded (Ahab's attempt to disguise himself served no purpose; a Syrian archer shot, not even knowing where he was shooting, and the Lord had the arrow and Ahab to meet in the same place).

35 And the battle increased that day: and the king was stayed up in his chariot against the Syrians, and died at evening: and the blood ran out of the wound into the midst of the chariot (the servants of Ahab propped him up in the chariot until he died).

36 And there went a proclamation throughout the host about the going down of the sun, saying, Every man to his city, and every man to his own country (it does not appear that Israel had been utterly defeated, or had suffered great loss; but their king was dead, so they now retreated).

37 So the king died, and was brought to Samaria; and they buried the king in Samaria (exactly as the Prophet Micaiah said would happen!).

38 And one washed the chariot in the pool of Samaria; and the dogs licked up his blood; and they washed his armour; according unto the Word of the LORD which He spoke (this prediction was given by Elijah [I Ki. 21:19]).

39 Now the rest of the acts of Ahab, and all that he did, and the ivory house which he made, and all the cities that he built, are they not written in the Book of the Chronicles of the Kings of Israel? (The Lord loved Ahab, and sought to save him again and again, but all in vain.)

40 So Ahab slept with his fathers; and Ahaziah his son reigned in his stead (the name "Ahaziah" means "whom Jehovah upholds"; Ahab giving his son this name suggests that, notwithstanding his idolatries, Ahab had knowledge of the Lord; however, despite the constant spiritual tug, he wouldn't serve the Lord).

JEHOSHAPHAT'S REIGN OVER JUDAH

41 And Jehoshaphat the son of Asa began to reign over Judah in the fourth year of Ahab king of Israel. (In this Book, Jehoshaphat's reign

is disposed of in 10 Verses, but 102 Verses are devoted to it in II Chronicles. The meaning is this:

To the unspiritual eye, Jehoshaphat would have been uninteresting beside the glitter of Ahab. But, to the spiritual eye, which is given in II Chronicles, Ahab is of no interest at all, with Jehoshaphat demanding God's attention. Both Books of Kings portray events as men saw them, with both Books of the Chronicles portraying events as God saw them.)

42 Jehoshaphat was thirty and five years old when he began to reign; and he reigned twenty and five years in Jerusalem. And his mother's name was Azubah the daughter of Shilhi.

43 And he walked in all the ways of Asa his father; he turned not aside from it, doing that which was right in the eyes of the LORD: nevertheless the high places were not taken away; for the people offered and burnt incense yet in the high places. *(There was to be only one place of Sacrifice, and that was to be at the Temple in Jerusalem. So, it seems that the Holy Spirit was displeased with Jehoshaphat's actions in not taking away the high places.)*

44 And Jehoshaphat made peace with the king of Israel. *(For some 70 years, from the date of their separation to the time of Asa's death, there had been little peace between Judah and Israel. Jehoshaphat seeks to remedy this situation, but, at times, as we have seen, by using methods that were displeasing to the Lord.)*

45 Now the rest of the acts of Jehoshaphat, and his might that he showed, and how he warred, are they not written in the Book of the Chronicles of the kings of Judah?

46 And the remnant of the sodomites, which remained in the days of his father Asa, he took out of the land. *(There seemed to have been only a few "sodomites" left; however, the Holy Spirit is quick to proclaim the fact that Jehoshaphat removed even these few. Too often the Child of God is willing to allow "the remnant" of evil to remain. The Holy Spirit demands that everything that is evil be "taken out," which can only be done by the Believer placing his Faith exclusively in Christ and the Cross, which then*

gives the Holy Spirit latitude to work within our lives, thereby bringing about the desired victory [Rom. 6:3-14; 8:1-2, 11; I Cor. 1:17-18, 21, 23; 2:2; Gal. 6:14].)

47 There was then no king in Edom: a deputy was king *(implies that this officer was appointed by the king of Judah; in other words, Judah controlled Edom).*

48 Jehoshaphat made ships of Tharshish to go to Ophir for gold: but they went not; for the ships were broken at Ezion-geber.

49 Then said Ahaziah the son of Ahab unto Jehoshaphat, Let my servants go with your servants in the ships. But Jehoshaphat would not. *(Jehoshaphat formed an alliance with Ahab's son, Ahaziah; however, the Lord was not pleased with this alliance and, thereby, destroyed the ships. Jehoshaphat would not permit Ahaziah to join him after that.)*

JEHOSHAPHAT'S DEATH

50 And Jehoshaphat slept with his fathers, and was buried with his fathers in the city of David his father: and Jehoram his son reigned in his stead *(all of this is important regarding the kings of Judah, because they were in the lineage of David, from which would come Christ the Redeemer [II Sam. 7:16]).*

AHAZIAH REIGNS OVER ISRAEL

51 Ahaziah the son of Ahab began to reign over Israel in Samaria the seventeenth year of Jehoshaphat king of Judah, and reigned two years over Israel.

52 And he did evil in the sight of the LORD, and walked in the way of his father, and in the way of his mother, and in the way of Jeroboam the son of Nebat, who made Israel to sin:

53 For he served Baal, and worshipped him, and provoked to anger the LORD God of Israel, according to all that his father had done. *(This was at least one of the reasons and, in fact, the primary reason, that the Lord was sorely displeased with Jehoshaphat forming an alliance with Ahaziah.)*

THE SECOND BOOK OF
THE KINGS

CHAPTER 1
(896 B.C.)
THE SICKNESS OF AHAZIAH

THEN Moab rebelled against Israel after the death of Ahab. *(Moab had originally been conquered by David [II Sam. 8:2; 23:20] and, after the division of Judah and Israel, it passed to Israel. The Moabites were greatly oppressed by Omri and Ahab and, on the death of Ahab, Mesha, king of Moab, rebelled and gained independence.)*

2 And Ahaziah fell down through a lattice in his upper chamber that was in Samaria, and was sick: and he sent messengers, and said unto them, Go, enquire of Baal-zebub the god of Ekron whether I shall recover of this disease. *(Ahaziah cast away the last remnant of faith in the Salvation afforded by the Lord and believed in by the Patriarchs of Israel, and consulted a foreign oracle, as if the Voice of God was silent in his own country.*

By and large, the sin of the modern Church is little different from the sin of Ahaziah. Having opted for the humanistic, even atheistic, fallacy of psychology, it has, by and large, forsaken the God of the Bible. It has tried to cover its sin by labeling its foray into modernism with the term, "Christian psychology." However, such does not exist. Psychology is not a true science; its various methods of treatment are worthy of a Roman circus. It has its roots in atheism, evolution, and humanism. It is the total opposite of the Bible. "Christian psychology," so-called, is no different whatsoever from any other type of psychology. The name "Christian" is given to it only to deceive a gullible Christian public that has, as well, by and large, forsaken the Bible.)

3 But the Angel of the LORD said to Elijah the Tishbite, Arise, go up to meet the messengers of the king of Samaria, and say unto them, Is it not because there is not a God in Israel, that you go to enquire of Baal-zebub the god of Ekron? *(The action of Ahaziah presents a complete and absolute denial of the Divinity of Jehovah. To consult a foreign oracle is equivalent to saying that the Voice of God is wholly silent in one's own land. This was going further in apostasy than Ahab had gone.*

As stated, the modern Church is doing the same thing in its acceptance of humanistic psychology. It does so under the farce of the guise that "all truth is God's truth." The meaning is: "If it is truth, it must come from God." However, let it ever be stated: truth is not a philosophy; it is a Person, and that Person is the Lord Jesus Christ [Jn. 14:6; 17:17; I Jn. 5:6]. The Word of God claims to hold the answer to all of man's spiritual problems, and the Word of God alone does this [II Pet. 1:3].)

4 Now therefore thus saith the LORD, You shall not come down from that bed on which you are gone up, but shall surely die. And Elijah departed. *(The word "therefore" is emphatic, and means "for this reason" or "on this account." Because Ahaziah had apostatized from God, the Lord sentenced him to die from the effects of his fall, and not recover. It is implied that he might have recovered, if he had acted otherwise.)*

5 And when the messengers turned back unto him, he said unto them, Why are you now turned back? *(When the messengers came back so soon to Ahaziah, he perceived that they could not have been to Ekron and come back in this amount of time. So, he asks them as to why they have come back so soon?)*

6 And they said unto him, There came a man up to meet us, and said unto us, Go, turn again unto the king who sent you, and say unto him, Thus saith the LORD, Is it not because there is not a God in Israel, that you send to enquire of Baal-zebub the god of Ekron? therefore you shall not come down from that bed on which you are gone up, but shall surely die.

7 And he said unto them, What manner of man was he which came up to meet you, and told you these words?

8 And they answered him, He was an hairy man, and girt with a girdle of leather about his loins. And he said, It is Elijah the Tishbite. *(He knew Elijah and all the miracles which this great Prophet had seen, but yet would not call him in, but rather would send for these heathenistic gods.*

"Jesus Christ and Him Crucified" is the answer for man's dilemma, and the only answer. But the trouble is, the modern Church little

believes in the Cross; therefore, it resorts to humanistic psychology, etc.)

9 Then the king sent unto him a captain of fifty with his fifty *(with 50 soldiers)*. And he went up to him: and, behold, he *(Elijah)* sat on the top of an hill. And he *(the captain)* spoke unto him, Thou man of God, the king has said, Come down.

10 And Elijah answered and said to the captain of fifty, If I be a man of God, then let fire come down from Heaven, and consume you and your fifty. And there came down fire from Heaven, and consumed him and his fifty. *(Elijah, within himself, had no power to do good or harm. He could but pray to the Lord and, in the Lord's Wisdom and Perfect Goodness, He could either grant or refuse the prayer. God's answer, in sending the fire, is His Response to Ahaziah and those who served him.)*

11 Again also he sent unto him another captain of fifty with his fifty. And he answered and said unto him, O man of God, thus has the king said, Come down quickly.

12 And Elijah answered and said unto them, If I be a man of God, let fire come down from Heaven, and consume you and your fifty. And the fire of God came down from Heaven, and consumed him and his fifty. *(If men do not trust the Lord and what He has done to redeem humanity, and I speak of Christ and the Cross, then ultimately the fire of judgment will fall upon them. It is inevitable!)*

13 And he sent again a captain of the third fifty with his fifty. And the third captain of fifty went up, and came and fell on his knees before Elijah, and besought him, and said unto him, O man of God, I pray you, let my life, and the life of these fifty your servants, be precious in your sight.

14 Behold, there came fire down from Heaven, and burnt up the two captains of the former fifties with their fifties: therefore let my life now be precious in your sight.

15 And the Angel of the LORD said unto Elijah *(this was the Lord Himself)*, Go down with him: be not afraid of him. And he arose, and went down with him unto the king.

16 And he said unto him, Thus saith the LORD, Forasmuch as you have sent messengers to enquire of Baal-zebub the god of Ekron, is it not because there is no God in Israel to enquire of His Word? therefore you shall not come down off that bed on which you are gone up, but shall surely die. *(Due to the fact that the Lord sent Elijah to Ahaziah, if the king had*

truly repented, it seems that, even at this late date, the sentence of death could have been altered; however, there was no Repentance!)

AHAZIAH'S DEATH

17 So he died according to the Word of the LORD which Elijah had spoken. And Jehoram reigned in his stead in the second year of Jehoram the son of Jehoshaphat king of Judah; because he had no son *(because Ahaziah had no son, he was succeeded by his younger brother, Jehoram).*

18 Now the rest of the acts of Ahaziah which he did, are they not written in the Book of the Chronicles of the Kings of Israel?

CHAPTER 2
(896 B.C.)
THE REVELATION OF ELIJAH'S TRANSLATION

AND it came to pass, when the LORD would take up Elijah into Heaven by a whirlwind, that Elijah went with Elisha from Gilgal. *(Elisha, since called of God, had now been with Elijah for approximately 10 years. The "Gilgal" mentioned here is not the Gilgal close to Jericho, but rather another Gilgal that was close to Shiloh in Samaria.)*

2 And Elijah said unto Elisha, Tarry here, I pray you; for the LORD has sent me to Beth-el. And Elisha said unto him, As the LORD lives, and as your soul lives, I will not leave you. So they went down to Beth-el. *(Elisha knew that Elijah was about to be taken, but probably, at this stage, not how he would be taken; consequently, he will not let the great Prophet out of his sight.)*

3 And the sons of the prophets who were at Beth-el came forth to Elisha, and said unto him, Knowest thou that the LORD will take away your master from your head to day? And he said, Yes, I know it; hold ye your peace *(how they knew this, we aren't told!).*

4 And Elijah said unto him, Elisha, tarry here, I pray you; for the LORD has sent me to Jericho. And he said, As the LORD lives, and as your soul lives, I will not leave you. So they came to Jericho *(it is the persistent soul who reaps the benefits of what Christ has done for us at Calvary, and only the persistent soul [Lk. 11:5-13]).*

5 And the sons of the prophets who were at Jericho came to Elisha, and said unto him,

Knowest thou that the LORD will take away your master from your head to day? And he answered, Yes, I know it; hold ye your peace.

6 And Elijah said unto him, Tarry, I pray you, here; for the LORD has sent me to Jordan. And he said, As the LORD lives, and as your soul lives, I will not leave you. And they two went on.

ELIJAH DIVIDES THE JORDAN

7 And fifty men of the sons of the prophets went, and stood to view afar off: and they two stood by Jordan.

8 And Elijah took his mantle, and wrapped it together, and smote the waters, and they were divided hither and thither, so that they two went over on dry ground (*by the Power of God, the Jordan River opened*).

THE DOUBLE PORTION

9 And it came to pass, when they were gone over, that Elijah said unto Elisha, Ask what I shall do for you, before I be taken away from you. And Elisha said, I pray you, let a double portion of your spirit be upon me (*in essence, a double portion of the Spirit of God which was on Elijah*).

10 And he said, You have asked a hard thing (*the word "hard," in the Hebrew, actually means "you have made a great claim"; the bane of the modern Church is that we make a much lesser claim, or no claim at all; as Believers, understanding that we are serving a great God, we should stake a great claim*): nevertheless, if you see me when I am taken from you, it shall be so unto you; but if not, It shall not be so. (*The great question should be, even to modern Believers, "What do you see?" Do we see the miracle-working Power of God, or do we see other things?*)

THE TRANSLATION OF ELIJAH

11 And it came to pass, as they still went on, and talked, that, behold, there appeared a chariot of fire, and horses of fire, and parted them both asunder; and Elijah went up by a whirlwind into Heaven (*in the original Hebrew, it says, "And Elijah went up in a storm into the Heavens"; there is no mention of a "whirlwind"; two only of the seed of Adam, Enoch and Elijah, have passed from Earth to Heaven without dying*).

12 And Elisha saw it, and he cried, My father, my father, the chariot of Israel, and the horsemen thereof (*Elijah had been the strength of Israel*). And he saw him no more: and he took hold of his own clothes, and rent them in two pieces (*Elisha tearing the clothes portrays the fact that he is no longer a learner, but now the Prophet*).

ELISHA DIVIDES THE JORDAN

13 He took up also the mantle (*the outer garment*) of Elijah that fell from him, and went back, and stood by the bank of Jordan (*probably where he and Elijah had crossed it a short time earlier*);

14 And he took the mantle of Elijah that fell from him, and smote the waters, and said, Where is the LORD God of Elijah? and when he also had smitten the waters, they parted hither and thither: and Elisha went over (*the Lord proclaimed to Elisha that He was with him by enabling him to repeat Elijah's last miracle, and thus gave him an assurance that He would be with him thenceforth in his Prophetic Ministry*).

15 And when the sons of the prophets which were to view at Jericho saw him, they said, The spirit of Elijah does rest on Elisha. And they came to meet him, and bowed themselves to the ground before him (*they recognized the Power of God upon him*).

16 And they said unto him, Behold now, there be with your servants fifty strong men; let them go, we pray you, and seek your master: lest peradventure the Spirit of the LORD has taken him up, and cast him upon some mountain, or into some valley. And he said, You shall not send (*evidently, they didn't understand what they saw regarding Elijah, that is, if they had seen anything at all; so they ventured the opinion that the body of Elijah would be found nearby, etc.*).

17 And when they urged him till he was ashamed, he said, Send. They sent therefore fifty men; and they sought three days, but found him not (*exactly as Elisha knew they would do*).

18 And when they came again to him, (for he tarried at Jericho,) he said unto them, Did I not say unto you, Go not? (*He waited at Jericho until the fifty men returned from their vain search, and then reminded them that his advice to them had been not to start on a useless errand.*)

JERICHO HEALED

19 And the men of the city said unto Elisha, Behold, I pray you, the situation of this city is pleasant, as my lord sees: but the water is naught *(poisoned)*, and the ground barren *(because of the poisoned water. Jericho is the city of the curse, and by God at that, simply because of its heathen worship in the days of Joshua. As well, the world is cursed, because of sin. In fact, it could be, as Jericho, a pleasant place; but instead, the water is poisoned and the ground barren).*

20 And he said, Bring me a new cruse *(this is symbolic of the sinless Body of the Lord Jesus Christ, because the cruse was made of clay),* and put salt therein *(the "salt" in it — a type of the incorruptible Word of God, that in its plenitude dwelt in Him — was the vehicle of this great healing power).* And they brought it to him.

21 And he went forth unto the spring of the waters, and cast the salt in there *(the Word of God must be cast into the poisoned spring; there is no other answer; that's the reason that it is imperative that this great Gospel of Jesus Christ be taken to the whole world [Mk. 16:15]),* and said, Thus saith the LORD, I have healed these waters; there shall not be from thence any more death or barren land *(Christ Alone can heal the broken heart, can set the captive free [Lk. 4:18-19]).*

22 So the waters were healed unto this day, according to the saying of Elisha which he spoke *(it was not a mere temporary, but a permanent, benefit which Elisha bestowed upon the town; when Christ comes in, there is "no more death or barren land").*

23 And he went up from thence unto Bethel: and as he was going up by the way, there came forth little children out of the city, and mocked him, and said unto him, Go up, you bald head; go up, you bald head *(the words, "little children," are probably an unfortunate translation; the Hebrew word is "na'ar"; it can mean anything up to 40 years old; as well, the words, "bald head," do not necessarily mean that Elisha had no hair on his head; it could have signified a "worthless fellow"; at any rate, it was a term of contempt).*

24 And he turned back, and looked on them, and cursed them in the Name of the LORD *(placed a curse on them).* And there came forth two she bears out of the wood, and tore forty and two children of them *(when they insulted the man of God, they, in effect, were insulting the Lord).*

25 And he went from thence to Mount Carmel, and from thence he returned to Samaria.

CHAPTER 3
(895 B.C.)
JEHORAM REIGNS OVER ISRAEL

NOW Jehoram the son of Ahab began to reign over Israel in Samaria the eighteenth year of Jehoshaphat king of Judah, and reigned twelve years.

2 And he wrought evil in the sight of the LORD; but not like his father, and like his mother: for he put away the image of Baal that his father had made.

3 Nevertheless he cleaved unto the sins of Jeroboam the son of Nebat, which made Israel to sin; he departed not therefrom. *(Jehoram removes the obscene idol erected by his father, but resolutely holds on to the great sin of Jeroboam, that is, the golden calf. In the Books of Kings, as in the first Epistle of John, "sin" principally means the substitution of a god other than the Lord Jesus, and "evil" means fidelity to that false god and false saviour.)*

ELISHA PREDICTS VICTORY OVER MOAB

4 And Mesha king of Moab was a sheepmaster, and rendered unto the king of Israel an hundred thousand lambs, and an hundred thousand rams, with the wool *(tribute rendered each year).*

5 But it came to pass, when Ahab was dead, that the king of Moab rebelled against the king of Israel.

6 And king Jehoram went out of Samaria the same time, and numbered all Israel *(prepared for war).*

7 And he went and sent to Jehoshaphat the king of Judah, saying, The king of Moab has rebelled against me: will you go with me against Moab to battle? And he said, I will go up: I am as you are, my people as your people, and my horses as your horses. *(These words were probably a common formula expressive of willingness to enter into the closest possible alliance.*

The incurable insubjection of the natural will, even in a Christian, to the Word of the Lord is seen in Jehoshaphat. Despite two severe lessons from God, he, for the third time, unites with the religious world in a "laudable" enterprise. The

result will be that he nearly loses his life.)

8 And he said, Which way shall we go up? And he answered, The way through the wilderness of Edom *(Edom, though under a native king, was a dependency of Judah [I Ki. 22:47]; so, this would be an easier route for invasion).*

9 So the king of Israel went, and the king of Judah, and the king of Edom: and they fetched a compass of seven days' journey: and there was no water for the host, and for the cattle that followed them *(the baggage animals).*

10 And the king of Israel said, Alas! that the LORD has called these three kings together, to deliver them into the hand of Moab! *(Even though an idol-worshipper, Jehoram blames the Lord for their predicament!)*

11 But Jehoshaphat said, Is there not here a prophet of the LORD, that we may enquire of the LORD by him? and one of the king of Israel's servants answered and said, Here is Elisha the son of Shaphat, which poured water on the hands of Elijah. *(Had Jehoshaphat enquired of such before he came, he would not now be in this predicament. Believers all too often seek the Lord after the die has been cast. It's best to seek Him beforehand, and for all things. It would save us much trouble.)*

12 And Jehoshaphat said, The Word of the LORD is with him. So the king of Israel and Jehoshaphat and the king of Edom went down to him *(went to the Prophet Elisha).*

13 And Elisha said unto the king of Israel, What have I to do with you? get thee to the prophets of your father, and to the prophets of your mother. And the king of Israel said unto him, No: for the LORD has called these three kings together, to deliver them into the hand of Moab *(Elisha regards it as incumbent on him to rebuke the Monarch from Israel, who, though he had "put away the image of Baal which his father had made," still "wrought evil in the sight of the Lord," and "cleaved to the sins of Jeroboam the son of Nebat" [2:2-3]; the King of Israel answered wisely!).*

14 And Elisha said, As the LORD of hosts lives, before Whom I stand, surely, were it not that I regard the presence of Jehoshaphat the king of Judah, I would not look toward you, nor see you *(this states that, in effect, Jehoram and the king of Edom owed their lives to Jehoshaphat).*

15 But now bring me a minstrel. And it came to pass, when the minstrel played, that the hand of the LORD came upon him *(most probably,*

these were musicians who came, sang, and played the Psalms; music which is touched by the Lord refreshes, heals, and delivers [I Sam. 16:23]).*

16 And he *(Elisha)* said, Thus saith the LORD, Make this valley full of ditches.

17 For thus saith the LORD, You shall not see wind, neither shall you see rain; yet that valley shall be filled with water, that you may drink, both you, and your cattle, and your beasts *(there would be rain, but it would be a distance away, actually out of sight, with the water running down into the valley and, thereby, filling the ditches).*

18 And this is but a light thing in the sight of the LORD *(God, the Author of nature, has full control over nature, and it is an easy matter for Him to produce at will any natural phenomena)*: he will deliver the Moabites also into your hand *(victory!).*

19 And you shall smite every fenced city, and every choice city, and shall fell every good tree, and stop all wells of water, and mar every good piece of land with stones *(in other words, Moab was to be scorched earth, because of her great wickedness against the Lord).*

20 And it came to pass in the morning, when the Meat Offering was offered, that, behold, there came water by the way of Edom, and the country was filled with water *(evidently, there were flash floods out of distance of the valley, but with the runoff filling the valley).*

MOAB DEFEATED

21 And when all the Moabites heard that the kings were come up to fight against them, they gathered all who were able to put on armour, and upward, and stood in the border *(a large army).*

22 And they rose up early in the morning, and the sun shone upon the water, and the Moabites saw the water on the other side as red as blood *(the Moabites concluded that the red-looking liquid was blood)*:

23 And they said, This is blood: the kings are surely slain, and they have smitten one another: now therefore, Moab, to the spoil *(they thought that Judah, Israel, and Edom had turned on each other, because there had been bad blood in the past between these countries).*

24 And when they came to the camp of Israel, the Israelites rose up and smote the Moabites, so that they fled before them: but they went forward smiting the Moabites, even in their country *(the smiting of the enemy can*

only be carried out by the Believer as Faith is evidenced in Christ and the Cross; the Holy Spirit, Who Alone can help, works entirely within the framework of the Finished Work of Christ).

25 And they beat down the cities, and on every good piece of land cast every man his stone, and filled it; and they stopped all the wells of water, and felled all the good trees: only in Kir-haraseth left they the stones thereof; howbeit the slingers went about it, and smote it *(fulfilling the predictions of Elisha).*

26 And when the king of Moab saw that the battle was too sore for him, he took with him seven hundred men who drew swords, to break through even unto the king of Edom: but they could not *(the attempt failed; Edom was too strong).*

27 Then he *(the king of Moab)* took his oldest son who should have reigned in his stead, and offered him for a burnt offering upon the wall *(human sacrifice was widely practiced by the idolatrous nations who bordered on Israel and Judah, and by none more than by the Moabites).* And there was great indignation against Israel *(by the Moabites)*: and they *(Judah, Samaria, and Edom)* departed from him *(from the Moabite king)*, and returned to their own land.

CHAPTER 4
(895 B.C.)
THE MIRACLE OF THE INCREASE OF THE WIDOW'S OIL

NOW there cried a certain woman of the wives of the sons of the prophets unto Elisha, saying, Your servant my husband is dead; and you know that your servant did fear the LORD: and the creditor is come to take unto him my two sons to be bondmen. *(There is some intimation that this woman's husband, one of the sons of the Prophets, was known to Elisha. Many a Christian is like this widow. There are depression, poverty, and bondage in the life, instead of joy, wealth, and liberty. The truth is: the plight of this home was not God's Will. It is God's Will that we be in health and prosper, even as our soul does prosper [III Jn., Vs. 2]. Satan never ceases in his efforts to deprive the Child of God of his rightful inheritance in Christ Jesus.)*

2 And Elisha said unto her, What shall I do for you? tell me, what have you in the house? And she said, Your handmaid has not any thing in the house, save a pot of oil *(for the Christian, the "house" is our physical body [I Cor. 3:16]; the Holy Spirit, represented by the "pot of oil," is supposed to fill the house; this woman had a small pot of oil, but nothing else).*

3 Then he said, Go, borrow thee vessels abroad of all your neighbours, even empty vessels; borrow not a few *(far too many are satisfied to subsist on meager spiritual rations, when, if we could provide more empty vessels, God would fill them up — "borrow not a few").*

4 And when you are come in, you shall shut the door upon you and upon your sons, and shall pour out into all those vessels, and you shall set aside that which is full *(the Holy Spirit, represented by the "oil," is inexhaustible; as long as there are "empty vessels," it will continue to "pour out").*

5 So she went from him, and shut the door upon her and upon her sons, who brought the vessels to her; and she poured out.

6 And it came to pass, when the vessels were full, that she said unto her son, Bring me yet a vessel. And he said unto her, There is not a vessel more. And the oil stayed *(our problem is that we gather too few vessels).*

7 Then she came and told the man of God. And he said, Go, sell the oil, and pay your debt, and you and your children live of the rest *(the Lord always gives enough and more!).*

HOSPITALITY OF THE GREAT WOMAN OF SHUNEM

8 And it fell on a day, that Elisha passed to Shunem, where was a great woman; and she constrained him to eat bread. And so it was, that as oft as he passed by, he turned in thither to eat bread *(this woman was wealthy, yet she did not allow her riches to lift her up in pride, as happens to so many, but rather allowed it to draw her closer to God).*

9 And she said unto her husband, Behold now, I perceive that this is an holy man of God, which passes by us continually.

10 Let us make a little chamber *(room)*, I pray you, on the wall; and let us set for him there a bed, and a table, and a stool, and a candlestick: and it shall be, when he comes to us, that he shall turn in thither *(she was wise; to bless the man of God, she, in effect, would bless herself, and greatly).*

11 And it fell on a day, that he came thither, and he turned into the chamber, and lay there *(used the room, as they requested).*

THE SHUNAMMITE WOMAN
IS PROMISED A SON

12 And he said to Gehazi his servant, Call this Shunammite. And when he had called her, she stood before him.

13 And he said unto him, Say now unto her, Behold, you have been careful for us with all this care; what is to be done for you? would you be spoken for to the king, or to the captain of the host? And she answered, I dwell among my own people.

14 And he said, What then is to be done for her? And Gehazi answered, Verily she has no child, and her husband is old *(if the woman will suggest nothing herself, can Gehazi suggest anything?)*.

15 And he said, Call her. And when he had called her, she stood in the door.

16 And he said, About this season, according to the time of life, you shall embrace a son. And she said, No, my lord, thou man of God, do not lie unto your handmaid *(like Sarah of old, the woman was incredulous; she could not believe the good tidings, and thought the Prophet was only raising hopes to disappoint them; but she would find out that the Lord never deceives anyone)*.

17 And the woman conceived, and bore a son at that season that Elisha had said unto her, according to the time of life *(a miracle!)*.

THE DEATH OF THE SON

18 And when the child was grown, it fell on a day, that he went out to his father to the reapers.

19 And he said unto his father, My head, my head. And he said to a lad, Carry him to his mother.

20 And when he had taken him, and brought him to his mother, he sat on her knees till noon, and then died *(evidently died of a sunstroke)*.

21 And she went up, and laid him on the bed of the man of God, and shut the door upon him, and went out *(she evidently reasoned that if the Lord through Elisha could give her the child, through Elisha the child could be raised from the dead)*.

THE MIRACLE OF THE BOY BEING
RAISED FROM THE DEAD

22 And she called unto her husband, and said, Send me, I pray you, one of the young men, and one of the asses, that I may run to the man of God, and come again.

23 And he said, Wherefore will you go to him to day? it is neither new moon, nor sabbath. And she said, It shall be well *(evidently, the father didn't know the child had died; the wife not telling him shows that she believed the child would be raised from the dead)*.

24 Then she saddled an ass, and said to her servant, Drive, and go forward; slack not your riding for me, except I bid you *(she would herself go to the Prophet)*.

25 So she went and came unto the man of God to Mount Carmel. And it came to pass, when the man of God saw her afar off, that he said to Gehazi his servant, Behold, yonder is that Shunammite *(the Prophet evidently knew her at a distance)*:

26 Run now, I pray you, to meet her, and say unto her, Is it well with you? is it well with your husband? is it well with the child? And she answered, It is well *(Elisha suspected that something was wrong; only faith could answer, "It is well"!)*.

27 And when she came to the man of God to the hill, she caught him by the feet: but Gehazi came near to thrust her away. And the man of God said, Let her alone; for her soul is vexed within her: and the LORD has hid it from me, and has not told me. *(He knew something was wrong, but he didn't know exactly what. Gehazi, who represents religion, "thrust her away," as religion must! But Elisha, who represents Grace, says, "Let her alone." Oh, that somehow we would turn from Gehazi to Elisha!)*

28 Then she said, Did I desire a son of my lord? did I not say, Do not deceive me? *(In other words, her son was given to her by the Lord, and she did not expect the Lord to take him away.)*

29 Then he said to Gehazi, Gird up your loins, and take my staff in your hand, and go your way: if you meet any man, salute him not; and if any salute you, answer him not again *(the object of all these injunctions is haste)*: and lay my staff upon the face of the child.

30 And the mother of the child said, As the LORD lives, and as your soul lives, I will not leave you. And he arose, and followed her *(she would not be satisfied with whatever the servant was to do; she wanted Elisha to go to where the child was; and so he did!)*.

31 And Gehazi passed on before them, and laid the staff upon the face of the child; but there was neither voice, nor hearing. Wherefore he went again to meet him, and told him, saying,

The child is not awaked. *(What purpose Elisha had in mind regarding the staff upon the child, we aren't told. Perhaps we could say that it represented ceremony, which means that a dead staff laid upon a dead face cannot give life. Religious ceremonies, however scriptural, are paralyzed in the presence of death. Religion has never set anyone free; ceremonies have never set anyone free. It is only the Power of Jesus Christ, made available to us through the Cross, and given by the Holy Spirit, that can bring life [Jn. 7:37-39].)*

32 And when Elisha was come into the house, behold, the child was dead, and laid upon his bed.

33 He went in therefore, and shut the door upon them twain *(that he may not be disturbed)*, and prayed unto the LORD.

34 And he went up, and lay upon the child, and put his mouth upon his mouth, and his eyes upon his eyes, and his hands upon his hands: and he stretched himself upon the child; and the flesh of the child waxed warm *(evidently, the Lord told him to do this)*.

35 Then he returned, and walked in the house to and fro; and went up, and stretched himself upon him: and the child sneezed seven times, and the child opened his eyes *(perhaps Elisha conducting himself as he did toward the dead child was meant to symbolize the fact that Jesus could not save mankind by passing a decree; He saved man by becoming one with man [Isa. 7:14]).*

36 And he called Gehazi, and said, Call this Shunammite. So he called her. And when she was come in unto him, he said, Take up your son *(one can only imagine the joy that filled this woman's heart at this time).*

37 Then she went in, and fell at his feet, and bowed herself to the ground, and took up her son, and went out.

THE POISONOUS POTTAGE

38 And Elisha came again to Gilgal: and there was a dearth in the land; and the sons of the prophets were sitting before him: and he said unto his servant, Set on the great pot, and seethe pottage for the sons of the prophets *(Elisha offers God's provision, for surely the Gospel occupies a great container).*

39 And one went into the field to gather herbs, and found a wild vine, and gathered thereof wild gourds his lap full, and came and shred them into the pot of pottage: for they knew them not. *(One man was not satisfied with that which the Lord had provided, so he* went out in the "field to gather herbs," and the herbs were from a "wild vine." These "herbs of the wild vine" represent all false doctrine. Men are ever trying to add to the Word of the God; it will only bring death.)*

40 So they poured out for the men to eat. And it came to pass, as they were eating of the pottage, that they cried out, and said, O thou man of God, there is death in the pot. And they could not eat thereof. *(The herbs were poison — all false doctrine brings death. Sadly, much, if not most, doctrine in the Church presently is unscriptural. In fact, if every doctrine is not built exclusively upon the Cross of Christ, then, in some way, it is spurious [I Pet. 1:18-20].)*

41 But he *(Elisha)* said, Then bring meal. And he cast it into the pot; and he said, Pour out for the people, that they may eat. And there was no harm in the pot. *(The meal is a Type of the Word of God, which was, and is, the only answer for the "death in the pot." When will we quit trying to take away or add to the Word of God? Every time, it brings "death.")*

A HUNDRED MEN FED MIRACULOUSLY

42 And there came a man from Baal-shalisha, and brought the man of God bread of the firstfruits, twenty loaves of barley, and full ears of corn in the husk thereof. And he *(Elisha)* said, Give unto the people, that they may eat.

43 And his servitor said, What, should I set this before an hundred men? He said again, Give the people, that they may eat: for thus saith the LORD, They shall eat, and shall leave thereof.

44 So he set it before them, and they did eat, and left thereof, according to the Word of the LORD. *(The same power that multiplied this food multiplied the loaves and fish regarding Christ. Men judge our Lord the same as the Prophet's servant judged the barley cakes. They do not believe that He can satisfy the hunger of their hearts; however, all that the world offers can never satisfy man's hunger. Jesus Alone can satisfy, and give even more. So, there was plenty, and there was even some left.)*

CHAPTER 5
(894 B.C.)
THE HEALING OF NAAMAN THE LEPER

NOW Naaman, captain of the host of the king of Syria, was a great man with his

master, and honourable, because by him the LORD had given deliverance unto Syria: he was also a mighty man in valour, but he was a leper. *(Leprosy in the Old Testament was a type of the spiritual condition of unregenerate man. There was no earthly cure for leprosy, just as there is no earthly cure for sin. All of these great things said about Naaman did not save or heal him; he was still a leper. And so are the untold millions in the world who think their state, status, and position mean something with God. They don't!)*

2 And the Syrians had gone out by companies, and had brought away captive out of the land of Israel a little maid; and she waited on Naaman's wife. *(This "little maid" would figure prominently in history. The Holy Spirit does not even give her name; however, her testimony will affect nations.*

It would have been very easy for her to have been bitter, morose, and angry toward God, for Him allowing her to be taken captive away from her land and family, and made a slave in Syria. But she exhibited none of these evil traits. She retained her testimony. The things she did not understand, she left in the Hands of God. What an example!)

3 And she said unto her mistress, Would God my lord were with the Prophet who is in Samaria! for he would recover him of his leprosy *(in effect, she said, "I know somebody, who knows somebody, who knows what to do for you!")*.

4 And one went in, and told his lord, saying, Thus and thus said the maid that is of the land of Israel *(should have been translated, "Naaman went in, and told his lord, Ben-hadad, the king of Syria")*.

5 And the king of Syria said, Go to, go, and I will send a letter unto the king of Israel. And he *(Naaman)* departed, and took with him ten talents of silver, and six thousand pieces of gold, and ten changes of raiment *(approximately $3 million, in 2004 currency; man has ever been trying to purchase something from God, when, in reality, the Lord has nothing for sale; it is all a free gift [Jn. 3:16])*.

6 And he brought the letter to the king of Israel, saying, Now when this letter is come unto you, behold, I have therewith sent Naaman my servant to you, that you may recover him of his leprosy.

7 And it came to pass, when the king of Israel had read the letter, that he rent his clothes, and said, Am I God, to kill and to make alive, that this man does send unto me to recover a man of his leprosy? wherefore consider, I pray you, and see how he seeks a quarrel against me. *(Unfortunately, much of the modern Church is trying to evangelize the world by political means, which are worse than useless. They are attempting to establish some type of "pseudo-Christian kingdom age philosophy." There is nothing in the Word of God that even remotely hints at such. Evangelism is carried on by the preaching of the Gospel, and by no other means [Mk. 16:15; I Cor. 1:17-18, 23; 2:2].)*

8 And it was so, when Elisha the man of God had heard that the king of Israel had rent his clothes, that he sent to the king, saying, Wherefore have you rent your clothes? let him come now to me, and he shall know that there is a Prophet in Israel *(evidently, it became obvious that the king of Israel was upset at such a request, so the news comes to Elisha; the Prophet says, in effect, "Send him to me!")*.

9 So Naaman came with his horses and with his chariot, and stood at the door of the house of Elisha *(the entire entourage)*.

10 And Elisha sent a messenger unto him, saying, Go and wash in Jordan seven times, and your flesh shall come again to you, and you shall be clean *(Naaman expects to be waited on, courted, and to receive every possible attention; but Elisha just sends a messenger out to him, and tells him what to do)*.

11 But Naaman was wroth *(very angry)*, and went away, and said, Behold, I thought, He will surely come out to me, and stand, and call on the Name of the LORD his God, and strike his hand over the place, and recover the leper *(Naaman was a powerful man and warranted, he thought, much more than this curt dismissal; entire nations trembled at his presence; after all, he was the mightiest military chieftain on the face of the Earth.*

All of this is pride, which is the crowning sin of the human race. It's the reason that most never receive from God. Every individual must come to the Lord the same way, the great, the rich, the poor, the small — they are all the same to the Lord — poor, wretched lepers.)

12 Are not Abana and Pharpar, rivers of Damascus, better than all the waters of Israel? may I not wash in them, and be clean? So he turned and went away in a rage. *(Actually, the two rivers, Abana and Pharpar, were some of the clearest streams in the world, so why this muddy Jordan?*

In fact, the Jordan, at least at this time, was a

Type of Calvary. Yes, it is muddy; yes, there are other rivers much more beautiful; however, there are no healing qualities in the other rivers, as beautiful as they may be, where there is total healing and cleansing in this Jordan, i.e., "Calvary.")

13 And his servants came near, and spoke unto him, and said, My father, if the Prophet had bid you do some great thing, would you not have done it? how much rather then, when he said to you, Wash, and be clean? *(Men are ever asking, "What can I do to earn Salvation?" Most of the world is trying to earn its salvation by good works; but, in reality, all one has to do, as it regards Calvary, is to "wash, and be clean.")*

14 Then went he down, and dipped himself seven times in Jordan, according to the saying of the man of God: and his flesh came again like unto the flesh of a little child, and he was clean. *(Why "seven"? There was nothing magical about the number, only that it denoted God's total and complete Redemption — in other words, a "finished work." Salvation makes a man whole. How many millions have dipped into the waters of Calvary, and have seen all of their sins washed away? Man is spiritually dirty. This "dirt" cannot be cleansed by the "soap" of this world, but only by the Precious Blood of Jesus Christ.)*

ELISHA REFUSES NAAMAN'S GIFTS

15 And he returned to the man of God, he and all his company, and came, and stood before him: and he said, Behold, now I know that there is no God in all the Earth, but in Israel: now therefore, I pray you, take a blessing of your servant *(he wanted to give Elisha an Offering).*

16 But he *(Elisha)* said, As the LORD lives, before Whom I stand, I will receive none. And he urged him to take it; but he refused. *(There is some evidence that Elisha did receive offerings at other times. So, why not this time?*

This entire episode was a picture portrayed by God of His Grace. One cannot purchase Grace. Money or good works are not the coin of this realm. If Elisha had taken money, it would instantly have nullified the work of Grace. It would have made a mockery of the Blood of Jesus Christ.)

17 And Naaman said, Shall there not then, I pray you, be given to your servant two mules' burden of earth? for your servant will henceforth offer neither Burnt Offering nor Sacrifice unto other gods, but unto the LORD

(Naaman now knew that the Lord of Israel was truly God, and not the heathen idols he had been worshipping in Syria; he desired to offer "Burnt Offerings" to the Lord of Israel, and felt that the soil of Syria was improper; inasmuch as Israel was "God's land," Naaman was far more theologically sound, at least at that time, than we might at first realize).

18 In this thing the LORD pardon your servant, that when my master *(the king of Syria)* goes into the house of Rimmon to worship there, and he leans on my hand, and I bow myself in the house of Rimmon *(to the god "Hadad")*: when I bow down myself in the house of Rimmon, the LORD pardon your servant in this thing.

19 And he *(Elisha)* said unto him *(Naaman)*, Go in peace. So he departed from him a little way *(Elisha approved of his request).*

THE SIN AND PUNISHMENT OF GEHAZI

20 But Gehazi, the servant of Elisha the man of God, said, Behold, my master has spared Naaman this Syrian, in not receiving at his hands that which he brought: but, as the LORD lives, I will run after him, and take somewhat of him. *(This proclaims the efforts of Gehazi to change the great Plan of Salvation from "the Grace of God" to "salvation by works." It was met, as we shall see, with severe and stern judgment.)*

21 So Gehazi followed after Naaman. And when Naaman saw him running after him, he lighted down from the chariot to meet him, and said, Is all well?

22 And he said, All is well. My master has sent me, saying, Behold, even now there be come to me from Mount Ephraim two young men of the sons of the prophets: give them, I pray you, a talent of silver, and two changes of garments *(his story was altogether most plausible, and his demand prudently moderate, at least as far as Naaman was concerned).*

23 And Naaman said, Be content, take two talents. And he urged him, and bound two talents of silver in two bags, with two changes of garments, and laid them upon two of his servants; and they bore them before him.

24 And when he came to the tower, he took them from their hand, and bestowed them in the house: and he let the men go, and they departed.

25 But he went in, and stood before his master. And Elisha said unto him, Whence comest thou, Gehazi? And he said, Your servant went

no whither *(he lied!)*.

26 And he said unto him, Went not my heart with you, when the man turned again from his chariot to meet you? Is it a time to receive money, and to receive garments, and olive-yards, and vineyards, and sheep, and oxen, and menservants, and maidservants? *(The same question could be asked presently! The world is dying without God, and so many modern Preachers are proclaiming a message of money. To be sure, their sin is no different than that of Gehazi.)*

27 The leprosy therefore of Naaman shall cleave unto you, and unto your seed for ever. And he went out from his presence a leper as white as snow. *(Gehazi's sin and his incurring of Naaman's leprosy is a type of man voiding the Grace of God by "works salvation." Gehazi's acceptance of money was, in effect, saying that Salvation could be purchased. He had made the Grace of God of none effect [Gal. 5:4].)*

CHAPTER 6
(893 B.C.)
THE AXE HEAD MADE TO FLOAT

AND the sons of the prophets said unto Elisha, Behold now, the place where we dwell with you is too strait for us. *(It seems that the unbelief registered in Chapter 2 concerning the sons of the prophets seems to at least have given way to some faith. Prayerfully, their association with Elisha had done much to direct them toward the Lord; however, there is little record that God used these individuals in much capacity.)*

2 Let us go, we pray you, unto Jordan, and take thence every man a beam, and let us make us a place there, where we may dwell. And he *(Elisha)* answered, Go ye *(of all the things that the sons of the prophets studied in this school, their association with Elisha was, by far, their greatest instruction)*.

3 And one said, Be content, I pray you, and go with your servants. And he answered, I will go *(one of the number was not satisfied with the Prophet's mere approval of the enterprise, but wished for his actual presence; Elisha acquiesced to the request)*.

4 So he went with them. And when they came to Jordan *(the river Jordan)*, they cut down wood.

5 But as one was felling a beam, the axe head fell into the water: and he cried, and said, Alas, master! for it was borrowed *(presently, the axe head seems an insignificant matter; however,*

in that day, it represented a sizable investment, and, thereby, a heavy loss).

6 And the man of God said, Where fell it? And he showed him the place. And he cut down a stick, and cast it in thither; and the iron did swim. *(The "stick," no matter how crude, was symbolic of the Cross of Jesus Christ. We learn from this the tremendous lesson of the power of Calvary. Every single blessing received by the Child of God comes through Calvary. Elisha applied the Cross to the problem. Regrettably, most in the modern Church have set the Cross aside, resorting to other things, which only bring death.)*

7 Therefore said he, Take it up to you. And he put out his hand, and took it. *(The Cross is a Finished Work. Consequently, all the Believer has to do is simply stretch out his hand and take it. All that the Cross represents is ours for the asking.)*

ELISHA AND THE SYRIANS

8 Then the king of Syria warred against Israel, and took counsel with his servants, saying, In such and such a place shall be my camp *(this was some time, even possibly several years, after the healing of Naaman)*.

9 And the man of God *(Elisha)* sent unto the king of Israel, saying, Beware that you pass not such a place; for thither the Syrians are come down. *(Despite Israel's spiritual degeneracy, the Lord helped them through Elisha. He disclosed three or more times the plans of the king of Syria.)*

10 And the king of Israel *(Jehoram)* sent to the place which the man of God told him and warned him of, and saved himself there, not once nor twice.

11 Therefore the heart of the king of Syria was sore troubled for this thing; and he called his servants, and said unto them, Will you not show me which of us is for the king of Israel? *(The Syrian king thought someone in his cabinet was relaying vital information to Israel.)*

12 And one of his servants said, None, my lord, O king: But Elisha, the Prophet that is in Israel, tells the king of Israel the words that you speak in your bedchamber. *(For this man to know this means that Elisha evidently made no secret of the instructions that he was giving to the king of Israel concerning the king of Syria. It seems from this that the king of Syria should have been convicted in his heart for his misdeeds, but he was not. Man's ability to resist*

God is simply amazing! In his stupidity, he sends his army to take Elisha.)

13 And he said, Go and spy where he *(Elisha)* is, that I may send and fetch him. And it was told him, saying, Behold, he is in Dothan.

14 Therefore sent he thither horses, and chariots, and a great host: and they came by night, and compassed the city about *(all for just one man)*.

15 And when the servant of the man of God was risen early, and gone forth, behold, an host compassed the city both with horses and chariots. And his servant said unto him, Alas, my master! how shall we do? *(The Holy Spirit is telling us here not to be daunted by that which appears on the surface. The Believer is not to walk "after the flesh," but rather "after the Spirit" [Rom. 8:1]. The trouble with most Christians is, they know what is happening, but they don't know what's going on.)*

16 And he *(Elisha)* answered, Fear not *(over 300 times in the Word of God, the Holy Spirit tells us, "Fear not")*: for they who be with us are more than they who be with them *(we should ever remember this; for the Promise applicable then is most assuredly applicable now!)*.

17 And Elisha prayed, and said, LORD, I pray Thee, open his eyes *(the eyes of the servant)*, that he may see. And the LORD opened the eyes of the young man; and he saw: and, behold, the mountain was full of horses and chariots of fire round about Elisha. *(The Holy Spirit allowed this to happen that you and I may understand by faith that we are surrounded by such, even though not seen by the natural eye. What an encouragement! In this Passage, we are given a glimpse into the spirit world of Righteousness.)*

18 And when they came down to him, Elisha prayed unto the LORD, and said, Smite this people, I pray you, with blindness. And he smote them with blindness according to the word of Elisha. *(The same Gospel that softens also hardens. As well, that which opens blinded eyes can close open eyes. The Gospel always has a powerful effect on anyone, whether it be positive or negative. The effect is according to the response of the individual.)*

19 And Elisha said unto them, This is not the way, neither is this the city: follow me, and I will bring you to the man whom you seek. But he led them to Samaria. *(No, this was not a lie. Their intention was to stop Elisha, because he was hindering them from getting to the king of Israel. The king of Israel was the one whom they were really seeking.)*

20 And it came to pass, when they were come into Samaria, that Elisha said, LORD, open the eyes of these men, that they may see. And the LORD opened their eyes, and they saw; and, behold, they were in the midst of Samaria.

21 And the king of Israel said unto Elisha, when he saw them, My father, shall I smite them? shall I smite them?

22 And he *(Elisha)* answered, You shall not smite them: would you smite those whom you have taken captive with your sword and with your bow? set bread and water before them, that they may eat and drink, and go to their master *(this Verse pictures a great work of Grace; the king of Israel would kill them; however, Elisha proclaims the love of God to them)*.

23 And he prepared great provision for them: and when they had eaten and drunk, he sent them away, and they went to their master. So the bands of Syria came no more into the land of Israel *(at least at that time!)*.

BEN-HADAD BESIEGES SAMARIA

24 And it came to pass after this *(several years have now passed)*, that Ben-hadad king of Syria gathered all his host, and went up, and besieged Samaria. *(This would never have happened had Ahab put Ben-hadad to death when he was in his power. The sufferings recorded in this Passage would have been avoided. This siege and its horrors fulfill the Prophecy then made to Ahab by the rebuking Prophet [I Ki. 20:31-34].)*

25 And there was a great famine in Samaria *(because of its sin)*: and, behold, they *(the Syrians)* besieged it *(the Lord allowed this to happen, because of Israel's sin)*, until an ass's head was sold for fourscore pieces of silver, and the fourth part of a cab of dove's dung for five pieces of silver.

26 And as the king of Israel was passing by upon the wall, there cried a woman unto him, saying, Help, my lord, O king.

27 And he said, If the LORD do not help you, whence shall I help you? out of the barnfloor, or out of the winepress? *(Do you suppose that I have stores of food at my disposal?)*

28 And the king said unto her, What ails you? And she answered, This woman said unto me, Give your son, that we may eat him to day, and we will eat my son to morrow.

29 So we boiled my son, and did eat him: and I said unto her on the next day, Give your son, that we may eat him: and she has hid her son. *(The siege had become so severe that the*

people of Israel, God's chosen People, had re-sorted to cannibalism. Moses had predicted that this would happen, if the people turned their backs upon God [Deut. 28:53-57].)

JEHORAM BLAMES ELISHA

30 And it came to pass, when the king heard the words of the woman, that he rent his clothes; and he passed by upon the wall, and the people looked, and, behold, he had sack-cloth within upon his flesh. (There was no Re-pentance on the part of Jehoram; the sackcloth was only a ceremony. While it was definitely a sign of his tremendous problems, it did not point to the cause of those problems, which was his terrible sin. In fact, the Church presently is loaded with similar ceremonies; however, the ceremo-nies are not based on the Cross and, therefore, aren't valid.)

31 Then he said, God do so and more also to me, if the head of Elisha the son of Shaphat shall stand on him this day. (His opposition to Elisha shows his spiritual condition. As well, Law will always attack Grace. Instead of the modern Church realizing the cause of its prob-lems, and thereby repenting, it attacks the ones who are preaching the answer, namely the Cross.)

32 But Elisha sat in his house, and the el-ders sat with him; and the king sent a man from before him: but ere the messenger came to him, he said to the elders, See you how this son of a murderer has sent to take away my head? look, when the messenger comes, shut the door, and hold him fast at the door: is not the sound of his master's feet behind him? (Elisha was supernaturally warned of what was about to take place — that an executioner was coming almost immediately to take away his life, and that the king himself would arrive shortly after.)

33 And while he yet talked with them, be-hold, the messenger came down unto him (to admit the king, for he had now arrived): and he (the king) said, Behold, this evil is of the LORD (now, Jehoram blames the Lord); what should I wait for the LORD any longer? (Jehoram had, apparently, to some extent repented of his hasty message, and had hurried after his messenger to give Elisha one further chance at life. We must understand that they had been in communica-tion previously on the subject of the siege, and that Elisha had encouraged the king to "wait for" an interposition of Jehovah. The king now urges that the time for waiting is over. In effect,

he says, "What use is there in waiting any longer? Why should he not break with Jehovah, behead the lying Prophet, and surrender the town? What has Elisha to say in reply?" — Pulpit.)

CHAPTER 7
(892 B.C.)
ELISHA'S PROPHECY

THEN Elisha said, Hear ye the Word of the LORD; Thus saith the LORD, To morrow about this time shall a measure of fine flour be sold for a shekel, and two measures of bar-ley for a shekel, in the gate of Samaria. (How amazing is Grace, that, in response to the mur-derous unbelief of the king's heart and the scorn-ful unbelief of the messenger, promised such an abundance of food, and so soon that it was to be had almost for nothing!)

2 Then a lord on whose hand the king leaned answered the man of God, and said, Behold, if the LORD would make windows in Heaven, might this thing be? And he (Elisha) said, Behold, you shall see it with your eyes, but shall not eat thereof (the reward of unbe-lief would be death, as the reward of unbelief is always death).

FOUR LEPERS

3 And there were four leprous men at the entering in of the gate: and they said one to another, Why sit we here until we die? (Lep-rosy in the Old Testament was a type of sin. Its horrid desperation was such that, in the eyes of Israel, a leper was hopeless. How many Chris-tians find themselves presently in such a peril-ous condition, a condition, we might add, so disastrous that there is no help from any quarter except God. Nevertheless, no condition is such that God cannot change it.

"Why sit we here until we die?" In these very words, you can feel Faith. How many Chris-tians have given up? How many have quit? Faith demands action. So, these four lepers act.)

4 If we say, We will enter into the city, then the famine is in the city, and we shall die there: and if we sit still here, we die also. Now there-fore come, and let us fall unto the host of the Syrians: if they save us alive, we shall live; and if they kill us, we shall but die (in other words, we have nothing to lose, because we are dying anyway).

5 And they rose up in the twilight (in the evening, near dark), to go unto the camp of the

Syrians: and when they were come to the uttermost part of the camp of Syria, behold, there was no man there *(the camp was empty, deserted)*.

THE CONFUSION AND FLIGHT OF THE SYRIANS

6 For the LORD had made the host of the Syrians to hear a noise of chariots, and a noise of horses, even the noise of a great host: and they said one to another, Lo, the king of Israel has hired against us the kings of the Hittites, and the kings of the Egyptians, to come upon us. *(The Syrians thought some powerful army from a higher nation was coming upon them and fled. How easy it is for the Lord to do anything. How so important it is for the Christian not to limit God and, sadly, how so much we do limit Him. Evidently, when these four lepers began to walk toward the camp of the Syrians, the Lord magnified their footsteps, until it sounded like the march of a mighty army. We exhibit Faith, and God does the rest; but what we do must be in the Will of God.)*

7 Wherefore they arose and fled in the twilight, and left their tents, and their horses, and their asses, even the camp as it was, and fled for their life.

8 And when these lepers came to the uttermost part of the camp, they went into one tent, and did eat and drink, and carried thence silver, and gold, and raiment, and went and hid it; and came again, and entered into another tent, and carried thence also, and went and hid it.

9 Then they said one to another, We do not well: this day is a day of good tidings, and we hold our peace: if we tarry till the morning light, some mischief will come upon us: now therefore come, that we may go and tell the king's household. *(The sun had set the day before on a day of disaster for Samaria, but the sun will now rise on one of the greatest days of blessing in her history. Faith in God would do this thing.*

In type, Samaria is a picture of the world with its hunger, starvation, pain, and agony. The lepers, as pitiful as they were, are a type of Preachers of the Gospel of Good News. The abundance that we have found is a product of the Gospel of Jesus Christ, which alone can satisfy the hunger and the craving of a starving world.

As the lepers, "we must not hold our peace." We have good news to bring, in fact, the greatest news than man has ever known. "Jesus saves, Jesus heals, Jesus baptizes with the Holy Spirit, Jesus delivers, and Jesus is coming again.")

10 So they came and called unto the porter of the city: and they told them, saying, We came to the camp of the Syrians, and, behold, there was no man there, neither voice of man, but horses tied, and asses tied, and the tents as they were.

11 And he called the porters; and they told it to the king's house within.

12 And the king arose in the night, and said unto his servants, I will now show you what the Syrians have done to us. They know that we be hungry; therefore are they gone out of the camp to hide themselves in the field, saying, When they come out of the city, we shall catch them alive, and get into the city *(unbelief always thinks the negative)*.

13 And one of his servants answered and said, Let some take, I pray you, five of the horses that remain, which are left in the city, (behold, they are as all the multitude of Israel who are left in it: behold, I say, they are even as all the multitude of the Israelites who are consumed:) and let us send and see.

14 They took therefore two chariot horses; and the king sent after the host of the Syrians, saying, Go and see.

15 And they went after them unto Jordan: and, lo, all the way was full of garments and vessels *(scattered about the way)*, which the Syrians had cast away in their haste. And the messengers returned, and told the king.

ELISHA'S PROPHECY OF PLENTY IS FULFILLED

16 And the people went out, and spoiled the tents of the Syrians. So a measure of fine flour was sold for a shekel, and two measures of barley for a shekel, according to the Word of the LORD.

17 And the king appointed the lord on whose hand he leaned to have the charge of the gate *(the man of unbelief of Verse 2)*: and the people trode upon him in the gate, and he died, as the man of God had said, who spoke when the king came down to him.

18 And it came to pass as the man of God had spoken to the king, saying, Two measures of barley for a shekel, and a measure of fine flour for a shekel, shall be to morrow about this time at the gate of Samaria:

19 And that lord answered the man of God,

and said, Now, behold, if the LORD should make windows in Heaven, might such a thing be? And he said, Behold, you shall see it with your eyes, but shall not eat thereof.

20 And so it fell out unto him: for the people trode upon him in the gate, and he died (they ran over him, trying to get to the food).

CHAPTER 8
(885 B.C.)
A SEVEN-YEAR FAMINE

THEN spoke Elisha unto the woman, whose son he had restored to life (4:18-37), saying, Arise, and go you and your household, and sojourn wheresoever you can sojourn: for the LORD has called for a famine; and it shall also come upon the land seven years. (Almost everything that happened to Elijah was doubled with Elisha, which pertained to the double portion received by Elisha. The famine in the days of Elijah was three and a half years, and this famine under Elisha is seven years. With the double blessings also came double judgment.)

2 And the woman arose, and did after the saying of the man of God: and she went with her household, and sojourned in the land of the Philistines seven years (the Lord sent the famine on Israel because of her sin; the famine did not include the land of the Philistines).

THE SHUNAMMITE'S INHERITANCE RESTORED

3 And it came to pass at the seven years' end, that the woman returned out of the land of the Philistines: and she went forth to cry unto the king for her house and for her land (evidently, other people had taken it over).

4 And the king talked with Gehazi the servant of the man of God, saying, Tell me, I pray you, all the great things that Elisha has done. (Yet all of these great things had not served the purpose to cause this king or Israel to repent. The king desired to hear the story of miracles, but nothing could be said of Righteousness, Temperance, or Judgment to come. Regrettably, it is the same presently!

Chapter 5 records Gehazi being stricken with leprosy. So, the account of the healing of Naaman may not have been given in chronological order. In other words, it is possible that it happened after this incident. If that is incorrect, then possibly Gehazi had been healed; however, there is no Scriptural record of such.)

5 And it came to pass, as he was telling the king how he had restored a dead body to life, that, behold, the woman, whose son he had restored to life, cried to the king for her house and for her land. And Gehazi said, My lord, O king, this is the woman, and this is her son, whom Elisha restored to life.

6 And when the king asked the woman, she told him. So the king appointed unto her a certain officer, saying, Restore all that was hers, and all the fruits of the field since the day that she left the land, even until now. (The Holy Spirit went to great lengths in relating this, for the express purpose of showing God's watchful care over this woman. The Lord had her come to the palace at exactly the same time that Gehazi was telling her story. For the good deed she had done to the Lord's Prophet, in building him an apartment onto her house some ten years earlier, the Lord would continue to bless her. Our gifts to Him are so fleeting. His Blessing to us is everlasting.)

HAZAEL BECOMES KING OF SYRIA

7 And Elisha came to Damascus; and Benhadad the king of Syria was sick; and it was told him, saying, The man of God is come hither (it seems that respect for Elisha had grown considerably, even in the heathen country of Syria).

8 And the king said unto Hazael, Take a present in your hand, and go, meet the man of God, and enquire of the LORD by him, saying, Shall I recover of this disease? (It's amazing how much faith a wicked king like Ben-hadad would have in Elisha, and in the Lord, as well, and still not repent of his wrongdoing.)

9 So Hazael went to meet him, and took a present with him, even of every good thing of Damascus, forty camels' burden, and came and stood before him, and said, Your son Benhadad king of Syria has sent me to you, saying, Shall I recover of this disease? (Whether Elisha received or accepted this gift is not known. To be sure, it was a gift of sizable proportions.)

10 And Elisha said unto him, Go, say unto him, You may certainly recover: howbeit the LORD has showed me that he shall surely die. (In other words, he could recover, but he won't. The reason? Hazael will kill him.)

11 And he (Hazael) settled his countenance stedfastly, until he was ashamed: and the man of God wept. (Elisha fixed on Hazael a long and meaning look, until Hazael felt embarrassed,

and his eyes fell. Elisha wept, because of the long series of calamities which Israel would suffer at the hands of Syria during Hazael's reign.)

12 And Hazael said, Why weeps my lord? And he answered, Because I know the evil that you will do unto the Children of Israel: their strong holds will you set on fire, and their young men will you slay with the sword, and will dash their children, and rip up their women with child.

13 And Hazael said, But what, is your servant a dog, that he should do this great thing? And Elisha answered, The LORD has showed me that you shall be king over Syria.

14 So he departed from Elisha, and came to his master; who said to him, What said Elisha to you? And he answered, He told me that you should surely recover.

15 And it came to pass on the morrow, that he took a thick cloth, and dipped it in water, and spread it on his *(Ben-hadad's)* face, so that he died: and Hazael reigned in his stead.

JEHORAM REIGNS OVER JUDAH

16 And in the fifth year of Joram the son of Ahab king of Israel, Jehoshaphat being then king of Judah, Jehoram the son of Jehoshaphat king of Judah began to reign. *(At this point, the history of the kingdom of Judah is taken up. Jehoram's reign was sometimes counted from the seventeenth year of his father, when he was given the royal title; sometimes from his father's twenty-third year, when he was associated; and sometimes, from his father's death, in his twenty-fifth year, when he became sole king. In other words, he reigned jointly with his father Jehoshaphat for a period of time.)*

17 Thirty and two years old was he when he began to reign; and he reigned eight years in Jerusalem.

18 And he walked in the way of the kings of Israel, as did the house of Ahab: for the daughter of Ahab was his wife: and he did evil in the sight of the LORD *(these Verses proclaim the result of Jehoshaphat's sin regarding his union with Ahab and that wicked family).*

19 Yet the LORD would not destroy Judah for David His servant's sake, as He promised him to give him always a light, and to his children. *(The "light" here refers to a king and a kingdom according to the Davidic Covenant of II Sam., Chpt. 7. A natural consequence of Jehoram's apostasy would have been the destruction of the house of David, and the starting of*

another dynasty, as in the case of Jeroboam [I Ki. 14:10], but the promises to David prevented this, and Jehoram was punished in other ways.)*

20 In his days Edom revolted from under the hand of Judah, and made a king over themselves.

21 So Joram *(because this king of Judah did evil in the sight of the Lord, the Holy Spirit excises from his name the Jehovah-syllable, reducing it to "Joram")* went over to Zair, and all the chariots with him: and he rose by night, and smote the Edomites which compassed him about, and the captains of the chariots: and the people fled into their tents.

22 Yet Edom revolted from under the hand of Judah unto this day. Then Libnah revolted at the same time *(all as a result of sin).*

23 And the rest of the acts of Joram, and all that he did, are they not written in the Book of the Chronicles of the kings of Judah?

24 And Joram slept with his fathers, and was buried with his fathers in the city of David: and Ahaziah his son reigned in his stead *(Joram died after an illness that lasted two years, of an incurable disease of his bowels; there was no regret at his death).*

AHAZIAH'S ONE-YEAR REIGN IN JUDAH

25 In the twelfth year of Joram the son of Ahab king of Israel did Ahaziah the son of Jehoram king of Judah begin to reign *(it is conjectured that he began to reign as viceroy to his father during his severe illness in Jehoram's eleventh year, and became sole king at his father's death in the year following).*

26 Two and twenty years old was Ahaziah when he began to reign; and he reigned one year in Jerusalem. And his mother's name was Athaliah, the daughter of Omri king of Israel.

27 And he walked in the way of the house of Ahab, and did evil in the sight of the LORD, as did the house of Ahab: for he was the son in law of the house of Ahab *(Jehoshaphat's sin of "unity" would take its deadly toll for years to come).*

28 And he went with Joram the son of Ahab to the war against Hazael king of Syria in Ramoth-gilead; and the Syrians wounded Joram.

29 And king Joram went back to be healed in Jezreel of the wounds which the Syrians had given him at Ramah, when he fought against Hazael king of Syria. And Ahaziah the son of Jehoram king of Judah went down to see Joram

the son of Ahab in Jezreel, because he was sick. *(This "Joram" is the king of Israel, while the "Joram" of Verse 21 was the king of Judah.)*

CHAPTER 9
(884 B.C.)
JEHU ANOINTED AS KING OF ISRAEL

AND Elisha the Prophet called one of the children of the prophets, and said unto him, Gird up your loins, and take this box of oil in your hand, and go to Ramoth-gilead *(the judgment of the house of Ahab now commences; Jehu is the Divine instrument chosen to execute that judgment; we will find that Jehu illustrates how zealous an unconverted man can be for God when it suits his personal interests and ambitions to attack national evils; what he did on behalf of Righteousness he did well and with energy; however, his zeal was carnal; he utterly destroyed Baal but permitted the golden calves to remain; this fact alone shows that his heart was a stranger to Divine Faith; he was an instrument of God's wrath, carrying out God's Will, at least in the destruction of Ahab and his family; but he never had a personal knowledge of God; so, now the second part of Elijah's prophecy those years earlier, concerning the anointing of Jehu as king over Israel, comes to pass [I Ki. 19:16]):*

2 And when you come thither, look out there Jehu the son of Jehoshaphat the son of Nimshi, and go in, and make him arise up from among his brethren, and carry him to an inner chamber *(secrecy was of extreme importance, lest Joram should get knowledge of what was happening, and prepare himself for resistance; had he not been taken by surprise, the result might have been a long and bloody civil war);*

3 Then take the box of oil, and pour it on his head, and say, Thus saith the LORD, I have anointed you king over Israel. Then open the door, and flee, and tarry not *(the conference was to be with closed doors, that no one might either hear or see what took place; and then the messenger was to leave instantly).*

4 So the young man, even the young man the prophet, went to Ramoth-gilead.

5 And when he came, behold, the captains of the host were sitting; and he said, I have an errand to you, O captain. And Jehu said, Unto which of all us? And he said, To you, O captain *(Jehu was thus singled out as the object of the message).*

6 And he arose, and went into the house; and he poured the oil on his head, and said unto him, Thus saith the LORD God of Israel, I have anointed you king over the people of the LORD, even over Israel *(even though Israel was in a sad state spiritually, the Lord still longingly referred to them as "His People").*

7 And you shall smite the house of Ahab your master, that I may avenge the blood of My servants the Prophets, and the blood of all the servants of the LORD, at the hand of Jezebel.

8 For the whole house of Ahab shall perish: and I will cut off from Ahab him who urinates against the wall, and him who is shut up and left in Israel:

9 And I will make the house of Ahab like the house of Jeroboam the son of Nebat, and like the house of Baasha the son of Ahijah:

10 And the dogs shall eat Jezebel in the portion of Jezreel, and there shall be none to bury her. And he opened the door, and fled *(all of this is plainly a command, and not a prophecy; Jehu is expressly ordered by God to "smite," to utterly destroy, the whole house of Ahab; in fact, Elijah had prophesied, years before, of the awful end of Jezebel [I Ki. 21:23]).*

11 Then Jehu came forth to the servants of his lord: and one said unto him, Is all well? wherefore came this mad fellow to you? And he said unto them, You know the man, and his communication *(the sudden appearance and disappearance of the messenger had evidently created an impression that all was not well).*

12 And they said, It is false; tell us now. And he said, Thus and thus spoke he to me, saying, Thus saith the LORD, I have anointed you king over Israel *(Jehu reveals to the others present what the young Prophet had said to him).*

13 Then they hasted, and took every man his garment, and put it under him on the top of the stairs, and blew with trumpets, saying, Jehu is king *(it seems that the captains threw themselves with ardor into his cause).*

JEHU KILLS JEHORAM (JORAM)

14 So Jehu the son of Jehoshaphat the son of Nimshi *(not the same Jehoshaphat who had been the king of Judah)* conspired against Joram. (Now Joram had kept Ramoth-gilead, he and all Israel, because of Hazael king of Syria.

15 But king Joram was returned to be healed in Jezreel of the wounds which the Syrians had given him, when he fought with Hazael king

of Syria.) And Jehu said, If it be your minds, then let none go forth nor escape out of the city to go to tell it in Jezreel *(as soon as he is proclaimed king, Jehu addresses himself to the captains, denoting that he has the military behind him, and proposes a policy; he swears everyone to secrecy).*

16 So Jehu rode in a chariot, and went to Jezreel; for Joram lay there. And Ahaziah king of Judah was come down to see Joram *(the great object of Jehu was to surprise Joram, and to kill or capture him before he could take any steps to organize a defense).*

17 And there stood a watchman on the tower in Jezreel, and he spied the company of Jehu as he came, and said, I see a company. And Joram said, Take an horseman, and send to meet them, and let him say, Is it peace?

18 So there went one on horseback to meet him, and said, Thus saith the king, Is it peace? And Jehu said, What have you to do with peace? turn thee behind me. And the watchman told, saying, The messenger came to them, but he comes not again *(in other words, the messenger was not allowed to take back any message whatsoever).*

19 Then he sent out a second on horseback, which came to them, and said, Thus saith the king, Is it peace? And Jehu answered, What have you to do with peace? turn you behind me *(the same was done with this messenger, as well).*

20 And the watchman told, saying, He came even unto them, and comes not again: and the driving is like the driving of Jehu the son of Nimshi; for he drives furiously *(the watchman on the wall conjectures that Jehu must be leading the company, since he had a character for impetuosity).*

21 And Joram said, Make ready. And his chariot was made ready. And Joram king of Israel and Ahaziah king of Judah went out, each in his chariot, and they went out against Jehu, and met him in the portion of Naboth the Jezreelite *(Divine providence has so ordered matters that vengeance for the sin of Ahab was exacted upon the very sin of his guilt regarding Naboth; the mills of God grind slowly, but they grind exceedingly fine; in other words, the Lord misses nothing).*

22 And it came to pass, when Joram saw Jehu, that he said, Is it peace, Jehu? And he answered, What peace, so long as the whoredoms of your mother Jezebel and her witchcrafts are so many? *("Whoredoms" mean idolatries, as so frequently*

used in the Old Testament [Lev. 19:29; 20:5; Jer. 3:2, 9; 13:17; Ezek. 16:17; etc.)*

23 And Joram turned his hands, and fled, and said to Ahaziah, There is treachery, O Ahaziah *(as Joram was king of Israel, Ahaziah was king of Judah).*

24 And Jehu drew a bow with his full strength, and smote Jehoram between his arms, and the arrow went out at his heart, and he sunk down in his chariot.

25 Then said Jehu to Bidkar his captain, Take up, and cast him in the portion of the field of Naboth the Jezreelite: for remember how that, when I and you rode together after Ahab his father, the LORD laid this burden upon him *(Jehu and Bidkar, who had personally ridden in the same chariot with Ahab, had heard the sentence of punishment addressed toward this evil king, as spoken by Elijah the Prophet [I Ki. 21:17-26]);*

26 Surely I have seen yesterday the blood of Naboth, and the blood of his sons, saith the LORD; and I will requite you in this plat, saith the LORD. Now therefore take and cast him into the plat of ground, according to the Word of the LORD *(the evil prophesied against Ahab had been formally and expressly deferred to the future days of his son, because of Ahab's Repentance [I Ki. 21:29]).*

JEHU SLAYS AHAZIAH, KING OF JUDAH

27 But when Ahaziah the king of Judah saw this, he fled by the way of the garden house. And Jehu followed after him, and said, Smite him also in the chariot. And they did so at the going up to Gur, which is by Ibleam. And he fled to Megiddo, and died there *(from a spiritual point of view, Jehu felt he could justify this act; the commission given to him [Vs. 7] was to smite all the house of Ahab, and Ahaziah was Ahab's grandson).*

28 And his servants carried him in a chariot to Jerusalem, and buried him in his sepulchre with his fathers in the city of David *(Ahaziah had reigned but a year [8:26]).*

29 And in the eleventh year of Joram the son of Ahab began Ahaziah to reign over Judah.

JEHU KILLS JEZEBEL

30 And when Jehu was come to Jezreel, Jezebel heard of it: and she painted her face, and tired *(tiered)* her head, and looked out at a window *(she looked out to see, but more so to*

be seen; it would not turn out well for her).

31 And as Jehu entered in at the gate, she said, Had Zimri peace, who slew his master? *(Ever how the question asked by Jezebel is to be interpreted, it seems that it is in a conciliatory attitude rather than that which is threatening.)*

32 And he *(Jehu)* lifted up his face to the window, and said, Who is on my side? who? And there looked out to him two or three eunuchs *(the eunuchs who "looked out" to Jehu were probably the chief eunuchs of the palace, who had authority over the others, and indeed over the court officials generally).*

33 And he said, Throw her down. So they threw her down: and some of her blood was sprinkled on the wall, and on the horses: and he trode her under foot *(there appears to have been no hesitation; the boldness of Jehu communicated itself to those whom he addressed; Jehu had his chariot driven over the prostrate corpse, so that the hoofs of his horses, and perhaps his own person, were sprinkled with her blood).*

34 And when he was come in, he did eat and drink, and said, Go, see now this cursed woman, and bury her: for she is a king's daughter *(he calls Jezebel "a cursed woman," not inappropriately; she had brought a curse on her husband, on her sons, and on her grandsons, as well as on the entirety of Israel and Judah; she had been the prime mover in a bloody persecution of the worshippers of Jehovah; so now, she must answer to the Lord, and that she has).*

35 And they went to bury her: but they found no more of her than the skull, and the feet, and the palms of her hands *(evidently, she was eaten by wild dogs).*

36 Wherefore they came again, and told him. And he said, This is the Word of the LORD, which He spoke by His servant Elijah the Tishbite, saying, In the portion of Jezreel shall dogs eat the flesh of Jezebel *(the Prophecy referred to is that recorded in I Kings 21:23):*

37 And the carcase of Jezebel shall be as dung upon the face of the field in the portion of Jezreel; so that they shall not say, This is Jezebel. *(The fragments of the body were so scattered that there could be no collective tomb, no place where admirers could congregate and say, "Here lies the great queen — here lies Jezebel." To rest in no tomb was viewed as a shame and a disgrace — Pulpit. And so concludes the life of this woman who had wrought such evil in both Israel and Judah. In one way or the other, all who reject Jesus Christ have an ignoble end. To die without God is the death of eternal darkness.)*

CHAPTER 10

(884 B.C.)

JEHU KILLS AHAB'S SONS

AND Ahab had seventy sons in Samaria. And Jehu wrote letters, and sent to Samaria, unto the rulers of Jezreel, to the elders, and to them who brought up Ahab's children, saying *(the word "sons" in the Hebrew being used as well for grandsons and even great-grandsons, most of these probably refer to his grandsons; however, Ahab showed he was doing all within his power to continue his dynasty.*

Jezreel is the scene of the cruel murder of Naboth and his sons, with it now becoming the theater of the just wrath of God upon Naboth's murderers. Here may be learned something of how God regards sin and judges it. If, in long-suffering Grace, He delays the judgment, this longsuffering heightens the terror of the Divine anger. In harmony with this, how appalling is the expression in the Book of Revelation, "the wrath of the Lamb" — not the wrath of the lion, but "the wrath of the Lamb"),

2 Now as soon as this letter comes to you, seeing your master's sons are with you, and there are with you chariots and horses, a fenced city also, and armour;

3 Look even out the best and meetest of your master's sons; and set him on his father's throne, and fight for your master's house.

4 But they were exceedingly afraid, and said, Behold, two kings stood not before him: how then shall we stand? *(The kings addressed are Joram and Ahaziah, who had confronted Jehu, and had met their deaths.)*

5 And he who was over the house, and he who was over the city, the elders also, and the bringers up of the children, sent to Jehu, saying, We are your servants, and will do all that you shall bid us; we will not make any king: do thou that which is good in your eyes.

6 Then he wrote a letter the second time to them, saying, If you be mine, and if you will hearken unto my voice, take ye the heads of the men your master's sons, and come to me to Jezreel by to morrow this time. Now the king's sons, being seventy persons, were with the great men of the city, which brought them up *(Jezreel was not more than twenty miles from Samaria).*

7 And it came to pass, when the letter came to them, that they took the king's sons, and slew seventy persons, and put their heads in baskets, and sent him them to Jezreel *(Jehu had told them to personally bring the heads to him; but this was a degradation to which they*

did not feel bound to submit; they, therefore, sent the heads by trusted messengers).

8 And there came a messenger, and told him, saying, They have brought the heads of the king's sons. And he said, Lay ye them in two heaps at the entering in of the gate until the morning *(thus, all who entered into the town or left the town would see them and, being struck by the ghastly spectacle, would make inquiry and learn the truth — Pulpit).*

9 And it came to pass in the morning, that he went out, and stood, and said to all the people, You be righteous: behold, I conspired against my master, and killed him: but who killed all these? *(Politically, Jehu seeks to absolve himself of blame concerning the deaths of these individuals.)*

10 Know now that there shall fall unto the earth nothing of the Word of the LORD, which the LORD spoke concerning the house of Ahab: for the LORD has done that which He spoke by His servant Elijah *(Jehu declares that what has been done has been according to the Word of the Lord, and so it was [I Ki. 21:19, 21, 28-29]).*

11 So Jehu slew all that remained of the house of Ahab in Jezreel, and all his great men, and his kinsfolks, and his priests, until he left him none remaining *(the entire Ahab faction was blotted out).*

JEHU KILLS THE PRINCES OF JUDAH, DESCENDANTS OF AHAB'S DAUGHTER

12 And he arose and departed, and came to Samaria *(the capital of Israel)*. And as he was at the shearing house in the way,

13 Jehu met with the brethren of Ahaziah king of Judah, and said, Who are you? And they answered, We are the brethren of Ahaziah *(who had been king of Judah)*; and we go down to salute the children of the king and the children of the queen *(hearing of the great unrest in Samaria, they had probably been sent to Athaliah to render any assistance that they could to the house of Ahab).*

14 And he said, Take them alive. And they took them alive, and killed them at the pit of the shearing house, even two and forty men; neither left he any of them *(as well, these were also descendants of Ahab).*

THE BALANCE OF AHAB'S HOUSE IN SAMARIA KILLED BY JEHU AS THE LORD INSTRUCTED

15 And when he was departed thence, he lighted on Jehonadab the son of Rechab coming to meet him: and he saluted him, and said to him, Is your heart right, as my heart is with your heart? And Jehonadab answered, It is. If it be, give me your hand. And he gave him his hand; and he took him up to him into the chariot *(Jehonadab was the founder of the sect of the Rechabites [Jer. 35:6-19]; he joins affinity with Jehu).*

16 And he said, Come with me, and see my zeal for the LORD. So they made him *(Jehonadab)* ride in his *(Jehu's)* chariot *(man can be very zealous for God, as Jehu, and yet not know Him, but this zeal only goes as far as it suits personal interests or religious and political pursuits; the zeal of such persons only lasts so long as it suits their purposes).*

17 And when he came to Samaria, he killed all that remained unto Ahab in Samaria, till he had destroyed him, according to the saying, of the LORD, which he spoke to Elijah *(I Ki. 21:17-22]).*

JEHU KILLS THE WORSHIPPERS OF BAAL

18 And Jehu gathered all the people together, and said unto them, Ahab served Baal a little; but Jehu shall serve him much *(probably, as yet, no suspicion had touched the public mind that Jehu would be a less zealous worshipper of Baal than his predecessor).*

19 Now therefore call unto me all the prophets of Baal, all his servants, and all his priests; let none be wanting: for I have a great sacrifice to do to Baal; whosoever shall be wanting, he shall not live. But Jehu did it in subtilty, to the intent that he might destroy the worshippers of Baal *("subtilty" was characteristic of Jehu, who always preferred to gain his ends by cunning rather than in a straightforward way).*

20 And Jehu said, Proclaim a solemn assembly for Baal. And they proclaimed it *(no opposition was made to the king's wish; however, they had no idea as to what he was about to do).*

21 And Jehu sent through all Israel: and all the worshippers of Baal came, so that there was not a man left that came not. And they came into the house of Baal; and the house of Baal was full from one end to another *(Ahab had erected a temple to Baal in Samaria shortly after his marriage to Jezebel [I Ki. 16:22]; so this is where they would gather).*

22 And he said unto him who was over the vestry, Bring forth vestments for all the worshippers of Baal. And he brought them forth

vestments *(the keeper of the wardrobe obeyed the order given him, and supplied the vestments to all the worshippers, whatever those vestments may have been)*.

23 And Jehu went, and Jehonadab the son of Rechab, into the house of Baal, and said unto the worshippers of Baal, Search, and look that there be here with you none of the servants of the LORD, but the worshippers of Baal only.

24 And when they went in to offer sacrifices and burnt offerings, Jehu appointed fourscore men without, and said, If any of the men whom I have brought into your hands escape, he who lets him go, his life shall be for the life of him.

25 And it came to pass, as soon as he had made an end of offering the burnt offering, that Jehu said to the guard and to the captains, Go in, and kill them; let none come forth. And they smote them with the edge of the sword; and the guard and the captains cast them out, and went to the city of the house of Baal *(they made their way into the inner sanctuary)*.

26 And they brought forth the images out of the house of Baal, and burned them *(they were evidently made of wood)*.

27 And they broke down the image of Baal, and broke down the house of Baal, and made it a draught house unto this day *(made it into a garbage dump)*.

28 Thus Jehu destroyed Baal out of Israel *(the measures taken were effective; the worship of Baal was put down, and is not said to have been revived in the kingdom of the ten tribes; regrettably, Moloch-worship seems to have taken its place — Pulpit)*.

29 Howbeit from the sins of Jeroboam the son of Nebat, who made Israel to sin, Jehu departed not from after them, to wit, the golden calves that were in Beth-el, and that were in Dan *(it seems that Jehu was not prepared to eradicate all idol worship in Israel; his "zeal for Jehovah" did not reach so far; thus his "reformation of religion" was but a half-reformation, a partial turning to Jehovah, which brought no permanent blessing upon the nation)*.

A SUMMARY OF JEHU'S KINGSHIP

30 And the LORD said unto Jehu, Because you have done well in executing that which is right in My eyes, and have done unto the house of Ahab according to all that was in My heart, your children of the fourth generation shall sit on the throne of Israel *(these four generations were: Jehoahaz [13:1-9], Joash [13:10-25;*

14:1-16], Jeroboam II [14:16-29], and Zechariah [14:28-29; 15:8-12]).

31 But Jehu took no heed to walk in the law of the LORD God of Israel with all his heart: for he departed not from the sins of Jeroboam, which made Israel to sin.

32 In those days the LORD began to cut Israel short: and Hazael smote them in all the coasts of Israel;

33 From Jordan eastward, all the land of Gilead, the Gadites, and the Reubenites, and the Manassites, from Aroer, which is by the river Arnon, even Gilead and Bashan. *(What a golden opportunity Jehu had to incur the blessings of God, but he had no real love for the Lord. Everything he did only suited himself. So now the Lord will allow troubles to begin in Israel, which will finally culminate in her ceasing to be as a nation, and all because of sin.)*

34 Now the rest of the acts of Jehu, and all that he did, and all his might, are they not written in the Book of the Chronicles of the kings of Israel?

35 And Jehu slept with his fathers: and they buried him in Samaria. And Jehoahaz his son reigned in his stead.

36 And the time that Jehu reigned over Israel in Samaria was twenty and eight years. *(Jehu's reign was the longest reign of an Israelite king, with the exception of Jeroboam II, who is said in 14:23 to have reigned 41 years. The kings of Judah, it seems, by and large, were longer-lived. In fact, not one single king of the northern confederation of Israel was said by the Lord to be Righteous.)*

CHAPTER 11
(878 B.C.)
ATHALIAH, AHAB'S DAUGHTER, DESTROYS THE ROYAL SEED

AND when Athaliah the mother of Ahaziah saw that her son was dead, she arose and destroyed all the seed royal. *(Once more, we see the terrible effects of Jehoshaphat's sin in attempting to align himself with idolatrous Israel. This woman, "Athaliah," was the only woman who ruled as a queen in Judah. She was the granddaughter of Omri [II Chron. 22:2], and the daughter of Ahab and Jezebel. The marriage between Jehoram, king of Judah, and Athaliah, daughter of Jezebel, was part of Satan's grand design to introduce idolatry into Judah so that Athaliah might do for Judah what Jezebel did for Israel.*

Jehoshaphat began this sordid situation by marrying his son to the idolatrous daughter of Israel's worst rulers, Ahab and Jezebel. Whatever were Jehoshaphat's ideas, Satan used them to work his devious design, which was to destroy the "seed of the woman," making it impossible for the Messiah to be born into the world.)

JOASH IS SAVED

2 But Jehosheba, the daughter of king Joram, sister of Ahaziah, took Joash the son of Ahaziah, and stole him from among the king's sons which were slain; and they hid him, even him and his nurse, in the bedchamber from Athaliah, so that he was not slain. *(Jehosheba, wife of Jehoiada the High Priest, was sister to the late king and, therefore, aunt to the infant Joash. She must have been a woman of nerve and ability. It was a courageous act on her part to enter such a slaughterhouse. It may be assumed that she did so to look with grief and horror upon her murdered nephews and cousins. The infant Joash lay among them, apparently dead; she found him still living, stole him, and hid him.)*

3 And he was with her hid in the house of the LORD six years. And Athaliah did reign over the land *(over Judah; she thought she had killed all the lineage of David, but such was not the case)*.

JEHOIADA, THE PRIEST, OVERTHROWS ATHALIAH; JOASH ANOINTED KING

4 And the seventh year Jehoiada sent and fetched the rulers over hundreds, with the captains and the guard, and brought them to him into the House of the LORD, and made a covenant with them, and took an oath of them in the House of the LORD, and showed them the king's son *(after waiting, impatiently, we may be sure, for six long years, and seeing the young prince grow from an infant to a boy of seven years of age, Jehoiada deemed that the time was now come, to act)*.

5 And he commanded them, saying, This is the thing that you shall do; A third part of you that enter in on the sabbath shall even be keepers of the watch of the king's house *(the object was to secure the palace, but not to prevent the queen from leaving it)*;

6 And a third part shall be at the gate of Sur; and a third part at the gate behind the guard: so shall you keep the watch of the house, that it be not broken down.

7 And two parts of all you who go forth on the sabbath, even they shall keep the watch of the house of the LORD about the king *(these Jehoiada commanded to enter the Temple and protect the young king)*.

8 And you shall compass the king round about, every man with his weapons in his hand: and he who comes within the ranges, let him be slain: and be ye with the king as he goes out and as he comes in.

9 And the captains over the hundreds did according to all things that Jehoiada the Priest commanded: and they took every man his men who were to come in on the sabbath, with them who should go out on the sabbath, and came to Jehoiada the Priest.

10 And to the captains over hundreds did the Priest give king David's spears and shields, that were in the Temple of the LORD.

11 And the guard stood, every man with his weapons in his hand, round about the king, from the right corner of the Temple to the left corner of the Temple, along by the Altar and the Temple *(the "Altar" of Burnt Offering, which stood in the great court, a little way from the porch right in front of it)*.

12 And he brought forth the king's son, and put the crown upon him, and gave him the Testimony *(either a copy of the Ten Commandments, or else a copy of the entirety of the Law of Moses, by which the young king should govern and mete out justice to the people)*; and they made him king, and anointed him; and they clapped their hands, and said, God save the king *(literally, "Long live the king!")*.

ATHALIAH IS SLAIN

13 And when Athaliah heard the noise of the guard and of the people, she came to the people into the Temple of the LORD *(it would seem that she was still unsuspicious of danger, and brought no guards with her, nor any large body of attendants)*.

14 And when she looked, behold, the king stood by a pillar, as the manner was, and the princes and the trumpeters by the king, and all the people of the land rejoiced, and blew with trumpets: and Athaliah rent her clothes, and cried, Treason, Treason *(there was treason all right, but it had been committed by this evil queen)*.

15 But Jehoiada the Priest commanded the captains of the hundreds, the officers of the host, and said unto them, Have her forth without

the ranges: and him who follows her kill with the sword. For the Priest had said, Let her not be slain in the House of the LORD (Jehoiada had previously given an order that her execution should take place outside the Temple).

16 And they laid hands on her; and she went by the way by the which the horses came into the king's house: and there was she slain.

REVIVAL UNDER JEHOIADA

17 And Jehoiada made a covenant between the LORD and the king and the people, that they should be the LORD's people; between the king also and the people (the meaning is that the High Priest renewed the Old Covenant understood to exist between king and people on the one hand, and God on the other; that they would be faithful to God, and God to them — that they would maintain His worship and that He would continue His Protection [Ex. 19:5-8; 24:3-8; 34:10-28]).

18 And all the people of the land went into the house of Baal, and broke it down; his altars and his images broke they in pieces thoroughly, and slew Mattan the priest of Baal before the altars. And the Priest (Jehoiada) appointed officers over the House of the LORD (Jehoiada re-established the regular courses and the worship).

19 And he took the rulers over hundreds, and the captains, and the guard, and all the people of the land; and they brought down the king from the house of the LORD, and came by the way of the gate of the guard to the king's house. And he sat on the throne of the kings (not till he had placed Joash on the royal throne of his ancestors, in the great throne-room of the palace, was Jehoiada content with the work of the day).

20 And all the people of the land rejoiced, and the city was in quiet: and they slew Athaliah with the sword beside the king's house (the intention of the writer is to connect the period of tranquility with the removal of Athaliah and, therefore, to point her out as the cause of Judah's great difficulties).

21 Seven years old was Jehoash (Joash) when he began to reign.

CHAPTER 12
(878 B.C.)
JOASH REIGNS OVER JUDAH

IN the seventh year of Jehu (who was king of Israel) Jehoash (Joash) began to reign (over the southern kingdom of Judah); and forty years reigned he in Jerusalem. And his mother's name was Zibiah of Beer-sheba.

2 And Jehoash did that which was right in the sight of the LORD all his days wherein Jehoiada the Priest instructed him (after Jehoiada died at the age of 130 years, Joash did evil in God's sight and brought judgment upon his people, as well as himself; the Godliness of Jehoiada was evidently a great influence upon Joash; consequently, the Lord allowed him to live long past the normal age).

3 But the high places were not taken away: the people still sacrificed and burnt incense in the high places (evidently, Jehoiada attempted to get Joash to remove these "high places," but was not successful; there was to be but one center of worship for Israel, as there is but one place of worship for the Christian, that is, Calvary; to Israel, Christ is "the Lamb slain from the foundation of the world"; to the Church, He is "the Lamb slain from before the foundation of the world" [I Pet. 1:20; Rev. 13:8]).

THE REPAIR OF THE TEMPLE

4 And Jehoash said to the Priests, All the money of the dedicated things that is brought into the House of the LORD, even the money of every one who passes the account, the money that every man is set at, and all the money that comes into any man's heart to bring into the House of the LORD (the Fourth Verse seems to imply that the Priests were little considered, with all the funds being designated toward repair).

5 Let the Priests take it to them, every man of his acquaintance: and let them repair the breaches of the house, wheresoever any breach shall be found (even though weak in other matters, it seems that Joash proved himself capable, as it regards this task).

6 But it was so, that in the three and twentieth year of king Jehoash the Priests had not repaired the breaches of the house (no charge is made against the Priests of embezzlement; they had simply been negligent, and probably because of lack of money).

7 Then king Jehoash called for Jehoiada the Priest, and the other Priests, and said unto them, Why repair ye not the breaches of the house? (This was, of course, the Temple.) now therefore receive no more money of your acquaintance, but deliver it for the breaches of the house (in other words, funds would be

8 And the Priests consented to receive no more money of the people, neither to repair the breaches of the house *(they consented to the new way)*.

9 But Jehoiada the Priest took a chest, and bored a hole in the lid of it, and set it beside the Altar *(the Brazen Altar)*, on the right side as one comes into the House of the LORD: and the Priests who kept the door put therein all the money that was brought into the House of the LORD *(the suggestion was probably that of Joash, but the Ecclesiastical and civil authorities worked harmoniously with the suggestion)*.

10 And it was so, when they saw that there was much money in the chest, that the king's scribe and the High Priest came up, and they put up in bags, and told the money that was found in the House of the LORD *(they counted the money that had been placed in the chest, put there for the repair of the Temple)*.

11 And they gave the money, being told, into the hands of them who did the work, that had the oversight of the House of the LORD: and they laid it out to the carpenters and builders, that wrought upon the House of the LORD *(it must be remembered that no coins existed as yet; and the lumps of silver which passed as shekels were of very uncertain weight; consequently, to know the value of the money in each bag, it was necessary not only to count the pieces, but to weigh each bag separately)*.

12 And to masons, and hewers of stone, and to buy timber and hewed stone to repair the breaches of the House of the LORD, and for all that was laid out for the house to repair it *(the Temple by now had been standing for a little over a hundred and fifty years; so it is obvious as to the needed repairs)*.

13 Howbeit there were not made for the House of the LORD bowls of silver, snuffers, basons, trumpets, any vessels of gold, or vessels of silver, of the money that was brought into the House of the LORD *(none of the money was used for the items listed, but was spent strictly on the repair of the structure; there is no contradiction between this statement and that of II Chronicles 24:14, which tells us that "after all of the repairs were completed," the surplus money was expended on the purchase of Temple vessels, etc.)*:

14 But they gave that to the workmen, and repaired therewith the House of the LORD *(used the money solely on repairs)*.

15 Moreover they reckoned not with the men, into whose hand they delivered the money to be bestowed on workmen: for they dealt faithfully *(the overseers of the project dealt faithfully with the money)*.

16 The trespass money and sin money was not brought into the House of the LORD: it was the Priests' *(this particular income went for the maintenance of the Priests and, consequently, was not used for the repair of the building)*.

JOASH PAYS RANSOM TO HAZAEL OF SYRIA

17 Then Hazael king of Syria went up, and fought against Gath, and took it: and Hazael set his face to go up to Jerusalem *(threatened to invade the city)*.

18 And Jehoash king of Judah took all the hallowed things that Jehoshaphat, and Jehoram, and Ahaziah, his fathers, kings of Judah, had dedicated, and his own hallowed things, and all the gold that was found in the treasures of the House of the LORD, and in the king's house, and sent it to Hazael king of Syria: and he went away from Jerusalem *(all of this happened after the death of the Godly Priest Jehoiada, after which Joash went into deep sin; while all trouble is definitely not caused by sin, much of it, in fact, is!)*.

JOASH'S DEATH; AMAZIAH REIGNS

19 And the rest of the acts of Joash, and all that he did, are they not written in the book of the chronicles of the kings of Judah?

20 And his servants arose, and made a conspiracy, and slew Joash in the house of Millo, which goes down to Silla *(this judgment came upon him because, as the writer of Chronicles says, "They had forsaken the LORD God of their fathers" [II Chron. 24:24-26])*.

21 For Jozachar the son of Shimeath, and Jehozabad the son of Shomer, his servants, smote him, and he died; and they buried him with his fathers in the city of David: and Amaziah his son reigned in his stead.

CHAPTER 13
(856 B.C.)
JEHOAHAZ REIGNS OVER ISRAEL

IN the three and twentieth year of Joash the son of Ahaziah king of Judah Jehoahaz the

son of Jehu began to reign over Israel in Samaria, and reigned seventeen years.

2 And he did that which was evil in the sight of the LORD, and followed the sins of Jeroboam the son of Nebat, which made Israel to sin; he departed not therefrom *(Jehoahaz kept up the worship of the calves, and in no way suffered this worship to decline).*

3 And the anger of the LORD was kindled against Israel, and He delivered them into the hand of Hazael king of Syria, and into the hand of Ben-hadad the son of Hazael, all their days *(Israel's troubles were strictly because of her sin; while righteous living doesn't forego all difficulties, it definitely foregoes most).*

4 And Jehoahaz besought the LORD, and the LORD hearkened unto him: for He saw the oppression of Israel, because the king of Syria oppressed them *(how much "oppression" do we encounter because of our sin? This one thing is clear, irrespective of what we have done or how bleak the situation, the only answer is, "And Jehoahaz besought the LORD").*

5 (And the LORD gave Israel a saviour, so that they went out from under the hand of the Syrians: and the Children of Israel dwelt in their tents, as beforetime. *[A "saviour" means a deliverer from the hand of the Syrians. The gift of Jehovah and the principle which turned away wrath and provided a Saviour was not the existence of any moral worthiness in Israel, for she had none, but the unconditional Covenant made with Abraham, as stated in Verse 23. In effect, it was "for Abraham's sake," and then, at times, "for David's sake," and then, "for Jonathan's sake." All illustrate the principle of Ephesians 4:32, "for Christ's sake." This great principle of Salvation gives all the glory to the Saviour and none to the person saved.]*

6 Nevertheless they departed not from the sins of the house of Jeroboam, who made Israel sin, but walked therein: and there remained the grove also in Samaria *[the devotion with which the ten Tribes worshipped the golden calf rebukes and instructs the Christian; it rebukes for, alas, how defective is the loyalty of even the most saintly person to Christ? — Williams].)*

7 Neither did he leave of the people to Jehoahaz but fifty horsemen, and ten chariots, and ten thousand footmen; for the king of Syria had destroyed them, and had made them like the dust by threshing *(before the "Saviour," Syria had laid Israel waste).*

THE DEATH OF JEHOAHAZ; JOASH HIS SUCCESSOR

8 Now the rest of the acts of Jehoahaz, and all that he did, and his might, are they not written in the book of the chronicles of the kings of Israel?

9 And Jehoahaz slept with his fathers; and they buried him in Samaria: and Joash his son reigned in his stead *(to rest with their fathers in the same royal sepulcher was to be duly honored at their death; to be excluded from it was a disgrace).*

JEHOASH REIGNS OVER ISRAEL

10 In the thirty and seventh year of Joash king of Judah began Jehoash the son of Jehoahaz to reign over Israel in Samaria, and reigned sixteen years *(he had the same name as the king of Judah; actually, the two Joashes were contemporary Monarchs for the space of three years).*

11 And he did that which was evil in the sight of the LORD; he departed not from all the sins of Jeroboam the son of Nebat, who made Israel sin: but he walked therein *(all of this tells us that Jehovah Elohim was not a Divinity invented by the Israelites, as some have claimed; for, had that been so, then would they have served Him faithfully; but the fact that they were continually forsaking Him, and turning to idols, and that there was perpetual contention between them and God, proves the testimony of the Bible, that the God of Israel is God over all, blessed forever).*

12 And the rest of the acts of Joash, and all that he did, and his might wherewith he fought against Amaziah king of Judah, are they not written in the book of the chronicles of the kings of Israel? *(The account of the war with Judah is found in II Chronicles 25:17-24.)*

13 And Joash slept with his fathers; and Jeroboam sat upon his throne: and Joash was buried in Samaria with the kings of Israel *(that Joash should call his eldest son Jeroboam, after the founder of the kingdom, indicated a thorough approval of that founder's policy and conduct, which, of course, were evil).*

ELISHA AND THE ARROW OF THE LORD

14 Now Elisha was fallen sick of his sickness whereof he died *(it is believed that Elisha was at least 80 years old at this time; his illness*

was probably the result of mere natural decay). And Joash the king of Israel came down unto him, and wept over his face, and said, O my father, my father, the chariot of Israel, and the horsemen thereof (it is amazing how Joash, as well as previous kings of Israel, knew of the worth of Elisha, but still would not serve Elisha's God; men love their sins!).

15 And Elisha said unto him, Take bow and arrows. And he took unto him bow and arrows (although not mentioned here, evidently, Joash had sought direction from the Lord through Elisha, as it regards the threat of Syrian domination; the Holy Spirit evidently tells Elisha what to do).

16 And he said to the king of Israel, Put your hand upon the bow. And he put his hand upon it: and Elisha put his hands upon the king's hands (the intention was, no doubt, to show that the power which would be manifested was not the king's own power, but "came from the Lord" through the mediation of His Prophet).

17 And he said, Open the window eastward (why eastward? The sun rose in the east; therefore, the Lord, through Elisha and this symbolism, was telling the king of Israel that if true Repentance would be forthcoming, Israel's sun would not be setting, but rather rising). And he opened it (thus far, the king operates in faith). Then Elisha said, Shoot. And he shot. And he said, The arrow of the LORD's deliverance, and the arrow of deliverance from Syria: for you shall smite the Syrians in Aphek, till you have consumed them (what a promise!).

18 And he (Elisha) said, Take the arrows. And he took them. And he said unto the king of Israel, Smite upon the ground (signifying the defeat of Syria). And he (the king of Israel) smote thrice, and stayed.

19 And the man of God was wroth with him, and said, You should have smitten five or six times; then had you smitten Syria till you had consumed it: whereas now you shall smite Syria but thrice. (The promise of total and complete victory over the Syrians had been given, but, because of lack of faith, Israel fell short. To the king of Israel, defeating the Syrians three times was big in his sight. However, the Lord was ready to give much more. How often do we fail to achieve God's best, simply because we stop short of total victory?)

DEATH OF ELISHA; THE MIRACLE AT HIS TOMB

20 And Elisha died, and they buried him.

And the bands of the Moabites invaded the land at the coming in of the year (Jerome says that the place of his sepulture was near Samaria; according to Josephus, his funeral was magnificent).

21 And it came to pass, as they (the Moabites) were burying a man, that, behold, they spied a band of men; and they cast the man (the corpse) into the sepulchre of Elisha: and when the man was let down, and touched the bones of Elisha, he revived, and stood up on his feet (this was the final miracle attributed to Elisha, even though he was now dead; this last miracle fulfilled the Promise of God, in that his ministry numbered twice as many Miracles as Elijah's, and some were twice as great; so the double portion held true, even to the very end [2:9-10]).

ISRAEL'S VICTORY OVER SYRIA

22 But Hazael king of Syria oppressed Israel all the days of Jehoahaz (the writer now returns to the subject of Syrian oppression).

23 And the LORD was gracious unto them (unto Israel), and had compassion on them, and had respect unto them, because of His Covenant with Abraham, Isaac, and Jacob, and would not destroy them, neither cast he them from His presence as yet (ultimately, they were cast away, rejected, and removed out of God's sight, because they continued to spurn His Mercy and Grace).

24 So Hazael king of Syria died; and Benhadad his son reigned in his stead (Hazael, the usurper, gave his eldest son the name of the Monarch whom he had murdered).

25 And Jehoash the son of Jehoahaz took again out of the hand of Ben-hadad the son of Hazael the cities, which he had taken out of the hand of Jehoahaz his father by war. Three times did Joash beat him, and recovered the cities of Israel (exactly as Elisha said would happen!).

CHAPTER 14
(839 B.C.)
AMAZIAH REIGNS OVER JUDAH

IN the second year of Joash son of Jehoahaz king of Israel reigned Amaziah the son of Joash king of Judah (this was the fourth good king in Judah, but with reservations).

2 He was twenty and five years old when he began to reign, and reigned twenty and nine years in Jerusalem. And his mother's name was Jehoaddan of Jerusalem.

3 And he did that which was right in the sight of the LORD, yet not like David his father *(his father, several times removed)*: he did according to all things as Joash his father did. *(David is ever used as the example, and that despite his sins and failures. God thinks of his true nature, faithful heart, and zeal for Jehovah in living free from idolatry and the gross wickedness of so many of the rulers in those days. David was a man after God's own heart, who loved Jehovah, considered Him, and obeyed Him when corrected.)*

4 Howbeit the high places were not taken away: as yet the people did sacrifice and burnt incense on the high places. *(Over and over again in the Sacred Text, the Holy Spirit points this out. The Temple in Jerusalem was to be the only place where the people were to offer sacrifice and burn incense, because the great Brazen Altar there was a Type of the Cross. Even though they burned sacrifice and incense to the Lord in these "high places," still, the Lord was displeased, because, in a sense, they pointed to "another Cross" [II Cor. 11:4].)*

Irrespective of our supposed worship, if it is not built supremely on the Cross of Christ, it is unacceptable to God. Regrettably, precious little worship today is, in fact, anchored in the Cross!)

5 And it came to pass, as soon as the kingdom was confirmed in his hand, that he slew his servants which had slain the king his father *(he put down the insurrectionists).*

6 But the children of the murderers he slew not: according unto that which is written in the Book of the Law of Moses, wherein the LORD commanded, saying, The fathers shall not be put to death for the children, nor the children be put to death for the fathers; but every man shall be put to death for his own sin *(Deut. 24:16; this was at the beginning of Amaziah's reign, and it seems that he was doing all within his power to obey the Word of God; had he continued thusly, great victory would have been his and Judah's; as Amaziah, so many begin well, and end poorly).*

7 He slew of Edom in the valley of salt ten thousand, and took Selah *(Petra)* by war, and called the name of it Joktheel unto this day *(this Verse proclaims his great victory in taking the almost impregnable Petra, called Selah; the name "Joktheel" means "subdued by God"; thus, he honored God, Who gave him the victory).*

AMAZIAH'S WARS AGAINST JOASH OF ISRAEL

8 Then Amaziah sent messengers to Jehoash, the son of Jehoahaz son of Jehu, king of Israel, saying, Come, let us look one another in the face *(Amaziah had a cause of complaint against Jehoash, the king of Israel, which does not appear in this narrative, but does in II Chron., Chpt. 25; however, Amaziah was wrong in doing this!).*

9 And Jehoash the king of Israel sent to Amaziah king of Judah, saying, The thistle that was in Lebanon sent to the cedar that was in Lebanon, saying, Give your daughter to my son to wife: and there passed by a wild beast that was in Lebanon, and trode down the thistle *(according to Josephus, the reply to the challenge was given in a formal letter, which was in the form of a parable).*

10 You have indeed smitten Edom, and your heart has lifted you up: glory of this, and tarry at home: for why should you meddle to your hurt, that you should fall, even you, and Judah with you? *(Your victory over Edom has caused you to be lifted up in pride.)*

11 But Amaziah would not hear. *(How many Christians have been given a "correct word" that was sent to them by the Lord, but "would not hear"?)* Therefore Jehoash king of Israel went up; and he and Amaziah king of Judah looked one another in the face at Beth-shemesh, which belongs to Judah *(went to battle!).*

12 And Judah was put to the worse before Israel; and they fled every man to their tents *(the complete account tells us that God allowed Judah to be defeated, because Amaziah had "sought after the gods of Edom" [II Chron. 25:20]).*

13 And Jehoash king of Israel took Amaziah king of Judah, the son of Jehoash the son of Ahaziah, at Beth-shemesh, and came to Jerusalem, and broke down the wall of Jerusalem from the gate of Ephraim unto the corner gate, four hundred cubits *(according to Josephus, Joash threatened his prisoner with death, unless the gates of Jerusalem were opened to him, and his army admitted into the town; the breach in the wall was, therefore, not the result of siege operations, but the act of a conqueror, who desired to leave his enemy as defenseless as possible).*

14 And he *(Joash, king of Israel)* took all the gold and silver, and all the vessels that were found in the House of the LORD, and in the treasures of the king's house, and hostages, and returned to Samaria *(because of Amaziah's*

pride, Judah lost the war, the protection of the wall of Jerusalem, all the public silver and gold, all the vessels of the Temple, and all the treasures of the king's house, and was completely humiliated before her enemies; it took years to recover what was lost in a few hours of time, all through pride and selfishness).

DEATH OF JEHOASH, KING OF ISRAEL

15 Now the rest of the acts of Jehoash which he did, and his might, and how he fought with Amaziah king of Judah, are they not written in the Book of the Chronicles of the kings of Israel?

16 And Jehoash slept with his fathers, and was buried in Samaria with the kings of Israel; and Jeroboam his son reigned in his stead (Jeroboam II).

DEATH OF AMAZIAH, KING OF JUDAH; AZARIAH (UZZIAH) HIS SUCCESSOR

17 And Amaziah the son of Joash king of Judah lived after the death of Jehoash son of Jehoahaz king of Israel fifteen years.

18 And the rest of the acts of Amaziah, are they not written in the Book of the Chronicles of the kings of Judah?

19 Now they made a conspiracy against him in Jerusalem: and he fled to Lachish; but they sent after him to Lachish, and slew him there (the author of Chronicles connects this conspiracy with the idolatry of which Amaziah was guilty [II Chron. 25:27]).

20 And they brought him on horses: and he was buried at Jerusalem with his fathers in the city of David (as stated, he began well, and ended poorly!).

21 And all the people of Judah took Azariah, which was sixteen years old, and made him king instead of his father Amaziah (this king was also known as "Uzziah").

22 He built Elath, and restored it to Judah, after that the king slept with his fathers (it was in the year that this king died that Isaiah had the great vision where he saw the Lord, which began his great prophecies [Isa., Chpt. 6]).

JEROBOAM II REIGNS OVER ISRAEL

23 In the fifteenth year of Amaziah the son of Joash king of Judah Jeroboam the son of Joash king of Israel began to reign in Samaria, and reigned forty and one years.

24 And he did that which was evil in the sight of the LORD; he departed not from all the sins of Jeroboam (after whom he was named) the son of Nebat, who made Israel to sin (judgments which had fallen upon Jehu and Jehoahaz on account of these sins did not teach any lesson, it seems, to Joash or Jeroboam II; the fatal taint, which was congenital with the Israelite Monarchy, could never be purged out; they clung to it until the end).

25 He restored the coast of Israel from the entering of Hamath unto the sea of the plain, according to the Word of the LORD God of Israel, which He spoke by the hand of His servant, Jonah, the son of Amittai, the Prophet, which was of Gath-hepher (this "Jonah" was the author of the Book of Jonah, who was commanded by God to go preach in the city of Nineveh; the victories of Jeroboam II were of the Lord, but not recognized as such by Jeroboam II).

26 For the LORD saw the affliction of Israel, that it was very bitter: for there was not any shut up, nor any left, nor any helper for Israel (the prosperous reign of Jeroboam II seemingly conflicts with the fact that he worshipped the golden calf; however, Verses 25-28 reveal the profound depths of Love and Grace in the heart of God toward His erring children; but still, Jeroboam II would not turn).

27 And the LORD said not that he would blot out the name of Israel from under Heaven: but he saved them by the hand of Jeroboam the son of Joash (even though Israel deserved to be "blotted out," on the contrary, the Lord gave the nation a breathing-space, a gleam of light, a second summer, so to speak, before the winter set in — a further opportunity of repenting, but all to no avail!).

28 Now the rest of the acts of Jeroboam, and all that he did, and his might, how he warred, and how he recovered Damascus, and Hamath, which belonged to Judah (had belonged to Judah during the times of David and Solomon), for Israel (recovered them for Israel), are they not written in the book of the chronicles of the kings of Israel?

29 And Jeroboam slept with his fathers, even with the kings of Israel; and Zachariah his son reigned in his stead. (Over and over again in these Passages concerning the kings of Israel and Judah, the Holy Spirit points out to us the reason for their blessings, which was the Grace of God, and the reason for their failure, which was sin. We would do well to heed this!)

CHAPTER 15
(772 B.C.)

AZARIAH'S (UZZIAH'S) LONG AND GOOD REIGN OVER JUDAH

IN the twenty and seventh year of Jeroboam king of Israel began Azariah son of Amaziah king of Judah to reign.

2 Sixteen years old was he when he began to reign, and he reigned two and fifty years in Jerusalem. And his mother's name was Jecholiah of Jerusalem.

3 And he did that which was right in the sight of the LORD, according to all that his father Amaziah had done (*how refreshing it is for the Holy Spirit to say, "And he did that which was right in the sight of the LORD"; but yet, even though he started well, as his father Amaziah, he finished poorly*);

4 Save that the high places were not removed: the people sacrificed and burnt incense still on the high places (*from this we should learn how it grieves the Holy Spirit to have any abiding sin within our lives; the constant repetition of these statements presents the Holy Spirit warning us by repetition of our own shortcomings*).

5 And the LORD smote the king, so that he was a leper unto the day of his death, and dwelt in a several house. And Jotham the king's son was over the house, judging the people of the land. (*We have to go to Chronicles for an explanation [II Chron. 26:16-23]. It was at this juncture that the Prophets Hosea, Joel, Amos, Micah, Isaiah, and Jonah exercised their ministries; consequently, their prophecies should be studied in connection with the history of these kings. They foretold the doom of both the northern and southern kingdoms.*)

6 And the rest of the acts of Azariah, and all that he did, are they not written in the book of the chronicles of the kings of Judah?

7 So Azariah slept with his fathers; and they buried him with his fathers in the city of David: and Jotham his son reigned in his stead. (*The writer of Chronicles gives us more detail. He was not buried in the rock-sepulcher which contained the bodies of the other kings, but in another part of the field wherein the sepulcher was situated. This was quite in keeping with the Jewish feeling with respect to the uncleanness of the leper [II Chron. 26:23].*)

ZACHARIAH REIGNS OVER ISRAEL

8 In the thirty and eighth year of Azariah king of Judah did Zachariah the son of Jeroboam reign over Israel in Samaria six months. (*We may wonder at the significance of all of this. However, let the Reader understand that everything that happened to Israel and Judah had to do with the great Plan of Redemption; accordingly, all of these happenings, be they good or bad, proclaim to us the means of God in bringing Redemption to the world, which would be through His Son, and our Saviour, the Lord Jesus Christ. All of these things played their part in this; consequently, this means that all of these happenings are of great significance.*)

9 And he did that which was evil in the sight of the LORD, as his fathers had done: he departed not from the sins of Jeroboam the son of Nebat, who made Israel to sin (*some 21 times the Holy Spirit solemnly records this terrible fact; the Lord can cancel out the effects of sin, but only through the Precious Blood of Jesus Christ, and our Faith in that Finished Work; however, Satan, thank God, cannot cancel out the effects of Righteousness*).

10 And Shallum the son of Jabesh conspired against him, and smote him before the people, and slew him, and reigned in his stead (*Zachariah reigned only six months*).

11 And the rest of the acts of Zachariah, behold, they are written in the Book of the Chronicles of the kings of Israel.

12 This was the Word of the LORD which He spoke unto Jehu, saying, Your sons shall sit on the throne of Israel unto the fourth generation. And so it came to pass (*this prophecy was fulfilled in the death of Zachariah [10:30]*).

SHALLUM REIGNS OVER ISRAEL FOR ONE MONTH

13 Shallum the son of Jabesh began to reign in the nine and thirtieth year of Uzziah (Azariah) king of Judah; and he reigned a full month in Samaria.

14 For Menahem the son of Gadi went up from Tirzah, and came to Samaria, and smote Shallum the son of Jabesh in Samaria, and slew him and reigned in his stead (*Josephus says that there was a battle in which Shallum was killed*).

15 And the rest of the acts of Shallum, and his conspiracy which he made, behold, they are written in the book of the chronicles of the kings of Israel.

MENAHEM'S TEN-YEAR REIGN OVER ISRAEL

16 Then Menahem smote Tiphsah, and all that were therein, and the coasts thereof from Tirzah: because they opened not to him, therefore he smote it; and all the women therein who were with child he ripped up (*one can see the depravity of this man regarding the type of sin that he committed*).

17 In the nine and thirtieth year of Azariah king of Judah began Menahem the son of Gadi to reign over Israel, and reigned ten years in Samaria.

18 And he did that which was evil in the sight of the LORD: he departed not all his days from the sins of Jeroboam the son of Nebat, who made Israel to sin.

19 And Pul the king of Assyria came against the land (*against the northern kingdom of Israel*): and Menahem gave Pul a thousand talents of silver, that his hand might be with him to confirm the kingdom in his hand (*it is not coincidence that the first distinct mention of Assyria in Scripture as an aggressive power immediately follows the account of the terrible sin of Menahem, even to the murdering of thousands of women and little children; by this time, Assyria had been rising to a great power for nearly a century, and had reached far beyond the River Euphrates, even to Egypt; from here on the history of the two kingdoms of Israel and Judah is linked with that of Assyria and Babylon*).

20 And Menahem exacted the money of Israel, even of all the mighty men of wealth, of each man fifty shekels of silver, to give to the king of Assyria. So the king of Assyria turned back, and stayed not there in the land (*Menahem bribed the king of Assyria in order that he not attack Israel*).

21 And the rest of the acts of Menahem, and all that he did, are they not written in the book of the chronicles of the kings of Israel?

22 And Menahem slept with his fathers; and Pekahiah his son reigned in his stead.

PEKAHIAH'S TWO-YEAR REIGN OVER ISRAEL

23 In the fiftieth year of Azariah king of Judah Pekahiah the son of Menahem began to reign over Israel in Samaria, and reigned two years.

24 And he did that which was evil in the sight of the LORD: he departed not from the sins of Jeroboam the son of Nebat, who made Israel to sin.

25 But Pekah the son of Remaliah, a captain of his, conspired against him, and smote him in Samaria, in the palace of the king's house, with Argob and Arieh, and with him fifty men of the Gileadites: and he killed him, and reigned in his room (*it does not appear that Pekah had any grievance; his crime seems to have been simply prompted by ambition*).

26 And the rest of the acts of Pekahiah, and all that he did, behold, they are written in the book of the chronicles of the kings of Israel.

PEKAH REIGNS OVER ISRAEL FOR TWENTY YEARS

27 In the two and fiftieth year of Azariah king of Judah Pekah the son of Remaliah began to reign over Israel in Samaria, and reigned twenty years.

28 And he did that which was evil in the sight of the LORD: he departed not from the sins of Jeroboam the son of Nebat, who made Israel to sin.

29 In the days of Pekah king of Israel came Tiglath-pileser king of Assyria, and took Ijon, and Abel-beth-maachah, and Janoah, and Kedesh, and Hazor, and Gilead, and Galilee, all the land of Naphtali, and carried them captive to Assyria (*this was the first carrying away of the Israelites into captivity; it continued until the ten-Tribe kingdom of Israel was destroyed*).

30 And Hoshea the son of Elah made a conspiracy against Pekah the son of Remaliah, and smote him, and slew him, and reigned in his stead, in the twentieth year of Jotham the son of Uzziah (*Azariah*).

31 And the rest of the acts of Pekah, and all that he did, behold, they are written in the book of the chronicles of the kings of Israel.

JOTHAM REIGNS OVER JUDAH

32 In the second year of Pekah the son of Remaliah king of Israel began Jotham the son of Uzziah king of Judah to reign.

33 Five and twenty years old was he when he began to reign, and he reigned sixteen years in Jerusalem. And his mother's name was Jerusha, the daughter of Zadok.

34 And he did that which was right in the sight of the LORD: he did according to all that his father Uzziah had done (*the author of Chronicles says the same, but adds, "Howbeit he*

entered not into the Temple of the Lord" — i.e., he did not repeat his father's act of impiety — Pulpit).

35 Howbeit the high places were not removed: the people sacrificed and burned incense still in the high places. He built the higher gate of the house of the LORD (*Azariah had paid great attention to the fortifying and arming of Jerusalem [II Chron. 26:9, 15], and his son now followed in his footsteps*).

36 Now the rest of the acts of Jotham, and all that he did, are they not written in the book of the chronicles of the kings of Judah?

37 In those days the LORD began to send against Judah Rezin the king of Syria, and Pekah the son of Remaliah. (*Because Jotham walked righteously before the Lord, the coming fury that would burst forth under sinful Ahaz was held off until that time. It is interesting to note the terminology, in that the Lord was the Author of what Syria did, even though Syria had no knowledge of such.*

Our obedience brings Blessings from God, while our sin brings chastisement from God in the form of judgment, in order that we may repent. Some few do repent; regrettably, most never do.)

38 And Jotham slept with his fathers, and was buried with his fathers in the city of David his father: and Ahaz his son reigned in his stead.

CHAPTER 16
(740 B.C.)
REIGN OF AHAZ OVER JUDAH

IN the seventeenth year of Pekah the son of Remaliah (*king of Israel*) Ahaz the son of Jotham king of Judah began to reign. (*Ahaz was one of the worst of all the kings of Judah. He imitated the worst of the kings of the ten Tribes — Ahab and Ahaziah — by establishing Baal worship in Judah, when it had been rooted out of the ten Tribes by Jehu [10:19-31], and out of Judah by Jehoiada [11:17-21]. Ahaz even made his sons to pass through the fire, according to all the abominations of the heathen.*)

2 Twenty years old was Ahaz when he began to reign, and reigned sixteen years in Jerusalem, and did not that which was right in the sight of the LORD his God, like David his father. (*In all that the Holy Spirit says about King Ahaz in the Books of Kings, Chronicles, and Isaiah, there is a throbbing of anguish, which the Reader can feel, and also a note of indignation,*

as, for example, in the words, "This is that King Ahaz" [II Chron. 28:22]. *His full name, as it appears in the Assyrian state records, was Jehoahaz, which means "the possession of Jehovah," but the Spirit of God strikes the Jehovah-syllable out of his name, and invariably calls him "Ahaz," which means "possession." Such was his life, for he was led, influenced, and possessed by anyone or anything except God.*)

3 But he walked in the way of the kings of Israel, yea, and made his son to pass through the fire, according to the abominations of the heathen, whom the LORD cast out from before the Children of Israel. (*This refers to the heathen idol, "Moloch," the god of fire. A fire would be built in its bulbous belly, until its outstretched arms became red-hot. Little children, as sacrifices to these demonic images, would be tied to its outstretched arms, and burned alive, while black-robed priests beat drums to drown out the screams of these little ones. The horror of Ahaz' sin knows no bounds.*)

4 And he sacrificed and burnt incense in the high places, and on the hills, and under every green tree.

5 Then Rezin king of Syria and Pekah son of Remaliah king of Israel came up to Jerusalem to war: and they besieged Ahaz, but could not overcome him (*no doubt, Ahaz was lifted up in pride because of his successful defense against the kings of Syria and Israel; however, his victory had nothing to do with his ability or righteousness, but, instead, was because of the promise that the Lord had made to the house of David*).

6 At that time Rezin king of Syria recovered Elath to Syria, and drove the Jews from Elath: and the Syrians came to Elath, and dwelt there unto this day.

AHAZ MAKES AN ALLIANCE
WITH ASSYRIA

7 So Ahaz sent messengers to Tiglath-pileser king of Assyria, saying, I am your servant and your son: come up, and save me out of the hand of the king of Syria, and out of the hand of the king of Israel, which rise up against me. (*The Lord through the Prophet Isaiah earnestly counseled him not to invite the king of Assyria to help him against the confederate kings of Israel and Damascus; however, he followed his own counsel with success, but with the ultimate result of ruin. His history illustrates how disastrous it is to the spiritual profit of a man*

when his own plans succeed.)

8 And Ahaz took the silver and gold that was found in the House of the LORD, and in the treasures of the king's house, and sent it for a present to the king of Assyria.

9 And the king of Assyria hearkened unto him: for the king of Assyria went up against Damascus, and took it, and carried the people of it captive to Kir, and slew Rezin.

AHAZ BUILDS A HEATHEN ALTAR

10 And king Ahaz went to Damascus to meet Tiglath-pileser king of Assyria, and saw an altar that was at Damascus: and king Ahaz sent to Urijah the Priest the fashion of the altar, and the pattern of it, according to all the workmanship thereof. *(Ahaz was not satisfied with the great Altar which sat in front of the Temple in Jerusalem, and which had been designed by the Lord, and which was a Type of Calvary. He desired a heathen altar, and the priesthood of Judah helped him carry out this evil design.*

This is the sin of modern Church. It has not totally forsaken the Altar, i.e., "the Cross," but has substituted another sacrifice, in fact, the same as did Cain of old [Gen., Chpt. 4].)

11 And Urijah the Priest built an altar according to all that king Ahaz had sent from Damascus: so Urijah the Priest made it against king Ahaz came from Damascus *(the modern Church is presently building its new altars; they go under the names of "psychological counseling," "Word of Faith," "seeker-sensitive," "the government of twelve," etc.).*

12 And when the king was come from Damascus, the king saw the altar; and the king approached to the altar, and offered thereon *(having no confidence in the Altar designed by the Lord, which typified the Cross, he would build his own altar, which was more to his liking; it is true that the Cross of Christ is an offense, but offense or not, the Cross of Christ alone can deliver men from sin; everything else is a mere window-dressing [Gal. 5:11]).*

13 And he burnt his burnt offering and his meat offering, and poured his drink offering, and sprinkled the blood of his peace offerings, upon the altar *(upon the heathen altar, which God would never accept, and will never accept).*

14 And he brought also the Brasen Altar *(the Altar designed by the Lord, on which alone sacrifices were to be offered),* which was before the LORD *(in front of the Temple),* from the forefront of the house, from between the altar and the House of the LORD, and put it *(put the Brazen Altar)* on the north side of the altar *(the heathen altar; so now he has two altars, but with the true Altar unused, which, again, so very much typifies the modern Church).*

15 And king Ahaz commanded Urijah the Priest, saying, Upon the great altar *(the heathen altar)* burn the morning burnt offering, and the evening meat offering, and the king's burnt sacrifice, and his meat offering, with the burnt offering of all the people of the land, and their meat offering, and their drink offerings; and sprinkle upon it all the blood of the burnt offering, and all the blood of the sacrifice: and the Brasen Altar *(the true Altar)* shall be for me to enquire by *(I shall hereafter determine what use, if any, it shall be put to; once again, this is the exact state of the modern Church; it hasn't totally abandoned the Cross, but it has set it aside, while the sacrifices are offered on the modern altars, which will ultimately bring the judgment of God).*

16 Thus did Urijah the Priest, according to all that king Ahaz commanded *(all too often the modern ministry apes Urijah of old!).*

17 And king Ahaz cut off the borders of the bases *(the stands of the ten brazen lavers),* and removed the laver *(ten brazen lavers)* from off them; and took down the sea *(the great Brazen Laver)* from off the brasen oxen that were under it, and put it upon the pavement of stones. *(The "Laver" is a Type of the Word of God. Even though it remained, the oxen, which had been designed by the Holy Spirit, on which it sat, were given away. The "oxen" represented the Power and Assurance of the Word of God.*

Basically, Ahaz is saying that he has no more confidence in the Word of God. All too often, the modern Church is saying the same thing. The Bible has not been completely thrown away; it has just been discarded to the place of "no confidence." The Church as a whole has turned to psychology. The degradation of the Laver illustrates the hostility of man's heart to the great Bible Doctrine of "Jesus Christ and Him Crucified" as the only answer for man's sin [Rom. 6:3-14; I Cor. 1:17-18, 21, 23; 2:2; Eph. 2:13-18; Gal. 6:14; Col. 2:14-15].)

18 And the covert for the sabbath that they had built in the house, and the king's entry without, turned he from the House of the LORD for the king of Assyria *(this appears to mean that a building inside the Temple area, having some relation to the Temple itself, was*

divorced from that purpose, and fitted up as a palace for the king of Assyria).

DEATH OF AHAZ; HEZEKIAH HIS SUCCESSOR OVER JUDAH

19 Now the rest of the acts of Ahaz which he did, are they not written in the book of the chronicles of the kings of Judah?

20 And Ahaz slept with his fathers, and was buried with his fathers in the city of David: and Hezekiah his son reigned in his stead. *(The writer of Chronicles tells us that even though this evil man was buried in Jerusalem, still, "they brought him not into the supulchres of the kings." Like Uzziah, he was not thought worthy of burial in the royal catacomb [II Chron. 28:27].)*

CHAPTER 17
(721 B.C.)
HOSHEA REIGNS OVER ISRAEL

IN the twelfth year of Ahaz king of Judah began Hoshea the son of Elah to reign in Samaria over Israel nine years.

2 And he did that which was evil in the sight of the LORD, but not as the kings of Israel that were before him. *(While Hoshea's general attitude towards Jehovah was much the same as that of the former kings of Israel, still, he was not guilty of any special wickedness; in other words, he set up no new idolatry.*

Regrettably, he turned a deaf ear to the teaching of the Prophets Hoshea [who had the same name] and Micah, who addressed their warnings to him.)

3 Against him came up Shalmaneser king of Assyria; and Hoshea became his servant, and gave him presents *(rendered him tribute; Hoshea had been placed on the throne by Tiglathpileser; upon this man's death, it seems that Hoshea revolted, and resumed his independence; Shalmaneser, having become king, came up against Hoshea and forced him to resume his position of Assyrian tributary).*

4 And the king of Assyria found conspiracy in Hoshea: for he *(Hoshea)* had sent messengers of So king of Egypt, and brought no present to the king of Assyria, as he had done year by year *(paid no tribute)*: therefore the king of Assyria shut him up, and bound him in prison *(evidently, Hoshea, at some point, ceased to pay tribute to the king of Assyria, and appealed to the king of Egypt to come to his rescue; his plan would not succeed).*

THE FALL OF SAMARIA AND THE CAPTIVITY OF ISRAEL

5 Then the king of Assyria came up throughout all the land, and went up to Samaria, and besieged it three years. *(Now the judgment begins. The ten Tribes of the Northern Kingdom will be ultimately carried "away into Assyria." Egypt would be of no help. Egypt, as a type of the world, is never any help.)*

6 In the ninth year of Hoshea the king of Assyria took Samaria, and carried Israel away into Assyria, and placed them in Halah and in Habor by the river of Gozan, and in the cities of the Medes.

7 For so it was, that the Children of Israel had sinned against the LORD their God, which had brought them up out of the land of Egypt, from under the hand of Pharaoh king of Egypt, and had feared other gods.

8 And walked in the statutes of the heathen, whom the LORD cast out from before the Children of Israel, and of the kings of Israel, which they had made.

9 And the Children of Israel did secretly those things that were not right against the LORD their God, and they built them high places in all their cities, from the tower of the watchmen to the fenced city.

10 And they set them up images and groves in every high hill, and under every green tree:

11 And there they burnt incense in all the high places, as did the heathen whom the LORD carried away before them; and wrought wicked things to provoke the LORD to anger:

12 For they served idols, whereof the LORD had said unto them, You shall not do this thing *(this Verse gives the reason, "For they served idols").*

13 Yet the LORD testified against Israel, and against Judah, by all the Prophets, and by all the Seers, saying, Turn ye from your evil ways *(repent)*, and keep My Commandments and My Statutes, according to all the Law which I commanded your fathers, and which I sent to you by My servants the Prophets *(they were sufficiently warned!).*

14 Notwithstanding they would not hear, but hardened their necks, like to the neck of their fathers, that did not believe in the LORD their God *(the problem then was "unbelief," and the problem now is "unbelief"; they did not believe in the Cross of Christ then, and they do not believe in the Cross of Christ now!).*

15 And they rejected His Statutes, and His

Covenant that He made with their fathers, and His Testimonies which He testified against them; and they followed vanity, and became vain, and went after the heathen who were round about them, concerning whom the LORD had charged them, that they should not do like them *(when Israel rejected God's Statutes, they adopted "the statutes of the heathen," and "walked in them"; if the Ways of the Lord are rejected, religious man must then adopt the ways of the world).*

16 And they left all the Commandments of the LORD their God, and made them molten images, even two calves, and made a grove, and worshipped all the host of heaven, and served Baal *(exactly as the heathen).*

17 And they caused their sons and their daughters to pass through the fire *(human sacrifice),* and used divination and enchantments, and sold themselves to do evil in the sight of the LORD, to provoke Him to anger *(willingly became slaves of Satan).*

18 Therefore the LORD was very angry with Israel, and removed them out of His sight: there was none left but the Tribe of Judah only *("the Tribe of Judah" stands for the kingdom of the two Tribes of Judah and Benjamin, into which the greater part of the Tribes of Dan and Simeon had also been absorbed; this became now, exclusively, God's "peculiar people," the object of His Love and of His Care).*

19 Also Judah kept not the Commandments of the LORD their God, but walked in the Statutes of Israel which they made *(even though Judah lasted for some 133 years longer, still, they ultimately lost their way, as well).*

20 And the LORD rejected all the seed of Israel *(which refers to both kingdoms of Israel and Judah),* and afflicted them, and delivered them into the hand of spoilers, until He had cast them out of His sight *(after the captivity of the ten Tribes, as recorded here, Judah, as well, went deeper into sin, and finally had to be destroyed and taken into captivity; all of this shows the total control of the Lord in all matters; He could deliver them into the hands of their enemies, or into the position of victory; whichever depended upon their disobedience or obedience).*

21 For He rent Israel from the House of David; and they made Jeroboam the son of Nebat king: and Jeroboam drove Israel from following the LORD, and made them sin a great sin. *(Without proper leadership, all is lost! One can be a religious leader, or one can be a Prophet. One cannot be both! The former* seeks to appease the people, while the latter seeks to obey God. Regrettably, we presently have far too many religious leaders.)

22 For the Children of Israel walked in all the sins of Jeroboam which he did; they departed not from them;

23 Until the LORD removed Israel out of His sight, as He had said by all His servants the Prophets. So was Israel carried away out of their own land to Assyria unto this day *(the time of the writing of this account, which was probably about 570 B.C., by which time the southern kingdom of Judah had also been carried away into captivity).*

THE BEGINNING OF THE SAMARITANS

24 And the king of Assyria brought men from Babylon and from Cuthah, and from Ava, and from Hamath, and from Sepharvaim, and placed them in the cities of Samaria instead of the Children of Israel: and they possessed Samaria, and dwelt in the cities thereof. *(This is the beginning of the New Testament Samaritans. These individuals subsequently intermixed with the Jews who returned from captivity; hence, this culminated in a mixed breed. The Jews in Jesus' day would basically have nothing to do with them.)*

25 And so it was at the beginning of their dwelling there, that they feared not the LORD: therefore the LORD sent lions among them, which slew some of them. *(The expulsion of the Israelites from God's pleasant land and the introduction of lions into it by God show that both the people and the land belonged to Him. Because the people were His People, He carried them away. Because the land was His Land, He brought the lions in. The Holy Spirit states that the lions were instruments of God's Discipline and Teaching.)*

26 Wherefore they spoke to the king of Assyria, saying, The nations which you have removed, and placed in the cities of Samaria, know not the manner of the God of the land: therefore He has sent lions among them, and, behold, they slay them, because they know not the manner of the God of the land *(it was the general belief of the heathen nations of antiquity that each country and nation had its own god or gods, who presided over its destinies, etc.; so they complained that they are not familiar with the manner of this God of Israel).*

27 Then the king of Assyria commanded, saying, Carry thither one of the priests whom

you brought from thence; and let them go and dwell there, and let him teach them the manner of the God of the land.

28 Then one of the Priests whom they had carried away from Samaria came and dwelt in Beth-el, and taught them now they should fear the LORD *(it seems that this Priest, even though from the northern kingdom, did have an understanding of the true worship of God, which he related, evidently, to the Samaritans).*

29 Howbeit every nation made gods of their own, and put them in the houses of the high places which the Samaritans had made, every nation in their cities wherein they dwelt *(along with "fearing the Lord," they also set up idol worship to their particular gods).*

30 And the men of Babylon made Succoth-benoth, and the men of Cuth made Nergal, and the men of Hamath made Ashima,

31 And the Avites made Nibhaz and Tartak, and the Sepharvites burnt their children in fire to Adrammelech and Anammelech, the gods of Sepharvaim *(these individuals, who had been brought from other countries and placed in the territory of the former northern kingdom of Israel, brought, as well, their heathen gods with them, which they continued to worship).*

32 So they feared the LORD, and made unto themselves of the lowest of them priests of the high places, which sacrificed for them in the houses of the high places *(with their idolatrous worship, they combined also the worship of Jehovah, which, of course, the Lord would not recognize).*

33 They feared the LORD, and served their own gods, after the manner of the nations whom they carried away from thence *(this means that they were afraid of Jehovah, but not enough to serve Him or keep His Laws).*

34 Unto this day they do after the former manners: they fear not the LORD *(meaning, as stated, that, while they did fear Him, they did not fear Him enough to serve Him),* neither do they after their statutes, or after their ordinances, or after the Law and Commandment which the LORD commanded the Children of Jacob, whom He named Israel *(their so-called worship of Jehovah did not include obedience to His Laws; unfortunately, that is basically the tenor of the modern Church, as well!);*

35 With whom the LORD had made a Covenant, and charged them, saying, You shall not fear other gods, nor bow yourselves to them, nor serve them, nor sacrifice to them *(for the "Covenant," see Exodus 19:5-8; 24:3-8):*

36 But the LORD, Who brought you up out of the land of Egypt with great power and a stretched out arm, Him shall you fear, and Him shall you worship, and to Him shall you do sacrifice *(true worship of God cannot be mixed with other things; we are to look to Him Alone as the Supplier of every need).*

37 And the Statutes, and the Ordinances, and the Law, and the Commandment, which He wrote for you, you shall observe to do for evermore; and you shall not fear other gods *(there is no need for "fear," providing we obey the Lord; presently, all of these Statutes and Laws have been kept in Christ, Who obeyed them perfectly; simple Faith in Him and what He did at the Cross automatically fulfills these Commands).*

38 And the Covenant that I have made with you you shall not forget; neither shall you fear other gods. *(The "Covenant" intended is not the Covenant of circumcision, which God made with Abraham [Gen. 17:9-14], but the Covenant of protection and obedience made at Sinai between God and the entirety of the people of Israel [Ex. 19:5-8], and most solemnly ratified by sprinkling with blood, and by a Covenant Feast, as is related in Exodus 24:3-11. This was the Covenant which Israel had been warned so frequently not to forget — Pulpit.)*

39 But the LORD your God you shall fear; and He shall deliver you out of the hand of all your enemies *(there was victory in every case declaring itself in favor of God's people, when they were faithful and obedient, while reverses always befell them in the contrary case [I Chron. 5:20-22; 10:13; 14:10-16; II Chron. 12:1-12; 13:4-18; 14:9-12; 20:5-30]).*

40 Howbeit they did not hearken, but they did after their former manner *(this mixed race, which now occupied the northern kingdom of Israel, with their mixed religion, though professing to be worshippers of Jehovah, paid no attention to the warnings and threatenings of the Law).*

41 So these nations feared the LORD, and served their graven images, both their children, and their children's children: as did their fathers, so do they unto this day. *(Continuing to speak of the Samaritans, this was certainly true up until the time this account was written. However, little by little, they began to forsake their idol gods and draw closer to Jehovah. In 409 B.C., they erected a Temple to Jehovah on Mount Gerizim, which, of course, the Lord couldn't recognize. However, they then laid aside their idols, accepting the Pentateuch as their*

religious Textbook, and began to attempt to observe the whole Law.

The Samaritans were ostracized by Israel as a whole, and thought of in a very negative manner; nevertheless, Jesus ministered to them extensively during His 3 1/2 years of public ministry.)

CHAPTER 18
(710 B.C.)
HEZEKIAH REIGNS OVER JUDAH

NOW it came to pass in the third year of Hoshea son of Elah king of Israel, that Hezekiah the son of Ahaz king of Judah began to reign *(so begins the reign of one of Judah's Godliest kings; he began his reign as a vassal of the king of Assyria, by whom he was placed upon the throne during the lifetime of his father Ahaz).*

2 Twenty and five years old was he when he began to reign; and he reigned twenty and nine years in Jerusalem. His mother's name also was Abi, the daughter of Zachariah *(Hezekiah's accession to the Throne may be placed almost certainly in 727 B.C.).*

3 And he did that which was right in the sight of the LORD, according to all that David his father did. *(Once again, David is used as the example. Few would come up to this example, as did Hezekiah. In fact, such unqualified praise is only assigned to two other kings of Judah — Asa [I Ki. 15:11] and Josiah [I Ki. 22:2]. It is curious that all three were the sons of wicked fathers. Hezekiah was probably, at an early age, brought under the influence of the Prophet Isaiah [Isa. 7:3-16].)*

4 He removed the high places, and broke the images, and cut down the groves *(over and over again, in previous Chapters, the Holy Spirit records that Israel yet sacrificed in the high places; but now, refreshingly, it records the very opposite),* and broke in pieces the brasen serpent that Moses had made: for unto those days the Children of Israel did burn incense to it: and he called it Nehushtan. *("Nehushtan" means "a piece of copper." Originally, the "brazen serpent" was set up by God as a symbol of the coming Redemption of Calvary. But so prone is the heart to idolatry that the Holy Spirit records here the action of Hezekiah with approval. Likewise, many in the modern Church have made idols out of water baptism, the Lord's Supper, particular religious denominations, etc. [I Cor. 1:17; Num. 21:9].)*

5 He trusted in the LORD God of Israel; so that after him was none like him among all the kings of Judah, nor any who were before him *(Hezekiah discarded trust in man and put his trust wholly in God; this was exactly what God required then, and exactly what He requires now [Isa. 30:1-7]).*

6 For he clave to the LORD, and departed not from following Him, but kept His Commandments, which the LORD commanded Moses *(this doesn't mean that Hezekiah was perfect, for no man is; it does mean that he tried with all of his heart to obey the Lord; and, when there was failure, he would take it to the Lord, even as did David).*

7 And the LORD was with him *(of no other King of Judah or Israel is this said, except only of David [II Sam. 5:10]; in fact, it's the greatest thing that can be said of anyone);* and he prospered whithersoever he went forth *(prosperity is dependent upon obedience):* and he rebelled against the king of Assyria, and served him not. *(The Child of God is to serve God Alone! However, as Assyria, do not expect Satan to go quietly! He seeks to dominate the Child of God, and will do so, if the Believer doesn't understand God's Prescribed Order of Victory, which is "Christ and Him Crucified," and our Faith in that Finished Work. Such Faith then gives latitude to the Holy Spirit, Who Works exclusively within the parameters of the Finished Work of Christ, to work mightily within our lives [Rom. 6:3-14; 8:1-2, 11].)*

8 He smote the Philistines, even unto Gaza, and the borders thereof, from the tower of the watchmen to the fenced city *(this victory over the Philistines, who were an internal enemy, and the later victory over the Assyrians, who were an external enemy, illustrate the fact that victory over both inward and outward temptation is promised to the overcomer [Rom. 6:14]).*

9 And it came to pass in the fourth year of king Hezekiah, which was the seventh year of Hoshea son of Elah king of Israel, that Shalmaneser king of Assyria came up against Samaria, and besieged it *(Verses 9-12 repeat the information already given in the previous Chapter; it is, no doubt, introduced designedly by the Holy Spirit as a solemn reminder to the House of David, and to Christian people of today, that God has the same controversy with evil, and will judge it with a like judgment, whether it be practiced by the followers of David or of Jeroboam).*

10 And at the end of three years they took it: even in the sixth year of Hezekiah, that is the ninth year of Hoshea king of Israel, Samaria was taken *(the fall of the northern kingdom).*

11 And the king of Assyria did carry away Israel unto Assyria, and put them in Halah and in Habor by the river of Gozan, and in the cities of the Medes:

12 Because they obeyed not the voice of the LORD their God, but transgressed His Covenant, and all that Moses the servant of the LORD commanded, and would not hear them, nor do them. *(This, and this alone, disobedience of the Word of the Lord, was the cause of the fall of the northern kingdom. Let the Reader understand that it is the same presently.*

How does the modern Christian properly obey?

We render obedience by placing our Faith and trust in Christ and the Cross exclusively, which then gives us the help of the Holy Spirit. This alone helps us to live a holy life. This, and this alone, is God's Prescribed Order of Victory [Rom. 6:3-14].)

SENNACHERIB, KING OF ASSYRIA, INVADES JUDAH

13 Now in the fourteenth year of king Hezekiah did Sennacherib king of Assyria come up against all the fenced cities of Judah, and took them. *(As stated, Satan does not go quietly! This was eight years after the captivity of the ten Tribes. If Hezekiah had yielded, Sennacherib, no doubt, would have taken the whole kingdom of Judah into captivity. As it was, at least for a period of time, he took the entirety of the nation, with the exception of Jerusalem. Ultimately, God gave Hezekiah victory over the Assyrians. It was not until some 125 years later that Judah fell, and then to the Babylonians.)*

HEZEKIAH PAYS TRIBUTE

14 And Hezekiah king of Judah sent to the king of Assyria to Lachish, saying, I have offended; return from me: that which you put on me I will bear. And the king of Assyria appointed unto Hezekiah king of Judah three hundred talents of silver and thirty talents of gold.

15 And Hezekiah gave him all the silver that was found in the House of the LORD *(the Temple)*, and in the treasures of the king's house.

16 At that time did Hezekiah cut off the gold from the doors of the Temple of the LORD, and from the pillars which Hezekiah king of Judah had overlaid, and gave it to the king of Assyria. *(The repetition of Hezekiah's name in Verse 16, after being given in the Fifteenth Verse, emphasizes a lesson. The very Hezekiah who overlaid the pillars of the Temple of Jehovah with gold was the very same Hezekiah who cut off the gold and sent it to the Assyrian king as tribute. Unbelief is costly, and compromise seldom delivers. Had Hezekiah at this time trusted fully in the Lord, he would not have suffered this abuse to the Temple of the Lord.)*

JUDAH INSULTED

17 And the king of Assyria sent Tartan and Rab-saris and Rab-shakeh from Lachish to king Hezekiah with a great host against Jerusalem *(the balance of Judah had already fallen)*. And they went up and came to Jerusalem. And when they were come up, they came and stood by the conduit of the upper pool, which is in the high way of the fuller's field. *(Irrespective of Hezekiah's efforts of compromise, it didn't work! It appears that Sennacherib, content with his tribute from Hezekiah, however, did go back to Nineveh. Hezekiah, left to himself, repented of his submission and commenced negotiations with Egypt, which implied treason against the king of Assyria; hence, the invasion. As well, Hezekiah should not have sought help from Egypt.*

As stated, no consecration is perfect. In fact, these enemies appeared because of Judah's unfaithfulness. So it is in the modern Believer's life.

Fidelity to the Lord and to His Word saves the Christian from those trials which a lack of fidelity surely brings. And yet, the pitying Love and Wisdom of God may use these very griefs as instruments of spiritual enrichment to those who, like Hezekiah, really love Him, even though that love, as with all of us, is imperfect.)

18 And when they had called to the king, there came out to them Eliakim the son of Hilkiah, which was over the household, and Shebna the scribe, and Joah the son of Asaph the recorder *(as Jerusalem was surrounded by Sennacherib, Hezekiah sends out three officials to address the general in command)*.

19 And Rab-shakeh said unto them, Speak you now to Hezekiah, Thus saith the great king, the king of Assyria *(Sennacherib)*, What confidence is this wherein you trust? *(Sennacherib is inquiring of Hezekiah, as to what strength on which does he rely? What is the ground of his confidence?)*

20 You say, (but they are but vain words,) I have counsel and strength for the war. Now

on whom do you trust, that you rebel against me? *(Sennacherib imagines that Hezekiah's real trust is in the "fleshly arm of Egypt." He could not be more wrong, even though Hezekiah may, in fact, have welcomed help from that source.)*

21 Now, behold, you trust upon the staff of this bruised reed, even upon Egypt, on which if a man lean, it will go into his hand, and pierce it: so is Pharaoh king of Egypt unto all who trust on him.

22 But if you say unto me, We trust in the LORD our God: is not that He, Whose high places and Whose altars Hezekiah has taken away, and has said to Judah and Jerusalem, You shall worship before this Altar in Jerusalem? *(The heathen monarch totally misunderstood what Hezekiah had done, as it regards the "high places," etc., being removed; he thought that Hezekiah had seriously offended the God of Israel by doing this.)*

23 Now therefore, I pray you, give pledges to my lord the king of Assyria *(so says Rabshakeh)*, and I will deliver thee two thousand horses, if you be able on your part to set riders upon them *(this is a strong expression of contempt for the military power of the Jews)*.

24 How then will you turn away the face of one captain of the least of my master's servants, and put your trust on Egypt for chariots and for horsemen?

25 Am I now come up without the LORD against this place to destroy it? The LORD said to me, Go up against this land, and destroy it. *(In effect, he is erroneously claiming the help of Jehovah. He no doubt does this based on the fact that Assyria, a short time earlier, had destroyed the northern kingdom of Israel, who purportedly served the same God as Judah. So, he reckoned he would do to Judah what he had done to Israel. These statements are meant as contempt of both Jehovah and Judah. In fact, he does feel very secure, considering that all of Judah has fallen to him, with the exception of Jerusalem. And now he will destroy it, or so he thinks!)*

JUDAH'S ANSWER

26 Then said Eliakim the son of Hilkiah, and Shebna, and Joah, unto Rab-shakeh, Speak, I pray you, to your servants in the Syrian language; for we understand it: and talk not with us in the Jews' language in the ears of the people who are on the wall.

RAB-SHAKEH OF ASSYRIA BOASTS AND INSULTS GOD

27 But Rab-shakeh said unto them, Has my master sent me to your master, and to you, to speak these words? has he not sent me to the men which sit on the wall, that they may eat their own dung, and drink their own urine with you? *(The contempt continues!)*

28 Then Rab-shakeh stood and cried with a loud voice in the Jews' language, and spoke, saying, Hear the word of the great king, the king of Assyria *(history scarcely presents any other instance of such coarse and barefaced effrontery)*:

29 Thus saith the king, Let not Hezekiah deceive you: for he shall not be able to deliver you out of his hand:

30 Neither let Hezekiah make you trust in the LORD, saying, The LORD will surely deliver us, and this city shall not be delivered into the hand of the king of Assyria *(Rabshakeh is appealing to the people of Jerusalem to surrender; it is useless, he continues, for them to depend on God!)*.

31 Hearken not to Hezekiah: for thus saith the king of Assyria, Make an agreement with me by a present *(make terms with me, but on my own demands)*, and come out to me, and then eat ye every man of his own vine, and every one of his fig tree, and drink ye every one the waters of his cistern *(you can avoid the war by coming under my control)*:

32 Until I come and take you away to a land like your own land, a land of corn and wine, a land of bread and vineyards, a land of oil olive and of honey, that you may live, and not die: and hearken not unto Hezekiah, when he persuades you, saying, The LORD will deliver us *(in other words, all of Jerusalem, as well as Judah, will be taken captive into a foreign land; evidently, Rabshakeh knew something of Jehovah, and of Hezekiah's faith)*.

33 Has any of the gods of the nations delivered at all his land out of the hand of the king of Assyria? *(Rabshakeh here equates Jehovah with the heathen gods of other countries which Assyria had defeated.)*

34 Where are the gods of Hamath, and of Arpad? where are the gods of Sepharvaim, Hena, and Ivah? have they delivered Samaria out of my hand? *(Rabshakeh is claiming that no god had hitherto delivered any city which the Assyrians had attacked.)*

35 Who are they among all the gods of the countries, that have delivered their country

out of my hand, that the LORD should deliver Jerusalem out of my hand? *("Produce an example of deliverance," Rabshakeh means to say, "before you speak of deliverance as probable, or even possible." This heathen field commander cannot conceive the idea that Jehovah is anything but a local god, on a par with all the other gods of the countries which incidentally Assyria had defeated.)*

36 But the people held their peace, and answered him not a word: for the king's commandment was, saying, Answer him not *(evidently, Hezekiah had expected something like this, so he forewarns the people).*

37 Then came Eliakim the son of Hilkiah, which was over the household, and Shebna the scribe, and Joah the son of Asaph the recorder, to Hezekiah with their clothes rent, and told him the words of Rab-shakeh *(they had rent their clothes, not so much in grief, or in alarm, as in horror at Rabshakeh's blasphemies).*

CHAPTER 19
(710 B.C.)
HEZEKIAH SEEKS HELP FROM GOD

A ND it came to pass, when king Hezekiah heard it, that he rent his clothes, and covered himself with sackcloth, and went into the House of the LORD. *(The "renting of the clothes" referred to a total lack of dependence on one's own ability, or in Judah's strength. The word "sackcloth" refers to his humbling himself in the sight of God. The "House of the Lord" refers to the Temple, where God dwelt in the Holy of Holies, between the Mercy Seat and the Cherubim. The only help for Judah was God; likewise, the only help for us today is God. But how so far removed are we from total dependence on Him? As well, our petition must be clothed in humility, or God will not heed.)*

2 And he sent Eliakim, which was over the household, and Shebna the scribe, and the elders of the Priests, covered with sackcloth, to Isaiah the Prophet the son of Amoz. *(This is the first mention of the Prophet Isaiah in the Bible. However, Hezekiah was the fourth king in whose reign Isaiah had prophesied [Isa. 1:1]. The Passages in the Book of Isaiah which refer to these events are 10:5-19; 14:24-27; 22:1-25; 36:1-37.)*

3 And they said unto him, Thus saith Hezekiah, This day is a day of trouble, and of rebuke, and blasphemy; for the children are come to the birth, and there is not strength to bring forth *(the idea is, within herself, Judah has no strength; they must look to the Lord!).*

4 It may be the LORD your God will hear all the words of Rab-shakeh, whom the king of Assyria his master has sent to reproach the Living God; and will reprove the words which the LORD your God has heard: wherefore lift up your prayer for the remnant who are left *(it is the prayer of Hezekiah that God has "heard" the blasphemy of Rabshakeh, would note it, and punish it).*

ISAIAH FORETELLS ASSYRIA'S DEFEAT

5 So the servants of king Hezekiah came to Isaiah *(regrettably, most of the modern Church is going to a humanistic psychologist!).*

6 And Isaiah said unto them, Thus shall you say to your master *(to Hezekiah)*, Thus saith the LORD, Be not afraid of the words which you have heard, with which the servants of the king of Assyria have blasphemed Me *(the Lord's word to His People is, "Be not afraid!").*

7 Behold, I will send a blast upon him, and he shall hear a rumour, and shall return to his own land; and I will cause him to fall by the sword in his own land *(all of this would be fulfilled to the letter, but over time).*

SENNACHERIB'S MESSAGE TO HEZEKIAH

8 So Rab-shakeh returned, and found the king of Assyria warring against Libnah: for he had heard that he was departed from Lachish *(Lachish had fallen).*

9 And when he heard say of Tirhakah king of Ethiopia, Behold, he is come out to fight against you: he sent messengers again unto Hezekiah, saying,

10 Thus shall you speak to Hezekiah king of Judah, saying, Let not your God in Whom you trust deceive you, saying, Jerusalem shall not be delivered into the hand of the king of Assyria *(in other words, because Egypt is coming against me, who was then ruled by a Pharaoh of Ethiopian birth, don't think this will help you).*

11 Behold, you have heard what the kings of Assyria have done to all lands, by destroying them utterly: and shall you be delivered?

12 Have the gods of the nations delivered them which my fathers have destroyed; as Gozan, and Haran, and Rezeph, and the children of Eden which were in Thelasar?

13 Where is the king of Hamath, and the king of Arpad, and the king of the city of Sepharvaim, of Hena, and Ivah? *(We have defeated the gods of all these other nations, so don't think that your Jehovah will save you. As we defeated them, we will defeat Him likewise!)*

THE PRAYER OF HEZEKIAH

14 And Hezekiah received the letter of the hand of the messengers, and read it: and Hezekiah went up into the House of the LORD, and spread it before the LORD *(Sennacherib had made all of these above statements in a letter sent to Hezekiah; so, Hezekiah takes this letter to the Temple, and "spreads it before the Lord").*

15 And Hezekiah prayed before the LORD, and said, O LORD God of Israel, which dwells between the Cherubims, You are the God, even You alone, of all the kingdoms of the Earth; You have made Heaven and Earth *(in other words, all these gods of the other nations mentioned by Sennacherib do not, in fact, even exist; Jehovah is God Alone, and the Creator of all things; hence, Hezekiah begins his prayer).*

16 LORD, bow down Your ear, and hear: open, LORD, Your Eyes, and see: and hear the words of Sennacherib, which has sent him *(it, the letter)* to reproach the Living God *(the tirade by the heathen monarch is against God, which was rightly so!).*

17 Of a truth, LORD, the kings of Assyria have destroyed the nations and their lands,

18 And have cast their gods into the fire: for they were no gods, but the work of men's hands, wood and stone: therefore they have destroyed them *(all the heathen gods were mere figments of men's imagination; and, if there was any power connected with such, it was always from demon spirits).*

19 Now therefore, O LORD our God, I beseech You, save Thou us out of his hand, that all the kingdoms of the Earth may know that You are the LORD God, even You only *(this was answered to the letter; after the great victory of Judah, "then said they among the heathen, The LORD has done great things for them" [Ps. 126:2]).*

ISAIAH'S PROPHECY OF DELIVERANCE

20 Then Isaiah the son of Amoz sent to Hezekiah, saying, Thus saith the LORD God of Israel, That which you have prayed to Me against Sennacherib king of Assyria I have heard *(while God certainly "hears" all things, still, the way the word "heard" is here used refers to the fact that the petition will be granted; it is "heard" in order to be answered).*

21 This is the word that the LORD has spoken concerning him *(concerning Sennacherib)*; The virgin the daughter of Zion has despised you, and laughed you to scorn; the daughter of Jerusalem has shaken her head at you *(now, the Lord as well uses scorn, sarcasm, and contempt, as it regards the boasts of Sennacherib).*

22 Whom have you reproached and blasphemed? and against Whom have you exalted your voice, and lifted up your eyes on high? even against the Holy One of Israel *(basically, the Lord is saying to Sennacherib, "You are not now addressing yourself to the little fake deities of these other nations, but rather to the Creator of the Ages").*

23 By your messengers you have reproached the LORD, and have said, With the multitude of my chariots I am come up to the height of the mountains, to the sides of Lebanon, and will cut down the tall cedar trees thereof, and the choice fir trees thereof: and I will enter into the lodgings of his borders, and into the forest of his Carmel *(Sennacherib had not actually said these words attributed to him, but he had thought them; and God accounts men's deliberate thoughts as their utterances).*

24 I have digged and drunk strange waters, and with the sole of my feet have I dried up all the rivers of besieged places *(Jehovah continues to read the thoughts and claims of the heathen monarch).*

25 Have you not heard long ago how I have done it, and of ancient times that I have formed it? now have I brought it to pass, that you should be to lay waste fenced cities into ruinous heaps *(now the Lord, in this Verse, switches from parroting Sennacherib to making statements of Himself).*

26 Therefore their inhabitants were of small power, they were dismayed and confounded; they were as the grass of the field, and as the green herb, as the grass on the house tops, and as corn blasted before it be grown up *(mighty nations are raised up by God and torn down by God; in fact, these nations are but "grass," which today is, and tomorrow is gone, all at the command of God).*

27 But I know your abode, and your going out, and your coming in, and your rage against Me *(human pride should stand abashed before*

such absolute knowledge).

28 Because your rage against Me and your tumult is come up into My ears, therefore I will put My hook in your nose, and My bridle in your lips, and I will turn you back by the way by which you came. *(Sculptures show that the kings of Assyria and Babylon actually put rings or fishhooks through the flesh of the captives, mostly through the lips, then attaching a throng or slender rope and, thereby, leading them about, as with a bridle. Thus, God threatens Sennacherib with a punishment he had inflicted on others many times. The Lord did not do this literally, so it expresses figuratively the complete defeat and humiliation of Sennacherib, whenever he would be judged by Jehovah.)*

29 And this shall be a sign unto you, You shall eat this year such things as grow of themselves, and in the second year that which springs of the same; and in the third year sow ye, and reap, and plant vineyards, and eat the fruits thereof *(this entire episode lasted for some two years, with the Children of Israel not planting crops because of the feared invasion; this tells Judah that they would be free from any siege, and could roam the fields to gather such food as grew of itself for the rest of this particular year and the next; after that, they would sow and reap again in a normal way).*

30 And the remnant that is escaped of the house of Judah shall yet again take root downward, and bear fruit upward *(be prosperous once again!).*

31 For out of Jerusalem shall go forth a remnant, and they that escape out of Mount Zion: the zeal of the LORD of Hosts shall do this *(the meaning is that God's zealous Love and Care for His People will effect their complete Restoration to prosperity and glory, difficult as it was at the time to imagine such a Restoration — Pulpit).*

32 Therefore thus saith the LORD concerning the king of Assyria, He shall not come into this city, nor shoot an arrow there, nor come before it with shield, nor cast a bank against it *(there shall be no siege).*

33 By the way that he came, by the same shall he return, and shall not come into this city, saith the LORD *(as he came, he will go, meaning there will be no victory for him).*

34 For I will defend this city, to save it, for My own sake, and for My servant David's sake *(it was not because of any moral beauty in Hezekiah that God delivered Jerusalem, but for His Own sake, and for David's sake — the true*

David, the Lord Jesus Christ).

GOD'S VENGEANCE ON ASSYRIA

35 And it came to pass that night, that the Angel of the LORD went out, and smote in the camp of the Assyrians an hundred fourscore and five thousand *(185,000)*: and when they arose early in the morning *(when the inhabitants of Jerusalem arose)*, behold, they *(the Assyrians)* were all dead corpses. *(Only one Angel did this! Such is the Power of God. How it was done, we aren't told!)*

36 So Sennacherib king of Assyria departed, and went and returned, and dwelt at Nineveh *(he came back to Nineveh without victory, which is the first time, it is believed, that such a thing happened; he was to find that Jehovah was not the same as these little tin-horned deities).*

37 And it came to pass, as he was worshipping in the house of Nisroch his god, that Adrammelech and Sharezer his sons smote him with the sword: and they escaped into the land of Armenia. And Esar-haddon his son reigned in his stead. *(Sennacherib promised the throne to his youngest son, Esar-haddon, instead of to the eldest. In fact, thinking he had offended his god, because of his terrible defeat regarding Jerusalem, he had promised to sacrifice his two older sons to that divinity. These two young men, prompted by fear on the one hand, and by jealousy on the other, murdered their father in December of that year. But then they had to flee to another country to escape their younger brother, Esar-haddon.)*

CHAPTER 20
(713 B.C.)
HEZEKIAH'S SICKNESS AND PROPHECY OF HEALING

IN those days was Hezekiah sick unto death. *(This was about the fourteenth year of his reign, which would have made Hezekiah about 39 years old. These events transpired some time in the two-year period of the invasion of Judah by the Assyrians, and immediately preceding the miraculous deliverance of the Nineteenth Chapter. So, this Chapter is not in chronological order.)* And the prophet Isaiah the son of Amoz came to him, and said unto him, Thus saith the LORD, Set your house in order; for you shall die, and not live. *(In this Passage, the reason is not given for Hezekiah's sickness; however, II Chron., Chpt. 32, in effect, says that*

Hezekiah, due to the Blessings of God, had become lifted up in pride. It seems that the people of Judah and Jerusalem had likewise gone into sin; therefore, the Assyrian invasion and Hezekiah's sickness, with threatened death, were the judgments of God because of sin. Hezekiah had begun his reign with one of the greatest spiritual reforms ever; consequently, God blessed him abundantly, and then the Blessing turned his head.)

2 Then he turned his face to the wall, and prayed unto the LORD, saying *(the Monarch turned his face away from all the riches, glory, and grandeur of Judah and Jerusalem; as well, he saw himself as undone, helpless, and totally dependent on the Mercy of God),*

3 I beseech you, O LORD, remember now how I have walked before You in truth and with a perfect heart, and have done that which is good in Your sight. And Hezekiah wept sore. *(It would seem here that the prayer of the king is somewhat prideful; however, he is merely saying to the Lord that he has tried to keep the Law of God to the very best of his ability. His "weeping" refers to the fact that he now understands that his diligent effort to keep the Law of God, as noble as it was, gained him no merit with God. Instead, he had allowed "justification by faith" to be turned into "justification by works," which generated pride in his heart, which such always does.)*

4 And it came to pass, afore Isaiah was gone out into the middle court, that the word of the LORD came to him, saying *(God will always respond to a broken heart),*

5 Turn again, and tell Hezekiah the captain of My people, Thus saith the LORD, the God of David your father, I have heard your prayer, I have seen your tears: behold, I will heal you: on the third day you shall go up unto the House of the LORD. *(The watchword of the Church once was, "You need Jesus." Now, sadly, the watchword of the Church is, "You need counseling." How so regrettably sad! Hezekiah could have been counseled forever, and there would have been no help from that source; however, he went to the Lord, and God turned an extremely ugly situation around. He is no respecter of persons. What he did for the Monarch, He will, as well, do for you and for me.)*

6 And will add unto your days fifteen years *(Hezekiah was one of the few men in history who knew basically the exact day on which he would die — fifteen years later)*; and I will deliver you and this city out of the hand of the king of Assyria; and I will defend this city for My Own sake, and for My servant David's sake *(for Jesus' sake, the Greater Son of David),*

7 And Isaiah said, Take a lump of figs. And they took and laid it on the boil, and he recovered. *(The critic may argue that if God healed him, why was the lump of figs needed as a poultice? Did God need the figs to complete the healing?*

The truth is: God needs nothing! Everything He does is always done for purpose, and is generally to generate Faith in the heart and life of the individual in question. God does nothing to cater to the pride of our heart, only to Faith.

As well, what difference does it make if God heals instantly, or uses a doctor, medicine, or other means, to bring about His desired effect? God's purposes are far greater than ours. Most of the time, we can only see the desired healing; God sees Spiritual Growth, as well, and will function accordingly.)

MIRACULOUS SIGNS OF HEZEKIAH'S HEALING: THE SUNDIAL GOES BACKWARD

8 And Hezekiah said unto Isaiah, What shall be the sign that the LORD will heal me, and that I shall go up into the House of the LORD the third day? *(The "third day" refers to the coming of the Messiah, and that he would rise from the dead on the third day. Considering that this "sign" had to do with the Messiah, neither the Lord nor the Prophet was angry at the request of Hezekiah.)*

9 And Isaiah said, This sign shall you have of the LORD, that the LORD will do the thing that He has spoken: shall the shadow go forward ten degrees, or go back ten degrees?

10 And Hezekiah answered, It is a light thing for the shadow to go down ten degrees *(forward)*; nay, but let the shadow return backward ten degrees *(both, going forward or backward, were impossible; however, going backward was even more impossible!).*

11 And Isaiah the Prophet cried unto the LORD: and He brought the shadow ten degrees backward, by which it had gone down in the dial of Ahaz. *(This was a notable miracle and would make a "long day"; the event of this "long day" was known over the world of that day.*

With the word of its origination having spread far and wide, inquiries came from Babylon to learn more about the God Who could not only stop the rotation of the Earth, but actually make

it go backwards for a period of time. Several centuries later, Greek historians informed Alexander the Great that this was one of the great wonders recorded in their scientific books.)

HEZEKIAH RECEIVES ENVOYS FROM BABYLON; ISAIAH'S PROPHECY OF JUDAH'S CAPTIVITY

12 At that time Berodach-baladan, the son of Baladan, king of Babylon, sent letters and a present unto Hezekiah: for he had heard that Hezekiah had been sick. *(Secular history relates that, at this moment in history, the king of Babylon was seeking allies to strengthen him against the king of Assyria; hence, this was one of his reasons for his embassage to Hezekiah.*

At this time, Babylon was not nearly the power that Nineveh was. So, the Prophecy that Isaiah would shortly give concerning the coming supremacy of Babylon would certainly not seem practical at this particular time; however, as are all Prophecies given by the Lord, they always come to pass exactly as stated.)

13 And Hezekiah hearkened unto them, and showed them all the house of his precious things, the silver, and the gold, and the spices, and the precious ointment, and all the house of his armour, and all that was found in his treasures: there was nothing in his house, nor in all his dominion, that Hezekiah showed them not. *(Although Hezekiah's object in showing the Babylonians the house of his armor and the house of his treasures was to convince these Ambassadors of the power of Judah, he would have done far better to have related to them the Grace and Glory of Jehovah!)*

14 Then came Isaiah the Prophet unto king Hezekiah, and said unto him, What said these men? and from whence came they unto you? And Hezekiah said, They are come from a far country, even from Babylon.

15 And he said, What have they seen in your house? And Hezekiah answered, All the things that are in my house have they seen: there is nothing among my treasures that I have not shown them. *(As stated, he did not show the Ambassadors from Babylon the things of God, but rather the riches of Judah. He will be rebuked for it. The greatest treasure of all, the Glory of God, it seems he mentioned not at all.)*

16 And Isaiah said unto Hezekiah, Hear the Word of the LORD.

17 Behold, the days come, that all that is in your house, and that which your fathers have laid up in store unto this day, shall be carried into Babylon: nothing shall be left, saith the LORD. *(This refers to the coming time, when Judah would completely lose her way with God, and be taken in chains to Babylon. It would be fulfilled about 125 years later.)*

18 And of your sons who shall issue from you, which you shall beget, shall they take away; and they shall be eunuchs in the palace of the king of Babylon. *(The whole Prophecy of Verses 17-18 was very remarkable, because, at that time, Babylon was a feeble kingdom.)*

19 Then said Hezekiah unto Isaiah, Good is the Word of the LORD which you have spoken. And he said, Is it not good, if peace and truth be in my days? *(Hezekiah accepts the rebuke, thereby acknowledging himself to have been in the wrong, and submits without remonstrance to his punishment. It is a relief, however, to hear that the blow will not fall during his lifetime.)*

DEATH OF HEZEKIAH; ACCESSION OF MANASSEH

20 And the rest of the acts of Hezekiah, and all his might, and how he made a pool, and a conduit, and brought water into the city, are they not written in the book of the chronicles of the kings of Judah? *(That conduit is still there. Up until 2003, it was claimed by some that Hezekiah was not the one who actually made this conduit underground; however, archaeologists discovered proof, in the latter part of 2003, which verifies the Scripture.*

The truth is: the Scripture doesn't need anything to verify it, while all such discoveries must have the Scripture to verify them.)

21 And Hezekiah slept with his fathers: and Manasseh his son reigned in his stead.

CHAPTER 21
(698 B.C.)
MANASSEH REIGNS OVER JUDAH

MANASSEH was twelve years old when he began to reign, and reigned fifty and five years in Jerusalem. And his mother's name was Hephzi-bah. *(As Hezekiah was at least one of the Godliest kings of Judah, his son Manasseh was the most ungodly — and then, strangely enough, he would reign the longest, 55 years. But, at the last, he would come to the Lord.)*

2 And he did that which was evil in the sight of the LORD, after the abominations of

the heathen, whom the LORD cast out before the Children of Israel.

3 For he built up again the high places which Hezekiah his father had destroyed; and he reared up altars for Baal *(the fire-god)*, and made a grove *(this was the "Asherah," the phallus; it is a Greek word, and means the male organ of procreation; it was the most debased of all forms of idolatry)*, as did Ahab king of Israel; and worshipped all the host of heaven, and served them *(the sun, moon, and stars)*.

4 And he built altars in the House of the LORD, of which the LORD said, In Jerusalem will I put My name *(he created altars to other gods in the very Temple of Jehovah; this was spiritual pollution beyond anything any other evil king had ever done)*.

5 And he built altars for all the host of heaven in the two courts of the House of the LORD *(idol gods were also set up in both the inner and outer Courts of the Temple)*.

6 And he made his son pass through the fire *(human sacrifice)*, and observed times, and used enchantments, and dealt with familiar spirits and wizards *(witchcraft)*: he wrought much wickedness in the sight of the LORD, to provoke Him to anger *(sin is the one thing which angers God)*.

7 And he set a graven image of the grove that he had made in the House, of which the LORD said to David, and to Solomon his son, In this House, and in Jerusalem, which I have chosen out of all Tribes of Israel, will I put My Name for ever *(Manasseh was not satisfied to introduce his new religions into the land; he went further and set up the most hideous of idols, the "Asherah," in the very Temple itself, and it is believed by some that he put it in the very Holy of Holies)*:

8 Neither will I make the feet of Israel move any more out of the land which I gave their fathers; only if they will observe to do according to all that I have commanded them, and according to all the Law that My servant Moses commanded them *(this Verse proclaims the Lord desiring to do great things for Israel, if only they would obey Him)*.

9 But they hearkened not: and Manasseh seduced them to do more evil than did the nations whom the LORD destroyed before the Children of Israel *("Manasseh seduced them"; this is not said of any other king of Judah; he not only sinned himself, but spent time and effort to seduce others to join him in his sinning)*.

PROPHECY OF JUDGMENT ON MANASSEH FOR HIS EVIL REIGN

10 And the LORD spoke by His servants the Prophets, saying,

11 Because Manasseh king of Judah has done these abominations, and has done wickedly above all that the Amorites did, which were before him, and has made Judah also to sin with his idols:

12 Therefore thus saith the LORD God of Israel, Behold, I am bringing such evil upon Jerusalem and Judah, that whosoever hears of it, both his ears shall tingle. *(Let it ever be known that sin will forever be punished, with such punishment falling upon Christ, which He took at the Cross of Calvary and, if rejected, upon the sinner — but fall it must!)*

13 And I will stretch over Jerusalem the line of Samaria, and the plummet of the house of Ahab: and I will wipe Jerusalem as a man wipes a dish, wiping it, and turning it upside down *(I will do to Jerusalem as I have done to Samaria; I will execute upon it a similar judgment; the metaphor of "wiping the dish" expresses contempt, as well as condemnation)*.

14 And I will forsake the remnant of My inheritance, and deliver them into the hand of their enemies; and they shall become a prey and a spoil to all their enemies *(the years which immediately followed the captivity were years of terrible suffering to the remnant whom Nebuchadnezzar left in the land; every petty power in the neighborhood felt itself at liberty to make incursions into Judah at its pleasure, to plunder and ravage, and drive off captives, or massacre them in cold blood, or commit any other atrocity)*;

15 Because they have done that which was evil in My sight, and have provoked Me to anger, since the day their fathers came forth out of Egypt, even unto this day *(the moral and spiritual depravity of Judah, though it only came to a head in the time of Manasseh, had its roots in a long-distant past)*.

16 Moreover Manasseh shed innocent blood very much, till he had filled Jerusalem from one end to another; beside his sin wherewith he made Judah to sin, in doing that which was evil in the sight of the LORD *(this was probably a bloody persecution of the faithful; Josephus declares positively that Manasseh "cruelly put to death all the righteous among the Hebrews, and did not even spare the Prophets"; a tradition,*

very widely received, declared Isaiah to have been one of the victims).

DEATH OF MANASSEH; AMON HIS SUCCESSOR

17 Now the rest of the acts of Manasseh, and all that he did, and his sin that he sinned, are they not written in the book of the chronicles of the kings of Judah? *(Even though it is not recorded here, the captivity and restoration of Manasseh are recorded in II Chron. 33:11-19. It is a remarkable story of the Grace of God; and it can only be explained by the Grace of God!)*

18 And Manasseh slept with his fathers, and was buried in the garden of his own house, in the garden of Uzza: and Amon his son reigned in his stead.

AMON'S EVIL TWO-YEAR REIGN OVER JUDAH

19 Amon was twenty and two years old when he began to reign, and he reigned two years in Jerusalem. And his mother's name was Meshullemeth, the daughter of Haruz of Jotbah.

20 And he did that which was evil in the sight of the LORD, as his father Manasseh did.

21 And he walked in all the way that his father walked in, and served the idols that his father served, and worshipped them:

22 And he forsook the LORD God of his fathers, and walked not in the way of the LORD *(he did not even maintain an outward observance of the Law of Moses, but set it wholly aside).*

DEATH OF AMON; JOSIAH HIS SUCCESSOR

23 And the servants of Amon conspired against him, and slew the king in his own house *(the Scripture doesn't say why).*

24 And the people of the land slew all them who had conspired against king Amon; and the people of the land made Josiah his son king in his stead *(after having punished the conspirators with death, they sought out the true heir and, having found him, though he was a boy of but 8 years of age, placed him upon his father's throne).*

25 Now the rest of the acts of Amon which he did, are they not written in the book of the chronicles of the kings of Judah?

26 And he was buried in his sepulchre in the garden of Uzza: and Josiah his son reigned in his stead *(in the same place as his father).*

CHAPTER 22
(641 B.C.)

JOSIAH REIGNS OVER JUDAH THIRTY-ONE YEARS; THE LAST GOOD KING OF JUDAH

JOSIAH was eight years old when he began to reign, and he reigned thirty and one years in Jerusalem. And his mother's name was Jedidah, the daughter of Adaiah of Boscath. *(Josiah was the second youngest king to begin his reign, with Joash being the youngest, at seven years old. Manasseh, Josiah's grandfather, was brought up under Godly Hezekiah, his father. Sadly, Manasseh became the worst king of all, but repented at the end. Josiah, the grandson of Manasseh, was brought up under his wicked father, Amon, but became one of the most Godly kings.)*

2 And he did that which was right in the sight of the LORD, and walked in all the way of David his father, and turned not aside to the right hand or to the left *(Josiah was predicted by name more than 300 years before his birth [I Ki. 13:2]; in noting the comments made by the Holy Spirit concerning these particular kings, it should give us pause regarding what He might be saying concerning us).*

THE TEMPLE REPAIRED

3 And it came to pass in the eighteenth year of king Josiah, that the king sent Shaphan the son of Azaliah, the son of Meshullam, the scribe, to the House of the LORD, saying *(the Prophet Jeremiah stood in the same relation to Josiah as Isaiah was to Hezekiah; there is a possibility that Josiah and Jeremiah were boys together, and that Jeremiah helped in the conversion of Josiah; in fact, his conversion took place when he was 16 years old [8 years into his reign]; Jeremiah was called to be a Prophet in the thirteenth year of Josiah's reign [Jer. 1:2], when Josiah was 21 years old),*

4 Go up to Hilkiah the High Priest, that he may sum the silver which is brought into the House of the LORD, which the keepers of the door have gathered of the people *(after the wicked doings of Manasseh and Amon, a renovation of the sacred building was required, and the money needed was being raised by a collection):*

5 And let them deliver it into the hand of the doers of the work, that have the oversight of the House of the LORD: and let them give it to the doers of the work which is in the House of the LORD, to repair the breaches of the House *(the "doers" are not the actual workmen, but the superintendents or overseers of the workmen)*,

6 Unto carpenters, and builders, and masons, and to buy timber and hewn stone to repair the House.

7 Howbeit there was no reckoning made with them of the money that was delivered into their hand, because they dealt faithfully *(the superintendents and overseers were impeccably honest)*.

THE BOOK OF THE LAW DISCOVERED

8 And Hilkiah the High Priest said unto Shaphan the scribe, I have found the Book of the Law in the House of the LORD. And Hilkiah gave the Book to Shaphan, and he read it. *(Actually, this was the original Pentateuch, which had been written by Moses, and had been laid up by the side of the Ark. It probably was hidden there during the reigns of Manasseh and Amon, because of their wickedness in turning against Jehovah. It had been written by Moses from the Mouth of God more than 800 years before Josiah was born. So, this was an incredible discovery.)*

9 And Shaphan the scribe came to the king, and brought the king word again, and said, Your servants have gathered the money that was found in the House, and have delivered it into the hand of them who do the work, who have the oversight of the House of the LORD *(we have carried out the king's orders exactly, in every particular)*.

10 And Shaphan the scribe showed the king, saying, Hilkiah the Priest has delivered me a Book. And Shaphan read it before the king *(exactly as to how much he read, we aren't told; however, it must have been a goodly portion; the Pentateuch consists of the first five Books of the Bible)*.

JOSIAH HEARS THE WORD OF GOD; REPENTS

11 And it came to pass, when the king had heard the words of the Book of the Law, that he rent his clothes *(it is easy for a man to know whether he has spiritual life or not if, when reading the Bible, he is neither comforted nor terrified; then it is evident that his soul is dead; Josiah was truly born from above, for he trembled exceedingly when hearing words written by God those many years before)*.

12 And the king commanded Hilkiah the Priest, and Ahikam the son of Shaphan, and Achbor the son of Michaiah, and Shaphan the scribe, and Asahiah a servant of the king's, saying,

13 Go ye, enquire of the LORD for me, and for the people, and for all Judah, concerning the words of this Book that is found: for great is the wrath of the LORD that is kindled against us, because our fathers have not hearkened unto the words of this book, to do according unto all that which is written concerning us *(Josiah recognized that Judah had done, and was still doing, exactly those things against which the threatenings of the Law were directed; Judah had forsaken Jehovah, gone after other gods, made to themselves high places, set up images, etc.)*.

14 So Hilkiah the Priest, and Ahikam, and Achbor, and Shaphan, and Asahiah, went unto Huldah the Prophetess, the wife of Shallum the son of Tikvah, the son of Harhas, keeper of the wardrobe; (now she dwelt in Jerusalem in the college;) and they communed with her. *(The word "college" has nothing to do with institutions of learning, but rather referred to "the lower city." The highest officers in the land were sent unto a woman Preacher. Why were they not commanded to go to the great men Preachers, Jeremiah and Zephaniah, who were, at this time, attached to the Court? No doubt the Holy Spirit, for whatever reason, moved upon Josiah to go to Huldah. There are other women Preachers mentioned in the Bible, as well: Miriam, Deborah, Isaiah's wife Nodiah, Anna, and Philip's daughters, together with many women Preachers forever framed in the letters of the Apostle Paul.)*

THE PROPHECY OF HULDAH: JUDGMENT ON JUDAH

15 And she said unto them, Thus saith the LORD God of Israel, Tell the man that sent you to me,

16 Thus saith the LORD, Behold, I will bring evil upon this place, and upon the inhabitants thereof, even all the words of the Book which the king of Judah has read:

17 Because they have forsaken Me, and have burned incense unto other gods, that they

might provoke Me to anger with all the works of their hands; therefore My wrath shall be kindled against this place, and shall not be quenched.

18 But to the king of Judah which sent you to enquire of the LORD, thus shall you say to him, Thus saith the LORD God of Israel, As touching the words which you have heard;

19 Because your heart was tender, and you have humbled yourself before the LORD, when you heard what I spoke against this place, and against the inhabitants thereof, that they should become a desolation and a curse, and have rent your clothes, and wept before Me; I also have heard you, saith the LORD (a true, sincere heart, broken before God, will always be recognized by the Heavenly Father; this which Josiah did is desperately that which the modern Church needs to do, as well!).

20 Behold therefore, I will gather you unto your fathers, and you shall be gathered into your grave in peace; and your eyes shall not see all the evil which I will bring upon this place. And they brought the king word again. (Josiah died in battle against the Egyptians, but was buried in peace, meaning that he did not see the terrible evil which came upon Judah, ultimately bringing about the destruction of the nation. While Josiah was Godly, Judah, by and large, continued on in her evil ways; consequently, judgment could not be withheld any longer, so the Lord took the Godly king into Paradise, even as we shall see in the following Chapter.)

CHAPTER 23
(624 B.C.)
THE LAW READ TO THE PEOPLE

AND the king sent, and they gathered unto him all the elders of Judah and of Jerusalem. (Josiah instituted one of the greatest spiritual reforms ever known to Judah; still, according to Jeremiah, even at the time that Josiah was destroying idolatry, the nation was secretly planning its Restoration, which was quickly effected after Josiah's death. But, still, Josiah did all that he could to bring the people back to the Bible.)

2 And the king went up into the House of the LORD, and all the men of Judah and all the inhabitants of Jerusalem with him, and the Priests, and the Prophets, and all the people, both small and great: and he read in their ears all the words of the Book of the Covenant which was found in the House of the LORD.

(This shows us that the Word of God is for everyone, and not just a privileged few. Regrettably, the Bible in the modern pulpit is basically used as window-dressing. Instead, the latest psychological fad is too often preached as gospel, when, in reality, it is no gospel at all.)

JOSIAH'S COVENANT

3 And the king stood by a pillar, and made a Covenant before the LORD, to walk after the LORD, and to keep His Commandments and His Testimonies and His Statutes with all their heart and all their soul, to perform the words of this Covenant that were written in this Book. And all the people stood to the Covenant (the terms expressed here include the totality of the Law, all its requirements, without exception).

JOSIAH'S REFORMS

4 And the king commanded Hilkiah the High Priest, and the Priests of the second order, and the keepers of the door, to bring forth out of the Temple of the LORD all the vessels that were made for Baal, and for the grove (worship of the Asherah, the male reproductive organ), and for all the host of heaven: and he burned them without Jerusalem in the fields of Kidron, and carried the ashes of them unto Beth-el (the ashes carried to Bethel to defile the altar of Jeroboam was predicted in I Ki. 13:2, where even the name of Josiah was mentioned, over 300 years before he was born, and nearly 350 years before the prediction was fulfilled; the Temple of the Lord had been turned into the abomination of idol worship).

5 And he put down the idolatrous priests, whom the kings of Judah had ordained to burn incense in the high places in the cities of Judah, and in the places round about Jerusalem; them also who burned incense unto Baal, to the sun, and to the moon, and to the planets, and to all the host of heaven (these were the black-robed priests instead of the white-robed Priests who belonged to God; they were not the "kohen" appointed by God, but "kemarim" appointed by man; each separate idol had its own priest, so there were then many orders of priests in Israel; the word "planets" referred to the twelve signs of the zodiac).

6 And he brought out the grove (Asherah) from the House of the LORD, without Jerusalem, unto the brook Kidron, and burned it at the brook Kidron, and stamped it small to

powder, and cast the powder thereof upon the graves of the children of the people *(the idea that such abomination was in the very House of God, where the Lord dwelt between the Mercy Seat and the Cherubim, is unthinkable; this shows how far down Judah had sunk).*

7 And he broke down the houses of the sodomites *(homosexuals),* who were by the House of the LORD, where the women wove hangings for the grove *(so we see here what God thinks of the terrible sin of homosexuality; to be sure, the same-sex marriages, so-called, presently being engaged in certain parts of the United States indicate the nation's downward slide, which will ultimately guarantee judgment).*

8 And he brought all the priests out of the cities of Judah, and defiled the high places where the priests *(ungodly priests)* had burned incense, from Geba to Beer-sheba, and broke down the high places of the gates that were in the entering in of the gate of Joshua the governor of the city, which were on a man's left hand at the gate of the city *(these "high places" were throughout the entire kingdom, both North and South; although God Alone was worshipped on most of them, still, the Law commanded that incense and sacrifice be confined to the one Altar at Jerusalem; as well, the modern Child of God has one Altar, which is Calvary; these priests who officiated in these "high places" were allowed to come to the Temple at Jerusalem and to officiate in some limited manner, but not at the Altar of Jehovah).*

9 Nevertheless the priests of the high places came not up to the Altar of the LORD in Jerusalem, but they did eat of the unleavened bread among their brethren *(as stated, they were given limited duties, which did not include the Altar of the Lord).*

10 And he defiled Topheth, which is in the valley of the children of Hinnom, that no man might make his son or his daughter to pass through the fire to Molech *(on this idol, little children were placed and tied to its arms; fire was then built in its bulbous belly, with the arms becoming red-hot; priests of this particular order would then loudly beat the drums, drowning out the screams of the dying child; this is how bad that Judah had become).*

11 And he took away the horses that the kings of Judah had given to the sun, at the entering in of the House of the LORD, by the chamber of Nathan-melech the chamberlain, which was in the suburbs, and burned the chariots of the sun with fire *(Josiah burnt all*

the material objects that had been desecrated by the idolatries; the persons and animals so desecrated he "removed," or deprived of their functions; this was a Persian practice, which had been adopted by Judah).*

12 And the altars that were on the top of the upper chamber of Ahaz, which the kings of Judah had made, and the altars which Manasseh had made in the two courts of the House of the LORD, did the king beat down, and broke them down from thence, and cast the dust of them into the brook Kidron *(as then, the modern Church seemingly has many altars; however, let it be remembered, there is only one Altar which God recognizes, and that is "Jesus Christ and Him Crucified" [I Cor. 1:23]).*

13 And the high places that were before Jerusalem, which were on the right hand of the Mount of corruption *(Mount of Olives),* which Solomon the king of Israel had builded for Ashtoreth the abomination of the Zidonians, and for Chemosh the abomination of the Moabites, and for Milcom the abomination of the children of Ammon, did the king defile.

14 And he broke in pieces the images, and cut down the groves, and filled their places with the bones of men *(all graves were considered to be unclean; therefore, all of this unclean refuse was deposited in graveyards, so to speak).*

15 Moreover the altar that was at Beth-el, and the high place which Jeroboam the son of Nebat, who made Israel to sin, had made, both that altar and the high place he broke down, and burned the high place, and stamped it small to powder, and burned the grove *(the Asherah; we see from all of this that Jerusalem was then literally filled with idols!).*

16 And as Josiah turned himself, he spied the sepulchres that were there in the mount, and sent, and took the bones out of the sepulchres, and burned them upon the altar, and polluted it, according to the Word of the LORD which the man of God proclaimed, who proclaimed these words *(I Kings 13:2; the meaning of the last phrase is that Josiah acted as he did, not in order to fulfill the Prophecy, but, that in thus acting, he unconsciously fulfilled it).*

17 Then he said, What title is that that I see? And the men of the city told him, It is the sepulchre of the man of God, which came from Judah, and proclaimed these things that you have done against the altar of Beth-el *(this Verse*

proves that Josiah did not actually know he was fulfilling Prophecy until after it was done).

18 And he said, Let him alone; let no man move his bones. So they let his bones alone, with the bones of the Prophet who came out of Samaria *(he would show honor to the "man of God" [I Ki., Chpt. 13]).*

19 And all the houses also of the high places that were in the cities of Samaria, which the kings of Israel had made to provoke the LORD to anger, Josiah took away, and did to them according to all the acts that he had done in Beth-el *(the cleansing process included the northern kingdom of Israel, which was now occupied by the Samaritans).*

20 And he slew all the priests of the high places who were there upon the altars, and burned men's bones upon them, and returned to Jerusalem *(the "priests" of these particular "high places" were different than those priests of Verses 8-9; the former were priests of idolatry; the latter were priests of God, but functioning in the wrong way).*

THE PASSOVER RESTORED

21 And the king commanded all the people, saying, Keep the Passover unto the LORD your God, as it is written in the Book of this Covenant *(Verses 21-23 record the greatest Passover ever conducted at Jerusalem).*

22 Surely there was not holden such a Passover from the days of the Judges who judged Israel, nor in all the days of the kings of Israel, nor of the kings of Judah *(in fact, the Word of God, as is overly obvious, had been sorely neglected);*

23 But in the eighteenth year of king Josiah, wherein this Passover was holden to the LORD in Jerusalem.

THE LORD'S ANGER AGAINST JUDAH

24 Moreover the workers with familiar spirits, and the wizards, and the images, and the idols, and all the abominations that were spied in the land of Judah and in Jerusalem, did Josiah put away, that he might perform the words of the Law which were written in the Book that Hilkiah the Priest found in the House of the LORD *(Laws against such practices as Josiah now put down are found in Ex. 22:18; Lev. 19:31; 20:27; Deut. 18:10-12).*

25 And like unto him was there no king before him, who turned to the LORD with all his heart, and with all his soul, and with all his might, according to all the Law of Moses; neither after him arose there any like him *(and it is the Holy Spirit Who said this!).*

26 Notwithstanding the LORD turned not from the fierceness of His great wrath, wherewith His anger was kindled against Judah, because of all the provocations that Manasseh had provoked Him withal *(regardless of the great Reformation of Josiah, the Lord did not see fit to turn away all His Wrath, for He knew the change would last only during the days of Josiah, and that Judah would follow the old pattern of most of the previous kings of Israel and Judah, by continuing to sin, and to sin grossly).*

27 And the LORD said, I will remove Judah also out of My sight, as I have removed Israel, and will cast off this city Jerusalem which I have chosen, and the House of which I said, My Name shall be there *(if there had been true Repentance on the part of the people of Judah, meaning that the people would turn away from their terrible sins, the Lord most assuredly would have turned away from His Wrath).*

28 Now the rest of the acts of Josiah, and all that he did, are they not written in the book of the chronicles of the kings of Judah?

DEATH OF JOSIAH; JEHOAHAZ HIS SUCCESSOR

29 In his days *(days of Josiah)* Pharaohnechoh king of Egypt went up against the king of Assyria to the river Euphrates: and king Josiah went against him; and he slew him *(Pharaoh killed Josiah in battle)* at Megiddo, when he had seen him *(as stated, the Lord allowed Josiah to be killed, not because of any wrongdoing on the part of Josiah, but because of the judgment that must come; it could not be delayed).*

30 And his servants carried him in a chariot dead from Megiddo, and brought him to Jerusalem, and buried him in his own sepulchre. And the people of the land took Jehoahaz the son of Josiah, and anointed him, and made him king in his father's stead *(even though he died in battle, he was buried in peace, because he had Peace with God; regrettably, Jehoahaz would not emulate his father).*

JEHOAHAZ REIGNS OVER JUDAH

31 Jehoahaz was twenty and three years old when he began to reign; and he reigned three

months in Jerusalem. And his mother's name was Hamutal, the daughter of Jeremiah of Libnah.

32 And he did that which was evil in the sight of the LORD, according to all that his fathers had done (*the three-month reign of Jehoahaz is briefly dismissed by the Holy Spirit by simply saying, "And he did evil in the sight of the LORD"*).

DEATH OF JEHOAHAZ; JEHOIAKIM HIS SUCCESSOR

33 And Pharaoh-nechoh put him in bands at Riblah in the land of Hamath, that he might not reign in Jerusalem; and put the land to a tribute of an hundred talents of silver, and a talent of gold (*Judah now becomes a vassal of Egypt*).

34 And Pharaoh-nechoh made Eliakim the son of Josiah king in the room of Josiah his father, and turned his name to Jehoiakim, and took Jehoahaz away: and he came to Egypt, and died there (*Nechoh required him to take a new name, as a mark of subjection*).

35 And Jehoiakim gave the silver and the gold to Pharaoh; but he taxed the land to give the money according to the commandment of Pharaoh: he exacted the silver and the gold of the people of the land, of every one according to his taxation, to give it unto Pharaoh-nechoh (*Judah now has to pay heavy tribute to Pharaoh, which was a great hardship on the people*).

JEHOIAKIM REIGNS OVER JUDAH

36 Jehoiakim was twenty and five years old when he began to reign; and he reigned eleven years in Jerusalem. And his mother's name was Zebudah, the daughter of Pedaiah of Rumah.

37 And he did that which was evil in the sight of the LORD, according to all that his fathers had done. (*Josephus calls him "an unjust man and an evildoer, neither pious in his relations towards God, nor equitable in his dealings with his fellowmen."*)

CHAPTER 24

(610 B.C.)

JEHOIAKIM SUBDUED BY NEBUCHADNEZZAR

IN his days Nebuchadnezzar king of Babylon came up, and Jehoiakim became his servant three years: then he turned and rebelled against him. (*In the Book of Daniel, God reveals the fact that He took the government of the world out of Israel's hand, and placed it in the hand of Nebuchadnezzar, to whom it was said: "You are this head of gold" [Dan. 2:38]. It was God's Will that unrepentant Judah be punished for her many sins, and that Nebuchadnezzar would be the chastening rod; consequently, when this Verse says that "he rebelled against him," this was very displeasing to the Lord.*)

2 And the LORD sent against him (*against Jehoiakim*) bands of the Chaldees, and bands of the Syrians, and bands of the Moabites, and bands of the children of Ammon, and sent them against Judah to destroy it, according to the Word of the LORD, which He spoke by His servants the Prophets (*God could command either way, whether judgment or Blessing; it all depends on obedience or disobedience*).

3 Surely at the Commandment of the LORD came this upon Judah, to remove them out of His sight, for the sins of Manasseh, according to all that he did (*the meaning is not that the nation was punished for the personal sins and crimes of the wicked Manasseh 40 or 50 years previously, but that the class of sins introduced by this king, being persisted in by the people, in other words, continuing, brought the stern judgments of God upon them — Pulpit*);

4 And also for the innocent blood that he shed: for he filled Jerusalem with innocent blood; which the LORD would not pardon (*like the other "sins of Manasseh," the shedding of innocent blood continued, both in the Moloch offerings [Jer. 7:31], and in the persecution of the righteous [Jer. 7:6, 9], etc.*).

DEATH OF JEHOIAKIM; SUCCEEDED BY JEHOIACHIN

5 Now the rest of the acts of Jehoiakim, and all that he did, are they not written in the book of the chronicles of the kings of Judah?

6 So Jehoiakim slept with his fathers: and Jehoiachin his son reigned in his stead (*it says nothing about him being buried, as would be normal, when, in fact, he was buried, but like an animal [Jer. 22:18-19]*).

7 And the king of Egypt came not again any more out of his land: for the king of Babylon had taken from the river of Egypt unto the river Euphrates all that pertained to the king of Egypt (*this speaks of the ascension of the mighty Babylonian Empire; in fact, Babylon had*

now conquered Egypt).

JEHOIACHIN'S REIGN; THE SECOND SEIZURE OF JERUSALEM

8 Jehoiachin was eighteen years old when he began to reign, and he reigned in Jerusalem three months. And his mother's name was Nehushta, the daughter of Elnathan of Jerusalem *(his mother was probably the ruling spirit of the time during her son's short reign).*

9 And he did that which was evil in the sight of the LORD, according to all that his father had done *(the Prophet Jeremiah calls him "a despised broken idol" and "a vessel wherein is no pleasure" [Jer. 22:28]).*

10 At that time the servants of Nebuchadnezzar king of Babylon came up against Jerusalem, and the city was besieged *(the short phrase, "at that time," refers to the reign of Jehoiachin).*

11 And Nebuchadnezzar king of Babylon came against the city, and his servants did besiege it *(while the siege conducted by his generals was still going on, Nebuchadnezzar made his appearance in person before the walls, which brought about the surrender of Jerusalem).*

12 And Jehoiachin the king of Judah went out to the king of Babylon, he, and his mother, and his servants, and his princes, and his officers: and the kings of Babylon took him in the eighth year of his reign *(the eighth year of Nebuchadnezzar's reign; this Verse portrays the surrender of Jerusalem).*

13 And he carried out thence all the treasures of the House of the LORD, and the treasures of the king's house, and cut in pieces all the vessels of gold which Solomon king of Israel had made in the Temple of the LORD, as the LORD had said *(thus the Prophecy by Isaiah to Hezekiah was fulfilled [20:17-18]).*

14 And he *(Nebuchadnezzar)* carried away all Jerusalem, and all the princes, and all the mighty men of valour, even ten thousand captives, and all the craftsmen and smiths: none remained, save the poorest sort of the people of the land *(in this first deportation were carried away Mordecai, Ezekiel, Daniel, and Nehemiah).*

JEHOIACHIN TAKEN CAPTIVE TO BABYLON

15 And he carried away Jehoiachin to Babylon, and the king's mother, and the king's wives, and his officers, and the mighty of the land, those carried he into captivity from Jerusalem to Babylon.

16 And all the men of might, even seven thousand, and craftsmen and smiths a thousand, all who were strong and apt for war, even them the king of Babylon brought captive to Babylon *(thus, the nation of Judah was left with no guiding force).*

REIGN OF ZEDEKIAH OVER JUDAH

17 And the king of Babylon made Mattaniah his father's brother king in his stead, and changed his name to Zedekiah.

18 Zedekiah was twenty and one years old when he began to reign, and he reigned eleven years in Jerusalem. And his mother's name was Hamutal, the daughter of Jeremiah of Libnah *(this was not Jeremiah the Prophet, who was at Anathoth).*

19 And he did that which was evil in the sight of the LORD, according to all that Jehoiakim had done *(among other things, he fell into the old error of "putting trust in Egypt," which was an act of rebellion against God, and against the Babylonian Empire).*

ZEDEKIAH REBELS AGAINST BABYLON

20 For through the anger of the LORD it came to pass in Jerusalem and Judah, until he had cast them out from His presence, that Zedekiah rebelled against the king of Babylon. *(God permitted Zedekiah to rebel, for it was determined that Judah should be destroyed at this time and go into captivity because of repeated sinning. Because of repeated rebellion against His Word, the anger of the Lord had risen to a white-hot pitch.)*

CHAPTER 25
(588 B.C.)
THE FALL OF JERUSALEM

AND it came to pass in the ninth year of his reign *(the reign of Zedekiah)*, in the tenth month, in the tenth day of the month, that Nebuchadnezzar king of Babylon came, he, and all his host, against Jerusalem, and pitched against it; and they built forts against it round about. *(The exact day of this siege was revealed to Ezekiel in a vision in faraway Babylonia [Ezek. 24:1]. The Holy Spirit records the exact day that this began, simply because of its significance. Israel, destined to be a light unto the world, lost*

her way, and would become a vassal state to heathen powers, which was never intended by God, but brought on because of Israel's persistent rebellion. God cannot condone sin, even if it is in His chosen People!)

2 And the city was besieged unto the eleventh year of king Zedekiah *(the writer omits all the details of the siege, and hastens to the final catastrophe).*

3 And on the ninth day of the fourth month the famine prevailed in the city, and there was no bread for the people of the land *(a third part of the inhabitants died of the famine, and the plague which grew out of it [Ezek. 5:12]; this could well have been nearly a half million people).*

4 And the city was broken up, and all the men of war fled by night by the way of the gate between two walls, which is by the king's garden: (now the Chaldees were against the city round about:) and the king went the way toward the plain *(Zedekiah tried to slip out of the city and avoid capture by the Babylonians; he would not be successful).*

5 And the army of the Chaldees pursued after the king, and overtook him in the plains of Jericho: and all his army were scattered from him *(it is probable, though not certain, that Zedekiah intended to cross the Jordan River, and seek a refuge in Moab, when he was apprehended).*

6 So they took the king, and brought him up to the king of Babylon to Riblah; and they gave judgment upon him *(as a rebel who had broken his covenant and his oath [Ezek. 17:16, 18], Zedekiah was brought to trial before Nebuchadnezzar and his great lords; while his life was spared, yet the judgment was still sufficiently severe).*

7 And they slew the sons of Zedekiah before his eyes, and put out the eyes of Zedekiah, and bound him with fetters of brass, and carried him to Babylon. *(The Prophets Jeremiah and Ezekiel predicted that Zedekiah should see the king of Babylon, but not the city of Babylon, and yet he would die there. So it came to pass. He saw the king of Babylon at Riblah, where his eyes were put out. He was then carried to Babylon. Being blind, he could not see the city. And he died there.)*

THE CAPTIVITY OF JUDAH; JERUSALEM AND THE TEMPLE DESTROYED

8 And in the fifth month, on the seventh day of the month, which is the nineteenth year of king Nebuchadnezzar king of Babylon, came Nebuzar-adan, captain of the guard, a servant of the king of Babylon, unto Jerusalem *(extreme exactness with respect to a date indicates the extreme importance of the event dated; in the whole range of the history contained in the two Books of the Kings, there is no instance of the year, month, and day being all given, except in this present Chapter, where we find this extreme exactness four times [Vss. 1, 3, 8, 27]):*

9 And he burnt the House of the LORD *(the Temple)*, and the king's house, and all the houses of Jerusalem, and every great man's house burnt he with fire *(the Temple, built by Solomon, had stood for some 470 years).*

10 And all the army of the Chaldees, that were with the captain of the guard, broke down the walls of Jerusalem round about *(it seems to be that they made breaches in the walls at given points).*

11 Now the rest of the people who were left in the city, and the fugitives who fell away to the king of Babylon, with the remnant of the multitude, did Nebuzar-adan the captain of the guard carry away.

12 But the captain of the guard left of the poor of the land to be vinedressers and husbandmen.

TEMPLE VESSELS AND METALS TAKEN TO BABYLON

13 And the pillars of brass that were in the House of the LORD, and the bases, and the Brasen Sea *(Brazen Laver)* that was in the House of the LORD, did the Chaldees break in pieces, and carried the brass of them to Babylon *(these giant copper pillars represented the people of God; there were two of them; they sat at the immediate front of the Temple; as these were no more God's people, these two symbols were broken up; likewise, the "Brazen Laver" was a Type of the Word of God; with the people refusing to obey the Word, the symbol was no longer needed; consequently, it was broken up along with the pillars).*

14 And the pots, and the shovels, and the snuffers, and the spoons, and all the vessels of brass wherewith they ministered, took they away. *(Vss. 13-17 have little interest for the unspiritual mind, but, to the heart which knows God, how full of agony they appear! These precious vessels and all this gathered wealth, designed by God Himself to express the Millennial*

Glories of Christ as King and Priest, were broken, dishonored, and carried to Babylon. This was a sad result of the unbelief of the elect nation to whom God had entrusted such glories.)

15 And the firepans, and the bowls, and such things as were of gold, in gold, and of silver, in silver, the captain of the guard took away.

16 The two pillars, one sea, and the bases which Solomon had made for the House of the LORD; the brass of all these vessels was without weight.

17 The height of the one pillar was eighteen cubits *(27 feet)*, and the chapiter upon it was brass: and the height of the chapiter three cubits *(4 1/2 feet)*; and the wreathen work, and pomegranates upon the chapiter round about, all of brass: and like unto these had the second pillar with wreathen work *(all of this was broken in pieces, aptly describing the Children of Israel, who were, as well, literally broken in pieces)*.

THE LEADERS OF JUDAH SLAIN

18 And the captain of the guard took Seraiah the chief priest, and Zephaniah the second priest, and the three keepers of the door:

19 And out of the city he took an officer who was set over the men of war, and five men of them who were in the king's presence, which were found in the city, and the principal scribe of the host, which mustered the people of the land, and threescore men of the people of the land who were found in the city:

20 And Nebuzar-adan captain of the guard took these, and brought them to the king of Babylon to Riblah:

21 And the king of Babylon smote them, and slew them at Riblah in the land of Hamath. So Judah was carried away out of their land *(the nation ceased to be, at least at that time)*.

GEDALIAH MADE GOVERNOR OF THE REMAINING JEWS; HIS ASSASSINATION

22 And as for the people who remained in the land of Judah, whom Nebuchadnezzar king of Babylon had left, even over them he made Gedaliah the son of Ahikam, the son of Shaphan, ruler *(Nebuchadnezzar's choice of Gedaliah for governor was probably made from some knowledge of his having sided with Jeremiah, whose persistent endeavors to make the Jews submit to the Babylonian yoke seemed to have been well-known, not only to the Jews, but*

to the Babylonians, as well).

23 And when all the captains of the armies, they and their men, heard that the king of Babylon had made Gedaliah governor, there came to Gedaliah to Mizpah, even Ishmael the son of Nethaniah, and Johanan the son of Careah, and Seraiah the son of Tanhumeth the Netophathite, and Jaazaniah the son of a Maachathite, they and their men *(the persons mentioned, that is, with the soldiers under them, came to Gedaliah at Mizpah, and placed themselves under him as his subjects — Pulpit)*.

24 And Gedaliah swore to them, and to their men, and said unto them, Fear not to be the servants of the Chaldees: dwell in the land, and serve the king of Babylon; and it shall be well with you.

25 But it came to pass in the seventh month, that Ishmael the son of Nethaniah, the son of Elishama, of the seed royal, came, and ten men with him, and smote Gedaliah, that he died, and the Jews and the Chaldees that were with him at Mizpah. *(Josephus says that Ishmael was a wicked and crafty man, who, during the siege of Jerusalem, had made his escape from the place, and fled for shelter to Baalim, king of Ammon, with whom he remained until the siege was over. Gedaliah had been warned about him, but treated the warning with little significance. He would pay dearly.)*

26 And all the people, both small and great, and the captains of the armies, arose, and came to Egypt: for they were afraid of the Chaldees. *(They went to Egypt in defiance of the Lord and His Prophets [Jer., Chpts. 42-43]. Jeremiah told them that Egypt would also be given to Nebuchadnezzar, and they, therefore, would still be in his dominion [Jer. 44:29-30].)*

JEHOIACHIN RESTORED AND HONORED IN BABYLON

27 And it came to pass in the seven and thirtieth year of the captivity of Jehoiachin king of Judah, in the twelfth month, on the seven and twentieth day of the month, that Evil-merodach king of Babylon in the year that he began to reign did lift up the head of Jehoiachin king of Judah out of prison;

28 And he spoke kindly to him, and set his throne above the throne of the kings who were with him in Babylon;

29 And changed his prison garments: and he did eat bread continually before him all the days of his life.

30 And his allowance was a continual allowance given him of the king, a daily rate for every day, all the days of his life. *(This event was intended as a comforting sign, to the whole of the captive people, that the Lord would one day put an end to their banishment, if they would acknowledge that it was a well-merited punishment for their sins that they had been driven away from before His Face, and would turn again*

to the Lord their God with all their hearts.

Thus, Jehovah's throne at Jerusalem was cast down, and man's throne at Babylon was set up and, strangely, God recognized it, and committed to it the government of the world. With it commences the "times of the Gentiles," which are to continue up to, and close with, the reign of the last great king of Babylon, the Antichrist [Lk. 21:24].)

THE FIRST BOOK OF THE
CHRONICLES

CHAPTER 1
(4004 B.C.)
GENEALOGIES FROM ADAM TO THE BABYLONIAN CAPTIVITY: DESCENDANTS OF ADAM TO NOAH

ADAM, Sheth (*Seth*), Enosh (*the Writer of Chronicles began abruptly with "Adam," supposing that His readers would understand from the First Book of the Bible about the origin of Adam, the first man from whom all other men have their beings [Gen. 1:26-31; 2:7]; this Divine Diary, for Chronicles is a Diary kept by God, begins with the First Adam, and carries on the story of Grace, in essence, to the Last Adam; in fact, this Book is placed as the last in the Hebrew Bible, and the reader passes at once to the First Chapter of Matthew*),

2 Kenan, Mahalaleel, Jered,

3 Henoch, Methuselah (*who lived longer than any other human being, 969 years*), Lamech,

4 Noah, Shem, Ham, and Japheth (*from these last three came all the descendants of planet Earth*).

DESCENDANTS OF JAPHETH

5 The sons of Japheth; Gomer, and Magog, and Madai, and Javan, and Tubal, and Meshech, and Tiras (*the descendants of Japheth populated Europe, some parts of the Far East, England, and eventually the United States*).

6 And the sons of Gomer; Ashchenaz, and Riphath, and Togarmah.

7 And the sons of Javan; Elishah, and Tarshish, Kittim, and Dodanim.

DESCENDANTS OF HAM

8 The sons of Ham; Cush, and Mizraim, Put, and Canaan (*the descendants of Ham first went into the Middle East, where they were exterminated or driven out by the "sons of Shem," and eventually populated Africa*).

9 And the sons of Cush; Seba, and Havilah, and Sabta, and Raamah, and Sabtecha. And the sons of Raamah: Sheba, and Dedan.

10 And Cush begat Nimrod (*it is believed that he led the first organized rebellion against God [Gen. 10:8-10]*): he began to be mighty upon the Earth.

11 And Mizraim begat Ludim, and Anamim, and Lehabim, and Naphtuhim,

12 And Pathrusim, and Casluhim, (*of whom came the Philistines,*) and Caphthorim (*the Philistines were ever a thorn in the side of Israel and, in some sense of the word, this continues even unto this very hour in modern Israel*).

13 And Canaan begat Zidon his firstborn, and Heth,

14 The Jebusite also, and the Amorite, and the Girgashite,

15 And the Hivite, and the Arkite, and the Sinite,

16 And the Arvadite, and the Zemarite, and the Hamathite (*in the taking of the land of Canaan, Israel opposed most of these Tribes; it was because of their great evil that they were allowed by God to be driven out; regrettably, just as we have studied in II Kings, Israel herself, because of great sin, was also driven out, and made captives of the Babylonians, where they remained for some 70 years before finally being allowed to come back into the land of Israel*).

DESCENDANTS OF SHEM

17 The sons of Shem; Elam; and Asshur, and Arphaxad, and Lud, and Aram, and Uz (*where Job resided [Job 1:1]*), and Hul, and Gether, and Meshech (*these "sons of Shem" ultimately overran the Middle East*).

18 And Arphaxad begat Shelah, and Shelah begat Eber.

19 And unto Eber were born two sons: the name of the one was Peleg; because in his days the Earth was divided: and his brother's name was Joktan (*it is believed that at one time in the distant past all the continents of the Earth were joined together; but during the days of Peleg, which was about 4,000 years ago, the continents were divided; this upheaval seemed to follow the Tower of Babel episode with the confusion of tongues, which scattered the people over the face of the Earth [Gen. 11:7-9]*).

20 And Joktan begat Almodad, and Sheleph, and Hazarmaveth, and Jerah,

21 Hadoram also, and Uzal, and Diklah,
22 And Ebal, and Abimael, and Sheba,
23 And Ophir, and Havilah, and Jobab. All these were the sons of Joktan.

THE LINE OF SHEM TO ABRAHAM

24 Shem, Arphaxad, Shelah,
25 Eber, Peleg, Reu,
26 Serug, Nahor, Terah,
27 Abram; the same is Abraham.

SONS OF ABRAHAM

28 The sons of Abraham; Isaac, and Ishmael *(Isaac, though younger than Ishmael, is placed first as the legitimate heir, since Sarah was the only true wife of Abraham; but in the genealogy which follows the sons of Ishmael and of Abraham's second wife are put first, so that the true line of the Messiah might be dealt with more fully, for that is the real purpose of all the genealogies).*

SONS OF ISHMAEL

29 These are their generations: The first-born of Ishmael, Nebaioth; then Kedar, and Adbeel, and Mibsam,
30 Mishma, and Dumah, Massa, Hadad, and Tema,
31 Jetur, Naphish, and Kedemah. These are the sons of Ishmael *(Ishmael, Abraham's son through Hagar, had twelve sons, as did Jacob; they were also the heads of twelve Tribes, making 24 Tribes which descended from Abraham through two of his sons).*

DESCENDANTS OF ABRAHAM AND KETURAH

32 Now the sons of Keturah, Abraham's concubine: she bore Zimran, and Jokshan, and Medan, and Midian, and Ishbak, and Shuah. And the sons of Jokshan; Sheba, and Dedan.
33 And the sons of Midian; Ephah, and Epher, and Henoch, and Abida, and Eldaah. All these are the sons of Keturah.

SONS OF ABRAHAM AND ISAAC

34 And Abraham begat Isaac. The sons of Isaac; Esau and Israel *(now, the Author comes back to Isaac and his seed, Esau and Jacob, and follows the main purpose of His writing, dealing briefly with the seed of Esau first before going into the more lengthy genealogies of the seed of Jacob or Israel; after this, He writes twelve Chapters recording the genealogies of Jacob's sons to the time of Saul and David).*

DESCENDANTS OF ESAU

35 The sons of Esau; Eliphaz *(this was the Eliphaz of the Book of Job, who was a Temanite [Job 2:11; 4:1]),* Reuel, and Jeush, and Jaalam, and Korah.
36 The son of Eliphaz; Teman, and Omar, Zephi, and Gatam, Kenaz, and Timna, and Amalek. *(This man, a descendant of Esau, was noted for his opposition to Israel. The Amalekites were the first to attack Israel as they came out of Egypt. For this God swore that they would have war from generation to generation and ultimately be destroyed. This was true; they were finally destroyed by Saul — all but a few. One of the reasons Saul was cut off was because he spared some of the Amalekites [I Sam., Chpt. 15]. They were a symbol of the flesh ever at war with the Spirit.)*
37 The sons of Reuel; Nahath, Zerah, Shammah, and Mizzah.
38 And the sons of Seir; Lotan, and Shobal, and Zibeon, and Anah, and Dishon, and Ezar, and Dishan.
39 And the sons of Lotan; Hori, and Homam: and Timna was Lotan's sister.
40 The sons of Shobal; Alian, and Manahath, and Ebal, Shephi, and Onam. And the sons of Zibeon; Aiah, and Anah.
41 The sons of Anah; Dishon. And the sons of Dishon; Amram, and Eshban, and Ithran, and Cheran.
42 The sons of Ezer; Bilhan, and Zavan, and Jakan. The sons of Dishan; Uz, and Aran.

KINGS OF EDOM BEFORE ISRAEL'S KINGS

43 Now these are the kings that reigned in the land of Edom before any king reigned over the Children of Israel; Bela the son of Beor: and the name of his city was Dinhabah.
44 And when Bela was dead, Jobab the son of Zerah of Bozrah reigned in his stead.
45 And when Jobab was dead, Husham of the land of the Temanites reigned in his stead.
46 And when Husham was dead, Hadad the son of Bedad, which smote Midian in the field of Moab, reigned in his stead: and the name of his city was Avith.

47 And when Hadad was dead, Samlah of Masrekah reigned in his stead.

48 And when Samlah was dead, Shaul of Rehoboth by the river reigned in his stead.

49 And when Shaul was dead, Baal-hanan the son of Achbor reigned in his stead.

50 And when Baal-hanan was dead, Hadad reigned in his stead: and the name of his city was Pai; and his wife's name was Mehetabel, the daughter of Matred, the daughter of Mezahab.

DUKES OF EDOM

51 Hadad died also. And the dukes of Edom were; duke Timnah, duke Aliah, duke Jetheth,

52 Duke Aholibamah, duke Elah, duke Pinon,

53 Duke Kenaz, duke Teman, duke Mibzar,

54 Duke Magdiel, duke Iram. These are the dukes of Edom.

CHAPTER 2
(1471 B.C.)
THE SONS OF ISRAEL (JACOB)

THESE are the sons of Israel; Reuben, Simeon, Levi, and Judah, Issachar, and Zebulun,

2 Dan, Joseph, and Benjamin, Naphtali, Gad, and Asher.

DESCENDANTS OF JUDAH

3 The sons of Judah; Er, and Onan, and Shelah: which three were born unto him of the daughter of Shua the Canaanitess. And Er, the firstborn of Judah, was evil in the sight of the LORD; and he slew him. (*As is obvious here, Judah is dealt with first. In fact, he was to be the chief and ruling Tribe of the twelve, and the Messiah was to come through him [Gen. 49:8-12].*

The evil thing that caused the Lord to slay Er was not recorded either in Genesis, Chapter 38, where this account is given, or elsewhere in Scripture. It could have been the same sin for which God killed Onan, as in Genesis 38:8-10 — that of refusing to have offspring. Incorporated in that, Er was the firstborn of Judah and, thereby, in the lineage of the coming Messiah. The evidence is: he cared not at all for that, and Satan endeavored to use him to stop the Plan of God; therefore, the reason for the actions of the Lord.)

4 And Tamar his daughter in law bore him Pharez and Zerah. All the sons of Judah were five.

5 The sons of Pharez; Hezron, and Hamul (*the line of the Messiah [Isa. 7:14] came through Pharez [Ruth 4:18; Lk. 3:23-38]; the kingly line also came through him [Mat. 1:1-17]*).

6 And the sons of Zerah; Zimri, and Ethan, and Heman, and Calcol, and Dara: five of them in all.

7 And the sons of Carmi; Achar, the troubler of Israel, who transgressed in the thing accursed (*this was Achan of Joshua 7:1*).

8 And the sons of Ethan; Azariah.

9 The sons also of Hezron, that were born unto him; Jerahmeel, and Ram, and Chelubai.

10 And Ram begat Amminadab; and Amminadab begat Nahshon, prince of the Children of Judah;

11 And Nahshon begat Salma, and Salma begat Boaz,

12 And Boaz begat Obed, and Obed begat Jesse,

13 And Jesse begat his firstborn Eliab, and Abinadab the second, and Shimma the third,

14 Nethaneel the fourth, Raddai the fifth,

15 Ozem the sixth, David the seventh (*actually, we know that Jesse, David's father, begat eight sons [I Sam. 16:6-11; 17:12-14]; here, only seven are numbered and named; David was the youngest [I Sam. 16:11], so the eighth may have died while young and without offspring; while it was proper to mention eight sons in the history, it was unnecessary to do so in the genealogy*):

16 Whose sisters were Zeruiah and Abigail. And the sons of Zeruiah; Abishai, and Joab, and Asahel, three (*these three nephews of David played important roles in David's kingdom, especially Joab, who was captain of the host until the death of David*).

17 And Abigail bore Amasa: and the father of Amasa was Jether the Ishmeelite.

18 And Caleb the son of Hezron begat children of Azubah his wife, and of Jerioth: her sons are these; Jesher, and Shobab, and Ardon.

19 And when Azubah was dead, Caleb took unto him Ephrath, which bore him Hur.

20 And Hur begat Uri, and Uri begat Bezaleel.

21 And afterward Hezron went in to the daughter of Machir the father of Gilead, whom he married when he was threescore years old; and she bore him Segub.

22 And Segub begat Jair, who had three and twenty cities in the land of Gilead.

23 And he took Geshur, and Aram, with the towns of Jair, from them with Kenath, and the towns thereof, even threescore cities. All these

belonged to the sons of Machir the father of Gilead.

24 And after that Hezron was dead in Caleb-ephratah, then Abiah Hezron's wife bore him Ashur the father of Tekoa.

25 And the sons of Jerahmeel the firstborn of Hezron were, Ram the firstborn, and Bunah, and Oren, and Ozem, and Ahijah.

26 Jerahmeel had also another wife, whose name was Atarah; she was the mother of Onam.

27 And the sons of Ram the firstborn of Jerahmeel were, Maaz, and Jamin, and Eker.

28 And the sons of Onam were, Shammai, and Jada. And the sons of Shammai; Nadab and Abishur.

29 And the name of the wife of Abishur was Abihail, and she bore him Ahban, and Molid.

30 And the sons of Nadab; Seled, and Appaim: but Seled died without children.

31 And the sons of Appaim; Ishi. And the sons of Ishi; Sheshan. And the children of Sheshan; Ahlai.

32 And the sons of Jada the brother of Shammai; Jether, and Jonathan: and Jether died without children.

33 And the sons of Jonathan; Peleth, and Zaza. These were the sons of Jerahmeel.

34 Now Sheshan had no sons, but daughters. And Sheshan had a servant, an Egyptian, whose name was Jarha.

35 And Sheshan gave his daughter to Jarha his servant to wife; and she bore him Attai.

36 And Attai begat Nathan, and Nathan begat Zabad,

37 And Zabad begat Ephlal, And Ephlal begat Obed,

38 And Obed begat Jehu, and Jehu begat Azariah,

39 And Azariah begat Helez, and Helez begat Eleasah,

40 And Eleasah begat Sisamai, and Sisamai begat Shallum,

41 And Shallum begat Jekamiah, and Jekamiah begat Elishama.

42 Now the sons of Caleb the brother of Jerahmeel were, Mesha his firstborn, which was the father of Ziph; and the sons of Mareshah the father of Hebron.

43 And the sons of Hebron; Korah, and Tappuah, and Rekem, and Shema.

44 And Shema begat Raham, the father of Jorkoam: and Rekem begat Shammai.

45 And the son of Shammai was Maon: and Maon was the father of Beth-zur.

46 And Ephah, Caleb's concubine, bore Haran, and Moza, and Gazez: and Haran begat Gazez.

47 And the sons of Jahdai; Regem, and Jotham, and Gesham, and Pelet, and Ephah, and Shaaph.

48 Maachah, Caleb's concubine, bore Sheber, and Tirhanah.

49 She bore also Shaaph the father of Madmannah, Sheva the father of Machbenah, and the father of Gibea: and the daughter of Caleb was Achsa.

50 These were the sons of Caleb the son of Hur, the firstborn of Ephratah; Shobal the father of Kirjath-jearim,

51 Salma the father of Beth-lehem, Hareph the father of Beth-gader.

52 And Shobal the father of Kirjath-jearim had sons; Haroeh, and half of the Manahethites.

53 And the families of Kirjath-jearim; the Ithrites, and the Puhites, and the Shumathites, and the Mishraites; of them came the Zare-athites, and the Eshtaulites.

54 The sons of Salma; Beth-lehem, and the Netophathites, Ataroth, the house of Joab, and half of the Manahethites, the Zorites.

55 And the families of the scribes which dwelt at Jabez; the Tirathites, the Shimeathites, and Suchathites. These are the Kenites that came of Hemath, the father of the house of Rechab (*the Kenites were the descendants of Jethro, father-in-law of Moses [Judg. 1:16; 4:11-17]; it is unusual that they should be alluded to as the descendants of Judah; this was because they were attached to the tribe of Judah, and had become intermixed with them for so many centuries*).

CHAPTER 3
(1053 B.C.)
DESCENDANTS OF DAVID

NOW these were the sons of David, which were born unto him in Hebron; the first-born Amnon, of Ahinoam the Jezreelitess; the second Daniel, of Abigail the Carmelitess (*the whole of this Chapter is occupied with the descendants of David, because through his family the Messiah would ultimately be born [II Sam., Chpt. 7]*):

2 The third, Absalom the son of Maachah the daughter of Talmai king of Geshur: the fourth, Adonijah the son of Haggith:

3 The fifth, Shephatiah of Abital: the sixth, Ithream by Eglah his wife.

4 These six were born unto him in Hebron; and there he reigned seven years and six months:

and in Jerusalem he reigned thirty and three years *(David reigned over the Tribe of Judah for seven and a half years, and over the entirety of Israel for thirty-three years, making a total of a little bit more than forty years).*

5 And these were born unto him in Jerusalem, Shimea, and Shobab, and Nathan *(this was Mary's family line [Lk. 3:23-38], through which the Messiah would actually come)*, and Solomon *(Joseph, Mary's husband, was of the kingly line through Solomon; so, the lineage of Christ was perfect, as it regards Him being the Son of David, for both Mary and Joseph went back to David in their lineage)*, four, of Bathshua *(Bath-sheba)* the daughter of Ammiel:

6 Ibhar also, and Elishama, and Eliphelet,

7 And Nogah, and Nepheg, and Japhia,

8 And Elishama, and Eliada, and Eliphelet, nine.

9 These were all the sons of David, beside the sons of the concubines, and Tamar their sister.

DESCENDANTS OF SOLOMON

10 And Solomon's son was Rehoboam, Abia his son, Asa his son, Jehoshaphat his son *(there were 21 royal descendants of David through Solomon who occupied the throne of Judah)*,

11 Joram his son, Ahaziah his son, Joash his son,

12 Amaziah his son, Azariah his son, Jotham his son,

13 Ahaz his son, Hezekiah his son, Manasseh his son,

14 Amon his son, Josiah his son.

15 And the sons of Josiah were, the first born Johanan, the second Jehoiakim, the third Zedekiah, the fourth Shallum.

16 And the sons of Jehoiakim: Jeconiah his son, Zedekiah his son.

17 And the sons of Jeconiah; Assir, Salathiel his son, *(He was also called "Jehoiachin" or "Coniah." Though Jehoiachin had eight sons, not one of them, nor any descendant of any one of them, could ever sit on the throne of David and rule in Jerusalem over Israel, for God had cursed him and his seed forever, cutting them off from kingship.*

The next king of Judah was not of his seed; he was an uncle.

All of these kings of Judah led up to the Messiah, and were intended to do so. This is the Incarnation, God becoming Man.

Jesus did not come through the kingly line, yet He had to obtain the throne rights through the kingly line to fulfill the Davidic Covenant regarding an eternal king of David's seed. However, this requirement was totally satisfied in Mary, the virgin mother of the Messiah, who came through Nathan, the son of David, who was not of the kingly line, and in Joseph, who was the legal heir to the throne through Solomon, the son of David.

When Joseph and Mary were married, Jesus, being the firstborn of the family, therefore, became the legal heir to the throne of David. And yet, He did not come through Jehoiachin [Coniah], so that the curse of Jeremiah 22:4-30 was literally fulfilled)

18 Malchiram also, and Pedaiah, and Shenazar, Jecamiah, Hoshama, and Nedabiah.

19 And the sons of Pedaiah were, Zerubbabel, and Shimei: and the sons of Zerubbabel; Meshullam, and Hananiah, and Shelomith their sister:

20 And Hashubah, and Ohel, and Berechiah, and Hasadiah, Jushab-hesed, five.

21 And the sons of Hananiah; Pelatiah, and Jesaiah: the sons of Rephaiah, the sons of Arnan, the sons of Obadiah, the sons of Shechaniah.

22 And the sons of Shechaniah; Shemaiah: and the sons of Shemaiah; Hattush, and Igeal, and Bariah, and Neariah, and Shaphat, six.

23 And the sons of Neariah; Elioenai, and Hezekiah, and Azrikam, three.

24 And the sons of Elioenai were, Hodaiah, and Eliashib, and Pelaiah, and Akkub, and Johanan and Dalaiah, and Anani seven.

CHAPTER 4
(1300 B.C.)
DESCENDANTS OF JUDAH

THE sons of Judah; Pharez, Hezron, and Carmi, and Hur, and Shobal.

2 And Reaiah the son of Shobal begat Jahath; and Jahath begat Ahumai, and Lahad. These are the families of the Zorathites.

3 And these were of the father of Etam; Jezreel, and Ishma, and Idbash: and the name of their sister was Hazelelponi:

4 And Penuel the father of Gedor, and Ezer the father of Hushah. These are the sons of Hur, the firstborn of Ephratah, the father of Beth-lehem.

5 And Ashur the father of Tekoa had two wives, Helah and Naarah.

6 And Naarah bore him Ahuzam, and

Hepher, and Temeni, and Haahashtari. These were the sons of Naarah.

7 And the sons of Helah were, Zereth, and Jezoar, and Ethnan.

8 And Coz begat Anub, and Zobebah, and the families of Aharhel the son of Harum.

9 And Jabez was more honourable than his brethren: and his mother called his name Jabez, saying, Because I bore him with sorrow. *(The Holy Spirit began the notation concerning Jabez by making the statement concerning him being more honorable. The reason was the trust in God and hunger for God which Jabez had.*

In Hebrew culture, the mother, with some few exceptions, always named the child. In that culture, the name was very important. If the Holy Spirit did not impress upon her the name that was to be given, as He sometimes did, she would name the child according to what she wanted him to be, or because of something that had happened in the family that was either a blessing or a curse [especially the boys]. This lady, in naming her little boy "Jabez," which means "he makes sorrow," either did not want him, or else felt she could not properly care for him; therefore, the child, by being given this name, would always be reminded of the negative circumstances of his birth. This severe hindrance could have turned him toward bitterness, which would have destroyed him, or toward God. Jabez allowed it to turn him toward God.

Every difficulty in the life of any person who knows the Lord, irrespective of its severity, can be turned into a blessing. In fact, God specializes in turning the curse into a blessing.)

10 And Jabez called on the God of Israel, saying, Oh that You would bless me indeed *(every Believer should ask the Lord for "the blessing," for God is a Blessing God)*, and enlarge my coast *(give me a greater vision)*, and that Your hand might be with me *(the Hand of God can do anything)*, and that You would keep me from evil, that it may not grieve me! *(This is the last entreaty of the prayer of Jabez, and is the largest and most far-seeing. It referred to "evil" in general but, more than that, it referred to evil which had evidently plagued his family in the past.)* And God granted him that which he requested *(He will do the same for all who will dare to believe Him, exactly as He did for Jabez).*

11 And Chelub the brother of Shuah begat Mehir, which was the father of Eshton.

12 And Eshton begat Beth-rapha, and Paseah, and Tehinnah the father of Ir-nahash. These are the men of Rechah.

13 And the sons of Kenaz; Othniel, and Seraiah: and the son of Othniel; Hathath.

14 And Meonothai begat Ophrah: and Seraiah begat Joab the father of the valley of Charashim; for they were craftsmen.

15 And the sons of Caleb the son of Jephunneh; Iru, Elah, and Naam: and the sons of Elah, even Kenaz.

16 And the sons of Jehaleleel; Ziph, and Ziphah, Tiria, and Asareel.

17 And the sons of Ezra were, Jether, and Mered, and Epher, and Jalon: and she bore Miriam, and Shammai, and Ishbah the father of Eshtemoa.

18 And his wife, Jehudijah bore Jered the father of Gedor, and Heber the father of Socho, and Jekuthiel the father of Zanoah. And these are the sons of Bithiah the daughter of Pharaoh, which Mered took. *(This Passage makes Bithiah, the daughter of Pharaoh, immortal! She was an Egyptian and, as well, the daughter of Pharaoh. She joined the people of God, thereby forsaking Egypt, and, as well, the high state and position she could have occupied in that culture, with the Lord giving her a new name, "Bithiah," which means "the daughter of Jehovah"!*

The proud daughter of the Egyptian monarch degrades herself [in Egypt's eyes] by becoming the wife of a Hebrew slave. No doubt, her name was, therefore, with ignominy, erased from the royal genealogy of Egypt, but — what eternal glory — engraved among the daughters of the royal family of Heaven!)

19 And the sons of his wife Hodiah the sister of Naham, the father of Keilah the Garmite, and Eshtemoa the Maachathite.

20 And the sons of Shimon were, Amnon, the Rinnah, Ben-hanah, and Tilon. And the sons of Ishi were, Zoheth, and Ben-zoheth.

21 The sons of Shelah the son of Judah were, Er the father of Lecah, and Laadah the father of Mareshah, and the families of the house of them that wrought fine linen, of the house of Ashbea,

22 And Jokim, and the men of Chozeba, and Joash, and Saraph, who had the dominion in Moab, and Jashubi-lehem. And these are ancient things.

23 These were the potters, and those that dwelt among plants and hedges: there they dwelt with the king for his work. *(Verses 22-23 may thus read: "Jokim and Saraph, who married in Moab, returned to Beth-lehem." [These records are ancient.]*

These were the potters who dwelt among plants and hedges with the king for his work. Like Ruth and Naomi [Ruth 1:19], they returned from Moab to Beth-lehem and were employed on the royal estate in a very humble position. The Holy Spirit seems to add with exquisite Grace that the work, though lowly, was work "for the king," and they dwelt there "with the king"!

Such is Grace that today points to some hidden ministries, and ennobles them by recording that "they dwell with the king for his work." To be sure, all Work·for the Lord Jesus Christ, irrespective as to what it might be, is of profound significance, even as brought out in these Passages.)

DESCENDANTS OF SIMEON

24 The sons of Simeon were, Nemuel, and Jamin, Jarib, Zerah, and Shaul:

25 Shallum his son, Mibsam his son, Mishma his son.

26 And the sons of Mishma; Hamuel his son, Zacchur his son, Shimei his son.

27 And Shimei had sixteen sons and six daughters; but his brethren had not many children, neither did all their family multiply, like to the Children of Judah.

28 And they dwelt at Beer-sheba, and Moladah, and Hazar-shual,

29 And at Bilhah, and at Ezem, and at Tolad,

30 And at Bethuel, and at Hormah, and at Ziklag,

31 And at Beth-marcaboth and Hazar-susim, and at Beth-birei, and at Shaaraim. These were their cities unto the reign of David.

32 And their villages were, Etam, and Ain, Rimmon, and Tochen, and Ashan, five cities:

33 And all their villages that were round about the same cities, unto Baal. These were their habitations, and their genealogy.

34 And Meshobab, and Jamlech, and Joshah, the son of Amaziah,

35 And Joel, and Jehu the son of Josibiah, the son of Seraiah, the son of Asiel,

36 And Elioenai, and Jaakobah, and Jeshohaiah, and Asaiah, and Adiel, and Jesimiel, and Benaiah,

37 And Ziza the son of Shiphi, the son of Allon, the son of Jedaiah, the son of Shimri, the son of Shemaiah;

38 These mentioned by their names were princes in their families: and the house of their fathers increased greatly.

39 And they went to the entrance of Gedor, even unto the east side of the valley, to seek pasture for their flocks.

40 And they found fat pasture and good, and the land was wide, and quiet, and peaceable; for they of Ham had dwelt there of old.

41 And these written by name came in the days of Hezekiah king of Judah, and smote their tents, and the habitations that were found there, and destroyed them utterly unto this day, and dwelt in their rooms: because there was pasture there for their flocks.

42 And some of them, even of the sons of Simeon, five hundred men, went to mount Seir, having for their captains Pelatiah, and Neariah, and Rephaiah, and Uzziel, the sons of Ishi.

43 And they smote the rest of the Amalekites that were escaped, and dwelt there unto this day.

CHAPTER 5
(1300 B.C.)
DESCENDANTS OF REUBEN

NOW the sons of Reuben the firstborn of Israel, (for he was the firstborn; but, forasmuch as he defiled his father's bed, his birthright was given unto the sons of Joseph the son of Israel *(Jacob)*: and the genealogy is not to be reckoned after the birthright. *(Reuben, being the firstborn of Jacob, should have had the birthright, but he forfeited it due to sin on his part [Gen. 35:22]. This is why his genealogy was not given first. In his place, Judah inherited the kingly rights [Gen. 49:10], and Joseph inherited the other blessings of the birthright [Jesus would be born of the Tribe of Judah].)*

2 For Judah prevailed above his brethren, and of him came the chief ruler; but the birthright was Joseph's *[the "chief ruler" was David and, in him, "David's greater Son and Lord"]*:)

3 The sons, I say, of Reuben the firstborn of Israel were Hanoch, and Pallu, Hezron, and Carmi.

4 The sons of Joel; Shemaiah his son, Gog his son, Shimei his son,

5 Micah his son, Reaia his son, Baal his son,

6 Beerah his son, whom Tilgath-pilneser king of Assyria carried away captive: he was prince of the Reubenites.

7 And his brethren by their families, when the genealogy of their generations was reckoned, were the chief, Jeiel, and Zechariah,

8 And Bela the son of Azaz, the son of Shema, the son of Joel, who dwelt in Aroer, even unto Nebo and Baal-meon:

9 And eastward he inhabited unto the

entering in of the wilderness from the river Euphrates: because their cattle were multiplied in the land of Gilead.

10 And in the days of Saul they made war with the Hagarites, who fell by their hand: and they dwelt in their tents throughout all the east land of Gilead.

DESCENDANTS OF GAD

11 And the children of Gad dwelt over against them, in the land of Bashan unto Salcah:

12 Joel the chief, and Shapham the next, and Jaanai, and Shaphat in Bashan.

13 And their brethren of the house of their father's were, Michael, and Meshullam, and Sheba, and Jorai, and Jachan, and Zia, and Heber, seven.

14 These are the children of Abihail the son of Huri, the son of Jaroah, the son of Gilead, the son of Michael, the son of Jeshishai, the son of Jahdo, the son of Buz;

15 Ahi the son of Abdiel, the son of Guni, chief of the house of their fathers.

16 And they dwelt in Gilead in Bashan, and in her towns, and in all the suburbs of Sharon, upon their borders.

17 All these were reckoned by genealogies in the days of Jotham king of Judah, and in the days of Jeroboam king of Israel.

LEADERS AND ACTIVITIES OF THE TWO-AND-A-HALF TRIBES

18 The sons of Reuben, and the Gadites, and half the Tribe of Manasseh, of valiant men, men able to bear buckler and sword, and to shoot with bow, and skillful in war, were four and forty thousand seven hundred and threescore, that went out to the war.

19 And they made war with the Hagarites, with Jetur, and Naphish, and Nodab.

20 And they were helped against them, and the Hagarites were delivered into their hand, and all that were with them: for they cried to God in the battle, and He was intreated of them; because they put their trust in Him (the simple words, "put their trust in Him," is the key to all victory).

21 And they took away their cattle; of their camels fifty thousand, and of sheep two hundred and fifty thousand, and of asses two thousand, and of men an hundred thousand.

22 For there fell down many slain, because the war was of God. And they dwelt in their steads until the captivity.

23 And the children of the half tribe of Manasseh dwelt in the land: they increased from Bashan unto Baal-hermon and Senir, and unto Mount Hermon.

24 And these were the heads of the house of their fathers, even Epher, and Ishi, and Eliel, and Azriel, and Jeremiah, and Hodaviah, and Jahdiel, mighty men of valour, famous men, and heads of the house of their fathers.

25 And they transgressed against the God of their fathers, and went a whoring after the gods of the people of the land, whom God destroyed before them (Israel went into idolatry).

26 And the God of Israel stirred up the spirit of Pul king of Assyria, and the spirit of Tilgath-pilneser king of Assyria, and he carried them away, even the Reubenites, and the Gadites, and the half tribe of Manasseh, and brought them unto Halah, and Habor, and Hara, and to the river Gozan, unto this day. (The heathen nation of "Assyria" was God's rod of chastisement. As it regards God's people, the methods that God chooses may vary, but it is still God.)

CHAPTER 6
(1280 B.C.)
SONS OF LEVI: THEIR HABITATIONS AND SERVICES

THE sons of Levi; Gershon, Kohath, and Merari (these three sons of Levi represented the three branches of the Levites, who were responsible for various services to the Tabernacle, and then to the Temple).

2 And the sons of Kohath; Amram, Izhar, and Hebron, and Uzziel.

3 And the children of Amram; Aaron, and Moses, and Miriam. The sons also of Aaron; Nadab, and Abihu, Eleazar, and Ithamar.

4 Eleazar begat Phinehas, Phinehas begat Abishua,

5 And Abishua begat Bukki, and Bukki begat Uzzi,

6 And Uzzi begat Zerahiah, and Zerahiah begat Meraioth,

7 Meraioth begat Amariah, and Amariah begat Ahitub,

8 And Ahitub begat Zadok, and Zadok begat Ahimaaz,

9 And Ahimaaz begat Azariah, and Azariah begat Johanan,

10 And Johanan begat Azariah, (he it is that executed the priest's office in the temple that

Solomon built in Jerusalem:)

11 And Azariah begat Amariah, and Amariah begat Ahitub,

12 And Ahitub begat Zadok, and Zadok begat Shallum,

13 And Shallum begat Hilkiah, and Hilkiah begat Azariah,

14 And Azariah begat Seraiah, and Seraiah begat Jehozadak,

15 And Jehozadak went into captivity, when the LORD carried away Judah and Jerusalem by the hand of Nebuchadnezzar.

16 The sons of Levi; Gershom; Kohath, and Merari.

17 And these be the names of the sons of Gershom; Libni, and Shimei.

18 And the sons of Kohath were, Amram, and Izhar, and Hebron, and Uzziel.

19 The sons of Merari; Mahli, and Mushi. And these are the families of the Levites according to their fathers.

20 Of Gershom; Libni his son, Jahath his son, Zimmah his son,

21 Joah his son, Iddo his son, Zerah his son, Jeaterai his son.

22 The sons of Kohath; Amminadab his son, Korah his son, Assir his son,

23 Elkanah his son, and Ebiasaph his son, and Assir his son,

24 Tahath his son, Uriel his son, Uzziah his son, and Shaul his son.

25 And the sons of Elkanah; Amasai, and Ahimoth.

26 As for Elkanah: the sons of Elkanah; Zophai his son, and Nahath his son,

27 Eliab his son, Jeroham his son, Elkanah his son.

28 And the sons of Samuel; the firstborn Vashni, and Abiah.

29 The sons of Merari; Mahli, Libni his son, Shimei his son, Uzza his son,

30 Shimea his son, Haggiah his son, Asaiah his son.

THE MINISTRY OF MUSIC

31 And these are they whom David set over the service of song in the House of the LORD, after that the Ark *(Ark of the Covenant)* had rest *(the great part that music plays in worship, by and large, had its beginning with David and the choirs).*

32 And they ministered before the dwelling place of the Tabernacle of the congregation with singing, until Solomon had built the House of the LORD in Jerusalem: and then they waited on their office according to their order. *(It is said that often, with some saying that it occurred every day, the various choirs, under three lead singers [Heman, Asaph, and Ethan], gathered at the site where the Temple would be built, and ministered in worship and singing. Some even said that this was done each day at the rising of the sun. This greeted Jerusalem at the beginning of each new day with worship and praise unto the Lord. Incidentally, Heman was Samuel's grandson — Verse 33.)*

33 And these are they that waited with their children. Of the sons of the Kohathites: Heman a singer, the son of Joel, the son of Shemuel,

34 The son of Elkanah, the son of Jeroham, the son of Eliel, the son of Toah,

35 The son of Zuph, the son of Elkanah, the son of Mahath, the son of Amasai,

36 The son of Elkanah, the son of Joel, the son of Azariah, the son of Zephaniah,

37 The son of Tahath, the son of Assir, the son of Ebiasaph, the son of Korah,

38 The son of Izhar, the son of Kohath, the son of Levi, the son of Israel.

39 And his brother Asaph, who stood on his right hand, even Asaph the son of Berachiah, the son of Shimea,

40 The son of Michael, the son of Baaseiah, the son of Malchiah,

41 The son of Ethni, the son of Zerah, the son of Adaiah,

42 The son of Ethan, the son of Zimmah, the son of Shimei,

43 The son of Jahath, the son of Gershom, the son of Levi.

44 And their brethren the sons of Merari stood on the left hand: Ethan the son of Kishi, the son of Abdi, the son of Malluch,

45 The son of Hashabiah, the son of Amaziah, the son of Hilkiah,

46 The son of Amzi, the son of Bani, the son of Shamer,

47 The son of Mahli, the son of Mushi, the son of Merari, the son of Levi.

48 Their brethren also the Levites were appointed unto all manner of service of the Tabernacle of the House of God.

DESCENDANTS OF AARON
AND THEIR SERVICES

49 But Aaron and his sons offered upon the

Altar of the Burnt Offering, and on the Altar of Incense, and were appointed for all the work of the place most holy, and to make an atonement for Israel, according to all that Moses the servant of God had commanded. *(Only the Priests were allowed to do this work, not the kings or Prophets, unless they were of the Tribe of Levi. Kings were never of this Tribe, being of the Tribe of Judah, but sometimes a Prophet would also be a Levite. All the Levites, whether Priests or choir directors, etc., came from one of the branches of "Gershon, Kohath, and Merari." The term "Levite" refers to the descendants of Levi.)*

50 And these are the sons of Aaron; Eleazar his son, Phinehas his son, Abishua his son,

51 Bukki his son, Uzzi his son, Zerahiah his son,

52 Meraioth his son, Amariah his son, Ahitub his son,

53 Zadok his son, Ahimaaz his son.

CITIES OF THE LEVITES

54 Now these are their dwelling places throughout their castles in their coasts, of the sons of Aaron, of the families of the Kohathites: for theirs was the lot.

55 And they gave them Hebron in the land of Judah, and the suburbs thereof round about it.

56 But the fields of the city, and the villages thereof, they gave to Caleb the son of Jephunneh.

57 And to the sons of Aaron they gave the cities of Judah, namely, Hebron the city of refuge, and Libnah with her suburbs, and Jattir, and Eshtemoa, with their suburbs,

58 And Hilen with her suburbs, Debir with her suburbs,

59 And Ashan with her suburbs, and Beth-shemesh with her suburbs:

60 And out of the Tribe of Benjamin; Geba with her suburbs, and Alemeth with her suburbs, and Anathoth with her suburbs. All their cities throughout their families were thirteen cities.

61 And unto the sons of Kohath, which were left of the family of that tribe, were cities given out of the half tribe, namely, out of the half tribe of Manasseh, by lot, ten cities.

62 And to the sons of Gershom throughout their families out of the tribe of Issachar, and out of the tribe of Asher, and out of the tribe of Naphtali, and out of the tribe of Manasseh in Bashan, thirteen cities.

63 Unto the sons of Merari were given by lot, throughout their families, out of the tribe of Reuben, and out of the tribe of Gad, and out of the tribe of Zebulun, twelve cities.

64 And the children of Israel gave to the Levites these cities with their suburbs.

65 And they gave by lot out of the tribe of the children of Judah, and out of the tribe of the children of Simeon, and out of the tribe of the children of Benjamin, these cities, which are called by their names.

66 And the residue of the families of the sons of Kohath had cities of their coasts out of the tribe of Ephraim.

67 And they gave unto them, of the cities of refuge, Shechem in mount Ephraim with her suburbs; they gave also Gezer with her suburbs,

68 And Jokmeam with her suburbs, and Beth-horon with her suburbs,

69 And Aijalon with her suburbs, and Gath-rimmon with her suburbs:

70 And out of the half tribe of Manasseh; Aner with her suburbs, and Bileam with her suburbs, for the family of the remnant of the sons of Kohath.

71 Unto the sons of Gershom were given out of the family of the half tribe of Manasseh, Golan in Bashan with her suburbs, and Ashtaroth with her suburbs:

72 And out of the tribe of Issachar; Kedesh with her suburbs, Daberath with her suburbs,

73 And Ramoth with her suburbs, and Anem with her suburbs:

74 And out of the tribe of Asher; Mashal with her suburbs, and Abdon with her suburbs,

75 And Hukok with her suburbs, and Rehob with her suburbs:

76 And out of the tribe of Naphtali; Kedesh in Galilee with her suburbs, and Hammon with her suburbs, and Kirjathaim with her suburbs.

77 Unto the rest of the children of Merari were given out of the tribe of Zebulun, Rimmon with her suburbs, Tabor with her suburbs:

78 And on the other side Jordan by Jericho, on the east side of Jordan, were given them out of the tribe of Reuben, Bezer in the wilderness with her suburbs, and Jahzah with her suburbs,

79 Kedemoth also with her suburbs, and Mephaath with her suburbs:

80 And out of the tribe of Gad; Ramoth in Gilead with her suburbs, and Mahanaim with her suburbs,

81 And Heshbon with her suburbs, and Jazer with her suburbs.

CHAPTER 7
(1400 B.C.)
DESCENDANTS OF ISSACHAR

NOW the sons of Issachar were, Tola, and Puah, Jashub, and Shimrom, four.

2 And the sons of Tola; Uzzi, and Rephaiah, and Jeriel, and Jahmai, and Jibsam, and Shemuel, heads of their father's house, to wit, of Tola: they were valiant men of might in their generations; whose number was in the days of David two and twenty thousand and six hundred.

3 And the sons of Uzzi; Izrahiah: and the sons of Izrahiah; Michael, and Obadiah, and Joel, Ishiah, five: all of them chief men.

4 And with them, by their generations, after the house of their fathers, were bands of soldiers for war, six and thirty thousand men: for they had many wives and sons.

5 And their brethren among all the families of Issachar were valiant men of might, reckoned in all by their genealogies fourscore and seven thousand.

DESCENDANTS OF BENJAMIN

6 The sons of Benjamin; Bela, and Becher, and Jediael, three.

7 And the sons of Bela; Ezbon, and Uzzi, and Uzziel, and Jerimoth, and Iri, five; heads of the house of their fathers, mighty men of valour; and were reckoned by their genealogies twenty and two thousand and thirty and four.

8 And the sons of Becher; Zemira, and Joash, and Eliezer, and Elioenai, and Omri, and Jerimoth, and Abiah, and Anathoth, and Alameth. All these are the sons of Becher.

9 And the number of them, after their genealogy by their generations, heads of the house of their fathers, mighty men of valour, was twenty thousand and two hundred.

10 The sons also of Jediael; Bilhan: and the sons of Bilhan; Jeush, and Benjamin, and Ehud, and Chenaanah, and Zethan, and Tharshish, and Ahishahar.

11 All these the sons of Jediael, by the heads of their fathers, mighty men of valour, were seventeen thousand and two hundred soldiers, fit to go out for war and battle.

12 Shuppim also, and Huppim, the children of Ir, and Hushim, the sons of Aher.

DESCENDANTS OF NAPHTALI

13 The sons of Naphtali; Jahziel, and Guni, and Jezer, and Shallum, the sons of Bilhah.

DESCENDANTS OF MANASSEH

14 The sons of Manasseh; Ashriel, whom she bore: (but his concubine the Aramitess bore Machir the father of Gilead:

15 And Machir took to wife the sister of Huppim and Shuppim, whose sister's name was Maachah;) and the name of the second was Zelophehad: and Zelophehad had daughters. *(Once again, this man is mentioned, with his fame being derived from the faith of his daughters [Num. 26:33]. God always honors Faith. Tragically, doubt never dies, unless washed by the Blood of Jesus; and, gloriously, Faith never dies, but extends its influence forever.)*

16 And Maachah the wife of Machir bore a son, and she called his name Peresh; and the name of his brother was Sheresh; and his sons were Ulam and Rakem.

17 And the sons of Ulam; Bedan. These were the sons of Gilead, the son of Machir, the son of Manasseh.

18 And his sister Hammoleketh bore Ishod, and Abiezer, and Mahalah.

19 And the sons of Shemidah were Ahian, and Shechem, and Likhi, and Aniam.

DESCENDANTS OF EPHRAIM

20 And the sons of Ephraim; Shuthelah, and Bered his son, and Tahath his son, and Eladah his son, and Tahath his son,

21 And Zabad his son, and Shuthelah his son, and Ezer, and Elead, whom the men of Gath that were born in that land slew, because they came down to take away their cattle.

22 And Ephraim their father mourned many days, and his brethren came to comfort him.

23 And when he went in to his wife, she conceived, and bore a son, and he called his name Beriah, because it went evil with his house.

24 (And his daughter was Sherah, who built Beth-horon the nether, and the upper, and Uzzen-sherah.)

25 And Rephah was his son, also Resheph, and Telah his son, and Tahan his son,

26 Laadan his son, Ammihud his son, Elishama his son,

27 Non his son, Jehoshuah his son.

28 And their possessions and habitations

were, Beth-el and the towns thereof, and eastward Naaran, and westward Gezer, with the towns thereof; Shechem also and the towns thereof:

29 And by the borders of the children of Manasseh, Beth-shean and her towns, Taanach and her towns, Megiddo and her towns, Dor and her towns. In these dwelt the children of Joseph the son of Israel.

DESCENDANTS OF ASHER

30 The sons of Asher; Imnah, and Isuah, and Ishuai, and Beriah, and Serah their sister.

31 And the sons of Beriah; Heber, and Malchiel, who is the father of Birzavith.

32 And Heber begat Japhlet, and Shomer, and Hotham, and Shua their sister.

33 And the sons of Japhlet; Pasach, and Bimhal, and Ashvath. These are the children of Japhlet.

34 And the sons of Shamer; Ahi, and Rohgah, Jehubbah, and Aram.

35 And the sons of his brother Helem; Zophah, and Imna, and Shelesh, and Amal.

36 The sons of Zophah; Suah, and Harnepher, and Shual, and Beri, and Imrah,

37 Bezer, and Hod, and Shamma, and Shilshah, and Ithran, and Beera.

38 And the sons of Jether; Jephunneh, and Pispah, and Ara.

39 And the sons of Ulla; Arah, and Haniel, and Rezia.

40 All these were the children of Asher, heads of their father's house, choice and mighty men of valour, chief of the princes. And the number throughout the genealogy of them that were apt to the war and to battle was twenty and six thousand men. *(Quite often in the Text, the Writer refers to some of the men of Israel being "choice and mighty men of valor," etc. The might and glory of Israel, when they were actually serving God, are almost beyond our comprehension. Regrettably, through sin, it was all lost!*

However, one day the glory of Israel will be re-established. It will be at the Coming of the Lord [Rom. 11:12].)

CHAPTER 8
(1400 B.C.)
DESCENDANTS OF BENJAMIN

NOW Benjamin begat Bela his firstborn, Ashbel the second, and Aharah the third, 2 Nohah the fourth, and Rapha the fifth.

3 And the sons of Bela were, Addar, and Gera, and Abihud,

4 And Abishua, and Naaman, and Ahoah,

5 And Gera, and Shephuphan, and Huram.

6 And these are the sons of Ehud: these are the heads of the fathers of the inhabitants of Geba, and they removed them to Manahath:

7 And Naaman, and Ahiah, and Gera, he removed them, and begat Uzza, and Ahihud.

8 And Shaharaim begat children in the country of Moab, after he had sent them away; Hushim and Baara were his wives.

9 And he begat of Hodesh his wife, Jobab, and Zibia, and Mesha, and Malcham,

10 And Jeuz, and Shachia, and Mirma. These were his sons, heads of the fathers.

11 And of Hushim he begat Abitub, and Elpaal.

12 The sons of Elpaal; Eber, and Misham, and Shamed, who built Ono, and Lod, with the towns thereof:

13 Beriah also, and Shema, who were heads of the fathers of the inhabitants of Aijalon, who drove away the inhabitants of Gath:

14 And Ahio, Shashak, and Jeremoth,

15 And Zebadiah, and Arad, and Ader,

16 And Michael, and Ispah, and Joha, the sons of Beriah;

17 And Zebadiah, and Meshullam, and Hezeki, and Heber,

18 Ishmerai also, and Jezliah, and Jobab, the sons of Elpaal;

19 And Jakim, and Zichri, and Zabdi,

20 And Elienai, and Zilthai, and Eliel,

21 And Adaiah, and Beraiah, and Shimrath, and sons of Shimhi;

22 And Ishpan, and Heber, and Eliel,

23 And Abdon, and Zichri, and Hanan,

24 And Hananiah, and Elam, and Antothijah,

25 And Iphedeiah, and Penuel, the sons of Shashak;

26 And Shamsherai, and Shehariah, and Athaliah,

27 And Jaresiah, and Eliah, and Zichri, the sons of Jeroham.

28 These were heads of the fathers, by their generations, chief men. These dwelt in Jerusalem. *(This proves that the Tribe of Benjamin adhered to the worship of the True God and remained loyal to Judah. As well, it seems that Simeon, whose inheritance was within the inheritance of Judah, had remained loyal also. We speak of the division of the kingdom, with Judah being the southern kingdom, and Israel the northern kingdom.)*

29 And at Gibeon dwelt the father of Gibeon; whose wife's name was Maachah:

30 And his firstborn son Abdon, and Zur, and Kish, and Baal, and Nadab,

31 And Gedor, and Ahio, and Zacher.

32 And Mikloth begat Shimeah. And these also dwelt with their brethren in Jerusalem, over against them.

DESCENDANTS OF SAUL

33 And Ner begat Kish, and Kish begat Saul, and Saul begat Jonathan, and Malchi-shua, and Abinadab, and Esh-baal.

34 And the son of Jonathan was Merib-baal; and Merib-baal begat Micah.

35 And the sons of Micah were Pithon, and Melech, and Tarea, and Ahaz.

36 And Ahaz begat Jehoadah; and Jehoadah begat Alemeth, and Azmaveth, and Zimri; and Zimri begat Moza,

37 And Moza begat Binea: Rapha was his son, Eleasah his son, Azel his son:

38 And Azel had six sons, whose names are these, Azrikam, Bocheru, and Ishmael, and Sheariah, and Obadiah, and Hanan. All these were the sons of Azel.

39 And the sons of Eshek his brother were, Ulam his firstborn, Jehush the second, and Eliphelet the third.

40 And the sons of Ulam were mighty men of valour, archers, and had many sons, and sons' sons, an hundred and fifty. All these are of the sons of Benjamin.

CHAPTER 9
(1200 B.C.)
SUMMARY OF THE GENEALOGIES OF THOSE RETURNING FROM BABYLONIAN CAPTIVITY

S O all Israel were reckoned by genealogies; and, behold, they were written in the book of the kings of Israel and Judah, who were carried away to Babylon for their transgression. *(This is a book which we do not now have, but which, no doubt, contained a complete record of the genealogies of every family in Israel. From this, the Author of Chronicles took only a part to serve His purpose of identifying certain key men in the history of the nation, by giving their background, so that something could be known of the coming Messiah's ancestors. During the time of Christ, the genealogy of every Tribe, and also of every family in Israel,* *was kept in the Temple. This was very important for several reasons:*

1. Each family in Israel could trace their ancestry all the way back to Abraham.

2. Each family could know to which Tribe they belonged.

3. As well, Israel knew that the Messiah was to come through the Tribe of Judah [Gen. 49:10], and that, if the kingly line of David from the Tribe of Judah had continued, Jesus would now be the king of Israel. So, there was no excuse for Israel not to know His identity.)

2 Now the first inhabitants who dwelt in their possessions in their cities were, the Israelites, the Priests, Levites, and the Nethinims. *(It is believed that the "Nethinims" were the descendants of the Gibeonites who deceived Joshua at the beginning of the occupation of Canaan, and who were made "hewers of wood and drawers of water unto all the congregation" [Josh. 9:21]. This referred to wood and water for the sacrifices at the Tabernacle, and then the Temple.)*

3 And in Jerusalem dwelt of the children of Judah, and of the children of Benjamin, and of the children of Ephraim, and Manasseh *(the children of the two Tribes of Ephraim and Manasseh were representative of the ten Tribes, for the northern ten-Tribe kingdom was often called "Ephraim");*

4 Uthai the son of Ammihud, the son of Omri, the son of Imri, the son of Omri, the son of Imri, the son of Bani, of the children of Pharez the son of Judah.

5 And of the Shilonites; Asaiah the firstborn, and his sons.

6 And of the sons of Zerah; Jeuel, and their brethren, six hundred and ninety.

7 And of the sons of Benjamin; Sallu the son of Meshullam, the son of Hodaviah, the son of Hasenuah,

8 And Ibneiah the son of Jeroham, and Elah the son of Uzzi, the son of Michri, and Meshullam the son of Shephathiah, the son of Reuel, the son of Ibnijah;

9 And their brethren, according to their generations, nine hundred and fifty and six. All these men were chief of the fathers in the house of their fathers.

PRIESTS AND LEVITES RETURNING FROM BABYLON

10 And of the priests; Jedaiah, and Jehoiarib, and Jachin,

11 And Azariah the son of Hilkiah, the son

of Meshullam, the son of Zadok, the son of Meraioth, the son of Ahitub, the ruler of the House of God;

12 And Adaiah the son of Jeroham, the son of Pashur, the son of Malchijah, and Maasiai the son of Adiel, the son of Jahzerah, the son of Meshullam, the son of Meshillemith, the son of Immer;

13 And their brethren, heads of the house of their fathers, a thousand and seven hundred and threescore; very able men for the work of the service of the House of God.

14 And of the Levites; Shemaiah the son of Hasshub, the son of Azrikam, the son of Hashabiah, of the sons of Merari;

15 And Bakbakkar, Heresh, and Galal, and Mattaniah the son of Micah, the son of Zichri, the son of Asaph;

16 And Obadiah the son of Shemaiah, the son of Galal, the son of Jeduthun, and Berechiah the son of Asa, the son of Elkanah, that dwelt in the villages of the Netophathites.

17 And the porters were Shallum, and Akkub, and Talmon, and Ahiman, and their brethren: Shallum was the chief;

18 Who hitherto waited in the king's gate eastward: they were porters in the companies of the children of Levi.

19 And Shallum the son of Kore, the son of Ebiasaph, the son of Korah, and his brethren, of the house of his father, the Korahites, were over the work of the service, keepers of the gates of the Tabernacle: and their fathers, being over the host of the LORD, were keepers of the entry.

20 And Phinehas the son of Eleazar was the ruler over them in time past, and the LORD was with him.

21 And Zechariah the son of Meshelemiah was porter of the door of the Tabernacle of the congregation.

22 All these which were chosen to be porters in the gates were two hundred and twelve. These were reckoned by their genealogy in their villages, whom David and Samuel the seer did ordain in their set office. *(Here we have proof that Samuel and David counseled together and received revelations of the coming Temple worship.)*

23 So they and their children had the oversight of the gates of the House of the LORD, namely, the House of the Tabernacle, by wards.

24 In four quarters were the porters, toward the east, west, north, and south.

25 And their brethren, which were in their villages, were to come after seven days from time to time with them.

26 For these Levites, the four chief porters, were in their set office, and were over the chambers and treasuries of the House of God.

27 And they lodged round about the House of God, because the charge was upon them, and the opening thereof every morning pertained to them.

28 And certain of them had the charge of the ministering vessels, that they should bring them in and out by tale.

29 Some of them also were appointed to oversee the vessels, and all the instruments of the sanctuary, and the fine flour, and the wine, and the oil, and the frankincense, and the spices.

30 And some of the sons of the priests made the ointment of the spices.

31 And Mattithiah, one of the Levites, who was the firstborn of Shallum the Korahite, had the set office over the things that were made in the pans.

32 And other of their brethren, of the sons of the Kohathites, were over the shewbread, to prepare it every sabbath.

33 And these are the singers, chief of the fathers of the Levites, who remaining in the chambers were free: for they were employed in that work day and night. *(This refers to the re-building of the Temple and Jerusalem after the captivity in Babylon. It seems that, at this time, great efforts were being made to carry on the worship of God as it had been instituted by David about 500 years before.)*

34 These chief fathers of the Levites were chief throughout their generations; these dwelt at Jerusalem.

SAUL'S DESCENDANTS

35 And in Gibeon dwelt the father of Gibeon, Jehiel, whose wife's name was Maachah:

36 And his firstborn son Abdon, then Zur, and Kish, and Baal, and Ner, and Nadab,

37 And Gedor, and Ahio, and Zechariah, and Mikloth.

38 And Mikloth begat Shimeam. And they also dwelt with their brethren at Jerusalem, over against their brethren.

39 And Ner begat Kish; and Kish begat Saul; and Saul begat Jonathan, and Malchi-shua, and Abinadab, and Esh-baal.

40 And the son of Jonathan was Merib-baal: and Merib-baal begat Micah.

41 And the sons of Micah were Pithon, and Melech, and Tahrea, and Ahaz.

42 And Ahaz begat Jarah; and Jarah begat Alemeth, and Azmaveth, and Zimri; and Zimri begat Moza;

43 And Moza begat Binea; and Rephaiah his son, Eleasah his son, Azel his son.

44 And Azel had six sons, whose names are these, Azrikam, Bocheru, and Ishmael, and Sheariah, and Obadiah, and Hanan: these were the sons of Azel.

CHAPTER 10
(1056 B.C.)
THE DEATH OF SAUL AND HIS SONS

NOW the Philistines fought against Israel; and the men of Israel fled from before the Philistines, and fell down slain in Mount Gilboa. *(The Holy Spirit, in the last ten Verses of the Ninth Chapter, recites the pedigree of King Saul, and then, in Chapter 10, repeats the circumstances of that monarch's death, which thus presents an introduction to the kingdom of David.)*

2 And the Philistines followed hard after Saul, and after his sons; and the Philistines slew Jonathan, and Abinadab, and Malchi-shua, the sons of Saul. *(These were the ones who accompanied him into the battle. There were other sons who stayed at home, and did not die. The Holy Spirit places Jonathan's name first. Of all of these, Jonathan was the only one who was Godly, at least that is known.)*

3 And the battle went sore against Saul, and the archers hit him, and he was wounded of the archers.

4 Then said Saul to his armourbearer, Draw your sword, and thrust me through therewith; lest these uncircumcised come and abuse me. But his armourbearer would not; for he was sore afraid. So Saul took a sword, and fell upon it. *(He committed suicide! He started so well, and concluded so poorly. He failed to defeat the enemies within, which were self-will, jealousy, and pride; therefore, the enemy without, "the Philistines," ultimately defeated him. This should be a lesson to us!)*

5 And when his armourbearer saw that Saul was dead, he fell likewise on the sword, and died.

6 So Saul died, and his three sons, and all his house died together.

7 And when all the men of Israel that were in the valley saw that they fled, and that Saul and his sons were dead, then they forsook their cities, and fled: and the Philistines came and dwelt in them. *(That which the Lord gave to Israel is now occupied by the Philistines. It is the same with us presently. Satan desires to inhabit that which God has given us; therefore, the battle ever rages, with the enemy trying to mar our inheritance.)*

8 And it came to pass on the morrow, when the Philistines came to strip the slain, that they found Saul and his sons fallen in Mount Gilboa. *(The evidence is obvious that Satan wants the last drop of blood. There can be no compromise with the evil one. We destroy him or he destroys us.)*

9 And when they had stripped him, they took his head, and his armour, and sent into the land of the Philistines round about, to carry tidings unto their idols, and to the people. *(It was customary to take the heads of conquered kings and make sport with them in the houses of the gods, and in the cities of their own people. But this was a tragedy, because these were God's people who were being so maltreated.)*

10 And they put his armour in the house of their gods, and fastened his head in the temple of Dagon *(thereby giving their gods credit for this victory).*

11 And when all Jabesh-gilead heard all that the Philistines had done to Saul,

12 They arose, all the valiant men, and took away the body of Saul, and the bodies of his sons, and brought them to Jabesh, and buried their bones under the oak in Jabesh, and fasted seven days. *(I Sam., Chpt. 31 records the fact of Saul's death. I Chron., Chpt. 10 records the reason. Men could see the outward historic event, but only the Spirit of God could reveal the cause of this event. The next Verse tells us the cause.)*

13 So Saul died for his transgression which he committed against the LORD, even against the Word of the LORD, which he kept not, and also for asking counsel of one who had a familiar spirit, to enquire of it;

14 And enquired not of the LORD: therefore he slew him, and turned the kingdom unto David the son of Jesse. *(In fact, Saul did enquire of the Lord [I Sam. 28:6]; however, it was an enquiry with no thought in mind of truly repenting. Had Saul truly repented at that time, the Lord definitely would have heard him and helped him. But man seems determined to insist upon his stubbornness and rebellion, even to his own death.)*

CHAPTER 11
(1047 B.C.)

DAVID MADE KING OVER ALL ISRAEL

THEN all Israel gathered themselves to David unto Hebron, saying, Behold, we are your bone and your flesh.

2 And moreover in time past, even when Saul was king, you were he that led out and brought in Israel: and the LORD your God said unto you, You shall feed My people Israel, and you shall be ruler over My people Israel. *(It was the Will of God that David be the first king of Israel, and not Saul. It is just as wrong to get ahead of God as it is to lag behind. Regrettably, Israel, despite the problems with Saul, and even though they knew that David had been anointed by the Lord to be king over Israel, did not, in fact, make him king until it was in their best interest to do so. Very few Believers will carry out the Will of God, if they erroneously feel that it's not in their best interests. The truth is, the Will of God, no matter what the circumstances may seem to be, is always the far better place for the Believer to be. There is no loss by abiding by the Will of God, and great loss by not doing so.)*

3 Therefore came all the elders of Israel to the king to Hebron; and David made a covenant with them in Hebron before the LORD; and they anointed David king over Israel, according to the Word of the LORD by Samuel. *(One can literally sense the Presence of God, even reading these words. It had taken some time, and much suffering and sorrow, but Israel has finally come around to God's Way.*

Thus David, the commanding figure of the First Book of Chronicles, is introduced. He is a Type of his greater Son, the Lord Jesus Christ. Characteristically, the first event of the Book is the deliverance of Jerusalem from the Jebusites, and David's ascension to the Throne of Jehovah on Zion. Such will be the action of Israel's great King in a future happy day.)

DAVID CAPTURES ZION

4 And David and all Israel went to Jerusalem, which is Jebus; where the Jebusites were, the inhabitants of the land. *(As a type, the Jebusites symbolize a stronghold that Satan erects within our hearts and lives. Saul never did defeat the Jebusites, who were within; consequently, the Philistines, who were without, eventually defeated him. Likewise, if we do not defeat the strongholds that are within our lives, strongholds of Satan, those without will ultimately overcome us. In connection with this, Paul said: "For the weapons of our warfare are not carnal, but mighty through God to the pulling down of strongholds" [II Cor. 10:4]. This is done, as it only can be done, by the Believer placing his Faith exclusively in Christ and what Christ has done for us at the Cross. That being the case, the Holy Spirit will then mightily help us, without Whom these great battles cannot be won [Rom. 8:1-2, 11].)*

5 And the inhabitants of Jebus said to David, You shall not come hither. Nevertheless David took the castle of Zion, which is the city of David. *(Satan will ever taunt us, declaring that since he has established this stronghold for so long, he cannot be dislodged. Through Christ and the Cross, every stronghold of Satan can be dislodged! [I Cor. 1:17-18].)*

6 And David said, Whosoever smites the Jebusites first shall be chief and captain. So Joab the son of Zeruiah went first up, and was chief *(thereby, became the Commander of the army of Israel).*

7 And David dwelt in the castle; therefore they called it the city of David *(the reason that Satan attempts to erect strongholds in our lives is because he knows that God intends for this to our strong point; so David, by the help of the Lord, took this, which had been inhabited by the enemy, and made it his Capital, i.e., "the city of David").*

8 And he built the city round about, even from Millo round about: and Joab repaired the rest of the city *(rid it of all enemies, that it might be a fit place for the Capital).*

9 So David waxed greater and greater: for the LORD of hosts was with him *(the victories were all tied to the Lord, as all victories are always tied to the Lord, and only to the Lord).*

DAVID'S MIGHTY MEN

10 These also are the chief of the mighty men whom David had, who strengthened themselves with him in his kingdom, and with all Israel, to make him king, according to the Word of the LORD concerning Israel. *(These men were "mighty" only because they came under the anointing of David, whom God had called for a particular task — to be the King of Israel. In fact, there would have been no "might," had they not functioned under David's anointing.*

To be sure, they had an anointing all of their

own, but it was predicated on them being in the Will of God, as it regarded David. Regrettably, far too many Christians don't understand this.

As a Believer, you should seek the Lord ardently about whom you are to follow, as it regards Preachers. If you guess wrong, or follow after the flesh, it will prove to be destructive. If you find the Mind of God, and it's not hard to find, He will lead you to that which you should follow, and then the anointing that's on that particular Ministry will also, in some way, the way God wants, be on you, as well.)

11 And this is the number of the mighty men whom David had; Jashobeam, an Hachmonite, the chief of the captains: he lifted up his spear against three hundred slain by him at one time *(I think it should be obvious that this man had to have the anointing of the Holy Spirit to perform such a mighty deed against God's enemies; however, had he and all the others not followed David, they would have never been used by God in any capacity).*

12 And after him was Eleazar the son of Dodo, the Ahohite, who was one of the three mighties *(also, it must ever be understood that God places His anointing only upon a man or a woman; he does not anoint denominations, church officials [just because they are church officials], committees, boards, or groups; there definitely may be individuals occupying these particular positions who are definitely called of God and perform a mighty service, but it's not because of that position).*

13 He was with David at Pas-dammim, and there the Philistines were gathered together to battle, where was a parcel of ground full of barley; and the people fled from before the Philistines. *(Barley, being the least of all the grains, many, perhaps, would have thought it not worthy to defend; however, God desires that Satan be rooted out of every part of our inheritance, no matter how seemingly insignificant. The reason? Little matters quickly grow into large matters!)*

14 And they set themselves in the midst of that parcel, and delivered it, and slew the Philistines; and the LORD saved them by a great deliverance. *(The people of God labored intensely to plant and cultivate these crops. And when they were ready to be harvested, the Philistines would swoop down and take what rightly belonged to Israel. This is a perfect example of what Satan attempts to do to the Believer. He attempts to rob you of your inheritance, and will do so, if you do not know how to properly follow the Lord, which*

is always by having Faith in Christ and the Cross, which then gives the Holy Spirit power to work on our behalf. To be sure, the Holy Spirit, Who is God, can do anything. But He is hindered so much of the time, simply because we are not following the Word of God, in effect, serving "another Jesus," which the Holy Spirit can never recognize. This refers to the fact that we are serving Christ, or claiming to do so, while eliminating the Cross, or ignoring it. If the Cross is ignored, then, pure and simple, we are serving "another Jesus," whom God can never recognize [Rom. 6:3-14; 8:1-2, 11; I Cor. 1:17-18, 21, 23; 2:2; Gal. 6:14; Col. 2:14-15].)*

15 Now three of the thirty captains went down to the rock to David, into the cave of Adullam; and the host of the Philistines encamped in the valley of Rephaim *(the valley of the Giants).*

16 And David was then in the hold, and the Philistines' garrison was then at Beth-lehem.

17 And David longed, and said, Oh that one would give me drink of the water of the well of Beth-lehem, that is at the gate!

18 And the three *(Vs. 15)* broke through the host of the Philistines, and drew water out of the well of Beth-lehem, that was by the gate, and took it, and brought it to David: but David would not drink of it, but poured it out to the LORD. *(Beth-lehem was where Jesus was born. The water being poured out by David was symbolic of Christ pouring out His Life on the Cross of Calvary, which guaranteed Salvation for all of mankind, at least all who will believe [Jn. 3:16]. How much David understood of this, we do not know; however, he probably understood far more than we presently realize.)*

19 And said, My God forbid it me, that I should do this thing: shall I drink the blood of these men who have put their lives in jeopardy? for with the jeopardy of their lives they brought it. Therefore he would not drink it. These things did these three mightiest. *(This means that the Sacrifice of Christ at Calvary's Cross is to never be used for personal aggrandizement, but always for what it was intended, which is the Salvation of souls, gained only by Christ pouring out His Life.*

This is, at least in part, what makes the "Word of Faith" doctrine, so-called, so wrong and false. It attempts to use Christ for personal gain, i.e., "riches." While it is certainly true that God does bless, and bless abundantly, He does so only on the basis of our Faith exclusively being in Christ and the Cross. The truth is, in that particular

false doctrine, the only ones getting rich are the Preachers, and that by subterfuge, and the perversion of Scripture.)

20 And Abishai the brother of Joab, he was chief of the three: for lifting up his spear against three hundred, he slew them, and had a name among the three.

21 Of the three, he was more honourable than the two; for he was their captain: howbeit he attained not to the first three *(nowhere in the world were there men like these, and all because of the anointing of the Holy Spirit which was upon them).*

22 Benaiah the son of Jehoiada, the son of a valiant man of Kabzeel, who had done many acts; he slew two lionlike men of Moab: also he went down and slew a lion in a pit in a snowy day.

23 And he slew an Egyptian, a man of great stature, five cubits high *(seven and a half feet)*; and in the Egyptian's hand was a spear like a weaver's beam; and he went down to him with a staff, and plucked the spear out of the Egyptian's hand, and slew him with his own spear *(once again, the anointing of the Spirit).*

24 These things did Benaiah the son of Jehoiada, and had the name among the three mighties. *(For time and eternity, their names are forever inscribed in the Word of God. What an honor! What a privilege! There is not one single Believer in the world today who cannot, in God's Way, attain to the same energy of power, if they will only truly follow the Lord.)*

25 Behold, he was honourable among the thirty, but attained not to the first three: and David set him over his guard. *(There is a great spiritual meaning here. Demon spirits, of which the defeated represent, will attempt to destroy the Child of God. We must "guard" ourselves from their encroachment, as "Benaiah did." In the "Name of Jesus," it can be done, and only in that mighty Name!)*

MORE MIGHTY MEN

26 Also the valiant men of the armies were, Asahel the brother of Joab, Elhanan the son of Dodo of Beth-lehem,

27 Shammoth the Harorite, Helez the Pelonite,

28 Ira the son of Ikkesh the Tekoite, Abiezer the Antothite,

29 Sibbecai the Hushathite, Ilai the Ahohite,

30 Maharai the Netophathite, Heled the son of Baanah the Netophathite,

31 Ithai the son of Ribai of Gibeah, that pertained to the children of Benjamin, Benaiah the Pirathonite,

32 Hurai of the brooks of Gaash, Abiel the Arbathite,

33 Azmaveth the Baharumite, Eliahba the Shaalbonite,

34 The sons of Hashem the Gizonite, Jonathan the son of Shage the Harorite,

35 Ahiam the son of Sacar the Harorite, Eliphal the son of Ur,

36 Hepher the Mecherathite, Ahijah the Pelonite,

37 Hezro the Carmelite, Naarai the son of Ezbai,

38 Joel the brother of Nathan, Mibhar the son of Haggeri,

39 Zelek the Ammonite, Naharai the Berothite, the armourbearer of Joab the son of Zeruiah,

40 Ira the Ithrite, Gareb the Ithrite,

41 Uriah the Hittite *(likewise, Uriah was listed in II Sam., Chpt. 23, although dead; an exception in listing him, even though dead, perhaps, was because of the connection with David, as the husband of the woman with whom David sinned; how tragic!),* Zabad the son of Ahlai,

42 Adina the son of Shiza the Reubenite, a captain of the Reubenites, and thirty with him,

43 Hanan the son of Maachah, and Joshaphat the Mithnite,

44 Uzzia the Ashterathite, Shama and Jehiel the sons of Hothan the Aroerite,

45 Jediael the son of Shimri, and Joha his brother, the Tizite,

46 Eliel the Mahavite, and Jeribai, and Joshaviah, the sons of Elnaam, and Ithmah the Moabite,

47 Eliel, and Obed, and Jasiel the Mesobaite.

CHAPTER 12
(1058 B.C.)

THE ARMY OF DAVID

NOW these are they who came to David to Ziklag, while he yet kept himself close because of Saul the son of Kish: and they were among the mighty men, helpers of the war. *(This is a glorious Chapter, as Israel finally begins to do God's Will. It begins with David's darkest days. It closes with unimaginable victory. The present need is "helpers of the war," for we are engaged in a war [II Cor. 10:3; I Tim. 1:18, 6:12; I Pet. 2:11]. However, this war must be fought God's Way, and it is a*

war of Faith, and that exclusively!)

2 They were armed with bows, and could use both the right hand and the left in hurling stones and shooting arrows out of a bow, even of Saul's brethren of Benjamin. *(Even though these were Benjamites, and consequently from Saul's Tribe, still, they knew the anointing of God rested on David, and not on Saul. How much faith did it take for these men to forsake Saul and come to David? How much faith does it take today for men to forsake man's religion and come to David, even though he is a fugitive, but has the Anointing of the Holy Spirit?)*

3 The chief was Ahiezer, then Joash, the sons of Shemaah the Gibeathite; and Jeziel, and Pelet, the sons of Azmaveth; and Berachah, and Jehu the Antothite.

4 And Ismaiah the Gibeonite, a mighty man among the thirty, and over the thirty; and Jeremiah, and Jahaziel, and Johanan, and Josabad the Gederathite,

5 Eluzai, and Jerimoth, and Bealiah, and Shemariah, and Shephatiah the Haruphite,

6 Elkanah, and Jesiah, and Azareel, and Joezer, and Jashobeam, the Korhites,

7 And Joelah, and Zebadiah the sons of Jeroham of Gedor.

8 And of the Gadites there separated themselves unto David into the hold to the wilderness men of might, and men of war fit for the battle, that could handle shield and buckler, whose faces were like the faces of lions, and were as swift as the roes *(deer)* upon the mountains *(in the spirit world, these men were so anointed by the Holy Spirit that their faces looked like "lions," and their swiftness was as "deer"; what do we look like to the spirit world?);*

9 Ezer the first, Obadiah the second, Eliab the third,

10 Mishmannah the fourth, Jeremiah the fifth,

11 Attai the sixth, Eliel the seventh,

12 Johanan the eighth, Elzabad the ninth,

13 Jeremiah the tenth, Machbanai the eleventh.

14 These were of the sons of Gad, captains of the host: one of the least was over an hundred, and the greatest over a thousand.

15 These are they who went over Jordan in the first month, when it had overflown all his banks; and they put to flight all them of the valleys, both toward the east, and toward the west. *(The Bible says, back up in the Eighth Verse, that the "Gadites [from the Tribe of Gad] there separated themselves unto David." There*

has to be a separation from man's way to God's Way. There would be hindrances to stop them, such as Jordan overflowing its banks; however, they did not allow this to stop them, and neither must we allow hindrances to stop us.)

16 And there came of the children of Benjamin and Judah to the hold *(where David was camped)* unto David.

17 And David went out to meet them, and answered and said unto them, If you be come peaceably unto me to help me, my heart shall be knit unto you: but if you be come to betray me to my enemies, seeing there is no wrong in my hands, the God of our fathers look thereon, and rebuke it.

18 Then the Spirit *(Holy Spirit)* came upon Amasai, who was chief of the captains, and he said, Yours are we, David, and on your side, you son of Jesse: peace, peace be unto you, and peace be to your helpers; for your God helps you. Then David received them, and made them captains of the band *(the phrase, "Yours are we, David, and on your side," must ever be the statement of any Child of God concerning the Lord Jesus Christ; as Amasai burned his bridges behind him, so to speak, we, as children of the Living God, must do the same in our service for Jesus Christ; Amasai was not looking back; we must not look back either).*

19 And there fell some of Manasseh to David, when he came with the Philistines against Saul to battle: but they helped them not: for the lords of the Philistines upon advisement sent him away, saying, He will fall to his master Saul to the jeopardy of our heads *(some of Manasseh coming to David implies, at the same time, that some did not come; regrettably, that seems to always be the case!).*

20 As he went to Ziklag, there fell to him of Manasseh, Adnah, and Jozabad, and Jediael, and Michael, and Jozabad, and Elihu, and Zilthai, captains of the thousands that were of Manasseh.

21 And they helped David against the band of the rovers: for they were all mighty men of valour, and were captains in the host.

22 For at that time day by day there came to David to help him, until it was a great host, like the host of God *(this was God's time for Israel; David was His man; consequently, all who were in the Will of God came to David; otherwise, they were out of the Will of God).*

23 And these are the numbers of the bands who were ready armed to the war, and came to David to Hebron, to turn the kingdom of Saul

to him, according to the Word of the LORD. *(They were not coming to be armed; they were "ready armed." So many today in modern Christendom are not armed and, therefore, are of no consequence to the Work of God.*

As well, they knew their mission. They were called of God. So many in the Church presently do not know their mission. Our mission is to take this "kingdom of Saul" [the world] and turn it over to our Heavenly David, because it is "according to the Word of the LORD.")

24 The children of Judah who bore shield and spear were six thousand and eight hundred, ready armed to the war.

25 Of the children of Simeon, mighty men of valour for the war, seven thousand and one hundred.

26 Of the children of Levi four thousand and six hundred.

27 And Jehoiada was the leader of the Aaronites, and with him were three thousand and seven hundred;

28 And Zadok, a young man mighty of valour, and of his father's house twenty and two captains.

29 And of the children of Benjamin, the kindred of Saul, three thousand: for hitherto the greatest part of them had kept the ward of the house of Saul.

30 And of the children of Ephraim twenty thousand and eight hundred, mighty men of valour, famous throughout the house of their fathers.

31 And of the half tribe of Manasseh eighteen thousand, which were expressed by name, to come and make David king *(these individuals were "expressed by name," and wanted everyone to know that they had "come to make David king"; they were not ashamed of their mission; they wanted all to know their purpose; these are the type who make a full consecration).*

32 And of the children of Issachar, which were men who had understanding of the times, to know what Israel ought to do; the heads of them were two hundred; and all their brethren were at their commandment *(if we follow the Holy Spirit like they were then doing, we will, as well, have "understanding of the times"; only those who truly follow the Lord will "know what the Church ought to do").*

33 Of Zebulun, such as went forth to battle, expert in war, with all instruments of war, fifty thousand, which could keep rank: they were not of double heart. *(Far too many Christians cannot keep rank simply because their hearts are divided between the world and the Lord Jesus Christ, or else between denominational religion and the Lord Jesus Christ. No matter the danger in battle, these men from Zebulun could keep rank.*

The "double heart" is also the bane of all of Christendom. The heart is divided between Christ and other pursuits. Our hearts must be single, meaning that all its devotion must be to Christ.)

34 And of Naphtali a thousand captains, and with them with shield and spear thirty and seven thousand. *(How is it that only 6,800 of Judah came [Vs. 24], and 50,000 of the Tribe of Zebulun came? The numbers denote accuracy and fidelity to present-day spiritual facts. Although David himself was of the Tribe of Judah, still, Judah would little respond. Benjamin, Simeon, and Levi were associated with Judah, as well, and the record will show small response. Likewise, these were the Tribes that crucified the Son of David, our Lord. So the seedbed of that crucifixion, which would take place about a thousand years later, was already being planted.)*

35 And of the Danites expert in war twenty and eight thousand and six hundred.

36 And of Asher, such as went forth to battle, expert in war, forty thousand.

37 And on the other side of Jordan, of the Reubenites, and the Gadites, and of the half tribe of Manasseh, with all manner of instruments of war for the battle, an hundred and twenty thousand.

38 All these men of war, who could keep rank, came with a perfect heart to Hebron, to make David king over all Israel: and all the rest also of Israel were of one heart to make David king *(Israel, at this time, is finally marching in tune with the Holy Spirit).*

39 And there they were with David three days, eating and drinking: for their brethren had prepared for them.

40 Moreover they who were near them, even unto Issachar and Zebulun and Naphtali, brought bread on asses, and on camels, and on mules, and on oxen, and meat, meal, cakes of figs, and bunches of raisins, and wine, and oil, and oxen, and sheep abundantly: for there was joy in Israel. *(Now there is "fellowship," there is "plenty," and there is "joy," all because Israel is now in the Will of God. It should be noted that in the entirety of this Chapter, the seven-and-a-half year reign in Hebron of David over Judah is not referred to once. It was God's Will for David to be king over all Israel, not just Judah; likewise, the Lord must be king over*

all our lives, not just part.)

CHAPTER 13
(1045 B.C.)
DAVID ATTEMPTS TO BRING
THE ARK TO JERUSALEM

AND David consulted with the captains of thousands and hundreds, and with every leader *(however, it doesn't say that David consulted with God; the results of such action would be disastrous).*

2 And David said unto all the congregation of Israel, If it seem good unto you, and that it be of the LORD our God, let us send abroad unto our brethren every where, who are left in all the land of Israel, and with them also to the Priests and Levites which are in their cities and suburbs, that they may gather themselves unto us *(there was much religious activity at this point, but very little, if any, leading of the Holy Spirit):*

3 And let us bring again the Ark of our God to us: for we enquired not at it in the days of Saul *(it is ironic that the entire motive for the bringing of the Ark was to "enquire of it," yet David did not enquire of the Lord concerning this all-important task).*

4 And all the congregation said that they would do so: for the thing was right in the eyes of all the people *(it was right in the Eyes of God, as well, but not in the way it was done).*

5 So David gathered all Israel together, from Shihor of Egypt even unto the entering of Hemath, to bring the Ark of God from Kirjath-jearim. *(How many times does the Church, with great fanfare, rush forward to carry out its bold plans, when, in reality, those plans will not bring life, but death? Great religious activity never denotes great spiritual depth; nevertheless, the clatter of religious machinery, combined with the noise of great religious profession, completely fool most people.)*

6 And David went up, and all Israel, to Baalah, that is, to Kirjath-jearim, which belonged to Judah, to bring up thence the Ark of God the LORD, Who dwells between the Cherubims, Whose name is called on it *(during the time of Saul, who was a work of the flesh, the Ark of God was ignored, because spiritual things had no value to Saul; I'm afraid the modern Church, at least for all practical purposes, is following the same course of ignoring the Will of God).*

7 And they carried the Ark of God in a new cart out of the house of Abinadab: and Uzza and Ahio drove the cart. *(The Ark of God, by the command of God, was to be carried on the shoulders of Priests, and not on a cart of any kind. The Priests were Types of Christ; the symbolism portrayed the fact that the Presence of God rested solely on Christ, and within Christ.*

It must be clearly noted that anything and everything instituted by man is always, and without exception, a "new cart." It is doomed to failure. All directions for all things are laid down in the Word of God [II Pet. 1:3]. Any deviation will always bring death [Ex. 37:5; Num. 4:15; Deut. 10:8; Josh. 3:8-14]. Regrettably, the Church presently is full of "new carts"!)

8 And David and all Israel played before God with all their might, and with singing, and with harps, and with psalteries, and with timbrels, and with cymbals, and with trumpets. *(How much does this characterize our modern-day Church? It is all very religious, but very wrong! It is all very loud, but very lost! It is all with great activity, but not by the Holy Spirit. If it's not according to the Word of God, then all the religious activity will not make it right, and death will be the result.)*

UZZA IS SMITTEN

9 And when they came unto the threshingfloor of Chidon, Uzza put forth his hand to hold the Ark; for the oxen stumbled *(there is always "a threshingfloor"; the threshingfloor was where the grain was separated from the husk; on this memorable day, the spiritual grain would be separated from the husk as well [Mat. 3:11-12]).*

10 And the anger of the LORD was kindled against Uzza, and He smote him, because he put his hand to the Ark: and there he died before God. *(Of all people, Uzza should have known better. The Ark had been at his place, for he was a son of Abinadab, where the Ark had been left many years before [I Sam. 7:1]; however, it seems he had not bothered to check out the Word of God, as to exactly what the disposition of the Ark should be.*

As well, millions presently think, as Uzza evidently did at that time, that David would be responsible, because he had delegated the responsibility to Uzza. Uzza was to find out differently.

Millions are in Hell presently, because they left responsibility up to a Preacher or a Priest. God demands that each individual know and understand the Word of God, and be responsible

accordingly. So, the idea that Believers are to obey someone in authority, and do so without question, irrespective as to whether it's right or wrong, is not taught in the Bible. In fact, the very opposite is taught [Ezek. 18:4].)

11 And David was displeased, because the LORD had made a breach upon Uzza: wherefore that place is called Perez-uzza to this day (the word "displeased" means "saddened"; David had a right to be sad, because he definitely was partly to blame).

12 And David was afraid of God that day, saying, How shall I bring the Ark of God home to me? (David's displeasure was quickly turned into acute fear. He realized how close he personally had come to death on this day. Sadly, most of the modern Church is only "displeased." There is very little "fear of God" left! Consequently, David's heart sobbed, "How shall I bring the Ark of God home to me?" All must be done God's Way.)

13 So David brought not the Ark home to himself to the city of David, but carried it aside into the house of Obed-edom the Gittite (undoubtedly, David was led by the Lord in leaving the Ark with Obed-edom; as the facts will prove, this man had a great heart for God, and knew how to treat the Ark, so to speak, even to a greater extent, it seems, than did David).

14 And the Ark of God remained with the family of Obed-edom in his house three months. And the LORD blessed the house of Obed-edom, and all that he had. (One man died because of ignoring the Word of God, and one man and his house are greatly blessed because of obeying the Word of God. That was the criteria then, obedience to the Word, and it is the criteria now!)

CHAPTER 14
(1043 B.C.)
HIRAM BUILDS DAVID A HOUSE

NOW Hiram king of Tyre sent messengers to David, and timber of cedars, with masons and carpenters, to build him an house.

2 And David perceived that the LORD had confirmed him king over Israel, for his kingdom was lifted up on high, because of his people Israel. (The first two Verses picture the coming day when Christ, the Shepherd of His people, shall be confirmed by God the Father as King over Israel, and when the Gentile princes, represented here by Hiram, shall bring their offerings to His feet.

David perceived that the Lord had established his kingdom because of this fact, but more so that Israel was the flock of God. Grace had elected that flock and had chosen David as its shepherd.)

DAVID'S FAMILY AT JERUSALEM

3 And David took more wives at Jerusalem: and David begat more sons and daughters (even though this was tolerated by the Lord, still, such was not His Will).

4 Now these are the names of his children which he had in Jerusalem; Shammua, and Shobab, Nathan, and Solomon (Mary, the mother of Christ, went back to David through Nathan, while Joseph went back to David through Solomon),

5 And Ibhar, and Elishua, and Elpalet,

6 And Nogah, and Nepheg, and Japhia,

7 And Elishama, and Beeliada, and Eliphalet.

DAVID'S VICTORY OVER THE PHILISTINES

8 And when the Philistines heard that David was anointed king over all Israel, all the Philistines went up to seek David. And David heard of it, and went out against them (the word "seek" means "to kill him"; the moment there is an "Anointing of the Spirit," Satan will come against it).

9 And the Philistines came and spread themselves in the valley of Rephaim (this was the valley of the giants; it must be clearly understood that the "flesh" cannot overcome these "giants"; they can be overcome only by "the Spirit of God"; the Philistines dwelt in the land; they illustrate the energies of sin that dwell in the Christian [Rom. 7:17]; whenever Christ is enthroned as king over the whole life, these energies gather themselves together to oppose Him in the Believer's heart, where Divine Faith and a child-like obedience have the upper hand; there must be complete victory over them [Rom. 8:1-2, 11]).

10 And David enquired of God, saying, Shall I go up against the Philistines? and will You deliver them into my hand? And the LORD said unto him, Go up; for I will deliver them into your hand (it seems that David now had learned his lesson well, concerning a lack of inquiry regarding the bringing up of the Ark; now, he would take nothing for granted; consequently, he would experience victory).

11 So they came up to Baal-perazim; and David smote them there. Then David said, God has broken in upon my enemies by my hand like the breaking forth of waters: therefore they called the name of that place Baal-perazim. *(The prefix on this place was called "Baal," which speaks of heathen gods. So, in effect, David is saying, "The Lord has broken through and defeated these idol gods." How many idol gods are in our lives?*

The "waters" typify the Word of God, which sweeps away these idol gods, and which must be swept away in our lives also. But we must remember they cannot be destroyed by human ingenuity, only by the Spirit of God!)

12 And when they had left their gods there, David gave a commandment, and they were burned with fire *(the fire of the Spirit is to burn the dross out of our lives [Mat. 3:11-12]).*

13 And the Philistines yet again spread themselves abroad in the valley *(our mistake is large, if we think Satan will not return; he probes for an opportunity; just because there has been great victory does not mean that he will not come "yet again"; however, the victory of the first day, and the methods which Grace counseled for the winning of it, are not to be rested upon in order to secure victory for the next day).*

14 Therefore David enquired again of God; and God said unto him, Go not up after them; turn away from them, and come upon them over against the mulberry trees. *(Had David thought it unnecessary to pray previous to the second battle, he would, no doubt, have been defeated. He learned that God cannot give victories to the "flesh." Flesh must be humbled! So David is commanded to run away from the Philistines, which was very humbling to so brave a warrior, who then learns to hide, wait, and listen for the Power and Leading of the Holy Spirit.*

No two victories are alike; hence, there must be definite exercises of heart and prayer, if the Philistine is to be defeated, not only the first time, but the second time, as well.)

15 And it shall be, when you shall hear a sound of going in the tops of the mulberry trees, that then you shall go out to battle: for God is gone forth before you to smite the host of the Philistines *(the "sound" which David heard was the coming of the Holy Spirit; He came to stay on the Day of Pentecost [Acts 2:2]).*

16 David therefore did as God commanded him: and they smote the host of the Philistines from Gibeon even to Gazer *(if we have the mind of the Lord, we will always have the victory which such affords).*

17 And the fame of David went out into all lands; and the LORD brought the fear of him upon all nations *(and so shall it be, when the Greater Son of David rules over the entirety of the planet, which will take place after the Second Coming).*

CHAPTER 15

(1042 B.C.)

ARRANGEMENTS FOR TRANSPORTING THE ARK

AND David made him houses in the city of David, and prepared a place for the Ark of God, and pitched for it a tent *(at this particular time, the Lord had not told David to do otherwise regarding the Ark; that would come later).*

2 Then David said, None ought to carry the Ark of God but the Levites: for them has the LORD chosen to carry the Ark of God, and to minister unto Him for ever *(David searched the Scriptures and learned how the Ark should be carried [Num. 4:15]; had he done that previously, a man would not have died; Priests were Types of Christ, hence they were ordained to carry the Ark).*

3 And David gathered all Israel together to Jerusalem, to bring up the Ark of the LORD unto his place, which he had prepared for it.

4 And David assembled the children of Aaron, and the Levites:

5 Of the sons of Kohath; Uriel the chief, and his brethren an hundred and twenty:

6 Of the sons of Merari; Asaiah the chief, and his brethren two hundred and twenty:

7 Of the son of Gershom; Joel the chief, and his brethren an hundred and thirty:

8 Of the sons of Elizaphan; Shemaiah the chief, and his brethren two hundred:

9 Of the sons of Hebron; Eliel the chief, and his brethren fourscore:

10 Of the sons of Uzziel; Amminadab the chief, and his brethren an hundred and twelve.

11 And David called for Zadok and Abiathar the Priests, and for the Levites, for Uriel, Asaiah, and Joel, Shemaiah, and Eliel, and Amminadab,

12 And said unto them, You are the chief of the fathers of the Levites: sanctify yourselves, both you and your brethren, that you may bring up the Ark of the LORD God of Israel unto the place that I have prepared for it.

13 For because you did it not at the first, the LORD our God made a breach upon us, for

that we sought Him not after the due order *(this Verse speaks of David admitting his sin of some three months earlier; he was speaking of the manner in which the Ark of God was to be transported).*

14 So the Priests and the Levites sanctified themselves to bring up the Ark of the LORD God of Israel.

15 And the children of the Levites bore the Ark of God upon their shoulders with the staves thereon, as Moses commanded according to the Word of the LORD.

SINGERS AND MUSICIANS APPOINTED BY DAVID TO PRAISE GOD BEFORE THE ARK

16 And David spoke to the chief of the Levites to appoint their brethren to be the singers with instruments of music, psalteries and harps and cymbals, sounding, by lifting up the voice with joy *(this time it will not be an empty profession; the joy will be real, because they are now abiding by the Word of God).*

17 So the Levites appointed Heman the son of Joel *(Samuel's grandson)*; and of his brethren, Asaph the son of Berechiah; and of the sons of Merari their brethren, Ethan the son of Kushaiah;

18 And with them their brethren of the second degree, Zechariah, Ben, and Jaaziel, and Shemiramoth, and Jehiel, and Unni, Eliab, and Benaiah, and Maaseiah, and Mattithiah, and Elipheleh, and Mikneiah, and Obed-edom, and Jeiel, the porters.

19 So the singers, Heman, Asaph, and Ethan, were appointed to sound with cymbals of brass;

20 And Zechariah, and Aziel, and Shemiramoth, and Jehiel, and Unni, and Eliab, and Maaseiah, and Benaiah, with psalteries on Alamoth;

21 And Mattithiah, and Elipheleh, and Mikneiah, and Obed-edom, and Jeiel, and Azaziah, with harps on the Sheminith to excel.

22 And Chenaniah, chief of the Levites, was for song: he instructed about the song, because he was skillful.

23 And Berechiah and Elkanah were doorkeepers for the Ark.

24 And Shebaniah, and Jehoshaphat, and Nethaneel, and Amasai, and Zechariah, and Benaiah, and Eliezer, the Priests, did blow with the trumpets before the Ark of God: and Obed-edom and Jehiah were doorkeepers for the Ark. *(The great processional that will go into*

Jerusalem with the Ark of God in its midst will be designed by the Holy Spirit. David seemingly wrote Psalm 68 to commemorate this great event. There were 862 Priests and Levites, plus others consecrated to bear the Ark and to offer Sacrifices.

Three choirs accompanied the Ark. The first choir was led by the Levites. The second choir was made up of maiden singers [Vs. 20]. The third choir was made up of the men singers [Vs. 21].

All three choirs are referred to in Psalms 68:25. The men's choir seemingly went before the musicians, who were following the maidens playing timbrels among or in-between the men singers and the musicians.)

DAVID BRINGS THE ARK TO JERUSALEM

25 So David, and the elders of Israel, and the captains over thousands, went to bring up the Ark of the Covenant of the LORD out of the house of Obed-edom with joy *(without proper leadership, such could never have been brought to pass).*

26 And it came to pass, when God helped the Levites who bore the Ark of the Covenant of the LORD, that they offered seven bullocks and seven rams *(the Sacrifices typified that all were based upon the shed Blood of the Lamb).*

27 And David was clothed with a robe of fine linen, and all the Levites who bore the Ark, and the singers, and Chenaniah the master of the song with the singers: David also had upon him an ephod of linen *(the "linen" represents the "Righteousness of the Saints," and, once again, a Righteousness that did not come from the merit of David, but from the merit of the slain Lamb — hence, the Sacrifices).*

28 Thus all Israel brought up the Ark of the Covenant of the LORD with shouting, and with sound of the cornet, and with trumpets, and with cymbals, making a noise with psalteries and harps *(we find here, as is obvious, all types of musical instruments, and all used for the Glory of God; in fact, the Book of Psalms is the longest Book in the Bible, showing us the emphasis that the Holy Spirit puts upon worship, as it regards music and singing).*

MICHAL'S SIN

29 And it came to pass, as the Ark of the Covenant of the LORD came to the city of David, that Michal the daughter of Saul looking out

at a window saw king David dancing and playing: and she despised him in her heart *(the "flesh" can never understand things of the "Spirit"; actually, the "flesh" despises all that which is of the "Spirit"; II Sam. 6:20-23 states that "she was childless to the day of her death"; likewise, if the Church disobeys the Word of God, there will be no joy, and the Church also will be barren).*

CHAPTER 16
(1042 B.C.)
THE SACRIFICES AND MUSIC

SO they brought the Ark of God, and set it in the midst of the tent that David had pitched for it: and they offered Burnt Sacrifices and Peace Offerings before God. *(Once again, the Holy Spirit calls attention to the Sacrifices, which typified Calvary. We aren't told where these Sacrifices were offered, whether at Gibeon, where the Brazen Altar was located, or whether a makeshift Altar was constructed nearby the Ark of the Covenant. At any rate, wherever they were offered at this time, everything seemed to be in the Will of God.)*

2 And when David had made an end of offering the Burnt Offerings and the Peace Offerings, he blessed the people in the Name of the LORD *(everything was built and ordered on the basis of the Cross, which the Sacrifices typified).*

3 And he dealt to every one of Israel, both man and woman, to every one a loaf of bread, and a good piece of flesh, and a flagon of wine. *(It is very difficult to explain to the Reader the significance of this moment in Israel's history. The "Ark of God" was symbolic of all of Israel's power, strength, and glory. With the "Ark," she was the most powerful nation on Earth; without the "Ark," she was nothing. David understood this; sadly, most of the kings who were to later come did not understand it.*

Likewise, the Presence of God in our Churches is the only thing of any real value. But sadly, most Churches are little more than a business. There is no Presence of God and, in fact, there never has been. The sacrificial meal denoted fellowship, joy, and communion.)

4 And he appointed certain of the Levites to minister before the Ark of the LORD, and to record, and to thank and praise the LORD God of Israel:

5 Asaph the chief, and next to him Zechariah, Jeiel, and Shemiramoth, and Jehiel, and Mattithiah, and Eliab, and Benaiah, and Obededom: and Jeiel with psalteries and with harps; but Asaph made a sound with cymbals;

6 Benaiah also and Jahaziel the priests with trumpets continually before the Ark of the Covenant of God. *(The word "continually" means both morning and evening, and at the time of the morning and evening sacrifices. This means that the choirs would worship the Lord by singing the Psalms each day at 9 a.m. [the time of the morning sacrifice] and 3 p.m. [the time of the evening sacrifice]. This would be done each day, with the exception of the Sabbath, which was the day of rest.)*

DAVID'S PSALM OF THANKSGIVING

7 Then on that day David delivered first this Psalm to thank the LORD into the hand of Asaph and his brethren. *(There are five great words which make up the entirety of this Psalm, which comprises praise and worship in our living for God. They are: "Give," "Sing," "Glory," "Seek," and "Remember.")*

8 Give thanks unto the LORD, call upon His Name, make known His deeds among the people *(the Believer must constantly give thanks).*

9 Sing unto Him, sing Psalms unto Him, talk ye of all His wondrous works *(we are to sing to Him, and the song should be about His wondrous Works).*

10 Glory ye in His Holy Name: let the heart of them rejoice who seek the LORD *(our "Glory" is to be in "His Holy Name," which incorporates His Character and Power; we then have the assurance that He will hear our prayers).*

11 Seek the LORD and His strength, seek His face continually *(and about everything!).*

12 Remember His marvelous works that He has done, His wonders, and the judgments of His mouth *(His Word and His Works are to ever be remembered);*

13 O ye seed of Israel His servant, ye children of Jacob, His chosen ones *(out of all the Earth, chosen!).*

14 He is the LORD our God; His judgments are in all the Earth *(He Alone is the Creator).*

15 Be ye mindful always of His Covenant; the Word which He commanded to a thousand generations *(in other words, unending!);*

16 Even of the Covenant which He made with Abraham, and of His oath unto Isaac *(Gen. 17:2; 26:3; 28:13; 35:11);*

17 And has confirmed the same to Jacob for a

Law, and to Israel for an Everlasting Covenant,

18 Saying, Unto you will I give the land of Canaan, the lot of your inheritance *(the Bible is the greatest title deed known to man; pure and simple, it allots here the "land of Canaan" to Israel, and not the so-called Palestinians, as claimed by the Muslims)*;

19 When you were but few, even a few, and strangers in it.

20 And when they went from nation to nation, and from one kingdom to another people *(before the land of Israel was occupied)*;

21 He suffered no man to do them wrong: yea, He reproved kings for their sakes *(Gen. 12:17; 20:3; Ex. 7:15-18)*,

22 Saying, Touch not My anointed, and do My Prophets no harm.

23 Sing unto the LORD, all the Earth; show forth from day to day His salvation.

24 Declare His glory among the heathen; His marvelous works among all nations *(evangelize the world!)*.

25 For great is the LORD, and greatly to be praised: He also is to be feared above all gods.

26 For all the gods of the people are idols: but the LORD made the Heavens *(there is One God, and only One, and He is the Creator of all things)*.

27 Glory and honour are in His presence; strength and gladness are in His place.

28 Give unto the LORD, you kindreds of the people, give unto the LORD glory and strength *(give Him the credit He is due)*.

29 Give unto the LORD the glory due unto His Name: bring an offering, and come before Him: worship the LORD in the beauty of Holiness.

30 Fear before Him, all the Earth: the world also shall be stable, that it be not moved *(that will one day be!)*.

31 Let the Heavens be glad, and let the Earth rejoice: and let men say among the nations, The LORD reigns *(in the coming Kingdom Age, this Scripture will be fulfilled)*.

32 Let the sea roar, and the fullness thereof: let the fields rejoice, and all that is therein *(rejoice in the Lord!)*.

33 Then shall the trees of the wood sing out at the presence of the LORD, because He comes to judge the Earth *(the coming Kingdom Age!)*.

34 O give thanks unto the LORD; for He is good; for His mercy endures for ever *(what a Promise!)*.

35 And say ye, Save us, O God of our Salvation, and gather us together, and deliver us from the heathen, that we may give thanks to Your Holy Name, and glory in Your praise.

36 Blessed be the LORD God of Israel for ever and ever. And all the people said, Amen, and praised the LORD *(the entirety of this Psalm can probably be summed up in the great phrase of Verse 25, "For great is the LORD, and greatly to be praised")*.

ATTENDANTS TO THE ARK

37 So he left there before the Ark of the Covenant of the LORD Asaph and his brethren, to minister before the Ark continually, as every day's work required *(the great celebration of worship was not to be discontinued after the installment of the Ark; it was to be "continually"; too often those who name the Name of Christ worship the Lord only on selected days or times; the Holy Spirit is saying here, "Every day, continually")*:

38 And Obed-edom with their brethren, threescore and eight; Obed-edom also the son of Jeduthun and Hosah to be porters *(this man, in whose house the Ark of God had been left by David for some three months, would forsake all that he had in order to be near the "Ark"; he would be associated with the singers and musicians; the Holy Spirit would be so pleased with his actions, dedication, and service that He would mention his name some 20 times throughout the Word of God, and always in a positive way; what an honor!)*:

39 And Zadok the Priest, and his brethren the Priests, before the Tabernacle of the LORD in the high place that was at Gibeon,

40 To offer Burnt Offerings unto the LORD upon the Altar of the Burnt Offering continually morning and evening, and to do according to all that is written in the Law of the LORD, which He commanded Israel *(the Ark was in Jerusalem, while the Brazen Altar was at Gibeon, about 5 miles northwest of Jerusalem; evidently, the Table of Shewbread, Golden Lampstand, and Altar of Incense were in Gibeon, as well! They would remain separated until the Temple was built, some years later)*;

41 And with them Heman and Jeduthun, and the rest who were chosen, who were expressed by name, to give thanks to the LORD, because His mercy endures for ever;

42 And with them Heman and Jeduthun with trumpets and cymbals for those who should make a sound, and with musical instruments of God. And the sons of Jeduthun

were porters *(under David, the great worship of God regarding musical instrumentation and choirs actually began; of course, he was led by the Lord to do so; the Book of Psalms was Earth's first songbook; David wrote at least half of those that are recorded, and possibly others that do not bear his name; in fact, some parts of the Psalm given in this Chapter are incorporated into Psalm 105).*

43 And all the people departed every man to his house: and David returned to bless his house.

CHAPTER 17
(1042 B.C.)
DAVID'S DESIRE TO BUILD THE TEMPLE

NOW it came to pass, as David sat in his house, that David said to Nathan the Prophet, Lo, I dwell in an house of cedars, but the Ark of the Covenant of the LORD remains under curtains *(David is here a Type of the Lord Jesus Christ residing in Jerusalem in the glories of the Kingdom Age; all enemies are defeated; David desires to build a house for the Lord; this pictures the beginning of the Kingdom Age, when the Lord Jesus, as a "greater than Solomon" will begin to build His "House").*

2 Then Nathan said unto David, Do all that is in your heart; for God is with you *(while the Lord definitely was with David, it was not the Will of God that David build the House; this tells us that irrespective as to who the person might be, even a Prophet such as Nathan, we must not assume that we know what God wants; we must seek His Face about everything, which Nathan did not then do).*

GOD'S COVENANT WITH DAVID

3 And it came to pass the same night, that the Word of God came to Nathan, saying *(as to how the Lord spoke to Nathan, we aren't told; however, the main thing is, Nathan was in such a spiritual condition that God could speak to him; regrettably, that isn't the case with most),*

4 Go and tell David My servant, Thus saith the LORD, you shall not build Me an house to dwell in *(the Hebrew marks the personal pronoun, "you," as emphatic; "you" shall not build):*

5 For I have not dwelt in an house since the day that I brought up Israel *(out of Egypt)* unto this day; but have gone from tent to tent, and from one tabernacle to another *(the Lord means*

to remind David how surely and faithfully He had shared the pilgrim lot and unsettledness of His people).*

6 Wheresoever I have walked with all Israel, spoke I a word to any of the Judges of Israel, whom I commanded to feed My people, saying, Why have you not built Me an house of cedars? *(The Lord had shared their lot, and had shared it unmurmuringly.)*

7 Now therefore thus shall you say unto My servant David, Thus saith the LORD of hosts, I took you from the sheepcote, even from following the sheep, that you should be ruler over My people Israel *(this Verse records the price of admission into this house; it is trust in the "slain Lamb," by the route of humility; as well, David was a shepherd, and the Lord Jesus Christ also would be a Shepherd [Heb. 13:20]):*

8 And I have been with you whithersoever you have walked, and have cut off all your enemies from before you, and have made you a name like the name of the great men who are in the Earth *(God will be with those who desire to be with Him).*

9 Also I will ordain a place for My people Israel, and will plant them, and they shall dwell in their place, and shall be moved no more; neither shall the children of wickedness waste them any more, as at the beginning *(this is God's unconditional Covenant with Israel; however, it must be stated that this unconditional Covenant is unconditional only in the sense that God will bring the Promises to pass irrespective; the only thing that is unconditional is the Covenant itself; to come into the blessing of the Covenant, one must meet its conditions, which is Faith in Christ and what Christ has done at the Cross; those Jews who do this will definitely dwell in the place ordained for them, which is the land of Israel; this includes all Jews who have accepted Christ before death, and all those who will accept Him at the Second Coming),*

10 And since the time that I commanded Judges to be over My people Israel. Moreover I will subdue all your enemies. Furthermore I tell you that the LORD will build you an house *(the more complete fulfillment of this Promise awaits the coming of the Messiah [Isa. 9:6-7; Rom. 11:25-27]).*

GOD PROMISES DAVID AN ETERNAL KINGDOM; HIS SON WILL BUILD THE TEMPLE

11 And it shall come to pass, when your

days be expired that you must go to be with your fathers, that I will raise up your seed after you, which shall be of your sons; and I will establish his kingdom *(this has a double application, with Solomon being spoken of in the immediate present, but far more so in the Lord Jesus Christ as the "Son of David").*

12 He shall build Me an house, and I will stablish his throne for ever *(the total fulfillment will be in Christ, Who will occupy this Throne in the coming Kingdom Age, and then forever).*

13 I will be his father, and he shall be My son: and I will not take My mercy away from him, as I took it from him *(Saul)* who was before you:

14 But I will settle him in My house and in My kingdom for ever: and his throne shall be established for evermore *(the Arabs should read these words, and consider them carefully; in fact, the entirety of the world needs to read them, and to consider them carefully).*

15 According to all these words, and according to all this vision, so did Nathan speak unto David.

DAVID'S PRAYER AND THANKSGIVING

16 And David the king came and sat before the LORD, and said, Who am I, O LORD God, and what is my house, that You have brought me hitherto? *(David now knows fully and beyond the shadow of a doubt that the Messiah will come through his lineage.)*

17 And yet this was a small thing in Your eyes, O God; for You have also spoken of Your servant's house for a great while to come, and have regarded me according to the estate of a man of high degree, O LORD God *(even though it is not recorded in this Chapter, still, in II Sam. 7:19, David says, "And is this the manner of man, O LORD God?" This refers to the Promise that the Seed of the woman shall bruise the serpent's head [Gen. 3:15]; that is, from David's line the Messiah will come, bringing eternal Salvation and reigning as the eternal King of the Earth; this would be the highest honor that God could show any man, i.e., "high degree").*

18 What can David speak more to You for the honour of Your servant? for You know Your servant *(meaning that David in no way could merit this great and high honor, even as no Child of God can merit the high honor of Salvation freely given by the Lord Jesus Christ).*

19 O LORD, for Your servant's sake, and according to Your own heart, have You done all this greatness, in making known all these great things *(once again, David exclaims the Glory of God, which is so much greater than what he at first thought; he wanted to build a house for the Lord; instead, the Lord tells David that He will build him a house, and it will be eternal).*

20 O LORD, there is none like You, neither is there any God beside You, according to all that we have heard with our ears *(no heathen god, which, in fact, was no god at all, but rather figments of men's imaginations, could compare with this!).*

21 And what one nation in the Earth is like Your people Israel, whom God went to redeem to be His own people, to make You a name of greatness and terribleness, by driving out nations from before Your people, whom You have redeemed out of Egypt? *(Israel constituted the only people on Earth who knew Jehovah, the Creator of the ages.)*

22 For Your people Israel did You make Your own people for ever; and You, LORD, became their God *(this meant that Israel was light-years, so to speak, above every other nation in the world).*

23 Therefore now, LORD, let the thing that You have spoken concerning Your servant and concerning his house be established for ever, and do as You have said *(this has only partially been fulfilled, but definitely will be fulfilled in the coming Kingdom Age).*

24 Let it even be established, that Your name may be magnified for ever, saying, The LORD of Hosts is the God of Israel, even a God to Israel: and let the House of David Your servant be established before You *(hence Jesus said to the woman at Jacob's well, "For Salvation is of the Jews" [Jn. 4:22]; it was through Israel that Jesus, the Saviour of the world, came!).*

25 For You, O my God, have told Your servant that You will build him an house: therefore Your servant has found in his heart to pray before You *(when prayers are found in the heart, they are the result of gratitude or the overflow of some desperate need).*

26 And now, LORD, You are God, and have promised this goodness unto Your servant *(God keeps His Promises!):*

27 Now therefore let it please You to bless the house of Your servant, that it may be before You for ever: for You bless, O LORD, and it shall be blessed for ever *(what God has blessed, nothing can curse [Num. 23:8, 20]).*

CHAPTER 18
(1040 B.C.)
EXPLOITS AND VICTORIES OF DAVID

NOW after this it came to pass, that David smote the Philistines, and subdued them, and took Gath and her towns out of the hand of the Philistines.

2 And he smote Moab; and the Moabites became David's servants, and brought gifts (this illustrates the moral fact, always true, that when Christ is set upon the throne of the heart, victory over both inward and outward enemies is assured; but the inward is always first conquered, as in the case of David and the Philistines in this Chapter, and then the outward will be conquered).

3 And David smote Hadarezer king of Zobah unto Hamath ("Hadarezer" means "my demon helper"; so, despite demon spirits helping this man, David, who was greater, "smote" them), as he went to stablish his dominion by the river Euphrates (this was the northeastern extremity of the kingdom promised to Abraham by the Lord [Gen. 15:18]; through our "Heavenly David," the Lord Jesus Christ, we can conquer and, in fact, must conquer, every part of our inheritance).

4 And David took from him a thousand chariots, and seven thousand horsemen, and twenty thousand footmen: David also houghed (made them unfit for chariot use) all the chariot horses, but reserved of them an hundred chariots (Israel's strength was not chariots, but rather the Lord!).

5 And when the Syrians of Damascus came to help Hadarezer king of Zobah, David slew of the Syrians two and twenty thousand men (all this is a Type of Christ, Who will defeat every enemy at the Cross [Col. 2:14-15]; when our Faith and trust are placed exclusively in Him and the Cross, His victory then becomes our victory!).

6 Then David put garrisons in Syria-damascus; and the Syrians became David's servants, and brought gifts. Thus the LORD preserved David whithersoever he went (it is the Will of God, and even the insistence of the Lord, that we subdue not just some of our spiritual enemies, but all; we must rule the sin nature, and not the sin nature ruling us [Rom. 6:3-14]).

DEDICATION TO THE LORD

7 And David took the shields of gold that were on the servants of Hadarezer, and brought them to Jerusalem (the wealth of Zobah was illustrated by the shields of gold; now this wealth belongs to the people of God, stipulating the coming Kingdom Age).

8 Likewise from Tibhath, and from Chun, cities of Hadarezer, brought David very much brass, wherewith Solomon made the Brasen Sea, and the Pillars, and the vessels of brass (all of this, formerly used for heathen idols, will now be used for God, as it regards the building of the Temple; this symbolizes the Believer, who is brought out of sin and darkness, brought to the Family of God, and made to be "a pillar in the Temple of My God" [Rev. 3:12]).

9 Now when Tou king of Hamath heard how David had smitten all the host of Hadarezer king of Zobah;

10 He sent Hadoram his son to king David, to enquire of his welfare, and to congratulate him, because he had fought against Hadarezer, and smitten him; (for Hadarezer had war with Tou;) and with him all manner of vessels of gold and silver and brass (portraying his submission to David).

11 Them also king David dedicated unto the LORD, with the silver and the gold that he brought from all these nations; from Edom, and from Moab, and from the children of Ammon, and from the Philistines, and from Amalek (if the Lord does see fit to bless us with worldly riches, it must, without fail, be "dedicated unto the LORD," and not to our own selfish desires).

12 Moreover Abishai the son of Zeruiah slew of the Edomites in the valley of salt eighteen thousand (those who were with David experienced, as well, David's anointing).

13 And he put garrisons in Edom; and all the Edomites became David's servants. Thus the LORD preserved David whithersoever he went (this statement is repeated from Verse 6, and with purpose; it is meant to impress upon all that the Lord was the Source of David's victories, and the Lord Alone!).

14 So David reigned over all Israel, and executed judgment and justice among all his people. (This means that no enemy occupied any part of the land. How many of us can say that we "reign over all the possession that God has given us"? It can be done only through Faith expressed in Christ and what Christ has done for us at the Cross, which then gives us the help of the Holy Spirit, without Whom nothing can be done [Rom. 8:1-2, 11].)

15 And Joab the son of Zeruiah was over the host *(general of the army)*; and Jehoshaphat the son of Ahilud, recorder.

16 And Zadok the son of Ahitub, and Abimelech the son of Abiathar, were the Priests; and Shavsha was scribe;

17 And Benaiah the son of Jehoiada was over the Cherethites and the Pelethites *(these last two groups were probably Philistines who served as David's bodyguards; they had, thereby, thrown in their lot with David, consequently forsaking their past, in effect, symbolic of all Believers)*; and the sons of David were chief about the king.

CHAPTER 19
(1037 B.C.)
DAVID'S MESSENGERS HUMILIATED AND INSULTED

NOW it came to pass after this, that Nahash *(means "shining serpent")* the king of the children of Ammon died, and his son reigned in his stead.

2 And David said, I will show kindness unto Hanun the son of Nahash, because his father showed kindness to me. And David sent messengers to comfort him concerning his father. So the servants of David came into the land of the children of Ammon to Hanun, to comfort him *(a perfect Type of our Heavenly David sending Godly Preachers and Teachers to the world to comfort them with the Gospel; this comfort alone is valid!)*.

3 But the princes of the children of Ammon said to Hanun, Thinkest thou that David does honour your father, that he has sent comforters unto you? are not his servants come unto you for to search, and to overthrow, and to spy out the land? *(Evil cannot discern righteousness, but rather sees evil in everything.)*

4 Wherefore Hanun took David's servants, and shaved them, and cut off their garments in the midst hard by their buttocks, and sent them away *(greatly humiliated them!)*.

5 Then there went certain, and told David how the men were served. And he sent to meet them: for the men were greatly ashamed. And the king said, Tarry at Jericho until your beards be grown, and then return.

DAVID DEFEATS AMMON

6 And when the children of Ammon saw that they had made themselves odious to David, Hanun and the children of Ammon sent a thousand talents of silver to hire them chariots and horsemen out of Mesopotamia, and out of Syria-maachah, and out of Zobah.

7 So they hired thirty and two thousand chariots, and the king of Maachah and his people; who came and pitched before Medeba. And the children of Ammon gathered themselves together from their cities, and came to battle *(this speaks in prophetic tones of the Antichrist, who will attempt, once and for all, to overthrow Christ and to destroy Israel; however, let the axis hosts be ever so strong, yet they cannot overcome the Divine energy which offered Grace and, that being rejected, now decrees Judgment)*.

8 And when David heard of it, he sent Joab, and all the host of the mighty men *(the Holy Spirit is quick to emphasize the fact that some of these men were "mighty")*.

9 And the children of Ammon came out, and put the battle in array before the gate of the city: and the kings who were come were by themselves in the field *(the heathen kings were together in a prominent place observing the battle)*.

10 Now when Joab saw that the battle was set against him before and behind, he chose out of all the choice of Israel, and put them in array against the Syrians *(set the "mighty men" against the Syrians)*.

11 And the rest of the people *(the army)* he delivered unto the hand of Abishai his brother, and they set themselves in array against the children of Ammon *(evidently, the Syrians were stronger than the Ammonites)*.

12 And he said, If the Syrians be too strong for me, then you shall help me: but if the children of Ammon be too strong for you, then I will help you.

13 Be of good courage, and let us behave ourselves valiantly for our people, and for the cities of our God: and let the LORD do that which is good in His sight.

14 So Joab and the people who were with him drew near before the Syrians unto the battle; and they fled before him *(resist Satan, and he will flee from you [James 4:7])*.

15 And when the children of Ammon saw that the Syrians were fled, they likewise fled before Abishai his *(Joab's)* brother, and entered into the city. Then Joab came to Jerusalem.

DAVID DEFEATS THE SYRIANS

16 And when the Syrians saw that they were

put to the worse before Israel, they sent messengers, and drew forth the Syrians who were beyond the river: and Shophach the captain of the host of Hadarezer went before them *(made another excursion)*.

17 And it was told David; and he gathered all Israel, and passed over Jordan, and came upon them, and set the battle in array against them. So when David had put the battle in array against the Syrians, they fought with him.

18 But the Syrians fled before Israel; and David slew of the Syrians seven thousand men which fought in chariots, and forty thousand footmen, and killed Shophach the captain of the host.

19 And when the servants of Hadarezer saw that they were put to the worse before Israel, they made peace with David, and became his servants: neither would the Syrians help the children of Ammon any more *(likewise, at the conclusion of the great Battle of Armageddon, with Jesus Christ reigning as the Lord of Heaven and Earth, the world will make peace with our Heavenly David and, in effect, will become His servant)*.

CHAPTER 20
(1017 B.C.)
AMMONITE WAR: JOAB AND DAVID CAPTURE RABBAH

AND it came to pass, that after the year was expired, at the time that kings go out to battle, Joab led forth the power of the army, and wasted the country of the children of Ammon, and came and besieged Rabbah. But David tarried at Jerusalem. And Joab smote Rabbah, and destroyed it. *(This Chapter coincides with II Sam., Chpt. 11, but with a glaring difference. David's sin with Bath-sheba and the sin concerning her husband are totally omitted. Why?*

I and II Samuel and I and II Kings give these accounts from the human standpoint; I and II Chronicles, from God's standpoint.

David had repented of these terrible sins [Ps. 51]. So now, as far as the Lord was concerned, it is as if David had never committed these sins, and so it is with all who place their sins at the foot of the Cross [I Jn. 1:7, 9].)

2 And David took the crown of their king from off his head, and found it to weigh a talent of gold *(about 75 pounds)*, and there were precious stones in it; and it was set upon David's head: and he brought also exceeding much spoil out of the city *(at Calvary, Jesus defeated Satan, and took the crown from his head; this victory is now ours [Col. 2:14-15])*.

3 And he brought out the people who were in it, and cut them with saws, and with harrows of iron, and with axes *(would have been better translated, "appointed them certain tasks," because the Hebrew word for "cut" is "sur," and does not literally mean to cut with something material)*. Even so dealt David with all the cities of the children of Ammon *(put them into submission to himself)*. And David and all the people *(army)* returned to Jerusalem.

PHILISTINE GIANTS SLAIN

4 And it came to pass after this, that there arose war at Gezer with the Philistines; at which time Sibbechai the Hushathite slew Sippai, that was of the children of the giant: and they were subdued *(II Sam. 21:18)*.

5 And there was war again with the Philistines; and Elhanan the son of Jair slew Lahmi the brother of Goliath the Gittite, whose spear staff was like a weaver's beam *(II Sam. 21:19)*.

6 And yet again there was war at Gath, where was a man of great stature, whose fingers and toes were four and twenty, six on each hand, and six on each foot: and he also was the son of the giant *(II Sam. 21:20)*.

7 But when he defied Israel, Jonathan the son of Shimea David's brother slew him.

8 These were born unto the giant in Gath, and they fell by the hand of David, and by the hand of his servants. *(In I Sam., Chpt. 17; II Sam., Chpt. 21; and, I Chron., Chpt. 20, some five giants are spoken of. It seems they were brothers [II Sam. 21:19-22]. These were the last of the mighty races of giants, who were the offspring of fallen angels and women, in Satan's efforts to pollute the human race, so that the Seed of the woman, the Lord Jesus Christ, might not be able to come into the world in order to redeem Adam's fallen race [Gen. 6:4].*

These also represent hindrances in our particular Christian lives, which seek to usurp authority over God's rule. Every Satanic "giant" in our lives must be destroyed. There is no room for compromise. The "flesh" must die, and the "Spirit" must reign supreme. This can be done only by the Believer placing his Faith exclusively in Christ and the Cross, which then gives the Holy Spirit latitude to work in our hearts and lives, bringing forth complete victory [Rom. 6:3-14; 8:1-2, 11].)

CHAPTER 21
(1017 B.C.)
DAVID'S SIN IN TAKING A CENSUS

AND Satan stood up against Israel, and provoked David to number Israel. *(II Sam. 24:1 says, "God moved David" to do such. Is there a contradiction?*

No. We learn from these Passages that Satan can do nothing against a Child of God, but that God allows it. He permits Satan a limited power in bringing merited judgment upon men. Why did the Lord allow this against David? The following Passages will tell us.)

2 And David said to Joab and to the rulers of the people, Go, number Israel from Beersheba even to Dan; and bring the number of them to me, that I may know it. *(What the Philistines, Ammonites, and Syrians failed to effect, this mental weapon of subtle temptation accomplished. It was "pride"!*

What could be more laudable than to verify the truthfulness of the promise made to Abraham that his children should exceed the stars in multitude? However, to seek to carnally verify a Divine Promise brings deadness to the soul! And such a desire leads not to the Bible, but from the Bible.)

3 And Joab answered, The LORD make his people an hundred times so many more as they be: but, my lord the king, are they not all my lord's servants? why then does my lord require this thing? why will he be a cause of trespass to Israel? *(It was not wrong to take a census; however, to do so, Exodus 30:12 demanded a half-shekel of silver be paid for each individual. It was referred to as "ransom money," meaning, in essence, that all the Children of Israel were purchased by the Blood of the Lamb, for "silver" was a type of Redemption in Old Testament terminology. In ignoring this command of the Lord to pay the ransom money, a half-shekel of the sanctuary for each person taken in the census, David was bypassing the Cross, which God can never allow!)*

4 Nevertheless the king's word prevailed against Joab. Wherefore Joab departed, and went throughout all Israel, and came to Jerusalem. *(It is doubtful that Joab would have known of the admonition of the payment of the half-shekel, but he felt that what David was doing was wrong, which it was. It seems, as well, that David never bothered to consult the Word, even as he didn't bother to consult the Word concerning the transportation of the Ark [Chpt. 13].*

God cannot abide a violation of the Word, even in His most choice servants, as David. The results will not be pleasant!)

5 And Joab gave the sum of the number of the people unto David. And all they of Israel were a thousand thousand and an hundred thousand men who drew sword: and Judah was four hundred threescore and ten thousand men who drew sword. *(The numbers do not tally with II Sam., Chpt. 24. The explanation is: Chronicles says, "All Israel were 1,100,000 men who drew sword," while II Samuel says, "800,000 valiant men who drew sword." Evidently, 300,000 were young soldiers that could not justly be deemed as "valiant." Similar details appear respecting Judah. II Samuel states that "the men of Judah were 500,000"; Chronicles records the number as "470,000." Evidently, therefore, the remaining 30,000 were either untrained men or non-combatants.)*

6 But Levi and Benjamin counted he not among them: for the king's word was abominable to Joab. *(Joab was a man of the world. He had not the spiritual insight of David; and yet, at times, such will have a better spiritual insight than a self-willed Believer. Such is the case here!)*

DAVID CHOOSES HIS PUNISHMENT

7 And God was displeased with this thing; therefore He smote Israel. *(The Lord was displeased because David had ignored, when taking the census, the payment of the ransom money of silver, which typified Redemption, which, of course, typified Calvary. The Lord will "smite" all who follow this course. In fact, He has no choice. It is the Judgment of God on Christ, which speaks of the Cross, or it's Judgment on the people. If the Cross is ignored, Judgment is the inevitable result.)*

8 And David said unto God, I have sinned greatly, because I have done this thing: but now, I beseech you, do away the iniquity of your servant; for I have done very foolishly. *(Let all know and understand, to treat the Cross with disdain is a "great sin." All who ignore the Cross do so "foolishly"!)*

9 And the LORD spoke unto Gad, David's seer, saying *(the Lord presently is speaking to His Prophets, at least what precious few there presently are; regrettably, the modern Church is not hearing and obeying the Message, as David did),*

10 Go and tell David, saying, Thus saith the LORD, I offer you three things: choose you

one of them, that I may do it unto you.

11 So Gad came to David, and said unto him, Thus saith the LORD, You choose

12 Either three years' famine; or three months to be destroyed before your foes, while that the sword of your enemies overtakes you; or else three days the sword of the LORD, even the pestilence, in the land, and the Angel of the LORD destroying throughout all the coast of Israel. Now therefore advise yourself what word I shall bring again to Him Who sent me. *(As stated, sin has to be addressed, whether in Christ and what He did for us at the Cross, or Judgment upon men. Let all understand, the only answer for sin is the Cross of Christ [Heb. 10:12].)*

13 And David said unto Gad, I am in a great strait *(sin does exactly that; it puts a person in a "great strait")*: let me fall now into the hand of the LORD; for very great are His mercies: but let me not fall into the hand of man *(very bad, at any rate, but an extremely wise choice!)*.

14 So the LORD sent pestilence upon Israel: and there fell of Israel seventy thousand men *(in Exodus 30:12, the Lord said there would be a "plague among them," if the "half-shekel" was not paid as ransom money for each person; it should be understood here that God means what He says; what type of "pestilence" it was, we aren't told!)*.

15 And God sent an Angel unto Jerusalem to destroy it: and as he was destroying, the LORD beheld, and He repented Him of the evil, and said to the Angel who destroyed, It is enough, stay now your hand. And the Angel of the LORD stood by the threshingfloor of Ornan the Jebusite. *(The word "repented," as used of the Lord, doesn't mean that God changes, for, in fact, He never changes [Mal. 3:6]; however, His Direction may vary according to the obedience or disobedience of man.*

It was not coincidental that the Angel "stood by the threshingfloor." As always, the wheat must be separated from the chaff, and it takes a threshingfloor to do that [Mat. 3:12].

We find from this Text that the sin of ignoring the Cross is at least one of the worst sins, if not the worst sin, that can be committed. The degree of judgment, 70,000 men dying, guarantees that fact.)

16 And David lifted up his eyes, and saw the Angel of the LORD stand between the Earth and the Heaven, having a drawn sword in his hand stretched out over Jerusalem. Then David and the elders of Israel, who were clothed in sackcloth, fell upon their faces *(the "sackcloth" denoted humility and Repentance; God has promised to look with favor at such [Isa. 66:2])*.

17 And David said unto God, Is it not I who commanded the people to be numbered? even I it is who has sinned and done evil indeed; but as for these sheep, what have they done? let Your hand, I pray You, O LORD my God, be on me, and on my father's house; but not on Your people, that they should be plagued. *(In a sense, David stood here similar to Moses, when the Lord was about to destroy them, as it regards the golden calf [Ex. 32:11-14]. As well, and even more importantly, David is here a Type of Christ, Who, at this moment, is interceding for all Believers [Heb. 7:25-26].)*

DAVID BUYS THE TEMPLE SITE; BUILDS AN ALTAR; MAKES ATONEMENT

18 Then the Angel of the LORD commanded Gad to say to David, that David should go up, and set up an Altar unto the LORD in the threshingfloor of Ornan the Jebusite. *(This would be the exact place where the Temple would be built. So, "where sin abounded, grace did much more abound" [Rom. 5:20]. That which David had ignored in taking the census, the "Altar," which typified the Cross, must be erected here. This is why Paul said, "We preach Christ Crucified" [I Cor. 1:23]. The modern Church presently casts about in its dilemma, trying to find a solution. The only solution is the Cross. The Church must go back to the Cross.)*

19 And David went up at the saying of Gad, which he spoke in the Name of the LORD *(the true Prophets of God are saying the same thing presently to the modern Church, "Build an Altar"; but, regrettably, they are little heeding)*.

20 And Ornan *(who owned the threshingfloor)* turned back, and saw the Angel; and his four sons with him hid themselves. Now Ornan was threshing wheat. *(The picture is striking: the wrath of God about to fall upon the city, the guilty king confessing his sin, the spotless Sacrifice slain, the judgment of God vindicated and honored.*

This Grace is the more apparent and all-embracing, when it is noticed that the ground upon which this most satisfactory Sacrifice was offered up belonged to a Gentile, Araunah, the Jebusite.)

21 And as David came to Ornan, Ornan looked and saw David, and went out of the

threshingfloor, and bowed himself to David with his face to the ground *(he was evidently surprised at seeing the king at this place).*

22 Then David said to Ornan, Grant me the place of this threshingfloor, that I may build an Altar therein unto the LORD: you shall grant it me for the full price: that the plague may be stayed from the people.

23 And Ornan said unto David, Take it to you, and let my lord the king do that which is good in his eyes: lo, I give you the oxen also for Burnt Offerings, and the threshing instruments for wood, and the wheat for the Meat Offering; I give it all *(it seems that this Jebusite was very well acquainted with the various Offerings of Israel).*

24 And king David said to Ornan, No; but I will verily buy it for the full price: for I will not take that which is yours for the LORD, nor offer Burnt Offerings without cost *(sin can never be atoned for without the "full price" of the Blood of Calvary; the problem with the Church is bloodless altars and a cross-less salvation; in fact, such do not exist; man cannot be redeemed by half measures; as stated, it has to be the "full price" — the Precious shed Blood of the Lord Jesus Christ [Jn. 3:16]).*

25 So David gave to Ornan for the place six hundred shekels of gold by weight *(about $60,000 in 2004 money).*

26 And David built there an Altar unto the LORD, and offered Burnt Offerings and Peace Offerings, and called upon the LORD; and He answered him from Heaven by fire upon the Altar of Burnt Offering. *(The lightning coming from Heaven and striking the Sacrifice is a picture of God's Judgment on sin — the Judgment, we may quickly add, that should have fallen on David, and on us, for that matter, but, instead, fell upon Christ. The choice belongs to man! Man can accept the Judgment that fell on Christ, and do so by accepting Christ, which sets the sinner free. Or he can rebel against Christ, and suffer the lightning-strike of Judgment upon himself. There is no alternative!).*

27 And the LORD commanded the Angel; and he put up his sword again into the sheath thereof *(the only thing that stands between Judgment of the entirety of this planet and God Almighty is the Cross of Christ).*

28 At that time when David saw that the LORD had answered him in the threshingfloor of Ornan the Jebusite, then he sacrificed there *(Verses 28-29 proclaim to us that the Lord told David that this site would now become the site*

of the Temple, soon to be constructed).

29 For the Tabernacle of the LORD, which Moses made in the wilderness, and the Altar of the Burnt Offering, were at that season in the high place at Gibeon *(about 5 miles northwest of Jerusalem).*

30 But David could not go before it to enquire of God: for he was afraid because of the sword of the Angel of the LORD *(the Tabernacle represented the Law, "but Grace and Truth came by Jesus Christ" [Jn. 1:17]).*

CHAPTER 22
(1017 B.C.)
PREPARATION FOR BUILDING
THE TEMPLE

THEN David said, This is the House of the LORD God, and this is the Altar of the Burnt Offering for Israel *(in other words, this is where the House of the Lord will be built).*

2 And David commanded to gather together the strangers who were in the land of Israel; and he set masons to hew wrought stones to build the House of God *(David's heart, until the day of his death, would be for the preparation of the Temple construction).*

3 And David prepared iron in abundance for the nails for the doors of the gates, and for the joinings; and brass in abundance without weight *(here we have the beginning of gathering the materials for the Temple — not counted in the 7 1/2 years of the actual construction by Solomon);*

4 Also cedar trees in abundance: for the Zidonians and they of Tyre brought much cedar wood to David.

5 And David said, Solomon my son is young and tender, and the House that is to be built for the LORD must be exceeding magnificent, of fame and of glory throughout all countries: I will therefore now make preparation for it. So David prepared abundantly before his death *(this "House" was to be "in type" the Millennial Glory of the Messiah, just as the Tabernacle had set forth His Mediatorial Glory).*

DAVID CHARGES SOLOMON
TO BUILD THE TEMPLE

6 Then he called for Solomon his son, and charged him to build an House for the LORD God of Israel *(Solomon was chosen by the Lord [I Ki. 1:30, 37, 39]).*

7 And David said to Solomon, My son, as

for me, it was in my mind to build an House unto the Name of the LORD my God:

8 But the Word of the LORD came to me saying, You have shed blood abundantly, and have made great wars: you shall not build an House unto My Name, because you have shed much blood upon the Earth in My sight *(David typifies Christ as a Man of war, destroying His enemies; Solomon, as Christ, the Prince of Peace, reigning over a kingdom free from these enemies)*.

9 Behold, a son shall be born to you, who shall be a man of rest; and I will give him rest from all his enemies round about: for his name shall be Solomon, and I will give peace and quietness unto Israel in his days *(this Verse proclaims that Solomon was named before he was born; he was one of the seven men in the Bible named before birth)*.

10 He shall build an House for My Name; and he shall be My son, and I will be his Father; and I will establish the throne of his kingdom over Israel for ever *(the complete fulfillment will be in Christ, and will take place in the coming Kingdom Age [Isa., Chpt. 11])*.

11 Now, my son, the LORD be with you; and prosper you, and build the House of the LORD your God, as He has said of you *(the charge by David given to Solomon)*.

12 Only the LORD give you wisdom and understanding, and give you charge concerning Israel, that you may keep the Law of the LORD your God *(these words said by David may have been the germ of Solomon's own prayer, which "pleased the Lord" [I Ki. 3:5-14; II Chron. 1:7-12])*.

13 Then shall you prosper, if you take heed to fulfill the Statutes and Judgments which the LORD charged Moses with concerning Israel: be strong, and of good courage; dread not, nor be dismayed *(basically, David quotes the very words given by the Lord to Joshua, which were given about 500 years earlier; however, a general Promise given by the Lord is applicable to anyone who will dare to believe!)*.

14 Now, behold, in my trouble I have prepared for the House of the LORD an hundred thousand talents of gold *(approximately $50 billion in 2004 currency)*, and a thousand thousand talents of silver *(approximately $100 million in 2004 currency)*; and of brass and iron without weight; for it is in abundance: timber also and stone have I prepared; and you may add thereto *(these words confirm what so often appears in the character of David, that all through his stormy life of warfare, his heart was* true to one great purpose, the establishment of the House of God, and the Peace of God in the midst of the people of God)*.

15 Moreover there are workmen with you in abundance, hewers and workers of stone and timber, and all manner of cunning men for every manner of work.

16 Of the gold, the silver, and the brass, and the iron, there is no number. Arise therefore, and be doing, and the LORD be with you *(this command, "Arise . . . and be doing," should be the criteria for every Believer, as well!)*.

17 David also commanded all the princes of Israel to help Solomon his son, saying,

18 Is not the LORD your God with you? and has He not given you rest on every side? for He has given the inhabitants of the land into my hand; and the land is subdued before the LORD, and before His people. *(At long last, every enemy has been defeated, and the great Promises of God have been brought to fulfillment. What a moment!)*

19 Now set your heart and your soul to seek the LORD your God; arise therefore, and build ye the Sanctuary of the LORD God, to bring the Ark of the Covenant of the LORD, and the holy vessels of God, into the House that is to be built to the Name of the LORD *(this is basically the same Word given by Christ in Mat. 6:33)*.

CHAPTER 23
(1015 B.C.)

DAVID MAKES SOLOMON KING

SO when David was old and full of days, he made Solomon his son king over Israel. *(As previously stated, David was a Type of Christ defeating all His enemies, and putting down Satan and all the minions of darkness, which He did at the Cross. Solomon is a Type of Christ resting in splendor and glory, victorious and triumphant over all enemies, reigning in the coming Kingdom Age, such as the world has never known.)*

2 And he gathered together all the princes of Israel, with the Priests and the Levites *(this is a foretype of the glorious day when the Lord Jesus Christ will reign supreme in Jerusalem, and will, as outlined by Ezek., Chpts. 40-48, gather the worship classes [Priests and Levites] together to establish the worship of God in Israel, and for the entire world, for that matter)*.

3 Now the Levites were numbered from the age of thirty years and upward: and their number by their polls, man by man, was thirty and

eight thousand *(this was changed to 25 years in Num. 8:24 and to 20 years by David in Verse 27; the reason for the lowering of the age was because of the need for greater numbers to service the Temple in the great Work for God).*

4 Of which, twenty and four thousand were to set forward the work of the House of the LORD; and six thousand were officers and judges:

5 Moreover four thousand were porters; and four thousand praised the LORD with the instruments which I made, said David, to praise therewith *(it is interesting to note that the workers and the worshippers are equal in number; consequently, we have here the tremendous emphasis placed by the Holy Spirit on worship; as well, the worship consisted of singing and music, which constitutes one of the greatest forms of praise and worship there is).*

6 And David divided them into courses among the sons of Levi, namely, Gershon, Kohath, and Merari *(all the many thousands of Levites who served in the Work of God came under one of these three designations).*

7 Of the Gershonites were, Laadan, and Shimei.

8 The sons of Laadan; the chief was Jehiel, and Zetham, and Joel, three.

9 The sons of Shimei; Shelomith, and Haziel, and Haran, three. These were the chief of the fathers of Laadan.

10 And the sons of Shimei were, Jahath, Zina, and Jeush, and Beriah. These four were the sons of Shimei.

11 And Jahath was the chief, and Zizah the second, but Jeush and Beriah had not many sons; therefore they were in one reckoning, according to their father's house.

12 The sons of Kohath; Amram, Izhar, Hebron, and Uzziel, four.

13 The sons of Amram; Aaron and Moses: and Aaron was separated, that he should sanctify the most holy things, he and his sons for ever, to burn incense before the LORD, to minister unto Him, and to bless in His Name for ever *(all the Priests were to be in the lineage of Aaron).*

14 Now concerning Moses the man of God, his sons were named of the Tribe of Levi.

15 The sons of Moses were, Gershom, and Eliezer.

16 Of the sons of Gershom, Shebuel was the chief.

17 And the sons of Eliezer were, Rehabiah the chief. And Eliezer had none other sons; but the sons of Rehabiah were very many.

18 Of the sons of Izhar; Shelomith the chief.

19 Of the sons of Hebron; Jeriah the first, Amariah the second, Jahaziel the third, and Jekameam the fourth.

20 Of the sons of Uzziel; Micah the first and Jesiah the second.

21 The sons of Merari; Mahli and Mushi. The sons of Mahli; Eleazar, and Kish.

22 And Eleazar died, and had no sons, but daughters: and their brethren the sons of Kish took them.

23 The sons of Mushi; Mahli, and Eder, and Jeremoth, three.

THE MINISTRY OF THE LEVITES

24 These were the sons of Levi after the house of their fathers; even the chief of the fathers, as they were counted by number of names by their polls, who did the work for the service of the House of the LORD, from the age of twenty years and upward *(this Verse and Verse 27 proclaim the lowering of the age for the Priests and the Levites to 20 years old and upward).*

25 For David said, The LORD God of Israel has given rest unto His people, that they may dwell in Jerusalem for ever *(regrettably, because of sin, they were driven from Jerusalem and all the Holy Land; but in the future, they will be restored, and will fulfill God's original purpose [Isa. 11:1-12]):*

26 And also unto the Levites; they shall no more carry the Tabernacle, nor any vessels of it for the service thereof *(because once the Temple is built, these Vessels will move no more).*

27 For by the last words of David the Levites were numbered from twenty years old and above *(included in his last instructions):*

28 Because their office was to wait on the sons of Aaron for the service of the House of the LORD, in the courts, and in the chambers, and in the purifying of all holy things, and the work of the service of the House of God;

29 Both for the shewbread, and for the fine flour for Meat Offering, and for the unleavened cakes, and for that which is baked in the pan, and for that which is fried, and for all manner of measure and size *(all these things were a constant necessity, meaning their work never ended; it did end when Jesus went to the Cross, thereby fulfilling all rudiments of the Law, plus its ceremonies and rituals);*

30 And to stand every morning to thank and praise the LORD, and likewise at evening

(seemingly, a choir met every morning at 9 a.m., and every evening at 3 p.m., at the time of the morning and evening sacrifices, in order to praise the Lord; this was done daily):

31 And to offer all Burnt Sacrifices unto the LORD in the sabbaths, in the new moons, and on the set feasts, by number, according to the order commanded unto them, continually before the LORD *(the Priests alone performed the actual sacrifices, which was done every day)*:

32 And that they should keep the charge of the Tabernacle of the congregation, and the charge of the Holy Place, and the charge of the sons of Aaron their brethren, in the service of the House of the LORD *(here the Priests are reminded of their representative character and position, and of the solemn responsibility which rested on them)*.

CHAPTER 24
(1015 B.C.)
THE GROUPING OF THE PRIESTS:
BY LOT INTO 24 COURSES

NOW these are the divisions of the sons of Aaron; The sons of Aaron; Nadab, and Abihu, Eleazar, and Ithamar *(these were the four sons of Aaron)*.

2 But Nadab and Abihu died before their father, and had no children *(were stricken dead by the Lord for offering "strange fire" [Lev. 10:1-2])*: therefore Eleazar and Ithamar executed the Priest's office *(from the two remaining sons, the order of Priests would derive their office)*.

3 And David distributed them, both Zadok of the sons of Eleazar, and Ahimelech of the sons of Ithamar, according to their offices in their service *(these two men were given the responsibility of these offices)*.

4 And there were more chief men found of the sons of Eleazar than of the sons of Ithamar, and thus were they divided. Among the sons of Eleazar there were sixteen chief men of the house of their fathers, and eight among the sons of Ithamar according to the house of their fathers *(these total 24; therefore, all the order of divisions of Priests would come from these original 24 sons, constituting 24 different orders)*.

5 Thus were they divided by lot, one sort with another; for the governors of the sanctuary, and governors of the House of God, were of the sons of Eleazar, and of the sons of Ithamar *(as stated, there were 24 courses, which had their origination in the 24 sons of Eleazar and Ithamar, who, incidentally, lived many years before)*.

6 And Shemaiah the son of Nethaneel the scribe, one of the Levites, wrote them before the king, and the princes, and Zadok the Priest, and Ahimelech the son of Abiathar, and before the chief of the fathers of the Priests and Levites; one principal household being taken for Eleazar, and one taken for Ithamar.

7 Now the first lot came forth to Jehoiarib, the second to Jedaiah *(the first order of Priests, consisting actually of many Priests, would have been the "Jehoiarib order or division"; the second, third, and so forth, would have been after their own respective names given in these Passages; the 24 chief men, who went by their respective names given, were governors of the House of the Lord in their own turn, one week at a time; each Priest would serve from Sabbath to Sabbath; Zechariah [Lk 1:5], the father of John the Baptist, belonged to the 8th course, which is the course of Abijah [Vs. 10]; it is interesting to learn from Lk. 1:5 how the Divine Son of David, through all the changes of Israel's history, watched over and maintained these courses of the Priests)*,

8 The third to Harim, the fourth to Seorim,

9 The fifth to Malchijah, the sixth of Mijamin,

10 The seventh to Hakkoz, the eighth to Abijah,

11 The ninth to Jeshuah, the tenth to Shecaniah,

12 The eleventh to Eliashib, the twelfth to Jakim,

13 The thirteenth to Huppah, the fourteenth to Jeshebeab,

14 The fifteenth to Bilgah, the sixteenth to Immer,

15 The seventeenth to Hezir, the eighteenth to Aphses,

16 The nineteenth to Pethahiah, the twentieth to Jehezekel,

17 The one and twentieth to Jachin, the two and twentieth to Gamul,

18 The three and twentieth to Delaiah, the four and twentieth to Maaziah.

19 These were the orderings of them in their service to come into the House of the LORD, according to their manner, under Aaron their father, as the LORD God of Israel had commanded him.

THE LEVITES ALSO DIVIDED BY LOT
INTO 24 COURSES

20 And the rest of the sons of Levi were these:

Of the sons of Amram; Shubael: of the sons of Shubael; Jehdeiah.

21 Concerning Rehabiah: of the sons of Rehabiah, the first was Isshiah.

22 Of the Izharites; Shelomoth: of the sons of Shelomoth; Jahath.

23 And the sons of Hebron; Jeriah the first, Amariah the second, Jahaziel the third, Jekameam the fourth.

24 Of the sons of Uzziel; Michah; of the sons of Michah, Shamir.

25 The brother of Michah was Isshiah: of the sons of Isshiah; Zechariah.

26 The sons of Merari were Mahli and Mushi: the sons of Jaaziah; Beno.

27 The sons of Merari by Jaaziah; Beno, and Shoham, and Zaccur, and Ibri.

28 Of Mahli came Eleazar, who had no sons.

29 Concerning Kish: the son of Kish was Jerahmeel.

30 The sons also of Mushi; Mahli, and Eder, and Jerimoth. These were the sons of the Levites after the house of their fathers.

31 These likewise cast lots over against their brethren the sons of Aaron in the presence of David the king, and Zadok, and Ahimelech, and the chief of the fathers of the Priests and Levites, even the principal fathers over against their younger brethren. *(The words "cast lots" refer to the Urim and the Thummim. In fact, absolutely nothing about the Temple, its furnishings, fixtures, design, the order of the Priests, as well as the Levites, was left to chance. Everything was ordered, guided, and directed by the Holy Spirit.*

Verses 20-31 give the order or courses of the Levites. They were 24 courses, as well. Whereas the Priests had to do with the Sacrifices [the Priests were also Levites], the balance of the Levites had to do with the worship, which concerned music and singing, along with maintenance of the Temple.)

CHAPTER 25

(1015 B.C.)

THE DIVISION OF THE MUSICIANS

MOREOVER David and the captains of the host separated to the service of the sons of Asaph, and of Heman, and of Jeduthun, who should prophesy with harps, with psalteries, and with cymbals: and the number of the workmen according to their service was *(we are now told of the division of the 4,000 singers into 24 courses or weekly periods; there was no such provision for song and worship in the Tabernacle in the wilderness, as in the Temple of Solomon; this was because the former spoke of a provided Redemption, the latter of an accomplished Salvation; as well, musical instrumentation which accompanies Spirit-led singing is constituted as "prophecy" [I Cor. 14:3]):*

2 Of the sons of Asaph; Zaccur, and Joseph, and Nethaniah, and Asarelah, the sons of Asaph under the hands of Asaph, which prophesied according to the order of the king.

3 Of Jeduthun: the sons of Jeduthun; Gedaliah, and Zeri, and Jeshaiah, Hashabiah, and Mattithiah, six, under the hands of their father Jeduthun, who prophesied with a harp, to give thanks and to praise the LORD.

4 Of Heman: the sons of Heman: Bukkiah, Mattaniah, Uzziel, Shebuel, and Jerimoth, Hananiah, Hanani, Eliathah, Giddalti, and Romamti-ezer, Joshbekashah, Mallothi, Hothir, and Mahazioth:

5 All these were the sons of Heman the king's seer in the words of God, to lit up the horn. And God gave to Heman fourteen sons and three daughters.

6 All these were under the hands of their father for song in the house of the LORD, with cymbals, psalteries, and harps, for the service of the House of God, according to the king's order to Asaph, Jeduthun, and Heman *(the overseership of this service seemed to be divided among the sons of Asaph, Jeduthun, and Heman).*

7 So the number of them, with their brethren who were instructed in the songs of the LORD, even all who were cunning, was two hundred fourscore and eight *(they were helped by 288 skilled musicians and skilled singers).*

8 And they cast lots, ward against ward, as well the small as the great, the teacher as the scholar.

9 Now the first lot came forth for Asaph to Joseph: the second to Gedaliah, who with his brethren and sons were twelve:

10 The third to Zaccur, he, his sons, and his brethren, were twelve:

11 The fourth to Izri, he, his sons, and his brethren, were twelve:

12 The fifth to Nethaniah, he, his sons, and his brethren, were twelve:

13 The sixth to Bukkiah, he, his sons, and his brethren, were twelve:

14 The seventh to Jesharelah, he, his sons, and his brethren, were twelve:

15 The eighth to Jeshaiah, he, his sons, and his brethren, were twelve:

16 The ninth to Mattaniah, he, his sons, and his brethren, were twelve:

17 The tenth to Shimei, he, his sons, and his brethren, were twelve:

18 The eleventh to Azareel, he, his sons, and his brethren, were twelve:

19 The twelfth to Hashabiah, he, his sons, and his brethren, were twelve:

20 The thirteenth to Shubael, he, his sons, and his brethren, were twelve:

21 The fourteenth to Mattithiah, he, his sons, and his brethren, were twelve:

22 The fifteenth to Jeremoth, he, his sons, and his brethren, were twelve:

23 The sixteenth to Hananiah, he, his sons, and his brethren, were twelve:

24 The seventeenth to Joshbekashah, he, his sons, and his brethren, were twelve:

25 The eighteenth to Hanani, he, his sons, and his brethren, were twelve:

26 The nineteenth to Mallothi, he, his sons, and his brethren, were twelve:

27 The twentieth to Eliathah, he, his sons, and his brethren, were twelve:

28 The one and twentieth of Hothir, he, his sons, and his brethren, were twelve:

29 The two and twentieth to Giddalti, he, his sons, and his brethren, were twelve:

30 The three and twentieth to Mahazioth, he, his sons, and his brethren, were twelve:

31 The four and twentieth to Romamti-ezer, he, his sons, and his brethren, were twelve.

CHAPTER 26

(1015 B.C.)

THE PORTERS AND OVERSEERS: DIVIDED BY LOT INTO 24 COURSES

CONCERNING the divisions of the porters *(there were 4,000 porters [23:5]; they were Levites, as well; they were divided into 24 courses, and were ruled by 93 chiefs; they were workers and helpers of the Temple service)*: Of the Korhites was Meshelemiah the son of Kore of the sons of Asaph. *(These were the descendants of Korah, who had led the rebellion against Moses, over 500 years before [Num., Chpt. 16]. We find from this that where sin abounded, Grace did much more abound. The sons of Korah are first chosen as doorkeepers, their duty being to prevent the presumption of which their father was guilty. Such are the ways of God! The sinful sons of a rebellious father are set on high by Him, and Heavenly things are committed to their hands. Such is Grace!)*

2 And the sons of Meshelemiah were, Zechariah the firstborn, Jediael the second, Zebadiah, the third, Jathniel the fourth,

3 Elam the fifth, Jehohanan the sixth, Elioenai the seventh.

4 Moreover the sons of Obed-edom were, Shemaiah the firstborn, Jehozabad the second, Joab the third, and Sacar the fourth, and Nethaneel the fifth.

5 Ammiel the sixth, Issachar the seventh, Peulthai the eighth: for God blessed him.

6 Also unto Shemaiah his son were sons born, that ruled throughout the house of their father: for they were mighty men of valour.

7 The sons of Shemaiah; Othni and Rephael, and Obed, Elzabad, whose brethren were strong men, Elihu, and Semachiah.

8 All these of the sons of Obed-edom: they and their sons and their brethren, able men for strength for the service, were threescore and two of Obed-edom. *(It is remarkable that the Holy Spirit will mention Obed-edom's name some 20 times throughout the Word of God, and it was all because of his love for the things of God [II Sam. 6:10-11].)*

9 And Meshelemiah had sons and brethren, strong men, eighteen.

10 Also Hosah, of the children of Merari, had sons; Simri the chief, (for though he was not the firstborn, yet his father made him the chief;)

11 Hilkiah the second, Tebaliah the third, Zechariah the fourth: all the sons and brethren of Hosah were thirteen.

12 Among these were the divisions of the porters, even among the chief men, having wards one against another, to minister in the House of the LORD.

PORTERS OF THE GATES

13 And they cast lots, as well the small as the great, according to the house of their fathers, for every gate.

14 And the lot eastward fell to Shelemiah. Then for Zechariah his son, a wise counsellor, they cast lots; and his lot came out northward.

15 To Obed-edom southward; and to his sons the house of Asuppim.

16 To Shuppim and Hosah the lot came forth westward, with the gate Shallecheth, by the causeway of the going up, ward against ward.

17 Eastward were six Levites, northward four a day, southward four a day, and toward

Asuppim two and two.

18 At Parbar westward, four at the causeway, and two at Parbar.

19 These are the divisions of the porters among the sons of Kore, and among the sons of Merari.

PORTERS OVER THE TREASURES

20 And of the Levites, Ahijah was over the treasures of the House of God, and over the treasures of the dedicated things.

21 As concerning the sons of Laadan; the sons of the Gershonite Laadan, chief fathers, even of Laadan the Gershonite, were Jehieli.

22 The sons of Jehieli; Zetham, and Joel his brother, which were over the treasures of the House of the LORD.

23 Of the Amramites, and the Izharites, the Hebronites, and the Uzzielites:

24 And Shebuel the son of Gershom, the son of Moses, was ruler of the treasures.

25 And his brethren by Eliezer; Rehabiah his son and Jeshaiah his son, and Joram his son, and Zichri his son, and Shelomith his son.

26 Which Shelomith and his brethren were over all the treasures of the dedicated things, which David the king, and the chief fathers, the captains over thousands and hundreds, and the captains of the host, had dedicated.

27 Out of the spoils won in battles did they dedicate to maintain the House of the LORD. *(This Passage recalls the oft-forgotten lesson that the Spiritual Temple of Jehovah must be built up with "spoils won in battle." There must be labor and prayer, battling with wicked spirits in Heavenly Places, and sharp encounters with the Devil and his human servants, if spoil, that is, souls, are to be won for Jesus Christ.)*

28 And all that Samuel the Seer, and Saul the son of Kish, and Abner the son of Ner, and Joab the son of Zeruiah, had dedicated; and whosoever had dedicated anything, it was under the hand of the Shelomith, and of his brethren *(the doorkeepers were to exclude evil, and treasure-keepers were to guard the Spiritual Wealth; this implies warfare; Paul told Timothy to "war a good warfare"; he was a "doorkeeper" and a "treasure-keeper" [I Tim. 1:3; 4:20]).*

THE PUBLIC ADMINISTRATORS

29 Of the Izharites, Chenaniah and his sons were for the outward business over Israel, for officers and judges.

30 And of the Hebronites, Hashabiah and his brethren, men of valour, a thousand and seven hundred, were officers among them of Israel on this side Jordan westward in all the business of the LORD, and in the service of the king.

31 Among the Hebronites was Jerijah the chief, even among the Hebronites, according to the generations of his fathers. In the fortieth year of the reign of David they were sought for, and there were found among them mighty men of valour at Jazer of Gilead.

32 And his brethren, men of valour, were two thousand and seven hundred chief fathers, whom king David made rulers over the Reubenites, the Gadites, and the half tribe of Manasseh, for every matter pertaining to God, and affairs of the king. *(Terms such as "mighty men of valor" and "men of valor" were used in connection with the appointment of these officers by David, as it regarded the administrative offices of the Kingdom. This shows that God honors and rewards proper business activity as a dedication to His Service. It is to be carried on with the same consecration and dedication to God, even as the Temple worship and service. We must conduct ourselves thusly today, as well!)*

CHAPTER 27
(1015 B.C.)
THE OFFICERS AND PRINCES OF THE TRIBES

NOW the Children of Israel after their number, to wit, the chief fathers and captains of thousands and hundreds, and their officers who served the king in any matter of the courses, which came in and went out month by month throughout all the months of the year, of every course were twenty and four thousand.

2 Over the first course for the first month was Jashobeam the son of Zabdiel: and in his course were twenty and four thousand.

3 Of the children of Perez was the chief of all the captains of the host for the first month.

4 And over the course of the second month was Dodai an Ahohite, and of his course was Mikloth also the ruler: in his course likewise were twenty and four thousand.

5 The third captain of the host for the third month was Benaiah the son of Jehoiada, a chief priest: and in his course were twenty and four thousand.

6 This is that Benaiah, who was mighty

among the thirty, and above the thirty: and in his course was Ammizabad his son.

7 The fourth captain for the fourth month was Asahel the brother of Joab, and Zebadiah his son after him: and in his course were twenty and four thousand.

8 The fifth captain for the fifth month was Shamhuth the Izrahite; and in his course were twenty and four thousand.

9 The sixth captain for the sixth month was Ira the son of Ikkesh the Tekoite: and in his course were twenty and four thousand.

10 The seventh captain for the seventh month was Helez the Pelonite, of the children of Ephraim: and in his course were twenty and four thousand.

11 The eighth captain for the eighth month was Sibbecai the Hushathite, of the Zarhites: and in his course were twenty and four thousand.

12 The ninth captain for the ninth month was Abiezer the Anetothite, of the Benjamites: and in his course were twenty and four thousand.

13 The tenth captain for the tenth month was Maharai the Netophathite, of the Zarhites: and in his course were twenty and four thousand.

14 The eleventh captain for the eleventh month was Benaiah the Pirathonite, of the children of Ephraim: and in his course were twenty and four thousand.

15 The twelfth captain for the twelfth month was Heldai the Netophathite, of Othniel: and in his course were twenty and four thousand.

(Verses 1-15 pertain to David's standing army, which numbered 288,000. These were divided into twelve monthly courses of 24,000 each. In other words, all 288,000 were not on duty at all times. Only 24,000, in their respective month, would stand duty, with the others going about their business in their homes, etc. Counting all the officers, leaders, and personal guard, the total number would have been approximately 300,000. Of course, during times of emergency, larger numbers than that could easily be marshaled.

It is interesting to note the exact manner in which the Holy Spirit appointed the army, as well as the exact manner in which it would stand guard.)

THE RULERS

16 Furthermore over the tribes of Israel: the ruler of the Reubenites was Eliezer the son of Zichri: of the Simeonites, Shephatiah the son of Maachah:

17 Of the Levites, Hashabiah the son of Kemuel: of the Aaronites, Zadok:

18 Of Judah, Elihu, one of the brethren of David: of Issachar, Omri the son of Michael.

19 Of Zebulun, Ishmaiah the son of Obadiah: of Naphtali, Jerimoth the son of Azriel:

20 Of the children of Ephraim, Hoshea the son of Azaziah: of the half tribe of Manasseh, Joel the son of Pedaiah:

21 Of the half tribe of Manasseh in Gilead, Iddo the son of Zechariah: of Benjamin, Jaasiel the son of Abner:

22 Of Dan, Azareel the son of Jeroham, These were the princes of the Tribes of Israel.

23 But David took not the number of them from twenty years old and under: because the LORD had said he would increase Israel like to the stars of the heavens.

24 Joab the son of Zeruiah began to number, but he finished not, because there fell wrath for it against Israel; neither was the number put in the account of the chronicles of king David. *(This wrath of God against Israel was all because of David disobeying the Word of God, and not supplying the half-shekel of silver of the Sanctuary, as he was commanded to do. This was failure to recognize that Israel's prosperity and protection depended solely upon the shed Blood of the Lamb [Ex. 30:11-16].*

Unfortunately, the modern Church is in the same position presently as was Israel at that time. The Cross is being ignored, or openly repudiated. As then, so now, judgment will be the ultimate result.)

ADMINISTRATIVE POSITIONS

25 And over the king's treasures was Azmaveth the son of Adiel: and over the storehouses in the fields, in the cities, and in the villages, and in the castles, was Jehonathan the son of Uzziah:

26 And over them that did the work of the field for tillage of the ground was Ezri the son of Chelub:

27 And over the vineyards was Shimei the Ramathite: over the increase of the vineyards for the wine cellars was Zabdi the Shiphmite:

28 And over the olive trees and the sycomore trees that were in the low plains was Baalhanan the Gederite: and over the cellars of oil was Joash:

29 And over the herds that fed in Sharon

was Shitrai the Sharonite: and over the herds that were in the valleys was Shaphat the son of Adlai:

30 Over the camels also was Obil the Ishmaelite: and over the asses was Jehdeiah the Meronothite:

31 And over the flocks was Jaziz the Hagerite. All these were the rulers of the substance which was king David's.

32 Also Jonathan David's uncle was a counsellor, a wise man, and a scribe: and Jehiel the son of Hachmoni was with the king's sons:

33 And Ahithophel was the king's counsellor: and Hushai the Archite was the king's companion:

34 And after Ahithophel was Jehoiada the son of Benaiah, and Abiathar: and the general of the king's army was Joab. *(Verses 33-34 mention "Ahithophel" and "Joab." This illustrates the sad truth that it is possible to have a very high official position in the spiritual household of the King of kings, and yet at heart be a rebel to the Lord Jesus Christ!)*

CHAPTER 28
(1015 B.C.)
DAVID'S COUNSEL TO ISRAEL

AND David assembled all the princes of Israel, the princes of the Tribes, and the captains of the companies who ministered to the king by course, and the captains over the thousands, and captains over the hundreds, and the stewards over all the substance and possession of the king, and of his sons, and with the officers, and with the mighty men, and with all the valiant men, unto Jerusalem *(this was David's last assembly for Israel).*

2 Then David the king stood up upon his feet, and said, Hear me, my brethren, and my people: As for me, I had in my heart to build an house of rest for the Ark of the Covenant of the LORD, and for the footstool of our God, and had made ready for the building *(this address will show that David, in his dying hour, was more concerned with the House of God than with anything else in his Kingdom)*:

3 But God said unto me, You shall not build an house for My Name, because you have been a man of war, and have shed blood.

4 Howbeit the LORD God of Israel chose me before all the house of my father to be king over Israel for ever *(his lineage, culminating in Christ)*: for He has chosen Judah to be the ruler *(Gen. 49:10)*; and of the house of

Judah, the house of my father *(of Jesse)*; and among the sons of my father He liked me to make me king over all Israel:

5 And of all my sons, (for the LORD has given me many sons,) He has chosen Solomon my son to sit upon the Throne of the Kingdom of the LORD over Israel *(this expression, not found in its entirety elsewhere, is an emphatic statement of the true theocracy, which should have ever prevailed among the people of Israel, but was set aside because of failure on the part of Israel; it is now paralleled by the kingship of our Lord in His Own Church).*

6 And He said unto me, Solomon your son, he shall build My House and My Courts: for I have chosen him to be My son, and I will be his father.

7 Moreover I will establish his kingdom for ever, if he be constant to do My Commandments and My Judgments, as at this day *(this provision is emphatically presented again to the attention of Solomon, when the time comes for the direct appeal of God to him [I Ki. 3:14; 8:61; 9:4]).*

8 Now therefore in the sight of all Israel the congregation of the LORD, and in the audience of our God, keep and seek for all the Commandments of the LORD your God: that you may possess this good land, and leave it for an inheritance for your children after you for ever. *(For a time, Solomon was a Child of God. He loved the Lord and walked in all His Statutes [I Ki. 3:3], and the Lord loved him [II Sam. 12:24]. However, in later life, Solomon grew cold toward Jehovah and loved many strange women, who turned his heart away from God [I Ki. 11:1-8]. The Lord then became angry with Solomon and turned against him in his backslidings [I Ki. 11:9-40]. The Lord then took his kingdom from him and finally destroyed it, all because of sin. The Kingdom will be renewed again when Israel comes to Repentance [Zech. 12:10]. Under the Messiah, this Kingdom shall continue eternally.)*

DAVID'S CHARGE TO SOLOMON

9 And you, Solomon my son, know thou the God of your father, and serve Him with a perfect heart and with a willing mind *(actually, this is the only thing that any individual can give to God)*: for the LORD searches all hearts, and understands all the imaginations of the thoughts *(the Lord sees all things and knows all things, past, present, and future)*: if

you seek Him, He will be found of you; but if you forsake Him, He will cast you off for ever. *(This is one of the greatest Promises found in the entirety of the Word of God. Irrespective of the disposition of the individual involved, if the person seeks the Lord will all his heart, the Lord will be found. What a consolation! Conversely, if we turn our back on the Lord, He will turn His back on us; consequently, this completely refutes the unscriptural doctrine of unconditional eternal security.)*

10 Take heed now; for the LORD has chosen you to build an house for the Sanctuary: be strong, and do it.

11 Then David gave to Solomon his son the pattern of the porch, and of the houses thereof, and of the treasuries thereof, and of the upper chambers thereof, and of the inner parlours thereof, and of the place of the Mercy Seat,

12 And the pattern of all that he had by the Spirit *(Holy Spirit)*, of the Courts of the House of the LORD, and of all the chambers round about, of the treasuries of the House of God, and of the treasuries of the dedicated things:

13 Also for the courses of the Priests and the Levites, and for all the work of the service of the House of the LORD, and for all the vessels of service in the House of the LORD. *(These Verses declare that the Temple of Solomon was wholly planned by God, and an absolutely full pattern of it and its vessels given to David — nothing was left to his or to Solomon's imagination.)*

EXACT MEASUREMENTS

14 He gave of gold by weight for things of gold, for all instruments of all manner of service; silver also for all instruments of silver by weight, for all instruments of every kind of service:

15 Even the weight for the candlesticks of gold, and for their lamps of gold, by weight for every candlestick, and for the lamps thereof: and for the candlesticks of silver by weight, both for the candlestick, and also for the lamps thereof, according to the use of every candlestick.

16 And by weight he gave gold for the tables of shewbread, for every table; and likewise silver for the tables of silver:

17 Also pure gold for the fleshhooks, and the bowls, and the cups: and for the golden basons he gave gold by weight for every bason; and likewise silver by weight for every bason of silver:

18 And for the Altar of Incense refined gold by weight; and gold for the pattern of the chariot of the cherubims, that spread out their wings, and covered the Ark of the Covenant of the LORD.

THE HAND OF THE LORD

19 All this, said David, the LORD made me understand in writing by His Hand upon me, even all the works of this pattern *(David says that this Divine Pattern was communicated to him by him being compelled by the Hand, or the Spirit, of Jehovah, to record it all in writing, which he did!)*.

20 And David said to Solomon his son, Be strong and of good courage, and do it: fear not, nor be dismayed: for the LORD God, even my God, will be with you; He will not fail you, nor forsake you, until you have finished all the work for the service of the House of the LORD.

21 And, behold, the courses of the Priests and the Levites, even they shall be with you for all the service of the House of the God: and there shall be with you for all manner of workmanship every willing skillful man, for any manner of service: also the princes and all the people will be wholly at your commandment. *(Nothing was left, as stated, to Solomon's or David's genius or taste. All was "by the Spirit"; all was Divine!)*

CHAPTER 29
(1015 B.C.)

DAVID EXHORTS THE PEOPLE TO GIVE OFFERINGS FOR THE TEMPLE

FURTHERMORE David the king said unto all the congregation, Solomon my son, whom alone God has chosen, is yet young and tender, and the work is great: for the palace is not for man, but for the LORD God. *(These Verses continue the account of what David said to the whole congregation respecting his son Solomon.)*

2 Now I have prepared with all my might for the House of my God the gold for things to be made of gold, and the silver for things of silver, and the brass for things of brass, the iron for things of iron, and wood for things of wood; onyx stones, and stones to be set, glistering stones, and of divers colours, and all manner of precious stones, and marble stones in abundance *(David's preparation was never for himself, but for God; however, if the Lord is*

put first, then blessings will come to such an individual [Mat. 6:33]).

3 Moreover, because I have set my affection to the House of my God, I have of my own proper good, of gold and silver, which I have given to the House of my God, over and above all that I have prepared for the Holy House *(in today's inflationary dollar, David would have personally given over $10 billion for the construction of the Temple [the cost of the Temple would be over $1 trillion in 2004 currency])*.

4 Even three thousand talents of gold, of the gold of Ophir, and seven thousand talents of refined silver, to overlay the walls of the houses withal *(this is among that which was given personally by David)*:

5 The gold for things of gold, and the silver for things of silver, and for all manner of work to be made by the hands of artificers. And who then is willing to consecrate his service this day unto the LORD? *(Our service to God is to always be on a voluntary basis. As well, the Lord accepts the consecration of all, both small and great. As God has freely given to us, will we freely give to Him?)*

6 Then the chief of the fathers and princes of the Tribes of Israel and the captains of thousands and of hundreds, with the rulers of the king's work, offered willingly,

7 And gave for the service of the House of God of gold five thousand talents and ten thousand drams, and of silver ten thousand talents, and of brass eighteen thousand talents, and one hundred thousand talents of iron *(they gave freely!)*.

8 And they with whom precious stones were found gave them to the treasure of the House of the LORD, by the hand of Jehiel the Gershonite.

9 Then the people rejoiced, for that they offered willingly, because with perfect heart they offered willingly to the LORD: and David the king also rejoiced with great joy *(the words "perfect heart" specify that their motivation was not one of greed; such giving always elicits "great joy!")*.

DAVID'S PRAISE AND PRAYER

10 Wherefore David blessed the LORD before all the congregation: and David said, Blessed be Thou, LORD God of Israel our father, for ever and ever *(the majesty of this prayer includes adoration, acknowledgment of the inherent nature of human dependence,* self-humiliation, confession, dedication of all the offerings, and prayer both for the whole people in general, and for Solomon in particular).

11 Thine, O LORD, is the greatness, and the power, and the glory, and the victory, and the majesty: for all that is in the Heaven and in the Earth is Thine; Thine is the Kingdom, O LORD, and You are exalted as Head above all *(similar to the Lord's prayer [Mat. 6:13])*.

12 Both riches and honour come of You, and You reign over all; and in Your hand is power and might; and in Your hand it is to make great, and to give strength unto all.

13 Now therefore, our God, we thank You, and praise Your glorious Name.

14 But who am I, and what is my people, that we should be able to offer so willingly after this sort? for all things come of You, and of Your Own have we given You *(even though they gave liberally to the Work of God, it was what God had given to them in the first place, as it is with all of us)*.

15 For we are strangers before You, and sojourners, as were all our fathers: our days on the Earth are as a shadow, and there is none abiding.

16 O LORD our God, all this store that we have prepared to build You an House for Your Holy Name comes of Your hand, and is all Your Own.

17 I know also, my God, that You try the heart, and have pleasure in uprightness. As for me, in the uprightness of my heart I have willingly offered all these things: and now have I seen with joy Your people, which are present here, to offer willingly unto You *(it may very well be possible that the stress with which David says here, "I know," has its special cause; the thought of God as One Who "tries the heart" is one often brought out in David's Psalms)*.

18 O LORD God of Abraham, Isaac, and of Israel, our fathers, keep this for ever in the imagination of the thoughts of the heart of Your people, and prepare their heart unto You *(constantly keep the thoughts of the Lord in our imagination and our heart)*:

19 And give unto Solomon my son a perfect heart, to keep Your Commandments, Your Testimonies, and Your Statutes, and to do all these things, and to build the palace, for the which I have made provision.

20 And David said to all the congregation, Now bless the LORD your God. And all the congregation blessed the LORD God of their fathers, and bowed down their heads, and

worshipped the LORD, and the king *(David worshipped, as well!).*

21 And they sacrificed Sacrifices unto the LORD, and offered Burnt Offerings unto the LORD, on the morrow after that day, even a thousand bullocks, a thousand rams, and a thousand lambs, with their Drink Offerings, and Sacrifices in abundance for all Israel *(most probably, these Sacrifices were offered on the threshingfloor of Araunah, the Jebusite, where the Temple would be built. All is ever anchored in Calvary. All the gold and silver given on this memorable occasion could not purchase Redemption of even one soul. This could only be brought about by the precious shed Blood of the Lord Jesus Christ. The giving of the people pointed toward Calvary; the Temple site pointed toward Calvary; the construction of the Temple itself would point toward Calvary.*

In fact, the entirety of the Temple site must have been saturated with blood. To the unspiritual eye, this would have been a gruesome and unacceptable sight. To those who know their Lord and His Love for lost mankind, it would speak of Redemption so glorious that it would beggar description):

SOLOMON MADE KING

22 And did eat and drink before the LORD on that day with great gladness *(whenever our worship is anchored in Calvary, there will always be "great gladness").* And they made Solomon the son of David king the second time, and anointed him unto the LORD to be the chief governor, and Zadok to be Priest *(the "second anointing" has reference to the first anointing, as is outlined in I Ki., Chpt. 1; however, this anointing is before the entirety of Israel).*

23 Then Solomon sat on the throne of the LORD as king instead of David his father, and prospered; and all Israel obeyed him.

24 And all the princes, and the mighty men, and all the sons likewise of king David, submitted themselves unto Solomon the king.

25 And the LORD magnified Solomon exceedingly in the sight of all Israel, and bestowed upon him such royal majesty as had not been on any king before him in Israel *(speaks of Solomon, but more particularly of the Greater than Solomon, the Lord Jesus Christ, which will come to pass in the coming Kingdom Age).*

THE DEATH OF DAVID

26 Thus David the son of Jesse reigned over all Israel.

27 And the time that he reigned over Israel was forty years; seven years reigned he in Hebron, and thirty and three years reigned he in Jerusalem.

28 And he died in a good old age, full of days, riches, and honour: and Solomon his son reigned in his stead. *(So concluded the life of one of the greatest men of God who ever lived. David wrote over half the Psalms, and he was given the plans for the Temple, which would be the greatest building ever constructed by the hand of man. Above all, he would be the ancestor of the Incarnation, of Whom the Son of David would be named. His name is the first human name in the New Testament [Mat. 1:1]; it is, as well, the last human name in the New Testament [Rev. 22:16].)*

29 Now the acts of David the king, first and last, behold, they are written in the Book of Samuel the Seer, and in the book of Nathan the Prophet, and in the book of Gad the Seer,

30 With all his reign and his might, and the times that went over him, and over Israel, and over all the kingdoms of the countries. *(And yet, his greatest time is yet to come. I speak of the coming Kingdom Age, when David will rule and reign over all of Israel, directly under the Lord Jesus Christ [Ezek. 37:24-25].)*

THE SECOND BOOK OF THE
CHRONICLES

CHAPTER 1
(1015 B.C.)
SOLOMON ESTABLISHED AS KING

AND Solomon the son of David was strengthened in his kingdom, and the LORD his God was with him, and magnified him exceedingly (*for a time, Solomon, as well, would magnify the Lord, and then would close his life by magnifying himself*).

2 Then Solomon spoke unto all Israel, to the captains of thousands and of hundreds, and to the judges, and to every governor in all Israel, the chief of the fathers (*rightly so; Solomon wanted the leaders of Israel to know and realize that their prosperity was based solely on the Blood of the Lamb, symbolized by the Sacrifices*).

3 So Solomon, and all the congregation with him, went to the high place that was at Gibeon; for there was the Tabernacle of the congregation of God, which Moses the servant of the LORD had made in the wilderness (*the "Tabernacle" was a type of the wilderness struggle; even though the wilderness struggle was long and hard, still, the Tabernacle remained; likewise, the Lord Jesus, of Which the Tabernacle is a Type, will "never leave us nor forsake us"*).

4 But the Ark of God had David brought up from Kirjath-jearim to the place which David had prepared for it: for he had pitched a tent for it at Jerusalem. (*The "Ark" was a type of the "land possessed"; it represents the Throne of God and victory in the inheritance. The "Temple" represents the glorious Kingdom Age to come; therefore, both mentioned in Chpts. 1-2 portray the Christian life.*)

5 Moreover the Brasen Altar, that Bezaleel the son of Uri, the son of Hur, had made, he put before the Tabernacle of the LORD: and Solomon and the congregation sought unto it (*there all of the great Sacrifices were offered*).

6 And Solomon went up thither to the Brasen Altar before the LORD, which was at the Tabernacle of the congregation, and offered a thousand Burnt Offerings upon it (*the first instance of the Whole Burnt Offering is Gen. 8:20; of the five Levitical Offerings, it was the chief, and was usually preceded by a "Sin Offering" [Ex. 29:36-38; Lev. 8:14]; how long it took to offer up a thousand Burnt Offerings, we aren't told!*).

SOLOMON PRAYS FOR WISDOM

7 In that night did God appear unto Solomon, and said unto him, Ask what I shall give you (*this is the night which followed the days of Sacrifices*).

8 And Solomon said unto God, You have showed great mercy unto David my father, and have made me to reign in his stead.

9 Now, O LORD God, let Your promise unto David my father be established: for You have made me king over a people like the dust of the earth in multitude.

10 Give me now wisdom and knowledge, that I may go out and come in before this people: for who can judge this Your people, that is so great? (*Many criticize Solomon for making such a request, claiming that he should have asked for other things.*)

11 And God said to Solomon, Because this was in your heart, and you have not asked riches, wealth, or honor, nor the life of your enemies (*to destroy enemies*), neither yet have asked long life; but have asked wisdom and knowledge for yourself, that you may judge My people, over whom I have made you king:

12 Wisdom and knowledge is granted unto you; and I will give you riches, and wealth, and honor, such as none of the kings have had who have been before you, neither shall there any after you have the like. (*Concerning this request, I Ki. 3:10 proclaims the Holy Spirit saying, "And the speech pleased the Lord, that Solomon had asked this thing." If the Holy Spirit said that God was pleased with it, and He did, surely it should be good enough for us.*)

SOLOMON'S WEALTH AND MIGHT

13 Then Solomon came from his journey to the high place that was at Gibeon to Jerusalem, from before the Tabernacle of the congregation, and reigned over Israel.

14 And Solomon gathered chariots and

horsemen: and he had a thousand and four hundred chariots, and twelve thousand horsemen, which he placed in the chariot cities, and with the king at Jerusalem.

15 And the king made silver and gold at Jerusalem as plenteous as stones, and cedar trees made he as the sycomore trees that are in the vale for abundance *(this is a type of the coming Kingdom Age, when prosperity will rule the Earth, completely ridding the world of all hunger and want, because our Lord will be reigning supreme from Jerusalem).*

16 And Solomon had horses brought out of Egypt, and linen yarn: the king's merchants received the linen yarn at a price.

17 And they fetched up, and brought forth out of Egypt a chariot for six hundred shekels of silver, and an horse for an hundred and fifty: and so brought they out horses for all the kings of the Hittites, and for the kings of Syria, by their means *(the Holy Spirit doesn't comment on these things, but merely mentions them).*

CHAPTER 2
(1015 B.C.)
PREPARATIONS FOR BUILDING
THE TEMPLE

AND Solomon determined to build an house for the Name of the LORD, and an house *(a royal residence for himself)* for his kingdom *(the wording of this Passage proclaims to us that Solomon's determination was even more than the prompting to do so by his father David; the Holy Spirit is, in fact, now helping him).*

2 And Solomon told out threescore and ten thousand men to bear burdens *(70,000)*, and fourscore thousand *(80,000)* to hew in the mountain, and three thousand and six hundred to oversee them. *(A total of 153,600. These were all foreigners, Gentiles, actually prisoners of war, justly condemned to hard labor for life. David could easily have put these men to death, as he might justly have done; for when they were captured, they had been attempting to kill David, destroy Israel, and the God of Israel. So, David allowing these people to remain alive was an act of mercy on his part.*

As well, any one of these individuals could have subscribed to the God of Abraham, Isaac, and Jacob, by submitting to the Law of Moses and to circumcision. They would have then become free men. Possibly, some of them did this.)

3 And Solomon sent to Huram the king of Tyre, saying, As you did deal with David my father, and did send him cedars to build him an house to dwell therein, even so deal with me *(this was not the Hiram of David's day, but the son of the Hiram of II Samuel 5:11).*

4 Behold, I build an house to the name of the LORD my God, to dedicate it to Him, and to burn before Him sweet incense, and for the continual shewbread, and for the Burnt Offerings morning and evening, on the sabbaths, and on the new moons, and on the solemn feasts of the LORD our God. This is an ordinance for ever to Israel *(the mention of these three particulars portray Christ; the "Sweet Incense" speaks of His glorious Presence; the "continual Shewbread" speaks of His continual life, for Jesus is the "Bread of Life"; the "Burnt Offerings" speak of His glorious Sacrifice at Calvary, that would forever atone for the sins of man in their Redemption).*

5 And the house which I build is great: for great is our God above all gods *(the testimony of Solomon, as to the greatness of God above the heathen entities of surrounding nations, is a witness to his boldness of testimony; he did not flinch from proclaiming the greatness of God over the insignificance of the god of Tyre).*

6 But who is able to build Him an house, seeing the Heaven and Heaven of Heavens cannot contain Him? who am I then, that I should build Him an house, save only to burn Sacrifice before Him? *(This refers back to the time that David desired to build a House for the Lord [I Chron., Chpt. 17], and the Lord, in effect, told David, "I do not want or need your house, and furthermore, I will build you a house" [I Chron. 17:10]. The major problem of the Church is that it tries to build the Lord a house. We are the ones who need the house, and that House is Jesus.)*

7 Send me now therefore a man cunning to work in gold, and in silver, and in brass, and in iron, and in purple, and crimson, and blue, and that can skill to grave with the cunning men who are with me in Judah and in Jerusalem, whom David my father did provide *(it is remarkable in Solomon's letter that nearly two-thirds extols the God of Glory, with only about one-third of it itemizing his request).*

8 Send me also cedar trees, fir trees, and algum trees, out of Lebanon: for I know that your servants can skill to cut timber in Lebanon; and, behold, my servants shall be with your servants,

9 Even to prepare me timber in abundance: for the house which I am about to build shall

be wonderful great *(it would be "wonderful great," because the Lord would occupy the House; otherwise, it would be just another house)*.

10 And, behold, I will give to your servants, the hewers who cut timber, twenty thousand measures of beaten wheat, and twenty thousand measures of barley, and twenty thousand baths of wine, and twenty thousand baths of oil *(a "measure" equals about 3 gallons, while a "bath" equals about 6 gallons)*.

HURAM AGREES TO HELP SOLOMON

11 Then Huram the king of Tyre answered in writing, which he sent to Solomon, Because the LORD has loved His people, He has made you king over them. *(This Verse and the following are also testimony to the indirect influences on surrounding nations of the knowledge of the One True Creator-God and Ruler-God, Who was domiciled by special Revelation and Oracle [Rom. 3:2] with Israel. Even when nations near were bitter foes, they often feared Israel's God.)*

12 Huram said moreover, Blessed be the LORD God of Israel, Who made Heaven and Earth, Who has given to David the king a wise son, endued with prudence and understanding, who might build an house for the LORD, and an house *(a palace for Solomon)* for his kingdom *(Hiram and the kingdom of Tyre will, no doubt, be greatly blessed, because of their participation in this great work for God)*.

13 And now I have sent a cunning man, endued with understanding, of Huram my father's,

14 The son of a woman of the daughters of Dan, and his father was a man of Tyre, skillful to work in gold, and in silver, in brass, in iron, in stone, and in timber, in purple, in blue, and in fine linen, and in crimson; also to grave any manner of graving, and to find out every device which shall be put to him, with your cunning men, and with the cunning men of my lord David your father.

15 Now therefore the wheat, and the barley, the oil, and the wine, which my lord has spoken of, let him send unto his servants:

16 And we will cut wood out of Lebanon, as much as you shall need: and we will bring it to you in floats by sea to Joppa; and you shall carry it up to Jerusalem *(from Joppa to Jerusalem was about 34 miles)*.

17 And Solomon numbered all the strangers who were in the land of Israel, after the numbering wherewith David his father had numbered them; and they were found an hundred and fifty thousand and three thousand and six hundred *(Vs. 2)*.

18 And he set threescore and ten thousand of them to be bearers of burdens, and fourscore thousand to be hewers in the mountain and three thousand and six hundred overseers to set the people a work.

CHAPTER 3
(1012 B.C.)
SOLOMON BEGINS TO BUILD THE TEMPLE

THEN Solomon began to build the House of the LORD at Jerusalem in Mount Moriah *(this is the first mention of Mount Moriah since Gen. 22:2; it is never mentioned after this; it is where Abraham was to offer up Isaac)*, where the LORD appeared unto David his father, in the place that David had prepared in the threshingfloor of Ornan the Jebusite *(a place of judgment, the destroying Angel [II Sam. 24:16], now turned into a place of Blessing, all by the Grace of God)*.

2 And he began to build in the second day of the second month, in the fourth year of his reign.

DIMENSIONS AND MATERIALS OF THE TEMPLE

3 Now these are the things wherein Solomon was instructed for the building of the House of God. The length by cubits after the first measure was threescore cubits *(90 feet long)*, and the breadth twenty cubits *(30 feet wide; however, this pertained only to the Temple proper; many rooms were also built on each side)*.

4 And the porch that was in the front of the house, the length of it was according to the breadth of the house, twenty cubits, and the height was an hundred and twenty *(the height is definitely a copyist error in one of the old manuscripts; this would make the Temple 180 feet high — twice as high as it was long; in I Ki. 6:2, it states that the height was 30 cubits, or 45 feet, counting 18 inches to the cubit; this would be normal for the highest part of the Temple, and for the three stories of chambers [I Ki. 6:8])*: and he overlaid it within with pure gold *(the "gold" signified the Deity of Christ, with every part of the Temple, in fact, portraying Christ, in either*

His Atoning, Mediatorial, or Intercessory Work).

5 And the greater house he cieled with fir tree, which he overlaid with fine gold, and set thereon palm trees and chains *(all of this was designed by the Holy Spirit, even down to the most minute detail; it must be adhered to strictly).*

6 And he garnished the house with precious stones for beauty: and the gold was gold of Parvaim *(the "precious stones" speak of the redeemed [Mal. 3:17]).*

7 He overlaid also the house, the beams, the posts, and the walls thereof, and the doors thereof, with gold; and graved cherubims on the walls. *(The "Cherubims" speak of God's Holiness. The "palm trees" of Verse 5 speak of the prefect rest found only in Christ, with the "chains" of that Verse speaking of the never-ceasing link of the Child of God with the Lord Jesus Christ.)*

THE HOLY OF HOLIES

8 And he made the most holy house *(the Holy of Holies, which contained the Ark of the Covenant),* the length whereof was according to the breadth of the house, twenty cubits *(30 feet),* and the breadth thereof twenty cubits *(30 feet; it was foursquare):* and he overlaid it with fine gold, amounting to six hundred talents *(about $300 million in 2004 currency).*

9 And the weight of the nails was fifty shekels of gold *(about $10,000).* And he overlaid the upper chambers with gold.

10 And in the most holy house *(Holy of Holies, where the Ark of the Covenant was)* he made two Cherubims of image work, and overlaid them with gold.

11 And the wings of the Cherubims were twenty cubits long *(30 feet):* one wing of the one cherub was five cubits *(7 1/2 feet),* reaching to the wall of the house: and the other wing was likewise five cubits, reaching to the wing of the other Cherub.

12 And one wing of the other Cherub was five cubits, reaching to the wall of the house: and the other wing was five cubits also, joining to the wing of the other Cherub.

13 The wings of these Cherubims spread themselves forth twenty cubits: and they stood on their feet, and their faces were inward. *(There is some indication that the word "inward" in the Hebrew, as used here, means "toward the house," in other words, outward.*

In Moses' Tabernacle, the Cherubim looked down upon the blood-sprinkled Mercy Seat, for only there could their eyes rest with satisfaction

all around, being under the reign of sin and death. But here the new Cherubim looked "outward" upon a kingdom governed in Righteousness by the King of Righteousness.)

14 And he made the Veil of blue *(signifying that Christ came from Heaven),* and purple *(signifying that Christ is the King),* and crimson *(signifying His shed Blood on the Cross of Calvary, which was necessary in order that man be redeemed),* and fine linen *(signifying His Perfect Righteousness),* and wrought Cherubims thereon *(signifying His Holiness. The Veil of the Temple is described here as being like that in the Tabernacle of Moses. It is not mentioned in I Kings at all. In I Ki. 6:31, the Holy Spirit records the fact that there were doors made of olive wood between the Most Holy Place and the Holy Place. It does not mention the Veil. In this Passage, it mentions "the Veil," but does not mention the doors. Quite possibly, the Veil hung immediately behind the doors. Therefore, when the doors were opened, the Veil would remain, and continue to hide the Holy of Holies from the inquisitive stare).*

THE TWO PILLARS

15 Also he made before the house two pillars of thirty and five cubits high *(52 1/2 feet high),* and the chapiter that was on the top of each of them was five cubits *(7 1/2 feet, making a total of 60 feet).*

16 And he made chains *(typifies our union with Christ),* as in the Oracle, and put them on the heads of the pillars; and made an hundred pomegranates *(typifying the Fruit of the Spirit),* and put them on the chains.

17 And he reared up the pillars before the Temple, one on the right hand, and the other on the left *(actually, these two pillars did not hold up anything; they were strictly for ornamentation, and signified Believers [Rev. 3:12]);* and called the name of that on the right hand Jachin *("he shall establish"),* and the name of that on the left Boaz *("in it is strength"; the actual meaning is "Believers shall be established in the Strength of the Lord").*

CHAPTER 4
(1012 B.C.)
THE FURNISHING OF THE TEMPLE:
THE BRAZEN ALTAR

MOREOVER he made an Altar of brass, twenty cubits the length thereof *(30 feet*

long), and twenty cubits the breadth thereof (*30 feet wide*), and ten cubits the height thereof (*15 feet high; this means that the Brazen Altar was the same dimensions as the Most Holy Place; the Altar portrayed God's Judgment on sin; the Holy of Holies portrayed His Mercy and Grace; therefore, God's Mercy and Grace are as large as His Judgment*).

2 Also he made a molten sea of ten cubits (*15 feet*) from brim to brim, round in compass, and five cubits the height thereof (*7 1/2 feet*); and a line of thirty cubits (*45 feet*) did compass it round about.

3 And under it was the similitude of oxen, which did compass it round about: ten in a cubit, compassing the sea round about. Two rows of oxen were cast, when it was cast.

4 It stood upon twelve oxen (*the number "twelve" signifies God's Government, while "oxen" symbolize the Word of God; so, God's Government is built entirely upon His Word, from which we must not deviate at all*), three looking toward the north, and three looking toward the west, and three looking toward the south, and three looking toward the east (*signifying that God's Government is the same throughout the entirety of the Earth; in other words, there is no such thing as a white man's gospel, or a black man's gospel, etc.; it is one Gospel for the entirety of mankind*): and the sea was set above upon them, and all their hinder parts were inward (*signifying that the strength of the oxen holds up the Great Laver, symbolizing the power of the Word of God*).

5 And the thickness of it was an handbreadth (*about 4 inches*), and the brim of it like the work of the brim of a cup, with flowers of lilies (*purity of Christ*); and it received and held three thousand baths (*about 18,000 gallons; I Ki. 7:27 says, "two thousand baths"; there is no contradiction; the three thousand baths were the maximum amount of water that the molten sea would hold; two thousand baths were the amount it generally held*).

LAVERS OF BRASS

6 He made also ten lavers, and put five on the right hand, and five on the left, to wash in them: such things as they offered for the Burnt Offering they washed in them (*these were used to wash the sacrifices before they were offered*); but the sea (*Brazen Laver*) was for the Priests to wash in (*which they had to do, washing both hands and feet, every time they went into the*

Temple; the Brazen Laver, as well, was a Type of the Word of God; as the Priests looked into the water, they would see their reflection, as in a mirror; likewise, when we read and study the Word of God, we see our reflection in the Word proclaiming to us what we are; the "oxen" stand for the indestructibility, power, and strength of the Word of God).

GOLDEN LAMPSTANDS

7 And he made ten candlesticks (*Lampstands*) of gold (*typifying the fact that Christ is the Light of the world*) according to their form, and set them in the Temple, five on the right hand, and five on the left.

8 He made also ten tables (*tables of Shewbread*), and placed them in the Temple, five on the right side, and five on the left (*there was only one Lampstand and one Table in the Tabernacle, but here there are ten of each*). And he made an hundred basons of gold (*the "tables" each held twelve loaves of bread, which had to be eaten by the Priests every Sabbath, with new loaves taking their place; the bread was a Type of Christ as the "Bread of Life" [Jn. 6:48]*).

THE COURTS AND DOORS

9 Furthermore he made the Court of the Priests, and the Great Court, and Doors for the Court, and overlaid the Doors of them with brass (*the "Doors" also typified Christ; He said, "I am the Door" [Jn. 10:9]; the "brass" signified the humanity of Christ*).

10 And he set the sea on the right side of the east end, over against the south (*the Brazen Laver, i.e., "the Sea," had its position as the Tabernacle Laver of old, which was between the Altar and the porch*).

SUMMARY OF HURAM'S METAL WORK

11 And Huram made the pots, and the shovels, and the basons. And Huram finished the work that he was to make for king Solomon for the House of God (*in a sense, Huram is a Type of the Holy Spirit, Who will finish the work regarding the Church, thereby presenting us faultless before the Throne of God [Jude, Vs. 24]*);

12 To wit, the two pillars, and the pommels (*shaped like a ball*), and the chapiters which were on the top of the two pillars, and the two wreaths (*chains*) to cover the two pommels of the chapiters which were on the top

of the pillars;

13 And four hundred pomegranates *(typical of the Fruit of the Spirit)* on the two wreaths *(chains, which typified our union with Christ)*; two rows of pomegranates on each wreath, to cover the two pommels of the chapiters which were upon the pillars.

14 He made also bases, and lavers made he upon the bases *(the ten Lavers [Vs. 6] were placed on the bases)*;

15 One sea, and twelve oxen under it.

16 The pots also, and the shovels, and the fleshhooks, and all their instruments, did Huram his father make to king Solomon for the House of the LORD of bright brass.

17 In the plain of Jordan did the king cast them, in the clay ground between Succoth and Zeredathah. *(This represents death and Resurrection. In a sense, there must be a death to the old self, with the new self raised in the identification of Christ. This means that all former identity for the Believer must be lost; what we were before Salvation is of no consequence. Truly, the Holy Spirit is making a "new creature," which can only be carried out by our understanding that we are "baptized into His death, buried with Him by baptism into death, and raised with Him in newness of life" [Rom. 6:3-4]. So, all of these heathen gold idols, along with the silver and the brass, had to be melted, which means they lost their old identity, and then fashioned into a new mold, in order to be of fit use for the Temple. This is a picture of what the Spirit of God does with us, which is carried out by and through the Cross [I Cor. 1:17-18, 23; 2:2].)*

18 Thus Solomon made all these vessels in great abundance: for the weight of the brass could not be found out.

19 And Solomon made all the vessels that were for the House of God, the golden Altar also *(this was the Altar of Incense, which stood immediately in front of the Holy of Holies)*, and the tables whereon the shewbread was set;

20 Moreover the candlesticks *(Lampstands)* with their lamps, that they should burn after the manner before the Oracle *(Holy of Holies)*, of pure gold *(the "pure gold" typified the Deity of Christ)*;

21 And the flowers, and the lamps, and the tongs, made he of gold, and that perfect gold *(meaning that it contained no alloy whatsoever)*;

22 And the snuffers, and the basons, and the spoons, and the censers, of pure gold: and the entry of the house, the inner doors thereof for the Most Holy Place, and the doors of the House of the Temple, were of gold *(there is no way into this "House of God" except through the Lord Jesus Christ, Who is the "Door" [Jn. 10:9])*.

CHAPTER 5
(1005 B.C.)
THE TEMPLE COMPLETED

THUS all the work that Solomon made for the House of the LORD was finished: and Solomon brought in all the things that David his father had dedicated; and the silver, and the gold, and all the instruments, put he among the treasures of the House of God. *(Solomon was seven years in building the Temple [I Ki. 6:38]. Now it is time for the dedication.)*

LEADERS ASSEMBLED FOR THE DEDICATION

2 Then Solomon assembled the elders of Israel, and all the heads of the Tribes, the chief of the fathers of the Children of Israel, unto Jerusalem, to bring up the Ark of the Covenant of the LORD out of the city of David, which is Zion.

3 Wherefore all the men of Israel assembled themselves unto the king in the Feast which was in the seventh month *(this was the Feast of Tabernacles, which convened in October [Lev. 23:33])*.

THE ARK BROUGHT INTO THE TEMPLE

4 And all the elders of Israel came; and the Levites took up the Ark *(these were Priests, who also were Levites, who were the only ones who could carry the Ark; they were types of Christ, Who Alone is the Door to the Throne of God, of which the Ark was a Type)*.

5 And they brought up the Ark, and the Tabernacle of the congregation, and all the holy vessels that were in the Tabernacle, these did the Priests and the Levites bring up *(all of these "holy vessels" were by now a little over 600 years old; they, no doubt, were put "among the treasures of the House of God" in a separate chamber)*.

6 Also king Solomon, and all the congregation of Israel who were assembled unto him before the Ark, sacrificed sheep and oxen, which could not be told nor numbered for multitude *(all the gold and precious stones in this magnificent Temple could not redeem one*

precious soul; only the Blood of Jesus could do such; consequently, the thousands of animals slaughtered, which soaked the ground with blood, were an eternal Type of the great price that would be paid at Calvary's Cross).

7 And the Priests brought in the Ark of the Covenant of the LORD unto his place, to the Oracle of the House, into the Most Holy Place, even under the wings of the Cherubims:

8 For the Cherubims spread forth their wings over the place of the Ark, and the Cherubims covered the Ark and the staves thereof above.

9 And they drew out the staves of the Ark, that the ends of the staves were seen from the Ark before the oracle *(signifying that it was to be moved no more)*; but they were not seen without. And there it is unto this day *(this proves that this section of II Chronicles was written before the destruction of the Temple).*

10 There was nothing in the Ark save the two tables *(Ten Commandments)* which Moses put therein at Horeb, when the LORD made a Covenant with the Children of Israel, when they came out of Egypt *(when Paul, in Heb. 9:4, mentioned the golden pot of Manna and Aaron's rod being in the Ark, he was speaking of the Ark while in the Tabernacle instead of the Temple; it is not known when these two things were removed).*

THE GLORY OF GOD APPEARS

11 And it came to pass, when the Priests were come out of the Holy Place: (for all the Priests who were present were sanctified, and did not then wait by course *[when the Priests had placed the Ark in the Most Holy Place, they left, never to enter this place again, except for the visit of the High Priest once a year, which was on the Great Day of Atonement]*:

12 Also the Levites which were the singers, all of them of Asaph, of Heman, of Jeduthun, with their sons and their brethren, being arrayed in white linen, having cymbals and psalteries and harps, stood at the east end of the Altar *[the Brazen Altar, which sat in front of the Temple]*, and with them an hundred and twenty Priests sounding with trumpets *[all of this signifies worship]*:)

13 It came even to pass, as the trumpeters and singers were as one, to make one sound to be heard in praising and thanking the LORD; and when they lifted up their voice with the trumpets and cymbals and instruments of music, and praised the LORD, saying, For He is good; for His mercy endures for ever: that then the House was filled with a Cloud, even the House of the LORD *(this was the Glory and the Power of God)*;

14 So that the Priests could not stand to minister by reason of the Cloud *(meaning that their knees buckled under them, and they fell to the floor, because of the magnitude of the Power of God being manifested)*: for the Glory of the LORD had filled the House of God. *(Paul says that now we are the Temple of God [I Cor. 3:16], and that the Spirit of God dwells in us. The next question is, "Is He allowed to have His Perfect Way within our lives?" If He is, then "the Glory of the Lord will fill this House of God," as well.)*

CHAPTER 6
(1004 B.C.)
SOLOMON'S MESSAGE

THEN said Solomon, The LORD has said that He would dwell in the thick darkness *(Solomon may have taken this idea from the fact of God's appearance in darkness at Sinai [Ex. 20:21]).*

2 But I have built an House of habitation for You, and a place for Your dwelling for ever *(after this Message, the Lord would, in fact, occupy this House).*

3 And the king turned his face, and blessed the whole congregation of Israel: and all the congregation of Israel stood *(this was a great moment in the history of Israel, as should be obvious!).*

4 And he said, Blessed be the LORD God of Israel, Who has with His hands fulfilled that which He spoke with His mouth to my father David, saying,

5 Since the day that I brought forth My people out of the land of Egypt I chose no city among all the Tribes of Israel to build an House in, that My Name might be there; neither chose I any man to be a ruler over My people Israel *(for approximately 500 years God had not chosen any particular place among Israel where a House should be built for Himself, nor had He chosen any man to be a permanent ruler over Israel. Now, He makes it clear that He has chosen Jerusalem as the place of His headquarters on Earth, and David as the one through whom all the future kings of Israel should come [II Sam., Chpt. 7; I Chron., Chpt. 17]. This makes it clear that God did not choose Saul as*

He chose David):

6 But I have chosen Jerusalem, that My Name might be there; and have chosen David to be over My people Israel.

7 Now it was in the heart of David my father to build an House for the Name of the LORD God of Israel.

8 But the LORD said to David my father, Forasmuch as it was in your heart to build an House for My Name, you did well in that it was in your heart *(the Lord was pleased with David's motives)*:

9 Notwithstanding you shall not build the house; but your son which shall come forth out of your loins, he shall build the house for My Name *(Solomon knew exactly what the Lord had told his father David)*.

10 The LORD therefore has performed His Word that He has spoken: for I am risen up in the room of David my father, and am set on the Throne of Israel, as the LORD promised, and have built the House for the Name of the LORD God of Israel.

11 And in it have I put the Ark, wherein is the Covenant of the LORD, that He made with the Children of Israel *(the Law of Moses)*.

SOLOMON'S PRAYER OF DEDICATION

12 And he stood before the Altar of the LORD *(Brazen Altar)* in the presence of all the congregation of Israel, and spread forth his hands:

13 For Solomon had made a brasen scaffold, of five cubits long *(7 1/2 feet)*, and five cubits broad *(7 1/2 feet)*, and three cubits high *(4 1/2 feet)*, and had set it in the midst of the Court: and upon it he stood, and kneeled down upon his knees before all the congregation of Israel, and spread forth his hands toward Heaven,

14 And said, O LORD God of Israel, there is no God like You in the Heaven, nor in the Earth; which keeps Covenant, and shows mercy unto Your servants, who walk before You with all their hearts *(no man will ever be able to say, in all eternity, that God has not kept His part of every agreement with men or that He has not fulfilled every Promise to them)*:

15 You Who have kept with Your servant David my father that which You have promised him; and spoke with Your mouth, and have fulfilled it with Your hand, as it is this day.

16 Now therefore, O LORD God of Israel, keep with Your servant David my father that

which You have promised him, saying, There shall not fail thee a man in My sight to sit upon the throne of Israel; yet so that your children take heed to their way to walk in My Law, as you have walked before Me *(regrettably, Solomon himself, even after praying this prayer, did not "take heed to walk in God's Law")*.

17 Now then, O LORD God of Israel, let Your Word be verified, which You have spoken unto Your servant David.

18 But will God in very deed dwell with men on the Earth? behold, Heaven and the Heaven of Heavens cannot contain You; how much less this house which I have built! *(Most definitely, the Lord will indeed dwell with men on this Earth. Rev., Chpts. 21-22 proclaim this fact.)*

19 Have respect therefore to the prayer of Your servant, and to his supplication, O LORD my God, to hearken unto the cry and the prayer which Your servant prays before You *(prayer includes every thought and word from the heart that is Godward)*:

20 That Your eyes may be open upon this house day and night, upon the place whereof You have said that You would put Your Name there; to hearken unto the prayer which Your servant prays toward this place.

MERCY AND GRACE

21 Hearken therefore unto the supplications of Your servant, and of Your people Israel, which they shall make toward this place: hear Thou from Your dwelling place, even from Heaven; and when You hear, forgive *(possibly one could say that the great thought of Solomon now is that the center and core of all worship is prayer)*.

22 If a man sin against his neighbour, and an oath be laid upon him to make him swear, and the oath come before Your Altar in this House;

23 Then hear Thou from Heaven, and do, and judge Your servants, by requiting the wicked, by recompensing his way upon his own head; and by justifying the righteous, by giving him according to his righteousness *(vindicate the righteous)*.

24 And if Your people Israel be put to the worse before the enemy, because they have sinned against You, and shall return and confess Your Name, and pray and make supplication before You in this House;

25 Then hear Thou from the Heavens and forgive the sin of Your people Israel, and bring

them again unto the land which You gave to them and to their fathers *(in this prayer, Solomon seems to sense the future of Israel prophetically; "sin" is the only reason that Israel was ever defeated; in fact, sin is to blame for all the troubles among men; as well, the Lord gave the land of Canaan to Israel, and not the Arabs, even as this Verse proclaims).*

26 When the Heaven is shut up, and there is no rain, because they have sinned against You; yet if they pray toward this place, and confess Your Name, and turn from their sin, when You do afflict them;

27 Then hear Thou from Heaven, and forgive the sin of Your servants, and of Your people Israel, when You have taught them the good way, wherein they should walk; and send rain upon Your land, which You have given unto Your people for an inheritance. *(Praying toward the Temple, Jerusalem, and this land is referred to eight times in this prayer. It was done so because, at that particular time, that is where God dwelt. Today, in this great dispensation of Grace, it doesn't really matter which direction a person faces while praying. The reason is that the Lord, through the Power of the Holy Spirit, now lives in the heart of Born-Again man [I Cor. 3:16], wherever such a man is, and not in some particular temple or building. This was all made possible by the Cross.*

As well, the land between the River Euphrates and the Mediterranean, and from the Red Sea on the south to Hamath on the north, is the only land promised in all Scripture for all the Tribes of Israel. Theories which teach that America and England are new Promised Lands for Israel are all error. There is no hint of such in Scripture.)

PESTILENCE

28 If there be dearth in the land, if there be pestilence, if there be blasting, or mildew, locusts, or caterpillers; if their enemies besiege them in the cities of their land; whatsoever sore or whatsoever sickness there be:

29 Then what prayer or what supplication soever shall be made of any man, or of all Your people Israel, when every one shall know his own sore and his own grief, and shall spread forth his hands in this House:

30 Then hear Thou from Heaven Your dwelling place, and forgive, and render unto every man according unto all his ways, whose heart You know; (for You only know the hearts of the children of men:)

31 That they may fear You, to walk in Your ways, so long as they live in the land which You gave unto our fathers *(in the absence of a healthy fear of God is involved the absence of a healing hopefulness).*

GENTILES

32 Moreover concerning the stranger *(Gentile)*, which is not of Your people Israel, but is come from a far country for Your great Name's sake, and Your mighty hand, and Your stretched out arm; if they come and pray in this House;

33 Then hear Thou from the Heavens, even from Your dwelling place, and do according to all that the stranger *(Gentile)* calls to You for; that all people of the Earth may know Your Name, and fear You, as does Your people Israel, and may know that this House which I have built is called by Your Name. *(Solomon, in his wisdom, did not forget the Gentiles, whom God had in mind to bless from the very beginning of His calling of Abraham, Isaac, and Jacob. All nations were to be blessed through Israel and their seed.*

As well, this would imply the preaching of the Gospel, for how could individuals come to the God of Israel, if they do not hear? [Rom. 10:9-17; I Cor. 1:18-24].

In fact, in the Millennium and the New Earth, all nations will go up to Jerusalem to pray and to worship, exactly as they do now [Isa. 2:2-4; Zech. 8:23].)

WAR

34 If Your people go out to war against their enemies by the way that You shall send them, and they pray unto You toward this city which You have chosen, and the House which I have built for Your Name;

35 Then hear Thou from the Heavens their prayer and their supplication, and maintain their cause *(God does maintain the cause of His people, as long as they live right, but when sin is committed, He Himself becomes their Judge and metes out the penalty for sin).*

36 If they sin against You, (for there is no man which sins not,) and You be angry with them, and deliver them over before their enemies, and they carry them away captives unto a land far off or near *(Solomon was right; all have sinned and come short of the Glory of God [Rom. 3:23]);*

37 Yet if they bethink themselves in the land where they are carried captive, and turn and pray unto You in the land of their captivity, saying, We have sinned, we have done amiss, and have dealt wickedly;

38 If they return to You with all their heart and with all their soul in the land of their captivity, whither they have carried them captives, and pray toward their land, which You gave unto their fathers, and toward the city *(Jerusalem)* which You have chosen, and toward the House which I have built for Your Name:

39 Then hear Thou from the Heavens, even from Your dwelling place, their prayer and their supplications, and maintain their cause, and forgive Your people which have sinned against You *(this speaks of true, heartfelt Repentance, which God will always honor!)*.

40 Now, my God, let, I beseech You, Your eyes be open, and let Your ears be attent unto the prayer that is made in this place.

41 Now therefore arise, O LORD God, into Your resting place, You, and the Ark of Your strength: let Your Priests, O LORD God, be clothed with Salvation, and let Your saints rejoice in goodness. *(The word "Saints" in the Hebrew reads "men of grace," that is, those who are subjects of the Grace of God. This plainly shows that those in Old Testament times were under Grace, as well as we are in New Testament times. Actually, everyone who has been saved has been saved by Grace, for there is no other way that an individual can be saved [Eph. 2:8]. And yet, Grace, as we know it under the New Dispensation, which came by Jesus Christ, means that it was all made possible by the Cross. Christ is always the Source, while the Cross is the Means.)*

42 O LORD God, turn not away the face of Your anointed *(God's Anointed is the Messiah; every blessing that we receive comes through the Lord Jesus Christ, and what He has done for us at the Cross)*: remember the mercies of David Your servant.

CHAPTER 7
(1004 B.C.)
GOD'S RESPONSE TO SOLOMON'S PRAYER: THE GLORY OF THE LORD FILLS THE TEMPLE

NOW when Solomon had made an end of praying, the fire came down from Heaven, and consumed the Burnt Offering and the Sacrifices; and the Glory of the LORD filled the House. *(This is additional to I Ki. 8:63-64, and shows the Divine acceptance by the Lord of the Sacrifices, until Christ should come to offer Himself as the one great eternal Sacrifice for all of humanity. The fire of God from Heaven has fallen several times on such occasions [Gen. 4:4; 15:17; Lev. 9:24; I Chron. 21:26; I Ki. 18:38].)*

2 And the Priests could not enter into the House of the LORD, because the Glory of the LORD had filled the LORD's House *(the "Glory of the Lord" can only come through Calvary)*.

3 And when all the Children of Israel saw how the fire came down, and the glory of the LORD upon the House, they bowed themselves with their faces to the ground upon the pavement, and worshipped, and praised the LORD, saying, For He is good; for His mercy endures for ever. *(On the Day of Pentecost, approximately a thousand years later, the fire fell from Heaven in a way that it had never fallen previously. In Old Testament times, it fell upon the Sacrifice. Now that The Sacrifice, the Lord Jesus Christ, has been offered, this same fire can now accompany the Holy Spirit into the heart and life of the Believer, but not with judgment, for the judgment has been expended on Christ. But yet, this "Pentecostal Fire" will definitely correct the Believer [Mat. 3:11-12; Acts 2:3].)*

THE SACRIFICES AND REJOICING

4 Then the king and all the people offered Sacrifices before the LORD.

5 And king Solomon offered a Sacrifice of twenty and two thousand oxen, and an hundred and twenty thousand sheep: so the king and all the people dedicated the House of God *(all of this showed Israel that her great blessing was built on the foundation of the shed Blood of Christ; even though the number of Sacrifices offered was staggering, still, it could not begin to portray Calvary; the blood of bulls and goats can never take away sin [Heb. 10:4]; nevertheless, those sacrifices did point to the Lamb of God, Who would take away all sin [Jn. 1:29])*.

6 And the Priests waited on their offices: the Levites also with instruments of music of the LORD, which David the king had made to praise the LORD, because His mercy endures for ever, when David praised by their ministry; and the Priests sounded trumpets before them, and all Israel stood *(the worship, heavily anchored in the Sacrifices, portrays the fact that Spirit-led music and singing accompany the Cross and, in fact, are made possible by the Cross)*.

7 Moreover Solomon hallowed the middle of the Court that was before the House of the LORD: for there he offered Burnt Offerings *(typified the perfection of Christ being given to the sinner)*, and the fat *(typifying the very best that God has in the offering up of His Son)* of the Peace Offerings *(this Offering typified that Peace had been restored, as a result of the Burnt Offering)*, because the Brasen Altar which Solomon had made was not able to receive the Burnt Offerings, and the Meat Offerings *(the Offering of Thanksgiving)*, and the fat *(the middle Court, which was the Court of women, had to also be used, because the area around the Brazen Altar was too small, considering the great number of Sacrifices being offered)*.

8 Also at the same time Solomon kept the Feast seven days, and all Israel with him, a very great congregation, from the entering in of Hamath unto the river of Egypt.

9 And in the eighth day they made a solemn assembly: for they kept the dedication of the Altar seven days, and the Feast seven days *(there was a Feast of Dedication of the Temple which was seven days long, and then Solomon also kept the Feast of Tabernacles, for an additional seven days, making altogether the fourteen days of feasting at this time)*.

10 And on the three and twentieth day of the seventh month he sent the people away into their tents, glad and merry in heart for the goodness that the LORD had shown unto David, and to Solomon, and to Israel His people *(joy always follows proper worship, which is always anchored in the Cross, typified by the Sacrifices)*.

11 Thus Solomon finished the House of the LORD, and the king's house *(the personal dwelling place of Solomon)*: and all that came into Solomon's heart to make in the House of the LORD, and in his own house, he prosperously effected *(carried forth to completion)*.

THE LORD APPEARS TO SOLOMON;
HIS COVENANT WITH SOLOMON

12 And the LORD appeared to Solomon by night, and said unto him, I have heard your prayer, and have chosen this place to Myself for an House of Sacrifice. *(The Lord not only answered Solomon's prayer by a manifestation of the fire falling from Heaven, but, as well, He portrayed what He will do, as it regards Solomon's petition, and in no uncertain terms. As well, we find here that the Lord referred to*

the Temple as a "House of Sacrifice." We should take note that the modern Church should fall into the same category, inasmuch as our Message should be, "Jesus Christ and Him Crucified" [I Cor. 1:23]. The Cross must be the primary Message [Rom. 6:3-14; I Cor. 2:2].)

13 If I shut up Heaven that there be no rain, or if I command the locusts to devour the land, or if I sent pestilence among My people *(if the Lord does such a thing, it will be because of sin, always because of sin)*;

14 If My people, which are called by My Name *(Believers)*, shall humble themselves *(humility)*, and pray, and seek My face *(the prayer of Repentance)*, and turn from their wicked ways *(which proclaims the manner of true Repentance)*; then will I hear from Heaven *(but not otherwise)*, and will forgive their sin, and will heal their land *(God's prescription for spiritual sickness)*.

15 Now My eyes shall be open, and My ears attent unto the prayer that is made in this place. *(As well, prayer from a distance being made toward this place would be answered.*

Due to what Christ did at the Cross, the Lord no longer resides in a building, but rather in the hearts and lives of Believers [I Cor. 3:16]. Now we pray to the Father up in Heaven, and do so in the Name of Jesus [Jn. 16:23].)

16 For now have I chosen and sanctified this House, that My Name may be there for ever: and My eyes and My heart shall be there perpetually *(literally, until the Cross; in general, forever, because the Lord now lives in our hearts and lives [I Cor. 3:16])*.

17 And as for you, if you will walk before Me, as David your father walked, and do according to all that I have commanded you, and shall observe My Statutes and My Judgments *(the conditions)*;

18 Then will I stablish the throne of your kingdom, according as I have covenanted with David your father, saying, There shall not fail you a man to be ruler in Israel *(is unconditional, for it contemplates Christ)*.

19 But if you turn away, and forsake My Statutes and My Commandments, which I have set before you, and shall go and serve other gods, and worship them;

20 Then will I pluck them up by the roots out of My land which I have given them; and this House, which I have sanctified for My Name, will I cast out of My sight, and will make it to be a proverb and a byword among all nations *(which is exactly what happened!)*.

21 And this House, which is high, shall be an astonishment to every one who passes by it; so that he shall say, Why has the LORD done thus unto this land, and unto this House?

22 And it shall be answered, Because they forsook the LORD God of their fathers, which brought them forth out of the land of Egypt, and laid hold on other gods, and worshipped them, and served them: therefore has He brought all this evil upon them. *(Verses 19-22 portray the Solomonic Covenant, which is conditional. In other words, if Solomon or his sons forsake the Lord, the Lord will forsake them.*

These two Covenants basically proclaim the correct scriptural teaching on predestination. It is predestined that God would have a nation called Israel [the Davidic Covenant]. This is, and man's acceptance, rejection, failure, or otherwise does not alter the fact. However, who will actually be a part of the Israel which is saved [the Solomonic Covenant] will depend on obedience. Actually, Paul said only a remnant would actually be saved [Rom. 9:27].)

CHAPTER 8
(992 B.C.)
SOLOMON'S BUILDING ACTIVITIES

AND it came to pass at the end of twenty years, wherein Solomon had built the House of the LORD, and his own house *(this Chapter in small measure pictures the peace and plenty which will characterize the Millennial Earth),*

2 That the cities which Huram had restored to Solomon, Solomon built them, and caused the Children of Israel to dwell there *(likewise, the coming Millennial Reign, of which all of this is a type, will see the greatest construction boom the world has ever known).*

3 And Solomon went to Hamath-zobah, and prevailed against it *(in the entirety of Solomon's reign, this was the only war that was fought; this typifies the scarcity of such in the coming Kingdom Age).*

4 And he built Tadmor in the wilderness, and all the store cities, which he built in Hamath.

5 Also he built Beth-horon the upper, and Beth-horon the nether, fenced cities, with walls, gates, and bars;

6 And Baalath, and all the store cities that Solomon had, and all the chariot cities, and the cities of the horsemen, and all that Solomon desired to build in Jerusalem, and in Lebanon, and throughout all the land of his dominion. *(So much of the world as designed by man has specialized in destruction instead of construction. However, during the coming Kingdom Age, when Jesus will reign supreme from Jerusalem, and over the entirety of the Earth, there will be no destruction except of that which is evil. Rather, there will be construction. For the first time, the world will see what the Earth could really be like under God's Government instead of man's flawed and faulty government.)*

7 As for all the people who were left of the Hittites, and the Amorites, and the Perizzites, and the Hivites, and the Jebusites, which were not of Israel,

8 But of their children, who were left after them in the land, whom the Children of Israel consumed not, them did Solomon make to pay tribute until this day *(likewise, in the coming Kingdom Age, the Gentile world will pay tribute to the Lord of Glory; but yet, it will not be in the form of ruinous taxation; in fact, it will gladly be paid, because of the great prosperity which will fill the entirety of the Earth).*

9 But of the Children of Israel did Solomon make no servants for his work; but they were men of war, and chief of his captains, and captains of his chariots and horsemen.

10 And these were the chief of king Solomon's officers, even two hundred and fifty, who bore rule over the people *(this typifies redeemed Israel and the blood-washed Saints of God in the coming Kingdom Age, who, under Christ, will carry out the Plan of God over the entirety of the Earth).*

11 And Solomon brought up the daughter of Pharaoh out of the city of David unto the house that he had built for her: for he said, My wife shall not dwell in the house of David king of Israel, because the places are holy, whereunto the Ark of the LORD has come *(with such a Gentile wife, Solomon was starting out the wrong way, and he did not learn the lesson he should have learned, for he later loved many foreign women, who turned his heart away from God [I Ki. 11:1-9]; Solomon, like all the other types, was a broken figure of Him Who is to come; nevertheless, the Antitype, Who is Christ, will be Perfect).*

SOLOMON'S FAITHFULNESS IN WORSHIP

12 Then Solomon offered Burnt Offerings unto the LORD on the Altar of the LORD, which he had built before the porch,

13 Even after a certain rate every day, offering according to the Commandment of Moses, on the Sabbaths, and on the new moons, and on the solemn Feasts, three times in the year, even in the Feast of Unleavened Bread (conducted in April), and in the Feast of Weeks (of Pentecost, in June), and in the Feast of Tabernacles (October; all the males of Israel were supposed to gather three times a year on these special Feasts [Ex. 23:14; Deut. 16:16]).

14 And he appointed, according to the order of David his father, the courses of the Priests to their service, and the Levites to their charges, to praise and minister before the Priests, as the duty of every day required: the porters also by their courses at every gate: for so had David the man of God commanded (this was the appointment of the 24 courses of the Priests in their services [I Chron., Chpt. 24], the 24 courses of the Levites to sing and play music regarding praise and worship [I Chron., Chpt. 25], and the 24 courses of the porters [I Chron., Chpt. 26]; all this had been revealed to David by the Holy Spirit, and now it is being obeyed as he had left instructions).

15 And they departed not from the Commandment of the king unto the Priests and Levites concerning any matter, or concerning the treasures (as well, we must not presently depart from the "Commandment of the King," the Lord Jesus Christ, i.e., His Word).

16 Now all the work of Solomon was prepared unto the day of the foundation of the House of the LORD, and until it was finished. So the House of the LORD was perfected (this is the desire and the work of the Holy Spirit — that He may "perfect the House of the LORD," that House now being our physical and spiritual persons, which are Temples of the Holy Spirit [I Cor. 3:16]; this is done by the Believer constantly exhibiting Faith in Christ, and what Christ has done at the Cross; the Holy Spirit, Who works exclusively within the parameters of the Finished Work of Christ, will then carry out the work within our lives [Rom. 8:1-2, 11]).

SOLOMON'S GREAT WEALTH

17 The went Solomon to Ezion-geber, and to Eloth, at the sea side in the land of Edom.

18 And Huram sent him by the hands of his servants ships, and servants that had knowledge of the sea; and they went with the servants of Solomon to Ophir, and took thence four hundred and fifty talents of gold, and

brought them to king Solomon (in fact, the entirety of the world, even as we shall see, beat a path to Solomon's door, exactly as the entirety of the world will come to Christ, availing themselves of His Perfect Wisdom, in the coming Kingdom Age, of which Solomon was a Type).

CHAPTER 9
(992 B.C.)
THE QUEEN OF SHEBA VISITS SOLOMON

AND when the Queen of Sheba heard of the fame of Solomon, she came to prove Solomon with hard questions at Jerusalem, with a very great company, and camels that bore spices, and gold in abundance, and precious stones: and when she was come to Solomon, she communed with him of all that was in her heart. (Solomon was a Type of Christ, albeit an imperfect type, as all types are. Jesus would say of Himself, "A greater than Solomon is here."

The Glory of the Lord having now risen upon Israel, the kings of the Gentiles come to that light, bringing their riches with them, and find there a glory and a wisdom such as the world had never seen. None of these monarchs are mentioned particularly except the Queen of Sheba, the Holy Spirit reserving that dignity for a woman. She is further honored by the Lord Himself in Mat. 12:42, where He predicts her reappearance in the Resurrection.

As well, Sheba communed with Solomon. Until one "communes with Christ," they can never know the glory and the splendor of all that Christ is and has. For anyone who cares to investigate, our Lord is waiting.)

2 And Solomon told her all her questions: and there was nothing hid from Solomon which he told her not (if the honest heart will earnestly seek, that which it desires will be revealed by the Lord Jesus Christ; the Word of God is His Voice).

3 And when the Queen of Sheba had seen the wisdom of Solomon, and the House that he had built (she saw the Glory of God),

4 And the meat of his table, and the sitting of his servants, and the attendance of his ministers, and their apparel; his cupbearers also, and their apparel; and his ascent by which he went up into the House of the LORD; there was no more spirit in her (splendor, in fact, greater than anything in the world; this is a comparison, at least as much as a comparison can

be in the natural realm, of the coming reign of the Lord Jesus Christ, in the coming Kingdom Age).

5 And she said to the king, It was a true report which I heard in my own land of your acts, and of your wisdom *(everything the Word of God says about the Lord Jesus Christ is "a true report")*:

6 Howbeit I believed not their words, until I came, and my eyes had seen it: and, behold, the one half of the greatness of your wisdom was not told me: for you exceed the fame that I heard *(the Lord Jesus invites inspection; His appeal to the hungry heart is, "Come . . .")*.

7 Happy are your men, and happy are these your servants, which stand continually before you, and hear your wisdom *(the only true happiness in the world is that which has been provided by the "greater than Solomon"; it is a happiness that is based on the Fruit of the Spirit, which is "joy")*.

8 Blessed be the LORD your God, which delights in you to set you on His Throne, to be king for the LORD your God: because your God loved Israel, to establish them for ever, therefore made He you king over them, to do judgment and justice *(due to the fact that the Queen spoke of the Lord as being Solomon's God, some have claimed that she really did not accept the Lord; however, the same terminology also suggests, at the same time, that she very well may have accepted the Lord, and probably did!)*.

9 And she gave the king an hundred and twenty talents of gold, and of spices great abundance, and precious stones: neither was there any such spice as the Queen of Sheba gave king Solomon *(what she gave him could be measured; what he gave her could not be measured)*.

10 And the servants also of Huram, and the servants of Solomon, which brought gold from Ophir, brought algum trees and precious stones.

11 And the king made of the algum trees terraces to the House of the LORD, and to the king's palace, and harps and psalteries for singers: and there were none such seen before in the land of Judah.

12 And king Solomon gave to the Queen of Sheba all her desire, whatsoever she asked, beside that which she had brought unto the king. So she turned, and went away to her own land, she and her servants *(our "greater than Solomon" admonishes us to ask of Him accordingly, and He will give [Lk., Chpt. 11])*.

SOLOMON'S RICHES, WISDOM, AND FAME RETOLD

13 Now the weight of gold that came to Solomon in one year was six hundred and threescore and six talents of gold *(666 talents of gold; Solomon, as well, had 6 steps to his throne; inasmuch as the number "six" is the number of man, and always, of course, comes short of "seven," which is the number of perfection, we find imperfection upon all his glory; man was created on the sixth day; despite all the glory given to Solomon, still, he was but a man, hence the number "six"; perfection comes only in and through the Lord Jesus Christ)*;

14 Beside that which chapmen and merchants brought. And all the kings of Arabia and governors of the country brought gold and silver to Solomon.

15 And king Solomon made two hundred targets *(large shields)* of beaten gold: six hundred shekels of beaten gold went to one target *(worth approximately $120,000 per target, according to 2004 money)*.

16 And three hundred shields made he of beaten gold: three hundred shekels of gold went to one shield *(about $60,000 per shield)*. And the king put them in the house of the forest of Lebanon.

17 Moreover the king made a great throne of ivory, and overlaid it with pure gold.

18 And there were six steps to the throne, with a footstool of gold, which were fastened to the throne, and stays on each side of the sitting place, and two lions standing by the stays:

19 And twelve lions stood there on the one side and on the other upon the six steps. There was not the like made in any kingdom.

20 And all the drinking vessels of king Solomon were of gold, and all the vessels of the house of the forest of Lebanon were of pure gold: none were of silver; it was not any thing accounted of in the days of Solomon *(this Verse symbolizes the great prosperity that will characterize the entirety of the planet when Jesus Christ comes back)*.

21 For the king's ships went to Tarshish with the servants of Huram: every three years once came the ships of Tarshish bringing gold, and silver, ivory, and apes, and peacocks.

22 And king Solomon passed all the kings of the Earth in riches and wisdom *(likewise, Jesus Christ, of Whom Solomon was a Type, when reigning from Jerusalem in the days of the coming Kingdom Age, will be the wisest King Who*

has ever lived and, thereby, will bring riches and prosperity to the entirety of the planet).

23 And all the kings of the Earth sought the presence of Solomon, to hear his wisdom, that God had put in his heart.

24 And they brought every man his present, vessels of silver, and vessels of gold, and raiment, harness, and spices, horses, and mules, a rate year by year (in fact, Israel, at this time, was the most powerful nation on the face of the Earth; however, it was not because of a mighty armed force, but because of the Grace of God).

25 And Solomon had four thousand stalls for horses and chariots, and twelve thousand horsemen; whom he bestowed in the chariot cities, and with the king at Jerusalem.

26 And he reigned over all the kings from the river even unto the land of the Philistines, and to the border of Egypt.

27 And the king made silver in Jerusalem as stones, and cedar trees made he as the sycomore trees that are in the low plains in abundance.

THE DEATH OF SOLOMON

28 And they brought unto Solomon horses out of Egypt, and out of all lands.

29 Now the rest of the acts of Solomon, first and last, are they not written in the book of Nathan the Prophet, and in the Prophecy of Ahijah the Shilonite, and in the visions of Iddo the Seer against Jeroboam the son of Nebat?

30 And Solomon reigned in Jerusalem over all Israel forty years.

31 And Solomon slept with his fathers, and he was buried in the city of David his father: and Rehoboam his son reigned in his stead. (The fact that God did not record the great sins of Solomon in his latter years is some indication that Solomon asked for and received Mercy, Forgiveness, and Grace. If so, these sins would have been washed away, and thereby unrecorded. This is about the only indication that we have that Solomon may have made things right with God before he died.)

CHAPTER 10
(975 B.C.)
REHOBOAM SUCCEEDS SOLOMON

AND Rehoboam went to Shechem: for to Shechem were all Israel come to make him king. (Jerusalem was where the Lord had placed His Name, and yet, for political purposes,

and without consulting the Lord, Rehoboam would go to Shechem. So much of what is today called "Christianity" is operated upon the rudiment of political expediency, and not according to the Word of the Lord.)

2 And it came to pass, when Jeroboam the son of Nebat, who was in Egypt, whither he had fled from the presence of Solomon the king, heard it, that Jeroboam returned out of Egypt (heard that Solomon had died.; it is instructive to point out the dissatisfaction of the nation with the glorious reign of Solomon, with all of its prosperity; in fact, much of Israel would elect Solomon's enemy as king; this is a perfect picture of Rev., Chpt. 20.

There it is foretold that although Christ will maintain an absolutely perfect and prosperous government over the entirety of the Earth for one thousand years, yet some of the world will be dissatisfied with that reign of Glory and Righteousness, and will call back Satan from exile, as Israel called back Jeroboam and, for a short time, will enthrone Satan as prince over at least a part of the Earth).

3 And they sent and called him. So Jeroboam and all Israel came and spoke to Rehoboam, saying,

4 Your father made our yoke grievous: now therefore ease thou somewhat the grievous servitude of your father, and his heavy yoke that he put upon us, and we will serve you (there is no Scriptural evidence of a "grievous servitude" or "heavy yoke").

5 And he said unto them, Come again unto me after three days. And the people departed.

6 And king Rehoboam took counsel with the old men who had stood before Solomon his father while he yet lived, saying, What counsel give you me to return answer to this people? (However, there is no place that it says that he took counsel with God. There seemed to be little desire for the Will of God. All was political expediency.)

7 And they spoke unto him, saying, If you be kind to this people, and please them, and speak good words to them, they will be your servants for ever (this was the counsel he should have taken!).

8 But he forsook the counsel which the old men gave him, and took counsel with the young men who were brought up with him, who stood before him (this would occasion much bloodshed!).

9 And he said unto them, What advice give you that we may return answer to this

people, which have spoken to me, saying, Ease somewhat the yoke that your father did put upon us?

10 And the young men who were brought up with him spoke unto him, saying, Thus shall you answer the people who spoke unto you, saying, Your father made our yoke heavy, but make thou it somewhat lighter for us; thus shall you say unto them, My little finger shall be thicker than my father's loins.

11 For whereas my father put a heavy yoke upon you, I will put more to your yoke: my father chastised you with whips, but I will chastise you with scorpions. *(No doubt, there was much more said than given here. They probably counseled him to conduct himself in a strong manner, etc. It was the worst advice he could have gotten!)*

REHOBOAM'S FOOLISH DECISION

12 So Jeroboam and all the people came to Rehoboam on the third day, as the king bade, saying, Come again to me on the third day.

13 And the king answered them roughly; and king Rehoboam forsook the counsel of the old men,

14 And answered them after the advice of the young men, saying, My father made your yoke heavy, but I will add thereto: my father chastised you with whips, but I will chastise you with scorpions.

15 So the king hearkened not unto the people: for the cause was of God, that the LORD might perform His Word, which He spoke by the hand of Ahijah the Shilonite to Jeroboam the son of Nebat *(I Ki. 11:29-39; Solomon, although dead, bears his full share of the responsibility of what Rehoboam was, and shortly came to show he was; the Lord didn't do this arbitrarily, but because of Judah's terrible idol-worship, which now characterized the country, and was instigated by Solomon).*

ISRAEL'S REVOLT

16 And when all Israel saw that the king would not hearken unto them, the people answered the king, saying, What portion have we in David? and we have none inheritance in the son of Jesse: every man to your tents, O Israel: and now, David, see to your own house. So all Israel went to their tents *(this was the beginning of over 250 years of division and strife between Israel, the northern kingdom, and Judah,*

the southern kingdom; this rupture would result in untold numbers of deaths).

17 But as for the Children of Israel who dwelt in the cities of Judah, Rehoboam reigned over them *(the northern kingdom under Jeroboam would be called by several names — Israel, Samaria, and Ephraim; some ten Tribes would be loyal to the northern confederacy; the southern confederacy, called Judah, would have some three Tribes that would remain loyal — Judah, Benjamin, and Levi; Shechem, and then Samaria, would be the capital of the northern confederacy, with Jerusalem being the capital of the southern confederacy).*

18 Then king Rehoboam sent Hadoram who was over the tribute *(taxes)*; and the Children of Israel stoned him with stones, that he died. But king Rehoboam made speed to get him up to his chariot, to flee to Jerusalem *(wherever Rehoboam was, he realized he was in acute danger, so he went speedily to Jerusalem).*

19 And Israel rebelled against the house of David unto this day.

CHAPTER 11
(974 B.C.)

REHOBOAM FORBIDDEN TO FIGHT ISRAEL

AND when Rehoboam was come to Jerusalem, he gathered of the house of Judah and Benjamin an hundred and fourscore thousand *(180,000)* chosen men, which were warriors, to fight against Israel, that he might bring the kingdom again to Rehoboam *(once again, Rehoboam did this thing without consulting the Lord; nevertheless, the Lord would consult him!).*

2 But the Word of the LORD came to Shemaiah the man of God, saying,

3 Speak unto Rehoboam the son of Solomon, king of Judah, and to all Israel in Judah and Benjamin, saying,

4 Thus saith the LORD, You shall not go up, nor fight against your brethren: return every man to his house: for this thing is done of Me. And they obeyed the words of the LORD, and returned from going against Jeroboam *(as God would not force Israel to serve Him, likewise, He will not force men to serve Him today; Salvation must always be from a "willing heart" [Rev. 22:17]).*

REHOBOAM FORTIFIES HIS KINGDOM

5 And Rehoboam dwelt in Jerusalem, and

built cities for defence in Judah.

6 He built even Beth-lehem, and Etam, and Tekoa,

7 And Beth-zur, and Shoco, and Adullam,

8 And Gath, and Mareshah, and Ziph,

9 And Adoraim, and Lachish, and Azekah,

10 And Zorah, and Aijalon, and Hebron, which are in Judah and in Benjamin fenced cities.

11 And he fortified the strongholds, and put captains in them, and store of victual, and of oil and wine.

12 And in every several city he put shields and spears, and made them exceeding strong having Judah and Benjamin on his side.

13 And the Priests and the Levites who were in all Israel *(the northern kingdom)* resorted to him out of all their coasts *(all worship of God had been discontinued in the northern confederacy; consequently, many Priests and Levites moved to Jerusalem)*.

THE PRIESTS AND LEVITES OF ISRAEL JOIN REHOBOAM BECAUSE OF JEROBOAM'S SINS

14 For the Levites left their suburbs and their possession, and came to Judah and Jerusalem: for Jeroboam and his sons had cast them off from executing the Priest's office unto the LORD *(living for God means forsaking all; it would seem farfetched to the carnal mind for individuals to leave their home, friends, and even family to go where God is moving; nevertheless, this has characterized true followers of the Lord from the very beginning)*:

15 And he ordained him priests for the high places, and for the devils, and for the calves which he had made. *(Because of worshipping Satan, the northern confederacy would be destroyed as a nation about 749 B.C. [II Sam., Chpt. 17]. A little over 130 years later [616 B.C.], Judah was also destroyed for her sins [I Ki., Chpts. 24-25]. Seventy years later [546 B.C.], the Godly of all the thirteen Tribes returned to make a nation again in the land of Israel.)*

16 And after them out of all the Tribes of Israel such as set their hearts to seek the LORD God of Israel came to Jerusalem, to sacrifice unto the LORD God of their fathers *(the Temple and the Altar were at Jerusalem; and this was the place that God had chosen, as it regards the site of His Temple)*.

17 So they strengthened the kingdom of Judah, and made Rehoboam the son of Solomon strong, three years: for three years they walked in the way of David and Solomon. *(This, of course, was speaking of the southern kingdom of Judah — but for only three years. It is amazing how the Holy Spirit delineated the time, down to almost the day. After this time, Rehoboam and Judah went into deep sin. As a result, God permitted Egypt to conquer them and take away all their treasures [12:2-12]. If Rehoboam had continued in the Godly Way, no kingdom or combination of kingdoms could have overcome him.)*

REHOBOAM'S FAMILY

18 And Rehoboam took him Mahalath the daughter of Jerimoth the son of David to wife, and Abihail the daughter of Eliab the son of Jesse;

19 Which bore him children; Jeush, and Shamariah, and Zaham.

20 And after her he took Maachah the daughter of Absalom; which bore him Abijah, and Attai, and Ziza, and Shelomith.

21 And Rehoboam loved Maachah the daughter of Absalom above all his wives and his concubines: (for he took eighteen wives, and threescore concubines; and begat twenty and eight sons, and threescore daughters *[Rehoboam was clearly wrong, according to Deut. 17:17].)*

22 And Rehoboam made Abijah the son of Maachah the chief, to be ruler among his brethren: for he thought to make him king.

23 And he dealt wisely, and dispersed of all his children throughout all the countries of Judah and Benjamin, unto every fenced city: and he gave them victual in abundance. And he desired many wives. *(The words in the Hebrew, "wise dealing," are an indication that his conscience was not quite at ease, and that he knew he was wrong. Nothing is so liable to blind judgment as personal affection — Pulpit.)*

CHAPTER 12
(972 B.C.)
REHOBOAM'S APOSTASY

AND it came to pass, when Rehoboam had established the kingdom, and had strengthened himself, he forsook the Law of the LORD, and all Israel *(Judah)* with him. *(Judah prospered. Regrettably, prosperity sometimes is not a blessing. Too many times when Believers are blessed, they do exactly as Rehoboam*

did. They "forsake the Law of the LORD.")

SHISHAK OF EGYPT INVADES JUDAH

2 And it came to pass, that in the fifth year of king Rehoboam Shishak king of Egypt came up against Jerusalem, because they had transgressed against the LORD *(in other words, the Lord allowed such, because of Judah's backsliding; the Lord allows such in order to cause people to appeal to Him; sometimes it works, and sometimes it doesn't!)*,

3 With twelve hundred chariots, and threescore thousand *(60,000)* horsemen: and the people were without number who came with him out of Egypt; the Lubims, the Sukkiims, and the Ethiopians *(the troops that accompanied the cavalry and the horse-soldiers were without number)*.

4 And he *(Shishak)* took the fenced cities which pertained to Judah, and came to Jerusalem *(the only way that Shishak could have taken Judah, and especially Jerusalem, was because Judah had forsaken the Lord; the Lord was their power and strength; as long as they kept His Commandments and Statutes, no nation in the world, nor confederation of nations, could defeat them; however, when they "forsook the Law of the LORD," defeat was inevitable)*.

5 Then came Shemaiah the Prophet to Rehoboam, and to the princes of Judah, who were gathered together to Jerusalem because of Shishak, and said unto them, Thus saith the LORD, You have forsaken Me, and therefore have I also left you in the hand of Shishak *(the Lord, in His Mercy, gives Judah warning; no warning could be more clear than this; if we follow the Lord, we will receive His Blessing; if we forsake the Lord, He will allow enemies to intrude upon us; our blessings are tied totally to Him)*.

6 Whereupon the princes of Israel and the king humbled themselves; and they said, The LORD is righteous *(regrettably, their Repentance was not very deep; nevertheless, the Lord would honor it; when they said, "The LORD is righteous," this means that they knew that He was justified in what He had done, and that they deserved it)*.

7 And when the LORD saw that they humbled themselves, the Word of the LORD came to Shemaiah, saying, They have humbled themselves; therefore I will not destroy them, but I will grant them some deliverance; and My wrath shall not be poured out upon Jerusalem by the hand of Shishak. *(Notice the words*

"some deliverance." They would not have a complete Deliverance, only partial. The reason? Their Repentance was partial; therefore, their Deliverance was partial.)*

8 Nevertheless they shall be his servants; that they may know My service, and the service of the kingdoms of the countries *(this meant that Judah must learn to obey and know the difference between serving God and serving ungodly nations; if they persisted in their ungodly ways, they would serve ungodly nations!)*.

9 So Shishak king of Egypt came up against Jerusalem, and took away the treasures of the House of the LORD, and the treasures of the king's house; he took all: he carried away also the shields of gold which Solomon had made. *(To be sure, considering the riches that Solomon had amassed, what Shishak took must have been astronomical. Let the Reader understand:*

Satan desires to take away our spiritual treasures, plus everything else. And he will definitely do so, unless we minutely follow the Lord, which means to minutely follow His Word.)

10 Instead of which king Rehoboam made shields of brass, and committed them to the hands of the chief of the guard, that kept the entrance of the king's house. *(The world robs the Church of Divine realities and public worship, and the Church tries to hide the loss by substituting imitation. How many Churches presently have "shields of brass" instead of "shields of gold"? The "shields of gold" represent Deity. They are symbolic of God's Glory, Protection, and Power. "Shields of brass" are symbolic of man and man's ways.)*

11 And when the king entered into the House of the LORD, the guard came and fetched them, and brought them again into the guard chamber.

12 And when he humbled himself, the wrath of the LORD turned from him, that he would not destroy him altogether: and also in Judah things went well *(humility is the only coin that will spend in God's economy [Isa. 66:2])*.

DEATH OF REHOBOAM

13 So king Rehoboam strengthened himself in Jerusalem, and reigned: for Rehoboam was one and forty years old when he began to reign, and he reigned seventeen years in Jerusalem, the city which the LORD had chosen out of all the Tribes of Israel, to put His Name there. And his mother's name was Naamah an Ammonitess.

14 And he did evil, because he prepared not his heart to seek the LORD. *(What an indictment! But yet how true of so many.)*

15 Now the acts of Rehoboam, first and last, are they not written in the book of Shemaiah the Prophet, and of Iddo the Seer concerning genealogies? *(A continued register of David's genealogies.)* And there were wars between Rehoboam and Jeroboam continually.

16 And Rehoboam slept with his fathers, and was buried in the city of David: And Abijah his son reigned in his stead.

CHAPTER 13
(957 B.C.)
ABIJAH REIGNS OVER JUDAH

NOW in the eighteenth year of king Jeroboam began Abijah to reign over Judah.

2 He reigned three years in Jerusalem. His mother's name also was Michaiah the daughter of Uriel of Gibeah. And there was war between Abijah and Jeroboam. *(The conflict between the northern and southern kingdoms of Israel and Judah continues, and will increase, even as we shall see.)*

WAR WITH JEROBOAM

3 And Abijah set the battle in array with an army of valiant men of war, even four hundred thousand chosen men: Jeroboam also set the battle in array against him with eight hundred thousand chosen men, being mighty men of valour. *(A few years before, Rehoboam could muster only 180,000 chosen men [11:1]. This indicates that many thousands of the northern confederacy had come down to become a part of the kingdom of Judah. The Holy Spirit wants us to note that even though these troops of Jeroboam were "mighty men of valor," still, they could not overcome what God had decreed otherwise!)*

4 And Abijah stood up upon Mount Zemaraim, which is in Mount Ephraim, and said, Hear me, thou Jeroboam, and all Israel;

5 Ought ye not to know that the LORD God of Israel gave the kingdom over Israel to David for ever, even to him and to his sons by a covenant of salt? *(A "covenant of salt" is mentioned two other times in the Word of God [Lev. 2:13; Num. 18:19]. This covenant became a symbol of the incorruptibility of God's Covenant, and the perpetuity of man's obligation to Him. This Covenant refers to the solemnizing of any inviolable covenant. In other words, Abijah is telling Jeroboam that he is attempting to destroy what God has ordained. All of this shows that Abijah had a tremendous knowledge of the Word of God.)*

6 Yet Jeroboam the son of Nebat, the servant of Solomon the son of David, is risen up, and has rebelled against his lord.

7 And there are gathered unto him vain men, the children of Belial, and have strengthened themselves against Rehoboam the son of Solomon, when Rehoboam was young and tenderhearted, and could not withstand them.

8 And now you think to withstand the kingdom of the LORD in the hand of the sons of David; and you be a great multitude, and there are with you golden calves, which Jeroboam made you for gods *(Abijah reminds Jeroboam of his worship of the "golden calves," which, in some measure, was the same as the religion of Egypt, and was totally detrimental to the Ways of the Lord).*

9 Have you not cast out the Priests of the LORD, the sons of Aaron, and the Levites, and have made you priests after the manner of the nations of other lands? so that whosoever comes to consecrate himself with a young bullock and seven rams, the same may be a priest of them that are no gods *(Jeroboam had substituted his own priesthood for God's Priesthood).*

10 But as for us, the LORD is our God, and we have not forsaken Him; and the Priests, which minister unto the LORD, are the sons of Aaron, and the Levites wait upon their business *(as the Lord had commanded in the Law of Moses):*

11 And they burn unto the LORD every morning and every evening Burnt Sacrifices and Sweet Incense: the shewbread also set they in order upon the pure Table; and the candlestick *(Lampstand)* of gold with the lamps thereof, to burn every evening: for we keep the charge of the LORD our God; but you have forsaken Him *(as stated, all of this proclaims an extensive knowledge of the Ways of the Lord and the Law of Moses).*

12 And, behold, God Himself is with us for our Captain, and His Priests with sounding trumpets to cry alarm against you. O Children of Israel, fight ye not against the LORD God of your fathers; for you shall not prosper *(the Lord anointed Abijah to say these things).*

ABIJAH DEFEATS JEROBOAM:
500,000 OF ISRAEL SLAIN

13 But Jeroboam caused an ambushment to

come about behind them: so they were before Judah, and the ambushment was behind them *(Jeroboam, because of having twice as many soldiers as Abijah, thinks his victory is certain; consequently, he ignores Abijah's message; in fact, he surrounded the army of Judah).*

14 And when Judah looked back, behold, the battle was before and behind: and they cried unto the LORD, and the Priests sounded with the trumpets *(man's only hope is to "cry unto the LORD"! But sadly, few do).*

15 Then the men of Judah gave a shout *(a shout of Faith)*: and as the men of Judah shouted, it came to pass, that God smote Jeroboam and all Israel before Abijah and Judah *(the Holy Spirit is careful to denote the cause of the victory as being God; in the natural there was no way that Abijah's 400,000 men could even hope to defeat Jeroboam's army of 800,000 men; but with God all things are possible!).*

16 And the Children of Israel fled before Judah: and God delivered them into their hand *(if God fights for us, the enemy cannot win).*

17 And Abijah and his people slew them with a great slaughter: so there fell down slain of Israel five hundred thousand chosen men *(the word "slain" in the Hebrew can also mean "wounded," which it no doubt means here; at any rate the victory was gargantuan!).*

18 Thus the Children of Israel were brought under at that time, and the Children of Judah prevailed, because they relied upon the LORD God of their fathers *(over and over again, the Holy Spirit makes it known that it is God Who is the Author of this victory; obedience brings blessing, while disobedience brings defeat).*

19 And Abijah pursued after Jeroboam, and took cities from him, Beth-el with the towns thereof, and Jeshanah with the towns thereof, and Ephrain with the towns thereof.

20 Neither did Jeroboam recover strength again in the days of Abijah: and the LORD struck him, and he died *(the Lord terminated his life, because he had set himself to do evil; how many others fall into the same category?).*

ABIJAH'S FAMILY

21 But Abijah waxed mighty, and married fourteen wives, and begat twenty and two sons, and sixteen daughters.

22 And the rest of the acts of Abijah, and his ways, and his sayings, are written in the story of the Prophet Iddo.

CHAPTER 14
(955 B.C.)

ASA REIGNS OVER JUDAH

SO Abijah slept with his fathers, and they buried him in the city of David: and Asa his son reigned in his stead. In his days the land was quiet ten years *(this was ten years without war, ten years of peace and prosperity).*

2 And Asa did that which was good and right in the eyes of the LORD his God *(this is the reason for the peace, quiet, and prosperity):*

3 For he took away the altars of the strange gods, and the high places, and broke down the images, and cut down the groves *(evidently, Judah, under Abijah, had been involved at least to some degree in idol worship, hence, the statement made about Abijah in I Ki., Chpt. 15):*

4 And commanded Judah to seek the LORD God of their fathers, and to do the Law and the Commandment *(Asa points Judah to the Bible; how so badly we need Preachers presently who will, as well, point people to the Bible; but all too often the people are pointed in every direction except the Bible).*

5 Also he took away out of all the cities of Judah the high places and the images: and the kingdom was quiet before him. *(This lesson should be plain to every Christian — that sin opens the door for strife, opposition, destruction, and all manner of turbulence, while seeking the Ways of God and following the Word of God insure serenity, rest, and peace. This doesn't mean that Satan will cease to oppose the true Child of God; however, it does mean victory and then peace when Satan does oppose.)*

ASA'S BUILDING PROGRAM

6 And he built fenced cities in Judah: for the land had rest, and he had no war in those years; because the LORD had given him rest *(when one properly follows the Lord, "rest" is guaranteed [Mat. 11:28-30]).*

7 Therefore he said unto Judah, Let us build these cities, and make about them walls, and towers, gates, and bars, while the land is yet before us; because we have sought the LORD our God, we have sought Him, and He has given us rest on every side. So they built and prospered *(five times in these first seven Verses of this Chapter, the Holy Spirit alludes to this great blessing of "rest").*

ASA'S ARMY

8 And Asa had an army of men who bore targets *(large shields)* and spears, out of Judah three hundred thousand; and out of Benjamin, who bore shields and drew bows, two hundred and fourscore thousand: all these were mighty men of valour *(the Holy Spirit here alludes to the power of Judah; when people are right with God, they have power over the enemy [Acts 1:8]).*

ASA'S VICTORY OVER ZERAH

9 And there came out against them Zerah the Ethiopian with an host of a thousand thousand *(one million men)*, and three hundred chariots; and came unto Mareshah.

10 Then Asa went out against him, and they set the battle in array in the valley of Zephathah at Mareshah.

11 And Asa cried unto the LORD his God, and said, LORD, it is nothing with you to help, whether with many, or with them who have no power: help us, O LORD our God; for we rest on You, and in Your Name we go against this multitude. O LORD, You are our God; let not man prevail against You. *(Even though Asa, in fact, did have a mighty army, still, he did not rely on such. He "cried unto the LORD." All too often blessing and prosperity, even though from God, can turn the hearts and the heads of men away from God, but Asa seems, at least at this time, to have trusted solely in the Lord. If God does bless us with money and numbers, fine, well, and good. However, we must never look to these things, but always, and only, to the Lord.)*

12 So the LORD smote the Ethiopians before Asa, and before Judah; and the Ethiopians fled *(the Holy Spirit is quick here to proclaim the fact that it was the Lord Who brought about this great victory).*

13 And Asa and the people who were with him pursued them unto Gerar: and the Ethiopians were overthrown, that they could not recover themselves; for they were destroyed before the LORD, and before His host; and they carried away very much spoil. *(This is the Way of the Lord! Instead of Satan taking all that we have in the Lord, we are to take all that he has. It can be done only if the Believer will place his Faith exclusively in Christ and the Cross. Then the Holy Spirit will Work mightily on our behalf, even as He did here for*

Asa [Rom. 8:1-2, 11].)

14 And they smote all the cities round about Gerar; for the fear of the LORD came upon them: and they spoiled all the cities; for there was exceeding much spoil in them. *(The area around Gerar constituted the extreme southern portion of Judah, in fact, that which bordered Egypt. If the Believer has forfeited any of his spiritual inheritance to Satan, it must be regained, and can be regained, and in totality.)*

15 They smote also the tents of cattle, and carried away sheep and camels in abundance, and returned to Jerusalem. *(This great victory dated the commencement of a period of comparative internal peace and reform for the kingdom of Judah, which lasted some twenty-one years, and all because of trust in God.)*

CHAPTER 15

(955 B.C.)

AZARIAH THE PROPHET GETS A MESSAGE FROM GOD FOR ASA

AND the Spirit of God came upon Azariah the son of Oded *(this is the only place that the Prophet Azariah is mentioned):*

2 And he went out to meet Asa, and said unto him, Hear ye me, Asa, and all Judah and Benjamin; The LORD is with you, while you be with Him; and if you seek Him, He will be found of you; but if you forsake Him, He will forsake you. *(Three things are here said: 1. The Lord is with you while you are with Him. 2. If you seek Him, He will be found of you. 3. If you forsake Him, He will forsake you. These eternal facts are true of an individual or a nation, Jews or Gentiles, people under Law or under Grace, in one age as well as another.)*

3 Now for a long season Israel has been without the true God, and without a teaching Priest, and without Law *(this, no doubt, refers to the last years of Solomon, the fourteen years of Rehoboam's reign [11:17; 12:1], and the three years of Abijah's reign [I Ki. 15:1-4]).*

4 But when they in their trouble did turn unto the LORD God of Israel, and sought Him, He was found of them *(this Promise is clear; God will not forsake those who turn to Him and seek Him; the Scripture is emphatic: "He was found of them").*

5 And in those times there was no peace to him who went out, nor to him who came in, but great vexations were upon all the inhabitants of the countries.

6 And nation was destroyed of nation, and city of city: for God did vex them with all adversity *(even though they were His chosen people, called of Him and loved of Him, still, when they turned their backs on Him, spiritually speaking, He would "vex them with all adversity"; God desires to bless us, but, if we desire to oppose Him, He will, instead, "vex us," and He does it in order to bring us to our spiritual senses).*

7 Be ye strong therefore, and let not your hands be weak: for your work shall be rewarded *(the admonishment by the Holy Spirit was then and now, "Be strong" [I Cor. 16:13; Eph. 6:10; II Tim. 2:1]).*

THE REFORMS UNDER ASA

8 And when Asa heard these words, and the Prophecy of Oded the Prophet *(evidently, Oded, the father of Azariah, prophesied to Asa, as well as his son),* he took courage, and put away the abominable idols out of all the land of Judah and Benjamin, and out of the cities which he had taken from Mount Ephraim, and renewed the Altar of the LORD, that was before the porch of the LORD *(any time there is a true Move of God, the Lord will bring the people back to the Cross, symbolized here by the "Altar").*

9 And he gathered all Judah and Benjamin, and the strangers with them out of Ephraim and Manasseh, and out of Simeon: for they fell to him out of Israel in abundance, when they saw that the LORD his God was with him *(tens of thousands from the northern kingdom of Israel moved to Judah when they saw that the Lord was with Asa).*

10 So they gathered themselves together at Jerusalem in the third month, in the fifteenth year of the reign of Asa *(this was probably the Feast of Pentecost, conducted in June).*

11 And they offered unto the LORD the same time, of the spoil which they had brought, seven hundred oxen and seven thousand sheep. *(According to Num. 31:25-54, the Lord's portion, concerning the spoil of war, was to be one animal out of every five hundred from the half that belonged to the men of war, and one out of every fifty of the other half of the spoils that belonged to the congregation. On this basis [eleven animals for the Lord out of every one thousand taken], the total spoil must have numbered approximately 63,000 oxen and 636,000 sheep. When the Fourteenth Verse of* the last Chapter said "exceeding much spoil," it meant exactly that.)

12 And they entered into a covenant to seek the LORD God of their fathers with all their heart and with all their soul;

13 That whosoever would not seek the LORD God of Israel should be put to death, whether small or great, whether man or woman *(this probably had to do with Ex. 22:20 and Deut. 13:6-11).*

14 And they swore unto the LORD with a loud voice, and with shouting, and with trumpets, and with cornets *(music has always accompanied Revival).*

15 And all Judah rejoiced at the oath: for they had sworn with all their heart, and sought Him with their whole desire; and He was found of them: and the LORD gave them rest round about *(what a great statement, "And He was found of them"; in fact, He can be found of anyone, if, with true sincerity, He is sought!).*

16 And also concerning Maachah the mother of Asa the king *(his grandmother),* he removed her from being queen, because she had made an idol in a grove: and Asa cut down her idol, and stamped it, and burnt it at the brook Kidron *(she was a worshipper of the Asherah, an idol carved in the likeness of the male reproductive organ).*

17 But the high places were not taken away out of Israel: nevertheless the heart of Asa was perfect all his days *(the word "perfect," as used here, does not mean sinless perfection, but that his heart was perfect as far as idolatry was concerned; the "high places," at least in this instance, would have been used to sacrifice to Jehovah; however, still, this was not in keeping with the Commandment of God that the Sacrifices be offered only at the Temple at Jerusalem; consequently, the Holy Spirit mentions the "high places" for a reason).*

18 And he brought into the House of God the things that his father had dedicated, and that he himself had dedicated, silver, and gold, and vessels.

19 And there was no more war unto the five and thirtieth year of the reign of Asa *(Asa had peace the first ten years of his reign [14:1]; then came the Ethiopian invasion of Judah [14:9-15]; after that, there was peace for twenty-five years [15:19]; then came war with Baasha, king of the northern confederacy of Israel [16:1-6]; because he trusted in Syria at that time instead of God, wars were pronounced upon him for the balance of his reign — six more years [16:9]).*

CHAPTER 16
(941 B.C.)
WAR WITH BAASHA: ASA'S UNHOLY ALLIANCE WITH BEN-HADAD

IN the six and thirtieth year of the reign of Asa Baasha king of Israel came up against Judah, and built Ramah, to the intent that he might let none go out or come in to Asa king of Judah. *(Tens of thousands of people from the northern kingdom of Israel were coming down to Judah, as stated, that they might worship God at the Temple. Baasha, king of Israel, was attempting to stop this flight by building this border city of Ramah.*

One of the sure signs that a doctrine, or a so-called gospel, is wrong is when the propagators try to stop people from hearing anything else. One of Satan's greatest ploys is to place the true worship of God "off limits," and to threaten by force anyone who would attempt to exceed those limits.)

2 Then Asa brought out silver and gold out of the treasures of the House of the LORD and of the king's house, and sent to Ben-hadad king of Syria, who dwelt at Damascus, saying *(rather than trust God to help him regarding Baasha, he hired the king of Syria. Asa's plan would succeed militarily, but fail spiritually. The success of self-made plans is always a spiritual disaster.*

It must be remembered that new victories cannot be won by the remembrance of old faith; there must be a fresh exercise of faith in every crisis),

3 There is a league between me and you, as there was between my father and your father: behold, I have sent you silver and gold; go, break your league with Baasha king of Israel, that he may depart from me *(Believers are never to join with unbelievers [II Cor. 6:14-18]).*

4 And Ben-hadad hearkened unto king Asa, and sent the captains of his armies against the cities of Israel; and they smote Ijon, and Dan, and Abel-maim, and all the store cities of Naphtali.

5 And it came to pass, when Baasha heard it, that he left off building of Ramah, and let his work cease.

6 Then Asa the king took all Judah; and they carried away the stones of Ramah, and the timber thereof, wherewith Baasha was building; and he built therewith Geba and Mizpah.

HANANI, THE PROPHET OF GOD, REBUKES ASA FOR RELYING ON SYRIA

7 And at that time Hanani the Seer came to Asa king of Judah, and said unto him, Because you have relied on the king of Syria, and not relied on the LORD your God, therefore is the host of the king of Syria escaped out of your hand *(is it possible that God makes plans for us which speak of great victory, and we forfeit those plans by our faithlessness? Rather than trusting Him, we trust man).*

8 Were not the Ethiopians and the Lubims a huge host, with very many chariots and horsemen? yet, because you did rely on the LORD, He delivered them into your hand *(why did Asa rely on the Lord then, and not rely on Him now? As stated, yesterday's faith will not suffice for today!).*

9 For the eyes of the LORD run to and fro throughout the whole Earth, to show Himself strong in the behalf of them whose heart is perfect toward Him. Herein you have done foolishly: therefore from henceforth you shall have wars *(when one considers that the Lord is ardently looking for individuals who will believe Him, so that He might "show Himself strong on their behalf," such should give us a very positive perspective on the Ways of the Lord; our Lord desires to help people, but they must evidence Faith in Him, and it must be a continuous Faith).*

10 Then Asa was wroth with the Seer, and put him in a prison house; for he was in a rage with him because of this thing. And Asa oppressed some of the people the same time. *(This is the same Asa who instituted the great Revival of Chapter 15. How the mighty have fallen! If Asa had truly repented as this time, thereby heeding the Prophet, more than likely the diseases of Verse 12 would not have come upon him and shortened his life.)*

11 And, behold, the acts of Asa, first and last *(the statement, "first and last," signifies that there was a difference in Asa in his last years),* lo, they are written in the book of the kings of Judah and Israel.

ASA'S SICKNESS AND DEATH

12 And Asa in the thirty and ninth year of his reign was diseased in his feet, until his disease was exceeding great: yet in his disease he sought not to the LORD, but to the

physicians. *(The Lord permitted this disease as a result of Asa's actions. I wonder how many presently fall into the same category?*

The idea of this Verse is that if Asa had sought the Lord, the Lord would have forgiven him and healed him.

The "physicians" who are spoken of here were probably Egyptian physicians, who were in high repute at foreign courts in ancient times, and who pretended to expel diseases by charms, incantations, and mystic arts. In other words, they were Satanic!)

13 And Asa slept with his fathers, and died in the one and fortieth year of his reign *(because of his faithlessness, Asa no doubt cut his life short!).*

14 And they buried him in his own sepulchres, which he had made for himself in the city of David, and laid him in the bed which was filled with sweet odours and divers kinds of spices prepared by the apothecaries' art: and they made a very great burning for him *(the burning of spices).*

CHAPTER 17
(912 B.C.)
JEHOSHAPHAT SUCCEEDS ASA

AND Jehoshaphat his son reigned in his stead, and strengthened himself against Israel. *(Jehoshaphat is a Godly man, yet with one glaring weakness — forming alliances with heathenistic Israel. Strangely enough, he would fortify himself greatly in a military sense against Israel, but, yet he will compromise his spiritual stand by forming an alliance with the same people.*

Far too often, the modern Church begins by opposing evil, and then compromises with evil.)

2 And he placed forces in all the fenced cities of Judah, and set garrisons in the land of Judah, and in the cities of Ephraim, which Asa his father had taken.

3 And the LORD was with Jehoshaphat *(the greatest thing that could ever be said of any man),* because he walked in the first ways of his father David, and sought not unto Baalim *(it is believed by some Scholars that the name of David is wrongly inserted here; as well, it is not in the Septuagint; most probably, the reference is to Asa, the father of Jehoshaphat; inasmuch as the terminology does not exactly fit David, it is my personal opinion also that the translation is incorrect here, with Asa being the correct name);*

4 But sought to the LORD God of his father, and walked in His Commandments, and not after the doings of Israel *(idolatry).*

5 Therefore the LORD stablished the kingdom in his hand; and all Judah brought to Jehoshaphat presents; and he had riches and honour in abundance *(blessings follow obedience!).*

REVIVAL UNDER JEHOSHAPHAT

6 And his heart was lifted up in the ways of the LORD: moreover he took away the high places and groves out of Judah. *(As previously stated, the people were not sacrificing to idols at these "high places and groves," but were sacrificing to Jehovah. Yet, this was against the Law of God inasmuch as they were supposed to sacrifice in Jerusalem. Almost invariably, the Sacrifices to Jehovah would eventually degenerate into sacrifices to idols. The reason for the one place of Sacrifice, and we speak of the Temple, is because there was to be but one Calvary.)*

7 Also in the third year of his reign he sent to his princes, even to Ben-hail, and to Obadiah, and to Zechariah *(not the Prophet),* and to Nethaneel, and to Michaiah, to teach in the cities of Judah *(this proclaims Jehoshaphat doing something that had never been done before — the teaching of the Law throughout Judah).*

8 And with them he sent Levites, even Shemaiah, and Nethaniah, and Zebadiah, and Asahel, and Shemiramoth, and Jehonathan, and Adonijah, and Tobijah, and Tob-adonijah, Levites; and with them Elishama and Jehoram, Priests.

9 And they taught in Judah, and had the Book of the Law of the LORD with them, and went about throughout all the cities of Judah, and taught the people *(this was the first great teaching mission instituted by any king of Israel; the Law of Moses was taken from city to city and taught to the people; the "Law of the LORD" was the Pentateuch — Genesis, Exodus, Leviticus, Numbers, and Deuteronomy; fidelity to the Word of God is the key to all blessing from God).*

JEHOSHAPHAT'S POWER AND PROSPERITY

10 And the fear of the LORD fell upon all the kingdoms of the lands that were round about Judah, so that they made no war against Jehoshaphat *(all of this shows that the Lord was immensely pleased with this which Jehoshaphat was doing; this Passage shows that God can stop*

enemies from making war, or He can cause them to make war; all depends on our faith and our consecration).

11 Also some of the Philistines brought Jehoshaphat presents, and tribute silver; and the Arabians brought him flocks, seven thousand and seven hundred rams, and seven thousand and seven hundred he goats *(this is the way it should be! Instead of Satan taking what we have, we should take what he has).*

12 And Jehoshaphat waxed great exceedingly; and he built in Judah castles, and cities of store.

13 And he had much business *(substance)* in the cities of Judah: and the men of war, mighty men of valour, were in Jerusalem.

14 And these are the numbers of them according to the house of their fathers: Of Judah, the captains of thousands; Adnah the chief, and with him mighty men of valour three hundred thousand.

15 And next to him was Jehohanan the captain, and with him two hundred and fourscore thousand.

16 And next him was Amasiah the son of Zichri, who willingly offered himself unto the LORD; and with him two hundred thousand mighty men of valour.

17 And of Benjamin; Eliada a mighty man of valour, and with him armed men with bow and shield two hundred thousand.

18 And next him was Jehozabad, and with him an hundred and fourscore thousand ready prepared for the war.

19 These waited on the king, beside those whom the king put in the fenced cities throughout all Judah *(very similar to David's "mighty men"!).*

CHAPTER 18
(897 B.C.)
JEHOSHAPHAT'S ALLIANCE WITH AHAB TO WAR AGAINST SYRIA

NOW Jehoshaphat had riches and honour in abundance, and joined affinity with Ahab. *(Oftentimes, riches and honor are more dangerous to the spiritual life than contempt and poverty. It is much better for the Preacher if most are cursing him instead of praising him. Probably the greatest danger to the Church is "joining affinity with the world." This leaven that Satan introduced into Judah would ultimately drench Jerusalem with blood.)*

2 And after certain years he went down to Ahab to Samaria. And Ahab killed sheep and oxen for him in abundance, and for the people who he had with him, and persuaded him to go up with him to Ramoth-gilead *(when the Believer "goes down" to the world, he is received with great hospitality, but immediately is made a tool of the world).*

3 And Ahab king of Israel said unto Jehoshaphat king of Judah, Will you go with me to Ramoth-gilead? And he answered him, I am as you are, and my people as your people; and we will be with you in the war *(Jehoshaphat answered falsely; he, in fact, was led by God, while Ahab was led by Satan; the people of Judah were worshippers of the True God, with the people of Israel worshipping Baal; in fact, there was no similarity between the two; the Lord was grossly displeased with Jehoshaphat making affinity with Ahab).*

AHAB'S FALSE PROPHETS

4 And Jehoshaphat said unto the king of Israel, Enquire, I pray you, at the Word of the LORD today *(if Jehoshaphat had enquired of the Lord previously, he would not even be here with Ahab).*

5 Therefore the king of Israel gathered together of prophets four hundred men *(false prophets)*, and said unto them, Shall we go to Ramoth-gilead to battle, or shall I forbear? And they said, Go up; for God will deliver it into the king's hand *(the modern Church abounds presently with this type of "prophet"; they prophesy continuously, but they prophesy out of their own minds, because precious few are actually from the Lord).*

6 But Jehoshaphat said, Is there not here a Prophet of the LORD besides, that we might enquire of him? *(At least, Jehoshaphat knew that their prophecies did not ring true; unfortunately, far too many of modern Christendom do not know the false from the true.)*

7 And the king of Israel said unto Jehoshaphat, There is yet one man, by whom we may enquire of the LORD: but I hate him; for he never prophesied good unto me, but always evil: the same is Micaiah the son of Imla. And Jehoshaphat said, Let not the king say so *(sadly, the ratio of 400-to-1 would pretty well hold true today; prophets abound on every corner, but precious few are actually from the Lord; the few who are from the Lord are "hated"; of this, one can be certain).*

8 And the king of Israel called for one of

his officers, and said, Fetch quickly Micaiah the son of Imla.

9 And the king of Israel and Jehoshaphat king of Judah sat either of them on his throne, clothed in their robes, and they say in a void place at the entering in of the gate of Samaria; and all the prophets *(false prophets)* prophesied before them *(if it is to be noticed, they were prophesying prosperity, exactly as is the modern brand)*.

10 And Zedekiah the son of Chenaanah had made him horns of iron, and said, Thus saith the LORD, With these you shall push Syria until they be consumed *(the false prophets were just as quick to cry, "Thus saith the LORD," but the truth was, what they were saying was not from the Lord!)*.

11 And all the prophets prophesied so, saying, Go up to Ramoth-gilead, and prosper: for the LORD shall deliver it into the hand of the king.

MICAIAH'S TRUE PROPHECY

12 And the messenger that went to call Micaiah spoke to him, saying, Behold, the words of the prophets declare good to the king with one assent; let your word therefore, I pray you, be like one of theirs, and speak thou good *(the times have changed; the demand has not; the apostate Church is still saying, "Speak thou good"; as Israel of old could not tolerate the truth, the modern Church cannot tolerate the truth, either)*.

13 And Micaiah said, As the LORD lives, even what my God says, that will I speak *(his determination to speak only what "Thus saith the LORD," would earn him continued imprisonment, the bread and water of affliction, and without Jehoshaphat lifting a hand to help him)*.

14 And when he was come to the king, the king said unto him, Micaiah, shall we go to Ramoth-gilead to battle, or shall I forbear? And he said, Go ye up, and prosper, and they shall be delivered into your hand *(Micaiah begins by answering a fool according to his folly; he answers in sarcasm, which is easily obvious)*.

15 And the king said to him, How many times shall I adjure you that you say nothing but the truth to me in the Name of the LORD? *(As the facts will prove, Ahab didn't want the truth!)*

16 Then he said, I did see all Israel scattered upon the mountains, as sheep that have no shepherd: and the LORD said, These have no master; let them return therefore every man to his house in peace *(this "word" must have hit like a bombshell in the ears of wicked Ahab)*.

17 And the king of Israel said to Jehoshaphat, Did I not tell you that he would not prophesy good unto me, but evil? *(Unfortunately, there are many false prophets presently, who are ready and willing to prophesy "good," irrespective of what the truth actually is.)*

18 Again he said, Therefore hear the Word of the LORD; I saw the LORD sitting upon His Throne, and all the Host of Heaven standing on His right hand and on His left *(we are now privy to one of the most astounding pictures of the Throne of God, and the manner in which Heavenly business is conducted)*.

19 And the LORD said, Who shall entice Ahab king of Israel, that he may go up and fall at Ramoth-gilead? And one spoke saying after this manner, and another saying after that manner *(if Ahab had repented, this scene would not have taken place; but despite the warning of the Lord, he will carry out his own self-will; it would be to his doom!)*.

20 Then there came out a spirit *(evil spirit)*, and stood before the LORD, and said, I will entice him. And the LORD said unto him, Wherewith? *(We learn from this, and from Job, Chpts. 1-2, that Satan, along with evil spirits, presently have access, at least at times, to the Throne of God. There will come a time, and shortly, when all such will be cast out of Heaven, and allowed no more entrance [Rev. 12:9-10]. In fact, just exactly why the Lord has allowed Satan and demon spirits such access is a mystery [Rev. 10:7].)*

21 And he said, I will go out, and be a lying spirit in the mouth of all his prophets *(Ahab's prophets; lying spirits still have access to the mouths of false prophets, even unto to this hour)*. And the LORD said, You shall entice him, and you shall also prevail: go out, and do even so *(the idea is, if men will not have the truth, the Lord will aid and abet their believing a lie)*.

22 Now therefore, behold, the LORD has put a lying spirit in the mouth of these your prophets, and the LORD has spoken evil against you *(we learn from this that God controls not only the Heavenly Host of Righteousness, but also the world of spiritual darkness; Satan can only do what God allows him to do)*.

23 Then Zedekiah the son of Chenaanah came near, and smote Micaiah upon the cheek, and said, Which way went the Spirit of the

LORD from me to speak unto you? *(Jehoshaphat saw this, and yet did not lift his hand to help the Prophet of God. Judah would pay dearly for Jehoshaphat's sin.)*

24 And Micaiah said, Behold, you shall see on that day when you shall go into an inner chamber to hide yourself *(which would take place when Ahab was killed!).*

25 Then the king of Israel said, Take ye Micaiah, and carry him back to Amon the governor of the city, and to Joash the king's son;

26 And say, Thus saith the king, Put this fellow in the prison, and feed him with bread of affliction and with water of affliction, until I return in peace *(as stated, Jehoshaphat didn't lift a hand to help him!).*

27 And Micaiah said, If you certainly return in peace, then has not the LORD spoken by me. And he said, Hearken, all ye people *(before Micaiah was led away to prison, he turned to all the people who were present, who had heard God's pronouncement, and warned them! Sadly, they did not hearken, and Ahab was killed).*

THE DEFEAT AND DEATH OF AHAB

28 So the king of Israel and Jehoshaphat the king of Judah went up to Ramoth-gilead *(Jehoshaphat was a foolish man, especially in the face of this prophecy, to accompany Ahab).*

29 And the king of Israel said unto Jehoshaphat, I will disguise myself, and I will go to the battle; but you put on your robes *(kingly robes).* So the king of Israel disguised himself; and they went to the battle *(stupid men! If men spent as much time trying to please God as they do trying to outwit God, how much better off they would be).*

30 Now the king of Syria had commanded the captains of the chariots that were with him, saying, Fight ye not with small or great, save only with the king of Israel *(the Lord had put it in the mind of the king of Syria to seek only Ahab).*

31 And it came to pass, when the captains of the chariots saw Jehoshaphat, that they said, It is the king of Israel *(because of his kingly robes).* Therefore they compassed about him to fight: but Jehoshaphat cried out, and the LORD helped him; and God moved them to depart from him *(otherwise, he would have been killed; only by the Mercy and Grace of God was he spared; he had no business being here).*

32 For it came to pass, that, when the captains of the chariots perceived that it was not the king of Israel, they turned back again from pursuing him.

33 And a certain man drew a bow at a venture *(in other words, he just shot an arrow, not especially aiming at anything),* and smote the king of Israel between the joints of the harness *(but God guided the arrow straight toward Ahab):* therefore he said to his chariot man, Turn your hand, that you may carry me out of the host; for I am wounded *(exactly as the Prophet Micaiah had said; the Word of God always comes to pass).*

34 And the battle increased that day: howbeit the king of Israel stayed himself up in his chariot against the Syrians until the evening: and about the time of the sun going down he died. *(The sun went "down" for Ahab in more ways than one. He not only lost his life; he lost his soul — despite the fact that God had attempted to show him Mercy and Grace. His death is a portrayal of rebellion — a rebellion that characterizes most of the human race. How many today are headed toward their doom, spurning the Love, Grace, and Mercy of God, along with repeated warnings? Their "sun is going down.")*

CHAPTER 19
(896 B.C.)

JEHU REBUKES JEHOSHAPHAT

AND Jehoshaphat the king of Judah returned to his house in peace to Jerusalem. *(This Chapter proclaims rebuke and Repentance. Jehoshaphat returned in peace, only because the Lord was merciful to him. The two kings, Ahab and Jehoshaphat, are perfect examples of rebellion against God, which brings death, and serving God, which brings life — and that despite Jehoshaphat's unfaithfulness.)*

2 And Jehu the son of Hanani the Seer went out to meet him, and said to king Jehoshaphat, Should you help the ungodly, and love them who hate the LORD? therefore is wrath upon you from before the LORD *(the Lord was very displeased with Jehoshaphat's alliance with Ahab, and there would be repercussions, even as the word "wrath" proclaims, and which we shall see; sin must never be taken lightly or with impunity; in fact, sin is so powerful that the only answer to this dilemma is the Cross [Heb. 10:12]).*

3 Nevertheless there are good things found in you, in that you have taken away the groves out of the land *(idols worship),* and have prepared your heart to seek God *(and it is the*

heart to which the Lord looks).

ADDITIONAL REFORMS UNDER JEHOSHAPHAT

4 And Jehoshaphat dwelt at Jerusalem: and he went out again through the people from Beer-sheba to Mount Ephraim, and brought them back unto the LORD God of their fathers *(the word "again," as used here, speaks of Repentance on the part of Jehoshaphat and, as well, the second revival of teaching the Law of Moses and bringing the people back to God; the "Word" must always be set before the people; there is no other refuge!).*

5 And he set judges in the land throughout all the fenced cities of Judah, city by city,

6 And said to the judges, Take heed what ye do: for ye judge not for man, but for the LORD, Who is with you in the judgment *(civil duties were to be carried out strictly according to the Word of the Lord).*

7 Wherefore now let the fear of the LORD be upon you; take heed and do it: for there is no iniquity with the LORD our God, nor respect of persons, nor taking of gifts *(the latter speaks of bribery; honest judgment by these Judges must be in the Name of the Lord, and all, as stated, according to God's Word).*

8 Moreover in Jerusalem did Jehoshaphat set of the Levites, and of the Priests, and of the chief of the fathers of Israel, for the judgment of the LORD, and for controversies, when they returned to Jerusalem. *(This concerned cases appealed to the higher court, actually the highest in Israel. There must be justice for the poor, and the rich must not be able to buy their way out of wrongdoing. All of this actually goes back to the Cross, in effect stating that sin cannot be assuaged by any other manner than the Cross [I Cor. 1:17-18, 23; 2:2].)*

9 And he charged them, saying, Thus shall you do in the fear of the LORD, faithfully, and with a perfect heart.

10 And what cause soever shall come to you of your brethren who dwell in your cities, between blood and blood, between Law and Commandments, Statutes and Judgments, you shall even warn them that they trespass not against the LORD, and so wrath come upon you, and upon your brethren: this do, and you shall not trespass *(pure and simple, Jehoshaphat warns these Judges that if they do not abide by the Word of the Lord, they will be committing sin, and the Wrath of God will be the result).*

11 And, behold, Amariah the Chief Priest is over you in all matters of the LORD *(the spiritual)*; and Zebadiah the son of Ishmael, the ruler of the House of Judah, for all the king's matters *(Civil duties)*: also the Levites shall be officers before you *(the Law)*. Deal courageously, and the LORD shall be with the good *(at the same time, the latter phrase is stating that the Lord cannot be with the bad).*

CHAPTER 20
(896 B.C.)

MOAB INVADES JUDAH

IT came to pass after this also, that the children of Moab, and the children of Ammon, and with them other beside the Ammonites, came against Jehoshaphat to battle *(this invasion was probably allowed by the Lord because of Jehoshaphat's previous alliance with Ahab, which, as stated, greatly displeased the Lord [19:2]).*

2 Then there came some who told Jehoshaphat, saying, There comes a great multitude against you from beyond the sea on this side Syria; and, behold, they be in Hazazon-tamar, which is En-gedi *(this was more than a skirmish; it was a concentrated effort by the powers of darkness to destroy Judah).*

JEHOSHAPHAT PRAYS FOR DELIVERANCE

3 And Jehoshaphat feared *(this is not the "spirit of fear" spoken of by Paul, but rather the type of fear that is supposed to drive us to the Lord, and which it did Jehoshaphat)*, and set himself to seek the LORD, and proclaimed a fast throughout all Judah.

4 And Judah gathered themselves together, to ask help of the LORD: even out of all the cities of Judah they came to seek the LORD *(regrettably, the modern Church is teaching the people to seek the help of humanistic psychologists; let it ever be known, there is no help whatsoever from that source; the Lord Alone can help!).*

5 And Jehoshaphat stood in the congregation of Judah and Jerusalem, in the House of the LORD, before the new court,

6 And said, O LORD God of our fathers, are not You God in Heaven? and rule not Thou over all the kingdoms of the heathen? and in Your hand is there not power and might, so that none is able to withstand You? *(Even though these heathen powers did not serve God,*

still, they could do nothing except that which the Lord allowed them to do. As well, while Satan may be mighty in some respects, God Alone is Almighty!)

7 Are not You our God, Who did drive out the inhabitants of this land before Your people Israel, and gave it to the seed of Abraham Your friend for ever? *(The Lord was Israel's God, and they were His Children. Now, Satan is attempting to take the possession and inheritance that was given by the Lord.*

The word "forever" signifies the fact that our inheritance is never to be taken from us by the powers of darkness. God intends for us to keep it forever. In fact, it can be forfeited only by rebellion against the Lord.)

8 And they dwelt therein, and have built You a Sanctuary therein for Your Name, saying *(it was a House of Sacrifices, hence the shed Blood of the Lamb being the defense, and the only true defense, of Israel [7:12])*,

9 If, when evil comes upon us, as the sword, judgment, or pestilence, or famine, we stand before this House, and in Your presence, (for Your Name is in this House,) and cry unto You in our affliction, then You will hear and help *(Solomon had prayed this prayer many years before [Chpt. 6]; the Lord had promised to answer, that is, if certain conditions were met [7:14])*.

10 And now, behold, the children of Ammon and Moab and Mount Seir, whom You would not let Israel invade, when they came out of the land of Egypt, but they turned from them, and destroyed them not *(all of this proclaims the fact that Jehoshaphat knew the Word)*;

11 Behold, I say, how they reward us, to come to cast us out of Your possession, which You have given us to inherit *(that which Satan ever attempts to do)*.

12 O our God, will You not judge them? for we have no might against this great company that comes against us; neither know we what to do: but our eyes are upon You *(within ourselves, we have no might against Satan, and that we must ever learn; our strength is totally in the Lord; as then, so now!)*.

JAHAZIEL PROMISES GOD'S DELIVERANCE

13 And all Judah stood before the LORD, with their little ones, their wives, and their children *(Jehoshaphat had called upon all to seek the Lord)*.

14 Then upon Jahaziel the son of Zechariah, the son of Benaiah, the son of Jeiel, the son of Mattaniah, a Levite of the sons of Asaph, came the Spirit of the LORD in the midst of the congregation *(the Spirit of the Lord is the answer, and the only answer [Zech. 4:6])*;

15 And he said, Hearken ye, all Judah, and ye inhabitants of Jerusalem, and thou king Jehoshaphat, Thus saith the LORD unto you, Be not afraid nor dismayed by reason of this great multitude; for the battle is not yours, but God's. *(If we try to fight the battle on our terms, we will lose; if we fight the battle on His terms, we will win. What are those terms?*

We have to trust in Christ, Who has already fought this battle and won, and did so at the Cross [Col. 2:14-15]. Doing that, the Holy Spirit will then guarantee us the victory of Christ [Rom. 8:1-2, 11].)

16 To morrow go ye down against them: behold, they come up by the cliff of Ziz; and you shall find them at the end of the brook, before the wilderness of Jeruel.

17 You shall not need to fight in this battle: set yourselves, stand ye still, and see the Salvation of the LORD with you, O Judah and Jerusalem *("stand still" refers to the ceasing and desisting of our own personal efforts, i.e., "the flesh," and thereby trusting the Lord completely, and what He has done for us at the Cross)*: fear not, nor be dismayed *(ever the Word given to us by the Lord)*; to morrow go out against them: for the LORD will be with you *(and if He is with us, who can be against us?)*.

18 And Jehoshaphat bowed his head with his face to the ground: and all Judah and the inhabitants of Jerusalem fell before the LORD, worshipping the LORD.

19 And the Levites, of the Children of the Kohathites, and of the Children of the Korhites, stood up to praise the LORD God of Israel with a loud voice on high *(indicative of a Pentecostal meeting!)*.

GOD FULFILLS HIS PROMISE

20 And they *(Judah)* rose early in the morning, and went forth into the wilderness of Tekoa: and as they went forth, Jehoshaphat stood and said, Hear me, O Judah, and you inhabitants of Jerusalem; Believe in the LORD your God *(have faith in Him)*, so shall you be established *(established in His Word)*; believe His prophets, so shall you prosper *(true Prophets!)*.

21 And when he had consulted with the people, he appointed singers unto the LORD *(told to do this by the Lord)*, and that should praise the Beauty of Holiness, as they went out before the army *(praise must precede our effort)*, and to say, Praise the LORD; for His Mercy endures for ever *(praise and worship through singing and music constitute the highest form of worship, that is if it is Spirit-directed; to be sure, modern contemporary Christian music, so-called, definitely does not fall into this category, and any Christian who thinks it does is only fooling himself)*.

22 And when they began to sing and to praise, the LORD set ambushments against the children of Ammon, Moab, and mount Seir, which were come against Judah; and they were smitten *(the Jewish Targums say that these ambushments were caused by Angels)*.

23 For the children of Ammon and Moab stood up against the inhabitants of mount Seir, utterly to slay and destroy them *(the children of Ammon and Moab became so confused that they began to destroy the Edomites instead of the Israelites)*: and when they had made an end of the inhabitants of Seir, every one helped to destroy another *(they then turned on each other — all of this caused by the Lord)*.

24 And when Judah came toward the watch tower in the wilderness, they looked unto the multitude, and, behold, they were dead bodies fallen to the earth, and none escaped *(all of this portrays to us, in type and shadow, the manner presently in which our battles must be fought and won; Paul said that these are examples for us [I Cor. 10:11])*.

25 And when Jehoshaphat and his people came to take away the spoil of them, they found among them in abundance both riches with the dead bodies, and precious jewels, which they stripped off for themselves, more than they could carry away: and they were three days in gathering of the spoil, it was so much *(this is the true position of the Child of God; the Lord intends for us to take the spoil of Satan, instead of him robbing us)*.

26 And on the fourth day they assembled themselves in the valley of Berachah; for there they blessed the LORD *(thanked Him for what He had done for them)*: therefore the name of the same place was called, The valley of Berachah, unto this day *(the "valley of Blessing")*.

27 Then they returned, every man of Judah and Jerusalem, and Jehoshaphat in the forefront of them, to go again to Jerusalem with joy; for the LORD had made them to rejoice over their enemies *(and this the Lord will enable all of us to do, providing we look to Christ as our Source and the Cross as the Means [Rom. 6:3-14; 8:1-2, 11; I Cor. 1:17-18, 23; 2:2; Gal. 6:14; Col. 2:14-15])*.

28 And they came to Jerusalem with psalteries and harps and trumpets unto the House of the LORD *(they were playing these instruments and praising the Lord as they came into Jerusalem, and unto the Temple)*.

29 And the fear of God was on all the kingdoms of those countries, when they had heard that the LORD fought against the enemies of Israel. *(Such a miraculous defeat of the Moabites, Ammonites, and Edomites was soon known by all nations round about. What a victory!)*

30 So the realm of Jehoshaphat was quiet: for his God gave him rest round about *(Mat. 11:28-30)*.

A SUMMARY OF JEHOSHAPHAT'S REIGN

31 And Jehoshaphat reigned over Judah: he was thirty and five years old when he began to reign, and he reigned twenty and five years in Jerusalem. And his mother's name was Azubah the daughter of Shilhi.

32 And he walked in the way of Asa his father, and departed not from it, doing that which was right in the sight of the LORD.

33 Howbeit the high places were not taken away *(even though Jehoshaphat had given instructions that this be done [17:6])*: for as yet the people had not prepared their hearts unto the God of their fathers *(despite the great miracle which they had just experienced in the defeat of their enemies; this shows that miracles do not necessarily turn one to God)*.

34 Now the rest of the acts of Jehoshaphat, first and last, behold, they are written in the book of Jehu the son of Hanani, who is mentioned in the book of the kings of Israel.

35 And after this did Jehoshaphat king of Judah join himself with Ahaziah king of Israel *(son of Ahab)*, who did very wickedly:

36 And he joined himself with him to make ships to go to Tarshish: and they made the ships in Ezion-gaber *(once again, Jehoshaphat will succumb to his old sin; an old sin is an easy sin)*.

37 Then Eliezer the son of Dodavah of Mareshah prophesied against Jehoshaphat, saying, Because you have joined yourself

with Ahaziah, the LORD has broken your works. And the ships were broken, that they were not able to go to Tarshish. *(The prosperity of Jehoshaphat was not to be found in wicked Ahaziah, but in the Lord, always in the Lord! When it says, in the Thirty-second Verse, that Jehoshaphat departed not from doing that which was right in the sight of the Lord, it was speaking of idol-worship. Despite his sin regarding alliances with the northern kingdom of Israel, he never succumbed in any manner to idol-worship.)*

CHAPTER 21

(896 B.C.)

THE REIGN OF WICKED JEHORAM OVER JUDAH

NOW Jehoshaphat slept with his fathers, and was buried with his fathers in the city of David. And Jehoram his son reigned in his stead.

2 And he had brethren the sons of Jehoshaphat, Azariah, and Jehiel, and Zechariah, and Azariah, and Michael, and Shephatiah: all these were the sons of Jehoshaphat king of Israel *(the word "Israel" being used instead of Judah is not an error in transcription; it does show that God recognized the faithful remnant of Judah as His entire people).*

3 And their father gave them great gifts of silver, and of gold, and of precious things, with fenced cities in Judah: but the kingdom gave he to Jehoram; because he was the firstborn *(Jehoram was one of the most wicked kings to sit on the throne of Judah; according to the last phrase of this Verse, the implication is that Jehoshaphat did not have the mind of the Lord regarding the selection of Jehoram; most of the time, the law of the firstborn held true even in throne rights, but not always; God overruled in some cases because the firstborn was not the suitable one for a position; to be sure, Jehoram was certainly not the suitable one here).*

4 Now when Jehoram was risen up to the kingdom of his father, he strengthened himself, and slew all his brethren with the sword, and divers also of the princes of Israel *(he killed all those of Verse 2; he strengthened himself by murder and ruthlessness, instead of doing it the way his Godly father had done, by the blessing of God).*

5 Jehoram was thirty and two years old when he began to reign, and he reigned eight years

in Jerusalem *(it was a dark time for Israel!).*

6 And he walked in the way of the kings of Israel, like as did the house of Ahab: for he had the daughter of Ahab to wife: and he wrought that which was evil in the eyes of the LORD *(we now see the leaven that was in the life of Jehoshaphat concerning his alliance with Ahab; the awful thing about sin is that it breeds more sin and, in fact, can only be stopped by Faith in Christ and what Christ did at the Cross).*

7 Howbeit the LORD would not destroy the house of David, because of the Covenant that He had made with David, and as He promised to give a light to him and to his sons for ever.

EDOM AND LIBNAH REVOLT

8 In his days the Edomites revolted from under the dominion of Judah, and made themselves a king.

9 Then Jehoram went forth with his princes, and all his chariots with him: and he rose up by night, and smote the Edomites which compassed him in, and the captains of the chariots.

10 So the Edomites revolted from under the hand of Judah unto this day. The same time also did Libnah revolt from under his hand; because he had forsaken the LORD God of his fathers *(over and over again, we see blessing coming because of adherence to the Word of God and, as well, judgment because of failure to adhere to the Word of God).*

ELIJAH'S PROPHECY OF THE SICKNESS AND DEATH OF JEHORAM

11 Moreover he made high places in the mountains of Judah and caused the inhabitants of Jerusalem to commit fornication, and compelled Judah thereto *(this was mostly the worship of the "Asherah"; it was the male sex organ, carved out of a tree trunk, and standing anywhere from 10 to 20 feet high; this, as the god of fertility, would be worshipped with all type of sexual sins being practiced).*

12 And there came a writing to him from Elijah the Prophet, saying, Thus saith the LORD God of David your father, Because you have not walked in the ways of Jehoshaphat your father, nor in the ways of Asa king of Judah,

13 But have walked in the way of the kings of Israel, and have made Judah and the inhabitants of Jerusalem to go a whoring, like to the whoredoms of the house of Ahab *(idol-worship)*, and also have slain your brethren of

your father's house, which were better than yourself:

14 Behold, with a great plague will the LORD smite your people, and your children, and your wives, and all your goods:

15 And you shall have great sickness by disease of your bowels, until your bowels fall out by reason of the sickness day by day. *(Even though Elijah was basically a Prophet to the northern kingdom of Israel, which was sometimes referred to as Samaria, still, the Lord gave him this great word for Jehoram. Had the king repented, all of this could have been avoided. But regrettably, he ignored the Word of the Lord from the Lord through Elijah the Prophet. The end result would be exactly as Elijah prophesied.)*

16 Moreover the LORD stirred up against Jehoram the spirit of the Philistines, and of the Arabians, who were near the Ethiopians *(we see the Lord's hand in everything, be it negative or positive, all based on disobedience or obedience)*:

17 And they came up into Judah, and broke into it, and carried away all the substance that was found in the king's house, and his sons also, and his wives; so that there was never a son left him, save Jehoahaz, the youngest of his sons *(this was the first of two times in this period that the royal line was cut off except for one boy — the line that would be in the lineage of Christ [22:10]).*

JEHORAM'S SUFFERING AND DEATH

18 And after all this the LORD smote him in his bowels with an incurable disease *(exactly as the Prophet Elijah had predicted, because of his gross wickedness; all sickness in Believers cannot be traced to sin in their lives; however, most definitely, some can!).*

19 And it came to pass, that in process of time, after the end of two years, his bowels fell out by reason of his sickness: so he died of sore diseases. And his people made no burning for him, like the burning of his fathers *(in essence, the Lord gave this wicked monarch "two years" in which to repent; but he didn't!).*

20 Thirty and two years old was he when he began to reign, and he reigned in Jerusalem eight years, and departed without being desired *(what an indictment!).* Howbeit they buried him in the city of David, but not in the sepulchres of the kings.

CHAPTER 22
(885 B.C.)
AHAZIAH'S WICKED REIGN
OVER JUDAH

AND the inhabitants of Jerusalem made Ahaziah his youngest son king in his stead: for the band of men that came with the Arabians to the camp had slain all the eldest. So Ahaziah the son of Jehoram king of Judah reigned. *(This king had three names: "Ahaziah," "Azariah," and "Jehoahaz." All have the same meaning in Hebrew, "Jehovah takes hold"; however, Jehovah had no opportunity to take hold in the life of this wicked king.*

As one reads these accounts, it becomes overly obvious that sin does not pay.)

2 Forty and two years old was Ahaziah when he began to reign, and he reigned one year in Jerusalem. His mother's name also was Athaliah the daughter of Omri *(the "leaven" that was in the life of Jehoshaphat concerning his alliance with Ahab will now continue its rot; Athaliah, the mother of Ahaziah, was actually the daughter of Ahab and Jezebel, which made her the granddaughter of Omri; the Hebrew language had no designation such as "granddaughter" or "grandson," etc.).*

3 He also walked in the ways of the house of Ahab: for his mother was his counsellor to do wickedly *(Jehoahaz followed his wicked father, Jehoram, who had also walked in all the wicked ways of Ahab and Jezebel; his mother killed all of her grandsons except one and seized the throne of Judah, which she kept for six years).*

4 Wherefore he did evil in the sight of the LORD like the house of Ahab: for they were his counsellors after the death of his father to his destruction.

5 He walked also after their counsel, and went with Jehoram the son of Ahab king of Israel to war against Hazael king of Syria at Ramoth-gilead: and the Syrians smote Joram *(Joram, the king of the northern confederacy of Israel, is the same as Jehoram).*

6 And he returned to be healed in Jezreel because of the wounds which were given him at Ramah, when he fought with Hazael king of Syria. And Azariah the son of Jehoram king of Judah went down to see Jehoram *(who was the king of Israel; he had the same name as Azariah's father)* the son of Ahab at Jezreel, because he was sick.

JEHU SLAYS AHAZIAH

7 And the destruction of Ahaziah was of God by coming to Joram: for when he was come, he went out with Jehoram against Jehu the son of Nimshi, whom the LORD had anointed to cut off the house of Ahab *(the Lord determined the destruction of Ahaziah because of his sins; it was brought about by Jehu, whom the Lord caused to be king of the ten Tribes; Jehu killed both Jehoram [Joram], king of the ten Tribes, and Ahaziah of Judah).*

8 And it came to pass, that, when Jehu was executing judgment upon the house of Ahab, and found the princes of Judah, and the sons of the brethren of Ahaziah, who ministered to Ahaziah, he slew them.

9 And he sought Ahaziah: and they caught him, (for he was hid in Samaria,) and brought him to Jehu: and when they had slain him, they buried him: Because, said they, he is the son of Jehoshaphat, who sought the LORD with all his heart. So the house of Ahaziah had no power to keep still the kingdom *(the last phrase in this Verse means that there was no one of the house of Ahaziah who could succeed him; the Hebrew Text does not say, "no one left," simply because Joash was the son of Ahaziah, but he was but an infant at the time).*

ATHALIAH USURPS THE THRONE

10 But when Athaliah the mother of Ahaziah saw that her son was dead, she arose and destroyed all the seed royal of the house of Judah *(one of the most wicked women ever!).*

11 But Jehoshabeath, the daughter of the king, took Joash the son of Ahaziah, and stole him from among the king's sons who were slain, and put him and his nurse in a bedchamber. So Jehoshabeath, the daughter of king Jehoram, the wife of Jehoiada the Priest, (for she was the sister of Ahaziah,) hid him from Athaliah, so that she slew him not *(evidently, this bloody woman thought she had killed them all, not realizing that the infant was not dead; from this bloodstained room, the daughter of Jehoram [Jehoshaphat's son] stole away baby Joash; he was the only one left in the lineage of Christ).*

12 And he was with them hid in the House of God six years: and Athaliah reigned over the land *(at this time, the Temple was not in use; the people were worshipping idols on the* mountaintops and other places; so, the "House of God" was the logical place for him to be hidden, so he wouldn't be murdered by this evil woman).*

CHAPTER 23

(878 B.C.)

JEHOIADA, THE PRIEST, SECURES THE CROWN FOR JOASH

AND in the seventh year Jehoiada *(the High Priest)* strengthened himself, and took the captains of hundreds, Azariah the son of Jeroham, and Ishmael the son of Jehohanan, and Azariah the son of Obed, and Maaseiah the son of Adaiah, and Elishaphat the son of Zichri, into covenant with him. *(The "seventh year" refers to the length of time between Ahaziah's assassination through the reign of the wicked queen Athaliah. Joash was now seven years old. The "covenant" had to do with making Joash king, who was the rightful heir to the throne. He was the only one left at this time in the lineage of David.)*

2 And they *(all of Verse 1)* went about in Judah, and gathered the Levites out of all the cities of Judah, and the chief of the fathers of Israel, and they came to Jerusalem.

3 And all the congregation made a covenant with the king in the House of God. And he said unto them, Behold, the king's son shall reign, as the LORD has said of the sons of David *(II Sam. 7:12).*

4 This is the thing that you shall do; A third part of you entering on the Sabbath, of the Priests and of the Levites, shall be porters of the doors *(keepers of the doors of the Temple [I Chron. 9:19]);*

5 And a third part shall be at the king's house; and a third part at the gate of the foundation: and all the people shall be in the courts of the House of the LORD *(to keep watch).*

6 But let none come into the House of the LORD, save the Priests, and they who minister of the Levites; they shall go in, for they are holy: but all the people shall keep the watch of the LORD *(the distinction between "the courts of the House of the Lord," which were outside the Temple, and "the House of the Lord," is quite apparent; none but the Priests could enter the Temple).*

7 And the Levites shall compass the king round about, every man with his weapons in his hand; and whosoever else comes into the house, he shall be put to death: but be ye with

the king when he comes in, and when he goes out *(the exception to the rule of no one entering the Temple but the Priests, at least at this time, was the boy king, Joash; he was to be surrounded by Priests and Levites when he was brought out of the Temple to the people).*

8 So the Levites and all Judah did according to all things that Jehoiada the Priest had commanded, and took every man his men who were to come in on the Sabbath, with them who were to go out on the Sabbath: for Jehoiada the Priest dismissed not the courses *(was going to set in motion once again the 24 courses ordained by David).*

9 Moreover Jehoiada the Priest delivered to the captains of hundreds spears, and bucklers, and shields, that had been king David's, which were in the House of God *(some think these may have been the shields of gold that king David took from the servants of Hadadezer [II Sam. 8:7, 11] — Pulpit).*

10 And he set all the people, every man having his weapon in his hand, from the right side of the Temple to the left side of the Temple, along by the Altar and the Temple, by the king round about *(Joash was placed by the Altar of Burnt Offerings, which typified Calvary, with rows of guards bristling with weapons before, behind, and round about him).*

11 Then they brought out the king's son *(Joash),* and put upon him the crown, and gave him the Testimony *(the Scrolls containing the Law — probably Exodus and Leviticus),* and made him king. And Jehoiada and his sons anointed him, and said, God save the king.

ATHALIAH IS SLAIN

12 Now when Athaliah *(the wicked queen)* heard the noise of the people running and praising the king, she came to the people into the House of the LORD *(unto the House of the Lord; she did not go into the Temple, but most definitely would have, had she not been restrained):*

13 And she looked, and, behold, the king stood at his pillar at the entering in, and the princes and the trumpets by the king: and all the people of the land rejoiced, and sounded with trumpets, also the singers with instruments of music, and such as taught to sing praise *(all of our music should be to render praise to the Lord).* Then Athaliah rent her clothes, and said, Treason, Treason *(it was treason directed at her, and of that she*

was right).

14 Then Jehoiada the Priest brought out the captains of hundreds who were set over the host, and said unto them, Have her forth of the ranges *(in the ranges or rows of soldiers):* and whoso follows her, let him be slain with the sword *(if anyone tries to go into the Temple).* For the Priest said, Slay her not in the House of the LORD *(in other words, they killed her before she could go into the Temple).*

15 So they laid hands on her; and when she was come to the entering of the horse gate by the king's house, they slew her there.

REVIVAL UNDER JEHOIADA, THE HIGH PRIEST

16 And Jehoiada made a covenant between him, and between all the people, and between the king, that they should be the LORD's people.

17 Then all the people went to the house of Baal, and broke it down, and broke his altars and his images in pieces, and slew Mattan the priest of Baal before the altars *(it seems that a building, dedicated to Baal, had been built alongside the Temple).*

18 Also Jehoiada appointed the offices of the House of the LORD by the hand of the Priests the Levites, whom David had distributed in the House of the LORD, to offer the Burnt Offerings of the LORD, as it is written in the Law of Moses, with rejoicing and with singing, as it was ordained by David *(all of the 24 courses ordained by David were reinstated, as well as all of the ceremonies of the Law of Moses).*

19 And he set the porters at the gates of the House of the LORD, that none which was unclean in any thing should enter in.

20 And he took the captains of hundreds, and the nobles, and the governors of the people, and all the people of the land, and brought down the king from the House of the LORD: and they came through the high gate into the king's house, and set the king upon the throne of the kingdom.

21 And all the people of the land rejoiced: and the city was quiet, after that they had slain Athaliah with the sword *(as the sword did rid Judah of this altogether evil influence, likewise, the sword of the Spirit, which is the Word of God, must, as well, rid every enemy of our souls from our lives [Heb. 12:1; Eph. 6:17]).*

CHAPTER 24
(878 B.C.)
JOASH REIGNS WELL AND LONG IN JUDAH

JOASH was seven years old when he began to reign, and he reigned forty years in Jerusalem. His mother's name also was Zibiah of Beer-sheba (if it is to be noticed, the mother's name is given, as it regards these kings, because the father often had several wives; Joash was the youngest king to reign in all Israel, and the fifth king to reign for 40 years; he is called "Jehoash" in II Ki. 12:2).

2 And Joash did that which was right in the sight of the LORD all the days of Jehoiada the Priest (but only during the lifetime of Jehoiada; under the tutelage of this Godly Priest, he had an excellent beginning; however, when Jehoiada died, Joash went into deep apostasy and sin; there is every indication that he died eternally lost).

3 And Jehoiada took for him two wives; and he begat sons and daughters (took two wives for Joash).

JOASH REPAIRS THE TEMPLE

4 And it came to pass after this, that Joash was minded to repair the House of the LORD (not having been used for years, it had fallen into a state of disrepair; presently, in the spiritual sense, there are many houses of the Lord which need repairing [I Cor. 3:16]).

5 And he gathered together the Priests and the Levites, and said to them, Go out unto the cities of Judah, and gather of all Israel money to repair the House of your God from year to year, and see that you hasten the ... est in some ... told ... beit the Levites ... for Jehoiada the ... the Levites to bring in out of Judah ... or Jerusalem the collection, according ... the Commandment of Moses the servant of the LORD, and of the congregation of Israel, for the Tabernacle of witness? (It seems that a census was to be taken in Judah, with a half-shekel for each person levied against all the people of Judah [Ex. 30:13-16]. This redemption money was to be used for the repair work. Organizing this, which was the responsibility of Jehoiada, seemed to cause the delay.)

7 For the sons of Athaliah, that wicked woman, had broken up the House of God; and also all the dedicated things of the House of the LORD did they bestow upon Baalim (most of the damage to the Temple came from wicked kings and, in this case, a wicked queen; likewise, most of the damage done to the Work of God presently is little done by the world, but, instead, by false doctrine in an apostate Church).

8 And at the king's commandment they made a chest, and set it without at the gate of the House of the LORD (where the census or ransom money would be collected).

9 And they made a proclamation through Judah and Jerusalem, to bring in to the LORD the collection that Moses the servant of God laid upon Israel in the wilderness (again, this was the ransom money of a half-shekel for each person that was to be paid when a census was taken; this money was to go for the upkeep of the Temple, etc.; this is why it was referred to as the "shekel of the Sanctuary" [Ex. 30:11-16]).

10 And all the princes and all the people rejoiced, and brought in, and cast into the chest, until they had made an end (when people start living right, people start giving; when people are not living right, people quit giving).

11 Now it came to pass, that at what time the chest was brought unto the king's office by the hand of the Levites, and when they saw that there was much money, the king's scribe and the High Priest's officer (an officer of Jehoiada) came and emptied the chest, and took it, and carried it to his place again. Thus they did day by day, and gathered money in abundance.

12 And the king and Jehoiada gave it to such as did the work of the service of the House of the LORD, and hired masons and carpenters to repair the House of the LORD, and also such as wrought iron and brass to mend the House of the LORD (the "House of the LORD" presently since the Cross] is the heart and life of each Believer [I Cor. 3:16]; the Holy Spirit is the One Who does the repairing, which, from time to time, is needed!).

13 So the workmen wrought, and the work was perfected by them, and they set the House of God in his state, and strengthened it.

14 And when they had finished it, they brought the rest of the money before the king and Jehoiada, whereof were made vessels for the House of the LORD, even vessels to minister, and to offer withal, and spoons, and vessels of gold and silver. And they offered Burnt Offerings in the House of the LORD continually

all the days of Jehoiada (*once again, the daily Sacrifices were established; however, when Jehoiada died, this too would stop*).

JEHOIADA, THE HIGH PRIEST, DIES

15 But Jehoiada waxed old, and was full of days when he died; an hundred and thirty years old was he when he died (*Jehoiada was born in Solomon's reign; he, therefore, lived through six reigns; as is obvious here, the Lord allowed him to live far beyond the normal time, all in order to guide Joash*).

16 And they buried him in the city of David among the kings, because he had done good in Israel, both toward God, and toward His House (*the Temple; what a testimony given by the Holy Spirit to the faithfulness of this man*).

JOASH TURNS TO IDOLATRY

17 Now after the death of Jehoiada came the princes of Judah, and made obeisance to the king. Then the king hearkened unto them (*at the commencement of his reign, Joash leaned on Jehoiada, who was a Godly man; afterwards, he leaned on the princes of Judah, who were wicked men; to lean on men, whether they be good or wicked, is disastrous; had the king leaned "only upon God," how different would have been his history!*).

18 And they left the House of the LORD God of their fathers, and served groves and idols: and wrath came upon Judah and Jerusalem for this their trespass. (*It was the prince of Judah this time who led into sin and apostasy. Usually the king led the princes and the people astray, but not here. The "wrath of God" must always come upon sin. God cannot abide such in any form; so the idea is:*

One can accept the wrath that came upon Christ at Calvary's Cross, which was for our sins, and definitely not His, for He had none, or one will experience the wrath of God upon oneself. There is no alternative!*)

19 Yet He (*the Lord*) sent Prophets to them, to bring them again unto the LORD; and they testified against them (*the Prophets testified against them*): but they (*the people and the princes*) would not give ear.

JOASH SLAYS ZECHARIAH, THE PRIEST

20 And the Spirit of God came upon Zechariah the son of Jehoiada the Priest (*who was now the High Priest himself*), which stood above the people, and said unto them, Thus saith God, Why transgress ye the Commandments of the LORD, that you cannot prosper? (*While a Believer who violates the Commandments of the Lord may occasionally prosper in the financial sense, he definitely cannot prosper in the spiritual sense*) because you have forsaken the LORD, He has also forsaken you (*the Spirit of the Lord spoke these words through Zechariah, and they are easy to understand; if we forsake the Lord, He will forsake us; if we uphold the Lord, He will uphold us!*).

21 And they conspired against him, and stoned him with stones at the Commandment of the king in the court of the House of the LORD (*this Zechariah who was stoned here was not the Prophet who wrote the Book of Zechariah, for the latter did not live until after the Babylonian captivities, which were over 150 years later [Zech. 1:1]; both men were stoned, one in the Court of the Temple, and the other between the Temple and the Altar [Mat. 23:35]*).

22 Thus Joash the king remembered not the kindness which Jehoiada his (*Zechariah's*) father had done to him, but slew his son. And when he died, he said, The LORD look upon it, and require it (*will require Judgment, and that by the Hand of the Lord*).

SYRIA INVADES AND DEFEATS JUDAH

23 And it came to pass at the end of the year, that the host of Syria came up against him: and they came to Judah and Jerusalem, and destroyed all the princes of the people from them, the Lord requi[...]

24 For the army of men, and delivered a very great host into their hand, because they had forsaken the LORD God of their fathers. So they executed judgment against Joash (*as stated, this "judgment" was caused by the Lord; even though Judah had a very large army, they were helpless to defeat the much smaller army of the Syrians, because the Lord decreed it so*).

DEATH OF JOASH

25 And when they were departed from him, (for they left him in great diseases [*the Syrians did not cause the diseases; the idea is, he was greatly ill at the time they invaded the land*],)

his own servants conspired against him for the blood of the sons of Jehoiada the Priest, and slew him on his bed, and he died: and they buried him in the city of David, but they buried him not in the sepulchres of the kings *(it says, "sons of Jehoiada"; however, the Bible only records one son, Zechariah; there may have been other sons, or other relations of Jehoiada covered by the word "sons")*.

26 And these are they who conspired against him; Zabad the son of Shimeath an Ammonitess, and Jehozabad the son of Shimrith a Moabitess *(the Holy Spirit emphasizes the fact that the two servants who killed him were heathen, which meant that his death was ignominious)*.

27 Now concerning his sons, and the greatness of the burdens laid upon him, and the repairing of the House of God, behold, they are written in the story of the book of the kings. And Amaziah his son reigned in his stead. *(From all of this, we see how obvious it is that the Blessings of God come upon Righteousness; as well, how obvious it is that the Judgment of God comes upon unrighteousness.)*

CHAPTER 25
(827 B.C.)
AMAZIAH REIGNS OVER JUDAH

AMAZIAH was twenty and five years old when he began to reign, and he reigned twenty and nine years in Jerusalem. And his mother's name was Jehoaddan of Jerusalem.

2 And he did that which was right in the sight of the LORD, but not with a perfect heart *(one might say that he had a divided heart; it would lead to his total ruin!)*.

3 Now it came to pass, when the kingdom was established to him, that he slew his servants who had killed the king his father.

4 But he slew not their children, but did as it is written in the Law in the Book of Moses, where the LORD commanded, saying, The fathers shall not die for the children, neither shall the children die for the fathers, but every man shall die for his own sin *(at the beginning of his reign, it seems that he tried to follow the Bible [Deut. 24:16])*.

AMAZIAH DEFEATS EDOM

5 Moreover Amaziah gathered Judah together, and made them captains over thousands, and captains over hundreds, according to the houses of their fathers, throughout all Judah and Benjamin: and he numbered them from twenty years old and above, and found them three hundred thousand choice men, able to go forth to war, who could handle spear and shield.

6 He hired also an hundred thousand mighty men of valour out of Israel for an hundred talents of silver.

7 But there came a man of God to him, saying, O king, let not the army of Israel go with you; for the LORD is not with Israel, to wit, with all the children of Ephraim *(the command is clear)*.

8 But if you will go *(go with Israel)*, do it, be strong for the battle *(no matter how strong you are)*: God shall make you fall before the enemy: for God has power to help, and to cast down *(the sum of Verses 7 and 8 may be translated: "Under no circumstances take Israel, and if you do take them, no matter how much you prepare, yet know that God shall destroy you")*.

9 And Amaziah said to the man of God, But what shall we do for the hundred talents which I have given to the army of Israel? And the man of God answered, The LORD is able to give you much more than this *(it seems that Amaziah was much more concerned about the money lost than obeying God; sadly, this is the concern of most people, even Christians; that which man deems so very important, the Lord brushes it aside as if nothing)*.

10 Then Amaziah separated them, to wit, the army that was come to him out of Ephraim, to go home again: wherefore their anger was greatly kindled against Judah, and they returned home in great anger *(this was in anticipation of plunder, which was now denied)*.

11 And Amaziah strengthened himself, and led forth his people, and went to the valley of salt, and smote of the children of Seir ten thousand.

12 And other ten thousand left alive did the children of Judah carry away captive, and brought them unto the top of the rock, and cast them down from the top of the rock, that they all were broken in pieces *(there is little doubt that this is Petra; it seems that he ruthlessly slaughtered 10,000 people)*.

13 But the soldiers of the army which Amaziah sent back, that they should not go with him to battle *(those from Israel)*, fell upon the cities of Judah, from Samaria even unto Beth-horon, and smote three thousand of them *(3,000 people)*, and took much spoil *(they satisfied their lust for plunder by ravaging Judah)*.

AMAZIAH IS REBUKED BY GOD FOR WORSHIPPING THE GODS OF EDOM

14 Now it came to pass, after that Amaziah was come from the slaughter of the Edomites, that he brought the gods of the children of Seir, and set them up to be his gods, and bowed down himself before them, and burned incense unto them *(how stupid!)*.

15 Wherefore the anger of the LORD was kindled against Amaziah, and He *(the Lord)* sent unto him a Prophet, which said unto him, Why have you sought after the gods of the people, which could not deliver their own people out of your hand? *(How utterly ridiculous! Amaziah will now worship the gods of the people he has just defeated. If they were so great, why didn't these gods help the Edomites? A modern parallel concerns Believers who will forsake the Presence of God for other things.)*

16 And it came to pass, as he *(the Prophet)* talked with him, that the king said unto him, Are you made of the king's counsel? *(Are you one of my advisors?)* forbear *(desist, away with your words)*; why should you be smitten? *(In other words, if you keep this up, I will kill you.)* Then the Prophet forbore *(except for one more statement)*, and said, I know that God has determined to destroy you, because you have done this, and have not hearkened unto my counsel.

AMAZIAH MAKES WAR ON ISRAEL

17 Then Amaziah king of Judah took advice *(took counsel from some of his advisors)*, and sent to Joash, the son of Jehoahaz, the son of Jehu, king of Israel, saying, Come, let us see one another in the face *(a threat!)*.

18 And Joash king of Israel sent to Amaziah king of Judah, saying, The thistle that was in Lebanon sent to the cedar that was in Lebanon, saying, Give your daughter to my son to wife: and there passed by a wild beast that was in Lebanon, and trode down the thistle *(in this parable, Joash likens Israel to a cedar, and Judah to a thistle; as well, he likens Israel to a "wild beast" that will ride roughshod over the thistle, i.e., "Judah")*.

19 You say, Lo, you have smitten the Edomites; and your heart lifts you up to boast: abide now at home; why should you meddle to your hurt, that you should fall, even you, and Judah with you?

AMAZIAH IS DEFEATED

20 But Amaziah would not hear; for it came of God, that He might deliver them into the hand of their enemies, because they sought after the gods of Edom *(because of idolatry, the Lord is now opposed to Judah)*.

21 So Joash the king of Israel went up; and they saw one another in the face, both he and Amaziah king of Judah, at Beth-shemesh, which belongs to Judah *(they went to battle, despite the warning of Joash, the king of Israel)*.

22 And Judah was put to the worse before Israel, and they fled every man to his tent *(with God against them, Judah couldn't win!)*.

23 And Joash the king of Israel took Amaziah king of Judah, the son of Joash, the son of Jehoahaz, at Beth-shemesh, and brought him to Jerusalem, and broke down the wall of Jerusalem from the gate of Ephraim to the corner gate, four hundred cubits *(about 600 feet)*.

24 And he took all the gold and the silver, and all the vessels that were found in the House of God with Obed-edom, and the treasures of the king's house, the hostages also, and returned to Samaria *(Obed-edom was a descendant of the Obed-edom of David's time [II Sam. 6:10; I Chron. 13:13], who was a custodian of the treasures in the House of God)*.

DEATH OF AMAZIAH

25 And Amaziah the son of Joash king of Judah lived after the death of Joash son of Jehoahaz king of Israel fifteen years.

26 Now the rest of the acts of Amaziah, first and last, behold, are they not written in the book of the kings of Judah and Israel?

27 Now after the time that Amaziah did turn away from following the LORD they made a conspiracy against him in Jerusalem; and he fled to Lachish: but they sent to Lachish after him, and slew him there *(the Holy Spirit will pinpoint the exact "time" that this happened; now he is at the mercy of Satan)*.

28 And they brought him upon horses, and buried him with his fathers in the city of Judah. *(When the king turned away from the Lord, the Holy Spirit declined to call his burial place by the lofty titles of "the city of David" or "Jerusalem," but instead, called it "the city of Judah." It seems that idol-worship and pride were the cause of Amaziah's fall. To be sure, idol-worship and pride are the cause of the fall of many Believers.)*

CHAPTER 26
(810 B.C.)
UZZIAH (AZARIAH) SUCCEEDS AMAZIAH

THEN all the people of Judah took Uzziah, who was sixteen years old, and made him king in the room of his father Amaziah *(Uzziah is named Azariah in II Kings)*.

2 He built Eloth, and restored it to Judah, after that the king *(Amaziah)* slept with his fathers.

3 Sixteen years old was Uzziah when he began to reign, and he reigned fifty and two years in Jerusalem. His mother's name also was Jecoliah of Jerusalem.

4 And he did that which was right in the sight of the LORD, according to all that his father Amaziah did *(the qualifier is, he started well, and ended poorly)*.

5 And he sought God in the days of Zechariah, who had understanding in the Visions of God *(this was not the "Zechariah," the son of Jehoiada, who lived some years prior; he was murdered by Joash, Uzziah's grandfather; neither was he the Zechariah who wrote the Book of Zechariah; all we know about this Zechariah is what is said here)*: and as long as he sought the LORD, God made him to prosper *(what a statement! The words, "sought the Lord," mean not only to desire what God desires, but to seek His Face incessantly; this is the secret of spiritual, domestic, financial, physical, and mental victory)*.

UZZIAH'S MILITARY SUCCESSES

6 And he went forth and warred against the Philistines, and broke down the wall of Gath, and the wall of Jabneh, and the wall of Ashdod, and built cities about Ashdod, and among the Philistines.

7 And God helped him against the Philistines, and against the Arabians who dwelt in Gur-baal, and the Mehunims.

8 And the Ammonites gave gifts to Uzziah: and his name spread abroad even to the entering in of Egypt; for he strengthened himself exceedingly *(he was able to strengthen himself, because "God helped him")*.

UZZIAH'S BUILDING PROGRAM, PROSPERITY, AND ARMY

9 Moreover Uzziah built towers in Jerusalem at the corner gate, and at the valley gate, and at the turning of the wall, and fortified them.

10 Also he built towers in the desert, and dug many wells: for he had much cattle, both in the low country, and in the plains: husbandmen also, and vine dressers in the mountains, and in Carmel: for he loved husbandry *(the king's partiality looked to agricultural and pastoral pursuits)*.

11 Moreover Uzziah had an host of fighting men, who went out to war by bands, according to the number of their account by the hand of Jeiel the scribe and Maaseiah the ruler, under the hand of Hananiah, one of the king's captains.

12 The whole number of the chief of the fathers of the mighty men of valour were two thousand and six hundred.

13 And under their hand was an army, three hundred thousand and seven thousand and five hundred, who made war with mighty power, to help the king against the enemy.

14 And Uzziah prepared for them throughout all the host shields, and spears, and helmets, and habergeons, and bows, and slings to cast stones.

15 And he made in Jerusalem engines, invented by cunning men, to be on the towers and upon the bulwarks, to shoot arrows and great stones withal. And his name spread far abroad; for he was marvellously helped, till he was strong *(this means that God prospered him so greatly that the people marveled; however, when he became strong, he entered into the zone of extreme danger)*.

UZZIAH'S SIN AND PUNISHMENT

16 But when he was strong, his heart was lifted up to his destruction *(with pride)*: for he transgressed against the LORD his God, and went into the Temple of the LORD to burn Incense upon the Altar of Incense. *(His transgression was far more serious than we realize. For him to attempt to burn incense upon the Altar of Incense proclaims the fact that he, in essence, was saying that he did not need a Saviour. The Priest, who alone could offer Incense, stood as a Type of Christ, as a mediator between God and man.*

As well, the sin of the modern Church is the sin of ignoring, or else outright denying, the Cross. Christ must be worshipped as the Saviour, and He is the Saviour through the Cross [I Cor. 1:17-18, 23; 2:2]. If Jesus is worshipped or sought after in any other manner, He becomes "another Jesus," which God can never accept [II Cor. 11:4; Ex. 25:6; 30:1, 7-8, 34, 37-38; Lev. 16:13].)

17 And Azariah the Priest *(High Priest)* went in after him *(into the Holy Place, where was the Altar of Incense)*, and with him fourscore *(80)* Priests of the LORD, who were valiant men *(brave men, who would stand up to the king)*:

18 And they withstood Uzziah the king, and said unto him, It appertains not unto you, Uzziah, to burn incense unto the LORD, but to the Priests the sons of Aaron, who are consecrated to burn Incense: go out of the Sanctuary *(in fact, no one was allowed in the Sanctuary except Priests)*; for you have trespassed; neither shall it be for your honour from the LORD God.

19 Then Uzziah was wroth, and had a censer in his hand to burn incense: and while he was wroth with the Priests, the leprosy even rose up in his forehead before the Priests in the House of the LORD, from beside the Incense Altar. *(Because he attempted to worship God without the intervention of an ongoing Saviour, the Lord smote him with leprosy. On the forehead of the High Priest was a golden plate with the words, "Holiness to the Lord"; on the forehead of Uzziah was "sinfulness" [leprosy]. We must ever remember that Christ is the Source of all things, as it pertains to the Believer, and the Cross is the Means by which all of these things come to us. If we attempt to obtain anything from the Lord by means other than the Cross, we have, in effect, like Uzziah, claimed to be our own Saviour.)*

20 And Azariah the Chief Priest, and all the Priests, looked upon him, and, behold, he was leprous in his forehead, and they thrust him out from thence; yea, himself hasted also to go out, because the LORD had smitten him. *(To be frank, he was afraid that the Lord would kill him and, but for the Mercy of God, this is exactly what would have happened. The leprosy started in his forehead, because, as stated, this was where the golden plate was worn by the High Priest, stipulating Holiness. Only Christ fits that designation. Man is holy only as he trusts Christ and what Christ did at the Cross. Upon proper trust in Christ, Righteousness and Holiness are instantly imputed to the individual. Otherwise, there is no Holiness!)*

21 And Uzziah the king was a leper unto the day of his death, and dwelt in a several house, being a leper; for he was cut off from the House of the LORD: and Jotham his son was over the king's house, judging the people of the land.

DEATH OF UZZIAH

22 Now the rest of the acts of Uzziah, first and last, did Isaiah the Prophet, the son of Amoz, write *(Isaiah the Prophet asserts that his prophetic inspiration was in Uzziah's time [Isa. 1:1; 6:1])*.

23 So Uzziah slept with his fathers, and they buried him with his fathers in the field of the burial which belonged to the kings; for they said, He is a leper: and Jotham his son reigned in his stead *(hopefully he repented, but there is no evidence that he did; the last thing the Holy Spirit said about him was, "He is a leper" — not "was," but rather "is")*.

CHAPTER 27
(758 B.C.)
JOTHAM REIGNS OVER JUDAH

JOTHAM was twenty and five years old when he began to reign, and he reigned sixteen years in Jerusalem. His mother's name also was Jerushah, the daughter of Zadok.

2 And he did that which was right in the sight of the LORD, according to all that his father Uzziah did *(the first ways of his father)*: howbeit he entered not into the Temple of the LORD. *(Williams says, "This probably means that, terrified by the fate of his father, he did not associate with the Temple at all. If this be so, then Uzziah, Jotham, and Ahaz illustrate how incurably diseased is the natural heart. The first king boldly intrudes into the Temple, the second timidly stands away from it, and the third shuts it up.")* And the people did yet corruptly *(this speaks of idol-worship)*.

3 He built the high gate of the House of the LORD, and on the wall of Ophel he built much.

4 Moreover he built cities in the mountains of Judah, and in the forests he built castles and towers *(if, instead of building these things, he had broken down the high places at which the people did corruptly, quite possibly it would have brought revival to Judah; regrettably, there has never been a perfect man; all, even when diligently trying to follow the Lord, are, it seems, freighted with failure; it is the Grace of God which gives us the victory, not our perfection)*.

JOTHAM'S VICTORY OVER AMMON

5 He fought also with the king of the Ammonites, and prevailed against them. And the children of Ammon gave him the same year

an hundred talents of silver, and ten thousand measures of wheat, and ten thousand of barley. So much did the children of Ammon pay unto him, both the second year, and the third.

6 So Jotham became mighty, because he prepared his ways before the LORD his God *(what a beautiful statement!)*.

DEATH OF JOTHAM

7 Now the rest of the acts of Jotham, and all his wars, and his ways, lo, they are written in the book of the kings of Israel and Judah.

8 He was five and twenty years old when he began to reign, and reigned sixteen years in Jerusalem *(evidently, he was 41 when he died)*.

9 And Jotham slept with his fathers, and they buried him in the city of David: and Ahaz his son reigned in his stead.

CHAPTER 28
(741 B.C.)
AHAZ REIGNS OVER JUDAH

AHAZ was twenty years old when he began to reign, and he reigned sixteen years in Jerusalem: but he did not that which was right in the sight of the LORD, like David his father *(in fact, Ahaz was one of the most ungodly kings who ever ruled over Judah)*:

2 For he walked in the ways of the kings of Israel, and made also molten images for Baalim *(this was a characteristic sin of Israel, but Judah had not previously been guilty of making molten images during the recent past)*.

3 Moreover he burnt incense in the valley of the son of Hinnom, and burnt his children in the fire *(human sacrifice)*, after the abominations of the heathen whom the LORD had cast out before the Children of Israel *(the intimation is, if Judah continued in this particular fashion, they would be cast out exactly as the heathen of old; in fact, that's exactly what ultimately happened!)*.

4 He sacrificed also and burnt incense in the high places, and on the hills, and under every green tree *(in other words, he engaged in idolatry to the hilt)*.

AHAZ CONQUERED BY ISRAEL
AND SYRIA

5 Wherefore the LORD his God delivered him into the hand of the king of Syria; and they smote him, and carried away a great multitude of them captives, and brought them to Damascus. And he was also delivered into the hand of the king of Israel, who smote him with a great slaughter.

6 For Pekah the son of Remaliah slew in Judah an hundred and twenty thousand in one day, which were all valiant men; because they had forsaken the LORD God of their fathers *(the reason for the judgment is obviously clear!)*.

7 And Zichri, a mighty man of Ephraim, slew Maaseiah the king's son, and Azrikam the governor of the house, and Elkanah who was next to the king.

8 And the Children of Israel carried away captive of their brethren *(of Judah)* two hundred thousand, women, sons, and daughters, and took also away much spoil from them, and brought the spoil to Samaria.

THE PROPHET

9 But a Prophet of the LORD was there, whose name was Oded: and he went out before the host who came to Samaria, and said unto them, Behold, because the LORD God of your fathers was wroth with Judah, He has delivered them into your hand, and you have slain them in a rage that reaches up unto Heaven *(the particular language in which this is set forth proclaims the inference of its abomination in God's sight)*.

10 And now you purpose to keep under the children of Judah and Jerusalem for bondmen and bondwomen unto you *(slaves)*: but are there not with you, even with you, sins against the LORD your God?

11 Now hear me therefore, and deliver the captives again, which you have taken captive of your brethren: for the fierce wrath of the LORD is upon you *(in other words, the Lord is going to do to you what you have done to Judah, if you do not quickly make amends)*.

12 Then certain of the heads of the children of Ephraim, Azariah the son of Johanan, Berechiah the son of Meshillemoth, and Jehizkiah the son of Shallum, and Amasa the son of Hadlai, stood up against them who came from the war,

13 And said unto them, You shall not bring in the captives hither: for whereas we have offended against the LORD already, you intend to add more to our sins and to our trespass: for our trespass is great, and there is fierce wrath against Israel *(for once, somebody heeded the Prophet of God!)*.

14 So the armed men left the captives and the spoil before the princes and all the congregation.

15 And the men which were expressed by name rose up, and took the captives, and with the spoil clothed all who were naked among them, and arrayed them, and shod them, and gave them to eat and to drink, and anointed them, and carried all the feeble of them upon asses, and brought them to Jericho, the city of palm trees, to their brethren: then they returned to Samaria.

EDOMITES AND PHILISTINES INVADE JUDAH

16 At that time did king Ahaz send unto the kings of Assyria to help him (after all the problems of being defeated by both Syria and Israel, still, Ahaz will not seek the Face of the Lord, but, instead, will lean on the arm of man, and heathen man, at that).

17 For again the Edomites had come and smitten Judah, and carried away captives.

18 The Philistines also had invaded the cities of the low country, and of the south of Judah, and had taken Beth-shemesh, and Ajalon, and Gederoth, and Shocho with the villages thereof, and Timnah with the villages thereof, Gimzo also and the villages thereof: and they dwelt there.

19 For the LORD brought Judah low because of Ahaz king of Israel ("Israel" is used in place of Judah, signifying the fact that the Lord looked at Judah as the legitimate Israel); for he made Judah naked (naked to the Judgment of God), and transgressed sore against the LORD (the judgment that the Lord brings is always redemptive in its application; it is intended to bring the person or the nation to repentance; in this case, it would not).

20 And Tilgath-pilneser king of Assyria came unto him, and distressed him, but strengthened him not (so, his effort to get the king of Assyria to help him only resulted in them walking on him, so to speak).

21 For Ahaz took away a portion out of the House of the LORD, and out of the house of the king, and of the princes, and gave it unto the king of Assyria: but he helped him not (they took advantage of him, knowing that he could not do anything about it).

22 And in the time of his distress did he trespass yet more against the LORD: this is that king Ahaz (the Holy Spirit uses this latter phrase in order to point him out; there are three especially branded transgressors in the Word of God; they are: Cain [Gen. 4:15], Dathan [Num. 26:9], and Ahaz [Vss. 22-25]).

23 For he sacrificed unto the gods of Damascus, which smote him: and he said, Because the gods of the kings of Syria help them, therefore will I sacrifice to them, that they may help me. But they were the ruin of him, and of all Israel (when we read the account of Ahaz, his plight because of his rebellion seems to be so clear, and yet most of the world, and even the Church, seek help from that other than God; I speak of witchcraft or humanistic psychology).

24 And Ahaz gathered together the vessels of the House of the God, and cut in pieces the vessels of the House of God, and shut up the doors of the House of the LORD, and he made him altars in the every corner of Jerusalem. (Tragically, the Church is presently shutting the covers of the Bible, the only revealed body of truth in the world. Most preaching and teaching of that which professes to be the Word of God is, rather, psychology. Psychology places the emphasis on the person or the problem instead of Christ and the Cross. There is no profit in the victim or the symptom; there is only profit in the Victor, Who is Christ.)

25 And in every several city of Judah he made high places to burn incense unto other gods, and provoked to anger the LORD God of his fathers (anything that departs from the Bible, be it the obvious evil of Ahaz or the subtle proposed solution of psychology, angers the Lord of Glory).

DEATH OF AHAZ

26 Now the rest of his acts and of all his ways, first and last, behold, they are written in the book of the kings of Judah and Israel.

27 And Ahaz slept with his fathers, and they buried him in the city, even in Jerusalem: but they brought him not into the sepulchres of the kings of Israel: and Hezekiah his son reigned in his stead (it is with great relief that the Holy Spirit closes out the sordid history of Ahaz; today he is in Hell, and will be there forever and forever!).

CHAPTER 29
(726 B.C.)

HEZEKIAH REIGNS OVER JUDAH

HEZEKIAH began to reign when he was five and twenty years old, and he reigned nine

and twenty years in Jerusalem. And his mother's name was Abijah, the daughter of Zechariah.

2 And he did that which was right in the sight of the LORD, according to all that David his father had done *(David was always used as the yardstick or example; that which is "right in the sight of God" is all that matters; unfortunately, the Church all too often cares little about what is right in God's eyes, making their own eyes the yardstick).*

REVIVAL UNDER HEZEKIAH

3 He in the first year of his reign, in the first month, opened the doors of the House of the LORD, and repaired them. *(Immediately upon becoming king, Hezekiah began to institute reform. He wasted no time! Under his evil father Ahaz, the doors to the House of the Lord had been closed, meaning that this House was no longer in use. He began to repair things.*

In our own spiritual lives, how much presently needs repairing?)

4 And he brought in the Priests and the Levites, and gathered them together into the east street,

5 And said unto them, Hear me, ye Levites, sanctify now yourselves, and sanctify the House of the LORD God of your fathers, and carry forth the filthiness out of the holy place. *(The word "sanctify" [or "Sanctification"] simply means in this case "to set apart for the exclusive use of God." In doing this, the "filthiness" would be carried out of the "Holy Place."*

Regarding our lives, when given the opportunity, the Holy Spirit will always clean us up. Paul said: "Let us cleanse ourselves from all filthiness of the flesh and spirit, perfecting holiness in the fear of God" [II Cor. 7:1].)

6 For our fathers have trespassed and done that which was evil in the eyes of the LORD our God, and have forsaken Him, and have turned away their faces from the habitation of the LORD, and turned their backs *(Repentance alone can reverse this situation; this means turning back to the Cross, for the Cross alone can address sin [Heb. 10:12]).*

7 Also they have shut up the doors of the porch *(Jesus is the Door)*, and put out the lamps *(the Golden Lampstand situated in the Holy Place, which typified Christ as the Light of the world)*, and have not burned Incense *(typifying the Intercession of Christ, all on our behalf)* nor offered Burnt Offerings *(typifying the Cross, where the perfection of Christ is given to the believing sinner)* in the Holy Place unto the God of Israel.

8 Wherefore the wrath of the LORD was upon Judah and Jerusalem, and He has delivered them to trouble, to astonishment, and to hissing, as you see with your eyes. *(The judgment was obvious! Because the Temple was symbolic of Christ and the Cross, when Christ and the Cross are forsaken, judgment is inevitable! There can be no other way.)*

9 For, lo, our fathers have fallen by the sword, and our sons and our daughters and our wives are in captivity for this *(sin puts people in captivity and it kills).*

10 Now it is in my heart to make a covenant with the LORD God of Israel, that His fierce wrath may turn away from us *(that Covenant would simply be to obey the Word of God).*

11 My sons, be not now negligent: for the LORD has chosen you to stand before Him, to serve Him, and that you should minister unto Him, and burn Incense *(Hezekiah is saying these things to the Priests and the Levites).*

THE TEMPLE IS CLEANSED AND PREPARED FOR WORSHIP

12 Then the Levites arose, Mahath the son of Amasai, and Joel the son of Azariah, of the sons of the Kohathites: and of the sons of Merari, Kish the son of Abdi, and Azariah the son of Jehalelel: and of the Gershonites; Joah the son of Zimmah, and Eden the son of Joah:

13 And of the sons of Elizaphan; Shimri, and Jeiel: and of the sons of Asaph; Zechariah, and Mattaniah:

14 And of the sons of Heman; Jehiel, and Shimei: and of the sons of Jeduthun; Shemaiah, and Uzziel *(the names of these fourteen Levites have no interest for the historians of this world, but such an interest for the Holy Spirit that they are all set out here, and they have been read already by hundreds of millions of people for nearly 2,800 years).*

15 And they gathered their brethren, and sanctified themselves, and came, according to the commandment of the king, by the Words of the LORD, to cleanse the House of the LORD *(the Words or Commands of the Lord are such as are written in Ex. 19:22 and Lev. 11:44; nothing can be spiritually cleansed, unless it is done according to the Word of the Lord).*

16 And the Priests went into the inner part of the House of the LORD, to cleanse it, and brought out all the uncleanness that they found

in the Temple of the LORD into the court of the House of the LORD. And the Levites took it, to carry it out abroad into the brook Kidron. *(Only the Priests could enter the Temple, while the Levites' sphere of work and service lay in the courts and round about the Temple.*

Spiritually, revival must begin in the "inner part," which means "the heart." It is unthinkable that the Temple was in this condition, but sadly it was. Is it possible that the modern Church is in the same condition now as the Temple of old?)

17 Now they began on the first day of the first month to sanctify, and on the eighth day of the month came they to the porch of the LORD: so they sanctified the House of the LORD in eight days; and in the sixteenth day of the first month they made an end.

18 Then they went in to Hezekiah the king, and said, We have cleansed all the House of the LORD, and the Altar of Burnt Offering, with all the vessels thereof, and the Shewbread Table, with all the vessels thereof *(the first thing that happens when Revival begins to take place is that things are cleaned up).*

19 Moreover all the vessels, which king Ahaz in his reign did cast away in his transgression, have we prepared and sanctified, and behold, they are before the Altar of the LORD.

TEMPLE WORSHIP IS RESTORED

20 Then Hezekiah the king rose early, and gathered the rulers of the city, and went up to the House of the LORD.

21 And they brought seven bullocks, and seven rams, and seven lambs, and seven he goats, for a Sin Offering for the kingdom, and for the Sanctuary, and for Judah. And he commanded the Priests the sons of Aaron to offer them on the Altar of the LORD. *(After the cleansing of the Temple, which made it serviceable, the first thing that is now done, in essence, is that Judah went back to the Cross. I must believe that the Holy Spirit urged Hezekiah to institute "seven" sacrifices each of the various animals. "Seven" signifies perfection, universality, and totality. It is God's number. It means that Israel was to have a complete cleansing. While the Temple could be cleansed of debris, it took the shed Blood of the Lamb to properly cleanse from sin. We as Believers can prepare the way, but only the Blood can cleanse [I Jn. 1:7].)*

22 So they killed the bullocks, and the Priests received the blood, and sprinkled it on the Altar *(the sprinkling of the blood marked*

the expiation of sin [Lev. 4:7, 18, 30; 5:9; 8:14-15; Heb. 9:12-14, 19-22]): likewise, when they had killed the rams, they sprinkled the blood upon the Altar: they killed also the lambs, and they sprinkled the blood upon the Altar.

23 And they brought forth the he goats for the Sin Offering before the king and the congregation; and they laid their hands upon them *(the laying of the hands on the head of the animal signified the transferring of the sins of the person offering the Sacrifice and, in this case, the entirety of the people of Judah, to the victim, which was a Type of Christ taking our sins on the Cross [Isa. 53:6]; this is what Paul was speaking of when he mentioned the "laying on of hands" in Heb. 6:2)*:

24 And the Priests killed them *(the animals, by slitting their throats)*, and they made reconciliation *(a Sin Offering)* with their blood upon the Altar, to make an Atonement *(a type of what Christ would do at the Cross)* for all Israel: for the king commanded that the Burnt Offering and the Sin Offering should be made for all Israel *(the Burnt Offering typified Christ giving His Perfection to the sinner; the Sin Offering typified the sinner giving his sin to Christ; He gives His Perfection to us; we give our sin to Him).*

25 And he set the Levites in the House of the LORD with cymbals, with psalteries, and with harps, according to the commandment of David, and of Gad the king's Seer, and Nathan the Prophet: for so was the Commandment of the LORD by His Prophets. *(Music and joy always accompany proper Faith in the Cross, because all sins have been washed away.*

The Bible does not distinguish between a "Seer" and a "Prophet." Sometimes both designations are used for the same individual [I Chron. 21:9; II Chron. 29:25].)

26 And the Levites stood with the instruments of David, and the Priests with the trumpets.

27 And Hezekiah commanded to offer the Burnt Offering upon the Altar. And when the Burnt Offering began, the song of the LORD began also with the trumpets, and with the instruments ordained by David king of Israel. *(When Faith is properly placed in Christ and the Cross, worship always follows, as it regards music and singing. Little Cross, little worship! Much Cross, much worship!)*

28 And all the congregation worshipped, and the singers sang, and the trumpeters sounded: and all this continued until the Burnt

Offering was finished.

29 And when they had made an end of offering, the king and all who were present with him bowed themselves, and worshipped.

30 Moreover Hezekiah the king and the princes commanded the Levites to sing praise unto the LORD with the words of David, and of Asaph the Seer *(the Psalms)*. And they sang praises with gladness, and they bowed their heads and worshipped.

31 Then Hezekiah answered and said, Now you have consecrated yourselves unto the LORD, come near and bring Sacrifices and Thank Offerings *(Meat Offerings)* into the House of the LORD. And the congregation brought in Sacrifices and Thank Offerings; and as many as were of a free heart Burnt Offerings.

32 And the number of the Burnt Offerings, which the congregation brought, was threescore and ten bullocks, an hundred rams, and two hundred lambs: all these were for a Burnt Offering to the LORD.

33 And the consecrated things were six hundred oxen and three thousand sheep *(dedicated to the Lord)*.

34 But the Priests were too few, so that they could not flay *(prepare properly)* all the Burnt Offerings: wherefore their brethren the Levites did help them, till the work was ended, and until the other Priests had sanctified themselves: for the Levites were more upright in heart to sanctify themselves than the Priests *(went about these duties with a greater consecration)*.

35 And also the Burnt Offerings were in abundance, with the fat of the Peace Offerings, and the Drink Offerings for every Burnt Offering *(the grape juice poured out on the Altar signified Christ pouring out His Life on the Cross)*. So the service of the House of the LORD was set in order.

36 And Hezekiah rejoiced, and all the people, that God had prepared the people: for the thing was done suddenly *(Heb. 4:7)*.

CHAPTER 30

(726 B.C.)

PREPARATION FOR THE PASSOVER

AND Hezekiah sent to all Israel and Judah, and wrote letters also to Ephraim and Manasseh, that they should come to the House of the LORD at Jerusalem, to keep the Passover unto the LORD God of Israel *(the Passover is a type of Calvary [Ex. 12:13])*.

2 For the king had taken counsel, and his princes, and all the congregation in Jerusalem, to keep the Passover in the second month.

3 For they could not keep it at that time *(the appointed season)*, because the Priests had not sanctified themselves sufficiently, neither had the people gathered themselves together to Jerusalem *(the Passover was supposed to be kept the first month [Ex. 12:2-3], but, because of all the things that needed to be done, they would have to take the Passover a month late, i.e., "the second month" [Vs. 2])*.

4 And the thing pleased the king and all the congregation.

5 So they established a decree to make proclamation throughout all Israel, from Beersheba even to Dan, that they should come to keep the Passover unto the LORD God of Israel at Jerusalem: for they had not done it of a long time in such sort as it was written *(in the multitude of an undivided and holy kingdom)*.

6 So the posts *(messengers)* went with the letters from the king and his princes throughout all Israel and Judah, and according to the commandment of the king, saying, You Children of Israel, turn again unto the LORD God of Abraham, Isaac, and Israel, and He will return to the remnant of you, that are escaped out of the hand of the kings of Assyria. *(The northern kingdom had by now fallen, and so the poorest of the poor had been left by Assyria in the land, with the elite taken out as captives; however, they were precious in God's sight just the same. Regrettably, as we shall see, most would not take this opportunity offered by Hezekiah.)*

7 And be not ye like your fathers, and like your brethren, which trespassed against the LORD God of their fathers, who therefore gave them up to desolation, as you see *(the desolation of the northern kingdom could easily be seen)*.

8 Now be ye not stiffnecked, as your fathers were, but yield yourselves unto the LORD, and enter into His Sanctuary, which He has sanctified for ever: and serve the LORD your God, that the fierceness of His wrath may turn away from you *(the only thing that assuages the wrath of God is Calvary; "His wrath" will either be turned toward the unrepentant Christian or Calvary; the price of sin must be paid; if we accept the price that He paid at Calvary, then His wrath has already been expended toward His Son, the Lord Jesus Christ; if we do not accept the price that was paid at Calvary, then His wrath is turned toward us)*.

9 For if you turn again unto the LORD, your brethren and your children shall find compassion before them that lead them captive, so that they shall come again into this land *(Hezekiah speaks of a possible restoration, but only if repentance is enjoined)*: for the LORD your God is gracious and merciful, and will not turn away His face from you, if you return unto Him *(sincerely repent!)*.

10 So the posts *(messengers)* passed from city to city through the country of Ephraim and Manasseh even unto Zebulun: but they laughed them to scorn, and mocked them *(these last two phrases speak significant description of the exact moral state in which Israel's Tribes were now to be found; sadly, far too many in the modern Church meet the Message of the Cross with "laughter, scorn, and mockery")*.

11 Nevertheless divers of Asher and Manasseh and of Zebulun humbled themselves, and came to Jerusalem *(while many will laugh and mock, many, as well, will accept and receive; it is to the latter we look!)*.

12 Also in Judah *(the former Verses pertain to the northern kingdom of Israel)* the hand of God was to give them one heart to do the commandment of the king and of the princes, by the Word of the LORD *(Judah was far more amenable to the Word of the Lord than Israel)*.

13 And there assembled at Jerusalem much people to keep the Feast of Unleavened Bread in the second month, a very great congregation. *(Three Feasts were to be conducted at this time: "Passover, Unleavened Bread, and Firstfruits." They took seven days. Passover commenced on the first day, Unleavened Bread would spread over the entire seven days, and Firstfruits took place the last day. Passover signified Calvary. Unleavened Bread signified the Perfect Life and Perfect Body of Christ, which would be offered in Sacrifice. Firstfruits typified His Resurrection.)*

14 And they arose and took away the altars that were in Jerusalem, and all the altars for incense took they away, and cast them into the brook Kidron *(idol altars)*.

THE PASSOVER OBSERVED

15 Then they killed the Passover on the fourteenth day of the second month: and the Priests and the Levites were ashamed, and sanctified themselves, and brought in the Burnt offerings into the House of the LORD *(speaks of Repentance on the part of the Priests and the Levites; judgment must begin at the House of God [I Pet. 4:17])*.

16 And they stood in their place after their manner, according to the Law of Moses the man of God: the Priests sprinkled the blood, which they received of the hand of the Levites.

17 For there were many in the congregation who were not sanctified: therefore the Levites had the charge of the killing of the Passovers for every one who was not clean, to sanctify them unto the LORD *(which affirms that the original directions of Moses were that the person who brought the victim to offer it was to kill it; but, in this case, the Levites mostly officiated)*.

18 For a multitude of the people, even many of Ephraim, and Manasseh, Issachar, and Zebulun, had not cleansed themselves, yet did they eat the Passover otherwise than it was written *(had not followed the proper procedure [Deut. 16:1-8])*. But Hezekiah prayed for them, saying, The good LORD pardon every one.

19 Who prepares his heart to seek God, the LORD God of his fathers, though he be not cleansed according to the purification of the Sanctuary *(the reason all of this was so serious is simply because it all pointed to Christ and what He would do to redeem humanity, which all led to the Cross)*.

20 And the LORD hearkened to Hezekiah, and healed the people *(there is no "healing" other than Calvary; all other cisterns are broken and "can hold no water" [Jer. 2:13])*.

FEAST OF UNLEAVENED BREAD RESTORED

21 And the Children of Israel who were present at Jerusalem kept the Feast of Unleavened Bread seven days with great gladness: and the Levites and the Priests praised the LORD day by day, singing with loud instruments unto the LORD *(once again, worship in the realm of music and singing always accompanies the Cross, and our Faith in that Finished Work)*.

22 And Hezekiah spoke comfortably unto all the Levites who taught the good knowledge of the LORD: and they did eat throughout the Feast seven days, offering Peace Offerings *(of which a part of this Offering was eaten by the offeror)*, and making confession to the LORD God of their fathers *(Repentance!)*.

THE FEAST CONTINUED FOR SEVEN MORE DAYS

23 And the whole assembly took counsel to

keep other seven days: and they kept other seven days with gladness *(making a total of fourteen days)*.

24 For Hezekiah king of Judah did give to the congregation a thousand bullocks and seven thousand sheep; and the princes gave to the congregation a thousand bullocks and ten thousand sheep: and a great number of Priests sanctified themselves *(the conduits carrying the blood from these many sacrifices from the Temple Mount would have caused the Brook Kidron, which ran between the Temple Mount and Olivet, to run red with blood; this is obnoxious and repulsive to the unspiritual eye, but, to those who know their God, Calvary is the greatest sight this side of Heaven; for it was there that man was liberated and set free [Col. 2:14-15])*.

25 And all the congregation of Judah, with the Priests and the Levites, and all the congregation that came out of Israel, and the strangers who came out of the land of Israel, and who dwelt in Judah, rejoiced.

26 So there was great joy in Jerusalem: for since the time of Solomon the son of David king of Israel there was not the like in Jerusalem *(Calvary alone brings "great joy"; nothing else will)*.

27 Then the Priests the Levites arose and blessed the people: and their voice was heard, and their prayer came up to His holy dwelling place, even unto Heaven *(the only prayer that God will hear is that which is anchored in Calvary's Cross)*.

CHAPTER 31
(726 B.C.)
THE IDOLS DESTROYED IN ALL ISRAEL

NOW when all this was finished, all Israel that were present went out to the cities of Judah, and broke the images in pieces, and cut down the groves, and threw down the high places and the altars out of all Judah and Benjamin, in Ephraim also and Manasseh, until they had utterly destroyed them all. Then all the Children of Israel returned, every man to his possession, into their own cities *(however, they returned with prosperity now made possible)*.

HEZEKIAH'S PROVISION FOR THE PRIESTS AND LEVITES

2 And Hezekiah appointed the courses of the Priests and the Levites after their courses, every man according to his service, the Priests and the Levites for Burnt Offerings and for Peace Offerings, to minister, and to give thanks, and to praise in the gates of the tents of the LORD *(this was thought of as so much foolishness by Ahaz; likewise, the carnal mind sees no profit in such, but the spiritual mind understands its value; if we ignore the Bible, we lose our love for God; if we love the Bible, we will love God; Hezekiah loved the Bible, so he would obey the Bible)*.

3 He appointed also the king's portion of his substance for the Burnt Offerings, to wit, for the morning and evening Burnt Offerings *(9 a.m. and 3 p.m.)*, and the Burnt Offerings for the Sabbaths, and for the new moons, and for the set Feasts, as it is written in the Law of the LORD *(Hezekiah did not evade his own responsibilities in the matter of contribution; his "portion" was the tithe)*.

4 Moreover he commanded the people who dwelt in Jerusalem to give the portion of the Priests and the Levites, that they might be encouraged in the Law of the LORD *(the king meant to set an example, which he did!)*.

5 And as soon as the commandment came abroad, the Children of Israel brought in abundance the firstfruits of corn, wine, and oil, and honey, and of all the increase of the field; and the tithe of all things brought they in abundantly *(whenever the Church is on fire for God, money is given liberally to the Work of God; otherwise, there is little giving)*.

6 And concerning the Children of Israel and Judah, that dwelt in the cities of Judah, they also brought in the tithe of oxen and sheep, and the tithe of the holy things which were consecrated unto the LORD their God, and laid them by heaps *(when we give in "heaps," the Lord gives it back to us even in "greater heaps" [Lk. 6:38])*.

7 In the third month they began to lay the foundation of the heaps, and finished them in the seventh month *(in the "third month" the Feast of Pentecost was conducted, while in the "seventh month" was conducted the Feast of Tabernacles)*.

8 And when Hezekiah and the princes came and saw the heaps, they blessed the LORD, and His people Israel.

9 Then Hezekiah questioned with the Priests and the Levites concerning the heaps *(the questioning probably had to do with how the superabundant contributions should be utilized or preserved — Pulpit)*.

THE BLESSINGS OF THE LORD

10 And Azariah the Chief Priest of the house of Zadok answered him, and said, Since the people began to bring the Offerings into the House of the LORD, we have had enough to eat, and have left plenty: for the LORD has blessed His people; and that which is left is this great store *(under the New Covenant, we have even greater Promises [Heb. 8:6]; if the Work of the Lord is put first, the Lord has promised that a "great store" will accrue to us as well [Mat. 6:33]).*

11 Then Hezekiah commanded to prepare chambers in the House of the LORD; and they prepared them,

12 And brought in the Offerings and the Tithes and the dedicated things faithfully: over which Cononiah the Levite was ruler, and Shimei his brother was the next.

13 And Jehiel, and Azaziah, and Nahath, and Asahel, and Jerimoth, and Jozabad, and Eliel, and Ismachiah, and Mahath, and Benaiah, were overseers under the hand of Cononiah and Shimei his brother, at the commandment of Hezekiah the king, and Azariah the ruler of the House of God.

14 And Kore the son of Imnah the Levite, the porter toward the east, was over the freewill offerings of God, to distribute the oblations of the LORD, and the most holy things.

15 And next him were Eden, and Miniamin, and Jeshua, and Shemaiah, Amariah, and Shecaniah, in the cities of the Priests, in their set office, to give to their brethren by courses, as well to the great as to the small *(the latter phrase portrays the fact that the duty had not always in the past been honestly discharged):*

16 Beside their genealogy of males, from three years old and upward, even unto every one that entered into the House of the LORD, his daily portion for their service in their charges according to their courses *(a picture of the little children being fed for the sake of their father's Sanctuary service is a pleasant glimpse);*

17 Both to the genealogy of the Priests by the House of their fathers, and the Levites from twenty years old and upward, in their charges by their courses;

18 And to the genealogy of all their little ones, their wives, and their sons, and their daughters, through all the congregation: for in their set office they sanctified themselves in Holiness *(according to the Word of the Lord):*

19 Also of the sons of Aaron the Priests, which were in the fields of the suburbs of their cities, in every several city, the men who were expressed by name, to give portions to all the males among the Priests, and to all who were reckoned by genealogies among the Levites *(all of this proclaims the fact that all the Priests and the Levites were remembered and carefully provided for, which is the way it was supposed to be).*

20 And thus did Hezekiah throughout all Judah, and wrought that which was good and right and truth before the LORD his God.

21 And in every work that he began in the service of the House of God, and in the Law, and in the Commandments, to seek his God, he did it with all his heart, and prospered *(true prosperity can only be found in faithfully following the Word of the Lord; this Hezekiah did!).*

CHAPTER 32

(710 B.C.)

SENNACHERIB, KING OF ASSYRIA, INVADES JUDAH

AFTER these things, and the establishment thereof, Sennacherib king of Assyria came, and entered into Judah, and encamped against the fenced cities, and thought to win them for himself. *("After these things" means after the great revival under Hezekiah. The king of Assyria then made war on Judah. He had already taken the ten Tribes into captivity, and now his heart was lifted up to take Judah also. In this, he overstepped himself, for he had been commissioned by the Lord, although unknown to him, to destroy the ten-Tribe kingdom only. God defeated the Assyrian's purpose and delivered Hezekiah after testing his faith by permitting Judah to be tested.)*

2 And when Hezekiah saw that Sennacherib was come, and that he was purposed to fight against Jerusalem *(according to II Ki. 18:13-16, Hezekiah had already given Sennacherib great quantities of gold and silver to stop the invasion; these bribes were not pleasing to the Lord; he came against Jerusalem anyway),*

3 He *(Hezekiah)* took counsel with his princes and his mighty men to stop the waters of the fountains which were without the city: and they did help him.

4 So there was gathered much people together, who stopped all the fountains, and the brook that ran through the midst of the land, saying, Why should the kings of Assyria come, and find much water? *(Hezekiah stopped*

the fountain which is now known as the "Virgin's Fount" on the east of Ophel. Through the conduit he made [II Ki. 20:20], the water from this fount was brought down to the lower Gihon [Pool of Siloam]. Now the upper Gihon was simply covered over and hidden from the enemy on the outside, making the water supply of Jerusalem safe by means of the two Gihons.)

5 Also he strengthened himself, and built up all the wall that was broken, and raised it up to the towers, and another wall without, and repaired Millo in the city of David, and made darts and shields in abundance *(he took all possible means to make himself, the people, and the city strong to withstand the invaders).*

6 And he set captains of war over the people, and gathered them together to him in the street of the gate of the city, and spoke comfortably to them, saying,

THE MESSAGE OF HEZEKIAH

7 Be strong and courageous, be not afraid nor dismayed for the king of Assyria, nor for all the multitude that is with him: for there be more with us than with him *(great Faith in a great God would come against a great enemy and win a great victory; as ever, Faith is the ingredient; let all Believers know that whatever Satan brings against us, God has more for us than Satan has against us):*

8 With him is an arm of flesh; but with us is the LORD our God to help us, and to fight our battles. And the people rested themselves upon the words of Hezekiah king of Judah *(our problem is that too often we attempt to defeat the flesh by the flesh; it cannot be done; our strength must be "the LORD our God").*

9 After this did Sennacherib king of Assyria send his servants to Jerusalem, (but he himself laid siege against Lachish, and all his power with him,) unto Hezekiah king of Judah, and unto all Judah who were at Jerusalem, saying,

THE MESSAGE OF SENNACHERIB

10 Thus saith Sennacherib king of Assyria, Whereon do you trust, that you abide in the siege in Jerusalem? *(In other words, the siege is going to be bad!)*

11 Does not Hezekiah persuade you to give over yourselves to die by famine and by thirst, saying, The LORD our God shall deliver us out of the hand of the king of Assyria? *(The emissaries of Sennacherib appealed to the people instead of to Hezekiah and his ministers of state, thinking to undermine their morale.)*

12 Has not the same Hezekiah taken away his high places and his altars, and commanded Judah and Jerusalem, saying, You shall worship before one altar, and burn incense upon it? *(This Verse illustrates the fact that wherever there is obedience to the teaching of the Bible, it will be misinterpreted by people of the world. The written Word commanded that there should be only one Altar in Israel; man approves of many. The emissaries of Sennacherib didn't know what they were talking about.)*

13 Know ye not what I and my fathers have done unto all the people of other lands? were the gods of the nations of those lands any ways able to deliver their lands out of my hand? *(This Passage portrays these emissaries boasting that their god was more powerful than all others, so it was vain to expect Jehovah to rescue the people, especially since He did not rescue their brethren in Samaria [II Ki., Chpt. 17].)*

14 Who was there among all the gods of those nations that my fathers utterly destroyed, that could deliver his people out of my hand, that your God should be able to deliver you out of my hand?

15 Now therefore let not Hezekiah deceive you, nor persuade you on this manner, neither yet believe him: for no god of any nation or kingdom was able to deliver his people out of my hand, and out of the hand of my fathers: how much less shall your God deliver you out of my hand? *(The mighty Sennacherib was soon to find out just Who the God of Judah actually was!)*

16 And his servants spoke yet more against the LORD God, and against His servant Hezekiah *(the Holy Spirit shows us here that the Lord is just as displeased with His servants being spoken against as "Himself").*

17 He wrote also letters to rail on the LORD God of Israel, and to speak against Him, saying, As the gods of the nations of other lands have not delivered their people out of my hand, so shall not the God of Hezekiah deliver His people out of my hand *(the emissaries of Sennacherib intended to intimidate the people of Jerusalem).*

18 Then they cried with a loud voice in the Jews' speech *(language)* unto the people of Jerusalem who were on the wall, to affright them, and to trouble them; that they might take the city.

19 And they spoke against the God of

Jerusalem, as against the gods of the people of the Earth, which were the work of the hands of man *(over and over again, Jehovah is grossly insulted! To be compared to the gods of other people, which were merely "the work of the hands of man," not only showed the ignorance of Sennacherib, but as well brought the blasphemy to a higher pitch).*

ISAIAH

20 And for this cause Hezekiah the king, and the Prophet Isaiah the son of Amoz, prayed and cried to Heaven *(too many in the modern Church no longer cry to God; instead, they resort to psychology, which has the same source as witchcraft — Satan).*

21 And the LORD sent an Angel, which cut off all the mighty men of valour, and the leaders and captains in the camp of the king of Assyria. So he returned with shame of face to his own land. And when he was come into the house of his god, they who came forth of his own bowels *(his sons)* slew him there with the sword *(with only one Angel, the Lord struck down 185,000 Assyrians in one night [II Ki. 19:35]; as a result, Sennacherib returned to Nineveh in shame; history records that he did not venture again even toward Judah; some years later, he was murdered by his own sons).*

22 Thus the LORD saved Hezekiah and the inhabitants of Jerusalem from the hand of Sennacherib the king of Assyria, and from the hand of all other, and guided them on every side. *(What a beautiful statement! The Holy Spirit will lead and guide us into all truth [Jn. 16:13].)*

23 And many brought gifts unto the LORD to Jerusalem, and presents to Hezekiah king of Judah: so that he was magnified in the sight of all nations from thenceforth *(Judah became one of the most powerful nations on the face of the Earth, all because of Hezekiah's faith, and the Blessings of God).*

HEZEKIAH'S SICKNESS AND RECOVERY

24 In those days Hezekiah was sick to the death, and prayed unto the LORD: and He spoke unto him, and He gave him a sign *(this was the sign of the sundial going backwards ten degrees, which was a miracle of unprecedented proportions; this means that the Earth literally went back on its axis, i.e., "its rotation," which brought about a "long day" [II Ki. 20:8-11]).*

25 But Hezekiah rendered not again according to the benefit done unto him; for his heart was lifted up: therefore there was wrath upon him, and upon Judah and Jerusalem *(someone has said that "praise and prosperity are the greatest obstacles for a Christian to overcome"; Hezekiah did not overcome them, but rather succumbed to them; this probably referred to him showing all his material riches to the Babylonians [II Ki. 20:12-15] instead of the riches of the God of Israel).*

26 Notwithstanding Hezekiah humbled himself for the pride of his heart *(showing that pride was his sin)*, both he and the inhabitants of Jerusalem, so that the wrath of the LORD came not upon them in the days of Hezekiah *(thankfully, Hezekiah repented, and the Lord healed him, giving him fifteen more years of life [II Ki. 20:1-7]).*

HEZEKIAH'S ACCOMPLISHMENTS

27 And Hezekiah had exceeding much riches and honour: and he made himself treasuries for silver, and for gold, and for precious stones, and for spices, and for shields, and for all manner of pleasant jewels;

28 Storehouses also for the increase of corn, and wine, and oil; and stalls for all manner of beasts, and cotes for flocks.

29 Moreover he provided him cities, and possessions of flocks and herds in abundance: for God had given him substance very much *(in other words, the Lord was the Author of all this prosperity).*

30 This same Hezekiah also stopped the upper watercourse of Gihon, and brought it straight down to the west side of the city of David. And Hezekiah prospered in all his works.

31 Howbeit in the business of the ambassadors of the princes of Babylon, who sent unto him to enquire of the wonder that was done in the land, God left him, to try him, that he *(Hezekiah)* might know all that was in his heart *(man, even the most dedicated and consecrated Believer, will invariably turn aside if "God leaves us" even for a moment; Hezekiah would find that "the heart is deceitful above all things, and desperately wicked: who can know it?" [Jer. 17:9]).*

THE DEATH OF HEZEKIAH

32 Now the rest of the acts of Hezekiah, and his goodness, behold, they are written in

the vision of Isaiah the Prophet, the son of Amoz, and in the book of the kings of Judah and Israel.

33 And Hezekiah slept with his fathers, and they buried him in the chiefest of the sepulchres of the sons of David: and all Judah and the inhabitants of Jerusalem did him honour at his death. And Manasseh his son reigned in his stead. *(Concerning his burial, such was not said of any man before or after this. It must have meant that he was buried next to David's tomb. Despite his failures, Hezekiah was one of the Godliest kings who ever reigned over Judah.)*

CHAPTER 33
(698 B.C.)
MANASSEH REIGNS OVER JUDAH

MANASSEH was twelve years old when he began to reign, and he reigned fifty and five years in Jerusalem *(Manasseh was one of the most wicked of all the 42 kings of Israel and Judah, yet he reigned longer than any other — 55 years; quite possibly the Lord allowed Manasseh to reign so long because He saw that this hard-riding Monarch would repent; everything that God does is an act of Mercy; even His Judgment is redemptive, if only the individual or the nation will allow it to be so)*:

2 But did that which was evil in the sight of the LORD, like unto the abominations of the heathen, whom the LORD had cast out before the Children of Israel *(not too many years from then, Judah would be cast out as well!)*.

3 For he built again the high places *(idol worship)* which Hezekiah his father had broken down, and he reared up altars for Baalim, and made groves *(the worship of the Asherah)*, and worshipped all the host of heaven *(the planetary bodies)*, and served them.

4 Also he built altars in the House of the LORD *(placed heathen altars in the very Temple itself)*, whereof the LORD had said, In Jerusalem shall My Name be for ever *(Deut. 12:11; I Ki. 9:3; II Chron. 6:6)*.

5 And he built altars for all the host of heaven in the two courts of the House of the LORD *(heathen altars built in the "court of Israel," which was the closest to the Temple, and the "court of women," which was immediately behind the court of Israel)*.

6 And he caused his children to pass through the fire in the valley of the son of Hinnom *(human sacrifice)*: also he observed times, and used enchantments, and used witchcraft, and dealt with a familiar spirit, and with wizards: he wrought much evil in the sight of the LORD, to provoke Him to anger.

7 And he set a carved image, the idol which he had made *(the Asherah, a statue of the male member)*, in the House of God *(some believe he put it in the very Holy of Holies)*, of which God had said to David and to Solomon his son, In this House, and in Jerusalem, which I have chosen before all the Tribes of Israel, will I put My Name for ever:

8 Neither will I any more remove the foot of Israel from out of the land which I have appointed for your fathers; so that they will take heed to do all that I have commanded them, according to the whole Law and the Statutes and the Ordinances by the hand of Moses *(for all the Blessings that the Lord had given Israel, all that He demanded of them was that they make every effort to keep the Law)*.

9 So Manasseh made Judah and the inhabitants of Jerusalem to err, and to do worse than the heathen, whom the LORD had destroyed before the Children of Israel *(in fact, sin by a Believer is always worse than that by the unredeemed, and for the obvious reasons)*.

10 And the LORD spoke to Manasseh, and to His people: but they would not hearken *(sadly, this is the story of untold millions; the Lord speaks in varied ways, but they will not hear, which refers to a willful rejection)*.

MANASSEH'S BABYLONIAN CAPTIVITY AND RESTORATION

11 Wherefore the LORD brought upon them the captains of the host of the king of Assyria, which took Manasseh among the thorns, and bound him with fetters, and carried him to Babylon *(this was an act of Mercy on the part of God, as He attempted to bring Manasseh to his senses; it accomplished its purpose)*.

12 And when he was in affliction, he besought the LORD his God, and humbled himself greatly before the God of his fathers *(this is evidently why the Lord allowed Manasseh to rule as long as he did; as well, and as stated, it was the reason the Lord allowed him to be taken captive to Babylon; it had the desired effect upon the Monarch; time and time again, the Lord chastises His children in attempting to bring them to a place of Repentance)*,

13 And prayed unto Him: and He was intreated of him, and heard his supplication,

and brought him again to Jerusalem into his kingdom. Then Manasseh knew that the LORD He was God *(there could be no more beautiful illustration of the Mercy and Grace of God than that which was extended to Manasseh; the great lesson learned here is that if the Lord would do that for this king, who had wrought more evil in Judah than any other king before him, He will do it for anyone else; there are only two requirements: to humble oneself, and to pray unto God).*

14 Now after this he built a wall without the city of David, on the west side of Gihon, in the valley, even to the entering in at the fish gate, and compassed about Ophel, and raised it up a very great height, and put captains of war in all the fenced cities of Judah.

REVIVAL UNDER MANASSEH

15 And he took away the strange gods, and the idol out of the House of the LORD, and all the altars that he had built in the mount of the House of the LORD, and in Jerusalem, and cast them out of the city.

16 And he repaired the Altar of the LORD *(the great Brazen Altar, on which the Sacrifices were offered)*, and sacrificed thereon Peace Offerings *(the "Peace Offerings" were generally offered after the Sin and Trespass Offerings, signifying that Peace with God had now been restored; this tells us that the Peace of God had now come to Manasseh)* and Thank Offerings *(to be sure, this king had much to be thankful for, hence the "Thank Offerings" and the emphasis on this by the Holy Spirit)*, and commanded Judah to serve the LORD God of Israel.

17 Nevertheless the people did sacrifice still in the high places, yet unto the LORD their God only *(the offering of Sacrifices to the Lord in the high places was contrary to the Word of God; there was to be one national worship in the one Temple, and the Offerings and Sacrifices on the one national Altar, which signified one Calvary).*

18 Now the rest of the acts of Manasseh, and his prayer unto his God, and the words of the Seers who spoke to him in the Name of the LORD God of Israel, behold, they are written in the book of the kings of Israel.

19 His prayer also, and how God was intreated of him, and all his sins, and his trespass, and the places wherein he built high places, and set up groves and graven images, before he was humbled: behold, they are written among the sayings of the Seers.

THE DEATH OF MANASSEH

20 So Manasseh slept with his fathers, and they buried him in his own house: and Amon his son reigned in his stead *(unlike some of the other kings, Manasseh began his reign as a wicked king, but ended it as a good one).*

THE REIGN OF AMON OVER JUDAH

21 Amon was two and twenty years old when he began to reign, and reigned two years in Jerusalem.

22 But he did that which was evil in the sight of the LORD, as did Manasseh his father: for Amon sacrificed unto all the carved images which Manasseh his father had made, and served them;

23 And humbled not himself before the LORD, as Manasseh his father had humbled himself *(proclaims the fact that the Lord evidently chastised Amon, trying to get him to repent, but to no avail)*; but Amon trespassed more and more *(actually, few humble themselves as Manasseh, with most hardening themselves as did Amon, and that despite the appeal of the Lord).*

THE DEATH OF AMON

24 And his servants conspired against him, and slew him in his own house.

25 But the people of the land slew all them who had conspired against king Amon; and the people of the land made Josiah his son king in his stead.

CHAPTER 34
(641 B.C.)
JOSIAH REIGNS OVER JUDAH

JOSIAH was eight years old when he began to reign, and he reigned in Jerusalem one and thirty years *(Josiah will be one of the most Godly; and yet, Judah's sun is beginning to set).*

2 And he did that which was right in the sight of the LORD, and walked in the ways of David his father, and declined neither to the right hand, nor to the left *(what a beautiful statement!).*

JOSIAH'S REFORMS

3 For in the eighth year of his reign, while he was yet young *(16 years old)*, he began to

seek after the God of David his father *(in other words, he was converted at 16)*: and in the twelfth year *(when he was 20 years old)* he began to purge Judah and Jerusalem from the high places, and the groves, and the carved images, and the molten images *(the Holy Spirit, no doubt, dealt with him greatly and inspired him to carry forth this great work)*.

4 And they broke down the altars of Baalim in his presence *(meaning that he personally saw to their destruction)*; and the images, that were on high above them, he cut down; and the groves, and the carved images, and the molten images, he broke in pieces, and made dust of them, and strowed it upon the graves of them who had sacrificed unto them.

5 And he burnt the bones of the Priests upon their altars, and cleansed Judah and Jerusalem. *(This is speaking of the ungodly priests who had burned incense on the altar at Bethel nearly 350 years before. A Prophet, at that time, came out of Judah and "cried against the Altar." He prophesied at that time that a "child shall be born unto the house of David, Josiah by name." In other words, the Holy Spirit through him called Josiah's name 320 years before Josiah was born [I Ki. 13:2])*.

6 And so did he in the cities of Manasseh, and Ephraim, and Simeon, even unto Naphtali, with their mattocks round about *(he extended this effort even into what had been the northern kingdom)*.

7 And when he had broken down the altars and the groves, and had beaten the graven images into powder, and cut down all the idols throughout all the land of Israel, he returned to Jerusalem *(which once again states that he attended to this task personally)*.

JOSIAH REPAIRS THE TEMPLE

8 Now in the eighteenth year of his reign *(when he was 26 years old)*, when he had purged the land, and the House *(the Temple)*, he sent Shaphan the son of Azaliah, and Maaseiah the governor of the city, and Joah the son of Joahaz the recorder, to repair the House of the LORD his God *(this was five or six years after Jeremiah began to prophesy [Jer. 2:2]; the great Prophet was, therefore, present at the time of these reformations and the great Passover Feast of these Chapters)*.

9 And when they came to Hilkiah the High Priest, they delivered the money that was brought into the House of God, which the Levites that kept the doors had gathered of the hand of Manasseh and Ephraim, and of all the remnant of Israel, and of all Judah and Benjamin; and they returned to Jerusalem *(the Levites had come back from the area occupied by the Tribes of Manasseh and Ephraim)*.

10 And they put it in the hand of the workmen who had the oversight of the House of the LORD, and they gave it to the workmen who wrought in the House of the LORD, to repair and amend the house:

11 Even to the artificers and builders gave they it, to buy hewn stone, and timber for couplings, and to floor the houses which the kings of Judah had destroyed *(there had been much negligence of the Temple, and even outright destruction)*.

12 And the men did the work faithfully: and the overseers of them were Jahath and Obadiah, the Levites, of the sons of Merari; and Zechariah and Meshullam, of the sons of the Kohathites, to set it forward; and other of the Levites, all who could skill of instruments of music *(it seems from this that the Levites played instruments and sang praises unto the Lord while the work on the Temple was being done)*.

13 Also they were over the bearers of burdens, and were overseers of all who wrought the work in any manner of service: and of the Levites there were scribes, and officers, and porters *(the Levites had the general oversight of all the work, and thereby filled the offices mentioned here)*.

THE BOOK OF THE LAW DISCOVERED

14 And when they brought out the money that was brought into the House of the LORD, Hilkiah the Priest found a Book of the Law of the LORD given by Moses *(this was no doubt the original Book of the Pentateuch — the one actually personally written by Moses [II Ki. 22:8]; the Hebrew should have been translated literally: "The actual engraving of the Law of the Ever-Living in the hand of Moses"; the Scrolls were nearly 850 years old; they had been hidden in the Temple, and were found somewhat by accident by Hilkiah the High Priest)*.

15 And Hilkiah answered and said to Shaphan the scribe, I have found the Book of the Law in the House of the LORD. And Hilkiah delivered the book to Shaphan.

16 And Shaphan carried the Book to the king, and brought the king word back again, saying, All that was committed to your servants,

they do it.

17 And they have gathered together the money that was found in the House of the LORD, and have delivered it into the hand of the overseers, and to the hand of the workmen.

18 Then Shaphan the scribe told the king, saying, Hilkiah the Priest has given me a Book. And Shaphan read it before the king *(or read a portion of it)*.

19 And it came to pass, when the king had heard the words of the Law, that he rent his clothes. *(The king rent his clothes in grief, because the practice of the nation had diverged so terribly from the ever-to-be-venerated Law. Learning from it how defective his reformation was, he proceeded with a thorough one.*

A cleansing of the heart and life under the searchlight of the Word of God differs vastly from a reformation initiated by the feeble light of conscience or by tradition.)

20 And the king commanded Hilkiah, and Ahikam the son of Shaphan, and Abdon the son of Micah, and Shaphan the scribe, and Asaiah a servant of the king's saying,

21 Go, enquire of the LORD for me, and for them who are left in Israel and in Judah, concerning the words of the book that is found: for great is the wrath of the LORD that is poured out upon us, because our fathers have not kept the Word of the LORD, to do after all that is written in this Book *(the words of the Book convicted Josiah)*.

22 And Hilkiah, and they whom the king had appointed, went to Huldah the Prophetess, the wife of Shallum the son of Tikvath, the son of Hasrah, keeper of the wardrobe; (now she dwelt in Jerusalem in the college *[a certain part of the city; has no relationship to academics]*;) and they spoke to her to that effect *(even though Jeremiah was serving in the office of the Prophet at that time, the Holy Spirit had the High Priest go to a woman, Huldah the Prophetess; in Christ, there is neither male nor female, and we speak of preference [Gal. 3:28])*.

23 And she answered them Thus saith the LORD God of Israel, Tell ye the man who sent you to me,

24 Thus saith the LORD, Behold, I will bring evil upon this place, and upon the inhabitants thereof, even all the curses that are written in the Book which they have read before the king of Judah *(Deut., Chpt. 28)*:

25 Because they have forsaken Me, and have burned incense unto other gods, that they might provoke Me to anger with all the works of their hands; therefore My wrath shall be poured out upon this place, and shall not be quenched *(this Judgment would come in a few years)*.

26 And as for the king of Judah *(Josiah)*, who sent you to enquire of the LORD, so shall you say unto him, Thus saith the LORD God of Israel concerning the words which you have heard;

27 Because your heart was tender, and you did humble yourself before God, when you heard His words against this place, and against the inhabitants thereof, and humbled yourself before Me, and did rend your clothes, and weep before Me; I have even heard you also, saith the LORD.

28 Behold, I will gather you to your fathers, and you shall be gathered to your grave in peace, neither shall your eyes see all the evil that I will bring upon this place, and upon the inhabitants of the same. So they brought the king word again. *(It seems from the pronouncement by the Lord against Judah that Josiah's reforms merely delayed the coming judgment. It did not halt it. In effect, the Lord told the Monarch that it would not come in his lifetime. His death would be "in peace," as it regards these judgments.)*

THE LAW READ AND THE COVENANT RENEWED

29 Then the king sent and gathered together all the elders of Judah and Jerusalem.

30 And the king went up into the House of the LORD, and all the men of Judah, and the inhabitants of Jerusalem, and the Priests, and the Levites, and all the people, great and small *(they gathered in the Court in front of the Temple)*: and he read in their ears all the Words of the Book of the Covenant that was found in the House of the LORD *(the Priests did read [Deut. 31:9])*.

31 And the king stood in his place, and made a Covenant before the LORD, to walk after the LORD, and to keep His Commandments, and His Testimonies, and His Statutes, with all his heart, and with all his soul, to perform the Words of the Covenant which are written in this Book.

32 And he caused all who were present in Jerusalem and Benjamin to stand to it. And the inhabitants of Jerusalem did according to the Covenant of God, the God of their fathers.

33 And Josiah took away all the abominations

out of all the countries that pertained to the Children of Israel, and made all who were present in Israel to serve, even to serve the LORD their God. And all his days they departed not from following the LORD, the God of their fathers *(every true revival is always, and without exception, based on the Word of God; the Bible is the only revealed Truth in the world and, in fact, ever has been; there is not a spiritual problem that is not addressed in the Word; there is not a difficulty for which it does not have a solution; there is not a question that it cannot answer; there is not a life that the God of its pages cannot change; there is not a broken heart that its Words cannot mend; there is not a darkness that its Light cannot dispel; not a sin that the Blood of its pages cannot wash away [Ps. 119:105])*.

CHAPTER 35
(623 B.C.)
THE PASSOVER IS KEPT

MOREOVER Josiah kept a Passover unto the LORD in Jerusalem: and they killed the Passover on the fourteenth day of the first month *(the "Passover" was the foundation of all Israel's worship and God's dealing with His People; it represents Israel's deliverance out of Egypt by the slain lamb and the shedding of innocent blood; likewise, the entirety of the Foundation of Christendom is founded on Calvary, of which the Passover is a type [Ex. 12:13])*.

2 And he set the Priests in their charges, and encouraged them to the service of the House of the LORD,

3 And said unto the Levites who taught all Israel, which were holy unto the LORD, Put the Holy Ark in the House which Solomon the son of David king of Israel did build; it shall not be a burden upon your shoulders: serve now the LORD your God, and His people Israel *(evidently, the Ark of the Covenant had been taken out of the Holy of Holies, quite possibly by Josiah's wicked father, Amon; it was to be placed in the Holy of Holies and intended to be moved no more)*.

4 And prepare yourselves by the houses of your fathers, after your courses, according to the writing of David king of Israel, and according to the writing of Solomon his son *(in other words, handle everything according to the Word of God)*.

5 And stand in the Holy Place *(to carry on the work of offering the Incense, keeping the*

Lamps lit, etc.) according to the divisions of the families of the fathers of your brethren the people, and after the division of the families of the Levites (according to the 24 courses).

6 So kill the Passover, and sanctify yourselves, and prepare your brethren, that they may do according to the Word of the LORD by the hand of Moses *(this records the fact that Josiah believed that Moses wrote the Pentateuch, and Verse 12 shows his acquaintanceship with the Book of Exodus — especially Chapter 12)*.

7 And Josiah gave to the people, of the flock, lambs and kids, all for the Passover Offerings, for all who were present, to the number of thirty thousand, and three thousand bullocks: these were of the king's substance *(these were to be offered up as Sacrifices according to the Word of the Lord, and it seems the animals were given to the people free of charge)*.

8 And his princes *(wealthy people)* gave willingly unto the people, to the Priests, and to the Levites: Hilkiah and Zechariah and Jehiel, rulers of the House of God, gave unto the Priests for the Passover offerings two thousand and six hundred small cattle *(probably sheep)* and three hundred oxen.

9 Conaniah also, and Shemaiah and Nethaneel, his brethren, and Hashabiah and Jeiel and Jozabad, chief of the Levites, gave unto the Levites for Passover Offerings five thousand small cattle, and five hundred oxen.

THE PASSOVER

10 So the service was prepared, and the Priests stood in their place, and the Levites in their courses, according to the king's commandment.

11 And they killed the Passover, and the Priests sprinkled the blood from their hands, and the Levites flayed them *(pulled the skin from their bodies)*.

12 And they removed the Burnt Offerings, that they might give according to the divisions of the families of the people, to offer unto the LORD, as it is written in the Book of Moses. And so did they with the oxen.

13 And they roasted the Passover with fire according to the Ordinance *(Ex. 12:8-9)*: but the other Holy Offerings sod they in pots, and in caldrons, and in pans, and divided them speedily among all the people *(all the people were carefully attended)*.

14 And afterward they made ready for themselves, and for the Priests: because the Priests

the sons of Aaron were busied in offering of Burnt Offerings and the fat until night; therefore the Levites prepared for themselves, and for the Priests the sons of Aaron.

15 And the singers the sons of Asaph were in their place, according to the Commandment of David, and Asaph, and Heman, and Jeduthun the king's Seer; and the porters waited at every gate; they might not depart from their service; for their brethren the Levites prepared for them. *(This Verse proclaims the fact that as the Sacrifices were offered, they were accompanied by music, singing, and worship. When Calvary is held up as the Foundation of the Faith, it always elicits joy. As well, the porters made certain that the Law of the Lord was adhered to regarding the Sacrifices. All of this shows Josiah's adherence to the Word of God.)*

16 So all the service of the LORD was prepared the same day, to keep the Passover, and to offer Burnt Offerings upon the Altar of the LORD, according to the commandment of king Josiah.

THE FEAST OF UNLEAVENED BREAD

17 And the Children of Israel who were present kept the Passover at that time, and the Feast of Unleavened Bread seven days *(the Passover was kept on the first day of the seven).*

18 And there was no Passover like to that kept in Israel from the days of Samuel the Prophet; neither did all the kings of Israel keep such a Passover as Josiah kept, and the Priests, and the Levites, and all Judah and Israel who were present, and the inhabitants of Jerusalem *(this was also said of Hezekiah's observance of the Passover; the statement is true in both cases, for Hezekiah kept the Passover such as had never been kept up unto his day [30:26], and here Josiah kept one that was greater than Hezekiah's).*

19 In the eighteenth year of the reign of Josiah was this Passover kept *(Josiah was now 26 years old).*

JOSIAH IS SLAIN IN BATTLE

20 After all this *(Josiah was 39 at this time),* when Josiah had prepared the Temple, Necho king of Egypt came up to fight against Charchemish by Euphrates: and Josiah went out against him.

21 But he *(Necho)* sent ambassadors to him *(to Josiah),* saying, What have I to do with you,

thou king of Judah? I come not against you this day, but against the house wherewith I have war: for God commanded me to make haste: forbear thee from meddling with God, Who is with me, that He destroy you not *(this is quite a statement coming from a heathen, but yet the Holy Spirit would ultimately say that he was right).*

22 Nevertheless Josiah would not turn his face from him, but disguised himself, that he might fight with him, and hearkened not unto the words of Necho from the Mouth of God, and came to fight in the valley of Megiddo *(every evidence is that Josiah was wrong in doing this).*

23 And the archers shot at king Josiah; and the king said to his servants, Have me away; for I am sore wounded.

24 His servants therefore took him out of that chariot, and put him in the second chariot that he had; and they brought him to Jerusalem, and he died, and was buried in one of the sepulchres of his fathers. And all Judah and Jerusalem mourned for Josiah. *(It has been argued from then until now as to why Josiah did this. Other than the information given here, the Scriptures are silent.*

Every evidence seems to point to the fact that the Lord tried to warn him; however, we can certainly understand Josiah paying no attention at all to a heathen who claimed to hear from God. He didn't and neither would we; therefore, with so little information given, we can only venture an opinion:

Despite Josiah's reforms, Judah, at heart, had little turned to the Lord; consequently, the Lord would take Josiah away, simply because it was time for Judgment to come. Isaiah said, possibly concerning such as this: "The righteous perishes, and no man lays it to heart: and merciful men are taken away, none considering that the righteous is taken away from the evil to come" [Isa. 57:1].)

LAMENT FOR JOSIAH

25 And Jeremiah lamented for Josiah: and all the singing men and the singing women spoke of Josiah in their lamentations to this day, and made them an ordinance in Israel: and, behold, they are written in the lamentations *(not the Book of Lamentations later written by Jeremiah).*

26 Now the rest of the acts of Josiah, and his goodness, according to that which was written

in the Law of the LORD *(this sentence pictures Josiah as a careful, loving student of the Word, to the end that he might become a "doer" of it)*,

27 And his deeds, first and last, behold, they are written in the book of the kings of Israel and Judah.

CHAPTER 36
(593 B.C.)
THE REIGN OF JEHOAHAZ

THEN the people of the land took Jehoahaz the son of Josiah, and made him king in his father's stead in Jerusalem.

2 Jehoahaz was twenty and three years old when he began to reign, and he reigned three months in Jerusalem *(this was the shortest of any reign in Judah; in II Kings 23:32, we read that he did that which was evil in the sight of God)*.

JEHOAHAZ IS DEFEATED: TAKEN CAPTIVE TO EGYPT BY NECHO

3 And the king of Egypt put him down at Jerusalem, and condemned the land in an hundred talents of silver and a talent of gold *(now Judah will become a vassal state of Egypt)*.

4 And the king of Egypt made Eliakim his brother king over Judah and Jerusalem, and turned his name to Jehoiakim. And Necho took Jehoahaz his brother, and carried him to Egypt.

JEHOIAKIM REIGNS OVER JUDAH

5 Jehoiakim was twenty and five years old when he began to reign, and he reigned eleven years in Jerusalem: and he did that which was evil in the sight of the LORD his God *(the words, "his God," mean that God fervently dealt with him to bring him to the true way; nevertheless, despite the heavy dealings by the Holy Spirit, Jehoiakim continued to "do evil")*.

JEHOIAKIM TAKEN CAPTIVE BY NEBUCHADNEZZAR TO BABYLON

6 Against him *(Jehoiakim)* came up Nebuchadnezzar king of Babylon, and bound him in fetters, to carry him to Babylon *(at this stage, Egypt begins to wane in power, which now sees the advent and rise of mighty Babylon)*.

7 Nebuchadnezzar also carried of the vessels of the House of the LORD to Babylon, and put them in his temple at Babylon. *(These articles were put in the temple of the god Bel [a derivative of Baal]. Inasmuch as there was no "god" in the Temple, Nebuchadnezzar no doubt took some of the Holy Vessels, such as the "Golden Lampstands," etc. This was the first deportation, which included Daniel and the three Hebrew children [II Ki. 24:14; Dan. 1:3-3].)*

8 Now the rest of the acts of Jehoiakim, and his abominations which he did, and that which was found in him, behold, they are written in the book of the kings of Israel and Judah: and Jehoiachin his son reigned in his stead.

THE REIGN AND CAPTIVITY OF JEHOIACHIN

9 Jehoiachin was eight years old when he began to reign *(should be "eighteen," as in II Kings 24:8; the error was made, no doubt, by a copyist)*, and he reigned three months and ten days in Jerusalem: and he did that which was evil in the sight of the LORD.

10 And when the year was expired, king Nebuchadnezzar sent, and brought him to Babylon, with the goodly vessels of the House of the LORD *(more of these Vessels, which had evidently been left)*, and made Zedekiah his brother king over Judah and Jerusalem *(this was the second deportation, which included Mordecai and Esther, as well as Ezekiel; they were taken to Babylon [II Ki. 24:10-16])*.

ZEDEKIAH REIGNS OVER JUDAH

11 Zedekiah was one and twenty years old when he began to reign, and reigned eleven years in Jerusalem.

12 And he did that which was evil in the sight of the LORD his God, and humbled not himself before Jeremiah the Prophet speaking from the Mouth of the LORD *(once again, the words, "his God," refer to the fact that the Holy Spirit through Jeremiah the Prophet dealt strongly with this man, but all to no avail! Millions presently fall into the same category, refusing to humble themselves before God)*.

THE REBELLION OF ZEDEKIAH

13 And he *(Zedekiah)* also rebelled against king Nebuchadnezzar, who had made him swear by God: but he stiffened his neck, and hardened his heart from turning unto the

LORD God of Israel *(the criticism by the Prophet Ezekiel concerning this oath violation on the part of Zedekiah is to be found in Ezek. 17:12-20 and 21:25).*

14 Moreover all the chief of the Priests, and the people, transgressed very much after all the abominations of the heathen; and polluted the House of the LORD which He had hallowed in Jerusalem. *(This, with the following three Verses, may be regarded as the formal and final indictment of the people of Judah. This Passage tells us that even the Priests practiced abominations!)*

15 And the LORD God of their fathers sent to them by His messengers, rising up betimes, and sending; because He had compassion on His people, and on His dwelling place *(however, as we shall see, God's compassion can be exhausted; the "messengers" addressed here could very well have been Isaiah, Jeremiah, and Ezekiel, with the emphasis on Jeremiah):*

16 But they mocked the messengers of God, and despised His Words, and misused His Prophets, until the wrath of the LORD arose against His people, till there was no remedy. *(It is one thing for man to say that there is no remedy, but quite something else altogether for the Lord to say, "Till there was no remedy." In these very words, one can feel the sob of the Holy Spirit!)*

17 Therefore he brought upon them the king of the Chaldees *(Nebuchadnezzar)*, who slew their young men with the sword in the House of their Sanctuary, and had no compassion upon young man or maiden, old man, or him who stooped for age: He *(the Lord)* gave them all into his hand.

18 And all the Vessels of the House of God, great and small, and the treasures of the House of the LORD, and the treasures of the king, and of his princes; all these he brought to Babylon *(this was the last deportation, with Jerusalem, as well as the Temple, being completely destroyed).*

19 And they burnt the House of God, and broke down the wall of Jerusalem, and burnt all the palaces thereof with fire, and destroyed all the goodly vessels thereof *(by the Lord allowing this, in effect, He was saying that Judah was no longer His people; now they belonged to the Babylonian king).*

20 And them who had escaped from the sword carried he away to Babylon; where they were servants to him and his sons until the reign of the kingdom of Persia *(a total of seventy years):*

21 To fulfill the Word of the LORD by the mouth of Jeremiah, until the land had enjoyed her Sabbaths: for as long as she lay desolate she kept Sabbath, to fulfill threescore and ten years. *(The Law of Moses had demanded that every seventh year the entirety of the land [Israel] should rest. It was called "a Sabbath of rest unto the land." On the seventh year, the Lord said, "You shall neither sow your field, nor prune your vineyard" [Lev. 25:3-4].*

For some 490 years, Israel ignored this Law of God; consequently, Israel "owed" the Lord 70 years of Sabbaths. Her deportation to Babylon would be for 70 years, thereby guaranteeing that the land would then lay fallow and would "enjoy her Sabbaths." God says what He means, and means what He says.)

THE DECREE OF CYRUS TO BUILD THE TEMPLE

22 Now in the first year of Cyrus king of Persia *(a period of about half a century had elapsed between the last date of the foregoing Verses and the date signalized here; as well, Cyrus was Esther's son)*, that the Word of the LORD spoken by the mouth of Jeremiah might be accomplished *(Jer. 29:10)*, the LORD stirred up the spirit of Cyrus king of Persia, that he made a proclamation throughout all his kingdom, and put it also in writing, saying,

23 Thus saith Cyrus king of Persia, All the kingdoms of the Earth has the LORD God of Heaven given me *(the Medo-Persian Empire had defeated the Babylonian Empire; no doubt, Cyrus had been greatly influenced by his Godly mother, Esther, in that he now recognizes that it is the Lord Who has raised up the Persian Empire)*; and He *(the Lord)* has charged me to build Him an house in Jerusalem, which is in Judah. Who is there among you of all His people? The LORD his God be with him, and let him go up. *(This concerned the re-building of the Temple under Ezra. All the Israelites were now free to go back to the land of Israel. Chapter 2 of Ezra gives us a list of the first group returning from captivity.)*

THE BOOK OF
EZRA

CHAPTER 1

(536 B.C.)

THE PROCLAMATION OF CYRUS

NOW in the first year of Cyrus king of Persia (*it is the first year of Cyrus as King of Babylon which is intended; it was 538 B.C.*), that the Word of the LORD by the mouth of Jeremiah might be fulfilled (*Jeremiah had prophesied not only the fact, but the date, of the return, assigning to the captivity a duration of "seventy years" [Jer. 29:10]*), the LORD stirred up the spirit of Cyrus king of Persia, that he made a proclamation throughout all his kingdom, and put it also in writing, saying (*this presents the Prophecy of Isaiah being fulfilled, which had been given over 200 years before [Isa. 44:28; 45:1-4]*),

2 Thus saith Cyrus king of Persia, The LORD God of Heaven has given me all the kingdoms of the Earth (*proclaims the Monarch giving praise to the Lord for his position*); and He has charged me to build Him an House (*Temple*) at Jerusalem, which is in Judah (*no doubt, his Godly mother Esther had exerted great influence over him for good; as well, he had been shown the Prophecies by Daniel, his aged Prime Minister, and thereby encouraged to befriend the Hebrews*).

3 Who is there among you of all His people? (*Proclaims the Monarch addressing himself to all the Tribes equally.*) his God be with him, and let him go up to Jerusalem, which is in Judah, and build the House of the LORD God of Israel, (He is the God,) which is in Jerusalem (*this latter statement emphatically declares that Jehovah of Israel is the One True God, beside Whom there is no other, which is quite an admission from a heathen monarch*).

4 And whosoever remains in any place where he sojourns, let the men of his place help him with silver, and with gold, and with goods, and with beasts, beside the freewill offering for the House of God that is in Jerusalem (*refers to the fact that he, from the king's treasury, is to give money in order to help this effort*).

PREPARATIONS FOR THE RETURN FROM BABYLON

5 Then rose up the chief of the fathers of Judah and Benjamin, and the Priests, and the Levites, with all them whose spirit God had raised, to go up to build the House of the LORD which is in Jerusalem (*their mission was laid out by the Lord, so there was no need for misunderstanding*).

6 And all they who were about them strengthened their hands with vessels of silver, with gold, with goods, and with beasts, and with precious things, beside all that was willingly offered (*in excess of the offerings which came from the kingdom treasury*).

7 Also Cyrus the king brought forth the vessels of the House of the LORD, which Nebuchadnezzar had brought forth out of Jerusalem, and had put them in the house of his gods (*refers to the Sacred Vessels which had been taken out of the Temple in Jerusalem before it was destroyed*);

8 Even those did Cyrus king of Persia bring forth by the hand of Mithredath the treasurer, and numbered them unto Sheshbazzar, the prince of Judah (*Sheshbazzar is, in fact, Zerubbabel; if the Davidic dynasty had continued, he would now be king; but because of the judgment pronounced upon Jehoiachin [Jer. 22:24-30], no king will sit on that throne until it is occupied at the beginning of the coming Kingdom Age by Jesus of Nazareth*).

9 And this is the number of them: thirty chargers of gold, a thousand chargers of silver, nine and twenty knives,

10 Thirty basons of gold, silver basons of a second sort four hundred and ten, and other vessels a thousand.

11 All the vessels of gold and of silver were five thousand and four hundred. All these did Sheshbazzar bring up with them of the captivity that were brought up from Babylon unto Jerusalem. (*The list of these vessels possess no interest for the natural heart. But how often must our Lord, as man, have read and reread these words! They were all precious to His Heart; and they are precious to the heart who loves Him.*)

CHAPTER 2

(536 B.C.)

THE FIRST GROUP RETURNING FROM CAPTIVITY UNDER ZERUBBABEL

NOW these are the children of the province who went up out of the captivity, of

those which had been carried away, whom Nebuchadnezzar the king of Babylon had carried away unto Babylon, and came again unto Jerusalem and Judah, every one unto his city *(many, if not most, of these had been born in captivity)*;

2 Which came with Zerubbabel: Jeshua, Nehemiah *(is not the same man who wrote the Book which bears that name)*, Seraiah, Reelaiah, Mordecai *(may very well have been the same man of the Book of Esther; actually, he was the cousin of Esther; since some came back who had seen the first Temple [3:12], Mordecai could have been one of these, for he was taken captive with Jehoiachin; it is possible that he could have lived through the 70 years of servitude)*, Bilshan, Mizpar, Bigvai, Rehum, Baanah. The number of the men of the people of Israel:

3 The children of Parosh, two thousand an hundred seventy and two.

4 The children of Shephatiah, three hundred seventy and two.

5 The children of Arah, seven hundred seventy and five.

6 The children of Pahath-moab, of the children of Jeshua and Joab, two thousand eight hundred and twelve.

7 The children of Elam, a thousand two hundred fifty and four.

8 The children of Zattu, nine hundred forty and five.

9 The children of Zaccai, seven hundred and threescore.

10 The children of Bani, six hundred forty and two.

11 The children of Bebai, six hundred twenty and three.

12 The children of Azgad, a thousand two hundred twenty and two.

13 The children of Adonikam, six hundred sixty and six.

14 The children of Bigvai, two thousand fifty and six.

15 The children of Adin, four hundred fifty and four.

16 The children of Ater of Hezekiah, ninety and eight.

17 The children of Bezai, three hundred twenty and three.

18 The children of Jorah, and hundred and twelve.

19 The children of Hashum, two hundred twenty and three.

20 The children of Gibbar, ninety and five.

21 The children of Beth-lehem, an hundred twenty and three.

22 The men of Netophah, fifty and six.

23 The men of Anathoth, an hundred twenty and eight.

24 The children of Azmaveth, forty and two.

25 The children of Kirjath-arim, Chephirah, and Beeroth, seven hundred and forty and three.

26 The children of Ramah and Gaba, six hundred twenty and one.

27 The men of Michmas, an hundred twenty and two.

28 The men of Beth-el and Ai, two hundred twenty and three.

29 The children of Nebo, fifty and two.

30 The children of Magbish, an hundred fifty and six.

31 The children of the other Elam, a thousand two hundred fifty and four.

32 The children of Harim, three hundred and twenty.

33 The children of Lod, Hadid, and Ono, seven hundred twenty and five.

34 The children of Jericho, three hundred forty and five.

35 The children of Senaah, three thousand and six hundred and thirty.

36 The Priests: the children of Jedaiah, of the house of Jeshua, nine hundred seventy and three.

37 The children of Immer, a thousand fifty and two.

38 The children of Pashur, a thousand two hundred forty and seven.

39 The children of Harim, a thousand and seventeen.

40 The Levites: the children of Jeshua and Kadmiel, of the children of Hodaviah, seventy and four.

41 The singers: the children of Asaph, an hundred twenty and eight.

42 The children of the porters: the children of Shallum, the children of Ater, the children of Talmon, the children of Akkub, the children of Hatita, the children of Shobai, in all an hundred thirty and nine.

43 The Nethinims: the children of Ziha, the children of Hasupha, the children of Tabbaoth,

44 The children of Keros, the children of Siaha, the children of Padon,

45 The children of Lebanah, the children of Hagabah, the children of Akkub,

46 The children of Hagab, the children of Shalmai, the children of Hanan,

47 The children of Giddel, the children of

Gahar, the children of Reaiah,

48 The children of Rezin, the children of Nekoda, the children of Gazzam,

49 The children of Uzza, the children of Paseah, the children of Besai,

50 The children of Asnah, the children of Mehunim, the children of Nephusim,

51 The children of Bakbuk, the children of Hakupha, the children of Harhur,

52 The children of Bazluth, the children of Mehida, the children of Harsha,

53 The children of Barkos, the children of Sisera, the children of Thamah,

54 The children of Neziah, the children of Hatipha.

55 The children of Solomon's servants: the children of Sotai, the children of Sophereth, the children of Peruda,

56 The children of Jaalah, the children of Darkon, the children of Giddel,

57 The children of Shephatiah, the children of Hattil, the children of Pochereth of Zebaim, the children of Ami.

58 All the Nethinims, and the children of Solomon's servants, were three hundred ninety and two.

59 And these were they which went up from Tel-melah, Tel-harsa, Cherub, Addan, and Immer: but they could not show their fathers' house, and their seed, whether they were of Israel:

60 The children of Delaiah, the children of Tobiah, the children of Nekoda, six hundred fifty and two. *(The total number returning from Babylon to Israel was 49,897. This included the servants and the singers, but not all are listed here.)*

THE PRIESTS

61 And of the children of the Priests: the children of Habaiah, the children of Koz, the children of Barzillai; which took a wife of the daughters of Barzillai the Gileadite, and was called after their name:

62 These sought their register among those who were reckoned by genealogy, but they were not found *(were not found in the genealogy)*: therefore were they, as polluted, put from the Priesthood *(some of those who claimed to be descendants of Aaron and, therefore, Priests, had also lost the evidence of their descent; this loss was held to disqualify them from the exercise of the Priestly office).*

63 And the Tirshatha *(Governor)* said unto them, that they should not eat of the most holy things, till there stood up a Priest with Urim and with Thummim *(Zerubbabel's expectation was disappointed; the gift of Urim and Thummim, forfeited by disobedience, was never recovered).*

64 The whole congregation together was forty and two thousand three hundred and threescore,

65 Beside their servants and their maids, of whom there were seven thousand three hundred thirty and seven: and there were among them two hundred singing men and singing women.

66 Their horses were seven hundred thirty and six; their mules, two hundred forty and five.

67 Their camels, four hundred thirty and five; their asses, six thousand seven hundred and twenty.

68 And some of the chief of the fathers, when they came to the house of the LORD which is at Jerusalem, offered freely for the House of God to set it up in his place:

69 They gave after their ability unto the treasure of the work threescore and one thousand drams of gold, and five thousand pound of silver, and one hundred Priests' garments.

70 So the Priests, and the Levites, and some of the people, and the singers, and the porters, and the Nethinims, dwelt in their cities, and all Israel in their cities.

CHAPTER 3
(536 B.C.)
RESTORATION OF WORSHIP

AND when the seventh month was come, and the Children of Israel were in the cities, the people gathered themselves together as one man to Jerusalem *(the "seventh month" corresponded nearly to our October; it commenced with a blowing of trumpets and a holy convocation on the first day [Lev. 23:24], which was followed on the tenth day by the solemn day of Atonement, and on the fifteenth day by the Feast of Tabernacles, or "Ingathering," which lasted until the twenty-second day, incorporating three Festivals: "Trumpets," "Atonement," and "Tabernacles").*

2 Then stood up Jeshua *(Joshua)* the son of Jozadak, and his brethren the Priests, and Zerubbabel the son of Shealtiel, and his brethren, and built the Altar of the God of Israel, to offer Burnt Offerings thereon, as it is written in the Law of Moses the man of God. *(The "Altar" was the first thing built upon the exiles*

returning, even before the Temple or the Wall. This proclaimed the fact that the Cross, of which the Altar was a Type, was the very foundation of all that Israel was. It is the same presently with the Church.

By building the Altar, where Burnt Offerings and Sin Offerings would be offered up, they thereby publicly confessed themselves to be guilty sinners, and that only by the shedding of atoning Blood could they be forgiven and brought back to God.)

3 And they set the Altar upon his bases *(means that they placed the new Altar upon the foundation of the old one, making it exactly conform to it)*; for fear was upon them because of the people of those countries: and they offered Burnt Offerings thereon unto the LORD, even Burnt Offerings morning and evening *(proclaims the fact that they were placing their Faith and confidence in the shed Blood of Christ, making that their defense against the heathen; in fact, this is what the Lord told them to do; thus, the daily "morning" and "evening" Sacrifices had begun).*

4 They kept also the Feast of Tabernacles *(presents the Feast which points toward, and promises, the Millennium, when all Israel shall be saved)*, as it is written *(Ex. 23:16)*, and offered the daily Burnt Offerings by number, according to the custom, as the duty of every day required *(presents the Offerings for each day of the Festival, as carefully laid down in Num. 29:13-38)*;

5 And afterward offered the continual Burnt Offering, both of the new moons, and of all the set Feasts of the LORD that were consecrated, and of every one who willingly offered a freewill offering unto the LORD *(pertains to those commanded in Num. 28:11-15, plus the offering up of Sacrifices anytime such Offerings were brought by individual Israelites).*

6 From the first day of the seventh month began they to offer Burnt Offerings unto the LORD *(presents their Faith in the shed Blood of Christ)*. But the foundation of the Temple of the LORD was not yet laid *(presents the fact that while everything about the Temple was of immense significance, still, the most significant of all was the "Altar," which typified the Cross).*

7 They gave money also unto the masons, and to the carpenters; and meat, and drink, and oil, unto them of Zidon, and to them of Tyre, to bring cedar trees from Lebanon to the sea of Joppa, according to the grant that they had of Cyrus king of Persia.

THE REBUILDING OF THE TEMPLE BEGUN

8 Now in the second year of their coming unto the House of God at Jerusalem, in the second month, began Zerubbabel the son of Shealtiel, and Jeshua *(Joshua)* the son of Jozadak, and the remnant of their brethren the Priests and the Levites, and all they who were come out of the captivity unto Jerusalem; and appointed the Levites, from twenty years old and upward, to set forward the work of the House of the LORD *(it was the second year after being in the land of Israel that work was begun on the Temple).*

9 Then stood Jeshua *(Joshua)* with his sons and his brethren, Kadmiel and his sons, the sons of Judah, together, to set forward the workmen in the House of God: the sons of Henadad, with their sons and their brethren the Levites *(Joshua [Jeshua] was then the High Priest; he was in charge of the work).*

10 And when the builders laid the foundation of the Temple of the LORD, they set the Priests in their apparel with trumpets, and the Levites the sons of Asaph with cymbals, to praise the LORD, after the Ordinance of David king of Israel.

11 And they sang together by course in praising and giving thanks unto the LORD; because He is good, for His mercy endures for ever toward Israel. And all the people shouted with a great shout, when they praised the LORD, because the foundation of the House of the LORD was laid *(this was certainly a time that rejoicing was most appropriate and, as well, it was centered up in music and singing, which the Holy Spirit had orchestrated through David many years before, and which is carried on even unto this present hour — at least with those who truly know the Lord).*

12 But many of the Priests and Levites and chief of the fathers, who were ancient men, who had seen the first house, when the foundation of this house was laid before their eyes, wept with a loud voice; and many shouted aloud for joy *(the Temple was not destroyed at the beginning of the seventy years captivity; in fact, it had probably been destroyed a little less than 50 years; consequently, there would be many who could remember its grandeur and glory)*:

13 So that the people could not discern the noise of the shout of joy from the noise of the weeping of the people: for the people shouted with a loud shout, and the noise was heard

afar off *(in fact, the Jewish people, in their displays of emotion, whether it was joy or sadness, were very demonstrative).*

CHAPTER 4
(535 B.C.)
ZERUBBABEL REFUSES THE HELP OF THEIR ADVERSARIES

NOW when the adversaries of Judah and Benjamin heard that the children of the captivity built the Temple unto the LORD God of Israel *(Satan now sends his adversaries, endeavoring to hinder the building of the Temple)*;

2 Then they came to Zerubbabel, and to the chief of the fathers, and said unto them, let us build with you: for we seek your God, as you do; and we do sacrifice unto Him since the days of Esar-haddon king of Assur *(Assyria)*, which brought us up hither *(these were the Samaritans, who occupied what was formerly referred to as the northern kingdom of Israel).*

3 But Zerubbabel, and Jeshua, and the rest of the chief of the fathers of Israel, said unto them, You have nothing to do with us to build an House unto our God; but we ourselves together will build unto the LORD God of Israel, as king Cyrus the king of Persia has commanded us *(the plan fomented here by Satan was designed to destroy the people of God; his proposal through the Samaritans for help, which was no doubt sorely needed, possibly seemed attractive on the surface; however, the Evil One had far more in mind than the Temple; he wanted to dilute the Jewish people by intermarriage with the Samaritans, thereby destroying the pure bloodline through which the Messiah must come).*

4 Then the people of the land weakened the hands of the people of Judah, and troubled them in building,

5 And hired counsellors against them, to frustrate their purpose, all the days of Cyrus king of Persia, even until the reign of Darius king of Persia *(the Lord allowed this opposition in order to test the faith of His people; regrettably, they failed; in fact, everything that happens to the Believer is, in essence, a test of faith).*

THE STOPPING OF THE WORK ON THE TEMPLE BY ARTAXERXES, THE KING

6 And in the reign of Ahasuerus, in the beginning of his reign, wrote they unto him an accusation against the inhabitants of Judah and Jerusalem *(a new king has taken the throne, so*

fresh representations were made to him by the "adversaries," lest the work of the Temple should continue).*

16 We certify the king that if this

7 And in the days of Artaxerxes wrote Bishlam, Mithredath, Tabeel, and the rest of their companions, unto Artaxerxes king of Persia; and the writing of the letter was written in the Syrian tongue, and interpreted in the Syrian tongue *(Artaxerxes now takes over the Persian kingdom, and the adversaries appeal to him, as well!).*

8 Rehum the chancellor and Shimshai the scribe wrote a letter against Jerusalem to Artaxerxes the king in this sort:

9 Then wrote Rehum the chancellor, and Shimshai the scribe and the rest of their companions; the Dinaites, the Apharsathchites, the Tarpelites, the Apharsites, the Archevites, the Babylonians, the Susanchites, the Dehavites, and the Elamites *(either the Samaritans were not now amalgamated into a single people, or else they thought, by listing all of these different names, that such would portray power and strength to the king, and he would, therefore, accede to their request),*

10 And the rest of the nations whom the great and noble Asnapper brought over, and set in the cities of Samaria, and the rest who are on this side the river, and at such a time *(who this "great and noble Asnapper" was, we aren't told; they were speaking of the "Jordan River").*

11 This is the copy of the letter that they sent unto him, even unto Artaxerxes the king; Your servants the men on this side the river, and at such a time.

12 Be it known unto the king, that the Jews which came up from thee to us are come unto Jerusalem, building the rebellious and the bad city, and have set up the walls thereof, and joined the foundations.

13 Be it known now unto the king, that, if this city be built, and the walls set up again, then will they not pay toll, tribute, and custom, and so you shall endamage the revenue of the kings.

14 Now because we have maintenance from the king's palace, and it was not meet for us to see the king's dishonour, therefore have we went and certified the king;

15 That search may be made in the book of the records of your fathers: so shall you find in the book of the records, and know that this city is a rebellious city, and hurtful unto kings and provinces, and that they have moved sedition

within the same of old time: for which cause was this city destroyed.

16 We certify the king that, if this city be built again, and the walls thereof set up, by this means you shall have no portion on this side the river. *(The enemies of the Lord told half-truths and outright lies, in order to hinder the rebuilding of the Temple.)*

THE ANSWER OF THE KING TO THE LETTER

17 Then sent the king *(Artaxerxes)* an answer unto Rehum the chancellor, and to Shimshai the scribe, and to the rest of their companions who dwell in Samaria, and unto the rest beyond the river *(east of the Jordan River)*, Peace, and at such a time.

18 The letter which you sent unto us has been plainly read before me.

19 And I commanded, and search has been made, and it is found that this city of old time has made insurrection against kings, and that rebellion and sedition have been made therein.

20 There have been mighty kings also over Jerusalem, which have ruled over all countries beyond the river; and too, tribute, and custom, was paid unto them.

21 Give ye now commandment to cause these men to cease, and that this city be not built, until another commandment shall be given from me.

22 Take heed now that you fail not to do this: why should damage grow to the hurt of the kings?

23 Now when the copy of king Artaxerxes' letter was read before Rehum, and Shimshai the scribe, and their companions, they went up in haste to Jerusalem unto the Jews, and made them to cease by force and power *(the "adversaries" lost no time in brandishing the letter from the Persian king, demanding that the work stop; by threatened force, the work did stop).*

24 Then ceased the work of the House of God which is at Jerusalem. So it ceased unto the second year of the reign of Darius king of Persia *(if the work was resumed early in Darius' second year, the entire period of suspension cannot have much exceeded a year and a half; however, the Jews allowed many other things to hinder, which stretched into approximately fifteen years of inactivity, as it regards the rebuilding of the Temple).*

CHAPTER 5
(520 B.C.)
THE REBUILDING STARTED AGAIN

THEN the Prophets, Haggai the Prophet, and Zechariah the son of Iddo, prophesied unto the Jews who were in Judah and Jerusalem in the Name of the God of Israel, even unto them *(the two Books of Haggai and Zechariah should be read in connection with this Chapter).*

2 Then rose up Zerubbabel the son of Shealtiel, and Jeshua the son of Jozadak, and began to build the House of God which is at Jerusalem: and with them were the Prophets of God helping them *(the Prophets now come on the scene, with the Word from the Lord that the work must be resumed, and speedily; the people had become so busy building their own houses and setting themselves up, that little thought was now given to the Temple; without true Prophets, the Church will languish).*

THE ENEMIES OF THE JEWS SEEK TO HINDER THE BUILDING AGAIN

3 At the same time came to them Tatnai, governor on this side the river, and Shethar-boznai and their companions, and said thus unto them, Who has commanded you to build this house, and to make up this wall? *(As the work proceeds, Satan will again rear his ugly head, but to no avail.)*

4 Then said we unto them after this manner, What are the names of the men who make this building? *(The text should read, "Then said they . . . .?")*

5 But the eye of their God was upon the elders of the Jews, that they could not cause them to cease, till the matter came to Darius: and then they returned answer by letter concerning this matter *(at this time, the Elders who presided over the workmen employed in the restoration were a special subject of God's watchful care, so that those who would fain have hindered them could not).*

A LETTER TO KING DARIUS SEEKING TO STOP THE WORK ON THE TEMPLE

6 The copy of the letter that Tatnai, governor on this side the river, and Shethar-boznai and his companions the Apharsachites, which were on this side the river, sent unto Darius the king *(Tatnai was a just Governor-general of the vast regions to the westward of the River*

Euphrates; he personally visited Jerusalem, rather than listen to the reports of Israel's adversaries):

7 They sent a letter unto him, wherein was written thus; Unto Darius the king, all peace.

8 Be it known unto the king, that we went into the province of Judea, to the house of the great God, which is builded with great stones, and timber is laid in the walls, and this work goes fast on, and prospered in their hands.

9 Then asked we those elders, and said unto them thus, Who commanded you to build this house, and to make up these walls?

10 We asked their names also, to certify you, that we might write the names of the men that were the chief of them.

11 And thus they returned us answer, saying, We are the servants of the God of Heaven and Earth, and build the house that was built these many years ago, which a great king of Israel built and set up.

12 But after that our fathers had provoked the God of Heaven unto wrath, He gave them into the hand of Nebuchadnezzar the king of Babylon, the Chaldean, who destroyed this house, and carried the people away into Babylon.

13 But in the first year of Cyrus the king of Babylon the same king Cyrus made a decree to build this house of God.

14 And the vessels also of gold and silver of the House of God, which Nebuchadnezzar took out of the Temple that was in Jerusalem, and brought them into the Temple of Babylon, those did Cyrus the king take out of the Temple of Babylon, and they were delivered unto one, whose name was Sheshbazzar, whom he had made governor;

15 And said unto him, Take these vessels, go, carry them into the Temple that is in Jerusalem, and let the House of God be built in his place.

16 Then came the same Sheshbazzar, and laid the foundation of the House of God which is in Jerusalem: and since that time even until now has it been in building, and yet it is not finished.

17 Now therefore, if it seem good to the king, let there be search made in the king's treasure house, which is there at Babylon, whether it be so, that a decree was made of Cyrus the king to build this House of God at Jerusalem, and let the king send his pleasure to us concerning this matter *(it is quite possible that this "decree of Cyrus" may still exist in the ruins of Babylon and will one day be discovered).*

CHAPTER 6
(515 B.C.)
DARIUS CONFIRMS THE DECREE OF CYRUS AND SUPPORTS THE REBUILDING

THEN Darius the king made a decree, and search was made in the house of the rolls, where the treasures were laid up in Babylon *(it seems that the application made to Darius received his immediate attention).*

2 And there was found at Achmetha, in the palace that is in the province of the Medes, a roll, and therein was a record thus written:

3 In the first year of Cyrus the king the same Cyrus the king made a decree concerning the House of God at Jerusalem, Let the house be built, the place where they offered Sacrifices, and let the foundations thereof be strongly laid; the height thereof threescore cubits, and the breadth thereof threescore cubits;

4 With three rows of great stones, and a row of new timber: and let the expenses be given out of the king's house:

5 And also let the golden and silver vessels of the House of God, which Nebuchadnezzar took forth out of the Temple which is at Jerusalem, and brought unto Babylon, be restored, and brought again unto the Temple which is at Jerusalem, every one to his place, and place them in the House of God.

6 Now therefore, Tatnai, governor beyond the river, Shethar-boznai, and your companions the Apharsachites, which are beyond the river, be ye far from thence:

7 Let the work of this House of God alone; let the governor of the Jews and the elders of the Jews build this House of God in his place *(as the trumpet had given no uncertain note, the Persian officials, Tatnai and Shethar-boznai, whatever their wishes may have been, had no choice as to their line of action; the king's word was law; they were to leave the Jews alone, and let them finish the work on the Temple).*

8 Moreover I make a decree what you shall do the elders of these Jews for the building of this House of God: that of the king's goods, even of the tribute beyond the river, forthwith expenses be given unto these men, that they be not hindered *(not only was permission given to continue the work, but, as well, the workmen on the Temple were to be paid out of the royal revenue, as well as the expenses of the Sacrifices; the money came out of the taxes levied by the Persians against Syria).*

9 And that which they have need of, both

young bullocks, and rams, and lambs, for the Burnt Offerings of the God of Heaven, wheat, salt, wine, and oil, according to the appointment of the Priests which are at Jerusalem, let it be given them day by day without fail:

10 That they may offer sacrifices of sweet savours unto the God of Heaven, and pray for the life of the king, and of his sons.

11 Also I have made a decree, that whosoever shall alter this word, let timber be pulled down from his house, and being set up, let him be hanged thereon; and let his house be made a dunghill for this.

12 And the God Who has caused His Name to dwell there destroy all kings and people, that shall put to their hand to alter and to destroy this House of God which is at Jerusalem. I Darius have made a decree; let it be done with speed *(Darius left absolutely no doubt as to what he was saying as it regards the building of the Temple; as well, he left absolutely no doubt as it regards the punishment that was to be inflicted if his decree was altered in any way)*.

THE TEMPLE COMPLETED

13 Then Tatnai, governor on this side the river, Shethar-boznai, and their companions, according to that which Darius the king had sent, so they did speedily *(the Persian authorities who dealt directly with the Jews showed no reluctance to obey)*.

14 And the elders of the Jews built, and they prospered through the prophesying of Haggai the Prophet and Zechariah the son of Iddo. And they built and finished it, according to the Commandment of the God of Israel, and according to the commandment of Cyrus, and Darius, and Artaxerxes king of Persia.

15 And this house was finished on the third day of the month Adar, which was in the sixth year of the reign of Darius the king. *(The prophesying of both Haggai and Zechariah contributed much toward the finishing of this edifice. The Temple had been approximately twenty-one years in building. Fifteen years of this time had been all but wasted.)*

THE TEMPLE DEDICATED WITH SACRIFICES AND JOY

16 And the Children of Israel, the Priests, and the Levites, and the rest of the children of the captivity, kept the dedication of this House of God with joy. *(If it is to be noticed, Ezra is careful to present the returned exiles as "Israel," and not merely "Judah." This indicates that some of all the Tribes of Israel had returned. As well, by the use of the words, "this House," it seems that Ezra does this to link the present with the past, the new Temple with the old, the restored faith with that of former times.)*

17 And offered at the dedication of this House of God an hundred bullocks, two hundred rams, four hundred lambs; and for a Sin Offering for all Israel, twelve he goats, according to the number of the Tribes of Israel *(all this proclaims the fact that Israel now rested on the foundation of the shed Blood of the Sacrifices, which pointed to the One Who was to come; the Cross of Christ is likewise the Foundation of the Church; regrettably, the modern Church seems to be forgetting this Scriptural fact)*.

18 And they set the Priests in their divisions, and the Levites in their courses, for the service of God, which is at Jerusalem; as it is written in the Book of Moses *(the respective Offices of these two orders, the Priests and the Levites, are given in Num. 3:6-10 and 8:6-26)*.

THE PASSOVER KEPT AGAIN

19 And the children of the captivity kept the Passover upon the fourteenth day of the first month *(Ex. 12:6)*.

20 For the Priests and the Levites were purified together, all of them were pure, and killed the Passover for all the children of the captivity, and for their brethren the Priests, and for themselves *(this is the first Passover mentioned in all the 21 years of the returned exiles; possibly they conducted other Passovers, but the Scripture does not say)*.

21 And the Children of Israel, which were come again out of captivity, and all such as had separated themselves unto them from the filthiness of the heathen of the land, to seek the LORD God of Israel, did eat,

22 And kept the Feast of Unleavened Bread seven days with joy: for the LORD had made them joyful, and turned the heart of the king of Assyria unto them, to strengthen their hands in the work of the House of God, the God of Israel *(as is obvious here, when Israel set about to carry out the Work of God, then the Lord began to work for them; He will do the same presently!)*.

CHAPTER 7
(457 B.C.)
THE SECOND GROUP OF EXILES RETURN TO JERUSALEM UNDER EZRA

NOW after these things (*over 50 years have passed between the happenings of the previous Chapter and this Chapter*), in the reign of Artaxerxes king of Persia (*this was Artaxerxes Longimanus, who is different than the Artaxerxes of 4:7*), Ezra the son of Seraiah, the son of Azariah, and son of Hilkiah,

2 The son of Shallum, the son of Zadok, the son of Ahitub,

3 The son of Amariah, the son of Azariah, the son of Meraioth,

4 The son of Zerahiah, the son of Uzzi, the son of Bukki,

5 The son of Abishua, the son of Phinehas, the son of Eleazar, the son of Aaron the Chief Priest (*Ezra, as proclaimed here, was a member of the High Priest's family, probably a third cousin to the existing High Priest, Eliashib*):

6 This Ezra went up from Babylon; and he was a ready Scribe in the Law of Moses, which the LORD God of Israel had given: and the king granted him all his request, according to the hand of the LORD his God upon him (*Ezra now comes from Babylon to Jerusalem; he was a student of the "Law of Moses," in effect, a Scholar; tradition says he was the president of the Great Synagogue, which settled the question of the Jewish Canon of Scripture and, as well, began building Synagogues in Jewish communities*).

7 And there went up some of the Children of Israel, and of the Priests, and the Levites, and the singers, and the porters, and the Nethinims, unto Jerusalem, in the seventh year of Artaxerxes the king (*Ezra came to Jerusalem in 458 B.C.*).

8 And he came to Jerusalem in the fifth month, which was in the seventh year of the king.

9 For upon the first day of the first month began he to go up from Babylon, and on the first day of the fifth month came he to Jerusalem, according to the good hand of his God upon him (*the journey from Babylon to Jerusalem by Ezra and his party took exactly four months, and the Lord was with him*).

10 For Ezra had prepared his heart to seek the Law of the LORD, and to do it, and to teach in Israel Statutes and Judgments (*"to teach Statutes and Judgments" is to inculcate both the ceremonial and the moral precepts of the Law;*

Ezra was a teacher of Righteousness [10:10-11; Neh. 8:2-18]).

KING ARTAXERXES' SUPPORT OF EZRA

11 Now this is the copy of the letter that the king Artaxerxes gave unto Ezra the Priest, the Scribe, even a Scribe of the words of the Commandments of the LORD, and of His Statutes to Israel (*the "letter" given by king Artaxerxes to Ezra gave him tremendous latitude regarding government, in fact, guaranteeing the might of the Persian Empire to back him up; actually, Ezra was invested with the chief authority over the whole district of Judah*).

12 Artaxerxes, king of kings, unto Ezra the Priest, a Scribe of the Law of the God of Heaven, perfect peace, and at such a time (*the phrase, "perfect peace, and at such a time," is meant to proclaim the fact that any obstruction or opposition to this letter which would destroy the peace, would, at the same time, fall out to the destruction of the individual who would be so foolish as to oppose Ezra; in other words, and as stated, he had the full support of the Persian king*).

13 I make a decree, that all they of the people of Israel, and of his Priests and Levites, in my realm, which are minded of their own freewill to go up to Jerusalem, go with you.

14 Forasmuch as you are sent of the king, and of his seven counsellors, to enquire concerning Judah and Jerusalem, according to the Law of your God which is in your hand (*the latter phrase proclaims the fact that Ezra was not ashamed to stand before the king, Bible in hand, and make known to him the Word of God*);

15 And to carry the silver and gold, which the king and his counsellors have freely offered unto the God of Israel, Whose habitation is in Jerusalem,

16 And all the silver and gold that you can find in all the province of Babylon, with the freewill offering of the people, and of the Priests, offering willingly for the House of their God which is in Jerusalem (*many Jews at that time did not desire to go back to Jerusalem; still, they gave freely of their means to supplement what was being given by the Persians*):

17 That you may buy speedily with this money bullocks, rams, lambs, with their Meat Offerings and their Drink Offerings, and offer them upon the Altar of the House of your God which is in Jerusalem (*the king seemed to have quite a bit of knowledge concerning the manner*

of worship of the Jews regarding their Sacrifices; evidently, Ezra had witnessed to him in depth).

18 And whatsoever shall seem good to you, and to your brethren, to do with the rest of the silver and the gold, that do after the will of your God *(the confidence vested in Ezra by the Persian king is exceptional, to say the least!).*

19 The vessels also that are given you for the service of the House of your God, those deliver thou before the God of Jerusalem *(these "Vessels" do not appear to be the Sacred Vessels, which had already been taken by Zerubbabel).*

20 And whatsoever more shall be needful for the House of your God, which you shall have occasion to bestow, bestow it out of the king's treasure house.

21 And I, even I Artaxerxes the king, do make a decree to all the treasurers which are beyond the river, that whatsoever Ezra the Priest, the Scribe of the Law of the God of Heaven, shall require of you, it be done speedily,

22 Unto an hundred talents of silver, and to an hundred measures of wheat, and to an hundred baths of wine, and to an hundred baths of oil, and salt without prescribing how much *(this is the limit as to how much Ezra could take from the treasury of Persia).*

23 Whatsoever is commanded by the God of Heaven, let it be diligently done for the House of the God of Heaven: for why should there be wrath against the realm of the king and his sons? *(This heathen Monarch had more fear of God even than most Believers; he was actually afraid not to do all that lay within his power and service toward the Temple and the worship of God.)*

24 Also we certify you, that touching any of the Priests and Levites, singers, porters, Nethinims, or ministers of this House of God, it shall not be lawful to impose toll, tribute, or custom, upon them *(all persons attached to the Temple service were to be exempt from taxation).*

25 And you, Ezra, after the wisdom of your God, Who is in your hand, set magistrates and judges, which may judge all the people who are beyond the river, all such as know the Laws of your God; and teach ye them who know them not *(Ezra was given the authority to appoint "Magistrates and Judges").*

26 And whosoever will not do the Law of your God, and the law of the king, let judgment be executed speedily upon him, whether it be unto death, or to banishment, or to confiscation of goods, or to imprisonment *(in effect, Ezra is given here the authority to act as*

the head of all Civil Government of the Jewish people, with power to fine, imprison, banish, or even to put to death offenders, as he might think right).

EZRA'S WORSHIP AND PRAISE TO GOD

27 Blessed be the LORD God of our fathers, which has put such a thing as this in the king's heart, to beautify the House of the LORD which is in Jerusalem *(Ezra doesn't credit the king with this largesse, but rather the "LORD God"):*

28 And has extended mercy unto me before the king, and his counsellors, and before all the king's mighty princes. And I was strengthened as the hand of the LORD my God was upon me, and I gathered together out of Israel chief men to go up with me *(there were some leading Jews in Babylon who would go to Jerusalem with Ezra).*

CHAPTER 8
(457 B.C.)

THE LIST OF THOSE WHO RETURNED

THESE are now the chief of their fathers, and this is the genealogy of them who went up with me from Babylon, in the reign of Artaxerxes the king *(this is the second expedition led from Babylon to Judah, with the first being led by Zerubbabel; there may have been other expeditions; however, only these two are mentioned in Ezra).*

2 Of the sons of Phinehas; Gershom: of the sons of the Ithamar; Daniel: of the sons of David; Hattush.

3 Of the sons of Shechaniah, of the sons of Pharosh, Zechariah: and with him were reckoned by genealogy of the males an hundred and fifty.

4 Of the sons of Pahath-moab; Elihoenai the son of Zerahiah, and with him two hundred males.

5 Of the sons of Shechaniah; the son of Jahaziel, and with him three hundred males.

6 Of the sons also Adin; Ebed the son of Jonathan, and with him fifty males.

7 And of the sons of Elam; Jeshaiah the son of Athaliah, and with him seventy males.

8 And of the sons of Shephatiah; Zebadiah the son of Michael, and with him fourscore males.

9 Of the sons of Joab; Obadiah the son of Jehiel, and with him two hundred and eighteen males.

10 And of the sons of Shelomith; the son of Josiphiah, and with him an hundred and three-score males.

11 And of the sons of Bebai; Zechariah the son of Bebai, and with him twenty and eight males.

12 And of the sons of Azgad; Johanan the son of Hakkatan, and with him an hundred and ten males.

13 And of the last sons of Adonikam, whose names are these, Eliphelet, Jeiel, and Shemaiah, and with them threescore males.

14 Of the sons also of Bigvai; Uthai, and Zabbud, and with them seventy males. (All these individuals named were guaranteed to be Jews, for their genealogy proves such. All of this was very important, because the Messiah would come through these people. Their going back to the land of Israel was extremely significant also, considering that this was the land which God had chosen for these people and, as stated, through whom the Messiah would come.)

EZRA SENDS FOR THE LEVITES

15 And I gathered them together to the river that runs to Ahava; and there abode we in tents three days: and I viewed the people, and the Priests, and found there none of the sons of Levi (as to why this slackness concerning the Levites, we aren't told; however, there certainly seemed to have been a special disinclination to return to Jerusalem on the part of most of the Levites; in fact, only 74 went up with Zerubbabel the years before, when, in fact, there were 4,289 Priests who did return [2:36-40]).

16 Then sent I for Eliezer, for Ariel, for Shemaiah, and for Elnathan, and for Jarib, and for Elnathan, and for Nathan, and for Zechariah, and for Meshullam, chief men; also for Joiarib, and for Elnathan, men of understanding.

17 And I sent them with commandment unto Iddo the chief at the place Casiphia, and I told them what they should say unto Iddo, and to his brethren the Nethinims, at the place Casiphia, that they should bring unto us ministers for the House of our God (persuade Levites to come, who were needed, as it regards the work for the Temple; if everything else in Israel was successful, but yet the House of God was unattended or not attended properly, then again ruin would come upon Israel).

18 And by the good hand of our God upon us they brought us a man of understanding, of the sons of Mahli, the son of Levi, the son of Israel; and Sherebiah, with his sons and his brethren, eighteen (with that "Good Hand," all things can be done and, without that "Good Hand," nothing can be done);

19 And Hashabiah, and with him Jeshaiah of the sons of Merari, his brethren and their sons, twenty;

20 Also of the Nethinims (the original Nethinims were the Gibeonites of Josh. 9:23), whom David and the princes had appointed for the service of the Levites, two hundred and twenty Nethinims: all of them were expressed by name (the Holy Spirit wants us to know that each individual person was of great significance, thereby "expressed by name").

EZRA PROCLAIMS A FAST

21 Then I proclaimed a fast there, at the river of Ahava, that we might afflict ourselves before our God, to seek of Him a right way for us, and for our little ones, and for all our substance (this "fast" was probably for one day, with the entire group giving themselves to seeking the Lord, as it regarded His Leading and Guidance pertaining to the long journey ahead of them in going from Babylon to Jerusalem).

22 For I was ashamed to require of the king a band of soldiers and horsemen to help us against the enemy in the way: because we had spoken unto the king, saying, The hand of our God is upon all them for good who seek Him; but His power and His wrath is against all them who forsake Him (Ezra had boasted to Artaxerxes, and rightly so, of the power and goodness of God, and had spoken of himself and his brethren as being assured of the Divine protection, hence him not asking for military help on the long journey; considering that this way was infested by robbers, this was a great step of faith).

23 So we fasted and besought our God for this: and He was intreated of us.

TWELVE PRIESTS CHOSEN AS
TREASURERS OF THE
TEMPLE RICHES

24 Then I separated twelve of the chief of the Priests, Sherebiah, Hashabiah, and ten of their brethren with them,

25 And weighed unto them the silver, and the gold, and the vessels, even the offering of the House of our God, which the king, and his counsellors, and his lords, and all Israel there present, had offered:

26 I even weighed unto their hand six hundred fifty talents of silver, and silver vessels an hundred talents, and of gold an hundred talents;

27 Also twenty basons of gold, of a thousand drams; and two vessels of fine copper, precious as gold. *(All of this was worth, in 2004 currency, approximately $100 million, or even more; so it is easy to understand how this would be a tempting target for robbers.)*

28 And I said unto them, You are holy unto the LORD *(the men appointed of Verse 24)*; the vessels are holy also; and the silver and the gold are a freewill offering unto the LORD God of your fathers.

29 Watch ye, and keep them, until you weigh them before the chief of the Priests and the Levites, and chief of the fathers of Israel, at Jerusalem, in the chambers of the House of the LORD.

30 So took the Priests and the Levites the weight of the silver, and the gold, and the vessels, to bring them to Jerusalem unto the House of our God *(consecrated to God by their Office, the Priests and Levites were the fitting custodians of consecrated things)*.

EZRA'S ARRIVAL IN JERUSALEM

31 Then we departed from the river of Ahava on the twelfth day of the first month, to go unto Jerusalem: and the hand of our God was upon us, and He delivered us from the hand of the enemy, and of such as lay in wait by the way *(robbers!)*.

32 And we came to Jerusalem, and abode there three days *(this tells us that they all arrived safely; in fact, more than likely most, if not all, of the people with Ezra had never seen Jerusalem, having been born in Babylon)*.

33 Now on the fourth day was the silver and the gold and the vessels weighed in the House of our God by the hand of Meremoth the son of Uriah the Priest; and with him was Eleazar the son of Phinehas; and with them was Jozabad the son of Jeshua, and Noadiah the son of Binnui, Levites *(Ezra's businesslike action should be followed by all Christian people in money matters, both secular and spiritual)*;

34 By number and by weight of every one: and all the weight was written at that time.

35 Also the children of those who had been carried away, which were come out of the captivity, offered Burnt Offerings unto the God of Israel, twelve bullocks for all Israel, ninety and six rams, seventy and seven lambs, twelve he goats for a Sin Offering: all this was a Burnt Offering unto the LORD *(on reaching Jerusalem, they hasted to offer up Burnt Offerings and Sin Offerings in great number; that is, they proclaimed that despite their faith, their praying, their fasting, and their costly donations to the Temple, yet were they great sinners, needing a great Saviour; the greatness and sufficiency of that Saviour were typified in the multitude of the animals slain)*.

36 And they delivered the king's commissions unto the king's lieutenants, and to the governors on this side the river *(the west side of Jordan)*: and they furthered the people, and the House of God.

CHAPTER 9
(457 B.C.)
SIN IS DISCOVERED AND
SORROW EXPRESSED

NOW when these things were done *(speaking of the things in the previous Verses)*, the princes came to me, saying, The people of Israel and the Priests, and the Levites, have not separated themselves from the people of the lands, doing according to their abominations, even of the Canaanites, the Hittites, the Perizzites, the Jebusites, the Ammonites, and Moabites, the Egyptians, and the Amorites *(the matter of the involvement of the people of Israel, as few as they were in the Land at that time, with the heathen around them, regarding "abominations," was serious)*.

2 For they have taken of their daughters for themselves, and for their sons *(of the heathen)*: so that the holy seed have mingled themselves with the people of those lands: yes, the hand of the princes and rulers has been chief in this trespass *(the term "holy seed" does not, in effect, say that the people committing these sins were holy, but rather that this is the designation that the Lord had given them as a people, and what He intended them to be, whether they were, in fact, that or not)*.

3 And when I heard this thing, I rent my garment and my mantle, and plucked off the hair of my head and of my beard, and sat down astonied *(astonished; rending the clothes was one of the most common Oriental modes of showing grief)*.

4 Then were assembled unto me every one who trembled at the Words of the God

of Israel, because of the transgression of those who had been carried away; and I sat astonied until the evening sacrifice (*Ezra chose the time of the evening Sacrifice [3 p.m.] to confess his sin and the sin of the nation, for the poured-out blood of the Sacrifices proclaimed forgiveness and atonement; divinely inspired Repentance always brings the soul to Calvary*).

EZRA'S PRAYER AND CONFESSION OF SIN

5 And at the evening Sacrifice I arose up from my heaviness; and having rent my garment and my mantle, I fell upon my knees, and spread out my hands unto the LORD my God (*the time of the Sacrifice, which represented the Cross, was the appropriate time for prayer, especially regarding prayer in which acknowledgment of sin was to form a large part*),

6 And said, O my God, I am ashamed and blush to lift up my face to You, my God: for our iniquities are increased over our head, and our trespass is grown up unto the Heavens (*Ezra, by the use of the pronoun "our," includes himself in this prayer of Repentance, as he also pleads for the entirety of Israel*).

7 Since the days of our fathers have we been in a great trespass unto this day; and for our iniquities have we, our kings, and our Priests, been delivered into the hand of the kings of the lands, to the sword, to captivity, and to a spoil, and to confusion of face, as it is this day (*Ezra goes straight to the point, labeling "sin" as the problem, as it regarded Israel, and all others for that matter, and for all time*).

8 And now for a little space grace has been showed from the LORD our God, to leave us a remnant to escape, and to give us a nail in His Holy Place, that our God may lighten our eyes, and give us a little reviving in our bondage (*the entirety of the statement given in this Verse proclaims the fact that Ezra is not claiming a full restoration; in other words, by his statement, he is saying that any Grace will be appreciated, for the truth is, they deserve no Grace at all*).

9 For we were bondmen; yet our God has not forsaken us in our bondage, but has extended mercy unto us in the sight of the kings of Persia, to give us a reviving, to set up the House of our God, and to repair the desolations thereof, and to give us a wall in Judah and in Jerusalem (*the phrase, "For we were bondmen," should have been translated, "For*

we are bondmen"; *the Jews had not recovered their independence and, in fact, would not do so; even now, the modern State of Israel is limited, and we speak of the Arabs, which occupy a good part of the Land of Israel*).

10 And now, O our God, what shall we say after this? for we have forsaken Your Commandments (*this Verse speaks to the fact that, when sin is committed, it is always, and without exception, against God*).

11 Which You have commanded by Your servants the Prophets, saying, The land, unto which you go to possess it, is an unclean land with the filthiness of the people of the lands, with their abominations, which have filled it from one end to another with their uncleanness (*in his prayer, Ezra is speaking of the corrupt character of the Canaanitish nations which formerly occupied the Land that later came to be called Israel*).

12 Now therefore give not your daughters unto their sons, neither take their daughters unto your sons, nor seek their peace or their wealth for ever: that you may be strong, and eat the good of the land, and leave it for an inheritance to your children for ever (*Ezra is quoting, at least in part, Deut. 7:3*).

13 And after all that is come upon us for our evil deeds, and for our great trespass, seeing that You our God have punished us less than our iniquities deserve, and have given us such deliverance as this (*the Lord always punishes less than we deserve; we should always remember this*);

14 Should we again break Your Commandments, and join in affinity with the people of these abominations? would not You be angry with us till You had consumed us, so that there should be no remnant nor escaping? (*Sadly, Israel did "again" fail the Lord, and did so miserably! They "joined" Rome and the "abomination" of the Crucifixion of Christ, which was the most horrifying abomination of all. As a result, the entire nation was destroyed, which took place in A.D. 70, and is only now beginning to come back, which began in 1948.*)

15 O LORD God of Israel, You are righteous: for we remain yet escaped, as it is this day: behold, we are before You in our trespasses: for we cannot stand before You because of this (*Righteousness, in its widest sense, includes Mercy; and so the meaning here may be: "You are good and gracious; of which Your having spared us is a proof"*).

CHAPTER 10
(457 B.C.)
REPENTANCE RESULTS IN
SEPARATION FROM SIN

NOW when Ezra had prayed, and when he had confessed, weeping and casting himself down before the House of God, there assembled unto him out of Israel a very great congregation of men and women and children: for the people wept very sore (in leading the way, Ezra spurred the people to Repentance as well!).

2 And Shechaniah the son of Jehiel, one of the sons of Elam, answered and said unto Ezra, We have trespassed against our God, and have taken strange wives of the people of the land: yet now there is hope in Israel concerning this thing (if sin is present, without fail, the Holy Spirit will point it out).

3 Now therefore let us make a Covenant with our God to put away all the wives, and such as are born of them (the children), according to the counsel of my lord, and of those who tremble at the Commandment of our God; and let it be done according to the Law (the "Covenant" proposed was that which addressed the problem of the heathen wives, and possibly, as well, the heathen husbands, also the children born to these unlawful unions [9:12]).

4 Arise; for this matter belongs unto you (Ezra): we also will be with you: be of good courage, and do it (the princes of Israel proclaimed to Ezra that he must take the lead in this thing, as distasteful as it was!).

5 Then arose Ezra, and made the Chief Priests, the Levites, and all Israel, to swear that they should do according to this word. And they swore (all of Israel was to act in the matter as Shechaniah had recommended and put away the adulterous wives).

6 Then Ezra rose up from before the House of God, and went into the chamber of Johanan the son of Eliashib: and when he came thither, he did eat no bread, nor drink water: for he mourned because of the transgression of them who had been carried away (the greater sin had to do with Satan's efforts through intermarriage to destroy the sacred bloodline through which the Messiah was to come, hence the mourning).

7 And they made proclamation throughout Judah and Jerusalem unto all the children of the captivity, that they should gather themselves together unto Jerusalem (Ezra and others had greatly sought the Lord; now they will put action to their prayers; they will call an assembly for all in Judah and Jerusalem);

8 And that whosoever would not come within three days, according to the counsel of the princes and the elders, all his substance should be forfeited, and himself separated from the congregation of those who had been carried away (the command was ironclad; all able-bodied men had to come to Jerusalem, irrespective as to where they lived in Judah).

9 Then all the men of Judah and Benjamin gathered themselves together unto Jerusalem within three days. It was the ninth month, on the twentieth day of the month; and all the people sat in the street of the House of God, trembling because of this matter, and for the great rain (they gathered in the month Chisleu, which corresponds somewhat with our December).

10 And Ezra the Priest stood up, and said unto them, You have transgressed, and have taken strange wives, to increase the trespass of Israel (the phrase, "to increase the trespass of Israel," refers to the fact that Israel must not again travel a strange path; the past 70 years of suffering should be warning enough; God's Word is not to be trifled with!).

11 Now therefore make confession unto the LORD God of your fathers, and do His pleasure: and separate yourselves from the people of the land, and from the strange wives (this sin had to be confessed before the Lord).

12 Then all the congregation answered and said with a loud voice, As you have said, so must we do.

13 But the people are many, and it is a time of much rain, and we are not able to stand without, neither is this a work of one day or two: for we are many who have transgressed in this thing (the phrase, "For we are many who have transgressed in this thing," should have been translated, "We have greatly offended in this thing").

14 Let now our rulers of all the congregation stand, and let all them which have taken strange wives in our cities come at appointed times, and with them the elders of every city, and the judges thereof, until the fierce wrath of our God for this matter be turned from us (each case had to be examined individually; in some cases, the foreign wives may have become proselytes, and the children may have been circumcised, and so accepted into the congregation, which would have given them a claim to remain, which would extend to the mothers as well).

15 Only Jonathan the son of Asahel and Jahaziah the son of Tikvah were employed about this matter: and Meshullam and Shabbethai the Levite helped them *(should have been translated, "Only Jonathan and Jahaziah stood up against this matter, or opposed it"; in other words, they were not happy about this "Covenant").*

16 And the children of the captivity did so. And Ezra the Priest, with certain chief of the fathers, after the house of their fathers, and all of them by their names, were separated, and sat down in the first day of the tenth month to examine the matter *(the people, despite the opposition of Jonathan and Jahaziah, acquiesced to Ezra's decision and acted accordingly).*

17 And they made an end with all the men who had taken strange wives by the first day of the first month *(it took about three months to do this).*

THE NAMES OF THOSE WHO HAD MARRIED STRANGE WIVES

18 And among the sons of the Priests there were found who had taken strange wives: namely, of the sons of Jeshua the son of Jozadak, and his brethren; Maaseiah, the Eliezer, and Jarib, and Gedaliah *(Ezra listed the offending Priests first of all, because, of all people, they should have known better than to take "strange wives").*

19 And they gave their hands that they would put away their wives; and being guilty, they offered a ram of the flock for their trespass *(the only answer for this sin was the Sacrifice, i.e., "the Cross," as the Cross is the only answer for any sin [I Jn. 1:7, 9]).*

20 And of the sons of Immer; Hanani, and Zebadiah.

21 And of the sons of Harim; Maaseiah, and Elijah, and Shemaiah, and Jehiel, and Uzziah.

22 And of the sons of Pashur; Elioenai, Maaseiah, Ishmael, Nethaneel, Jozabad, and Elasah.

23 Also of the Levites; Jozabad, and Shimei, and Kelaiah, (the same is Kelita,) Pethahiah, Judah, and Eliezer.

24 Of the singers also; Eliashib: and of the porters; Shallum, and Telem, and Uri.

25 Moreover of Israel: of the sons of Parosh; Ramiah, and Jeziah, and Malchiah, and Miamin, and Eleazar, and Malchijah, and Benaiah.

26 And of the sons of Elam; Mattaniah, Zechariah, and Jehiel, and Abdi, and Jeremoth, and Eliah.

27 And of the sons of Zattu; Elioenai, Eliashib, Mattaniah, And Jeremoth, and Zabad, and Aziza.

28 Of the sons also of Bebai; Jehohanan, Hananiah, Zabbai, and Athlai.

29 And of the sons of Bani; Meshullam, Malluch, and Adaiah, Jashub, and Sheal, and Ramoth.

30 And of the sons of Pahath-moab; Adna, and Chelal, Benaiah, Maaseiah, Mattaniah, Bezaleel, and Binnui, and Manasseh.

31 And of the sons of Harim; Eliezer, Ishijah, Malchiah, Shemaiah, Shimeon,

32 Benjamin, Malluch, and Shemariah.

33 Of the sons of Hashum; Mattenai, Mattathah, Zabad, Eliphelet, Jeremai, Manasseh, and Shimei.

34 Of the sons of Bani; Maadai, Amram, and Uel,

35 Benaiah, Bedeiah, Chelluh,

36 Vaniah, Meremoth, Eliashib,

37 Mattaniah, Mattenai, and Jaasau,

38 And Bani, and Binnui, Shimei,

39 And Shelemiah, and Nathan, and Adaiah,

40 Machnadebai, Shashai, Sharai,

41 Azareel, and Shelemiah, Shemariah,

42 Shallum, Amariah, and Joseph.

43 Of the sons of Nebo; Jeiel, Mattithiah, Zabad, Zebina, Jadau, and Joel, Benaiah.

44 All these had taken strange wives: and some of them had wives by whom they had children. *(One may wonder why the necessity of these individuals and their families being listed, even as Ezra did? However, the Holy Spirit wanted this done in order that we may all understand how awful sin really is, and of any description.)*

THE BOOK OF
NEHEMIAH

CHAPTER 1
(446 B.C.)
THE BAD NEWS FROM JERUSALEM

THE words of Nehemiah the son of Hachaliah. And it came to pass in the month Chisleu *(December)*, in the twentieth year *(the 20th year of the reign of Artaxerxes Longimanus)*, as I was in Shushan the palace *(where Daniel saw the vision of the ram with two horns [Dan. 8:2], and Ahasuerus [Xerxes] made his great feast to all his princes and servants [Esther 1:3])*,

2 That Hanani, one of my brethren, came, he and certain men of Judah; and I asked them concerning the Jews who had escaped, which were left of the captivity, and concerning Jerusalem *(Hanani was later given the charge of the gates of Jerusalem by Nehemiah [7:2])*.

3 And they said unto me, The remnant who are left of the captivity there in the province are in great affliction and reproach: the wall of Jerusalem also is broken down, and the gates thereof are burned with fire *(Hanani and certain others had come from Jerusalem to the Persian Capital, and Nehemiah questions them regarding certain conditions in Jerusalem; he is told that the wall is broken down, and the gates are burned with fire; this is some years after the first group had returned under Ezra)*.

NEHEMIAH'S PRAYER FOR JERUSALEM

4 And it came to pass, when I heard these words, that I sat down and wept, and mourned certain days, and fasted, and prayed before the God of Heaven *(the revelation of the actual condition of Jerusalem, especially after all this time, came upon Nehemiah with a shock; so he took the situation to the Lord!)*,

5 And said, I beseech You, O LORD God of Heaven, the great and terrible God, Who keeps Covenant and Mercy for them who love Him and observe His Commandments *(Nehemiah's words are very similar to the prayer prayed by Daniel [Dan. 9:4])*:

6 Let Your ear now be attentive, and Your eyes open, that You may hear the prayer of Your servant, which I pray before You now, day and night, for the Children of Israel Your servants, and confess the sins of the Children of Israel, which we have sinned against You: both I and my father's house have sinned *(as Ezra, Nehemiah includes himself in the need for Repentance [Ezra 9:6])*.

7 We have dealt very corruptly against You, and have not kept the Commandments, nor the Statutes, nor the Judgments, which You commanded Your servant Moses *(the Ordinances of the Law are frequently summed up under these three headings [Deut. 5:31; 6:1; 11:1])*.

8 Remember, I beseech You, the Word that You commanded Your servant Moses, saying, If you transgress, I will scatter you abroad among the nations *(this is not a quotation of a particular Verse, but a reference to the general sense of various Passages; in fact, many of the sacred historians habitually referred to the older Scriptures in this way, quoting the spirit of the text rather than the letter)*:

9 But if you turn unto Me, and keep My Commandments, and do them; though there were of you cast out unto the uttermost part of the Heaven, yet will I gather them from thence, and will bring them unto the place that I have chosen to set My Name there *(national Repentance is the one great condition of national Restoration)*.

10 Now these are Your servants and Your people, whom You have redeemed by Your great power, and by Your strong hand *(the reference is especially to the deliverance from Egypt)*.

11 O LORD, I beseech You, let now Your ear be attentive to the prayer of Your servant *(Nehemiah)*, and to the prayer of Your servants, who desire to fear Your name: and prosper, I pray You, Your servant this day, and grant him mercy in the sight of this man *(Artaxerxes)*. For I was the king's cupbearer *(not his sole cupbearer, but one of many; therefore, he had access to the king)*.

CHAPTER 2
(445 B.C.)
NEHEMIAH'S REQUEST OF
KING ARTAXERXES

AND it came to pass in the month Nisan *(April)*, in the twentieth year of Artaxerxes

the king, that wine was before him: and I took up the wine, and gave it unto the king. Now I had not been beforetime sad in his presence *(hitherto I had always worn a cheerful countenance before him — now it was otherwise — my sorrow showed itself despite me — Pulpit).*

2 Wherefore the king said unto me, Why is your countenance sad, seeing you are not sick? this is nothing else but sorrow of heart. Then I was very sore afraid *(those who showed sorrow in the presence of the king were liable to be executed; however, Artaxerxes Longimanus feels compassion, and wishes to assuage the grief of his servant),*

3 And said unto the king, Let the king live for ever: why should not my countenance be sad, when the city, the place of my fathers' sepulchres, lies waste, and the gates thereof are consumed with fire? *(Nehemiah, though holding a high position in the imperial court, did not set his heart upon the glorious city of Shushan, but on the ruined city of Jerusalem. He loved it and its people because both belonged to God.)*

4 Then the king said unto me, For what do you make request? So I prayed to the God of Heaven *(upon the king asking this question, it seems that Nehemiah prayed silently and quickly for the Lord to be with him in making his request; how so must we as well emulate his example!).*

5 And I said unto the king, If it please the king, and if your servant have found favour in your sight, that you would send me unto Judah, unto the city of my fathers' sepulchres, that I may build it *(speaking of the wall and the gates; it was quite a request!).*

6 And the king said unto me, (the queen also sitting by him,) For how long shall your journey be? and when will you return? So it pleased the king to send me; and I set him a time *(the queen's name was "Damaspia"; Nehemiah probably mentioned some such time as a year or two years; he stayed away, however, as he tells us [5:14], twelve years, obtaining no doubt from time to time an extension of his leave).*

7 Moreover I said unto the king, If it please the king, let letters be given me to the governors beyond the river, that they may convey me over till I come into Judah;

8 And a letter unto Asaph the keeper of the king's forest, that he may give me timber to make beams for the gates of the palace which appertain to the house *(Temple)*, and for the wall of the city, and for the house that I shall enter into *(the governor's residence)*. And the king granted me, according to the good hand of my God upon me.

NEHEMIAH GOES FROM BABYLON TO JERUSALEM

9 Then I came to the governors beyond the river, and gave them the king's letters. Now the king had sent captains of the army and horsemen with me.

10 When Sanballat the Horonite and Tobiah the servant, the Ammonite, heard of it, it grieved them exceedingly that there was come a man to seek the welfare of the Children of Israel *(all who venture, in any way, to forward the interests of the Kingdom of Heaven are sure to meet with opposition from the world, and discouragement from the Church; Nehemiah found it to be so; I speak of the opposition offered by Sanballat and his friends, and the discouragement by the men of Judah [4:10; 6:10-19]).*

11 So I came to Jerusalem, and was there three days *(after the long journey, three days of rest).*

INSPECTING THE WALLS

12 And I arose in the night, I and some few men with me; neither told I any man what my God had put in my heart to do at Jerusalem: neither was there any beast with me, save the beast that I rode upon *(all the arrangements are made to avoid notice).*

13 And I went out by night by the gate of the valley, even before the dragon well *(the pool of Siloam)*, and to the dung port, and viewed the walls of Jerusalem, which were broken down, and the gates thereof were consumed with fire.

14 Then I went on to the gate of the fountain, and to the king's pool: but there was no place for the beast that was under me to pass.

15 Then went I up in the night by the brook, and viewed the wall, and turned back, and entered by the gate of the valley, and so returned.

16 And the rulers knew not whither I went, or what I did; neither had I as yet told it to the Jews, nor to the Priests, nor to the nobles, nor to the rulers, nor to the rest who did the work.

WORK BEGUN ON THE WALLS OF JERUSALEM

17 Then said I unto them, You see the distress that we are in, how Jerusalem lies waste, and the gates thereof are burned with fire:

come, and let us build up the wall of Jerusalem, that we be no more a reproach (*sadly, the walls of the Church, in many cases, are broken down; I speak of the wall of prayer, the wall of strict adherence to the Scriptures and, above all, the wall of Faith in Christ and what He has done for us at the Cross; as Jerusalem was then a reproach, I'm concerned that the Church presently falls into the same category, at least in the Eyes of God [Rev. 3:14-22]*).

18 Then I told them of the hand of my God which was good upon me; as also the king's words that he had spoken unto me. And they said, Let us rise up and build. So they strengthened their hands for this good work (*the original Text says, "And they strengthened their hands for good"; is the Holy Spirit presently saying to us, "Let us rise up and build," as it concerns the great Work of God?*).

RIDICULE BY THEIR ENEMIES

19 But when Sanballat the Horonite, and Tobiah the servant, the Ammonite, and Geshem the Arabian, heard it, they laughed us to scorn, and despised us, and said, What is this thing that you do? will you rebel against the king? (*The world, of which Sanballat was a type, continues to laugh to scorn those who truly serve God.*)

20 Then answered I them, and said unto them, The God of Heaven, He will prosper us; therefore we His servants will arise and build: but you have no portion, nor right, nor memorial, in Jerusalem (*Nehemiah claims a Divine sanction for his proceedings; he avoids opposition by concealment as long as he can; but, when opposition nevertheless appears, he meets it with defiance; the world has no part nor place in the Work of God!*).

CHAPTER 3
(445 B.C.)
THE BUILDERS OF THE WALLS
AND GATES

T HEN Eliashib the High Priest rose up with his brethren the Priests, and they built the sheep gate; they sanctified it, and set up the doors of it; even unto the tower of Meah they sanctified it, unto the tower of Hananeel (*it was called the "Sheep Gate," because through it entered the sheep destined for Sacrifice; this Jerusalem had twelve gates; so shall the future city*).

2 And next unto him built the men of Jericho. And next to them built Zaccur the son of Imri.

3 But the fish gate did the sons of Hassenaah build, who also laid the beams thereof, and set up the doors thereof, the locks thereof, and the bars thereof.

4 And next unto them repaired Meremoth the son of Urijah, the son of Koz. And next unto them repaired Meshullam the son of Berechiah, the son of Meshezabeel. And next unto them repaired Zadok the son of Baana.

5 And next unto them the Tekoites repaired; but their nobles put not their necks to the work of their LORD. (*This Chapter may be regarded as a specimen page from God's Book of remembrance. It is, therefore, to be noted that Meremoth appears twice [Vss. 4, 21], and that the nobles did not put their necks to the work. Had these nobles known that their dereliction of duty would be read by millions down through the ages, they possibly would have done differently. We should look at ourselves in this same light.*)

6 Moreover the old gate repaired Jehoiada the son of Paseah, and Meshullam the son of Besodeiah; they laid the beams thereof, and set up the doors thereof, and the locks thereof, and the bars thereof.

7 And next unto them repaired Melatiah the Gibeonite, and Jadon the Meronothite, the men of Gibeon, and of Mizpah, unto the throne of the governor on this side the river.

8 Next unto him repaired Uzziel the son of Harhaiah, of the goldsmiths. Next unto him also repaired Hananiah the son of one of the apothecaries, and they fortified Jerusalem unto the broad wall.

9 And next unto them repaired Rephaiah the son of Hur, the ruler of the half part of Jerusalem.

10 And next unto them repaired Jedaiah the son of Harumaph, even over against his house. And next unto him repaired Hattush the son of Hashabniah.

11 Malchijah the son of Harim, and Hashub the son of Pahath-moab, repaired the other piece, and the tower of the furnaces.

12 And next unto him repaired Shallum the son of Halohesh, the ruler of the half part of Jerusalem, he and his daughters (*these young ladies had a share in this great Work for God as well*).

13 The valley gate repaired Hanun, and the inhabitants of Zanoah; they built it, and set up

the doors thereof, the locks thereof, and the bars thereof, and a thousand cubits on the wall unto the dung gate.

14 But the dung gate repaired Malchiah the son of Rechab, the ruler of part of Beth-haccerem; he built it, and set up the doors thereof, the locks thereof, and the bars thereof.

15 But the gate of the fountain repaired Shallun the son of Col-hozeh, the ruler of part of Mizpah; he built it, and covered it, and set up the doors thereof, the locks thereof, and the bars thereof, and the wall of the pool of Siloah by the king's garden, and unto the stairs that go down from the city of David.

16 After him repaired Nehemiah the son of Azbuk, the ruler of the half part of Beth-zur, unto the place over against the sepulchres of David, and to the pool that was made, and unto the house of the mighty.

17 After him repaired the Levites, Rehum the son of Bani. Next unto him repaired Hashabiah, the ruler of the half part of Keilah, in his part.

18 After him repaired their brethren, Bavai the son of Henadad, the ruler of the half part of Keilah.

19 And next to him repaired Ezer the son of Jeshua, the ruler of Mizpah, another piece over against the going up to the armoury at the turning of the wall.

20 After him Baruch the son of Zabbai earnestly repaired the other piece, from the turning of the wall unto the door of the house of Eliashib the High Priest *(Baruch, to his undying fame, is recorded to have repaired "earnestly"; little did this man think, as he zealously labored amid the sneers and taunts of the enemy, that 2,500 years later millions of men and women would read about him).*

21 After him repaired Meremoth the son of Urijah the son of Koz another piece, from the door of the house of Eliashib even to the end of the house of Eliashib.

22 And after him repaired the Priests, the men of the plain.

23 After him repaired Benjamin and Hashub over against their house. After him repaired Azariah the son of Maaseiah the son of Ananiah by his house.

24 After him repaired Binnui the son of Henadad another piece, from the house of Azariah unto the turning of the wall, even unto the corner.

25 Palal the son of Uzai, over against the turning of the wall, and the tower which lies out from the king's high house, that was by the court of the prison. After him Pedaiah the son of Parosh.

26 Moreover the Nethinims dwelt in Ophel, unto the place over against the water gate toward the east, and the tower that lies out.

27 After them the Tekoites repaired another piece, over against the great tower that lies out, even unto the wall of Ophel.

28 From above the horse gate repaired the Priests, every one over against his house.

29 After them repaired Zadok the son of Immer over against his house. After him repaired also Shemaiah the son of Shechaniah, the keeper of the east gate.

30 After him repaired Hananiah the son of Shelemiah, and Hanun the sixth son of Zalaph, Meshullam the son of Berechiah over against his chamber.

31 After him repaired Malchiah the goldsmith's son unto the place of the Nethinims, and of the merchants, over against the gate Miphkad, and to the going up of the corner.

32 And between the going up of the corner unto the sheep gate repaired the goldsmiths and the merchants. *(As is obvious, and as it regards all of these people and their particular occupations, each one contributed his part, showing that the Work of God needs all people from all walks of life.)*

CHAPTER 4
(445 B.C.)
NEHEMIAH OPPOSED AND RIDICULED

BUT it came to pass, that when Sanballat heard that we built the wall, he was wroth, and took great indignation, and mocked the Jews. *(Contempt and violence from the enemy and cowardice from the men of Judah [Vss. 3, 8, 10, 12] were defeated by praying and watching [Vss. 4-5, 9]. As stated, all Christian workers must expect opposition from the world and discouragement from the Church; but prayer and watchfulness always bring victory.)*

2 And he spoke before his brethren and the army of Samaria, and said, What do these feeble Jews? will they fortify themselves? will they sacrifice? will they make an end in a day? will they revive the stones out of the heaps of the rubbish which are burned? *(And that's exactly what they did! They took the "burnt stones" and built the wall. There are millions of "burnt stones" in Christendom, whom the Devil has made believe that they can no longer*

be used in the Work of God. These Passages prove the contrary!)

3 Now Tobiah the Ammonite was by him, and he said, Even that which they build, if a fox go up, he shall even break down their stone wall.

PRAYER AND WORK IN THE FACE OF CONTINUED OPPOSITION

4 Hear, O our God; for we are despised: and turn their reproach upon their own head, and give them for a prey in the land of captivity:

5 And cover not their iniquity, and let not their sin be blotted out from before You: for they have provoked You to anger before the builders. *(Some have criticized Nehemiah for his prayer. However, it is perfectly Scriptural. These were individuals who were attempting to destroy the Work of God. In fact, the prayer of Nehemiah, if anything, was restrained.)*

6 So built we the wall; and all the wall was joined together unto the half thereof: for the people had a mind to work *(it seemed that insult and gibe stimulated them rather than daunted them)*.

7 But it came to pass, that when Sanballat, and Tobiah, and the Arabians, and the Ammonites, and the Ashdodites, heard that the walls of Jerusalem were made up, and that the breaches began to be stopped, then they were very wroth,

8 And conspired all of them together to come and to fight against Jerusalem, and to hinder it *(as well, as the Lord carefully noted the labor expended by individual Jews, He also notes carefully the taunts and threats of the adversaries; no man, at least in his right mind, wants to be crossways with the Lord!)*.

9 Nevertheless we made our prayer unto our God, and set a watch against them day and night, because of them *("watch and pray" [Mat. 26:41])*.

10 And Judah said, The strength of the bearers of burdens is decayed, and there is much rubbish; so that we are not able to build the wall *(it is never easy to clean up the rubbish, i.e., "to oppose false doctrine"; consequently, there are few who perform this task)*.

11 And our adversaries said, They shall not know, neither see, till we come in the midst among them, and slay them, and cause the work to cease.

12 And it came to pass, that when the Jews which dwelt by them came, they said unto us ten times, From all places whence you shall return unto us they will be upon you *(these Jews from other parts of Judah came repeatedly to Jerusalem to warn Nehemiah of the enemy's designs)*.

13 Therefore set I in the lower places behind the wall, and on the higher places, I even set the people after their families with their swords, their spears, and their bows.

14 And I looked, and rose up, and said unto the nobles, and to the rulers, and to the rest of the people, Be not ye afraid of them: remember the LORD, which is great and terrible, and fight for your brethren, your sons, and your daughters, your wives, and your houses *(spiritually speaking, all Believers must "fight" for the Salvation of their loved ones; this fight is "the good fight of Faith" [I Tim. 6:12])*.

15 And it came to pass, when our enemies heard that it was known unto us, and God had brought their counsel to nought, that we returned all of us to the wall, every one unto his work *(Nehemiah divided the people into two bodies, one of which labored at the wall, while the other kept guard fully armed)*.

16 And it came to pass from that time forth, that the half of my servants wrought in the work, and the other half of them held both the spears, the shields, and the bows, and the habergeons; and the rulers were behind all the house of Judah *(in order to direct the battle if such occurred)*.

17 They which built on the wall, and they who bore burdens, with those who laded, every one with one of his hands wrought in the work, and with the other hand held a weapon.

18 For the builders, every one had his sword girded by his side, and so built. And he who sounded the trumpet was by me *(whether a "builder" or a "burden-bearer," the Believer is in equal danger, and cannot dispense with the "Sword of the Spirit")*.

19 And I said unto the nobles, and to the rulers, and to the rest of the people, The work is great and large, and we are separated upon the wall, one far from another.

20 In what place therefore you hear the sound of the trumpet, resort ye thither unto us: our God shall fight for us *(Justification is the Holy Spirit fighting "for" us, while Sanctification is the Holy Spirit fighting "in" us!)*.

21 So we laboured in the work: and half of them held the spears from the rising of the morning till the stars appeared.

22 Likewise at the same time said I unto the

people, Let every one with his servant lodge within Jerusalem, that in the night they may be a guard to us, and labour on the day.

23 So neither I, nor my brethren, nor my servants, nor the men of the guard which followed me, none of us put off our clothes, saving that every one put them off for washing. *(As is obvious, Nehemiah meant to get this work done. He was no doubt moved upon by the Holy Spirit in all of this. Every Believer should be as conscientious for the Work of God, whatever task the Lord has assigned to us, as was Nehemiah!)*

CHAPTER 5
(445 B.C.)
OPPRESSION

AND there was a great cry of the people and of their wives against their brethren the Jews *(the reason for this "cry" was because of rich Jews loaning money to poor Jews at a high interest rate, when they were not supposed to charge any interest at all, as it regarded fellow Jews [Lev. 25:35-38]; as a result, many were going into bondage, serving in a sense as slaves, to pay off the debt).*

2 For there were who said, We, our sons, and our daughters, are many *(many poor)*: therefore we take up corn for them, that we may eat, and live *(food for which they did not have money to purchase).*

3 Some also there were who said, We have mortgaged our lands, vineyards, and houses, that we might buy corn, because of the dearth *(drought; inclement weather conditions were normally caused by Israel not properly obeying the Word of God).*

4 There were also who said, We have borrowed money for the king's tribute, and that upon our lands and vineyards *(to pay taxes to the Persians, of which they were a vassal State).*

5 Yet now our flesh is as the flesh of our brethren, our children as their children: and, lo, we bring into bondage our sons and our daughters to be servants, and some of our daughters are brought unto bondage already: neither is it in our power to redeem them; for other men have our lands and vineyards *(due to not being able to pay off the loans, their sons and daughters had to pay off the debts by working for the people to whom money was owed; as stated, in a sense, this was a form of slavery; so they were appealing to Nehemiah for help).*

THE PAYMENT OF INTEREST ABOLISHED

6 And I was very angry when I heard their cry and these words *(speaks of Nehemiah; certain ones were breaking the Law of God, which said, "You shall not oppress one another" [Lev. 25:14-19]).*

7 Then I consulted with myself *(my heart told me that what was being done was wrong)*, and I rebuked the nobles, and the rulers, and said unto them, You exact usury *(ruinous interest)*, every one of his brother. And I set a great assembly against them *(the rich Jews paid no heed to Nehemiah, when he demanded a change; therefore, he called a "great assembly," in order to discuss the situation with all the people).*

8 And I said unto them, We after our ability have redeemed our brethren the Jews, which were sold unto the heathen; and will you even sell your brethren? or shall they be sold unto us? Then held they their peace, and found nothing to answer *(the Lord had delivered Israel from Persian bondage, and now some of the rich Jews were putting some of the people back into bondage; when Nehemiah put it in this manner, the guilty parties had no answer).*

9 Also I said, It is not good that ye do: ought ye not to walk in the fear of our God because of the reproach of the heathen our enemies? *(To silence the nobles was not enough. To shame them was not enough. What was wanted was to persuade them. He did so by calling to account the potential wrath of God upon such actions.)*

10 I likewise, and my brethren, and my servants, might exact of them money and corn: I pray you, let us leave off this usury *(you who are able should loan your poorer brethren money without interest; and be lenient with their repayment).*

11 Restore, I pray you, to them, even this day, their lands, their vineyards, their oliveyards, and their houses, also the hundredth part of the money, and of the corn, the wine, and the oil, that you exact of them. *(Give back the interest that you have illegally taken. As well, give them back their lands and houses so that they might make a living. And let them repay you as they can. This is God's Way.*

All of this was meant to serve as a type of what the Lord has done for us — forgiven us all things, meaning that we should show leniency and mercy to others likewise. And yet, there is no hint here in the Text of the condoning of laziness. As Paul said, "If they don't work, they don't eat" [II Thess. 3:10].)

12 Then said they, We will restore them, and will require nothing of them; so will we do as you say. Then I called the Priests, and took an oath of them, that they should do according to this promise (*the nobles agreed to restore all*).

13 Also I shook my lap (*a Jewish custom*), and said, So God shake out every man from his house, and from his labour, who performs not this promise, even thus be he shaken out, and emptied (*in a sense, Nehemiah called a curse upon the nobles who would fail to obey this promise*). And all the congregation said, Amen, and praised the LORD. And the people did according to this promise (*the nobles obeyed!*).

NEHEMIAH'S UNSELFISHNESS AND LEADERSHIP

14 Moreover from the time that I was appointed to be their governor in the land of Judah, from the twentieth year even unto the two and thirtieth year of Artaxerxes the king, that is, twelve years, I and my brethren have not eaten the bread of the governor (*"I, and those who serve under me in the realm of government, have not taxed you at all for our upkeep," even though he was entitled to do so; in other words, what he was asking the nobles to do, he had done, and was doing, himself*).

15 But the former governors who had been before me were chargeable unto the people, and had taken of them bread and wine, beside forty shekels of silver; yes, even their servants bore rule over the people: but so did not I, because of the fear of God (*Nehemiah wasn't condemning these former governors; only two are known, Zerubbabel and Ezra, although there may have been others; he is merely stating what the Lord wanted him personally to do; Jesus said we must "render to Caesar the things which are Caesar's, and to God that which belongs to God" [Mk. 12:17]*).

16 Yea, also I continued in the work of this wall, neither bought we any land: and all my servants were gathered thither unto the work (*I have donated my time and services to build up Israel, not to do otherwise*).

17 Moreover there were at my table an hundred and fifty of the Jews and rulers, beside those who came unto us from among the heathen who are about us (*he set a public table daily for over 150 people who were serving in government, and paid for it himself*).

18 Now that which was prepared for me daily was one ox and six choice sheep; also

fowls were prepared for me; and once in ten days store of all sorts of wine: yet for all this required not I the bread of the governor, because the bondage was heavy upon this people (*as stated, even though he had the power to tax the people to pay for all of this, he did nothing of the sort*).

19 Think upon me, my God, for good, according to all that I have done for this people (*and, to be sure, the Lord will always think upon such for good*).

CHAPTER 6
(445 B.C.)

CONTINUED OPPOSITION BY SANBALLAT, TOBIAH, AND GESHEM

NOW it came to pass, when Sanballat and Tobiah, and Geshem the Arabian, and the rest of our enemies, heard that I had built the wall, and that there was no breach left therein; (though at that time I had not set up the doors upon the gates;)

2 That Sanballat and Geshem sent unto me, saying, Come, let us meet together in some one of the villages in the plain of Ono. But they thought to do me mischief (*the Hebrew Text bears it out that they were plotting to murder Nehemiah*).

3 And I sent messengers unto them, saying, I am doing a great work, so that I cannot come down: why should the work cease, while I leave it, and come down to you? (*The Lord evidently informed Nehemiah of this snare of treachery.*)

4 Yet they sent unto me four times after this sort; and I answered them after the same manner.

5 Then sent Sanballat his servant unto me in like manner the fifth time with an open letter in his hand (*in that culture, to have addressed an "open letter" to a state Governor was a designed insult*);

6 Wherein was written, It is reported among the heathen, and Gashmu said it, that you and the Jews think to rebel: for which cause you build the wall, that you may be their king, according to these words (*all of this was a lie!*).

7 And you have also appointed Prophets to preach of you at Jerusalem, saying, There is a king in Judah: and now shall it be reported to the king according to these words. Come now therefore, and let us take counsel together (*none of that happened, or else a Prophecy was*

misinterpreted by this heathen).

8 Then I sent unto him, saying, There are no such things done as you say, but you feign them out of your own heart.

9 For they all made us afraid *(sought to make us afraid)*, saying, Their hands shall be weakened from the work, that it be not done. Now therefore, O God, strengthen my hands *(which the Lord did).*

10 Afterward I came unto the house of Shemaiah the son of Delaiah the son of Mehetabeel, who was shut up; and he said, Let us meet together in the House of God, within the Temple, and let us shut the doors of the Temple: for they will come to slay you; yea, in the night will they come to slay you *(the Divine Word forbade Nehemiah, being a prince of the Tribe of Judah, and not a Priest of the Tribe of Levi, to enter the Temple; thus was Shemaiah shown to be a false Prophet; his message contradicted the Bible; every other professed Prophet should be judged accordingly; is what is being said in accordance with the Bible?).*

11 And I said, Should such a man as I flee? and who is there, that, being as I am, would go into the Temple to save his life? I will not go in *(I will not even go into the Temple to save my life, because I, not being a Levite, would be disobeying the Word of God to do so).*

12 And, lo, I perceived that God had not sent him *(this Jew was a false prophet)*; but that he pronounced this prophecy against me: for Tobiah and Sanballat had hired him *(Nehemiah evidently found this out a short time later).*

13 Therefore was he hired, that I should be afraid, and do so, and sin, and that they might have matter for an evil report, that they might reproach me *(unfortunately, even as we have seen, God's people joined with the world in attempting to destroy the man of God; sadly, this is not the only time this has happened!).*

14 My God, think Thou upon Tobiah and Sanballat according to these their works, and on the prophetess Noadiah, and the rest of the prophets, that would have put me in fear. *(Evidently, quite a few of the prophets, along with this particular woman, had joined the world against Nehemiah. In fact, the far greater harm always comes from inside the Church. But let it always be understood: if dates and times are put on a prophecy and it doesn't come to pass, or else what is being said is not according to the Word of God, it should be known and understood that those who give forth such are false prophets. In these modern times, the world abounds with*

false prophets, and the Church seems to be disinclined to call anyone to account.)

THE WALLS AND GATES OF JERUSALEM FINISHED

15 So the wall was finished in the twenty and fifth day of the month Elul *(September)*, in fifty and two days.

16 And it came to pass, that when all our enemies heard thereof, and all the heathen who were about us saw these things, they were much cast down in their own eyes: for they perceived that this work was wrought of our God *(even many of the enemies of Nehemiah and of Israel had to admit that the Lord was helping Israel).*

17 Moreover in those days the nobles of Judah sent many letters unto Tobiah, and the letters of Tobiah came unto them *(as stated, it seems that many of the powerful men in Israel were friends of Sanballat and Tobiah).*

18 For there were many in Judah sworn unto him, because he was the son in law of Shechaniah the son of Arah; and his son Johanan had taken the daughter of Meshullam the son of Berechiah. *(Why in the world would some of these Jews throw in their lot with these heathen, who were trying to stop the work? Regrettably, it hasn't changed from then until now. Many in the Church oppose the true Work of God!)*

19 Also they reported his good deeds before me, and uttered my words to him. And Tobiah sent letters to put me in fear. *(The Holy Spirit carefully brings all of this out, so that future Believers will not make the same mistake of siding with those who seek to hinder the Work of God. But regrettably, few heed!)*

CHAPTER 7
(445 B.C.)

NEHEMIAH APPOINTS NEW RULERS: HANANI AND HANANIAH

NOW it came to pass, when the wall was built, and I had set up the doors, and the porters and the singers and the Levites were appointed *(Nehemiah is preparing things, because he is about to leave and go back to Persia).*

2 That I gave my brother Hanani *(his personal blood brother)*, and Hanani the ruler of the palace, charge over Jerusalem: for he was a faithful man, and feared God above many *(they were given equal charge, with one man over one-half of Jerusalem and the other man over the other*

half; the reason was their fear and love for God).

3 And I said unto them, Let not the gates of Jerusalem be opened until the sun be hot; and while they stand by, let them shut the doors, and bar them: and appoint watches of the inhabitants of Jerusalem, every one in his watch, and every one to be over against his house *(he set up a systemized order regarding protection and business)*.

4 Now the city was large and great: but the people were few therein, and the houses were not built *(over a hundred years before, it had been destroyed by Nebuchadnezzar; there were still many areas in the city which had not been rebuilt)*.

LIST OF THE RETURNED EXILES

5 And my God put into my heart to gather together the nobles, and the rulers, and the people, that they might be reckoned by genealogy. And I found a register of the genealogy of them which came up at the first, and found written therein *(this pertains to the genealogy of Ezra, Chpt. 8)*,

6 These are the children of the province, who went up out of the captivity, of those that had been carried away, whom Nebuchadnezzar the king of Babylon had carried away, and came again to Jerusalem and to Judah, every one unto his city;

7 Who came with Zerubbabel, Jeshua, Nehemiah, Azariah, Raamiah, Nahamani, Mordecai, Bilshan, Mispereth, Bigvai, Nehum, Baanah. The number, I say, of the men of the people of Israel was this;

8 The children of Parosh, two thousand an hundred seventy and two.

9 The children of Shephatiah, three hundred seventy and two.

10 The children of Arah, six hundred fifty and two.

11 The children of Pahath-moab, of the children of Jeshua and Joab, two thousand and eight hundred and eighteen.

12 The children of Elam, a thousand two hundred fifty and four.

13 The children of Zattu, eight hundred forty and five.

14 The children of Zaccai, seven hundred and threescore.

15 The children of Binnui, six hundred forty and eight.

16 The children of Bebai, six hundred twenty and eight.

17 The children of Azgad, two thousand three hundred twenty and two.

18 The children of Adonikam, six hundred threescore and seven.

19 The children of Bigvai, two thousand threescore and seven.

20 The children of Adin, six hundred fifty and five.

21 The children of Ater of Hezekiah, ninety and eight.

22 The children of Hashum, three hundred twenty and eight.

23 The children of Bezai, three hundred twenty and four.

24 The children of Hariph, an hundred and twelve.

25 The children of Gibeon, ninety and five.

26 The men of Beth-lehem and Netophah, an hundred fourscore and eight.

27 The men of Anathoth, an hundred twenty and eight.

28 The men of Beth-azmaveth, forty and two.

29 The men of Kirjath-jearim, Chephirah, and Beeroth, seven hundred forty and three.

30 The men of Ramah and Gaba, six hundred twenty and one.

31 The men of Michmas, an hundred and twenty and two.

32 The men of Beth-el and Ai, an hundred and twenty and three.

33 The men of the other Nebo, fifty and two.

34 The children of the other Elam, a thousand two hundred fifty and four.

35 The children of Harim, three hundred and twenty.

36 The children of Jericho, three hundred forty and five.

37 The children of Lod, Hadid, and Ono, seven hundred twenty and one.

38 The children of Senaah, three thousand nine hundred and thirty.

39 The Priests: the children of Jedaiah, of the house of Jeshua, nine hundred seventy and three.

40 The children of Immer, a thousand fifty and two.

41 The children of Pashur, a thousand two hundred forty and seven.

42 The children of Harim, a thousand the seventeen.

43 The Levites: the children of Jeshua, of Kadmiel, and of the children of Hodevah, seventy and four.

44 The singers: the children of Asaph, an hundred forty and eight.

45 The porters: the children of Shallum,

the children of Ater, the children of Talmon, the children of Akkub, the children of Hatita, the children of Shobai, and hundred thirty and eight.

46 The Nethinims: the children of Ziha, the children of Hashupha, the children of Tabbaoth,

47 The children of Keros, the children of Sia, the children of Padon,

48 The children of Lebana, the children of Hagaba, the children of Shalmai,

49 The children of Hanan, the children of Giddel, the children of Gahar,

50 The children of Reaiah, the children of Rezin, the children of Nekoda,

51 The children of Gazzam, the children of Uzza, the children of Phaseah,

52 The children of Besai, the children of Meunim, the children of Nephishesim,

53 The children of Bakbuk, the children of Hakupha, the children of Harhur,

54 The children of Bazlith, the children of Mehida, the children of Harsha,

55 The children of Barkos, the children of Sisera, the children of Tamah,

56 The children of Neziah, the children of Hatipha.

57 The children of Solomon's servants: the children of Sotai, the children of Sophereth, the children of Perida,

58 The children of Jaala, the children of Darkon, the children of Giddel,

59 The children of Shephatiah, the children of Hattil, the children of Pochereth of Zebaim, the children of Amon.

60 All the Nethinims, and the children of Solomon's servants, were three hundred ninety and two.

THE ONES WHO COULDN'T PROVE THEIR GENEALOGY

61 And these were they which went up also from Tel-melah, Tel-haresha, Cherub, Addon, and Immer: but they could not show their father's house, nor their seed, whether they were of Israel.

62 The children of Delaiah, the children of Tobiah, the children of Nekoda, six hundred forty and two.

63 And of the Priests: the children of Habaiah, the children of Koz, the children of Barzillai, which took one of the daughters of Barzillai the Gileadite to wife, and was called after their name.

64 These sought their register among those that were reckoned by genealogy, but it was not found: therefore were they, as polluted, put from the Priesthood.

65 And the Tirshatha *(Governor)* said unto them, that they should not eat of the most holy things *(speaking of the Priests who had been disallowed because of not being able to prove their genealogy)*, till there stood up a Priest with Urim and Thummim *(which could prove that they were actually Jews; there is no record that the "Urim and Thummim" were ever brought back; we are not told in Scripture as to exactly what they were; it is believed that they were two in number, possibly two small stones, with the word "yes" on one, and the word "no" on the other; they were carried behind the Breastplate of the High Priest, and were used to divine the Will of God [Ex. 28:30; Lev. 8:8; Num. 27:21])*.

66 The whole congregation together was forty and two thousand three hundred and threescore,

67 Beside their manservants and their maidservants, of whom there were seven thousand three hundred thirty and seven: and they had two hundred forty and five singing women.

68 Their horses, seven hundred thirty and six: their mules, two hundred forty and five:

69 Their camels, four hundred thirty and five: six thousand seven hundred and twenty asses.

70 And some of the chief of the fathers gave unto the work. The Tirshatha gave to the treasure of thousand drams of gold, fifty basons, five hundred and thirty Priests' garments.

71 And some of the chief of the fathers gave to the treasure of the work twenty thousand drams of gold, and two thousand and two hundred pound of silver.

72 And that which the rest of the people gave was twenty thousand drams of gold, and two thousand pound of silver, and threescore and seven Priests' garments.

73 So the Priests, and the Levites, and the porters, and the singers, and some of the people, and the Nethinims, and all Israel, dwelt in their cities; and when the seventh month came, the children of Israel were in their cities.

CHAPTER 8
(445 B.C.)
EZRA READS AND EXPLAINS THE WORD OF GOD

A ND all the people gathered themselves together as one man into the street that was

before the water gate; and they spoke unto Ezra the Scribe to bring the Book of the Law of Moses, which the LORD had commanded to Israel. *(Blessed people! They are asking for instruction from the Bible, and they have an instinctive feeling that to hear God's Word will help them. Most definitely it did, and most definitely it will!)*

2 And Ezra the Priest brought the Law before the congregation both of men and women, and all who could hear with understanding *(even little children)*, upon the first day of the seventh month *(our October, the time then of the Feast of Tabernacles)*.

3 And he read therein before the street that was before the water gate from the morning until midday *(about 6 hours)*, before the men and the women, and those who could understand; and the ears of all the people were attentive unto the Book of the Law *(the meaning is: "The ears of all the people were to the Book," fixed on that, and on nothing else)*.

4 And Ezra the Scribe stood upon a pulpit of wood, which they had made for the purpose; and beside him stood Mattithiah, and Shema, and Anaiah, and Urijah, and Hilkiah, and Maaseiah, on his right hand; and on his left hand, Pedaiah, and Mishael, and Malchiah, and Hashum, and Hashbadana, Zechariah, and Meshullam *(these men stood with Ezra, evidently, to support him; how many presently are standing with the man of God?)*.

5 And Ezra opened the Book in the sight of all the people; (for he was above all the people *[standing on an upraised platform]*;) and when he opened it, all the people stood up *(the Jews commonly sat to hear and stood up to pray; but in hearing they occasionally stood up to do great honor to the person or the occasion; it is not to be supposed that they stood during the whole of the six hours that Ezra's reading lasted)*:

6 And Ezra blessed the LORD, the great God. And all the people answered, Amen, Amen, with lifting up their hands: and they bowed their heads, and worshipped the LORD with their faces to the ground *(very similar to modern worship, and we speak of that which is truly of the Spirit)*.

7 Also Jeshua, and Bani, and Sherebiah, Jamin, Akkub, Shabbethai, Hodijah, Maaseiah, Kelita, Azariah, Jozabad, Hanan, Pelaiah, and the Levites, caused the people to understand the Law *(expounded it during pauses in the reading)*: and the people stood in their place *(this doesn't mean that the people stood all of this time, but that they kept their place all of this time, whatever their posture)*.

8 So they read in the Book in the Law of God distinctly, and gave the sense, and caused them to understand the reading *(identically as true Preachers of the Gospel are to do presently; this is expository teaching, the only kind which will help people to understand the Word; it simply means that the Scripture is read and then explained)*.

9 And Nehemiah, which is the Tirshatha *(Governor)*, and Ezra the Priest the Scribe *(who wrote the Book of Ezra)*, and the Levites who taught the people, said unto all the people, This day is holy unto the LORD your God; mourn not, nor weep. For all the people wept, when they heard the Words of the Law *(people wept, for they recognized how deeply they had sinned against so loving a God; it was hearing the Words of the Book that awoke them to this consciousness; however, the weeping, which was contrition for sin, now occasions joy, even as it always does)*.

10 Then he said unto them, Go your way, eat the fat, and drink the sweet *(in other words, rejoice in the Lord)*, and send portions unto them for whom nothing is prepared *(share with those who have nothing)*: for this day is holy unto our LORD: neither be ye sorry *(the Lord has forgiven you, so there is no more need to be sorry)*; for the Joy of the LORD is your strength. *(They were now encouraged to rejoice, because God was rejoicing in them. This was the Joy that filled God's heart because of their obedience, which meant both strength and safety to them. If we presently follow their example, we too will experience the Joy of the Lord, and it will be our strength. Remember, this is God's Joy, which we are privileged to share.)*

11 So the Levites stilled all the people, saying, Hold your peace, for the day is holy; neither be ye grieved.

12 And all the people went their way to eat, and to drink, and to send portions, and to make great mirth, because they had understood the Words that were declared unto them *("great rejoicing")*.

THE FEAST OF TABERNACLES RESTORED

13 And on the second day were gathered together the chief of the fathers of all the people, the Priests, and the Levites, unto Ezra the Scribe, even to understand the Words of the Law *(only the leaders gathered on this day, all*

in order to study further the Word of God).

14 And they found written in the Law which the LORD had commanded by Moses, that the Children of Israel should dwell in booths in the Feast of the seventh month (Feast of Tabernacles).

15 And that they should publish and proclaim in all their cities, and in Jerusalem, saying, Go forth unto the mount, and fetch olive branches, and pine branches, and myrtle branches, and palm branches, and branches of thick trees, to make booths, as it is written.

16 So the people went forth, and brought them, and made themselves booths, every one upon the roof of his house (roofs are flat in that part of the world), and in their courts, and in the courts of the House of God, and in the street of the water gate, and in the street of the gate of Ephraim (those who lived away from Jerusalem made themselves booths in these particular places).

17 And all the congregation of them who were come again out of the captivity made booths, and sat under the booths: for since the days of Jeshua (Joshua) the son of Nun unto that day had not the Children of Israel done so. And there was very great gladness (it is not to be understood that there had been no previous compliance of this Feast, but only that there had been no such joy and general celebration of the Festival; it is the "very great gladness" that is especially insisted upon — Pulpit).

18 Also day by day, from the first day unto the last day, he read in the Book of the Law of God. And they kept the Feast seven days; and on the eighth day was a solemn assembly, according unto the manner (according to the Scripture [Lev. 23:33-43]).

CHAPTER 9
(445 B.C.)
THE PEOPLE FAST AND REPENT

NOW in the twenty and fourth day of this month the Children of Israel were assembled with fasting, and with sackclothes, and earth upon them (actually, the Law commanded that all of Israel fast on the 10th day of October, which was the Great Day of Atonement; however, for reasons unexplained here, they chose the 24th day of the month to do this [Lev. 23:26-32]).

2 And the seed of Israel separated themselves from all strangers, and stood and confessed their sins, and the iniquities of their fathers (their confession shows how attentively they had read the Bible, how well they had learned the lessons of man's total corruption and of God's amazing Grace — Williams).

3 And they stood up in their place, and read in the Book of the Law of the LORD their God one fourth part of the day; and another fourth part they confessed, and worshipped the LORD their God (three hours were given to Bible reading, and three hours to confession, prayer, and worship).

PRAYER AND CONFESSION
OF THE LEVITES

4 Then stood up upon the stairs (platform), of the Levites, Jeshua (Joshua), and Bani, Kadmiel, Shebaniah, Bunni, Sherebiah, Bani, and Chenani, and cried with a loud voice unto the LORD their God.

5 Then the Levites, Jeshua, and Kadmiel, Bani, Hashabniah, Sherebiah, Hodijah, Shebaniah, and Pethahiah, said, Stand up and bless the LORD your God for ever and ever: and blessed be Your glorious name, which is exalted above all blessing and praise (the high honor due to the "Name" of God is taught by the sacred writers with one uniform voice from Moses [Ex. 20:7] to the last surviving original Apostle [Rev. 15:4]).

6 You, even You, are LORD alone; You have made Heaven, the Heaven of Heavens, with all their host, the Earth, and all things that are therein, the seas, and all that is therein, and You preserved them all; and the host of Heaven worships You (the Lord is the Creator of all things, which completely debunks the baseless prattle of evolution).

7 You are the LORD the God, Who did choose Abram, and brought him forth out of Ur of the Chaldees, and gave him the name of Abraham (the Lord chose Abraham, because Abraham had chosen the Lord; predestination is taught in the Bible as a determination of certain things [Rom. 8:29], but those who enter into those things are based on "whosoever will" [Rev. 22:17]; the Bible doesn't teach that God predestines some to be lost and some to be saved, and that they have no choice in the matter; when Jesus died on Calvary, He died for the entirety of the world, not just for a select, chosen few [Jn. 3:16]; Paul said, "For whosoever [and that means anyone, not just certain ones the Lord selects] shall call upon the Name of the Lord shall be saved" [Rom. 10:13]);

8 And found his heart faithful before You *(a faithful heart toward God is one of the greatest things that could be said about any individual)*, and made a covenant with him to give the land of the Canaanites, the Hittites, the Amorites, and the Perizzites, and the Jebusites, and the Girgashites, to give it, I say, to his seed, and have performed Your Words; for You are righteous *(the Lord dispossessed these people from the land of Canaan, because of their terrible evil; the nations driven out were actually "seven" in number [Deut. 7:1]; it is a common figure of speech to put the part for the whole; the other nation omitted is the Hivites)*:

9 And did see the affliction of our fathers in Egypt, and heard their cry by the Red Sea *(Ex. 2:23-25; 14:10)*;

10 And showed signs and wonders upon Pharaoh, and on all his servants, and on all the people of his land: for You knew that they dealt proudly against them. So did You get You a name, as it is this day *(Ex., Chpts. 7-10, 12, 14; 18:11; Jer. 32:20)*.

11 And You did divide the Sea before them, so that they went through the midst of the Sea on the dry land; and their persecutors You threw into the deeps, as a stone into the mighty waters *(Ex. 14:21; 15:5; Ps. 78:13)*.

12 Moreover You led them in the day by a cloudy pillar; and in the night by a pillar of fire, to give them light in the way wherein they should go.

13 You came down also upon Mount Sinai, and spoke with them from Heaven, and gave them right Judgments, and true Laws, good Statutes and Commandments *(they were "right," "true," and "good," not only because God said it, but because they were, in fact, "right," "true," and "good")*:

14 And made known unto them Your Holy Sabbath, and commanded them Precepts, Statutes, and Laws, by the hand of Moses Your servant:

15 And gave them bread from Heaven for their hunger, and brought forth water for them out of the rock for their thirst, and promised them that they should go in to possess the land which You had sworn to give them.

16 But they and our fathers dealt proudly, and hardened their necks, and hearkened not to Your Commandments,

17 And refused to obey, neither were mindful of Your wonders that You did among them; but hardened their necks, and in their rebellion appointed a captain to return to their bondage *(someone other than Moses [Num. 14:4])*: but You are a God ready to pardon, gracious and merciful, slow to anger, and of great kindness, and forsook them not *(the Hebrew actually says, "A God of pardons")*.

18 Yes, when they had made them a molten calf, and said, This is your God Who brought you up out of Egypt, and had wrought great provocations *(Ex. 32:4)*;

19 Yet You in Your manifold mercies forsook them not in the wilderness *(even though the Lord knew they would continue to rebel against Him, which they did, with that entire generation dying in the wilderness because of unbelief [Heb. 4:2-6])*: the pillar of the cloud departed not from them by day, to lead them in the way; neither the pillar of fire by night, to show them light, and the way wherein they should go.

20 You gave also Your good Spirit *(Holy Spirit)* to instruct them *(Ex. 17:6)*, and withheld not Your manna from their mouth, and gave them water for their thirst.

THE CONTINUED BLESSINGS
OF THE LORD

21 Yes, forty years did You sustain them in the wilderness, so that they lacked nothing; their clothes waxed not old, and their feet swelled not *(Deut. 2:7; 8:4; 29:5)*.

22 Moreover You gave them kingdoms and nations, and did divide them into corners *(put them in every corner of the Holy Land)*: so they possessed the land of Sihon, and the land of the king of Heshbon, and the land of Og king of Bashan *(even though these were giants)*.

23 Their children also multiplied You as the stars of Heaven, and brought them into the land, concerning which You had promised to their fathers, that they should go in to possess it.

24 So the children went in and possessed the land, and You subdued before them the inhabitants of the land, the Canaanites, and gave them into their hands, with their kings, and the people of the land, that they might do with them as they would.

25 And they took strong cities, and a fat land, and possessed houses full of all goods, wells digged, vineyards, and oliveyards, and fruit trees in abundance: so they did eat, and were filled, and became fat, and delighted themselves in Your great goodness *(the actual statement in the Hebrew is: "They grew wanton and self-indulgent")*.

26 Nevertheless they were disobedient, and rebelled against You, and cast Your Law behind their backs, and killed Your Prophets which testified against them to turn them to You, and they wrought great provocations *(Judg. 2:11; I Ki. 14:9; 18:4; Ps. 50:17)*.

27 Therefore You delivered them into the hand of their enemies, who vexed them: and in the time of their trouble, when they cried unto You, You heard them from Heaven; and according to Your manifold mercies You gave them saviours, who saved them out of the hand of their enemies *(the writer seems to have the history of "Judges" primarily in mind)*.

28 But after they had rest, they did evil again before You: therefore You left them in the hand of their enemies, so that they had the dominion over them *(the enemies had dominion over Israel)*: yet when they returned, and cried unto You, You heard them from Heaven; and many times did You deliver them according to Your mercies;

29 And testified against them, that You might bring them again unto Your Law; yet they dealt proudly, and hearkened not unto Your Commandments, but sinned against Your judgments, (which if a man do, he shall live in them *[shall be subject to their penalty (Rom. 10:5)]*;) and withdrew the shoulder, and hardened their neck, and would not hear.

30 Yet many years did You forbear them, and testified against them by Your Spirit *(the Holy Spirit)* in Your Prophets: yet would they not give ear: therefore You gave them into the hand of the people of the lands.

31 Nevertheless for Your great mercies' sake You did not utterly consume them, nor forsake them; for You are a gracious and merciful God *(Jer. 4:27)*.

32 Now therefore, our God, the great, the mighty, and the terrible God, Who keeps Covenant and Mercy, let not all the trouble seem little before You, that has come upon us, on our kings, on our princes, and on our Priests, and on our Prophets, and on our fathers, and on all Your people, since the time of the kings of Assyria unto this day *(the kings of Assyria, in the strict sense of the word, had been God's original instrument for punishing His rebellious people [II Ki., Chpt. 17])*.

33 Howbeit You are just in all that is brought upon us; for You have done right, but we have done wickedly *(the spirit which true Repentance demands)*:

34 Neither have our kings, our princes, our Priests, nor our fathers, kept Your Law, nor hearkened unto Your Commandments and Your Testimonies, wherewith You did testify against them.

35 For they have not served You in their kingdom, and in Your great goodness that You gave them, and in the large and fat land which You gave before them, neither turned they from their wicked works.

36 Behold, we are servants this day, and for the land that You gave unto our fathers to eat the fruit thereof and the good thereof, behold, we are servants in it *(we have now no kingdom, the Persian is our master; as we would not be God's servants, we are handed over to him; "the service of God" and "the service of the kingdoms of the countries" are contrasted)*:

37 And it yields much increase unto the kings *(heathen kings)* whom You have set over us because of our sins *(the "increase" should have gone to Israel, but instead, because of Israel's sin, went to the heathen)*: also they have dominion over our bodies, and over our cattle, at their pleasure, and we are in great distress *(distress brought upon Israel because of her failure to live for God, despite repeated warnings)*.

38 And because of all this we make a sure Covenant, and write it; and our princes, Levites, and Priests, seal unto it. *(True Repentance leads to action. They signed a pledge to walk in God's Law. Unfortunately, they broke this Covenant as well!)*

CHAPTER 10
(445 B.C.)
THE SIGNERS OF THE COVENANT

NOW those who sealed were, Nehemiah, the Tirshatha *(the Governor)*, the son of Hachaliah, and Zidkijah,

2 Seraiah, Azariah, Jeremiah,

3 Pashur, Amariah, Malchijah,

4 Hattush, Shebaniah, Malluch,

5 Harim, Meremoth, Obadiah,

6 Daniel, Ginnethon, Baruch,

7 Meshullam, Abijah, Mijamin,

8 Maaziah, Bilgai, Shemaiah: these were the Priests.

9 And the Levites: both Jeshua the son of Azaniah, Binnui of the sons of Henadad, Kadmiel;

10 And their brethren, Shebaniah, Hodijah, Kelita, Pelaiah, Hanan,

11 Micha, Rehob, Hashabiah,

12 Zaccur, Sherebiah, Shebaniah,

13 Hodijah, Bani, Beninu.

14 The chief of the people; Parosh, Pahath-moab, Elam, Zatthu, Bani,

15 Bunni, Azgad, Bebai,

16 Adonijah, Bigvai, Adin,

17 Ater, Hizkijah, Azzur,

18 Hodijah, Hashum, Bezai,

19 Hariph, Anathoth, Nebai,

20 Magpiash, Meshullam, Hezir,

21 Meshezabeel, Zadok, Jaddua,

22 Pelatiah, Hanan, Anaiah,

23 Hoshea, Hananiah, Hashub,

24 Hallohesh, Pileha, Shobek,

25 Rehum, Hashabnah, Maaseiah,

26 And Ahijah, Hanan, Anan,

27 Malluch, Harim, Baanah. *(God honors those who honor His Book. Accordingly, a role of honor opens this Chapter. None of these men dreamed that 2,500 years after their deaths millions of people would read their names with praise to God.)*

TERMS OF THE COVENANT: TO REMAIN A SEPARATED AND PECULIAR PEOPLE

28 And the rest of the people, the Priests, the Levites, the porters, the singers, the Nethinims, and all they who had separated themselves from the people of the lands unto the Law of God, their wives, their sons, and their daughters, every one having knowledge, and having understanding *(all who were of age to understand the nature of the Covenant and what was meant by sealing it — not a special "intelligent" or "learned" class)*;

29 They clave to their brethren, their nobles, and entered into a curse, and into an oath, to walk in God's Law, which was given by Moses the servant of God, and to observe and do all the Commandments of the LORD our Lord, and His Judgments and His Statutes *(the important statement of this Chapter is the acceptance by the restored Israelites of the written Word of God as the sole authority for conduct and worship; they did not say that the Bible belonged to a past age and was now out-of-date; but, on the contrary, they confessed its teaching to be living and binding)*;

30 And that we would not give our daughters unto the people of the land, nor take their daughters for our sons *(referring to the mixed marriages so soon after the reformation of Ezra [Ex. 34:16; Deut. 7:3; Ezra 9:12])*:

31 And if the people of the land bring ware or any victuals on the Sabbath day to sell, that we would not buy it of them on the Sabbath, or on the holy day: and that we would leave the seventh year, and the exaction of every debt *(this precept of the Law, leaving the land fallow every seventh year, had been frequently neglected during the times of the monarchy, and its neglect was one of the sins which the captivity was expressly intended to punish [II Chron. 36:21])*.

OFFERINGS GIVEN FOR WORSHIP IN THE TEMPLE

32 Also we made Ordinances for us, to charge ourselves yearly with the third part of the shekel for the service of the House of our God *(to keep up the Temple and its Services)*;

33 For the Shewbread, and for the continual Meat Offering *(Thank Offering)*, and for the continual Burnt Offering *(the daily morning and evening Offerings)*, of the Sabbaths, of the new moons, for the set Feasts *(three times a year)*, and for the holy things, and for the Sin Offerings to make an Atonement for Israel, and for all the work of the House of our God *(this is the service of which Nehemiah speaks in Verse 32)*.

TITHES AND OFFERINGS FOR THE PRIESTS AND LEVITES

34 And we cast the lots among the Priests, the Levites, and the people, for the wood offering *(first time this is mentioned; the people were to bring in wood for the fire of the Sacrifices)*, to bring it into the House of our God, after the houses of our fathers, at times appointed year by year *(certain times to bring it in)*, to burn upon the Altar of the LORD our God, as it is written in the Law:

35 And to bring the firstfruits of our ground, and the firstfruits of all fruit of all trees, year by year, unto the House of the LORD *(it is believed that "firstfruits" referred to a tenth, or a tithe)*:

36 Also the firstborn of our sons *(firstborn sons were to be "redeemed" [Ex. 22:29; 34:19], which meant that five shekels had to be given to the Sanctuary [Num. 18:15-16])*, and of our cattle, as it is written in the Law, and the firstlings of our herds and of our flocks, to bring to the House of our God, unto the Priests who minister in the House of our God:

37 And that we should bring the firstfruits of our dough, and our offerings, and the fruit of all manner of trees, of wine and of oil,

unto the Priests, to the chambers of the House of our God; and the Tithes of our ground unto the Levites, that the same Levites might have the Tithes in all the cities of our tillage *(Tithing is first mentioned in the Bible with Abraham paying Tithe to Melchizedek; this was long before the Law; this means that Tithing was meant to continue in the Plan of God, even in the New Covenant, for we are all children of Abraham [Gal. 3:7]; also, Melchizedek was a Type of Christ [Heb. 5:5-6, 10], which means that we presently are supposed to continue to pay Tithe in support of the Work of God, headed up by Christ [Col. 1:16-21]).*

38 And the Priest the son of Aaron shall be with the Levites, when the Levites take Tithes *(meaning that the Priests were to share with the Levites, inasmuch as the "Tithes" were given for this purpose):* and the Levites shall bring up the Tithe of the Tithes into the House of our God, to the chambers, unto the treasure house *(the Tithes were to go for the support of the Priests and the Levites; however, the Priests and Levites were as well to take a tenth of that which was given to them and put it in the Temple treasury for the maintenance of the Temple proper).*

39 For the Children of Israel and the children of Levi shall bring the offering of the corn, of the new wine, and the oil, unto the chambers, where are the vessels of the Sanctuary, and the Priests who minister, and the porters, and the singers: and we will not forsake the House of our God *(to be sure, all of this was the Will of God!).*

CHAPTER 11
(445 B.C.)
THE RESIDENTS OF JERUSALEM

AND the rulers of the people dwelt at Jerusalem: the rest of the people also cast lots, to bring one of ten to dwell in Jerusalem the Holy City, and nine parts to dwell in other cites *(for the first time in the Word of God, Jerusalem is now called "the Holy City" by the Holy Spirit; it was not so called in the days of Israel's kingdom and glory; the Spirit of God delights to ennoble and to recognize fidelity to the Word of God in circumstances of weakness, fear, and danger).*

2 And the people blessed all the men, who willingly offered themselves to dwell at Jerusalem *(Jerusalem was the focal point of greatest danger; and, therefore, the Holy Spirit honors in this Chapter the brave men who garrisoned*

it; *this Chapter, therefore, may be regarded as another specimen page from the Book of Life).*

3 Now these are the chief of the province that dwelt in Jerusalem: but in the cities of Judah dwelt every one in his possession in their cities, to wit, Israel, the Priests, and the Levites, and the Nethinims, and the children of Solomon's servants.

4 And at Jerusalem dwelt certain of the Children of Judah, and of the children of Benjamin. Of the Children of Judah; Athaiah the son of Uzziah, the son of Zechariah, the son of Amariah, the son of Shephatiah, the son of Mahalaleel, of the children of Perez,

5 And Maaseiah the son of Baruch, the son of Col-hozeh, the son of Hazaiah, the son of Adaiah, the son of Joiarib, the son of Zechariah, the son of Shiloni.

6 All the sons of Perez that dwelt at Jerusalem were four hundred threescore and eight valiant men.

7 And these are the son of Benjamin; Sallu the son of Meshullam, the son of Joed, the son of Pedaiah, the son of Kolaiah, the son of Maaseiah, the son of Ithiel, the son of Jesaiah.

8 And after him Gabbai, Sallai, nine hundred twenty and eight.

9 And Joel the son of Zichri was their overseer: and Judah the son of Senuah was second of the city.

10 Of the Priests: Jedaiah the son of Joiarib, Jachin.

11 Seraiah the son of Hilkiah, the son of Meshullam, the son of Zadok, the son of Meraioth, the son of Ahitub, was the ruler of the House of God.

12 And their brethren that did the work of the house were eight hundred twenty and two: and Adaiah the son of Jeroham, the son of Pelaliah, the son of Amzi, the son of Zechariah, the son of Pashur, the son of Malchiah,

13 And his brethren, chief of the fathers, two hundred forty and two: and Amashai the son of Azareel, the son of Ahasai, the son of Meshillemoth, the son of Immer,

14 And their brethren, mighty men of valour, an hundred twenty and eight: and their overseer was Zabdiel, the son of one of the great men.

15 Also of the Levites: Shemaiah the son of Hashub, the son of Azrikam, the son of Hashabiah, the son of Bunni;

16 And Shabbethai and Jozabad, of the chief of the Levites, had the oversight of the outward business of the House of God *(the outward*

business of the Temple was committed to two chief-
tains of Levi).

17 And Mattaniah the son of Micha, the son of Zabdi, the son of Asaph, was the principal to begin the thanksgiving in prayer: and Bakbukiah the second among his brethren, and Abda the son of Shammua, the son of Galal, the son of Jeduthun.

18 All the Levites in the holy city were two hundred fourscore and four.

19 Moreover the porters, Akkub, Talmon, the their brethren that kept the gates, were an hundred seventy and two.

THOSE DWELLING IN OTHER CITIES

20 And the residue of Israel, of the Priests, and the Levites, were in all the cities of Judah, every one in his inheritance.

21 But the Nethinims dwelt in Ophel: and Ziha and Gispa were over the Nethinims.

22 The overseer also of the Levites at Jerusalem was Uzzi the son of Bani, the son of Hashabiah, the son of Mattaniah, the son of Micha. Of the sons of Asaph, the singers were over the business of the House of God. *(The inward business of the Temple was given to the singers, the sons of Asaph.*

When in captivity [Ps. 137], the hand that should have awakened the song upon the pleasant harp was used to hang it upon the willow tree. But now, restored to Zion, Israel could sing!

The Christian life is outward and inward. The singing is to be inward. If the song of God is not in the heart, there will be neither melody nor power in the life.)

23 For it was the king's commandment concerning them, that a certain portion should be for the singers, due for every day *(the Grace that placed the singers within the House of God provided in tender love for their daily bread, and, accordingly, the Persian Monarch was moved to apportion them a fitting maintenance; how admirable is the love of God in making a mighty king supply bread to an obscure Psalm-singer!).*

24 And Pethahiah the son of Meshezabeel, of the children of Zerah the son of Judah, was at the king's hand in all matters concerning the people.

25 And for the villages, with their fields, some of the children of Judah dwelt at Kirjath-arba, and in the villages thereof, and at Dibon, and in the villages thereof, and at Jekabzeel, and in the villages thereof,

26 And at Jeshua, and at Moladah, and at Beth-phelet,

27 And at Hazar-shual, and at Beer-sheba, and in the villages thereof,

28 And at Ziklag, and at Mekonah, and in the villages thereof,

29 And at En-rimmon, and at Zareah, and at Jarmuth,

30 Zanoah, Adullam, and in their villages, at Lachish, and the fields thereof, at Azekah, and in the villages thereof. And they dwelt from Beer-sheba unto the valley of Hinnom.

31 The children also of Benjamin from Geba dwelt at Michmash, and Aija, and Beth-el, and in their villages.

32 And at Anathoth, Knob, Ananiah;

33 Hazor, Ramah, Gittaim,

34 Hadid, Zeboim, Neballat,

35 Lod, and Ono, the valley of craftsmen.

36 And of the Levites were divisions in Judah, and in Benjamin. *(These individuals listed were to protect the city. Jerusalem having been recovered from the enemy, and surrounded by a wall, it had now to be garrisoned and held against him. There is a spiritual energy which wins a position for God, but which takes no steps to hold it for God. Nehemiah recognized the necessity of holding what had been won.)*

CHAPTER 12
(536 B.C.)
THE PRIESTS AND LEVITES WHO RETURNED FROM CAPTIVITY WITH ZERUBBABEL

NOW these are the Priests and the Levites who went up with Zerubbabel the son of Shealtiel, and Joshua: Seraiah, Jeremiah, and Ezra *(these last two are not the same as the Prophet Jeremiah or Ezra the Scribe, but are persons of whom nothing more is known to us.*

God and the Bible form the center around which the returned captives gathered, hence the prominence given in the Books of Ezra and Nehemiah to the Priests and Levites. The Priests with their Sacrifices typified worship through the Atonement and Intercession of Christ; the Levites were the public teachers of the Law.

Worship and meditation upon the Holy Scriptures form the foundation of the Christian life in the individual, the family, or the Church. If these be destroyed, the Church disappears),

2 Amariah, Malluch, Hattush,

3 Shechaniah, Rehum, Meremoth,

4 Iddo, Ginnetho, Abijah,

5 Miamin, Maadiah, Bilgah,

6 Shemaiah, and Joiarib, Jedaiah,

7 Sallu, Amok, Hilkiah, Jedaiah. These were the chief of the Priests and of their brethren in the days of Jeshua.

8 Moreover the Levites: Jeshua, Binnui, Kadmiel, Sherebiah, Judah, and Mattaniah, which was over the thanksgiving, he and his brethren.

9 Also Bakbukiah and Unni, their brethren, were over against them in the watches.

10 And Jeshua begat Joiakim, Joiakim also begat Eliashib, and Eliashib begat Joiada,

11 And Joiada begat Jonathan, and Jonathan, begat Jaddua.

12 And in the days of Joiakim were Priests, the chief of the fathers: of Seraiah, Meraiah; of Jeremiah, Hananiah;

13 Of Ezra, Meshullam; of Amariah, Jehohanan;

14 Of Melicu, Jonathan; of Shebaniah, Joseph;

15 Of Harim, Adna; of Meraioth, Helkai;

16 Of Iddo, Zechariah; of Ginnethon, Meshullam;

17 Of Abijah, Zichri; of Miniamin, of Moadiah, Piltai;

18 Of Bilgah, Shammua; of Shemaiah, Jehonathan;

19 And of Joiarib, Mattenai, of Jedaiah, Uzzi;

20 Of Sallai, Kallai; of Amok, Eber;

21 Of Hilkiah, Hashabiah; of Jedaiah, Nethaneel.

22 The Levites in the days of Eliashib, Joiada, and Johanan, and Jaddua, were recorded chief of the fathers: also the Priests, to the reign of Darius the Persian.

23 The sons of Levi, the chief of the fathers, were written in the book of chronicles, even until the days of Johanan the son of Eliashib.

24 And the chief of the Levites: Hashabiah, Sherebiah, and Jeshua the son of Kadmiel, with their brethren over against them to praise and to give thanks, according to the commandment of David the man of God, ward over against ward.

25 Mattaniah, and Bakbukiah, Obadiah, Meshullam, Talmon, Akkub, were porters keeping the ward at the thresholds of the gates.

26 These were in the days of Joiakim the son of Jeshua, the son of Jozadak, and in the days of Nehemiah the governor, and of Ezra the Priest, the Scribe. *(The first twenty-six Verses of this Chapter are very important, not only as they relate to the spiritual facts which we addressed in Verse 1, but also because these so registered secured the purity of the pedigree of the Aaronic Priesthood. Since the nation was no longer governed by kings, the High Priests marked the chronology of the people up to the advent of the Messiah.)*

THE DEDICATION OF THE WALLS OF JERUSALEM

27 And at the dedication of the wall of Jerusalem they sought the Levites out of all their places, to bring them to Jerusalem, to keep the dedication with gladness, both with thanksgivings, and with singing, with cymbals, psalteries, and with harps.

28 And the sons of the singers gathered themselves together, both out of the plain country round about Jerusalem, and from the villages of Netophathi;

29 Also from the house of Gilgal, and out of the fields of Geba and Azmaveth: for the singers had built them villages round about Jerusalem.

30 And the Priests and the Levites purified themselves, and purified the people, and the gates, and the wall.

31 Then I brought up the princes of Judah upon the wall, and appointed two great companies of them that gave thanks, whereof one went on the right hand upon the wall toward the dung gate *(the wall, having been completed, was now dedicated; the entire praise for its erection was given to God and none to the builders; the whole multitude was parted into two companies; headed by a choir, each company moved, one to the right and the other to the left, to make, with sounding of cymbals and of song, the half-circuit, respectively, of the wall; the dual march was so planned that the two companies met again upon the wall opposite the Temple, even as we shall see):*

32 And after them went Hoshaiah, and half of the princes of Judah,

33 And Azariah, Ezra, and Meshullam,

34 Judah, and Benjamin, and Shemaiah, and Jeremiah.

35 And certain of the Priests' sons with trumpets; namely, Zechariah the son of Jonathan, the son of Shemaiah, the son of Mattaniah, the son of Michaiah, the son of Zaccur, the son of Asaph:

36 And his brethren, Shemaiah, and Azarael, Milalai, Gilalai, Maai, Nethaneel, and Judah, Hanani, with the musical instruments of David the man of God, and Ezra the Scribe before them.

37 And at the fountain gate, which was over

against them, they went up by the stairs of the city of David, at the going up of the wall, above the house of David, even unto the water gate eastward.

38 And the other company of them that gave thanks went over against them, and I after them, and the half of the people upon the wall, from beyond the tower of the furnaces even unto the broad wall;

39 And from above the gate of Ephraim, and above the old gate, and above the fish gate, and the tower of Hananeel, and the tower of Meah, even unto the sheep gate: and they stood still in the prison gate.

40 So stood the two companies of them that gave thanks in the house of God, and I, and the half of the rulers with me:

41 And the Priests; Eliakim, Maaseiah, Miniamin, Michaiah, Elioenai, Zechariah, and Hananiah, with trumpets;

42 And Maaseiah, and Shemaiah, and Eleazar, and Uzzi, and Jehohanan, and Malchijah, and Elam, and Ezer. And the singers sang loud, with Jezrahiah their overseer.

43 Also that day they offered great sacrifices, and rejoiced: for God had made them rejoice with great joy: the wives also and the children rejoiced: so that the joy of Jerusalem was heard even afar off *(the united choirs "sang aloud," while the Priests offered Sacrifices; so all rejoiced, even the little children; one might say, without the fear of contradiction, this was a Campmeeting, and rightly so!).*

THE TEMPLE OFFICERS RESTORED

44 And at that time were some appointed over the chambers for the treasures, for the offerings, for the firstfruits, and for the tithes, to gather into them out of the fields of the cities the portions of the Law for the Priests and Levites: for Judah rejoiced for the Priests and for the Levites who waited.

45 And both the singers and the porters kept the ward of their God, and the ward of the purification, according to the commandment of David, and of Solomon his son.

46 For in the days of David and Asaph of old there were chief of the singers, and songs of praise and thanksgiving unto God *(as stated, music and singing for the Glory of God constitute one of the highest forms of worship; when a Church is in tune with the Lord, singing and music will always be the result).*

47 And all Israel in the days of Zerubbabel, and in the days of Nehemiah, gave the portions of the singers and the porters, every day his portion: and they sanctified holy things unto the Levites; and the Levites sanctified them unto the children of Aaron. *(The words in Verse 44, "Judah rejoiced for the Priests and for the Levites who waited," mean that Judah gave with joy the Tithes for the Priests, etc. The words in Verse 47, "They sanctified for the Levites, and the Levites sanctified for the sons of Aaron," mean that the people gave Tithes for the Levites, and the Levites, in their turn, gave a Tithe of these Tithes to the Priests [Num., Chpt. 18].)*

CHAPTER 13
(445 B.C.)
NEHEMIAH'S REFORMS: SEPARATION OF FOREIGNERS FROM WORSHIP

O N that day they read in the Book of Moses in the audience of the people; and therein was found written, that the Ammonite and the Moabite should not come into the congregation of God for ever *(Deut. 31:11-12; II Ki. 23:2; Isa. 34:16);*

2 Because they met not the Children of Israel with bread and with water, but hired Balaam against them: that he should curse them: howbeit our God turned the curse into a blessing *(Num. 22:5; 23:11; 24:10; Deut. 23:5; Josh. 24:9-10).*

3 Now it came to pass, when they had heard the Law, that they separated from Israel all the mixed multitude. *(On reaching Deut., Chpt. 23 in the course of the public reading of the Scriptures, the returned captives, directly they heard the command of Verses 3-6, obeyed it.*

The "mixed multitude" had always been a snare [Num., Chpt. 11] to the Israel of God under the First Covenant; and this snare remains to the present day under the Second Covenant.)

4 And before this, Eliashib the Priest, having the oversight of the chamber of the House of our God, was allied unto Tobiah:

5 And he had prepared for him a great chamber *(connected to the Temple),* where aforetime they laid the Meat Offerings, the frankincense, and the vessels, and the Tithes of the corn, the new wine, and the oil, which was commanded to be given to the Levites, and the singers, and the porters; and the offerings of the Priests. *(Tobiah was an Ammonite. This ruling concerning the Ammonite could be relaxed, that is, if they became a proselyte Jew, as did Ruth. But, to be sure, Tobiah definitely*

did not fit that bill. And yet, the High Priest had formed a close association with him, even giving him a chamber connected with the Temple.

In the first place, the High Priest, or any Israelite for that matter, should not have desired to have anything to do with this Ammonite, who had tried extremely so to hurt the Work of God. Such should be shunned in the modern Church, as well!)

CLEANSING OF THE TEMPLE

6 But in all this time was not I at Jerusalem: for in the two and thirtieth year of Artaxerxes king of Babylon came I unto the king, and after certain days obtained I leave of the king *(after the dedication of the wall, Nehemiah returned to the Persian court; but after some time, possibly two years, he obtained leave of absence and returned to Jerusalem, because, it may be assumed, he had heard of the faithlessness of the High Priest and the nobles to the Covenant to which they had subscribed [Chpt. 10])*:

7 And I came to Jerusalem, and understood of the evil that Eliashib *(the High Priest)* did for Tobiah *(the Ammonite)*, in preparing him a chamber in the courts of the House of God.

8 And it grieved me sore: therefore I cast forth all the household stuff of Tobiah out of the chamber *(Tobiah had furnished his "chamber" as a dwelling-house)*.

9 Then I commanded, and they cleansed the chambers: and thither brought I again the vessels of the House of God, with the Meat Offering and the Frankincense *(how often in the history of an individual or a Church has "the great chamber," which should be filled with Christ and His Preciousness, been fitted up for the Ammonite and his loathsomeness! But now the Temple was cleansed)*.

THE SUPPORT OF THE
LEVITES RESTORED

10 And I perceived that the portions of the Levites had not been given them: for the Levites and the singers, who did the work, were fled every one to his field. *(The people had been lax with their Tithes. With the High Priest conducting himself as he did, one can understand the faithlessness of the entirety of the nation. As the leadership goes, so goes all else.)*

11 Then contended I with the rulers, and said, Why is the House of God forsaken? and I gathered them together, and set them in their place *(Nehemiah gathered all the rulers together, for they are the ones who had ceased paying their Tithes)*.

12 Then brought all Judah the tithe of the corn and the new wine and the oil unto the treasuries *(with proper leadership, namely Nehemiah, the Work of God again begins to function)*.

13 And I made treasurers over the treasuries, Shelemiah the Priest, and Zadok the Scribe, and of the Levites, Pedaiah: and next to them was Hanan the son of Zaccur, the son of Mattaniah: for they were counted faithful, and their office was to distribute unto their brethren *(which seemingly, due to their faithfulness, they could be counted on to do)*.

14 Remember me, O my God, concerning this, and wipe not out my good deeds that I have done for the House of my God, and for the offices thereof *(Nehemiah did not ask his countrymen to do anything for him, to erect a statue to his honor, or recompense him for his public services; he sought the honor that comes from God only)*.

SABBATH OBSERVANCE RESTORED

15 In those days saw I in Judah some treading wine presses on the Sabbath, and bringing in sheaves, and lading asses; as also wine, grapes, and figs, and all manner of burdens, which they brought into Jerusalem on the Sabbath day: and I testified against them in the day wherein they sold victuals *(the "Sabbath," which was a Saturday, was to be a day of "rest"; it typified Christ, in Whom Alone true rest can be found [Mat. 11:28-30])*.

16 There dwelt men of Tyre also therein, which brought fish, and all manner of ware, and sold on the Sabbath unto the Children of Judah, and in Jerusalem.

17 Then I contended with the nobles of Judah, and said unto them, What evil thing is this that you do, and profane the Sabbath day?

18 Did not your fathers thus, and did not our God bring all this evil upon us, and upon this city? yet you bring more wrath upon Israel by profaning the Sabbath *(fidelity to the Sabbath characterized the Old Covenant, while fidelity to Christ, of which the Sabbath was a symbol, proclaims fidelity to the New Covenant)*.

19 And it came to pass, that when the gates of Jerusalem began to be dark before the Sabbath, I commanded that the gates should be shut, and charged that they should not be

opened till after the Sabbath: and some of my servants set I at the gates, that there should no burden be brought in on the Sabbath day.

20 So the merchants and sellers of all kind of ware lodged without Jerusalem once or twice.

21 Then I testified against them, and said unto them, Why lodge you about the wall? if you do so again, I will lay hands on you. From that time forth came they no more on the Sabbath. *(The merchants could not leave their wares unguarded. Thus, a crowd had collected about the gates, which caused disturbance and excitement, which were unsuitable for the Sabbath. To prevent this, Nehemiah threatened to arrest the merchants, whereupon the practice was discontinued.)*

22 And I commanded the Levites that they should cleanse themselves, and that they should come and keep the gates, to sanctify the Sabbath Day. Remember me, O my God, concerning this also, and spare me according to the greatness of Your mercy *(Nehemiah's plea for Salvation was based upon the greatness of God's Mercy, and not upon the merit of his own works).*

MIXED MARRIAGES DEALT WITH

23 In those days also saw I Jews who had married wives of Ashdod, of Ammon, and of Moab:

24 And their children spoke half in the speech of Ashdod, and could not speak in the Jews' language, but according to the language of each people *(once again, we point to the laxness of the High Priest! When suitable leadership is lacking, almost all the time the people will be spiritually lax as well).*

25 And I contended with them *(false doctrine must be addressed, and openly)*, and cursed them *(reviled them)*, and smote certain of them, and plucked off their hair, and made them swear by God, saying, You shall not give your daughters unto their sons, nor take their daughters unto your sons, or for yourselves *(Nehemiah made them swear not to intermarry with the heathen; if they did, the curse of God should fall upon them).*

26 Did not Solomon king of Israel sin by these things? yet among many nations was there no king like him, who was beloved of his God, and God made him king over all Israel: nevertheless even him did outlandish women cause to sin *(the idea is, if the Lord would be bitterly opposed to Solomon, whom He loved very much, concerning these things, then Israel presently couldn't hope to escape [I Ki. 11:1-40]).*

27 Shall we then hearken unto you to do all this great evil, to transgress against our God in marrying strange wives? *(Shall we give way to you, thus transgressing against God, and provoking Him to destroy us? Surely not! Solomon's example is enough to deter us.)*

28 And one of the sons of Joiada, the son of Eliashib the High Priest, was son in law to Sanballat the Horonite: therefore I chased him from me *(we may suppose that the son of the High Priest, who had married the Samaritan, refused to repudiate his foreign wife, and, therefore, he left Jerusalem at the insistence of Nehemiah, and went to Samaria).*

29 Remember them, O my God, because they have defiled the Priesthood, and the covenant of the Priesthood, and of the Levites *(once again, corrupted leadership leads to a corrupted people).*

SUMMARY

30 Thus cleansed I them from all strangers, and appointed the wards of the Priests and the Levites, every one in his business *(the "cleansing" probably resembled the process adopted by Ezra [Ezra 10:5-17]; Nehemiah also assigned the offices to the various Priests and Levites);*

31 And for the wood offering, at times appointed, and for the firstfruits. Remember me, O my God, for good. *(And to be sure, the Lord definitely did. The account of Nehemiah was recorded by the Holy Spirit for the Word of God and, accordingly, has been read by untold millions. Because it is the Word of God, it will stand forever!)*

THE BOOK OF
ESTHER

CHAPTER 1
(521 B.C.)

AHASUERUS MAKES A ROYAL FEAST

NOW it came to pass in the days of Ahasuerus, (this is Ahasuerus which reigned, from India even unto Ethiopia, over an hundred and seven and twenty provinces *[Ahasuerus is a kingly title, and could have applied to several individuals.*

The Book of Esther presents to the Reader the captives of Israel scattered among the Gentiles under the just judgment of Hosea 1:9, and yet loved and cared for, in secret, by God. Being "Lo-ammi," He could not publicly recognize them. That recognition could only be given to the Gentile, to whom the Lord had committed supreme power. Without revoking the judgment pronounced through Hosea, the Lord secretly watched over them and, without displaying Himself, shaped public affairs in their interests. They had lost all title to His Protection and, therefore, it is an extremely important and comforting study to observe in this Book how the Lord's hidden Hand prepared and directed everything for a people, in themselves unlovely, but beloved for the fathers' sake. Hence the Holy Spirit, with design, is careful not to let the Name of God appear in the Book, though it lies concealed in the Hebrew Text.

As well, the absence, therefore, of that Name is a great encouragement to faith, for the argument and the lesson which its omission conveys is that, behind the visible events of history, there is an Almighty and Faithful Love that cherishes and protects the broken and scattered people of God — Williams]:)

2 That in those days, when the king Ahasuerus sat on the throne of his kingdom, which was in Shushan the palace,

3 In the third year of his reign, he made a feast unto all his princes and his servants; the power of Persia and Media, the nobles and princes of the provinces, being before him *(he was the master of the world of that day; this position was given to him by God, even though he did not recognize such)*:

4 When he showed the riches of his glorious kingdom and the honour of his excellent majesty many days, even an hundred and fourscore days *(many believe this particular Ahasuerus was Xerxes; this festivity lasted for six months)*.

5 And when these days were expired, the king made a feast unto all the people who were present in Shushan the palace, both unto great and small, seven days, in the court of the garden of the king's palace *(from Verse 9, we gather that this was a feast for men only)*;

6 Where were white, green, and blue, hangings, fastened with cords of fine linen and purple to silver rings and pillars of marble: the beds were of gold and silver, upon a pavement of red, and blue, and white, and black, marble *(this was a mosaic pavement of four different hues, no doubt, exquisitely beautiful)*.

7 And they gave them drink in vessels of gold, (the vessels being diverse one from another,) and royal wine in abundance, according to the state of the king.

8 And the drinking was according to the law; none did compel: for so the king had appointed to all the officers of his house, that they should do according to every man's pleasure *(for this particular feast, the men could drink or not drink; it was their choice)*.

9 Also Vashti the Queen made a feast for the women in the royal house which belonged to king Ahasuerus *(evidently, this particular feast was for women only)*.

QUEEN VASHTI REFUSES TO OBEY THE KING

10 On the seventh day, when the heart of the king was merry with wine, he commanded Mehuman, Biztha, Harbona, Bigtha, and Abagtha, Zethar, and Carcas, the seven chamberlains who served in the presence of Ahasuerus the king,

11 To bring Vashti the Queen before the king with the crown royal, to show the people and the princes her beauty: for she was fair to look on *(this practice was not entirely unusual for kings of that day)*.

12 But the Queen Vashti refused to come at the king's commandment by his chamberlains: therefore was the king very wroth *(angry)*, and

his anger burned in him *(Vashti, in this instance, was justified in her actions; had she complied, she would have lost the respect not only of the Persian nation, but of the king himself)*.

VASHTI'S PUNISHMENT

13 Then the king said to the wise men, which knew the times, (for so was the king's manner toward all who knew law and judgment *[the law of the Medes and the Persians]*:

14 And the next unto him was Carshena, Shethar, Admatha, Tarshish, Meres, Marsena, and Memucan, the seven princes of Persia and Media, which saw the king's face, and which sat the first in the kingdom *[these individuals seemed to have access to the Monarch at all times]*;)

15 What shall we do unto the Queen Vashti according to law, because she has not performed the commandment of the king Ahasuerus by the chamberlains?

16 And Memucan answered before the king and the princes, Vashti the Queen has not done wrong to the king only, but also to all the princes, and to all the people who are in all the provinces of the king Ahasuerus. *(From this man's reply, we realize that there was no Persian law which provided for a penalty for such a case. The idea seems to be that they will now make up a law, which, of course, was unjust.*

However, even though the Lord did not cause these events to take place, He most definitely did take advantage of the events, even as we shall see.)

17 For this deed of the Queen shall come abroad unto all women, so that they shall despise their husbands in their eyes, when it shall be reported, The king Ahasuerus commanded Vashti the Queen to be brought in before him, but she came not *(all of it is a trumped up charge!)*.

18 Likewise shall the ladies of Persia and Media say this day unto all the king's princes, which have heard of the deed of the Queen. Thus shall there arise too much contempt and wrath.

19 If it please the king, let there go a royal commandment from him, and let it be written among the laws of the Persians and the Medes, that it be not altered, That Vashti come no more before king Ahasuerus; and let the king giver her royal estate unto another who is better than she.

20 And when the king's decree which he shall make shall be published throughout all his empire, (for it is great,) all the wives shall give to their husbands honour, both to great and small.

21 And the saying pleased the king and the princes; and the king did according to the word of Memucan:

22 For he sent letters into all the king's provinces, into every province according to the writing thereof, and to every people after their language, that every man should bear rule in his own house, and that it should be published according to the language of every people *(besides publishing the decree, Ahasuerus sent letters prescribing certain things)*.

CHAPTER 2
(518 B.C.)
THE SEARCH FOR A NEW QUEEN

AFTER these things, when the wrath of king Ahasuerus was appeased, he remembered Vashti, and what she had done, and what was decreed against her *(the idea seems to be that the king somewhat regretted what he had done concerning Vashti; however, the die was now cast, and he must follow through)*.

2 Then said the king's servants who ministered unto him, Let there be fair young virgins sought for the king:

3 And let the king appoint officers in all the provinces of his kingdom, that they may gather together all the fair young virgins unto Shushan the palace, to the house of the women, unto the custody of Hege the king's chamberlain, keeper of the women; and let their things for purification be given them:

4 And let the maiden which pleases the king be queen instead of Vashti. And the thing pleased the king; and he did so.

ESTHER'S ANCESTRY

5 Now in Shushan the palace there was a certain Jew, whose name was Mordecai, the son of Jair, the son of Shimei, the son of Kish, a Benjamite *(Mordecai was with Nehemiah, an exile in Shushan; he held a high position in the palace; at the same time, Daniel was exiled in Babylon, about 200 miles due west of Shushan, with Ezekiel exiled in some other part of Babylonia, of which the exact location is unknown)*;

6 Who had been carried away from Jerusalem with the captivity which had been carried away with Jeconiah king of Judah, whom

Nebuchadnezzar the king of Babylon had carried away. *(This was the second deportation, which took place in 597 B.C. The first deportation took place in 605 B.C., when Daniel was deported. The third deportation took place in 586 B.C., and Jerusalem was then burned and the Temple completely destroyed — all under Nebuchadnezzar.)*

7 And he *(Mordecai)* brought up Hadassah *(her Hebrew name)*, that is, Esther *(her Persian name)*, his uncle's daughter *(his own first cousin, but probably much younger than he)*: for she had neither father nor mother, and the maid was fair and beautiful; whom Mordecai, when her father and mother were dead, took for his own daughter *(not perhaps by a formal adoption, but by taking her to live with him, and treating her as if she had been his own child; from this, we know that the man was kindly and benevolent)*.

8 So it came to pass, when the king's commandment and his decree was heard, and when many maidens were gathered together unto Shushan the palace, to the custody of Hegai *(who was in charge of all of this)*, that Esther was brought also unto the king's house, to the custody of the Hegai, keeper of the women *(evidently, because of her beauty, she was chosen among many others as a possible choice to be the new queen)*.

9 And the maiden pleased him *(Hegai)*, and she obtained kindness of him; and he speedily gave her her things for purification, with such things as belonged to her, and seven maidens, which were meet to be given her *(as attendants)*, out of the king's house: and he preferred her and her maids unto the best place of the house of the women *(she obtained the favor of this man, which no doubt was all guided by the Lord)*.

10 Esther had not showed her people nor her kindred *(had not divulged that she was Jewish)*: for Mordecai had charged her that she should not show it *(because of possible prejudice)*.

11 And Mordecai walked every day before the court of the women's house, to know how Esther did, and what should become of her.

ESTHER CHOSEN TO BE QUEEN

12 Now when every maid's turn was come to go in to king Ahasuerus, after that she had been twelve months, according to the manner of the women, (for so were the days of their purifications accomplished, to wit, six months with oil of myrrh, and six months with sweet odours, and with other things for the purifying of the women *[a year's purification was considered necessary before any maiden could approach the king]*;)

13 Then thus came every maiden unto the king; whatsoever she desired was given her to go with her out of the house of the women unto the king's house *(any maiden was entitled to demand anything that she liked, in the way of dress or ornaments, and it had to be given her, so she might look her best, or what she thought was her best)*.

14 In the evening she went, and on the morrow she returned into the second house of the women, to the custody of Shaashgaz, the king's chamberlain, which kept the concubines: she came in unto the king no more, except the king delighted in her, and that she were called by name *(this was a ritual which was incumbent upon each woman)*.

15 Now when the turn of Esther, the daughter of Abihail the uncle of Mordecai, who had taken her for his daughter, was come to go in unto the king, she required nothing but what Hegai the king's chamberlain, the keeper of the women, appointed *(Esther would not trust to ostentatious dress or ornaments, but would leave it up to Hegai as to what she should wear, which evidently portrayed her natural beauty)*. And Esther obtained favour in the sight of all them who looked upon her *(she stood out above all the rest)*.

16 So Esther was taken unto king Ahasuerus into his house royal in the tenth month, which is the month Tebeth, in the seventh year of his reign *(1:3, coupled with this Verse, proclaim to us that four years had elapsed between the degradation of Vashti and the enthronement of Esther)*.

17 And the king loved Esther above all the women, and she obtained grace and favour in his sight more than all the virgins; so that he set the royal crown upon her head, and made her queen instead of Vashti. *(Thus, in the providence of God, and by His overruling of human folly, Esther was seated upon the throne at the very time that Satan made a supreme effort to destroy every member of the Tribe of Judah in particular, and the Israelites in general, so as to make impossible the advent of the promised Redeemer.*

He was defeated by the hidden Hand of God. The judgment threatened in Deut. 31:16-18 — "I will hide My Face" — came to pass; but,

though Israel proved faithless to Him, He abode faithful to her, for He could not deny Himself and, though He hid Himself, yet was the Lord's care over them as real as ever — Williams.)

18 Then the king made a great feast unto all his princes and his servants, even Esther's feast *(in her honor)*; and he made a release to the provinces *(relaxation from taxes for a short period of time)*, and gave gifts, according to the state of the king *(in celebration of his new Queen)*.

MORDECAI SAVES THE KING'S LIFE

19 And when the virgins were gathered together the second time *(evidently, some type of Persian ritual)*, then Mordecai sat in the king's gate *(signifying place, position, and authority, all in the realm of government)*.

20 Esther had not yet shown her kindred nor her people *(none knew that she was Jewish)*; as Mordecai had charged her: for Esther did the commandment of Mordecai, like as when she was brought up with him *(despite the fact that she was now Queen, she still heeded the counsel of Mordecai, as always, and rightly so!)*.

21 In those days, while Mordecai sat in the king's gate, two of the king's chamberlains, Bigthan and Teresh, of those which kept the door *(a position of the highest possible trust)*, were wroth, and sought to lay hands on the king Ahasuerus.

22 And the thing was known to Mordecai *(Josephus says that a certain man by the name of Pharnabazus, a slave of one of the conspirators, betrayed them to Mordecai)*, who told it unto Esther the Queen; and Esther certified the king thereof in Mordecai's name *(Esther revealed to the king that Mordecai had relayed to her this information, which would save the king's life)*.

23 And when inquisition was made of the matter, it was found out; therefore they were both hanged on a tree *(Bigthan and Teresh)*: and it was written in the book of the chronicles before the king *(and so the king's life was saved because of Mordecai and Esther)*.

CHAPTER 3
(510 B.C.)
HAMAN'S EXALTATION; AND
HATRED OF MORDECAI

A FTER these things did king Ahasuerus promote Haman the son of Hammedatha the Agagite, and advanced him, and set his seat above all the princes who were with him *(it is believed that Haman was an Amalekite)*.

2 And all the king's servants, who were in the king's gate *(government employees, so to speak)*, bowed, and reverenced Haman: for the king had so commanded concerning him. But Mordecai bowed not, nor did him reverence *(prostration was, in the mind of Mordecai, an act of worship, and it was not proper to worship anyone except God [Rev. 22:9])*.

3 Then the king's servants, which were in the king's gate, said unto Mordecai, Why do you transgress the king's commandment? *(Mordecai seems, at last, to have explained to them what his objection was, and to have said that, as a Jew, he was precluded from prostrating himself before a man.)*

4 Now it came to pass, when they spoke daily unto him, and he hearkened not unto them, that they told Haman, to see whether Mordecai's matters would stand: for he had told them that the was a Jew. *(Mordecai explained to the palace officials that his not reverencing Haman was not due to discourtesy to Haman, or disobedience to the king, but because he was a Hebrew; that is, he worshipped the One and Only True and Living God.*

Refusal to give this homage brought Daniel into the den of lions, and the three princes into the fiery furnace. It may justly, therefore, be assumed from Mordecai's statement that he was a worthy companion of Daniel and the three Hebrew children.

In fact, Haman, as stated, was an Amalekite. As such, he was an enemy to God, and Jehovah had sworn to have war with him forever [Ex. 17:16]. God's enemies were Mordecai's enemies, for Mordecai was a servant of God. This fact representing Haman was an added reason why faithfulness to God demanded this seeming discourtesy to Haman.)

5 And when Haman saw that Mordecai bowed not, nor did him reverence, then was Haman full of wrath *(apparently, Mordecai's disrespect had not been observed by Haman until the "king's servants" called his attention to it)*.

HAMAN PLOTS TO KILL ALL THE JEWS

6 And he thought scorn to lay hands on Mordecai alone; for they had showed him the people of Mordecai *(that they were Jews)*: wherefore Haman sought to destroy all the Jews who were throughout the whole kingdom

of Ahasuerus, even the people of Mordecai *(in the mind of this evil man, Mordecai, as a Jew, had insulted him, and the Jews, and that meant all the Jews, would pay the penalty)*.

7 In the first month, that is, the month Nisan, in the twelfth year of king Ahasuerus, they cast Pur, that is, the lot, before Haman from day to day, and from month to month, to the twelfth month, that is, the month Adar *(this Verse does not mean that twelve months were employed in seeking, by means of the lot, a propitious day for the slaughter of the Jews; it means that the diviners [astrologers] sought for a favorable day, month by month, and at last chose the 13th day of the 12th month as promising success, as outlined in Verse 13)*.

8 And Haman said unto king Ahasuerus, There is a certain people scattered abroad and dispersed among the people in all the provinces of your kingdom; and their laws are diverse from all people; neither keep they the king's laws: therefore it is not for the king's profit to suffer them *(the basic thrust of all of this was a "lie"; there might be an occasional royal edict which a Jew could not obey, but that was rare; anyway, as long as it didn't hurt the kingdom, the Persians allowed all the conquered nations to retain their own laws and usages)*.

9 If it please the king, let it be written that they may be destroyed: and I will pay ten thousand talents of silver to the hands of those who have the charge of the business, to bring it into the king's treasuries *(to pay the expenses of those who would carry out the terrible deed)*.

10 And the king took his ring from his hand, and gave it unto Haman the son of Hammedatha the Agagite, the Jews' enemy *(this was the royal seal, and gave Haman liberty to do about whatever he desired)*.

11 And the king said unto Haman, The silver is given to you *(whatever wealth the Jews had, after they were slaughtered, Haman could take that for himself)*, the people also, to do with them as it seems good to you *(you can do whatever you like to these people, i.e., "the Jews")*.

THE DECREE TO DESTROY THE JEWS

12 Then were the king's scribes called on the thirteenth day of the first month, and there was written according to all that Haman had commanded unto the king's lieutenants, and to the governors that were over every province, and to the rulers of every people of every province according to the writing thereof, and

to every people after their language; in the name of king Ahasuerus was it written, and sealed with the king's ring *(all edicts were in the king's name, even when a subject had been allowed to issue them, as Haman)*.

13 And the letters were sent by posts *(messengers)* into all the king's provinces, to destroy, to kill, and to cause to perish, all Jews, both young and old, little children and women, in one day, even upon the thirteenth day of the twelfth month, which is the month Adar, and to take the spoil of them for a prey *(the command was explicit, all were to be killed; as stated, this was Satan's plan to destroy the possibility of the Messiah being born into the world, Who had to come through the Jewish people and, more specifically, the Tribe of Judah [Gen. 49:10])*.

14 The copy of the writing for a commandment to be given in every province was published unto all people, that they should be ready against that day *(the 13th day of the 12th month, which was March)*.

15 The posts *(messengers)* went out, being hastened by the king's commandment, and the decree was given in Shushan the palace. And the king and Haman sat down to drink; but the city Shushan was perplexed. *(These two, having assigned an entire nation to destruction, proceeded to enjoy themselves at "a banquet of wine."*

The city of Susa being perplexed had to do with the widespread feeling, among many of other nationalities, that the precedent now being set was a dangerous one. They couldn't see the justice of this, not at all, and were thereby confused.

As well, almost every time in the Bible that we see alcoholic beverage being used, it is always, as here, in a negative sense.)

CHAPTER 4

(510 B.C.)

FASTING AND PRAYING
AMONG THE JEWS

WHEN Mordecai perceived all that was done, Mordecai rent his clothes, and put on sackcloth with ashes, and went out into the midst of the city, and cried with a loud and a bitter cry *(this was not totally uncommon for that particular time)*;

2 And came even before the king's gate: for none might enter into the king's gate clothed with sackcloth *(due to his manner of dress, he was not allowed to pass through the gate into the palace)*.

3 And in every province, whithersoever the

king's commandment and his decree came, there was great mourning among the Jews, and fasting, and weeping, and wailing; and many lay in sackcloth and ashes *(and no wonder!)*.

ESTHER AND MORDECAI CONFER

4 So Esther's maids and her chamberlains came and told it her *(about Mordecai)*. Then was the queen exceedingly grieved; and she sent raiment to clothe Mordecai, and to take away his sackcloth from him: but he received it not.

5 Then called Esther for Hatach, one of the king's chamberlains, whom he had appointed to attend upon her, and gave him a commandment to Mordecai, to know what it was, and why it was *(Esther, in the seclusion of the harem, knew nothing of what the king and Haman had determined to carry forth; so, as stated, she didn't know the reason for Mordecai's great consternation)*.

6 So Hatach went forth to Mordecai unto the street of the city, which was before the king's gate.

7 And Mordecai told him of all that had happened unto him, and of the sum of the money that Haman had promised to pay to the king's treasuries for the Jews, to destroy them.

8 Also he gave him the copy of the writing of the decree that was given at Shushan to destroy them, to show it unto Esther, and to declare it unto her, and to charge her that she should go in unto the king, to make supplication unto him, and to make request before him for her people *(Esther's marriage took place in the seventh year of the reign of Ahasuerus [2:16]; this murderous decree was issued five years later [3:7])*.

9 And Hatach came and told Esther the words of Mordecai.

10 Again Esther spoke unto Hatach, and gave him commandment unto Mordecai;

11 All the king's servants, and the people of the king's provinces, do know, that whosoever, whether man or woman, shall come unto the king into the inner court, who is not called, there is one law of his to put him to death, except such to whom the king shall hold out the golden sceptre, that he may live: but I have not been called to come in unto the king these thirty days *(she did not realize that these past thirty days had been spent by Haman in persuading the king to kill all the Jews)*.

12 And they told to Mordecai Esther's words.

MORDECAI'S CHARGE TO ESTHER

13 Then Mordecai commanded to answer Esther, Think not with yourself that you shall escape in the king's house, more than all the Jews *("Due to the fact that you are Jewish," Mordecai says, "you will die as well!")*.

14 For if you altogether hold your peace at this time, then shall there enlargement and deliverance arise to the Jews from another place *(Mordecai is confident that God will not allow the destruction of His People)*; but you and your father's house shall be destroyed *(even though the Lord will spare the nation someway, still, many Jews will die, and you and I will definitely be among them)*: and who knows whether you are come to the kingdom for such a time as this? *(And, to be sure, this is exactly why the Lord had raised up Esther to this particular position. The Lord knows all things, past, present, and future; therefore, He functions accordingly. Inasmuch as He is also Almighty, He can basically do whatever He likes, without violating the free moral agency of anyone.)*

ESTHER DECIDES TO FACE PERSONAL DANGER FOR THE SAKE OF HER PEOPLE

15 Then Esther bade them return Mordecai this answer,

16 Go, gather together all the Jews who are present in Shushan, and fast ye for me, and neither eat nor drink three days, night or day: I also and my maidens will fast likewise *(her request that a prayer-meeting, lasting for three days and three nights, should be held outside the palace, in unison with a similar prayer-meeting inside, showed her belief that God hears prayer, and that He is a very present help in time of trouble)*; and so will I go in unto the king, which is not according to the law: and if I perish, I perish *(this noble woman resolved, if necessary, to sacrifice her life for the sake of her people)*.

17 So Mordecai went his way, and did according to all that Esther had commanded him *(unfortunately, far too many modern Believers, in a time of trouble, are taught to turn to anything and everything except the Lord!)*.

CHAPTER 5
(510 B.C.)
THE COURAGE OF ESTHER

NOW it came to pass on the third day *(the third day of the fast)*, that Esther put on

her royal apparel, and stood in the inner court of the king's house, over against the king's house: and the king sat upon his royal throne in the royal house, over against the gate of the house *(where the king could see her)*.

2 And it was so, when the king saw Esther the Queen standing in the court, that she obtained favour in his sight: and the king held out to Esther the golden sceptre that was in his hand. So Esther drew near, and touched the top of the sceptre *(this was, no doubt, the customary act by which the king's grace was, as it were, accepted and appropriated)*.

3 Then said the king under her, What will you, Queen Esther? and what is your request? it shall be even given you to the half of the kingdom.

4 And Esther answered, If it seem good unto the king, let the king and Haman come this day unto the banquet that I have prepared for him. *(Concerning this, Williams says, "Esther's intelligence and tact were admirable. Her life and that of her people hung on a thread. She was playing with edged tools, and the slightest mistake would have been fatal. To invite the king to a banquet was a master-stroke of policy; and to include his favorite minister, Haman, in the invitation was not only an added evidence of skill and of a deep knowledge of human nature, but it was, at the same time, a clever plan for getting Haman into her power." No doubt, the Lord had told her exactly what to do.)*

5 Then the king said, Cause Haman to make haste, that he may do as Esther has said. So the king and Haman came to the banquet that Esther had prepared.

6 And the king said unto Esther at the banquet of wine, What is your petition? and it shall be granted you: and what is your request? even to the half of the kingdom it shall be performed *(the king sensed that Esther had something more in mind that what was now being done; he knew that she must have a request, a real favor that she wants him to grant; therefore, he repeats the inquiry and the promise that he had made previously)*.

7 Then answered Esther, and said, My petition and my request is;

8 If I have found favour in the sight of the king, and if it please the king to grant my petition, and to perform my request, let the king and Haman come to the banquet that I shall prepare for them, and I will do to morrow as the king has said. *("I will make known tomorrow my actual request." The repetition of her*

invitation showed extraordinary wisdom. At the first banquet, the king rightly divined that some important matter lay behind the invitation; else, why should Esther risk her life by coming uninvited into his presence? It was surely not merely to invite him and Haman to a dinner. Esther, by repeating the invitation and postponing the secret petition, enhanced its importance while, at the same time, she increased her personal interest in the king's affections and more deeply excited his curiosity. Furthermore, she more effectually threw Haman off his guard and so secured his fall.)*

HAMAN'S JOY AND PRIDE

9 Then went Haman forth that day joyful and with a glad heart: but when Haman saw Mordecai in the king's gate, that he stood not up, nor moved for him, he was full of indignation against Mordecai *(Mordecai showed his utter contempt for Haman by not even acknowledging his presence; such infuriated Haman!)*.

10 Nevertheless Haman refrained himself: and when he came home, he sent and called for his friends, and Zeresh his wife *(it was a plot to know what to do with Mordecai; in other words, killing would not be enough; he wanted his death to be a spectacle)*.

11 And Haman told them of the glory of his riches, and the multitude of his children, and all the things wherein the king had promoted him, and how he had advanced him above the princes and servants of the king.

12 Haman said moreover, Yea, Esther the Queen did let no man come in with the king unto the banquet that she had prepared but myself; and to morrow am I invited unto her also with the king.

HAMAN'S PLAN TO HANG MORDECAI

13 Yet all this avails me nothing, so long as I see Mordecai the Jew sitting at the king's gate *(he will find his wife holds the solution to his problem, or so he thinks!)*.

14 Then said Zeresh his wife and all his friends unto him, Let a gallows be made of fifty cubits high *(75 feet)*, and to morrow speak thou unto the king that Mordecai may be hanged thereon: then go thou in merrily with the king unto the banquet *(your problem has been solved)*. And the thing pleased Haman; and he caused the gallows to be made *(he was very sure of himself)*.

CHAPTER 6
(510 B.C.)
THE KING BECOMES AWARE OF MORDECAI'S SERVICE

ON that night could not the king sleep *(and so ordered by the Lord)*, and he commanded to bring the book of records of the chronicles; and they were read before the king *(the Holy Spirit no doubt placed this in the king's mind, as well, to have the record read)*.

2 And it was found written, that Mordecai had told of Bigthana and Teresh, two of the king's chamberlains, the keepers of the door, who sought to lay hand on the king Ahasuerus.

3 And the king said, What honour and dignity have been done to Mordecai for this? Then said the king's servants that ministered unto him, There is nothing done for him *(had Mordecai complained at the time that he saved the king's life [2:21-23] of the non-recognition of his services, he would have lost the extraordinary honors recorded in this Chapter; it is always better and more dignified not to seek for human recognition but to walk in fellowship with God, doing one's duty, and waiting for the honor that comes from above; and it will surely come, as this Chapter proves)*.

HAMAN IS FORCED TO
HONOR MORDECAI

4 And the king said, Who is in the court? Now Haman was come into the outward court of the king's house *(which was no doubt the next morning)*, to speak unto the king to hang Mordecai on the gallows that he had prepared for him.

5 And the king's servants said unto him, Behold, Haman stands in the court. And the king said, Let him come in.

6 So Haman came in. And the king said unto him, What shall be done unto the man whom the king delights to honour? Now Haman thought in his heart *(literally, "said in his heart")*, To whom would the king delight to do honour more than to myself?

7 And Haman answered the king, For the man whom the king delights to honour,

8 Let the royal apparel be brought which the king uses to wear, and the horse that the king rides upon, and the crown royal which is set upon his head *(the insignia of the crown on the horse's head, not the head of the man)*:

9 And let this apparel and horse be delivered to the hand of one of the king's most noble princes, that they may array the man withal whom the king delights to honour, and bring him on horseback through the street of the city, and proclaim before him, Thus shall it be done to the man whom the king delights to honour *(if Haman only knew!)*.

10 Then the king said to Haman, Make haste, and take the apparel and the horse, as you have said, and do even so to Mordecai the Jew, who sits at the king's gate: let nothing fail of all that you have spoken. *(What must have been Haman's thoughts, when the king said this should be done to Mordecai, when all the time he thought it was for himself? Considering some of the things the Lord does, and He definitely did this, we must come to the conclusion that the Lord has a sense of humor. Only the Lord could work out a situation in this manner.)*

11 Then took Haman the apparel and the horse, and arrayed Mordecai, and brought him on horseback through the street of the city, and proclaimed before him, Thus shall it be done unto the man whom the king delights to honour *(Haman had backed himself into a corner; there was no ground on which he could decline this task thrust upon him; so, he does exactly what the king has commanded to be done, as galling as it must have been; also, Mordecai must have been just as pleasantly surprised as Haman had been dismally dejected)*.

HAMAN'S FALL PREDICTED

12 And Mordecai came again to the king's gate. But Haman hasted to his house mourning, and having his head covered *(a sign of acute dejection)*.

13 And Haman told Zeresh his wife and all his friends every thing that had befallen him. Then said his wise men and Zeresh his wife unto him, If Mordecai be of the seed of the Jews, before whom you have begun to fall, you shall not prevail against him, but shall surely fall before him *(for one time, these "wise men" were right!)*.

14 And while they were yet talking with him, came the king's chamberlains, and hasted to bring Haman unto the banquet that Esther had prepared *(this was normal for servants to be sent to escort guests of importance from their own homes to the place of entertainment)*.

CHAPTER 7
(510 B.C.)
ESTHER'S BANQUET FOR THE KING

So the king and Haman came to banquet with Esther the Queen.

2 And the king said again unto Esther on the second day at the banquet of wine, What is your petition, Queen Esther? and it shall be granted you: and what is your request? and it shall be performed, even to the half of the kingdom (the king, obviously, is very pleasantly curious).

ESTHER'S REQUEST FOR HER LIFE AND THE LIFE OF THE JEWS

3 Then Esther the Queen answered and said, If I have found favour in your sight, O king, and if it please the king, let my life be given me at my petition, and my people at my request:

4 For we are sold, I and my people, to be destroyed, to be slain, and to perish. But if we had been sold for bondmen and bondwomen, I had held my tongue, although the enemy could not countervail the king's damage (even in the case of the latter, with all the Jews made into slaves, the king's revenues would have been injured beyond compensation; so the empire was going to lose in every capacity, at least if this thing be carried out).

5 Then the king Ahasuerus answered and said unto Esther the Queen, Who is he, and where is he, who does presume in his heart to do so?

6 And Esther said, The adversary and enemy is this wicked Haman. Then Haman was afraid before the king and the Queen (Esther adds the word "enemy" to the list, with the insinuation that, in actuality, Haman was an enemy of the king also; in other words, he was playing the king for all he could get, and was being very successful, at least up until now).

THE KING'S WRATH AND HAMAN'S PLEA FOR MERCY

7 And the king arising from the banquet of wine in his wrath went into the palace garden: and Haman stood up to make request for his life to Esther the Queen; for he saw that there was evil determined against him by the king.

8 Then the king returned out of the palace garden into the place of the banquet of wine; and Haman was fallen upon the bed whereon Esther was (actually, reclining on a couch, as was the custom then at banquets). Then said the king, Will he force the Queen also before me in the house? As the word went out of the king's mouth, they covered Haman's face. (In his pleading with Esther for his life, he, more than likely, sought to grasp her feet or her garments, as was usual with supplicants in the east. At that moment, the king returned. Misunderstanding Haman's action, or pretending to do so, the king accused Haman of attacking the Queen. At that moment, at the king's command, guards standing nearby covered Haman's face, which meant that he was doomed.

To be sure, the Lord orchestrated all of this, even for the king to come back in at the exact moment he did.)

HAMAN IS HUNG ON THE GALLOWS HE MADE FOR MORDECAI

9 And Harbonah, one of the chamberlains (eunuchs), said before the king, Behold also, the gallows fifty cubits high (75 feet), which Haman had made for Mordecai, who had spoken good for the king, stands in the house of Haman. Then the king said, Hang him thereon (evidently, Haman had erected the gallows within the compound of his home, which no doubt was quite large and included many acres of gardens, etc.; now he will hang on his own gallows).

10 So they hanged Haman on the gallows that he had prepared for Mordecai. Then was the king's wrath pacified (the king realized that Haman had made a fool of him; so, he determines to settle the score in the worst way of all, which he did).

CHAPTER 8
(510 B.C.)
MORDECAI ADVANCED AND HONORED

On that day did the king Ahasuerus give the house of Haman the Jews' enemy unto Esther the Queen (to be sure, it was considerable, because Haman had been one of the richest men in the empire; now it all belongs to Esther, and Haman is dead, all orchestrated by the Lord). And Mordecai came before the king; for Esther had told what he was unto her (her uncle).

2 And the king took off his ring, which he had taken from Haman, and gave it unto Mordecai. And Esther set Mordecai over the house of Haman. (In effect, the king made

Mordecai his Prime Minister. Joseph and Daniel were also Prime Ministers to heathen princes.

If God, in the pursuit of His Purposes, places one of His Servants in such a high position, He will give him Grace and Wisdom to glorify the Lord in that position. But an ambitious Christian, who, by his energy and talent and in order to gratify himself, grasps at such a post, cannot count upon God to deliver him from its snares and temptations — Williams.)

ESTHER'S PLEA FOR THE LIFE OF HER PEOPLE

3 And Esther spoke yet again before the king, and fell down at his feet, and besought him with tears to put away the mischief of Haman the Agagite, and his device that he had devised against the Jews.

4 Then the king held out the golden sceptre toward Esther. So Esther arose, and stood before the king *(the golden scepter was held out simply to express a readiness to do as Esther desired)*,

5 And said, If it please the king, and if I have found favour in his sight, and the thing seem right before the king, and I be pleasing in his eyes, let it be written to reverse the letters devised by Haman the son of Hammedatha the Agagite, which he wrote to destroy the Jews which are in all the king's provinces:

6 For how can I endure to see the evil that shall come unto my people? or how can I endure to see the destruction of my kindred? *(The laws of the Medes and Persians being irrevocable, the king could not recall his decree; but he could issue a fresh one authorizing Esther's people to defend themselves against all who should attack them.)*

A NEW DECREE AUTHORIZES THE JEWS TO RESIST AND SPOIL THEIR ENEMIES

7 Then the king Ahasuerus said unto Esther the Queen and to Mordecai the Jew, Behold, I have given Esther the house of Haman, and him they have hanged upon the gallows, because he laid his hand upon the Jews *(Mordecai is now included in the king's response)*.

8 Write you also for the Jews, as it liketh you, in the king's name, and seal it with the king's ring: for the writing which is written in the king's name, and sealed with the king's ring, may no man reverse *(in effect, he is saying to Mordecai, "Surely you can devise something which will save your people without calling on me to retract my own words, which would break a great principle of Persian law")*.

9 Then were the king's scribes called at the time in the third month, that is, the month Sivan *(June)*, on the three and twentieth day thereof; and it was written according to all that Mordecai commanded unto the Jews, and to the lieutenants, and the deputies and rulers of the provinces which are from India unto Ethiopia, an hundred twenty and seven provinces, unto every province according to the writing thereof, and unto every people after their language, and to the Jews according to their writing, and according to their language *(it seems that copies of the former edict had not been sent especially to the Jews; they had been left to learn their danger indirectly from the people among whom they dwelt; but Mordecai took care that they should be informed directly of their right of defense)*.

10 And he wrote in the king Ahasuerus' name, and sealed it with the king's ring, and sent letters by posts *(messengers)* on horseback, and riders on mules, camels, and young dromedaries *(it seems that the older Manuscripts do not contain the words mules, camels, etc., but rather thoroughbred horses exclusively, which no doubt is correct; that would be the fastest mode of transportation in those days)*:

11 Wherein the king granted the Jews which were in every city to gather themselves together, and to stand for their life, to destroy, to slay, and to cause to perish, all the power of the people and province that would assault them, both little ones and women, and to take the spoil of them for a prey *(the earlier edict had given permission to the Jews' enemies to kill and to take; the new law, while not forbidding the former, as well gives the Jews the same privilege, and in every respect)*,

12 Upon one day in all the provinces of king Ahasuerus, namely, upon the thirteenth day of the twelfth month, which is the month Adar *(the month of March; this was the day designated by the former edict to be carried out; now, on this day, the Jews have been given the freedom to protect themselves; so that day, which was determined to be a day of infamy regarding the Jews, would turn out to be the opposite, all because of what the Lord had done)*.

13 The copy of the writing for a commandment to be given in every province was published unto all people, and that the Jews should be ready against that day to avenge themselves on their enemies.

14 So the posts *(messengers)* who rode upon mules and camels went out *(should have been translated "royal studs," in other words, the very fastest horses in the kingdom)*, being hastened and pressed on by the king's commandment. And the decree was given at Shushan the palace.

MORDECAI AND THE JEWS EXALTED

15 And Mordecai went out from the presence of the king in royal apparel of blue and white, and with a great crown of gold, and with a garment of fine linen and purple: and the city of Shushan rejoiced and was glad *(as the capital city had been perplexed at the first, concerning the original edict, they now rejoiced at the second)*.

16 The Jews had light, and gladness, and joy, and honour.

17 And in every province, and in every city, whithersoever the king's commandment and his decree came, the Jews had joy and gladness, a feast and a good day. And many of the people of the land became Jews *(proselyte Jews, which means they adopted the Mosaic Law, and thereby the worship of Jehovah as the One True God)*; for the fear of the Jews fell upon them *(because of all that had happened!)*.

CHAPTER 9
(510 B.C.)
THE JEWS DESTROY THEIR ENEMIES

NOW in the twelfth month, that is, the month Adar *(March)*, on the thirteenth day of the same, when the king's commandment and his decree drew near to be put in execution, in the day that the enemies of the Jews hoped to have power over them, (though it was turned to the contrary, that the Jews had rule over them who hated them;)

2 The Jews gathered themselves together in their cities throughout all the provinces of the king Ahasuerus, to lay hand on such as sought their hurt: and no man could withstand them; for the fear of them fell upon all people *(the number "thirteen," which is so feared by the superstitious children of this world, is a gladsome number to the people of God, for, on that day in March, the Amalekite and all his allies were destroyed)*.

3 And all the rulers of the provinces, and the lieutenants, and the deputies, and officers of the king, helped the Jews; because the fear

of Mordecai fell upon them *(due to the fact that he was now Prime Minister, which refers to one who actually runs the government)*.

4 For Mordecai was great in the king's house, and his fame went out throughout all the provinces: for this man Mordecai waxed greater and greater.

5 Thus the Jews smote all their enemies with the stroke of the sword, and slaughter, and destruction, and did what they would unto those who hated them *(who would have killed the Jews, had the former edict remained in place)*.

6 And in Shushan the palace the Jews slew and destroyed five hundred men *(actually refers to the upper city where the palace was)*.

7 And Parshandatha, and Dalphon, and Aspatha,

8 And Poratha, and Adalia, and Aridatha,

9 And Parmashta, and Arisai, and Aridai, and Vajezatha,

10 The ten sons of Haman the son of Hammedatha, the enemy of the Jews, slew they; but on the spoil laid they not their hand. *(All of this was looked at by the Lord as war. It is the same as when Joshua or David overcame the enemy, killing, at times, thousands of them. Presently, the United States has the Scriptural right to put down any nation in the world that is seeking to take peace from the world. Such is sanctioned by the Word of God, but only as a matter of last resort [Rom. 13:1-7].)*

11 On that day the number of those who were slain in Shushan the palace was brought before the king *(it was customary in all wars for the number of the slain to be carefully made out and recorded)*.

12 And the king said unto Esther the Queen. The Jews have slain and destroyed five hundred men in Shushan the palace, and the ten sons of Haman *(have arrested these ten, with the intention of executing them)*; what have they done in the rest of the king's provinces? now what is your petition? and it shall be granted you: or what is your request further? and it shall be done.

13 Then said Esther, If it please the king, let it be granted to the Jews which are in Shushan to do to morrow also according unto this day's decree, and let Haman's ten sons be hanged upon the gallows *(this was the manner in which they would be executed)*.

14 And the king commanded it so to be done: and the decree was given at Shushan; and they hanged Haman's ten sons.

15 For the Jews who were in Shushan gathered

themselves together on the fourteenth day also of the month Adar, and slew three hundred men at Shushan; but on the prey they laid not their hand *(notwithstanding the clause in the edict which allowed the Jews "to take the spoil of their enemies for a prey," neither in the capital nor in the provinces did the triumphant Israelites touch the property of those opposed to them [8:11]; this was an evident wish to show that they were not motivated by greed, but simply desirous of securing themselves from future harm).*

16 But the other Jews who were in the king's provinces gathered themselves together, and stood for their lives, and had rest from their enemies, and slew of their foes seventy and five thousand, but they laid not their hands on the prey. *(Some of the older manuscripts had the number "15,000," which is probably the correct number. There are no original copies of Biblical Scrolls left, as would be obvious. However, there are tens of thousands of copies of the entirety, or individual Books, of the Bible. When making copies, sometimes an error would be made, mostly in numbers. In both the Hebrew and the Greek languages there were no such thing as numbers, with letters actually standing for numbers, making it even easier to make a mistake.)*

17 On the thirteenth day of the month Adar; and on the fourteenth day of the same rested they, and made it a day of feasting and gladness *(the Jews would have lived in daily fear of the vengeance of these men, if they had not been destroyed; Esther's wise conduct gave perfect peace to her people and, at the same time, punished with death men worthy of death).*

18 But the Jews who were at Shushan assembled together on the thirteenth day thereof, and on the fourteenth thereof; and on the fifteenth day of the same they rested, and made it a day of feasting and gladness.

19 Therefore the Jews of the villages, who dwelt in the unwalled towns, made the fourteenth day of the month Adar a day of gladness and feasting, and a good day, and of sending portions one to another.

THE FEAST OF PURIM INSTITUTED

20 And Mordecai wrote these things, and sent letters unto all the Jews who were in all the provinces of the king Ahasuerus, both near and far,

21 To stablish this among them, that they should keep the fourteenth day of the month Adar, and the fifteenth day of the same, yearly,

22 As the days wherein the Jews rested from their enemies, and the month which was turned unto them from sorrow to joy, and from mourning into a good day: that they should make them days of feasting and joy, and of sending portions one to another, and gifts to the poor.

23 And the Jews undertook to do as they had begun, and as Mordecai had written unto them;

24 Because Haman the son of Hammedatha, the Agagite, the enemy of all the Jews, had devised against the Jews to destroy them, and had cast Pur, that is, the lot, to consume them, and to destroy them;

25 But when Esther came before the king, he commanded by letters that his wicked device, which he devised against the Jews, should return upon his own head, and that he and his sons should be hanged on the gallows.

26 Wherefore they called these days Purim after the name of Pur. Therefore for all the words of this letter, and of that which they had seen concerning this matter, and which had come unto them,

27 The Jews ordained, and took upon them, and upon their seed, and upon all such as joined themselves unto them, so as it should not fail, that they would keep these two days according to their writing, and according to their appointed time every year;

28 And that these days should be remembered and kept throughout every generation, every family, every province, and every city; and that these days of Purim should not fail from among the Jews, nor the memorial of them perish from their seed *(in fact, this feast has continued among the Jews, at least in some form, even unto this day).*

29 Then Esther the Queen, the daughter of Abihail, and Mordecai the Jew, wrote with all authority, to confirm this second letter of Purim *(the first letter is the one which is mentioned in Verses 20 and 26; a "second letter" of Purim was now issued, "confirming" and establishing the observance; it went forth, not as an edict, or in the king's name, but as a letter, and in the names of Esther and Mordecai).*

30 And he sent the letters unto all the Jews, to the hundred twenty and seven provinces of the kingdom of Ahasuerus, with words of peace and truth,

31 To confirm these days of Purim in their times appointed, according as Mordecai the Jew and Esther the Queen had enjoined them,

and as they had decreed for themselves and for their seed, the matters of the fastings and their cry *(sort of a history as to what had happened)*.

32 And the decree of Esther confirmed these matters of Purim; and it was written in the book.

CHAPTER 10
(509 B.C.)
MORDECAI'S GREATNESS

AND the king Ahasuerus laid a tribute *(tax)* upon the land, and upon the isles of the sea.

2 And all the acts of his power and of his might, and the declaration of the greatness of Mordecai, whereunto the king advanced him, are they not written in the book of the chronicles of the kings of Media and Persia?

3 For Mordecai the Jew was next unto king Ahasuerus, and great among the Jews, and accepted of the multitude of his brethren, seeking the wealth of his people, and speaking peace to all his seed *(promoting their peace and safety, guaranteeing them, so long as he lived and ruled, a quiet and peaceful existence — Pulpit)*.

THE BOOK OF
JOB

CHAPTER 1
(1520 B.C.)
JOB'S CHARACTER AND RICHES

THERE was a man in the land of Uz (probably located between Edom and Saudi Arabia), whose name was Job (the son of Issachar, which means that Jacob was his grandfather); and that man was perfect and upright, and one who feared God, and eschewed (hated) evil. (The word "perfect" here doesn't mean sinless perfection, but rather perfect in his efforts in doing all he could to please the Lord.

In fact, the Book of Job is the oldest book in the world. It was probably written by Moses [Lk. 24:27, 44]. It explains the problem of why good men are afflicted. It is in order to effect their Sanctification. It is interesting that this difficult question should be the first taken up and answered in the Bible.)

2 And there were born unto him seven sons and three daughters.

3 His substance also was seven thousand sheep, and three thousand camels, and five hundred yoke of oxen, and five hundred she asses, and a very great household; so that this man was the greatest of all the men of the east (which means that he was one of the richest men in the world; in other words, God had blessed him greatly).

4 And his sons went and feasted in their houses, every one his day (every one on his birthday); and sent and called for their three sisters to eat and to drink with them.

5 And it was so, when the days of their feasting were gone about (came around), that Job sent and sanctified them, and rose up early in the morning, and offered Burnt Offerings according to the number of them all: for Job said, It may be that my sons have sinned, and cursed God in their hearts. Thus did Job continually. (Before the giving of the Law, the father of the family was the Priest of the family. It was his responsibility to bless, purify, and offer Sacrifice.

The offering up of these Sacrifices, a ram for each Burnt Offering, and one for each son and daughter, proclaimed the fact that Job had placed his Faith and trust in the Sacrifice of Christ.

However, the offering up of these Sacrifices, although a great blessing to him, could not atone for the sins of his sons and daughters, unless they personally placed their faith in such. There is no evidence they did!)

SATAN PERMITTED TO TEST JOB

6 Now there was a day when the sons of God came to present themselves before the LORD (used in this sense, it always speaks of Angels, whether righteous or fallen [Gen. 6:2]; this meeting took place in Heaven, at the Throne of God), and Satan came also among them. (In the Hebrew, the definite article is before Satan, meaning that it reads "the Satan," specifying the leader of evil. This tells us that these angelic ministers appear at appointed seasons to give account of their actions to God. This is the first instance in the Bible of this mighty angel being named "Satan," or "the Adversary." Some time in eternity past, he led a revolution against God, with one-third of the Angels throwing in their lot with him [Rev. 12:4, 7-11]. From the time of that revolution unto the present, this war between good and evil, between righteousness and unrighteousness, has raged. However, it is not long before this battle will end [Rev. 20:1-3, 7-10].)

7 And the LORD said unto Satan, Where have you been? (Of course, the Lord already knew the answer to that.) Then Satan answered the LORD, and said, From going to and fro in the Earth, and from walking up and down in it. (Pulpit says, "Satan searches the whole Earth continually, never pausing, never resting, but 'going about,' as Peter said [I Pet. 5:8], 'like a roaring lion, seeking whom he may devour.'" As stated, the end of his darkness and destruction is very soon [Rev. 20:1-2].)

8 And the LORD said unto Satan, Have you considered My servant Job, that there is none like him in the Earth, a perfect and an upright man, one who fears God, and escheweth (hates) evil? (While it doesn't say that Job at that time is the only one on Earth living for God, it does say that he is closer to God than anyone else. We learn from this of the minute attention given by the Lord of all those who love and follow Him.

It is a sobering thought to realize that conversations may be conducted in Heaven, even by the Lord Himself, as it regards some of His children. What is He saying about me? About you?)

9 Then Satan answered the LORD, and said, Does Job fear God for nought? *(Satan insinuates that Job's motive is purely selfish. He intimates that Job is serving God, not out of love for God, but for what he gets out of it. Regrettably, that just might be true concerning some, hence, Satan asking this question.)*

10 Have You not made an hedge about him, and about his house, and about all that he has on every side? You have blessed the work of his hands, and his substance is increased in the land *(this Verse proves how absolutely secure from Satanic malignity are the Children of God, unless the Lord purposely allows certain things; in other words, Satan can only do, whatever it might be, whatever the Lord allows him to do).*

11 But put forth Your hand now, and touch all that he has, and he will curse You to Your face *(the Lord would not do this, but He gave Satan permission to do certain things; again, we state: Satan had to have permission).*

12 And the LORD said unto Satan, Behold, all that he has is in your power; only upon himself put not forth your hand. So Satan went forth from the Presence of the LORD. *(There were limitations placed on what Satan could do, as there are with all Believers. Concerning this, Williams says: "Job does not symbolize an unconverted, but a converted, man. It was necessary that one of God's children should be chosen for this trial; for the subject of the Book is not the conversion of the sinner, but the consecration of the Saint. It is evident that an unconverted man needs to be brought to the end of himself; but that a man who feared God, who was perfect, and who hated evil should also need this is not so clear.*

"We find in this Book that God uses Satan, calamity, and sickness to be His instruments in creating character and making men partakers of His Holiness. Such were the instruments; but the Hand that used them was God's; and the facts of this Book explain to Christian people, who, like Job, are conscious of personal integrity, why calamities, sorrows, and diseases are permitted to afflict them.")

JOB LOSES HIS WEALTH, SERVANTS, AND CHILDREN

13 And there was a day when his sons and his daughters were eating and drinking wine in their eldest brother's house *(one of the birthdays, probably the eldest brother's):*

14 And there came a messenger unto Job, and said, The oxen were plowing, and the asses feeding beside them:

15 And the Sabeans fell upon them, and took them away; yea, they have slain the servants with the edge of the sword; and I only am escaped alone to tell you.

16 While he was yet speaking, there came also another, and said, The fire of God is fallen from Heaven, and has burned up the sheep, and the servants, and consumed them; and I only am escaped alone to tell you.

17 While he was yet speaking, there came also another, and said, The Chaldeans made out three bands, and fell upon the camels, and have carried them away, yea, and slain the servants with the edge of the sword; and I only am escaped alone to tell you. *(All of this shows that this is exactly what would happen to every Believer if the Lord allowed such. Satan's hatred would demand this. But, as stated, the Evil One can only do what the Lord allows him to do.)*

18 While he was yet speaking, there came also another, and said, Your sons and your daughters were eating and drinking wine in their eldest brother's house:

19 And, behold, there came a great wind from the wilderness, and smote the four corners of the house, and it fell upon the young men, and they are dead; and I only am escaped alone to tell you. *(The loss of property is one thing; however, the loss of one's family is something else altogether. Why did the Lord allow the latter?*

The Lord did not choose to directly tell us. However, if it is to be noted, the only thing that was said about those sons and daughters was that they were "eating and drinking." I think it is clear that the consecration of Job definitely was not their consecration. Having little, if any, desire for the Lord, they were taken away. This we do know:

Whatever the Lord does is right. It's not right just because He does it, but because, in fact, it is right.)

20 Then Job arose, and rent his mantle, and shaved his head, and fell down upon the ground, and worshipped *(while this blow was almost enough to kill a man, still, we see here the depths of his consecration by his worship of the Lord, even at this terrible time; in times like these,*

only a few worship, while most blame God!),

21 And said, Naked came I out of my mother's womb, and naked shall I return thither *(return unto the earth)*: the LORD gave, and the LORD has taken away; blessed be the Name of the LORD. *(Satan said that Job would curse God to His Face, if such calamity fell upon him. However, before the entirety of the spirit world, the Lord proved that this would not be the case. In fact, all of us are "compassed about with so great a cloud of witnesses" [Heb. 12:1]. What type of testimony are we giving to the spirit world?)*

22 In all this Job sinned not, nor charged God foolishly. *(Some foolishly claim that Job was not showing faith regarding his words of Verse 21; however, the Holy Spirit says the very opposite!)*

CHAPTER 2
(1520 B.C.)
SATAN GRANTED PERMISSION TO TEST JOB FURTHER

AGAIN there was a day when the sons of God came to present themselves before the LORD, and Satan came also among them to present himself before the LORD *(regrettably, Satan always comes "again")*.

2 And the LORD said unto Satan, From where do you come? And Satan answered the LORD, and said, From going to and fro in the Earth, and from walking up and down in it *(1:7)*.

3 And the LORD said unto Satan, Have you considered My servant Job, that there is none like him in the Earth, a perfect and an upright man, one who fears God, and hates evil? and still he holds fast his integrity, although you moved Me against him to destroy him without cause *(the Lord reminds Satan that Job did not do what Satan said he would do, which was to curse God [1:11])*.

4 And Satan answered the LORD, and said, Skin for skin, yea, all that a man has will he give for his life *(while that is true for most, it definitely isn't true for all, even as it wasn't true for Job)*.

5 But put forth Your hand now, and touch his bone and his flesh, and he will curse You to Your face *(the trial deepens!)*.

6 And the LORD said unto Satan, Behold, he is in your hand; but save his life *(once again, the Lord sets the limits; Job's health can be affected, and severely so, but Satan cannot*

take his life; again we state: all of this shows that Satan can only do what the Lord allows him to do).*

7 So went Satan forth from the presence of the LORD, and smote Job with sore boils from the sole of his foot unto his crown *(it is believed that this disease was "elephantiasis," which is a strongly developed form of leprosy; while it is a non-contagious disease, it is extremely painful, coming from a burning and ulcerous swelling; generally, it attacks only a certain part of the body; however, Job was afflicted over the entirety of his body, which was not only notoriously painful, but, as well, terribly humiliating, as would be obvious).*

8 And he took him a potsherd to scrape himself withal; and he sat down among the ashes *(the sores, it is said, emit a fluid with an offensive odor; Job used the potsherd to scrape it away).*

JOB AND HIS WIFE

9 Then said his wife unto him, Do you still retain your integrity? curse God, and die *(in essence, Job's wife said, "Why do you hold on to your religious profession? Throw your idol god aside; there is no eternity; you need not be afraid to die; there is nothing behind death. This religion of Abel, Noah, and Abraham is a fairy tale!").*

10 But he said unto her, You speak as one of the foolish women speaks. What? shall we receive good at the hand of God, and shall we not receive evil? In all this did not Job sin with his lips *(this man, who had been the richest man in the east, which means he had been the most powerful, now is reduced to total poverty, his body full of sores, with even his wife condemning him; but yet he did not blame God; what an example!).*

JOB AND HIS THREE FRIENDS

11 Now when Job's three friends heard of all this evil that was come upon him, they came every one from his own place; Eliphaz the Temanite, and Bildad the Shuhite, and Zophar the Naamathite: for they had made an appointment together to come to mourn with him and to comfort him *(these three men represent the world of religion that attempts to serve God by means other than Christ and the Cross; the truth is, they were very religious, but very lost, because their faith, even as we shall see,*

was in the wrong things).

12 And when they lifted up their eyes afar off, and knew him not, they lifted up their voice, and wept; and they rent every one his mantle, and sprinkled dust upon their heads toward Heaven *(Job was so disfigured by the disease that they failed to recognize him; when he was recognized, they instantly realized that the situation was far worse than they could even begin to contemplate).*

13 So they sat down with him upon the ground seven days and seven nights, and none spoke a word unto him: for they saw that his grief was very great *(we must remember that Job, at least at this time, had absolutely no knowledge as to what was going on; so the questions must have loomed large and furious in his mind; in fact, this was one of the greatest tests of Faith that one has ever engaged).*

CHAPTER 3
(1520 B.C.)
JOB BEWAILS HIS BIRTH

AFTER this *(seven days and seven nights)* opened Job his mouth, and cursed his day *(cursed his birthday; the word "cursed" doesn't speak of profanity, but rather a negativism regarding his birth).*

2 And Job spoke, and said,

3 Let the day perish wherein I was born, and the night in which it was said, There is a man child conceived *(in other words, he is saying that the birth of a baby boy should have been a great blessing, but it seems it wasn't; Job could not have been more wrong!).*

4 Let that day be darkness; let not God regard it from above, neither let the light shine upon it.

5 Let darkness and the shadow of death stain it; let a cloud dwell upon it; let the blackness of the day terrify it.

6 As for that night, let darkness seize upon it; let it not be joined unto the days of the year, let it not come into the number of the months *(Job wishes the day of his birth and the night of his conception to be utterly blotted out from the calendar; but, aware that this is impossible, he subsides into a milder class of imprecations — Pulpit).*

7 Lo, let that night be solitary, let no joyful voice come therein. *("Considering what has happened to me, my birth was definitely not the cause of joy." But again, how wrong Job was! All of this is meant to show us, as Believers,*

that we cannot look at circumstances, irrespective as to how negative they may presently seem to be.)

8 Let them curse it who curse the day, who are ready to raise up their mourning *(in essence, Job is saying, "Let those who curse life add my name to the list").*

9 Let the stars of the twilight thereof be dark; let it look for light, but have none; neither let it see the dawning of the day *("everything is dark," for that's exactly the way it looked to Job):*

10 Because it shut not up the doors of my mother's womb, nor hid sorrow from my eyes *(the light of the day did not prevent the darkness!).*

JOB LAMENTS HIS INFANCY

11 Why died I not from the womb? whey did I not give up the ghost when I came out of the belly? *(Perhaps this one word, "Why?", looms as the largest word in any language!*

The Holy Spirit allows the "Why?" because this teaches us trust. With God, everything is a lesson. His desire is that we learn the lesson. All of us desire immediate answers; nevertheless, they are not always immediately forthcoming. True love will truly trust [I Jn. 4:18].)

12 Why did the knees prevent *(receive)* me? *(The culture of that time placed a new-born child upon the knees of the father, which means he accepted it as his own, and pledged himself to provide for it.)* or why the breasts that I should suck?

13 For now should I have lain still and been quiet, I should have slept: then had I been at rest *(if I had died, I would now be at rest),*

14 With kings and counsellors of the Earth, which build desolate places for themselves *(that built on the Earth ultimately comes to desolation);*

15 Or with princes who had gold, who filled their houses with silver *(none of this can stop the sorrow):*

16 Or as an hidden untimely birth I had not been; as infants which never saw light *(I wish I had been born dead!).*

17 There the wicked cease from troubling; and there the weary be at rest *(but only if they make the Lord their eternal Saviour; otherwise, no matter how bad life has been, at death the real Hell begins!).*

18 There the prisoners rest together; they hear not the voice of the oppressor *(again, if*

they know the Lord).

19 The small and great are there; and the servant is free from his master *(true freedom is found only in Christ, of which Job would have had only a dim view at that time).*

HIS MANHOOD LAMENTED

20 Wherefore is light given to him who is in misery, and life unto the bitter in soul *(why would the Lord give life, if it's going to be such misery? Due to his circumstances, I would surely trust that one can understand Job's present frame of mind);*

21 Which long for death, but it comes not; and dig for it more than for hid treasures *(some of God's greatest have longed for death; however, they were not right in doing so!);*

22 Which rejoice exceedingly, and are glad, when they can find the grave? *(Inspiration guarantees that Job made these statements, but inspiration does not guarantee that they are right. In fact, much of what Job is saying here is wrong. The Holy Spirit allowed it to be put in the Sacred Text in order that we as Believers may understand that something is always behind what is taking place. We presently have the benefit of Job's experience, whereas Job didn't have that benefit. So, we shouldn't be hard on him.)*

23 Why is light given to a man whose way is hid, and whom God has hedged in? *(The idea is, Job doesn't know what to do!)*

24 For my sighing comes before I eat, and my roarings are poured out like the waters.

25 For the thing which I greatly feared is come upon me, and that which I was afraid of is come unto me *(many have claimed that it was "fear" which caused Job's problems; however, the Bible doesn't say such; in fact, there is no hint that Job did anything that caused the hedge to come down; it was purely a matter of God allowing the test and the trial, which would be of great benefit to coming generations, and would, as well, turn out to be a great blessing to Job).*

26 I was not in safety, neither had I rest, neither was I quiet; yet trouble came *(the idea is, "I don't know why this has happened to me!").*

CHAPTER 4
(1520 B.C.)

ELIPHAZ REBUKES JOB: "INNOCENT PEOPLE AREN'T PUNISHED," HE SAYS!

THEN Eliphaz the Temanite answered and said,

2 If we assay to commune with you, will you be grieved? but who can withhold himself from speaking? *(Eliphaz' argument will be from human experience, which will prove to be totally wrong.)*

3 Behold, you have instructed many, and you have strengthened the weak hands *(it is true that Job did this when he was the most powerful man of the east; now Eliphaz is telling him that what he counseled was wrong; however, it is Eliphaz who is wrong!).*

4 Your words have upholden him who was falling, and you have strengthened the feeble knees.

5 But now it is come upon you, and you faint; it touches you, and you are troubled *("your condition," Eliphaz says, "proves that you were wrong, or else this trouble would not have come upon you").*

6 Is not this your fear, your confidence, your hope, and the uprightness of your ways? *(Eliphaz puts words in Job's mouth, in essence saying, "Your confidence is gone!")*

7 Remember, I pray you, who ever perished, being innocent? or where were the righteous cut off? *(Eliphaz, upon hearing Job curse the day that he was born, had heard enough to convince him that, regardless of Job's past outward goodness in helping the poor, instructing the needy, and upholding the weak, he was a wicked man, who had committed many sinful acts in secret, and now was reaping what he had sown.*

Consequently, this "friend" argues that all of Job's past, public, and private acts of goodness were for show, and to cover up his real self. He called attention to the fact that, by observing what had happened to other wicked men, one could see that Job's reaping was only normal, and something to be expected.)

8 Even as I have seen, they who plow iniquity, and sow wickedness, reap the same *(that much is true! However, many times problems come to those, as Job, who have not "plowed iniquity" or "sown wickedness" [II Corinthians 11:23-27]).*

9 By the blast of God they perish, and by the breath of His nostrils are they consumed *(this statement can be true; however, the Lord is "longsuffering to us-ward, not willing that any should perish, but that all should come to Repentance" [II Pet. 3:9]).*

10 The roaring of the lion, and the voice of the fierce lion, and the teeth of the young lions, are broken *(the Lord is stronger than*

lions, which should be obvious).

11 The old lion perishes for lack of prey, and the stout lion's whelps are scattered abroad *(in essence, Eliphaz is referring to Job as an "old lion," who is about done in; in fact, Job is 70 years old at the time, and will live to be 210; so, whatever now seems to be the case is not the case; in fact, every Believer should take a lesson from this).*

ELIPHAZ CONCLUDES THAT GOD IS JUST IN PUNISHING JOB

12 Now a thing was secretly brought to me, and my ear received a little thereof *(Eliphaz will now relate a personal experience).*

13 In thoughts from the visions of the night, when deep sleep falls on men,

14 Fear came upon me, and trembling, which made all my bones to shake.

15 Then a spirit passed before my face; the hair of my flesh stood up *(this no doubt happened)*:

16 It stood still, but I could not discern the form thereof: an image was before my eyes, there was silence, and I heard a voice, saying,

17 Shall mortal man be more just than God? shall a man be more pure than his Maker? *(Was this vision that Eliphaz had from the Lord, or from an evil spirit? The Fifteenth Verse says that it was "a spirit," which means that it was not of God. To be sure, Satan and his spirits at times tell the truth, but only to make a big lie bigger. And that's what is happening here.)*

18 Behold, He put no trust in His servants; and His angels He charged with folly *(this "spirit" continues to say these things to Eliphaz)*:

19 How much less in them who dwell in houses of clay, whose foundation is in the dust, which are crushed before the moth? *(Meaning that he is saying that man is much less than Angels.)*

20 They are destroyed from morning to evening: they perish for ever without any regarding it.

21 Does not their excellency which is in them go away? they die, even without wisdom. *(As we shall see at the end of this Book, the direction of all of Job's friends is totally wrong. While they may say some right things, their right things basically come from human wisdom, and not from a true knowledge of God.)*

CHAPTER 5
(1520 B.C.)

JOB IS CONCLUDED BY ELIPHAZ TO BE WICKED

CALL now, if there be any who will answer you; and to which of the Saints will you turn? *(Certain ones in Roman Catholicism have tried to use this Verse to authorize prayers to the Saints. The argument, however, of this Verse is to show the uselessness of such prayer.*

Eliphaz' argument will now become more pointed, more direct, more cutting. He will now pour sarcasm upon Job. He is taunting Job, claiming that it's not even possible for Job to get his prayers answered. In other words, Job has sinned so terribly, he says, that God will not even hear him any longer.

As well, there is not another believer [Saint] to whom he can turn. All the Saints, according to Eliphaz, know of Job's hypocrisy.)

2 For wrath kills the foolish man, and envy slays the silly one *(Job is foolish and silly, according to Eliphaz, if he thinks that anyone will hear him now!).*

3 I have seen the foolish taking root: but suddenly I cursed his habitation.

4 His children are far from safety, and they are crushed in the gate, neither is there any to deliver them. *(Inasmuch as Job's ten children were instantly killed, in effect, Eliphaz is saying that Job is to blame.*

To judge what seems to be obvious is, most of the time, wrong, just as here.).

5 Whose harvest the hungry eats up, and takes it even out of the thorns, and the robber swallows up their substance *(once again implying that Job has come to this condition because of his wickedness).*

6 Although affliction comes not forth of the dust, neither does trouble spring out of the ground *(in other words, he is saying that Job is in the condition he's in simply because he has been secretly wicked)*;

7 Yet man is born unto trouble, as the sparks fly upward *(this is true, but it is because of man's corrupt nature, due to the Fall).*

ELIPHAZ CLAIMS THAT JOB MUST CONFESS HIS SINS

8 I would seek unto God, and unto God would I commit my cause *(in other words, Job should confess to God what he really is)*:

9 Which does great things and unsearchable;

marvellous things without number:

10 Who gives rain upon the Earth, and sends waters upon the fields:

11 To set up on high those who be low; that those which mourn may be exalted to safety.

12 He disappoints the devices of the crafty, so that their hands cannot perform their enterprise *(Job is judged here to be "crafty," but God, so says Eliphaz, sees through Job's craftiness)*.

13 He takes the wise in their own craftiness: and the counsel of the froward is carried headlong.

14 They meet with darkness in the daytime, and grope in the noonday as in the night *(which is what is now happening to Job!)*.

15 But he saves the poor from the sword, from their mouth, and from the hand of the mighty *(Job wasn't poor, so this doesn't apply to him, according to Eliphaz)*.

16 So the poor has hope, and iniquity stops her mouth *(Job's mouth has now been stopped, and the "poor" can rest in ease; the truth is, Job had been a great benefactor to the poor)*.

17 Behold, happy is the man whom God corrects: therefore despise not thou the chastening of the Almighty *(true! However, the Lord is not really correcting Job, at least not as Eliphaz thinks)*:

18 For He makes sore, and binds up: He wounds, and His hands make whole.

19 He shall deliver you in six troubles: yea, in seven there shall no evil touch you *(once again, the idea is, at least as expressed by Eliphaz, that if one is walking in righteousness that "no evil will touch you"; so, Job is judged to be unrighteous!)*.

20 In famine He shall redeem you from death: and in war from the power of the sword.

21 You shall be hid from the scourge of the tongue *(therefore, since many people are now speaking evil of Job, this means that Job must be wicked)*: neither shall you be afraid of destruction when it comes *(Job is afraid, so this means that something is badly wrong with him in a spiritual sense)*.

22 At destruction and famine you shall laugh: neither shall you be afraid of the beasts of the Earth.

23 For you shall be in league with the stones of the field: and the beasts of the field shall be at peace with you.

24 And you shall know that your tabernacle shall be in peace; and you shall visit your habitation, and shall not sin *(it's very obvious that Job now has no peace, so that means he, according*

to Eliphaz, has sinned; however, the Lord has said differently *[1:10, 22]*).

25 You shall know also that your seed shall be great, and your offspring as the grass of the Earth *(inasmuch as Job's ten children were killed, this only furnishes more proof of Job's wickedness, according to Eliphaz)*.

26 You shall come to your grave in a full age, like as a shock of corn comes in in his season.

27 Lo this, we have searched it, so it is; hear it, and know you it for your good *(Eliphaz claims that his word is law and gospel; the truth is, it is anything but)*.

CHAPTER 6
(1520 B.C.)
JOB'S REPLY TO ELIPHAZ

BUT Job answered and said,
2 Oh that my grief were throughly weighed, and my calamity laid in the balances together!

3 For now it would be heavier than the sand of the sea: therefore my words are swallowed up. *(Job struggles to find words to express his sorrow. He has no understanding as to the reasons for these happenings in his life. And, at this time, God does not choose to reveal to him the cause or the reason. He will later.*

It would seem to the unbeliever, or even to the carnal Christian, that the Almighty is unjust and cruel for allowing such to happen to Job. And make no mistake about it, God was the One Who allowed Satan to do these things.

The reasons were many. First of all, Job had to discover the worthlessness of self. Then, he had to discover the worthfulness of Christ. And that he would!)

4 For the arrows of the Almighty are within me, the poison whereof drinks up my spirit: the terrors of God do set themselves in array against me *(there is fear now in Job's heart, and no wonder!)*.

5 Does the wild ass bray when he has grass? or loweth the ox over his fodder?

6 Can that which is unsavoury be eaten without salt: or is there any taste in the white of an egg?

7 The things that my soul refused to touch are as my sorrowful meat *(Job says he will only go so far in his complaints)*.

8 Oh that I might have my request; and that God would grant me the thing that I long for! *(Many Christians are pressed to the point that they will request of God that which is not God's Will. Job wanted to die; that was his*

request. *God would not answer this prayer. He had something far better for Job than death.*)

9 Even that it would please God to destroy me; that He would let loose His hand, and cut me off!

10 Then should I yet have comfort; yes, I would harden myself in sorrow: let Him not spare; for I have not concealed the words of the Holy One. (*Job falls back on the Word of God. While none of it had yet been written as of this time [that began with Moses, who was probably then alive, and maybe even helped Job write this Book], still, all the great things of the Lord had been passed down from the very beginning by word of mouth, which could be repeated word for word and in detail.*)

11 What is my strength, that I should hope? and what is my end, that I should prolong my life? (*In effect, he says he has nothing left for which to live.*)

12 Is my strength the strength of stones: or is my flesh of brass? (*"There is only so much a human being can stand," is the thought of Job.*)

13 Is not my help in me? and is wisdom driven quite from me? (*He is at the end of his resources and, considering what the man has been through, it is no wonder! And yet, all of this is necessary in order to bring Job to the end of himself. Satan had one thing in mind, but God had entirely another. Through Job, and the terrible trial which he endured, we will learn God's Way, which is not man's way.*)

JOB REPROVES HIS FRIENDS

14 To him who is afflicted pity should be shown from his friend; but he forsakes the fear of the Almighty. (*Job looked for pity from his friend, but found none. The Patriarch says that his friend has overstepped his bounds, and has shown, by his attitude, that he has no fear of God. Regrettably, most of Christendom thinks little of roundly accusing or condemning that of which it has no knowledge and no understanding. They do so because they, as well, have precious little fear of God. The reason is self-righteousness.*)

15 My brethren have dealt deceitfully as a brook, and as the stream of brooks they pass away (*these individuals came to Job as if they desired to comfort and to help him; instead, they accused and condemned him*);

16 Which are blackish by reason of the ice, and wherein the snow is hid (*toward me they are cold*):

17 What time they wax warm, they vanish: when it is hot, they are consumed out of their place (*if they try to say something good, their warmth soon vanishes*).

18 The paths of their way are turned aside; they go to nothing, and perish (*what they are saying has no merit*).

19 The troops of Tema looked, the companies of Sheba waited for them (*however, these friends could not be trusted*).

20 They were confounded because they had hoped; they came thither, and were ashamed (*Job implies that he is ashamed of having looked for compassion and kindness from his friends; he should have been wiser and known better*).

21 For now you are nothing; you see my casting down, and are afraid (*these friends thought that Job was an object of Divine vengeance, and feared, if they would show him sympathy, they might involve themselves in his punishment*).

JOB MAINTAINS HIS INDEPENDENCE

22 Did I say, Bring unto me? or, Give a reward for me of your substance? (*Have I asked you for help?*)

23 Or, Deliver me from the enemy's hand? or, Redeem me from the hand of the mighty? (*Job had not called on his friends to do any of these things.*)

24 Teach me, and I will hold my tongue: and cause me to understand wherein I have erred (*they claim he has sinned, so they should tell him what he has done!*).

25 How forcible are right words! but what does your arguing reprove? (*If your words were right, that would be something else; however, they aren't right!*)

26 Do you imagine to reprove words, and the speeches of one who is desperate, which are as wind? (*Your words and accusations should not be dignified by a response.*)

27 Yea, you overwhelm the fatherless, and you dig a pit for your friend (*all of this tells us, when one is down, condemnation is of no value; a helping hand is what is needed [Gal. 6:1-2]*).

28 Now therefore be content, look upon me; for it is evident unto you if I lie (*what Job desires is that his friends would look him straight in the face; then they would not be able to doubt him; they would see that he is telling the truth*).

29 Return, I pray you, let it not be iniquity, yea, return again, my righteousness is in it (*if my cause be well considered, despite how things look, it will be seen that I am in*

no way blameworthy).

30 Is there iniquity in my tongue? cannot my taste discern perverse things? *(Job will ultimately find that there is iniquity in his tongue, as there is with all; however, it has nothing to do with these "friends," and what they have said.)*

CHAPTER 7
(1520 B.C.)
THE DIFFICULTIES OF LIFE

IS there not an appointed time to man upon Earth? are not his days also like the days of an hireling? *(Job, under tremendous pressure, now resorts to cynicism. He has asked to die, and now he thinks he really will die; and, to die in this state makes it seem as though his life has had no purpose. He sees nothing except destruction and hurt, little knowing what is taking place in the spirit world.*

I doubt that there has ever been another human being whom the Lord has tested as He did Job. So this means that it was not only for Job's benefit, but for ours, as well. There is far more here than meets the eye.)

2 As a servant earnestly desires the shadow, and as an hireling looks for the reward of his work:

3 So am I made to possess months of vanity, and wearisome nights are appointed to me.

4 When I lie down, I say, When shall I arise, and the night be gone? and I am full of tossings to and from unto the dawning of the day *(one can well imagine the consternation which filled Job's heart and mind, as it regarded his situation; there was no rest night or day).*

5 My flesh is clothed with worms and clods of dust; my skin is broken, and become loathsome *(regarding the type of disease which gripped Job, tumors would develop on the skin, followed by a discharge of a virulent and loathsome character).*

6 My days are swifter than a weaver's shuttle, and are spent without hope *(regarding his loathsome situation, physically, domestically, and financially, he reasons that there is no hope!).*

7 O remember that my life is wind: my eye shall no more see good *(he was wrong on all counts; through Job's situation, the Lord is showing us that no matter how bad the situation might be, if we know the Lord, there is nothing that He cannot change).*

8 The eye of him who has seen me shall see me no more: your eyes are upon me, and

I am not *(the rich, famous, powerful Job which once existed is no more and, he thinks, will never be again!).*

9 As the cloud is consumed and vanishes away: so he that goes down to the grave shall come up no more *(all that Job can see ahead of him is death! Little does he realize that, in a sense, his life is just beginning).*

10 He shall return no more to his house, neither shall his place know him any more *(that which he was, rich, powerful, and famous, he thinks, is forever over).*

JOB SPEAKS TO THE LORD

11 Therefore I will not refrain my mouth; I will speak in the anguish of my spirit; I will complain in the bitterness of my soul. *(In other words, "What difference does it now make what I say?" Perhaps this is the trying point for all Christians. Lacking understanding in the happenings of our life, we are prone to give vent to our emotions. Every time this happens, it is a lack of faith because of unbelief. And yet, the Lord will have amazing patience with Job, and with us.)*

12 Am I a sea, or a whale, that You set a watch over me? *(A set of physical impediments which leave me no freedom of action.)*

13 When I say, My bed shall comfort me, my couch shall ease my complaint;

14 Then You scare me with dreams, and terrify me through visions *(along with the terrible affliction of his body, and the loss of all his material goods, Satan, no doubt, terrified Job with demonic dreams and visions; Job thought it was God doing it and, in effect, the Lord was allowing Satan to use this method; so, Job's terrible predicament was not only the loss of his possessions and his physical health, but also the terror of his soul):*

15 So that my soul chooses strangling, and death rather than my life *("I am reduced to nothing — my life is vanity").*

16 I loathe it; I would not live alway: let me alone; for my days are vanity *(fortunately, the Lord will not let us alone, and thank God He won't! If He did, we would be eternally lost).*

17 What is man, that You should magnify him? and that You should set Your heart upon him? *(This great question of life would ultimately be answered by God. It would be given to David about 600 years later [Ps. 8:4-6].*

It was very difficult for Job to see God's ultimate purpose in the creation of man, especially when

he sat in an ash heap with sore boils all over his body, scraping himself with a potsherd.)

18 And that You should visit him every morning, and try him every moment? *(Our whole life is a probation, not merely particular parts of it. God "tries us every moment." Everything is a test!)*

19 How long will You not depart from me, nor let me alone till I swallow down my spittle? *(To the natural mind, the thought is intolerable that God's watchful eye should scrutinize every action, but, to the mind enlightened by and subjected to the Holy Spirit, the fact is delightful.)*

20 I have sinned; what shall I do unto You, O You preserver *(Observer)* of men? why have You set me as a mark against You, so that I am a burden to myself? *(A continuation of the complaint that God's Eye is always upon him.)*

21 And why do You not pardon my transgression, and take away my iniquity? for now shall I sleep in the dust; and You shall seek me in the morning, but I shall not be. *(Whatever the problem, in Job's mind, it is now too late! However, let the Reader understand that with God, at least as long as there is breath, it is never too late!)*

CHAPTER 8
(1520 B.C.)
BILDAD: ANOTHER *"FRIEND!"*

THEN answered Bildad the Shuhite, and said *(as Eliphaz argued from the position of "experience," Bildad argues from the position of "tradition"; he would have nothing good to say about Job),*

2 How long will you speak these things? and how long shall the words of your mouth be like a strong wind? *(It was not very encouraging for Job, while sitting in an ash heap, to hear this man say that his words were no more than "hot air.")*

3 Does God pervert judgment? or does the Almighty pervert justice? *(As Eliphaz, this man knew some things about God, but not the things that really matter.)*

4 If your children have sinned against Him, and He has cast them away for their transgression;

5 If you would seek unto God betimes, and make your supplication to the Almighty;

6 If you were pure and upright; surely now He would awake for you, and make the habitation of your righteousness prosperous.

(Bildad was really saying that if Job were as pure and upright as he [Bildad] was; then he too would be prosperous, and not in this condition. If one will notice carefully, the entirety of the discourses of these three "friends" will subtly extol their righteousness while proclaiming Job's unrighteousness. In truth, Job was "pure and upright," but only in the Eyes of God. Still, isn't that all that counts?)

7 Though your beginning was small, yet your latter end should greatly increase *("your 'latter end,'" says Bildad, "shows that your 'beginning' was all wrong as well").*

8 For enquire, I pray you, of the former age, and prepare yourself to the search of their fathers *(Bildad was speaking of "human tradition"; some traditions are good; most are not [Mat. 15:6]):*

9 (For we are but of yesterday, and know nothing, because our days upon Earth are a shadow *[pontificating words, meant to make Bildad seem very wise]*:)

10 Shall not they teach you, and tell you, and utter words out of their heart? *(In other words, "Job, if you had even a modicum of intelligence, you would know the answer to your questions.")*

11 Can the rush grow up without mire? can the flag grow without water?

12 While it is yet in his greenness, and not cut down, it withers before any other herb *(both images represent the prosperity of the wicked, and were probably proverbial).*

BILDAD CONSIDERS JOB A HYPOCRITE

13 So are the paths of all who forget God; and the hypocrite's hope shall perish *(bluntly, Bildad calls Job a "hypocrite. The truth of the matter was that Job was no hypocrite, but Eliphaz, Bildad, and Zophar were. Their hypocrisy was the hypocrisy of self-righteousness, which is the worst hypocrisy of all. Men are fond of judging their righteousness by comparing it to others. It made Bildad feel superior to point out Job's alleged shortcomings. He did not dream that while he was judging Job, God was judging him):*

14 Whose hope shall be cut off, and whose trust shall be a spider's web.

15 He shall lean upon his house, but it shall not stand: he shall hold it fast, but it shall not endure.

16 He is green before the sun, and his branch shoots forth in his garden.

17 His roots are wrapped about the heap,

and sees the place of stones.

18 If he destroy him from his place, then it shall deny him, saying, I have not seen you. (*"Even the Earth will deny that Job has ever lived here!"*)

19 Behold, this is the joy of his way, and out of the Earth shall others grow (*"Job's destruction leaves room for something better to follow," says Bildad!*).

20 Behold, God will not cast away a perfect man, neither will He help the evil doers (*how ironclad his argument, he thinks; if Job had been a "perfect man," God would not have cast him away; likewise, God not helping him proves that he is an "evil doer"; how smug Bildad feels in his summation*):

21 Till He fill your mouth with laughing, and your lips with rejoicing (*in other words, Bildad is saying to Job, "If you will confess your evil, the Lord will fill your mouth with laughing"*).

22 They who hate you shall be clothed with shame; and the dwelling place of the wicked shall come to nought. (*Whenever man working from human reasoning begins to judge, almost invariably he will call "unholy" what God calls "holy," and "holy" what God calls "unholy"!*)

CHAPTER 9
(1520 B.C.)
JOB'S REPLY TO BILDAD

THEN Job answered and said,

2 I know it is so of a truth: but how should man be just with God? (*The answer to this question is found in Rom., Chpt. 3.*)

3 If he will contend with Him, he cannot answer Him one of a thousand (*if God questions us, we cannot even answer one question of a thousand, at least out of our own ability, no matter how educated we might be*).

4 He is wise in heart, and mighty in strength: who has hardened himself against Him, and has prospered? (*No man can win fighting against God!*)

5 Which removes the mountains, and they know not: which overturns them in His anger.

6 Which shakes the Earth out of her place, and the pillars thereof tremble.

7 Which commands the sun, and it rises not; and seals up the stars.

8 Which alone spreads out the Heavens, and treads upon the waves of the sea (*God is the Creator of all things, and thereby has control of all things, and can change their function as He so desires*).

9 Which makes Arcturus, Orion, and Pleiades, and the chambers of the south (*this Verse shows that the rotundity of the Earth was known at that time, which was about 3,700 years ago*).

10 Which does great things past finding out; yea, and wonders without number.

11 Lo, He goes by me, and I see Him not: He passes on also, but I perceive Him not. (*Job says these things in the heat of this tremendous trial. Some things he says are right and some are wrong. In fact, Job does perceive the Lord, but he is now questioning his own experience. In other words, he is saying, "Considering what has happened to me, I'm not sure if my perception is right or not."*)

12 Behold, He takes away, who can hinder Him? who will say unto Him, What doest Thou? (*Job is saying that the Lord has taken away all that he has and, in a sense, that is true, and there was nothing that Job could do to stop or change the situation. Furthermore, he doesn't even know why!*)

JOB CANNOT ANSWER GOD
BUT WILL PRAY TO HIM

13 If God will not withdraw His anger, the proud helpers do stoop under Him. (*Considering Job's circumstances, surely God, he thinks, must be angry with him. So, all of this tells us that it's very difficult for us to discern the Lord or His Ways. Unless He reveals His Purpose to us, as He did to Job a little later, almost all the time our assumptions are wrong.*)

14 How much less shall I answer Him, and choose out my words to reason with Him? (*Job is saying that he did not know how to pray; in fact, he didn't even know what to say. Living under the Old Covenant, Job did not have the privilege of the infilling of the Holy Spirit as we do today under the New Covenant. Truly our New Covenant is based on better Promises [Heb. 8:6].*)

15 Whom, though I were righteous, yet would I not answer, but I would make supplication to my Judge (*God is my Judge; prayer is the only rightful attitude of even the best man before his Maker — prayer for Mercy, pardon, Grace, prayer for advance in holiness*).

16 If I had called, and He had answered me; yet would I not believe that He had hearkened unto my voice (*Job reasons, and wrongly we might add, that due to his condition, God would not hearken unto him*).

17 For He breaks me with a tempest, and

multiplies my wounds without cause *(there was a cause, but not in the realm which Job could comprehend, or anyone else at that time for that matter; the "cause" was not Job or anything he had done, but rather the "spirit world")*.

18 He will not suffer me to take my breath, but fills me with bitterness *(in other words, one blow after the other!)*.

19 If I speak of strength, lo, He is strong: and if of judgment, who shall set me a time to plead?

20 If I justify myself, my own mouth shall condemn me: if I say, I am perfect, it shall also prove me perverse *(about ourselves, there is nothing we can say; in fact, it's what God says that counts; He had already made a gracious statement about Job, but unknown to the Patriarch [2:3])*.

21 Though I were perfect, yet would I not know my soul: I would despise my life *(Job is closer to the truth now than he realizes)*.

22 This is one thing, therefore I said it, He destroys the perfect and the wicked *(while Job is not concluding himself to be perfect, in effect, he is saying, "It wouldn't matter if I were, it would do me no good"; in that he is wrong!)*.

23 If the scourge slay suddenly, He will laugh at the trial of the innocent *(in other words, God laughs at those who claim they are innocent)*.

24 The Earth is given into the hand of the wicked: He covers the faces of the judges thereof; if not, where, and who is he? *(Inasmuch as God has to allow things to be done before they can be done, and irrespective as to what they are, still, there is a reason why God does all things, and that reason is valid; the Judge of all the Earth will do right! [Gen. 18:25].)*

JOB'S COMPLAINT AGAINST GOD

25 Now my days are swifter than a post *(a messenger who quickly comes and goes)*: they flee away, they see no good *(but yet, despite how things now look, there is a better day coming)*.

26 They are passed away as the swift ships: as the eagle that hasteth to the prey.

27 If I say, I will forget my complaint, I will leave off my heaviness, and comfort myself:

28 I am afraid of all my sorrows, I know that You will not hold me innocent *("if all of this is happening to me, then it stands to reason that I'm not innocent"; specifically, he was right; particularly, he was wrong!)*.

29 If I be wicked, why then labour I in vain? *("Why do I try to live right?")*

30 If I wash myself with snow water, and make my hands never so clean;

31 Yet shall You plunge me in the ditch, and my own clothes shall abhor me. *("It doesn't matter what I have done to try to live right, the only conclusion to which I can arrive is that 'the Lord abhors me.'" Once again, the great Patriarch was looking at circumstances. He knew what was happening, but he didn't know what was going on.)*

32 For He is not a man, as I am, that I should answer Him, and we should come together in judgment. *(What a plea for the coming Redeemer! True, God is not a man, but God would become Man, and then God and Man would "come together in Judgment.")*

33 Neither is there any daysman betwixt us, that might lay his hand upon us both. *(Job did not understand the coming Work of Christ as Mediator between God and man [I Tim. 2:4-5], but he knew in his heart that the need for such was great. Thank God Jesus Christ has come as the Mediator, i.e., "Daysman.")*

34 Let Him take His rod away from me, and let not His fear terrify me *(little did Job realize that this prayer, no doubt half uttered, would be answered so fully and wondrously in Christ)*:

35 Then would I speak, and not fear Him; but it is not so with me *(but with the coming Christ, it would be so!)*.

CHAPTER 10
(1520 B.C.)
JOB BEWAILS HIS CONDITION

MY soul is weary of my life; I will leave my complaint upon myself; I will speak in the bitterness of my soul *(it is very easy to condemn Job for his statements and actions; however, if any one of us had been placed in his position, would we have done any better, or even as well?)*.

2 I will say unto God, Do not condemn me; show me wherefore You contend with me. *("Why do You contend with me?" Very shortly, the Lord will answer that prayer, and in a far greater way than Job can now imagine.)*

3 Is it good unto You that You should oppress, that You should despise the work of Your hands, and shine upon the counsel of the wicked? *(The Lord was not despising Job's work; in effect, He was refining it.)*

4 Have You eyes of flesh? or do You see as man sees? *(The Lord does not see as man sees, but infinitely greater, which means that He*

knows all things.)

5 Are Your days as the days of man? are Your years as man's days,

6 That You enquire after my iniquity, and search after my sin? *(Search out things for which to punish Job?)*

7 You know that I am not wicked; and there is none who can deliver out of Your hand *(Job makes his case, and in this he is right!).*

8 Your hands have made me and fashioned me together round about; yet You do destroy me *(there are times when it seems that God is destroying us; during these times, Satan desires that we throw up our hands and quit and, in effect, "curse God"; God desires that we throw ourselves at the foot of the Cross and draw ever closer to Him, which is what the trial is all about).*

9 Remember, I beseech You, that You have made me as the clay; and will You bring me into dust again? *(Job has already stated that God can deliver him if He do desires, or else He can kill him. He has the power to do both. Which will it be?)*

10 Have You not poured me out as milk, and curdled me like cheese?

11 You have clothed me with skin and flesh, and have fenced me with bones and sinews.

12 You have granted me life and favour, and Your visitation has preserved my spirit *(in fact, this is a man who has walked with God, who has experienced countless "visitations," and who has known God's Power and even God's Grace; he has been favored, but only because he favored God).*

13 And these things have You hid in Your heart: I know that this is with You *("Have You all the time intended to destroy me?").*

14 If I sin, then You mark me, and You will not acquit me from my iniquity *(God forgives only on the basis of one's faith in the Atonement of Christ, which was symbolized in the Sacrifices of Job's day).*

15 If I be wicked, woe unto me; and if I be righteous, yet will I not lift up my head. I am full of confusion; therefore see Thou my affliction *(at the end, the Lord does not condemn Job for his confusion; Job was asked to undergo what few, if any, had ever undergone; he was asked to do so without explanation; his confusion is understandable);*

16 For it increases, You hunt me as a fierce lion: and again You show Yourself marvellous upon me *(marvelous means of destruction, and of that Job was right).*

17 You renew Your witnesses against me, and increase Your indignation upon me;

changes and war are against me *(one blow after the other).*

JOB LAMENTS HIS BIRTH AND DREADS HIS DEATH

18 Wherefore then have You brought me forth out of the womb? Oh that I had given up the ghost, and no eye had seen me! *("I wish I had died at birth.")*

19 I should have been as though I had not been; I should have been carried from the womb to the grave.

20 Are not my days few? cease then, and let me alone, that I may take comfort a little *(this is a prayer that Job would be very glad the Lord didn't answer),*

21 Before I go whence I shall not return, even to the land of darkness and the shadow of death *(at that time, the understanding of the Resurrection was very dim);*

22 A land of darkness, as darkness itself; and of the shadow of death, without any order, and where the light is as darkness *(at this stage, Job sees nothing but darkness).*

CHAPTER 11
(1520 B.C.)

ZOPHAR SPEAKS: ACCUSES JOB OF BEING A LYING HYPOCRITE

THEN answered Zophar the Naamathite, and said *(this man argues from the position of "human merit"),*

2 Should not the multitude of words be answered? and should a man full of talk be justified? *(So now, Zophar accuses Job of being full of hot air.)*

3 Should your lies make men hold their peace? and when you mock, shall no man make you ashamed? *(Job has been called a hypocrite; now he is called a liar.)*

4 For you have said, My doctrine is pure, and I am clean in your eyes *(to self-righteousness, Job's claims are a joke).*

5 But oh that God would speak, and open His lips against you *(ultimately, the Lord will speak, but it will not be against Job);*

6 And that He would show you the secrets of wisdom, that they are double to that which is! Know therefore that God exacts of you less than your iniquity deserves *(Zophar knew nothing of Job's life, and yet he felt perfectly free to claim that Job was some kind of great sinner).*

ZOPHAR ATTEMPTS TO EXPLAIN
WHO GOD IS

7 Can you by searching find out God? can you find out the Almighty unto perfection? *(These questions are sometimes used as proof that God is so great that the most learned cannot comprehend Him, but this is an improper use of the questions. While one cannot learn about God by scientific methods, so-called, one can definitely learn about Him from His Word, and by Revelation.)*

8 It is as high as Heaven; what can you do? deeper than Hell; what can you know?

9 The measure thereof is longer than the Earth, and broader than the sea.

10 If He cut off, and shut up, or gather together, then who can hinder Him?

11 For He knows vain men: He sees wickedness also; will He not then consider it? *(The idea is, God is so great that there is no point in men trying to find out anything about Him. Were that true, the Lord would not have given us His Word, or sent the Messiah!)*

12 For vain men would be wise, though man be born like a wild ass's colt *(in this statement, Zophar refers to Job as "vain").*

JOB IS URGED TO REPENT
AND QUIT SINNING

13 If you prepare your heart, and stretch out your hands toward Him *(here, as always, we have the self-righteous telling the righteous how to seek the Lord; what a travesty!)*;

14 If iniquity be in your hand, put it far away, and let not wickedness dwell in your tabernacles *(Zophar so much believes that Job is full of iniquity; self-righteousness always assumes such; the facts are that Zophar is full of iniquity, and Job is not).*

15 For then shall you lift up your face without spot; yea, you shall be stedfast, and shall not fear *(Zophar implies that Job cannot lift up his face without spot)*:

16 Because you shall forget your misery, and remember it as waters that pass away *(if Job would only repent, so says his "friend")*:

17 And your age shall be clearer than the noonday: you shall shine forth, you shall be as the morning.

18 And you shall be secure, because there is hope; yea, you shall dig about you, and you shall take your rest in safety.

19 Also you shall lie down, and none shall make you afraid; yes, many shall make suit unto you.

20 But the eyes of the wicked shall fail, and they shall not escape, and their hope shall be as the giving up of the ghost. *(Zophar declares that Job must be wicked or he would not be suffering like the wicked. What conceit! What self-righteousness!)*

CHAPTER 12
(1520 B.C.)
JOB'S REPLY: HE IS INNOCENT

AND Job answered and said,
2 No doubt but you are the people, and wisdom shall die with you *(Job uses sarcasm, actually saying the opposite of what he means).*

3 But I have understanding as well as you; I am not inferior to you: yea, who knows not such things as these? *(These men had treated Job as though he had no understanding of God's Ways and God's Actions. While it was true that Job did not understand the present situation, still, quite possibly at this present time, there were few men on the face of the Earth, if any, who had the knowledge of God and the relationship with God that Job had.)*

4 I am as one mocked of his neighbour, who calls upon God, and He answers him: the just upright man is laughed to scorn *(such comes about even presently, because the modern Church, as then, little understands "Justification by Faith").*

5 He who is ready to slip with his feet is as a lamp despised in the thought of him that is at ease *(this Verse may be read: "A lamp is for him who is ready to fall, but is despised by him who thinks himself safe"; this was a rebuke to the self-confidence and self-righteousness of his "three friends").*

6 The tabernacles of robbers prosper, and they who provoke God are secure; into whose hand God brings abundantly *(these "three friends" asserted that prosperity would always follow the one who was right with God; Job replies to this assertion by pointing out that robbers and rebels often prosper).*

JOB ACKNOWLEDGES GOD'S
OMNIPOTENCE

7 But ask now the beasts, and they shall teach you; and the fowls of the air, and they shall tell you:

8 Or speak to the Earth, and it shall teach you: and the fishes of the sea shall declare unto you.

9 Who knows not in all these that the hand of the LORD has wrought this?

10 In Whose hand is the soul of every living thing, and the breath of all mankind (*all of Creation shows that there is a Creator*).

11 Does not the ear try words? and the mouth taste his meat? (*The Lord made them that way.*)

12 With the ancient is wisdom; and in length of days understanding (*wisdom comes slowly, if at all!*).

13 With Him is wisdom and strength, He has counsel and understanding (*with God dwell wisdom and strength essentially*).

14 Behold, He breaks down, and it cannot be built again: He shuts up a man, and there can be no opening (*no other power can give release*).

15 Behold, He withholds the waters, and they dry up: also He sends them out, and they overturn the Earth.

16 With Him is strength and wisdom: the deceived and the deceiver are His (*God has not only the wisdom to design the course of events, but the power and ability to carry out all that He designs*).

17 He leads counsellors away spoiled, and makes the judges fools (*the wise of the Earth cannot resist or escape Him; He frustrates their designs and overthrows them*).

18 He looses the bond of kings, and girds their loins with a girdle.

19 He leads princes away spoiled, and overthrows the mighty (*while some men may be mighty, God is Almighty; there is a vast difference!*).

20 He removes away the speech of the trusty, and takes away the understanding of the aged (*because they have forsaken Him*).

21 He pours contempt upon princes, and weakens the strength of the mighty (*he holds in contempt those who would come against Him*).

22 He discovers deep things out of darkness, and brings out to light the shadow of death (*God, at times, reveals truths to men which are beyond their power of understanding*).

23 He increases the nations, and destroys them: He enlarges the nations, and straitens them again (*the Lord sets up some kingdoms, and then tears down some kingdoms; all are at His Mercy*).

24 He takes away the heart of the chief of the people of the Earth, and causes them to wander in a wilderness where there is no way (*despite all their claimed wisdom*).

25 They grope in the dark without light, and He makes them to stagger like a drunken man (*to pursue a devious course instead of a straight one, because they have forsaken Him*).

CHAPTER 13
(1520 B.C.)
JOB ACCUSES HIS FRIENDS
OF LYING

LO, my eye has seen all this, my ear has heard and understood it.

2 What you know, the same do I know also: I am not inferior unto you (*whatever they claim to know about God, he knows as well; actually, Job is far superior in knowledge!*).

3 Surely I would speak to the Almighty, and I desire to reason with God (*Job, realizing that God is his only hope, addresses himself to that conclusion; these "friends" cannot help*).

4 But you are forgers of lies, you are all physicians of no value (*any Preacher who stands behind a pulpit and holds up anything but the Lord Jesus Christ, and what He did at the Cross, as the answer to the ills of man falls into the same category*).

5 O that you would altogether hold your peace! and it should be your wisdom (*what a statement!*).

6 Hear now my reasoning, and hearken to the pleadings of my lips (*as his friends have not kept silence, but have spoken, Job claims the right also to be heard!*).

7 Will you speak wickedly for God? and talk deceitfully for Him? (*It is sad but true that the majority of those who stand behind pulpits "speak wickedly for God" and "talk deceitfully for Him." They do so because they substitute their own human reasoning for the Word of God.*)

8 Will you accept His person? will you contend for God? (*Claiming that what you say is of God?*)

9 Is it good that He should search you out? or as one man mocks another, do you so mock Him? (*You may impose on a man by so acting, but you will not impose on God.*)

10 He will surely reprove you, if you do secretly accept persons (*curry favor!*).

11 Shall not His excellency make you afraid? and His dread fall upon you? (*God, Who is no respecter of persons, will hold you accountable*

for what you are now saying and doing.)

12 Your remembrances are like unto ashes, your bodies to bodies of clay *(you think what you are saying is of God, but in reality it is of human origin).*

13 Hold your peace, let me alone, that I may speak, and let come on me what will *(I don't know much, but you don't know anything).*

JOB DEFENDS HIS INTEGRITY

14 Wherefore do I take my flesh in my teeth, and put my life in my hand? *(The appeal is now to God; but Job prefaces it by excusing his boldness.)*

15 Though He slay me, yet will I trust in Him: but I will maintain my own ways before Him *(a tremendous statement of faith).*

16 He also shall be my salvation: for an hypocrite shall not come before Him *(meaning that these "friends" hold no salvation for him; as well, he states here that he is not a hypocrite, as they have contended).*

17 Hear diligently my speech, and my declaration with your ears.

18 Behold now, I have ordered my cause; I know that I shall be justified *(faith is rising!).*

JOB PRAYS TO THE LORD

19 Who is he who will plead with me? for now, if I hold my tongue, I shall give up the ghost *(Job says that he has nothing to lose; he will make his case).*

20 Only do not two things unto me: then will I not hide myself from You.

21 Withdraw Your hand far from me *(take away the physical pain)*: and let not Your dread make me afraid *(help me not to fear, and my greatest fear is that I have displeased You).*

22 Then You call, and I will answer: or let me speak, and You answer me *(Job is asking for an audience, irrespective of the outcome).*

23 How many are my iniquities and sins? make me to know my transgression and my sin *(these "friends" have claimed that I am a great sinner; I will only take Your Word for that, not theirs).*

24 Wherefore hidest Thou Your face, and holdest me for Your enemy? *(Job believes that the Lord will vindicate him; but he asks if there is a present alienation, and desires to be made acquainted with the cause of it, if, in fact, it does exist.)*

25 Will You break a leaf driven to and fro? and will You pursue the dry stubble? *(Job compares himself to two of the weakest things in nature — a withered leaf and a morsel of dry stubble.)*

26 For You write bitter things against me, and make me to possess the iniquities of my youth *(in considering what the indictment against him might be, he can only suppose that these old and long-forsaken sins are being remembered and brought up against him).*

27 You put my feet also in the stocks, and look narrowly unto all my paths; You set a print upon the heels of my feet *(this was a figure of speech on Job's part, meaning that it seemed as if God had made him a captive to his terrible plight).*

28 And he *(Job)*, as a rotten thing, consumes, as a garment that is moth eaten *(an allusion to the character of the disease from which he is suffering).*

CHAPTER 14
(1520 B.C.)
JOB SPEAKS OF LIFE'S WOES

MAN who is born of a woman is of few days and full of trouble *(due to the Fall in the Garden of Eden by our original parents, this is true).*

2 He comes forth like a flower, and is cut down: he flees also as a shadow, and continues not *(the first phrase is used quite frequently in Scripture [Ps. 103:15; Isa. 28:1, 4; James 1:10-11; I Pet. 1:24]).*

3 And do You open Your eyes upon such an one, and bring me into judgment with You? *(This question is actually the age-old question of man. Why would God, Who is able to create whatever He desires, go to such lengths and trouble to redeem "such an one"?)*

4 Who can bring a clean thing out of an unclean? not one. *(This question and the answer direct themselves to the inability of man to save himself; therefore, Salvation had to be outside of man, and that it was, in Christ Jesus.)*

5 Seeing his days are determined, the number of his months are with You, You have appointed his bounds that he cannot pass *(the life span of every individual is fixed by God; however, it can be cut short or prolonged, according to disobedience or obedience);*

6 Turn from him, that he may rest, till he shall accomplish, as an hireling, his day *(the idea is, when his life span is over, he should have accomplished that which was intended;*

regrettably, only a precious few actually accomplish their appointed task).

7 For there is hope of a tree, if it be cut down, that it will sprout again, and that the tender branch thereof will not cease *(in this one Verse, we are told that even if man does fall on hard times, if he will believe God, the fallen tree can sprout and grow again),*

8 Though the root thereof wax old in the earth, and the stock thereof die in the ground;

9 Yet through the scent of water it will bud, and bring forth boughs like a plant *(the water of the Word can bring it back).*

10 But man dies, and wastes away: yea, man gives up the ghost and where is he? *(Before Christ, and even before the Law, the eternal abode of man was only dimly understood.)*

11 As the waters fail from the sea, and the flood decays and dries up:

12 So man lies down, and rises not: till the Heavens be no more, they shall not awake, nor be raised out of their sleep *(Job is not addressing himself to the Resurrection, but rather the brevity of this life).*

13 O that You would hide me in the grave, that You would keep me secret, until Your wrath be past, that You would appoint me a set time, and remember me! *(Due to what has happened to him, Job is confused here, and is asking for relief, even the relief of death.)*

14 If a man die, shall he live again? all the days of my appointed time will I wait, till my change come *(plainly, this Passage proclaims the coming Resurrection, although dimly understood; correct understanding would come only with Christ and the Truth He would ultimately give to the Apostle Paul [I Cor. 15:51-57]).*

15 You shall call, and I will answer You; You will have a desire to the work of Your hands *(this one Passage tells us that the great creation of God, as it regards man, will not be lost; that which the Lord originally intended will ultimately be carried out).*

16 For now You number my steps: do You not watch over my sin? *(The Lord minutely records and catalogs everything about man.)*

17 My transgression is sealed up in a bag, and You sew up my iniquity *(the transgression of man can be erased only by Faith in the shed Blood of Christ [Eph. 2:13-18]).*

18 And surely the mountains falling come to nought, and the rock is removed out of his place.

19 The waters wear the stones: You wash away the things which grow out of the dust of the earth; and you destroy the hope of man *(hopes which aren't anchored solidly in the Word of God).*

20 You prevail for ever against him, and he passes: You change his countenance, and send him away *(man cannot prevail against God, irrespective as to what he might do).*

21 His sons come to honour, and he knows it not; and they are brought low, but he perceives it not of them *(this Passage answers the question of whether the Saints of God in Heaven know what is transpiring with their loved ones on Earth; in effect, it says they know nothing of the things that happen on Earth; so this destroys the Catholic myth of praying to Saints in Heaven).*

22 But his flesh upon him shall have pain, and his soul within him shall mourn. *(This statement is based on Job's present situation. Inspiration guarantees that these things were said, and by the ones to whom they are attributed. However, Inspiration does not guarantee that all that is said is true. In fact, virtually all that is said by the friends of Job would have to be concluded as being incorrect. Most of what Job says is true.)*

CHAPTER 15
(1520 B.C.)
THE SECOND SPEECH OF ELIPHAZ

THEN answered Eliphaz the Temanite, and said,

2 Should a wise man utter vain knowledge, and fill his belly with the east wind? *(Eliphaz says here that everything that Job has said is nothing but wind.)*

3 Should he reason with unprofitable talk? or with speeches wherewith he can do no good?

4 Yes, you cast off fear, and restrain prayer before God *(Eliphaz now belittles Job's faith).*

5 For your mouth utters your iniquity, and you choose the tongue of the crafty *(he is accusing Job now of being deceitful).*

6 Your own mouth condemns you, and not I: yea, your own lips testify against you *(he is repeatedly condemning Job while claiming he isn't; the self-righteous enjoy putting words into the mouths of those whom they condemn).*

7 Are you the first man who was born? or were you made before the hills?

8 Have you heard the secret of God? and do you restrain wisdom to yourself? *("Are you claiming to have an 'in' with God?")*

9 What do you know, that we don't know? what understanding do you have, which is not in us? *(Eliphaz is plainly agitated at the statements made by Job.)*

10 With us are both the grayheaded and very aged men, much elder than your father *(he is here saying that these "friends" are wiser than Job).*

11 Are the consolations of God small with you? is there any secret thing with you? *(The man is claiming that they have been consoling Job, but that he doesn't seem to appreciate it.)*

12 Why does your heart carry you away? and what do your eyes wink at *(in other words, "Don't you see your true condition?")*

13 That you turn your spirit against God, and let such words go out of your mouth? *(They never say to what particular words they object.)*

14 What is man, that he should be clean? and he which is born of a woman, that he should be righteous? *(In other words, Job's sins are so grievous that his punishment is just, or so they say!)*

15 Behold, He *(the Lord)* puts no trust in His Saints; yea, the Heavens are not clean in His sight *(the first phrase is untrue, while the second phrase is true; however, the Heavens and the Earth are going to be cleansed [II Pet. 3:7-13]).*

16 How much more abominable and filthy is man, which drinks iniquity like water? *(It cannot be doubted that Job is individually pointed at here, and not mankind in general. Eliphaz could not be more wrong.)*

THE FACT THAT JOB IS SUFFERING JUDGMENT IS A SURE SIGN, SAYS ELIPHAZ, THAT HE MUST BE WICKED

17 I will show you, hear me; and that which I have seen I will declare *(Eliphaz now proclaims his judgment upon Job)*;

18 Which wise men have told from their fathers, and have not hid it *(however, this was worldly wisdom, and not wisdom from above [James 3:15])*:

19 Unto whom alone the Earth was given, and no stranger passed among them *(to dilute their worldly wisdom).*

20 The wicked man travails with pain all his days, and the number of years is hidden to the oppressor *(clearly an overstatement of the truth).*

21 A dreadful sound is in his ears: in prosperity the destroyer shall come upon him *(this is directed toward Job).*

22 He believes not that he shall return out of darkness, and he is waited for of the sword.

23 He wanders abroad for bread, saying, Where is it? he knows that the day of darkness is ready at his hand.

24 Trouble and anguish shall make him afraid; they shall prevail against him, as a king ready to the battle.

25 For he stretches out his hand against God, and strengthens himself against the Almighty *(Job is accused of being against God).*

26 He runs upon him, even on his neck, upon the thick bosses of his bucklers:

27 Because he covers his face with his fatness, and makes collops of fat on his flanks.

28 And he dwells in desolate cities, and in houses which no man inhabits, which are ready to become heaps.

29 He shall not be rich, neither shall his substance continue, neither shall he prolong the perfection thereof upon the Earth *(the hypocrisy of Job is now being found out, according to Eliphaz!).*

30 He shall not depart out of darkness; the flame shall dry up his branches, and by the breath of his mouth shall he go away *(there is no hope for Job, says Eliphaz).*

31 Let not him who is deceived trust in vanity: for vanity shall be his recompence *(Job is deceived, says Eliphaz, and so all his trust and faith are of no consequence).*

32 It shall be accomplished before his time, and his branch shall not be green.

33 He shall shake off his unripe grape as the vine, and shall cast off his flower as the olive.

34 For the congregation of hypocrites shall be desolate, and fire shall consume the tabernacles of bribery *(once again, Job is accused of being a hypocrite; some friends!).*

35 They conceive mischief, and bring forth vanity, and their belly prepares deceit *(the Lord allowed the prattle of these "friends" to be included in the Sacred Text, even as wrong as it was, in order to show us that circumstances rarely present the true picture; understanding this, we had best withhold judgment).*

CHAPTER 16
(1520 B.C.)
JOB'S REPLY TO ELIPHAZ

THEN Job answered and said,

2 I have heard many such things: miserable comforters are you all *(and so they were!).*

3 Shall vain words have an end? or what

emboldens you that you answer? *(Job was right; their words were "vain.")*

4 I also could speak as you do: if your soul were in my soul's stead, I could heap up words against you, and shake my head at you *(you have accused me of wickedness, when there is much dirt in your house, as well!).*

5 But I would strengthen you with my mouth, and the moving of my lips should asswage your grief *(from what the Lord said about Job [42:7], there is every evidence, if the tables were reversed, that he would truly have comforted them).*

6 Though I speak, my grief is not asswaged: and though I forbear, what am I eased? *(Speaking or silent, my grief is the same.)*

7 But now He *(the Lord)* has made me weary: You have made desolate all my company.

8 And You have filled me with wrinkles, which is a witness against me: and my leanness rising up in me bears witness to my face.

9 He *(the Lord)* tears me in His wrath, Who hates me: He gnashes upon me with His teeth; my enemy sharpens his eyes upon me *(Job is incorrect in all of this; there was no wrath of God against Job, which he will ultimately see).*

10 They *(these friends and others)* have gaped upon me with their mouth: they have smitten me upon the cheek reproachfully; they have gathered themselves together against me *(which was true! These statements are very similar to some used about the Lord [Ps. 35:16; 37:12]).*

11 God has delivered me to the ungodly, and turned me over into the hands of the wicked *(this is only partially true).*

12 I was at ease, but He *(the Lord)* has broken me asunder: He has also taken me by my neck, and shaken me to pieces, and set me up for His mark *(partially true!).*

13 His archers compass me round about, He cleaves my reins asunder, and does not spare; He pours out my gall upon the ground.

14 He breaks me with breach upon breach, He runs upon me like a giant *(while it was Satan who actually did these things, the Lord allowed him to do so; so, in essence, Job wasn't wrong in this particular statement).*

JOB MAINTAINS HIS INNOCENCE

15 I have sewed sackcloth upon my skin, and defiled my horn in the dust *(he doesn't see any way out).*

16 My face is foul with weeping, and on my eyelids is the shadow of death *(he thought he was dying);*

17 Not for any injustice in my hands: also my prayer is pure *(Job repudiates the charge of rapine and robbery which Eliphaz had brought against him [15:28, 34]; neither has he been guilty of hypocrisy).*

18 O Earth, do not cover my blood, and let my cry have no place *(after he is dead, he wants the Earth to cry out against the injustice done to him, typifying that of Abel [Gen. 4:10]).*

19 Also now, behold, my witness is in Heaven, and my record is on high *(believes that he will be vindicated, even if it's after his death).*

20 My friends scorn me: but my eye pours out tears unto God *(God Alone is his refuge).*

21 O that one might plead for a man with God, as a man pleads for his neighbour! *(Job once again pleads for a true Mediator. That prayer will ultimately be answered in Christ.)*

22 When a few years are come, then I shall go the way whence I shall not return *(Job thinks he is dying).*

CHAPTER 17
(1520 B.C.)
JOB APPEALS TO GOD

MY breath is corrupt, my days are extinct, the graves are ready for me.

2 Are there not mockers with me? and does not my eye continue in their provocation? *(The accusations of these "friends" were contributing as much as his physical disability toward Job's possible death. We as Believers should take a lesson from all of this.)*

3 Lay down now, put me in a surety with You; who is he who will strike hands with me? *(In other words, "Lord, You are the only One to Whom I can look.")*

4 For You have hid their heart from understanding: therefore shall You not exalt them *("Lord, I know that You will not honor their words").*

5 He who speaks flattery to his friends, even the eyes of his children shall fail *(these "friends" will pay for what they have done).*

6 He has made me also a byword of the people; and aforetime I was as a tabret *(in other words, Job had become a joke in the entirety of that part of the world).*

7 My eye also is dim by reason of sorrow, and all my members are as a shadow *("I cannot defend myself!").*

8 Upright men shall be astonied at this, and the innocent shall stir up himself against

the hypocrite. *(Job is saying that even upright men, upon viewing his terrible plight, will be astonished and will surely think him guilty. Even the innocent [little children] will think he is a hypocrite. Perhaps this was the heaviest load of all to bear.)*

9 The righteous also shall hold on his way, and he who has clean hands shall be stronger and stronger. *(These words are uttered by faith. Job will not allow these individuals, whoever they might be, to deter him from his hold on God. In fact, the accusations will only make his Faith stronger.)*

10 But as for you all, do you return, and come now: for I cannot find one wise man among you *(in effect, he is saying that these "friends" can repeat their arguments as often as they wish; even so, not a wise word has yet been uttered, because it was not the Word of God).*

11 My days are past, my purposes are broken off, even the thoughts of my heart *("Anymore, I really don't care what others say").*

12 They change the night into day: the light is short because of darkness *(doubt, unbelief, accusations, and condemnation, as offered by these "friends," actually do the work of Satan).*

13 If I wait, the grave is my house: I have made my bed in the darkness. *(He is saying that if he listens to these people, their words will kill him. Are our words to others a blessing or a curse?)*

14 I have said to corruption, You are my father: to the worm, You are my mother, and my sister *(once again, he is saying that he is ready to die).*

15 And where is now my hope? as for my hope, who shall see it? *(His "friends" are saying that he has no hope in God. There is no greater sin that a person can commit than the sin of denying the hope of the Word of God to any individual.)*

16 They shall go down to the bars of the pit, when our rest together is in the dust *(they will not be satisfied until they have killed me).*

CHAPTER 18
(1520 B.C.)
BILDAD'S SECOND SPEECH

THEN answered Bildad the Shuhite, and said,

2 How long will it be ere you make an end of words? mark, and afterwards we will speak *(in other words, "What you say is of no consequence, and what we say is the only wisdom being spoken here").*

3 Wherefore are we counted as beasts, and reputed vile in your sight? *(Job had not said that these "friends" were "unclean." Bildad, therefore, misrepresents him. But what else is new!)*

4 He tears himself in his anger: shall the Earth be forsaken for you? and shall the rock be removed out of his place? *(In 16:9, Job complained that God was tearing him in His anger. Bildad says that Job was tearing himself in his bad temper, and asked him if he expected natural and physical laws to be convulsed in support of his pretended innocency?)*

5 Yea, the light of the wicked shall be put out, and the spark of his fire shall not shine *(Bildad is saying, "Job, you are wicked, and your pretended light shall be extinguished").*

6 The light shall be dark in his tabernacle, and his candle shall be put out with him *(no hope for Job, says Bildad).*

7 The steps of his strength shall be straitened, and his own counsel shall cast him down *(Job is very unwise by not heeding our counsel).*

8 For he is cast into a net by his own feet, and he walks upon a snare.

9 The gin shall take him by the heel, and the robber shall prevail against him *(and why not! Considering that he is so wicked!).*

10 The snare is laid for him in the ground, and a trap for him in the way.

11 Terrors shall make him afraid on every side, and shall drive him to his feet.

12 His strength shall be hungerbitten, and destruction shall be ready at his side.

13 It shall devour the strength of his skin: even the first born of death shall devour his strength *(imagine how Job must have felt listening to this!).*

14 His confidence shall be rooted out of his tabernacle, and it shall bring him to the king of terrors *(in other words, he will die lost).*

15 It shall dwell in his tabernacle, because it is none of his: brimstone shall be scattered upon his habitation.

16 His roots shall be dried up beneath, and above shall his branch be cut off.

17 His remembrance shall perish from the Earth, and he shall have no name in the street. *(Job not only has not been forgotten, but, to the contrary. Few men on the face of the Earth, and through all time, have been remembered as Job is remembered, because he placed his trust and Faith in God, and not in man. No name? To the contrary, Job's name is famous, because it is linked to patience, faith, and trust in God. He*

is looked to as an example by every single person who has ever had to undergo a trial of any nature — and that includes the entirety of the human race.)

18 He shall be driven from light into darkness, and chased out of the world.

19 He shall neither have son nor nephew among his people, nor any remaining in his dwellings (quite the contrary; the Lord gave Job "seven more sons and three more daughters" [42:13]).

20 They who come after him shall be astonied at his day, as they who went before were affrighted (Job will be a byword, so Bildad says; however, it was the opposite!).

21 Surely such are the dwellings of the wicked, and this is the place of him who knows not God. (How difficult it must have been for Job, especially in his weakened condition, to hear his "friend" say to him that he did not know God. The only thing that a man really has is his faith. And now all will deny that faith. Thankfully, even though they tried, Job never lost his faith.)

CHAPTER 19
(1520 B.C.)
JOB'S REPLY

THEN Job answered and said,

2 How long will you vex my soul, and break me in pieces with words? (This statement implies that the accusations and the condemnation of his "friends" only added to his hurt.)

3 These ten times have you reproached me: you are not ashamed that you make yourselves strange to me (this must be a figurative expression meaning a number of times, for literally they have not answered him ten times).

4 And be it indeed that I have erred, my error remains with myself (Job at no time maintains his impeccability).

5 If indeed you will magnify yourselves against me, and plead against me my reproach:

6 Know now that God has overthrown me, and has compassed me with His net (Bildad insinuates that Job has fallen into his own snare [18:7-9]; Job replies that the snare in which he is taken is from God; and in that he was right).

7 Behold, I cry out of wrong, but I am not heard: I cry aloud, but there is no judgment (up to now, all Job's appeals to God have elicited no reply from Him).

8 He has fenced up my way that I cannot pass, and He has set darkness in my paths

(nothing vexes him so much as his inability to understand why he is so afflicted).

9 He has stripped me of my glory, and taken the crown from my head (that the Lord did, but in order to give him something better).

10 He has destroyed me on every side, and I am gone: and my hope has He removed like a tree (but yet, Job has recently said, "For there is hope of a tree, if it be cut down, that it will sprout again" [14:7]).

11 He has also kindled His wrath against me, and He counts me unto Him as one of His enemies (the actual afflictions take second place to the cause of why he is afflicted, which he thinks is the wrath of God; it isn't!).

12 His troops come together, and raise up their way against me, and encamp round about my tabernacle.

13 He has put my brethren far from me, and my acquaintance are verily estranged from me (Job had actual "brothers" [42:11], who forsook him and "dealt deceitfully" with him [6:15] during the time of his adversity).

14 My kinsfolk have failed, and my familiar friends have forgotten me (no one wanted to have anything to do with him, neither his relatives, nor even his friends; in their thinking he was surely under the judgment of God and, consequently, had done terrible things; therefore, they too joined in with accusations).

15 They who dwell in my house, and my maids, count me for a stranger: I am an alien in their sight (all, his kinfolk and even his servants, condemned him; there was not one person who stood up for him except God; what a lesson for us when we begin to judge others, especially of things that we know little or nothing about).

16 I called my servant, and he gave me no answer; I intreated him with my mouth (in eastern culture, this would have been the insult of all insults).

17 My breath is strange to my wife, though I intreated for the children's sake of my own body (his own wife turned against him; the last phrase either speaks of his children which are now dead, or else, as some Scholars claim, his personal brothers and sisters, who also turned against him).

18 Yea, young children despised me; I arose, and they spoke against me (young children, no doubt, had heard their parents speak against Job, so they followed suit).

19 All my inward friends abhorred me: and they whom I loved are turned against me (the

rejection was total!).

20 My bone cleaves to my skin and to my flesh, and I am escaped with the skin of my teeth *(so far, he has escaped death!).*

JOB APPEALS FOR PITY

21 Have pity upon me, have pity upon me, O ye my friends; for the hand of God has touched me *(this pathetic appeal should have elicited sympathy, but it did not).*

22 Why do you persecute me as God, and are not satisfied with my flesh? *("Isn't my condition enough punishment? Why do you want to persecute me more?")*

23 Oh that my words were now written! oh that they were printed in a book! *(Job would have his prayer answered. The Book of Job, and all of its detail that would give future generations untold direction and counsel, would be the result of his prayer.)*

24 That they were graven with an iron pen and lead in the rock for ever! *(Even greater than that! They were placed as a part of the Word of God.)*

JOB REAFFIRMS HIS FAITH

25 For I know that my redeemer liveth, and that He shall stand at the latter day upon the Earth *(even though Job would not have understood the term, "the Lord Jesus Christ," actually, this is the One of Whom he was speaking; he knew the Redeemer was coming, even though he knew nothing about particulars):*

26 And though after my skin worms destroy this body, yet in my flesh shall I see God *(Job portrays here the fact of the Resurrection and the glorified body; this proves that God had made to primitive man a wonderfully full revelation of some New Testament Truth):*

27 Whom I shall see for myself, and my eyes shall behold, and not another; though my reins be consumed within me *("not by proxy, or merely through faith, or in a vision, but really, actually, I shall see Him for myself"; once again, Job proclaims the Resurrection).*

28 But you should say, Why persecute we him, seeing the root of the matter is found in me? *(In other words, Job tells these "friends" that they had better be careful as to what they say about him.)*

29 Be ye afraid of the sword: for wrath brings the punishments of the sword, that you may know there is a judgment *(the sword of God's*

justice will assuredly smite you, if you persecute an innocent man).

CHAPTER 20
(1520 B.C.)

ZOPHAR'S SECOND SPEECH

THEN answered Zophar the Naamathite, and said,

2 Therefore do my thoughts cause me to answer, and for this I make haste *(he brushes aside Job's warnings concerning judgment, and hastens to answer, again with venom).*

3 I have heard the check of my reproach, and the spirit of my understanding causes me to answer *(in his self-righteousness, he says that he admits he has reproached Job, but not nearly to the degree that he should have been reproached; also, because he has great understanding of these matters, he has no choice but to answer).*

4 Knowest thou not this of old, since man was placed upon Earth,

5 That the triumphing of the wicked is short, and the joy of the hypocrite but for a moment? *(So he continues to refer to Job as a "hypocrite.")*

6 Though his excellency mount up to the Heavens, and his head reach unto the clouds;

7 Yet he shall perish for ever like his own dung: they which have seen him shall say, Where is he? *(Zophar insults Job, and further says that future generations will ask, "What has become of him?")*

8 He shall fly away as a dream, and shall not be found: yea, he shall be chased away as a vision of the night.

9 The eye also which saw him shall see him no more; neither shall his place any more behold him.

10 His children shall seek to please the poor, and his hands shall restore their goods *(he now accuses Job of having gained his former riches by oppressing the poor).*

11 His bones are full of the sin of his youth, which shall lie down with him in the dust.

12 Though wickedness be sweet in his mouth, though he hide it under his tongue;

13 Though he spare it, and forsake it not; but keep it still within his mouth *(even though he won't admit to evil, Job, Zophar says, is full of evil):*

14 Yet his meat in his bowels is turned, it is the gall of asps within him *(Job is now referred to as a snake, and a poisonous one at that).*

15 He has swallowed down riches, and he

shall vomit them up again: God shall cast them out of his belly *(the wicked man shall be made to disgorge his ill-gotten gains, which he claims that Job has had to do)*.

16 He shall suck the poison of asps: the viper's tongue shall slay him *(Satan will take him out)*.

17 He shall not see the rivers, the floods, the brooks of honey and butter *(he may have once seen such, says Zophar, but he will see it no more)*.

18 That which he laboured for shall he restore, and shall not swallow it down: according to his substance shall the restitution be, and he shall not rejoice therein.

19 Because he has oppressed and has forsaken the poor; because he has violently taken away an house which he built not *(once again, Job is accused of having gained his former riches by deceit and fraud, and especially by oppressing the poor)*;

20 Surely he shall not feel quietness in his belly, he shall not save of that which he desired *(Job was never satisfied, says Zophar, in that he continued to oppress the poor long after he was extremely wealthy)*.

21 There shall none of his meat be left; therefore shall no man look for his goods *(in other words, the Lord has taken everything away because of his terrible sin)*.

22 In the fulness of his sufficiency he shall be in straits: every hand of the wicked shall come upon him *(because he is so wicked, says Zophar!)*.

23 When he is about to fill his belly, God shall cast the fury of his wrath upon him, and shall rain it upon him while he is eating *(many, like Zophar, seem to enjoy calling down the wrath of God on others)*.

24 He shall flee from the iron weapon, and the bow of steel shall strike him through.

25 It is drawn, and comes out of the body; yea, the glittering sword comes out of his gall: terrors are upon him.

26 All darkness shall be hid in his secret places: a fire not blown shall consume him; it shall go ill with him that is left in his tabernacle *(anyone around him is also going to suffer judgment)*.

27 The Heaven shall reveal his iniquity; and the Earth shall rise up against him *(actually, the very opposite happened; Heaven revealed his Righteousness, and men once again sought his help and advice)*.

28 The increase of his house shall depart, and his goods shall flow away in the day of his wrath *(once again, the very opposite happened!)*.

29 This is the portion of a wicked man from God, and the heritage appointed unto him by God. *(Zophar's arguments seemed plausible, enough so that the entirety of all who knew Job agreed with this summation and, therefore, soundly condemned Job themselves. Once again, it shows that the majority are not always right — in fact, they seldom are.)*

CHAPTER 21
(1520 B.C.)
JOB'S REPLY TO ZOPHAR

BUT Job answered and said,
2 Hear diligently my speech, and let this be your consolations.

3 Suffer me that I may speak; and after that I have spoken, mock on *("hear what I have to say and, if you do not agree, 'mock on'"; and that's exactly what they did)*.

4 As for me, is my complaint to man? and if it were so, why should not my spirit be troubled? *("I'm not looking to man," says Job, "but rather to God!")*

5 Mark me, and be astonished, and lay your hand upon your mouth *(in other words, "hear me out")*.

6 Even when I remember I am afraid, and trembling takes hold on my flesh *("when I think of what has happened to me, I tremble with fear")*.

7 Wherefore do the wicked live, become old, yea, are mighty in power? *(Job says that sometimes the wicked live as long as the righteous, and are mighty in power, as well. So the argument of his "friends" doesn't hold water.)*

8 Their seed is established in their sight with them, and their offspring before their eyes *(oftentimes the children of the wicked are blessed, at least with worldly goods)*.

9 Their houses are safe from fear, neither is the rod of God upon them *(and that is true)*.

10 Their bull genders, and fails not; their cow calves, and casts not her calf.

11 They send forth their little ones like a flock, and their children dance.

12 They take the timbrel and harp, and rejoice at the sound of the organ.

13 They spend their days in wealth, and in a moment go down to the grave *(they die without suffering from any prolonged or severe illness)*.

14 Therefore they say unto God, Depart from us; for we desire not the knowledge of

Your ways *(this pretty well characterizes the at-titude of most of the world; hundreds of millions are steeped in heathenistic idolatry; other hundreds of millions know about God, but do not want any part of Him).*

15 What is the Almighty, that we should serve Him? and what profit should we have, if we pray unto Him? *(The love of money being the root of all evil [I Tim. 6:10], unconverted man only thinks in terms of "profit." Not being spiritually minded, he has no idea as to the "profit" found in serving God and praying unto Him. In fact, this is the greatest "profit" of all.)*

16 Lo, their good is not in their hand: the counsel of the wicked is far from me *(Job says that the wicked sometimes prosper without being judged by God in this life any more than the righteous; so the reasoning that he was a wicked man because of suffering the judgments of the wicked prove nothing in his case).*

17 How oft is the candle of the wicked put out! and how oft comes their destruction upon them? God distributes sorrows in His anger *(this is actually a question; God at times does distribute sorrow upon the wicked; however, only at times; the real sorrow comes after death, when Hell awaits them, and from that there will be no reprieve).*

18 They are as stubble before the wind, and as chaff that the storm carries away.

19 God lays up His iniquity for his children: He rewards him *(with evil),* and he shall know it. *("God," Job's opponents may say, "punishes the wicked through their children." Job does not deny that the Lord may do so, but suggests a better course in the latter phrase. Judgment at times is sent by the Lord on the wicked; oftentimes, in fact!)*

20 His eyes shall see his destruction, and he shall drink of the wrath of the Almighty *(and so many do).*

21 For what pleasure has he in his house after him, when the number of his months is cut off in the midst? *(The wicked, normally, little care about the fate of their children.)*

22 Shall any teach God knowledge? seeing He judges those who are high *(no matter how powerful a man may be on this Earth, God is above him).*

23 One dies in his full strength, being wholly at ease and quiet.

24 His breasts are full of milk, and his bones are moistened with marrow *(continuing to speak of the wicked).*

25 And another dies in the bitterness of his soul, and never eats with pleasure *(others have to suffer terribly before death comes to them, and their spirit is embittered by their misfortunes).*

26 They shall lie down alike in the dust, and the worms shall cover them *(however different the circumstances of their lives, men are alike in their death; all die, and become the prey of worms).*

JOB APPEALS TO HIS FRIENDS TO CONSIDER WHAT THEY SAY

27 Behold, I know your thoughts, and the devices which you wrongfully imagine against me *("I know," Job says, "what you think of me").*

28 For you say, Where is the house of the prince? and where are the dwelling places of the wicked? *(The barb is directed against Job.)*

29 Have you not asked them who go by the way? and do you not know their tokens *(if they will admit it, they will have to agree that Job is right regarding what he has said about the wicked),*

30 That the wicked is reserved to the day of destruction? they shall be brought forth to the day of wrath *(irrespective as to what type of life the wicked may enjoy on this Earth, destruction in eternity awaits them, unless they get right with God).*

31 Who shall declare his way to his face? and who shall repay him what he has done? *(Being castigated neither by God nor man, the wicked, at times, seem to enjoy complete impunity.)*

32 Yet shall he be brought to the grave, and shall remain in the tomb.

33 The clods of the valley shall be sweet unto him, and every man shall draw after him, as there are innumerable before him *(they reckon without eternity and Heaven or Hell).*

34 How then comfort ye me in vain, seeing in your answers there remaineth falsehood? *(Your position, that the Godly always prosper, while the wicked always are afflicted and brought low, by experience, in other words by your own reckoning, prove false.)*

CHAPTER 22
(1520 B.C.)
ELIPHAZ'S THIRD SPEECH

THEN Eliphaz the Temanite answered and said,

2 Can a man be profitable unto God, as he who is wise may be profitable unto himself? *(Eliphaz, annoyed by the introduction*

of inconvenient facts, becomes abusive and, whereas in his first two speeches he only hinted at Job's alleged evil conduct, in this, his last speech, he directly accuses Job of wickedness and wrongdoing.)

3 Is it any pleasure to the Almighty, that you are righteous? or is it gain to Him, that you make your ways perfect? *(In reply to Job's facts, Eliphaz advances the theory that man's goodness does not add to, nor man's badness take from, God's economy; therefore, God does not prosper some and afflict others for His Own advantage. The cause, therefore, of such action must be found in men themselves, so Job's calamities clearly prove his guilt.)*

4 Will He reprove you for fear of you? will He enter with you into judgment? *(In other words, the fact of your reproof is sure evidence of the fact of your guilt.)*

5 Is not your wickedness great? and your iniquities infinite?

6 For you have taken a pledge from your brother for nought, and stripped the naked of their clothing.

7 You have not given water to the weary to drink, and you have withheld bread from the hungry *(he now openly accuses Job of the worst types of sin).*

8 But as for the mighty man, he had the Earth; and the honourable man dwelt in it *(Job, this man says, favors the mighty and oppresses the poor).*

9 You have sent widows away empty, and the arms of the fatherless have been broken *(when "friends" conduct themselves in this fashion, the truth is, this has been in their hearts all along).*

10 Therefore snares are round about you, and sudden fear troubles you;

11 Or darkness, that you cannot see; and abundance of waters cover you *(judgment covers you, and rightly so!).*

12 Is not God in the height of Heaven? and behold the height of the stars, how high they are! *(Eliphaz now brings God into his denunciation of Job.)*

13 And you say, How does God know? can He judge through the dark cloud? *(Job had never said any such thing, but it suits Eliphaz' purpose to malign and misrepresent Job.)*

14 Thick clouds are a covering to Him, that He sees not; and He walks in the circuit of Heaven.

15 Have you marked the old way which wicked men have trod? *(Now Eliphaz puts Job*

into the seed of Cain before the Flood, who "corrupted their way" [Gen. 6:12].)*

16 Which were cut down out of time, whose foundation was overflown with a flood *(Noah's flood):*

17 Which said unto God, Depart from us: and what can the Almighty do for them? *(Eliphaz places Job among the most evil, whom God had to destroy with a flood.)*

18 Yet He filled their houses with good things: but the counsel of the wicked is far from me *("even though those particular wicked prospered, I will not have," Eliphaz says, "any part with them," thereby holding himself up as pious).*

19 The righteous see it, and are glad: and the innocent laugh them to scorn *(in other words, "it is righteous of me to condemn you!").*

20 Whereas our substance is not cut down, but the remnant of them the fire consumes *("because I am blessed," Eliphaz says, "and you are severely cursed, proves my statements").*

JOB IS FURTHER INSULTED

21 Acquaint now your self with Him, and be at peace: thereby good shall come unto you *(Eliphaz implores Job now to repent).*

22 Receive, I pray you, the law from His mouth, and lay up His words in your heart *(for Job to be insulted by Eliphaz in this manner must have been a bitter pill to swallow).*

23 If you return to the Almighty, you shall be built up, you shall put away iniquity far from your tabernacles.

24 Then shall you lay up gold as dust, and the gold of Ophir as the stones of the brooks *("you'll get rich again," Eliphaz says, "if you will only repent"; so, judgment was equated with poverty, while blessing was equated with riches).*

25 Yes, the Almighty shall be your defence, and you shall have plenty of silver *("reduced to poverty," Eliphaz says, "proves, Job, that God is against you").*

26 For then shall you have your delight in the Almighty, and shall lift up your face unto God *(it's interesting that Eliphaz placed the entirety of his theology on riches and poverty; how so much like some presently).*

27 You shall make your prayer unto Him, and He shall hear you, and you shall pay your vows *("if you'll repent, God will hear you").*

28 You shall also decree a thing, and it shall be established unto you: and the light shall shine upon your ways.

29 When men are cast down, then you shall say, There is lifting up; and He shall save the humble person (*continuing to imply that Job has oppressed the poor*).

30 He shall deliver the island of the innocent: and it is delivered by the pureness of your hands (*little did Eliphaz realize that shortly Job would deliver these "friends" from the wrath of God by his intercession [42:7-9]*).

CHAPTER 23
(1520 B.C.)
JOB'S REPLY TO ELIPHAZ

THEN Job answered and said,

2 Even to day is my complaint bitter: my stroke is heavier than my groaning (*Job's situation at present is so acute, and seemingly growing worse by the moment, that if God doesn't do something quickly, he cannot last much longer*).

3 Oh that I knew where I might find Him! that I might come even to His seat! (*There is despair in these words. Job knows now that he will receive no help from his "friends," or even his loved ones. The only help that he will receive will come from God. Therefore, he longs for an audience.*)

4 I would order my cause before Him, and fill my mouth with arguments. (*A short time later, the Lord will give Job exactly that which he has requested. However, his conduct will be far different from what he had imagined. Actually he will little "order his cause before Him."*)

5 I would know the words which He would answer me, and understand what He would say unto me (*actually, the words that the Lord will say will be far beyond Job's ability to grasp or understand; however, the "words" will be words of comfort, strength, and deliverance, totally different from his "friends"*).

6 Will He plead against me with His great power? No; but He would put strength in me (*in fact, God will do exactly what Job had prophesied*).

7 There the righteous might dispute with Him; so should I be delivered for ever from my Judge (*Job is confident that, if he can bring his cause before God, he will obtain an acquittal and deliverance*).

GOD KNOWS MAN'S WAYS

8 Behold, I go forward, but He is not there; and backward, but I cannot perceive Him:

9 On the left hand, where He does work, but I cannot behold Him; He hides Himself on the right hand, that I cannot see Him (*for every Believer, there are times when it seems that God has hidden Himself from us*):

10 But He knows the way that I take: when He has tried me, I shall come forth as gold. (*This is one of the greatest statements made in the entirety of the Word of God. In effect, Job is saying, "Even though I cannot 'perceive Him,' and it seems like He 'hides Himself,' still, He knows exactly what is happening to me and, when this trial is over, I shall come forth as gold!"*)

11 My foot has held His steps, His way have I kept, and not declined (*Job continues to maintain his rightful direction, and rightly so!*).

12 Neither have I gone back from the Commandment of His lips; I have esteemed the words of His mouth more than my necessary food (*to Job, the most important thing in the world was the "Commandment of the Lord"; so there you have it, "His Will and His Word"*).

13 But He is in one mind, and who can turn Him? and what His soul desires, even that He does (*in other words, Job is saying he is not quite certain as to what the Lord is going to do with him, but he knows, whatever it is, he will "come forth as gold"; Job is right!*).

14 For He performs the thing that is appointed for me: and many such things are with Him (*He will assuredly accomplish whatever He has decreed for me*).

15 Therefore am I troubled at His presence: when I consider, I am afraid of Him (*Job means that the fear of an Eternal Being Who has an eternal plan, which we cannot doubt, is wise, even though it is inscrutable to us; it is fear mingled with confidence, as we go into the future*).

16 For God makes my heart soft, and the Almighty troubles me (*"due to what has happened to me, I fear the Lord now more than ever"*):

17 Because I was not cut off before the darkness, neither has He covered the darkness from my face (*Job doesn't understand the severity of this trial, and no wonder!*).

CHAPTER 24
(1520 B.C.)
JOB'S COMPLAINTS

WHY, seeing times are not hidden from the Almighty, do they who know Him not see His days? (*To make the language more clear to us, Job is asking the question as to why the Almighty does not have set times to judge, or why His followers often do not see His interventions.*)

2 Some remove the landmarks; they violently take away flocks, and feed thereof.

3 They drive away the ass of the fatherless, they take the widow's ox for a pledge.

4 They turn the needy out of the way: the poor of the Earth hide themselves together.

5 Behold, as wild asses in the desert, go they forth to their work; rising betimes for a prey: the wilderness yields food for them and for their children.

6 They reap every one his corn in the field: and they gather the vintage of the wicked.

7 They cause the naked to lodge without clothing, that they have no covering in the cold.

8 They are wet with the showers of the mountains, and embrace the rock for want of a shelter.

9 They pluck the fatherless from the breast, and take a pledge of the poor.

10 They cause him to go naked without clothing, and they take away the sheaf from the hungry;

11 Which make oil within their walls, and tread their winepresses, and suffer thirst.

12 Men groan from out of the city, and the soul of the wounded cries out: yet God lays not folly to them *(this means that God, at times, does not seem to punish wickedness quickly; and yet, God's judgment will ultimately come for those who persist in their wickedness; it may be in this life or the next life, but come it will)*.

13 They are of those who rebel against the light; they know not the ways thereof, nor abide in the paths thereof *(they will not know, will not have anything to do with, the law of moral restraint)*.

14 The murderer rising with the light kills the poor and needy, and in the night is as a thief.

15 The eye also of the adulterer waits for the twilight, saying, No eye shall see me: and disguises his face.

16 In the dark they dig through houses, which they had marked for themselves in the daytime: they know not the light *(they have no desire to know the Way of the Lord)*.

GOD'S PUNISHMENT OF THE WICKED IS SOMETIMES DEFERRED

17 For the morning is to them even as the shadow of death: if one know them, they are in the terrors of the shadow of death *(they tempt death!)*.

18 He is swift as the waters; their portion is cursed in the earth: he beholds not the way of the vineyards.

19 Drought and heat consume the snow waters: so does the grave those which have sinned.

20 The womb shall forget him; the worm shall feed sweetly on him; he shall be no more remembered; and wickedness shall be broken as a tree *(wickedness may thrive for a season, but ultimately it will be called to account)*.

21 He evil entreats the barren who bears not: and does not good to the widow *(which, in that culture, was reprehensible)*.

22 He draws also the mighty with his power: he rises up, and no man is sure of life *(the wicked, at times, seem to overcome all obstacles)*.

23 Though it be given him to be in safety, whereon he rests; yet His *(God's)* eyes are upon their ways *(Job is saying that at times it seems like even the most wicked are in safety, and they rest in that safety; he then says that it seems that God for a time watches the cruelties of oppressors without interference; in other words, He does not immediately punish their wicked conduct)*.

24 They are exalted for a little while, but are gone and brought low; they are taken out of the way as all other, and cut off as the tops of the ears of corn *(this means that many of the wicked live out their lives seemingly experiencing no interference from God, and even die as the righteous do — they die a natural death)*.

25 And if it be not so now, who will make me a liar, and make my speech nothing worth? *(Job is saying that his words are true, and that even his three friends know it. In fact, Job's statements are correct. God will not contradict him. But, at last, when He does appear, He will contradict Job's three "friends."*

God deals with each person on an individual basis, be they righteous or unrighteous. In effect, the Lord tells us that it is not our business how He deals with others.)

CHAPTER 25
(1520 B.C.)
BILDAD'S THIRD SPEECH

THEN answered Bildad the Shuhite, and said,

2 Dominion and fear are with Him, He makes peace in His high places *(the idea is, Bildad is saying that Job cannot hope to reach God, considering who Job is, and considering Who God is)*.

3 Is there any number of His armies? and

upon whom does not His light arise?

4 How then can man be justified with God? or how can he be clean who is born of a woman? *(By faith in God, which Job surely evidenced, a man could be justified, but which Bildad evidently didn't believe.)*

5 Behold even to the moon, and it shines not; yea, the stars are not pure in His sight.

6 How much less man, that is a worm? and the son of man, which is a worm? *(Job, I'm sure, gets the point. He is being referred to by Bildad as a "worm.")*

CHAPTER 26
(1520 B.C.)
JOB'S REPLY

BUT Job answered and said,
2 How have you helped him who is without power? how do save the arm that has no strength?

3 How have you counselled him who has no wisdom? and how have you plentifully declared the thing as it is? *(Job is using irony. He rebukes the worthlessness of Bildad's human reasoning. In fact, all human reasoning, as it regards the Lord and His Work, is worthless.)*

4 To whom have you uttered words? and whose spirit came from you? *(The facts are that there is no inspiration on any words that come from man, even though so intellectual or lofty, unless they come from the Word of God. And, to be sure, the words of Bildad, and the other "friends" as well, didn't come from God, but rather out of their own minds, as does so much presently.)*

5 Dead things are formed from under the waters, and the inhabitants thereof *(the "dead things" here addressed refer to the Rephaim, which was the result of the union of fallen angels and women [Gen. 6:4]).*

6 Hell is naked before Him, and destruction has no covering *(whereas the statements of Bildad and the other "friends" were not inspired, these particular statements concerning God, as given by Job, definitely are inspired).*

7 He stretches out the north over the empty place, and hangs the Earth upon nothing *(this means that it is the Power of God, evidenced in His fixed laws, which upholds the Earth, and that alone).*

8 He binds up the waters in His thick clouds, and the cloud is not rent under them. *(Clouds have no texture, but yet they hold great volumes of water. How? By the Power of God,*

once again, evidenced in fixed laws.)

9 He holds back the face of His throne, and spreads His cloud upon it *(to where that man can only fathom a few of these laws; the evidence is, in the coming Kingdom Age, all of God's laws of creation will be revealed [Isa. 11:9-19]).*

10 He has compassed the waters with bounds, until the day and night come to an end *(speaks of the firmament [Gen. 1:6]).*

11 The pillars of Heaven tremble and are astonished at His reproof *(great mountains tremble at His Presence [Ex. 20:18]).*

12 He divides the sea with His power, and by His understanding He smites through the proud *(fixes the bounds of the sea).*

13 By His Spirit He has garnished the Heavens; His hand has formed the crooked serpent *(should be translated, "His hand has pierced the swift serpent," which refers to the defeat of Satan at the Cross, although that was then yet future; however, so sure was this coming event, that the Lord could speak of it in the past tense).*

14 Lo, these are parts of His ways: but how little a portion is heard of Him? but the thunder of His power who can understand? *(Job implies that he has not enumerated one-half of God's great works — he has just hinted at them.)*

CHAPTER 27
(1520 B.C.)
JOB SUMS UP HIS SITUATION

MOREOVER Job continued his parable, and said *(the word "parable," as used here, refers to a comparison of one thing with another, thereby making it simpler to understand),*

2 As God lives, Who has taken away my judgment; and the Almighty, Who has vexed my soul *(which is obvious, but yet Job still doesn't know the reason);*

3 All the while my breath is in me, and the Spirit of God is in my nostrils *(despite his calamity, he is still alive and the Spirit of God is still in him; he will now give a ringing defense of his own position);*

4 My lips shall not speak wickedness, nor my tongue utter deceit *(he maintains his correctness of position, even from the beginning; when the Lord did finally appear, He did not contradict Job's statement).*

5 God forbid that I should justify you: till I die I will not remove my integrity from me *(the certainty of a position, irrespective of circumstances, can be maintained only if it is fully based on the Word of God).*

6 My righteousness I hold fast, and will not let it go: my heart shall not reproach me so long as I live *(Job says to his "friends" that they have reproached him, but his heart hasn't)*.

7 Let my enemy be as the wicked, and he who rises up against me as the unrighteous *(this is a bold statement, but Job is right; the truth of the matter is that the three "friends" were the wicked and, therefore, unrighteous)*.

THE HOPELESSNESS OF THE HYPOCRITE

8 For what is the hope of the hypocrite, though he has gained, when God takes away his soul? *("What shall it profit a man, if he shall gain the whole world, and lose his own soul?" [Mk. 8:36].)*

9 Will God hear his cry when trouble comes upon him? *(Only if he truly repents!)*

10 Will he delight himself in the Almighty? Will he always call upon God? *(Hypocrisy alienates God from us, and alienates us from God. Such cannot "delight in the Almighty.")*

11 I will teach you by the hand of God: that which is with the Almighty will I not conceal *(Job claims his words now are inspired of the Lord)*.

12 Behold, all ye yourselves have seen it; why then are you thus altogether vain? *(Therefore, his "friends" should know better.)*

13 This is the portion of a wicked man with God, and the heritage of oppressors, which they shall receive of the Almighty *(those who oppose the Lord will ultimately be judged)*.

14 If his children be multiplied, it is for the sword: and his offspring shall not be satisfied with bread. *(Some claim that these Passages contradict what Job said in Chapter 24. They do not! Chapter 24 proclaims what it often looks like outwardly regarding the wicked. Chapter 27 tells us what is really happening.)*

15 Those who remain of him shall be buried in death: and his widows shall not weep *(forgotten in death)*.

16 Though he heap up silver as the dust, and prepare raiment as the clay;

17 He may prepare it, but the just shall put it on, and the innocent shall divide the silver *(a perfect example is the blessing of the United States versus nations of heathenism)*.

18 He builds his house as a moth, and as a booth that the keeper makes *(a house that will not stand, despite all the effort put into such)*.

19 The rich man shall lie down, but he shall not be gathered: he opens his eyes,

and he is not *(riches flee away much faster than they come)*.

20 Terrors take hold on him as waters, a tempest steals him away in the night *(this is what is really going on in the heart of the unbeliever who has set himself against God)*.

21 The east wind carries him away, and he departs: and as a storm hurls him out of his place *(he has no protection from calamities, for the Lord is not his Father)*.

22 For God shall cast upon him, and not spare: he would fain flee out of His hand *(he will not be able to escape God)*.

23 Men shall clap their hands at him, and shall hiss him out of his place *(the greed that got his riches is also in the hearts of others who will rejoice at his downfall, which happens constantly)*.

CHAPTER 28
(1520 B.C.)

THE FEAR OF THE LORD
IS TRUE WISDOM

SURELY there is a vein for the silver, and a place for gold where they fine it.

2 Iron is taken out of the Earth, and brass is molten out of the stone *(however, the wisdom of God cannot be found in this manner)*.

3 He sets an end to darkness, and searches out all perfection: the stones of darkness, and the shadow of death *(men mine for precious metals both day and night; if they would do so for such, surely we should be as diligent to find the things of the Lord, which can only be found in His Word)*.

4 The flood breaks out from the inhabitant: even the waters forgotten of the foot: they are dried up, they are gone away from men *(the miner goes to great lengths to find precious metals; likewise, we should do no less in searching out the things of God)*.

5 As for the earth, out of it comes bread: and under it is turned up as it were fire *(fire is used to separate the gold from other metals; likewise, the fire of the Holy Spirit is used to burn the chaff out of our lives [Mat. 3:11-12])*.

6 The stones of it are the place of sapphires: and it has dust of gold *(for those who ardently seek the Lord, they will find spiritual sapphires and spiritual gold)*.

7 There is a path which no fowl knows, and which the vulture's eye has not seen *(this is the "path of life," which demons cannot penetrate [Ps. 16:11])*:

8 The lion's whelps have not trodden it, nor the fierce lion passed by it (the one who comes as a "roaring lion," namely Satan, will not be able to trod it or pass by it; this is "the secret place of the Most High" [Ps. 91:1]).

9 He (man) puts forth his hand upon the rock; he overturns the mountains by the roots.

10 He cuts out rivers among the rocks; and his eye sees every precious thing.

11 He binds the floods from overflowing; and the thing that is hid brings he forth to light (all of this in an effort to find precious metals).

12 But where shall wisdom be found? And where is the place of understanding? (As clever as man is in bringing to the light the wealth hidden in the darkness of the mine, he fails altogether to find out the place of wisdom, because the wisdom of God cannot be found out by such methods.)

13 Man knows not the price thereof; neither is it found in the land of the living (the real value of Heavenly Wisdom cannot be estimated in terms of ordinary human calculations; in fact, a person is not truly educated until he is first educated in the Bible).

14 The depth saith, It is not in me; and the sea saith, It is not with me.

15 It cannot be gotten for gold, neither shall silver be weighed for the price thereof.

16 It (wisdom) cannot be valued with the gold of Ophir, with the precious onyx, or the sapphire.

17 The gold and the crystal cannot equal it: and the exchange of it shall not be for jewels of fine gold (the proper understanding of the Word of God is of far greater value than all gold, silver, and jewels).

18 No mention shall be made of coral, or of pearls: for the price of wisdom is above rubies.

19 The topaz of Ethiopia shall not equal it, neither shall it be valued with pure gold.

20 Whence then comes wisdom? and where is the place of understanding? (It is found only in the Word of God!)

21 Seeing it is hid from the eyes of all living, and kept close from the fowls of the air (human intelligence cannot come by this wisdom; it is revealed by the Spirit [I Cor. 2:7-12]).

22 Destruction and death say, We have heard the fame thereof without ears (Heavenly Wisdom, i.e., "the Word of God," alone answers the questions of death and destruction).

23 God understands the way thereof, and he knows the place thereof (God alone understands what true wisdom is, and it is found in His Word).

24 For He looks to the ends of the Earth, and sees under the whole Heaven (God is Omniscient, meaning that He knows everything);

25 To make the weight for the winds; and He weighs the waters by measure (all according to the laws of creation, which He has made, and, to be sure, everything functions according to those laws).

26 When He made a decree for the rain, and a way for the lightning of the thunder (means that God placed the fall of rain under fixed and unalterable laws):

27 Then did he see it, and declare it; he prepares it, yea, and searched it out (God foresaw all that was necessary to maintain His universe in perfect order).

28 And unto man he said, Behold, and fear of the LORD, that is wisdom; and to depart from evil is understanding (no amount of intelligence, no amount of cleverness, or of information or knowledge, or of worldly or scientific wisdom, will be of any true avail to man, unless he starts with this "beginning" [Ps. 111:10; Prov. 1:7]).

CHAPTER 29

(1520 B.C.)

JOB SPEAKS OF HIS LIFE
BEFORE THE TRIAL

MOREOVER Job continued his parable, and said,

2 Oh that I were as in months past, as in the days when God preserved me (Job had yet to learn that "self" must die, whether it be prosperous self, afflicted self, or innocent self, and that he had to be brought to abhor himself, whether innocent or guilty; entrance into the life more abundant can only be experienced when religious self is as heartily abhorred as irreligious self);

3 When His candle shined upon my head, and when by His light I walked through darkness (there is no light other than the Gospel of Jesus Christ; all else is darkness);

4 As I was in the days of my youth, when the secret of God was upon my tabernacle (the "secret of God" was the "light of God," which was the "Word of God," which was passed down then by word of mouth);

5 When the Almighty was yet with me, when my children were about me (although Job does not now know it, the Almighty is with him now even more than ever);

6 When I washed my steps with butter, and

the rock poured me out rivers of oil *(Job had been very wealthy)*;

7 When I went out to the gate through the city, when I prepared my seat in the street! *(It was customary for elders of the city to sit in the open place at the entrance of the gates. Judgment was meted out here, and many other activities were carried on, as well.)*

8 The young men saw me, and hid themselves: and the aged arose, and stood up *(all deferred to Job, and rightly so; the touch of God on his life was obvious and evident to all).*

9 The princes refrained talking, and laid their hand on their mouth *(they would not be so foolish as to speak when Job was present).*

10 The nobles held their peace, and their tongue cleaved to the roof of their mouth *(whatever it is they knew, Job knew more).*

11 When the ear heard me, then it blessed me; and when the eye saw me, it gave witness to me *(knowing that Job would be fair in his judgment):*

12 Because I delivered the poor who cried, and the fatherless, and him who had none to help him.

13 The blessing of him who was ready to perish came upon me: and I caused the widow's heart to sing for joy. *(And yet, none of these "poor," or "fatherless," or "widows," would now speak a kind word for him. No doubt, he had helped thousands, or maybe even tens of thousands, but none remembered his kindness to them. Such is humanity!)*

14 I put on righteousness, and it clothed me: my judgment was as a robe and a diadem *(the Word of the Lord was his garment).*

15 I was eyes to the blind, and feet was I to the lame.

16 I was a father to the poor: and the cause which I knew not I searched out.

17 And I broke the jaws of the wicked, and plucked the spoil out of his teeth *(if the wicked were going to defraud the poor, they would have to answer to Job!).*

18 Then I said, I shall die in my nest, and I shall multiply my days as the sand *(there was then no cloud on the horizon).*

19 My root was spread out by the waters, and the dew lay all night upon my branch *(it seemed that nothing could destroy Job).*

20 My glory was fresh in me, and my bow was renewed in my hand *(unfailing strength).*

21 Unto me men gave ear, and waited, and kept silence at my counsel *(Job had the last word, because he had the wise word).*

22 After my words they spoke not again; and my speech dropped upon them *(his judgments could not be improved upon).*

23 And they waited for me as for the rain; and they opened their mouth wide as for the latter rain *(knowing that Job could help them).*

24 If I laughed on them, they believed it not; and the light of my countenance they cast not down *(when Job smiled on anyone, they were signally honored and blessed).*

25 I chose out their way, and sat chief, and dwelt as a king in the army, as one who comforts the mourners *(Job was the one to whom all looked in times of distress).*

CHAPTER 30
(1520 B.C.)
JOB'S PRESENT POVERTY
AND CALAMITIES

BUT now they who are younger than I have me in derision, whose fathers I would have disdained to have set with the dogs of my flock *(as high as he had been in the estimation of others, as low he has fallen).*

2 Yea, whereto might the strength of their hands profit me, in whom old age was perished? *(Job is saying that now it is as if he is so old he is of no more worth.)*

3 For want and famine they were solitary; fleeing into the wilderness in former time desolate and waste *(he looks at himself as "desolate and waste").*

4 Who cut up mallows by the bushes, and juniper roots for their meat *(from a king's table, Job is reduced to eating scraps).*

5 They were driven forth from among men, (they cried after them as after a thief *[Job is looked at as no more than human flotsam];)*

6 To dwell in the cliffs of the valleys, in caves of the earth, and in the rocks *(from a mansion to a cave!).*

7 Among the bushes they brayed; under the nettles they were gathered together *(Job has been reduced to scavenging).*

8 They were children of fools, yea, children of base men: they were viler than the earth *(as stated, the flotsam of humanity!).*

9 And now am I their song, yea, I am their byword *(the lowest of the low ridiculed Job).*

10 They abhor me, they flee far from me, and spare not to spit in my face. *(They mocked the Patriarch with ribald songs. Standing at a distance, they spat on him. Because God had loosed His scourge and afflicted him, they too*

cast off all restraint in their persecution of him. As rabble they stood at his right hand to accuse him. They gave him no standing room in any court of justice and laid snares for him. They did their best to add to his sufferings, even though doing so brought them no personal profit.)

11 Because He has loosed my cord, and afflicted me, they have also let loose the bridle before me *(they reasoned that if God had turned His back upon Job, then he was now "fair game").*

12 Upon my right hand rise the youth; they push away my feet, and they raise up against me the ways of their destruction.

13 They mar my path, they set forward my calamity, they have no helper *(they made sport of Job!).*

14 They came upon me as a wide breaking in of waters: in the desolation they rolled themselves upon me *(when one began to taunt Job, then they all began to taunt him).*

15 Terrors are turned upon me: they pursue my soul as the wind: and my welfare passes away as a cloud *(not only is his physical and financial welfare impugned, but he fears now for his soul).*

16 And now my soul is poured out upon me; the days of affliction have taken hold upon me.

17 My bones are pierced in me in the night season: and my sinews take no rest *(gnawing pain).*

18 By the great force of my disease is my garment changed: it binds me about as the collar of my coat *(along with the insults, Job's physical condition seems to be deteriorating by the hour).*

19 He has cast me into the mire, and I am become like dust and ashes *(perhaps it is not possible for God to sanctify "carnal self" without the individual, in some way, experiencing the "dust and ashes").*

20 I cry unto You, and You do not hear me: I stand up, and You regard me not *(it is the worst of all calamities to be God-forsaken, as Job believed himself to be; however, he will soon find out that the Lord had not forsaken him).*

21 You are become cruel to me: with Your strong hand You oppose Yourself against me *(it looked like that to Job).*

22 You lifted me up to the wind; you caused me to ride upon it, and dissolved my substance *(the wind of adversity was allowed to blow against him in full force).*

23 For I know that You will bring me to death, and to the house appointed for all living *(Job fully expects to die!).*

24 Howbeit he will not stretch out his hand to the grave, though they cry in his destruction *(one part of him wants death, and another part is trying to stop death).*

25 Did not I weep for him who was in trouble? Was not my soul grieved for the poor? *(But none wept for him!)*

26 When I looked for good, then evil came unto me: and when I waited for light, there came darkness *(I have been thinking the situation would change, but instead it has only gotten worse).*

27 My bowels boiled, and rested not: the days of affliction prevented me *(there was no respite).*

28 I went mourning without the sun: I stood up, and I cried in the congregation *(but no one cared or heard).*

29 I am a brother to dragons, and a companion to owls *(as they are awake at night, so am I).*

30 My skin is black upon me, and my bones are burned with heat *(terrible physical affliction).*

31 My harp also is turned to mourning, and my organ into the voice of them who weep *(there is no more music in his soul!).*

CHAPTER 31
(1520 B.C.)
JOB'S FINAL DEFENSE

I made a covenant with my eyes: why then should I think upon a maid? *(Job says here that he's not guilty of the sin of lust.)*

2 For what portion of God is there from above? and what inheritance of the Almighty from on high? *(What would the Lord say about such sin? The next Verse tells us.)*

3 Is not destruction to the wicked? and a strange punishment to the workers of iniquity? *(This is what sin does — ruin both of soul and body.)*

4 Does not He see my ways, and count all my steps? *(The Lord sees all!)*

5 If I have walked with vanity, or if my foot has hasted to deceit *(in this Passage, Job claims that he is not guilty of deceit);*

6 Let me be weighed in an even balance, that God may know my integrity *(in fact, the only "even balance" in the universe is that which is of God; all else is spurious).*

7 If my step has turned out of the way, and my heart walked after my eyes, and if any blot

has cleaved to my hands (*it is to be remembered that Job has the testimony of God Himself to the fact that he was "a perfect and an upright man, one who feared God, and hated evil" [2:3]; this doesn't mean that Job was sinlessly perfect, for he wasn't; but it does mean that he was attempting to follow the Lord as closely as possible*);

8 Then let me sow, and let another eat; yea, let my offspring be rooted out (*"if the Lord says I'm guilty, then I will accept my punishment"*).

9 If my heart has been deceived by a woman, or if I have laid wait at my neighbour's door (*I have not committed adultery*);

10 Then let my wife grind unto another, and let others bow down upon her (*if adultery is committed by a husband, the wife suffers, and suffers unjustly*).

11 For this is an heinous crime; yea, it is an iniquity to be punished by the judges (*the crime of adultery subverts the family relation on which it has pleased God to erect the entire fabric of human society*).

12 For it is a fire that consumes to destruction, and would root out all my increase (*the sin of adultery, lacking Repentance, will bring down the wrath of God upon the person who commits such*).

JOB IS NOT GUILTY OF
OPPRESSING OTHERS

13 If I did despise the cause of my manservant or of my maidservant, when they contended with me (*Job now disclaims the oppression of his dependants; of which he had been accused by Eliphaz [22:5-9]*);

14 What then shall I do when God rises up? and when He visits, what shall I answer Him?

15 Did not He Who made me in the womb make him? and did not One fashion us in the womb? (*Here the Spirit of God through Job proclaims the equality of all men, irrespective of race, creed, or color.*)

16 If I have withheld the poor from their desire, or have caused the eyes of the widow to fail;

17 Or have eaten my morsel myself alone, and the fatherless has not eaten thereof (*Job claims to have always shared his bread with orphans and made them partakers of his abundance*);

18 (For from my youth he was brought up with me, as with a father, and I have guided her from my mother's womb;)

19 If I have seen any perish for want of clothing, or any poor without covering;

20 If his loins have not blessed me, and if he were not warmed with the fleece of my sheep;

21 If I have lifted up my hand against the fatherless, when I saw my help in the gate (*in other words, "I have done everything for the poor and the helpless that I had the power to do"*):

22 Then let my arm fall from my shoulder blade, and my arm be broken from the bone.

23 For destruction from God was a terror to me, and by reason of His highness I could not endure (*"I could not have committed the sins of which I am accused, because of my fear of God"*).

JOB'S HOPE WAS NOT IN MONEY

24 If I have made gold my hope, or have said to the fine gold, You are my confidence;

25 If I rejoice because my wealth was great, and because my hand had gotten much (*Job feels that it is wrong even to care greatly for wealth*);

JOB IS NOT GUILTY OF IDOLATRY

26 If I beheld the sun when it shined, or the moon walking in brightness (*not guilty of idolatry*);

27 And my heart has been secretly enticed, or my mouth has kissed my hand (*a part of the process of the worship of planetary bodies*):

28 This also were an iniquity to be punished by the judge: for I should have denied the God Who is above (*the worship of any other god besides the supreme God is tantamount to atheism*).

JOB DOES NOT REJOICE AT THE
DOWNFALL OF OTHERS

29 If I rejoiced at the destruction of him who hated me, or lifted up myself when evil found him:

30 Neither have I suffered my mouth to sin by wishing a curse to his soul (*Job left all others to the Lord [Rom. 12:17-21]*).

31 If the men of my tabernacle said not, Oh that we had of his flesh! we cannot be satisfied (*all were satisfied with Job's hospitality*).

32 The stranger did not lodge in the street: but I opened my doors to the traveller.

33 If I covered my transgressions as Adam, by hiding my iniquity in my bosom (*Adam tried to hide the true state of his heart from God [Gen. 3:8]*):

34 Did I fear a great multitude, or did the contempt of families terrify me, that I kept

silence, and went not out of the door? (*Because of his integrity, Job had no fear of facing people.*)

35 Oh that one would hear me! behold, my desire is, that the Almighty would answer me, and that my adversary had written a book (*to be sure, the Lord was definitely hearing Job, and noting all that was said by his adversaries*).

36 Surely I would take it upon my shoulder, and bind it as a crown to me (*"I am this sure of my integrity"*).

37 I would declare unto him (*my adversary*) the number of my steps; as a prince would I go near unto him (*I can face any man without a guilty conscience*).

38 If my land cry against me, or that the furrows likewise thereof complain;

39 If I have eaten the fruits thereof without money, or have caused the owners thereof to lose their life:

40 Let thistles grow instead of wheat, and cockle instead of barley. The words of Job are ended (*Job is not trying here to justify himself before God, but merely answering the charges made against him by his "friends"*).

CHAPTER 32
(1520 B.C.)
ELIHU SPEAKS

So these three men ceased to answer Job, because he was righteous in his own eyes (*it should be noted that this is what these "three men" said, and not God; actually, the reverse is true; it is the "three friends" who are "righteous in their own eyes," not Job*).

2 Then was kindled the wrath of Elihu the son of Barachel the Buzite, of the kindred of Ram: against Job was his wrath kindled, because he justified himself rather than God (*Job was not trying to justify himself in the Eyes of God, but rather he was stating his case; as it regards Elihu, it was his self-righteousness which caused his anger against Job*).

3 Also against his three friends was his wrath kindled, because they had found no answer, and yet had condemned Job (*Elihu sets himself up as above all who are there, including Job*).

4 Now Elihu had waited till Job had spoken, because they were older than he (*he would have been wiser yet to have said nothing*).

5 When Elihu saw that there was no answer in the mouth of these three men, then his wrath was kindled (*fools walk where angels fear to tread*).

6 And Elihu the son of Barachel the Buzite answered and said, I am young, and you are very old; wherefore I was afraid, and did not show you my opinion.

7 I said, Days should speak, and multitude of years should teach wisdom (*"you are older than I am, so you should have more wisdom, but you don't"*).

8 But there is a spirit in man: and the inspiration of the Almighty gives them understanding (*Elihu claims great understanding from God*).

9 Great men are not always wise: neither do the aged understand judgment (*in other words, "even though I am younger, I understand more than you do"; what impertinence!*).

10 Therefore I said, Hearken to me; I also will show my opinion (*some claim that Elihu was a type of Christ; however, that is contradicted by his statement; the Lord does not give "His opinion," but only "Thus saith the Lord"*).

ELIHU'S IMPERTINENCE

11 Behold, I waited for your words; I gave ear to your reasons, while you searched out what to say (*to the three friends, "I have heard all that you have said"*).

12 Yes, I attended unto you, and behold, there was none of you who convinced Job, or who answered his words (*no doubt, there were many others present who also heard this entire exchange*):

13 Lest you should say, We have found out wisdom: God thrusts him down, not man (*this latter phrase is true; God will have the last say, and not man*).

14 Now he (*Job*) has not directed his words against me: neither will I answer him with your speeches (*I will bring forward fresh arguments*).

15 They were amazed, they answered no more: they left off speaking (*the three "friends" were amazed at this young man's impertinence; so they answered him by saying nothing*).

16 When I had waited, (for they spoke not, but stood still, and answered no more [*he waited for them to answer, but they said nothing*];)

17 I said, I will answer also my part, I also will show my opinion (*in other words, "it's now my turn"!*).

18 For I am full of matter (*words*), the spirit within me constrains me (*"I must speak!" To be sure, it was his spirit and not God's Spirit*).

19 Behold, my belly is as wine which has no vent; it is ready to burst like new bottles (*only*)

youth would make such foolish statements).

20 I will speak, that I may be refreshed: I will open my lips and answer.

21 Let me not, I pray you, accept any man's person, neither let me give flattering titles unto man *(in other words, he's not going to show Job any respect).*

22 For I know not to give flattering titles; in so doing my Maker would soon take me away *(here, he puts himself spiritually above Job).*

CHAPTER 33
(1520 B.C.)
ELIHU SPEAKS TO JOB

WHEREFORE, Job, I pray you, hear my speeches, and hearken to all my words *(the truth is, Elihu has nothing to say, so God will ignore all that he will say, thereby tendering the worst insult of all; his own self-righteousness screams as loud as the three "friends" or even louder).*

2 Behold, now I have opened my mouth, my tongue has spoken in my mouth.

3 My words shall be of the uprightness of my heart: and my lips shall utter knowledge clearly *(he evidently has a high opinion of himself).*

4 The Spirit of God has made me, and the breath of the Almighty has given me life *(he is coming close here to saying that the words he will utter are from the Lord).*

5 If you can answer me, set your words in order before me, stand up *(Job will not answer him, even as he should not have).*

6 Behold, I am according to your wish in God's stead: I also am formed out of the clay *(in other words, "even though I am only a man, I can give you all the answers for which you have sought!").*

7 Behold, my terror shall not make you afraid, neither shall my hand be heavy upon you *(how foolish to insinuate that Job would be afraid of him).*

8 Surely you have spoken in my hearing, and I have heard the voice of your words, saying,

9 I am clean without transgression, I am innocent; neither is there iniquity in me *(Job had not said these things).*

10 Behold, He *(the Lord)* finds occasions against me, He counts me for His enemy,

11 He puts my feet in the stocks, He marks all my paths *(Job did say these things [16:9; 19:11; 31:2, 6, 28, 35-37; 31:4]).*

12 Behold, in this you are not just: I will answer you, that God is greater than man *(it is*

a poor way to justify God by urging that He is all-powerful, and may do what He likes).

13 Why do you strive against Him? for He gives not account of any of His matters *(Job had not striven against the Lord).*

ELIHU CONTINUES TO PONTIFICATE

14 For God speaks once, yea twice, yet man perceives it not *(in a sense, Elihu is claiming that God has spoken to Job, but that Job is so lacking in spirituality that he didn't perceive it).*

15 In a dream, in a vision of the night, when deep sleep falls upon men, in slumberings upon the bed;

16 Then He opens the ears of men, and seals their instruction,

17 That He may withdraw man from his purpose, and hide pride from man *(here, Elihu claims that Job is unduly proud of his integrity).*

18 He keeps back his soul from the pit, and his life from perishing by the sword.

19 He is chastened also with pain upon his bed, and the multitude of his bones with strong pain *(so he is saying here that Job is being chastened by the Lord; that is not correct):*

20 So that his life abhors bread, and his soul dainty meat.

21 His flesh is consumed away, that it cannot be seen; and his bones that were not seen stick out *(he is now referring to Job's "chastisement," regarding his physical sickness).*

22 Yea, his soul draws near unto the grave, and his life to the destroyers.

23 If there be a messenger with him, an interpreter, one among a thousand, to show unto man his uprightness *(in effect, Elihu is telling Job that he is the "messenger" with the "interpretation" of Job's problems; he is saying, "I am one among a thousand"; only youthfulness, with its immaturity and ignorance, would dare make such a statement):*

24 Then he is gracious unto him *(Elihu says that he will be gracious to Job),* and says, Deliver him from going down to the pit: I have found a ransom *(if Job will listen to him, says Elihu, his soul will be settled, his physical body will be healed, and his joy will return).*

25 His flesh shall be fresher than a child's: he shall return to the days of his youth:

26 He shall pray unto God, and He will be favourable unto him: and he shall see His face with joy: for He will render unto man His righteousness *(so, to obtain God's Righteousness, all Job has to do is to listen to Elihu; such*

words sound greatly familiar!).

27 He looks upon men, and if any say, I have sinned, and perverted that which was right, and it profited me not *(if Job would only repent . . .);*

28 He will deliver his soul from going into the pit, and his life shall see the light *(so, to keep from going to Hell, Job should listen to Elihu).*

29 Lo, all these things works God oftentimes with man *(in essence, Elihu is saying that Job's situation is not uncommon. He could not be more wrong! How many men in history have been the subject of a contest between God and Satan? Perhaps some, but not many!),*

30 To bring back his soul from the pit, to be enlightened with the light of the living.

31 Mark well, O Job, hearken unto me: hold your peace, and I will speak *(it seems that Job, at this juncture, may have attempted to answer the impertinence of this young man, but he is told by Elihu to keep quiet).*

32 If you have any thing to say, answer me: speak, for I desire to justify you *(when Elihu claims that he is able to justify Job, Job evidently realizes that it would be foolish to dignify this young man's statements with an answer).*

33 If not, hearken unto me: hold your peace, and I shall teach you wisdom. *(What arrogance! Especially in his notion that he could "teach Job wisdom.")*

CHAPTER 34
(1520 B.C.)
ELIHU'S ARROGANCE CONTINUES

FURTHERMORE, Elihu answered and said, 2 Hear my words, O ye wise men; and give ear unto me, you who have knowledge *(the first fifteen Verses of this Chapter are spoken to the "three friends," with the remaining Verses spoken to Job).*

3 For the ear tries words, as the mouth tastes meat *(this was a proverbial expression; it meant, "it is as much the business of the ear to discriminate between wise and foolish words, as of the palate to distinguish between wholesome and unwholesome food").*

4 Let us choose to us judgment: let us know among ourselves what is good.

5 For Job has said, I am righteous: and God has taken away my judgment *(while it was true that Job maintained his "righteousness" in a certain sense, still, he had not maintained his sinfulness).*

6 Should I lie against my right? my wound is incurable without transgression *(Job had in fact maintained that transgressions were not the cause of his terrible condition).*

7 What man is like Job, who drinks up scorning like water? *(Job had not scorned the Lord.)*

8 Which goes in company with the workers of iniquity, and walks with wicked men *(this was totally untrue!).*

9 For he has said, It profits a man nothing that he should delight himself with God *(Job had not said this!).*

ELIHU PONTIFICATES ABOUT GOD, OF WHOM HE HAS LITTLE TRUE UNDERSTANDING

10 Therefore hearken unto me, you men of understanding: far be it from God, that He should do wickedness; and from the Almighty, that He should commit iniquity *(to say that God is not wicked should be obvious!).*

11 For the work of a man shall He render unto him, and cause every man to find according to his ways.

12 Yes, surely God will not do wickedly, neither will the Almighty pervert judgment.

13 Who has given Him a charge over the Earth? or who has discovered the whole world?

14 If He *(the Lord)* set His heart upon man, if He gather unto Himself His Spirit and His breath:

15 All flesh shall perish together, and man shall turn again unto dust. *(Why did the Lord desire that the ramblings of this man be placed in the Sacred Text? Among other reasons, He did so to show us that intellectualism is not the answer. In fact, without a true Revelation from the Lord, one cannot understand the Lord or His Word [I Cor. 2:9-10].)*

ELIHU NOW SPEAKS DIRECTLY TO JOB

16 If now you have understanding, hear this: hearken to the voice of my words *(the young man insults Job by saying that his words will be so wise that Job possibly will not be able to understand them; in fact, they will actually be the opposite).*

17 Shall even he who hates right govern? and will you condemn him who is most just? *(Elihu now accuses Job of condemning God.)*

18 Is it fit to say to a king, You are wicked? and to princes, You are ungodly?

19 How much less to Him Who accepts not

the persons of princes, nor regards the rich more than the poor? for they all are the work of His hands.

20 In a moment shall they die, and the people shall be troubled at midnight, and pass away: and the mighty shall be taken away without hand.

21 For His eyes are upon the ways of man, and He sees all his goings (*now Elihu tells Job that the Lord has seen everything that he [Job] has done*).

22 There is no darkness, nor shadow of death, where the workers of iniquity may hide themselves (*he accuses Job of being full of iniquity and, therefore, trying to hide himself from God*).

23 For He will not lay upon man more than right; that he should enter into judgment with God (*so, according to Elihu, what the Lord has done to Job is "right," because Job is so wicked*).

24 He shall break in pieces mighty men without number, and set others in their stead (*so Job was once mighty, and the Lord has now broken him in pieces; that is true, but not for the reasons that Elihu or the three friends have said*).

25 Therefore He knows their works, and He overturns them in the night, so that they are destroyed.

26 He strikes them as wicked men in the open sight of others (*and thus he describes Job, or so he thinks*);

27 Because they turned back from Him, and would not consider any of His ways (*now he accuses Job of forsaking the Ways of God*):

28 So that they cause the cry of the poor to come unto Him, and He hears the cry of the afflicted (*as the three "friends," Elihu accuses Job of oppressing the poor*).

29 When He gives quietness, who then can make trouble? and when He hides His face, who then can behold Him? whether it be done against a nation, or against a man only (*Elihu accuses Job of trying to escape the wrath of God*):

30 That the hypocrite reign not, lest the people be ensnared (*now he calls the great Patriarch a hypocrite*).

ELIHU CONTINUES TO REPROVE JOB

31 Surely it is meet to be said unto God, I have borne chastisement, I will not offend any more (*he now tells Job to repent*):

32 That which I see not teach thou me: if I have done iniquity, I will do no more.

33 Should it be according to your mind? He

will recompense it, whether you refuse, or whether you choose; and not I: therefore speak what you know (*in his feigned piousness, Elihu gives an altar call for Job to get right with God*).

34 Let men of understanding tell me, and let a wise man hearken unto me (*in other words, he tells Job that "if you have any wisdom, you will hearken unto my words"*).

35 Job has spoken without knowledge, and his words were without wisdom (*what arrogance!*).

36 My desire is that Job may be tried unto the end because of his answers for wicked men (*after the manner of wicked men; he wants Job to be afflicted even more*).

37 For he (*Job*) adds rebellion unto his sin, he claps his hands among us, and multiplies his words against God (*so now, he becomes more bold and more rash in his accusations against Job*).

CHAPTER 35
(1520 B.C.)
ELIHU CONTINUES

ELIHU spoke moreover, and said,

2 Do you think this to be right, that you said, My righteousness is more than God's? (*Job had said no such thing.*)

3 For you said, What advantage will it be unto you? and, What profit shall I have, if I be cleansed from my sin? (*Once again, he twists Job's words.*)

4 I will answer you, and your companions with you (*so now, Elihu, at least in his own eyes, is wiser than all who are there*).

5 Look unto the Heavens, and see; and behold the clouds which are higher than you (*that should be obvious to all*).

6 If you sin, what do you against Him? of if your transgressions be multiplied, what do you unto Him?

7 If you be righteous, what do you give Him? or what receives He of your hand? (*Once again, all of these things should be known by any sincere Believer.*)

8 Your wickedness may hurt a man as you are; and your righteousness may profit the son of man (*the meaning is, "We cannot add to God, or take from Him, irrespective of our obedience or disobedience," which all Believers should know*).

9 By reason of the multitude of oppressions they make the oppressed to cry: they cry out by reason of the arm of the mighty (*once

again, Job is accused of oppressing others).

10 But none says, Where is God my Maker, Who gives songs in the night;

11 Who teaches us more than the beasts of the earth, and makes us wiser than the fowls of Heaven?

12 There they cry, but none gives answer, because of the pride of evil men.

13 Surely God will not hear vanity, neither will the Almighty regard it *(now, Elihu accuses Job of being "vain").*

14 Although you say you shall not see Him, yet judgment is before Him; therefore trust thou in Him *(in other words, "you are in the condition you are in, because you have not trusted the Lord").*

15 But now, because it is not so, He has visited in His anger; yet He knows it not in great extremity *(while God is angry at Job, so says Elihu, due to Job's wickedness, He should have been much more angry):*

16 Therefore does Job open his mouth in vain; he multiplies words without knowledge *(it is Elihu and the three friends who have multiplied words without knowledge, not Job).*

CHAPTER 36
(1520 B.C.)
ELIHU CLAIMS TO BE PERFECT IN KNOWLEDGE

ELIHU also proceeded, and said *(if Elihu had been led by the Holy Spirit, he would not have even begun, much less proceeded),*

2 Suffer me a little, and I will show you that I have yet to speak on God's behalf *(so now, Elihu professes to speak for God).*

3 I will fetch my knowledge from afar, and will ascribe righteousness to my Maker.

4 For truly my words shall not be false: he who is perfect in knowledge is with you *(what an arrogant statement!).*

5 Behold, God is mighty, and despises not any: He is mighty in strength and wisdom.

6 He preserves not the life of the wicked: but gives right to the poor *(he tells Job that his life is not going to be preserved; in other words, Job is going to die; the truth is, Job would live another 140 years, for a total of 210 years [42:16]).*

7 He withdraws not His eyes from the righteous: but with kings are they on the throne; yes, He does establish them for ever, and they are exalted *(the Lord has the power to raise up one and pull down another; He has pulled down Job, so says Elihu).*

8 And it they be bound in fetters, and be holden in cords of affliction;

9 Then He shows them their work, and their transgression that they have exceeded.

10 He opens also their ear to discipline, and commands that they return from iniquity.

11 If they obey and serve Him, they shall spend their days in prosperity, and their years in pleasures *(in fact, the Righteous are told to expect tribulations and persecutions [Jn. 16:33; Acts 14:22; II Tim. 3:12; Heb. 12:1-11; I Pet. 4:12-13]).*

12 But if they obey not, they shall perish by the sword, and they shall die without knowledge.

13 But the hypocrites in heart heap up wrath: they cry not when He binds them *(Elihu continues to call Job a hypocrite).*

14 They die in youth, and their life is among the unclean.

15 He delivers the poor in his affliction, and opens their ears in oppression.

16 Even so would He have removed you out of the strait into a broad place, where there is no straitness: and that which should be set on your table should be full of fatness *("if you would only repent!").*

17 But you have fulfilled the judgment of the wicked: judgment and justice take hold on you.

18 Because there is wrath, beware lest He take you away with His stroke: then a great ransom cannot deliver you. *(Elihu is saying that God is so angry with Job that He has taken away all his possessions, plus his health, and is now very close to taking his life — and there is nothing Job can do to stop it.*

First of all, there was no wrath with God concerning Job; however, there definitely would be wrath from God concerning these individuals who judged Job [42:7].)

19 Will He esteem your riches? no, not gold, nor all the forces of strength.

20 Desire not the night, when people are cut off in their place.

21 Take heed, regard not iniquity: for this have you chosen rather than affliction. *(He accuses Job of choosing iniquity. The tragedy of Eliphaz, Bildad, Zophar, and Elihu is that they actually were doing the work of Satan. All their accusations, judgmental attitudes, and approaches to Job were far more in keeping with the destructive work of Satan than of God.)*

22 Behold, God exalts by His power: who teaches like Him?

23 Who has enjoined Him His way? or who

can say, You have wrought iniquity?

24 Remember that you magnify His work, which men behold (but instead, Elihu says that Job is magnifying other things).

25 Every man may see it; man may behold it afar off (in other words, anybody can see how wrong that Job is, so says Elihu).

ELIHU CONTINUES HIS EFFORTS TO EXPLAIN GOD

26 Behold, God is great, and we know Him not, neither can the number of His years be searched out.

27 For He makes small the drops of water: they pour down rain according to the vapour thereof (all of this is from intellectualism; it shows not at all any relationship with the Lord; regrettably, it is the state of many modern professing Believers):

28 Which the clouds do drop and distil upon man abundantly.

29 Also can any understand the spreadings of the clouds, or the noise of His tabernacle?

30 Behold, He spreads His light upon it, and covers the bottom of the sea (Elihu says many words, but in reality he says nothing!).

31 For by them judges He the people; He gives meat in abundance.

32 With clouds He covers the light; and commands it not to shine by the cloud that comes betwixt.

33 The noise thereof shows concerning it, the cattle also concerning the vapour (could be translated: "The cattle also are facing the storm").

CHAPTER 37
(1520 B.C.)
ELIHU SPEAKS MANY WORDS, BUT ACTUALLY HAS VERY LITTLE KNOWLEDGE OF GOD

AT this also my heart trembles, and is moved out of his place (it seems that Elihu's fear of God was somewhat misplaced; he seems to be far more concerned about God's "acts" than of God Himself).

2 Hear attentively the noise of His voice, and the sound that goes out of His mouth (the facts were that Job had heard; neither Elihu nor the three friends had; they were judging from outward appearance, as all judging is done; that's the reason we are told not to judge [Mat. 7:1-2]).

3 He directs it under the whole Heaven, and His lightning unto the ends of the Earth.

4 After it a voice roars: He thunders with the voice of His excellency; and He will not stay them when His voice is heard.

5 God thunders marvellously with His voice; great things does He, which we cannot comprehend (if it is to be noticed, all of this says what every Believer knows).

6 For He saith to the snow, Be thou on the Earth; likewise to the small rain, and to the great rain of His strength.

7 He seals up the hand of every man; that all men may know His work.

8 Then the beasts go into dens, and remain in their places.

9 Out of the south comes the whirlwind: and cold out of the north.

10 By the breath of God frost is given: and the breadth of the waters is straitened (please remember, Inspiration guarantees that what is said was actually said, and by the person to whom it is attributed; however, that doesn't mean that it is true; in fact, much of what the "three friends" and Elihu said was completely untrue).

11 Also by watering He wearies the thick cloud: He scatters His bright cloud:

12 And it is turned round about by His counsels: that they may do whatsoever He commands them upon the face of the world in the Earth.

13 He causes it to come, whether for correction, or for his land, or for mercy.

14 Hearken unto this, O Job: stand still, and consider the wondrous works of God (Elihu felt perfectly comfortable in admonishing Job; there was a time that the mightiest of men held their tongues when in Job's presence; now, even this youthful Elihu harshly commands Job to "listen").

15 Do you know when God disposed them, and caused the light of His cloud to shine?

16 Do you know the balancings of the clouds, the wondrous works of Him which is perfect in knowledge?

17 How your garments are warm, when He quiets the Earth by the south wind?

18 Have you with Him spread out the sky, which is strong, and as a molten looking glass?

19 Teach us what we shall say unto Him, for we cannot order our speech by reason of darkness.

20 Shall it be told him that I speak? if a man speak, surely he shall be swallowed up (Elihu should have heeded carefully his own statement; God, being God, would certainly

hear his prattling, but would totally ignore him).

21 And now men see not the bright light which is in the clouds: but the wind passes, and cleanses them.

22 Fair weather comes out of the north: with God is terrible majesty.

23 Touching the Almighty, we cannot find Him out: He is excellent in power, and in judgment, and in plenty of justice: He will not afflict.

24 Men do therefore fear Him: He respects not any who are wise of heart *(so, by his own words, Elihu is ruled out!).*

CHAPTER 38
(1520 B.C.)
THE INFINITE GOD, THE
CREATOR SPEAKS

THEN the LORD answered Job out of the whirlwind, and said *(the Lord, it seems, appeared suddenly and without warning; He did so with some type of atmospheric disturbance; His appearing would have been cataclysmic, startling, and absolutely overwhelming),*

2 Who is this who darkens counsel by words without knowledge? *(The Lord is not speaking of Job, but rather these "three friends" and Elihu. The Lord said of Job that he had "spoken of Me the thing that is right" [42:7].)*

3 Gird up now your loins like a man *(He now speaks to Job)*; for I will demand of you, and answer thou Me *(even though Job has been reduced to the most humiliating position, still, God will demand that he stand while being spoken to; in fact, this command of God is the beginning of Job's Restoration; God picks men up; He does not put men down, unless He has no choice but to do so).*

4 Where were you when I laid the foundations of the Earth? declare, if you have understanding. *(The truth that God made all things is obvious according to the creation. A creation must have a Creator. Therefore, the alleged theory of evolution is a farce. Evolution, in fact, cannot even be honestly called a "theory," because a theory has to have at least some rudiments of facts to buttress its claims. Evolution has no facts whatsoever.)*

5 Who has laid the measures thereof, if you know? or who has stretched the line upon it? *(The idea is that God has planned and created the Universe, down to the most fine detail.)*

6 Whereupon are the foundations thereof fastened? or who laid the corner stone thereof *(in fact, the worlds are held up by the Word of God [Heb. 11:3])*;

7 When the morning stars sang together, and all the sons of God shouted for joy? *(The Lord is speaking here of the completion of the Earth and the Universe, and of the celebration that followed by the Angels of Heaven.*

Lucifer, before his Fall, was called the "son of the morning" [Isa. 14:12].

There is a possibility that these "morning stars" who "sang together" were led in their worship and celebration by Lucifer, the "son of the morning.")

8 Or who shut up the sea with doors, when it broke forth, as if it had issued out of the womb? *(The Lord put boundaries on the mighty oceans. So the fact of global warming, etc., will not noticeably alter those boundaries.)*

9 When I made the cloud the garment thereof, and thick darkness a swaddlingband for it,

10 And broke up for it my decreed place, and set bars and doors,

11 And said, Hitherto shall you come, but no further: and here shall your proud waves be stayed? *(Again, we are told that the oceans have boundaries, and boundaries set by the Lord Himself.)*

12 Have you commanded the morning since your days; and caused the dayspring to know his place *(all days and nights are fixed by the Lord, and are ruled by the sun, moon, and stars [Gen. 1:14-19; 8:22])*;

13 That it might take hold of the ends of the Earth, that the wicked might be shaken out of it? *(The idea is, the "wicked" cannot do anything about God's order.)*

14 It is turned as clay to the seal; and they stand as a garment *(everything is obvious as to its function, but not so obvious as to exactly how it functions).*

15 And from the wicked their light is withholden, and the high arm shall be broken *(the Lord will allow the "wicked" to go only so far, before He steps in and breaks their arms, which He has done many times in the past, and will yet do in the future).*

16 Have you entered into the springs of the sea? or have you walked in the search of the depth? *(Can man go to the bottom of anything, explore its secrets, and explain its cause and origin?)*

17 Have the gates of death been opened unto you? or have you seen the doors of the shadow of death? *(This reveals openings and doors to Hell and Death [Rev. 1:18].)*

THE LORD CONTINUES WITH HIS DESCRIPTION OF CREATION

18 Have you perceived the breadth of the Earth? declare if you know it all. *(As we read these things said by the Almighty, we wonder how they relate to Job's condition? The reason for the Lord giving this information is many-fold; however, in essence, the Lord is saying to Job, "If I can do all of this, don't you realize how easy it is for Me to change your situation?")*

19 Where is the way where light dwells? and as for darkness, where is the place thereof *(in fact, Light is a thing quite distinct from the sun [Gen. 1:3, 16]),*

20 That you should take it to the bound thereof, and that you should know the paths to the house thereof? *(No man can!)*

21 Do you know it, because you were then born? or because the number of your days is great? *(In other words, "Job, are you as old as I am?")*

22 Have you entered into the treasures of the snow? or have you seen the treasures of the hail *(no two flakes of snow or two pieces of hail are alike),*

23 Which I have reserved against the time of trouble, against the day of battle and war? *(Many times the Lord has used the elements against His enemies [Ex. 9:22-26; Josh. 10:11; Ps. 18:12-13]. In the future, hail will fall again as a part of judgment [Rev. 8:7; 11:19; 16:21].)*

24 By what way is the light parted, which scatters the east wind upon the Earth?

25 Who has divided a watercourse for the overflowing of waters, or a way for the lightning of thunder;

26 To cause it to rain on the Earth, where no man is; on the wilderness, wherein there is no man *(the animals need rain as well);*

27 To satisfy the desolate and waste ground; and to cause the bud of the tender herb to spring forth? *(Plants also need the rain.)*

28 Has the rain a father? or who has begotten the drops of dew? *(God is the Father of rain and dew, etc.)*

29 Out of whose womb came the ice? and the hoary frost of Heaven, who has gendered it?

30 The waters are hid as with a stone, and the face of the deep is frozen *(the Arctic and the Antarctic).*

31 Can you bind the sweet influences of Pleiades, or loose the bands of Orion?

32 Can you bring forth Mazzaroth in his season? or can you guide Arcturus with his sons?

33 Knowest thou the ordinances of Heaven? can you set the dominion thereof in the Earth? *(The "sweet influences of the Pleiades" are appealed to as a matter of common knowledge at that time. Modern astronomers do not know very much about them at present.*

The ancient Greeks called them the "Seven Stars" and named them the "Pleiades," because their appearance indicated a favorable time for sea voyages. The Chaldaic name means a "pivot," and astronomers, some time ago, claimed to have discovered that the largest of these stars form a pivot around which the solar system revolves.

When it is remembered that the Sun is more than 3,000 billion miles away from the Pleiades, some idea is arrived at of the amazing "influence" of these seven stars in swinging this vast Universe — the Earth included — at the rate of more than 150 million miles a year in an orbit so vast that one revolution occupies thousands of years to make, and yet does so with unvarying regularity and smoothness.

Thus, this remote Verse in what is generally accepted to be the oldest Book in the world speaks of the influences of these stars as a matter of everyday knowledge, and it is remarkable that the expression "sweet" is employed — the very word which engineers use in describing the smooth working of complex machinery.

"Orion" is the constellation commonly known as "the Giant." The space in the sword of the Giant alone is estimated to be two trillion two hundred billion [2,200,000,000,000] times larger than the Sun.

"Mazzaroth" means the twelve signs of the Zodiac; it is only mentioned here in Scripture.)

34 Can you lift up your voice to the clouds, that abundance of waters may cover you?

35 Can you send lightnings, that they may go and say unto you, Here we are?

36 Who has put wisdom in the inward parts? or who has given understanding to the heart?

37 Who can number the clouds in wisdom? or who can stay the bottles of Heaven *(this tells us that all the clouds, coming and going, we might quickly add, are numbered by the Lord),*

38 When the dust grows into hardness, and the clods cleave fast together?

39 Will you hunt the prey for the lion? or fill the appetite of the young lions,

40 When they couch in their dens, and abide in the covert to lie in wait?

41 Who provides for the raven his food? when his young ones cry unto God, they wander for lack of meat *(God provides for all, even*

the lowliest of creation; if He does this for them, how much more will He care for us, "O ye of little faith" [Mat. 6:30]).

CHAPTER 39
(1520 B.C.)
THE LORD CONTINUES TO DESCRIBE HIS CREATION

KNOWEST thou the time when the wild goats of the rock bring forth? or can you mark when the hinds do calve?

2 Can you number the months that they fulfill? or knowest thou the time when they bring forth?

3 They bow themselves, they bring forth their young ones, they cast out their sorrows.

4 Their young ones are in good liking, they grow up with corn; they go forth, and return not unto them.

5 Who has sent out the wild ass free? or who has loosed the bands of the wild ass? *(The first two words of this Chapter, "knowest thou," pretty well tell the story. The fact is that man does not know. Man is able to study each animal and to understand its basic instincts, as well as its habits, strength, or peculiarities; nevertheless, man is totally unable to even begin to understand the manner in which God created the animal kingdom. This we do know:*

The Bible declares that, after its own kind [some ten times in Gen., Chpt. 1], everything created by God was given power to reproduce "its own kind." No one thing could break this law and produce any other kind [Gen. 1:20-28]. Now, after more than six thousand years, the law of reproduction is still unbroken, and the fact is that it will remain that way.)

6 Whose house I have made the wilderness, and the barren land his dwellings.

7 He scorns the multitude of the city, neither regards he the crying of the driver *(nothing will induce the wild ass to submit to domestication).*

8 The range of the mountains is his pasture, and he searches after every green thing.

9 Will the unicorn be willing to serve you, or abide by your crib? *(The word "unicorn" is an unfortunate translation, since there is no word correspondent to "unicorn" in the original. It actually pertains to the wild bull.)*

10 Can you bind the unicorn with his band in the furrow? or will he harrow the valleys after you? *(In fact, the type of wild bull mentioned here cannot be harnessed.)*

11 Will you trust him, because his strength is great? or will you leave your labour to him? *(As stated, he cannot be domesticated.)*

12 Will you believe him, that he will bring home your seed, and gather it into your barn?

13 Gavest thou the goodly wings unto the peacocks? or wings and feathers unto the ostrich?

14 Which leaves her eggs in the earth, and warms them in dust,

15 And forgets that the foot may crush them, or that the wild beast may break them.

16 She is hardened against her young ones, as though they were not hers: her labour is in vain without fear;

17 Because God has deprived her of wisdom, neither has He imparted to her understanding.

18 What time she lifts up herself on high, she scorns the horse and his rider *(at full pace, the fastest horse can little catch, if at all, the ostrich, at least when she starts to fly).*

19 Have you given the horse strength? have you clothed his neck with thunder?

20 Can you make him afraid as a grasshopper? the glory of his nostrils is terrible.

21 He paweth in the valley, and rejoiceth in his strength: he goes on to meet the armed men.

22 He mocks at fear, and is not affrighted; neither turns he back from the sword.

23 The quiver rattles against him, the glittering spear and the shield.

24 He swalloweth the ground with fierceness and rage: neither believes he that it is the sound of the trumpet.

25 He saith among the trumpets, Ha, ha; and he smells the battle afar off, the thunder of the captains, and the shouting *(and yet the horse eats only grass or such like feed, and yet is as strong as he is).*

26 Does the hawk fly by your wisdom, and stretch her wings toward the south?

27 Does the eagle mount up at your command, and make her nest on high?

28 She dwells and abides on the rock, upon the crag of the rock, and the strong place.

29 From thence she seeks the prey, and her eyes behold afar off.

30 Her young ones also suck up blood: and where the slain are, there is she.

CHAPTER 40
(1520 B.C.)
JOB ANSWERS THE LORD

MOREOVER the LORD answered Job, and said,

2 Shall he who contends with the Almighty instruct Him? he who reproves God, let him answer it *(the basic sin of the human race is "contending with the Almighty"; men have a tendency to blame God for the terrible problems of mankind).*

3 Then Job answered the LORD, and said,

4 Behold, I am vile; what shall I answer You? I will lay my hand upon my mouth. *(Job, convicted of his ignorance, his impotence, and his sinfulness, at last learns the lesson that it seems none of us can learn without at least some such trial. As a son of Adam, he was a total moral wreck and, consequently, he loathed himself, though he had done all he could to live right.*

He did not learn this humiliating lesson so long as he confronted the Church, i.e., his "three friends," but he learned it directly when he entered into the sinless light of the presence of God. That light showed his comeliness to actually be corruption, and his righteousness to be as filthy rags.)

5 Once have I spoken; but I will not answer: yea, twice; but I will proceed no further *(Job now realizes the futility, and even foolishness, of his arguments).*

THE LORD ANSWERS JOB

6 Then answered the LORD unto Job out of the whirlwind, and said,

7 Gird up your loins now like man: I will demand of you, and declare thou unto Me. *(Job is given every opportunity of making good his pleas before God. If he has anything to say that he really wishes to urge, God is ready, even anxious, to hear him — Pulpit.)*

8 Will you also disannul My judgment? will you condemn Me, that you may be righteous? *(Men have been trying to disannul the judgment of God from the very beginning. God's Judgment is His Word.)*

9 Have you an arm like God? or can you thunder with a voice like Him?

10 Deck yourself now with majesty and excellency; and array yourself with glory and beauty *(of course, Job could not do that, but the Lord could do it for Job and, in fact, ultimately did!).*

11 Cast abroad the rage of your wrath: and behold every one who is proud, and abase him.

12 Look on every one who is proud, and bring him low; and tread down the wicked in their place *(in other words, Job is a mere mortal, and he cannot do what God Alone can do,*

and neither can any other man).*

13 Hide them in the dust together; and bind their faces in secret *(which only God can do!).*

14 Then will I also confess unto you that your own right hand can save you *(man's problem has ever been that he thinks that he can save himself; there is only one answer for man, and that is "Jesus Christ and Him Crucified" [I Cor. 1:23]).*

15 Behold now behemoth, which I made with you; he eats grass as an ox *(the "behemoth" is probably the hippo; this particular animal eats grass).*

16 Lo now, his strength is in his loins, and his force is in the navel of his belly.

17 He moves his tail like a cedar: the sinews of his stones are wrapped together.

18 His bones are as strong pieces of brass; his bones are like bars of iron.

19 He is the chief of the ways of God: He Who made him can make his sword to approach unto him *(in that day, God Alone could bring down such a beast).*

20 Surely the mountains bring him forth food, where all the beasts of the field play.

21 He lies under the shady trees, in the covert of the reed, and fens *(this is exactly descriptive of the hippopotamus, and far less so of the elephant, or any other such like animal).*

22 The shady trees cover him with their shadow; the willows of the brook compass him about.

23 Behold, he drinks up a river, and hastes not: he trusts that he can draw up Jordan into his mouth.

24 He takes it with his eyes: his nose pierces through snares. *(Once again, why would the Lord address these things which seem to have no bearing whatsoever on Job's situation? The idea is, this great contest, with Job caught in the middle between God and Satan, is being played out before the entire spirit world. Among other things, the Lord desires to show the futility of man, or even Satan and fallen angels, contending with Him. It cannot successfully be done.)*

CHAPTER 41
(1520 B.C.)
THE LEVIATHAN

CAN you draw out leviathan with an hook? or his tongue with a cord which you let down? *(This Chapter is, no doubt, one of the most misunderstood in the entirety of the Word of God. Many have ascertained the description*

as to refer to some type of huge animal; however, there are certain things said that make us understand that God was not speaking of some such creature, but rather this is a description given of Satan. He is portrayed as a great dragon who is the enemy of both God and man.)

2 Can you put an hook into his nose? or bore his jaw through with a thorn? (The Lord is telling man here that, within himself, he cannot subdue Satan. The battle is not physical, mental, or financial; the battle is spiritual.)

3 Will he make many supplications unto you? will he speak soft words unto you? (Satan plies the heart of man continually, seeking to deceive him and, thereby, to lead him astray. Deception is his greatest weapon. He uses "soft words" to carry it through to its successful conclusion.)

4 Will he make a covenant with you? will you take him for a servant for ever? (Satan strongly desires to make a covenant with man. He will promise riches, power, influence, fame, etc. Inasmuch as he is a liar and the father of it, he will make any covenant that man likes, knowing that he will not keep his side of the bargain.)

5 Will you play with him as with a bird? or will you bind him for your maidens? (Unfortunately, untold millions attempt to do this very thing each day; however, they soon find out that Satan and sin are not playthings.)

6 Shall the companions make a banquet of him? shall they part him among the merchants? (How many hundreds of millions through the centuries have thought that they were man or woman enough to defeat Satan in their own strength? They found out the hard way that they couldn't!)

7 Can you fill his skin with barbed irons? or his head with fish spears? (Satan does not respond to natural weapons.)

8 Lay your hand upon him, remember the battle, do no more. (In effect, the Lord is saying, "When man attempts to do battle with Satan, he should remember that he has lost all these conflicts in the past. Consequently, he should desire to 'do no more' in this capacity." The Lord Jesus Christ has defeated Satan; He did so at Calvary's Cross.)

9 Behold, the hope of him is in vain: shall not one be cast down even at the sight of him? (No one can bargain with Satan. Every effort is in vain. The one who attempts to do business with him will be 'cast down.')

10 None is so fierce who dare stir him up (the foolishness of one who dares to think he can beat the game of sin will meet with none other than the fierceness of Satan): who then is able to stand before Me? (The Lord is referring in this last phrase to Himself. Man cannot defeat Satan, but God can and, in effect, has, by the death, burial, and Resurrection of the Lord Jesus Christ, which atoned for all sin, thereby completely defeating the Evil One.)

11 Who has prevented Me, that I should repay him? whatsoever is under the whole Heaven is Mine (all things belong to God; one day, the Lord will make an end of Satan; the Bible tells us so [Rev. 20:1-3]).

12 I will not conceal his parts, nor his power, nor his comely proportion (in effect, God created him, but not as a fallen angel, but rather the beautiful Angel, Lucifer, who in fact served God in righteous and holiness for an undetermined period of time [Ezek. 28:11-19]).

13 Who can discover the face of his garment? or who can come to him with his double bridle?

14 Who can open the doors of his face? his teeth are terrible round about (Satan is very successful at making that which is ugly seem beautiful; that which is wicked seem righteous; that which is evil seem not evil; but behind "his face" is terrible destruction).

15 His scales are his pride, shut up together as with a close seal.

16 One is so near to another, that no air can come between them (the idea of all of this pertains to man being unable to oppose Satan, as he would other creatures).

17 They are joined one to another, they stick together, that they cannot be sundered.

18 By his neesings (sneezings) a light does shine, and his eyes are like the eyelids of the morning.

19 Out of his mouth go burning lamps, and sparks of fire leap out.

20 Out of his nostrils goes smoke, as out of a seething pot or caldron.

21 His breath kindles coals, and a flame goes out of his mouth.

22 In his neck remains strength, and sorrow is turned into joy before him.

23 The flakes of his flesh are joined together: they are firm in themselves; they cannot be moved.

24 His heart is a firm as a stone; yea, as hard as a piece of the nether millstone.

25 When he raised up himself, the mighty are afraid: by reason of breakings they purify themselves (Lucifer was probably the most powerful of all the angels ever created by God).

26 The sword of him who lays at him cannot hold: the spear, the dart, nor the habergeon *(no natural weapon will suffice against him).*

27 He esteems iron as straw, and brass as rotten wood.

28 The arrow cannot make him flee: slingstones are turned with him into stubble.

29 Darts are counted as stubble: he laughs at the shaking of a spear.

30 Sharp stones are under him: he spreads sharp pointed things upon the mire *(Satan cannot be opposed as other creatures).*

31 He makes the deep to boil like a pot: he makes the sea like a pot of ointment.

32 He makes a path to shine after him; one would think the deep to be hoary *(while the path shines, still, it is deception).*

33 Upon earth there is not his like, who is made without fear.

34 He beholds all high things: he is a king over all the children of pride. *(Pride is the crowning sin that besets the human race; it is the foundation sin of all sin; it is the "good side" of the "tree of the knowledge of good and evil." Behind every sin, one ultimately will find pride. It is that which God cannot abide. It is the sin that caused the downfall of Lucifer to begin with [Ezek. 28:17]. Pride is the sin that caused the Fall of Adam and Eve in the Garden of Eden [Gen. 3:5-7]. Pride is the sin that God hates more than any other sin, "a proud look" [Prov. 6:16-17].)*

CHAPTER 42
(1520 B.C.)
JOB'S REPLY

THEN Job answered the LORD, and said, 2 I know that You can do every thing, and that no thought can be withheld from You *(from the Lord's questions to Job, he knows that God is Omnipotent [all-powerful]; as well as Omniscient [all-knowing]).*

3 Who is he who hides counsel without knowledge? therefore have I uttered that I understood not; things too wonderful for me, which I knew not *(even though it seems that God did not directly accuse Job of such, still, after Job saw and heard the Lord, he realized how woeful that his knowledge of God actually was).*

4 Hear, I beseech You, and I will speak: I will demand of You, and declare You unto me *(many times in the last few months, Job had longed for this opportunity to speak to God; now the opportunity presents itself; what he will say*

after seeing the Lord will not be nearly what he thought he would say; he had spoken of how he would demand of God, but now he falls silent, and rightly so).

5 I have heard of You by the hearing of the ear: but now my eye sees You *(from this we must believe that God made a visible appearance to Job, and that he was able to see His bodily shape; as well, we must conclude that God is a literal Person with a Spirit Body).*

6 Wherefore I abhor myself, and repent in dust and ashes. *(In effect, Job had previously reported that he had not abhorred himself, but, on the contrary, thought well of himself and had held fast to his moral excellency. The discovery of the deep corruption of the heart is the most painful and humbling that a man can make.*

So the Patriarch had to crucify all his goodness as truly as all his badness, and sit in wood ashes as a public confession that he merited death because of his sin-defiled nature.

This moral principle governs the Salvation of the sinner as well as the Sanctification of the Saint.)

JOB PRAYS FOR HIS FRIENDS

7 And it was so, that after the LORD had spoken these words unto Job, the LORD said to Eliphaz the Temanite, My wrath is kindled against you, and against your two friends *(the Lord completely ignores Elihu):* for you have not spoken of Me the thing that is right, as My servant Job has. *(We will find that even though the Lord has spoken well of Job, still, everyone had to change except God! This is a crowning truth that all must understand and believe. It is not God Who needs to change; we do.)*

8 Therefore take unto you now seven bullocks and seven rams, and go to my servant Job, and offer up for yourselves a Burnt Offering; and My servant Job shall pray for you: for him will I accept: lest I deal with you after your folly, in that you have not spoken of Me the thing which is right, like My servant Job. *(The answer to Job's "three friends" was Calvary, as Calvary is the answer to all. The number "seven" speaks of the perfect offering of the Lord Jesus Christ at Calvary by the offering of Himself.)*

9 So Eliphaz the Temanite and Bildad the Shuhite and Zophar the Naamathite went, and did according as the LORD commanded them: the LORD also accepted Job *(the Lord*

accepted the intercession of Job on behalf of his "three friends"; Job is thus a Type of Christ, not merely in his sufferings, but also in his mediatorial character).

10 And the LORD turned the captivity of Job, when he prayed for his friends *(Job had to humble himself and pray for God to bless these three chieftains who had so despitefully used him and persecuted him, and the three princes themselves had to confess themselves worthy of death and seek forgiveness from God through the Precious Blood of Christ, as foreshadowed in Verse 8, and acceptance before God in the Person of Christ, as typified in Verse 9):* **also the LORD gave Job twice as much as he had before** *(added to all that had been Job's to the double; thus this Book sets off the action of God in leading His children into a higher Christian experience; the subject of this Book is not how God justifies a sinner so much as it is how God sanctifies a Saint; hence, none but a good man such as Job could have been chosen for the process or profited by it).*

11 Then came there unto him all his brethren, and all his sisters, and all they who had been of his acquaintance before, and did eat bread with him in his house: and they bemoaned him, and comforted him over all the evil that the LORD had brought upon him *(had allowed to be brought upon him):* **every man also gave him a piece of money, and every one an earring of gold** *(all of those who had previously spoken so harshly of him will change their minds now that God has appeared; public opinion is fickle and always according to appearances and circumstances; now they would attempt to atone for their judgmental attitudes by giving Job an offering).*

12 So the LORD blessed the latter end of Job more than his beginning: **for he had fourteen thousand sheep, and six thousand camels, and a thousand yoke of oxen, and a thousand she asses.** *(All goodness and beauty which men recognize in themselves and in others must be nailed in death to the Cross, and the only Man Who is to live must be the risen Man, Christ Jesus.*

True self-abhorrence comes not from self-examination, but in looking away from Self to Jesus, the Perfecter, as well as the Author of Faith. Job was very much satisfied with himself until he saw God. "Self" is very enticing to man, especially religious Self, and self-examination is an interesting occupation and, accordingly, it is found very difficult to learn the lesson to crucify it, and to find that victory is enjoyed only when Self is ignored and Christ adored — Williams.)

13 He had also seven sons and three daughters *(the Lord replaced what he had lost, and much, much more!).*

14 And he called the name of the first, Jemima; and the name of the second, Kezia; and the name of the third, Keren-happuch.

15 And in all the land were no women found so fair as the daughters of Job: and their father gave them inheritance among their brethren.

16 After this lived Job an hundred and forty years, and saw his sons, and his sons' sons, even four generations. *(It has been concluded from this statement, combined with that at the close of Verse 10, that Job was exactly seventy years of age when his calamities fell upon him. That being the case, Job would have lived to the age of 210.)*

17 So Job died, being old and full of days. *(In effect, the Book of Job reveals the death of self, the risen life, the school of God, the emptiness of the world, the ugliness of self-righteousness and, above all, the fullness of Christ.)*

THE BOOK OF
PSALMS

PSALM 1

THE GENESIS BOOK:
THE BLESSEDNESS OF CHRIST

BLESSED *(happy)* is the Man *(Christ Jesus, Who is our Representative Man [I Cor. 15:47])* Who walks *(orders His lifestyle)* not in the counsel of the ungodly *(but according to the Word of God)*, nor stands in the way of sinners *(doesn't trod the evil path of sin)*, nor sits in the seat of the scornful *(but rather evidences Faith in God. All 150 Psalms point to Christ, with the exception of the parts that point to the Evil One and his followers. As the Gospels proclaim the acts of Christ, the Psalms portray His Heart, in either His Atoning, Mediatorial, or Intercessory Work)*.

2 But His *(our Lord's)* delight is in the Law of the LORD *(God's Word [119:97-108])*; and in His Law does He meditate day and night *(this was the manner of Christ as our Representative Man in His Earthly sojourn; as our example, it is meant to be our practice as well)*.

3 And He shall be like a tree planted by the rivers of water *(symbol of the Holy Spirit [Jn. 7:37-39])*, that brings forth His fruit in His season *(Jn. 15:1-8)*; his leaf also shall not wither; and whatsoever He does shall prosper *("His Leaf" corresponds with the "Tree of Life"; everything that man does dies; everything Jesus does lives forever and is blessed)*.

THE MISERY OF THE UNRIGHTEOUS

4 The ungodly are not so *(speaks primarily of the Antichrist; however, it includes all who follow Satan)*: but are like the chaff which the wind drives away *(no matter how rich, famous, or powerful the ungodly might be, the Lord refers to them as "chaff")*.

5 Therefore the ungodly *(the Antichrist)* shall not stand in the judgment *(will not be able to pass muster, so to speak)*, nor sinners in the congregation of the righteous *(only those who follow the "Blessed Man," Who is Christ, are judged as righteous)*.

6 For the LORD knows the way of the righteous *(Christ and all who follow Him)*: but the way of the ungodly *(the Antichrist)* shall perish *(it's either Christ or the Antichrist!)*.

PSALM 2

A PSALM OF DAVID:
MESSIAH'S KINGSHIP AND KINGDOM

WHY do the heathen rage, and the people imagine a vain thing? *(This is the great gathering of the mighty armies of the Antichrist against Christ in Rev., Chpt. 17.)*

2 The kings of the Earth set themselves, and the rulers take counsel together, against the LORD, and against His Anointed *(the Lord Jesus Christ; this is the Battle of Armageddon)*, saying,

3 Let us break their bands asunder, and cast away their cords from us *(man has ever tried to disassociate himself from God; the first organized effort was the building of the Tower of Babel [Gen., Chpt. 11]; this last great organized effort will be the Antichrist, who will seek to overcome Christ once and for all; as the first failed, so will the last)*.

4 He who sits in the Heavens shall laugh *(man's great efforts against Christ only produce a "laugh" on the part of the Creator)*: the LORD shall have them in derision *(holds them in contempt)*.

5 Then shall He speak unto them in His wrath, and vex them in His sore displeasure *(this pertains to the Second Coming)*.

6 Yet have I set My king upon My Holy Hill of Zion *(which will take place immediately after the Second Coming; the "Blessed Man" of Psalm 1, and the "Crowned King" of Psalm 2 are the One and Same Divine Person, the Messiah, the Son of Man, the Son of God; in both Psalms, He stands in contrast to the first Adam as Man and King in the Earth and over the Earth)*.

7 I will declare the decree *(the Father gives the Son sovereign power over the Universe)*: the LORD has said unto Me, You are My Son *(the Lord Jesus Christ)*; this day have I begotten You. *(What day? The day this was decreed in Heaven, even before the foundation of the world. It speaks of the Plan of God to redeem humanity, by God becoming Man, and going to the Cross [I Pet. 1:18-20].)*

8 Ask of Me, and I shall give you the heathen for your inheritance *(speaks of two things: the defeat of the Antichrist at the Battle of Armageddon, and the evangelization of the world)*, and the uttermost parts of the Earth for Your possession *(Christ will rule the entirety of the world in the Kingdom Age, and not the Antichrist)*.

9 You shall break them with a rod of iron; You shall dash them in pieces like a potter's vessel *(meaning that the Kingdom Age will come in with great violence; it pertains to the Second Coming, when the Lord will smite the nations [Ezek., Chpts. 38-39; Dan. 2:34-35])*.

10 Be wise now therefore, O ye kings: be instructed, you judges of the Earth *(in other words, let this be a warning to you; don't side with the Antichrist)*.

11 Serve the LORD with fear, and rejoice with trembling *(the idea is, the Lord is going to win out)*.

12 Kiss the Son *(the Lord Jesus, meaning to embrace Him)*, lest He be angry, and you perish from the way, when His wrath is kindled but a little *(once again, it speaks of the coming Battle of Armageddon)*. Blessed are all they who put their trust in Him *(which holds for all people for all time)*.

PSALM 3

A PSALM OF DAVID:
A PRAYER OF CONFIDENCE IN THE LORD

LORD, how are they increased who trouble Me! many are they who rise up against Me. *(The Holy Spirit put these words into David's mouth the morning after his flight from Jerusalem because of Absalom's unnatural rebellion. David is seen here as a Type of the Messiah rejected by His Own people. Though surrounded by enemies, he slept in confidence upon the mountainside beneath Jehovah's sheltering wing, and in the assurance of faith declared that God would lift up his head and destroy his foes. So, even though many of these Psalms speak of David, they more so speak of our Greater David, the Lord Jesus Christ. In other words, David was a Type of Christ.)*

2 Many there be which say of My soul, There is no help for Him in God. Selah. *(As Israel said this of David, likewise, they said it of the Lord Jesus Christ [Mat. 27:43].)*

3 But You, O LORD, are a shield for me; my glory, and the lifter up of my head *(the latter phrase proclaims the fact that it is the Lord Who put David on the throne, and the Lord will keep him on the throne)*.

4 I cried unto the LORD with my voice, and He heard me out of His holy hill. Selah. *(David believed in prayer, and so should we!)*

5 I laid me down and slept; I awaked; for the LORD sustained me *(even though in the midst of a terrible problem, with Absalom trying to kill him, David knew that the Lord was in control)*.

6 I will not be afraid of ten thousands of people, who have set themselves against me round about *(the Lord, with one man who believes in Him, is a majority [Rom. 8:31])*.

7 Arise, O LORD; save me, O my God: for You have smitten all my enemies upon the cheek bone; You have broken the teeth of the ungodly *(a euphemism or allegory portraying the Lord discomfiting our enemies; the idea is, if we are truly right with God, the enemies of the Lord are also our enemies!)*.

8 Salvation belongs unto the LORD *(He Alone can save)*: Your blessing is upon Your people. Selah. *(The blessings surely aren't on God's enemies.)*

PSALM 4

A PSALM OF DAVID:
AN EVENING PRAYER OF TRUST IN GOD

HEAR me when I call, O God of my righteousness: You have enlarged me when I was in distress; have mercy upon me, and hear my prayer *(this Psalm was composed by David on the same occasion as Psalm 3, when Absalom rebelled; as David cried to the Lord, likewise, the Lord Jesus cried to God in the same manner when the Scribes and Pharisees, in the spirit of Absalom, came against Him)*.

2 O ye sons of men, how long will you turn my glory into shame? how long will you love vanity, and seek after leasing? Selah. *(Leasing means lying. The sins listed in this Verse are the reason that Absalom rebelled against his father; the Scribes and Pharisees rebelled against Christ; and all men rebel against God.)*

3 But know that the LORD has set apart him who is Godly for Himself: the LORD will hear when I call unto Him *(the Lord has set aside Christ as His very Own — made Him a special subject of Grace and providence; He will do the same for all who properly follow Christ)*.

4 Stand in awe, and sin not: commune with

your own heart upon your bed, and be still. **Selah.** *(This was perhaps addressed to David's faithful followers, advising them to check their wrath [II Sam. 16:9; 18:5-15]. As well, when reviled, Jesus did not revile again [I Pet. 2:23].)*

5 **Offer the sacrifices of righteousness, and put your trust in the LORD** *(in effect, Jesus is saying that He counsels the Pharisees to commune with their own hearts, to be silent in true conversion, and to offer righteous sacrifices and not vain oblations).*

6 **There be many who say, Who will show us any good? LORD, lift Thou up the light of Your Countenance upon us** *(men are always seeking for good while not actually knowing what their true good is; the true good is to have the light of God's Countenance shining on us).*

7 **You have put gladness in my heart, more than in the time that their corn and their wine increased** *(the greater Blessings are spiritual rather than material).*

8 **I will both lay me down in peace, and sleep: for You, LORD, only make me dwell in safety** *(even in the face of acute trouble, David did, and the Lord likewise, lay down in perfect peace, and went immediately to sleep, for He was the Prince and Perfecter of Faith [Lk. 21:37; Heb. 12:2]).*

PSALM 5

A PSALM OF DAVID:
A PRAYER FOR PROTECTION

GIVE **ear to my words, O LORD, consider my meditation.** *(As the Fourth Psalm was an evening Psalm, a prayer to the Lord concerning the coming night, the Fifth Psalm is a morning Psalm. David awakens to meditate upon God and pray. This pertains likewise to Christ [Isa. 50:4].)*

2 **Hearken unto the voice of my cry, my King, and my God: for unto You will I pray** *(we learn from these Psalms just how strong was David's prayer life, and likewise our Saviour's).*

3 **My voice shall You hear in the morning, O LORD; in the morning will I direct my prayer unto You, and will look up** *(he will "look up," simply because his help comes from above; we must never forget that).*

4 **For You are not a God Who has pleasure in wickedness: neither shall evil dwell with You** *(there was no wickedness or evil in the Messiah; there was terrible wickedness and evil in Israel).*

5 **The foolish shall not stand in Your sight: You hate all workers of iniquity** *(Israel played the fool and rejected the Messiah; consequently, they could not stand in God's sight; God cannot abide wickedness or evil, even in those He calls His "chosen").*

6 **You shall destroy them who speak leasing** *(lies)*: **the LORD will abhor the bloody and deceitful man** *(this has a double meaning; the first speaks of Ahithophel, who betrayed David; he was David's closest advisor; the second and foremost speaks of Judas, the Lord's Disciple, who betrayed Him).*

7 **But as for me, I will come into Your house in the multitude of Your mercy: and in Your fear will I worship toward Your Holy Temple** *(the "Temple" referred to here is speaking of the Heavenly Temple toward which David prayed and the Earthly Temple into which Jesus went [Jn. 2:16]; so, He came into this "house" in "mercy" and "fear" and cleansed the Temple of its traffickers).*

8 **Lead me, O LORD, in Your righteousness because of my enemies; make your way straight before my face** *(when Jesus cleansed the Temple, He did not fear His "enemies," because He was led by the Holy Spirit because of Righteousness).*

9 **For there is no faithfulness in their mouth** *(the Pharisees)*; **their inward part is very wickedness; their throat is an open sepulchre** *(the Sadducees)*; **they flatter with their tongue** *(the Herodians).*

10 **Destroy Thou them, O God; let them fall by their own counsels; cast them out in the multitude of their transgressions; for they have rebelled against You** *(in all cases, this prayer was answered; Ahithophel died of suicide, Absalom was killed in the battle to overthrow David; likewise, Judas died of suicide, and the whole of Israel was destroyed in A.D. 70).*

11 **But let all those who put their trust in You rejoice: let them ever shout for joy, because You defend them: let them also who love Your Name be joyful in You** *(this Passage speaks of the Resurrection of the Lord Jesus Christ, and also the Resurrection of David, who was resurrected from potential destruction; David placed his trust in Jehovah, and the Lord restored him to the throne).*

12 **For You, LORD, will bless the righteous; with favour will You compass him as with a shield.** *(The "shield" addressed here is the largest size, which covers the entire body. This shield here is the favor and Grace of Jehovah.*

The "Righteous" is the Lord Jesus. All who are in Him are likewise blessed.)

PSALM 6

A PSALM OF DAVID:
THE INTERCESSORY PRAYER OF CHRIST

O LORD, rebuke me not in Your anger, neither chasten me in Your hot displeasure. *(This is an example of the complete advocacy of Christ in Intercession. He, though Himself sinless, declares Himself in these Psalms to be the Advocate. And He expresses to God the abhorrence of sin, accompanied by the Repentance and sorrow which man ought to feel and express, but will not and cannot. Similarly, the faith, love, obedience, and worship which man fails to give, He perfectly renders.*

Thus, as the High Priest of His People, He, the True Advocate, charges Himself with the guilt of our sins, declares them to be His Own, confesses them, repents of them, declaring at the same time His Own sinlessness, and atones for them. Thus, those Psalms in which the speaker declares his sinfulness and his sinlessness become quite clear of comprehension when it is recognized Who the Speaker is — Williams.)

2 Have mercy upon me, O LORD; for I am weak: O LORD, heal me; for my bones are vexed. *(As David cried these words to the Lord, he was saying that which the Son of David cried for Israel, and as well for every Saint of God. In fact, these particular Psalms constitute the Intercession of Christ on our behalf. So, when you read these words, apply them to yourself, for they were given for you and me.)*

3 My soul is also sore vexed: but You, O LORD, how long? *(In essence, Jesus repeated these words later in His Ministry, when He said, "Now is My soul troubled" [Jn. 12:27].)*

4 Return, O LORD, deliver my soul: oh save me for Your mercies' sake *(it is only by and through the Mercy of God that we are saved or helped; for certain, we do not deserve such!).*

5 For in death there is no remembrance of You: in the grave who shall give You thanks? *(This means simply that after death there is no more opportunity to be saved.)*

6 I am weary with my groaning; all the night make I my bed to swim; I water my couch with my tears *(on this particular night, and no doubt on many other nights, Christ in secret wept bitterly over the guilty city, as that day He had wept aloud over it in public [Lk. 19:41]).*

7 My eye is consumed because of grief; it waxes old because of all my enemies *(David's enemies were myriad because David was a Type of Christ, Who as well would be surrounded by many enemies — the Pharisees, etc.).*

8 Depart from me, all you workers of iniquity; for the LORD has heard the voice of my weeping. *(For three and one half years of public ministry, the Lord importuned the leaders of Israel to return to God; however, they persisted in their iniquity and rebellion. Soon He would depart for Glory, and soon they would depart for eternal darkness [Jn. 7:34].)*

9 The LORD has heard my supplication; the LORD will receive my prayer *(the LORD always hears the prayers of the Messiah; He always heeds His Supplication).*

10 Let all my enemies be ashamed and sore vexed: let them return and be ashamed suddenly *(this prayer regarding Christ has not yet been answered; it will be answered in the not-too-distant future [Zech. 12:10]).*

PSALM 7

A PSALM OF DAVID:
A PETITION FOR PROTECTION

O LORD my God, in You do I put my trust: save me from all them who persecute me, and deliver me *(David more than likely wrote this Psalm [song] while Saul was attempting to kill him; however, in a greater way, this Psalm refers to the suffering of the Messiah in sympathy with the elect remnant of Israel under the persecution of the Antichrist.*

I think it would be obvious in all of these Psalms written by David that his personal experiences and moral character were much below the language of the Psalm. It is, therefore, prophetic of the Messiah):

2 Lest he tear my soul like a lion, rending it in pieces, while there is none to deliver *(all of this answers to these some twenty-one attempts of Saul to kill David [I Sam. 18:1-26:2]).*

3 O LORD my God, If I have done this; if there be iniquity in my hands *(David was accused by Saul of seeking the kingdom and the opportunity to kill the king; David denies these charges here before God, offering to lay down his life if such be true);*

4 If I have reward evil unto him who was at peace with me; (yea, I have delivered him who without cause is my enemy *[David denies that he has either injured a friend or requited evil to a foe]:)*

5 Let the enemy persecute my soul, and take it; yea, let him tread down my life upon

the Earth, and lay my honour in the dust. Selah.

6 Arise, O LORD, in Your anger, lift up Yourself because of the rage of my enemies: and awake for me to the judgment that You have commanded (*in other words, "Lord, I desperately need Your help"*).

7 So shall the congregation of the people compass You about: for their sakes therefore return Thou on high (*"Lord, come down and do something, and then return to Heaven"*).

8 The LORD shall judge the people: judge me, O LORD, according to my righteousness, and according to my integrity that is in me (*our Faith in Christ gives us His Righteousness and His Integrity*).

9 Oh let the wickedness of the wicked come to an end; but establish the just: for the righteous God tries the hearts and reins (*it is not so much the removal of the wicked, but the removal of their wickedness, that David desires*).

10 My defence is of God, which saves the upright in heart (*one can be "upright in heart" only by trust in Christ!*).

11 God judges the righteous, and God is angry with the wicked every day (*God's anger continues against the wicked as long as their wickedness continues [I Pet. 4:17]*).

12 If He turn not, He will whet His sword; He has bent His bow, and made it ready (*every new transgression sets a fresh edge to God's sword*).

13 He has also prepared for Him the instruments of death; He ordains His arrows against the persecutors (*what one sows, one will reap [Gal. 6:7]*).

14 Behold, he (*the persecutors*) travails with iniquity, and has conceived mischief, and brought forth falsehood (*in particular, it pictures Saul and, in general, the Antichrist*).

15 He made a pit, and digged it, and is fallen into the ditch which he made (*the fall of both Saul and the Antichrist*).

16 His mischief shall return upon his own head, and his violent dealing shall come down upon his own pate (*this was fulfilled in Saul when he died fighting the Philistines, and will be fulfilled in particular when the Antichrist is subdued by Christ at the Second Coming [Ezek., Chpts. 38-39]*).

17 I will praise the LORD according to His righteousness: and will sing praise to the Name of the LORD most high (*the phrase, "Most High," in the Hebrew, is "Elyon," which means "Possessor of Heaven and Earth; the dispenser of God's Blessings in the Earth"; it is one of the titles of the Messiah as "Most High" over all the Earth*).

PSALM 8

A PSALM OF DAVID:
THE SOVEREIGNTY OF THE SON OF MAN

O LORD, our Lord, how excellent is Your name in all the Earth! who has set Your glory above the Heavens (*this Psalm pictures the happiness that is to fill the Earth when, after the destruction of the Antichrist and his followers, the Messiah will establish His Kingdom of Righteousness and Peace, and His right to ascend the Throne*).

2 Out of the mouth of babes and sucklings have You ordained strength because of Your enemies, that You might still the enemy and the avenger (*the word "babes" is figurative and portrays the redeemed; the redeemed will praise Him because He has "stilled the enemy and the avenger" — namely Satan*).

3 When I consider Your Heavens, the work of Your fingers, the moon and the stars, which You have ordained (*the argument of Verses 3-8 is the amazing love of Christ in coming forth from the Highest Glory to redeem a being so insignificant as man*);

4 What is man, that You are mindful of him? and the son of man, that You visit him? (*God became man and went to Calvary in order to redeem fallen humanity. The price that was paid for that Redemption proclaims to us the worth of man, which in fact is God's highest creation.*)

5 For You have made him a little lower than the Angels, and have crowned him with glory and honor (*the Hebrew word "Elohim" here translated "angels" should have been translated "God," for that's what the word actually means; there is no place in the Old Testament where "Elohim" means "angels"; this means that man was originally created higher than the Angels, and through Christ will be restored to that lofty position [Rom. 8:14-17]*).

6 You made him to have dominion over the works of Your hands; You have put all things under His feet (*in their fullness, these words given here are only true of the God-Man, Jesus Christ [Mat. 28:18]; Christ has been exalted to a place higher than Angels or any other being except the Father; redeemed man is to be raised up to that exalted position with Him [Eph. 2:6-7]*):

7 All sheep and oxen, yea, and the beasts of the field;

8 The fowl of the air, and the fish of the sea, and whatsoever passes through the paths of the seas (*man was made to have dominion over*

all this).

9 O LORD, our Lord, how excellent is Your name in all the Earth! *(Christ is the Head of the Church, which is His Body; ultimately, that which is given by Promise will, upon the Resurrection of Life, be carried to its ultimate victorious conclusion.)*

PSALM 9

A PSALM OF DAVID:
PRAISE TO GOD, THE GREAT DELIVERER

I will praise You, O LORD, with my whole heart; I will show forth all Your marvelous works *(David praises the Lord for victory; however, the greater fulfillment is praise to the Lord for the victory of Christ over the Antichrist in the coming Battle of Armageddon).*

2 I will be glad and rejoice in You: I will sing praise to Your Name, O Thou Most High *(Possessor of Heaven and Earth).*

3 When my enemies are turned back, they shall fall and perish at Your presence *(once again, proclaims the defeat of the Antichrist).*

4 For You have maintained my right and my cause; You sat in the Throne judging right *(it is the Lord Who decided the victory!).*

5 You have rebuked the heathen, You have destroyed the wicked, You have put out their name for ever and ever *(once again, victory over the Antichrist).*

6 O thou enemy, destructions are come to a perpetual end: and you have destroyed cities; their memorial is perished with them *("you, the Antichrist, will destroy no more").*

7 But the LORD shall endure for ever: He has prepared His throne for judgment *(the beginning of the Kingdom Age, which will commence immediately after the defeat of the Antichrist).*

8 And He shall judge the world in righteousness, He shall minister judgment to the people in uprightness *(the government of the world will be upon His shoulder [Isa. 9:6]).*

9 The LORD also will be a refuge for the oppressed, a refuge in times of trouble *(the "oppressed" will no longer be oppressed).*

10 And they who know Your Name will put their trust in You: for You, LORD, have not forsaken them who seek You *(the Lord forsakes not His Saints; we are preserved forever [Ps. 38:28]).*

11 Sing praises to the LORD, which dwells in Zion: declare among the people His doings *(this is the Kingdom Age, when the Lord reigns supreme from Jerusalem).*

12 When He makes inquisition for blood, He remembers them: He forgets not the cry of the humble *(God will eventually avenge all the righteous and punish oppressors and criminals; this will take place at the beginning of the Kingdom Age).*

13 Have mercy upon me, O LORD; consider my trouble which I suffer of them who hate me, You Who lifts me up from the gates of death *(the Lord will deliver Israel from the Antichrist when they are at the very "gates of death"):*

14 That I may show forth all Your praise in the gates of the daughter of Zion: I will rejoice in Your salvation *(Israel will then accept Christ as Saviour and Lord [Zech. 13:1]).*

15 The heathen are sunk down in the pit that they made: in the net which they hid is their own foot taken *(the Antichrist will set a trap for the whole of Israel; however, he will be snared in his own "net").*

16 The LORD is known by the judgment which He executes: the wicked is snared in the work of his own hands. Higgaion. Selah. *(The last two words speak of meditation on what has been said.)*

17 The wicked shall be turned into Hell, and all the nations that forget God *(every nation that sides with the Antichrist will, in effect, have turned their back on God, and as well will be "turned into Hell").*

18 For the needy *(Israel)* shall not alway be forgotten: the expectation of the poor *(Israel)* shall not perish for ever *(in the midst of the Battle of Armageddon, the Lord will come to the rescue of Israel).*

19 Arise, O LORD; let not man *(the Antichrist)* prevail: let the heathen be judged in Your sight.

20 Put them in fear, O LORD: that the nations may know themselves to be but men. Selah. *(Despite the fact that the Antichrist and his followers will strut like gods, the truth is, they are but men; and up beside the Power of God, they are nothing!)*

PSALM 10

AN APPEAL TO PUNISH THE WICKED

WHY do You stand afar off, O LORD? why do You hide Yourself in times of trouble? *(This is referring to "Jacob's trouble," speaking of the Great Tribulation [Jer. 30:7].)*

2 The wicked *(the Antichrist)* in his pride does persecute the poor *(Israel)*: let them be taken in the devices that they have imagined *(they imagined to destroy Israel, but instead they will be destroyed)*.

3 For the wicked boasts of his heart's desire, and blesses the covetous, whom the LORD abhors *(Paul referred to the Antichrist as "the wicked" [II Thess. 2:8])*.

4 The wicked, through the pride of his countenance, will not seek after God: God is not in all his thoughts *(in the pride of the Antichrist, he will declare that there is no God, or that, if there is, He takes no interest in human affairs)*.

5 His ways are always grievous; Your judgments are far above out of his sight: as for all his enemies, he puffs at them *(the Antichrist will declare that the judgment of God cannot reach him)*.

6 He has said in his heart, I shall not be moved: for I shall never be in adversity *(the Antichrist will think himself unbeatable, unstoppable, and immovable)*.

7 His mouth is full of cursing and deceit and fraud: under his tongue is mischief and vanity *(all his faculties will be employed in his efforts to destroy Israel)*.

8 He sits in the lurking places of the villages: in the secret places does he murder the innocent: his eyes are privily set against the poor *(refers to his efforts to destroy the "holy people," Israel)*.

9 He lies in wait secretly as a lion in his den: he lies in wait to catch the poor: he does catch the poor, when he draws him into his net.

10 He crouches, and humbles himself, that the poor may fall by his strong ones *(all of this to destroy Israel; the Antichrist will think to do what Haman, Herod, and Hitler could not do!)*.

11 He has said in his heart, God has forgotten: He hides His face; He will never see it *(Daniel said, "And He shall speak great words against the Most High" [Dan. 7:25])*.

A PETITION FOR HELP

12 Arise, O LORD; O God, lift up Your hand: forget not the humble *(the "humble" refers to Israel in the Battle of Armageddon, when it seems as if she will suffer total loss)*.

13 Wherefore does the wicked contemn God? he has said in his heart, You will not require it *(the Antichrist will think himself above God)*.

14 You have seen it; for You behold mischief and spite, to requite it with Your hand: the poor commits himself unto You; You are the helper of the fatherless *(at long last "the poor" [Israel] will commit herself unto the Lord; this is the primary purpose of the Great Tribulation — to bring Israel to Christ)*.

15 Break Thou the arm of the wicked and the evil man: seek out his wickedness till You find none *("Lord, destroy the Antichrist"; and that's exactly what will happen)*.

16 The LORD is King for ever and ever *(not the Antichrist)*: the heathen are perished out of His land *(the Antichrist and his army will be destroyed in Israel, and taken out [Ezek., Chpts. 38-39])*.

17 LORD, You have heard the desire of the humble: You will prepare their heart, You will cause Your ear to hear *(at that time, the Battle of Armageddon, Israel will call upon the Lord, and He will hear)*.

18 To judge the fatherless and the oppressed, that the man of the Earth may no more oppress *(the apparition of the Messiah will so effectually destroy the Antichrist that he will be no more [Rev., Chpt. 19])*.

PSALM 11

A PSALM OF DAVID:
THE LORD IS OUR FAITHFUL DEFENDER

IN the LORD put I my trust: how say ye to my soul, Flee as a bird to your mountain? *(Even though there is no sure way of knowing, this Psalm was probably written when Saul was constantly threatening David with death. To the Lord Alone could David look.)*

2 For, lo, the wicked bend their bow, they make ready their arrow upon the string, that they may privily shoot at the upright in heart *(as this possibly represented Saul in his effort to destroy David, even more so it represents the Antichrist, who will make every effort to destroy Israel; it will be during the time of the Great Tribulation [Jer. 30:7])*.

3 If the foundations be destroyed, what can the righteous do? *(World law, whether the participants realize it or not, is based at least in part on the Bible; however, the Antichrist will do all within his power to abolish these foundations of law and replace them with lawlessness. Righteous men will then have no legal remedy.)*

4 The LORD is in His Holy Temple, the LORD's Throne is in Heaven: His eyes behold,

His eyelids try, the children of men (*even during the times when it seems as if the Lord is doing nothing, He sees all, both good and bad*).

5 The LORD tries the righteous: but the wicked and him who loves violence His soul hates (*the Faith of the righteous must be tested, and great Faith must be tested greatly*).

6 Upon the wicked He shall rain snares, fire and brimstone, and an horrible tempest: this shall be the portion of their cup (*true, in general, but particularly to the Antichrist*).

7 For the righteous LORD loves righteousness; His countenance does behold the upright (*"Righteousness" is simply that which is "right"; however, its standard is God's standard and not man's*).

PSALM 12

A PSALM OF DAVID:
THE RIGHTEOUS ARE DELIVERED

HELP, LORD; for the Godly man ceases; for the faithful fail from among the children of men. (*This Psalm as well was probably written during the time of persecution by Saul. Violence and falsehood are Satan's two greatest weapons against the servants of God. The violence of the false Messiah is the theme in the previous Chapter, with falsehood being the theme in this Chapter.*)

2 They speak vanity every one with his neighbour: with flattering lips and with a double heart do they speak (*whenever the Bible is displaced by human teaching, a logical result is that righteous men will be persecuted*).

3 The LORD shall cut off all flattering lips, and the tongue that speaks proud things (*all who do not believe the Word of God will ultimately be "cut off"*):

4 Who have said, With our tongue will we prevail; our lips are our own: who is lord over us? (*In the Great Tribulation when the Antichrist prevails, false teachers will abound. They will boast that they are their own masters controlled by no God of the Heavens. They will say that their lips are their own; that their teaching originates with themselves.*)

5 For the oppression of the poor (*Israel*), for the sighing of the needy (*Israel*), now will I arise, saith the LORD; I will set him in safety from him who puffs at him (*speaks of David, but more than all of the Lord's protection of Israel in the coming Great Tribulation*).

6 The words of the LORD are pure words:

as silver tried in a furnace of earth, purified seven times (*the Word of God is perfectly pure*).

7 You shall keep them, O LORD, You shall preserve them from this generation for ever (*the time of the Great Tribulation will be Israel's greatest trial; they will be preserved by the Second Coming, and thereby forever [Mat. 24:21]*).

8 The wicked walk on every side, when the vilest men are exalted (*pertains to Saul, but more than all to the Antichrist*).

PSALM 13

A PSALM OF DAVID:
A PRAYER OF DISTRESS AND FAITH

HOW long will You forget me, O LORD? for ever? how long will you hide Your face from me? (*Some think this Psalm was written by David during the time of Saul, with others believing that David wrote it after committing the sin concerning Bath-sheba and her husband Uriah.*

Even though David here cries for help, the far greater picture pertains to the coming sufferings of Israel during the "times of trouble" under the reign of the false messiah [Jer. 30:7]. However, the ultimate portrayal is the Greater Israel, the Lord Jesus Christ, interceding for Israel and as Israel.)

2 How long shall I take counsel in my soul, having sorrow in my heart daily? how long shall my enemy be exalted over me? (*Once again, this pertains to David and also to Israel during the coming Great Tribulation. As well, it must be understood that these Psalms are applicable to us as individuals!*)

3 Consider and hear me, O LORD my God: lighten my eyes, lest I sleep the sleep of death (*symbolized by David, this will be the prayer prayed by Israel when it looks like the Antichrist will completely destroy them; actually, you are reading the very words here which will precipitate the Second Coming*);

4 Lest my enemy say, I have prevailed against him; and those who trouble me rejoice when I am moved (*false apostles always rejoice when true Apostles suffer trouble*).

5 But I have trusted in Your mercy; my heart shall rejoice in Your Salvation (*perhaps these words were written immediately after the writing of the Fifty-first Psalm*).

6 I will sing unto the LORD, because He has dealt bountifully with me (*the word "bountifully" can be translated "compensated"; it thus

reaffirms what so often appears in the Scriptures, that the overcomer will be compensated both here and in the future state for all troubles and sufferings, and that he will learn that perfect wisdom and infinite love will permit and overrule every trial).

PSALM 14

A PSALM OF DAVID:
THE FOOLISHNESS OF MEN

THE fool has said in his heart, There is no God. They are corrupt, they have done abominable works, there is none who does good *(the "fool" is the Antichrist, along with all who will follow him; despite all of their promises to "do good," they will do no good at all, only great harm).*

2 The LORD looked down from Heaven upon the children of men, to see if there were any who did understand, and seek God. *(During the Great Tribulation, due to the fact that the Church has been raptured away, there will not be many on Earth living for God, at least according to the entirety of the population.*

The word "looked" means literally to bow Himself over to get a better and closer examination of men and their wicked ways.

Most of these Psalms have a threefold application: 1. They apply to the matter at hand, whatever it might be; 2. They apply to every Believer who reads them; and, 3. They have a prophetic meaning, with many of them pointing toward the coming Antichrist and Israel's coming problems.).

3 They are all gone aside, they are all together become filthy: there is none who does good, no, not one *(applies to the whole human race, with the only solution being Christ and what He did at the Cross).*

4 Have all the workers of iniquity no knowledge? who eat up My people as they eat bread, and call not upon the LORD *(even though "My people" has a general application, more particularly it speaks of Israel in the coming Great Tribulation).*

5 There were they in great fear: for God is in the generation of the righteous *(God's people cannot be attacked without provoking Him; we are in Him, and He in us; He will assuredly come to our relief).*

6 You have shamed the counsel of the poor, because the LORD is his refuge *(the "poor" pictures Israel and her coming troubles, with*

the statement presented that Israel will have no help from any other nation in the world, except the Lord).*

7 Oh that the salvation of Israel were come out of Zion! when the LORD brings back the captivity of His people, Jacob shall rejoice, and Israel shall be glad *(this speaks of the Second Coming, when Israel will then be redeemed [Zech., Chpt. 14]).*

PSALM 15

A PSALM OF DAVID:
WHO SHALL DWELL IN YOUR HOLY HILL?

LORD, who shall abide in Your tabernacle? who shall dwell in Your Holy Hill? *(The Messiah Alone satisfies the requirements of Verses 2 through 5.)*

2 He who walks uprightly, and works righteousness, and speaks the truth in His heart. *(Verses 2 through 5 pertain to the Perfect Man Who perfectly keeps and perfectly kept God's Perfect Law. He lives blamelessly and always did so live; He practices Righteousness and never practices ought. This is Christ, and Christ Alone!)*

3 He who backbites not with his tongue, nor does evil to his neighbour, nor takes up a reproach against his neighbour.

4 In whose eyes a vile person is contemned *(condemned)*; but He honours them who fear the LORD. He who swears to his own hurt, and changes not *(Christ swore to keep the Law; He did so, and suffered Crucifixion [119:106]).*

5 He who puts not out his money to usury, nor takes reward against the innocent. He who does these things shall never be moved. *(We were not purchased with such corruptible things as silver or gold, but by the Precious Blood of Christ [I Pet. 1:18-20].*

God's requirement for eternal life is perfection. No one except the Lord Jesus Christ has ever met that standard and no one ever will; nevertheless, the moment we accept Christ as our Saviour, He becomes our Substitute in all things. Then His perfection becomes our perfection, and we shall sit with Christ in Heavenly Places [Eph. 2:6].)

PSALM 16

A PSALM OF DAVID:
THE COMING DAVIDIC KING

PRESERVE me, O God: for in You do I put my trust *(all of the Verses of this Psalm*

refer to the Messiah, with the first four Verses referring also to David).

2 O my soul, You have said unto the LORD, You are my LORD; my goodness extends not to You (could be translated, "You are my Lord, I have no good beyond and apart from You; You are my highest and only good");

3 But to the Saints who are in the Earth, and to the excellent, in whom is all my delight (thus the Messiah appears as a Man in His relation to God and as a Brother in His relation to Israel and the Church).

4 Their sorrows shall be multiplied who hasten after another god: their drink offerings of blood will I not offer, nor take up their names into my lips (anything other than "Christ and Him Crucified" is "another god," i.e., "another Jesus" [II Cor. 11:4]).

5 The LORD is the portion of my inheritance and of my cup: You maintain my lot (this Verse expresses the Mission and characterizes the Ministry given to the Messiah and declared by Him to be pleasant and goodly — the Redemption of man).

6 The lines are fallen unto me in pleasant places; yea, I have a goodly heritage (the Messiah's heritage is the Redemption of man and the Restoration of the Earth to God, all made possible by the Cross [Eph. 1:10; Rev., Chpts. 21-22]).

7 I will bless the LORD, Who has given me counsel: my reins also instruct me in the night seasons (Christ, by dwelling in a human body, "learned obedience" [Heb. 5:8]; He did not have to learn to be obedient, for that would imply that He was a sinner by nature, but He "learned obedience," which is quite another thing).

8 I have set the LORD always before me: because He is at my right hand. I shall not be moved (pertains to the Mission of Redemption).

9 Therefore my heart is glad, and my glory rejoices: my flesh also shall rest in hope.

10 For You will not leave my soul in Hell (pertains to Paradise, and not the burning side of Hell as some teach; Jesus never went to that place); neither will You suffer Your Holy One to see corruption (Christ saw no corruption in the grave simply because He atoned for all sin; therefore, there was no doubt about Him being raised from the dead).

11 You will show me the path of life (the Resurrection): in Your Presence is fulness of joy (Christ would be elevated to the very Throne of God [Heb. 1:3]); at Your right hand there are pleasures for evermore (where He ever lives to make Intercession for the Saints [Heb. 7:26-27]).

PSALM 17

A PSALM OF DAVID:
A PRAYER FOR PROTECTION

HEAR the right, O LORD, attend unto my cry, give ear unto my prayer, that goes not out of feigned lips. (Even though uttered by David, it is a prayer more so of the Greater Son of David. If we lack understanding regarding His Incarnation, it will be difficult for us to understand His praying, as this Psalm proclaims. As He prays, He associates His people with Himself.)

2 Let my sentence come forth from Your presence: let Your eyes behold the things that are equal (could be translated, "Let sentence in my favor be pronounced by You, for Your eyes discern upright actions").

3 You have proved my heart; You have visited me in the night; You have tried me, and shall find nothing; I am purposed that my mouth shall not transgress (Satan found no imperfection in Christ, and God found nothing but perfection in Him).

4 Concerning the works of men, by the word of Your lips I have kept me from the paths of the destroyer.

5 Hold up my goings in Your paths, that my footsteps slip not (the "paths of the destroyer" and the "paths of Jehovah" are contrasted in Verses 4 through 5, and the statement is made that preservation from the one and perseverance in the other alone are secured by allegiance to the Scriptures).

6 I have called upon You, for You will hear me, O God: incline Your ear unto me, and hear my speech (this is concentrated intercessory prayer, which is almost unheard of presently!).

7 Show Your marvellous lovingkindness, O Thou Who saves by Your right hand them which put their trust in You from those who rise up against them (in Verses 7 through 14, the Son of David associates His People with Himself; we have the same enemies, and we have the same Deliverer).

8 Keep me as the apple of the eye, hide me under the shadow of Your wings (the "apple of the eye" is the pupil of the eye; it means that as God looks at His People, figuratively speaking, He can see only His People),

9 From the wicked who oppress me, from my deadly enemies, who compass me about.

10 They are inclosed in their own fat: with their mouth they speak proudly.

11 They have now compassed us in our steps: they have set their eyes bowing down to the earth.

12 Like as a lion that is greedy of his prey, and as it were a young lion lurking in secret places (*Satan comes as a "roaring lion, seeking whom he may devour" [I Pet. 5:8]; he is the enemy of Christ and the enemy of every Child of God*).

13 Arise, O LORD, disappoint him, cast him down: deliver my soul from the wicked, which is Your sword (*while this speaks of David, as well as every other Believer, it more pointedly speaks to the Antichrist; Israel must be delivered from him, and will be delivered*).

14 From men which are Your hand, O LORD, from men of the world, which have their portion in this life, and whose belly You fill with Your hid treasure: they are full of children, and leave the rest of their substance to their babes (*in Verse 13, the enemy is Satan, while in Verse 14, the enemy is men; they are those of the world who have no concern for Heavenly things, and they are full of children, meaning that scores seek to emulate them*).

15 As for me, I will behold Your face in righteousness: I shall be satisfied, when I awake, with Your likeness (*this statement expresses the highest joy of the spiritual nature; it is the one absorbing desire to see God's Face, and to be like Him*).

PSALM 18

A PSALM OF DAVID:
A HYMN OF THANKSGIVING

I will love You, O LORD, my strength. (*This is virtually the same Psalm recorded in II Sam., Chpt. 22. David spoke these words to the Lord on the day that the Lord delivered him from the hand of all his enemies from the hand of Saul.*)

2 The LORD is my rock, and my fortress, and my Deliverer: my God, my strength, in Whom I will trust; my Buckler, and the Horn of my Salvation, and my High Tower (*the Lord is all of this through the Cross; Christ is the Source, while the Cross is the means [I Cor. 1:17-18]*).

3 I will call upon the LORD, Who is worthy to be praised: so shall I be saved from my enemies.

4 The sorrows of death compassed me, and the floods of ungodly men made me afraid (*in these Verses, David thinks of Saul in his efforts to destroy him*).

5 The sorrows of Hell compass me about: the snares of death prevented me (*the idea is, Saul would have banned David to Hell if he could have done so; as well, those presently in the apostate Church would do the same to those in the True Church — if they had the power*).

6 In my distress I called upon the LORD, and cried unto my God: He heard my voice out of His temple, and my cry came before Him, even into His ears (*these Passages go far beyond David; even more so, they describe the mysterious sufferings of the Messiah at the Cross of Calvary*).

7 Then the Earth shook and trembled; the foundations also of the hills moved and were shaken, because He was wroth (*when Jesus died on Calvary, an earthquake rent the area of Jerusalem [Mat. 27:51]*).

8 There went up a smoke out of His nostrils, and fire out of His mouth devoured: coals were kindled by it (*this describes God's anger, not at His Son, but at the sin which had caused all of this*).

9 He bowed the Heavens also, and came down: and darkness was under His feet (*Matthew said, at the time of the Cross, there was "darkness over all the land" [Mat. 27:45]*).

10 And He rode upon a Cherub, and did fly: yea, He did fly upon the wings of the wind.

11 He made darkness His secret place; His pavilion round about Him were dark waters and thick clouds of the skies.

12 At the brightness that was before Him His thick clouds passed, hail stones and coals of fire.

13 The LORD also thundered in the Heavens, and the Highest gave His voice; hail stones and coals of fire.

14 Yea, He sent out His arrows, and scattered them; and He shot out lightnings, and discomfited them.

15 Then the channels of waters were seen, and the foundations of the world were discovered at Your rebuke, O LORD, at the blast of the breath of Your nostrils.

16 He sent from above, He took me, He drew me out of many waters.

17 He delivered me from my strong enemy, and from them which hated me: for they were too strong for me.

18 They prevented me in the day of my calamity: but the LORD was my stay.

19 He brought me forth also into a large place; He delivered me; because He delighted in me (*all of these previous Verses portray the*

actions of the Heavenly Father as it regards Christ and concerning the Cross of Calvary; these things, whatever they represent, took place in the spirit world).

20 The LORD rewarded me according to my righteousness; according to the cleanness of my hands has He recompensed me *(Satan had no claim on Jesus, because He had never sinned; therefore, death could not defeat Him and, in fact, He defeated both Satan and death, because He atoned for all sin [Col. 2:14-15]).*

21 For I have kept the ways of the LORD, and have not wickedly departed from my God *(Christ was the Perfect Sacrifice, and that He had to be in order to be accepted by the Father).*

22 For all His Judgments were before me, and I did not put away His Statutes from me *(the Lord abided by, and kept, every single Statute, Law, and Commandment, failing not even one time [Rom. 10:4]).*

23 I was also upright before Him, and I kept myself from my iniquity *(the words, "my iniquity," do not mean that Christ had a besetting sin, nor may they be understood here as intending the iniquity of the Elect whom He had made His own, but they point to a form of iniquity especially planned by Satan for Him, and to which He Alone could be tempted; the third temptation in the wilderness is an example [Lk. 4:9]).*

24 Therefore has the LORD recompensed me according to my righteousness, according to the cleanness of my hands in His eyesight *(Christ, as the Second Man, did what the first man, Adam, failed to do, which was to render a perfect obedience to God; likewise, such a perfect obedience, upon our Faith registered in Him and what He did at the Cross, becomes our perfect obedience).*

25 With the merciful You will show Yourself merciful; with an upright man You will show Yourself upright *(Mat. 5:7);*

26 With the pure You will show Yourself pure; and with the froward You will show Yourself froward *(the pure will be met with purity, and the froward will be met with adversity).*

27 For You will save the afflicted people; but will bring down high looks *(the Lord gives grace to the humble, but resists the proud [I Pet. 5:5]).*

28 For You will light my candle: the LORD my God will enlighten my darkness *(the true lamp which enlightens the darkness is the "light of God's Countenance").*

29 For by You I have run through a troop; and by my God have I leaped over a wall *(an euphemism for victory).*

30 As for God, His way is perfect: the Word of the LORD is tried: He is a buckler to all those who trust in Him *(God's Word is tried in the fire; it has stood all tests; it has never failed those who have pleaded its Promises and met its terms before its Author).*

31 For Who is God save the LORD? or Who is a Rock save our God? *(Absolute confidence may be placed in the Lord, Who is able to protect and preserve to the uttermost all who serve Him.)*

GOD'S BLESSINGS

32 It is God Who girds me with strength, and makes my way perfect *(perfection is found only in Christ; in the Sin-Offering, the sin of the sinner is given to Christ; in the Burnt-Offering, the Perfection of Christ is given to the sinner).*

33 He makes my feet like hinds' feet, and sets me upon my high places *(He gives me secure possessions).*

34 He teaches my hands to war, so that a bow of steel is broken by my arms *(the language is figurative; when the Herodians, the Pharisees, the Scribes, and the Sadducees warred against Him with their bows of steel, He bent their bows and broke them; He showed the folly of their hard questions and confounded them).*

35 You have also given me the shield of Your Salvation; and Your right hand has held me up, and Your gentleness has made me great *(the "right hand" speaks of power).*

36 You have enlarged my steps under me, that my feet did not slip *(pertains to David in the final alternative, but to Christ in totality; His Feet never slipped even one time!).*

37 I have pursued my enemies, and overtaken them: neither did I turn again till they were consumed *(every sin was atoned for at Calvary; none were left hanging).*

38 I have wounded them that they were not able to rise: they are fallen under my feet *(considering that Believers are the Body of Christ, this means that all enemies are under our feet, because, first of all, they were put under His Feet [Col 1:16-20]).*

39 For You have girded me with strength unto the battle: You have subdued under me those who rose up against me.

40 You have also given me the necks of my enemies; that I might destroy them who hate me *(and that He did at the Cross).*

41 They cried, but there was none to save them, even unto the LORD, but He answered them not *(this speaks of the Pharisees, who cried*

to the Lord against Christ, but a prayer, of course, which could not be answered; no matter how religious man may be, if he opposes Christ and the Cross, God will not answer his prayer).

42 Then did I beat them small as the dust before the wind: I did cast them out as the dirt in the streets.

43 You have delivered me from the strivings of the people; and You have made me the head of the heathen: a people whom I have not known shall serve me *(due to the Cross, the Gentile world has come to Christ; that obedience will be total in the coming Millennium).*

44 As soon as they hear of me, they shall obey me: the strangers shall submit themselves unto me *(to the Apostle Paul was given the responsibility of taking the Message of Redemption to the Gentile world; from that time, untold millions have accepted Christ).*

45 The strangers shall fade away, and be afraid out of their close places *(which will take place in the coming Millennium).*

46 The LORD lives; and blessed be my Rock; and let the God of my Salvation be exalted *(at long last, in the Millennial Reign, sin will be put down, Satan will be locked away, and the song of the world will be "The Lord liveth . . .").*

47 It is God Who avenges me, and subdues the people under me.

48 He delivers me from my enemies: yes, You did lift me up above those who rose up against me: you have delivered me from the violent man *(while David was delivered from Saul, Christ was delivered from all His enemies).*

49 Therefore will I give thanks unto You, O LORD, among the heathen, and sing praises unto Your name *(at this moment, untold millions in the Gentile world sing praises to the Lord).*

50 Great deliverance gives He to His king; and shows mercy to His anointed, to David, and to his seed for evermore *(this speaks not only of David and the great victory that God gave him, but it speaks even more so of "His Anointed," meaning the Son of David; also, this same victory is promised to all of us because of the "Son of David," for it says, "To His seed forever more").*

PSALM 19

A PSALM OF DAVID:
THE WONDERFUL CREATION AND
COVENANTS OF GOD

THE Heavens declare the Glory of God; and the firmament shows His handywork *(this*

Passage means that there is no excuse for man not to believe in God, for we are plainly told here that "the Heavens declare the Glory of God").

2 Day unto day utters speech, and night unto night shows knowledge.

3 There is no speech nor language, where their voice is not heard. *(This means that the material Earth is the sphere in which the Heavenly message operates, and the message itself is addressed to the inhabited "world." There is no limitation. All nations are embraced in this gracious revelation. Even though such knowledge does not bring one Salvation, it is the first step toward the acknowledgment of God, and all that pertains to God, which leaves man without excuse.)*

4 Their line *(teaching)* is gone out through all the Earth, and their words to the end of the world. In them has He set a tabernacle for the sun *(this means the Heavens and the constellations keep continually pouring forth teaching respecting the Glory of God, so that all nations are without excuse [Rom. 1:19-20]; modern science has discovered that the sun is enclosed in an envelope of fire, but this fact was shown in this Psalm about three thousand years ago),*

5 Which is as a bridegroom coming out of his chamber, and rejoices as a strong man to run a race *(pictures the sun).*

6 His going forth is from the end of the Heaven, and his circuit unto the ends of it: and there is nothing hid from the heat thereof *(many things are hidden from the light of the sun, but nothing from its "heat," which is the vital force whence the whole Earth receives life and energy, incidentally given here in the Bible first of all).*

7 The Law of the LORD is perfect, converting the soul: the Testimony of the LORD is sure, making wise the simple *(this tells us that the Bible is Perfect; in fact, the Bible is the only revealed Truth in the world, and in fact ever has been; it alone can "make wise the simple").*

8 The Statutes of the LORD are right, rejoicing the heart: the Commandment of the LORD is pure, enlightening the eyes *(they are "right," not merely because they are of the Lord, but because they, in fact, are right).*

9 The fear of the LORD is clean, enduring for ever: the judgments of the LORD are true and righteous altogether *(this is the instruction afforded by God for fearing Him).*

10 More to be desired are they than gold, yea, than much fine gold: sweeter also than honey and the honeycomb *(God's Word is a*

far greater good to man and, therefore, far more to be desired, than any amount of riches).

11 Moreover by them is Your servant warned: and in keeping of them there is great reward *(one might say that Jesus dwelt in the Scriptures as the sun dwells in the Heavens; they "warned" Him, they admonished and taught Him).*

12 Who can understand his errors? cleanse Thou me from secret faults *(the only way that one can understand his errors is by going to the Word of God; as well, the only thing that will probe deep into the heart of man, locating the "secret faults," is the Word of God).*

13 Keep back Your servant also from presumptuous sins; let them not have dominion over me: then shall I be upright, and I shall be innocent from the great transgression *(the "great transgression" spoken of in this Verse is that of declaring the Word of God insufficient for the problems at hand; this is what makes humanistic psychology so wrong, the embracing of such is a statement that says the Word of God is insufficient).*

14 Let the words of my mouth, and the meditation of my heart, be acceptable in Your sight, O LORD, my strength, and my redeemer *(our words can only be acceptable unto Him, along with the meditation of our heart, so long as they remain constant in the Word of God).*

PSALM 20

A PSALM OF DAVID:
A PSALM OF TRUST: PRAYER FOR VICTORY

THE LORD *(will)* hear you in the day of trouble; the Name of the God of Jacob *(will)* defend you *(in effect, the Holy Spirit prays through David here, stating that the LORD will hear the Messiah regarding His petition; "the Name of the God of Jacob" means the God Who met Jacob when he had nothing and deserved nothing [but wrath] and Who gave him everything; it is the equivalent of the New Testament "God of all Grace" [I Pet. 5:10]);*

2 Send You help from the sanctuary, and strengthen You out of Zion *(when on Earth, even though our Lord was not normally close to the Sanctuary, nevertheless, He received great help from what it represented, hence the cleansing of it two times);*

3 Remember all Your offerings, and accept Your Burnt Sacrifice, Selah. *(Our Lord is praying that the Sacrifice of His sinless Life and atoning death will be accepted.)*

4 Grant You according to Your Own heart, and fulfil all Your counsel *(most probably these were the words of the High Priest to the people after offering their Sacrifices; likewise, the Lord cried that His petition would be fulfilled).*

5 We will rejoice in Your Salvation, and in the Name of our God we will set up our banners: the LORD fulfil all Your petitions *(the idea is, if the great Sacrifice of Christ is accepted, and it definitely was, then the Salvation of all who put their trust in Christ will be accepted; therefore, we will rejoice).*

6 Now know I that the LORD saves His Anointed *(Christ)*; He will hear Him from His Holy Heaven with the saving strength of His right hand *(the words, "His Anointed," always speak of "His Messiah"; when He prays, God the Father always hears and always grants Him the "saving strength of His right hand").*

7 Some trust in chariots, and some in horses: but we will remember the Name of the LORD our God *(the Antichrist, by trusting in chariots and horses, will be defeated, but the Lord Jesus Christ, by trusting in the Name of the LORD God, will be victorious).*

8 They are brought down and fallen: but we are risen, and stand upright *(all who follow Satan will ultimately be brought down, but all who follow Christ will rise and stand upright).*

9 Save, LORD: let the king hear us when we call. *(Verses 1-6 refer to the Messiah's calling to God. Verses 7-9 refer to Israel in the Battle of Armageddon calling to the God of Glory and to the King, Who will be the Lord Jesus Christ. God will hear when they call. He will "save.")*

PSALM 21

A PSALM OF DAVID:
THANKS AND PRAISE FOR VICTORY

THE king shall joy in Your strength, O LORD; and in Your salvation how greatly shall He rejoice! *(This Psalm presents the exaltation and crowning of the Messiah as King over all the Earth, and His appointment as the Source and Channel of blessing to all nations.)*

2 You have given Him His heart's desire, and have not withheld the request of His lips. Selah. *(This was partially fulfilled in David, but is to be completely fulfilled in David's Son — the Messiah.)*

3 For You prevent *(anticipate)* Him with the blessings of goodness *(You give Him blessings before He asks, and more than He asks)*: You set

a crown of pure gold on His head *(no doubt, this happened to David when he became king of the whole of Israel; however, in a greater measure it refers to the Lord of Glory, Who will begin His Kingdom Reign as the rightful King that He is).*

4 He asked life of You, and You gave it Him, even length of days for ever and ever *(this pertains to the Resurrection of Christ, and it pertains to Believers enjoying the same thing through Christ — eternal life).*

5 His glory is great in Your salvation: honour and majesty have You laid upon Him *(the Lord Jesus Christ is given a Name that is above every name [Phil. 2:9]).*

6 For You have made Him most blessed for ever: You have made Him exceeding glad with Your countenance *(Jesus Christ will bless the entirety of the world during the Millennial Reign; in effect, He has done so already, at least for those who will believe [Jn. 3:16]).*

7 For the King trusts in the LORD, and through the mercy of the Most High He shall not be moved *(this King, the Lord Jesus Christ, will not be voted out of office, neither shall He grow old and die; "He shall not be moved").*

8 Your hand shall find out all Your enemies: Your right hand shall find out those who hate You *(during the coming Kingdom Age, it will be easily discernible as to who loves the Lord and who hates Him).*

9 You shall make them as a fiery oven in the time of Your anger: the LORD shall swallow them up in His wrath, and the fire shall devour them *(evil will not be tolerated in the coming Kingdom Age).*

10 Their fruit shall You destroy from the Earth, and their seed from among the children of men *(evil will not be allowed to gain a foothold).*

11 For they intended evil against You: they imagined a mischievous device, which they are not able to perform *(this Passage pertains to the Battle of Armageddon, when the Antichrist will literally declare war on Christ, and do so by attacking God's People, Israel; however, the Antichrist will not be able to perform that which he intends).*

12 Therefore shall You make them turn their back, when You shall make ready Your arrows upon Your strings against the face of them *(this is the Second Coming [Ezek., Chpts. 38-39]).*

13 Be Thou exalted. LORD, in Your own strength: so will we sing and praise Your power *(in the coming Kingdom Age, evil will not be exalted, Jesus Christ will).*

PSALM 22

A PSALM OF DAVID: CHRIST'S SUFFERING AND COMING GLORY

MY God, My God, why have You forsaken Me? why are You so far from helping Me, and from the words of My roaring? *(The stark reality of this Psalm portrays the Crucifixion of the Lord Jesus Christ. The Gospels narrate the fact of the Crucifixion, this Psalm the feelings of the Crucified.*

Jesus cried this Word while hanging on the Cross [Mat. 27:46]. This portrayal glorifies Him as the Sin-Offering.

It presents a sinless Man, the Lord Jesus Christ, forsaken by God, but only in the sense that God allowed Him to die. Such a fact is unique in history and will never need to be repeated. This sinless Man — Himself God manifest in the flesh — was made to be a Sin-Offering, in effect, the penalty of sin, which, in this case, was physical death [II Cor. 5:21], and thereby pierced with a sword of Divine Wrath [Zech. 13:7]. In that judgment, God dealt infinitely with sin and, in so dealing with it in the Person of His Beloved Son, showed His wrath against sin and His love for the sinner. Thus, He vindicated Himself and, as well, redeemed man. God revealed Himself at Calvary as in no other place or way.

What the depth of horror was to which the sinless soul of Jesus sank under the Wrath of God as the Sin-Offering is unfathomable for men or angels; therefore, our efforts to explain these sufferings will, of necessity, fall short of that which He really experienced.)

2 O My God, I cry in the daytime, but You hear not; and in the night season, and am not silent *(as a Sin-Offering and Perfect, still, God could not hear or answer prayer from such, at least at this particular time, but could only pour His judgment as He had done so through the centuries on the slain lamb).*

3 But You are Holy, O Thou Who inhabits the praises of Israel. *(This is the closest that the Scripture comes to the statement, "God inhabits the praises of His people." During Christ's Earthly Ministry, He spoke of God as His "Father," and resumed the title after He had triumphantly shouted, "Finished." But while suffering Divine Wrath as the Sin-Offering, He addressed Him as "God." Because God is so Holy, He could not even look upon this particular "Sin-Offering," much less hear and answer prayer,*

but only for the time when He was bearing the sin penalty on the Cross [Mk. 15:33-34].)

4 Our fathers trusted in You: they trusted, and You did deliver them. *(However, Christ could not be delivered from this terrible act. Had He been delivered, humanity could not be delivered.*

Had the Messiah been only Man, He would have put His physical sufferings first, and His spiritual sufferings last. But to Him, as the only begotten Son of God, there was no anguish so infinite as the hiding of the Father's face.)

5 They cried unto You, and were delivered: they trusted in You, and were not confounded *(this teaches God's people to cling in confidence to the Lord when circumstances seem to say that God has abandoned them; the infinite care of God for us is made possible by what Christ did for us at the Cross, and by no other means).*

6 But I am a worm, and no man; a reproach of men, and despised of the people *(the word "worm," as used here by Christ, means that He took the lowest place among men, to be rejected, scorned, spit upon, and even humiliated in infamy and shame [I Pet. 2:24; Isa. 49:7; 52:14; 53:1-12]).*

7 All they who see Me laugh Me to scorn: they shoot out the lip, they shake the head, saying *(this was done by His Own people while He hung on the Cross in bitter suffering; they had no kind word for Him; they only laughed and mocked Him [Mat. 27:39-43]),*

8 He trusted on the LORD that He would deliver Him: let Him deliver Him, seeing He delighted in Him *(at the Cross, the enemies of Christ, His Own people, actually used the very words as recorded in this Eighth Verse [Mat. 27:43]).*

9 But You are He Who took Me out of the womb: You did make Me hope when I was upon My mother's breasts *(these two Verses [9-10] show the relationship between the Father and the Son, even from the womb of the Virgin Mary; and yet, this relationship that had never before been broken would now be broken, at least for a short period of time, because He was bearing the sin penalty of the world).*

10 I was cast upon You from the womb: You are My God from My mother's belly *(in a certain sense, this is true of all; but, of the Holy Child, it was most true [Lk. 2:40, 49, 52]).*

11 Be not far from Me; for trouble is near; for there is none to help *("all the Disciples forsook Him and fled" [Mat. 26:56] — He was truly One Who "had no helper").*

12 Many bulls have compassed Me: strong bulls of Bashan have beset Me round *("bulls" here symbolize the demon-possessed religious leaders of Israel, who were determined to kill the Messiah [Mat. 27:1-66; Acts 2:36]).*

13 They gaped upon Me with their mouths, as a ravening and a roaring lion.

14 I am poured out like water, and all My bones are out of joint: My heart is like wax; it is melted in the midst of My bowels *(Crucifixion was one of the most, if not the most, horrible forms of death ever devised by evil men; coupling that with the spiritual torture, which was even far worse, we have suffering that is unimaginable).*

15 My strength is dried up like a potsherd; and My tongue cleaves to My jaws; and You have brought Me into the dust of death *(but yet, His death would be totally unlike any other death that had ever been experienced; it would be the death of a Perfect One, Who purposely laid down His Life as a Sacrifice).*

16 For dogs have compassed Me *(refers to the Gentiles, who carried out the Crucifixion):* the assembly of the wicked have inclosed Me *(refers to the Scribes, Priests, and the Pharisees, actually, the religious leaders of Israel):* they pierced My hands and My feet *(nailing Him to the Cross).*

17 I may tell all My bones: they look and stare upon Me *(Christ hung on the Cross in complete humiliation, in other words, totally naked).*

18 They part My garments among them, and cast lots upon My vesture *(uttered a thousand years before the fact, Mat. 27:35, Mk. 15:24, Lk. 23:34, and Jn. 19:24 all record its fulfillment).*

19 But be not Thou far from Me, O LORD: O My strength, haste Thee to help Me. *(Jesus was placed on the Cross at 9 a.m. [Mk. 15:25]. From 12 noon until 3 p.m., the latter being the time when Jesus Died and also the time of the evening sacrifice, darkness covered the land for that three-hour period — the period when Jesus was bearing the sin penalty of the world [Mat. 27:45]. During that three-hour period, the Lord would not answer the prayers of Christ, nor help Him in any way; however, at the moment He died, the sin penalty was paid [Mat. 27:51], and the Lord could, and in fact most definitely did, answer His prayers from that moment on [Jn. 19:30; Lk. 23:46].)*

20 Deliver My soul from the sword; My darling *(My soul)* from the power of the dog *(the Gentiles, and more particularly Pilate).*

21 Save Me from the lion's mouth *(religious*

leaders of Israel): **for You have heard Me from the horns of the unicorns** (wild bulls, again typifying the religious leaders of Israel).

22 I will declare Your name unto My brethren: in the midst of the congregation will I praise You. (Verses 1-21 present to us the sufferings of the Messiah, while Verses 22 through 31 present to us the Exaltation and Glory of the Messiah. We are to declare His Name all over the world, and praise Him for what He has done in redeeming man.)

23 You who fear the LORD, praise Him; all ye the seed of Jacob, glorify Him; and fear Him, all ye the seed of Israel (all Believers are to praise the Lord for what He has done; Jesus is the Source, and the Cross is the Means).

24 For He (God the Father) **has not despised nor abhorred the affliction** (suffering) **of the afflicted** (His Only Begotten Son); **neither has He hid His face from Him** (not permanently, actually for only about three hours); **but when He** (our Saviour) **cried unto Him** (God the Father), **He heard** (cried out of the death world, and the Lord heard Him, and raised Him from the dead).

25 My praise shall be of You in the great congregation (every Saint is to praise God for what Jesus has done for us at the Cross): **I will pay My vows** (devotions) **before them who fear Him.**

26 The meek shall eat and be satisfied: they shall praise the LORD who seek Him: your heart shall live for ever (the Cross afforded us eternal life).

27 All the ends of the world shall remember and turn unto the LORD: and all the kindreds of the nations shall worship before You (when Jesus died on the Cross, He died not only for Israel, but for the entirety of mankind).

28 For the kingdom is the LORD's: and He is the governor among the nations (this privilege is afforded Him because of Calvary).

29 All they that be fat upon Earth shall eat and worship: all they who go down to the dust shall bow before Him: and none can keep alive his own soul (life is Christ's gift; the soul cannot be kept spiritually alive except through Him, by His quickening Spirit [Jn. 6:53, 63]).

30 A seed shall serve Him; it shall be accounted to the LORD for a generation (what Jesus did at the Cross shall be told of the Lord to generation after generation).

31 They shall come, and shall declare His righteousness unto a people who shall be born, that He has done this (the words, "that He has done this," speak of the great price He paid for man's Redemption; it is done; "It is Finished" [Jn. 19:30]; this shall be told from generation to generation, and so has it been).

PSALM 23

A PSALM OF DAVID:
THE SHEPHERD PSALM

THE LORD is My shepherd; I shall not want. (Even though this beautiful Psalm applied to David, and to all Believers as well, more than all it applied to Christ.

Williams says, "Only one voice sang this Psalm in perfect tune. It was the voice of Jesus. When walking through the dark valley of His Earthly life, Jehovah was His Shepherd. There is no suggestion of sin in the Psalm. Its great theme is not so much what Jehovah gives, or does, as What or Who He is."

And yet, at the same time, as Christ presents Himself as the Sheep, He is also presented as the Great Shepherd of His People, for He was raised from the dead in order to be such [Heb. 13:20].)

2 He makes Me to lie down in green pastures (any other voice that is followed will lead only to barren pastures): **He leads Me beside the still waters.** (The 23rd Psalm makes it abundantly clear that the Church is not the Saviour, neither is religious hierarchy the Saviour, neither are rules and regulations the Saviour. Only the Lord is. We can follow Him, or we can follow other things; we cannot follow both.)

3 He restoreth My soul (when the sheep skin their forehead foraging for grass, the shepherd would pour oil over the wounds): **He leads Me in the paths of righteousness for His name's sake.** (At times the lamb will leave the appointed path, even doing so several times, being retrieved each time by the Shepherd. But if it leaves too many times, the Shepherd, upon retrieving it from the rocky crevices, will take His staff and break one of the legs. He then carefully "sets" the leg, and then lays the lamb on His Shoulder close to His Heart. He carries it until the wound is healed. That is a symbol of chastisement [Heb. 12:5-11]).

4 Yea, though I walk through the valley of the shadow of death, I will fear no evil (the powers of darkness, constituting powerful attacks by Satan): **for You are with Me; Your rod and Your staff they comfort Me.** (The ideal position for the "lamb" is to allow the Shepherd to fight for him. In fact, the only

fight we are told to fight is the "good fight of Faith" [I Tim. 6:12].

What a comfort it is to know that the "rod" and "staff" are constantly beating back the powers of darkness on our behalf.)

5 You prepare a table before Me in the presence of My enemies *(and these "enemies" cannot touch this "prepared table"):* You anoint My head with oil *(a Type of the Holy Spirit);* My cup runs over *(a figure of speech that refers to abundance).*

6 Surely goodness and mercy shall follow Me all the days of My life *("goodness" gives us green pastures and still waters; "mercy" retrieves us when we foolishly leave the "paths of righteousness"):* and I will dwell in the House of the LORD for ever *(as long as the Lord is our Shepherd, we can expect all of this, "all the days of our lives").*

PSALM 24

A PSALM OF DAVID: THE KING OF GLORY

THE Earth is the LORD's, and the fulness thereof; the world, and they who dwell therein *(God created the Earth, so it legally belongs to Him; sadly, it is now in rebellion against Him, being dominated more or less by Satan and evil spirit forces [II Cor. 4:4; Eph. 2:2; I Jn. 5:19]; however, with the Second Coming, all of this will be rectified).*

2 For He has founded it upon the seas, and established it upon the floods *(founded and established it above . . .).*

3 Who shall ascend into the hill of the LORD? or who shall stand in His Holy Place? *(Speaks of the time that Christ will enter Jerusalem and take His Place as the Ruler of the entirety of the world.)*

4 He Who has clean hands, and a pure heart; Who has not lifted up His soul unto vanity, nor sworn deceitfully *(only the Lord Jesus Christ could fit this description).*

5 He shall receive the blessing from the LORD, and righteousness from the God of His salvation *(in effect, God can only bless His Son, the Lord Jesus Christ; He blesses us when we are properly in Christ, and only when we are properly in Christ [Jn. 14:20; 15:5], which we can only be by and through the Cross [Gal., Chpt. 5).*

6 This is the generation of them who seek Him, who seek Your face, O Jacob. Selah. *(Jacob is used as an example, because by faith Jacob*

received everything good, when truly he only merited condemnation [Gen. 28:12-15; 48:16].)

7 Lift up your heads, O ye gates; and be ye lift up, ye everlasting doors; and the King of Glory shall come in *(this is Christ making His entrance into Jerusalem at the beginning of the Kingdom Age; as the previous Psalm proclaims, Israel must first accept Christ as the Shepherd, even as the Song of Solomon proclaims, before they can have Him as King).*

8 Who is this King of Glory? *(The Lord Jesus Christ, the only One with clean hands.)* The LORD strong and mighty, the LORD mighty in battle *(meaning that He fought the battle at Calvary as the Good Shepherd, and did so for all of mankind).*

9 Lift up your heads, O ye gates; even lift them up, ye everlasting doors; and the King of Glory shall come in *(the triumphant entry of Jesus into Jerusalem, which will take place immediately after the Second Coming [Zech., Chpt. 14]).*

10 Who is this King of Glory? The LORD of Hosts, He is the King of Glory. Selah. *(The answer is: "Jesus Jehovah.")*

PSALM 25

A PSALM OF DAVID: A PRAYER OF DISTRESS

UNTO Thee, O LORD, do I lift up My soul *(while this is a prayer of distress from David, and can be for us as well, more particularly, it is a prayer of distress from the Messiah serving as the Intercessor for His People [Heb. 7:26-27]).*

2 O My God, I trust in You: let Me not be ashamed, let not My enemies triumph over Me *(the theme of the entirety of the Book of Psalms is "trust in God").*

3 Yea, let none who wait on You be ashamed *(though the Lord, at times, tarries long, ultimately He will answer):* let them be ashamed which transgress without cause *(who will not wait on the Lord).*

4 Show Me Your ways, O LORD; teach Me Your paths *(few Christians seek the "Ways of the Lord"; most seek His Acts [Ex. 33:13]).*

5 Lead Me in Your truth, and teach Me: for You are the God of My salvation; on You do I wait all the day *(again, they who wait on the Lord will not be ashamed).*

6 Remember, O LORD, Your tender mercies and Your lovingkindnesses; for they

have been ever of old *(past mercies form a ground for the expectation of future blessings; God's Character cannot change; His action at one time will always be consistent with His action at another).*

7 Remember not the sins of My youth, nor My transgressions: according to Your mercy remember Thou Me for Your goodness' sake, O LORD *(an Earthly father does not remember youthful sins against his son; how much less will our Heavenly Father!).*

8 Good and upright is the LORD: therefore will He teach sinners in the way *(this Verse is a barrier to those who would insist upon teaching sinless perfection; truly the Child of God should hate sin and strive to follow wholly after the Lord; but, at the same time, the very nature of "the flesh" causes error; however, the Blood cleanses and Grace covers [I Jn. 1:7; 2:1-2]).*

9 The meek will He guide in judgment: and the meek will He teach His way *(the coin that will spend in God's economy is "meekness and humility").*

10 All the paths of the LORD are mercy and truth unto such as keep His Covenant and His Testimonies *(this can be done only as the Believer looks exclusively to Christ and the Cross; then, and then alone, will the Holy Spirit help, without Whom we cannot keep anything [I Cor. 1:17-18, 23; Rom. 8:1-2, 11]).*

11 For Your Name's sake, O LORD, pardon My iniquity; for it is great. *(Our Great High Priest, when confessing His People's iniquity as His Own, asks for pardon on two grounds: 1. The magnitude of the sin; and, 2. The Name and Character of God as a pardoning God. Man tries to belittle his sin and magnify his penitence; he pleads for pardon, because the one is so small and the other is so great. However, the Great High Priest, the Lord Jesus Christ, rightly estimates all sin as being great and urges its magnitude as grounds for pardon.)*

12 What man is he who fears the LORD? him shall He teach in the way that he shall choose *(the Lord shall make His Way plain to the God-fearing man).*

13 His soul shall dwell at ease; and his seed shall inherit the Earth *(Righteousness will ultimately prevail!).*

14 The secret of the LORD is with them who fear Him; and He will show them His Covenant *(the Word of the Lord will be opened to the Believer who truly fears the Lord).*

15 My eyes are ever toward the LORD; for He shall pluck My feet out of the net *(the Lord Alone can keep one out of the net, or pull one out of the net, which refers to sin's entanglement).*

16 Turn Thee unto Me, and have mercy upon Me; for I am desolate and afflicted *(the cause doesn't matter, as long as we truly turn to Him for help).*

17 The troubles of My heart are enlarged: O bring Thou Me out of My distresses *(once again, the Lord Alone can do this).*

18 Look upon My affliction and My pain; and forgive all My sins *(once again, we point to the Intercessory Work of Christ, which is carried out merely by His Presence before the Throne of God [Heb. 7:25]).*

19 Consider My enemies; for they are many; and they hate Me with cruel hatred *(the greatest hatred will come from the apostate Church).*

20 O keep My soul, and deliver Me; let Me not be ashamed; for I put My trust in You.

21 Let integrity and uprightness preserve Me; for I wait on You *(only our Saviour can claim "integrity and uprightness").*

22 Redeem Israel, O God, out of all his troubles. *(This prayer has not yet been answered, not because of the Intercessor, but because of Israel's rebellion. Ultimately, it will be answered in all its totality. Israel will be redeemed. The same can be said for every Child of God who puts his faith and trust in the Lord.)*

PSALM 26

A PSALM OF DAVID:
A PETITION FOR EXONERATION

JUDGE Me, O LORD; for I have walked in My integrity; I have trusted also in the LORD; therefore I shall not slide. *(This presents David pleading regarding his own petitions. But more than all, it presents the Son of David pleading for Israel and also for you and me. If one will read theses Psalms with not only David's petition in mind, but also the petition of the Greater Petitioner, our Intercessor, the Psalm will become much more understandable.*

In effect, our LORD is telling Jehovah to judge Him rather than us. The integrity of which He speaks is His Own and not ours.).

2 Examine Me, O LORD, and prove Me; try My reins and My heart *(every Child of God should urge the Holy Spirit to probe deep within the heart to "prove me" — to see that we are abiding in the Word of God and not in a man-made gospel).*

3 For Your lovingkindness is before My

eyes: and I have walked in Your truth. *(Only the Lord Jesus Christ could actually say such; only He has constantly "walked in Your truth."*

This Psalm is rich with instruction for the people of God in all Dispensations, but two facts full of consolation are especially prominent: 1. That help is sure to be given in response to such a Pleader and to such a plea; and, 2. That this Divine Priest is willing and able to live His blameless Life in whosoever will trust Him.)

4 I have not sat with vain persons, neither will I go in with dissemblers *(the only way a Believer can rise to such spiritual height is through Christ; He becomes our Substitute, and our identification with Him gives us His Perfection).*

5 I have hated the congregation of evildoers; and will not sit with the wicked *(those who are opposed to the true Gospel of Christ; with those our Lord will not participate).*

6 I will wash My hands in innocency: so will I compass Your altar, O LORD *(the only way that we can attain to the Righteousness of Christ is by fully trusting in the Cross and what Jesus did there, symbolized here by the "Altar"):*

7 That I may publish with the voice of thanksgiving, and tell of all Your wondrous works *(the Believer is to ever keep these wondrous works in mind, and to constantly thank the Lord for such; then those "wondrous works" will become a part of our lives).*

8 LORD, I have loved the habitation of Your house, and the place where Your honour dwells *(presently, this speaks of the Holy Spirit abiding in us personally [I Cor. 3:16]).*

9 Gather not my soul with sinners, nor my life with bloody men:

10 In whose hands is mischief, and their right hand is full of bribes. *(Unfortunately, David, in committing adultery with Bath-sheba, and then the cold-blooded murder of her husband, Uriah, and in his efforts to cover these terrible sins, became the very thing which he cried against. But God forgave him, as the Lord will forgive all who sincerely repent. In one way or the other, all of us with David fall into the same category.)*

11 But as for Me, I will walk in My integrity: redeem Me, and be merciful unto Me *(we can "walk in integrity" only in Christ; we do this by constantly expressing Faith in Him and the Cross, which then gives the Holy Spirit latitude to work within our lives [Rom. 8:1-2, 11]).*

12 My foot stands in an even place: in the congregations will I bless the LORD. *(As* the Intercessor, His Foot was planted upon the smooth, righteous pavement of the Divine audience chamber, and the Foot itself was as "even" as the pavement on which it stood, for, as prefigured in the Meat-Offering, there was an evenness in His Life among men that all their hatred, treachery, and snares failed to roughen. In Christ Alone, and through His Cross, can our "foot stand in an even place.")*

PSALM 27

A PSALM OF DAVID:
TRUST AND COMMITMENT TO GOD

THE LORD is My Light and My Salvation; whom shall I fear? the LORD is the Strength of My life; of whom shall I be afraid? *(This portrays Christ in the Garden of Gethsemane and on His Way to Calvary. As He looked through the darkness, seeing the lanterns and torches held by those who were coming to seize Him, His heart sang of the quiet confidence of an assured Faith.)*

2 When the wicked, even My enemies and My foes, came upon Me to eat up My flesh, they stumbled and fell *(this pertains to the scores who came to arrest Jesus in the Garden of Gethsemane; Jesus asked them, "Whom seek ye?" They answered, "Jesus of Nazareth." He then answered, "I am He," and, when He said that, the Scripture says, "They went backward and fell to the ground," thereby fulfilling this statement by David a thousand years earlier [Jn. 18:6]).*

3 Though an host should encamp against Me, My heart shall not fear: though war should rise against Me, in this will I be confident *(there is torment in fear, but Jesus had no torment at all, simply because there was no fear).*

4 One thing have I desired of the LORD, that will I seek after; that I may dwell in the House of the LORD all the days of My life, to behold the beauty of the LORD, and to enquire in His Temple *(the doctrine of this Psalm is that the Messiah is an all-sufficient High Priest for His People, and that He can, by His example, by His Ministry, and by His Spirit in us, carry us triumphantly through the sharpest trials and through death itself [Heb. 4:14]).*

5 For in the time of trouble He shall hide Me in His pavilion: in the secret of His tabernacle shall He hide Me; He shall set Me up upon a rock.

6 And now shall My head be lifted up above

My enemies round about Me: therefore will I offer in His Tabernacle Sacrifices of joy; I will sing, yea, I will sing praises unto the LORD. *(As David cried these words, little did he realize that He was saying what the Messiah would say. Verses 5-6 reveal the unshakable confidence of Christ in His Father, and His conviction as to Resurrection, and He consequently pledges Himself to sing loud praises in the Heavenly Temple. These were among the joys that the Father set before Him, because of which He endured the Cross, despising its shame [Heb. 12:2].)*

7 Hear, O LORD, when I cry with My voice: have mercy also upon Me, and answer Me. *(Verses 7-10 belong to the moment of His arrest and the abandonment of His Disciples.)*

8 When You said, Seek ye My face; My heart said unto You, Your Face, LORD, will I seek *(Christ looked to the Heavenly Father Alone, for none other could help; it is the same presently with all Believers!).*

9 Hide not Your face far from Me; put not Your servant away in anger: You have been My help; leave Me not, neither forsake Me, O God of My Salvation *(a petition of Christ to the Father, which was fully answered).*

10 When My father and My mother forsake Me, then the LORD will take Me up *(in fact, at the Crucifixion, all forsook Christ, all except the Lord!).*

11 Teach Me Your way, O LORD, and lead Me in a plain path, because of My enemies *(that "path" was Calvary; it is the same path presently, that which the Lord teaches [Lk. 9:23-24]).*

12 Deliver Me not over unto the will of My enemies: for false witnesses are risen up against Me, and such as breathe out cruelty *(this speaks of the trial of Christ, when the religious leaders of Israel sentenced Him to die).*

13 I had fainted, unless I had believed to see the goodness of the LORD in the land of the living *(He believed that though crucified, yet would He be raised from the dead, and, on the way to Pilate's judgment hall, He addressed the words of the next Verse to His own heart).*

14 Wait on the LORD: be of good courage, and He shall strengthen your heart: wait, I say, on the LORD. *(The word "courage" means "be encouraged." What a statement to make when on the way to Calvary! Due to the agony of the Garden and Satan's efforts to kill Him, He was strengthened in His heart by "waiting on the Lord." What a lesson for us!)*

PSALM 28

A PSALM OF DAVID:
A PRAYER FOR GOD'S HELP

UNTO You will I cry, O LORD My rock; be not silent to Me: lest, if You be silent to Me, I become like them who go down into the pit. *(This is a prayer of David, but more importantly, the prayer of the Son of David, and again as an Intercessor on our part. What comfort it is to feel the heartthrob of His Petition, as He becomes One with us!)*

2 Hear the voice of My supplications, when I cry unto You, when I lift up My hands toward Your holy oracle. *(In the Old Testament, the "Holy Oracle" was the "Most Holy Place," which contained the Ark of the Covenant, where God dwelt between the Mercy Seat and the Cherubim.*

Under the New Covenant, we are to petition the Father in Heaven in the Name of Jesus Christ [Jn. 16:23].)

3 Draw Me not away with the wicked, and with the workers of iniquity, which speak peace to their neighbours, but mischief is in their hearts. *(Verses 1-2 proclaim the great chasm that divides the Child of God from the wicked, which are described in Verses 3-5. The wicked actually love their sins, because "mischief is in their hearts.")*

4 Give them according to their deeds, and according to the wickedness of their endeavours: give them after the work of their hands; render to them their desert *(when one considers that this is the prayer of the Son of God, Who gave Himself for a wicked world, then one should realize the thoughts of God for those who will not repent).*

5 Because they regard not the works of the LORD, nor the operation of His hands, He shall destroy them, and not build them up *(most of the world falls into the category of Verses 3-5).*

6 Blessed be the LORD, because He has heard the voice of My supplications. *(Now, Christ acts as the Great High Priest in the perfection of the Faith, of which He is the Author and Finisher, by declaring that His Supplications have been heard. God always hears the Intercession of the Great Intercessor, the Lord Jesus Christ. In Verse 2, we have the petition that God will "hear the supplications." In Verse 6, we have the assurance that He has "heard the supplications" — and for all time.*

While Christ is now beside the Father making

Intercession for us [Heb. 1:3; 7:25], the Inter- cession that He has made, which stands for time and eternity, is found in these Psalms. In fact, no other Intercession is needed.

So, His very Presence at the Throne of God means that He and His Intercession have been accepted, which means it is a "Finished Work.")

7 The LORD is My strength and My shield; My heart trusted in Him, and I am helped: therefore My heart greatly rejoices; and with My song will I praise Him. *(Let it ever be said, "There is no other help.")*

8 The LORD is their strength and He is the saving strength of His Anointed. *(This Passage declares the Trinity. He Who anoints is God the Father, and He Who is anointed is God the Son; the oil with which He is anointed is symbolic of God the Holy Spirit.)*

9 Save Your people, and bless Your inherit- ance: feed them also, and lift them up for ever. *(Now that the Lord has heard this petition, and the sin of the Believer has been washed away because of the Intercession of Christ made pos- sible by the Cross [that which is given to us in Psalm 22], we are no longer in the "pit," but now we are as sheep in "green pastures" and beside the "still waters" with Him feeding us. He has promised to do so "forever.")*

PSALM 29

A PSALM OF DAVID:
THE VOICE OF GOD

GIVE unto the LORD, O ye mighty *(the mightiest Angels)*, give unto the LORD glory and strength. *(The Divine Psalmist calls upon the Angels to worship Jehovah. In this Psalm, the Messiah takes us to a higher level of praise, and rightly so, now that our sins have been forgiven, even as the last Psalm proclaims.)*

2 Give unto the LORD the glory due unto His Name; worship the LORD in the beauty of holiness. *(He can only be worshipped in the "beauty of holiness," which means "in Spirit and in Truth" [Jn. 4:24]. All Holiness is in Christ. We obtain such by having Faith in Him and what He has done for us at the Cross, and by that way alone [I Cor. 1:17-18].)*

3 The voice of the LORD is upon the wa- ters: the God of glory thunders: the LORD is upon many waters.

4 The voice of the LORD is powerful; the voice of the LORD is full of majesty.

5 The voice of the LORD breaks the cedars;

yea, the LORD breaks the cedars of Lebanon.

6 He makes them also to skip like a calf; Lebanon and Sirion like a young unicorn.

7 The voice of the LORD divides the flames of fire.

8 The voice of the LORD shakes the wil- derness; the LORD shakes the wilderness of Kadesh.

9 The voice of the LORD makes the hinds to calve, and discovers the forest: and in His Temple does every one speak of His glory. *(The actual Hebrew rendering is, "Does everyone say, 'Glory.'" If the voice of the Lord carries out all of these many things described by David, and more than all described by the Greater Son of David, surely we can give our little voice to Him in praise.)*

10 The LORD sits upon the flood *(Noah's flood)*; yea, the LORD sits King for ever. *(The doctrine of this Psalm is that Jehovah is mightier than the Angels of His might; that He is stron- ger than the forces of nature; that He is Al- mighty; and that all this limitless strength is at the disposition of His weakest child. The forces against us may be mighty, but He Who loves and cares for us is mightier than they.)*

11 The LORD will give strength unto His people; the LORD will bless His people with peace *(this means that the Lord gives His Own strength and peace to us).*

PSALM 30

A PSALM OF DAVID:
PRAISE FOR DELIVERANCE

I will extol You, O LORD; for You have lifted me up, and have not made my foes to re- joice over me. *(This is a prayer-praise song that was sung at the dedication of the House of David. As well, it will be sung at the dedication of the future Millennial Temple, and by the Messiah.)*

2 O LORD my God, I cried unto You, and You have healed me *(this pertains to Israel at the dawn of the Great Millennial Day, when, at long last, she will be healed).*

3 O LORD, You have brought up my soul from the grave: You have kept me alive, that I should not go down to the pit *(down through the many centuries, it has looked as if Israel would be totally destroyed, especially during World War II, when Hitler's killing machine slaughtered over six million Jews. The greater Hitler, the Antichrist, will go even further by taking Israel to the edge of extinction, but the*

Lord will actually bring their "soul from the grave," and against impossible odds will "keep them alive").

4 Sing unto the LORD, O ye saints of His, and give thanks at the remembrance of His Holiness *(this should be the song of every Child of God, but more pointedly it will be the song of redeemed Israel at the conclusion of the Battle of Armageddon, when they, at long last, return from their spiritual exile).*

5 For His anger endures but a moment; in His favour is life: weeping may endure for a night, but joy comes in the morning. *(Many Saints of God have gathered strength from this Passage, and rightly so. But more pointedly, this points to Israel's rebellion and God's Anger. Even though His Anger against Israel has lasted now for some 2,500 years, in the light of eternity, the Holy Spirit calls it but "a moment."*

Israel's "night" has now lasted for about 2,000 years. However, the "morning" is about to break over the horizon. This speaks of that Millennial morn, when Israel will, at long last, accept the Lord Jesus as her Messiah. And then this "morning" will last forever.)

6 And in my prosperity I said, I shall never be moved *(the prosperity continued as long as Israel's obedience continued; when her obedience faltered, the prosperity faltered).*

7 LORD, by Your favour You have made my mountain to stand strong: You did hide Your face, and I was troubled *(it is the Lord Who made Israel strong, actually like a mountain; but then Israel rebelled, and the Lord hid His Face).*

8 I cried to You, O LORD; and unto the LORD I made supplication *(one of the great purposes of the Great Tribulation is to bring Israel back to God; the Lord will then push her to the place to where she will "cry to the Lord" [Zech. 12:10]).*

9 What profit is there in my blood, when I go down to the pit? Shall the dust praise You? shall it declare Your truth? *(Israel's argument is that there is only profit to God in Israel's Salvation, not in her destruction.)*

10 Hear, O LORD, and have mercy upon me: LORD, be Thou my helper *(God will hear this cry, as He will hear the cry of anyone who petitions Him thusly; at long last, Israel's pride is broken; she no longer stands haughty; she cries for mercy, and pleads with the Lord that He once again be her "helper").*

11 You have turned for me my mourning into dancing: You have put off my sackcloth,

and girded me with gladness *(this speaks of the coming of the Lord, and His Deliverance of Israel in the Battle of Armageddon; Israel will then accept Christ as Saviour and Lord, and be "girded with gladness");*

12 To the end that my glory may sing praise to You, and not be silent O LORD my God, I will give thanks unto You for ever *(Israel is saying that never again will she discontinue singing praise to the Lord).*

PSALM 31

A PSALM OF DAVID:
PRAYER FOR VICTORY OVER ENEMIES

IN You, O LORD, do I put My trust; let Me never be ashamed: deliver Me in Your righteousness. *(The theme of this Psalm is trust in God. Its doctrine is that the Messiah was tested in all points, yet was without sin; that as Captain of His People's Salvation, He was perfected through suffering; He was a Man of Sorrows and acquainted with grief, and was hated, despised, and rejected of men [Isa., Chpt. 53].)*

2 Bow down Your ear to Me; deliver Me speedily: be Thou My strong Rock, for an house of defence to save Me *(in fact, in these first two Verses, our Lord prays to be rescued from the Scribes, Pharisees, and Herodians, who were seeking His life).*

3 For You are my Rock and My fortress; therefore for Your Name's sake lead Me, and guide Me *(considering the number of enemies who surrounded Him, if He were to fully obey the Father and carry out His mission, He would say, "Lead Me, and guide Me").*

4 Pull Me out of the net that they have laid privily for Me: for You are My strength *(the Pharisees, along with Scribes and Herodians, constantly attempted to entangle Him in His talk; He cried for deliverance).*

5 Into Your hand I commit My Spirit: You have redeemed Me, O LORD God of truth *(on the Cross, He uttered aloud the first sentence of this Verse).*

6 I have hated them who regard lying vanities: but I trust in the LORD *(the "lying vanities" spoken of here refer to idols that Israel had worshipped in centuries past, which caused her so many troubles and, as well, the "idols" of ritualistic religion of the present time).*

7 I will be glad and rejoice in Your mercy: for You have considered My trouble; You have known My soul in adversities *(if it were*

possible, Immanuel was more precious to God when in adversity, trouble, and danger than at any other time; man refuses generally to recognize a companion when in adversity, but God did not so act toward His Servant; He actually recognized both Him and His adversities);

8 And have not shut Me up into the hand of the enemy: You have set my feet in a large room *(the "large room" pertains to Calvary, where the greatest victory of all time was won, and afforded Christ a "Name that is above every name" [Phil. 2:9-11])*.

9 Have mercy upon Me, O LORD, for I am in trouble: My eye is consumed with grief, yea, My soul and My belly *(the "grief" that He experienced as He came unto His Own, and His Own received Him not, can only be measured imperfectly by mere mortals)*.

10 For My life is spent with grief, and My years with sighing: My strength fails because of My iniquity, and My bones are consumed *(this in no way means that He had sinned or failed; it means that He took our iniquity as His Own. What a statement!)*.

11 I was a reproach among all My enemies, but especially among My neighbours, and a fear to My acquaintance: they that did see Me without fled from Me *(He was a joke to His enemies and a derision to His neighbors; His relatives abandoned Him through fear of being put out of the Synagogue)*.

12 I am forgotten as a dead man out of mind: I am like a broken vessel *(Israel flatly refused to believe that He was the Messiah; He did not carry their credentials, neither did He fit their description)*.

13 For I have heard the slander of many: fear was on every side: while they took counsel together against Me, they devised to take away My life *("slander" is one of Satan's favorite tactics; actually the name "Satan" means "slanderer")*.

14 But I trusted in You, O LORD: I said, You are My God *(as David did not attempt to defend himself, the Son of David did not attempt to defend Himself either; the matter, as severe as it was, was placed in the Hands of the Lord. What an example for us to follow!)*.

15 My times are in Your hand: deliver Me from the hand of My enemies, and from them who persecute Me *(the Master's Faith was not broken; He kept believing that His times and His mission were not in man's hands, but in God's [Lk. 13:33])*.

16 Make Your face to shine upon Your servant: save Me for Your mercies' sake *(the Face of the LORD shining upon anyone, as it most definitely did upon our Saviour and God's Son, is a sure sign of great favor and great blessings)*.

17 Let Me not be ashamed, O LORD; for I have called upon You: let the wicked be ashamed, and let them be silent in the grave *(for sure, death would silence the lying lips of those who opposed the Son of God, even as it ultimately did — but after this, the judgment [Heb. 9:27])*.

18 Let the lying lips be put to silence; which speak grievous things proudly and contemptuously against the righteous *(it was religious pride that opposed Christ; it was religious pride that nailed Him to the Cross; religious pride showed Him nothing but contempt)*.

19 Oh how great is Your goodness, which You have laid up for them who fear You; which You have wrought for them who trust in You before the sons of men! *(To serve the Lord will bring untold blessings; to oppose Him will bring ultimate judgment.)*

20 You shall hide them in the secret of Your presence from the pride of man: You shall keep them secretly in a pavilion from the strife of tongues *("the secret place of the Most High" [91:1])*.

21 Blessed be the LORD: for He has showed me His marvellous kindness in a strong city *(when in Jerusalem, the Pharisees showed Christ no respect at all, but the Father showed Christ "His marvelous kindness")*.

22 For I said in My haste, I am cut off from before Your eyes: nevertheless You heard the voice of My supplications when I cried unto You *(the Son of Man knew that except for God it was impossible for Him to be delivered)*.

23 O love the LORD, all ye His saints: for the LORD preserves the faithful, and plentifully rewards the proud doer *(as the Lord preserves the faithful, He will, at the same time, judge the "proud doer")*.

24 Be of good courage, and He shall strengthen your heart, all ye who hope in the LORD *(in the very face of the enemy, the Lord will strengthen us)*.

PSALM 32

A PSALM OF DAVID:
THE BLESSEDNESS OF FORGIVENESS

BLESSED is he whose transgression is forgiven, whose sin is covered. *(This Psalm*

speaks of the terror of unconfessed sin, and then of the blessing of confessed sin. David probably wrote this Psalm immediately after the sin with Bath-sheba, and shortly before the coming of Nathan the Prophet.

Once again, the Reader will be taken into the heart of God, resulting in the Intercessory Work of Christ, our Great High Priest.

In this Psalm, the Lord will speak in His Own Name, as the Great High Priest of His People, on our behalf, as if He Himself were the guilty transgressor.

What a consolation it is to have a Priest Who thus makes Himself One with the repentant sinner, pleads and prays as the sinner ought to plead and pray but cannot, and uses the very words which will be acceptable to God. Such an High Priest becomes repentant man.)

2 Blessed is the man unto whom the LORD imputes not iniquity, and in whose spirit there is no guile *(although we are guilty, the Lord will not impute iniquity to us, providing our Faith is in Christ, Who has taken the guilt of penalty upon Himself, all at the Cross of Calvary).*

3 When I kept silence, my bones waxed old through my roaring all the day long *(no load is heavier to bear than unconfessed sin).*

4 For day and night Your hand was heavy upon me: my moisture is turned into the drought of summer. Selah. *(No night is so black as when the Hand of God is held over one's face to shut out the light because of unconfessed sin.)*

5 I acknowledged my sin unto You, and my iniquity have I not hid. I said, I will confess my transgressions unto the LORD; and You forgave the iniquity of my sin. Selah. *(Verse 5 proclaims the joy of sins forgiven versus the misery of the unconfessed sin of Verse 4.)*

6 For this shall every one who is Godly pray unto You in a time when You may be found: surely in the floods of great waters they shall not come near unto him *(the term "Godly" means one to whom God shows Mercy; it expresses the attitude of God toward the repentant sinner, rather than the moral worthiness of the repentant sinner toward God).*

7 You are my hiding place; You shall preserve me from trouble; You shall compass me about with songs of deliverance. Selah. *(Unconfessed sin stifles the song; forgiveness and Deliverance bring on the song.)*

8 I will instruct you and teach you in the way which you shall go: I will guide you with My eye *(with such instruction, teaching, and guidance, we cannot fail!).*

9 Be ye not as the horse, or as the mule, which have no understanding: whose mouth must be held in with bit and bridle, lest they come near unto You *(as these animals must be restrained, so must the willful Christian be constrained).*

10 Many sorrows shall be to the wicked: but he who trusts in the LORD, mercy shall compass him about *(there is precious little mercy with man, but with the Lord there is abundant Mercy).*

11 Be glad in the LORD, and rejoice, ye righteous: and shout for joy, all ye who are upright in heart *(the true Believer in this world is the only one who has anything to truly shout about!).*

PSALM 33

PROBABLY WRITTEN BY DAVID: PRAISE TO THE LORD

REJOICE in the LORD, O ye righteous: for praise is comely for the upright *(the word "rejoice" actually means "shout for joy"; consequently, "praise" should be in the heart of every Child of God constantly).*

2 Praise the LORD with harp: sing unto Him with the psaltery and an instrument of ten strings *(music is an undeniable part of the worship of God; it is at this time, and will be forever, even in Heaven [Rev. 5:8]).*

3 Sing unto Him a new song; play skillfully with a loud noise *(this "new song" is spoken of some seven times in the Old Testament and once in the New [Rev. 14:3]; it pertains to present Salvation and also to the coming Millennial Reign).*

4 For the Word of the LORD is right; and all His works are done in truth *(the Holy Spirit is telling us here that what the "Word of the Lord" says about God's Creation is correct).*

5 He loves righteousness and judgment: the Earth is full of the goodness of the LORD *(the "Righteousness" that God is speaking of here is the Righteousness of His Son, Jesus Christ, which is freely given to the believing sinner upon faith — Faith in Christ and the Cross [Eph. 2:8-9]).*

6 By the Word of the LORD were the Heavens made; and all the host of them by the breath of His mouth *(the "Word of the Lord" speaks of the Lord Jesus Christ [Jn. 1:1-5]; "of the LORD" speaks of Jehovah, with "the breath of His Mouth" speaking of the Holy Spirit; consequently, we have the Trinity outlined in this Passage).*

7 He gathers the waters of the sea together as an heap: He lays up the depth in storehouses *(in this Passage, we are told of tremendous forces that would, in fact, destroy the Earth, were they not held in check by the "Word of the Lord").*

8 Let all the Earth fear the LORD: let all the inhabitants of the world stand in awe of Him *(in fact, the Earth as a whole does not "fear the LORD"; precious few "stand in awe of Him"; nevertheless, the day is soon to come when this Scripture will be literally fulfilled).*

9 For He spoke, and it was done; He commanded, and it stood fast *(this is the way the Earth and the Universe were created [Heb. 11:3]).*

10 The LORD brings the counsel of the heathen to nought: He makes the devices of the people of none effect *(if the Lord didn't stop the "counsel" and "devices" of the heathen, the world would have been destroyed a long time ago).*

11 The counsel of the LORD stands for ever, the thoughts of His heart to all generations *(the latter phrase speaks of the Bible; because it is the Word of the Lord, it will stand forever).*

12 Blessed is the nation whose God is the LORD; and the people whom He has chosen for His Own inheritance *(it was once Israel, but now it is the Church — the True Church).*

13 The LORD looks from Heaven: He beholds all the sons of men *(He numbers the very hairs of our heads, and notes every sparrow's fall [Lk. 12:6-7]).*

14 From the place of His habitation He looks upon all the inhabitants of the Earth *(everything is under His control).*

15 He fashions their hearts alike; He considers all their works *(in other words, God did not fashion some hearts to be evil and some to be righteous; all are equal, and all have the power of choice; upon man's choice, God considers man's works).*

16 There is no king saved by the multitude of an host: a mighty man is not delivered by much strength *(irrespective as to who the man might be, the only sure protection is God).*

17 An horse is a vain thing for safety: neither shall he deliver any by his great strength.

18 Behold, the eye of the LORD is upon them who fear Him, upon them who hope in His mercy;

19 To deliver their soul from death, and to keep them alive in famine *(for sure protection, man must look to the Lord!).*

20 Our soul waits for the LORD: He is our help and our shield.

21 For our heart shall rejoice in Him, because we have trusted in His Holy Name.

22 Let Your mercy, O LORD, be upon us, according as we hope in You *(proper hope in the Lord will always bring mercy).*

PSALM 34

A PSALM OF DAVID:
THANKS FOR DELIVERANCE

I will bless the LORD at all times: His praise shall continually be in my mouth *(while these words are those of David, they are more so of the Greater Son of David; according to this Verse, we should praise the Lord continually).*

2 My soul shall make her boast in the LORD: the humble shall hear thereof, and be glad. *(The word "humble" is the key word that unlocks the mystery of this Psalm. That the Holy Spirit should give this to David immediately after his degrading conduct in Gath is incomprehensible to the self-righteous and to strangers of the Spiritual Life. Verse 18 will explain it when we arrive at that Passage.)*

3 O magnify the LORD with me, and let us exalt His name together *(the purpose of the schooling is to so humble the Saint that he will trust the Lord, praising and magnifying Jehovah).*

4 I sought the LORD, and He heard me, and delivered me from all my fears *(when the Believer is mortified, ashamed, broken, contrite in spirit, and amazed that such a wretch should find pardon and deliverance, then the soul is restored and fresh revelation is given respecting the Divine David, Who found deliverance, not by deceiving man, but in trusting God).*

5 They looked unto Him, and were lightened: and their faces were not ashamed *(such will always be the case).*

6 This poor man cried, and the LORD heard him, and saved him out of all his troubles. *(Here the Messiah portrays Himself as a "poor man," because all mankind falls into the same category. We cannot save ourselves. We cannot deliver ourselves. In fact, self cannot improve self, irrespective of the efforts made.*

To look at self clothes the face with misery; to look at man clothes it with distraction; to look at God makes it shine. So it was with Moses [II Cor., Chpt. 3].)

7 The Angel of the LORD encamps round about them who fear Him, and delivers them *(the Hebrew word for "encamp" is related to the name "Mahanaim," meaning "two camps"*

[Gen. 32:1-2]; one was Jacob's feeble camp; the other, the encompassing camp of God's mighty Angels [II Ki. 6:17]).

8 O taste and see that the LORD is good: blessed is the man who trusts in Him *(here the eternal invitation is given to all that if they will only "taste," then they will "see" that "the LORD is good"; regrettably, most will not "taste").*

9 O fear the LORD, ye His saints: for there is no want to them who fear Him *(this means that we understand that the Lord says what He means, and means what He says).*

10 The young lions do lack, and suffer hunger: but they who seek the LORD shall not want any good thing *(what a promise!).*

11 Come, ye children, hearken unto Me: I will teach you the fear of the LORD *(we are told that the "fear of the LORD" is the secret of receiving good things; now we are told that the Holy Spirit will "teach us how to fear the Lord").*

12 What man is he who desires life, and loves many days, that he may see good? *(The next two Verses tell us how.)*

13 Keep your tongue from evil, and your lips from speaking guile *(this can only be done as the Believer places his Faith exclusively in Christ and the Cross, which then gives him the help of the Holy Spirit, Who Alone can tame the tongue [I Cor. 1:18; James, Chpt. 3]).*

14 Depart from evil, and do good; seek peace, and pursue it.

15 The eyes of the LORD are upon the righteous, and His ears are open unto their cry *(His "eyes" are watching us, and His "ears" are listening to us; He is waiting for us to call on Him).*

16 The face of the LORD is against them who do evil, to cut off the remembrance of them from the Earth *(which will ultimately be done!).*

17 The righteous cry, and the LORD hears, and delivers them out of all their troubles *(take the problem to the Lord).*

18 The LORD is near unto them who are of a broken heart; and saves such as be of a contrite spirit *(man is naturally proud and, with pride being the foundational sin of all sin, man is not easily brought to the place of the "broken heart" and "contrite spirit"; the word "contrite" means "broken and crushed"; the Lord would bring David to this state despite his failure of faith).*

19 Many are the afflictions of the righteous: but the LORD delivers him out of them all *(the Lord doesn't promise us a trouble-free existence, but He does promise to deliver us).*

20 He keeps all his bones: not one of them is broken *(Satan may do some damage, but it will not be lethal!).*

21 Evil shall slay the wicked: and they who hate the righteous shall be desolate *(because the Lord is with the righteous).*

22 The LORD redeems the soul of His servants: and none of them who trust in Him shall be desolate *(the latter phrase actually says "shall be held guilty" or "shall be condemned"; those whom God has redeemed He justifies and saves from all condemnation [Rom. 8:1-2]).*

PSALM 35

A PSALM OF DAVID:
A PRAYER FOR DELIVERANCE

PLEAD My cause, O LORD, with them who strive with Me: fight against them who fight against Me. *(Even though written by David, more than all it presents Christ, the Lamb of God, surrounded by the wolves of Satan and his followers [Jn. 15:20-25]. This Psalm, which is more a Prophecy than a petition, relates to His rejection and Crucifixion. It reveals the love of God's Heart to man, and the hatred of man's heart to God.)*

2 Take hold of shield and buckler, and stand up for My help.

3 Draw out also the spear, and stop the way against them who persecute Me: say unto My soul, I am Your Salvation.

4 Let them be confounded and put to shame who seek after My soul: let them be turned back and brought to confusion who devise My hurt *(they who persecute Christ and His followers can ultimately expect the following Verses to apply to them).*

5 Let them be as chaff before the wind: and let the angel of the LORD chase them.

6 Let their way be dark and slippery: and let the angel of the LORD persecute them *(it would be improper for David or any other sinful man to present such petitions to God; but, in such Psalms, the Petitioner is the Sinless Man, Christ Jesus, and He fittingly calls for the Divine Judgment upon those who hate Him, for, in hating Him, they hate God and His People, and also goodness, righteousness, and truth).*

7 For without cause have they hid for Me their net in a pit, which without cause they have digged for My soul *(when people rebel against the Lord or against true followers of the Lord, it is always, and without exception, "without cause").*

8 Let destruction come upon him at unawares; and let his net that he has hid catch

himself: into that very destruction let him fall *(while it is not fitting for any Believer to pray accordingly, it is definitely fitting for Christ to cry for vengeance upon His tormentors, and it is most fitting for Him to do so in our interests, as well).*

9 And My soul shall be joyful in the LORD: it shall rejoice in His Salvation.

10 All My bones shall say, LORD, who is like unto You, which delivers the poor from him who is too strong for him, yea, the poor and the needy from him who spoils him? *(As in Verse 6 of Psalm 34, likewise, the Messiah, along with David and the Believer, are called "the poor"; and they who are arrayed against us are "too strong for us"; however, the Lord will help us, and we will praise His Name.)*

11 False witnesses did rise up; they laid to My charge things that I knew not *(as David was accused, Christ was also accused; the very name "Satan" means "slanderer"; it should be wisely considered that when Christians accuse other Christians, they are becoming tools of Satan).*

12 They rewarded Me evil for good to the spoiling of My soul *(as David had done nothing but good for his enemies and for Israel, likewise, the Son of David).*

13 But as for Me, when they were sick, My clothing was sackcloth: I humbled My soul with fasting; and My prayer returned into My own bosom *(who this was that David was speaking of is not known).*

14 I behaved Myself as though he had been My friend or brother: I bowed down heavily, as one who mourns for his mother *(likewise, the Lord Jesus Christ clothed Himself in "sackcloth" [the Incarnation] over Israel and the lost world; His "fasting" included the denial of all that He had previously known, in order that He might "humble Himself" for the souls of man).*

15 But in My adversity they rejoiced, and gathered themselves together: yea, the abjects gathered themselves together against Me, and I knew it not; they did tear Me, and ceased not *(Why? They do no less presently! All true followers of Christ can basically expect the same):*

16 With hypocritical mockers in feasts, they gnashed upon Me with their teeth *(when David needed help, these for whom he had cried to God on their behalf turned against him and rejoiced over his suffering; they did the same with Christ; as they hurled at David every accusation, even more so they hurled at Christ the venom of the pit).*

17 LORD, how long will You look on? rescue My soul from their destructions, My darling from the lions *(the "lions" refer to the demon powers of darkness, who registered themselves in the lives of the Pharisees and Sadducees, who would destroy Christ).*

18 I will give You thanks in the great congregation: I will praise You among much people *(David is saying that he will not allow such to stop his praises to God, and the Messiah claims the fact that His Victory is in His Praises to God — and so is our victory!).*

19 Let not them who are My enemies wrongfully rejoice over Me: neither let them wink with the eye who hate Me without a cause *(the horror is this: those who did this to Him were not the harlots or the thieves, but those who called themselves religious, and thereby righteous; however, they were self-righteous; this was the Church of Jesus' day; it also characterizes the modern Church).*

20 For they speak not peace: but they devise deceitful matters against them who are quiet in the land.

21 Yea, they opened their mouth wide against Me, and said Aha, aha, our eye has seen it *(our eye has seen his downfall, which probably spoke of David at the time of Absalom's rebellion; it would have been the same with Jesus and Judas).*

22 This You have seen, O LORD: keep not silence: O LORD, be not far from Me.

23 Stir up Yourself, and awake to My judgment, even unto My cause, My God and My LORD.

24 Judge Me, O LORD My God, according to Your righteousness; and let them not rejoice over Me.

25 Let them not say in their hearts, Ah, so would we have it: let them not say, We have swallowed Him up.

26 Let them be ashamed and brought to confusion together who rejoice at My hurt: let them be clothed with shame and dishonour who magnify themselves against Me. *(The entirety of this Petition, from Verse 17 through Verse 26, was answered regarding both David and the Messiah. It will be honored regarding every true Child of God, as well.)*

27 Let them shout for joy, and be glad, who favour My righteous cause: yes, let them say continually, Let the LORD be magnified, which has pleasure in the prosperity of His servant *(this Passage is powerful; it is saying that only those who favor His "righteous cause" will "shout for joy, and be glad").*

28 And My tongue shall speak of Your righteousness and of Your praise all the day long.

PSALM 36

A PSALM OF DAVID:
THE STEADFAST LOVE AND
FAITHFULNESS OF GOD

THE transgression of the wicked says within my heart, that there is no fear of God before his eyes (*the first thing that happens to the wicked is the loss of "the fear of God"*).

2 For he flatters himself in his own eyes, until his iniquity be found to be hateful (*dealing from a wicked heart, the transgressor makes himself believe that he is capable of carrying out any wickedness; however, his iniquity will not come out the way he thinks*).

3 The words of his mouth are iniquity and deceit: he has left off to be wise, and to do good (*all who do not follow the Lord and adhere to His Word fall into this category*).

4 He devises mischief upon his bed; he sets himself in a way that is not good; he abhors not evil (*this Fourth Verse, in simple and few words, proclaims to us the reason for the misery of the world*).

5 Your mercy, O LORD, is in the Heavens; and Your faithfulness reaches unto the clouds (*a man who is so described in Verses 1-4 would find no compassion on Earth, but the Grace that is born in the Heavens and written upon the clouds, as exhibited in these Passages, can pity and save such a sinner; to those who will come to Him, God is "faithful" to show "mercy"*).

6 Your Righteousness is like the great mountains; Your Judgments are a great deep: O LORD, You preserve man and beast. (*Man has no righteousness on his own and, in fact, cannot attain any by his own merit, work, or effort. But God has Righteousness that is so abundant, it stands like "great mountains."*

"Your Judgments" speak of God's Word. Irrespective of how much man may probe into the depths of the Bible, still, he cannot scale its heights or plumb its depths. In other words, its riches are inexhaustible.)

7 How excellent is Your lovingkindness, O God! therefore the children of men put their trust under the shadow of Your wings (*God is pictured by Satan as brutal, judgmental, harsh, and destructive; the Holy Spirit tells us rather that God is "lovingkindness"*).

8 They shall be abundantly satisfied with the fatness of Your house; and You shall make them drink of the river of Your pleasures (*anyone who follows Christ is "abundantly satisfied," which is the only true satisfaction there is*).

9 For with You is the fountain of life: in Your light shall we see light (*there is no "life" outside of God; all else is death; likewise, there is no true knowledge, wisdom, or understanding other than the illumination of His "light," which is found in His Word*).

10 O continue Your lovingkindness unto them who know You; and Your righteousness to the upright in heart (*which the Lord will most abundantly do, providing the Believer continues to look to Christ and the Cross [I Cor. 1:17]*).

11 Let not the foot of pride come against me, and let not the hand of the wicked remove me (*pride is the foundation sin of all sin, and the sin of which the Believer must be most aware; if pride overtakes the Believer, the hand of the wicked against the Believer can then cause great harm*).

12 There are the workers of iniquity fallen: they are cast down, and shall not be able to rise (*this refers to the place or state of pride in which the wicked fall and will not rise again; it was pride that caused Lucifer to fall [Ezek. 28:11-17]*).

PSALM 37

A PSALM OF DAVID:
THE RIGHTEOUS VINDICATED

FRET not yourself because of evildoers, neither be thou envious against the workers of iniquity. (*This Psalm anticipates the two principle difficulties which confuse and discourage beginners in the Christian life. That they should be hated by their fellowmen because they have become followers of Christ is unexpected and painful, and that evil doers should prosper is confounding. However, the Holy Spirit tells us regarding these things, "Don't fret yourself."*)

2 For they shall soon be cut down like the grass, and wither as the green herb (*in other words, the wicked may prosper for a time, but only for a time*).

3 Trust in the LORD, and do good; so shall you dwell in the land, and verily you shall be fed (*in other words, don't look to the wicked or at the wicked, but rather "the Lord," and in Him put your "trust"*).

4 Delight yourself also in the LORD: and He shall give you the desires of your heart (*what a Promise!*).

5 Commit your way unto the LORD; trust also in Him; and He shall bring it to pass.

6 And He shall bring forth your righteousness as the light, and your judgment as the noonday (these things will ultimately be rewarded).

7 Rest in the LORD, and wait patiently for Him: fret not yourself because of him who prospers in his way, because of the man who brings wicked devices to pass (in Verses 3-7, we have the four keys to a victorious life: "Trust," "Delight," "Commit," and "Rest").

8 Cease from anger, and forsake wrath: fret not yourself in any wise to do evil (never turn to that which is evil to remedy the situation, whatever the situation might be; continue to "trust, delight, commit, and rest").

9 For evildoers shall be cut off: but those who wait upon the LORD, they shall inherit the Earth (always, and without exception, the righteous will come out on top, because the righteous have prepared for eternity).

10 For yet a little while, and the wicked shall not be: yes, you shall diligently consider his place, and it shall not be (this speaks of the coming Kingdom Age).

11 But the meek shall inherit the Earth (again, the Kingdom Age); and shall delight themselves in the abundance of peace (Isa. 2:4).

THE GOOD AND THE WICKED CONTRASTED

12 The wicked plots against the just, and gnashes upon him with his teeth (Christ is the "Just").

13 The LORD shall laugh at him: for He sees that his day (the wicked) is coming (there will be a judgment [Rev. 20:11-15]).

14 The wicked have drawn out the sword, and have bent their bow, to cast down the poor and needy, and to slay such as be of upright conversation (the one who is poor and needy is Christ; as well, "conversation" means "lifestyle").

15 Their sword shall enter into their own heart, and their bows shall be broken (Israel also comes under the heading of the "poor and needy," with the "broken bow" referring to the Battle of Armageddon and the Second Coming).

16 A little that a righteous man has is better than the riches of many wicked (too often the righteous are deceived into seeking the same rewards that the wicked seek out; if money and riches are the goal in the Christian's life, he will pierce himself through with many sorrows

[I Tim. 6:10]; even though most Christians have only a "little" of this world's goods, still, this is better than the abundance of the wicked, because the Blessings of the Lord are upon the "little").

17 For the arms of the wicked shall be broken: but the LORD upholds the righteous.

18 The LORD knows the days of the upright: and their inheritance shall be for ever.

19 They shall not be ashamed in the evil time: and in the days of famine they shall be satisfied (we have His Promise; He keeps His Promises).

20 But the wicked shall perish, and the enemies of the LORD shall be as the fat of lambs: they shall consume; into smoke shall they consume away.

21 The wicked borrows, and pays not again: but the righteous shows mercy, and gives (the difference in the economy of the world and the economy of God).

22 For such as be blessed of Him shall inherit the Earth; and they who be cursed of Him shall be cut off (the pronouns "Him" refer to Christ).

23 The steps of a good man are ordered by the LORD: and he delights in his way (the "Good Man" is the Lord Jesus Christ).

24 Though he fall, he shall not be utterly cast down: for the LORD upholds him with His hand (this Passage tells us that what God is promising is not an uneventful life; there will be difficulties along the way; in fact, at times the Believer looks as though he will be defeated and "utterly cast down"; but we have the Promise of the Lord that He will pick us up and start us again on our way).

25 I have been young, and now am old; yet have I not seen the righteous forsaken, nor his seed begging bread. (What a Promise! God's Word is true. If our steps are "ordered by the Lord," we will never be forsaken, nor will we suffer want. Such will be until the Lord calls us home [Heb. 11:35-40].)

26 He is ever merciful, and lends; and his seed is blessed.

27 Depart from evil, and do good; and dwell for evermore.

28 For the LORD loves judgment, and forsakes not His Saints; they are preserved for ever: but the seed of the wicked shall be cut off (the word "Judgment," as rendered here, refers to the Bible; in other words, God loves His Word).

29 The righteous shall inherit the land, and dwell therein for ever (the coming Kingdom

Age, and then forever [Rev., Chpts. 21-22]).

30 The mouth of the righteous speaks wisdom, and his tongue talks of judgment *(talks of the Word of God).*

31 The law of his God is in his heart; none of his steps shall slide *(speaks of Christ, and all who truly follow Christ, which can only be done by taking up the Cross daily [Lk. 9:23-24]).*

32 The wicked watch the righteous, and seek to slay him *(refers to Christ!).*

33 The LORD will not leave him in his hand, nor condemn him when he is judged *(again, speaks of Christ).*

34 Wait on the LORD, and keep His way, and He shall exalt you to inherit the land: when the wicked are cut off, you shall see it. *(The lessons taught here are to wait "on" God, and to wait "for" God, when perplexed by the prosperity of evil doers and when oppressed by them.*

The Messiah Himself, in the days of His flesh, when in the midst of His foes, perfectly learned and lived the lessons of this Psalm.)

35 I have seen the wicked in great power, and spreading himself like a green bay tree *(thus did the Pharisees and Sadducees during the time of Christ).*

36 Yet he passed away, and, lo, he was not: yes, I sought him, but he could not be found *(prophesied a thousand years before it happened, Jerusalem, i.e., "the Pharisees and Sadducees" were totally destroyed in A.D. 70).*

37 Mark the perfect man, and behold the upright: for the end of that man is peace *(Christ is the "Perfect Man").*

38 But the transgressors shall be destroyed together: the end of the wicked shall be cut off.

39 But the salvation of the righteous is of the LORD: He is their strength in the time of trouble *(Verses 38-39 speak of the Battle of Armageddon, and the destruction of Israel's enemies).*

40 And the LORD shall help them, and deliver them: He shall deliver them from the wicked *(from the Antichrist),* and save them, because they trust in Him *(at that day they shall and will be saved [Zech. 13:1]).*

PSALM 38

A PSALM OF DAVID:
THE PRAYER OF A PENITENT HEART

O LORD, rebuke Me not in Your wrath: neither chasten Me in Your hot displeasure. *(Although picturing David as pleading to God in regard to his sin and asking for help,*

even in a greater measure it pictures the Messiah, by revealing the thoughts that filled His heart up to and while upon the Cross. It describes His sympathetic Intercession for His People, for whom He was suffering the Wrath of God because of their sin. As well, it records the hatred and ingratitude of those who ought to have loved Him.)*

2 For Your arrows stick fast in Me, and Your hand presses Me sore. *(Himself sinless, here He loads Himself with the Believer's sins, makes full confession of them, admits the justice of the Divine Wrath upon them, and utters no reproach against those members of His nation who sought to destroy Him.*

What a possession it is to have a Priest Who can perfectly fulfill the Divine requirements, and Who can furnish to His People in all Dispensations the fitting vehicle of language with which to approach God in confession and prayer!

As He takes upon Himself the sin of the world [II Cor. 5:21], He knows that the Wrath of God will be directed at Him instead of the ones who rightly deserved it — namely you and me.)

3 There is no soundness in My flesh because of Your anger; neither is there any rest in My bones because of My sin. *(It is difficult for the Believer to fully understand the total Intercession of Christ on our behalf, as He literally takes our sin unto Himself — "My sin." In order for the great price of Redemption to be paid and for man to go free, our sin must become "His sin." Consequently, the "rebuke," the "chastening," and the "anger" of God must be directed at Him — the Redeemer.)*

4 For My iniquities are gone over My head: as an heavy burden they are too heavy for Me *(they were "heavy" because He bore the sin of the entirety of the world).*

5 My wounds stink and are corrupt because of My foolishness *(sin is truly foolishness; every sin is committed by a fool; foolishness it is, and yet God gave Heaven's best to redeem man from this "foolishness").*

6 I am troubled; I am bowed down greatly; I go mourning all the day long *(while on the Cross!).*

7 For My loins are filled with a loathsome disease: and there is no soundness in My flesh *(the words, "a loathsome disease," should have been translated "a burning fever," for, in the Hebrew, the word "loathsome" means "burning"; as He hung on the Cross, a burning fever wracked His Body, even as this Perfect Body was being offered as the Perfect Sacrifice)*

8 I am feeble and sore broken: I have roared by reason of the disquietness of My heart.

9 LORD, all My desire is before You; and My groaning is not hid from You *(while He was on the Cross!).*

10 My heart pants, My strength fails Me: as for the light of My eyes, it also is gone from Me *(the "light" of His Eyes was His Heavenly Father; the Lord pulled the blinds on this horrible scene, and refused to look at His Only Son, because He was bearing the sin of the whole world).*

11 My lovers and My friends stand aloof from My sore; and My kinsmen stand afar off *(at the Crucifixion, all forsook Him).*

12 They also who seek after My life lay snares for Me: and they who seek My hurt speak mischievous things, and imagine deceits all the day long *(this pertains to the Pharisees and the Sadducees, plus virtually the entire religious hierarchy of Israel).*

13 But I, as a deaf man, heard not; and I was as a dumb man who opens not his mouth *(our Lord conducted Himself as though He did not hear their taunts; likewise, He did not open His Mouth in His Own defense).*

14 Thus I was as a man who hears not, and in whose mouth are no reproofs.

15 For in You, O LORD, do I hope: You will hear, O LORD My God *(He would let the LORD God fight His battles).*

16 For I said, Hear Me, lest otherwise they should rejoice over Me: when My foot slips *(when He was put on the Cross),* they magnify themselves against Me.

17 For I am ready to halt *(to be offered),* and My sorrow is continually before Me.

18 For I will declare My iniquity; I will be sorry for My sin. *(These were the words of David. Possibly he was speaking of the terrible sin with Bath-sheba.*

But yet, it portrays Christ, as well, in His great Intercessory Work. He literally took our sin as His Own "sin.")

19 But My enemies are lively, and they are strong: and they who hate Me wrongfully are multiplied *(this Verse proclaims the terrible opposition by Satan leveled against Christ because of His redeeming the whole of mankind).*

20 They also who render evil for good are My adversaries; because I follow the thing that good is *(anyone who opposes Christ or those who truly follow Christ oppose the good).*

21 Forsake Me not, O LORD: O My God, be not far from Me.

22 Make haste to help Me, O LORD My

Salvation *(and thus the Father did, in raising Christ from the dead!).*

PSALM 39

A PSALM OF DAVID:
HUMAN FRAILTY

I said, I will take heed to My ways, that I sin not with My tongue: I will keep My mouth with a bridle, while the wicked is before Me *(there was only one Man Who could bridle His Tongue and Who did not sin with His Lips; He was the sinless Son of Man).*

2 I was dumb with silence, I held My peace, even from good; and My sorrow was stirred. *(It must have been a great temptation to pronounce a curse upon the Pharisees, Sadducees, and Scribes, who so bitterly opposed Him. But, He did not do so. He literally put a "bridle on His Mouth."*

His enemies would think that His silence bespoke a lack of intelligence; however, His "silence" was the Mercy and Grace of God. Had He spoken Judgment, they would have been instantly destroyed.)

3 My heart was hot within Me, while I was musing the fire burned: then spoke I with My tongue, *(It is difficult for the Bible student to imagine the humanity of the Son of God. There was temptation to step outside of the Will of God in respect to His enemies. The anger of righteous indignation burned within His heart; however, to have done so would have been disastrous.)*

4 LORD, make Me to know My end, and the measure of My days, what it is; that I may know how frail I am *(in this we see the totality of the Incarnation [God becoming Man]; as God, He was unlimited; as Man, He was very much limited, i.e., "frail" [II Cor. 13:14]).*

5 Behold, You have made My days as an handbreadth; and My age is as nothing before You: verily every man at his best state is altogether vanity. Selah. *(What a rebuke to the greedy, demanding, preening pride of arrogant man!)*

6 Surely every man walks in a vain show: surely they are disquieted in vain: he heaps up riches, and knows not who shall gather them *(outside of Christ, "every man" walks in vanity).*

7 And now, LORD, what wait I for? My hope is in You *(in other words, "What is My purpose in life?" The question is asked, and the answer is given, "My hope is in You").*

8 Deliver Me from all My transgressions:

make Me not the reproach of the foolish. *(In other Psalms, it says that the wicked spoke "mischievous things" against Him. And yet He, in the wonders of His Grace, took upon Himself the very sin which they committed in thus falsely accusing Him, and confessed it as His Own!*

Although He could have confounded them with a fitting "good" reply [Vs. 2], yet He remained dumb before them [Vs. 1]. His heart was stirred with sorrow for them [Vs. 2], while, at the same time, it felt the biting flame of their cruel words [Vs. 3]. But though dumb before men, He was eloquent before God.)

9 **I was dumb, I opened not My mouth; because You did it** *(it was the Will of God for Him not to answer His accusers).*

10 **Remove Your stroke away from Me: I am consumed by the blow of Your hand.** *(The knowledge He had, which was given to Him by the Father, did not make Him insensible or stoical. If so, He would not have been human, and He was fully human. Accordingly, He cried for relief from the pressure of that afflicting hand, while recognizing its justice and citing His Own preciousness to God. He prayed for strength to pursue this path of affliction until the day dawned when He would go back to the Glory from whence He came, and then would be no more afflicted.)*

11 **When You with rebukes do correct man for iniquity, You make his beauty to consume away like a moth: surely every man is vanity. Selah.** *(If He were to be truly Man, He would have to take the "rebukes" that justice demanded. Under these "rebukes," there would be "no beauty that we should desire Him" [Isa. 53:2].)*

12 **Hear My prayer, O LORD, and give ear unto My cry; hold not Your peace at My tears: for I am a stranger with You, and a sojourner, as all My fathers were** *(these same words that we often cry to the Father have already been laid at His Feet by His Only Son, Who stands in our place).*

13 **O spare Me, that I may recover strength, before I go hence, and be no more** *(as David pleaded for "strength," likewise, the Son of David pleads to the Father for strength for Himself, which, in reality, is for us; without that "strength," we could not make it).*

PSALM 40

A PSALM OF DAVID:
PRAISE FOR ANSWERED PRAYER

I waited patiently for the LORD; and He inclined unto Me, and heard My cry. *(The word*

"patiently" directs our attention to the thought that God, at times, does not answer immediately; however, the latter portion of this Verse encourages us that ultimately He will answer and "hear my cry."

The theme is threefold: 1. As the Redeemer: As our Redeemer, He atones for our sins, having loaded them upon Himself and having confessed them as His Own; 2. As our High Priest: He burdens Himself with our sorrows, encourages us to follow Him in His life of absolute confidence in God, teaching us to believe in Promises which never fail, and furnishes us with perfect forms of confession, prayer, and praise; and, 3. As our Commander: As such, He engages to deliver us from the powers of darkness, which, in fact, He has already done at the Cross [Col. 2:14-15].)

2 **He brought Me up also out of an horrible pit, out of the miry clay, and set My feet upon a rock, and established My goings** *(the words here are figurative of the state of sin and death out of which God Alone can save; He does so by the means of the Cross; trying to extricate ourselves by our own means, we only seek deeper into the "miry clay"; trusting in Him and what He did at the Cross will bring us out).*

3 **And He has put a new song in My mouth, even praise unto our God: many shall see it, and fear, and shall trust in the LORD** *(the doctrine of this Psalm is Christ's Perfect Obedience to the Will of God as the Sin-bearer of His People, and His Perfect Patience in waiting on and for God to deliver Him and them out of all afflictions).*

4 **Blessed is that man that makes the LORD his trust, and respects not the proud, nor such as turn aside to lies** *(trust placed in anything other than "Jesus Christ and Him Crucified" is trust placed in a lie [I Cor. 3:23]).*

5 **Many, O LORD My God, are Your wonderful works which You have done, and Your thoughts which are to usward: they cannot be reckoned up in order unto You: if I would declare and speak of them, they are more than can be numbered** *(it is strange that much of the modern Church declares that modern man faces problems that are not addressed in the Bible; and yet the Psalmist says that the "wonderful works" of God are so many, and His "thoughts" [counsel and cure for our plight] are so numerous, addressing themselves to far more than we would ever need, or that mere mortals could ever begin to enumerate, that only the Messiah could both declare them and speak of them).*

6 **Sacrifice and offering You did not desire;**

My ears have You opened: Burnt Offering and Sin Offering have You not required (the Divine displeasure with animal sacrifices and offerings is defined in Hebrews, Chapter 10 as displeasure with them as types and symbols; animal blood simply would not suffice [Heb. 10:4]; and yet this does not conflict with God's infinite delight in the one great Sacrifice of Calvary; the contrast, on the contrary, heightens that delight).

7 Then said I, Lo, I come: in the volume of the Book it is written of Me (the words, "Lo, I come," signal His Incarnation, and the word "Book" is the Bible; in that Book, it was "engraved" concerning Him that He was to be born as a Man and suffer as a Sacrifice; regrettably, the world attempts to manufacture another god, while the Church attempts to manufacture another sacrifice),

8 I delight to do Your will, O My God: yea, Your Law is within My heart (the Incarnation and Atonement were necessary as predicted of Him and prescribed to Him in the Scriptures, and the statement is made that He delighted to obey these prescriptions, for they were not only in the "Book," but also in His "heart").

9 I have preached righteousness in the great congregation: lo, I have not refrained My lips, O LORD, You know.

10 I have not hid Your righteousness within My heart; I have declared Your faithfulness and Your salvation: I have not concealed Your lovingkindness and Your truth from the great congregation (Christ was faithful to deliver the entirety of the Word of God).

11 Withhold not Thou Your tender mercies from Me, O LORD: let Your lovingkindness and Your truth continually preserve Me (sadly, man would show the Messiah no "mercy" or "lovingkindness"; the only thing that preserved Him was "Your Truth").

12 For innumerable evils have compassed Me about: My iniquities have taken hold upon Me, so that I am not able to look up; they are more than the hairs of My head: therefore My heart fails Me (calamities and afflictions in the sense of "evils" and "iniquities" result from sin; however, these sorrows and troubles did not result from the Messiah's sins, for He had none, but from the sins of those whom He came to save; these griefs so bent Him down that He was not able to look up, and they enfeebled His physical powers so that His heart fainted; in fact, never was there sorrow in this world comparable to His! [Mk 14:34]).

13 Be pleased, O LORD, to deliver Me: O LORD, make haste to help Me (man gave Him "no help"; even His Own Disciples would not associate themselves with His suffering or His dying; His Own kindred forsook Him; if these Passages do not proclaim the depravity of man, nothing does!).

14 Let them be ashamed and confounded together who seek after My soul to destroy it; let them be driven backward and put to shame who wish Me evil (the religious men of Jesus' day desired that the only truly good Man Whoever lived lose His soul; let this ever be a lesson to mankind; the true Child of God must ever be wary of the world and doubly wary of organized religion).

15 Let them be desolate for a reward of their shame who say unto Me, Aha, aha (these Verses are a prediction foretelling the doom of the haters of the Messiah, just as Verse 16 predicts the Salvation and felicity of those who love Him).

16 Let all those who seek You rejoice and be glad in You: let such as love Your salvation say continually, The LORD be magnified (the contrast is outstanding; those who reject Him will be "driven backward"; those who seek Him and accept Him will "rejoice and be glad").

17 But I am poor and needy; yet the LORD thinks upon Me: You are My help and My deliverer; make no tarrying, O My God. (Some are "poor" and some are "needy," but only One was, in the fullest sense, poor and needy at the same time.

The words, "make no tarrying, O My God," refer to the speedy conclusion of the Sacrifice that must be offered, not because of the pain of the "poor and needy," but rather because of the hurried necessity of the Redemption of man.

As we have stated, every one of these Psalms speaks of Christ in some way, whether in His Atoning, Mediatorial, or Intercessory Work.)

PSALM 41

A PSALM OF DAVID:
A PRAYER FOR DELIVERANCE

BLESSED is he who considers the poor: the LORD will deliver him in time of trouble. (This Psalm concludes the first Book of Psalms, or what is called the "Genesis Book." As Genesis opens with the first Adam in blessing and closes with his children in affliction, so this first Book of the Psalms opens with the Second Man in blessing and closes with His people in affliction. The Pharaoh of Israel's first affliction [the

Book of Exodus] prefigures the Antichrist of Israel's future and last affliction.)

2 The LORD will preserve him, and keep him alive: and he shall be blessed upon the Earth: and You will not deliver him unto the will of his enemies (this Verse has a triple meaning: 1. It speaks of the Lord preserving David when Absalom sought to overthrow him and even kill him; 2. It speaks of Christ in His Earthly Ministry Whom the religious leaders desired to kill, even before the Crucifixion; and, 3. It speaks of Israel being weak and faint in the Great Tribulation Period, and then delivered by the Second Coming).

3 The LORD will strengthen him upon the bed of languishing: You will make all his bed in his sickness (God's future loving sympathy to the fainting elect of Israel is contrasted here with man's duplicity and heartlessness [Vss. 5-8]).

4 I said, LORD, be merciful unto me: heal my soul: for I have sinned against You (as David prays this prayer, he knows that the terrible difficulties that are now coming against him, due to the rebellion of his son Absalom, are permitted by God because of his [David's] sins; likewise, God will permit judgment against Israel by the Antichrist due to Israel's terrible denial of her own Son and Saviour, the Lord Jesus Christ; as well, it speaks of Christ interceding for Israel, making her rebellion His own).

5 My enemies speak evil of me, When shall he die, and his name perish? (The Messiah defines the conduct of Israel's enemies as hatred against Himself. And yet Israel desired the death of Christ and for His Name to perish. In fact, they have fought that Name for nearly two thousand years, despite the fact that He Alone is their Saviour; however, they will not know this until the Second Coming.)

6 And if he come to see me, he speaks vanity: his heart gathers iniquity to itself; when he goes abroad, he tells it. (This Passage has a triple meaning: 1. It speaks of David and those who would attempt to destroy him; 2. It speaks of Israel and their terrible opposition to their Messiah, Jesus Christ; and, 3. It speaks of the world and also the apostate Church that hates both Christ and His People. They desire the destruction of both. They treat them with falsehood, malice, and slander. While the apostate Church speaks favorably of Christ, it is, in reality, another Christ [II Cor. 11:4].)

7 All who hate me whisper together against me: against me do they devise my hurt (there is no doubt of a double fulfillment in these Verses

of both David and Christ; every statement could be understood of both men; Ahithophel, David's trusted advisor, led the rebellion against David; Judas, likewise, led such against Christ).

8 An evil disease, say they, cleaves fast unto him: and now that he lies he shall rise up no more (multiple tens of thousands in Israel, led by Ahithophel and Absalom, claimed that David had an evil heart [evil disease]; they attributed all types of malignity to him; they claimed that it would be impossible for him to overcome it, and so they concluded him to be finished and, therefore, "fair game"; they said the same of Christ, but both David and Christ rose again).

9 Yea, my own familiar friend, in whom I trusted, which did eat of my bread, has lifted up his heel against me (this speaks of Ahithophel and his betrayal of David; in an even greater sense, it speaks of Judas, and shows to what extent he was a familiar friend of Christ [Acts 1:25]).

10 But You, O LORD, be merciful unto me, and raise me up, that I may requite them (this is the prayer of David that he will be raised up from the deep humiliation and seeming defeat experienced as he fled from Absalom and was betrayed by Ahithophel [II Sam. 15:31]; but in an even greater sense, this speaks of the great Resurrection of the Lord Jesus Christ, when, on the third day, He came out of the tomb).

11 By this (the Resurrection) **I know that You favor me, because my enemy does not triumph over me** (Ahithophel, along with treacherous Absalom, did not triumph over David; likewise, Judas and the evil elders of Israel did not triumph over Christ; even more so, the "enemy," Death, did not triumph over the Lord; at Calvary, Jesus broke the back of sin and death, which was verified by the Resurrection).

12 And as for me, You uphold me in my integrity, and set me before Your face for ever. (How could David speak of his "integrity," especially after his terrible sin with Bath-sheba? He could do so because the "integrity" of which he spoke was not man's integrity, but God's. The Lord sat David before "His face forever," because David's sin had been forgiven forever.

As well, in this Passage, Christ is asserting that, because of His sinlessness [integrity], He would be seated upon the Throne of Glory forever. Now that His sinlessness has become our sinlessness, which is God's true "integrity," we are seated together with Christ in the Heavenlies [Eph. 2:6] — "before Your face.")

13 Blessed be the LORD God of Israel from everlasting, and to everlasting. Amen, and

Amen. *(This Psalm closes the Genesis Book of the five Books of the Psalms. It closes with a fitting "Amen, and Amen.")*

PSALM 42

THE EXODUS BOOK
PROBABLY WRITTEN BY DAVID:
AN INTENSE LONGING FOR GOD

AS the hart *(deer)* pants after the water brooks, so pants my soul after You, O God. *(This is the First Psalm of the Exodus Book. As the Book of Exodus opens with an oppressed people longing for deliverance, likewise, this Psalm opens with David being oppressed and longing for deliverance.*

This is the first of some ten Psalms written for the sons of Korah. It doesn't really say that these sons of Korah wrote the Psalms, but more implies that they sang them. Even though it is not stated, probably David wrote this Psalm, and maybe some or all of the others of Korah.

Korah himself died under the wrath of God [Num. 16:31], but his children were spared [Num. 26:11]. These special Psalms, therefore, sing of redeeming Grace.

This was probably composed when David was fleeing Absalom. He was cut off from worship at the Tabernacle in Jerusalem, where the Ark of God resided. At this stage he likely had no knowledge if he would be restored to the throne or not. As the Psalm is begun, we feel the heart's cry of a man who wants God more than anything else.)

2 My soul thirsts for God, for the living God: when shall I come and appear before God? *(This Psalm gives a forepicture of Israel when out of Covenant relationship with Jehovah and suffering the oppression of the Antichrist. At that time, she will cast herself for Deliverance upon God as Elohim.*

This means that the Messiah, for that's Who this Psalm portrays, cries for Israel and, as the Redeemer, He cries for us.)

3 My tears have been my meat day and night, while they continually say unto me, Where is your God? *(This was said of David in his darkest hour, and also of Christ by the religious leaders of Israel, when He was on the Cross. Moreover, this very taunt will be addressed to the unhappy sons of Israel by the Antichrist and his minions in the coming "Time of Jacob's Trouble" [Joel 2:17].)*

4 When I remember these things, I pour out my soul in me: for I had gone with the multitude, I went with them to the House of God, with the voice of joy and praise, with a multitude who kept holyday *(David said, "I remember"! As well, it speaks of Christ remembering all the times of worship before His public Ministry began, and with it the rejection of Israel!).*

5 Why are you cast down, O my soul? And why are you disquieted in me? Hope thou in God: for I shall yet praise Him for the help of His countenance *(David has faith and confidence that he will be restored to the throne, and so he was!).*

6 O my God, my soul is cast down within me: therefore will I remember You from the land of Jordan, and of the Hermonites, from the hill Mizar *("the hill Mizar" lies between Mount Hermon and the Jordan River, a long ways from Jerusalem; no matter how far away from the Tabernacle, he would continue to remember and worship).*

7 Deep calls unto deep at the noise of your waterspouts: all your waves and your billows are gone over me *(in effect, David is saying by this statement that at times we must be brought into deep distress before we can be brought to the deep things of God; when this deep distress happens, it is as though we have been thrown into a "waterspout," with such spewing us up and tumbling us head over heels; we are defenseless, but yet this is necessary, that is, if we are to be brought to the place of total consecration).*

8 Yet the LORD will command His lovingkindness in the daytime, and in the night His song shall be with me, and my prayer unto the God of my life *(during the day, David felt the kindness of the Lord, and continuously; in the night, he sang the Psalms, and then prayed himself to sleep).*

9 I will say unto God my Rock, Why have You forgotten me? Why do I go mourning because of the oppression of the enemy? *(This Verse not only pictures David's troubles, but also the coming future suffering of Israel under the Antichrist; in fact, the suffering will be so severe that they will think the Promises made by God to Abraham, Isaac, and Jacob are forgotten.)*

10 As with a sword in my bones, my enemies reproach me; while they say daily unto me, Where is your God? *(Not only did David's enemies say this of him, "Where is your God?", but it was also said to Christ while He was on the Cross. It will also be said to Israel by the Antichrist during the Battle of Armageddon, when it seems like the chosen people will be completely annihilated. And finally, the same presently is at times said to us.)*

11 Why are you cast down, O my soul? And why are you disquieted within me? hope thou in God: for I shall yet praise Him, Who is the health of my countenance, and my God. *(By Faith, David claims restoration, i.e., "health." Likewise, at the Second Coming, the Lord will bring Israel back to "health." He will do the same for all who will trust Him.)*

PSALM 43

THE EXODUS BOOK
PROBABLY WRITTEN BY DAVID:
PRAYER FOR DELIVERANCE FROM
THE UNGODLY

JUDGE me, O God, and plead my cause against an ungodly nation: O deliver me from the deceitful and unjust man. *(This Psalm also has three basic meanings: 1. David crying to God to be delivered from Absalom; 2. The Greater Son of David crying to God to be delivered from the evil religious leaders of Israel; and, 3. The Messiah crying to God in Israel's place during the time of the Great Tribulation, with threatened destruction from the "deceitful and unjust man," the Antichrist.)*

2 For You are the God of my strength: why do You cast me off? Why go I mourning because of the oppression of the enemy? *(In other words, "Lord, Why have You allowed this?")*

3 O send out Your light and Your truth: let them lead me; let them bring me unto Your holy hill, and to Your tabernacles *(a petition for the Lord to lead us will be answered favorably).*

4 Then will I go unto the Altar of God, unto God my exceeding joy: yea, upon the harp will I praise You, O God my God *(despite the terrible distress, David never lost his song).*

5 Why are you cast down, O my soul? And why are you disquieted within me? hope in God: for I shall yet praise Him, Who is the health of my countenance, and my God. *(This Psalm ends exactly as the previous Psalm. David is praising the Lord now, but he will "yet praise Him" on the "holy hill" and in the "Tabernacle.")*

PSALM 44

AUTHOR UNKNOWN, IT DOESN'T
APPEAR TO BE DAVIDIC:
A CRY FOR HELP

WE have heard with our ears, O God, our fathers have told us, what work You did in their days, in the times of old. *(Whoever the writer was, it seems that the Holy Spirit took him back in spirit to the great Deliverance by God of Israel under Joshua. As well, the latter part of the Psalm seems to include Israel under the trying days of the Antichrist, and her cry for Deliverance.)*

2 How You did drive out the heathen with Your hand, and planted them: how You did afflict the people, and cast them out *(this is a reference to the Lord casting the heathen nations out of the Promised Land; as well, it is a physical example of the spiritual experience in our own lives, with the Lord driving out the works of the flesh).*

3 For they got not the land in possession by their own sword, neither did their own arm save them: but Your right hand, and Your arm, and the light of Your countenance, because You had a favor unto them *(as it was not possible for Israel to gain their inheritance by "their own sword," likewise, it is not possible for us to obtain our spiritual inheritance by the works of the flesh; it can only be done by our Faith in Christ and what He did for us at the Cross, which gives the Holy Spirit latitude to work on our behalf [Rom. 8:1-2, 11]).*

4 You are my King, O God: command deliverances for Jacob *(being King, You have a right to command; we pray that, at this present time, You will command our deliverance).*

5 Through You will we push down our enemies: through Your name will we tread them under who rise up against us *(only through the Lord can victory be ours; as well, this victory can come only by Faith in Christ and the Cross [Rom. 6:3-14]).*

6 For I will not trust in my bow, neither shall my sword save me *(human ability, no matter how strong, is woefully insufficient as it regards victory over the world, the flesh, and the Devil [Gal., Chpt. 5]).*

7 But You have saved us from our enemies, and have put them to shame who hate us *(some think that Hezekiah may have written this Psalm; if so, he rejoices in the enemies of Israel being defeated).*

8 In God we boast all the day long, and praise Your name for ever. Selah. *(Paul said, "God forbid that I glory [boast] save in the Cross of our Lord Jesus Christ, by Whom the world is crucified unto me, and I unto the world" [Gal. 6:14].)*

9 But You have cast off, and put us to shame; and go not forth with our armies.

(Prophetically, this Psalm is a forepicture of the affliction of the believing remnant of Israel under the oppression of the Antichrist. Presently, it speaks of every Christian who, at one time or the other, due to failure, suffers chastisement at the hands of God. Nevertheless, God's chastisement is never punitive, but rather redemptive.)

10 You make us to turn back from the enemy: and they which hate us spoil for themselves.

11 You have given us like sheep appointed for meat; and have scattered us among the heathen *(this happened in A.D. 70, and continues in a sense unto this hour).*

12 You sold Your people for nought, and do not increase Your wealth by their price *(the wealth of the Kingdom of God was not increased by this necessary act, but actually decreased).*

13 You make us a reproach to our neighbours, a scorn and a derision to them who are round about us.

14 You make us a byword among the heathen, a shaking of the head among the people *(and that's exactly what has happened!).*

15 My confusion is continually before me, and the shame of my face has covered me,

16 For the voice of him who reproaches and blasphemes; by reason of the enemy and avenger *(Israel is reproached and blasphemed, and yet the Lord seems to do nothing about it).*

17 All this is come upon us: yet have we not forgotten You, neither have we dealt falsely in Your Covenant *(at the beginning of the Great Tribulation, Israel will cry these words, but they are false).*

18 Our heart is not turned back, neither have our steps declined from Your way;

19 Though You have sore broken us in the place of dragons, and covered us with the shadow of death. *(Here, Israel is admitting that God has rightly broken them because they had, for a long period of time, forgotten Him with their hearts turned back from Him.*

The "place of dragons" concerns that terrible time when Israel will accept the Antichrist and think he is, in fact, the Messiah. Because of this, they will be brought to the "shadow of death." The Antichrist will declare war on them, with Israel at that time coming close to total annihilation [Jn. 5:43].)

20 If we have forgotten the Name of our God, or stretched out our hands to a strange god *(in fact, they did "forget the Name of their God," and they did "stretch out their hands to a strange god" [Dan. 11:39]; the Antichrist, who Israel at*

the beginning will think is the Messiah, will actually be a "strange god");

21 Shall not God search this out? for He knows the secrets of the heart.

22 Yea, for Your sake are we killed all the day long; we are counted as sheep for the slaughter *(Paul quoted this Passage in Romans 8:36; the Holy Spirit through Paul uses this Passage in the correct sense, basically stating that the things God allows to come upon us are meant to bring us closer to God; rather than separating us from God, they are designed to bring us into compliance with His Will).*

23 Awake, why do You sleep, O Lord? Arise, cast us not off for ever. *(This will be the cry of Israel during the closing days of the Battle of Armageddon, when it looks like they will be annihilated. In a sense, it is Christ interceding for Israel, which He no doubt will do at that time!)*

24 Wherefore do You hide Your face, and forget our affliction and our oppression? *(During the Battle of Armageddon, Israel will be pressed beyond measure, with no visible hope in sight.)*

25 For our soul is bowed down to the dust: our belly cleaves unto the Earth *(this will be the darkest hour of Israel's history, when, as Zechariah prophesied, they will come close to extinction [Zech. 14:1-3]).*

26 Arise for our help, and redeem us for Your mercies' sake. *(This prayer will be answered after so many years of spiritual declension. Zechariah said so [Zech. 14:3].*

The reason God will answer is because of "Thy Mercies' sake.")

PSALM 45

AUTHOR UNKNOWN:
THE KING; MESSIAH'S MAJESTY
AND POWER

MY heart is inditing a good matter: I speak of the things which I have made touching the king: my tongue is the pen of a ready writer. *(This Psalm is actually the answer to the prayer and petition of the last four Verses of the previous Psalm.*

Its setting could have actually been about Solomon and his Queen. Solomon was a Type of Christ in the Millennial Reign. Israel is portrayed here as the Queen in the coming Kingdom Age.)

2 You are fairer than the children of men: grace is poured into Your lips: therefore God has blessed You for ever *(this speaks of Israel's praises of Christ after they have accepted Him,*

which will take place at the Second Coming).

3 Gird Your sword upon Your thigh, O most mighty, with Your glory and Your majesty *(at this time, Jesus will have become a mighty Man of War in defeating the Antichrist and, in fact, all of Israel's enemies).*

4 And in Your majesty ride prosperously because of truth and meekness and righteousness: and Your right hand shall teach You terrible things *(the Lord will be "prosperous" in His attack upon the Antichrist).*

5 Your arrows are sharp in the heart of the king's enemies; where by the people fall under You *(these "enemies" include the Antichrist and all his armies).*

6 Your Throne, O God is for ever and ever: the scepter of Your kingdom is a right sceptre *(among other things, this Scripture proves the Deity of Jesus Christ as God).*

7 You love righteousness, and hate wickedness: therefore God, Your God, has anointed You with the oil of gladness above Your fellows *(Jesus was anointed by the Holy Spirit to a greater degree than any ever has been or ever will be [Lk. 4:18-19; Jn. 3:34]).*

8 All Your garments smell of myrrh, and aloes, and cassia, out of the ivory palaces, whereby they have made You glad *(pictures the Glory of Christ!).*

9 Kings' daughters were among Your honourable women: upon Your right hand did stand the Queen in gold of Ophir *(speaks of Israel during the coming Kingdom Age, when they will have accepted Christ, having finally reached their privileged position).*

10 Hearken, O daughter, and consider, and incline your ear: forget also your own people, and your father's house *(Israel's golden day has now dawned; consequently, they are to forget the past [Acts 1:6-7]);*

11 So shall the king greatly desire your beauty: for He is your Lord: and worship thou Him *("the King" is the Lord Jesus Christ; at long last, Israel will recognize and worship Him).*

12 And the daughter of Tyre shall be there with a gift; even the rich among the people shall intreat your favour *(this stands for the Gentile nations, which will come with their "gifts").*

13 The King's daughter is all glorious within: her clothing is of wrought gold *(glorious Israel!).*

14 She shall be brought unto the King in raiment of needlework: the virgins her companions who follow her shall be brought unto you *(at long last, Israel accepts Christ as "the*

King"; in turn, He will gloriously adorn her).*

15 With gladness and rejoicing shall they be brought: they shall enter into the King's palace *(Solomon's Palace was glorious; likewise, the "King's Palace" will be even more glorious, of which Solomon's was a Type).*

16 Instead of your fathers shall be your children, whom you may make princes in all the Earth *(the fathers of old rejected Christ, but their children will accept Him, which speaks of the future).*

17 I will make your name to be remembered in all generations: therefore shall the people praise you for ever and ever *(Christ will never again be rejected and, consequently, the people shall "praise Him forever and ever," which includes both the Gentiles and the Jews).*

PSALM 46

MAY HAVE BEEN WRITTEN BY HEZEKIAH: GOD IS OUR REFUGE AND STRENGTH

GOD is our refuge and strength, a very present help in trouble. *(There is some evidence that this Psalm was written during the siege of Jerusalem by the Assyrians. It is quite possible that the Holy Spirit gave it at that time through Isaiah to Hezekiah at Jerusalem.*

If that, in fact, is the case, it addresses itself as well to the siege of Jerusalem which will take place by the Antichrist in the Battle of Armageddon [Zech. 14:1-3].)

2 Therefore will not we fear, though the Earth be removed, and though the mountains be carried into the midst of the sea *(this statement addresses itself to "fear," which plagues every Christian at one time or another);*

3 Though the waters therefore roar and be troubled, though the mountains shake with the swelling thereof: Selah. *(By the use of descriptive statements, the Holy Spirit outlines just how strong this effort of Satan was.)*

4 There is a river, the streams whereof shall make glad the city of God, the Holy Place of the Tabernacles of the Most High *(this reaches forward to the coming Kingdom Age, when a veritable river will flow out of the Temple, by the Altar, toward the Dead Sea, with a branch going into the Mediterranean; consequently, the Dead Sea [as it is now called] will no longer be dead, but will teem with life; in a sense, that river will be symbolic of the Holy Spirit, Who Alone brings life, with Christ as its Source, and the Cross as its means*

[Col. 2:14-15]).

5 God is in the midst of her; she shall not be moved: God shall help her, and that right early *(this speaks of the invasion of the Assyrians under Sennacherib, and also of the Antichrist, of which the latter is yet future).*

6 The heathen raged, and kingdoms were moved: He uttered His voice, and Earth melted. *(Isaiah, Chpt. 37 records the rage of this "heathen." As stated, it speaks of Sennacherib. Still, it speaks of an even greater fulfillment during the Battle of Armageddon, when the Lord will utter His Voice before His armies and defeat the raging nations surrounding Jerusalem [Zech., Chpt. 14; Rev. 19:11-21].)*

7 The LORD of Hosts is with us; the God of Jacob is our refuge. Selah. *(The reason for Israel's victory is the "LORD of Hosts." It is the same presently, but in a little different way. Presently, the victory has already been won at Calvary. Faith in that Finished Work guarantees the victory afforded by the Cross.)*

8 Come, behold the works of the LORD, what desolations He has made in the Earth *(this has to do with the Great Tribulation, and pertains to the "seven seals," "seven trumpets," etc.).*

9 He makes wars to cease unto the end of the Earth: He breaks the bow, and cuts the spear in sunder: He burns the chariot in the fire *(this will happen at the beginning of the Kingdom Age; Jesus Christ is the Prince of Peace; He Alone can bring peace [Isa. 2:2-4; Mic. 4:1-8]).*

10 Be still, and know that I am God: I will be exalted among the heathen, I will be exalted in the Earth *(this is exactly what happened with Sennacherib, and will be exactly what will happen at the Second Coming).*

11 The LORD of Hosts is with us; the God of Jacob is our refuge. Selah. *(To the self-righteous mind, it would seem that God should speak of Himself as the "God of Israel" instead of the "God of Jacob," considering what the name Jacob means. However, "Jacob" is what we are; "Israel" is what only God can make of us.)*

PSALM 47

IT IS BELIEVED IT MAY HAVE BEEN WRITTEN BY EITHER HEZEKIAH OR ISAIAH: GOD REIGNS OVER ALL THE EARTH

O clap your hands, all ye people; shout unto God with the voice of triumph. *(This is the only place in the Bible that commands us to clap our hands respecting praise to God; other places in the Bible allude to it [II Ki. 11:12; Ps. 98:8; Isa. 55:12].*

If it was written by Hezekiah or Isaiah, it was during the time immediately following the great victory over Sennacherib, brought about entirely by the Lord. It is a time of praise!)

2 For the LORD Most High is terrible: He is a great King over all the Earth *(Sennacherib had made his boasts, and now the Holy Spirit through the people of Jerusalem makes His boast, which proclaims the "LORD Most High" as "King over all the Earth").*

3 He shall subdue the people under us, and the nations under our feet *(He has, and He will!).*

4 He shall choose our inheritance for us, the excellency of Jacob whom He loved. Selah. *(The "excellency of Jacob" means the supremacy of Jacob over the nations, which will take place in the coming Kingdom Age.)*

5 God is gone up with a shout, the LORD with the sound of a trumpet *(even though this speaks of the victory over the Assyrians, it also speaks of the great victory yet to come over the Antichrist, which will take place at the Second Coming).*

6 Sing praises to God, sing praises: sing praises unto our King, sing praises *(the closer to God that one gets, the more the song of praises becomes prominent).*

7 For God is the King of all the Earth: sing ye praises with understanding *(the Holy Spirit is saying that we should have "understanding" regarding this matter; "Jesus Christ is King of all the Earth," and not the Antichrist).*

8 God reigns over the heathen: God sits upon the throne of His Holiness *(in the coming Millennial Reign, the Lord of Glory will reign over the entirety of the Earth, and will do so Personally from Jerusalem).*

9 The princes of the people are gathered together, even the people of the God of Abraham: for the shields of the Earth belong unto God: He is greatly exalted. *(This pertains to the great victory of the Lord defeating the army of the Assyrians in one night with one Angel [II Ki. 19:35; Isa. 37:36]. In a greater sense, it speaks of the tremendous victory of the Lord Jesus Christ over the Antichrist, which, of course, is yet future. But as surely as the previous victory took place, as surely will this victory take place!)*

PSALM 48

AS WELL, THIS PSALM COULD HAVE BEEN
WRITTEN BY EITHER ISAIAH
OR HEZEKIAH:
ZION, THE CITY OF THE GREAT KING

GREAT is the LORD, and greatly to be praised in the city of our God, in the mountain of His holiness. (*The celebration over the Assyrians continues. As well, these same Passages speak in prophetic tones of the coming victory over the Antichrist. As stated, as surely as the previous, most definitely will be the future.*)

2 Beautiful for situation, the joy of the whole Earth, is mount Zion, on the sides of the north, the city of the great King. (*Jerusalem is situated in the exact geographical center of the Earth. In the coming Kingdom Age, Jerusalem will be what God has always intended, "The Joy of the Whole Earth."*)

3 God is known in her palaces for a refuge (*in the great cities and the governmental centers of the world, men are known; but, in this great city and palace, God will be known*).

4 For, lo, the kings were assembled, they passed by together. (*This speaks of the kings of the Earth during Hezekiah's day, who assembled to destroy Jerusalem. They felt they could not lose, but lose they did! It will be the same during the days of the Antichrist!*)

5 They saw it, and so they marveled; they were troubled, and hasted away. (*Why did they run? They ran because the Lord, with one Angel, in one night, killed 185,000 Assyrians, completely decimating their army [II Ki. 19:35; Isa. 37:36].*)

6 Fear took hold upon them there, and pain, as of a woman in travail. (*And no wonder! For the first time in their history, they came up against the God of Glory!*)

7 You break the ships of Tarshish with an east wind. (*If Hezekiah wrote this Psalm, he probably little understood the full meaning of this Verse given to him by the Holy Spirit. Its greater fulfillment will be at the Battle of Armageddon, with the Antichrist having great warships anchored in the Mediterranean, aiding his great strike against Israel. The Lord will break those ships, and do so with "an east wind," whatever that actually means.*)

8 As we have heard, so have we seen in the city of the LORD of Hosts, in the city of our God: God will establish it for ever. Selah. (*During the time of Hezekiah, Judah saw what the Lord could do. At the Second Coming, which will end the Battle of Armageddon, Israel will once again see what the Lord can do. And so will the entirety of the world!*)

9 We have thought of Your lovingkindness, O God, in the midst of Your temple (*the writer is referring to the times of prayer in "the Temple," when the enemy was at the gate*).

10 According to Your Name, O God, so is Your praise unto the ends of the Earth: Your right hand is full of righteousness (*God's action being ever in harmony with His Character, His fame, therefore, extends and will extend to the very ends of the Earth*).

11 Let mount Zion rejoice, let the daughters of Judah be glad, because of Your Judgments (*while Judah rejoiced at the great victory over Sennacherib, still, this pertains to the even greater victory over the coming Antichrist, of which the victory over Sennacherib was a symbol*).

12 Walk about Zion, and go round about her: tell the towers thereof (*the idea is, peace now reigns because the Prince of Peace now reigns*).

13 Mark ye well her bulwarks, consider her palaces: that you may tell it to the generation following. (*This Psalm is sung in testimony of the great victory won by the Lord in the sending of His Angel to defeat the Assyrians, and which should be told forever. And so it has been! And so it shall be!*)

14 For this God is our God for ever and ever: He will be our guide even unto death. (*This Psalm had its limitations when sung by Hezekiah. It will have no limitations when sung by the people of God at the beginning of the great Millennial Reign. Jesus Christ will then be "Our Guide." Thank God! Ultimately, there will be no more death [Rev. 21:4].*)

PSALM 49

AS WELL, THIS PSALM MAY HAVE BEEN
WRITTEN BY EITHER ISAIAH
OR HEZEKIAH:
TRUST IN GOD, NOT RICHES

HEAR this, all ye people, give ear, all ye inhabitants of the world (*As stated, it is not known exactly who wrote this Psalm; however its theme is Salvation, then from the Assyrians, and now from sin. The Speaker, in effect, is the Lord Jesus Christ. In these first four Verses, He proposes an enigma, and invites all the nations of the Earth to hear His solution of it.*)

The enigma is: man, being without understanding and without power, how can he redeem himself from the dominion of death?):

2 Both low and high, rich and poor, together *(all are in the same condition, in desperate need of a Redeemer).*

3 My mouth shall speak of wisdom; and the meditation of my heart shall be of understanding *(the "wisdom" given here is from Heaven; likewise, the Lord of Glory is the only One Who has "understanding" of Death, Hell, and what it takes to redeem man from such).*

4 I will incline my ear to a parable: I will open my dark saying upon the harp *(through this Psalm set to music, the answer will be given; likewise, if our modern Christian music doesn't extol Christ and the price He paid at the Cross, it is of no worth).*

5 Wherefore should I fear in the days of evil, when the iniquity of my heels shall compass me about? *(This Psalm will support Israel's faith in her future suffering under the oppression of the false messiah, just as in the past its truth sustained her while oppressed by the Assyrian.)*

6 They who trust in their wealth, and boast themselves in the multitude of their riches;

7 None of them can by any means redeem his brother, nor give to God a ransom for him *(the Holy Spirit through Peter plainly tells us that man cannot be redeemed by silver or gold; it takes the priceless Blood of Jesus to redeem fallen humanity, and that alone [I Pet. 1:18-20]):*

8 (For the redemption of their soul is precious, and it ceases for ever *[after death, the efforts by the Lord to redeem souls will "cease forever"; there is no such thing as purgatory; such is not taught in the Bible]:)*

9 That he should still live for ever, and not see corruption *(this can be brought about, eternal life, only by Faith in Christ and what Christ has done for us at the Cross [Jn. 3:3-16; Eph. 2:13-18]).*

10 For he sees that wise men die, likewise the fool and the brutish person perish, and leave their wealth to others *(if the rich man dies trusting in his riches to save him, he will die as a fool; only the redeeming Blood of the Lord Jesus Christ can be taken with us in death [Eph. 2:13-18]).*

11 Their inward thought is, that their houses shall continue for ever, and their dwelling places to all generations; they call their lands after their own names *(such individuals think, by calling "their lands after their own names," that they will perpetuate their memory; irrespective, they are soon forgotten).*

12 Nevertheless man being in honour abides not: he is like the beasts that perish *(man cannot perpetuate himself except in the new birth and by the Lord Jesus Christ; all else is folly; if he thinks otherwise, his thinking is no higher than "the beasts that perish").*

13 This their way is their folly: yet their posterity approve their sayings. Selah. *(No matter the plans made to perpetuate the names and memories, even though their children attempt to carry it out, and we speak of the wicked, the Holy Spirit says, "Their way is their folly.")*

14 Like sheep they are laid in the grave; death shall feed on them; and the upright shall have dominion over them in the morning; and their beauty shall consume in the grave from their dwelling *(all the riches and power of the wicked are consumed in the grave; conversely, the Godly shall be resurrected, and with their Faith in Christ, will have "dominion").*

15 But God will redeem my soul from the power of the grave: for He shall receive me. Selah. *(This refers to the Great Resurrection of Life, which will take place at the Rapture of the Saints [I Thess. 4:13-18].)*

16 Be not thou afraid when one is made rich, when the glory of his house is increased *(this speaks of the wicked);*

17 For when he dies he shall carry nothing away: his glory shall not descend after him *(riches, fame, power, and glory count as nothing after death, only Salvation, which is in Christ).*

18 Though while he lived he blessed his soul: and men will praise you, when you do well to yourself *(none of this has any effect on eternity).*

19 He shall go to the generation of his fathers; they shall never see light *(this means that irrespective of his riches and power, the wicked will ultimately die; as well, they will be cast into outer darkness [Mat. 8:12; 25:30; Jude, Vs. 13]).*

20 Man who is in honour, and understands not, is like the beasts that perish. *(The lesson taught in this Psalm is very simple: man cannot redeem himself, irrespective of his might, majesty, or wealth. Christ is the only One Who can redeem the soul, and He does so by His Precious Shed Blood, which requires faith by the believing sinner [Eph. 2:8-9].*

Regrettably, the far greater majority of the human race has chosen to disbelieve the Word of the Lord, and instead has believed in frail, poor, flawed man, despite the never-ceasing failure of all.)

PSALM 50

A PSALM OF ASAPH:
GOD IS THE JUDGE

THE mighty God, even the LORD, has spoken, and called the Earth from the rising of the sun unto the going down thereof. *(As far as we know, Asaph wrote twelve Psalms, of which this is the first.*

The doctrine of this Verse is: "The God of gods, even Jehovah Messiah, summons the Earth to judgment." The certitude of this judgment is so sure that it is spoken of as a present fact. The extent of this judgment from the "rising of the sun" to "its going down" is repeated in Matthew 24:27.)

2 Out of Zion, the perfection of beauty, God has shined *(immediately prior to the appearance of the Messiah at the Second Coming, Israel will be reduced to the lowest possible depth of misery and well-nigh extinction as a nation; but, at that moment, her Deliverer will appear on Mount Zion with all the accompaniments of terrific majesty, as at Sinai, and He will summon the whole Earth to judgment).*

3 Our God shall come, and shall not keep silence: a fire shall devour before Him, and it shall be very tempestuous round about Him *(this speaks as well of His Second Coming during the Battle of Armageddon; He came the first time as a Lamb; He will come the second time as the conquering King of kings and Lord and lords [Rev. 19:11-21]).*

4 He shall call to the Heavens from above, and to the Earth, that He may judge His people *("His people" refer to the Jewish people, who have rejected Him for all these many centuries; Zechariah spoke of this moment [Zech. 12:10-14]).*

5 Gather My saints together unto Me: those who have made a covenant with Me by Sacrifice. *(The term here, "My Saints," does not refer to the Blood-bought Church that has already been raptured some seven years earlier, but rather to the Jewish people, as designated by their "Covenant of Sacrifice."*

The term "Saints" does not express the Believer's moral attitude toward God, but God's attitude toward the Believer.

This "Covenant" made by Sacrifice, as it refers to Israel, was typified in Exodus 24:8, explained in Hebrews 9:20, and fulfilled in I Corinthians 5:7. It pointed toward Calvary and is illustrated in Genesis 15:9-21.)

6 And the Heavens shall declare His righteousness: for God is Judge Himself. Selah. *(This refers to the judgment of the nations, as to how they opposed Israel or helped Israel [Mat. 25:31-46].)*

7 Hear, O My people, and I will speak; O Israel, and I will testify against you: I am God, even your God *(this is the Messiah, the Lord Jesus Christ, addressing Israel; His "testimony against them" will concern their rejection of Him at His First Advent; they, at that time, rejected Him as the Messiah; now He is telling them "I am God, even your God").*

8 I will not reprove you for your Sacrifices or your Burnt Offerings, to have been continually before Me *(the Lord is saying that His reproof that He will give to Israel does not concern the true Sacrifices that they should have offered before Him continually, but will be for the sacrifices that were offered not for their true rightful purpose [Atonement], but those which constituted "works" alone, as though they were feeding a hungry God, which was the method of the heathen).*

9 I will take no bullock out of your house, nor he goats out of your folds *(in essence, "I need no bullocks or goats").*

10 For every beast of the forest is Mine, and the cattle upon a thousand hills *(in other words, "I do not need your animals; I have plenty of My Own").*

11 I know all the fowls of the mountains: and the wild beasts of the field are Mine.

12 If I were hungry, I would not tell you: for the world is Mine, and the fullness thereof *(this refers back to the heathen gods to which the Pagans offered sacrifices in order to appease their hunger; God is saying, in effect, "Don't class Me as a heathen god or treat Me thusly").*

13 Will I eat the flesh of bulls, or drink the blood of goats? *(Israel lost the true purpose of what the Sacrifices really meant, and conducted themselves as heathen offering up their sacrifices to appease Jehovah.)*

14 Offer unto God thanksgiving; and pay your vows unto the Most High *(now He alludes to the correct manner in which the Sacrifices should have been offered; they should have been offered in "thanksgiving" for the "Way" that God had made for His People to have their sins covered; they were to serve as a symbol of the Redeemer Who was to come into the world, Who would give His Life for fallen humanity; sacrifices offered for any other purpose would be rejected out of hand):*

15 And call upon Me in the day of trouble: I

will deliver you, and you shall glorify Me *(offering the Sacrifices in the right way, which symbolized the coming Redeemer and the price that He would pay on Calvary's Cross, guaranteed deliverance).*

16 But unto the wicked God says, What have you to do to declare My Statutes, or that you should take My Covenant in your mouth? *(Every nation of the world that has rejected the true Sacrifice of Christ has persecuted Israel. They will now answer!)*

17 Seeing you hate instruction, and cast My words behind you *(to most nations of the world, the Word of God means little; now they will answer!).*

18 When you saw a thief, then you consented with him, and have been partaker with adulterers *(the Lord is saying to the nations that opposed Israel [before His Coming] that they joined in with "thieves" in their treatment of Israel; this means that they sought to take away from Israel that which God had rightly promised her; as well, they consorted with idol-worshippers [adulterers] in their ill-treatment of these ancient people).*

19 You gave your mouth to evil, and your tongue framed deceit.

20 You sit and speak against your brother: you slander your own mother's son *(here, He speaks directly to the Arab world; Ishmael was Isaac's brother; so, in effect, the Arabs have slandered their own mother's son; even though Sarah was Isaac's mother, and Hagar was Ishmael's mother, still, Sarah was looked at as the foster mother of Ishmael; because Hagar was Sarah's servant, she could only bear the son according to Sarah's wishes [Gen. 16:1-6]).*

21 These things have you done, and I kept silence: you thought that I was altogether such an one as yourself: but I will reprove you, and set them in order before your eyes *(due to the false religion of Islam, the Arabs have thought that they were praying to God, and that He was "one" with them; they will now know they have been wrong; the Promise was not through Ishmael, but through Isaac [Gen. 17:18-19]; they have mistaken God's "silence" for approval; at this coming day, prophesied about 3,000 years ago, the world of Islam will then answer).*

22 Now consider this, you who forget God, lest I tear you in pieces, and there be none to deliver *(the Lord is saying here that the Arab world of Islam, which has substituted this false religion in the place of God, is now in danger*

of being "torn to pieces" with none being able to "deliver them").*

23 Whoso offers praise glorifies Me: and to him who orders his conversation *(manner of behavior)* aright will I show the Salvation of God *(the idea seems to be that the nations of the world which have opposed God and His Plan will now be given an opportunity to repent; to those who do, Salvation will be afforded them; otherwise, judgment! This will be at the beginning of the Kingdom Age).*

PSALM 51

A PSALM OF DAVID:
A PRAYER FOR FORGIVENESS
AND CLEANSING

HAVE mercy upon me, O God, according to Your lovingkindness: according unto the multitude of Your tender mercies blot out my transgressions. *(This is a Psalm of David, written when Nathan the Prophet came unto him after the sin with Bath-sheba and the murder of her husband Uriah [II Sam., Chpt. 12]. This Psalm was given by the Holy Spirit to David when, his heart broken and contrite because of his sin against God, he pleaded for pardon through the Atoning Blood of the Lamb of God, foreshadowed in Exodus, Chapter 12. Thus, he was not only fittingly provided with a vehicle of expression in Repentance and faith, but he was also used as a channel of prophetic communication.*

David, in his sin, Repentance, and Restoration, is a forepicture of Israel. For as he forsook the Law and was guilty of adultery and murder, so Israel despised the Covenant, turned aside to idolatry [spiritual adultery], and murdered the Messiah.

Thus the scope and structure of this Psalm goes far beyond David. It predicts the future confession and forgiveness of Israel in the day of the Messiah's Second Coming, when, looking upon Him Whom they pierced, they shall mourn and weep [Zech., Chpts. 12-13].

As well, this is even more perfectly a vivid portrayal of the Intercessory Work of Christ on behalf of His People. Even though David prayed this prayer, the Son of David would make David's sin [as well as ours] His Own, and pray through him that which must be said.

This means that this is the truest prayer of Repentance ever prayed, because it symbolizes the Intercessory Work of the Son of David.)

2 Wash me thoroughly from my iniquity,

and cleanse me from my sin *(man's problem is sin, and man must admit that; the only remedy for sin is "Jesus Christ and Him Crucified," to which David, in essence, appealed [Heb. 10:12]; the Blood of Jesus Christ alone cleanses from all sin [I Jn. 1:7]).*

3 For I acknowledge my transgressions: and my sin is ever before me *(the acknowledgement of Verses 3 through 4 is the condition of Divine forgiveness; all sin, in essence, is committed against God; therefore, God demands that the transgressions be acknowledged, placing the blame where it rightfully belongs — on the perpetrator; He cannot and, in fact, will not, forgive sin that is not acknowledged and for which no responsibility is taken).*

4 Against You, You only, have I sinned, and done this evil in Your sight: that You might be justified when You speak, and be clear when You judge. *(While David's sins were against Bath-sheba, her husband Uriah, and all of Israel, still, the ultimate direction of sin, perfected by Satan, is always against God.*

All sin is a departure from God's Ways to man's ways.

David is saying that God is always "justified" in any action that He takes, and His "judgment" is always perfect.).

5 Behold, I was shaped in iniquity; and in sin did my mother conceive me. *(Unequivocally, this Verse proclaims the fact of original sin. This Passage states that all are born in sin, and as a result of Adam's Fall in the Garden of Eden.*

When Adam, as the federal head of the human race, failed, this means that all of humanity failed. It means that all who would be born would, in effect, be born lost.

As a result of this, the Second Man, the Last Adam, the Lord Jesus Christ, had to come into this world, in effect, God becoming Man, to undo what the original Adam did. He would have to keep the Law of God perfectly, which He did, all as our Substitute, and then pay the penalty for the terrible sin debt owed by all of mankind, for all had broken the Law, which He did by giving Himself on the Cross of Calvary [Jn. 3:16].

To escape the judgment of original sin, man must be "born again," which is carried out by the believing sinner expressing Faith in Christ and what Christ did at the Cross [Jn. 3:3; Eph. 2:8-9].)

6 Behold, You desire truth in the inward parts: and in the hidden part You shall make me to know wisdom *(man can only deal with the externals, and even that not very well; God Alone can deal with the "inward parts" of man, which is the source of sin, which speaks of the heart; in other words, the heart has to be changed, which the Lord Alone can do [Mat. 5:8]).*

7 Purge me with hyssop, and I shall be clean: wash me, and I shall be whiter than snow. *(The petition, "purge me with hyssop," expresses a figure of speech. "Purge me with the blood which on that night in Egypt was sprinkled on the doorposts with a bunch of hyssop" [Ex. 12:13, 22] portrays David's dependence on "the Blood of the Lamb."*

David had no recourse in the Law, even as no one has recourse in the Law. The Law can only condemn. All recourse is found exclusively in Christ and what He did for us at the Cross, of which the slain lamb and the blood on the doorposts in Egypt were symbols [Ex. 12:13].)

8 Make me to hear joy and gladness; that the bones which You have broken may rejoice. *(Forgiveness for the past never exhausts the fullness of pardon. There is provision for the future.*

The expression, "bones which You have broken," presents a figure of speech meaning that one cannot proceed until things have been made right with God. It is as though a man's leg is broken, and he cannot walk. Unforgiven sin immobilizes the soul the same as a broken bone immobilizes the body.)

9 Hide Your face from my sins, and blot out all my iniquities. *(Unforgiven sin stares in the Face of God. This can only be stopped when the sins are put away, which can only be done by proper Confession and Repentance, with the Blood of Jesus being applied by faith. When this is done, the "iniquities" are "blotted out" as though they had never existed. This is "Justification by Faith" [Rom. 5:1].)*

10 Create in me a clean heart, O God: and renew a right spirit within me. *(David's heart was unclean. Sin makes the heart unclean. The word "create" is interesting. It means the old heart is infected by sin, is diseased, and cannot be salvaged. God must, spiritually speaking, "create a clean heart" [Ezek. 18:31].*

Also, it is impossible for any individual to have a "right spirit" if there is unconfessed sin.)

11 Cast me not away from Your presence; and take not Your Holy Spirit from me. *(If sin is unconfessed and rebellion persists, God will ultimately "cast away" the individual "from His Presence." He will also "take the Holy Spirit" from the person. This refutes the doctrine of*

Unconditional Eternal Security.)

12 Restore unto me the joy of Your salvation; and uphold me with Your free spirit. *(Part of the business of the Holy Spirit is "restoration," but only if the individual meets God's conditions, as David did, and as we must do. With unconfessed sin, all "joy" is lost. With sin confessed, cleansed, and put away, the "joy of Salvation" returns. A clean heart, a willing spirit, and a steadfast will are then given by the Holy Spirit.)*

13 Then will I teach transgressors Your ways; and sinners shall be converted unto You. *(Before Repentance, David was in no condition to proclaim God's truth to "transgressors," because he was a transgressor himself.*

Upon true Repentance, David was now ready to teach and to preach, and the Holy Spirit attested to that.)

14 Deliver me from blood guiltiness, O God, Thou God of my salvation: and my tongue shall sing aloud of Your righteousness. *(This refers to the terrible sin of having Uriah, the husband of Bath-sheba, killed [II Sam. 11:14-21].*

Only the consciously pardoned sinner can "sing aloud" of God's Righteousness. Unpardoned men can speak of His Mercy, but their thoughts about it are unholy thoughts.)

15 O LORD, open Thou my lips; and my mouth shall show forth Your praise. *(Proper praise to the Lord cannot go forth as long as there is unconfessed sin. This is the reason for such little praise in most Churches, and far too often the praise which actually is offered is hollow. True praise can only come from a true heart!)*

16 For You desire not Sacrifice; else would I give it: You delight not in Burnt Offering. *(No penance, sacraments, or costly gifts of Churches or men, regarding expiation of past sins, are desired or accepted by God. Only Faith and trust in Christ and what He has done for us at the Cross can be accepted by the Lord.*

Unfortunately, the world tries to create a new god, while the Church tries to create another sacrifice. There is only one Sacrifice for sin [Heb. 10:12].)

17 The sacrifices of God are a broken spirit: a broken and a contrite heart, O God, You will not despise. *(True Repentance will always include a "broken spirit" and a "broken and contrite heart." Such alone will accept Christ and what Christ has done at the Cross. God will accept nothing less.)*

18 Do good in Your good pleasure unto Zion: build Thou the walls of Jerusalem.

(Verses 18-19 are not, as some think, a meaningless addition to the Psalm by some later writer. They both belong to the structure and prophetic scope of the Psalm.

David's sin, confession, and Restoration illustrate this future chapter in Israel's history. With their idolatry [spiritual adultery] and murder forgiven, they will go forth as messengers of the Gospel to win other nations to wholehearted faith and service in and for Christ.

Upon Israel's Repentance, the Lord will once again "build Thou the walls of Jerusalem.")

19 Then shall You be pleased with the sacrifices of righteousness, with Burnt Offering and Whole Burnt Offering: then shall they offer bullocks upon Your Altar. *(The sacrificial program under the old system was lawful, because it pointed to the coming Redeemer. Since Christ and the Cross, they are no longer necessary, and for all the obvious reasons. Why the symbol when the substance is available?*

During the Millennial Reign, the sacrificial system will be restored, but only as a memorial of what Christ has done at the Cross [Ezek., Chpts. 40-48].)

PSALM 52

A PSALM OF DAVID:
THE DOOM OF THE WICKED

WHY boastest thou yourself in mischief, O mighty man? the goodness of God endures continually. *(This Psalm was written by David at the time when Doeg the Edomite caused David much harm.*

Even though the Psalm concerns itself with David, even more so it concerns itself with the Antichrist, who will declare war with Israel at the midpoint of the Great Tribulation; therefore, David is a Type of Christ in this Psalm, and Doeg is a type of the Antichrist.

The Holy Spirit uses this occasion to portray not only that which had happened, but also that which will come in the distant future during the Great Tribulation [Mat. 24:21].)

2 The tongue devises mischief; like a sharp razor, working deceitfully. *(There are few people in the Bible who were more treacherous or evil than Doeg the Edomite. He falsely accused the High Priest and his family, who were true to David, which resulted in them losing their lives.*

During the latter half of the Great Tribulation, the Antichrist will totally fulfill this Passage. Daniel said, "He shall speak great words

against the Most High" [Dan. 7:25].

James addressed the tongue, saying, "It is full of deadly poison" [James 3:8]. Only the Holy Spirit can tame the tongue.)

3 You love evil more than good; and lying rather than to speak righteousness. Selah. (This fits Doeg, and it fits the Antichrist.)

4 You love all devouring words, O thou deceitful tongue. (Doeg illustrates the Antichrist. He plotted the destruction of David; he loved evil rather than good; he falsely accused the High Priest, Ahimelech; and he rejoiced at Saul's murderous command authorizing him to destroy Ahimelech's entire family plus many other Priests [I Sam. 22:9-23].)

5 God shall likewise destroy you for ever, He shall take you away, and pluck you out of your dwelling place, and root you out of the land of the living. Selah. (This speaks of both Doeg and the Antichrist, of which Doeg was a type.)

6 The righteous also shall see, and fear, and shall laugh at him (these words are but an indication of the laughter of Israel concerning the Antichrist, when he is destroyed by the Lord Jesus Christ at the Lord's Second Coming; Israel is called here "the righteous," and so they will be when they accept the Lord Jesus Christ as their Saviour at His Second Advent):

7 Lo, this is the man who made not God his strength; but trusted in the abundance of his riches, and strengthened himself in his wickedness. (No doubt, Saul made Doeg rich; however, the gold and silver given to him by Saul could in no way protect him in his "wickedness."

Likewise, the Antichrist will have great riches [Dan. 11:43]. However, those who trust in "riches" instead of trusting in "God" will ultimately fail.)

8 But I am like a green olive tree in the House of God: I trust in the mercy of God for ever and ever. (As Verses 8 and 9 portray David at that particular time, they even more portray the Messiah in the coming Day. Jesus Christ perfectly and eternally trusts. He is the "green olive tree.")

9 I will praise You for ever, because You have done it: and I will wait on Your Name; for it is good before Your saints. (David praises the Name of the Lord for his victory over the efforts of Satan to destroy him.

In its fuller meaning, it pertains to the Messiah as He praises God in the execution of His Wrath upon the Antichrist. It is this Divine action which is pointed to in the word "it.")

PSALM 53

A PSALM OF DAVID:
THE FOOLISHNESS OF MAN

THE fool has said in his heart, There is no God, Corrupt are they, and have done abominable iniquity: there is none who does good. (This Psalm is very similar to Psalm 14; however, even though similar, still, they are different.

For instance, in Psalm 14 the attention of the Reader is directed to the suffering of the Messiah and His servants and, therefore, is private.

The Fifty-third Psalm is given respecting the judgment of the oppressor [the Antichrist] and the deliverance of the oppressed; consequently, it is for public use.

The "fool" who is spoken of here actually refers to the Antichrist. He is a fool because he says, "There is no God." Despite all the "good" that he will promise the world, there will be no "good" that is done, but rather evil.)

2 God looked down from Heaven upon the children of men, to see if there were any who did understand, that did seek God. (This refers to the Great Tribulation Period and will signal the rise of the Antichrist. At this time, God will pour out tremendous plagues and judgments on this planet; however, He will search planet Earth to see if such can be avoided, being true to His nature as a God of Mercy. Regrettably, He will find none at all who will cry out after God; all will in fact refuse to repent [Rev. 9:20-21].)

3 Every one of them is gone back: they are altogether become filthy; there is none who does good, no, not one. (Paul quoted this Passage in Romans 3:10-18. Going to the bottom line, all who follow the Antichrist will be "filthy," with none doing "good.")

4 Have the workers of iniquity no knowledge? who eat up My people as they eat bread: they have not called upon God. (These "workers of iniquity" included those who followed Saul. They attempted, at Saul's command, to kill David. David "called upon God"; they did not.

In a greater way, it refers to the followers of the Antichrist, who have "no knowledge of God." They are all "workers of iniquity" [Dan. 8:24].)

5 There were they in great fear, where no fear was: for God has scattered the bones of him who encamps against you (against Israel): you have put them to shame, because God has despised them. (This Verse proclaims the destruction of the Antichrist. When the power of

God explodes against the "man of sin," the Antichrist will then be "in great fear." The statement, "where no fear was," refers to the Antichrist thinking that God will not take action against him, but now he sees that God has come on the scene and will completely destroy him.

This Verse and the last Verse point to the place and predict the time of the destruction of this fool and his followers. His folly is described in II Thessalonians 2:4, as well as in Verse 1 of this Psalm.

The "scattering of the bones" refers to the conclusion of the Battle of Armageddon, when Israel will spend some seven months burying the dead [Ezek. 39:11-12].

The "shame" of the defeat of the Antichrist and his followers will be obvious to the whole world, "because God has despised them.")

6 Oh that the salvation of Israel were come out of Zion! When God brings back the captivity of His people, Jacob shall rejoice, and Israel shall be glad. (This will be fulfilled at the Second Advent of Christ. At long last, the "captivity" of Israel will be ended. Then "Jacob shall rejoice, and Israel shall be glad" [Zech. 14:20-21].)

PSALM 54

A PSALM OF DAVID:
A CRY FOR HELP

SAVE me, O God, by Your Name, and judge me by Your strength. (This is a Psalm of David, which was written when the Ziphites intended to betray him to Saul [I Sam., Chpt. 23]. David is a Type of Christ. He delivered certain people, but yet they betrayed him; likewise, Christ has delivered the world, and yet they betray Him.

In either case, David did not attempt to avenge himself [Rom. 12:19]. He knew that vengeance belongs to God, and that the trusting servant, when tried, does not take matters into his own hands, but relies on his Master to rescue him.)

2 Hear my prayer, O God; give ear to the words of my mouth. (The answer to any problem that any Believer may have is to "take it to the Lord in prayer.")

3 For strangers are risen up against me, and oppressors seek after my soul: they have not set God before them. Selah. (The "strangers" were the men of Keilah, and the "oppressors" were Saul and his henchmen. Why would they seek David's destruction? They did so because "they have not set God before them.")

When it comes to God, men cannot be neutral. They are either opposed to Him or in favor of Him.

As this spoke of David, it also spoke of the Greater Son of David!)

4 Behold, God is my helper: the LORD is with them who uphold my soul. (This means that the few who did seek to help David would be immeasurably blessed by "the Lord.")

5 He shall reward evil unto my enemies: cut them off in Your truth. (This ultimately happened exactly as David prayed. His "enemies" were ultimately "cut off." The reason is obvious. It was because of "Thy Truth." Men should find out what "God's Truth" is and follow it. His "Truth" is His Word.)

6 I will freely sacrifice unto You: I will praise Your Name, O LORD, for it is good. (This "Sacrifice" was offered in faith; likewise, "praise" was also offered in faith. Despite the difficulties and circumstances, David knew that God would ultimately deliver him.)

7 For He has delivered me out of all trouble: and my eye has seen His desire upon my enemies. (Most probably this was written by faith. He called those things that were not as though they were — and that day of victory ultimately came!

The setting of this Psalm is aptly described; however, prophetically, it concerns the Messiah and the minority of the Jews who will, in the last days, believe on Him — possibly even the 144,000.

Jesus asked for a just punishment upon their enemies. Being Himself sinless as Man and righteous as God, He can demand a fitting judgment. He claims a just sentence upon these convicted transgressors.)

PSALM 55

A PSALM OF DAVID:
BETRAYAL

GIVE ear to my prayer, O God; and hide not Yourself from my supplication. (This Psalm was written by David during the time when his son, Absalom, and his most trusted advisor, Ahithophel, rebelled against him by seeking to take his throne and thereby turn the hearts of Israel against him. It was no doubt the most awful time in David's life.

It also portrays the Lord Jesus Christ, Who was betrayed by His personal Disciple and chosen Apostle, Judas.

Even though this Psalm concerns David's time, still, it more so concerns the hatred and treachery which the Messiah suffered Personally in the days of His flesh, and which He now suffers and will yet suffer in sympathy with His people [Col. 1:24].

How wonderful it is to be permitted to hear Christ speaking to His Father! The Gospels record the words and acts of Christ; the Psalms reveal His prayers and thoughts.)

2 **Attend unto me, and hear me: I mourn in my complaint, and make a noise** (*the cry of the Messiah to God was because of the attitude of Israel against Him; He would come unto His Own, and His Own would receive Him not [Jn. 1:11]*);

3 **Because of the voice of the enemy, because of the oppression of the wicked: for they cast iniquity upon me, and in wrath they hate me.** (*While this concerns David and those who would take his throne and his life, still, in a greater way, it concerns Israel, who hated Christ. Why did they hate Him? They did so because their deeds were evil.*

Absalom and Ahithophel felt justified in their actions. David said, "They cast iniquity upon me." They felt that because of David's sin with Bath-sheba and against Uriah that they not only could, but in fact should, take his throne.

In the first place, David was, in God's great Mercy and Forgiveness, the same after his sin as he had been before; however, self-righteousness can never see this. In their minds, David had forfeited his crown and his place, so they took matters into their own hands. They did not recognize God's Mercy, Grace, or Love. They only saw their own jaded, selfish ambition.

Men would do well to heed the words of this Psalm. If they, as Absalom and Ahithophel, deny forgiveness to David, likewise, it will be denied to them.

As stated, in its greater fulfillment, this Psalm speaks of Christ in His Earthly Ministry. David had sinned, so his enemies felt they had cause against him. Jesus never sinned, so His enemies would manufacture deceit against Him.)

4 **My heart is sore pained within me: and the terrors of death are fallen upon me.** (*David felt this way at this lowest of times. In the greater fulfillment by the Son of David, He would in no way be at fault, and yet He would take all the fault unto Himself, suffering the "terrors of death" as though he had sinned.)*

5 **Fearfulness and trembling are come upon me, and horror has overwhelmed me.** (*To fuel this "fearfulness and trembling" was the realization that he had sinned, and terribly so! True, God had put away his sin, but yet the nagging fear was there that perhaps God would allow Absalom and Ahithophel to have their way.*

Prophetically, Christ would enter into the same agony because He would enter into our place and position. That's the reason that He Alone can be the True Intercessor. Only One Who had never sinned could fill this place, and Christ Alone fits this description.)

6 **And I said, Oh that I had wings like a dove! for then would I fly away, and be at rest.** (*Historically, David is symbolized by this dove, but prophetically, it means the Messiah. The unnatural rebellion of Absalom and the treachery of Ahithophel foreshadow the rebellion of Israel and the betrayal of Judas.)*

7 **Lo, then would I wander far off, and remain in the wilderness. Selah.** (*There seemed to be no answer to David's dilemma.)*

8 **I would hasten my escape from the windy storm and tempest.** (*He "would," but he couldn't! The only escape is in Christ!)*

9 **Destroy, O LORD, and divide their tongues: for I have seen violence and strife in the city.** (*David prays that the excellent advice of Ahithophel will be "divided." This prayer was answered [II Sam. 15:31].)*

10 **Day and night they go about it upon the walls thereof; mischief also and sorrow are in the midst of it.** (*This refers to the leaders of the plot to overthrow David and put Absalom on the throne.)*

11 **Wickedness is in the midst thereof: deceit and guile depart not from her streets.** (*"Deceit" is Satan's greatest weapon. His ambition is to make people believe that what is of God, isn't, and that what is not of God, is. He is amazingly successful.)*

12 **For it was not an enemy who reproached me; then I could have borne it: neither was it he who hated me who did magnify himself against me; then I would have hid myself from him** (*David is speaking here of the betrayal of Ahithophel; in a greater fulfillment, it speaks of the betrayal of the Messiah by Judas; so, when one reads the words of this Twelfth Verse, one is actually reading the thoughts of Christ concerning Judas):*

13 **But it was you, a man my equal, my guide, and my acquaintance.** (*The words, "equal," "guide," and "acquaintance," as applied to Judas, may be translated "My chosen," for Jesus elected him an Apostle, "My fellow tribesman," as Judas was the only member of the Twelve,*

who, like the Lord, was of the Tribe of Judah.)

14 We took sweet counsel together, and walked unto the House of God in company. *(David is speaking of the times that he went into the Tabernacle to worship God with Ahithophel. For three and a half years, Judas walked with Jesus. This tells us that association, environment, and participation do not save one. Salvation must come from the heart, and Ahithophel had not fully given his heart to David. Judas, above all, had not fully given his heart to Christ.)*

15 Let death seize upon them, and let them go down quick into Hell: for wickedness is in their dwellings, and among them. *(This is exactly what happened! David could only say this by the Spirit of God. Thus, in reality, it is the Greater Son of David Who utters these words. In His perfection, He is qualified to do so, and He Alone!)*

16 As for me, I will call upon God; and the LORD shall save me. *(There is no other solution! And yet most of the modern Church opts for humanistic psychology.)*

17 Evening, and morning, and at noon, will I pray, and cry aloud: and He shall hear my voice. *(Three times a day David prays.)*

18 He has delivered my soul in peace from the battle that was against me: for there were many with me. *(The Lord assures David that He will "deliver his soul." He has "peace" that the victory will be his. The "many" to whom David refers are the Host who are with God. As well, such is available to every true Believer, and for all time.)*

19 God shall hear, and afflict them, even He Who abides of old. Selah. Because they have no changes, therefore they fear not God. *(Unregenerate man, in his stubbornness, will not change. In fact, he cannot change, unless he turns solely to the Lord. Most won't do that, because they have no fear of God.)*

20 He has put forth his hands against such as be at peace with him: he has broken his covenant. *(Whenever Ahithophel rebelled against David, and thereby the Lord, he actually broke a spiritual Covenant that he had made to support David and the Work of God. Judas did the same thing.)*

21 The words of his mouth were smoother than butter, but war was in his heart: his words were softer than oil, yet were they drawn swords. *(This refers to both Ahithophel and Judas, and even more so to the Antichrist.)*

22 Cast your burden upon the LORD, and He shall sustain you: He shall never suffer the righteous to be moved. *(This should be a tremendous encouragement to all true Believers. Take your burden to the Lord and leave it there!)*

23 But You, O God, shall bring them down into the pit of destruction: bloody and deceitful men shall not live out half their days; but I will trust in You. *(Be it ever remembered that God's Way will ultimately win out. Those who trusted Ahithophel went "down into the pit of destruction." Those who trusted Judas did likewise. Those who trust the Antichrist, in that coming day, will also be destroyed; however, those who put their trust in the Lord will ever gain the victory.)*

PSALM 56

A PSALM OF DAVID:
PRAYER FOR DELIVERANCE

BE merciful unto me, O God, for man would swallow me up; he fighting daily oppresses me. *(This Psalm was written by David when Saul was trying to kill him, and he joined the Philistines in Gath [I Sam., Chpts. 21, 27]. As expressed here, David's terrible problem, with Saul trying to kill him, was a "daily" battle.)*

2 My enemies would daily swallow me up: for they be many who fight against me, O Thou Most High. *(David's experiences while far from his Father's house and in exile among those who hated him occasioned this Psalm. Nevertheless, he was inspired to write it, but its full theme is the experience of the Messiah when living in this world among sinners, and far from the glory which He had with the Father before the world was. Actually, Christ is the Speaker; His are the petitions; and His are the expressions of faith and confidence.)*

3 What time I am afraid, I will trust in You. *(David did not deny the presence of fear; however, through him the Holy Spirit tells us here the antidote for fear, and all other problems, for that matter. "I will trust in You.")*

4 In God I will praise His Word, in God I have put my trust; I will not fear what flesh can do unto me. *(Confidence in man and his word never gives occasion for praise. Confidence in God and His Word gives constant occasion for praise.)*

5 Every day they wrest my words: all their thoughts are against me for evil. *(This describes the constant pursuits and plots against David by Saul and his men. As well, and even more so, this pertains to the Scribes and Pharisees,*

who conducted themselves in the same manner against Christ.)

6 They gather themselves together, they hide themselves, they mark my steps, when they wait for my soul. *(The Scribes and Pharisees pounced on every Word Jesus said, attempting to trap Him in His speech; incidentally, they were never able to do so.)*

7 Shall they escape by iniquity? in Your anger cast down the people, O God. *(This prayer sets itself against those who would set themselves against God.)*

8 You tell my wanderings: put Thou my tears into Your bottle: are they not in Your book? *(The Holy Spirit through David is saying that despite David's "wanderings" and his attempts to escape from Saul, God knew at all times exactly where he was. The "tears in the bottle" proclaim an ancient custom that spoke of tremendous pathos and pain. Whenever the Believer sets out to carry out the Will of God for his life, Satan will do all he can to oppose these efforts. And the Lord allows the Evil One certain latitude in order that we may learn to have Faith and to place our trust exclusively in the Word of God.)*

9 When I cry unto You, then shall my enemies turn back: this I know; for God is for me. *(The phrase, "this I know," is a most precious declaration of the Perfect Faith of God's Beloved Son.)*

10 In God will I praise His Word: in the LORD will I praise His Word. *(God's Word is the only body of revealed Truth in the world today, and in fact ever has been; consequently, every Christian should make it his life's work to learn the "Word."*

The double statement in this Verse is not an oversight. It was done by the Holy Spirit in order for us to understand the significance that God places on His Word.)

11 In God have I put my trust: I will not be afraid what man can do unto me. *(Once again, the Holy Spirit is telling us that in order to gain the strength and confidence we must have in life's journey, we must "put our trust in God." Then the fear of man leaves.)*

12 Your vows are upon me, O God: I will render praises unto You. *(This is not God making vows, but David vowing to be God's servant, to give his whole life to Him, and to render praises for His benefits.)*

13 For You have delivered my soul from death: will not You deliver my feet from falling, that I may walk before God in the light of

the living? *(The sense of this Verse is that God will surely deliver the Messiah's soul out of the death world and His Body out of the grave. The word "falling" has, in the Hebrew Text, no moral significance. It means a thrusting down. Man proposed to thrust Christ's dishonored Body down into the Earth. God placed It in an honored tomb instead, raised It in glory, and caused Him to walk in Resurrection Life.*

In His Incarnation, He was an "ear" [perfect obedience]; in Resurrection, He was a "foot" [perfect walk], for His enemies will be made a footstool for His Feet and, in that day of universal dominion, His feet shall stand upon the Mount of Olives [Zech., Chpt. 14].)

PSALM 57

A PSALM OF DAVID:
GOD DELIVERS DAVID FROM KING SAUL

BE merciful unto me, O God, be merciful unto me: for my soul trusts in You: yea, in the shadow of Your wings will I make my refuge, until these calamities be overpast. *(This was probably written by David when he was being chased by Saul, and was in the cave of Engedi. It was one of the most critical times in David's life. The sweet singer of Israel could not trust in any man to save him. If he was to be saved, the Lord Alone would have to do it; consequently, David's trust in the Lord is overwhelmingly obvious here. It most definitely must be a lesson to us.)*

2 I will cry unto God Most High; unto God Who performs all things for me. *(The words, "all things," are not in the original Hebrew Text; therefore, the Verse is a blank check. In other words, whatever is needed, God will do; however, we must keep our petitions in the scope of His Will.)*

3 He shall send from Heaven, and save me from the reproach of him who would swallow me up. Selah. God shall send forth His mercy and His truth. *(Even though this is a Psalm of David, even more so it is a Psalm of the Greater Son, the Lord Jesus Christ. This Verse proclaims Christ's descent into the realm of the dead. It also proclaims His glorious Resurrection from the grave.*

Actually, the entire Psalm is the language of the Messiah, with the exception of Verses 5 and 11, which are addressed to him by the Holy Spirit.)

4 My soul is among lions: and I lie even among them who are set on fire, even the sons of men, whose teeth are spears and arrows,

and their tongue a sharp sword. *(In His Earthly Ministry, our Lord was constantly beset by the opposition of demon spirits.*

The latter part of this Verse speaks of the hatred of man directed toward the Messiah. There was no distinction or difference in the vehemence of their hatred from the hatred of demons; actually, the hatred within the Scribes and Pharisees was placed there by demon spirits. In fact, Christ met with almost universal hatred.)

5 Be Thou exalted, O God, above the Heavens; let Your Glory be above all the Earth. *(In this Verse, the Holy Spirit addresses the Lord Jesus Christ, and does so as God. The imperative sense of the Hebrew verb employed here implies the certainty of the desired exaltation, and so marks the contrast with the sufferings described in Verse 4.)*

6 They have prepared a net for my steps; my soul is bowed down: they have dug a pit before me, into the midst whereof they are fallen themselves. Selah. *(As Saul and his henchmen hated David, likewise, the Scribes and Pharisees hated the Lord Jesus Christ.*

Every Christian should allow this Psalm to be a warning that if he moves his tongue against that which God has truly anointed, or lifts his hand against the same, it will ultimately destroy him.)

7 My heart is fixed, O God, my heart is fixed: I will sing and give praise. *(No matter what happened, David would not lose his song and, thereby, would not lose his praise for God. What a testimony!)*

8 Awake up, my glory; awake, psaltery and harp: I myself will awake early. *(David will "awake early" in order to have time with the Lord in communion and fellowship. At times, this was accompanied with the harp and him singing the Psalms.)*

9 I will praise You, O Lord, among the people: I will sing unto You among the nations. *(In the cave of Engedi, little did he realize how prophetic this statement was. These Psalms have been sung by untold millions from then until now, and in fact will ever be sung.)*

10 For Your mercy is great unto the Heavens, and Your truth unto the clouds. *(What would he sing? He would sing of God's "mercy" and His "truth." There could be nothing greater to sing about.)*

11 Be Thou exalted, O God, above the Heavens: let Your Glory be above all the Earth. *(Once again, and even in double measure, the Holy Spirit proclaims Jesus Christ as "God." One*

day His "Glory will be above all the Earth." In fact, this will be fulfilled in the coming Millennial Reign.)*

PSALM 58

A PSALM OF DAVID:
THE DEPRAVITY OF THE WICKED

DO you indeed speak righteousness O congregation? do you judge uprightly, O you sons of men? *(This Psalm speaks of the leaders of Israel during David's day aligning themselves with Saul, and trying to destroy David, who was God's anointed.*

Likewise, the Psalm characterizes the leaders of Israel during Christ's Earthly sojourn. They are "the wicked" of Verses 3 and 4.

The Psalm also speaks of the Antichrist coming against Israel in the last half of the Great Tribulation, attempting to destroy her.)

2 Yea, in heart you work wickedness; you weigh the violence of your hands in the Earth. *(The hearts of those under Saul who opposed David were "wicked." They lived by "violence." The same could be said even more so about the oppressors of the Messiah. As well, it speaks of the "evil hearts" of the Antichrist and his followers.)*

3 The wicked are estranged from the womb: they go astray as soon as they be born, speaking lies. *(In general, this speaks of the total depravity of man. More particularly, it speaks of the Antichrist and his followers.)*

4 Their poison is like the poison of a serpent: they are like the deaf adder that stops her ear *(while this speaks of all who would oppose Christ, prophetically, it applies to the Antichrist; he will poison the world against Israel by "speaking lies");*

5 Which will not hearken to the voice of charmers, charming never so wisely. *(The "adder" is said to be "deaf," and consequently very difficult to charm. The idea is, in the coming Great Tribulation, all other forms of evil must give way to the Antichrist. He will not be deterred from his path.)*

6 Break their teeth, O God, in their mouth: break out the great teeth of the young lions, O LORD. *(This speaks of those who opposed David and who opposed Christ. As well, it speaks of those who will oppose Israel at the Battle of Armageddon.)*

7 Let them melt away as waters which run continually: when He bends his bow to shoot his arrows, let them be as cut in pieces *(this*

was fulfilled concerning David and Christ; prophetically, it will be fulfilled at the Battle of Armageddon, when the Antichrist will be defeated by the coming of the Lord.)

8 As a snail which melts, let every one of them pass away: like the untimely birth of a woman, that they may not see the sun. *(In short, everyone who opposes Christ will ultimately "pass away.")*

9 Before your pots can feel the thorns, He shall take them away as with a whirlwind, both living, and in His wrath. *(Prophetically, this speaks of the Antichrist and his followers being completely destroyed by the Wrath of God.)*

10 The righteous *(Israel)* shall rejoice when he sees the vengeance: he *(Israel)* shall wash his feet in the blood of the wicked *(speaks of the defeat of the Antichrist at the Battle of Armageddon [Ezek., Chpts. 38-39]).*

11 So that a man shall say, Verily there is a reward for the righteous: verily He is a God Who judges in the Earth. *(Regarding those who trust the Lord, even as David, ultimately they will prevail. Prophetically, it speaks of the Lord judging the Earth in the realm of defeating the Antichrist and all who follow him.)*

PSALM 59

A PSALM OF DAVID:
A PRAYER FOR PROTECTION
AND PUNISHMENT

DELIVER me from my enemies, O my God: defend me from them who rise up against me. *(The occasion of this Psalm is found in I Sam., Chpt. 19, when Saul tried to apprehend David in order to kill him.*

This Psalm is very similar to the previous Psalm, portraying David being delivered from the murderous hatred of his encircling enemies. It also typifies the deliverance of the Messiah from the acute hatred of the religious leaders of Israel, as they tried to kill Him before His time in order to prevent Calvary.

It also typifies the deliverance of Israel from the Antichrist during the latter half of the Great Tribulation, and at the Battle of Armageddon.)

2 Deliver me from the workers of iniquity, and save me from bloody men.

3 For, lo, they lie in wait for my soul: the mighty are gathered against me; not for my transgression, nor for my sin, O LORD. *(Saul is attempting to kill David, not because of any "transgression" or "sin" against Saul, but because*

of Saul's great evil. It does not mean that David had never sinned; it simply means that Saul's anger with him was not because of any sin or transgression against him on David's part.

As well, Israel hated Christ, not because of any "transgression" or "sin" on His part, but because of their own "transgression and sin.")

4 They run and prepare themselves without my fault: awake to help me, and behold. *(It seemed to David that the Lord was asleep; but, of course, that was incorrect. The Lord was watching over David minutely, even as He watches over every single one of His children.)*

5 You therefore, O LORD God of Hosts, the God of Israel, awake to visit all the heathen: be not merciful to any wicked transgressors. Selah. *(The "heathen" refer to the nations which will surround Jerusalem during the Battle of Armageddon. This Prophecy relates to the last hours of that time. Verses 13 and 16 point to this fact.*

The believing remnant of Israel is pictured as shut up in Jerusalem by the nations and by certain wicked transgressors. The Messiah, in Spirit, takes His place in their midst, cheers them with the assurance of deliverance, and prays for the destruction of their besiegers. Judgment, consequently, in the keynote of this Psalm.)

6 They return at evening: they make a noise like a dog, and go round about the city. *(This refers to the Antichrist and his armies attempting to take Jerusalem. In fact, half of the city will fall to the Antichrist, which will take place immediately before the Second Coming [Zech. 14:2-3].)*

7 Behold, they belch out with their mouth: swords are in their lips: for who, say they, does hear? *(At this time, Israel will cry to God for deliverance, because they realize that now the Messiah is their only hope. The Antichrist will taunt their appeal!)*

8 But You, O LORD, shall laugh at them; You shall have all the heathen in derision. *(The Lord's disdain for the Antichrist is referred to with the brief comment, "laugh at them.")*

9 Because of his strength will I wait upon You: for God is my defence. *(As David says these words, so will Israel at that coming time.)*

10 The God of my mercy shall prevent me: God shall let me see my desire upon my enemies. *(This was fulfilled in David's life. It will have a greater fulfillment regarding Israel in the Last Days. At the time of this writing [2004], most of the world could be constituted as an enemy of Israel. No matter! Israel will ultimately prevail, because she will cry to the*

Lord, and He will come to her rescue. It is the Second Coming!)

11 Slay them not, lest my people forget: scatter them by Your power: and bring them down, O LORD our shield. (In other words, David's prayer is that the Lord will defeat the enemy in such a fashion that all will know that it is the Lord Who has done such. To be sure, this is exactly what will happen at the Battle of Armageddon.)

12 For the sin of their mouth and the words of their lips let them even be taken in their pride: and for cursing and lying which they speak. (It should be noticed that the sin of all three, Saul, the religious leaders of Israel, and the Antichrist, is "pride.")

13 Consume them in wrath, consume them, that they may not be: and let them know that God rules in Jacob unto the ends of the Earth. Selah. (God doesn't rule in "Jacob" presently; however, that is going to change in the not-too-distant future. As an aside, it doesn't say that God rules in Muhammad, etc.)

14 And at evening let them return; and let them make a noise like a dog, and go round about the city. (This Verse is very similar to Verse 6.)

15 Let them wander up and down for meat, and grudge if they be not satisfied. (This Verse speaks of the near victory by the Antichrist over Jerusalem. Even though some two-thirds of Israel will have already been destroyed [Zech. 13:8], still, the Antichrist will "grudge" and "be not satisfied," until all Israel is destroyed. He will be sorely disappointed.)

16 But I will sing of Your power; yea, I will sing aloud of Your mercy in the morning: for You have been my defence and refuge in the day of my trouble. (Prophetically, this speaks of the "Day of Jacob's Trouble" [Jer. 30:7]. Despite the power of the Antichrist, the "power" of the Lord will be much greater. Therefore, David, as well as the Messiah, will sing of such.)

17 Unto You, O my strength, will I sing: for God is my defence, and the God of my mercy. (This is a beautiful Passage, signifying God's "strength" and "defense," which He gives not only to Israel, but to all who love Him and proclaim His Name.)

PSALM 60

A PSALM OF DAVID:
A PRAYER FOR ISRAEL'S DELIVERANCE

O God, You have cast us off, You have scattered us, You have been displeased; O turn Yourself to us again. (This Psalm was written by David when he fought the enemy in a place called "Zobah," which is in Mesopotamia [I Chron. 18:1-5]. While David fought up north, Joab was fighting in the south, and it took him some six months to defeat the enemy. David cries to the Lord because of these problems.)

2 You have made the Earth to tremble; You have broken it: heal the breaches thereof; for it shakes. (The greater fulfillment of this prayer and prophecy will be during the time of Jacob's Trouble, and his deliverance out of it. During the Great Tribulation, the Earth will literally "tremble.")

3 You have showed Your people hard things: You have made us to drink the wine of astonishment. (Regarding David, he was astonished that it took Joab so long to win the victory over the Edomites; however, the greater fulfillment pertains to Israel, who will be reduced to "astonishment" when the Antichrist breaks his seven-year covenant with them, declares war, and threatens their very existence.)

4 You have given a banner to them who fear You, that it may be displayed because of the truth. Selah. (Prophetically, this speaks of the Battle of Armageddon, when the Messiah will be Israel's Jehovah-Nissi [the Lord our Banner]. Israel's only hope in this Battle will be this "banner." Little by little, she will draw around this "banner," and so should God's servants in all times and in all circumstances [Ex. 17:8-16].)

5 That Your beloved may be delivered; save with Your right hand, and hear me. (To be sure, the Lord will hear Israel, and she will be delivered from the Antichrist.)

6 God has spoken in His holiness; I will rejoice, I will divide Shechem, and mete out the valley of Succoth.

7 Gilead is Mine, and Manasseh is Mine; Ephraim also is the strength of My head; Judah is My lawgiver (these Passages dogmatically proclaim the fact that God has drawn the boundaries for Israel; this means that this area doesn't belong to the Arabs, or anyone else);

8 Moab is My washpot; over Edom will I cast out My shoe: Philistia, triumph thou because of Me. ("Moab" and "Edom" now make up modern Jordan. The Philistines have long since ceased to exist, with the Palestinians, so-called, occupying the Gaza strip, which is a small part of the area that the Philistines once occupied.

The Lord is saying here that the enemies of

Israel will all be defeated, and will be forced to recognize Israel's place and position, all because of the Lord Jesus Christ.

David was having problems with these areas, and the Lord is merely telling him that the day is coming when these problems would be ended, and forever.)

9 Who will bring Me into the strong city? who will lead Me into Edom? *(This refers to the Antichrist breaking his covenant with Israel at the midpoint of the Great Tribulation, and actually declaring war on her. Israel will then flee to "the strong city," which is located in ancient "Edom," and which corresponds to the present day Petra.)*

10 Will not You, O God, which had cast us off? and You, O God, which did not go out with our armies? *(The Tenth Verse actually answers the questions of Verse 9. Because of Israel's backsliding, God has "cast them off"; however, at this prophetical time, the situation is about to change.)*

11 Give us the help from trouble: for vain is the help of man. *(The "trouble" referred to here is the seven-year Great Tribulation, which Jesus said would be the worst ever [Mat. 24:21]. At that time, it seems that no nation in the world will come to the help of Israel. However, in a sense, this is the Plan of God. With no one to help her, Israel will then cry out to God.)*

12 Through God we shall do valiantly: for He it is Who shall tread down our enemies. *(This speaks of the Lord coming to Israel's rescue during the Battle of Armageddon [Rev., Chpt. 19] in order to "tread down our enemies." He Alone can do such! As well, both Verses 11 and 12 apply to, and should be heeded by, every Believer. Truly, God is our refuge, and He Alone can overcome the powers of darkness; in fact, He already has at Calvary's Cross [Col. 2:14-15].)*

PSALM 61

A PSALM OF DAVID:
A HYMN OF TRUST AND CONFIDENCE

HEAR My cry, O God; attend unto My prayer. *(The words are David's, but the Speaker is actually the Messiah. The doctrine of this and similar Psalms is the perfection of the Faith of the Messiah. As Man, He had to undergo every form of hatred, affliction, and adversity. The sharper these became, the more He trusted. So, His moral glory as the Servant of Jehovah shines through all. He voluntarily took upon Himself*

this position of dependence and suffering in union with and on behalf of His People.)

2 From the end of the Earth will I cry unto You, when My heart is overwhelmed: lead Me to the rock that is higher than I. *(The petitions of the Messiah are evident in the four Gospels, as He, over and over again, resorts to a private place of prayer [Mat. 14:23; 26:36; Mk. 6:46; Lk. 9:28; Jn., Chpt. 17]. The "Rock" was His Father [Deut. 32:4, 15, 18, 31; I Sam. 2:2]. Irrespective of how high our problems may be, "the Rock is higher.")*

3 For You have been a shelter for Me, and a strong tower from the enemy. *(The "Shelter" for the Messiah was God the Father. He must be our "Shelter" as well. As dependent Man, He prayed to be led to a Rock Shelter that was Divine; as sinless Man, He conceived of no higher joy than to perpetually dwell in the presence of God.)*

4 I will abide in Your tabernacle for ever: I will trust in the covert of Your wings. Selah. *(The instigation of the Holy Spirit is to pull the Believer into total "trust" in God. This refers to "trust" for every facet and walk of life.)*

5 For You, O God, have heard My vows: You have given Me the heritage of those who fear Your Name. *(David had made "vows" unto the Lord. He failed in some of these vows; however, the Greater Son of David did not fail in any of His "vows." He said, "I will always do those things that please Him" [Jn. 8:29].*

He has not received His "heritage" as of yet. It will be forthcoming shortly at the Rapture of the Church, and when Israel is gathered to Him at the beginning of the Kingdom Age.)

6 You will prolong the King's life: and His years as many generations. *(David died at 70 years of age; however, his life was "prolonged" through the life of the Messiah, that is, in fact, unending.)*

7 He shall abide before God for ever: O prepare mercy and truth, which may preserve Him. *(Today, Christ is seated by the right hand of the Father and will "abide before God forever.")*

8 So will I sing praise unto Your Name for ever, that I may daily perform my vows. *(David was the first one of whom we know who actually and continually sang praises "unto Your Name forever." If he did that under the Old Covenant of Law, how could we do less under the New Covenant of Grace?*

The statement, "daily perform my vows," actually means to trust God at all times.)

PSALM 62

A PSALM OF DAVID:
A PSALM OF LONGING AND TRUST

TRULY My soul waits upon God: from Him comes My salvation. *(As the last Psalm, while David says the words, the actual Speaker is the Messiah.)*

2 He only is My Rock and My Salvation; He is My defence; I shall not be greatly moved. *(Man's hatred of the Messiah occupies the first four Verses of the Psalm. Man's hatred of God's People occupies the following six. If we take up our own "defense," we will fail. If He is our "defense," we cannot fail.)*

3 How long will you imagine mischief against a man? you shall be slain all of you: as a bowing wall shall you be, and as a tottering fence. *(Matthew 16:27 and Acts 17:31 make it evident that the Messiah is the Man of Verse 3 and the God of Verse 12. The religious leaders of Israel looked at Jesus as One so feeble that they could easily dispense with Him. They hungered for His Life, and their hearts were enflamed with the very hatred of Hell. These were the men who shouted, "Crucify Him! Crucify Him!".*

The Prophecy, "you shall be slain all of you," happened exactly as predicted. In A.D. 70, Rome completely destroyed Jerusalem and the Temple. Over one million Jews died in that carnage, with other hundreds of thousands sold as slaves.)

4 They only consult to cast Him down from His excellency: they delight in lies: they bless with their mouth, but they curse inwardly. Selah. *(The Scribes, Pharisees, and Sadducees were liars like their father, the Devil [Jn. 8:44-55]. It is impossible for the self-righteous to truly love God or those who truly follow the Lord.)*

5 My soul, wait thou only upon God; for my expectation is from him. *(When man has been disappointed enough by other men, he will then "wait only upon God." No "expectation" should be looked to from other men. The Lord Alone will provide.)*

6 He only is my rock and my salvation: He is my defence; I shall not be moved. *(David, as well as the Greater Son of David, once again uses the word "only" concerning his "Rock" and "defense." From this position, he says, "I shall not be moved.")*

7 In God is my salvation and my glory: the Rock of my strength, and my refuge, is in God. *(Over and over again in the Psalms, the Holy Spirit repeats these statements in one form or the other. It is done so for our benefit.)*

8 Trust in Him at all times; you people, pour out your heart before Him: God is a refuge for us. Selah.

9 Surely men of low degree are vanity, and men of high degree are a lie: to be laid in the balance, they are altogether lighter than vanity. *(The idea is, if we as Believers trust in men in any capacity, we will be disappointed. We must fully trust in the Lord.)*

10 Trust not in oppression, and become not vain in robbery: if riches increase, set not your heart upon them. *(Our hearts must at all times be on God and His Word, and never on the things of this world, no matter what they might be.)*

11 God has spoken once; twice have I heard this; that power belongs unto God. *(It is "not by human might, nor by human power, but by My Spirit, saith the Lord of Hosts" [Zech. 4:6].)*

12 Also unto You, O LORD, belongs mercy: for You render to every man according to his work. *(He blesses us according to our work, but He does not judge us because of failure, as He might, and because of His "Mercy.")*

PSALM 63

A PSALM OF DAVID:
THE PRAYER OF A THIRSTING SOUL

O God, You are my God; early will I seek You: my soul thirsts for You, my flesh longs for You in a dry and thirsty land, where no water is *(this Psalm was written by David while he was in the wilderness of Judah, fleeing from Saul; it was a dark time in his life.*

The statement, "early will I seek You," seems to have been a habit with David [Ps. 57:8-9]. The statement, "my soul thirsts for You," was also a statement often repeated by David [Ps. 42:1-2]. This gives us an insight into David's consecration. How many hearts really "thirst" for God?);

2 To see Your power and Your glory, so as I have seen You in the Sanctuary. *(The phrase, "a dry and thirsty land, where no water is," of Verse 1, pertains to the fact that David, while fleeing from Saul, did not have access to the Sanctuary. It was a spiritual dryness of which he spoke.)*

3 Because Your lovingkindness is better than life, my lips shall praise You. *(David could easily have blamed the Lord for his predicament, but he never resorted to such. He never*

allowed the present situation, no matter how dark it may have been, to steal his worship of God. What a lesson for us!)

4 Thus will I bless You while I live: I will lift up my hands in Your Name. *(The first ten Verses sing of the First Advent of David's Son and Lord. The Eleventh Verse speaks of His Second Advent [Rev., Chpt. 19]. In His First Advent, He found this world a wilderness, a dry and weary land, without one stream of moral refreshment, and His heart longed for the joys He had tasted from all eternity in His Father's bosom.*

But if He found this world to be a thirsty wilderness, yet He found God to be a satisfying Source of perfect joy and happiness.)

5 My soul shall be satisfied as with marrow and fatness; and my mouth shall praise You with joyful lips *(when you read these words of David, you are also reading the words of the Greater Son of David):*

6 When I remember You upon my bed, and meditate on You in the night watches *("meditation" on the Word of God [both day and night] will cure one of fear, stress, and, thereby, most sicknesses).*

7 Because You have been my help, therefore in the shadow of Your wings will I rejoice *(quite possibly, David had before him the Scroll of the 91st Psalm, which had been written by Moses about 500 years before [Ps. 91:1-4]).*

8 My soul follows hard after You: Your right hand upholds me. *(David's statement means that no matter what the situation, or where it leads, he will follow. Many Christians follow if it is profitable [or if they think it is]. Many, when facing difficult times, cease to follow.)*

9 But those who seek my soul, to destroy it, shall go into the lower parts of the Earth. *(David is speaking of Saul and those who would ally themselves with him. The Greater Son of David is speaking of the Scribes, Pharisees, and Sadducees. Those who rejected Him all died and went to Hell. It is the same now, and in fact always has been, for all who reject Him [Jn. 14:6].)*

10 They shall fall by the sword: they shall be a portion for foxes. *(Exactly as the Holy Spirit predicted, it was brought to pass. Saul "fell by the sword." In A.D. 70, all of Jerusalem "fell by the sword.")*

11 But the King shall rejoice in God; every one who swears by Him shall glory: but the mouth of them who speak lies shall be stopped. *(This speaks of David, and it came to pass exactly as stated; however, it speaks even in greater*

measure of the Greater Son of David and His Second Coming [Rev., Chpt. 19].)

PSALM 64

A PSALM OF DAVID:
PRAYER FOR PROTECTION

HEAR my voice, O God, in my prayer: preserve my life from fear of the enemy. *(The leaders of the Jews composed in private crafty questions for the Lord, so as to entangle Him in His teaching, and thus to be in a position to accuse Him either to the Sanhedrin or the Roman Government as a heretic or an insurgent, and consequently condemn Him to execution.)*

2 Hide me from the secret counsel of the wicked; from the insurrection of the workers of iniquity *(be it known that the greatest "iniquity" of all is found in the realm of religion. [Religion is anything that is man-devised; Salvation is that which is God-devised, and is found only in the Word of God.] Shockingly, "the wicked" were actually the Church of Jesus' day):*

3 Who whet their tongue like a sword, and bend their bows to shoot their arrows, even bitter words *(as is recorded in Mat., Chpt. 22 and Lk., Chpt. 11, these "wicked" religious leaders devised their entanglements, and then in public rudely and vehemently proposed their questions to Him. In this Psalm are found His comments about their conduct and His appeal to God about it):*

4 That they may shoot in secret at the perfect: suddenly do they shoot at Him, and fear not. *(Jesus Christ was "the Perfect." They had lost all "fear" of God. The terrible sin of not fearing God is the product of self-righteousness, which plagued the religious rulers of Israel and, sadly, plagues the majority of the modern Church.)*

5 They encourage themselves in an evil matter: they commune of laying snares privily: they say, Who shall see them? *(Encouraging themselves in their evil purpose, the Scribes and Pharisees suddenly sprang their questions upon Christ, secreting themselves under an assumption of moral earnestness and patriotism.)*

6 They search out iniquities; they accomplish a diligent search: both the inward thought of every one of them, and the heart, is deep. *("Iniquities" here mean "iniquitous questions" – questions which they hoped would involve Him with the Jewish or Roman Governments. They were so clever and crafty in their questions that they were sure, they thought, to accomplish the*

desired purpose.

Christ, Who read their thoughts and knew their hearts, gives in this Verse His judgment on both. He says that their hearts were deep, meaning deep with "iniquity.")

7 But God shall shoot at them with an arrow; suddenly shall they be wounded. *(With many arrows, they tried in vain to wound Him, but God shall without fail suddenly and fatally wound them with only one arrow, which is His Word. And He did!)*

8 So they shall make their own tongue to fall upon themselves: all who see them shall flee away. *(When they stand before God in the Judgment, the bitter slanders of their tongues shall rise in judgment against them and cause them to perish.)*

9 And all men shall fear, and shall declare the work of God; for they shall wisely consider of His doing. *(There will come an hour when the entirety of mankind will praise the Lord for all He has done, even judging the rebels.)*

10 The righteous shall be glad in the LORD, and shall trust in Him; and all the upright in heart shall glory. *(At the very time that this just judgment shall fall upon the enemy, the Lord, Who is both Perfect and Righteous, shall be glorified together with the upright — He upon His Throne, and we round about it.)*

PSALM 65

A PSALM OF DAVID:
PRAISE AND THANKSGIVING TO GOD

PRAISE waits for You, O God, in Sion: and unto You shall the vow be performed. *(Written by David, this Psalm involves itself in the Blessings of God that come upon those who place their trust in the Lord and stand upon His Promises.*

It also points to the coming Kingdom Age, when Christ will reign over a happy Earth. At that time, Israel will perform her vow of praise, as well as every Believer. Then the converted nations will unite with Israel in the worship of the Messiah. Then the Gentiles will rejoice with His people [Rom. 15:10]. Christ will reign, not only in Zion, but also over the entire Earth, and will fill it with happiness and joy.)

2 O Thou Who hears prayer, unto You shall all flesh come. *(This Verse proclaims a promise to all that God hears our believing petitions. As well, this Scripture speaks of the coming Kingdom Age, when ambassadors from all over the world will come to the Lord Jesus, Who will be governing from Jerusalem, and will present their petitions unto Him. He will give them instant answers, which will revolutionize their countries, people, and circumstances.)*

3 Iniquities prevail against me: as for our transgressions, You shall purge them away. *(David is saying here that iniquitous actions prevail against him by his enemies. But he then says that his heart, contrited by the Holy Spirit, does not speak further of man's transgressions against him, but only of his own transgressions against God. His faith looks forward for purging to Calvary, as our faith now looks back to Calvary. Faith then said, "You shall purge"; faith now says, "You have purged.")*

4 Blessed is the man whom You choose, and cause to approach unto You, that he may dwell in Your courts: we shall be satisfied with the goodness of Your house, even of Your Holy Temple. *(The Lord chooses those who choose Him.)*

5 By terrible things in righteousness will You answer us, O God of our salvation; Who are the confidence of all the ends of the Earth, and of them who are afar off upon the sea *(at the time of this writing and for all the years of the distant past, God has not been "the confidence" of all people; however, He is worthy of such, and this statement proclaims by faith that this definitely will be the case in the eternal future):*

6 Which by His strength sets fast the mountains; being girded with power *(with His "strength," He will still the tumult of the people, and so establish universal peace; this will begin at the Second Coming):*

7 Which stills the noise of the seas, the noise of their waves, and the tumult of the people *(there is an unsettling spirit that has always plagued the Earth; this unsettling spirit has been caused by man's estrangement from God; when Jesus reigns, this unsettled spirit will vanish).*

8 They also who dwell in the uttermost parts are afraid at Your tokens: You make the outgoings of the morning and evening to rejoice. *(The demonstration of our Lord over nature and over man will compel all who dwell even in the uttermost parts of the Earth to worship Him. The rejoicing will not stop, continually going from morning to evening. And no wonder! Jesus reigns!)*

9 You visit the Earth, and water it: You greatly enrich it with the river of God, which is full of water: You prepare them corn, when

You have so provided for it. *(The watering of the Earth has to do not only with great fertility being brought back to the entirety of the planet, even with the deserts blossoming as a rose, but, as well, speaks of the Blessings and Presence of God which will "visit the Earth," and will be the cause of all the blessings.)*

10 You water the ridges thereof abundantly: You settle the furrows thereof: You make it soft with showers: You bless the springing thereof. *(This Passage is so freighted with blessing that it is difficult to put the entirety of the meaning given by the Holy Spirit into English [or any other language]. It means that years as well as days will be crowned with goodness. Hill and vale will wave with golden grain, the pastures will be clothed with flocks, and Earth's happy inhabitants will be constrained to sing aloud and shout for joy. It will be a time of Heaven on Earth. It is called the one-thousand-year Millennial Reign [Rev., Chpt. 20]. Then Jesus Christ will reign supreme from Jerusalem as the Premier of the Earth.)*

11 You crown the year with Your goodness; and Your paths drop fatness. *(Men have ever looked to the beginning of each new year with hope and anticipation; they are always disappointed. However, with the Advent of the Son of Man, each year will come forth with promise, "crowned" with His "goodness.")*

12 They drop upon the pastures of the wilderness: and the little hills rejoice on every side. *(Even the "wilderness" parts of the Earth will rejoice with great blessing, and "on every side.")*

13 The pastures are clothed with flocks; the valleys also are covered over with corn; they shout for joy, they also sing. *(The Hebrew Text is very emphatic, and actually says, "They shall most certainly sing."*

This 65th Psalm is one of David's greatest songs of blessing. It was, no doubt, later sung many times by the great choirs at the Temple in anticipation of the coming Glory. It should be sung by every Child of God presently; it definitely will be sung by every Child of God tomorrow.)

PSALM 66

THE WRITER IS UNKNOWN: A SONG OF PRAISE AND WORSHIP

MAKE a joyful noise unto God, all ye lands *(this Psalm will be sung by Israel and the Messiah at the opening of the Millennium):*

2 Sing forth the honour of His Name: make His praise glorious. *(The "Name" of the Lord Jesus Christ has never been honored in the Earth. Actually, it was never even honored by Israel, but, in fact, was blasphemed. Now, at long last, at the beginning of the great Kingdom Age, the "Name" of the Messiah will be honored all over the world, and all men will sing His praises. The "Glory of His Name" will be universal.)*

3 Say unto God, How terrible are You in Your works! through the greatness of Your power shall Your enemies submit themselves unto You. *(The word "terrible" has reference to the "greatness of Your Power." The Lord is not just mighty, but Almighty. Due to this "Power," all "enemies" on the Earth will "submit themselves unto Him.")*

4 All the Earth shall worship You, and shall sing unto You; they shall sing to Your Name. Selah. *(This speaks of the coming Kingdom Age, which will be a time of universal praise and universal worship.)*

5 Come and see the works of God: He is terrible in His doing toward the children of men *(in the coming Kingdom Age, the topic of conversation on every tongue, and all over the world, will be "the works of God").*

6 He turned the sea into dry land: they went through the flood on foot: there did we rejoice in Him *(the sense of this Verse is that if one doubts what God will do in the future, one should look back at what He has done in the past).*

7 He rules by His power for ever; His eyes behold the nations: let not the rebellious exalt themselves. Selah. *(Let every nation realize that God rules in the affairs of men. His Way will ultimately triumph. "Let not the rebellious" think that they can overcome Him.)*

8 O bless our God, you people, and make the voice of His praise to be heard *(is His Praise heard from your lips? From your Church?):*

9 Which holds our soul in life, and suffers not our feet to be moved *("holding our soul in life" means the preserving of our Salvation).*

10 For You, O God, have proved us: You have tried us, as silver is tried *(Faith must be tested, and great Faith must be tested greatly; it is absolutely necessary for our consecration).*

11 You brought us into the net; You laid affliction upon our loins *(at times affliction is necessary in order to bring us to the place spiritually that we ought to be).*

12 You have caused men to ride over our heads; we went through fire and through water: but You brought us out into a wealthy

place. ("Some through the waters and some through the flood, some through the fire, but all through the Blood!" But it's worth it to be brought to the "wealthy place.")

13 I will go into Your house with Burnt Offerings: I will pay You my vows (every Believer must be brought to Calvary, in that he understands that everything that comes to him from the Lord comes exclusively through Christ as the Source and the Cross as the means; the "Burnt Offerings" are symbolic of the Cross),

14 Which my lips have uttered, and my mouth has spoken, when I was in trouble (our "lips" must ever speak of the price that He paid, which alone has given us victory over the "trouble" of sin).

15 I will offer unto You Burnt Sacrifices of fatlings, with the incense of rams; I will offer bullocks with goats. Selah. (All are symbolic of Calvary, which alone opens the door. The only way to God the Father is through Christ [Jn. 14:6]. The only way to Christ is through the Cross. And the only way to the Cross is by denial of self [Lk. 9:23-24].)

16 Come and hear, all ye who fear God, and I will declare what He has done for my soul (the greatest witness in the world is a redeemed soul giving a testimony to others, telling what the Lord has done for them).

17 I cried unto him with my mouth, and He was extolled with my tongue (our "tongue" should be used always to praise the Lord, and never used for slander or gossip).

18 If I regard iniquity in my heart, the LORD will not hear me (the reason most prayers are never heard and answered is because individuals will not confess the sin that lurks within their hearts and repent of it being there):

19 But verily God has heard me; He has attended to the voice of my prayer (the writer is saying that God has heard him, proving that he had not held on to, or loved, iniquity in his heart).

20 Blessed be God, which has not turned away my prayer, nor His mercy from me (the channel to God can only be kept open if we depend on Calvary and forsake all sin, as the Lord lives in us [Gal. 2:20]).

PSALM 67

THE WRITER IS UNKNOWN:
LET ALL THE PEOPLE PRAISE YOU

GOD be merciful unto us, and bless us; and cause His face to shine upon us;

Selah. (The "shining of God's Face upon us" is one of the most beautiful Passages found in the Bible. It signifies the Blessings of God upon the person or the people in question.)

2 That Your way may be known upon Earth, Your saving health among all nations. (The Prophetic Doctrine that the Salvation of the world depends upon the Restoration of Israel [Rom., Chpt. 11] is repeated in the last two Verses, as it is affirmed in these first two Verses. This repetition emphasizes its importance.)

3 Let the people praise You, O God; let all the people praise You (as prosperity covers the entirety of the Earth, and in every capacity, and we speak of the Kingdom Age, all the people will then definitely praise the Lord).

4 O let the nations be glad and sing for joy: for You shall judge the people righteously, and govern the nations upon Earth. Selah. (Many nations of the world presently are in deep poverty. All of that will change when Jesus rules and reigns Personally from Jerusalem.)

5 Let the people praise You, O God; let all the people praise You. (This is a repetition of Verse 3, given by the Holy Spirit in a double manner that all may know the significance that God places on His people praising Him.

At this time, only a very small number of people throughout the Earth praise the Lord. In fact, only a small number in the Church praise the Lord. In the Millennial Kingdom, the entirety of the Earth ["all people"] shall "praise You.")

6 Then shall the Earth yield her increase; and God, even our own God, shall bless us. (A most remarkable revelation is given to us in this Passage. Much of the world presently is plagued by drought, famine, and starvation.

With Israel in her proper place, and the kingdoms of this world praising the Lord, then the "Earth will yield her increase," and there will be abundance for all!)

7 God shall bless us; and all the ends of the Earth shall fear Him. (To use an old Pentecostal phrase, "It's Blessing Time!")

PSALM 68

A PSALM OF DAVID:
A SONG OF TRIUMPH

LET God arise, let His enemies be scattered: let them also who hate Him flee before Him. (This statement, originated by the Holy Spirit through Moses [Num. 10:35], was used by David as he composed the entirety of this Psalm,

which was more than likely sung as the Ark was being brought into Jerusalem. The Ark of the Covenant represented the Presence of God, which was reached only through the Cross, represented by the Brazen Altar. All "enemies" flee before the shed Blood of Christ [Eph. 2:13-18].)

2 As smoke is driven away, so drive them away: as wax melts before the fire, so let the wicked perish at the Presence of God. (The "Presence of God," here represented by the Ark, is the key to all things. This can be had only as the Believer places his faith and trust exclusively in Christ and what Christ did at the Cross, which then gives the Holy Spirit latitude to work. The Holy Spirit will respond to nothing else, only the Cross [Rom. 8:1-2, 11].)

3 But let the righteous be glad; let them rejoice before God: yea, let them exceedingly rejoice. (The "righteous" need have no fear of Satan providing the "Presence of God" is present. Let us state it again:

We must ever realize that Christ is always the Source, while the Cross is always the Means.)

4 Sing unto God, sing praises to His Name: extol Him Who rides upon the Heavens by His Name JAH, and rejoice before Him. (According to the Psalms, Spirit-anointed music is the highest form of praise there is.

"JAH" is an abbreviation of Jehovah, the Self-Existent One – He Who is, and was, and is to come. This is the only place in the Bible that this name is used in this fashion.)

5 A father of the fatherless, and a judge of the widows, is God in His holy habitation. (This tells us that this Almighty God, in His distant habitation, and in the sinless essence of His Being, is a Father of the fatherless and a Guardian of the widow. As well, He restores and enriches rebellious sinners, if they will only yield to Him.)

6 God sets the solitary in families: He brings out those which are bound with chains; but the rebellious dwell in a dry land. (The word "solitary" means singular, or one. In the Hebrew, the word is "yachid," which means that the one will unite.

God oftentimes has one person in a family who is serving Him; consequently, the Salvation of the entirety of the family is dependent upon that one person.

If the light is given by the solitary one, and it is rebuked, the Lord says, "The rebellious shall dwell in a dry land.")

7 O God, when You went forth before Your people, when You did march through the wilderness; Selah (David recalls the wilderness experience):

8 The Earth shook, the Heavens also dropped at the Presence of God: even Sinai itself was moved at the Presence of God, the God of Israel (this Passage is a clear reference to the time when Israel received the Law at Sinai [Ex. 19:16-25]).

9 You, O God, did send a plentiful rain, whereby You did confirm Your inheritance, when it was weary (this refers to the Manna and the quails "raining" upon Israel from Heaven, and the water which flowed for them from the Smitten Rock).

10 Your congregation has dwelt therein: You, O God, have prepared of Your goodness for the poor (without God, Israel, while in the wilderness, was "poor" indeed; but God had "prepared" for them).

11 The Lord gave the Word: great was the company of those who published it (the "Word" that is spoken of here concerns the Law given on Mount Sinai; it has been "published" ever since).

12 Kings of armies did flee apace: and she who tarried at home divided the spoil. (This speaks of the conquest of the Promised Land by Joshua. More so, even as the previous Verses, it speaks of the Coming of the Lord at the Battle of Armageddon. The Antichrist will attempt to "flee." Israel will then "divide the spoil." The Prophet Zechariah said: "The wealth of all the heathen round about shall be gathered together" [Zech. 14:14].)

13 Though you have lien among the pots, yet shall you be as the wings of a dove covered with silver, and her feathers with yellow gold. (The idea here is that Israel, who had been living in slavery in Egypt, would come forth as a beautiful dove covered with silver and with feathers tipped in gold.

The greater fulfillment will be in the Millennial Reign in her future restoration as the head of all nations on Earth. This thrown-away "pot" will come to Jesus and be saved, and will finally realize her place and position, but only in Christ.)

14 When the Almighty scattered kings in it, it was white as snow in Salmon (the sense of this terminology, even as it speaks of Israel's victories under Joshua, even more so pertains to the Lord dispersing the armies of Israel's enemies during the Battle of Armageddon; the scattering of these armies will be like snowflakes driven by a storm against the dark wooded slopes of Mount Salmon near Shechem)

15 The hill of God is as the hill of Bashan; an high hill as the hill of Bashan. *(In this Passage, God is laying claim to Israel as His Land. He calls it "the Hill of God." Because of this statement, the battle has raged from the time that God gave this land to Abraham. It rages even today. The Antichrist will attempt to take this "hill." He will fail!)*

16 Why leap ye, ye high hills? this is the hill which God desires to dwell in; yea, the LORD will dwell in it for ever. *(This Land of Israel, referred to as "the Hill," is where God desires to dwell, and will do so forever. The Muslim world, and all of the world for that matter, should understand that. It belongs to Israel, not the Arabs.)*

17 The chariots of God are twenty thousand, even thousands of Angels: the Lord is among them, as in Sinai, in the Holy Place. *(This speaks of the Coming of the Lord Jesus Christ [Rev., Chpt. 19]. If we are to take this Passage literally, it means that there will be over 20 million "chariots of God" occupied by Angels involved in the Second Coming. It further says, "The Lord will be among them.")*

18 You have ascended on high, You have led captivity captive: You have received gifts for men; yea, for the rebellious also, that the LORD God might dwell among them. *(Paul quoted this Scripture in Ephesians 4:8-10. It refers to Christ just before His Resurrection going down into Paradise and liberating all the Old Testament Saints, who, in fact, had been held captive by Satan, hence the term "have led captivity captive," and taking all of them with Him to Glory. Now, when a Believer dies, instead of being taken to the heart of the Earth, which was the destination before the Cross, he is now instantly taken to Heaven, and all because of the Cross [Ps. 16:10; Mat. 12:40; Heb. 2:14-15; Lk. 16:19-31; II Cor. 5:8; Phil. 1:21-24; Rev. 6:9-11].)*

19 Blessed be the LORD, who daily loads us with benefits, even the God of our salvation. Selah. *(Every single "benefit" comes to us by the means of the Cross, with Christ as the Source.)*

20 He Who is our God is the God of Salvation; and unto God the Lord belong the issues from death. *(Two things are here said: (1) Only the Lord can save. (2) Only the Lord can redeem man from spiritual "death.")*

21 But God shall wound the head of His enemies, and the hairy scalp of such an one as goes on still in his trespasses. *(This was done at the Cross of Calvary [Col. 2:14-15].)*

22 The LORD said, I will bring again from Bashan, I will bring My people again from the depths of the sea *(this speaks of the regathering of Israel at the beginning of the Kingdom Age)*:

23 That your foot may be dipped in the blood of Your enemies, and the tongue of Your dogs in the same *(this speaks of the Battle of Armageddon, when the great Gentile armies will be defeated, along with the Antichrist, referred to as "dogs").*

24 They have seen Your goings, O God; even the goings of my God, my King, in the Sanctuary *(when the world government under Christ is set up in Jerusalem at the beginning of the Kingdom Age, the entire world will "know" and "see").*

25 The singers went before, the players on instruments followed after; among them were the damsels playing with timbrels. *(When David wrote this Psalm, and when it was sung as the Ark was being brought into Jerusalem, he was referring to the worship of the "singers" and the "musicians."*

In its greater fulfillment, it refers to the Lord Jesus Christ going into Jerusalem, possibly even through the Eastern Gate. This will be at the beginning of the Millennial Reign. It will be a time of such rejoicing as the world has never seen before.)

26 Bless ye God in the congregations, even the Lord, from the fountain of Israel. *(This simply has reference to Israel's praising God as a nation. They will then finally accept Jesus Christ as Messiah. Then "the fountain of Israel" will bubble forth with praises of the Lord.)*

27 There is little Benjamin with their ruler, the princes of Judah and their council, the princes of Zebulun, and the princes of Naphtali. *(As David sings this song while watching the Ark of God being carried on the shoulders of the Priests into Jerusalem, his eyes scan the representatives of the various Tribes.*

The greater fulfillment will be when Jesus Christ, the Greater Son of David, comes into Jerusalem to begin the one-thousand-year Millennial Reign. All the Tribes, in fact, will be there.

Incidentally, Benjamin was the least of the Tribes and the last on the jasper stone of Aaron's Breastplate; however, jasper is the first stone in the foundations of the Holy City [Rev. 21:19].)

28 Your God has commanded Your strength: strengthen, O God, that which You have wrought for us. *(When David wrote these words, Israel, as commanded by God, was well on its way to becoming the premier nation on the face*

of the Earth. However, the prophetical meaning of this Passage is the greater blessing of Israel in the Millennial Reign.)

29 Because of Your Temple at Jerusalem shall kings bring presents unto You. *(When David wrote these words, the Temple had not yet been built. When it would be built by Solomon, David's son, kings from all over the world would bring presents to Solomon.*

The greater fulfillment will be when representatives from all nations in the world come to Jerusalem to bring "presents" to the Lord Jesus Christ. Solomon was a Type of the Greater than Solomon.)

30 Rebuke the company of spearmen, the multitude of the bulls, with the calves of the people, till every one submit himself with pieces of silver: scatter Thou the people who delight in war. *(The future supremacy of Israel over all Earthly monarchs is compared here, as in Daniel, to wild beasts, and predicted in the last stirring stanza of this song [Vss. 28-35]. Then, because of the Almighty Power of Jesus Christ, the nations of the world will be "rebuked.")*

31 Princes shall come out of Egypt; Ethiopia shall soon stretch out her hands unto God. *(All of this happened in a measure during the reign of Solomon. It will happen on a worldwide basis when the Greater than Solomon reigns in Jerusalem.)*

32 Sing unto God, you kingdoms of the Earth; O sing praises unto the Lord; Selah *(in view of the great happenings which will take place all over the world in the Millennial Reign, all the "kingdoms of the Earth" will "sing unto God," and rightly so!):*

33 To Him Who rides upon the heavens of heavens, which were of old; lo, He does send out His voice, and that a mighty voice *(the meaning of the Verse is that, as God has reigned supreme within the heavens, He will then reign supreme upon the Earth; His "mighty voice" will be heard in every nation of the world).*

34 Ascribe ye strength unto God: His excellency is over Israel, and His strength is in the clouds *(the idea is, God has the strength to do what He has promised, and that He will do).*

35 O God, You are terrible out of Your Holy Places: the God of Israel is He Who gives strength and power unto His people. Blessed be God. *(Not only is God great in His "Holy Places," but, as well, He will show the world that He is great in every facet of life and living, irrespective as to what it might be.)*

PSALM 69

A PSALM OF DAVID: THE SUFFERING SERVANT

SAVE **me, O God; for the waters are come in unto my soul.** *(Eight quotations from the New Testament establish the relationship of this Psalm to the Messiah [Mat. 27:34; Mk. 15:23; Jn. 2:17; 15:25; 19:29; Rom. 11:9; 15:3; II Cor. 6:2]. The voice is, therefore, that of the Man of Sorrows, excepting Verses 22-28, which record the prediction of the Holy Spirit of temporary wrath upon Israel because of its supreme sin in the Crucifixion of their King and Redeemer [Rom. 11:9-12].*

The Psalm throbs with unspeakable agony. Jesus at Calvary, as the great Trespass Offering, restored that which He took not away, that is, He perfectly restored to God the love and obedience of which man had robbed God, at the same time He voluntarily charged Himself with man's foolishness and guiltiness, and called them His Own, thereby declaring Himself to be the guilty Person.)

2 I sink in deep mire, where there is no standing: I am come into deep waters, where the floods overflow me. *(David is speaking of the terrible difficulties that his failure regarding Bath-sheba has brought upon him. From these Passages, we understand the horror of sin. Truly the words, "deep mire," perfectly describe sin. There is no way that one can extricate himself from such without the Power of God. In fact, only the Cross can extricate one from the "deep mire.")*

3 I am weary of my crying: my throat is dried: my eyes fail while I wait for my God. *(All of us, at one time or the other, have failed God. Our concern and attitude certainly should be the same as David's. This speaks of true Repentance.)*

4 They who hate Me without a cause are more than the hairs of My head: they who would destroy Me, being my enemies wrongfully, are mighty: then I restored that which I took not away. *(This is quoted by Christ in St. John 15:25. He, through His death on Calvary, "restored" that which man lost by his rebellion against God. Because of sinful hearts, men hated him "without a cause.")*

5 O God, You know my foolishness; and my sins are not hid from You. *(Even though David uttered these words, it more so points to Christ in His Intercessory Work, Who takes our sins as His*

Own and prays to the Father for us, as though He is asking for Mercy and Pardon for His Own sin, when in fact He has never sinned. Actually, when one reads these Psalms, one is reading the Intercessory Work of Christ. These words stand for time and eternity, meaning that Christ does not presently have to say anything else. His very Presence at the Throne of God guarantees that His Intercession is accepted by the Father, all on our behalf [Heb. 1:3; 7:25-27].)

6 Let not them who wait on You, O Lord GOD of Hosts, be ashamed for My sake: let not those who seek You be confounded for My sake, O God of Israel. *(The meaning of Verses 6 and 7 is that God's abandonment, so to speak, of His Beloved Son at Calvary might upset the faith of those who confide in God for Deliverance from human or Satanic hatred. He prayed that they might understand that He, as the Trespass Offering, should be so forsaken.)*

7 Because for Your sake I have borne reproach; shame has covered My face. *(Bearing the sin penalty on the Cross, our Lord suffered untold reproach and shame.)*

8 I am become a stranger unto My brethren, and an alien unto My mother's children. *(This Prophecy refutes the lie of the Catholic Church that Mary had no other children but Christ. The Gospels are replete with the fact that His Own "Brethren" [His half-brothers] did not believe in Him, at least before the Cross [Jn. 7:5].)*

9 For the zeal of Your house has eaten Me up; and the reproaches of them that reproached You are fallen upon Me. *(Our Lord quoted this Passage in St. John 2:17. All the rebellion of the evil hearts of men against God was directed at the Lord Jesus Christ.)*

10 When I wept, and chastened My soul with fasting, that was to My reproach. *(Even though all of these Passages refer to David in some manner, their basic intent is to portray Christ. No human being ever suffered the "reproach" that Christ suffered, not even remotely so!)*

11 I made sackcloth also My garment; and I became a proverb to them. *(There is no record that Christ literally wore "sackcloth"; therefore, this Passage proclaims that which Christ gave up and became for lost humanity. It is referred to as the self-emptying of Christ [Phil. 2:5-8].)*

12 They who sit in the gate speak against Me; and I was the song of the drunkards. *(The short phrase, "sit in the gate," speaks of those who held positions of authority. Ridicule was heaped upon David, because of the incident with Bath-sheba. But with Christ there was no wrong, and yet the religious leaders of Israel spoke vehemently against Him, and they did all within their power to make the Name of Christ a reproach until it was "the song of the drunkards.")*

13 But as for Me, My prayer is unto You, O LORD, in an acceptable time: O God, in the multitude of Your mercy hear Me, in the truth of Your salvation. *(This speaks of David as a Type of Christ. Both, David and Christ, cried to God incessantly. David, as a Type of Christ, knew that God was his only hope. The Greater Son of David would likewise cry to God for leading and guidance.*

This should be an example to us. God is the only One Who can protect us and can, in fact, change our situation, whatever it might be.)

14 Deliver Me out of the mire, and let Me not sink: let Me be delivered from them who hate Me, and out of the deep waters. *(David is speaking in this Passage of the terrible "mire" of sin he has fallen into, regarding Bath-sheba. His enemies, of which he seemed to have many, greatly used this as a weapon against him.*

The same could be said for Christ in an even greater way, except He committed no sin; however, He would so much take our sin upon Himself, becoming one with its penalty, that He would suffer the full effects of its horror, even though He Himself never failed even one time.)

15 Let not the waterflood overflow Me, neither let the deep swallow Me up, and let not the pit shut her mouth upon Me. *(This terminology inspired by the Holy Spirit is a perfect picture of the efforts of Satan to destroy an individual. These Passages could well apply to the horror of Gethsemane, when Satan attempted to kill Christ before He could go to the Cross. Only God's intervention saved His Life [Lk. 22:43-44].)*

16 Hear Me, O LORD, for Your lovingkindness is good: turn unto Me according to the multitude of Your tender mercies. *(The Hebrew word translated "lovingkindness" means "grace," and as "tender mercies," it signifies the same tender affection that mothers show their offspring. If it is to be noticed, it is used quite often in the Psalms.)*

17 And hide not Your face from Your servant; for I am in trouble: hear Me speedily. *(The only relief from "trouble" is for the Believer to express Faith in Christ and the Cross, which will then give the Holy Spirit the latitude to apply the Word and its effect to your heart and life.)*

18 Draw near unto My soul, and redeem it:

deliver Me because of My enemies. *(Anyone who is truly called of God will experience the opposition of these "enemies." These will come from three sources: the world, the apostate Church, and demon spirits.)*

19 You have known My reproach, and My shame, and My dishonour: My adversaries are all before You. *(Most of the adversaries against Christ were those of the religious leaders of His day.)*

20 Reproach has broken My heart; and I am full of heaviness: and I looked for some to take pity, but there was none; and for comforters, but I found none. *(This spoke of David, but far more of Christ. It probably refers to His trial and the terrible ordeal on the Cross. He actually died of a "broken heart" [Jn. 19:34].)*

21 They gave me also gall for My meat; and in My thirst they gave Me vinegar to drink. *(This was fulfilled at the Crucifixion [Mat. 27:48]. It must be remembered that those who did this were not the drunks, the thieves, or the harlots who nailed Christ to a Cross, but, instead, it was the religious leaders of that day. Regrettably, it has not changed from then until now.)*

22 Let their table become a snare before them: and that which should have been for their welfare, let it become a trap. *(The "table" that is referred to here is actually that which the Lord prepares for His Own [Psalm 23]. Judas did not want the "table" that the Lord had prepared; he desired another "table." It would become a "snare." Along with Judas, this also speaks of the Priests who opposed Christ, and most did!)*

23 Let their eyes be darkened that they see not; and make their loins continually to shake. *(They refused "light," so now they will have "darkness." This "darkness" will bring a fear that will cause them "continually to shake." And so it did!)*

24 Pour out Your indignation upon them, and let Your wrathful anger take hold of them. *(Judas committed suicide, as did Caiaphas, the High Priest. Also, Jerusalem, some thirty-seven years later [A.D. 70], was totally destroyed by the Roman army.)*

25 Let their habitation be desolate; and let none dwell in their tents. *(This was quoted about Judas in Acts 1:20. It was also quoted in part by Christ concerning Israel and Jerusalem [Lk. 13:34-35].)*

26 For they persecute Him whom You have smitten; and they talk to the grief of those whom You have wounded. *(The Father Himself smote the Son, which speaks of the Cross [Isa. 53:4].*

27 Add iniquity unto their iniquity: and let them not come into Your Righteousness. *(This speaks of Judas and the religious leaders of Israel blaspheming the Holy Spirit. They added this "iniquity unto their iniquity.")*

28 Let them be blotted out of the Book of the living, and not be written with the righteous. *(This proves that names can be blotted out of the Book of Life. The same thing is said in other places of the Bible, as well [Ex. 32:33; Rev. 3:5; 22:19]. That this is the Book of Life is clear from the fact that it is the Book wherein the names of the righteous are written.)*

29 But I am poor and sorrowful: let Your salvation, O God, set Me up on high. *(The religious leaders of Israel would not set Christ "on high," meaning they would not recognize Him for Who He actually was; however, the Father most definitely did "set Him upon high.")*

30 I will praise the Name of God with a song, and will magnify Him with thanksgiving. *(David was noted for praising the Name of the Lord "with a song." As well, Jesus and His Disciples sang a song at the Last Supper [Mat. 26:30].)*

31 This also shall please the LORD better than an ox or bullock that has horns and hoofs. *(David is saying that praise to the Name of the Lord in song and thanksgiving pleases the Lord better than animal sacrifices. In a greater measure, it speaks of the Greater Sacrifice of Christ on the Cross, which was better than animal sacrifices.)*

32 The humble shall see this, and be glad: and your heart shall live that seek God. *(Even though the "humble" refers to all Believers in a general sense, even more so it speaks of Christ.)*

33 For the LORD hears the poor, and despises not His prisoners. *(The word "poor" refers to Christ. "His prisoners" refer to those who follow Him. The Lord will always hear Christ, and those who follow Him will never be "despised by God.")*

34 Let the Heaven and Earth praise Him, the seas, and every thing that moves therein. *(The One Who is called "humble" and "poor" will ultimately see the entirety of the Heavens and the Earth praising Him. This will be fulfilled in the Millennial Reign, and forever.)*

35 For God will save Zion, and will build the cities of Judah: that they may dwell there, and have it in possession. *(This speaks of the coming Kingdom Age. As well, it tells us, by the use of the word "Zion," which is strictly*

Jewish, that the Land of Israel belongs to the Jews, and not to the Arabs. It is their possession, and given to them by the Lord [Gen. 17:19, 21].)

36 The seed also of his servants shall inherit it: and they who love his name shall dwell therein. *(Here, Jesus is called "the Seed." Paul wrote, "And to thy Seed, which is Christ" [Gal. 3:16]. At the beginning of the Kingdom Age, the dispute concerning the Land of Israel will forever end. "The Lord Jesus Christ shall inherit it.")*

PSALM 70

A PSALM OF DAVID:
A CRY FOR HELP

MAKE haste, O God, to deliver me; make haste to help me, O LORD. *(The majority of this Psalm is almost identical to Verses 13-17 of Psalm 40. The theme of that in the Fortieth Psalm is the Messiah's Personal sufferings in His First Advent; that of this Psalm, His sympathetic sufferings with His People immediately prior to His Second Advent.)*

2 Let them be ashamed and confounded who seek after my soul: let them be turned backward, and put to confusion, who desire my hurt. *(Israel will cry these words in the closing days of the Tribulation [the time of Jacob's Trouble]. In effect, the Son of David, as portrayed here, will have already prayed this prayer on their behalf. This Second Verse will be fulfilled at the Second Coming.)*

3 Let them be turned back for a reward of their shame who say, Aha, aha. *(During the Battle of Armageddon, the Antichrist will think surely that victory is within his grasp; however, he will be put to "shame" at the Coming of the Lord Jesus.)*

4 Let all those who seek You rejoice and be glad in You: and let such as love Your salvation say continually, Let God be magnified. *(This refers in general to anyone who would "seek the Lord." It refers more pointedly to Israel in the last days when they will, at long last, "seek God.")*

5 But I am poor and needy: make haste unto me, O God: You are my help and my deliverer: O LORD, make no tarrying. *(The words, "make no tarrying," refer to the Battle of Armageddon, when it seems as though all hope is gone. In fact, Israel's only hope at that time will be the Coming of the Messiah. He will hear this prayer and answer it.)*

PSALM 71

DAVID PROBABLY WROTE THIS PSALM:
A PRAYER FOR GOD'S HELP
IN OLD AGE

IN You, O LORD, do I put my trust: let me never be put to confusion. *(Even though there is no proof of the authorship of this Psalm, however, there is a good possibility that it was given to David for the purpose of refreshing his heart during the dark days of Absalom's rebellion. It must also have refreshed the heart of the Greater Son of David when He was suffering man's hatred, and it will feed the faith of Israel in the future and darkest day of her history.)*

2 Deliver me in Your righteousness, and cause me to escape: incline Your ear unto me, and save me. *(This seems to be language that David would have used at the time of Absalom's rebellion. It would refer at a later day to the Lord Jesus Christ, as well, and to Israel, who will face the Antichrist in the last days.)*

3 Be Thou my strong habitation, whereunto I may continually resort: You have given commandment to save me; for You are my rock and my fortress. *(Trust exclusively in the Lord guarantees the "Commandment" to save us. This Commandment cannot be abrogated by the powers of darkness. The reason is, God is a "Rock" and a "Fortress," and, as well, "my Rock" and "my Fortress.")*

4 Deliver me, O my God, out of the hand of the wicked, out of the hand of the unrighteous and cruel man. *(This is the cry of the true Israel, the Lord Jesus Christ, as He intercedes on behalf of His People, that they be delivered out of the hands of the Antichrist. To be sure, this prayer will most definitely be answered.)*

5 For You are my hope, O Lord God: You are my trust from my youth. *(Once again, "trust" in God is the theme. Man can either "hope" in other men or "hope" in God. He cannot place "hope" in both.)*

6 By You have I been holden up from the womb: You are He Who took me out of my mother's bowels: my praise shall be continually of You. *(This speaks of David and, as well, of the Incarnation of Christ. It also speaks of Israel, which was born from Sarah's womb.)*

7 I am as a wonder unto many; but You are my strong refuge. *(The meaning of this Verse is that due to David's, the Messiah's, and Israel's many enemies, it was "a wonder" that each survived. They did so because God was*

their "strong refuge.")

8 Let my mouth be filled with Your praise and with Your honour all the day. *(David and the Messiah fulfilled this Passage in its entirety. Israel one day will fill her mouth with praise of the Lord Jesus Christ "all the day." As well, this should hold true for every Believer.)*

9 Cast me not off in the time of old age; forsake me not when my strength fails. *(Most particularly, this speaks of Israel in the last half of the Great Tribulation. At that time, her strength will fail. So, she pleads with God to not forsake her. The pleading is that God should not forsake her because of her great sin; therefore, God will not forsake her and will come to her rescue.)*

10 For my enemies speak against me; and they who lay wait for my soul take counsel together *(these "enemies" of David and the Messiah were all religious; the greater enemies of Israel are the Muslims, and all of that, of course, is religious; religion, which is man-devised, has ever been the nemesis of God),*

11 Saying, God has forsaken him: persecute and take him; for there is none to deliver him. *(Absalom and his cohorts would say this of David because of the situation with Bath-sheba. Israel thought and said the same thing of Christ at His trial and Crucifixion. The Antichrist will say the same to Israel during the latter half of the Great Tribulation [Mat. 7:1-2].)*

12 O God, be not far from me: O my God, make haste for my help. *(This cry came from David at the most critical time in his life, during Absalom's rebellion. This cry came from Christ, as well, while on the Cross. Prophetically, it will come from Israel during the Battle of Armageddon, when it seems that all is lost.)*

13 Let them be confounded and consumed who are adversaries to my soul; let them be covered with reproach and dishonour who seek my hurt. *(This prayer was answered in totality. Absalom was killed, Israel was ultimately destroyed, and the Antichrist will be defeated and killed at the Battle of Armageddon by the Coming of the Lord.)*

14 But I will hope continually, and will yet praise You more and more. *(In Psalms 70 and 71, the word "continually" is used three times: 1. "Say continually, let God be magnified" [Ps. 70:4]; 2. "Continually resort to my strong habitation," which is God [71:3]; and, 3. "But I will hope continually" [71:14].)*

15 My mouth shall show forth Your righteousness and Your salvation all the day; for I know not the numbers thereof. *(The expression, "I know not the numbers," is a figure denoting infinitude [without number].)*

16 I will go in the strength of the Lord GOD: I will make mention of Your righteousness, even of Yours only. *(The Righteousness of Christ Alone is recognized by God, which is made possible to us through the Cross and our Faith in that Finished Work. All else is self-righteousness, which God can never accept [Gal. 2:21].)*

17 O God, You have taught me from my youth: and hitherto have I declared Your wondrous works. *(Of course, both David and the Messiah "declared" His "wondrous works." Israel will also do this in the Kingdom Age.)*

18 Now also when I am old and greyheaded, O God, forsake me not; until I have shown Your strength unto this generation, and Your power to every one who is to come. *(David most certainly said these words of himself, desiring strongly that he finish the work God had called him to do. But, its greater fulfillment pertains to Israel. She is now old, but the Lord is going to give her another opportunity, of which she will take full advantage, meaning that this prayer will be answered. In the coming Kingdom Age, Israel will "show the strength of the Lord to that generation.")*

19 Your righteousness also, O God, is very high, Who has done great things: O God, Who is like unto You! *(The righteousness of man is very low. The righteousness of God "is very high." Men keep trying to earn their own righteousness, which is impossible, especially when it's free from God for the asking. Righteousness comes exclusively by Christ, with Him as the Source, but the Cross as the means. Simple Faith in what He has done for us at the Cross guarantees instant imputed Righteousness.)*

20 You, which have showed me great and sore troubles, shall quicken me again, and shall bring me up again from the depths of the Earth. *(This speaks of the Resurrection of Christ; because He lives, we shall live also [Rom. 6:3-5].)*

21 You shall increase my greatness, and comfort me on every side. *(All of this applies to David, Christ, and Israel. It, as well, applies to every Christian.)*

22 I will also praise You with the psaltery, even Your truth, O my God: unto You will I sing with the harp, O You Holy One of Israel. *(This Passage gives further proof that David was the author. Music is an integral part of worship. In fact, music and singing present the highest form of praise.)*

23 My lips shall greatly rejoice when I sing unto You; and my soul, which You have redeemed. *(David says that he would sing of God's great redemptive power and more specifically about the Redemption of his own soul.)*

24 My tongue also shall talk of Your righteousness all the day long: for they are confounded, for they are brought unto shame, who seek my hurt. *(Either David said these words by faith concerning Absalom or else this latter portion was written after the defeat of Absalom. As well, they were "brought to shame" who sought the hurt of the Messiah. They will be brought to shame who seek the "hurt" of Israel in the Battle of Armageddon.)*

PSALM 72

A PSALM OF DAVID:
PRAYER FOR SOLOMON

G IVE the king Your judgments, O God, and Your righteousness unto the king's son. *(The Lord gave David this Psalm when Solomon was appointed to the Throne, which would have been very shortly before David died.)*

2 He shall judge Your people with righteousness, and Your poor with judgment. *(Solomon would do this, and, above all, the Greater than Solomon, of Whom Solomon was a type, will carry this forth in the coming Kingdom Age.)*

3 The mountains shall bring peace to the people, and the little hills, by righteousness. *(This speaks of the coming Kingdom Age, when "righteousness shall cover the Earth, as waters cover the sea.")*

4 He shall judge the poor of the people, He shall save the children of the needy, and shall break in pieces the oppressor. *(This speaks of Christ coming to the aid of the "poor and needy," which, in this case, is Israel, and defeating, on their behalf, the Antichrist, who is the oppressor.)*

5 They shall fear You as long as the sun and moon endure, throughout all generations. *(In effect, the coming Kingdom Age will never end [Ps. 89:29; Jer. 31:35-36].)*

6 He shall come down like rain upon the mown grass: as showers that water the Earth *(the Blessings of Christ in the coming Kingdom Age will be abundant over the entirety of the Earth).*

7 In his days shall the righteous flourish; and abundance of peace so long as the moon endures *(speaking of Solomon, who was a Type of Christ, but more particularly of Christ Himself).*

8 He shall have dominion also from sea to sea, and from the river unto the ends of the Earth *(this speaks of the entirety of planet Earth).*

9 They who dwell in the wilderness shall bow before Him; and His enemies shall lick the dust *(the phrase, "shall lick the dust," is always a picture of complete submission of enemies).*

10 The kings of Tarshish and of the isles shall bring presents: the kings of Sheba and Seba shall offer gifts *(this happened in measure to Solomon, who was a Type of Christ; however, the type only pointed toward the future glory that will encompass the entirety of the Earth in the coming Kingdom Age).*

11 Yea, all kings shall fall down before Him: all nations shall serve Him. *(This speaks of the coming Kingdom Age, when Christ will rule over the entirety of the world, and do so from Jerusalem [Ezek. 48:35].)*

12 For He shall deliver the needy when he cries; the poor also, and him who has no helper. *(This speaks of Israel in her coming Restoration [Rom. 11:26].)*

13 He shall spare the poor and needy, and shall save the souls of the needy. *(This will be the time that Israel accepts Christ as their Saviour and their Lord [Zech. 13:1].)*

14 He shall redeem their soul from deceit and violence: and precious shall their blood be in His sight. *(The "deceit and violence" will be practiced on Israel by the Antichrist and, in fact, by much of the world. But all will learn in that day just how precious before God is the blood of all of the Children of Israel.)*

15 And He shall live, and to Him shall be given the gold of Sheba: prayer also shall be made for Him continually; and daily shall He be praised. *(This Prophecy was partially fulfilled when the Queen of Sheba came to Solomon. It will be totally fulfilled in the coming Kingdom Age, when the Lord Jesus Christ will solve every problem, thereby making the world what it ought to be.)*

16 There shall be an handful of corn in the Earth upon the top of the mountains; the fruit thereof shall shake like Lebanon: and they of the city shall flourish like grass of the Earth. *(The idea is, a handful of seed will bring forth such a crop as to defy all description, thereby doing away with all hunger in the world, and on a grand scale.)*

17 His name shall endure for ever: His Name shall be continued as long as the sun: and men shall be blessed in Him: all nations shall call Him blessed. *(In Jesus Alone will this be done. This rules out Muhammad, Joseph Smith, and any other fake luminary.)*

18 Blessed be the LORD God, the God of Israel, Who Only does wondrous things. *(He always has done "wondrous things," and He always will do "wondrous things"!)*

19 And blessed be His glorious name for ever: and let the whole Earth be filled with His glory; Amen, and Amen. *(Today the Earth is not filled with "His Glory." In that day, the Kingdom Age and forever, the entirety of the Earth, with no part excluded, will be filled with the "Glory" of Jesus Christ. A double "Amen" is given, proclaiming the certitude of its fulfillment.)*

20 The prayers of David the son of Jesse are ended. *(More than likely, this was the last Psalm written by David. When the Psalms were chronologically organized, no doubt, the Holy Spirit inspired the placement of each Psalm. As previously stated, the 150 Psalms [songs] are comprised into five Books corresponding to the five Books of the Pentateuch. Each Psalm was placed exactly where the Holy Spirit desired it, irrespective of the order in which He inspired it to be written.)*

PSALM 73

THE LEVITICUS BOOK
A PSALM OF ASAPH:
THE PROSPERITY OF THE WICKED
AND THEIR END

TRULY God is good to Israel, even to such as are of a clean heart. *(This is the third Book of the Psalms, referred to as "The Leviticus Book." Its subject is the Sanctuary, as that of the first Book was the Blessed Man [Christ], and that of the second, Israel [His People].*

Israel, as a worshipper in her future time of trouble, is the subject of this Book rather than the Messiah and the Remnant, which are that of the first two Books. Most definitely, God was good to Israel.)

2 But as for me *(Asaph)*, my feet were almost gone; my steps had well nigh slipped. *(Asaph was the leader of the choral worship under David [I Chron. 16:4-5]. So he held a very high spiritual position in Israel.)*

3 For I was envious at the foolish, when I saw the prosperity of the wicked. *(Asaph, perplexed with the problem that the ungodly prosper and the children of the Kingdom suffer, learns the lesson that outside the Sanctuary, the mind is distracted and the heart fermented, but that inside, all is peace. Looking in confounds; looking out confuses; looking up comforts.*

Asaph's problem was "self." Preoccupation with "self" always leads to spiritual distraction. Men have ever tried to improve self; men have ever failed. Even Christian man fails, when endeavoring to improve "self." "Self" can only be conquered when it is hidden in Christ [Jn. 14:20].)

4 For there are no bands in their death: but their strength is firm. *(When one becomes enamored with "self," then one's spiritual judgment becomes flawed. Asaph fell into the age-old trap. First of all, "prosperity" is not the purpose of Redemption; Salvation is.*

Second, Asaph is wrong about the "death" of the wicked. It is anything but positive.)

5 They are not in trouble as other men; neither are they plagued like other men. *(The truth is, the system of this world is not of God, but of Satan; consequently, the Child of God is constantly "plagued" by that system.*

But considering that, still, the life of the follower of Christ is, by far, the most rewarding life there is. If there were no eternity, living for God would still be, by far, the greater choice.)

6 Therefore pride compasses them about as a chain, violence covers them as a garment. *(Asaph is saying that "the wicked" constantly engage themselves in "violence," with few negative results. They are filled with "pride," and, instead of it bringing destruction, it seems to reward them.)*

7 Their eyes stand out with fatness: they have more than heart could wish. *(These statements show that Asaph has given this much thought. Due to his preoccupation with "self," Satan has made great inroads into his soul. One of Satan's greatest weapons is to make the Christian think that, by living for God, he is truly missing out. However, we must always remember that Satan is a liar and the father of lies. Actually, the opposite is true.)*

8 They are corrupt, and speak wickedly concerning oppression: they speak loftily. *(The speech of the wicked is lofty concerning how they will oppress people, and no harm seems to come to them.)*

9 They set their mouth against the Heavens, and their tongue walks through the Earth.

(Everything they say is in opposition to the Word of God. They boast of what they will do, evil as it may be, and they seem to be able to do it without hindrance.)

10 Therefore his people return hither: and waters of a full cup are wrung out to them. *(They cause men who have been converted from a life of covetousness to return to it.)*

11 And they say, How does God know? and is there knowledge in the Most High? *(In other words, they laugh at God, thinking they are getting by with their wickedness.)*

12 Behold, these are the ungodly, who prosper in the world; they increase in riches. *(It is true that some of the ungodly "prosper" [financially], but, as a whole, it is not true. In fact, it is seldom true. Taking the whole world into consideration, for every one prosperous wicked man there are ten thousand who are the very opposite.)*

13 Verily I have cleansed my heart in vain, and washed my hands in innocency. *(Every attack that Satan levels against a Believer, irrespective of its direction, is for one purpose: to destroy the faith of the individual. In other words, Asaph is saying that there is no profit in living for God.*

How wrong he is! The rewards of the wicked, such as they are, are fleeting and temporal. The rewards of the righteous are eternal.)

14 For all the day long have I been plagued, and chastened every morning. *(The Lord is sorely displeased with complaints. This is the opposite of faith and appreciation for what the Lord has done for us. And yet, so many of us are guilty of this sin — thanklessness.)*

15 If I say, I will speak thus; behold, I should offend against the generation of Your children. *(He knew that the evidence was against him. Wickedness was not profitable, and living for God is.)*

16 When I thought to know this, it was too painful for me *(now Asaph realizes he is wrong; he knows he is sliding down a path that leads only to destruction; still, he does not know the answer to his dilemma);*

17 Until I went into the Sanctuary of God; then understood I their end. *(How could the Sanctuary give him the answers? Because the Sanctuary is where God dwelt. Now, he no longer sees the alleged prosperity of the wicked, but the Glory of God. Then and only then do the flaws of the wicked become obvious. As well, when he sees the Lord, he no longer sees himself.)*

18 Surely You did set them *(the wicked)* in slippery places: You cast them down into destruction. *(On the surface, the road of the wicked may look prosperous; however, upon closer inspection, it is easy to see that it is "slippery." Being so, they will fall to their own "destruction.")*

19 How are they brought into desolation, as in a moment! they are utterly consumed with terrors. *(Now Asaph begins to see what the situation really is. The wicked look as though they are so prosperous, and then, all of a sudden, they are bankrupt and "brought into desolation" — "as in a moment!"*

Now he sees that all of their boasting and clamor against God is but a facade. In a moment, they are "utterly consumed with terrors.")

20 As a dream when one awakes; so, O Lord, when You awake, You shall despise their image. *(At times, it may seem as though the Lord is asleep; however, after a short period, the Lord will "awake." Then He will intrude into their "evil dream.")*

21 Thus my heart was grieved, and I was pricked in my reins. *(Now that Asaph has seen the Lord, he has come under Holy Spirit conviction. He is "grieved," because of his sin. What he has done now dawns upon him, and he is cut to the core of his being.)*

22 So foolish was I, and ignorant: I was as a beast before You. *(The Holy Spirit causes Asaph to see that the direction he had been traveling was foolish indeed! In fact, one of the chief ministries of the Spirit is to smite with conviction. Were it not that, the Christian would too often get off course, and would not know how to get back on course.)*

23 Nevertheless I am continually with You: You have held me by my right hand. *(The Lord does not cast us off when we begin to go astray. Rather, He deals with us, speaks to us, and attempts to pull us back to the right direction. In doing so, He will literally, spiritually speaking, hold us by the hand.)*

24 You shall guide me with Your counsel, and afterward receive me to glory. *(Asaph had previously been listening to the "counsel" of self-will. Now he tells the Lord, "I will listen to Your counsel." God's "counsel" is His Word.)*

25 Whom have I in Heaven but You? and there is none upon Earth that I desire beside You. *(After seeing the Lord and receiving a fresh touch from Glory, he realizes that his salvation is not money, place, or position, but Christ. He now knows that Christ satisfies all.)*

26 My flesh and my heart fails: but God is the strength of my heart, and my portion for

ever. *(When Asaph begins to lean on his own strength, which is woefully inadequate, he "fails." But now he realizes that "God is his strength." Also, he now knows that anything and everything he needs can be provided by God — "my portion forever.")*

27 For, lo, they who are far from You shall perish: You have destroyed all them who go a whoring from You. *(He now fully sees the position of the wicked. They "shall perish.")*

28 But it is good for me to draw near to God: I have put my trust in the Lord GOD, that I may declare all Your works. *(Some bad things have happened, but some "good" is coming out of this, as well. His perilous situation has caused him to "draw near to God." Now, his "trust" is in the Lord, and not in the things of the world. Asaph vows that he will no longer talk about the prosperity of the wicked, but now will "declare all Your works." This should be a great lesson to us!)*

PSALM 74

A PSALM OF ASAPH:
THE DEVASTATION OF MOUNT ZION

O God, why have You cast us off for ever? why does Your anger smoke against the sheep of Your pasture? *(The question is asked by the Psalmist concerning the anger of God against Israel. The "anger" was not without cause. Israel had repeatedly gone into deep sin and rebellion, and that despite the repeated efforts by the Lord to bring them to the Altar of Repentance. Then and only then did God's "anger smoke against the sheep of His pasture.")*

2 Remember Your congregation, which You have purchased of old; the rod of Your inheritance, which You have redeemed; this Mount Zion, wherein You have dwelt. *(This Psalm could also refer to the Intercessory Ministry of Christ on behalf of His People. Little can the pleadings of the sinner, as sincere as they may be, assuage the terrible wrong that has been done against God. Coupled with contrition and humility must be Christ's Intercessory Work [Heb. 7:25]. In effect, everything the Believer receives from God comes through His Son, Christ Jesus, and the means is always the Cross. In fact, God cannot really bless poor fallen man, even though he is redeemed. He can only bless Christ within us.)*

3 Lift up your feet unto the perpetual desolations; even all that the enemy has done wickedly in the sanctuary. *(This refers to "the abomination of desolation, spoken of by Daniel the Prophet, standing in the Holy Place" [Mat. 24:15], and refers to the Antichrist placing his image in the Jewish Temple at Jerusalem for the last three and a half years of the Great Tribulation.)*

4 Your enemies roar in the midst of Your congregations; they set up their ensigns for signs. *(The word "ensigns" means "standard." It refers to the Antichrist's image that will be set up in the rebuilt Temple at Jerusalem [Dan. 8:9-14; 9:27; 11:45; Rev. 13:1-18; 14:9-11; 20:4-6].)*

5 A man was famous according as he had lifted up axes upon the thick trees. *(Verses 5 and 6 are meant to contrast each other. Verse 5 refers to the building of the Temple. Verse 6 refers to its destruction.)*

6 But now they break down the carved work thereof at once with axes and hammers.

7 They have cast fire into Your sanctuary, they have defiled by casting down the dwelling place of Your name to the ground. *(The Lord, when foretelling the destruction of the Temple by the Romans, in substance repeated Verses 7 and 8 of this Psalm. They cast it down to the ground; they did not leave one stone upon another; and history says they also burned all the Synagogues in Israel [Lk. 21:6].)*

8 They said in their hearts, Let us destroy them together: they have burned up all the Synagogues of God in the land. *(This is the first mention of "Synagogues" in the Old Testament. It was a place of religious assemblies. Jesus preached extensively in the Synagogues in the first two years of His Earthly Ministry. By and large, He was banned from most, if not all, of the Synagogues during the last year of His public Ministry. Now it becomes somewhat obvious as to why God allowed them to be "burned.")*

9 We see not our signs: there is no more any prophet: neither is there among us any who knows how long. *(This refers to the time between Malachi and John the Baptist, when there was no Prophet for a period of approximately 400 years. Then, after the rejection of the Lord Jesus Christ, Who was the True Prophet, Israel has now gone for about 2,000 years with "no Prophet" and "no signs.")*

10 O God, how long shall the adversary reproach? shall the enemy blaspheme Your name for ever? *(This Passage certainly had meaning concerning the destruction of Judah by Nebuchadnezzar, but much more so it refers to the Great Tribulation, when the Antichrist, as the "adversary," will "reproach." He, as no other,*

will "blaspheme" the Name of the Lord.)

11 Why do You withdraw Your hand, even Your right hand? pluck it out of Your bosom. *(This prayer will be answered at the Battle of Armageddon, when God will take His "Right Hand" [the Lord Jesus Christ] out of His "bosom" and dethrone the Antichrist.)*

12 For God is my King of old, working salvation in the midst of the Earth. *(Verses 12 through 17 proclaim by the Psalmist the greatness and glory of God. It is a plea for God to exert Himself and come to the rescue of His people.)*

13 You did divide the sea by Your strength: You broke the heads of the dragons in the waters. *(This refers to the great deliverance of Israel from Egyptian bondage, with the opening of the Red Sea. Here, the majesty of Egypt, "the dragons," was broken.)*

14 You broke the heads of leviathan in pieces, and gave him to be meat to the people inhabiting the wilderness. *(The word "leviathan" is a symbol for Satan. The language here is figurative of the defeat of Satanic powers.)*

15 You did cleave the fountain and the flood: You dried up mighty rivers. *(The first part of this Verse seems to refer to the water that came out of the Rock, when it was smitten by Moses [Ex. 17:6]. The latter portion refers to the drying up of the Jordan River when Joshua crossed with the Children of Israel into the Promised Land [Josh. 3:13-17].)*

16 The day is Yours, the night also is Yours: You have prepared the light and the sun *(proclaims the fact that God is the Creator of all things; as well, He also has the power to protect what He has created).*

17 You have set all the borders of the Earth: You have made summer and winter. *(This Verse refers to God making the seasons, such as summer and winter, which are eternal [Gen. 1:14-18; 8:22].)*

18 Remember this, that the enemy has reproached, O LORD, and that the foolish people have blasphemed Your name. *(This speaks of those who have opposed the people of God down through the many centuries; however, its greater fulfillment will be when the Antichrist attempts to destroy Israel.)*

19 O deliver not the soul of Your turtledove unto the multitude of the wicked: forget not the congregation of Your poor for ever. *(Both statements, "Your turtledove" and "Your poor," refer to Israel. The Intercessor, Who now reverts from His role of Creator to that of pleading for*

His People, will ask the Father that they not be turned over to "the wicked." Paul called him "that wicked" [II Thess. 2:8] — the Antichrist.)

20 Have respect unto the covenant: for the dark places of the Earth are full of the habitations of cruelty. *(The "Covenant" that is spoken of here refers to the Promises that were made to the Prophets of old. It is referred to by Christ in the Lord's prayer, "Thy Kingdom come, Thy Will be done, in Earth as it is in Heaven" [Mat. 6:9-10].)*

21 O let not the oppressed return ashamed: let the poor and needy praise Your name. *(The plea is for the "oppressed" [Israel] to win this conflict with the Antichrist. Israel, as well, is referred to as "the poor" and "needy.")*

22 Arise, O God, plead Your Own cause: remember how the foolish man reproaches You daily. *(There are two points made in this Verse; both are beautiful: 1. Israel's Advocate presses this condition of His People [poor and needy] as a reason why they should be delivered and 2. He identifies their interests with God; hence, their Advocate, the Lord Jesus Christ, calls on God to arise and plead His Own cause.)*

23 Forget not the voice of Your enemies: the tumult of those who rise up against You increases continually. *(The clamor by the Antichrist will increase in intensity in the Battle of Armageddon. It seems there is no way he can lose, but lose he will, because the Lord will "arise and plead His Own cause" [Rev., Chpt. 19].)*

PSALM 75

A SONG OF ASAPH:
A WARNING TO THE WICKED

UNTO You, O God, do we give thanks, unto You do we give thanks: for that Your Name is near Your wondrous works declare. *(The speaker of this Verse is the Redeemed; the Messiah Himself is the Speaker in the remaining Verses. He is addressed as God. The expression, "Your Name is near," refers to His manifested appearance in His future Coming.)*

2 When I shall receive the congregation I will judge uprightly. *(This speaks of the Second Coming, when the Lord will then set up His government, which will cover the entirety of the Earth.)*

3 The Earth and all the inhabitants thereof are dissolved: I bear up the pillars of it. Selah. *(This predicts the termination in confusion and guilt of man's government, as well as the firm*

establishment of the Messiah's rule. The latter portion of this Verse speaks of all creations that are upheld by God through Christ [Heb. 1:3].)

4 I said unto the fools, Deal not foolishly: and to the wicked, Lift not up the horn *(eastern women once wore a protruding ornament on the forehead called "a horn"; as sons were born, the horn was raised, hence the expression, "to lift up the horn"; it means to become proud; it addresses itself to all who would be lifted up in pride, and specifically to the Antichrist):*

5 Lift not up your horn on high: speak not with a stiff neck. *(The coming Antichrist will lift himself up greatly [II Thess. 2:4].)*

6 For promotion comes neither from the east, nor from the west, nor from the south. *(The Antichrist will claim great things. In actuality, he will be able to do nothing, at least that is lasting. As well, if it is to be noticed, the "north" is not mentioned, proclaiming the fact that promotion does come from the north, which has to do with the direction of Heaven and, consequently, the Throne of God.)*

7 But God is the judge: He puts down one, and sets up another. *(Regrettably, men, even in the modern Church, look to other men for promotion. They little remember that "God is the Judge." In effect, God is saying that He is the One Who will "lift up the horn," not man. If man does such, it will only breed pride. If God does such, it breeds humility.*

In the strict interpretation of this Verse, it means that the Lord will "put down" the Antichrist, and "set up" the Lord Jesus Christ.)

8 For in the hand of the LORD there is a cup, and the wine is red; it is full of mixture; and He pours out of the same: but the dregs thereof, all the wicked of the Earth shall wring them out, and drink them. *(This speaks of the judgment that is coming upon the Earth during the time of the Great Tribulation. Jesus said it would be worse than any time had ever been in history [Mat. 24:21].)*

9 But I will declare for ever; I will sing praises to the God of Jacob. *(The Lord blessed Jacob, when, in fact, Jacob deserved nothing good; consequently, the beautiful phrase, "God of Jacob," tells us that the Lord will so honor anyone who will meet His conditions. Those conditions are Faith in Christ and what Christ did at the Cross [Lk. 9:23-24; Gal., Chpt. 5].)*

10 All the horns of the wicked also will I cut off; but the horns of the righteous shall be exalted. *(Evil will not take best; Righteousness will take best!)*

PSALM 76

A PSALM OF ASAPH: A SONG OF DELIVERANCE

I N Judah is God known: His Name is great in Israel. *(At the time of the writing, God was known in "Judah." He is not known there now; however, He will be known there in the near future. As well, His Name will be "great in Israel."*

Psalm 74 speaks of the enemy in the Sanctuary. Psalm 75 speaks of the Messiah in the Sanctuary. Psalm 76 speaks of Messiah's destruction of the haters of the Sanctuary. Its fulfillment belongs to the predictions of Zech., Chpts. 12 and 14, along with Rev., Chpt. 19, and other similar Prophecies.)

2 In Salem also is His Tabernacle, and His dwelling place in Zion. *("Salem" is Jerusalem. "Zion" is where the Tabernacle was located, near where the Temple would later be built. God then dwelt in the Tabernacle in the Holy of Holies, between the Mercy Seat and the Cherubim. Due to the Cross, He now dwells in the hearts and lives of Believers [I Cor. 3:16].)*

3 There broke He the arrows of the bow, the shield, and the sword, and the battle. Selah. *(This speaks of the Battle of Armageddon, when the Lord will break in pieces the weapons of the Antichrist [Ezek. 39:9].)*

4 You are more glorious and excellent than the mountains of prey. *(Man must learn that God is greater than His creation. The Verse also speaks of the future days of the Antichrist, when he will invade Israel, taking it for "prey." He will there learn that God is more glorious in battle than in any other manner [Zech. 14:1-3].)*

5 The stouthearted are spoiled, they have slept their sleep: and none of the men of might have found their hands. *(This Passage has a double meaning: 1. It speaks of the defeat of the Jebusites by God under David and 2. It speaks prophetically of the Antichrist, when he too will not be able to "find his hands," with his armies being defeated [Rev., Chpt. 19].*

6 At Your rebuke, O God of Jacob, both the chariot and horse are cast into a dead sleep. *(This refers to both the Jebusites, whose army was slaughtered, and the Antichrist, whose armies will be slaughtered [Ezek. 39:11-29].)*

7 You, even You, are to be feared: and who may stand in Your sight when once You are angry? *(Once again, this refers to the Jebusites, and prophetically to the Antichrist. It says, "For*

the great day of His [God's] Wrath is come; and who shall be able to stand?" [Rev. 6:17].)

8 You did cause judgment to be heard from Heaven; the Earth feared, and was still (this reveals that Israel had some difficulty in taking the stronghold of Zion from the Jebusites, and might not have done so if God had not helped; as well, it refers to His Second Coming, when half of Jerusalem will fall to the Antichrist [Zech., Chpt. 14]),

9 When God arose to judgment, to save all the meek of the Earth. Selah. (The "meek of the Earth," refers to Israel when the Antichrist will seek to destroy them totally. At that time, God will "arise to judgment.")

10 Surely the wrath of man shall praise You: the remainder of wrath shall You restrain. (The "wrath of man" refers to the wrath of the Antichrist. "The remainder of wrath" refers to the Antichrist being halted in his efforts to destroy Israel and the subsequent dominion of the Earth by the Coming of the Lord [Rev., Chpt. 19].)

11 Vow, and pay unto the LORD your God: let all who be round about Him bring presents unto Him Who ought to be feared. (Under David and Solomon, this was partially fulfilled [II Chron. 9:13-14]. It will be completely fulfilled in the Millennial Reign, when Christ rules from Jerusalem [Zech. 14:14].)

12 He shall cut off the spirit of princes: He is terrible to the kings of the Earth. (This means that, in the days of the Millennial Reign, men will rule only under Christ. If they refuse to carry out His Commands, the price will be "terrible" [Zech. 14:16-19].)

PSALM 77

A PSALM OF ASAPH:
THE GREATNESS OF GOD

I cried unto God with my voice, even unto God with my voice; and He gave ear unto me. (This Psalm has a double meaning: 1. It refers to any Believer who calls on the Lord and 2. It is a prophetic portrayal of Israel in the last half of the Great Tribulation, when it seems that she will be completely destroyed by the Antichrist. No doubt, Israel will refer repeatedly to this Psalm during that particular time.)

2 In the day of my trouble I sought the LORD: my sore ran in the night, and ceased not: my soul refused to be comforted. (Unfortunately, the modern Church is presently being taught to look elsewhere than to the Lord. But,

let it be known, He Alone can help!)

3 I remembered God, and was troubled: I complained, and my spirit was overwhelmed. Selah. (The meaning of this Verse is that Asaph felt God could have prevented him from getting into this trouble and, therefore, he "complains." When he did so, his spirit "was overwhelmed." Complaining is never in the Will of God!)

4 You hold my eyes waking: I am so troubled that I cannot speak. (Fear overwhelms him, and he registers doubt.)

5 I have considered the days of old, the years of ancient times. (Israel will, in the days of "Jacob's Trouble," do the same thing. They will remember God's opening of the Red Sea, the waters of Jordan, and the fighting of their battles. They will hunger for Him to do it again.)

6 I call to remembrance my song in the night: I commune with my own heart: and my spirit made diligent search. (Asaph now begins to search his own heart.)

7 Will the Lord cast off for ever? and will He be favourable no more? (At times, the Lord allows such to take place, all designed to teach us Faith and Trust.)

8 Is His mercy clean gone for ever? does His promise fail for evermore? (This will be the thoughts of Israel at the latter half of the Great Tribulation. The Antichrist will have turned on her, and she faces extinction!)

9 Has God forgotten to be gracious? has He in anger shut up His tender mercies? Selah. (Preoccupation with self only leads to these questions and to doubt. When an individual comes to this place, doubt has degenerated to despair. As stated, Israel will cry these words in the last half of the Great Tribulation. Their only hope is God, but it seems as though the Heavens are brass, and He will not answer.)

10 And I said, This is my infirmity: but I will remember the years of the right hand of the Most High. (Here, the Psalmist ceases his dejected self-occupation, and becomes occupied with God. Consequently, his despondency vanishes. This is the only cure for misery and despair.

He first of all says, "I will remember," and speaks of the years of past blessings. He will account them and speak of them in his mind.)

11 I will remember the works of the LORD: surely I will remember Your wonders of old. ("The works of the LORD" pertain to the things that the Lord has done in one's life. These things are to be remembered and accounted.)

12 I will meditate also of all Your work, and talk of Your doings. (Not only are we to

remember what the Lord has done, but we should meditate on it, and then, at every chance, talk about "Your doings." If we "talk" of God's doings, then we cannot talk of doubt and unbelief.

God's Word and Ways are timeless. As it worked for Asaph, it will work for anyone who will embark upon that which was tendered by the Holy Spirit.

1. Remember His ancient Works, and those done personally for us; 2. Meditate on His great Works; and, 3. Talk of His great Works.)

13 Your way, O God, is in the Sanctuary: Who is so great a God as our God? (Occupation of heart with others outside the Sanctuary and occupation of heart with self inside the Sanctuary both produce misery, but occupation of heart with God inside the Sanctuary gives comfort and victory. Despite our circumstances, "God is Great!")

14 You are the God Who does wonders: You have declared Your strength among the people. (The "Strength of God" is gained by the Believer evidencing Faith in Christ and what Christ has done at the Cross [I Cor. 1:18].)

15 You have with Your arm redeemed Your people, the sons of Jacob and Joseph. Selah. (As the Lord has redeemed His People in times past, He most definitely will do so during the time of the coming Great Tribulation. In fact, this is a Prophecy which says that He will.)

16 The waters saw You, O God, the waters saw You; they were afraid: the depths also were troubled. (This speaks of the Red Sea, and the Lord opening that body of water on behalf of His Children, when they were delivered out of Egypt [Ex. 14:21-31].)

17 The clouds poured out water: the skies sent out a sound: Your arrows also went abroad. (Due to the fact that the Lord delivered His People in ancient times, He will also do so at the Battle of Armageddon, to which this Verse pertains.)

18 The voice of Your thunder was in the Heaven: the lightnings lightened the world: the Earth trembled and shook. (This, as well, refers to the coming Battle of Armageddon.)

19 Your way is in the sea, and Your path in the great waters, and Your footsteps are not known. (The sense of this Passage is that as "footsteps" are not left in the sea, neither is the "Way" of God so easily tracked. God's "Way" is His Word. It is not man's way. Man does not understand it and, in fact, within himself, cannot understand it [Rom. 11:33].)

20 You led Your people like a flock by the hand of Moses and Aaron. (The names, Jacob,

Joseph, Moses, and Aaron, are significant. Moses and Aaron typify Christ as King and Priest. A flock thus doubly led is surely led. Jacob and Joseph [Vs. 15] express how doubly precious to God is the flock itself, because the sheep are the sons of these fathers so beloved of God.)

PSALM 78

WRITTEN BY ASAPH:
GOD'S DEALINGS WITH HIS
PEOPLE ISRAEL

GIVE ear, O My people, to My law: incline your ears to the words of My mouth. (Jesus called Asaph "a Prophet" [Mat. 13:35]. In fact, all who wrote the Psalms must be placed in that category.

This Verse presents an Old Testament command to obey the Law of Moses. In fact, the statement, "Give ear to My Law," is found some 32 times in the Old Testament, but not once in the New. The reason is simple:

Jesus fulfilled all the Law, and Faith in Him and what He has done at the Cross makes Believers dead to the Law [Rom. 7:4].)

2 I will open My mouth in a parable: I will utter dark sayings of old (this was quoted by Matthew concerning Christ [Mat. 13:35]. The puzzle here is not in the expression of mystery or in words hard to understand, but in great wonderment of how these many miraculous things happened to Israel. This Verse refers strictly to Christ):

3 Which we have heard and known, and our fathers have told us (these great happenings, which God performed from the very beginning, were remembered, and then began to be written down by Moses [Lk. 24:27]).

4 We will not hide them from their children, showing to the generation to come the praises of the LORD, and His strength, and His wonderful works that He has done (the Holy Spirit is saying here that it is extremely important for parents to recount the "wonderful works of God" to "their children").

5 For He established a testimony in Jacob, and appointed a law in Israel, which He commanded our fathers, that they should make them known to their children. (That the children should be taught the Word of God by the fathers was not a suggestion; it was a "command." The "Testimony in Jacob" was the Lord's Personal dealings with the Patriarch; He would change him from Jacob, the schemer, to Israel,

the Prince with God.

The "Law in Israel" was that which was given by God to Moses.

Concerning these two things, Israel was to constantly relate them to their children. Incidentally, it was not a suggestion, but rather a command.)

6 That the generation to come might know them, even the children which should be born; who should arise and declare them to their children (a Move of God is actually limited to the present generation unless that generation proclaims the Truth to the coming generation):

7 That they might set their hope in God, and not forget the works of God, but keep His Commandments (this is the only way to a successful life and living):

8 And might not be as their fathers, a stubborn and rebellious generation; a generation that set not their heart aright, and whose spirit was not stedfast with God (the idea is, if the children aren't properly taught, everything will be lost).

9 The children of Ephraim, being armed, and carrying bows, turned back in the day of battle (he is probably speaking of the northern kingdom of Israel, which sometime went under the name of "Ephraim").

10 They kept not the Covenant of God, and refused to walk in His Law (this is the reason for the lack of victory regarding Ephraim, and it is the reason for the lack of victory now);

11 And forgot His works, and His wonders that He had shown them (these "works" and "wonders" were not properly shown and related to the children).

12 Marvellous things did He in the sight of their fathers, in the land of Egypt, in the field of Zoan.

13 He divided the sea, and caused them to pass through; and He made the waters to stand as an heap (the miracle of the Red Sea crossing).

14 In the daytime also He led them with a cloud, and all the night with a light of fire.

15 He clave the rocks in the wilderness, and gave them drink as out of the great depths (the water out of the Rock).

16 He brought streams also out of the rock, and caused waters to run down like rivers (this means that this was no slight trickle that came out of the Rock, but rather a small river — enough to slake the thirst of some three million people, plus all of the animals).

17 And they sinned yet more against Him by provoking the Most High in the wilderness.

(Miracles do not produce Faith; only the Word of God can produce Faith [Rom. 10:17]. During the time of Christ, Israel had the greatest array of miracles the world had ever known, but to no avail. They crucified their Lord!)

18 And they tempted God in their heart by asking meat for their lust (in other words, they were not satisfied with the Manna).

19 Yea, they spoke against God; they said, Can God furnish a table in the wilderness? (He could, and He did!)

20 Behold, He smote the rock, that the waters gushed out, and the streams overflowed; can He give bread also? can He provide flesh for His people? (Even though these people saw the miracle of bringing water out of the Rock, which was actually a Type of the great Eternal Life that Christ would provide for the whole world, still, these faithless people not only did not understand its meaning, but also held it with contempt.)

21 Therefore the LORD heard this, and was wroth: so a fire was kindled against Jacob, and anger also came up against Israel (let it ever be understood that God cannot condone sin in His Chosen any more than He can in those who do not profess His Name);

22 Because they believed not in God, and trusted not in His salvation (their sin was unbelief. It is, as well, the sin of the modern Church. I speak of a lack of Faith in Christ and the Cross):

23 Though He had commanded the clouds from above, and opened the doors of Heaven,

24 And had rained down Manna upon them to eat, and had given them of the corn of Heaven.

25 Man did eat Angels' food: He sent them meat to the full (we are told here that the Manna was "Angels' food").

26 He caused an east wind to blow in the Heaven: and by His power He brought in the south wind.

27 He rained flesh also upon them as dust, and feathered fowls like as the sand of the sea (the quail [Num. 11:20]):

28 And He let it fall (the quail) in the midst of their camp, round about their habitations.

29 So they did eat, and were well filled: for He gave them their own desire (if it is to be noticed, it was "their desire" and not God's);

30 They were not estranged from their lust. But while their meat was yet in their mouths,

31 The wrath of God came upon them, and slew the fattest of them, and smote down the

chosen men of Israel. *(Israel's lust and complaints angered God, so His wrath fell on them. We should allow this to be a lesson to us, as well.)*

32 For all this they sinned still, and believed not for His wondrous works. *(Ultimately, they died in this wilderness, and never did see the Promised Land; all of this was because of unbelief.)*

33 Therefore their days did He consume in vanity, and their years in trouble. *(And unbelief was the reason!)*

34 When He slew them, then they sought Him: and they returned and enquired early after God. *(Sometimes it takes the Judgment of God to get people to repent.)*

35 And they remembered that God was their Rock, and the high God their Redeemer. *(Still, their attitude was to "use God" rather than to "serve God.")*

36 Nevertheless they did flatter Him with their mouth, and they lied unto Him with their tongues. *(What a foolish thing to do, considering that God knows the thoughts and hearts of men!)*

37 For their heart was not right with Him, neither were they stedfast in His Covenant. *(This was the problem. It was a "heart" problem. It was not a question of understanding or of knowledge. It was a question of "an evil heart of unbelief.")*

38 But He, being full of compassion, forgave their iniquity, and destroyed them not: yea, many a time turned He His anger away, and did not stir up all His wrath. *(In this Passage, we are given a most beautiful description of the Love of God.)*

39 For He remembered that they were but flesh; a wind that passes away, and comes not again. *(In other words, the Lord knows the frailty of the flesh and, due to the fall of man, the constant pressure of the sin nature.)*

40 How oft did they provoke Him in the wilderness, and grieve Him in the desert! *(Actually, they provoked Him some ten times in approximately two years [Num. 14:22].)*

41 Yea, they turned back and tempted God, and limited the Holy One of Israel. *(We limit God when we fail to take Him at His Word.)*

42 They remembered not His hand, nor the day when He delivered them from the enemy. *(The Holy Spirit is telling us that Israel had no faith, because they forgot the great miracles the Lord had performed for them in the past. Over and over again, the Holy Spirit admonishes us to constantly meditate and talk about the things He has done in the past. This is His Word; it builds faith [Ps. 77:10-12].)*

43 How He had wrought his signs in Egypt, and His wonders in the field of Zoan *(Verses 43 through 58 proclaim the great miracles and wonders of God performed in Egypt, as well as in the Promised Land)*:

44 And had turned their rivers into blood; and their floods, that they could not drink.

45 He sent divers sorts of flies among them, which devoured them; and frogs, which destroyed them.

46 He gave also their increase unto the caterpiller, and their labour unto the locust. *(This is what the Lord did to Egypt, because they refused to let God's People go.)*

47 He destroyed their vines with hail, and their sycomore trees with frost.

48 He gave up their cattle also to the hail, and their flocks to hot thunderbolts.

49 He cast upon them the fierceness of His anger, wrath, and indignation, and trouble, by sending evil angels among them. *(These were probably righteous Angels who carried out the intended results of God's "anger, wrath, indignation, and trouble," referred to as "evil.")*

50 He made a way to His anger; He spared not their soul from death, but gave their life over to the pestilence;

51 And smote all the firstborn in Egypt; the chief of their strength in the tabernacles of Ham:

52 But made His own people to go forth like sheep, and guided them in the wilderness like a flock. *(The Holy Spirit, through Asaph, outlines the tender leading of Israel by Jehovah. In fact, He became their Shepherd.)*

53 And He led them on safely, so that they feared not: but the sea overwhelmed their enemies *(the Red Sea)*.

54 And He brought them to the border of His Sanctuary, even to this mountain, which His right hand had purchased *(the Land of Israel)*.

55 He cast out the heathen also before them, and divided them an inheritance by line, and made the Tribes of Israel to dwell in their tents *(this Passage means that the Holy Spirit drew the boundaries in this Land for each particular Tribe)*.

56 Yet they tempted and provoked the Most High God, and kept not His Testimonies:

57 But turned back, and dealt unfaithfully like their fathers: they were turned aside like a deceitful bow *(this is a bow which flips back and harms the person trying to shoot it)*.

58 For they provoked Him to anger with

their high places, and moved Him to jealousy with their graven images *(upon arriving in the Promised Land, Israel quickly took upon herself the practices of the heathen round about her).*

59 When God heard this, He was wroth, and greatly abhorred Israel *(because of their sin):*

60 So that He forsook the Tabernacle of Shiloh, the Tent which He placed among men *(the Lord could no longer live among Israel);*

61 And delivered His strength into captivity, and His glory into the enemy's hand *(the Ark of God, for a period of time, was taken by the Philistines [I Sam. 4:11]).*

62 He gave His people over also unto the sword; and was wroth with His inheritance.

63 The fire consumed their young men; and their maidens were not given to marriage.

64 Their Priests fell by the sword; and their widows made no lamentation *(Hophni and Phinehas fell by the sword and their widows made no lamentation; Phinehas' wife, when dying, bewailed the loss of the Ark more than the loss of her husband [I Sam. 4:17-18]).*

65 Then the Lord awaked as one out of sleep, and like a mighty man who shouts by reason of wine *(this refers to the defeat of the Philistines by Israel [I Sam. 7:7-14]).*

66 And He smote His enemies in the hinder parts: He put them to a perpetual reproach.

67 Moreover He refused the Tabernacle of Joseph, and chose not the Tribe of Ephraim *(the "Tabernacle of Joseph" is the Sanctuary at Shiloh, which was north of Bethel, and thus within the limits of the Tribe of Ephraim):*

68 But chose the Tribe of Judah, the Mount Zion which He loved. *(When a permanent site was to be assigned to the Tabernacle and the Ark, God did not choose for them the position of Shiloh, but rather that of Jerusalem. The choice was made when David was, by God's command, anointed to be king [I Sam. 16:1-12].)*

69 And He build His Sanctuary like high palaces, like the Earth which He has established for ever. *(This was the place where the great Temple was ultimately built, with the plans given to David, but with David's son, Solomon, actually building the structure.)*

70 He chose David also His servant, and took him from the sheepfolds *(Saul was man's choice, while David was God's choice; He took David from humble beginnings; David started out by feeding sheep; he was promoted to feeding God's people):*

71 From following the ewes great with young He brought him to feed Jacob His people, and Israel His inheritance.

72 So he fed them according to the integrity of his heart; and guided them by the skilfulness of his hands. *(The Lord, through David, fed Israel, because David had "integrity of heart." However, the "integrity" that David had was God's integrity, and not man's.*

Let it ever be known that only those who have God's "integrity" will be the shepherds that God desires, guiding God's sheep "by the skillfulness of His hands" — the Holy Spirit.)

PSALM 79

A PSALM OF ASAPH:
A PRAYER FOR THE DESTRUCTION OF HEATHEN ENEMIES

O God, the heathen are come into Your inheritance; Your Holy Temple have they defiled; they have laid Jerusalem on heaps. *(The Psalm has a triple meaning: 1. It speaks of the time when Nebuchadnezzar would take Jerusalem, destroying the Temple; 2. It refers to Titus, the Roman General, who destroyed Jerusalem and the Temple in A.D. 70; and, 3. It refers to the future Temple, which will be defiled by the Antichrist at the midway point of the Great Tribulation.)*

2 The dead bodies of Your servants have they given to be meat unto the fowls of the Heaven, the flesh of Your Saints unto the beasts of the Earth. *(Daniel said that the Antichrist would "destroy the mighty and the holy people" [Dan. 8:24].)*

3 Their blood have they shed like water round about Jerusalem; and there was none to bury them.

4 We are become a reproach to our neighbours, a scorn and derision to them who are round about us. *(This happened in the past, and it will also happen in the future [Lam. 2:15-16].)*

5 How long, LORD? will You be angry for ever? shall Your jealousy burn like fire? *(These questions were, no doubt, asked many times in the past; however, they will be asked with even greater intensity during the latter half of the Great Tribulation, called "The Time of Jacob's Trouble" [Jer. 30:7].)*

6 Pour out Your wrath upon the heathen who have not known You, and upon the kingdoms that have not called upon Your Name *(considering that Israel has a long history with Jehovah, she wonders as to why the Lord is not*

pouring out His wrath upon the heathen, who care not at all for Him?).

7 For they have devoured Jacob, and laid waste His dwelling place *(even though happening many times in the past, once again it refers to the coming Great Tribulation, when the Antichrist will lay waste Jerusalem and the Temple).*

8 O remember not against us former iniquities: let Your tender mercies speedily prevent us: for we are brought very low. *(During the latter half of the Great Tribulation, two-thirds of the population of Israel will be killed [Zech. 13:8]. It will look as if they will be totally annihilated. They realize that they have sinned greatly in the past. They are now pleading with the Lord not to remember "their former iniquities." This is a true prayer of Repentance and one that Israel has seldom prayed. It is a prayer that will be heard and answered.)*

9 Help us, O God of our Salvation, for the glory of Your Name: and deliver us, and purge away our sins, for Your Name's sake. *(This moment, even though futuristic, is so holy that one is brought to tears even while reading the words.*

As this will be the prayer of Israel during the Battle of Armageddon, likewise, it should be the prayer of the entirety of the modern Church. It is a prayer of true Repentance.)

10 Wherefore should the heathen say, Where is their God? let Him be known among the heathen in our sight by the revenging of the blood of Your servants which is shed. *(And that's exactly what the Lord will do. It is called the "Second Coming"!)*

11 Let the sighing of the prisoner come before You; according to the greatness of Your power preserve Thou those who are appointed to die *(the Lord will answer this prayer; Zechariah prophesied, "Then shall the LORD go forth, and fight against those nations, as when He fought in the day of battle" [Zech. 14:3]);*

12 And render unto our neighbours sevenfold into their bosom their reproach, wherewith they have reproached You, O Lord. *(And that's exactly what will happen [Ezek. 38:18].)*

13 So we Your people and sheep of Your pasture will give You thanks for ever: we will show forth Your praise to all generations. *(This Passage lets us know that the Prophecy given in this Psalm pertains more to the coming Great Tribulation and the Second Coming of the Lord. Then, Israel will truly give the Lord "thanks forever." They have never done that in the past. They will do so in the future!)*

PSALM 80

A PSALM OF ASAPH:
A PRAYER FOR RESTORATION

GIVE ear, O Shepherd of Israel, Thou Who led Joseph like a flock; Thou Who dwelt between the Cherubims, shine forth. *(The blessing of Joseph [Gen. 49:22-26] uses the figures of the "Shepherd" and the "Vine, whose fruitful branches run over the wall." Hence, the nation is here called Joseph, and the Messiah is addressed as its Shepherd. This Psalm, as the previous, delineates Israel's history and future.)*

2 Before Ephraim and Benjamin and Manasseh stir up Your strength, and come and save us. *(When the cloud was taken up from Israel in the wilderness, the Tribes journeyed. Following the Kohathites, who were bearing the Sanctuary and the Ark, came Ephraim, Benjamin, and Manasseh. Accordingly, in this Psalm, they occupy this position in relation to the Ark. These Tribes were the Children of Rachel.)*

3 Turn us again, O God, and cause Your face to shine; and we shall be saved. *(In Ezekiel, we are told of the Glory of God departing from Jerusalem and the Temple [Ezek. 11:22-23]. Ezekiel also saw the Glory of God returning [Ezek. 43:1-5]. The latter will be during the opening days of the Millennial Reign.*

The Psalmist, and actually Christ as the Intercessor, prays for that Glory to return. In fact, it will return when the Messiah returns, to the discomfiture of Israel's oppressors, and thus will recover and replant His Vine.)

4 O LORD God of Hosts, how long will You be angry against the prayer of Your people? *(The anger of God against His People, because they killed the Messiah, has lasted now for nearly 2,000 years.)*

5 You feed them with the bread of tears; and give them tears to drink in great measure. *(No people on Earth have shed tears as long as Israel has, due to the great sorrow brought upon them because of their rejection of their Messiah and the world's Saviour, the Lord Jesus Christ.)*

6 You make us a strife unto our neighbours: and our enemies laugh among themselves. *(This has happened many times in Israel's history; it is happening even now with Israel's neighbors, Saudi Arabia, Jordan, Syria, Egypt, Iraq, Iran, etc. The greater meaning has to do with the Time of Jacob's Trouble, when it looks like Israel will be totally destroyed by the Antichrist. Her enemies will then "laugh among themselves.")*

7 Turn us again, O God of Hosts, and cause Your face to shine; and we shall be saved. *(This is a petition for Israel to be restored to nationhood and to the worship of God in the Sanctuary. In complete form, this will not be done until the Second Coming.)*

8 You have brought a Vine out of Egypt: You have cast out the heathen, and planted it *(that "Vine" is Israel).*

9 You prepared room before it, and did cause it to take deep root, and it filled the land *(the Land of Promise).*

10 The hills were covered with the shadow of it, and the boughs thereof were like the goodly cedars *(great growth!).*

11 She sent out her boughs unto the sea, and her branches unto the river *(extended to the Mediterranean Sea and the Euphrates River).*

12 Why have You then broken down her hedges, so that all they which pass by the way do pluck her? *(The Lord allowed this to happen to Israel because of her rebellion against Him.)*

13 The boar out of the wood does waste it, and the wild beast of the field does devour it *(basically, this refers to Rome and her subjugation of Israel, which took place before the First Advent of Christ).*

14 Return, we beseech You, O God of Hosts: look down from Heaven, and behold, and visit this vine *(the words, "once more," should be supplied in these petitions, because that meaning is found in the Hebrew Text; it actually says, "Once more look down from Heaven! Once more behold! Once more visit this Vine!");*

15 And the vineyard which Your right hand has planted, and the branch that You made strong for Yourself *(in fact, this prayer ultimately will be answered; God will restore Israel [Rom., Chpt. 11]).*

16 It is burned with fire, it is cut down: they perish at the rebuke of Your countenance. *(This means that the shining of His Countenance will save His People; its rebuking will destroy their foes. This Verse should read, "They [the destroyers of the Vine] shall perish at the rebuke of Your Countenance.")*

17 Let Your hand be upon the man of Your right hand, upon the son of man whom You made strong for Yourself. *(The Chaldee reads, "King Messiah," the Man upon God's Right Hand. It is possibly to this Verse and Prophecy that the Lord pointed when claiming for Himself the title, "Son of Man.")*

18 So will not we go back from You: quicken us, and we will call upon Your Name. *(The*

moral results of the Messiah's entrance into the Sanctuary are seen in this Verse. Whenever Jesus enters into the Millennial Temple, Israel will never again turn their back on Him.)*

19 Turn us again, O LORD God of Hosts, cause Your face to shine; and we shall be saved. *(For the soul into which He shines, there is no going back; whomever He quickens, He eternally attaches to His Name. With Him Alone is there Salvation.)*

PSALM 81

WRITTEN BY ASAPH: GOD'S GOODNESS AND MAN'S WAYWARDNESS

SING aloud unto God our strength: make a joyful noise unto the God of Jacob. *(The expression, "God of Jacob," means the "God of all Grace." These are His Old Testament and New Testament titles. Israel's Messiah is the Speaker in this Psalm. In it are the tender thoughts and loving purposes of His Heart for His Sheep [Mat. 23:37; Lk. 19:42].)*

2 Take a Psalm, and bring hither the timbrel, the pleasant harp with the psaltery. *(As many other Passages do, this Passage proclaims not only the approval, but actually the creation, of musical instruments for the worship of God. Such was done at that time, is being done now, and actually will be done forever in eternity, in praise to God [Rev. 5:8-9].)*

3 Blow up the trumpet in the new moon, in the time appointed, on our solemn feast day. *(The terms, "new moon" and "solemn feast day," all have to do with the Law of Moses, which was all fulfilled in Christ, and in actuality is no more. But that which it represented, the worship of God, most definitely continues, and will ever continue.)*

4 For this was a Statute for Israel, and a Law of the God of Jacob. *(Under the Old Covenant, Israel was the only nation on Earth that had the "Law of God.")*

5 This He ordained in Joseph for a Testimony, when He went out through the land of Egypt: where I heard a language that I understood not. *(This does not mean that the Great Shepherd did not understand the Egyptian language, but that He did not acknowledge the Egyptians as His Sheep. The Hebrew verb here should be translated "acknowledge," as in Psalms 32:5, instead of the word "understood.")*

6 I removed his *(Israel's)* shoulder from

the burden: his hands were delivered from the pots *(this refers to Israel's deliverance as slaves from Egyptian bondage).*

7 You called in trouble, and I delivered you; I answered you in the secret place of thunder: I proved you at the waters of Meribah. Selah. *(This means that the "waters of Meribah," etc., [waters of murmuring and strife] were a test [Ex. 17:7]. In fact, everything, as it regards the Child of God, is a test.)*

8 Hear, O My people, and I will testify unto You: O Israel, if you will hearken unto Me *(Verses 8 through 10 may be understood as having been addressed to Israel upon leaving Egypt);*

9 There shall no strange god be in you; neither shall you worship any strange god. *(The "strange god" expressed here refers to heathenistic idols, which were actually representations of demon spirits. Regrettably, many "strange gods" abide in the modern Church. Modern psychology is a "strange god." So is "philosophy," which is "vain deceit" [Col. 2:8]. In fact, anything that is not "Jesus Christ and Him Crucified," and that exclusively, presents a "strange god.")*

10 I am the LORD your God, which brought you out of the land of Egypt: open your mouth wide, and I will fill it *(this meant that every desire and need of Israel would be fulfilled, if they would only believe God).*

11 But My people would not hearken to My voice; and Israel would none of Me. *(Is the modern Church presently in the same spiritual condition?)*

12 So I gave them up unto their own hearts' lust: and they walked in their own counsels. *(If Believers do not desire God's "Counsel," which is His Word, and that exclusively, then He will allow such Believers to walk in their "own counsels." Such presents disaster!)*

13 Oh that My people had hearkened unto Me, and Israel had walked in My ways! *(The Ministry of the Holy Spirit is to straighten out man's walk, which can only be done as we evidence Faith in Christ and what Christ did for us at the Cross; this is the Faith through which the Holy Spirit exclusively works [Rom. 8:1-2, 11].)*

14 I should soon have subdued their enemies, and turned My hand against their adversaries. *(The "adversaries" came whenever Israel turned to her own ways instead of God's Way.)*

15 The haters of the LORD should have submitted themselves unto Him: but their time should have endured for ever. *(The Lord is saying that He would have subdued these "haters," if only Israel would have "submitted themselves unto Him — God." If they had done so, Israel would have never been defeated, and would have, in fact, "endured forever.")*

16 He should have fed them also with the finest of the wheat: and with honey out of the rock should I have satisfied you. *(These are affectionate terms, with "wheat" speaking of prosperity and "honey out of the rock" speaking of God's special additional Blessings.)*

PSALM 82

A PSALM OF ASAPH:
GOD THE RIGHTEOUS JUDGE

GOD stands in the congregation of the mighty; He judges among the gods. *(The first four Verses of this Psalm are an account of the Lord Jesus standing in the Temple in the midst of what was the congregation of God and judging the rulers of the people. He fulfilled the first four Verses [Mat., Chpts. 21-23; Jn., Chpts. 8-10].)*

2 How long will you judge unjustly, and accept the persons of the wicked? Selah. *(Israel was designed by God to be His representative in the Earth and judge of the nations. Hence, her magistrates were termed "gods" — representatives of God.*

Israel failed to fulfill this Divine Purpose; therefore, the prediction of this Psalm is that the Messiah will take up this Divine Purpose and perfectly fulfill it as Judge of Israel and of all nations — through His Body, the Church [Eph. 1:20-23].)

3 Defend the poor and fatherless: do justice to the afflicted and needy. *(When religious leaders leave the way of God and devise their own ways, the people then become pawns. True and righteous judgment demands that true Servants of God serve the people [Jn. 13:12-17]. When religion prevails, the way of God is turned upside down, with the people washing the feet of religious leaders.)*

4 Deliver the poor and needy: rid them out of the hand of the wicked. *(Deliverance can be effected only by looking to Christ as the Source, and the Cross as the means [Lk. 4:18].)*

5 They know not, neither will they understand; they walk on in darkness: all the foundations of the Earth are out of course. *(These wicked religious leaders of Israel would not hear Christ; therefore, they continued in darkness until the nation was finally destroyed, with the Gospel then being given to the Gentiles.)*

6 I have said, You are gods; and all of you are children of the Most High. *(The statement means that God had appointed Israel as judges [gods], simply because they were chosen of God and, therefore, the Children of God; however, Israel failed to fulfill this purpose and ultimately was destroyed.)*

7 But you shall die like men, and fall like one of the princes. *(Israel was so lifted up in herself, that she felt she merited righteousness. The Lord's pronouncements, in effect, told them they would die and die lost [Mat., Chpt. 23]. Even though they were called a "prince," or a representative of God, still, they would "fall." And that they did!)*

8 Arise, O God, judge the Earth: for You shall inherit all nations. *(Israel failed, but Jesus Christ will never fail. The Messiah has taken up this Divine Purpose, and will perfectly fulfill it as Judge of Israel and of all nations.)*

PSALM 83

A PSALM OF ASAPH:
A PRAYER FOR THE DESTRUCTION OF ISRAEL'S ENEMIES

KEEP not Thou silence, O God: hold not Your peace, and be not still, O God. *(As the previous Psalm proclaimed the destruction of Israel by the Messiah because of their terrible rebellion, this Psalm reflects the efforts of the Antichrist to completely annihilate Israel.)*

2 For, lo, your *(Israel's)* enemies make a tumult: and they who hate you have lifted up the head. *(This "head," representing ten nations, as outlined by Daniel [Dan. 7:7; Rev. 13:1], will join with the Antichrist in opposing Israel.)*

3 They have taken crafty counsel against Your people, and consulted against Your hidden ones. *(The "crafty counsel" means that the seven-year pact that the Antichrist will make with Israel will be broken at the midpoint. The term, "hidden ones," means that the Antichrist will think that God no longer cares for Israel. His Care has been somewhat "hidden," but will now come forth to full bloom.)*

4 They have said, Come, and let us cut them off from being a nation; that the name of Israel may be no more in remembrance. *(This is the "evil thought" of Ezek. 38:10.)*

5 For they have consulted together with one consent: they are confederate against You *(these who are "confederate" are the ten horns of Dan. 7:7; John said these kings would be confederate*

with the Antichrist [the beast — Rev. 17:12]):*

6 The tabernacles of Edom, and the Ishmaelites; of Moab, and the Hagarenes;

7 Gebal, and Ammon, and Amalek; the Philistines with the inhabitants of Tyre;

8 Assur also is joined with them: they have helped the children of Lot. Selah.

9 Do unto them as unto the Midianites; as to Sisera, as to Jabin, at the brook of Kison:

10 Which perished at En-dor; they became as dung for the Earth.

11 Make their nobles like Oreb, and like Zeeb: yea, all their princes as Zebah, and as Zalmunna *(these nations listed were confederates against Israel, and are representative of the ten nations in the last days which, under the Antichrist, will oppose and persecute Israel greatly):*

12 Who said, Let us take to ourselves the houses of God in possession. *(This speaks of the Antichrist, who will take over the rebuilt Temple at the midpoint of his seven-year pact with Israel. He will do this by setting up his own statue in the "House of God," and will demand worship [II Thess. 2:4].)*

13 O my God, make them like a wheel; as the stubble before the wind.

14 As the fire burns a wood, and as the flame sets the mountains on fire;

15 So persecute them with Your tempest, and make them afraid with Your storm.

16 Fill their faces with shame; that they may seek Your Name, O LORD.

17 Let them be confounded and troubled for ever; yea, let them be put to shame, and perish *(and all of this will most definitely happen at the Second Coming):*

18 That men may know that You, Whose name alone is JEHOVAH, are the Most High over all the Earth. *(Ezekiel said concerning God's Deliverance of Israel in the Battle of Armageddon, "The heathen shall know that I am the LORD, the Holy One in Israel" [Ezek. 39:7].)*

PSALM 84

AUTHOR UNKNOWN:
THE BLESSING

HOW amiable are Your Tabernacles, O LORD of Hosts! *(The word "Tabernacles," in the Hebrew, is "Mishkan." It means "dwellingplace" or "where God dwells." The word is also the plural of "majesty," expressing the greatness and glory of the Sanctuary. The doctrine of this Psalm is that the Sanctuary*

is a home of pure and satisfying bliss, and that the road to it is a highway of happiness, even though it passes through a valley of weeping.)

2 My soul longs, yea, even faints for the courts of the LORD: my heart and my flesh cries out for the living God. *(The Psalm is somewhat Davidic. It is possible that it was written by David when he was being chased by Saul. Only those who have the longing of Verse 2 will reap the blessing of Verse 11.)*

3 Yea, the sparrow has found an house, and the swallow a nest for herself, where she may lay her young, even Your altars, O LORD of Hosts, my King, and my God. *(The Psalmist is saying that as the "sparrow" and the "swallow" have a house and a nest, likewise, until man finds God and God's dwellingplace, man will have no home. That home can be found only by trust in Christ and the Cross, of which the "Altars" were a Type.)*

4 Blessed are they who dwell in Your house: they will be still praising You. Selah. *(Unceasing praise [I Chron. 9:33] fills the hearts and clothes the lips of those who dwell with God.)*

5 Blessed is the man whose strength is in You; in whose heart are the ways of them. *(Over and over again, the ways of God are contrasted with the ways of man. "Blessed is the man" who follows the ways of God [His Way is in His Word]. There is no blessing to the man who follows the ways of man.)*

6 Who passing through the valley of Baca make it a well; the rain also fills the pools. *(The "valley of Baca" actually means "the valley of weeping." It produces a well of tears. If the spirit of the Believer is carnal, this valley will only be a valley of weeping, but to the spiritual heart, it will be a new nature and unfailing reservoir of strength and refreshment.)*

7 They go from strength to strength, every one of them in Zion appears before God. *(The expression, "strength to strength," refers to enough "strength" for the day but not the morrow. There will be a fresh supply of "strength" awaiting at that time.)*

8 O LORD God of Hosts, hear my prayer: give ear, O God of Jacob. Selah. *(Now that the weary traveler has come through the "valley of Baca" and has made it a "well," going from "strength to strength," he finally stands before the "God of Jacob.")*

9 Behold, O God our shield, and look upon the face of Your anointed. *(The Lord here is referred to as "our shield," meaning that He has protected us on this trying journey, in effect, the*

journey of life. Now He will let us see "the face of Your Anointed" — the Lord Jesus Christ. He is the only Mediator between God and man [I Tim. 2:5]. Now that we have this Mediator [Your Anointed], we are given assurance of our audience with God.)

10 For a day in Your courts is better than a thousand. I had rather be a doorkeeper in the house of my God, than to dwell in the tents of wickedness. *(Now that the Sanctuary has been reached and we are able to stand before the Lord and see His "face," the conclusion is easily reached. A few moments in the Presence of God is greater than anything Satan or the world would have to offer a thousand times over. It is worth a "thousand valleys of Baca" to have this short time in the Presence of God.)*

11 For the LORD God is a Sun and Shield: the LORD will give grace and glory: no good thing will He withhold from them who walk uprightly. *(We must not make the mistake in this Passage of assuming that we know what the good things are! We must allow Him to give us the "good things" that He desires to give.)*

12 O LORD of Hosts, blessed is the man who trusts in You. *(The man who places his trust in God will always be "blessed.")*

PSALM 85

AUTHOR UNKNOWN:
GOD'S ANGER REMOVED FROM ISRAEL

LORD, You have been favourable unto Your land: You have brought back the captivity of Jacob. *(Again, the Scripture states that the Land of Israel belongs to God, and He has given it to Jacob. The "captivity of Jacob" will end at the Second Coming, when Israel will then accept Christ as Saviour and Lord [Zech. 13:6].)*

2 You have forgiven the iniquity of Your people, You have covered all their sin. Selah. *(At the Second Coming, Israel will pray the great prayer of David's Repentance [Ps. 51], and will be forgiven their sins.)*

3 You have taken away all Your wrath: You have turned Yourself from the fierceness of Your anger. *(This will be brought to pass when Israel accepts Christ, Whom they rejected so long ago.)*

4 Turn us, O God of our Salvation, and cause Your anger toward us to cease. *(The expression, "turn us," actually speaks of Repentance.)*

5 Will You be angry with us for ever? will You draw out Your anger to all generations?

(The "generations" addressed here refer to the long period of time that has passed between the First Advent of Christ to the moment of reconciliation — now approximately 2,000 years.)

6 Will You not revive us again: that Your people may rejoice in You? *(The prayer, "revive us again," as it will be prayed by Israel at the Second Coming, should be prayed now by the Church!)*

7 Show us Your mercy, O LORD, and grant us Your salvation. *(In His Intercessory role, the Greater Son of David will, no doubt, pray this prayer on behalf of Israel. In fact, they could never be accepted otherwise. Israel does not ask for justice, but for "mercy" — and even more so, "Your Mercy.")*

8 I will hear what God the LORD will speak: for He will speak peace unto His people, and to His Saints: but let them not turn again to folly. *(If David prayed this prayer regarding Israel's great sin in joining Absalom's rebellion, the Lord will answer by telling them not to "turn again to folly." Sadly, they did not heed the Lord the first time. In the Latter Day, they will heed Him and never again "turn to folly.")*

9 Surely His salvation is near them who fear Him; that glory may dwell in our land. *(When Jesus Christ dwells in Jerusalem, which He most surely shall, "glory will dwell in our land.")*

10 Mercy and Truth are met together; Righteousness and Peace have kissed each other. *(Under the Law, "Mercy" and "Truth" could not meet. "Righteousness" and "Peace" could not kiss or greet each other. However, in Christ, the two will meet.*

Jesus satisfied the Law and did so in every capacity. He did so at the Cross. Christ is the Source and the Cross is the Means.)

11 Truth shall spring out of the Earth; and Righteousness shall look down from Heaven. *(This Passage means that only a Heaven-born Righteousness could undertake the justification of guilty men. The foundation of this Salvation was laid at Golgotha, where, in the Cross of Jesus, Verse 10 was fulfilled. There, Truth and Righteousness judged sin in the Person of Christ, and with that one and only question between God and man now settled, Mercy and Peace flowed freely to sinners.)*

12 Yea, the LORD shall give that which is good; and our land shall yield her increase. *(When Israel gets right with God, this will trigger an abundance of blessings throughout the entirety of the Earth [Rom. 11:15].)*

13 Righteousness shall go before Him; and shall set us in the way of His steps. *(Two thousand years ago, Jesus Christ asked Israel to "follow Me." They refused to do so. Now, at long last, they shall follow "the way of His Steps.")*

PSALM 86

A PSALM OF DAVID:
A PSALM OF PETITION, PENITENCE, AND PRAISE

BOW down Your ear, O LORD, hear Me: for I am poor and needy. *(Actually, the title of this Psalm is "A Prayer of David." More so, it is an Intercession by the Messiah on behalf of His People; therefore, He will take their place and pray the prayer they need to pray by saying, "I am poor and needy."*

The occasion was probably when David was forgiven of his great sin with Bath-sheba, was delivered from Absalom's rebellion, and was restored to his throne.

Its greater occasion will be the Intercession of Christ on behalf of Israel, a prayer which will be answered at the Second Coming.)

2 Preserve My soul; for I am holy: O You My God; save Your Servant who trusts in You. *(The Virgin Mary, in Verse 16, emphasizes the fact that Christ became truly Man; otherwise, He could not be an Advocate for men. It was necessary that, as Man, He should be tempted in all points [Heb. 4:15]. It was equally necessary that, as an Intercessor, He should be sinless; hence, He, the True David, could say what David himself could never say, "I am holy.")*

3 Be merciful unto Me, O Lord: for I cry unto You daily. *(As David cried "daily" for deliverance from the powers of darkness that sought to destroy him, likewise, our Heavenly Intercessor, the Lord Jesus Christ, intercedes on our behalf "daily." He pleads for mercy [Heb. 7:25].)*

4 Rejoice the soul of Your Servant: for unto You, O Lord, do I lift up My soul. *(David can rejoice and the Greater Son of David can rejoice, because the Lord has answered this prayer.)*

5 For You, Lord, are good, and ready to forgive; and plenteous in mercy unto all them who call upon You. *(The Lord is ready to do all these things upon proper confession of sin.)*

6 Give ear, O LORD, unto My prayer; and attend to the voice of My supplications. *("Prayer" is the great bulwark of the Christian. Sadly, few engage in its blessed Promises [James 5:13].)*

7 In the day of My trouble I will call upon You: for You will answer Me. *(Three things are said here: 1. Trouble will come; 2. When it comes, call on God; and, 3. God will answer.)*

8 Among the gods there is none like unto You, O Lord; neither are there any works like unto Your works. *(The title "gods" actually refers to heathenistic "gods," which are actually demon spirits. There is no God but Jehovah!)*

9 All nations whom You have made shall come and worship before You, O Lord; and shall glorify Your Name. *(This is yet unfulfilled. It will be totally fulfilled in the Millennial Reign.)*

10 For You are great, and do wondrous things: You are God Alone. *(On the entirety of the planet, when Christ comes back, He will be "God Alone." Muhammad will be no more; Buddha will be no more. Likewise, all other pretenders will vanish into oblivion.)*

11 Teach Me Your way, O LORD; I will walk in Your truth: unite My heart to fear Your name. *(David prays these words, as we should. More so, the Messiah, as the Intercessor, will pray them on behalf of Israel.)*

12 I will praise You, O Lord My God, with all My heart: and I will glorify Your name for evermore. *(Praise should be a continuous occupation for every Child of God.)*

13 For great is Your mercy toward Me: and You have delivered My soul from the lowest Hell. *(The Lord was gracious to David in forgiving him his great sin, so that he did not die eternally lost. In a greater way, this is the petition of the Son of God praying for His Resurrection, a prayer which was carried out a thousand years before the fact. During the three days and nights that Christ was in the heart of the Earth, He preached to the spirits in prison, which were fallen angels, and He delivered every righteous soul out of Paradise [I Pet. 3:19; Eph. 4:8-9]. All of the underworld is referred to as "Hell," including Paradise. There is no Scriptural record of Jesus going to the burning side of Hell.)*

14 O God, the proud are risen against Me, and the assemblies of violent men have sought after My soul; and have not set You before them. *("The proud" spoken of here refer to the Scribes, Pharisees, and Sadducees. "The assemblies of violent men" are the Sanhedrin. At the trial of Jesus, God had no part in their proceedings; they "have not set You before them." Consequently, they would perform their hellish deed.)*

15 But You, O LORD, are a God full of compassion, and gracious, longsuffering, and plenteous in mercy and truth. *(The world says that God is "cruel," while the Word of God says the opposite.)*

16 O turn unto Me, and have mercy upon Me; give Your strength unto Your Servant, and save the Son of Your handmaid. *(Israel would not save the "Son" of the Virgin Mary, "Your handmaid"; however, God will save "the Son" and, in effect, ultimately will save Israel.)*

17 Show Me a token for good; that they which hate Me may see it, and be ashamed: because You, LORD, have helped Me, and comforted Me. *(The "token for good" that was shown Him was His Resurrection. Those who hated Him saw it. They were not ashamed then, but, at the Second Coming, they will be ashamed [Zech. 12:10].)*

PSALM 87

AUTHOR UNKNOWN:
THE GLORIES OF ZION

HIS foundation is in the holy mountains. *(Even though this Psalm was written "for the sons of Korah," it could very well have been penned by David. It was probably given by the Spirit on the occasion of the bringing up of the Ark to Jerusalem [II Sam., Chpt. 6]. The "holy mountains" probably refer to those of Jerusalem, or possibly the entirety of the Land of Israel.)*

2 The LORD loves the gates of Zion more than all the dwellings of Jacob. *(This means that the Lord has chosen Zion as His chief habitation in Israel [Isa. 8:18; Ps. 48:2; 50:2; 78:68]. This Passage plainly tells us that the Muslims will not occupy Zion much longer.)*

3 Glorious things are spoken of you, O city of God. Selah. *(This speaks of Jerusalem.)*

4 I will make mention of Rahab and Babylon to them who know me: behold Philistia, and Tyre, with Ethiopia; this man was born there. *(Psalms 22:27 will possibly help explain Verse 4. The two names given here by the Holy Spirit, "Rahab" [meaning Egypt] and "Babylon", are expressed in Hebrew, "arrogance" and "confusion." The two terms fitly portray the nature of human government.*

In the coming Kingdom Age, Jerusalem will be the princely city of the nations of the world. It will be that for many reasons, but the greatest reason of all is that Jesus was born there. [Bethlehem may be accounted as a suburb of Jerusalem.]

Coupled with Calvary and the Resurrection,

there is no event that supercedes this. Zion's greatness is attributed to the birth of Christ and not to His Crucifixion. The Crucifixion was the most foul murder ever carried out by wicked hearts. It, as well, was carried out in "Zion."

But, inasmuch as this great event of Psalm 87 takes place in the Millennial Reign, this terrible sin committed by the people of Zion will no longer be remembered by God and, in fact, will be blotted out, even as all sins are blotted out, once the person is washed in the Blood of the Lamb [Eph. 2:13-18].)

5 And of Zion it shall be said, This and that man was born in her: and the Highest Himself shall establish her (Jerusalem D.C. [David's Capital]).

6 The LORD shall count, when He writes up the people, that this man was born there. Selah. (Irrespective of who may have been born in Jerusalem down through the centuries, as mentioned in Verse 5, the only one Who really counts is "this Man," i.e., "the Lord Jesus Christ.")

7 As well the singers as the players on instruments shall be there: all my springs are in you. (All blessings will flow out of Zion [Isa. 2:2-4].)

PSALM 88

AUTHOR UNKNOWN:
THE CRY OF A DESPERATE MAN

O LORD God of My salvation, I have cried day and night before You (as the Holy Spirit has given to the world the words of Jonah's prayer [Jonah, Chpt. 2], so has He given in this Psalm the words of the Messiah's prayer. How amazing that the Spirit of Truth should here invite men to contemplate the eternal Son of God when shut up in the abyss, and should communicate to them the very words of the prayer which He from thence addressed to God!):

2 Let My prayer come before You: incline Your ear unto My cry (just as our Saviour trusted God during His lifetime and when hanging upon the Cross, so He trusted Him when imprisoned in Sheol. He truly believed that God would deliver Him; God did!);

3 For My soul is full of troubles: and My life draws near unto the grave. (This Psalm could as well be a part of the prayer that Jesus prayed in the Garden of Gethsemane.)

4 I am counted with them who go down into the pit: I am as a man who has no strength (He had much "strength" to deliver others. He had no "strength" to deliver Himself. For had He delivered Himself, He could not have delivered others.

The "pit" refers to the Paradise part of Hell, where all the righteous souls were held captive from Abel to the Resurrection of Christ. Christ had to go down into that "pit" and "led captivity captive" [Eph. 4:8]):

5 Free among the dead, like the slain who lie in the grave, whom You remember no more: and they are cut off from Your hand. (When Jesus died on Calvary, no one, not even His most ardent Disciples, believed He would rise from the dead [Lk., Chpt. 24]. He was put in the "grave" [the tomb] to be "remembered no more."

The phrase, "And they are cut off from Your hand," refers to Jesus being "smitten of God and afflicted" [Isa. 53:4]. The Disciples could not understand how He could be "cut off" and be the Messiah at the same time! They lacked understanding, because they lacked knowledge of the Word [Lk. 24:25-27]. They did not, at the time, realize that His being "cut off" meant that we would not be "cut off.")

6 You have laid Me in the lowest pit, in darkness, in the deeps. (Jesus breached this "lowest pit" and "darkness in the deeps" that we have no fear. The first Adam caused the darkness; the Last Adam conquered the darkness.)

7 Your wrath lies hard upon Me, and You have afflicted Me with all Your waves. Selah. (He took the "wrath" that I should have justly received. In taking this "wrath," He had to be "afflicted" by God [Isa. 53:4].)

8 You have put away My acquaintance far from Me; You have made Me an abomination unto them: I am shut up, and I cannot come forth. (The "acquaintance" that He speaks of here pertains to all — His Disciples, His Own relatives, even God and the Holy Angels. Truly He was "made an abomination unto them," because he was bearing the sin of the world [II Cor. 5:21].)

9 My eye mourns by reason of affliction: LORD, I have called daily upon You, I have stretched out My hands unto You. (This Passage proves the truth of Christ's Personal helplessness. The secret of His total Victory was His "calling daily upon You." The "stretching out the hands unto God" refers to a total dependence upon God [Jn. 8:28-29].)

10 Will You show wonders to the dead? shall the dead arise and praise You? Selah. (Truly, God would "show wonders to the dead," i.e., "Christ," and raise Him from the dead. Truly,

He would "arise and praise You.")

11 Shall Your lovingkindness be declared in the grave? or Your faithfulness in destruction? *(Truly, God's "lovingkindness" was "declared in the grave" by raising Christ from the dead. These Passages are some of the most miraculous and wonderful in Scripture. The great victory won by Jesus Christ guarantees to every Believer victory as well!)*

12 Shall Your wonders be known in the dark? and Your righteousness in the land of forgetfulness? *(Satan taunted Christ with these questions.)*

13 But unto You have I cried, O LORD; and in the morning shall My prayer prevent You. *(The Messiah took these accusations of Satan to the Father. In effect, He is saying that, on the third "morning," He will be resurrected from the dead. In this Passage, we are given this Promise from the Father.)*

14 LORD, why do You cast off My soul? why do You hide Your face from Me? *(God would do this, because there was no other choice. The Saviour was bearing the curse of sin for the whole world. This was the fulfillment of the Prophecy of John the Baptist, "Behold the Lamb of God, Who takes away the sin of the world" [Jn. 1:29].*

Isaiah prophesied these words, "And we hid as it were our faces from Him" [Isa. 53:3].)

15 I am afflicted and ready to die from My youth up: while I suffer Your terrors I am distracted. *(Christ's Mission on Earth was to die on Calvary. This was why He came, and "from My youth up." When He was twelve years old, He said these words, "Do you not know that I must be about My Father's business?" [Lk. 2:49]. What was His Father's business? It was many things, but the primary business was to die on Calvary, in order that man might be redeemed [I Pet. 1:18-20].)*

16 Your fierce wrath goes over Me; Your terrors have cut Me off. *(God's "wrath" had to be poured out on Him, that is, if we were to be redeemed. God cannot abide sin in any form, even on His Only Son, despite the fact that His Son had never sinned. But, still, He became one with my sin and failure, taking the full penalty upon Himself. That penalty was the wrath of God that culminated in His Death on the Cross.)*

17 They came round about Me daily like water; they compassed Me about together. *(The meaning of this Verse is that the enemies of Christ constantly swarmed around Him and attempted to catch Him in His speech, or even to kill Him*

before He would go to Calvary. As water, when poured out, runs over someone or something, likewise, these enemies did the same.)

18 Lover and friend have You put far from Me, and My acquaintance into darkness. *(When Jesus went to the Cross, both those who loved Him and those who were considered friends forsook Him. The Scripture says that "all forsook Him and fled" [Mat. 26:56].)*

PSALM 89

PROBABLY WRITTEN BY ETHAN: PRAISE FOR THE LORD

I will sing of the Mercies of the LORD for ever: with my mouth will I make known Your faithfulness to all generations. *(Williams says, "The Messiah, in the confidence of Coronation and of the fulfillment of the sure Promises made to Him as David [Acts 13:34], recites these Promises, voices the lament of His people at their seeming breach, and then closes the Psalm as He began it, with praise to Jehovah.*

Thus, during His life of sorrow, His death of shame, and His arrest in Sheol, nothing is seen in Him but perfection — perfection of faith toward God and of love toward man.")

2 For I have said, Mercy shall be built up for ever: Your faithfulness shall You establish in the very heavens. *(The Law came by Moses, but Grace and Truth came by Jesus Christ [Jn. 1:17].)*

3 I have made a Covenant with My chosen, I have sworn unto David My servant.

4 Your seed will I establish for ever, and build up your throne to all generations. Selah. *(II Sam., Chpt. 7, records the Davidic Covenant, promising David an Eternal Seed and Throne. Jesus Christ is the Root of David and will reign supremely forever. That was the intention of the Davidic Covenant, and it will yet be realized.)*

5 And the Heavens shall praise Your wonders, O LORD: Your faithfulness also in the congregation of the Saints. *(This Chapter is replete with the "faithfulness" of God. The word occurs seven times [Vss. 1, 2, 5, 8, 24, 33, 49]. Actually, the word "lovingkindness" in Verse 49 could have been translated "faithfulness.")*

6 For who in the Heaven can be compared unto the LORD? who among the sons of the mighty can be likened unto the LORD? *(These "sons of the mighty" are Angels, plainly stating that no Angel "in the Heaven" can be compared unto the Lord. So, on both Earth and*

Heaven, there is nothing to compare with the Lord Jesus Christ.)

7 God is greatly to be feared in the assembly of the Saints, and to be had in reverence of all them who are about Him. *(Sadly, there is not much "reverence" for Christ in this present world. Shortly, this will change.)*

8 O LORD God of hosts, who is a strong LORD like unto You? or to Your faithfulness round about You? *(Quite possibly, Jesus had this Scripture in mind when He talked about the stronger man [Himself] overcoming the strong man [Satan] and spoiling his house [Mat. 12:29].)*

9 You rule the raging of the sea: when the waves thereof arise, You still them. *(The spirit world of darkness is likened to "the raging of the sea." Only Jesus can "still them." How foolish it is for poor fallen man to think that pitiful humanistic psychology, or such like, can still these "waves"!)*

10 You have broken Rahab *(Egypt)* in pieces, as one that is slain; You have scattered Your Enemies with Your strong Arm. *("Rahab" is a poetic name for Egypt, and means "boastful," or "arrogant." The Lord, in delivering the Children of Israel from Egyptian bondage, "broke Rahab.")*

11 The heavens are Yours, the Earth also is Yours: as for the world and the fulness thereof, You have founded them. *(This declares that the Heavens and the Earth and all in them are the creation of God, and not a product of evolution.)*

12 The north and the south You have created them: Tabor and Hermon shall rejoice in Your name. *(As Verse 11 refers to the entirety of the Earth, Verse 12 refers to Israel. As the battle has raged for the world in general, it has raged even more regarding Israel. In the Abrahamic Covenant, God promised the Land to Abraham's descendant, Isaac. Instead, Ishmael, a product of the flesh, has attempted to wrest this Land from Isaac. The contest rages even today. This Verse is a statement that says, in effect, that Isaac will be the recipient of the Land, according to the Covenant. This means that it will not go to the Arabs.)*

13 You have a mighty Arm: strong is Your Hand, and high is Your Right Hand. *(In the Twelfth Verse, the Promise is made that Satan will not obtain the Land of Israel, and in this Thirteenth Verse, the statement is made that God has "a mighty army" and a "strong hand" to carry out that which He has promised. "High is Your right hand" means that there is no one stron-*

ger.)

14 Justice and judgment are the habitation of Your throne: mercy and truth shall go before Your face. *(The Lord is strong because of four qualities: 1. "Justice"; 2. "Judgment"; 3. "Mercy"; and, 4. "Truth.")*

15 Blessed is the people who know the joyful sound: they shall walk, O LORD, in the light of Your countenance. *(The "joyful sound" in this instance concerns the people who live in the Millennium and hear the "joyful sound" of the trumpet on the morning of Jubilee, which will proclaim deliverance to the captives and restoration of their forfeited estates. Then the Davidic Covenant will be fulfilled in all its totality. Israel will be the supreme nation on the face of the Earth. Its people will be "blessed.")*

16 In Your Name shall they rejoice all the day: and in Your righteousness shall they be exalted. *(There are many names given to our Lord in the Old Testament; however, the greatest name ever is that which was spoken by the Angel Gabriel, "You shall call His Name JESUS: for He shall save His people from their sins" [Mat. 1:21].)*

17 For You are the glory of their strength: and in Your favour our horn shall be exalted. *(The word "horn" in the Scriptures refers to kings [Dan. 7:7-8, 19-24; Rev. 17:12-17]. This refers to David ruling over Israel in the coming Kingdom Age, but even more so to the King of kings, the Lord Jesus Christ.)*

18 For the LORD is our defence; and the Holy One of Israel is our king *(the Lord Jesus Christ)*.

19 Then You spoke in vision to Your Holy One, and said, I have laid help upon One Who is mighty; I have exalted One chosen out of the people. *(The "vision" that is spoken of here concerns the many Prophecies that are given concerning the coming of the Redeemer, beginning with Gen. 3:15. Jesus spoke of these in Lk. 24:27.)*

20 I have found David My servant; with My holy oil have I anointed him. *(This refers to Samuel anointing David with oil as the future king of Israel, even while Saul was then king [I Sam., Chpt. 16]. Christ would come through David's family [II Sam., Chpt. 7].)*

21 With whom My hand shall be established: My arm also shall strengthen him *(and the Lord did exactly that!)*.

22 The enemy shall not exact upon him; nor the son of wickedness afflict him. *(In many ways, Satan endeavored to kill David, but this Passage tells us that the Lord protected him.)*

23 And I will beat down his foes before his face, and plague them who hate him. *(The struggle lasted for nearly 15 years, but ultimately Saul was killed on Mount Gilboa. Saul's mission to destroy David, inspired by Satan, was a fruitless effort because God was on David's side.*

Likewise, those who oppose Christ, which has been and will be.)

24 But My faithfulness and My mercy shall be with him: and in My name shall His horn be exalted. *("His horn" refers to the Messiah, Who would come through David [II Sam. 7:12-17; Rev. 22:16].)*

25 I will set his hand also in the sea, and his right hand in the rivers. *(This refers to David conquering all from the Mediterranean to the Euphrates. Powerful armies opposed him; none succeeded.)*

26 He shall cry unto Me, You are my Father, my God, and the Rock of my Salvation. *(David referred to the Lord by three titles: "my Father," "my God," and "the Rock of my Salvation.")*

27 Also I will make Him My Firstborn, higher than the kings of the Earth. *(After these statements concerning David, the next prediction is that David's Son, the Messiah, shall also be the Son of the Heavenly Father — the Firstborn and only truly Begotten Son of God, Whom God is to exalt higher than all kings of the Earth.)*

28 My mercy will I keep for him for evermore, and My Covenant shall stand fast with him. *(The Text now reverts back to David and the Davidic Covenant, which is unconditional, because it is anchored in the Greater Son of David.)*

29 His seed also will I make to endure for ever, and his throne as the days of Heaven. *(After referring to the Messiah in Verse 27, God resumes His predictions concerning David and the Davidic Covenant. This means that the throne of David will exist forever. Even though Israel ultimately lost her way, still, God will bring her back and restore her with the throne of David once again becoming supreme and lasting forever.)*

30 If his children forsake My Law, and walk not in My Judgments;

31 If they break My Statutes, and keep not My Commandments;

32 Then will I visit their transgression with the rod, and their iniquity with stripes *(in other words, God will chastise those He loves).*

33 Nevertheless My lovingkindness will I not utterly take from him, nor suffer My faithfulness to fail. *(The Lord means that even though David or particular individuals in his lineage would sin, and even though He would have to visit their transgression with the rod, still, He would follow the lineage through to Christ, which He did. God's "faithfulness did not fail," as it cannot fail.)*

34 My Covenant will I not break, nor alter the thing that is gone out of My lips. *(This was the Promise that was given approximately a thousand years before Christ. Satan did everything within Hell's power to break this "Covenant." At one time, the only person in the lineage who was left was baby Joash, with all the others of the lineage being killed by the wicked Queen, Athaliah [II Chron. 22:10]. However, this little baby boy survived and became the king of Judah, with the lineage continuing until the Birth of Christ.)*

35 Once have I sworn by My holiness that I will not lie unto David. *(This Passage refers to the events that transpired in II Sam., Chpt. 7. God's Promises are sure.)*

36 His seed shall endure for ever, and his throne as the sun before Me. *(God guarantees this Covenant with David, as He guaranteed the Solaric Covenant.)*

37 It shall be established for ever as the moon, and as a faithful witness in Heaven. Selah. *(This means that, at the Second Coming of Christ, David, and every Saint of God who has ever lived, will come back to reign on Earth forever. At that time, David will once again be established as king over Israel. He will serve under Christ, along with all the Glorified Saints. This will be during the one-thousand-year Millennial Reign, and then in the New Heaven and the New Earth forever.)*

38 But You have cast off and abhorred, You have been wroth with Your anointed. *(This speaks of David. Verses 38 through 46 refer back to Verses 31 through 32. David sinned greatly [Bath-sheba and Uriah] and so did Solomon and all of his kingly descendants. As a result, God did exactly what He said He would do, as He always will [Vs. 32].)*

39 You have made void the covenant of Your servant: You have profaned his crown by casting it to the ground. *(If Ethan the Ezrahite actually wrote this Psalm, then his statement here is prophetic, because it refers to the dispersion of Israel to Babylon, and then even to the final dispersion, after Titus the Roman General destroyed Jerusalem in A.D. 70.*

The statement, "Made void the covenant of Your servant," is not a contradiction of the Thirty-fourth Verse, where is says, "My Covenant will I not break." It means this:

Even though Israel was totally dispersed in A.D. 70, actually ceasing to be a nation for nearly 2,000 years, still, the Covenant will be brought back to fruition at the conclusion of the Great Tribulation. For this length of time it has been "made void"; however, it has not been broken, and will be reestablished at the Second Coming of Christ.)

40 You have broken down all his hedges; You have brought his strong holds to ruin. *(This came to pass in the Babylonian dispersion, as well as the total destruction in A.D. 70.)*

41 All who pass by the way spoil him: he is a reproach to his neighbours. *(During the dispersion to Babylon, the Prophet Ezekiel mentioned these nations that would "spoil" Israel. They were Ammon, Edom, Moab, Philistia, Tyre, and others [Ezek., Chpts. 25-26].)*

42 You have set up the right hand of his adversaries; You have made all his enemies to rejoice. *(Whereas God so many times in the past had fought for Israel, now He fights against Israel, and all because of sin.)*

43 You have also turned the edge of his sword, and have not made him to stand in the battle.

44 You have made his glory to cease, and cast his throne down to the ground. *(Jeremiah refers to this in his Lamentations [Lam. 2:17].)*

45 The days of his youth have You shortened: You have covered him with shame. Selah. *(The meaning of this Verse pertains to both David and Judah. The glory of David and the power of Judah were cut short in comparison to what they might have been. Sin was the cause; consequently, they were "covered with shame.")*

46 How long, LORD? will You hide Yourself for ever? shall Your wrath burn like fire? *(It has now been nearly 2,000 years since the Lord has hidden His Face from Israel. They have suffered untold agony, and all because they rejected their Messiah, the Lord Jesus Christ, and accepted a worldly king [Jn. 19:15].)*

47 Remember how short my time is: wherefore have You made all men in vain? *(The Psalmist now laments the present status of Israel. In this Passage, we see that man is more concerned with his own circumstances than with God's glory and how He has been offended. God's interests are generally last. True Repentance little laments our plight, but, instead, our terrible sin against God and how we have defrauded Him.)*

48 What man is he who lives, and shall not see death? shall he deliver his soul from the hand of the grave? Selah. *(The Psalmist seems to be asking, in view of the fact that men sin and die, how is it that God can keep His Covenant with David?)*

49 Lord, where are Your former lovingkindnesses, which You swore unto David in Your truth? *(The plea is for the Lord to bring Israel back to her place of greatness.)*

50 Remember, Lord, the reproach of Your servants; how I do bear in my bosom the reproach of all the mighty people *(truly Israel has definitely suffered terrible reproach; however, the fault is that of Israel alone, and not at all of God; they desired Caesar, and that proved to be a very unwise choice);*

51 Wherewith Your enemies have reproached, O LORD; wherewith they have reproached the footsteps of Your anointed. *(The Holy Spirit, due to God's great Promises to Israel, still refers to them as "Your anointed." They have been away from God for a long time, but the Scripture says they are coming home.)*

52 Blessed be the LORD for evermore. Amen, and Amen. *(This closes the Leviticus Book of Psalms, with the Holy Spirit saying that regardless of the way the situation looks, the Lord is "blessed." As well, the suffering spoken of in Verses 50 through 51 are those suffered by Christ as High Priest in sympathy with the sufferings of His People. This is an effective picture of the identification of a True Advocate with the miseries and sorrows of those He represents.)*

PSALM 90

THE NUMBERS BOOK
THE AUTHOR IS MOSES:
THE EVERLASTING GOD

LORD, You have been our dwelling place in all generations. *(Moses is saying that the Lord is our "dwellingplace," and so it is "in all generations." This is the same as "in Him we live, and move, and have our being" [Acts 17:28]. In other words, we look to God for everything.)*

2 Before the mountains were brought forth, or ever You had formed the Earth and the world, even from everlasting to everlasting, You are God. *(Those who pass through life depending on their own strength find it a way of labor and sorrow; those who lean on the arm of Adonai, Who is Eternal, find it a way of joy and rejoicing — even in the wilderness.)*

3 You turn man to destruction; and say, Return, you children of men. *(Whereas the*

Second Verse speaks of Creation, the Third Verse speaks of the Fall. God gave man the choice of eating of the Tree of the Knowledge of Good and Evil, or not eating of it. They were told not to, but if so, they would suffer the consequence, which was eternal death [Gen. 2:17]. The latter part of this Verse is an appeal for man to return to God.)

4 For a thousand years in Your sight are but as yesterday when it is past, and as a watch in the night. (Man should look at eternity as God looks at eternity. In other words, we should base our actions on the eternal, instead of the temporal. Sadly, the majority of the world sells out for the temporal.)

5 You carry them away as with a flood; they are as a sleep: in the morning they are like grass which grows up. (Verse 2 speaks of Creation, Verse 3 speaks of the Fall, and Verse 5 speaks of Noah's Flood. In its broader meaning, it speaks of death as "a flood." It speaks of life as "grass," which flourishes for a short while and then is gone.)

6 In the morning it flourishes, and grows up; in the evening it is cut down, and withers. (This is the way that the Holy Spirit describes man's life.)

7 For we are consumed by Your anger, and by Your wrath are we troubled. (The "anger" and "wrath" mentioned here speaks of the curse that God placed upon the human race because of the Fall. God cannot abide sin in any form.)

8 You have set our iniquities before You, our secret sins in the light of Your countenance. (This Passage means that God will judge sins, both secret and open.)

9 For all our days are passed away in Your wrath: we spend our years as a tale that is told. (This Ninth Verse speaks of the pride of man's heart being broken, its self-sufficiency banished, and its energies governed by wisdom.)

10 The days of our years are threescore years and ten; and if by reason of strength they be fourscore years, yet is their strength labour and sorrow; for it is soon cut off, and we fly away. (For all of man's vaunted modern prowess, the lifespan is basically, on the average, between 70 and 80 years old.)

11 Who knows the power of Your anger? even according to Your fear, so is Your wrath. (For the most part, men do not fear God. Many do not even believe there is a God. Nevertheless, there is a God, and He will do exactly as He has said in His Word. His Power is absolute but not arbitrary.)

12 So teach us to number our days, that we may apply our hearts unto wisdom. (In view of man's perilous condition and his short life-span, Moses pleads with the Lord to "teach us." This Verse should sum up the cry of the human heart, but, regrettably, it little does.)

13 Return, O LORD, how long? and let it repent You concerning Your servants. (The dark background of Verses 3 through 12 makes the doctrine of Verses 13 through 17 the more precious to faith. The doctrine is that the only hope for the Earth and its inhabitants is in the coming of the Messiah. His Advent will compensate for all the calamities of the wilderness in this night of misery and pain, and He will endow man with a new moral nature, so that the works of man's hands will be only good.)

14 O satisfy us early with Your mercy; that we may rejoice and be glad all our days. (The sense of this Verse is that there is no satisfaction other than with the "Mercy" of God. Only when we are recipients of such may we "rejoice and be glad all our days.")

15 Make us glad according to the days wherein You have afflicted us, and the years wherein we have seen evil. (This should be the cry of every man, even the most consecrated Christian. Moses is asking that the days of affliction be no more than the days of gladness.)

16 Let Your work appear unto Your servants, and Your glory unto their children. (The sense of this Verse is far more reaching than we at first realize. It is as follows: 1. That our failures not stop "Your Work" and 2. That the next generation would know "Your Glory.")

17 And let the beauty of the LORD our God be upon us: and establish Thou the work of our hands upon us; yea, the work of our hands establish Thou it. (The sense of this Verse is that there is no "beauty" on the Earth other than that which is given by the Lord. As well, the "work of our hands" is nothing unless it is established by God.)

PSALM 91

PROBABLY WRITTEN BY MOSES: GOD IS A REFUGE AND A FORTRESS

HE who dwells in the secret place of the Most High shall abide under the shadow of the Almighty. (The previous Psalm introduced the Wilderness and contrasted the misery and happiness of travelers in it who trust self or God. This Psalm points to the one Man Who passed

through it undefiled, unhurt, and trusting and loving God in perfection.

The absence of a superscription suggests that the Psalm was written by Moses, for the previous one was written by him. If this be so, then all the Scriptures quoted in the temptation in the desert [Mat., Chpt. 4] were Mosaic.

That the Messiah is the great figure of this Psalm is decided by Mat. 4:6.)

2 I will say of the LORD, He is my Refuge and my Fortress: my God; in Him will I trust. *(As Christ enters the "secret place of the Most High," the Holy Spirit assures Him that companionship with God will be a safe refuge from Satan's power and from all the dangers of the way.)*

3 Surely He shall deliver you from the snare of the fowler, and from the noisome pestilence. *(The "snare of the fowler" was the demon forces of darkness that opposed Christ, either through the evil religious leaders of Jesus' day, or in their own capacity. They came in such quantity that they were called the "noisome pestilence," which means a "rushing calamity" — one that sweeps everything before it. Christ had the promise of the Holy Spirit that He would be delivered, and so He was!)*

4 He shall cover you with His feathers, and under His wings shall You trust: His truth shall be your shield and buckler. *(This Passage has to do with the Holy of Holies. It speaks of where God dwelt between the Cherubim and the Mercy Seat. He invited Christ to dwell there with Him. In turn, Christ paid the price for us, that the Holy Spirit may dwell in us [I Cor. 3:16].)*

5 You shall not be afraid for the terror by night; nor for the arrow that flies by day *(the "terror by night" speaks of the spiritual darkness of Satan. The "arrow that flies by day" refers to the deliberate effort by Satan to destroy the soul. The Evil One devises a temptation, oppression, or trap for the Believer, and then shoots it like an "arrow." The only thing that can stop it is the "Shield and Buckler" of Verse 4);*

6 Nor for the pestilence that walks in darkness; nor for the destruction that wastes at noonday. *("The pestilence that walks in darkness" pertains to every scourge of Satanic darkness. The "destruction that wastes at noonday" refers to Satan's destroying great multitudes, yet not touching the Child of God, who is dwelling in the "secret place of the Most High.")*

7 A thousand shall fall at your side, and ten thousand at your right hand; but it shall not come near you. *(Untold millions are being destroyed by the powers of darkness; but the Be-*

liever who puts his trust in God is promised that "it shall not come near you.")

8 Only with Your eyes shall you behold and see the reward of the wicked. *(The results of living without God are overly obvious!)*

9 Because you have made the LORD, which is my refuge, even the Most High, your habitation *(the Holy Spirit here is the Speaker. The Messiah is assured victory by the Holy Spirit only because He "has made the Lord His refuge." Since Christ is our Substitute, the Lord can be our "habitation" as well);*

10 There shall no evil befall you, neither shall any plague come near your dwelling. *(Because His "dwelling" is in the "secret place of the Most High," it is impossible for "evil" to befall you. Verses 11 through 12 were quoted by Satan, and his quoting them showed his intelligence in recognizing that the Psalm applied to Jesus [Mat. 4:6].)*

11 For He shall give His Angels charge over you, to keep you in all your ways. *(This shows how much Satan knows the Bible, but yet he still thinks he can circumvent the Word of God. Angels did constantly help Christ [Mat. 4:11; Lk. 4:10-11]. However, Satan corrupted the Scripture by omitting "in all your ways," and inserting in its place "at any time." The Messiah's path through the desert of the Wilderness was one of dependence upon God. Satan's effort in the temptation was to move Him to independence, but he failed. Christ walked a path of perfect submission, obedience, and dependence; likewise, all those who walk after Him in like dependence and faith can be assured of His Victory.)*

12 They shall bear you up in their hands, lest you dash your foot against a stone. *(Satan attempted to get Christ to commit the sin of presumption, which means to twist the Word of God in order that it mean something that God did not intend.)*

13 You shall tread upon the lion and adder: the young lion and the dragon shall you trample under feet. *(Satan quoted Verses 11 through 12 in the temptation of Christ, but he did not dare quote Verse 13, because it promised his defeat [Gen. 3:15].)*

14 Because he has set his love upon Me, therefore will I deliver him: I will set him on high, because he has known My name. *(These are the words of the Father. How amazing that sinful men should be permitted to hear the sweet converse of the Three Persons of the Trinity!)*

15 He shall call upon Me, and I will answer him: I will be with him in trouble; I will de-

liver him, and honour him. *(Christ has been greatly honored for what He did at the Cross by being given a Name that is above every name [Phil. 2:9].)*

16 With long life will I satisfy him, and show him My salvation. *(This speaks of Christ, but even more so, it speaks of the man who trusts Christ, and thereby reaps the benefits of what Jesus did at Calvary, all on our behalf.)*

PSALM 92

AUTHOR UNKNOWN:
A SONG FOR THE SABBATH DAY

IT is a good thing to give thanks unto the LORD, and to sing praises unto Your Name, O Most High *(this is a Wilderness Psalm, which proclaims the Sabbath as God's Rest for His People. The Sabbath was symbolic of the "rest" that is found only in Christ. Here, Israel sings of Him and addresses Him as "Jehovah" [the LORD] and "Elyon" [Most High]. Consistently, the Holy Spirit proclaims the "good thing" of thanking and praising the Lord):*

2 To show forth Your lovingkindness in the morning, and Your faithfulness every night. *(This proclaims constant praises both "morning" and "night." The Lord is portrayed in "lovingkindness" and "faithfulness.")*

3 Upon an instrument of ten strings, and upon the psaltery; upon the harp with a solemn sound. *(The Holy Spirit through David orchestrated the worship of God through musical instruments, choirs, songs, and singers; therefore, all true worship of God in any and all Churches would come from the Root of David.)*

4 For You, LORD, have made me glad through Your work: I will triumph in the works of Your hands. *(The praises are rendered to God for what the Lord has done for Israel.)*

5 O LORD, how great are Your works! and Your thoughts are very deep. *(When we revert back to the helplessness of man in Psalm 90, realizing what God has done for us, then how can we help but praise Him!)*

6 A brutish man knows not; neither does a fool understand this. *(God calls "fools" those who do not understand worship toward God. At the Fall, man did descend toward the animal kingdom. At the New Birth, he is made a New Creature, consequently becoming more like God. In other words, God is saying that those who do not know nor understand the worship of God are little more than brute beasts.)*

7 When the wicked spring as the grass, and when all the workers of iniquity do flourish; it is that they shall be destroyed for ever *(ultimately, the righteous will be blessed, and ultimately the wicked will be destroyed):*

8 But You, LORD, are Most High for evermore. *(This Verse actually means that Jehovah will be enthroned forever. This statement, preceded and followed by declarations as to the destruction of the wicked, makes terribly clear the doctrine that the eternity of His Government necessitates the eternity of their misery. For as long as His Government lasts, a rebellion and recovery by them will be impossible.)*

9 For, lo, Your enemies, O LORD, for, lo, Your enemies shall perish; all the workers of iniquity shall be scattered. *(Israel looked at her enemies as God's enemies, and so they were!)*

10 But my horn shall You exalt like the horn of an unicorn: I shall be anointed with fresh oil. *(The word "horn" refers to Israel's future exaltation as the premier nation of the world, which will take place in the Millennial Reign. At that time, she will be brought back to God, will accept Jesus Christ, and will be "anointed with fresh oil.")*

11 My eye also shall see my desire on my enemies, and my ears shall hear my desire of the wicked who rise up against me. *(Every Promise given here to Israel can be accepted and enjoyed by the modern Believer, except those Promises which are Dispensational, and thereby affect Israel only.)*

12 The righteous shall flourish like the palm tree: he shall grow like a cedar in Lebanon. *(The Believer is comparable to a palm and to a cedar. The one grows in a sandy plain, the other on a rugged mountain. The one has a taproot that draws nourishment from beneath, the other is refreshed from above. The one is beautiful, the other strong. The Christian has a secret source of life; he receives blessing from beneath and from above, and he is morally beautiful and strong.)*

13 Those who be planted in the House of the LORD shall flourish in the courts of our God. *(The inference in this Verse is that "the wicked" of Verse 7 may flourish for a while, but then they will be cut off. Nevertheless, those who are "planted" in God's Grace will eternally "flourish.")*

14 They shall still bring forth fruit in old age; they shall be fat and flourishing *(this speaks of all Believers, but primarily of Israel in her "old age"; having been away from God for so*

long and finally brought back to Him, she will then begin to "bring forth fruit"; during the Great Millennial Reign, she "shall be fat and flourishing");

15 To show that the LORD is upright: He is my Rock, and there is no unrighteousness in Him. (The fruit and strength of the Spirit exhibited in the Christian life is an effective testimony to the moral glory of the Lord Jesus Christ. Finally recognizing that moral glory, Israel will shout with exultation, "He is my Rock — there is no unrighteousness in Him!")

PSALM 93

AUTHOR UNKNOWN:
THE LORD IS CLOTHED WITH MAJESTY

THE LORD reigns, He is clothed with majesty; the LORD is clothed with strength, wherewith He has girded Himself: the world also is stablished, that it cannot be moved. (The great price at Calvary has been paid, and the Holy Spirit can now abide in the hearts of believing, born-again men. It can now also be said that "the world also is stablished." Now that this great price has been paid and the "lion, adder, and the dragon" defeated [Ps. 91:13], there is no doubt of the outcome. "It cannot be moved.")

2 Your throne is established of old: You are from everlasting. (All human history, in its final settlement, is comprised in the brief compass of this Psalm. It sets out the Majesty of the King's Person and the stability of His Kingdom [Vs. 1], plus the antiquity of His Throne, and the eternity of His Being.)

3 The floods have lifted up, O LORD, the floods have lifted up their voice; the floods lift up their waves. (This presents a picture of Millennial Glory. The angry nations [Rev. 11:18], likened to the raging waves of the storm-tossed ocean, are subdued, and the Messiah, mightier than they, is seen seated upon His Throne.)

4 The LORD on high is mightier than the noise of many waters, yea, than the mighty waves of the sea. (This is likened to Christ stilling the raging of the Galilean Sea [Jn. 6:16], as He will still the future raging of the hostile nations and will establish universal peace.)

5 Your Testimonies are very sure: holiness becomes Your House, O LORD, for ever. ("Your Testimonies" refer to God's Word in its various Revelations of Truth, while the foundation of God's House is "Holiness," as the foundation of man's house is unholiness.)

PSALM 94

AUTHOR UNKNOWN:
A PRAYER FOR VENGEANCE
ON THE OPPRESSORS

O LORD God, to Whom vengeance belongs; O God, to Whom vengeance belongs, show Yourself. (This Psalm corresponds with the time of "Jacob's Trouble" [Jer. 30:7], and will introduce the Antichrist, who will be the greatest work of the flesh ever devised by Satan.

In the latter half of the Great Tribulation, Israel will cry to God as never before. When it seems that she faces annihilation, she will plead with the Lord, "show Yourself.")

2 Lift up Yourself, Thou judge of the Earth: render a reward to the proud. (Israel, upon realizing that no nation in the world will lift a hand to save her, and we speak of the coming Great Tribulation, will cry for the Messiah to come. He is her only hope. The "proud" spoken of here pertains to the man of sin, the Antichrist.)

3 LORD, how long shall the wicked, how long shall the wicked triumph? (How long before the Lord works vengeance on the Antichrist?)

4 How long shall they utter and speak hard things? and all the workers of iniquity boast themselves? (The followers of the Antichrist will boast of what looks like the annihilation of Israel.)

5 They break in pieces Your people, O LORD, and afflict Your heritage. (This concerns the Antichrist breaking his seven-year Covenant with Israel at the midpoint. He will then set out to systematically destroy "Your heritage.")

6 They slay the widow and the stranger, and murder the fatherless. (The Antichrist will attempt to do what Hitler failed to do. He will have no mercy on any. He will hate Israel with a passion, thinking that if he can destroy them, the entirety of the Word of God will fall to the ground.)

7 Yet they say, the LORD shall not see, neither shall the God of Jacob regard it. (In effect, the Antichrist will blaspheme the Lord of Glory, proclaiming that God can do nothing to stop him. As well, he will blaspheme the Old Testament, claiming that the "God of Jacob does not regard it."

What he does not know is that the very words he is using, "the God of Jacob," specifically refer to the God Who met Jacob when he had nothing and deserved nothing, and gave him Grace

and the Promise of every known blessing of life [Gen., Chpt. 28]. Likewise, this same God will once again come to the rescue of "Jacob" [Israel] when she has nothing and deserves nothing good and, in effect, will give Israel Grace and certain victory over the man of sin.)

8 Understand, you brutish among the people: and you fools, when will you be wise? *(In this Passage, the Holy Spirit calls the Antichrist and those who follow him "fools"!)*

9 He who plants the ear, shall He not hear? He Who forms the eye, shall He not see? *(The Holy Spirit is informing the Antichrist that God sees all and hears all.)*

10 He Who chastises the heathen, shall not He correct? He Who teaches man knowledge, shall not He know? *(The Holy Spirit is saying that, as the Lord chastised the heathen of the past, He will likewise chastise the heathen of the present, meaning the Antichrist.)*

11 The LORD knows the thoughts of man, that they are vanity. *(The Lord will conclude all the great thoughts and claims of the Antichrist as being "vanity," which means "empty nothings.")*

12 Blessed is the man whom You chasten, O LORD, and teach him out of Your Law *(the sense of this Verse is that the Great Tribulation is Israel's chastening, and that, through this chastening, she will be brought back to "Your Law" [Jer. 30:7]);*

13 That You may give him rest from the days of adversity, until the pit be digged for the wicked. *(Israel will ultimately be given "rest"; the Antichrist ultimately will fall into the "pit" [II Thess. 2:8].)*

14 For the LORD will not cast off His people, neither will He forsake His inheritance. *(The Lord has made many Promises that Israel will be brought to restoration. This Passage is but one of those many.)*

15 But judgment shall return unto righteousness: and all the upright in heart shall follow it. *(Judgment divorced from righteousness entails oppression. When the Son of Man returns to judge the Earth, the judgment will return to Righteousness and all the upright in heart will gladly follow in its train.)*

16 Who will rise up for me against the evildoers? or who will stand up for me against the workers of iniquity? *(The confession of Verses 16 through 19 is that the Messiah Alone could protect defenseless Israel.)*

17 Unless the LORD had been my help, my soul had almost dwelt in silence. *(At that time*

[the Battle of Armageddon], it will seem that no nation on Earth will come to Israel's rescue. But the Lord will come to her aid!)

18 When I said, My foot slips; Your mercy, O LORD, held me up. *(When it looks like Israel has surely lost, and that the Antichrist will gain the victory, she will cry, "Have mercy, O LORD, hold me up!" And that He shall do [Zech. 14:3-4].)*

19 In the multitude of my thoughts within me Your comforts delight my soul. *(This means that at this critical juncture in Israel's long history, the only "comforts" she will have are the Promises of God, which will "delight my soul.")*

20 Shall the throne of iniquity have fellowship with You, which frames mischief by a law? *(In this Passage, Israel contrasts the Earth under the Antichrist versus the Earth under Christ. Daniel said that the Antichrist would "think to change times and laws" [Dan. 7:25]. Actually, this has ever been man's problem. He continues to try to change God's Laws into his own manmade laws; this always bring "mischief.")*

21 They gather themselves together against the soul of the righteous, and condemn the innocent blood. *(Here Israel is called "the righteous," because they are the ancient people of the Book. The Antichrist will "condemn" them to death. Instead, he will die.)*

22 But the LORD is my defence; and my God is the Rock of my refuge. *(After so many years in the wilderness, Israel is finally coming home. She now realizes that her own strength cannot save her, nor the strength of any other nation, since none will come to her aid. She now knows that God Alone is her "Rock.")*

23 And He shall bring upon them their own iniquity, and shall cut them off in their own wickedness; yea, the LORD our God shall cut them off. *(Ezek., Chpts. 38-39, proclaim exactly how the Lord will do this.)*

PSALM 95

A PSALM OF DAVID:
A PSALM OF PRAISE TO GOD

O come, let us sing unto the LORD: let us make a joyful noise to the Rock of our Salvation. *(Psalm 94 portrayed the wilderness journey. Now the first fingers of dawn are about to break upon the Millennial morn. The long night of Israel's weeping is about to come to an end. Israel has seen the Earth under the Antichrist. Now she will see the Earth under Christ.*

The "joyful noise" that we are to make is the singing of hymns of praise [96:1-3].)

2 Let us come before His presence with thanksgiving, and make a joyful noise unto Him with Psalms. *(We are given here a wonderful directive by the Holy Spirit concerning the approach of the Believer to the Lord. It is to be with "thanksgiving" and "singing.")*

3 For the LORD is a great God, and a great King above all gods. *(Creation Rest, Redemption Rest, and Millennial Rest are all based upon the Person and Work of Christ. Faith brings us into these Rests; unbelief excludes us.)*

4 In His hand are the deep places of the Earth: the strength of the hills is His also. *(This means that God is Lord over Hell, and also over the entirety of the Earth.)*

5 The sea is His, and He made it: and His hands formed the dry land. *(Over and over again, the Holy Spirit refutes the lie of evolution. God is the Creator of all, and He deserves worship by all.)*

6 O come, let us worship and bow down: let us kneel before the LORD our Maker. *(This Verse is the great invitation to come to Jesus. He is God's Rest — an ineffable Rest. How wonderful is the Grace that invites sinners to share God's Rest! This is a Rest that never can be disturbed; its wonders are developed by the God of Glory [Heb., Chpts. 3-4].)*

7 For He is our God; and we are the people of His pasture, and the sheep of His hand. Today if you will hear His voice. *(This Passage is quoted in Hebrews 3:7-11 and 4:7.*

What a privilege to say, "He is our God" and that "we are the people of His Pasture"! As well, the expression, "the sheep of His Hand," refers to our being made by Him. It has a far greater meaning than if a shepherd purchases sheep. In this instance, it means that God created the sheep — "the sheep of His Hand."

Accordingly, we are admonished to "hear His Voice," the voice of the Shepherd.)

8 Harden not your heart, as in the provocation, and as in the day of temptation in the wilderness *(the wilderness was a proving time for Israel; regrettably, they failed!):*

9 When your fathers tempted Me, proved Me, and saw My work. *(Israel tempted the Lord in the wilderness, and refused to believe, even though they "saw His Work.")*

10 Forty years long was I grieved with this generation, and said, It is a people who do err in their heart, and they have not known My ways *(Israel challenged God to provide a* table for them in the desert and, when it was provided, declared that Pharaoh's was better, so they desired to appoint a captain to return to Egypt! [Num. 14:3-4]):*

11 Unto whom I swore in My wrath that they should not enter into My rest. *(The greatest sin of all just may be the sin of faithlessness. The entire fabric of the Plan of God demands Faith. Men forsake God because they don't believe God. In the Wilderness, Israel showed unbelief. They died because of that unbelief and "could not enter into God's rest.")*

PSALM 96

POSSIBLY WRITTEN BY DAVID: A NEW SONG OF PRAISE TO THE LORD

O **Sing unto the LORD a new song: sing unto the LORD, all the Earth.** *(The setting of this song seems to be at the beginning of the Millennial Reign. Israel, having sung the previous Psalm, now invites the nations to join her in "a new song." Psalm 97 will be that song. This "new song" belongs to the day when the kingdoms of the world shall become the Kingdom of Jehovah and of His Christ [Rev. 11:15; 12:10].)*

2 Sing unto the LORD, bless His name, show forth His salvation from day to day. *(The doctrine of this Psalm is that the Advent of the Messiah into the world will make it a Paradise, and that His Rule alone can eliminate dissension, war, misery, and injustice, and furthermore will establish society in an enduring brotherhood — "His Salvation.")*

3 Declare His glory among the heathen, His wonders among all people. *(Men may test the reality and credibility of this Prophecy by surrendering their sinful hearts to the government of Immanuel. They will then experience love, peace, and a moral power that their hearts were strangers to, previous to conversion.*

Much of the world is presently steeped in demonic Islam, Hinduism, spiritism, and other works of darkness; however, during the great Kingdom Age to come, the whole world will finally know of His Glory.)

4 For the LORD is great, and greatly to be praised: He is to be feared above all gods. *(Satan's great contest with God has always been to make himself God instead of Jehovah. He has sought to do this through demon spirits, idol worship, false religions, etc. Paul addressed himself to this in II Cor., Chpt. 11.)*

5 For all the gods of the nations are idols:

but the LORD made the Heavens *("idols," in the Hebrew, is "elilim," and means "nothings, vanities, emptiness, things of nought"; regrettably, the far greater majority of the world serves these "nothings" instead of the Lord Who created all things).*

6 Honour and majesty are before Him: strength and beauty are in His Sanctuary. *(The emphasis is on the pronoun "His." There are many other sanctuaries at present in the world, but they are false. As just stated, they are "nothings." The only "strength" and "beauty" in the world are in "His Sanctuary," which now refers to born-again Believers serving as the Temple of the Holy Spirit [I Cor. 3:16].)*

7 Give unto the LORD, O ye kindreds of the people, give unto the LORD glory and strength. *(The nations of the world are invited to share in this "strength" and "beauty." They are invited to give the "LORD" the "glory" due His Name, instead of wasting it on "idols.")*

8 Give unto the LORD the glory due unto His Name: bring an offering, and come into His courts. *(The latter half of this Verse, concerning the bringing of Offerings, refers to the Prophecies of Zechariah. In the coming Kingdom Age, the nations of the world will come to Jerusalem to keep the "Feast of Tabernacles" [Zech. 14:16-19].)*

9 O worship the LORD in the beauty of holiness: fear before Him, all the Earth. *(In the coming Kingdom Age, everything will be "holiness," even the "bells of the horses" [Zech. 14:20].)*

10 Say among the heathen that the LORD reigns: the world also shall be established that it shall not be moved: He shall judge the people righteously. *(For the first time, the world in its entirety will know government that is not corrupt, because "the LORD reigns.")*

11 Let the heavens rejoice, and let the Earth be glad; let the sea roar, and the fulness thereof. *(When Jesus Christ reigns over the entirety of planet Earth in the glorious Kingdom Age, then the Heavens can rejoice and the Earth can be glad. The sea will roar, not with anger, but with praises unto the Lord.)*

12 Let the field be joyful, and all that is therein: then shall all the trees of the wood rejoice. *(For the first time since Lucifer's original Fall, planet Earth will be in union with God, because Jesus Christ reigns.)*

13 Before the LORD: for He comes, for He comes to judge the Earth: He shall judge the world with righteousness, and the people with His truth. *(This is the judgment of the nations during the coming Kingdom Age [Mat. 25:31-46].)*

PSALM 97

AUTHOR UNKNOWN: THE LORD REIGNS: REJOICE

THE LORD reigns; let the Earth rejoice; let the multitude of isles be glad thereof. *(As the previous Psalm gave the invitation, this Psalm proclaims its fulfillment. This is the "new song" that is spoken of in 96:1. It is new for Earth, but not for Heaven. It sings of a new day for humanity — a day of Righteousness, peace, and brotherhood. It will dawn when God causes His First Begotten to return to the Earth on that Great Millennial Morn and commands all the Angels to worship Him [Heb. 1:6].)*

2 Clouds and darkness are round about Him: righteousness and judgment are the habitation of His Throne. *(The reason for the great "gladness" on Earth is because "Righteousness and Judgment are the habitation of His Throne.")*

3 A fire goes before Him, and burns up His enemies round about. *(This will be the Second Coming at the Battle of Armageddon [II Thess. 1:7-8].)*

4 His lightnings enlightened the world: the Earth saw, and trembled. *(His Second Coming will be with such manifestations as the world has never seen before. The very Heavens will dance with joy [Mat. 24:27, 29-30].)*

5 The hills melted like wax at the presence of the LORD, at the presence of the Lord of the whole Earth. *(According to the Prophecies, the Second Coming will be the most phenomenal event that has ever transpired on planet Earth.)*

6 The Heavens declare His righteousness, and all the people see His glory. *(There is a good possibility that the Second Coming will be flashed by television all over the world. There is no doubt that hundreds, if not thousands, of television cameras, representing every network in the world, will be recording the Battle of Armageddon. Thus, they will be there at the moment of the Second Coming.)*

7 Confounded be all they who serve graven images, that boast themselves of idols: worship Him, all ye gods. *(Then, and beyond the shadow of a doubt, the world will know that Jesus is God, and not idols or false religions.)*

8 Zion heard, and was glad; and the daughters of Judah rejoiced because of Your judgments, O LORD. *(Israel will now accept Jesus Christ as both Saviour and Lord.)*

9 For You, LORD, are high above all the

Earth: You are exalted far above all gods. *(At long last, the Holy Spirit is telling us that at the time of the Kingdom Age, all false worship will be ended. The Lord Alone will be worshipped!)*

10 You who love the LORD, hate evil: He preserves the souls of His saints; He delivers them out of the hand of the wicked. *(Particularly, this refers to the deliverance of Israel from the Antichrist during the Battle of Armageddon. In general, it refers to all Believers who place their Faith and trust in Christ and what He has done for us at the Cross [Gal. 1:4].)*

11 Light is sown for the righteous, and gladness for the upright in heart. *(By and large, the world has known nothing but spiritual darkness. Now it will know "light." The Coming of the Lord will bring "gladness" to the entirety of the planet.)*

12 Rejoice in the LORD, you righteous; and give thanks at the remembrance of His holiness. *(The word "Holiness" really means that everything will be set apart for His Service. And we mean everything!)*

PSALM 98

AUTHOR UNKNOWN:
PRAISE TO GOD FOR HIS SALVATION

O sing unto the LORD a new song; for He has done marvellous things: His right hand, and His holy arm, has gotten Him the victory. *(This glorious "new song" will salute Jehovah Messiah on that Millennial Morn, and will have three voices: 1. Restored Israel will now have a "new song"; 2. The Gentile nations will as well sing this song; well may men sing at the prospect of such a rule!; they have never enjoyed a government exhibiting righteousness and equity; now they will; and, 3. Nature, for the first time since the Fall, will respond to its Creator in harmony [Rom. 8:22].)*

2 The LORD has made known His salvation: His righteousness has He openly shown in the sight of the heathen. *(The word "Salvation" refers to Deliverance from the powers of sin, Satan, and darkness. Only Jesus Christ can set men free. He is the Source, and the Cross is the means [Rom. 6:3-14].)*

3 He has remembered His mercy and His truth toward the house of Israel: all the ends of the Earth have seen the salvation of our God. *(As the nations of the world in olden times witnessed with wonder the birth of the Twelve Tribes, so they will see with astonishment their Restora-*

tion. This will take place at the Second Coming.)*

4 Make a joyful noise unto the LORD, all the Earth: make a loud noise, and rejoice, and sing praise. *(The world has ever attempted its celebrations; however, they ring with a hollow sound. Now, and at long last, there is a true "joyful noise," because the Lord Himself is the Author of this celebration.)*

5 Sing unto the LORD with the harp; with the harp, and the voice of a Psalm.

6 With trumpets and sound of cornets make a joyful noise before the LORD, the King. *(The very structure of music, which was originally created by the Lord, has within it the incorporation of the Divine Trinity. It is combined under three headings, all given by God: 1. Melody: this refers to an ordered structure of sound; 2. Harmony: this has to do with the accompanying voices or instruments regarding the different parts of music, such as lead, alto, bass, or tenor; and, 3. Rhythm: this has to do with measured beats of which many of the Psalms were written.*

During the coming Kingdom Age, the world will be filled with music — but music unto God, even as it was originally intended. In fact, in a sense, "the LORD, the King" will be the conductor.)

7 Let the sea roar, and the fulness thereof; the world, and they who dwell therein.

8 Let the floods clap their hands: let the hills be joyful together. *(The harmony of nature was interrupted at the Fall [Gen., Chpt. 3; Ps. 8]. Now, for the first time in history, Nature is at one with God.)*

9 Before the LORD; for He comes to judge the Earth: with righteousness shall He judge the world, and the people with equity. *(For the first time, the entirety of the world will have a fair judgment.)*

PSALM 99

AUTHOR UNKNOWN:
ADMONITIONS TO FEAR, PRAISE, AND WORSHIP GOD

THE LORD reigns; let the people tremble: He sits between the Cherubims; let the Earth be moved. *(This will take place at the beginning of the Kingdom Age.)*

2 The LORD is great in Zion; and He is high above all the people. *(Animated by this great vision, the pilgrim company joyfully shouts, "Jehovah takes the Kingdom." The meaning of the statement, "high above all the people," refers to the Deity of the Messiah. While it is true*

He is Very Man, still, He is also Very God.)

3 Let them praise Your great and terrible Name; for it is Holy *(meaning without impurity of any nature).*

4 The King's strength also loves judgment; You do establish equity, You execute judgment and righteousness in Jacob. *(This Verse promises that the power of the King shall be employed on behalf of judgment, equity, and Righteousness. This is not true of Earthly governments and monarchs.*

If one will notice, the word "equity" is used repeatedly by the Holy Spirit in these Psalms, meaning that the Lord of Glory will at long last bring equality on Earth.)

5 Exalt ye the LORD our God, and worship at His footstool; for He is Holy. *(In the Third Verse, it says, "His Name is Holy," and in this Verse it says, "He is Holy.")*

6 Moses and Aaron among His Priests, and Samuel among them who call upon His Name; they called upon the LORD, and He answered them. *(Moses actually exercised the Office of Priest before Aaron [Ex. 24:6-8]. So, both Moses and Aaron were among His Priests. Samuel represents the Prophets.*

The Holy Spirit recognizes and brings forward those who in the past were true to His communications, despite national and ecclesiastical apostasy.

These men figure together all who loved and trusted the Messiah in the past and who were faithful to His Word. Even though they died thousands of years ago, true to His Promise, they will appear with our Lord in the glory of His Kingdom, and along with them all whom they represent and who exercised the faith that they exercised.)

7 He spoke unto them in the cloudy pillar: they kept His testimonies, and the ordinance that He gave them. *(We are told here that the Holy Spirit judged all before the Cross in the light of justification by faith and called them righteous when, in fact, they had no righteousness. This means that they entered into His Victory, and were accorded the same as the New Testament Saints.)*

8 You answered them, O LORD our God: You were a God Who forgave them, though You took vengeance of their inventions. *(Two great Divine principles appear in this Verse: 1. That God forgives confessed sin and 2. That He judges its action.)*

9 Exalt the LORD our God, and worship at His holy hill; for the LORD our God is holy.

(The Fifth Verse extols Israel to worship the Lord; this Ninth Verse extols the nations of the world to praise Israel's God and Lord.)

PSALM 100

AUTHOR UNKNOWN:
A CALL TO PRAISE THE LORD

MAKE a joyful noise unto the LORD, all ye lands. *(Seven times in these Psalms, men are commanded to make a "joyful noise unto the Lord" [66:1; 81:1; 95:1-2; 98:4-6; 100:1]. "Seven" is God's number, speaking of totality, completion, perfection, fulfillment, and universality. This speaks of Christ reigning supreme in the Kingdom Age. Every country in the world will then serve Him.)*

2 Serve the LORD with gladness: come before His presence with singing. *(Then the theme of the world will be "gladness and singing.")*

3 Know ye that the LORD He is God: it is He Who has made us, and not we ourselves; we are His people, and the sheep of His pasture. *(Several things are said in this Verse: 1. Jesus Christ is God, not Buddha, Muhammad, etc.; 2. We are the product of His Hand, not a product of senseless, mindless evolution; 3. He saved us; we could not save ourselves; 4. We are His People; and, 5. We will forage in His pasture, and a wonderful pasture it is!)*

4 Enter into His gates with thanksgiving, and into His courts with praise: be thankful unto Him, and bless His Name. *(Even though this Verse refers to the old economy of God, in essence it means that every Believer, when coming into our Lord's Presence in prayer, should begin with "thanksgiving" and "praise.")*

5 For the LORD is good; His mercy is everlasting; and His truth endures to all generations. *(Everything else falls by the wayside, while "His Truth" marches on, and does so forever.)*

PSALM 101

A PSALM OF DAVID:
THE KING'S MANIFESTO

I will sing of mercy and judgment: unto You, O LORD, will I sing. *(This Psalm portrays the character and capacity of the King to Whom is to be given the Kingdom. This Psalm, plus several which follow, show how Christ was to be tested by suffering, whether Personal or sympathetic. David, who wrote this Psalm, and was a*

Type of Him, was also tested by suffering. His Personal Perfection is the subject of the first two Verses),

2 I will behave myself wisely in a perfect way, O when will You come unto me? I will walk within my house with a perfect heart. *(The expression, "behave myself wisely," was said of David several times, while he was with Saul, and when Saul was attempting to kill him [I Sam. 18:5, 14-15]. As well, the Greater Son of David behaved Himself wisely. David's way was not perfect; however, the way of the Son of Man was "a perfect way," because He had a "perfect heart." David could only desire these things; Christ was these things.)*

3 I will set no wicked thing before my eyes: I hate the work of them who turn aside; it shall not cleave to me. *(This was the heart of David, although not always his actions.*

The "turning aside" has to do with deviating from the Word of God. The Sadducees denied the Word of God. The Pharisees twisted the Word of God, as well as adding to it. Christ said that He hated their work.)

4 A froward heart shall depart from me: I will not know a wicked person. *(The word "froward" means "perverse" or "wicked." The sense of this Verse is that Christ would never agree to, or place approval upon, the perverseness of the Scribes, Sadducees, and Pharisees. They were classified as "a wicked person.")*

5 Whoso privily slanders his neighbour, him will I cut off: him who has a high look and a proud heart will not I suffer. *(In general, this applies to anyone; however, its greater fulfillment pertains to the action of the Scribes, Sadducees, and Pharisees, who slandered Christ.)*

6 My eyes shall be upon the faithful of the land, that they may dwell with me: he who walks in a perfect way, he shall serve me. *(Christ here says that He would put His eyes upon the "faithful of the land," instead of upon the ruling religious hierarchy.)*

7 He who works deceit shall not dwell within my house: he who tells lies shall not tarry in my sight. *(Regrettably, most organized religion works from a foundation of "deceit." As its master, Satan, it functions by "telling lies."*

8 I will early destroy all the wicked of the land; that I may cut off all wicked doers from the city of the LORD. *(At the very beginning of the Millennial Reign, Christ will put down the "wicked of the land.")*

PSALM 102

AUTHOR UNKNOWN:
A PRAYER OF PENITENCE

HEAR My prayer, O LORD, and let My cry come unto You. *(The subject of this Psalm is twofold. The glories of Christ as the Great King are contrasted with His sufferings as the Rejected Man. Here, as in so many other Scriptures, His sufferings and glories are brought together, and always in that order. It was necessary that He should be both the Man of Sorrows and the Mighty God. As the One, He is equipped with Mercy; as the other, with Judgment. He is the Afflicted One of this Psalm.)*

2 Hide not Your face from Me in the day when I am in trouble; incline Your ear unto Me: in the day when I call answer Me speedily. *(Both Verses 1 and 2 pertain to Christ as Very Man, although never ceasing to be Very God, yet the Perfect Sacrifice.)*

3 For My days are consumed like smoke, and My bones are burned as an hearth. *(The sufferings He endured from the opposition of virtually all of Israel, especially the religious hierarchy, literally consumed Him.)*

4 My heart is smitten, and withered like grass; so that I forget to eat My bread. *(As Christ dealt with a lost world, brokenhearted over its destitute spiritual condition, it says of Him, "In the mean while His Disciples prayed Him, saying, Master, eat" [Jn. 4:31].)*

5 By reason of the voice of My groaning My bones cleave to My skin. *(This Passage tells us that the entirety of His Earthly Ministry was filled with such consternation because of the terrible sin of the people, especially the religious leaders.)*

6 I am like a pelican of the wilderness: I am like an owl of the desert. *(Both the "pelican" and the "owl" were unclean fowls and, thereby, unacceptable. Christ was treated by the religious hierarchy like an unclean fowl.)*

7 I watch, and am as a sparrow alone upon the house top. *(A sparrow was seldom alone, unless its mate was killed. There was no one who could enter into the sufferings of Christ, and for all the obvious reasons.)*

8 My enemies reproach Me all the day; and they who are mad against Me are sworn against Me. *(The Scribes and Pharisees, as is evident from this Verse, bound themselves by an oath to destroy Him.)*

9 For I have eaten ashes like bread, and

mingled My drink with weeping. *(The great sorrow of our Lord was twofold: 1. Israel's rejection of Him and 2. What it would mean to them.)*

10 Because of Your indignation and Your wrath: for You have lifted Me up, and cast Me down. *(On the Mount of Transfiguration, He was "lifted up," for the Voice said, "This is My Beloved Son"; and on the Mount of Condemnation [Calvary], He was "cast down," for He cried, "Why have You forsaken Me?")*

11 My days are like a shadow that declines; and I am withered like grass. *(He did not come to live, He came to die. But in His Death, He bought eternal life.)*

12 But You, O LORD, shall endure for ever; and Your remembrance unto all generations. *(Whereas Verses 1 through 11 speak of His First Advent, Verses 12 through 22 speak of His Second Advent. As the First was in suffering and sorrow, the Second shall be in glory and victory.)*

13 You shall arise, and have mercy upon Zion: for the time to favour her, yea, the set time, is come. *(The "set time" for Israel began in 1948, when she was restored, at least partially, as a nation. It will come to fruition in the Battle of Armageddon, when it seems that Israel and Jerusalem will be completely destroyed. At that time, Israel will cry out to God for her Messiah. He will then "arise" and "have mercy upon Zion" [Rev., Chpt. 19].)*

14 For Your servants take pleasure in her stones, and favour the dust thereof. *(Modern Israel desires the world to look at Jerusalem as her capital, but with the United States, as well as most other nations, not doing so for fear of offending the Arabs. All need to read these Verses.)*

15 So the heathen shall fear the Name of the LORD, and all the kings of the Earth Your glory. *(This will take place in the coming Kingdom Age.)*

16 When the LORD shall build up Zion, He shall appear in His glory. *(Israel is God's prophetic time clock. The Lord has already begun to build up Zion, so this tells us that we are living in the very last of the last days, regarding the Church Age.)*

17 He will regard the prayer of the destitute, and not despise their prayer. *(The "destitute" here pertains to Israel in the Battle of Armageddon. God will hear their prayer and will answer it.)*

18 This shall be written for the generation to come: and the people which shall be created shall praise the LORD. *(This speaks of those who will be born in the coming Kingdom Age.)*

19 For He has looked down from the height of His Sanctuary; from Heaven did the LORD behold the Earth *(the specific meaning of this Passage, through Verse 22, is that God will see Israel's plight in the latter half of the Great Tribulation, and especially in the Battle of Armageddon, when He will come to their rescue);*

20 To hear the groaning of the prisoner; to loose those that are appointed to death *(this pertains to the efforts by the Antichrist to completely annihilate Israel);*

21 To declare the Name of the LORD in Zion, and His praise in Jerusalem *(when Israel rejected Christ in His First Advent, the Lord withdrew from visible protection of that nation. For nearly 2,000 years now, they have wandered throughout the nations of the world. In the latter half of the Great Tribulation, and especially during the Battle of Armageddon, the Lord will once again begin to visibly show Himself, and upon His Second Advent will actually set up His Earthly headquarters in Jerusalem);*

22 When the people are gathered together, and the kingdoms, to serve the LORD. *(The sense of this Verse is the glory of the Millennial Morn. Satan's day is over.)*

23 He weakened My strength in the way; He shortened My days.

24 I said, O My God, take Me not away in the midst of My days: Your years are throughout all generations. *(First of all, these two Passages refer to the Messiah in His Earthly Ministry and the price He paid for the Deliverance of humanity. Second, it refers to Israel, when her days were shortened because of sin. She was meant to be a light "throughout all generations," but she herself extinguished that light. However, that light will be restored, and Israel will faithfully serve the Lord "throughout all generations.")*

25 Of old have You laid the foundation of the Earth: and the Heavens are the work of Your hands. *(Not mindless evolution!)*

26 They shall perish, but You shall endure: yea, all of them shall wax old like a garment; as a vesture shall You change them, and they shall be changed *(this means that the Heavens and the Earth will ultimately be changed. The idea here is that they are being affected by sin and the bondage of corruption. They will be renewed and liberated from this corrupt state to a new and eternal state and be kept eternally new when all sin is put down [I Cor. 15:24-28], with everything then restored as before the curse. There will be no more curse or bondage of*

corruption after this [Rom. 8:21-24; Heb. 1:10-12; Rev. 21:1; 22:3]):

27 But You are the same, and Your years shall have no end. *(The material creations that have been cursed and brought under the bondage of corruption to wax old will, of necessity, be renewed and changed to the state of eternal newness. God will never wax old nor need to be renewed. He is eternally the same.)*

28 The children of Your servants shall continue, and their seed shall be established before You. *(This has a twofold meaning: 1. It refers to Israel, which will be restored and will worship God forever and 2. It means that eternal generations of natural people shall continue upon planet Earth forever, and will be established. In other words, the Plan of God for the human race was not cancelled by the Fall [Gen., Chpt. 3], but was only delayed.)*

PSALM 103

DAVID IS THE AUTHOR:
THANKSGIVING TO THE LORD

BLESS the LORD, O my soul: and all that is within me, bless His holy name. *(The subject of this Psalm is Redemption. It begins with thanksgiving unto the Lord for all that He has done. In essence, it refers to the "benefits" of the Cross.)*

2 Bless the LORD, O my soul, and forget not all His benefits *(while Christ is the Source of all benefits, the Cross is the means):*

3 Who forgives all your iniquities; Who heals all your diseases *(the Lord Alone can forgive sin [I Jn. 1:9]; the Lord Alone can heal [I Pet. 2:24]);*

4 Who redeems your life from destruction; Who crowns you with lovingkindness and tender mercies *(the word "redeemed" means to purchase something back that has been lost through death, default, or failure to pay; Jesus did so by the means of the Cross [Eph. 2:13-18]);*

5 Who satisfies your mouth with good things; so that your youth is renewed like the eagle's. *(The "eagle" was used by the Holy Spirit as an example. Once a year, eagles cast off their old feathers and receive new ones; therefore, despite their age, they have the continued look of youthfulness. Likewise, upon acceptance of Christ, and the individual becoming a new creature with the guilt of sin removed, the redeemed one always has a youthful spirit!)*

6 The LORD executes righteousness and

judgment for all who are oppressed. *(The word "oppressed" has to do with Satan's heavy hand upon the human race. The Lord Alone can deliver those who are oppressed by the Devil. He does so through our Faith in Him and what He has done for us at the Cross [Acts 10:38].)*

7 He made known His ways unto Moses, His acts unto the Children of Israel. *(Natural intelligence can recognize Divine "acts," but only to the spiritual mind does God make known His "Ways.")*

8 The LORD is merciful and gracious, slow to anger, and plenteous in mercy. *(In this and the following Verses, God outlines His dealings with Israel while in the wilderness, and even in the Land. His dealings are thusly with us.)*

9 He will not always chide: neither will He keep His anger for ever. *(Irrespective of what has happened, if the Believer will humble himself and confess his wrongdoing, the Lord will discontinue His admonishment and cool His anger. God does not hold grudges.)*

10 He has not dealt with us after our sins; nor rewarded us according to our iniquities. *(This is the reason God takes a stern attitude toward Believers who will not show mercy nor be quick to forgive. He expects us to conduct ourselves toward others as He has conducted Himself toward us.)*

11 For as the Heaven is high above the Earth, so great is His mercy toward them who fear Him. *(This refers to unlimited Mercy, but with a condition. The condition is that we "fear Him." If we do, there will be less iniquities.)*

12 As far as the east is from the west, so far has he removed our transgressions from us. *(This is equivalent to "blotting out our sins" [Acts 3:19; Isa. 43:25; 44:22]. It is impossible to bring the east and the west together; so it is impossible to bring the forgiven sinner and his forgiven sins together. This Divine fact gives to those who believe it a peace which nothing can destroy.)*

13 Like as a father pities his children, so the LORD pities them who fear Him *(as a result, He has great Mercy on us).*

14 For He knows our frame; He remembers that we are dust. *(God remembers what man forgets [our infirmities]; man remembers what God forgets [our sins].)*

15 As for man, his days are as grass: as a flower of the field, so he flourishes. *(As a flower is beautiful for a short time, so is man. But then. . . .)*

16 For the wind passes over it, and it is gone;

and the place thereof shall know it no more. *(As a flower blooms and then is shortly gone, so man passes away. One cannot tell where the flower had been, and one can little tell where man has been, irrespective of how great he formerly was!)*

17 But the mercy of the LORD is from everlasting to everlasting upon them who fear him, and His righteousness unto children's children *(the sense of this Verse has to do with the previous Verses; there is no dependability in man, but there is great dependability in "the Mercy of the Lord");*

18 To such as keep His Covenant, and to those who remember His Commandments to do them. *(God will not and, in fact, cannot, show His Mercy to those who flout His Word.)*

19 The LORD has prepared His Throne in the Heavens; and His kingdom rules over all. *(This will come to fruition in the coming Kingdom Age. Then the Lord's Prayer will be answered, "Your Will be done on Earth as it is in Heaven.")*

20 Bless the LORD, you His angels, who excel in strength, who do His Commandments, hearkening unto the voice of His Word. *(All the righteous Angels praise Him, and so should we, especially considering that we have experienced Redemption, which Angels have never known.)*

21 Bless ye the LORD, all ye His hosts; ye ministers of His, who do His pleasure. *(Angels are called here "Ministers," meaning that they carry out His Will according to "His pleasure.")*

22 Bless the LORD, all His works in all places of His dominion: bless the LORD, O my soul. *(The Psalm ends as it begins, with an admonishment for us to ever kneel in reverence and respect to the Lord of Glory, Who has given us all good things, despite the fact that we are poor, frail, flawed, and fallen human beings made of dust.)*

PSALM 104

AUTHOR UNKNOWN:
PRAISE TO GOD THE CREATOR

BLESS the LORD, O my soul. O LORD my God, You are very great; You are clothed with honour and majesty. *(This Psalm will show that the conception of Deity and of creative power is not human, but Divine, and the language is that of pure science. None of the great religions of the world, either ancient or modern, approach this portrayal in sublimity or accuracy.)*

2 Who covers Yourself with light as with a garment: Who stretches out the Heavens like a curtain *(this refers to the great light in which God dwells that no man can approach unto [I Tim. 6:16]. In this Passage, light appears like in Genesis, Chapter 1, as the first attribute and evidence of the Creator. The word "curtain" means "tabernacle" and should have been so translated):*

3 Who lays the beams of His chambers in the waters: Who makes the clouds His chariot: Who walks upon the wings of the wind *(the sense of this Verse is that creation serves the Creator):*

4 Who makes His angels spirits; His ministers a flaming fire *(as the previous two Verses show the Lord's wisdom as Creator of the Heavens, this Verse shows His supremacy over the Angels):*

5 Who laid the foundations of the Earth, that it should not be removed for ever *(creation demands a Creator).*

6 You cover it with the deep as with a garment: the waters stood above the mountains. *(This refers to the first universal flood, as described in Gen. 1:2, which was the result of Lucifer's Fall. It does not refer to Noah's flood.)*

7 At Your rebuke they fled; at the voice of Your thunder they hasted away *(this refers to Gen. 1:2).*

8 They go up by the mountains; they go down by the valleys unto the place which You have founded for them.

9 You have set a bound that they may not pass over; that they turn not again to cover the Earth. *(In Gen. 1:2, the waters covered the entirety of the Earth. Verses 7 through 9 simply mean that God appointed the waters certain places and the dry land certain places.)*

10 He sends the springs into the valleys, which run among the hills. *(This simply means that the Lord is the Creator of every river, lake, and even the springs, whether above ground or underground.)*

11 They give drink to every beast of the field: the wild asses quench their thirst.

12 By them shall the fowls of the Heaven have their habitation, which sing among the branches.

13 He waters the hills from His chambers: the Earth is satisfied with the fruit of Your works.

14 He causes the grass to grow for the cattle, and herb for the service of man: that He may

bring forth food out of the earth (all of these present the Laws of God regarding plant life, and also the animal kingdom, all for the "service of man");

15 And wine that makes glad the heart of man, and oil to make his face to shine, and bread which strengthens man's heart (all are created by God, and according to certain Laws).

16 The trees of the LORD are full of sap; the cedars of Lebanon, which He has planted (the Lord planted them by the decree of His Word, which is a continuing process, with new trees coming forth from the seed of the old);

17 Where the birds make their nests: as for the stork, the fir trees are her house.

18 The high hills are a refuge for the wild goats; and the rocks for the conies. (The previous two Verses declare God as the Creator of fowls as well as animals and all their dwellingplaces.)

19 He appointed the moon for seasons: the sun knows his going down. (The reference to "the moon" is another reference to the Solaric Covenant [Gen. 1:14-19; 8:22; Jer. 33:20; Dan. 2:21]. The reference made about the sun "going down" is a figure of speech. In fact, the sun does not really move. It is the Earth that moves — one rotation every twenty-four hours.)

20 You make darkness, and it is night: wherein all the beasts of the forest do creep forth.

21 The young lions roar after their prey, and seek their meat from God. (The manner of creation of the animals is given here. Certain types of beasts, such as the "lions," feed at night.)

22 The sun arises, they gather themselves together, and lay them down in their dens.

23 Man goes forth unto his work and to his labour until the evening. (Many animals do much of their work at night, while man does his work during the day.)

24 O LORD, how manifold are Your works! in wisdom have You made them all: the Earth is full of Your riches. (No wonder that Paul said, "O the depth of the riches both of the wisdom and knowledge of God! How unsearchable are His Judgments, and His Ways past finding out!" [Rom. 11:33].)

25 So is this great and wide sea, wherein are things creeping innumerable, both small and great beasts. (The continents of this planet have been minutely inspected for precious metals, etc., at least as far as modern technology allows such to be done; however, the riches of the great oceans of the world have little been tapped. That awaits the Coming of the Lord.)

26 There go the ships: there is that leviathan, whom You have made to play therein. (The word "leviathan," in the Hebrew, is "livyathan," which means "a great sea serpent." It is also a symbol of Satan [Job, Chpt. 41].)

27 These wait all upon You; that You may give them their meat in due season. (All of creation, whatever it might be, is totally dependent upon God for sustenance regarding daily life and living.)

28 That You give them they gather: You open Your hand, they are filled with good (while the Lord gives the sustenance, man must gather it, which he does in various ways).

29 You hide Your face, they are troubled: You take away their breath, they die, and return to their dust. (Death is a result of the curse. While God never originally intended for man to die, we have no Biblical knowledge as it regards His intentions concerning the animal kingdom, at least in this respect [Gen. 3:14-21].)

30 You send forth Your Spirit, they are created: and You renew the face of the Earth. (The sense of this Verse is that God upholds this planet and all of His Creation by "His Spirit." In other words, the Spirit of God, Who originally moved upon the face of the waters [Gen. 1:2], from that time continues to move in order to insure God's Creation. Therefore, the prognostications by some that this Earth will be destroyed by the "greenhouse effect," "ozone depletion," or other similar theories, hold no Scriptural or literal reality.)

31 The glory of the LORD shall endure for ever: the LORD shall rejoice in His works. (As long as the Glory of the Lord endures, and it will endure forever, His Creation will also endure forever.)

32 He looks on the Earth, and it trembles: He touches the hills, and they smoke. (The sense of this Verse is that God has such awesome Power that He is able to do with His Creation what He desires.)

33 I will sing unto the LORD as long as I live: I will sing praise to my God while I have my being.

34 My meditation of Him shall be sweet: I will be glad in the LORD. (Singing of the Lord's wonderful works and meditating on those works are the cure for fear, worry, and anxiety.)

35 Let the sinners be consumed out of the Earth, and let the wicked be no more. Bless thou the LORD, O my soul. Praise ye the LORD. (The word translated "praise" here should have been translated "Hallelujah." In fact, this

is the first time the word "Hallelujah" is used in the Old Testament. It is interesting that it is connected with the overthrow of the wicked, which guarantees the such will ultimately be done. The actual fulfillment will be at the Second Coming.)

PSALM 105

AUTHOR UNKNOWN: GOD'S WONDROUS WORKS ON BEHALF OF ISRAEL

O give thanks unto the LORD; call upon His Name: make known His deeds among the people. (In this Psalm, we will find that the action of the Messiah with Israel is a picture and a Promise of His future action with the world. The Covenant consummated at Calvary will be the basis of His Millennial rule, and the Promises of that Covenant will then be performed and fulfilled. In fact, all of these Promises constitute the benefits of the Cross.)

2 Sing unto Him, sing psalms unto Him: talk ye of all His wondrous works. (As it is the Holy Spirit Who is the Speaker in this Psalm, then we must realize how absolutely significant are these words! Every Believer should "sing" of all the wondrous works of the Lord, and do so constantly. As well, we must constantly "talk" of all these great works. This builds Faith!)

3 Glory ye in His holy name: let the heart of them rejoice who seek the LORD. (We are told here that seeking the Lord brings rejoicing, because seeking Him brings forth wondrous things, all on our behalf.)

4 Seek the LORD, and His strength: seek His face evermore. (Seek the Lord about every problem. This is the answer to man's dilemma and, in fact, the only answer. This plainly tells us that humanistic psychology has no place in the thinking of the true Believer.)

5 Remember His marvellous works that He has done; His wonders, and the judgments of His mouth (this pertains to the Word of God, which every Believer ought to study minutely);

6 O ye seed of Abraham His servant, you children of Jacob His chosen. (Every Believer, whether Jew or Gentile, is the "Seed of Abraham" [Gal. 3:7]; however, the ultimate Seed is the Lord Jesus Christ [Gal. 3:16]. "Jacob" pertains strictly to Israel, as God's chosen People.)

7 He is the LORD our God: His judgments are in all the Earth. (His "Judgments" refer to His Law and Word. At this moment, this Passage

has not yet been fulfilled. It will be fulfilled in the coming Kingdom Age.)

8 He has remembered His Covenant for ever, the Word which He commanded to a thousand generations. (The Lord entered into a Covenant with Israel, and that Covenant still holds good. He has not forgotten it, and will never forget it. In essence, it has been suspended for approximately 2,000 years, but will once again flower into full potential at the Second Coming. At that time, Israel will fully accept the Lord Jesus as Saviour and Lord. The Covenant will actually be the New Covenant, to which the Old Covenant always pointed. And this New Covenant is "The Everlasting Covenant," meaning that it will never have to be suspended or amended [Heb. 13:20].)

9 Which Covenant He made with Abraham (Justification by Faith [Gal. 3:14-29]), and His oath unto Isaac (pertains to the supremacy of Israel and the coming Kingdom Age, as well as the Land of Israel [Gen. 22:17-18; 26:2-4]);

10 And confirmed the same unto Jacob for a Law, and to Israel for an Everlasting Covenant (this Covenant of the Land of Israel belonging to the sons of Jacob cannot be abrogated):

11 Saying, Unto you will I give the land of Canaan, the lot of your inheritance (the Arabs should read this and believe it [Gen 13:15; 15:18]):

12 When they were but a few men in number; yea, very few, and strangers in it. (When Abraham and his family were called to the land of Canaan, they were truly few in number, by comparison to the inhabitants of the land [Gen. 34:20; Deut. 7:7; Heb. 11:9].)

13 When they went from one nation to another, from one kingdom to another people (they sojourned among the Philistines [Gen., Chpt. 20] and the Egyptians [Gen., Chpts. 46-50]);

14 He suffered no man to do them wrong: yea, he reproved kings for their sakes (Pharaoh and Abimelech were threatened with death if they touched them [Gen. 12:17; 20:3; 26:11]);

15 Saying, Touch not My anointed, and do My Prophets no harm. (Regarding those who are truly Prophets of the Lord, this admonition had better be heeded!)

16 Moreover He called for a famine upon the land: He broke the whole staff of bread. (The length that God will go to ensure His Covenant with His People, which we will study in succeeding Verses, should make us realize that His every Word will come to pass exactly as spoken.)

17 He sent a man before them, even Joseph, who was sold for a servant *(God had nothing to do with Joseph's brothers, regarding their hate and their ungodliness; yet God would use the situation to bring about His intended results):*

18 Whose feet they hurt with fetters: he was laid in iron *(Gen., Chpt. 39, gives us the account):*

19 Until the time that His Word came: the Word of the LORD tried him. *(Regarding the mission that God had for Joseph, which Joseph was not even aware of, he would have to be put to the test. Faith must be tested, and great Faith must be tested greatly.)*

20 The king sent and loosed him; even the ruler of the people, and let him go free *(Gen. 41:14).*

21 He made him lord of his house, and ruler of all his substance *(Gen. 41:40):*

22 To bind his princes at his pleasure; and teach his senators wisdom. *(At this time, Egypt was the most powerful nation on the face of the Earth; consequently, the advisors to Pharaoh, here called "senators," would now be taught by an ex-convict. Only the Lord could work out such a thing.)*

23 Israel also came into Egypt; and Jacob sojourned in the land of Ham *(which the Lord told the Patriarch to do [Gen. 46:6]).*

24 And He *(the Lord)* increased His people *(Israel)* greatly; and made them stronger than their enemies *(stronger than Egypt).*

25 He turned their heart to hate His people, to deal subtilly with His servants. *(This does not mean that God forced Egypt to hate the Israelites. It does mean that God provided the opportunity for them to do so; however, this was done by their own free will. Had this not happened, the Israelites would not have desired to leave Egypt and go to Canaan, which was the original intention of the Lord.)*

26 He sent Moses His servant; and Aaron whom He had chosen. *(The Lord chose Moses, while Moses chose Aaron [Ex. 3:10].)*

27 They *(Moses and Aaron)* showed His *(the Lord's)* signs among them *(among the Egyptians)*, and wonders in the land of Ham *(Ex., Chpts. 7-12).*

28 He sent darkness, and made it dark; and they rebelled not against His Word. *(The close connection between the plague of darkness and the compelled submission of the Egyptians is very striking. God sent the darkness, and the Egyptians let the Hebrews go. This alludes possibly to the ninth plague, but, as a substantive statement, the word "darkness" is to be understood as a covering term expressive of the entire period of the Divine punitive action upon Pharaoh. It was indeed a time of darkness for him, and it lasted several months.)*

29 He turned their waters into blood, and slew their fish *(Ex. 7:20).*

30 Their land brought forth frogs in abundance, in the chambers of their kings *(Ex. 8:6).*

31 He spoke, and there came divers sorts of flies, and lice in all their coasts *(Ex. 8:17).*

32 He gave them hail for rain, and flaming fire in their land *(turned the rain to hail).*

33 He smote their vines also and their fig trees; and broke the trees of their coasts *(Ps. 78:47).*

34 He spoke, and the locusts came, and caterpillers, and that without number *(Ex. 10:4),*

35 And did eat up all the herbs in their land, and devoured the fruit of their ground.

36 He smote also all the first born in their land, the chief of all their strength *(Ex. 12:29).*

37 He brought them forth also with silver and gold: and there was not one feeble person among their tribes. *(The "silver and gold" mentioned here was payment for the many years of slavery. It may seem to some that God is not keeping account; however, when His payday does come, and it will come, it will be done as only He can do.*

As well, He healed all the sick who were among them and gave them strength, even unto the eldest.)

38 Egypt was glad when they departed: for the fear of them fell upon them *(Ex. 12:33).*

39 He spread a cloud for a covering; and fire to give light in the night *(Ex. 13:21).*

40 The people asked, and He brought quails, and satisfied them with the bread of heaven *(Ex. 16:12).*

41 He opened the rock, and the waters gushed out; they ran in the dry places like a river. *(The "Rock" was a Type of Christ. The "waters" that "gushed out" were a type of the eternal life being given according to the price He paid at Calvary. The "dry places" are symbolic of this world and the barrenness of its spiritual obligation. The "river" symbolized the magnitude of this great gift of God. It was not a trickle of water that came out of this Rock, but a veritable "river" — enough to satisfy some three million Israelites, with all their cattle, sheep, and other livestock. As well, there is enough to satisfy the thirst of every heart that comes to this life-giving stream.)*

42 For He remembered His holy promise, and Abraham His servant. *(These were the Promises that God gave to Abraham [Gen. 12:1-3; 13:14-18; 15:18-21; 17:1-8].)*

43 And He brought forth His people with joy, and His chosen with gladness *(also, we should ever rejoice and praise His Holy Name, realizing that He has delivered us from the terrible bondages of darkness. What "joy" we should have! What "gladness" should characterize our hearts and lives!)*:

44 And gave them the lands of the heathen: and they inherited the labour of the people *(as well, the great inheritance that God has given us is carved out of that which Satan intended for the destruction of our lives)*;

45 That they might observe His Statutes, and keep His Laws. Praise ye the LORD. *(Once again, the word "praise" here should have been translated "Hallelujah," for that's what it means in the Hebrew. Psalm 104 also closes accordingly.)*

PSALM 106

AUTHOR UNKNOWN:
ISRAEL'S SINS AND GOD'S MERCY

PRAISE ye the LORD. O give thanks unto the LORD; for He is good: for His mercy endures forever. *(This is the last Psalm of that which is commonly called "The Numbers Book," or Book No. 4 — Psalms 90 through 106.*

This Psalm predicts with confidence that Christ will establish a just understanding and a gracious government over man, and that He will change the Earth, at present a wilderness, into a paradise.

In view of this, the Psalm begins with "Hallelujah" [Praise].)

2 Who can utter the mighty acts of the LORD? who can show forth all His praise? *(The answer is that no one can exhaustively analyze, understand, or show the meaning and purpose of Divine actions, or adequately praise such actions. But the Messiah can, and He will show forth all God's praises.)*

3 Blessed are they who keep judgment, and he who does righteousness at all times. *(This Passage shows us that spiritual intelligence will always recognize Divine actions and bow and worship because of such actions. Spiritual intelligence also results only from subjection of the mind to the Scriptures and from an unvarying life of righteous conduct. Only Christ could*

fit this description!)

4 Remember me, O LORD, with the favour that You bear unto Your people: O visit me with Your salvation *(the author requests two things, "favor," and "Salvation")*;

5 That I may see the good of Your chosen, that I may rejoice in the gladness of Your nation, that I may glory with Your inheritance. *(Love delights in possession, hence the terms "Your people," "Your chosen," "Your nation," "Your inheritance.")*

6 We have sinned with our fathers, we have committed iniquity, we have done wickedly. *(The nature of evil is seen in the terms "sin," "iniquity," and "wickedness.")*

7 Our fathers understood not Your wonders in Egypt; they remembered not the multitude of Your mercies; but provoked Him at the sea, even at the Red Sea. *(Israel did not wish to understand, nor take the trouble to study the ten plagues, nor wish to remember the countless mercies of their Great Shepherd. Forty hours took Israel out of Egypt, but forty years did not take Egypt out of Israel.)*

8 Nevertheless He saved them for His Name's sake, that He might make His mighty power to be known. *(If one will notice, God did not save Israel because of their righteousness or morality, but for "His Name's sake.")*

9 He rebuked the Red Sea also, and it was dried up: so He led them through the depths, as through the wilderness. *(The waters that stood up like two walls on both sides of the Children of Israel were symbolic of the great weight of sin binding the sinner. When Jesus Christ died on Calvary, He opened a path through that great "depth" of sin, so that all who will may come. The sinner little knows how lost he is, and the Christian little knows how saved he is.)*

10 And He saved them from the hand of him who hated them, and redeemed them from the hand of the enemy. *(The enemy in this case was Egypt, whose sponsor was Satan. Israel could have only been extricated by God. No military force in the world could have carried this out; only God could and did.)*

11 And the waters covered their enemies: there was not one of them left. *(As every Egyptian in that army drowned, from their mightiest generals to their lowliest foot soldiers, likewise, every single enemy of our soul has been defeated at Calvary.)*

12 Then believed they His words; they sang His praise. *(When the Believer truly knows the Lord, he will "sing His praise." When he begins*

13 They soon forgot His works; they waited not for His counsel (*unfortunately, this fits the modern Church, as well*):

14 But lusted exceedingly in the wilderness, and tempted God in the desert (*doubt can never see God, even when He is in the very midst; Faith always sees God*).

15 And He gave them their request; but sent leanness into their soul. (*Israel wanted things, but not Christ. The modern Church wants things, but not Christ. Everything but Christ brings "leanness."*)

16 They envied Moses also in the camp, and Aaron the Saint of the LORD. (*The example is found in Num., Chpts. 12, 16-17.*)

17 The Earth opened and swallowed up Dathan and covered the company of Abiram. (*Num., Chpt. 16, gives the account of this episode. The warning is clear.*)

18 And a fire was kindled in their company; the flame burned up the wicked. (*Men will have Holy Ghost fire, or else they will have the fire of God's judgment.*)

19 They made a calf in Horeb, and worshipped the molten image. (*The sacred name of Horeb is given to Sinai so as to heighten the sin of representing the God of Glory by a beast that eats grass.*)

20 Thus they changed their glory into the similitude of an ox that eats grass. (*This Passage portrays the fact that the idol worship of Egypt was still ingrained in the Israelites.*)

21 They forgot God their Saviour which had done great things in Egypt (*this is speaking of the mighty plagues that God brought upon the Egyptians; Israel forgot that He was their Saviour, not man!*);

22 Wondrous works in the land of Ham, and terrible things by the Red Sea. (*Egypt is referred to here as the descendants of Noah's son, Ham. These Passages show the incurable evil of the human heart.*)

23 Therefore He said that He would destroy them, had not Moses His chosen stood before Him in the breach, to turn away His wrath, lest He should destroy them. (*None of us would be here, irrespective of past experiences in the Lord, were it not for our Heavenly Moses, the Lord Jesus Christ. He turns away the wrath of God from us.*)

24 Yea, they despised the pleasant land, they believed not His Word (*the cause of all error, sin, failure, wrong direction, incorrect leading, and straying from God is because of failure to believe the Bible*):

25 But murmured in their tents, and hearkened not unto the voice of the LORD. (*Murmuring and complaining has to be one of the greatest sins in the life of any Believer. Such action always marks faithlessness.*)

26 Therefore He lifted up His hand against them, to overthrow them in the wilderness (*the Lord considered the unbelief of the Children of Israel at least as great a sin as the making of the golden calf*):

27 To overthrow their seed also among the nations, and to scatter them in the lands. (*This was done twice: 1. The dispersion into Babylon; and 2. The destruction of Jerusalem by Titus in A.D. 70.*)

28 They joined themselves also unto Baalpeor, and ate the sacrifices of the dead. (*The Baal cults affected and challenged the worship of the Lord throughout Israelite history. Little by little, Israel switched her allegiance from the God of Heaven, Who was her "Master" and "Husband," to Baal, by referring to him by the same names.*

The "sacrifices of the dead" have to do with communicating with the dead. This cannot be done, and all such efforts are in the realm of witchcraft.)

29 Thus they provoked Him to anger with their inventions: and the plague broke in upon them. (*The word "inventions" has to do with new ways of committing sin. All sin ultimately invites, and will entertain, "plague." America and Canada are today "plagued" because of sin. These "plagues" consist of alcoholism, drug addiction, AIDS, homosexuality, etc., all resulting in untold heartache, suffering, and sorrow for the people.*)

30 Then stood up Phinehas, and executed judgment: and so the plague was stayed. (*Men are ever seeking to stop the "plague" by human means. It is not possible to do so. Only one thing can stop the plague, "Fidelity to the Bible."*)

31 And that was counted unto him for righteousness unto all generations for evermore. (*Phinehas became the third High Priest. God gave him an everlasting Priesthood because of his zeal for righteousness in slaying the rebels. He will be an everlasting Priest like all the Redeemed, who are made Kings and Priests to reign on Earth [Rev. 1:5-6; 5:10; 20:4-6; 22:4-5].*)

32 They angered Him also at the waters of strife, so that it went ill with Moses for their sakes (*the Children of Israel who did this thing comprised the group who were to go into the*

Promised Land. The old unbelieving genera-tion had now died off. So, in fact, the evil heart of unbelief that resided in their fathers resided in them as well. They complained, they murmured, they blamed their plight on Moses. Man's complaints, like these, are usu-ally senseless):

33 Because they provoked his spirit, so that he spoke unadvisedly with his lips. *(The sin that Moses committed was in striking the Rock the second time, when God had told him just to speak to it. The Rock was a Type of Christ [I Cor. 10:4]. It had already been previously smitten once, which was a Type of Christ's dying at Calvary [Ex. 17:5-7].*

When Moses smote the Rock the second time, in effect, and by symbolism, he was saying that the first smiting of the Rock, symbolizing Jesus' dying on Calvary, did not suffice for the sins of man, so Christ needed to be crucified again. This was a grievous sin in the mind of God.)

34 They did not destroy the nations, con-cerning whom the LORD commanded them *(this speaks of the Jebusites, the Hivites, and oth-ers [Deut. 7:2; Judg. 1:21; 2:2]):*

35 But were mingled among the heathen, and learned their works. *(As Israel did not come to terms with these idol worshippers, like-wise, we cannot come to terms with hindrances within our lives. If we do not defeat them, they will defeat us. As well, we can only defeat them by looking exclusively to Christ and what He did for us at the Cross [Judg. 3:5-6].)*

36 And they served their idols: which were a snare unto them. *(These heathen people did not become acclimated to Israel's God, but, rather, Israel became acclimated to their gods [idols]. This is the law of regression. If one rotten apple is placed in a barrel of good apples, the rotten apple does not become healthy as the good apples. The opposite happens.)*

37 Yea, they sacrificed their sons and their daughters unto devils,

38 And shed innocent blood, even the blood of their sons and of their daughters, whom they sacrificed unto the idols of Canaan: and the land was polluted with blood. *(Israel sank to the lowest depths of sinful bondage. They actually began to engage in human sacri-fice, offering their sons and daughters to these idol gods.)*

39 Thus were they defiled with their own works, and went a whoring with their own in-ventions. *(They went ever deeper into sin, actu-ally inventing new ways to sin.)*

40 Therefore was the wrath of the LORD kindled against His people, insomuch that He abhorred His own inheritance *(because of their deep, deep sin, and their refusing to turn to Him, despite the many warnings; Jesus addressed this as well [Mat. 23:37]).*

41 And He gave them into the hand of the heathen, and they who hated them ruled over them. *(He did not do so until all avenues of Mercy and Grace were exhausted [Jer. 7:25-26].)*

42 Their enemies also oppressed them, and they were brought into subjection under their hand. *(When Israel was living for God, her enemies made no headway whatsoever against her; however, when Israel turned away from God, then God allowed her enemies to "oppress them.")*

43 Many times did He deliver them; but they provoked Him with their counsel, and were brought low for their iniquity. *(All be-cause of sin!)*

44 Nevertheless He regarded their afflic-tion, when He heard their cry *(the Lord an-swered this, as it regards His answer to Solomon [II Chron. 7:14]):*

45 And He remembered for them His Cov-enant, and repented according to the multi-tude of His mercies. *(The Lord was always ready to forgive Israel and deliver them, if they would only meet His righteous terms of the Covenant.)*

46 He made them also to be pitied of all those who carried them captives. *(In other words, God gave Israel favor in the eyes of their captors [II Ki., Chpt. 25; Dan. 1:19; 6:2].)*

47 Save us, O LORD our God, and gather us from among the heathen, to give thanks unto Your holy name, and to triumph in Your praise. *(This request and prayer were answered in re-gards to the dispersion at Babylon. It has not been answered concerning their dispersion in A.D. 70, because Israel, since the Crucifixion of Christ, has not truly repented. They will at the Second Coming.)*

48 Blessed be the LORD God of Israel from everlasting to everlasting: and let all the people say, Amen. Praise ye the LORD. *(This fourth Book closes with the expected "Amen," but the repeated "Amen" is changed to "Halle-lujah" here. This harmonizes with the theme of the Book. "Amen" expresses the desire that the wilderness journey should end and the Kingdom should be established. "Hallelu-jah" joyfully announces the gratification of both desires.)*

PSALM 107

THE DEUTERONOMY BOOK
AUTHOR UNKNOWN:
PRAISE TO GOD FOR DELIVERANCE

O give thanks unto the LORD, for He is good: for His mercy endures for ever. *(This is the first Psalm of the fifth Book of Psalms, which corresponds to the Fifth Book of the Pentateuch [Deuteronomy].*

Prosperity is shown to be dependent upon acceptance of the Word of God as the rule of life. But the Message is not now directed to a new and untried people, but, instead, to a tested, rebellious, and fallen people.

Therefore, this fifth Book presents the beauteous picture of the Messiah coming as the Word of God with healing and help to those who, by disobedience to that Word, had brought themselves to ruin.)

2 Let the redeemed of the LORD say so, whom He has redeemed from the hand of the enemy *(the "enemy" is the Antichrist, and the "redeemed" pictures Israel immediately after the Second Coming, at which time they will accept the Lord; as well, all redeemed, and in every Dispensation, should "say so");*

3 And gathered them out of the lands, from the east, and from the west, from the north, and from the south. *(This will be completely fulfilled after the Second Coming.)*

4 They wandered in the wilderness in a solitary way; they found no city to dwell in.

5 Hungry and thirsty, their soul fainted in them. *(The entirety of the world has by and large become a wilderness to the Jews since their rejection of Christ. Here they are grouped into four companies: wanderers, prisoners, fools, and homeless.)*

6 Then they cried unto the LORD in their trouble, and He delivered them out of their distresses. *(This Verse, in a few simple words, proclaims the Coming of the Lord. It will be during the Battle of Armageddon.)*

7 And He led them forth by the right way, that they might go to a city of habitation. *(This speaks of the Lord's great victory at Armageddon [Ezek., Chpts. 38-39]. The "city of habitation" is Jerusalem. Now, and at long last, it will be safely inhabited.)*

8 Oh that men would praise the LORD for His goodness, and for His wonderful works to the children of men! *(The entirety of this Psalm is a paean of praise to God for*
the great Deliverance He has brought, which speaks of the defeat of the Antichrist at the Battle of Armageddon.)*

9 For He satisfies the longing soul, and fills the hungry soul with goodness. *(Someone has said, "The soul of man is so big that only God can fill it up.")*

10 Such as sit in darkness and in the shadow of death, being bound in affliction and iron *(pointedly, this Verse refers to Israel in her great Redemption from the terrible bondage which resulted from their rejection of the Word of God; in general, the Passage speaks to all who are without Christ, and man's foolishness of futility of trying to save himself);*

11 Because they rebelled against the Words of God, and contemned the counsel of the Most High *(this pertains to the rejection of Jesus Christ by Israel):*

12 Therefore He brought down their heart with labour; they fell down, and there was none to help. *(When Israel rejected Jesus Christ, there remained no more remedy for them. As well, it pertains to all who fall into this category. One cannot help but weep as one reads this Scripture.)*

13 Then they cried unto the LORD in their trouble, and He saved them out of their distresses. *(The "trouble" spoken of here is the time of "Jacob's Trouble" [Jer. 30:7]. The "distress" speaks to the terrible latter half of the Great Tribulation, when the Antichrist will turn on Israel. The Lord will save them by the Second Coming.)*

14 He brought them out of darkness and the shadow of death, and broke their bands in sunder. *(Israel has walked in darkness, and even the shadow of death, since they rejected Christ. At the Second Coming, the Lord will "break their bands asunder" [Ps. 2:3].)*

15 Oh that men would praise the LORD for His goodness, and for His wonderful works to the children of men! *(This same Verse is repeated four times [Vss. 8, 15, 21, 31]. When the Holy Spirit repeats Himself in this fashion, it is not without purpose.)*

16 For He has broken the gates of brass, and cut the bars of iron in sunder. *(The bondages of Satan on human beings are spoken of as "brass" and "iron." How foolish of man to think that humanistic psychology, or anything else for that matter, can break this bondage! The truth is, it was broken at Calvary, and our Faith in Christ and His Finished Work gives us freedom, and that alone gives us freedom.)*

17 Fools because of their transgression, and because of their iniquities, are afflicted. *(The word "fools" means those who are perverse, those depending upon their own wisdom, which is foolishness to God [I Cor. 1:20-25].)*

18 Their soul abhors all manner of meat; and they draw near unto the gates of death. *(The "meat" spoken of here refers to the "meat" of the Word of God [I Cor. 3:2; 10:3; Heb. 5:12, 14].)*

19 Then they cry unto the LORD in their trouble, and He saves them out of their distresses. *(This is the very nature of the Lord. Poor man stumbles after his own foolish wisdom and, with his back to the wall, he cries to the Lord. Then, with Mercy and Grace, the Lord saves us. How wonderful is our Lord!)*

20 He sent His Word, and healed them, and delivered them from their destructions. *(This can only be done by Christ being the only Source and the Cross being the only means. The Holy Spirit will work in no other fashion [Rom. 8:2].)*

21 Oh that men would praise the LORD for His goodness, and for His wonderful works to the children of men! *(Praise to the Lord should be constant!)*

22 And let them sacrifice the sacrifices of thanksgiving, and declare His works with rejoicing. *(Any time the word "sacrifice" is mentioned in the Scriptures, it has its root in the Cross. So this Verse tells us that all of our "thanksgiving" to Him should be based exclusively on the Cross, for that's where the great Sacrifice was offered.)*

23 They who go down to the sea in ships, who do business in great waters *(knowing that the Lord has created all things, He is the One we should look to in order to find protection; of course, every person should do all that is within their power to take advantage of every protecting source, with the final alternative always being the Lord);*

24 These see the works of the LORD, and His wonders in the deep. *(All of this shows that the Lord is mightily concerned about all the activity of His children.)*

25 For He commands, and raises the stormy wind, which lifts up the waves thereof. *(Irrespective if it's Satan who causes the storm, the Lord is the One Who has the final say. In other words, Satan has to get permission from Him to do whatever he does.)*

26 They mount up to the Heaven, they go down again to the depths: their soul is melted because of trouble. *(Due to modern technology, man is very sure of himself; however, in a moment's time, by using the power of nature, God can make man realize how absolutely helpless he actually is.)*

27 They reel to and fro, and stagger like a drunken man, and are at their wit's end.

28 Then they cry unto the LORD in their trouble, and He brings them out of their distresses. *(We are admonished to ask God for help exactly as the Disciples asked the Lord for help in the storm that threatened them on the Sea of Galilee.)*

29 He makes the storm a calm, so that the waves thereof are still. *(This shows us that it is God's Power that governs nature.)*

30 Then are they glad because they be quiet; so He brings them unto their desired haven. *(All should teach trust in the Lord, and thereby seek Him for the desired result.)*

31 Oh that men would praise the LORD for His goodness, and for His wonderful works to the children of men! *(This is the fourth repetition of this Passage by the Holy Spirit. He wishes to impress upon us our absolute helplessness and God's absolute Power, and that we should continually praise Him for His goodness extended to us.)*

32 Let them exalt Him also in the congregation of the people, and praise Him in the assembly of the elders. *(This means that gatherings of Christians should be filled with praise to the Lord.)*

33 He turns rivers into a wilderness, and the watersprings into dry ground;

34 A fruitful land into barrenness, for the wickedness of them who dwell therein. *(In these two Scriptures, we are given the reason for the hunger, starvation, famine, want, and poverty in all countries of the world. It is because of "the wickedness of them who dwell therein.")*

35 He turns the wilderness into a standing water, and dry ground into watersprings. *(Conversely, upon Repentance, the Holy Spirit informs us that God can reverse a desperate situation.)*

36 And there He makes the hungry to dwell, that they may prepare a city for habitation *(much of the world at this present time goes to bed hungry each night; only God has the answer to these problems; but, regrettably, the far greater majority of the human race little looks to Him);*

37 And sow the fields, and plant vineyards, which may yield fruits of increase. *(This will happen on a worldwide basis in the Millennial Reign, when Christ reigns supreme.)*

38 He blesses them also, so that they are

multiplied greatly; and suffers not their cattle to decrease. *(That which belongs to the Child of God should be an oasis in the midst of a desert. With Faith in God and in His Word, even now this can be so.)*

39 Again, they are minished and brought low through oppression, affliction, and sorrow. *(Once again, the Holy Spirit calls our attention to the wages of sin.)*

40 He pours contempt upon princes, and causes them to wander in the wilderness, where there is no way. *(These Verses emphasize the ruin to nature and to man that results from disobedience to God's Law.)*

41 Yet sets He the poor on high from affliction, and makes Him families like a flock. *(This is God's Message to "the poor" of the world. If they will seek the Lord, He has promised to hear and answer.)*

42 The righteous shall see it, and rejoice: and all iniquity shall stop her mouth. *(The Holy Spirit emphasizes to us that if we will but follow the Word of the Lord, the Lord will set His People on high, above the reach of calamity, unless He has other Plans [Heb. 11:32-40].)*

43 Whoso is wise, and will observe these things, even they shall understand the lovingkindness of the LORD. *(The Holy Spirit has so carefully laid out the path to ruin and the path to Redemption and, as well, the paths of both poverty and plenty. It's up to us to follow the right path.)*

PSALM 108

A PSALM OF DAVID:
ISRAEL LOOKS TO GOD FOR HELP

O God, My heart is fixed; I will sing and give praise, even with My glory. *(The Speaker here is the Messiah. His heart is "fixed" in order to obtain the Will of God regarding the Salvation of mankind, the Restoration of Israel, and the Restoration of all things. Even though not yet an accomplished fact, in the heart of God it is, nevertheless, thought of as such; therefore, the Messiah "will sing and give praise" as though it is already accomplished. He will do it even with "My glory," signifying that the Glory of God rests upon the fulfillment of these Divine Promises.)*

2 Awake, psaltery and harp: I myself will awake early. *(David is saying here that he would arise early in order to spend time alone with God. He would worship with both praise and music.)*

3 I will praise You, O LORD, among the people: and I will sing praises unto You among the nations. *(Little did David realize that the Psalms God had given him would actually be sung "among the nations." However, its greater fulfillment will be in the coming days of the Millennial Reign, when David will truly sing these Psalms in every nation of the world.)*

4 For Your mercy is great above the Heavens: and Your truth reaches unto the clouds. *(Here, "Mercy" is linked to "Truth." These are the two great attributes of God and speak of the Messiah. He is "Mercy" in living form and is "Truth" in visible proclamation [Jn. 1:1-5].)*

5 Be Thou exalted, O God, above the Heavens: and Your glory above all the Earth *(this is a prayer that is, in effect, a Prophecy; God has never been truly exalted; however, at the Advent of the soon-coming Kingdom Age, He will then be exalted throughout the entirety of planet Earth)*;

6 That Your beloved may be delivered: save with Your right hand, and answer me. *("Your Beloved" speaks of the Messiah. The petition, approximately a thousand years before the Incarnation, was that He may be able to accomplish His Task and be delivered from the powers of darkness.)*

7 God has spoken in His holiness; I will rejoice, I will divide Shechem, and mete out the valley of Succoth. *(To the petition of Verse 6, the answer is forthcoming, "God has spoken in His holiness"; therefore, the Messiah "will rejoice." Israel will be restored!)*

8 Gilead is Mine; Manasseh is Mine; Ephraim also is the strength of My head; Judah is My Lawgiver *(Judah is called the "Lawgiver," because it was from the Tribe of Judah that Christ came)*;

9 Moab is My washpot; over Edom will I cast out My shoe; over Philistia will I triumph. *(In these Passages, the Messiah predicts the future supremacy of Israel and the subjugation of the Gentiles.)*

10 Who will bring Me into the strong city? who will lead Me into Edom? *(The "strong city" is referring to "Sela" or "Petra.")*

11 Will not You, O God, Who has cast us off? and will not You, O God, go forth with our hosts? *(This Verse pertains to the flight of Israel to Petra, when she will flee from the Antichrist in the second half of the Great Tribulation. There the Lord will protect them for 1,260 days [Mat. 24:15-22; Rev. 12:6, 14].)*

12 Give us help from trouble: for vain is the help of man. *(The "trouble" addressed here is the full-scale attack by the Antichrist in order to destroy Israel, which will take place, as stated, in the second half of the Great Tribulation. At that time, there will be no fellow nations to help Israel.)*

13 Through God we shall do valiantly: for He it is Who shall tread down our enemies. *(The major reason for the Great Tribulation is that Israel might be brought back to God. At that time, they will be placed in such a position, with no nation in the world to help them, staring annihilation in the face, that they will then call upon God. He will answer, and His Answer will be the Second Coming. To be sure, at that time, "He it is Who shall tread down our enemies" [Rev., Chpt. 19].)*

PSALM 109

THE AUTHOR IS DAVID:
A PSALM OF VENGEANCE ON ENEMIES

HOLD not Your peace, O God, of my praise *(the Holy Spirit is the Author of this Psalm [Acts 1:16-22]. The Speaker is the Messiah. The instrument is David. Consequently, it has a double fulfillment in David and the Messiah);*

2 For the mouth of the wicked and the mouth of the deceitful are opened against me: they have spoken against me with a lying tongue. *(This speaks of the mouths of both Ahithophel, who raised up against David, and Judas, against Christ. They lied because there was nothing derogatory they could truthfully say about David or the Messiah.)*

3 They compassed me about also with words of hatred; and fought against me without a cause. *(The Holy Spirit emphasizes the words, "without a cause.")*

4 For my love they are my adversaries: but I give myself unto prayer. *(The meaning of this Verse is that both David and the Messiah gave their love to both Ahithophel and Judas. Sadly, both became adversaries. Neither David nor Christ lifted their hands against these adversaries. Instead, they took it to the Lord in prayer. What a lesson for us!)*

5 And they have rewarded me evil for good, and hatred for my love. *(The Holy Spirit, once again, emphasizes the gravity of this sin.)*

6 Set thou a wicked man over him: and let Satan stand at his right hand. *(Accordingly, the language of this Psalm is judicial and prophetic.*

All enemies of the Word of God will be judged.)

7 When he shall be judged, let him be condemned: and let his prayer become sin. *(If a person does not truly repent, condemnation is the only conclusion.)*

8 Let his days be few; and let another take his office. *(The days of Judas were few. He was probably in his late twenties or early thirties when he committed suicide. As well, another took his office [Acts 1:23-26].)*

9 Let his children be fatherless, and his wife a widow. *(And this is exactly what happened!)*

10 Let his children be continually vagabonds, and beg: let them seek their bread also out of their desolate places. *(True Repentance on the part of these addressed will turn this around, but only true Repentance. The Lord does not make children pay for the sins of their fathers, unless they continue on the same path [Ezek. 18:4, 20].)*

11 Let the extortioner catch all that he has; and let the strangers spoil his labour. *(This Passage, at least in part, was fulfilled when the Priests refused to take back the blood money [thirty pieces of silver], thereby desiring no part of him thereafter [Mat., Chpt. 27].)*

12 Let there be none to extend mercy unto him: neither let there be any to favour his fatherless children. *(The evidence is, the wife and children of Judas continued in rebellion.)*

13 Let his posterity be cut off; and in the generation following let their name be blotted out. *(The idea is, if he had children, let them die without offspring. This would mean that their family would come to an end, which it, no doubt, did.)*

14 Let the iniquity of his fathers be remembered with the LORD; and let not the sin of his mother be blotted out. *(There is some evidence that the mother of Judas was a co-conspirator in the plot. As well, due to the action of Judas, the sins of his fathers would be visited upon him [Ex. 20:5].)*

15 Let them be before the LORD continually, that he may cut off the memory of them from the Earth. *(Sins unrepented are always before the Lord continually. As well, it would seem that the children of Judas were cut off in death before marriage, thereby leaving no posterity. Consequently, there is no memory, because they do not exist.)*

16 Because that he remembered not to show mercy, but persecuted the poor and needy man, that he might even slay the broken in heart. *(Christ was the Poor and Needy Man. His was*

17 As he loved cursing, so let it come unto him: as he delighted not in blessing, so let it be far from him. *(The cursing spoken of here has little, if anything, to do with profanity. It is speaking of the terrible curse of sin. In other words, Judas delighted not in the blessing that Christ would bring as the Giver of eternal life. He loved sin and desired to continue therein. In fact, this Verse speaks of both Ahithophel and Judas.)*

18 As he clothed himself with cursing like as with his garment, so let it come into his bowels like water, and like oil into his bones. *(Sin is not an external matter only; it penetrates the very heart and vitals of the sinner.)*

19 Let it be unto him as the garment which covers him, and for a girdle wherewith he is girded continually. *(At this moment, Judas Iscariot is in Hell. That is a somber thought, but true. He could have been an Apostle of the Lord Jesus Christ forever, ruling and reigning with Him. His name could have been inscribed on the foundations of that city built foursquare [Rev. 21:14]. Instead, he is in Hell, and the garment of sin covers him. It will squeeze him like a girdle forever.)*

20 Let this be the reward of my adversaries from the LORD, and of them who speak evil against my soul. *(This is not only concerning the fate of Judas and Ahithophel, but is also the fate of all who spurn, refuse, and reject the Mercy, Grace, and extended Love of the Lord Jesus Christ.)*

21 But do Thou for me, O GOD the Lord, for Your Name's sake: because Your mercy is good, deliver Thou me. *(The efforts of both Judas and Ahithophel were to murder Christ and David. The plea here is for Deliverance from their evil actions. The prayer was answered.)*

22 For I am poor and needy, and my heart is wounded within me. *(There is no hurt like the hurt of a broken heart.)*

23 I am gone like the shadow when it declines: I am tossed up and down as the locust. *(These are the words of David, when set upon by his son, Absalom, and his most trusted advisor, Ahithophel. They are the words of Christ, as well, in using none of His great Power to defend Himself against the traitor, Judas Iscariot.)*

24 My knees are weak through fasting; and my flesh fails of fatness. *(These were the words of David, no doubt, in seeking God regarding the great rebellion that had been brought against him by both Absalom and Ahithophel.*

There is no record that Christ fasted while in His Earthly Ministry, other than the temptation in the wilderness.)

25 I became also a reproach unto them: when they looked upon me they shook their heads. *(This speaks of Christ being on the Cross. The pronoun "them" refers not to the drunks, drug addicts, or harlots, but rather to the religious leaders of that day.)*

26 Help me, O LORD my God: O save me according to Your mercy *(there was no one to whom either David or Christ could turn but God; there was no man to help)*:

27 That they may know that this is Your hand; that You, LORD, have done it. *(The prayer of both David and the Messiah was that God would act so powerfully on their behalf that there would be no doubt as to Who had accomplished their Deliverance. Even their worst enemies would have to know that it was God. And that's exactly what happened!)*

28 Let them curse, but bless You: when they arise, let them be ashamed; but let Your servant rejoice. *(The sense of this Verse is that despite the curse that was willed upon them by their adversaries, it would not and, in fact, could not, stop the Blessings of the Lord.)*

29 Let my adversaries be clothed with shame, and let them cover themselves with their own confusion, as with a mantle. *(Sin and rebellion confuse men. The cause of the loss of both of these men, Judas and Ahithophel, is because they rejected God's only solution for sin, which is Christ and the Cross [Jn. 6:53-71].)*

30 I will greatly praise the LORD with my mouth; yea, I will praise Him among the multitude. *(David, by faith, cries to God, and by faith he praises God. It is a praise of victory, although, at that time, victory had not yet come. But victory would come, as victory did.)*

31 For he shall stand at the right hand of the poor, to save him from those who condemn his soul. *(In Psalm 109, Jehovah stands at the right hand of the Poor Man, the Lord Jesus Christ. In Psalm 110, the Poor Man sits at the right hand of Jehovah.)*

PSALM 110

DAVID IS THE AUTHOR:
THE ETERNAL KING AND PRIEST

THE LORD *(Jehovah)* **said unto my** *(David's)* **Lord** *(here it is translated "Adonai," but should have been translated "Jehovah")*, **Sit Thou**

at My right hand *(Heb. 1:3)*, until I make Your enemies Your footstool. *(This Verse covers the whole of the present period of time from Acts 1:9 to II Thess. 1:7. It will be fulfilled at the Second Coming.)*

2 The LORD shall send the rod of Your strength out of Zion: rule Thou in the midst of Your enemies. *(This Verse pictures the enthronement of Christ in Zion, and the committal to His Hand of the sceptre of strength, emblem of His worldwide dominion. This is speaking of the Millennial Reign.)*

3 Your people shall be willing in the day of Your power, in the beauties of holiness from the womb of the morning: You have the dew of Your youth. *(Both statements in this Verse refer to the Resurrection — the one to its occasion, the other to its continuance.)*

4 The LORD has sworn, and will not repent, You are a Priest for ever after the order of Melchizedek. *(This is addressed in Heb. 5:6 and 6:20. Christ is the Eternal Priest. The Priestly "Order of Melchizedek" was different from the Levitical or the Aaronic Priesthood. The Melchizedek Order was eternal, with the Aaronic Order being temporary [Gen. 14:17-20].)*

5 The Lord at Your right hand shall strike through kings in the day of His wrath.

6 He shall judge among the heathen, He shall fill the places with the dead bodies; He shall wound the heads over many countries. *(Both Verses 5 and 6 predict the triumph of the Messiah over the Antichrist and his followers [Ezek., Chpts. 38-39].)*

7 He shall drink of the brook in the way: therefore shall He lift up the head. *(The "lifting up of the head" means that Christ will be exalted over the nations of the world and, as the only Head, He will rule in Righteousness, Holiness, and Judgment [Isa. 2:2-4; Dan. 2:44-45; Zech., Chpt. 14; Rev. 20:4-6].)*

PSALM 111

AUTHOR UNKNOWN:
PRAISE TO THE LORD

PRAISE ye the LORD. I will praise the LORD with my whole heart, in the assembly of the upright, and in the congregation. *(This and the two following Psalms are the three Hallelujah Psalms, which Israel will sing to the Messiah on the day of His enthronement in Zion. Psalm 111 claims the perfection of His Works; Psalm 112, the perfection of His Ways; Psalm 113,*

the perfection of His Person.)

2 The works of the LORD are great, sought out of all them who have pleasure therein. *(This Verse pertains to the great Works of God studied with great pleasure by those who fear Him.)*

3 His work is honourable and glorious: and His righteousness endures for ever. *(The only work that is honorable is that which is done for God and is of God.)*

4 He has made His wonderful works to be remembered: the LORD is gracious and full of compassion. *(Verses 2 through 4 extol the glory of His Works. Actually, mere words could never plumb the depths nor scale the heights of that which He has done.)*

5 He has given meat unto them who fear Him: He will ever be mindful of His Covenant. *(There has always been a breakdown on man's side of the Covenant. For everywhere that man is placed, man fails; nevertheless, the viability of the Covenant is in Christ and not man. Consequently, there is no fear or even possibility of the Covenant being broken. It is all in Christ [Gal. 3:11-18].)*

6 He has shown His people the power of His works, that He may give them the heritage of the heathen. *(In other words, the Lord is always able to carry out what He has promised.)*

7 The works of His hands are verity and judgment; all His Commandments are sure. *(The word "verity" means "truth." All of this is given in contrast to man's works and laws, which are flawed, faulty, and soon perish.)*

8 They stand fast for ever and ever, and are done in truth and uprightness. *(The Works of the Lord are eternal, because they are of the Lord.)*

9 He sent redemption unto His people: He has commanded His Covenant for ever: holy and reverend is His Name. *(Men are to ever reverence God and His Word.)*

10 The fear of the LORD is the beginning of wisdom: a good understanding have all they who do His Commandments: His praise endures for ever. *(When men lose "the fear of the LORD," which means they ignore His Word, they lose wisdom.)*

PSALM 112

AUTHOR UNKNOWN:
BLESSED IS THE MAN WHO
FEARS THE LORD

PRAISE ye the LORD. Blessed is the man who fears the LORD, who delights greatly

in His Commandments. *(This Song is an expansion of the last Verse of the previous Psalm. It praises the Messiah because of His Ways on Earth, and because He molds men into His Own moral image.)*

2 His seed shall be mighty upon Earth: the generation of the upright shall be blessed. *(If we delight greatly in the Word of the Lord, we shall be greatly blessed.)*

3 Wealth and riches shall be in His house: and His righteousness endures for ever. *(It is into "His House" that we are invited, where wealth and riches abide.)*

4 Unto the upright there ariseth light in the darkness: He is gracious, and full of compassion, and righteous. *(The word "upright" in Verse 2 is singular in the Hebrew Text, and thereby applies to the Messiah. The word "upright" in this Verse is plural in the Hebrew Text, and thereby applies to His servants. Thus is the argument illustrated that He can make His servants like Himself.)*

5 A good man shows favour, and lends: he will guide his affairs with discretion. *(The Blessings of the Lord make it possible for the "good man" to "lend.")*

6 Surely he shall not be moved for ever: the righteous shall be in everlasting remembrance. *(Prosperity, at times, comes even to the unrighteous, but is fleeting and ultimately goes away. The contrast given by the Holy Spirit concerning the righteous is that their prosperity shall last forever, because it is anchored in Christ.)*

7 He shall not be afraid of evil tidings: his heart is fixed, trusting in the LORD.

8 His heart is established, he shall not be afraid, until he see his desire upon his enemies. *(Evil tidings shall not put the Believer in fear, for he knows the Lord will undertake.)*

9 He has dispersed, he has given to the poor; his righteousness endures for ever; his horn shall be exalted with honour. *(This Verse speaks directly of the Messiah. He enriches, His benefits never end, and He triumphs.)*

10 The wicked shall see it, and be grieved; he shall gnash with his teeth, and melt away: the desire of the wicked shall perish. *("Wicked" in the first line of this Verse is singular in the Hebrew Text. It means the lawless one of Dan. 11:36 and II Thess. 2:8. "Wicked" in the last line of this Verse is plural in the Hebrew Text, and means the lawless ones, i.e., the followers of the Antichrist.*

Thus, the great picture is drawn. The Antichrist

and those who hope in him will perish, while those whose expectation is based on Christ will triumph.)*

PSALM 113

AUTHOR UNKNOWN: PRAISE TO GOD

PRAISE ye the LORD. Praise, O you servants of the LORD, praise the Name of the LORD. *(It brings these Psalms very near to the heart, when one remembers that they [113-118] were sung by the Lord Himself on the night of His betrayal.*

Only those who are the servants of God can worship God. What the Messiah Personally is, as already stated, is the theme of this Psalm.)

2 Blessed be the Name of the LORD from this time forth and for evermore. *(The words, "from this time forth," relate to the occasion of His future enthronement in Zion. The duration of that Kingdom is foretold in this Verse, "forevermore.")*

3 From the rising of the sun unto the going down of the same the LORD's Name is to be praised. *(Concerning the world, the extent of His Kingdom is predicted here — worldwide.)*

4 The LORD is high above all nations, and His glory above the Heavens. *(As Verse 3 proclaimed the extent of His reign, Verse 4 proclaims its universality.)*

5 Who is like unto the LORD our God, Who dwells on high. *(The Hebrew Text says, "Who has enthroned Himself on high." God enthrones Himself, for there is none greater than He.)*

6 Who humbles Himself to behold the things that are in Heaven, and in the Earth! *(To interest Himself in the Heavens is wonderful condescension, but to descend in His affection still lower to the Earth is Amazing Grace [Gen. 1:1].)*

7 He raises up the poor out of the dust, and lifts the needy out of the dunghill *(the Lord delights to help the poor, the hurting, the suffering — if they will only trust Him);*

8 That He may set him with princes, even with the princes of his people. *(If trusted, the Lord leads one into great blessings.)*

9 He makes the barren woman to keep house, and to be a joyful mother of children. Praise ye the LORD. *(The "barren woman" speaks of Israel in her glorious Restoration. The Psalm begins with "Hallelujah" [Praise]. It ends with "Hallelujah.")*

PSALM 114

AUTHOR UNKNOWN:
GOD'S POWER DEMONSTRATED
IN THE EXODUS

W HEN Israel went out of Egypt, the house of Jacob from a people of strange language *(this Verse commemorates the powerful, even the all-powerful, Deliverance of Israel from Egyptian bondage. The name "Jacob" is used here and in Verse 7 to emphasize that Grace, not merit, forms the basis of past and future Deliverance for Israel, as well as all Believers, and for all time);*

2 Judah was His sanctuary, and Israel His dominion. *(Evidently, this Psalm was written after the Kingdom was divided [II Ki., Chpt. 17].)*

3 The sea saw it, and fled: Jordan was driven back.

4 The mountains skipped like rams, and the little hills like lambs. *(The argument of this Psalm is, as to the past, that if nature, represented by the Red Sea, Sinai, and Jordan, trembled at the manifestation of God, how much more should the sinners of Canaan tremble before Him?)*

5 What ailed you, O thou sea, that you fled? thou Jordan, that you were driven back?

6 You mountains, that you skipped like rams; and you little hills, like lambs? *(The Holy Spirit draws our attention to the great Power of God, to which even nature must respond accordingly.)*

7 Tremble, thou Earth, at the presence of the Lord, at the presence of the God of Jacob *(the "Presence of the Lord" means His parousia or Revelation — that is, His future coming in Power and great Glory. The word "Lord," in this Verse, is "Adon." The idea is, if the Lord shows such kindness and affection for His ancient People, then so much fearful doom will fall upon all who ill-treat them [Mat. 25:31-46]. The Arabs, and all other nations for that matter, should read these words very carefully. It says "The God of Jacob," not the god of Muhammad);*

8 Which turned the rock into a standing water, the flint into a fountain of waters. *(The sense of the Verse is that the Rock was Christ [I Cor. 10:4]. It actually refers to the waters from the Smitten Rock [Ex. 17:6; Num. 20:11]. "The flint" stands for the stony heart of men, which is melted by the Grace of God and turned into "a fountain of waters" [Jn. 4:13-14].)*

PSALM 115

AUTHOR UNKNOWN:
PRAISE TO GOD WHO IS OUR
HELP AND SHIELD

N OT unto us, O LORD, not unto us, but unto Your Name give glory, for Your mercy, and for Your truth's sake. *(This Song has to do with the beginning of the Millennial Reign. On the happy morning of Israel's Restoration, she will ascribe to the Messiah the Glory of the Deliverance sung in the previous Psalm.)*

2 Wherefore should the heathen say, Where is now their God? *(All the world will then see Israel's God.)*

3 But our God is in the Heavens: He has done whatsoever He has pleased. *(In this Passage, Israel is saying that her God is in the Heavens, and is, therefore, invisible, and not a visible god of wood or stone in the Earth, as viewed by the heathen.)*

4 Their idols are silver and gold, the work of men's hands. *(These Verses contrast Jehovah with the helplessness of idols and idolatry.)*

5 They have mouths, but they speak not: eyes have they, but they see not:

6 They have ears, but they hear not: noses have they, but they smell not:

7 They have hands, but they handle not: feet have they, but they walk not: neither speak they through their throat. *(The Holy Spirit is speaking of objects made by the hands of men and, therefore, dead.)*

8 They who make them are like unto them; so is every one who trusts in them. *(This Verse states what has been, and it continues to be true to the fact that the worshippers of idols become like the idols which they worship — senseless, cruel, and impure. Multitudes presently worship idols made with their own hands or within their minds. An idol is an idol, whether it be made manually or mentally, and to worship God under the similitude of metal, stone, bread, or mind is idolatry — such as are many religious activities in both Catholic and Protestant Churches.)*

9 O Israel, trust thou in the LORD: He is their help and their shield. *(As Israel of old could not trust in the Lord and idols at the same time, likewise, the modern Church cannot trust in psychology, education, therapy, or counseling, and the Lord at the same time.)*

10 O house of Aaron, trust in the LORD: He is their help and their shield. *(The "House of*

Aaron" pertains to the Ministry. If the Priesthood placed its trust in the Lord, basically the majority of the people would follow suit.)

11 Ye who fear the LORD, trust in the LORD: He is their help and their shield. *(The Holy Spirit pinpoints here the admonition of trusting the Lord, even down to the specific individual.)*

12 The LORD has been mindful of us: He will bless us; He will bless the House of Israel; He will bless the house of Aaron. *(This means that the Lord will greatly bless the Ministry, of which Aaron is a symbol, if the Ministry will only place their Faith and trust exclusively in Him.)*

13 He will bless them who fear the LORD, both small and great. *(This refers even to the individual.)*

14 The LORD shall increase you more and more, you and your children. *(The very word "blessing" means "increase.")*

15 You are blessed of the LORD which made Heaven and Earth. *(Over and over again, the Bible proclaims the Lord as the Creator of all things; and He didn't use evolution to do such.)*

16 The Heaven, even the Heavens, are the LORD's: but the Earth has He given to the children of men. *(In the Garden of Eden, God gave dominion of planet Earth to Adam [Gen. 1:26]. So this Verse tells us that other planets, regardless of modern technology, will never be seriously inhabited.)*

17 The dead praise not the LORD, neither any who go down into silence. *(This speaks of the spiritually dead, those who died without knowing the Lord.)*

18 But we will bless the LORD from this time forth and for evermore. Praise the LORD. *(All Believers, totally unlike unbelievers, will praise the Lord forever.)*

PSALM 116

DAVID IS THE AUTHOR:
PRAISE TO GOD FOR DELIVERANCE

I love the LORD, because He has heard my voice and my supplications. *(This might be called the Resurrection Psalm. The comforting message to faith in this Song is that the Resurrection of Christ is a pledge and assurance of the Resurrection of His People, and that as God carried Him victoriously through the sorrows of life and of death, so will He triumphantly carry those who, by faith, are united to Him. Hence, our Resurrection is based upon and connected with His Resurrection.)*

2 Because He has inclined His ear unto me, therefore will I call upon Him as long as I live. *(This Psalm, sung by Him and His little flock on the eve of His Crucifixion, will be sung again by Him in the midst of the great congregation on the morn of His Coronation.)*

3 The sorrows of death compassed me, and the pains of Hell got hold upon me: I found trouble and sorrow. *(The first section of this Psalm [Vss. 3-11] presents the Messiah's recalling of His First Advent while in weakness and atonement. In Verses 12 through 19, He anticipates His Second Advent in Power and Glory, and He praises and worships Jehovah in respect to both.)*

4 Then called I upon the Name of the LORD, O LORD, I beseech You, deliver my soul. *(His sorrows in the death world and His prayer when there are the subject of Verses 3-6, and His joyful testimony on the morning of His Resurrection is the theme of Verses 7-11.)*

5 Gracious is the LORD, and righteous; yea, our God is merciful. *(As should be understood, the Messiah spoke more of His petitions, supplications, prayers, and victories through David than through any other Psalmist. This was because it was through David's lineage that the Messiah would come [II Sam., Chpt. 7].)*

6 The LORD preserves the simple: I was brought low, and He helped me. *(The word "simple" refers to "sinless"; because He was such, He was guarded safely when in Sheol.)*

7 Return unto Your rest, O my soul: for the LORD has dealt bountifully with You. *(The "rest" intended in this Verse is that of St. John 17:4-5. Having accomplished Redemption, our Lord returned to the repose of the Father's bosom.)*

8 For You have delivered my soul from death, my eyes from tears, and my feet from falling. *(The word "falling" has no moral significance here, for it is impossible for the Messiah to morally stumble. The Hebrew word means "a thrusting down.")*

9 I will walk before the LORD in the land of the living. *(Delivered from being "thrust down," in Death, He is now raised up in Resurrection.)*

10 I believed, therefore have I spoken: I was greatly afflicted *(this faith of Verse 10 is most striking, for it was exercised by the Messiah when in the regions of death, and is now exercised by Him in Resurrection):*

11 I said in my haste, All men are liars. *(The word "haste," in the Hebrew, does not mean*

"hastily," but "hasting on." No one thought that Christ would be raised from the dead, not even His closest Disciples. Concerning the Resurrection, at least after He was crucified, all were liars.)

12 What shall I render unto the LORD for all His benefits toward me? *(We cannot render anything. In fact, the Lord has nothing for sale. It is all a Gift.)*

13 I will take the cup of Salvation, and call upon the name of the LORD. *(Being saved, we have the right to petition our Heavenly Father and expect an answer [I Jn. 5:14].)*

14 I will pay my vows unto the LORD now in the presence of all His people. *(What Christ did in the Redemption of man was done "in the presence of all" [Ps. 40:7].)*

15 Precious in the sight of the LORD is the death of His saints. *(The word "precious" means "costly." It is costly to the Work of God upon the passing of any of His Saints. The only light in the world is the Light of Christ which reposes in the lives of the Saints.)*

16 O LORD, truly I am Your servant; I am Your servant, and the son of Your handmaid: You have loosed my bonds. *(The sense of this Verse is twofold — it speaks of both David and the Messiah. Its message is humility. The word "handmaid," likewise, has a double meaning. It refers both to Mary and to Israel, for Jesus was born of both the Virgin and of Israel. His Father loosed Him from the bonds of death and raised Him from the dead.)*

17 I will offer to You the sacrifice of thanksgiving, and will call upon the Name of the LORD. *(We must understand that from this Verse we learn that all "thanksgiving" is based upon the Sacrifice of Christ.)*

18 I will pay my vows unto the LORD now in the presence of all His people. *(This is the second time this Verse is given to us verbatim, but not without cause. It refers to the tremendous victories won by the Lord Jesus Christ on behalf of a world that was loved by Him, but yet a world altogether unlovely.)*

19 In the courts of the LORD's house, in the midst of you, O Jerusalem. Praise ye the LORD. *(This will be fulfilled at the beginning of and throughout the great Kingdom Age. At that time, and continually all over the world, the great victories bought and paid for by the Lord Jesus Christ will be heralded "in the presence of all His people." No wonder the world at that time will say, "Praise ye the LORD.")*

PSALM 117

AUTHOR UNKNOWN:
PRAISE THE LORD

O praise the LORD, all ye nations: praise Him, all ye people. *(The Apostle Paul quotes this Verse in Rom. 15:11. This short Song proclaims the beginning of the great Millennial Reign. Israel now invites the nations of the world to unite with her in praising the Messiah, and the reason is set out in the Second Verse.)*

2 For His merciful kindness is great toward us: and the truth of the LORD endures for ever. Praise ye the LORD. *(The phrase, "is great toward," should read "has prevailed over." This tells us that the Lord will fulfill to Israel the Promise of the Kingdom and, in His abounding Grace, which will prevail over all their misconduct, He will forgive their sins.)*

PSALM 118

AUTHOR UNKNOWN:
THANKSGIVING FOR THE
LORD'S SALVATION

O give thanks unto the LORD; for He is good: because His mercy endures for ever. *(This was the last Song sang at the Pascal Supper, as stated by the Hebrew historians. It gives it an added preciousness to the heart who knows the Lord to picture Him singing it immediately before setting out for Gethsemane.)*

2 Let Israel now say, that His mercy endures for ever. *(Israel will repeatedly say this because of the constant failure that checkers her past through her present. Therefore, they realize that it is only by the Mercy of God that they have been spared.)*

3 Let the house of Aaron now say, that His mercy endures for ever. *(As well, the Priesthood constantly failed and failed constantly; therefore, any act of Grace extended toward them by the Messiah can only be attributed to "His Mercy.")*

4 Let them now who fear the LORD say, that His mercy endures for ever. *(Those who properly fear the Lord will see that "His mercy endures forever.")*

5 I called upon the LORD in distress: the LORD answered me, and set me in a large place. *(In the coming Great Tribulation, and especially in the Battle of Armageddon, Israel will call on the Lord, and He will answer her.*

It is remarkable in the fact that He has not answered her in over 2,000 years. But then He will answer; then He will set her "in a large place.")

6 The LORD is on my side; I will not fear: what can man do unto me? *(Once Israel realizes that God has heard her and is coming to her rescue, which pertains to the Second Coming, then all fear is dispelled [Zech. 14:1-3].)*

7 The LORD takes my part with them who help me: therefore shall I see my desire upon them who hate me. *(Israel, at long last, realizes that to have the Lord on her side and take her part is better than all men in their riches.)*

8 It is better to trust in the LORD than to put confidence in man. *(Confidence in man was Israel's great problem, and it is the problem of the modern Church, as well.)*

9 It is better to trust in the LORD than to put confidence in princes. *(Some think that because a person is rich and powerful that they can truly help. Most will not and, if they do, it is the Lord Who moves upon them to do so.)*

10 All nations compassed me about: but in the name of the LORD will I destroy them. *(This speaks of the nations of the world that will gather at the Battle of Armageddon.)*

11 They compassed me about; yea, they compassed me about: but in the Name of the LORD I will destroy them. *(Regardless of the number of nations arrayed against Israel during the Battle of Armageddon, they will go down in defeat.)*

12 They compassed me about like bees; they are quenched as the fire of thorns: for in the Name of the LORD I will destroy them. *(The hundreds of thousands of men gathered at Armageddon will push at Israel "like bees." Regardless of the number, they will be defeated.)*

13 You have thrust sore at me that I might fall: but the LORD helped me. *(The pronoun "you" is important because it refers to Satan. He energized the enemies of Verses 7-12.)*

14 The LORD is my strength and song, and is become my Salvation. *(Israel confesses here that her Restoration apart from the once-rejected Messiah is impossible.)*

15 The voice of rejoicing and Salvation is in the tabernacles of the righteous: the right hand of the LORD does valiantly. *(This rejoicing will take place at the Second Coming, when the Lord then vanquishes all of Israel's enemies.)*

16 The right hand of the LORD is exalted: the right hand of the LORD does valiantly. *(The right hand of Jehovah is symbolic of His Power [Ex. 15:6; Ps. 17:7; 20:6; 44:3].)*

17 I shall not die, but live, and declare the works of the LORD. *(During the Battle of Armageddon, it looks like Israel will die; but the Second Coming will change that.)*

18 The LORD has chastened me sore: but He has not given me over unto death. *(Israel now acknowledges the wisdom and love which permitted her sufferings at the hands of man. She approves these moral lessons. When the Believer comes to this place, he can expect the same type of Deliverance that God will give to Israel.)*

19 Open to me the gates of righteousness: I will go into them, and I will praise the LORD *(the "Gates of Righteousness" were opened to her upon the First Advent of Christ; she refused to walk through those gates; now, the Lord has given her a second opportunity):*

20 This gate of the LORD, into which the righteous shall enter. *(Israel, on her own, could never claim righteousness. Neither can we! Now, she accepts the Righteousness that the Lord freely gives unto her, which she rejected so long ago in favor of her own righteousness [Rom. 10:3].)*

21 I will praise You: for You have heard me, and are become my Salvation. *(Now, Israel proclaims that the once-rejected Saviour is her God and Redeemer.)*

22 The stone which the builders refused is become the Head Stone of the corner. *(The Lord Jesus is the Stone, and furthermore, "the Head Stone." This was quoted and referred to in Mat. 21:42, Mk. 12:10-11, Lk. 20:17, Acts 4:11, and I Pet. 2:4-8.)*

23 This is the LORD's doing; it is marvellous in our eyes. *(The whole of Salvation is from the Lord. None of it pertains to man in the realm of its origin. All pertains to God.)*

24 This is the day which the LORD has made; we will rejoice and be glad in it. *(This refers to Israel's great day of Restoration. She will then acknowledge that it is all of the Lord and none of her. Consequently, it will be a day of rejoicing and gladness.)*

25 Save now, I beseech You, O LORD: O LORD, I beseech You, send now prosperity. *(These words were sung by Christ, when He made His entrance into Jerusalem [Mat. 21:9]. Prophetically, it pertains to Israel's glad day, when, at the Feast of Tabernacles, at the beginning of and throughout the Millennial Reign, she will not only ask the Lord for prosperity, but will also rejoice in a prosperity already sent, because Jesus Christ is that prosperity.)*

26 Blessed be He Who comes in the Name of the LORD: we have blessed you out of the House of the LORD. *(At the beginning of the*

Great Millennial Reign, Christ will once again come into Jerusalem, and Israel will shout these words all over again. The difference will be that now Israel is a Redeemed Israel, and they now know Who He is.)

27 God is the LORD, which has shown us light: bind the Sacrifice with cords, even unto the horns of the Altar. *(At this time, the Kingdom Age, Israel will proclaim to the world that they now understand the meaning of the Sacrifices of old. When the Sacrifice was bound with cords to the Altar, likewise, Jesus Christ died on Calvary for Israel and the whole of humanity.)*

28 You are my God, and I will praise You: You are my God, I will exalt You. *(Here, after some 2,000 years, Israel will exalt Christ. They will proclaim to the whole world that "Messiah is my God.")*

29 O give thanks unto the LORD; for He is good: for His mercy endures for ever. *(Thus, Israel closes this grand and great Psalm even as it was opened. It was opened with Mercy. It closes with Mercy. Israel will then proclaim to the whole world that "God is good.")*

PSALM 119

AUTHOR UNKNOWN:
ALEPH,
BLESSINGS OF THE WORD OF GOD

BLESSED are the undefiled in the Way, who walk in the Law of the LORD. *(There are twenty-two Stanzas in this Psalm, as there are twenty-two letters [words] in the Hebrew alphabet. Consequently, the first Stanza begins with the first letter of the Hebrew alphabet, going all through the twenty-two Stanzas, with each beginning with the corresponding Hebrew letter.*

The word "undefiled" [perfect] can only be spoken of the Messiah. He Alone walked perfectly in the Law of the Lord.)

2 Blessed are they who keep His Testimonies, and who seek Him with the whole heart. *(Also, there are ten different words used throughout this Psalm, which are each a word for the Bible, actually in all 176 Verses, with the exception of four: 90, 121, 122, and 132. The words are , "Way, Testimonies, Commandments, Word, Statutes, Precepts, Judgments, Laws, Truth, Ordinances." We are to seek Him "with the whole heart" and not a divided heart.)*

3 They also do no iniquity: they walk in His Ways. *("To do no iniquity" is the goal. The Messiah Alone did this.)*

4 You have commanded us to keep Your precepts diligently. *(This is to be the whole duty of man [Eccl. 12:13].)*

5 O that my ways were directed to keep Your Statutes! *(Due to the Fall, the ways of man are the opposite of the Ways of God. Since the Cross, Born-Again man now has a Divine Nature. Therefore, upon Faith directed toward Christ and the Cross, a person has the help of the Holy Spirit and, through Christ, the "Statutes" are kept.)*

6 Then shall I not be ashamed, when I have respect unto all Your Commandments. *(Unless we respect "all" of God's Commandments, there will be shame within our hearts, and rightly so.)*

7 I will praise You with uprightness of heart, when I shall have learned Your righteous judgments. *(The moral condition of the heart is decided by obedience to the Word of God; consequently, true worship depends upon true knowledge of the Word.)*

8 I will keep Your Statutes: O forsake me not utterly. *(The sense of this Verse is: "Do not in any case take away this Lamp in which I am trusting, else I shall stumble in the darkness and fall.")*

BETH,
PERSONAL HOLINESS THROUGH
THE WORD

9 Wherewithal shall a young man cleanse his way? by taking heed thereto according to Your Word. *(The applied Word alone can cleanse.)*

10 With my whole heart have I sought You: O let me not wander from Your Commandments. *(The Messiah Alone could say that He always sought the Lord with His whole heart and never did wander from the Commandments of the Lord.)*

11 Your Word have I hid in my heart, that I might not sin against You. *(Before the lips can fitly declare the teaching of the Scripture, the heart must be home to the Scriptures. Its Words form the rule of Faith, and subjection to its Judgments is the secret of a life of victory.)*

12 Blessed are You, O LORD: teach me Your Statutes. *(Revelation knowledge of the Bible is the only true knowledge of the Word there is. This comes about by the Lord teaching us, which He does through the fivefold Ministry [Eph. 4:11], or directly by the Holy Spirit [Gal. 1:12].)*

13 With my lips have I declared all the Judgments of Your mouth. *(This is the obligation of*

every Believer, and especially the Preacher. Regrettably, with many, some Judgments are declared, but not all. The Messiah declared them all, even though it aroused great anger in the hearts of the religious hierarchy.)

14 I have rejoiced in the way of Your Testimonies, as much as in all riches. *(Our learning and understanding of the Word of God must be placed at the very top of all things sought. It is by far the most important.)*

15 I will meditate in Your Precepts, and have respect unto Your Ways. *(The phrase, "meditate in Your Precepts," is the secret of life.)*

16 I will delight myself in Your Statutes: I will not forget Your Word. *(The Messiah delighted Himself constantly in the Word of God. This was His delight. What is your delight?)*

GIMEL,
PRAYER AND HUNGER FOR
ENLIGHTENMENT

17 Deal bountifully with Your servant, that I may live, and keep Your Word. *(The Reader will find that the first four Verses of this Stanza express the activities of the heart toward God excited by the study of, and the obedience to, His Word. The second four Verses express the contempt and hatred that an obedient person receives from man.)*

18 Open Thou my eyes, that I may behold wondrous things out of Your Law. *(There are wondrous things in the Word, but the eyes must be unveiled in order to see them. To see them, the Reader must sit where Mary of Bethany sat [Lk. 10:38-42].)*

19 I am a stranger in the Earth: hide not Your Commandments from me. *(The Bible makes its lover a stranger in this world, but it is a satisfying companion for the lonely exile. The Bible-lover will find no companionship among those who deny its contents.)*

20 My soul breaks for the longing that it has unto Your judgments at all times. *(This is an expression used of deep passion or intense longing, and shows to what extent the Psalmist hungered for Righteousness [Mat. 5:6].)*

21 You have rebuked the proud who are cursed, which do err from Your Commandments. *(Those who are too proud to subject their wills to the teaching of the Scriptures bring a curse, and not a blessing, upon themselves, and become the bitter persecutors of those who make the Scriptures their delight.)*

22 Remove from me reproach and contempt;

for I have kept Your Testimonies. *(The sense of this Verse is for the lover of the Bible not to allow reproach and contempt to weaken his love for the Word of God.)*

23 Princes also did sit and speak against me: but Your servant did meditate in Your Statutes. *(All of these Passages speak of Christ as our example. The mightiest in Israel spoke against Christ, but His solace was "Your Statutes.")*

24 Your Testimonies also are my delight and my counsellors. *(What a rebuke to a worldly Church that seeks the counsel of men from a man-made philosophy with its man-made answers. The Word of God Alone should be our Counselor.)*

DALETH,
GETTING INSTRUCTION
FROM THE WORD

25 My soul cleaves unto the dust: quicken Thou me according to Your Word. *(The Messiah's love for the Bible and His Perfect Obedience to its teaching alone illustrate the statements of this Stanza. The idea is, the soul will fall into the dust [defeat], unless it is quickened by the Word of God.)*

26 I have declared my ways, and You heard me: teach me Your Statutes. *(Such a heart attempts to hide nothing from God.)*

27 Make me to understand the way of Your Precepts: so shall I talk of Your wondrous works. *(The entire life, inward and outward, must be subjected to the searchlight of the Holy Scriptures.)*

28 My soul melts for heaviness: strengthen Thou me according unto Your Word. *(Once again, the Holy Spirit calls our attention to the difficulties of the way, and that "strength" can come only through "Your Word.")*

29 Remove from me the way of lying: and grant me Your Law graciously. *(This is a request by the Messiah, and it also should be our request that all falsity, prevarication, and everything that is contrary to Truth, or that is the opposite of the Way of the Truth, would be removed from us.)*

30 I have chosen the way of Truth: Your Judgments have I laid before me. *(The "Way of Truth" is the Bible.)*

31 I have stuck unto Your Testimonies: O LORD, put me not to shame. *(The word "stuck" actually means "I have been glued to." Let it be known that being glued to "Your Testimonies" is not one way of victory, but the only way.)*

32 I will run the way of Your Commandments, when You shall enlarge my heart. *("To enlarge the heart" means "to arouse its moral affections." To understand and profit by the Scriptures, contrition of heart, rather than cleverness of head, is necessary.)*

HE,
GIVE ME UNDERSTANDING

33 Teach me, O LORD, the way of Your Statutes; and I shall keep it unto the end. *(Allow me to remind the Bible Student that these petitions are the heartthrob and cry of the Messiah; therefore, if they are of Him, they should be of us.)*

34 Give me understanding, and I shall keep Your Law; yea, I shall observe it with my whole heart. *(This Stanza teaches that if the Bible Student disassociates the Book from its Author, his eyes will be unopened, his mind uninstructed, his heart unaffected, and his feet unled.)*

35 Make me to go in the path of Your Commandments; for therein do I delight. *(The sense of this Verse is that the human heart is so turned away from the paths of God that the Holy Spirit must use power to bring us back to the correct path, and will do so only upon the petitioning cry of the searching heart.)*

36 Incline my heart unto Your Testimonies, and not to covetousness. *(The Bible is more precious that gold. It can fill the broken heart with hope and strength. That is something money cannot do.)*

37 Turn away my eyes from beholding vanity; and quicken Thou me in Your Way. *(Any teaching that does not harmonize with the Bible is "vanity.")*

38 Stablish Your Word unto Your servant, who is devoted to Your fear. *(There is little devotion to the Word of God when there is little devotion to the "fear of God.")*

39 Turn away my reproach which I fear: for Your judgments are good. *(The Lord Alone can turn away the reproach of sin.)*

40 Behold, I have longed after Your precepts: quicken me in Your righteousness. *(The "Righteousness" spoken of is God's Righteousness, which He imputes to Believers.)*

VAU,
I TRUST IN YOUR WORD

41 Let Your mercies come also unto me, O LORD, even Your Salvation, according to Your Word. *(A Salvation which is not according to God's Word is a false salvation. It can neither silence mockers, nor influence kings.)*

42 So shall I have wherewith to answer him who reproaches me: for I trust in Your Word. *(The world reproaches those who trust solely in the Word of God.)*

43 And take not the word of Truth utterly out of my mouth; for I have hoped in Your Judgments. *(The Psalmist is actually saying that the Word of God is his only hope, at it is likewise our only hope.)*

44 So shall I keep Your Law continually for ever and ever. *(Only the Messiah could say such.)*

45 And I will walk at liberty: for I seek Your Precepts. *(The Bible alone brings liberty.)*

46 I will speak of Your testimonies also before kings, and will not be ashamed. *(Multitudes believe that a life shut in-between the covers of the Bible must necessarily be a narrow one. The opposite is found by experience to be the truth.)*

47 And I will delight myself in Your Commandments, which I have loved. *(The love and delight of the Psalmist comes from "Your Commandments," and not the things of the world.)*

48 My hands also will I lift up unto Your Commandments, which I have loved; and I will meditate in Your Statutes. *(Over and over, the Holy Spirit draws our attention to "mediating in His Statutes." This is the answer for stress, nervous disorders, emotional disturbances, and all other such problems.)*

ZAIN,
GOD'S WORD, THE SOURCE
OF COMFORT

49 Remember the Word unto Your servant, upon which You have caused me to hope. *(The Messiah expresses to Jehovah the fact of total dependence being placed in the Word.)*

50 This is my comfort in my affliction: for Your Word has quickened me. *(The Messiah does not deny affliction, nor does He offer any direction that guarantees no affliction, but He does offer hope in the Word of God, which "quickens me.")*

51 The proud have had me greatly in derision: yet have I not declined from Your Law. *(The proud deride the Promises of the Bible, but the humble rest upon them and hold fast to them.)*

52 I remembered Your Judgments of old, O LORD; and have comforted myself. *(The comfort that every soul needs can only be derived from the Bible.)*

53 Horror has taken hold upon me because of the wicked who forsake Your Law. *(A holy anger and a just indignation become the true witness for God and for His Truth.)*

54 Your Statutes have been my songs in the house of my pilgrimage. *(The word "songs" is an indication that David may have been the author of this Psalm.)*

55 I have remembered Your name, O LORD, in the night, and have kept Your Law. *(This speaks of meditation on the "Word" and the "Name" in the night of problems.)*

56 This I had, because I kept Your Precepts. *(The Messiah Alone satisfies the language of this section, as He Alone illustrates the faith, loyalty, and love of all the other sections of this Psalm.)*

CHETH,
SATISFACTION BY THE WORD

57 You are my portion, O LORD: I have said that I would keep Your Words. *(The bane of the modern Church is that "portions" devised by man attempt to usurp authority over the "portions" given by God.)*

58 I intreated Your favour with my whole heart: be merciful unto me according to Your Word. *("Favor" means the conscious Presence of God.)*

59 I thought on my ways, and turned my feet unto Your Testimonies. *(Turn to the Bible, always turn to the Bible!)*

60 I made haste, and delayed not to keep Your Commandments. *(This could only be said of the Messiah.)*

61 The bands of the wicked have robbed me: but I have not forgotten Your Law. *(The perfect keeping of the perfect Law did not keep away the bands of the wicked, nor their insidious activity, but it did give a comfort that nothing else could give.)*

62 At midnight I will rise to give thanks unto You because of Your righteous Judgments. *(The sense of this Psalm and this Passage is that neither suffering nor ease could weaken the affection of the heart for the Scriptures.)*

63 I am a companion of all them who fear You, and of them who keep Your Precepts. *(The companions of the Messiah were not the religious leaders of His day.)*

64 The Earth, O LORD, is full of Your mercy: teach Me Your Statutes. *(As the adversity of Verse Sixty-one failed to turn the Messiah away from the Bible, so neither did the prosperity of Verse Sixty-four weaken His fidelity to it.)*

TETH,
TEACH ME GOOD JUDGMENT

65 You have dealt well with Your servant, O LORD, according unto Your Word. *(Fidelity to "Your Word" ensures Blessings from the Lord. He honors nothing else.)*

66 Teach me good judgment and knowledge: for I have believed Your Commandments. *(According to the Bible, immediately upon conversion, intelligence instantly increases.)*

67 Before I was afflicted I went astray: but now have I kept Your Word. *(As a True Priest and Advocate, Christ presents Himself as the guilty One and, at the same time, credits us with the perfection of the obedience which only He Personally rendered to the Word of God.)*

68 You are good, and do good, teach me Your Statutes. *(The Statutes of God fill the Earth with goodness.)*

69 The proud have forged a lie against me: but I will keep Your Precepts with my whole heart. *(The hatred of the proud against the lover of the Bible makes the Bible more precious to the meek.)*

70 Their heart is as fat as grease; but I delight in Your Law. *(A heart "as fat as grease" is insensible and stupid. Such a heart is incompetent to judge the Commandments of God.)*

71 It is good for me that I have been afflicted; that I might learn Your Statutes. *(Chastening and discipline make the Bible more precious and the life more fruitful. They are helpful Bible teachers.)*

72 The Law of Your mouth is better unto me than thousands of gold and silver. *(The possession of the Scriptures is greater wealth than all the treasure the world contains.)*

JOD,
RIGHTEOUSNESS OF THE WORD

73 Your hands have made me and fashioned me: give me understanding, that I may learn Your Commandments. *(The True Speaker is Christ, and the words apply to Him in perfection, as they apply to others of necessity only in part.)*

74 They who fear You will be glad when they see me; because I have hoped in Your Word. *(Israel will be glad in the coming day, when they see Christ.)*

75 I know, O LORD, that Your Judgments are right, and that You in faithfulness have afflicted me. *(In the most strict interpretation,*

this Passage applies to Christ in His Incarnation.)

76 Let, I pray You, Your merciful kindness be for my comfort, according to Your Word unto Your servant. *(If one will notice, the Messiah here does not pray for the removal of these afflictions, but instead for the enjoyment of compensating comforts, but only such comforts as accorded with God's Word.)*

77 Let Your tender mercies come unto me, that I may live: for Your Law is my delight. *("Delight" in the Hebrew Text stands in the plural number and, therefore, means "supreme delight.")*

78 Let the proud be ashamed; for they dealt perversely with me without a cause: but I will meditate in Your Precepts. *(This pertains to the Scribes and Pharisees, who dealt perversely with Christ. He retreated to the Word of the Lord.)*

79 Let those who fear You turn unto me, and those who have known Your Testimonies. *(Those who feared God turned to the Messiah. Those who did not fear God turned to the "proud" [Pharisees].)*

80 Let my heart be sound in Your Statutes; that I be not ashamed. *(Soundness in the Word of God is the criteria.)*

CAPH,
ALL YOUR COMMANDMENTS
ARE FAITHFUL

81 My soul faints for Your Salvation: but I hope in Your Word. *(No man who longs for and faints for Salvation from God will go unheard [Mat. 5:6].)*

82 My eyes fail for Your Word, saying, When will You comfort me? *(The first part of this Scripture could be translated, "I will not stop looking for the fulfillment of Your Word and, in fact, will look, if necessary, until I go blind.")*

83 For I am become like a bottle in the smoke; yet do I not forget Your Statutes. *(This pertains to Israel's rejection of Christ and the constant persecution heaped upon Him by the Pharisees. His hope was in the Word.)*

84 How many are the days of Your servant? when will You execute Judgment on them who persecute me? *(Christ, as Lord, could, at any moment, have destroyed His persecutors, but, as Man, He would not take vengeance into His Own hands, for vengeance belongs unto God [Rom. 12:19].)*

85 The proud have dug pits for me, which are not after Your Law. *(The "proud" are the self-righteous Pharisees. Mat., Chpt. 15, records*

some of the pits that the proud dug for Him.)

86 All Your Commandments are faithful: they persecute me wrongfully; help Thou me. *(The sense of the first part of this Passage is that even though God did not deem it desirable to lift the persecution, still, the Word of God would see Him through.)*

87 They had almost consumed me upon earth; but I forsook not Your Precepts. *("Almost" means "quickly." The sense of the Verse is: they wished to quickly make an end of me.)*

88 Quicken me after Your lovingkindness; so shall I keep the Testimony of Your mouth. *(The word "quicken" means "make alive.")*

LAMED,
GOD'S WORD IS ETERNAL

89 For ever, O LORD, Your Word is settled in Heaven. *(God's Word is eternal.)*

90 Your faithfulness is unto all generations: You have established the Earth, and it abides. *(All man-made religious laws change, and change constantly. The Word of God never changes.)*

91 They continue this day according to Your Ordinances: for all are Your servants. *(The Heavens are God's creation, and are upheld by His Word [Heb. 11:3].)*

92 Unless Your law had been my delights, I should then have perished in my affliction. *(God's Law was the Messiah's "delights," meaning the supreme joy of His Heart.)*

93 I will never forget Your Precepts: for with them You have quickened me. *(The Messiah gives all the credit to the Bible for victory, sustenance, power, and for keeping Him alive.)*

94 I am Yours, save me; for I have sought Your Precepts. *(The word "save" signifies preservation through trial and opposition.)*

95 The wicked have waited for me to destroy me: but I will consider Your Testimonies. *("The wicked" in the Messiah's day referred to the Pharisees.)*

96 I have seen an end of all perfection: but Your Commandment is exceeding broad. *(There is an end or boundary to the extent of God's Work in Creation, but no boundary to His Word in Revelation — it is infinite and eternal.)*

MEM,
I LOVE YOUR LAW

97 O how I love Your Law! it is my meditation all the day. *(Even though all the Passages in this Psalm refer to the Messiah and His love*

for God's Word, still, the Holy Spirit lifts the Greater Son of David to a higher exclamation in this thirteenth chorus than all previously given. Once again, we are drawn to His constant "meditation.")

98 You through Your Commandments have made me wiser than my enemies: for they are ever with me. *(The pronoun "they" refers to the "Commandments.")*

99 I have more understanding than all my teachers: for Your testimonies are my meditation. *(Even as a young boy, Jesus knew more about the Word of God than His teachers [Lk. 2:40-49].)*

100 I understand more than the ancients, because I keep Your Precepts. *(The claim is made, and accurately so, that Christ understood more about God and His Word than even the great Patriarchs and Prophets of the past — all because of the knowledge of and the keeping of "Your Precepts.")*

101 I have refrained my feet from every evil way, that I might keep Your Word. *(Only Christ could make such a statement!)*

102 I have not departed from Your Judgments: for You have taught me. *(In previous choruses of this One Hundred Nineteenth Psalm, we have witnessed the petition of the Holy Spirit to serve as Teacher. We have here the exclamation that the petition was heard and granted.)*

103 How sweet are Your Words unto my taste? yea, sweeter than honey to my mouth! *(As in the previous Stanza, the Messiah sang of the strength of God's Word, so here He sings of its sweetness.)*

104 Through Your precepts I get understanding: therefore I hate every false way. *(This Stanza closes with the statement that the wisdom which flows from the Scriptures destroys all desire for false teaching.)*

NUN,
GOD'S WORD IS A LAMP AND A LIGHT

105 Your Word is a Lamp unto my feet, and a Light unto my path. *(The only "Lamp" in the world that produces "true Spiritual Light" is the Bible.)*

106 I have sworn, and I will perform it, that I will keep Your righteous Judgments. *(The Messiah has sworn His fidelity to the Word, and by no less than Himself.)*

107 I am afflicted very much: quicken me, O LORD, according unto Your Word. *(Even though the Path did lighten and gladden, still, it was a Path of affliction from God. Some modern doctrines have attempted to make the Path golden. It is not! It is a Path that is freighted with tests. The tests are from God.)*

108 Accept, I beseech You, the freewill offerings of my mouth, O LORD, and teach me Your Judgments. *(The "freewill Offering" spoken of here is "the Sacrifice of Praise" [Heb. 13:15].)*

109 My soul is continually in my hand: yet do I not forget Your Law. *(To have "the life in the hand" means to be in deadly danger. This danger was from the Pharisees.)*

110 The wicked have laid a snare for me: yet I erred not from Your Precepts. *(These "snares" were laid by the Pharisees [Mat. 26:3-4].)*

111 Your Testimonies have I taken as an heritage for ever: for they are the rejoicing of my heart. *(The Bible was not only a present help for the Messiah, but, in fact, stands as His security forever, because it never changes.)*

112 I have inclined my heart to perform Your Statutes alway, even unto the end. *(A lamp is useless unless used.)*

SAMECH,
GOD'S WORD IS A REFUGE
AND A SHIELD

113 I hate vain thoughts: but Your Law do I love. *(The statement, "I hate vain thoughts," means "I hate false teaching.")*

114 You are my hiding place and my shield: I hope in Your Word. *(The Law inspired the confidence of the Messiah, and its Author, the Holy Spirit, was His hiding place and shield.)*

115 Depart from me, you evildoers: for I will keep the Commandments of my God. *(The choice then, and the choice now, is either man's ways or God's Ways.)*

116 Uphold me according unto Your Word, that I may live: and let me not be ashamed of my hope.

117 Hold Thou me up, and I shall be safe: and I will have respect unto Your Statutes continually. *("Uphold me" and "hold me up" are noteworthy verbs in the Hebrew Text. They represent God's supporting the Believer from both above and beneath — carried and, at the same time, held by the hand.)*

118 You have trodden down all them who err from Your Statutes: for their deceit is falsehood. *(The Messiah gives the Glory to God for the failure of these false teachers to detach Him from the Bible.)*

119 You put away all the wicked of the Earth like dross: therefore I love Your Testimonies.

120 My flesh trembles for fear of You; and I am afraid of Your Judgments. *(These two Scriptures are clear: all false teachers and false teaching will ultimately be doomed.)*

AIN,
THE PSALMIST HAS OBEYED
GOD'S LAWS

121 I have done judgment and justice: leave me not to my oppressors. *(Christ, being perfect, affirms in this Stanza the moral perfection of the Bible and declares it to be His Rule of life.)*

122 Be surety for Your Servant for good: let not the proud oppress me. *(Here, He prays for deliverance from His detractors and bases His claim to be delivered from them on His integrity, as is outlined in the previous Verse, on His Relationship to God, and on His Loyalty to the Scriptures.)*

123 My eyes fail for Your Salvation, and for the Word of Your Righteousness. *(The word "fail" expresses longing and desire.)*

124 Deal with Your servant according unto Your mercy, and teach me Your Statutes.

125 I am Your servant; give me understanding, that I may know Your Testimonies. *(Twice in these two Verses the Messiah implores the Holy Spirit to teach Him the Word of God. In the Incarnate state, therefore, as Man, He had to learn exactly as we do.)*

126 It is time for You, LORD, to work: for they have made void Your Law. *(The words, "to work," mean "to intervene.")*

127 Therefore I love Your Commandments above gold; yea, above fine gold. *(He Who was Himself the Incarnate Word of God reveals here His Affection for the Written Word of God.)*

128 Therefore I esteem all Your precepts concerning all things to be right; and I hate every false way. *(In this Verse, the Messiah testifies to the inspiration, moral perfection, inerrancy, and authority of the Bible, and declares that its effect as a moral teacher is to beget hostility to evil. He says that all its Precepts concerning all things are right.)*

PE,
THE ENTRANCE OF YOUR
WORDS GIVES LIGHT

129 Your Testimonies are wonderful: therefore does my soul keep them. *(Immanuel's love for the Scriptures and His grief because men*

ignore them are the keynotes of this Stanza.)*

130 The entrance of Your Words gives light; it gives understanding unto the simple. *(The word "simple" means "sincere." To the sincere heart God will reveal Himself.)*

131 I opened my mouth, and panted: for I longed for Your Commandments. *(This Passage exemplifies the absolute thirst for the Word of God by the Messiah.)*

132 Look thou upon me, and be merciful unto me, as You used to do unto those who love Your name. *(Should be translated, "as You give judgment to those who love Your Name.")*

133 Order my steps in Your Word: and let not any iniquity have dominion over me. *(Could be translated: "Guide my steps by Your Word, cause my conduct to harmonize with the Bible, and let not any iniquitous action of man have power against me.")*

134 Deliver me from the oppression of man: so will I keep Your Precepts. *(His prayer for deliverance from oppression was not in order that He might have leisure to enjoy Himself, but liberty to practice the teachings of the Bible.)*

135 Make Your face to shine upon Your servant; and teach me Your Statutes. *(The phrase, "Make Your face to shine," means "Give me Your Favor or Grace.")*

136 Rivers of waters run down my eyes, because they keep not Your Law. *(In a previous Stanza [Vs. 126], the Messiah mourned because men made void His Father's Law; here He weeps because they did not prize and obey it.)*

TZADDI,
YOUR WORD IS VERY PURE

137 Righteous are You, O LORD, and upright are Your Judgments. *(The extolling of the Word of God in these Passages is a wonder to behold, and by the Messiah, at that!)*

138 Your Testimonies that You have commanded are righteous and very faithful. *(In fact, these are the only true Testimonies in the world, and actually ever have been.)*

139 My zeal has consumed me, because my enemies have forgotten Your Words. *(Here the Messiah pours out His Grief because men forget God's Word.)*

140 Your Word is very pure: therefore Your servant loves it. *(Only the Word of God is pure, with man's word never being pure.)*

141 I am small and despised: yet do not I forget Your Precepts. *(The word "small" means "insignificant.")*

142 Your righteousness is an everlasting righteousness, and Your Law is the truth. *(The Righteousness of the Divine Essence and the Righteousness of His Testimonies are one and the same Righteousness. As a consequence, all the Statements and Doctrines of the Bible are free from error.)*

143 Trouble and anguish have taken hold on me: yet Your Commandments are my delights. *(The sense of this Verse is: "I have trouble and anguish, but they do not cause me to turn from You or Your Word.")*

144 The righteousness of Your Testimonies is everlasting: give me understanding, and I shall live. *(The only "Righteousness" is found in the Word of God, which denies all man-made righteousness.)*

KOPH,
GOD'S WORD IS A SOURCE
OF STRENGTH

145 I cried with my whole heart, hear me, O LORD: I will keep Your Statutes. *(His cry to God to help Him in His fidelity to the Word ensured the keeping of that Word. The word "cried" refers to a heart-longing desire akin to physical hunger or thirst.)*

146 I cried unto You; save me, and I shall keep Your Testimonies.

147 I prevented the dawning of the morning, and cried: I hope in Your Word.

148 My eyes prevent the night watches, that I might meditate in Your Word. *(These two Verses portray Christ studying the Word both morning and night.)*

149 Hear my voice according unto Your lovingkindness: O LORD, quicken me according to Your Judgment. *(The Messiah desired that the Scriptures be the instrument and channel of refreshment and vivification to His Mind and Faith. He prayed to be kept within the banks of that channel.)*

150 They draw near who follow after mischief: they are far from Your Law. *(How strange it was that the Pharisees were so near Him, yet did not know Him, because they did not know God's Word!)*

151 You are near, O LORD; and all Your Commandments are Truth. *(This Passage tells us that God hovers near all fidelity to His Word.)*

152 Concerning Your Testimonies, I have known of old that You have founded them for ever. *(The last Verse in this chorus proclaims the Messiah testifying to the inspiration and antiquity of the Sacred Scriptures. He declares God to be their Author, and predicts that they will endure forever [Mat. 24:35].)*

RESH,
GOD'S WORD IS A SOURCE
OF DELIVERANCE

153 Consider my affliction, and deliver me: for I do not forget Your law. *(The word "deliver," in the Hebrew, as used here, is "halaz," and means "to rescue with a gentle hand.")*

154 Plead my cause, and deliver me: quicken me according to Your Word. *(When suffering injustice, most men defend themselves, but the Messiah resigned Himself to God, pleading for His deliverance.)*

155 Salvation is far from the wicked: for they seek not Your Statutes. *(Deliverance was near to this dependent Man because He loved the Bible, but was far from the self-reliant because they despised it.)*

156 Great are Your tender mercies, O LORD: quicken me according to Your Judgments. *(The name "LORD" refers to "Covenant" and promises such.)*

157 Many are my persecutors and my enemies; yet do I not decline from Your Testimonies. *(Their every effort was to push Him away from the Bible. Instead, it drew Him closer.)*

158 I beheld the transgressors, and was grieved; because they kept not Your Word. *(This Passage could be translated, "I looked upon the traitors and loathed them because they kept not Your Word.")*

159 Consider how I love Your Precepts: quicken me, O LORD, according to Your lovingkindness. *(In contrast to the treachery of the Pharisees to that Holy Law, He could truthfully exclaim, "Consider how I love it!")*

160 Your Word is true from the beginning: and every one of Your righteous Judgments endures for ever. *(In this Verse, He repeats the testimony of Verse One Hundred Fifty-two, but especially urges the inerrancy of this Sacred Volume.)*

SCHIN,
GREAT PEACE HAVE THEY WHICH
LOVE YOUR LAW

161 Princes have persecuted me without a cause: but my heart stands in awe of Your Word. *(This Verse refers to the persecution of Christ by the rulers and leaders of Israel.)*

162 I rejoice at Your Word, as one who finds

great spoil. *(The greatest treasure of all is found in "Your Word," and will produce exhilarating rejoicing.)*

163 I hate and abhor lying: but Your Law do I love. *(The sense of this Verse is that the persecutors of Christ were liars, as are all those who vacillate from God's Word.)*

164 Seven times a day do I praise You because of Your righteous Judgments. *(The word "seven" signifies completion, fulfillment, totality, and perfection. It means that the "praise" of the Messiah was perfect and unceasing.)*

165 Great peace have they which love Your Law: and nothing shall offend them. *("Great peace" follows fidelity to and love of "Your Law.")*

166 LORD, I have hoped for Your Salvation, and done Your Commandments.

167 My soul has kept Your Testimonies; and I love them exceedingly.

168 I have kept Your Precepts and Your Testimonies: for all my ways are before You. *(Only a perfect Believer could make the statements of these last three Verses. Such a Believer was Jesus of Nazareth.)*

TAU,
YOUR LAW IS MY DELIGHT

169 Let my cry come near before You, O LORD: give me understanding according to Your Word. *(This is the Twenty-second and final Stanza. If possible, it increases in intensity the Messiah's extolling the Word of God. It opens with a "cry" for the "understanding" of the Bible.)*

170 Let my supplication come before You: deliver me according to Your Word. *(This word "deliver," in the Hebrew, is "nazal," which means "to pluck out of the hands of the enemy; to recover.")*

171 My lips shall utter praise, when You have taught me Your Statutes. *(The word "utter" means "to bubble over with." The effect of Heaven's legislation is to make Earthly lips overflow with praise.)*

172 My tongue shall speak of Your Word: for all Your Commandments are righteousness. *(In these last two Verses, we have "praise" and "testimony." His utterance to God was "praise." His utterance to man was "testimony," or "Your Word.")*

173 Let Your hand help me; for I have chosen Your Precepts. *(Neither the deliverance by man's hand nor the prosperity of his ways were desired by Christ, but God's Salvation and His Word were.)*

174 I have longed for Your Salvation, O LORD; and Your Law is my delight. *(The word "Salvation," hinged with God's Covenant ["O LORD"], guarantee total deliverance, victory, development, and fulfillment.)*

175 Let my soul live, and it shall praise You; and let Your Judgments help me. *(We "live not by bread alone, but by every Word that proceeds out of the mouth of God" [Mat. 4:4].)*

176 I have gone astray like a lost sheep; seek Your servant; for I do not forget Your Commandments. *(To wander as a lost sheep here expresses defenselessness and loneliness, and not moral defection.)*

PSALM 120

AUTHOR UNKNOWN:
PRAYER OF DISTRESS

IN my distress I cried unto the LORD, and He heard me. *(In the great One Hundred Nineteenth Psalm, with its twenty-two Stanzas, the Messiah sang of the Lamp [the Bible] that lightens the celestial way. In these next fifteen Psalms, which are called the "Songs of Degrees" or "Ascents," He will sing of that way, for it is an ascending way — it leads up to God.)*

2 Deliver my soul, O LORD, from lying lips, and from a deceitful tongue. *(The slanderous tongues of the Pharisees attested to the innocency of the Messiah.)*

3 What shall be given unto You? or what shall be done unto You, You false tongue? *(The sense of this Verse is that the Lord called the Pharisees "a false tongue.")*

4 Sharp arrows of the mighty, with coals of juniper. *(The idea is, the "tongues" of the Scribes and Pharisees would burn in the fires of Hell.)*

5 Woe is me, that I sojourn in Mesech, that I dwell in the tents of Kedar! *(Mesech and Kedar were sons of Ishmael. They represent the Scribes and Pharisees, who were indeed of the seed of Abraham, but born after the flesh.)*

6 My soul has long dwelt with him who hates peace. *(The Lord's Earthly life was a short one, yet it was so filled with sorrows that, measured by suffering, it could truthfully be recorded as a long one.)*

7 I am for peace: but when I speak, they are for war. *(The True Messiah was Peace Personified and was rejected by Israel. The false messiah will promise peace but will bring war.)*

PSALM 121

AUTHOR UNKNOWN:
A SONG OF DEGREES, GOD'S
SUSTAINING POWER

I will lift up my eyes unto the hills, from whence comes my help. *(The Messiah here is not saying that His help comes from the hills. The next Verse explains it.)*

2 My help comes from the LORD, which made Heaven and Earth. *(In other words, my help comes from the Lord, Who made the hills, and, in fact, all of Heaven and Earth.)*

3 He will not suffer your foot to be moved: He Who keeps you will not slumber. *(As long as our foot is anchored on the path of His Word, He will see to it that nothing can move it off.)*

4 Behold, He Who keeps Israel shall neither slumber nor sleep. *(The Lord watched over us constantly and forever. He never sleeps!)*

5 The LORD is your keeper: the LORD is your shade upon your right hand. *(The "right hand" was considered the hand of strength. God will protect our strength.)*

6 The sun shall not smite you by day, nor the moon by night. *(This simply means that the Lord will not permit His Creation to work against us, but actually on our behalf.)*

7 The LORD shall preserve You from all evil: He shall preserve your soul. *(Presently, the Lord does such by our abiding Faith in Christ and the Cross, which then gives us the help and Power of the Holy Spirit [Rom. 8:1-2, 11].)*

8 The LORD shall preserve your going out and your coming in from this time forth, and even for evermore. *(This is an ironclad contract that requires only "trust in the Lord," which now refers to Trust in Christ and the Cross. Christ is always the Source, while the Cross is always the Means.)*

PSALM 122

THE AUTHOR IS DAVID:
PRAY FOR THE PEACE OF JERUSALEM

I was glad when they said unto me, Let us go into the House of the LORD. *(The Messiah's heart, saddened by the long centuries of Israel's unbelief, is now gladdened by their cry, "Let us go into the House of Jehovah.")*

2 Our feet shall stand within your gates, O Jerusalem. *(The Vision belongs to the future, but faith makes present what Grace promises.)*

3 Jerusalem is built as a city that is compact together *(this statement in abbreviated form exclaims the fact of Jerusalem's tremendous troubles of the past, which are now over)*:

4 Whither the Tribes go up, the Tribes of the LORD, unto the testimony of Israel, to give thanks unto the Name of the LORD. *(Here in Jerusalem, and we speak of the coming Kingdom Age, Israel's twelve Tribes, redeemed and with new hearts, are presented as worshippers.)*

5 For there are set Thrones of Judgment, the Thrones of the House of David. *(This Throne will be placed in Jerusalem. It signifies the government of the world that will be upon the Shoulder of the Messiah [Isa. 9:6].)*

6 Pray for the peace of Jerusalem: they shall prosper who love you. *(This command by the Holy Spirit should be obeyed by all Christians. Prosperity is promised to all who obey it [Gen. 12:3].)*

7 Peace be within your walls, and prosperity within your palaces. *(The Holy Spirit in Verse 6 not only tells us to pray for the peace of Jerusalem, but also gives us the prayer that we ought to pray. It is this Seventh Verse.)*

8 For my brethren and companions' sakes, I will now say, Peace be within you. *(Two perfections of the Messiah's heart appear in the last two Verses — its sensitivity to the voice of the Holy Spirit and its affection for the people of God's choice.)*

9 Because of the House of the LORD our God I will seek your good. *(This Song is for David. It relates to David, that is, to the True David, the Messiah.)*

PSALM 123

AUTHOR UNKNOWN:
PRAYER FOR MERCY

UNTO You lift I up my eyes, O Thou Who dwells in the heavens. *(The contrast is shown here between the great King of the heavens and the proud but puny king of the nations, evidenced in Verse 4.)*

2 Behold, as the eyes of the servants look unto the hand of their masters, and as the eyes of a maiden unto the hand of her mistress; so our eyes wait upon the LORD our God, until that He have mercy upon us. *(In the east, in ancient times, masters directed their servants with the hand rather than with the voice. Servants, therefore, watched the hand of their masters; likewise, God's Hand directs, supplies,*

protects, comforts, caresses, corrects, and rewards His servants.)

3 Have mercy upon us, O LORD, have mercy upon us: for we are exceedingly filled with contempt. *(Even though Israel is held in contempt, the Lord will hear her cry during the coming Battle of Armageddon and have Mercy upon her.)*

4 Our soul is exceedingly filled with the scorning of those who are at ease, and with the contempt of the proud. *(The one called "the proud" will be the Antichrist. He will be "at ease," thinking that victory is his. He will find, to his dismay, that will not be the case.)*

PSALM 124

THE AUTHOR IS DAVID:
PRAISE FOR DELIVERANCE

I F it had not been the LORD who was on our side, now may Israel say *(the folly of seeking the trembling hand of man is folly indeed! The Lord Alone is the Saviour)*:

2 If it had not been the LORD Who was on our side, when men rose up against us *(Satan uses men; almost always they are men of religion; they do the work of their father, the Devil)*:

3 Then they had swallowed us up quick, when their wrath was kindled against us *(the Lord, when calling past victories to remembrance, animates Israel to trust for present ones)*:

4 Then the waters had overwhelmed us, the stream had gone over our soul:

5 Then the proud waters had gone over our soul. *(The enemy here is compared to a raging flood.)*

6 Blessed be the LORD, Who has not given us as a prey to their teeth.

7 Our soul is escaped as a bird out of the snare of the fowlers: the snare is broken, and we are escaped. *(In a vainglorious cylinder of Sennacherib's, now in the British Museum in London, the proud monarch records that he shut up Hezekiah in Jerusalem "as a bird in a cage." But the Scriptures of Truth relate that the snare of the fowler was broken and the bird escaped [II Chron., Chpt. 32]. As well, the Holy Spirit through David wrote this hundreds of years before the fact.)*

8 Our help is in the name of the LORD, Who made Heaven and Earth. *(How so much the Holy Spirit implores us to look to the Lord, and not man!)*

PSALM 125

AUTHOR UNKNOWN:
GOD SURROUNDS AND PROTECTS
HIS PEOPLE

T HEY who trust in the LORD shall be as Mount Zion, which cannot be removed, but abides for ever. *(Despite Satan's repeated attacks, God has promised that Zion will always remain. He speaks of Jerusalem. The Muslims should read this!)*

2 As the mountains are round about Jerusalem, so the LORD is round about His people from henceforth even for ever. *(The word "henceforth" defines the time of the fulfillment of this Prophecy. It will be the morn of Christ's Millennial Reign.)*

3 For the rod of the wicked shall not rest upon the lot of the righteous: lest the righteous put forth their hands unto iniquity. *(This Passage would have been better translated, "The Sceptre of the lawless one [Dan. 11:36; II Thess. 2:8] shall not remain upon the lot of the righteous." The "righteous" are Christ and all who follow Him. The place is Israel. This Verse predicts the close of the Antichrist's reign and of his possession of God's pleasant land.)*

4 Do good, O LORD, unto those who be good, and to them who are upright in their hearts.

5 As for such as turn aside unto their crooked ways, the LORD shall lead them forth with the workers of iniquity: but peace shall be upon Israel. *(Righteousness will be rewarded, while wickedness will be judged.)*

PSALM 126

AUTHOR UNKNOWN:
DELIVERANCE FROM CAPTIVITY

W HEN the LORD turned again the captivity of Zion, we were like them who dream. *(This pictures the deliverance of Jerusalem from Sennacherib. It was so glorious that it all seemed like a dream [II Ki. 19:20-35].)*

2 Then was our mouth filled with laughter, and our tongue with singing: then said they among the heathen, The LORD has done great things for them. *(The deliverance of Jerusalem was so outstanding that it was noticed by all the heathen round about, with them giving glory to God. The Lord sent one Angel and destroyed 185,000 Assyrians in one night [II Ki. 19:35].)*

3 The LORD has done great things for us;

whereof we are glad.

4 Turn again our captivity, O LORD, as the streams in the south. *("To turn again our captivity" is a figure of speech for the restoration of prosperity.)*

5 They who sow in tears shall reap in joy.

6 He who goes forth and weeps, bearing precious seed, shall doubtless come again with rejoicing, bringing his sheaves with him. *(Paul said, "This Seed is Christ" [Gal. 3:16]. The "sheaves" are symbolic of the harvest which, at long last, is Righteousness.)*

PSALM 127

WRITTEN BY SOLOMON:
TRUSTING GOD IS FRUITFUL

EXCEPT the LORD build the house, they labour in vain who build it: except the LORD keep the city, the watchman wakes but in vain. *(The sense of this Verse is that faith contrasts the sufficiency of God with the insufficiency of man.)*

2 It is vain for you to rise up early, to sit up late, to eat the bread of sorrows: for so He gives His beloved sleep. *(The argument of this Verse is that God gives to His loved ones, while asleep, treasures that men toil for early and late in vain.)*

3 Lo, children are an heritage of the LORD: and the fruit of the womb is His reward. *(The "house" built by the Lord will be full of children, built of living stones — a multitude of redeemed sinners that no man can number [I Pet. 2:5; Rev. 7:9].)*

4 As arrows are in the hand of a mighty man, so are children of the youth. *(God is building a spiritual house of sons. The "Mighty Man" is the Lord Jesus Christ. These sons, loved and energized by Him, become more than conquerors.)*

5 Happy is the man who has his quiver full of them: they shall not be ashamed, but they shall speak with the enemies in the gate. *("The Man" is Jesus Christ. The great price paid at Calvary was not in vain. Millions have flocked and will flock to His banner, and the gates of Hell shall not prevail against them [Mat. 16:18].)*

PSALM 128

WRITER UNKNOWN:
THE REWARDS OF FAITHFULNESS

BLESSED is every one who fears the LORD; who walks in His ways. *(This is fulfilled now in part; it will be fulfilled totally in the coming Kingdom Age.)*

2 For You shall eat the labour of your hands: happy shall you be, and it shall be well with you. *(This speaks of the coming Kingdom Age, when the deserts will blossom like the rose.)*

3 Your wife shall be as a fruitful vine by the sides of your house: your children like olive plants round about your table.

4 Behold, that thus shall the man be blessed who fears the LORD. *("Your wife" refers to Israel, who is no longer the "wife of whoredoms." As well, the "children" will not be "children of whoredoms"; they came from the wayward wife, but this "wife," a fully restored Israel, shall be a "fruitful vine" [Hos. 1:2; Chpt. 14].)*

5 The LORD shall bless you out of Zion: and you shall see the good of Jerusalem all the days of your life.

6 Yea, you shall see your children's children, and peace upon Israel. *(This will take place in the coming Kingdom Age, and will most definitely be fulfilled to the letter.)*

PSALM 129

AUTHOR UNKNOWN:
A PRAYER FOR JUDGMENT FOR THOSE
WHO AFFLICT ISRAEL

MANY a time have they afflicted me from my youth, may Israel now say *(the Speaker here is the Messiah; here He recalls Israel's struggles in her beginnings as a nation):*

2 Many a time have they afflicted me from my youth: yet they have not prevailed against me. *(The Hamans, the Herods, and the Hitlers have repeatedly tried to destroy Israel. They have all failed!)*

3 The plowers plowed upon my back: they made long their furrows. *(This pertains to Israel while in Egyptian slavery [Ex. 2:23-24].)*

4 The LORD is righteous: He has cut asunder the cords of the wicked. *(This statement, "Jehovah is righteous," is placed in the center of this Psalm. It vindicates His actions in permitting the past and future afflictions of His People.)*

5 Let them all be confounded and turned back who hate Zion. *(This prayer was prayed by the Messiah and is, therefore, guaranteed of fulfillment.)*

6 Let them be as the grass upon the housetops, which withers afore it grows up. *(The prediction is clear — all who oppose Israel,*

including the Antichrist, will "wither.")

7 Wherewith the mower fills not his hand; nor he who binds sheaves his bosom. *(In this Passage, the Antichrist is likened to "the mower." He will not fill his hand nor gather profit from his invasion of Israel, which will take place in the middle of the Great Tribulation, and at its conclusion.)*

8 Neither do they which go by say, The blessing of the LORD be upon you: we bless you in the name of the LORD. *(The sense of this Verse is that even though Israel has long strayed from God, still, their oppressor will have no blessing from the Lord.)*

PSALM 130

AUTHOR UNKNOWN:
MY SOUL WAITS FOR THE LORD

OUT of the depths have I cried unto You, O LORD. *("The depths" relate to the depth of affliction which Israel will suffer under the false messiah, which will be the just punishment of her rejection of the True Messiah.)*

2 Lord, hear my voice: let Your ears be attentive to the voice of my supplications. *(The Messiah requests that Jehovah hear His voice on behalf of His people.)*

3 If You, LORD, should mark iniquities, O Lord, who shall stand? *(The depravity of all men is declared in this Verse.)*

4 But there is forgiveness with You, that You may be feared. *(The cry for forgiveness of sins must be addressed to God, for He Alone can forgive. As well, a cry for deliverance from oppression is to be made to Him, for He is mighty to save.)*

5 I wait for the LORD, my soul does wait, and in His Word do I hope.

6 My soul waits for the Lord more than they who watch for the morning: I say, more than they who watch for the morning. *(This is a faith that waits "on" God and that waits "for" God. Saul was willing to wait "on" God, but not to wait "for" God, and so he lost the Kingdom [I Sam. 10:8; 13:8-14].)*

7 Let Israel hope in the LORD: for with the LORD there is mercy, and with Him is plenteous redemption.

8 And He shall redeem Israel from all his iniquities. *(This Song of Trust gives abundant hope, not only for Israel, but for all who would take advantage of God's great Salvation Plan.)*

PSALM 131

THE AUTHOR IS DAVID:
HUMILITY BEFORE THE LORD

LORD, my heart is not haughty, nor my eyes lofty: neither do I exercise myself in great matters, or in things too high for me. *(This is a Song of Triumph. It speaks of humility, which is, in fact, the greatest Triumph of all.)*

2 Surely I have behaved and quieted myself, as a child that is weaned of his mother: my soul is even as a weaned child. *(Even though David wrote these Words, the Messiah is the Speaker and, thereby, the Subject of this Song. The sense of this Verse is that, as a weaned child submits its will to that of its mother, so will the Messiah, as God's perfect king, be wholly subject to God; by ruling in His fear, this will form a contrast to self-willed human kings.)*

3 Let Israel hope in the LORD from henceforth and for ever. *(She is to do this because the character of the King is such that a perfect government will be enjoyed by His subjects, and Israel will dwell in peace.)*

PSALM 132

THE AUTHOR IS DAVID:
WORSHIP AND BLESSINGS WITH THE
RETURN OF THE ARK

LORD, remember David, and all his afflictions *(this Psalm contains a Prayer and a Promise and, as always, the Promise exceeds the Prayer in Grace)*:

2 How he swore unto the LORD, and vowed unto the mighty God of Jacob *(the "Vow" that David makes concerns the bringing of the Ark of the Covenant to Jerusalem)*;

3 Surely I will not come into the tabernacle of my house, nor go up into my bed;

4 I will not give sleep to my eyes, or slumber to my eyelids,

5 Until I find out a place for the LORD, an habitation for the Mighty God of Jacob. *(It is obvious that David has placed the business of Israel and his own occupation aside, with his total attention being given to the bringing of the Ark to Jerusalem.)*

6 Lo, we heard of it at Ephratah: we found it in the fields of the wood. *(If this is to be taken literally, the implications are woeful and give us an indication of the terrible spiritual*

plight of Israel under Saul. It seems it was little known at this time as to exactly where the Ark of the Covenant actually was.)

7 We will go into His tabernacles: we will worship at His footstool. *(This is the indication that God has chosen Jerusalem as the appointed place for His Name. This is the first time the Ark will reside in Zion at Jerusalem.)*

8 Arise, O LORD, into Your rest; You, and the Ark of Your strength. *(David, no doubt, was referring to the great Prophecy of Moses, as given in Num. 10:35-36.)*

9 Let Your Priests be clothed with Righteousness; and let Your Saints shout for joy. *(There can be tremendous religious activity without the presence of the Ark, but there can be no real "joy." Only His Presence provides such.)*

10 For Your servant David's sake turn not away the face of your anointed. *(Three men were prominently associated with the Ark of Israel: Eli, the Priest; Samuel, the Prophet; and David, the King. They all sinned and failed, but in Him Whom they typified there is not, nor can there be, sin or failure.)*

11 The LORD has sworn in truth unto David; He will not turn from it; Of the fruit of your body will I set upon your throne.

12 If your children will keep My Covenant and My Testimony that I shall teach them, their children shall also sit upon your throne for evermore. *(This will be fulfilled in totality in the coming Kingdom Age, and will continue forever.)*

13 For the LORD has chosen Zion; He has desired it for His habitation.

14 This is My rest for ever: here will I dwell; for I have desired it. *(Satan has ever contested this Promise of God concerning Zion and Jerusalem. Presently, the Muslims claim the city for Muhammad. The Jews claim it for the Promises, of which this is but one. While the contest may be fierce, nevertheless, the following Verses will be fulfilled.)*

15 I will abundantly bless her provision: I will satisfy her poor with bread. *(This is a Promise that the Government of the Lord will prosper. This will take place during the coming Kingdom Age, when Christ rules in Zion.)*

16 I will also clothe her Priests with salvation: and her Saints shall shout aloud for joy. *(In Verse Fifteen, we have the Promise of material and financial prosperity concerning the coming days of Jerusalem. In this Verse, we have the Promise of coming Holy Spirit Revival. That which Israel rejected on the Day of Pentecost,*

they will now accept.)

17 There will I make the horn of David to bud: I have ordained a lamp for My Anointed. *(The word "horn" represents power and authority that will be held by Jesus Christ. "My Anointed" refers directly to Christ.)*

18 His enemies will I clothe with shame: but upon Himself shall His crown flourish. *(We are told here that the prosperity of the Son of David will be forever, and His dominion will be likewise [Dan. 2:35].)*

PSALM 133

THE AUTHOR IS DAVID:
THE JOY OF BROTHERHOOD
AND HARMONY

BEHOLD, how good and how pleasant it is for brethren to dwell together in unity! *(There are two types of unity: the man-made variety, and that which can only be given by God, which will always have the Cross as its foundation.)*

2 It is like the precious ointment upon the head, that ran down upon the beard, even Aaron's beard: that went down to the skirts of his garments;

3 As the dew of Hermon, and as the dew that descended upon the mountains of Zion: for there the LORD commanded the blessing, even life for evermore. *(Faith can sing in days of sorrow, "All will be well." Most probably this Psalm was sung by Hezekiah and the people of Jerusalem in their day of disunion and distress.*

The unity predicted in this Prophecy will be the creation of the Holy Spirit, and yet cannot be effected until the Coming of the Lord.

A lack of unity is because of a lack of fidelity to the Bible. Fidelity to the Bible "commands the Blessing of the Lord.")

PSALM 134

DAVID IS PROBABLY THE AUTHOR:
AN EXHORTATION TO PRAISE

BEHOLD, bless ye the LORD, all ye servants of the LORD, which by night stand in the House of the LORD. *(This is the last of the Songs of Degrees or Ascents and is, therefore, a Song of Triumph. It is a scene of Millennial peace and glory, for Christ now reigns in Jerusalem. The Holy Spirit now invites the servants*

of Jehovah to praise Jehovah in the House of Jehovah.)

2 Lift up your hands in the Sanctuary, and bless the LORD. (It is difficult for us to imagine at the present time the praise and worship that will characterize Jerusalem in that day, especially at the Temple site [Ezek., Chpts. 40-48].)

3 The LORD Who made Heaven and Earth bless you out of Zion. (As the first two Verses invited the servants of Jehovah to praise Him, Verse 3 is the response to the invitation. In the Millennial Day, men will bless Him, and He will bless men.)

PSALM 135

PROBABLY WRITTEN BY DAVID: PRAISE TO GOD FOR HIS GREATNESS

PRAISE ye the LORD. Praise ye the Name of the LORD; praise Him, O ye servants of the LORD. (The word "praise," in the Hebrew, means "Hallelujah!" Therefore, this Psalm begins with "Hallelujah" and closes with "Hallelujah.")

2 You who stand in the House of the LORD, in the courts of the House of our God. (These "courts" are in front of the Temple, and are where the people worship.)

3 Praise the LORD; for the LORD is good: sing praises unto His Name; for it is pleasant. (Singing praises unto the Lord is one of the highest forms of worship.)

4 For the LORD has chosen Jacob unto Himself, and Israel for His peculiar treasure. (This Psalm points toward the time that the Messiah will dwell in Jerusalem. The Song will then be sung by redeemed Israel at the Coronation of the Great King in Zion.)

5 For I know that the LORD is great, and that our Lord is above all gods (that which is inspired by Satan and the depraved figments of men's imagination).

6 Whatsoever the LORD pleased, that did He in Heaven, and in Earth, in the seas, and all deep places. (This Passage extols the Lord as Creator of the Heavens and the Earth, and all that is therein.)

7 He causes the vapours to ascend from the ends of the Earth; He makes lightnings for the rain; He brings the wind out of His treasuries. (The heathen worshipped idols in order to secure good weather for their crops, etc. We are told here that God controls the weather.)

8 Who smote the first born of Egypt, both of man and beast. (The great deliverance of Israel from Egyptian bondage is ever portrayed by the Holy Spirit as an example of the Power of God.)

9 Who sent tokens and wonders into the midst of you, O Egypt, upon Pharaoh, and upon all his servants. (In the Eyes of God, Pharaoh is placed no higher than his servants. All answer to God!)

10 Who smote great nations, and slew mighty kings;

11 Sihon king of the Amorites, and Og king of Bashan, and all the kingdoms of Canaan (these kings and kingdoms were emissaries of Satan, resplendent with his power; they were placed there and energized by Satan for the very purpose of hindering the Children of Israel from taking their inheritance):

12 And gave their land for an heritage, an heritage unto Israel His people. (Instead of Satan taking that which is rightfully ours, we are intended by the Lord to take from Satan. It can be done if we look to Christ and the Cross, and do so exclusively, which gives the Holy Spirit latitude to work within our lives [Rom. 8:1-2, 11].)

13 Your Name, O LORD, endures for ever; and Your memorial, O LORD, throughout all generations. (Satan does not fear us as personalities; however, he does fear "the Name of the Lord," and greatly so!)

14 For the LORD will judge His people, and He will repent Himself concerning His servants. (The sense of this Verse is that the Lord will judge the righteous after the Rapture [I Cor. 3:11-15]. This pertains to works and not sins, which were already judged at Calvary.)

15 The idols of the heathen are silver and gold, the work of men's hands. (The term, "work of men's hands," has to do with all religious work. The meaning of the word "religion," in its strictest spiritual sense, is that it is man-made and not God-made.)

16 They have mouths, but they speak not; eyes have they, but they see not;

17 They have ears, but they hear not; neither is there any breath in their mouths. (The Word of God has "Life." As well, it has "Light." All which is made by man, irrespective of its religious content, have no "Life" or "Light.")

18 They who make them are like unto them: so is every one who trusts in them. (The worshippers of idols take upon themselves the character of these idols, i.e., "religion." Thus, the followers of the religion of Islam take upon themselves the character of that religion, which is

hate and murder.)

19 Bless the LORD, O House of Israel: bless the LORD, O House of Aaron:

20 Bless the LORD, O House of Levi: ye who fear the LORD, bless the LORD. *(The impotency of idols and of everyone who trusts in them is contrasted with the Almightiness of the Messiah and the happiness of those who trust in Him.)*

21 Blessed be the LORD out of Zion, which dwells at Jerusalem. Praise ye the LORD. *(As stated, this Psalm is prophetic, with its fulfillment pointing toward the coming Kingdom Age.)*

PSALM 136

AUTHOR UNKNOWN:
PRAISE AND THANKSGIVING TO GOD

O give thanks unto the LORD; for He is good: for His mercy endures for ever. *(We must never forget that "God is good!" Therefore, He is merciful.)*

2 O give thanks unto the God of gods: for His mercy endures for ever. *(The Hebrew for "God of gods" is "Elohim of the Elohim." He is speaking here of the Trinity of which all are equal. In the Trinity, "His Mercy endures forever.")*

3 O give thanks to the Lord of lords: for His mercy endures for ever. *(The Hebrew is "Adonim of the Adonim," which means "Sovereign of the sovereigns; Master of the masters; Ruler of the rulers.")*

4 To Him Who Alone does great wonders: for His mercy endures for ever. *(God Alone can perform constructive miracles.)*

5 To Him Who by wisdom made the Heavens: for His mercy endures for ever. *(This ascribes to God all the planetary systems.)*

6 To Him Who stretched out the Earth above the waters: for His mercy endures for ever *(who separated the land and the seas; the attention which the Holy Spirit gives to the Mercy of God in all of these Verses is beautifully amazing, and rightly so!).*

7 To Him Who made great lights: for His mercy endures for ever *(God is "Light," so the creation of Light is a natural result of His Divine Person):*

8 The sun to rule by day: for His mercy endures for ever:

9 The moon and stars to rule by night: for His mercy endures for ever. *(The Holy Spirit is telling us here that all of Creation, and its ordered existence, is a result of the Mercy of God.)*

10 To Him Who smote Egypt in their firstborn: for His mercy endures for ever *(this tells us that all Judgments poured out on Egypt were a result of Mercy; the Lord could have smitten Egypt at the beginning; however, He sent Judgments, including the death of the firstborn, all in order to get them to repent, but to no avail):*

11 And brought out Israel from among them: for His mercy endures for ever *(to bring Israel out was not only an act of Mercy for Israel, but for Egypt as well):*

12 With a strong hand, and with a stretched out arm: for His mercy endures for ever. *(The "strong hand" and the "stretched out arm," which God used to deliver Israel, were all because of Mercy.)*

13 To Him which divided the Red Sea into parts: for His mercy endures for ever *(this Passage destroys the myth that the Red Sea, at the place of the crossing, was only a few inches deep):*

14 And made Israel to pass through the midst of it: for His Mercy endures for ever *(it took Faith for Israel to pass through; they had to believe that God, Who had made this path through the Sea, would, as well, continue to defy the laws of gravity by holding the water up like two walls on either side):*

15 But overthrew Pharaoh and his host in the Red Sea: for His mercy endures for ever. *(The indication here is that Pharaoh drowned along with his army.)*

16 To Him which led His people through the wilderness: for His mercy endures for ever. *(God intended for the stay in the wilderness to be of short duration — a few months to two years at the most. The forty years was because of Israel's unbelief and rebellion.)*

17 To Him which smote great kings: for His mercy endures for ever *(this speaks of Pharaoh as well as the kings mentioned in following Verses):*

18 And slew famous kings: for His mercy endures for ever:

19 Sihon king of the Amorites: for His mercy endures for ever:

20 And Og the king of Bashan: for His mercy endures for ever *(tradition says that Sihon was the brother of king Og; both were Amorites; they were giants of the race of the Rephaim at the time of the conquest of Palestine):*

21 And gave their land for an heritage: for His mercy endures for ever:

22 Even an heritage unto Israel His servant: for His mercy endures for ever. *(Og's territory was given to the half-Tribe of Manasseh*

[Deut. 3:13]. Sihon's territory was given to the Tribes of Reuben and Gad [Num. 32:23-38; Josh. 13:10].)

23 Who remembered us in our low estate: for His mercy endures for ever (God remembers His Mercy and Grace and forgets our sins; man forgets God's Mercy and Grace and remembers our sins):

24 And has redeemed us from our enemies: for His mercy endures for ever. (The word "redeemed" means to rescue and to break the power of the one who has us bound, namely Satan. This Redemption is so powerful that it not only redeems us, but also destroys our enemies.)

25 Who gives food to all flesh: for His mercy endures for ever. (The "food" addressed here pertains not only to spiritual food, but also to natural food.)

26 O give thanks unto the God of Heaven: for His mercy endures for ever. (As "His mercy endures forever," likewise, our "thanks unto Him" should endure forever.)

PSALM 137

AUTHOR UNKNOWN:
THE MOURNING OF THE EXILES
IN BABYLON

BY the rivers of Babylon, there we sat down, yea, we wept, when we remembered Zion. (The two cities of Jerusalem and Babylon are opposed. The one is God's city; the other, man's. The one figures truth; the other, falsehood. The one represents the Kingdom of Light; the other, that of darkness. These cities exist today as principles.)

2 We hanged our harps upon the willows in the midst thereof. (Captivity to the world paralyzes both hand and tongue so that it is impossible in such an atmosphere to sing the Lord's Song.)

3 For there they who carried us away captive required of us a song; and they who wasted us required of us mirth, saying, Sing us one of the songs of Zion. (The word "there" emphasizes the hostile environment.)

4 How shall we sing the LORD's song in a strange land? (As well as typifying the historical narrative of an actual event, this Verse also portrays the Christian who has lost his way.)

5 If I forget you, O Jerusalem, let my right hand forget her cunning. (The harpist is saying that even though he is not playing his harp, he has not forgotten how. As well, even though he

is not in Jerusalem, he will not forget her glory and her joys.)

6 If I do not remember you, let my tongue cleave to the roof of my mouth; if I prefer not Jerusalem above my chief joy. (The Psalmist realizes what he has lost and what he must regain. He has faith that it will be regained.)

7 Remember, O LORD, the children of Edom in the day of Jerusalem; who said, Rase it, rase it, even to the foundation thereof. (Inasmuch as Edom rejoiced in the day of Jerusalem's defeat, probably the lament of this Psalm refers to Nebuchadnezzar's destruction of Jerusalem.)

8 O daughter of Babylon, who is to be destroyed; happy shall he be, who rewards you as you have served us. (It seems this Prophecy was given before Babylon was destroyed and promised its destruction.)

9 Happy shall he be, who takes and dashes your little ones against the stones. (The language is figurative. Babylon represents idolatry; her children are the idol images beloved by her. To destroy these is indeed happiness to the servants of Truth.)

PSALM 138

THE AUTHOR IS DAVID:
I WILL PRAISE YOU WITH MY
WHOLE HEART

I will praise You with my whole heart: before the gods will I sing praise unto You. (The predictions in Verses 4 through 6 relate to the time when all the kings of the Earth — the gods of this Verse — will become subject to the Words of the Messiah's mouth.)

2 I will worship toward Your holy temple, and praise Your name for Your lovingkindness and for Your truth: for You have magnified Your Word above all Your name. (His Name means His Reputation and Character for faithfulness and goodness. His Word is His Promise. In that future day, His Performance will exceed His Promise, thereby magnifying His Word above all His Name.)

3 In the day when I cried You answered me, and strengthened me with strength in my soul. (On the Millennial Morn, Israel will proclaim in song that all her expectations founded upon the Promises of God will be surpassed by their performance.)

4 All the kings of the Earth shall praise You, O LORD, when they hear the words of Your mouth.

5 Yea, they shall sing in the ways of the LORD: for great is the glory of the LORD. *(Such praise, which is presently foreign, will, at that time, the Kingdom Age, be common.)*

6 Though the LORD be high, yet has He respect unto the lowly: but the proud He knows afar off. *(He, as the Self-humbled One [Phil. 2:8], will be enthroned; the proud one [the Antichrist — Isa. 10:13; Dan. 11:36] will be afar off in the Lake of Fire [Rev. 19:20].)*

7 Though I walk in the midst of trouble, You will revive me: You shall stretch forth Your hand against the wrath of my enemies, and Your right hand shall save me.

8 The LORD will perfect that which concerns me: your mercy, O LORD, endures for ever: forsake not the works of Your own hands. *(The confidence of the Messiah and His People in the trustworthiness of the Promises of God is expressed in these last two Verses. He and His People are one; hence, He walks with them in the midst of trouble.)*

PSALM 139

THE AUTHOR IS DAVID: THE PRESENCE AND POWER OF GOD

O LORD, You have searched me, and known me. *(There is absolute harmony here between the Incarnate Word of God [the Lord Jesus Christ] and the Written Word of God. This Psalm is, therefore, fittingly placed in this Deuteronomy Book of the Psalms, for it reveals the perfect submission and obedience of Christ's human nature to the Word of God.)*

2 You know my downsitting and my uprising, You understand my thoughts afar off. *(God, by searching and trying the heart, finds out such.)*

3 You compass my path and my lying down, and are acquainted with all my ways. *(The word "compass" means "scrutinize." Therefore, God scrutinized the path of the Messiah and inspected all His Ways. He found nothing but perfection.)*

4 For there is not a word in my tongue, but, lo, O LORD, You know it altogether. *(God knew all about the Words of the Messiah, His Ways, and even His Thoughts, while they were being formed. He found all to be perfect [I Pet. 2:22; 3:10].)*

5 You have beset me behind and before, and laid Your hand upon me. *(The words, "to lay," signify to lay protectingly, while "beset" means "to guard.")*

6 Such knowledge is too wonderful for me; it is high, I cannot attain unto it. *(The sense of this Verse is that the Messiah greatly admired God's infinite Intelligence and Love and rejoiced that it was impossible to get outside of them. He lived and moved and had His being in God.)*

7 Where shall I go from Your Spirit? or where shall I flee from Your Presence? *(The Messiah exalted in the knowledge that the greatest distance could not separate Him from God, nor the darkest night hide Him from the Father's loving Eye.)*

8 If I ascend up into Heaven, You are there: if I make my bed in Hell, behold, You are there. *(Jesus is now in Heaven by the right hand of the Father [Heb. 1:3]. As well, He went down into the Paradise-side of Hell at the time of His Death, and also preached to the fallen angels held there in prison. There is no record that He went into the burning side of Hell [I Pet. 3:19].)*

9 If I take the wings of the morning, and dwell in the uttermost parts of the sea;

10 Even there shall Your hand lead me, and Your right hand shall hold me. *(Our Lord became our Substitute in all of these things and, therefore, guaranteed the Father's help to us exactly as it was to Him, for we are joint-heirs with Him [Rom. 8:17].)*

11 If I say, Surely the darkness shall cover me; even the night shall be light about me.

12 Yea, the darkness hides not from You; but the night shines as the day: the darkness and the light are both alike to you. *(The meaning of these two Verses is that all is open before God.)*

13 For You have possessed my reins: You have covered me in my mother's womb. *(This Passage pertains to the Incarnation of Christ. The words "possess" and "cover" mean here "to collect and to knit together"; "reins" is a comprehensive term embracing the human body both physically and emotionally.)*

14 I will praise You; for I am fearfully and wonderfully made: marvellous are Your works; and that my soul knows right well. *(This Passage certainly refers to every human being; yet it particularly refers to the Messiah. The miraculous nature of His birth and His full testimony to it form the subjects for praise. "Fearfully" signifies "miraculously.")*

15 My substance was not hid from You, when I was made in secret, and curiously wrought in the lowest parts of the Earth. *(This means that our Lord's human body was skillfully made from the dust of the ground.)*

16 Your eyes did see my substance, yet being

unperfect; and in Your book all my members were written, which in continuance were fashioned, when as yet there was none of them. *(This pertains to the Perfect Body created for the Son of God. The members of that sinless body were not "imperfect" but "unperfect," which means "unformed in fact," but all its parts were inscribed from eternity.)*

17 How precious also are Your thoughts unto me, O God! how great is the sum of them! *(The Messiah was made of the same material as the First Adam, which emphasizes the fact that His Body was human and not angelic. In fact, His human Body was the supreme Work of God's Own hands [Heb. 10:5].)*

18 If I should count them, they are more in number than the sand: when I awake, I am still with You. *(This Verse speaks of Christ's Death and Resurrection, and the continual preciousness of the Incarnation, even during those times.)*

19 Surely You will slay the wicked, O God: depart from me therefore, you bloody men.

20 For they speak against You wickedly, and Your enemies take Your name in vain. *(These Passages speak of the absolute sinless perfection of this human body that was developed by God for the Incarnation and, therefore, for the Redemption of man, by providing a perfect Sacrifice. It was never tainted by sin, not even the slightest!)*

21 Do not I hate them, O LORD, who hate You? and am not I grieved with those who rise up against You?

22 I hate them with perfect hatred: I count them my enemies. *(The "hatred" expressed here is a perfect hatred, not a sinful hatred. This demands a sinless nature, which Christians do not now have.)*

23 Search me, O God, and know my heart: try me, and know my thoughts:

24 And see if there be any wicked way in me, and lead me in the way everlasting. *(These Passages refer not only to all Believers, but more particularly to the Messiah. The Perfect One was to be searched by God in a manner that no human heart has ever been searched; nothing but perfection was found.)*

PSALM 140

THE AUTHOR IS DAVID:
PRAYER FOR DELIVERANCE FROM
ONE'S ENEMIES

DELIVER me, O LORD, from the evil man: preserve me from the violent man *(the "evil man" and the "violent man" pertain to the Pharisees, Sadducees, and the Herodians, with their snares, nets, and gins, as in Mat., Chpt. 22);*

2 Which imagine mischiefs in their heart; continually are they gathered together for war. *(The four Gospels record these "mischiefs.")*

3 They have sharpened their tongues like a serpent; adders' poison is under their lips. Selah. *(It is remarkable that all of these statements pertain to the religious elite of Israel at the time of Christ. In fact, Satan's greatest effort is from within the Church.)*

4 Keep me, O LORD, from the hands of the wicked; preserve me from the violent man; who have purposed to overthrow my goings. *(Every intention of "these wicked" was to stop the mission of Christ. It is the same presently. The Lord Alone is our help!)*

5 The proud have hid a snare for me, and cords; they have spread a net by the wayside; they have set gins for me. Selah. *(The Pharisees and Sadducees and their followers are called "the proud." All religion has pride as its foundation. This pride always produces self-righteousness.)*

6 I said unto the LORD, You are my God: hear the voice of my supplications, O LORD. *(The Messiah's defense was His Heavenly Father, as our defense must be our Heavenly Father.)*

7 O God the Lord, the strength of my salvation, You have covered my head in the day of battle. *(The Messiah attributed to His Father the Source of all His Strength. As well, during the horror of Calvary, His Head [Headship] was covered and protected by the Father, while the head of the enemy was uncovered and, thereby, bruised [Gen. 3:15].)*

8 Grant not, O LORD, the desires of the wicked: further not his wicked device; lest they exalt themselves. Selah. *(While Verses 1 through 5 address themselves to the Pharisees and Sadducees, Verses 8 through 11 pertain to the Antichrist and the False Prophet.)*

9 As for the head of those who compass me about, let the mischief of their own lips cover them. *(There is a possibility that David was speaking of Absalom, regarding his rebellion. If so, this Passage was fulfilled. It was also fulfilled in the Pharisees and Sadducees, who persecuted Christ. It will be fulfilled in the Antichrist and the False Prophet at the Second Coming.)*

10 Let burning coals fall upon them; let them be cast into the fire; into deep pits, that they rise not up again. *(We are told in this*

Passage concerning the Antichrist and his followers that "they rise not up again.")

11 Let not an evil speaker be established in the Earth: evil shall hunt the violent man to overthrow him. *(The "evil speaker" could have referred to Absalom, as well as Judas, and all who oppose the Lord. But more particularly it concerns the Antichrist.)*

12 I know that the LORD will maintain the cause of the afflicted, and the right of the poor.

13 Surely the righteous shall give thanks unto Your name: the upright shall dwell in Your presence. *(The words, "afflicted," "poor," "righteous," and "upright," all refer to the Messiah. God will maintain no cause except that of the Messiah, so our faith, without fail, must be in Him [Jn. 14:6].)*

PSALM 141

THE AUTHOR IS DAVID: PRAYER TO BE KEPT FROM SIN AND TEMPTATION

LORD, I cry unto You: make haste unto me; give ear unto my voice, when I cry unto You. *(This is a Psalm of David, and yet the voice of the Messiah. The tenor of this Verse tells us that the Father was the Messiah's total dependence. He sought help only from Him.)*

2 Let my prayer be set forth before You as incense; and the lifting up of my hands as the evening Sacrifice. *(The "Incense" had to do with the Golden Altar, with it being offered up at least twice a day. The "evening Sacrifice" took place at 3 p.m., the exact time that Jesus died on the Cross.)*

3 Set a watch, O LORD, before my mouth; keep the door of my lips. *(The Messiah is the only One of Whom it can be said that His Heart was Perfect before God; consequently, everything that came from His Lips was edifying and holy.)*

4 Incline not my heart to any evil thing, to practice wicked works with men who work iniquity: and let me not eat of their dainties. *(The separation from evil which characterized Christ when on Earth also characterizes those in whom He dwells.)*

5 Let the Righteous smite me; it shall be a kindness: and let Him reprove me; it shall be an excellent oil, which shall not break my head: for yet my prayer also shall be in their calamities. *("The Righteous" could only refer to the Heavenly Father. God does not allow fellow Christians to smite each other. Vengeance*

belongs to Him, and no one else. It is proper for the Lord to chastise us, but not proper for anyone else to do so [Heb. 12:5-11]. If anyone else attempts to chastise a Christian, "calamity" will come upon them.)*

6 When their judges are overthrown in stony places, they shall hear my words; for they are sweet. *(The words, "in stony places," in the Hebrew, read "the hands of the rock." This refers to Christ. The religious leaders were overthrown by the "Rock," and then the common people heard the "sweet words" of Christ [Jn. 7:46].)*

7 Our bones are scattered at the grave's mouth, as when one cuts and cleaves wood upon the Earth. *(This Passage shows the hatred of man's heart to the Messiah and His followers.)*

8 But my eyes are unto you, O GOD the Lord: in You is my trust; leave not my soul destitute. *(Protection from these "judges" [self-righteous Pharisees, Vs. 6] can be given only by God.)*

9 Keep me from the snares which they have laid for me, and the gins of the workers of iniquity. *(So the "hands of the Rock" of Verse 6 overthrew those who had planned that the hands of the snare should overthrow Him. The Hebrew word used here shows that the Rock is an immovable Rock [Mat. 16:18].)*

10 Let the wicked fall into their own nets, while that I withal escape. *(The sense of this Verse is that the Pharisees, Sadducees, and the Herodians were caught in their own snares, but the Messiah passed safely through and over them.)*

PSALM 142

THE AUTHOR IS DAVID: DAVID'S PRAYER IN THE CAVE OF ADULLAM

I cried unto the LORD with my voice; with my voice unto the LORD did I make my supplication. *(Even though this Psalm portrays the heart of David, even more so it portrays the Messiah, when He was shut up in the prison-house of Sheol.)*

2 I poured out my complaint before Him; I showed before Him my trouble. *(As David poured out his complaints to God and David's Greater Son poured out His to the Father, likewise we are given an example which we are to follow.)*

3 When my spirit was overwhelmed within me, then You knew my path. In the way

wherein I walked have they privily laid a snare for me. (*The sense of this Verse is that when the Messiah's Spirit was overwhelmed within Him, then He was supported by the remembrance that God knew His life of sorrow. This implies conscious sinlessness. He invited God to scrutinize His conduct from the cradle to the Cross. It was a life of constant and bitter trial, but it was a sinless life. He was tested daily by snares laid for Him, but He never sinned. Men hated Him, but He was unspeakably precious to God.*)

4 I looked on my right hand, and beheld, but there was no man who would know me: refuge failed me; no man cared for my soul.

5 I cried unto You, O LORD: I said, You are my refuge and my portion in the land of the living. (*This speaks of the time when Christ went to the Cross. The phrase, "No man cared for my soul," has reference to His dying on the Cross and, thereby, being made a curse by God. In reality, while He was made a curse by God, it was not because of His sin, for He had none, but because of our sin [Gal. 3:13].*)

6 Attend unto my cry; for I am brought very low: deliver me from my persecutors; for they are stronger than I. (*Shut up in the prison-house of Sheol, into which He descended from Golgotha, He trusts, prays, and believes. He cries for deliverance and predicts the triumph which His Resurrection will bring to the righteous.*)

7 Bring my soul out of prison, that I may praise Your name: the righteous shall compass me about; for You shall deal bountifully with me. (*Here the Messiah prays that He will be delivered out of the death world. He knows that His prayer will be answered and the subsequent joy that His Resurrection will bring to His People.*)

PSALM 143

DAVID IS THE AUTHOR:
A PRAYER IN THE HOUR OF DARKNESS AND DISTRESS

HEAR my prayer, O LORD, give ear to my supplications: in Your faithfulness answer me, and in Your righteousness. (*While this Psalm speaks of David, in a greater way, it points to the Messiah, Who prays out of the depths and darkness of Sheol. The Holy Spirit allows us, thereby, to see inside this dark moment.*)

2 And enter not into judgment with Your servant: for in Your sight shall no man living be justified. (*In this Verse, David and the Greater Son of David declare the Righteousness of God and the unrighteousness of man. As Jehovah's Atoning Servant, He occupies the center of the Verse as the Mediator or the Daysman. The idea is, man cannot justify himself, but God will freely justify man upon believing Faith, which pertains to believing exclusively in Christ.*)

3 For the enemy has persecuted my soul; he has smitten my life down to the ground; he has made me to dwell in darkness, as those who have been long dead. (*The "enemy" of both Verses 3 and 4 is death, the last enemy that is to be destroyed. He who has the power of death is Satan. The Messiah's death on the Cross is foretold in these two Verses.*)

4 Therefore is my spirit overwhelmed within me; my heart within me is desolate. (*The extremity of horror which Christ suffered in the death world is revealed in the statements that He dwelt in darkness. The very fact of death constituted this horror.*)

5 I remember the days of old; I meditate on all Your works; I muse on the work of Your hands. (*The depth of this anguish was deepened by the remembrance of the Glory which He had with the Father before and at Creation.*)

6 I stretch forth my hands unto You: my soul thirsts after You, as a thirsty land. Selah. (*The language of intense suffering, a full subjection of will, and of confident expectation of the Promised Resurrection are all expressed in Verses 6 through 11.*)

7 Hear me speedily, O LORD: my spirit fails: hide not Your face from me, lest I be like unto them who go down into the pit. (*In effect, this Verse tells us that Jesus did not go into the burning side of Hell, as some teach. As well, He did not die a lost soul, as some also teach. The Lord does not hear nor answer the prayers of a lost soul in Hell. To be sure, Jehovah heard the prayers of Christ and answered them, even while He was in the death world.*)

8 Cause me to hear Your lovingkindness in the morning; for in You do I trust: cause me to know the way wherein I should walk; for I lift up my soul unto You. (*He prayed for the Father to raise Him in the morning. And that He did!*)

9 Deliver me, O LORD, from my enemies: I flee unto You to hide me. (*Now, with the great price of Redemption paid, the Father will answer this prayer and deliver Christ from the enemy of death.*)

10 Teach me to do Your will; for You are my God: Your Spirit is good; lead me into the

land of uprightness. *(The "land of upright-ness" refers to the Resurrection.)*

11 Quicken me, O LORD, for Your name's sake: for Your righteousness' sake bring my soul out of trouble. *(The words, "quicken me," actually mean "make me alive," which refers to the Resurrection. This prayer was answered, and for "Your Name's sake.")*

12 And of Your mercy cut off my enemies, and destroy all them who afflict my soul: for I am Your servant. *(The prayer of this Verse has been answered partially; it will be answered to-tally at the conclusion of the Millennial Reign. Of that one can be sure!)*

PSALM 144

THE AUTHOR IS DAVID: I WILL SING A NEW SONG

BLESSED be the LORD my strength which teaches my hands to war, and my fingers to fight *(the time of this writing was probably after the putting down of the rebellion of Absalom [II Sam., Chpt. 18].*

The two previous Psalms, which preserve the prayer of the Messiah when in the darkness of the grave, are followed in this Psalm by the triumph and sunshine of the Resurrection and Millennial mornings. These glorious mornings are brought together here, as they are in so many Passages in the Bible.

The "fight" we are now to fight is the "good fight of Faith," and that alone [I Tim. 6:12]):

2 My goodness, and my fortress; my high tower, and my deliverer; my shield, and He in Whom I trust; Who subdues my people un-der me. *(The Lord is all of this to the Believer, and even more. To obtain this help, the Believer must simply place his Faith exclusively in Christ and what Christ has done for us at the Cross, which then gives the Holy Spirit latitude to work in our lives [Rom. 8:1-2, 11].)*

3 LORD, what is man, that You take knowl-edge of him! or the son of man, that You make account of him!

4 Man is like to vanity: his days are as a shadow that passes away. *(That the Mighty God should so concern Himself with man, who is as a breath and a shadow, as to send His Beloved Son to redeem him, fills the heart with wonder and praise.)*

5 Bow Your Heavens, O LORD, and come down: touch the mountains, and they shall smoke.

6 Cast forth lightning, and scatter them: shoot out Your arrows, and destroy them. *(David is referring here to the might and maj-esty of God, relative to His appearance on Mount Sinai [Ex. 19:16-19]. If the Lord could do all of that, then the Lord could deliver him, and so He did!)*

7 Send Your hand from above; rid me, and deliver me out of great waters, from the hand of strange children;

8 Whose mouth speaks vanity, and their right hand is a right hand of falsehood. *(David was delivered, and the Messiah was delivered. This speaks of David being placed on the Throne and Christ being Resurrected.)*

9 I will sing a new song unto You, O God: upon a psaltery and an instrument of ten strings will I sing praises unto You.

10 It is He Who gives salvation unto kings: Who delivers David His servant from the hurt-ful sword. *(In all this, David was a Type of the Messiah, Who, having been raised from the dead, promised to sing a new song on mounting His Millennial Throne.)*

11 Rid me, and deliver me from the hand of strange children, whose mouth speaks vanity, and their right hand is a right hand of false-hood *(in both Verses 7 and 11, the word "strange" is derived from a Hebrew root signifying "to know and not to know"; the Messiah's enemies in His First Advent knew Him and yet refused to know Him [Jn. 7:28]):*

12 That our sons may be as plants grown up in their youth; that our daughters may be as corner stones, polished after the similitude of a palace:

13 That our garners may be full, afford-ing all manner of store: that our sheep may bring forth thousands and ten thousands in our streets:

14 That our oxen may be strong to labour; that there be no breaking in, nor going out; that there be no complaining in our streets. *(This prayer has not yet been fulfilled in to-tality, only in part. It will be fully brought about and fulfilled when Jesus reigns in Jerusa-lem. This speaks of the Kingdom Age, which is yet to come.)*

15 Happy is that people, that is in such a case: yea, happy is that people, whose God is the LORD. *(Down through the many, vast cen-turies, men have longed for David's prayer to be answered. On that glad morning when Jesus comes back, it will then be answered, and hap-piness will be the order of the day for all people,*

everywhere, and for all time [Rev., Chpt. 19; Isa. 9:6-7].)

PSALM 145

THE AUTHOR IS DAVID:
GREAT IS THE LORD, AND GREATLY
TO BE PRAISED

I will extol You, my God, O King; and I will bless Your name for ever and ever. *(Even though this pertains to David, even more so it pertains to the Greater Son of David, Who will lead this Song on the Millennial Morn, with all enemies defeated, and the great congregation of Israel and the Glorified Saints will respond.)*

2 Every day will I bless You; and I will praise Your name for ever and ever. *(Praise to the Lord is the hallmark of every true Believer.)*

3 Great is the LORD, and greatly to be praised; and His greatness is unsearchable. *(On that Millennial morn, the world will look out upon a landscape that, for the first time in human history, is bathed in peace. The praise for such will be given to "the Lord.")*

4 One generation shall praise Your works to another, and shall declare Your mighty acts. *(In the Kingdom Age to come, the greater topic of conversation will always be "Your works" and "Your mighty acts." Thus, the conversation will not be on sports, entertainment, the stock market, etc.)*

5 I will speak of the glorious honour of Your majesty, and of Your wondrous works. *(In these Passages, Christ extols the Father, while the people extol the Messiah.)*

6 And men shall speak of the might of Your terrible acts: and I will declare Your greatness.

7 They shall abundantly utter the memory of Your great goodness, and shall sing of Your righteousness. *(In that day, men will speak of God's great Power, and also of the great Goodness of God.)*

8 The LORD is gracious, and full of compassion; slow to anger, and of great mercy.

9 The LORD is good to all: and His tender mercies are over all His works. *(Verses 8 through 9 are the Song. The Song concerns the character of Jehovah.)*

10 All Your works shall praise You, O LORD; and Your saints shall bless You. *(The great price that was paid at Calvary for the Redemption of man is called here "Your works." For that we will ever praise Him.)*

11 They shall speak of the glory of Your kingdom, and talk of Your power *(such will be the topic of all conversation)*;

12 To make known to the sons of men His mighty acts, and the glorious majesty of His kingdom. *(During the Millennial Reign, the priority of Jehovah will be the evangelization of the world.)*

13 Your kingdom is an everlasting kingdom, and Your dominion endures throughout all generations. *(This Kingdom proclaims the interpretation by Daniel of the dream which was given much later to Nebuchadnezzar [Dan. 2:44-45].)*

14 The LORD upholds all who fall, and raises up all those who be bowed down. *(Because of sin, man has ever been "bowed down." In the coming Kingdom Age, by the Power of God, he will be "raised up.")*

15 The eyes of all wait upon You; and You give them their meat in due season. *(The eyes of the whole world in that day will be directed toward the Messiah. Because of this, the Earth will then yield her increase, which will guarantee a world without hunger, want, or poverty.)*

16 You open Your hand, and satisfy the desire of every living thing. *(As Jesus touched the bread and fed the great multitudes and they were all satisfied, he will, likewise, satisfy the righteous hunger of every heart.)*

17 The LORD is righteous in all His ways, and holy in all His works. *(In that coming day, the entirety of the world will admit that "His Ways" are right and "His Works" are Holy.)*

18 The LORD is near unto all them who call upon Him, to all who call upon Him in truth. *(In this Passage, we are told that all of the servants of God may presently foretaste, on a personal basis, in their hearts the sweetness and power of Christ's future perfect Earthly government.)*

19 He will fulfill the desire of them who fear Him: He also will hear their cry, and will save them. *(Not only will the Lord do this in the coming Kingdom Age, but also, and as always, He will do so now, that is, if men will only believe Him.)*

20 The LORD preserves all them who love Him: but all the wicked will He destroy. *(This tells us that in the end Righteousness will prevail.)*

21 My mouth shall speak the praise of the LORD: and let all flesh bless His holy name for ever and ever. *(This was David's commitment; it should be our commitment as well. However, its greater fulfillment will come during the Kingdom Age.)*

PSALM 146

AUTHOR UNKNOWN:
PRAISE TO GOD, MIGHTY CREATOR

PRAISE ye the LORD. Praise the LORD, O my soul. (*As the five Books of the Psalms correspond to the five Books of the Pentateuch, so the five closing Hallelujah Psalms also correspond. This Psalm is, therefore, the "Genesis Psalm." It recalls the forming of man and the creation of the worlds.*)

2 While I live will I praise the LORD: I will sing praises unto my God while I have any being. (*Each Psalm begins and ends in the Hebrew Text with the word, "Hallelujah." They will be sung by the happy subjects of Christ's future Kingdom.*)

3 Put not your trust in princes, nor in the son of man, in whom there is no help.

4 His breath goes forth, he returns to his Earth; in that very day his thoughts perish. (*The great struggle in the Christian is always concerning the trusting of man or God. These very Verses tell us that modern, humanistic psychology holds no help.*)

5 Happy is he who has the God of Jacob for his help, whose hope is in the LORD his God. (*The singer contrasts man and the Messiah, showing the inability of the one and the sufficiency of The Other as the Saviour. Thus, man: faithless, powerless, and mortal; Messiah: Faithful, All-Powerful, Eternal.*

The Old Testament title, "God of Jacob," corresponds to the New Testament title, "God of all Grace." He met Jacob when he deserved nothing and promised him everything.)

6 Which made Heaven, and Earth, the sea, and all that therein is: which keeps truth for ever (*Verses 6 through 10 contrast what God can do versus what man can do*):

7 Which executes judgment for the oppressed: which gives food to the hungry. The LORD looses the prisoners (*God uses His Power to lift up man and set him free, while man, if he has any power, generally uses it to enrich himself*):

8 The LORD opens the eyes of the blind: the LORD raises them who are bowed down: the LORD loves the righteous (*since this Passage is very similar to Verse 14 of the previous Psalm, and inasmuch as David wrote that Psalm, quite possibly he wrote this one, as well*):

9 The LORD preserves the strangers; He relieves the fatherless and widow: but the way of the wicked He turns upside down. (*All*

that is portrayed in these Passages could have been the way of Earth for all these millennia. Instead, man, in his rebellion, has made it mostly a Hell instead of a Heaven. However, the "way of the wicked" is just about over, and then "the Way of the Lord" will be the covering of the entire world.*)

10 The LORD shall reign for ever, even your God, O Zion, unto all generations, Praise ye the LORD. (*This Kingdom that is soon to come will not be the government of man, which comes and goes, but will, in effect, last forever.*)

PSALM 147

AUTHOR UNKNOWN:
GREAT IS OUR GOD

PRAISE ye the LORD: for it is good to sing praises unto our God; for it is pleasant, and praise is comely. (*As Psalm 146 was a symbol of the Book of Genesis, likewise, this Psalm is symbolic of the Book of Exodus, which portrays Israel's great Deliverance, and which points to her even greater Deliverance from the Antichrist in the coming Great Tribulation. This is a Millennial Song, which will be sung on that Millennial Morn.*)

2 The LORD does build up Jerusalem: He gathers together the outcasts of Israel. (*Israel, for nearly 2,000 years, has lived as "outcasts" all over the world. In the coming Kingdom Age, all of that will change.*)

3 He heals the broken in heart, and binds up their wounds. (*When Jesus healed the man born blind [Jn., Chpt. 9], this was a type of Israel in her blindness and Israel which will wash and finally be able to see. Again, this will take place in the coming Kingdom Age.*)

4 He tells the number of the stars; he calls them all by their names. (*If we take this literally, and we certainly should, this means that God calls all the stars by name.*

In the 1950's, astronomers claimed that there were about 40 sextillion stars in the vast universe, which are suns to other planets. They have presently increased that number, but have left it open-ended. [Forty sextillion is the number 40 followed by twenty-one zeros.] At any rate, God knows the exact number, for He made them [Isa. 45:18].

It is said that there are approximately 500,000 words in Webster's Unabridged Dictionary. If all the names of all the stars were put in books of this size, it would take 80 quadrillion books

to list the name of every star. *[Eighty quadrillion is the number 80 followed by 15 zeros.])*

5 Great is our LORD, and of great power; His understanding is infinite. *(Considering Verse 4, the phrase, "Great is our LORD," has to be summed up as a gross understatement.)*

6 The LORD lifts up the meek: He casts the wicked down to the ground. *(The strict interpretation of this Passage portrays Israel as "the meek." The Antichrist is portrayed as "the wicked.")*

7 Sing unto the LORD with thanksgiving; sing praise upon the harp unto our God *(the Millennial Reign, in which this Song will be sung, will be a time of music)*:

8 Who covers the Heaven with clouds, Who prepares rain for the Earth, Who makes grass to grow upon the mountains. *(We have here the regulation by God of His Creation.)*

9 He gives to the beast his food, and to the young ravens which cry. *(The animal kingdom is portrayed here as not only created by God, but, as well, superintended by God.)*

10 He delights not in the strength of the horse: He takes not pleasure in the legs of a man. *(The sense of this Passage is that God takes no delight in those things in which man trusts.)*

11 The LORD takes pleasure in them who fear Him, in those who hope in His mercy. *(If we want to know what pleases God, we find it in this Verse.)*

12 Praise the LORD, O Jerusalem; praise your God, O Zion. *(Now restored Israel can truly praise the Lord.)*

13 For He has strengthened the bars of your gates; He has blessed your children within you. *(Israel could have had this at the First Advent, but their rejection of Christ destroyed the "bars of their gates." Their acceptance of Christ at the beginning of the Kingdom Age will restore all that has been lost.)*

14 He makes peace in your borders, and fills you with the finest of the wheat. *(God delights in giving good things to His children.)*

15 He sends forth His Commandment upon Earth: His Word runs very swiftly. *("His Commandment" is the Bible. Within its pages is the wisdom of the ages. It alone contains the only Revealed Truth in the world today and, in fact, ever has been.)*

16 He gives snow like wool: He scatters the hoarfrost like ashes. *(All of this is superintended by God.)*

17 He casts forth His ice like morsels: who can stand before His cold? *(All of this functions according to God's Word.)*

18 He sends out His Word, and melts them: He causes His wind to blow, and the waters flow. *(We are told here that everything is held up by the glorious and beauteous Word of God. This means that the world does not have to fear a coming "greenhouse" effect, etc.)*

19 He shows His Word unto Jacob, His Statutes and His Judgments unto Israel. *(His election of Israel as the depository of His Word and as the channel of its communication to the world moved both Moses and Paul to wonder and worship [Deut. 4:8; Rom. 3:2; 11:33].)*

20 He has not dealt so with any nation: and as for His Judgments, they have not known them. Praise ye the LORD. *(Israel was chosen by God to give the world the Word of God, which they did, and to serve as the womb of the Messiah, which they also did. They were also destined to evangelize the world, which they have not yet done, but will do in the coming Kingdom Age [Isa. 66:19-20].)*

PSALM 148

AUTHOR UNKNOWN:
LET ALL CREATION PRAISE GOD

PRAISE ye the LORD. Praise ye the LORD from the heavens: praise Him in the heights. *(This is the third of the five Hallelujah Psalms. It corresponds to the Leviticus Book of the Pentateuch, and as such ordains Worship as the subject of that Book. The reach of this worship is vast. It reaches from the depths beneath the Earth [Vs. 7[to the heights above the heavens.)*

2 Praise ye Him, all His angels: praise ye Him, all His Hosts. *(In the coming Kingdom Age, for the first time, the entirety of God's vast creation will praise Him and continue to praise Him.)*

3 Praise ye Him, sun and moon: praise Him, all ye stars of light.

4 Praise Him, ye Heavens of Heavens, and ye waters that be above the Heavens. *(All these things praise Him by functioning in the orderly manner in which they were created.)*

5 Let them praise the Name of the LORD: for He commanded, and they were created.

6 He has also stablished them for ever and ever: He has made a decree which shall not pass. *(This present Earth little recognizes such. Instead, school children are taught the mindless drivel of evolution as the origin of all things.*

To the contrary, on the coming Kingdom Day, the entirety of the world will know and understand Who God is, what He has done, and His greatness.)

7 Praise the LORD from the Earth, you dragons, and all deeps:

8 Fire, and hail; snow, and vapours; stormy wind fulfilling His Word:

9 Mountains, and all hills; fruitful trees, and all cedars:

10 Beasts, and all cattle; creeping things, and flying fowl *(then, and we speak of the coming Kingdom Age, all creation will function exactly as God originally intended, which will be different than the present time, because the Fall has adversely affected everything):*

11 Kings of the Earth, and all people; princes, and all judges of the Earth:

12 Both young men, and maidens; old men, and children *(these two Verses speak of all people, both small and great, praising the Lord):*

13 Let them praise the Name of the LORD: for His Name alone is excellent; His glory is above the Earth and Heaven.

14 He also exalts the horn of his people, the praise of all His saints; even of the children of Israel, a people near unto Him. Praise ye the LORD. *(Verse 14 reveals that this Mighty God, Whom both the heavens and the Earth are eternally to adore, is the Messiah, the God of Israel. The heavens are to adore Him because He created them, and He maintains them. At long last, and we speak of the Kingdom Age, the Earth will follow suit.*

The phrase, "the Earth and Heaven," is noteworthy. This order is only found here and in Gen. 2:4. It is connected with the Divine title, "Jehovah Elohim" [the Eternal Creator]. This title, as it occurs in Gen. 2:4 and Verse 13 [the LORD], expresses God's relationship as a Redeeming Saviour. The Earth is, therefore, made to precede the heavens.)

PSALM 149

AUTHOR UNKNOWN: LET ALL THE SAINTS PRAISE GOD

PRAISE ye the LORD. Sing unto the LORD a new song, and His praise in the congregation of Saints. *(This is the fourth Hallelujah Psalm and corresponds to the Book of Numbers. At the close of that Book, Israel stood at the entrance of Canaan, her brows wreathed with the victory over the Moabites and the Amorites.*

In this Psalm, she stands at the entrance of the Millennial Kingdom, crowned with victory over the Antichrist and the False Prophet.

The "new song" can be entered into, because there has been a "new creation" [II Cor. 5:17].)

2 Let Israel rejoice in Him Who made him: let the children of Zion be joyful in their King. *(The whole of this Passage is a prophetical prayer for God's People and applies to their Restoration and reign with the Messiah.)*

3 Let them praise His Name in the dance: let them sing praises unto Him with the timbrel and harp. *(Israel's worship was always demonstrative.)*

4 For the LORD takes pleasure in His people: He will beautify the meek with salvation. *(The last phrase could be translated, "He will adorn the meek with victory." "Meekness" is the criteria, which can only be reached by one's Faith being placed entirely in Christ and the Cross [Mat. 11:28-30].)*

5 Let the Saints be joyful in glory: let them sing aloud upon their beds. *(The word "beds," or couches of glory, here refer to "thrones." In one sense, this section [Vss. 5-9] foretells the efficiency, the piety, and the equity of the Government which Israel will exercise over the nations of the Earth.)*

6 Let the high praises of God be in their mouth, and a two-edged sword in their hand *(this Government will be efficient because of the two-edged sword; it will be pious, for the high praises of God will be in their mouths; it will be just, for it will exact vengeance; it will be impartial, for it will bind kings; it will be legal, for it will execute the judgment written in the Statute Books of Heaven);*

7 To execute vengeance upon the heathen, and punishments upon the people;

8 To bind their kings with chains, and their nobles with fetters of iron;

9 To execute upon them the judgment written: this honour have all His saints. Praise ye the LORD. *(In the coming glorious day of the Millennial Reign, the twelve Apostles will sit upon twelve Thrones judging the twelve Tribes of Israel. As is evident, Israel will sit on thrones judging the nations of the Earth, along with the glorified Saints. In the Millennium, the nations of the Earth will be allocated by God in correspondence with and in relation to the boundaries of the sons of Jacob [Deut. 32:8].*

That the Church will reign with Christ is plainly taught in Scripture as well [II Tim. 2:12; Rev. 5:10].)

PSALM 150

AUTHOR UNKNOWN:
FINAL DOXOLOGY

PRAISE ye the LORD. Praise God in His Sanctuary: praise Him in the firmament of His power. (*This is the fifth and, therefore, last Hallelujah Psalm. As well, it should be described as the "Deuteronomy Psalm" of the Deuteronomy Book.*

In this glad day of the Kingdom Age, with Christ reigning supreme in Jerusalem, praise will be offered unto God continually all over the world.

The Divine titles in this Psalm are "El" and "Jah." "El" is essentially the Almighty, and "Jah" signifies the Ever-existing One, for example, Jesus Christ, the same yesterday, today, and forever.)

2 Praise Him for His mighty acts: praise Him according to His excellent greatness. (*The theme of praise will be twofold: 1. What He does — His mighty Acts and 2. What He is — His excellent Greatness. These express His Glory as Creator, as Redeemer, as the Lamb of God, and as the Son of God. The scene of worship in the Book of Revelation is Heaven; in this Psalm, it is the Earth in unison with Heaven.*)

3 Praise Him with the sound of the trumpet: praise Him with the psaltery and harp.

4 Praise Him with the timbrel and dance: Praise Him with stringed instruments and organs.

5 Praise Him upon the loud cymbals: praise Him upon the high sounding cymbals. (*These praises portray to us the fact that the worship is not only spontaneous, but orchestrated, exactly as it is now in praise and worship. By and large, the musicians of the world have formerly dedicated their talents to the Evil One. Now these talents will be dedicated exclusively to God's Glory.*)

6 Let every thing that has breath praise the LORD. Praise ye the LORD. (*The very first Psalm calls the Messiah "the Blessed Man." In this last Psalm He is worshipped as "the Blessed God." All of the 148 intervening Psalms sing of the countless perfections of His Nature and of His Actions, as both Son of Man and Son of God.*

The cry here is that everything that has breath must praise the Lord. In the coming Kingdom Age, this will be brought about. Men will have nothing but praise for Him.

The Book of Psalms assures this. Its pages are wet with tears, and its music broken with sighs, but its last Song is a burst of satisfied rapture. Its five Volumes fitly close with a loud "Hallelujah!")

THE
PROVERBS

CHAPTER 1
(1000 B.C.)
TITLE

THE proverbs of Solomon the son of David, king of Israel (*the Wisdom in this Book is not human sagacity, cleverness, or ability, but the application to the smallest details of human life of the Wisdom that built the Heavens and the Earth and maintains them in being*);

PURPOSE OF THE BOOK

2 To know wisdom and instruction; to perceive the words of understanding (*the theme of this Verse is "to know"; that which we are instructed to know could be categorized as "the Bible," which is "Wisdom"*);

3 To receive the instruction of wisdom, justice, and judgment, and equity (*the theme of this Verse is "to receive"; therefore, if we "know" the Bible, we will then "receive" its instruction*);

4 To give subtilty to the simple, to the young man knowledge and discretion. (*If we "know" the Bible and then "receive" its instruction, we will then be able to "give" the benefit of our knowledge to others.*)

5 A wise man will hear, and will increase learning; and a man of understanding shall attain unto wise counsels (*if we know the Bible, the Holy Spirit then considers us "wise," and we will, thereby, continue to "increase learning" through His wise counsels*):

6 To understand a proverb, and the interpretation; the words of the wise, and their dark sayings. (*The natural man receives not the things of the Spirit [I Cor. 2:14]. Therefore, we are told in the following Verse how this understanding can come about.*)

A WARNING

7 The fear of the LORD is the beginning of knowledge: but fools despise wisdom and instruction. (*So, the beginning of this God-breathed road is "the fear of the LORD." Men do not fear Him because most do not believe Him.*)

8 My son, hear the instruction of your father, and forsake not the law of your mother:

9 For they shall be an ornament of grace unto your head, and chains about your neck. (*The Book opens with a double statement that fear of God [Vs. 7] and obedience to parents form the foundation of a just relationship to God and man.*

Chains of gold about the neck indicate political dignity; therefore, the sense of the Passage is that rulership of men must be preceded by fidelity to God's Commands, showing consecration of parents to God's Word, and submission by children to Godly parents.)

10 My son, if sinners entice you, consent thou not. (*This tells us that if parents have not been properly guided by the Word that they may properly instruct their sons and daughters, then the enticement of sinners will be successful in its allurement; this, sadly, is the lot of most.*)

11 If they say, Come with us, let us lay wait for blood, let us lurk privily for the innocent without cause (*Verses 11 through 14 suggest the evil enticement fomented by Satan that lurks in the path of every young man and young lady. To be sure, these enticements are deadly, characterized by the words "blood," "grave," and "the pit"*):

12 Let us swallow them up alive as the grave; and whole, as those who go down into the pit (*as a result of lacking the Wisdom of God, the land is filled with blood, the graves cannot be dug fast enough, and Hell opens her mouth without measure*):

13 We shall find all precious substance, we shall fill our houses with spoil (*Satan lies, and men love to believe his lies; he is the master of deception; there is no precious substance that can be obtained by such measures; and, if there is, it brings no satisfaction*):

14 Cast in your lot among us; let us all have one purse (*this "purse" carries wages of sin, which is death*):

15 My son, walk not thou in the way with them; refrain your foot from their path (*the reference is that it is impossible to make the right decision concerning the right path unless the solidity of the Bible is our foundation*):

16 For their feet run to evil, and make haste to shed blood (*the spirit of this Passage ensconces itself in the heart of every Bible rejecter*).

17 Surely in vain the net is spread in the

sight of any bird *(the argument of this Verse is that as a bird with its eyes open flies into a net spread for its destruction, so evil men rush with their eyes wide open into death).*

18 And they lay wait for their own blood; they lurk privily for their own lives *(they seek to kill others for ill-gotten gain; in the killing of others, they also kill themselves).*

19 So are the ways of every one who is greedy of gain; which takes away the life of the owners thereof *(the far greater majority of the world is "greedy of gain," and will do anything up to and including murder to accomplish their purpose).*

WISDOM SPEAKS

20 Wisdom cries without; she utters her voice in the streets *(in Lk. 7:35, the Lord Jesus says, "Wisdom is justified of all her children"; the Wisdom who speaks here to Solomon and to all men invites them to become her sons):*

21 She cries in the chief place of concourse, in the openings of the gates: in the city she utters her words, saying *(although Righteousness is not nearly as proliferated as evil, still, the crying of Wisdom which God gives is ample enough that it will appeal even to the "simple"),*

22 How long, you simple ones, will you love simplicity? and the scorners delight in their scorning, and fools hate knowledge? *(The terms, "simple," "scorner," and "fool," mark regression. The man who treats Wisdom with good humor and polite inattention presently becomes a mocker and finally a hater.*

So it was with the Pharisees and the rulers of the Synagogue. At first, they politely permitted the Lord to read the Scriptures in the Synagogue and to preach; but very soon they began to mock Him; and, finally, they hated and crucified Him.)

23 Turn you at My reproof: behold, I will pour out My Spirit unto you, I will make known My Words unto you. *(Wisdom speaks and pleads with the frivolous, the mockers, and the hostile, promising them that if they would "turn," she would abundantly enrich them with her own spirit and with understanding. But such is conditional upon conversion, and conversion is repugnant to man, because it humbles him.)*

24 Because I have called, and you refused; I have stretched out My hand, and no man regarded *(the whole of humanity is set apart in two camps: those who follow God-given Wisdom, i.e., the Bible, and those who reject God-given Wisdom);*

25 But you have set at nought all My counsel, and would none of My reproof *(the implication is that man willingly and deliberately sets aside "God's counsel"; then the "reproofs" come; they are but signposts directing our attention to the coming catastrophe; most mock and continue on):*

26 I also will laugh at your calamity; I will mock when your fear comes *(this Verse does not mean that Wisdom will actually deride her rejecters; it is the language of idiomatic argument; the rejecters laughed and mocked at Wisdom; when, therefore, calamities came upon them, which Wisdom predicted, their laughter and mocking turned upon themselves, and so Wisdom may be justly said to deride their calamity);*

27 When your fear comes as desolation, and your destruction comes as a whirlwind; when distress and anguish comes upon you. *(Some may argue that such does not come to all who ignore God; however, they are only looking at the physical and the material. Spiritually, it is definite.)*

28 Then shall they call upon Me, but I will not answer; they shall seek Me early, but they shall not find Me *(while it is certainly true that God will hear any and all who earnestly cry out to Him, still, the sense of this Passage is that a late call cannot undo the irreparable harm done in a misspent life):*

29 For that they hated knowledge, and did not choose the fear of the LORD *(there is a "choice" that everyone has to make; those who "choose" the wrong path do so because they "hate knowledge," i.e., "the Bible"):*

30 They would none of My counsel: they despised all My reproof. *(The almost identical repetition of this Passage from Verse 25 is not by accident, but by design. If men reject the "counsel" of God and "despise His reproof," then the following Passage must come to pass.)*

31 Therefore shall they eat of the fruit of their own way, and be filled with their own devices. *(Man's problem is "his own way" and "his own devices." It is either God's Way, which brings life, or our way, which brings death.)*

32 For the turning away of the simple shall slay them, and the prosperity of fools shall destroy them. *(The "simple" turns away from God and is, thereby, destroyed. Likewise, the "prosperity of fools" does not bring the gain that they anticipated in Verse 19, but instead destruction.)*

33 But whoso hearkens unto Me shall dwell safely, and shall be quiet from fear of evil. *(In this First Chapter of Proverbs, written by Solomon, we are given the blueprint for living: God's Way versus our way. Those who listen to Him shall "dwell safely" and shall have no "fear.")*

CHAPTER 2
(1000 B.C.)
THE BLESSINGS AND REWARDS OF HEEDING WISDOM

MY son, if you will receive My Words, and hide My Commandments with you *(God gives His "Words" and "Commandments," but does not force men to receive them)*;

2 So that you incline your ear unto wisdom, and apply your heart to understanding *(the words "incline" and "apply" simply speak of priority)*;

3 Yea, if you cry after knowledge, and lift up your voice for understanding *(this speaks of a conscious unending effort that sets one's heart to earnestly seek for God's "knowledge" and "understanding")*;

4 If you seek her as silver, and search for her as for hid treasures *(the Holy Spirit points to the earnest efforts of men in seeking wealth; if one will do the same in seeking after the things of God, our quest will not be fruitless, as it is for the far greater majority of those who seek for gold)*;

5 Then shall you understand the fear of the LORD, and find the knowledge of God. *(The "knowledge of God" is the Bible.)*

6 For the LORD gives wisdom: out of His mouth comes knowledge and understanding. *(If we do what the Lord has told us to do, He will give what He has promised.)*

7 He lays up sound wisdom for the righteous: He is a buckler to them who walk uprightly. *("Sound wisdom" is from God. All the wisdom of the world is sensual and is, therefore, devilish [James 3:15]. Consequently, it can only destroy.)*

8 He keeps the paths of judgment, and preserves the way of His Saints. *(The added bonus of those who have the Wisdom of God is that God watches over and protects all such Disciples.)*

9 Then shall you understand righteousness, and judgment, and equity; yea, every good path. *(Verse 3 in the previous Chapter says that we would "receive" such, with this Passage saying that we would "understand" such.)*

10 When wisdom enters into your heart, and knowledge is pleasant unto your soul;

11 Discretion shall preserve you, understanding shall keep you *(how little "discretion" and "understanding" we have today, even in the ranks of the Church)*:

12 To deliver you from the way of the evil man, from the man who speaks froward things *(the sense of this Passage is that the world is filled with such a vortex of evil that it is impossible not to be sucked into this maelstrom without the "Wisdom" and "Knowledge" that God Alone gives)*;

13 Who leave the paths of uprightness, to walk in the ways of darkness;

14 Who rejoice to do evil, and delight in the frowardness of the wicked;

15 Whose ways are crooked, and they froward in their paths *(actually, this characterizes the entirety of the world — "crooked"; conversely, only that which is of God is "straight")*:

16 To deliver you from the strange woman, even from the stranger which flatters with her words;

17 Which forsakes the guide of her youth, and forgets the covenant of her God.

18 For her house inclines unto death, and her paths unto the dead.

19 None who go unto her return again, neither take they hold of the paths of life. *(The Hebrew word for "strange woman" is "zur," which means an apostate or foreign religion. Religious teachers who lead people away from the Scriptures are likened in these Passages to women who are faithless to their husbands.*

The words, "strange" and "stranger," are different in the Hebrew Text. The first means "apostate"; the second, "foreign." They suggest that a faithless wife ceases to be of Israel and makes herself an alien.)

20 That you may walk in the way of good men, and keep the paths of the righteous. *(In this Chapter, we have "evil men," "strange women," and now "good men." The choice is ours. What shall it be?)*

21 For the upright shall dwell in the land, and the perfect shall remain in it. *(The "upright" and the "perfect" is Christ.)*

22 But the wicked shall be cut off from the Earth, and the transgressors shall be rooted out of it. *(Both Verses 21 and 22 allude to the coming Kingdom Age, and to every Child of God who can claim by faith the glory and the possession of these glad promises, even now.)*

CHAPTER 3
(1000 B.C.)

AN EXHORTATION TO OBEDIENCE

MY son, forget not My Law; but let your heart keep My Commandments:

2 For length of days, and long life, and peace, shall they add to you. (*In Chapter 1 we have the foundation laid for true prosperity and life, which is Wisdom. This Wisdom is the Word of God.*

Chapter 2 tells us how to receive such.

Chapter 3 now tells us that when prosperity comes, we must not forget from whence it came — "forget not My Law.")

3 Let not mercy and truth forsake you: bind them about your neck; write them upon the table of your heart:

4 So shall you find favour and good understanding in the sight of God and man. (*The Holy Spirit is informing us here that finding favor with God must come first. If such is done with God, it will automatically come about with man. Too often, religious man seeks to find favor with other religious men. The end result is that favor is ultimately found with neither God nor man.*)

5 Trust in the LORD with all your heart; and lean not unto your own understanding.

6 In all your ways acknowledge Him, and He shall direct your paths. (*Man's problem has always been man's will, whether Christian or otherwise. In these Passages, we are told here that we do not have the self-sufficiency to run this race alone.*)

7 Be not wise in your own eyes: fear the LORD, and depart from evil.

8 It shall be health to your navel, and marrow to your bones. (*The phrase, "Be not wise in your own eyes," is, as we have mentioned in the previous Passage, the bane, blight, and terminal flaw of man.*)

9 Honour the LORD with your substance, and with the firstfruits of all your increase:

10 So shall your barns be filled with plenty, and your presses shall burst out with new wine. (*The word "firstfruits" speaks of the tenth, and, therefore, tithing. Tithing is carried over into the New Testament, as well. The Melchizedek Priesthood is eternal and must be supported by the children of Abraham, which include every Believer [Heb. 6:20; 7:1-11].*)

11 My son, despise not the chastening of the LORD; neither be weary of His correction:

12 For whom the LORD loves He corrects; even as a father the son in whom he delights. (*We find from this Text that Wisdom shows her love as much in rebuking as in enriching.*)

13 Happy is the man who finds wisdom, and the man who gets understanding. (*Happiness and joy are two different things. The first pertains to externals and can, therefore, be enjoyed even by the ungodly. The latter pertains to that which is within, and can only be enjoyed by those who know the Lord and, thereby, have this precious Fruit of the Spirit [Gal. 5:22-23].*)

14 For the merchandise of it is better than the merchandise of silver, and the gain thereof than fine gold. (*Precious few, even Christians, understand that knowledge of the Word of God is of more value than even silver and gold.*)

15 She is more precious than rubies: and all the things you can desire are not to be compared unto her. (*Most, if not all, Christians would agree with this statement, but yet they little believe it in their hearts. If they did, they would devote more attention to this all-important aspect of life — the study of the Word.*)

16 Length of days is in her right hand; and in her left hand riches and honour. (*The Holy Spirit is telling us here that the very thing we think we must spend all of our time and attention to acquire, namely silver and gold, will, in fact, come to us if we will place the Word of God first!*)

17 Her ways are ways of pleasantness, and all her paths are peace. (*Most everything that one does in life has its negatives; however, the Holy Spirit tells us here that the study and pursuit of the Word of God has no negatives whatsoever.*)

18 She is a tree of life to them who lay hold upon her: and happy is every one who retains her. (*The phrase, "tree of life," is interesting. It is spoken of in Gen. 2:9, and portrays man's losing access to it. It is spoken of again in the Book of Revelation [Rev. 2:7; 22:2, 14]; it is there regained. Therefore, between the loss and the restoration, we are given this Promise of access. The key is the Bible.*)

19 The LORD by wisdom has founded the Earth; by understanding has He established the Heavens.

20 By His knowledge the depths are broken up, and the clouds drop down the dew. (*This Wisdom delights to order and prosper the smallest details of a man's private and public life.*)

21 My son, let not them depart from your eyes: keep sound wisdom and discretion:

22 So shall they be life unto your soul, and grace to your neck. (*In effect, this tells us that*

what the soul is truly looking for, and that alone which will satisfy, is the Bible. For in the Bible, and in the Bible alone, are found all of these attributes.)

23 Then shall you walk in your way safely, and your foot shall not stumble. (Billions of dollars are spent each year on seminars, convocations, and motivational clinics that try to do what this Passage promises. All fail, because God and His Word Alone give the security that the heart craves.)

24 When you lie down, you shall not be afraid: yea, you shall lie down, and your sleep shall be sweet. (The safety, security, and well-being that one craves can only be derived by going God's Way. His Way is His Word.)

25 Be not afraid of sudden fear, neither of the desolation of the wicked, when it comes.

26 For the LORD shall be your confidence, and shall keep your foot from being taken. (The Word of God not only guards from stumbling, but delivers from fear by keeping the soul in fellowship with God.)

TREATMENT OF NEIGHBORS

27 Withhold not good from them to whom it is due, when it is in the power of your hand to do it. (This is the kindness that all Christians should show to other Christians, and even to the wicked, for that matter. It is the Spirit of Christ that should characterize all of the Godly.)

28 Say not unto your neighbour, Go, and come again, and to morrow I will give; when you have it by you. (This Passage is very much akin to the Sermon on the Mount [Mat. 5:42].)

29 Devise not evil against your neighbour, seeing he dwells securely by you. (In essence, the Lord addressed this Text [Mat. 5:44].)

30 Strive not with a man without cause, if he have done you no harm. (The idea here is "without cause.")

31 Envy thou not the oppressor, and choose none of his ways. (The spirit of "oppression" characterizes the human family. Too often Christians choose the "ways" of the oppressor, thinking to get gain. Wrong choice!)

32 For the froward is abomination to the LORD: but His secret is with the righteous. (The word "froward" means "perverse" or "one who turns aside." This refers to one who follows his own ways, instead of God's Ways.)

33 The curse of the LORD is in the house of the wicked: but He blesses the habitation of the just. (The sense of this Passage is that the "curse of the LORD" is in the house of the wicked the world over, and for all time. As well, a Christian can bring such a curse upon himself by forsaking the True Word of God, and embracing false doctrine [Gal. 1:8-9].)

34 Surely He scorns the scorners: but He gives grace unto the lowly. (This is another one of the many Passages in the Bible that tell us that God greatly opposes pride, while giving Grace to the humble. He will not give Grace to the proud. Therefore, Paul was numbered, as would be obvious, with the "lowly" [II Cor. 12:9].)

35 The wise shall inherit glory: but shame shall be the promotion of fools. (The wise shall "inherit," not "merit," glory. Fools, clothed with shame, shall "merit" judgment and go into everlasting contempt [Dan. 12:2].)

CHAPTER 4
(1000 B.C.)
A FATHER'S WISDOM AND ADVICE

HEAR, you children, the instruction of a father, and attend to know understanding. (We will now learn the source of this great Wisdom, which will prove extremely interesting.)

2 For I give you good doctrine, forsake ye not my law.

3 For I was my father's son, tender and only beloved in the sight of my mother. (Solomon was speaking of his father, David, and his mother, Bath-sheba. He claims to have received the "doctrine" and the "Law" from David; therefore, in these Passages we have the manner in which the Holy Spirit chose regarding Solomon's great Wisdom. Along with what David taught him, which, of course, was generated by the Holy Spirit, likewise, the Lord gave Solomon the great Gift of Wisdom [I Ki. 3:9-15].)

4 He taught me also, and said unto me, Let your heart retain my words: keep my commandments, and live. (Solomon recalls the countless hours that David painstakingly taught him the Ways of the Lord.)

5 Get wisdom, get understanding: forget it not; neither decline from the words of my mouth. (This "Wisdom" consisted of what David taught his son, Solomon, which was derived from the Word of God. At this time, David would have had as his Bible the Pentateuch [Genesis through Deuteronomy], as well as Joshua, Judges, and possibly Ruth. There is every evidence that Solomon was well versed in the great Law of Moses.)

6 Forsake her not, and she shall preserve

you: love her, and she shall keep you. *(Solomon would heed these words for the greater part of his life; however, in the latter part of his reign, he would do what David had admonished him not to do, which was to forget and forsake the Ways of the Lord [I Ki. 11:4].)*

7 Wisdom is the principal thing; therefore get wisdom: and with all your getting get understanding. *(There are six different Hebrew words translated "Wisdom." We have likened "Wisdom" and the "Bible" as one and the same; however, in the strict and narrow interpretation of the word, this would not be totally correct. It would more so apply to the comprehension and understanding of the Bible. Still, without the Bible, there can be no Wisdom.)*

8 Exalt her, and she shall promote you: she shall bring you to honour, when you do embrace her.

9 She shall give to your head an ornament of grace: a crown of glory shall she deliver to you. *(Without fail, we are told that "Wisdom" [the Bible] will fulfill the cry of the human heart. It is sad when even the Church little exalts the Bible, but, rather, promotes the works of man.)*

10 Hear, O my son, and receive my sayings; and the years of your life shall be many. *(While it is certainly true that things seen with the eye are important, still, the way the Gospel is imparted is by the hearing of the ear [Mat. 11:15].)*

11 I have taught you in the way of wisdom; I have led you in right paths. *(The "Way of Wisdom" and the "Right Paths" are the Bible. The tragedy is that no one but Christ has ever faithfully walked the "Right Paths.")*

12 When you go, your steps shall not be straitened; and when you run, you shall not stumble. *(This Verse should read, "When you walk" and "if you run." To walk is obligatory; to run is optional. Wisdom secures both. When walking, the way opens — it is not "straitened"; if running, the feet are guarded from stumbling [Jude, Vs. 24].)*

13 Take fast hold of instruction; let her not go: keep her; for she is your life. *(This refers to the Truth that the Bible, and the Bible alone, holds the secret of eternal life.)*

14 Enter not into the path of the wicked, and go not in the way of evil men. *(The inference is that "the path of the wicked" constantly beckons.)*

15 Avoid it, pass not by it, turn from it, and pass away. *(The Holy Spirit is emphatic in giving us a fourfold warning.)*

16 For they sleep not, except they have done mischief; and their sleep is taken away, unless they cause some to fall. *(We are told here that spiritual vigilance is ever required.)*

17 For they eat the bread of wickedness, and drink the wine of violence. *(Such who follow this path of evil always conclude in "wickedness" and "violence.")*

18 But the path of the just is as the shining light, that shines more and more unto the perfect day. *(The Word of God alone leads to that "perfect day.")*

19 The way of the wicked is as darkness: they know not at what they stumble. *(The Bible is the only Light [Ps. 119:105]. Everything else is darkness, irrespective of its claims, and induces stumbling.)*

20 My son, attend to my words; incline your ear unto my sayings.

21 Let them not depart from your eyes; keep them in the midst of your heart. *(We are admonished here to continue to read the Bible and to study it daily. As well, its teachings are to embed themselves into our hearts.)*

22 For they are life unto those who find them, and health to all their flesh. *(In these Passages, we learn the secret of life. The Word of God is "Life" and "Health.")*

23 Keep your heart with all diligence; for out of it are the issues of life. *(The "issues of life" speak of the Foundation of the Faith, which is "Jesus Christ and Him Crucified" [I Cor. 1:23].)*

24 Put away from you a froward mouth, and perverse lips put far from you. *(The word "froward" means to be habitually disposed toward disobedience and opposition to the Word of God. The word "perverse" means basically the same. So we are told here not to question the Bible, find fault with it, or oppose it.)*

25 Let your eyes look right on, and let your eyelids look straight before you. *(Irrespective of the attractions that may try to draw us away, our "eyes" must continue to look to the Word of God.)*

26 Ponder the path of your feet, and let all your ways be established.

27 Turn not to the right hand nor to the left: remove your foot from evil. *(The word "ponder" means to "prayerfully weigh," that is, not to enter hastily upon any course of conduct.)*

CHAPTER 5
(1000 B.C.)

WARNINGS AGAINST THE PURVEYORS OF FALSE DOCTRINE

MY son, attend unto my wisdom, and bow your ear to my understanding:

2 That you may regard discretion, and that your lips may keep knowledge. *(Wisdom and understanding are distinct, one from the other. Understanding is the discrimination which recognizes Wisdom. A child, not having understanding, cannot discriminate between a glass ball and a diamond. So, to discern between the gaudy glass of folly and the simple beauty of Wisdom, understanding is needed.)*

3 For the lips of a strange woman drop as an honeycomb, and her mouth is smoother than oil:

4 But her end is bitter as wormwood, sharp as a two edged sword.

5 Her feet go down to death; her steps take hold on Hell.

6 Lest you should ponder the path of life, her ways are moveable, that you can not know them. *(Wisdom [the Bible], the true Woman, pictures true Salvation; the strange woman represents false religion. The strange woman [apostasy] is Wisdom's enemy and rival.*

The teaching of the inspired Scriptures always has been, and is, unacceptable to man. False teaching [I Jn. 4:5] has been, and is, to him as the droppings of a honeycomb, but the honey is poisoned and ends in death.)

7 Hear me now therefore, O ye children, and depart not from the words of my mouth. *(Over and over again, warnings are given concerning departure from the Word of God.)*

8 Remove your way far from her, and come not near the door of her house *(Israel was forbidden even to look at false worship, and Wisdom warns against approaching idolatry's door; obedience to this injunction will save Christians from being lured into apostasy):*

9 Lest you give your honour unto others, and your years unto the cruel *(the physical suffering which follows upon vice is a fearful picture of the wreckage wrought in the soul by false religion):*

10 Lest strangers be filled with your wealth; and your labours be in the house of a stranger;

11 And you mourn at the last, when your flesh and your body are consumed *(the problem of the Church is the "strange woman," which speaks of false doctrine; as an example, modern psychology is the HIV of the modern Church),*

12 And say, How have I hated instruction, and my heart despised reproof *(departure from God's Word is quickly followed by enslavement to evil);*

13 And have not obeyed the voice of my teachers, nor inclined my ear to them who instructed me! *(Without fail, the Lord will provide a Godly voice. If we do not hear, we are without excuse [Rom. 1:20].)*

14 I was almost in all evil in the midst of the congregation and assembly. *(It seems strange that one would lose his way in "the midst of the congregation." And yet, this is Satan's greatest field of endeavor. Sadly, most lose their way in Church because of false doctrine that it taught from behind the pulpit.)*

15 Drink waters out of your own cistern, and running waters out of your own well. *(The "cistern" here is the Bible. Years later, Jeremiah would refer to this very Passage [Jer. 2:13].)*

16 Let your fountains be dispersed abroad, and rivers of waters in the streets. *(It is insensible for man to turn from Wisdom to folly; from the Word of God to man-made religions.)*

17 Let them be only your own and not strangers' with you. *(The word "strangers" once again refers to false doctrine, false apostles, and idol worship.)*

18 Let your fountain be blessed: and rejoice with the wife of your youth.

19 Let her be as the loving hind and pleasant roe; let her breasts satisfy you at all times; and be thou ravished always with her love. *(Solomon is enjoining, as his father David enjoined him, to not forsake Jehovah, Who is responsible for all blessings. Regrettably, Solomon would not heed his own injunction. The God of Glory, Who touched him in his youth, would be forsaken in Solomon's old age.)*

20 And why will you, my son, be ravished with a strange woman, and embrace the bosom of a stranger? *(The Holy Spirit once again gives warning concerning the "strange woman" [false doctrine, false apostles, and idol worship].)*

21 For the ways of man are before the eyes of the LORD, and He ponders all his goings. *(A record is kept by the Lord of every sparrow that falls to the ground, and every hair lost from the head of each person [Mat. 10:29-30].)*

22 His own iniquities shall take the wicked himself, and he shall be holden with the cords of his sins.

23 He shall die without instruction; and in the greatness of his folly he shall go astray. *(The word "take" in Verse 22 means "entrap." The statement, "cords of his sins," refers to bondage. It is a bondage that man, within himself, cannot break. It can be broken only by the Power of God through the Blood of the Lord Jesus Christ, and our Faith in that Finished Work [Eph. 2:13-18; Gal. 2:20]. The gist of all of this is that*

religion is the greatest entrapment of all. Deliverance from religion can be effected only by the Power of the Holy Spirit, which functions on the basis of Christ and His Finished Work of the Cross [Rom. 6:3-5, 14; 8:1-2, 11].)

CHAPTER 6
(1000 B.C.)
ADVICE AGAINST GUARANTEEING
A DEBT

MY son, if you be surety for your friend, if you have stricken your hand with a stranger,

2 You are snared with the words of your mouth, you are taken with the words of your mouth. *(This Passage pertains to standing good for the debts of another. While it does not absolutely forbid it, it does strongly suggest the wisdom of thinking very carefully before such is done. The word "friend" means a neighbor who is a "stranger.")*

3 Do this now, my son, and deliver yourself, when you are come into the hand of your friend: go, humble yourself, and make sure your friend.

4 Give not sleep to your eyes, nor slumber to your eyelids.

5 Deliver yourself as a roe from the hand of the hunter, and as a bird from the hand of the fowler. *(On the surface, this would speak to the entanglement of guaranteeing the debt of others and the freeing of oneself from such as quickly as possible.)*

THE ANT AND THE SLUGGARD:
LAZINESS CONDEMNED

6 Go to the ant, thou sluggard: consider her ways, and be wise:

7 Which having no guide, overseer, or ruler,

8 Provides her meat in the summer, and gathers her food in the harvest. *(That the Holy Spirit chose the ant as the example portrays the minute detail which God gave to even the most delicate of His glorious Creation.)*

9 How long will you sleep, O sluggard? When will you arise out of your sleep?

10 Yet a little sleep, a little slumber, a little folding of the hands to sleep:

11 So shall your poverty come as one who travels, and your want as an armed man. *(As the Holy Spirit speaks to the lack of diligence concerning the affairs of life, even more so, He speaks to the danger of spiritual lethargy. The*

balance of the Chapter effectively bears this out.)

12 A naughty person, a wicked man, walks with a froward mouth.

13 He winks with his eyes, he speaks with his feet, he teaches with his fingers *(the word "naughty" means "worthless" or "a man of Belial" [Satan]; the word "froward" means "a lying mouth");*

14 Frowardness is in his heart, he devises mischief continually; he sows discord.

15 Therefore shall his calamity come suddenly; suddenly shall he be broken without remedy. *(This would appear to be the "apostate" [stranger] of Verse 1. As the Holy Spirit divulges the heart of such individuals, He is, at the same time, portraying the heart of those who proclaim false doctrine — anything that turns one away from the Word of God.)*

SEVEN SINS OF THE WICKED

16 These six things does the LORD hate: yea, seven are an abomination unto Him *(the phrase, "six things, yea, seven," is a figure of speech arresting attention and signifying that the list is not exhaustive):*

17 A proud look *(pride leads the list)*, a lying tongue *(such always follows "a proud look")*, and hands that shed innocent blood *(this pertains to murderers; however, it also pertains to those who murder someone's character),*

18 An heart that devises wicked imaginations *(the "heart" of the "proud" devises "wicked imaginations" because the heart has not been changed)*, feet that be swift in running to mischief *(as pride is deceptive, this sin is, therefore, cloaked; it actually believes it is doing right),*

19 A false witness that speaks lies *(the difference in the "lying tongue" of Verse 17 and the "false witness" of Verse 19 is that the "lying tongue" will only tell the truth if it suits his advantage; otherwise, he will lie; the "false witness" premeditates lies; he concocts schemes that are made up of lies, in order to carry out a perfidious evil design)*, and he who sows discord among brethren *(individuals who "sow discord" do so for the purpose of carrying out schemes).*

WARNINGS AGAINST SPIRITUAL
ADULTERY

20 My son, keep your father's commandment, and forsake not the law of your mother *(religious, rather than moral, evil is warned*

against in this fourth, and last, section of the Chapter [Vss. 20-35]):

21 Bind them continually upon your heart, and tie them about your neck. *(The Bible governs the heart and adorns the neck. It gives outward beauty of life and inward wealth of principle.)*

22 When you go, it shall lead you; when you sleep, it shall keep you; and when you awake, it shall talk with you. *(The three Persons of the Trinity appear in this Verse. God the Father guides [Ps. 32:8; Jer. 3:4]. God the Son guards [Ps. 121:4]. God the Holy Spirit teaches [Lk. 12:12; Jn. 14:26].)*

23 For the commandment is a lamp; and the law is light; and reproofs of instruction are the way of life *(this Verse repeats the triplet; the Lamp guides, the Light guards, and reproof teaches; there is no "Lamp" or "Light" in the world other than the Bible):*

24 To keep you from the evil woman, from the flattery of the tongue of a strange woman. *(There is an attraction to false teaching as is outlined in this Passage.)*

25 Lust not after her beauty in your heart; neither let her take you with her eyelids. *(False religious teaching always has an amazing attraction. The majority of the world follows this "strange woman," with only a few following the Bible [Mat. 7:14].)*

26 For by means of a whorish woman a man is brought to a piece of bread: and the adultress will hunt for the precious life. *(As immorality leads to destruction, so does a false way of salvation; hence, the term used is "the precious life.")*

27 Can a man take fire in his bosom, and his clothes not be burned?

28 Can one go upon hot coals, and his feet not be burned?

29 So he who goes in to his neighbour's wife; whosoever touches her shall not be innocent. *(Once again, the Holy Spirit likens the infidelity of marriage vows being broken to spiritual immorality [Rom. 7:1-4].)*

30 Men do not despise a thief, if he steal to satisfy his soul when he is hungry;

31 But if he be found, he shall restore sevenfold; he shall give all the substance of his house. *(In Verses 30 through 35, the Holy Spirit presents an argument that is irrefutable.)*

32 But whoso commits adultery with a woman lacks understanding: he who does it destroys his own soul. *(While this Passage definitely addresses itself to physical adultery, still, the true meaning has to do with spiritual*

adultery, i.e., "forsaking Christ and the Cross for another way" [Rom., Chpts 1-4].)*

33 A wound and dishonour shall he get; and his reproach shall not be wiped away.

34 For jealousy is the rage of a man: therefore he will not spare in the day of vengeance.

35 He will not regard any ransom; neither will he rest content, though you give many gifts. *(This illustration vividly pictures the spiritual ruin which results from turning away from Christ to "another gospel" [Gal. 1:6; II Cor. 11:4; Rom. 7:1-4].)*

CHAPTER 7
(1000 B.C.)

THE STRANGE WOMAN

MY son, keep my words, and lay up my commandments with you. *(This Chapter dramatically illustrates the seducing power of false teaching, as is illustrated here by the figure of a treacherous wife, who, in the absence of her husband, allures a youth to do evil.)*

2 Keep my commandments, and live; and my law as the apple of your eye. *(The Bible is the Word of God and, therefore, contains the only teaching that leads to life.*

The phrase, "the apple of your eye," presents the pupil of the eye, which is very tender and delicate. The implication is that we should treat the Bible as we do this sensitive part of our body.)

3 Bind them upon your fingers, write them upon the table of your heart. *(The implication is that the Bible should be used by all Christians with the same frequency that they use their fingers.)*

4 Say unto wisdom, You are my sister; and call understanding your kinswoman *(the terms, "my sister" and "your kinswoman," refer to very close relatives; the implication is that we should treat the Bible as much a part of our family as our own blood relatives):*

5 That they may keep you from the strange woman, from the stranger which flatters with her words. *("Strange woman," in the Hebrew, refers to an Israelite woman gone over to the idolatrous impurities of heathen religion. "The stranger" refers to a purely foreign woman, who does not worship Israel's God, and is, in fact, a worshipper of heathenistic idols. Both represent false doctrine.)*

6 For at the window of my house I looked through my casement,

7 And beheld among the simple ones, I discerned among the youths, a young man void

of understanding,

8 Passing through the street near her corner; and he went the way to her house,

9 In the twilight, in the evening, in the black and dark night (*the "young man void of understanding" does not refer to one who is young in age, but one who is young in the Word of God*):

10 And, behold, there met him a woman with the attire of an harlot, and subtil of heart. (*This "woman" is the "strange woman" or the "stranger" of Verse 5. This young man, having precious little knowledge of the Bible, does not recognize what he sees, which is the case with so many modern Christians.*)

11 (She is loud and stubborn; her feet abide not in her house [*"loud and stubborn" refer to the tenacity and insistence of the peddler of false doctrine*]:

12 Now is she without, now in the streets, and lies in wait at every corner [*the sense of this Verse is that there is no place in the world that is safe from this "strange woman," except "the secret place of the Most High," which is Christ and the Cross (Ps. 91:1; I Cor. 1:23)*].)

13 So she caught him, and kissed him, and with an impudent face said unto him (*so many have been "caught" by this "strange woman"; she will treat her devotees very kindly, putting on "an impudent face," which means a friendly, confident, and sincere face; it is appealing, and many fall for it*),

14 I have peace offerings with me; this day have I payed my vows. (*In this Verse is the key to the deception. This "strange woman" mentions "Peace Offerings," but no "Burnt Offerings." The "Burnt Offering" signified Calvary, which alone could guarantee Peace with God. In effect, this "strange woman" claims that she can have Peace with God without Calvary, hence, no mention of a Burnt Offering.*

The starting point of all false doctrine is an improper understanding of the Cross.)

15 Therefore came I forth to meet you, diligently to seek your face, and I have found you. (*The purveyors of false doctrine, which mean they are false apostles and thereby Satan's ministers [II Cor. 11:12-15], are always diligent to seek out those who are ignorant of the Word of God.*)

16 I have decked my bed with coverings of tapestry, with carved works, with fine linen of Egypt (*to get in "bed" with false apostles is the general idea*).

17 I have perfumed my bed with myrrh, aloes, and cinnamon. (*The description given here*

is very similar to that given in Psalms 45:8. The description in Psalms is of Christ; hence, this "strange woman" claims to present Christ. However, it is a Christ without Calvary, which means it is "another Jesus" [II Cor. 11:4].)

18 Come, let us take our fill of love until the morning: let us solace ourselves with loves. (*In these false doctrines, "love" is usually center stage. The word "loves" is also used because it is plural, going in many directions, and seeking many affections. The Love of God is pure and singular.*)

19 For the goodman is not at home, he is gone a long journey (*the "goodman" is the same as the Watchman or the Master; he should be "earnestly contending for the Faith" [Jude, Vs. 3], but, in fact, other things demand his attention; how so sadly true of so many modern Preachers*):

20 He has taken a bag of money with him, and will come home at the day appointed. (*The things of this world demand the time and the attention of the "goodman," and he, therefore, neglects his true calling [II Tim. 2:4].*)

21 With her much fair speech she caused him to yield, with the flattering of her lips she forced him. (*False doctrine is so subtle. Its appeal is tantalizing, and its power is strong, because it is the power of Satan.*)

22 He goes after her straightway, as an ox goes to the slaughter, or as a fool to the correction of the stocks (*the statement given here by the Holy Spirit is clear; even though the promises of false doctrine and false apostles are tantalizing, their only conclusion will be "slaughter"; those who follow them become "a fool"*);

23 Till a dart strike through his liver; as a bird hastes to the snare, and knows not that it is for his life. (*The analogy is compelling. No matter how wonderful the false doctrine sounds, if it is not "Jesus Christ and Him Crucified," the end result will be death.*)

24 Hearken unto me now therefore, O ye children, and attend to the words of my mouth. (*The implication should be clear. The "children" are those who are true followers of the Lord; irrespective, they are not immune. In fact, they are the very ones whom the "strange woman" seeks after.*)

25 Let not your heart decline to her ways, go not astray in her paths. (*The warning is clear!*)

26 For she has cast down many wounded: yea, many strong men have been slain by her. (*This "strange woman" has been extremely successful in her bid for the souls of men. Many*

mighty ones have gone down before her wiles.)

27 Her house is the way to Hell, going down to the chambers of death. *(There is nothing worse than a false way of salvation. This "strange woman" pictures all such false ways. To make it easy to understand, "false ways" pertain to any way that is not "Jesus Christ and Him Crucified" [I Cor. 1:23].)*

CHAPTER 8
(1000 B.C.)
WISDOM IS PERSONIFIED

DOES not wisdom cry? and understanding put forth her voice? *(The entirety of this Chapter is devoted to "Wisdom," which is the Word of God. So, the True Gospel makes its appeal to men exactly as the false.)*

2 She stands in the top of high places, by the way in the places of the paths.

3 She cries at the gates, at the entry of the city, at the coming in at the doors. *(This emphasizes the truth that the Holy Spirit is seeking at every intersection of life to put forth the Word of God.)*

4 Unto you, O men, I call; and my voice is to the sons of man. *(This means the old and young alike.)*

5 O ye simple, understand wisdom: and, you fools, be ye of an understanding heart. *(The implication is that men are "simple" because they do not understand the Bible; they are "fools" simply because they do not have a heart that seeks after the Word of God.)*

6 Hear; for I will speak of excellent things; and the opening of my lips shall be right things. *(This means that if it's not truly Biblical, then it's not truly right!)*

7 For my mouth shall speak truth; and wickedness is an abomination to my lips. *(The only revealed Truth in the world is the Bible. It alone sets the standard for morality and righteousness.)*

8 All the words of my mouth are in righteousness; there is nothing froward or perverse in them. *(The only "Righteousness" that God will recognize is taught in the Bible.)*

9 They are all plain to him who understands, and right to them who find knowledge. *(God's Word is plain and clear concerning understanding, to those who truly desire Biblical Knowledge.)*

10 Receive my instruction, and not silver; and knowledge rather than choice gold.

11 For wisdom is better than rubies; and all the things that may be desired are not to be compared to it. *(How many Christians place the Bible and the knowledge of it superior to gold and silver?)*

12 I wisdom dwell with prudence, and find out knowledge of witty inventions. *(The phrase, "witty inventions," refers to the great questions of life that seem to have no answers, but, in fact, are given to us in the Bible, namely, "Where did man come from?" "Where is man now?" and "Where is man going in the future?")*

13 The fear of the LORD is to hate evil: pride, and arrogancy, and the evil way, and the froward mouth, do I hate. *(The "evil way" is all that is not truly of the Bible.)*

14 Counsel is mine, and sound wisdom: I am understanding; I have strength. *(In this Passage, the Lord is saying that He really doesn't "have" Counsel, but, in fact, He "is" Counsel, etc.)*

15 By me kings reign, and princes decree justice.

16 By me princes rule, and nobles, even all the judges of the Earth. *(The spirit of the world proclaims that only those of simple mind would believe and peruse the Bible. The Holy Spirit here says otherwise.)*

17 I love them who love me; and those that seek me early shall find me. *(The Lord promises here that if anyone seeks to know and understand His Word, thereby finding Wisdom, He guarantees that it will be found.)*

18 Riches and honour are with me; yea, durable riches and righteousness. *(The riches given by the Word of God are durable and do not flee away as gold and silver.)*

19 My fruit is better than gold, yea, than fine gold; and my revenue than choice silver. *(Once again, the Holy Spirit emphasizes the fact that if we place the seeking of silver and gold ahead of the Bible, we have made a very poor choice.)*

20 I lead in the way of righteousness, in the midst of the paths of judgment *(the Bible, and the Bible alone, tells us of "the way of righteousness"; it also shows us [and it alone] "the paths of judgment"):*

21 That I may cause those who love me to inherit substance; and I will fill their treasures. *(And so the proclamation is to all that the path to success, honor, durable riches, Righteousness, and judgment is found in the treasure house of the Bible.)*

WISDOM IS EVERLASTING

22 The LORD possessed me in the beginning of His way, before His works of old. *(This*

speaks of the beginning of His Creation, which was all carried out by His Word [Heb. 11:3].)

23 I was set up from everlasting, from the beginning, or ever the Earth was. (These Passages illustrate the Truth that the Word of God did not come about as a result of God's Creation, but, in fact, is the cause of His Creation.)

24 When there were no depths, I was brought forth; when there were no fountains abounding with water.

25 Before the mountains were settled, before the hills was I brought forth (the Lord, with His Word, brought forth all these things):

26 While as yet He had not made the Earth, nor the fields, nor the highest part of the dust of the world. (The "highest part of the dust" refers to "the first particle of matter — the primitive atom.")

27 When He prepared the Heavens, I was there: when He set a compass upon the face of the depth (Christ, Who is the Word, Who is Wisdom, was with the Father in preparation of the Creation, and, in fact, created all things [Jn. 1:1-3]):

28 When He established the clouds above: when He strengthened the fountains of the deep:

29 When He gave to the sea His decree, that the waters should not pass His Commandment: when He appointed the foundations of the Earth (it was all done by the Word of God!):

30 Then I was by Him, as one brought up with Him: and I was daily His delight, rejoicing always before Him;

31 Rejoicing in the habitable part of His Earth; and my delights were with the sons of men. (This speaks of Christ, Who is Wisdom, Who is the Word, and Who was with God, i.e., "Him" [Jn. 1:1-3].)

INVITATION TO SEEK WISDOM

32 Now therefore hearken unto me, O ye children: for blessed are they who keep my ways. (Man has the choice of his own ways, which really are Satan's ways, or God's Ways. God's Ways are ensconced in His Word.)

33 Hear instruction, and be wise, and refuse it not. (The wise accept this instruction; the unwise refuse it.)

34 Blessed is the man who hears me, watching daily at my gates, waiting at the posts of my doors. (Wisdom will not come uninvited to any man.)

35 For whoso finds me finds life, and shall obtain favour of the LORD. (Any life promised by anything other than what we find in the Bible is a lie.)

36 But he who sins against me wrongs his own soul: all they who hate me love death. (If we sin against the Bible, which is disobeying or ignoring its instructions, we have sinned against our souls.)

CHAPTER 9
(1000 B.C.)

AN INVITATION TO WISDOM'S BANQUET

WISDOM has built her house, she has hewn out her seven pillars ("seven" is God's number of perfection, totality, completion, and universality; it's the same Church for all of mankind):

2 She has killed her beasts (animal sacrifices before the Cross); she has mingled her wine (joy which comes with Salvation); she has also furnished her table (made provision for all things).

3 She has sent forth her maidens (the word in the Hebrew refers to both young men and young women sent as missionaries over the world): she cries upon the highest places of the city (uses every means to get out the Gospel),

4 Whoso is simple, let him turn in hither: as for him who wants understanding, she says to him. (Verses 4 through 6 present the invitation of Wisdom to the lost, in comparison to the invitation extended by the "strange woman" of Chapter 7.)

5 Come, eat of my bread, and drink of the wine which I have mingled (the "bread" and the "wine" symbolize the broken Body of our Lord, along with His shed Blood [Mat. 26:26-30; I Cor. 10:16-17]).

6 Forsake the foolish, and live; and go in the way of understanding (the Holy Spirit is telling us to turn a deaf ear to the "strange woman" [false doctrine and false apostles] and go the way of the Bible, which is true understanding).

7 He who reproves a scorner gets to himself shame: and he who rebukes a wicked man gets himself a blot. (In this Passage, the Preachers of Verse 3 are told of the reception they will receive. Scorners will mock them, and the violent will injure them.)

8 Reprove not a scorner, lest he hate you: rebuke a wise man, and he will love you. (Those who live by ways and means other than

the Bible do not know how to take a kind rebuke.)

9 Give instruction to a wise man, and he will be yet wiser: teach a just man, and he will increase in learning. (We are told in this Passage that irrespective as to how "wise" one may be, the Bible will make him "yet wiser.")

10 The fear of the LORD is the beginning of wisdom: and the knowledge of the holy is understanding. (Once again, the Holy Spirit tells us that all of our knowledge is futile, unless we have the "fear of the LORD." That is the "beginning of wisdom," and that alone!)

11 For by me your days shall be multiplied, and the years of your life shall be increased. (Length of physical life is not necessarily intended in this Verse, but rather fullness and usefulness of Spiritual Life.)

12 If you be wise, you shall be wise for yourself: but if you scorn, you alone shall bear it. (The idea is that the rejecter of the Gospel Message must personally suffer the consequences of his rejection.)

AVOID FALSE DOCTRINE AT ALL COST

13 A foolish woman is clamorous: she is simple, and knows nothing. (The "foolish woman" is similar to the "strange woman" of 7:5. It is remarkable the number of times the Holy Spirit likens the infidelity of the female gender to spiritual adultery [Rom. 7:1-4].)

14 For she sits at the door of her house, on a seat in the high places of the city,

15 To call passengers who go right on their ways (as the Holy Spirit sends His Messengers and they "cry upon the high places of the city" [preaching the Gospel], likewise, those who peddle their false doctrine also utilize the same "high places"):

16 Whoso is simple, let him turn in hither: and as for him who wants understanding, she says to him (the "simple" of Verse 4 are appealed to by the Holy Spirit; they are also appealed to by the "foolish woman"),

17 Stolen waters are sweet, and bread eaten in secret is pleasant. (Wisdom's last cry is, "Forsake the foolish, and live!" [Vs. 6]. The last cry of the "foolish woman" is, "Stolen waters are sweet!")

18 But he knows not that the dead are there; and that her guests are in the depths of Hell. (The conclusion of all false doctrine propagated by false apostles, of which the "foolish woman" is symbolic, is "spiritual death.")

CHAPTER 10
(1000 B.C.)
THE WISE AND THE FOOLISH CONTRASTED

THE proverbs of Solomon. A wise son makes a glad father: but a foolish son is the heaviness of his mother. (The "wise son" is the one who follows the Word of God, which will make glad his earthly father and his Heavenly Father. Such is contrasted with the "foolish son," who is the opposite.)

2 Treasures of wickedness profit nothing: but righteousness delivers from death. (There are some who may tend to disagree with this statement; however, the type of "profit" of which the Holy Spirit is speaking is that which is eternal in value and consequence.)

3 The LORD will not suffer the soul of the righteous to famish: but He casts away the substance of the wicked. (This speaks of the Lord taking care of the "righteous" regarding material needs, and serving as a shield regarding Satanic attacks [Gen. 15:1].)

4 He becomes poor who deals with a slack hand: but the hand of the diligent makes rich. (The words, "slack hand," actually mean "deceitful hand.")

5 He who gathers in summer is a wise son: but he who sleeps in harvest is a son who causes shame. (This Proverb illustrates "diligence.")

6 Blessings are upon the head of the just: but violence covers the mouth of the wicked.

7 The memory of the just is blessed: but the name of the wicked shall rot. (The argument of Verses 6 through 7 is that a righteous person is a fount of blessing to society, but an unrighteous person is a source of injury, even though he tries to hide the fact with honeyed words.)

8 The wise in heart will receive commandments: but a prating fool shall fall. (The "wise" are those who follow the Commandments of the Lord.)

9 He who walks uprightly walks surely: but he who perverts his ways shall be known. (Such a person is never afraid of detection, because he never acts in deceit.)

10 He who winks with the eye causes sorrow: but a prating fool shall fall. ("To wink with the eye," in the east as well as other parts of the world, is a method of signaling a bribe to a judge or, in general society, of injuring the character of an acquaintance.)

11 The mouth of a righteous man is a well of life: but violence covers the mouth of the

wicked. *(The only "life" in this world is that which is given by Christ. Ideally, the "mouth" of such a one becomes a fount of blessing.)*

12 Hatred stirs up strifes: but love covers all sins. *(Those who love to stir up the failing of others, while hiding their own, show that their hearts are filled with "hatred.")*

13 In the lips of him who has understanding wisdom is found: but a rod is for the back of him who is void of understanding. *(Those who understand and believe the Bible become a fount of wisdom; however, for the Believer who strays from the Bible, chastisement from God will be forthcoming [Heb. 12:5-8].)*

14 Wise men lay up knowledge: but the mouth of the foolish is near destruction. *(Those who truly know the Bible will not repeat the negative things they hear about others; conversely, the fool repeats them everywhere, and causes strife.)*

15 The rich man's wealth is his strong city: the destruction of the poor is their poverty. *(The rich, in order to become richer and to accumulate even more, will oftentimes destroy the poor.)*

16 The labour of the righteous tends to life: the fruit of the wicked to sin. *(In many and varied ways, the Holy Spirit proclaims the desired direction, which gives life. He also points out the way of the wicked, which brings death.)*

17 He is in the way of life who keeps instruction: but he who refuses reproof errs. *(The "instruction" that is spoken of here is the Bible, and it points to "the way of life.")*

18 He who hides hatred with lying lips, and he who utters a slander, is a fool. *("Hypocrisy" deals with the first part of this Verse, while "gossip" deals with the latter part.)*

19 In the multitude of words there wants not sin: but he who refrains his lips is wise. *(Those who talk a lot, especially about other people, will usually sin with their tongues.)*

20 The tongue of the just is as choice silver: the heart of the wicked is little worth. *(The "tongue of the just" will be quick to hear and slow to speak.)*

21 The lips of the righteous feed many: but fools die for want of wisdom. *(The "righteous" bless, while the unrighteous curse.)*

22 The blessing of the LORD, it makes rich, and He adds no sorrow with it. *(Those who ignore the Word of God may, for a time, be blessed, but the sorrow that comes with it is so expensive that none can afford it.)*

23 It is as sport to a fool to do mischief: but a man of understanding has wisdom. *(The essence of this Proverb is that one who does not know or abide by the Bible will do mischief and cause great harm.)*

24 The fear of the wicked, it shall come upon him: but the desire of the righteous shall be granted. *(Wickedness carries its own "fear," while Righteousness dispels all fear.)*

25 As the whirlwind passes, so is the wicked no more: but the righteous is an everlasting foundation. *(This Proverb portrays the house built upon the sand, and the house built upon the Rock [Mat. 7:24-27].)*

26 As vinegar to the teeth, and as smoke to the eyes, so is the sluggard to them who send him. *(The Holy Spirit labels as "sluggards" all who do not know and abide by the Bible; they will ultimately prove no good to those who employ their services.)*

27 The fear of the LORD prolongs days: but the years of the wicked shall be shortened. *(To "fear the LORD" and to serve Him prolong our lives.)*

28 The hope of the righteous shall be gladness: but the expectation of the wicked shall perish. *(Outside of Christ, there is no hope!)*

29 The way of the LORD is strength to the upright: but destruction shall be to the workers of iniquity. *(To follow the "Way of the Lord" is to constantly gain strength.)*

30 The righteous shall never be removed: but the wicked shall not inhabit the Earth. *(This points to the coming Kingdom Age [Mat. 5:5].)*

31 The mouth of the just brings forth wisdom: but the froward tongue shall be cut out. *(All of the boasts of the "froward" [crooked] tongue will come to naught, irrespective of how strong such presently looks. However, that which is said by "the just" will ultimately be realized.)*

32 The lips of the righteous know what is acceptable: but the mouth of the wicked speaks frowardness. *(The righteous know, because they know what the Bible says; however, the wicked speak crookedly, because they do not know or believe the Bible.)*

CHAPTER 11
(1000 B.C.)

THE CONTRAST OF THE WISE
AND THE FOOLISH

A false balance is abomination to the LORD: but a just weight is his delight. *(The tender Love of God for men, and especially for the poor, appears in these Proverbs, for, if they were obeyed, injustice, dishonesty, fraud, and cruelty*

would cease to exist. Four times it is stated that fraud in business is abominable in God's sight [11:1; 16:11; 20:10, 23].)

2 When pride comes, then comes shame: but with the lowly is wisdom. *(Over and over again, the Holy Spirit portrays humility as the example [Isa. 66:2].)*

3 The integrity of the upright shall guide them: but the perverseness of transgressors shall destroy them. *(The word "perverseness" means treacherous and unfaithful. The "integrity" addressed here is God's integrity, which is His Word.)*

4 Riches profit not in the day of wrath: but righteousness delivers from death. *(Among men, riches can do wonders; with God, they purchase nothing.)*

5 The righteousness of the perfect shall direct his way: but the wicked shall fall by his own wickedness. *(The word "perfect" here means "blameless." This is the age-old contest between man's righteousness and God's Righteousness.)*

6 The righteousness of the upright shall deliver them: but transgressors shall be taken in their own naughtiness. *(There are two types of righteousness: 1. Imputed Righteousness, which comes from the Lord, and is given to Believers upon Faith in Christ and the Cross; and, 2. Self-righteousness, which comes about by works, which God will not recognize.)*

7 When a wicked man dies, his expectation shall perish: and the hope of unjust men perishes. *(Irrespective of how rich, powerful, strong, or great the wicked are, they will always come to a hopeless end.)*

8 The righteous is delivered out of trouble, and the wicked comes in his stead. *(Daniel and his wicked accusers illustrate this Verse.)*

9 An hypocrite with his mouth destroys his neighbour: but through knowledge shall the just be delivered. *(Jesus exposed those who were quick to point out the faults of others while ignoring their own [Mat. 7:1-5] by calling them "hypocrites.")*

10 When it goes well with the righteous, the city rejoices: and when the wicked perish, there is shouting. *(Mordecai and Haman illustrate this Verse.)*

11 By the blessing of the upright the city is exalted: but it is overthrown by the mouth of the wicked. *(Unfortunately, the "upright" in any city are seldom noticed, but rather are oftentimes opposed and even persecuted. "The wicked" little know that the ones they are persecuting are the reason for their blessing!)*

12 He who is void of wisdom despises his neighbour: but a man of understanding holds his peace. *(Having to live beside a neighbor constantly, it is best to hold our peace regarding many things of which we might like to speak a word. If a man has "understanding," which comes from the Bible alone, he will use such wisdom.)*

13 A talebearer reveals secrets: but he who is of a faithful spirit conceals the matter. *(In the Hebrew, the word "talebearer" is "holechrachil," which means "a peddler of scandal." Doeg is a good example of such talebearing [I Sam. 21:7].)*

14 Where no counsel is, the people fall: but in the multitude of counsellors there is safety. *(The "counsel" addressed here concerns that which comes from the Bible, and the Bible alone.)*

15 He who is surety for a stranger shall smart for it: and he who hates suretiship is sure. *("Stranger" signifies "one who has forsaken truth." Such is man. Christ, in His Love for man, became man's surety; as a consequence, He was sorely broken at Calvary.)*

16 A gracious woman retains honour: and strong men retain riches. *(Two things are addressed in this Proverb — a woman who has grace, and men who have strength. The Lord is the giver of both.)*

17 The merciful man does good to his own soul: but he who is cruel troubles his own flesh. *(In this one Proverb is found the key to much sickness.)*

18 The wicked works a deceitful work: but to him who sows righteousness shall be a sure reward. *(Sadly, almost all of the world is made up of "the wicked." Consequently, almost everything in the world that is done should come under the heading of "a deceitful work." That is the reason for most of the sorrow in the world.)*

19 As righteousness tends to life: so he who pursues evil pursues it to his own death. *(In this Proverb, "life" and "death" are set before us, and the cause for both.)*

20 They who are of a froward heart are abomination to the LORD: but such as are upright in their way are His delight. *(The word "froward" refers to one who is disobedient and rebellious. This speaks of one who constantly opposes God's Will.)*

21 Though hand join in hand, the wicked shall not be unpunished: but the seed of the righteous shall be delivered. *(There is no way that "the wicked" can avoid the coming punishment, irrespective of their strength or agreements. The "Righteous" is Christ, while the "seed" refers to those who serve Christ.)*

22 As a jewel of gold in a swine's snout, so is a fair woman which is without discretion. *(This refers to a beautiful woman who has no "discretion." Her beauty is wasted, as a "jewel of gold" would be wasted in the nose of a pig.)*

23 The desire of the righteous is only good: but the expectation of the wicked is wrath. *(The word "desire" is a strong word which characterizes the whole of humanity, whether good or bad.)*

24 There is that scatters, and yet increases; and there is that withholds more than is meet, but it tends to poverty. *(In the abbreviated meaning, the statement is, "What you give, you gain; what you keep, you lose" [Lk. 6:38; II Cor. 8:15; 9:6; Gal. 6:7-8].)*

25 The liberal soul shall be made fat: and he who waters shall be watered also himself. *(Who is the "liberal soul"? It is he who "scatters" [gives liberally] into that which is definitely of God, and not "false apostles or deceitful workers.")*

26 He who withholds corn, the people shall curse him: but blessing shall be upon the head of him who sells it. *(This speaks of trouble and difficulty that comes to a community when individuals take advantage of such by increasing the price of the item that is needed, irrespective of the suffering of the people.)*

27 He who diligently seeks good procures favour: but he who seeks mischief, it shall come unto him. *(This speaks of seeking the "good" of others.)*

28 He who trusts in his riches shall fall; but the righteous shall flourish as a branch. *(Those who trust in God are described as a beautiful branch which continues to grow into a full flower.)*

29 He who troubles his own house shall inherit the wind: and the fool shall be servant to the wise of heart. *(This speaks of those who ignore these Proverbs and travel in directions of their own making. They shall "inherit the wind.")*

30 The fruit of the righteous is a tree of life; and he who wins souls is wise. *(He who tells others about Christ is, in effect, presenting to them "a tree of life.")*

31 Behold, the righteous shall be recompensed in the Earth: much more the wicked and the sinner. *(This simply means that all will reap what they sow.)*

CHAPTER 12
(1000 B.C.)
FOOLISH AND WISE CONTRASTED

WHOSO loves instruction loves knowledge: but he who hates reproof is brutish.

(The Bible gives instruction which generates knowledge. This has to do with the true knowledge of life. Much knowledge is generated in other capacities, and may or may not be true; however, the knowledge that pertains to life is found only in the Bible.)

2 A good man obtains favour of the LORD: but a man of wicked devices will He condemn. *("Favor of the LORD" is the highest attainment of any seeker. It is stated that only a "good man" can secure such; however, the "goodness" is only that which God gives. There is a "goodness" devised by the world, and even at times by the Church, that God will neither accept nor recognize. He will accept only that which comes from Himself.)*

3 A man shall not be established by wickedness: but the root of the righteous shall not be moved. *(Irrespective of money, power, or position, a man who has built such by "wickedness" will know no lasting security.)*

4 A virtuous woman is a crown to her husband: but she who makes ashamed is as rottenness in his bones. *(Ruth is an excellent example of "a virtuous woman" [Ruth 3:11].)*

5 The thoughts of the righteous are right: but the counsels of the wicked are deceit. *(So much is said here in such a short Verse. The troubles of the entirety of the world are wrapped up in this Proverb. Regrettably, there are precious few who are "righteous," with many who are "wicked." Consequently, "deceit" characterizes the dealings of man.)*

6 The words of the wicked are to lie in wait for blood: but the mouth of the upright shall deliver them. *(Upright men benefit society, but evil men destroy a nation.)*

7 The wicked are overthrown, and are not: but the house of the righteous shall stand. *(The "house of the righteous" refers to that which is built upon the Rock, Who is the Lord Jesus Christ [Mat. 7:24].)*

8 A man shall be commended according to his wisdom: but he who is of perverse heart shall be despised. *(To get "His Wisdom," we must learn "His Word.")*

9 He who is despised, and has a servant, is better than he who honours himself, and lacks bread. *(The one "despised" in this Verse is different than the one "despised" in Verse 8. The one in Verse 8 is "despised" by God. In this Verse, he is commended by God. God despises those who do not adhere to His Word, and the world despises those who do.)*

10 A righteous man regards the life of his

beast: but the tender mercies of the wicked are cruel. *(The Holy Spirit regards animals and contends that "a righteous man" will have mercy.)*

11 He who tills his land shall be satisfied with bread: but he who follows vain persons is void of understanding. *(The Bible extols the value of honest labor. Absence of the Bible promotes vanity and lack of understanding.)*

12 The wicked desire the net of evil men: but the root of the righteous yields fruit. *("The net of evil men" denotes what is caught in it. Consequently, hundreds of thousands, or even millions, of young people desire what is caught in the net of the drug pushers or of Hollywood. They envy these supposed high dividends and desire the same. However, the fruit that is produced comes from a "corrupt tree" and produces "evil fruit" [Mat. 7:17].*

The good tree, which is "the righteous" yields "good fruit.")

13 The wicked is snared by the transgression of his lips: but the just shall come out of trouble. *(God does not promise an absence of trouble for those who follow the teachings of the Bible; however, He does promise that "the just" shall be delivered out of the trouble.)*

14 A man shall be satisfied with good by the fruit of his mouth: and the recompence of a man's hands shall be rendered unto him. *(The "man" addressed here is "the just" of Verse 13. The "fruit of his mouth" will be "good" because it comes from "Wisdom," which is the Bible [Vs. 8].)*

15 The way of a fool is right in his own eyes: but he who hearkens unto counsel is wise.

16 A fool's wrath is presently known: but a prudent man covers shame. *(The "fool" is the one who does not believe the Bible. He trusts his own "way." God calls him "a fool."*

The Sixteenth Verse means that a fool will make his wrath known at once when he is offended, but a wise man will hold his peace.)

17 He who speaks truth shows forth righteousness: but a false witness deceit. *(The only "truth" that can be addressed is that which is of Christ. He Alone "shows forth righteousness." All else is a "false witness" and spawns "deceit.")*

18 There is that speaks like the piercings of a sword: but the tongue of the wise is health. *(Thank God for the few Preachers who have "the tongue of the wise," which is the Bible, which gives spiritual "health.")*

19 The lip of truth shall be established for ever: but a lying tongue is but for a moment.

(Those who forsake the Bible have a "lying tongue." What they say only lasts for a moment, because it changes with the telling.)

20 Deceit is in the heart of them who imagine evil: but to the counsellors of peace is joy. *(Deception is Satan's greatest weapon, and his children "imagine evil" because "deceit is in their hearts.")*

21 There shall no evil happen to the just: but the wicked shall be filled with mischief. *(This means that no "evil" can come from the "Wisdom" of the Bible. There is no fear of such in its "counsel.")*

22 Lying lips are abomination to the LORD: but they who deal truly are His delight. *(It is impossible to "deal truly" and, thereby, be a "delight" to the Lord without abiding by the Bible. Anything other than the Bible results in "lying lips" and is an "abomination to the LORD.")*

23 A prudent man conceals knowledge: but the heart of fools proclaims foolishness. *(The "prudent man conceals knowledge" because the world is little interested in his "knowledge," because his "knowledge" comes from the Bible; consequently, the world feeds on "foolishness.")*

24 The hand of the diligent shall bear rule: but the slothful shall be under tribute. *(Those who adhere to the work ethic of the Bible will prosper. Those who do not adhere to the work ethic of the Bible will find themselves in debt.)*

25 Heaviness in the heart of man makes it stoop: but a good word makes it glad. *(The "good word" that is truly spoken of here is the Word of God. Only it can truly make the heart "glad.")*

26 The righteous is more excellent than his neighbour: but the way of the wicked seduces them. *("The righteous," who comes from Christ, blesses his neighbor, while "the wicked" seduces his neighbor.)*

27 The slothful man roasts not that which he took in hunting: but the substance of a diligent man is precious. *("The slothful man," who attempts to make his living by devious means, contributes nothing to the community. Conversely, the "diligent man" provides substance, which is "precious" for the community.)*

28 In the way of righteousness is life: and in the pathway thereof there is no death. *(The "Way of Righteousness" is the "Way of the Bible." It alone brings "life," which stems from Christ.)*

CHAPTER 13
(1000 B.C.)
PROVERBS OF TEMPORAL AND ETERNAL GOOD

A wise son hears his father's instruction: but a scorner hears not rebuke. *(The surface meaning of this Passage is obvious; constructive criticism by the wise is needed. Those who are not wise scorn the rebuke and continue on in their erroneous way.)*

2 A man shall eat good by the fruit of his mouth: but the soul of the transgressors shall eat violence.

3 He who keeps his mouth keeps his life: but he who opens wide his lips shall have destruction. *(In the spiritual sense, the "fruit of our mouth" should be the Word of God.)*

4 The soul of the sluggard desires, and has nothing: but the soul of the diligent shall be made fat. *(This Passage proclaims the blessing of the work ethic and the poverty of the lazy.)*

5 A righteous man hates lying: but a wicked man is loathsome, and comes to shame. *(The entirety of the world's system, which is Godless, is based on "lying," hence, all the problems.)*

6 Righteousness keeps him who is upright in the way: but wickedness overthrows the sinner. *(The obvious sense is that "wickedness" will ultimately bring the "sinner" to ruin, and that "Righteousness," which can only be supplied by Christ and is freely imputed by Him, will guarantee success.)*

7 There is that makes himself rich, yet has nothing: there is that makes himself poor, yet has great riches. *(This speaks of those who have much money, but yet they are poor, simply because they are selfish and give no help to anyone.*

Then there are those who use what comes into their hands as a blessing to others. In the things that really count, they have "great riches.")

8 The ransom of a man's life are his riches: but the poor hears not rebuke. *(The sense of this Passage is that the hoarding of wealth makes a man's life his "ransom." In other words, because of his riches, he is a target in many respects.)*

9 The light of the righteous rejoices: but the lamp of the wicked shall be put out. *(The "light" of "the righteous" is the "light" that comes from the Bible. It is the "light" that Christ produces in the lives of His followers. Such brings rejoicing.)*

10 Only by pride comes contention: but with the well advised is wisdom. *("Pride" is the foundation sin of all sin [6:16-17]. It stems from Satan, as humility stems from Christ. "Pride" breeds "contention," because it is ever seeking its own. Humility, which can only be given by Christ, generates "wisdom." The Holy Spirit calls such "well advised.")*

11 Wealth gotten by vanity shall be diminished: but he who gathers by labour shall increase. *(The sense of the Passage is that "wealth" gathered by labor benefits society, but "wealth" obtained by gambling, crime, or any other means is "a vanity." It is useless to the well-being of the community.)*

12 Hope deferred makes the heart sick: but when the desire comes, it is a tree of life. *(All "hope" outside of Christ is never realized. All "hope" in Christ is ever realized.)*

13 Whoso despises the word shall be destroyed: but he who fears the commandment shall be rewarded. *(The "Word of God" is the only answer for the ills of man. As well, one can only know the Word if one also knows its Author.)*

14 The law of the wise is a fountain of life, to depart from the snares of death. *(The "wise" to whom the Holy Spirit refers are those who adhere to the Word of God. God has ordained it a "Law" that such will be "a fountain of life." Everything outside of the Bible is "a snare of death.")*

15 Good understanding gives favour: but the way of transgressors is hard. *(Those who transgress the Word of God will find their way "hard.")*

16 Every prudent man deals with knowledge: but a fool lays open his folly. *(The spiritual sense of this Proverb is that all true "knowledge" comes from the Bible, and the man who seeks this "knowledge" is "prudent" [wise].)*

17 A wicked messenger falls into mischief: but a faithful ambassador is health. *(If an "ambassador" is "faithful" to the Bible, he will bring messages of "health"; if not, then "mischief.")*

18 Poverty and shame shall be to him who refuses instruction: but he who regards reproof shall be honoured. *(If the individual faithfully follows the instruction given by the Word of God, he will, at the same time, highly regard the "reproof" of those who try to instruct him for the better.)*

19 The desire accomplished is sweet to the soul: but it is abomination to fools to depart from evil. *(To obtain what is really desirable demands self-denial. But it is most distasteful to a fool to obtain anything worthful by the surrender of worthless and injurious pleasures.)*

20 He who walks with wise men shall be wise: but a companion of fools shall be destroyed. *(Every Christian should diligently search for the Preacher who preaches the whole Counsel of God. If he does otherwise, he is associating with "fools" and will come to destruction.)*

21 Evil pursues sinners: but to the righteous good shall be repaid. *(God's Law is that if a person wills evil, God wills evil unto him. If he wills "good," the Lord also wills "good" to him [Gal. 6:7].)*

22 A good man leaves an inheritance to his children's children: and the wealth of the sinner is laid up for the just. *(The term "laid up," as it pertains to the "wealth of the sinner," refers to the coming Kingdom Age, when the meek will inherit the Earth [Mat. 5:5].)*

23 Much food is in the tillage of the poor: but there is that is destroyed for want of judgment. *(The sense of this Proverb is that "the poor" are in their state partly because of bad management. They have very little foresight. When they get something, they quickly spend it and very seldom endeavor to plan ahead.)*

24 He who spares his rod hates his son: but he who loves him chastens him betimes. *(Hatred spares the rod; love uses it.)*

25 The righteous eats to the satisfying of his soul: but the belly of the wicked shall want. *(This, as well, constitutes a Law of God: "the righteous" are content with moderate desires and pleased with their lot in life. Conversely, "the wicked," regardless of how much they have, are never satisfied.)*

CHAPTER 14
(1000 B.C.)
THE RIGHTEOUS AND THE WICKED CONTRASTED

EVERY wise woman builds her house: but the foolish pluck it down with her hands. *(Over and over again, the Holy Spirit alludes to the "woman," whether "strange," "evil," "foolish," "gracious," or "virtuous." In this Verse, He speaks of both the "wise" and "foolish" woman in the building of their "house.")*

2 He who walks in his uprightness fears the LORD: but he who is perverse in his ways despises Him. *(Once again, our attention is called to the "fear of the LORD" or the lack of such. We learn from this and many other similar Scriptures that the Holy Spirit puts great stock in the "fear of the LORD.")*

3 In the mouth of the foolish is a rod of pride: but the lips of the wise shall preserve them. *("Pride" is the foundation of all sin. It produces the fountainhead of sin, which is unbelief. Those who speak in a prideful way are called "foolish" by the Holy Spirit. The conversation of the "wise" is of humility and, thereby, preserves them.)*

4 Where no oxen are, the crib is clean: but much increase is by the strength of the ox. *(The sense of the Passage is that "you can't make an omelet without breaking some eggs." As long as there is activity, there's going to be some untidiness, but there will also be increase.)*

5 A faithful witness will not lie; but a false witness will utter lies. *(Men are not liars because they lie; they lie because they are liars.)*

6 A scorner seeks wisdom, and finds it not: but knowledge is easy unto him who understands. *(The scornful Pharisee professed to seek wisdom and found nothing; to the understanding Ethiopian, knowledge was easy [Acts, Chpt. 8]. Jesus is Wisdom. He was a stumbling-stone to the Pharisee, but a stepping-stone to the Ethiopian.)*

7 Go from the presence of a foolish man, when you perceive not in him the lips of knowledge. *(This is the Law of Separation [II Cor. 6:14-18]. The only "lips of knowledge" are those that know the Word of God.)*

8 The wisdom of the prudent is to understand his way: but the folly of fools is deceit. *(The only way that one can "understand his way" is to know the Bible. Such is spoken of by the Holy Spirit as "wise and prudent.")*

9 Fools make a mock at sin: but among the righteous there is favour. *(Fools mock the Sin Offering [the Atonement], but among the righteous it is prized.)*

10 The heart knows his own bitterness; and a stranger does not intermeddle with his joy. *(The "heart" that is spoken of here is the "heart" of a Christian. One who is a "stranger" to God and His Ways has no knowledge of the burden that is carried or the "joy" that resides in the heart of a true Christian.)*

11 The house of the wicked shall be overthrown: but the tabernacle of the upright shall flourish. *(The "upright" is a pilgrim, and as such has no "house," but rather a tent. This world is not his home, and he is seeking a city whose Builder and Maker is God. To the unspiritual eye, such looks not at all stable. But the Holy Spirit says the opposite.)*

12 There is a way which seems right unto a man, but the end thereof are the ways of death.

(Salvation by sacraments and personal merit [in other words, any way other than the Cross] is to most men an acceptable way to eternal life, but, in reality, it leads to death. The right way is "Jesus Christ and Him Crucified," and that alone [I Cor. 1:23].)

13 Even in laughter the heart is sorrowful; and the end of that mirth is heaviness. *(A false way of salvation, of which many abound, may bring momentary surface "laughter." But it will not, and in fact cannot, satisfy the hunger and craving of the human heart. When it's all over, the "heart" is "sorrowful" and "heavy.")*

14 The backslider in heart shall be filled with his own ways: and a good man shall be satisfied from himself. *(This speaks of the fact that the "backslider" does so "in heart" before it becomes outwardly observable.)*

15 The simple believe every word: but the prudent man looks well to his going. *(Two individuals are placed before us; "the simple" and "the prudent." Irrespective of their education, God calls "simple" those who "believe every word" except the Bible. The Holy Spirit calls "prudent" the one who "looks well to his going," which refers to searching out the Bible for its direction.)*

16 A wise man fears, and departs from evil: but the fool rages, and is confident. *(The "wise man" believes the Bible, fears God, and "departs from evil.")*

17 He who is soon angry deals foolishly: and a man of wicked devices is hated. *(The quickly-angered will always deal foolishly. As well, the cool-tempered intriguer is the opposite of the above, but his coolness under pressure does not denote piety, but rather a scheming for personal gain.*

Both the quick-tempered and the intriguer are led by their own impulses and not by God. Both will lead to wrong paths.)

18 The simple inherit folly: but the prudent are crowned with knowledge. *(To the unspiritual ear, Verse 18 seems to be but a repetition of Verse 15; however, the Holy Spirit, from many directions, attempts to get us to understand that He calls those who do not believe the Bible "the simple," irrespective of their otherwise so-called education.)*

19 The evil bow before the good; and the wicked at the gates of the righteous. *(Good will ultimately triumph, even though at present it seems impossible.)*

20 The poor is hated even of his own neighbour: but the rich has many friends.

(Consequently, Jesus was despised and hated [Isa., Chpt. 53].)

21 He who despises his neighbour sins: but he who has mercy on the poor, happy is he. *(In this Proverb, the Lord tells us that He will look after the "poor" who trust in Him.)*

22 Do they not err who devise evil? but mercy and truth shall be to them who devise good. *(Concerning the affairs of life, all that is devised outside of the Bible is "evil." All the truly "good" that is devised comes from the Bible, and will give "Mercy and Truth.")*

23 In all labour there is profit: but the talk of the lips tends only to penury. *(There are many who talk much, but do nothing. Those who truly "labor" will know "profit" [Mat. 6:7].)*

24 The crown of the wise is their riches: but the foolishness of fools is folly. *(Riches do not make a fool cease his foolishness; even though he is rich, he is still a "fool.")*

25 A true witness delivers souls: but a deceitful witness speaks lies. *(A Preacher of the True Gospel of Jesus Christ is a true witness and greatly helps men; the Preacher of "modern thought" and "another gospel" propagates falsehood and, thereby, leads men to destruction [II Cor. 11:4].)*

26 In the fear of the LORD is strong confidence: and his children shall have a place of refuge. *(Once again, the Holy Spirit points to the "fear of the LORD." Such is the foundation of true Righteousness.)*

27 The fear of the LORD is a fountain of life, to depart from the snares of death. *(To escape eternal death and be united to life, there is one sure and only way; it is to fear Jehovah. That means to love, serve, and follow the Lord Jesus Christ [Lk. 9:23-24].)*

28 In the multitude of people is the king's honour: but in the want of people is the destruction of the prince. *(At the present, "the King" [the Lord Jesus Christ] does not have "the multitude" on His Side. In the coming glad day of the Kingdom Age, this will change, and all will serve Him.)*

29 He who is slow to wrath is of great understanding: but he who is hasty of spirit exalts folly. *(The quick-tempered are that way for a reason: such shows pride and, thereby, a lack of trust in God. The one who is "slow to wrath" and is, thereby, "of great understanding" shows that his dependence is in the Lord and not in himself.)*

30 A sound heart is the life of the flesh: but envy the rottenness of the bones. *(In this

Proverb, the Holy Spirit is portraying to us the secret of good health. A "sound heart" is the heart that is right with God. No envy, jealousy, pride, malice, greed, or hatred abides there. If such abides, we are told it will "rot the bones.")

31 He who oppresses the poor reproaches his Maker: but he who honours Him has mercy on the poor. *(Most of the world oppress the poor and thereby reproach God, because God made all men, whether they be rich or poor. Then the Holy Spirit plainly tells us that if we honor God, we will have "mercy on the poor.")*

32 The wicked is driven away in his wickedness: but the righteous has hope in his death. *(Belshazzar illustrates the first line of this Verse; the Apostle Paul, the second line.)*

33 Wisdom rests in the heart of him who has understanding: but that which is in the midst of fools is made known. *(The sense of this Proverb is that a wise man does not display his wisdom, but a fool parades all he knows.)*

34 Righteousness exalts a nation: but sin is a reproach to any people. *(This holds true for any nation. "Much Bible, much freedom; little Bible, little freedom; no Bible, no freedom.")*

35 The king's favour is toward a wise servant: but his wrath is against him who causes shame. *(The "wise servant" will know his Bible, and consequently "has understanding.")*

CHAPTER 15
(1000 B.C.)
THE USE OF THE TONGUE

A soft answer turns away wrath: but grievous words stir up anger. *(Even one grievous word stirs up anger. Any discussion that becomes heated automatically becomes an uncontrolled discussion, which will only lead to more "wrath."*

Self is the cause of heated exchanges. Only when self is properly hidden in Christ is the "soft answer" possible [Gal. 2:20].)

2 The tongue of the wise uses knowledge aright: but the mouth of fools pours out foolishness. *(The "wise" are those who know their Bibles. "Fools" are those who do not know their Bibles. The first "uses knowledge aright," while the latter "pours out foolishness.")*

3 The eyes of the LORD are in every place, beholding the evil and the good. *(This Proverb portrays the Omnipresence of God, meaning that He is everywhere. Such constant observation is terribly unsettling to the unspiritual heart, but, to those who know and love their Redeemer, such*

knowledge is invigorating to the spirit and comforting to the soul.)

4 A wholesome tongue is a tree of life: but perverseness therein is a breach in the spirit. *(The gist of the Proverb is that the Christ-controlled life is "a tree of life," while the life that is not controlled by Christ is "perverse" and becomes a broken tree [Gal. 2:20].)*

5 A fool despises his father's instruction: but he who regards reproof is prudent. *(The unteachable spirit is one where self rules, and Christ does not rule.)*

CONTRASTS BETWEEN THE RIGHTEOUS AND THE WICKED

6 In the house of the righteous is much treasure: but in the revenues of the wicked is trouble. *("Much treasure" is the unsearchable riches of Christ.)*

7 The lips of the wise disperse knowledge: but the heart of the foolish does not so. *(In many and varied ways, the Holy Spirit constantly calls attention to "the wise," whose "knowledge" is from the Bible; conversely, He calls "fools" those who do not adhere to the Word of God.)*

8 The sacrifice of the wicked is an abomination to the LORD: but the prayer of the upright is his delight.

9 The way of the wicked is an abomination unto the LORD: but He loves him who follows after righteousness.

10 Correction is grievous unto him who forsakes the way: and he who hates reproof shall die. *(The worship of the self-willed [Vs. 8] and the way [the conduct] of the self-willed [Vs. 9] are both abominable. Such was Cain's worship and conduct. Abel illustrates the prayer of the upright and God's Way of Righteousness.)*

11 Hell and destruction are before the LORD: how much more then the hearts of the children of men? *(This Proverb, like Verse 3, proclaims all open to the Lord, as well as the unseen world. Also, only God knows the hearts of men!)*

12 A scorner loves not one who reproves him: neither will he go unto the wise. *(The "scorner" holds the "wise" in disdain, because he feels his way is right and, therefore, does not need correction or reproof. Such an intractable spirit will not abide by the Bible.)*

13 A merry heart makes a cheerful countenance: but by sorrow of the heart the spirit is broken. *(The true "merry heart" can only come about by Christ abiding in the heart and having*

complete control. Then the "heart" is not moved by good or bad news, but its joy is in the Lord.)

14 The heart of him who has understanding seeks knowledge: but the mouth of fools feeds on foolishness. *(The Holy Spirit, once again, calls our attention to the fact that the Bible is the fountainhead of knowledge, and we speak of the way that life should be lived.)*

15 All the days of the afflicted are evil: but he who is of a merry heart has a continual feast. *(The "merry heart" has to do with total occupation by Christ.)*

16 Better is little with the fear of the LORD than great treasure and trouble therewith. *(Christ is a Substitute for every good thing; nothing is a substitute for Him.)*

17 Better is a dinner of herbs where love is, than a stalled ox and hatred therewith. *(Better is a poor man's dinner where love is than a rich man's feast where hatred and strife are.)*

18 A wrathful man stirs up strife: but he who is slow to anger appeases strife. *(Anger only stirs up more anger; he who shows coolness under fire calms the strife.)*

19 The way of the slothful man is as an hedge of thorns: but the way of the righteous is made plain. *(The knowledge of the Word of God alone, and it applied to our hearts and lives, can keep us from the unnecessary thorns.)*

20 A wise son makes a glad father: but a foolish man despises his mother. *(A wise son honors his parents, but a foolish one despises them.)*

21 Folly is joy to him who is destitute of wisdom: but a man of understanding walks uprightly. *("Understanding" is joy to the upright, while "folly" is joy to the fool.)*

22 Without counsel purposes are disappointed: but in the multitude of counsellors they are established. *(The "multitude of counselors" are the Books of the Bible.)*

23 A man has joy by the answer of his mouth: and a word spoken in due season, how good is it! *(The only safe "word" is the "Word of God." It is good in any "season." It always brings "joy." It should always be the "answer of the mouth.")*

24 The way of life is above to the wise, that he may depart from Hell beneath. *(Only this "way of life," which is Christ and Him Crucified, will spare one from "Hell beneath.")*

25 The LORD will destroy the house of the proud: but he will establish the border of the widow. *(The "widow" is used as symbolism for the humbled and abased. God will exalt*

humility and abase pride [Lk. 18:14].)

26 The thoughts of the wicked are an abomination to the LORD: but the words of the pure are pleasant words. *("Pleasant words" come from the Bible. They are sure to be "pure." The Blood of Jesus, along with the Word of God, bring purity, and that alone.)*

27 He who is greedy of gain troubles his own house; but he who hates gifts shall live. *(The love of money is the root of all evil. This means that the present-day greed message "troubles" God's house.)*

28 The heart of the righteous studies to answer: but the mouth of the wicked pours out evil things. *("The righteous" studies his heart to know what the Bible says about any particular question.)*

29 The LORD is far from the wicked: but He hears the prayer of the righteous. *(To those who have the imputed Righteousness of the Lord, as well, it is guaranteed that their prayers will be heard. What a comfort!)*

30 The light of the eyes rejoices the heart: and a good report makes the bones fat. *(The light and glad tidings of the Gospel rejoice the heart and make fat the bones.)*

31 The ear that hears the reproof of life abides among the wise. *(The "reproof of life" is the Word of God, and the Word of God alone!)*

32 He who refuses instruction despises his own soul: but he who hears reproof gets understanding. *(The "instruction" that the Bible gives is not only for man's good, but, in effect, is the only way of Salvation. If it is refused, it is a sin against one's own soul.)*

33 The fear of the LORD is the instruction of wisdom; and before honour is humility. *("Humility" is the foundation of all Christlikeness. The only personal thing that Christ said about Himself was, "I am meek and lowly in heart" [Mat. 11:29].)*

CHAPTER 16
(1000 B.C.)

THE FEAR OF THE LORD
AND OBEDIENCE

THE preparations of the heart in man, and the answer of the tongue, is from the LORD. *(As the Proverbs of Chapters 10 through 15 affect man's relationships with his fellowman, so the Proverbs of Chapters 16 through 19 concern man's relationship to God.*

One might say that man proposes, but God disposes, and that is the doctrine of this Proverb.)

2 All the ways of a man are clean in his own eyes; but the LORD weighs the spirits. *(Conscience is a blind guide unless enlightened by the Word of God.)*

3 Commit your works unto the LORD, and your thoughts shall be established. *(Faith in Christ and what He has done for us at the Cross will help us to "walk after the Spirit," thereby with all thoughts properly established [Rom. 8:1-2, 11].)*

4 The LORD has made all things for Himself: yea, even the wicked for the day of evil. *(The sense of this Proverb is that God's Plan was designed for and by Himself. In this Plan is the Truth that the "wicked" will suffer for their evil unless they repent.)*

5 Every one who is proud in heart is an abomination to the LORD: though hand join in hand, he shall not be unpunished. *(Pride is the foundation sin of all sin. It breeds unbelief.*

God has pledged that even though the proud join "hand in hand," and despite all of their power and riches, still, they will not go unpunished.)

6 By mercy and truth iniquity is purged: and by the fear of the LORD men depart from evil. *("Purged" denotes "covered" or "atoned for." Mercy and Truth atoned for iniquity at Calvary. The moral effect of this great fact and Doctrine is to cause men to fear God and depart from evil.)*

7 When a man's ways please the LORD, he makes even his enemies to be at peace with him. *(The idea of the Proverb is that even though the "enemies" remain "enemies," they realize that God is with this man, and there is nothing they can do to cause him harm. Therefore, they make peace.)*

8 Better is a little with righteousness than great revenues without right. *(The song says: "Little is much if God be in it.")*

9 A man's heart devises his way: but the LORD directs his steps. *(The idea of the Lord directing one's steps is glorious beyond compare. Irrespective of the seeming dangers, the steps will be sure and the way will be secure.)*

10 A divine sentence is in the lips of the king: his mouth transgresses not in judgment. *(The phrase, "a Divine sentence," refers to the king or magistrate of any nature using the Bible as the guide for all judgment.)*

11 A just weight and balance are the LORD'S: all the weights of the bag are His work. *(In this Proverb, as well as others similar, the Holy Spirit impresses upon everyone God's demand for honesty.)*

12 It is an abomination to kings to commit wickedness: for the throne is established by righteousness. *(If bribery, deceit, and calumny are practiced by the leadership of any country, state, city or organization, it will ultimately result in the whole being adversely affected. This is the reason God calls it an "abomination.")*

13 Righteous lips are the delight of kings; and they love him who speaks right. *(The only way that any king or leader can have "righteous lips" [to speak that which is right] is to speak according to the Bible.)*

14 The wrath of a king is as messengers of death: but a wise man will pacify it. *(In these Passages, the monarchical form of government is being addressed; however, it would apply to the democratic form, as well. Advisors are supposed to pacify the anger of the leader.)*

15 In the light of the king's countenance is life; and his favour is as a cloud of the latter rain. *(If men would make as much effort to win the favor of God as they do the favor of monarchs or political leaders, their blessing would be unlimited.)*

16 How much better is it to get wisdom than gold! and to get understanding rather to be chosen than silver! *(The "wisdom" and "understanding" referred to here is that which comes from the Bible. Despite the fact that the Holy Spirit tells us that this is so much better than "gold or silver," still, most spend far more of their time and effort to obtain money rather than the knowledge of the Word of God.)*

17 The highway of the upright is to depart from evil: he who keeps his way preserves his soul. *(There is no way that any Christian can continue to live "in evil" and "preserve his soul.")*

18 Pride goes before destruction, and an haughty spirit before a fall. *(Pride is the foundational cause of man's lost condition. It is the principal sin of self-righteousness. It was such that nailed Christ to the Cross.)*

19 Better it is to be of an humble spirit with the lowly, than to divide the spoil with the proud. *(This Proverb characterizes Christ. He never in any manner associated with the proud Pharisees. He rather associated Himself with "the lowly," and, in fact, chose fishermen and a lowly tax collector as His Disciples.)*

20 He who handles a matter wisely shall find good: and whoso trusts in the LORD, happy is he. *(This Proverb could be translated: "He who gives heed unto the Word of God shall find good; and he who trusts in Jehovah, Oh how happy is he!")*

21 The wise in heart shall be called prudent: and the sweetness of the lips increases learning. *(There is no way that one can be "wise in heart" without allowing the Bible to be his teacher and guide.)*

22 Understanding is a wellspring of life unto him who has it: but the instruction of fools is folly. *(This Proverb can easily be abbreviated and explained by saying, "If one understands the Bible, it will be to him 'a wellspring of life.'")*

23 The heart of the wise teaches his mouth, and adds learning to his lips. *(The "wise" person is the one who knows the Bible and is, therefore, wise in the things of God, which are the things that really matter.)*

24 Pleasant words are as an honeycomb, sweet to the soul, and health to the bones. *("Pleasant words" speak of kind words, which have their foundation in the Bible.)*

THE BROAD ROAD THAT
LEADS TO DEATH

25 There is a way that seems right unto a man, but the end thereof are the ways of death. *(This same Proverb is quoted in 14:12. It is given thusly by the Holy Spirit by design. The entirety of the problems of the human family is because of wrong direction. The only "true way" is "Jesus Christ and Him Crucified" [I Cor. 1:14-18, 21, 23; 2:2].)*

26 He who labours labours for himself; for his mouth craves it of him. *(This speaks of selfish labor, which has no basis or foundation in the Work or Word of God. Such is done to satisfy some appetite or meet some alleged need in life; therefore, this means that selfishness and greed characterize the far greater majority of the human family.)*

27 An ungodly man digs up evil: and in his lips there is as a burning fire. *(As an example, Ham uncovered the nakedness of his father, Noah, while Shem and Japheth covered the nakedness of their father [Gen. 9:22-23].)*

28 A froward man sows strife: and a whisperer separates chief friends. *(The word "froward" means one who is habitually disobedient. Such a one loves to spread gossip and rumors about others.)*

29 A violent man entices his neighbour, and leads him into the way that is not good. *(The "violent man" pertains to those who are willing to commit any act to get what they want.)*

30 He shuts his eyes to devise froward things: moving his lips he brings evil to pass. *(The pronoun "he" refers to the "violent man" of Verse 29. He is constantly devising evil things.)*

31 The hoary head is a crown of glory, if it be found in the way of righteousness. *(The "hoary head" speaks of age; however, it is a "crown of glory" only if it adheres to the "way of righteousness.")*

32 He who is slow to anger is better than the mighty; and he who rules his spirit than he who takes a city. *(True self-control can only be given by the Holy Spirit. It comes through Christ, and our Faith in Him and what He has done for us at the Cross [Gal. 2:20-21].)*

33 The lot is cast into the lap; but the whole disposing thereof is of the LORD. *(The sense of this Passage is that the Lord is the One Who gives the direction, and that man should seek to be led by the Lord in all things.)*

CHAPTER 17
(1000 B.C.)
GOOD AND EVIL SPEECH

BETTER is a dry morsel, and quietness therewith, than an house full of sacrifices with strife. *(Poverty with peace and contentment is better than plenty with strife. As well, great religious activity is often accompanied by "strife.")*

2 A wise servant shall have rule over a son who causes shame, and shall have part of the inheritance among the brethren. *(The Holy Spirit is saying that irrespective of a person's status in life, if he will wholly follow the Lord and make himself "wise" through the Bible, then God will promote him.)*

3 The fining pot is for silver, and the furnace for gold: but the LORD tries the hearts. *(The Holy Spirit is saying that inasmuch as "silver and gold" are precious, they are both placed in the furnace to remove the impurities. At times, the Believer has to go through the "fiery trial" in order to remove moral and spiritual impurities [James 1:2; I Pet. 1:7; 4:12; Rev. 3:18].)*

4 A wicked doer gives heed to false lips; and a liar gives ear to a naughty tongue. *(God calls those who enjoy hearing gossip "liars." Likewise, the "liar" loves to hear and pass on the gossip of other "liars.")*

5 Whoso mocks the poor reproaches his Maker: and he who is glad at calamities shall not be unpunished. *(In this Proverb, the Lord plainly states that whosoever takes advantage of the poor reproaches the Lord. God has promised that such "shall not be unpunished.")*

6 Children's children are the crown of old men; and the glory of children are their fathers. *(One of the happiest things in the life of a grandfather is the grandchildren.)*

7 Excellent speech becomes not a fool: much less do lying lips a prince. *(The sense of this Proverb is that we should not expect a prince to lie anymore than we would expect a fool to use "excellent speech.")*

8 A gift is as a precious stone in the eyes of him who has it: whithersoever it turns, it prospers. *(If one will find his "gift," thank the Lord for it, and use it for God's Glory, then prosperity will come.)*

9 He who covers a transgression seeks love; but he who repeats a matter separates very friends. *(Transgressions which have been forgiven are to be covered.)*

10 A reproof enters more into a wise man than an hundred stripes into a fool. *(A mild "reproof" will be instantly picked up by a "wise man," and he will take it to heart and correct the situation.)*

11 An evil man seeks only rebellion: therefore a cruel messenger shall be sent against him. *(Those who would foment "rebellion" against Righteousness will sooner or later come to grief.)*

MORAL VIRTUES AND CONTRARY VICES

12 Let a bear robbed of her whelps meet a man, rather than a fool in his folly. *(Who are these fools? They are those who do not regard the Bible as the Word of God, consequently ignoring its contents.)*

13 Whoso rewards evil for good, evil shall not depart from his house. *(As is obvious, evil cannot be rewarded by God. It must be forsaken and, thereby, forgiven.)*

14 The beginning of strife is as when one lets out water: therefore leave off contention, before it be meddled with. *(The Holy Spirit compares the "beginning of strife" to a small crack in a dam.)*

15 He who justifies the wicked, and he who condemns the just, even they both are abomination to the LORD. *(Self-righteousness will always justify the wickedness of those who agree with its concepts. Self-righteousness will also condemn the just, i.e., "those who trust exclusively in Christ.")*

16 Wherefore is there a price in the hand of a fool to get wisdom, seeing he has no heart to it? *(A "fool" is one who does not know God*

and, thereby, ignores God's Word.)*

17 A friend loves at all times, and a brother is born for adversity. *(There are many fair-weather friends; when the storms come, they leave. However, a true friend will continue to "love," irrespective of the circumstances and situations. These are few and far between.)*

18 A man void of understanding strikes hands, and becomes surety in the presence of his friend. *(This concerns a man who makes foolish bargains, or else he stands good for the debt of another.)*

19 He loves transgression who loves strife: and he who exalts his gate seeks destruction. *("Strife" will sooner or later lead to sin. That's the reason we are told in Verse 14 to "leave off contention," which causes strife.)*

20 He who has a froward heart finds no good: and he who has a perverse tongue falls into mischief. *(The evil heart and lying tongue will come to "no good." Such are all who do not fear God and keep His Word.)*

21 He who begets a fool does it to his sorrow: and the father of a fool has no joy. *("The begetting of a fool" has to do with raising a child outside the boundaries of God and His Word.)*

22 A merry heart does good like a medicine: but a broken spirit dries the bones. *(A "merry heart" can only be brought about by total trust in the Lord.)*

23 A wicked man takes a gift out of the bosom to pervert the ways of judgment. *(True "judgment" is sidestepped by the bribe.)*

24 Wisdom is before him who has understanding; but the eyes of a fool are in the ends of the Earth. *(Men are running even to the "ends of the Earth," attempting to find Wisdom, understanding, or the "pearl of great price." They little know that all that they seek is right at their fingertips, and it's in a Book called "the Bible.")*

25 A foolish son is a grief to his father, and bitterness to her who bore him. *(The father and mother who raise a son without God and without the Bible are raising a "fool.")*

26 Also to punish the just is not good, nor to strike princes for equity. *(To punish one who has truly repented of sin, and is now just, and made so by the Grace of God, presents a gross injustice. It is the same as anarchy, which leads to the ruin for a community or a nation.)*

27 He who has knowledge spares his words: and a man of understanding is of an excellent spirit. *(One who truly has "knowledge" [Bible knowledge] will not have a know-it-all attitude.*

He will "spare his words.")

28 Even a fool, when he holds his peace, is counted wise: and he who shuts his lips is esteemed a man of understanding. *(From this, we certainly should learn that hasty words only bring regret, contention, and sorrow. They never show us to be people of "wisdom and understanding.")*

CHAPTER 18
(1000 B.C.)
FOOLISH AND WISE WORDS

THROUGH desire a man, having separated himself, seeks and intermeddles with all wisdom. *(Multiple tens of million the world over separate themselves and seek to learn the wisdom of the ages without the Bible. Such presents itself as a fruitless exercise.)*

2 A fool has no delight in understanding, but that his heart may discover itself. *(The "fool" of this Proverb is the one who constantly tries to find "himself." Proper "understanding" of one's self can only be found in the Bible.)*

3 When the wicked comes, then comes also contempt, and with ignominy reproach. *(The less one values the Bible, the less "contempt" one will have for the way of "the wicked.")*

4 The words of a man's mouth are as deep waters, and the wellspring of wisdom as a flowing brook. *(The worldly wisdom of man is like a brackish pool that quickly dries up; however, for the man who knows and understands the Bible, his "mouth" will be as "deep waters.")*

5 It is not good to accept the person of the wicked, to overthrow the righteous in judgment. *(The only correct "judgment" in the world is that which comes from "the righteous." Mostly, and with great loss, they are ignored.)*

6 A fool's lips enter into contention, and his mouth calls for strokes.

7 A fool's mouth is his destruction, and his lips are the snare of his soul. *(Spiritually, the "fool" is the one who does not know the Bible; because of his lack of true knowledge, he will quickly find trouble. His "mouth" will guarantee his destruction.)*

8 The words of a talebearer are as wounds, and they go down into the innermost parts of the belly. *(A "talebearer" in this Passage is likened to a slanderer. His "words" are as morsels that go down into the heart of the listener and cause "wounds.")*

9 He also who is slothful in his work is brother to him who is a great waster. *(The*

"great waster" is one who does not properly care for that which is entrusted to him.)

10 The name of the LORD is a strong tower: the righteous runs into it, and is safe. *(The correct spiritual posture for the Christian is to fear Satan and in no way attempt to face him in one's own strength, but, instead, quickly run to Christ. Only there is one guaranteed safety.)*

11 The rich man's wealth is his strong city, and as an high wall in his own conceit. *(Verse 11 contrasts with Verse 10. Verse 10 is fact and Verse 11 is fiction. Only the one who runs to "the Lord" will be safe. The one who runs to riches does so out of "his own conceit," and ultimately comes to destruction.)*

12 Before destruction the heart of man is haughty, and before honour is humility. *(The spirit of the world is pride and "haughtiness." It ultimately leads to destruction. The Spirit of Christ is "humility"; it ultimately leads to "honor.")*

13 He who answers a matter before he hears it, it is folly and shame unto him. *(The Holy Spirit is telling us here that no man, at least within himself, can be so brilliant or intelligent that he can make the proper decision before hearing all the matter!)*

14 The spirit of a man will sustain his infirmity; but a wounded spirit who can bear? *(The world, and even the Church, are full of man-made solutions to "the wounded spirit." Faith in Christ and His Atoning Work is the only answer [Gal. 5:4].)*

15 The heart of the prudent gets knowledge; and the ear of the wise seeks knowledge. *(The only true "knowledge" of life is the Bible.)*

16 A man's gift makes room for him, and brings him before great men. *(The idea the Holy Spirit imposes is that the individual is there, not because of himself, but due to his "gift." The possessor of such must never forget that the Giver of this "Gift" is God.)*

17 He who is first in his own cause seems just; but his neighbour comes and searches him. *(The Holy Spirit is telling us that we should not jump to conclusions upon hearing the first witness.)*

18 The lot causes contentions to cease, and parts between the mighty. *(The "lot" has to do with the Old Testament "Urim and Thummim." They were used to divine the Will of the Lord in specific matters.*

This tells us that we must seek God's Will in all matters, for He Alone holds the solution.)

19 A brother offended is harder to be won than a strong city: and their contentions are

like the bars of a castle. *(The word "offended" should have been translated "injured.")*

20 A man's belly shall be satisfied with the fruit of his mouth; and with the increase of his lips shall he be filled. *(If the "fruit of the mouth" and the "increase of the lips" be Heavenly, then there is inward contentment; if not, then there is inward desolation.)*

21 Death and life are in the power of the tongue: and they who love it shall eat the fruit thereof. *(Christians who constantly talk doubt, in effect, talk "death." Those who speak the Word of God speak "life.")*

22 Whoso finds a wife finds a good thing, and obtains favour of the LORD. *(This Passage tells us that celibacy for Believers is not required, and marriage is honorable in all [Heb. 13:4].)*

23 The poor uses intreaties, but the rich answers roughly. *(Sadly, this Proverb has been true for all time. The "poor" and needy cry to the rich for the necessities of life, but all too often they are answered roughly. One day Jesus is coming back, and then these terrible wrongs will be made right!)*

24 A man who has friends must show himself friendly: and there is a friend who sticks closer than a brother. *(The greatest "Friend" of all is the Lord Jesus Christ. He will never leave you nor forsake you [Heb. 13:5].)*

CHAPTER 19
(1000 B.C.)
PROVERBS OF PERSONAL CHARACTER

BETTER is the poor who walks in his integrity, than he who is perverse in his lips, and is a fool. *(The intention of this Proverb is that poverty with integrity is better than wealth with dishonesty.)*

2 Also, that the soul be without knowledge, it is not good; and he who hastens with his feet sins. *(If the "soul" be without the "knowledge" of the Bible, it cannot come to "good.")*

3 The foolishness of man perverts his way: and his heart frets against the LORD. *(Self-will causes men to make fools of themselves.)*

4 Wealth makes many friends; but the poor is separated from his neighbour. *(Money attracts many friends, but most are fair-weather ones. "The poor," by not having any money, also have few friends.)*

5 A false witness shall not be unpunished, and he who speaks lies shall not escape. *(God hates a "lying tongue" and a "false witness." Considering that, judgment will ultimately come*

on those who practice such.)*

6 Many will intreat the favour of the prince: and every man is a friend to him who gives gifts. *(The heart of man is basically hypocritical, and is shown in these efforts.)*

7 All the brethren of the poor do hate him: how much more do his friends go far from him? he pursues them with words, yet they are wanting to him. *(While the "prince" is in power, everyone is his "friend." However, when he is out of office and can no longer bestow "gifts," possibly because of reversal of fortunes, and becomes "poor," those who formerly swore allegiance to their dying day now "hate him.")*

8 He who gets wisdom loves his own soul: he who keeps understanding shall find good. *(The "Wisdom" and "understanding" of this Proverb mean Heavenly Knowledge, which can only come from the Bible.)*

9 A false witness shall not be unpunished, and he who speaks lies shall perish. *(Verse 9 is not a needless repetition of Verse 5. The latter Verse defines the punishment announced in the former; the repetition emphasizes God's just anger against falsehood and His love for humanity, especially for the oppressed.)*

10 Delight is not seemly for a fool; much less for a servant to have rule over princes. *(The first part of this Proverb refers to a "fool" who is of royal birth and enjoys luxury, rank, and honor. His rule brings no "delight."*

The second part refers to a "servant" who somehow finds himself in a position of authority. Generally when this happens, he is cruel and tyrannical.)

11 The discretion of a man defers his anger; and it is his glory to pass over a transgression. *(A forgiving spirit marks the true man of God under both the First and Second Covenants.)*

12 The king's wrath is as the roaring of a lion; but his favour is as dew upon the grass. *(Opposition to lawful government ensures just suffering, but obedience secures prosperity.)*

13 A foolish son is the calamity of his father: and the contentions of a wife are a continual dropping. *(An example is the Chinese water torture. A drop of water dropped on a person's head causes little difficulty, but, if perpetually continued, will drive one to insanity.)*

14 House and riches are the inheritance of fathers: and a prudent wife is from the LORD. *(This woman is the utter contrast to the one in Verse 13. She may have many causes for complaint, but she avoids them all.)*

15 Slothfulness casts into a deep sleep; and

an idle soul shall suffer hunger. *(In the Bible, laziness is, as by now should be obvious, roundly condemned.)*

16 He who keeps the commandment keeps his own soul; but he who despises his ways shall die. *(He who cherishes "the Commandment" [the Bible] safeguards his life; indifference to Divine teaching [His Ways] causes spiritual death.)*

17 He who has pity upon the poor lends unto the LORD; and that which he has given will he pay him again. *(In this Proverb, God guarantees the "gift" or the debt.)*

18 Chasten your son while there is hope, and let not your soul spare for his crying. *(This speaks of proper discipline.)*

19 A man of great wrath shall suffer punishment: for if you deliver him, yet you must do it again. *(The need of such a man is for his "great wrath" to be throttled, not for someone to pay his fine.)*

COUNSEL AND INSTRUCTION

20 Hear counsel, and receive instruction, that you may be wise in your latter end. *(The "counsel" and "instruction" spoken of here pertain to the Bible.)*

21 There are many devices in a man's heart; nevertheless the counsel of the LORD, that shall stand. *(The Bible alone will stand, because it is the Word, i.e., "the Counsel of the LORD.")*

22 The desire of a man is his kindness: and a poor man is better than a liar. *(The latter portion of this Proverb means that a little kindness received from a poor man is better than the false promises of a rich liar.)*

23 The fear of the LORD tends to life: and he who has it shall abide satisfied; he shall not be visited with evil. *(To love and serve the Lord Jesus Christ leads to an endless life of abiding bliss; not to do so results in everlasting misery.)*

24 A slothful man hides his hand in his bosom, and will not so much as bring it to his mouth again. *(The "slothful" is constantly claiming to be sick [hiding his hand in his bosom] when, in fact, he is only lazy and wants somebody to put food in "his mouth." If it is done once, he will want it done "again" and "again." That's the reason Paul said, "If they don't work, they don't eat" [II Thess. 3:10].)*

25 Smite a scorner, and the simple will beware: and reprove one who has understanding, and he will understand knowledge. *(Some claim that punishment for crime is no deterrent! While it is true that it is not the best deterrent, which is the conversion of the soul, still, judgment of evil is definitely a deterrent.)*

26 He who wastes his father, and chases away his mother, is a son who causes shame, and brings reproach. *(This speaks of a son who wastes the father's goods, and then, upon the father's death, refuses to allow the aged mother to live with him, or else to provide for her necessities.)*

27 Cease, my son, to hear the instruction that causes to err from the words of knowledge. *(All the Proverbs spoken to "My son" are from the Lord to Solomon. Anything that steers a person away from the Bible is called "error" by the Holy Spirit.)*

28 An ungodly witness scorns judgment: and the mouth of the wicked devours iniquity. *(The "ungodly witness" is similar to the "false witness" of 19:9. God has promised that such would not be unpunished.)*

29 Judgments are prepared for scorners, and stripes for the back of fools. *(The Holy Spirit states unequivocally that despite the scorning "mouth" of "the wicked," judgments are prepared by God for these "scorners.")*

CHAPTER 20
(1000 B.C.)
MORAL VIRTUES AND CONTRARY VICES CONTINUED

WINE is a mocker, strong drink is raging: and whosoever is deceived thereby is not wise. *(The Holy Spirit here says that "wine mocks," and it causes a "raging" in the hearts and lives of all who imbibe. As well, it is a great "deceiver." This means that every Believer ought to be a teetotaler.)*

2 The fear of a king is as the roaring of a lion: whoso provokes him to anger sins against his own soul. *(Righteous government is to be obeyed.)*

3 It is an honour for a man to cease from strife: but every fool will be meddling. *(Everything short of violating the Word of God is to be done to stop "strife." Those who do not do so are called "fools" by the Lord.)*

4 The sluggard will not plow by reason of the cold; therefore shall he beg in harvest, and have nothing. *(If we allow hindrances to stop us doing what needs to be done, then nothing will ever be done, and we will come to poverty.)*

5 Counsel in the heart of man is like deep water; but a man of understanding will draw it out. *(At the beginning of inquiry men will not*

usually reveal what they really think or want. They generally talk around the edges. Consequently, only those who truly know the Bible have proper "understanding," and can, therefore, normally draw out what needs to be known.)

6 Most men will proclaim every one his own goodness: but a faithful man who can find? (Boasters can readily be found on every side, but trustworthy men must be sought for.)

7 The just man walks in his integrity: his children are blessed after him. (The "integrity" addressed here is the "integrity" that God gives.)

8 A king who sits in the throne of judgment scatters away all evil with his eyes. (A righteous king judges evil, disclaims personal moral perfection and, in fellowship with God, protects the poor against the injustice of evildoers.)

9 Who can say, I have made my heart clean, I am pure from my sin? (The only way that purity can be brought about is by Faith and trust in Christ and what He has done for us at the Cross. Only then can all sins be washed away [I Jn. 1:7].)

10 Divers weights, and divers measures, both of them are alike abomination to the LORD. ("Divers" refers to that which is fraudulent. All dishonesty is an abomination to the LORD.)

11 Even a child is known by his doings, whether his work be pure, and whether it be right. (Most of the world attempts to replace the Bible with secular education. The results are obvious.)

12 The hearing ear, and the seeing eye, the LORD has made even both of them. (The "hearing ear" is meant to hear only the Lord, and the "seeing eye" meant to observe only what the Lord wants, namely His Word to be obeyed.)

13 Love not sleep, lest you come to poverty; open your eyes, and you shall be satisfied with bread. (Over and over again, the Holy Spirit lauds industry, while condemning laziness.)

14 It is naught, it is naught, saith the buyer: but when he is gone his way, then he boasts. (Men attempt to belittle the object of their proposed purchase in order to get it at a cheaper price; after it is purchased, they boast as to its quality and at their bargain.)

15 There is gold, and a multitude of rubies: but the lips of knowledge are a precious jewel. (The "knowledge" spoken of is that which comes exclusively from the Bible.)

16 Take his garment that is surety for a stranger: and take a pledge of him for a strange woman. (The sense of the Proverb is that those who are of heathenistic religions, and those who serve a corrupt Christianity, cannot be trusted.)

17 Bread of deceit is sweet to a man; but afterwards his mouth shall be filled with gravel. ("Bread of deceit" means wealth obtained by falsehood.)

18 Every purpose is established by counsel: and with good advice make war. (In other words, we should "look before we leap.")

19 He who goes about as a talebearer reveals secrets: therefore meddle not with him who flatters with his lips. (The sense of this Proverb is that some individuals are "talebearers" by disposition. As such, they will flatter a person to get him to reveal "secrets." They will then proceed to spread the "secrets" far and wide. The Holy Spirit is saying that we should not have any association with these type of people.)

20 Whoso curses his father or his mother, his lamp shall be put out in obscure darkness. (There are three Laws given in Verses 20 through 22. They are given by God and are, therefore, unfailing.)

21 An inheritance may be gotten hastily at the beginning; but the end thereof shall not be blessed. (Money that we do not have to work for generally brings no blessing.)

22 Say not thou, I will recompense evil; but wait on the LORD, and He shall save you. (To recompense evil for evil will not be blessed of the Lord, but those who trust God to reward evil in His Own time will see such vengeance brought about by His Hand [Rom. 12:19].)

23 Divers weights are an abomination unto the LORD; and a false balance is not good. (This Proverb is very similar to Verse 10 by design. Such is repeated in Deut. 25:13 and in Prov. 11:1 and 16:11. Due to the repetition, I think it should be obvious that the Holy Spirit places great stock in honesty.)

24 Man's going are of the LORD; how can a man then understand his own way? (This Proverb holds the key to man's success or failure. Man's goings are to be "of the LORD" and not the mindless claptrap of evolution, psychology, or other of man's absurdities!)

25 It is a snare to the man who devours that which is holy, and after vows to make enquiry. (Most of the world is in a "snare" because they have taken that which is "holy," namely their lives, and used them for the pursuit of self.)

26 A wise king scatters the wicked, and brings the wheel over them. (A nation is blessed which has a leader who will protect it from "the wicked" and who will bring such evil

to punishment.)

27 The spirit of man is the candle of the LORD, searching all the inward parts of the belly. (Man can have contact with the Lord only by and through his spirit; therefore, they who worship Him must worship Him in spirit and in truth [Jn. 4:24].)

28 Mercy and truth preserve the king: and his throne is upholden by mercy.

29 The glory of young men is their strength: and the beauty of old men is the grey head. (What is presented here is contrasted glory. The truth is, the "glory" of both young and old should be their knowledge of the Word of God. "Strength" soon fades and the "gray head" is soon to die; the Word of God endures forever!)

30 The blueness of a wound cleanses away evil: so do stripes the inward parts of the belly. (This speaks of the correction of the child. It is amazing that man made by God thinks he knows more than God! Such arrogancy is the result of man's pride.

As a man-made adage says, "When all else fails, read the instructions," i.e., "the Bible.")

CHAPTER 21
(1000 B.C.)
MORAL, ETHICAL, AND SPIRITUAL TEACHINGS CONTINUED

THE king's heart is in the hand of the LORD, as the rivers of water: He turns it whithersoever He will. (The general sense of this Proverb is that "kings" or leaders may think that because of their position they are not controlled by God. This Proverb tells us differently.)

2 Every way of a man is right in his own eyes: but the LORD ponders the hearts. (This comes under the heading of: "Man looks at the outward appearance, but the Lord looks on the heart" [I Sam. 16:7].)

3 To do justice and judgment is more acceptable to the LORD than sacrifice. (The idea is that even though "Sacrifice" is certainly "acceptable to the LORD," still, "to do justice and judgment," in other words to simply do right, which requires no "Sacrifice," is "more acceptable to the LORD." "To obey is better than to Sacrifice" [I Sam. 15:22].)

4 An high look and a proud heart, and the plowing of the wicked, is sin. (This means that the "proud" do not consider such as sin, and they see no need for a "Sin Offering.")

5 The thoughts of the diligent tend only to plenteousness; but of every one who is hasty only to want. (The "diligent" will count the cost before they begin work on the tower [Lk. 14:28].)

6 The getting of treasures by a lying tongue is a vanity tossed to and fro of them who seek death. (Treasures obtained by a "lying tongue" are, likewise, taken away by a "lying tongue.")

7 The robbery of the wicked shall destroy them; because they refused to do judgment. (Those who refuse God's "Judgment" [Righteousness] are given Satan's wickedness by default. What we sow, we reap [Gal. 6:7].)

8 The way of man is froward and strange: but as for the pure, his work is right. (The straightness of the one man is contrasted with the crookedness of the other.)

9 It is better to dwell in a corner of the housetop, than with a brawling woman in a wide house. (There are several Passages that are very similar to this Proverb [19:13; 25:24; 27:15]. The repetition was by design and given by the Holy Spirit.)

10 The soul of the wicked desires evil: his neighbour finds no favour in his eyes. (All are called "the wicked" who do not believe in God or His Word. Such cannot be trusted by anyone, even "his neighbor.")

11 When the scorner is punished, the simple is made wise: and when the wise is instructed, he receives knowledge. (The "wise" are instructed by the Bible, which is "knowledge.")

12 The righteous man wisely considers the house of the wicked: but God overthrows the wicked for their wickedness. (In Verse 10, the wicked have no sympathy for anyone, even their neighbors; however, in this Verse, "the Righteous" have sympathy for "the wicked.")

13 Whoso stops his ears at the cry of the poor, he also shall cry himself, but shall not be heard. (What we sow, we reap [Gal. 6:7].)

14 A gift in secret pacifies anger: and a reward in the bosom strong wrath. (Upright men act justly under all circumstances and refuse to shield themselves from public or private hostility by trying to bribe their way out of scandal or the revelation of wrongdoing!)

15 It is joy to the just to do judgment: but destruction shall be to the workers of iniquity. (This Proverb proves the folly of the previous Verse in attempting to pacify anger with bribery. The truly "just" will accept the true "Judgment" of God. Actually, it will be a "joy" to him, because God's "Judgment" is always corrective and never punitive.)

16 The man who wanders out of the way of

understanding shall remain in the congregation of the dead. *(The "way of understanding" is the way of the Bible. To leave that "Way" is to leave life.)*

17 He who loves pleasure shall be a poor man: he who loves wine and oil shall not be rich. *(Lack of diligence and lack of responsibility produce laziness and are roundly condemned by the Bible.)*

18 The wicked shall be a ransom for the righteous, and the transgressor for the upright. *(At present, it might look like "the wicked" and "the transgressor" shall be the winners in this game of life; however, God says that "the wicked" shall be ultimately cut off by God's Judgment in order to preserve the Righteous.)*

19 It is better to dwell in the wilderness, than with a contentious and an angry woman. *(While it is true that men become as easily embroiled in contention as women, still, men are much quicker to let the matter rest. Women have a greater tendency not to do so.)*

20 There is treasure to be desired and oil in the dwelling of the wise; but a foolish man spends it up. *(The "wise" are those who know their Bibles and will consequently conserve what God gives them.)*

21 He who follows after righteousness and mercy finds life, righteousness, and honour. *(This somewhat coincides with Jesus' statement, "Blessed are they which do hunger and thirst after Righteousness: for they shall be filled" [Mat. 5:6].)*

22 A wise man scales the city of the mighty, and casts down the strength of the confidence thereof. *(The Holy Spirit in this Proverb tells us that Wisdom [knowledge of the Bible and how to use it] is greater than "might.")*

23 Whoso keeps his mouth and his tongue keeps his soul from troubles. *(How so many times all of us have proven this Proverb absolutely correct! We talk when we should have been listening.)*

24 Proud and haughty scorner is his name, who deals in proud wrath. *(This concerns the man who treats his fellowman with pride, contempt, and violence. He merits an opprobrious name.)*

25 The desire of the slothful kills him; for his hands refuse to labour. *(The "desire" of the lazy is that he be able to eat, drink, be clothed, and be housed without working for it.)*

26 He covets greedily all the day long: but the righteous gives and spares not. *(Because "the slothful" will not work ["his hands refuse*

to labor"], he "covets" that which the righteous have, and "greedily" at that, thereby breaking the Tenth Commandment [Ex. 20:17].)*

27 The sacrifice of the wicked is abomination: how much more, when he brings it with a wicked mind? *(Many during the time of Israel thought that the Sacrifices atoned for their sin, when they actually had no intention of quitting the sin business. God calls this an "abomination.")*

28 A false witness shall perish: but the man who hears speaks constantly. *(The testimony of a truthful witness stands, but that of an untruthful one will ultimately be found out, and he will "perish.")*

29 A wicked man hardens his face: but as for the upright, he directed his way. *(A "wicked man" makes bold his face and statements in order to hide his guilt, which will ultimately be found out.)*

30 There is no wisdom nor understanding nor counsel against the LORD. *(What a beautiful Promise! Irrespective of the opposition, with all of its earthly wisdom and understanding, if it is fighting against God, it cannot win [Rom. 8:31].)*

31 The horse is prepared against the day of battle: but safety is of the LORD. *(The "safety" of the United States is the Lord. We must never forget that!)*

CHAPTER 22
(1000 B.C.)
CHOOSING A GOOD NAME

A good name is rather to be chosen than great riches, and loving favour rather than silver and gold. *(The sense of this Proverb is that most men would sacrifice anything and everything, even their "good name," in order to obtain "riches." Such is a sorry choice! To do so deems the right way of God as less than the way of "riches.")*

2 The rich and poor meet together: the LORD is the maker of them all. *(This doesn't mean that God made some men to be rich and some to be poor, but rather that He is the Maker of all, regardless as to whether they are rich or poor. Moreover, since they are equal before God, they should be the same before a king or leader.)*

3 A prudent man foresees the evil, and hides himself: but the simple pass on, and are punished. *(The "prudent man" is the one who lives his life by the Bible and, therefore, "foresees evil." He can, therefore, protect himself*

from its environment.

The "simple" can be likened to those who do not know or believe the Bible and are, therefore, ignorant of the vicissitudes of the spirit world.)

4 **By humility and the fear of the LORD are riches, and honour, and life.** *(Verse 4 is contrasted with Verse 1. These are the true "riches, and honor, and life.")*

5 **Thorns and snares are in the way of the froward: he who does keep his soul shall be far from them.** *(The word "froward" is often used by the Holy Spirit in these Proverbs. It means "to be habitually disposed to disobedience and opposition." Such will find their way beset by "thorns and snares.")*

6 **Train up a child in the way he should go: and when he is old, he will not depart from it.** *(The words, "train up," mean to "hedge up" or "hedge in." It is like building a fence around a child; however, what are to be fenced in must be two things, "the child and the Bible." This is the "way he should go.")*

7 **The rich rule over the poor, and the borrower is servant to the lender.** *(It is not wrong to borrow money as long as our capabilities are such that we can easily repay; however, if those capabilities are ever diminished, the "borrower" will learn, to his dismay, the truth of this statement.)*

8 **He who sows iniquity shall reap vanity: and the rod of his anger shall fail.** *(This is the law of sowing and reaping [Lk. 6:38; Gal. 6:7-8].)*

9 **He who has a bountiful eye shall be blessed; for he gives of his bread to the poor.** *(Most people go through life desiring to be "getters" and consequently are discontented. The true Christian goes through life as a "giver" and consequently is happy, because "giving" is God's economy [Jn. 3:16].)*

10 **Cast out the scorner, and contention shall go out; yea, strife and reproach shall cease.** *(The "scorner" is one who scorns the Bible and sets his own course. Wherever he is, "strife and reproach" will be also.)*

11 **He who loves pureness of heart, for the grace of his lips the king shall be his friend.** *(There is never any friction between just men and just governments.)*

12 **The eyes of the LORD preserve knowledge, and He overthrows the words of the transgressor.** *(God prospers truth but overthrows false teaching.)*

13 **The slothful man says, There is a lion without, I shall be slain in the streets.** *(This Proverb illustrates the truth of the absurdities that the "slothful" come up with to keep from working!)*

14 **The mouth of strange women is a deep pit: he who is abhorred of the LORD shall fall therein.** *(The Hebrew word for "strange women" is "zur," and means "a Hebrew woman who has turned apostate by leaving Jehovah and going to a foreign religion." Such refers to all false religion and false doctrine.)*

15 **Foolishness is bound in the heart of a child; but the rod of correction shall drive it far from him.** *(The word "foolishness" in the Hebrew is "ivveleth," which means "silliness, perverseness, careless of body and soul."*

This does not refer to the sin nature, but instead to the by-product of the Fall, which is a perverted or erroneous way.

The "rod of correction" cannot subdue a sin nature, but it can subdue foolishness, and even "drive such from him.")

16 **He who oppresses the poor to increase his riches, and he who gives to the rich, shall surely come to want.** *(The "want" that God says will come to the "oppressor" is not always material want. Above all, it is spiritual want.*

Giving to the "rich" in order to curry favor will not come out with the intended results. In fact, such gifts are wasted, and the giver is that much more impoverished.

Men are importuned to look to God for their sustenance and not to rich people or any other source [Mk. 11:24].)

17 **Bow down your ear, and hear the words of the wise, and apply your heart unto my knowledge.** *(Strangely enough, the Gospel is not given by seeing, but by hearing [Rom. 10:17].)*

18 **For it is a pleasant thing if you keep them within you; they shall withal be fitted in your lips.** *(The Holy Spirit frames the words perfectly. Diligence given to the Word of God and the making of it a part of our very being is not laborious, but rather "pleasant.")*

19 **That your trust may be in the LORD, I have made known to you this day, even to you.** *(It is impossible to have "trust" in the Lord, unless one adequately knows His Word [Rom. 10:17].)*

20 **Have not I written to you excellent things in counsels and knowledge,**

21 **That I might make you know the certainty of the words of truth; that you might answer the words of truth to them who send unto you?** *(The word "excellent" in the Hebrew is "shalishim," which means "threefold" or "three."*

There is no distinct proof exactly as to what

this means if it does not refer to the three writings of Solomon: Proverbs, Ecclesiastes, and Song of Solomon.

God's Word is "truth." It does not merely "contain" truth, but in fact "is" Truth.)

22 Rob not the poor, because he is poor: neither oppress the afflicted in the gate:

23 For the LORD will plead their cause, and spoil the soul of those who spoiled them. *(By now it should be obvious that God looks very sternly at those who would "oppress the afflicted.")*

24 Make no friendship with an angry man; and with a furious man you shall not go:

25 Lest you learn his ways, and get a snare to your soul. *(Association breeds similarity.*

Such anger addressed here is a Godless direction and means to get what it desires at any cost, whether to others or self. It does not know the Will of God and does not want the Will of God. It is a pursuit that characterizes most of the world. It means to step on as many people as one has to in order to get where one is going.

Believers should not associate with such individuals.)

26 Be not thou one of them who strike hands, or of them who are sureties for debts.

27 If you have nothing to pay, why should he take away your bed from under you? *(The "striking of hands" has to do with the making of contracts. In other words, "Don't be quick to do so unless you know exactly what you're doing."*

"Sureties for debts" refers to standing good for someone else's debt. Never go into such an agreement unless you are prepared to pay the debt yourself, for that is what you will probably have to do.)

28 Remove not the ancient landmark, which your fathers have set. *("Landmarks" of old separated fields and properties and served as boundaries. If they were movable objects such as stones, some people were tempted to gradually move the stones over, especially if the property was owned by those who were living elsewhere or were incapacitated, thereby stealing their land.*

The Lord is saying that He observes all things, even to the moving of a stone. Honesty in all matters is demanded by the Holy Spirit.)

29 Seest thou a man diligent in his business? he shall stand before kings; he shall not stand before mean men. *(The Hebrew word for "mean" is "chashok," which means "men of no repute."*

The Holy Spirit is saying that those who are not "diligent" concerning their affairs can rest

assured that they will never see advancement; conversely, they shall forever deal with men of no repute.)

CHAPTER 23
(1000 B.C.)
GLUTTONY

WHEN you sit to eat with a ruler, consider diligently what is before you *(the sense of this Proverb is "deceit" [Vs. 3]):*

2 And put a knife to your throat, if you be a man given to appetite. *(This Verse should read, "For you will put a knife to your throat," meaning to ruin yourself.*

The phrase, "given to appetite," has little to do with food. It is speaking of the desire for gain, such as property, advancement, money, etc.)

3 Be not desirous of his dainties: for they are deceitful meat. *(This type of "ruler," and all such like, are said by the Holy Spirit to be "deceitful." So, if anything he has is desired, one should know what to expect — in other words, don't desire it.)*

4 Labour not to be rich: cease from your own wisdom. *(The "ceasing from your own wisdom" refers to a course and path that is not laid out by God. The Holy Spirit is saying, "Trust the Lord and let Him be your Wisdom."*

The Apostle Paul probably drew from this Proverb regarding I Tim. 6:9.)

5 Will you set your eyes upon that which is not? for riches certainly make themselves wings; they fly away as an eagle toward Heaven. *("Riches are temporary, so don't set your eyes on such, but rather set your eyes on the Lord.")*

6 Eat thou not the bread of him who has an evil eye, neither desire thou his dainty meats:

7 For as he thinks in his heart, so is he: Eat and drink, says he to you; but his heart is not with you.

8 The morsel which you have eaten shall you vomit up, and lose your sweet words. *(In these three Verses, the Holy Spirit is saying that Christians who have a desire to be rich will be thrown very soon into the company of those who have an "evil eye." Consequently, the end result will not be good.)*

9 Speak not in the ears of a fool: for he will despise the wisdom of your words. *(The "fool" is one who does not desire the instruction of the Bible and will not adhere to its Wisdom.*

It may have been in the wisdom of this Proverb that the True Solomon refused to speak to Herod. He also, when sitting with rulers and

rich men, observed the counsel of Verses 1 through 3 and 6 through 8.)

10 Remove not the old landmark; and enter not into the fields of the fatherless *(this Verse is not a meaningless repetition of Verse 28 in the previous Chapter; the first refers to an unwise changing of a father's previous arrangement of property; the other to a dishonest seizure of that which belongs to the defenseless):*

11 For their redeemer is mighty; he shall plead their cause with you. *(Basically, as the word "redeemer" is used here, it refers to "kinsman redeemer.")*

12 Apply your heart unto instruction, and your ears to the words of knowledge. *("Instruction" and "knowledge," as they regard life, come strictly from the Bible.)*

13 Withhold not correction from the child: for if you beat him with the rod, he shall not die.

14 You shall beat him with the rod, and shall deliver his soul from Hell. *(Erroneous and harmful habits uncorrected in a child will only become more perverted upon adulthood. They have caused countless numbers to be eternally lost.*

Proper correction is not child abuse. It is a proclamation to the child that the parent loves it enough to correct it.

Real child abuse is when a child is raised without the benefit of the instruction and guidance of the Bible. That is the greatest child abuse of all.)

PARENTS' DESIRE FOR A SON: WISDOM

15 My son, if your heart be wise, my heart shall rejoice, even mine.

16 Yea, my reins shall rejoice, when your lips speak right things. *(A son or daughter on erroneous paths and uncorrected will bring great grief to the heart of parents. A "wise son" will bring great pleasure to parents.*

The word "reins" refers to the heart or the soul and spirit.)

17 Let not your heart envy sinners: but be thou in the fear of the LORD all the day long.

18 For surely there is an end; and your expectation shall not be cut off. *(Sometimes "sinners" prosper and Christians envy them, especially when they seem to have abundance.*

The Holy Spirit is telling us here that our eyes, hearts, and minds should not be on "sinners," regarding their prosperity or anything of the like, but instead should dwell "in the fear

of the LORD all the day long."

As well, "an end" or conclusion is coming, and for the "sinner," it is not going to be pleasant. But the recompense for those who love and follow Christ is that their "expectation shall not be cut off." They will be rewarded by being with Christ forever [Rev., Chpt. 22].)

19 Hear thou, my son, and be wise, and guide your heart in the way.

20 Be not among winebibbers; among riotous eaters of flesh:

21 For the drunkard and the glutton shall come to poverty: and drowsiness shall clothe a man with rags. *(The "wise" one of Verse 19 is the one who allows his life to be guided by the Bible. He is contrasted with the slaves of appetite in Verse 20 and the poverty and misery of Verse 21.)*

22 Hearken unto your father who begat you, and despise not your mother when she is old. *(The child is to "hearken" unto the father as long as the father guides the child by the way of the Word of God.)*

23 Buy the truth, and sell it not; also wisdom, and instruction, and understanding. *(Such action is placed at far greater value than silver or gold. All pertain to the Word of God.)*

24 The father of the righteous shall greatly rejoice: and he who begets a wise child shall have joy of him.

25 Your father and your mother shall be glad, and she who bore you shall rejoice. *(This Proverb informs us as to what the ambition of the parents should be regarding their child. He is to be a "wise child," one who makes the Bible his instructor and guide. Only this will bring joy and gladness to a parent.)*

26 My son, give me your heart, and let your eyes observe my ways.

27 For a whore is a deep ditch; and a strange woman is a narrow pit.

28 She also lies in wait as for a prey, and increases the transgressors among men. *(The "strange woman" of Verse 27 refers to an Israelite who has gone over to a foreign religion. In effect, the Holy Spirit says here that she is committing spiritual adultery.*

Presently, every Believer who makes something other than Christ and the Cross the object of his faith is committing spiritual adultery [Rom. 7:1-4].)

29 Who has woe? who has sorrow? who has contentions? who has babbling? who has wounds without cause? who has redness of eyes?

30 They who tarry long at the wine; they who go to seek mixed wine. *(The "wine" addressed here is fermented wine, the kind that will make one drunk. Its effects are given in these Verses.)*

31 Look not thou upon the wine when it is red, when it gives his colour in the cup, when it moves itself aright. *(The allurement of intoxicating beverage is given here by the Holy Spirit. This Verse, within itself, proclaims the futility, and even the stupidity, of those who maintain the harmlessness, as they put it, of moderate drinking. There is no such thing.)*

32 At the last it bites like a serpent, and stings like an adder. *(If one wants to know what the Holy Spirit thinks about intoxicating beverages, this Passage is an adequate description. It likens it to the bite of a poisonous snake.)*

33 Your eyes shall behold strange women, and your heart shall utter perverse things. *(The "strange women" of this Proverb is the same as in Verse 27, and refers to apostate religion.*

In this Passage, we are told that false doctrine and intoxicants go hand in hand.)

34 Yea, you shall be as he who lies down in the midst of the sea, or as he who lies upon the top of a mast. *(False doctrines and alcoholic beverages are similar. Both lead to foolish directions. Let such a person not think that the end result will be anything but catastrophic.*

Anyone who would "lie upon the top of a mast," and be so foolish as to think they will not fall off, is likened to those who are embroiled in false doctrine.)

35 They have stricken me, shall you say, and I was not sick; they have beaten me, and I felt it not: when shall I awake? I will seek it yet again. *(Like those who are addicted to alcohol, those addicted to false doctrine and apostasy will "seek it yet again," despite the terrible discomfort and sickness always brought on by this evil.*

False doctrine and the apostate way have the same type of hold on their victims. They are exploited, "stricken," emotionally "beaten," and still they come back for more. Satan is a hard taskmaster. God gives, Satan takes!)

CHAPTER 24
(1000 B.C.)
WISE LIVING

BE not thou envious against evil men, neither desire to be with them.

2 For their heart studies destruction, and their lips talk of mischief. *(No matter how prosperous the evil man may be, the Believer is never to be envious of him or the things he has, especially considering that what the Believer has is far more.)*

3 Through wisdom is an house built; and by understanding it is established *(the "Wisdom" that is spoken of here pertains to the teaching of the Bible; there is no other "Wisdom")*:

4 And by knowledge shall the chambers be filled with all precious and pleasant riches. *(The enduring prosperity of Verses 3 through 4 is contrasted with the temporary prosperity of Verses 1 and 2, which is based on earthly scheming. Only the prosperity that comes from Christ is of lasting consequence.)*

5 A wise man is strong; yea, a man of knowledge increases strength. *(Only those who know their Bibles are both "wise" and "strong.")*

6 For by wise counsel you shall make your war: and in multitude of counsellors there is safety. *(The "counsel" addressed here pertains to the Bible. As well, its Books are "Counselors.")*

7 Wisdom is too high for a fool: he opens not his mouth in the gate. *(The term, "in the gate," refers to the action of a city magistrate, who, in days of old, had his judicial and civic buildings near the gate of the city.*

If a community gives leadership to one who is not wise in the Bible, the Lord calls such a "fool." He will not open his mouth to any good. Tragically, too many "fools" sit in seats of government!)

8 He who devises to do evil shall be called a mischievous person. *(The words, "mischievous person," have to do with a schemer of plots. Regrettably, many of these occupy positions "in the gate.")*

9 The thought of foolishness is sin: and the scorner is an abomination to men. *(The foolishness addressed here speaks of that which is "perverse." The word in the Hebrew is "evveleth." Such foolishness makes one corrupt.)*

10 If you faint in the day of adversity, your strength is small. *(Moral strength based upon earthly wisdom fails when tested, but Heavenly Wisdom gives a "strength" based on the Bible, which cannot fail.)*

11 If you forbear to deliver them who are drawn unto death, and those who are ready to be slain;

12 If you say, Behold, we knew it not; does not He Who ponders the heart consider it? and He Who keeps your soul, does not He know it? and shall not He render to every

man according to his works? *(This Proverb has two meanings:*

1. It is incumbent upon governments to protect the innocent from punishment and death.

2. It is the obligation of every Christian to rescue the perishing and to do his utmost to save all who are on the way to eternal death. Inaction in this matter entails the Judgment of God — "render to every man.")

ADVICE TO A SON

13 My son, eat thou honey, because it is good; and the honeycomb, which is sweet to your taste:

14 So shall the knowledge of wisdom be unto your soul: when you have found it, then there shall be a reward, and your expectation shall not be cut off. *(The Holy Spirit tells us that "Wisdom" [the Word of God] shall be to the taste the same as "honey."*

As well, those who spend their lives studying and understanding the Bible will always, and without fail, reap its great blessings.)

15 Lay not wait, O wicked man, against the dwelling of the righteous; spoil not his resting place:

16 For a just man falls seven times, and rises up again: but the wicked shall fall into mischief. *(The sense of this Proverb is that calamity may well overtake an honest man. Bad things do happen, at times, to good people.*

However, any who would attempt to take advantage of such an occurrence will be looked at by God as "a wicked man."

The Holy Spirit says that this "just man" will "rise up again," and his oppressor will be overthrown beyond recovery. The "wicked" cannot ultimately succeed, while the "just" cannot ultimately lose.)

17 Rejoice not when your enemy falls, and let not your heart be glad when he stumbles:

18 Lest the LORD see it, and it displease Him, and He turn away His wrath from him. *(The sense is that whatever has caused our "enemy" to fall resides also, in some measure, in us; consequently, if our "heart be glad" at his discomfiture, then we have an improper understanding of our own righteousness, or lack thereof.)*

19 Fret not yourself because of evil men, neither be thou envious at the wicked;

20 For there shall be no reward to the evil man; the candle of the wicked shall be put out. *(Christians, at times, are "envious at the wicked." We should remember that their prosperity is only*

temporary, and their punishment, unless they turn to God, eternal. No matter how it looks now, their "candle shall be put out.")*

21 My son, fear thou the LORD and the king: and meddle not with them who are given to change:

22 For their calamity shall rise suddenly; and who knows the ruin of them both? *(Those "given to change" speak of anarchy. The spirit of anarchy is one of the most, if not the most, dangerous spirits that can get hold of men [II Pet. 2:10].*

Men are to render to Caesar the things which are Caesar's and unto God the things that are God's [Mat. 22:21].

In this Proverb, the Holy Spirit commands us to respect civil government [Rom. 13:1-7].)

ADVICE AND COMMANDS

23 These things also belong to the wise. It is not good to have respect of persons in judgment.

24 He who says unto the wicked, You are righteous; him shall the people curse, nations shall abhor him:

25 But to them who rebuke him shall be delight, and a good blessing shall come upon them.

26 Every man shall kiss his lips who gives a right answer. *(We must not have respect of persons in judgment.*

Because of money or other things, when leaders refer to the "wicked" as "righteous," this will ultimately lead to the wreckage of a nation.

In a spiritual sense, when Preachers condone wrongdoing, proverbially speaking, so as not to rock the boat, this will also lead to the wreckage of Christianity. Leaders who follow the command of the Lord will be blessed, irrespective of the present circumstances.)

27 Prepare your work without, and make it fit for yourself in the field; and afterwards build your house. *("Take care first to attend to the business, and the business will 'build the house.'")*

28 Be not a witness against your neighbour without cause; and deceive not with your lips. *(Extra care must be taken regarding one's "neighbor," simply because he is your "neighbor," and one must continue to live beside him; consequently, all must be done, even to the taking of a loss, to "remain on good terms.")*

29 Say not, I will do so to him as he has done to me: I will render to the man according to his work. *(The Christian is to never pay "kind for kind." Instead, he is to "bless those who curse him" [Mat. 5:44]. When we are reviled,*

we are to revile not again [I Pet. 2:23].)

30 I went by the field of the slothful, and by the vineyard of the man void of understanding;

31 And, lo, it was all grown over with thorns, and nettles had covered the face thereof, and the stone wall thereof was broken down.

32 Then I saw, and considered it well: I looked upon it, and received instruction.

33 Yet a little sleep, a little slumber, a little folding of the hands to sleep:

34 So shall your poverty come as one who travels; and your want as an armed man. *(This is an exceptionally long Proverb; however, its lesson will be the Salvation of all who follow its precepts.*

To be brief, the Holy Spirit once again greatly condemns slothfulness.)

CHAPTER 25
(700 B.C.)
COMPARISONS, INSTRUCTIONS, AND WARNINGS

THESE are also proverbs of Solomon, which the men of Hezekiah king of Judah copied out. *(The word "also" makes it clear that the preceding Proverbs are Solomon's, as well.*

These Proverbs were copied by the men of Hezekiah — not imagined or remembered, but actually copied from the original manuscript.)

2 It is the glory of God to conceal a thing: but the honour of kings is to search out a matter. *(God conceals just how bad man really is because of His Mercy and Grace.*

Conversely, authorities are honored when they investigate a matter and bring it to a righteous and lawful conclusion.

The reason for the juxtaposition is because man knows only the external actions of others, while only God knows the heart.)

3 The Heaven for height, and the Earth for depth, and the heart of kings is unsearchable. *(The idea is the instability, changeableness, and the variableness of man, even "kings."*

Conversely, God can be depended upon to do the same thing in every situation every time [James 1:17].)

4 Take away the dross from the silver, and there shall come forth a vessel for the finer.

5 Take away the wicked from before the king, and his throne shall be established in righteousness. *(As it is impossible to have pure "silver" unless the "dross" is taken away, likewise, "wicked counselors" must be "taken away" from the king or leader. Until such is*

done, there will be no "Righteousness" in his government.)

6 Put not forth yourself in the presence of the king, and stand not in the place of great men:

7 For better it is that it be said unto you, Come up hither; than that you should be put lower in the presence of the prince whom your eyes have seen. *(The sense of this Proverb is that we are not to promote ourselves. If we do, sooner or later, someone will demote us. The essence is that we let God do the promoting.)*

8 Go not forth hastily to strive, lest you know not what to do in the end thereof, when your neighbour has put you to shame.

9 Debate your cause with your neighbour himself; and discover not a secret to another:

10 Lest he who hears it put you to shame, and your infamy turn not away. *(Every effort should be made to put down "strife" regarding one's "neighbor." The simple reason is that you have to live next door to him. This could go, as well, for a fellow Church member, fellow employee, etc.*

Jesus mentioned this [Mat. 18:15].)

11 A word fitly spoken is like apples of gold in pictures of silver. *(The word "pictures" should be translated "baskets."*

"Fitly spoken" is a phrase that means "timely" or "appropriate."

The only True "Word" that fits the description of "apples of gold" is the Bible. How so much Wisdom God has given to man, and how so little man takes advantage of it! Mostly, it is ignored.)

12 As an earring of gold, and an ornament of fine gold, so is a wise reprover upon an obedient ear. *(The "wise reprover" is the one who knows his Bible and kindly imparts its Wisdom to others.*

The "obedient ear" is the one who takes the advice of the Proverb and commentary of Verse 11. The Holy Spirit likens such instruction to "gold" that is being given unto the "obedient ear.")

13 As the cold of snow in the time of harvest, so is a faithful messenger to them who send him: for he refreshes the soul of his masters. *(During winter, when the snow fell in Judea, some of it would be taken deep into caves where the temperature was very cool. If it were correctly stored in these certain places, it would not melt.*

Therefore, during the "time of harvest," when the sun was hot, water that was cooled by "snow" was brought from the place of storage and was very refreshing.

As such is refreshing, so is a "faithful messenger" bearing good news. This could be likened to the Gospel being taken to those who have not had the privilege to hear.)

14 Whoso boasts himself of a false gift is like clouds and wind without rain. *(As parched ground in dire need of rain is denied such by "clouds" that give none, likewise, so is a "boaster" who promises large gifts but, in fact, gives nothing!)*

15 By long forbearing is a prince persuaded, and a soft tongue breaks the bone. *(The "prince" in this case is a "judge" or "magistrate." Very seldom will a hard tongue break down his resistance. The Holy Spirit says here that a "soft tongue" or a gentle approach will subdue the most obstinate and turn away wrath.)*

16 Have you found honey? eat so much as is sufficient for you, lest you be filled therewith, and vomit it. *(Because of the sweetness of "honey," the temptation is to eat more than we need.*

Such is the same regarding any good thing. In all walks of life, if we would subdue greed and heed this Proverb, then the good will remain good.)

17 Withdraw your foot from your neighbour's house; lest he be weary of you, and so hate you. *(In other words, "Don't wear out your welcome!")*

18 A man who bears false witness against his neighbour is a maul, and a sword, and a sharp arrow. *(All the weapons listed are weapons of destruction. Such is a "false witness." Regrettably, if a man is a "false witness," he seldom changes. To put confidence in such is not only a wasted effort, but it is also a very hurtful one.)*

19 Confidence in an unfaithful man in time of trouble is like a broken tooth, and a foot out of joint. *(When one is in "trouble," one desires someone in whom "confidence" can be placed.*

To place "confidence" in "an unfaithful man," especially in a "time of trouble," is like trying to eat with a "broken tooth" or run with a "foot out of joint.")

20 As he who takes away a garment in cold weather, and as vinegar upon nitre, so is he who sings songs to an heavy heart. *(Too often in modern religious society, a world that has a broken heart is approached by the gospel of entertainment. Such will not heal the broken or "heavy heart."*

There is one thing, or rather Person, Who will. His Name is Jesus. He, and He Alone, can heal the "heavy heart" [Lk. 4:18].)

21 If your enemy be hungry, give him bread to eat; and if he be thirsty, give him water to drink:

22 For you shall heap coals of fire upon his head, and the LORD shall reward you. *(This was quoted by the Apostle Paul in Rom. 12:20. As fire melts the hardest metal, so love melts the hardest heart.)*

23 The north wind drives away rain: so does an angry countenance a backbiting tongue. *(Whenever a "backbiting tongue" is rebuked, it stops. If more Christians would show displeasure at gossip and slander, there would be less of such.)*

24 It is better to dwell in the corner of the housetop, than with a brawling woman and in a wide house. *(The Holy Spirit is saying here that it is better to dwell in that small room which houses only a few Believers in the Word of God than to dwell in a "wide house" with many people and the "brawling woman" of false doctrine.)*

25 As cold waters to a thirsty soul, so is good news from a far country. *(This Proverb is similar to Verse 13.*

The "good news" is the Gospel being taken to a lost world.)

26 A righteous man falling down before the wicked is as a troubled fountain, and a corrupt spring. *(As the purest spring becomes contaminated if trampled upon, so do Christians, if they permit themselves to be influenced by the world, or if they fall into sin and disobedience.)*

27 It is not good to eat much honey: so for men to search their own glory is not glory. *(As eating too much "honey" makes one ill, so men searching for "their own glory" proves to be no "glory" at all.)*

28 He who has no rule over his own spirit is like a city that is broken down, and without walls. *(In ancient times, cities that were "without walls" were virtually defenseless; likewise, so is a person who has no control over his passions or temper. Such control can only be had by Faith exhibited constantly in Christ and the Cross, which then gives the Holy Spirit latitude to work in our lives [Rom. 8:1-2, 11].)*

CHAPTER 26
(700 B.C.)
THE ARGUMENTS OF A FOOL

AS snow in summer, and as rain in harvest, so honour is not seemly for a fool. *(To be blunt, the Lord labels as "fools" all those who*

do not know and abide by His Word.)

2 As the bird by wandering, as the swallow by flying, so the curse causeless shall not come. *(There is a "cause," and it is the failure to know and abide by the Word.)*

3 A whip for the horse, a bridle for the ass, and a rod for the fool's back. *(Because of the repeated breaking of God's Laws, the "fool" always finds himself in difficult straits.)*

4 Answer not a fool according to his folly, lest you also be like unto him.

5 Answer a fool according to his folly, lest he be wise in his own conceit. *(Verse 5 seems, at first sight, to be antagonistic to the purport of the preceding Verse, but it is not really so. In this case, the words, "according to his folly," mean "as his folly deserves." In other words, he is to be exposed and shamed, which will hopefully bring him to a better mind. This is to be done "lest he be wise in his own conceit.")*

6 He who sends a message by the hand of a fool cuts off the feet, and drinks damage. *(He who transacts business by the hand of a fool is like the man who cuts off his own feet; he renders himself helpless.)*

7 The legs of the lame are not equal: so is a parable in the mouth of fools. *(This means that a "fool" affecting Wisdom is as manifestly absurd as a lame man affecting a graceful manner of walking.)*

8 As he who binds a stone in a sling, so is he who gives honour to a fool. *(Once again, the "fool" is the person who does not believe in, nor abide by, the Word of God. Regrettably, the world is full of this kind, and always has been. This the reason for all the heartache in the world presently, and always has been.)*

9 As a thorn goes up into the hand of a drunkard, so is a parable in the mouth of fools. *(A "drunkard," in his inebriation, is insensitive to a "thorn" that pricks his hand; likewise, a "fool" has absolutely no idea of the true worth of the knowledge of the Bible.)*

10 The great God Who formed all things both rewards the fool, and rewards transgressors. *(The word for "God" in this Verse is "rab," and may mean either the great God or a great man. It probably refers to "man" instead of "God," and means this:*

"A master craftsman makes or forms all things well, but he who hires a fool hires a transgressor who will spoil the work.")

11 As a dog returns to his vomit, so a fool returns to his folly. *(Peter referred to this Proverb by using it in reference to backsliders who*

go back into sin [II Pet. 2:22]. This shows that Peter was a student of the Proverbs.)*

12 Seest thou a man wise in his own conceit? there is more hope of a fool than of him. *(In these Passages, the only one whom God puts on a lower level than a "fool" is a "conceited fool." This is a lesson on self-conceit, self-importance, and self-exaltation. Such is the opposite of Christlikeness.)*

13 The slothful man says, There is a lion in the way; a lion is in the streets. *(This Proverb is very similar to 22:13. The idea is that a lazy man will use any excuse, no matter how preposterous, to keep from having to work.)*

14 As the door turns upon his hinges, so does the slothful upon his bed. *(A door always turns in the same place, and a sluggard moves about but never advances; he suggests any excuse for inactivity.)*

15 The slothful hides his hand in his bosom; it grieves him to bring it again to his mouth. *(The meaning is that the lazy man hides his hand in his bosom and is too lazy to take it out, dip into the dish, and put food into his mouth. Paul addressed this [II Thess. 3:10].)*

16 The sluggard is wiser in his own conceit than seven men that can render a reason. *(Someone has said that "lack of knowledge is when you don't know. Ignorance is when you don't know that you don't know."*

The "slothful" are ignorant.)

17 He who passes by, and meddles with strife belonging not to him, is like one who takes a dog by the ears. *(Some dogs, when held up by the ears, will become very angry and, when let go, will turn on the one doing so to them.)*

18 As a mad man who casts firebrands, arrows, and death,

19 So is the man who deceives his neighbour, and says, Am not I in sport? *(This pertains to a hypocritical and affected interest in a neighbor's business, and in meddling in his affairs. Such a one is pretending to help, but is, in fact, "deceiving" the neighbor.)*

20 Where no wood is, there the fire goes out: so where there is no talebearer, the strife ceases. *(A fire cannot be kept going without fuel.)*

21 As coals are to burning coals, and wood to fire; so is a contentious man to kindle strife. *(A "talebearer" is a "contentious man" [or woman]. Such "kindles [stirs] strife.")*

22 The words of a talebearer are as wounds, and they go down into the innermost parts of the belly. *(When the "tale receiver" hears the words of the "talebearer," they at first taste like*

delicious morsels; however, soon he will find that these very "words" will cause a spiritual sickness in his innermost being.)

23 Burning lips and a wicked heart are like a potsherd covered with silver dross. *(This Proverb speaks of hypocrisy. Even though a broken piece of pottery may have a thin silver covering, still, it is worthless, and it will soon reveal itself to be so.)*

24 He who hates dissembles with his lips, and lays up deceit within him. *(As well, this also describes a hypocrite. The word "dissembles" means "to hide under a false appearance." Such a person is saying things with his mouth that he does not mean within his heart; while his lips proclaim blessing, his heart is devising wickedness [deceit].)*

25 When he speaks fair, believe him not: for there are seven abominations in his heart. *(It doesn't matter how "fair" [well] that this hypocrite speaks, his "heart" is wicked. As well, the Lord uses the number "seven," which speaks of totality and completeness, i.e., "complete wickedness.")*

26 Whose hatred is covered by deceit, his wickedness shall be showed before the whole congregation. *("Hatred" drives this individual, and is the fuel for his hypocrisy. Why the hatred? Men hate because of alleged wrongdoing carried out against them, because of jealousy, envy, or for any variety of evil reasons. True Believers must "forget" what others have done to them and turn it over to the Lord.)*

27 Whoso digs a pit shall fall therein: and he who rolls a stone, it will return upon him. *(This Proverb points to Jacob, who deceived with a kid of the goats, and was deceived by a kid of the goats; to David, who slew with the sword, and mourned his son slain by the sword. Every Christian should heed well these words: "it will return upon him.")*

28 A lying tongue hates those who are afflicted by it; and a flattering mouth works ruin. *(This is a Law of God. Liars hate their victims, as robbers hate their victims. Only in Christ can this Law be broken.*

The injured forgive, but the injurer, never.)

CHAPTER 27
(700 B.C.)
INSTRUCTIONS AND ADMONITIONS
FOR SONS

BOAST not yourself of tomorrow; for you know not what a day may bring forth. *(A Christian should not "boast," period! The rich*

fool of Lk. 12:20 boasted of the morrow, but that night his soul was required of him. [Not all fools are poor; some are rich!])

2 Let another man praise you, and not your own mouth; a stranger, and not your own lips. *(Self-praise denotes pride.)*

3 A stone is heavy, and the sand weighty; but a fool's wrath is heavier than them both. *(The "fool" loses his temper, hindering and hurting all around him, and he doesn't even have sense enough to know the damage that he is causing.)*

4 Wrath is cruel, and anger is outrageous; but who is able to stand before envy? *(The word "envy," as used here, would have probably been better translated "jealousy." The sense of this Proverb is that a "cruel" temper is destructive, but is not as deadly as the hatred of "jealousy.")*

5 Open rebuke is better than secret love. *(A love that says and does nothing is not as valuable as an affection that rebukes.)*

6 Faithful are the wounds of a friend; but the kisses of an enemy are deceitful. *(A "friend" who will kindly tell you of your mistakes or faults is not destructive, but rather helpful [faithful]. Conversely, the one who flatters and "kisses," proclaiming everything to be wonderful and well, when, in reality, it is not, is said by God to be "deceitful" and, therefore, an "enemy.")*

7 The full soul loathes an honeycomb; but to the hungry soul every bitter thing is sweet. *(The one who has come by riches without having to earn them does not understand what he has and, thereby, does not appreciate them. Conversely, the "hungry soul," whether rich or poor, having earned what he has, finds value in that which does not even seem to have value.)*

8 As a bird that wanders from her nest, so is a man who wanders from his place. *(The "place" that God proposes for each person, if vacated, is done so because of self-will. To "wander" in self-will is as the little bird that wanders from its nest away from the care of its parent and, therefore, exposes itself to great danger.)*

9 Ointment and perfume rejoice the heart: so does the sweetness of a man's friend by hearty counsel. *("Hearty counsel" speaks of the sincere counsel of the soul. Such "counsel" comes from the Bible.)*

10 Your own friend, and your father's friend, forsake not; neither go into your brother's house in the day of your calamity: for better is a neighbour that is near than a brother far off. *(The moment a person comes*

to Christ, his allegiance, affection, and relationships change. As a result, fellow followers of Christ become even closer than one's own blood relatives [relatives who do not know the Lord].)

11 My son, be wise, and make my heart glad, that I may answer him who reproaches me. (In this Proverb, the Holy Spirit is speaking directly to Solomon, and likewise to everyone. The Bible is the only Book of teaching or instruction that can produce character. Most of the world reproaches the Bible, but, when they do so, they reproach Him [the Holy Spirit] Who inspired it. As well, whenever Preachers use anything but the Bible, they are reproaching the Holy Spirit.)

12 A prudent man foresees the evil, and hides himself; but the simple pass on, and are punished. (God calls "prudent" those who know, understand, and live by the Bible. God calls "simple" those who do not believe the Bible, or else do not take the time to study its contents.)

13 Take his garment that is surety for a stranger, and take a pledge of him for a strange woman. (The simple meaning of this Proverb is that neither the one who worships strange gods nor the one who has forsaken the True God can be trusted. The intent of the Holy Spirit is to impress upon the Bible student the simple truth that the only honesty in the world is that which is taught by the Bible and given by Jesus Christ.)

14 He who blesses his friend with a loud voice, rising early in the morning, it shall be counted a curse to him. (Its reason is self-seeking and deceitful.)

15 A continual dropping in a very rainy day and a contentious woman are alike.

16 Whosoever hides her hides the wind, and the ointment of his right hand, which betrays itself. (The word "contention" means "rivalry, competition, and discord." It means one who exhibits an often perverse and wearisome tendency to quarrels and disputes. It is the opposite of being peaceable.

As the smell of "ointment" on the hand cannot be hidden, likewise the "contentious woman" cannot be hidden. She will quickly make herself known.

The "contentious woman" has some relationship to the "strange woman" of Verse 13, which speaks of false doctrine and the part of Christianity which is apostate.)

17 Iron sharpens iron; so a man sharpens the countenance of his friend. (It takes an iron file to sharpen an ax. Likewise, it takes a man with strong courage, holy ambition, and with a strong moral and Spiritual Life, to "sharpen" or affect the lives of his friends and others.)

18 Whoso keeps the fig tree shall eat the fruit thereof: so he who waits on his master shall be honoured. (If the "fig tree" is carefully tended, surely some of the fruit will go to the one responsible. Likewise, if a man is faithful in his responsibilities and duties, it should be noticed and proper recognition and reward given.)

19 As in water face answers to face, so the heart of man to man. (This Proverb should humble all of us; it declares that, upon looking into the heart of the vilest criminal, one finds his own heart reflected. There is no difference, for all have sinned. Jesus Christ Alone is the only answer [Jn. 14:6].)

20 Hell and destruction are never full; so the eyes of man are never satisfied. (This Proverb portrays the "unsatisfied man," who typifies almost all of the human family. Men are not satisfied, because they seek that which cannot satisfy. Only Christ can satisfy the soul.)

21 As the fining pot for silver, and the furnace for gold; so is a man to his praise. (Silver and gold are tested by fire, and man is tested by praise. Few endure the test; they are wise whom praise affects not.)

22 Though you should bray a fool in a mortar among wheat with a pestle, yet will not his foolishness depart from him. (The sense of this Proverb is that "foolishness" cannot be educated out of a "fool." The "fool" is one who has no desire for God or His Word.)

23 Be thou diligent to know the state of your flocks, and look well to your herds. (In this Proverb, the Holy Spirit proclaims the necessity for "diligence." Whatever is given to us, we are to care for it diligently.)

24 For riches are not for ever: and does the crown endure to every generation? (The "crown" speaks of a king. He is being told that the day is coming when he will no longer be king and, therefore, he must make sure, concerning his "flocks" and "herds," that he may have something to live on. The present state of his prosperity may not last forever!)

25 The hay appears, and the tender grass shows itself, and herbs of the mountains are gathered. (In other words, "Make hay while the sun shines.")

26 The lambs are for your clothing, and the goats are the price of the field.

27 And you shall have goats' milk enough for your food, for the food of your household, and for the maintenance for your maidens.

(This principle governs the spiritual as well as the business life.)

CHAPTER 28
(700 B.C.)
MORE COMPARISONS

THE wicked flee when no man pursues: but the righteous are bold as a lion. *(This posture is such because the "wicked" have done wrong and, thereby, see harm coming from every direction. Conversely, the "righteous" have harmed no one, and consequently fear no one; they are "bold" because of a clear conscience. The "righteous" are those who follow the Lord and His Word.)*

2 For the transgression of a land many are the princes thereof: but by a man of understanding and knowledge the state thereof shall be prolonged. *(The "understanding and knowledge" spoken of here are derived from the Bible. Any country, state, city, or community that would be so blessed as to have such a man of the Bible at its helm is blessed indeed!)*

3 A poor man who oppresses the poor is like a sweeping rain which leaves no food. *(Tragically, this Proverb is rather the rule than the exception. Seemingly, the "poor," if given the opportunity to serve in even the least position of authority, will usually "oppress" their fellow poor.)*

4 They who forsake the law praise the wicked: but such as keep the law contend with them. *(They who forsake the Bible applaud the enemies of the Bible, but lovers of the Bible oppose and condemn them.)*

5 Evil men understand not judgment: but they who seek the LORD understand all things. *(Ahab accused Elijah of being the author of the Divine Judgment resting on the land. Being evil, Ahab was not willing to understand Judgment, and that, in effect, he [Ahab] was the cause of the "Judgment.")*

6 Better is the poor who walks in his uprightness, than he who is perverse in his ways, though he be rich. *(It is better to be poor and righteous than to be rich and wicked. Wealth does not excuse sin; poverty cannot effect goodness.)*

7 Whoso keeps the law is a wise son: but he who is a companion of riotous men shames his father. *(An appetite for the Bible is contrasted here with greediness for human teaching. The latter causes shame.)*

8 He who by usury and unjust gain increases his substance, he shall gather it for him who will pity the poor. *(The Lord is the One Who does "pity the poor," and He will see to it that, ultimately, a just accounting will be forthcoming.)*

9 He who turns away his ear from hearing the law, even his prayer shall be abomination. *(Outward worship, where the heart refuses obedience to the Gospel, is an abomination to God.)*

10 Whoso causes the righteous to go astray in an evil way, he shall fall himself into his own pit: but the upright shall have good things in possession. *(The "good things" spoken of in this Passage have to do with that which makes a person "upright," which is the "Righteousness of Christ." That which was Abel's "possession" could not be taken away by Cain, nor did death take it away either [I Jn. 3:12].*

Ultimately, all who forsake the Way of God for their own way will fall into "his own pit.")

11 The rich man is wise in his own conceit; but the poor who has understanding searches him out. *(Belshazzar was wise in his own eyes, but a poor man, Daniel, exposed his folly [Dan., Chpt. 5].)*

12 When righteous men do rejoice, there is great glory: but when the wicked rise, a man is hidden. *(Any nation, city, or community that is privileged to have "righteous men" in positions of leadership will see "rejoicing," and this will bring "great glory."*

Conversely, when "the wicked rise" to positions of leadership, as is often the case, righteous men must hide.)

13 He who covers his sins shall not prosper: but whoso confesses and forsakes them shall have mercy. *(Achan covered his transgressions [Josh., Chpt. 7], and neither he nor Israel prospered until he was found out and justly judged. Had he voluntarily confessed his sin and forsaken it, he would have found Mercy. Many are willing to confess their sins, at least after a fashion, but few are willing to forsake them.)*

14 Happy is the man who fears always: but he who hardens his heart shall fall into mischief. *(The broken and contrite spirit produces a "happiness" that only God can give. The "hardened heart" cannot be dealt with by the Holy Spirit. Such hearts will go astray.)*

15 As a roaring lion, and a ranging bear; so is a wicked ruler over the poor people. *("Roaring" would have probably been better translated "growling." A lion growls when devouring its prey, and a bear prowls when seeking its prey. Both actions express the conduct of a wicked prince to his defenseless people, and especially*

the "poor people.")

16 The prince who wants understanding is also a great oppressor: but he who hates covetousness shall prolong his days. *(The word "wants" would have been better translated "lacks." Such a man lacks understanding of the Bible; consequently, he oppresses the people because of covetousness.*

The closer to the Bible that a ruler follows, the longer will be his days in office.)

17 A man who does violence to the blood of any person shall flee to the pit; let no man stay him. *(This speaks of one who is guilty of murder. No one is to help such a "person.")*

18 Whoso walks uprightly shall be saved: but he who is perverse in his ways shall fall at once. *(The sense of this Proverb is that straight paths lead to prosperity, both materially and spiritually. The double-minded direction speaks of two ways, both good and bad, with the person attempting to walk both ways at the same time. Obviously, he will fall and "at once.")*

19 He who tills his land shall have plenty of bread: but he who follows after vain persons shall have poverty enough. *(This Proverb characterizes one who works for what he gets and the other who tries to gain what he wants by illicit means.)*

20 A faithful man shall abound with blessings: but he who makes haste to be rich shall not be innocent. *(The one who "makes haste to be rich" implies fraud.)*

21 To have respect of persons is not good: but for a piece of bread that man will transgress. *(The word "man" in the Hebrew implies a "strong man"; this points to the humbling fact that if a "strong man" has "respect of persons," he is, at the same time, for sale to the highest bidder.)*

22 He who hastens to be rich has an evil eye, and considers not that poverty shall come upon him. *(The Holy Spirit has much to say about those who strive to "be rich" [I Tim. 6:9-10].)*

23 He who rebukes a man afterwards shall find more favour than he who flatters with the tongue. *(A "flatterer" seeks not the truth, but rather to impress an individual in order to obtain something. Such never bodes any good.)*

24 Whoso robs his father or his mother, and says, It is no transgression; the same is the companion of a destroyer. *(Hebrew Law declared property to belong to the entirety of the family; therefore, undutiful children, at times, might take money or goods and declare it to not be a "transgression". But Heavenly Wisdom*

declares such a person to be a thief and a "destroyer." Scrupulous honesty is demanded by the Lord in all matters.)

25 He who is of a proud heart stirs up strife: but he who puts his trust in the LORD shall be made fat. *(The "proud heart" is the bane of all people, but especially the Christian. Such pertains to a greedy disposition. It will always "stir up strife," because it is never satisfied with the path that God has laid out, but rather seeks its own direction.)*

26 He who trusts in his own heart is a fool: but whoso walks wisely, he shall be delivered. *(The one who "walks wisely" is the one who follows the Bible. He alone "shall be delivered.")*

27 He who gives unto the poor shall not lack: but he who hides his eyes shall have many a curse. *(To "hide the eyes" means to divert attention from the misery of "the poor." The Holy Spirit commands that attention be given to the poor.)*

28 When the wicked rise, men hide themselves: but when they perish, the righteous increase. *(In this world, too much and too often the "wicked" rule, hence, the condition of much of mankind!)*

CHAPTER 29
(700 B.C.)
COMPARISONS CONTINUED

HE, who being often reproved hardens his neck, shall suddenly be destroyed, and that without remedy. *(Whenever one will not accept the "reproof" of the Lord, then there is no other remedy.)*

2 When the righteous are in authority, the people rejoice: but when the wicked bear rule, the people mourn. *(Every good government since the dawn of time owes such to the "authority" of the Bible. It is an unfailing Law: much Bible, much freedom; little Bible, little freedom; no Bible, no freedom.)*

3 Whoso loves wisdom rejoices his father: but he who keeps company with harlots spends his substance. *(The "Wisdom" spoken of here refers to "Heavenly Wisdom," which pertains to the Word of God. This "Wisdom" has stated that immorality will "spend the substance," both economically and spiritually.)*

4 The king by judgment establishes the land: but he who receives gifts overthrows it. *(The bane of any nation is political leaders who are "for sale.")*

5 A man who flatters his neighbour spreads

a net for his feet. *("Flattery" is another form of lying.)*

6 In the transgression of an evil man there is a snare: but the righteous do sing and rejoice. *(Wrongdoing leads to trouble, but right doing to gladness.)*

7 The righteous consider the cause of the poor: but the wicked regard not to know it. *(All who are "righteous" will ever be concerned about the plight of the "poor." The Holy Spirit, over and over again, tells us that they are not to be ignored and, thereby, forgotten. The Lord will hold all accountable who do so.)*

8 Scornful men bring a city into a snare: but wise men turn away wrath. *(Had there been even ten wise men in Sodom, Divine wrath would have been turned away, but the city being filled with scoffers [Gen. 19:14] caused it to be set aflame.)*

9 If a wise man contends with a foolish man, whether he rage or laugh, there is no rest. *(The "wise men" are those who love the Bible and derive "Wisdom" from it. The "foolish man" is the one who scorns the Word of God and goes his own way; consequently, whatever he does will be wrong, whether it be anger or laughter.)*

10 The bloodthirsty hate the upright: but the just seek his soul. *(Jezebel, in her hatred of Naboth and Elijah, illustrates this Proverb.)*

11 A fool utters all his mind: but a wise man keeps it in till afterwards. *(The "fool" is one who ignores the Bible and, thereby, gives "his mind," which is not the mind of Christ, and is, thereby, spurious. His wisdom is earthly wisdom, which will bless no one.*

Conversely, the "wise man" is the one who knows his Bible and attempts to live by it.)

12 If a ruler hearken to lies, all his servants are wicked. *(If a political leader surrounds himself with those who are wicked, the advice he gets from them will be distorted, i.e., "lies." A corrupt tree cannot produce good fruit.)*

13 The poor and the deceitful man meet together: the LORD lightens both their eyes. *(Even though both "the poor" and "the deceitful" are totally different, still, the Lord knows the hearts of both. All will ultimately be brought to account. The "deceiver" may deceive the "poor," but he cannot "deceive" God.)*

14 The king who faithfully judges the poor, his throne shall be established for ever. *(The coming, future Kingdom of the Messiah is described in this Proverb.)*

15 The rod and reproof give wisdom: but a child left to himself brings his mother to shame. *(Man's natural depravity and constitutional bias to evil is demonstrated in this Proverb.*

A flower, if left to itself, becomes beautiful. A child, if left to himself and undisciplined, brings shame upon his mother.)

16 When the wicked are multiplied, transgression increases: but the righteous shall see their fall. *(Ultimately, Righteousness will prevail! [Mat. 5:5])*

17 Correct your son, and he shall give you rest; yea, he shall give delight unto your soul. *(Some five times in the Book of Proverbs the Holy Spirit counsels the wise and necessary discipline of children.)*

18 Where there is no vision, the people perish: but he who keeps the Law, happy is he. *(The "Vision" and the "Law" point to the Bible, always the Bible!)*

19 A servant will not be corrected by words: for though he understand he will not answer. *(The word "answer" should have been translated "obey." A disobedient servant must be corrected with something sterner than mere words [Heb. 12:5-11].)*

20 Seest thou a man who is hasty in his words? there is more hope of a fool than of him. *(The man with the "hasty words" implies a "fiery-tempered man." Such portrays that "self" is ruling instead of Christ. Self never bodes well.)*

21 He who delicately brings up his servant from a child shall have him become his son at the length. *(The implication is that such a "servant," brought up from a child with all responsibility, will ultimately conduct himself as "a son."*

Eliezer, who was a servant born in Abraham's house [Gen. 15:2-3], is a perfect example of this Proverb.)

22 An angry man stirs up strife, and a furious man abounds in transgression. *(Both the "angry" and the "furious" are led by "self," and not by the Holy Spirit.)*

23 A man's pride shall bring him low: but honour shall uphold the humble in spirit. *(Self always breeds "pride," while the "humble" always breed "honor.")*

24 Whoso is partner with a thief hates his own soul: he hears cursing, and betrays it not. *(The individual who conceals the evil plotting of a "thief," under the guise of not wanting to become involved, actually becomes a "partner" with the "thief," and is doing terrible damage to "his own soul.")*

25 The fear of man brings a snare: but whoso puts his trust in the LORD shall be safe. *(The Believer can either "fear man" or "fear the Lord." He cannot fear both. If he fears man, he will be made a slave of man and will always find himself in a "snare." "Safety" is guaranteed only to him "who puts his trust in the LORD.")*

26 Many seek the ruler's favour; but every man's judgment comes from the LORD. *(An earthly ruler may err and oftentimes does in dispensing favors, but Emmanuel the Prince will exercise discriminating judgment infallibly.)*

27 An unjust man is an abomination to the just: and he who is upright in the way is abomination to the wicked. *(These two cannot walk together, because they cannot be agreed.)*

CHAPTER 30
(700 B.C.)
THE SAYINGS OF AGUR

THE words of Agur the son of Jakeh, even the prophecy: the man spoke unto Ithiel, even unto Ithiel and Ucal *(the Jewish Talmud says that Solomon was referred to by several names, "Agur" being one of them; that being the case, "Jakeh" was another name for David; actually, Ithiel and Ucal may have been disciples of Agur [Solomon]),*

2 Surely I am more brutish than any man, and have not the understanding of a man.

3 I neither learned wisdom, nor have the knowledge of the holy. *(Solomon did not consider himself special, because the Wisdom which he had was given to him by God.*

In Verses 2-3, it should be possible for us to see why God loved Solomon so much [II Sam. 12:24].

The greatest commodity in the halls of Heaven is humility. Solomon, in these two Verses, portrays a humility seldom seen. This man characterized such in his early years and was blessed by God as few men have ever been blessed.)

4 Who has ascended up into Heaven, or descended? who has gathered the wind in his fists? who has bound the waters in a garment? who has established all the ends of the Earth? what is his name, and what is his son's name, if you can tell? *(This Verse exclaims tremendous "knowledge of the holy," and yet it is not a contradiction of Verse 3. The "knowledge" that is evidenced in this Verse, which is phenomenal, came through the Wisdom given to him by God and not through education and knowledge acquired by the normal means of study. It was a Revelation from God.)*

5 Every Word of God is pure: He is a shield unto them who put their trust in Him. *(This tells us that "every Word" in the Bible is ordained and inspired of God [Mat. 4:4].)*

6 Add thou not unto His Words, lest He reprove you, and you be found a liar. *(Unfortunately, this is the sin of the Church. Men either take away or add to the Word of God.)*

7 Two things have I required of you; deny me them not before I die *(Solomon asked for only two things in life. What would we request if such an opportunity presented itself?):*

8 Remove far from me vanity and lies: give me neither poverty nor riches; feed me with food convenient for me *(in other words, Solomon is saying: 1. That everything should be removed from him except the Bible; all else is "vanity and lies"; and, 2. He asks that God would be the dispenser of what He wanted him to have; in other words, he would leave such in the Hands of the Lord):*

9 Lest I be full, and deny You, and say, Who is the LORD? or lest I be poor, and steal, and take the name of my God in vain. *(These two requests show not only great Wisdom, but also tremendous consecration.)*

10 Accuse not a servant unto his master, lest he curse you, and you be found guilty. *(One of the reasons that God takes such a dim view of this sin is because there is no defense against a lie.)*

11 There is a generation that curses their father, and does not bless their mother. *(Sadly, this present "generation" falls into this category. If one is raised without the influence of the Bible, no less can be expected.)*

12 There is a generation that are pure in their own eyes, and yet is not washed from their filthiness. *(As well, this characterizes this present generation. It speaks of a present self-righteous Church. Self-righteousness justifies one's self. It is "pure in its own eyes," but, in reality, is "filthy" in the sight of God.)*

13 There is a generation, O how lofty are their eyes! and their eyelids are lifted up. *(This speaks of a "generation" that is full of vanity, pride, and insolence [Ps. 10:4; Dan. 4:37; I Jn. 2:16].)*

14 There is a generation, whose teeth are as swords, and their jaw teeth as knives, to devour the poor from off the Earth, and the needy from among men. *(The Pharisees are described adequately in this Verse as they attempted to "devour" the "poor and needy" Man from among men. That Man was Christ Jesus.*

There is nothing in the world more cruel than man-made religion.)

15 The horseleach has two daughters, crying, Give, give. There are three things that are never satisfied, yea, four things say not, It is enough *(this speaks of a generation that never has enough and who will prey on their neighbor to gain even more)*:

16 The grave; and the barren womb; the Earth that is not filled with water; and the fire that says not, It is enough. *("Grave" should have been translated "Hell." This place is never full despite the fact that the majority of the human race has gone there. As well, the barren womb always craves a child, even as the dry earth longs for water to quench its parched surface. The fire is also greedy for everything that will burn.)*

17 The eye that mocks at his father, and despises to obey his mother, the ravens of the valley shall pick it out, and the young eagles shall eat it. *(The "father" and "mother" spoken of in this Proverb pertain to those who follow the Bible. If they are "mocked" and "despised," destruction is sure.)*

18 There be three things which are too wonderful for me, yea, four which I know not *(to show one the difference in man's wisdom and God's Wisdom, if man had written such, he would have written about things that he had devised, made, or perfected; as well, it would have been dated almost by the time the words were written; conversely, the "wonderful" things mentioned by the Holy Spirit cease to be no less "wonderful" now than some 3,000 years ago when this Proverb was first written)*:

19 The way of an eagle in the air; the way of a serpent upon a rock; the way of a ship in the midst of the sea; and the way of a man with a maid. *(All four speak of that which leaves no trace of its path.)*

20 Such is the way of an adulterous woman; she eats, and wipes her mouth, and says, I have done no wickedness. *(The "adulterous woman" attempts to leave no trace. She claims, "I have done no wickedness," because there seems to be no trace of what she has done.*

However, the Holy Spirit is saying that even though there may be no discernible trace of where the eagle has flown, still, God knows this, and also He knows every action of the "adulterous woman.")

21 For three things the Earth is disquieted, and for four which it cannot bear *(from the throne to the kitchen, all is unrest and confusion when God is not recognized and served)*:

22 For a servant when he reigns; and a fool when he is filled with meat;

23 For an odious woman when she is married; and an handmaid that is heir to her mistress. *(When a "servant" reigns, he will lord it over all who have the misfortune to be in his employ or kingdom.*

The "fool" thinks his stomach is filled because of his great wisdom.

The Holy Spirit says that if a woman is "odious" before marriage, so will she be after marriage.

The "handmaid," as proclaimed here, falls into the same category as the "servant.")

24 There be four things which are little upon the Earth, but they are exceeding wise *(these things that are mentioned are feeble and defenseless, but, because of wisdom, they have food, security, government, and dignity)*:

25 The ants are a people not strong, yet they prepare their meat in the summer *(as small as they are, the ant has a systemized government; the Holy Spirit says that men would do well to observe it)*;

26 The conies are but a feeble folk, yet make they their houses in the rocks *(the "conies" are so observant and wary that they are almost impossible to apprehend)*;

27 The locusts have no king, yet go they forth all of them by bands *(there is power in unity, even as the locusts portray)*;

28 The spider takes hold with her hands, and is in kings' palaces *(for their size, spiders have an amazing ability to fend for themselves; the Holy Spirit implores us to at least use the wisdom given to these little creatures)*.

29 There be three things which go well, yea, four are comely in going *(the four things mentioned are graceful in their actions)*:

30 A lion which is strongest among beasts, and turns not away for any *(the "lion" has been called the "king of the beasts"; he alone is the leader)*;

31 A greyhound; an he goat also; and a king, against whom there is no rising up *(the "greyhound" runs races, and is very graceful in his action; the "he goat" stands at the head, the majestic head, of the sheep; a "king" who deals honestly and correctly with his subjects cannot be toppled)*.

32 If you have done foolishly in lifting up yourself, or if you have thought evil, lay your hand upon your mouth. *("Confess your sins unto the Lord, Who forgives, and not to man, who will not forgive.")*

33 Surely the churning of milk brings forth butter, and the wringing of the nose brings forth blood: so the forcing of wrath brings forth strife. *(The "forcing of wrath" speaks of self-will. It is angry because it has not had its way. Man's way always ends in "strife" and confusion. God's Way always ends in fulfillment, development, rejoicing, and Righteousness.)*

CHAPTER 31
(1015 B.C.)
THE WORDS OF KING LEMUEL

T HE words of king Lemuel, the prophecy that his mother taught him. *("Lemuel" was another name for Solomon. His mother was Bath-sheba. The sense of this Proverb is that his mother kept teaching him continually.)*

2 What, my son? and what, the son of my womb? and what, the son of my vows? *(From this Passage, we know that Bath-sheba dedicated Solomon to God before his birth. He was a child of Repentance and Faith.)*

3 Give not your strength unto women, nor your ways to that which destroys kings. *(The obviousness of immorality is apparent in this Passage; however, its deeper meaning pertains to the false woman, idolatry, as is contrasted with the True Woman, the Gospel.)*

4 It is not for kings, O Lemuel, it is not for kings to drink wine; nor for princes strong drink *(the admonition of the Holy Spirit through Bath-sheba to her son Solomon is clear and plain: "Leave strong drink alone!"):*

5 Lest they drink, and forget the Law, and pervert the judgment of any of the afflicted. *(The pain of "strong drink," even moderately consumed, causes men to "forget the Law," which means to forget the Word of God; consequently, "Judgment" is perverted in such a case, and in whatever capacity.)*

6 Give strong drink unto him who is ready to perish, and wine unto those who be of heavy hearts.

7 Let him drink, and forget his poverty, and remember his misery no more. *(This pertains possibly to one ready to be executed, or another in extreme difficulties. The same is done in modern times, with certain drugs prescribed by doctors.)*

8 Open your mouth for the dumb in the cause of all such as are appointed to destruction. *(Bath-sheba seems to have a premonition that God will graciously open the Heavens regarding Wisdom that would be given to her*

son Solomon. *She seemed to know and understand that the helpless, afflicted, and defenseless would come to him in order for him to champion their "cause.")*

9 Open your mouth, judge righteously, and plead the cause of the poor and needy. *(Solomon was a Type of Christ and, as such, he was instructed, through his mother Bath-sheba by the Holy Spirit, to "judge righteously.")*

10 Who can find a virtuous woman? for her price is far above rubies. *(The word "virtuous" is not limited in Hebrew, as in English, in its meaning; it is a covering term suggesting character and ability. Spiritually, the dialogue concerning the "virtuous woman" can also apply to the Church and what it ought to be.)*

11 The heart of her husband does safely trust in her, so that he shall have no need of spoil. *(He has absolute confidence in her faithfulness.)*

12 She will do him good and not evil all the days of her life. *(He is blessed by her tireless and unfailing industry, which will last all the days of her life.)*

13 She seeks wool, and flax, and works willingly with her hands. *(She goes to every length to save money, even "working willingly with her hands." There is no hint of laziness about her.)*

14 She is like the merchants' ships; she brings her food from afar. *(If she buys something, she does so with the idea in mind of using some of it and selling the other to pay for that which she has used.)*

15 She rises also while it is yet night, and gives meat to her household, and a portion to her maidens. *(She takes the lead in guiding the house, and expects all who are in the household to follow her example, which they do.)*

16 She considers a field, and buys it: with the fruit of her hands she plants a vineyard. *(She is constantly planning as to how to provide for her growing family.)*

17 She girds her loins with strength, and strengthens her arms. *(She keeps herself and her family in good health with proper food and clothing.)*

18 She perceives that her merchandise is good: her candle goes not out by night. *(She produces quality product.)*

19 She lays her hands to the spindle, and her hands hold the distaff. *(All of this was a part of the spinning wheel, showing her industriousness and ability.)*

20 She stretches out her hand to the poor; yea, she reaches forth her hands to the needy. *(Even though she works hard for her money,*

she does not fail to help the "poor" and the "needy." She does so because she knows that God honors such.)

21 She is not afraid of the snow for her household: for all her household are clothed with scarlet. *(She has prepared for the coming winter with suitable clothing for all of her household. She thinks ahead. Coming difficulties do not catch her shortsighted.)*

22 She makes herself coverings of tapestry; her clothing is silk and purple. *(Even though she is very conservative, still, money is not her God. Therefore, she does not skimp in providing the furniture for her home, or for her own personal clothing. It is such that befits her station in life, as one who is blessed by God and is a Child of God.)*

23 Her husband is known in the gates, when he sits among the elders of the land. *(As her husband was guided in his choice of her, likewise, she was guided by the Holy Spirit in her choice of him. He is a leader in the community.)*

24 She makes fine linen, and sells it; and delivers girdles unto the merchant. *(Once again, her business ability places her on a par with her husband. The Holy Spirit gives her no lesser position. She is capable of being a captain of industry and a maker of excellent decisions.)*

25 Strength and honour are her clothing; and she shall rejoice in time to come. *(All that she manufactures is done so with quality. Her goods are sought the world over.)*

26 She opens her mouth with wisdom; and in her tongue is the law of kindness. *(Even though this virtuous woman, whose price is far above rubies, is said by the Holy Spirit to be a captain of industry with striking and startling abilities, still, her "mouth" is a mouth of "Wisdom." Despite all her qualities and riches, still, her "tongue" is not harsh, but always "kind.")*

27 She looks well to the ways of her household, and eats not the bread of idleness. *(Even though she is now greatly blessed, still, there is no place for "idleness" in her thinking or doing. In essence, industry never stops.)*

28 Her children arise up, and call her blessed; her husband also, and he praises her. *(Such women could not be praised too highly.*

Bath-sheba was truly led by the Holy Spirit and inspired greatly to write the instruction that she did for her son Solomon. She was quite a lady!)

29 Many daughters have done virtuously, but you excel them all. *(It seems that the husband of this "virtuous woman" speaks in this Verse. He claims that many have done "virtuously," but that this one whom God has given him, his lovely wife, "excels them all."*

If this is to be carried to its conclusion, David spoke these words about Bath-sheba. Such is God; such is Grace.)

30 Favour is deceitful, and beauty is vain, but a woman who fears the LORD, she shall be praised.

31 Give her of the fruit of her hands; and let her own works praise her in the gates. *(These two closing Verses of this Chapter are the Holy Spirit's conclusion, not only to the Chapter itself, but to the Message of the entirety of the Book of Proverbs. That Message is: the fear of the Lord secures abiding favor, moral beauty, public approbation, and eternal recompense.)*

THE BOOK OF
ECCLESIASTES

CHAPTER 1

(977 B.C.)

INTRODUCTION AND THEME

THE words of the Preacher, the son of David, king in Jerusalem. *(The beginning of this Book has a majesty that defies description. The title, "son of David," not only applies to Solomon, but also to the Greater Son of David, the Lord Jesus Christ [Mat. 1:1].*

In fact, the title, "Son of David," contains, within itself, no majesty whatsoever, but rather shame, until it is attached to the King of kings and Lord of lords. Only then does it sparkle with majesty.)

2 Vanity of vanities, saith the Preacher, vanity of vanities; all is vanity. *(The Holy Spirit says here that all that man is and has done, irrespective of his riches, beauty, power, or glory, can never satisfy the cravings of the human heart.*

The word "vanity" means "empty nothings." Ironically enough, Solomon, when he wrote this Book, was not right with God.)

3 What profit has a man of all his labour which he takes under the sun? *(This Book discusses "labor" as man's proposed "end" or ideal of happiness. The Book argues that, as an end, it is unsatisfying, however profitable it may be as a means.)*

4 One generation passes away, and another generation comes: but the Earth abides forever. *(The brevity of human life is contrasted with the age of the Earth. The word "forever" is comparative, not absolute.)*

5 The sun also arises, and the sun goes down, and hastes to his place where he arose. *(The anguish of Verses 5 through 11 is that all things move in an appointed circle, and so there is, to man, the dissatisfaction of recurrence.)*

6 The wind goes toward the south, and turns about unto the north; it whirls about continually, and the wind returns again according to his circuits.

7 All the rivers run into the sea; yet the sea is not full; unto the place from whence the rivers come, thither they return again.

8 All things are full of labour; man cannot utter it: the eye is not satisfied with seeing, nor the ear filled with hearing. *(The lesson the Holy Spirit is portraying to us is that any and all that the "eye" sees or the "ear" hears can never satisfy the craving of the human heart.*

Man thinks that if he can just obtain what he sees, it will bring fulfillment and satisfaction. It never does, because things cannot satisfy.)

9 The thing that has been, it is that which shall be; and that which is done is that which shall be done: and there is no new thing under the sun.

10 Is there any thing whereof it may be said, See, this is new? it has been already of old time, which was before us. *(There is, in reality, "nothing new"; that is, nothing occurs or can occur which can transport man into a new world or give him new joys or new emotions. Modern inventions are only "new" in a comparative, and not in an absolute, sense.)*

11 There is no remembrance of former things; neither shall there be any remembrance of things that are to come with those that shall come after. *(This Verse says that the records of the antediluvian world are totally destroyed, except for the information that is given to us in the Bible [from the time of Adam to Noah's flood]. God destroyed it all, thereby saying that man did nothing worthwhile. In fact, what man did was grossly evil, so evil that it had to be destroyed.)*

12 I the Preacher was king over Israel in Jerusalem. *(Solomon called himself a "Preacher," and so he was. He was called of God to be such.)*

13 And I gave my heart to seek and search out by wisdom concerning all things that are done under Heaven: this sore travail has God given to the sons of man to be exercised therewith. *(All that science can do is to recognize the vanity of all of man's efforts to turn Earth into a Heaven without God.)*

14 I have seen all the works that are done under the sun; and, behold, all is vanity and vexation of spirit. *(The gist of this Passage is that man cannot solve man's problem. That problem is a sinful, fallen nature that is in rebellion against God.)*

15 That which is crooked cannot be made straight: and that which is wanting cannot be numbered. *(Man's inability to straighten what has been made morally crooked and to furnish*

what is defective is insisted on with Truth in this entire Book.)

16 I communed with my own heart, saying, Lo, I am come to great estate, and have gotten more wisdom than all they who have been before me in Jerusalem: yea, my heart had great experience of wisdom and knowledge. *(No man in the world ever has had the "Wisdom" or the "Knowledge" that Solomon had. As well, his great "Wisdom" was given to him by God. In other words, it was a Gift of God.*

However, this did not bring Salvation and, in fact, could not bring Salvation. Solomon's experience bore this out as no other man who has ever lived.)

17 And I gave my heart to know wisdom, and to know madness and folly: I perceived that this also is vexation of spirit. *(Solomon had the money and the power to do what millions would like to do but simply cannot afford to do. But after it was done, he said, "This also is vexation of spirit.")*

18 For in much wisdom is much grief: and he who increases knowledge increases sorrow. *("Wisdom" without God only brings "grief." "Knowledge" without God only brings "sorrow."*

This is not to say that these attributes are disapproved of by the Lord. The meaning is that even these lofty ideals will bring no satisfaction without Christ.)

CHAPTER 2
(977 B.C.)
PLEASURE IS VAIN

I said in my heart, Go to now, I will prove you with mirth, therefore enjoy pleasure: and, behold, this also is vanity. *(The dissatisfaction and vexation of spirit which Solomon experienced in testing the insufficiency of industry, philosophy, and pleasure were the more painful because of his possession of the superhuman wisdom which remained with him, for the greater the capacity of enjoyment, the greater the disappointment and vexation. His misery was, therefore, greater than that of any who preceded or succeeded him because of his unique gift of wisdom. If ordinary intelligence finds everything "under the sun" to be vanity, extraordinary intelligence finds it to be "vanity of vanities.")*

2 I said of laughter, It is mad: and of mirth, What good does it? *(The finest comedians of the land were brought in. After the laughter subsided, the question still remained, "What good does it?")*

3 I sought in my heart to give myself unto wine, yet acquainting my heart with wisdom; and to lay hold on folly, till I might see what was that good for the sons of men, which they should do under the Heaven all the days of their life. *(That which is "good for the sons of men" is that which is found only in the Bible. It is amazing how man will try everything except the Bible.*

Solomon wrote the Proverbs and knew what the Holy Spirit told him concerning "wine.")

GREAT WORKS ARE VAIN

4 I made me great works; I built me houses; I planted me vineyards:

5 I made me gardens and orchards, and I planted trees in them of all kind of fruits:

6 I made me pools of water, to water therewith the wood that brings forth trees *(Millions say, "My work is my life." If so, they will find that the last day on the job will be the most unrewarding of all.*

Only if one says, "Christ is my life," will true satisfaction, fulfillment and realization be attained!):

7 I got me servants and maidens, and had servants born in my house; also I had great possessions of great and small cattle above all that were in Jerusalem before me *(self says that it will be rewarded and served if it has many "servants" to command; as well, great herds of "cattle" seem to be the craving of the empty heart)*:

8 I gathered me also silver and gold, and the peculiar treasure of kings and of the provinces: I got me men singers and women singers, and the delights of the sons of men, as musical instruments, and that of all sorts. *(Great riches and the pomp of court would have made this court the greatest in the history of man in times past, present, or future.*

Few have been the kingdoms where wealth was no object. And the few that have had abundant wealth have had little wisdom. Solomon had both!)

9 So I was great, and increased more than all who were before me in Jerusalem: also my wisdom remained with me. *(In His love, God has placed this Book in the Bible for the warning and instruction of His Children; in His Goodness, He denies them the means of making the woeful experiment which Solomon found so bitter.)*

10 And whatsoever my eyes desired I kept not from them, I withheld not my heart from

any joy; for my heart rejoiced in all my labour: and this was my portion of all my labour. *(Only one man in history was able to get all that his heart desired and all that his eyes beheld. That man was Solomon. He found it to be vanity.)*

11 Then I looked on all the works that my hands had wrought, and on the labour that I had laboured to do: and, behold, all was vanity and vexation of spirit, and there was no profit under the sun. *(All of this was done with an attempt to take the place of the Lord. As someone has well said, "The soul of man is so big, that only God can fill it up.")*

12 And I turned myself to behold wisdom, and madness, and folly: for what can the man do who comes after the king? even that which has been already done. *(No one ever was, or will be, as efficiently equipped as Solomon was for this terrible experience.)*

13 Then I saw that wisdom excels folly, as far as light excels darkness. *(Solomon once knew God in a great and personal way. The Lord even gave him a special name, "Jedidiah," which means "beloved of Jehovah."*

So, why would anyone leave such glory and grandeur for "folly"?

The answer to that "Why?" shows the incurable evil of the human heart which resulted from the Fall of man in the Garden of Eden.)

14 The wise man's eyes are in his head; but the fool walks in darkness: and I myself perceived also that one event happens to them all. *(In Verses 12 through 17, Solomon set himself to "behold wisdom" [to study philosophy], with the result that he observed that death no more respected the wise man than the fool. Thus, he discovered philosophy also to be vanity.)*

15 Then said I in my heart, As it happens to the fool, so it happens even to me; and why was I then more wise? Then I said in my heart, that this also is vanity. *(In essence, Solomon is saying that riches, wisdom, and power cannot change the things that really matter. Solomon said, "It happens to the fool, and it happens even to me."*

The Holy Spirit is impressing upon us the futility of this present life, that is, if it is lived without Christ.)

16 For there is no remembrance of the wise more than of the fool for ever; seeing that which now is in the days to come shall all be forgotten. And how dies the wise man? as the fool. *(Everything that is done, irrespective of its seeming worth, will be "forgotten," except that which is done for God. Such lasts forever.)*

17 Therefore I hated life; because the work that is wrought under the sun is grievous unto me: for all is vanity and vexation of spirit. *(The only One Who can make life worth living is Christ Jesus. A life totally immersed in Him, irrespective of its circumstances, will bring fulfillment, satisfaction, and contentment, as well as "joy unspeakable and full of glory" — but only in Christ [Jn. 10:10].)*

18 Yea, I hated all my labour which I had taken under the sun: because I should leave it unto the man who shall be after me. *(If Solomon had used the great Wisdom that God have given him [greater than any man had ever had or would ever have] to fill the land with the Word of God, the future might have been far different. Instead, he used his great Wisdom to enrich himself and Israel. That which looks so beautiful to the natural eye was taken so easily by the king of Egypt very shortly thereafter.)*

19 And who knows whether he shall be a wise man or a fool? yet shall he have rule over all my labour wherein I have laboured, and wherein I have showed myself wise under the sun. This is also vanity. *(His son, Rehoboam, was his successor, and he was a "fool.")*

20 Therefore I went about to cause my heart to despair of all the labour which I took under the sun. *(Anything and everything tied to this present world that is done other than for God, and that which is built strictly by man, no matter how grandiose, will lead one to "despair.")*

21 For there is a man whose labour is in wisdom, and in knowledge, and in equity; yet to a man who has not laboured therein shall he leave it for his portion. This also is vanity and a great evil. *(The wise man's "portion" or share is labor, difficulty, and sometimes great sorrow, but his foolish successor's share is the possession without effort of all that his father painfully toiled to bring into being.)*

22 For what has man of all his labour, and of the vexation of his heart, wherein he has laboured under the sun? *(Jesus answered this by giving us the statement recorded in Mat. 6:19-21.)*

23 For all his days are sorrows, and his travail grief; yea, his heart takes not rest in the night. This is also vanity. *(The Holy Spirit is informing us in a grand manner that the only thing that is not "vanity" is the labor carried out for the Work of God.)*

24 There is nothing better for a man, than that he should eat and drink, and that he should make his soul enjoy good in his labour. This also I saw, that it was from the hand of God.

(Life is meant to be a pleasure, not a rat race. Paul said, "But Godliness with contentment is great gain" [I Tim. 6:6].)

25 For who can eat, or who else can hasten hereunto, more than I? *(Solomon verified that a life of honest labor ministers a happiness appointed by the Hand of God. In this Verse, "eat and drink" are to be understood as enjoyment of needful food with an appetite quickened by honest "labor.")*

26 For God gives to a man that is good in His sight wisdom, and knowledge, and joy: but to the sinner He gives travail, to gather and to heap up, that he may give to him that is good before God. This also is vanity and vexation of spirit. *(He who thus works for his daily bread in obedience to the Divine Will, to him God recompenses wisdom, knowledge, and joy. But to the disobedient, He gives the fruitless toil of amassing wealth that brings no enjoyment, as honest labor does to the Godly man.)*

CHAPTER 3
(977 B.C.)
A TIME FOR EVERYTHING

TO every thing there is a season, and a time to every purpose under the Heaven *(to misunderstand this Chapter is to misunderstand the purpose of God):*

2 A time to be born, and a time to die; a time to plant, and a time to pluck up that which is planted;

3 A time to kill, and a time to heal; a time to break down, and a time to build up;

4 A time to weep, and a time to laugh; a time to mourn, and a time to dance;

5 A time to cast away stones, and a time to gather stones together; a time to embrace, and a time to refrain from embracing;

6 A time to get, and a time to lose; a time to keep, and a time to cast away;

7 A time to rend, and a time to sew; a time to keep silence, and a time to speak;

8 A time to love, and a time to hate; a time of war, and a time of peace. *(One can only know and understand these respective "times," if one properly "walks after the Spirit" [Rom. 8:1]. This can be done only by the Believer exhibiting Faith in Christ as the Source, and the Cross as the Means, and maintaining his Faith in that capacity. The Holy Spirit works entirely within the framework of the Finished Work of Christ. He demands of us, which is precious little to demand, that our Faith ever be in that*

Finished Work. That being done, the Spirit of God will work in our lives, leading and guiding us [Jn. 16:13-15; Rom. 8:2, 11].)

9 What profit has he who works in that wherein he labours? *(If, in fact, man labors only for this present world, there is no "profit." However, if man's "labor" is engaged to provide the necessities of life and to do the Work of God to help take the Gospel to the world, then the "profit" will be eternal.)*

10 I have seen the travail, which God has given to the sons of men to be exercised in it. *(God has given labor to man as a discipline and not as an end. Consequently, to make the actions of labor the chief end of life is to seek a profitless object.)*

11 He has made every thing beautiful in His time: also He has set the world in their heart, so that no man can find out the work that God makes from the beginning to the end. *(In this Verse, the word "world" should have been translated "eternity." God has made everything beautiful in its season and, at the same time, given to man the consciousness of "eternity." But He has limited this intelligence so that man cannot review or criticize the whole of God's actions as they embrace the past and the future. This is done in order to humble man and to teach him to trust God.)*

12 I know that here is no good in them, but for a man to rejoice, and to do good in his life. *(Man is meant to rejoice in God's creation, as all of this was created for the good of man.)*

13 And also that every man should eat and drink, and enjoy the good of all his labour, it is the gift of God. *(The eating, drinking, and toiling, and the enjoyment resulting from such, mean that legitimate labor is man's daily duty, but it is not the end or purpose of his being.)*

14 I know that, whatsoever God does, it shall be for ever: nothing can be put to it, nor any thing taken from it: and God does it, that men should fear before Him. *(The immutability and unchangeableness of God's actions and purposes awaken reverential fear, holy love, and worship in all who are born of the Spirit.)*

15 That which has been is now; and that which is to be has already been; and God requires that which is past. *(The sense of this Passage is that God's Word is immutable, and that in the coming Judgment, whether at the Great White Throne or at the Judgment Seat of Christ, God will require obedience to His Word which was given in the "past.")*

16 And moreover I saw under the sun the

place of judgment, that wickedness was there; and the place of righteousness, that iniquity was there. *(A difficulty is presented in this Verse, but answered in Verse 17. The difficulty is: if God governs human affairs, why is injustice found where justice is enthroned? The answer is that God permits this folly on the part of man in order to humble him, and He will then, in a future life, judge him for his wrongdoing.)*

17 I said in my heart, God shall judge the righteous and the wicked: for there is a time there for every purpose and for every work. *(The word "there" means in the world beyond the grave, that is, in the great day of future judgment. Two judgments are mentioned here, "the Judgment Seat of Christ" [Rom. 14:10; I Cor. 3:11-15] and "the Great White Throne Judgment" [Rev. 20:13-15].*

At the first, only Believers will be present, and will be judged only for their actions and motives on Earth, and not for their sins, which were judged at Calvary. At the second judgment, only unbelievers will be there. Each will include all.)

18 I said in my heart concerning the estate of the sons of men, that God might manifest them, and that they might see that they themselves are beasts. *(Solomon is not teaching evolution, but that men and beasts alike have bodies that die and go back to dust.*

As well, it is also true that men can become bestial in lust and conduct.

In the Fall, man lost God-consciousness and fell to the far lower level of self-consciousness.)

19 For that which befalls the sons of men befalls beasts; even one thing befalls them: as the one dies, so dies the other; yea, they have all one breath; so that a man has no preeminence above a beast: for all is vanity. *(Both man and beast live and die; however, it was not originally the Plan of God that man should die. This came about through the Fall. It will be rectified in the coming Resurrection [I Cor., Chpt. 15].)*

20 All go unto one place; all are of the dust, and all turn to dust again. *(This speaks of the body only, which is made of "dust," and which goes back to "dust." It does not speak of the soul or spirit, which are indestructible.*

The bodies of both men and animals go back to dust from which they were made.)

21 Who knows the spirit of man that goes upward, and the spirit of the beast that goes downward to the Earth? *(As the previous Verse spoke of the body, this Verse speaks of the "spirit"*

of both man and beast.

While it is obvious that the spirit of the redeemed goes upward, the only way that it can be said that the spirit of the unredeemed goes upward is in view of the fact that God is in control of both the righteous and unrighteous. At His Command, the spirit of the unredeemed goes downward into the pit [Ezek. 31:14; Lk. 16:23-31].)

22 Wherefore I perceive that there is nothing better, than that a man should rejoice in his own works; for that is his portion: for who shall bring him to see what shall be after him? *(Man's happiness is in making the best of the present and cheerfully enjoying what the Lord offers without anxious care for the future; nevertheless, only one who has made his peace with God and has entrusted his past, present, and future into the Hands of the Saviour can rest in complete assurance.)*

CHAPTER 4

(977 B.C.)

**OPPRESSIONS BY OTHERS
INCREASE VANITY**

SO I returned, and considered all the oppressions that are done under the sun: and behold the tears of such as were oppressed, and they had no comforter; and on the side of their oppressors there was power; but they had no comforter. *(This Chapter portrays a world that has banished God from its life; consequently, there is confusion, ignorance, and misery. Such characterizes most of the present world.*

The words, "so I returned," mean "I resumed my investigation.")

2 Wherefore I praised the dead which are already dead more than the living which are yet alive. *(The tragedy is that the "dead," without God, do not end their oppression but, in actuality, it increases, and forever.)*

3 Yea, better is he than both they, which has not yet been, who has not seen the evil work that is done under the sun. *(Solomon reasons, and despite his great Wisdom, that it would be better that man not even be born; however, all of this is reasoning without God. If, in fact, there were no God, no Saviour, and no "Comforter," then the argument would be valid; however, there is a "Comforter," and He is the Holy Spirit [Jn. 14:16].)*

4 Again, I considered all travail, and every right work, that for this a man is envied of his neighbour. This is also vanity and vexation of spirit. *(Any work for God should be met with*

approval; however, it is almost always, if not always, met with opposition. The reason is "envy" or control. Men cannot control that which is of God; therefore, they oppose it.)

THE INCREASE OF VANITY

5 The fool folds his hands together, and eats his own flesh. *(Solomon observed that the man who, with grasping hand, enriched himself by promoting himself, or else by robbing others, was a fool, for he ate his own flesh, that is, opposed that which could have been a blessing even to him.)*

6 Better is an handful with quietness, than both the hands full with travail and vexation of spirit. *(Men are too quick to trade inner peace for "things" that add nothing to one's life, but rather destroy it [Lk., Chpt. 15].)*

7 Then I returned, and I saw vanity under the sun. *(The Book of Ecclesiastes, more than any other book, proclaims the "vanity, foolishness, and folly" of all of man's efforts.)*

8 There is one alone, and there is not a second; yea, he has neither child nor brother: yet is there no end of all his labour; neither is his eye satisfied with riches; neither saith he, For whom do I labour, and bereave my soul of good? This is also vanity, yea, it is a sore travail. *(Solomon then observed what this constant quest of life without God ultimately brought about. It brought an acute selfishness.)*

9 Two are better than one; because they have a good reward for their labour. *(In the action of this Verse, we further learn that it is not good for man to be alone [Gen. 2:18].)*

10 For if they fall, the one will lift up his fellow: but woe to him who is alone when he falls; for he has not another to help him up. *(The Holy Spirit through Solomon says, "Help him up.")*

11 Again, if two lie together, then they have heat: but how can one be warm alone? *(Every effort is made by the Holy Spirit to show the value of two rather than one. In all of the travels of the Apostle Paul, he almost always took one or more with him, and for the obvious reasons.)*

12 And if one prevail against him, two shall withstand him; and a threefold cord is not quickly broken. *(The "threefold cord" proclaims the truth that the spiritual power of two is more than double. That's the reason it is so important for two or more to agree together in prayer [Mat. 18:19-20].)*

13 Better is a poor and a wise child than an old and foolish king, who will no more be admonished. *(The words that were given by Solomon in Verses 13 through 16 were actually a prophecy of what would happen to himself; to his son, Rehoboam; and to his servant, Jeroboam.*

He became the "old and foolish king" who refused to listen to the Divine admonition [I Ki. 3:14; 9:3-9; 11:9-40].)

14 For out of prison he comes to reign; whereas also he who is born in his kingdom becomes poor. *(Jeroboam was the poor but clever youth who came out of prison and was made king. The great nation of Israel, then the greatest on the face of the Earth, would now be split.)*

15 I considered all the living which walk under the sun, with the second child that shall stand up in his stead. *(As Solomon considered his son, Rehoboam, perhaps even then he knew that Rehoboam had little relationship, if any, with the Lord, and consequently would come to ruin, which he did.)*

16 There is no end of all the people, even of all who have been before them: they also who come after shall not rejoice in him. Surely this also is vanity and vexation of spirit. *(If the investigator limits his observations to what takes place "under the sun," then is the conclusion indeed a just one that "all is vanity" and a feeding upon wind.*

But the Christian recognizes that God exists, that there is a future life, and that having been gifted with free will, it is reasonable that God should permit man liberty of action. Although such liberty involves suffering, the misery is overruled by God for the ultimate good of His People, and for the discipline, humbling, and moral enrichment of man.)

CHAPTER 5
(977 B.C.)
CAUTION AGAINST HASTY VOWS

KEEP your foot when you go to the House of God, and be more ready to hear than to give the sacrifice of fools: for they consider not that they do evil. *("Keep your foot" means to be reverent. The "House of God" refers to the Presence of God. "To hear" means to obey.*

Cain offered the "sacrifice of fools" [Gen. 4:3-5]. Most of that which calls itself "Church" falls into the same category.

The only Sacrifice that God will accept is the Sacrifice of His Son, Christ Jesus. This is what Abel's offering typified.

Any message that does not make Christ the

Source and the Cross the Means is a "sacrifice of fools.")

2 Be not rash with your mouth, and let not your heart be hasty to utter any thing before God: for God is in Heaven, and you upon Earth: therefore let your words be few. *(This Verse points to loud religious profession with the lips.)*

3 For a dream comes through the multitude of business; and a fool's voice is known by multitude of words. *(The first part of this Verse speaks of busy activity that oftentimes causes one to have dreams which cannot be remembered the next morning.*

As well, the man who constantly prattles at the mouth is called "a fool" by God, and his words are like the "dream" that cannot be remembered.)

4 When you vow a vow unto God, defer not to pay it; for He has no pleasure in fools: pay that which you have vowed. *(In no uncertain terms, the Holy Spirit has told us to be very careful about making a "vow." However, if one is made, we are to keep it.)*

5 Better is it that you should not vow, than that you should vow and not pay. *(If a person makes a "vow," he should do all within his power and ability to keep that "vow." However, if a person makes a rash "vow," and it turns out that it is impossible to keep, one should plead with the Lord to forgive such rashness, and then lay the "vow" aside.)*

6 Suffer not your mouth to cause your flesh to sin; neither say thou before the Angel, that it was an error: wherefore should God be angry at your voice, and destroy the work of your hands? *(The "mouth" too often causes the "flesh to sin." This Verse should make us understand how serious that God takes "vows.")*

7 For in the multitude of dreams and many words there are also divers vanities: but fear thou God. *(The professors of ceremonial religion construct a worship of dreams, vanities, and many words. God calls it "empty nothings," which characterize all the religions of the world. Religion is a man-made system used in place of a God-given Salvation. A true experience with God is a personal relationship with God, which can only come through an acceptance of Jesus Christ and what He did for us at the Cross [Lk. 9:23].)*

8 If you see the oppression of the poor, and violent perverting of judgment and justice in a province, marvel not at the matter: for he who is higher than the highest regards; and there be higher than they. *(The argument of this Verse is: if God, Who is higher than the kings of the Earth, temporarily permits oppression, His Child is not to be stumbled or be confused by this fact, but to accept the Divine purpose, realizing that God will ultimately call to justice those who "pervert judgment." No matter how high the king, president, etc., may be, God is "higher.")*

9 Moreover the profit of the Earth is for all: the king himself is served by the field. *(The Earth has the potential, we are told, to feed 100 billion people. Because of religion and the powers of darkness, it strains at present with the approximate 6 1/2 billion population. In the coming Kingdom Age, all of that will change.)*

10 He who loves silver shall not be satisfied with silver; nor he who loves abundance with increase: this is also vanity. *(Why? As man is a physical being, he is also a spiritual being. The soul and the spirit of man can only be satisfied by God, and not by silver or gold.)*

11 When goods increase, they are increased who eat them: and what good is there to the owners thereof, saving the beholding of them with their eyes? *(Other than the food we eat, the clothes we wear, and a home to live in, plus whatever physical or material needs we may have, what actual good is there in great accumulation of properties and things? All that one can do is look at them.)*

12 The sleep of a labouring man is sweet, whether he eat little or much: but the abundance of the rich will not suffer him to sleep. *(The "rich" are constantly concerned about their abundance, so sleep oftentimes escapes their eyes.)*

13 There is a sore evil which I have seen under the sun, namely, riches kept for the owners thereof to their hurt. *(This is the tragic story of so many!)*

14 But those riches perish by evil travail: and he begets a son, and there is nothing in his hand. *(If riches are all that a father can give a son, then he has really given him nothing. The greatest thing that one can give is Christ.)*

15 As he came forth of his mother's womb, naked shall he return to go as he came, and shall take nothing of his labour, which he may carry away in his hand. *(A very wealthy man died. As the funeral train passed, someone was heard to ask, "How much did he leave?" Another who stood nearby answered immediately, "He left it all"!)*

16 And this also is a sore evil, that in all points as he came, so shall he go: and what

profit has he who has laboured for the wind? *(Man is born naked, and he leaves naked. If he has all of this world's goods and none of God, he will have "labored for the wind." Such characterizes almost all of humanity. That is the reason that Jesus instead told us to lay up treasures in Heaven [Mat. 6:19-20].)*

17 All his days also he eats in darkness, and he has much sorrow and wrath with his sickness. *(The Lord calls the grasping after riches a "sickness." He says that those who follow this course, no matter how rich they may be, are in "darkness.")*

18 Behold that which I have seen: it is good and comely for one to eat and to drink, and to enjoy the good of all his labour that he takes under the sun all the days of his life, which God gives him: for it is his portion. *(God means for men to enjoy life, "to enjoy the good." Such can be, but only if men will seek after the Lord, obey His Word, and seek His Will.*

The "enjoyment" comes because of what God puts in the heart, and not what the person has accumulated or gathered.)

19 Every man also to whom God has given riches and wealth, and has given him power to eat thereof, and to take his portion, and to rejoice in his labour; this is the gift of God. *(In this Passage, we are told that God does in fact give some people "riches and wealth." Those to whom the Lord has given such must understand that it was done in order that such a person may bless the Kingdom of God.)*

20 For he shall not much remember the days of his life; because God answers him in the joy of his heart. *(The only things of his life that will be worth remembering are those things that are done for God.)*

CHAPTER 6
(977 B.C.)
THE VANITY AND EVILS OF LIFE

THERE is an evil which I have seen under the sun, and it is common among men:

2 A man to whom God has given riches, wealth, and honour, so that he wants nothing for his soul of all that he desires, yet God gives him not power to eat thereof, but a stranger eats it: this is vanity, and it is an evil disease. *(The word "common" should read "heavy," for the misery described in Verses 2 through 7 is peculiar to the miser, and not to all men. The rich man of Verse 2 is to be distinguished from the rich man of 5:19. The one uses the given*

wealth legitimately; the other hoards it.

The moral of this statement is that any individual who seeks riches without God, of whom there are many, is laboring only for "vanity," which is "empty nothings.")

3 If a man beget an hundred children, and live many years, so that the days of his years be many, and his soul be not filled with good, and also that he have no burial; I say, that an untimely birth is better than he. *(The moral of this is that only God can make life what it ought to be.)*

4 For he comes in with vanity, and departs in darkness, and his name shall be covered with darkness.

5 Moreover he has not seen the sun, nor known any thing: this has more rest than the other. *(Three things are said in these two Verses: 1. Man "comes in with vanity," which is a result of the Fall; 2. "And departs in darkness," that is, if he doesn't know the Lord; and, 3. "And his name shall be covered with darkness." This means forever. Whether rich or poor, this is the state of the human race without God.)*

6 Yea, though he live a thousand years twice told, yet has he seen no good: do not all go to one place? *(The sense of this Passage is that irrespective of the length of life, without God, this will only point to wasted opportunities. He will go to the same "place" where every Christ-rejecter has gone!)*

7 All the labour of man is for his mouth, and yet the appetite is not filled. *(Man without God is never satisfied because all that he seeks to obtain cannot satisfy. Only Jesus can satisfy the soul [Jn. 4:13-14].)*

8 For what has the wise more than the fool? what has the poor, who knows to walk before the living? *(In both cases, the word "advantage" should be supplied after the word "what." The "wise" is one who knows the Lord, so his advantage is great, to say the least!)*

9 Better is the sight of the eyes than the wandering of the desire: this is also vanity and vexation of spirit. *(The unspiritual heart is never satisfied and is, therefore, ever the victim of "the wandering of the desire." He keeps thinking that if such-and-such can be obtained, then satisfaction and fulfillment will come. It won't!)*

10 That which has been is named already, and it is known that it is man: neither may he contend with him who is mightier than he. *(This Verse can be paraphrased: "Whatsoever he be, whether rich or poor, his name was given*

him long ago, and is known to be Adam" [a morsel of red dust]. So how can such a one contend with his Creator?)

11 Seeing there be many things that increase vanity, what is man the better? *(Irrespective of the fact that man uses "many words" in disputation with his Maker, such words only increase vanity and fail to better him.)*

12 For who knows what is good for man in this life, all the days of his vain life which he spends as a shadow? for who can tell a man what shall be after him under the sun? *(The Lord Alone can supply such answers; otherwise, there is no answer.)*

CHAPTER 7
(977 B.C.)
CHOOSE THE BETTER THINGS

A good name is better than precious ointment; and the day of death than the day of one's birth. *(The only truly "good name" is the Name of Christ, and the only ones who can truly say they have a "good name" are those who take the Name of Christ upon themselves.*

To him who has this "good name," but only such a one, is the death-day better than the birthday, for it introduces him to a blissful and perfect life "above the sun" [Phil. 1:23].)

2 It is better to go to the house of mourning, than to go to the house of feasting: for that is the end of all men; and the living will lay it to his heart. *(To the flesh, this Passage seems wrong; however, the "house of mourning" has a tendency to show to us our true selves, to help us think more highly of others and, thereby, to humble us, which is better.)*

3 Sorrow is better than laughter: for by the sadness of the countenance the heart is made better. *("Sorrow" has a tendency to drive people to their knees. "Laughter" has a tendency to exalt self.)*

4 The heart of the wise is in the house of mourning; but the heart of fools is in the house of mirth. *(The "wise" are those who know their Bibles and, therefore, understand the gravity of the situation; consequently, to the "wise," the "house of mourning" speaks of intercessory and travailing prayer.)*

5 It is better to hear the rebuke of the wise, than for a man to hear the song of fools. *(Man, and religious man above all, does not like to be rebuked, so he seeks out the "song of fools," which speaks of false doctrine.)*

6 For as the crackling of thorns under a pot, so is the laughter of the fool: this also is vanity. *(A fire of thorns makes a great noise, but lasts only a short time; likewise, the "laughter of the fool" makes a great noise, but dies just as quickly.)*

7 Surely oppression makes a wise man mad; and a gift destroys the heart. *(The "wise man" is one who knows and understands the Bible. If such a one begins to "oppress" others and, at the same time, overlooks injustice done to another because he has taken bribes, he will then ultimately be driven to "madness." Sin against light is the worst sin of all.)*

8 Better is the end of a thing than the beginning thereof: and the patient in spirit is better than the proud in spirit. *(The sense of Verses 7 and 8 is that the follower of the Lord begins to look to the world and, thereby, ceases to look to the Lord, for both cannot be looked upon at the same time. By looking at the world, he begins to feel that he is not getting his just due, and that his living for God has not brought the prosperity he desires. So he succumbs to the wiles of the world.)*

WISDOM IS BETTER THAN WEALTH

9 Be not hasty in your spirit to be angry: for anger rests in the bosom of fools. *(All things done to us, irrespective as to how bad they might be, must be quickly turned over to the Lord. Let Him take care of the situation [Rom. 12:18-21].)*

10 Say not thou, What is the cause that the former days were better than these? for you do not enquire wisely concerning this. *(In this Passage, the Holy Spirit warns us not to complain of having fallen upon difficult days, for such irritation shows a want of Heavenly Wisdom and a questioning of the love that plans all things for man's good.)*

11 Wisdom is good with an inheritance: and by it there is profit to them who see the sun. *(The "wisdom" that is spoken of is that which is derived from the Word of God. An "inheritance" without such "wisdom" will bring no "profit.")*

12 For wisdom is a defence, and money is a defence: but the excellency of knowledge is, that wisdom gives life to them who have it. *(This Passage tells us that "wisdom" is greater than "money." Wisdom shields from the ills of life, and so does money; however, money can be lost, but wisdom, never.)*

13 Consider the work of God: for who can make that straight, which He has made

crooked? *(The argument of these Verses is: if God sends adversity [makes a thing crooked], who can reverse His Decree and defeat His Will? Heavenly Wisdom teaches a joyful acceptance of His Will, if He grants prosperity; and a approbation of His Will, if He ordains adversity.)*

14 In the day of prosperity be joyful, but in the day of adversity consider: God also has set the one over against the other, to the end that man should find nothing after him. *(This Passage may be rendered in this way: "In the day of prosperity be joyful, and in the day of adversity be thankful. Consider that God has even made or set the one side by side with the other, so that man shall not find any cause of complaint against Him.")*

SELF-RIGHTEOUSNESS

15 All things have I seen in the days of my vanity: there is a just man who perishes in his righteousness, and there is a wicked man who prolongs his life in his wickedness. *(First of all, this Passage does not mean that a man perishes because he is righteous; neither does it mean that a wicked man prolongs his life by being wicked. It does mean that some just men die at an early age, even though "righteous." As well, some men, despite their wickedness, live long lives.*

We must leave such things in the Hands of God!)

16 Be not righteous over much; neither make yourself over wise: why should you destroy yourself? *(There must not be any self-righteousness in the heart of the Believer, for such will destroy.)*

17 Be not over much wicked, neither be thou foolish: why should you die before your time? *(This is not meant that it is satisfactory in the Eyes of God to be "wicked" in a small degree. It does mean that our situation is already perilous, and to aggravate our sinfulness could bring upon us the wrath of God, with our life cut short.)*

18 It is good that you should take hold of this; yes, also from this withdraw not your hand: for he who fears God shall come forth of them all. *(A proper fear of God will destroy all self-righteousness.)*

DO NOT TRUST IN MIGHT

19 Wisdom strengthens the wise more than ten mighty men which are in the city. *(A city*

is far better off having ten wise men than ten mighty men; regrettably, the world has many "mighty men" and precious few "wise men.")*

20 For there is not a just man upon Earth, who does good, and sins not. *(The moral of this Passage is that men, within themselves, are fatally flawed.*

I wonder when the Church will look at these Verses and realize that humanistic psychology has no answer? Jesus Christ Alone, and what He did for us at the Cross, is the only answer [I Cor. 1:23; 2:2; Jn. 3:16].)

21 Also take no heed unto all words that are spoken; lest you hear your servant curse you *(we are importuned here to have a forbearing and forgiving spirit):*

22 For oftentimes also your own heart knows that you yourself likewise have cursed others. *(Such instruction humbles us with a consciousness that all hearts are diseased by sin and are, in this sense, alike.)*

DISCOVERIES OF A BACKSLIDER

23 All this have I proved by wisdom: I said, I will be wise; but it was far from me. *(Even with his great wisdom, wisdom given by God, Solomon still could not find a way to slake the thirst of the human heart outside of God.)*

24 That which is far off, and exceeding deep, who can find it out? *(That which is far off and exceeding deep is Heavenly Wisdom. It is impossible to be found out by Earthly wisdom.)*

25 I applied my heart to know, and to search, and to seek out wisdom, and the reason of things, and to know the wickedness of folly, even of foolishness and madness *(this Verse can be thus rendered: "I resumed by investigations, and I determined to ascertain and learn the cause of actions [the actions of self-righteousness on the one hand and of debauchery on the other], and to know the wickedness of folly and the extravagance of foolishness." No man in history has ever had the means to do this as Solomon had; therefore, God would turn his backslidings into instruction. Even with all of his "wisdom," he was unable to find the answers to the great questions of life outside of God, because there are no answers outside of God):*

26 And I find more bitter than death the woman, whose heart is snares and nets, and her hands as bands: whoso pleases God shall escape from her; but the sinner shall be taken by her. *(In this Verse, the cause of self-righteousness and of profligacy is found to be idolatry. This is*

symbolized by a woman. Salvation by personal merit and immorality characterize idolatrous nations and people.)

27 Behold, this have I found, says the preacher, counting one by one, to find out the account (all of this is so given by the Holy Spirit that we may be instructed by Solomon's failures):

28 Which yet my soul seeks, but I find not: one man among a thousand have I found; but a woman among all those have I not found. (This all resulted from his exercise of self-will. He chose idolatrous women, and they corrupted him. Had he sought Divine guidance in the matter, God would have given him one wife, and he would have lived the experience that "he who finds a God-given wife finds a good thing."

Probably the one honest man of which he speaks was the Prophet Ahijah [I Ki. 11:29], but, doubtless, this is a prophetic utterance and points to the only human being Who was Perfect, the True Man, the Man, Christ Jesus.)

29 Lo, this only have I found, that God has made man upright; but they have sought out many inventions. (The declaration of this Verse is that God made Adam and Eve upright, but they and their children introduced many inventions, the most popular of which are idolatry and polygamy. Solomon suffered from these two.)

CHAPTER 8
(977 B.C.)
RESPECT FOR RULERS

WHO is as the wise man? and who knows the interpretation of a thing? a man's wisdom makes his face to shine, and the boldness of his face shall be changed. (When Christ, Who is Wisdom, lives by the Power of the Holy Spirit in the heart of man, man is made intelligent, and his face, naturally discontented and gloomy, is made bright and peaceful [Gal. 2:20].)

2 I counsel you to keep the king's commandment, and that in regard of the oath of God. (This basically has to do with Psalm 89:35. Verses 3 through 5 prove that the Messiah is intended. The "King" is Christ!)

3 Be not hasty to go out of His sight: stand not in an evil thing; for He does whatsoever pleases Him. (We should seek to please Christ in all things, which we can do only by constantly exhibiting Faith in Christ and what He has done for us at the Cross [Rom., Chpt. 6]. As well, Christ has the Power to do "whatsoever pleases Him," not whatsoever pleases us!)

4 Where the word of a King is, there is power: and who may say unto Him, What do You? (Even though God will not answer the questions of prideful conceit, still, He will answer the questions of the broken, contrite, searching heart [Isa. 66:2].)

5 Whoso keeps the commandment shall feel no evil thing: and a wise man's heart discerns both time and judgment. (The Christian, though he knows there will be a day of judgment, feels no terror, because all has been committed to "the King.")

THE INEQUITIES OF LIFE

6 Because to every purpose there is time and judgment, therefore the misery of man is great upon him. (The "misery of man" is the guilt of unpardoned sin and the knowledge that a future day of reckoning is coming. That "misery" can only be assuaged at the Cross of Christ.)

7 For he knows not that which shall be: for who can tell him when it shall be? (No man knows "when" that time of judgment will come; however, the righteous man is not troubled, because he has committed the judgment to Christ.)

8 There is no man that has power over the spirit to retain the spirit; neither has he power in the day of death: and there is no discharge in that war; neither shall wickedness deliver those who are given to it. ("Wickedness" here means a way of salvation other than God's Way. Human priests offer dying men a salvation which they themselves have invented, and many Preachers also offer a salvation other than the Bible. Such "wickedness" will not deliver those who trust it.)

9 All this have I seen, and applied my heart unto every work that is done under the sun: there is a time wherein one man rules over another to his own hurt. (To rule over another in the things of the Lord will ultimately bring hurt — both to the ruler and to the ruled. This is "the doctrine of the Nicolaitanes," which the Lord hates [Rev. 2:15].)

10 And so I saw the wicked buried, who had come and gone from the place of the holy, and they were forgotten in the city where they had so done: this is also vanity. (This pertains to the "wicked" dying in the false hope of a false plan of salvation.)

11 Because sentence against an evil work is not executed speedily, therefore the heart of the sons of men is fully set in them to do evil. (The government is morally and spiritually obligated to put down all "evil work," whether in

the hearts and lives of individuals or in entire nations. To not do so will only increase the evil.)

12 Though a sinner do evil an hundred times, and his days be prolonged, yet surely I know that it shall be well with them who fear God, which fear before Him *(the "sinner" placed in his best position cannot begin to compare with the "well-being" of those who "fear God"):*

13 But it shall not be well with the wicked, neither shall he prolong his days, which are as a shadow; because he fears not before God. *(Even though the days of the "wicked" can be prolonged, nevertheless, there will come a day that it will all end.)*

14 There is a vanity which is done upon the Earth; that there be just men, unto whom it happens according to the work of the wicked; again, there be wicked men, to whom it happens according to the work of the righteous: I said that this also is vanity. *(Irrespective as to how things may look on the surface, it is eternity to which one must look.)*

15 Then I commended mirth, because a man has no better thing under the sun, than to eat, and to drink, and to be merry: for that shall abide with him of his labour the days of his life, which God gives him under the sun. *(The argument and teaching of the Book of Ecclesiastes is that going the opposite direction of the Lord is folly, for God exists and will bring every action into judgment.)*

16 When I applied my heart to know wisdom, and to see the business that is done upon the Earth: (for also there is that neither day nor night sees sleep with his eyes *[some are so engrossed in their business that they cannot even sleep at night, which means there is no enjoyment in their business]*:)

17 Then I beheld all the work of God, that a man cannot find out the work that is done under the sun: because though a man labour to seek it out, yet he shall not find it; yea farther; though a wise man think to know it, yet shall he not be able to find it. *(To understand everything about God, even the wisest man is unable to do so. Neither are we meant to do so. We can know many things, but the only true thing worthwhile of knowing is that our soul is right with God.)*

CHAPTER 9
(977 B.C.)
ALL THINGS COME ALIKE TO ALL

F OR all this I considered in my heart even to declare all this, that the righteous, and

the wise, and their works, are in the hand of God: no man knows either love or hatred by all that is before them. *(The contrast between the "work of God" in Verse 17 of the previous Chapter and the "works of man" in this Verse expresses the whole philosophy of life. All the "works" of both "the righteous" and "the wicked" "are in the Hand of God"; the Lord has total control, with all "love" and "hatred" measured by Him.)*

2 All things come alike to all: there is one event to the righteous, and to the wicked; to the good and to the clean, and to the unclean; to him who sacrifices, and to him who sacrifices not: as is the good, so is the sinner; and he who swears, as he who fears an oath. *(The modern confession message has attempted to do away with all the vicissitudes of life; it fails, as it must, because some trials are the Will of God.)*

3 This is an evil among all things that are done under the sun, that there is one event unto all: yea, also the heart of the sons of men is full of evil, and madness is in their heart while they live, and after that they go to the dead. *(The "one event" that Solomon is speaking of is death. It comes to all, irrespective of their being rich, poor, great, or small. Yet, despite this fact, men's hearts are filled with evil and madness, so long as they live without God.)*

4 For to him who is joined to all the living there is hope: for a living dog is better than a dead lion. *(There is hope for Salvation only while the individual is alive. All opportunities for Salvation are on this side of the grave.)*

5 For the living know that they shall die: but the dead know not any thing, neither have they any more a reward; for the memory of them is forgotten.

6 Also their love, and their hatred, and their envy, is now perished; neither have they any more a portion for ever in any thing that is done under the sun. *(When the life on this Earth is ended, the soul and the spirit, whether of the wicked or the righteous dead, have no more earthly involvement, at least at this time.)*

PRINCIPLES FOR LIVING

7 Go your way, eat your bread with joy, and drink your wine with a merry heart; for God now accepts your works. *(The sense of this Verse is that in view of man's rebellion in the Garden of Eden, God has designed this life and existence and the hereafter accordingly. If man will understand that and give his heart to God,*

and, thereby, seek the Will of God for his life and existence, God will "accept his works." Consequently, there will be "joy" and a "merry heart.")

8 Let your garments be always white; and let your head lack no ointment. *(Such can be done only in Christ!)*

9 Live joyfully with the wife whom you love all the days of the life of your vanity, which he has given you under the sun, all the days of your vanity: for that is your portion in this life, and in your labour which you take under the sun. *(There is no profit in this life other than God. All else, irrespective of its seeming glory, riches, or grandeur, is "vanity." Over and over again, Solomon comes back to the futility of this life without God.)*

10 Whatsoever your hand finds to do, do it with your might; for there is no work, nor device, nor knowledge, nor wisdom, in the grave, where you go. *(The word "grave" really speaks of "Sheol" or "Hell." This means that no earthly activity necessary to human life on this planet is carried on in Hell. Our Christianity should not be just a part of our lives, but all of our lives. "Do it with your might.")*

11 I returned, and saw under the sun, that the race is not to the swift, nor the battle to the strong, neither yet bread to the wise, nor yet riches to men of understanding, nor yet favour to men of skill; but time and chance happens to them all. *(The words, "I returned," mean "I resumed my investigations." The moral is that the only sure thing is a life lived for God.)*

12 For man also knows not his time: as the fishes that are taken in an evil net, and as the birds that are caught in the snare; so are the sons of men snared in an evil time, when it falls suddenly upon them. *(The statement of this Verse is that man is suddenly ensnared by death, as birds and fish are by a net. This fact reveals his ignorance and his helplessness. How uncertain life is without God!)*

WISDOM IS BETTER THAN STRENGTH

13 This wisdom have I seen also under the sun, and it seemed great unto me *(the "wisdom" of which he will now speak is from the Lord and brings about great good; but yet, it will be little appreciated; such is the Bible!)*:

14 There was a little city, and few men within it; and there came a great king against it, and besieged it, and built great bulwarks against it:

15 Now there was found in it a poor wise man, and he by his wisdom delivered the city;

yet no man remembered that same poor man. *(This is a perfect analogy of the Word of God and its Power to deliver, and of the world, which quickly forgets that delivering Power.)*

16 Then said I, Wisdom is better than strength: nevertheless the poor man's wisdom is despised, and his words are not heard. *(There is no true "wisdom" outside of God. But sadly, this "wisdom" is despised, and its words are not heard.)*

17 The words of wise men are heard in quiet more than the cry of him who rules among fools. *(The Lord Jesus Christ, by His Wisdom, i.e., "the Cross," delivered man from the power of "the great king" [Satan], and yet He is forgotten and despised by men.)*

18 Wisdom is better than weapons of war: but one sinner destroys much good. *(The "wisdom" addressed here is the Bible. It is better than "weapons of war."*

However, as more and more men and women who do not know God and who do not believe His Word are installed in government, little by little, one can see them "destroying much good.")

CHAPTER 10
(977 B.C.)
WISDOM AND FOLLY

DEAD flies cause the ointment of the apothecary to send forth a stinking savour: so does a little folly him who is in reputation for wisdom and honour. *(One little inconsistency in the character of a renowned Believer destroys his testimony as effectually as a dead fly destroys the fragrance of a precious ointment. The greater the renown, the greater the damage.)*

2 A wise man's heart is at his right hand; but a fool's heart at his left.

3 Yea also, when he who is a fool walks by the way, his wisdom fails him, and he says to every one that he is a fool. *(Two types of wisdom are portrayed in these two Verses: 1. Wisdom that comes from the Bible alone and 2. Wisdom that comes from the world. The "right hand" speaks of power [Mat. 26:64] and, therefore, wisdom that comes from God. The "left hand" speaks of the power of this world; God says that all who follow it are "fools.")*

4 If the spirit of the ruler rise up against you, leave not your place; for yielding pacifies great offences. *(The words, "leave not your place," mean that one does not assert oneself when attacked, but, by using gentleness, escapes*

worse evils. *The true Christian will yield even in the face of great offenses, unless the offenses demand violation of the Word of God. If that be the case, he cannot "yield.")*

5 There is an evil which I have seen under the sun, as an error which proceeds from the ruler. *(Solomon now speaks of "rulers" who do not use the wisdom of God in their appointments of people to high places. Such is the bane of society.)*

6 Folly is set in great dignity, and the rich sit in low place. *(This is portrayed by king Ahasuerus' promoting of Haman to a place of "great dignity," while Mordecai, who was rich in wisdom and who had, in fact, saved the king's life, "sits in a low place," i.e., has a small place in government [Esther 3:1-2].)*

7 I have seen servants upon horses, and princes walking as servants upon the Earth. *(Solomon had seen these things and instantly recognized the stupidity of rulers who did not wisely appoint their officials. Such all too often characterizes man's government.)*

8 He who digs a pit shall fall into it; and whoso breaks an hedge, a serpent shall bite him.

9 Whoso removes stones shall be hurt therewith; and he who cleaves wood shall be endangered thereby.

10 If the iron be blunt, and he do not whet the edge, then must he put to more strength: but wisdom is profitable to direct. *(We should make the Lord a part of all of our doings, even those things which only seem to be menial.)*

WISE MEN AND FOOLS

11 Surely the serpent will bite without enchantment; and a babbler is no better. *(The argument of this Verse is that both a slanderer and a serpent should be skillfully avoided. The slanderer is looked at by the Lord the same as a snake.)*

12 The words of a wise man's mouth are gracious; but the lips of a fool will swallow up himself.

13 The beginning of the words of his mouth is foolishness: and the end of his talk is mischievous madness.

14 A fool also is full of words: a man cannot tell what shall be; and what shall be after him, who can tell him? *(Human science multiplies books and theories and wearies itself in such labor. But its uselessness and ignorance concerning the great questions of life are demonstrated by its inability to declare the future.)*

15 The labour of the foolish wearies every one of them, because he knows not how to go to the city. *("To go to the city" proverbially expresses the inability of a fool to find his way to even so conspicuous a place. Man is mentally and spiritually incapable of finding his way to the Holy City, hence the necessity of Divine Revelation.)*

FOLLY IN HIGH PLACES

16 Woe to you, O land, when your king is a child, and your princes eat in the morning! *(In the East, this speaks of neglect of duty, for that is the time that princes are supposed to have ministered justice at the gate of the city.)*

17 Blessed are you, O land, when your king is the son of nobles, and your princes eat in due season, for strength, and not for drunkenness! *(The words, "eat in due season," mean that one is not to neglect duty in order to indulge appetite. Too many times public officials forget that they are servants of the people and use their office for personal gain as well as to engage in vice [drunkenness].)*

18 By much slothfulness the building decays; and through idleness of the hands the house drops through. *(The fabric of government and of the state are compared here to a neglected house which suffers serious damage when members of the government neglect duty and give themselves over to debauchery and pleasure. Such is the condition of too many countries in the world.)*

19 A feast is made for laughter, and wine makes merry: but money answers all things. *(This means "money responds to all things"; that is, money can procure all the luxuries needed for banquetings and revelings.*

This Verse can be understood as a drunken reply of the princely revelers to the rebuke contained in Verse 18.)

20 Curse not the king, no not in your thought; and curse not the rich in your bedchamber: for a bird of the air shall carry the voice, and that which has wings shall tell the matter. *(Solomon, being a king, knew how that things said by others easily found way to his ears. We should take a lesson from such, which means to keep our mouths closed.)*

CHAPTER 11
(977 B.C.)
DOING GOOD THINGS

CAST your bread upon the waters: for you shall find it after many days. *(We have*

here the Promise of the Lord that every Blessing Promised will be fulfilled, even though some of the fulfillment may be "after many days." We are not to lose faith. The guarantee has been given.)

2 Give a portion to seven, and also to eight; for you know not what evil shall be upon the Earth. *(The number "seven" is God's number of Perfection. We are to give this Perfect Gospel to others. The number "eight" is the number of Resurrection. There is only one Gospel in the world that will guarantee a Resurrection, and I speak of the immediate life and the life to come, and that is the Gospel of Jesus Christ. To do what we can to take this Gospel to others must never be predicated on the "evil" that pervades the Earth. It is our business to "occupy" until He comes.)*

3 If the clouds be full of rain, they empty themselves upon the Earth: and if the tree fall toward the south, or toward the north, in the place where the tree falls, there it shall be. *(Whatever position in which the Christian finds himself is an opportunity for the Blessings of the Lord, irrespective as to what that position might be. Many Christians always try to put themselves in another place. In other words, if they were in the other place, God could bless; however, the Holy Spirit tells us that it doesn't matter which way the tree falls, God is able to move in that particular situation. Believe Him and receive!)*

4 He who observes the wind shall not sow; and he who regards the clouds shall not reap. *(The Christian who looks at circumstances, adverse situations, negatives, or any other so-called hindrance, is not exercising faith. We should "sow" and expect to "reap.")*

5 As you know not what is the way of the spirit, nor how the bones do grow in the womb of her who is with child: even so you know not the works of God Who makes all. *(In this Verse, the Holy Spirit tells us that it is useless to try to find out exactly how God does things. His Power is infinite.*

We do not know how "bones" can grow from sperm "in the womb of her who is with child." However, it happens, because God is the God of the impossible [Mat. 19:26]. So, believe Him despite circumstances.)

6 In the morning sow your seed, and in the evening withhold not your hand: for you know not whether shall prosper, either this or that, or whether they both shall be alike good. *(Men exhibit great faith in the system of this world,*

even though they have absolutely no certainty of success or prosperity. "Surely," the Holy Spirit says, "we can exhibit as much faith in God!")

7 Truly the light is sweet, and a pleasant thing it is for the eyes to behold the sun:

8 But if a man live many years, and rejoice in them all: yet let him remember the days of darkness; for they shall be many. All that comes is vanity. *(These Verses testify that youth and mature age, however richly provided with pleasures, are bound to lead to decrepitude and death; they are, therefore, vanity of vanities, if God be excluded.)*

LIVE IN VIEW OF COMING JUDGMENT

9 Rejoice, O young man, in your youth; and let your heart cheer you in the days of your youth, and walk in the ways of your heart, and in the sight of your eyes: but know thou, that for all these things God will bring you into judgment. *(While the young man is to rejoice in his youth, he is to always remember that sooner or later a "Judgment Day" is coming. Consequently, one should live one's life with that Judgment Day ever in view.)*

10 Therefore remove sorrow from your heart, and put away evil from your flesh: for childhood and youth are vanity. *(All dreams of early childhood outside of the Lord are vanity.)*

CHAPTER 12
(977 B.C.)
REMEMBER YOUR CREATOR

REMEMBER now your Creator in the days of your youth, while the evil days come not, nor the years draw nigh, when you shall say, I have no pleasure in them *(in the "days of one's youth," how so few remember the Creator, and how so few are saved!)*;

2 While the sun, or the light, or the moon, or the stars, be not darkened, nor the clouds return after the rain *(in youth, life appears all bright; if there is rain, sunshine quickly follows; but it is not so in old age; clouds then return after the rain; similarly, the mind loses its power of recovery and cheerfulness)*:

3 In the day when the keepers of the house shall tremble, and the strong men shall bow themselves, and the grinders cease because they are few, and those who look out of the windows be darkened. *(More than once in the Bible, "the house" figures the human body.)*

4 And the doors shall be shut in the streets,

when the sound of the grinding is low, and he shall rise up at the voice of the bird, and all the daughters of musick shall be brought low *(the cry of a bird causes the aged to start; the power to distinguish melodies is lost; the nerve to climb, or even to walk, is broken; the hair turns white; the lightest load becomes a burden)*;

5 Also when they shall be afraid of that which is high, and fears shall be in the way, and the almond tree shall flourish, and the grasshopper shall be a burden, and desire shall fail: because man goes to his long home, and the mourners go about the streets *(if the Creator is not remembered in the days of one's youth, then there will be a fear to meet God. What will that "long home" be? Will it be Heaven, or will it be Hell?)*:

6 Or ever the silver cord be loosed, or the golden bowl be broken, or the pitcher be broken at the fountain, or the wheel broken at the cistern. *(All of this pictures the human body, which ultimately wears out.)*

7 Then shall the dust return to the Earth as it was: and the spirit shall return unto God Who gave it. *(The human body is made of dust, and goes back to dust at death; however, the human spirit then becomes the property of God. If redeemed, it will go to Heaven [II Cor. 5:8; Phil. 1:21-24; Heb. 12:22-23; Rev. 6:9-11]; if unredeemed, to Hell [Isa. 14:9; Lk. 16:19-31].)*

HEED THE WORDS OF THE WISE

8 Vanity of vanities, saith the Preacher; all is vanity. *(Solomon, as "the Preacher," although in the later years losing his way with God, nevertheless, preached the most powerful evangelistic message ever preached, as recorded in this Book of Ecclesiastes.*

Such are the disappointments, miseries, and mournful end of life, as viewed "under the sun" and independent of God; exceptional intelligence fittingly declares it all to be "vanity of vanities." The whole world should take notice!)

9 And moreover, because the Preacher was wise, he still taught the people knowledge; yea, he gave good heed, and sought out, and set in order many Proverbs. *(Solomon wrote some 3,000 Proverbs [I Ki. 4:32], of which less than 1,000 are included in the Book of Proverbs. Those that are in the Book are inspired of God and are the Wisdom of God. The others are the wisdom of Solomon and, thereby, not deemed worthy, even though no doubt brilliant, to be included*

among the Words of God.

The "knowledge" that Solomon "taught the people" was the "knowledge of God," which made Israel the greatest nation on the face of the Earth.)

10 The Preacher sought to find out acceptable words: and that which was written was upright, even words of truth. *(The eternal value of Sacred Writings is contrasted in Verses 9 through 12 with the worthlessness of human writings.)*

11 The words of the wise are as goads, and as nails fastened by the masters of assemblies, which are given from one shepherd. *(These are "Words" that one can depend on. They are called the "Words of the Wise," and are labeled as such throughout Proverbs and Ecclesiastes.*

Today, these "Words" span from Genesis through Revelation. They begin with, "In the beginning God" [Gen. 1:1]. They end with the words, "The Grace of our Lord Jesus Christ be with you all. Amen." [Rev. 22:21].)

12 And further, by these, my son, be admonished: of making many books there is no end; and much study is a weariness of the flesh. *(Human writings, however numerous, lead nowhere and only produce weariness. The Divine Writings lead to Christ and to Heaven. They are Words of delight; they refresh and do not weary.)*

CONCLUSION: THE CHIEF DUTIES OF MAN

13 Let us hear the conclusion of the whole matter: Fear God, and keep His Commandments: for this is the whole duty of man. *(Having heard all that can be said in favor of trying to secure happiness in this life by the use of material agents, the conclusion is:*

It is impossible; the only happy life is one in fellowship with God and the Bible; such fellowship produces the ideal man; any other life is madness, because there is a day coming when every action, however hidden, will be brought into the unsparing light of the Throne of God and judged, unless cleansed and covered by the Blood [I Jn. 1:7].)

14 For God shall bring every work into judgment, with every secret thing, whether it be good, or whether it be evil. *(The subject then of this Book is the folly of seeking happiness and fulfillment "under the sun," and that the possession of exceptional intelligence only renders more evident the folly and unhappiness of this quest.)*

THE SONG OF
SOLOMON

CHAPTER 1
(1014 B.C.)
THE LOVE OF THE SHULAMITE
FOR THE SHEPHERD

THE song of songs, which is Solomon's. *(The interpretation of this "Song" belongs to Israel. She, as the unfaithful wife of the prophecies of Jeremiah and Ezekiel, has been judged. But she is to be new born as a pure virgin [Hos., Chpt. 2] and, as such, be betrothed to the Divine Solomon, become the wife of the Lamb, and reign with Him over the Millennial Earth. Consequently, the fulfillment of this Song belongs to that future time.*

As in Ecclesiastes all is emptiness, so in the Song of Songs all is fullness. Christ and the world are contrasted.

In the one Book, the heart is too large for the portion; in the other, the portion is too large for the heart.

If in the Sacred Scriptures one Book may be spoken of as more sacred than another, then this Book could possibly be called the most sacred of all. It is the Holy of Holies of Communion with God. Although expressing Israel, it also carries the figure of a Bride and a Bridegroom, which is expressed in the love of Christ to the Believer and of the Believer to Christ. There is no sin and, therefore, no shame.)

2 Let him kiss me with the kisses of his mouth: for your love is better than wine. *(The beautiful Shulamite speaks of her shepherd betrothed. To "kiss with the mouth" implies betrothal. The Reader must study this Book with the understanding that sin and shame are no more and, therefore, the love is pure.)*

3 Because of the savour of your good ointments your name is as ointment poured forth, therefore do the virgins love you. *(In effect, the phrase, "Your Name is as ointment poured forth," refers to Christ.)*

4 Draw me, we will run after you: the king has brought me into his chambers: we will be glad and rejoice in you, we will remember your love more than wine: the upright love you. *(Israel is portrayed here in this Song as the Bride of Christ, for Solomon is here a Type of Christ, which, needless to say, will not interfere with the Church. Also, in the coming Kingdom Age, Israel fits the harmony of other great allegories and Prophecies concerning the sons of Jacob.)*

5 I am black, but comely, O ye daughters of Jerusalem, as the tents of Kedar, as the curtains of Solomon. *(As this Shulamite speaks, she is now addressing the daughters of Jerusalem. She confesses that she is as unlovely as the "tents of Kedar," [meaning the black tent of the Arab]. But through the comeliness that has been put upon her, she is as the curtains of Solomon. So is the Believer in himself and in Christ.)*

6 Look not upon me, because I am black, because the sun has looked upon me: my mother's children were angry with me; they made me the keeper of the vineyards; but my own vineyard have I not kept. *(Likewise, Israel's relatives, such as the Moabites and the Ammonites, treated her with disdain. In fact, such continues even unto this hour in the form of the Palestinians.)*

7 Tell me, O thou whom my soul loves, where you feed, where you make your flock to rest at noon: for why should I be as one who turns aside by the flocks of your companions? *(In this Verse, the Bride cries out for a fellowship sweeter than that of her companions. Christian fellowship is sweet, but it is "veiled"; the heart desires the sweeter fellowship of the Bridegroom Himself.)*

8 If you know not, O thou fairest among women, go your way forth by the footsteps of the flock, and feed your kids beside the shepherds' tents. *(As the Shulamite speaks of her shepherd lover, the court ladies answer her. In her request as to where he is, they encourage her to be a little bolder and take her small flock of sheep to where he may be tending his sheep.*

The scenario is as follows:

Both Solomon and the shepherd are types of Christ. The beautiful Shulamite girl is a type of Israel. So how can both be types of Christ?

The moral is this: before Israel can have Messiah King, she must accept Messiah Shepherd. This she would not do at the First Coming. But this she will do at the Second Coming.)

9 I have compared you, O my love, to a company of horses in Pharaoh's chariots.

10 Your cheeks are comely with rows of jewels, your neck with chains of gold.

11 We will make you borders of gold with studs of silver. *(Solomon is now speaking, using terminology appropriate for that time. He declares her to be the fairest among women, and adds words of admiring love. He tells her that he will be most quickly found in the places of daily duty.)*

THE SHULAMITE AND THE
SHEPHERD TOGETHER

12 While the king sits at his table, my spikenard sends forth the smell thereof.

13 A bundle of myrrh is my wellbeloved unto me; he shall lie all night betwixt my breasts.

14 My beloved is unto me as a cluster of camphire in the vineyards of En-gedi. *(In these three Verses, the Shulamite [the Bride] speaks to her shepherd lover. She has not responded to Solomon's overtures to her. Her heart responds rather to the young shepherd with whom she is deeply in love.)*

15 Behold, you are fair, my love; behold, you are fair; you have doves' eyes. *(Now the lowly shepherd speaks. He insists on the loveliness of the Bride in his eyes, repeating the declaration — emphasis being laid on the word "behold" and on the word "are.")*

16 Behold, you are fair, my beloved, yea, pleasant: also our bed is green.

17 The beams of our house are cedar, and our rafters of fir. *(Now the Bride cries in response, "Behold, you are fair," intimating that he alone was fair and she herself was unlovely.*

In the east at noontide, shepherds rest upon a bed of green grass beneath the shade of pleasant trees, both cedar and fir. This is spoken of in these two Verses.)

CHAPTER 2
(1014 B.C.)
THE SHULAMITE AND THE SHEPHERD
SPEAK OF THEIR MUTUAL LOVE

I am the rose of Sharon, and the lily of the valleys. *(Having spoken of the beauty of her Bridegroom and of this house of the forest, she humbly adds that she is no better than the rose of Sharon or the lily of the valley. These were the most common flowers of the field.*

The Church is fond of referring to Christ as the "Rose of Sharon" and the "Lily of the Valley."

And so He is! Everything that Christ will be to Israel in the coming glad day, so He is to the Church, and more. Therefore, every sweet expression that is applied by the Holy Spirit to Israel and Christ can be said, as well, of the Church and Christ.)

2 As the lily among thorns, so is my love among the daughters. *(In response to the statement of the Bride that she is a common field-flower, the Bridegroom replies that as beautiful as the daughters of Jerusalem may be, they are, in comparison with her, no better than thorns; she is, in his eyes, as a lily.*

One lily, but many thorns! So it is; and so it has always been. God's People are a little flock, comparable to one lily; the unconverted are without number and are comparable to many thorns.)

3 As the apple tree among the trees of the wood, so is my beloved among the sons. I sat down under his shadow with great delight, and his fruit was sweet to my taste. *(The following is that which is given to the Believer upon the acceptance of Christ:*

1. "I sat down": in union with Him, there is rest.

2. "With great delight": there is joy.

3. "His shadow": there is shelter from the heat.

4. "His fruit was sweet to my taste": in Christ, there is ample sustenance.)

4 He brought me to the banqueting house, and his banner over me was love. *(Christian experience knows the truth of this, for all that the Bridegroom here is to the Bride, Christ is to the Believer.)*

5 Stay me with flagons, comfort me with apples: for I am sick of love. *(It is impossible to describe a love for and to Christ that contains such emotion that one is so overcome he must cry out to be strengthened under such spiritual emotion.)*

6 His left hand is under my head, and his right hand does embrace me. *(Such is the nature of communion. A word, or a look, or a thought suffices to break it, and the Bride resting here in a restful sleep upon the arm of the beloved is a very lovely picture of the Believer's communion with Christ.)*

THE LOVERS ARE SEPARATED; THEY SEEK
AND FIND EACH OTHER

7 I charge you, O ye daughters of Jerusalem, by the roes, and by the hinds of the field, that you stir not up, nor awake my love, till he please.

8 The voice of my beloved! behold, he comes leaping upon the mountains, skipping upon the hills. *(The strength of the love of the shepherd for the Shulamite is evidenced by his speedily overcoming all hindrances. He will run hastily to her.)*

9 My beloved is like a roe or a young hart: behold, he stands behind our wall, he looks forth at the windows, showing himself through the lattice. *(As Christ comes to us, sometimes His Face is dimmed; He is behind the lattice. Our thoughts are that if He were only near, the problems would vanish; however, there is a glorious purpose to His method. The next Verse tells us what that purpose is.)*

10 My beloved spoke, and said unto me, Rise up, my love, my fair one, and come away. *(Him not showing Himself clearly [behind the lattice] is in order that we may come unto Him.)*

11 For, lo, the winter is past, the rain is over and gone. *(The shepherd is telling his betrothed that hindrances such as the rains are now "over and gone." He is attempting to draw her near.)*

12 The flowers appear on the earth; the time of the singing of birds is come, and the voice of the turtle is heard in our land *("turtle" should read "turtle dove"; the entirety of this Passage speaks of the beginning of the great Kingdom Age; the "winter" [signifying terrible war and tribulation] is past, now "flowers appear on the Earth");*

13 The fig tree puts forth her green figs, and the vines with the tender grape give a good smell. Arise, my love, my fair one, and come away. *(This speaks of the coming of the Lord [Mat. 24:28-31]. At that time, the Lord will bid Israel to come to Him, which she will. Zechariah, as possibly no other Prophet, spoke of this moment [Zech. 13:8-9].)*

14 O my dove, who is in the clefts of the rock, in the secret places of the stairs, let me see your countenance, let me hear your voice; for sweet is your voice, and your countenance is comely. *(These are the tender words that Christ will speak unto wayward Israel at His Second Coming. These same words are given to the Church, as well.*

That Christ should declare the Believer's face to be comely and the voice sweet is amazing love. He desires first to see the face and then to hear the voice. This is a tremendous encouragement to prayer. He loves to see His People drawing near to Him, and He loves to hear them speaking to Him.)

15 Take us the foxes, the little foxes, that spoil the vines: for our vines have tender grapes. *(Now, the Bride is speaking. Directly the Lord makes a manifestation of Himself to the soul, at once there is a conscious recognition of the little sins [little foxes] that hinder the grapes of testimony, and there is the desire to bring Christ practically into the daily life in order to set it right.*

Only this type of nearness to Christ can point out the flaws that are otherwise hidden.)

16 My beloved is mine, and I am his: he feeds among the lilies.

17 Until the day break, and the shadows flee away, turn my beloved, and be thou like a roe or a young hart upon the mountains of Bether. *(The Bride now establishes her heart in the knowledge of her union with him and where she will be sure of fellowship with him. She then prays that at dawn of day he will return quickly as a roe or a young hart over the mountains that then separate them.*

Israel in that coming glad day will speak tenderly and kindly of the Lowly Shepherd Whom she once spurned.)

CHAPTER 3
(1014 B.C.)
SHE TELLS OF HER SEARCH

BY night on my bed I sought him whom my soul loves: I sought him, but I found him not. *(Once the Lowly Shepherd, Christ, sought Israel; now Israel seeks "Him.")*

2 I will rise now, and go about the city in the streets, and in the broad ways I will seek him whom my soul loves: I sought him, but I found him not. *(In the coming latter half of the Great Tribulation, Israel will greatly search for the Messiah, but, until the Second Coming, she will have to say, "I found Him not.")*

3 The watchmen who go about the city found me: to whom I said, Saw ye him whom my soul loves? *(Her full heart, like Mary's at the sepulcher, she assumes that everybody is interested in her beloved. She, therefore, does not mention his name to the watchmen. Just as the Angels at the tomb were uninteresting to Mary, so were the watchmen to the Bride. She rather sought "Him.")*

4 It was but a little that I passed from them, but I found him whom my soul loves: I held him, and would not let him go, until I had brought him into my mother's house, and into the chamber of her who conceived me. *(At long last, the Bride finds the Bridegroom. Two*

thousand years ago, she did not realize Who He was and rejected Him. Now, she knows Who He is and "will not let Him go.")

5 I charge you, O you daughters of Jerusalem, by the roes, and by the hinds of the field, that you stir not up, nor awake my love, till he please. *(Truly, Israel will go through a dark night of Tribulation during the time of "Jacob's Trouble" [Jer. 30:7]. Now that communion is restored and the heart brought into the joy, confidence, and rest of union with Christ, it is His Will that nothing should interrupt that rest.)*

THE ARRIVAL OF HER BELOVED

6 Who is this who comes out of the wilderness like pillars of smoke, perfumed with myrrh and frankincense, with all powders of the merchant? *(The scene now changes from the Shepherd to Solomon. Verses 6 through 11 portray Solomon's procession back to Jerusalem from Shunem, the home of the Shulamite. With Solomon in his procession is the young Shulamite. He will endeavor to win her over with flatteries.)*

7 Behold his bed, which is Solomon's; threescore valiant men are about it, of the valiant of Israel. *(Sixty of the most valiant men of all Israel surround Solomon as his bodyguards. The word "bed" should have been translated "car of state" or "chariot.")*

8 They all hold swords, being expert in war: every man has his sword upon his thigh because of fear in the night. *(Despite the greatness and glory of Solomon and of Israel, still, there was "fear in the night." Men's hearts are unspeakably evil; therefore, men who were "expert in war" were needed as guards.*

However, in the coming glorious Kingdom Age, when Christ will reign supreme over the entirety of the world, there will be no "fear in the night" [Isa. 54:14].)

9 King Solomon made himself a chariot of the wood of Lebanon.

10 He made the pillars thereof of silver, the bottom thereof of gold, the covering of it of purple, the midst thereof being paved with love, for the daughters of Jerusalem. *(This chariot, no doubt, was a wonder to behold!)*

11 Go forth, O ye daughters of Zion, and behold king Solomon with the crown wherewith his mother crowned him in the day of his espousals, and in the day of the gladness of his heart. *(In the coming Kingdom Age, this scene, with Solomon now as a Type of Christ, will no*

doubt be repeated many times and in many variations. The coming and going of Christ, Who will no doubt often travel all over the world, will be marked by striking celebration everywhere He goes.)

CHAPTER 4
(1014 B.C.)

THE SHEPHERD ADORES HIS BELOVED

BEHOLD, you are fair, my love; behold, you are fair; you have doves' eyes within your locks: your hair is as a flock of goats, that appear from mount Gilead. *(All of this Chapter, with the exception of the Sixth and final Verses, pertains to Solomon, as he attempts to win the hand of the beautiful Shulamite.)*

2 Your teeth are like a flock of sheep that are even shorn, which came up from the washing; whereof every one bear twins, and none is barren among them. *(This speaks of Israel at the beginning of the Kingdom Age and immediately after recognizing Christ as the Messiah and being washed of all her past iniquity [Zech. 13:1].*

It is interesting that the Holy Spirit through Solomon would mention the phrase, "your teeth," concerning "sheep."

Sheep have no teeth except on the bottom jaw; therefore, they cannot tear flesh, but can only eat grass and the like. Therefore, at long last, Israel is docile, kind, and gracious. The warlike, rebellious spirit of Satan is now gone, and gone forever.

As well, all will be fruitful and productive with "none barren among them." Heretofore, almost all were "barren.")

3 Your lips are like a thread of scarlet, and your speech is comely: your temples are like a piece of a pomegranate within your locks. *(The reddened "lips" speak of Israel's acceptance of Christ's sacrificial offering of Himself at Calvary. Whereas the "temples" of their foreheads were once hard like granite [Ps. 78:8], now, they are soft like a "pomegranate.")*

4 Your neck is like the tower of David built for an armoury, whereon there hang a thousand bucklers, all shields of mighty men. *(The "bucklers" and "shields of mighty men" speak of Israel during the coming Kingdom Age, when she will, at long last, be the mightiest nation in the world.)*

5 Your two breasts are like two young roes that are twins, which feed among the lilies. *(A gazelle feeds not on, but among, the lilies. The best pasture is found there. This Verse not only*

points to the beauty of the Bride's form, but to the softness and gentleness of her character.)

6 Until the day break, and the shadows flee away, I will get me to the mountain of myrrh, and to the hill of frankincense. (The speaker here is not Solomon, but the Shulamite. Her answer to all of his praises is modesty.)

7 You are all fair, my love; there is no spot in you. (Christ will have said these words to the Church a short time earlier [Eph. 5:27]. Now He will say these words to Israel.)

8 Come with me from Lebanon, my spouse, with me from Lebanon: look from the top of Amana, from the top of Shenir and Hermon, from the lions' dens, from the mountains of the leopards. (Christ's call demands a forsaking of everything in order to be His.)

9 You have ravished my heart, my sister, my spouse; you have ravished my heart with one of your eyes, with one chain of your neck. (The word "ravished" probably should have been rendered "emboldened." It means to "make courageous." Love in the beginning overpowers, but the general idea must be that of "smitten" or "captured.")

10 How fair is your love, my sister, my spouse! how much better is your love than wine! and the smell of your ointments than all spices! (Actually, these are the words of the Greater Son of David as He utters them to Israel, which will take place at the beginning of the Kingdom Age.)

11 Your lips, O my spouse, drop as the honeycomb: honey and milk are under your tongue; and the smell of your garments is like the smell of Lebanon. (The use of the term, "the smell of Lebanon," is interesting. It refers to the great cedars of Lebanon that grew in abundance. They were huge trees that were used for many purposes, not the least of which was to provide the great foundation timbers for the Temple.

However, what is being referred to here is something else entirely.

This type of tree gives forth a "smell" that is not at all offensive to the human nose and is actually very sweet and pleasant, but it has the very opposite effect upon serpents and certain types of insects. In other words, there are no snakes where these trees are!

The "smell" of religion, education, riches, or personal achievement is no offense at all to the Evil One, but the "smell of Lebanon," he cannot stand. That glorious aroma is Christ.)

12 A garden inclosed is my sister, my spouse; a spring shut up, a fountain sealed. (The idea of a paradise or garden is carried from the beginning of Scripture to the end, this symbol of perfect blessedness. It is found only in Christ, as Israel will ultimately see.)

13 Your plants are an orchard of pomegranates, with pleasant fruits; camphire, with spikenard,

14 Spikenard and saffron; calamus and cinnamon, with all trees of frankincense; myrrh and aloes, with all the chief spices:

15 A fountain of gardens, a well of living waters, and streams from Lebanon. (Solomon continues to speak. The fragrances mentioned here speak of prayer, relationship, and worship [Ex. 30:23-25, 34-35].)

The "fountain of gardens" speaks of a life that produces fruit that is a holy and pleasant fragrance to the nostrils of our Lord.

The "well of living waters" speaks of the "well of water" springing up into "everlasting life" [Jn. 4:13-14].

The "streams from Lebanon" speak of the mighty Baptism with the Holy Spirit.)

16 Awake, O north wind; and come, thou south; blow upon my garden, that the spices thereof may flow out. Let my beloved come into his garden, and eat his pleasant fruits. (This is the answer of the Bride to the lavish praises of Solomon. The north and south winds represent various influences from different quarters that flow gently over the garden and call forth the fragrance and fruits. There is a rich suggestion in such words.

However, the "spices" do not flow out except under extreme pressure, whether by cold or by heat, which speaks of the coming Great Tribulation, which will bring Israel to Christ [Mat. 24:21].)

CHAPTER 5
(1014 B.C.)

THE SHULAMITE AND HER BELOVED

I am come into my garden, my sister, my spouse: I have gathered my myrrh with my spice; I have eaten my honeycomb with my honey; I have drunk my wine with my milk: eat, O friends; drink, yea, drink abundantly, O beloved. (Now Solomon responds to the invitation of the last Verse of the last Chapter. He comes into the "garden." This symbolizes Christ coming to Israel at the beginning of the great Kingdom Age, after Israel has invited Him.

Whereas the first part of this Verse was spoken by Solomon, the last two lines are spoken by the Shulamite. The "friends" referred to here speak

of all the Gentile world, who, at the beginning of the Kingdom Age, are invited to come and "drink, yea, drink abundantly" of the water of life freely [Rev. 22:17].)

2 I sleep, but my heart wakes: it is the voice of my beloved who knocks, saying, Open to me, my sister, my love, my dove, my undefiled: for my head is filled with dew, and my locks with the drops of the night. *(The lowly shepherd is now knocking. The Shulamite is now speaking, and referring back to her searchings of Chapter 3, Verses 1 through 4. She has been greatly moved by Solomon's appeal, but now her heart goes back to her lowly shepherd, who seeks her hand. This beautiful Passage speaks not only to Israel, but as well to the Church.)*

3 I have put off my coat; how shall I put it on? I have washed my feet; how shall I defile them? *(The meaning is, "I have retired to rest; do not disturb me." Sloth, reluctance, ease, and lethargy here keep her back. How so true of both the individual soul and of the Church in spiritual decline!*

Yes, she "washed her feet," but Christ did not wash them; consequently, in His Eyes, Whose Eyes alone matter, they are not clean.

How so much it portrays Israel of some 2,000 years ago; she was so holy in her own eyes that she refused her Messiah, the Lowly Shepherd, and accepted a robber [Jn. 18:40].)

4 My beloved put in his hand by the hole of the door, and my bowels were moved for him. *(The doors of ancient homes had in them a doorhole. If someone was anticipated, the bolt or lock could be left in the open position, where, by pressing it, the door would open.*

How much the lowly shepherd loved her! How he tried to come to her!

As applied to the Saviour, what infinite suggestiveness! He would be with us; He not only knocks at the door, but is impatient to enter. He tries the lock and too often finds it locked. He is repelled. He is resisted. He is coldly excluded.

The four Gospels portray Christ trying in vain to reach Israel, but they would not. Too sadly, it describes the Church, as well.

The phrase, "my bowels were moved for him," could have been translated, "my heart was moved for him.")

5 I rose up to open to my beloved; and my hands dropped with myrrh, and my fingers with sweet smelling myrrh, upon the handles of the lock. *(She should have been expecting him and, thereby, had the door open; however, it was locked. As well, she was asleep and did not*

hear the cry, "Behold, the Bridegroom cometh" [Mat. 25:5-6].

When she finally did arise, she laded herself with all the accoutrements of religion. To her, it was "sweet smelling," but to the Lord it was not. How so much we make our preparations, and so much they are unacceptable to Him!)

6 I opened to my beloved; but my beloved had withdrawn himself, and was gone: my soul failed when he spoke: I sought him, but I could not find him; I called him, but he gave me no answer. *(She took so long to open the door that whenever it finally was opened, he had "withdrawn himself." He was not interested in her religious preparations, but only in her.)*

7 The watchmen who went about the city found me, they smote me, they wounded me; the keepers of the walls took away my veil from me. *(The "watchmen" in this case were the soldiers of the mighty Roman army, who "went about the city." That "city" was Jerusalem.*

"They took my veil from me" speaks of Israel, who could have been the Bride of Christ. But, in that day of so long ago, she refused Him. Her "veil" was taken from her and she was made to wander from nation to nation exactly as Moses had prophesied that she would do [Deut. 28:64].)

8 I charge you, O daughters of Jerusalem, if you find my beloved, that you tell him, that I am sick of love. *(Israel's cry for some 2,000 years, while scattered all over the world, was "next year, Jerusalem."*

The phrase, "sick of love," refers to the hurt that has come to her because her love for Him has not been returned. In other words, "as He once sought me, I now seek Him."

This will happen in the last half of the Great Tribulation, when it looks like Israel will be totally annihilated by the Antichrist. She will then realize that her only Salvation is the coming of the Messiah. He will come!)

9 What is your beloved more than another beloved, O thou fairest among women? what is your beloved more than another beloved, that you do so charge us? *(The court ladies, the "daughters of Jerusalem," answer her with sarcasm. Her "beloved" is the Lord Jesus Christ, Who they little recognize; consequently, the nations of the world have treated Israel this last 2,000 years with sarcasm and with disdain.*

Even though the following Passages glowingly describe Him and are beautifully accurate, still, she does not realize that her beloved, the Lowly Shepherd, and the Great King are One and the Same.)

10 My beloved is white and ruddy, the chiefest among ten thousand. *(The Shulamite now speaks of her lowly shepherd. Strangely enough, the word "white" actually means "dark red," and corresponds to the Vision that John saw on the Isle of Patmos.*

Truly, He is the "fairest among ten thousand.")

11 His head is as the most fine gold, his locks are bushy, and black as a raven.

12 His eyes are as the eyes of doves by the rivers of waters, washed with milk, and fitly set.

13 His cheeks are as a bed of spices, as sweet flowers: his lips like lilies, dropping sweet smelling myrrh.

14 His hands are as gold rings set with the beryl: his belly is as bright ivory overlaid with sapphires.

15 His legs are as pillars of marble, set upon sockets of fine gold: his countenance is as Lebanon, excellent as the cedars.

16 His mouth is most sweet: yea, he is altogether lovely. This is my beloved, and this is my friend, O daughters of Jerusalem. *(This description corresponds somewhat with the Visions of Daniel and John the Beloved in the Book of Revelation [Dan. 7:13-14; Rev. 1:12-16]. There are ten corporeal excellencies enumerated in this description; however, all of this, plus one thousand more, could not adequately portray the attributes of greatness and beauty in the Son of Man.*

On a coming glad day, at the beginning of the Kingdom Age when Christ returns, Israel will then say to the "daughters of Jerusalem," whoever they may be, speaking of Christ, the One Who has nail-prints in His Hands, "this is my Beloved, this is my Friend.")

CHAPTER 6

(1014 B.C.)

MUTUAL PLEASURE

WHITHER is your beloved gone, O thou fairest among women? whither is your beloved turned aside? that we may seek him with you. *(This Verse portrays the nations of the world who now are seeking after Christ. This will be at the beginning of the great Kingdom Age, when Israel [the Shulamite] finally accepts the Lowly Shepherd of Israel, the Lord Jesus Christ.)*

2 My beloved is gone down into his garden, to the beds of spices, to feed in the gardens, and to gather lilies.

3 I am my beloved's, and my beloved is mine: he feeds among the lilies. *(In 2:16, the*

Bride joyfully said, "My beloved is mine." But in this Third Verse, she says, with deeper and chastened intelligence and no longer able to think with satisfaction of her love to him, "I am my beloved's." She speaks not of Solomon, but of the lowly shepherd. This marks very real progress in the Spiritual Life and establishes the heart in the assurance of Salvation.*

Two thousand years ago, Israel spoke of Christ in terms of hatred, anger, and murder. She accused Him to being an imposter. Now she says the very opposite.

To "feed in the gardens" speaks of the Second Adam, Who was, and is, the Tree of Life. In the first Garden, the Tree of the Knowledge of Good and Evil was unfaithfully attended and, thereby, the Garden was destroyed. Now, the True Tree of Life, the Lord Jesus Christ, will be faithfully attended, and the Garden will be preserved forever.)

THE KING'S APPEAL

4 You are beautiful, O my love, as Tirzah, comely as Jerusalem, terrible as an army with banners. *(Now Solomon, in all his splendor and glory, comes on the scene. He will once again attempt to draw the Shulamite away from her lowly shepherd betrothed.*

He tells her how beautiful she is, likening her to the beauty of Jerusalem, which, to the Jewish heart, was unexcelled. He will use all his wiles to pull her away. He will not succeed, despite his riches, wisdom, splendor, and glory. In this beautiful spiritual soliloquy, she must accept the lowly shepherd.

Even though this incident no doubt happened to Solomon, with every incident being very real, still, the Holy Spirit used it to draw a picture of Israel's future. Israel would reject her Lowly Shepherd, the Lord Jesus Christ, and even crucify Him. Therefore, to be accepted by the Lord, she must, and without reservation, finally accept this Lowly Shepherd Whom she once spurned.

Even though in this soliloquy the lowly shepherd and Solomon are very different people, nevertheless, in the mind of the Spirit they are one and the same. Both are types of Christ. One figures the Shepherd, Who gave His Life for the world, including Israel, even though rejected and spurned by Israel. The other figures the victorious Christ, triumphant over all, as evidenced by Solomon.

In the spiritual sense, Israel must accept the Shepherd before she can have the King, and that

she will do at the Second Coming.)

5 Turn away your eyes from me, for they have overcome me: your hair is as a flock of goats that appear from Gilead. *(Solomon uses all of his flattery to appeal to her. He speaks of the beauty of her "eyes," because now she truly can see. The Shepherd came to "open the eyes of the blind" [Lk. 4:18].)*

6 Your teeth are as a flock of sheep which go up from the washing, whereof every one bears twins, and there is not one barren among them. *(Solomon now speaks to her as he did previously [4:2]. Israel in that coming glad day will be like a lamb, not like a bear or a lion. The Holy Spirit draws this analogy to show that Israel, in fact, had the spirit of a carnivorous animal when Jesus first came, but now has the spirit of a lamb.*

7 As a piece of a pomegranate are your temples within your locks. *(The forehead of Israel was once hard as granite, but now it is soft and tender like a "pomegranate.")*

8 There are threescore queens, and fourscore concubines, and virgins without number. *(These represent the Gentile nations that will flock to Christ in the Kingdom Age. But to Israel, and to Israel alone, He says the following:)*

9 My dove, my undefiled is but one; she is the only one of her mother, she is the choice one of her who bore her. The daughters saw her, and blessed her; yea, the queens and the concubines, and they praised her. *(Then Israel will be very special to Christ and to the world. The Gentile nations [daughters and concubines] will "bless her and praise her." Of the nations of the world in the coming Kingdom Age, she will be "the choice."*

The phrase, "She is the only one of her mother," speaks of Isaac. That was the only one whom God called "your Seed," which actually spoke of Christ [Gen. 21:12].)

10 Who is she who looks forth as the morning, fair as the moon, clear as the sun, and terrible as an army with banners? *(Israel has suffered much these past 2,000 years, actually more than any other nation has ever suffered. The world has not understood her role; neither has she understood her role.*

However, the many Promises that God made to the Patriarchs, as well as to the Prophets, will finally be realized in that coming glad day. When she stands before Christ, she will be "fair as the moon, clear as the sun, and terrible as an army with banners.")

11 I went down into the garden of nuts to see the fruits of the valley, and to see whether the vine flourished and the pomegranates budded. *(Verses 11 through 12 are spoken by the Shulamite. Solomon is making his boldest appeal, but without success. In effect, the Shulamite is telling Solomon that she is seeking her beloved lowly shepherd. As stated, in the spiritual sense, this must be done. Israel must accept the Lowly One before she can accept the Glorious One.)*

12 Or ever I was aware, my soul made me like the chariots of Ammi-nadib. *(She is saying that she is "aware" of Solomon's appeal to her, but that her "soul" is not bonded to Solomon. Instead, it is bonded to the lowly shepherd.)*

13 Return, return, O Shulamite; return, return, that we may look upon you. What will you see in the Shulamite? As it were the company of two armies. *(Here Solomon begs her to return so that he, as well as all his court, may look upon her beauty. It is the strongest appeal yet.*

He will make one more appeal, as recorded in the next Chapter. She will spurn that as well.)

CHAPTER 7
(1014 B.C.)
THE KING'S APPEAL CONTINUED

HOW beautiful are your feet with shoes, O prince's daughter! the joints of your thighs are like jewels, the work of the hands of a cunning workman. *(Solomon will now make his last and most powerful appeal to the Shulamite. He will address words of admiring love to the Bride. She is altogether perfect. The most minute scrutiny discovers no blemish in her.*

To the pure in mind, this is sacred and precious. This section of the Song helps the Believer to realize how beautiful he is in the eyes of Christ; but it also fills him with humility, for he knows that his moral beauty is not his own, but rather Christ's comeliness put upon him.)

2 Your navel is like a round goblet, which wants not liquor: your belly is like an heap of wheat set about with lilies. *(If one will notice, the exclamation is totally different from that of sensual statements! As Verse 1 speaks of the creation of Israel [Gen. 12:1-3], Verse 2 describes Israel's form.)*

3 Your two breasts are like two young roes that are twins. *(Israel, before Christ, could not nourish her children. Her spiritual condition was one of destitution, emaciation, and death. Jeremiah addressed this [Jer. 4:31].*

Now Israel, because of her acceptance of Christ, will have what she could have had all along!)

4 Your neck is as a tower of ivory; your eyes like the fishpools in Heshbon, by the gate of Bath-rabbim: your nose is as the tower of Lebanon which looks toward Damascus.

5 Your head upon you is like Carmel, and the hair of your head like purple; the king is held in the galleries. *(If one is to notice, Israel's geography as a nation is described here.)*

6 How fair and how pleasant are you, O love, for delights! *(In a sense, Jesus said the same thing to Israel at His First Advent. Tragically, Israel at that time was neither "fair" nor "pleasant," but rather evil. Even though He spoke kindly to them, they spoke harshly to Him [Jn. 8:48].*

Thankfully and grandly, they will respond favorably on the coming glad Millennial Day, but only after much sorrow and trouble [Jer. 30:7].)

7 This your stature is like to a palm tree, and your breasts to clusters of grapes. *(In ancient times, the Palm Tree denoted the emblem of love, which characterizes Christ.*

The "breasts" speak of the bearing of nourishing fruit, hence, "clusters of grapes" [Jn., Chpt. 15]. On that coming glad day of the Kingdom Age, Israel will at long last function according to her creation, which is to nourish the entirety of the world, which can only be done in Christ.)

8 I said, I will go up to the palm tree, I will take hold of the boughs thereof: now also your breasts shall be as clusters of the vine, and the smell of your nose like apples. *(The Lord delights in these "fruits of righteousness," which come forth from the life and love of His People. They will be the true adornment of Israel, and are to be the true adornment of the Church at present.*

The people of God are never so beautiful in the eyes of their Saviour as when they are covered with gifts and graces that are their active expression in the world. Then it is when He Himself fills presently His Church, and then Israel, with His Presence.)

9 And the roof of your mouth like the best wine for my beloved, that goes down sweetly, causing the lips of those who are asleep to speak. *(This Verse speaks of very intimate and close communion. The sense of this Passage is that even with the most intimate contact, there is no hint of disorder, vulgarity, uncleanliness, or distaste.*

Only Christ can make one so lovely, so clean, so pure, and so holy.

When we read this Ninth Verse, we are reading the difference between man's broken cisterns that can hold no water [Jer. 2:13] and the Purity, Holiness, and Righteousness that only Christ can give.

In the coming Millennial Day, everyone will exclaim Israel's beauty. It will be the "beauty of holiness" [Ps. 29:2].)

THE SHEPHERD AND THE MAIDEN LOVER REUNITED

10 I am my beloved's, and his desire is toward me. *(Solomon, with all his glory, riches, wisdom, and power, has made his most extravagant appeal to the Shulamite. She has spurned him, as she must.*

Israel's major problem upon the First Advent of Christ was her desire for exaltation. She was not looking for a Lowly Peasant Shepherd Messiah. Instead, she wanted, and even demanded, a Triumphant Messiah [Jn. 6:15]. Consequently, she rejected her Messiah, crucified Him on the Cross, and thereby destroyed herself.

Nevertheless, the Promises of God made to the Patriarchs and Prophets remain firm. Those Prophecies concerning Israel's glad and future Restoration must be fulfilled [Isa. 4:2-4], but can be fulfilled only when she accepts the Lowly Shepherd, which she will at the Second Coming. Then she can be exalted.)

11 Come, my beloved, let us go forth into the field; let us lodge in the villages. *(The Shulamite now turns her back on all of Solomon's riches, glory, and beauty. She accepts the lowly station of the "field" and "villages."*

These Verses also point forward to the time when Israel will go forth with Immanuel in this certainty and communion of His Love to enjoy the fruit of the Millennial Earth. It is the way of humility instead of the way of pride. It is the way that all must come; hence, not many mighty or noble are called! [I Cor. 1:26].)

12 Let us get up early to the vineyards; let us see if the vine flourish, whether the tender grape appear, and the pomegranates bud forth: there will I give you my loves. *(In the coming glad Millennial Day, all manner of precious fruit, new and old, will appear in restored Israel to delight the heart of Him Whom she at first rejected.*

Now she understands her reason for being. As well, the follower of Christ should hear His Words in John, Chpt. 15, concerning the bearing of fruit and watching the "Vine" flourish.

We, like Israel, continue to try to bear fruit apart from the Vine. It cannot be done [Jn. 15:5].)

13 The mandrakes give a smell, and at our gates are all manner of pleasant fruits, new and old, which I have laid up for you, O my beloved. *(The "mandrakes" were called "love flowers" or "love fruit." Now, as the Shulamite gives the "pleasant fruits" to "my beloved," likewise, Israel will one day finally give such to Christ. Israel thought that to be great she must be powerful. Now she learns that to be great she must be lowly.*

So it is with the Christian. Then we will bear "much fruit.")

CHAPTER 8
(1014 B.C.)

THE LOVERS SPEAK; THE HAPPY ENDING

O that you were as my brother, who sucked the breasts of my mother! when I should find you without, I would kiss you; yes, I should not be despised. *(It seems that in Verses 1 through 4 the Shulamite is speaking to Solomon concerning his appeal to her. In the spiritual sense, one can see the transformation that will take place in Israel. The desire will no longer be for glory and grandeur, but rather for the true love that she will find in her Lowly Shepherd. What a beautiful picture the Holy Spirit paints of Israel's coming Salvation!)*

2 I would lead you, and bring you into my mother's house, who would instruct me: I would cause you to drink of spiced wine of the juice of my pomegranate. *(She would further desire that Solomon allow her to take him to her "mother's house," which harks back to the Patriarchs, and what the Lord originally intended Israel to be, and which she will be in the coming Kingdom Age.)*

3 His left hand should be under my head, and his right hand should embrace me. *(In effect, she is saying that she will allow such affection only in the presence of her mother. So it says that Israel can have such intimate relationship with Christ only as they go back to the spirit of the Patriarchs.)*

4 I charge you, O daughters of Jerusalem, that you stir not up, nor awake my love, until he please. *(She calls to the "daughters of Jerusalem" that they seek no more her hand for Solomon. With kindness, yet firmly, she has made her decision. She will take the hand of the lowly peasant shepherd.*

On that day when she charged the "daughters of Jerusalem" regarding the lowly shepherd, she painted a picture in type that would take thousands of years to fulfill, but would be as certain as God Himself, because He was actually the One Who painted this glorious and beautiful portrait. It is very soon to come to pass in totality.)*

5 Who is this who comes up from the wilderness, leaning upon her beloved? I raised you up under the apple tree: there your mother brought you forth: there she brought you forth who bore you. *(The question of Verse 5 is asked by the "daughters of Jerusalem," that is, by the nations who will be redeemed in relationship with Jerusalem.*

The picture presented in Verses 5 through 7 is most touching and gracious. The Bridegroom and the Bride are presented coming together up out of the wilderness; she is leaning upon Him, and we are permitted to hear their sweet converse. Hers is the weakness and His the strength. She leans on Him.

They have their backs to the wilderness and their faces toward the spice mountains. She is not alone. He accompanies her. Such is the relationship between Christ and the Believer.)

6 Set me as a seal upon your heart, as a seal upon your arm: for love is strong as death; jealousy is cruel as the grave: the coals thereof are coals of fire, which has a most vehement flame. *(The speaker in Verses 5 through 7 is the Beloved. He first reminds the Bride of where [in His Grace] He found her [Gen., Chpt. 3], and then gently hints at her past unfaithfulness in having given her heart and her arm to others, thus causing Him to suffer the bitter pains of a holy jealousy. He urges that for the future her heart and arm might be sealed for Him.*

The "seal" is the signet ring, which means to "impress." It was sometimes carried by a string around the neck and on the breast and would, therefore, be near the heart [Gen. 38:18]. It was sometimes worn on the finger, as well.

The true Believer understands well such language. He knows that the maintenance of devout affection is not a matter of mere desire and will. The Lord Himself must help us with His blessed Gifts, the influence of His gracious Spirit, to overcome the feebleness and fickleness of a fallen heart. We want to be close to the heart of the Saviour. We want to be constantly in His Eye, so diligently employed in His Service, and so closely associated with the Work of His mighty Arm that we shall be ever receiving from Him the signs and evidences of His Approval and Affection. The priceless value of such love is described in I Cor. 13:3. It is an unquenchable

flame; nothing can resist it.)

7 Many waters cannot quench love, neither can the floods drown it: if a man would give all the substance of his house for love, it would utterly be contemned. *(This is the love of Christ setting its affections upon an object wholly unworthy of such affection. The corrupt Christian Church teaches that Divine love can be purchased by works of merit and that God's Justice and Pity can be bought with a sufficiency of money and so induce Him to release His suffering Children from the pains of a supposed purgatory that does not even exist.*

The last line of this Verse may be understood to read, "he and it would utterly be condemned," that is, both the man and his money would be rejected in the effort to purchase the love of God.)

8 We have a little sister, and she has no breasts: what shall we do for our sister in the day when she shall be spoken for? *(Now the Shulamite's brothers will speak. They see her coming back on the arm of the lowly shepherd. They proclaim that they have known her all her life. They recall when she was "little" and had "no breasts," meaning no maturity.*

The words of both Verses 8 through 9 do not seem to be words of endearment, but rather of sarcasm and contempt. These sons of her mother do not at all see in her what the Beloved sees. Likewise, the world little sees in the Believer what Christ sees!)

9 If she be a wall, we will build upon her a palace of silver: and if she be a door, we will inclose her with boards of cedar. *(The brothers of the Shulamite were not speaking kindly of their sister. The word "little" in Verse 8 does not have an affectionate meaning. They claimed that she was neither "a wall" nor "a door" [of no use to exclude or to admit], that is, she was good for nothing.*

However, what the nations of the world, represented by these brothers, could not see in Israel, Christ did, and what the world does not see in us, Christ does!)

10 I am a wall, and my breasts like towers: then was I in his eyes as one who found favour. *(Now the Shulamite speaks. She exalts in the consciousness that even though she is despised by her brothers, the children of their common mother, yet she is beautiful in the eyes of her Beloved.*

Thus will Israel be beautiful in the eyes of her Beloved, Christ Jesus.

Only Grace can say, "I was in His Eyes as one who found favor."

In that coming glad day when Christ rescues

Israel from the onslaught of Satan and finally restores her to a position of glory, it will not be because Israel was beautiful, lovely, or merited such. In fact, she merits nothing! Only Grace can function in such a climate.

The scene is now reversed. Christ originally came "despised and rejected of men" [Isa. 53:3], and Israel rejected Him.

Now, Israel will be "despised and rejected of men"; however, Christ will not reject her, but instead "in His Eyes they will find favor.")

11 Solomon had a vineyard at Baal-hamon; he let out the vineyard unto keepers; every one for the fruit thereof was to bring a thousand pieces of silver.

12 My vineyard, which is mine, is before me: you, O Solomon, must have a thousand, and those that keep the fruit thereof two hundred. *(The contrast between the compulsion of Law and the compelling of love is set out in Verses 11 and 12. Solomon's tenants were bound to furnish the legal rent of the vineyard hired out to them, but love constrained the Bride to give the produce of her vineyard, while at the same time not forgetting what was justly due to the laborer.)*

13 You who dwell in the gardens, the companions hearken to your voice: cause me to hear it. *(Now her Beloved Shepherd Bridegroom speaks. He says, "Your companions in the vineyard hear your voice. That is good, but speak to Me, 'cause Me to hear it!'"*

Such is Christ's complaint today. Many speak to their companions in testimony and in the necessary ordering of Christian service, but they neglect private prayer and secret communion.

He wants to hear our voice! This is the second time that He has requested such, emphasizing the strong desire [2:14].

The word "jealousy," as found in Verse 6, is set in order in this Passage as well. While it is true that others needed to hear her story, still, more than all, He says, "cause Me to hear it."

That He would even want to hear our voice is beyond our pale of understanding. What do we have to say to Him that could be of interest? Quite possibly it is not so much what we say, but the love with which we must say it!)

14 Make haste, my beloved, and be thou like to a roe or to a young hart upon the mountains of spices. *(The Song closes with the ardent cry of the Bride to the Bridegroom to hasten His return, to come as a roe or a young hart, that is, to come quickly.*

Thus, this Book, the last of the poetic Books, corresponds to, and closes like, the Book of Revelation,

the last of the Prophetic Books.

There the Bride says, "Come!" [Rev. 22:17]. And the Bridegroom answers, "Yes, I am coming." And the Bride repeats, "Do so! Come, Lord Jesus!"

The principal personages and the circumstances in the two Books are similar. The Bride, Israel, is despised and ill-treated by the sons, the nations. She and they are children of a common mother [compare 8:5 with Gen., Chpt. 3 and Ezek., Chpt. 16].

The Bridegroom is the Messiah. The Bride's vineyard is the Land of Israel. The Divine Solomon's vineyard is the Gentile world.

In the Book of Revelation, as in the Song of Songs, the Bridegroom descends into the wilderness, rescues His Bride from her persecutors, celebrates His marriage with her, establishes His Kingdom, and makes her His companion in His Glory.

All of this tells us that Christ Alone can satisfy the deepest longings of the human heart.)

THE BOOK OF THE PROPHET
ISAIAH

CHAPTER 1
(760 B.C.)
INTRODUCTION

THE vision of Isaiah the son of Amoz, which he saw concerning Judah and Jerusalem in the days of Uzziah, Jotham, Ahaz, and Hezekiah, kings of Judah. *(Isaiah was a contemporary of Jonah, Amos, Hosea, and Micah. It is thought that he began to preach at about 15 years of age and died at about 85. Tradition says that Manasseh placed Isaiah in a hollow log and cut him in two [Heb. 11:37]. This great Book which bears his name was written about 800 years before Christ.*

His Prophecies covered the entire or the partial reign of some four kings, as listed in the Text. [Every message was primarily related to Judah, Jerusalem, or to the Jews and their Holy City.]

He is called "the Millennial Prophet," having given more Prophecies concerning that coming grand day than any other Prophet. As well, he was quoted by Christ more than any other Prophet.

Of the four kings under whom Isaiah prophesied, "Hezekiah" was the Godliest.)

GOD'S CASE AGAINST JUDAH

2 Hear, O heavens, and give ear, O Earth: for the LORD has spoken, I have nourished and brought up children, and they have rebelled against Me. *(In this Verse, all nature is invoked to hear Jehovah make complaint of the ingratitude of His People. The invocation is cast in the same form which is so common in Deuteronomy [Deut. 4:26; 30:19; 31:28; 32:1] and seems to indicate familiarity with that Book.*

To step out of the Song of Solomon into Isaiah is to pass from sunshine to shadow. The love that exults in the one laments in the other.

Actually, Isaiah is not the One actually speaking here, but rather Jehovah. The Prophet is only His mouthpiece.)

3 The ox knows his owner, and the ass his master's crib: but Israel does not know, My people do not consider. *(The meaning of this Verse seems to be, "My people do not consider Me, do not reflect on My relation to them as Lord and Master.")*

4 Ah sinful nation, a people laden with iniquity, a seed of evildoers, children who are corrupters: they have forsaken the LORD, they have provoked the Holy One of Israel unto anger, they are gone away backward. *(According to Isaiah, holiness is the most essential element of God's nature; hence, he would call Him "the Holy One of Israel."*

In their forsaking the Lord, Judah did not renounce His worship, but actually continued it; however, it was reduced to a mere formality. The people "honored Him with their lips, while their hearts were far from Him" [Isa. 29:13].)

5 Why should you be stricken any more? you will revolt more and more: the whole head is sick, and the whole heart faint.

6 From the sole of the foot even unto the head there is no soundness in it; but wounds, and bruises, and putrifying sores: they have not been closed, neither bound up, neither mollified with ointment. *(The statement of Verses 5 and 6 not only describes moral character, or rather the lack thereof, but also the severity of future just but unavailing punishment. Israel refused to repent notwithstanding such punishment.*

The "head" and "heart" of Israel respectively represented the intellectual and moral natures. Israel had turned away from God in both her mind and heart.

The deadly "bruises" and "sores" of Israel, while but a spiritual analogy, still, could not be cured by anything except the Lord.)

7 Your country is desolate, your cities are burned with fire: your land, strangers devour it in your presence, and it is desolate, as overthrown by strangers.

8 And the daughter of Zion is left as a cottage in a vineyard, as a lodge in a garden of cucumbers, as a besieged city. *(The descriptions given in these two Verses were literally fulfilled about 175 years after this stern prediction; however, a prelude to its destruction by Babylon was rendered by the Edomites and the Philistines, who invaded Judea in the time of Ahaz [II Chron. 28:17-18].)*

A CALL TO REPENTANCE

9 Except the LORD of hosts had left unto

us a very small remnant, we should have been as Sodom, and we should have been like unto Gomorrah. *(In a sense, there were always two Israels. There was the "remnant" which served the Lord, and which was always very small; and the balance of Israel, which rebelled against the Lord. It is the same in the modern Church; consequently, every blessing experienced by Israel, whatever it may have been, was because of that "small remnant." Once again, it is the same in the modern Church.)*

10 Hear the Word of the LORD, you rulers of Sodom; give ear unto the Law of our God, you people of Gomorrah. *(The Holy Spirit likens Israel to "Sodom and Gomorrah." However, the people will meet the Prophecy of Isaiah with an appeal to the fact that they maintain all the outward ordinances of religion as required by the Law, and are, therefore, blameless. In response to this, the Prophet denounces such a pretense of religion as an aggravation of their sin, and then characterizes their whole worship as an "abomination.")*

11 To what purpose is the multitude of your sacrifices unto Me? saith the LORD: I am full of the Burnt Offerings of rams, and the fat of fed beasts; and I delight not in the blood of bullocks, or of lambs, or of he goats. *(The very worship which God Himself had commanded was debased by them and became an abomination in His Sight, because they looked to the ceremony instead of what the ceremony represented, namely, "Jesus Christ and Him Crucified.")*

12 When you come to appear before Me, who has required this at your hand, to tread My courts? *(The Lord required more than mere bodily attendance and a trampling of His Courts with their feet, when their hearts were far from Him.)*

13 Bring no more vain oblations; incense is an abomination unto Me; the new moons and sabbaths, the calling of assemblies, I cannot away with; it is iniquity, even the solemn meeting. *(All the religious activity, which in fact was genuine and actually God-given, still, was emptied of all its significance and became hateful to God — a mere form; consequently, it was, as stated, an "abomination.")*

14 Your new moons and your appointed feasts My soul hates: they are a trouble unto Me; I am weary to bear them. *(The Hebrew word for "weary" is "la'ah," which means "to be disgusted, grieved, loathe.")*

15 And when you spread forth your hands, I will hide My eyes from you: yea, when you make many prayers, I will not hear: your hands are full of blood. *(If their hands had been "spread forth" with a broken heart and with Repentance, the Lord would not have hidden His Eyes.)*

GOD'S DEMANDS

16 Wash you, make you clean; put away the evil of your doings from before My eyes; cease to do evil *(sin defiles, hence the need for a spiritual "washing"; defilement has always been felt by men universally wherever there has been any sense of sin; only the Blood of Jesus Christ, which in fact was symbolized by the animal sacrifices, can take away sin; however, Israel did not trust in what the sacrifices represented, but rather the ceremony itself, which God could never tolerate)*;

17 Learn to do well; seek judgment, relieve the oppressed, judge the fatherless, plead for the widow. *(The idea is, if a person is truly right with God, they will also treat their fellow man right.)*

18 Come now, and let us reason together, saith the LORD: though your sins be as scarlet, they shall be as white as snow; though they be red like crimson, they shall be as wool. *(There is no greater invitation found in the Bible than this one given by the Holy Spirit through the Prophet Isaiah.*

In this Passage, sins are spoken of as "scarlet." Such has a reference to blood-guiltiness. All sin is murder in some form, hence the blood-guiltiness.

This glorious Passage illustrates to us the eternal Truth that irrespective of the evil, wickedness, deception, and weight of sin, the Lord stands ready, upon proper confession and Repentance, to forgive all and, therefore, to cleanse all. As stated, this is done exclusively by Faith in Christ and His shed Blood [Eph. 2:13-18].)

19 If you be willing and obedient, you shall eat the good of the land:

20 But if you refuse and rebel, you shall be devoured with the sword: for the mouth of the LORD has spoken it. *(This means, "If you consent in your wills and are also obedient in your actions."*

The "eating of the good of the land" refers to blessing and Satan's not devouring the increase.

The idea is that God controls all. If we obey Him, blessing will be ours. If we do not obey Him, He will allow enemies to come in and "devour with a sword.")

21 How is the faithful city become an harlot!

it was full of judgment; righteousness lodged in it; but now murderers. *(The word "judgment" does not refer here to the negative, but rather to the positive. It spoke of right doing and doing right which could only come from the Lord.*

Jerusalem is not called here an idolatress, but rather one who has left her first love and turned to other attractions. Faithful once to her Lord, she has now cast Him off — she is as an adulterous wife; she no longer obeys or loves her husband.

This is identical to the modern Christian who makes something other than the Cross of Christ the object of his faith. The Holy Spirit through Paul referred to such as "spiritual adulterers" [Rom. 7:1-4].)

22 Your silver is become dross, your wine mixed with water *(this means that the great men of Israel had deteriorated)*:

23 Your princes are rebellious, and companions of thieves: every one loves gifts, and follows after rewards: they judge not the fatherless, neither does the cause of the widow come unto them. *("Gifts" mean "bribes." God's Love perpetually appears throughout the Bible in indignant denunciation of injustice and hardness of heart toward the widow and fatherless.)*

PROMISED RESTORATION

24 Therefore saith the Lord, the LORD of Hosts, the Mighty One of Israel, Ah, I will ease Me of My adversaries, and avenge Me of My enemies *(the title, "Mighty One of Israel," is peculiar to Isaiah; Verses 24 through 27 speak of the day, which is even yet to come, when Israel will be completely restored; it is the coming Kingdom Age)*:

25 And I will turn my hand upon you, and purely purge away your dross, and take away all your tin *(this Promise has to do with the Prophecy of Zechariah [Zech. 12:10]; it will take place at the Second Coming)*:

26 And I will restore your judges as at the first, and your counsellors as at the beginning: afterward you shall be called, The city of righteousness, the faithful city. *(The Lord is promising to bring back the time when the nation will renew its first love and be as it was in the days of David and the early days of Solomon. As stated, this will take place at the Second Coming, when Israel will then accept Christ as Saviour and Lord. However, it cannot happen until Jesus is accepted.)*

27 Zion shall be redeemed with judgment, and her converts with righteousness. *(Jerusalem and Zion are the names of the only city that God has promised to redeem and to make His eternal, earthly capital. This will take place at the Second Advent of Christ.)*

JUDAH'S JUDGMENT

28 And the destruction of the transgressors and of the sinners shall be together, and they who forsake the LORD shall be consumed. *(This Passage, among many others, completely refutes the doctrine of "Unconditional Eternal Security." This clearly refers to those who no longer have faith in the Lord, thereby rejecting Him, and doing so to the point of being destroyed. Men are warned not to forsake God [Deut. 12:19; 14:27].)*

29 For they shall be ashamed of the oaks which you have desired, and you shall be confounded for the gardens that you have chosen. *(The reference in Verses 29 through 31 is to idolatry. It is figured by "oaks" and "gardens." The garden probably was an imitation of the Garden of Eden, and the oak, of the Tree of Life.)*

30 For you shall be as an oak whose leaf fades, and as a garden that has no water. *(This is to be contrasted with the Godly, whose "leaf shall not wither" [Ps. 1:3].)*

31 And the strong shall be as tow, and the maker of it as a spark, and they shall both burn together, and none shall quench them. *("Tow" referred to the fiber of flax or hemp, which had the idea of being fragile.*

The word "maker" refers to the makers of pillars, or Asherahs, as idols.

This Verse speaks of eternal Hell, where all who rebel against God shall go [Ps. 9:17].)

CHAPTER 2
(760 B.C.)
IMMEDIATE JUDGMENT; FUTURE GLORY; THE MILLENNIUM

THE word that Isaiah the son of Amoz saw concerning Judah and Jerusalem. *(The word "saw," as used here by Isaiah, basically means the same thing as "Vision.")*

2 And it shall come to pass in the last days, that the mountain of the LORD's house shall be established in the top of the mountains, and shall be exalted above the hills; and all nations shall flow unto it. *(Verses 2 through 4*

in this Chapter correspond to Mic. 4:1-3. Micah's Prophecy was 17 years later than Isaiah's. Some wonder if the latter Prophet borrowed from the former, but this shows a want of intelligence. When God repeats a message, the repetition emphasizes its preciousness to Him and its importance to man.

In both of the Prophecies, Isaiah and Micah, the Lord reveals the character of the Kingdom He proposed to set up on the Earth; in the latter, it is repeated to the nations. All of this will take place in the coming Kingdom Age.)

3 And many people shall go and say, Come ye, and let us go up to the mountain of the LORD, to the House of the God of Jacob; and He will teach us of His ways, and we will walk in His paths: for out of Zion shall go forth the Law, and the Word of the LORD from Jerusalem. *(The "Law," as referred to here, has no reference to the Law of Moses, but rather to instruction, direction, and teaching. Again, this is the coming Kingdom Age, when the Messiah, "The Greater than Solomon," will rule the world by Wisdom, Grace, and Love.)*

4 And He shall judge among the nations, and shall rebuke many people: and they shall beat their swords into plowshares, and their spears into pruninghooks: nation shall not lift up sword against nation, neither shall they learn war any more. *(The words, "judge among," should read "arbitrate between", and "rebuke" would have been better translated "decide the disputes of." Man's courts of arbitration are doomed to failure, but, to Messiah's Court, success is promised here.)*

JUDGMENT AND CHASTISEMENT BEFORE BLESSING

5 O house of Jacob, come ye, and let us walk in the light of the LORD. *(Jacob was an unlovely person, who deserved nothing good and had nothing to offer, but was given everything by Christ. Such is Grace! The "light" mentioned here is God's moral teaching. It is the teaching of the Bible.)*

6 Therefore You have forsaken Your people the House of Jacob, because they be replenished from the east, and are soothsayers like the Philistines, and they please themselves in the children of strangers. *(Instead of Judah being a "light" to the rest of the world, the world has now darkened Judah's "light." Instead of surrounding nations taking on Judah's ways of Godliness, which the Lord intended, Judah has*

taken on the world's ways of ungodliness.)

7 Their land also is full of silver and gold, neither is there any end of their treasures; their land is also full of horses, neither is there any end of their chariots *(the overaccumulation of wealth, the striking of partnerships with heathen nations, the multiplication of horses, and the making of idols were all strictly forbidden by the Mosaic Law)*:

8 Their land also is full of idols; they worship the work of their own hands, that which their own fingers have made *(the sacred historians declare that both Uzziah and Jotham maintained the worship of Jehovah and disallowed idolatry [II Ki. 15:3, 34; II Chron. 26:4; 27:2], so what is spoken of here of private devotion is idol-worship)*:

9 And the mean man bows down, and the great man humbles himself: therefore forgive them not. *(The bowing down and humbling of this Verse refer to the adoration of images; "the mean man" and "the great man" figure all ranks of society. While outwardly loyal to the Law [1:11-15], they, like the Pharisees, were private idolaters [Lk. 16:14; Col. 3:5].)*

THE DAY OF THE LORD

10 Enter into the rock, and hide thee in the dust, for fear of the LORD, and for the glory of His majesty. *(This proclamation is intended to humble the proud "mean man" and the proud "great man.")*

11 The lofty looks of man shall be humbled, and the haughtiness of men shall be bowed down, and the LORD alone shall be exalted in that day. *("In that day" refers to the Second Advent. The "man with the lofty looks" is the Antichrist. He "shall be humbled." Jesus Christ Alone will "be exalted in that day.")*

12 For the day of the LORD of Hosts shall be upon every one who is proud and lofty, and upon every one who is lifted up; and he shall be brought low *(the very nature of the Antichrist and all who follow him will be "proud and lofty"; the Holy Spirit says, "he shall be brought low" [Rev., Chpt 19])*:

13 And upon all the cedars of Lebanon, that are high and lifted up, and upon all the oaks of Bashan *(these "cedars" and "oaks" are symbolic of mighty and powerful men who will throw in their lot with the "man of sin," attempting to annihilate Israel and take over the world; again, the Holy Spirit says that they will be brought down)*,

14 And upon all the high mountains, and upon all the hills that are lifted up *(once again, the "mountains" and "hills" stand for nations, kingdoms, and powers ruled by the great men of Verse 13; a blanket condemnation of all of man's efforts is enjoined here)*,

15 And upon every high tower, and upon every fenced wall *(this speaks of the preparations, war efforts, and military armaments amassed for Israel's annihilation)*,

16 And upon all the ships of Tarshish, and upon all pleasant pictures. *(This refers to the mighty navies of the Antichrist and all preparations for war.*

The "pleasant pictures" refer to their idols, which shall all be utterly destroyed.)

17 And the loftiness of man shall be bowed down, and the haughtiness of men shall be made low: and the LORD alone shall be exalted in that day. *(This Passage is very similar to Verse 11, and is so intended by the Holy Spirit. The very nature of the Antichrist and his followers will be "pride." But he and all his minions "shall be made low.")*

IDOLATRY ABOLISHED

18 And the idols he shall utterly abolish. *(The "idol" spawning the "idols" will be the Antichrist, and all will be "utterly abolished," which will take place at the Second Coming.)*

19 And they shall go into the holes of the rocks, and into the caves of the Earth, for fear of the LORD, and for the glory of His majesty, when He arises to shake terribly the Earth. *(This speaks of the Second Coming.)*

20 In that day a man shall cast his idols of silver, and his idols of gold, which they made each one for himself to worship, to the moles and to the bats;

21 To go into the clefts of the rocks, and into the tops of the ragged rocks, for fear of the LORD, and for the glory of His majesty, when He arises to shake terribly the Earth. *(For emphasis, the Holy Spirit repeats the admonition of the Nineteenth Verse in the latter portion of the Twenty-first Verse. The coming of the Lord will definitely "shake terribly the Earth." It will, and without doubt, be the most cataclysmic and momentous happening ever experienced on the face of this planet.)*

22 Cease ye from man, whose breath is in his nostrils: for wherein is he to be accounted of? *(The judgment of Verses 12 through 21 had a partial fulfillment in the destruction of Jerusalem* by the Babylonians. *But its plenary fulfillment is described in Rev., Chpt. 6.*

The first Verse, Verse 10, and the last Verse of this Message give the import which is the folly of dependence upon man and the wisdom of trusting the Messiah. As for man, he is the feeble creature of a moment, but the Messiah is an all-sufficient and eternal refuge.)

CHAPTER 3
(760 B.C.)

JUDGMENT ON JUDAH

FOR, behold, the Lord, the LORD of hosts, does take away from Jerusalem and from Judah the stay and the staff, the whole stay of bread, and the whole stay of water. *(The entirety of this particular Chapter refers to the coming Judgment, with Babylon used as God's instrument. The Prophecy would be fulfilled about 150 years into the future, even though Judah and Jerusalem did not know, at this time, exactly when it would come.)*

2 The mighty man, and the man of war, the judge, and the prophet, and the prudent, and the ancient. *(The idea is once again presented that man is not to be trusted, but rather the Lord.)*

3 The captain of fifty, and the honourable man, and the counsellor, and the cunning artificer, and the eloquent orator. *(The Holy Spirit says to Judah and Jerusalem that irrespective of the talents and ability of the man in question, nevertheless, man, even the "honorable man," will fail. Once again, "trust God!")*

4 And I will give children to be their princes, and babes shall rule over them. *(The word "children" would have been better translated "youths." This came to pass exactly as the Holy Spirit said:*

The extreme youth of the later kings of Judah at that date of their accession is very remarkable. After Hezekiah, only one was as much as 25 years old when he came to the throne. Jehoahaz was 23 [II Ki. 24:18]; Jehoiachin, 18 [II Ki. 24:8]; Manasseh was 12 years old when he became king [II Ki. 21:1]; and Josiah was but 8 [II Ki. 22:1].)

5 And the people shall be oppressed, every one by another, and every one by his neighbour: the child shall behave himself proudly against the ancient, and the base against the honourable. *(Isaiah said that respect for the aged would disappear. Youths would set at naught the counsel of the aged.)*

6 When a man shall take hold of his brother of the house of his father, saying, You have clothing, be thou our ruler, and let this ruin be under your hand *(the Prophecy was that the day would come when no one would want to serve in positions of leadership, because the situation seemed hopeless):*

7 In that day shall he swear, saying, I will not be an healer; for in my house is neither bread nor clothing; make me not a ruler of the people. *(And it came to pass exactly as the Holy Spirit predicted.)*

8 For Jerusalem is ruined, and Judah is fallen: because their tongue and their doings are against the LORD, to provoke the eyes of His glory. *(The reason for this "ruin" is hereby given: "their tongue and their doings are against the LORD."*

Backsliding is seldom, if ever, brought about by an explosion, but rather by leakage.)

9 The show of their countenance does witness against them; and they declare their sin as Sodom, they hide it not. Woe unto their soul! for they have rewarded evil unto themselves. *(Rebellion will quickly show itself on the "countenance," for all sin, in its final form, is rebellion against God.*

The phrase, "they have rewarded evil unto themselves," refers to the "Ways of God" being perverted and turned by being compromised and diluted.)

10 Say ye to the righteous, that it shall be well with him: for they shall eat the fruit of their doings.

11 Woe unto the wicked! it shall be ill with him: for the reward of his hands shall be given him. *(The contrast is given here between the "righteous" and the "wicked." God will reward the "righteous," while bringing judgment upon the "wicked."*

This portrays the fact that the Ways of the Lord are very clear and simple: obey and be blessed; disobey and be judged.)

12 As for My people, children are their oppressors, and women rule over them. O My people, they which lead you cause you to err, and destroy the way of your paths.

13 The LORD stands up to plead, and stands to judge the people. *("To destroy [swallow up] the way of your paths" means to do away with the Bible as the rule of moral conduct. "Your paths" denote the "paths of righteousness" designed by God for His People [Ps. 23:3].)*

14 The LORD will enter into judgment with the ancients of His people, and the princes thereof: for you have eaten up the vineyard; the spoil of the poor is in your houses.

15 What mean ye that ye beat my people to pieces, and grind the faces of the poor? saith the Lord GOD of Hosts. *(In these Passages, the Lord holds the leadership responsible for the oppression of the people, and especially of the poor.)*

16 Moreover the LORD says, Because the daughters of Zion are haughty, and walk with stretched forth necks and wanton eyes, walking and mincing as they go, and making a tinkling with their feet *("the daughters of Zion" are the female inhabitants of Jerusalem; the word "haughty" means that they are "proud"; the statement, "stretched forth necks and wanton eyes," indicates the desire to attract men's attention; they were shameless and immodest in this effort):*

17 Therefore the Lord will smite with a scab the crown of the head of the daughters of Zion, and the LORD will discover their secret parts. *(Basically, this refers to war, and the clothing being taken away by the victors, which would cause the women to suffer great shame and indignities.)*

18 In that day the Lord will take away the bravery of their tinkling ornaments about their feet, and their cauls, and their round tires like the moon,

19 The chains, and the bracelets, and the mufflers,

20 The bonnets, and the ornaments of the legs, and the headbands, and the tablets, and the earrings,

21 The rings, and nose jewels,

22 The changeable suits of apparel, and the mantles, and the wimples, and the crisping pins,

23 The glasses, and the fine linen, and the hoods, and the vails. *(Judah and Jerusalem suffered all of these indignities when Nebuchadnezzar sacked Jerusalem and led God's people into captivity. This would happen about 150 years later.*

However, due to the words, "in that day," the main thrust of this Prophecy refers to the coming Great Tribulation, when Israel will face threatened annihilation by the Antichrist [Mat. 24:21].)

24 And it shall come to pass, that instead of sweet smell there shall be stink; and instead of a girdle a rent; and instead of well set hair baldness; and instead of a stomacher a girding of sackcloth; and burning instead of beauty. *(The words, "in that day," continue to refer to*

the coming Great Tribulation. But again, it also happened during the siege by Nebuchadnezzar.)

25 Your men shall fall by the sword, and your mighty in the war,

26 And her gates shall lament and mourn; and she being desolate shall sit upon the ground. *(Inasmuch as the words, "in that day," are given in Verse 18 and continued in Verse 1 of the following Chapter, which describes the coming Millennium, it is certain that the future fulfillment of this Prophecy concerns that coming terrible and yet glad day — terrible because of the horrible suffering that will come to Israel, and glad because of the resultant acceptance of the Saviour by Israel. It will be the time of the Second Coming of Jesus.)*

CHAPTER 4
(760 B.C.)
JERUSALEM'S GLORIOUS FUTURE:
THE MILLENNIUM

AND in that day seven women shall take hold of one man, saying, We will eat our own bread, and wear our own apparel: only let us be called by your name, to take away our reproach. *(Verses 1 and 2 refer to the Great Tribulation that is soon to come upon this Earth [Mat. 24:21], as well as the coming glorious Millennium.*

As Isaiah's Prophecy continues, the Holy Spirit, after giving the horrors of the yet to come Great Tribulation, now continues with a glorious Word of Mercy.)

MESSIAH REIGNING

2 In that day shall the Branch of the LORD be beautiful and glorious, and the fruit of the Earth shall be excellent and comely for them who are escaped of Israel. *(This is the coming Millennial Reign. The phrase, "are escaped of Israel," refers to the remnant which shall escape the future Tribulation and the Battle of Armageddon. The "branch of the LORD" is Christ.)*

A HOLY PEOPLE

3 And it shall come to pass, that he who is left in Zion, and he who remains in Jerusalem, shall be called holy, even every one that is written among the living in Jerusalem *(Israel, after a long night of thousands of years, will finally come home, but at great price [Zech. 14:16-21]):*

4 When the Lord shall have washed away the filth of the daughters of Zion, and shall have purged the blood of Jerusalem from the midst thereof by the Spirit of Judgment, and by the Spirit of Burning. *(This speaks of the conversion of the Remnant, immediately after the Battle of Armageddon and the Second Coming. Israel, at that time, will be saved by accepting Jesus as Saviour.*

The "Spirit of Judgment" and the "Spirit of Burning" have to do with the Office Work of the Holy Spirit. He will deal with Israel in Him bringing them to Christ in exactly the same manner that He has dealt with all men.)

GOD'S GLORY RESTORED

5 And the LORD will create upon every dwelling place of mount Zion, and upon her assemblies, a cloud and smoke by day, and the shining of a flaming fire by night: for upon all the glory shall be a defence. *(In that coming Glad Day, Jerusalem, and especially the Temple area, will be totally different from anything the world has ever known.*

Hovering over Mount Zion will be a "pillar of cloud by day" and "fire by night," which will be eternal symbols and manifestations of His Presence. As Ezekiel said, "The LORD is there" [Ezek. 48:35].)

6 And there shall be a tabernacle for a shadow in the daytime from the heat, and for a place of refuge, and for a covert from storm and from rain. *(All of this is Christ: the "Tabernacle," the "Shadow," the "Place of Refuge," and the "Covert."*

All of this proves that Israel is going to be restored. In fact, the Church Age has almost come to its conclusion. It is being phased out, which will conclude with the Rapture, and Israel will be restored [Rom., Chpt. 11].)

CHAPTER 5
(760 B.C.)
SONG OF GOD'S VINEYARD:
A PARABLE OF JUDGMENT

NOW will I sing to My wellbeloved a song of My beloved touching His vineyard. My wellbeloved has a vineyard in a very fruitful hill *(the first four Chapters were one complete Prophecy; now a new Prophecy by Isaiah begins; it has no connection to the previous Prophecy except in Message; the "vineyard" is Israel; the singer is "Elohim" and the "Beloved"*

is His Beloved Son [Lk., Chpt. 20]):

2 And He fenced it, and gathered out the stones thereof, and planted it with the choicest vine, and built a tower in the midst of it, and also made a winepress therein: and He looked that it should bring forth grapes, and it brought forth wild grapes. *(Isaiah is using metaphors to describe the "vineyard," i.e., "Israel." Despite all the work done regarding this vineyard, "it brought forth wild grapes." It should have been the choicest of fruit, but, instead, it brought forth a worthless product.)*

3 And now, O inhabitants of Jerusalem, and men of Judah, judge, I pray you, betwixt Me and My vineyard.

4 What could have been done more to My vineyard, that I have not done in it? wherefore, when I looked that it should bring forth grapes, brought it forth wild grapes? *(In these Passages is an awful finality. When the Lord said there is nothing more He could do, this denotes an effort of retrieval that is far beyond our capacity to grasp or understand!)*

5 And now go to; I will tell you what I will do to My vineyard: I will take away the hedge thereof, and it shall be eaten up; and break down the wall thereof, and it shall be trodden down:

6 And I will lay it waste: it shall not be pruned, nor digged; but there shall come up briers and thorns: I will also command the clouds that they rain no rain upon it. *(As is obvious, there is now a change in the Message; the style becomes abrupt, the tone fierce and menacing. Consequently, the Lord did exactly what He said He would do. During the time of Nebuchadnezzar, and then in A.D. 70, all of this came to pass, and in most horrifying detail.*

The "rain" spoken of concerns spiritual renewal. Since Israel's rejection of Christ, there has been no spiritual "rain" in any capacity. As well, she has brought forth "briars and thorns" in the spiritual sense.)

SIN OF JUDAH: GREED

7 For the vineyard of the LORD of Hosts is the House of Israel, and the men of Judah His pleasant plant: and He looked for judgment, but behold oppression; for righteousness, but behold a cry. *(Instead of this "vineyard of the LORD" producing good and pleasant plants, it produced instead "oppression" and wickedness.)*

8 Woe unto them who join house to house, who lay field to field, till there be no place, that they may be placed alone in the midst of the Earth! *(The expression " field to field" refers to covetousness. They were coveting more fields until they would own them all, so as to be great in the Earth. This is the first "Woe!")*

9 In My ears said the LORD of Hosts, Of a truth many houses shall be desolate, even great and fair, without inhabitant.

10 Yea, ten acres of vineyard shall yield one bath, and the seed of an homer shall yield an ephah. *(The Lord had promised in the beginning that Israel would be a land of "milk and honey." Now, because of sin and rebellion, He promises "desolation."*

Incidentally, the word "ephah" has reference concerning its total fulfillment in the Prophecy of Zechariah. It concerns Babylon being rebuilt "in the land of Shinar" [Zech. 5:5-11].

This is all because of the spiritual declension and fall of Israel. Even though this Prophecy was given nearly 2,800 years ago, truly the beginning of its fulfillment has already begun. Babylon will be rebuilt, whether the city or the system [Rev., Chpt. 18].)

DRUNKEN INDULGENCE

11 Woe unto them who rise up early in the morning, that they may follow strong drink, that continue until night, till wine inflame them! *(As the first "Woe!" was pronounced on covetousness, now a second "Woe!" is pronounced on pleasure-seekers. As well, this mirrors the modern Church [II Tim. 3:1-5].)*

12 And the harp, and the viol, the tabret, and pipe, and wine, are in their feast: but they regard not the work of the LORD, neither consider the operation of His Hands. *(The instruments of music are not condemned, but their wrong use is. The Blessings of God are the source of all the good things which have happened to us, but presently, even in the Churches, we no longer "consider the operation of His Hands.")*

13 Therefore My people are gone into captivity, because they have no knowledge: and their honourable men are famished, and their multitude dried up with thirst. *(The "captivity" of which Isaiah speaks is a spiritual captivity that was already pandemic in the nation. The reason:*

They had no "knowledge" of the Word of God.

If the modern Believer doesn't understand the Message of the Cross, which in effect is the story of the Bible, then spiritual captivity is the result. Freedom over the world, the flesh, and the

Devil can be brought about only by Christ and what Christ did at the Cross, which gives the Holy Spirit latitude to work in one's life. All that is required of the Believer is to exhibit Faith in Christ and what Christ did at the Cross, and this on a perpetual basis [Rom. 6:3-14]. But the truth is that the modern Church has "knowledge" of many things, but little at all as it regards the Word of God.)

14 Therefore Hell has enlarged herself, and opened her mouth without measure: and their glory, and their multitude, and their pomp, and he who rejoices, shall descend into it. *(The end result of this "captivity" is eternal Hell; consequently, the bottom line reads, "Jesus Christ and Him Crucified" or eternal Hell.)*

15 And the mean man shall be brought down, and the mighty man shall be humbled, and the eyes of the lofty shall be humbled *(the sense of this Passage is that "pride" is the cause of Israel's sins, as well as our sins)*:

16 But the LORD of Hosts shall be exalted in judgment, and God Who is holy shall be sanctified in Righteousness. *(This Passage means that the Holy God shows Himself to be Holy by Righteousness; by executing this righteous judgment on Jerusalem, the Holy God shows His Holiness. God must judge sin, either in Christ on the Cross, which is its rightful place, or else in the individual, which spells doom.)*

17 Then shall the lambs feed after their manner, and the waste places of the fat ones shall strangers eat. *(The meaning is that human habitations will become pastures for animals, which is exactly what happened to the Holy Land.)*

INIQUITIES AND APOSTASY

18 Woe unto them who draw iniquity with cords of vanity, and sin as it were with a cart rope *(now the third "Woe!" is pronounced against those who openly pile up sin upon sin and scoff at God)*:

19 Who say, Let Him make speed, and hasten His work, that we may see it: and let the counsel of the Holy One of Israel draw nigh and come, that we may know it! *(The implication of this Passage is chilling! Isaiah's Prophecies are being mocked by the inhabitants of Judah and Jerusalem. They use one of Isaiah's favorite titles of God, not from any belief in Him, but rather in a mocking spirit.)*

20 Woe unto them who call evil good, and good evil; who put darkness for light, and light for darkness; who put bitter for sweet, and sweet for bitter! *(This is the fourth "Woe!" The idea is that Israel had so perverted the Scripture that anymore they didn't know right from wrong. Does it sound familiar?)*

PRIDE, INTEMPERANCE, AND INJUSTICE

21 Woe unto them who are wise in their own eyes, and prudent in their own sight! *(This is the fifth "Woe!" Self-conceit is the antithesis of humility; as humility is, in a certain sense, the crowning virtue, so is self-conceit a sort of finishing touch put to vice.)*

22 Woe unto them who are mighty to drink wine, and men of strength to mingle strong drink:

23 Which justify the wicked for reward, and take away the righteousness of the righteous from him! *(This is the sixth "Woe!" This seems to be a repetition of the second "Woe!" However, there is a marked difference!*

This "Woe!" concerns the leaders of Judah. They are drinkers but do not succumb to their liquor; therefore, this sixth "Woe!" may be considered to be pronounced more upon their corruption than upon their drinking, and so is really quite distinct from the previous "Woe!")

GOD WILL BRING JUDGMENT ON JUDAH

24 Therefore as the fire devours the stubble, and the flame consumes the chaff, so their root shall be as rottenness, and their blossom shall go up as dust: because they have cast away the Law of the LORD of Hosts, and despised the Word of the Holy One of Israel. *(Judgment is now pronounced, and will come in two directions — a judgment of ruin and destruction.*

The phrase, "despised the Word," does not refer to the "written Word," but to the declarations of God by the mouth of His Prophets; however, in effect, much of what the Prophets said was included in the written Text.)

25 Therefore is the anger of the LORD kindled against His people, and He has stretched forth His hand against them, and has smitten them: and the hills did tremble, and their carcases were torn in the midst of the streets. For all this His anger is not turned away, but His hand is stretched out still. *(These words imply that God's judgment upon Judah will not be a single stroke, but a continuous smiting, covering some considerable era of time.*

The language used is meant to portray the

coming horror in cataclysmic terms. There is to be no mistake concerning God's intentions.)

26 And He will lift up an ensign to the nations from far, and will hiss unto them from the end of the Earth: and, behold, they shall come with speed swiftly *(these Verses through Verse 30 portray the coming judgment by Babylon)*:

27 None shall be weary nor stumble among them; none shall slumber nor sleep; neither shall the girdle of their loins be loosed, nor the latchet of their shoes be broken *(the metaphor is meant to describe the power and fierceness of the attack of the enemy)*:

28 Whose arrows are sharp, and all their bows bent, their horses' hoofs shall be counted like flint, and their wheels like a whirlwind *(the Holy Spirit, looking ahead some 150 years into the future, would proclaim by Prophecy to Isaiah the coming judgment; all of this was given at this time in order that Judah might turn and repent; but sadly they did not, because they would not!)*:

29 Their roaring shall be like a lion, they shall roar like young lions: yea, they shall roar, and lay hold of the prey, and shall carry it away safe, and none shall deliver it. *(Again, this is meant to denote the fierceness of the intruder.)*

30 And in that day they shall roar against them like the roaring of the sea: and if one look unto the land, behold darkness and sorrow, and the light is darkened in the Heavens thereof. *("In that day" when the judgment proceeds and Judah looks to her own self for deliverance, she will behold nothing but "darkness and sorrow."*

Judah's only help was God. Without Him, they had no hope. It is the same presently with individual Believers.)

CHAPTER 6
(760 B.C.)
ISAIAH'S VISION AND COMMISSION

I N the year that king Uzziah died I saw also the LORD sitting upon a Throne, high and lifted up, and His train filled the temple. *(That which Isaiah saw, Who is Jehovah, was actually a preincarnate appearance of the Lord Jesus Christ, and is declared so by the Holy Spirit in Jn. 12:37-41. It places Jehovah, Jesus the Saviour, in the midst of guilty and lost men, just as He is seen at Golgotha, for there they crucified two thieves with Him, placing Him in their midst.*

It is believed that king Uzziah died in 759 B.C.)

2 Above it stood the Seraphims: each one had six wings; with twain he covered his face, and with twain he covered his feet, and with twain he did fly. *(The word "Seraphim" means "fiery ones." This is the only mention of these celestial beings in Scripture. These Seraphim were stationed above the Throne of God and appear to have led in Divine Worship.*

In the light of the Throne, Isaiah learned that he was a moral leper, that his people were moral lepers, and that they altogether were as vile as king Uzziah.

If the sinless Seraphim, in the Presence of the Thrice-Holy Lord of Hosts, had to veil both their faces and their feet, then how hopeless was it for a moral leper such as Isaiah to stand in such a light!)

3 And one cried unto another, and said, Holy, holy, holy, is the LORD of Hosts: the whole Earth is full of His glory. *(The phrase, "one cried," means "kept crying." Day and night they are saying, "Holy, Holy, Holy." The triple repetition of "Holy, Holy, Holy" has been understood in all ages of the Church as connected with the Doctrine of the Trinity.)*

4 And the posts of the door moved at the voice of him who cried, and the house was filled with smoke. *(First of all, let us look at the energy of the worship conducted here. So vigorous was this act that the thresholds of the Divine Temple shook, and the Holy Place was filled with smoke.)*

5 Then said I, Woe is me! for I am undone; because I am a man of unclean lips, and I dwell in the midst of a people of unclean lips: for my eyes have seen the King, the LORD of Hosts. *(In Chpt. 5, Isaiah had pronounced six "Woes!" upon Judah; now he pronounces one on himself!*

The sinless King of this Verse is to be contrasted with the leprous king of Verse 1.

The word "undone" means "justly doomed to death." Such thought is the product of true Repentance. What Isaiah saw produced in him a deep feeling of unworthiness.)

6 Then flew one of the Seraphims unto me, having a live coal in his hand, which he had taken with the tongs from off the Altar *(Isaiah needed a cleansing and a covering of his sin. The living coal from off the Altar of Burnt Offering, symbolizing the fire of the Wrath of God and the Blood of the Lamb of God, when brought in contact with his "unclean lips," removed his iniquity and expiated his sin.*

The "Altar" represented Calvary, to which sinful man be exposed before he can be cleansed and saved. The essence of true conviction is a

deep overwhelming concern over what I am, not so much what I have done or not done. It is more important what man is than what he has done, and man is a sinner.

Genuine moral cleansing must be carried out in the heart of the sinner in order to be saved, and that can only be accomplished by Faith in the shed Blood of Christ, of which this was a symbol [Rom. 3:24-25; Heb. 9:22; I Pet. 1:18-23; I Jn. 1:7-9]):

7 And he laid it upon my mouth, and said, Lo, this has touched your lips; and your iniquity is taken away, and your sin purged. *(There is no other way to be cleansed and expiated than through the Wrath of God and the Atoning Blood of Christ. These are revealed and glorified at Calvary. There, God judged sin infinitely and eternally in the Person of Christ, and His Precious Blood shed there is the one and only and perfect expiation for cleansing of sin.)*

8 Also I heard the voice of the Lord, saying, Whom shall I send, and who will go for Us? Then said I, Here am I; send me. *(As in the case of Saul of Tarsus on the road to Damascus [Acts, Chpt. 9], true conversion manifested itself here in surrender and activity.*

The pronoun "Us" suggests the Trinity.)

9 And He said, Go, and tell this people, Hear ye indeed, but understand not; and see ye indeed, but perceive not. *(The command was, "Go, and tell.")*

10 Make the heart of this people fat, and make their ears heavy, and shut their eyes; lest they see with their eyes, and hear with their ears, and understand with their heart, and convert, and be healed. *(Isaiah is commanded to effect, by his preaching, that which his preaching would in fact bring about. It would not awaken the people out of their apathy; it would not stir them to Repentance. Instead, it would only harden and deaden them. These words have a national as well as an individual application.*

He was commanded to "Go," but yet he is told that there will be no favorable response.)

11 Then said I, Lord, how long? And He answered, Until the cities be wasted without inhabitant, and the houses without man, and the land be utterly desolate. *(The answer to the question of this Verse is found in Rom. 11:25. It is faith alone that could ask this question. This blindness will rest on Israel's heart until the consummation of the judgment inflicted on her.)*

12 And the LORD have removed men far away, and there be a great forsaking in the midst of the land. *(This was fulfilled in totality.*

In A.D. 70, Israel was totally destroyed, with millions of Jews scattered all over the world, and remaining in that posture until 1948.)*

13 But yet in it shall be a tenth, and it shall return, and shall be eaten: as a teil tree, and as an oak, whose substance is in them, when they cast their leaves: so the holy seed shall be the substance thereof. *(The meaning of the first part of this Verse is that if there be only a tenth of the population left in the country, then this, too, shall be destined to further judgment and destruction. Yet there is a Holy Promise in this Passage!*

The "teil tree" and the "oak tree" are types of trees which shoot up again from the stump after being cut down. There will remain a "holy seed" that will be hidden, a living root cherished by Israel's faithful God, and the day will come when that root will spring up into a greater and fairer tree than it ever was in the past [Rom. 11:16-18, 23-27].)

CHAPTER 7
(742 B.C.)
THE ALLIANCE OF SYRIA AND ISRAEL AGAINST JUDAH

AND it came to pass in the days of Ahaz the son of Jotham, the son of Uzziah, king of Judah, that Rezin the king of Syria, and Pekah the son of Remaliah, king of Israel, went up toward Jerusalem to war against it, but could not prevail against it. *(Ahaz was one of the most wicked kings who reigned in Judah, yet God would repeatedly speak to him, endeavoring to bring him to Repentance, but without success.*

Pekah, the king of the Northern Kingdom of Israel, had the last prosperous reign in the ten-Tribe Kingdom of Israel. It began two years before Uzziah died and continued to the third year of the reign of Ahaz.

Rezin and Pekah desired to place on the throne of Judah a person in whom they could thoroughly depend. It was not really their design to conquer Judah, but only to change the king. But the Holy Spirit says, "They could not prevail against it.")

2 And it was told the House of David, saying, Syria is confederate with Ephraim *(another name for the Northern Kingdom of Israel)*. And his heart was moved, and the heart of his people, as the trees of the wood are moved with the wind. *(The statement, "it was told the House of David," refers to the Promises that God made to David concerning his*

lineage continuing on the Throne unto the coming of the Messiah. Even though Judah completely lost her way and was taken over by the Babylonians, still, the Throne was preserved exactly as predicted.)

GOD'S PROMISE OF DELIVERANCE
TO AHAZ

3 Then said the LORD unto Isaiah, Go forth now to meet Ahaz, you, and Shearjashub your son, at the end of the conduit of the upper pool in the highway of the fuller's field *(Isaiah's child was to accompany him as a symbol in order that his name might carry a message of judgment and grace to the heart of king Ahaz. The little boy's name is "Shearjashub," which means "a remnant shall return." It is thought that the Lord had told Isaiah by Revelation to give his son this name; it was given in order to testify of his faith, both in the threats and in the promises of which he had been made the mouthpiece);*

4 And say unto him, Take heed, and be quiet; fear not, neither be fainthearted for the two tails of these smoking firebrands, for the fierce anger of Rezin with Syria, and of the son of Remaliah. *(To an energetic, warlike, and capable monarch like Ahaz, king of the Southern Kingdom of Judah, the injunction to do nothing but believe was both trying and irritating.*

To predict the destruction of both the Northern Kingdom of Israel and Syria within 65 years was the purpose of this Prophecy.

Also, to call the king of Israel merely "the son of Remaliah" was a sign of contempt by the Lord.)

5 Because Syria, Ephraim, and the son of Remaliah, have taken evil counsel against you, saying,

6 Let us go up against Judah, and vex it, and let us make a breach therein for us, and set a king in the midst of it, even the son of Tabeal *(the Scripture does not say who the son of Tabeal was, but no doubt he was a prince chosen by the kings of Syria and Ephraim to be king of Jerusalem and, thereby, their servant. This was the effort of Satan to do away with the lineage of David and replace him with their own king. Satan's design was to foil the Prophecy given to David concerning the Messiah coming through his family [II Sam. 7:12, 16].*

In fact, until Judah was taken captive by Babylon nearly 200 years later, David's heirs continued to occupy the throne; however, even though David's house no longer occupied the

throne after the Babylonian captivity, because there was no throne, the lineage continued. So Satan's attempt was foiled):

7 Thus saith the Lord GOD, It shall not stand, neither shall it come to pass. *(Actually, the statement says, "The Lord Jehovah declares it shall not stand," meaning that the plans of Syria and Israel against Judah would not succeed.)*

8 For the head of Syria is Damascus, and the head of Damascus is Rezin; and within threescore and five years shall Ephraim be broken, that it be not a people.

9 And the head of Ephraim is Samaria, and the head of Samaria is Remaliah's son. If you will not believe, surely you shall not be established. *(The implication here is that Syria and Ephraim [Israel] have merely human heads — the one, Rezin; the other, Pekah — but Judah, it is implied, has a Divine Head, even Jehovah.*

Ahaz is given an opportunity to believe God and turn loose of the frail "arm of flesh" on which he was prone to trust. Yet the offer was given by the Lord in a somewhat negative way, since the Lord knew the evil heart of king Ahaz.

Distrust of this promise would lead him to take steps which would not tend to "establish" him, but would make his position even more insecure [II Ki. 16:7-18; II Chron. 28:16-20].)

10 Moreover the LORD spoke again unto Ahaz, saying,

11 Ask thee a sign of the LORD your God; ask it either in the depth, or in the height above. *(Ahaz had no faith in God, so he would not ask for a sign. He really desired to have help from Assyria and, thereby, to continue in idolatry [II Ki. 16:7-8].)*

12 But Ahaz said, I will not ask, neither will I tempt the LORD. *(Such is "the flesh." It refuses a sign when offered one and demands a sign when refused one [Mk. 8:12].)*

SIGN OF THE VIRGIN BIRTH;
IMMANUEL: GOD WITH US

13 And he said, Hear ye now, O house of David; Is it a small thing for you to weary men, but will you weary my God also? *(To "weary" a man is to doubt his promises. Ahaz is in such a weak spiritual condition that he neither realizes nor understands the threat of Satan. It is not against Ahaz only, but also against the "House of David." Evil men are conspiring to move the "House of David.")*

14 Therefore the Lord Himself shall give you a sign; Behold, a virgin shall conceive, and bear a son, and shall call His Name Immanuel. *(Without a doubt, this Prophecy is one of the greatest, if not the greatest, in the Bible.*

In Hebrew, the word "virgin" is "haalmah," which means "the virgin — the only one that ever was or ever will be a mother in this way."

The "Son" Who would be born would be the "Son of God." The word "Immanuel" means "God with us." Such was fulfilled in Christ.

This Prophecy was given by God as a rebuttal to the efforts of Satan working through the kings of Syria and Israel to unseat Ahaz. In other words, their efforts to make void the Promise of God given to David would come to naught.)

15 Butter and honey shall he eat, that he may know to refuse the evil, and choose the good. *(The Prophecy actually was twofold: first of all, Isaiah's little son, a mere suckling of a child who was then present, served as the immediate sign. That sign pertained to the destruction of the kings of Syria and Ephraim, which would take place about 3 years later.*

The greater part of the Prophecy concerned the virgin-born Child, Who would be born about 750 years later, Who in effect would be the Messiah.)

16 For before the child shall know to refuse the evil, and choose the good, the land that you abhor shall be forsaken of both her kings. *(The prediction here is that the two kings of Syria and Israel will be killed. This happened, as stated, about 3 years later [II Ki. 15:30].)*

INVASION OF JUDAH BY ASSYRIA

17 The LORD shall bring upon you, and upon your people, and upon your father's house, days that have not come, from the day that Ephraim departed from Judah; even the king of Assyria. *(God, Who could read Ahaz's heart and its plans, addressed to him personally the message of this Verse. He tells him plainly that great as were the miseries suffered by the kingdoms since the disruption [the separation of Israel and Judah], they would be exceeded by those now about to come.)*

18 And it shall come to pass in that day, that the LORD shall hiss for the fly that is in the uttermost part of the rivers of Egypt, and for the bee that is in the land of Assyria. *(The phrase, "in that day," does not pertain here to the Millennium, as it often does, but speaks of Assyria and Egypt invading Judah.)*

19 And they shall come, and shall rest all of them in the desolate valleys, and in the holes of the rocks, and upon all thorns, and upon all bushes. *(The colorful description characterizes the totality of the overflowing army respecting its invasion of Judah.)*

20 In the same day shall the Lord shave with a razor that is hired, namely, by them beyond the river, by the king of Assyria, the head, and the hair of the feet: and it shall also consume the beard. *(All of this refers to total destruction upon Judah.)*

21 And it shall come to pass in that day, that a man shall nourish a young cow, and two sheep;

22 And it shall come to pass, for the abundance of milk that they shall give he shall eat butter: for butter and honey shall every one eat who is left in the land. *(At first glance, these Passages seem to indicate abundance; however, they are really denoting poverty.*

In his inscriptions, Tiglath-Pileser, the Assyria king, mentions his carrying off many thousands of horned cattle and sheep from the countries which he overran or conquered, which refers to these two Verses.)

23 And it shall come to pass in that day, that every place shall be, where there were a thousand vines at a thousand silverlings, it shall even be for briers and thorns. *(The general meaning seems to be that not even the best vineyards would be cultivated at that time [after the invasion of Assyria], but would lie in waste and grow only "briers and thorns.")*

24 With arrows and with bows shall men come thither; because all the land shall become briers and thorns. *(The references are to the land being depopulated because of war and its population being taken as slaves; therefore, desolation will rule.*

What a sad commentary on the land that once flowed with "milk and honey"; a land that was God's choice land; a land that was the joy of the whole Earth. All of this was because of sin.)

25 And on all hills that shall be dug with the mattock, there shall not come thither the fear of briers and thorns: but it shall be for the sending forth of oxen, and for the treading of lesser cattle. *(The sense of this Verse is that the "briers and thorns" will be so thick in some areas of Judah that it will be difficult for one to even walk. Men will send their cattle into these places, as they alone will be able to penetrate such a congestion without harm.)*

CHAPTER 8

(742 B.C.)

INVASION OF SYRIA AND ISRAEL BY ASSYRIA; THE PROPHETIC NAMES OF ISAIAH'S SONS

MOREOVER the LORD said unto me, Take thee a great roll, and write in it with a man's pen concerning Maher-shal'al-hash-baz. *(Isaiah was to write upon the roll that he was to have another son, and that this little boy was to be a sign to Israel. His name, which is the longest in the Bible, literally means "plunder speeds, spoil hastens."*

The tablet posted in a conspicuous place was to be read by all.)

2 And I took unto me faithful witnesses to record, Uriah the Priest, and Zechariah the son of Jeberechiah. *(Uriah the High Priest was Ahaz's colleague in idolatry [II Ki. 16:16]. Him attaching his signature to the tablet predicting the birth of Isaiah's symbolic child made the denial of the circumstances of the birth and its prediction impossible.*

All of this shows that association with Godliness does not guarantee Godliness. Uriah the High Priest is intimately associated here with one of the greatest Prophets who ever lived, namely Isaiah, yet he would know none of Isaiah's Righteousness.)

3 And I went unto the Prophetess; and she conceived, and bore a son. Then said the LORD to me, Call his name Maher-shal'al-hash-baz. *(Even though the term "the Prophetess" does not necessarily mean here that the wife of Isaiah uttered Prophecies, still, more than likely, the Lord did use her in this capacity.)*

4 For before the child shall have knowledge to cry, My father, and my mother, the riches of Damascus and the spoil of Samaria shall be taken away before the king of Assyria. *(All of this was fulfilled a little bit short of two years after it was uttered. Even though the Scripture does not record this foray into Samaria, still, the inscriptions of Tiglath-Pileser, the Assyrian king, supplied the deficiency. They state that this monarch "sent the population, the goods of the people of Beth-Omri, and their furniture to the land of Assyria." This place was Samaria, i.e., "Israel.")*

5 The LORD spoke also unto me again, saying *(in view of the pointed and direct Prophecies of Isaiah given to him by the Lord, there was no excuse for Judah's continued rebellion against God. Proper Repentance on the part of Ahaz*

and Judah would have secured the help of the Lord rather than His judgment),

6 Forasmuch as this people refuses the waters of Shiloah that go softly, and rejoice in Rezin and Remaliah's son *(in essence, the Lord is saying that inasmuch as the Northern Kingdom of Israel preferred the Syrians, He would give them even more, the Assyrians; however, it would not be a pleasant trip.*

The waters "that go softly" speak of Christ, as the "river strong and many" of Assyria speaks of Satan.

As well, Verses 7 and 8 also point forward to the time in the future when the Assyrian, i.e., the Antichrist, will conquer Immanuel's land [Dan. 11:45]);

7 Now therefore, behold, the Lord brings up upon them the waters of the river, strong and many, even the king of Assyria, and all his glory: and he shall come up over all his channels, and go over all his banks *("the river" is the Euphrates. The overflow of the latter portion of the Verse speaks not only of the coming invasion by the Assyrians of Judah, but also looks forward to the coming Antichrist, who will attempt to completely destroy Israel):*

JUDAH INVADED ALSO

8 And he shall pass through Judah; he shall overflow and go over, he shall reach even to the neck; and the stretching out of his wings shall fill the breadth of your land, O Immanuel. *(This Prophecy as well has not only a near meaning, but also reaches into the far distant future of the Antichrist. The use of the word "Immanuel" speaks of the Antichrist, who will attempt to make this land his land. He will fail!*

The statement, "He shall reach even to the neck," refers to the Assyrian attack stopping short of destroying Judah. The flood shall not submerge the head, but only rise as high as the neck. This was fulfilled under Hezekiah, when the Assyrians took most of Judah, but failed to take Jerusalem, the head.)

FALSE AND TRUE DEPENDENCE

9 Associate yourselves, O ye people, and you shall be broken in pieces; and give ear, all you of far countries: gird yourselves, and you shall be broken in pieces; gird yourselves, and you shall be broken in pieces. *("Give ear, all you of far countries" refers to the outlying nations that are to witness the discomfiture of*

the Assyrian boast [II Chron. 32:21-23]. The Prophecy was fulfilled exactly as the Lord spoke through Isaiah.)

10 Take counsel together, and it shall come to nought; speak the word, and it shall not stand: for God is with us. (No matter how clever the plan of the opposition against God's People, such would come to naught.)

11 For the LORD spoke thus to me with a strong hand, and instructed me that I should not walk in the way of this people, saying (it was not merely idolatry against which Isaiah was warned, but that the whole spirit and tone of the society of his day was in conflict with Jehovah),

12 Say ye not, A confederacy, to all them to whom this people shall say, A confederacy; neither fear ye their fear, nor be afraid. (The word "ye" implies a transition from the singular to the plural. It implies that Isaiah did not stand totally alone, but had at least some followers, a "little flock."

The idea of the Verse is that the majority of the people favored an alliance with Assyria and, therefore, would accuse Isaiah and others of treason who did not support this cause, but in effect proclaimed trust in the Lord.)

13 Sanctify the LORD of Hosts Himself; and let Him be your fear, and let Him be your dread. (God is "sanctified" by being trusted [Num. 20:12]. These who feared Rezin of Syria and Pekah of Samaria, despite God's assurances that their designs should fail, did not believe in Him, and so did not "sanctify" Him.)

14 And He shall be for a Sanctuary; but for a Stone of stumbling and for a Rock of offence to both the houses of Israel, for a gin and for a snare to the inhabitants of Jerusalem. (A "Sanctuary" is a refuge, and something more. It is a Holy Refuge, a place which is a refuge because of its holiness.

The Prophecy is that both the "houses" of Israel and Judah would ultimately forsake Jehovah and find in Him a "snare" and a "Rock of offense."

As well, it is a direct Prophecy of the coming of the Messiah and His Ministry in Israel.

Christ is the "Sanctuary" to those who will believe Him — a place of safety. He would also be the "Stone of stumbling" and the "Rock of offense.")

15 And many among them shall stumble, and fall, and be broken, and be snared, and be taken. (This refers to Israel's destruction by Titus in A.D. 70.)

16 Bind up the Testimony, seal the Law

among My disciples. (These Words are still those of Jehovah and are addressed to His servant, Isaiah.

God commands that the Prophecy shall be written on a Scroll, which is then to be carefully tied with a string and sealed for future use. It is yet for an appointed time to be fulfilled.)

17 And I will wait upon the LORD, Who hides His face from the House of Jacob, and I will look for Him.

18 Behold, I and the children whom the LORD has given me are for signs and for wonders in Israel from the LORD of hosts, which dwells in Mount Zion. (The phrase, "from the LORD of hosts, which dwells in Mount Zion," means that God had not left Zion. The Shechinah still rested between the Cherubim and the Holy of Holies. While this is so, God is still with His People — "Immanuel." Sadly, Judah took little advantage of the Glory and Grace that were in their midst.)

19 And when they shall say unto you, Seek unto them that have familiar spirits, and unto wizards that peep, and that mutter: should not a people seek unto their God? for the living to the dead? (Isaiah was speaking of those in Judah who were attempting to contact departed loved ones and claiming communication with the dead.

The question is: should not these individuals seek a Living God rather than dead people?)

20 To the Law and to the Testimony: if they speak not according to this Word, it is because there is no light in them. (The great question should always be, and about any situation, "Is it Biblical?")

21 And they shall pass through it, hardly bestead and hungry: and it shall come to pass, that when they shall be hungry, they shall fret themselves, and curse their king and their God, and look upward. (The prediction is that Judah would not blame themselves for their problems, but would rather blame God.)

22 And they shall look unto the Earth; and behold trouble and darkness, dimness of anguish; and they shall be driven to darkness. (This "darkness" refers here to demon spirits.)

CHAPTER 9
(771 B.C.)

THE PROMISE OF THE COMING MESSIAH

NEVERTHELESS the dimness shall not be such as was in her vexation, when at the first He lightly afflicted the land of Zebulun

and the land of Naphtali, and afterward did more grievously afflict her by the way of the sea, beyond Jordan, in Galilee of the nations. *(The translation from the Hebrew to the English is thought by some Scholars not to have been as sufficient as it could have been.*

The major weakness in the translation of this Verse seems to be the latter part where it says, "and afterward did more grievously afflict her." This should have been translated, "So, in the latter time, He has brought honor on the way of the sea."

Actually, the "way of the sea" has reference to the "Sea of Galilee," where Christ carried out most of His Ministry.

The "Galilee of the nations" refers to the district where the far greater number of His Miracles were performed.)

2 The people who walked in darkness have seen a great light: they who dwell in the land of the shadow of death, upon them has the light shined. *(To the end of this Verse the Prophecy concerns itself with the First Advent. As well, Verses 1 and 2 were quoted by Matthew concerning Christ [Mat. 4:15-16].*

The "darkness" spoken of here is called "the shadow of death." Such pictures acute bondage. The only panacea for this "darkness" is the "great light" of Christ.

This powerful Passage closes with the Word, "upon them has the light shined." How many are there in the world who do not fall into this category? How many are there who have never seen any "light"?

How many?)

3 You have multiplied the nation, and not increased the joy: they joy before you according to the joy in harvest, and as men rejoice when they divide the spoil. *(The basic intent of this Verse pertains to Israel's coming rejection of the Lord Jesus Christ. They saw the "great light," but would not accept the "great light," and in fact crucified their Lord.*

At the coming of Christ, the nation truly was "multiplied"; however, the "joy" was not increased, because the religious leadership of Israel rejected Christ. They could have had tremendous "joy," but they refused the Giver of joy and lost their way.)

4 For you have broken the yoke of his burden, and the staff of his shoulder, the rod of his oppressor, as in the day of Midian. *(When Christ came, He would break the yoke of Satan off their shoulders, at least for those who would believe. The "yoke" addressed here is sin. The*

"oppressor" is the prince of darkness, who had well nigh brought all mankind under his dominion when Christ came.)

5 For every battle of the warrior is with confused noise, and garments rolled in blood; but this shall be with burning and fuel of fire. *(The Holy Spirit is telling Judah here to take their eyes off of military power, and look to the Lord. He Alone holds the answer!)*

6 For unto us a Child is born, unto us a Son is given: and the Government shall be upon His Shoulder: and His Name shall be called Wonderful, Counsellor, The Mighty God, The Everlasting Father, The Prince of Peace. *(This glorious Promise pertains not only to the First Advent, but to the Second Advent, as well.*

The pronoun "us" refers to Israel. From the Seed of Abraham, which spawned the Jewish people, and hence ultimately the Messiah, the greatest Promise of all time would finally be fulfilled.

The phrase, "Government on His Shoulder," refers to the coming Kingdom Age, when Christ will rule and reign over the entirety of the Earth [Dan. 7:13-14; I Cor. 15:24-28; Rev. 11:15; 20:4-10].)

7 Of the increase of His Government and peace there shall be no end, upon the throne of David, and upon His Kingdom, to order it, and to establish it with judgment and with justice from henceforth even for ever. The zeal of the LORD of Hosts will perform this. *(The last phrase guarantees that what the Lord has promised, He will perform.*

The first part of this Verse has reference to the fact that there will not be an immediate subjugation of the Earth upon the Lord's return, but that the Messiah's Kingdom shall ever increase more and more until it ultimately fills the world.)

JUDGMENT ON ISRAEL

8 The Lord sent a word into Jacob, and it has lighted upon Israel. *(The Holy Spirit here resumes the history of the nation from Chpt. 5.*

At the close of Chpt. 5, the national history is interrupted in order to introduce the Messiah, for He was to spring out of Judah, that is, out of the Southern Kingdom.

The last section of this Prophecy [10:33; 12:6] presents the Messiah destroying the Antichrist and establishing the Kingdom of God in the Earth.)

9 And all the people shall know, even Ephraim and the inhabitant of Samaria, who say in the pride and stoutness of heart *(in this Passage, we find the cause of Israel's sin and*

rebellion against the Lord; the sin was "pride"; such is the foundation of all sin),

10 The bricks are fallen down, but we will build with hewn stones: the sycomores are cut down, but we will change them into cedars. *(In this Verse, we have the defiance of the people against the judgments of God.*

In effect, they are saying, "We have suffered moderate damage, but we will more than make up for it; we will replace all our losses with something better.")

11 Therefore the LORD shall set up the adversaries of Rezin against him, and join his enemies together *(the "adversaries" of Rezin, king of Damascus, were the Assyrians.*

The pronoun "him" refers to Israel [Ephraim].

The "joining of the enemies together," which meant in opposition to Israel, was, in effect, the Lord's "confederation");

12 The Syrians before, and the Philistines behind; and they shall devour Israel with open mouth. For all this His anger is not turned away, but His hand is stretched out still. *(This speaks of the Syrians coming from the east and the Philistines coming from the west.*

The "stretched out hand" refers to either mercy or judgment. If they had repented, the judgment would have ceased. Inasmuch as they continued impenitent, the "hand" was "stretched out," not to save, but to smite.)

13 For the people turned not unto Him Who smote them, neither do they seek the LORD of Hosts. *("Conversion," i.e., "turning around," ensures blessing, and speaks of Repentance; to refuse to turn around makes wrath certain.*

Israel set herself to seek after Baal from the time of Ahab [I Ki. 16:31]. The reform of Jehu [II Ki. 10:28] had gone but skin-deep, for Baal was still "sought to" rather than Jehovah, when the final judgment came [II Ki. 17:16; Hos. 2:13].)

14 Therefore the LORD will cut off from Israel head and tail, branch and rush, in one day. *(This colorful expression refers to the whole nation, from the highest to the lowest.)*

15 The ancient and honourable, he is the head; and the prophet who teaches lies, he is the tail.

16 For the leaders of this people cause them to err; and they who are led of them are destroyed. *("Leaders" in Verse 16 should read "flatterers"; these are the prophets of Verse 15. Like many Preachers of the present day, they flatter their congregations by preaching what the people like to hear instead of what God said.)*

THE EVIL CONSEQUENCES OF SIN

17 Therefore the Lord shall have no joy in their young men, neither shall have mercy on their fatherless and widows: for every one is an hypocrite and an evildoer, and every mouth speaks folly. For all this His anger is not turned away, but His hand is stretched out still. *(The phrase, "His hand is stretched out still," is found some five times in the Book of Isaiah. It indicates that God's Anger is still strong and that His People had not responded to mercy or judgment; therefore, other judgments would have to come [5:25; 9:12, 17, 21; 10:4]. Each time a series of punishments is mentioned, it ends with this statement.)*

18 For wickedness burns as the fire: it shall devour the briers and thorns, and shall kindle in the thickets of the forest, and they shall mount up like the lifting up of smoke. *(As the "wickedness" is total, likewise, the judgment will be total!)*

19 Through the wrath of the LORD of Hosts is the land darkened, and the people shall be as the fuel of the fire: no man shall spare his brother. *(The "land darkened" is not used in this fashion elsewhere in Scripture. The light they rejected will now turn to darkness.)*

20 And he shall snatch on the right hand, and be hungry; and he shall eat on the left hand, and they shall not be satisfied: they shall eat every man the flesh of his own arm *(this Passage refers to the spirit and lust for blood that is permeating the entirety of the land; it is a time of looting, stealing, robbing, and murder, even of one's neighbors, as Israel had never seen):*

21 Manasseh, Ephraim; and Ephraim, Manasseh: and they together shall be against Judah. For all this His anger is not turned away, but His hand is stretched out still. *(These two are mentioned as the two principal Tribes of the Northern Kingdom [I Chron. 9:3; II Chron. 30:1]. The meaning is that they would fight each other and then "join together against Judah.")*

CHAPTER 10
(713 B.C.)
SINS OF LEADERS

WOE unto them who decree unrighteous decrees, and who write grievousness which they have prescribed;

2 To turn aside the needy from judgment, and to take away the right from the poor of

My people, that widows may be their prey, and that they may rob the fatherless! *(The Holy Spirit in these two Verses calls attention to the perversion of justice. The "poor" and the "widows" who were helpless were the classes who were the chief sufferers of this perversion of justice, and all caused by the declension of the spiritual leaders.*

They were very careful to be legal in their doings, but the Lord truly saw their hearts and His answer was, "Woe unto them!")

JUDGMENT ON SIN

3 And what will you do in the day of visitation, and in the desolation which shall come from far? to whom will you flee for help? and where will you leave your glory? *(The "day of visitation" referred to the coming Judgment. Then there will be no one to help; the Lord through the Prophet is speaking of these religious leaders.)*

4 Without Me they shall bow down under the prisoners, and they shall fall under the slain. For all this His anger is not turned away, but His hand is stretched out still. *(The feebleness and misery of these unrighteous magistrates portrayed in Verses 1 and 2 are vividly pictured by viewing them as bowing down even to prisoners and falling before deadly, wounded men.*

The Lord is saying that these "crooks" will have nowhere to flee, unless they shall crouch amid the captives who are being carried off or fall amid the slain.

The final phrase of this Fourth Verse is used several times by the Holy Spirit to denote the serious and severity of the situation.)

ASSYRIA, GOD'S ROD OF CHASTENING ON ISRAEL: ASSYRIA'S JUDGMENT FORETOLD

5 O Assyrian, the rod of My anger, and the staff in their hand is My indignation. *(A new Prophecy begins with this Verse. Assyria, after being God's instrument to punish Israel, shall herself be punished in turn.)*

6 I will send him against an hypocritical nation, and against the people of My wrath will I give him a charge, to take the spoil, and to take the prey, and to tread them down like the mire of the streets. *(The "hypocritical nation" mentioned here is Ephraim, sometimes referred to as Samaria, or Israel, which was the ten-Tribe Northern Kingdom.)*

7 Howbeit he means not so, neither does his heart think so; but it is in his heart to destroy and cut off nations not a few. *(The monuments record that "the nations not a few" that the Assyrian leader proposed to cut off were the Egyptians, the Libyans, and the Ethiopians. He believed himself to be a free agent, but it is shown here that he was but an instrument in the Hands of God. He exalted himself and meant to go beyond what God charged him to do; therefore, God destroyed him.)*

8 For he said, Are not my princes altogether kings? *(One mark of the superiority of Assyria to other countries was to be seen in the fact that her king had not mere officers, but vassal kings, under him, hence, the title "king of kings" assumed by so many Assyrian Monarchs.)*

9 Is not Calno as Carchemish? is not Hamath as Arpad? is not Samaria as Damascus? *(This Verse should read, "Is not Calno as much mine as Carchemish?")*

10 As my hand has found the kingdoms of the idols, and whose graven images did excel them of Jerusalem and of Samaria *(it is quite in accordance with Syrian ideas that the conquered countries should be called "kingdoms of the idols" [literally, "no gods"]. The Assyrian Monarchs regarded their own gods alone as really deserving of the name. Consequently, they made war very much with the object of proving the superiority of their deities over those of their neighbors — hence, their practice of carrying off the idols from the various cities which they conquered, or else of inscribing on them "the praises of Asshur");*

11 Shall I not, as I have done unto Samaria and her idols, so do to Jerusalem and her idols? *(This Prophecy was probably uttered during the reign of Ahaz, when that wicked king and all Judah had turned to idols, which was about 30 years before the Assyrian invasion. This Prophecy attests the inspiration of the Bible. No political forecast, however clever, could predict with such minuteness the actions and words of a king these years beforehand.)*

12 Wherefore it shall come to pass, that when the Lord has performed His whole work upon Mount Zion and on Jerusalem, I will punish the fruit of the stout heart of the king of Assyria, and the glory of his high looks. *(The "work" assigned to Assyria by the Lord was the destruction of the Northern Kingdom of Israel, and a share in the trial, punishment, and discipline of Judah. The last task seems to have been the humiliation of Manasseh, which brought*

about his Repentance [II Chron. 33:11-13].

However, the king of Assyria overstepped his bounds, and so the Lord promised to destroy him, which He ultimately did.)

13 For he said, By the strength of my hand I have done it, and by my wisdom; for I am prudent: and I have removed the bounds of the people, and have robbed their treasures, and I have put down the inhabitants like a valiant man *(the vainglorious language of the Assyrian king corresponds with that found on the monuments; this is one of the numberless, undesigned testimonies to the antiquity and truthfulness of the Book of Isaiah):*

14 And my hand has found as a nest the riches of the people: and as one gathers eggs that are left, have I gathered all the Earth; and there was none that moved the wing, or opened the mouth, or peeped. *(The Assyrians were fond of comparing their enemies to birds. The word "peeped" refers to the inhabitants of these particular nations who offered not so much as even a feeble resistance that a bird would make when its nest is robbed.)*

15 Shall the axe boast itself against him who hews therewith? or shall the saw magnify itself against him who shakes it? as if the rod should shake itself against them who lift it up, or as if the staff should lift up itself, as if it were no wood. *(For Assyria to assert herself as if she were independent of God is like a rod attempting to sway the hand that holds it.)*

16 Therefore shall the Lord, the Lord of Hosts, send among his fat ones leanness; and under his glory he shall kindle a burning like the burning of a fire. *(In this Passage, the Lord says that the glory and pride of the king of Assyria shall be destroyed like a great fire consuming the fuel.)*

17 And the light of Israel shall be for a fire, and his Holy One for a flame: and it shall burn and devour his thorns and his briers in one day *(the "Light of Israel" is a Messianic title. The phrase, "In one day," refers to the destroying by an Angel of the Lord of 185,000 of Assyria's best soldiers, and all in one day. Therefore, it came to pass exactly as prophesied [II Ki. 19:35]. Israel's [Judah's] "Light" was not an idol made of stone or wood, but instead was Jehovah);*

18 And shall consume the glory of his forest, and of his fruitful field, both soul and body: and they shall be as when a standardbearer faints. *(Here it is predicted about 30 years beforehand the manner of the death which struck the Assyrian host at Lachish.)*

19 And the rest of the trees of his forest shall be few, that a child may write them. *(Both Verses 18 and 19 refer to the Angel of the Lord smiting the 185,000 of the Assyrian army in one night and of few being left. Actually, the Prophecy says, and it was carried out, that so few survived that a lad could count them.)*

20 And it shall come to pass in that day, that the remnant of Israel, and such as are escaped of the house of Jacob, shall no more again stay upon him who smote them; but shall stay upon the LORD, the Holy One of Israel, in Truth. *(All of these Passages, beginning with Verse 5, have reference to the Assyrian Monarch, Sennacherib. They will as well have reference to the coming Antichrist.*

The pronoun "him" refers to the Assyrian king. Judah leaned upon him [Sennacherib] in the past, and will lean upon him [Antichrist] in the future, but never again, for she will lean upon the Messiah in Truth, i.e., sincerely. He Alone is Jehovah, the Holy One of Israel.)

21 The remnant shall return, even the remnant of Jacob, unto the Mighty God. *(The Messiah is entitled here "The Mighty God," because He is "The Mighty God."*

The "remnant" refers to the Jews who will be left after the Battle of Armageddon. They will come to the Lord.)

22 For though your people Israel be as the sand of the sea, yet a remnant of them shall return: the consumption decreed shall overflow with righteousness. *(Verses 22 and 23 are exegetical of the term "remnant" and bring out its full force. The Promise had been made to Abraham that his seed should be "like the sand of the sea for multitude" [Gen. 22:17]. This Promise had been fulfilled [I Ki. 4:20], but now the sins of the people would produce a reversal of it. It would be a "remnant," and only a "remnant," of the nation who would escape. Judah, in the time of Hezekiah and in the time of the Coming of the Lord, would have to make a fresh start, as from a new beginning [Ezra 2:64].)*

23 For the Lord GOD of Hosts shall make a consumption, even determined, in the midst of all the land. *(This will take place at the Second Coming.)*

24 Therefore thus saith the Lord GOD of Hosts, O My people who dwell in Zion, be not afraid of the Assyrian: he shall smite you with a rod, and shall lift up his staff against you, after the manner of Egypt. *(This Passage speaks of the invasion of Sennacherib and also of the future invasion of the Antichrist.)*

25 For yet a very little while, and the indignation shall cease, and My anger in their destruction. *(This refers to the coming Great Tribulation, and that it will be only for a very short time in duration.*

The "anger" and "destruction" spoken of here refer to God's "anger" against the Antichrist and God's "destruction" of this evil one.)

26 And the LORD of Hosts shall stir up a scourge for him according to the slaughter of Midian at the rock of Oreb: and as his rod was upon the sea, so shall he lift it up after the manner of Egypt. *(The word "Scourge" should be printed with a capital "S," for it is here a Messianic title. Christ will be a "Scourge" against the Antichrist [II Thess. 2:8].)*

27 And it shall come to pass in that day, that his burden shall be taken away from off your shoulder, and his yoke from off your neck, and the yoke shall be destroyed because of the anointing. *(The words, "because of the anointing," should have been translated "by reason of the appearing of the Anointed One," Christ.)*

28 He is come to Aiath, he is passed to Migron; at Michmash he has laid up his carriages *(in a Passage of magnificent poetic Prophesy in Verses 28 through 32, Isaiah, in a vision, describes the approach of the Antichrist and his hosts against Jerusalem. The march of Sennacherib and his army in the days of Hezekiah was a foreshadowing of this greater future danger):*

29 They are gone over the passage: they have taken up their lodging at Geba; Ramah is afraid; Gibeah of Saul is fled.

30 Lift up your voice, O daughter of Gallim: cause it to be heard unto Laish, O poor Anathoth. *(Anathoth was Jeremiah's birthplace. These too were near Jerusalem, which no doubt the Antichrist will occupy upon his invasion of Jerusalem [Ezek., Chpts. 38-39].)*

31 Madmenah is removed; the inhabitants of Gebim gather themselves to flee. *(These villages were near Jerusalem toward the north. Their inhabitants flee as the Assyrian [Antichrist] approaches.)*

32 As yet shall he remain at Nob that day: he shall shake his hand against the mount of the daughter of Zion, the hill of Jerusalem. *(It is believed that "Nob," which was a city of Priests, and only a few miles from Jerusalem, will be the headquarters of the Antichrist while he is seeking to take Jerusalem [Zech. 14:1-5; Lk. 21:20-24; Rev. 11:1-2]. This is where he will shake his fist at Mount Zion.)*

33 Behold, the Lord, the LORD of hosts, shall lop the bough with terror: and the high ones of stature shall be hewn down, and the haughty shall be humbled. *(The "haughty" speaks of the Antichrist and how he will be "humbled" by the Lord Jesus Christ.)*

34 And He shall cut down the thickets of the forest with iron, and Lebanon shall fall by a Mighty One. *("He" refers to Jehovah. "A Mighty One" refers to the "the Anointed One."*

The word "Lebanon" refers to its great cedar trees, which the Antichrist envisions himself like; however, he will "fall.")

CHAPTER 11
(713 B.C.)
THE RIGHTEOUS REIGN OF THE BRANCH (THE MESSIAH) OUT OF JESSE'S ROOTS

AND there shall come forth a Rod out of the stem of Jesse, and a Branch shall grow out of his roots *(this Verse has to do with the Incarnation, with the balance of the Chapter referring to the glorious reign of Christ during the Millennium. The word "Rod," in this instance, refers to a "tender branch," which means a tender shoot sprouting out of the root of a dead, fallen tree, referring both to humanity in general and Israel in particular. Jesse was David's father, and through this family the Messiah would come; and so He did!):*

2 And the Spirit of the LORD shall rest upon Him *(upon Christ)*, the Spirit of Wisdom and Understanding, the Spirit of Counsel and Might, the Spirit of Knowledge and of the Fear of the LORD *(this proclaims the Perfection of the Holy Spirit in all His attributes listed here resting upon the Messiah);*

3 And shall make Him of quick understanding in the Fear of the LORD: and He shall not judge after the sight of His eyes, neither reprove after the hearing of His ears *(the words, "quick understanding," would probably have been better translated "the breath of His nostrils shall be in the Fear of the LORD." It suggests a disposition instinct with delight in God and fragrant with God [Gen. 8:21]. As a result, His Judgment of all things will be perfect):*

4 But with Righteousness shall He judge the poor, and reprove with equity for the meek of the Earth: and He shall smite the Earth with the rod of His Mouth, and with the breath of His Lips shall He slay the wicked. *(The "smiting of the Earth" might be better stated "the oppressor of the land," referring to the Antichrist.*

The word "reprove" means "to set right with equity" or "to administer justice on behalf of the meek.")

5 And Righteousness shall be the girdle of His loins, and Faithfulness the girdle of His reins. *(This Verse presents Immanuel as Priest. The "loins" speak of the physical, with the "reins" speaking of the heart and, therefore, the spiritual. For the first time, the human family in Christ will witness perfection. In fact, the Man Christ Jesus will be girdled with Perfection.)*

CONDITIONS DURING THE MILLENNIUM

6 The wolf also shall dwell with the lamb, and the leopard shall lie down with the kid; and the calf and the young lion and the fatling together; and a little child shall lead them. *(The character and nature of the planet, including its occupants and even the animal creation, will revert to their posture as before the Fall.)*

7 And the cow and the bear shall feed *(feed together)*; their young ones shall lie down together: and the lion shall eat straw like the ox. *(This Passage plainly tells us that the carnivorous nature of the animal kingdom will be totally and eternally changed.)*

8 And the sucking child shall play on the hole of the asp, and the weaned child shall put his hand on the cockatrice' den. *(Even though some of the curse will remain on the serpent in the Millennium, in that he continues to writhe in the dust, still, the deadly part will be removed [Gen. 3:14].)*

EXTENT OF MESSIAH'S REIGN

9 They shall not hurt nor destroy in all My holy mountain: for the Earth shall be full of the knowledge of the LORD, as the waters cover the sea. *(The "holy mountain" refers to the dwelling place of Christ during the Kingdom Age, which will be Jerusalem. And from that vantage point shall go out the "knowledge of the LORD," which will cover the entirety of the Earth.)*

10 And in that day there shall be a root of Jesse, which shall stand for an ensign of the people; to it shall the Gentiles seek: and His rest shall be glorious. *(The words, "in that day," as in most cases, refer to the Great Tribulation, the Battle of Armageddon, the Second Coming of the Lord, and the coming Kingdom Age.*

The "root of Jesse" refers to David and the Promise made by the Lord to David in II Sam., Chpt. 7.

Hence, Christ is really the "root of Jesse," "the Son of David.")

ISRAEL, GOD'S PEOPLE, TO BE RESTORED

11 And it shall come to pass in that day, that the Lord shall set His hand again the second time to recover the remnant of His people, which shall be left, from Assyria, and from Egypt, and from Pathros, and from Cush, and from Elam, and from Shinar, and from Hamath, and from the islands of the sea. *(Once again, "in that day," refers to Christ reigning Personally in Jerusalem. The first gathering of the "remnant," as it refers to Israel, took place when Israel was gathered out of the Medo-Persian Empire and brought back to the Promised Land. In a sense, the second gathering began in 1948. It will be fulfilled in totality at the beginning of the Kingdom Age, when Jews all over the world will recognize Christ as the their Messiah and, thereby, desire to come to Israel and live near Him.)*

12 And He shall set up an ensign for the nations, and shall assemble the outcasts of Israel, and gather together the dispersed of Judah from the four corners of the Earth. *(Here, Israel is called "outcasts," and they have been such ever since their rejection of Christ and the destruction of Jerusalem by Titus in A.D. 70.*

The central theme of this Verse is Christ. Israel will now [during the Kingdom Age] recognize Him, and Him Alone, as their True Messiah. Jerusalem, the place of His Crucifixion, will now be the place of His Glory. The Jews will come to this Glory from "the four corners of the Earth.")

13 The envy also of Ephraim shall depart, and the adversaries of Judah shall be cut off: Ephraim shall not envy Judah, and Judah shall not vex Ephraim. *(This pertains to the splitting of Israel into two nations, with the ten Tribes forming the Northern Kingdom called "Ephraim," and the two Tribes of "Judah" and "Benjamin" making up the Southern Kingdom. The Holy Spirit is saying that the old "envy" between the two will be forever dissipated. The nation will be one again, but only in Christ.)*

14 But they shall fly upon the shoulders of the Philistines toward the west; they shall spoil them of the east together: they shall lay their hand upon Edom and Moab; and the children of Ammon shall obey them. *(This Passage refers to the long and continued fight over possession of the Promised Land. This Verse*

proclaims the fact that this land that was promised to Israel by the Lord will finally be realized [Gen. 15:7; Num. 34:1-12; Isa. 60:12; Ezek. 47:13; 48:35].)

15 And the LORD shall utterly destroy the tongue of the Egyptian sea; and with His mighty wind shall He shake His hand over the river, and shall smite it in the seven streams, and make men go over dryshod.

16 And there shall be an highway for the remnant of His people, which shall be left, from Assyria; like as it was to Israel in the day that He came up out of the land of Egypt. (From this Passage, it seems that the Euphrates River in that day will be made by the Hand of the Lord into "seven rivers." They very well could turn the Arabian Peninsula, which is now a desert, into a garden.

The whole of this part of the world is presently gripped in the Satanic maw of Islam. The prediction is that not only will the topography of the Middle East be changed, but the demonic control of the region will be dispelled, as well.)

CHAPTER 12
(713 B.C.)
A PSALM OF PRAISE; MILLENNIAL WORSHIP

AND in that day you shall say, O LORD, I will praise You: though You were angry with me, Your anger is turned away, and You comfort me. (Israel is saying that even though the Lord had been "angry" with her because of her Crucifixion of Christ, nevertheless, "Your anger is turned away.")

2 Behold, God is my salvation; I will trust, and not be afraid: for the LORD JEHOVAH is my strength and my song; He also is become my salvation. (A part of this is from the "Song of Moses" [Ex. 15:2]. As Moses sang this song on the shores of the Red Sea after Israel's great Deliverance, Israel, likewise, will once again sing this great "song" and call it "my song." From what looked like certain annihilation at the hands of the Antichrist, she has been delivered, and the Antichrist, like Pharaoh, has been destroyed.)

3 Therefore with joy shall you draw water out of the wells of salvation. (The "wells of salvation" speak of a constant, flowing, neverending source — not a cistern — for unfailing assurance, consolation, hope, and victory.)

4 And in that day shall you say, Praise the LORD, call upon His name, declare His doings

among the people, make mention that His name is exalted. (Four things are listed here that Israel will then do, and which Believers should do now: 1. Praise the Lord constantly; 2. Call upon His Name constantly; 3. Declare His doings among the people constantly; and, 4. Make mention that His Name is exalted constantly.)

5 Sing unto the LORD; for He has done excellent things: this is known in all the Earth. (In the coming Kingdom Age, Christ will be the theme "in all the Earth.")

6 Cry out and shout, you inhabitant of Zion: for great is the Holy One of Israel in the midst of you. (This refers to a constant Campmeeting, when Christ finally reigns upon this Earth.)

CHAPTER 13
(712 B.C.)
THE DOOM OF BABYLON PREDICTED

THE burden of Babylon, which Isaiah the son of Amoz did see. (According to Isaiah's Prophecies, Babylon is the first city or empire to be judged. And so she was! She has been, is, and will be, the great enemy. She is Satan's city in opposition to Jerusalem, which is the Messiah's city.)

2 Lift ye up a banner upon the high mountain, exalt the voice unto them, shake the hand, that they may go into the gates of the nobles. (This Passage has to do with the capture of Babylon by the Medes, but, even more so, it symbolizes the calling of the nations to gather to fight at Armageddon.)

3 I have commanded My sanctified ones, I have also called My mighty ones for My anger, even them who rejoice in My highness. (This refers to the Second Coming, which will destroy the Antichrist.)

4 The noise of a multitude in the mountains, like as of a great people; a tumultuous noise of the kingdoms of nations gathered together: the LORD of Hosts musters the Host of the battle. (Once again, this refers to the Battle of Armageddon and the destruction of the Antichrist, which will take place at the Second Coming.)

5 They come from a far country, from the end of the Heaven, even the LORD, and the weapons of His indignation, to destroy the whole land. (At this time, and we continue to speak of Armageddon, the Lord will lead this charge.)

JUDGMENT IN THE DAY OF THE LORD

6 Howl ye; for the day of the LORD is at hand; it shall come as a destruction from the Almighty. *(The "howling" refers to Israel's destitute condition during the Battle of Armageddon, immediately before the Second Coming of Christ; however, the Lord will definitely then come, with the Antichrist then destroyed.)*

7 Therefore shall all hands be faint, and every man's heart shall melt *(even though this pertains to the near destruction of Babylon by Cyrus, it portrays in an even greater way the helplessness of the Antichrist and his armies at the Second Coming of Christ)*:

8 And they shall be afraid: pangs and sorrows shall take hold of them; they shall be in pain as a woman who travails: they shall be amazed one at another; their faces shall be as flames. *(This speaks of Israel's condition just before the Second Coming [I Thess. 5:2-3].)*

9 Behold, the day of the LORD comes, cruel both with wrath and fierce anger, to lay the land desolate: and He shall destroy the sinners thereof out of it. *(While these Passages have a limited reference to the near destruction of Babylon by the Medes and Persians, their total fulfillment awaits the coming Battle of Armageddon and the Second Coming of the Lord.)*

10 For the stars of Heaven and the constellations thereof shall not give their light: the sun shall be darkened in his going forth, and the moon shall not cause her light to shine. *(As is obvious, none of this happened during the first destruction of Babylon; however, it will happen in the last half of the Great Tribulation and at the Second Coming [Mat. 24:29].)*

11 And I will punish the world for their evil, and the wicked for their iniquity: and I will cause the arrogancy of the proud to cease, and will lay low the haughtiness of the terrible. *("The proud" and "the terrible" refer to the Antichrist in particular and to all his followers in general.)*

12 I will make a man more precious than fine gold; even a man than the golden wedge of Ophir. *(So great will be the destruction, and so many men will be killed that they will be as scarce as "the golden wedge of Ophir" [Ezek., Chpts. 38-39].)*

13 Therefore I will shake the heavens, and the Earth shall remove out of her place, in the wrath of the LORD of Hosts, and in the day of His fierce anger. *(For the last nearly 2,000 years, the world has little known the "wrath" or "anger" of God. During the last half of the Great Tribulation, and especially during the Battle of Armageddon, His "wrath" and "anger" will most definitely be directed toward the Earth.)*

14 And it shall be as the chased roe, and as a sheep that no man takes up: they shall every man turn to his own people, and flee every one into his own land. *(This speaks of the great fear of the people at the exhibition of the "wrath" and "anger" of the Lord, which will take place, as stated, in the latter half of the Great Tribulation.)*

15 Every one who is found shall be thrust through; and every one who is joined unto them shall fall by the sword. *(This Passage is saying that all in the armies of the Antichrist who do not flee will perish.)*

16 Their children also shall be dashed to pieces before their eyes; their houses shall be spoiled, and their wives ravished. *(This refers to the Prophecies of Zechariah, which will be fulfilled in totality at the Battle of Armageddon [Zech. 14:2].)*

17 Behold, I will stir up the Medes against them, which shall not regard silver; and as for gold, they shall not delight in it. *(This Passage, as is obvious, refers to the Medes and the Persians attacking Babylon and taking the city. Their object was not plunder, but rather conquest and the extension of dominion.)*

18 Their bows also shall dash the young men to pieces; and they shall have no pity on the fruit of the womb; their eyes shall not spare children. *(Isaiah now predicts a great slaughter concerning the coming invasion of Babylon by the Medes, which would take place about 200 years from the time of Isaiah.)*

FINAL DESOLATION OF BABYLON

19 And Babylon, the glory of kingdoms, the beauty of the Chaldees' excellency, shall be as when God overthrew Sodom and Gomorrah. *(Verses 19 through 22 relate to the judgment described in Rev. 16:6 and 18:1-2; therefore, this Passage does not refer to the invasion by the Medes.)*

20 It shall never be inhabited, neither shall it be dwelt in from generation to generation: neither shall the Arabian pitch tent there; neither shall the shepherds make their fold there. *(After the destruction of Babylon near the close of the Great Tribulation [Rev., Chpt. 18], the area shall never be inhabited again. This could*

not be said of the destruction of Babylon in the past; in fact, the city continued for several centuries.)

21 But wild beasts of the desert shall lie there; and their houses shall be full of doleful creatures; and owls shall dwell there, and satyrs shall dance there.

22 And the wild beasts of the islands shall cry in their desolate houses, and dragons in their pleasant palaces: and her time is near to come, and her days shall not be prolonged. *(In the coming Millennium, and even into the New Earth [Rev., Chpts. 21-22], there will be certain openings in the Earth where men can actually see into eternal Hell. Some have suggested that this spot [Babylon] so long used as a site of rebellion against God will be one of those openings.*

If so, the words, "satyrs" and "dragons," could refer to demon spirits which, at that time, will be visible as one looks down into these openings.)

CHAPTER 14
(712 B.C.)
IN THE MILLENNIUM: ISRAEL RESTORED AND EXALTED

FOR the LORD will have mercy on Jacob, and will yet choose Israel, and set them in their own land: and the strangers shall be joined with them, and they shall cleave to the house of Jacob. *(The entirety of this Chapter concerns itself with the Restoration of Israel, which actually began in 1948, and will be completed shortly after the Second Coming.)*

2 And the people shall take them, and bring them to their place: and the house of Israel shall possess them in the land of the LORD for servants and handmaids: and they shall take them captives, whose captives they were; and they shall rule over their oppressors. *(The nations of the world that have caused Israel great sorrow and trouble will see the roles reversed, and we speak of the coming Kingdom Age. Whereas the "oppressors" once ruled over them, now Israel will rule over the "oppressors.")*

3 And it shall come to pass in the day that the LORD shall give you rest from your sorrow, and from your fear, and from the hard bondage wherein you were made to serve. *(Israel could have had this "rest" all along, but for their rebellion against the Lord.)*

ISRAEL'S SONG OF TRIUMPH

4 That you shall take up this Proverb against the king of Babylon, and say, How has the oppressor ceased! the golden city ceased! *(This will come to pass at the Second Coming, with this song then, no doubt, being sung, because Israel will have then accepted Christ.)*

5 The LORD has broken the staff of the wicked, and the sceptre of the rulers. *(The Antichrist is called here "the wicked." Paul addressed him as such, as well [II Thess. 2:8]. At the Battle of Armageddon, he will be "broken," along with his cohorts [Ezek., Chpts. 38-39].)*

6 He who smote the people in wrath with a continual stroke, he who ruled the nations in anger, is persecuted, and none hinders. *(The phrase, "none hinders," refers to the nations of the world, which will have no power against the Lord of Glory when He comes back. The "people" in this Passage basically refer to Israel, and the efforts of the Antichrist to completely destroy them.)*

7 The whole Earth is at rest, and is quiet: they break forth into singing.

8 Yea, the fir trees rejoice at You, and the cedars of Lebanon, saying, Since You are laid down, no feller is come up against us. *(The tranquility of this Verse results from the doom of the Antichrist.)*

9 Hell from beneath is moved for you to meet you at your coming: it stirs up the dead for you, even all the chief ones of the Earth; it has raised up from their thrones all the kings of the nations. *(That this place called "Hell" is literal cannot be denied by any honest investigation of Scripture. The most powerful one to enter that place will be the Antichrist; however, his just doom will be the same as all others.)*

10 All they shall speak and say unto you, Are you also become weak as we? are you become like unto us? *(This one Passage should be a warning to all who think their power, pomp, and prestige will reserve some special place for them in God's eternity. It will not!)*

11 Your pomp is brought down to the grave, and the noise of your viols: the worm is spread under you, and the worms cover you. *(The "dead" spoken of in Verse 9 refer to the "Rephaim," the giants who once inhabited certain parts of the Earth, and who were the results of the ungodly union of fallen angels and women [Gen. 6:4].*

The "viols" speak of the pomp and ceremony that once accompanied the Antichrist.

The "worm" is spoken of in a figurative sense here of the never-dying consciousness of men in Hell [Mk. 9:44-46].)

12 How are you fallen from Heaven, O

Lucifer, son of the morning! how are you cut down to the ground, which did weaken the nations! *(Isaiah's Prophecy now switches from the Antichrist to his unholy sponsor, Satan himself.*

"Lucifer" is the name of Satan. Actually, he is an angel, originally created by God, who served the Lord in righteousness for an undetermined period of time.

When he fell, he led a revolution against God, with about one-third of the angels, it seems, throwing in their lot with him [Rev. 12:4]. Therefore, all the pain, suffering, misery, heartache, death, and deception which have ruled the nations from the very beginning can be laid at the doorstep of this revolution headed up by Satan.)

13 For you have said in your heart, I will ascend into Heaven, I will exalt my throne above the stars of God: I will sit also upon the mount of the congregation, in the sides of the north:

14 I will ascend above the heights of the clouds; I will be like the Most High. *(In these two Verses, we see the foment of Satan's rebellion and revolution against God. It seems that Lucifer, while true to the Lord, was given dominion of the Earth, which was before Adam. After his fall, he worked deceitfully to get other angelic rulers to follow him in his war against God.)*

15 Yet you shall be brought down to Hell, to the sides of the pit. *(This would be the lot of Satan and all who seek to be like God, but in a wrong way, in effect, by making themselves god.)*

16 They who see you shall narrowly look upon you, and consider you, saying, Is this the man who made the Earth to tremble, who did shake kingdoms *(now the Prophecy reverts back to the Antichrist; we know this because it addresses him by saying, "Is this the man. . .?");*

17 Who made the world as a wilderness, and destroyed the cities thereof; who opened not the house of his prisoners? *(The debut of the Antichrist, which will take place shortly after the Rapture of the Church, will not bring the promised peace and prosperity, but instead will make the world a prison.)*

18 All the kings of the nations, even all of them, lie in glory, every one in his own house.

19 But you are cast out of your grave like an abominable branch, and as the raiment of those who are slain, thrust through with a sword, who go down to the stones of the pit; as a carcase trodden under feet. *(Despite the fact that the Antichrist will come closer than any man to conquering the entirety of the world, still, his final end will be ignominious, degrading, and despicable. He will be killed by the Lord at the Battle of Armageddon.)*

20 You shall not be joined with them in burial, because you have destroyed your land, and slain your people: the seed of evildoers shall never be renowned. *(In this Verse, we have some proof that the Antichrist will be an apostate Jew, because it uses the words, "your land" and "your people." Some even think, because of the Prophecies of Jacob, that the Antichrist will come from the Tribe of Dan [Gen. 49:17].)*

DESOLATION OF BABYLON

21 Prepare slaughter for his children for the iniquity of their fathers; that they do not rise, nor possess the land, nor fill the face of the world with cities. *(Verses 21 through 23 pertain to the destruction and the desolation of rebuilt Babylon [Rev., Chpt. 18].)*

22 For I will rise up against them, saith the LORD of Hosts, and cut off from Babylon the name, and remnant, and son, and nephew, saith the LORD. *("Babylon" is man's city and, hence, of Satan. It was built by Nimrod as a sign of rebellion against God [Gen. 10:8-10]. It, in its rebellion, will be no more.)*

23 I will also make it a possession for the bittern, and pools of water: and I will sweep it with the besom of destruction, saith the LORD of Hosts. *(The destruction by the Lord of this city will be like something that is swept clean.)*

24 The LORD of Hosts has sworn, saying, Surely as I have thought, so shall it come to pass; and as I have purposed, so shall it stand *(the word "thought" would have been better translated "intended"; Verses 24 through 27 contain a sixfold oath by the Lord to destroy the Antichrist):*

25 That I will break the Assyrian in My land, and upon My mountains tread him under foot: then shall his yoke depart from off them, and his burden depart from off their shoulders. *(The inference is that the "yoke" of the Antichrist is so strong that neither Israel nor the nations can throw it off in their own power. But the Lord will definitely throw it off.)*

26 This is the purpose that is purposed upon the whole Earth: and this is the hand that is stretched out upon all the nations. *(Satan has contested God for dominion of this "Earth" and its inhabitants from the beginning. At the Second Coming, the contest will end. Instead of iniquity, Righteousness will then cover the entirety of the whole Earth.)*

27 For the LORD of Hosts has purposed, and who shall disannul it? and His hand is stretched out, and who shall turn it back? *(In this Passage, we have the emphatic Promise that all of this will be done by "the LORD of Hosts." The prediction will not fail!)*

28 In the year that king Ahaz died was this burden. *(As was to be expected, Babylon, an immense religious system and the political and world opponent of the Throne of David, was first judged. The other nations hostile to Israel now enter the Prophetic scene, even as we shall see.)*

THE WARNING TO PALESTINE

29 Rejoice not thou, whole Palestina, because the rod of him who smote you is broken: for out of the serpent's root shall come forth a cockatrice, and his fruit shall be a fiery flying serpent. *(The immediate fulfillment concerned the defeat of Philistia by Uzziah [II Ki. 15:1-7; II Chron. 28:16-21]; however, the total fulfillment has to do with the present time, even as it regards modern Israel and the Palestinians. In other words, the Palestinians will not win.)*

30 And the firstborn of the poor shall feed, and the needy shall lie down in safety: and I will kill your root with famine, and he shall slay your remnant. *(II Kings, Chpt. 18, records the fulfillment of this Prophecy in the immediate future. Its total fulfillment concerns the distant future. The "poor" and "needy" refer to Judah, i.e., "Israel," who will be protected by the Lord and will "lie down in safety.")*

31 Howl, O gate; cry, O city; you, whole Palestina, are dissolved: for there shall come from the north a smoke, and none shall be alone in his appointed times. *(The word "Palestina" refers to the Philistines. The land addressed here extends along the Mediterranean from Gaza on the south to Lydda on the north. As stated, the problem rages even unto this modern time. But, in this Passage, we are told that the Palestinian problem will be solved at the Second Coming.)*

32 What shall one then answer the messengers of the nation? That the LORD has founded Zion, and the poor of His people shall trust in it. *(The sense of the entirety of this Prophecy [Vss. 28-32] pertains to the land that God promised Israel. It has been contested from that moment until now. The prediction is that those who contested it will not have it. It belongs to Israel, referred to as "the poor of His people.")*

CHAPTER 15
(726 B.C.)
MOAB'S DESTRUCTION DESCRIBED

THE burden of Moab. Because in the night Ar of Moab is laid waste, and brought to silence; because in the night Kir of Moab is laid waste, and brought to silence *(this Prophecy was uttered in the year that king Ahaz died [14:28] and had a primary fulfillment three years later; however, its exhaustive fulfillment awaits the future.*

Moab, Ammon, and Edom are part of present-day Jordan, which means that these Prophecies not only pertain to Isaiah's day, but also have a future fulfillment, even as we shall see);

2 He is gone up to Bajith, and to Dibon, the high places, to weep: Moab shall howl over Nebo, and over Medeba: on all their heads shall be baldness, and every beard cut off. *(These "high places" were centers of idolatrous worship; the two most important were upon Nebo and Medeba. The Prophet, in Vision, sees the terror-stricken Moabites hastening up these mountains to seek help from their god, Chemosh, but in vain.*

The "baldness" of the heads consisted of the practice of cutting off the hair because of mourning.)

3 In their streets they shall gird themselves with sackcloth: on the tops of their houses, and in their streets, every one shall howl, weeping abundantly. *(This Prophecy speaks of the coming invasion by Assyria of Moab, which would take place about three years from this time.*

Through the Prophecies of Isaiah, the Lord gave them ample time for Repentance, but to no avail. They continued to appeal to their idol gods.)

4 And Heshbon shall cry, and Elealeh: their voices shall be heard even unto Jahaz: therefore the armed soldiers of Moab shall cry out; his life shall be grievous unto him. *(The last statement, "his life shall be grievous," personifies the Moabite people and the terrible judgment that was coming.)*

5 My heart shall cry out for Moab; his fugitives shall flee unto Zoar, an heifer of three years old: for by the mounting up of Luhith with weeping shall they go it up; for in the way of Horonaim they shall raise up a cry of destruction. *(Isaiah, upon seeing the terrible judgment in his Vision that was coming upon idol-worshipping Moab, cried out for them. He sympathizes with the sufferings of Moab as a kindred people [Gen. 19:37], and perhaps as having, in the person of Ruth, furnished an*

ancestress to the Messiah [Mat. 1:5].)

6 For the waters of Nimrim shall be desolate: for the hay is withered away, the grass fails, there is no green thing. *(This Verse speaks of the desolation that is coming to this land.)*

7 Therefore the abundance they have gotten, and that which they have laid up, shall they carry away to the brook of the willows. *("The abundance" speaks of the property that the people will endeavor to carry with them when they flee the enemy.)*

8 For the cry is gone round about the borders of Moab; the howling thereof unto Eglaim, and the howling thereof unto Beer-elim. *(A hope had been entertained of the pursuit slackening, but it is disappointed.)*

9 For the waters of Dimon shall be full of blood: for I will bring more upon Dimon, lions upon him who escapes of Moab, and upon the remnant of the land. *(The Prophecy is that so many people will die that the "waters of Dimon" will run red with blood. Of those who escape the enemies' lance, "lions" and wild animals will help destroy the majority of the remnant of Moab.)*

CHAPTER 16
(726 B.C.)
MOAB THE PROTECTOR OF ISRAEL IN THE TRIBULATION

SEND ye the lamb to the ruler of the land from Sela *(Petra)* to the wilderness, unto the mount of the daughter of Zion. *(The "lamb" refers to Israel. At the midpoint of the Great Tribulation, when the Antichrist attacks Israel, showing his true colors, Israel will then flee to Moab, which is modern-day Jordan [Mat. 24:15-24; Rev. 12:6, 14].)*

2 For it shall be, that, as a wandering bird cast out of the nest, so the daughters of Moab shall be at the fords of Arnon. *(The "wandering bird" speaks of Moab, who will be highly disturbed at the events that are taking place when the Antichrist suddenly attacks Israel, and Israel is forced to flee. Moab [Jordan] will welcome Israel at that time.)*

3 Take counsel, execute judgment; make your shadow as the night in the midst of the noonday; hide the outcasts; bewray not him who wanders. *(Once again, Israel is referred to as "the outcasts." Moab is instructed to hide these outcasts, and not to betray them.)*

4 Let my outcasts dwell with you, Moab; be thou a covert to them from the face of the spoiler *(the Antichrist):* for the extortioner is at an end, the spoiler ceases, the oppressors are consumed out of the land. *(The "extortioner," the "spoiler," and the "oppressor" are all names for the Antichrist.*

The Holy Spirit requests of "Moab" at the time of the invasion by the Antichrist that His "outcasts" dwell with them. The place that is being spoken of is Petra, which is in present-day Jordan. For this reason, the Holy Spirit will cause the country of Jordan to escape out of the hand of the Antichrist [Dan. 11:40-45].)

5 And in mercy shall the throne be established: and he shall sit upon it in truth in the tabernacle of David, judging, and seeking judgment, and hasting righteousness. *(We are emphatically told here that the "Tabernacle of David" shall be once again set up, which will take place after the Church Age [Acts 15:13-18].)*

MOAB'S SINS: PRIDE, ARROGANCE, AND INSOLENCE; LAMENT FOR MOAB

6 We have heard of the pride of Moab; he is very proud; even of his haughtiness, and his pride, and his wrath: but his lies shall not be so. *(The immediate judgment upon Moab is again taken up in Verses 6 through 12. These Prophecies as well compare with the Prophecies in Chapter 15. This concerns the soon coming invasion by Assyria.)*

7 Therefore shall Moab howl for Moab, every one shall howl: for the foundations of Kir-hareseth shall ye mourn; surely they are stricken. *(This speaks of the judgment that shall come upon the entirety of the nation, and not on just a few.)*

8 For the field of Heshbon languish, and the vine of Sibmah: the lords of the heathen have broken down the principal plants thereof, they are come even unto Jazer, they wandered through the wilderness: her branches are stretched out, they are gone over the sea. *("The lords of the heathen" are probably the Assyrians, who made a practice of destroying the fruit trees in enemy country for the mere purpose of doing mischief.)*

9 Therefore I will bewail with the weeping of Jazer the vine of Sibmah: I will water you with my tears, O Heshbon, and Elealeh: for the shouting for your summer fruits and for your harvest is fallen. *(This Verse portrays the great sorrow and mourning over the destruction of the country and the wasting of its crops.)*

10 And gladness is taken away, and joy out

of the plentiful field; and in the vineyards there shall be no singing, neither shall there be shouting: the treaders shall tread out no wine in their presses; I have made their vintage shouting to cease. *(At the grape harvest, there were times of great celebration and joy; however, all of this would be taken away, says the Holy Spirit.)*

11 Wherefore my bowels shall sound like an harp for Moab, and my inward parts for Kir-haresh. *(In his Vision, seeing the coming destruction, Isaiah was moved with deep compassion for these people.)*

12 And it shall come to pass, when it is seen that Moab is weary on the high place, that he shall come to his sanctuary to pray; but he shall not prevail. *(This Verse pictures the Moabites presenting themselves before their idol, and, like the worshippers of Baal at Carmel, they wearied themselves in their fruitless cries to him.)*

13 This is the Word that the LORD has spoken concerning Moab since that time. *(The words, "since that time," refer to the Prophecy of 15:1.)*

14 But now the LORD has spoken, saying, Within three years, as the years of an hireling, and the glory of Moab shall be contemned, with all that great multitude; and the remnant shall be very small and feeble. *(Concerning some of the heathen people, the annihilation was to be absolute, but Moab would have a remnant, very small and of little account; however, this remnant is to be redeemed in the latter days, and in fact presently occupies modern Jordan, and for the express purpose of protecting Israel, which she will do in the latter half of the Great Tribulation.)*

CHAPTER 17
(741 B.C.)
AN ORACLE CONCERNING THE RUIN OF DAMASCUS

THE burden of Damascus. Behold, Damascus is taken away from being a city, and it shall be a ruinous heap. *(The defeat of Rezin and the destruction of Damascus was fulfilled by the Assyrians [II Ki. 16:5-8].)*

2 The cities of Aroer are forsaken: they shall be for flocks, which shall lie down, and none shall make them afraid. *(The destruction of these cities was to be so complete that cattle would pasture on their former sites; there would be no man to drive them away.)*

3 The fortress also shall cease from Ephraim, and the kingdom from Damascus, and the remnant of Syria: they shall be as the glory of the children of Israel, saith the LORD of Hosts. *(The Prophecy was that "Ephraim" was to be destroyed. Sargon did not destroy Samaria on the occasion of his first capture, but he says that he "reduced it to a heap of ruins" on the occasion of his second capture.*

In effect, when the Lord speaks of the "remnant of Syria" being "as the glory of the Children of Israel," He is using irony.)

4 And in that day it shall come to pass, that the glory of Jacob shall be made thin, and the fatness of his flesh shall wax lean. *(The Holy Spirit continues to speak of the destruction of the Northern Kingdom of Israel.)*

5 And it shall be as when the harvestman gathers the corn, and reaps the ears with his arm; and it shall be as he who gathers ears in the valley of Rephaim. *(Death is the "harvestman" here and gathers the Israelites by shocks or sheaves into his garner. It is a dire Prophecy.)*

6 Yet gleaning grapes shall be left in it, as the shaking of an olive tree, two or three berries in the top of the uppermost bough, four or five in the outmost fruitful branches thereof, saith the LORD God of Israel. *(Due to the great destruction by the Assyrians, the remnant of Syria and Ephraim would be small.)*

7 At that day shall a man look to his Maker, and his eyes shall have respect to the Holy One of Israel. *(After the terrible chastisement, the remnant left had a tendency to look to the Lord instead of their idols. This took place about 75 years after Isaiah's Prophecy.)*

8 And he shall not look to the altars, the work of his hands, neither shall respect that which his fingers have made, either the groves, or the images. *(In this Verse, we are told that Israel finally ceased their idol-worship.)*

9 In that day shall his strong cities be as a forsaken bough, and an uppermost branch, which they left because of the Children of Israel: and there shall be desolation. *(Normally the phrase, "in that day," applies to the Endtime, and especially the Millennium; however, it rather applied here to the destruction by the Assyrians, which would take place not too many years distant.)*

10 Because you have forgotten the God of your Salvation, and have not been mindful of the Rock of your strength, therefore shall you plant pleasant plants, and shall set it with strange slips *(the reasons are here given for*

the great chastisement of the Northern Kingdom of Israel):

11 In the day shall you make your plant to grow, and in the morning shall you make your seed to flourish: but the harvest shall be a heap in the day of grief and of desperate sorrow. *(Again, the Holy Spirit speaks of this coming time when even the crops would be destroyed.)*

12 Woe to the multitude of many people, which make a noise like the noise of the seas; and to the rushing of nations, that make a rushing like the rushing of mighty waters! *(The Prophecy, although continuing, no longer refers to Israel's present problems, but to a later time; actually, Verses 12 through 14 refer to the coming Tribulation, the rise of the Antichrist, and the Battle of Armageddon.)*

13 The nations shall rush like the rushing of many waters: but God shall rebuke them, and they shall flee far off, and shall be chased as the chaff of the mountains before the wind, and like a rolling thing before the whirlwind.

14 And behold at eveningtide trouble; and before the morning he is not. This is the portion of them who spoil us, and the lot of them who rob us. *(This pictures the gathering of many nations against Israel at the Battle of Armageddon. It will be at that time when God will rebuke them and fight for Israel [Ezek., Chpts. 38-39; Joel, Chpt. 3; Zech., Chpt. 14; Rev., Chpt. 19].)*

CHAPTER 18
(714 B.C.)
THE DOWNFALL OF ETHIOPIA

WOE to the land shadowing with wings, which is beyond the rivers of Ethiopia *(the word, "Woe," is used here of judgment; the Prophecy given here regarding "Ethiopia" does not concern Israel's present judgments during the time of Isaiah, but rather the latter days, as in Verses 12 through 14 of the previous Chapter):*

2 Who sends ambassadors by the sea, even in vessels of bulrushes upon the waters, saying, Go, you swift messengers, to a nation scattered and peeled, to a people terrible from their beginning hitherto; a nation meted out and trodden down, whose land the rivers have spoiled! *(Some Scholars contend that the entirety of Verse 2 refers to Ethiopia. While that may be true, still, the language expressed does not seem to fit Ethiopia, but rather Israel.)*

JUDGMENT DESCRIBED

3 All ye inhabitants of the world, and dwellers on the Earth, see ye, when He lifts up an ensign on the mountains; and when He blows a trumpet, hear ye. *(The entirety of the "world" is called to attention regarding that which the Lord will do at the Battle of Armageddon. The pronoun "He" refers to Jehovah. The "Ensign" that He will lift up is the Messiah.*

It seems that the Lord Himself will "blow a trumpet" at the Second Coming of Christ [Joel 2:1; Zech. 9:14; I Thess. 4:16].)

4 For so the LORD said unto me, I will take My rest, and I will consider in My dwelling place like a clear heat upon herbs, and like a cloud of dew in the heat of harvest. *(The action of the Messiah during the entire period of Israel's rejection and up to "the time" of Verse 7 is declared in Verses 4 through 6. His silence concerning Israel during this time, which now numbers approximately 2,000 years, is predicted in this Verse. In effect, He says, "I will be inactive; yet will I keep looking for My dwellingplace; I will be to them like sunshine after rain, and like a cloud of dew in the heat of harvest."*

He is saying that He will neither cease to love nor lose sight of His ancient People.)

5 For afore the harvest, when the bud is perfect, and the sour grape is ripening in the flower, He shall both cut off the sprigs with pruning hooks, and take away and cut down the branches. *("He" is the Divine Vine-Dresser, the Messiah. His instrument will be the Antichrist.)*

6 They shall be left together unto the fowls of the mountains, and to the beasts of the Earth: and the fowls shall summer upon them, and all the beasts of the Earth shall winter upon them. *(If Israel's faithful Redeemer likens His People to a Vine, so does He liken their enemies to ravenous vultures and wild beasts.)*

FUTURE RESTORATION

7 In that time shall the present be brought unto the LORD of Hosts of a people scattered and peeled, and from a people terrible from their beginning hitherto; a nation meted out and trodden under foot, whose land the rivers have spoiled, to the place of the name of the LORD of Hosts, the Mount Zion. *("In that time" refers to the Antichrist's armies, which will be destroyed in the Battle of Armageddon. Then the Millennium will begin. Israel, at that time, will offer herself as a "present" to the*

Messiah, and, at the same time, the Gentile nations will offer her as a "present" to Him. The gift will be made upon "Mount Zion.")

CHAPTER 19
(714 B.C.)
THE FALL OF EGYPT

THE burden of Egypt. Behold, the LORD rides upon a swift cloud, and shall come into Egypt: and the idols of Egypt shall be moved at His presence, and the heart of Egypt shall melt in the midst of it. *(This Verse mentions the "idols of Egypt." Egypt has always been symbolic of the world. The Deliverance of the Children of Israel out of Egypt symbolizes the Born-Again experience, as well as victory over Satan, concerning the Child of God.*

This speaks of the Second Coming, when Egypt will accept the Lord.)

2 And I will set the Egyptians against the Egyptians: and they shall fight every one against his brother, and every one against his neighbour; city against city, and kingdom against kingdom. *(When this civil war in Egypt will take place in connection with these last-day events is not stated, but it is clear that at Armageddon men will be so confused that they will turn on each other [Zech. 14:13-14].)*

3 And the spirit of Egypt shall fail in the midst thereof; and I will destroy the counsel thereof; and they shall seek to the idols, and to the charmers, and to them who have familiar spirits, and to the wizards. *(Egypt, except for the short time under Joseph [Gen., Chpt. 41], has always been ruled, at least indirectly, by demon spirits. At the time of the Antichrist, they will consult these spirits, but all in vain.)*

4 And the Egyptians will I give over into the hand of a cruel lord; and a fierce king shall rule over them, saith the LORD, the LORD of Hosts. *(This Passage tells us that the Lord will allow Egypt to be defeated by the Antichrist. This will happen at approximately the outset of the Great Tribulation.)*

DESOLATION

5 And the waters shall fail from the sea, and the river shall be wasted and dried up. *(The "sea" referred to here is probably the Nile. The "rivers" wasted and dried up refer, no doubt, to a phenomenon of nature brought about by the Lord, which will take place during the time of the Great Tribulation, beginning possibly with*

the invasion of the Antichrist.)

6 And they shall turn the rivers far away; and the brooks of defence shall be emptied and dried up: the reeds and flags shall wither.

7 The paper reeds by the brooks, by the mouth of the brooks, and every thing sown by the brooks, shall wither, be driven away, and be no more. *(During the time of the Great Tribulation, which will last for some seven years, the Lord Himself will disturb the planetary bodies, causing tremendous disturbance on Earth. Egypt will probably be greatly affected by this [Rev. 6:12-17].)*

8 The fishers also shall mourn, and all they who cast angle into the brooks shall lament, and they who spread nets upon the waters shall languish.

9 Moreover they who work in fine flax, and they who weave networks, shall be confounded.

10 And they shall be broken in the purposes thereof, all who make sluices and ponds for fish. *(These Verses merely reflect the fact of industries being brought to a standstill during the time of the Great Tribulation.)*

CAUSE OF DESTRUCTION

11 Surely the princes of Zoan are fools, the counsel of the wise counsellors of Pharaoh is become brutish: how say ye unto Pharaoh, I am the son of the wise, the son of ancient kings? *("The princes" of Verses 11 through 13 refer to the priests-princes. They were a travesty of God's kings and priests. They claimed superhuman knowledge and royal descent.)*

12 Where are they? where are your wise men? and let them tell you now, and let them know what the LORD of Hosts has purposed upon Egypt. *(This is a tremendous challenge! The Prophets of Jehovah addressed it more than once to the prophets of idolatry, for only God can foretell what will surely happen!)*

13 The princes of Zoan are become fools, the princes of Noph are deceived; they have also seduced Egypt, even they who are the stay of the tribes thereof. *("Zoan" was the seat of the Egyptian Court. It was there that Moses announced the ten plagues. Once again, God calls the leaders of Egypt "deceived fools." They are deceived because they listen to these "counselors" who receive their information from demon spirits.)*

14 The LORD has mingled a perverse spirit in the midst thereof: and they have caused Egypt to err in every work thereof, as a drunken

man staggers in his vomit. *(While the leaders of Egypt will not understand it, still, the cause of their problems is demon spirits. It is the same presently in many nations of the world.)*

15 Neither shall there be any work for Egypt, which the head or tail, branch or rush, may do. *(In ancient times, Egypt was supposed to be the center of wisdom. There will be no wisdom in the coming day of the Great Tribulation. There will be nothing but confusion.)*

EGYPT'S ULTIMATE DELIVERANCE; MILLENNIAL BLESSINGS, PEACE

16 In that day shall Egypt be like unto women: and it shall be afraid and fear because of the shaking of the hand of the LORD of Hosts, which He shakes over it. *(This Verse is the portrayal of wrath and judgment that shall come "in that day." It pertains basically to the Battle of Armageddon, which will cause Egypt much more trouble than normal, due to the fact that the "LORD of Hosts" will express a particular anger toward it, because of Egypt's perverseness toward Israel.)*

17 And the land of Judah shall be a terror unto Egypt, every one who makes mention thereof shall be afraid in himself, because of the counsel of the LORD of Hosts, which He has determined against it. *(In the coming Battle of Armageddon, Judah will have the "counsel of the LORD of Hosts," while Egypt will be trusting in demon spirits. The outcome is inevitable!)*

18 In that day shall five cities in the land of Egypt speak the language of Canaan, and swear to the LORD of Hosts; one shall be called, The city of destruction. *(The five great cities of ancient Egypt were originally cities of unrighteousness. Here, they will be turned to cities of Righteousness. This will be in the Kingdom Age, after the Second Coming.)*

19 In that day shall there be an Altar to the LORD in the midst of the land of Egypt, and a Pillar at the border thereof to the LORD. *("An Altar" and "a Pillar," not "altars" and "pillars," for there is only one way of Redemption and one Testimony. Obviously, this "Altar" will be for men to offer Sacrifices to God in the Millennium, like the one to be used in Jerusalem for the same purpose during this period.*

The "Pillar" is to be used only as a sign and witness to commemorate an event, which speaks of Egypt's Deliverance by the Lord from the Antichrist.)

20 And it shall be for a sign and for a witness unto the LORD of Hosts in the land of Egypt: for they shall cry unto the LORD because of the oppressors, and He shall send them a Saviour, and a Great One, and He shall deliver them. *(The "Saviour" and "Great One" will be none other than the Lord Jesus Christ. Only He can "deliver.")*

21 And the LORD shall be known to Egypt, and the Egyptians shall know the LORD in that day, and shall do sacrifice and oblation; yea, they shall vow a vow unto the LORD, and perform it. *(Now, the Glory of the Lord will cover Egypt, and they will gladly serve Him.*

Upon this "Altar" mentioned in Verse 19, they will "do sacrifice and oblation." This will be in the Kingdom Age.)

22 And the LORD shall smite Egypt: He shall smite and heal it: and they shall return even to the LORD, and He shall be intreated of them, and shall heal them. *(Before the "healing" can come, the "smiting" must come first, which it shall!)*

23 In that day shall there be a highway out of Egypt to Assyria, and the Assyrian shall come into Egypt, and the Egyptian into Assyria, and the Egyptians shall serve with the Assyrians. *("In that day" refers to the Millennium. Consequently, the animosity, hatred, and anger which have characterized this area of the world since the dawn of time have now finally been wrested away from Satan, and the land will then be ruled by the Lord of Glory. The hatred is now gone.)*

24 In that day shall Israel be the third with Egypt and with Assyria, even a blessing in the midst of the Land *(these three nations speak of Noah's three sons, which refer to the entire world, and will become servants to Jehovah; the human race consists of these three great families: Assyria, Israel, and Egypt, i.e., Japheth, Shem, and Ham [Gen. 9:27]; these three countries, "Israel," "Egypt," and "Assyria" [modern Iraq], instead of being a curse, will now be a "blessing"):*

25 Whom the LORD of Hosts shall bless, saying, Blessed be Egypt My people, and Assyria the work of My hands, and Israel My inheritance. *(This tells us that the Arabs will ultimately come to Christ, thereby disavowing the religion of Islam. Actually, it will be no more, as well as all the other religions of the world. In that Glad Day, there will be One Saviour, Who is the world's Redeemer, Who is the Lord Jesus Christ.)*

CHAPTER 20
(714 B.C.)
EGYPT'S IMMEDIATE CONQUEST
BY ASSYRIA

IN the year that Tartan came unto Ashdod, (when Sargon the king of Assyria sent him,) and fought against Ashdod, and took it *(this Prophecy is different from the Prophecy of the previous Chapter, which is obvious; its lesson for Israel was the bitter fruit that the servants of God must taste when the arm of flesh is leaned upon and not the Arm of God);*

2 At the same time spoke the LORD by Isaiah the son of Amoz, saying, Go and loose the sackcloth from off your loins, and put off your shoe from your foot. And he did so, walking naked and barefoot. *(Jehovah was the Speaker and Isaiah was His Instrument. The Prophet was not naked, as we think of such, simply laying aside his peculiar prophetic garment.)*

3 And the LORD said, Like as My servant Isaiah has walked naked and barefoot three years for a sign and wonder upon Egypt and upon Ethiopia. *(The "three years" mentioned here probably refer to the same number mentioned in 16:14. Within three years, Moab, Egypt, and Ethiopia were to be destroyed, which they were.)*

4 So shall the king of Assyria lead away the Egyptians prisoners, and the Ethiopians captives, young and old, naked and barefoot, even with their buttocks uncovered, to the shame of Egypt. *(Such was meant the object lesson of Isaiah of Verse 2 to portray. So complete and abject would be the enslavement of the Egyptian warriors that they would not even be given loin cloths to wrap around their naked bodies. Such showed the utter defeat and humiliation of the Egyptians.)*

5 And they shall be afraid and ashamed of Ethiopia their expectation, and of Egypt their glory. *(The Prophet is telling Judah not to look to "Ethiopia" or "Egypt" for help, because none would be forthcoming from these sectors, due to the fact that they themselves would be completely destroyed.)*

6 And the inhabitant of this isle shall say in that day, Behold, such is our expectation, whither we flee for help to be delivered from the king of Assyria: and how shall we escape? *(Judah would ask the question, "How shall we escape?" If they cannot get the help of Ethiopia and Egypt, what can they do?*

They would learn that their escape was the

Lord of Hosts; He sent an Angel, who killed 185,000 Assyrians and caused the others to flee [Isa. 37:36-38].)*

CHAPTER 21
(714 B.C.)
THE FALL OF BABYLON, MEDO-PERSIA
THE SPOILER

THE burden of the desert of the sea. As whirlwinds in the south pass through; so it comes from the desert, from a terrible land. *(The phrase, "the desert of the sea," refers to Babylon.)*

2 A grievous vision is declared unto me; the treacherous dealer deals treacherously, and the spoiler spoils. Go up, O Elam: besiege, O Media; all the sighing thereof have I made to cease. *(The primal occasion of the fulfillment of this Prophecy was the destruction of Babylon some 200 years later by the Medes and Persians on the night that Belshazzar was slain. This means that the command to Elam and to Media to go up and besiege Babylon was a Divine command. This was done because of Babylon's treatment of Israel.)*

3 Therefore are my loins filled with pain: pangs have taken hold upon me, as the pangs of a woman who travails: I was bowed down at the hearing of it; I was dismayed at the seeing of it. *(The Prophet is horror-stricken at the devastation, the ruin, the carnage.)*

4 My heart panted, fearfulness affrighted me: the night of my pleasure has he turned into fear unto me. *(This was no doubt the night of the handwriting on the wall, which saw the fall of Babylon to the Medes and Persians [Dan., Chpt. 5].)*

5 Prepare the table, watch in the watchtower, eat, drink: arise, you princes, and anoint the shield. *(This speaks of war and destruction, when the Medes and the Persians would break through and take the city.)*

6 For thus has the Lord said unto me, Go, set a watchman, let him declare what he sees. *(The Holy Spirit will, in effect, give Isaiah a ringside seat as to what he will observe. These are the judgments which will come upon Babylon.)*

7 And he saw a chariot with a couple of horsemen, a chariot of asses, and a chariot of camels; and he hearkened diligently with much heed. *(Isaiah saw something that would happen many years into the future. Such pinpoint accuracy should provide information to anyone who desires to know of the Hand of God, even*

minutely so, in world affairs!)

8 And he cried, A lion: My lord, I stand continually upon the watchtower in the daytime, and I am set in my ward whole nights *(the sense of the Verse is that the Prophet cried as a "lion"; he can contain himself no longer)*:

9 And, behold, here comes a chariot of men, with a couple of horsemen. And he answered and said, Babylon is fallen, is fallen; and all the graven images of her gods He has broken unto the ground. *(The masses of infantry and cavalry seen by the watchman in Vision were the hosts of Media and Elam. The repetition of the word "fallen" and the use of the present tense emphasize the sure fulfillment of the Prophecy. It, in fact, happened exactly as stated!)*

10 O my threshing, and the corn of my floor: that which I have heard of the LORD of Hosts, the God of Israel, have I declared unto you. *(The "bruised corn" of the threshingfloor describes Israel as oppressed by the Babylonians. The Lord identifies Himself here with these hapless slaves and is not ashamed to call them "His people.")*

THE MESSAGE TO DUMAH (EDOM)

11 The burden of Dumah. He calls to me out of Seir, Watchman, what of the night? Watchman, what of the night? *(The word "Dumah" refers to Idumea or Edom. There is a play here upon words, for "Dumah" means "silence." The Prophecy foretold an eternal silence for the sons of Esau.*

Evidently, the Edomites appealed to the Prophet as to their future. The answer would not be to their liking.)

12 The watchman said, The morning comes, and also the night: if you will enquire, enquire ye: return, come. *(In essence, Isaiah says: "For Israel, the morning is indeed coming, but for Edom, the night"; and yet, in the tender compassion of the Holy Spirit, He adds, "If you are in earnest and are inquiring sincerely, then turn away from your idols and come to the Light." But Edom refused the gracious invitation and has passed away into the eternal night.)*

THE FATE OF ARABIA

13 The burden upon Arabia. In the forest in Arabia shall you lodge, O ye travelling companies of Dedanim. *(There is a play upon the word "Arabia." It has to do with the word "sunset." For the sons of Ishmael, there is an evening of sorrow as they "lodge in the forest," but not a*

night of eternal silence. And so they have continued unto this day!)

14 The inhabitants of the land of Tema brought water to him who was thirsty, they prevented with their bread him who fled. *(The fleeing Dedanites are helped by the descendants of Abraham as they pass through. They are given bread and water.)*

15 For they fled from the swords, from the drawn sword, and from the bent bow, and from the grievousness of war. *(This Prophecy pertains to the invasion by Assyria, which would happen very shortly. Isaiah sees the defeat of the Arabians, as well as their fleeing for their lives and from the heartache of war.)*

16 For thus has the Lord said unto me. Within a year, according to the years of an hireling, and all the glory of Kedar shall fail *(the word "Kedar" refers to another part of Arabia; the Prophet says that the judgment upon Arabia will take place "within a year"; this pertains to the invasion by Assyria)*:

17 And the residue of the number of archers, the mighty men of the children of Kedar, shall be diminished: for the LORD God of Israel has spoken it. *(These people glory, not only in their wealth, but in their "number of archers" and their "mighty men." They felt secure!*

However, they have sinned greatly, and now they were sinning against Light, because the Holy Spirit through the Prophet was pinpointing to them exactly what was going to take place in the near future, even in a year.)

CHAPTER 22
(712 B.C.)
THE FALL OF JERUSALEM

THE burden of the valley of vision. What ails you now, that you are wholly gone up to the housetops? *("The valley of vision" is Jerusalem. Just as Babylon, her great rival, is pictured in the prior Chapter as "the wilderness of the sea," so Jerusalem is named here "the valley of vision." Man's city is morally, intellectually, and spiritually a "desert"; God's City is a center of Vision, i.e., of Divine Revelation.*

The "housetops" pertain to the Jews looking from this vantage point for the approaching Assyrians, even though at this time only a spearhead was coming from Sennacherib.)

2 You who are full of stirs, a tumultuous city, a joyous city: your slain men are not slain with the sword, nor dead in battle. *(Hezekiah is revealed in this episode as sincere*

in his Repentance and Faith; however, his people, as revealed in this Prophecy, were insincere.

The phrase, "your slain men, not dead in battle," refers to a blockade rather than a siege.)

3 All your rulers are fled together, they are bound by the archers: all who are found in you are bound together, which have fled from far. *(This Verse expresses the idea that the people in Jerusalem were benumbed by fear, and were helpless against the great army of the Assyrians, which demanded surrendered.)*

4 Therefore said I, Look away from me; I will weep bitterly, labour not to comfort me, because of the spoiling of the daughter of my people. *(The burden that Isaiah expresses is the true burden that comes only to Godly men, and to those who understand the gravity of the situation. Isaiah will "weep bitterly.")*

5 For it is a day of trouble, and of treading down, and of perplexity by the Lord GOD of Hosts in the valley of vision, breaking down the walls, and of crying to the mountains. *(Isaiah proclaims the fact that the "Lord GOD of Hosts" is allowing such to happen to Judah because of sin.*

The phrase, "crying to the mountains," has not been adequately translated by the Scholars. It probably refers to idols in those areas, which, of course, could do Judah no good whatsoever!)

6 And Elam bore the quiver with chariots of men and horsemen, and Kir uncovered the shield. *(This Verse indicates that the Medes and the Persians accompanied the Assyrian army.)*

7 And it shall come to pass, that your choicest valleys shall be full of chariots, and the horsemen shall set themselves in array at the gate. *(At times, the Lord allows Satan certain latitude against us, making the situation so hopeless that we will be forced to turn to the Lord. It is a shame that God's People have to be brought to this place, but, seemingly, most of us do at one time or the other!)*

8 And he discovered the covering of Judah, and you did look in that day to the armour of the house of the forest. *(The "covering of Judah" refers to that which hid their weakness either from themselves or from the enemy — probably the former. God drew this aside, and they suddenly saw their danger and began to think how they could best defend themselves against the coming Assyrians.)*

9 You have seen also the breaches of the city of David, that they are many: and you gathered together the waters of the lower pool. *(This portrays Hezekiah attempting to repair any*

place in the wall that might afford any type of advantage for the enemy.)*

10 And you have numbered the houses of Jerusalem, and the houses have you broken down to fortify the wall. *(Certain "houses" in Jerusalem, built of stone and no doubt luxurious and beautiful, were marked for destruction in order that the stones could be used to repair the walls.)*

11 You made also a ditch between the two walls for the water of the old pool: but you have not looked unto the Maker thereof, neither had respect unto Him Who fashioned it long ago. *(The pronoun "Him" refers to Jehovah. However intelligent Hezekiah's efforts may have been, the people did not really lean upon God for Deliverance, nor did they recognize that this chastening was from Him, that Sennacherib was His Instrument, and that God had "done" and "fashioned" this trial long beforehand.)*

12 And in that day did the Lord GOD of Hosts call to weeping, and to mourning, and to baldness, and to girding with sackcloth *(even though the Message is from Isaiah, it is actually sent by "the Lord GOD of Hosts"; He calls the people to Repentance)*:

13 And behold joy and gladness, slaying oxen, and killing sheep, eating flesh, and drinking wine: let us eat and drink; for to morrow we shall die. *(God called them to "weeping and mourning" for their sins, but instead He received merriment, revelry, joking, and partying.)*

14 And it was revealed in my ears by the LORD of Hosts, Surely this iniquity shall not be purged from you till you die, saith the Lord GOD of Hosts. *(The people mocked, it seems, the Spirit of God, hence the fearful doom pronounced in this Verse.)*

SHEBNA REMOVED FROM OFFICE

15 Thus saith the Lord GOD of Hosts, Go, get you unto this treasurer, even unto Shebna, which is over the house, and say *(it seems that "Shebna," the appointed "treasurer" of the nation and, therefore, in Hezekiah's cabinet, was himself a stranger to the Grace of God; the people held fast to their sins and pleasures, with "Shebna" as their leader in such rebellion)*,

16 What have you here? and whom have you here, that you have hewed you out a sepulchre here, as he who hews him out a sepulchre on high, and who graves an habitation for himself in a rock? *(Shebna had made great preparations for his burial. He was to be disappointed.*

He would be taken captive and buried in a foreign land.)

17 Behold, the LORD will carry you away with a mighty captivity, and will surely cover you. *(The words, "cover you," seem to indicate that Shebna had scoffed at the appeal by the Lord for Repentance.)*

18 He will surely violently turn and toss you like a ball into a large country: there shall you die, and there the chariots of your glory shall be the shame of your Lord's house. *("Your Lord" refers to Hezekiah, but more so to the Lord of Glory. This man would be the shame of Hezekiah's governmental cabinet.)*

19 And I will drive you from your station, and from your state shall he pull you down. *(The pronoun "he" refers to Hezekiah. It seems that Hezekiah, upon the advice of Isaiah, dispossessed Shebna from public office.)*

ELIAKIM PLACED IN OFFICE

20 And it shall come to pass in that day, that I will call My servant Eliakim the son of Hilkiah *(the office of "treasurer" and of prefect of the palace was taken from Shebna and given to "My servant Eliakim"; no higher honor could God pay any man that to give him the simple title of "My servant"; this He bestowed upon "Eliakim"):*

21 And I will clothe Him with your robe, and strengthen Him with your girdle, and I will commit your government into His hand: and He shall be a father to the inhabitants of Jerusalem, and to the house of Judah. *(Such terminology could only describe God's Son and our Saviour. Whereas Judah had been plagued with "Shebnas," she will now, at long last, be led by "My Servant." Then the "government shall be upon His shoulder" [Isa. 9:6].)*

22 And the key of the house of David will I lay upon His shoulder; so He shall open, and none shall shut; and He shall shut, and none shall open. *(The spiritual "key" of the house of David had to do with the Promise that God made to David concerning the coming of the Messiah, and that the Messiah would come through his family [II Sam., Chpt. 7].*

So as to make it unmistakably perfect, David's lineage to the birth of Jesus concluded in both Joseph and Mary, making the claim irrefutable.)

23 And I will fasten Him as a Nail in a sure place; and He shall be for a glorious throne to His Father's House. *(Christ is Jehovah's sure Nail, fastened in a sure place, i.e., the heavenlies; no one who is suspended upon Him shall ever*

be confounded, but, on the contrary, shall be ennobled.)

24 And they shall hang upon Him all the glory of His Father's House, the offspring and the issue, all vessels of small quantity, from the vessels of cups, even to all the vessels of flagons. *(Multiple millions can say that upon that "Nail" they have hung their eternal hopes for a golden tomorrow and blissful future. None will be disappointed!)*

25 In that day, saith the LORD of Hosts, shall the Nail that is fastened in the sure place be removed, and be cut down, and fall; and the burden that was upon it shall be cut off: for the LORD has spoken it. *(The "Nail" in the sure place is Christ. At His Crucifixion, He was "cut down," but not for Himself, but rather for lost humanity [I Pet. 2:24; I Jn. 2:2; II Cor. 5:19; Eph. 2:16; Col. 2:14]. Through His Resurrection, however, the Nail is put back firmly in place and will never be removed.)*

CHAPTER 23
(715 B.C.)
THE MESSAGE TO TYRE: DESOLATION

THE burden of Tyre. Howl, you ships of Tarshish; for it is laid waste, so that there is no house, no entering in: from the land of Chittim it is revealed to them. *("Tyre," in its early days, was a great stronghold. "Tarshish" refers to Spain and "Chittim" refers to Cyprus.)*

2 Be still, you inhabitants of the isle; you whom the merchants of Zidon, who pass over the sea, have replenished. *(The general meaning of the words, "have replenished," concern Zidon, which was secondary to Tyre and, for the most part, acquiesced to Tyrian supremacy.)*

3 And by great waters the seed of Sihor, the harvest of the river, is her revenue; and she is a mart of nations. *("Sihor" is another name for the Nile River in Egypt. The phrase, "mart of nations," has to do with Tyre's being somewhat of a clearinghouse for great cargo vessels from Egypt and other countries.)*

4 Be thou ashamed, O Zidon: for the sea has spoken, even the strength of the sea, saying, I travail not, nor bring forth children, neither do I nourish up young men, nor bring up virgins. *(This Passage has to do with Zidon's statement respecting Tyre. Even though Tyre was the stronger of the two cities, it seems that Zidon in essence had founded this great trade mart; so Zidon was considered to be Tyre's mother. Zidon would be so weakened by Tyre's fall that she*

declared that she would never found or begin another city.)

5 As at the report concerning Egypt, so shall they be sorely pained at the report of Tyre. *(The Egyptians bore no great affection towards foreign nations. They were a people whose charity began and ended at home. But the fall of Tyre was always a shock to them and they felt it portended evil to themselves.)*

6 Pass ye over to Tarshish; howl, you inhabitants of the isle. *(When Nebuchadnezzar would lay siege to the city, approximately 100 years into the future, many of the inhabitants would flee, taking their wealth with them. So when the city was finally taken, even after a thirteen-year siege, Nebuchadnezzar found very little of value. It so enraged him that he destroyed the place completely.)*

7 Is this your joyous city, whose antiquity is of ancient days? her own feet shall carry her afar off to sojourn. *(The "feet" of Tyre were her ships. As a man flees upon his feet, so the Tyrians would flee upon their ships.)*

8 Who has taken this counsel against Tyre, the crowning city, whose merchants are princes, whose traffickers are the honourable of the Earth? *(The question as to "Who has taken this counsel against Tyre?" will be answered in the next Verse.)*

9 The LORD of Hosts has purposed it, to stain the pride of all glory, and to bring into contempt all the honourable of the Earth. *(This Verse tells us that God was the One Who took "counsel against Tyre." It presents the judgment of Tyre as an earnest of the universal judgment yet to come upon the world, which will abase the pride of all human glory and cover with contempt the great ones of the Earth.)*

10 Pass through your land as a river, O daughter of Tarshish: there is no more strength. *(The announcement is here given by the Holy Spirit that colony cities, such as "Tarshish," were no more to be subject to the bonds of Tyre.)*

11 He stretched out His hand over the sea, He shook the kingdoms: the LORD has given a commandment against the merchant city, to destroy the strongholds thereof. *("He" is the Lord of Glory. "He" would give instructions for the destruction of the city, because of her pride.)*

12 And he said, You shall no more rejoice, O you oppressed virgin, daughter of Zidon: arise, pass over to Chittim; there also shall you have no rest. *(The meaning of the Passage is that once the quest by the Babylonians commences,*

they will not cease until they have accomplished their intended purpose.)*

13 Behold the land of the Chaldeans; this people was not, till the Assyrian founded it for them who dwell in the wilderness: they set up the towers thereof, they raised up the palaces thereof; and he brought it to ruin. *(The Prophet points to Assyria, a stronger and much more ancient government, and urged that it would fall before the king of the Chaldeans. How much more surely would Tyre fall!)*

14 Howl, you ships of Tarshish: for your strength is laid waste. *(Alexander's destruction of the city was the final and complete fulfillment of the Prophecy. So the Prophecy would be several hundreds of years in its total fulfillment. "The mills of God grind slowly, but they grind exceedingly fine.")*

RESTORATION AFTER SEVENTY YEARS

15 And it shall come to pass in that day, that Tyre shall be forgotten seventy years, according to the days of one king: after the end of seventy years shall Tyre sing as an harlot. *(The phrase, "the days of one king," means the duration of the Babylonian kingdom. It lasted exactly seventy years. During the seventy years, Jerusalem was a captive and Tyre, a desolation [Jer. 25:11].)*

16 Take an harp, go about the city, you harlot who has been forgotten; make sweet melody, sing many songs, that you may be remembered. *(In addressing Tyre as a harlot, the Prophet does not seem to mean more than that her aims were, or at any rate had been, selfish and worldly — such as to sever man and God. Hers had been the covetousness which is "idolatry" [Col. 3:5].)*

17 And it shall come to pass after the end of seventy years, that the LORD will visit Tyre, and she shall turn to her hire, and shall commit fornication with all the kingdoms of the world upon the face of the Earth. *(While Tyre regained her power, wealth, and fame, even as here recorded, the new city was taken by Alexander the Great, which was about 250 years after the former one had been destroyed by Nebuchadnezzar.)*

18 And her merchandise and her hire shall be holiness to the LORD: it shall not be treasured nor laid up; for her merchandise shall be for them who dwell before the LORD, to eat sufficiently, and for durable clothing. *(Oftentimes, the Holy Spirit will give Prophecies*

that will span from one age to the other without a break in the sentence. Such is the case, evidently, in this particular Prophecy.

In essence, this Verse looks forward to the coming Millennium, when Tyre will then be blessed by Christ, with the old times then forgotten.)

CHAPTER 24

(712 B.C.)

THE TRIBULATION: CHAOS, WASTE, JUDGMENT

BEHOLD, the LORD makes the Earth empty, and makes it waste, and turns it upside down, and scatters abroad the inhabitants thereof. *(The intention of the Holy Spirit is for the hearer of this Prophecy to understand that as Israel is affected, so, at least in some measure, is the entirety of the Earth. This Verse could read, "Behold, Jehovah shall make the Land of Palestine empty, and shall make it waste, and shall turn it upside down, and shall scatter abroad its inhabitants.")*

2 And it shall be, as with the people, so with the Priest; as with the servant, so with his master; as with the maid, so with her mistress; as with the buyer, so with the seller; as with the lender, so with the borrower; as with the taker of usury, so with the giver of usury to him. *(The inhabitants in this Passage are divided into six groups doubled. "Six" in the Scriptures is the number of man and expresses his imperfection, for it comes short of the perfect number "seven." Man was created on the sixth day, and the number of the future superman will be "666."*

These Passages, in some limited way, have had fulfillment in the past; however, their greater fulfillment concerns the Great Tribulation yet to come and the Battle of Armageddon.)

3 The land shall be utterly emptied, and utterly spoiled: for the LORD has spoken this Word. *(With the emphasis placed on "the LORD has spoken this Word," we are given an idea of the unchangeable position of God. Perfection doesn't need to change.)*

4 The Earth mourns and fades away, the world languishes and fades away, the haughty people of the Earth do languish. *(When the word "Earth" is here used, the manifold thrust of the Passage is toward Israel; however, during this time of the Great Tribulation, the judgments of God, even though centered up in the Middle East, will also affect the entirety of the Earth [Mat. 24:21; Rev., Chpt. 6].)*

5 The Earth also is defiled under the inhabitants thereof; because they have transgressed the laws, changed the ordinance, broken the Everlasting Covenant. *(The reason for the Great Tribulation that is to come is because of the acute violation of the Word of God [Mat. 24:21].)*

6 Therefore has the curse devoured the Earth, and they who dwell therein are desolate: therefore the inhabitants of the Earth are burned, and few men left. *(The justice of this Divine action is stated in Verses 5 and 6. This Passage basically speaks of the Second Coming of Christ, when so many men will be killed that blood will run to the horses' bridles [Rev. 14:20; Ezek. 38:22].)*

7 The new wine mourns, the vine languishes, all the merryhearted do sigh. *(In olden times, the harvest constituted days of merrymaking. It was the grandest time of the year. But at this coming time, there will be no "merryhearted," but only those who "do sigh.")*

8 The mirth of tabrets ceases, the noise of them who rejoice ends, the joy of the harp ceases. *(All is dismay and wretchedness — desolation in the present and worse desolation expected in the future.)*

9 They shall not drink wine with a song; strong drink shall be bitter to them who drink it. *(This Passage does not mean that men will cease drinking alcohol; they will probably drink even more, yet without any accompanying merriment that usually corresponds with such action.*

During the last three and a half years of the Great Tribulation, there will be no more "joy" in Israel.)

10 The city of confusion is broken down: every house is shut up, that no man may come in. *(This probably addresses Jerusalem. Chaos reigns. There is no civic life, no government, no order, and nothing but confusion [Zech. 14:2].)*

11 There is a crying for wine in the streets; all joy is darkened, the mirth of the land is gone. *(During the Great Tribulation, there is implication that great amounts of alcohol will be consumed. They will desire its opiate for the oblivion it brings when drunk to excess.)*

12 In the city is left desolation, and the gate is smitten with destruction. *(No amount of negotiations, diplomacy, or treaty agreements can halt the inevitable march of this coming doom, because the Third Verse says, "The LORD has spoken this Word."*

Even though this judgment is horrifying, still, it is not meant by the Lord to be punitive, but

JEWISH REMNANT REJOICES

13 When thus it shall be in the midst of the land among the people, there shall be as the shaking of an olive tree, and as the gleaning grapes when the vintage is done. *(The idea of this Verse is to portray the tremendous number of Jews who will be killed in the latter half of the Great Tribulation and at the Battle of Armageddon. Zechariah said that two-thirds would die [Zech. 13:8]. There are approximately 5 million Jews in Israel presently. The death of two-thirds would leave about 1.6 million alive. As stated, it won't be a pleasant time!)*

14 They shall lift up their voice, they shall sing for the majesty of the LORD, they shall cry aloud from the sea. *(This refers to the remnant that is left at the beginning of the Kingdom Age, after Christ has returned, and those remaining in Israel have accepted Him as Saviour and Lord. There will be great rejoicing [Zech. 13:9].)*

15 Wherefore glorify ye the LORD in the fires, even the name of the LORD God of Israel in the isles of the sea. *(It seems that the word "fires" is an unfortunate translation. The rendering which the Hebrew seems to suggest is that the "Lord" will be glorified even to the borders of Israel.*

"Crying aloud from the sea" refers to the border on the west, which is the Mediterranean.)

A NEW AGE FOLLOWING JUDGMENT

16 From the uttermost part of the Earth have we heard songs, even glory to the righteous. But I said, My leanness, my leanness, woe unto me! the treacherous dealers have dealt treacherously; yea, the treacherous dealers have dealt very treacherously. *(The "Righteous" is the "Messiah." Israel rejected the "Righteous One" and accepted the "treacherous dealers," which brought a terrible "leanness." Now they will have finally realized their tragic mistake, and, at long last, will glorify "the Righteous," i.e., "Christ.")*

17 Fear, and the pit, and the snare, are upon you, O inhabitant of the Earth. *(The Prophecy now reverts back to the time of the Great Tribulation. "Fear" will captivate the entirety of mankind and even the atmosphere.)*

18 And it shall come to pass, that he who flees from the noise of the fear shall fall into the pit; and he who comes up out of the midst of the pit shall be taken in the snare: for the windows from on high are open, and the foundations of the Earth do shake. *(These great judgments in the coming Great Tribulation will affect the entirety of the Earth [Rev. 6:12-17; 11:13; 16:17-21].)*

19 The Earth is utterly broken down, the Earth is clean dissolved, the Earth is moved exceedingly. *(The implication from the Scholars is that the English translation is very feeble compared to the original. Giant earthquakes, greater than the world has ever seen before, will no doubt be instrumental in this great calamity [Rev. 16:18].)*

20 The Earth shall reel to and fro like a drunkard, and shall be removed like a cottage; and the transgression thereof shall be heavy upon it; and it shall fall, and not rise again. *(The phrase, "shall be removed like a cottage," means to sway to and fro like a hammock. During this time, one can well imagine what will happen to the tides, mountains, and even vast continents! [Rev. 16:16-21].)*

21 And it shall come to pass in that day, that the LORD shall punish the host of the high ones who are on high, and the kings of the Earth upon the Earth. *(The words, "in that day," refer to the Battle of Armageddon. Then, all the mighty men on Earth, plus Satan, demon spirits, and fallen angels, will be dealt with by the Lord at the Second Coming [Rev. 19:19-21; 20:1-10].)*

22 And they shall be gathered together, as prisoners are gathered in the pit, and shall be shut up in the prison, and after many days shall they be visited. *(Satan and all fallen angels and demon spirits will be locked in the bottomless pit for a thousand years [Rev. 20:17]. At the end of that thousand years will be the second resurrection of damnation, when every unsaved person who has ever lived will stand before God at the Great White Throne Judgment. There will be no reprieve.*

So, Jesus Christ can be your Saviour today or your Judge tomorrow; but one way or the other, all will face Christ [Rev. 20:11-15].)

THE MILLENNIAL REIGN OF THE MESSIAH

23 Then the moon shall be confounded, and the sun ashamed, when the LORD of Hosts shall reign in Mount Zion, and in

Jerusalem, and before His ancients gloriously. *(The Chapter closes with the glorious Promise of the coming Kingdom Age.)*

CHAPTER 25
(712 B.C.)
MILLENNIAL WORSHIP: PRAISE FOR GOD'S PAST RIGHTEOUS JUDGMENTS

O LORD, You are my God; I will exalt You, I will praise Your name; for You have done wonderful things; Your counsels of old are faithfulness and truth. *(This Chapter pertains to the coming Millennial morn, when the cause of all suffering will be put away and the cause of all life will be enthroned. He is Christ. The Promises are glorious and they will surely come to pass.)*

2 For You have made of a city an heap; of a defenced city a ruin: a palace of strangers to be no city; it shall never be built. *(The things outlined in this Chapter include the destruction of Babylon, which represents all of man's rebellion against God. It will never be rebuilt. Sin and rebellion have had their day; Righteousness now prevails.)*

3 Therefore shall the strong people glorify You *(Babylon)*, the city of the terrible nations shall fear You. *(Babylon, whether the actual city or the system, is the city indicated in Verse 2; it will be rebuilt by the Antichrist, who will head it up; it will express all the opposition to the True Prince of this world from the day of its foundation by Nimrod. But now all of that will have its end, and will never rise again.)*

4 For You have been a strength to the poor, a strength to the needy in his distress, a refuge from the storm, a shadow from the heat, when the blast of the terrible ones is as a storm against the wall. *(The "poor" and "needy" in this Passage refer to Israel in particular and to all who follow the Lord in all ages, in opposition to the "strong people" and "terrible nations" in Verse 3, which oppose God's People.*

While the efforts by the Evil One against the Child of God are mighty, still, the protection by the Righteous One is Almighty!)

5 You shall bring down the noise of strangers, as the heat in a dry place; even the heat with the shadow of a cloud: the branch of the terrible ones shall be brought low. *(The Prophecy now reverts from the Millennial Reign back to the Battle of Armageddon and the defeat of the Antichrist.)*

PRAISE FOR BLESSINGS TO GOD'S PEOPLE AND JUDGMENT ON ENEMIES

6 And in this mountain shall the LORD of Hosts make unto all people a feast of fat things, a feast of wines on the lees, of fat things full of marrow, of wines on the lees well refined. *(The greatness of this "feast" is vividly suggested by the way the words are heaped together. This is even more apparent in the Hebrew Text.*

The Kingdom Age will be the grandest time the world has ever known. For the first time, planet Earth will be at rest from all war, starvation, pain, and sickness.)

7 And He will destroy in this mountain the face of the covering cast over all people, and the vail that is spread over all nations. *("In this mountain" refers to the headquarters of Christ on Earth, which will be Jerusalem and Mount Zion.*

Since Adam's Fall, no one has ever seen the world, or man for that matter, as God originally created them. When Christ comes back, for the first time things will be as they ought to be, because Christ reigns.)

8 He will swallow up death in victory; and the Lord GOD will wipe away tears from off all faces; and the rebuke of His people shall He take away from off all the Earth: for the LORD has spoken it. *(The "swallowing up of death in victory" has to do with the First Resurrection of life. While death will not be taken away totally from the Earth during the Kingdom Age, it definitely will be taken away totally for all who know Christ.*

Hosea, who was a contemporary of Isaiah, was the first one to mention the abolishment of death. Other than that, this Passage by Isaiah was the first announcement that death was to disappear and cease to be a possibility. To have such an announcement as this was an enormous advance on the dim and vague conceptions of a future life current to that time. Hitherto, men had been "through fear of death all their lives subject to bondage" [Heb. 2:14]. Now, they were taught that in the Resurrection-life there would be no fear and no possibility of death.

The joyous outburst of the Apostle Paul, when he quotes the present Passage [I Cor. 15:54], is the natural thanksgiving song of reassured humanity from recognizing its final Deliverance from the unspeakable terror of death and the

unknown beyond.

This great pronouncement is closed by the words, *"The LORD has spoken it."* There can be no retraction. The blessings promised are certain to be obtained. As stated, this will be during the Millennial Reign.)

9 And it shall be said in that day, Lo, this is our God; we have waited for Him, and He will save us: this is the LORD; we have waited for Him, we will be glad and rejoice in His Salvation. *(The words, "in that day," place the time factor of this great pronouncement in the Millennium, which is the same as the "Kingdom Age."*

The phrase, "this is our God," means "this Man is Jehovah," speaking of Christ.

The words, "He will save us," refer to the Second Coming, when the Lord of Glory, the One they first rejected, will come and save them. He is the only One Who can save them.)

10 For in this mountain shall the hand of the LORD rest, and Moab shall be trodden down under Him, even as straw is trodden down for the dunghill. *(Once again, "this mountain" refers to Mount Zion in Jerusalem. The first nine Verses of this Chapter contain the song that is to be sung; the last three, faith's subscription as the certitude of its being sung.*

"Moab" is representative of every form of human hostility. In fact, the Moabites in ancient times were the bitterest of all the adversaries of Israel [II Ki. 24:2; Ezek. 25:8-11]. Therefore, they are regarded as the fittest representatives of the human adversaries of God.)

11 And He shall spread forth His hands in the midst of them, as He Who swims spreads forth His hands to swim: and He shall bring down their pride together with the spoils of their hands. *(Christ will only have to order the decree and it shall be done; that refers to whatever is needed. All enemies of Righteousness will be put down, and forever.)*

12 And the fortress of the high fort of your walls shall He bring down, lay low, and bring to the ground, even to the dust. *("Your walls" refer to both Babylon and Moab. Thus, Babylon and Moab are morally united in this Prophecy. Babylon often appears as a political oppressor and Moab as a spiritual corruptor [Num., Chpts. 22-24].*

The idea is that this "fortress" of Satan will be brought down to the ground, even to the dust, which insures certain, total, and absolute defeat, never to rise again.)

CHAPTER 26
(712 B.C.)

A MILLENNIAL SONG: PRAISE FOR THE SALVATION OF THE RIGHTEOUS AND PUNISHMENT OF THE WICKED

IN that day shall this song be sung in the land of Judah; We have a strong city; salvation will God appoint for walls and bulwarks. *(The entirety of this Chapter is a Millennial song to be sung by Judah as a song of triumph in that coming Glad Day.*

The "night" of Israel's captivity and subjection [Vs. 9] is to be succeeded by the "day" of her Restoration and glory.

"The lofty city" [Babylon, Vs. 5], representative of Satan's whole power, will be destroyed, and the "strong city" [Jerusalem] will be beautified and fortified by Jehovah, its Salvation.

The words, "in that day," signify the coming Millennium, and consequently have not yet been fulfilled.)

2 Open ye the gates, that the righteous nation which keeps the truth may enter in. *(Israel has never fully kept "the Truth," but now will do so. "The Truth" is the Word of God.)*

3 You will keep him in perfect peace, whose mind is stayed on You: because he trusts in You. *(The keynote of this Passage is "Peace." It speaks of the coming Glad Day of the Millennium, when Christ, the Prince of Peace, reigns supremely on Earth.*

As well, every Believer can presently enjoy the tremendous fruit of this Promise by keeping our minds centered on Christ and what Christ has done for us at the Cross. This shows total and complete "trust.")

4 Trust ye in the LORD for ever: for in the LORD JEHOVAH is everlasting strength *(Jehovah is the Rock of Ages, the Undefeatable One, the Eternal Strong One. The implication of this Verse is that whereas men, even faithful men, will sometimes prove unfaithful, the Lord can be trusted "forever." He will not change or vary in direction. What He says today, He will say tomorrow):*

5 For He brings down them who dwell on high; the lofty city, He lays it low; He lays it low, even to the ground; He brings it even to the dust. *("The lofty city" is Babylon. It speaks of Satan's efforts through man from the beginning, and it will never rise again. Immediately before or at the Second Coming, the Lord will "lay it low.")*

6 The foot shall tread it down, even the

feet of the poor, and the steps of the needy. *(The "poor" and "needy" constitute Israel. Now, energized by Christ, she shall tread down the glory and power of the enemy.)*

THE WAY OF THE RIGHTEOUS

7 The way of the just is uprightness: You, Most Upright, do weigh the path of the just. *(The way of the just can be described with one word — uprightness. The "Most Upright" is Christ. He is the One Who makes level the "path of the just." As well, one can be "just" only in Christ and Faith in what He did for us at the Cross.)*

8 Yea, in the way of Your judgments, O LORD, have we waited for You; the desire of our soul is to Your name, and to the remembrance of You. *(The righteous nation and the righteous person do not follow the judgments of their own wisdom, but walk in the way of Divine Judgments, and in the energy of true affection for the absent but expected Messiah.)*

9 With my soul have I desired You in the night; yea, with my spirit within me will I seek You early: for when Your judgments are in the Earth, the inhabitants of the world will learn righteousness. *(This is similar to a portion of the Lord's prayer, "Your Will be done on Earth as it is in Heaven" [Mat. 6:10]. That prayer has yet to be answered, but most surely it will be answered!)*

THE WAY OF THE WICKED

10 Let favour be shown to the wicked, yet will he not learn righteousness: in the land of uprightness will he deal unjustly, and will not behold the majesty of the LORD. *(This Verse foretells the present dispensation of Grace and predicts man's rejection of it. Verses 9 and 11 point to the day of wrath that is to succeed it. Then man will learn that God is faithful to His People and righteous in His punishment of their adversaries.)*

11 LORD, when Your hand is lifted up, they will not see: but they shall see, and be ashamed for their envy at the people; yea, the fire of Your enemies shall devour them. *(This Verse may be thus understood: "Lord, Your Hand is lifted up in indignation in defense of Your People, Israel; yet the wicked nations do not recognize it; but they shall see Your Zeal for Your ancient People and shall be ashamed; and the fire reserved for Your Adversaries shall devour them."*

If men will not yield to God's Grace, they must bow to His Wrath!)

THE PRAYER OF GOD'S PEOPLE ANSWERED

12 LORD, You will ordain peace for us: for You also have wrought all our works in us. *(As it is with Israel, so it is with Believers; our Salvation is ordained and accomplished by God Alone.)*

13 O LORD our God, other lords beside You have had dominion over us; but by You only will we make mention of Your name. *(The "other lords" were the oppressors of the past. But it is the Lord Alone Who holds the answers.)*

14 They are dead, they shall not live; they are deceased, they shall not rise: therefore have You visited and destroyed them, and made all their memory to perish. *(Those who oppressed Israel, Isaiah says, are "dead" and "deceased," and shall not rise and live in the First Resurrection [Rev. 20:6]; however, they shall rise in the second resurrection of damnation [Rev. 20:14-15], and then they shall be punished, destroyed, and all their memory caused to perish.)*

15 You have increased the nation, O LORD, You have increased the nation: You are glorified: You have removed it far unto all the ends of the Earth. *(The Lord increased Israel, and then removed it, because of rebellion against Righteousness. But Israel will be restored.)*

16 LORD, in trouble have they visited You, they poured out a prayer when Your chastening was upon them. *(Israel has done this many times in the past, but will do it even in a greater way during the last half of the Great Tribulation. At that time, they will truly be "in trouble" [Jer. 20:1-9; Dan. 12:1; Rev., Chpt. 12].)*

17 Like as a woman with child, who draws near the time of her delivery, is in pain, and cries out in her pangs; so have we been in Your sight, O LORD. *(Paul alluded to this in I Thess. 5:3. Israel will then find out that the Antichrist is not really the Messiah, but an imposter, meaning that the last half of the Great Tribulation is going to be a terrible time for Israel, actually more terrible than she has every known before [Mat. 24:21].)*

18 We have been with child, we have been in pain, we have as it were brought forth wind; we have not wrought any deliverance in the Earth; neither have the inhabitants of the world fallen. *(In effect, the Holy Spirit is saying through Isaiah that Israel has brought forth nothing in the world but "wind." They did not bring*

any "deliverance to the Earth," as God intended, because they became too lifted up in their own self-righteousness. "The inhabitants of the world," namely the Gentiles, did not bow to Israel's God, but instead continued to worship idols [Rom. 10:1-3].)

RESURRECTION OF THE JUST; PUNISHMENT OF THE UNJUST

19 Your dead men shall live, together with my dead body shall they arise. Awake and sing, you who dwell in dust: for your dew is as the dew of herbs, and the Earth shall cast out the dead. (The Holy Spirit in this Passage declares the Truth of the coming Resurrection of Life [I Thess. 4:16-18]. The phrase, "And the Earth shall cast out the dead," refers to the giants, or the Rephaim, which the Earth will not yield up in Resurrection. This concerns fallen angels who cohabited with women, bringing forth a race of giants [Gen. 6:4].)

20 Come, My people, enter thou into your chambers, and shut your doors about you: hide yourself as it were for a little moment, until the indignation be overpast. (This speaks of the latter half of the Great Tribulation, and comprises about three and a half years. At this time, when Israel is invaded by the Antichrist, she will flee to Petra, which is in modern-day Jordan, comprising the area once known as Edom and Moab.)

21 For, behold, the LORD comes out of His place to punish the inhabitants of the Earth for their iniquity: the Earth also shall disclose her blood, and shall no more cover her slain. (This proclaims the Wrath of God being poured out upon the Earth in the coming Great Tribulation. It refers, as well, to the Battle of Armageddon, which will take place at the very conclusion of the Great Tribulation.)

CHAPTER 27
(712 B.C.)
SATAN DEFEATED AT ARMAGEDDON

IN that day the LORD with His sore and great and strong sword shall punish Leviathan the piercing serpent, even Leviathan that crooked serpent; and He shall slay the dragon that is in the sea. (The words, "in that day," refer to the Great Tribulation and the Millennium. As well, "Leviathan" refers to Satan. Victory over this "Evil One" will take place at the Battle of Armageddon [Rev., Chpt. 19].)

A MILLENNIAL SONG

2 In that day sing ye unto her, A vineyard of red wine. (This refers to the Millennium, when this "Vineyard" called Israel will, at long last, bring forth the proper fruit, and in copious amounts!)

3 I the LORD do keep it; I will water it every moment: lest any hurt it, I will keep it night and day. (This guarantees that Israel will never again wander, but rather will walk close to the Lord, and forever.)

4 Fury is not in Me: who would set the briers and thorns against Me in battle? I would go through them, I would burn them together. (The anger of the Lord toward Judah has been eternally abated, because they have accepted Him as Saviour and Lord. As well, He will allow no "briers and thorns" to grow in this Vineyard. In effect, it will be a pure Vineyard.)

5 Or let him take hold of My strength, that he may make peace with Me, and he shall make peace with Me. (Now the Lord addresses the nations of the world that have previously thrown in their lot with the Antichrist. The Lord will invite these nations to "make peace with Me." Every indication is that they will!)

6 He shall cause them who come of Jacob to take root: Israel shall blossom and bud, and fill the face of the world with fruit. (Israel being now in her rightful place will insure the blessing of the entirety of the world [Ps. 67].)

7 Has He smitten him, as He smote those who smote him? or is he slain according to the slaughter of them who are slain by Him? (The question of this Verse is: "Did God chasten Israel in the same measure that He smote her oppressors?" The following Verse supplies the answer. It is "No!")

8 In measure, when it shoots forth, you will debate with it: he stays his rough wind in the day of the east wind. (The words, "in measure," refer to the purging of Israel, but not to its destruction. The words, "when it shoots forth," refer to the stroke of judgment which was for correction and not for destruction. The "rough wind" was tempered as well as the tempestuous and violent "east wind."

Israel is the mystery people of the ages. By all logical accounts, they should have gone into the dark night long ago; nevertheless, despite the ferocious attacks by the enemy, they have remained a viable people. It is because of this one Verse!)

9 By this therefore shall the iniquity of

Jacob be purged; and this is all the fruit to take away his sin; when he makes all the stones of the Altar as chalkstones that are beaten in sunder, the groves and images shall not stand up. *(The cleansing effect of this purging of the Vine is declared. In this Verse, the word "fruit" means "results." The result of chastening is that iniquity is purged and sin taken away.*

This is not necessarily the expiation of guilt by the Atonement of Christ, for that has already been done, but it is the purging of a branch already in the True Vine [Zech. 13:1; Jn., Chpt. 15].)

10 Yet the defenced city shall be desolate, and the habitation forsaken, and left like a wilderness: there shall the calf feed, and there shall he lie down, and consume the branches thereof. *(The "defensed city" is Jerusalem. Isaiah now comes back to his present day, and speaks of the coming destruction of Jerusalem by Nebuchadnezzar. This would happen a little over a hundred years later. Jerusalem was destroyed again in A.D. 70. And even though it was inhabited, and has been from then until now, still, for the last 2,000 years, as far as God is concerned, spiritually it is "left like a wilderness.")*

11 When the boughs thereof are withered, they shall be broken off: the women come, and set them on fire: for it is a people of no understanding: therefore He Who made them will not have mercy on them, and He Who formed them will show them no favour. *(A little over a hundred years after this Prophecy, Israel was "broken off," exactly as was prophesied by Isaiah.)*

ISRAEL WILL BE REGATHERED
TO MOUNT ZION

12 And it shall come to pass in that day, that the LORD shall beat off from the channel of the river unto the stream of Egypt, and you shall be gathered one by one, O ye children of Israel. *(The words, "in that day," as usual, speak of the Millennium. After Israel accepts Jesus as their Saviour and Lord, which they will immediately after the Second Coming, there will be a great migration of Jews from all over the world to Israel, and with great joy.)*

13 And it shall come to pass in that day, that the great trumpet shall be blown, and they shall come which were ready to perish in the land of Assyria, and the outcasts in the land of Egypt, and shall worship the LORD in the Holy Mount at Jerusalem. *("The great*

trumpet" will be the Jubilee Trump, summoning all Israel to the Feast of Tabernacles, which will be celebrated to and with the Messiah at Jerusalem. When the "trumpet" blows, "the outcasts" will finally come home!)

CHAPTER 28
(725 B.C.)
WOE TO EPHRAIM

WOE to the crown of pride, to the drunkards of Ephraim, whose glorious beauty is a fading flower, which are on the head of the fat valleys of them who are overcome with wine! *(Chapters 28 through 35 may be regarded as one continuous Prophecy. Its "woes" are contrasted with the "burdens" of the preceding section. In these "woes," the Divine purpose is alternately thrown into sharp contrast.*

The men of Ephraim [the Northern Kingdom] were drunkards, both actually and morally. They were intoxicated with the strong wine of idolatry.)

2 Behold, the Lord has a mighty and strong one, which as a tempest of hail and a destroying storm, as a flood of mighty waters overflowing, shall cast down to the Earth with the hand. *(The "mighty and strong one" pertains to the king of Assyria, who was to destroy the Northern Kingdom and, thereby, take the Ten Tribes into captivity [II Ki., Chpt. 17].*

As well, after "cast down," supply the words, "drunkards of Ephraim.")

3 The crown of pride, the drunkards of Ephraim, shall be trodden under feet *(this "crown of pride" is the self-complacency and boastful spirit of the Israelite people, who will be "trodden under feet" by the Assyrians):*

4 And the glorious beauty, which is on the head of the fat valley, shall be a fading flower, and as the hasty fruit before the summer; which when he who looks upon it sees, while it is yet in his hand he eats it up. *(Figs ripen in August, but some which ripen in June are considered a great delicacy. Immediately, they are plucked then and eaten. So would Sennacherib, the Assyrian prince, quickly and thoroughly swallow up Samaria.)*

5 In that day shall the LORD of Hosts be for a crown of glory, and for a diadem of beauty, unto the residue of His people. *(Across the gloom of this Chapter is cast the bright ray of Verses 5 and 6. The Prophecy of these two Verses pertains to Isaiah's day, as well as the coming Millennium.)*

6 And for a spirit of judgment to him who sits in judgment, and for strength to them who turn the battle to the gate. *(Hezekiah came to the throne of Judah only three years before the fatal siege of Samaria, the Northern Kingdom, began. It was the dawn of a day of promise for the Southern Kingdom, such as the Prophet seems to point to in these two Verses. Under Hezekiah, the Lord would bring back "a spirit of judgment," which pertains to the following of the Bible.*

The "strength" addressed here pertains to Hezekiah smiting the Philistines, etc. [II Ki. 18:8].)

WOE TO JUDAH

7 But they also *(Judah)* have erred through wine, and through strong drink are out of the way; the Priest and the Prophet have erred through strong drink, they are swallowed up of wine, they are out of the way through strong drink; they err in vision, they stumble in judgment. *(The magistrates were "Priests." The Preachers were "Prophets." These were drunk in the pulpit ["they reel in Vision"] and were tipsy while on the bench ["they stumble in judgment"]. This tells us that the reformation effected by Hezekiah was but a half-reformation. It put away idolatry, but it left untouched a variety of moral evils.)*

8 For all tables are full of vomit and filthiness, so that there is no place clean. *(Isaiah says, "There is no place," referring to the fact that every part of Judah, from the ruling order to the Priestly order, was contaminated. It was quite an indictment!)*

9 Whom shall he teach knowledge? and whom shall he make to understand doctrine? them who are weaned from the milk, and drawn from the breasts. *(This Verse is meant to be understood as the mocking words of the scornful men of Jerusalem [Vs. 14]. They taunted Isaiah with his own words, "knowledge" and "doctrine," insinuating that they were mere "catch-words."*

The term translated "doctrine" properly means "tidings," and involves the idea that the Prophet obtained the teachings so designated by direct Revelation from God.)

10 For precept must be upon precept, precept upon precept; line upon line, line upon line; here a little, and there a little *(the Hebrew word for "precept" is "tsav" and means "injunction" or "commandment." The second "precept" is from the Hebrew word "tsavah," which means "to enjoin" or "to appoint, charge, set in order."*

The Hebrew for "line" is "qav," which means "a rule, measuring cord, here a little and there a little."

The idea is that everything must be measured by the Word of God. No other "measurement" will be accepted. To be sure, Judah fell woefully short):

11 For with stammering lips and another tongue will He speak to this people. *(The phrase, "stammering lips," refers to a proper language being spoken, but yet the people hearing it would not understand it. Paul quoted this same Passage as it regards the Gift of Tongues as a sign to unbelievers [I Cor. 14:21-22]. Oftentimes, the Holy Spirit used strange circumstances to present Prophecy proclaiming tremendously important coming events, even as this Prophecy does.*

Such also was the Prophecy given through Isaiah of the Birth of Christ through a "virgin" [Isa. 7:14]. The occasion would be the unbelief, ridicule, and scorn of wicked Ahaz.

Therefore, it seems that the Holy Spirit designed both these Prophecies [the Virgin Birth of Christ and the Baptism with the Holy Spirit], to occasion faith in Believers and unbelief in mockers!)

12 To whom He said, This is the rest wherewith you may cause the weary to rest; and this is the refreshing: yet they would not hear. *(Coupled with Verse 11, this tells us that speaking with other tongues brings about a "rest" from the tiredness of the journey of life. As well, speaking with other tongues brings about a "refreshing," which rejuvenates the person. Many people ask, "What good is there in speaking with other tongues?" This mentioned by Isaiah presents two blessings, of which there are many. Regrettably, despite this tremendous gift given to the people of God, at least to those who will believe, like Judah of old, most "will not hear," even as Paul quoted Isaiah [I Cor. 14:21].)*

13 But the Word of the LORD was unto them precept upon precept, precept upon precept; line upon line, line upon line; here a little, and there a little; that they might go, and fall backward, and be broken, and snared, and taken. *(The meaning is that because they would not hear, therefore, by a just judgment, will the simplicity of the Gospel become a stumbling-block to them, resulting in their captivity.*

While this "captivity" pertained to Judah of old, it also pertains to modern Christians who "will not hear.")

JERUSALEM WARNED

14 Wherefore hear the Word of the LORD, you scornful men, who rule this people which is in Jerusalem. *(Isaiah now turns from a denunciation of the Priests and Prophets, who especially opposed his teaching, to a threatening of the great men who guided the course of public affairs. He called them "scornful men.")*

15 Because you have said, We have made a covenant with death, and with Hell are we at agreement; when the overflowing scourge shall pass through, it shall not come unto us: for we have made lies our refuge, and under falsehood have we hid ourselves *(the "covenant of death" that Isaiah was speaking of was probably Judah's agreement with Egypt. It also refers to the "covenant" that Israel will make with the Antichrist at the beginning of the Great Tribulation.*

It is very interesting to see the terminology used by the Holy Spirit. Truly the "covenant" that Judah had made, whatever it was, was with "death" and "Hell");

16 Therefore thus saith the Lord GOD, Behold, I lay in Zion for a foundation a Stone, a tried Stone, a precious Corner Stone, a sure Foundation: he who believes shall not make haste. *(This Passage speaks of the Lord Jesus Christ. As Zion was not itself the Corner Stone, so the Church is not the Saviour. Christ is the "Stone," but sadly almost the entirety of the world stumbles over this "tried Stone."*

Every "foundation" that is not "Jesus Christ and Him Crucified" is built upon "lies" and "falsehood.")

17 Judgment also will I lay to the line, and righteousness to the plummet: and the hail shall sweep away the refuge of lies, and the waters shall overflow the hiding place. *(A "plummet" is a piece of metal on a string that makes a straight line of its own weight as it hangs down. Not only is the Messiah the Foundation, He is also the "Plummet," i.e., He is the standard of Righteousness that will stand in the judgment. All who stand there will be measured by this Divine Line and Plummet, and those who are not found as perfect and sinless as He will be rejected.)*

18 And your covenant with death shall be disannulled, and your agreement with Hell shall not stand; when the overflowing scourge shall pass through, then you shall be trodden down by it. *(The Assyrians, like an overflowing scourge, would go through Judah. The Holy*

Spirit is saying that the entire clever arrangement by which Judah thought to avert the danger from themselves will come to naught.)

19 From the time that it goes forth it shall take you: for morning by morning shall it pass over, by day and by night: and it shall be a vexation only to understand the report. *(The words, "to understand the report," are an allusion to Verse 9. They had scorned Isaiah's "doctrine," when he taught them by word of mouth; they will understand it too well and find it "nothing but a terror," when it is impressed upon them by its actual fulfillment.)*

20 For the bed is shorter than that a man can stretch himself on it: and the covering narrower than that he can wrap himself in it. *(The Jews will have made themselves a bed in which they can have no comfort or ease, and consequently no rest. But they will only have themselves to blame! This also has reference to the Plumbline. The righteousness produced by man is woefully inadequate.)*

21 For the LORD shall rise up as in Mount Perazim, He shall be wroth as in the valley of Gibeon, that He may do His work, His strange work; and bring to pass His act, His strange act. *(Just as God broke forth at Gibeon and at Perazim [II Sam. 5:20], so He was about to break forth upon His Own People; but, He adds with anguish in His tone, to act against them would be for Him a foreign and an unwanted action, i.e., "a strange work."*

It was Judah's strange conduct which caused God's strange action. They had become, as it were, Philistines.)

22 Now therefore be ye not mockers, lest your bands be made strong: for I have heard from the Lord GOD of Hosts a consumption, even determined upon the whole Earth. *(The Holy Spirit through the Prophet now entreats Judah to repent.)*

AN ILLUSTRATION OF THE FARMER

23 Give ye ear, and hear My voice; hearken, and hear My speech. *(Judah at this time would in fact partially hear. Because of the intercession of Hezekiah and Isaiah, God would send an Angel who would kill 185,000 Assyrian soldiers. Thus, Jerusalem and Judah would be spared, at least for now.)*

24 Does the plowman plow all day to sow? does he open and break the clods of his ground? *(Using a farmer as an example, the Lord in effect says that He will try again to bring*

Judah to the place she ought to be.)

25 When he has made plain the face thereof, does he not cast abroad the fitches, and scatter the cummin, and cast in the principal wheat and the appointed barley and the rie in their place? *(The detail to which the Holy Spirit went in describing how the farmer protects his land and plants the seed illustrates the detail with which God had prepared the spiritual soil of Judah.)*

26 For his God does instruct him to discretion, and does teach him. *(That which taught man then, and that which teaches man now, is the Word of God.)*

27 For the fitches are not threshed with a threshing instrument, neither is a cart wheel turned about upon the cummin; but the fitches are beaten out with a staff, and the cummin with a rod.

28 Bread corn is bruised; because he will not ever be threshing it, nor break it with the wheel of his cart, nor bruise it with his horsemen. *(The idea is that the farmer will not continue always threshing the grain nor crunching it with his cart wheel and with his horses. In other words, he will not bruise it.*

The afflictions which God sends upon His People are adapted to their strengths or the lack thereof, and to their needs. In no case are they used to crush and injure; only such violence is used that is required to detach the good seed from the husk. Where the process is most severe, still, the "bread corn" is not "bruised.")

29 This also comes forth from the LORD of Hosts, which is wonderful in counsel, and excellent in working. *(The Prophet goes no further, but leaves his disciples to draw the conclusion that God's Own method of working will be similar to the farmer threshing the grain [Prov. 8:14].)*

CHAPTER 29
(712 B.C.)
JUDGMENT ON JERUSALEM

WOE to Ariel, to Ariel, the city where David dwelt! add ye year to year; let them kill sacrifices. *(The word "Ariel" means "the Lion of God," which is another name for Jerusalem.*

Judah thought that their religious activity [the offering of the Sacrifices] would cancel the judgment that was determined upon Jerusalem; however, their experience was ceremony only, with no relationship with the Lord.)

2 Yet I will distress Ariel, and there shall be heaviness and sorrow: and it shall be unto me as Ariel. *(Two things are said here: 1. The religious activity, for all the obvious reasons, would not stop God's Hand of Judgment and 2. Despite what will happen, Jerusalem will ultimately be the "Lion of God."*

3 And I will camp against you round about, and will lay siege against you with a mount, and I will raise forts against you. *(These things did not happen when Sennacherib invaded Judah and threatened Jerusalem. So, the coming Tribulation will see its total fulfillment.)*

4 And you shall be brought down, and shall speak out of the ground, and your speech shall be low out of the dust, and your voice shall be, as of one who has a familiar spirit, out of the ground, and your speech shall whisper out of the dust. *(This Passage has to do with the Antichrist breaking his seven-year covenant with Israel at the midpoint and actually invading the land.*

The "familiar spirit" that is spoken of here speaks of the Antichrist setting up his statue in the Temple and demanding worship [II Thess. 2:4].)

5 Moreover the multitude of your strangers shall be like small dust, and the multitude of the terrible ones shall be as chaff that pass away: yea, it shall be at an instant suddenly. *(The "strangers" speak of the hordes who are with the Antichrist when he comes into Israel at the end of the seven-year period, determined to completely destroy the holy people.*

Even though the Antichrist will have so many men in his army that they are likened by the Holy Spirit as "small dust," still, they will "pass away" as "chaff." Isaiah also said it would be done "suddenly," which will take place at the Coming of the Lord.)

6 You shall be visited of the LORD of Hosts with thunder, and with earthquake, and great noise, with storm and tempest, and the flame of devouring fire. *(This will no doubt be the greatest phenomenon the world has ever known. At times in the past, the Lord has used the elements; however, He will use them here as never before [Ezek. 38:17-23].)*

JUDGMENT ON HER ENEMIES

7 And the multitude of all the nations that fight against Ariel, even all who fight against her and her munition, and that distress her, shall be as a dream of a night vision. *(Both Verses 7 and 8 continue to speak of the coming*

Battle of Armageddon, but also have reference to Jerusalem's Deliverance from the Assyrian horde.

Most, if not all, of Psalm 126 is devoted to the miraculous deliverance of Jerusalem from the Assyrian.)

8 It shall even be as when an hungry man dreams, and, behold, he eats; but he awakes, and his soul is empty: or as when a thirsty man dreams, and, behold, he drinks; but he awakes, and, behold, he is faint, and his soul has appetite: so shall the multitude of all the nations be, that fight against Mount Zion. *(The idea is, the Antichrist will feel certain that he is going to take Jerusalem and destroy every Jew down to the last man.*

He is like a "hungry man" who dreams he has eaten a full meal, and awakens and finds that, in fact, he has not eaten anything, but rather is "empty." Contrary to his thoughts, his efforts as well are going to come up "empty.")

THE BLINDNESS OF ISRAEL

9 Stay yourselves, and wonder; cry ye out, and cry: they are drunken, but not with wine; they stagger, but not with strong drink. *(This Verse should read: "Be ye amazed and you shall be amazed! Blind yourselves and you shall become blind!" — that is, a judicial blindness would descend upon them, and they would be amazed at God's Action toward them.*

But these Verses actually belong to the future. Because Israel shut her eyes to the Work and Person of the Messiah at His First Advent, the Book of God and its Vision have ever since been covered with a veil to them and will so remain up to the Second Advent.)

10 For the LORD has poured out upon you the spirit of deep sleep, and has closed your eyes: the Prophets and your rulers, the seers has He covered. *(The "deep sleep" spoken of here refers to a spiritual deadness and impassiveness — an inability to appreciate or even to understand spiritual warnings.)*

11 And the Vision of all is become unto you as the words of a book that is sealed, which men deliver to one who is learned, saying, Read this, I pray you: and he says, I cannot; for it is sealed *(these were "learned" men; in other words, they were knowledgeable in the Word of God; these were the spiritual leaders of Israel, and yet they were totally without spiritual understanding; they were devoid of spiritual discernment; even the rulers were but "blind leaders of the blind"):*

12 And the book is delivered to him who is not learned, saying, Read this, I pray you: and he said, I am not learned. *(The thrust of this Message has little to do with academic excellence. Isaiah is speaking of the spiritual deadness of the people, irrespective of their ability to read or write.)*

13 Wherefore the Lord said, Forasmuch as this people draw near Me with their mouth, and with their lips do honour Me, but have removed their heart far from Me, and their fear toward Me is taught by the precept of men *(this Passage was quoted by Christ [Mat. 15:7-9]; there are four causes of spiritual blindness recorded here: 1. Drawing near to God with the mouth only; 2. Honoring Him with the lips only; 3. Removing the heart far from Him; and, 4. Fearing Him only after the precept of men):*

14 Therefore, behold, I will proceed to do a marvellous work among this people, even a marvellous work and a wonder: for the wisdom of their wise men shall perish, and the understanding of their prudent men shall be hid. *(The idea of the Passage is that despite the unbelief of men, God's Work would nevertheless be carried out. While it is true that the unbelief would cause millions to die eternally lost, still, some would accept. Those who accept will receive Eternal Life.)*

15 Woe unto them who seek deep to hide their counsel from the LORD, and their works are in the dark, and they say, Who sees us? and who knows us? *(In particular, this Passage applies to the secret negotiations between the rulers in Jerusalem and the king of Egypt. They conducted themselves as if the Lord did not know their actions.)*

16 Surely your turning of things upside down shall be esteemed as the potter's clay: for shall the work say of him who made it, He made me not? or shall the thing framed say of him who framed it, He had no understanding? *(These people were so perverse and wrong-headed that they inverted the relation in which they stood to God and God to them. In their thinking, God was to be passive, or merely given opportunities of action; they were to mold, or so they thought, their own plans and carve out their own destinies. Taking their destinies into their own hands was equivalent to saying that they were their own masters, which they could not be if God made them.*

To refuse to take counsel of God and to direct the national policy by the light of their own reason was to tax God with having no understanding.)

THE REDEMPTION OF ISRAEL

17 Is it not yet a very little while, and Lebanon shall be turned into a fruitful field, and the fruitful field shall be esteemed as a forest? *(The Holy Spirit through Isaiah leaps ahead, leaving behind the unbelief, the doubting, and the spiritual obstinacy of Judah. The time that He now speaks of is the coming Kingdom Age, which has not even yet come to pass, but most surely will.)*

18 And in that day shall the deaf hear the words of the Book, and the eyes of the blind shall see out of obscurity, and out of darkness. *(The words, "in that day," at least as far as total fulfillment is concerned, refer to the coming Millennial Reign.)*

19 The meek also shall increase their joy in the LORD, and the poor among men shall rejoice in the Holy One of Israel. *(In effect, the Holy Spirit is saying that even though the men of Judah would not hear the "Holy One of Israel," nevertheless, the "meek" and the "poor" among men, referring to the Gentiles, would "rejoice in the Holy One of Israel."*

This is a veiled reference to the Church, which even Isaiah himself probably did not understand.)

20 For the terrible one is brought to nought, and the scorner is consumed, and all who watch for iniquity are cut off *(this refers to the Battle of Armageddon, when the Antichrist will be killed, with all the scorners at that time set straight; this, of course, will take place at the Second Coming)*:

21 That make a man an offender for a word, and lay a snare for him who reproves in the gate, and turn aside the just for a thing of nought. *(This is the spirit of self-righteousness, which prevailed upon the First Advent of Christ. The Pharisees laid many "snares" for Christ; still, they never caught Him. As well, Christ was the Only Truly "Just" Individual Who ever lived. Israel "turned Him aside for a thing of nought." In other words, for no reason at all!)*

22 Therefore thus saith the LORD, Who redeemed Abraham, concerning the house of Jacob, Jacob shall not now be ashamed, neither shall his face now wax pale. *(In the coming Kingdom Age, Israel will finally conduct herself as she should, because of her acceptance of Christ. This means that "Jacob" will no longer be ashamed.)*

23 But when he sees his children, the work of My hands, in the midst of him, they shall sanctify My name, and sanctify the Holy One

of Jacob, and shall fear the God of Israel. *(This will take place during the coming Kingdom Age, when Israel will accept the Christ Whom they so long rejected. At that time, they will "sanctify the Holy One of Jacob" [Zech. 13:1].)*

24 They also who erred in spirit shall come to understanding, and they who murmured shall learn doctrine. *(The "murmuring" speaks of doubt and unbelief. The phrase, "shall learn doctrine," means that they will willingly receive the teaching of God's Prophets and profit by it.)*

CHAPTER 30

(713 B.C.)

THE FUTILITY OF TRUSTING EGYPT AND THE PHARAOH

WOE to the rebellious children, saith the LORD, who take counsel, but not of Me, and who cover with a covering, but not of My Spirit, that they may add sin to sin *(in the preceding Chapter, the design of the Jewish rulers to seek the alliance of Egypt was covertly looked at and condemned; now it is openly declared and rebuked.*

"Counsel" which is not of the Word of God is also not from God.

As well, only the Spirit of God can cover someone, which He does through the Word, which speaks of what Jesus did for us at the Cross. Actually, the "covering" comes for each Believer through Christ, Who Alone can actually cover. And He does so by the Spirit through the Cross. Christ is the Source, while the Cross is the Means.

Any poor mortal who thinks he can be the "covering" for another presents spiritual and Scriptural ignorance):

2 That walk to go down into Egypt, and have not asked at My mouth; to strengthen themselves in the strength of Pharaoh, and to trust in the shadow of Egypt? *(Egypt symbolized the world. The words, "who walk," insinuate that either the Jewish ambassadors had already started for Egypt or the Prophet sees them as if starting.*

The words, "have not asked at My mouth," refer to the fact that Hezekiah, or at least the nobles of Judah, had not taken this matter to the Lord as they ought to have done [Num. 27:21].)

3 Therefore shall the strength of Pharaoh be your shame, and the trust in the shadow of Egypt your confusion. *(It is a "shame" for God's People to place their trust in man and not in God. The "confusion" is obvious. God's People are supposed to only seek the Lord for help and*

not the ways of the world, which are actually of Satan.)

4 For his princes were at Zoan, and his ambassadors came to Hanes. ("Zoan" was one of the principal cities of ancient Egypt, and it was probably the same as "Tanis." "Hanes" was probably not very far from "Zoan." To this place came Hezekiah's ambassadors. They would seek the help of the Egyptians against Assyria; however, we already know what the Lord has said about this!)

5 They were all ashamed of a people who could not profit them, nor be an help nor profit, but a shame, and also a reproach. (From this proposed alliance, Judah would be "put to shame" and become "also a reproach," which will always be the case for those who turn to the world instead of to the Lord.)

6 The burden of the beasts of the south: into the land of trouble and anguish, from whence come the young and old lion, the viper and fiery flying serpent, they will carry their riches upon the shoulders of young asses, and their treasures upon the bunches of camels, to a people who shall not profit them.

7 For the Egyptians shall help in vain, and to no purpose: therefore have I cried concerning this, Their strength is to sit still. (The intent of the Holy Spirit is to portray the great efforts being made by Judah to appeal to Egypt, even to going through the howling desert; they would not so much as seek the Lord, even though He was with them in Jerusalem.)

GOD WILL JUDGE ISRAEL FOR REBELLION

8 Now go, write it before them in a table, and note it in a book, that it may be for the time to come for ever and ever (Isaiah was told to write an account of this happening in a "Book." It was to be a warning to others, and so it was! As well, it became a part of the Bible):

9 That this is a rebellious people, lying children, children who will not hear the Law of the LORD (the leaders of Judah were both rebels and liars. Not being a fashionable Preacher like many today, Isaiah did not hesitate to tell them so. How they must have hated him! They were rebels, for they rebelled against the Law, and they were liars, because they claimed to keep it):

10 Which say to the seers, See not; and to the Prophets, Prophesy not unto us right things, speak unto us smooth things, prophesy deceits

(the lips of the false prophets did not use the words of Verses 10 through 11; but their hearts did, and God, Who reads the heart, can expose its hatred and folly.

Now, almost all the modern pulpits speak "smooth things" and "prophesy deceits." They aren't hard to find; most any Church on Sunday morning will suffice):

11 Get you out of the way, turn aside out of the path, cause the Holy One of Israel to cease from before us. (The irreligious Jews were weary of this constant iteration and wished to hear no more concerning the "Holy One," Whose very Holiness was a reproach to them.)

12 Wherefore thus saith the Holy One of Israel, Because you despise this word, and trust in oppression and perverseness, and stay thereon. ("This Word" was the Word of God given by the Prophet. The people despised it! He plainly told them that looking to Egypt was in vain. It was a message they did not want to hear.)

13 Therefore this iniquity shall be to you as a breach ready to fall, swelling out in a high wall, whose breaking comes suddenly at an instant. (The Holy Spirit told them through Isaiah that they were building a wall [lack of trust in God] which looked strong on the outside, but would suddenly break "at an instant.")

14 And he shall break it as the breaking of the potters' vessel that is broken in pieces; he shall not spare: so that there shall not be found in the bursting of it a sherd to take fire from the hearth, or to take water withal out of the pit. (The implication is that the destruction would be so complete that there wouldn't be left even a piece large enough to carry water from a pit. The ruin would be total.)

15 For thus saith the Lord GOD, the Holy One of Israel; In returning and rest shall you be saved; in quietness and in confidence shall be your strength: and you would not. ("In returning and rest" refers to their turning back from their proposed embassage to Egypt and their resting in the Promises of God. This would result in Deliverance.

However, the admonition, "and you would not," not only held true then, but sadly holds true now.)

16 But you said, No; for we will flee upon horses; therefore shall you flee: and, We will ride upon the swift; therefore shall they who pursue you be swift. (Rather than come to God and allow Him to have His Way in their lives, they would rather allow Jerusalem to be destroyed and themselves rendered homeless. Their

flippant answer was, "We will flee upon horses.")

17 One thousand shall flee at the rebuke of one; at the rebuke of five shall you flee: till you be left as a beacon upon the top of a mountain, and as an ensign on an hill. *(A pole upon the top of a mountain and a flagstaff on a hill are duplicated figures expressing loneliness and depopulation.)*

SPIRITUAL AND MATERIAL BLESSINGS IN THE MILLENNIUM

18 And therefore will the LORD wait, that He may be gracious unto you, and therefore will He be exalted, that He may have mercy upon you: for the LORD is a God of Judgment: blessed are all they who wait for Him. *(Verses 18 through 26 portray a renewal of Promise. The denunciations of the preceding Passages had been so terrible that, without some counterpose of Promise, they would have produced a general despair.*

This was not the Divine purpose! Judah's probation still continued; therefore, it was not necessary to let it be seen that the Divine longsuffering was not yet exhausted — there were still conditions under which God would be gracious to His People. The conditions were "crying to the Lord" and the entire abolition of idolatry.)

19 For the people shall dwell in Zion at Jerusalem: you shall weep no more: He will be very gracious unto you at the voice of your cry; when He shall hear it, He will answer you. *(This has to do with the Battle of Armageddon, when Israel will cry to the Lord, and also to the Millennium; however, it also applies to any and all, and for all time, who will "cry" unto Him.)*

20 And though the Lord give you the bread of adversity, and the water of affliction, yet shall not your teachers be removed into a corner any more, but your eyes shall see your teachers *(the "teachers being removed into a corner" referred to the Prophets who were sent by the Lord to Israel, but who were so maltreated that they had to hide in a "corner," i.e., flee for their lives. The "bread of adversity" and the "water of affliction," which are chastisements given by the Lord, are always given in love):*

21 And your ears shall hear a word behind you, saying, This is the way, walk ye in it, when you turn to the right hand, and when you turn to the left. *(This pertains to the coming Kingdom Age, when Israel will finally be led by the Lord, and in totality!)*

22 You shall defile also the covering of your graven images of silver, and the ornament of your molten images of gold: you shall cast them away as a menstruous cloth; you shall say unto it, Get thee hence. *(When the Holy Spirit has His Way, He will cleanse our lives of all "graven images" of self-will and rebellion. Once He begins to speak to us and deal with us, we will then begin to see sin and rebellion as filthy as they really are — "a menstruous cloth.")*

23 Then shall He give the rain of your seed, that you shall sow the ground withal; and bread of the increase of the Earth, and it shall be fat and plenteous: in that day shall your cattle feed in large pastures. *(This will take place with Israel in the coming Kingdom Age, but it can take place even now in the heart and life of every Christian who will dare to follow the Lord and do things His Way. Note the contrast of the "bread of adversity" in Verse 20 to the "bread of increase" in this Verse.)*

24 The oxen likewise and the young asses that ear the ground shall eat clean provender, which has been winnowed with the shovel and with the fan. *(The Passage speaks of victory!)*

25 And there shall be upon every high mountain, and upon every high hill, rivers and streams of waters in the day of the great slaughter, when the towers fall. *(This exhibition of Amazing Grace will synchronize with an exhibition of appalling judgment. It will be the day of destruction of the Antichrist, symbolized by the slaughter and destruction of mighty men ["towers"]; in Isaiah's day, this included the annihilation of the Assyrians and their generals [Isa. 37:36].)*

26 Moreover the light of the moon shall be as the light of the sun, and the light of the sun shall be sevenfold, as the light of seven days, in the day that the LORD binds up the breach of His people, and heals the stroke of their wound. *(This will be literal, and will take place in the coming Kingdom Age. The extended "light" of the moon and of the sun speaks of healing, for "light" heals. Such will heal not only Israel, but the entirety of the Earth.)*

JUDGMENT ON ISRAEL'S ENEMIES

27 Behold, the name of the LORD comes from far, burning with His anger, and the burden thereof is heavy: His lips are full of indignation, and His tongue as a devouring fire *(this is a description of the Second Coming, when the Lord will completely destroy the Antichrist and the totality of his army [Ezek., Chpts. 38-39]):*

28 And His breath, as an overflowing stream, shall reach to the midst of the neck, to sift the nations with the sieve of vanity: and there shall be a bridle in the jaws of the people, causing them to err. *(This statement is a metaphor describing the fierceness of God's Judgment. It will reach to the "midst of the neck," meaning that it will be so deep that men cannot walk against it.*

During the Battle of Armageddon, many "nations" will throw in their lot with the Antichrist, thinking not only to destroy all Jews, but also to take over the entirety of the world. Their "vanity" will bring on their destruction. The Lord will "sift" them with the "sieve" of their own "vanity," meaning that the snare they did lay for Israel will catch them instead.)

29 You shall have a song, as in the night when a holy solemnity is kept; and gladness of heart, as when one goes with a pipe to come into the mountain of the LORD, to the Mighty One of Israel. *(After the defeat of the Antichrist, Israel will now sing. Their song will be "to the Mighty One of Israel." At His First Advent, they crucified Him; at His Second Advent, they will sing to Him.)*

30 And the LORD shall cause His glorious voice to be heard, and shall show the lighting down of His arm, with the indignation of His anger, and with the flame of a devouring fire, with scattering, and tempest, and hailstones. *(This was prophesied by Ezekiel, as well [Ezek. 38:17-21]. This Passage refers to the Battle of Armageddon, with the "Assyrian" [Sennacherib] serving as a symbol.)*

31 For through the voice of the LORD shall the Assyrian be beaten down, which smote with a rod. *(The "Assyrian" refers to the Sennacherib, as well as to the coming Antichrist. The "glorious voice" of the Messiah was not "heard" when He first came; however, it will very well now be heard.)*

32 And in every place where the grounded staff shall pass, which the LORD shall lay upon him, it shall be with tabrets and harps: and in battles of shaking will He fight with it. *(As the Lord snatches certain victory out of certain defeat, as the tide instantly turns in favor of His People [the Second Coming], and as the strokes of the Divine Rod smite that wicked king [the Antichrist], God's People will play upon "tabrets and harps.")*

33 For Tophet is ordained of old; yea for the king it is prepared; he has made it deep and large: the pile thereof is fire and much wood;

the breath of the LORD, like a stream of brimstone, does kindle it. *(This Passage speaks of the instant defeat of the Antichrist, a defeat so total that it will be absolutely complete.)*

CHAPTER 31
(713 B.C.)
THE FOLLY OF TRUSTING EGYPT

WOE to them Who go down to Egypt for help; and stay on horses, and trust in chariots, because they are many; and in horsemen, because they are very strong; but they look not unto the Holy One of Israel, neither seek the LORD! *(This Chapter is one of warning, yet also of victory. The people go "down" into Egypt, both geographically and morally; in their fear of the Assyrians, they put their trust in the wisdom and cavalry of the Egyptians instead of in the Lord.)*

2 Yet He also is wise, and will bring evil, and will not call back His words: but will arise against the house of the evildoers, and against the help of them who work iniquity. *(In this Verse, the Holy Spirit is using intense irony. He is saying that "wisdom is not wholly confined to the human counselors whose advice Judah follows. He [Jehovah] is 'wise,' too, and could give prudent counsel, if His Advice were asked."*

By making the statement in this fashion, the Holy Spirit is attempting to bring Judah to the place of comparing God's Wisdom, as opposed to the wisdom of the Egyptians.

The "house of the evildoers" is Jerusalem, "the workers of iniquity" are the men of Judah, and their "help" is the Egyptians.)

3 Now the Egyptians are men, and not God; and their horses flesh, and not Spirit. When the LORD shall stretch out His hand, both he who helps shall fall, and he who is helped shall fall down, and they all shall fail together. *(In this Verse, the comparison is made between the "flesh" and the "Spirit." The "Egyptians" had nothing but the arm of "flesh," while Judah had the Power of the "Spirit," that is, if they would only use it. And that's the problem with the modern Church, as well! As Judah, it resorts to the ways of the world, instead of the Lord. What a sorry trade!)*

GOD PROMISES PROTECTION TO HIS PEOPLE; HE CALLS FOR THEIR TRUST

4 For thus has the LORD spoken unto me, Like as the lion and the young lion roaring on

his prey, when a multitude of shepherds is called forth against him, he will not be afraid of their voice, nor abase himself for the noise of them: so shall the LORD of Hosts come down to fight for Mount Zion, and for the hill thereof. *(Verse Four points to the Might of the God of Israel and Verse Five to His Love. His Might is illustrated by a strong lion putting evil shepherds to flight, and His Love by the action of a bird hovering over its nest in order to protect its brood from the hawk.*

The image of these proposals is best explained as representing Jehovah standing over and keeping guard on Jerusalem, which He will allow no one to rend from Him.)

5 As birds flying, so will the LORD of Hosts defend Jerusalem; defending also He will deliver it; and passing over He will preserve it. *(The Prophecy of this Chapter definitely refers to Isaiah's day, and the Deliverance of Jerusalem from the Assyrians; however, more particularly, it is directed to a future day when the Antichrist will attempt to destroy Israel and Jerusalem, but will be stopped by the Coming of the Lord.)*

6 Turn ye unto Him from Whom the children of Israel have deeply revolted. *(There is a great tenderness in this appeal. It pertained to Israel then, and it pertains to Israel of a coming day. Israel, at the beginning of the Great Tribulation, will accept the false messiah. This is what the Lord means by "deeply revolted.")*

7 For in that day every man shall cast away his idols of silver, and his idols of gold, which your own hands have made unto you for a sin. *(The words, "in that day," speak of Israel's conversion, when she will return unto Jehovah, for true conversion is marked by a turning away from all "idols" and by the destruction of everything that disputes God's Kingdom in the soul.)*

8 Then shall the Assyrian fall with the sword, not of a mighty man; and the sword not of a mean man, shall devour him: but he shall flee from the sword, and his young men shall be discomfited. *(The destruction of the Assyrian host in one night at Lachish by the Lord sending one Angel is predicted in Verses 8 and 9, but that did not exhaust the prediction of this Prophecy. Its total fulfillment awaits the destruction of the Antichrist and his host.*

The Assyrian did not fall with the sword of a "mighty man" or of a "mean man"; he, like the future Assyrian, was "broken without hand," for a plague destroyed his army [Dan. 8:25].)

9 And he shall pass over to his strong hold for fear, and his princes shall be afraid of the Ensign, saith the LORD, Whose fire is in Zion, and His furnace in Jerusalem. *(As stated, the entirety of this Prophecy refers to both Sennacherib, who even then was bearing down upon Jerusalem, and to the Antichrist, who is yet to come.*

The "Ensign" is the Holy Spirit. He dwelt between the Mercy Seat and the Cherubim, and could send "fire" out from that thrice-Holy Place if necessary [II Chron. 7:1].)

CHAPTER 32
(713 B.C.)

THE COMING MILLENNIAL REIGN OF THE RIGHTEOUS KING, THE MESSIAH

BEHOLD, a King shall reign in righteousness, and princes shall rule in judgment. *(The flavor of the Prophecy continues from the previous Chapter. The Antichrist, the false king, is now defeated, and the true "King" now "reigns in righteousness" over the entirety of the world. This "King" is the "Lord Jesus Christ."*

The "princes" refer to the resurrected Saints of all time, who will be kings and priests in the coming Kingdom Age [Dan. 7:19; I Cor. 6:1-3; Zech. 14:5; II Tim. 2:12; Rev. 5:10; 12:5; 20:1-10; 22:4-5].)

2 And a man shall be as an hiding place from the wind, and a covert from the tempest; as rivers of water in a dry place, as the shadow of a great rock in a weary land. *(This "Man" is "The Man Christ Jesus." As well, the world is a "dry place," spiritually speaking. He will be "rivers of water" that will cover this world with the knowledge of the Lord, as the waters cover the sea [Isa. 11:9]. Christ is the "Great Rock," and His "Shadow" will cover the entirety of the Earth.)*

3 And the eyes of them who see shall not be dim, and the ears of them who hear shall hearken. *(Heretofore, it has been very difficult for people to "see" and "hear" the Gospel. But, in that coming day, the Kingdom Age, all "eyes" shall "see," and all "ears" shall "hear" and "hearken," meaning that most will hear and believe.)*

4 The heart also of the rash shall understand knowledge, and the tongue of the stammerers shall be ready to speak plainly. *(Those who are "rash" refer to the ones who would not give themselves time to understand the warnings addressed to them, or to think of the real character of their actions. Then, they will be given a different "heart" and "shall understand knowledge," meaning the Bible.*

The "tongue of the stammerers" speaks of

Preachers of the Gospel, who will then have perfect knowledge of the Word of God and the anointing to deliver it. They "shall be ready to speak plainly.")

5 The vile person shall be no more called liberal, nor the churl said to be bountiful. (The "vile person" of this Verse refers to the modern Preachers of today who are fools and "churls." They are admired as "liberal" [i.e., broadminded] and "bountiful," [i.e., emancipated], but the Holy Spirit calls such Preachers and their preaching "folly," "iniquity," "profaneness," and "error."

The world and most of the Church calls them "liberal" and "bountiful." God calls them "vile persons.")

6 For the vile person will speak villany, and his heart will work iniquity, to practise hypocrisy, and to utter error against the LORD, to make empty the soul of the hungry, and he will cause the drink of the thirsty to fail. (This speaks of false prophets in Isaiah's day, false apostles in Paul's day [II Cor. 11:13-15], and false Preachers in our day.

Consequently, those who are spiritually "hungry" are not fed, and those who are spiritually "thirsty" do not have their thirst slaked. Such characterizes the far greater majority of modern Christendom.)

7 The instruments also of the churl are evil: he devises wicked devices to destroy the poor with lying words, even when the needy speaks right. (The "instruments" [i.e., the arguments or teaching] of the "false apostle" are also evil; they impoverish and destroy the seekers with lying words, though opposed by "the needy" [i.e., Christ's servants] who speak the right [i.e., "plead Truth."])

8 But the liberal devises liberal things; and by liberal things shall he stand. (The "liberal," in the spiritual sense [and good sense, we might add], refers here to the Preacher of the Gospel who truly preaches the Word of God. In the minds of people at the present, the word "liberal" is the same as in Verse 5. For example, the modernists, who do not believe the Word of God, are presently called "liberal." As we have previously stated, God calls them "vile.")

WARNING TO THE WOMEN
OF JERUSALEM

9 Rise up, you women who are at ease; hear my voice, you careless daughters; give ear unto my speech. (The "women" and "daughters" symbolize here the Hebrew people. In essence, the entirety of the population of Judah is admonished to hear what the Lord is saying through the Prophet.)

10 Many days and years shall you be troubled, you careless women: for the vintage shall fail, the gathering shall not come. (The portend of this Verse is frightening! The "vintage" definitely did "fail." The "gathering," which speaks of the harvest, "shall not come." A little over a hundred years from this time, Judah was destroyed and Jerusalem taken by Nebuchadnezzar and the Babylonians. They remained captive for some seventy years.)

11 Tremble, you women who are at ease; be troubled, you careless ones: strip you, and make you bare, and gird sackcloth upon your loins. (The repetition of this Verse is, as usual, emphatic; its object is to impress those whom the Prophet is addressing with a certainty of the coming Judgment.

The "sackcloth" speaks of extreme suffering and sorrow. . . . Still, Judah would not repent!)

12 They shall lament for the teats, for the pleasant fields, for the fruitful vine. (This says that everything will be barren in Israel — and all because of sin!)

13 Upon the land of My people shall come up thorns and briers; yea, upon all the houses of joy in the joyous city (this was literally fulfilled! Sennacherib carried off approximately 200,000 captives from Judea before he was turned back by the visitation of the Angel. "The joyous city" has the sense of unholy mirth; in other words, "Eat and drink, for tomorrow we die!"):

14 Because the palaces shall be forsaken; the multitude of the city shall be left; the forts and towers shall be for dens for ever, a joy of wild asses, a pasture of flocks (in Vision, the Prophet sees Jerusalem deserted by her inhabitants, the grand houses of the rich empty, the strongholds haunted by wild beasts, and the slopes of the hills fed on by sheep, etc.

The Scholars say that the entirety of this Passage is "grammatically strange, the language becoming more complicated, disjointed, and difficult." It is as if there is no language in which the Holy Spirit can properly express Himself, at least that human beings can properly understand);

15 Until the Spirit be poured upon us from on high, and the wilderness be a fruitful field, and the fruitful field be counted for a forest. (The "Holy Spirit" being poured out upon Israel, and in fact the entirety of the world, which will make "the wilderness a fruitful field," will happen at the very end of the Great Tribulation,

after the Battle of Armageddon, immediately after the return of Christ [Zech. 12:10-13:1].)

16 Then judgment shall dwell in the wilderness, and righteousness remain in the fruitful field. *(The word "then" signifies when the "Spirit" is poured out upon Israel and the world "from on high." Then "judgment" and "righteousness" will "remain." Everything that God does is attended by the "Holy Spirit.")*

17 And the work of righteousness shall be peace; and the effect of righteousness quietness and assurance for ever. *(The word "forever" in this Passage means "forever, eternity without end." The "Righteousness" which will cover the Earth then, without fail and perpetually, will be the "Righteousness of Christ," which is made possible by what He did at the Cross.)*

18 And My people shall dwell in a peaceable habitation, and in sure dwellings, and in quiet resting places *(the picture is one of total security; war has forever ended; the boundaries and "dwellings" are "sure," i.e., secure.*

The world has ever tried to bring this about, but with no success, because the world cannot bring such about; it can only come through Christ);

19 When it shall hail, coming down on the forest; and the city shall be low in a low place. *(Babylon, which has always symbolized man's rebellion against God and which is yet to be rebuilt on or close to its ancient site, will be completely destroyed at the conclusion of the Great Tribulation. It is necessary for the intrusion of this Passage in order to portray the demise of man's efforts and the victory of the Holy Spirit.)*

20 Blessed are you who sow beside all waters, who send forth thither the feet of the ox and the ass. *(During the Millennium, seedtime and harvest will be times of happiness, and not of apprehension, as now. The idea is that every effort of prosperity will be "blessed." No effort will be fruitless; all will be bountiful!*

The Glorious One, Whom the world now scorns, will be the One Who brings peace, prosperity, and great glory to the entirety of the world. His Name is Jesus.)

CHAPTER 33
(713 B.C.)
WOE TO THE ANTICHRIST

WOE to thee who spoils, and you were not spoiled; and dealt treacherously, and they dealt not treacherously with you! when you shall cease to spoil, you shall be spoiled; and when you shall make an end to deal treacherously, they shall deal treacherously with you. *(The whole of this Chapter contrasts Christ with the Antichrist. The one king is willful, a spoiler, a traitor, a devastator, and a murderer. The Other came not to do His Own Will; He enriches with abundance of Salvation, Wisdom, and Knowledge; He is faithful; He fills the land with plenty; and He abolishes sickness and death.*

The first "they" of Verse 1 means the servants of Hezekiah; the second "they," the sons and servants of Sennacherib.)

2 O LORD, be gracious unto us; we have waited for You: be Thou their arm every morning, our salvation also in the time of trouble. *(The Spirit of Christ in Isaiah pleads with and for the sons of Israel; hence, the change of pronoun from "we" to "their." The word "arm" means "defense.")*

3 At the noise of the tumult the people fled; at the lifting up of yourself the nations were scattered. *(The "tumult" spoken of refers to the night of terror, when the host of the Assyrians was destroyed by the coming of the Angel; 185,000 Assyrians died that night. More particularly, it speaks of the "tumult" that will prevail when Jesus Christ comes back in the Battle of Armageddon and destroys the Antichrist. At this time, "the nations will be scattered.")*

4 And your spoil shall be gathered like the gathering of the caterpiller: as the running to and fro of locusts shall he run upon them. *(Upon the coming of the Angel who killed 185,000 Assyrian soldiers, the Israelites gathered the "spoil" as locusts leap upon and gather every green thing. Likewise, when Jesus Christ abruptly intervenes in the Battle of Armageddon, the armies of the Antichrist will be destroyed and much spoil gathered [Zech. 14:14].)*

5 The LORD is exalted; for He dwells on high: He has filled Zion with Judgment and Righteousness. *(On this night in question when the Angel was sent, Jehovah did indeed lift up Himself; hence, He is declared to be "exalted." And yet, the total exaltation awaits a future fulfillment.)*

6 And wisdom and knowledge shall be the stability of Your times, and strength of salvation: the fear of the LORD is His treasure. *(The "stability of Your times" is a beautiful statement which the world has little enjoyed. It refers to the Messiah as the true Hezekiah. In His times, there shall be a boundless Salvation; the wealth which will distinguish Him will be His*

fear of Jehovah.)

7 Behold, their valiant ones shall cry without: the ambassadors of peace shall weep bitterly. *(The "ambassadors of peace," sent by Hezekiah to Sennacherib to beg him to respect the covenant, were refused admission to the king's presence and had to remain "without." As well, this is a portend of the coming Great Tribulation, when Israel will try to make peace with the Antichrist, but to no avail [Dan. 7:19-25; 8:20-25; 9:27; 12:7].)*

8 The highways lie waste, the wayfaring man ceases: he has broken the covenant, he has despised the cities, he regards no man. *(Hezekiah stripped the Temple of its wealth and gave it to Sennacherib. The Assyrian king took the money, broke the covenant that had been made, and devastated the country. All this suffering, as well as the Temple sacrilege, would have been avoided, if only Hezekiah had obeyed the Bible and not followed his own counsel. All of this was totally unnecessary!)*

9 The Earth mourns and languishes: Lebanon is ashamed and hewn down: Sharon is like a wilderness; and Bashan and Carmel shake off their fruits. *(Man now being at his extremity of misery and helplessness, Grace can act and Judgment fall — Grace to God's People and Wrath to their foes — but sadly, most have to come to the extremity of misery before Grace can work.)*

10 Now will I rise, saith the LORD; now will I be exalted; now will I lift up Myself. *(The word "now" gives us the time. Sennacherib has robbed Judah, insulted God, and now threatens Jerusalem. The Lord will "lift Himself up" by sending one Angel, who will destroy 185,000 of the troops of Sennacherib.)*

11 You shall conceive chaff, you shall bring forth stubble: your breath, as fire, shall devour you. *(All the Assyrian plans against Jerusalem shall be mere "chaff" and "stubble." They shall all come to naught. On an even greater scale, this will happen to the Antichrist and all who are with him.)*

12 And the people shall be as the burnings of lime: as thorns cut up shall they be burned in the fire. *("Thorns" and "lime" burn very hot but are consumed very quickly. Such will be the brevity of time that God will use to stop Sennacherib.)*

MESSIAH'S MILLENNIAL REIGN

13 Hear, ye who are far off, what I have done;

and, ye who are near, acknowledge my might. *(The great miracle that God brought about by the sending of an Angel and destroying 185,000 of the Assyrian army in one night was definitely heard "far off." As well, it was acknowledged that it was the Hand of the Lord and not of man [II Chron. 32:23].)*

14 The sinners in Zion are afraid; fearfulness has surprised the hypocrites. Who among us shall dwell with the devouring fire? who among us shall dwell with everlasting burnings? *(The Jews who desired to go down into Egypt and seek their help were now "afraid." The Holy Spirit called them "sinners" and "hypocrites." The "devouring fire" spoken of here is the "Wrath of God." The "everlasting burnings" have to do with the Judgment of God, which would come upon them next, as well as eternal Hell-fire. Although "in Zion," yet were they Godless, i.e., without God and unlike God, that is, unconverted. Similarly, multitudes today are in that which professes to be the City of God, but their hearts are strangers to Christ.)*

15 He who walks righteously, and speaks uprightly; he that despises the gain of oppressions, who shakes his hands from holding of bribes, who stops his ears from hearing of blood, and shuts his eyes from seeing evil *(if a person really knows the Lord, Righteousness is going to be their lifestyle, which will be obvious; in other words, when a person comes to Christ, they are gloriously changed; otherwise, they haven't really come to Christ!);*

16 He shall dwell on high: his place of defence shall be the munitions of rocks: bread shall be given him; his waters shall be sure. *(In today's terminology, to "dwell on high" refers to being "raised up together, and made to sit together in Heavenly Places in Christ Jesus" [Eph. 2:6].*

The "munitions of Rocks" refer to Christ. Paul said, "That Rock was Christ" [I Cor. 10:4].

The "Bread that is given" is the "Bread of Life," which is the True Bread, Christ Jesus [Jn. 6:32, 35].

The "sure waters" refer to the mighty Baptism with the Holy Spirit [Jn. 7:37-39].)

A VISION OF JERUSALEM UNDER THE MESSIAH: AT PEACE, RESTORED

17 Your eyes shall see the King in His beauty: they shall behold the land that is very far off. *(At this time, Jerusalem saw Hezekiah in sackcloth, but the day is coming when they will see*

the Messiah, the King, in His "beauty.")

18 Your heart shall meditate terror. Where is the scribe? where is the receiver? where is he who counts the towers? *(God's Wrath, as exhibited with terror in the destruction of the Assyrian host, shook with terror the heart of the unconverted in Zion, but was a subject of profitable meditation for the heart of the converted. The faithful, when musing on the destruction of the enemy, exultingly ask, "Where now are these unbelieving officials?")*

19 You shall not see a fierce people, a people of a deeper speech than you can perceive; of a stammering tongue, that you cannot understand. *(That generation did no longer see the Assyrians; however, the Verse has a far greater meaning. The greater meaning goes all the way to the Antichrist. The word "not" is to be understood in the sense of "never again." Israel's enemies will never again be seen, for war in the Kingdom Age will now be a thing of the past [Isa. 2:2-4].)*

20 Look upon Zion, the city of our solemnities: your eyes shall see Jerusalem a quiet habitation, a tabernacle that shall not be taken down; not one of the stakes thereof shall ever be removed, neither shall any of the cords thereof be broken. *(Sennacherib thought to reduce "Zion" to ashes, destroying its Temple. Instead, he was destroyed. More particularly, this Passage refers to the coming Glad Day when Christ will reign supreme in Jerusalem. The Believer will feast his eyes upon the King and upon His Kingdom.)*

21 But there the glorious LORD will be unto us a place of broad rivers and streams; wherein shall go no galley with oars, neither shall gallant ship pass thereby. *(Great rivers were the foundation of wealth and strength for Assyria and Egypt, the greatest Monarchies of that day; however, the Messiah, and not rivers, etc., will be the foundation of all wealth and strength in the coming Millennial Day. The Lord will be to all as broad and deep streams of Grace and Glory. On such streams, no warship will ever sail; for there will be no war, because the Messiah will be Judge, Lawgiver, and King. He will be an Almighty Saviour.)*

22 For the LORD is our Judge, the LORD is our Lawgiver, the LORD is our King; He will save us. *(Jesus Christ is everything!)*

23 Your tacklings are loosed; they could not well strengthen their mast, they could not spread the sail: then is the prey of a great spoil divided; the lame take the prey. *(The overthrow of the enemy is compared to a shipwreck and to a ruin so complete that even cripples would become victors. The spoil at Armageddon will be in great abundance, and those who were thought to have been defeated will "take the prey." This refers to Israel.)*

24 And the inhabitant shall not say, I am sick: the people who dwell therein shall be forgiven their iniquity. *(When sin is abolished, sickness shall no more exist. The one is the cause; the other, the effect. This will be the blessing of the coming Kingdom Age, when Christ will reign Personally and Supreme.)*

CHAPTER 34
(713 B.C.)
ARMAGEDDON; GOD'S WRATH ON THE NATIONS

COME near, you nations, to hear; and hearken, you people: let the Earth hear, and all that is therein; the world, and all things that come forth of it. *(Chapters 34 and 35 form one Prophecy. Chapter 34 pertains to the Great Tribulation, while Chapter 35 pertains to the coming Millennium.*

In this Prophecy, as throughout the Bible, the evening of judgment precedes the morning of blessing. Man, in his energies, must be judged and broken before the Kingdom of God can be established.)

2 For the indignation of the LORD is upon all nations, and His fury upon all their armies; He has utterly destroyed them, He has delivered them to the slaughter. *(This speaks of the nations and the armies that will be gathered at Jerusalem in order to destroy that city and to annihilate the Jews. The Lord will meet this with "His fury.")*

3 Their slain also shall be cast out, and their stink shall come up out of their carcases, and the mountains shall be melted with their blood. *(Concerning statements such as "the mountains shall be melted with their blood," some have accused Isaiah of lapsing into hyperbole; however, Isaiah is merely speaking the words of the Holy Spirit, and it is certain that He would not resort to such!*

Actually, the entirety of the army of the Antichrist will be destroyed, with the exception of one-sixth, and this will happen in one day [Ezek. 39:2; Zech. 14:1-15; Rev. 19:11-21].)

4 And all the host of Heaven shall be dissolved, and the Heavens shall be rolled together as a scroll: and all their host shall fall

down, as the leaf falls off from the vine, and as a falling fig from the fig tree. *(This speaks of the Great Tribulation, which will last for seven years. During this time, "the host of Heaven," which includes the stars and planetary bodies, will be greatly affected. The word "dissolved" seems to imply that their orderly conduct will be interrupted, which will cause tremendous upheaval on the Earth [Rev. 8:7-12].)*

5 For My sword shall be bathed in Heaven: behold, it shall come down upon Idumea, and upon the people of My curse, to judgment. *("Idumea" is the same as "Edom," and symbolizes all who are opposed to Zion. It represents "all the nations," "Edom" and "Adam" being the same word.*

"The sword bathed in Heaven" is the Wrath of God purposed in Heaven and descending upon guilty man like the fire fell out of Heaven upon Sodom.

The statement, "the people of My curse," literally means "the people on whom I have laid a curse" — the Edomites. To be cursed is one thing, but to be cursed by God is something else altogether.)

6 The sword of the LORD is filled with blood, it is made fat with fatness, and with the blood of lambs and goats, with the fat of the kidneys of rams: for the LORD has a sacrifice in Bozrah, and a great slaughter in the land of Idumea. *(The "Sacrifices" are mentioned because they are used as an example of the coming "slaughter." This will be in the Great Tribulation and at the Battle of Armageddon.*

At that time, the Lord, in effect, will perform major surgery on planet Earth; otherwise, Earth would be destroyed.)

7 And the unicorns shall come down with them, and the bullocks with the bulls; and their land shall be soaked with blood, and their dust made fat with fatness. *(All the power of man, as symbolized by the strong animals of this Verse, shall be destroyed in that day.)*

8 For it is the day of the LORD's vengeance, and the year of recompences for the controversy of Zion. *(The "controversy of Zion" relates not only to the hostility of the nations to Israel, but also to the age-long war of man against God. This war has raged since the Fall of Adam and Eve in the Garden of Eden. All of this will come to a head in the Great Tribulation [Mat. 24:21].)*

9 And the streams thereof shall be turned into pitch, and the dust thereof into brimstone, and the land thereof shall become burning pitch.

10 It shall not be quenched night nor day; the smoke thereof shall go up for ever: from generation to generation it shall lie waste; none shall pass through it for ever and ever. *(These two Verses seem to describe one of the openings in the Earth where men will be able to see down into Hell, which will exist during the entirety of the Millennial Reign.)*

11 But the cormorant and the bittern shall possess it; the owl also and the raven shall dwell in it: and he shall stretch out upon it the line of confusion, and the stones of emptiness. *(This continues to describe the opening in the Earth, which could well be the site of Babylon [Isa. 66:22-24].)*

12 They shall call the nobles thereof to the kingdom, but none shall be there, and all her princes shall be nothing. *(This speaks of all the "nobles" who have lived down through the ages but refused to serve God. Irrespective of their nobility and their lofty station in life, they will not gain entrance into the "Kingdom.")*

13 And thorns shall come up in her palaces, nettles and brambles in the fortresses thereof: and it shall be an habitation of dragons, and a court for owls. *(This tells us what the Lord says about those things in which man placed such stock; they are good for nothing except to grow "nettles and brambles.")*

14 The wild beasts of the desert shall also meet with the wild beasts of the island, and the satyr shall cry to his fellow; the screech owl also shall rest there, and find for herself a place of rest. *(In Lev. 17:7, the word "satyr" is used for "devils," and probably means this here. The idea of this Passage is that on this particular site, wherever it may be [probably where Babylon once existed], the sounds that come from it will be debilitating, to say the least. The "screeching" and "crying" will characterize the horror of eternal Hell, which it represents [Mat. 8:12].)*

15 There shall the great owl make her nest, and lay, and hatch, and gather under her shadow: there shall the vultures also be gathered, every one with her mate. *(The type of animals and fowls that are mentioned here come under the heading of "unclean." Such will characterize this place.*

Many may ask the question, "Why would the Lord have such a place or opening to Hell in the Earth?" Perhaps the purpose of this opening will be to cause coming generations to abhor sin and its consequences. When natural men can actually see into eternal Hell, it will be a

great warning to them to walk in the Ways of God. Not only men on the New Earth, but Angels also, and all other beings will be able to look into this place and see how horrible the punishment of sin is [Rev. 14:9-11].

Horrifying as the thought may be, the view may be God's best method of keeping eternal generations in line with His Laws and Commandments, as they progress in the New Earth in the eternal future.)

16 Seek ye out of the Book of the LORD, and read: no one of these shall fail, none shall want her mate: for My mouth it has commanded, and His Spirit it has gathered them. (It seems as if the Holy Spirit senses the unbelief of men regarding these predictions and proclaims to all that "no one of these shall fail." Mankind is ordered to "seek ye out of the Book of the LORD, and read" and understand that of all the things predicted, all shall come to pass.)

17 And He has cast the lot for them, and His hand has divided it unto them by line: they shall possess it for ever, from generation to generation shall they dwell therein. (The words, "He has cast the lot for them," refer to the fact that God allots to all nations of the Earth their particular destiny. It all has to do with their acceptance or rejection of Him. It is said that "His Hand" draws the line of their habitation; consequently, He has said, "The wicked shall be turned into Hell, and all the nations that forget God" [Ps. 9:17].)

CHAPTER 35
(713 B.C.)
MILLENNIUM: LAND RESTORED; PEOPLE HEALED; HIGHWAY OF HOLINESS

THE wilderness and the solitary place shall be glad for them; and the desert shall rejoice, and blossom as the rose. (This pertains to the coming Kingdom Age. The previous Chapter, which was the first part of this Prophecy, proclaims the cause of all sorrow, pain, heartache, and destruction, which is sin and man's rebellion against God, which will be destroyed by the Lord Jesus Christ; this Chapter, the concluding part of the Prophecy, portrays what God can do in a heart and life that is yielded to Him. As the spiritual renewal takes place in hearts and lives, the material, economic, domestic, and physical renewal will take place over the entirety of the Earth.)

2 It shall blossom abundantly, and rejoice even with joy and singing: the glory of Lebanon shall be given unto it, the excellency of Carmel and Sharon, they shall see the glory of the LORD, and the excellency of our God. ("The glory of the LORD, and the excellency of our God" is the cause of the "abundant blossoming" and the "rejoicing even with joy and singing.")

3 Strengthen ye the weak hands, and confirm the feeble knees. (With these exceeding great and precious Promises, the servants of Truth are commanded to strengthen trembling and apprehensive Believers. With the "Glory of the LORD" now paramount, even the "weak" gain "strength," and "feeble knees" are no longer so.)

4 Say to them who are of a fearful heart, Be strong, fear not: behold, your God will come with vengeance, even God with a recompence; He will come and save you. (This Passage expresses again the Doctrine of the Coming of the Lord Jesus Christ. As well, this Verse points to the period predicted in II Peter 3:10 and Rev. 19:11-21. However, we greatly shortchange the Scriptures if we limit this Passage only to the Second Coming of Christ. Its words are pointed at every Child of God in every period.

The sentence, "He will come and save you," actually says, "He will come Himself to save you." There is One Alone Who can save, and He must do it Himself; to do it, He must "come" to us.)

5 Then the eyes of the blind shall be opened, and the ears of the deaf shall be unstopped. (Verses 5 and 6 had a fulfillment in the Messiah's First Advent, but their moral and plenary fulfillment belong to His Second and future Advent. Christ did not work miracles in His First Advent as mere wonders, but because it was predicted here that when He came, He would work miracles of this nature; hence, His performing these particular Miracles proved Him to be the predicted Messiah. But His rejection postponed to the future the wonders and blessings of this entire Chapter.)

6 Then shall the lame man leap as an hart, and the tongue of the dumb sing: for in the wilderness shall waters break out, and streams in the desert. (The entire complexion of that future Glad Day [the Millennium] will be changed. Sickness and disease will be at an end. "Then" the "lame man" will not only be able to walk, but will have such freedom of movement that he will be able to "leap as an hart." "Then" the "bound tongue" will not only be able to speak, but "sing," as well!

However, in the spiritual sense, this has even a greater meaning! Due to the Fall, men have been "spiritually lame" as well as "spiritually dumb." "Then" all such will "dance in the Spirit" and "sing His praises"!

Due to the Fall, the world is a "wilderness." But at that time, the "waters" and "streams," signifying the Holy Spirit, will make the "desert blossom as the rose.")

7 And the parched ground shall become a pool, and the thirsty land springs of water: in the habitation of dragons, where each lay, shall be grass with reeds and rushes. *("Jackals" make their home in the sandy desert. They will be banished and their haunts turned into verdant meadows. Many nations of the world presently cannot now feed themselves due to "parched ground." This Passage proclaims the fact that all the Earth will then become fertile. "Springs of water" will burst through the desert floor, which will then be turned into a garden. Areas deserted and given over to desolation will then be "fat pastures" grazed by cattle.)*

8 And an highway shall be there, and a way, and it shall be called The way of holiness; the unclean shall not pass over it; but it shall be for those: the wayfaring men, though fools, shall not err therein. *(The Scripture definitely predicts a literal "highway" that will be built from Egypt through Israel to Assyria [Isa. 11:6; 19:23-25]; however, these Passages do not refer to that particular "highway," but to "The way of Holiness."*

It is proclaimed by the Holy Spirit that the "way" is "holiness." Holiness characterizes all that God is and does.)

9 No lion shall be there, nor any ravenous beast shall go up thereon, it shall not be found there; but the redeemed shall walk there *(such proclaims the Truth that Satan, as a "roaring lion," shall not have access to "The way of holiness"; demon spirits, i.e., "ravenous beasts" also "shall not be found there"; therefore, the victory that every true Child of God earnestly desires is found in "The way of holiness."*

Its complete fulfillment portrays the Millennial Reign, when Satan and all his minions of darkness will be locked away; consequently, only the "redeemed" shall occupy this "highway"):

10 And the ransomed of the LORD shall return, and come to Zion with songs and everlasting joy upon their heads: they shall obtain joy and gladness, and sorrow and sighing shall flee away. *(Verses 8 through 10 can be summed up by saying, "The unclean shall not pass over*

it, for He shall be with them walking in the way; so even the simple shall not go astray therein." It shall be the Way of the Lord [Mal. 3:1] and, therefore, not only will His companionship exclude evil and assure arrival, but it will protect from peril.

With such a Keeper on the way and such a harbor at the close, it is not to be wondered at that the ransomed of the Lord shall be characterized by songs, joy, and by gladness.

"Sorrow and sighing shall flee away," that is, the bliss of the redeemed shall not in the perfect state be liable to be broken as was the innocent joy of Eden's Garden.)

CHAPTER 36
(710 B.C.)
HISTORICAL INTERLUDE: ASSYRIA'S INVASION OF JUDAH

NOW it came to pass in the fourteenth year of king Hezekiah, that Sennacherib king of Assyria came up against all the defenced cities of Judah, and took them. *(This is the third time that the Holy Spirit records the facts relating to Hezekiah and the proposed attack by Assyria against Jerusalem, thereby denoting its significance. Its significance lies in the fact that this episode is a symbol of the future invasion of Israel by the Antichrist. As Sennacherib was stopped, so will the Antichrist.)*

2 And the king of Assyria sent Rabshakeh from Lachish to Jerusalem unto king Hezekiah with a great army. And he stood by the conduit of the upper pool in the highway of the fuller's field. *("Rabshakeh," seemingly, was the head of the Assyrian expedition against Jerusalem. He is there to demand the surrender of Jerusalem. "The conduit of the upper pool" is the same place Isaiah stood with Ahaz about 28 years before [7:3].)*

3 Then came forth unto him Eliakim, Hilkiah's son, which was over the house, and Shebna the Scribe, and Joah, Asaph's son, the Recorder. *("Eliakim" and "Shebna" were sent outside the city to meet with Rabshakeh; this is the same "Shebna" whom Isaiah prophesied against in Chapter 22.)*

AN INSULTING MESSAGE TO HEZEKIAH OF JUDAH

4 And Rabshakeh said unto them, Say ye now to Hezekiah, Thus saith the great king, the king of Assyria, What confidence is this

wherein you trust? *(Of the three Assyrian envoys, Rabshakeh alone obtains mention in Isaiah, because he was the spokesman. He was probably chosen for such because he could speak Hebrew fluently.*

He refers to the king of Assyria as "the great king." This is meant to insinuate that no king anywhere in the world is as great as "the king of Assyria." However, "Rabshakeh" is to find, to his dismay, that his king, Sennacherib, is subservient to another King, "the LORD of Glory."

Rabshakeh chides Hezekiah about his trust being placed in Egypt. This tells us that trusting man rather than God exposes the Christian to the contempt of the world.)

5 I say, sayest thou, (but they are but vain words) I have counsel and strength for war: now on whom do you trust, that you rebel against me? *(It seems that Rabshakeh had obtained a copy of the proposed agreement between Judah and Egypt, or that the very words had been verbally reported to him.)*

6 Lo, you trust in the staff of this broken reed, on Egypt; whereon if a man lean, it will go into his hand, and pierce it: so is Pharaoh king of Egypt to all who trust in him. *(When the Assyrian spoke of this "broken reed," namely "Egypt," he was speaking from knowledge instead of merely boasting.)*

7 But if you say to me, We trust in the LORD our God: is it not He, Whose high places and Whose altars Hezekiah has taken away, and said to Judah and to Jerusalem, You shall worship before this Altar? *(To destroy the fashionable materials and corrupt ceremonies of worldly religion is misunderstood by the world and accounted sacrilege. Rabshakeh was totally ignorant of the Ways of God and had misunderstood Hezekiah's destruction of the idol groves, thinking he had offended the God of Judah.)*

8 Now therefore give pledges, I pray you, to my master the king of Assyria, and I will give you two thousand horses, if you be able on your part to set riders upon them. *(Rabshakeh continues to reproach Judah.)*

9 How then will you turn away the face of one captain of the least of my master's servants, and put your trust on Egypt for chariots and for horsemen? *(Judah's true weakness was her lack of dependence on God, not her lack of military preparation.)*

10 And am I now come up without the LORD against this land to destroy it? the LORD said unto me, Go up against this land, and destroy it. *(Rabshakeh's statements make*

it obvious that the Prophesy given by Isaiah some years before had been read or seen by him. Its use by him was a clever ruse to persuade the people to disobey Jehovah. When unconverted men quote the Bible in support of their projects or doctrines, they contradict themselves and expose their ignorance of the Scriptures and their hatred of God.*

Neither Sennacherib nor his captain, Rabshakeh, believed in Jehovah. Their statements are made from the viewpoint of ego. They imagined themselves to be so high and mighty that if there is a God, they are His princely ones in the Earth.

Sennacherib misunderstood Isaiah's Prophecy. It was certainly true that God did ordain the Assyrians [without them being aware of such] to overthrow certain countries, which included the Northern Kingdom of Israel, and also to chasten Judah; however, He never gave them a commission to destroy Judah. So, in this, they were overstepping their bounds, and would face dire consequences.)

JUDAH'S ANSWER

11 Then said Eliakim and Shebna and Joah unto Rabshakeh, Speak, I pray you, unto your servants in the Syrian language; for we understand it: and speak not to us in the Jews' language, in the ears of the people who are on the wall. *(Rabshakeh spoke in Hebrew, desiring that the people hear his words, as well as their leaders, in order to weaken their will to resist. The request of the Jews will be ignored.*

Incidentally, regarding the three Jews addressed here, "Eliakim" and "Shebna" stand in contrast. "Eliakim" is a Type of Christ; hence, he is symbolic of the Spirit. "Shebna" is a type of Satan; hence, he is a type of the flesh [Isa. 22:15-24].

"Shebna" strongly encourages seeking the help of the Egyptians, while "Eliakim" strongly urges trust in God. The majority in Jerusalem at that time followed "Shebna," while a small remnant followed Isaiah and "Eliakim" [Isa. 1:9]. In fact, almost all the religious leaders of Jerusalem followed the carnal path of "Shebna.")

MESSAGE TO THE PEOPLE

12 But Rabshakeh said, Has my master sent me to your master and to you to speak these words? has he not sent me to the men who sit upon the wall, that they may eat their own dung, and drink their own urine with you? *(The language used by Rabshakeh shows his*

contempt for Judah.)

13 Then Rabshakeh stood, and cried with a loud voice in the Jews' language, and said, Hear ye the words of the great king, the king of Assyria. *(Satan always cries with a "loud voice." He also says it in the "language" that we easily understand.)*

14 Thus saith the king, Let not Hezekiah deceive you: for he shall not be able to deliver you. *(Rabshakeh claims to speak for "the king," Sennacherib. Satan has plenty of envoys. Therefore, the people had a choice; they could believe Rabshakeh or "Hezekiah."*

If the people had not had strong spiritual leadership in the persons of "Hezekiah" and "Isaiah," they would no doubt have acquiesced to Rabshakeh.)

15 Neither let Hezekiah make you trust in the LORD, saying, The LORD will surely deliver us: this city shall not be delivered into the hand of the king of Assyria. *(The words of Isaiah given to Hezekiah no doubt had come to the ears of Sennacherib. So now we have the Word of the Lord versus the word of Sennacherib.)*

16 Hearken not to Hezekiah: for thus saith the king of Assyria, Make an agreement with me by a present, and come out to me: and eat ye every one of his vine, and every one of his fig tree, and drink ye every one the waters of his own cistern *(in other words, the war will cease if you will "make an agreement with me"; this has ever been Satan's ploy; the message is "compromise," which is never of God!);*

17 Until I come and take you away to a land like your own land, a land of corn and wine, a land of bread and vineyards. *(Despite the golden promises, the plan was to take Judah captive into Assyria, as they had already taken Ephraim. This is Satan's plan for the modern Christian, as well! He promises everything, but only gives captivity.)*

18 Beware lest Hezekiah persuade you, saying, The LORD will deliver us. Has any of the gods of the nations delivered his land out of the hand of the king of Assyria? *(The boast of Rabshakeh was not hollow, at least regarding the "gods" of the nations. As far as the Assyrians were concerned, this was a religious war. Their success in the religious character of their wars justified this boast.)*

19 Where are the gods of Hamath and Arphad? where are the gods of Sepharvaim? and have they delivered Samaria out of my hand? *(In this Passage, Rabshakeh boasts of his god, Asshur, over "the gods of Hamath and* Arphad." *Sennacherib sees no distinction between the cities where Jehovah was worshipped, as supposedly in Samaria, than those which acknowledged other gods. As Samaria fell, which supposedly worshipped Jehovah, why should not Jerusalem fall? Therefore, he equates Samaria's God with Judah's.)*

20 Who are they among all the gods of these lands, that have delivered their land out of my hand, that the LORD should deliver Jerusalem out of my hand? *(In this statement, Rabshakeh places Jehovah in the same category as the idol gods of other nations. That Jehovah would deliver Judah, there was no doubt! However, the manner in which He delivered them was because of this insult. He would humiliate them so greatly that Sennacherib would not recover. As well, Jerusalem would not suffer the loss of one single person or even an arrow being shot against its wall. So much for the god, Asshur!)*

21 But they held their peace, and answered him not a word: for the king's commandment was, saying, Answer him not. *(There are occasions when faith's most effective reply to insulting language is the dignity of silence, and her best refuge is prayer.)*

22 Then came Eliakim, the son of Hilkiah, who was over the household, and Shebna the Scribe, and Joah, the son of Asaph, the Recorder, to Hezekiah with their clothes rent, and told him the words of Rabshakeh. *(If one will notice, "Shebna the Scribe" was dressed in sackcloth the same as "Eliakim." There the similarity ended. Eliakim wanted the Will of God, while Shebna wanted his place and position salvaged. This describes far too many Christians!)*

CHAPTER 37
(710 B.C.)

HEZEKIAH DISTRESSED; ASKS ISAIAH TO PRAY

AND it came to pass, when king Hezekiah heard it, that he rent his clothes, and covered himself with sackcloth, and went into the House of the LORD. *(This Chapter is actually a continuation of the previous; therefore, the two constitute but one narrative. Whatever difficulties of faithlessness that had previously plagued Hezekiah have now been thrown off, and he is doing what he should have done all along. He is taking his difficulties to the Lord. The Assyrians are threatening his destruction, and he realizes there is no hope except in God.)*

2 And he sent Eliakim, who was over the household, and Shebna the Scribe, and the elders of the Priests covered with sackcloth, unto Isaiah the Prophet the son of Amoz. *(They should have done this at the beginning!)*

3 And they said unto him, Thus saith Hezekiah, This day is a day of trouble, and of rebuke, and of blasphemy: for the children are come to the birth, and there is not strength to bring forth. *(The Passage, "the children are come to the birth . . . etc.," was a proverbial phrase for a time of extreme difficulty. Judah was in sore trouble and was expecting deliverance; however, it seemed now as if she would not have enough strength to go through the crisis, but would perish through weakness.)*

4 It may be the LORD your God will hear the words of Rabshakeh, whom the king of Assyria his master has sent to reproach the Living God, and will reprove the words which the LORD your God has heard: wherefore lift up your prayer for the remnant that is left. *(Notice the manner in this Verse in which Hezekiah couches his terminology. He doesn't plead with the Lord regarding the merit of Judah, but rather the blasphemy of "Rabshakeh." He knows that neither he nor Judah have any merit with God. This attitude should be a model for us, as well.*

"The remnant that is left" refers to the great number of Judaeans who have already been taken captive from the other cities of Judah, with only those who are in Jerusalem remaining.)

GOD PROMISES DELIVERANCE

5 So the servants of king Hezekiah came to Isaiah.

6 And Isaiah said unto them, Thus shall you say unto your master, Thus saith the LORD, Be not afraid of the words that you have heard, wherewith the servants of the king of Assyria have blasphemed Me. *(The blasphemy of Rabshakeh was against the Lord, and would be answered in kind.)*

7 Behold, I will send a blast upon him, and he shall hear a rumour, and return to his own land; and I will cause him to fall by the sword in his own land. *(The words, "I will send a blast upon him," rather mean "I will put a spirit within him," i.e., "I will remove from him the spirit of pride and arrogancy and instead will infuse into his heart a spirit of hesitation and fear." When the Lord takes a hand in a situation, this Verse gives us the proof of the ample*

provision that He has to do whatever He desires.

The "blast" was the sending of an Angel from Heaven, who would kill 185,000 Assyrian soldiers in one night. Sennacherib would give up his plans for the destruction of Jerusalem and return to his own land. Ultimately, he was killed by his own sons.)

ASSYRIA'S ARROGANT ATTITUDE, MORE INSULTS TO GOD AND JUDAH

8 So Rabshakeh returned, and found the king of Assyria warring against Libnah: for he had heard that he was departed from Lachish. *(After Rabshakeh concluded his mission, not realizing the wheels he had set in motion, he returned to Sennacherib, for he found him attempting to destroy "Libnah." It seems that this was the next stronghold on the way to Egypt.)*

9 And he heard say concerning Tirhakah king of Ethiopia, He is come forth to make war with you. And when he heard it, he sent messengers to Hezekiah, saying *("Tirhakah king of Ethiopia" is among the most famous of the Monarchs belonging to this period; it seems this king had defeated Egypt and now ruled both Ethiopia and Egypt; the movement of Tirhakah provoked rather than alarmed Sennacherib, who had already defeated one Egyptian army a short time before; he was confident of success against any effort that the Egyptians might make)*,

10 Thus shall you speak to Hezekiah king of Judah, saying, Let not your God, in Whom you trust, deceive you, saying, Jerusalem shall not be given into the hand of the king of Assyria. *(Sennacherib recognized Jehovah as a God, the God of the Jews, but put Him on the same par with the other "gods of the nations," for whom he had no respect.)*

11 Behold, you have heard what the kings of Assyria have done to all lands by destroying them utterly; and shall you be delivered? *(In fact, Sennacherib at this time was the most powerful Monarch on the face of the Earth; therefore, these boasts were not hollow threats!)*

12 Have the gods of the nations delivered them which my fathers have destroyed, as Gozan, and Haran, and Rezeph, and the children of Eden which were in Telassar? *(He enumerates here areas which had been taken by the Assyrians.)*

13 Where is the king of Hamath, and the king of Arphad, and the king of the city of Sepharvaim, Hena, and Ivah? *(Sennacherib,*

like Satan, delights in boasting of his victories.)

HEZEKIAH PRAYS TO GOD FOR HELP

14 And Hezekiah received the letter from the hand of the messengers, and read it: and Hezekiah went up unto the House of the LORD, and spread it before the LORD. *(This last message was sent to Hezekiah in a "letter." In II Chron. 32:17, the word "letters" is used, signifying plurality and indicating an arrogant, insulting, and boastful letter. The "spreading" of the letter "before the LORD" did not imply on Hezekiah's part that God did not know its contents previously, but was designed thusly that Sennacherib's reproach of the God of Judah would be ever before the Lord.)*

15 And Hezekiah prayed unto the LORD, saying *(this is the answer!)*,

16 O LORD of Hosts, God of Israel, Who dwells between the Cherubims, You are the God, even You Alone, of all the kingdoms of the Earth: You have made Heaven and Earth. *(Hezekiah's prayer is very interesting and well worth our attention. It would be the same that we would pray today, with one exception. Now, we are admonished to pray to the Lord in the Name of Jesus [Jn. 16:23].)*

17 Incline Your ear, O LORD, and hear; open Your eyes, O LORD, and see: and hear all the words of Sennacherib, which has sent to reproach the Living God. *(This is a conscious pleading of the Promise made to Solomon [II Chron. 7:15]. Hezekiah is calling to account this Promise, as we can also call to account the many Promises made in the Word of God [Mk. 9:23; Mat. 18:18; Jn. 14:14; 15:7].*

Petition that is offered to the Lord without being based on the Word of God is a fruitless petition.)

18 Of a truth, LORD, the kings of Assyria have laid waste all the nations, and their countries. *(Actually, this was fact which was impossible to deny.)*

19 And have cast their gods into the fire: for they were no gods but the work of men's hands, wood and stone: therefore they have destroyed them. *(If one will notice, Hezekiah did not deny the existence or even the power of the Assyrians. Let it be known, like here, that the confession of existing problems does not show a lack of faith and that the denial of certain difficulties does not make them any less real.)*

20 Now therefore, O LORD our God, save us from his hand, that all the kingdoms of the Earth may know that you are the LORD, even You only. *(Every petition that is made to the Lord, like Hezekiah's, should not be for deliverance or triumph over enemies for our own sakes, or the sake of others, but rather for the "Glory of God.")*

GOD'S ANSWER: SENNACHERIB WILL BE CRUSHED

21 Then Isaiah the son of Amoz sent unto Hezekiah, saying, Thus saith the LORD God of Israel, Whereas you have prayed to Me against Sennacherib king of Assyria *(either Isaiah knew that Hezekiah was seeking the Lord concerning the Assyrian threat, or else the Lord revealed it to him; the Promise had already been given by the Lord through Isaiah that Sennacherib would not be successful in this venture [37:7], so it would seem that Hezekiah was showing a lack of faith by continuing to plead when the Promise had already been given; but not necessarily so!; in truth, our faith has to be constantly reassured; hence, David would repeatedly cry to the Lord for reassurance, despite the fact that the Lord had said that he would be king of Israel [I Sam. 16:1, 12-13; Ps. 13]):*

22 This is the word which the LORD has spoken concerning him; The virgin, the daughter of Zion, has despised you, and laughed you to scorn; the daughter of Jerusalem has shaken her head at you. *(The expression, "virgin daughter," represents Jerusalem as a tender maiden, weak and delicate, yet still bold enough to stand up against Sennacherib and all his hosts and bid him defiance. Confident that the Lord will protect her, she "laughs him to scorn." This is God's answer to the boasts of Sennacherib, and, due to its source, it must be taken extremely seriously.)*

23 Whom have you reproached and blasphemed? and against Whom have you exalted your voice, and lifted up your eyes on high? even against the Holy One of Israel. *(This proclaims the fact that Sennacherib is fighting against God. It is a battle that he cannot hope to win!)*

24 By your servants have you reproached the Lord, and have said, By the multitude of my chariots am I come up to the height of the mountains, to the sides of Lebanon; and I will cut down the tall cedars thereof, and the choice fir trees thereof: and I will enter into the height of his border, and the forest of his Carmel. *(In this Passage, the Holy Spirit is not claiming that Sennacherib has actually uttered these words*

with his mouth, but that he has thought them within his heart.)

25 I have dug and drunk water; and with the sole of my feet have I dried up all the rivers of the besieged places. *(The Lord continues to proclaim the boasts of Sennacherib.)*

26 Have you not heard long ago, how I have done it; and of ancient times, that I have formed it? now have I brought it to pass, that you should be to lay waste defenced cities into ruinous heaps. *(In this Passage, Isaiah, after speaking as the person of Sennacherib, breaks off without warning and returns to speaking as the person of Jehovah. In this Passage, Sennacherib is reproached by the Holy Spirit for not knowing what he ought to have known and might have known, if he had only listened to the voice of conscience and reason. The words, "now have I brought it to pass," refer to the fact that all that Sennacherib had done, he had done as God's instrument, by God's permission — even by His aid; however, Sennacherib had become so lifted up in his own pride that he thought his victories were due to his own ability, tactical designs, and military expertise.)*

27 Therefore their inhabitants were of small power, they were dismayed and confounded: they were as the grass of the field, and as the green herb, as the grass on the housetops, and as corn blasted before it be grown up. *(God, having decreed the success of the Assyrians, effected them [in part] by infusing weakness into the nations that were their adversaries. Sennacherib thought it was his military prowess that effected his victories, when God now says the opposite.)*

28 But I know your abode, and your going out, and your coming in, and your rage against Me. *(Sennacherib, even though an unwitting instrument in the Hands of God, still, could have known all he needed to know about God, if he had only taken the time and the trouble to learn. Verse 26 says so! So, for not taking the time to learn about God and, therefore, to understand the secret of his victories, he would incur the Wrath of God.)*

29 Because your rage against Me, and your tumult, is come up into My ears, therefore will I put My hook in your nose, and My bridle in your lips, and I will turn you back by the way by which you came. *(Sennacherib proposed the shocking cruelty of this Verse for Hezekiah and his people, but, figuratively, he was made to suffer it himself.)*

30 And this shall be a sign unto you, You shall eat this year such as grow of itself; and the second year that which springs of the same: and in the third year sow ye, and reap, and plant vineyards, and eat the fruit thereof. *(Agriculture had been impossible for the two prior years, because of the invasion of the Assyrians. But now God encourages the remnant of His People to go out of the city into the country and till the ground, for He promised that the Assyrian king should never return to injure them. Therefore, it seems that the acute danger lasted for about two years.)*

31 And the remnant that is escaped of the House of Judah shall again take root downward, and bear fruit upward *(the Blessing of God is now upon Judah; in a short time, she recovered her ancient vigor so that under Josiah she was able to extend her dominion over almost the whole of the old Israelite territory [II Chron. 34:6, 18]):*

32 For out of Jerusalem shall go forth a remnant, and they who escape out of Mount Zion: the zeal of the LORD of Hosts shall do this. *(The "remnant" speaks of those who escaped the incursion of the last two years. In fact, many had died or had been taken captive.*

The phrase, "the zeal of the LORD of Hosts," is used by the Holy Spirit to insure the fulfillment of what has been promised. God's People will be blessed and grow strong once again.)

33 Therefore thus saith the LORD concerning the king of Assyria, He shall not come into this city, nor shoot an arrow there, nor come before it with shields, nor cast a bank against it. *(Sennacherib had planned all along to lay siege against Jerusalem. The Holy Spirit through Isaiah says that no siege will be laid against the city.)*

34 By the way that he came, by the same shall he return, and shall not come into this city, saith the LORD. *(This Promise assured Hezekiah that he would not be confronted with this enemy.)*

35 For I will defend this city to save it for My Own sake, and for My servant David's sake. *(Hezekiah is told here by no less than the Holy Spirit that he could not boast that the beauty or fervor of his prayer purchased the victory, for God told him that He would deliver the city, not for Hezekiah's sake, but for David's sake, i.e., "for the Messiah's sake."*

The phrase, "I will defend his city," literally means "I will cover over this city, as a bird covers its young with its wings.")

THE FULFILLMENT OF
GOD'S PROMISE

36 Then the Angel of LORD went forth, and smote in the camp of the Assyrians a hundred and fourscore and five thousand: and when they *(those in Judah)* arose early in the morning, behold, they *(the Assyrians)* were all dead corpses. *(The scene of the account was probably about 25 miles from Jerusalem. Word would have come quickly to Jerusalem concerning the "dead bodies" that were lying everywhere.*

This great Miracle instituted by the Lord ranks in the same category as the opening of the Red Sea and the destruction of the Egyptian army, as well as the opening of the Jordan and the falling of the walls of Jericho!)

37 So Sennacherib king of Assyria departed, and went and returned, and dwelt at Nineveh. *(In this Passage, the Holy Spirit, and with short shift, dispenses with "Sennacherib." The word "departed" has the same meaning as a dog leaving with its tail between its legs. He went back to his capital, "Nineveh."*

He lived for some 18 or 20 years longer after this and made other military expeditions elsewhere; however, he made no further expeditions toward Jerusalem, or even toward Egypt. The Jews had peace so far as the Assyrians were concerned.

In his military life, he tackled many little tin gods; however, when he faced Jerusalem, he faced the God of the ages, his Creator. It was to be an experience he would never forget!)

38 And it came to pass, as he was worshipping in the house of Nisroch his god, that Adrammelech and Sharezer his sons smote him with the sword; and they escaped into the land of Armenia: and Esar-haddon his son reigned in his stead. *(Ancient history records that Sennacherib bequeathed his throne to his youngest son, Esar-haddon. In order to gain the favor of his god, he promised to sacrifice the two elder sons to that divinity, so-called. These sons, doubtless prompted by fear on the one hand and by jealousy on the other, murdered their father in December of that year. But six months later, they were obliged to flee to Armenia to escape the vengeance of Esar-haddon.*

Sennacherib had the opportunity to accept the God of Israel, but instead he attempted to destroy God's People. In turn, he was destroyed himself.)

CHAPTER 38
(713 B.C.)
HEZEKIAH'S SICKNESS AND RECOVERY

IN those days was Hezekiah sick unto death. And Isaiah the Prophet the son of Amoz came unto him, and said unto him, Thus saith the LORD, Set your house in order: for you shall die, and not live. *(The words, "in those days," refer to the fourteenth year of Hezekiah's reign; consequently, his sickness took place during the time of the Assyrian invasion and prior to the final Deliverance of Jerusalem.*

It seems from II Chron. 32:25 that Hezekiah's sickness was brought on by his heart that was filled with pride.

In the previous Chapter, we see Sennacherib humbled because of his pride. In this Chapter, we see God's Own [Hezekiah] humbled because of his pride. God cannot tolerate such in His Own no more than He can in the heathen.)

2 Then Hezekiah turned his face toward the wall, and prayed unto the LORD *(the "turning of his face to the wall" denotes a turning away from all his accomplishments, supposed merit, and things he held so dear; it also spoke of his helplessness; it is that which is demanded by God of everyone who comes to Him, irrespective of the cause or reason),*

3 And said, Remember now, O LORD, I beseech You, how I have walked before You in truth and with a perfect heart, and have done that which is good in Your sight. And Hezekiah wept sore. *(Hezekiah was only 39 years old. As yet, he had no son to succeed him. When he died at the age of 54, his son Manasseh, who succeeded him, was but 12 [II Ki. 21:1; II Chron. 33:1].*

The "perfect heart" must be understood in this manner:

From his statement in Verse 17, we know that he was not claiming sinlessness. He was referring to his efforts to put away idol worship out of Judah and to restore true Temple Worship, which had been discontinued by his evil father, Ahaz [II Chron., Chpts. 29-31].

The Holy Spirit said that "Hezekiah wept sore," which denotes his humbling himself before the Lord; such humbling is always demanded by God.)

4 Then came the Word of the LORD to Isaiah, saying *(Hezekiah's Repentance was quick and with a sincere heart),*

5 Go, and say to Hezekiah, Thus saith the LORD, the God of David your father, I have

heard your prayer, I have seen your tears: behold, I will add unto your days fifteen years. *(As far as we know, this is the only time that the Lord ever informed one as to exactly how much longer they would live. He was 39 years old when this Promise of 15 more years was given. Therefore, he died at the age of 54, exactly as the Lord said.)*

6 And I will deliver you and this city out of the hand of the king of Assyria: and I will defend this city. *(This points to the two-year period when the Assyrians were threatening Jerusalem. The Promise must have been very sweet to his ears. His life would be extended, and Jerusalem would be delivered.)*

7 And this shall be a sign unto you from the LORD, that the LORD will do this thing that He has spoken *(it seems from Verse 22 that Hezekiah had asked for a "sign" that it was now proper for him to "go up to the House of the Lord."*

Possibly, before his Repentance, he may have felt that he was unclean and, thereby, unworthy. In response to his request for such a "sign," the Lord will give him far more in the way of a "sign" than he had envisioned);

8 Behold, I will bring again the shadow of the degrees, which is gone down in the sun dial of Ahaz, ten degrees backward. So the sun returned ten degrees, by which degrees it was gone down. *(The sign would be powerful indeed! It concerned the rotation of the Earth on its axis. Such an outstanding sign seemed to speak to the lack of faith in Hezekiah's heart.*

The Scripture emphasizes that this was the "sun dial of Ahaz." Ahaz was so unbelieving and so lacking in desire to serve God that he ignored the offer of the Lord as it regarded a "sign." Now, the Lord will give Hezekiah, Ahaz's son, a "sign" on the same sun dial.

The sun dial going ten degrees backward would constitute a "long day.")

9 The writing of Hezekiah king of Judah, when he had been sick, and was recovered of his sickness *(the "writing" spoken of here is a Psalm written by Hezekiah concerning the great Miracle the Lord had performed for him):*

10 I said in the cutting off of my days, I shall go to the gates of the grave: I am deprived of the residue of my years. *(The words, "I am deprived of the residue of my years," speak of his work being cut short, even in the middle of it. He feels that his work is not finished, and yet he is dying!)*

11 I said, I shall not see the LORD, even the LORD, in the land of the living: I shall behold man no more with the inhabitants of the world. *(In effect, he is saying that if he died, he would not be able to see and worship the Lord, "as I do now in the land of the living.")*

12 My age is departed, and is removed from me as a shepherd's tent: I have cut off like a weaver my life: he will cut me off with pining sickness: from day even to night will you make an end of me. *(The entirety of the Text seems to be not so much the fear of dying, but of being cutoff in the midst of his days, not being able to finish the work that God had called him to do.)*

13 I reckoned till morning, that, as a lion, so will He break all my bones: from day even to night will You make an end of me. *(His terminology implies that he has disobeyed God and, in doing so, has angered Jehovah.)*

14 Like a crane or a swallow, so did I chatter: I did mourn as a dove: my eyes fail with looking upward: O LORD, I am oppressed; undertake for me. *(He is proclaiming the fact that he cannot approach the Lord from the basis of personal merit, for he has none. He can only appeal to God's Mercy and Grace and, therefore, weakly request, "Undertake for me.")*

15 What shall I say? He has both spoken unto me, and Himself has done it: I shall go softly all my years in the bitterness of my soul. *(The Lord heard his petition and answered him. His prayer has been answered. As well, he is at a loss to express his wonder and gratitude. He gives the Lord all the praise and glory by saying, "and Himself has done it."*

The phrase, "I shall go softly all my years," refers to walking "softly" before the Lord. The added "years" that the Lord will give him, he intends to walk humbly before Jehovah.)

16 O LORD, by these things men live, and in all these things is the life of my spirit: so will You recover me, and make me to live. *(In effect, Hezekiah is revealing somewhat of his failure, and his revival. He is saying that man lives by "these things," meaning "The Word of God"; in such, "is the life of my spirit.")*

17 Behold, for peace I had great bitterness: but You have in love to my soul delivered it from the pit of corruption: for You have cast all my sins behind Your back. *(This proclaims the fact that Hezekiah in Verse 3 was speaking only of the work that he had attempted for the Lord, and not of his own personal life. Now, he says, "All my sins" are gone, and are "behind Your back," and can be seen by You no more.)*

18 For the grave cannot praise You, death

can not celebrate You: they who go down into the pit cannot hope for Your truth. *(Hezekiah is speaking of the work that we are able to do for the Lord in this life. When death comes, our work is ended.)*

19 The living, the living, he shall praise You, as I do this day: the father to the children shall make known Your truth. *(His statement is this: As You, Lord, have given me the privilege to continue to "live," I will spend this "life" by "praising You.")*

20 The LORD was ready to save me: therefore we will sing my songs to the stringed instruments all the days of our life in the House of the LORD. *(The words, "The LORD was ready to save me," mean "He came to my rescue, came and saved me.")*

21 For Isaiah had said, Let them take a lump of figs, and lay it for a plaister upon the boil, and he shall recover. *(The "boil" symbolized the sinful corruption that been in his life. The "lump of figs" made into a "plaister" and "laid upon the boil" symbolized the Healing Power of God, Who Alone can remove the corruption of sin, which caused the sickness in the first place.)*

22 Hezekiah also had said, What is the sign that I shall go up to the House of the LORD? *(Through the symbolism of this "plaister," portraying the Power of God, laid upon the "boil," which symbolized his sinful corruption, and it being taken away, he knew now that his sins were forgiven and washed, and that he could "go up to the House of the LORD.")*

CHAPTER 39

(712 B.C.)

HEZEKIAH'S MISTAKE

AT that time Merodach-baladan, the son of Baladan, king of Babylon, sent letters and a present to Hezekiah: for he had heard that he had been sick, and was recovered. *(The words, "at that time," refer to the time after the healing of Hezekiah, probably within the year. The Babylonian Empire was just now beginning to flex its muscles and was, therefore, breaking loose from the mighty Assyrian Empire.*

Isaiah, Chpt. 37, records Hezekiah receiving a "letter" from the Assyrian, threatening his destruction. This "letter" that he now receives from the hand of the "king of Babylon" is filled with sympathy. The first letter sent him to God; this letter pulled him from God. Satan's persecution is to be feared much less than his offer of compromise.)

2 And Hezekiah was glad of them, and showed them the house of his precious things, the silver, and the gold, and the spices, and the precious ointment, and all the house of his armour, and all that was found in his treasures: there was nothing in his house, nor in all his dominion, that Hezekiah showed them not. *(The words, "and" and "his," occur each five times in this Verse. They call attention to, and emphasize, Hezekiah's childish ostentation in directing attention to the wonders of his palace rather than to the "wonders" of God's action in retiring the shadow of the sun, and in healing the king's sickness.)*

BABYLONIAN CAPTIVITY FORETOLD

3 Then came Isaiah the Prophet unto king Hezekiah, and said unto him, What said these men? and from whence came they unto you? And Hezekiah said, They are come from a far country unto me, even from Babylon. *(Isaiah was not sent for! He came unbidden to rebuke the king. This bold attitude was one which Prophets were entitled to take by virtue of their office, which called upon them to bear testimony, even before kings, and to have no respect of persons.*

Isaiah said, "What said these men?" It was actually said with contempt. He receives little answer from Hezekiah.)

4 Then said he, What have they seen in your house? And Hezekiah answered, All that is in my house have they seen: there is nothing among my treasures that I have not shown them. *(Hezekiah does not withhold from him the information, because he is not ashamed of the act, but rather glories in it. Once again, pride is the culprit. He desires that the envoy from Babylon see all of his great riches and power, and, thereby, desire his alliance.*

The trap by Satan is subtly set.)

5 Then said Isaiah to Hezekiah, Hear the Word of the LORD of Hosts *(there is no indication that the Lord punished Hezekiah for this deed, even though the sin was great; however, II Chron. 32:31 addresses itself to this which Hezekiah did)*:

6 Behold, the days come, that all who are in your house, and that which your fathers have laid up in store until this day shall be carried to Babylon: nothing shall be left, saith the LORD. *(Isaiah was a true and brave servant of the Gospel; he did not fear to warn even kings of the Wrath of God.)*

7 And of your sons who shall issue from

you, which you shall beget, shall they take away; and they shall be eunuchs in the palace of the king of Babylon. *(When Isaiah said this, Hezekiah had no sons. Manasseh was born about three years later [II Ki. 20:20; 21:1].*

Judah was later carried to Babylon because of her rejection of the Law, and beyond Babylon because of her rejection of the Law-giver, the Lord Jesus Christ [I Ki. 14:15; Amos 5:27; Lev. 26:33; Deut. 28:64; Acts 7:43].)

8 Then said Hezekiah to Isaiah, Good is the Word of the LORD which you have spoken. He said moreover, For there shall be peace and truth in my days. *(II Chron. 32:26 shows that the king's Repentance was sincere and accepted by the Lord. The words, "For there shall be peace and truth in my days," are not said with a lack of concern for the future, but that God has forgiven him of this sin, and will not bring judgment upon Judah in "my days.")*

CHAPTER 40
(712 B.C.)
THE LORD, THE MESSIAH, TO COME

COMFORT ye, comfort ye My people, saith your God. *(In this First Verse, Judah's faithful God hastens, beforehand, to assure the exiles [when they are later banished to Babylon], prophetically, that He will not forget nor lose sight of them.*

The Assyrian struggle is over. The Prophet has accepted into the depths of his spirit God's announcement that the true spoiler, "the rod of His Anger, and the staff of His Indignation," is no more Assyria, but rather Babylon. The Prophet has accepted the sentence that his people, because of their sin [in fact continued sin] and refusal to repent, are to go into captivity.)

2 Speak ye comfortably to Jerusalem, and cry unto her, that her warfare is accomplished, that her iniquity is pardoned: for she has received of the LORD's hand double for all her sins. *(This Passage leaps ahead until after the captivity, which will be many years in the future.*

The phrase, "double for her sins," actually refers to the practice of "possessing the double."

If a Jew went bankrupt, he was to list all of his indebtedness on a skin and nail it in a conspicuous place, where it could be seen by all. At times, a benefactor would stand good for the entirety of the debt, take down the skin, double it over [hence, "the double"], and write his name on the front, meaning that he would pay all indebtedness.

When Jesus died on the Cross, He took the penalty for all of our sins upon Himself, and then doubled over the account, meaning the sins can no longer be seen, because they are gone, and wrote His Name on the front, meaning that He has paid the price. So, we can also say, even though Gentiles, that through Christ and what He did at the Cross, that we "possess the double.")

3 The voice of him who cries in the wilderness, Prepare ye the way of the LORD, make straight in the desert a highway for our God. *(The "voice" of this Verse was partially fulfilled in John the Baptist, but will be totally fulfilled in the coming ministry of Elijah [Mal. 4:5-6]. His ministry will immediately precede Christ's apparition in Glory. Morally, John the Baptist was Elijah to his generation, and introduced the Redemption Glory of the Messiah, exhibited at Calvary, and perfected in His First Advent.*

The "wilderness" and "desert" represent the world. As well, it represented Israel that had lost her way; therefore, the Promise is for the Restoration of that nation, which will yet take place.)

4 Every valley shall be exalted, and every mountain and hill shall be made low: and the crooked shall be made straight, and the rough places plain *(when Christ comes the Second Time, "every valley" in the world, filled with its hurting and weeping, will at that time "be exalted." The "mountain" and "hill" represent the oppressors of the world. They will be brought down from their exalted position, and "shall be made low." Only Christ can make the "crooked" "straight," and the "rough places plain," and that He shall do!):*

5 And the Glory of the LORD shall be revealed, and all flesh shall see it together: for the mouth of the LORD has spoken it. *("The Glory of the Lord" is Jesus Christ. At the Second Coming, "all flesh shall see it together.")*

6 The voice said, Cry. And he said, What shall I cry? All flesh is grass, and all the goodliness thereof is as the flower of the field *(the "voice" in this Passage is that of the Holy Spirit. He instructs the Prophet what to proclaim. The message is, and will ever be, a humbling one; but its acceptance by man is a fundamental of Salvation):*

7 The grass withers, the flower fades: because the Spirit of the LORD blows upon it: surely the people is grass. *(Man, as symbolized here by the word "grass," has no moral worth. To prove that, "the Spirit of the LORD blows upon it," exposing all deadly flaws.)*

8 The grass withers, the flower fades: but

the Word of our God shall stand for ever. (*The Love and Truth which tell man of his moral ruin reveal to him, at the same time, an ever-living Saviour Whose Word is infallible and eternal.*)

9 O Zion, that brings good tidings, get thee up into the high mountain; O Jerusalem, that bring good tidings, lift up your voice with strength; lift it up, be not afraid; say unto the cities of Judah, Behold your God! (*Isaiah is saying that the Preacher is to point Israel to Jesus of Nazareth and cry, "Behold your God!"*)

10 Behold, the Lord GOD will come with strong hand, and His arm shall rule for Him: behold, His reward is with Him, and His work before Him. (*His title as "Adonai-Jehovah" expresses His claim as King of all the Earth. The phrase, "His arm shall rule for Him," means that Christ will not need to lean on another's arm for governmental powers. Moreover, when He comes, He will "reward" His People and "recompense" His enemies.*)

11 He shall feed His flock like a shepherd: He shall gather the lambs with His arm, and carry them in His bosom, and shall gently lead those who are with young. (*The Perfection of His Love as a Shepherd is set out in this Verse with exquisite beauty.*)

GOD'S MIGHTY POWER AND MAJESTY

12 Who has measured the waters in the hollow of His hand, and meted out Heaven with the span, and comprehended the dust of the Earth in a measure, and weighed the mountains in scales, and the hills in a balance? (*Verses 12 through 31 concern the Might and the Greatness of God contrasted with the weakness of man and the futility of idols.*)

13 Who has directed the Spirit of the LORD, or being His counselor has taught Him? (*This was quoted by Paul in Rom. 11:34 and referred to in I Cor. 2:16. In this Passage, Isaiah seems to shift from God the Father to God the Holy Spirit. The direction mentioned was ordered by the "Spirit of the LORD." But who, Isaiah asks, "directed" [or "regulated"] the Spirit Himself? The answer is instant and obvious — "no one" — making Him indivisible with God the Father.*)

14 With whom took He counsel, and who instructed Him, and taught Him in the path of Judgment, and taught Him Knowledge, and showed to Him the Way of Understanding? (*God instructs, because He knows all; therefore, none "can instruct Him." Likewise, He teaches, and does not need to be "taught," because He knows all.*)

15 Behold, the nations are as a drop of a bucket, and are counted as the small dust of the balance: behold, He takes up the isles as a very little thing. (*As God weighs mountains and hills in His balance, so He can take up in His Own Hands "lands" or "countries," with all their inhabitants, and do with them as seems to Him good. They are of no burden to Him.*)

16 And Lebanon is not sufficient to burn, nor the beasts thereof sufficient for a Burnt Offering. (*In this Passage, God is in effect saying that if all the "beasts" in Lebanon were offered as Sacrifice and all the great forests of this country, which were noted for their great Firs and Cedars, were used for wood for the fires of the Sacrifices, such would not be "sufficient." But Christ was sufficient!*)

17 All nations before Him are as nothing; and they are counted to Him less than nothing, and vanity. (*In Verse 15, individual "nations" had been declared to be of no account; now the same is said of all the nations of the Earth collectively.*)

18 To whom then will you liken God? or what likeness will you compare unto Him? (*This great God and Saviour, Jesus Christ, is contrasted here with idols in Verses 18 through 26.*)

19 The workman melts a graven image, and the goldsmith spreads it over with gold, and casts silver chains. (*The Holy Spirit through Isaiah now employs ridicule, and the first ground of His ridicule is the formation of an image. It is made by man himself out of known material substance. Can it be supposed that such things are "likenesses" of God, or that He is comparable to them?*)

20 He who is so impoverished that he has no oblation chooses a tree that will not rot; he seeks unto him a cunning workman to prepare a graven image, that shall not be moved. (*As someone has said, "The thing carries its own satire" in the mere plain description of it. Is such a thing comparable to God?*)

21 Have you not known? Have you not heard? Has it not been told you from the beginning? Have you not understood from the foundations of the Earth? (*That God made a Revelation of Himself to man at, and from, the beginning is clear from this Verse and Rom. 1:19-21. Therefore, man has no excuse for the worship of idols, religion, or the works of his own hands.*

Modern man has the Bible, which is the Word of God and, thereby, fully explains itself so that

man has no excuse.)

22 It is He who sits upon the circle of the Earth, and the inhabitants thereof are as grass hoppers; Who stretches out the Heavens as a curtain, and spreads them out as a tent to dwell in *(the word "upon" would better read "above." The words, "the circle of the Earth," reveal that the Earth is round. The "curtain" speaks of the atmosphere surrounding the Earth, which protects it from violent rays coming from the Sun. While the Bible is not a scientific Textbook, and is not meant to be, still, whatever it does say about science is impeccably correct)*:

23 That brings the princes to nothing; He makes the judges of the Earth as vanity. *(Men who think of themselves as mighty count as nothing to God. Men rule, but God overrules!)*

24 Yea, they shall not be planted; yea, they shall not be sown: yea, their stock shall not take root in the Earth: and He shall also blow upon them, and they shall wither, and the whirlwind shall take them away as stubble. *(The idea of this Passage is: all of man's efforts, no matter how powerful he may think he is, in his opposition to God, sow the seed of his own destruction.)*

25 To whom then will you liken Me, or shall I be equal? saith the Holy One. *(Once again, the Holy Spirit asks the question. This is a summary to conclude the section, as Verse 18 concludes the preceding one. If God is paramount over idols, over nature, and over humanity, to whom can He be likened? Is He not altogether unique and incomparable?)*

26 Lift up your eyes on high, and behold Who has created these things, that brings out their host by number: He calls them all by names by the greatness of His might, for that He is strong in power; not one fails. *(Some 50 years ago, it was claimed by Astronomers that there were over 40 sextillion [40,000,000,000,000,000,000,000] stars in the Universe. There are as well approximately 500,000 entries in the Webster's Unabridged Dictionary. If every one of these stars were named, there would be enough names to fill approximately 80 quadrillion [80,000,000,000,000,000] books of this size. To understand that the Supreme Being has created all of these stars, and calls them each by name, is beyond our comprehension!)*

27 Why sayest thou, O Jacob, and speakest, O Israel, My way is hid from the LORD, and my judgment is passed over from my God? *(Understanding, at least somewhat, of the Greatness of God, and then to think that we can hide things from Him, presents foolishness*

of the highest order.)

28 Have you not known? Have you not heard, that the everlasting God, the LORD, the Creator of the ends of the Earth, faints not, neither is weary? There is no searching of His understanding. *(In this Verse, the Lord tells Israel and us that He never fails or wearies in upholding the feeblest of His people, nor does He ever tire of our circumstances, nor grow uninterested in our affairs. On the contrary, far from fainting in His Action on our behalf, He, as the next Verse tells us, gives power to those who do faint among us. The strongest men grow feeble in effort and interest, but the "Great Shepherd" never!)*

29 He gives power to the faint; and to them who have no might He increases strength. *(So far is He from being "faint" Himself that He has superabundant energy to impart to any who are faint among His servants. What a Promise!)*

30 Even the youths shall faint and be weary, and the young men shall utterly fall *(this has reference to the fact that even the most vigorous and powerful men will faint under enough strain and eventually fall; man's strength is grossly limited, even the strength of the strongman; however, those who trust the Lord, as the next Verse tells us, will not "fall")*:

31 But they who wait upon the LORD shall renew their strength; they shall mount up with wings as eagles; they shall run, and not be weary; and they shall walk, and not faint. *(The word "wait," in the Hebrew, is "qavah," and means "to bind together by twisting." The sense is that if we really "wait upon the LORD," we will be constantly seeking His Face and, being bound together with Him, we will be desirous of carrying out His Will.*

The Holy Spirit uses "eagles" as an example. "Eagles" do not stay perpetually young, but do in fact periodically take on a luster on their wings that gives them a perpetual youthful appearance. Such is intended here!

God promises to give strength for the journey in order that we may "run" and "not be weary.")

CHAPTER 41
(712 B.C.)
THE SOVEREIGNTY OF GOD
OVER THE NATIONS

KEEP silence before Me, O islands; and let the people renew their strength: let them come near; then let them speak : let us come near together to judgment. *(Through Isaiah,*

God is the Speaker. The idea of this Passage is that before God man has no argument; hence, "Keep silence before Me.")

2 Who raised up the righteous man from the east, called him to his foot, gave the nations before him, and made him rule over kings? He gave them as the dust to his sword, and as driven stubble to his bow. *(It seems from Verse 8 that this "righteous man" is "Abraham, My friend." He was called from the east in Righteousness to Jehovah's foot; for God said to him, "Walk before Me and be thou perfect" [Gen. 17:1]. He made him ruler over kings; for they became as dust to his sword and as stubble to his bow.)*

3 He pursued them, and passed safely; even by the way that he had not gone with his feet. *("He pursued them" refers to Abraham rescuing Lot when he was taken captive by the four kings, as outlined in Gen. 14:1-3. His "passing safely by the way that he had not gone with his feet" refers to him refusing to take anything from "the king of Sodom" [Gen. 14:21-24]. He won the battle with the four kings with "his feet." He won the battle with the king of Sodom with his spirit. All by the Power of the Holy Spirit, the latter victory was greater even that the former!)*

4 Who has wrought and done it, calling the generations from the beginning? I the LORD, the first, and with the last; I am He. *(The generations chosen from the beginning were the children of Abraham; for they were all in their father's loins when God chose him [Heb. 7:10].*

"I, Jehovah, the first, and with the Last — I Am." This glorious title occurs three times in Isaiah and three times in the Book of Revelation.)

5 The isles saw it, and feared; the ends of the Earth were afraid, drew near, and came. *(This refers to Israel, as is evident in Verse 8, and the seven nations of idolaters in Canaan, and their appeal to their idols for salvation from the victorious soldiers of Joshua. Rahab declared that the hearts of the inhabitants of the land were melting with terror [Josh. 2:9-11]. Thus, again, the folly of idolatry is evidenced.)*

6 They helped every one his neighbour; and every one said to his brother, Be of good courage. *(The courage of the confederate nations which tried to stop Joshua was of no consequence with the Lord.)*

7 So the carpenter encouraged the goldsmith, and he who smooths with the hammer him who smote the anvil, saying, It is ready for the soldering: and he fastened it with nails, that it should not be moved. *(As they would make their idol, they would then need to "solder" and "nail" it so that the wretched object might be kept erect and not show its weakness by falling over. Such is the spiritual dumbness of man!)*

ISRAEL IS GOD'S SOVEREIGN CHOICE

8 But you, Israel, are My servant, Jacob whom I have chosen, the seed of Abraham My friend. *(In Verses 8 through 20, the existence and love of an irresistible Power of the God of Israel are set out. The name "Israel" means "Prince with God," while "Jacob" means "schemer." God's ever purpose was to change "Jacob, the schemer" into "Israel, the Prince with God," which He did!)*

9 You whom I have taken from the ends of the Earth, and called you from the chief men thereof, and said unto you, You are My servant; I have chosen you, and not cast you away. *(Concerning the "chief men thereof," the idea is that God had the ability to choose anyone. He had His pick of the "chief men." However, it was Abraham whom He chose, i.e., "Jacob.")*

GOD WILL GIVE ISRAEL VICTORY;
HE WILL BLESS HIS PEOPLE

10 Fear thou not; for I am with you: be not dismayed; for I am your God: I will strengthen you; yea, I will help you; yea, I will uphold you with the right hand of My righteousness. *(The progression in this Verse is most precious: "I am with you"; but He comes yet nearer: "I will strengthen you"; and still closer: "I will help you"; and finally, He throws His arms around His Child and says, "I will uphold you.")*

11 Behold, all they who were incensed against you shall be ashamed and confounded: they shall be as nothing; and they who strive with thee shall perish.

12 You shall seek them, and shall not find them, even them who contended with you: they who war against you shall be as nothing, and as a thing of nought. *(The order, as given here, is one of climax. Similarly, with each augmentation of the hostility, there is an augmentation of the sentence of punishment. In essence, the Holy Spirit through Isaiah is saying that all who trust the Lord will be vindicated.)*

13 For I the LORD your God will hold your right hand, saying unto you, Fear not; I will help you. *(God Himself will be their [our] strength, courage, power, and their glory, and*

will *Personally interfere on their behalf, taking them, as it were, by their right hand. As an adult leads a little child, thereby giving it protection, the Lord promises to do the same for Israel, and for us!)*

14 Fear not, thou worm Jacob, and you men of Israel; I will help you, saith the LORD, and your Redeemer, the Holy One of Israel. *(It is the "worm Jacob" that is to become a "new sharp threshing instrument having teeth," and who is to break in pieces the great nations and the lesser nations, here compared to mountains and hills.*

The Passage, "worm Jacob," is given here so that Israel will recognize that such is done, not because they are good, but because God is good.)

15 Behold, I will make you a new sharp threshing instrument having teeth: you shall thresh the mountains, and beat them small, and shall make the hills as chaff. *(Israel is to be more than just sustained here. Strength is to be given her to take the aggressive, and to subdue her enemies under her. This will occur when Jesus comes back. Then every Promise that God made to the Patriarchs and Prophets will be brought to pass.)*

16 You shall fan them, and the wind shall carry them away, and the whirlwind shall scatter them: and you shall rejoice in the LORD, and shall glory in the Holy One of Israel. *(Israel in the past has little "rejoiced" or "gloried" in the "LORD." However, her strength has always been derived from this Source, and this Source Alone!)*

17 When the poor and needy seek water, and there is none, and their tongue fails for thirst, I the LORD will hear them, I the God of Israel will not forsake them. *(The "poor and needy" represent Israel. The "water" represents the "Water of Life." Israel doesn't have this "Water of Life," so her "thirst" continues; however, in the Battle of Armageddon, the Lord will hear their cries, and that "thirst" will be forever slaked.)*

18 I will open rivers in the high places, and fountains in the midst of the valleys: I will make the wilderness a pool of water, and the dry land springs of water. *(Often the Holy Spirit likens the spiritual rejuvenation to the "wilderness" being made fertile, and that by ample irrigation. Life is a "wilderness," and can enjoy fertility only in Christ. How so much, and so often, does man attempt to make the "wilderness" fertile, but fail he does, as fail he must! Only Christ can do such!)*

19 I will plant in the wilderness the cedar, the shittah tree, and the myrtle, and the oil tree; I will set in the desert the fir tree, and the pine, the box tree together *(the trees named are the choicest in Israel; the idea is that we have a deep relationship with the One Who does the planting; in fact, Isaiah will later say that we are "the planting of the Lord" [61:3]):*

20 That they may see, and know, and consider, and understand together, that the hand of the LORD has done this, and the Holy One of Israel has created it. *(In that future day of blessing, Israel, now barren and stony, will become beauteous and fertile as the Garden of the Lord; and the nations of the Earth will recognize that these wonders are the Work of God and not idols.)*

THE LORD IS THE ONE WHO DECLARES THE FUTURE

21 Produce your cause, saith the LORD; bring forth your strong reasons, saith the King of Jacob. *(In view of all of this that the Lord will do, Isaiah once again compares Jehovah with idols. He says, "Produce your cause," etc., i.e., "state your case in favor of idolatry; bring forth your weighty arguments," etc.)*

22 Let them bring them forth, and shew us what shall happen: let them shew the former things, what they be, that we may consider them, and know the latter end of them; or declare us things for to come. *(The words, "Let them bring them forth," is basically the same as "Produce your cause." God claims that the power of predicting the future is His Own inalienable prerogative. He defies the idol-gods and their votaries to give any clear prediction of future events.*

The Bible alone proclaims future events, which means all the other so-called holy books are mere works of men's hands — "idols.")

23 Shew the things that are to come hereafter, that we may know that you are gods: yea, do good, or do evil, that we may be dismayed, and behold it together. *(In effect, the Lord is saying, concerning these idols, "If you cannot prophesy, what can you do? In actuality, you cannot do 'good' or 'evil.'" In effect, He is saying, "You have no power to do anything.")*

24 Behold, you are of nothing, and your work of nought: an abomination is he who chooses you. *(This Scripture declares an idol to be an abomination. Hence, an idolater becomes an abomination; not only abominable, but worse, an abomination; for a man becomes morally like that which he worships, and idolatry and obscenity are one. As the false god is abomination, so the True God, the Messiah, is Righteousness; not*

only Righteous, but Righteousness itself.)

25 I have raised up one from the north, and he shall come: from the rising of the sun shall he call upon My name: and he shall come upon princes as upon morter, and as the potter treads clay. *(Cyrus was the one raised up by God to fulfill His Word concerning the punishment of Babylon and the freeing of Israel]Jer., Chpt. 25; Dan. 1:21; 6:28; Ezra, Chpt. 1]. This Prophecy was fulfilled about 140 years later. Abraham was the man from the east, Cyrus, the man from the north; both are types of the Son of Man, Who, in His Second Advent, will destroy all idols and all idolaters.)*

26 Who has declared from the beginning, that we may know? And before time, that we may say, He is righteous? Yea, there is none who shews, yea, there is none who declares, yea, there is none who hears your words. *(Said in contrast to this prediction as to Cyrus, the challenge is repeated to the dumb idols to produce such a prediction on their part, thus demonstrating their trustworthiness. But the Verse closes with the statement that not one of the countless idols that men worship could "declare" anything, or "reveal" anything, or could even utter one word. They were all dumb!)*

27 The first shall say to Zion, Behold, behold them: and I will give to Jerusalem one who brings good tidings. *(The Messiah speaks here and calls to Zion to behold the fulfillment of His Prediction. Idols bring nothing, while the Lord always brings "Good Tidings.")*

28 For I beheld, and there was no man; even among them, and there was no counselor, that, when I asked of them, could answer a word. *(Not only are the idols themselves dumb, but their worshippers, when challenged to defend them, are dumb also; and the inability of the idols to act, as to speak, is again pointed to in this Verse.*

Let it ever be understood that outside of the Bible there is "no counselor.")

29 Behold, they are all vanity; their works are nothing: their molten images are wind and confusion. *("Wind and confusion" adequately describe anything and everything that is not of the Lord. This final "outburst of scorn" is directed primarily against the idol-worshippers and, only through them, against the idols.)*

CHAPTER 42
(712 B.C.)
MESSIAH'S FIRST ADVENT

BEHOLD My servant, Whom I uphold; My elect, in Whom My soul delights; I have put My spirit upon Him: He shall bring forth judgment to the Gentiles. *(Almost the entirety of this Chapter concerns itself with Prophecy extolling the coming of the Messiah in both His First and Second Advents. As well, Israel is addressed in her rejection of Christ in His First Advent.*

God had only one Perfect Servant on Earth, His Own and well-beloved Son, in Whom His soul delighted. He speaks of Him in the Scriptures as "My Servant."

The Holy Spirit in Mat. 12:9-23 declares the Servant of this Prophecy to be Jehovah Messiah.)

2 He shall not cry, nor lift up, nor cause His voice to be heard in the street. *("Cry" here means "to claim His rights.")*

3 A bruised reed shall He not break, and the smoking flax shall He not quench: He shall bring forth judgment unto truth. *(This presents the image of the weak and depressed in spirit, the lowly and dejected. Christ would deal tenderly with such, not violently.*

Where the flame of devotion burns at all, however feebly and dimly, the Messiah will take care not to quench it; rather, He will tend it, trim it, give it fresh oil, and cause it to burn more brightly.)

4 He shall not fail nor be discouraged, till He have set judgment in the Earth: and the isles shall wait for His Law. *(In a sense, this Verse is the exact opposite of the previous. Compared to those whom He helps, He will Himself show no signs of the weakness with which He is compassionate with others. As a "Light," He will burn brightly and strongly; as a "Reed" or "Rod," He will be firm and unbroken.)*

5 Thus saith God the LORD, He Who created the heavens, and stretched them out; He Who spread forth the Earth, and that which comes out of it; He Who gives breath unto the people upon it, and Spirit to them who walk therein *(the phrase, "Thus saith God the LORD," literally means "Thus saith the One God Jehovah." Actually, the entirety of the utterance beginning with the first word of the First Verse is the utterance of God; however, the Prophet suddenly stops, and seemingly makes a new beginning. The Holy Spirit wants it to be perfectly clear that the announcement of the "Servant of the Lord" [Christ] and His mission is from the Almighty, and that He is able to do what He has predicted)*:

6 I the LORD have called You in righteousness, and will hold Your hand, and will keep You, and give You for a covenant of the people, for a light of the Gentiles *(all statements in*

Verses 6 and 7 refer to the Messiah, as well as Verses 1 through 4. In the humiliation and grace of His First Coming, it is predicted that He would not assert His rights nor judge His enemies, but that, on the contrary, He would introduce the New Covenant of Salvation for Israel, and for the Gentiles, and illuminate and liberate alike through the preaching of the Gospel [I Cor. 1:21]);

7 To open the blind eyes, to bring out the prisoners from the prison, and them who sit in darkness out of the prison house. *("To open the blind eyes" refers to spiritual blindness [Lk. 4:18-19]. Christ Alone can deliver, and He does so through the Means of the Cross, and through that Means alone [I Cor. 1:17-18, 23; 2:2].)*

8 I am the LORD: that is My Name: and My glory will I not give to another, neither My praise to graven images. *(The phrase actually says, "I the Lord. I Who am all that the Name "Jehovah" signifies — self-existent, eternal, self-sufficing, independent, omnipotent, omniscient, and, therefore, unique, One Whose Glory cannot be shared with any other being that exists — least of all with images which are mere vanity and nothingness.")*

9 Behold, the former things are come to pass, and new things do I declare: before they spring forth I tell you of them. *(In Verses 5 through 8, God speaks to the Messiah; and in Verses 9 through 12, He points to the fulfillment of "former things," i.e., Prophecies, and predicts "new things," i.e., new Prophecies.*

The point is that only God can do such things! The "former things" came to pass and, therefore, the "new things" will also come to pass.)

GIVE GLORY TO GOD

10 Sing unto the LORD a new song, and His praise from the end of the Earth, you who go down to the sea, and all who are therein; the isles, and the inhabitants thereof. *(The words, "new song," have reference to the coming Kingdom Age, when Christ will rule and reign supremely over the entirety of the Earth, totally changing its government, bringing everything into subjection unto Him, which will give to the entirety of the world a "new song."*

As well, every single Believer can presently have that "new song," which is given freely according to our Faith evidenced in Christ and what He has done for us at the Cross [I Cor. 1:23].)

11 Let the wilderness and the cities thereof lift up their voice, the villages that Kedar does inhabit: let the inhabitants of the rock sing, let them shout from the top of the mountains. *(This Passage continues the results of the "new song." Hitherto, the "wilderness" has had little to shout about. Now the "wilderness," because of Christ, will be turned into a garden.)*

12 Let them give glory unto the LORD, and declare His praise in the islands. *(Glory is to be given to the Lord over the entirety of the Earth, and in the Kingdom Age most definitely will be done!)*

MESSIAH'S SECOND ADVENT; JUDGMENT AND RESTORATION

13 The LORD shall go forth as a mighty man, He shall stir up jealousy like a man of war: He shall cry, yea, roar; He shall prevail against His enemies. *(This pertains to His Second Coming, and the carrying out of that which has been predicted.)*

14 I have long time held My peace; I have been still, and refrained Myself: now will I cry like a travailing woman; I will destroy and devour at once. *(Righteous men have long wondered, "Why did not God step in and take a hand in the Hell that this world has become?" The answer is that now, and for His Own reasons which are valid and right, He is "holding His peace." The sense of the Verse is that He has chafed, as it were, under the necessity of inaction, and has with difficulty "refrained Himself." Now He will "refrain" no longer.)*

15 I will make waste mountains and hills, and dry up all their herbs; and I will make the rivers islands, and I will dry up the pools. *(The result of God's "stirring up His Jealousy" and giving a free vent to His Feelings will be the destruction of the great and mighty ones of the Earth. The "mountains and hills" of fortifications, wealth, and power gathered by the Antichrist will be "made waste.")*

16 And I will bring the blind by a way that they knew not; I will lead them in paths that they have not known: I will make darkness light before them, and crooked things straight. These things will I do unto them, and not forsake them. *("The blind" here can only mean captive Israel, about to be destroyed by the Antichrist. Because of her long rejection of her Messiah, the Lord Jesus Christ, she is still dim-sighted from the effect of her old sins against Light and, therefore, greatly needing God's guidance. God promises to "bring them" out of captivity "by a way not hitherto known to them" — the way of voluntary release by the favor of the new King,*

the Lord Jesus Christ.

Two thousand years ago, with the rejection of Christ, Israel chose "crooked things." Now these "crooked things" shall be made "straight," because the "straight One" is Christ.)

17 They shall be turned back, they shall be greatly ashamed, who trust in graven images, who say to the molten images, You are our gods. *(In the past, Israel trusted in "graven images," their own self-righteousness; they will, in fact, accept the false messiah and say to him, "You are our god," i.e., messiah. At the coming of the Lord, they will then be "greatly ashamed" that they did this!)*

18 Hear, you deaf; and look you blind, that you may see. *(Previously, because of their rejection of Christ, Israel has been "deaf" and "blind." Now, and we speak of the Second Coming, Israel will then "hear" and "see.")*

19 Who is blind, but My servant? or deaf, as My messenger whom I sent? Who is blind as he who is perfect, and blind as the LORD's servant? *(This Verse speaks of Israel, but as well of the Church. Israel then was "His servant" and "His messenger." The Church is now such. Apostate Israel refused their True Messiah, the Lord Jesus Christ, and will accept a false messiah, the Antichrist. Tragically, the apostate Church also refuses the Lord Jesus Christ and the Cross, and will accept a false christ, the Antichrist.)*

20 Seeing many things, but you observe not; opening the ears, but he hears not. *(Israel had seen so many things that were sent from God; the miracles, the Law, the Prophets, and then even the Messiah, "but you observe not." Jesus ministered unto their "ears," but "they heard not." There is no blindness like willful blindness! In God's Eyes, this is perhaps the worst sin of all!)*

21 The LORD is well pleased for His righteousness' sake; He will magnify the Law, and make it honourable. *(Despite the fact that Israel would not honor the Law, the Lord most definitely did. In fact, His Righteousness demanded such!)*

22 But this is a people robbed and spoiled; they are all of them snared in holes, and they are hid in prison houses: they are for a prey, and none delivers; for a spoil, and none says, Restore. *(God's True Messenger, the Messiah, did not fail. He lived and preached the Law, and made the teaching great and glorious, totally unlike what the Pharisees had done. But yet they would not accept Him.*

By not accepting Christ and His Way, "they

are all of them snared in holes." They could have had a Heaven, but instead were put in "holes," i.e., "death camps.")*

23 Who among you will give ear to this? Who will hearken and hear for the time to come? *(The Holy Spirit through Isaiah says, "Surely there are some among you, less hardened than the rest, who will take advantage of My warning and repent at this, the eleventh hour.")*

24 Who gave Jacob for a spoil, and Israel to the robbers? Did not the LORD, He against Whom we have sinned? For they would not walk in His ways, neither were they obedient unto His Law. *(Even though "Israel" was God's Chosen, still, the Lord could not tolerate their self-way in them, any more than He could in the heathen. Therefore, He gave "Jacob" to the "robbers.")*

25 Therefore He has poured upon him the fury of His anger, and the strength of battle: and it has set him on fire round about, yet he knew not; and it burned him, yet he laid it not to heart. *(God's chastisement is meant to draw us back to Himself. He does it for "our profit, that we might be partakers of His Holiness" [Heb. 12:10]. If that fails, there is no hope!)*

CHAPTER 43
(712 B.C.)
GOD HAS REDEEMED HIS PEOPLE

BUT now thus saith the LORD Who created you, O Jacob, and He Who formed you, O Israel, Fear not: for I have redeemed you, I have called you by your name; you are Mine. *(In this Chapter, the Holy Spirit through Isaiah portrays two things: Israel's purpose and God's greatness! The last Verse of the previous Chapter portrays Israel's refusal to repent. Set over against this impenitence, ignorance, and rebellion are displayed the Grace, Power, and Love of the Messiah.)*

2 When you pass through the waters, I will be with you; and through the rivers, they shall not overflow you: when you walk through the fire, you shall not be burned; neither shall the flame kindle upon you. *(Israel's past history affords striking proofs of the truthfulness of this Verse. The future will reveal yet more striking proofs of its truth. Such Prophecies not only apply to Israel, but any follower of the Lord.)*

3 For I am the LORD your God, the Holy One of Israel, your Saviour: I gave Egypt for your ransom, Ethiopia and Seba for you. *(Particular countries which would have destroyed*

Israel were instead destroyed by the Lord, which is referred to as "your ransom." As well, the Lord paid the ransom on the Cross, which was demanded by God, which was the giving of His Life, that whosoever will, may find life [Jn. 3:16].)

4 Since you were precious in My sight, you have been honourable, and I have loved you: therefore will I give men for you, and people for your life. *(Israel became "precious" from the time that the Promise was given to Jacob that in his seed all the nations of the Earth should be blessed [Gen. 28:14]. Henceforward, God placed the interests of Israel above those of "men" generally and markedly above those of any other "people."*

The only reason they have suffered such defeat and failure is because of their rejection of God and their Saviour, the Lord Jesus Christ.)

5 Fear not: for I am with you: I will bring your seed from the east, and gather you from the west *(Verses 1 through 4 portray the preservation of Israel, while Verses 5 through 7 portray the gathering of Israel, which in essence began in 1948 and will be finished at the Second Coming);*

6 I will say to the north, Give up; and to the south, Keep not back: bring my sons from far, and my daughters from the ends of the Earth *(as stated, this will take place on a worldwide scale immediately after the Second Coming, because Israel will have then made Christ her Saviour and her Lord);*

7 Even every one who is called by My name: for I have created him for My glory, I have formed him; yea, I have made him. *(The very name of "Israel" means "Prince of God" or "Soldier of God," and thus every Israelite was "called by God's Name.")*

8 Bring forth the blind people who have eyes, and the deaf who have ears. *(Israel is described here as "blind people who have eyes"; in other words, a people long blind, who have now, to some extent, recovered their sight and are ready to witness for God. As stated, this will take place in the Kingdom Age.)*

9 Let all the nations be gathered together, and let the people be assembled: who among them can declare this, and shew us former things? let them bring forth their witnesses, that they may be justified: or let them hear, and say, It is truth. *(This of which the Lord will do, and we speak of the Restoration of Israel, will be of such magnitude that the Lord will gather the nations of the world that they may observe "and say, It is truth.")*

ISRAEL'S MISSION

10 You are My witnesses, saith the LORD, and My servant whom I have chosen: that you may know and believe Me, and understand that I am He: before Me there was no God formed, neither shall there be after Me. *(As in the previous Verse, the nations are invited to come together and challenged once more to vindicate their idols by fulfilled Prophecy. But it is in vain that they will seek for witnesses! But the Messiah will bring forth His witnesses, even His Servant Israel to prove that there is no God but the God of Israel; that He "declares" and "saves" and "shows"; that He is from everlasting; and that He is Almighty.)*

11 I, even I, am the LORD; and beside Me there is no Saviour. *(None but God can save men. Man cannot make atonement for his followers. In this Passage is found the telling point of the Gospel, and the contention arousing Satan's anger. Emphatically, it is declared that the Lord is the only "Saviour." Satan deceives men into believing otherwise.)*

12 I have declared, and have saved, and I have shewed, when there was no strange god among you: therefore you are My witnesses, saith the LORD, that I am God. *(It could be translated, "I did what the idol-gods cannot do — announced Deliverance and effected it, and further proclaimed [or published] it at the time when you Israelites had no idolatry among you." Therefore, He is saying, "There is no excuse for you not to believe.")*

DECLARATIONS OF GOD TO ISRAEL

13 Yea, before the day was I am He; and there is none that can deliver out of My hand: I will work, and who shall let it? *(The first part of this Verse, "before the day was I am He," refers to the Truth that God was just as powerful before He delivered Judah from Sennacherib as He was at the time of their Deliverance. God does not change! He says, "I will work, and who can stop it?")*

14 Thus saith the LORD, your Redeemer, the Holy One of Israel; For your sake I have sent to Babylon, and have brought down all their nobles, and the Chaldeans, whose cry is in the ships. *(Now the Prophecy is given concerning the coming destruction of Babylon. It would happen approximately 170 years in the future.*

The "ships" speak of the "Chaldeans," a special ruling group of Babylonians, who would

attempt to escape. Instead of the "ships" becoming their saviour, they would be tombs; hence, the "cry."

The words, "for your sake," speak of Israel's Restoration, which would take place in the Medo-Persian Empire; however, its greater fulfillment awaits the coming Kingdom Age.)

15 I am the LORD, your Holy One, the creator of Israel, your King. (In this Passage, we are told that the "LORD" is the only One Who can make such predictions as are outlined in the previous Verse and unfailingly make them come to pass. He tells them here that He is "their King." Sadly, some 750 years later, they would say, "We have no king but Caesar" [Jn. 19:15].)

16 Thus saith the LORD, which makes a way in the sea, and a path in the mighty waters (this has reference to God's Deliverance of Israel out of Egypt by the "way in the sea"; these "mighty waters" would be pushed back, with a "path" made through them for Israel's safe crossing);

17 Which brings forth the chariot and horse, the army and the power; they shall lie down together, they shall not rise: they are extinct, they are quenched as tow. (The Chaldeans were to perish as completely as the Egyptians did in the Red Sea. The words, "quenched as tow," refer to the wick that was made of flax; it was very flimsy and, thereby, easily extinguished. The Lord is saying that the Babylonians will be extinguished as easily.)

18 Remember ye not the former things, neither consider the things of old. (The Holy Spirit is saying that the old Deliverance will be as nothing compared with the new. Israel must cast its eye forwards, not backwards.)

19 Behold, I will do a new thing; now it shall spring forth; shall you not know it? I will even make a way in the wilderness, and rivers in the desert. (This refers to the Millennial Reign, when Christ will reign supreme from Jerusalem, and Israel, at long last, will accept Him as Lord and Saviour.)

20 The beast of the field shall honour Me, the dragons and the owls: because I give waters in the wilderness, and rivers in the desert, to give drink to My people, My chosen. (These wild beasts and fowls of this Verse may possibly figure the Gentile nations. Many will come to Christ, because of His Power to save.)

21 This people have I formed for Myself; they shall shew forth My praise. (Finally, and at long last, "this people," i.e., Israel, "shall show forth My praise.")

22 But you have not called upon Me, O

Jacob; but you have been weary of Me, O Israel. (Constantly, the Holy Spirit contrasts "Jacob" and "Israel." He attempts to make them into "Israel, the Prince of God," while they insist upon being "Jacob, the schemer and supplanter.")

23 You have not brought Me the small cattle of your Burnt Offerings; neither have you honoured Me with your sacrifices. I have not caused you to serve with an Offering, nor wearied you with Incense. (In these Passages, we are witnessing a loving parent pleading with his children; and with pity, compassion, love, and tenderness!)

24 You have bought Me no sweet cane with money, neither have you filled Me with the fat of your Sacrifices: but you have made Me to serve with your sins, you have wearied Me with your iniquities. (It is actually "sweet calamus" referred to here by the Lord using the term "sweet cane." It was used in the Incense that was poured on the Golden Altar [Ex. 30:23; Ezek. 27:19].

It seems that Israel had grown weary of offering the Incense, and also of the Sacrifices; consequently, the "fat," symbolic of God's best given for humanity, i.e., "the Lord Jesus Christ," was no longer burned on the Altar. They forgot the source of their prosperity.

When one no longer makes the Cross the object of one's faith, of which the Sacrifices were a symbol, one then also does not define sin as one should!)

25 I, even I, am He Who blots out your transgressions for My Own sake, and will not remember your sins. (The recital of Israel's contempt of and disobedience to the Law is cleft in two and seemingly disjointed and interrupted by the declaration of this Verse. Such is the heart of God! When sin reaches its climax, as it did at Calvary, and becomes unbearable, Grace puts away the sin instead of putting away the sinner!

As man under the First Covenant despised the spotless Lamb and its atoning Blood — God's Way of Salvation in type — so man today denies and despises the Divine Way of the Cross as it refers to Justification and Sanctification through the Precious Blood of Christ, the Lamb without blemish and without spot.)

26 Put Me in remembrance, let us plead together: declare thou, that you may be justified. (The answer is: "I cannot produce any defense." When man is brought to this consciousness, he listens with wonder to the glad tidings offering him a spotless Righteousness in and through Christ and what He did for us at the Cross!)

27 Your first father has sinned, and your

teachers have transgressed against Me. *(The "first father" refers to Abraham. "Your teachers" refer to the Priests and Levites of the Sanctuary, who also sinned! The idea of this Passage is that Israel cannot fall back upon merit.)*

28 Therefore I have profaned the princes of the Sanctuary, and have given Jacob to the curse, and Israel to reproaches. *(The "profaning of the princes of the Sanctuary" refers to the captivity, when the Babylonians took Jerusalem and destroyed the Temple. It refers to the principal members of the Priesthood who were carried into captivity with the rest of the people [II Ki. 25:18].*

Israel, at that time, was "given to the curse" of a severe bondage, and to the "reproaches" of the neighboring nations.)

CHAPTER 44
(712 B.C.)
GOD'S SPIRIT TO BE ON ISRAEL, HIS SERVANT-NATION

YET now hear, O Jacob My servant; and Israel, whom I have chosen *(the Lord is saying, "Be not dismayed at what has been said; listen a little longer"):*

2 Thus saith the LORD Who made you, and formed you from the womb, which will help you; Fear not, O Jacob, My servant; and you, Jesurun, whom I have chosen. *(After proclaiming to Israel exactly what they were — sinners, the Lord now assures them of His Love and Grace. He introduces this message with: "Yet now hear."*

The words, "from the womb," are used here for increased emphasis. They emphasize that no man had anything to do with the bringing forth of these people called "Israel." They were strictly a Work of God and, as such, will be strictly restored. The name "Jesurun" refers to something special.)

3 For I will pour water upon him who is thirsty, and floods upon the dry ground: I will pour My Spirit upon your seed, and My blessing upon your offspring *(this Promise had a fulfillment at Pentecost; but the future only will bring the total fulfillment.*

The "water" here is a figure of the Holy Spirit; the "willows," a figure of the sons of Israel.

This is the Promise to which Peter pointed in Acts 2:39. It is a Promise to Israel and to her children. As such, and as other Scriptures show, it was to overflow from Israel to all the nations of the Earth. It will yet do so!):

4 And they shall spring up as among the grass, as willows by the water courses. *(Israel rejected their "Pentecost" some 2,000 years ago. But now at the Second Advent of Christ they will accept, and gladly! At this time, He will "pour water upon him who is thirsty, and floods upon the dry ground."*

This infusion of the Holy Spirit upon and within Israel shall cause them to blossom as "willows by the water courses.")

5 One shall say, I am the LORD's and another shall call himself by the name of Jacob; and another shall subscribe with his hand unto the LORD, and surname himself by the name of Israel. *(The idea of this Passage is that untold thousands of Gentiles, seeing the blessings of the Lord upon Israel, will no doubt take as a surname the "name of Israel."*

This means that the heathen nations, instead of looking scornfully on and uttering gibes and jeers, even as they have done for thousands of years, will hasten to enroll themselves among the worshippers of Jehovah, and do so through Israel.)

THE FOLLY OF IDOLATRY

6 Thus saith the LORD the King of Israel, and His Redeemer the LORD of Hosts; I am the First, and I am the Last; and beside Me there is no God. *(Let all know and understand: there is no "Redeemer" but the Lord! There is One God, manifest in Three Persons: God the Father, God the Son, and God the Holy Spirit, Who are all One in essence [I Cor. 8:6; Eph. 4:3-6; Heb. 1:8; Jn. 1:1-2; 20:28; Acts 5:3-4; II Jn. 3; Acts 2:34].)*

7 And who, as I, shall call, and shall declare it, and set it in order for Me, since I appointed the ancient people? and the things that are coming, and shall come, let them shew unto them. *(The pronoun "them" in the last sentence refers to idolaters. They are challenged to declare the things that are coming, and that shall come, as only the Lord can do!)*

8 Fear ye not, neither be afraid: have not I told you from that time, and have declared it? you are even My witnesses, Is there a God beside Me? yes, there is no God; I know not any. *(Israel's Saviour keeps assuring His People here that they are His; that they always have been His; that they always shall be His; that He will never forget them; that though all other nations may perish, they never shall.*

"From that time" refers to the time that God appointed [i.e., elected] His ancient people.

The statement, "Beside Me there is no God,"

literally means: "There is no Rock"; i.e., "no sure ground of trust or confidence in anything else.")

9 They who make a graven image are all of them vanity; and their delectable things shall not profit; and they are their own witnesses; they see not, nor know; that they may be ashamed. *(The idolaters, as witnesses to the supposed existence and power of their idols, are themselves like the idols. They neither see nor know; they have neither vision nor intelligence. Hence, the reason [idolatry] for the terrible problems which beset planet Earth!)*

10 Who has formed a god, or molten a graven image that is profitable for nothing? *(The meaning of the Passage is: "Who has been so foolish as to do so — to take so much trouble about a thing which cannot possibly profit anyone?"*

So it can truthfully be said that all who do not serve the Lord Jesus Christ "have formed their own god.")

11 Behold, all his fellows shall be ashamed: and the workmen, they are of men: let them all be gathered together, let them stand up; yet they shall fear, and they shall be ashamed together. *(The essence of this Verse is: Even if all the worshippers and makers of idols should all be "gathered together" and "stand up" to help one another, yet would they be unable to effect anything. Gathered together against God, they would "tremble and be ashamed.")*

12 The smith with the tongs both works in the coals, and fashions it with hammers, and works it with the strength of his arms: yea, he is hungry, and his strength fails: he drinks no water, and is faint. *(The Holy Spirit uses sarcasm in these Passages, speaking of the smith who makes an ax for the carpenter with which he can cut down a strong tree and fashion it into the figure of a handsome man, or whatever, that it may stand in the house; and that is all that it can do, for it cannot provide food and drink for the fainting smith or famished carpenter.)*

13 The carpenter stretches out his rule; he marks it out with a line; he fits it with planes, and he marks it out with the compass, and makes it after the figure of a man, according to the beauty of a man; that it may remain in the house. *(Idolatry blinds the senses that a man will cook his food with one-half of a tree and bow down and worship the other half as a god able to deliver him. He worships a god whom he himself makes!)*

14 He hews him down cedars, and takes the cypress and the oak, which he strengthens for himself among the trees of the forest: he plants an ash, and the rain does nourish it. *(The idea of this Passage is that God made the trees of any and all varieties; then senseless man, deceived by Satan, takes one and proposes to make a god of it. How stupid!)*

15 Then shall it be for a man to burn: for he will take thereof, and warm himself; yea, he kindles it, and bakes bread; yea, he makes a god, and worships it; he makes it a graven image, and falls down thereto. *(He worships what he makes. Again, I say, "How stupid!" He doesn't seem to realize that he has to be more intelligent than what he has made. So why worship something that is less intelligent than the maker?)*

16 He burns part thereof in the fire; with part thereof he eats flesh; he roasts roast, and is satisfied: yea, he warms himself, and says, Aha, I am warm, I have seen the fire *(he takes part of the tree and uses the wood to build a fire, thereby preparing his meal; with the other half, he fashions a god. Hence, men take on the nature of that which they worship. In this case, it is a dumb idol; consequently, its maker becomes more dumb!):*

17 And the residue thereof he makes a god, even his graven image: he falls down unto it, and worships it, and prays unto it, and says, Deliver me; for you are my god. *(The Harvard graduate would smile at such ignorance; and yet, if the graduate knows not the Lord Jesus Christ, he is himself an idolater, functioning in the same capacity as the one he ridicules!)*

18 They have not known nor understood: for He has shut their eyes, that they cannot see; and their hearts, that they cannot understand. *(The word "shut" means to be daubed with clay. When anyone turns from the Revelation God has given of Himself in Scriptures and bows down to idols, or places something else ahead of God, a judicial blindness from God descends upon him.)*

19 And none considers in his heart, neither is there knowledge nor understanding to say, I have burned part of it in the fire; yea, also I have baked bread upon the coals thereof; I have roasted flesh, and eaten it: and shall I make the residue thereof an abomination? shall I fall down to the stock of a tree? *(The phrase, "none considers in his heart," refers to the fact that the idolaters had once had it in their power to think and reason justly upon the absurdity of such conduct as that which was now habitual to them. But they have lost the power. They had suffered themselves little by little to be deluded.*

This is the reason that religious bondage is the worst bondage of all, for this is the type of bondage of which the Holy Spirit through Isaiah speaks.)

20 He feeds on ashes: a deceived heart has turned him aside, that he cannot deliver his soul, nor say, Is there not a lie in my right hand? *(Anything and everything apart from God and His Word is a lie!)*

THE LORD THE REDEEMER OF ISRAEL

21 Remember these, O Jacob and Israel; for you are My servant: I have formed you; you are My servant: O Israel, you shall not be forgotten of Me. *(The things that He desires Israel to "remember" is the futility of idol worship. He says the same to us today!*

The words, "I have formed you," pertain to the duty of absolute and unquestioning obedience contained in the relation of that which is formed to that which has formed it.)

22 I have blotted out, as a thick cloud, your transgressions, and, as a cloud, your sins: return unto Me; for I have redeemed you. *(The phrase, "Return unto Me," is the underlying condition of both Restoration and forgiveness. It signals Repentance! Then, and then only, can the "sins" be "blotted out.")*

23 Sing, O ye Heavens; for the LORD has done it: shout, you lower parts of the Earth: break forth into singing, you mountains, O forest, and every tree therein: for the LORD has redeemed Jacob, and glorified Himself in Israel. *(The implication of this Passage is that if Israel is right with God, the "Heavens will sing," the lower parts of the Earth will "shout," etc.*

Conversely, if Israel is depressed, as she now is, the Earth must "mourn and languish." At the coming Kingdom Age, Israel will no longer languish!)

24 Thus saith the LORD, your Redeemer, and He Who formed you from the womb, I am the LORD Who makes all things; Who stretches forth the Heavens alone; Who spreads abroad the Earth by Myself *(not only is the Deliverance absolutely determined in God's Counsels, but the Deliverer Himself is always chosen and designated; that Deliverer is Christ, which He has done through the Cross);*

25 Who frustrates the tokens of the liars, and makes diviners mad; Who turns wise men backward, and makes their knowledge foolish *(the world today is full of psychics, mediums, prognosticators, channelers, new-agers, and*

pretenders to knowledge of the future, etc. God calls them "liars"!);

26 Who confirms the word of the His servant, and performs the counsel of His messengers; Who says to Jerusalem, You shall be inhabited; and to the cities of Judah, You shall be built, and I will raise up the decayed places thereof *(this was fulfilled approximately 200 years later, when Cyrus, king of Persia, made a decree that Jews could return to their own land and rebuild their City and Temple [II Chron. 36:22-23]):*

27 Who says to the deep, Be dry, and I will dry up your rivers *(this proclaims, approximately 200 years before it happened, how the riverbed of the Euphrates would be dried up so that Cyrus could take the city of Babylon):*

28 Who says of Cyrus, He is My shepherd, and shall perform all My pleasure: even saying to Jerusalem, You shall be built; and to the temple, Your foundation shall be laid. *(Amazingly enough, the Lord calls Cyrus by name approximately 150 years before he was born, and about 200 years before these things came to pass.)*

CHAPTER 45
(712 B.C.)
GOD HAS CHOSEN CYRUS AND WILL HELP HIM

THUS saith the LORD to His anointed, to Cyrus, whose right hand I have held, to subdue nations before him; and I will loose the loins of kings, to open before him the two leaved gates; and the gates shall not be shut *(this Chapter gives us a direct address of God to a heathen king, which is without parallel in Scripture.*

The phrase, "His anointed," as it pertains to Cyrus, refers to what Cyrus would do, and not to holiness and character.

The "two leaved gates" refer to the great gates which went down into the Euphrates River, built to keep out intruders. They were left unlocked, which made it possible for the army of Cyrus to take Babylon. As stated, these predictions were given about 200 years before they actually happened);

2 I will go before you, and make the crooked places straight: I will break in pieces the gates of brass, and cut in sunder the bars of iron *(on the night that Belshazzar was slain, these gates, by a strange oversight, were left open; the Medes had diverted the course of the river, and so the soldiers marched up its dried bed and entered the city through the open gates,*

thus becoming masters of Babylon after a siege of two years. Belshazzar and his government had thought the city impregnable, but God said differently!):

3 And I will give you the treasures of darkness, and hidden riches of secret places, that you may know that I, the LORD, which call you by your name, am the God of Israel. *(This pertained to the treasures and riches of Babylon.)*

4 For Jacob My servant's sake, and Israel My elect, I have even called you by your name: I have surnamed you, though you have not known Me. *(The conqueror's name was Agradetes, but God surnamed him Cyrus; and, as predicted in these Verses, he has ever since been known by this name.*

Josephus said that this Prophecy was pointed out to Cyrus on his conquest of Babylon, and he thereupon determined to fulfill what was written; however, he probably already knew about it from his mother, Esther.)

5 I am the LORD, and there is none else, there is no God beside Me: I girded you, though you have not known Me *(the Holy Spirit is calling to attention the fact that none but "the LORD" could forecast such minute detail concerning something that would happen approximately 200 years in the future):*

6 That they may know from the rising of the sun, and from the west, that there is none beside Me. I am the LORD, and there is none else. *(The phrase, "from the rising of the sun, and from the west," is meant to call attention to all the world, from the extreme east to the extreme west, to these wonderful occurrences, so that Jehovah's Hand in them would be perceived and His sole Godhead would be acknowledged; for only Jehovah could do such a thing!)*

THE LORD THE CREATOR

7 I form the light, and create darkness: I make peace, and create evil: I the LORD do all these things. *(All of this debunks the stupidity of evolution. The phrase, "I create evil," is rendered according to the following: the Hebrew word used here for "evil" is "ra," and is never rendered "sin," but rather "calamity, diversity, distress and trouble." This "evil" is meant to be directed by God at the enemies of His People.)*

8 Drop down, you heavens, from above, and let the skies pour down righteousness: let the Earth open, and let them bring forth salvation, and let righteousness spring up together; I the LORD have created it. *(The Holy Spirit,*

upon proclaiming Israel's release from captivity, when in fact they have not even yet gone into captivity, leaps ahead to the coming Glad Day, when "the LORD" will reign supreme in the world, and Israel will finally come to the place of God's intentions. At this prospect, the Prophecy is that "the heavens will come down to Earth," and consequently, "the skies will pour down righteousness.")*

9 Woe unto him who strives with his Maker! Let the potsherd strive with the potsherds of the Earth. Shall the clay say to Him Who fashions it, What do you make? or your work, He has no hands? *(The "woe" announced in Verses 9 through 13 is directed against those in Isaiah's day among the Hebrews who criticized the action of God in choosing a heathen prince as the deliverer of His People. These objectors are compared to potsherds objecting to the action of the potter.*

The idea of this Passage is that man is no more entitled to lift up his voice against his Maker than the vessel to rebel against the man who shapes it.)

10 Woe unto him who says unto his father, What do you beget? or to the woman, What have you brought forth? *(This Verse is to be understood in the light of the angry utterance of a son and heir at the birth of a brother. It illustrates the anger and jealousy of the people of Israel at the Divine action in choosing and blessing the Gentiles.)*

11 Thus saith the LORD, the Holy One of Israel, and his Maker, Ask Me of things to come concerning My sons, and concerning the work of My hands command you Me. *(This Passage has been misunderstood by many, thinking it gave the right to the pottery to command the potter. The merit of the entirety of this Chapter [and more particularly Verses 7 through 12] speaks to the Omnipotence and Omniscience of God, and the folly of the individual "striving with his Maker"!*

There should have been a question mark at the end of the sentence.)

12 I have made the Earth, and created man upon it: I, even My hands, have stretched out the heavens, and all their host have I commanded. *(The idea of all of this is: God is saying, "I do the commanding, and not you!")*

13 I have raised him up in righteousness, and I will direct all his ways: he shall build My city, and he shall let go My captives, not for price nor reward, saith the LORD of Hosts. *(The pronoun "him" refers to Cyrus, and to him*

being raised up by the Lord for a special task and mission. The phrase, "in righteousness," means "to carry out My righteous purposes." "Directing all his ways" means making it possible for him to do what needs to be done. The "captives" refer to Israel.)

AN EVERLASTING SALVATION FOR ISRAEL

14 Thus saith the LORD, The labour of Egypt, and merchandise of Ethiopia and of the Sabeans, men of stature, shall come over unto you, and they shall be yours: they shall come after you; in chains they shall come over, and they shall fall down unto you, they shall make supplication unto you, saying, Surely God is in you; and there is none else, there is no God. *(This Passage refers to the fact that the Gentiles robbed the sons of Israel and carried them away in fetters of iron and brass; but they will, in the future day of Restoration, come up to Jerusalem in chains of love and Repentance, bringing their wealth with them, and confessing that there is but One True and Living God, Jehovah, Messiah, the God of Israel.*

The latter phrase, "There is no God," actually says, "There is no other God.")

15 Verily You are a God Who hides Yourself, O God of Israel, the Saviour. *(In the coming Kingdom Age, the Gentile world will exclaim that the Lord is now visible to all. As well, this Text means that the Lord hides many of His Plans from men, even though He is still our Saviour. Such is designed by the Holy Spirit so that man will develop trust and dependence on God, instead of having to be told everything that the Lord will do.)*

16 They shall be ashamed, and also confounded, all of them: they shall go to confusion together who are makers of idols. *(This pertains to the coming Kingdom Age, when all religions will be ashamed in the Face of Christ.)*

17 But Israel shall be saved in the LORD with an everlasting Salvation: you shall not be ashamed nor confounded world without end. *(The "Everlasting Salvation" means one which will continue age after age. The general sense of the Passage is that those who trust in the Lord shall be vindicated, and shall never "be ashamed nor confounded.")*

GOD THE CREATOR AND SAVIOUR

18 For thus saith the LORD Who created the Heavens; God Himself Who formed the Earth

and made it; He has established it, He created it not in vain, He formed it to be inhabited: I am the LORD; and there is none else. *(The heaping together of the terms of this Verse shows how much more the Scriptures tell us about the creation of the worlds than the professors of modern science. The terms, "created," "formed," "made," and "established," are terms of exact science. The prognosticators of the lie of evolution have never been able to determine the "first cause" of all things. This Verse and so many others tell us that God is the "First Cause.")*

19 I have not spoken in secret, in a dark place of the Earth: I said not unto the seed of Jacob, Seek ye Me in vain: I the LORD speak righteousness, I declare things that are right. *(Things are not right merely because the Lord declares such, but because in fact they "are right.")*

20 Assemble yourselves and come; draw near together, you who are escaped of the nations: they have no knowledge who set up the wood of their graven image, and pray unto a god who cannot save. *(The statement, "and pray unto a god who cannot save," is a heart-rending word! Sadly, it incorporates most of the world.)*

21 Tell ye, and bring them near; yea, let them take counsel together: who has declared this from ancient time? who has told it from that time? have not I the LORD? and there is no God else beside Me; a just God and a Saviour; there is none beside Me. *(This Verse could be thusly stated: "Tell ye [O Israel] and bring forth the Prophecy of Isaiah; let them [the idolaters] confer together, and then ask them who declared this Prophecy 200 years ago? Who predicted it from that time?"*

To this there could be but one answer: the Only True and Living God.)

22 Look unto Me, and be ye saved, all the ends of the Earth: for I am God, and there is none else. *(Truth, having in the previous Verse confounded the idolaters, Grace, in this Verse, offers them without exception a sure and eternal Salvation in the words, "Look unto Me. . . .")*

23 I have sworn by Myself, the Word is gone out of My mouth in righteousness, and shall not return, That unto Me every knee shall bow, every tongue shall swear. *(God swears "by Himself," because He can swear by no greater peer [Heb. 6:13]. He condescends, for man's sake, to confirm in this way Promises that are exceedingly precious.*

He said that His Word "shall not return." In other words, it will not be withdrawn or retracted.

God's Gifts and Promises are "without Repentance" [Rom. 11:29].

"Every knee bowing" and "every tongue confessing" refer to the universal turning to God, which will take place in the coming Kingdom Age.)

24 Surely, shall one say, in the LORD have I righteousness and strength: even to Him shall men come; and all who are incensed against Him shall be ashamed. *(All of this is ascribed to Christ, so asserting His Deity, that He is Jehovah, and that all men shall worship Him as God by bowing the knee to Him.)*

25 In the LORD shall all the seed of Israel be justified, and shall glory. *(Self-justification, as practiced by Israel, brought self-righteousness, and resulted in pride and misery. God's Justification, which is by Faith, and which is in Christ and what Christ has done for us at the Cross, always brings "glory," which is the "Glory of God," and not the glory of man.)*

CHAPTER 46
(712 B.C.)
THE IDOLS OF BABYLON ARE POWERLESS

BEL bows down, Nebo stoops, their idols were upon the beasts, and upon the cattle: your carriages were heavy laden; they are a burden to the weary beast. *(The fall of the gods of Babylon is among the direct consequences of the victories of Cyrus. The Prophet expresses the downfall of material imagery, graphically describing the fate of the idols themselves. The latter portion of the Verse refers to the many idols being torn from their pedestals, seized as spoils, and carried off by the soldiers of Cyrus.)*

2 They stoop, they bow down together; they could not deliver the burden, but themselves are gone into captivity. *(The meaning of this Passage is that these gods were, in each case, unable to deliver or save from capture. Consequently, they were carried off on the backs of "weary beasts."*

As they held men in superstitious "captivity," likewise, they "themselves are gone into captivity.")

GOD IS OMNIPOTENT

3 Hearken unto Me, O house of Jacob, and all the remnant of the House of Israel, which are borne by Me from the belly, which are carried from the womb *(even though this Prophecy was given some 200 years before the fact, still, the Holy Spirit is addressing Israel at the time of*

their Restoration from Babylon. He says, "Hearken unto Me." The very reason they had to undergo some 70 years of captivity was because they did not "hearken" unto Him!):

4 And even to your old age I am He; and even to hoar hairs will I carry you: I have made, and I will bear; even I will carry, and will deliver you. *(The implication is this: The mother carries the child for a while, but soon tires of carrying him and leaves him to shift for himself. But God's tender Care for His People lasts from their infancy through their boyhood and manhood to their old age. The Everlasting Arms never weary. God's watchfulness, His Providence, and His Protection never fail.*

The statement, "I have made, and I will bear," refers to the creation of the Creator, and that He will see it through to ultimate victory.)

5 To whom will you liken Me, and make Me equal, and compare Me, that we may be like? *(There is no equal to the Lord! There is only one image of God that is favored by the Holy Spirit. Paul said: "For whom He did foreknow, He also did predestinate to be conformed to the Image of His Son, that He might be the firstborn among many brethren" [Rom. 8:29]. He wants us to be in the Image of Christ! Actually, the entire mission of the Holy Spirit is to "conform us" to that Image.)*

6 They lavish gold out of the bag, and weigh silver in the balance, and hire a goldsmith; and he makes it a god: they fall down, yea, they worship. *(Once again, the Holy Spirit puts forth the fallacy of worshipping something inferior to the one who made it.)*

7 They bear him upon the shoulder, they carry him, and set him in his place, and he stands; from his place shall he not remove: yea, one shall cry unto him, yet can he not answer, nor save him out of his trouble. *(Let it ever be known that if it's not Christ, it is an idol and, as such, it "cannot answer, nor save out of trouble.")*

8 Remember this, and shew yourselves men: bring it again to mind, O ye transgressors. *(It could be translated, "Remember, and keep remembering this fact, and show yourselves men against idolatry." In other words, "quit acting like a beast, which can neither consider nor understand, and act like the 'man' that God made you!")*

9 Remember the former things of old: for I am God, and there is none else; I am God, and there is none like Me *(the things that the Lord has done in the past, and will do in the*

present for those who believe Him, prove Him to be God in a sense in which the Word cannot be applied to any other. The Word, "I am God," in the original, is "I am El . . . I am Elohim." "El" is "The Mighty One," "The Omnipotent"; Elohim, "the Godhead in all its fullness."

How touching to the heart that God, Who made the worlds and created man, that He would condescend to plead with poor mortals to investigate Him and prove His claims),

10 Declaring the end from the beginning, and from ancient times the things that are not yet done, saying, My counsel shall stand, and I will do all My pleasure *(all of this declares that God has a distinct, Divine Plan; to be sure, that Plan will be carried through to completion):*

11 Calling a ravenous bird from the east, the man who executes My counsel from a far country: yea, I have spoken it, I will also bring it to pass; I have purposed it, I will also do it. *(At this time, it was strange to Jewish ears that God would use a heathen, a Gentile, and "from a far country." But this is exactly what the Lord did, as it regards Cyrus, whom He refers to as a "ravenous bird.")*

RESTORATION OF ISRAEL

12 Hearken unto Me, you stouthearted, who are far from righteousness *(the transgressors of Verse 8 and the "stouthearted" of this Verse were those Hebrews who desired to retain the worship of idols together with the worship of Jehovah. Man, by nature, is "far from righteousness"; hence, in order to save him, God must bring near His Righteousness):*

13 I bring near My Righteousness; it shall not be far off, and My Salvation shall not tarry: and I will place Salvation in Zion for Israel My Glory. *(Salvation is found alone in Zion, i.e., in Christ; and it is found in Him with eternal Glory [II Tim. 2:10].*

The implication of this Passage is that if any individual desires the "Righteousness of God," then "it shall not be far off." If one will earnestly seek, then "His Salvation will not tarry."

What a glorious Promise to all who are in trouble and cry to Him for help!)

CHAPTER 47
(712 B.C.)

JUDGMENT ON BABYLON

COME down and sit in the dust, O virgin daughter of Babylon, sit on the ground:

there is no throne, O daughter of the Chaldeans: for you shall no more be called tender and delicate. *(These Passages predict the fall of Babylon, and have a twofold fulfillment:*

The entirety of this Chapter should be read in connection with Rev., Chpt. 18. Both Chapters predict the future doom of the city of Babylon. The city was founded by Nimrod, the first Antichrist, and will be restored with great magnificence by the last Antichrist.

Babylon, in the Scripture, symbolizes corruption of Divine Truth, developed into the enemy of Truth. So the entirety of this Chapter presents Babylon as a proud queen degraded to the lowest form of slavery.

The words, "sit on the ground," should read "sit throneless on the ground."

The words, "virgin daughter," mean "hitherto uncaptured" or "impregnable." So this Chapter concerns the destruction of Babylon by Cyrus, and then, in the future day, the destruction of Babylon by an earthquake [Rev. 16:17-21].)

2 Take the millstones, and grind meal: uncover your locks, make bare the leg, uncover the thigh, pass over the rivers. *(In Verses 2 and 3, grinding corn and fetching water express the most abject slavery. The phrase, "Make bare the leg, uncover the thigh, pass over the rivers," refers to long lines of men and women being taken from their city into captivity. In so doing, they would have to wade through streams, and would expose parts of their person which delicacy required to be concealed. The idea is of total defeat!)*

3 Your nakedness shall be uncovered, yea, your shame shall be seen: I will take vengeance, and I will not meet you as a man. *(The idea of this Verse is that the Lord will spare, or give quarter, to no one. The "vengeance" guaranteed would have to do with Babylon's treatment of the Jews.)*

4 As for our Redeemer, the LORD of Hosts is His Name, the Holy One of Israel. *(The essence of this Verse is that Babylon has no "Redeemer," because of her worship of idols, but Israel has a "Redeemer," even in times of distress. "The LORD of Hosts is His Name.")*

5 Sit thou silent, and get thee into darkness, O daughter of the Chaldeans: for you shall no more be called, The lady of kingdoms. *(The "lady of kingdoms" could possibly be better expressed as "the mistress of kingdoms." The phrase, "Sit thou silent, and get thee into darkness," refers to this fallen people hiding in shame and silence, as well as in darkness, as*

disgraced persons who shrink from being seen by their fellows.)

6 I was wroth with My people, I have polluted My inheritance, and given them into your hand: you did shew them no mercy; upon the ancient have you very heavily laid your yoke. *(The Holy Spirit saying that Israel was shown no "mercy" implies that the Lord wanted "mercy" to be shown!)*

7 And you said, I shall be a lady for ever: so that you did not lay these things to your heart, neither did remember the latter end of it. *(Babylon should have reasoned that if God punished His Own people so severely because of idolatry, how much more severely would He punish them, "the Chaldeans," because of their wickedness, and how terrible would be their end.*

The phrase, "I shall be a lady forever," pertains to what Babylon says, but the Lord says otherwise.)

8 Therefore hear now this, you who are given to pleasures, who dwells carelessly, who says in your heart, I am, and none else beside me; I shall not sit as a widow, neither shall I know the loss of children *(among Babylon's sins, she said in her heart, "I am, and there is none else beside me." She here assumes a Divine title; however, she would come to know exactly, as it regards Jehovah, as to what Divinity actually meant):*

9 But these two things shall come to you in a moment in one day, the loss of children, and widowhood: they shall come upon you in their perfection for the multitude of your sorceries, and for the great abundance of your enchantments. *(This was partially fulfilled by Cyrus; however, the total fulfillment of this Passage remains to the last days of the Great Tribulation, when Babylon will be destroyed in one day, exactly as predicted here [Rev. 18:1-24].)*

10 For you have trusted in your wickedness: you have said, None sees me. Your wisdom and your knowledge, it has perverted you; and you have said in your heart, I am, and none else beside me. *(Once again, the Holy Spirit emphasizes the fact that the Babylonian Monarch claimed that he was the kingly substitute of God on Earth. The "wisdom" and "knowledge" which "perverted them" refers to astrology, which, when once entered upon, seduces the mind from all genuine and fruitful study of the celestial phenomena, and leads into a labyrinth of absurdities.)*

11 Therefore shall evil come upon you; you shall not know from whence it rises: and

mischief shall fall upon you; you shall not be able to put it off: and desolation shall come upon you suddenly, which you shall not know. *(The implication of this Verse is that the "evil" that will come upon them, which in fact would be sent by God, could not be warded off or charmed away by "sorceries" or "enchantments.")*

12 Stand now with your enchantments, and with the multitude of your sorceries, wherein you have laboured from your youth; if so be you shall be able to profit, if so be you may prevail. *(The Holy Spirit now uses sarcasm. In effect, He is saying, "For many centuries, you have relied upon your enchantments and sorceries. See if they will help you now!")*

13 You are wearied in the multitude of your counsels. Let now the astrologers, the stargazers, the monthly prognosticators, stand up, and save you from these things that shall come upon you. *(The Holy Spirit through Isaiah invites Babylon's best, whoever they might be, to stop the course of events that were going to come, because they were ordained by God.)*

14 Behold, they shall be as stubble; the fire shall burn them; they shall not deliver themselves from the power of the flame: there shall not be a coal to warm at, nor fire to sit before it. *(The last line of this Verse means that these diviners were to be totally destroyed, and that the doom that should fall upon them would not be as a little fire that one could comfortably sit at, but a devouring fire of horror and death.)*

15 Thus shall they be unto you with whom you have laboured, even your merchants, from your youth: they shall wander every one to his quarter; none shall save you. *(The sense of this Verse is that the powerful influence that Babylon had, which involved itself with every nation in the world of that day, would be destroyed along with all commerce and activity. In other words, destruction would be complete!)*

CHAPTER 48
(712 B.C.)
ISRAEL'S UNFAITHFULNESS REBUKED

HEAR ye this, O house of Jacob, which are called by the name of Israel, and are come forth out of the waters of Judah, which swear by the name of the LORD, and make mention of the God of Israel, but not in truth, nor in righteousness. *("Jacob" is the nation's natural name; "Israel" is the spiritual name. "To swear by the name of Jehovah" is an idiom expressive of worship. The phrase, "But not in truth,*

nor in righteousness," expresses the thought of worshipping, but neither in sincerity nor pure from idolatry.)

2 For they call themselves of the Holy City, and stay themselves upon the God of Israel; The LORD of Hosts is His Name. (The essence of this Verse is the idea that Judah put great dependence and store upon the outward and formal, as the fact of their belonging to the "Holy City," Jerusalem. Compare the boasts of the Jews in our Lord's time, "We be Abraham's seed" [Jn. 8:33].)

3 I have declared the former things from the beginning; and they went forth out of My mouth, and I shewed them; I did them suddenly, and they came to pass. ("The former things" concern the predicted birth of Isaac and the foretold exodus from Egypt. The words, "showed" and "declared," as well as "suddenly," refer to the Deliverance from Egypt, and that there was nothing to indicate its coming, and yet it came "suddenly.")

4 Because I knew that you are obstinate, and your neck is an iron sinew, and your brow brass (the argument of Verses 4 through 8 is that God, knowing beforehand the obstinacy with which His People would cling to idols and attribute all their good fortune to them, here announces, some two hundred years in advance, what should happen in the days of Cyrus; this would make it impossible for the people to credit their idols with this happy change in their circumstances);

5 I have even from the beginning declared it to you; before it came to pass I shewed it you: lest you should say, My idol has done them, and my graven image, and my molten image, have commanded them. (It has been already observed that there was a strong tendency to idolatry among the Jews, not only before, but also during, the captivity! [Ezek. 20:32].)

6 You have heard, see all this; and will not you declare it? I have shewed you new things from this time, even hidden things, and you did not know them. (The "new things" contrasted with the "former things" of Verse 3 mean the Prophecies respecting Cyrus and the restoration.)

7 They are created now, and not from the beginning; even before the day when you heard them not; lest you should say, Behold, I knew them. (The words, "they are created now," do not mean that God is hastily formulating a new plan, but that what has lain in secret in God's counsels from all eternity is now being revealed to man.)

8 Yea, you heard not; yea, you knew not;

yea, from that time that your ear was not opened: for I knew that you would deal very treacherously, and were called a transgressor from the womb. (Israel had ears, but they would not "hear," and consequently they did not "know." It was a willful deadness and, thereby, a willful ignorance!)

GOD'S FORBEARANCE: HIS APPEAL TO ISRAEL

9 For My name's sake will I defer My anger, and for My praise will I refrain for you, that I cut you not off. (Israel's annihilation was not escaped from because of their goodness, but because of the Glory of Jehovah's Name and Praise.)

10 Behold, I have refined you, but not with silver; I have chosen you in the furnace of affliction. (Israel was "refined" in Egypt, and was to be "refined" after Isaiah's day in Babylon, and will be "refined" during the coming Great Tribulation. The "furnace of affliction" always has to do with wrongdoing on the part of the individual or nation. The Lord allows the affliction, hopefully, that it will bring the person or nation to Repentance! Consequently, Israel still has one great "furnace of affliction" to go through!)

11 For My Own sake, even for My Own sake, will I do it: for how should My name be polluted? and I will not give My glory unto another. (Had the Lord not deferred His Anger and had He cut Israel off, then would His Name have been profaned and His Glory would have been given to another god.)

12 Hearken unto Me, O Jacob and Israel, My called; I am He; I am the First, I also am the Last. (The Holy Spirit is impressing upon Israel the seriousness of the situation by considering Who it is by Whom they have been called — "I am He" — i.e., "I am the absolute and eternally unchangeable One, the Alpha and Omega of all history." "The First and also The Last" means "from Whom and to Whom are all things" [Rom. 11:36].)

13 My hand also has laid the foundation of the Earth, and My right hand has spanned the Heavens; when I call unto them, they stand up together. (Heaven and Earth and all things that are in them, except man, are prompt to perform God's Will and rise up at once at His Call to show their readiness.)

14 All ye, assemble yourselves, and hear; which among them has declared these things? The LORD has loved him; he will do his pleasure on Babylon, and his arm shall be on the

Chaldeans. *(This is all the more startling when one realizes that the Babylonian Empire, at the time of Isaiah's Prophecy, had not even come into being, much less a settled power in the world! So, such Prophecies proclaim the inexhaustible Power of God, plus His Omniscience, i.e., "the knowledge of all things, past, present, and future.")*

15 I, even I, have spoken; yea, I have called him: I have brought him, and he shall make his way prosperous. *(Cyrus is represented as raised up by God, "called" by Him and commissioned by Him "to do all his pleasure.")*

16 Come ye near unto Me, hear ye this; I have not spoken in secret from the beginning; from the time that it was, there am I: and now the Lord GOD, and His Spirit, has sent Me. *(God, "from the beginning" and from His first dealings with Israel, had raised up a succession of Prophets who had declared His Will, not "in secret," or ambiguously, but openly and plainly, so that all who heard might understand.*

The pronoun "Me," the last word of this Verse, pertains to the Coming Messiah.)

ISRAEL'S REGATHERING FROM BABYLON

17 Thus saith the LORD, your Redeemer, the Holy One of Israel; I am the LORD your God which teaches you to profit, which leads you by the way that you should go. *(The Promise of this Scripture is absolutely phenomenal! The Word of God is extolled here; if the Word is followed, the result will be tremendous "profit," and in every capacity.)*

18 O that you had hearkened to My Commandments! then had your peace been as a river, and your righteousness as the waves of the sea *(the idea of this Passage is that Israel should try to keep the Commandments to the very best of their ability. In truth, they were not capable of doing so, but they were supposed to try. Had they sincerely tried, the Lord would have abundantly blessed them):*

19 Your seed also had been as the sand, and the offspring of your bowels like the gravel thereof; his name should not have been cut off nor destroyed from before Me. *(This Prophecy looks ahead some two hundred years when Israel will be coming back from dispersion, and then it looks ahead even unto the present hour. Due to Israel's Crucifixion of Christ, they cut themselves off from God; as a nation, they went into oblivion and actually were scattered all over the world.)*

20 Go ye forth of Babylon, flee ye from the Chaldeans, with a voice of singing declare ye, tell this, utter it even to the end of the Earth; say ye, The LORD has redeemed His servant Jacob. *(The sons of Israel were to forsake Babylon and her idols and to testify to the ends of the Earth that their Deliverance was due to Jehovah Messiah, and not to any false god.)*

21 And they thirsted not when he led them through the deserts: he caused the waters to flow out of the rock for them: he clave the rock also, and the waters gushed out. *(The Promise is that God would superintend their passage exactly as He did their forefathers those many centuries before. The Holy Spirit is saying, "As the 'Rock' was Christ for Israel coming out of Egypt, the 'Rock' was Christ as they would come out of Babylon.")*

22 There is no peace, saith the LORD, unto the wicked. *(This Prophecy closes with a tremendous Promise and tremendous warning! Those who follow Him will never "thirst," while those who do not follow Him will have "no peace." As eternal is the flowing water of life from the "Smitten Rock," eternal is the misery of the "wicked."*

The world does not have a choice regarding its Saviour. It is Jesus Christ and Eternal Life or wickedness and eternal misery! There is no in-between.)

CHAPTER 49
(712 B.C.)
MESSIAH'S CALL AND COMMISSION

LISTEN, O isles, unto Me; and hearken, you people, from far; The LORD has called Me from the womb; from the bowels of My mother has He made mention of My name. *(The Speaker in Verses 1 through 6 is the Messiah; He invites the inhabitants of the "Isles" and the people, that is, the whole Gentile world, to listen to Him.*

The phrase, "The LORD has called Me from the womb," speaks of the Incarnation. In order to save the human family, God would have to become Man. He would be called "Immanuel," which means "God with us" [Isa. 7:14].)

2 And He has made My mouth like a sharp sword; in the shadow of His hand has He hid Me, and made Me a polished shaft; in His quiver has He hid Me *(no one knew the Word like Christ; in fact, He was, and is, the "the Living Word" [Jn. 1:1].*

The imagery recurs in the Book of Revelation, when John said, "And out of His mouth went a

sharp twoedged sword" [Rev. 1:16].

The phrase, "In the shadow of His hand has He hid Me," means that He was reserved until the time that He would be revealed to the world, and even then would be guided and protected by the Hand of God);

3 And said unto me, You are My servant, O Israel, in Whom I will be glorified. *(The word "Servant" is used concerning the Messiah. He Alone portrayed the true "Servant spirit." The Prophecy is that now Christ, addressed as "Israel," would stand as a new federal head to the Nation, which would be summed up in Him. Moreover, Christ would be, in a truer sense than any other, the "Israel" or "Prince with God." In fact, Jesus is the True Man, the True Israel, and the True Church.)*

4 Then I said, I have laboured in vain, I have spent My strength for nought, and in vain: yet surely My judgment is with the LORD, and My work with My God. *(From the Exodus to Pentecost, He labored and spent Himself for Israel, but in vain; yet His "judgment," i.e., vindication, was with Jehovah, and His "work," i.e., His reward, with His God.)*

5 And now, saith the LORD Who formed Me from the womb to be His Servant, to bring Jacob again to Him, Though Israel be not gathered, yet shall I be glorious in the eyes of the LORD, and My God shall be My strength. *(This Verse predicts that Christ will gather Israel to God; that the ability enabling Him to do so will be God's; and that He Himself shall always be glorious in the Eyes of Jehovah.*

The words, "Though Israel be not gathered," in the Hebrew, actually mean "though Israel be not yet gathered," and point to temporary disappointments owing to Israel's unbelief, but that the Messiah will ultimately not only bring back all the Tribes of Jacob to Jehovah, but, in addition and in union with them, will bring back to God the whole of rebellious humanity, at least those who will believe Him.)

6 And He said, It is a light thing that You should be my Servant to raise up the Tribes of Jacob, and to restore the preserved of Israel: I will also give You for a light to the Gentiles, that You may be My salvation unto the end of the Earth. *(The phrase, "It is a light thing," refers to the fact that God considers the "raising up of the Tribes of Jacob" and the "Restoration of the preserved of Israel" as a small thing in comparison to what else the Messiah will do.*

As well, He will also be a "light to the Gentiles," i.e., "the whole world"!)

MESSIAH'S HUMILIATION AND EXALTATION

7 Thus saith the LORD, the Redeemer of Israel, and His Holy One, to Him Whom man despises, to Him Whom the nation abhors, to a servant of rulers, Kings shall see and arise, princes also shall worship, because of the LORD Who is faithful, and the Holy One of Israel, and He shall choose You. *(This Passage gives our Lord's humiliation and exaltation. The Speaker in Verses 7 through 12 is Jehovah, and the One spoken to [His Holy One] is "Immanuel" — despised by man and abhorred by Israel. Such was He in His First Advent. But, in His Second Advent, kings, when they see Him, shall stand in awe because of Him, and princes shall fall and worship Him.*

This is the first place in the Prophecies of Isaiah where this note of the Messiah being "despised" is brought forward. It is found earlier in the Psalms [Ps. 22:6].)

HIS MINISTRY

8 Thus saith the LORD, In an acceptable time have I heard You, and in a day of salvation have I helped You: and I will preserve You, and give You for a Covenant of the people, to establish the Earth, to cause to inherit the desolate heritages *(the Father helped the Son throughout His Earthly Ministry; however, the "acceptable time" and "day of Salvation" refer to Calvary and the Resurrection, where at Calvary every foe was defeated [Col. 2:14-15].*

The phrase, "To establish the Earth," is powerful indeed! Through what Jesus did at the Cross, the "Earth" will be brought back to its original place as before the Fall. This will cause the "desolate heritage" to once again become fruitful!);

9 That you may say to the prisoners, Go forth; to them who are in darkness, Shew yourselves. They shall feed in the ways, and their pastures shall be in all high places. *(Due to what Christ did at the Cross, the prisoners can be released from the prison house of darkness. Coming out to the Light, "they shall feed in the ways" and have great "pastures.")*

10 They shall not hunger nor thirst; neither shall the heat nor sun smite them: for He Who has mercy on them shall lead them, even by the springs of water shall He guide them. *(Verses 9 through 13 picture the Great Shepherd, the Lord Jesus Christ, leading His sheep*

to Zion. In particular, Verses 9 and 10 speak of Israel; in general, they speak of all who accept Christ.)

11 And I will make all My mountains a way, and My highways shall be exalted. (Satan endeavors to make the Christian think that even though he might make it, still, it's going to be so difficult that the journey will not be worth the effort! Conversely, the Holy Spirit tells us that Christ, despite the "mountains of difficulties," will make it a happy, joyous, and glorious "way," and an "exalted highway.")

12 Behold, these shall come from far: and, lo, these from the north and from the west; and these from the land of Sinim. (The four points of the compass appear in this Verse, with the word "far" representing the south, and the word "Sinim" representing, as many Scholars believe, China and, therefore, the east.

In any case, this reference is not to the dispersed Jews, but to the remote Gentiles, who will pass from all quarters of the Earth into the Kingdom of the Redeemer.)

RESTORATION OF ISRAEL

13 Sing, O heavens; and be joyful, O Earth; and break forth into singing, O mountains: for the LORD has comforted His people, and will have mercy upon His afflicted. (The exclamations of both the "heavens" and the "Earth" are given here at the Restoration of Israel and the fulfillment of these great Promises! This is happening because Israel, who has been so long "afflicted" because of their sins, has now come back to the Lord and is "comforted.")

14 But Zion said, The LORD has forsaken me, and my Lord has forgotten me. (At her most terrible time, with Jerusalem falling and the Antichrist pressing for total destruction, Israel will realize that the Messiah is her only hope; and yet it seems from events "the LORD has forsaken me, and my Lord has forgotten me." But the following Passages address this cry of Israel!)

15 Can a woman forget her sucking child, that she should not have compassion on the son of her womb? yea, they may forget, yet will I not forget you. (The Lord speaks of Israel as His "child." The analogy is drawn of a woman who loves her child, "the son of her womb." She loves it, no matter how it looks, or what it has done!

The Holy Spirit then says that God's Love is far greater than that; even though some mothers

"may forget," yet He says, "I will not forget you.")

16 Behold, I have graven you upon the palms of My hands; your walls are continually before Me. (It is said that there was a custom among pilgrims to Jerusalem to have representations of the city or Temple tattooed on their hands and arms to remind them of the sacred places. They were called "ensigns of Jerusalem."

The Lord uses this analogy, which would have been easily understood by the Jews.

The Lord uses the "walls" as the symbol that is to be "graven" or "portrayed." Such speaks of Divine protection. In other words, the walls, which have long since fallen down, spiritually speaking, will be rebuilt. David mentioned this in his prayer of Repentance [Ps. 51:18].)

17 Your children shall make haste; your destroyers and they who made you waste shall go forth of you. (This speaks of the Second Coming of Christ, with the defeat of the Antichrist and Israel finally accepting the Lord as their Saviour. When this happens, Jews from all over the world will "make haste" to come to Israel.)

18 Lift up your eyes round about, and behold: all these gather themselves together, and come to Thee. As I live, saith the LORD, You shall surely clothe Thee with them all, as with an ornament, and bind them on Thee, as a bride does. (The phrase, "All these," continues to refer to "Your children" of Verse 17. There will be an astonishment in Israel, as well as in the entirety of the world, at the number of Jews who will come from all over the world to Israel; all will be welcome.)

19 For your waste and your desolate places, and the land of your destruction, shall even now be too narrow by reason of the inhabitants, and they who swallowed you up shall be far away. ("The land of your destruction" refers to Israel, which has become a graveyard for the entirety of the Jewish people. Now it will be the opposite! All those who threatened to "swallow you up" surely "shall be far away," even in Hell itself, at least as far as the Antichrist is concerned!

At the beginning of the Kingdom Age, so many Jews will come to Israel that even the "waste" and "desolate places" will be fully used; still, room will be at a premium.)

20 The children which you shall have, after you have lost the other, shall say again in your ears, The place is too strait for me: give place to me that I may dwell. (As stated, the Holy Spirit continues to speak of the millions of Jews who will come to Israel from all parts of the

world at the beginning of the Kingdom Age.)

21 Then shall you say in your heart, Who has begotten me these, seeing I have lost my children, and am desolate, a captive, and removing to and fro? and who has brought up these? Behold, I was left alone; these, where had they been? *(At the very conclusion of the Battle of Armageddon, and at the return of Christ, after losing so many millions in this terrible conflict, the leaders of Israel will wonder if they have enough people to once again be a viable nation. But then millions will begin to come from all over the world, with Israel then asking the question, "Where have they been?")*

ISRAEL'S ENEMIES DESTROYED

22 Thus saith the Lord GOD, Behold, I will lift up My hand to the Gentiles, and set up My standard to the people: and they shall bring your sons in their arms, and your daughters shall be carried upon their shoulders. *(The "Standard" that the Lord will set up is Jesus Christ. Not only will the Jews be rallying to "My Standard," but the "Gentiles," as well!*

The Gentile world, realizing that Israel is God's Chosen People, and that they have finally accepted Christ as their Messiah, and knowing that God will bless all who favor His People, will do everything they can to provide aid, comfort, money, and help regarding their relocation to the Land of Israel.)

23 And kings shall be your nursing fathers, and their queens your nursing mothers: they shall bow down to you with their face toward the Earth, and lick up the dust of your feet; and you shall know that I am the LORD: for they shall not be ashamed who wait for Me. *(The phrase, "Lick up the dust," is an expression of complete submission. "Kings and queens," i.e., world leaders, will "bow down to you." This will be done, not so much because of the Jew himself, but rather because of the "LORD of Glory," and Israel's relationship with Him.)*

24 Shall the prey be taken from the mighty, or the lawful captive delivered? *(The mighty and terrible one of Verses 24 and 25 is the Antichrist. His "prey" and lawful captives will be the sons of Israel. They will have accepted him as the messiah, as predicted in John 5:43 and will, consequently, be his lawful captives. Concerning this, the next Verse tells us what Christ will do.)*

25 But thus saith the LORD, Even the captives of the mighty shall be taken away, and the prey of the terrible shall be delivered: for I will contend with him who contends with you, and I will save your children. *(The "Deliverance" that will come to Israel, even at the last minute, will be the Second Coming of Christ. At that time, the "prey," i.e., Israel, "shall be delivered."*

Even though the Antichrist will be "terrible," still, Christ will be far "more terrible."

The phrase, "I will contend with him who contends with you," should be well noted! That holds true for all time, not only for Israel, but also for every Believer.)

26 And I will feed them who oppress you with their own flesh; and they shall be drunk with their own blood, as with sweet wine: and all flesh shall know that I the LORD am your Saviour and your Redeemer, the Mighty One of Jacob. *(This Passage proclaims the destruction of the Antichrist and all who oppose Israel in that coming day of the Battle of Armageddon. At that time, and we continue to speak of the Second Coming, the entirety of the world will know that "the LORD is Israel's Saviour and her Redeemer." He is "the Mighty One of Jacob.")*

CHAPTER 50
(712 B.C.)
UNFAITHFUL ISRAEL DIVORCED BY GOD

THUS saith the LORD, Where is the bill of your mother's divorcement, whom I have put away? or which of My creditors is it to whom I have sold you? Behold, for your iniquities have you sold yourselves, and for your transgressions is your mother put away. *(In fact, the Lord had "put away," "written a bill of divorcement," concerning the Northern Kingdom of Israel; however, concerning Judah, He had not so done, and her children were wrong to suppose themselves altogether cast off.*

They had, in fact, "by their transgressions," especially their idolatries, willfully divorced themselves, or at any rate separated themselves, from God. But no sentence had gone forth from Him to bar reconciliation and return.

Neither had He sold them to a "creditor." Consequently, the Babylonians are not thus their rightful owners — they are still God's Children, His Property, and the object of His Care.)

2 Wherefore, when I came, was there no man? when I called, was there none to answer? Is My hand shortened at all, that it cannot redeem? or have I no power to deliver? behold, at My rebuke I dry up the sea, I make

the rivers a wilderness: their fish stink, because there is no water, and die for thirst. *(The Prophecy now jumps from Judah's present difficulties to a future day when He Who is Himself the Mighty God came from Heaven to Earth to seek and bless her. But no one would receive Him or open the door to Him when He knocked [Jn. 1:11; Acts 13:46; 28:28]. His dignity as God is declared in this Verse. He proclaims that if Judah will only believe Him, He can "redeem" her from all the difficulties brought on by her sins. In fact, by using the words, "Is My hand shortened at all, that it cannot redeem?" He proclaims the Truth that He is able to deliver from any and all situations, if men will only believe Him.)*

3 I clothe the Heavens with blackness, and I make sackcloth their covering. *(The assertion here is that if He so chooses, He could leave all nature in absolute darkness — a power necessarily belonging only to Him Who said, "Let there be light; and there was light" [Gen. 1:3].)*

MESSIAH, THE OBEDIENT SERVANT

4 The Lord GOD has given Me the tongue of the learned, that I should know how to speak a Word in season to him who is weary: He wakens morning by morning, He wakens My ear to hear as the learned. *(The intent of the Holy Spirit in this Chapter is to portray to man the inexhaustible Power of God that could, if He so chose, use that Power in any capacity, but rather chose to send His Only Son to "redeem" not only Israel, but the entirety of mankind.*

In this Verse, He is presented as the Perfect Disciple. He only spoke the Words which were given Him by God ["that I should know how to speak"]. He asserted this seven times when on Earth [Jn. 7:16; 8:28, 46-47; 14:10, 24; 17:8].

The phrase, "He wakens morning by morning, He wakens My ear to hear as the learned," refers to the fact that God held immediate and constant communication with the "Servant" — not enlightening Him occasionally, as He did the Prophets by dreams and visions, but continually whispering in His Ear.

In fact, the phrase, "Morning by morning," is not to be narrowed to the bare literal meaning, but to be taken in the sense of "uninterruptedly." All of this was not necessarily for His Own benefit, but rather that "He should know how to speak a Word in season to him who is weary.")

5 The Lord GOD has opened My ear, and I was not rebellious, neither turned away back. *(This Verse pertains to the entire willingness of Christ to hear the Father, and to do so as the True Servant, as contrasted with the professed servant, or Children of Israel.*

The phrase, "Neither turned away back," refers to Him being most tried. Even in the Garden of Gethsemane, His final Word was, "Not My Will, but Thine, be done" [Lk. 22:42].)

HIS SUFFERING AND HELP

6 I gave My back to the smiters, and My cheeks to them who plucked off the hair: I hid not My face from shame and spitting. *(This Verse addresses itself to the hours before the Crucifixion. Mat. 26:67 and 27:26 fulfill this Passage.*

That our Lord, of such power as is described in Verse 3, could contain Himself, when His Own People would treat Him thusly, is beyond comprehension! Their response to His Love was their hate. They whipped Him, pulled His beard from His Face, and spit on Him.

Their doing it was no surprise. By His Omniscience, He knew before He came what the results would be. And yet, He came anyway!)

7 For the Lord GOD will help Me; therefore shall I not be confounded: therefore have I set My face like a flint, and I know that I shall not be ashamed. *(Lk. 9:31, 51 fulfill this Verse. The "help" that His Father gave Him was that He might finish the task of redeeming mankind. The idea of redeeming someone who responds only with hate cannot be comprehended by the mortal mind, especially when one considers what that Redemption costs!*

The phrase, "I set My face like a flint," refers to the resolve of accomplishing a certain thing despite all the scorn and hatred.)

8 He is near Who justifies Me; who will contend with Me? let us stand together: who is My adversary? let him come near to Me. *(The idea of this Verse is that those who "contend with Me," i.e., accuse Me, will have to answer to the One Who "justifies Me," namely "The Lord GOD.")*

9 Behold, the Lord GOD will help Me; who is he who shall condemn Me? lo, they all shall wax old as a garment; the moth shall eat them up. *(The only One Who can truly help is "the Lord GOD.")*

COMMAND TO TRUST THE LORD

10 Who is among you who fears the LORD,

who obeys the voice of His servant, who walks in darkness, and has no light? let him trust in the name of the LORD, and stay upon His God. *(There are times of darkness in every Believer's experience; but light will surely be had if the Voice of Jehovah's Servant be obeyed. And the "Servant" is Christ.)*

11 Behold, all ye who kindle a fire, who compass yourselves about with sparks: walk in the light of your fire, and in the sparks that you have kindled. This shall you have of My hand; you shall lie down in sorrow. *(The idea of this Verse is that all enemies who kindle their own fires of accusation and judgment against the Messiah shall reap what they sow to their own sorrow.)*

CHAPTER 51
(712 B.C.)
TRUST GOD; HIS MERCY BESTOWED ON ABRAHAM'S SEED

HEARKEN to Me, you who follow after righteousness, you who seek the LORD: look unto the Rock whence you are hewn, and to the hole of the pit whence you are digged. *(Abraham and Sarah are referred to as "the Rock" from which Israel was hewn. The "hole of the pit" refers to idolatry from whence Abraham and Sarah were brought, for they were idolaters when they came to the Lord.*

The idea of this Verse is: Israel was raised up from an aged man and a barren woman and made into a numerous nation, a multitude like the sand of the sea.)

2 Look unto Abraham your father, and unto Sarah who bore you: for I called him alone, and blessed him, and increased him. *(The idea is: If God could multiply the progeny of one man, how much more could He make a flourishing nation out of the exiles, who, though but a "Remnant" of the pre-captivity Israel, were yet many thousands in number, that is, if Judah would only believe Him.)*

COMFORT PROMISED: ZION AND WASTE PLACES WILL BE RESTORED

3 For the LORD shall comfort Zion: He will comfort all her waste places; and He will make her wilderness like Eden, and her desert like the garden of the LORD; joy and gladness shall be found therein, thanksgiving, and the voice of melody. *(The Promise of this Verse has several applications. It certainly referred* to Judah after the captivity, if they would only believe the Lord; it, as well, refers to Israel upon the Second Advent of the Lord. But these Promises also picture the perpetual bliss promised to all who listen to and obey the Lord Jesus Christ.)*

CALL TO ISRAEL

4 Hearken unto Me, My people; and give ear unto Me, O My nation: for a law shall proceed from Me, and I will make My judgment to rest for a light of the people. *(The spiritual life is sustained, as well as initiated, by the principle of "hearing." The Divine provision for this is the Bible. That is the "Law," which has proceeded from God; and that is the "Judgment" established to be the "light of the nations.")*

5 My righteousness is near; My salvation is gone forth, and My arms shall judge the people; the isles shall wait upon Me, and on My arm shall they trust. *(Christ is both "Righteousness" and "Salvation." As "Salvation," He has gone forth, and, as "Righteousness," He has come near. He is, therefore, within the reach of all sinners; and all who come to Him, sincerely seeking Him, will find exactly what He has promised!)*

6 Lift up your eyes to the Heavens, and look upon the Earth beneath: for the Heavens shall vanish away like smoke, and the Earth shall wax old like a garment, and they who dwell therein shall die in like manner: but My salvation shall be for ever, and My righteousness shall not be abolished. *(The Lord uses the most stable illustration to be found, His Own Creation. As glorious and stable as this Creation is, still, it will one day have to be refurbished; however, His "Salvation" and "Righteousness," which refer to His Word, shall be forever, and shall not be abolished.)*

7 Hearken unto Me, you who know righteousness, the people in whose heart is My law; fear ye not the reproach of men, neither be ye afraid of their revilings. *(Progress in the Christian life entails increasing hostility from the world, and even from the Church.)*

8 For the moth shall eat them up like a garment, and the worm shall eat them like wool: but My righteousness shall be for ever, and My salvation from generation to generation. *(If men themselves never wholly pass away, yet it is otherwise with their judgments. These perish absolutely, disappear, and are utterly forgotten. In other words, the taunts will come to a speedy end, while those whose will and affections are governed by the Scriptures will live forever.)*

9 Awake, awake, put on strength, O arm of the LORD; awake, as in the ancient days, in the generations of old. Are you not it who has cut Rahab, and wounded the dragon? *(The phrase, "Awake, awake," is a cry of faith and desire addressed to the Messiah by those who hearken unto Him, and in whose heart is His Law. "Rahab" is a symbolic expression for Egypt. The name actually means "pride" or "the proud one." The phrase, "Wounded the dragon," refers to Egypt's power and such being destroyed at the Red Sea.)*

10 Are you not it which has dried the sea, the waters of the great deep; who has made the depths of the sea a way for the ransomed to pass over? *(This Passage pertains to the Deliverance of the Children of Israel from Egypt and the opening of the Red Sea.)*

11 Therefore the redeemed of the LORD shall return, and come with singing unto Zion; and everlasting joy shall be upon their head: they shall obtain gladness and joy; and sorrow and mourning shall flee away. *(This speaks of Israel's acceptance of Christ as the Messiah and, as such, will be "redeemed." At that time, and we speak of the beginning of the Kingdom Age, and from all over the world, they shall come to "Zion" with "singing and everlasting joy." Then, the "sorrow and mourning" of thousands of years "shall flee away.")*

COMFORT AND RESTORATION PROMISED

12 I, even I, am He Who comforts you: who are you, that you should be afraid of a man that shall die, and of the son of man which shall be made as grass *("I, even I" refers to Christ as the only One Who can "comfort you." The "man" referred to in this Verse is the oppressor, the Antichrist. Under his oppression, Israel will reach the lowest depth of misery. They are admonished here to not "be afraid" of him, but to look to the Lord)*;

13 And forget the LORD your Maker, Who has stretched forth the Heavens, and laid the foundations of the Earth; and has feared continually every day because of the fury of the oppressor, as if he were ready to destroy? and where is the fury of the oppressor? *(The Lord chastises Israel for forgetting Him Who has created all things, and then living in fear of the oppressor, whoever the oppressor might be.*

In this Verse, the gauntlet is laid down. Believers can trust the Lord or fear man. You can't do both.)

14 The captive exile hastens that he may be loosed, and that he should not die in the pit, nor that his bread should fail. *(In a strict sense, "the captive exile" refers to Israel in the latter half of the Great Tribulation, and more particularly in the Battle of Armageddon, when bottled up by the Antichrist, facing extermination. The Promise by God is that Israel, by the Second Coming of the Lord, will be "loosed" and will not "die in the pit." As well, her sustenance will not fail; the Lord will see to that.*

In general, the Promise is to all who will dare to believe God, whoever they might be!)

15 But I am the LORD your God, Who divided the sea, Whose waves roared: the LORD of Hosts is His Name. *(The reference is once more to the great miracle wrought at the Exodus, when the Red Sea was "divided" before the host of Israelites [Ex. 14:21].)*

16 And I have put My words in your mouth, and I have covered you in the shadow of My hand, that I may plant the Heavens, and lay the foundations of the Earth, and say unto Zion, You are My people. *(Regarding its total fulfillment, this pertains to the Millennium, when Israel will be converted under the Messiah, and will trust, love, and serve Him. For the last two thousand years, God has refused to say concerning Israel, "You are My People." Now, because of their turning to Him, this will all change.)*

CALL TO JERUSALEM

17 Awake, awake, stand up, O Jerusalem, which has drunk at the hand of the LORD the cup of His fury; you have drunk the dregs of the cup of trembling, and wrung them out. *(This speaks of the Battle of Armageddon, when the Antichrist will attempt to annihilate the Jews. As well, it refers to "Jerusalem" when it fell to Babylonian captivity, but its greater fulfillment pertains to the coming time of Jacob's trouble [Jer. 30:7].)*

18 There is none to guide her among all the sons whom she has brought forth; neither is there any who takes her by the hand of all the sons that she has brought up. *(There was no one to help Israel during the time of the Babylonian siege. Neither will there be anyone to help during the time of the Battle of Armageddon, when it seems that every nation in the world will either side with the Antichrist or else remain neutral.)*

19 These two things are come unto you; who shall be sorry for you? desolation, and destruction, and the famine, and the sword:

by whom shall I comfort you? *(There is only One Who can comfort Israel, and that is the Lord Jesus Christ, and that He will do at the Second Coming.)*

20 Your sons have fainted, they lie at the head of all the streets, as a wild bull in a net: they are full of the fury of the LORD, the rebuke of your God. *(This speaks of both the invasion by Nebuchadnezzar and by the Antichrist. The difference is this: Israel was not rescued during the siege by the Babylonians, but will be rescued at the siege of the Antichrist. But not without great destruction!*

The phrase, "Full of the fury of the LORD," refers to God's Wrath being poured upon Israel, because of their great sins and refusal to accept Him as their Saviour.

Only when Israel is destitute, trapped like a "wild bull in a net," panting, exhausted, and incapable of the least resistance, will they finally turn to the Lord. Then, the "fury" that has been turned upon them will now be turned upon their adversaries.)

21 Therefore hear now this, you afflicted, and drunken, but not with wine *(rebellion against God has such an effect upon individuals that it is as if they are drunk, when in fact they have not taken any intoxicating beverage at all)*:

22 Thus saith your Lord the LORD, and your God Who pleads the cause of His people, Behold, I have taken out of your hand the cup of trembling, even the dregs of the cup of My fury; you shall no more drink it again *(their punishment will now be complete! They had asked for Caesar as their king and had received Caesar, along with "desolation, destruction, famine, and the sword."*

Now, their True Messiah, the Lord Jesus Christ, the One they rejected, upon hearing their cry, will come to their rescue. It will be the greatest phenomenon the world has ever known! It will be at the Battle of Armageddon, with Christ coming Himself, leading His great Army, which will include every Saint of God who has ever lived.

When He rescues Israel, He will take the "cup of trembling out of their hands" for them to "no more drink it again"):

23 But I will put it into the hand of them who afflict you; which have said to your soul, Bow down, that we may go over: and you have laid your body as the ground, and as the street, to them who went over. *(The Antichrist will make his boasts that he is going to so completely destroy Israel that nothing will*

be left. However, his "certain victory" will be turned into "certain defeat," by the return of the Lord Jesus Christ, the Saviour of Israel.

Instead of the Antichrist walking on Israel, his "body" will be laid "on the ground," and conquering feet will tread upon it.

He demanded that Israel "bow down." Instead, he will "bow down," because his evil sponsor, Satan, "bowed down" to Christ at Calvary.)

CHAPTER 52
(712 B.C.)
THE LORD WILL DELIVER ZION FROM CAPTIVITY

AWAKE; awake; put on your strength, O Zion; put on your beautiful garments, O Jerusalem, the Holy City: for henceforth there shall no more come into you the uncircumcised and the unclean. *(This Chapter speaks of Israel's Restoration, as well as the First and Second Advents of the Messiah. The admonition to "Zion" is to "awake." This concerns the coming in of the Messiah, and of her preparation for Him.*

When Christ comes back, Jerusalem will no more be a contested city, even as it has been for so many centuries, but will be then what its name means, "peace.")

2 Shake yourself from the dust; arise, and sit down, O Jerusalem: loose yourself from the bands of your neck, O captive daughter of Zion. *(The essence of this Verse concerns itself with the long history of Israel's rebellion against God, and their resultant captivities.*

The phrase, "Shake yourself from the dust," refers to Israel wandering among the nations for so long, even as an outcast. Now, at the Second Coming, she will "arise" from her position of debasement, and will "sit down" in a seat of authority, but all under Christ.)

3 For thus saith the LORD, you have sold yourselves for nought; and you shall be redeemed without money. *(The essence of this Scripture is: God received nothing when He allowed His People to become slaves of the Babylonians and others. He took no price for them and, therefore, is free to claim them back without payment. He has but to say the Word, and He is about to say it!)*

4 For thus saith the Lord GOD, My people went down aforetime into Egypt to sojourn there; and the Assyrian oppressed them without cause. *(For many years, the title "Assyrian" was generally assumed to be an error in the Hebrew Text, but excavations about the turn of the*

Twentieth Century proved that the Pharaoh of the oppression was, by race, Assyrian. He was a type of Israel's last great oppressor, who will also be an Assyrian [a Jewish Assyrian].)

5 Now therefore, what have I here, saith the LORD, that My people is taken away for nought? they who rule over them make them to howl, saith the LORD; and My name continually every day is blasphemed. *(Cruel taskmasters vexed the captive Israelites by insulting their God. When God's People are brutally treated and insulted, in effect, God is brutally treated and insulted!)*

6 Therefore My people shall know My name: therefore they shall know in that day that I am He Who does speak: behold, it is I. *(This speaks of the Deliverance of the Children of Israel from Egypt, with a Strong and Mighty Hand, as well as their Deliverance from Babylon, by the overthrow of Belshazzar by Cyrus the Mede, whom God had raised up. As well, it refers to the coming day, when the Antichrist will seek to once and for all destroy Israel, but will instead be destroyed himself by Christ. It will be the day that the Lord speaks, and He says, "Behold, it is I." The "I" is emphatic, proclaiming enough Power to destroy the future Assyrian many times over!)*

7 How beautiful upon the mountains are the feet of Him who brings good tidings, Who publishes peace; Who brings good tidings of good, Who publishes salvation; Who says unto Zion, Your God reigns! *(The "beautiful feet" are those of the Messiah. This Verse is often misapplied to the proclamation of the Gospel by Preachers. As a secondary meaning, it certainly could refer to such; however, the overflowing application concerns itself only with the Messiah. Only His "feet" are "beautiful." Only He "brings good tidings." Only He "publishes peace." Only He "publishes Salvation."*

When He comes, the entirety of the world will say, "Your God reigns!" [Ps. 97:1].)

8 Your watchmen shall lift up the voice; with the voice together shall they sing: for they shall see eye to eye, when the LORD shall bring again Zion. *(The evidence is: during the Battle of Armageddon, "watchmen" will be stationed at particular points in Jerusalem, looking up to the Heavens in anticipation of His Coming. He will not disappoint them!*

As they see Him coming, these "watchmen" will proclaim His Coming with gladness of heart and a cry of triumph.

It will not be an apparition, but rather a Coming visible to all, and even "eye to eye" with the watchmen.)

9 Break forth into joy, sing together, you waste places of Jerusalem: for the LORD has comforted His people, He has redeemed Jerusalem. *(The struggle has always been between Satan's city, "Babylon," and God's city, "Jerusalem." However, Babylon is now destroyed, and "Jerusalem" is "redeemed" from the hands of the enemy, never again to fall into such a state. It will take place at the Second Coming.)*

10 The LORD has made bare His holy arm in the eyes of all the nations; and all the ends of the Earth shall see the salvation of our God. *(This speaks of the Coming of the Lord, with the Antichrist being defeated, and defeated before the entirety of the world.)*

11 Depart ye, depart ye, go ye out from thence, touch no unclean thing; go ye out of the midst of her; be ye clean, who bear the vessels of the LORD. *(While the Bible does not teach isolation for the Believer, it definitely does teach separation, and we speak of separation from the world, symbolized by Babylon.)*

12 For you shall not go out with haste, nor go by flight: for the LORD will go before you; and the God of Israel will be your rereward. *(When Israel forsook Babylon at the end of their 70 years of captivity, they did not need to flee, "go out with haste," for the way was prepared for them. Not only was the way prepared, but the Lord also was their "rereward," referring to their "rear guard." Obedience, either for Israel or the modern Believer, guarantees God's total protection.)*

THE SUFFERING OF THE LORD'S "SERVANT," THE MESSIAH

13 Behold, My servant shall deal prudently, He shall be exalted and extolled, and be very high. *("My Servant" is the Lord Jesus Christ. The phrase, "Shall deal prudently," means to be circumspect and intelligent. "Extolled" means to be lifted up, honored, magnified, and respected, with the words, "very high," referring to Christ being exalted higher than any and all else [Eph. 1:20-23; Phil. 2:9-11; Col. 1:15-18; Heb. 1:3; I Pet. 3:22].)*

14 As many were astonied at You; His visage was so marred more than any man, and His form more than the sons of men *(this Prophecy predicts the sufferings of Christ in His First Advent, and the glories that shall follow in His Second [I Pet. 1:11].*

In these Passages, Isaiah seems to sit at the foot of the Cross of Calvary; he views the Redeemer as He hung upon the accursed tree, after He had been buffeted, crowned with thorns, smitten, scourged, and crucified, when His Face was covered with bruises and gore, His Frame and Features distorted with agony):

15 So shall He sprinkle many nations; the kings shall shut their mouths at Him: for that which had not been told them shall they see; and that which they had not heard shall they consider. *(The "as" of Verse 14 corresponds with the "so" of Verse 15. The statement is: That just as the Messiah astonished men by the humiliation of His First Advent, so will He astonish them by the Glory of His Second. For as in His First Coming, the basest of men mocked Him, so in His Second, the chiefest of men will stand in silent awe before Him.*

The phrase, "And that which they had not heard shall they consider," refers to the facts of Christ's Humiliation, Sufferings, Death, Resurrection, and Ascension to Heaven — events that had never entered into the hearts of men to conceive, and of which, therefore, no tongue had ever spoken.)

CHAPTER 53
(712 B.C.)
THE SUFFERING SERVANT: THE
MESSIAH, JESUS CHRIST

WHO has believed our report? and to whom is the arm of the LORD revealed? *(The phrase, "Our report," refers to this very Prophecy, as well as the other Messianic Prophecies delivered by Isaiah. To Israel was "the arm of the LORD revealed." And to Israel is ascribed the "unbelief," which destroyed them.*

The Revelation of "the arm of the LORD" requires the eye of faith to see it. Unbelief can always assign the most plainly providential arrangements to happy accident. It takes faith to believe the report that is revealed.)

2 For He shall grow up before Him as a tender plant, and as a root out of a dry ground: He has no form nor comeliness; and when we shall see Him, there is no beauty that we should desire Him. *(To God's Eye, Israel, and the entirety of the Earth for that matter, were a "dry ground," but that Eye rested with delight upon one tender plant which had a living root. It was Jesus!*

The Hebrew verbs in these Verses [through Verse 7] are to be regarded as "perfects of prophetic certitude." This means that in the mind

of God all has been finished before the foundation of the world and done so in the Divine Counsels [I Pet. 1:18-20].

The words, "Before Him," mean "before Jehovah" — under the fostering care of Jehovah. God the Father had His Eye fixed upon the Son with a watchfulness and tenderness and love.

This "sapling" from the house of David shall become the "root" out of which His Church will grow. The Messiah will be a fresh sprout from the stump of a tree that had been felled, i.e., from the destroyed Davidic Monarchy.

The words, "He has no form nor comeliness," refer to the fact that He had none during His sufferings, but now He has it more than anyone else except the Father and the Holy Spirit [Eph. 1:20-23; Phil. 2:9-11; Col. 1:15-18; I Pet. 3:22].

The words, "There is no beauty that we should desire Him," refer to His sufferings, which include His peasant upbringing and, as a consequence, His poverty, as well as His lack of association with the aristocracy!)

3 He is despised and rejected of men; a man of sorrows, and acquainted with grief: and we hid as it were our faces from Him; He was despised, and we esteemed Him not. *(Him being "rejected of men" means "One from Whom men held themselves aloof." Why? He was pure Holiness and they were pure corruption.*

The phrase, "A man of sorrows," refers to Jesus taking all the sorrows of humanity upon Himself.

The phrase, "Acquainted with grief," actually refers to diseases and sicknesses, for that's what the word "grief" in the Hebrew means.

The phrase, "And we hid as it were our faces from Him," describes the treatment of the Servant by His fellowmen. Again, Why? He was not the type of Messiah they wanted!

The phrase, "He was despised, and we esteemed Him not," refers to the fact that the religious leadership of Israel esteemed Him not at all. He came to deliver men from sin, but that wasn't the type of deliverance they desired!)

4 Surely He has borne our griefs, and carried our sorrows: yet we did esteem Him stricken, smitten of God, and afflicted. *(Twelve times within the space of nine Verses the Prophet asserts, with the most emphatic reiteration, that all the Servant's sufferings were vicarious; i.e., borne for man to save him from the consequences of his sins, to enable him to escape punishment. In other words, Jesus did this all for us.*

The phrase, "Yet we did esteem Him stricken, smitten of God, and afflicted," proclaims the fact that because He died on a Cross, Israel assumed

that He died under the curse of God, because Moses had said, "For he who is hanged is accursed of God" [Deut. 21:23].

What they did not understand was that He was not accursed, neither in Himself was cursed, but in fact was "made a curse for us."

Israel assumed He was "smitten of God," and, in a sense, He was. He suffered in our stead, actually as our Substitute, which means that the blow that should have come to us instead went to Him. But yet, it was not for His sins, because He had none, but instead was for our sins. He was "afflicted" for us. As stated, He was our Substitute.)

5 But He was wounded for our transgressions, He was bruised for our iniquities: the chastisement of our peace was upon Him; and with His stripes we are healed. (The phrase, "He was wounded for our transgressions," pertains to the manner in which He died, which was the price He paid for the Redemption of humanity.

The phrase, "He was bruised for our iniquities," means that what He suffered was not at all for Himself, but all for us. It was for our iniquities. Look at the Cross, and then say, "My sin did this."

The phrase, "The chastisement of our peace was upon Him," means that if peace between God and man was to be restored, all which Adam lost, then Jesus would have to bring it about. Here is the simple doctrine of the Gospel — the death of Christ. All other founders of religions base their claims upon their life and their teaching — their death was a calamity, and without significance. But the death of Christ was His Glory, and forms the imperishable foundation of the one and only Salvation. His purpose in coming was to die.

The phrase, "And with His stripes we are healed," definitely pertains to physical healing, but is far greater in meaning than that. Its greater meaning refers to being healed of the terrible malady of sin.)

6 All we like sheep have gone astray; we have turned every one to his own way; and the LORD has laid on Him the iniquity of us all. (Sheep without a shepherd get lost easily. Man as sheep has wandered from the right path; he has become so hopelessly lost that it is impossible for him, within his own means, to come back to the right path. Therefore, the Lord had to come from Heaven down to this wilderness called Earth and, thereby, seek and save man, who is lost.

The phrase, "We have turned every one to his own way," refers to the fact that the whole world, collectively and individually, has sinned and come short of the Glory of God. This "erroneous way" has led to death, suffering, sorrow, heartache, loneliness, despair, and pain. This is the reason that everything that man touches dies! Whereas everything that God touches lives! So man desperately needs God's Touch, i.e., "the Atonement of Calvary."

The phrase, "And the LORD has laid on Him the iniquity of us all," refers to the total price He paid for our total Salvation. The penalty for every sin for all of humanity and for all time was laid on Christ. God the Father, as the primary disposer of all things, lays upon the Son the burden which the Son voluntarily accepts. He comes into the world to do the Father's Will, and the Father's Will is to secure the Salvation of man, as least for those who will believe.)

7 He was oppressed, and He was afflicted, yet He opened not His mouth: He is brought as a lamb to the slaughter, and as a sheep before her shearers is dumb, so He opens not His mouth. (The first phrase refers to all that was done to Him in His humiliation, suffering, and agony. He could so easily have vindicated Himself from every charge; therefore, He self-abased Himself.

It seemed like an admission of guilt, and in fact was, but not His guilt, but the guilt of those who were accusing Him, as well as the entirety of the world.

Of all the Levitical Offerings [five total], the "lamb" was the animal most used; hence, John the Baptist would say, "Behold the Lamb of God, which takes away the sin of the world" [Jn. 1:29].)

8 He was taken from prison and from judgment: and who shall declare His generation? for He was cut off out of the land of the living: for the transgression of My people was He stricken. (The phrase, "He was taken from prison and from judgment," refers to a violence which cloaked itself under the formalities of a legal process.

The phrase, "And who shall declare His generation," refers to the fact of Him being "cut off" [Dan. 9:26], which means that He would have no posterity.

The phrase, "For the transgression of My people was He stricken," can be summed up in what He suffered, and all on our behalf. This must never be forgotten: Every single thing He suffered was not at all for Himself, or for Heaven in any capacity, but all for sinners.)

9 And He made His grave with the wicked,

and with the rich in His death; because He had done no violence, neither was any deceit in His mouth. *(The phrase, "And He made His grave with the wicked," means that he was appointed such by the religious hierarchy of Israel, but Joseph of Arimathea, a rich man, asked that Jesus be buried in his personal tomb instead, and so He was. The phrase, "Because He had done no violence, neither was any deceit in His mouth," proclaims the sinlessness of Christ, and forms the main argument in the Epistle to the Hebrews for the superiority of the New Covenant over the Old [Heb. 7:26-28; 9:14].*

As no other man was ever without sin, it follows that the Servant of this present Chapter is, and can be no other than, Christ.)

10 Yet it pleased the LORD to bruise Him; He has put Him to grief: when You shall make His soul an offering for sin, He shall see His seed, He shall prolong His days, and the pleasure of the LORD shall prosper in His hand. *(The phrase, "Yet it pleased the LORD to bruise Him," refers to the sufferings of Christ, which proceeded from the "determinate counsel and foreknowledge of God" [Acts 2:23], and which, being permitted by Him, were in some way His doing. It "pleased Him" moreover that they should be undergone, for the Father saw with satisfaction the Son's self-sacrifice, and He witnessed with joy man's Redemption and Deliverance effected thereby.*

The phrase, "He has put Him to grief," actually says "He has put Him to sicknesses" or "He has made Him sick." This spoke of the time He was on the Cross bearing our sins and "sicknesses" [Mat. 8:16-17; I Pet. 2:24]. And yet, while all sin and sickness were atoned at the Cross, the total effects of such will not be completely dissipated until the coming Resurrection [Rom. 8:23].

The phrase, "When You shall make His soul an offering for sin," is powerful indeed! The word "offering" in the Hebrew is "Asham," and means "a Trespass Offering," an "offering for sin."

Offerings for sin, or "guilt offerings," were distinct from "sin offerings." The object of the former was "satisfaction"; of the latter, "expiation." The Servant of Jehovah was, however, to be both. He was both the "Sin Offering" and the "Guilt Offering."

This completely destroys the idea that Jesus died spiritually on the Cross, meaning that He became a sinner on the Cross, and died and went to Hell as all sinners, and was born again in Hell after three days and nights of suffering,

etc. *None of that is in the Word of God. While Jesus definitely was a "Sin Offering," He was not a sinner, and did not become a sinner on the Cross. To have done so would have destroyed His Perfection of Sacrifice, which was demanded by God. In other words, the Sacrifice had to be perfect, and He was perfect in every respect.*

The phrase, "He shall see His seed," refers to all His "true followers," which include all who have ever been Born-Again.

The phrase, "He shall prolong His days," refers to His Resurrection.

The phrase, "And the pleasure of the LORD shall prosper in His hand," refers to the great victory that He would win at Calvary, which will ultimately restore everything that Adam lost.)

11 He shall see of the travail of His soul, and shall be satisfied: by His knowledge shall My righteous Servant justify many; for He shall bear their iniquities. *(The "travail of His soul" pertains to His Sacrifice for sin, which has resulted in the Restoration of man, at least for those who will believe.*

The phrase, "And shall be satisfied," refers to the fact that even though the price was high, actually beyond comprehension, still, it was worth the Redemption it accomplished.

What Jesus did at the Cross made it possible for man to be fully and totally "justified" in the Eyes of God, which comes about by man exhibiting Faith in Christ and what Christ did at the Cross.)

12 Therefore will I divide Him a portion with the great, and He shall divide the spoil with the strong; because He has poured out His soul unto death: and He was numbered with the transgressors; and He bore the sin of many, and made intercession for the transgressors. *(To be appointed with the great and to divide the spoil with the strong is figurative language expressive of full victory. It means here that Christ, by His Death, delivers from Satan mankind who was held captive.*

The phrase, "Because He has poured out His soul unto death," means that Christ not only died for man, but, as it were, "poured out His soul" with His Own Hand to the last drop. The expression emphasizes the duration and the voluntariness of the Messiah's sufferings. In other words, He laid down His Own life and no man took it from Him [Jn. 10:18].

The phrase, "And He was numbered with the transgressors," refers to the actions of the Jews toward Him. He was crucified between two thieves. He was condemned as a "blasphemer"

[Mat. 26:65], *crucified with malefactors [Lk. 23:32], called "that deceiver" [Mat. 27:63], and regarded generally by the Jews as accursed [Deut. 21:23].*

The phrase, "And He bore the sin of many, and made Intercession for the transgressors," is, in the Hebrew, an act, though begun in the past, not yet completed. The "Intercession for transgressors" was begun on the Cross with the compassionate words, "Father, forgive them; for they know not what they do" [Lk. 23:34]. This Intercession for Believers has continued ever since and will ever continue [Rom. 8:34; Heb. 7:25]; such Intercession is made possible by what Christ did at the Cross.)

CHAPTER 54
(712 B.C.)
GOD'S EVERLASTING LOVE FOR ISRAEL

S ING, O barren, you who did not bear; break forth into singing, and cry aloud, you who did not travail with child: for more are the children of the desolate than the children of the married wife, saith the LORD. (*The singing of this Chapter will be the moral result of the weeping of the prior one. The Tribes of Israel, having wailed because of Him, will then sing because of Him. This is a great moral principle. Before the heart can taste the joy of God's Salvation, there must be the recognition and confession of its guilt and its rejection of Christ.*

The "barren" woman, at least in this case, is Israel. Two periods of her history are pointed to: 1. As the married wife, i.e., when in official relationship with God and 2. When out of relationship as the "desolate" woman.

During the first period of her history, she gave birth to many sons; but during the second period, which is yet to come, she will give birth to a countless multitude.

As well, Paul quoted this very Passage, using it to prove that more will be saved under the New Covenant than under the Old [Gal. 4:27]. As such, the Church has many more "children," i.e., followers of the Lord, than Israel of old! Moreover, the Gentiles, who were once "barren," can now "sing," because of having been included in the great Salvation plan [Jn. 3:16]. So, in essence, this Passage, as given, has two meanings.)

2 Enlarge the place of your tent, and let them stretch forth the curtains of your habitations: spare not, lengthen your cords, and strengthen your stakes (*the entirety of this Chapter speaks of the coming Glad Day, when Israel*

will have prayed the 51st Psalm and, thereby, blotted out the terrible sin of crucifying Christ, as is outlined in the previous Chapter, and has finally accepted Christ as their Messiah and Saviour. As such, they will "sing" and then be blessed in a manner that is beyond description);

3 For you shall break forth on the right hand and on the left; and Your seed shall inherit the Gentiles, and make the desolate cities to be inhabited. (*The first phrase speaks of Israel's Restoration, which will take place in the coming Kingdom Age.*

The phrase, "And Your Seed shall inherit the Gentiles," refers to Christ as the "Seed" settling the dispute between Israel and the Gentiles concerning the Land of Israel. This means that this dispute, which rages at the present, will not be settled until the Second Coming.)

4 Fear not; for you shall not be ashamed: neither be thou confounded; for you shall not be put to shame: for you shall forget the shame of your youth, and shall not remember the reproach of your widowhood any more. (*The shame of Israel's "youth" was idolatry, with the "reproach" of her "widowhood," her present rejection. This "reproach" has lasted now for about 2,000 years.*

The words, "fear not," have to do with Israel, when she realizes that the Christ she crucified is truly her Messiah. Realizing that He has just destroyed the Antichrist, what will He in turn do to her? The answer will be extremely comforting.

He will not only not hurt them, but instead will forgive them, wash them, cleanse them, and renew His Covenant with them.)

5 For your Maker is your husband; the LORD of Hosts is His name; and your Redeemer the Holy One of Israel; The God of the whole Earth shall He be called. (*The words, "Maker" and "Husband," refer to the Lord as being such to Israel.*

At the present time, Jesus is not recognized as God by the world. However, when He comes back in the clouds of Heaven in Power and Glory and restores Israel, which He shall, He will then be recognized as "The God of the whole Earth," which refers not only to the Jews, but to the Gentiles, as well [Rom. 3:29].)

6 For the LORD has called you as a woman forsaken and grieved in spirit, and a wife of youth, when you were refused, saith your God. (*The word "called" is actually "recalled," i.e., recall you to Himself — summon you to return and once more resume the office of the wife.*

The words, "When you were refused," refer to Israel being cast off, and Jehovah taking her back into the old relationship as a man takes back "the wife of his youth," when she had been for a long time "cast off." This will take place in the Kingdom Age.)

7 For a small moment have I forsaken you; but with great mercies will I gather you.

8 In a little wrath I hid My face from you for a moment; but with everlasting kindness will I have mercy on you, saith the LORD your Redeemer. *(Regarding eternity, it has only been a "small moment" respecting Israel's lost condition. As well, the words, "little wrath," seem inappropriate; however, compared to what God could have done, He rather restrained Himself.*

Compared to the "kindness" which the Lord will show Israel, which is "everlasting," His Wrath is truly only "for a moment." This is indicative of God's manner [Ps. 30:5].)

9 For this is as the waters of Noah unto Me: for as I have sworn that the waters of Noah should no more go over the Earth; so have I sworn that I would not be wroth with you, nor rebuke you. *(The Promise of this Verse is: as God assured Noah that He would never again destroy the Earth with a flood, so does He promise Israel that He will never again rebuke her with His Wrath. This speaks of the coming Millennial Reign, when Israel will have come back to Him and repented of her past. The Lord will not use wrath again, because there will be no need for such to be done, due to Israel's continued faithfulness.)*

10 For the mountains shall depart, and the hills be removed; but My kindness shall not depart from you, neither shall the covenant of My peace be removed, saith the LORD Who has mercy on you. *(This will take place at the Second Coming, when Israel will then accept Christ as Saviour and Lord [Zech. 13:1].)*

11 O thou afflicted, tossed with tempest, and not comforted, behold, I will lay your stones with fair colours, and lay your foundations with sapphires. *(The present condition of Jerusalem is that of the first part of this Verse, and the remainder of the Verse, with those following, picture her future happiness and glory.)*

12 And I will make your windows of agates, and your gates of carbuncles, and all your borders of pleasant stones. *(One should compare Jerusalem's present with her future and realize that her future could have been her present. This beauty is because of Christ; without Christ, such*

is impossible!)

13 And all your children shall be taught of the LORD; and great shall be the peace of your children. *(The Messiah Himself, in Jn. 6:45, quoted this Verse. The truth of this Verse was not the case in His First Advent, but it will be so in His Second.)*

14 In righteousness shall you be established: you shall be far from oppression; for you shall not fear: and from terror; for it shall not come near you. *(In that coming Glad Day, when Israel accepts Christ as her Messiah, she then will be totally and completely free from "oppression," "fear," and "terror."*

Such can be said in the Christian heart, and at the present, for all whose "Righteousness" is "established" in Christ and not in self, which can only be done by the Believer exhibiting Faith constantly in Christ and the Cross [Lk. 9:23-24].)

15 Behold, they shall surely gather together, but not by Me: whosoever shall gather together against you shall fall for your sake. *(The words, "But not by Me," address themselves to the many times in the past that God had had to bring chastisement upon Israel, and for her many sins.*

The Prophet is referring here to Satan being loosed from the pit at the conclusion of the Kingdom Age, and going out to deceive the nations of the Earth.

In effect, the Lord is saying, "This will happen, but it will not be from Me," and will be quickly stopped, for Israel's sake.)

16 Behold, I have created the smith who blows the coals in the fire, and who brings forth an instrument for his work; and I have created the waster to destroy.

17 No weapon that is formed against you shall prosper; and every tongue that shall rise against you in judgment you shall condemn. This is the heritage of the servants of the LORD, and their righteousness is of Me, saith the LORD. *(Irrespective of the efforts made by Satan to come against the people of God, it must ever be remembered that the Lord is in control of all things. This means that "no weapon that is formed against the Believer shall prosper." More particularly, it refers to Israel, but, in general, it refers to all who trust the Lord, because "this is the heritage of the servants of the LORD," and that includes all Believers, and for all time. However, it must be remembered that it is alone the "Righteousness" of the Lord which closes the door to every enemy and "weapon.")*

CHAPTER 55
(712 B.C.)
GOD'S PROMISE TO ALL

HO, every one who thirsts, come ye to the waters, and he who has no money; come ye, buy, and eat; yea, come, buy wine and milk without money and without price. *(With Chapter 53 proclaiming the great price that was paid at Calvary, and Chapter 54 proclaiming the coming grand and glorious Kingdom Age, now the inhabitants of the entirety of the world are invited to come and partake of the One Who guarantees entrance into that Kingdom.*

Three times in this one Passage the word "come" is used. It corresponds to Rev. 22:17; it is used three times there as well! The triple invitation corresponds to the Trinity: "God the Father," "God the Son," and "God the Holy Spirit." All are participants in the great Salvation Plan.

The four articles of purchase, as are outlined in Verses 1 and 2 are: "water, bread, wine, and milk." Such expresses the plenitude of Grace in the Saviour, as exhibited in the four Gospels.

The word "buy" is used, and yet the purchase price is not "money." Were it so, most could never obtain the treasure. Therefore, the price that is demanded is the heart of man! [Rom. 10:9-10].

Then the phrase is used, "and eat." Men must partake of Christ before they can become a part of Christ, which can be done only by Faith in Christ and what He has done for us at the Cross.)

2 Wherefore do you spend money for that which is not bread? and your labour for that which satisfies not? hearken diligently unto Me, and eat ye that which is good, and let your soul delight itself in fatness. *(Accepting the Spirit's invitation through the Prophet will satisfy fully. As someone has well said, "The soul of man is so big that only God can fill it up.")*

3 Incline your ear, and come unto Me: hear, and your soul shall live; and I will make an everlasting covenant with you, even the sure mercies of David. *(The phrase, "Incline your ear," refers to the Words given by Christ, when He said, "he who has ears to here, let him hear" [Mk. 4:9].*

The "Everlasting Covenant" refers to the "New Covenant," the Divine David, the Lord Jesus Christ. It is called "the sure mercies of David," referring to God becoming Man, the Incarnation [Heb. 13:20; Isa. 7:14].)

4 Behold, I have given Him for a witness to the people, a leader and commander to the people. *(The pronoun "Him" refers to Christ.*

He Alone is the "witness to the people." He "came to bear witness to the Truth" [Jn. 18:37].

As well, He is "Leader and Commander to the people." He "feeds and leads" His People [Rev. 7:17], and is the "Commander" under Whose banner they serve [II Tim. 2:3-4].

The word "people," in the Hebrew, is actually "peoples," and rather refers to the entirety of mankind, at least those who will believe in Him.)

5 Behold, You shall call a nation that You knew not, and nations who knew not You shall run unto You because of the LORD Your God, and for the Holy One of Israel; for He has glorified You. *(The first phrase refers to the calling and Salvation of the Gentiles, which Christ afforded by what He did at the Cross [Mat. 21:33-44; Jn. 10:16].*

The phrase, "Because of the LORD Your God," refers to "God" as the Father of the Messiah. God gave "Him" not only for Israel, but for the entirety of mankind.

The "Holy One of Israel" refers to the fact that God always intended for "Israel" to be the bearer of this great Message of Eternal Life, and to the entirety of mankind, but "Israel" refused!

The phrase, "For He has glorified You," refers to Jehovah glorifying the Messiah, which was done at His Resurrection, because of what He did to bring Redemption to mankind — all of mankind.)

REPENTANT SINNERS TOLD
TO SEEK THE LORD

6 Seek ye the LORD while He may be found, call ye upon Him while He is near *(the entirety of this Verse, as given by the Holy Spirit, has rather a tone of reproach. Israel, as well as all, must "seek the Lord" without delay, or the opportunity will be past. Therefore, the admonition in this Verse is one of warning, proclaiming to us the fact that there can come a time when God cannot be found!):*

7 Let the wicked forsake his way, and the unrighteous man his thoughts: and let him return unto the LORD, and He will have mercy upon him; and to our God, for He will abundantly pardon. *(A general promise of forgiveness of sin upon Repentance and amendment of life was implied by the Lord from the very beginning [Gen. 4:4], but was actually given to Israel through Solomon [II Chron. 7:14]. The Doctrine is largely preached by the Prophet, but is nowhere so distinctly and emphatically laid down as in this place. God's Will is to "multiply*

pardon," if man will only turn to Him.

The words, "abundantly pardon," have the idea of "Justification by Faith." God sets the sin aside as though it never happened, which can only be brought about by Faith in Christ and what Christ did at the Cross, of which the Sacrifices in Isaiah's day were symbols.)

8 For My thoughts are not your thoughts, neither are your ways My ways, saith the LORD. *(The idea of this Passage is that the "thoughts" of God and the "Ways" of God are so far above the comprehension of man, that man must take these statements by Faith. However, Verse 8, in essence, points toward the Sacrifice of Christ, which would be nearly 800 years into the future, and which would bring about the Redemption of mankind, at least for those who will believe.)*

9 For as the Heavens are higher than the Earth, so are My ways higher than your ways, and My thoughts than your thoughts. *(Through the Word of God we are given some of the "thoughts" and "Ways" of God; however, so few Believers actually take advantage of this treasure trove of wisdom.)*

10 For as the rain comes down, and the snow from Heaven, and returns not thither, but waters the Earth, and makes it bring forth and bud, that it may give seed to the sower, and bread to the eater *(the sense of this Passage is not in its direction, but in its mission)*:

11 So shall My word be that goes forth out of My mouth: it shall not return unto Me void, but it shall accomplish that which I please, and it shall prosper in the thing whereto I sent it. *(God's Word is creative. With the utterance, the result is achieved. It is given not for just a special time, but for the benefit of the people of God in all ages.)*

THE REDEEMED WILL LIVE IN JOY

12 For you shall go out with joy, and be led forth with peace: the mountains and the hills shall break forth before you into singing, and all the trees of the field shall clap their hands. *(The idea of this Verse is that the captives of Jacob will ultimately be led forth from captivity by the Leader and Commander of Verse 4. When Israel is finally restored by Christ, because they have finally accepted Him as Saviour and Messiah, the entirety of the world will be grandly blessed [Rom. 11:12].)*

13 Instead of the thorn shall come up the fir tree, and instead of the brier shall come up the myrtle tree: and it shall be to the LORD for a name, for an everlasting sign that shall not be cut off. *(Sinful man is born morally a "thorn" and a "brier." But the Messiah and Saviour can recreate him as a "fir tree" and a "myrtle."*

A sincere thirst for forgiveness of sins and for communion with God is marked by a separation from all known sin, and by a subjection and attachment of heart and will to the Lord Jesus Christ, in Whom are found Salvation and Righteousness, and Who is Himself the Saviour of the New Covenant [Lk. 22:20], which was made possible by the Cross [Eph. 2:13-18].)

CHAPTER 56
(712 B.C.)
DO JUSTICE; KEEP GOD'S JUDGMENTS; GOD'S CONCERN INCLUDES THE GENTILES

THUS saith the LORD, Keep ye judgment, and do justice: for My salvation is near to come, and My righteousness to be revealed. *("Judgment" and "Justice" have to do with the Word of God. In essence, Christ is all of this and more. He is the Salvation which would come, and in fact did come, and the Righteousness which was to be revealed, and in fact was revealed.)*

2 Blessed is the man who does this, and the Son of Man who lays hold on it; who keeps the sabbath from polluting it, and keeps his hand from doing any evil. *(Jesus Christ is God's True Sabbath. Worshipping and serving Him thereby "keeps the Sabbath.")*

3 Neither let the son of the stranger, who has joined himself to the LORD, speak, saying, The LORD has utterly separated me from His people: neither let the eunuch say, Behold, I am a dry tree. *(The idea of this Passage, continuing to refer to the coming Kingdom Age, is that under the New Covenant none are excluded.)*

4 For thus saith the LORD unto the eunuchs who keep My sabbaths, and choose the things that please Me, and take hold of My covenant *(certain individuals, such as "eunuchs," were denied certain privileges in the official life of Israel, because those in positions of leadership were to be types of Christ [Deut. 23:1]; however, this did not preclude their Salvation, but only their service. Under the New Covenant, no such restriction is allowed, because Christ has already come! As well, in the coming Kingdom Age, when the Law of Moses, at least to a certain degree, will be reinstituted, the old restrictions will not be binding, because Christ is present);*

5 Even unto them will I give in My house and within My walls a place and a name better than of sons and of daughters: I will give them an everlasting name, that shall not be cut off. (*The phrase, "Even unto them," refers to any and all who will accept Christ as Saviour, irrespective of their nationality, race, or handicap, as being accepted with full rights and privileges! Such is the New Covenant [Rev. 22:17].*

The phrase, "Sons and daughters" refers to Israel; the acceptance of Christ, irrespective as to who the person might be, gives them a place and position better than Israel had under the Old Covenant.)

6 Also the sons of the stranger, who join themselves to the LORD, to serve Him, and to love the name of the LORD, to be His servants, every one who keeps the sabbath from polluting it, and takes hold of My covenant (*"My Covenant" refers to "The Everlasting Name," which refers to Christ. It is the New Covenant!*);

7 Even them will I bring to My holy mountain, and make them joyful in My house of prayer: their Burnt Offerings and their sacrifices shall be accepted upon My altar; for My house shall be called an house of prayer for all people. (*The House of Prayer, the Burnt Offerings, the Sacrifices, the Altar, and the Sabbath will all be restored in the coming Kingdom Age, and so point back to Christ and to Calvary; prior to the First Advent, they pointed forward to them [Ezek., Chpts. 40-48].*

Jesus addressed Himself to the phrase, "an House of Prayer for all people," [Mk. 11:17]. In His day, it was made a "house of merchandise." In the coming Glad Day, it will fulfill that which God originally intended.)

8 The Lord GOD which gathers the outcasts of Israel says, Yet will I gather others to Him, beside those who are gathered unto Him. (*"The others" that Adonai Jehovah will gather to Israel will be the "other sheep" of which He Himself speaks in Jn. 10:16, i.e., the Gentiles. They were to be brought in, and in fact have already been brought in. Thus, there is one flock and One Shepherd.*)

9 All ye beasts of the field, come to devour, yea, all ye beasts in the forest. (*In the last four Verses of this Chapter and the first two of the next, Israel is compared to a flock of sheep neglected by unfaithful shepherds, who feed themselves and persecute the Godly. Such was the moral condition which caused Israel to become an outcast.*

When shepherds are unfaithful, wild beasts ravage the flocks. The beasts of this Verse symbolize the Gentile princes who will press the Israelites — past, present, and future.)

BLIND WATCHMEN REPROVED

10 His watchmen are blind: they are all ignorant, they are all dumb dogs, they cannot bark; sleeping, lying down, loving to slumber. (*The idea, as presented by the Holy Spirit, is that Israel lost her way because of these "blind watchmen," i.e., Preachers! Israel forfeited all the great Promises because of these "dumb dogs" that "cannot bark," which means they do not preach the Truth or warn of false doctrine.*)

11 Yea, they are greedy dogs which can never have enough, and they are shepherds who cannot understand: they all look to their own way, every one for his gain, from his quarter. (*In Jesus' day, these "watchmen" were called "blind guides" of the Gospel [Mat. 15:14; Lk. 6:39]. They did not have the spiritual discernment which would enable them to lead people aright. Instead of acting as faithful watchdogs who give warning of the approach of danger by their barking, they remain apathetic and utter no warning at all. It is as if they pass their lives in sleep.*

Not only do they fail in the way of neglect of duty, but they are actively culpable. Being worldly and not spiritually minded, they are "greedy" after gain, i.e., "greedy dogs.")

12 Come ye, say they, I will fetch wine, and we will fill ourselves with strong drink; and to morrow shall be as this day, and much more abundant. (*The Prophets of Isaiah's time, as well as the time of Christ, were not only negligent of their duty, and covetous, but they were given to excess regarding entertainment.*

Such crucified their Saviour when He came, and such today reject their Saviour Who has come!)

CHAPTER 57
(698 B.C.)
GOD'S CARE FOR THE RIGHTEOUS

THE righteous perish and no man lays it to heart: and merciful men are taken away, none considering that the righteous is taken away from the evil to come. (*The word translated "perish" does not imply violence, but the context implies a premature death. The righteous disappear — are taken from the Earth before their natural time.*

The Text is so structured that, in effect, the

Holy Spirit is saying that inasmuch as these "righteous" were not appreciated, but rather hated for their Godly walk, and as such were a rebuke to ungodly but religious Israel, the Lord prematurely took them away in death.

The phrase, "No man lays it to heart," refers to the fact that no one asked what it means — no one is disturbed, no one grieves.

The phrase, "And merciful men are taken away," implies that "mercy" was found only in these few "righteous." When these were taken, very little "mercy" was left in the religious heart of spiritually demented Israel!

The phrase, "None considering that the righteous is taken away from the evil to come," refers to the fact that God may permit the premature death of His servants as an escape from calamities worse than death [I Ki. 14:13; II Ki. 22:20].)

2 He shall enter into peace: they shall rest in their beds, each one walking in his uprightness. (The pronoun "he" refers to the "righteous man" of Verse 1, while the pronoun "they" refers to the same. The phrase, "He shall enter into peace," refers to "a state of peace." The phrase, "walking in his uprightness," has to do with walking according to the Word of God, and not according to public opinion, or the false paths of these religious hypocrites.)

THE WICKED AND UNFAITHFUL REBUKED

3 But draw near hither, ye sons of the sorceress, the seed of the adulterer and the whore. ("Sorcery" has to do with seeking leading and guidance from anything other than the Word of God. As well, the words, "adulterer and the whore," refer to Israel being unfaithful to God, Who was actually their Husband, and taking up with idols.

Paul referred to Believers who placed their trust and faith in anything except Christ and Him Crucified as "spiritual adulterers." It is basically the same as this which Isaiah says [Rom. 7:1-4].)

4 Against whom do you sport yourselves? against whom do you make a wide mouth, and draw out the tongue? are you not children of transgression, a seed of falsehood. (The first phrase of this Verse refers to the fact that this opposition was against God, even though it was directed at the true Prophets [Mat. 25:40]. The "wide mouth" is a statement expressing scorn. The phrase, "A seed of falsehood," refers to the parents who lived a lie and

consequently brought forth a lie, referring to their children! [Prov. 22:6].)

5 Enflaming yourselves with idols under every green tree, slaying the children in the valleys under the clifts of the rocks? (The intent of this Verse is beyond belief! The phrase, "Enflaming yourselves with idols under every green tree," pertains to a practice so despicable that it defies description! The reference is to the "orgiastic cults in the sacred groves of Palestinian heathenism," which was accompanied by every type of immorality.

The passage, "slaying the children in the valleys under the clifts of the rocks," spoke of children offered in sacrifice to the god Moloch. This is how far Judah had fallen!)

6 Among the smooth stones of the stream is your portion; they, they are your lot: even to them have you poured a drink offering, you have offered a meat offering. Should I receive comfort in these? (The question, "Should I receive comfort in these?" actually says, "Shall I endure with patience such cruelties and abominations?" or "Can I, Jehovah, be comforted, when My people indulge in such practices?")

7 Upon a lofty and high mountain have you set your bed: even thither went you up to offer sacrifice. (The word "bed" refers to altars, with sacrifices offered to idols.)

8 Behind the doors also and the posts have you set up your remembrance: for you have discovered yourself to another than Me, and are gone up; you have enlarged your bed, and made you a covenant with them; you loved their bed where you saw it. (The words, "your remembrance," have to do with idolatrous pictures. God commanded His People to put Text of Scripture upon the walls of their rooms. The Hebrews removed these and replaced them with idolatrous emblems, just as today it is the fashion to banish from homes a Bible Text, and instead hang up pictures of the Madonna and child, and ornament the rooms with crosses and crucifixes [Deut. 6:9; 11:20].

The phrase, "You have enlarged your bed," refers to introducing the worship of every false god.

The phrase, "You loved their bed where you saw it," refers to the altars that were set up even in the homes of the people, and even in very conspicuous places. In other words, they paraded their false worship, wanting all to know of their brazen rebellion!)

9 And you went to the king with ointment, and did increase your perfumes, and did send your messengers far off, and did

debase yourself even unto Hell. *(The phrase, "Went to the king," refers to Moloch, which in Hebrew means "the king." This idol was worshipped with ointments and perfumes.*

The phrase, "And did send your messengers far off," refers to ambassadors sent to distant countries to secure the alliance of idolaters and to bring back their idols and set them up in the Temple of God at Jerusalem.

The phrase, "And did debase yourself even unto Hell," refers to taking on the yoke of groveling superstition, which debased them to the lowest point conceivable, with the ultimate destination being "Hell.")

10 You are wearied in the greatness of your way; yet said you not, There is no hope: you have found the life of your hand; therefore you were not grieved. *(Judah, in straying so far from the Lord, and seeking aid from all quarters, seemingly would have been "wearied" with her quest; but she would not confess her weariness, even though it never brought forth any positive results, even as sin and sinners never bring forth positive results.)*

11 And of whom have you been afraid or feared, that you have lied, and have not remembered Me, nor laid it to your heart? have not I held My peace even of old, and you feared Me not? *(The phrase, "And of whom have you been afraid or feared," refers to the fact that Judah feared man, especially Assyria.*

The phrase, "Have not I held My peace," refers to the Lord suffering them to "go on still in their wickedness" — not interposing on them severe judgment. Therefore, they had ceased to fear Him, and had feared men instead!

The phrase, "That you have lied," refers to their professed loyalty to Jehovah, but in fact they did not remember Him, nor heartily record His past Goodness and Power; and they misused His long-continued gentleness in not punishing them.)

12 I will declare your righteousness, and your works; for they shall not profit you. *(The word "declare" refers to the fact that God would expose their hypocritical righteousness and their useless works. He would show that their righteousness, so-called, was in fact unrighteousness.*

The phrase, "For they shall not profit you," refers to the eternal Truth that there is no "profit" in anything other than obedience to God's Word.)

THE PENITENT ARE REFRESHED; NO PEACE FOR THE WICKED

13 When you cry, let your companies deliver you; but the wind shall carry them all away; vanity shall take them: but he who puts his trust in Me shall possess the land, and shall inherit My holy mountain *(in effect, the Holy Spirit uses sarcasm in telling Judah to "cry" to their idol gods, and see if they will deliver her!*

The words, "Let your companies deliver you," refer to the mixture of gods, that if one could not deliver, possibly several could; however, no matter how many gods they produced, all will fail utterly — so utterly, that "the wind," or rather a breath, "shall carry them all away."

Even at this late hour, He says, "he who puts his trust in Me shall possess the land," which means "to inherit the Promises." This corresponds with Christ's great invitation [Mat. 11:28-30]);

14 And shall say, Cast ye up, cast ye up, prepare the way, take up the stumblingblock out of the way of My people. *(The appeal is to the religious leaders of Judah. The Holy Spirit says, "Remove the stumblingblock out of the way of My people." The "stumblingblock" actually was the religious leaders themselves.*

It was not an idle threat! Sadly, they would not repent, and this "stumblingblock" was taken out of the way by Nebuchadnezzar, when he destroyed Jerusalem and the Temple, and took these individuals captive into Babylon.

The same thing happened when Israel rejected Christ. The "stumblingblock" was then removed, and in such a way that Israel would be without a nation, and would wander as outcasts all over the world for nearly 2,000 years.)

15 For thus saith the high and lofty One Who inhabits eternity, Whose Name is Holy; I dwell in the high and holy place, with him also that is of a contrite and humble spirit, to revive the spirit of the humble, and to revive the heart of the contrite ones. *(The phrase, "Who inhabits eternity," refers to the fact that God has lived in all the eternity past — before the ages of time as we know them now [II Pet., Chpt. 3].*

The words, "Whose Name is Holy," refer to God's true Nature.

The Lord condescends to dwell only with those who are "humble" and have a "contrite spirit." To be sure, His Presence is a well of life, springing up within the soul to Everlasting Life [Jn. 4:14].)

16 For I will not contend for ever, neither will I be always wroth: for the spirit should fail before Me, and the souls which I have made. *(The meaning of the Passage is beautiful! The idea given by the Holy Spirit, "For I will not contend forever," refers to God's Anger that quickly abates. If He were "extreme to mark*

what is done amiss," none could abide it [Ps. 130:3]. If it were otherwise, man's "spirit should fail before Me." In other words, man, utterly unable to justify himself, would faint and fade away before the Divine fury. If such were the case, the "souls which He has made" would all fail, and all likewise perish.

Every effort by the Lord is always with patience, love, compassion, gentleness, and kindness. Every effort is made to restore the wayward one!)

17 For the iniquity of his covetousness was I wroth, and smote him: I hid Me, and was wroth, and he went on frowardly in the way of his heart. (The word "covetousness" speaks of idolatry here, but yet idolatry that took a different turn.

The words, "I hid Me and was wroth," refers to the fact that God, in His dealings with Israel, time and time again, did not unleash His full fury when He "smote him," i.e., Israel, but gave many warnings before the final catastrophe.

The "froward" manner speaks of perverseness and wrong-headedness! Such was Judah's "heart" and such was the cause of their downfall.)

18 I have seen his ways, and will heal him: I will lead him also, and restore comforts unto him and to his mourners. (So long as Israel practiced idolatry there was no healing; it is only promised to a Repentance which forsakes sin. The action of the statement, "I have seen his ways, and will heal him," refers to the fact that God, even though seeing the perverse ways of Israel, still had pity on them, and stood ready to heal them the moment they would turn to Him. The Good Shepherd follows and recalls the wanderers of the flock.)

19 I create the fruit of the lips; Peace, peace to him who is far off, and to him who is near, saith the LORD; and I will heal him. (Here God proclaimed "peace" to the Gentiles, who were "far off," and to the Jews, who were "near" [Eph. 2:13-17]. The message of perfect peace is a Divine Message. It is not of human origination or imagination.

When the Lord "heals him," then "the fruit of the lips" will be praise and thanksgiving.)

20 But the wicked are like the troubled sea, when it cannot rest, whose waters cast up mire and dirt. (The statement is: the sea is never at rest; it continually casts up mud and dirt. Therefore, it is a true picture of the enemies of Truth. To these there is, and shall be, no peace.)

21 There is no peace, saith my God, to the wicked. (The Divine Title here is "Elohim,"

not "Jehovah."

"Peace," which God Alone gives, refers to the enmity that has been removed between Him and sinful man, and was done so by and through Christ and what He did for us at the Cross; therefore, this glorious "peace" can only be obtained by the Believer exhibiting Faith in Christ and what Christ did at the Cross [Rom. 6:3-5; I Cor. 1:17-18, 23; 2:2].)

CHAPTER 58

(698 B.C.)

A DESCRIPTION OF TRUE SALVATION

CRY aloud, spare not, lift up your voice like a trumpet, and show My people their transgression, and the house of Jacob their sins. (In this Verse, God directly addresses His People. He begins with the question of sin. Isaiah was commanded to "cry aloud," referring to sin and, thereby, the guilt of Judah. He was to "lift up his voice like a trumpet," which means that he was to speak in no uncertain terms.

Such a message will never be met by approval, and the greatest disapproval of all will come from the religious community; consequently, there are very few whom God can find to deliver such a Message!)

2 Yet they seek Me daily, and delight to know My ways, as a nation that did righteousness, and forsook not the ordinance of their God; they ask of Me the ordinances of justice; they take delight in approaching to God. (The phrase, "Yet they seek Me daily, and delight to know My ways," presents that which is all outward. We have here the representation of people honoring God with their lips, but whose hearts were far from Him.

The phrase, "As a nation that did righteousness," actually speaks of a legal righteousness, which always promotes self-righteousness.

In doing these things, they felt that all requirements were met, and that God delighted in them! The phrases, "They ask of Me the ordinances of justice" and "they take delight in approaching to God," refer to their claim, at God's Hands, of righteous judgments on their enemies. They thought surely He would do so, because of their outward piety!)

3 Wherefore have we fasted, say they, and You see not? wherefore have we afflicted our soul, and You take no knowledge? Behold, in the day of your fast you find pleasure, and exact all your labours. (The fasting spoken of is probably that of the Great Day of Atonement,

the only fasting demanded in the Law, which consisted of only one day [Lev. 16:29, 31].

Actually, the "worshippers" regarded their religious observances as "not merely pleasing to God [which they actually were not], but as laying Him under a binding obligation, and almost compelling Him to grant the requests of the worshipper.")

4 Behold, you fast for strife and debate, and to smite with the fist of wickedness; you shall not fast as you do this day, to make your voice to be heard on high. *(The phrases, "Fast for strife and contention" and "smite with the fist of wickedness," mean to use religion as an instrument for oppression. Pointblank God proclaims that He will not hear such prayer nor honor such a fast. Such endeavors to earn its way with God, which God will never accept.)*

5 Is it such a fast that I have chosen? a day for a man to afflict his soul? is it to bow down his head as a bulrush, and to spread sackcloth and ashes under him? will you call this a fast, and an acceptable day to the LORD? *(The Holy Spirit through Isaiah probes deep here into the hypocrisy of Judah by asking the question, "Is it such a fast that I have chosen?" The Holy Spirit says that the "fast that I have chosen" is a "day for a man to afflict his soul." It is not outward show, but inward inspection!)*

6 Is not this the fast that I have chosen? to loose the bands of wickedness, to undo the heavy burdens, and to let the oppressed go free, and that you break every yoke? *(The Lord was telling Judah through Isaiah that if they really loved Him, and truly desired to serve Him, the ritualistic observances would be secondary to the "weightier matters of the Law," such as "judgment, mercy, and faith" [Mat. 23:23]. Jesus called those who fasted for show "hypocrites"! He was no doubt referring to this very Verse.)*

7 Is it not to deal your bread to the hungry, and that you bring the poor who are cast out to your house? when you see the naked, that you cover him; and that you hide not yourself from your own flesh? *(The phrase, "Hide not yourself from your own flesh," refers to these "ritual keepers," who strictly observed, or thought they did, the Law, while hiding themselves from the hurting, hungry, wounded, and needy. They were so holy, at least in their own eyes, that they could not dirty their hands with such activities.)*

8 Then shall your light break forth as the morning, and your health shall spring forth speedily: and your righteousness shall go before you; the glory of the LORD shall be your

rereward. *(To go God's Way, which is the Way of His Word, brings about a true experience with the Lord, i.e., "then shall your light break forth as the morning."*

In effect, the Lord is saying that prayers will no longer go unanswered, or Covenant Promises left in abeyance.)

9 Then shall you call, and the LORD shall answer; you shall cry, and He shall say, Here I am. If you take away from the midst of you the yoke, the putting forth of the finger, and speaking vanity. *(In these Passages, the Lord pleads with His People, explaining to them, as He would explain such to a child, the reasons their prayers are not answered.*

The phrase, "If you take away from the midst of you the yoke," refers to the ruling class of Judah making virtual slaves out of those who were less privileged.

The phrase, "The putting forth of the finger," speaks of bribery. The officials, by moving their "finger" a certain way, would let certain ones know that they could be bought!

The phrase, "and speaking vanity," rather speaks of plotting evil against others. It spoke primarily of perjury. Truth had fallen in the street!)

10 And if you draw out your soul to the hungry, and satisfy the afflicted soul; then shall your light rise in obscurity, and your darkness be as the noon day. *(The idea of this Passage is that their profession must translate into righteous action, which meant to help the poor and hungry, etc.)*

11 And the LORD shall guide you continually, and satisfy your soul in drought, and make fat your bones: and you shall be like a watered garden, and like a spring of water, whose waters fail not. *(It should be easy to see that the great things promised by the Lord are so much more than the few things that He asks of Judah. It is the same with us today. What little He asks of us is nothing in comparison with what He promises us, and always delivers! And yet, men are loathe to trust Him.)*

12 And they who shall be of you shall build the old waste places: you shall raise up the foundations of many generations; and you shall be called, The repairer of the breach, The restorer of paths to dwell in. *(The "old waste places" refer to that which had been ruined by sin. A revival of the heart will change all of this.*

The phrase, "You shall raise up the foundations of many generations," refers to the fact that all the great Promises of God given in past years will now be brought to pass, because of the

present Move of God.

The phrase, "The repairer of the breach, the restorer of paths to dwell in," proclaims the Preacher directing the people back to the Bible.)

THE OBSERVANCE OF THE SABBATH

13 If you turn away your foot from the sabbath, from doing your pleasure on My holy day; and call the sabbath a delight, the holy of the LORD, honourable, and shall honour him, not doing your own ways, nor finding your own pleasure, nor speaking your own words *(under the Old Covenant, Israel was commanded to keep the seventh day, which was Saturday. It was to be a day of rest rather than so much as a day of worship. Under the New Covenant, Jesus is the True Sabbath; therefore, denying ourselves and following Him, and taking up the Cross daily, constitutes Sabbath-keeping [Mat. 11:28-30])*:

14 Then shall you delight yourself in the LORD; and I will cause you to ride upon the high places of the Earth, and feed you with the heritage of Jacob your Father: for the mouth of the LORD has spoken it. *(The words, "Then shall you delight yourself in the LORD," refer to the Truth that if the relationship is heartfelt instead of ritualistic, communion with Jehovah will be a real pleasure. Blessings will always come to such a one.*

The phrase, "And feed you with the heritage of Jacob your Father," refers to the Truth, as promised by the Holy Spirit, that Israel will ultimately be restored [Rom., Chpt. 11].

The "heritage of Jacob," although long delayed by their own rebellion, will ultimately be realized! Israel will eventually be the premier nation in the world, but only when Christ is received, and Redemption is experienced. This will happen at the Second Coming.

The words, "For the mouth of the LORD has spoken it," is a formula declaring that these Statements and Promises were not originated by the Prophet, but were the utterances of God Himself.)

CHAPTER 59
(698 B.C.)
ISRAEL'S SINS RECOUNTED

BEHOLD, the LORD's hand is not shortened, that it cannot save; neither His ear heavy, that it cannot hear *(the Lord can "do," and the Lord can "hear," and will do such, but only if His People follow His Way)*:

2 But your iniquities have separated between you and your God, and your sins have hid His face from you, that He will not hear. *(The problem is not God's inability to save, or that He cannot hear, but rather that Judah has sinned, which always separates man from God.)*

3 For your hands are defiled with blood, and your fingers with iniquity; your lips have spoken lies, your tongue has muttered perverseness. *(In this Verse and following, the Holy Spirit, in graphic detail, explains exactly what these "iniquities" are!)*

4 None calls for justice, nor any pleads for truth: they trust in vanity, and speak lies; they conceive mischief, and bring forth iniquity. *(The Lord is speaking here of people, who, while ceremonially religious, were morally unrighteous. The idea of the Verse is that the whole basis of dealings between man and man were unsound, corrupt, and chaotic. Where truth and plain dealing are set aside, all shortly become ruin and confusion.)*

5 They hatch cockatrice's eggs, and weave the spider's web: he who eats of their eggs die, and that which is crushed breaks out into a viper. *(The accusation by the Holy Spirit is astonishing here! He uses three dangerous examples to describe the people of Judah. In fact, this one Verse describes the entirety of the world.)*

6 Their webs shall not become garments, neither shall they cover themselves with their works: their works are works of iniquity, and the act of violence is in their hands. *(The idea of this Passage is that evil hearts cannot produce Righteousness. The "act of violence in their hands" refers to the fact that violence creates nothing, and, at best, destroys. And yet, the world is bathed in "violence" [Jn. 10:10].)*

7 Their feet run to evil, and they make haste to shed innocent blood: their thoughts are thoughts of iniquity; wasting and destruction are in their paths. *(Paul quoted this in Rom. 3:15-16. He was speaking of the corruption of the human heart, and how, within itself, it cannot transform itself, neither can it produce Righteousness. Its "feet" can only "run to evil."*

The outline of the human family is given here, as stated, in these Verses. It is the cause of the ills of the world, i.e., the corrupt, evil, wicked hearts of men. It tells us why God does not move nor hear.)

8 The way of peace they know not; and there is no judgment in their goings: they have made them crooked paths: whosoever goes therein shall not know peace. *(This is a*

principle which applies to all periods of human history, thereby resulting in human misery. The subject in this Verse is "peace," because the world does not have such.

The phrase, "And there is no judgment in their goings," refers to the fact that their decisions are faulty, and their "judgment" unsure, resulting in confusion.

The phrase, "They have made them crooked paths," refers to great and elaborate schemes of "peace" based on a rotten foundation, i.e., "crooked paths."

"Peace" is not a philosophy, creed, dogma, theory, or doctrine. It is a Person, and that Person is Christ.)

ISRAEL'S CONFESSION OF SIN

9 Therefore is judgment far from us, neither does justice overtake us: we wait for light, but behold obscurity; for brightness, but we walk in darkness. *(The acceptance of Christ, and only the acceptance of Christ, which refers to the following of His Will and Way, will instantly reverse all these actions, and bring about that which the Lord Alone can give, which is the miraculous! But men, it seems, would desire to continue in "darkness.")*

10 We grope for the wall like the blind, and we grope as if we had no eyes: we stumble at noon day as in the night; we are in desolate places as dead men. *(The Holy Spirit in these Passages is saying about Judah what they would never admit to themselves. It is not that light is wanting, but that they had no eyes to behold it. This speaks of "willful blindness." It is the same type of "blindness" that grips almost all the world.)*

11 We roar all like bears, and mourn sore like doves: we look for judgment, but there is none; for Salvation, but it is far off from us. *(The phrase, "We roar all like bears," uses the same verb that is used commonly of the "roaring" of the sea. It, along with the "dove," represents the constant, never-ending murmur of discontent, sorrow, and unhappiness.*

They look for "judgment" [justice] and "Salvation," but, in order to receive these, do not want to depart from their sins.)

12 For our transgressions are multiplied before you, and our sins testify against us: for our transgressions are with us; and as for our iniquities, we know them *(this Passage illuminates the fact that Israel's blindness of Verse 10 is a willful blindness. The "transgressions are*

multiplied" and yet Judah wanted to continue in them. Even though their "sins testify against them," they do not want to stop their sins. They know what their "transgressions" are, as well as their "iniquities." They emphatically state, "We know them!");

13 In transgressing and lying against the LORD, and departing away from our God, speaking oppression and revolt, conceiving and uttering from the heart words of falsehood. *(In this Scripture, we are told where the trouble lies. It is the "heart"! [Mat. 15:19])*

14 And judgment is turned away backward, and justice stands afar off: for truth is fallen in the street, and equity cannot enter. *(As a consequence, every facet of the person, and even of the entirety of a nation, suffers an inversion. Things are upside down, and consequently do not, and in fact cannot, work right.*

The phrase, "Judgment is turned away backward," refers to Righteousness being out, while unrighteousness is in.)

15 Yea, truth fails; and he who departs from evil makes himself a prey: and the LORD saw it, and it displeased Him that there was no judgment. *("A prey" means a victim of persecution. This fact is true of all ages. The few who are faithful to the doctrinal and moral teaching of God's Word are despised, derided, and persecuted by religious professors, and by the world.*

The word "judgment" means "Righteousness," as in Verse 14.

The words, "Truth fails," should have been translated "Truth is lacking," for Truth never fails.

The phrase, "And the LORD saw it," refers to the lack of justice between man and man. No one thought of pronouncing just judgments. The circumstances were such as to invite a Divine interposition.

Sadly, this evil would rise to such a crescendo that the Lord "Himself" would become "a prey," i.e., be crucified!)

RESTORATION BY THE MESSIAH; MESSIAH'S SECOND ADVENT AND COVENANT

16 And He saw that there was no man, and wondered that there was no intercessor: therefore His arm brought salvation unto him; and His righteousness, it sustained him. *(The entirety of this Passage, down through the final Verse of this Chapter, belongs to the future Second Advent, when the Messiah will appear, clothed with vengeance, to recompense*

tribulation to the adversaries of His Ancient People, but rest to them [II Thess., Chpt. 1].

The phrase, "And He saw that there was no man, and wondered that there was no intercessor," refers to the lack in Judah of spiritual leadership who would occupy the Throne.

The phrase, "Therefore His arm brought Salvation unto him; and His Righteousness, it sustained him," probably refers to Josiah, who, from the time of Isaiah unto Christ, was the only king to occupy the Throne who proclaimed Righteousness [II Chron. 34:2].

It seems that Josiah attempted to be the "intercessor," but the Holy Spirit, in effect, said that Judah had gone too far down the path of sin and evil to be turned around now [II Ki. 23:26].

A short time later, Josiah was killed. The Lord knew that despite Josiah's righteous efforts, Judah would not turn; therefore, the Lord took him out of the way, exactly as Isaiah had prophesied in 57:1.)

17 For He put on righteousness as a breastplate, and an helmet of salvation upon His head; and He put on the garments of vengeance for clothing, and was clad with zeal as a cloak. *(Paul will somewhat speak of this Passage in Eph. 6:10-18. It is strange, yet beautiful, that the Divine panoply takes no offensive weapon, with the exception of the "Spirit of the LORD," as is outlined in Verse 19.*

From Verse 15, commencing with the words, "And Jehovah saw it," and reading to the end of Verse 21, there is the predicted return of the Messiah appearing for the deliverance of Israel, and for the taking of vengeance upon their persecutors. He will do so now, because Israel will repent, which describes the future, and the Second Coming.

The Seventeenth Verse describes Christ in His victorious posture, as the Fifty-third Chapter describes Him in His suffering posture.)

18 According to their deeds, accordingly He will repay, fury to His adversaries, recompence to His enemies; to the islands He will repay recompence. *(This speaks of the defeat of the Antichrist and all of his followers at the Second Coming.)*

19 So shall they fear the name of the LORD from the west, and His glory from the rising of the sun. When the enemy shall come in like a flood, the Spirit of the LORD shall lift up a standard against him. *(The "Standard" is Christ! The "Spirit of the LORD" anointed Christ to set the captive free [Lk. 4:18]. That "Anointing," which could have saved Israel then, and*

has consequently saved tens of millions since then, will now, and finally, save Israel.

As He attempted to proclaim the "acceptable year of the LORD" at His First Advent, and was refused, He will now declare the "acceptable year of the LORD" at His Second Advent, and be accepted.)

20 And the Redeemer shall come to Zion, and unto them who turn from transgression in Jacob, saith the LORD. *(The "Redeemer" is Christ, and He shall "come to Zion." Paul quoted this in Rom. 11:26. All the "transgressions" mentioned in Verse 12 and corresponding Scriptures will now, and finally, be brought to the Redeemer. Then "Jacob" will finally become "Israel, the Prince with God.")*

21 As for Me, this is My Covenant with them, saith the LORD; My Spirit that is upon you, and My Words which I have put in Your mouth, shall not depart out of Your mouth, nor out of the mouth of Your seed, nor out of the mouth of Your seed's seed, saith the LORD, from henceforth and for ever. *(The words, "As for Me," refer to Jehovah speaking, and not Isaiah. This Scripture proclaims the Divine Trinity: 1. The One speaking is Jehovah; 2. The Redeemer is the Messiah; and, 3. My Spirit, i.e., the Holy Spirit, Who is sent by Jehovah, is still yet another Person [Jn. 14:16, 26].*

The words, "My Covenant," refer to the New Testament, i.e., New Covenant, which Israel would not accept the first time, but will now accept!

"My Words" refer to the entirety of the Bible. Israel, even though used by God to bring it into the world, still, never really did abide by it. Now they shall, and it "shall not depart out of your mouth."

As well, the Holy Spirit declares that all succeeding generations will continue to follow the Lord, as referred to by "Your seed's seed." This will all take place during the coming Kingdom Age.)

CHAPTER 60
(698 B.C.)
THE FUTURE GLORY OF ZION

ARISE, shine; for your light is come, and the glory of the LORD is risen upon you. *(The Speaker here is the Holy Spirit; the person spoken to is Israel. The words, "Arise, shine," refer not necessarily to Israel's light, for she has no light; rather she reflects the streams of Light that pour from the Person of Jehovah Whose Name is Christ. This Passage refers back to Psalm 67:1.*

The phrase, "And the glory of the LORD is risen upon you," refers to Israel's Repentance.)

2 For, behold, the darkness shall cover the Earth, and gross darkness the people: but the LORD shall arise upon you, and His glory shall be seen upon you. *(The "darkness" mentioned here speaks of the Great Tribulation, when the Church will have been Raptured away, thereby leaving the world without "Light" [I Thess. 4:13-18]; however, the "darkness" will be expelled by the Coming of the Lord, and the destination of the "Glory" will be Israel.)*

GENTILES WILL WORSHIP ISRAEL'S GOD

3 And the Gentiles shall come to your light, and kings to the brightness of your rising. *(The phrase, "your light," does not mean that such originated with Israel, but is to be poured upon her. Because of this, and it being overly obvious, the nations of the world will come to Israel; however, as always, that "Light" is Christ.)*

4 Lift up your eyes round about, and see: all they gather themselves together, they come to you: your sons shall come from far, and your daughters shall be nursed at your side. *("Your sons" and "your daughters" refer to Israelites still scattered among the nations, and then being gathered back to Judah. As stated, this will take place at the beginning of the Kingdom Age.*

The words, "shall be nursed at your side," speak of the hurts, wounds, suffering, and pains of the last 2,000 and more years. During this time, they have blamed Christ for their troubles. Now they will realize how wrong they were, and be healed of their stubbornness and rebellion, and know that Christ is the Source of their blessing, and not their bondage!)

5 Then you shall see, and flow together, and your heart shall fear, and be enlarged; because the abundance of the sea shall be converted unto you, the forces of the Gentiles shall come unto you. *(The word "fear" should have been translated "rejoice" or "tremble," i.e., "tremble with holy joy." Verses 5 through 7 proclaim the "abundance" of material prosperity that will come to Israel as well.*

The phrase, "The abundance of the sea shall be converted unto you," does not refer to maritime prosperity, but rather to the multitude of "Gentiles," who will show great favor to Israel.)

6 The multitude of camels shall cover you, the dromedaries of Midian and Ephah; all they from Sheba shall come: they shall bring gold and incense; and they shall shew forth the praises of the LORD. *(The phrase, "Multitude of camels," refers to a continual stream of caravans, implying that Jerusalem is not only the center of spiritual Glory, but also of economic power.*

The phrase, "And they shall show forth the Praises of the LORD," tells us that the prosperity of the world is tied to "the Praises of the LORD.")

7 All the flocks of Kedar shall be gathered together unto you, the rams of Nebaioth shall minister unto you: they shall come up with acceptance on My Altar, and I will glorify the house of My Glory. *(The phrase, "And I will glorify the house of My Glory," should read "I will beautify My beautiful house," that is, the palace at Jerusalem, which is to be built. It will be beautiful beyond words!)*

8 Who are these who fly as a cloud, and as the doves to their windows? *(This refers to ships coming from all over the world to Israel, which, as stated, will take place in the coming Kingdom Age.)*

9 Surely the isles shall wait for Me, and the ships of Tarshish first, to bring your sons from far, their silver and their gold with them, unto the name of the LORD your God, and to the Holy One of Israel, because He has glorified you. *(The phrase, "Surely the isles [maritime countries] shall wait for Me," refers to Christ being the focal point of all that is done. Once again, Israel's blessing is totally dependent upon the Lord, as in fact all blessing is totally dependent on the Lord!)*

MILLENNIAL GLORY; GOD'S BLESSINGS

10 And the sons of strangers shall build up your walls, and their kings shall minister unto you: for in My wrath I smote you, but in My favour have I had mercy on you. *(The "sons of strangers" refer to the allegiance of the Gentiles concerning their favor toward Israel. The words, "In My wrath I smote you," refer to Titus, who in A.D. 70 destroyed Jerusalem, killing over one million Jews. From that point on, they were scattered all over the world as outcasts.*

The phrase, "But in My favor have I had mercy on you," strongly implies that the "mercy" was not deserved, and in fact cannot be deserved.)

11 Therefore your gates shall be open continually; they shall not be shut day nor night; that men may bring unto you the forces of the Gentiles, and that their kings may be brought. *(The "forces of the Gentiles" speak of the wealth*

of the Gentiles. The phrase, "And that their kings may be brought," refers to the leaders of nations coming to Israel and actually being forced to come by their subjects, who know that their own prosperity is involved in complete submission to Christ in Zion. They will, therefore, compel their kings to come and render their homage in person, so there will be no doubt about their allegiance!)

12 For the nation and kingdom that will not serve you shall perish; yea, those nations shall be utterly wasted. *(The implication is that some nations and kingdoms possibly will not desire to serve the Lord; however, there will be no opportunity for them to respond. They shall "perish" and "be utterly wasted." How the Lord will do this, regarding these nations, we aren't told; however, to be sure, it will happen exactly as predicted.)*

13 The glory of Lebanon shall come unto you, the fir tree, the pine tree, and the box together, to beautify the place of My sanctuary; and I will make the place of My feet glorious. *(The phrase, "And I will make the place of My feet glorious," refers to Christ literally walking on Earth, and in this beautiful capital building, which will be befitting of His Presence [Ezek. 43:7; Zech. 14:4].)*

14 The sons also of them who afflicted you shall come bending unto you; and all they who despised you shall bow themselves down at the soles of your feet; and they shall call you, The city of the LORD, The Zion of the Holy One of Israel. *(The phrase, "Of them who afflicted you," concerns the nations of the world that have grandly opposed Israel; however, those nations "shall come bending unto you." The phrase, "At the soles of your feet," guarantees total submission; however, it will not be a forced submission, but a voluntary submission!*

The last phrase refers to the enemies of Jerusalem, which once bestowed disparaging names on her, such as "forsaken" or "desolate." Now they will substitute for such names titles of honor, such as "City of Jehovah" and "Zion of Israel's Holy One." In fact, the "Holy One" is the cause of all blessing and prosperity!)

15 Whereas you have been forsaken and hated, so that no man went through you, I will make you an eternal excellency, a joy of many generations. *(Israel has been "hated" from her very beginning in the days of Abraham, because of animosity against the Lord. Tragically, the True Israel, i.e., Christ, was "hated" upon His First Advent; however, all of this will change in the coming Kingdom Age.)*

16 You shall also suck the milk of the Gentiles, and shall suck the breast of kings: and you shall know that I the LORD am your Saviour and your Redeemer, the Mighty One of Jacob. *(The phrase, "Suck the milk of the Gentiles," refers to a continual stream of material sustenance to help in the restoration of Jerusalem and all of Israel, and to carry on the universal missionary program of the Millennium [Zech. 8:12].*

The continuous emphasis by the Holy Spirit relates Israel's blessings to "the LORD your Saviour." This is the Lord Jesus Christ, "your Redeemer." Only He can redeem!)

17 For brass I will bring gold, and for iron I will bring silver, and for wood brass, and for stones iron: I will also make your officers peace, and your exactors righteousness. *(The material splendor throughout the whole description is, no doubt, typical in the main of spiritual glories and excellencies, as well.*

The phrase, "I will also make your officers peace, and your exactors righteousness," refers to the rulers of Israel, who will be officers of peace, and the tax collectors, who will be honest, equitable, and righteous.)

18 Violence shall no more be heard in your land, wasting nor destruction within your borders; but you shall call your walls Salvation, and your gates Praise. *(The entire cessation of war and violence is one of the most characteristic features of the Kingdom Age, when swords shall be beaten into plowshares and spears into pruninghooks. "The Prince of Peace" shall ultimately establish peace.*

"Your Land" refers to Israel. It is emphasized because it has known nothing but war almost from its very beginning. Only during the times of Solomon did it know peace, because Solomon was a Type of Christ, and the Israel of that day, a type of the coming Kingdom Age.

During that coming time, even the very walls will be called "Salvation," and the gates "Praise," because of such perfect conditions.)

19 The sun shall be no more your light by day; neither for brightness shall the moon give light unto you: but the LORD shall be unto you an everlasting light, and your God your glory. *(The splendor of such will make Jerusalem the joy of the whole world. While the "sun" and "moon" will continue to shine as always, still, the Glory of the Lord will be of such magnificence that the light of those orbs will go unnoticed!)*

20 Your sun shall no more go down; neither shall your moon withdraw itself: for the LORD shall be your Everlasting Light, and the days of your mourning shall be ended. (*The phrase, "Your sun shall no more go down," does not mean that the rotation of the Earth will cease, but rather that its rising and its setting will not be noticed at all, due to the Glory of God filling the city with light both day and night. As well, this "Light" will be an "Everlasting Light."*

The phrase, "And the days of your mourning shall be ended," means exactly what it says!)

21 Your people also shall be all righteous: they shall inherit the land for ever, the branch of My planting, the work of My hands, that I may be glorified. (*The reason for the suffering being ended is because "your people also shall be all righteous." Now, the Land that was promised to Abraham in the beginning will be theirs "forever." It is called "the branch of My planting, the Work of My Hands." Their full occupation of it, with His Blessings, will also bless the entirety of the world.*

All of this will "glorify the Lord," because it proclaims His Word coming to pass in totality.)

22 A little one shall become a thousand, and a small one a strong nation: I the LORD will hasten it in His time. (*The "little one" refers to the "little flock" who will ultimately inherit the Kingdom [Lk. 12:32]. This "little one" will grow into a countless multitude [Rev. 7:9]. The phrase, "In His time," refers to the fixed time in God's Counsels for the final establishment of Christ's Kingdom. If it is to be noticed, it doesn't say "in our time," but rather "in His time," meaning that "the times and the seasons are in the Power of the Father," and not in the power of the Church, etc. [Acts 1:6-7].*)

CHAPTER 61
(698 B.C.)
MESSIAH'S FIRST ADVENT

THE Spirit of the Lord GOD is upon Me; because the LORD has anointed Me to preach good tidings unto the meek; He has sent Me to bind up the brokenhearted, to proclaim liberty to the captives, and the opening of the prison to them who are bound (*the first nine Verses of this Chapter present the Messiah and His People. Actually, the Speaker in Verse 1 is the Messiah Himself, as He proclaims His First and Second Comings. That the Speaker is the Messiah is proved by Lk. 4:16-21.*

The "Anointing" of Jesus was the Sanctification

of His human nature by the Holy Spirit, which commenced in the womb of the Blessed Virgin [Lk. 1:35], which continued as He grew to manhood [Lk. 2:40, 52], which was openly manifested at His Baptism, and never ceased till He took His Glorified Body and Soul to Heaven.

That which the Father anointed Him to do addressed itself to every aspect of life and living. In Truth, Christ Alone can address these problems, which means that humanistic psychology holds no answers);

2 To proclaim the acceptable year of the LORD, and the day of vengeance of our God; to comfort all who mourn (*this is the Year of Jubilee, as proclaimed in Lev. 25:9. Such was brought about every Fiftieth year, according to the Law of Moses. Scholars point out that the reading of this Verse by the Lord in the Synagogue of Nazareth took place on the first Sabbath of the Year of Jubilee.*

The year of "acceptance" contrasts with the day of "vengeance." Nearly 2,000 years have already intervened between this "year" and that "day," though only separated by a comma in the Text.

The Lord, when reading these Verses at Nazareth, stopped in the middle of the second line, and did not go on to read "of the day of vengeance." Thus, He rightly divided the Word of Truth; for the year of acceptance is the present period of Grace connected with His First Coming, and the "day of vengeance," the future day of Wrath connected with His Second Coming. Hence, "He closed the Book," on reaching the Name "Jehovah."

At His Second Coming, He will truly "comfort all who mourn," respecting Israel, who has finally come home to Him [Zech. 12:11-14]);

MESSIAH'S SECOND ADVENT; ZION, WASTEPLACES REBUILT

3 To appoint unto them who mourn in Zion, to give unto them beauty for ashes, the oil of joy for mourning, the garment of praise for the spirit of heaviness; that they might be called trees of righteousness, the planting of the LORD, that He might be glorified. (*"Beauty" refers to a nuptial crown. Wood ashes placed upon the head expressed mourning, a nuptial garland signified gladness. The "trees" of this Verse are the redeemed of 60:21. It should be noticed that no praise is to be given to the beauteous trees, but all praise will be given to their wondrous Planter.*

All of this will come to Israel on that coming

Glad Day, which in fact they could have had 2,000 years ago, had they only accepted Christ.)

4 And they shall build the old wastes, they shall raise up the former desolations, and they shall repair the waste cities, the desolations of many generations. *(To assure the reality of these statements, they are repeated. Thus, the first and third lines of the Verse predict the rebuilding of the deserted cities, and the second and fourth lines foretell the fertility of the desolate fields.*

Such speaks of the coming Kingdom Age, and in a literal and material sense, but even more so speaks of the spiritual rejuvenation that takes place in the hearts and lives of Believers.

The words, "build," "raise," and "repair," are used to signify the material resurgence, but even more so, the spiritual renewal in the life of the Believer.

The words, "waste" and "desolations," characterize the unbeliever.)

5 And strangers shall stand and feed your flocks, and the sons of the alien shall be your plowmen and your vinedressers. *(To the proud nations of the past and present, it was, and is, a degradation to be associated thus with the Jew; but in the future it will be an honor, but only because of Israel's acceptance of Christ.)*

6 But you shall be named the Priests of the LORD: men shall call you the Ministers of our God: you shall eat the riches of the Gentiles, and in their glory shall you boast yourselves. *(In that day of Restoration, the entire nation of Israel will be a nation of Priests and Ministers, and will act as such in relation to God and the inhabited world. Actually, what God intended for Israel to be at the beginning, they shall now be! [Ex. 19:6]. In brief, Ezekiel proclaims this in the last nine Chapters of his Book.)*

7 For your shame you shall have double; and for confusion they shall rejoice in their portion: therefore in their land they shall possess the double: everlasting joy shall be unto them. *("Possessing the double" pertained to the following:*

In ancient times, if someone in Israel went bankrupt, they were to list all their indebtedness on a skin, and have it posted in a conspicuous place for all to see. At times, a wealthy benefactor would come to the rescue and pay all the indebtedness. He would take down the skin, double it over, hence hiding all of the indebtedness, and then write his name on the front. He would post it as well in a conspicuous place, and all could come to him for payment.

When Jesus died on the Cross, He atoned for all sin. Upon Faith in Him, He took down the list of all our sins, doubled it over, where these sins could no longer be seen, and wrote His Name on the front, meaning that all the indebtedness was settled; therefore, every single Believer in the world has the privilege of "possessing the double.")

8 For I the LORD love judgment, I hate robbery for Burnt Offering; and I will direct their work in Truth, and I will make an Everlasting Covenant with them. *(The word "judgment" here is "justice." Hence, the Lord loves fairness, equality, correct measures, honesty, integrity, truthfulness, and rightness. The phrase, "I hate robbery for Burnt Offering," refers to nations that robbed Israel of her status and thereby stopped the "Burnt Offerings," which typified Calvary.*

The phrase, "And I will direct their work in Truth," refers to the Lord directing the work, and it, thereby, being guaranteed of Truth. The phrase also means "as they have been wronged, they shall be righted; they shall be faithfully and exactly compensated for what they have suffered." As they have "Everlasting Joy," they now also have an "Everlasting Covenant.")

9 And their seed shall be known among the Gentiles, and their offspring among the people: all who see them shall acknowledge them, that they are the seed which the LORD has blessed. *(In that day, the restored sons of Jacob will be a testimony to the moral glory of the Messiah. The "Seed" actually refers to Christ [Gal. 3:16]. The phrase, "The seed which the LORD has blessed," unequivocally states that one cannot be blessed without Christ. Even in redeemed men, it is Christ within men Who is blessed!)*

HYMN OF PRAISE TO GOD

10 I will greatly rejoice in the LORD, My soul shall be joyful in My God; for He has clothed Me with the garments of salvation, He has covered Me with the robe of righteousness, as a bridegroom decks himself with ornaments, and as a bride adorns herself with her jewels. *(This speaks of Christ and His ornamentation by the Father. In the Incarnation, He lived as a Peasant, and was despised and rejected of men; still, the Lord has blessed this "Seed," and has made His "soul to be joyful in His God."*

All of this tells us that "Salvation and Righteousness" belong strictly to Christ.

Whereas He was formerly "decked" with the "form of a servant" [Phil. 2:7], now He is "decked" with "Ornaments and Jewels." These "Jewels" are the Church [Mal. 3:17].

These "Jewels" are strictly "Ornaments," and, as such, are not actually needed by the Messiah, and in fact add no beauty to Him, but He rather adds beauty to them.

So, He decks and adorns Himself with that which He does not need, not in order that it beautify Him, but rather that He beautify us! His Name truly is Wonderful!)

11 For as the Earth brings forth her bud, and as the garden causes the things that are sown in it to spring forth; so the Lord GOD will cause righteousness and praise to spring forth before all the nations. *("Adonai-Jehovah" will introduce a government which will evoke praise. Until then, all man's efforts to set up a praise-worthy rule in the Earth will be fruitless. At the present, wickedness, blasphemy, profanity, and vulgarity spring forth from the nations; however, this will soon change! Ultimately and even-tually, "everything that has breath will praise the LORD" [Ps. 150:6].)*

CHAPTER 62
(698 B.C.)
THE RESTORATION OF ZION
AND ITS GLORY

FOR Zion's sake will I not hold My peace, and for Jerusalem's sake I will not rest, until the righteousness thereof go forth as brightness, and the salvation thereof as a lamp that burns. *(The Speaker in this Chapter is the Messiah; in Verses 1 through 9, He speaks to Israel; in Verses 10 through 12, to the nations of the world. He is a faithful High Priest. He pleads unceasingly for His People, and is, at the same time, their Righteousness and their Salva-tion. If it is to be noticed, Zion, Jerusalem, and Judah are the ones around which all Prophecy revolves. Washington, London, or any other city are not referred to in these predictions.*

The phrase, "For Zion's sake will I not hold My peace," implies that in the past God has kept silent. The nations of the world have been al-lowed to continue their oppression unchecked; however, this will now change. He will do it "for Jerusalem's sake.")

2 And the Gentiles shall see Your Righ-teousness, and all kings Your Glory: and you shall be called by a new name, which the Mouth of the LORD shall name. *(The entirety*

of the world, i.e., the Gentiles, shall easily "see your Righteousness." Instead of the "kings" re-belling against it, they will rather accept it, and, thereby, rejoice in it! What they will see will be the Righteousness and Glory of Israel's High Priest, the Lord Jesus Christ.

The "new name" that will be given will be "Hephzibah," which means "delight" or "in whom is My delight." This "name" is given to her by the "mouth of the LORD," and not man.)

3 You shall also be a Crown of Glory in the Hand of the LORD, and a royal diadem in the Hand of Your God. *(This Divine Priest can transform defiled and degraded sinners into royal diadems and crowns of glory. In that day, the Lord will exhibit Israel to an admiring world, as a man might exhibit a "crown" or "diadem," which he held in his hand.)*

4 You shall no more be termed Forsaken; neither shall your land any more be termed Desolate: but you shall be called Hephzibah, and your land Beulah: for the LORD delights in you, and your land shall be married. *(The phrase, "You shall no more be termed Forsaken," refers to the fact that Judah had believed herself "forsaken" of God, and had actually been, in a certain sense, forsaken "for a small moment" [54:7]. Her enemies, it would seem, had gone so far as to give her this name in derision.*

"You shall be called Hephzibah" was the name of Hezekiah's Queen, Manasseh's mother [II Ki. 21:1]. The meaning is this:

As Hezekiah's wife mothered evil Manasseh, not necessarily through any fault of her own, with this boy ultimately inspired by Satan in order to sully the coming Promise, the Holy Spirit through the Prophecy of Isaiah proclaims the certitude of Righteousness prevailing, and not evil, as was symbolized in Manasseh.

Beautifully enough, Manasseh, "when he was in affliction," humbled himself before the Lord and repented; therefore, he symbolized Jerusa-lem, which would go into great evil, but which would come back to God and be restored to great-ness and glory.)

5 For as a young man marries a virgin, so shall your sons marry you: and as the bride-groom rejoices over the bride, so shall your God rejoice over you. *(By changing the vowel points [which are not inspired] in the Hebrew Text of the phrase, "your sons," it would read "your builders," i.e., the plural of majesty for "your Restorer." Thus, the correspondence with the Name of God in the last line would be pre-served. To be sure, He will definitely be the*

Restorer of Jerusalem and, in essence, be said to marry her.)

6 I have set watchmen upon your walls, O Jerusalem, which shall never hold their peace day nor night: you who make mention of the LORD, keep not silence. *(The "watchmen" addressed here can refer to either "Prophets" or "Priests," or even "Angelic Beings." They were to keep perpetual watch, and not hold their peace, but continually cry out until the full restoration of Jerusalem would take place.*

Concerning every Promise of God, every Believer should do the same.)

7 And give Him no rest, till He establish, and till He make Jerusalem a praise in the Earth. *(Faithful watchmen upon the walls of an eastern city keep calling out day and night all matters of interest or of danger. The figure expresses the watchful love and care of Immanuel, and those in fellowship with Him, for His oppressed People.*

The idea is not that the Lord forgets, or that we have to badger Him to bring forth results, but is designed accordingly that our faith may be strengthened.)

8 The LORD has sworn by His right hand, and by the arm of His strength, Surely I will no more give your corn to be meat for your enemies; and the sons of the stranger shall not drink your wine, for the which you have laboured *(the phrase, "The LORD has sworn," is strong indeed! God solemnly binds Himself by an oath to come to the relief of His People, to restore them to their own land, and to give them the enjoyment of its fruits in peace.*

The phrase, "By His Right Hand, and by the Arm of His Strength," is employed nowhere else in Scripture. God swears "by Himself," because He can swear by no greater than Himself. The "hand and arm" were emblems of His Power to act. This great Promise has behind it the surety of God's Power to carry out what He has promised. No Promise could be greater!):

9 But they who have gathered it shall eat it, and praise the LORD; and they who have brought it together shall drink it in the courts of My holiness. *(The idea is that the enemy will not "eat it," but that the Child of God will enjoy the increase of his labor. He will do it, "praising the LORD." This implies fellowship and communion restored, which can only be done upon proper Repentance.)*

10 Go through, go through the gates; prepare ye the way of the people; cast up, cast up the highway; gather out the stones; lift up a Standard for the people. *(This Passage, looking forward to the future, concerns itself with the Second Coming of the Lord. The statement, "Go through, go through the gates," refers to Israel coming back to the Holy Land, after the Second Coming of Christ, and then filling Jerusalem.*

The phrase, "Cast up, cast up the highway," refers to a way being made for Jews to come back from all over the world. Every hindrance is to be removed, hence the phrase, "gather out the stones." All of this is being done because of the last line of this Verse, "lift up a Standard for the people." That "Standard" is Christ! They are coming solely because of Him, and every Blessing, as well, is because of Him, i.e., Christ.)

11 Behold, the LORD has proclaimed unto the end of the world, Say ye to the daughter of Zion, Behold, your salvation comes; behold, His reward is with Him, and His work before Him. *(Zion's "Salvation" is Jehovah. He will return to her bringing both rewards and recompenses with Him — rewards for those who love Him, and recompenses for those who hate Him [II Thess., Chpt. 1].)*

12 And they shall call them, The holy people, The redeemed of the LORD: and you shall be called, Sought out, A city not forsaken. *(All of this speaks of the coming Kingdom Age, when Christ will reign supreme, with Israel having accepted Him, not only as their Saviour, but as their Messiah. As a result, all over the world they will be called "The holy people, The redeemed of the LORD."*

The phrase, "A city not forsaken," characterizes the Jerusalem of so many centuries. It was "forsaken" by God, because Jerusalem had forsaken Him! Now they have accepted Him; therefore, it is "A city not forsaken," meaning that God has placed His approval upon it, by making it the capital of planet Earth, and the domicile of the Saviour.)

CHAPTER 63
(698 B.C.)
MESSIAH'S SECOND ADVENT: VENGEANCE ON ISRAEL'S ENEMIES

WHO is this Who comes from Edom, with dyed garments from Bozrah? He Who is glorious in His apparel, travelling in the greatness of His strength? I Who speak in Righteousness, mighty to save. *(The question, "Who is this Who comes from Edom?" refers to Christ. This pertains to the Second Coming, with the*

description in Verses 1 through 6 pertaining to the Battle of Armageddon.

Some have thought that this Vision, concerning the garments dyed with blood, is descriptive of Christ as Saviour; however, this Vision, as the language states, concerns vengeance, which is the opposite of Grace, and it belongs to His future Second Coming in Judgment.)

2 Wherefore are You red in your apparel, and Your garments like him who treads in the winefat? *(The phrase, "And Your garments like him who treads in the winefat," has to do with one in olden times who treaded down grapes, and, therefore, had his garments splattered with the juice. Such typifies what Christ will do at Armageddon.)*

3 I have trodden the winepress alone; and of the people there was none with Me: for I will tread them in My anger, and trample them in My fury; and their blood shall be sprinkled upon My garments, and I will stain all My raiment. *(The "winepress" speaks of the terrible carnage and bloodletting at Armageddon. Quite possibly millions will die at this particular time.*

The phrase, "And of the people there was none with Me," refers to the nations of the world, which had joined in opposition to Israel in favor of the Antichrist. None sided with Israel, i.e., Christ. Consequently, He "will tread them in My anger, and trample them in My fury.")

4 For the day of vengeance is in My heart, and the year of My redeemed is come. *(This is the time that the Lord will once again, as Zechariah prophesied, "fight against those nations as when He fought in the day of battle" [Zech. 14:3]. As well, this will be the time of Israel's restoration.)*

5 And I looked, and there was none to help; and I wondered that there was none to uphold: therefore My Own arm brought salvation unto Me; and My fury, it upheld Me. *(Those who had no helper and no upholder are the sons of Jacob, who, at the time of Messiah's Second Coming, will be suffering most cruel persecution. However, the Lord will come back in Power and Glory — in fact, such Power and Glory as the world has never seen before. Consequently, He will bring victory to His chosen People.)*

6 And I will tread down the people in My anger, and make them drunk in My fury, and I will bring down their strength to the Earth. *(The phrase, "The people," should have been translated "the nations." The destruction is to be so complete that it will be absolutely and utterly overwhelming. There will be no recovery for the*

Antichrist and those who follow him. They will all be destroyed!)*

GOD'S FAVOR SHOWN ISRAEL; PRAISE FOR PAST BLESSINGS

7 I will mention the lovingkindnesses of the LORD, and the praises of the LORD, according to all that the LORD has bestowed on us, and the great goodness toward the house of Israel, which He has bestowed on them according to His mercies, and according to the multitude of His lovingkindnesses. *(As praise for present blessings followed the First Advent [61:1-11], so praise for past blessings [Vss. 7-14] here follows the Second Advent, and rightly so!)*

8 For He said, Surely they are My people, children who will not lie: so He was their Saviour. *(This harks back to the deliverance of the Children of Israel from Egyptian bondage. The Lord at that time was their Saviour.)*

9 In all their affliction He was afflicted, and the Angel of His Presence saved them: in His love and in His pity He redeemed them; and He bore them, and carried them all the days of old. *(The phrase, "the Angel of His Presence," occurs nowhere but in this place. It is probably equivalent to "the Angel of God" [Ex. 19:19; Judg. 15:6; Acts 27:23]. It either designates the Second Person of the Trinity, or the highest of the Angelic company, who seems, at least in this instance, to be the Archangel Michael.*

Such refers not only to their deliverance from Egypt, but their preservation in the wilderness.)

10 But they rebelled, and vexed His Holy Spirit: therefore He was turned to be their enemy, and He fought against them. *(Any rebellion against the Lord or His Word always, and without fail, "vexes the Holy Spirit," without Whom we simply cannot succeed or survive.*

The phrase, "Therefore He was turned to be their enemy," was brought about because of Israel's sin and rebellion. Consequently, "He fought against them," which is a sad state of affairs, to say the least! The Lord, Who desired to fight for them, was forced to fight against them.)

11 Then He remembered the days of old, Moses, and His people, saying, Where is He Who brought them up out of the sea with the shepherd of His flock? where is He Who put his Holy Spirit within him? *(The scene now changes from the ancient deliverance of Israel to the coming Battle of Armageddon. Then the Lord will "remember the days of old." He will*

remember His Covenants and deal with them again [Lev. 26:33-43; Deut. 30:1-10].)

12 Who led them by the right hand of Moses with His glorious arm, dividing the water before them, to make Himself an Everlasting Name? (This speaks of the mighty miracle of the opening of the Red Sea, which the Lord now once again calls to account.

The phrase, "To make Himself an Everlasting Name," is one of the main purposes of the entire series of miracles wrought in Egypt: "that God's Name might be declared throughout all the Earth" [Ex. 9:16].)

13 Who led them through the deep, as an horse in the wilderness, that they should not stumble? (What a sight this must have been! Some 5 to 6 million people coming through this created path, with a wall of water standing up on either side of them, and the way so smooth that not one of them "should stumble.")

14 As a beast goes down into the valley, the Spirit of the LORD caused him to rest: so did You lead Your people, to make Yourself a glorious name. (The Glory of all these past blessings is ascribed not to Israel, but to Israel's Great Shepherd — all to make Himself "a Glorious Name," not for egotistical or selfish purposes, but that men throughout the Earth may know that all Blessings and Deliverance come from God, and from God Alone!)

PRAYER FOR DELIVERANCE

15 Look down from Heaven, and behold from the habitation of Your holiness and of Your glory: where is Your zeal and Your strength, the sounding of Your bowels and of Your mercies toward me? are they restrained? (This prayer, in effect, will be prayed by Israel, or rather the Believing Remnant of Israel, prior to the Second Coming.

The faith, attachment, and anguish of the prayer are most effecting, and are made the more so by the way in which the Holy Spirit lends Himself to the feelings of a dependent and desolate heart, recalling past blessings, expressing present distress, acknowledging sin and the justice of God's judicial blinding, but pleading for Deliverance, not because of the Repentance and Faith of the supplicants, but nevertheless required, but because of the election of God and the immutability of His Nature.)

16 Doubtless You are our Father, though Abraham be ignorant of us, and Israel acknowledge us not: You, O LORD, are our Father, our Redeemer; Your name is from everlasting. (The Pharisee based his expectation of Salvation upon his relation to Abraham, but the spiritual Israelite bases his upon his relation to God. When facing Christ at His First Advent, they boasted that they were children of Abraham [Jn. 8:39]. Now at the eve of His Second Advent, they boast no more, but rather confess that Abraham would not even own them, i.e., "be ignorant of us."

They now admit that Israel, i.e., Jacob, would not even "acknowledge them."

The phrase, "Doubtless You are our Father," rather says, "If You will not be our Father, then we have no Father!" This is the ground of their appeal to God. They acknowledge that their ancient relationship to Abraham and Jacob cannot redeem them. If the Lord does not claim them and redeem them, they are eternally lost!)

17 O LORD, why have You made us to err from Your ways, and hardened our heart from Your fear? Return for Your servants' sake, the tribes of Your inheritance. (This Verse should read: "O Jehovah, why have You suffered us to err from Your Ways? And why have You let us harden our hearts to Your fear?" Thus, true Repentance confesses that God justly gives men over to a hardened heart when they resist His Will. At the same time, faith holds to it that the Tribes of Jacob were God's inheritance and His holy people.

The phrase, "Hardened our heart from Your fear," refers to the fact that when men have scornfully and obstinately rejected the Grace of God, God withdraws it from them judicially, giving them up to their wanderings, which makes their heart incapable of faith.

The phrase, "Return for Your servants' sake," speaks of humility, and no longer of a hardened heart.)

18 The people of Your holiness have possessed it but a little while: our adversaries have trodden down Your Sanctuary. (The great "inheritance" that God gave unto His People was "possessed by them only a little while." As a result of their sin, "our adversaries have trodden down Your Sanctuary." They are referring to the destruction by Nebuchadnezzar and by Titus, the Roman General. But more than all they are speaking of the Antichrist, whom they erroneously thought was the Messiah, but who turned on them and did "trod down their Sanctuary" [Dan. 9:27].)

19 We are Yours: You never bore rule over them; they were not called by Your name.

(There is no "Thine" [Yours] in the original, and so important a word could not possibly be supplied from without. Therefore, the translation should read, "We are as those over whom You have not ruled from of old, as those upon whom Your Name has not been called; i.e., we have lost all our privileges — we have become in God's sight no better than the heathen — He has forgotten that we were ever His People.")

CHAPTER 64

(698 B.C.)

A PRAYER FOR HELP AGAINST THEIR ENEMIES

OH that You would rend the Heavens, that You would come down, that the mountains might flow down at Your presence *(in this Chapter, Israel's prayer continues and concludes. As she asks the Lord to look upon them once more with favor, Israel now asks for a manifestation of the Divine Presence, such as they have experienced in the times of old, and such as shall suffice to strike terror into the hearts of their enemies. Their prayer will be answered!),*

2 As when the melting fire burns, the fire causes the waters to boil, to make Your name known to Your adversaries, that the nations may tremble at Your presence! *(His Coming, as described in Rev., Chpt. 19, will be so cataclysmic in nature, so powerful in actual fact, with such a sure defeat of God's enemies, that "His Name will surely be known to His adversaries." Truly, "the nations will tremble at His Presence!")*

3 When You did terrible things which we looked not for, You came down, the mountains flowed down at Your presence. *(The inference is that God did exceedingly more than Israel ever dreamed He would do, respecting their deliverance from Egypt. His actions transcended their utmost expectations.)*

4 For since the beginning of the world men have not heard, nor perceived by the ear, neither has the eye seen, O God, beside You, what He has prepared for him who waits for Him. *(The Apostle Paul, in I Cor. 2:9, alludes to this Verse and states that, under the Second Covenant, the wonders prepared for Believers are revealed. Here Faith declares that neither has the eye seen, nor the ear heard of, a God doing such wonders as the God of Israel did.*

In Israel's prayer, and at a most destitute time, such pleadings proclaim Israel's return to God and the Bible. Now Faith begins to come forth, Faith that was lacking upon the First Advent.)

5 You meet him who rejoices and works righteousness, those who remember You in Your ways: behold, You are wroth; for we have sinned: in those is continuance, and we shall be saved. *(The provisions of the Gospel, "prepared" under the First Covenant and "revealed" under the Second Covenant, are foreshadowed in this Verse. God's Way of pardoning and justifying the sinner is opposed to man's way. First, there is the belief of His Revelation respecting sin and its eternal doom, and then the acceptance of the atoning Saviour, Who said, "I am the Way." Such is the Salvation afforded by Christ, and such is the only Salvation that saves!)*

CONFESSION OF SIN

6 But we are all as an unclean thing, and all our righteousnesses are as filthy rags; and we all do fade as a leaf; and our iniquities, like the wind, have taken us away. *(Here Israel confesses the reason for their desperate condition. At long last, they own up as to exactly what it is, "our iniquities."*

The phrase, "But we are all as an unclean thing," is actually saying before God that they are a spiritual leper. They now recognize that their self-righteousness is no more than "filthy rags," which refer to the menstrual flux of a woman regarding her monthly period.

It is very difficult for men, and especially religious men, to admit to such! Hence, not many religious men are saved!)

7 And there is none who calls upon Your name, who stirs up himself to take hold of You: for You have hid Your face from us, and have consumed us, because of our iniquities. *(Once again, Israel admits that it is her "iniquities" which have brought about the judgment of God upon her. She has only herself to blame!)*

8 But now, O LORD, you are our Father; we are the clay, and You our potter; and we all are the work of Your hand. *(In this Passage is the gist of the great Salvation Message of Christianity. Only God can change the shape of the clay, thereby molding the vessel into the shape and design that is desired, thereby mending the flaws and weaknesses.)*

9 Be not wroth very sore, O LORD, neither remember iniquity for ever: behold, see, we beseech You, we are all Your people. *(The appeal here is for God to begin all over again, like the potter with the clay. The idea of the phrase, "Be not wroth very sore," refers to the fact that God had become very angry with His People.*

The reason for that anger was sin on the part of Israel. God cannot abide sin in the lives of His Own People any more than He can in the wicked.)

10 Your holy cities are a wilderness, Zion is a wilderness, Jerusalem a desolation. *(As we have stated, the entirety of this prayer of Repentance, which began in the Fifteenth Verse of the previous Chapter, will be prayed by Israel at the end of the Great Tribulation — at the Second Advent of Christ.)*

11 Our holy and our beautiful house, where our fathers praised You, is burned up with fire: and all our pleasant things are laid waste. *(This speaks of the Temple that is yet to be built in Jerusalem. In fact, when the Antichrist turns on Israel, he will make their Temple his religious headquarters, committing every act of vileness that one could think.)*

12 Will You refrain Yourself for these things, O LORD? will You hold Your peace, and afflict us very sore? *(Israel first repents of her terrible sins, pleading God's Mercy, Grace, and Love. They then bring to His attention the terrible plight of the "holy cities," and of "Jerusalem." Last of all, they proclaim to Him the destruction of the Temple.*

They then ask, "Will You refrain Yourself for these things, O LORD?"

The answer is certain. He will not refrain Himself! He will not hold His peace!)

CHAPTER 65
(698 B.C.)

GOD'S PROPHETIC ANSWER:
A REVIEW OF ISRAEL

I am sought of them who asked not for Me; I am found of them who sought Me not: I said, Behold Me, behold Me, unto a nation that was not called by My name. *(The phrase, "I am sought of them who asked not for Me," refers to the Gentiles coming to Christ and the establishment of the Church, when Israel crucified her Saviour.*

The phrase, "Behold Me, behold Me," refers to the Call of God to the Gentiles. The Apostle Paul, called "the Apostle to the Gentiles," was used by God signally in this great prophetic Plan [Rom 11:13].

The phrase, "To a nation that was not called by My Name," refers to all except Israel. At that time, the only nation in the world that was called by His Name was Israel. Now, there are many nations that are called by His Name!)

2 I have spread out My hands all the day

unto a rebellious people, which walks in a way that was not good, after their own thoughts *(even though the Lord will give Israel great Promises in His Answer to them, nevertheless, He takes this occasion to once again remind them of the terrible sin they have committed. He calls them "a rebellious people."*

The "spreading out of His Hands" was a longing, kind appeal to them to mend their ways. In effect, He is saying to them that the cause of their troubles was not His lack of attention toward them, but because they "walked in a way that was not good, after their own thoughts");

3 A people who provokes Me to anger continually to My face; who sacrifices in gardens, and burns incense upon altars of brick *(although Israel during the time of Christ had outwardly rejected idolatry, yet that evil spirit had returned to its garnished house, bringing other spirits worse than itself and, hence, Stephen charged them, as does the Prophet in this Chapter, with being not only Christ-rejecters, but idolaters [Acts 7:51-53]. They did all of this in the "face" of God, as all sin is performed in the "face" of God, in defiance of Him!):*

4 Which remain among the graves, and lodge in the monuments, which eat swine's flesh, and broth of abominable things is in their vessels *(when people who have once known God rebel against Him, and go their own way, the spiritual depths to which they sink, even as Israel of old, are worse than any);*

5 Which say, Stand by yourself, come not near to me; for I am holier than you. These are a smoke in My nose, a fire that burns all the day. *(Israel's initiation into heathen mysteries was thought to confer on the initiated a holiness unattainable otherwise. Thus, the heathenized Jew claimed to be holier than the true servants of Jehovah.*

In effect, the Lord says this is repugnant to Him. Their sin was like "smoke in My nose," caused by a fire that "burns all the day," sending up its offensive odor.)

6 Behold, it is written before Me: I will not keep silence, but will recompense, even recompense into their bosom. *(The implication is that the Book lies open "before Him," so that their sin is ever in His sight. He would "recompense" accordingly!*

As well, it would be a personal "recompense," even "into their bosom.")

7 Your iniquities, and the iniquities of your fathers together, saith the LORD, which have burned incense upon the mountains, and

blasphemed Me upon the hills: therefore will I measure their former work into their bosom. *(This Verse links together into one guilty company the idolaters of the past and the Pharisees of the present. Both are Christ-rejecters. Therefore, the conduct of the former will be judged in bosom of the latter.*

In all of this, the Lord reminds Israel, in graphic terms, as to exactly what the cause of their previous state had been. There must not be a mistake in their understanding this.)

A SEED PROMISED

8 Thus saith the LORD, As the new wine is found in the cluster, and one says, Destroy it not; for a blessing is in it: so will I do for My servants' sakes, that I may not destroy them all. *(The phrase, "As the new wine is found in the cluster," refers to even a single cluster of grapes on the vine-stem. The vine-pruners would say one to another, "Destroy not that stem, but spare it." As well, God will refrain from destroying those stalks in His vineyard which give even a small promise of bearing good fruit.*

Therefore, the Lord uses this as an example that He will preserve a Remnant of Israel to be blessed in the eternal society under the Messiah [Rom. 9:27].)

9 And I will bring forth a Seed out of Jacob, and out of Judah an Inheritor of My mountains: and My elect shall inherit it, and My servants shall dwell there. *(The "Seed out of Jacob" actually refers to Christ [Gal. 3:16]. The "Inheritor of My mountains" is also the Messiah. The "elect" concerns the Remnant of Israel left after the Battle of Armageddon, which will accept Christ as their Saviour and Messiah. They are as well called "My servants" and "shall dwell there." They are "elected" by Him, because they choose to be "servants.")*

10 And Sharon shall be a fold of flocks, and the valley of Achor a place for the herds to lie down in, for My people who have sought Me. *(Achor was the place near Jericho where Achan was put to death [Josh. 7:24; 15:7; Hos. 2:15]. In effect, the Grace of God will turn the valley of Achor, which was a scene of Wrath, into a door of hope, while those that were Israel after the flesh shall perish.)*

REBELS AND APOSTATES WILL BE PURGED FROM ISRAEL

11 But you are they who forsake the LORD, who forget My holy mountain, who prepare a table for that troop, and who furnish the drink offering unto that number. *(The word "troop," in the Hebrew, has reference to "the god," or rather "the god of fortune," which had to do with the planet Jupiter. The phrase, "That number," has to do with the goddess "Destiny," that is, the planet Venus.*

All of this referred to the astrological charts that originated with Babylon. The Israelites furnished the sacrifices and drink offerings to these heathenistic gods in order to secure what they believed would be good fortune.)

12 Therefore will I number you to the sword, and you shall all bow down to the slaughter: because when I called, you did not answer; when I spoke, you did not hear; but did evil before My eyes, and did choose that wherein I delighted not. *(As Israel looked to the "numbers," responding to their "god of fortune," i.e., "chance," the Lord says, "Therefore will I number you to the sword." With Israel seeking help from demon spirits, they were, in effect, forfeiting the help that God could give, and also actually making God their enemy, Who would fight against them.*

The phrase, "Because when I called, you did not answer; when I spoke, you did not hear," refers to Israel that had the opportunity to hear either demon spirits, i.e., the "god of fortune," or else the "God of Heaven." Sadly and regrettably, they chose to hear the "god of fortune," and refused to "answer" or "hear" the God of Heaven.

As a result, "you shall all bow down to the slaughter.")

13 Therefore thus saith the Lord GOD, Behold, My servants shall eat, but you shall be hungry: behold, My servants shall drink, but you shall be thirsty: behold, My servants shall rejoice, but you shall be ashamed. *(The idea of this Passage is this:*

There would be, as always, a small Remnant who would not choose the way of evil, and as a result, and in all places, would be sustained with spiritual food and "rejoice and sing for joy of heart."

Conversely, those who stake their claim on the "god of chance" would everywhere feel a craving for the "meat" and "drink" which alone satisfy the soul, and would instead be oppressed with care and with a sense of shame and, thereby, suffer anguish of spirit!)

14 Behold, My servants shall sing for joy of heart, but you shall cry for sorrow of heart, and shall howl for vexation of spirit. *(Solomon*

said that all such was a "vanity and vexation of spirit," implying that even if there was so-called "good fortune," it would still result in "empty nothings." For that's what the words, "vanity and vexation," actually mean!)

15 And you shall leave your name for a curse unto My chosen: for the Lord GOD shall slay you, and call His servants by another name *(because of Israel's rebellion against God, their very name has been cursed. As well, instead of protecting them, the Lord, because they didn't want Him, has allowed them to be slain by their enemies, which have been many.*

The phrase, "And call His servants by another name," refers to the Church, which was grafted in because of Israel's failure [Rom. 11:17]):

16 That he who blesses himself in the Earth shall bless himself in the God of Truth; and he who swears in the Earth shall swear by the God of Truth; because the former troubles are forgotten, and because they are hid from My eyes. *(The idea of this Passage is that if one is truly blessed, it will be by "the God of Truth." The phrase, "And he who swears in the Earth shall swear by the God of Truth," refers to God, Who keeps Covenant and Promise, to which the strongest formula of consent is the word "Amen" [Num. 5:22; Deut. 27:15-26; I Ki. 1:36].*

The phrase, "Because the former troubles are forgotten," speaks of the coming Kingdom Age, when all of the rebellion of Israel will be "forgotten."

The phrase, "And because they are hid from My eyes," refers to the fact of Israel being washed in the Blood of the Lamb, which means their sins are no more [Zech. 13:1].)

17 For, behold, I create new heavens and a new Earth: and the former shall not be remembered, nor come into mind. *(This Scripture, as given by the Holy Spirit through Isaiah, leaps ahead, even beyond the coming Millennium, to the time of the "new heavens and new Earth." The phrase, "And the former shall not be remembered, nor come into mind," means that the Glory of the new heavens and Earth will be such that the absolving of the former ones will not only not be regretted, but will not even be had in remembrance. No one will so much as even think of them!)*

18 But be ye glad and rejoice for ever in that which I create: for, behold, I create Jerusalem a rejoicing, and her people a joy. *(Whereas the Holy Spirit in Verse 17 spoke of the coming "new heavens and new Earth," now He, through Isaiah, beginning with this Verse and continuing through the end of the Chapter, proclaims the Glory of the coming Kingdom Age, when Christ will reign Personally and supremely from Jerusalem.*

Actually, this is the reason that "Jerusalem" will be a city of "rejoicing, and her people a joy.")

19 And I will rejoice in Jerusalem, and joy in My people: and the voice of weeping shall be no more heard in her, nor the voice of crying. *(In fact, Jerusalem has been a place of "weeping and crying." It, as no other city in the world, has known war, heartache, sadness, and sorrow! Satan has contested God's ownership of this city from the very beginning.*

But with the coming of the Lord, all of this will be passed. "Weeping" and "crying" will be "heard" no more. Such will be because of Christ, and only because of Christ and what He has done for mankind through the Cross.)

20 There shall be no more thence an infant of days, nor an old man who has not filled his days: for the child shall die an hundred years old; but the sinner being an hundred years old shall be accursed. *(During the coming Millennium, the Redeemed, with glorified bodies, and even those who have given their hearts to Christ at that time, will experience no death whatsoever. Even among the unredeemed, longevity of life, possibly even for hundreds of years, will be restored.*

The phrase, "But the sinner being an hundred years old shall be accursed," means that any person living at that time who hasn't given his heart and life to Christ by the time he is 100 years old will be "accursed," meaning that, in all likelihood, he will not be saved.")

21 And they shall build houses, and inhabit them; and they shall plant vineyards, and eat the fruit of them. *(This proves that ordinary natural life and living conditions on the Earth will continue in the Millennium. The idea of this Passage is that work and labor will bring forth fruit and not be cut off by death, sickness, or sin, as at the present. Men, then, can build, construct, labor, and enjoy the fruit of their labor.)*

22 They shall not build, and another inhabit; they shall not plant, and another eat: for as the days of a tree are the days of My people, and My elect shall long enjoy the work of their hands. *(The phrase, "My elect," speaks of Israel, but also of all who have accepted Christ as their Saviour. The phrase, "Shall long enjoy the work of their hands," actually speaks of eternity. The "enjoyment" will never cease.*

The phrase, "For as the days of a tree are the days of My people," refers to the longevity of certain types of trees, which are actually thousands of years old.

As is alluded to in this Passage, death will continue through the 1000-year Reign of Christ on Earth, but only for those who refuse to accept Christ and who commit sins worthy of death. If such is the case, they will be executed, for the "Law will go forth from Zion and the Word of the LORD from Jerusalem" [Isa. 2:3].)

23 They shall not labour in vain, nor bring forth for trouble; for they are the seed of the blessed of the LORD, and their offspring with them. *(The phrase, "Their offspring with them," tells us that children will be born during the Kingdom Age, and actually will be born forever, even in the "new Earth." This will not pertain to the glorified Saints, but rather to the redeemed who are not glorified, meaning they didn't have part in the First Resurrection, but will keep alive forever by means of the Tree of Life [Rev. 22:1-3]. These will bring forth offspring.)*

24 And it shall come to pass, that before they call, I will answer; and while they are yet speaking, I will hear. *(This Scripture proclaims the Truth that Christ will be the One Who will solve all problems, answer all questions, meet all needs, and right all wrongs. The answer will not be delayed, hindered, or denied!)*

25 The wolf and the lamb shall feed together, and the lion shall eat straw like the bullock: and dust shall be the serpent's meat. They shall not hurt nor destroy in all My holy mountain, saith the LORD. *(Rom. 8:19-22 is based upon the last Verse of this Chapter. The animal creation will enjoy the beneficence of the Messiah's government; but the serpent, i.e., Satan, shall be made to "eat the dust." This is a fine and striking idiom expressing his perpetual impotency and degradation [the language is figurative]. However, the snake, even though not having the curse lifted, will be rendered harmless, and instead of preying upon beasts, birds, or reptiles, shall be content with the food assigned it in the primeval decree.*

The phrase, "They shall not hurt nor destroy in all My holy mountain, saith the LORD," is repeated from 11:9 word for word. In either case, we should not regard the subject of the sentence as limited to the animals only. The meaning is that there shall be no violence of any kind, done either by man or beast, in the happy period described.)

CHAPTER 66
(698 B.C.)
THE RIGHTEOUS RESPECTED; SINNERS DOOMED

THUS saith the LORD, The Heaven is My throne, and the Earth is My footstool: where is the house that you build unto Me? and where is the place of My rest? *(This Chapter takes up and reviews all the prior Chapters concerning this particular Prophesy. The Messiah's First Advent and the judgment which followed it are the subject of the first six Verses; His Second Advent and the judgment which will follow it occupy the rest of the Chapter.*

The Chapter opens by contrasting Herod's Temple with that of the Universe — the one so puny and the other so vast.)

2 For all those things have My hand made, and all those things have been, saith the LORD: but to this man will I look, even to him who is poor and of a contrite spirit, and trembles at My Word. *(The Great Temple fashioned by Jehovah's Hand, i.e., the heavens and the Earth, is contrasted in Verse 2, and the statement is made that God's true Temple is the heart that trembles at His Word.*

The "contrite man" is one with a broken, crushed, contrite spirit. The only One Who actually fits this description is Christ; therefore, for the Lord to properly look at us, one must be properly in Christ [Rom. 6:3-5].)

3 He who kills an ox is as if he slew a man; he who sacrifices a lamb, as if he cut off a dog's neck; he who offers an oblation, as if he offered swine's blood; he who burns incense, as if he blessed an idol. Yea, they have chosen their own ways, and their soul delights in their abominations. *(The Sacrifices which the Pharisees offered so zealously are declared in this Verse to be abominable to God, as if they offered up human sacrifice, or dogs, or swine, and their worship is stated to be as offensive as if addressed to an idol.*

Man, tutored by Satan as a minister of righteousness, has succeeded in all times in corrupting the Divine revelation and ordinances. This is very apparent in the modern Church, so that religious services and ceremonies, which are very beautiful to man's judgment and which appeal to his religious feeling, are declared by God to be abominable. The reason?

Simply because the object of faith is something other than Christ and the Cross, which God will not tolerate [I Cor. 1:17-18, 23; 2:2].)

4 I also will choose their delusions, and will bring their fears upon them; because when I called, none did answer; when I spoke, they did nor hear: But they did evil before My eyes, and chose that in which I delighted not. *(Israel's rejection of Christ at His First Coming is recorded in this Verse, and the persecution of His Disciples predicted in the next Verse.*

The choice and delight of the Pharisees are contrasted with the choice and delight of the Messiah.)

ISRAEL'S FUTURE TRAVAIL

5 Hear the Word of the LORD, you who tremble at His Word; Your brethren who hated you, who cast you out for My name's sake, said, Let the LORD be glorified: but He shall appear to your joy, and they shall be ashamed. *(The phrase, "Hear the Word of the LORD," is an admonishment to the Church to not hear the word of man. The words, "You who tremble at His Word," refer to those who are of a "poor and contrite spirit." The prideful never "tremble at His Word," but rather substitute their own word. The phrase, "Your brethren who hated you, who cast you out for My Name's sake," refers to a formal excommunication, or at least to a renunciation of fellowship. This speaks of persecution by an apostate Church.*

The phrase, "Let the LORD be glorified," is actually a sarcastic statement from these false brethren! This was the sarcastic challenge of the Pharisees. It means: "Let Jehovah manifest His Power and favor in Your behalf." This, in effect, is what they said to Christ when he was hanging on the Cross.

The phrase, "But He shall appear to your joy, and they shall be ashamed," refers to the fact that God, even though He tarry long, will ultimately vindicate your trust in Him.)

6 A voice of noise from the city, a voice from the temple, a voice of the LORD Who renders recompence to his enemies. *(After rebuking the hypocrisy of the wicked, God addressed the righteous, promising that they would be blessed in the end, and declared that He would recompense their enemies in due time.)*

7 Before she travailed, she brought forth; before her pain came, she was delivered of a man child. *(As the Sixth Verse speaks of the Second Coming, this Verse speaks of the events immediately preceding that all-important occasion.*

Verses 7 through 17 speak not only of the travail of Israel, which will take place during the Great Tribulation, but as well of her redemption.

The phrase, "she was delivered of a man child," refers to the 144,000 Jews who will be saved during the first half of the Great Tribulation [Rev. 7:4-8].)

8 Who has heard such a thing? who has seen such things? Shall the Earth be made to bring forth in one day? or shall a nation be born at once? for as soon as Zion travailed, she brought forth her children. *(It is as if the Holy Spirit, anticipating the incredulity of the Reader, asks, "Who has heard such a thing?"*

The statement, "For as soon as Zion travailed, she brought forth her children," refers to the terrible horror of the latter half of the Great Tribulation, and especially the Battle of Armageddon, when it looks like Israel will be totally annihilated. In this terrible judgment, producing great "travail," Israel will be brought back to God. These birth pangs of Israel are referred to here and in the following [Dan. 12:1; Zech 12:10-13:1; Mat. 24:8, 15-22; Rev. 12:1-6, 14].)

9 Shall I bring to the birth, and not cause to bring forth? saith the LORD: shall I cause to bring forth, and shut the womb? says your God. *(No matter how it looks, the Lord is emphatically stating that Israel will be brought back, irrespective as to how negative her situation may seem. To emphasize the strength of His statement, the Lord uses the analogy of a pregnant woman: "Shall I cause to bring forth, and shut the womb?" In other words, after the gestation period of nine months has run its course, nothing can stop the birth of the child. As well, it will not be stillborn, but a healthy, vibrant child!*

[This birth that is spoken of has nothing to do with the "man child" of the Seventh Verse, as the two are separate incidents.])

A NEW AGE OF PEACE AND PROSPERITY

10 Rejoice ye with Jerusalem, and be glad with her, all ye who love her: rejoice for joy with her, all ye who mourn for her *(the Holy Spirit through Isaiah is contemplating, especially due to the strength of His pronouncements, that the Reader must believe what is said and, therefore, "Rejoice ye with Jerusalem, and be glad with her"):*

11 That you may suck, and be satisfied with the breasts of her consolations; that you may milk out, and be delighted with the abundance of her glory. *(The Holy Spirit now uses another strong analogy, and does so by using the mother who has now brought forth a child, by saying,*

"That you may suck, and be satisfied with the breasts of her consolations." In other words, by Israel's restoration, the entirety of the world will be blessed, and abundantly!)

12 For thus saith the LORD, Behold, I will extend peace to her like a river, and the glory of the Gentiles like a flowing stream: then shall you suck, you shall be borne upon her sides, and be dandled upon her knees. *(The sudden and vast enlargement of the nation of Israel, with her glory, her spiritual wealth, her consolation, and her headship over the nations, and all because of Christ, are pictured in these Verses, and will accompany the Messiah's Second Advent.*

The phrase, "You shall be borne upon her sides," refers to the fact that Jerusalem will at that time, and we speak of the Kingdom Age, be the nurturer of the world. That may seem strange, but it will all be because of Christ!)

13 As one whom his mother comforts, so will I comfort you; and you shall be comforted in Jerusalem. *(The phrase, "As one whom his mother comforts," continues the analogy used by the Holy Spirit concerning the birth [Vs. 9]. Now Israel is presented as a full-grown man. The words, "So will I comfort you," refer to the Lord Himself comforting this man, i.e., Israel.)*

14 And when you see this, your heart shall rejoice, and your bones shall flourish like an herb: and the hand of the LORD shall be known toward His servants, and His indignation toward His enemies. *(The Passage, "And your bones shall flourish like an herb," refers to the fact that in times past Israel's "bones had been consumed" [Ps. 31:10], and "waxed old" [Ps. 32:3]. Now they shall enjoy a time of refreshing from the Lord. New life shall enter them, and health and growth shall follow. Ezekiel proclaimed this in his Thirty-seventh Chapter.*

The phrase, "And the hand of the LORD shall be known," refers to a two-pronged thrust. There will be blessing toward Israel and all who serve the Lord, and "indignation toward His enemies.")

THE PUNISHMENT OF THE WICKED

15 For, behold, the LORD will come with fire, and with His chariots like a whirlwind, to render His anger with fury, and His rebuke with flames of fire. *(These Passages are not symbolic, but literal. This is the Second Coming, which Ezekiel describes in detail [Ezek. 38:18-23].)*

16 For by fire and by His sword will the LORD plead with all flesh: and the slain of the LORD shall be many. *(The entirety of the army of the Antichrist will be killed, with the exception of a one-sixth part [Ezek. 39:2]. This, of course, continues to speak of the Second Coming.)*

17 They who sanctify themselves, and purify themselves in the gardens behind one tree in the midst, eating swine's flesh, and the abomination, and the mouse, shall be consumed together, saith the LORD. *(This Verse signifies that all idolatry in Israel will now end. That abominable day is forever over.)*

MILLENNIUM: JEW AND GENTILE TOGETHER GLORIFY GOD

18 For I know their works and their thoughts: it shall come, that I will gather all nations and tongues; and they shall come, and see My Glory. *(Verses 18 through 21 portray the greatest move of Evangelism the world will have ever known! It is during this time that hundreds of million, or even billions, will accept Christ as their eternal Saviour. The Scripture says, "they shall come, and they shall see." What they will see will be the "Glory of God as it resides in Christ.")*

19 And I will set a sign among them, and I will send those who escape of them unto the nations, to Tarshish, Pul, and Lud, who draw the bow, to Tubal, and Javan, to the isles afar off, who have not heard My fame, neither have seen My glory; and they shall declare My glory among the Gentiles. *(The phrase, "And I will set a sign among them," actually pertains to Christ. He will be the sign!*

The phrase, "And I will send those who escape of them unto the nations," refers to the two-thirds who will be killed during the latter half of the Great Tribulation and the Battle of Armageddon, who did not want or desire Christ. The one-third of Israel remaining [Zech. 13:8-9] will then be sent as missionaries to the nations of the world to proclaim Messiah's Glory. They will do so with such success that entire nations will be converted even in "one day" [Vs. 8]. Then Israel will finally fulfill her intended purpose to serve as a light to the world.)

20 And they shall bring all your brethren for an offering unto the LORD out of all nations upon horses, and in chariots, and in litters, and upon mules, and upon swift beasts, to My holy mountain Jerusalem, saith the LORD, as the Children of Israel bring an

offering in a clean vessel into the house of the LORD. *(The implication of the Verse is this:*

The Gentile world, including all nations, realizing the Glory of Christ and that the blessing resides in His People, will provide every necessary means to help Israel fulfill her obligations to the Lord.

The phrase, "As the Children of Israel bring an offering in a clean vessel into the house of the Lord," refers to the Gentiles strongly desiring Israel to adhere strictly to the Commandments of the Lord. The reason is explained in the following Verse.)

21 And I will also take of them for Priests and Levites, saith the LORD. *(The reason that the Gentiles will be so eager to help Israel is because the intermediary between Christ and the Gentile world will be, at least in some small way, the "Priests," who come from the Tribe of "Levi." This does not mean that they will serve as mediators between Christ and man, but that the channel and flow of blessings going to the Gentile nations will pertain in some sense to the Levitical Order, which, according to Ezekiel, will be restored.*

As well, it is believed by some that quite possibly proselyte Gentiles will be allowed to serve as "Priests," and thereby taken into the Tribe of "Levi," thereby becoming "Levites.")

NEW HEAVENS AND NEW EARTH; THE WICKED IN HELL

22 For as the new heavens and the New Earth, which I will make, shall remain before Me, saith the LORD, so shall your seed and your name remain. *(In other words, the order that the Lord will set up "shall remain before*

Me." This signifies that it will never be overthrown as it was in the past in the Garden of Eden. That which He is going to do will exist and remain forever.)

23 And it shall come to pass, that from one new moon to another, and from one sabbath to another, shall all flesh come to worship before Me, saith the LORD. *(This Passage merely reflects the thought that the worship of the Lord will go on from month to month, and forever!*

The phrase, "Shall all flesh come to worship before Me, saith the LORD," refers to the entirety of the Earth. Then it will no longer be a mere "Remnant," as it has been through the ages, but now "all" will "worship before Me." This Passage guarantees the perpetuity of God's Kingdom, with Satan locked away forever, with no possibility of rebellion ever again taking place!)

24 And they shall go forth, and look upon the carcases of the men who have transgressed against Me: for their worm shall not die, neither shall their fire be quenched; and they shall be an abhorring unto all flesh. *(The eternal doom pronounced in this Verse is confirmed by the Messiah Himself when He said, "Where their worm dies not, and the fire is not quenched" [Mk. 9:48]. Isaiah commences with a gracious invitation [1:18], and closes with a solemn warning!*

This Passage proclaims the fact, which Isaiah has previously mentioned, that there will be certain openings in the Earth into which men can gaze and look upon those who are in eternal Hell.

To the natural mind, this may be horrifying. Yet, this will no doubt serve as the greatest example ever of the horrors of sin, that it must never happen again!)

THE BOOK OF THE PROPHET
JEREMIAH

CHAPTER 1

(629 B.C.)

INTRODUCTION

THE words of Jeremiah the son of Hilkiah, of the Priests who were in Anathoth in the land of Benjamin *(the name "Jeremiah" means "Jehovah is high, Jehovah raises up or launches out." As we shall see, the Ministry of Jeremiah was, in many ways, typical of the Ministry of Christ)*:

2 To whom the Word of the LORD came in the days of Josiah the son of Amon king of Judah, in the thirteenth year of his reign. *(From that time to the fall of Jerusalem was approximately 40 years. No doubt, Jeremiah was greatly encouraged at the beginning of his ministry, in view of the fact that "Josiah" was one of the Godliest kings that ever graced the Throne of Judah [II Ki. 22:2]. But yet Josiah will be cut down in his prime, possibly fulfilling the Prophecy of Isaiah [Isa. 57:1].)*

3 It came also in the days of Jehoiakim the son of Josiah king of Judah, unto the end of the eleventh year of Zedekiah the son of Josiah king of Judah, unto the carrying away of Jerusalem captive in the fifth month. *(In this Verse, we have the fulfillment of the Prophecies of Moses, as well as others [Deut. 28:36-37]. The length of the time mentioned in this Verse was approximately 40 years, during which Jeremiah continued to prophesy. As well, he prophesied even after the fall of Jerusalem [Jer. 40:1; 42:7; 43:1-44:30].)*

GOD CALLS JEREMIAH

4 Then the Word of the LORD came unto me, saying *(this is the first Prophecy that is given in this Book, and concerns itself with the call of Jeremiah)*

5 Before I formed you in the belly I knew you; and before you came forth out of the womb I sanctified you, and I ordained you a Prophet unto the nations. *(In this, one can easily see the doctrine of predestination. But only that the Lord through foreknowledge "knew" what kind of man that Jeremiah would be, and not that Jeremiah had been denied the power of choice*

and had been forced by God into a certain course of action.

The words, "I sanctified you," refer to the call of Jeremiah, that he had been set apart for this particular use.

The words, "Ordained you a Prophet unto the nations," rather mean "appointed." His message would involve not only Israel, but also those nations which had to do with Israel.)

6 Then said I, Ah, Lord GOD! behold, I cannot speak: for I am a child. *(This does not speak of a preteen child, but a young man ranging from that of a teenager to twenty-five or thirty years of age.)*

7 But the LORD said unto me, Say not, I am a child: for you shall go to all that I shall send you, and whatsoever I command you you shall speak. *(Almost immediately upon God's Commands, the flesh, lacking faith, withdraws. So did Moses and Jonah. The call demanded absolute leading and absolute obedience!)*

8 Be not afraid of their faces: for I am with you to deliver you, saith the LORD. *(This Verse implies, and by the Lord at that, that Jeremiah will face great opposition; however, he had the Promise of the Lord to deliver him, but only if Jeremiah fully obeyed.)*

9 Then the LORD put forth His hand, and touched my mouth. And the LORD said unto me, Behold, I have put My words in your mouth. *(The phrase, "I have put My Words in your mouth," explains Inspiration. The mouth was Jeremiah's, the Words were God's [Acts 3:21; II Tim. 3:16-17; II Pet. 1:21].)*

10 See, I have this day set you over the nations and over the kingdoms, to root out, and to pull down, and to destroy, and to throw down, to build, and to plant. *(As there is so much more threat than promise in Jeremiah's writings, the destructive side of his activity is expressed by four verbs; the constructive, only by two.)*

VISION OF ALMOND TREE BRANCH

11 Moreover the Word of the LORD came unto me, saying, Jeremiah, what do you see? And I said, I see a rod of an almond tree. *(The "almond tree" is, in the east, the first to awake*

after the sleep of winter. It, therefore, symbolized the nearness of the predicted event.)

12 Then said the LORD unto me. You have well seen: for I will hasten My Word to perform it. *(The urgency was impressed upon Jeremiah that inasmuch as his call was given, that the Prophecies must begin, because the time of their fulfillment was at hand! It would be some thirty-five or more years, at least concerning Jerusalem and Judah, regarding the fulfillment, but the warnings were to begin immediately.)*

VISION OF A SEETHING POT

13 And the Word of the LORD came unto me the second time, saying, What do you see? And I said, I see a seething pot; and the face thereof is toward the north. *(The "seething pot" symbolized the eruption of the Babylonians into Judah.)*

14 Then the LORD said unto me, Out of the north an evil shall break forth upon all the inhabitants of the land. *(The phrase, "Out of the north," refers to the invasion route. Actually, Babylon was due east of Judah. However, the caravan road which the Chaldean armies had to take entered Judah at Dan, which was due north of Jerusalem.*

The words, "an evil," refer to the calamity which in deepening gloom forms the burden of the Prophet's discourses.)

15 For, lo, I will call all the families of the kingdoms of the north, saith the LORD; and they shall come, and they shall set every one his throne at the entering of the gates of Jerusalem, and against all the walls thereof round about, and against all the cities of Judah. *(This was fulfilled approximately thirty-five years later. The word "against" occurs eight times in this Chapter. This emphasizes the fact that man is estranged from God. Scriptural teaching is, therefore, opposed to human teaching. Doctrines which appeal to the natural heart, and which are in harmony with the "assured results" of modern thought, must, therefore, be false; for the natural mind is enmity against God, and is not appealed to by Divine teaching [Rom. 8:7].*

The prediction in this Verse is that the kings and generals of the mighty Babylonian Empire would set up the high seat of power and judicial authority near the gate of the city of Jerusalem. And so it ultimately happened [II Ki. 24:12].)

16 And I will utter My judgments against them *(against Judah)* touching all their wickedness, who have forsaken Me, and have burned incense unto other gods, and worshipped the works of their own hands. *(God always makes clear the reasons for His judgments in time for men to avoid them, if they will only listen. Jeremiah did not go into the detail as did Isaiah concerning these idol gods. It is as if the Lord is weary of His explanations being rejected; therefore, He only alludes to these "other gods," as if to say that if Jerusalem and Judah do not now know better, there is nothing else He can say!)*

17 Thou therefore gird up your loins, and arise, and speak unto them all that I command you: be not dismayed at their faces, lest I confound you before them. *(A Promise and a warning is given in this Verse. The Promise is that God would give him the Words that he is to say. The warning is that if there is a want of confidence on Jeremiah's part, his enemies would utterly discomfit him.)*

18 For, behold, I have made you this day a defenced city, and an iron pillar, and brasen walls against the whole land, against the kings of Judah, against the princes thereof, against the priests thereof, and against the people of the land. *(The Lord would give Jeremiah the strength to stand against the king, the Priesthood, and the people of the land, but only if he stood strong.)*

19 And they shall fight against you; but they shall not prevail against you; for I am with you, saith the LORD, to deliver you. *(The opposition of the land was predicted. To be sure, the opposition by the modern Church against true prophetic utterance is almost always the case; however, the Promise of deliverance for the Prophet against this opposition is given here, at least until the Message has been properly delivered.)*

CHAPTER 2
(629 B.C.)
THE WICKEDNESS OF ISRAEL

MOREOVER the Word of the LORD came to me, saying *(this "Word" given by Jeremiah is thought by some to be the first oracle delivered in public),*

2 Go and cry in the ears of Jerusalem, saying, Thus saith the LORD, I remember you, the kindness of your youth, the love of your espousals, when you went after Me in the wilderness, in a land that was not sown. *(This Message was addressed to Judah, but, as it did not flatter them, it was rejected, and its rejection shows that the revival of 629 B.C. did not*

last [3:10].

The phrase, "I remember for your good the kindness of your youth," speaks of that of God toward the people, rather than the people toward God.

The phrase, "Your espousals," refers to Israel's beginnings, the bridal state.

The phrase, "When you went after Me," refers to the forty years in the wilderness, and the tremendous miracles wrought by the Lord in response to His People.)

3 Israel was holiness unto the LORD, and the first fruits of His increase: all who devour him shall offend; evil shall come upon them, saith the LORD. (The phrase, "Israel was holiness unto the LORD," refers to their being a consecrated people. This does not necessarily imply a personal holiness, and in fact definitely did not imply such, but rather an imputed holiness. It is as if the Holy Spirit was attempting to pressure the people to be what they should have been.

The phrase, "The firstfruits of His increase," is compared to the firstfruits of the land, which were devoted to the House of the Lord [Ex. 23:19; Num. 18:12-13].

The phrase, "All who devour him shall offend," refers to enemies attempting to hurt or even destroy Israel. By attempting such, they would incur the Wrath of God. Such foreign nations or tribes became guilty of a most serious trespass, having invaded the rights of Jehovah.)

4 Hear ye the Word of the LORD, O house of Jacob, and all the families of the House of Israel (now the Holy Spirit through Jeremiah will begin a long litany of grievances against Judah. The pleadings by the Holy Spirit present the pathos of a broken heart — the broken heart of God!):

5 Thus saith the LORD, What iniquity have your fathers found in Me, that they are gone far from Me, and have walked after vanity, and are become vain? (This Passage refers to God, Who never fails and always keeps Covenants and Promises. Of course, there is no "iniquity" in the Lord! If a man leaves God, it is always wrongdoing on the part of the man, and never on the part of God.

"Have walked after vanity" refers to idols. In the wilderness, they walked after Jehovah; in Canaan, they walked after Moloch and became "vain," for man becomes morally like that which he worships.)

6 Neither said they, Where is the LORD Who brought us up out of the land of Egypt, Who led us through the wilderness, through a land of deserts and of pits, through a land of drought, and of the shadow of death, through a land that no man passed through, and where no man dwelt? (The words, "Neither said they," refer to lack of inquiry on the part of Judah. Even though the Lord had done so many great things for them, they were little interested in recounting His mighty exploits. They did not want Him now; therefore, they had no desire to recount past blessings.)

7 And I brought you into a plentiful country, to eat the fruit thereof and the goodness thereof, but when you entered, you defiled My land, and made My heritage an abomination. (This Verse simply speaks of the glory of the Land of Israel. It was a "garden-land." If one is to notice, the Holy Spirit says, "My Land," denoting the fact that the Land of Israel belongs to the Lord. He has never relinquished ownership, and in fact never will.)

8 The Priests said not, Where is the LORD? And they who handle the Law knew Me not: the pastors also transgressed against Me, and the Prophets prophesied by Baal, and walked after things that do not profit. (The Priests, the Magistrates, and the Prophets, i.e., the whole nation, apostatized from God to Baal. Only that which comes from the Lord and His Word is profitable. All else "does not profit.")

9 Wherefore I will yet plead with you, saith the LORD, and with your children's children will I plead. (In modern terminology, the Holy Spirit pleads with people. The pleading is always for them to get right with God and draw closer to Him. The word "plead" also refers to chastisement, for the Lord chastises those He loves [Heb. 12:5-11].)

10 For pass over the isles of Chittim, and see; and send unto Kedar, and consider diligently, and see if there be such a thing. (Chittim lay to the west and Kedar to the east of Jerusalem. The challenge here was to find, if possible, either east or west, a nation that had changed its gods. Such a quest would be fruitless.

Here is found an unanswerable argument in support of the credibility of the Bible and in refutation of the popular theory that Jehovah was just another trifle god invented by the Hebrews themselves.

Had such been so, they never would have forsaken Him, but would have clung to Him with the same devotion with which all nations cling to the gods and goddesses of their own creation.)

11 Has a nation changed their gods, which

are yet no gods? But My people have changed their glory for that which does not profit. *(The question, "Has a nation changed their gods?" actually asks, "Has any heathen nation ever changed its idol god for another?"*

Actually, Judah never ceased worshipping Jehovah altogether, but rather incorporated heathen religions in with their worship of the True God. Neither did they wholly forsake the Law, but rather added their own man-made laws to the Law of God. Is the modern Church guilty of the same thing?

The phrase, "But My people have changed their glory," refers to the fact that they no longer worship God, but rather idols.)

12 Be astonished, O ye heavens, at this, and be horribly afraid, be ye very desolate, saith the LORD. *(Judah at this time should have been trembling with fear, especially considering the awful doom that was soon to break upon them! The "heavens" were afraid, but not Judah! With Judah and Jerusalem, it was business as usual, even with the storm clouds gathering on the horizon.)*

13 For My people have committed two evils; they have forsake Me the Fountain of Living Waters, and hewed them out cisterns, broken cisterns, that can hold no water. *(When one forsakes God, they always do such for that which is far, far less! The answer for every problem is found in the Word of God; however, the modern Church has by and large forsaken the Word, and rather resorted to humanistic psychology, which can be defined as nothing other than a "broken cistern.")*

THE CONSEQUENCES OF ISRAEL'S SINS: THE COMING CAPTIVITY

14 Is Israel a servant? is he a homeborn slave? Why is he spoiled? *(Israel was a son, not a slave, yet they were about to become slaves! In fact, Israel had become a "servant," i.e., slave, to the heathenistic gods. As a result, they would soon become a slave to a foreign power.*

The question, "Is he a homeborn slave?", is interesting indeed! It has reference to an animal in a zoo. An animal was made by God to be free and unfettered. However, if born in a zoo and knowing nothing but the confines of such, it is a slave without really knowing it. Such was Israel, and such are so many modern Believers!

The question, "Why is he spoiled?", refers to Judah, which had sinned so long with impunity

that there was no fear of Divine retribution.)

15 The young lions roared upon him, and yelled, and they made his land waste: his cities are burned without inhabitant. *(The Prophet will now speak of future events as if they had already happened. Actually, Verse 15 also applied in the past tense to the Northern Kingdom of Israel, which had fallen to Assyria nearly a hundred years earlier. The Holy Spirit uses it as an example of what is going to happen in the near future to Judah.)*

16 Also the children of Noph and Tahapanes have broken the crown of your head. *(The implication in this Passage is that despite the reforms of Godly Josiah, the Lord, knowing the unrepentant heart of Judah, took Josiah, "the righteous man" [Isa. 57:1], out of the way in order to hasten Judah's judgment. When Josiah was killed, in effect, the Egyptians "broke the crown of your head.")*

17 Have you not procured this unto yourself, in that you have forsaken the LORD your God, when He led you to the way? *(So long as God leads, there is sonship, liberty, and dignity, but self-will insures slavery.)*

18 And now what have you to do in the way of Egypt, to drink the waters of Sihor? Or what have you to do in the way of Assyria, to drink the waters of the river? *(The "waters of Sihor," referring to Egypt, and the "waters of the river" [Euphrates], referring to Assyria, are what the Holy Spirit is speaking of in Verse 13, when He mentions "broken cisterns." Judah forsook the Lord for that!)*

19 Your own wickedness shall correct you, and your backslidings shall reprove you: know therefore and see that it is an evil thing and bitter, that you have forsaken the LORD your God, and that My fear is not in you, saith the Lord GOD of Hosts. *(The suffering that comes upon men results from their own self-will, and is not justly chargeable to God. So, the idea, as claimed by humanistic psychology, that Believers should "forgive God," borders on blasphemy!)*

20 For of old time I have broken your yoke, and burst your bands; and you said, I will not transgress; when upon every high hill and under every green tree you wandered, playing the harlot. *(The phrase, "For of old time I have broken your yoke," refers to their deliverance from Egyptian bondage. The phrase, "Playing the harlot," is a descriptive term used by the Holy Spirit, referring to idolatry.)*

21 Yet I had planted you a noble vine, wholly a right seed: how then are you turned into the

degenerate plant of a strange vine unto Me? *(The implication is that the type of "Vine" planted by the Lord was a "noble Vine," which came from the "right Seed," with the inference referring to Christ and, thereby, designed to bring forth much fruit.*

Nevertheless, despite the Lord Himself serving as the Gardener, this "noble Vine" turned into a "strange vine.")

THE GUILT CANNOT BE WASHED AWAY

22 For though you wash yourself with nitre, and take you much soap, yet your iniquity is marked before Me, saith the Lord GOD. *(The inference by the Holy Spirit is that all of man's efforts cannot take away "your iniquity." Such can only be done by the Blood of Christ. The problem of the modern Church is that it treats the results of man's sin instead of the cause of man's sin! Man doesn't need to be saved nearly so much for what he has done as for what he is — a sinner.)*

23 How can you say, I am not polluted, I have not gone after Baalim? See your way in the valley, know what you have done: you are a swift dromedary traversing her ways *(sin deadens and blinds the conscience — here the Prophet indignantly points to the valley of Hinnom, which was filled with idolatrous altars. Judah's fault was not in neglecting the public worship of Jehovah in His appointed Temple, but in superadding these idolatrous rites, which were anathema to the teaching of the Bible. Such is the problem in the modern Church today!*

The phrase, "You are a swift dromedary traversing her ways," refers to a young she-camel which has not yet had a foal, and is running backwards and forwards at the impulse of passion. In other words, Israel did not know where she was going!);

24 A wild ass used to the wilderness, that snuffs up the wind at her pleasure; in her occasion who can turn her away? All they who seek her will not weary themselves; in her month they shall find her. *(In Verses 23 through 25, Judah is compared to the camel and to the ass, which, in the mating season, run hither and thither after the males, so that these need not weary themselves in searching for them. Thus, Judah ran after idols!)*

25 Withhold your foot from being unshod, and your throat from thirst: but you said, There is no hope: no; for I have loved strangers, and after them will I go. *(Concerning her*

love for God, Judah said, "No, I love strange gods, and after them will I go"; but the result was shame to their kings, their princes, their Priests, and their Prophets.)*

ISRAEL'S IDOLATRY

26 As the thief is ashamed when he is found, so is the House of Israel ashamed; they, their kings, their princes, and their Priests, and their Prophets *(the blame for Judah's plight is laid at the feet of her spiritual leaders),*

27 Saying to a stock, You are my father; and to a stone, You have brought me forth: for they have turned their back unto Me, and not their face: but in the time of their trouble they will say, Arise, and save us. *(Judah forsook God as their Father, and worshipped idols. These idols were given credit for Israel's inheritance, as modern psychology is given credit today! The Holy Spirit warns that "a time of trouble" is coming, and then "they will say, Arise, and save us." However, it will then be too late!)*

28 But where are your gods that you have made for yourself? Let them arise, if they can save you in the time of your trouble: for according to the number of your cities are your gods, O Judah. *(The impotency of idols and the mental degradation of idolaters are the sad burden of Verses 27 and 28.)*

PUNISHMENT IS AT HAND

29 Wherefore will ye plead with Me? ye all have transgressed against Me, saith the LORD. *(The question, "Wherefore will you plead with Me?" refers to Judah's audacity at attempting to justify herself!)*

30 In vain have I smitten your children; they received no correction: your own sword has devoured your Prophets, like a destroying lion. *(The phrase, "In vain have I smitten your children," refers to the fact that the Lord brought corrective judgments on Judah, but to no avail! However, "they received no correction," meaning that Judah, despite their chastisements, would not be corrected. Instead, they killed the very ones, i.e., "your Prophets," sent to warn them. As well, their attitude was like a "destroying lion," implying that they did such with a hatred, a vengeance, and malice, which ultimately resulted in their murder of the Messiah.)*

31 O generation, see ye the Word of the LORD. Have I been a wilderness unto Israel? A land of darkness? Wherefore say My people,

We are lords; we will come no more unto You? *(The Lord is asking Judah the question, "Did He lead them into privation and misery?" Of course not! God does not lead His People in lowliness and darkness, but into light and fellowship. The last line of this Verse, "We are lords; we will come no more unto You?" refers to Judah's independence of God. In other words, they were saying, "We are our own master; we prefer the religion of Moloch to that of Jehovah!")*

32 Can a maid forget her ornaments, or a bride her attire? Yet My people have forgotten Me days without number. *(It was completely contrary to nature for Judah to forget God.)*

33 Why do you trim your way to seek love? Therefore have you also taught the wicked ones your ways. *(The "wicked ones" actually mean "wicked women." The idolatrous nations are here compared to debauched women having Judah as their teacher in vileness. It is a sad fact that the rejecter of Biblical Truth falls to a lower moral level than those who have never heard the Gospel.)*

34 Also in your skirts is found the blood of the souls of the poor innocents: I have not found it by secret search, but upon all these. *(The "poor innocents" refer to the "helpless." The accusation is: the evidence of Judah's guilt as the destroyer of God's servants is so visible that a search is not needed.)*

35 Yet you say, Because I am innocent, surely His anger shall turn from me. Behold, I will plead with you, because you say, I have not sinned. *(Someone has said, "A revival which is not based upon conviction of sin and the certainty of God's Wrath is a false revival!" Even at this late date, with the cup of iniquity running over, Judah claims "innocence," and then brazenly says, "I have not sinned.")*

36 Why do you gad about so much to change your way? You also shall be ashamed of Egypt, as you were ashamed of Assyria. *(The question, "Why do you gad about in order to change your way?" refers to the different political parties in Judah, which were seeking alliances, first in this place and then in another. In other words, Judah is no longer being led by the Lord, but rather by men.*

The phrase, "You also shall be ashamed of Egypt," refers to such efforts bringing no lasting solid results.)

37 Yea, you shall go forth from him, and your hands upon your head: for the LORD has rejected your confidences, and you shall not prosper in them. *(Confident schemes which repose upon human promises and which ignore God never prosper. The phrase, "For the LORD has rejected your confidences," refers to the fact that God will not allow these alliances, or proposed alliances, to prosper. They were not of Him, so He would not sanction them. Such is God with all the schemes of men!)*

CHAPTER 3
(629 B.C.)

THE PEOPLE REFUSE TO REPENT

THEY say, If a man put away his wife, and she go from him, and become another man's, shall he return unto her again? Shall not that land be greatly polluted? But you have played the harlot with many lovers; yet return again to Me, saith the LORD. *(The question, ". . . and become another man's, shall he return unto her again?", refers to the Command in Deut. 24:1-4. The Holy Spirit is likening Judah to a "harlot" who has gone to "many lovers," i.e., idols, and puts her in the same class as the forbidden one of Deut. 24:1-4. Yet Judah was invited to return! Did God then propose to violate His Own Law?*

The answer is found in Rom. 7:1-4. This Passage reveals the Divine method of Sanctification, and sets out its impossibility under the bondage of Law and its certainty under the freedom of Grace.

The argument here is: just as the death of the Saviour is the only force that can liberate from the claims of sin, so is it the only force that can liberate from the claims of the Law.

Paul, in Rom. 7:1-4, illustrates two husbands — the Law and Christ. Union with the Law is bondage and brings forth "fruit unto death," while union with Christ is freedom and brings forth fruit unto God.

The Law does not die, neither is its Divine authority affected. On the contrary, its righteous requirements are satisfied by the fruit brought forth under the Grace of God, made possible by the death of Christ, and the Believer's death in Christ [Rom. 6:3-5].

The old Israel was to die, and a new Israel to be created; and thus the foul harlot of this Chapter shall become the spotless Bride of Rev. 19:7-8.

Jesus satisfied the demands of the Law in that He died, suffering its judgment for our transgression and, therefore, satisfied its penalty. Now, in Christ, I am free, and so can Israel be free. On the basis of the price that Christ paid, the Lord can now say to Israel, and by faith

then could say, "yet return again to Me, saith the LORD.")

2 Lift up your eyes unto the high places, and see where you have not been lien with. In the ways have you sat for them, as the Arabian in the wilderness; and you have polluted the land with your whoredoms and with your wickedness. *(The phrase, "As the Arabian in the wilderness," refers to their thirst for plunder, and is likened to Israel's thirst for idolatry.)*

3 Therefore the showers have been withheld, and there has been no latter rain; and you had a whore's forehead, you refused to be ashamed. *(The Lord withheld the rains, thereby stunting the crops, trying to get Judah to repent, but to no avail! In effect, the Holy Spirit is saying that Judah is so far gone that they now have a "whore's forehead," meaning that they were so spiritually obstinate and stubborn that they had no inclination to turn to the Lord.)*

4 Will you not from this time cry unto Me, my Father, You are the guide of my youth? *(The language, "My Father," was insincere.)*

5 Will He reserve His anger for ever? Will He keep it to the end? Behold, you have spoken and done evil things as you could. *(These Passages probe deep into the heart of wayward Judah, revealing not only her actions, but her thoughts, and even the intent of her thoughts. The power of such preaching was enough to turn anyone to God, but Judah still would not heed the admonition of the Lord to "return.")*

JUDAH'S SIN AND BACKSLIDING

6 The LORD said also unto me in the days of Josiah the king, Have you seen that which backsliding Israel has done? She is gone up upon every high mountain and under every green tree, and there has played the harlot. *(In Verses 6 through 11, the Northern Kingdom is contrasted with the Southern, and the latter is charged with deeper guilt than the former because she added treachery to apostasy.*

The warning is: Judah sits in the same seat of judgment as her wayward sister of years past!)

7 And I said after she had done all these things, Turn thou unto Me. But she returned not. And her treacherous sister Judah saw it. *(Judah had been an observer to all that had happened in the Northern Kingdom. She heard, saw, witnessed, and experienced the appeal made to Ephraim. She saw her destruction, and knew the reason why! Therefore, her sin was against light, which is the greatest sin of all!)*

8 And I saw, when for all the causes whereby backsliding Israel committed adultery I had put her away, and given her a bill of divorce; yet her treacherous sister Judah feared not, but went and played the harlot also. *(The "adultery" named here is "spiritual adultery," i.e., in this case, consorting with idols. As stated, in Rom. 7:1-4, the Apostle Paul likens the Believer who makes the object of his faith something other than Christ as a "spiritual adulterer."*

The phrase, "And given her a bill of divorce," refers to the fact that the Northern Kingdom of Israel forsook the Lord, and not that the Lord forsook them.)

9 And it came to pass through the lightness of her whoredom, that she defiled the land, and committed adultery with stones and with stocks. *(The phrase, "Committed adultery with stones and with stocks," refers to the worship of idols, some of which were made of "stone." The word "stocks" refers to the manner in which the idols were worshipped.*

Is the Lord presently accusing the modern Church of "committing spiritual adultery"? To be sure, if the object of faith for the Believer is anything other than Christ and Him Crucified, then "spiritual adultery" is definitely being committed [Rom. 7:1-4].)

10 And yet for all this her treacherous sister Judah has not turned unto Me with her whole heart, but feignedly, saith the LORD. *(Judah professed attachment to the Law, but it was a feigned loyalty; and, untaught by the judgment that had fallen upon the Ten Tribes, she secretly and even openly practiced idolatry.*

The phrase, "Whole heart," gives us the manner, and in fact the only manner, which God will accept! He will not accept a repentance that continues sinning with impunity!)

11 And the LORD said unto me, The backsliding Israel has justified herself more than treacherous Judah. *(The reason for Judah's treacherous condition was because of the great light that had been given to her by the advent of at least some Godly kings, when in fact Israel did not have a single Godly king! To whom much is given, much is required.)*

REPENTANCE WILL RELEASE GOD'S MERCY

12 Go and proclaim these words toward the north, and say, Return, thou backsliding Israel, saith the LORD; and I will not cause My anger to fall upon you: for I am merciful,

saith the LORD, and I will not keep anger for ever. *(This second prophetic Message was sent by the Holy Spirit through Jeremiah to the Ten Tribes, then and now, in captivity. It assured them that the proclamation of Cyrus, which would be given about 100 years later, would embrace them as well as the exiles of Judah. It must have nourished the faith of those in that dispersion who feared God and loved His Word. The amazing love, pity, and Grace of God for those captives appear in every sentence of this Message.)*

13 Only acknowledge your iniquity, that you have transgressed against the LORD your God, and have scattered your ways to the strangers under every green tree, and you have not obeyed My voice, saith the LORD. *(The one condition of acceptance is the acknowledgment of one's guilt and a sincere desire to break with sin, which is repeated in each Verse [Vss. 13, 21, 4:1]. This is, in all dispensations, the one fundamental condition accompanying true Repentance.)*

14 Turn, O backsliding children, saith the LORD; for I am married unto you: and I will take you one of a city, and two of a family, and I will bring you to Zion *(this thrice repeated invitation has never yet been fully responded to by the Ten Tribes, but will be in the future, and then God will bring to Zion all who accept it.*

The statement, "I am married to the backslider," is derived from this Verse. Here, Jehovah repeats His invitation, assuring Israel that He does not consider the marriage bonds broken. But yet, every indication is that unless they return, they will be eternally lost! This Passage, therefore, destroys the erroneous idea of unconditional eternal security):

15 And I will give you pastors according to My heart, which shall feed you with knowledge and understanding. *(This will take place in the coming Kingdom Age, but not before.)*

16 And it shall come to pass, when you be multiplied and increased in the land, in those days, saith the LORD, they shall say no more, The Ark of the Covenant of the LORD: neither shall it come to mind: neither shall they remember it; neither shall they visit it; neither shall that be done any more. *(The phrase, "In those days," refers to the future time of Restoration. The "Ark," which was a symbol, will be replaced by Christ Himself, i.e., the Throne, which will be the reality. The Ark and the Glory which shone above* it characterize the First Covenant; the Throne, with the Messiah sitting on it, will characterize the Second.

The phrase, "Neither shall they visit it," should have been translated "miss it." The "Ark" will no longer be needed as a symbol of God's Personal Presence, for the Lord Himself will be Personally present [Ezek. 34:7; Zech. 14:9; Rev. 11:15; 21:3-6; 22:4-5]. This will take place in the coming Kingdom Age.)

17 At that time they shall call Jerusalem the Throne of the LORD; and all the nations shall be gathered unto it, to the Name of the LORD, to Jerusalem: neither shall they walk any more after the imagination of their evil heart. *(The words, "At that time," refer to the coming Kingdom Age, when Christ will reign supreme from Jerusalem. Actually, this city will serve as His "Throne.")*

18 In those days the House of Judah shall walk with the House of Israel, and they shall come together out of the land of the north to the land that I have given for an inheritance unto your fathers. *(In the coming Kingdom Age, Israel will be no more divided as it was in the days of Jeremiah, but will again become one nation.)*

19 But I said, How shall I put you among the children, and give you a pleasant land, a goodly heritage of the hosts of nations? And I said, You shall call Me, my Father; and shall not turn away from Me. *(The question, "How shall I put you among the children, and give you a pleasant land?", refers to God's great question in bringing Israel to a place of Repentance in order that He can fulfill the Everlasting Covenants with them, and give them the land as originally promised!*

This will be accomplished, but not without great tribulation, suffering, and sorrow, which will take place in the coming Great Tribulation [Mat. 24:21].)

A CALL FOR CONFESSION OF SIN

20 Surely as a wife treacherously departs from her husband, so have you dealt treacherously with Me, O House of Israel, saith the LORD. *(In this Passage, the Lord bluntly reminds Israel of her former "treachery." He uses as an example the "unfaithful wife." He likens Himself to Israel's "Husband.")*

21 A voice was heard upon the high places, weeping and supplications of the Children of Israel: for they have perverted their way, and

they have forgotten the LORD their God. *(Verses 12 through 20 are spoken by the Messiah; Verse 21, by the returning supplicants; the first part of Verse 22, by the Messiah again; and the rest of the Chapter, by the returning exiles.*

The phrase, "They have forgotten the LORD their God," refers now to some 2,600 years. It is a long time to forget the Lord; during this time, Israel has suffered as few have suffered!)

22 Return, you backsliding children, and I will heal your backslidings. Behold, we come unto You; for You are the LORD our God. *(This will be the call of the Messiah to wayward Israel, immediately after His Second Coming. Finally, their response will be positive.)*

23 Truly in vain is salvation hoped for from the hills, and from the multitude of mountains: truly in the LORD our God is the Salvation of Israel. *(The argument of this Verse is that as surely as deliverance is vainly hoped for from the multitude of idols placed on the hills and mountains, so surely is Salvation a certitude when sought from Jehovah.*

Hence, the Psalmist said he would not lift up his eyes to the hills, that is, to the idols on the hills, for no Salvation was to be obtained from them, but he would lift up his eyes to Jehovah [Ps. 121:1].)

24 For shame has devoured the labour of our fathers from our youth; their flocks and their herds, their sons and their daughters. *(Serving God enriches and ennobles; serving idols degrades and impoverishes. The "flocks and herds" refer to animals being offered in sacrifice to idols. As well, "sons and daughters," during the time of these "backslidings," were offered as human sacrifice to idols [Lev. 18:21; 20:2-5; II Ki. 23:10; Jer. 32:35].)*

25 We lie down in our shame, and our confusion covers us: for we have sinned against the LORD our God, we and our fathers, from our youth even unto this day, and have not obeyed the voice of the LORD our God. *(In the Fall, man took control of his life out of the Hands of God, placing it into his own domain, i.e., Satan. "Shame" and "confusion" are the result! Now Israel confesses her sin and rebellion, even from the beginning. Now there is no hedging or efforts at self-justification. A free and open admission of sin and failure is tendered: "and have not obeyed the voice of the LORD our God."*

This prayer and action of Repentance will take place immediately after the Second Coming of the Lord.)

CHAPTER 4
(612 B.C.)
GOD CALLED ISRAEL BY HIS PROMISE

IF you will return, O Israel, saith the LORD, return unto Me: and if you will put away your abominations out of My sight, then shall you not remove.

2 And you shall swear, The LORD lives, in Truth, in Judgment, and in Righteousness; and the nations shall bless themselves in Him, and in Him shall they glory. *(The Lord Jesus Christ Himself is Salvation. The closing words of this Prophecy could well be paraphrased: "If you shall put away your abominations out of My sight, and will not wander from Me, and will worship Me, the Living God, sincerely, justly, and righteously, then shall the nations bless themselves in Him [the Messiah] and in Him shall they glory.")*

3 For thus saith the LORD to the men of Judah and Jerusalem, Break up your fallow ground, and sow not among thorns. *(The previous Prophecy has ended; a new one commences. "Fallow ground" is ground that is unbroken, in a natural state, covered with briars and weeds. It pictures the natural heart of man, which must be broken and contrite before it can receive the good seed of the Kingdom. The call here was to break up their idols. This was a necessary condition of Forgiveness and Deliverance.)*

4 Circumcise yourselves to the LORD, and take away the foreskins of your heart, you men of Judah and inhabitants of Jerusalem: lest My fury come forth like fire, and burn that none can quench it, because of the evil of your doings. *(Circumcision of the heart is spoken of three times in the Old Testament, here and in Deut. 10:16 and 30:6. It is frequently met with in the New Testament [Rom. 2:28-29; Phil. 3:3; Col. 2:11]. Such is meant by the Holy Spirit to move the people away from mere religious ceremony to a true heart experience.)*

JUDAH THREATENED WITH JUDGMENT

5 Declare ye in Judah, and publish in Jerusalem; and say, Blow ye the trumpet in the land: cry, gather together, and say, Assemble yourselves, and let us go into the defenced cities. *(The Holy Spirit through Jeremiah looks ahead some 15 years to the coming calamity of Judah's and Jerusalem's fall and proclaims what they will do! Along with a portrait, the Holy Spirit cries for Repentance on the part of the people,*

which would avoid this coming catastrophe! Sadly, it will not be heeded.)

6 Set up the standard toward Zion: retire, stay not: for I will bring evil from the north, and a great destruction. *(The phrase, "Set up the standard toward Zion," referred to a tall pole with a flag, pointing in the direction of Zion, for the guidance of fugitives. They would be running away from the coming Babylonians, hoping to find safety in Jerusalem.*

The words, "Retire, stay not," refer to the fact that they should not linger, but rather hurry!

The "evil from the north" refers to the coming invasion by Nebuchadnezzar.

The "great destruction" was carried out in totality. The streets of Jerusalem ran red with blood, with the Temple being totally destroyed!)

7 The lion is come up from his thicket, and the destroyer of the Gentiles is on his way; he is gone forth from his place to make your land desolate; and your cities shall be laid waste, without an inhabitant. *("The lion" was Nebuchadnezzar. His invasion was so certain that the Prophet speaks of him here as already issued from his lair and on his way to destroy Jerusalem.)*

8 For this gird you with sackcloth, lament and howl: for the fierce anger of the LORD is not turned back from us. *(The first phrase of the Scripture refers to that which will take place during the time of the coming judgment; however, the time of Repentance is now, for then it will be too late! As far as personal Salvation is concerned, it is never too late for men to repent; nevertheless, Repentance can be delayed too long for judgment to be stopped, even though personal Salvation is given! Regrettably, with Judah, there was very little Repentance enjoined.)*

9 And it shall come to pass at that day, saith the LORD, that the heart of the king shall perish, and the heart of the princes; and the Priests shall be astonished, and the Prophets shall wonder. *("The heart" in Old Testament language is the center of intellectual as well as of moral life. The phrase, "At that day," refers to the time of the coming invasion by the Babylonians. The phrase, "And the Priests shall be astonished, and the Prophets shall wonder," refers to those who thought that surely, because of their sacred positions as "God's chosen people," judgment would never come! These "Priests" and "Prophets" busily engaged in their constant religious pursuits, paid no heed to Jeremiah, but actually held him in scorn. The idea that they needed Repentance, at least in their thinking,*

was laughable!)

10 Then said I, Ah, Lord GOD! surely You have greatly deceived this people and Jerusalem, saying, You shall have peace; whereas the sword reaches unto the soul. *(Although somewhat cluttered in the translation, the meaning of this statement concerns the preaching of the false prophets. In contrast to Jeremiah's Prophecies, they were saying to the people, "You shall have peace." In this, they greatly deceived the people and Jerusalem.*

The meaning is that God permitted these false prophets to greatly deceive the people. This was just judgment pronounced by the Lord, because the people refused to listen to the truth, and they preferred falsehood. If they preferred such, and they did, God allowed them to have such.)

11 At that time shall it be said to this people and to Jerusalem, A dry wind of the high places in the wilderness toward the daughter of My people, not to fan, nor to cleanse. *(In Verses 11 through 13, the Chaldean army is compared to a hurricane from the wilderness. It would be sanctioned by the Lord as God's instrument of Wrath.)*

12 Even a full wind from those places shall come unto Me: now also will I give sentence against them. *(The phrase, "Now also will I give sentence against them," actually says, "as they [Judah] have sinned against Me, so will I also now hold a court of justice upon them.")*

13 Behold, he shall come up as clouds, and his chariots shall be as a whirlwind: his horses are swifter than eagles. Woe unto us! for we are spoiled. *(This Verse signals the coming invasion by Nebuchadnezzar.)*

JUDAH CALLED TO REPENTANCE

14 O Jerusalem, wash your heart from wickedness, that you may be saved. How long shall your vain thoughts lodge within you? *(The "vain thoughts" concern the idea that their idols would save them, or that the Egyptians would deliver them from the Chaldeans. They were not looking to God, but rather to man. They would find it a poor choice!)*

15 For a voice declares from Dan, and publishes affliction from Mount Ephraim. *(Verses 15 through 17 describe the messengers from the northern towns reporting the advance of the Chaldeans, and then their invasion of Jerusalem. The Prophet sees this as happening at present, even though it will be some 15 years in the future. The Holy Spirit does it in this fashion*

hopefully to get the people to repent. But sadly, there was no Repentance!)

16 Make ye mention to the nations; behold, publish against Jerusalem, that watchers come from a far country, and give out their voice against the cities of Judah. *(The phrase, "Make ye mention to the nations," refers to the surrounding nations that border Judah. They would not escape this carnage either! The phrase, "Behold, publish against Jerusalem," refers to judgment that is determined against this city, even though it is the City of God. It is because of the wickedness of the "heart," as listed in Verse 14.*

The "watchers" refer to the Babylonian besiegers, who watched for people to come from besieged Jerusalem, as well as from other cities, in order to kill them.)

17 As keepers of a field, are they against her round about; because she has been rebellious against Me, saith the LORD. *(The phrase, "As keepers of a field," refers to individuals who guard crops and vineyards. The Babylonian army would lay siege to Jerusalem in the same manner.)*

18 Your way and your doings have procured these things unto you; this is your wickedness, because it is bitter, because it reaches unto your heart. *(The cause of all this is not God, but "your wickedness." The Fourteenth Verse records the cure!)*

JEREMIAH LAMENTS OVER JUDAH

19 My bowels, my bowels! I am pained at my very heart; my heart makes a noise in me; I cannot hold my peace, because you have heard, O my soul, the sound of the trumpet, the alarm of war. *(The phrase, "My bowels, my bowels!" proclaims the intensity with which Jeremiah felt the pain of what he was being told. The phrase, "Because you have heard, O my soul," means that Jeremiah actually saw in his spirit the coming destruction and "heard" the din of battle and the literal screams of the people. He felt it to the depths of his "soul." Such is the true Prophet; such is the true Preacher!)*

20 Destruction upon destruction is cried; for the whole land is spoiled: suddenly are My tents spoiled, and My curtains in a moment. *(The phrase, "Destruction upon destruction is cried," refers to the Prophet seeing such devastation as defies description. Nothing is spared! The words, "And My curtains in a moment," refer to the door or flap of the entrance to the tent, meaning that the Babylonian soldiers would even come into the very tents in order to kill the wounded.)*

21 How long shall I see the standard, and hear the sound of the trumpet? *(The idea of this Passage is that the Babylonians will not stop until their purpose is carried out, which is the destruction, total destruction, of Judah and Jerusalem.)*

22 For My people is foolish, they have not known Me; they are sottish children, and they have none understanding: they are wise to do evil, but to do good they have no knowledge. *(The last phrase, "They are wise to do evil, but to do good they have no knowledge," is striking! They would manufacture many ways to sin, i.e., "wise to do evil," but they had no knowledge of God, despite the fact that they were God's chosen People. Their lack of "knowledge" was because of their abandonment of the Bible. The knowledge to "do good" is found in the Bible, and only in the Bible!)*

23 I beheld the Earth, and, lo, it was without form, and void; and the Heavens, and they had no light. *(It is thought by some that Verses 23 through 26 pertain to the chaos of the original Earth after the rebellion of Lucifer. As such, it would apply to the first part of Gen. 1:2. No doubt this is what the Holy Spirit had in mind, and He would use this as an example of what was going to happen to Judah and Jerusalem!)*

24 I beheld the mountains, and, lo, they trembled, and all the hills moved lightly. *(As stated, this took place at the rebellion of Lucifer, which involved at least one-third of the angels, who attempted to usurp authority over God [Isa. 14:12-15].)*

25 I beheld, and, lo, there was no man, and all the birds of the Heavens were fled. *(If, in fact, this does apply to Lucifer's rebellion, then this Verse tells us that there were men on the Earth in the original creation, before Lucifer's fall, and consequently before Adam and Eve. If that is correct, we then have here the origin of demons, which are the spirits of the race that lived on the Earth before Lucifer's rebellion, and their throwing in their lot with him.)*

26 I beheld, and, lo, the fruitful place was a wilderness, and all the cities thereof were broken down at the Presence of the LORD, and by His fierce anger. *(If these Verses 23 through 26 do speak to a pre-Adamic civilization, then not only were there men on the Earth at that time, but also "cities," as would be logical. Therefore, if we rightly divide the Word of Truth, we should associate Jer. 4:23-26 with Gen. 1:2 and II Pet. 3:5-6, recognizing that the terminology fits nothing else.)*

JUDGMENT COMING BECAUSE OF SIN

27 For thus has the LORD said, The whole land shall be desolate; yet will I not make a full end. *(Whereas the previous four Verses spoke of the pre-Adamic creation and its destruction, this Verse now brings the Bible student back to the problem at hand, the coming judgment upon Judah and Jerusalem.)*

28 For this shall the Earth mourn, and the Heavens above be black: because I have spoken it, I have purposed it, and will not repent, neither will I turn back from it. *(The statement, "I have purposed it, and will not repent, neither will I turn back from it," states, in effect, that short of Repentance on the part of Judah and Jerusalem, nothing will deter this coming judgment!*

The statement, "For this shall the Earth mourn, and the Heavens above be black," refers to the spiritual light that was given to the world by Israel, but which will now be stifled! The only nation in the world to point the heathen to God was Israel, and now that light is to be extinguished. Consequently, the Earth will "mourn.")

29 The whole city shall flee for the noise of the horsemen and bowmen; they shall go into thickets, and climb up upon the rocks: every city shall be forsaken, and not a man dwell therein. *(The "whole city" speaks of Jerusalem.)*

30 And when you are spoiled, what will you do? Though you clothe yourself with crimson, though you deck yourself with ornaments of gold, though you rent your face with painting, in vain shall you make yourself fair; your lovers will despise you, they will seek your life. *(The phrase, "Your lovers," refers to heathen powers courted by Judah and Jerusalem, which did not come to their help, and which now hold Jerusalem in contempt. Jerusalem courted the heathen, but she would not court the Lord. He would have given her life, while these "lovers" took "your life.")*

31 For I have heard a voice as of a woman in travail, and the anguish as of her who brings forth her first child, the voice of the daughter of Zion, who bewails herself, who spreads her hands, saying, Woe is me now! For my soul is wearied because of murderers. *(Thus, Zion's soul "fainted before the murderers," i.e., the Babylonians. The "woman in travail" is Jerusalem, who weeps over her destruction and the slaughter of her inhabitants. The Holy Spirit likens it to birth pains, but, in reality, it will be death pains. Her cry is, "Woe is me now!" At* any time, she could have said, "Forgive me now," and the prayer would have been instantly answered, and this catastrophe avoided!)*

CHAPTER 5
(612 B.C.)
THE SINS AND PERVERSENESS OF JUDAH

RUN ye to and fro through the streets of Jerusalem, and see now, and know, and seek in the broad places thereof, if you can find a man, if there be any who execute judgment, who seek the truth; and I will pardon it. *(Other than Jeremiah's little flock, there seemed to be no one in Jerusalem, be they Priest or Prophet, who "executed judgment and sought the truth." Jerusalem was that far gone, and yet precious few would have even remotely considered such!*

Other than Jeremiah and his little flock, there was not a single "man" who sought the ways of the Lord. What an indictment!)

2 And though they say, The LORD lives; surely they swear falsely. *(The words, "swear falsely," mean "to worship insincerely." Their worship was false, and they even associated idols with the Lord.)*

3 O LORD, are not Your eyes upon the truth? You have stricken them, but they have not grieved; You have consumed them, but they have refused to receive correction: they have made their faces harder than a rock; they have refused to return. *(The phrase, "O LORD, are not Your eyes upon the Truth?", refers to the Bible. Judah had forsaken the truth, and would not "receive correction.")*

4 Therefore I said, Surely these are poor; they are foolish: for they know not the way of the LORD, nor the judgment of their God. *(The words, "surely these are poor," refer to Jerusalem being poverty-stricken in a spiritual sense, while very wealthy in a material sense. How much such mirrors the modern Church!)*

5 I will get Me unto the great men, and will speak unto them; for they have known the way of the LORD, and the judgment of their God: but these have altogether broken the yoke, and burst the bonds. *(The "yoke" and "bonds" refer to the Bible. These "great men" rejected the Law of God as a binding authority, as corrupt Christendom does today.)*

6 Wherefore a lion out of the forest shall slay them, and a wolf of the evenings shall spoil them, a leopard shall watch over their cities: every one who goes out thence shall be

torn in pieces: because their transgressions are many, and their backslidings are increased. *(Foreign powers are given the names of wild animals, which would overrun and destroy Jerusalem. Because the sin was great, the Lord would not protect Judah from these enemies. The Lord Alone was their Protector. When they forsook Him, He in turn would have to forsake them. He would have no choice!)*

7 How shall I pardon you for this? your children have forsaken Me, and sworn by them that are no gods: when I had fed them to the full, they then committed adultery, and assembled themselves by troops in the harlots' houses. *(The words, "When I had fed them to the full," refer to the Lord giving a full Revelation in the Pentateuch, and yet Israel practiced idolatry in response; they assembled themselves by troops in the temples of idols. The Lord could not pardon them for this, because they did not seek pardon, but rather went deeper into sin.)*

8 They were as fed horses in the morning: every one neighed after his neighbour's wife. *(This Verse could read: "They were as fed [lustful] horses roaming at large, every one seeking his neighbor's god." The implication in these Verses does not pertain to literal adultery, although they were certainly guilty of such, but rather to forsaking the Word of God and resorting to other things.)*

9 Shall I not visit for these things? saith the LORD: and shall not My soul be avenged on such a nation as this? *(In this Verse, the Lord is speaking of the idol worship of Verses 7 and 8.)*

10 Go ye up upon her walls, and destroy; but make not a full end: take away her battlements; for they are not the LORD's. *(The phrase, "But make not a full end," refers to Judah's degenerate members, who were to be removed, but the vine-stock, i.e., the believing kernel of the nation was to be left. It is the keynote of that which Jeremiah spoke of in 4:27.)*

GOD WILL CONSUME JUDAH

11 For the House of Israel and the House of Judah have dealt very treacherously against Me, saith the LORD. *(Here the Lord speaks of both "Israel" and "Judah," even though Israel had been completely destroyed a little over 100 years before. He concluded both to have committed spiritual high treason. He uses the words, "against Me," referring to the fact that all sin is directed by Satan against God.)*

12 They have belied the LORD, and said, It is not He; neither shall evil come upon us; neither shall we see sword nor famine *(the phrase, "It is not He," refers to the fact that Judah denied that God was speaking through Jeremiah.*

The phrase, "They have belied the LORD," means to give a false representation of something, or to contradict):

13 And the Prophets shall become wind, and the word is not in them: thus shall it be done unto them. *(Verses 12 and 13 could be paraphrased: "They have contradicted Jehovah, and said, 'Not He!' Neither shall calamity come upon us, neither shall we see sword nor famine; for the Prophets [i.e. Jehovah's True Prophets] are windbags, and the Word [of God] is not in them; and the miseries which they threaten will come upon themselves!"*

Thus, the popular Preachers of that time, as at the present day, said that God never punishes sin and sinners; that He never casts anyone into the Lake of Fire; that, in fact, there is no Lake of Fire; and that those Preachers who announce His coming Wrath belie His Character and talk nonsense.)

14 Wherefore thus saith the LORD God of Hosts, Because you speak this word, behold, I will make My words in your mouth fire, and this people wood, and it shall devour them. *(The "fire" that would "devour them" would be the anointing of the Holy Spirit upon Jeremiah. Yet for all this, Judah would not turn.)*

15 Lo, I will bring a nation upon you from far, O House of Israel, saith the LORD: it is a mighty nation, it is an ancient nation, a nation whose language you know not, neither understand what they say. *(This nation speaks of the mighty Babylonian Empire.)*

16 Their quiver is as a open sepulcher, they are all mighty men. *(The idea of this Passage, as given by the Holy Spirit, is to portray the cruelty and the power of the Babylonian invader, all used as the instruments of the Lord.)*

17 And they shall eat up your harvest, and your bread, which your sons and your daughters should eat: they shall eat up your flocks and your herds: they shall eat up your vines and your fig trees: they shall impoverish your fenced cities, wherein you trusted, with the sword. *(The phrase, "Which your sons and your daughters should eat," in the original Hebrew actually says, "they shall eat your sons and your daughters," meaning they would be killed!)*

18 Nevertheless in those days, saith the

LORD, I will not make a full end with you. *(God's tender pity for guilty men is revealed in the sentences: "I will pardon her" [Vs. 1], but "not make a full end" [Vs. 10], and "I will not make a full end with you" [Vs. 18].)*

19 And it shall come to pass, when you shall say, Wherefore does the LORD our God all these things unto us? then shall you answer them, Like as you have forsaken Me, and served strange gods in your land, so shall you serve strangers in a land that is not yours. *(The intent of this Passage is that inasmuch as the Jews served foreign gods in Jehovah's Land, they shall become the slaves of foreigners in a land that is not theirs.)*

SPIRITUAL AND CIVIL CORRUPTION BRINGS JUDGMENT AND PUNISHMENT

20 Declare this in the house of Jacob, and publish it in Judah, saying *(Jeremiah is told to proclaim this Message to the people of Judah. It is to be "published," meaning to be proliferated among the people),*

21 Hear now this, O foolish people, and without understanding, which have eyes, and see not; which have ears, and hear not. *(The phrase, "Without understanding," actually means "without heart." It means that the people have no heart toward God. They have set a course of deliberate sin, which always perverts a man's moral perceptions. The Prophet first of all states the result, and then the cause.*

The statement, "Which have eyes and see not," refers to judicial blindness. In other words, they desired to be such!)

22 Fear ye not Me? saith the LORD: will you not tremble at My presence, which have placed the sand for the bound of the sea by a perpetual decree, that it cannot pass it: and though the waves thereof toss themselves, yet can they not prevail; though they roar, yet can they not pass over it? *(The sense of the Passage is that the sands of the seashore obey God, but His People disobey Him. They disobey Him because they have no "fear" of Him!)*

23 But this people has a revolting and a rebellious heart, they are revolted and gone. *(The "heart" is the center of the moral and spiritual life, virtually equivalent to "the will." The phrase, "A rebellious heart," refers to actively defying and opposing the Lord. "A revolting heart" refers to turning back from God's Law and service.)*

24 Neither say they in their heart, Let us now fear the LORD our God, Who gives rain, both the former and the latter, in His season: He reserves unto us the appointed weeks of the harvest. *(In this Verse, we have another "perpetual decree," as outlined in Verse 22. This one is the "rain" and "appointed weeks of the harvest." The word "perpetual" in Verse 22 means that these Laws are eternal, and consequently the seasons are eternal and unchangeable, and made so by God's decree [Gen. 8:22]. The "appointed weeks" are the seven weeks which elapse from the second day of the Passover to the "Feast of Pentecost" [Ex. 23:16; 34:22; Deut. 16:9-10].)*

25 Your iniquities have turned away these things, and your sins have withheld good things from you. *(Let the Reader understand that as "sin withheld good things from Judah," likewise, sin withholds good things from any and all.)*

26 For among My people are found wicked men: they lay wait, as he who sets snares; they set a trap, they catch men. *(Who are these wicked men? They are the "Priests, Pastors, and Prophets" of 2:8. They, in their religious schemes, have no desire to carry out the Will of God, but rather to "catch men" in their web in order to sustain their lavish lifestyles. How so similar to the modern "Word of Faith" doctrine or "greed gospel"!)*

27 As a cage is full of birds, so are their houses full of deceit: therefore they are become great, and waxed rich. *(This Verse could be paraphrased: "As a cage is full of birds caught in traps, so their houses are full of riches secured by deceit." God is not opposed to greatness or riches as such, but is deadly opposed to such obtained by spiritual fraud and spiritual deceit.)*

28 They are waxed fat, they shine: yea, they overpass the deeds of the wicked: they judge not the cause, the cause of the fatherless, yet they prosper; and the right of the needy do they not judge. *(The phrase, "Yea, they overpass the deeds of the wicked," literally means "they overpass the common measure of wickedness." This was the sin that opposed Christ, the sin of the Pharisees.*

The phrase, "They judge not the cause, the cause of the fatherless," refers to the fact that their prosperity was at the expense of the poor, and even the poorest of the poor!)

29 Shall I not visit for these things? saith the LORD, shall not My soul be avenged on such a nation as this? *(This Verse is a repetition of Verse 9, in order to impress the severity*

of the situation! This, as Verse 9, carries powerful weight, because it answers the charges of the preceding Verses.)

30 **A wonderful and horrible thing is committed in the land** *(the words, "wonderful and horrible," could have been translated "appalling and horrible." The word "appalling" means "stupefying");*

31 **The Prophets prophesy falsely, and the Priests bear rule by their means; and My people love to have it so: and what will you do in the end thereof?** *(The Priests were appointed to teach the Law. They failed to do so! God then raised up the Prophets to teach the people, but Satan sent out false prophets to oppose and confuse the Truth, and the Priests united with them.)*

CHAPTER 6
(612 B.C.)
THE DESTRUCTION OF JERUSALEM
PROPHESIED

O you children of Benjamin, gather yourselves to flee out of the midst of Jerusalem, and blow the trumpet in Tekoa, and set up a sign of fire in Beth-haccerem: for evil appears out of the north, and great destruction. *(The phrase, "O you children of Benjamin," refers to the Tribe of Benjamin, which bordered the Tribe of Judah. Strangely enough, Jerusalem was not locally a city of Judah, at all. In fact, it belonged, strictly speaking, to the Tribe of Benjamin.*

The "evil that appeared out of the north" referred to the Babylonian armies.)

2 **I have likened the daughter of Zion to a comely and delicate woman.** *(The Lord likened Israel, Jerusalem, Zion, and Judah unto a woman. As such, she was called His wife, and He, her Husband [3:1, 8; 31:32; Isa. 54:5]. He also likened her departure to idols unto unfaithfulness, and called it "adultery," i.e., "spiritual adultery.")*

3 **The shepherds with their flocks shall come unto her; they shall pitch their tents against her round about; they shall feed every one in his place.** *(The shepherds and their flocks were the Babylonian generals and their soldiers. They would surround Jerusalem, laying siege to the city.)*

4 **Prepare ye war against her; arise, and let us go up at noon. Woe unto us! for the day goes away, for the shadows of the evening are stretched out.** *(The Babylonians are the speakers of Verses 4 and 5. In their eagerness to*

capture Jerusalem, they fight in the burning heat of the midday, lament that the evening hinders their operations, and resolve to fight by night and destroy her palaces. And so it came to pass.

The phrase, "Woe unto us!" presents the Holy Spirit attempting to impress upon Judah the lateness of the hour! The "day" of Repentance is fast slipping away, with the "shadows" of the "evening" growing longer by the moment. Judah simply does not have much time left!)

5 **Arise, and let us go by night, and let us destroy her palaces.** *(The Holy Spirit would proclaim, a little more than 15 years before the actual happening, the actual terminology of the Babylonians and their intent.)*

6 **For thus has the LORD of Hosts said, Hew ye down trees, and cast a mount against Jerusalem: this is the city to be visited; she is wholly oppression in the midst of her.** *(The phrase, "This is the city to be visited," means "punished." The reason for this punishment is given in the words, "she is wholly oppression in the midst of her," referring to the oppression by the strong and the mighty against the poor, helpless, and dispossessed.)*

7 **As a fountain casts out her waters, so she casts out her wickedness: violence and spoil is heard in her; before Me continually is grief and wounds.** *(The "grief and wounds" were afflicted on the poor by their rich oppressors. The words, "Before Me," mean rather "before My face." God sees it, and is determined to take vengeance on the oppressors!)*

8 **Be thou instructed, O Jerusalem, lest My soul depart from you; lest I make you desolate, a land not inhabited.** *(The words, "Be thou instructed, O Jerusalem," actually mean "Let yourself be corrected." It means to accept the warning conveyed in the Divine admonition.)*

9 **Thus saith the LORD of Hosts, They shall thoroughly glean the remnant of Israel as a vine: turn back your hand as a grapegatherer into the baskets.** *(As a grapegatherer keeps putting the grapes into his basket and causes his hand to return to the basket until he has gleaned all the grapes, so is it predicted here that Nebuchadnezzar would keep returning to Jerusalem until he had taken away all of its inhabitants.)*

10 **To whom shall I speak, and give warning, that they may hear? Behold, their ear is uncircumcised, and they cannot hearken: behold, the Word of the LORD is unto them a reproach; they have no delight in it.** *(The words, "Behold, their ear is uncircumcised," tell*

us the reason for their spiritual impotence. They had forsaken the Word of God.)

11 Therefore I am full of the fury of the LORD; I am weary with holding in: I will pour it out upon the children abroad, and upon the assembly of young men together: for even the husband with the wife shall be taken, the aged with him who is full of days. *(The phrase, "Therefore I am full of the fury of the LORD," refers to Jeremiah personally. The phrase, "I am weary with holding in," refers to Jeremiah sincerely attempting to keep his personal feelings out of that which he was to deliver. He here proclaims that he could no longer do so!)*

12 And their houses shall be turned unto others, with their fields and wives together: for I will stretch out My hand upon the inhabitants of the land, saith the LORD. *(The judgment of this Verse was that predicted in Deut. 28:30.)*

13 For from the least of them even unto the greatest of them every one is given to covetousness, and from the prophet even unto the priest every one deals falsely. *(This indictment by the Holy Spirit is severe indeed! The words, "given to covetousness," mean "gaineth gain." However, the word rendered here "gain" implies that it is unrighteous gain. The root means "to tear," referring to taking things by force from the helpless.*

The "prophet" and the "priest" are included in this group! In other words, money had become their pursuit instead of God.)

14 They have healed also the hurt of the daughter of My people slightly, saying, Peace, peace; when there is no peace. *(When an unconverted man is disquieted [hurt] about death and the judgment sure to follow [Heb. 11:27], fashionable Preachers heal "the hurt" with a false peace-plaster. They assure him that there is no judgment to come and, thus, they deal falsely. But they themselves shall perish with their dupes, as is told us in the next Verse.)*

15 Were they ashamed when they had committed abomination? Nay, they were not at all ashamed, neither could they blush: therefore they shall fall among them who fall: at the time that I visit them they shall be cast down, saith the LORD. *(The phrase, "Therefore they shall fall among them who fall," refers to the "Prophets and Priests" of Verse 13, who would fall with their dupes. All would go down!*

The question, "Were they ashamed?" referring to their "abominations," refers to the fact that they were not only not ashamed, but attempted

to make the Lord a part of their terrible sin by claiming that He was blessing them, regarding their ill-gotten gains from "covetousness.")

16 Thus saith the LORD, Stand ye in the ways, and see, and ask for the old paths, where is the good way, and walk therein, and you shall find rest for your souls. But they said, We will not walk therein. *(True rest and healing is to be found in "the old paths" and "the good way," that is, the Gospel as taught in the Bible. The phrase, "Stand ye in the ways," refers to the ardent seeking of the Ways of God.)*

17 Also I set watchmen over you, saying, Hearken to the sound of the trumpet. But they said, We will not hearken. *(With the word "watchmen," a metaphor is used by the Holy Spirit describing the high watchtower [Hab. 2:1], from which the "watchmen," i.e., Prophets, scrutinized the horizon for the first appearance of danger, and gave warning of it by blowing a trumpet.*

Once again, the Holy Spirit gives an Altar Call, "But they said, We will not hearken.")

18 Therefore hear, you nations, and know, O congregation, what is among them. *(The nations surrounding Judah were to hear this Message, as well!)*

19 Hear, O Earth: behold, I will bring evil upon this people, even the fruit of their thoughts, because they have not hearkened unto My words, nor to My Law, but rejected it. *(The phrase, "Behold, I will bring evil upon this people," is because of their refusal and rejection of the Bible. The phrase, "The fruit of their thoughts," is strong indeed! It refers to the determination of the people not to hearken to the Word of the Lord.)*

20 To what purpose comes there to Me incense from Sheba, and the sweet cane from a far country? Your burnt offerings are not acceptable, nor your sacrifices sweet unto Me. *(When the Holy Scriptures are thrust aside, incense and burnt offerings become abominable to God. Placing faith in the ceremony instead of in what the ceremony represented, namely, Christ and Him Crucified, presents the wrong object of faith, which God can never accept.)*

21 Therefore thus saith the LORD, Behold, I will lay stumblingblocks before this people, and the fathers and the sons together shall fall upon them; the neighbour and his friend shall perish. *(The phrase, "Behold, I will lay stumblingblocks before this people," refers to the coming invader, the Babylonians.)*

22 Thus saith the LORD, Behold, a people

comes from the north country, and a great nation shall be raised from the sides of the Earth. *(This refers to the Babylonians.)*

23 They shall lay hold on bow and spear; they are cruel, and have no mercy; their voice roars like the sea; and they ride upon horses, set in array as men for war against you, O daughter of Zion. *(The Holy Spirit in this Passage goes to great lengths to explain to Judah and Jerusalem exactly as to the "cruelty" and lack of "mercy" among the Babylonians.)*

24 We have heard the fame thereof: our hands wax feeble: anguish has taken hold of us, and pain, as of a woman in travail. *(The horror will know no bounds!)*

25 Go not forth into the field, nor walk by the way; for the sword of the enemy and fear is on every side. *(When this time comes, if the people feel they can escape by fleeing the city, this Passage proclaims the opposite!)*

26 O daughter of My people, gird thee with sackcloth, and wallow yourself in ashes: make thee mourning, as for an only son, most bitter lamentation: for the spoiler shall suddenly come upon us. *(Yet again in this Verse, a love which calls these idolaters and oppressors, "My people," cries aloud to them to repent, but in vain. "The spoiler" is Nebuchadnezzar.)*

27 I have set you for a tower and a fortress among My people, that you may know and try their way. *(In Verses 27 through 30, God speaks Personally to Jeremiah and, under the figure of an assayer of metals, commands him to expose the corruption of the people, and so demonstrate that they refused to yield to Truth and were morally "refuse-silver." "Tower" and "fortress" should read "assayer" and "examiner" or "scrutinizer.")*

28 They are all grievous revolters, walking with slanders: they are brass and iron; they are all corrupters. *(The phrase, "They are all corrupters," refers to the fact that not only are they corrupted, but they seek to corrupt all others, as well!)*

29 The bellows are burned, the lead is consumed of the fire; the founder melts in vain: for the wicked are not plucked away. *(The assayer has spared no trouble, all the rules of his art have been obeyed, but no silver appears as a result of the process.)*

30 Reprobate silver shall men call them, because the LORD has rejected them. *(So was it with Israel! The furnace of affliction, though very hot, failed to separate the dross, with the result that God adjudged the nation as refuse-silver.)*

CHAPTER 7
(600 B.C.)
JEREMIAH CALLS FOR REPENTANCE

THE word that came to Jeremiah from the LORD, saying *(the date of the original utterance of this Prophecy seems to have been either the early years or at the midpoint of the reign of Jehoiakim. If that, in fact, is the case, this Prophecy was probably about 5 to 7 years before the first excursion by Nebuchadnezzar)*,

2 Stand in the gate of the LORD's house, and proclaim there this word, and say, Hear the word of the LORD, all ye of Judah, who enter in at these gates to worship the LORD. *(The phrase, "Who enter in at these gates to worship the LORD," bespoke the idea that people were constantly coming and going regarding their worship of God, but, in reality, it was "worship" that God would not accept.)*

3 Thus saith the LORD of Hosts, the God of Israel, Amend your ways and your doings, and I will cause you to dwell in this place. *(Once again, the Holy Spirit gives an Altar Call. The phrase, "And I will cause you to dwell in this place," referred to Jerusalem, and the inheritance that he had originally given them. Once again, the choice is placed before them! Once again, they refused to heed!)*

4 Trust ye not in lying words, saying, The Temple of the LORD, The Temple of the LORD, The Temple of the LORD, are these. *(The Temple was of Divine ordination. The men of Judah and Jerusalem had an idolatrous pride in it. They believed that its presence in their city secured their national independence and safety, and that its worship could be made to harmonize with the idolatry and injustice of Verses 6, 9, and 30.*

The "lying words" of Verses 4 and 8 were: that the Temple, being the Temple of Jehovah, no calamity would come upon them.)

5 For if you thoroughly amend your ways and your doings; if you thoroughly execute judgment between a man and his neighbour *(here the word "thoroughly" is introduced before the word "amend," lending more credence to the statement, and also saying that a partial repentance would not be accepted)*;

6 If you oppress not the stranger, the fatherless, and the widow, and shed not innocent blood in this place, neither walk, after other gods to your hurt *(the Holy Spirit once again portrays the love and concern of the Lord for the helpless)*:

7 Then will I cause you to dwell in this place, in the land that I gave to your fathers, for ever and ever. *(The words, "I will cause you to dwell in this place," as in Verse 3, have the addition in this Verse "forever and ever.")*

SINS OF JUDAH

8 Behold, you trust in lying words, that cannot profit. *(As stated, the "lying words" spoke of the claims of the religious leaders of Jerusalem, who asserted that by maintaining Temple worship, they would be protected from all evil. In the broader sense, "lying words" refer to anything and everything apart from the Bible. The Holy Spirit emphatically states that such "cannot profit"!)*

9 Will you steal, murder, and commit adultery, and swear falsely, and burn incense unto Baal, and walk after other gods whom you know not *(the Passage may be thus read: "Is this your way of life — course of theft, murder, lying, and adultery?");*

10 And come and stand before Me in this house, which is called by My name, and say, We are delivered to do all these abominations? *("This house" refers to the Temple. The words, "Stand before Me," refer to God knowing not only the actions of these false worshippers, but also the thoughts and intent of their hearts.*

The words, "And say, We are delivered to do all these abominations," refer to their erroneous thinking that their actions cleansed them from all past sins, and they were, therefore, free to continue in their present lifestyles.)

11 Is this house, which is called by My name, become a den of robbers in your eyes? Behold, even I have seen it, saith the LORD. *(The phrase, "A den of robbers," is that which the Lord calls the people of Jerusalem. They were treating "His House" as a group of thieves would treat a gathering place where they congregated in order to drink, carouse, and even plan robberies.)*

12 But go ye now unto my place which was in Shiloh, where I set My name at the first, and see what I did to it for the wickedness of My people Israel. *("Shiloh" was to Israel during the time of the Judges what Jerusalem was to them during the Kings. The Lord destroyed it, because of Israel's sin.)*

JUDGMENT ON SIN

13 And now, because ye have done all these works, saith the LORD, and I spoke unto you, rising up early and speaking, but you heard not; and I called you, but you answered not *(the phrase, "Rising up early and speaking," refers to speaking zealously and continually, but yet without favorable response);*

14 Therefore will I do unto this house, which is called by My name, wherein you trust, and unto the place which I gave to you and to your fathers, as I have done to Shiloh. *(The Prophet pointed to the ruin of Shiloh as illustrating the Wrath of God, which, when corruption enters, falls upon that which He Himself sets up; and He predicted a sure destruction for the Temple.)*

15 And I will cast you out of My sight, as I have cast out all your brethren, even the whole seed of Ephraim. *(The expulsion of Ten Tribes over 100 years earlier should have warned Jerusalem; but it did not.)*

JUDAH'S IDOLATRY

16 Therefore pray not thou for this people, neither lift up cry nor prayer for them, neither make intercession to Me: for I will not hear you. *(To substitute the idols of man's religious will in place of Christ is the sin unto death of I Jn. 5:16. In this Verse, the Lord does not say that He would not forgive them, if they, in fact, came to Him with a broken heart in contrite Repentance! What He does say is that neither Jeremiah's intercession nor the intercession of anyone else would cause Him to change His Mind about their destruction, barring their Repentance.)*

17 Do you not see what they do in the cities of Judah and in the streets of Jerusalem? *(Their sin had become open and without shame! Man becomes what he worships.)*

18 The children gather wood, and the fathers kindle the fire, and the women knead their dough, to make cakes to the queen of heaven, and to pour out drink offerings unto other gods, that they may provoke Me to anger. *(All ages, as represented by the "children, fathers, and women," were involved in these idolatrous acts, thus justifying the sweeping character of the Judgment, as described in 6:11. The word "queen" in "queen of heaven" is probably the Phoenician title of "Astarte." The Jews concluded that inasmuch as Jehovah created the heavens, the worship of that which He created was the same as worshipping Him [Rom. 1:25].)*

19 Do they provoke Me to anger? Saith the

LORD: do they not provoke themselves to the confusion of their own faces? *(The phrase, "Do they not provoke themselves to the confusion of their own faces?", refers to their confusing the Creator with the created; hence, they "changed the Truth of God into a lie.")*

PUNISHMENT FOR JUDAH'S REBELLION

20 Therefore thus saith the Lord GOD; Behold, My anger and My fury shall be poured out upon this place, upon man, and upon beast, and upon the trees of the field, and upon the fruit of the ground; and it shall burn, and shall not be quenched. *(Man's rebellion against God brings suffering upon the animal creation and blight upon the vegetable kingdom, hence the plight of this present world.)*

21 Thus saith the LORD of Hosts, the God of Israel; Put your burnt offerings unto your sacrifices, and eat flesh. *(The flesh of the Burnt Offering was forbidden to be eaten by the worshipper [Lev., Chpt. 1], but that of some of the other Offerings permitted [Lev., Chpt. 4]. This Verse means that, so far as God was concerned, the Sacrifices had become hypocrisies, and they might eat them all, if they like; God accepted none of them.)*

22 For I spoke not unto your fathers, nor commanded them in the day that I brought them out of the land of Egypt, concerning burnt offerings or sacrifices *(the Jews were attempting to make the Sacrifices into a rite of Salvation within themselves. They had lost all understanding as to what these Sacrifices represented, namely, the Coming Redeemer [Heb. 10:4]):*

23 But this thing commanded I them, saying, Obey My voice, and I will be your God, and you shall be My people: and walk ye in all the ways that I have commanded you, that it may be well unto you. *(The condition for acceptance is obedience.)*

24 But they hearkened not, nor inclined their ear, but walked in the counsels and in the imagination of their evil heart, and went backward, and not forward. *(Whenever man follows his own counsel, he always "goes backward and not forward." However, in the "imagination of his evil heart," he surely thinks he is improving upon God!)*

25 Since the day that your fathers came forth out of the land of Egypt unto this day I have even sent unto you all My servants the Prophets, daily rising up early and sending them *(the phrase, "daily rising up early and sending them," refers to the most opportune time, in order that the greatest number of people would hear and be given every opportunity):*

26 Yet they hearkened not unto Me, nor inclined their ear, but hardened their neck: they did worse than their fathers. *("They hearkened not" is their indictment!)*

27 Therefore you shall speak all these words unto them; but they will not hearken to you: you shall also call unto them; but they will not answer you. *(Through foreknowledge, God knew that they "would not hearken to Jeremiah." He knew what the outcome would be, and yet He continued to call and plead, knowing it was useless, but doing so anyway!)*

28 But you shall say unto them, This is a nation that obeys not the voice of the LORD their God, nor receives correction: truth is perished; and is cut off from their mouth. *(As they trusted in "lying words" [Vs. 8], they then lost the "Truth.")*

29 Cut off your hair, O Jerusalem, and cast it away, and take up a lamentation on high places; for the LORD has rejected and forsaken the generation of His wrath. *(The "cutting off of the hair" was a practice of the women of that day when they were rejected and forsaken. The phrase, "And take up a lamentation on high places," refers to the fact that they worshipped idols there, so they should add the cut hair to their devotional offerings. The Lord is, of course, using sarcasm.*

"The generation of His Wrath" refers to the generation on which His Wrath is to be poured out.)

30 For the children of Judah have done evil in My sight, saith the LORD: they have set their abominations in the house which is called by My name, to pollute it. *(The "abominations" spoken of here included, no doubt, the heathen altars set up by Ahaz in place of the Brazen Altar [II Ki. 16:10-18], plus the altars which Manasseh built [for all the hosts of Heaven in the two courts of the House of Jehovah], and especially the image of the Canaanitish goddess Asherah, which he set up in the Temple itself [II Ki. 21:5-7].)*

31 And they have built the high places of Tophet, which is in the valley of the son of Hinnom, to burn their sons and their daughters in the fire; which I commanded them not, neither came it into My heart. *(At these "high places," child sacrifices were offered by fire to the deity Molech. This hideous practice is beyond comprehension!)*

32 Therefore, behold, the days come, saith

the LORD, that it shall no more be called Tophet, not the valley of the son of Hinnom, but the valley of slaughter: for they shall bury in Tophet, till there be no place. *(In essence, the Holy Spirit is saying that if they desire to sacrifice humans here, then humans would be sacrificed here, and to a degree and in a manner that would stagger the imagination, i.e., "the Babylonians would do such!")*

33 And the carcases of this people shall be meat for the fowls of the Heaven, and for the beasts of the Earth; and none shall fray them away. *(The word "fray" means "frighten." The phrase, "And the carcasses of this people," refers to a scene so desolate that it beggars description!)*

34 Then will I cause to cease from the cities of Judah, and from the streets of Jerusalem, the voice of mirth, and the voice of gladness, the voice of the bridegroom, and the voice of the bride: for the land shall be desolate. *(The phrase, "For the land shall be desolate," rather means "shall become a waste.")*

CHAPTER 8
(600 B.C.)
JUDGMENT ON JUDAH

AT that time, saith the LORD, they shall bring out the bones of the kings of Judah, and the bones of his princes, and the bones of the Priests, and the bones of the Prophets, and the bones of the inhabitants of Jerusalem, out of their graves *(the phrase, "At that time," refers to the sack of Jerusalem by the Chaldeans. The repetition of the word "bones" is important. Not only are the objects of their idolatrous worship designated, but also the fact that every class of society had apostatized from Jehovah.*

The phrase, "Out of their graves," refers to the sack of all the tombs, with the Babylonians looking, no doubt, for valuable objects):

2 And they shall spread them before the sun, and the moon, and all the host of Heaven, whom they have loved, and whom they have served, and after whom they have walked, and whom they have sought, and whom they have worshipped: they shall not be gathered, not be buried; they shall be for dung upon the face of the Earth. *(The phrase, "And they shall spread them . . . ," refers to the Babylonians leaving the bones on the ground before the planetary bodies which Israel had worshipped. The phrase, "They shall be for dung on the face of the Earth," portrays God's thoughts and actions concerning the bones of these unhappy idol worshippers!*

While their souls were in Hell, their remains were desecrated, and by fellow idol worshippers, at that!)

3 And death shall be chosen rather than life by all the residue of them who remain of this evil family, which remain in all the places where I have driven them, saith the LORD of Hosts. *(So great would be the misery of the living in their captivity that they would prefer to die.)*

SINS OF JUDAH

4 Moreover you shall say unto them, Thus saith the LORD; Shall they fall, and not arise? shall He turn away, and not return? *(In this prophetic utterance, the anguish of the speaker reveals the love of God to rebellious man; and the rejection of the Message proves the hatred of rebellious man to God.)*

5 Why then is this people of Jerusalem slidden back by a perpetual backsliding? they hold fast deceit, they refuse to return. *(The words, "perpetual backsliding," refer to a continuous backsliding, ever going deeper into sin. There was no halting of their spiritual decline. Not once did they make an attempt to turn toward God.)*

6 I hearkened and heard, but they spoke not aright: no man repented him of his wickedness, saying, What have I done? Every one turned to his course, as the horse rushes into the battle. *(The words, "They spoke not aright," refer to their expression of repentance not being sincere, for no man questioned the character of his actions, but continued to rush toward evil.)*

7 Yea, the stork in the Heaven knows her appointed times; and the turtle and the crane and the swallow observe the time of their coming; but My people know not the judgment of the LORD. *(Migratory birds have more intelligence than unconverted men. They obey the migratory instinct, and so escape famine and death. Man disobeys his conscience and the Word of God, and so he perishes.)*

8 How do you say, We are wise, and the Law of the LORD is with us? Lo, certainly in vain made he it; the pen of the scribes is in vain. *(The question posed by Jeremiah, "How do you say, We are wise?", is directed toward the Priests and the Prophets, whom he so constantly described as among the chief causes of Judah's ruin, as such is the ruin of the modern Church. As these individuals in Isaiah's day regarded it as an unwarrantable assumption on the part of*

that Prophet to pretend to instruct them in their duty [Isa. 28:9], likewise, Jeremiah was looked at with ridicule.

The answer of these Priests and Prophets was: "The Law of the LORD is with us." In giving this answer, they bade him keep his exhortations to himself, seeing that they themselves were wise and the divinely appointed teachers of the people.)

9 The wise men are ashamed, they are dismayed and taken: lo, they have rejected the Word of the LORD; and what wisdom is in them? (The phrase, "The wise men are ashamed," actually looks forward to the coming calamity and says, "the wise men will be ashamed.")

JUDGMENT COMING

10 Therefore will I give their wives unto others, and their fields to them who shall inherit them: for every one from the least even unto the greatest is given to covetousness, from the Prophet even unto the Priest every one deals falsely. (Verses 10 through 12 show that the Prophet Jeremiah, like the Prophet of Nazareth, was not ashamed to repeat the words given him by God. The Holy Spirit through Jeremiah is saying that if Jerusalem follows these "wise men," terrible things will happen. The phrase, "Them who shall inherit them," actually means "to them who shall take possession of them by violence.")

11 For they have healed the hurt of the daughter of My people slightly, saying, Peace, peace; when there is no peace. (The Holy Spirit says, "There is no peace," and yet they choose to believe liars and their lies rather than the Holy Spirit and His Truth.)

12 Were they ashamed when they had committed abomination? Nay, they were not at all ashamed, neither could they blush: therefore shall they fall among them who fall: in the time of their visitation they shall be cast down, saith the LORD. (Israel had had a "time of visitation" of Righteousness under Josiah, but had rejected it. Now they will have a "time of visitation" of Judgment.)

13 I will surely consume them, saith the LORD: there shall be no grapes on the vine, nor figs on the fig tree, and the leaf shall fade; and the things that I have given them shall pass away from them. (Israel in the Scriptures is presented as a vine, as a fig tree, and as an olive tree. These express Divine relationships. Judah is compared to a vine with bad grapes [2:21]; here the vine does not even pretend to bear fruit.

The words, "And the things that I have given

them shall pass away from them," refer to their possession and inheritance of the Land of Israel, plus the prosperity and blessings. All of these blessings, plus the land, would be taken from them by the Babylonians.

They gave idols credit for their blessings and prosperity; therefore, the Lord would give their blessings and prosperity to idol worshippers, i.e., the Babylonians.)

BABYLONIAN INVASION OF JUDAH FORETOLD

14 Why do we sit still? assemble yourselves, and let us enter into the defenced cities, and let us be silent there: for the LORD our God has put us to silence, and given us water of gall to drink, because we have sinned against the LORD. (The phrase, "For the LORD our God has put us to silence," refers to being decreed to utter destruction. The word "silent" means that there is no defense! The phrase, "And give us water of gall to drink," is a symbolism of Judgment. It is bitter water, extremely bitter, and they by no means desire to drink it, but have no choice!

The phrase, "Because we have sinned against the LORD," presents the cause of all trouble and calamity on Earth.)

15 We looked for peace, but no good came; and for a time of health, and behold trouble! (The Prophet enters into the minds of the people, expressing their thoughts when this time of terror comes! The phrase, "We looked for peace, but no good came," refers back to Verse 11, when these "wise men," in contradiction to Jeremiah's Prophecies, said, "Peace, peace." Instead, they find the opposite, which is war! They were told by the false prophets that "good times" were coming, but instead "no good came.")

16 The snorting of his horses was heard from Dan: the whole land trembled at the sound of the neighing of his strong one; for they are come, and have devoured the land, and all that is in it; the city, and those who dwell therein. (This Scripture pictures the coming invasion of the Babylonians, which also symbolizes the yet future Antichrist, who will come from the same direction, and who will "devour the land" in the same manner!)

17 For, behold, I will send serpents, cockatrices, among you, which will not be charmed, and they shall bite you, saith the LORD. (The Chaldeans will be so terrible that they are compared to serpents and adders, and so fierce that to placate them would be impossible.)

JEREMIAH'S SORROW

18 When I would comfort myself against sorrow, my heart is faint in me. *(The obvious consternation of Jeremiah is expressed in this Passage!)*

19 Behold the voice of the cry of the daughter of My people, because of them that dwell in a far country, Is not the LORD in Zion? Is not her king in her? Why have they provoked Me to anger with their graven images, and with strange vanities? *(Almost as if in answer to Jeremiah's great "sorrow," the Voice of the Lord explains His Own sadness. The expression, "The daughter of My people," applied to this nation of idolaters, liars, and oppressors, strikingly exhibits the amazing love and pity of God, and proclaims His willingness to forgive the greatest sinners, if they will but turn to Him.)*

20 The harvest is past, the summer is ended, and we are not saved. *(This statement is projected into the future, at the time of the siege of Jerusalem by the Babylonians, and presents the cry, or rather the forlorn expression, of the people. The phrase, "The summer is ended," spoke of late summer and the fall of the year, just before the winter rains set it. They were expecting the Egyptian army to come to their rescue, but the time for armies to march is now ended. Winter is coming on and "we are not saved.")*

21 For the hurt of the daughter of My people am I hurt; I am black; astonishment has taken hold on Me. *(The phrase, "I am black," refers to mourning in sackcloth and ashes, and does not mean the color of his skin. The phrase, "Astonishment has taken hold on me," refers to the horror that is even greater than he had previously anticipated.)*

22 Is there no balm in Gilead; is there no physician there? Why then is not the health of the daughter of My people recovered? *(The questions asked by the Lord are meant to receive a negative answer. No Earthly "physician" could "recover the health of the people of Judah." Just as no Earthly mortal can recover the health of hurting, dying humanity; however, the "Physician" would ultimately come to Gilead, and He would be the Lord Jesus Christ.)*

CHAPTER 9
(600 B.C.)

JEREMIAH'S LAMENT FOR THE PEOPLE'S SIN AND THE PENDING JUDGMENT

OH that my head were waters, and my eyes a fountain of tears, that I might weep day and night for the slain of the daughter of my people! *(Jeremiah was called "the weeping Prophet," and for good reason! After seeing what is coming upon his people, he cannot help but weep, even "day and night." The "slain" will be many!)*

2 Oh that I had in the wilderness a lodging place of wayfaring men; that I might leave my people, and go from them! for they be all adulterers, an assembly of treacherous men. *(Because of the vileness of Jerusalem, the Prophet wanted to "go from them," but yet he could not go, because he was the only one standing between them and total destruction. However, they did not regard him at all, and in fact desired to kill him, and would have succeeded were it not for the delivering Power of the Lord.*

The word "treacherous" is used because they actually committed spiritual high treason!)

3 And they bend their tongues like their bow for lies: but they are not valiant for the truth upon the Earth; for they proceed from evil to evil, and they know not Me, saith the LORD. *(This Verse could be translated, "They bend their tongues as it were their bow for falsehoods; and they are grown rich in the land, but not by speaking truth; for they proceed from evil to evil, and they refuse to recognize Me, saith Jehovah.")*

4 Take ye heed every one of his neighbour, and trust ye not in any brother: for every brother will utterly supplant, and every neighbour will walk with slanders. *(The phrase, "For every brother will utterly supplant," has reference to Jacob, who was a supplanter, or a deceiver. This was before Jacob, by the Power of God, was changed to Israel, the Prince with God.*

"Slanders" have to do with tale-bearing, whether true or false.)

5 And they will deceive every one his neighbour, and will not speak the truth: they have taught their tongue to speak lies, and weary themselves to commit iniquity. *(The phrase, "And they will deceive every one his neighbor," speaks of the utter disposition of the entirety of the people. They were deceived, so it was easy for them to be deceivers. Such are Satan and his followers!*

The phrase, "They have taught their tongue to speak lies," is an intimation of the unnaturalness of vice. Not only did they lie, but they practiced lying.)

6 Your habitation is in the midst of deceit; through deceit they refuse to know Me, saith the LORD. *(The idea of this Passage is that*

some of these individuals may feign an appreciation for Jeremiah and his Message; nevertheless, the Holy Spirit tells him here that these individuals cannot "speak the Truth," and should not be trusted.

The phrase, "Through deceit they refuse to know Me," means that they refused to be converted to the Lord, because that would cost them the loss of the money gained by fraud.)

7 Therefore thus saith the LORD of Hosts, Behold, I will melt them, and try them; for how shall I do for the daughter of My people? *(The furnace for the "melting," at least in this instance, would be the 70-year captivity in Babylon. The question, "For how shall I do for the daughter of My people?", rather asks the question, "How shall I act?" or "How otherwise should I act?", referring to Jehovah!)*

8 Their tongue is as an arrow shot out; it speaks deceit: one speaks peaceably to his neighbour with his mouth, but in heart he lays his wait. *(The phrase, "Their tongue is as an arrow shot out," refers to their tongue being a sharpened arrow designed to destroy. The phrase, "It speaks deceit," refers to the fact that it can speak nothing else!)*

9 Shall I not visit them for these things? saith the LORD: shall not My soul be avenged on such a nation as this? *(The word "visit" means to punish.)*

10 For the mountains will I take up a weeping and wailing, and for the habitations of the wilderness a lamentation, because they are burned up, so that none can pass through them; neither can men hear the voice of the cattle; both the fowl of the Heavens and the beast are fled; they are gone. *(The word "habitations" refers to pastures. The exclamation of this Verse is of a desolation so total that even the birds cannot find subsistence. The phrase, "They are gone," speaks of a denuding of Judah so severe that nothing is left!)*

11 And I will make Jerusalem heaps, and a den of dragons; and I will make the cities of Judah desolate, without an inhabitant. *(Once again, the Holy Spirit uses the words, "I will," referring to his total control over what was to be done to Judah and Jerusalem.)*

12 Who is the wise man, who may understand this? and who is he to whom the mouth of the LORD has spoken, that he may declare it, for what the land perishes and is burned up like a wilderness, that none passes through? *(The question, "Who is the wise man, who may understand this?", refers to the fact that there*

were many men in Jerusalem who were worldly-wise, but none who were spiritually wise.)

13 And the LORD says, Because they have forsaken My Law which I set before them, and have not obeyed My voice, neither walked therein *(the doctrine of this Verse, and several of the following, is that unrenewed men, however, intelligent, are incapable of recognizing the Hand of God in the private or public calamities that come upon them; that it needs a Revelation from the Holy Spirit to awake them to the fact that such calamities are God's just Judgment; and that those who are thus enlightened are responsible to declare and explain the true nature and the cause of the suffering experienced);*

14 But have walked after the imagination of their own heart, and after Baalim, which their fathers taught them *(this Scripture tells us that the Word of God, and not the "teaching of the Fathers," is the only authoritative and infallible rule of faith and obedience; for "the Fathers" can oppose Truth, and in fact often do, and consequently perish with their pupils):*

15 Therefore thus saith the LORD of Hosts, the God of Israel; Behold, I will feed them, even this people, with wormwood, and give them water of gall to drink. *(The "Water of gall to drink" is a fluid secreted by the liver, which is extremely bitter!)*

16 I will scatter them also among the heathen, whom neither they nor their fathers have known: and I will send a sword after them, till I have consumed them. *(The pronoun "them" refers to those who follow "the imagination of their own heart," and not the Law of God. The error taught by "their Fathers" will now have its bitter result in captivity.)*

17 Thus saith the LORD of Hosts, Consider ye, and call for the mourning women, that they may come; and send for cunning women, that they may come *(the sense of this Passage is that so many are going to die that the usual practice of hiring individuals to weep and wail at funerals would have to be increased manyfold):*

18 And let them make haste, and take up a wailing for us, that our eyes may run down with tears, and our eyelids gush out with waters. *(The idea of this Passage is that the "mourning women" will weep, not because they are paid for such, but because of the agony and destruction that is everywhere.)*

19 For a voice of wailing is heard out of Zion, How are we spoiled! we are greatly confounded, because we have forsaken the land, because our dwellings have cast us out. *(When*

the time of destruction would come, which would be about 5 to 7 years in the future, instead of then ridiculing Jeremiah, "a voice of wailing is heard out of Zion," because of the terrible destruction.)

20 Yet hear the word of the LORD, O ye women, and let your ear receive the word of His mouth, and teach your daughters wailing, and every one her neighbour lamentation. (The first word of Verse 20 could very well have read, "Yea"; for it was just that the women should share in the suffering, because they had urged their husbands to be idolaters.)

21 For death is come up into our windows, and is entered into our palaces, to cut off the children from without, and the young men from the streets. (The statement is hyperbole. No one would really be hired to weep, because every family in Judah would be weeping uncontrollably. But such is given by the Holy Spirit accordingly that it may impress upon the listener the severity of that which is coming.)

22 Speak, Thus saith the LORD, Even the carcases of men shall fall as dung upon the open field, and as the handful after the harvestman, and none shall gather them. (In this Verse, the proud Hebrews are compared to dung, and to grains of corn trampled into the ground by the feet of the harvestman and, therefore, worthless to be gleaned.)

KNOWLEDGE OF GOD IS MAN'S GLORY

23 Thus saith the LORD, Let not the wise man glory in his wisdom, neither let the mighty man glory in his might, let not the rich man glory in his riches:

24 But let him who glories glory in this, that he understands and knows Me, that I am the LORD which exercise lovingkindness, judgment, and righteousness, in the Earth: for in these things I delight, saith the LORD. (Verse 23 proclaims the fact that nothing that man has, irrespective of its seeming power, will do in the time of adversity; however, Verse 24 tells us that which will stand the test, and that alone, which is the Word of God!)

25 Behold, the days come, saith the LORD, that I will punish all them which are circumcised with the uncircumcised (the idea is that these were circumcised in the flesh, but not in the heart);

26 Egypt, and Judah, and Edom, and the children of Ammon, and Moab, and all who are in the utmost corners, who dwell in the wilderness: for all these nations are uncircumcised, and all the House of Israel are uncircumcised in the heart. (The prediction here was that the Cup of Wrath for the people of Judah would have this added bitterness of having to be drunk in fellowship with the neighboring nations whom they so despised. These nations practiced circumcision, as Judah did; and, like Judah, they were uncircumcised in heart.)

CHAPTER 10
(600 B.C.)
THE VANITY OF IDOLS

HEAR ye the word which the LORD speaks unto you, O House of Israel (the phrase, "House of Israel," is actually the Kingdom of Judah. It is called such here because of being the only part of Israel that is left. The phrase, "The LORD speaks unto you," is not only intended to address Israel collectively as a nation, but also personally as to each individual):

2 Thus saith the LORD, learn not the way of the heathen, and be not dismayed at the signs of heaven; for the heathen are dismayed at them. (The phrase, "The way of the heathen," actually refers to "the religion of the heathen." The phrase, "The signs of heaven," refers, in this case, to the astrological calculations based upon extraordinary appearances in the sky, or the signs of the zodiac. Israel was commanded by the Lord to pay no heed to these things, because, in reality, they hold no answers whatsoever!)

3 For the customs of the people are vain: for one cuts a tree out of the forest, the work of the hands of the workman, with the axe. (The word "customs" refers to the "images of wood," i.e., "idols." The word "people" refers to heathen nations. The "vanity" addressed here, concerning the "cutting of the tree out of the forest," is meant by the Holy Spirit to portray the absurdity of thinking that something fashioned by the hands of man could be greater than the hands which fashioned it.)

4 They deck it with silver and with gold; they fasten it with nails and with hammers, that it move not. (This making of an idol is the same as described in Isa. 41:7 and 44:13-17, which could very well have been read by Jeremiah, with the Holy Spirit impressing him strongly to emphasize this great sin once more. Such does not show a weakness in the Text, but rather an emphasis placed by the Holy Spirit on that which He considers to be very important. And if He considers it to be very important, by all means,

we should, as well!

These Passages are sometimes taken to mean the modern Christmas tree, but actually the tree referred to had no branches left on it at all. This refers to a tree trunk being made into an idol, not the Christmas tree.)

5 They are upright as the palm tree, but speak not: they must needs be borne, because they cannot go. Be not afraid of them; for they cannot do evil, neither also is it in them to do good. *(These absurd man-made idols, which "speak not" and which have to be carried about because of having no mobility of their own, are not something to be "afraid of." They don't have the power to do "evil" or "good.")*

PROOFS OF THE TRUE AND LIVING GOD

6 Forasmuch as there is none like unto You, O LORD, You are great, and Your name is great in might. *(Verses 6 and 7 contrast God with these blocks of wood.)*

7 Who would not fear You, O King of nations? for to You does it appertain: forasmuch as among all the wise men of the nations, and in all their kingdoms, there is none like unto You. *(In this Verse, Jeremiah enlarges on the Truth that God is God not only of Israel, but rather the entirety of the world, i.e., "King of nations.")*

8 But they are altogether brutish and foolish: the stock is a doctrine of vanities. *(The phrase, "Doctrine of vanities," is the teaching that such an absurdity is the true god of the nations, which could protect them, etc.)*

9 Silver spread into plates is brought from Tarshish, and gold from Uphaz, the work of the workman, and of the hands of the founder: blue and purple is their clothing: they are all the work of cunning men. *(The idea of this Passage is that the maker of these gods had it in mind that the more valuable the metal, such as "silver and gold," applied to the idol, and the more elaborate its appointments, such as "blue and purple," and the more talented its craftsmen, "cunning men," then surely the more powerful the idol! How foolish the ideas of unregenerate men!)*

10 But the LORD is the true God, He is the Living God, and an Everlasting King: at His Wrath the Earth shall tremble, and the nations shall not be able to abide His indignation. *(Verses 10 through 13 again contrast God with idols. The phrase, "The True God," literally means "a God in Truth." It is given in this vein to*

emphasize the idea of "Truth." Only God and His Ways are Truth, with all else being a fabrication and, thereby, inspired by Satan. The phrase, "He is the Living God," emphasizes that He is alive by contrast to these idols that have no life. As well, He is "an Everlasting King.")

11 Thus shall you say unto them, The gods that have not made the Heavens and the Earth, even they shall perish from the Earth, and from under these Heavens. *(This Verse alone in the original Text is written in Chaldee. It provided the Godly exiles with the reply that they were to make to their Babylonian captors when pointing out the impotency and folly of idols.)*

12 He has made the Earth by His power, He has established the world by His wisdom, and has stretched out the Heavens by His discretion. *(Throughout the Bible, the Holy Spirit declares Jehovah as the Creator of "the Earth." His Almighty Power "made the Earth" and "His Wisdom" established a set of fixed laws which govern its seasons, rotation, and productivity. As well, all the Heavens (Universes) were made according to His understanding and symbolize a fixed order of events each playing their part in the order of things. In other words, nothing that pertains to His Creation is by chance, happenstance, or confusion. Therefore, the idea of evolution is absurd, to say the least, and ludicrous in its explanation.)*

13 When He utters His voice, there is a multitude of waters in the Heavens, and He causes the vapours to ascend from the ends of the Earth; He makes lightnings with rain, and brings forth the wind out of His treasures. *(The phrase, "When He utters His voice," emphasizes the Truth that these fixed Laws which govern the Earth, concerning rain and the evaporation process, "vapors to ascend from the ends of the Earth," which in the process causes "lightnings" and "wind," were actually spoken into existence. He decreed them in the same manner that He said, "Let there be light" [Gen. 1:3].)*

THE STUPIDITY OF IDOLS

14 Every man is brutish in his knowledge: every founder is confounded by the graven image: for his molten image is falsehood, and there is no breath in them. *(The phrase, "Every man is brutish in his knowledge," emphasizes the point that except for those who have been enlightened by Revelation knowledge, i.e., the Lord, all others are without knowledge. In other words, they have no insight into the origin and*

*meaning of the world and all creation; hence,
the absurdity of evolution.)*

15 They are vanity, and the work of errors:
in the time of their visitation they shall perish. *(The word "vanity" means "empty nothings." The phrase, "Work of errors," refers to
the rewards of disappointment. The phrase, "In
the time of their visitation," refers mostly to
coming Judgment. The sense of the Passage is
that not only will the idols perish, but their worshippers, as well.)*

16 The portion of Jacob is not like them: for
He is the former of all things; and Israel is the
rod of His inheritance: The LORD of Hosts is
His Name. *("The portion of Jacob" was totally
unlike the portion of the heathen, who did not
know God, and had not, as Israel, experienced
any Revelation from God. The phrase, "For He
is the former of all things," literally means that
Jehovah is the "Maker" of Israel, whereas He was
not the "Maker" of these heathen nations, at
least as far as their religion was concerned!*

*The word "Rod" should have been trans-
lated "Tribe.")*

FLEE THE COMING JUDGMENT

17 Gather up your wares out of the land, O
inhabitant of the fortress. *(The unhappy captives, when setting out for Babylonia from Jerusalem, would be permitted to take nothing with
them but what they could carry by hand.)*

18 For thus saith the LORD, Behold, I will
sling out the inhabitants of the land at this
once, and will distress them, that they may
find it so. *(The Passage refers to the violence of
the expulsion!)*

19 Woe is me for my hurt! my wound is
grievous; but I said, Truly this is a grief, and I
must bear it. *(In Verses 19 through 22, Judah
and Jerusalem speak through the mouth of the
Prophet. Jeremiah takes up the cry of Judah,
which was to suffer this great distress, hurt,
wound, and grief.)*

20 My tabernacle is spoiled, and all My cords
are broken: My children are gone forth of Me,
and they are not: there is none to stretch forth
My tent any more, and to set up My curtains.
*(The phrase, "All My cords are broken," refers
to the Law and Sacrifices, that even though adhered to outwardly, were not in fact adhered to
at all as far as God was concerned. Despite the
presence of the Temple, the "cords were broken."
The words, "My children are gone forth of Me,
and they are not," spoke of those who truly loved*

*His Word, and attempted to follow His Ways,
who are now dead, with none to take their place!
"They are not!")*

21 For the pastors are become brutish, and
have not sought the LORD: therefore they shall
not prosper, and all their flocks shall be scattered. *(The "Pastors" or "Shepherds" refer to
Jehoiakim and the Princes. The phrase, "And
all their flocks shall be scattered," referred to
him being taken captive by Nebuchadnezzar to
Babylon, which no doubt included other notables
of Judah as well, hence, "scattered.")*

22 Behold, the noise of the bruit is come,
and a great commotion out of the north country, to make the cities of Judah desolate, and a
den of dragons. *(The Babylonians entered Israel from the north. Zion refused to listen to
the Voice of God, and so was compelled to listen
to the voice of the Chaldeans.)*

23 O LORD, I know that the way of man is
not in himself: it is not in man who walks to
direct his steps. *(Man is a spiritual being, tied
to his Creator, Who is God. Without the direction that only God can give, man wanders helplessly! However, man is loathe to admit such.)*

24 O LORD, correct me, but with judgment;
not in Your anger, lest You bring me to nothing. *(The idea of this Passage is that if full and
total correction was given, Judah and Jerusalem would be totally destroyed. As well, the
idea presents itself that total destruction is what
Judah and Jerusalem deserved. But the plea is
for Mercy!)*

25 Pour out Your fury upon the heathen who
know You not, and upon the families who call
not on Your name: for they have eaten up
Jacob, and devoured him, and consumed him,
and have made his habitation desolate. *(The
sense of the Passage is that even though Judah
has sinned and certainly deserved Judgment, still,
these heathen Babylonians must not be allowed
to remain in their idolatry; they also must suffer Judgment!*

*Such was true and, therefore, allowed to be
prayed by Judah through Jeremiah, and was ultimately answered.)*

CHAPTER 11
(608 B.C.)

JUDAH HAS BROKEN THE COVENANT

T HE word that came to Jeremiah from the
LORD, saying *(some have said this is
Jeremiah's fourth Commission. "The word" be-
gins this First Verse, which came from the Lord,*

and which could have been the salvation of the nation, but they would not hear),

2 Hear ye the words of this Covenant, and speak unto the men of Judah, and to the inhabitants of Jerusalem *("this Covenant" refers to the Book of the Law that had been found in the Temple some years previously during the reign of King Josiah, and which originated the revival proposed by that good Monarch. Immediately following his death, the nation restored idolatry [Vss. 9-10]);*

3 And say thou unto them, Thus saith the LORD God of Israel; Cursed be the man who obeys not the words of this Covenant. *(The word "cursed," describing the Law, means "condemned to death." This is the function of Law; it cannot give life to dead men. It condemns lawbreakers! The Law was given to make man conscious of his moral condition as a sinner and of his need for a Saviour. The Tabernacle, and its Sacrifices which accompanied the Law, revealed that Saviour in symbol.)*

4 Which I commanded your fathers in the day that I brought them forth out of the land of Egypt, from the iron furnace, saying, Obey My voice, and do them, according to all which I command you: so shall you be My people, and I will be your God *(God does not ask men to obey Him as a selfish and tyrannical master orders a slave in order to gratify his own cruel temper, but He commands man's obedience in order to secure man's happiness. Egypt was likened to an "iron furnace" from which the people were delivered, but yet they seemed determined to go back into this "iron furnace"!):*

5 That I may perform the oath which I have sworn unto your fathers, to give them a land flowing with milk and honey, as it is this day. Then answered I, and said, So be it, O LORD. *("A land flowing with milk and honey" is found fifteen times in the Pentateuch, and some five times elsewhere. The Lord kept His Promise, as He always keeps His Promises, and gave them the land; however, His children did not keep their promises to Him. In truth, man fails in every test to which he is exposed; therefore, it was imperative that God become man, which He did in the Person of Christ, and did for man what man could not do for himself.)*

6 Then the LORD said unto me, Proclaim all these words in the cities of Judah, and in the streets of Jerusalem, saying, Hear ye the words of this Covenant, and do them. *(In effect, the Lord was telling Jeremiah to be a street Preacher, both in Jerusalem and in the cities of Judah. He carried in his hand the Bible, and caused the people to hear its words, and urged his followers to believe and obey them. The urgency of this action by the Holy Spirit portrays the near catastrophe!)*

7 For I earnestly protested unto your fathers in the day that I brought them up out of the land of Egypt, even unto this day, rising early and protesting, saying, Obey My voice. *(The sense of the Passage is that the protesting did not begin with Jeremiah, but in fact has been needful from the time they were delivered "from Egypt." The cup is now full — not only full, but running over! All He asked was, "Obey My Voice," and this is all He asks today!)*

8 Yet they obeyed not, nor inclined their ear, but walked every one in the imagination of their evil heart: therefore I will bring upon them all the words of this Covenant, which I commanded them to do: but they did them not. *(Jeremiah contrasted the teachings of the Bible with those of the human imagination, and declared the latter to be evil, and that the wrath predicted in the Bible would certainly strike those who accepted this religion of the imagination.)*

9 And the LORD said unto me, A conspiracy is found among the men of Judah, and among the inhabitants of Jerusalem. *(It is clear from Verses 9 and 10 that King Josiah's subjects secretly decided to return to idolatry, and to set aside the Bible at the first favorable opportunity. This is the "conspiracy.")*

10 They are turned back to the iniquities of their forefathers, which refused to hear My words; and they went after other gods to serve them: the House of Israel and the House of Judah have broken My Covenant which I made with their fathers. *(The phrase, "Their forefathers," refers back to the sins of the Israelites in the wilderness and in Canaan under the Judges. The righteous Prophets were constantly pointing their hearers back to those early times, either for warning [as here] or for encouragement.*

The phrase, "And they went after other gods to serve them," refers not to the past, but to the present. They broke the "Covenant" which the Lord had made with them.)

11 Therefore thus saith the LORD, Behold, I will bring evil upon them, which they shall not be able to escape, and though they shall cry unto Me, I will not hearken unto them. *(The words, "I will," once again emphasize the fact that the Lord controls all. The phrase, "They shall not be able to escape," refers to the idea in the minds of the people of Judah that if*

the Prophecies of Jeremiah perchance are right, they will find a way of escape, namely Egypt. When the terrible time came, they found no way of escape.)

12 Then shall the cities of Judah and inhabitants of Jerusalem go, and cry unto the gods unto whom they offer incense: but they shall not save them at all in the time of their trouble. *(The impotency of idols to protect idolaters is declared in Verses 11 through 14. History attests this fact, for the people of Judah were overthrown by the Chaldeans and carried captive into Babylon.)*

13 For according to the number of your cities were your gods, O Judah, and according to the number of the streets of Jerusalem have you set up altars to that shameful thing, even altars to burn incense unto Baal. *(Not only does idolatry bring shame upon idolaters, but the most popular idol of that time was so shameful that a description of it is impossible.)*

14 Therefore pray not thou for this people, neither lift up a cry or prayer for them: for I will not hear them in the time that they cry unto Me for their trouble. *(The die has already been cast! There is no hope for their deliverance. It does not mean that if they truly repented, the Lord would not hear! Actually, He definitely would hear in such a case. But it does mean that there is no chance of them doing such! So there is no point in interceding for them. The implication is that they will "cry unto Me" when the Babylonians come, but then it will be too late!)*

15 What has My beloved to do in My house, seeing she has wrought lewdness with many, and the holy flesh is passed from you? when you do evil, then you rejoice. *(The Jews, it would seem, came to the Temple to pray, but their prayer is not accepted because it is associated with unholy practices. Actually, they were not truly praying, but only going through the form.*

The phrase, "When you do evil, then you rejoice," refers to two things: 1. They "rejoiced" in their idol worship, foolishly thinking that such would deliver them; and, 2. They "rejoiced" in the thought that by their Temple ritual they had paid their debt to Jehovah, and could, therefore, continue in their evil.)

16 The LORD called your name, A green olive tree, fair, and of goodly fruit: with the noise of a great tumult He has kindled fire upon it, and the branches of it are broken. *("The green olive tree" was Israel; the "tumult" was the Chaldean invasion, symbolized here by a*

thunderstorm with lightning. The storm destroys the tree, and the lightning sets it on fire.)

17 For the LORD of Hosts, Who planted you, has pronounced evil against you, for the evil of the House of Israel and of the House of Judah, which they have done against themselves to provoke Me to anger in offering incense unto Baal. *(The phrase, "For the LORD of Hosts, Who planted you," refers to Israel being a peculiar people under the Lord, as no other people or nation. He was their Sponsor in the sense that He has never been the sponsor of any other people.*

The phrase, "Against themselves," refers to men sinning to their own hurt. The idea is that God is not the cause of this, but they themselves.)

THE PLOT AGAINST JEREMIAH

18 And the LORD has given me knowledge of it, and I know it: then You showed me their doings. *(The phrase, "And the LORD has given me knowledge of it," refers to a plot against Jeremiah's life, and by his own brethren, at that! How the Lord showed him this is not known.*

"Their doings" referred to murderous intent against the Prophet, because they could not stand the strength and power of his preaching. Scripturally, they could not refute the Message; therefore, they sought to destroy the Messenger.)

19 But I was like a lamb or an ox that is brought to the slaughter, and I knew not that they had devised devices against me, saying, Let us destroy the tree with the fruit thereof, and let us cut him off from the land of the living, that his name may be no more remembered. *(Jeremiah came unto his own and his own received him not. They resolved to kill him though he was to them as a gentle lamb, and his only crime was that he prophesied to them in the Name of the Lord. Anathoth was his native village. It belonged to the Priests and they, together with the members of the Prophet's family, joined in the plot to destroy him.*

So was it with the Messiah, of Whom Jeremiah is here a Type.)

20 But, O LORD of Hosts, Who judges righteously, Who tries the reins and the heart, let me see Your vengeance on them: for unto You have I revealed my cause. *(The prayer of this Verse concerns the conflict between Truth and Righteousness versus falsehood and evil. It corresponds to similar language on the lips of David and of the Apostle Paul [Gal. 1:8; I Cor. 16:22].*

Jeremiah would not take vengeance into his

own hands, but gave place unto wrath, i.e., stepped aside so as to give room for the Wrath of God to act [Rom. 12:19].)

21 Therefore thus saith the LORD of the men of Anathoth, who seek your life, saying, Prophesy not in the Name of the LORD, that you die not by our hand (now that the plot is revealed, the demand is that he stop prophesying. Their anger was because of his Message):

22 Therefore thus saith the LORD of Hosts, Behold, I will punish them: the young men shall die by the sword; their sons and their daughters shall die by famine (Verses 22 and 23 record the answer to Jeremiah's prayer. The Lord said, "Behold, I will punish them." However, this punishment would consist of the destruction that was coming by the hand of the Babylonians, and did not necessarily include any extra punishment, unless it contained a guarantee that the perpetrators would be included in "the sword" and "the famine."

The question in many hearts is, "If these had sincerely repented before Jeremiah and before the Lord, would their Repentance have been accepted?"

Most definitely it would have! But sadly, no Repentance was forthcoming):

23 And there shall be no remnant of them: for I will bring evil upon the men of Anathoth, even the year of their visitation. (To touch God's is to touch God! As Anathoth was where many Priests resided, this was a special judgment on the Priesthood, who had been so instrumental in steering Judah and Jerusalem into paths of unrighteousness. Therefore, God's Anger against them was twofold: 1. Because of leading Judah and Jerusalem astray; and 2. Because of the plot against Jeremiah.)

CHAPTER 12
(608 B.C.)
JEREMIAH'S PRAYER AND COMPLAINT

RIGHTEOUS are You, O LORD, when I plead with You: yet let me talk with You of Your judgments: Wherefore does the way of the wicked prosper? Wherefore are all they happy who deal very treacherously? (The words, "Righteous are You, O LORD," present the answer of Jeremiah, as he hastens to vindicate God, even in the midst of his sorrows and dangers. The Lord judged righteously and was Himself Righteous, yet the Prophet desired to reason with the Lord of His Action in permitting evil, or so it seemed, to prosper. Such is the question of many!

The questions of Jeremiah are proof that those who are the recipients of special Divine Revelations and who are in close communion with the Lord are not precluded from having doubting thoughts and spiritual distress.)

2 You have planted them, yea, they have taken root: they grow, yea, they bring forth fruit: You are near in their mouth, and far from their reins. (The phrase, "You have planted them," refers to 11:17. Jeremiah reasons that if God "planted them," and in fact Israel "took root" and became a great nation, i.e., "brought forth fruit," why did they not glorify Him instead of being doers of evil? Instead they brought forth evil fruit [Mat. 7:17]. The answer is found in that last phrase. The words, "You are near in their mouth, and far from their reins," refer to the Priests who mouth the services, but their hearts were bound to their idols and to their sins.)

3 But You, O LORD, know me: You have seen me, and tried my heart toward You: pull them out like sheep for the slaughter, and prepare them for the day of slaughter. (In this Scripture, we are delving into the innermost chamber of the heart of Jeremiah. For such, the Lord will carefully and patiently rebuke him.)

4 How long shall the land mourn, and the herbs of every field wither, for the wickedness of them who dwell therein? The beasts are consumed, and the birds; because they said, He shall not see our last end. (The phrase, "He shall not see our last end," refers to the Prophet's enemies, who were confident of a successful future for themselves and for Jerusalem, but were determined that Jeremiah should not see their good fortune, nor share in it, for they determined to kill him.

In this Passage, we have the prophetic doctrine that because of "the wickedness of them who dwell therein," the "land mourns," the crops do not grow as they should, and the "beasts and birds" suffer! In this one Verse is easily seen the cause of all the problems which plague humanity. It is "wickedness.")

GOD'S ANSWER TO JEREMIAH

5 If you have run with the footmen, and they have wearied you, then how can you contend with horses? And if in the land of peace, wherein you trusted, they wearied you, then how will you do in the swelling of Jordan? (Jeremiah has been speaking in the first four Verses, with the Lord now speaking in the remainder. Now comes the Lord's gentle rebuke

to the Prophet. The "footmen" represent the men of Anathoth; the "horsemen," the rulers of Jerusalem, whose hatred and blood-thirst would be far worse than Anathoth's. "The land of peace," in which he thought himself secure, was his own village; "the swelling of Jordan," the wild fury that he would have to face in the capital city.)

6 For even your brethren, and the house of your father, even they have dealt treacherously with you; yes, they have called a multitude after you: believe them not, though they speak fair words unto you. (The phrase, "Though they speak fair words unto you," seems to imply that the Lord is imparting information to Jeremiah that he has not previously had. He now informs him that in the plot to take his life, his own "brethren," and even "the house of his father," which would imply his nearest of kin, are involved. His family urges those who are opposed to Jeremiah to murder him, but to his face they spoke fair words. This Divine Revelation to him of the treachery of his relatives must have deeply pained his heart.

Thus, the Prophet was trained to feel how bitter was the pain that hurt the Heart of God when sinful men, in response to the Messiah's love, met Him with hatred and murder.)

7 I have forsaken My house, I have left My heritage, I have given the dearly beloved of My soul into the hand of her enemies. (Now the Lord speaks His Heart, as Jeremiah has spoken his. These Verses, beginning with the Seventh Verse on to the end of the Chapter, apply to Judah and Jerusalem and are, therefore, to be distinguished from those of the previous section, which relate solely to Anathoth.

This Verse even supplies more answers to Verse 1. When God, for reasons satisfactory to Himself, withdraws from active interference in the affairs of men and leaves them to their own Hell-bent desire, the result is oppression of the weak by the strong and the robbery of the poor by the rich. Evil and violent men prosper, and good men suffer.)

8 My heritage is unto Me as a lion in the forest; it cries out against Me: therefore have I hated it. (So degraded and hostile had idolatry made Judah that they are compared in Verses 8 and 9 to an angry lion and a fierce vulture. Such is man's moral response to God's wondrous love!

The word "hated" in this Verse means "less cared for" or "less favored." The Hebrew verb is not the same as the verb which means "to hate with malice," but signifies "to love less." For example, "Jacob have I loved, but Esau have I hated," i.e., "preferred less.")

9 My heritage is unto Me as a speckled bird, the birds round about are against her; come ye, assemble all the beast of the field, come to devour. (The phrase, "My heritage is unto Me as a speckled bird," refers to a bird of beautiful bright plumage which arouses the animosity of its less brilliant contemporaries, who gather around to pull it to pieces. The prosperity of Judah no doubt had long been a source of wonder to the surrounding nations! They witnessed her prosperity, greatness, blessing, and grandeur, knowing there was a difference, and a great difference at that, but not quite understanding what the difference was!)

10 Many pastors have destroyed My vineyard, they have trodden My portion under foot, they have made My pleasant portion a desolate wilderness. (The "Pastors" here are not as we normally think of such, but rather civil rulers, even heathen rulers at that! Actually, the Passage is speaking of Nebuchadnezzar and the leaders under him who would come into Judah and "trod My portion underfoot.")

11 They have made it desolate, and being desolate it mourns unto Me; the whole land is made desolate, because no man lays it to heart. (The Holy Spirit, Who has been speaking in the future tense since Verse 7, speaks now as though in the past tense. Through foreknowledge, He knows that despite Jeremiah's continued Prophecies, Judah will not repent; consequently, the awful finality comes through.)

12 The spoilers are come upon all high places through the wilderness: for the sword of the LORD shall devour from the one end of the land even to the other end of the land: no flesh shall have peace. ("The spoilers" are definitely the Babylonians, with "the sword of the LORD," at least in this case, being Nebuchadnezzar. In other words, Nebuchadnezzar, although unwitting, will be an instrument in God's Hands to carry out God's Will.)

13 They have sown wheat, but shall reap thorns: they have put themselves to pain, but shall not profit: and they shall be ashamed of your revenues because of the fierce anger of the LORD. (The sense of this Verse is: Judah thought surely they were "sowing wheat," regarding their man-made religious worship. In their minds, they were appeasing Jehovah, especially by continuing to offer Sacrifices along with the Temple ritual, as well as the other gods by their idol worship. They had also constructed

for themselves a fall-back position by looking to Egypt. It was all man-devised and, therefore, God-rejected! Consequently, instead of reaping wheat, they would "reap thorns.")

14 Thus saith the LORD against all My evil neighbours, who touch the inheritance which I have caused My people Israel to inherit; Behold, I will pluck them out of their land, and pluck out the House of Judah from among them. (These "evil neighbors" are Egypt, Edom, Philistia, Ammon, Moab, and Syria. Due to these nations seeking to take advantage of Judah's problems, the Lord would bring judgment upon them. All this makes the unchangeable Love of God and the unbreakable nature of His Faithfulness clear to His ancient people. He has designed Israel as the center of all Earthly governments. This national system is now in confusion because of Israel's fall, for she is the keystone. Her restoration will be their [the other nations] recovery. The Lord Jesus Christ, as Man and Messiah, will unite in His Person the headship of man and the dominion of Israel, which will take place in the coming Kingdom Age.)

15 And it shall come to pass, after that I have plucked them out I will return, and have compassion on them, and will bring them again, every man to his heritage, and every man to his land. (As stated, this will take place in the coming Kingdom Age.)

16 And it shall come to pass, if they will diligently learn the ways of My people, to swear by My Name, The LORD lives, as they taught My people to swear by Baal; then shall they be built in the midst of My people. ("The ways of My people" mean "the Divine Way of Salvation" revealed and committed to Israel. "To swear by My Name," saying "Jehovah lives," is to worship God through Jesus Christ; for "Jesus" is God's Greatest Name.)

17 But if they will not obey, I will utterly pluck up and destroy that nation, saith the LORD. (Some of the nations mentioned in Verse 14 will, in fact, not obey and will be destroyed. Those destroyed were Edom, Philistia, Ammon, and Moab. Three of these areas are now occupied by modern Jordan, with Philistia being occupied by Israel and the Palestinians. Egypt and Syria continue, and in fact will be greatly blessed by God during the coming Kingdom Age because of their acceptance of the Lord Jesus Christ [Isa. 19:23-25]. The area known as modern Syria, in fact, will be incorporated into Israel in the coming Kingdom Age.)

CHAPTER 13
(602 B.C.)

THE SIGN OF THE LINEN GIRDLE

THUS saith the LORD unto me, Go and get you a linen girdle, and put it upon your loins, and put it not in water. (In symbolic language, the Holy Spirit through Jeremiah will describe a Divinely-commanded action indicative of the approaching ruin of the people of Judah. This Message was addressed to King Jehoiachin, who was about 18 years of age, to the Queen Mother Nehushta, and to the Priests and people of Jerusalem. The Speaker is Emmanuel, not Jeremiah; he was a mere instrument.)

2 So I got a girdle according to the Word of the LORD, and put it on my loins. (It was a "Linen Girdle" and, therefore, meant to be beautiful and ornate.)

3 And the Word of the LORD came unto me the second time, saying (this, as with the "Linen Girdle" and many other instances in the Bible, lets us know that God's leading is thus by design; such teaches continued faith, leading, leaning, and trust),

4 Take the girdle that you have got, which is upon your loins, and arise, go to Euphrates, and hide it there in a hole of the rock. (Due to the phrase, "The second time," in the Third Verse, Jeremiah probably wore the girdle for quite some time. The Holy Spirit evidently meant for the people of Jerusalem to see this girdle on Jeremiah in order that they may ultimately know what it meant. So, Jeremiah makes this long trip of about 400 miles to the Euphrates, which he would have reached first at Carchemish.)

5 So I went, and hid it by Euphrates, as the LORD commanded me. (Even as this time, it seems that Jeremiah still had little knowledge as to what the Lord was going to do with such a symbol; however, he faithfully obeys.)

6 And it came to pass after many days, that the LORD said unto me, Arise, go to Euphrates, and take the girdle from thence, which I commanded you to hide there. (The "many days" of this Verse do not tell us of the length of time, but it definitely could refer to several years.)

7 Then I went to Euphrates, and digged, and took the girdle from the place where I had hid it: and, behold, the girdle was marred, it was profitable for nothing. (The original beautiful girdle was used as a touching symbol to teach Israel how Emmanuel had bound her upon His Heart, and worn her as an ornament, the fine linen expressing her purity. Such was His

Love for her. But her disobedience compelled the Lord to remove the girdle and bury it at the Euphrates, where it became marred and worthless, showing Judah's present spiritual condition!

This symbolic action foretold the captivity of 70 years in the Euphrates Valley.)

THE APPLICATION TO ALL ISRAEL

8 Then the Word of the LORD came unto me, saying,

9 Thus saith the LORD, after this manner will I mar the pride of Judah, and the great pride of Jerusalem. *(The words, "After this manner," refer to the girdle and its marred condition. As the girdle had been so beautiful and is now so marred, so will be Judah and Jerusalem. The cause was "pride.")*

10 This evil people, which refuse to hear My words, which walk in the imagination of their heart, and walk after other gods, to serve them, and to worship them, shall even be as this girdle, which is good for nothing. *(The "great pride" of the previous Verse has produced "this evil people.")*

11 For as the girdle cleaves to the loins of a man, so have I caused to cleave unto Me the whole House of Israel and the whole House of Judah, saith the LORD, that they might be unto Me for a people, and for a name, and for a praise, and for a glory: but they would not hear. *(Both Israel and Judah lost their "glory" because of sin and because "they would not hear" the Word of the Lord.)*

THE LESSON FROM THE FILLED BOTTLES; APPLICATION TO JUDAH

12 Therefore you shall speak unto them this word; Thus saith the LORD God of Israel, Every bottle shall be filled with wine: and they shall say unto you, Do we not certainly know that every bottle shall be filled with wine? *(The "bottle" was a large wineskin made from a lamb's skin or a cowhide. Upon instruction from the Holy Spirit, Jeremiah took several wineskins and hung them up in a straight line. They were then to be filled with wine.)*

13 Then shall you say unto them, Thus saith the LORD, Behold, I will fill all the inhabitants of this land, even the kings who sit upon David's Throne, and the Priests, and the Prophets, and all the inhabitants of Jerusalem, with drunkenness. *(The "drunkenness" spoken of here is symbolic. The people were symbolized by*

the bottles and the wine symbolized the Wrath of God against them.)

14 And I will dash them one against another, even the fathers and the sons together, saith the LORD: I will not pity, nor spare, nor have mercy, but destroy them. *(The words, "I will dash them one against another," refer to the Lord allowing them to follow their own "imaginations," resulting in utter confusion!)*

15 Hear ye, and give ear; be not proud: for the LORD has spoken. *(As is obvious, the Lord admonishes Judah to "hear.")*

16 Give glory to the LORD your God, before He cause darkness, and before your feet stumble upon the dark mountains, and, while you look for light, He turn it into the shadow of death, and make it gross darkness. *(The light that Judah now has, which is the Word of the LORD through the Prophet Jeremiah, will soon give way to "darkness," because the Light is the Lord and not Judah's foolish imagination. All of these "other gods" are "darkness and death.")*

17 But if you will not hear it, my soul shall weep in secret places for your pride; and My eye shall weep sore, and run down with tears, because the LORD's flock is carried away captive. *(As the Lord was speaking in previous Verses, Jeremiah speaks in Verses 15 through 17. The Lord is very clear in dealing with His People; therefore, there are no excuses for misunderstanding. Here the cause, which is sin, is plainly outlined; the cure, which is Repentance, is plainly given! If they do not hear, it is because they do not want to hear.)*

18 Say unto the king and to the queen, Humble yourselves, sit down: for your principalities shall come down, even the crown of your glory. *(The fulfillment of this is found in II Ki. 24:15. After a reign of three months, Jehoiachin, who was only 18 years old, and his mother, the reigning Queen named Nehushta, were taken captive by Nebuchadnezzar, along with all Jehoiachin's court.)*

19 The cities of the south shall be shut up, and none shall open them: Judah shall be carried away captive all of it, it shall be wholly carried away captive. *(This was fulfilled about 12 years later. The captivity being still a thing of the future, the Prophet seeks to awaken the conscience of this king and his mother, but to no avail.)*

20 Lift up your eyes, and behold them who come from the north: where is the flock that was given you, your beautiful flock? *(Even though Babylon lay due east, the invasion route*

was "from the north." "The flock that was given you" refers to the people of Judah. The implication is: if the king and his mother would have led the people in a spiritual revival, this "beautiful flock" possibly would have followed; however, they had no desire for spiritual things, and their people had no desire for this "son of David" to wholly follow the Lord.)

21 What will you say when He shall punish you? For you have taught them to be captains, and as chief over you: shall not sorrows take you, as a woman in travail? *(The sense of this Verse is that the military captains and civil rulers of Nebuchadnezzar will now be "chief over you." Judah would not have the Lord be "captain and chief"; therefore, a heathen Monarch with no pity would serve in this capacity.)*

22 And if you say in your heart, Wherefore come these things upon me? For the greatness of your iniquity are your skirts discovered, and your heels made bare. *("Iniquity," i.e., idolatry, caused this just judgment. Nakedness and bare feet express slavery. Upon the coming catastrophe, Judah will exclaim, "Wherefore come these things upon me?" The Holy Spirit tells us the reason. It is "the greatness of your iniquity.")*

23 Can the Ethiopian change his skin, or the leopard his spots? Then may you also do good, who are accustomed to do evil. *(This Passage refutes any and all ideas that man can change himself. He cannot, yet he keeps trying!)*

24 Therefore will I scatter them as the stubble that passes away by the wind of the wilderness. *(This refers to the chaff that is separated from the wheat on the threshingfloor. The "wind of the wilderness" refers to great trouble that was coming upon Judah, which in fact would be the scattering process.)*

25 This is your lot, the portion of your measures from Me, saith the LORD; because you have forgotten Me, and trusted in falsehood. *(What type of "falsehood" is being spoken of in this Passage? In this case, it pertained to idols; however, in any case, it pertains to "false doctrine" perpetrated by "false apostles, deceitful workers, and Satan's ministers" [II Cor. 11:13-15].)*

26 Therefore will I discover your skirts upon your face, that your shame may appear. *(The spirit of the Text is that Judah has "shamed" the Lord, and now He will "shame" them!)*

27 I have seen your adulteries, and your neighings, the lewdness of your whoredom, and your abominations on the hills in the fields. Woe unto you, O Jerusalem! Will you not be made clean? when shall it once be? *(In this Passage, as in many others, Judah is likened to Jehovah's wife. As such, she has committed spiritual adultery. And these "whoredoms and abominations" have not been slight, but rather as evil as possible!)*

CHAPTER 14
(601 B.C.)
THE LESSON ON THE FAMINE; JUDAH DESOLATE

THE Word of the LORD that came to Jeremiah concerning the dearth. *(The word "dearth," which means "drought," is plural in the Hebrew, i.e., "droughts," actually referring to the length of time the drought lasted. This was an act of Judgment sent by God.)*

2 Judah mourns, and the gates thereof languish; they are black unto the ground; and the cry of Jerusalem is gone up. *(This drought should not have been unexpected, because God had promised such if Israel went into sin [Lev. 26:19; Deut. 28:23]. Therefore, what He says He will do, He will do!)*

3 And their nobles have sent their little ones to the waters: they came to the pits, and found no water; they returned with their vessels empty; they were ashamed and confounded, and covered their heads. *(The "nobles" referred to the upper classes of Judah and Jerusalem. The "little ones" do not refer to children, but to their servants, or even "the common people." Verses 3 through 6 portray the futility of their efforts. There is no water, and they are "ashamed and confounded," to come back empty-handed; therefore, "they covered their heads.")*

4 Because the ground is chapt, for there was no rain in the Earth, the plowmen were ashamed, they covered their heads. *(The word "chapt" spoke of the ground being parched, dry, and barren. This means that the physical drought was symbolic of the spiritual drought!*

The "plowmen" are symbolic of Jeremiah, who has no crops, i.e., harvest. The people do not respond to his Altar Calls, because of their hardened hearts, which are symbolized by the seed put into the ground by the "plowmen," which will not germinate for lack of water.)

5 Yea, the hind also calved in the field, and forsook it, because there was no grass. *(The "hind" is a young deer. It is noted for its devotion to its offspring, and yet the drought is so severe that it "forsakes it." It does so because there is no grass.)*

6 And the wild asses did stand in the high

places, they snuffed up the wind like dragons; their eyes did fail, because there was no grass. *(The phrase, "Their eyes did fail," speaking of the animals, refers to the lack of ability to find "grass," and the weakness that ultimately overtakes them.)*

JEREMIAH'S CONFESSION

7 O LORD, though our iniquities testify against us, do Thou it for Your Names' sake: for our backslidings are many; we have sinned against You. *(In this Passage, Jeremiah begins to intercede for the people. The words, "iniquities," "backslidings," and "sins," express the moral character and worthlessness of man, however high may be his religious privileges. Hence, forgiveness can only be prayed for His Name's sake, i.e. in the Name of Jesus. That Name being Perfection, it secures a perfect pardon; however, Judah of old would not trust in that Blessed Name, of which the Sacrifices were a Type.)*

8 O the hope of Israel, the saviour thereof in time of trouble, why should you be as a stranger in the land, and as a wayfaring man who turns aside to tarry for a night? *(The question, "Why should you be as a stranger in the land, and as a wayfaring man who turns aside to tarry for a night?", refers to an individual who is a "foreigner" in the land, someone who was only passing through, and consequently would only stay the night. As such, because they were not citizens, they enjoyed no rights, and had no say-so whatsoever regarding the manner in which the nation conducted itself.*

Such was the Lord! Judah treated Him as if He was a foreigner, a stranger, and One Who had no say-so in the affairs of State.)

9 Why should You be as a man astonied, as a mighty Man Who cannot save? Yet You, O LORD, are in the midst of us, and we are called by Your name; leave us not. *(Jeremiah soberly asks the question of the Lord, "Why should You be as a man astonied?" The phrase means, "As one struck dumb." In these words which came from Jeremiah's heart, and also inspired by the Holy Spirit, one can easily see the broken heart of the Lord of Glory. He is "struck dumb" at Judah's reaction toward Him.*

The continuing of the question, "As a mighty Man Who cannot save?" refers to One, in this case, the Lord, Who has the might to save Judah, but, in effect, "cannot save" them, because they will not allow Him to save them [Jn. 5:40].)

10 Thus saith the LORD unto this people,

Thus have they loved to wander, they have not refrained their feet, therefore the LORD does not accept them; He will now remember their iniquity, and visit their sins. *(Beginning with the word "therefore," Jeremiah quotes verbatim from Hos. 8:13; therefore, what the Holy Spirit said through Hosea to the Northern Kingdom those many years past, and by now long since in dispersion, He now says identically to the Southern Kingdom of Judah.)*

GOD DECLARES THAT JUDGMENT IS COMING

11 Then said the LORD unto me, Pray not for this people for their good. *(This is the third time that the Lord has told Jeremiah to "pray not for this people" [7:16; 11:14]. The seriousness of this cannot be overemphasized!)*

12 When they fast, I will not hear their cry; and when they offer Burnt Offering and an oblation, I will not accept them: but I will consume them by the sword, and by the famine, and by the pestilence. *(This Scripture does not present the idea that God will not respond to a truly sincere broken heart, crying to Him for Mercy and Forgiveness, but that He was rejecting Judah's heartless formalism and insincerity.)*

JEREMIAH COMPLAINS; GOD ANSWERS: THE PROPHETS LIED; JUDGMENT IS COMING

13 Then said I, Ah, Lord GOD! behold, the Prophets say unto them, You shall not see the sword, neither shall you have famine; but I will give you assured peace in this place. *("The Prophets" spoken of here were "false prophets." Their message was the exact opposite of Jeremiah's, who stood alone in his pronouncements. In fact, as fast as he proclaimed the Word of God to Judah and Jerusalem, it was contradicted by these false prophets. He was prophesying judgment while they were prophesying "peace.")*

14 Then the LORD said unto me, The Prophets prophesy lies in My name: I sent them not, neither have I commanded them, neither spoke unto them: they prophesy unto you a false vision and divination, and a thing of nought, and the deceit of their heart. *(The closing Verses [13-18] predicted the doom of the false prophets, and God's denunciation of them. In fact, the blight of the modern Church is "those prophets who prophesy lies in My Name.")*

15 Therefore thus saith the LORD concerning

the Prophets who prophesy in My name, and I sent them not, yet they say, Sword and famine shall not be in this land; By sword and famine shall those prophets be consumed. *(The pronouncement by the Lord in this Passage is chilling! "Those Prophets" then and "those Prophets" now will be consumed by the false message they proclaim.)*

16 And the people to whom they prophesy shall be cast out in the streets of Jerusalem because of the famine and the sword; and they shall have none to bury them, them, their wives, nor their sons, nor their daughters: for I will pour their wickedness upon them. *(Not only will the false preacher be consumed, but those who listen to him will be consumed as well. This is the tragedy and horror of this Truth.)*

17 Therefore you shall say this word unto them; Let my eyes run down with tears night and day, and let them not cease: for the virgin daughter of My people is broken with a great breach, with a very grievous blow. *(The True Prophet, Christ, faithfully told men of their sins and of the wrath to come, but He did so with sobs and tears. Every Preacher controlled by the Holy Spirit, in like manner, warns men with tears [Acts 20:31], either secret or public.)*

18 If I go forth into the field, then behold the slain with the sword! And if I enter into the city, then behold them who are sick with famine! yea, both the Prophet and the Priest go about into a land that they know not. *(Jeremiah now jumps ahead to the coming destruction. He proclaims that both those "in the field" and "in the city" are stricken! They are either "slain" or "sick." Therefore, these false prophets would be shown up to be as the liars they are!*

The phrase, "Yea, both the Prophet and the Priest go about into a land that they know not," is strong indeed! It means that these false prophets, who were once idolized by the people but who are now shown to be what they really are, are "begging their way" into an unknown land — Babylon — at least the few who have not been killed by the sword or who have not died by famine.)

19 Have you utterly rejected Judah? Has Your soul loathed Zion? why have you smitten us, and there is no healing for us? we looked for peace, and there is no good; and for the time of healing, and behold trouble! *(As a true intercessor, Jeremiah identifies himself with those for whom he intercedes; hence the "us," the "we," and the "our" of his prayer.)*

20 We acknowledge, O LORD, our wickedness, and the iniquity of our fathers: for we have sinned against You. *(True Intercession functions in the same manner as the Great Intercessor, Christ. Jeremiah associated himself with Judah's sin, as Christ associates Himself with us in our sin. Consequently, in that Intercession, Christ pleads as if He sinned, which, of course, He did not. But on our behalf, He truly enters into our failure [Heb. 7:25].*

The Intercession of which we speak has already been carried out, and is cataloged in most of the Psalms; consequently, the Presence of the Lord before the Father is now all that is required for Intercession, because Calvary paid it all [Heb. 1:3].)

21 Do not abhor us, for Your Name's sake, do not disgrace the throne of Your glory: remember, break not Your covenant with us. *(These efforts made by Jeremiah are given to us by the Holy Spirit in order that we may see the heart of this man. Despite the opposition of the people, Prophets, and Priests to him, he still cries to God on their behalf. Yet, he does not know the depths of their sin as Jehovah does!)*

22 Are there any among the vanities of the Gentiles who can cause rain? Or can the Heavens give showers? Are not You He, O LORD our God? therefore we will wait upon You: for You have made all these things. *("Vanities" refer to the false gods of the heathen. The inference is that many in Jerusalem were appealing to false gods to bring rain instead of seeking the "LORD our God." They, in effect, have said that they would not "wait upon Him any longer," while Jeremiah exclaims, "We will wait upon You."*

The last phrase, "For You have made all these things," refers to the uselessness of appealing to these false gods, when, in reality, the Lord is the Creator of all! Therefore, He, and He Alone, can assuage the terrible problems of the drought and all other problems, for that matter!)

CHAPTER 15
(601 B.C.)
JUDAH IS REJECTED AND
FACES JUDGMENT

THEN said the LORD unto me, Though Moses and Samuel stood before Me, yet My mind could not be toward this people: cast them out of My sight, and let them go forth. *(The phrase, "Though Moses and Samuel stood before Me," suggests that these two through intercession had persuaded the Lord to change His*

direction regarding appointed destruction of the people of Israel. It does not mean that God changes His Mind, for He changes not, but that He has designed in His Plan the potential of proper intercession, and, by the proper people, the possibility of a different direction!

The phrase, "Cast them out of My sight," is the command to the Prophet to do what he has been commissioned to foretell, i.e., their expulsion from the Promised Land, and their exile in Babylon.)

2 And it shall come to pass, if they say unto you, Whither shall we go forth? Then you shall tell them, Thus saith the LORD; Such as are for death, to death; and such as are for the sword, to the sword; and such as are for the famine, to the famine; and such as are for the captivity, to the captivity. *(In this Verse, we find that three-fourths of the people were doomed to death, and one-fourth to slavery, and all because of sin!)*

3 And I will appoint over them four kinds, saith the LORD: the sword to slay, and the dogs to tear, and the fowls of the heaven, and the beasts of the Earth, to devour and destroy. *(The judgment of this Verse was a just one, for the people of Judah worshipped the gods of war, the vultures of the heavens, and the wild beasts of the Earth. The phrase, "And I will appoint over them," means that the full Power of God will be pressed into service in order to bring about the Judgment.)*

4 And I will cause them to be removed into all kingdoms of the Earth, because of Manasseh the son of Hezekiah king of Judah, for that which he did in Jerusalem. *(Manasseh repented of his evil conduct, and was wondrously cleansed and forgiven by the Lord, and is today in Heaven; however, the bitter fruits of his evil conduct prior to his humbling before the Lord remained and occasioned the Wrath of God some 80 years later [II Ki. 21:1-16].*

Judah's being "removed into all kingdoms of the Earth" took place several years later upon the invasion of the Babylonians. The kingdoms of the Earth of which the Lord spoke were then ruled by Babylon.)

5 For who shall have pity upon you, O Jerusalem? Or who shall bemoan you? Or who shall go aside to ask how you do? *(The implication of this Verse is that "Jerusalem" would fall, suffering horribly, and no one would care. The surrounding nations not only would not care, but would themselves "come to devour" [12:9].)*

6 You have forsaken Me, saith the LORD,

you are gone backward: therefore will I stretch out My hand against you, and destroy you; I am weary with repenting. *(The phrase, "I am weary with repenting," refers to the Lord, and not to Judah. He had, over and over again, delayed the Judgment [repented of what He was about to do], and now says He will no longer delay, for the cup of iniquity has long since spilled over, and she must be judged.)*

7 And I will fan them with a fan in the gates of the land; I will bereave them of children, I will destroy My people, since they return not from their ways. *(The phrase, "In the gates of the land," refers to the fortresses commanding the entrance into Judah, hence, the people being taken captive into Babylon close by these very fortresses designed to protect them.*

The phrase, "Since they return not from their ways," speaks of the cause of not only Judah's problems, but the cause of the problems of the entirety of mankind! Men want "their ways" instead of "God's Ways.")

8 Their widows are increased to Me above the sand of the seas: I have brought upon them against the mother of the young men a spoiler at noonday: I have caused him to fall upon it suddenly, and terrors upon the city. *(The "spoiler" is Nebuchadnezzar. He will come at "noonday," referring to his powerful strength, which makes known what he will do, and has the power to carry it out.)*

9 She who has borne seven languishes: she has given up the ghost; her sun is gone down while it was yet day: she has been ashamed and confounded: and the residue of them will I deliver to the sword before their enemies, saith the LORD. *(So wholesale would be the destruction of life that a mother of seven sons would not have one left to comfort her. Upon hearing these Prophecies, the people thought them to be lunatic and, therefore, they cursed Jeremiah, as will be proclaimed in the next Verse.)*

10 Woe is me, my mother, that you have borne me a man of strife and a man of contention to the whole Earth! I have neither lent on usury, nor men have lent to me on usury; yet every one of them does curse me. *(The Spirit of Christ expresses Itself in Jeremiah. In Christ, the expression is perfect; in Jeremiah, imperfect, because the Prophet was only a man, and sinful. He loved the people, bore their sorrows upon his heart, confessed their sins, suffered in sympathy their judgments; and yet they hated him.*

He seems to not be able to comprehend the cause of their tremendous opposition — even

to the taking of his life, if the Lord had allowed them!)

THE WICKED ARE JUDGED;
A REMNANT SPARED

11 The LORD said, Verily it shall be well with your remnant; verily I will cause the enemy to intreat you well in the time of evil and in the time of affliction. *(The phrase, "Your Remnant," shows that there were a few who heeded Jeremiah's words and, therefore, followed him, as he followed the Lord. [The Remnant could also refer to the small number left in the land as caretakers after the fall of Judah.]*

The "enemy" was the Babylonians, and they truly would treat Jeremiah "well in the time of evil and in the time of affliction." He was treated well by these, but not his own, which prefigured Christ being crucified by His Own, but rather received by the Gentiles [Mat. 12:21].)

12 Shall iron break the northern iron and the steel? *(The "iron" is Judah, while the "northern iron" is the Chaldeans. The figure expresses the impossibility of Judah, at least within their own power, defeating the Chaldeans.)*

13 Your substance and your treasures will I give to the spoil without price, and that for all your sins, even in all your borders. *(This Verse proclaims the "substance and treasures" of Judah being given as "spoil" to the Babylonians.)*

14 And I will make you to pass with your enemies into a land which you know not: for a fire is kindled in My anger, which shall burn upon you. *(Jeremiah, in this Verse, at least in part, is quoting from Deut. 32:22. "To pass with your enemies" refers to being taken to Babylon. The phrase, "For a fire is kindled in My anger," speaks of the fire stirred up in the heart of God because of the sins of the people.)*

JEREMIAH'S PERSONAL LAMENT

15 O LORD, You know: remember me, and visit me, and revenge me of my persecutors; take me not away in Your longsuffering: know that for Your sake I have suffered rebuke. *(The Prophet in this Passage prays for the Remnant. In the Spirit of Christ, he calls their persecutors his persecutors, and pleads that God, in His longsuffering to the persecutors, will not allow the persecuted to perish; adding that in his identification of himself with the Remnant he, therefore, suffered reproach. Verse 19 will enlighten this interpretation even more.)*

16 Your words were found, and I did eat them; and Your Word was unto me the joy and rejoicing of my heart: for I am called by Your Name, O LORD God of Hosts. *(The Bible was found in the Eighteenth year of King Josiah, and its Divine Words were the joy and rejoicing of the Prophet's heart. In this Verse, the Prophet is a marked Type of Christ.*

The phrase, "Your Words were found, and I did eat them," reveals Jeremiah's great love for the Word of God.)

17 I sat not in the assembly of the mockers, nor rejoiced; I sat alone because of Your hand: for You have filled me with indignation. *(As his Message was rejected, so was he rejected and, therefore, he "sat not in the assembly of the mockers." "Mockers" mocked his Message and laughed at him; consequently, he was "alone," save the small Remnant. Actually, his own family turned against him [12:6], along with all the Priests and Prophets. From this source, there was no encouraging voice.)*

18 Why is my pain perpetual, and my wound incurable, which refuses to be healed? Will You be altogether unto me as a liar, and as waters that fail? *(His indignation against sin, his perpetual pain for the sinner, his consciousness of a moral hopelessness of the nation, all marked the energy and intelligence of the Divine life and love in his soul.*

When he asked the question, "Will You be altogether unto me as a liar?", he was referring to God's Promises of protection to him. From the anger of the people, who did continually curse him [Vs. 10], he was fearful for his life, and afraid that God had changed His Mind about his preservation. He asked the question, because his future looked hopeless!)

GOD PROMISES TO PRESERVE
JEREMIAH IN THE TROUBLE

19 Therefore thus saith the LORD, If you return, then will I bring you again, and you shall stand before Me: and if you take forth the precious from the vile, you shall be as My mouth: let them return unto you; but return not thou unto them. *(In the last three Verses, the Prophet is addressed as the representative of the Remnant. The Remnant was first to return to Jehovah, thereby separating the precious from the vile; and second, to invite the nation to come over to them — but they were not to return to the nation.*

As a result, the Remnant should enjoy protection

and deliverance. All this, Daniel and his companions found to be true.)

20 And I will make you unto this people a fenced brasen wall: and they shall fight against you, but they shall not prevail against you: for I am with you to save you and to deliver you, saith the LORD. *(In effect, the Lord is saying that as He delivered Jeremiah from these staggering odds, He, as well, could have, and in fact would have, delivered Judah from the Babylonians, if they had only trusted Him and served Him.)*

21 And I will deliver you out of the hand of the wicked, and I will redeem you out of the hand of the terrible. *(These individuals would have killed Jeremiah in a moment but for the Hand of the Lord. Their hearts are so wicked, and their intentions so evil, that the Holy Spirit describes them as "wicked" and "terrible.")*

CHAPTER 16
(601 B.C.)
JEREMIAH TO REMAIN
UNMARRIED AS A SIGN

THE Word of the LORD came also unto me, saying *(in the giving of this Prophecy, Jeremiah is no doubt referring back some 20 years earlier when the Prophecy was first give to him by the Lord; he is just now relating to Judah what was said),*

2 You shall not take thee a wife, neither shall you have sons or daughters in this place. *(So certain and so imminent was the coming Wrath of God that Jeremiah was commanded not to marry [Vs. 2], not to mourn [Vs. 5], and not to feast [Vs. 8].)*

3 For thus saith the LORD concerning the sons and concerning the daughters who are born in this place, and concerning their mothers who bore them, and concerning their fathers that begat them in this land *(normally, the dearest thing to parents is their children; therefore, to be told that their children were going to die in the coming catastrophe, and for them to pay no heed, only shows the depths of their unbelief and wickedness!);*

4 They shall die of grievous deaths; they shall not be lamented; neither shall they be buried; but they shall be as dung upon the face of the Earth: and they shall be consumed by the sword, and by famine; and their carcases shall be meat for the fowls of Heaven, and for the beasts of the Earth. *(The words, "grievous deaths," mean deadly diseases, starvation, and sword. The phrase, "They shall not be lamented," refers to parents or loved ones who are actually glad that the child or children are dead, simply because death will relieve them of the pain, suffering, and starvation. The phrase, "Neither shall they be buried," refers to the lack of burial places, due to the Babylonians surrounding the city.)*

5 For thus saith the LORD, Enter not into the house of mourning, neither go to lament nor bemoan them: for I have taken away My peace from this people, saith the LORD, even lovingkindness and mercies. *("The house of mourning" actually means "the house of screaming." Such denotes the extensive horror that is going to take place! The phrase, "For I have taken away My peace from this people," refers to the Lord, Who had protected them, but now will allow the Babylonians to wage war and succeed. The people showed no restraint in their worshipping of idols, therefore, idol worshippers will show no restraint upon them!)*

6 Both the great and the small shall die in this land: they shall not be buried, neither shall men lament for them, nor cut themselves, nor make themselves bald for them *("the great and the small" signify that none shall escape! As well, none of the usual mourning for the dead would be practiced, because so many will have died):*

7 Neither shall men tear themselves for them in mourning, to comfort them for the dead; neither shall men give them the cup of consolation to drink for their father or for their mother.

8 You shall not also go into the house of feasting, to sit with them to eat and to drink. *(In a time of crisis, a true Servant of God must become a personal witness for God, and thus will he best help his perishing fellowmen. Jeremiah's action in withdrawing from sympathizing with his fellow countrymen in either their sorrows or their joys was an announcement of the wrath to come, which they were compelled to hear. But they refused to believe it, and the terrific doom announced against them came to pass, and actually, in a sense, is still in operation.)*

9 For thus saith the LORD of Hosts, the God of Israel; Behold, I will cause to cease out of this place in your eyes, and in your days, the voice of mirth, and the voice of gladness, the voice of the bridegroom, and the voice of the bride. *(When Jeremiah gave these Prophecies, Judah and Jerusalem were in a time of great prosperity! His "voice of judgment" sounded foreign to their "voice of mirth," and*

his "voice of sadness" sounded bitter to their "voice of gladness.")

10 And it shall come to pass, when you shall show this people all these words, and they shall say unto you, Wherefore has the LORD pronounced all this great evil against us? or what is our iniquity? or what is our sin that we have committed against the LORD our God? *(In this Passage, we learn that sin deadens the conscience.)*

11 Then shall you say unto them, Because your fathers have forsaken Me, saith the LORD, and have walked after other gods, and have served them, and have worshipped them, and have forsaken Me, and have not kept My Law *(the answer to the sarcastic questions which will be asked by the people of Judah and Jerusalem is now given by the Lord. This Scripture proclaims the fact that the cup of judgment has been building for a long time. Twice in this one Verse the Lord says, "have forsaken Me");*

12 And you have done worse than your fathers; for, behold, you walk every one after the imagination of his evil heart, that they may not hearken unto Me *(the pronoun "you" is emphatic, meaning to emphasize strongly. In effect, the Lord is saying, "And as for you . . . ." As bad as the "fathers" were, these "have done worse"! Even after being repeatedly shown their sin, with continued pleading for Repentance, Judah stubbornly refused to yield):*

13 Therefore will I cast you out of this land into a land that you know not, neither you nor your fathers; and there shall you serve other gods day and night; where I will not show you favour. *(The phrase, "Therefore will I cast you out of this land," refers to the twofold investment by the Lord, referring to both the people and the land. The Land was very special to Him, and had been chosen especially for His People. It was a Land flowing with milk and honey, and had been called "The Promised Land."*

The phrase, "A land that you know not," is Babylon.

The phrase, "And there shall you serve other gods day and night," means to be compelled by torture to serve [Dan., Chpts. 3, 6].

The phrase, "Where I will not show you favor," refers to His Divine leading. Such, with some few exceptions, will be lifted during the exile.)

14 Therefore, behold, the days come, saith the LORD, that it shall no more be said, The LORD lives, Who brought up the Children of Israel out of the land of Egypt *(as the darkness of a tunnel may be realized by contrast with the bright burst of sunshine on issuing from its mouth, so the sunshine of Verses 14 and 15 reveal the darkness of Verses 13 and 16 through 18. Great as was the suffering in Egypt, and great as was the deliverance therefrom, so much greater is Israel's present affliction, and so much more wonderful will be her future Deliverance, that the wonders of the former redemption will be obscured by those of the future);*

15 But, The LORD lives, Who brought up the Children of Israel from the land of the north, and from all the lands whither He had driven them: and I will bring them again into their land that I gave unto their fathers. *(Plainly and beautifully, the Lord says that Israel will not be destroyed, but only severely chastised. It is evident that the restoration from Babylon did not fulfill the language of this Verse, because this proposes the recovery of all the Children of Israel out of all the countries in which they are presently dispersed. This will take place in the coming Kingdom Age.)*

16 Behold, I will send for many fishers, saith the LORD, and they shall fish them; and after will I send for many hunters, and they shall hunt them from every mountain, and from every hill, and out of the holes of the rocks. *(The "fishers" and the "hunters" refer to the individuals [possibly even Angels] who will search the entirety of the world in order to bring every single Jew to the Holy Land. This will be after the Second Coming of Christ.)*

17 For My eyes are upon all their ways: they are not hid from My face, neither is their iniquity hid from My eyes. *(The sense of this Verse is that God notes all the ways of Israel, both good and bad, as He also does with every Believer!)*

18 And first I will recompense their iniquity and their sin double; because they have defiled My land, they have filled My inheritance with the carcases of their detestable and abominable things. *(The words, "And first I will recompense," mean "But first of all." The phrase, "I will recompense their iniquity and their sin double," does not have the same meaning as Isa. 61:7. There it refers to Mercy and Forgiveness, while here it means punishment, even double punishment. The reason? "They have defiled My Land.")*

19 O LORD, my strength, and my fortress, and my refuge in the day of affliction, the Gentiles shall come unto You from the ends of the Earth, and shall say, Surely our fathers have inherited lies, vanity, and things wherein there is no profit. *(The Restoration of Israel*

during the coming Kingdom Age will ensure the Salvation of the Gentiles. They and the sons of Israel will cast away their idols and learn once for all and forever of the existence and might of Jehovah.

The phrase, "Day of affliction," refers to all such times, but more particularly to the coming Great Tribulation, which in essence will serve to bring Israel back to God.)

20 Shall a man make gods unto himself, and they are no gods? *(The absurdity of the creature forming the Creator is finally expressed in this Verse. All of these false religions are called "gods," and are said to be man-made and therefore useless!)*

21 Therefore, behold, I will this once cause them to know, I will cause them to know My hand and My might; and they shall know that My name is The LORD. *(The phrase, "Therefore, behold, I will this once cause them to know," means that "once for all," which refers to the coming Great Tribulation and Jehovah's Deliverance of Israel, which will settle for all time Who Jehovah is!)*

CHAPTER 17
(601 B.C.)
THE SIN OF JUDAH

THE sin of Judah is written with a pen of iron, and with the point of a diamond: it is graven upon the table of their heart, and upon the horns of your altars *(the phrase, "Written with a pen of iron, and with the point of a diamond," signifies that the "heart" has become so hard that it takes a "pen" made of "iron," with its tip made of diamond, one of the hardest substances known to man, in order to penetrate such a hard heart.*

Such portrays the utter foolishness of man's flimsy self-help programs for bringing about change! Only the Power of God can set such a captive free!);

2 While their children remember their altars and their groves by the green trees upon the high hills. *(The children remembered other children who had been offered as human sacrifice to these horrible and hideous idols. Such would create a horror in the minds of these children, as they wondered if they would be next, or as they grieved over the loss of loved ones. Such further portrays the hardness of heart of the parents, who left Jehovah, the God of Love and Mercy, and instead served these heathen gods.)*

3 O My mountain in the field, I will give your substance and all your treasures to the spoil, and your high places for sin, throughout all your borders. *(The phrase, "O My mountain in the field," refers to Mount Zion, the site of the Temple. "Your substance" and "your treasures" refer to the holy utensils, such as the Brazen Altar, the Brazen Laver, and the Golden Lampstand, etc., which would be taken by Nebuchadnezzar as "spoil." As well, all of their heathen idols on the "high places for sin" throughout the entirety of the Judah would also be taken!)*

4 And you, even yourself, shall discontinue from your heritage that I gave you; and I will cause you to serve your enemies in the land which you know not: for you have kindled a fire in My anger, which shall burn for ever. *(The phrase, "And I will cause you to serve your enemies," refers to being taken to Babylon and serving Nebuchadnezzar. They now revert to the slavery from which they were delivered when they came out of Egypt.*

The phrase, "You have kindled a fire in My anger," refers to God's just "anger" regarding sin and the judicial judgment that always follows.

The phrase, "Which shall burn forever," means that God will forever conduct Himself accordingly toward willful rebellion and disobedience.)

TRUST IN GOD IS THE ONLY HOPE

5 Thus saith the LORD; Cursed be the man who trusts in man, and makes flesh his arm, and whose heart departs from the LORD. *(The people of Judah at this time proposed an alliance with the Egyptians as a protection from the Chaldeans. The folly of trusting them and not Jehovah and the wisdom of trusting Jehovah and not them are contrasted in Verses 5 through 8; and [Vs. 9] the nature of the heart — incurably diseased with deceit — which proposed this alliance is exposed. In a sense, Paul's statement in Gal. 1:8-9 is the same as here.)*

6 For he shall be like the heath in the desert, and shall not see when good comes; but shall inhabit the parched places in the wilderness, in a salt land and not inhabited. *("The heath" is insensible and fruitless. Such is the Christless man insensible of good, fruitless in life, and a stranger to real fellowship. The sense of this Verse is that inasmuch as the people of Israel treated the Promised Land as they did, they would now "inhabit the parched places in the wilderness, in a salt land and not [previously] inhabited.")*

7 Blessed is the man who trusts in the LORD, and whose hope the LORD is. *(Verse 5*

says that the man who does not trust in the Lord is "cursed," while this Verse says that the man who trusts in the Lord is "blessed." There you have it! This is where the die is cast.)

8 For he shall be as a tree planted by the waters, and that spreads out her roots by the river, and shall not see when heat comes, but her leaf shall be green; and shall not be careful in the year of drought, neither shall cease from yielding fruit. *(To trust in the Lord gives one the "fruit of the Spirit." To trust man is to be "cursed by the Lord." The modern Church should note this in her acceptance of humanistic psychology in place of the Word of God.)*

9 The heart is deceitful above all things, and desperately wicked: who can know it? *(God knows the hopeless corruption of the natural heart, and so He said to Nicodemus that no one, however cultured and moral, can either see or enter into the Kingdom of God. There must be a new birth.)*

10 I the LORD search the heart, I try the reins, even to give every man according to his ways, and according to the fruit of his doings. *(The phrase, "I the LORD search the heart," refers to the fact that only God knows the heart. The phrase, "I try the reins," refers to the Lord allowing certain particulars to take place, according to the disposition of the individual involved, in order to bring out what is actually there. The Lord through Omniscience already knows all things, in other words, what is in the heart of man, even before man knows it. But in order that man not be able to say that he is unjustly judged, the Lord allows events to transpire, uncaused or caused by Him, which always reveal exactly what is in the heart, whether good or bad. This is done in order that the Judgment Day will be fair and impartial, and that the record of such actions can be shown in black and white to the individual, who, at that time, will be without argument. Therefore, his judgment will be "according to his ways, and according to the fruit of his doings.")*

11 As the partridge sits on eggs, and hatches them not; so he who gets riches, and not by right, shall leave them in the midst of his days, and at his end shall be a fool. *(The sense of this Verse is that whoever trusts in wealth is a fool. To trust man [Vs. 5], to trust one's own heart [Vs. 9], or to trust wealth [Vs. 11] ensures ruin.)*

12 A glorious high throne from the beginning is the place of Our sanctuary. *(In Verses 12 through 14, the wisdom of trusting Jehovah,*

the Hope of Israel, and the happiness which results are contrasted with the folly and misery of confidence in human saviours. The pronoun "Our" in the phrase, "Our Sanctuary," is emphatic. The word "Sanctuary" speaks of a place of sacred security; that place is glorious, it is set on high above the reach of calamity, and is long established. It is for the one who trusts exclusively in the Lord!)

13 O LORD, the hope of Israel, all who forsake you shall be ashamed, and they who depart from Me shall be written in the Earth, because they have forsaken the LORD, the Fountain of Living Waters. *(This refers to the "Fountain of Life," which ever flows forth, in contrast to the "parched places" of Verse 6.)*

14 Heal me, O LORD, and I shall be healed; save me, and I shall be saved: for You are my praise. *(In this Verse, the Prophet, pleading on behalf of the people as their representative and identifying himself with them, prays that their incurably sick hearts may be healed. How can a wicked and deceitful heart be trusted? He pleads that God, not the Egyptian Monarch, should save them from the impending danger.)*

15 Behold, they say unto me, Where is the word of the LORD? let it come now. *(The people for whom Jeremiah prayed ridiculed the Divine Judgment which the Prophet announced, and, with skeptical contempt, demanded an immediate demonstration of it.)*

16 As for me, I have not hastened from being a Pastor to follow You: neither have I desired the woeful day; You know: that which came out of my lips was right before You. *(Jeremiah, like a true Minister of the Gospel, did not in self-will choose to be a Preacher, nor, when bravely and faithfully announcing the coming Day of Judgment, did he desire that day; and he can sincerely state that the Truth he preached was uttered in the conscious Presence of God.)*

17 Be not a terror unto me: You are my hope in the day of evil. *(The words, "Be not a terror unto me," refer to the possibility that the Lord could forsake him, as threatened in 1:17. Thus he appealed to God for protection and vindication.)*

18 Let them be confounded who persecute me, but let not me be confounded: let them be dismayed, but let not me be dismayed: bring upon them the day of evil, and destroy them with double destruction. *(Jeremiah now sees the necessity of such destruction and, in effect, sees as God sees!)*

KEEPING THE SABBATH

19 Thus said the LORD unto me; Go and stand in the gate of the children of the people, whereby the kings of Judah come in, and by the which they go out, and in all the gates of Jerusalem *(this was to be done so that everyone would hear and so no one would be able to say, "I did not know")*;

20 And say unto them, Hear ye the word of the LORD, you kings of Judah, and all Judah, and all the inhabitants of Jerusalem, who enter in by these gates *(one can well imagine Jeremiah standing first at one gate and then the next, and possibly holding up a Scroll of the Pentateuch, saying, "Hear ye the Word of the Lord." His Message, sadly, was not received favorably, but rather was scorned with skepticism and bold opposition)*:

21 Thus saith the LORD; Take heed to yourselves, and bear no burden on the sabbath day, nor bring it in by the gates of Jerusalem *(the people have evidently claimed that they had already repented, or else they needed no repentance. At any rate, one test of professed Repentance was proposed to them, the observance of the Sabbath)*;

22 Neither carry forth a burden out of your houses on the sabbath day, neither do ye any work, but hallow ye the sabbath day, as I commanded your fathers. *(The length of the captivity — 70 years — was made to correspond with each seventh year, which was supposed to be kept as a Sabbath for the entire year, which they had defiled during the entirety of their 490 years of history from Saul to the exile [Lev. 26:34-35; II Chron. 36:21]. So the Lord would collect His Sabbaths, which numbered exactly 70 years.)*

23 But they obeyed not, neither inclined their ear, but made their neck stiff, that they might not hear, nor receive instruction. *(All God has ever required is "obedience." The phrase, "But made their neck stiff," refers to an unbowing [unbending], which manifests itself in the average sinner of all races in all ages. The phrase, "Nor receive instruction," refers to the fact that the Lord stands ready to give "instruction.")*

24 And it shall come to pass, if you diligently hearken unto Me, saith the LORD, to bring in no burden through the gates of this city on the sabbath day, but hallow the sabbath day, to do no work therein *(which means to use the day not only to rest, but to understand that it is God Who has given this for the good of man and, therefore, that He be praised)*;

25 Then shall there enter into the gates of this city Kings and Princes sitting upon the throne of David, riding in chariots and on horses, they, and their Princes, the men of Judah, and the inhabitants of Jerusalem: and this city shall remain for ever. *(This Prophecy was given no doubt several times, and to as many Kings. Sadly, it was rejected! And yet Grace outlined a picture of glory and happiness for them; for God in His longsuffering, even at the last moment, opened the door of Repentance to them and to their King. But they refused!)*

26 And they shall come from the cities of Judah, and from the places about Jerusalem, and from the land of Benjamin, and from the plain, and from the mountains, and from the south, bringing Burnt Offerings, and Sacrifices, and Meat Offerings, and Incense, and bringing Sacrifices of Praise, unto the House of the LORD. *(Verse 26 tells us that "the House of the LORD" is the principal interest after Repentance. Verse 21 proclaims the pleasing of themselves, while Verse 26 proclaims the pleasing of God.)*

27 But if you will not hearken unto Me to hallow the sabbath day, and not to bear a burden, even entering in at the gates of Jerusalem on the sabbath day; then will I kindle a fire in the gates thereof, and it shall devour the palaces of Jerusalem, and it shall not be quenched. *(Christ is God's Sabbath. To burden that Sabbath with sacerdotalism and its ceremonies and doctrines is to desecrate and destroy it. In other words, under the New Covenant, serving Christ, Who is the True Sabbath, constitutes "keeping the Sabbath.")*

CHAPTER 18

(605 B.C.)

THE LESSON FROM THE POTTER

THE Word which came to Jeremiah from the LORD, saying *(the offer of Repentance will again be enjoined, but with no success. In fact, greater opposition will be plotted against the Prophet)*,

2 Arise, and go down to the potter's house, and there I will cause you to hear My words. *(The "potter's house" was where various utensils were made of clay.)*

3 Then I went down to the potter's house, and, behold, he wrought a work on the wheels. *(Jeremiah was to behold the work of the potter; the lesson would concern Judah.)*

4 And the vessel that he made of clay was marred in the hand of the potter: so he made

it again another vessel, as seemed good to the potter to make it. *(The lesson of the potter's house is that God never mends what man mars. He creates something new. Man attempts to mend the vessel, i.e., "rehabilitation," which is impossible.)*

5 Then the word of the LORD came to me, saying *(this "Word" will concern the lesson learned)*,

6 O House of Israel, cannot I do with you as this potter? saith the LORD. Behold, as the clay is in the potter's hand, so are you in My hand, O House of Israel. *(The interpretation of this symbol belongs to the "House of Israel." The Verse beginning and closing as it does with these words decides the interpretation of the symbol; but its application is general. God's liberty of action is absolute. There is, and can be, no moral change in Him; but the moral changes in man are recognized by Him, and He, therefore, in His sovereignty, judges or forgives them accordingly. Plainly this symbol proclaims the glaring fact that God can change the person or the situation; however, He must do it in His Own Way.)*

7 At what instant I shall speak concerning a nation, and concerning a kingdom, to pluck up, and to pull down, and to destroy it *(the idea is: Judah, or any nation for that matter, even on the brink of destruction, with judgment already pronounced, if they will repent, as is outlined in the next Verse, "God will repent," i.e., change His direction about what He had previously thought to do! It is not so much that God changes, but rather that men change through Repentance)*;

8 If that nation, against whom I have pronounced, turn from their evil, I will repent of the evil that I thought to do unto them. *(True heartfelt Repentance on the part of men brings about the change on the part of God. Without that Repentance, judgment will continue.)*

9 And at what instant I shall speak concerning a nation, and concerning a kingdom, to build and to plant it *(the "instant" spoken of in this Passage concerns the moment the Gospel is proclaimed to that "nation"; according to its rejection or acceptance, the Lord will either do "evil" or "good")*;

10 If it do evil in My sight, that it obey not My voice, then I will repent of the good, wherewith I said I would benefit them. *(The Lord desires to do good to any and all, but what He does depends upon the "obedience" of the individual or individuals involved.)*

11 Now therefore go to, speak to the men of Judah, and to the inhabitants of Jerusalem, saying, Thus saith the LORD; Behold, I frame evil against you, and devise a device against you: return ye now every one from his evil way, and make your ways and your doings good. *(The phrase, "Behold, I frame evil against you, and devise a device against you," refers to the calamity that God was framing against them at this time, which was the Chaldean invasion.*

Again, this Passage implies that God either frames "evil" or "good" against His Children according to their disobedience or obedience!)

12 And they said, There is no hope: but we will walk after our own devices, and we will every one do the imagination of his evil heart. *(Coupling this Verse with Verse 18, the words, "There is no hope," mean: "There is no hope in your preaching! You are a killjoy Prophet! You say our hearts are evil as well as our religious plans, but we deny both charges. Despite all that you are predicting, the Law will not perish from the Priests.")*

13 Therefore thus saith the LORD; Ask ye now among the heathen, who has heard such things: the virgin of Israel has done a very horrible thing. *(The "very horrible thing" of this Verse was Israel's forsaking Jehovah for Baal. The phrase, "The virgin of Israel," has to do with what Israel should have been instead of what she actually was. As well, the word "virgin" had to do with Israel being the only nation in the world who knew the True God.)*

14 Will a man leave the snow of Lebanon which comes from the rock of the field? or shall the cold flowing waters that come from another place be forsaken? *(In this symbol, Christ is compared to the cool and pure waters which flow from the summit of Lebanon; and man's religion, to the muddy waters of the trampled field. Tragically, Christ has been "forsaken"!)*

15 Because My people have forgotten Me, they have burned incense to vanity, and they have caused them to stumble in their ways from the ancient paths, to walk in paths, in a way not cast up *(the word "vanity" actually means "empty nothings." Whenever God is forsaken, men receive nothing for their trade; however, these "nothings" are made very enticing, because men are easily deceived. The "ancient paths" refer to the Bible)*;

16 To make their land desolate, and a perpetual hissing; every one who passes thereby shall be astonished, and wag his head. *(As the forsaking of the Bible "made their land desolate,"*

it is making America desolate, as well! Jerusalem, which had been the city of gold, would now be destroyed, and so completely that passersby would be "astonished" and "wag their heads.")

17 I will scatter them as with an east wind before the enemy; I will show them the back, and not the face, in the day of their calamity. *(The "east wind" was a stormy wind and was used as symbolism regarding the "scattering" of Judah "before the enemy." This refers to the Babylonian invasion, with the terminology portraying the fact that God, not Nebuchadnezzar, designed all!*

The phrase, "I will show them the back, and not the face," refers to Judgment and not Blessing.)

18 Then said they, Come, and let us devise devices against Jeremiah; for the Law shall not perish from the Priest, nor counsel from the wise, nor the word from the Prophet. Come, and let us smite him with the tongue, and let us not give heed to any of his words. *(This Verse is the answer of the people to Jeremiah's Prophecies!)*

JEREMIAH'S PRAYER

19 Give heed to me, O LORD, and hearken to the voice of them who contend with me. *(The Speaker in Verses 19 through 23 is Christ. His Spirit in Jeremiah thus prays. It is not a prayer for the gratification of personal vengeance, such as fallen human nature would use, but the prayer of a crowned-counsel justly demanding a righteous judgment upon evildoers in the interest of truth and society. If it is right for God to punish evildoers, then it is right to pray Him to do so; and such men having been forewarned of the consequences to them and to their families, no charge of injustice can be brought against God for carrying out the decrees of these righteous Laws.*

This and similar prayers in the Bible belong to the past dispensation of Law and the future dispensation of Righteousness — not to the present dispensation of Grace.)

20 Shall evil be recompensed for good? For they have digged a pit for my soul. Remember that I stood before You to speak good for them, and to turn away Your wrath from them. *(The "good" spoken of by Jeremiah was the Word of God given to them and the intercession he made to the Lord on their behalf.)*

21 Therefore deliver up their children to the famine, and pour out their blood by the force of the sword; and let their wives be bereaved of their children, and be widows; and let their men be put to death; let their young men be slain by the sword in battle. *(The action of this prayer, allowed by the Holy Spirit, is that Judah and Jerusalem desired such, and such they would have! If man wills evil, God wills further evil to him. They had denied the veracity of Jeremiah's Prophecies; therefore, there was nothing left for them but "famine," "blood," and "death.")*

22 Let a cry be heard from their houses, when You shall bring a troop suddenly upon them: for they have digged a pit to take me, and hid snares for my feet. *(The petition of this Verse is that they themselves fall into the "pit they have digged for Jeremiah"!)*

23 Yet, LORD, You know all their counsel against me to slay me: forgive not their iniquity, neither blot out their sin from Your sight, but let them be overthrown before You; deal thus with them in the time of Your anger. *(These individuals hated the Prophet so much that they "took counsel against him to kill him." They were not satisfied to reject the Message; they wanted to destroy the Messenger, as well! Such has been the case throughout the ages.*

The Lord could not "forgive their iniquity, nor blot out their sin from His sight," because they did not desire such. God cannot forgive sins that are unconfessed, with the person, thereby, unrepentant! He can only forgive those who come to Him in humble contrition, who earnestly seek His Mercy and Grace; from such He has promised to never turn away [I Jn. 1:9].)

CHAPTER 19
(605 B.C.)
THE LESSON FROM THE BROKEN POTTERY

THUS saith the LORD, Go and get a potter's earthen bottle, and take of the ancients of the people, and of the ancients of the Priests *(the "earthen bottle" was a bottle made of clay, and, therefore, easily broken. Jeremiah was to take this "earthen bottle" to the "ancients of the people, and the ancients of the Priests," and, after pronouncing judgment, break the bottle in their sight, symbolizing therewith the breaking and destruction of Judah and Jerusalem);*

2 And go forth unto the valley of the son of Hinnom, which is by the entry of the east gate, and proclaim there the words that I shall tell you *(it was to this valley, its worm, and its fire to which our Lord pointed when preaching about Hell; but He added that in that dread place*

[Hell] the worm should not die nor the fire be quenched, because that on which they feed shall never be annihilated; thereby will Hell be different from the valley of Hinnom [Mk. 9:48]),

3 And say, Hear ye the Word of the LORD, O kings of Judah, and inhabitants of Jerusalem; Thus saith the LORD of Hosts, the God of Israel; Behold, I will bring evil upon this place, the which whosoever hears, his ears shall tingle. *(The implication is that the king[s] would enjoy no more respite than the people. As one, so the other! Therefore, no deal could be struck with the King of Babylon ensuring the safety of the Nobles.*

The phrase, "I will bring evil," refers to the sovereignty and ability of God, which are unlimited. It speaks of His total control over all things. Nebuchadnezzar, the heathen monarch, would think the plan is his; but, in reality, he was but a tool!)

4 Because they have forsaken Me, and have estranged this place, and have burned incense in it unto other gods, whom neither they nor their fathers have known, nor the kings of Judah, and have filled this place with the blood of innocents *(the phrase, "And have estranged this place," means to devote their worship to strange divinities. The phrase, "And have filled this place with the blood of innocents," is chilling indeed! It referred to the slaughter of little children, offered up in sacrifice to Moloch);*

5 They have built also the high places of Baal, to burn their sons with fire for burnt offerings unto Baal, which I commanded not, nor spoke it, neither came it into My mind *(the Spirit of God in Jeremiah, as afterwards in Christ, did not hesitate to repeat His Messages, so Verses 5 through 6 repeat 7:31-32):*

6 Therefore, behold, the days come, saith the LORD, that this place shall no more be called Tophet, nor The valley of the son of Hinnom, but The valley of slaughter. *("The valley of slaughter" referred to this same valley of "Hinnom," where these awful human sacrifices were carried out. As they had made it a "valley of slaughter," God would now make it a "valley of slaughter," and even on a far greater scale! Jesus plainly said, "With what measure you mete, it shall be measured to you again" [Mat. 7:2].)*

7 And I will make void the counsel of Judah and Jerusalem in this place; and I will cause them to fall by the sword before their enemies, and by the hands of them who seek their lives: and their carcases will I give to be meat for the fowls of the Heaven, and for the beasts of the Earth. *(The "counsel of Judah and Jerusalem" was their plan to defeat the Chaldeans by means of the Egyptian alliance. But, in that very valley of Hinnom, the folly of that plan would be demonstrated by the appalling slaughter carried out by the Chaldeans on the men who made it. There were they justly punished for the blood of the tortured children burned alive in sacrifice to Moloch. Such cruelty to children, especially by God's chosen People, never was contemplated by the loving heart of God.)*

8 And I will make this city desolate, and an hissing; every one who passes thereby shall be astonished and hiss because of all the plagues thereof. *(The response to Jeremiah's Message was met with "hissing"; therefore, the Lord would "make this city an hissing.")*

9 And I will cause them to eat the flesh of their sons and the flesh of their daughters, and they shall eat every one the flesh of his friend in the siege and straitness, wherewith their enemies, and they who seek their lives, shall straiten them. *(This Ninth Verse is quoted almost verbatim from Deut. 28:53. The words, "in the siege," refer to the coming siege of Jerusalem by Nebuchadnezzar. As a result, the city was shut up tight, with no traffic coming in or out. The food, therefore, quickly ran out!)*

10 Then shall you break the bottle in the sight of the men who go with you. *(Once again, the Lord will use apt symbolism to make His point! The breaking of the bottle signified the destruction of Judah and Jerusalem that was soon to come.)*

11 And shall say unto them, Thus saith the LORD of Hosts; Even so will I break this people and this city, as one breaks a potter's vessel, that cannot be made whole again: and they shall bury them in Tophet, till there be no place to bury. *(By using this type of vessel, the Lord portrays to Judah and Jerusalem their utter worthlessness as far as He was concerned! Conversely, they no doubt had a very high opinion of themselves.*

The phrase, "That cannot be made whole again," refers to the utter destruction of Judah and Jerusalem. In fact, they have never been "whole" from that day until this!)

12 Thus will I do unto this place, saith the LORD, and to the inhabitants thereof, and even make this city as Tophet:

13 And the houses of Jerusalem, and the houses of the kings of Judah, shall be defiled as the place of Tophet, because of all the houses

upon whose roofs they have burned incense unto all the host of heaven, and have poured out drink offerings unto other gods. *(The worship of the "host of heaven" was especially forbidden in Deut. 4:19. These "other gods" were either Baal or a derivative of Baal, such as Chemosh, etc.)*

14 Then came Jeremiah from Tophet, whither the LORD had sent him to prophesy; and he stood in the court of the LORD's House; and said to all the people *(Jeremiah, having finished his mission in the "valley of Hinnom," now goes, according to the direction of the Lord, to the "court of the LORD's House." This is at the Temple. The Holy Spirit, no doubt, desires to draw attention to the fact that while the people are "pouring out drink offerings unto other gods," they are also worshipping Jehovah in the Temple! In their minds, because of doing this, they are even more religious; but in God's Mind, they are abominable!),*

15 Thus saith the LORD of Hosts, the God of Israel; Behold, I will bring upon this city and upon all her towns all the evil that I have pronounced against it, because they have hardened their necks, that they might not hear My words. *(To "harden the neck" in order not to hear means to refuse to turn the head to a speaker so as to listen to him. Consequently, Jeremiah's words fell upon deaf ears. They ignored him as if he was not there.)*

CHAPTER 20
(605 B.C.)
JEREMIAH'S IMPRISONMENT

NOW Pashur the son of Immer the Priest, who was also chief governor in the House of the LORD, heard that Jeremiah prophesied these things. *(As evil as this man was, he was still "chief governor in the House of the LORD." Too much and too often the religious hierarchy, typified by "Pashur," persecutes the true followers of the Lord, typified by "Jeremiah." This evil man felt he had to stop the preaching of Jeremiah.)*

2 Then Pashur smote Jeremiah the Prophet, and put him in the stocks that were in the high gate of Benjamin, which was by the House of the LORD. *(Pashur, the chief officer of the Temple, scourged Jeremiah, as the Apostle Paul afterwards was scourged, and then, without any Scriptural warrant, condemned him, for about twenty-four hours, to the torture of the stocks. This was a beam of timber with five holes in it, through which the head, the hands, and the feet*

were thrust, thus bending the body so as to cause great suffering.

So it was with Christ! His greatest enemies were the ruling religious order of His day. They opposed Him bitterly then, and they oppose Him bitterly now!)

3 And it came to pass on the morrow, that Pashur brought forth Jeremiah out of the stocks. Then said Jeremiah unto him, The LORD has not called your name Pashur, but Magor-missabib. *("Pashur" means "security on every side," while "Magor-missabib" means "terror on every side." The words of Verses 3 through 6 were not the hot-tempered utterance of the Prophet, but the solemn warnings of Jehovah.)*

4 For thus saith the LORD, Behold, I will make you a terror to yourself, and to all your friends: and they shall fall by the sword of their enemies, and your eyes shall behold it: and I will give all Judah into the hand of the king of Babylon, and he shall carry them captive into Babylon, and shall slay them with the sword. *(The phrase, "I will make you a terror to yourself, and to all your friends," refers to the coming Judgment heaped upon those who listen to "Pashur" rather than to "Jeremiah.")*

5 Moreover I will deliver all the strength of the city, and all the labours thereof, and all the precious things thereof, and all the treasures of the kings of Judah will I give into the hand of their enemies, which shall spoil them, and take them, and carry them to Babylon. *(The "strength" and "labor" pertain to the wealth obtained by the people of Judah and Jerusalem. It would all be forfeited to "the king of Babylon." Therefore, they would now lose all the things for which they sold their souls, as all such things are always lost!)*

6 And you, Pashur, and all who dwell in your house shall go into captivity: and you shall come to Babylon, and there you shall die, and shall be buried there, you, and all your friends, to whom you have prophesied lies. *(The terrible punishment inflicted upon Jeremiah by Pashur little quenched the ardor of the Prophet. His Message is as straightforward now as it was before, and even more so, if possible! This time the Message is directed to "Pashur" and pulls no punches.)*

JEREMIAH'S COMPLAINT

7 O LORD, You have deceived me, and I was deceived; You are stronger than I, and have prevailed: I am in derision daily, every one

mocks me. *(The twice-used word "deceived," in the Hebrew, is "patha," which would have been better translated "persuaded," as it was in Prov. 25:15. Jeremiah is referring to his original call and the powerful persuasive force used by the Lord regarding his call.)*

8 For since I spoke, I cried out, I cried violence and spoil; because the Word of the LORD was made a reproach unto me, and a derision, daily. *(The subject of his preaching is expressed in the two words, "violence" and "spoil." This oppression and robbery of the poor so deeply stirred him that he shouted aloud against it, but the only response to his outcries was that he was had in derision daily, and everyone laughed at him.)*

9 Then I said, I will not make mention of Him, nor speak any more in His name. But His Word was in my heart as a burning fire shut up in my bones, and I was weary with forbearing, and I could not stay. *(In view of the terrible opposition, even bodily harm, the Prophet actually stopped preaching, at least for a while. The cause of the opposition was "Him" and "His Name."*

However, he found it impossible to cease from preaching. The fire of the Divine Wrath against sin burned so fiercely within him that he could not help but resume his work.)

10 For I heard the defaming of many, fear on every side. Report, say they, and we will report it. All my familiars watched for my halting, saying, Peradventure he will be enticed, and we shall prevail against him, and we shall take our revenge on him. *(The "defaming" and "fear" have relation to the Prophet. "Denounce" and "we will denounce him" are the words of his enemies encouraging one another and his pretended friends to "entice him" to a moral lapse or a charge of heresy against the Law of Moses, and so to denounce him to the judges and have him put to death, or at least destroy any influence he may have.)*

11 But the LORD is with me as a mighty terrible One: therefore my persecutors shall stumble, and they shall not prevail: they shall be greatly ashamed; for they shall not prosper: their everlasting confusion shall never be forgotten. *(The idea of this Verse is that the persecution of Jeremiah by his enemies hastened their destruction and deepened their punishment. As such, the Holy Spirit says it "shall never be forgotten"!)*

12 But, O LORD of Hosts, Who tries the righteous, and sees the reins and the heart, let me see Your vengeance on them: for unto You have I opened my cause. *(The words, "You try the righteous, and see the reins and the heart," refer back to his severe persecutions and why they were allowed to take place. This phraseology proves that Jeremiah understands, at least as far as one can understand, the Ways of the Lord in allowing such persecution.)*

13 Sing unto the LORD, praise ye the LORD: for He has delivered the soul of the poor from the hand of evildoers. *(Here, Faith gives the victory, foresees the judgment, and sings.)*

14 Cursed be the day wherein I was born: let not the day wherein my mother bore me be blessed. *(Verses 14 through 18, as far as the time frame is concerned, do not follow Verse 13, but in fact precede it. These words were uttered by the Prophet most probably when suffering the torment of the stocks.)*

15 Cursed be the man who brought tidings to my father, saying, A man child is born unto you; making him very glad.

16 And let that man be as the cities which the LORD overthrew, and repented not: and let him hear the cry in the morning, and the shouting at noontide *(Jeremiah is quoting from Job 3:3-12. Deep emotion expresses itself in the language suggested by the moment. The Prophet, even though retouching the discourses, would leave much of the original expression.*

The modern Christian, filled with Faith, would have a tendency to demean the Prophet for uttering such words; however, in every human life, even the Godliest, there must be some encouragement in order for the effort to continue. Jeremiah had none! No one complimented him on his Message! Even those who claimed friendship, as outlined in Verse 10, were secretly plotting his overthrow!

Therefore, the question does not pertain itself to the venting of discouragement by the Prophet, but rather that he was able to do as well as he did!);

17 Because He slew me not from the womb; or that my mother might have been my grave, and her womb to be always great with me. *(The idea is that inasmuch as they were going to kill him anyhow, it would be better, or so he thought, had he died "in the womb." As stated, this was no doubt said while he was in the stocks and after having experienced the terrible beating. At this time, his faith is sorely tested. He is wondering if God has forgotten His Promise made to him — that over him "his enemies would not prevail" [1:19].)*

18 Wherefore came I forth out of the womb to see labour and sorrow, that my days should be consumed with shame? *(This Verse is not a statement but rather a question, and it is answered in the Thirteenth Verse.)*

CHAPTER 21
(589 B.C.)
ZEDEKIAH'S INQUIRY

THE Word which came unto Jeremiah from the LORD, when king Zedekiah sent unto him Pashur the son of Melchiah, and Zephaniah the son of Maaseiah the Priest, saying *(Chapters 21 through 24 are an entirely different set of Prophecies than those ending with the last Verse of the Twentieth Chapter. This Chapter records the Divine Wrath upon Jerusalem, announced on the eve of the fall of the city, and the following Chapters show the justice of that Wrath.*

The "Pashur" of this Chapter is not Pashur the son of Immer of Chapter 20. Some Nineteen years separate the Prophecies addressed to these two Priests),

2 Enquire, I pray you, of the LORD for us: for Nebuchadnezzar king of Babylon makes war against us; if so be that the LORD will deal with us according to all His wondrous works, that He may go up from us. *(The phrase, used by king Zedekiah, "That the LORD will deal with us according to all His wondrous works," portrays man using religious language when he is in trouble and talking of God's "wondrous works." But yet, they can remain, like Zedekiah and the Priests and Princes, unconverted and rebellious.*

This illustrates the great Bible doctrine that man is a moral wreck, comparable to a broken vessel of pottery and, therefore, impossible of rehabilitation; hence, he must be re-made [II Cor. 5:17].)

THE DESTRUCTION OF JERUSALEM
FORETOLD

3 Then said Jeremiah unto them, Thus shall you say to Zedekiah *(many men, when preaching before a king, are careful only to say what the king would like to hear. But it was not thus with this brave and faithful man of God. The Word of the Lord is the same whether delivered to a president or a pauper)*:

4 Thus saith the LORD God of Israel; Behold, I will turn back the weapons of war that are in your hands, wherewith you fight against the king of Babylon, and against the Chaldeans, which besiege you without the walls, and I will assemble them into the midst of this city. *(The message is straight to the point! The Lord, instead of fighting for His People, will fight rather against His People.)*

5 And I Myself will fight against you with an outstretched hand and with a strong arm, even in anger, and in fury, and in great wrath. *(Every indication is that true Repentance at this late date, even though always accepted by God, and which would have definitely saved their souls, still, would not have effected a turn of events. After repeated offers of Mercy and Pardon, which were repeatedly spurned, the sands of time are speedily running out!)*

6 And I will smite the inhabitants of this city, both man and beast: they shall die of a great pestilence. *(The Holy Spirit through His Prophet presents the Message in crystal clarity. There is to be no misunderstanding as to what the Lord intends; therefore, their rebellion is inexcusable. To sin is bad; to sin against Light is worse; and Judah and Jerusalem sinned against Light!)*

7 And afterward, saith the LORD, I will deliver Zedekiah king of Judah, and his servants, and the people, and such as are left in this city from the pestilence, from the sword, and from the famine, into the hand of Nebuchadnezzar king of Babylon, and into the hand of their enemies, and into the hand of those who seek their life: and he shall smite them with the edge of the sword; he shall not spare them, neither have pity, nor have mercy. *(King Zedekiah of Judah need not think that he can work a deal with "Nebuchadnezzar" and, thereby, escape punishment! Actually, there will be no "pity" or "mercy" shown whatsoever.)*

8 And unto this people you shall say, Thus saith the LORD; Behold, I set before you the way of life, and the way of death. *(God, in His Love and Grace, has always offered life to these stout rebels, even at the eleventh hour; however, the deliverance guaranteed is far less than that originally promised. The people had spurned the Call of God for so long that time was rapidly running out. Several years before the offer of Deliverance upon Repentance was of far greater margin. They were virtually guaranteed enduring blessing [17:24-26], whereas now the offer only includes the saving of life.)*

9 He who abides in this city shall die by the sword, and by the famine, and by the pestilence: but he who goes out, and falls to the Chaldeans who besiege you, he shall live, and his life shall be unto him for a prey. *(The words, "His life shall be unto him for a prey," refer to*

the fact of losing both property and liberty, but not life. Some accepted this offer. Those who believed and acted on this promise are referred to in 39:9 and 52:15.)

10 For I have set My face against this city for evil, and not for good, saith the LORD: it shall be given into the hand of the king of Babylon, and he shall burn it with fire. *(At this time, Judah thinks she will be saved by Egypt. Consequently, the entire energies of the city were spent in this pursuit. They reasoned that inasmuch as the Temple was in their midst, God surely would not allow anything to happen in a negative way. The other cities of Judah, in their thinking, may fall, but not Jerusalem! However, the Lord says differently.)*

COMMANDS TO ZEDEKIAH, KING OF JUDAH

11 And touching the house of the king of Judah, say, Hear ye the Word of the LORD *(Zedekiah had repeatedly heard the word of men. It was prolific, abundant, beautiful in its prose, and promising in its application; however, it was a lie! Now, he is to hear the "Word of the LORD");*

12 O house of David, thus saith the LORD; Execute judgment in the morning, and deliver him who is spoiled out of the hand of the oppressor, lest My fury go out like fire, and burn that none can quench it, because of the evil of your doings. *(Even at the time that the city was being besieged by the Chaldeans, the rich kept oppressing and robbing the poor. God pities the oppressed, and His fury burns like fire against the oppressors. Ultimately, the oppressors have to answer!)*

13 Behold, I am against you, O inhabitant of the valley, and rock of the plain, saith the LORD; which say, Who shall come down against us? or who shall enter into our habitations? *(They have boastingly claimed that the Babylonian army cannot take the city. The boast had come from king to people; however, the boast was in opposition to the Word of the Lord. As such, despite all efforts, it could not stand!)*

14 But I will punish you according to the fruit of your doings, saith the LORD: and I will kindle a fire in the forest thereof, and it shall devour all things round about it. *(To their questions, the Lord gives His answer. Instead of peace and prosperity, He says, "I will punish you according to the fruit of your doings." This "fruit" was their opposition to the Word of the Lord as given by Jeremiah.)*

CHAPTER 22
(609 B.C.)
GOD WILL YET SPARE JUDAH: CONDITIONS TO BE MET; OTHERWISE JUDGMENT

THUS saith the LORD; Go down to the house of the king of Judah, and speak there this word,

2 And say, Hear the Word of the LORD, O king of Judah, who sits upon the throne of David, you, and your servants, and your people who enter in by these gates *(in this Chapter and the prior one, the four kings who hastened and presided at the ruin of their people is contrasted with the Righteous King, Who will restore and bless His people [23:5-6]. These four kings were Jehoahaz [also called Shallum], Jehoiakim, Jehoiachin, and Zedekiah. The king whom Jeremiah addresses in Verses 1 and 2 is Jehoiakim):*

3 Thus saith the LORD; Execute ye judgment and righteousness, and deliver the spoiled out of the hand of the oppressor: and do no wrong, do no violence to the stranger, the fatherless, nor the widow, neither shed innocent blood in this place. *(The Message from the Lord was simple, to the point, with absolutely no reason that it be misunderstood.)*

4 For if you do this thing indeed, then shall there enter in by the gates of this house kings sitting upon the throne of David, riding in chariots and on horses, he, and his servants, and his people. *(This Promise is almost identical to the same Promise given previously [17:25].)*

5 But if you will not hear these words, I swear by Myself, saith the LORD, that this house shall become a desolation. *(The phrase, "I swear by Myself, saith the LORD," is a solemn oath synonymous with the expression, "As I live, says Jehovah," and refers to the certitude of the Word being carried out.)*

6 For thus saith the LORD unto the king's house of Judah; You are Gilead unto Me, and the head of Lebanon; yet surely I will make you a wilderness, and cities which are not inhabited. *(The phrase, "You are Gilead unto Me, and the head of Lebanon," refers to the beauty of Judah. The phrase, "Yet surely I will make you a wilderness, and cities which are not inhabited," has a terrible significance. It was carried out in totality.)*

7 And I will prepare destroyers against you, every one with his weapons: and they shall cut down your choice cedars, and cast them into

the fire. *(The "destroyers" were the Chaldeans. The "choice cedars" actually referred to the palaces erected by the king and his nobles. They were built of cedar. As well, they were "burned" by the Chaldeans.)*

8 And many nations shall pass by this city, and they shall say every man to this neighbour, Wherefore has the LORD done thus unto this great city? *(Nebuchadnezzar no doubt thought that it was his military power that "did this unto this great city," Jerusalem; however, he was only an instrument in the Hands of the "LORD.")*

9 Then they shall answer, Because they have forsaken the Covenant of the LORD their God, and worshipped other gods, and served them. *(The people of Judah traded the "LORD their God" for "other gods." The "Covenant" was the Bible, and it was "forsaken.")*

PROPHECY AGAINST SHALLUM (JEHOAHAZ)

10 Weep ye not for the dead, neither bemoan him: but weep sore for him who goes away: for he shall return no more, nor see his native country. *(The phrase, "Weep ye not for the dead, neither bemoan him," refers to Josiah [II Chron. 35:24-25]. They had a reason to weep for him, because he was the last Godly king on the throne of David. The phrase, "But weep sore for him who goes away," refers to king Jehoahaz [Shallum; II Ki. 23:30-34]. The phrase, "For he shall return no more, nor see his native country," refers to Jehoahaz being taken captive "unto the land of Egypt" [Ezek. 19:1-4]. He only reigned three months and was the youngest son of Josiah.)*

11 For thus saith the LORD touching Shallum the son of Josiah king of Judah, which reigned instead of Josiah his father, which went forth out of this place; He shall not return thither any more *(it seems that Shallum [Jehoahaz], although younger, was preferred above his brother Jehoiakim. Pharaoh-Neco preferred his brother to him; therefore, after only a three-month reign, he took him to Egypt, where he died! This was approximately 20 years before the total destruction of Judah and Jerusalem by Nebuchadnezzar):*

12 But he shall die in the place whither they have led him captive, and shall see this land no more. *(Jehoahaz was two years younger than his brother Jehoiakim, and by right should not have had the throne after the death of his*

father Josiah. However, it seems from II Chron. 36:1 that the people preferred him over Jehoiakim; therefore, he would become king, but only for some three months. As stated, he was taken to Egypt by Pharaoh, and there he died.)*

PROPHECY AGAINST JEHOIAKIM

13 Woe unto him who builds his house by unrighteousness, and his chambers by wrong; who uses his neighbour's service without wages, and gives him not for his work *(this speaks of Jehoiakim, who took the place of Jehoahaz, and to whom Jeremiah was sent by the Lord, recorded at the beginning of this Chapter. He reigned for eleven years and was marked by the worst characteristics of idolatry and despotism);*

14 That saith, I will build me a wide house and large chambers, and cuts him out windows; and it is ceiled with cedar, and painted with vermilion. *(This is but one example of palatial excellence being built at the expense of the poor, fatherless, and widowed.)*

15 Shall you reign, because you closest yourself in cedar? did not your father eat and drink, and do judgment and justice, and then it was well with him? *(The way this palace was built by Jehoiakim violated Lev. 19:13 and Deut. 24:14-15. The question, "Shall you reign. . . ?", rather asks, "Do you prove your royal qualities because you live in a cedar palace?" This tells us that his government was for the benefit of himself and his lackeys around him, and not for the people.*

"Your father" refers to Josiah.)*

16 He *(Josiah)* judged the cause of the poor and needy; then it was well with him: was not this to know Me? saith the LORD. *(Because Josiah did these things, the Holy Spirit says, and two times at that, "Then it was well with him." What he did pleased the Lord; therefore, he had the Blessings of God.)*

17 But your eyes and your heart are not but for your covetousness, and for to shed innocent blood, and for oppression, and for violence, to do it. *(In this Passage, we see that Jehoiakim was the total opposite of his father Josiah!)*

18 Therefore thus saith the LORD concerning Jehoiakim the son of Josiah king of Judah; They shall not lament for him, saying, Ah my brother! Or, Ah sister! They shall not lament for him, saying, Ah lord! Or, Ah his glory! *(It is noteworthy that II Ki. 24:6 omits the usual*

mention of the burial of this deceased king. II Chron. 36:6 records that he was bound in fetters in order to be carried to Babylon, but it does not state that he ever reached that city. Here and in 36:30 his miserable end is predicted, and most certainly the Prophecy came to pass.)

19 He shall be buried with the burial of an ass, drawn and cast forth beyond the gates of Jerusalem. *(It is strange that the man, even the king, would hear this type of Prophecy, knowing that it was speaking of him, and in no uncertain terms, and still reject it!)*

PROPHECY AGAINST CONIAH, WHO WAS ALSO CALLED JEHOIACHIN OR JECHONIAH

20 Go up to Lebanon, and cry; and lift up your voice in Bashan, and cry from the passages: for all your lovers are destroyed. *(As the Nineteenth Verse finished with Jehoiakim, this Verse deals with his son and successor, Jehoiachin. The phrase, "Your lovers are destroyed," refers to the nations to which Judah looked, but which did not help her.)*

21 I spoke unto you in your prosperity; but you said, I will not hear. This has been your manner from your youth, that you obeyed not My voice. *(Even though Jehoiachin [Coniah] will be addressed momentarily, at this point the Holy Spirit is speaking directly to Judah.)*

22 The wind shall eat up all your Pastors, and your lovers shall go into captivity: surely then shall you be ashamed and confounded for all your wickedness. *(The "Pastors" referred to here actually speak of rulers of all kinds. It does not refer to Pastors of Churches, as we know such today! The "wind" spoken of is the armed force of Nebuchadnezzar, who would either kill or take into captivity all of these individuals.)*

23 O inhabitant of Lebanon, who makes your nest in the cedars, how gracious shall you be when pangs come upon you, the pain as of a woman in travail! *(Even though it seems as if Jeremiah is speaking of "Lebanon," he actually is speaking of the nobles of Jerusalem, who built their homes out of the great cedar trees of Lebanon.)*

24 As I live, saith the LORD, though Coniah the son of Jehoiakim king of Judah were the signet upon My right hand, yet would I pluck you thence *(in fact, due to him being the "king of Judah," and, thereby, the leader of God's chosen People, he, in effect, was "the signet upon*

God's right Hand." However, the Lord had disowned him, i.e., "yet will I pluck you thence," signifying that the scepter of power would pass from Judah to another, in this case, to the heathen Monarch Nebuchadnezzar);

25 And I will give you into the hand of them who seek your life, and into the hand of them whose face you fear, even into the hand of Nebuchadnezzar king of Babylon, and into the hand of the Chaldeans.

26 And I will cast you out, and your mother who bore you, into another country, where you were not born; and there shall you die. *(Jehoiachin [Coniah] and his mother Nehushta died in Babylon. The mentioning of her, and by the Holy Spirit at that, shows that she was rather influential and had no doubt encouraged Coniah in his rebellion.)*

27 But to the land whereunto they desire to return, thither shall they not return. *(The words, "they desire to return," no doubt indicate that their stay in Babylon was not a happy one; furthermore, they would never again see the "land" given to them by God, which had been polluted by their sin.)*

28 Is this man Coniah a despised broken idol? Is he a vessel wherein is no pleasure? Wherefore are they cast out, he and his seed, and are cast into a land which they know not? *(The question, "Is this man Coniah a despised broken idol?", is strong indeed! The word "idol" means a despised earthen vessel; the potter has no pleasure in it and, therefore, breaks it.)*

29 O Earth, Earth, Earth, hear the Word of the LORD. *(The declaration of this Verse is solemn! With the fall of Judah, there would be no nation left in the world who knew anything about Jehovah; consequently, the entirety of the world would suffer as a result of her fall.)*

30 Thus saith the LORD, Write ye this man childless, a man who shall not prosper in his days: for no man of his seed shall prosper, sitting upon the throne of David, and ruling any more in Judah. *(And so it came to pass! Though Coniah had descendents, not one of them ever sat upon the throne at Jerusalem. Great attention is given to this king, even though he reigned only a very short time, because he was the last in the Davidic line of kings; so it ended in him.*

While it is true that Zedekiah succeeded him, he was only his uncle. Therefore, not being in the direct lineage of David, he was not actually looked at by God as king, at least in the lineage of David.)

CHAPTER 23
(599 B.C.)
WOE TO FAITHLESS PASTORS

WOE be unto the Pastors who destroy and scatter the sheep of My pasture! saith the LORD. *(This Chapter is actually divided into two parts, with the first eight Verses dealing with the faithless civil leaders, i.e., kings [Pastors], and the remainder of the Chapter dealing with the faithless Prophets.)*

2 Therefore thus saith the LORD God of Israel against the Pastors who feed My people; You have scattered My flock, and driven them away, and have not visited them: behold, I will visit upon you the evil of your doings, saith the LORD. *(The phrase, "The LORD God of Israel against the Pastors," refers to the Lord as the Great Shepherd of Israel, with the kings serving as under-shepherds. Because of their sins, He sets Himself "against these Pastors," because they did not "feed My people.")*

RESTORATION UNDER THE MESSIAH

3 And I will gather the remnant of My flock out of all countries whither I have driven them, and will bring them again to their folds; and they shall be fruitful and increase. *(Verses 3 through 8 proclaim the regathering of all Israel. In these Verses, the Holy Spirit forges ahead even unto the coming Kingdom Age, when these great Prophecies will then be fulfilled.)*

4 And I will set up shepherds over them which shall feed them: and they shall fear no more, nor be dismayed, neither shall they be lacking, saith the LORD. *("Shepherds" are the same as the "Pastors" of Verse 1.)*

5 Behold, the days come, saith the LORD, that I will raise unto David a Righteous Branch, and a King shall reign and prosper, and shall execute judgment and justice in the Earth. *(This "Righteous Branch" is the Messiah. The justice and benevolence of His Rule here stand in contrast to the injustice and selfishness of that of the four kings who succeeded Godly king Josiah.*

The beautiful title, "The Branch," is given to Him four times in the Old Testament, thus foreshadowing the four Gospels and the necessity that there should be four: the Branch, the King [Matthew]; the Branch, the Servant [Mark]; the Branch, the Man [Luke]; and the Branch, Jehovah [John].)

6 In His days Judah shall be saved, and Israel shall dwell safely: and this is His name whereby He shall be called, THE LORD OUR RIGHTEOUSNESS. *(The phrase, "In His days," refers to the days of the Messiah, which will be the Millennial Reign. The phrase, "Judah shall be saved," is in contrast to Judah now being lost!)*

7 Therefore, behold, the days come, saith the LORD, that they shall no more say, The LORD lives, which brought up the Children of Israel out of the land of Egypt *(during the coming Kingdom Age, the Children of Israel will then exclaim the great Deliverance by Christ from the Antichrist);*

8 But, the LORD lives, which brought up and which led the seed of the House of Israel out of the north country, and from all countries whither I had driven them; and they shall dwell in their own land. *(The "north country" contains most of the countries where Israel wandered as outcasts for nearly 2,000 years. At the beginning of the Kingdom Age, all Jews will come from these countries to the Land of Israel.)*

FALSE PROPHETS

9 My heart within me is broken because of the Prophets; all my bones shake; I am like a drunken man, and like a man whom wine has overcome, because of the LORD, and because of the words of His Holiness. *(As Verses 1 and 2 concerned themselves with the kings of Judah, Verses 9 through 40 concern the false prophets.)*

10 For the land is full of adulterers; for because of swearing the land mourns; the pleasant places of the wilderness are dried up, and their course is evil, and their force is not right. *(The phrase, "For the land is full of adulterers," refers to idolaters. While no doubt immorality was rampant, still, the idolatry was even worse, which the Lord describes as "adultery," i.e., "spiritual adultery" [Rom. 7:1-4].*

The phrase, "For because of swearing the land mourns," refers to idol worship. It actually means "because of the curse." Beside the original curse on the Earth, as described in Gen. 3:17, the Holy Spirit describes a further deepening of the curse because of added sin.)

11 For both Prophet and Priest are profane; yea, in My house have I found their wickedness, saith the LORD. *(The material misery and moral corruption which resulted from the teaching of these false prophets appear in the statement that it did not produce that which was right and that it occasioned a physical drought. The Priests, it seems, set up idols even in the Temple.)*

12 Wherefore their way shall be unto them as slippery ways in the darkness: they shall be driven on, and fall therein: for I will bring evil upon them, even the year of their visitation, saith the LORD. *("Their way" refers to their fashionable religion. The phrase, "The year of their visitation," pertains to the punishment that is to be brought by Nebuchadnezzar.)*

13 And I have seen folly in the prophets of Samaria; they prophesied in Baal, and caused My people Israel to err. *(The Holy Spirit through Jeremiah now reverts back well over 100 years to the fall of "Samaria." They had their "prophets" as well!*

Incidentally, the Hebrew name for "Baal" was "Ba'al," which means "husband." Therefore, in Israel's mind, they were still worshipping Jehovah, Whom they called "Husband," but they had substituted some figure [idol] that could be touched, held, and felt. In fact, the Baal cults affected and challenged the worship of Jehovah throughout Israelite history.)

14 I have seen also in the Prophets of Jerusalem an horrible thing: they commit adultery, and walk in lies: they strengthen also the hands of evildoers, that none does return from his wickedness; they are all of them unto Me as Sodom, and the inhabitants thereof as Gomorrah. *(The guilt of the Prophets of Jerusalem is declared to be greater than that of the Prophets of Samaria. Their "adultery," as stated, was idol worship; consequently, the Lord placed "all of them" in the same status as "Sodom" and "Gomorrah." There could be no worse description!)*

15 Therefore thus saith the LORD of Hosts concerning the Prophets; Behold, I will feed them with wormwood, and make them drink the water of gall: for from the Prophets of Jerusalem is profaneness gone forth into all the land. *(The moral condition of a nation results from the character of the spiritual teaching given to it. In this Scripture, Judgment is guaranteed to all who claim to be preaching the Word of God but who, in reality, are not!)*

16 Thus saith the LORD of Hosts, Hearken not unto the words of the Prophets who prophesy unto you: they make you vain: they speak a vision of their own heart, and not out of the mouth of the LORD. *(The "mouth of the LORD" refers to Inspiration. As false prophets wrecked the Northern Kingdom of Israel and the Southern Kingdom of Judah, likewise, false prophets are destroying the Church in America, as well!)*

17 They say still unto them who despise Me, The LORD has said, You shall have peace; and they say unto every one who walks after the imagination of his own heart, No evil shall come upon you. *(These individuals, even on the eve of destruction, preached a false feel-good gospel which promoted self-esteem.)*

18 For who has stood in the counsel of the LORD, and has perceived and heard His Word? who has marked His Word, and heard it? *(The phrase, "For who has stood in the counsel of the LORD," actually refers back to Verse 16. This Verse gives the reason the false prophets were not to be believed. They did not have the Mind of the Lord and, therefore, were not given anything from the Lord; however, they said what the people wanted to hear and, therefore, they were paid well!)*

19 Behold, a whirlwind of the LORD is gone forth in fury, even a grievous whirlwind: it shall fall grievously upon the head of the wicked. *(The false prophets were announcing peace and prosperity, while the Lord through Jeremiah spoke of the soon-to-come "whirlwind." Furthermore, it was "a whirlwind of the LORD" and it had already begun "in fury."*

"The wicked" addressed here not only included the false prophets, but all who listened to them.)

20 The anger of the LORD shall not return, until He have executed, and till He have performed the thoughts of His heart: in the latter days you shall consider it perfectly. *(The "latter days" mentioned here refer to some years later, with the exiles in Babylon, who would then understand perfectly that Jeremiah had preached the Truth from the Mouth of the Lord, and that his opponents had preached falsehood out of the imagination of their own hearts.*

As well, it refers to Israel, which in the last days will accept the false messiah, the Antichrist, and then realize they have been deceived.

This Verse also portrays God as an emotional Being exhibiting "anger" and having "thoughts." Such shows an active involvement in the everyday lives of His People. Sin, and upon the refusal to repent, and even after repeated warnings, brings about "the anger of the LORD."

The phrase, "Thoughts of His Heart," refers to the Word of God.)

21 I have not sent these Prophets, yet they ran: I have not spoken to them, yet they prophesied. *(That which angered Him was that they "prophesied" in His Name when, in reality, He had not "sent them" or "spoken to them.")*

22 But if they had stood in My counsel, and had caused My people to hear My words, then they should have turned them from their evil

way, and from the evil of their doings. *(The idea of this Verse is that at least some of these Prophets had once known God and had been truly called by Him; however, for whatever reason, they had lost their way!)*

23 Am I a God at hand, saith the LORD, and not a God afar off? *(The impossibility of false teachers hiding themselves and their doctrines from God is declared in Verses 23 through 27. The implication of this Verse is that God is always "at hand," meaning that He notes all that is being done, whether good or bad. As well, He does so whether near or far.)*

24 Can any hide himself in secret places that I shall not see him? saith the LORD. Do not I fill Heaven and Earth? saith the LORD. *(This Verse proclaims the Omnipresence of God. In other words, He is everywhere and, thereby, sees everything.)*

25 I have heard what the Prophets said, who prophesy lies in My Name, saying, I have dreamed, I have dreamed. *(The Prophet of Verse 18 is God's Prophet in contrast with man's prophet of Verse 25; and the dream of Verse 28, as opposed to that of Verse 25.)*

26 How long shall this be in the heart of the prophets who prophesy lies? yea, they are prophets of the deceit of their own heart *(it is certain that these Prophecies by Jeremiah concerning these false prophets were not met with approbation, but rather with anger! Especially that the Holy Spirit through the Prophet called them liars!)*;

27 Which think to cause My people to forget My name by their dreams which they tell every man to his neighbour, as their fathers have forgotten My name for Baal. *(As the people of Israel called the Lord "Master" or "Husband" and called "Baal" by the same name, they no longer could distinguish between the two. Consequently, in modern religion, the Catholic Church equates Mary with the Lord, while too many of their Protestant counterparts equate their religious denominations with the Lord.)*

28 The Prophet who has a dream, let him tell a dream; and he who has My Word, let him speak My Word faithfully. What is the chaff to the wheat? saith the LORD. *(This Verse contrasts the two prophets: false and true. The former one has a "false dream," which is likened to "chaff," while the latter has "God's Word," which is likened to "wheat.")*

29 Is not My Word like as a fire? saith the LORD; and like a hammer that breaks the rock in pieces? *(In this Passage, the Word of God is likened to a "fire" and a "hammer"; a*

fire to burn, a hammer to break. Thus, the doctrine preached reveals the truth or falseness of the Preacher. Preaching which leaves out or denies the Wrath to come is false; and such a Preacher is false.)*

30 Therefore, behold, I am against the prophets, saith the LORD, who steal My Words every one from his neighbour. *(The words, "Behold, I am against," respecting these false prophets, are repeated three times in as many Verses. The thrice-repeated admonition proclaims the just anger of God, which will ultimately result in their destruction.*

The phrase, "Who steal My Words, every one from his neighbor," refers to them stealing Jeremiah's methods. They listened greedily to the discourses of the true Prophet, not with a view to spiritual profit, but to making their own utterances more effective.)

31 Behold, I am against the prophets, saith the LORD, who use their tongues, and say, He says. *(In other words, they preface their prophecies with "Thus saith the LORD," adopting the same forms as the true Prophet, but to them only forms.)*

32 Behold, I am against them who prophesy false dreams, saith the LORD, and do tell them, and cause My people to err by their lies, and by their lightness; yet I sent them not, nor commanded them: therefore they shall not profit this people at all, saith the LORD. *(This Passage proclaims to us the fact of a plethora of false prophets attempting to countermand the true Prophecies of Jeremiah.*

The phrase, "By their lightness," implies arrogance and boastfulness.)

33 And when this people, or the prophet, or a priest, shall ask you, saying, What is the burden of the LORD? you shall then say unto them, What burden? I will even forsake you, saith the LORD.

34 And as for the prophet, and the priest, and the people, who shall say, The burden of the LORD, I will even punish that man and his house. *(They were not content to merely reject the Message, they must mock it! However, they would rue the day that they did this!)*

35 Thus shall you say every one to his neighbour, and every one to his brother, What has the LORD answered? and, What has the LORD spoken? *(This Verse proclaims the Holy Spirit through Jeremiah patiently explaining to the people that their mocking the Word of the Lord by saying, "The burden of the LORD," was placing them in very dangerous circumstances.*

While it was satisfactory for them to ask the questions, they must never do so in a mocking tone, which they evidently were doing!)

36 And the burden of the LORD shall you mention no more: for every man's word shall be his burden; for you have perverted the Words of the Living God, of the LORD of Hosts our God. *(By the people using the phrase, "The burden of the LORD," and doing so in a mocking tone, they were making light of Jeremiah's Prophecies. He was speaking of coming war and judgment, while they were speaking of peace and prosperity; therefore, they made a joke of what he was saying.)*

37 Thus shall you say to the Prophet, What has the LORD answered you? and, What has the LORD spoken? *(The Holy Spirit comes back to the same admonishment of Verse 35, imploring the people to hear what the Lord says, and not what these false prophets say! As well, only Jeremiah had the Word of the Lord.)*

38 But since you say, The burden of the LORD; therefore thus saith the LORD, Because you say this word, The burden of the LORD, and I have sent unto you, saying, You shall not say, The burden of the LORD *(the phrase, "But since you say," implies that they ignored the admonishment of the Lord and continued to mock!)*;

39 Therefore, behold, I, even I, will utterly forget you, and I will forsake you, and the city that I gave you and your fathers, and cast you out of My presence. *(The pronoun "I" is emphatic, emphasizing the solemnity of the moment! The phrase, "I will utterly forget you," means He will utterly remove them. The "casting out" was so complete that not only were they taken away and the city totally destroyed by Nebuchadnezzar, but the Lord also departed, as seen by the Prophet Ezekiel [Ezek: 11:23], who incidentally was prophesying in Babylonia.)*

40 And I will bring an everlasting reproach upon you, and a perpetual shame, which shall not be forgotten. *(This "everlasting reproach" rested upon Israel until the coming of the Messiah and, due to their rejection of Him, deepened even more! They have suffered this "everlasting reproach" now for some 2,500 years. Sadly, their very name is "a perpetual shame.")*

CHAPTER 24
(598 B.C.)
THE BASKETS OF GOOD AND BAD FIGS

THE LORD showed me, and, behold, two baskets of figs were set before the Temple of the LORD, after that Nebuchadnezzar king of Babylon had carried away captive Jeconiah the son of Jehoiakim king of Judah, and the princes of Judah, with the carpenters and smiths, from Jerusalem, and had brought them to Babylon. *(This is the second deportation under Jehoiachin, which included Mordecai and Esther, who were taken to Babylon [Esther 2:5-6]. The first deportation was under Jehoiakim, which included Daniel and the three Hebrew children. The second deportation took place in 597 B.C.*

The two deportations before the final and complete destruction were another way of the Lord attempting to warn Judah and Jerusalem to repent, but to no avail!)

2 One basket had very good figs, even like the figs that are first ripe: and the other basket had very naughty figs, which could not be eaten, they were so bad. *(The two baskets of figs were a symbolism of the two classes of people in Judah and Jerusalem. The "very good figs" represented the few Godly in the nation and the city, who, for the most part, were deported to Babylon. The "very naughty figs" represented the ungodly, who would be left in Judah and Jerusalem and, thereby, slated for destruction.*

However, the unspiritual minds of the ungodly thought surely that because they were spared deportation [the first two deportations], this surely was a sign of their Godliness and, thereby, the Blessings of God. They no doubt ridiculed those who were taken away, having no spiritual understanding at all of the intentions of the Lord.

When men, even in modern times, do not follow the Bible, they seriously mistake God's intentions and read into His Hand the very opposite of His Plan.)

3 Then said the LORD unto me, What do you see, Jeremiah? And I said, Figs; the good figs, very good; and the evil, very evil, that cannot be eaten, they are so evil. *(As Jeremiah observes these "figs," he is allowed to see, at least in part, that which God sees.)*

APPLICATION OF THE GOOD FIGS

4 Again the Word of the LORD came unto me, saying,

5 Thus saith the LORD, the God of Israel; Like these good figs, so will I acknowledge them who are carried away captive of Judah, whom I have sent out of this place into the land of the Chaldeans for their good. *(Everything that happens to a true follower of the Lord is always caused or allowed by the Lord, i.e.,*

"for their good.")

6 For I will set My eyes upon them for good, and I will bring them again to this land: and I will build them, and not pull them down; and I will plant them, and not pluck them up.

7 And I will give them an heart to know Me, that I am the LORD: and they shall be My people, and I will be their God: for they shall return unto Me with their whole heart. *(The "whole heart," which speaks of total consecration, is the key to all these Promises!)*

APPLICATION OF THE BAD FIGS

8 And as the evil figs, which cannot be eaten, they are so evil; surely thus saith the LORD, So will I give Zedekiah the king of Judah, and his princes, and the residue of Jerusalem, who remain in this land, and them who dwell in the land of Egypt *(as the Blessing was pronounced on those taken to Babylon, who obeyed the Commands of the Lord and diligently attempted to follow Him, conversely, the curse is now pronounced upon the "evil figs," symbolizing "Zedekiah," as well as "his princes" and all "who remained in the land," as well as those who were in the "land of Egypt")*:

9 And I will deliver them to be removed into all the kingdoms of the Earth for their hurt, to be a reproach and a proverb, a taunt and a curse, in all places whither I shall drive them. *(As the Lord would deliver the former to blessing, He now delivers the latter to destruction. It would soon come.)*

10 And I will send the sword, the famine, and the pestilence, among them, till they be consumed from off the land that I gave unto them and to their fathers. *(The Lord had slated Judah and Jerusalem for judgment, all because of their sin and refusal to repent. Babylon would be the instrument that He would use. The preaching of Jeremiah demanded that they yield to Babylon. But instead the leaders of Judah claimed deliverance by the hand of the Egyptians or even that the Lord would deliver them. But the Lord says here the opposite will occur, and in a very destructive way.)*

CHAPTER 25
(606 B.C.)
THE REBELLION OF JUDAH

THE word that came to Jeremiah concerning all the people of Judah in the fourth year of Jehoiakim the son of Josiah king of Judah, that was the first year of Nebuchadnezzar king of Babylon *(this Chapter records the great Prophecy of the 70 years servitude in Babylon. It also predicts the overthrow of Babylon by the nations whom she had enslaved. However, the Prophecy goes much further than the judgment of ancient Babylon, for the principle of universal judgment is also developed and foretold. The repetition of the Judgment of Verse 10 in Rev. 18:23 shows that the predictions of this Chapter were not exhausted by the destruction of the Chaldean Empire in the days of Cyrus)*;

2 The which Jeremiah the Prophet spoke unto all the people of Judah, and to all the inhabitants of Jerusalem, saying *(the expression, "Jeremiah the Prophet," is given in this manner to emphasize the fact that this Prophet is the one to whom God is speaking concerning the future of the "people of Judah and to all the inhabitants of Jerusalem")*,

3 From the thirteenth year of Josiah the son of Amon king of Judah, even unto this day, that is the three and twentieth year, the Word of the LORD has come unto me, and I have spoken unto you, rising early and speaking; but you have not hearkened. *(Jeremiah had been a Prophet from the Thirteenth year of Josiah, which now totaled about twenty-three years. This was eighteen years under Josiah, 3 months under Jehoahaz, and 4 years under Jehoiakim.)*

4 And the LORD has sent unto you all his servants the Prophets, rising early and sending them; but you have not hearkened, nor inclined your ear to hear. *(This actually refers to all the Prophets who had come before Jeremiah. Israel little heard them, as well!)*

5 They said, Turn ye again now every one from his evil way, and from the evil of your doings, and dwell in the land that the LORD has given unto you and to your fathers for ever and ever *(settlement in the Land of Promise was contingent upon obedience)*:

6 And go not after other gods to serve them, and to worship them, and provoke Me not to anger with the works of your hands; and I will do you no hurt. *(Upon relationship with the Lord, the ancient as well as the modern Believer can either gladden the heart of God or "anger Him." Such shows a direct and total involvement in the lives of those who claim His Name.)*

7 Yet you have not hearkened unto Me, saith the LORD; that you might provoke Me to anger with the works of your hands to your own hurt. *(It was not a matter of not hearing or understanding what the Lord was saying, but*

a matter of not believing what He was saying. Such also is the modern Church!)

SEVENTY YEARS CAPTIVITY FORETOLD

8 Therefore thus saith the LORD of Hosts; Because you have not heard My words *(God's Words were given through Jeremiah, but yet they had all been given before in the Bible. In fact, the Book of Deuteronomy was basically the foundation of all of Jeremiah's Prophecies [Deut., Chpt. 28]),*

9 Behold, I will send and take all the families of the north, saith the LORD, and Nebuchadnezzar the king of Babylon, My servant, and will bring them against this land, and against the inhabitants thereof, and against all these nations round about, and will utterly destroy them, and make them an astonishment, and an hissing, and perpetual desolations. *(The "families of the north" consist of Nebuchadnezzar plus all those who followed him. The phrase, "My servant," concerning Nebuchadnezzar, does not refer to relationship, but rather as an instrument of punishment.)*

10 Moreover I will take from them the voice of mirth, and the voice of gladness, the voice of the bridegroom, and the voice of the bride, the sound of the millstones, and the light of the candle. *(The phrase, "Moreover I will take from them," refers to total "desolations," and in fact "perpetual desolations," meaning "long-continued.")*

11 And this whole land shall be a desolation, and an astonishment; and these nations shall serve the king of Babylon seventy years. *(The Lord sentenced Judah to "seventy years" of service to the king of Babylon, because she had ignored the yearly Sabbath that was supposed to be conducted every seventh year. In fact, they had gone for about 490 years without keeping this yearly Sabbath, which amounted to 70 years they owed the Lord, which He would now collect. However, the fact of the judgment was because of continued unrepented sin. The length of time was for the reason given [Lev. 25:1-7; II Chron., Chpts. 20-21].)*

JUDGMENT ON BABYLON

12 And it shall come to pass, when seventy years are accomplished, that I will punish the king of Babylon, and that nation, saith the LORD, for their iniquity, and the land of the Chaldeans, and will make it perpetual desolations. *(The "king of Babylon" at that time was Belshazzar. The kings used by God to "punish him" were "Darius the Mede" and "Cyrus the Persian.")*

13 And I will bring upon that land all My words which I have pronounced against it, even all that is written in this Book which Jeremiah has prophesied against all the nations. *(The phrase, "My Words written in this Book," are God's Words, and they were written in a Book of the Bible, i.e., the Book of Jeremiah, the very Book we now hold in our hands. Such is Inspiration! [I Pet. 1:11].)*

14 For many nations and great kings shall serve themselves of them also: and I will recompense them according to their deeds, and according to the works of their own hands. *(Although certain nations were commissioned by the Lord to punish Judah and Jerusalem, still, every indication is that they carried this commission too far regarding cruelty and oppression. Now, the Lord will call them to account, as well!)*

THE CUP OF WRATH FOR ALL NATIONS

15 For thus saith the LORD God of Israel unto me; Take the wine cup of this fury at My hand, and cause all the nations, to whom I send you, to drink it. *(This part of the Prophecy leaps ahead to the future, and in fact has not yet been fulfilled. The fulfillment will come in the Great Tribulation [Rev. 16:19].)*

16 And they shall drink, and be moved, and be mad, because of the sword that I will send among them. *(This refers not only to the coming destruction of Babylon by Darius and Cyrus, but as well to the Great Tribulation when the Antichrist will "take peace from the Earth" [Rev. 6:4].)*

17 Then took I the cup at the LORD's hand, and made all the nations to drink, unto whom the LORD had sent me *(this would have proper fulfillment in Jeremiah's near future, and would include all the nations surrounding Judah. But yet, the words, "The cup at the LORD's Hand," jump ahead to the Book of Revelation [Rev. 14:10]):*

18 To wit, Jerusalem, and the cities of Judah, and the kings thereof, and the princes thereof, to make them a desolation, an astonishment, an hissing, and a curse; as it is this day *(judgment was to begin at Jerusalem because it is the House of God [I Pet. 4:17], and it will end with Babylon [Rev., Chpt. 18]);*

19 Pharaoh king of Egypt, and his servants, and his princes, and all his people (after Judah, mighty "Egypt" is addressed first of all. "Pharaoh" is especially signaled out, because of Egypt's supposed strength, and because of "Pharaoh" being worshipped as Deity. Egypt as well as others to be listed will all taste of the Wrath of God!);

20 And all the mingled people, and all the kings of the land of Uz, and all the kings of the land of the Philistines, and Ashkelon, and Azzah, and Ekron, and the remnant of Ashdod (it is interesting that the "land of Uz" is mentioned, inasmuch as it was the home of Job about 1,000 years before),

21 Edom, and Moab, and the children of Ammon (this is the area that makes up present day Jordan. Strangely enough, this area will escape the hand of the Antichrist in that coming terrible day of Judgment, to which Israel will flee after being invaded and defeated by the Antichrist [Isa. 26:20; Rev., Chpt. 12]),

22 And all the kings of Tyrus, and all the kings of Zidon, and the kings of the isles which are beyond the sea (these two cities, "Tyrus" and "Zidon," situated on the Mediterranean, were to become two of the most powerful cities of commerce in the world of that day. Tyre would become so rich and lifted up with pride that the Holy Spirit would use her king as a symbol of Satan [Ezek., Chpt. 28]),

23 Dedan, and Tema, and Buz, and all who are in the utmost corners ("Dedan" is on the border of Edom, while "Tema" is the area that Eliphaz came from, regarding one of Job's "friends" [Job 2:11]. "Buz" is the place that Elihu came from, who was the last one to admonish Job, and whom God totally ignored [Job 32:2]),

24 And all the kings of Arabia, and all the kings of the mingled people who dwell in the desert (all are singled out because of their association with Judah, whether near or far),

25 And all the kings of Zimri, and all the kings of Elam, and all the kings of the Medes,

26 And all the kings of the north, far and near, one with another, and all the kingdoms of the world, which are upon the face of the Earth: and the king of Sheshach shall drink after them. (Many of the statements, such as "All the kingdoms of the world," prove that this Prophecy belongs to the future. It speaks to the coming Great Tribulation.)

27 Therefore you shall say unto them, Thus saith the LORD of Hosts, the God of Israel; Drink ye, and be drunken, and spue, and fall, and rise no more, because of the sword which I will send among you. (The phrase, "Because of the sword which I will send among you," refers to God's total control over all the nations of the world.)

28 And it shall be, if they refuse to take the cup at your hand to drink, then shall you say unto them, Thus saith the LORD of Hosts; You shall certainly drink. (The phrase, "You shall certainly drink," portrays these nations reaping what they have sown [Gal. 6:7-8].)

29 For, lo, I begin to bring evil on the city which is called by My Name, and should you be utterly unpunished? You shall not be unpunished: for I will call for a sword upon all the inhabitants of the Earth, saith the LORD of Hosts. ("The city which is called by My Name" is Jerusalem.)

30 Therefore prophesy thou against them all these words, and say unto them, The LORD shall roar from on high, and utter His voice from His holy habitation; He shall mightily roar upon His habitation; He shall give a shout, as they who tread the grapes, against all the inhabitants of the Earth. (This Prophecy speaks of the forthcoming glee of the surrounding nations at the destruction of Judah; however, their glee shall be short-lived! As well, the phrase, "Against all the inhabitants of the Earth," proclaims the fact that the fall of Judah would adversely affect the entirety of the world. However, the world was entirely ignorant of that.)

31 A noise shall come even to the ends of the Earth; for the LORD has a controversy with the nations, He will plead with all flesh; He will give them who are wicked to the sword, saith the LORD. (The word "plead" means "to judge." The Prophecy now extends from Jeremiah's day to the coming Great Tribulation, and even the Battle of Armageddon [Rev. 14:20].)

32 Thus saith the LORD of Hosts, Behold, evil shall go forth from nation to nation, and a great whirlwind shall be raised up from the coasts of the Earth. (All of this refers to Rev. 16:13-14.)

33 And the slain of the LORD shall be at that day from one end of the Earth even unto the other end of the Earth: they shall not be lamented, neither gathered, nor buried; they shall be dung upon the ground. (The phrase, "From one end of the Earth even unto the other end of the Earth," refers to the Antichrist "taking peace from the Earth," which will take place in the coming Great Tribulation [Rev. 6:4].)

34 Howl, you shepherds, and cry; and wallow yourselves in the ashes, you principal of

the flock: for the days of your slaughter and of your dispersions are accomplished; and you shall fall like a pleasant vessel. *(The Prophecy now reverts back to Jeremiah's time. These "shepherds" were Zedekiah and his ministers and men of war. The "pleasant vessel" refers to Judah. When a precious but fragile vessel falls, it breaks in pieces beyond repair. Such was Israel, a pleasant vessel, now broken, and never to be repaired. However, a new Israel, a "pleasant vessel" never to be broken, will be made by the Heavenly Potter, which will take place immediately after the Second Coming [Zech. 13:1].)*

35 And the shepherds shall have no way to flee, nor the principal of the flock to escape. *(The last kings of Judah, Jehoiakim, Jehoiachin, and Zedekiah, all came to a miserable end [II Ki. 23:34-24:16; 25:7].)*

36 A voice of the cry of the shepherds, and an howling of the principal of the flock, shall be heard: for the LORD has spoiled their pasture. *("His habitation," i.e., "His pasture," is now "their pasture," because disowned by Him.)*

37 And the peaceable habitations are cut down because of the fierce anger of the LORD. *(We learn from all of this that the Lord can abide sin in His Own no more than He can in the heathen — in fact, not nearly as much!)*

38 He has forsaken His covert, as the lion: for their land is desolate because of the fierceness of the oppressor, and because of His fierce anger. *(The "oppressor" is the Chaldean, while "His fierce anger" is "God's anger.")*

CHAPTER 26
(609 B.C.)
JEREMIAH THREATENED WITH DEATH

IN the beginning of the reign of Jehoiakim the son of Josiah king of Judah came this word from the LORD, saying *(this Prophecy takes us back some 22 years before the Babylonian captivity [II Ki. 23:36; 24:18]. All that happened, at least concerning Judah, as portrayed in the previous Chapter, could have been avoided if the words of the Prophet had been heeded at this early time),*

2 Thus saith the LORD; Stand in the court of the LORD's house, and speak unto all the cities of Judah, which come to worship in the LORD's house, all the words that I command you to speak unto them; diminish not a word *(as today, so then, people were willing to attend religious services, but not to abandon their sins. In fact, almost all who came to "worship" did*

not know the Lord)*:

3 If so be they will hearken, and turn every man from his evil way, that I may repent Me of the evil, which I purpose to do unto them because of the evil of their doings. *(The word "turn" means "to repent." This Message was spoken to the religious elite of Judah. Such are the hardest to bring to Repentance.)*

4 And you shall say unto them, Thus saith the LORD; If you will not hearken to Me, to walk in My law, which I have set before you *(the criteria was "My Law," i.e., the Mosaic Law. While the Mosaic Law has been completely fulfilled in Christ, presently the criteria still is the Bible and will always be the Bible),*

5 To hearken to the words of My servants the Prophets, whom I sent unto you, both rising up early, and sending them, but you have not hearkened *(the idea is: due to the persistence of the Lord, Judah was without excuse!);*

6 Then will I make this house like Shiloh, and will make this city a curse to all the nations of the Earth. *("Shiloh" was the place where the Tabernacle of Moses was located during the time of the Judges. Because of Israel's great sin in those days, the Lord allowed the Philistines to spoil that place and its worship.)*

7 So the Priests and the Prophets and all the people heard Jeremiah speaking these words in the House of the LORD. *(As Jeremiah prophesied the destruction of the Temple and the city of Jerusalem, and did so in the very Temple itself, such a prediction must have been startling to all who heard it. But to those who placed their confidence in the mere existence of this consecrated building, it was like a blow aimed at their life. In fact, the "Priests" and the "Prophets" were preaching the very opposite of Jeremiah.)*

8 Now it came to pass, when Jeremiah had made an end of speaking all that the LORD had commanded him to speak unto all the people, that the Priests and the Prophets and all the people took him, saying, You shall surely die. *(Jeremiah is placed under arrest because of what he is now preaching.)*

9 Why have you prophesied in the Name of the LORD, saying, This house shall be like Shiloh, and this city shall be desolate without an inhabitant? And all the people were gathered against Jeremiah in the House of the LORD. *(The phrase, "And all the people were gathered against Jeremiah in the House of the LORD," all too often characterizes the response to all true Prophets. They did not like what he preached, so they were determined to silence him.)*

10 When the princes of Judah heard these things, then they came up from the king's house unto the House of the LORD, and sat down in the entry of the new gate of the LORD's House. *(The "Princes of Judah" referred to the members of the various branches of the royal family, who acted as Judges and Magistrates. Their "sitting down in the entry of the new gate of the LORD's House" refers to Jeremiah being put on trial for his life.)*

11 Then spoke the Priests and the Prophets unto the princes and to all the people, saying, This man is worthy to die; for he has prophesied against this city, as you have heard with your ears. *(The accusations of these "Priests" and "Prophets" to the royal Judges fly thick and fast. They want Jeremiah's life!)*

JEREMIAH'S ANSWER

12 Then spoke Jeremiah unto all the princes and to all the people, saying, The LORD sent me to prophesy against this house and against this city all the words that you have heard. *(In reply to their accusations, Jeremiah little defends himself, but rather uses the occasion to continue his Message. He claims "The LORD" as his sponsor. As well, he claims that his very "Words" that have been "heard" by the people were given to him by the Lord.)*

13 Therefore now amend your ways and your doings, and obey the voice of the LORD your God; and the LORD will repent Him of the evil that He has pronounced against you. *(In effect, Jeremiah will now give an Altar Call! However, it will do little good.)*

14 As for me, behold, I am in your hand: do with me as seems good and meet unto you. *(With this statement, he puts himself in the hands of God, but does make the following statement:)*

15 But know ye for certain, that if you put me to death, you shall surely bring innocent blood upon yourselves, and upon this city, and upon the inhabitants thereof: for of a truth the LORD has sent me unto you to speak all these words in your ears. *(Jeremiah's statement must have sent fear into the hearts of these Magistrates, "the princes," because they would not take Jeremiah's side. No doubt, the Lord used these words to speak to their hearts.)*

CONTENTION OVER JEREMIAH

16 Then said the princes and all the people unto the Priests and to the Prophets; This man is not worthy to die: for he has spoken to us in the name of the LORD our God. *(It is amazing that these men admitted that "he has spoken to us in the Name of the LORD our God," but yet they would not obey the admonition to repent!)*

17 Then rose up certain of the elders of the land, and spoke to all the assembly of the people, saying *(the "elders of the land" were originally the heads of powerful families in Israel, and probably had their foundation in the fixed number of 70, as described in Ex. 24:1),*

18 Micah the Morasthite prophesied in the days of Hezekiah king of Judah, and spoke to all the people of Judah, saying, Thus saith the LORD of Hosts; Zion shall be plowed like a field, and Jerusalem shall become heaps, and the mountain of the house as the high places of a forest. *(The "Prophet Micah" was a contemporary with Hosea, Amos, and Isaiah. His Prophecy is recorded in his Book, Micah 1:1 and 3:12. At this time, the Prophecy was over 100 years old.)*

19 Did Hezekiah king of Judah and all Judah put him at all to death? did he not fear the LORD, and besought the LORD, and the LORD repented him of the evil which He had pronounced against them? Thus might we procure great evil against our souls. *(The elders used "Hezekiah king of Judah" as an example of Righteousness; however, there was a world of difference in Hezekiah and Jehoiakim, who was now the reigning king. By the statement, "Thus might we procure great evil against our souls," the elders seemed to understand, at least in part, their precarious spiritual condition. But yet, because of their fear of man, it seems they did little about it, at least regarding Repentance.)*

20 And there was also a man who prophesied in the Name of the LORD, Urijah the son of Shemaiah of Kirjath-jearim, who prophesied against this city and against this land according to all the words of Jeremiah. *(Other than this incident, the Scripture is silent concerning the "Prophet Urijah.")*

21 And when Jehoiakim the king, with all his mighty men, and all the princes, heard his words, the king sought to put him to death: but when Urijah heard it, he was afraid, and fled, and went into Egypt *(this will show that it is disastrous for a servant of God to take shelter in the shadow of Egypt rather than in the secret place of the Most High. The path of duty is usually the path of safety);*

22 And Jehoiakim the king sent men into Egypt, namely, Elnathan the son of Achbor, and

certain men with him into Egypt. ("Jehoiakim" was not satisfied to stop the voice of the Prophet Urijah, who evidently was prophesying at the same time as Jeremiah, but he had to kill him, as well! Consequently, he would send his henchmen into Egypt to secure that Prophet.)

23 And they fetched forth Urijah out of Egypt, and brought him unto Jehoiakim the king; who slew him with the sword, and cast his dead body into the graves of the common people. (His casting "His dead body into the graves of the common people" was the answer of Jehoiakim to Urijah's Prophecies. Such actions show Jehoiakim's contempt! However, what he did to the Prophet likewise would be done to him [Jer. 22:19].)

24 Nevertheless the hand of Ahikam the son of Shaphan was with Jeremiah, that they should not give him into the hand of the people to put him to death. (Ahikam was one of those who found the original Scroll of the Pentateuch [II Ki. 22:12] and seemed to have some affinity for that Great Book, as well as for God's Prophet Jeremiah.)

CHAPTER 27

(598 B.C.)

THE LESSON OF THE YOKES: SERVITUDE TO BABYLON

IN the beginning of the reign of Jehoiakim the son of Josiah king of Judah came this word unto Jeremiah from the LORD, saying (even though this Prophecy was given to Jeremiah at the "beginning of the reign of Jehoiakim," still, it was not to be delivered until some years later, which was at this particular time, the reign of "Zedekiah"),

2 Thus saith the LORD to me; Make you bonds and yokes, and put them upon your neck (the word "yokes," in the Hebrew, is plural. This shows that the article was literally constructed as a symbol and a vehicle of doctrine. The yokes expressed a condition of slavery, and the Prophecy symbolized by them was fulfilled),

3 And send them to the king of Edom, and to the king of Moab, and to the king of the Ammonites, and to the king of Tyrus, and to the king of Zidon, by the hand of the messengers which come to Jerusalem unto Zedekiah king of Judah (these "yokes" were made and sent to the various nations by messengers from these nations who came to visit Zedekiah in the ninth year of his reign, when he rebelled against the king of Babylon. These visitors were perhaps discussing a common defense with Judah against what they all felt would be an invasion from Babylon.

Using the "yoke" as a symbol of submission to the Will of God and subjection to the king of Babylon, they were told by Jeremiah what they must do. They were to come under the yoke of the Babylonian Empire. And had they obeyed, they would have saved themselves untold bloodshed);

4 And command them to say unto their masters, Thus saith the LORD of Hosts, the God of Israel; Thus shall you say unto your masters (all of these countries mentioned in Verse 3 were idol worshippers; therefore, what must have been their thoughts when they were given this Message by "the God of Israel"?);

5 I have made the Earth, the man and the beast that are upon the ground, by My great power and by My outstretched arm, and have given it unto whom it seemed meet unto Me. (The declaration of Verses 5 through 11 was such as Gentile princes could easily understand — the Being and Almighty Power of God; His purpose in giving the supreme government to Nebuchadnezzar [Vs. 6]; the punishment of those who should rebel against Him [Vs. 8]; the tranquility of those who would submit [Vs. 11]; and the future doom of Babylon itself [Vs. 7].)

6 And now have I given all these lands into the hand of Nebuchadnezzar the king of Babylon, My servant; and the beasts of the field have I given him also to serve him. (The phrase, "My servant," concerning Nebuchadnezzar, referred to him as an instrument, not to relationship. The phrase, "And the beasts of the field have I given him also to serve him," indicates the unlimited character of Nebuchadnezzar's power.)

7 And all nations shall serve him, and his son, and his son's son, until the very time of his land come: and then many nations and great kings shall serve themselves of him. (The phrase, "And then many nations and great kings shall serve themselves of him," refers to Babylon being overthrown by the great kings of Medo-Persia. History testifies to the accuracy of this prediction, for Nabonidus was co-regent with his son Belshazzar when the Babylonian Empire was overthrown.)

8 And it shall come to pass, that the nation and kingdom which will not serve the same Nebuchadnezzar the king of Babylon, and that will not put their neck under the yoke of the king of Babylon, that nation will

I punish, saith the LORD, with the sword, and with the famine, and with the pestilence, until I have consumed them by his hand. *(Tragically, these other nations, as Judah, would not listen and were "consumed," irrespective of the great Promise given to them by God in Verse 11.)*

CONCERNING LYING PROPHETS

9 Therefore hearken not ye to your prophets, nor to your diviners, nor to your dreamers, nor to your enchanters, nor to your sorcerers, which speak unto you, saying, You shall not serve the king of Babylon *(Through Jeremiah, the leaders of these nations were being told that their prophets, so-called, would speak the very opposite of what Jeremiah was saying. They must not heed them, but tragically they did!)*:

10 For they prophesy a lie unto you, to remove you far from your land; and that I should drive you out, and you should perish. *(These "enchanters" prophesied "lies" to the kings of these nations, as the false prophets prophesied lies to the kings and people of Judah.)*

11 But the nations that bring their neck under the yoke of the king of Babylon, and serve him, those will I let remain still in their own land, saith the LORD; and they shall till it, and dwell therein. *(If they submitted to the Word of God, they would continue to remain "in their own land," but with their land under the control of the king of Babylon. If they did not yield to the "king of Babylon," they would, for God's Own Divine purposes, suffer destruction.)*

COMMANDS TO ZEDEKIAH, KING OF JUDAH

12 I spoke also to Zedekiah king of Judah according to all these words, saying, Bring your necks under the yoke of the king of Babylon, and serve him and his people, and live. *(The Message is unequivocally clear!)*

13 Why will you die, you and your people, by the sword, by the famine, and by the pestilence, as the LORD has spoken against the nation that will not serve the king of Babylon? *(The question, "Why will you die?", proclaims every word beating hotly with the Love of God. So Judah and all these surrounding nations had no excuse for their rebellion. The Word of the Lord came to them most clearly!)*

14 Therefore hearken not unto the words of the Prophets who speak unto you, saying, You shall not serve the king of Babylon: for they prophesy a lie unto you. *(The same words the Holy Spirit had said through Jeremiah to the heathen, He now says to Judah.)*

15 For I have not sent them, saith the LORD, yet they prophesy a lie in My Name; that I might drive you out, and that you might perish, ye, and the Prophets who prophesy unto you. *(This is very similar to the statement given to the heathen kings in Verse 10; however, there was a difference. Whereas the "sorcerers" of Verse 9 prophesied from the realm of demon spirits, these false prophets in Judah and Jerusalem were "prophesying a lie in God's Name." They attempted to give authenticity to their lies by using the Name of the Lord. As such, they only deepened their great sin; in fact, they blasphemed by attempting to make God a part of their lying schemes. Consequently, they would "perish," as well!)*

COMMANDS TO ALL JUDAH

16 Also I spoke to the Priests and to all this people, saying, Thus saith the LORD: Hearken not to the words of your prophets who prophesy unto you, saying, Behold, the vessels of the LORD's house shall now shortly be brought again from Babylon: for they prophesy a lie unto you. *(The "vessels" in question were those taken by Nebuchadnezzar in his first two excursions into Jerusalem. They were taken from the House of the Lord [II Ki. 24:13; II Chron. 36:7-10; Dan. 1:1-2].)*

17 Hearken not unto them; serve the king of Babylon, and live: wherefore should this city be laid waste? *(The words, "Hearken not unto them," concerning the false prophets, were not only valid for Jeremiah's day, but are also just as valid presently [Gal. 1:8-9].)*

18 But if they be prophets, and if the word of the LORD be with them, let them now make intercession to the LORD of Hosts, that the vessels which are left in the House of the LORD, and in the house of the king of Judah, and at Jerusalem, go not to Babylon. *(The false prophets were claiming that the vessels from the Temple which had been taken to Babylon in the first two excursions by Nebuchadnezzar would be brought back, while Jeremiah was saying that not only were the remaining vessels going to be taken to Babylon, but the Temple and the city would also be totally destroyed. Jeremiah says that if these individuals are true prophets, let them pray that what he has said would not happen. If it does not happen, it will show that they are true and he is false.)*

19 For thus saith the LORD of Hosts concerning the Pillars, and concerning the Sea *(Brazen Laver)*, and concerning the Bases *(that on which the smaller Brazen Lavers sat)*, and concerning the residue of the vessels that remain in this city,

20 Which Nebuchadnezzar king of Babylon took not, when he carried away captive Jeconiah the son of Jehoiakim king of Judah from Jerusalem to Babylon, and all the nobles of Judah and Jerusalem *(the carrying away of a number of the vessels of the Temple as well as some of the people of Judah and Jerusalem should have been a warning to the people and to the nobles that they must repent; however, those things seemed to have no effect!)*;

21 Yea, thus saith the LORD of Hosts, the God of Israel, concerning the vessels that remain in the House of the LORD, and in the house of the king of Judah and of Jerusalem *(these "vessels" were very important, simply because they were a part of the worship of God regarding the Temple at Jerusalem. The Lord allowing such to be removed was, in effect, allowing a part of the means of their worship to be removed, with the prediction that if they didn't repent, all of it would be removed, including themselves)*;

22 They shall be carried to Babylon, and there shall they be until the day that I visit them, saith the LORD; then will I bring them up, and restore them to this place. *(In fact, these vessels in Babylon were to be restored, but at a much later date, and by Cyrus; they would be brought to Jerusalem by Ezra [Ezra 1:7, 13]. By using the words, "until the day that I visit them," the Lord is saying that these vessels will be brought back, but only when He says so, not when those false prophets say so! They were to be "restored to this place," but only after the Lord had carried out that which He desired to do, which was the captivity of the people of Judah and Jerusalem, with them suffering the punishment they deserved.)*

CHAPTER 28
(596 B.C.)
THE FALSE PROPHECY OF HANANIAH

AND it came to pass the same year, in the beginning of the reign of Zedekiah king of Judah, in the fourth year, and in the fifth month, that Hananiah the son of Azur the Prophet, which was of Gibeon, spoke unto me in the House of the LORD, in the presence of the Priests and of all the people, saying *(in this Chapter, we find the reason, at least in part, for Zedekiah's rebellion against Babylon. He was listening to the false prophecies of "Hananiah." Actually, the entirety of this Chapter consists of the confrontation between this false prophet and Jeremiah. Hananiah seemed to be the leader of those who opposed Jeremiah. Most probably he was a Priest, just as was Jeremiah)*,

2 Thus speaks the LORD of Hosts, the God of Israel, saying, I have broken the yoke of the king of Babylon. *(If one is to notice, the terminology being used by this false prophet, i.e., "Thus speaks the LORD of Hosts, the God of Israel," is very similar to the terminology used by Jeremiah. In this false prophecy he contradicts the true Prophet.)*

3 Within two full years will I bring again into this place all the vessels of the LORD's House, that Nebuchadnezzar king of Babylon took away from this place, and carried them to Babylon *(Jeremiah had prophesied that the vessels would be returned, but only after a long period of time [27:21-22]. This false prophet claims they will be returned within two years)*:

4 And I will bring again to this place Jeconiah the son of Jehoiakim king of Judah, with all the captives of Judah, who went into Babylon, saith the LORD: for I will break the yoke of the king of Babylon. *(The phrase, "And I will bring again," concerning "Jeconiah," directly contradicts the Prophecy of Jeremiah that this king would die in a foreign land [22:26-27]. The deportation which took away "Jeconiah" [Jehoiachin] also took away Mordecai and Esther, as well as many others. This false prophet claims they all will be brought back.)*

JEREMIAH'S ANSWER

5 Then the Prophet Jeremiah said unto the Prophet Hananiah in the presence of the Priests, and in the presence of all the people who stood in the House of the LORD *(in modern times, I wonder what the "unity crowd" would think of Jeremiah! Virtually all of Judah and Jerusalem are in unity, with the exception of this lone Prophet Jeremiah. He alone disturbs this unity! However, unity at the expense of compromise is man's way, and not God's Way)*,

6 Even the Prophet Jeremiah said, Amen: the LORD do so: the LORD perform your words which you have prophesied, to bring again the vessels of the LORD's house, and all that is carried away captive, from Babylon into

this place. (*The phrase, "Even the Prophet Jeremiah said, Amen," simply means that he wishes such were true!*)

7 Nevertheless hear thou now this word that I speak in your ears, and in the ears of all the people;

8 The Prophets who have been before me and before you of old prophesied both against many countries, and against great kingdoms, of war, and of evil, and of pestilence. (*Jeremiah now refers to the Prophets of old who prophesied as he, and who had also been opposed by false prophets foretelling peace.*)

9 The prophet which prophesies of peace, when the word of the prophet shall come to pass, then shall the prophet be known, that the LORD has truly sent him. (*Jeremiah is probably referring to Deut. 18:22.*)

HANANIAH BREAKS JEREMIAH'S YOKE

10 Then Hananiah the prophet took the yoke from off the Prophet Jeremiah's neck, and broke it. (*As Jeremiah stands with a "yoke" of wood about his neck, symbolizing the Babylonian yoke that would remain and even intensify upon Judah, Hananiah no doubt ridicules the stupidity of such and holds up Jeremiah to derision. He then proceeds to take the "yoke" from off "Jeremiah's neck," and then he "breaks it." It was probably done with much favorable response from the people.*)

11 And Hananiah spoke in the presence of all the people, saying, Thus saith the LORD; Even so will I break the yoke of Nebuchadnezzar king of Babylon from the neck of all nations within the space of two full years. And the Prophet Jeremiah went his way. (*However, the Lord has not said anything to Hananiah. The phrase, "And the Prophet Jeremiah went his way," probably means that he walked out alone, maybe even with the jeers of the people ringing in his ears.*)

THE TRUE PROPHECY OF JEREMIAH; PREDICTS HANANIAH'S DEATH

12 Then the word of the LORD came unto Jeremiah the Prophet, after that Hananiah the Prophet had broken the yoke from off the neck of the Prophet Jeremiah, saying (*the phrase, "Then the word of the LORD came unto Jeremiah the Prophet," refers to a lapse of time of possibly several days or even weeks. It is obvious that the Holy Spirit was grossly offended by Hananiah*

forcibly taking the "yoke" off the neck of the true Prophet and then breaking it. This man set himself to oppose the Word of the Lord, and such is always a dangerous occupation*),

13 Go and tell Hananiah, saying, Thus saith the LORD; You have broken the yokes of wood; but you shall make for them yokes of iron. (*The phrase, "You shall make for them," refers to the people! By listening to the false prophecies of Hananiah and others, they were only making the yokes heavier and harder, i.e., "yokes of iron."*)

14 For thus saith the LORD of Hosts, the God of Israel; I have put a yoke of iron upon the neck of all these nations, that they may serve Nebuchadnezzar king of Babylon; and they shall serve him: and I have given him the beasts of the field also. (*The Message that Jeremiah now delivers is not softened whatsoever, but is rather hardened. It was a "yoke of wood," and now it is a "yoke of iron."*)

15 Then said the Prophet Jeremiah unto Hananiah the prophet, Hear now, Hananiah; The LORD has not sent you; but you make this people to trust in a lie. (*The phrase, "But you make this people to trust in a lie," seems to indicate that people were present when Jeremiah spoke these words to Hananiah. The true Prophet pulled no punches!*)

16 Therefore thus saith the LORD; Behold, I will cast you from off the face of the Earth: this year you shall die, because you have taught rebellion against the LORD. (*As it regards this false prophet, the chilling announcement was "this year you shall die"! In the phrase, "This year," there is ample room for Repentance, but there is no evidence whatsoever that Hananiah did repent; actually, the evidence is that he did not.*

The phrase, "Because you have taught rebellion against the LORD," is also a powerful statement to any and all Preachers. In fact, most of the preaching presently is actually "rebellion against the LORD," i.e., "against His Word.")

17 So Hananiah the Prophet died the same year in the seventh month. (*Hananiah promised the people deliverance within two years, but he was himself struck down by death within two months; however, even that seemed not to turn the people toward God!*)

CHAPTER 29
(599 B.C.)

JEREMIAH'S LETTER TO THE CAPTIVES

NOW these are the words of the letter that Jeremiah the Prophet sent from Jerusalem

unto the residue of the elders which were carried away captives, and to the Priests, and to the Prophets, and to all the people whom Nebuchadnezzar had carried away captive from Jerusalem to Babylon (*the problem with the false prophets in Jerusalem was the same among the captives in Babylon. There were false prophets there, as well, proclaiming that the yoke of Babylon would be thrown off, thereby giving the people there a false hope. Ezekiel was the major exception in Babylon. Jeremiah sent a letter to these captives declaring the opposite of what these false prophets were proclaiming. The captivity, Jeremiah said, was going to be long, even 70 years*);

2 (After that Jeconiah the king, and the queen, and the eunuchs, the princes of Judah and Jerusalem, and the carpenters, and the smiths, were departed from Jerusalem [*Jehoiachin, who was the same king as "Jeconiah," only reigned for three months and ten days before he was taken captive along with others; this "letter" also will be given to him*];)

3 By the hand of Elasah the son of Shaphan, and Gemariah the son of Hilkiah, (whom Zedekiah king of Judah sent unto Babylon to Nebuchadnezzar king of Babylon) saying (*"Elasah" and "Gemariah" were the sons of the good men who found the original Scroll of the Pentateuch [II Ki., Chpts. 22-23; II Chron. 34:35-38]; no doubt they willingly carried Jeremiah's letter to the captives*),

4 Thus saith the LORD of Hosts, the God of Israel, unto all who are carried away captives, whom I have caused to be carried away from Jerusalem unto Babylon (*intelligence in the Ways and Counsels of God, as revealed in His Word, submission to those Counsels, and a recognition of His just Judgments upon unfaithfulness, together with a blameless life and prayer for the peace of the Earthly government ordained by God, bring a measure of tranquility and prosperity to the obedient, but suffering and punishment to the disobedient*);

5 Build ye houses, and dwell in them; and plant gardens, and eat the fruit of them (*evidently, these unhappy captives had not been doing such, thinking, according to the false prophecies given by the false prophets, that they would be restored any day to Judah. Jeremiah's letter would say the very opposite, and in no uncertain terms*);

6 Take ye wives, and beget sons and daughters; and take wives for your sons, and give your daughters to husbands, that they may bear sons and daughters; that you may be increased there, and not diminished. (*The phrase, "That you may be increased there, and not diminished," pertains to the fact that the nation is to be kept alive.*)

7 And seek the peace of the city whither I have caused you to be carried away captives, and pray unto the LORD for it: for in the peace thereof shall you have peace. (*The phrase, "And seek the peace of the city," refers to Babylon and the blessing that God's People, even though under chastisement, could be to their host city and country. This proclaims the power of God's People.*)

8 For thus saith the LORD of Hosts, the God of Israel; Let not your Prophets and your diviners, who be in the midst of you, deceive you, neither hearken to your dreams which you cause to be dreamed. (*Recognition of God's Judgment upon unfaithfulness was necessary in order to explain why the Divine Promise of Supremacy to the Throne of David seemed to be forgotten. The popular preachers of Verses 8 and 9 could point to certain Bible Promises; with a show of spirituality and fidelity, they consoled the people with them. But the true Prophets of Jehovah recognized the temporary forfeiture of these Promises because of sin and they announced the coming Wrath of God; for in the spiritual as in the physical realm, the night precedes the day.*)

9 For they prophesy falsely unto you in My Name: I have not sent them saith the LORD. (*How did the people know what to believe, especially in view of the fact that Ezekiel in Babylonia stood alone, as Jeremiah in Jerusalem stood alone? They were to do as Jesus later said, "Check the fruit" [Mat. 7:15-20].*)

THE PROMISE OF RESTORATION
AFTER SEVENTY YEARS

10 For thus saith the LORD, That after seventy years be accomplished at Babylon I will visit you, and perform My good word toward you, in causing you to return to this place. (*The "seventy years" began with the first deportation, which took place in 605 B.C., with the captivity ending in 536 B.C., for a total of 70 years. The phrase, "I will visit you," refers to the Lord paying heed to His People and restoring them to Judah and Jerusalem, which would be done after the seventy-year period of time.*)

11 For I know the thoughts that I think toward you, saith the LORD, thoughts of peace,

and not of evil, to give you an expected end. *(Upon obedience to the Lord, with a sincere attempt to follow His Ways and Word, His "thoughts toward us" are always "thoughts of peace, and not of evil.")*

12 Then shall you call upon Me, and you shall go and pray unto Me, and I will hearken unto you. *(The Restoration under Cyrus fulfilled the Prophecy of Verses 10 through 14. That Restoration was an earnest of the yet greater one of the future.)*

13 And you shall seek Me, and find Me, when you shall search for Me with all your heart. *(This glorious Promise is given to any and to all, and for all time!)*

14 And I will be found of you, saith the LORD: and I will turn away your captivity, and I will gather you from all the nations, and from all the places whither I have driven you, saith the LORD; and I will bring you again into the place whence I caused you to be carried away captive. *(Verses 13 and 14 are a carte blanche invitation to any and all, irrespective of the need, to come to the Lord for help. And yet, so few take advantage of these great Promises!)*

15 Because you have said, The LORD has raised us up prophets in Babylon *(other than Ezekiel in Babylonia, there is no record that there were other true Prophets, which means the ones among the captives who were prophesying peace were not sent by the LORD)*;

16 Know that thus saith the LORD of the king who sits upon the throne of David, and of all the people who dwell in this city, and of your brethren who are not gone forth with you into captivity *(with startling clarity, the Holy Spirit will once again proclaim the Truth to those in Judah and Babylon)*;

17 Thus saith the LORD of Hosts; Behold, I will send upon them the sword, the famine, and the pestilence, and will make them like vile figs, that cannot be eaten, they are so evil. *(The Holy Spirit has repeatedly attempted to get the people to submit to the righteous judgment upon them and thus yield to the Babylonian Empire, but to no avail! Had they yielded to the Command of the Lord, they might have been able to stay in their own land, although subservient to Babylon; however, they would not heed the Word of God, even after two deportations, which were a harbinger which was to come. Despite the Word of the Lord, they resisted until Nebuchadnezzar completely destroyed them.)*

18 And I will persecute them with the sword, with the famine, and with the pestilence, and will deliver them to be removed to all the kingdoms of the Earth, to be a curse, and an astonishment, and an hissing, and a reproach, among all the nations whither I have driven them *(These people, the sons of Jacob, were meant by the Lord to be a blessing to the entirety of the world, but instead they were, because of sin, "a curse, and an astonishment, and an hissing, and a reproach")*:

19 Because they have not hearkened to My words, saith the LORD, which I sent unto them by My servants the Prophets, rising up early and sending them; but you would not hear, saith the LORD. *(The phrase, "But you would not hear, saith the LORD," pertains to the spiritual insensibility that had resulted from a hardened heart [Heb. 3:13].)*

JUDGMENT ON THE FALSE PROPHETS IN BABYLON

20 Hear ye therefore the word of the LORD, all ye of the captivity, whom I have sent from Jerusalem to Babylon *(those in "captivity" had been hearing false prophets, and now they are admonished to "hear ye therefore the word of the LORD." They were to understand that they were in Babylonia because God had sent them there; consequently, neither the disposition of Egypt nor who was ruling in Babylon really mattered. Their situation was unchangeable because the Lord was the Author)*:

21 Thus saith the LORD of Hosts, the God of Israel, of Ahab the son of Kolaiah, and of Zedekiah the son of Maaseiah, which prophesy a lie unto you in My Name; Behold, I will deliver them into the hand of Nebuchadnezzar king of Babylon; and he shall slay them before your eyes *(this "Ahab" was not the same as king Ahab who lived many years before Jeremiah's time, nor was this "Zedekiah" the king of Judah. They both were false prophets. As well, the Holy Spirit through Jeremiah called their names and pronounced doom upon them for their false prophecies. They were to be killed by Nebuchadnezzar. So, this puts to rest the idea that true Prophets should not call the names of those who are false)*;

22 And of them shall be taken up a curse by all the captivity of Judah which are in Babylon, saying, The LORD make you like Zedekiah and like Ahab, whom the king of Babylon roasted in the fire *(the phrase, "Roasted in the fire," seems to imply that these false prophets were cast into the midst of a burning fiery furnace. The Lord would deliver the three Hebrew*

Children [Dan., Chpt. 3] but would not deliver these false prophets. As well, this Passage implies that if the people believe the lies of these false prophets, a "curse" would be upon them);

23 Because they have committed villany in Israel, and have committed adultery with their neighbours' wives, and have spoken lying words in My name, which I have not commanded them; even I know, and am a witness, saith the LORD. (The phrase, "Even I know, and am a witness, saith the LORD," is chilling indeed! It refers to the fact that the Lord knows all and sees all, i.e., is "a witness.")

24 Thus shall you also speak to Shemaiah the Nehelamite, saying (this man "Shemaiah" seems to have been the leader of the false prophets in Babylon. Thus, Jeremiah again publicly calls the name of another false prophet),

25 Thus speaks the LORD of Hosts, the God of Israel, saying, Because you have sent letters in your name unto all the people who are at Jerusalem, and to Zephaniah the son of Maaseiah the Priests, and to all the Priests, saying (the letters of Shemaiah will seek the harm of Jeremiah),

26 The LORD has made you Priest in the stead of Jehoiada the Priest, that you should be officers in the House of the LORD, for every man who is mad, and makes himself a prophet, that you should put him in prison, and in the stocks. (Shemaiah was demanding that the High Priest "put Jeremiah in prison" and "in the stocks." By using the phrase, "And makes himself a Prophet," he was claiming that Jeremiah was not truly a Prophet of the Lord. He is calling on "Zephaniah" to stop this madman, as he refers to Jeremiah!)

27 Now therefore why have you not reproved Jeremiah of Anathoth, which makes himself a Prophet to you? (These false prophets were not content to oppose the Lord's Message; they also desired to attack the Messenger!)

28 For therefore he sent unto us in Babylon, saying, This captivity is long: build ye houses, and dwell in them; and plant gardens, and eat the fruit of them. (Jeremiah was saying the very opposite of the false prophets. He was saying, "the captivity is long," i.e., "seventy years," while the false prophets were claiming that it was about over.)

29 And Zephaniah the Priest read this letter in the ears of Jeremiah the Prophet. (This man "Shemaiah" had stated that it was the duty before God for Zephaniah the High Priest to arrest and imprison Jeremiah; that Jeremiah was a madman and a self-ordained Preacher. However, his command that Jeremiah should be shut up in the prison was met by Divine Judgment, which rather shut him and his children out of restored Jerusalem, as we shall soon see!)

30 Then came the Word of the LORD unto Jeremiah, saying (surely these false prophets had learned what had happened to "Hananiah the prophet" [28:17], "Ahab" and "Zedekiah"! Nevertheless, in the face of sure judgment, they persisted!),

31 Send to all them of the captivity, saying, Thus saith the LORD concerning Shemaiah the Nehelamite; Because that Shemaiah has prophesied unto you, and I sent him not, and he caused you to trust in a lie (this Verse outlines the responsibility of the Preacher of the Gospel to proclaim the Word of God without fear or favor. How many thousands of Preachers presently "cause people to trust in a lie" and, thereby, cause them to be eternally lost? Judah and Jerusalem would suffer terror at least in part because of these false prophets. Due to the fact that the Gospel of Jesus Christ is the most important and the most serious thing there is, true Preachers must not only preach the Truth, but they also must serve as watchmen and point out error, even calling the names of those who are preaching a false message, exactly as did Jeremiah. To be sure, such will be met by the anger of much of the Church; nevertheless, it must be done!):

32 Therefore thus saith the LORD; Behold, I will punish Shemaiah the Nehelamite, and his seed: he shall not have a man to dwell among this people; neither shall he behold the good that I will do for My people, saith the LORD, because he has taught rebellion against the LORD. (To "teach rebellion against the LORD" is to teach that which is contrary to God's Word. The Apostle Paul dealt with this in Gal. 1:8-9.

The phrase, "He shall not have a man to dwell among this people," actually referred to a curse placed upon him by the Lord. It meant his posterity would be cut off, which meant that no sons would be born to him; or else, if he already had sons, none would be born to them. Or it could mean that all would be killed!)

CHAPTER 30
(606 B.C.)
THE PROMISED RETURN OF THE CAPTIVES; REGATHERING OF JUDAH AND ISRAEL TO PALESTINE

THE Word that came to Jeremiah from the LORD, saying (Chapters 30 and 31 are as

an oasis in the midst of a swamp. They shine out among all Jeremiah's Prophecies. This Chapter proclaims the drawing together of both Israel and Judah into one. God is One, so His People are one. As well, this Chapter proclaims the restoration of Judah to her Land, which will demand a new heart, which will demand a New Covenant),

2 Thus speaks the LORD God of Israel, saying, Write thee all the words that I have spoken unto you in a Book. *(The "Book" spoken of is the part of the Bible we now have in our possession, the Book of Jeremiah.)*

3 For, lo, the days come, saith the LORD, that I will bring again the captivity of My people Israel and Judah, saith the LORD: and I will cause them to return to the land that I gave to their fathers, and they shall possess it. *(While Israel would partially fulfill this after the dispersion into Babylon, still, its total fulfillment awaits the coming Kingdom Age.)*

THE GREAT TRIBULATION

4 And these are the words that the LORD spoke concerning Israel and concerning Judah. *(Again, the Holy Spirit speaks of both "Israel" and "Judah" as being one. In other words, all the Promises that concern one concern both!)*

5 For thus saith the LORD; We have heard a voice of trembling, of fear, and not of peace. *(Verses 4 through 7 refer to the coming Great Tribulation and the Battle of Armageddon; consequently, they leap over the soon-to-come destruction of Jerusalem by Nebuchadnezzar and go into the future, even beyond our present day.)*

6 Ask ye now, and see whether a man does travail with child? Wherefore do I see every man with his hands on his loins, as a woman in travail, and all faces are turned into paleness? *(The phrase, "And all faces are turned into paleness," refers to Israel's shock when she realizes that she has been played for a fool! The Antichrist is really not the Messiah, but an imposter! Israel has been deceived! Consequently, there seems to be no way out of their dilemma and they face what looks like certain annihilation.)*

7 Alas! For that day is great, so that none is like it: it is even the time of Jacob's trouble; but he shall be saved out of it. *(The glory of Israel's restoration, as is proclaimed in the previous Verses, will be preceded by the horror of "the time of Jacob's Trouble." It will be the last three and a half years of the Great Tribulation. Jesus addressed this when He said it would be* the worst that has ever been, so bad that it would never happen again [Mat. 24:21].)*

REGATHERING OF ISRAEL
UNDER THE MESSIAH

8 For it shall come to pass in that day, saith the LORD of Hosts, that I will break his yoke from off your neck, and will burst your bonds, and strangers shall no more serve themselves of him *(the phrase, "I will break his yoke," refers to the last king of Babylon — the Antichrist. This will be done during the Battle of Armageddon, when Jesus Christ comes back)*:

9 But they shall serve the LORD their God, and David their king, whom I will raise up unto them. *("The LORD their God" is the Lord Jesus Christ. The phrase, "And David their king, whom I will raise up unto them," refers to David being resurrected, along with all the Saints, and given a glorified body. He will then serve, and we speak of the coming Kingdom Age, as the king of Israel, and do so under Christ.)*

10 Therefore fear thou not, O My servant Jacob, saith the LORD; neither be dismayed, O Israel: for, lo, I will save you from afar, and your seed from the land of their captivity; and Jacob shall return, and shall be in rest, and be quiet, and none shall make him afraid. *(This speaks of Israel's restoration at the beginning of the Kingdom Age. In fact, the phrase, "And Jacob shall return," began to be fulfilled in 1948, when a part of the original Promised Land was declared by the United Nations as the recognized State of Israel; however, it will not be completely fulfilled until the Second Coming of Christ, when all Jews will return from all over the world.)*

11 For I am with you, saith the LORD, to save you: though I make a full end of all nations whither I have scattered you, yet I will not make a full end of you: but I will correct you in measure, and will not leave you altogether unpunished. *(The phrase, "Though I make a full end of all nations whither I have scattered you," refers to nations and empires such as Babylon, Medo-Persia, the Grecian Empire, and the Roman Empire. These nations and empires, despite their might and power, are no more; yet, Israel remains!*

The phrase, "Yet will I not make a full end of you," means that the Lord will not destroy them completely, as He has destroyed mighty nations and empires in the past; however, they have suffered and they will yet suffer greatly, fulfilling the phrase, "And will not leave you altogether

unpunished.")

12 For thus saith the LORD, Your bruise is incurable, and your wound is grievous. *(The sense of this Verse is that the "bruise" which Israel has is "incurable," i.e., cannot be cured by the world, but only by the Lord, which will be done at the Second Coming. The only cure for this "wound" is the Cross of Christ, as this is the only cure for any such wound [Zech. 13:1].)*

13 There is none to plead your cause, that you may be bound up: you have no healing medicines. *(Upon Israel's abandonment of Christ, there is "none to plead your cause." Consequently, the only "healing medicines" are those which come from the Lord, and not from the system of the world.)*

14 All your lovers have forgotten you: they seek you not: for I have wounded you with the wound of an enemy, with the chastisement of a cruel one, for the multitude of your iniquity; because your sins were increased. *(The "cruel one" is the Antichrist. When he turns on them, breaking his covenant in the middle of the week [seven years], they will then see that "all your lovers have forgotten you." Every nation will then turn against Israel [Dan. 9:27; Zech. 12:3].*

The Lord will bring this to pass "for the multitude of your iniquity." This concerns their rejection of Christ! [Jn. 5:43].)

15 Why do you cry for your affliction? your sorrow is incurable for the multitude of your iniquity: because your sins were increased, I have done these things unto you. *(The question, "Why do you cry for your affliction?", refers to them "mourning for Him" when they realize that the One they crucified was actually their Messiah, the Lord of Glory [Zech. 12:10-11].*

The phrase, "I have done these things unto you," expresses the Lord's total control. Why? "Because your sins were increased," which states the reasons for the chastisement.)

16 Therefore all they who devour you shall be devoured: and all your adversaries, every one of them, shall go into captivity; and they who spoil you shall be a spoil, and all who prey upon you will I give for a prey. *(This refers to every nation in the world which has opposed Israel, which is opposing Israel at the present, and which will oppose Israel under the Antichrist in the future. They should read these words very carefully!)*

17 For I will restore health unto you, and I will heal you of your wounds, saith the LORD; because they called you an Outcast, saying, This is Zion, whom no man seeks after. *(In this Passage, as well as so many others, the "restoration to health" is promised here! Even though no one else in the world could heal the "grievous wound" of Israel, nevertheless, the Lord says, "I will heal you of your wounds.")*

REBUILDING OF JERUSALEM

18 Thus saith the LORD; Behold, I will bring again the captivity of Jacob's tents, and have mercy on his dwellingplaces; and the city shall be built upon her own heap, and the palace shall remain after the manner thereof. *("The palace" refers to the Temple, which will be built in Jerusalem upon the Second Coming of Christ. It shall be inhabited and have a style befitting its glory [Ezek., Chpts. 40-48].)*

BLESSINGS ON ISRAEL

19 And out of them shall proceed thanksgiving and the voice of them who make merry: and I will multiply them, and they shall not be few; I will also glorify them, and they shall not be small. *(The phrase, "I will multiply them, and they shall not be few," refers to their smallness now, but their greatness then. Israel will then grow into a great nation, with David as their king and Christ as their Messiah. As such, they will be the premier nation of the world, which will bring untold blessings to the entirety of the world.)*

20 Their children also shall be as aforetime, and their congregation shall be established before Me, and I will punish all who oppress them. *(The phrase, "And I will punish all who oppress them," is the same as the original Abrahamic Covenant [Gen. 12:1-3]. The phrase, "And their congregation shall be established before Me," refers to all being in Christ. It can only be established in Him, and not otherwise! To be sure, they tried to establish it without Him, but to no avail!)*

21 And their nobles shall be of themselves, and their governor shall proceed from the midst of them; and I will cause him to draw near, and he shall approach unto Me: for who is this who engaged his heart to approach unto Me? saith the LORD. *(The phrase, "And their nobles shall be of themselves," refers to the Gentiles no longer lording it over Israel as they have done for centuries, for "the times of the Gentiles" will be ended [Lk. 21:24; Rom. 11:25-29].*

The phrase, "And their governors shall proceed from the midst of them," signifies the Gentile

world looking to Israel for leadership instead of the opposite.

The phrase, "And I will cause him to draw near, and he shall approach unto Me," refers to Christ finally being accepted as Jacob's Priest. As such, He pledged His life at Calvary in order to put away sin, opened the way to God, and so enabled His People, in fellowship with Himself, to approach the Throne of Grace, not with timidity, but with boldness [Heb. 4:16].)

22 And you shall be My people, and I will be your God. (All of this will have been made possible by the Cross [Zech. 13:1].)

THE GREAT TRIBULATION

23 Behold, the whirlwind of the LORD goes forth with fury, a continuing whirlwind: it shall fall with pain upon the head of the wicked. (The "whirlwind" pictures Divine Judgment on the nations of the world that have set themselves to foil the Plan of God. The purpose will be to "fall with pain upon the head of the wicked," which specifically points to the Antichrist [II Thess. 2:8].)

24 The fierce anger of the LORD shall not return, until He have done it, and until He have performed the intents of His heart: in the latter days you shall consider it. (The phrase, "The fierce anger of the LORD shall not return, until He have done it," refers to the fact that evil will be dealt with in the Great Tribulation and at the Second Coming. This is a guarantee!)

CHAPTER 31
(606 B.C.)
RESTORATION OF ISRAEL

AT the same time, saith the LORD, will I be the God of all the families of Israel, and they shall be My people. (The phrase, "Of all the families of Israel," pertains to the fact that Israel will be no more divided, but in truth will be one nation. The statement, "At the same time," refers to the defeat of the Antichrist at Armageddon and the fact that Israel has now accepted Christ as her Saviour and Messiah. At that "time," He will be their "God," and "they shall be My People.")

2 Thus saith the LORD, The people which were left of the sword found grace in the wilderness, even Israel, when I went to cause him to rest. ("The sword" concerns the murderous cruelty of Pharaoh. "Grace in the wilderness"

pertains to the many miracles performed by the Lord in this howling wasteland in order to provide for His People.

"When I went" refers to leading them with the Cloud by day and the Pillar of Fire by night!

The words, "To cause him to rest," speak to the establishment of Israel in the Promised Land.)

3 The LORD has appeared of old unto me, saying, Yea, I have loved you with an everlasting love: therefore with lovingkindness have I drawn you. (The argument is: God chose to love Israel with a love from all eternity; therefore, He kept exhibiting proofs of that love with unwearied affection.)

4 Again I will build you, and you shall be built, O virgin of Israel: you shall again be adorned with your tabrets, and shall go forth in the dances of them who make merry. (The phrase, "O virgin of Israel," is beautiful indeed! It signals Justification by Faith, which Israel will finally understand and accept at the coming Kingdom Age.

The "tabrets" and "dances" refer to David's victory over Goliath and the rejoicing that followed [I Sam. 18:6]. Goliath was a type of Satan, while David was a Type of Christ. The great rejoicing that will take place on that coming Glad Day when Jesus Christ is enthroned in Jerusalem will be because of the defeat of the future Goliath, the Antichrist.)

5 You shall yet plant vines upon the mountains of Samaria: the planters shall plant, and shall eat them as common things. (Under the Law, the vine-owner had to wait five years before he could gather for himself the fruit of his vineyard [Lev. 19:23-25; Deut. 20:6; 29:30]. Consequently, he might never enjoy its produce because of the insecurity of the times; however, in the coming Restoration there will be perfect government, and so his enjoyment of the fruit of his labor will be assured.)

6 For there shall be a day, that the watchman upon the Mount Ephraim shall cry, Arise ye, and let us go up to Zion unto the LORD our God. (In Ephraim's sad past, the watchman summoned the people to go up to Bethel or up to Dan to worship an idol; but, in the happy future, they will be summoned to go up to Zion unto Jehovah the Messiah.)

7 For thus saith the LORD; Sing with gladness for Jacob, and shout among the chief of the nations: publish ye, praise ye, and say, O LORD, save Your people, the remnant of Israel. ("The chief of the nations" is Israel. The phrase, "Publish ye, praise ye," refers to the

proclamation of this great Truth by Faith, look-ing forward to its fulfillment.

The phrase, "O LORD, save Your people, the remnant of Israel," means that so certain is Sal-vation sure to those who call upon the Lord that it can be published and praised in advance.)

8 Behold, I will bring them from the north country, and gather them from the coast of the Earth, and with them the blind and the lame, the woman with child and her who travails with child together: a great company shall return thither. *(This refers to the beginning of the Kingdom Age, when every Jew on the face of the Earth will be brought to the Land of Israel, and gladly so!)*

9 They shall come with weeping, and with supplications will I lead them: I will cause them to walk by the rivers of waters in a straight way, wherein they shall not stumble: for I am a father to Israel, and Ephraim is My firstborn. *(The phrase, "They shall come with weeping," does not speak of a sorrowful return, but actually a mixture of joy and sorrow. They will sorrow when they think of their spiritual blindness that lasted so long, and yet the tears of joy shall flow because of their Redemption.*

The "rivers of waters" speak of the miracle river which will flow from the Temple in Jerusa-lem, out from under the threshold at the "south side of the Altar." As it flows, it will widen until it is "a river that cannot be passed over."

After it leaves the Temple, it will divide, with part going toward the Mediterranean and part toward the Dead Sea, which will be dead no longer [Ezek. 47:1, 5, 9; Zech. 14:8].

The words, "My firstborn," have a very special meaning, at least in this instance! In the Israel-ite ritual, the firstborn of man and beast had a special place. The male firstborn belonged to the Lord [Ex. 13:2; 22:29-30; Num. 3:13]. This was underlined by Israel's deliverance in the fi-nal plague upon Egypt.

There were accompanying privileges associated with the firstborn, which included a larger in-heritance, a special paternal blessing, family leadership, and an honored place at meal times; consequently, Israel, being "My Firstborn" is guaranteed these privileges among the nations, hence her being "chief of nations" [Gen. 25:5-6; 27:35-36; 37:21; 42:37; 43:33; Deut. 21:15-17].)

THE BLESSINGS OF ISRAEL

10 Hear the Word of the LORD, O ye na-tions, and declare it in the isles afar off, and say, He who scatters Israel will gather him, and keep him, as a shepherd does his flock. *(The first phrase emphasizes the fact that the res-toration of the chosen people will be so great an event that it will be of worldwide significance.)*

11 For the LORD has redeemed Jacob, and ransomed him from the hand of him who was stronger than he. *(This refers to the Antichrist, who will be much "stronger" than Israel; but, above all, it refers to his sponsor, Satan. Jesus will defeat the Antichrist at the Second Coming and will also ransom Israel.)*

12 Therefore they shall come and sing in the height of Zion, and shall flow together to the goodness of the LORD, for wheat, and for wine, and for oil, and for the young of the flock and of the herd: and their soul shall be as a watered garden; and they shall not sorrow any more at all. *(The "height of Zion" refers to the Temple. For nearly 2,000 years, they have had no song; now, "they shall come and sing." The phrase, "And shall flow together to the good-ness of the LORD," pertains to the fact of divi-sions in the past, but which now will be healed of that breach, and "shall flow together."*

The phrase, "And they shall not sorrow any more at all," refers to the terrible sorrow of the past, but the absence of this malady at the present, and as well for the future.)

13 Then shall the virgin rejoice in the dance, both young men and old together: for I will turn their mourning into joy, and will comfort them, and make them rejoice from their sor-row. *(The phrase, "For I will turn their mourn-ing into joy," refers to the "great mourning" that will take place in Jerusalem and through-out Israel, regarding what they had previously done to the Messiah; they now realize the ter-rible mistake they made and the horrible sin they committed!)*

14 And I will satiate the soul of the Priests with fatness, and My people shall be satisfied with My goodness, saith the LORD. *(This tells us that in the coming age of Righteousness that the office of the "Priest" will be restored, as well.)*

ADMONITION TO CEASE WEEPING

15 Thus saith the LORD; A voice was heard in Ramah, lamentation, and bitter weeping; Rahel *(Rachel)* weeping for her children re-fused to be comforted for her children, be-cause they were not. *(Rachel was one of the two wives of Jacob. She was the mother of Joseph and Benjamin and, therefore, of the two kingdoms*

and the two peoples. She wept for her children, figuratively speaking, when they were carried captive to Babylon and again when they were slain by Herod. Thus, to this extent was the Prophecy fulfilled, as stated in Mat. 2:17-18; but the weeping and the Promise of Verses 16 and 17 belong to the future, and pertain to the coming Great Tribulation [Zech. 12:10-13:1, 9; Rom. 11:25-29].)

16 Thus saith the LORD; Refrain your voice from weeping, and your eyes from tears: for your work shall be rewarded, saith the LORD; and they shall come again from the land of the enemy. *(The phrase, "To come again from the land of the enemy," means to be gathered from all over the world, after some 2,000 years of dispersion.)*

17 And there is hope in your end, saith the LORD, that your children shall come again to their own border. *(The phrase, "And there is hope in your end," is the Lord telling Rachel that her death was not one of darkness and despair, but rather of "hope." In effect, the Lord is saying, "Rachel, you died and left your children, but you will see them again, and your children shall come again to their own border," i.e., Israel.)*

REPENTANCE OF ISRAEL

18 I have surely heard Ephraim bemoaning himself thus; You have chastised me, and I was chastised, as a bullock unaccustomed to the yoke: turn thou me, and I shall be turned; for you are the LORD my God. *(True conversion has God as its Agent and is occasioned by Repentance, which Ephraim will do immediately after the Second Coming.)*

19 Surely after that I was turned, I repented; and after that I was instructed, I smote upon my thigh: I was ashamed, yea, even confounded, because I did bear the reproach of my youth. *(The phrase, "Surely after that I was turned," proclaims the act performed that was requested in the previous Verse. Ephraim could not totally turn himself, but he needed the help of the Lord, which was given!)*

20 Is Ephraim My dear son? is he a pleasant child? for since I spoke against him, I do earnestly remember him still: therefore My bowels are troubled for him; I will surely have mercy upon him, saith the LORD. *(In this Verse, the Love of the Heart of God throbs for "Ephraim." He asks the question, "Is Ephraim My dear son?" This is the voice of the Divine Speaker, Who asks if Ephraim, who has so flagrantly sinned again Him, can really be His "dear son," His "pleasant child"?*

The phrase, "I do earnestly remember him still," refers to the Promises made regarding Ephraim's restoration.

The words, "Therefore My bowels are troubled for him," literally means to moan. It is something akin to human grief in the Heart of God for Ephraim. Such is the humility of the Lord of the ages [Ps. 18:35].)

21 Set thee up waymarks, make thee high heaps: set your heart toward the highway, even the way which you went: turn again, O virgin of Israel, turn again to these your cities. *(The idea is: Travel the "way" of Repentance; to be sure, there are "waymarks" all along the way, so you will not be confused.)*

22 How long will you go about, O thou backsliding daughter? for the LORD has created a new thing in the Earth, A woman shall compass a man. *(The question, "How long will you go about, O thou backsliding daughter?", refers to "the virgin of Israel" in the previous Verse. Actually, the two terms do not go together. They are contradictory. However, the "virgin of Israel" is what the Lord will make of this "backsliding daughter" upon her Repentance. It is called "Justification by Faith" [Rom. 5:1].)*

JUDAH TO BE RESTORED

23 Thus saith the LORD of Hosts, the God of Israel; As yet they shall use this speech in the land of Judah and in the cities thereof, when I shall bring again their captivity; The LORD bless you, O habitation of justice, and mountain of holiness. *(It seems that Israel never quite knew or understood the purpose of the Sacrifices, which pointed to a coming Redeemer, or the purpose of the Temple, which was the habitation of God, and which pointed to another habitation, i.e., our bodies, hearts, and lives [I Cor. 3:16]. Because of her proper Repentance, she now fully understands what the Lord is doing, and she eagerly desires to follow Him. She will then clearly understand that the Lord is "a habitation of justice" and "mountain of holiness." "Justice" is His Word, and "Holiness" is His Person.)*

24 And there shall dwell in Judah itself, and in all the cities thereof together, husbandmen, and they who go forth with flocks. *(The idea of this Verse is to proclaim the utter serenity and peace which will envelope "Judah" and "all the cities thereof.")*

25 For I have satiated the weary soul, and I have replenished every sorrowful soul. *(The phrase, "For I have satiated," literally means "I have watered," speaking of the "weary soul.")*

26 Upon this I awaked, and beheld; and my sleep was sweet unto me. *(The phrase, "Upon this I awaked, and beheld," means that these words of encouragement concerning Israel's future day of great victory have given Jeremiah great hope. Now he has something to hold to, even though it may be well into the future. As a result, "my sleep was sweet unto me.")*

27 Behold, the days come, saith the LORD, that I will sow the House of Israel and the House of Judah with the seed of man, and with the seed of beast. *(The idea is: Israel will once again become a great nation with a large population.)*

28 And it shall come to pass, that like as I have watched over them, to pluck up, and to break down, and to throw down, and to destroy, and to afflict; so will I watch over them, to build, and to plant, saith the LORD. *(The phrase, "As I have watched over them," refers to continued surveillance, even in their dispersion, and even some protection so that they are not totally destroyed.*

Now, as the Lord once had to destroy them because of sin, His energy will be spent on "rebuilding." This will take place in the coming Kingdom Age!)

29 In those days they shall say no more, The fathers have eaten a sour grape, and the children's teeth are set on edge. *(By the use of this Proverb, the people were saying that the cause of their present difficulty was not because of their own sins, but because of the sins of their fathers. They absolved themselves of blame! But during the coming Millennium, this Proverb will be no more!)*

30 But every one shall die for his own iniquity: every man who eats the sour grape, his teeth shall be set on edge. *(The sense of this Verse is that in the coming day of the Millennium, with Christ Personally ruling, the failure to take responsibility for one's own sins will no longer be possible. There will be perfect judgment and justice in the Earth.)*

THE NEW COVENANT

31 Behold, the days come, saith the LORD, that I will make a New Covenant with the House of Israel, and with the House of Judah. *(The "New Covenant" mentioned here is the New Testament, that for which Jesus died. Israel would not accept it at that time, but they will accept it in the coming Kingdom Age.)*

32 Not according to the Covenant that I made with their fathers in the day that I took them by the hand to bring them out of the land of Egypt; which My Covenant they broke, although I was an husband unto them, saith the LORD *(Paul quotes these Passages in Heb. 8:7-13. The Lord is referring to the Old Law of Moses, which Israel did not keep):*

33 But this shall be the Covenant that I will make with the House of Israel; After those days, saith the LORD, I will put My Law in their inward parts, and write it in their hearts; and will be their God, and they shall be My people. *("The Covenant" spoken of here, as stated, is the "New Covenant," that which we have in our present Bibles. The phrase, "After those days, saith the LORD," refers to the intervening time from the days of Jeremiah even unto the Second Coming, at which time Israel will then accept the New Covenant, i.e., "Christ.")*

34 And they shall teach no more every man his neighbour, and every man his brother, saying, Know the LORD: for they shall all know Me, from the least of them unto the greatest of them, saith the LORD: for I will forgive their iniquity, and I will remember their sin no more. *(This Verse speaks of the coming Millennial Reign; at its beginning, Israel will accept Christ and what He did for them at Calvary. This will occasion their forgiveness and cleansing [Zech. 13:1].)*

35 Thus saith the LORD, which gives the sun for a light by day, and the ordinances of the moon and of the stars for a light by night, which divides the sea when the waves thereof roar; The LORD of Hosts is His Name *(this Verse is given in this manner to proclaim the fact that the Lord, Who is the Creator of all things, has the Power to do what He says He will do):*

36 If those ordinances depart from before Me, saith the LORD, then the seed of Israel also shall cease from being a nation before Me for ever. *(The Promise of Verses 31 through 34 is that of a new moral nature; and the argument of Verses 35 through 37 is the impossibility of God ceasing to love His ancient people or casting them away because of their past misconduct.)*

37 Thus saith the LORD; If Heaven above can be measured, and the foundations of the Earth searched out beneath, I will also cast off all the seed of Israel for all that they have done, saith the LORD. *(In this Scripture, the Holy Spirit uses an anomaly, which means*

something that deviates in excess of normal varia-
tion [Ps. 99:1].)

JERUSALEM TO BE HOLY UNTO
THE LORD FOREVER

38 Behold, the days come, saith the LORD, that the city shall be built to the LORD from the tower of Hananeel unto the gate of the corner. *(This refers to the coming Kingdom Age.)*

39 And the measuring line shall yet go forth over against it upon the hill Gareb, and shall compass about to Goath. *(In this Passage, "The measuring line" only describes a part of the city, with Ezekiel giving its entirety as "18,000 measures" [43 miles all the way around; Ezek. 48:30-35].)*

40 And the whole valley of the dead bodies, and of the ashes, and all the fields unto the brook of Kidron, unto the corner of the horse gate toward the east, shall be holy unto the LORD; it shall not be plucked up, nor thrown down any more for ever. *(The idea is that all of these areas in Jerusalem which had been so polluted by Satan will now be cleansed, never again to be corrupted; they will forever more be "holy unto the LORD.")*

CHAPTER 32
(590 B.C.)
JEREMIAH BUYS A FIELD AT ANATHOTH:
A SIGN OF ISRAEL'S REDEMPTION

THE Word that came to Jeremiah from the LORD in the tenth year of Zedekiah king of Judah, which was the eighteenth year of Nebuchadnezzar. *(This signifies the very eve of Jerusalem's destruction. In fact, the City will be destroyed in approximately one year. Actually, the siege had begun the preceding year [39:1], but had been temporarily raised on the approach of an Egyptian army [37:5, 11].)*

2 For then the king of Babylon's army besieged Jerusalem: and Jeremiah the Prophet was shut up in the court of the prison, which was in the king of Judah's house. *(Jeremiah was in prison because he foretold the capture of the city by the Chaldeans. When the Babylonian siege was raised by the Egyptian army, such must have exposed the Prophet and his Message to public ridicule. In fact, the false prophets were proclaiming that the Egyptians would come to their rescue and the Babylonians would be forced to flee. However, the Egyptians army would prove to be insufficient for the task, with the*

Babylonians once again resuming the siege. This proved the validity of Jeremiah's Message.)

3 For Zedekiah king of Judah had shut him up, saying, Wherefore do you prophesy, and say, Thus saith the LORD, Behold, I will give this city into the hand of the king of Babylon, and he shall take it *(Jeremiah's answer to the approaching Egyptians and their supposed relief was, in effect, that nothing had changed. The Babylonians, despite the Egyptians, would take the city);*

4 And Zedekiah king of Judah shall not escape out of the hand of the Chaldeans, but shall surely be delivered into the hand of the king of Babylon, and shall speak with him mouth to mouth, and his eyes shall behold his eyes *(Zedekiah's eyes saw the Chaldean Monarch at Riblah; his eyes were then put out, and he was carried to Babylon, where he died. Thus, as predicted by the Prophet Ezekiel, he died in Babylon and yet never saw it [II Ki. 25:6-7; Ezek. 12:13; Jer. 34:3]);*

5 And he shall lead Zedekiah to Babylon, and there shall he be until I visit him, saith the LORD: though you fight with the Chaldeans, you shall not prosper. *(There is some indication in this Verse, considering the words, "And there shall he be until I visit him," that Zedekiah at the last repented before the LORD, even though it was too late to save Judah and Jerusalem.)*

6 And Jeremiah said, The word of the LORD came unto me, saying *(Verses 2 through 5 being somewhat of a parenthesis, the account resumes following Verse 1),*

7 Behold, Hanameel the son of Shallum your uncle shall come unto you, saying, Buy thee my field that is in Anathoth: for the right of redemption is yours to buy it. *(The Law concerning the Redemption of Land is found in Lev., Chpt. 25 and Ruth, Chpt. 4.)*

8 So Hanameel my uncle's son came to me in the court of the prison according to the word of the LORD, and said unto me, Buy my field, I pray you, that is in Anathoth, which is in the country of Benjamin: for the right of inheritance is yours, and the redemption is yours; buy it for yourself. Then I knew that this was the Word of the LORD. *(The phrase, "Then I knew that this was the Word of the LORD," seems to imply that Jeremiah was not quite certain that the Lord had really told him this until his cousin "came to the court of the prison.")*

9 And I bought the field of Hanameel my uncle's son, who was in Anathoth, and weighed

him the money, even seventeen shekels of silver. *(Even though the amount of money was small, still, the symbolism for which the Holy Spirit desired to use this was very special in the sight of God. It was to serve as notice that houses, fields, and vineyards would be possessed by the Jews again after many days — actually some seventy years after the beginning of the captivity, and in this very place.)*

10 And I subscribed the evidence, and sealed it, and took witnesses, and weighed him the money in the balances.

11 So I took the evidence of the purchase, both that which was sealed according to the Law and custom, and that which was open:

12 And I gave the evidence of the purchase unto Baruch the son of Neriah, the son of Maaseiah, in the sight of Hanameel my uncle's son, and in the presence of the witnesses who subscribed the book of the purchase, before all the Jews who sat in the court of the prison. *("Baruch the son of Neriah" was the brother of Seraiah, the quartermaster to king Zedekiah. Josephus says that he was of noble family. He was a faithful attendant to the Prophet Jeremiah.)*

13 And I charged Baruch before them, saying,

14 Thus saith the LORD of Hosts, the God of Israel; Take these evidences, this evidence of the purchase, both which is sealed, and this evidence which is open; and put them in an earthen vessel, that they may continue many days. *(The "many days" refer to the seventy years of captivity of 25:9-14, of which some eighteen years had already passed. As such, the Prophecy was not meant to be negative, but rather positive, meaning that the Jews would be restored to this very land at the end of the seventy-year period.)*

15 For thus saith the LORD of Hosts, the God of Israel; Houses and fields and vineyards shall be possessed again in this land. *(The purchase of this land served as a symbolism and also demonstrated the Prophet's belief in the Divine Promise of Restoration.)*

JEREMIAH'S PRAYER

16 Now when I had delivered the evidence of the purchase unto Baruch the son of Neriah, I prayed unto the LORD, saying,

17 Ah Lord GOD! behold, You have made the Heaven and the Earth by Your great power and stretched out arm, and there is nothing too hard for You *(Jeremiah's prayer would have been identical to those prayed today, with one exception. Since the Advent of Christ, Believers now pray to the Father in the Name of Jesus [Jn. 16:23]):*

18 You show lovingkindness unto thousands, and recompense the iniquity of the fathers into the bosom of their children after them: the Great, the Mighty God, the LORD of Hosts, is His Name *(the conjunction of love to thousands and of suffering to children because of their parents' sin is an offense to the carnal mind; however, the reasons should be overly obvious),*

19 Great in counsel, and mighty in work: for Your eyes are open upon all the ways of the sons of men: to give every one according to his ways, and according to the fruit of his doings *(the phrase, "To give every one according to his ways, and according to the fruit of his doings," is the same as "with what measure you mete, it shall be measured to you again" [Mat. 7:2]):*

20 Which have set signs and wonders in the land of Egypt, even unto this day, and in Israel, and among other men; and have made You a name, as at this day *(the phrase, "As at this day," refers to signs and wonders continuing to be performed, equal to those wrought in Egypt and elsewhere);*

21 And have brought forth Your people Israel out of the land of Egypt with signs, and with wonders and with a strong hand, and with a stretched out arm, and with great terror *(God is a miracle-working God!);*

22 And have given them this land, which You did swear to their fathers to give them, a land flowing with milk and honey *("this land" given to them by the Lord was now about to be taken away from them by the Lord!);*

23 And they came in, and possessed it; but they obeyed not Your voice, neither walked in Your Law; they have done nothing of all that You commanded them to do: therefore You have caused all this evil to come upon them *(this Verse tells us there were conditions for maintaining the "possession"):*

24 Behold the mounts, they are come unto the city to take it; and the city is given into the hand of the Chaldeans, who fight against it, because of the sword, and of the famine, and of the pestilence: and what You have spoken is come to pass; and, behold, You see it. *(The phrase, "And the city is given into the hand of the Chaldeans," refers to the act already performed, at least in the Mind of God; actually, the city had not yet fallen to the "Chaldeans," but its fall a foregone conclusion.)*

25 And You have said unto me, O Lord GOD, Buy thee the field for money, and take witnesses; for the city is given into the hand of the Chaldeans. *(The purchase, as stated, was designated by the Holy Spirit to serve as a symbolism that, despite the present circumstances, there ultimately would be a restoration.)*

JUDGMENT ON ISRAEL AND JUDAH

26 Then came the Word of the LORD unto Jeremiah, saying,

27 Behold, I am the LORD, the God of all flesh: is there any thing too hard for Me? *(In this Verse and those following, the Lord exclaims His Power to do whatever is necessary to bring about His intended results. The question, "Is there anything too hard for Me?", implies that not only is there nothing "too hard for Him," but that there is not even anything "hard" for Him to do!)*

28 Therefore thus saith the LORD; Behold, I will give this city into the hand of the Chaldeans, and into the hand of Nebuchadnezzar king of Babylon, and he shall take it *(this Passage denotes the sovereignty of God and His ability to do that which needs to be done. At this juncture, world leadership would pass from the faltering hands of the kings of Judah to the Gentiles, where it has remained ever since [Lk. 21:24]):*

29 And the Chaldeans, who fight against this city, shall come and set fire on this city, and burn it with the houses, upon whose roofs they *(the Israelites)* have offered incense unto Baal, and poured out drink offerings unto other gods, to provoke Me to anger. *(Since the Hebrews had substituted Moloch, the god of fire, in the place of Jehovah, it was a just judgment which burned their houses with fire [Deut. 3:6].)*

30 For the Children of Israel and the Children of Judah have only done evil before Me from their youth: for the Children of Israel have only provoked Me to anger with the work of their hands, saith the LORD. *(In the reply to the Prophet's prayer, the two foundation doctrines find expression: the incurable depravity of human nature, even in the most favorable moral conditions; and the necessity of a new Spiritual birth. However, these two doctrines deeply offend moralists.)*

31 For this city has been to Me as a provocation of My anger and of My fury from the day that they built it even unto this day; that I should remove it from before My face *(Solomon, who beautified Jerusalem, also established idolatry in it [I Ki. 11:1-9]. Therefore, the problem of "provocation" persisted from the very beginning, and only increased in intensity as the years passed. Now, the Lord will "remove it from before His Face"),*

32 Because of all the evil of the Children of Israel and of the Children of Judah, which they have done to provoke Me to anger, they, their kings, their princes, their Priests, and their Prophets, and the men of Judah, and the inhabitants of Jerusalem. *(This Passage tells us that iniquity had permeated every part and parcel of Jewish society.)*

33 And they have turned unto Me the back, and not the face: though I taught them, rising up early and teaching them, yet they have not hearkened to receive instruction. *(The phrase, "Have turned unto Me the back, and not the face," signifies a refusal of God's Word.)*

34 But they set their abominations in the house, which is called by My Name, to defile it. *(This could have referred to the altars which Manasseh built "for all the host of heaven in the two courts of the House of Jehovah," and especially to the image of the Canaanitish goddess Asherah, which he set up in the Temple itself, and which was most abominable [II Ki. 21:5, 7].)*

35 And they built the high places of Baal, which are in the valley of the son of Hinnom, to cause their sons and their daughters to pass through the fire unto Molech; which I commanded them not, neither came it into My mind, that they should do this abomination, to cause Judah to sin. *(The worship of Molech seems to have been associated with the sacrifice of children in the fire. The Law of Moses demanded the death of anyone who offered his child to Molech or as a sacrifice [Lev. 8:21; 20:2-5].*

The phrase, "Neither came it into My mind, that they should do this abomination, to cause Judah to sin," refers to the fact that even Omniscience is surprised by such action. The phrase does not imply a lack of knowledge.)

36 And now therefore thus saith the LORD, the God of Israel, concerning this city, whereof you say, It shall be delivered into the hand of the king of Babylon by the sword, and by the famine, and by the pestilence *(the carnal mind passes easily from presumption to despair. But when man is brought to despair, Grace can intervene to infinitely and permanently bless him. Thus, man's incurable sinfulness must be fully demonstrated in order to provide a field of action for the operations of Grace);*

REGATHERING OF ISRAEL

37 Behold, I will gather them out of all countries, whither I have driven them in My anger, and in My fury, and in great wrath; and I will bring them again unto this place, and I will cause them to dwell safely *(the Holy Spirit through Jeremiah now jumps ahead to the coming Kingdom Age, when virtually every Jew from all over the world will be brought to Israel)*:

38 And they shall be My people, and I will be their God *(this, God has always intended, and this will ultimately be)*:

39 And I will give them one heart, and one way, that they may fear Me for ever, for the good of them, and of their children after them *(the phrase, "I will give them one heart," speaks of conversion, which can only be brought about by the Holy Spirit and Faith in Christ. Such is the New Covenant, i.e., New Testament, given by Christ, now enjoyed for some 2,000 years, but not by Israel!)*:

40 And I will make an Everlasting Covenant with them, that I will not turn away from them, to do them good; but I will put My fear in their hearts, that they shall not depart from Me. *(After Israel's acceptance of Christ at the Second Coming, there is no record in the Bible that one single Hebrew will in the future turn their back upon Christ, but they will continue along with their children to serve Him forever.)*

41 Yea, I will rejoice over them to do them good, and I will plant them in this land assuredly with My whole heart and with My whole soul. *(In the coming Kingdom Age, the Jews are not only promised a new heart and untold blessings, but also the geographical Land of Israel. In fact, the Palestinians and the rest of the world should read this.)*

42 For thus saith the LORD; Like as I have brought all this great evil upon this people, so will I bring upon them all the good that I have promised them. *(The "good" and the "evil" are carried out by the Lord on the basis of obedience or disobedience.)*

43 And fields shall be bought in this land, whereof you say, It is desolate without man or beast; it is given into the hand of the Chaldeans. *(The idea is: after the destruction by Nebuchadnezzar, many will say that it can never be restored; however, the Lord has said it would be restored. And so it was!)*

44 Men shall buy fields for money, and subscribe evidences, and seal them, and take witnesses in the land of Benjamin, and in the places about Jerusalem, and in the cities of Judah, and in the cities of the mountains, and in the cities of the valley, and in the cities of the south: for I will cause their captivity to return, saith the LORD. *(Hebrew Scholars instance this Verse as illustrating the full force and beauty of the Infinite Absolute in emphasizing the certain fulfillment of its several predictions.)*

CHAPTER 33

(590 B.C.)

DESOLATION TO BE FOLLOWED BY RESTORATION

MOREOVER the Word of the LORD came unto Jeremiah the second time, while he was yet shut up in the court of the prison, saying *(the phrase, "The second time," concerned the second Prophecy given by Jeremiah while "shut up in the court of the prison." This was the same incarceration given at the beginning of the previous Chapter. It was probably about nine months to a year before the fall of Jerusalem and the final captivity of Jews to Babylon [II Ki. 25:1-2])*,

2 Thus saith the LORD the Maker thereof, the LORD Who formed it, to establish it; the LORD is His Name *(this Chapter predicts the Restoration of the people; the prior one foretold the restoration of the land)*;

3 Call unto Me, and I will answer you, and show you great and mighty things, which you know not. *(This great Promise, although given specifically to Judah, definitely applies also to any and all Believers [Mat. 21:22; Mk. 11:23-24; Lk. 11:9-13; Jn. 14:14; 15:7].)*

4 For thus saith the LORD, the God of Israel, concerning the houses of this city, and concerning the houses of the kings of Judah, which are thrown down by the mounts, and by the sword *(the statement appears to be that the houses proposed to be demolished in order to form barricades against the Chaldeans, on the contrary, were destined by the Lord to be filled with the dead bodies of Hebrew soldiers)*;

5 They come to fight with the Chaldeans, but it is to fill them with the dead bodies of men, whom I have slain in My anger and in My fury, and for all whose wickedness I have hid My face from this city. *(The "houses of this city" and the "houses of the kings of Judah" referred to the beautiful homes of the wealthiest, and even the palaces of the kings. These were to be filled with multiple thousands of dead bodies stacked up like cordwood.*

The "anger" and the "fury" of the Lord are expressed here against "wickedness," which caused Him to "hide His face from this city.")

6 Behold, I will bring it health and cure, and I will cure them, and will reveal unto them the abundance of peace and truth. *(Without a break in stride, as if the Holy Spirit desired to hurriedly proclaim the restoration of Judah and Jerusalem, even in the face of their destruction, He then promises "health and cure." However, between Verses 5 and 6 lie a gap that has not even yet been bridged, but which most surely will be. We speak of the coming Kingdom Age.)*

7 And I will cause the captivity of Judah and the captivity of Israel to return, and will build them, as at the first.

8 And I will cleanse them from all their iniquity, whereby they have sinned against Me; and I will pardon all their iniquities, whereby they have sinned, and whereby they have transgressed against Me.

9 And it shall be to Me a name of joy, a praise and an honour before all the nations of the Earth, which shall hear all the good that I do unto them: and they shall fear and tremble for all the goodness and for all the prosperity that I procure unto it. *(The blessing at that coming time will be total!)*

10 Thus saith the LORD; Again there shall be heard in this place, which you say shall be desolate without man and without beast, even in the cities of Judah, and in the streets of Jerusalem, that are desolate, without man, and without inhabitant, and without beast *(what a joy these words must have been to Jeremiah! Through the eye of faith, the Lord invites the Prophet to look ahead, past the soon-to-come "desolation," and then see that which the Lord will ultimately do, which speaks of untold blessing)*,

11 The voice of joy, and the voice of gladness, the voice of the bridegroom, and the voice of the bride, the voice of them who shall say, Praise the LORD of Hosts: for the LORD is good; for His mercy endures forever: and of them who shall bring the sacrifice of praise into the House of the LORD. For I will cause to return the captivity of the land, as at the first, saith the LORD. *("The Sacrifice of Praise" refers to praise unto the Lord which is anchored in the Cross of Christ, hence the "Sacrifice." That's the reason that most praise presently is not accepted by the Lord. It is because it's not anchored in the Cross.)*

12 Thus saith the LORD of Hosts; Again in this place, which is desolate without man and

without beast, and in all the cities thereof, shall be an habitation of shepherds causing their flocks to lie down. *(The idea of this Verse is to portray the certain peace that is coming in contrast to the terrible war about to take place. While this serenity is future, to be sure, it is also certain.)*

13 In the cities of the mountains, in the cities of the vale, and in the cities of the south, and in the land of Benjamin, and in the places about Jerusalem, and in the cities of Judah, shall the flocks pass again under the hands of Him Who tells them, saith the LORD. *(Not only will the Peace of God fill Jerusalem, and we continue to speak of the coming Kingdom Age, but also throughout the entirety of the Land of Israel shall Peace prevail!*

The phrase, "Shall the flocks pass again under the hands of Him Who tells them, saith the LORD," refers actually to the Great Shepherd, the Lord Jesus Christ [Heb. 13:20-21].)

REIGN OF THE MESSIAH

14 Behold, the days come, saith the LORD, that I will perform that good thing which I have promised unto the House of Israel and to the House of Judah. *("That good thing which I have promised" refers to the coming Messiah and full Redemption and Restoration under Him.)*

15 In those days, and at that time, will I cause the Branch of Righteousness to grow up unto David; and He shall execute Judgment and Righteousness in the land. *(The phrase, "In those days, and at that time," refers to the coming Kingdom Age. As well, "the Branch of Righteousness" is none other than the Lord Jesus Christ.*

The phrase, "To grow up unto David," refers to the Throne of David, which was broken off with Jehoiachin [II Ki. 24:10-16], and has been unoccupied from that day until now, and will remain unoccupied until Christ occupies it on His return, with David in his glorified body ruling under Him.)

16 In those days shall Judah be saved, and Jerusalem shall dwell safely: and this is the name wherewith she shall be called, The LORD our Righteousness. *(The Messiah's Name is here declared to be "Jehovah-Tsidkenu." This is the Name which will be given to the New Israel. "Tsidkenu" means "Righteousness.")*

17 For thus saith the LORD; David shall never want a man to sit upon the throne of the House of Israel *(this proclaims the Promise given by God to David, which shall be fulfilled*

in the coming Kingdom Age [II Sam. 7:12-14]);

18 Neither shall the Priests the Levites want a man before Me to offer Burnt Offerings, and to kindle Meat Offerings, and to do sacrifice continually. *(Again, we continue with the Kingdom Age. Sacrifices before Christ pointed to the coming Redeemer; now, they point backward to the Redeemer Who has already come. In the Kingdom Age, Sacrifices will be offered constantly, but only as a reminder, a symbolism, and a memorial.)*

DAVIDIC COVENANT CONFIRMED AS ETERNAL

19 And the Word of the LORD came unto Jeremiah, saying,

20 Thus saith the LORD; If you can break My Covenant of the day and My Covenant of the night, and that there should not be day and night in their season *(the "Covenant" addressed here is the "Solaric Covenant" made by the Lord as recorded in Gen. 1:14-19 and 8:22);*

21 Then may also My Covenant be broken with David My servant, that he should not have a son to reign upon his throne; and with the Levites the Priests, My ministers. *(This Verse could be thus paraphrased: "If anyone is powerful enough to affect the assigned position and duty of the planetary bodies, including the rotation of the Earth, then may he break My Covenant with David My servant".)*

22 As the Host of Heaven cannot be numbered, neither the sand of the sea measured: so will I multiply the seed of David My servant, and the Levites who minister unto Me. *(The Promise of this Scripture has to do with the coming Kingdom Age and the premiership of Israel as a nation; in fact, she will serve as "Chief of Nations" [31:7].)*

GOD'S COVENANT WITH ISRAEL ETERNAL

23 Moreover the Word of the LORD came to Jeremiah, saying,

24 Consider thou not what this people have spoken, saying, The two families which the LORD has chosen, He has even cast them off? thus they have despised My people, that they should be no more a nation before them. *(The phrase, "The two families which the LORD has chosen," refers to both Judah and Israel. The phrase, "This people," pertains to the people of Judah, who regarded the Promises of God as*

worthless. These were unworthy Jews in Jeremiah's day, who, seeing their nation fallen from its high estate, despaired of its deliverance and regeneration.)

25 Thus saith the LORD; If My Covenant be not with day and night, and if I have not appointed the ordinances of Heaven and Earth *(the Solaric Covenant is once again brought back as an example, but with added emphasis! The words, "And if I have not appointed the ordinances of Heaven and Earth," in effect state that those who do not believe in the future restoration of Israel must also deny the Solaric Covenant);*

26 Then will I cast away the seed of Jacob, and David My servant, so that I will not take any of his seed to be rulers over the seed of Abraham, Isaac, and Jacob: for I will cause their captivity to return, and have mercy on them. *(The sorrows and rejection of the Messiah are not the subject of Jeremiah's Prophecies, but rather the guilt of the nation at that time, the resulting judgments, and the Grace which promised a Restoration. This Grace will be exercised by the Messiah; the Restoration, with all its wealth of Mercy and Blessing, will be based upon His Person and Atoning Work.)*

CHAPTER 34
(591 B.C.)
ZEDEKIAH'S OVERTHROW AND CAPTIVITY

THE Word which came unto Jeremiah from the LORD, when Nebuchadnezzar king of Babylon, and all his army, and all the kingdoms of the Earth of his dominion, and all the people, fought against Jerusalem, and against all the cities thereof, saying *(this Prophecy was given by Jeremiah after Nebuchadnezzar had laid siege to Jerusalem and other cities in Judah),*

2 Thus saith the LORD, the God of Israel; Go and speak to Zedekiah king of Judah, and tell him, Thus saith the LORD; Behold, I will give this city into the hand of the king of Babylon, and he shall burn it with fire *(shortly before Nebuchadnezzar's time, Egypt had ruled all the country up to the River Euphrates. However, when Nebuchadnezzar came to the throne, he defeated the Egyptians at the Battle of Carchemish. Therefore, there was great animosity between Egypt and Babylon. Consequently, Zedekiah thought that Egypt might come to his rescue. Jeremiah tells him that this will not happen):*

3 And you shall not escape out of his hand,

but shall surely be taken, and delivered into his hand; and your eyes shall behold the eyes of the king of Babylon, and he shall speak with you mouth to mouth, and you shall go to Babylon. *(Not only is the future of the city foretold, but Zedekiah's future, as well!)*

4 Yet hear the Word of the LORD, O Zedekiah king of Judah; Thus saith the LORD of you, You shall not die by the sword *(meaning that he would be taken prisoner to Babylon, which he was)*:

5 But you shall die in peace: and with the burnings of your fathers, the former kings which were before you, so shall they burn odors for you; and they will lament you, saying, Ah lord! for I have pronounced the Word, saith the LORD. *(The words, "But you shall die in peace," lends some credence to the possibility that Zedekiah, in the misery of his blindness and captivity in Babylon [for he was blinded by his captors], experienced a true conversion.)*

6 Then Jeremiah the Prophet spoke all these words unto Zedekiah king of Judah in Jerusalem. *(Even though he took his life in his hands by telling the king these words, still, Jeremiah was true to his calling in delivering the Message from the Lord to this king of Judah.)*

7 When the king of Babylon's army fought against Jerusalem, and against all the cities of Judah that were left, against Lachish, and against Azekah: for these defenced cities remained of the cities of Judah. *(Nebuchadnezzar's plan in taking the cities of "Lachish" and "Azekah" was to guard against Egypt.)*

THE BROKEN COVENANT
CONCERNING SERVANTS

8 This is the Word that came unto Jeremiah from the LORD, after that the king Zedekiah had made a covenant with all the people which were at Jerusalem to proclaim liberty unto them *(it seems that Zedekiah now tried to press fairness and justice for all, even the poorest of the poor, which the Lord demanded, but which was too little, too late!)*;

9 That every man should let his manservant, and every man his maidservant, being an Hebrew or an Hebrewess, go free; that none should serve himself of them, to wit, of a Jew his brother. *(The command was that every Hebrew, whether man or woman, be instantly released from their servitude, which seems not to have been done for many years. In other words, thousands of poorer Jews had literally been pressed* into the service of slavery, with others growing very rich at their expense.)*

10 Now when all the princes, and all the people, which had entered into the covenant, heard that every one should let his manservant, and every one his maidservant, go free, that none should serve themselves of them any more, then they obeyed, and let them go. *(It was probably hoped that the slaves, being freed, would now more heartily help in resisting the enemy, etc. The next Verse will show that the repentance of the nobles was not true heart Repentance, but rather the necessity of the moment.)*

11 But afterward they turned, and caused the servants and the handmaids, whom they had let go free, to return, and brought them into subjection for servants and for handmaids. *(In the summer of the same year, when the siege was made, and also the covenant was, therefore, made to let the slaves go free in obedience to God's Word, the Egyptians began to advance to the rescue of Jerusalem; so Nebuchadnezzar withdrew to meet their attack.*

Seeing their immediate danger lessened and what looked like certain rescue by the Egyptians, the nobles at once forced the slaves back into service. Then God sent Jeremiah with his Message of rebuke and prediction that the Chaldean army would return to complete the destruction of Jerusalem.)

12 Therefore the word of the LORD came to Jeremiah from the LORD, saying *(the absolute lack of sincerity on the part of the people, even in the face of certain judgment, is staggering in its concept and fearful in its principle; consequently, one can readily see the reason for the necessary judgment)*,

13 Thus saith the LORD, the God of Israel; I made a covenant with your fathers in the day that I brought them forth out of the land of Egypt, out of the house of bondmen, saying *(the Lord reminds them that He had "brought them forth out of the land of Egypt," in effect, delivering them from their slavery, and now, because of their rebellion, the entire nation was about to go back into slavery. The "Covenant" of which the Lord speaks is found in Lev. 25:10, 39-46 and Deut. 15:12-18)*,

14 At the end of seven years you let go every man his brother an Hebrew, which has been sold unto you; and when he has served you six years, you shall let him go free from you: but your fathers hearkened not unto Me, neither inclined their ear. *(The implication is: this Covenant had been ignored by the people for*

many, many years, which had caused great hardship for many of, if not most of, the people of Judah and Jerusalem.)

15 And you were now turned, and had done right in My sight, in proclaiming liberty every man to his neighbour; and you had made a covenant before Me in the house which is called by My Name *(the phrase, "In the House which is called by My Name," shows that the Covenant was made in the Temple. But the people had broken it):*

GOD'S CONDEMNATION AND JUDGMENT

16 But you turned and polluted My Name, and caused every man his servant, and every man his handmaid, whom he had set at liberty at their pleasure, to return, and brought them into subjection, to be unto you for servants and for handmaids.

17 Therefore thus saith the LORD; You have not hearkened unto Me, in proclaiming liberty, every one to his brother, and every man to his neighbour: behold, I proclaim a liberty for you, saith the LORD, to the sword, to the pestilence, and to the famine; and I will make you to be removed into all the kingdoms of the Earth. *(God having delivered the Hebrews from slavery, the cruelty of their action in enslaving others was, therefore, made more inexcusable. The phrase, "Behold, I proclaim a liberty for you," is an antithesis, which means the opposite of what is said.)*

18 And I will give the men who have transgressed My Covenant, which have not performed the words of the Covenant which they had made before Me, when they cut the calf in twain, and passed between the parts thereof *(this was called "cutting the covenant." A calf was killed and cut into two parts, with the contracting parties then walking between the parts. The idea was that if anyone broke the covenant, they would be cut in two pieces, just like the calf [Gen. 15:9-17]),*

19 The princes of Judah, and the princes of Jerusalem, the eunuchs, and the Priests, and all the people of the land, which passed between the parts of the calf *(a distinction and guilt appears to be drawn here between those who originate evil and those who are, through weakness of character, led into evil. The former [Vss. 19-20] were doomed to the major punishment of death; the latter [Vs. 21], i.e., Zedekiah and his princes, to the punishment of slavery);*

20 I will even give them into the hand of their enemies, and into the hand of them who seek their life: and their dead bodies shall be for meat unto the fowls of the Heaven, and to the beasts of the Earth. *(They had broken the covenant which they had solemnly made; therefore, they would pay the penalty.*

The phrase, "I will even give them," proclaims the totality of God's judgment and rule. And yet, His People conducted themselves toward Him as if He had no control over their lives.)

21 And Zedekiah king of Judah and his princes will I give into the hand of their enemies, and into the hand of them who seek their life, and into the hand of the king of Babylon's army, which are gone up from you. *(As stated, a distinction was made by the Lord between the guilty parties. Some were condemned to slavery, while others were condemned to death. God Alone knows the human heart; therefore, He Alone can pronounce judgment that is equitable and right.)*

22 Behold, I will command, saith the LORD, and cause them *(the Babylonians)* to return to this city; and they shall fight against it, and take it, and burn it with fire: and I will make the cities of Judah a desolation without an inhabitant. *(Due to the rumored approach of the Egyptian army, the Babylonians lifted their siege from Jerusalem. As a consequence, the covenant made by Zedekiah, the Priestly Order, and the Nobles of Jerusalem was broken. The slaves who had been "set at liberty" were quickly pressed back into slavery. Such greatly angered the Lord, and judgment was pronounced, as is evident in this Chapter.)*

CHAPTER 35
(607 B.C.)

THE OBEDIENCE OF THE RECHABITES

THE Word which came unto Jeremiah from the LORD in the days of Jehoiakim the son of Josiah king of Judah, saying *(as the Prophecy in the previous Chapter came just months before the fall of Jerusalem, this Prophecy in Chapter 35 came "in the days of Jehoiakim," which was approximately 20 years earlier),*

2 Go unto the house of the Rechabites, and speak unto them, and bring them into the House of the LORD, into one of the chambers, and give them wine to drink. *(The "House of the LORD" refers to the Temple, with "one of the chambers" referring to one of the many rooms in Solomon's Temple.*

The phrase, "And give them wine to drink," refers to intoxicating beverage. This might seem strange coming from the Lord; however, in the light of the entire episode, we will find this is not so.)

3 Then I took Jaazaniah the son of Jeremiah, the son of Habaziniah, and his brethren, and all his sons, and the whole house of the Rechabites *(the "Jeremiah" spoken of here was not the Prophet Jeremiah, but rather one of the Rechabite rulers)*;

4 And I brought them into the House of the LORD, into the chamber of the sons of Hanan, the son of Igdaliah, a man of God, which was by the chamber of the princes, which was above the chamber of Maaseiah the son of Shallum, the keeper of the door *(whoever these "sons of Hanan" were, Jeremiah calls one of their group "the son of Igdaliah, a man of God")*:

5 And I set before the sons of the house of the Rechabites pots full of wine, and cups, and I said unto them, Drink ye wine.

6 But they said, We will drink no wine: for Jonadab the son of Rechab our father commanded us, saying, You shall drink no wine, neither ye, nor your sons for ever *("Jonadab" was a Kenite, one of the descendants of the father-in-law of Moses. He lived during the time of Jehu, king of the Northern Confederacy of Israel. There is some small evidence that he may have helped Jehu in his extermination of the evil family of Ahab [II Ki. 10:15, 17]. At any rate, he definitely was not an idol worshipper, and seemed to have a zeal for the Lord. He "commanded" that his sons "nor your sons forever" not drink intoxicating wine or "dwell in houses." These commands were binding from generation to generation, and it seems they had been kept, at least up to this time)*:

7 Neither shall you build house, nor sow seed, nor plant vineyard, nor have any: but all your days you shall dwell in tents; that you may live many days in the land where you be strangers. *(The reason for these two commands [the drinking of no wine and not living in houses, but rather tents] seemed to have something to do with the religion of Baal, which was prominent in the time of Jonadab. Seeing this debauchery, it seems that Jonadab chose the very opposite lifestyle. From this account, it seems to have been approved greatly by the Lord, even to the using of Jonadab's descendants as a Godly example to Judah. It should be an example to us, as well!)*

8 Thus have we obeyed the voice of Jonadab the son of Rechab our father in all that he has charged us, to drink no wine all our days, we, our wives, our sons, nor our daughters *(as stated here, Jonadab impressed this "charge" upon all his descendants)*;

9 Nor to build houses for us to dwell in: neither have we vineyard, nor field, nor seed:

10 But we have dwelt in tents, and have obeyed, and done according to all that Jonadab our father commanded us. *(Little did these people realize that the Lord was taking careful note of all their activities; therefore, when the time came for them to be used of the Lord as an example of faith and obedience, they were ready.)*

11 But it came to pass, when Nebuchadnezzar king of Babylon came up into the land, that we said, Come, and let us go to Jerusalem for fear of the army of the Chaldeans, and for fear of the army of the Syrians: so we dwell at Jerusalem. *(Inasmuch as every room in Jerusalem no doubt was filled, the "tents" of the Rechabites may have then been the better mode of accommodation.)*

12 Then came the word of the LORD unto Jeremiah, saying,

13 Thus saith the LORD of Hosts, the God of Israel; Go and tell the men of Judah and the inhabitants of Jerusalem, Will you not receive instruction to hearken to My words? saith the LORD. *(All of this portrays the "hurt" felt by the Lord of Glory at the spiritual condition of His People.)*

14 The words of Jonadab the son of Rechab, that he commanded his sons not to drink wine, are performed; for unto this day they drink none, but obey their father's commandment: notwithstanding I have spoken unto you, rising early and speaking; but you hearkened not unto Me. *(The Holy Spirit is actually asking, "If the sons of Jonadab would heed his words, why would not God's 'sons' heed His Words?")*

15 I have sent also unto you all My servants the Prophets, rising up early and sending them, saying, Return ye now every man from his evil way, and amend your doings, and go not after other gods to serve them, and you shall dwell in the land which I have given to you and to your fathers: but you have not inclined your ear, nor hearkened unto Me. *(Three times in this one Chapter the Lord uses the phrase, "nor hearkened unto Me" [Vss. 14, 15, and 16]. The repetition portrays to the Reader the significance of this command.)*

16 Because the sons of Jonadab the son of Rechab have performed the commandment of

their father, which He commanded them; but this people has not hearkened unto Me (once again, the Holy Spirit points to the comparison of the "Rechabites" and God's People. The Rechabites obeyed, while Judah would not!):

17 Therefore thus saith the LORD God of Hosts, the God of Israel; Behold, I will bring upon Judah and upon all the inhabitants of Jerusalem all the evil that I have pronounced against them: because I have spoken unto them, but they have not heard; and I have called unto them, but they have not answered. (The wickedness of Israel's disobedience is emphasized by the Title, "Jehovah Elohim Zabaoth Elohim of Israel." The full and most solemn use of this Divine Title occurs three times in this Book [35:17; 38:17; 44:7].)

GOD'S COVENANT WITH THE RECHABITES

18 And Jeremiah said unto the house of the Rechabites, Thus saith the LORD of Hosts, the God of Israel; Because you have obeyed the commandment of Jonadab your father, and kept all his precepts, and done according unto all that he has commanded you:

19 Therefore thus saith the LORD of Hosts, the God of Israel; Jonadab the son of Rechab shall not want a man to stand before Me for ever. (The form of this Promise is remarkable. Exactly what the Lord meant by this is not clearly stated. This we do know: it was a favor to be compared only to that accorded to His most honored servants among the Israelites — the Patriarchs, the Priests, and the Prophets.

Incidentally, they refused the command to drink the wine, even as the Lord knew they would, and even as they should have refused.)

CHAPTER 36
(607 B.C.)
JEREMIAH'S WORD FROM GOD OF JUDGMENTS WRITTEN DOWN BY BARUCH

AND it came to pass in the fourth year of Jehoiakim the son of Josiah king of Judah, that this Word came unto Jeremiah from the LORD, saying (the phrase, "The fourth year of Jehoiakim," takes us back to about 18 years before the destruction of Jerusalem),

2 Take thee a roll of a book, and write therein all the words that I have spoken unto you against Israel, and against Judah, and

against all the nations, from the day I spoke unto you, from the days of Josiah, even unto this day. (This refers to the Prophecies of some 23 years. It actually formed the part of our Bible that we know as the Book of Jeremiah, at least up to this point, with the balance added as time went by.)

3 It may be that the House of Judah will hear all the evil which I purpose to do unto them; that they may return every man from his evil way; that I may forgive their iniquity and their sin. (The phrase, "It may be," does not imply a lack of knowledge on God's part, for He is Omniscient, meaning "all-knowing." It does imply that God, in His Love to sinners, warns them beforehand of their danger, even though He knows they will not repent.)

4 Then Jeremiah called Baruch the son of Neriah: and Baruch wrote from the mouth of Jeremiah all the words of the LORD, which He had spoken unto him, upon a roll of a book. (Baruch was Jeremiah's faithful attendant [32:12]. Josephus, the Jewish historian, said that he was of high rank in the government of Judah. Baruch served as a Scribe for Jeremiah.)

THE BOOK OF JUDGMENTS READ TO JUDAH

5 And Jeremiah commanded Baruch, saying, I am shut up; I cannot go into the House of the LORD (some have claimed that the words, "I am shut up," referred to him being in prison, as described in 33:1; however, that imprisonment was under Zedekiah, which would have been some years later. So, if this meant that he actually was now in prison, the incident was not recorded):

6 Therefore go thou, and read in the roll, which you have written from my mouth, the words of the LORD in the ears of the people in the LORD's House upon the fasting day: and also you shall read them in the ears of all Judah that come out of their cities. (One of God's objects in writing the Bible is that it should be read to the people and by the people, and that the moral effect of reading it should be amendment of life, and consequently an escape from the Wrath to come.)

7 It may be they will present their supplication before the LORD, and will return every one from his evil way: for great is the anger and the fury that the LORD has pronounced against this people. (This Verse is very similar to Verse 3 in that the Holy Spirit through the

Prophet earnestly solicits the repentance of Judah and Jerusalem, but to no avail!)

8 And Baruch the son of Neriah did according to all that Jeremiah the Prophet commanded him, reading in the Book the words of the LORD in the LORD's House. *("Baruch" was faithful in doing that which was commanded of the Lord, in "reading the Words of the LORD in the LORD's House." It was demanded that the people hear, even though they did not receive it favorably.)*

9 And it came to pass in the fifth year of Jehoiakim the son of Josiah king of Judah, in the ninth month, that they proclaimed a fast before the LORD to all the people in Jerusalem, and to all the people who came from the cities of Judah unto Jerusalem. *(The Lord had repeatedly demanded Repentance, and the people responded with "a fast." However, it was a mere religious ordinance; it was not accompanied by repentance and, therefore, it was of no consequence to God and did not turn away the anger of God.)*

10 Then read Baruch in the Book the words of Jeremiah in the House of the LORD, in the chamber of Gemariah the son of Shaphan the Scribe, in the higher court, at the entry of the new gate of the LORD's House, in the ears of all the people. *(Some think that "Gemariah" was a friend to Jeremiah and allowed "Baruch" to read "the words of Jeremiah" at the "entry of the new gate of the LORD's House, in the ears of all the people.")*

EFFECT ON MICHAIAH AND THE PRINCES

11 When Michaiah the son of Gemariah, the son of Shaphan, had heard out of the Book all the words of the LORD,

12 Then he went down into the king's house, into the Scribe's chamber: and, lo, all the princes sat there, even Elishama the Scribe, and Delaiah the son of Shemaiah, and Elnathan the son of Achbor, and Gemariah the son of Shaphan, and Zedekiah the son of Hananiah, and all the princes. *(All these individuals listed in this Scripture are called "princes"; they were no doubt a part of the ruling aristocracy of Judah and Jerusalem.)*

13 Then Michaiah declared unto them all the words that he had heard, when Baruch read the Book in the ears of the people. *("Michaiah" was the son of "Gemariah." The "Book" referred to was that which we now know as the "Book of*

Jeremiah," at least almost the first half.)

14 Therefore all the princes sent Jehudi the son of Nethaniah, the son of Shelemiah, the son of Cushi, unto Baruch, saying, Take in your hand the roll wherein you have read in the ears of the people, and come. So Baruch the son of Neriah took the roll in his hand, and came unto them. *(This refers to the Prophecies ultimately being read to the king of Judah.)*

15 And they said unto him, Sit down now, and read it in our ears. So Baruch read it in their ears. *(That which the princes were hearing could save their souls, their lives, their city, and their country, but most of them would little heed its words.)*

16 Now it came to pass, when they had heard all the words, they were afraid both one and other, and said unto Baruch, We will surely tell the king of all these words. *(The phrase, "They were afraid both one and other," means rather "they turned shudderingly one to another.")*

17 And they asked Baruch, saying, Tell us now, How did you write all these words at his mouth? *(The phrase, "Tell us now," implies their natural curiosity as to how these Prophecies came, and how Baruch had them all in one large Scroll.)*

18 Then Baruch answered them, He pronounced all these words unto me with his mouth, and I wrote them with ink in the Book. *(This implies that Jeremiah read them no doubt from existing parchments, with Baruch writing them down "with ink in the Book," actually on one long Scroll.)*

19 Then said the princes unto Baruch, Go, hide thee, you and Jeremiah; and let no man know where you be. *(The Prophecies were so startling, pronouncing the doom of both Judah and Jerusalem if they did not repent, that these "princes" felt that, upon hearing such pronouncements, some might try to do the Prophet and his Scribe bodily harm.)*

JEHOIAKIM BURNS THE SCROLL

20 And they went in to the king into the court, but they laid up the roll in the chamber of Elishama the Scribe, and told all the words in the ears of the king. *(The "princes" did not, at least not at the first, take the Scroll with them when they went into the presence of the king, but rather left it in a safe place. They then "told all the words in the ears of the king," which he met with sarcasm.)*

21 So the king sent Jehudi to fetch the roll:

and he took it out of Elishama the Scribe's chamber. And Jehudi read it in the ears of the king, and in the ears of all the princes which stood beside the king. *(Now the Prophecies will be read to the king by an individual named "Jehudi.")*

22 Now the king sat in the winterhouse in the ninth month: and there was a fire on the hearth burning before him. *(This was December. Jerusalem, being nearly a half mile above sea level, can get quite cool in the winter months.)*

23 And it came to pass, that when Jehudi had read three or four leaves, he cut it with the penknife, and cast it into the fire that was on the hearth, until all the roll was consumed in the fire that was on the hearth. *(The entirety of the scenario implies that as the Scroll was read by Jehudi, certain parts would infuriate the king, who, therefore, out of contempt, commanded that it be cut and thrown into the fire. How many presently, in one way or the other, are doing the same thing with the Word of God? They ignore what they don't like.)*

24 Yet they were not afraid, nor rent their garments, neither the king, nor any of his servants who heard all these words. *(These individuals showed no "fear" of God, only contempt. There was no evidence of Repentance, only rebellion!)*

25 Nevertheless Elnathan and Delaiah and Gemariah had made intercession to the king that he would not burn the roll: but he would not hear them. *(Regrettably, the greater majority of the human family falls into the same category; they "will not hear"!)*

26 But the king commanded Jerahmeel the son of Hammelech, and Seraiah the son of Azriel, and Shelemiah the son of Abdeel, to take Baruch the Scribe and Jeremiah the Prophet: but the LORD hid them. *(The phrase, "The LORD hid them," is interesting indeed! Jeremiah and Baruch had already been told by the three of Verse 25 and by others to hide themselves and "let no man know where you be." No doubt, these individuals had the Mind of the Lord when this was done.)*

THE BOOK REWRITTEN; JUDGMENTS ADDED; JEHOIAKIM SENTENCED

27 Then the word of the LORD came to Jeremiah, after that the king had burned the roll, and the words which Baruch wrote at the mouth of Jeremiah, saying *(even after the Holy Spirit had been insulted and degraded, still,*

He would make another attempt to reach this wicked king),

28 Take thee again another roll, and write in it all the former words that were in the first roll, which Jehoiakim the king of Judah has burned. *(The Holy Spirit denotes the seriousness of the king's act by saying, "which Jehoiakim the king of Judah has burned.")*

29 And you shall say to Jehoiakim king of Judah, Thus saith the LORD; You have burned this roll, saying, Why have you written therein, saying, The king of Babylon shall certainly come and destroy this land, and shall cause to cease from thence man and beast? *(The king is to be made to know that the very reason for the coming destruction is the rebellion and wickedness registered by "Jehoiakim." His was a representative rebellion of all the people!)*

30 Therefore thus saith the LORD of Jehoiakim king of Judah; He shall have none to sit upon the throne of David: and his dead body shall be cast out in the day to the heat, and in the night to the frost. *(Jehoiakim was only 36 years old when he died on December 6th, 598 B.C. It seems that his death occurred on the way to captivity [II Chron. 36:6], apparently at the instigation of Nebuchadnezzar, who, according to the Jewish historian Josephus, had his body thrown outside the city wall, as prophesied by Jeremiah [22:18]. Evidently, he was not buried, but allowed to be prey for beasts and vultures.*

Such is the ultimate end of Christ-rejecters, and they have no one but themselves to blame!)

31 And I will punish him and his seed and his servants for their iniquity; and I will bring upon them, and upon the inhabitants of Jerusalem, and upon the men of Judah, all the evil that I have pronounced against them; but they hearkened not. *("All the evil that I have pronounced against them" came to pass exactly as the Lord said it would. Few were spared, because few repented!)*

32 Then took Jeremiah another roll, and gave it to Baruch the Scribe, the son of Neriah; who wrote therein from the mouth of Jeremiah all the words of the Book which Jehoiakim king of Judah had burned in the fire: and there were added besides unto them many like words. *(Whether Jehoiakim was given the pronouncement of this second Scroll is not known! Nevertheless, his sinful actions did not stop the Word of God, because "another roll" was written containing all that had been, and more was added. As stated, this was the very Book in your*

Bible called "the Book of Jeremiah.")

CHAPTER 37
(590 B.C.)
ZEDEKIAH'S ACCESSION TO THE THRONE; THE KING REQUESTS PRAYER

AND king Zedekiah the son of Josiah reigned instead of Coniah the son of Jehoiakim, whom Nebuchadnezzar king of Babylon made king in the land of Judah. *("Zedekiah" was Josiah's son, but not in the kingly line. For instance, Nathan was David's son, but not, as Solomon, in the kingly line.*

"Coniah" was Jehoiachin, son of Jehoiakim. In fact, Jehoiachin was the last son of David to reign on the Throne of Judah [22:30]. Thus, the Davidic line of kings came to an end in him. The next King to reign upon that Throne will be the Messiah, the Eternal King of David's seed, and this He will do at His Second Advent.)

2 But neither he *(Zedekiah)*, nor his servants, nor the people of the land, did hearken unto the words of the LORD, which He spoke by the Prophet Jeremiah. *(Zedekiah and his cabinet ministers, like many today, were willing that God's servants should pray for them [Vs. 3], but determined to continue to disobey the Word of the Lord. The Holy Spirit is emphatic that basically the entirety of the land of Judah would not heed Jeremiah.)*

3 And Zedekiah the king sent Jehucal the son of Shelemiah and Zephaniah the son of Maaseiah the Priest to the Prophet Jeremiah, saying, Pray now unto the LORD our God for us. *(Quite possibly, Zedekiah, in sending this embassy to Jeremiah, was doing so as Hezekiah had sent such to Isaiah many years earlier in view of Sennacherib's invasion. The king expected Jeremiah to pray for the city to be spared as Isaiah had done [Isa. 37:6]; however, it was God's Will for Jerusalem to be spared during the time of Hezekiah, but not His Will for the land or the city to be spared at this time.)*

4 Now Jeremiah came in and went out among the people: for they had not put him into prison. *(Even though he was not in prison now, the situation would soon change [he would be incarcerated]. His prison experiences are as follows:*

1. He was put in prison for the first time on false charges [37:11-15].

2. He was released, but confined to the court of the prison [37:21]. Chronologically, Chapter

37 precedes Chapter 32, where Jeremiah was in prison, which was at the close of Zedekiah's reign.

3. He was imprisoned again in a miry dungeon [38:1-6].

4. He was released again as before [38:13-28].

5. He was carried away in chains by Nebuchadnezzar [40:1].

6. He was released from chains in Ramah [40:1-4].)

THE CHALDEANS DEPART JERUSALEM; THEY WILL RETURN

5 Then Pharaoh's army was come forth out of Egypt: and when the Chaldeans that besieged Jerusalem heard tidings of them, they departed from Jerusalem. *(At this time, Jeremiah was no doubt ridiculed greatly by the people, because it seemed like the predictions of the false prophets concerning the Salvation of Jerusalem were correct. Jeremiah had constantly prophesied that no help would be forthcoming from Egypt, and that Judah and Jerusalem would not be spared. For a short period of time, it looked like he was wrong!)*

6 Then came the word of the LORD unto the Prophet Jeremiah saying,

7 Thus saith the LORD, the God of Israel; Thus shall you say to the king of Judah, who sent you unto Me to enquire of Me; Behold, Pharaoh's army, which is come forth to help you, shall return to Egypt into their own land. *(Court Preachers are careful to say what kings wish to hear; however, it was not so with Jeremiah.)*

8 And the Chaldeans shall come again, and fight against this city, and take it, and burn it with fire. *(Jehoiakim had taken the leaves of the Bible and thrown them into the fire; now the "Chaldeans" shall take Jerusalem "and burn it with fire." What we sow, we reap!)*

9 Thus saith the LORD; Deceive not yourselves, saying, The Chaldeans shall surely depart from us: for they shall not depart. *(Inasmuch as the army of Nebuchadnezzar had withdrawn to fight the Egyptians, the false prophets, and hence the people, were having a field day exclaiming the veracity of their false prophecies while denouncing Jeremiah. They were doing exactly as the Holy Spirit said, "Deceiving themselves.")*

10 For though you had smitten the whole army of the Chaldeans who fight against you, and there remained but wounded men among them, yet should they rise up every man in his tent, and burn this city with fire. *(The idea*

is: *nothing can stop the Prophecies of Jeremiah from being fulfilled.*)

JEREMIAH ARRESTED AND ACCUSED

11 And it came to pass, that when the army of the Chaldeans was broken up from Jerusalem for fear of Pharaoh's army *(the "Pharaoh" referred to was Hophra, the Apries of Herodotus, the Uah-ab-ra of the monuments. The retreat of the Chaldean army would prove to be short-lived, with the Egyptian army being quickly defeated, and the siege of "Jerusalem" recommencing),*

12 Then Jeremiah went forth out of Jerusalem to go into the land of Benjamin, to separate himself thence in the midst of the people. *(When the Chaldean army began to retreat in the face of the coming Egyptians, the situation for Jeremiah must have become unbearable.)*

13 And when he was in the gate of Benjamin, a captain of the ward was there, whose name was Irijah, the son of Shelemiah, the son of Hananiah; and he took Jeremiah the Prophet, saying, You fall away to the Chaldeans. *("Irijah" was the grandson of Hananiah, who was probably the same Hananiah of Chapter 28. If so, this would explain Irijah's action. He would now falsely accuse the Prophet, claiming his defection to the "Chaldeans.")*

14 Then said Jeremiah, It is false; I fall not away to the Chaldeans. But he hearkened not to him: so Irijah took Jeremiah, and brought him to the princes. *(In other words, Irijah arrested the great Prophet.)*

JEREMIAH CAST INTO A DUNGEON

15 Wherefore the princes were wroth with Jeremiah, and smote him, and put him in prison in the house of Jonathan the Scribe: for they made that the prison. *(They accused him of being a traitor.)*

16 When Jeremiah was entered into the dungeon, and into the cabins, and Jeremiah had remained there many days *(the word "dungeon" refers to an underground excavation, with the word "cabins" possibly referring to particular vaults or cells in this place, with Jeremiah put in one of them. He probably remained there for several weeks, or even several months);*

JEREMIAH RELEASED; PLEADS
FOR MERCY

17 Then Zedekiah the king sent, and took him out: and the king asked him secretly in his house, and said, Is there any word from the LORD? And Jeremiah said, There is: for, said he, you shall be delivered into the hand of the king of Babylon. *(The question asked by Zedekiah, "Is there any word from the LORD?" shows that this man knew in his heart that Jeremiah was a true Prophet of God. But yet he was not strong enough to stand up and do that which was right. The answer to the question was not to the king's liking.)*

18 Moreover Jeremiah said unto king Zedekiah, What have I offended against you, or against your servants, or against this people, that you have put me in prison?

19 Where are now your prophets which prophesied unto you, saying, The king of Babylon shall not come against you, nor against this land? *(These false prophets waxed bold upon the coming of the Egyptian army, which resulted in the retreat of the Babylonian army. Jeremiah's name then became a joke! But now, the table has turned. The Egyptians are defeated, with the Babylonians once again laying siege to the city. The false prophets are no longer to be heard. The fallacy of their prophecies has silenced them.)*

20 Therefore hear now, I pray you, O my lord the king: let my supplication, I pray you, be accepted before you; that you cause me not to return to the house of Jonathan the Scribe, lest I die there. *(Jeremiah's pathetic appeal not to be left to die of starvation in the dungeon, while showing his natural fear of death, makes his courage and testimony the more remarkable, and the result proves that honest reproof sometimes gains more favor than flattery.*

Jeremiah was a faithful Preacher of the Divine Message. He most earnestly and affectionately warned the king of the sure Wrath of God and begged him to accept the Grace of God that promised absolute safety from that Wrath. But the king, like most today, chose death rather than life.)

JEREMIAH CONFINED TO
THE PRISON COURT

21 Then Zedekiah the king commanded that they should commit Jeremiah into the court of the prison, and that they should give him daily a piece of bread out of the bakers' street, until all the bread in the city were spent. Thus Jeremiah remained in the court of the prison. *(The city, now under siege by the Babylonians,*

quickly runs out of food! Hence, if Zedekiah had not "commanded" that Jeremiah be allowed to remain in the "court of the prison," and that they should "give him daily a piece of bread," he would have starved to death.)

CHAPTER 38
(589 B.C.)
THE PRINCES ACCUSE JEREMIAH; DEMAND DEATH

THEN Shephatiah the son of Mattan, and Gedaliah the son of Pashur, and Jucal the son of Shelemiah, and Pashur the son of Malchiah, heard the words that Jeremiah had spoken unto all the people, saying *(the individuals mentioned in this Verse were high up in government circles; setting themselves against the Will of God, they demanded the life of Jeremiah. They would go to any lengths to stop his voice)*,

2 Thus saith the LORD, He who remains in this city shall die by the sword, by the famine, and by the pestilence: but he who goes forth to the Chaldeans shall live, for he shall have his life for a prey, and shall live. *(There was absolutely no doubt as to what the Message said or its intent; therefore, the Leaders of Judah, as well as the people, were without excuse.)*

3 Thus saith the LORD, This city shall surely be given into the hand of the king of Babylon's army, which shall take it.

4 Therefore the princes said unto the king, We beseech you, let this man be put to death: for thus he weakens the hands of the men of war who remain in this city, and the hands of all the people, in speaking such words unto them: for this man seeks not the welfare of this people, but the hurt. *(One must say this: even in the face of what looked like possible death, Jeremiah never compromised his Message.)*

JEREMIAH CAST INTO A MIRY DUNGEON

5 Then Zedekiah the king said, Behold, he is in your hand: for the king is not he who can do any thing against you. *(As is obvious, Zedekiah was a weak king, fearful to stand up for that which was right.)*

6 Then took they Jeremiah, and cast him into the dungeon of Malchiah the son of Hammelech, that was in the court of the prison: and they let down Jeremiah with cords. And in the dungeon there was no water, but mire: so Jeremiah sunk in the mire. *(Jeremiah sank*

in the mire physically, but Zedekiah sank in it morally. The mire to the one was a mantle of glory; to the other, a vesture of shame. Jeremiah was left in this terrible predicament to die of hunger. Such was the cruelty of the haters of Truth; servants of God must not think it a strange thing if God permits such suffering to befall them.)

JEREMIAH RESCUED BY AN ETHIOPIAN

7 Now when Ebed-melech the Ethiopian, one of the eunuchs which was in the king's house, heard that they had put Jeremiah in the dungeon; the king then sitting in the gate of Benjamin *("Ebed-melech the Ethiopian" was the king's slave and no doubt a Negro. He was used greatly of God in saving Jeremiah's life and, no doubt, was a convert to Israel's God. For doing this thing, his life would be spared at the sack of Jerusalem [39:15-18])*;

8 Ebed-melech went forth out of the king's house, and spoke to the king saying *(to do this, he was taking his life in his hands!)*,

9 My lord the king, these men have done evil in all that they have done to Jeremiah the Prophet, whom they have cast into the dungeon; and he is like to die for hunger in the place where he is: for there is no more bread in the city. *(This man showed no fear regarding these "princes" who had determined Jeremiah's death. He calls it exactly as it is: "evil." In effect, he is making the "king" culpable, as well!)*

10 Then the king commanded Ebed-melech the Ethiopian, saying, Take from hence thirty men with you, and take up Jeremiah the Prophet out of the dungeon, before he die. *(The courage of this Ethiopian stands here in contrast with the cowardice of the king. He boldly and publicly braved the anger of both princes and people and so shamed the king that he obtained authority to deliver the Prophet. So dangerous was this mission that he needed thirty soldiers as a protecting guard.)*

11 So Ebed-melech took the men with him, and went into the house of the king under the treasury, and took thence old cast clouts and old rotten rags, and let them down by cords into the dungeon to Jeremiah. *(This "dungeon" was a place where water was normally kept, but from which the water had recently been used, leaving nothing but sediment, muck, and mire, which was probably several feet thick. In this "gook," Jeremiah had sunk.)*

12 And Ebed-melech the Ethiopian said

unto Jeremiah, Put now these old cast clouts and rotten rags under your armholes under the cords. And Jeremiah did so.

13 So they drew up Jeremiah with cords, and took him up out of the dungeon: and Jeremiah remained in the court of the prison. *(The "court of the prison" certainly was not paradise, but still, it was far, far better than this "dungeon.")*

ZEDEKIAH SEEKS ADVICE FROM JEREMIAH

14 Then Zedekiah the king sent, and took Jeremiah the Prophet unto him into the third entry that is in the house of the LORD: and the king said unto Jeremiah, I will ask you a thing; hide nothing from me. *(Zedekiah knew that Jeremiah was God's Prophet and that the words he spoke were from the Lord. But yet, he would not heed them, "for he loved the praise of men more than the praise of God" [Jn. 12:43].)*

15 Then Jeremiah said unto Zedekiah, If I declare it unto you, will you not surely put me to death? and if I give you counsel, will you not hearken unto me? *(The nobility and elevation of Jeremiah's character appear in this, that in his interview with the king, he did not indignantly denounce the brutality of his enemies and demand their just punishment; neither did he in righteous anger rebuke the king for his cowardly conduct in the matter. On the contrary, he earnestly and affectionately urged the king to save his life and theirs by obeying the Word of the Lord and surrendering to the Chaldeans.)*

16 So Zedekiah the king swore secretly unto Jeremiah, saying, As the LORD lives, Who made us this soul, I will not put you to death, neither will I give you into the hand of these men who seek your life. *(The phrase, "Who made us this soul," means "May God take my life if I take yours.")*

A CONDITIONAL PROPHECY

17 Then said Jeremiah unto Zedekiah, Thus saith the LORD, the God of Hosts, the God of Israel; If you will assuredly go forth unto the king of Babylon's princes, then your soul shall live, and this city shall not be burned with fire; and you shall live, and your house:

18 But if you will not go forth to the king of Babylon's princes, then shall this city be given into the hand of the Chaldeans, and they shall burn it with fire, and you shall not escape out of their hand. *(The choice is crystal clear.)*

19 And Zedekiah the king said unto Jeremiah, I am afraid of the Jews who are fallen to the Chaldeans, lest they deliver me into their hand, and they mock me. *(Zedekiah, as millions, feared man more than he feared God. As a result, he had neither the help of man or God.)*

20 But Jeremiah said, They shall not deliver you. Obey, I beseech you, the voice of the LORD, which I speak unto you: so it shall be well unto you, and your soul shall live.

21 But if you refuse to go forth, this is the word that the LORD has shown me *(the words, "But if you refuse to go forth," proclaim man's free moral agency. The Lord will proclaim the right way to the individual, but will never force a person's will. The very nature of obedience demands free moral agency, or else it is not obedience, but rather slavery.*

However, to disobey God sets oneself against God's perfect order of creation and the Restoration of all things. Catastrophe is always the result!):

22 And, behold, all the women who are left in the king of Judah's house shall be brought forth to the king of Babylon's princes, and those women shall say, Your friends have set you on, and have prevailed against you: your feet are sunk in the mire, and they are turned away back. *(That which the Holy Spirit was attempting to impress upon Zedekiah [and upon all, for the principle holds] is that the very thing we fear, and which causes us not to obey God, will, in our disobedience, bring the thing feared upon us, and even in a far greater measure.)*

23 So they shall bring out all your wives and your children to the Chaldeans: and you shall not escape out of their hand, but shall be taken by the hand of the king of Babylon: and you shall cause this city to be burned with fire. *(The rewards for obedience, which have already been enumerated, are grand, while the judgment for disobedience is awful; and yet, Zedekiah, as most, still would not obey.)*

ZEDEKIAH FEARS THE PRINCES

24 Then said Zedekiah unto Jeremiah, Let no man know of these words, and you shall not die. *(Public opinion was not on the side of Jeremiah, hence Zedekiah's fear. Actually, public opinion is seldom, if ever, on the side of the Word of God.)*

25 But if the princes hear that I have talked with you, and they come unto you, and say unto you, Declare unto us now what you have said unto the king, hide it not from us, and we

will not put you to death; also what the king said unto you *(in his weakness, the king could not stand up to the princes; therefore, he does not want them to know that he seeks the Word of the Lord from the Prophet):*

26 Then you shall say unto them, I presented my supplication before the king, that he would not cause me to return to Jonathan's house, to die there.

27 Then came all the princes unto Jeremiah, and asked him: and he told them according to all these words that the king had commanded. So they left off speaking with him; for the matter was not perceived. *(Some have claimed that Jeremiah was not altogether truthful by not relating to these murderers the entirety of the conversation; however, he was under no Scriptural obligation to reveal to these men the entirety of the personal words exchanged between him and Zedekiah.)*

28 So Jeremiah abode in the court of the prison until the day that Jerusalem was taken: and he was there when Jerusalem was taken. *(The "court of the prison" meant that he was under house arrest, but still had some small measure of freedom.*

Regrettably, Zedekiah would not heed the words given to him from the Lord by Jeremiah; as a result, he would suffer terrible loss, as would the entirety of the city and its people.)

CHAPTER 39
(590 B.C.)
THE FALL OF JERUSALEM

IN the ninth year of Zedekiah king of Judah, in the tenth month, came Nebuchadnezzar king of Babylon and all his army against Jerusalem, and they besieged it. *(In the fourth month of the eleventh year of "Zedekiah," the city was taken. The last siege lasted about 16 months; the first siege lasted about 8 months [before the Egyptian army came]; the combined sieges lasted about 2 years.)*

2 And in the eleventh year of Zedekiah, in the fourth month, the ninth day of the month, the city was broken up. *(The Holy Spirit inspires these words with the sob of a broken heart.)*

3 And all the princes of the king of Babylon came in, and sat in the middle gate, even Nergal-sharezer, Samgar-nebo, Sarsechim, Rab-saris, Nergal-sharezer, Rab-mag, with all the residue of the princes of the king of Babylon. *(The "middle gate" has reference to the separation of the city. The northern end of*

Jerusalem was separated from the southern by an interior wall in which was a gate called "the middle gate." The Chaldeans captured that portion of the city, and then took up their position ["sat in"] opposite the middle gate in order to force it. Having these individuals of high rank and title present at the overthrow of Jerusalem no doubt portrayed the significance placed on its capture by Nebuchadnezzar.)

4 And it came to pass, that when Zedekiah the king of Judah saw them, and all the men of war, then they fled, and went forth out of the city by night, by the way of the king's garden, by the gate betwixt the two walls: and he went out the way of the plain. *(All through his unbelief, disobedience, and cowardice, Zedekiah kept up an outward show of religion. He acted as men do presently. He was practically an unbeliever; up to the very end, he thought he could defeat the Word of the Lord by breaking a passage through the south wall of the city, thus escaping from the Chaldeans [Ezek. 12:1-16]. But he was defeated and captured at Jericho.)*

JUDGMENT ON ZEDEKIAH

5 But the Chaldeans' army pursued after them, and overtook Zedekiah in the plains of Jericho: and when they had taken him, they brought him up to Nebuchadnezzar king of Babylon to Riblah in the land of Hamath, where he gave judgment upon him. *(Ironically enough, the ancient city of Jericho, which witnessed Israel's first victory, now witnesses its last defeat. The Scripture says, "They brought him up to Nebuchadnezzar king of Babylon to Riblah," thus fulfilling the Prophecy about Zedekiah seeing the king of Babylon eye to eye and speaking to him mouth to mouth, as predicted in 32:4 and 34:3.)*

6 Then the king of Babylon slew the sons of Zedekiah in Riblah before his eyes: also the king of Babylon slew all the nobles of Judah.

7 Moreover he put out Zedekiah's eyes, and bound him with chains, to carry him to Babylon. *(Thus, as predicted in Ezek. 12:13 and Jer. 32:4, Zedekiah's eyes saw the eyes of the Babylonian Monarch, but not the Babylonian capital, though he died there, because he was blind. This was what the Holy Spirit through Jeremiah had pleaded with Zedekiah to avoid. But the king, fearful of his nobles, refused to obey and suffered the horror here represented.)*

JERUSALEM DESTROYED; THE PEOPLE DEPORTED

8 And the Chaldeans burned the king's house, and the houses of the people, with fire, and broke down the walls of Jerusalem. *(Nebuchadnezzar was incensed at Jerusalem's obstinacy and refusal to surrender; therefore, he turned it into a smoking ruin. Thus ended its nearly 500-year reign as the premier city in the world. It would now be subject to Gentile powers, as it is, at least in part, unto this very day.)*

9 Then Nebuzar-adan the captain of the guard carried away captive into Babylon the remnant of the people who remained in the city, and those who fell away, who fell to him, with the rest of the people who remained. *(The phrase, "The remnant of the people who remained in the city," referred to the small number left in Jerusalem after the slaughter had subsided. This fulfilled the predictions of the Prophet.*

Those who remained, at least the ones selected, were "carried away captive into Babylon." This was the third and final deportation.)

A REMNANT LEFT

10 But Nebuzar-adan the captain of the guard left of the poor of the people, which had nothing, in the land of Judah, and gave them vineyards and fields at the same time. *(The "poor of the people" no doubt consisted of many who had virtually been made slaves by the nobles of Judah in Jerusalem. In Chapter 34, the Holy Spirit had pleaded through Jeremiah for these hapless individuals to be set free from their lives of servitude to the Nobles of the land. The pleadings of the Holy Spirit were ignored.*

For this disobedience, the former slaves are now given "the vineyards and fields" where they once toiled, and as their own possessions. Thus, the law of sowing and reaping was carried out [Mat. 7:2].

We must understand that God says what He means and means what He says!)

NEBUCHADNEZZAR'S CARE FOR JEREMIAH

11 Now Nebuchadnezzar king of Babylon gave charge concerning Jeremiah to Nebuzar-adan the captain of the guard, saying,

12 Take him, and look well to him, and do him no harm; but do unto him even as he shall say unto you. *(God sometimes moves heathen princes to honor faithful Preachers of His Word. Jeremiah was thus honored, for the highest officers of the empire were commanded to attend him, remove his fetters [40:1], and do all that he wished.)*

13 So Nebuzar-adan the captain of the guard sent, and Nebushasban, Rab-saris, and Nergal-sharezer, Rab-mag, and all the king of Babylon's princes;

14 Even they sent, and took Jeremiah out of the court of the prison, and committed him unto Gedaliah the son of Ahikam the son of Shaphan, that he should carry him home: so he dwelt among the people. *(The phrase, "And committed him unto Gedaliah the son of Ahikam," was in effect committing him to a friend. Whether the Babylonians knew of this friendship between "Gedaliah" and "Jeremiah" is not known.)*

GOD'S PROMISE OF DELIVERANCE TO EBED-MELECH, THE ETHIOPIAN

15 Now the word of the LORD came unto Jeremiah, while he was shut up in the court of the prison, saying *(the time frame of this "Word of the LORD," as well as the remainder of the Chapter, goes back several months, but is introduced here because it pertains to God's Promise of Deliverance to "Ebed-melech the Ethiopian"),*

16 Go and speak to Ebed-melech the Ethiopian, saying, Thus saith the LORD of Hosts, the God of Israel; Behold, I will bring My words upon this city for evil, and not for good; and they shall be accomplished in that day before you. *(Jeremiah was God's Prophet; therefore, all who befriended and helped him were, in turn, befriended and helped by the Lord.)*

17 But I will deliver you in that day, saith the LORD: and you shall not be given into the hand of the men of whom you are afraid.

18 For I will surely deliver you, and you shall not fall by the sword, but your life shall be for a prey unto you: because you have put your trust in Me, saith the LORD. *("Peace through believing" is illustrated by Ebed-melech. He feared the vengeance of the princes of Judah and he feared the sword of the Chaldeans. But this double fear was dismissed by the Lord's "I will deliver you," "Yea, I will surely deliver you." This Divine Promise was made to him because of his faith.)*

CHAPTER 40
(588 B.C.)
JEREMIAH LIBERATED

THE Word that came to Jeremiah from the LORD, after that Nebuzar-adan the captain of the guard had let him go from Ramah, when he had taken him being bound in chains among all who were carried away captive of Jerusalem and Judah, which were carried away captive unto Babylon. (According to this Verse, we learn that war and captivity cannot prevent the Great Shepherd from speaking to His Own.)

2 And the captain of the guard took Jeremiah, and said unto him, The LORD your God has pronounced this evil upon this place. (The statement of the "captain of the guard," concerning "The LORD your God has pronounced evil upon this place," shows the clear vision of the heathen prince, in contrast with the blindness of the men of Judah.

The terminology used by this Babylonian proclaims his interest as more than casual. It seems that he had carefully studied the Prophecies of Jeremiah, and he understood perfectly why judgment had come upon Judah and Jerusalem.)

3 Now the LORD has brought it, and done according as He has said: because you have sinned against the LORD, and have not obeyed His voice, therefore this thing is come upon you. (Once again, we must derive from the terminology used by this man that he had a far greater knowledge of Jehovah than most; there is even some evidence that he may possibly have accepted Jehovah as his God, thereby denouncing the Babylonian deities.)

4 And now, behold, I loose you this day from the chains which were upon your hand. If it seem good unto you to come with me into Babylon, come; and I will look well unto you: but if it seem ill unto you to come with me into Babylon, forbear: behold, all the land is before you: whither it seems good and convenient for you to go, thither go. (Jeremiah, seemingly, is set aside from the other prisoners and is given his choice respecting "Babylon" or the whole of Judah and Jerusalem.)

5 Now while he was not yet gone back, he said, Go back also to Gedaliah the son of Ahikam the son of Shaphan, whom the king of Babylon has made governor over the cities of Judah, and dwell with him among the people: or go wheresoever it seems convenient unto you to go. So the captain of the guard gave him victuals and a reward, and let him go. (The phrase, "Now while he was not yet gone back," refers to Jeremiah hesitating in respect to his decision as to what he should do. The "reward" mentioned here was probably money, but without any specified amount made known. More than likely, the Prophet was financially destitute; therefore, the financial help given, if in fact it was financial help, was no doubt greatly needed!)

6 Then went Jeremiah unto Gedaliah the son of Ahikam to Mizpah; and dwelt with him among the people who were left in the land. (This Passage shows that the Prophet preferred poverty and obscurity with the hostile and degenerate Hebrews to the fame and comfort among the admiring Chaldeans.)

REGATHERING OF THE JEWS

7 Now when all the captains of the forces which were in the fields, even they and their men, heard that the king of Babylon had made Gedaliah the son of Ahikam governor in the land, and had committed unto him men, and women, and children, and of the poor of the land, of them who were not carried away captive to Babylon (these were probably individuals who had escaped from the city during the siege or during its actual break-up and who were now filtering back in. Some would prove to be of evil heart);

8 Then they came to Gedaliah to Mizpah, even Ishmael the son of Nethaniah, and Johanan and Jonathan the sons of Kareah, and Seraiah the son of Tanhumeth, and the sons of Ephai the Netophathite, and Jezaniah the son of Maachathite, they and their men. (These men had come to meet with Gedaliah, the appointed governor.)

9 And Gedaliah the son of Ahikam the son of Shaphan swore unto them and to their men, saying, Fear not to serve the Chaldeans: dwell in the land, and serve the king of Babylon, and it shall be well with you. ("Gedaliah" here professes the validity of the Prophecy of Jeremiah [27:11]. The phrase, "And it shall be well with you," implies that it is the Will of God for them to serve the Chaldeans. If they did such, things would go well; if not, not well at all!)

10 As for me, behold, I will dwell at Mizpah, to serve the Chaldeans, which will come unto us: but you, gather ye wine, and summer fruits, and oil, and put them in your vessels, and dwell in your cities that you have taken. ("Mizpah" is to be the headquarters of the occupation of Judah,

because Jerusalem is destroyed. The phrase, "The Chaldeans, which will come unto us," refers to the occupation forces from Babylon that will soon occupy the land.)

11 Likewise when all the Jews who were in Moab, and among the Ammonites, and in Edom, and who were in all the countries, heard that the king of Babylon had left a remnant of Judah, and that he had set over them Gedaliah the son of Ahikam the son of Shaphan;

12 Even all the Jews returned out of all places whither they were driven, and came to the land of Judah, to Gedaliah, unto Mizpah, and gathered wine and summer fruits very much. *(When Jerusalem was threatened by Nebuchadnezzar, it seems that many "Jews" fled to surrounding countries seeking asylum. Now they begin to filter back into the Land.)*

ISHMAEL'S CONSPIRACY

13 Moreover Johanan the son of Kareah, and all the captains of the forces who were in the fields, came to Gedaliah to Mizpah,

14 And said unto him, Do you certainly know that Baalis the king of the Ammonites has sent Ishmael the son of Nethaniah to slay you? But Gedaliah the son of Ahikam believed them not. *(The situation, as evidenced in these Verses, proclaims the spirit of the world, as men jockey for power. "Baalis the king of the Ammonites" desires to kill Gedaliah, but the reason is not here given. At any rate, he finds a ready accomplice in "Ishmael," who may have been angry at Gedaliah because he had sided with Jeremiah. Perhaps Ishmael thought that he should be governor in place of Gedaliah, which was probably the case!)*

15 Then Johanan the son of Kareah spoke to Gedaliah in Mizpah secretly, saying, Let me go, I pray you, and I will slay Ishmael the son of Nethaniah, and no man shall know it: wherefore should he slay you, that all the Jews which are gathered unto you should be scattered, and the remnant in Judah perish? *(Why "Johanan" did not suggest incarceration is not known. Irrespective, his fear concerning future difficulties, especially with "Ishmael," was well-founded. Satan no doubt engineered this scenario in that "Gedaliah" was a good man, determined to rule with fairness and justice. As well, he was a friend of Jeremiah's, and would have benefited greatly from the Prophet's influence. But sadly, because of perfidy and wickedness, this was not to be.)*

16 But Gedaliah the son of Ahikam said unto Johanan the son of Kareah, You shall not do this thing: for you speak falsely of Ishmael. *(It seems that Gedaliah did not seek counsel from Jeremiah concerning this thing. Had he done so, the outcome would no doubt have been far different.)*

CHAPTER 41
(588 B.C.)

ISHMAEL SLAYS GEDALIAH

NOW it came to pass in the seventh month, that Ishmael the son of Nethaniah the son of Elishama, of the seed royal, and the princes of the king, even ten men with him, came unto Gedaliah the son of Ahikam to Mizpah; and there they did eat bread together in Mizpah. *(The phrase, "Of the seed royal," tells us that "Ishmael" was no doubt moved by jealousy to murder Gedaliah because he had been made viceroy.)*

2 Then arose Ishmael the son of Nethaniah, and the ten men who were with him, and smote Gedaliah the son of Ahikam the son of Shaphan with the sword, and slew him, whom the king of Babylon had made governor over the land. *(In this Chapter, Jeremiah is unseen yet present, but unsought! Gedaliah's not seeking the counsel of the great Prophet would prove to be disastrous!)*

3 Ishmael also slew all the Jews who were with him, even with Gedaliah, at Mizpah, and the Chaldeans who were found there, and the men of war.

4 And it came to pass the second day after he had slain Gedaliah, and no man knew it *(no one knew who had done it),*

5 That there came certain from Shechem, from Shiloh, and from Samaria, even fourscore men, having their beards shaven, and their clothes rent, and having cut themselves, with offerings and incense in their hand, to bring them to the House of the LORD. *(This portrays individuals coming to the Temple site, although destroyed, in order to worship God. Faith recognized and approved the appalling judgments that had fallen upon them. They turned not from, but to, Him Who had poured out those judgments and brought Him Thank Offerings of the abundance which Grace provided. While 70 of these men were permitted to perish, still, theirs was the faith that overcomes.)*

6 And Ishmael the son of Nethaniah went forth from Mizpah to meet them, weeping all

along as he went: and it came to pass, as he met them, he said unto them, Come to Gedaliah the son of Ahikam. *(A carnal Church has no desire for the true worship of God; therefore, it will seek to kill, as "Ishmael" did, all participants. Its agenda does not include "Offerings" which speak of Calvary, nor "Incense" which speaks of Godly worship. Actually, it is upon these two rocks, Calvary and worship of God, that the true Church stands, but which the apostate Church regards not at all!)*

7 And it was so, when they came into the midst of the city, that Ishmael the son of Nethaniah slew them, and cast them into the midst of the pit, he, and the men who were with him. *(As well, those who are led by "Ishmael" will be destroyed and "cast into the midst of the pit," i.e., "Hell fire.")*

8 But ten men were found among them who said unto Ishmael, Slay us not: for we have treasures in the field, of wheat, and of barley, and of oil, and of honey. So he forbore, and slew them not among their brethren. *(Along with the thirst for power and control, "Ishmael" also desired "treasures." So these "ten men" traded their treasures for their lives!)*

9 Now the pit wherein Ishmael had cast all the dead bodies of the men, whom he had slain because of Gedaliah, was it which Asa the king had made for fear of Baasha king of Israel: and Ishmael the son of Nethaniah filled it with them who were slain. *(This symbolizes the many Godly people through the centuries who have been slain by the religious "Ishmaels.")*

10 Then Ishmael carried away captive all the residue of the people who were in Mizpah, even the king's daughters, and all the people who remained in Mizpah, whom Nebuzaradan the captain of the guard had committed to Gedaliah the son of Ahikam: and Ishmael the son of Nethaniah carried them away captive, and departed to go over to the Ammonites. *(Evidently, the Babylonians had not occupied the land, that is, if they ever did!)*

JOHANAN BECOMES LEADER

11 But when Johanan the son of Kareah, and all the captains of the forces who were with him, heard of all the evil that Ishmael the son of Nethaniah had done,

12 Then they took all the men, and went to fight with Ishmael the son of Nethaniah, and found him by the great waters that are in Gibeon. *(The struggle continues, with "Johanan"* the son of Kareah entering the picture, whose comport was little better than Ishmael's. None are led by God. In fact, "Johanan" will ultimately, at least in part, be responsible for the death of Jeremiah. Tradition says that Jeremiah was killed in Egypt by his own people, who, at least at first, were led by "Johanan.")*

13 Now it came to pass, that when all the people which were with Ishmael saw Johanan the son of Kareah, and all the captains of the forces that were with him, then they were glad. *(They had a right to be "glad," because their lives were probably spared by the action of "Johanan." However, they were merely trading one dead Church for another. Their "gladness" was not rooted in proper soil; therefore, they would come to no satisfactory conclusion.)*

14 So all the people that Ishmael had carried away captive from Mizpah cast about and returned, and went unto Johanan the son of Kareah. *(The intent of the Holy Spirit, among other things, is to portray a people who should have been depending on God, but who were continuing to depend upon themselves, therefore, floundering without sense of purpose or direction.)*

15 But Ishmael the son of Nethaniah escaped from Johanan with eight men, and went to the Ammonites. *(This man "went to the Ammonites" because he had a murderous heart identical to these rebels against God. "Ishmael" was in fact in the lineage of David; but he knew David's God not at all, showing that natural birth, even from the Godly, does not make one a true "son of David." God has no grandchildren!)*

16 Then took Johanan the son of Kareah, and all the captains of the forces that were with him, all the remnant of the people whom he had recovered from Ishmael the son of Nethaniah, from Mizpah, after that he had slain Gedaliah the son of Ahikam, even mighty men of war, and the women, and the children, and the eunuchs, whom he had brought again from Gibeon *(the group that was with "Johanan" probably was the cream of the remnant left in the whole of Judah. Events will show that these individuals will make a pretense at seeking the Will of God by consulting Jeremiah, but the truth will out that their hearts were not after God, but toward Egypt. They did not know the Lord; they would not believe His Prophet; and they had no desire for His Will)*:

17 And they departed, and dwelt in the habitation of Chimham, which is by Beth-lehem,

to go to enter into Egypt *(while they would consult with Jeremiah, theirs minds had already been made up "to enter into Egypt"),*

18 Because of the Chaldeans: for they were afraid of them, because Ishmael the son of Nethaniah had slain Gedaliah the son of Ahikam, whom the king of Babylon made governor in the land. *("Fear" linked with self-will because of unspiritual hearts would lead them to make a rash and terrible decision. They would attempt to escape the hand of "the king of Babylon," but, even though in Egypt, they would not escape it at all! Had they put their trust in God, depending on Him for protection, guidance, and security, they would have been protected, blessed, led, guided, helped, and looked after as only the Lord can do.)*

CHAPTER 42

(588 B.C.)

JEREMIAH COUNSELS JOHANAN

THEN all the captains of the forces, and Johanan the son of Kareah, and Jezaniah the son of Hoshaiah, and all the people from the least even unto the greatest, came near *(the treachery and cruelty of Ishmael and his companions and the hypocrisy, obstinacy, rebellion, and unbelief of Johanan and the people revealed the moral condition of the nation and the justness of the calamities which came upon them. Ishmael illustrates the ugliness of the "flesh," and Johanan illustrates its unbelief. For that which is born of the flesh is flesh, and the carnal mind is enmity against God as much when making a show of religion as when shedding blood. Cain illustrates this fact, for he was just as hostile to God when worshipping at his aesthetic altar as he was when murdering his brother. The Holy Spirit [I Jn. 3:12] says that Cain's religious works were evil),*

2 And said unto Jeremiah the Prophet, Let, we beseech you, our supplication be accepted before you, and pray for us unto the LORD your God, even for all this remnant; (for we are left but a few of many, as your eyes do behold us *[unconverted people use very pious and very humble language, but the humility of the natural man is as abhorrent to God as the pride of the natural man (Col. 2:18, 23)]:)*

3 That the LORD your God may show us the way wherein we may walk, and the thing that we may do. *(They wanted the Lord to "show them the way," but only if it was the way they had already selected and chosen.)*

JEREMIAH PRAYS FOR DIRECTION; THE JEWS PROMISE OBEDIENCE

4 Then Jeremiah the Prophet said unto them, I have heard you; behold, I will pray unto the LORD your God according to your words; and it shall come to pass, that whatsoever thing the LORD shall answer you, I will declare it unto you; I will keep nothing back from you. *(In asking Jeremiah to seek the Lord on their behalf, the people were at the threshold of blessing and prosperity; nevertheless, they were expected by the Lord to obey Him and to follow exactly what He desired. They came so close; and yet, because of their obstinacy and self-will, they were so far away.)*

5 Then they said to Jeremiah, The LORD be a true and faithful witness between us, if we do not even according to all things for the which the LORD your God shall send you to us. *(Men are very quick to make promises to God, even with an oath: "The Lord be a true and faithful witness between us." In other words, they were saying that if they broke their promise, Jehovah was to "witness against them" by punishing them.)*

6 Whether it be good, or whether it be evil, we will obey the voice of the LORD our God, to Whom we send you; that it may be well with us, when we obey the voice of the LORD our God. *(They spoke with great resolve, but the words only came from their mouths and not from their hearts.)*

GOD'S MESSAGE: SAFETY IN JUDAH; DESTRUCTION IF THEY GO TO EGYPT

7 And it came to pass after ten days, that the Word of the LORD came unto Jeremiah.

8 Then called he Johanan the son of Kareah, and all the captains of the forces which were with him, and all the people from the least even to the greatest.

9 And said unto them, Thus saith the LORD, the God of Israel, unto Whom you sent me to present your supplication before Him;

10 If you will still abide in this land, then will I build you, and not pull you down, and I will plant you, and not pluck you up: for I repent Me of the evil that I have done unto you. *(In 41:18, it says that they feared the Chaldeans. But in this Passage, the Lord tells them that the Babylonians are not pulling the strings, so to speak; He is!)*

11 Be not afraid of the king of Babylon, of

whom you are afraid; be not afraid of him, saith the LORD: for I am with you to save you, and to deliver you from his hand. *(What a delight to serve One Who is subservient to no person or thing. He answers to no one, while all answer to Him. How foolish it is to serve anyone or anything else! Only the Lord can "save," and only the Lord can "deliver." Men rule, but God overrules!)*

12 And I will show mercies unto you, that he may have mercy upon you, and cause you to return to your own land. *(The Truth given in this Verse is that everything that happens to a Believer is either caused or allowed by the Lord.)*

13 But if you say, We will not dwell in this land, neither obey the voice of the LORD your God *(if one will notice, far more attention is given to the negatives than to the positives because of the propensity of man to go astray. Three Verses are devoted to the Promise of God's great blessings, while nine Verses are devoted to solemn warnings. This same method is employed in Deut., Chpt. 28),*

14 Saying, No; but we will go into the land of Egypt, where we shall see no war, nor hear the sound of the trumpet, nor have hunger of bread; and there will we dwell *(whatever their reasons, it seems the major cause of the failure of the remnant was their lack of trust in God):*

15 And now therefore hear the word of the LORD, you remnant of Judah; Thus saith the LORD of Hosts, the God of Israel; If you wholly set your faces to enter into Egypt, and go to sojourn there *(the exclamation, "Thus saith the LORD of Hosts, the God of Israel," is meant to impress upon the "remnant" the Power and Omniscience of God);*

16 Then it shall come to pass, that the sword, which you feared, shall overtake you there in the land of Egypt, and the famine, whereof you were afraid, shall follow close after you there in Egypt; and there you shall die *(in fact, Nebuchadnezzar would shortly invade Egypt, even though that was not known at the present. Therefore, if they went to Egypt, the very war they were seeking to avoid would be brought to them, which is exactly what happened!),*

17 So shall it be with all the men who set their faces to go into Egypt to sojourn there; they shall die by the sword, by the famine, and by the pestilence: and none of them shall remain or escape from the evil that I will bring upon them. *(The predictions of this Verse all came to pass, but none could say that they were not warned!)*

18 For thus saith the LORD of Hosts, the God of Israel; As My anger and My fury has been poured forth upon the inhabitants of Jerusalem; so shall My fury be poured forth upon you, when you shall enter into Egypt: and you shall be an execration, and an astonishment, and a curse, and a reproach; and you shall see this place no more. *(It is folly for men to deny the fact of the Wrath of God.)*

19 The LORD has said concerning you, O ye remnant of Judah; Go ye not into Egypt: know certainly that I have admonished you this day. *(So what they did was not out of ignorance, but out of abject disobedience and rebellion. To sin against light is the worse sin of all.)*

20 For you dissembled in your hearts, when you sent me unto the LORD your God, saying, Pray for us unto the LORD our God; and according unto all that the LORD our God shall say, so declare unto us, and we will do it. *(The Lord, knowing their hearts, plainly predicts what their choice will be. Human intelligence is incapable of the knowledge shown in Verses 20 and 21. The Holy Spirit revealed to the Prophet the hypocrisy of the petitioners and their pre-determined resolve to disobey the voice of the God.*

The word "dissembled" means "to hide under a false appearance" or "to conceal facts and intentions." The Lord's knowing the "hearts of the remnant of Judah" and His predicting the resultant outcome show the folly of attempting to lie to God.)

21 And now I have this day declared it to you; but you have not obeyed the voice of the LORD your God, nor any thing for the which He has sent me unto you. *("You have not obeyed," i.e., "you have not intended to obey.")*

22 Now therefore know certainly that you shall die by the sword, by the famine, and by the pestilence, in the place whither you desire to go and to sojourn. *(The words, "Know certainly that you shall die," could not be stronger. And yet even in the face of full disclosure, the remnant determined to disobey, which they did, and brought upon themselves "certain death.")*

CHAPTER 43
(588 B.C.)
REBELLION OF THE REMNANT

AND it came to pass, that when Jeremiah had made an end of speaking unto all the people all the Words of the LORD their God, for which the LORD their God had sent

him to them, even all these Words *(the phrase, "All the words of the LORD their God," represented life or death for these people, all according to their obedience or disobedience. Regrettably, they disobeyed!),*

2 Then spoke Azariah the son of Hoshaiah, and Johanan the son of Kareah, and all the proud men, saying unto Jeremiah, You speak falsely: the LORD our God has not sent you to say, Go not into Egypt to sojourn there *(it is positive that all these individuals were well aware of the Prophecies Jeremiah had given for many years. Before their very eyes, they had seen these Prophecies come true. Judah was a desolation, and Jerusalem a smoking ruin, exactly as Jeremiah had prophesied. Yet they now accuse him of lying!*

What could make the heart of man so intractable, obstinate, stubborn, unyielding, and unbelieving? The Holy Spirit tells us by calling them "proud men"):

3 But Baruch the son of Neriah sets you on against us, for to deliver us into the hand of the Chaldeans, that they might put us to death, and carry us away captives into Babylon.

4 So Johanan the son of Kareah, and all the captains of the forces, and all the people, obeyed not the voice of the LORD, to dwell in the land of Judah. *(If they had "dwelled in the land of Judah," as demanded by the Lord, they would have been blessed, and greatly so!)*

THE MIGRATION TO EGYPT

5 But Johanan the son of Kareah, and all the captains of the forces, took all the remnant of Judah, that were returned from all nations, whither they had been driven, to dwell in the land of Judah *("Johanan the son of Kareah" seems to have been the ring-leader of this rebellion against God);*

6 Even men, and women, and children, and the king's daughters, and every person that Nebuzar-adan the captain of the guard had left with Gedaliah the son of Ahikam the son of Shaphan, and Jeremiah the Prophet, and Baruch the son of Neriah. *(As portrayed here, "Jeremiah the Prophet" and "Baruch the son of Neriah" are forced to go into Egypt with this rebellious group.)*

7 So they came into the land of Egypt: for they obeyed not the voice of the LORD: thus came they even to Tahpanhes. *("Tahpanhes" was a fortress on the Syrian frontier of Egypt. It was a royal palace.*

The phrase, "So they came into the land of Egypt," is recorded by the Holy Spirit for a greater purpose than mere historical narrative. They had been delivered out of Egyptian bondage many centuries before, and now they will go back into Egyptian bondage. This shows their total trust in man, i.e., the flesh, Egypt; and likewise their total distrust of the Lord.)

NEBUCHADNEZZAR TO CONQUER EGYPT

8 Then came the Word of the LORD unto Jeremiah in Tahpanhes, saying *(these rebels, if they had not wanted to hear the Word of the LORD, would have been much better off to have left Jeremiah in Judah),*

9 Take great stones in your hand, and hide them in the clay in the brickkiln, which is at the entry of Pharaoh's house in Tahpanhes, in the sight of the men of Judah *(the phrase, "Take great stones," was to represent a symbolic act. Jeremiah is directed to take these stones and embed them in the mortar in the brick pavement [brickkiln] at the entry to the palace. When the events predicted came to pass, these stones would testify that Jeremiah had predicted them. This "brick platform" or "brick pavement" was discovered by a man named "Petrie" in 1886);*

10 And say unto them, Thus saith the LORD of Hosts, the God of Israel; Behold, I will send and take Nebuchadnezzar the king of Babylon, My servant, and will set his throne upon these stones that I have hid; and he shall spread his royal pavilion over them. *(Josephus, the Jewish historian, records the fact that this was done by Nebuchadnezzar, exactly as Jeremiah had prophesied.)*

11 And when he comes, he shall smite the land of Egypt, and deliver such as are for death to death; and such as are for captivity to captivity; and such as are for the sword to the sword. *(Seated there, Nebuchadnezzar condemned to slavery or death the captives brought before him, which included those from Judah.)*

12 And I will kindle a fire in the houses of the gods of Egypt; and he shall burn them, and carry them away captives: and he shall array himself with the land of Egypt, as a shepherd puts on his garment; and he shall go forth from thence in peace. *(The phrase, "He shall burn them," referred to the gorgeous and imposing temples which filled Egypt, dedicated to her many gods, and the idols in them made of wood.*

The phrase, "He shall array himself with the

land of Egypt," refers to Nebuchadnezzar grasping Egypt with his hand, so to speak, and flinging it around him like an easily managed garment, in order to leave the land as an absolute conqueror clothed in this attire of booty, in peace, without an enemy.)

13 He shall break also the images of Bethshemesh, that is in the land of Egypt; and the houses of the gods of the Egyptians shall he burn with fire. *(The sinking of the Egyptians' great stones and the brick pavement, as characterized in Verse 9, and the setting of the Chaldean Throne upon them [Vs. 10] symbolize the downfall of the Egyptian monarchy and the supremacy of the Chaldean, which, as stated, was fulfillment to the letter concerning Jeremiah's Prophecies.)*

CHAPTER 44
(587 B.C.)
THE JEWISH REFUGEES TO PERISH IN EGYPT

THE word that came to Jeremiah concerning all the Jews which dwell in the land of Egypt, which dwell at Migdol, and at Tahpanhes, and at Noph, and in the country of Pathros, saying *(the Jews, after arriving in Egypt, had spread over the land, some going north and some south. It seems that the occasion for this Prophecy by Jeremiah was at some type of festival that drew representatives of the Jews from all over Egypt, if not most Egyptians, as well! This is Jeremiah's last Prophecy relating to Israel. The remaining Prophecies of the Book concern the Gentiles.*

The Jews lived in hopes of being able to return to Judah soon. But, because of their unbelief and rebellion against God, only a few would actually see Judah again),

2 Thus saith the LORD of Hosts, the God of Israel; You have seen all the evil that I have brought upon Jerusalem, and upon all the cities of Judah; and, behold, this day they are a desolation, and no man dwells therein *(this Scripture refers to the righteous judgment of God against His chosen People because of their gross idolatry and rebellion. The word "evil" means "judgment"!),*

3 Because of their wickedness which they have committed to provoke Me to anger, in that they went to burn incense, and to serve other gods, whom they knew not, neither they, ye, nor your fathers. *(Although the destruction of Jerusalem and Judah was a fact that could not be denied, yet these obstinate unbelievers* refused to recognize its cause. On the contrary, they declared that their misfortunes arose from their lack of devotion to the Queen of Heaven, i.e., the Great Mother of God [Vss. 17-19].)

4 Howbeit I sent unto you all My servants the Prophets, rising early and sending them, saying, Oh, do not this abominable thing that I hate. *(The phrase, "Oh, do not this abominable thing that I hate," is a plaintive cry from the Holy Spirit, breathing an agony that only Divine Love could feel and utter.)*

5 But they hearkened not, nor inclined their ear to turn from their wickedness, to burn no incense unto other gods. *(Even though the Lord is speaking in the past tense here, future Passages will show that this sin was still prevalent among the remnant, even while in Egypt.)*

6 Wherefore My fury and My anger was poured forth, and was kindled in the cities of Judah and in the streets of Jerusalem; and they are wasted and desolate, as at this day. *(The words, "wasted and desolate," aptly describe the results of sin.)*

7 Therefore now thus saith the LORD, the God of Hosts, the God of Israel; Wherefore commit ye this great evil against your souls, to cut off from you man and woman, child and suckling, out of Judah, to leave you none to remain *(the phrase, "To cut off from you . . . ," refers to Judah and Jerusalem, which have already been denuded; this present sin will destroy even the remnant);*

8 In that you provoke Me unto wrath with the works of your hands, burning incense unto other gods in the land of Egypt, whither you be gone to dwell, that you might cut yourselves off, and that you might be a curse and a reproach among all the nations of the Earth? *(The words, "In that you provoke Me unto wrath with the works of your hands," suggest that the sinning of the people was more than failure; it was a dare to God. It was as though they were daring Him to do anything about their rebellion.)*

9 Have you forgotten the wickedness of your fathers, and the wickedness of the kings of Judah, and the wickedness of their wives, and your own wickedness, and the wickedness of your wives, which they have committed in the land of Judah, and in the streets of Jerusalem? *(The Holy Spirit here points out the culpability of the "wives" as well as their husbands, showing that the wives of nobles, princes, and kings have been, in the past, and at times in the present, the most active introducers of idolatry. Instead of helping each other toward Heaven,*

husband and wife often ripen each other for Hell.)

10 They are not humbled even unto this day, neither have they feared, nor walked in My Law, nor in My Statutes, that I set before you and before your fathers. *(The change from the third to the second person is designed to express how idolatry alienates from God.)*

11 Therefore thus saith the LORD of Hosts, the God of Israel; Behold, I will set My face against you for evil, and to cut off all Judah. *(These individuals no doubt believe that by putting aside the Bible and worshipping the Egyptian gods, they would secure a prosperous return to their native land, while those who surrendered to the Chaldeans, who rejected idolatry, and who clung to the Bible would perish. The exact opposite, however, is a historic fact.)*

12 And I will take the remnant of Judah, that have set their faces to go into the land of Egypt to sojourn there, and they shall all be consumed, and fall in the land of Egypt; they shall even be consumed by the sword and by the famine: they shall die, from the least even unto the greatest, by the sword and by the famine: and they shall be an execration, and an astonishment, and a curse, and a reproach. *(Once again, these rebels hear the same Prophecy as was given by Jeremiah just before they left Judah [42:17].)*

13 For I will punish them who dwell in the land of Egypt, as I have punished Jerusalem, by the sword, by the famine, and by the pestilence *(this prediction is given again because these people, no doubt, thought they were totally safe in Egypt. They paid absolutely no attention to Jeremiah's Prophecies, because they had already formed their opinion, which was contrary to the statement of the Lord):*

14 So that none of the remnant of Judah, which are gone into the land of Egypt to sojourn there, shall escape or remain, that they should return into the land of Judah, to the which they have a desire to return to dwell there: for none shall return but such as shall escape. *(The phrase, "But such as shall escape," must have referred to those who, like "Jeremiah" and "Baruch," refused to burn incense to the idol. God always has, and always has had, His "few" [Mat. 7:14; I Pet. 3:20; Rev. 3:4]. The awakened heart cries: "O to be one of that few!")*

15 Then all the men which knew that their wives had burned incense unto other gods, and all the women who stood by, a great multitude, even all the people who dwelt in the land of Egypt, in Pathros, answered Jeremiah, saying *(the phrase, "Had burned incense," really means "were burning incense," because the practice was still going on. Here we have the formal commitment of Israel in Egypt to the moon goddess instead of Jehovah. Thus, they made their choice and, in effect, signed their own death warrant),*

16 As for the word that you have spoken unto us in the Name of the LORD, we will not hearken unto you. *(Their answer, "we will not hearken unto you," while directed to the Prophet, was actually spoken to the Lord.)*

17 But we will certainly do whatsoever thing goes forth out of our own mouth, to burn incense unto the Queen of Heaven, and to pour out drink offerings unto her, as we have done, we, and our fathers, our kings, and our princes, in the cities of Judah, and in the streets of Jerusalem: for then had we plenty of victuals, and were well, and saw no evil. *(The phrase, "Queen of Heaven," was the name given to the moon goddess by these rebels of Judah, but was called "Ashtoreth" or "Astarte," the wife of Baal, or "Molech," who was called the King of Heaven by the Phoenicians. The male and female pair of deities symbolized the generative powers of nature; hence, the introduction of prostitution in connection with such worship.*

The Babylonians worshipped the goddess as "Mylitta" [generative]. The moon became the symbol of female productiveness, and all women converts were to submit to immorality at least once in this worship.)

18 But since we left off to burn incense to the Queen of Heaven, and to pour out drink offerings unto her, we have wanted all things, and have been consumed by the sword and by the famine. *(Unregenerate men are incapable of recognizing the Hand of God in calamities.)*

19 And when we burned incense to the Queen of Heaven, and poured out drink offerings unto her, did we make her cakes to worship her, and pour out drink offerings unto her, without our men? *(If one will notice, their boldness in their sin is characterized here by their open confession of idol worship. The slide downward into sin is accelerated by each act performed, with a searing of the conscience and a deadening of the soul. Now they have no shame whatsoever!)*

20 Then Jeremiah said unto all the people, to the men, and to the women, and to all the people which had given him that answer, saying *(the Lord would answer through His Prophet, but it would be not at all what the people desired to hear),*

21 The incense that you burned in the cities of Judah, and in the streets of Jerusalem, you, and your fathers, your kings, and your princes, and the people of the land, did not the LORD remember them, and came it not into His mind? *(The phrase, "And came it not into His mind?", refers back to the Prophecy of 32:35. In that Prophecy, He was referring to human sacrifice; He is referring now to the worship of the "Queen of Heaven." Both have their origination in demon spirits!*

Judah went far deeper into sin than could be contemplated by the natural mind.)

22 So that the LORD could not longer bear, because of the evil of your doings, and because of the abominations which you have committed; therefore is your land a desolation, and an astonishment, and a curse, without an inhabitant, as at this day. *(According to these Passages and many similar others, the Truth is proclaimed that all disfavor shown by God resulting in judgment or chastisement is due to sin, i.e., "the evil of your doings.")*

23 Because you have burned incense, and because you have sinned against the LORD, and have not obeyed the voice of the LORD, nor walked in His Law, nor in His Statutes, nor in His Testimonies; therefore this evil is happened unto you, as at this day. *(The Lord exclaims to these people that they can claim as much as they desire that their problems were caused by their "leaving off to burn incense to the Queen of Heaven," but in truth their problems have been brought about "because you have sinned against the Lord.")*

24 Moreover Jeremiah said unto all the people, and to all the women, Hear the word of the LORD, all Judah that are in the land of Egypt *(I think it is obvious that while Satan hates both men and women, he hates women in particular. It was the woman he first approached in the Garden of Eden, and the hatred intensified when the Lord told him, "And I will put enmity [hatred] between you and the woman, and between your seed [mankind which doesn't serve God] and her Seed [the Lord Jesus Christ]; it [He] shall bruise your head [what Jesus did at the Cross], and you shall bruise His heel" [the sufferings of Calvary; Gen. 3:15]):*

25 Thus saith the LORD of Hosts, the God of Israel, saying: You and your wives have both spoken with your mouths, and fulfilled with your hand, saying, We will surely perform our vows that we have vowed, to burn incense to the Queen of Heaven, and to pour our drink offerings unto her: you will surely accomplish your vows, and surely perform your vows. *(If these people were determined to accomplish their vows of evil, God, on His part, was resolved to perform His in their destruction.)*

26 Therefore hear ye the Word of the LORD, all Judah that dwell in the land of Egypt; Behold, I have sworn by My great Name, saith the LORD, that My Name shall no more be named in the mouth of any man of Judah in all the land of Egypt, saying, The Lord GOD lives. *(The vows of these rebels had been given with sarcasm; but this vow of the Lord is given with a cold finality. The idea is: no Jews will be left alive in Egypt, with the exception of a small number that will escape — probably those who did not succumb to the sin of idolatry. The others would die tragically!)*

27 Behold, I will watch over them for evil, and not for good: and all the men of Judah who are in the land of Egypt shall be consumed by the sword and by the famine, until there be an end of them. *(This is the worst judgment that could be imagined!)*

28 Yet a small number who escape the sword shall return out of the land of Egypt into the land of Judah, and all the remnant of Judah, who are gone into the land of Egypt to sojourn there, shall know whose words shall stand, Mine, or theirs. *(It is not known who was in this "small number who escaped the sword and returned to Judah," nor how many were in it, but it is believed that it consisted of those who refused to offer incense to this "Queen of Heaven," and who did not join in the sarcastic answer to the Lord.)*

29 And this shall be a sign unto you, saith the LORD, that I will punish you in this place, that you may know that My words shall surely stand against you for evil:

30 Thus saith the LORD; Behold, I will give Pharaoh-hophra king of Egypt into the hand of his enemies, and into the hand of them who seek his life; as I gave Zedekiah king of Judah into the hand of Nebuchadnezzar king of Babylon, his enemy, and who sought his life. *(History records the miserable end of Pharaoh-hophra at the hand of his enemies, led by Amasis, a rebel. The civil war which this man provoked facilitated the conquest of Egypt by Nebuchadnezzar. It is said that the Egyptians who were "his enemies" took him and strangled him. Therefore, the Lord punished Pharaoh for his opening Egypt to the*

rebellious remnant of Judah.

I suspect this statement, "Whose words shall stand, Mine or theirs," rang in the ears of these hapless rebels on the eve of their life.)

CHAPTER 45
(607 B.C.)
PROPHECY TO BARUCH, JEREMIAH'S SCRIBE

THE word that Jeremiah the Prophet spoke unto Baruch the son of Neriah, when he had written these words in a Book at the mouth of Jeremiah, in the fourth year of Jehoiakim the son of Josiah king of Judah, saying *(this Prophecy was given about 18 years before the destruction of Jerusalem by Nebuchadnezzar [II Ki. 23:36; 24:18]. We see in the five short Verses of this Chapter the care and concern the Heavenly Father has for all His Children. In the midst of His efforts to save the entirety of a nation, He would not forget one lone worker, namely "Baruch"!),*

2 Thus saith the LORD, the God of Israel, unto you, O Baruch *(with the words, "O Baruch," the Holy Spirit proclaims a distinctive care, as well as a slight reprimand!)*;

3 You did say, Woe is me now! For the LORD has added grief to my sorrow; I fainted in my sighing, and I find no rest. *(Baruch's grief, added to his sorrow, was possibly his grief at the burning of the Roll and his sorrow at being suspected of treason. The admonishment by the Holy Spirit, "You did say," suggested to him that he should have rejoiced rather than sighed because he was deemed worthy to suffer shame for Jehovah's Name.)*

4 Thus shall you say unto him, The LORD saith thus; Behold, that which I have built will I break down, and that which I have planted I will pluck up, even this whole land. *(At least part of the reason for Baruch's sorrow and sighing is that he is griefstricken at what is going to happen to Judah and Jerusalem.)*

5 And seekest thou great things for yourself? Seek them not: for, behold, I will bring evil upon all flesh, saith the LORD: but your life will I give unto you for a prey in all places whither you go. *("Thou" is emphatic. When the eye keeps steadfastly fastened on God's judgments upon a guilty world and upon His assured Promise of personal Salvation, then the heart is delivered from Earthly expectations and is, at the same time, prepared to suffer calamities in sympathy with national distress.)*

CHAPTER 46
(607 B.C.)
PROPHECIES CONCERNING EGYPT

THE Word of the LORD which came to Jeremiah the Prophet against the Gentiles *(the next six Chapters contain Prophecies concerning the Gentile nations, with the last Chapter of Jeremiah given further historical narrative concerning the destruction of Jerusalem. In these Prophecies, ten Gentile powers are addressed under the headship of Babylon.*

The phrase, "Against the Gentiles," means "concerning the nations");

2 Against Egypt, against the army of Pharaoh-necho king of Egypt, which was by the river Euphrates in Carchemish, which Nebuchadnezzar king of Babylon smote in the fourth year of Jehoiakim the son of Josiah king of Judah. *(The word "against" would have been better translated "concerning Egypt." This Prophecy was delivered after the death of king Josiah in the Battle of Megiddo [II Chron. 35:20-25], and four years prior to the Battle of Carchemish on the Euphrates, where Nebuchadnezzar defeated Pharaoh-necho. This battle took place in May-June 606 B.C.)*

3 Order ye the buckler and shield, and draw near to battle. *(This proclaims the total control by the Lord regarding the direction and destiny of nations.)*

4 Harness the horses; and get up, you horsemen, and stand forth with your helmets; furbish the spears, and put on the brigandines. *(Verses 3 and 4 portray Egypt's preparations for battle. From the description, it seems that they prepared with the idea of certain victory; however, the Lord, Who controls all, would deem it otherwise!)*

5 Wherefore have I seen them dismayed and turned away back? And their mighty ones are beaten down, and are fled apace, and look not back: for fear was round about, saith the LORD. *(The question, "Wherefore have I seen them dismayed and turned away back?", concerns itself with what Jeremiah saw in the Spirit, even some time before it actually happened!*

The phrase, "And their mighty ones are beaten down," portrays their boastfulness at defeating the Babylonians; but they were instead defeated themselves.)

6 Let not the swift flee away, nor the mighty man escape; they shall stumble, and fall toward the north by the river Euphrates. *(The mobilization and march of the Egyptian army*

are pictured in Verses 3 and 4; its defeat in Verses 5 and 6; its self-confidence in Verses 7 through 9; its destruction, as ordained by God, in Verse 10; its hopelessness of recovery in Verse 11; and the worldwide knowledge of its destruction in Verse 12.)

7 Who is this who comes up as a flood, whose waters are moved as the rivers? *(This question in Verse 7 is asked by the Holy Spirit and refers to the boastfulness of Egypt.)*

8 Egypt rises up like a flood, and his waters are moved like the rivers; and he says, I will go up, and will cover the Earth; I will destroy the city and the inhabitants thereof. *(The Holy Spirit delineates this boastfulness of Egypt, because it was in direct conflict with the Will of God. Egypt, of course, would have had little knowledge of Jehovah, and would have considered her gods as superior, because king Josiah of Judah had been defeated a short time previously. Consequently, they felt very secure in their boastfulness, not realizing it was God's Will that the Babylonians reign supreme.)*

9 Come up, you horses; and rage, you chariots; and let the mighty men come forth; the Ethiopians and the Libyans, who handle the shield; and the Lydians, who handle and bend the bow. *(We find here that the "Ethiopians," the "Libyans," and the "Lydians" are confederates of Egypt, which makes Egypt's power invincible, or so they think!)*

10 For this is the day of the Lord GOD of Hosts, a day of vengeance, that He may avenge Him of His adversaries: and the sword shall devour, and it shall be satiate and made drunk with their blood: for the Lord GOD of Hosts has a sacrifice in the north country by the River Euphrates. *(This "vengeance" refers to judgment on Pharaoh-necho, who, a short time before, had killed Godly king Josiah [II Chron. 35:20-24].*

The last phrase of the Verse represents the self-revealing side of the Divine Nature; it is not merely poetical ornamentation, but corresponds to terrible, objective reality. Divine vengeance exists and must exercise itself on all who oppose the Divine Will.

The word "sacrifice" is the purpose for which this immense host "rolls up from Africa" — it is that it may fall by the Euphrates as proof of God's justice and warning to transgressors.)

11 Go up into Gilead, and take balm, O virgin, the daughter of Egypt: in vain shall you use many medicines; for you shall not be cured. *(The idea is that Egypt, at least as a world power, is destroyed and, thereby, needs medicine.)*

12 The nations have heard of your shame, and your cry has filled the land: for the mighty man has stumbled against the mighty, and they are fallen both together. *(Egypt's defeat would be so severe that it would be the talk of all surrounding "nations.")*

13 The word that the LORD spoke to Jeremiah the Prophet, how Nebuchadnezzar king of Babylon should come and smite the land of Egypt. *(The conquest of Egypt by Nebuchadnezzar is foretold in Verses 13-26.)*

14 Declare ye in Egypt, and publish in Migdol, and publish in Noph and in Tahpanhes: say ye, Stand fast, and prepare thee; for the sword shall devour round about you. *(The Prophecy directs itself to the great cities in Egypt, as they are called upon to prepare to meet the foe, but in vain!)*

15 Why are your valiant men swept away? They stood not, because the LORD did drive them. *(It seems that the Holy Spirit through the Prophet is referring to Apis, the sacred bull in which the Egyptians believed the supreme god Osiris was incarnate. For this Apis [bull] to be "swept away" like ordinary plunder or "cast down" in the slaughtering-trough was a token indeed that the glory of Egypt had departed.)*

16 He made many to fall, yea, one fell upon another: and they said, Arise, and let us go again to our own people, and to the land of our nativity, from the oppressing sword. *(This refers to the mercenaries hired to fight for Egypt, but who now, due to the great slaughter, had lost their ardor and were proposing desertion.)*

17 They did cry there, Pharaoh king of Egypt is but a noise; he has passed the time appointed. *(The phrase, "Pharaoh king of Egypt is but a noise," is spoken by Egyptians rather than the mercenaries. They were actually saying, "Call ye the name of Pharaoh king of Egypt, desolation," meaning that he is now a fallen monarch.)*

18 As I live, saith the King, Whose Name is the LORD of Hosts, Surely as Tabor is among the mountains, and as Carmel by the sea, so shall he come. *(The Lord points to "Tabor" and "Carmel," two prominent mountains in Israel, and claims that as surely as they exist, Nebuchadnezzar will invade Egypt.)*

19 O thou daughter dwelling in Egypt, furnish yourself to go into captivity: for Noph shall be waste and desolate without an inhabitant.

20 Egypt is like a very fair heifer, but destruction comes; it comes out of the north.

21 Also her hired men are in the midst of

her like fatted bullocks; for they also are turned back, and are fled away together: they did not stand, because the day of their calamity was come upon them, and the time of their visitation. *(The Lord had marked Egypt for destruction, and irrespective as to what precautions they might take, all would be to no avail!)*

22 The voice thereof shall go like a serpent; for they shall march with an army, and come against her with axes, as hewers of wood. *(The "axes" have to do with battleaxes, which will be used by the Babylonians against the Egyptians, chopping them as they would chop wood. It is not a pretty picture!)*

23 They shall cut down her forest, saith the LORD, though it cannot be searched; because they are more than the grasshoppers, and are innumerable. *(The phrase, "They shall cut down her forest," speaks of Egypt's army being cut down by the Babylonians.)*

24 The daughter of Egypt shall be confounded; she shall be delivered into the hand of the people of the north. *(The phrase, "She shall be," is emphatic, stating the certitude of the action — that God will deliver them up to Babylon.)*

25 The LORD of Hosts, the God of Israel, saith; Behold, I will punish the multitude of No, and Pharaoh, and Egypt, with their gods, and their kings; even Pharaoh, and all them who trust in him *(the idea is that the gods of Egypt have come up against "The LORD of Hosts, the God of Israel"; consequently the viability of Jehovah will be obvious to all)*:

26 And I will deliver them into the hand of those who seek their lives, and into the hand of Nebuchadnezzar king of Babylon, and into the hand of his servants, and afterward it shall be inhabited, as in the days of old, saith the LORD. *(The words, "And afterward it shall be inhabited," refer to the coming Millennial Reign; this, of course, has not yet been fulfilled. However, as surely as the former was fulfilled, the latter will come to fruition as well!)*

JEREMIAH COMFORTS THE JEWS: ISRAEL TO BE RESTORED

27 But fear not thou, O My servant Jacob, and be not dismayed, O Israel: for, behold, I will save you from afar off, and your seed from the land of their captivity; and Jacob shall return, and be in rest and at ease, and none shall make him afraid. *(Admonition as well as consolation is the Message of Verses 27 and 28. They*

assured the safety and restoration of the captive Jews in Babylon and, by implication, the doom of the self-willed exiles in Egypt [Chpt. 44].*

Thus God, amid the welter of warring nations, watches over and guards His People, using public calamities as instruments for their discipline.)

28 Fear thou not, O Jacob My servant, saith the LORD: for I am with you; for I will make a full end of all the nations whither I have driven you: but I will not make a full end of you, but correct you in measure; yet will I not leave you wholly unpunished. *(In looking at the might and power of Babylon and other kingdoms that followed her, Israel could little understand her survival against such power. However, they are told here by the Lord that these empires will come and go, "but I will not make a full end of you," meaning that He would chastise them greatly, but also would guarantee their survival, "correct you in measure.")*

CHAPTER 47
(600 B.C.)
PROPHECY AGAINST THE PHILISTINES

THE Word of the LORD that came to Jeremiah the Prophet against the Philistines, before that Pharaoh smote Gaza. *(God did not wish that even one Philistine should perish. So, in His Love, He warned them to flee from the coming wrath. But they refused to listen and obey.)*

2 Thus saith the LORD; Behold, waters rise up out of the north, and shall be an overflowing flood, and shall overflow the land, and all that is therein; the city, and them who dwell therein: then the men shall cry, and all the inhabitants of the land shall howl. *(The word "waters" in this Verse refers to the Chaldeans. Babylon would defeat the Philistines as well!)*

3 At the noise of the stamping of the hoofs of his strong horses, at the rushing of his chariots, and at the rumbling of his wheels, the fathers shall not look back to their children for feebleness of hands *("the rushing of his chariots" refers to the speed of conquest of the Babylonians and the din of battle)*;

4 Because of the day that comes to spoil all the Philistines, and to cut off from Tyrus and Zidon every helper who remains: for the LORD will spoil the Philistines, the remnant of the country of Caphtor. *(Three lessons are taught by this Prophecy concerning Philistia: the Wrath of God upon sinners; the inability of man*

to save himself or his fellows from this Wrath; and the Grace of God in warning sinners of its coming so they may repent and escape.

The phrase, "Of the country of Caphtor," probably refers to where the Philistines originated, which many Scholars believe to have been a province of lower Egypt.)

5 Baldness is come upon Gaza; Ashkelon is cut off with the remnant of their valley: how long will you cut yourself? (The ancients, especially in the Middle East, when in extreme grief, plucked out their hair and cut themselves.)

6 O thou sword of the LORD, how long will it be ere you be quiet? Put up yourself into your scabbard, rest, and be still. (The sword of Babylon is here called the "sword of the LORD.")

7 How can it be quiet, seeing the LORD has given it a charge against Ashkelon, and against the sea shore? There has He appointed it. (The phrase, "There has He appointed it," refers to that being carried out exactly as the Lord designs. Men rule, while God overrules!)

CHAPTER 48
(600 B.C.)
PROPHECY CONCERNING MOAB:
INVASION BY BABYLON

AGAINST Moab thus saith the LORD of Hosts, the God of Israel; Woe unto Nebo! For it is spoiled: Kiriathaim is confounded and taken: Misgab is confounded and dismayed. (This Prophecy was given about 23 years before the overthrow of Moab by the Babylonians. Moab was in modern day Jordan, actually bordering the southern extremity of the Dead Sea.)

2 There shall be no more praise of Moab: in Heshbon they have devised evil against it; come, and let us cut it off from being a nation. Also you shall be cut down, O Madmen; the sword shall pursue you. (The phrase, "There shall be no more praise of Moab," refers to her military power and courage.)

3 A voice of crying shall be from Horonaim, spoiling and great destruction. (The city "Horonaim" was probably located on the border of Edom. Heshbon being on the opposite border shows the scope of the desolation that would afflict Moab.)

4 Moab is destroyed; her little ones have caused a cry to be heard. ("Her little ones" refer to children. They would suffer greatly!)

5 For in the going up of Luhith continual weeping shall go up; for in the going down of Horonaim the enemies have heard a cry of destruction. (A little over a hundred years before, as prophesied by Isaiah, Moab was subdued by Assyria and compelled to pay tribute [Isa., Chpts. 15-16]. But after Assyria fell, Moab was free again, but only until the Babylonians overran it. Therefore, the Moabites had been warned by God on at least two occasions regarding coming judgment, but they would heed neither warning!)

FLIGHT OF MOAB

6 Flee, save your lives, and be like the heath in the wilderness. (The phrase, "Flee, save your lives," could be literally translated: "Flee, save your souls." The statement is actually a plea by the Holy Spirit through the Prophet for Moab to get right with God. Proper Repentance, if not stopping the Babylonians, would at least have guaranteed favorable treatment, ensured by the Lord. In fact, this Prophecy is actually given for that very reason, that Moab may hear and, thereby, heed the Words of the Lord. It would have saved them terrible suffering and agony had they done so.)

7 For because you have trusted in your works and in your treasures, you shall also be taken: and Chemosh shall go forth into captivity with his priests and his princes together. (The urge for Repentance in the Sixth Verse is followed by the reason for the great need of Repentance. It speaks of their trust in idols, in this case, "Chemosh." Moab is called the land of the "people of Chemosh," the patron-god, the king and lord, of this people. This was a most hideous, heathenistic god, with the sacrifice of children as a burnt offering being a part of their worship of him [II Ki. 3:27]. All of this, and we speak of this system of worship, would be destroyed by the Babylonians.)

8 And the spoiler shall come upon every city, and no city shall escape: the valley also shall perish, and the plain shall be destroyed, as the LORD has spoken. ("The spoiler" is the Babylonian army.)

9 Give wings unto Moab, that it may flee and get away: for the cities thereof shall be desolate, without any to dwell therein. (The spirit of this Verse is the haste with which the Moabites will attempt to flee from their cities because of the attacking Babylonians.)

10 Cursed be he who does the work of the LORD deceitfully, and cursed be he who keeps back his sword from blood. (Babylon has been appointed by the Lord as the instrument

of chastisement for Moab. They are admonished not to "keep back the sword from blood"; hence, the fleeing of the Moabites from the cities!)

THE DESOLATION OF MOAB

11 Moab has been at ease from his youth, and he has settled on his lees, and has not been emptied from vessel to vessel, neither has he gone into captivity: therefore his taste remained in him, and his scent is not changed. *(Moab derived its name from a son of Lot who was born by an incestuous union between Lot and his older daughter [Gen. 19:37]. Moab is here likened to wine, and the Babylonian Monarch to a pourer-out of wine.)*

12 Therefore, behold, the days come, saith the LORD, that I will send unto him wanderers, that shall cause him to wander, and shall empty his vessels, and break their bottles. *(This speaks of the Babylonians pouring out the wine, i.e., the prosperity of Moab.)*

13 And Moab shall be ashamed of Chemosh, as the House of Israel was ashamed of Beth-el their confidence. *(The phrase, "As the House of Israel was ashamed of Beth-el their confidence," refers to Jeroboam, who set up a golden calf at Beth-el as a symbol of the strong God Jehovah. Even though symbolizing Jehovah, God called it idolatry, and it was odious in His sight.*

The Lord is here saying that as the "calf" was helpless to deliver Israel, likewise, "Chemosh" will be just as helpless.)

14 How say ye, We are mighty and strong men for the war? *(The Holy Spirit here belittles the supposed power of Moab.)*

15 Moab is spoiled, and gone up out of her cities, and his chosen young men are gone down to the slaughter, saith the King, Whose Name is the LORD of Hosts. *(The phrase, "Saith the King, Whose Name is the LORD of Hosts," refers to the boasts of the king of Moab versus the acclamation of the "King of Glory."*

The Holy Spirit is emphatic in this statement comparing "Kings": the absolute helplessness of the one and the absolute Sovereignty of the Other.)

16 The calamity of Moab is near to come, and his affliction hastes fast. *(Even though the Holy Spirit uses the phrases, "Near to come" and "Hastes fast," it would still be approximately 20 years before "the calamity of Moab." And yet, when the destruction would come, it would seem as though the time had passed*

very quickly.)

17 All ye who are about him, bemoan him; and all ye who know his name, say, How is the strong staff broken, and the beautiful rod! *(This expresses the sympathy extended by the surrounding nations concerning Moab's destruction. The country they thought was impregnable is destroyed by the Babylonians.)*

18 Thou daughter who does inhabit Dibon, come down from your glory, and sit in thirst; for the spoiler of Moab shall come upon you, and he shall destroy your strong holds. *(The phrase, "Sit in thirst," actually refers to sitting in the dust of defeat. Incidentally, "Dibon" was where the famous Moabite stone containing the inscription of king Mesha was found [II. 3:4]. This account commemorated the revolt of the king of Moab against Israel and his subsequent rebuilding of many important towns. This occurred approximately 300 years before Jeremiah [II Ki. 3:4-5].*

The stone was found on August 19, 1868 by the Rev. F. Klein, a German Missionary working with the Church Missionary Society. The great importance of the inscription on the stone linguistically, religiously, and historically lies in its close relation to the Old Testament.)

19 O inhabitant of Aroer, stand by the way, and espy; ask him who flees, and her who escapes, and say, What is done? *(It is interesting that "the way" was probably the king's highway, over which Moses had requested passage about 800 years before, but was refused [Deut. 2:27-30]. It is now traveled by Moabite fugitives fleeing for their lives from the Babylonian army.)*

20 Moab is confounded; for it is broken down: howl and cry; tell ye it in Arnon, that Moab is spoiled *(the word "confounded" means "to be brought to shame"),*

21 And judgment is come upon the plain country, upon Holon, and upon Jahazah, and upon Mephaath,

22 And upon Dibon, and upon Nebo, and upon Beth-diblathaim,

23 And upon Kiriathaim, and upon Beth-gamul, and upon Beth-meon,

24 And upon Kerioth, and upon Bozrah, and upon all the cities of the land of Moab, far or near. *(The purpose of these Verses is to portray the total destruction brought upon the entirety of Moab.)*

25 The horn of Moab is cut off, and his arm is broken, saith the LORD. *("The horn of Moab" refers to the "king of Moab.")*

REASONS FOR JUDGMENT

26 Make ye him drunken: for he magnified himself against the LORD: Moab also shall wallow in his vomit, and he also shall be in derision. *(The phrase, "For he magnified himself against the LORD," indicates a further reason for the judgment. At any earlier point, the Prophet said it was the callousness produced by long prosperity [Vs. 11]; but here another sin is mentioned — Moab's haughty contempt for Jehovah.*

In effect, this says that offenses against Israel, God's chosen People, irrespective of their spiritual condition, were also offenses against Israel's God. For instance, Moab laughed with derision when the Assyrians carried the Ten Tribes into captivity.)

27 For was not Israel a derision unto you? Was he found among thieves? For since you spoke of him, you skipped for joy. *(The question, "For was not Israel a derision unto you?", pertains to the unwarranted animosity of Moab for Israel, primarily because they were the people of Jehovah.)*

28 O ye who dwell in Moab, leave the cities, and dwell in the rock, and be like the dove that makes her nest in the sides of the hole's mouth. *(Upon the advance of the Babylonians, the Moabites would try to hide in the rocks and caves.)*

29 We have heard the pride of Moab, (he is exceeding proud) his loftiness, and his arrogancy, and his pride, and the haughtiness of his heart. *(The major cause of this "pride" which God hated was the worship of their heathenistic god, "Chemosh." They prided themselves that their god was greater than all others, even greater than the God of Israel and Judah. They were not content to merely believe this; they, as well, voiced it, and loudly! Hence, all the prosperity they attributed to Chemosh would be taken away by Jehovah of Judah.)*

30 I know his wrath, saith the LORD; but is shall not be so; his lies shall not so effect it. *(The phrase, "I know his wrath, saith the LORD," refers to Moab's railings against Jehovah.)*

LAMENT FOR MOAB

31 Therefore will I howl for Moab, and I will cry out for all Moab; my heart shall mourn for the men of Kir-heres. *(The judgment against Moab is to be so severe that Jeremiah, while understanding the justness of that judgment, still cannot help but be greatly moved, and "cry out for all Moab.")*

32 O vine of Sibmah, I will weep for you with the weeping of Jazer: your plants are gone over the sea, they reach even to the sea of Jazer: the spoiler is fallen upon your summer fruits and upon your vintage. *(This that they boasted Chemosh had given them is now to be taken away, and Chemosh will be helpless to stop it.)*

33 And joy and gladness is taken from the plentiful field, and from the land of Moab; and I have caused wine to fail from the winepresses: none shall tread with shouting; their shouting shall be no shouting. *(The phrase, "Their shouting shall be no shouting," means that there will be shouting, but not that of the peaceful vintagers at their work; instead, it will be the "shouting" of pain and sorrow.)*

34 From the cry of Heshbon even unto Elealeh, and even unto Jahaz, have they uttered their voice, from Zoar even unto Horonaim, as an heifer of three years old: for the waters also of Nimrim shall be desolate. *(This Passage speaks of the beautiful valleys of Moab which, because of their solitude, were thought to be beyond the grasp of the Babylonians. Such was not to be!)*

35 Moreover I will cause to cease in Moab, saith the LORD, him who offers in the high places, and him who burns incense to his gods. *(This speaks of the idol worship of Moab. The abominable "offerings in the high places" included the sacrifice of little baby boys and all its attendant horror! Therefore, the phrase, "I will cause to cease," irrespective of the manner, is welcomed by the honest heart.)*

36 Therefore my heart shall sound for Moab like pipes, and my heart shall sound like pipes for the men of Kir-heres: because the riches that he has gotten are perished. *(This refers to what was given, they claimed, by Chemosh, but would now be taken away by Jehovah.)*

37 For every head shall be bald, and every beard clipped: upon all the hands shall be cuttings, and upon the loins sackcloth. *(Cutting the hair, lacerating the hands, and wearing sackcloth were expressions of mourning in that society of long ago.)*

38 There shall be lamentation generally upon all the housetops of Moab, and in the streets thereof: for I have broken Moab like a vessel wherein is no pleasure, saith the LORD. *(Moab's usefulness as a nation has come to an end. Because of its many sins, it has reached the place that it must be excised, like a surgeon*

removing a cancer from a patient.)

39 They shall howl, saying, How is it broken down! How has Moab turned the back with shame! So shall Moab be a derision and a dismaying to all them about him. *(This Verse proclaims the end of the pride of Verse 29. Instead of pride, "Moab now has turned the back with shame!")*

REASON FOR BABYLONIAN INVASION

40 For thus saith the LORD; Behold, he shall fly as an eagle, and shall spread his wings over Moab. *(The pronoun "he" refers to Nebuchadnezzar, and the Verse refers to his speed in overrunning Moab, i.e., "fly as an eagle.")*

41 Kerioth is taken, and the strong holds are surprised, and the mighty men's hearts in Moab at that day shall be as the heart of a woman in her pangs. *(The hearts of her "mighty men," who had heretofore boasted of their invincibility, now palpitate as "the heart of a woman in her pangs.")*

42 And Moab shall be destroyed from being a people, because he has magnified himself against the LORD. *(The phrase, "Has magnified himself against the LORD," expresses the cause of the demise of all who ignore the Book, i.e., "the Bible.")*

43 Fear, and the pit, and the snare, shall be upon you, O inhabitant of Moab, saith the LORD. *(This Scripture proclaims the fact that "Chemosh" has not saved his people and in fact cannot save his people.)*

44 He who flees from the fear shall fall into the pit; and he who gets up out of the pit shall be taken in the snare: for I will bring upon it, even upon Moab, the year of their visitation, saith the LORD. *(This refers to a particular time that judgment would come upon Moab if they did not repent.)*

45 They who fled stood under the shadow of Heshbon because of the force: but a fire shall come forth out of Heshbon, and a flame from the midst of Sihon, and shall devour the corner of Moab, and the crown of the head of the tumultuous ones. *(This is quoted from Num. 21:28. But, whereas it meant one thing then [the conquest of Moab by Sihon, the giant king of the Amorites, some 800 years before], it now refers to Moab's destruction by the Babylonians.)*

46 Woe be unto you, O Moab! The people of Chemosh perish: for your sons are taken captives, and your daughters captives. *(This Passage is based on Num. 21:29. They had offered "sons" and "daughters" to this god in human sacrifice, and now their "sons" and "daughters" would be taken captive by the Babylonians.)*

FUTURE RESTORATION OF MOAB

47 Yet will I bring again the captivity of Moab in the latter days, saith the LORD. Thus far is the judgment of Moab. *(In all forty-seven Verses of this Chapter, this is the only mention of the coming Restoration of these ancient people called "Moabites." It will take place at the Second Coming.)*

CHAPTER 49
(600 B.C.)
PROPHECY CONCERNING THE AMMONITES

CONCERNING the Ammonites, thus saith the LORD; Has Israel no sons? Has he no heir? Why then does their king inherit Gad, and his people dwell in his cities? *(The "Ammonites" are the descendants of Ben-ammi, Lot's younger son by his daughter [an incestuous union], born in a cave near Zoar [Gen. 19:38]. They were regarded as relatives of the Israelites, who were commanded to treat them kindly [Deut. 2:19]. This country was on the east side of the Jordan River, and bordered Moab on the south.*

The Ammonites worshipped Molech [I Ki. 11:1, 5, 7, 33]. This worship was associated with the sacrifice of children in the fire [II Ki. 17:31; 23:10; Jer. 32:35].

The question, "Has Israel no sons?", refers to a part of Israel which the Ammonites were occupying, but which actually was owned by the Tribe of Gad.

The question, "Has he no heir?", concerns the following generation of Gadites, who should have inherited the land, but instead it was taken by the Ammonites.)

2 Therefore, behold, the days come, saith the LORD, that I will cause an alarm of war to be heard in Rabbah of the Ammonites; and it shall be a desolate heap, and her daughters shall be burned with fire: then shall Israel be heir unto them who were his heirs, saith the LORD. *(The chief city of Ammon was "Rabbah," which the Babylonians would make a "desolate heap.")*

3 How, O Heshbon, for Ai is spoiled: cry, you daughters of Rabbah, gird you with sackcloth; lament, and run to and fro by the hedges; for their king shall go into captivity, and his priests and his princes together. *(The phrase,*

"for their king shall go into captivity," refers to their idol god, "Molech."

The phrase, "How, O Heshbon," refers to the same city, Heshbon, mentioned in the previous Chapter, which was on the Moabite and Ammonite border, and whose ownership was constantly contested between the two countries.)

4 Wherefore gloriest thou in the valleys, your flowing valley, O backsliding daughter? who trusted in her treasures, saying, Who shall come unto me? (The question, "Who shall come unto me?", is now answered by the Prophet. The Ammonites will not escape the approaching Babylonian horde.)

5 Behold, I will bring a fear upon you, saith the Lord GOD of Hosts, from all those who be about you; and you shall be driven out every man right forth; and none shall gather up him who wanders. (When Jeremiah gave this Prophecy, which was approximately 20 years before its fulfillment, the Ammonites had only that long to exist as a cohesive country. But still, just as the Moabites, they refused to repent!)

6 And afterward I will bring again the captivity of the Children of Ammon, saith the LORD. (This statement is very similar to the prediction concerning the Moabites, which, in effect, states that Ammon will also be restored in the coming Kingdom Age. Perhaps it will be because of "righteous Lot" [II Pet. 2:7-8].)

PROPHECY AGAINST EDOM: DESOLATION

7 Concerning Edom, thus saith the LORD of Hosts; Is wisdom no more in Teman? is counsel perished from the prudent? is their wisdom vanished? (This Prophecy concerning Edom, which began with Esau and his country Idumea, should be read in the light of Heb. 12:16, where the Holy Spirit speaks of him as "a profane person." Hence his judgment as a nation will be as final as that of Sodom and Gomorrah. Edom was situated south of Moab, with its northern extremity touching the southern end of the Dead Sea.

The idea of this Verse is that for all the vaunted "wisdom" of the Edomites, they could not halt the coming Babylonians.)

8 Flee ye, turn back, dwell deep, O inhabitants of Dedan; for I will bring the calamity of Esau upon him, the time that I will visit him. (Edom had long been a bitter enemy of Israel, and would rejoice over the destruction of Jerusalem by the Chaldeans. They also showed great cruelty to the Jews who fled to them for refuge during that time. The Prophet is telling them that their rejoicing will be short-lived, because shortly after the fall of Jerusalem, Nebuchadnezzar will take out the countries east of the Jordan River, as well!)

9 If grapegatherers come to you, would they not leave some gleaning grapes? if thieves by night, they will destroy till they have enough. (The argument of Verses 9 and 10 is that a grapegatherer might leave a few grapes, or a housebreaker some pieces of property; but God, in His just severity, would absolutely extinguish Edom.)

10 But I have made Esau bare, I have uncovered his secret places, and he shall not be able to hide himself: his seed is spoiled, and his brethren, and his neighbours, and he is not. ("His secret places" referred to Petra and other mountain strongholds. The phrase, "And he is not," means that Edom shall cease to exist as a nation, even as Isaiah had also prophesied!)

11 Leave your fatherless children, I will preserve them alive; and let your widows trust in Me. (There is a promise here that the Lord will somewhat protect the women and children of Edom, a promise that was not given to Moab.)

12 For thus saith the LORD; Behold, they whose judgment was not to drink of the cup have assuredly drunken; and are you he who shall altogether go unpunished? You shall not go unpunished, but you shall surely drink of it. (The Lord did not plan for Israel to have to "drink of the cup of judgment." However, due to their forsaking Him and going into idol worship, they "have assuredly drunken."

The Lord then asks the question, "If I have punished My Own, shall you go unpunished?" He then answers His Own question by saying, "but you shall surely drink of it!")

13 For I have sworn by Myself, saith the LORD, that Bozrah shall become a desolation, a reproach, a waste, and a curse; and all the cities thereof shall be perpetual wastes. (Bozrah, a hill city, seems to have been the capital of Edom at one time.)

INVASION BY BABYLON; JUDGMENT AND FUTURE DESOLATION

14 I have heard a rumour from the LORD, and an ambassador is sent unto the heathen, saying, Gather ye together, and come against her, and rise up to the battle. (The result of these Prophecies will be the coming Babylonian horde.)

15 For lo, I will make you small among the heathen, and despised among men. (*Edom, for all her boasts, will be humbled, and even extinguished.*)

16 Your terribleness has deceived you, and the pride of your heart, O thou who dwells in the clefts of the rock, who holds the height of the hill: though you should make your nest as high as the eagle, I will bring you down from thence, saith the LORD. (*The phrase, "Your terribleness has deceived you," refers to the worship of her idol god, "Molech." The phrase, "O thou who dwells in the clefts of the rock," refers to Petra, which was a secure place for Edom for many centuries, and in fact was impregnable — until the Babylonians came!*)

17 Also Edom shall be a desolation: every one who goes by it shall be astonished, and shall hiss at all the plagues thereof. (*The "astonishment" is the reversal of this once flourishing kingdom.*)

18 As in the overthrow of Sodom and Gomorrah and the neighbour cities thereof, saith the LORD, no man shall abide there, neither shall a son of man dwell in it. (*The sense of this Verse does not mean that fire and brimstone will be the agents of destruction for Edom, but that the desolate appearance of Edom will remind one of the area around the Dead Sea [Isa. 13:19; Amos 4:11].*)

19 Behold, he shall come up like a lion from the swelling of Jordan against the habitation of the strong: but I will suddenly make him run away from her: and who is a chosen man, that I may appoint over her? For who is like Me? and who will appoint Me the time? And who is that shepherd who will stand before Me? (*The "he" in the first phrase is Nebuchadnezzar. The phrase, "But I will suddenly make him [Nebuchadnezzar] run away from her," does not imply this Monarch being defeated; instead it actually means that he will conquer Edom speedily and then go on to other conquests.*

The questions of this Verse are meant to point to the total inadequacy of the heathenistic god, Molech, while calling attention to the total supremacy of Jehovah.)

20 Therefore hear the counsel of the LORD, that He has taken against Edom; and His purposes that He (*the Lord*) has purposed against the inhabitants of Teman: Surely the least of the flock shall draw them out: surely he (*Nebuchadnezzar*) shall make their habitations desolate with them. (*The phrase, "The counsel of the LORD," is meant to imply that such*

is "framed" from eternity [Isa. 22:11; 37:26]; therefore, the statement does not imply a hastily called meeting, which would be incongruous to Deity.*)

21 The Earth is moved at the noise of their fall, at the cry the noise thereof was heard in the Red Sea. (*The phrase, "The Earth is moved," refers to the extinction of Edom as a nation, with no chance of restoration.*)

22 Behold, he (*Nebuchadnezzar*) shall come up and fly as the eagle, and spread his wings over Bozrah: and at that day shall the heart of the mighty men of Edom be as the heart of a woman in her pangs. (*Therefore, the last Scripture of the Prophecy concerning Edom does not close with a promised Restoration, as with Moab and Ammon, but with pain and suffering.*)

PROPHECY AGAINST DAMASCUS

23 Concerning Damascus, Hamath is confounded, and Arpad: for they have heard evil tidings: they are fainthearted; there is sorrow on the sea; it cannot be quiet. (*Damascus is the capital city of Syria, one of the oldest cities in the world [Isa. 7:8]. The "evil tidings," which produce the "fainthearted" spirit, are caused by the coming Babylonians. Syria will not escape. The phrase, "There is sorrow on the sea; it cannot be quiet," probably refers to the Mediterranean, which Syria then bordered on the west.*)

24 Damascus is waxed feeble, and turns herself to flee, and fear has seized on her: anguish and sorrows have taken her, as a woman in travail. (*The picture drawn by the Holy Spirit is one of extreme anxiety, which reached from border to border.*)

25 How is the city of praise not left, the city of My joy! (*The helplessness of Damascus is the subject of the lamentation.*)

26 Therefore her young men shall fall in her streets, and all the men of war shall be cut off in that day, saith the LORD of Hosts. (*The phrase, "And all the men of war shall be cut off in that day, saith the LORD of Hosts," refers not only to the Babylonian invasion, but to the coming Antichrist, as well. Every indication, according to Daniel's Prophecies, is that the Antichrist will be a "Syrian Jew" [Dan. 7:24-25; 8:9; 11:40-45].*)

27 And I will kindle a fire in the wall of Damascus, and it shall consume the palaces of Ben-hadad. (*The name "Ben-hadad" was the official title of the kings of Syria [I Ki. 15:18; II Ki. 13:3].*)

PROPHECY CONCERNING
KEDAR AND HAZOR

28 Concerning Kedar, and concerning the kingdoms of Hazor, which Nebuchadnezzar king of Babylon shall smite, thus saith the LORD; Arise ye, go up to Kedar, and spoil the men of the east. *(The implication of this Verse is that the idea in the mind of Nebuchadnezzar regarding the destruction of both "Kedar" and "Hazor" was placed there by the Lord, though unknown to the Monarch.)*

29 Their tents and their flocks shall they take away: they shall take to themselves their curtains, and all their vessels, and their camels; and they shall cry unto them, Fear is on every side. *(Everything will be taken by the Babylonians, including "their tents and their flocks.")*

30 Flee, get you far off, dwell deep, O ye inhabitants of Hazor, saith the LORD; for Nebuchadnezzar king of Babylon has taken counsel against you, and has conceived a purpose against you. *(The "purpose against you" refers to the Will of God placed, unknown to him, in the mind of Nebuchadnezzar. His plans were no doubt different from the Lord's, but God's "purposes" were carried out!)*

31 Arise, get you up unto the wealthy nation, that dwells without care, saith the LORD, which have neither gates nor bars, which dwell alone. *(It was unusual in those days for cities to not have walls, but "Kedar" had none. They thought their peaceful intentions would preserve them from all harm. They were to be greatly disappointed!)*

32 And their camels shall be a booty, and the multitude of their cattle a spoil: and I will scatter into all winds them who are in the utmost corners; and I will bring their calamity from all sides thereof, saith the LORD. *(Repentance could have greatly lessened the blow, with Babylon even possibly granting these people a degree of autonomy. However, Repentance was not forthcoming. Therefore, judgment came, because "thus saith the LORD.")*

33 And Hazor shall be a dwelling for dragons, and a desolation for ever: there shall no man abide there, nor any son of man dwell in it. *(Nothing is said of the future of "Kedar," while "Hazor" is consigned to "desolation forever.")*

PROPHECY CONCERNING ELAM:
DESTRUCTION AND DISPERSION
BY BABYLON

34 The word of the LORD that came to Jeremiah the Prophet against Elam in the beginning of the reign of Zedekiah king of Judah, saying *("Elam" was the name of the country originally possessed by the Persians, named after Elam, son of Shem [Gen. 10:22], which is present-day Iran. As this Prophecy predicted, it was subjected by Nebuchadnezzar, along with all other countries round about Babylon [Dan. 2:37-38].*

The phrase, "In the beginning of the reign of Zedekiah king of Judah," tells us that this Prophecy was given about 11 years before Jerusalem was destroyed. In fact, Elam probably fell before the destruction of Jerusalem),

35 Thus saith the LORD of Hosts; Behold, I will break the bow of Elam, the chief of their might. *(The archers of Elam were famous for their accuracy with the bow; however, this would not help them! They would be defeated by Nebuchadnezzar.)*

36 And upon Elam will I bring the four winds from the four quarters of Heaven, and will scatter them toward all those winds; and there shall be no nation whither the outcasts of Elam shall not come. *(Upon her defeat, the phrase says, "And there shall be no nation whither the outcasts of Elam shall not come." Elam will be defeated by the Babylonians, with her people fleeing to all the surrounding nations, just as many in Judah attempted to do.)*

DISMAY AS JUDGMENT COMES

37 For I will cause Elam to be dismayed before their enemies, and before them who seek their life: and I will bring evil upon them, even My fierce anger, saith the LORD; and I will send the sword after them, till I have consumed them *(the word "evil" means "judgment" because of the "fierce anger" of the Lord, caused by their sins, which were no doubt the same as the others, i.e., "idol worship," etc.):*

38 And I will set My throne in Elam, and will destroy from thence the king and the princes, saith the LORD. *(The phrase, "And I will set My throne in Elam," refers to the throne of Nebuchadnezzar, because it was God Who was giving the kingdom to the Babylonian Monarch. As a result, the leadership of Elam will be no more!)*

FUTURE RESTORATION OF ELAM

39 But if shall come to pass in the latter days, that I will bring again the captivity of Elam, saith the LORD. *(Elam is another of*

several nations God has promised to restore in the latter days, which will be the time of the Kingdom Age.)

CHAPTER 50
(595 B.C.)
PROPHECY CONCERNING BABYLON: INVASION BY MEDO-PERSIA

THE Word that the LORD spoke against Babylon and against the land of the Chaldeans by Jeremiah the Prophet. *(According to Gen. 10:10, Nimrod founded Babylon as his capital. The name "Babylon" comes from the Hebrew word "Babel," and was derived from the action of the Lord in "confounding their language." "Babel" means "confusion," which had to do with the confusion of languages, but more so with the confusion of man tendered by the Fall. Therefore, "Babylon," throughout its history, became a symbol of the pride of man in his inevitable Fall.)*

2 Declare ye among the nations, and publish, and set up a standard; publish, and conceal not: say, Babylon is taken, Bel is confounded, Merodach is broken in pieces; her idols are confounded, her images are broken in pieces. *(When Isaiah, well over 100 years before, predicted the rise of Babylon and its subsequent fall, it was, at that time, of little consequence. It actually was a vassal state of the Assyrian Empire, of which Nineveh was the capital city. Therefore, to the carnal ear, Isaiah's Prophecies would have been ludicrous!*

As well, Jeremiah's Prophecies concerning the fall of this mighty Empire, which was then the greatest in the world, would have been just as unbelievable.)

3 For out of the north there comes up a nation against her, which shall make her land desolate, and none shall dwell therein: they shall remove, they shall depart, both man and beast. *(The phrase, "Out of the north," refers to the Medes and the Persians, who would come from the north. The phrase, "And none shall dwell therein," has not actually been fulfilled, at least according to the Bible. While it is true that it is "desolate" today, and has been for quite some time, still, the Scripture tells us that it will be rebuilt in the last days, and then completely destroyed [Rev., Chpt. 18].)*

THE REGATHERING OF ISRAEL

4 In those days, and in that time, saith the LORD, the children of Israel shall come, they and the children of Judah together, going and weeping: they shall go, and seek the LORD their God. *(The phrase, "In those days, and in that time," has a double meaning! It refers, first of all, to the fall of Babylon at the hands of the conquering Medes and Persians, which allowed Israel to be restored to her land again. However, the greater fulfillment of this Verse pertains to the Second Coming of Christ, when Israel will be completely restored.)*

5 They shall ask the way to Zion with their faces thitherward, saying, Come, and let us join ourselves to the LORD in a perpetual covenant that shall not be forgotten. *(This will take place at the Second Coming of Christ.)*

6 My people have been lost sheep: their shepherds have caused them to go astray, they have turned them away on the mountains: they have gone from mountain to hill, they have forgotten their restingplace. *(This Passage will have its complete fulfillment in the coming Great Tribulation. At that time, a "foolish shepherd," i.e., the Antichrist [Zech. 11:15], will deceive the ancient people, Israel, with them believing he is the Messiah. This shepherd will "cause them to go astray." They will do so because "they have forgotten their restingplace," i.e., "Jehovah and the Bible.")*

7 All who found them have devoured them: and, their adversaries said, We offend not, because they have sinned against the LORD, the habitation of justice, even the LORD, the hope of their fathers. *(The phrase, "We offend not," pertains to Israel's enemies. They thought that because Israel had "sinned against the LORD" and had in fact been slated for judgment, their actions would be condoned. However, these enemies overstepped their bounds and did "offend God." By such, they incurred wrath upon themselves.)*

INVASION OF BABYLON

8 Remove out of the midst of Babylon, and go forth out of the land of the Chaldeans, and be as the he goats before the flocks. *(This Passage is telling Israel to be ready to leave when the change of government — from the Babylonians to the Medes and the Persians — takes place. Even though this Prophecy was given at the beginning of the dispersion, it would no doubt be a source of great encouragement to the exiles awaiting its fulfillment.)*

9 For, lo, I will raise and cause to come up

against Babylon an assembly of great nations from the north country: and they shall set themselves in array against her; from thence she shall be taken: their arrows shall be as of a mighty expert man; none shall return in vain. *(This refers to the Medes, the Persians, and other nations which came against Babylon and defeated her. The "mighty expert man" was Darius, who headed up the Medes, and Cyrus, who headed up the Persians. It is said that both were present at the fall of Babylon; therefore, either one could have fulfilled the Prophecy.)*

10 And Chaldea shall be spoil: all who spoil her shall be satisfied, saith the LORD. *(Babylon was so rich that all the invaders filled themselves to the full with the "spoil.")*

11 Because you were glad, because you rejoiced, O ye destroyers of My heritage, because you are grown fat as the heifer at grass, and bellow as bulls *(the phrase, "Because you were glad, because you rejoiced," refers to Babylon taking her commission too far as the "destroyers of My heritage." While it is true these idols worshippers were used by God as an instrument of chastisement, they did not do it with pity, but with rejoicing, which brought the judgment of God upon their own heads)*;

12 Your mother shall be sore confounded; she who bore you shall be ashamed: behold, the hindermost of the nations shall be a wilderness, a dry land, and a desert. *(The phrase, "Your mother shall be sore confounded," refers to the city of Babylon as the nourisher of the kingdom, but with the area gradually diminishing until it finally became "a wilderness, a dry land, and a desert," which it is presently.)*

13 Because of the wrath of the LORD it shall not be inhabited, but it shall be wholly desolate: every one who goes by Babylon shall be astonished, and hiss at all her plagues. *(For it to be fully understood, this Passage must be linked to Verses 39 and 40. Its total fulfillment awaits a future day, actually at the conclusion of the Great Tribulation [Rev., Chpt. 18].)*

14 Put yourselves in array against Babylon round about: all ye who bend the bow, shoot at her, spare no arrows: for she has sinned against the LORD. *(The phrase, "For she has sinned against the LORD," refers to the sins of Verse 11, which were the reason for the success of the Medes and the Persians, even though they would have had no knowledge of such.)*

15 Shout against her round about: she has given her hand: her foundations are fallen, her walls are thrown down: for it is the vengeance of the LORD: take vengeance upon her; as she has done, do unto her. *(What Babylon did to Judah would be done to her; and so it was. It is the same thing as said by Christ, "And with what measure you mete, it shall be measured to you again" [Mat. 7:2].)*

16 Cut off the sower from Babylon, and him who handles the sickle in the time of harvest: for fear of the oppressing sword they shall turn every one to his people, and they shall flee every one to his own land. *(This Verse expresses the thought that upon the invasion by the Medes and the Persians, many of the people from other countries who were in Babylon, whether slaves or high officials, would take the opportunity to flee.)*

BABYLON PUNISHED; ISRAEL TO BE RESTORED TO HER LAND

17 Israel is a scattered sheep; the lions have driven him away: first the king of Assyria has devoured him; and last this Nebuchadnezzar king of Babylon has broken his bones. *(Ironically, the emblem of both the Assyrians and the Babylonians, who greatly persecuted both the Northern Kingdom of Israel and the Southern Kingdom of Judah, was the "lion.")*

18 Therefore thus saith the LORD of Hosts, the God of Israel: Behold, I will punish the king of Babylon and his land, as I have punished the king of Assyria. *(The phrase, "Thus saith the LORD of Hosts, the God of Israel," is often used in these Passages to denote the power of Jehovah.)*

19 And I will bring Israel again to his habitation, and he shall feed on Carmel and Bashan, and his soul shall be satisfied upon Mount Ephraim and Gilead. *(This Passage goes beyond the Restoration of Israel after the dispersion; it leaps ahead to the Second Coming of Christ and Israel's acceptance of Him as Messiah and Lord, which will take place in the coming Kingdom Age.)*

20 In those days, and in that time, saith the LORD, the iniquity of Israel shall be sought for, and there shall be none; and the sins of Judah, and they shall not be found: for I will pardon them whom I reserve. *(The phrase, "In those days," refers to the final Restoration of Israel at the Second Coming of Christ [Zech. 13:1].)*

COMMAND TO DESTROY BABYLON

21 Go up against the land of Merathaim,

even against it, and against the inhabitants of Pekod: waste and utterly destroy after them, saith the LORD, and do according to all that I have commanded you. *(Through the Prophet, the Holy Spirit actually gives Babylon three symbolic names:*

1. Merathaim: it means "doubly rebellious."

2. Pekod: the word means "visitation" or "punishment."

3. Sheshach: the name conveys the meaning of "humiliation," meaning that God would humiliate Babylon, even as He did!)

22 A sound of battle is in the land, and of great destruction. *(These Passages pertain not only to the destruction of Babylon by the Medes and the Persians, but also point to the coming Battle of Armageddon in the closing days of the Great Tribulation.)*

23 How is the hammer of the whole Earth cut asunder and broken! how is Babylon become a desolation among the nations! *(Babylon, i.e., "Nebuchadnezzar," was God's "hammer" to break the nations; but judgment fell upon her because she rejected the Divine Revelation given to her through Daniel, when she exceeded her instructions [Dan. 5:17-23; Isa. 47:5-6; Zech. 1:15]. And yet, there is some small evidence that ultimately Nebuchadnezzar actually accepted the Lord [Dan. 4:34-35].)*

24 I have laid a snare for you, and you are also taken, O Babylon, and you were not aware: you are found, and also caught, because you have striven against the LORD. *(The phrase, "I have laid a snare for you, and you are also taken, O Babylon," refers to Cyrus diverting the Euphrates so he could use the river-bed as an entrance into the city.)*

25 The LORD has opened His armoury, and has brought forth the weapons of His indignation: for this is the work of the Lord GOD of Hosts in the land of the Chaldeans. *(This Passage refers to the fact that the Lord has the ability to use whatever He desires — be it nations, the elements, Angels, or individuals — in order to carry out His Work!)*

26 Come against her from the utmost border, open her storehouses: cast her up as heaps, and destroy her utterly: let nothing of her be left. *(The greater fulfillment will have to do with the coming Great Tribulation. Babylon is left to the last because it represents the entire rebellion against God. Its founder was Nimrod, whose name in the Hebrew is "Marad," which means "to rebel," or "we will rebel," and which points to a violent and open rebellion against*

God. *In fact, he established the first kingdom and the first great universal false religion opposing God.)*

27 Slay all her bullocks; let them go down to the slaughter: woe unto them! For their day is come, the time of their visitation. *(The phrase, "Slay all her bullocks," does not refer to cattle, but rather "Princes"!)*

28 The voice of them who flee and escape out of the land of Babylon, to declare in Zion the vengeance of the LORD our God, the vengeance of His Temple. *(The phrase, "To declare in Zion," refers to the remnant of Jews who will be allowed to return to the Land of Israel after the overthrow of "Babylon," who will tell of the destruction of that kingdom.*

The phrase, "The vengeance of the LORD our God, the vengeance of His Temple," is recorded in Dan. 5:1-5, which records the dishonor done to the Temple of Jehovah, when Belshazzar and his nobles drank wine out of the sacred vessels of the Temple, which then would cry aloud for vengeance. Of all the sins that Belshazzar committed, this was the worst!)

29 Call together the archers against Babylon: all ye who bend the bow, camp against it round about; let none thereof escape: recompense her according to her work; according to all that she has done, do unto her: for she has been proud against the LORD, against the Holy One of Israel. *(Even though Babylon was commissioned as God's hand of judgment against His Own People, she took the commission too far and engaged in wanton destruction and cruelty. Now her kingdom would be destroyed.)*

30 Therefore shall her young men fall in the streets, and all her men of war shall be cut off in that day, saith the LORD. *(When God fights, the efforts of resistance are useless!)*

31 Behold, I am against you, O thou most proud, saith the Lord GOD of Hosts: for your day is come, the time that I will visit you. *(The phrase, "O thou most proud," actually says, in the Hebrew, "O Pride"! As she represents the whole of mankind in his rebellion against God, "pride" is her crowning sin.)*

32 And the most proud shall stumble and fall, and none shall raise him up: and I will kindle a fire in his cities, and it shall devour all round about him. *(The phrase, "And the most proud shall stumble and fall," refers to Belshazzar, who was slain the very night the handwriting appeared on the wall [Dan. 5:30].*

In this Verse, the pronoun "him" is used because it refers not only to Belshazzar, but also to

the Antichrist. In the other Scriptures, Babylon is feminine in its translation, but here it is masculine, hence agreeing with "pride" and the Antichrist.)

33 Thus saith the LORD of Hosts; The children of Israel and the children of Judah were oppressed together: and all who took them captives held them fast; they refused to let them go. *(The statement, "They refused to let them go," refers to the Assyrians, who refused to release the captives of the Northern Kingdom, just as the Babylonians refused to release the captives of the Southern Kingdom of Judah. However, the Lord would terminate this captivity at His time, irrespective of the wishes of the captors.)*

34 Their Redeemer is strong; the LORD of Hosts is His Name: He shall thoroughly plead their cause, that He may give rest to the land, and disquiet the inhabitants of Babylon. *(The phrase, "He shall thoroughly plead their cause," refers to the Deliverance of the Children of Israel by God coming about not by mere power, but by Righteousness. For He pleads their cause, the plea being the Person and Atoning Work of their High Priest and Saviour, the Lord Jesus Christ.)*

IMMEDIATE JUDGMENT

35 A sword is upon the Chaldeans, saith the LORD, and upon the inhabitants of Babylon, and upon her princes, and upon her wise men. *(The "sword" is called by their "Strong Redeemer," and refers not only to the Medes and Persians, but also to the coming Battle of Armageddon.)*

36 A sword is upon the liars; and they shall dote: a sword is upon her mighty men; and they shall be dismayed. *(The Chaldeans claimed to be wise men. They especially boasted of their astrological knowledge. But, in this Verse, they are declared to be "liars," who shall be shown to be foolish by the nonfulfillment of their prognostications.)*

37 A sword is upon their horses, and upon their chariots, and upon all the mingled people who are in the midst of her; and they shall become as women: a sword is upon her treasures; and they shall be robbed. *(It was the duty of her "wise men," who were astronomers and astrologers at the various observatories in Babylonia, to submit monthly reports of the appearances in the sky, which were regarded as having an occult political significance. However, in their demon-inspired prognostications,*

they did not see the "sword," because God did not allow them to see the truth, but instead to see a lie and, thereby, "be robbed.")

38 A drought is upon her waters; and they shall be dried up: for it is the land of graven images, and they are made upon their idols. *(The phrase, "And they are made upon their idols," refers to their "terror" at realizing their idols and prognostications from their vaunted astrological predictions have fooled them, and in fact they are going to be destroyed!)*

FUTURE JUDGMENT

39 Therefore the wild beasts of the desert with the wild beasts of the islands shall dwell there, and the owls shall dwell therein: and it shall be no more inhabited for ever; neither shall it be dwelt in from generation to generation. *(This Verse pertains to Babylon, which will be rebuilt [Rev., Chpt. 18], and then completely and totally destroyed in the last weeks of the Great Tribulation, never to rise again [Isa. 13:6, 9, 19-22; Rev. 16:17-21; 18:1-24].)*

40 As God overthrew Sodom and Gomorrah and the neighbour cities thereof, saith the LORD; so shall no man abide there, neither shall any son of man dwell therein. *(When the Medes and Persians overthrew the Babylonian Empire, it was not at that time destroyed, as were "Sodom and Gomorrah," but in fact continued to exist as a city for some 500 more years. However, Rev. 16:19 does record the destruction of future Babylon as "Sodom and Gomorrah"!)*

41 Behold, a people shall come from the north, and a great nation, and many kings shall be raised up from the coast of the Earth. *(The "people from the north" are the Medes and Persians. The Holy Spirit now reverts back to the destruction of Babylon at the time of Daniel.)*

42 They shall hold the bow and the lance: they are cruel, and will not show mercy: their voice shall roar like the sea, and they shall ride upon horses, every one put in array, like a man to the battle, against thee, O daughter of Babylon. *(History records that the Medes and Persians "showed no mercy.")*

43 The king of Babylon has heard the report of them, and his hands waxed feeble: anguish took hold of him, and pangs as of a woman in travail. *(The phrase, "And his hands waxed feeble," refers to Belshazzar, of whom Daniel said was discomfited [Dan. 5:6], referring to the handwriting on the wall which foretold his defeat by the opposing army.)*

44 Behold, he shall come up like a lion from the swelling of Jordan unto the habitation of the strong: but I will make them suddenly run away from her: and who is a chosen man, that I may appoint over her? For who is like Me? and who will appoint Me the time? And who is that shepherd who will stand before Me? *(Who will do what I want to be done?)*

45 Therefore hear ye the counsel of the LORD, that He has taken against Babylon; and His purposes, that He has purposed against the land of the Chaldeans: Surely the least of the flock shall draw them out: surely He shall make their habitation desolate with them. *("The Counsel of the LORD" is that Babylon must be destroyed!)*

46 At the noise of the taking of Babylon the Earth is moved, and the cry is heard among the nations. *(Babylon was considered by the other nations of the world to be impregnable. Therefore, its destruction by Cyrus was hailed as one of the great feats of arms of that time, and by all nations.)*

CHAPTER 51
(595 B.C.)
THE LORD'S JUDGMENT ON BABYLON

T HUS saith the LORD; Behold, I will raise up against Babylon, and against them who dwell in the midst of them who rise up against Me, a destroying wind *(the essence of this Verse is: the Word of the Lord had been given to the Babylonian leaders by Daniel, the Hebrew children, and possibly others, but it was rejected; in fact, for the most part, it was greatly opposed!*

The phrase, "A destroying wind," referred to the coming Medes and Persians);

2 And will send unto Babylon fanners, who shall fan her, and shall empty her land: for in the day of trouble they shall be against her round about. *(The phrase, "And will send unto Babylon fanners," has reference to the threshing-floor, where the grain was separated from the chaff. The violent crushing of the stalk preceded this, typifying the destruction of Babylon.)*

3 Against him who bends let the archer bend his bow, and against him who lifts himself up in his brigandine: and spare ye not her young men; destroy ye utterly all her host. *(The idea of this Verse is that the expert "archers" of the Medes and Persians will find that their marksmanship is even more accurate, inasmuch as the Lord will actually help them, even though they will not be aware of such!)*

4 Thus the slain shall fall in the land of the Chaldeans, and they who are thrust through in her streets. *("Thrust through" has to do with the accuracy of the "archers" of Verse 3.)*

JUDAH AND ISRAEL STILL GOD'S CHOSEN PEOPLE

5 For Israel has not been forsaken, nor Judah of his God, of the LORD of Hosts; though their land was filled with sin against the Holy One of Israel. *(The phrase, "Though their land was filled with sin," means to be full of desolation in consequence of their guilt. The argument is that although the desolation of Israel seemed to evidence Jehovah's desertion of His People, the destruction of Babylon proved the contrary, hence the importance of the word "For.")*

FUTURE DESTRUCTION OF BABYLON

6 Flee out of the midst of Babylon, and deliver every man his soul: be not cut off in her iniquity; for this is the time of the LORD's vengence; He will render unto her a recompence. *(The command to flee out of Babylon actually pertains to Rev. 18:4.)*

7 Babylon has been a golden cup in the LORD's hand, that made all the Earth drunken: the nations have drunken of her wine; therefore the nations are mad. *(Babylon was the head of gold [Dan. 2:38], and the golden cup of dominion in the Earth was committed to her princes. But they filled that pure and costly vessel with the maddening wine of idolatry; hence, the justice of their doom.*

The phrase, "That made all the Earth drunken," refers to man's efforts to rebuild the Garden of Eden without the Tree of Life in its midst, i.e., "Christ."

Once again, this points to the coming Great Tribulation.)

8 Babylon is suddenly fallen and destroyed: howl for her; take balm for her pain, if so be she may be healed. *(The prediction of this Verse yet awaits fulfillment, for ancient Babylon was slowly, not suddenly, destroyed. Restored Babylon will perish like Sodom [Rev. 16:19; Chpts. 17-18].)*

IMMEDIATE DESTRUCTION

9 We would have healed Babylon, but she is not healed: forsake her, and let us go every one into his own country: for her judgment

reaches unto Heaven, and is lifted up even to the skies. *(The phrase, "We would have healed Babylon," refers to Daniel and the Hebrew children, plus others, attempting to turn Babylon from her evil ways, but to no avail. Similarly, the efforts of God's present people have also failed to heal corrupt Christendom, the modern spiritual Babylon. Hence, Paul would say, "Come out from among them" [II Cor. 6:17].)*

10 The LORD has brought forth our righteousness: come, and let us declare in Zion the work of the LORD our God. *(This Verse pertains to the Deliverance of the exiles, as well as their Restoration at a future day. In other words, it reaches even unto the coming Kingdom Age, which will see the last great Restoration.)*

11 Make bright the arrows; gather the shields: the LORD has raised up the spirit of the kings of the Medes: for his device is against Babylon, to destroy it; because it is the vengeance of the LORD, the vengeance of His Temple. *(The argument of Verses 11 through 14 is the uselessness of a military defense of Babylon, for God has purposed and would accomplish her destruction.)*

12 Set up the standard upon the walls of Babylon, make the watch strong, set up the watchmen, prepare the ambushes: for the LORD has both devised and done that which He spoke against the inhabitants of Babylon. *(God's dealings with this world concern two things: His children and His Plan. Consequently, anything that impacts His Children, as did Babylon, also involves His Plan and is, therefore, given to us in the Bible.)*

13 O thou who dwells upon many waters, abundant in treasures, your end is come, and the measure of your covetousness. *(The future reference of this Passage has to do with the efforts of the Antichrist to take over the world, which he will be well on his way to doing. In fact, he would succeed, but for the Coming of the Lord. However, the Second Coming will "cut him off.")*

14 The LORD of Hosts has sworn by Himself, saying, Surely I will fill you with men, as with caterpillars; and they shall lift up a shout against you. *(No doubt, Babylon's population during the siege by the Medes and the Persians swelled to possibly even several hundreds of thousands of people. But still, the great numbers would do no good, because the opposing force would be larger, and would "lift up a shout against you," i.e., a "victory shout.")*

15 He has made the Earth by His power; He has established the world by His wisdom, and has stretched out the Heaven by His understanding. *(The creative Power, Glory, and Wisdom of God are contrasted with the ignorance of idolaters and the vanity of their idols. The indication of this Verse is this:*

The Earth was made by the Lord and consequently belongs to Him. As well, "He has established" all its laws regarding its governance. This includes "the Heavens," i.e., the Universes, as well!

As such, He has the right to perform the necessary acts to save it from those who would destroy it; consequently, every system that is not of His making will ultimately be eliminated.)

16 When He utters His voice, there is a multitude of waters in the Heavens; and He causes the vapours to ascend from the ends of the Earth: He makes lightnings with rain, and brings forth the wind out of His treasures. *(This Verse says: The Lord controls the elements and does so by "uttering His Voice"; the elements instantly obey, but rebellious man will not obey!)*

17 Every man is brutish by his knowledge; every founder is confounded by the graven image; for his molten image is falsehood, and there is no breath in them. *(The phrase, "Every founder is confounded by the graven image," means that the worshipper of idols becomes like the idols. "His molten image is falsehood"; therefore, this "brutish man" is a lie and lives a lie. Such is the world without God!)*

18 They are vanity, the work of errors: in the time of their visitation they shall perish. *(The phrase, "They are vanity," speaks of all the works of man. Because of the way man fell in the Garden of Eden, and because of his unlawful quest to be like God [or, in fact, to be God], he has tried to fashion his own salvation. It is a "work of errors.")*

19 The portion of Jacob is not like them; for He is the former of all things: and Israel is the rod of His inheritance: the LORD of Hosts is His Name. *(The phrase, "The portion of Jacob," refers to Emmanuel. When the "Portion" is not Christ Alone, Babylon swallows the Church, even as Babylon has swallowed the Church.*

As "Israel" was the "rod," i.e., scepter, "of His inheritance," so today is the Church. The phrase means that Israel, as a son, will ultimately inherit the total kingdom.)

THE MEDES, GOD'S INSTRUMENT AGAINST BABYLON

20 You are My battle axe and weapons of

war: for with you will I break in pieces the nations, and with you will I destroy kingdoms (the phrase, "You are My battle axe and weapons of war," refers to Cyrus as the head of the Medes and Persians, who would execute God's vengeance and "destroy kingdoms");

21 And with you will I break in pieces the horse and his rider; and with you will I break in pieces the chariot and his rider (while the Medes and the Persians would be the instruments, Jehovah would be the Author);

22 With you also will I break in pieces man and woman, and with you will I break in pieces old and young; and with you will I break in pieces the young man and the maid (the judgment was just because all were involved in the rebellion against God. Cyrus, as stated, was to be this instrument);

23 I will also break in pieces with you the shepherd and his flock; and with you will I break in pieces the husbandman and his yoke of oxen; and with you will I break in pieces captains and rulers.

24 And I will render unto Babylon and to all the inhabitants of Chaldea all their evil that they have done in Zion in your sight, saith the LORD. (The commission given to Cyrus reveals the justice which inflicted on Babylon miseries similar to those that she inflicted on others.)

25 Behold, I am against you, O destroying mountain, saith the LORD, which destroyed all the Earth: and I will stretch out My hand upon you, and roll you down from the rocks, and will make you a burnt mountain. (In the Bible, great empires are addressed as "mountains," with the phrase, "Destroying mountain," referring to all the conquests of the Babylonian Empire. However, despite all of its power, the Lord said that He would make it a "burnt mountain." And so He did!)

BABYLON TO BE DESOLATE FOREVER

26 And they shall not take of you a stone for a corner, nor a stone for foundations; but you shall be desolate for ever, saith the LORD. (Once again, this Passage reaches forward to the coming Great Tribulation, when Babylon, the rebuilt city, will then be totally and completely destroyed, and done so instantly, one might say [Rev., Chpt. 18].)

27 Set ye up a standard in the land, blow the trumpet among the nations, prepare the nations against her, call together against her the kingdoms of Ararat, Minni, and Ashchenaz; appoint a captain against her; cause the horses to come up as the rough caterpillars. (The countries represented in this Passage are modern Armenia and Asia Minor. Verses 17 through 33 are another call for the immediate destruction of Babylon by the Medes and Persians, but with certain phrases referring to the coming Great Tribulation.)

28 Prepare against her the nations with the kings of the Medes, the captains thereof, and all the rulers thereof, and all the land of his dominion. (Jeremiah is giving this Prophecy about 50 years before the fall of Babylon, and yet the Lord proclaims the fact that it will be the "Medes" who will overcome this mighty Empire.)

29 And the land shall tremble and sorrow: for every purpose of the LORD shall be performed against Babylon, to make the land of Babylon a desolation without an inhabitant. (Once again, the essence of the Text leaps forward to the coming Great Tribulation.)

30 The mighty men of Babylon have forborne to fight, they have remained in their holds: their might has failed; they became as women: they have burned her dwellingplaces; her bars are broken. (This Passage predicts the coming softness of Babylon because of corruption. When the Medes and the Persians laid siege to the city, Babylon was no longer depending on her mighty army, but rather on the defenses of the impregnable city; impregnable they thought! Its leaders and military had grown lazy, corrupt, soft, and effeminate. Consequently, the Scripture aptly describes them when it says, "they became as women.")

31 One post shall run to meet another, and one messenger to meet another, to show the king of Babylon that his city is taken at one end (the phrase, "That his city is taken at one end," refers to the eastern portion being taken, after which the western portion fell!),

32 And that the passages are stopped, and the reeds they have burned with fire, and the men of war are affrighted. (Cyrus diverted the river, marched his soldiers down the dry bed, and seized the boats or ferries at each gate. He found the gates unlocked, which should have been closed to keep invaders out of the city. But through negligence, the gates were left open. Verses 30 through 32 proclaim this fact some 50 years before it actually happened.)

33 For thus saith the LORD of Hosts, the God of Israel; The daughter of Babylon is like a threshingfloor, it is time to thresh her: yet a little while, and the time of her harvest shall

come. (The phrase, "For thus saith the LORD of Hosts, the God of Israel," portrays the absolute control held by the Lord regarding the disposition of men, nations, and empires.)

ISRAEL'S COMPLAINT

34 Nebuchadnezzar the king of Babylon has devoured me, he has crushed me, he has made me an empty vessel, he has swallowed me up like a dragon, he has filled his belly with my delicates, he has cast me out. (Even though Nebuchadnezzar was commissioned by God to destroy Judah and Jerusalem, still, it seems he carried his commission too far, engaging Judah and Jerusalem with great cruelty.

But yet, the Lord dealt greatly with "Nebuchadnezzar" through the Prophet Daniel, with some indication that he made Jehovah his Saviour [Dan. 4:37].)

35 The violence done to me and to my flesh be upon Babylon, shall the inhabitant of Zion say; and my blood upon the inhabitants of Chaldea, shall Jerusalem say. (As "violence was done to me," i.e., Judah and Jerusalem, likewise, "violence" will be done to Babylon.)

GOD WILL AVENGE ISRAEL

36 Therefore thus saith the LORD; Behold, I will plead your cause, and take vengeance for you; and I will dry up her sea, and make her springs dry. (The phrase, "And I will dry up her sea," refers to Cyrus diverting the Euphrates, which enabled him to take the city. In this, the Lord would "plead the cause" of Israel.)

37 And Babylon shall become heaps, a dwellingplace for dragons, an astonishment, and an hissing, without an inhabitant. (The total fulfillment of this Passage awaits its future rebuilding and subsequent destruction, which will be done instantly [Rev., Chpt. 18].)

38 They shall roar together like lions: they shall yell as lions' whelps. (Babylon is symbolized by the Holy Spirit as a "lion" [Dan. 7:4]. However, their "roar," when attacked by the invader, will be as a little cub and, therefore, unable to defend themselves.)

39 In their heat I will make their feasts, and I will make them drunken, that they may rejoice, and sleep a perpetual sleep, and not wake, saith the LORD. (The drunken and boastful feast of Belshazzar is pictured in Verses 38 through 40. Historians suggest it was celebrated in honor of the great goddess "Shac," and was accompanied by grossly obscene ceremonies. The introduction of the Temple vessels [Dan. 5:2] into such an orgy of idolatry and impurity emphasizes the bold vileness of the Babylonian Monarch. That night they died!)

40 I will bring them down like lambs to the slaughter, like rams with he goats. (As Jerusalem was a "lamb to the slaughter," likewise was Babylon!)

41 How is Sheshach taken! and how is the praise of the whole Earth surprised! How is Babylon become an astonishment among the nations! (There is some evidence that one of the goddesses of the Babylonians was "Shac," i.e., "Sheshach."

The phrase, "The whole Earth surprised," refers to the supposed impregnability of Babylon and its subduction by Cyrus. As such, it "became an astonishment among the nations.")

42 The sea is come up upon Babylon: she is covered with the multitude of the waves thereof. (The "sea" and the "waves" are metaphors referring to the Medes and the Persians.)

43 Her cities are a desolation, a dry land, and a wilderness, a land wherein no man dwells, neither does any son of man pass thereby. (Once again, this pertains to the coming Great Tribulation, when rebuilt Babylon will be totally decimated, and in the time of one hour [Rev. 18:10].)

44 And I will punish Bel in Babylon, and I will bring forth out of his mouth that which he has swallowed up: and the nations shall not flow together any more unto him: yea, the wall of Babylon shall fall. ("Bel" was the patron deity of Babylon. The wall of Babylon was 300 feet high, 90 feet wide, and 60 miles long. It formed a square having 25 huge gates of brass and 250 towers on each face — in all, 100 brazen gates and 1,000 towers. However, these great walls were breached by the Medes and the Persians.)

COMMAND TO LEAVE BABYLON; JUDGMENT COMING

45 My people, go ye out of the midst of her, and deliver ye every man his soul from the fierce anger of the LORD. (If possible, the captive Jews were to leave the city at the time of the siege by the Medes and the Persians, because it was sure to fall and result in a great slaughter.)

46 And lest your heart faint, and you fear for the rumour that shall be heard in the land; a rumour shall both come one year, and after

than in another year shall come a rumour, and violence in the land, ruler against ruler. *(History records that the first year a rumor reached Babylon of the Median preparations for invasion; in the second year, a rumor arrived announcing that the Medes had set out on the expedition; and the following year, which was the third year of Belshazzar, they captured the city.)*

47 Therefore, behold, the days come, that I will do judgment upon the graven images of Babylon: and her whole land shall be confounded, and all her slain shall fall in the midst of her. *(Some 50 years before it actually happened, the Lord warned of the coming "judgment" because of Babylon's continued idol worship. Not only was this warning given here, but it was also given by Daniel and the Hebrew children, even at a later time. Therefore, Babylon was without excuse.)*

48 Then the Heaven and the Earth, and all that is therein, shall sing for Babylon: for the spoilers shall come unto her from the north, saith the LORD. *(The phrase, "Shall sing for Babylon," refers to rejoicing in both "Heaven" and "Earth" because of her destruction. This speaks of the coming Great Tribulation, when Babylon will be destroyed under the Seventh Vial [Rev., Chpt. 18].)*

49 As Babylon has caused the slain of Israel to fall, so at Babylon shall fall the slain of all the Earth. *(This Passage refers to the coming destruction of Babylon, as stated, under the Seventh Vial [Rev. 16:17-21]. In the last half of the Great Tribulation, Israel will face what looks like certain annihilation. Babylon, i.e., the Antichrist, will press for her destruction and come very close to succeeding, and would succeed, but for the Coming of the Lord; this Coming will occasion the slaying of possibly millions [Ezek., Chpts. 38-39].)*

COMMAND TO RETURN TO ZION

50 You who have escaped the sword, go away, stand not still: remember the LORD afar off, and let Jerusalem come into your mind. *(The phrase, "You who have escaped the sword," refers to the fact that possibly some of the exiles were killed in Babylon by the invasion by Cyrus. The exiles were to plan to return to Jerusalem just as soon as Cyrus gave the command [Ezra 1:1-4].*

The phrase, "Remember the LORD afar off," referred to His desired dwellingplace in Jerusalem. Hence, this was to be on their "mind.")

51 We are confounded, because we have heard reproach: shame has covered our faces: for strangers are come into the sanctuaries of the LORD's House. *(This refers to the soldiers of Nebuchadnezzar, who, when taking Jerusalem, went into the Temple, taking all its treasures, and then destroying the building.*

As a result, because of their 70 years of captivity, they have suffered "reproach" and "shame has covered our faces.")

JUDGMENT ON BABYLON

52 Wherefore, behold, the days come, saith the LORD, that I will do judgment upon her graven images: and through all her land the wounded shall groan. *(And that day did come, and the Babylonian Kingdom fell!)*

53 Though Babylon should mount up to Heaven, and though she should fortify the height of her strength, yet from Me shall spoilers come unto her, saith the LORD. *(The "height of her strength" refers to her walls being fortified, but to no avail! She would not recognize God; therefore, He sent "spoilers unto her," which spelled out trouble of every description, until finally she fell to the Medes and the Persians.)*

54 A sound of a cry comes from Babylon, and great destruction, from the land of the Chaldeans *(this was the "cry of defeat"!)*:

55 Because the LORD has spoiled Babylon, and destroyed out of her the great voice; when her waves do roar like great waters, a noise of their voice is uttered *(the "great voice" and "waves" were the loud boastings of Babylon. The boastings were silenced!)*:

56 Because the spoiler is come upon her, even upon Babylon, and her mighty men are taken, every one of their bows is broken: for the LORD God of recompences shall surely requite. *(The phrase, "For the LORD God of recompences shall surely requite," proclaims that which is true of not only God's dealings with ancient Babylon, but in every other circumstance, as well! [Mat. 7:2].)*

57 And I will make drunk her princes, and her wise men, her captains, and her rulers, and her mighty men: and they shall sleep a perpetual sleep, and not wake, saith the King, Whose Name is the LORD of Hosts. *(The "perpetual sleep" refers to the phrase, "In that night was Belshazzar the king of the Chaldeans slain" [Dan. 5:30]. The title "king" concerning Belshazzar is compared with the title "King, Whose Name is the LORD of Hosts." Of the two Kings,*

there is no comparison.)

58 Thus saith the LORD of Hosts; The broad walls of Babylon shall be utterly broken, and her high gates shall be burned with fire; and the people shall labour in vain, and the folk in the fire, and they shall be weary. *(Immense multitudes of slaves were employed in building the mighty walls and fashioning in the fire the brazen gates of Babylon; but their labor was in vain, and only secured weariness. This result is emphatically declared twice in Verses 58 and 64. Such is the one and only and invariable result of human toil, whether religious or physical, without God.*

Thus, this Fifty-eighth Verse concludes the Prophecy given to Jeremiah concerning Babylon and its destruction, which, as stated, was given about 50 years before the actual fact. It came true in totality, even as every Word of the Lord is true in totality!)

59 The word which Jeremiah the Prophet commanded Seraiah the son of Neriah, the son of Maaseiah, when he went with Zedekiah the king of Judah into Babylon in the fourth year of his reign. And this Seraiah was a quiet prince. *(The phrase, "In the fourth year of his reign," refers to the reign of Zedekiah, when he and Seraiah went to renew vows of allegiance to Babylon. However, soon after returning home, Zedekiah broke his vows and rebelled against the king of Babylon [II Ki. 24:17-20].*

"Seraiah" was probably in charge of the gifts that were to be made to the king of Babylon.)

60 So Jeremiah wrote in a Book all the evil that should come upon Babylon, even all these words that are written against Babylon. *(This Volume of Prophecies concerning Babylon was dispatched to that city some 6 years before the destruction of Jerusalem by the Babylonians. The exiles were instructed to read the Prophecies carefully, which no doubt strengthened them greatly, even in the time of their supreme calamity.)*

61 And Jeremiah said to Seraiah, When you come to Babylon, and shall see, and shall read all these words *(upon hearing these Prophecies read, the exiles probably wondered how such could even begin to come to pass; and yet those with faith knew that most assuredly they would come to pass);*

62 Then shall you say, O LORD, You have spoken against this place, to cut it off, that none shall remain in it, neither man nor beast, but that it shall be desolate for ever. *(What a statement, especially in view of the present splendor of Babylon! Only God could predict*

such, and many years before the fact, and bring it to pass.)

63 And it shall be, when you have made an end of reading this Book, that you shall bind a stone to it, and cast it into the midst of Euphrates:

64 And you shall say, Thus shall Babylon sink, and shall not rise from the evil that I will bring upon her: and they shall be weary. Thus far are the words of Jeremiah. *(The sinking of the stone with the Prophecies attached portrayed Babylon's demise. As well, this world's system, symbolized by Babylon of old, is going to "sink" and will "not rise from the evil [judgment] that God will bring upon her." This will happen at the Second Coming!)*

CHAPTER 52
(588 B.C.)
THE REIGN OF ZEDEKIAH

ZEDEKIAH was one and twenty years old when he began to reign, and he reigned eleven years in Jerusalem. And his mother's name was Hamutal the daughter of Jeremiah of Libnah. *(It is not known if Jeremiah is the author of this final Chapter, as the closing words of the last Verse of the previous Chapter might very well affirm that those words closed his Prophecies.*

The capture of Jerusalem and the deportation of its people have little interest for historians, but so great an interest for God that the event is narrated four times with considerable detail [II Ki. 24:25; II Chron., Chpt. 36; Jer. 29:52]. Incidentally, the Jeremiah of this Verse is not the Jeremiah of this Book.)

2 And he did that which was evil in the eyes of the LORD, according to all that Jehoiakim had done. *(Irrespective of God's Love, appalling chastisement must visit aggravated sinfulness. Therefore, Judah and Jerusalem were taken into captivity.*

Actually, Zedekiah was not of the royal line of David and, therefore, the last king to grace the throne who was in the royal line of David was Jehoiachin [Coniah].)

3 For through the anger of the LORD it came to pass in Jerusalem and Judah, till He had cast them out from His presence, that Zedekiah rebelled against the king of Babylon. *(The first part of this Verse refers to sin as the reason, which God cannot abide. "Zedekiah rebelled against the king of Babylon" because he thought Egypt would come to his rescue.*

Actually, Zedekiah rebelled against the Lord.)

THE FALL OF JERUSALEM

4 And it came to pass in the ninth year of his reign, in the tenth month, in the tenth day of the month, that Nebuchadnezzar king of Babylon came, he and all his army, against Jerusalem, and pitched against it, and built forts against it round about. *(The Holy Spirit records the exact day of the siege, because it was "against Jerusalem," which was His City and the place of His Dwelling. However, He would now leave it, as recorded in Ezek. 11:23.)*

5 So the city was besieged unto the eleventh year of king Zedekiah. *(Jerusalem, in her backsliding, did not understand Who her Saviour was and, therefore, trusted in Egypt, who could not even save herself, much less Judah and Jerusalem! Therefore, the Holy Spirit proclaims, "the city was besieged.")*

6 And in the fourth month, in the ninth day of the month, the famine was sore in the city, so that there was no bread for the people of the land. *(Exactly what Moses said in Deut., Chpt. 28, was now coming to pass.)*

7 Then the city was broken up, and all the men of war fled, and went forth out of the city by night by the way of the gate between the two walls, which was by the king's garden; (now the Chaldeans were by the city round about:) and they went by the way of the plain. *(For some 40 years, Jeremiah had warned of this time, pleading with the people to repent, but to no avail! Now, and exactly as the Holy Spirit through the Prophet had said, all comes to pass. How this must have crushed the already broken heart of the Prophet!)*

JUDGMENT ON ZEDEKIAH

8 But the army of the Chaldeans pursued after the king, and overtook Zedekiah in the plains of Jericho; and all his army was scattered from him. *(No amount of skill or sagacity can defeat the purposes and judgments of God. Zedekiah and his soldiers thought to escape by making a hole in the city wall at night-time; but they were defeated and captured at the very scene of Israel's first victory many hundreds of years before, which was "Jericho.")*

9 Then they took the king, and carried him up unto the king of Babylon to Riblah in the land of Hamath; where he gave judgment upon him. *(The "king of Babylon" was*

Nebuchadnezzar. The phrase, "Where he gave judgment upon him," refers to a terrible severity.)

10 And the king of Babylon slew the sons of Zedekiah before his eyes: he slew also all the princes of Judah in Riblah.

11 Then he put out the eyes of Zedekiah; and the king of Babylon bound him in chains, and carried him to Babylon, and put him in prison till the day of his death. *(The prison was a house of hard labor. And yet, there is some small evidence that Zedekiah came to the Lord while in this "prison.")*

JERUSALEM DESTROYED;
FINAL CAPTIVITY OF JUDAH;
A REMNANT LEFT

12 Now in the fifth month, in the tenth day of the month, which was the nineteenth year of Nebuchadnezzar king of Babylon, came Nebuzar-adan, captain of the guard, which served the king of Babylon, into Jerusalem *(II Ki. 25:8 says, "The seventh day of the month." However, there is no discrepancy. II Kings uses the words, "unto Jerusalem," whereas the words here are "into Jerusalem." The two are not the same; the former refers to the approach to the city, while the latter refers to actually entering the city. Evidently, "Nebuzar-adan" needed some three days of preparation after arriving outside the city before entering it),*

13 And burned the House of the LORD, and the king's house; and all the houses of Jerusalem, and all the houses of the great men, burned he with fire *(the Lord allowed "His House" to be burned because His People had discredited it):*

14 And all the army of the Chaldeans, who were with the captain of the guard, broke down all the walls of Jerusalem round about. *(Their protection and security depended on their obedience to God. Upon obedience, no power on Earth could defeat them. Upon disobedience, the Lord lifted His Hand of protection, and the walls were broken.)*

15 Then Nebuzar-adan the captain of the guard carried away captive certain of the poor of the people, and the residue of the people who remained in the city, and those who fell away, who fell to the king of Babylon, and the rest of the multitude. *(Upon the advent of disobedience, the Lord's Hand is lifted, and the end result is the same as then, i.e., captive of Satan.)*

16 But Nebuzar-adan the captain of the guard left certain of the poor of the land for

vinedressers and for husbandmen. *(The "poor of the land" refers to those who had been slaves, or else nearly so, and had consequently been denied ownership of property, but now would be the possessors of the finest "land" and "vineyards" in Judah.)*

TEMPLE RICHES TAKEN

17 Also the pillars of brass that were in the House of the LORD, and the bases, and the Brazen Sea that was in the House of the LORD, the Chaldeans broke, and carried all the brass of them to Babylon. *(The breaking of these symbols and the carrying of them to "Babylon" would sadly signify the victory of the flesh over the Spirit. Such was the ruin of Judah, and such is the ruin of the modern Believer.)*

18 The caldrons also, and the shovels, and the snuffers, and the bowls, and the spoons, and all the vessels of brass wherewith they ministered, took they away. *(These words could hold little meaning to the carnal mind, but are given here with a sob by the Holy Spirit. These symbols of worship were removed, because the people no longer worshipped God, but rather idols.)*

19 And the basons, and the firepans, and the bowls, and the caldrons, and the candlesticks, and the spoons, and the cups; that which was of gold in gold, and that which was of silver in silver, took the captain of the guard away. *(These beauteous and precious vessels and pillars pictured the Power and Glories of Christ, which Judah no longer desired. So they lost them!)*

20 The two pillars, one sea, and twelve brazen bulls that were under the bases, which king Solomon had made in the House of the LORD: the brass of all these vessels was without weight. *(These "twelve brazen bulls" or oxen were designed by the Holy Spirit, with the design given to David, and he to Solomon. They represented the Word of God [I Ki. 7:25-26]. These oxen or "bulls" were placed three to the side, portraying the Word of God as applicable to all directions: north, south, east, and west.)*

21 And concerning the pillars, the height of one pillar was eighteen cubits; and a fillet of twelve cubits did compass it; and the thickness thereof was four fingers: it was hollow.

22 And a chapiter of brass was upon it; and the height of one chapiter was five cubits, with network and pomegranates upon the chapiters round about, all of brass. The second pillar also and the pomegranates were like unto these. *("Pomegranates" are fruit, and thus symbolized*

the fruitfulness of the Child of God [Jn. 15:1-5]. In the Passage in St. John, He says, "Every branch in Me that bears not fruit, He takes away," symbolizing the removal carried out by Babylon.)*

23 And there were ninety and six pomegranates on a side; and all the pomegranates upon the network were an hundred round about. *(Such symbolized the "much fruit" spoken of by Christ in Jn. 15:5. Each "pomegranate" was precious to Him, and should be precious to us, as well!)*

PRIESTS AND PRINCES EXECUTED

24 And the captain of the guard took Seraiah the Chief Priest, and Zephaniah the second Priest, and the three keepers of the door *(the "three keepers of the door" were taken and executed, because they did not truly "keep the door." The Preacher of the Gospel is the "keeper of the door," and if he does not keep Babylon from it, Babylon will come into it)*:

25 He took also out of the city an eunuch, which had the charge of the men of war; and seven men of them who were near the king's person, which were found in the city; and the principal scribe of the host, who mustered the people of the land; and threescore men of the people of the land, who were found in the midst of the city. *(II Ki. 25:19 records "five men." This marks accuracy and not error, for the greater includes the less, and since Riblah was many days journey from Jerusalem, two of the captives may have escaped or died during the journey.)*

26 So Nebuzar-adan the captain of the guard took them, and brought them to the king of Babylon to Riblah.

27 And the king of Babylon smote them, and put them to death in Riblah in the land of Hamath. Thus Judah was carried away captive out of his own land. *(Of all the captivity spread out over a number of years, the captivity of this Verse is actually the great captivity when Jerusalem was destroyed.)*

THREE DEPORTATIONS TO BABYLON

28 This is the people whom Nebuchadnezzar carried away captive: in the seventh year three thousand Jews and three and twenty *(the Hebrews and the Babylonians did not reckon time in exactly the same manner. Hence, the seventh year of Nebuchadnezzar according to the*

one reckoning would be the eighth according to the other [II Ki. 24:12, 14, 16]. This is the first deportation, which was under Jehoiakim. During this time, Daniel and the three Hebrew children were taken to Babylon, with many others):

29 In the eighteenth year of Nebuchadnezzar he carried away captive from Jerusalem eight hundred thirty and two persons *(this would have been the second deportation under Jehoiachin. In this, Mordecai and Esther were taken to Babylon [Esther 2:5-6]):*

30 In the three and twentieth year of Nebuchadnezzar Nebuzar-adan the captain of the guard carried away captive of the Jews seven hundred forty and five persons: all the persons were four thousand and six hundred. *(This was the last deportation, which was under Zedekiah, during which time Jerusalem was completely destroyed, including the Temple.)*

JEHOIACHIN RELEASED IN BABYLON

31 And it came to pass in the seven and thirtieth year of the captivity of Jehoiachin king of Judah, in the twelfth month, in the five and twentieth day of the month, that Evil-merodach king of Babylon in the first year of his reign lifted up the head of Jehoiachin king of Judah, and brought him forth out of prison.

("Jehoiachin" was only 18 years old when he began to reign, and actually only reigned for "three months and ten days in Jerusalem." As well, Jehoiachin was the last king in the Davidic line, as Zedekiah, although of the royal family, was not in the kingly line, being only an uncle of Jehoiachin.

Jehoiachin was in captivity for 37 years; thus, he would have been 55 years old at the time he was freed from prison.)

32 And spoke kindly unto him, and set his throne above the throne of the kings who were with him in Babylon *(these were perhaps captive kings who had been taken in the many campaigns of Nebuchadnezzar),*

33 And changed his prison garments: and he did continually eat bread before him all the days of his life. *(It is not known why Jehoiachin was favored by the king of Babylon. As well, nothing is known of his spiritual condition.)*

34 And for his diet, there was a continual diet given him of the king of Babylon, every day a portion until the day of his death, all the days of his life. *("Evil-merodach" was the son of Nebuchadnezzar. Perhaps his favorable treatment of "Jehoiachin" was the result of the influence of his father Nebuchadnezzar, who showed some inclination in his closing years of turning to Jehovah.)*

THE
LAMENTATIONS
OF JEREMIAH

CHAPTER 1
(588 B.C.)
SORROW OVER JERUSALEM'S DESOLATE STATE

HOW does the city sit solitary, that was full of people! how is she become as a widow! she that was great among the nations, and Princess among the provinces, how is she become tributary! *(The word "How" opens the "Lamentations of Jeremiah." What makes the word so amazing is that it is asked by the Holy Spirit, not as a question, but as an exclamation! How could this have happened to Jerusalem? These, who are now on their way to captivity in Babylon, are the People of God. This ruined city is His City! The Temple where He once dwelt now lies a smoking ruin. How could this have happened?!)*

2 She weeps sore in the night, and her tears are on her cheeks: among all her lovers she has none to comfort her: all her friends have dealt treacherously with her, they are become her enemies. *(Who are these "lovers" and "friends" who have "dealt treacherously with her" and "become her enemies"? These are the Edomites, Ammonites, Moabites, etc. These are the neighboring nations with which Judah formed alliances, which included Egypt, as well! The Holy Spirit brings it out that she preferred these to Jehovah. As well, their gods were made her gods. But where are they now?*

The spirit of the Text is that trust must never be placed in man, but in God Alone [Prov. 18:24].)

3 Judah is gone into captivity because of affliction, and because of great servitude: she dwells among the heathen, she finds no rest: all her persecutors overtook her between the straits. *(Judah's captivity was to be an exile of "affliction" and "great servitude." She served heathen gods; now she must serve their master, Satan. She will find him a hard taskmaster! "She now dwells among the heathen." She desired their ways, and now she is given nothing but their ways. Consequently, she "finds no rest.")*

4 The ways of Zion do mourn, because none come to the solemn feasts: all her gates are desolate: her Priests sigh, her virgins are afflicted, and she is in bitterness. *(The "ways of Zion" were the Ways of God; however, Judah forsook those Ways for the world. But she found only "bitterness.")*

5 Her adversaries are the chief, her enemies prosper; for the LORD has afflicted her for the multitude of her transgressions: her children are gone into captivity before the enemy. *(Long before Judah was a people or Jerusalem was a city, Moses had said that this would happen if she turned her back on God [Deut., Chpt. 28].)*

6 And from the daughter of Zion all her beauty is departed: her princes are become like harts that find no pasture, and they are gone without strength before the pursuer. *(The phrase, "All her beauty is departed," refers to "her glory." This "glory" was God, Who is now "departed." The "pursuer" is Satan, and Judah has no "strength" to resist him.)*

JERUSALEM'S PAST MEMORIES

7 Jerusalem remembered in the days of her affliction and of her miseries all her pleasant things that she had in the days of old, when her people fell into the hand of the enemy, and none did help her: the adversaries saw her, and did mock at her sabbaths. *(The "days of old" refer to the times when God was paramount, and Judah and Jerusalem enjoyed His Blessings. These are "pleasant things." Now they are gone! As she suffers in "affliction and misery," she can only "remember"!)*

8 Jerusalem has grievously sinned; therefore she is removed: all who honoured her despise her, because they have seen her nakedness: yea, she sighs, and turns backward. *(Sin was the procuring cause of the city's ruin. She had "grievously sinned." As a result of her refusing to repent, "she is removed." Those who once "honored her" now "despise her."*

Satan does that! He uses a person up, and then he throws them aside.)

9 Her filthiness is in her skirts; she remembers not her last end; therefore she came down

wonderfully: she had no comforter. O LORD, behold My affliction: for the enemy has magnified himself. *(The phrase, "Her filthiness is in her skirts," means that for a period of time her defilement was hidden underneath her skirts [Jer. 13:22]. Now these skirts have been removed, and her "nakedness" is obvious to all!*

The expression, "O LORD, behold My affliction," is the Messiah impersonating Jerusalem. Now, their affliction becomes His affliction. Such Love one cannot understand! Such is His Intercessory role, not only then, but now [Heb. 7:25].)

10 The adversary has spread out his hand upon all her pleasant things: for she has seen that the heathen entered into her Sanctuary, whom You did command that they should not enter into Your congregation. *(The phrase, "The heathen entered into her Sanctuary," refers to the soldiers of Nebuchadnezzar entering into the Temple, and even into the Holy of Holies, and all because Judah had long since lost the meaning of these things [Deut. 23:3; Ezek. 44:9].)*

11 All her people sigh, they seek bread; they have given their pleasant things for meat to relieve the soul: see, O LORD, and consider; for I am become vile. *(The phrase, "They seek bread," refers to natural food, which was in short supply. They had come to this place, the place of starvation, because they forsook the "spiritual bread," i.e., the Word of God.)*

JERUSALEM'S SORROW; JUDGMENTS

12 Is it nothing to you, all you who pass by? behold, and see if there be any sorrow like unto my sorrow, which is done unto me, wherewith the LORD has afflicted me in the day of His fierce anger. *(The Holy Spirit desires the Reader to know and understand that it is not Nebuchadnezzar who brought this on, but "the LORD." His "anger" was "fierce" because Judah's sin was "fierce.")*

13 From above has He sent fire into my bones, and it prevails against them: He has spread a net for my feet, He has turned me back: He has made me desolate and faint all the day. *(When the Messiah's soul was made an Offering for sin upon the Altar of Calvary [Isa. 53:10], then Verses 12 through 15 were fulfilled; for although these words have an application to Jerusalem, their interpretation belongs to Him.)*

14 The yoke of my transgressions is bound by His hand: they are wreathed, and come up upon my neck: He has made my strength to fall, the LORD has delivered me into their hands, from whom I am not able to rise up. *(As stated, Jerusalem is addressed, but Christ is intended. As God compelled Judah to bear the punishment of her sins like wearing a yoke or wreath around her neck, likewise, He compelled Christ to do the same in order to deliver man [II Cor. 5:21].*

The Lord did such to Jerusalem because they would not heed His clarion call to repent, and He did it to Christ in order that man may be delivered from the terrible, crushing blow of sin. The load was so heavy that they were "not able to rise up"; however, the Lord, i.e., "Adonai," raised Christ from the dead, and He will yet restore Judah and Jerusalem.)

15 The LORD has trodden under foot all my mighty men in the midst of me: He has called an assembly against me to crush my young men: the LORD has trodden the virgin, the daughter of Judah, as in a winepress. *(This Verse proclaims the fact that Judah trusted in her "mighty men" and her "young men" rather than God. As a result, "the LORD has trodden under foot" all those on whom Judah depended.)*

16 For these things I weep; my eye, my eye runs down with water, because the comforter that should relieve my soul is far from me: my children are desolate, because the enemy prevailed. *(If Judah had wept as Jeremiah now "weeps," the "enemy" would never have "prevailed.")*

17 Zion spreads forth her hands, and there is none to comfort her: the LORD has commanded concerning Jacob, that his adversaries should be round about him: Jerusalem is as a menstruous woman among them. *(Judah spurned the call so long, until "the LORD has commanded concerning Jacob" that judgment must come; and judgment did come! As a "menstruous woman," Jerusalem must go through her period of uncleanliness and, thereby, become purified before she will be acceptable. This will happen as the Second Coming. The Prophet Zechariah said so [Zech. 13:1].)*

18 The LORD is righteous; for I have rebelled against His commandment: hear, I pray you, all people, and behold my sorrow: my virgins and my young men are gone into captivity. *(True Repentance vindicates God and condemns self!)*

19 I called for my lovers, but they deceived me: my Priests and my Elders gave up the ghost in the city, while they sought their meat to relieve their souls. *(These "lovers" were the surrounding nations, who had proclaimed their*

devotion to Judah, but in fact "deceived me." Judgment was poured out upon the "Priests" and "Elders" as well! In fact, they were singled out, because they led the parade of rebellion against God and against His Word.)

JEREMIAH'S DISTRESS

20 Behold, O LORD; for I am in distress: my bowels are troubled; my heart is turned within me; for I have grievously rebelled: abroad the sword bereaves, at home there is as death. (The Holy Spirit here proclaims to us the fact of Judah's "distress," her "trouble," and her "broken heart." All of this is because they have "grievously rebelled" against God.)

21 They have heard that I sigh: there is none to comfort me: all my enemies have heard of my trouble; they are glad that You have done it: You will bring the day that You have called, and they shall be like unto me. (The phrase, "They are glad that You have done it," refers to the gloating of Judah's enemies over her destruction. Jehovah shows His People that their safety, security, and protection never were in these nations or alliances with them, but in Jehovah. It's a lesson the modern Church desperately needs to learn!)

22 Let all their wickedness come before You; and do unto them, as You have done unto me for all my transgressions: for my sighs are many, and my heart is faint. (The terms of this proclamation are found in Jer., Chpts. 50-51, which declare that the Medes will inflict the same cruelty upon Babylon which Babylon inflicted upon Jerusalem. From this fact may be learned the lesson not to rejoice when calamity falls upon an enemy. The evil which brought judgment upon him also dwells in us! As such, none has any right to boast, but rather to mourn.)

CHAPTER 2
(588 B.C.)
ZION UNDER JUDGMENT

HOW has the LORD covered the daughter of Zion with a cloud in His anger, and cast down from heaven unto the Earth the beauty of Israel, and remembered not His footstool in the day of His anger! (The deep sorrow of this Chapter is occasioned by the recognition of the fact that the wrath which overthrew the Temple was Divine Wrath. Never had there been, therefore, such sorrow. But this foreshadowed the Wrath which smote the True Temple at Calvary. That was sorrow indeed, for that Temple was without blemish and undefiled, while the Temple at Jerusalem, which God had planned and set up, had been polluted by man.)

2 The LORD has swallowed up all the habitations of Jacob, and has not pitied: He has thrown down in His wrath the strongholds of the daughter of Judah; He has brought them down to the ground: He has polluted the kingdom and the princes thereof. (These Verses plainly proclaim the fact that God was the sole Source of Judah's blessings, as He is the sole Source of the blessings of the Church. If He is repeatedly insulted by sin, with a refusal to repent, He will "throw down" the Church "in His Wrath," exactly as He did Jerusalem of old. Paul said so [Rom. 11:18-22].)

3 He has cut off in His fierce anger all the horn of Israel: He has drawn back His right hand from before the enemy, and He burned against Jacob like a flaming fire, which devours round about. (The phrase, "The horn of Israel," refers to the kings of Israel. He had "cut them off in His fierce anger" because of sin. The phrase, "He has drawn back His right hand from before the enemy," refers to the Lord lifting His Hand of protection over Israel, permitting the enemy to destroy His People. Repentance would have stopped this, but, despite Prophet after Prophet being sent by the Lord, with Jeremiah being the last, Jacob would not repent [Mat. 23:37].)

4 He has bent His bow like an enemy: He stood with His right hand as an adversary, and slew all who were pleasant to the eye in the Tabernacle of the daughter of Zion: He poured out His fury like fire. (Even though Nebuchadnezzar was the instrument, the Lord was the Author. He actually became Israel's "Adversary.")

5 The LORD was as an enemy: He has swallowed up Israel, He has swallowed up all her palaces: He has destroyed His strongholds, and has increased in the daughter of Judah mourning and lamentation. (The phrase, "The LORD was as an enemy," does not actually say that He was an enemy, but "as an enemy." In other words, He Who was accustomed to blessing Israel now does them harm, as an enemy would do, again, because they would not repent.)

6 And He has violently taken away His tabernacle, as if it were of a garden: He has destroyed His places of the assembly: the LORD has caused the solemn Feasts and Sabbaths to be forgotten in Zion, and has despised in the

indignation of His anger the king and the Priest. *(This Verse proclaims the apparatus of the entire worship of God being taken away. It included "His Tabernacle," which pertained to all the Holy Vessels, which symbolized the Coming Redeemer. In fact, He took everything away, because Israel had grossly polluted it.)*

7 The LORD has cast off His Altar, He has abhorred His Sanctuary, He has given up into the hand of the enemy the walls of her palaces; they have made a noise in the House of the LORD, as in the day of a solemn feast. *(The phrase, "The LORD has cast off His Altar," is awful indeed! This was the Brazen Altar, which was a type of Calvary. They didn't want the "Cross," so the Lord took the "Cross" away!)*

8 The LORD has purposed to destroy the wall of the daughter of Zion: He has stretched out a line, He has not withdrawn His hand from destroying: therefore He made the rampart and the wall to lament; they languished together. *(The phrase, "He has stretched out a line," expressed unsparing demolition [II Ki. 21:13].)*

ZION'S HUMILIATION

9 Her gates are sunk into the ground; He has destroyed and broken her bars: her king and her princes are among the Gentiles: the Law is no more; her Prophets also find no vision from the LORD. *(The phrase, "The Law is no more," is devastating! A material Temple was indispensable to its continued existence and enforcement; however, the Temple was destroyed and the Sacrifices were stopped! The only Light was now extinguished!)*

10 The elders of the daughter of Zion sit upon the ground, and keep silence: they have cast up dust upon their heads; they have girded themselves with sackcloth: the virgins of Jerusalem hang down their heads to the ground. *(If the action of this Verse had been done when the Lord commanded them to repent, the horror of this time would never have happened!)*

11 My eyes do fail with tears, my bowels are troubled, my liver is poured upon the Earth, for the destruction of the daughter of my people; because the children and the sucklings swoon in the streets of the city. *(This speaks of acute shortage of food, with the children staggering because of physical weakness. Israel was brought to this state, with some of them even becoming cannibals and eating their own sons and daughters, because of their sinfulness against* Jehovah. This was predicted by Moses [Lev. 26:29; Deut. 28:53].)*

12 They say to their mothers, Where is corn and wine? when they swooned as the wounded in the streets of the city, when their soul was poured out into their mothers' bosom.

13 What thing shall I take to witness for you? what thing shall I liken to you, O daughter of Jerusalem? what shall I equal to you, that I may comfort you, O virgin daughter of Zion? for your breach is great like the sea: who can heal you? *(The statement of this Verse is that it is impossible to console Jerusalem by pointing to others in a like affliction, for her misery was greater than there had ever been, and for the obvious reasons. In fact, her misery was so bad that only the Lord could heal such!)*

14 Your prophets have seen vain and foolish things for you: and they have not discovered your iniquity, to turn away your captivity; but have seen for you false burdens and causes of banishment. *(The phrase, "And they have not discovered your iniquity," means that these false prophets would not point out Israel's sins; they rather preached what Israel wanted to hear. The words, "false burdens," refer to false prophecies. The Holy Spirit here says that the "false prophets" led this parade, which led to total destruction.)*

15 All who pass by clap their hands at you; they hiss and wag their head at the daughter of Jerusalem, saying, Is this the city that men call The perfection of beauty, The joy of the whole Earth? *(Jerusalem had been the capital of the "whole Earth," because the Lord Himself dwelt in Jerusalem, actually in the Temple between the Mercy Seat and the Cherubim. But now all of that is gone!)*

16 All your enemies have opened their mouth against you; they hiss and gnash the teeth: they say, We have swallowed her up: certainly this is the day that we looked for; we have found, we have seen it. *(These "enemies" are some of the nations that Judah and Jerusalem thought were her friends. Jerusalem embraced their gods and, thereby, forsook Jehovah. All the time these "friends" were secretly "hissing and gnashing their teeth in anger"; they hated Judah and Jerusalem.*

The world is not our friend!)

JUDGMENT ON JUDAH;
ADMONITION TO PRAY

17 The LORD has done that which He had

devised; He has fulfilled His Word that He had commanded in the days of old: He has thrown down, and has not pitied: and He has caused your enemy to rejoice over you, He has set up the horn of your adversaries. *(The phrase, "The LORD has done that which He had devised," refers to the fulfilling of His Word which He had given to the Prophets many years before, and many times. So Israel had no excuse!)*

18 Their heart cried unto the LORD, O wall of the daughter of Zion, let tears run down like a river day and night: give yourself no rest; let not the apple of your eye cease. *(While it is true that Judah and Jerusalem are under the judging Hand of God, still, the Holy Spirit through the Prophet implores the people to come before the Lord with a broken heart, and Mercy, at least in some respect, will be given.)*

19 Arise, cry out in the night: in the beginning of the watches pour out your heart like water before the face of the LORD: lift up your hands toward Him for the life of your young children, who faint for hunger in the top of every street. *(Despite the anger of the Lord against Judah and Jerusalem [because they would not repent], still, the Lord was their only hope, as He had always been their only hope. So, they were exhorted to "cry out in the night" to Him. Even though Judah and Jerusalem could not be spared, as is now obvious, still, the Lord tells these hapless survivors that He can help, and He in fact will help, if they will only seek His Face.)*

JEREMIAH'S PRAYER

20 Behold, O LORD, and consider to whom You have done this. Shall the women eat their fruit, and children of a span long? shall the priest and the prophet be slain in the Sanctuary of the LORD? *(Even though Judah and Jerusalem have grievously sinned and refused to repent, which is the cause of all this problem, Jeremiah pleads for help. Inasmuch as the Holy Spirit allowed this to be recorded, the indication is that the Lord would "consider" and show Mercy.)*

21 The young and the old lie on the ground in the streets: my virgins and my young men are fallen by the sword; You have slain them in the day of Your anger; You have killed, and not pitied. *(The idea of this petition in this Verse is that Jeremiah pleads to the Lord that great judgment has already been carried out on the people, with many killed and others in a state of acute*

starvation, so now surely the Lord will show Mercy. The phrase, "You have killed, and not pitied," portrays the past tense; surely at the present "pity" can be shown!)*

22 You have called as in a solemn day my terrors round about, so that in the day of the LORD's anger none escaped nor remained: those whom I have swaddled and brought up has my enemy consumed. *(The phrase, "Those whom I have swaddled and brought up has my enemy consumed," seems to refer to the possibility of some of Jeremiah's relatives being killed in the carnage. If in fact this did happen, it would have been a just vengeance carried out by the Lord, because these very individuals, Jeremiah's family, had sought his life because they did not like what he preached [Jer. 12:6].)*

CHAPTER 3
(588 B.C.)

LAMENT OVER JERUSALEM'S DOWNFALL

I am the man who has seen affliction by the rod of His Wrath. *(The Prophet speaks here as a representative of the nation. He speaks as a true Intercessor, thereby associating with the sin of the people, even though he himself had not sinned.*

Such was Christ. He Who knew no sin entered into the penalty of our sin in order to make proper Intercession for the Believer, which He does by simply being in the Presence of the Father [Heb. 1:3; 7:25]. Everything which makes possible Intercession on our behalf was done and finished at Calvary.)

2 He has led me, and brought me into darkness, but not into light. *(The idea is: if a person wills Light, God wills Light unto him; however, if he wills darkness, such is willed unto him!)*

3 Surely against me is He turned; He turns His hand against me all the day. *(Upon obedience, "His hand is for me." Upon disobedience, "His hand is against me.")*

4 My flesh and my skin has He made old; He has broken my bones. *(The Lord promised healing to His People as long as they followed Him [Ex. 15:26; Ps. 103:3]. Conversely, if they did not follow Him, there would be no healing.)*

5 He has built against me, and compassed me with gall and travail. *(The idea is: the Lord can "compass" us with blessing or trouble, all dependent upon our obedience or disobedience!)*

6 He has set me in dark places, as they that be dead of old. *(Even though these were God's chosen People, still, sin would destroy them just*

as readily as it destroyed the heathen of old, i.e., "the flood.")

7 He has hedged me about, that I cannot get out: He has made my chain heavy. *(The phrase, "He has made my chain heavy," corresponds to the "chain" or the "weight" [sin] that we are admonished to lay aside, which we can do only by looking to Christ and the Cross [Heb. 12:1]. If we do not look to Christ and the Cross, it cannot be laid aside, and it will become heavier and heavier until we are imprisoned.)*

8 Also when I cry and shout, He shuts out my prayer. *(The Psalmist said, "If I regard iniquity in my heart, the Lord will not hear me" [Ps. 66:18].)*

9 He has inclosed my ways with hewn stone, He has made my paths crooked. *(As the Lord had taken great measures to bless His People, now He takes great measures to do the very opposite. However, it is meant to be corrective rather than destructive.)*

10 He was unto me as a bear lying in wait, and as a lion in secret places. *("Bears" and "lions" are carnivorous animals, fierce by nature. Therefore, for the Lord to position Himself in this manner regarding His Children demonstrates His use of measures of extremity. Instead of Him being the Shepherd, He now turns to be the Destroyer of the sheep, as Judah woefully found out!)*

11 He has turned aside my ways, and pulled me in pieces: He has made me desolate. *(In just judgment, the Divine Hand has broken to pieces the nation which that same Hand had established. What He builds up, He is able to pull down.)*

12 He has bent His bow, and set me as a mark for the arrow. *(The target once was Israel's enemies. Now Israel has turned to be the enemy of God and, therefore, the "mark for His arrow.")*

13 He has caused the arrows of his quiver to enter into my reins. *(The "reins" speak of the very seat of one's being. The Lord shoots the arrow to the place where the sin begins, which is the heart.)*

14 I was a derision to all my people; and their song all the day. *(The phrase would probably have been better translated, "I was a derision to all people," referring to the surrounding nations, as they looked upon the destruction of Judah and Jerusalem.*

The phrase, "And their song all the day," refers to songs of mockery and derision by the heathen regarding the destruction of God's People.)

15 He has filled me with bitterness, He has made me drunken with wormwood. *(The word "bitterness" means "bitter troubles." The word "wormwood" actually means "to curse." Instead of the Lord blessing Judah, He now curses Judah.)*

16 He has also broken my teeth with gravel stones, He has covered me with ashes. *(The phrase, "He has covered me with ashes," is a figurative expression of great humiliation.)*

17 And You have removed my soul far off from peace: I forgot prosperity. *(This may have been a quotation from Ps. 88:14. The "prosperity" addressed here is spiritual prosperity, which results in all other prosperity, as well!)*

18 And I said, My strength and my hope is perished from the LORD *(Judah, because of spiritual declension, forgot that her "strength" and "hope" were in the Lord. He was the Source of all her blessings. But being lifted up in pride, she began to think that Jehovah would not and could not abandon her, because of her unique place and position as His special People. They would find that the Lord could not abide sin, irrespective as to who the people were):*

19 Remembering my affliction and my misery, the wormwood and the gall. *(The word "remembering" is the state to which the Holy Spirit desires to draw the person. He wants the person to remember the cause of the "affliction" and "misery" resulting in "the wormwood and the gall.")*

20 My soul has them still in remembrance, and is humbled in me. *(Verses 19 and 20 are very similar to Ps. 42:5. Now the individual, or in this case Judah, remembers why she is in this condition, "and is humbled.")*

HOPE THROUGH GOD'S MERCY

21 This I recall to my mind, therefore have I hope. *(This Verse could well have been taken from Ps. 42:4. Jeremiah's statements thus far concerning Judah have been of despair, but now God's Promises of Mercy and Grace come to his "mind." Only this can give him "hope," as this is the only sure "hope" for anyone!)*

22 It is of the LORD's mercies that we are not consumed, because His compassions fail not. *(As the Prophet enters the Intercessory role, he will now learn that God Himself, in the absence of all outward spiritual fellowship, is a sufficing portion for Faith, and even in the face of what looks like catastrophic defeat.*

The Holy Spirit directs Jeremiah's attention, and hence Judah's, away from their plight to

"the LORD's Mercies.")

23 They are new every morning: great is Your faithfulness. *(In a sense, God's Mercy cannot be exhausted, because it begins "anew each and every morning." As well, one can be certain that this will never change, because the Holy Spirit says, "Great is Your faithfulness.")*

24 The LORD is my portion, says my soul; therefore will I hope in Him. *(The phrase, "The LORD is my portion," proclaims the fact that anything and everything that one truly needs is found in the Lord, and only in the Lord [II Pet. 1:3-4; Ps. 16:5].)*

25 The LORD is good unto them who wait for Him, to the soul that seeks Him. *(The intimation is: if we properly "seek Him," even though it may take some time, we will "find Him" [Lk. 11:5-13].)*

26 It is good that a man should both hope and quietly wait for the salvation of the LORD. *(It means to wait in travail, and with great burden of soul. Of necessity, it is placed beside "quietly wait," which speaks of serenity. Therefore, this waiting will incorporate times of travail interspersed with times of serenity.)*

27 It is good for a man that he bear the yoke of his youth. *(This Verse may have been derived from Ps. 119:71.)*

28 He sits alone and keeps silence, because He has borne it upon him. *(The idea is: the individual should not blame God for the problem, neither should he complain about his woeful situation, but instead "keep silence" and "bear it with patience," believing that most surely the Lord will come to his rescue and deliver him.*

Also, he will learn the lesson that the affliction is designed to teach, thereby, coming out the better man for the trial.)

29 He puts his mouth in the dust; if so be there may be hope. *(The phrase, "He puts his mouth in the dust," is an oriental manner of expressing submission, which is one of the lessons the Holy Spirit desires to teach.)*

30 He gives his cheek to Him Who smites him: he is filled full with reproach. *(The phrase, "He gives his cheek to Him Who smites him," means that he bears the affliction with patience, attempting to learn the reason from the Lord and to profit thereby. Even though "he is filled full with reproach," and, as Job, is ridiculed by others, still, he knows the Lord is in control, and that victory most assuredly will come.)*

31 For the LORD will not cast off forever *(the Lord will not afflict forever, meaning that it will come to an end, if we will only trust Him):*

32 But though He cause grief, yet will He have compassion according to the multitude of His mercies. *(We have the assurance that any "grief" He causes is brought about for our good, and is done with "Compassion" and "Mercy." What a wonderful Lord we serve!)*

33 For He does not afflict willingly nor grieve the children of men. *(God does not afflict in a malicious spirit, as man does. Men afflict others in order to hurt. God afflicts in order to help, i.e., "to bring us to a place of maturity.")*

34 To crush under His feet all the prisoners of the Earth. *(In this instance, the "prisoners of the Earth" refer to the unhappy Jewish captives of the Babylonians. Even though they had terribly sinned and were, therefore, under the just judgment of God, still, He would not allow them to be "crushed." Ultimately, He would deliver them.)*

35 To turn aside the right of a man before the face of the Most High *(the idea is: the "Most High" is the Heavenly Supreme Court. Irrespective of what the individual has done, as Judah, if they will sincerely repent, the Lord will guarantee Deliverance and Restoration, and will not "turn aside the right of that man"),*

36 To subvert a man in his cause, the LORD approves not. *("His cause" refers to the Word of God being applied to a person's life and his trust in it. "To subvert a man" refers to those who claim God will no longer show Mercy, etc. The phrase, "The LORD approves not," means that irrespective of what unbelievers may say, the Lord will not "approve" of their denial of Mercy and Grace to anyone who meets God's conditions.)*

37 Who is he who says, and it comes to pass, when the LORD commands it not? *(The Holy Spirit asks the question through Jeremiah, "Who is he who says it cannot, when God says it can?", or "Who is he who says it can, when God says it cannot?" It is what "the LORD commands," not man!)*

38 Out of the mouth of the Most High proceeds not evil and good? *(The Lord does not say He will, when He won't! Neither does He say He won't, when He will! [James 3:9-11].)*

JEREMIAH'S CONFESSION AND REPENTANCE FOR ZION

39 Wherefore does a living man complain, a man for the punishment of his sins? *(Judah is not to complain of her present condition, because it is "punishment for her sins." As such, it*

should be suffered with dignity, realizing it is just, but also tempered with Mercy. The next Verse tells Judah, as well as all others, exactly what must be done!)

40 Let us search and try our ways, and turn again to the LORD. *(The purpose of the affliction allowed by the Lord is given in this Verse. The phrase, "And turn again to the LORD," means that we have been turning to other than the Lord. Self-will is always the cause of this, which leads one astray from the Bible and, thereby, from God.*

The word "search" means to ferret out that which has been concealed. Our troubles being caused by our sins, let us search them out and allow the Lord to correct them.)

41 Let us lift up our heart with our hands unto God in the Heavens. *(If one is to notice, the mere "lifting up of the hands," within itself, is not enough! The "heart," with its corresponding action of Repentance, must accompany the physical gesture.)*

42 We have transgressed and have rebelled: You have not pardoned. *(The pronouns, "we" and "You," as expressed in the Hebrew, are meant to be spoken with heavy emphasis. Such acknowledges the sin and takes responsibility for wrongdoing, and is correspondent with I John 1:9.*

The phrase, "You have not pardoned," does not have reference to forgiveness of sin, but rather has reference to the effect of that sin, which has continued. Thus, the affliction.)

43 You have covered with anger, and persecuted us: You have slain, You have not pitied. *(These are the just results of their sin. The "anger" represents a long pent-up anger that is finally released because of constant transgression, rebellion, and refusal to repent, as recorded in Verse 42.*

The phrase, "Persecuted us," refers to Judah's enemies having their way with her.)

44 You have covered Yourself with a cloud, that our prayer should not pass through. *(Prayer cannot "pass through" to God if sin is being harbored, with a refusal to repent, which was the situation in Judah and Jerusalem.)*

45 You have made us as the offscouring and refuse in the midst of the people. *(If the Lord builds up, He can also tear down. If He plants, He can also uproot. As He is the Author of one, He is also the Author of the other!)*

46 All our enemies have opened their mouths against us. *(When Judah was walking with the Lord, these "enemies" did not dare do such! Now that God is no longer with her because of her*

sins, these "enemies" feel free to say and do whatever they desire. Consequently, their scorn and sarcasm knew no bounds!)

47 Fear and a snare is come upon us, desolation and destruction. *(All of this is brought on by sin and a refusal to repent!)*

48 My eye runs down with rivers of water for the destruction of the daughter of my people. *(In this Verse, Jeremiah returns to his own personal grief over the terrible condition of both Judah and Jerusalem. He was called the Weeping Prophet, and not without reason! For about 40 years, he had prophesied of the coming destruction, and had watched that destruction come closer and closer. Still, the people would not repent, but instead grew worse in their obstinacy and rebellion. And then he was an eyewitness to the actual destruction, seeing exactly what he had prophesied come to pass, which brought about the deaths of tens of thousands of people, etc.)*

49 My eye trickles down, and ceases not, without any intermission. *(The phrase, "Trickles down," in the Hebrew instead says, "pours down." Therefore, this Passage speaks of the burden of a broken heart so heavy that it even threatens the life of the Prophet. It was a burden "without any intermission.")*

50 Till the LORD look down, and behold from Heaven. *(As far as is known, Jeremiah is one of a precious few who interceded for Judah and Jerusalem.)*

51 My eye affects my heart because of all the daughters of my city. *(The Babylonians had no mercy, not even on the women and children.)*

PRAYER FOR VENGEANCE ON ENEMIES

52 My enemies chased me sore, like a bird, without cause. *(This Prophet of God had many "enemies," who constantly attempted to silence his voice, therefore, "chasing him like a bird." Furthermore, it was "without cause," just as the anger and actions of the Pharisees against Christ were "without cause," of which this a type.)*

53 They have cut off my life in the dungeon, and cast a stone upon me. *(This incarceration is given in Jer. 38:6. The phrase, "They have cut off my life," means that they intended for Jeremiah to die in this dungeon, which would have happened, had the Lord not intervened.)*

54 Waters flowed over my head; then I said, I am cut off. *(Even though there was no water actually in this dungeon [Jer. 38:6], still, his enemies no doubt removed at times the stone and*

poured water, which was probably filthy, into the dungeon, which "flowed over Jeremiah's head.")

55 I called upon Your Name, O LORD, out of the low dungeon. *(In any and every situation, the Lord is the only One Who can truly help. For whatever problem, we need to always call upon "His Name." At this terrible time, Jeremiah no doubt reminded the Lord of the Promise made to him at the very beginning of his Prophetic Ministry [Jer. 1;19].)*

56 You have heard my voice: hide not Your ear at my breathing, at my cry. *(With us, at times, even as with Jeremiah, the Lord will allow adverse things to take place in our lives in order that we may learn to trust Him, to believe Him, and to call on Him. Everything the Lord does and allows in our lives is for a purpose; to be sure, He guides everything. In other words, nothing happens to a Believer but that the Lord causes it or allows it, and all is for our good.*

Verse 56 portrays the physical weakness of Jeremiah while in this dungeon, but yet his great spiritual strength.)

57 You drew near in the day that I called upon You: You said, Fear not. *(In this terrible situation, when Jeremiah called upon the Lord, the Word of the Lord came back, "Fear not." That Word, as it was given to Jeremiah, is also given to every true Believer.)*

58 O LORD, You have pleaded the causes of my soul; You have redeemed my life. *(To do this, to redeem the life of the great Prophet, the Lord would use "Ebed-melech the Ethiopian.")*

59 O LORD, You have seen my wrong: You judge my cause. *(The phrase, "O LORD, You have seen my wrong," does not necessarily mean that Jeremiah had committed a wrong, but that the Lord was implored to search his life. Jeremiah believed that the Lord would find no "wrong." On that basis, he would ask that the Lord would "judge his cause," which the Lord definitely did, and delivered him.)*

60 You have seen all their vengeance and all their imaginations against me. *(It is certain that the Lord sees all; recompense will be made according to the evil deeds of all concerned.)*

61 You have heard their reproach, O LORD, and all their imaginations against me *(this pertains to the plans that these individuals had devised in order to harm or even kill Jeremiah);*

62 The lips of those who rose up against me, and their device against me all the day. *(It was very easy to speak against Jeremiah during the 35 years of his prophesying before Jerusalem fell. No one believed in him. But, to be sure, the*

Lord heard every derogatory thing these people said against the Prophet.)

63 Behold their sitting down, and their rising up; I am their music. *(The phrase, "I am their music," speaks of the ribald songs of scorn and ridicule they made up and sang concerning him.)*

64 Render unto them a recompence, O LORD, according to the work of their hands. *(This prayer, at least this part, is derived from Ps. 28:4, which was also a prayer of David. Such a prayer is not wrong and can be prayed presently by Christians, providing their heart is clean before God. Jeremiah is speaking of people here who refused to repent.)*

65 Give them sorrow of heart, Your curse upon them. *(The phrase, "Your curse upon them," is not known or understood by most Christians. However, Deut., Chpt. 28, proclaims the Truth that God blesses obedience while cursing disobedience. Even though this is the day of Grace, the principle now is the same as then.)*

66 Persecute and destroy them in anger from under the Heavens of the LORD. *(And that's exactly what happened! Once again, "what we sow, we reap.")*

CHAPTER 4
(588 B.C.)
JERUSALEM'S FORMER GLORY
AND LATTER CONDITION

HOW is the gold become dim! how is the most fine gold changed! the stones of the Sanctuary are poured out in the top of every street. *(The "gold" in this Verse is figurative. It stands for the greatness and glory of the Temple in Jerusalem, and signifies Deity. It being "dim" proclaims the fact that Jehovah, while having left Judah and Jerusalem, still watches over her from afar.*

The phrase, "How is the fine gold changed!" refers to the Lord's changed manner of operation, typified by the Sanctuary being torn down, stone by stone.)

2 The precious sons of Zion, comparable to fine gold, how are they esteemed as earthen pitchers, the work of the hands of the potter! *(The People of God, typified as "the precious sons of Zion," and compared to "fine gold," have now been reduced to no more than a cheap "earthen pitcher," which is easily broken and thrown away.*

In regard to this, we might ask ourselves the question, "How does the Lord look at us." Does

He see "fine gold" or a cheap "earthen pitcher"?)

3 Even the sea monsters draw out the breast, they give suck to their young ones: the daughter of My people is become cruel, like the ostriches in the wilderness. *(The phrase, "Sea monsters," would have been better translated "jackals." The idea is: the people of God had so lost their way until cruelty was the norm.)*

4 The tongue of the sucking child cleaves to the roof of his mouth for thirst: the young children ask bread, and no man breaks it unto them. *(This Verse proclaims the fact that little children at the time of the siege were begging for bread, and the adults who had bread would share none with them. Their hearts had grown so hard and cold that they could see a child staggering in the street for want of food and show no concern.)*

5 They who did feed delicately are desolate in the streets: they who were brought up in scarlet embrace dunghills. *(The Prophet speaks of the Nobles of Jerusalem, once rich, but now scavenging the streets for a little food. All of this could have been avoided, if, at any time during the many years of Jeremiah's Prophecies, they had only heeded the Word of the Lord.)*

6 For the punishment of the iniquity of the daughter of my people is greater than the punishment of the sin of Sodom, that was overthrown as in a moment, and no hands stayed on her. *(Sodom sinned greatly and had to be destroyed; however, Judah sinned against Light, which is far worse! As such, they became worse than the surrounding heathen!)*

7 Her Nazarites were purer than snow, they were whiter than milk, they were more ruddy in body than rubies, their polishing was of sapphire *(Jeremiah now alludes to Judah and Jerusalem as they once were, when they lived for God and consequently were greatly blessed by Him)*:

8 Their visage is blacker than a coal; they are not known in the streets: their skin cleaves to their bones; it is withered, it is become like a stick. *(Jeremiah, having thought back to the Jerusalem of the past, now portrays their present condition!)*

9 They that be slain with the sword are better than they that be slain with hunger: for these pine away, stricken through for want of the fruits of the field. *(Exactly as the Prophet had predicted, the living now are worse off than the dead.)*

10 The hands of the pitiful women have sodden their own children: they were their meat in the destruction of the daughter of my people. *(Moses, about a thousand years earlier, had prophesied that if Israel turned her back on God, the people would sink to the level of eating their own children. And that's exactly what happened! [Deut. 28:57].)*

11 The LORD has accomplished His fury; He has poured out His fierce anger, and has kindled a fire in Zion, and it has devoured the foundations thereof. *(God cannot abide sin in any form, nor in any people. It must be judged. Wondrously so, it has been judged in Christ and what He did at the Cross. However, if men do not accept His Atoning Sacrifice, they will themselves become a sacrifice, but a sacrifice which will not atone.)*

12 The kings of the Earth, and all the inhabitants of the world, would not have believed that the adversary and the enemy should have entered into the gates of Jerusalem. *(The miraculous acts of God among His People were legend among the nations of the world of that day. Even though they would not serve Him, they knew of His great Power. But when God's People sinned against Him and refused to repent, even after repeated warnings, all that was great had to be destroyed.)*

REASONS FOR THE JUDGMENT

13 For the sins of her prophets, and the iniquities of her priests, who have shed the blood of the just in the midst of her *(the blame is laid at the feet of the spiritual leaders, so-called, of Jerusalem, i.e., her prophets who prophesied falsely and her priests who perverted the Law. It is the same presently in the modern Church!)*,

14 They have wandered as blind men in the streets, they have polluted themselves with blood, so that men could not touch their garments. *(They were the blind leading the blind, and all fell in the ditch [Mat. 15:14]. The phrase, "They have polluted themselves with blood," means that the blood of the people lost because of their false preaching would be required at their hands [Ezek. 3:17-18].)*

15 They cried unto them, Depart ye; it is unclean; depart, depart, touch not: when they fled away and wandered, they said among the heathen, They shall no more sojourn there. *(The idea of this Verse concerns the Jews who left the city for foreign lands before and after the fall of Jerusalem. They would be maltreated at*

each place they would go, with the people of that particular country saying, "Depart ye."

The phrase, "It is unclean," has the same idea as the leper who was unclean. In other words, in all these foreign countries, the Jews were treated as "lepers.")

16 The anger of the LORD has divided them; he will no more regard them: they respected not the persons of the Priests, they favoured not the Elders. (This refers to the fact that Judah had shown favor to the heathen priests of the idol gods who came to Jerusalem, but now, as they fled from the Babylonian horde, Judah's Priests were shown no respect or favor by these heathen.)

17 As for us, our eyes as yet failed for our vain help: in our watching we have watched for a nation that could not save us. ("The nation that could not save us" was Egypt. If they had sought the Lord, they would have been saved!

The phrase, "Vain help," adequately describes what Egypt provided; it also describes all that man can do in any circumstances or at any time!

These words should be read by those in the modern Church who advocate humanistic psychology as the answer to the perversions of man!)

18 They hunt our steps, that we cannot go in our streets: our end is near, our days are fulfilled; for our end is come. (The word "they" refers to the Chaldeans. Jeremiah now takes the Reader back to the moment of the fall of Jerusalem.)

19 Our persecutors are swifter than the eagles of the Heaven: they pursued us upon the mountains, they laid wait for us in the wilderness. (The Jews who tried to escape the city at the time of the siege were easily caught by the Chaldeans.)

20 The breath of our nostrils, the anointed of the LORD, was taken in their pits, of whom we said, Under his shadow we shall live among the heathen. ("The anointed of the LORD" probably refers to king Zedekiah. He was the last king of Judah. The idea was probably held by some Jews that they could escape to a "heathen country" and live there under their own king. Such thinking was foolish!)

21 Rejoice and be glad, O daughter of Edom, that dwells in the land of Uz; the cup also shall pass through unto you: you shall be drunken, and shall make yourself naked. ("Edom," a neighbor of Judah, rejoiced when Judah fell. However, the Prophet says that they would suffer the same judgment that Judah suffered. And so they did!)

FINAL RESTORATION OF JUDAH

22 The punishment of your iniquity is accomplished, O daughter of Zion; He will no more carry you away into captivity; He will visit your iniquity, O daughter of Edom; He will discover your sins. (For Edom, there is no promise of Restoration, but, on the contrary, a disclosure of her sins; for Zion, a full judgment, but a covering up of her sin, which will ultimately result in a complete Restoration, which will take place at the Second Coming.)

CHAPTER 5
(588 B.C.)
PRAYER: CONFESSION OF GUILT AND REPENTANCE

REMEMBER, O LORD, what is come upon us: consider, and behold our reproach. (As in the Psalms, so in these Elegies, the Spirit of God expresses His Thoughts through those whom He chooses as vessels of His testimony in circumstances exhibiting the judgment of God on that which He had Himself founded.

This is one of the beauties and marvels of Inspiration. The Spirit Himself furnishes a picture of His Own activities in the hearts of evil men. Such is His Love for them. He hearkens to their sighs, records their fears, and registers their victories. Tragically, there is no victory here, only "reproach."

This prayer would be answered, with the Lord not only beholding their reproach, but also beholding them in view of future Restoration. Therefore, the lesson is learned that the Lord does indeed "consider," and He constantly works for the Restoration of the chastised one.)

2 Our inheritance is turned to strangers, our houses to aliens. (The "inheritance" spoke of their land which had been "given" to Abraham [Gen. 13:25; 17:8], and was consequently inherited by Abraham's posterity. Consequently, this was God's Land and God's People; and yet, it was "turned to strangers.")

3 We are orphans and fatherless, our mothers are as widows. (Without the Lord, they definitely were "orphans.")

4 We have drunken our water for money; our wood is sold unto us. (Spiritually speaking, their inheritance had been reduced to "water" and "wood." And even that was horrendously scarce!)

5 Our necks are under persecution: we labour, and have no rest. (They have now

become slaves of the Babylonians. As such, they were forced into hard labor, with the slightest infraction resulting in beatings.)

6 We have given the hand to the Egyptians, and to the Assyrians, to be satisfied with bread. (The idea of this Verse is: now, instead of looking to the Lord, they had to look to the Egyptians or Assyrians for food. To "give the hand" means to beg. And these were God's chosen People!)

7 Our fathers have sinned, and are not; and we have borne their iniquities. (This Verse tells us that the iniquity of Judah had spanned many generations.)

8 Servants have ruled over us: there is none that does deliver us out of their hand. (The Egyptians were the children of Ham, and it is thought that the Assyrians and the Chaldeans may have been, as well! As such, they were "servants" and, according to the Prophecy of Noah, should not have ruled over the sons of Shem [Gen. 9:27].)

9 We got our bread with the peril of our lives because of the sword of the wilderness. (The people of God are now prey to anyone who desires to take what little they have left!)

10 Our skin was black like an oven because of the terrible famine. (The word "black" probably should have been translated "glows," which is the feverish glow produced by gnawing hunger, which is what is actually meant.)

11 They ravished the women in Zion, and the maids in the cities of Judah. (When the Babylonians took the city, the women and the young girls of the city were fair game for the animal passion of drunken soldiers.)

12 Princes are hanged up by their hand: the faces of elders were not honored. (None were respected at the fall of Jerusalem. The "Princes" and "Elders" were treated as brutally as any and all.)

13 They took the young men to grind, and the children fell under the wood. (What men were left were reduced to slavery, with even the children put to work gathering wood.)

14 The Elders have ceased from the gate, the young men from their musick. ("The gate" was a term used for the buildings at the main entrance of the city where legal proceedings were conducted. Such have ceased! Most of the "Elders" are dead, and there are no legal proceedings to conduct.

As well, the "music" has ceased, unless it is a funeral dirge.)

15 The joy of our heart is ceased; our dance is turned into mourning.

16 The crown is fallen from our head: woe unto us, that we have sinned! (The phrase, "The crown is fallen from our head," refers to the supremacy of Judah and Jerusalem for nearly 500 years. No nation in the world was their equal. No city compared to Jerusalem. They were God's chosen, but have now forfeited everything, and all because of sin!)

JEREMIAH'S APPEAL FOR MERCY

17 For this our heart is faint; for these things our eyes are dim.

18 Because of the mountain of Zion, which is desolate, the foxes walk upon it. ("Zion" was where the Temple was located. And now it is trod upon by jackals. These jackals were the Babylonians!)

19 Thou, O LORD, remain for ever; Your Throne from generation to generation. (In effect, the Holy Spirit through the Prophet is saying that even though Judah and the Temple are no more, still, "the LORD remains forever." As great as His "Throne" was yesterday, as great it is today, that is, if men will only believe Him, and shall be "from generation to generation.")

20 Wherefore do You forget us for ever, and forsake us so long time? (The idea is: Jehovah's Power is unbroken, and consequently He can restore Israel. And that He shall [Rom., Chpt. 11].)

21 Turn Thou us unto You, O LORD, and we shall be turned; renew our days as of old. (The phrase, "Turn Thou us unto You," shows that true conversion is a Divine and not a human action. The phrase, "And we shall be turned," speaks of true heartfelt Repentance, which must be enjoined before Salvation is granted. This, Israel will do in the coming Day, when Jesus comes back [Zech. 13:1].)

22 But You have utterly rejected us; You are very wroth against us. (It may seem that the Book of Lamentations concludes on a very negative note. However, the Prophet turns from the fulfillment of the Promises at a future day back to the present. Now they are "utterly rejected." Now the anger of God still burns hot against them. This simply says that the present must be dealt with before the future can be guaranteed.)

THE BOOK OF THE PROPHET
EZEKIEL

CHAPTER 1
(595 B.C.)
EZEKIEL'S VISION OF GOD'S GLORY

NOW it came to pass in the thirtieth year, in the fourth month, in the fifth day of the month, as I was among the captives by the river of Chebar, that the heavens were opened, and I saw visions of God. *("The thirtieth year" probably refers to the thirtieth year of the Babylonian Empire. The phrase, "By the river of Chebar," does not exactly tell us where Ezekiel was. Some think that this is the river now known as Khabour, which flows into the Euphrates about 200 miles north of Babylon. At any rate, it was somewhere in Babylonia.*

The phrase, "That the heavens were opened," signifies the beginning of Ezekiel's Prophetic Ministry.)

2 In the fifth day of the month, which was the fifth year of king Jehoiachin's captivity *(at this time, Ezekiel had been in captivity approximately five years. At this time, the false prophets of Judah were prophesying of the overthrow of Babylon and the return of Jehoiachin within two years [Jer. 28:3]. The expectations thus raised were probably shared by many of Ezekiel's companions in exile. However, Ezekiel knew better, adhering to the counsels of the letter which Jeremiah had sent to the Jews of the captivity [Jer. 29:1-23]. Thus, in this atmosphere he began his Prophecies)*,

3 The Word of the LORD came expressly unto Ezekiel the Priest, the son of Buzi, in the land of the Chaldeans by the river Chebar; and the hand of the LORD was there upon him. *(The phrase, "The Word of the LORD came expressly unto Ezekiel," means "in reality" or "without doubt." The phrase, "In the land of the Chaldeans," refers to the Divine Truth that wherever a searching heart is, God will be found. Actually, the deeper the darkness, the brighter the Light.)*

4 And I looked, and, behold, a whirlwind came out of the north, a great cloud, and a fire infolding itself, and a brightness was about it, and out of the midst thereof as the colour of amber, out of the midst of the fire. *(The phrase, "And I looked, and, behold," refers to the fact that what was described could be seen. In other words, it was not a figment of Ezekiel's imagination.*

The phrase, "A whirlwind came out of the north," refers to the Holy Spirit. It was the same "rushing wind" that came on the Day of Pentecost [Acts 2:2]. Actually, Ezekiel is given a vision of the traveling Throne of God, one might say.)

5 Also out of the midst thereof came the likeness of four living creatures. And this was their appearance; they had the likeness of a man. *(We learn from 10:1 that these "Living Creatures" are Cherubims.)*

6 And every one had four faces, and every one had four wings. *(Their hands and their wings were in proportion, which means that equal intelligence indwelt their entire being, and the One Spirit energized them all.)*

7 And their feet were straight feet; and the sole of their feet was like the sole of a calf's foot: and they sparkled like the colour of burnished brass. *(The phrase, "Straight feet," means they were shaped like those of an ox, which emphasizes the fact that they did not move by walking. Even though like an ox, there their similarity ended.)*

8 And they had the hands of a man under their wings on their four sides; and they four had their faces and their wings. *(The number "four" is not without intense meaning. Four refers to fourfold and, therefore, "completion," i.e., complete within itself, which can only speak of the Creator, and not the Creation. These Creatures attend the Throne of God [Rev. 4:6-8].)*

9 Their wings were joined one to another; they turned not when they went; they went every one straight forward. *(When adding Verses 11 and 24, two of the wings were always down, and, when the Living Creatures moved, two were extended upwards, so that their tips touched, and were in this sense "joined." When at rest, these were let down again.*

The phrase, "They turned not when they went," refers to the fact that the four wings were not in motion as wings normally are when the Cherubim moved. In other words, their power of movement was not in the wings.)

10 As for the likeness of their faces, they

four had the face of a man, and the face of a lion, on the right side: and they four had the face of an ox on the left side; they four also had the face of an eagle. *(First of all, it is impossible to exhaust the meaning of the symbolism given here. One can connect all of this with the human face of the Son of Man, Who shared in the Glory of the Father: the Ox, with that of His Sacrifice; the Lion, with that of His Sovereignty, as the Lion of the Tribe of Judah [Rev. 5:5]; the Eagle, with that of His bearing His People, as on Eagles' Wings unto the highest heavens [Ex. 19:4; Deut. 32:11].)*

11 Thus were their faces: and their wings were stretched upward; two wings of every one were joined one to another, and two covered their bodies. *(The phrase, "Thus were their faces," seems to imply that the Holy Spirit desired for us to understand the symbolism, at least as far as is possible for man to do!)*

12 And they went every one straight forward: whither the Spirit was to go, they went; and they turned not when they went. *(The phrase, "And they went every one straight forward," seems to imply that from point to point, they always traveled in a straight line, thereby denoting perfect knowledge of direction and perfect ability to travel the designated course.*

The phrase, "Whither the Spirit was to go, they went," refers to the Holy Spirit giving direction, which the Cherubim instantly obeyed. [The Hebrew word for "Spirit" is a noun, and should have been translated "the Spirit," as in Gen. 1:2.])

13 As for the likeness of the Living Creatures, their appearance was like burning coals of fire, and like the appearance of lamps: it went up and down among the Living Creatures; and the fire was bright, and out of the fire went forth lightning. *(It seems that these "Living Creatures" were bathed, as it were, in the fire that played around them, yet were not consumed. "Fire," as distinct from "Light," seems to be the symbol of the Power of God, as manifested against evil [Deut. 4:24; Heb. 12:29].)*

14 And the Living Creatures ran and returned as the appearance of a flash of lightning. *(The idea is of speed incomprehensible to the human mind and overwhelming in brightness. Perhaps one can say that they traveled with the "speed of thought.")*

15 Now as I beheld the Living Creatures, behold one wheel upon the Earth by the Living Creatures, with his four faces. *(The "wheels" represent direction, hence the "eyes" of Verse 18.)*

16 The appearance of the wheels and their work was like unto the colour of a beryl: and they four had one likeness: and their appearance and their work was as it were a wheel in the middle of a wheel. *(Strangely enough, and as we shall see, these "wheels" which accompanied the Cherubim were not attached in any way. The phrase, "A wheel in the middle of a wheel," seems to imply two wheels in one.)*

17 When they went, they went upon their four sides: and they turned not when they went. *(The phrase, "And they turned not when they went," probably indicates that they traveled in a straight line and that the "wheels" did not turn as wheels normally do. This suggests the idea of orderly and harmonious working.)*

18 As for their rings, they were so high that they were dreadful; and their rings were full of eyes round about them four. *(John the Beloved, on the Isle of Patmos, described the Living Creatures he saw as "full of eyes before and behind" [Rev. 4:6], whereas Ezekiel describes his as the "rings [rims of the wheels] full of eyes round about them four." These "eyes" see all of the Holiness of God [Rev. 4:8].)*

19 And when the Living Creatures went, the wheels went by them: and when the Living Creatures were lifted up from the Earth, the wheels were lifted up. *(First of all, we should understand the laws of nature have absolutely nothing to do with these Cherubims. They seem to be subject to no laws except the sphere pertaining to their own creation and design by God.)*

20 Whithersoever the Spirit was to go, they went, thither was their spirit to go; and the wheels were lifted up over against them: for the spirit of the living creature was in the wheels. *(The phrase, "Whithersoever the Spirit was to go," refers to the Holy Spirit, and should have been capitalized in the English translation. As well, the phrase, "Thither was their spirit to go," implies their own personal spirit, soul, and body, regarding these "Living Creatures." However, it should be emphasized that their body is not physical, but rather a "spirit body."*

The phrase, "For the spirit of the Living Creature was in the wheels," seems to have to do with the "eyes" and concerns their ability to "know.")

21 When those went, these went; and when those stood, these stood; and when those were lifted up from the Earth, the wheels were lifted up over against them: for the spirit of the Living Creature was in the wheels. *(This Verse is very similar to Verse 20. Laws indigenous to man are only a part of the laws created by God.*

We are now seeing the laws of the Heavenly creation, which are far ahead of anything we presently know. We will know these laws after the Resurrection of Life, when we are given Glorified Bodies.)

22 And the likeness of the firmament upon the heads of the Living Creature was as the colour of the terrible crystal, stretched forth over their heads above.

23 And under the firmament were their wings straight, the one toward the other: every one had two, which covered on this side, and every one had two, which covered on that side, their bodies. *(According to Verse 9, when the Cherubim moved, their wings were straight up with the tips touching. When they stopped, they were let down pointing straight forward with the tips continuing to touch. The other pair "covered their bodies.")*

24 And when they went, I heard the noise of their wings, like the noise of great waters, as the voice of the Almighty, the voice of speech, as the noise of an host: when they stood, they let down their wings. *(Even though there is no evidence that the "wings" moved except from a vertical to a horizontal position when stopped, still, he "heard the noise of their wings." The only explanation is that their movement signified great praise to God [Rev. 19:6].)*

25 And there was a voice from the firmament that was over their heads, when they stood, and had let down their wings. *(This is the Voice of God, even though we are not told what was said.)*

26 And above the firmament that was over their heads was the likeness of a throne, as the appearance of a sapphire stone: and upon the likeness of the throne was the likeness as the appearance of a man above upon it. *(Ezekiel sees the appearance of God here, which was similar to a "Man," but with a spirit body.)*

27 And I saw as the colour of amber, as the appearance of fire round about within it, from the appearance of His loins even upward, and from the appearance of His loins even downward, I saw as it were the appearance of fire, and it had brightness round about. *(Ezekiel did not say that God was clothed in fire, but "the appearance of fire round about within it." In other words, there was a glow which made the Lord's Spirit Body seem as if it was on fire.)*

28 As the appearance of the bow that is in the cloud in the day of rain, so was the appearance of the brightness round about. This was the appearance of the likeness of the Glory of the LORD. And when I saw it, I fell upon my face, and I heard a voice of one who spoke. *(Ezekiel saw a rainbow round about the Throne of God exactly as did John in his vision [Rev. 4:2-3]. The "Glory of God" denotes the revelation of God's being, nature, and presence to mankind, sometimes with material and spiritual phenomena, as here.*

The phrase, "And when I saw it [the Glory of God], I fell upon my face," portrays the experience of most under these circumstances [Mat. 17:1-8; Mk. 9:2-8; Lk. 9:28-36; Gen. 17:3; Ex. 3:1-6; Num. 22:31; Josh. 5:14; Dan. 8:17; Jn. 18:6; Acts 9:4]. This proclaims the fact that "being slain in the Spirit" is Scriptural.)

CHAPTER 2
(595 B.C.)
EZEKIEL'S COMMISSION

AND He said unto me, Son of man, stand upon your feet, and I will speak unto you. *(Apart from the four Gospels, the term, "Son of man," is not used in the New Testament; and apart from Ezekiel, it is found only in Dan. 8:17.*

The entire Glory of God is outlined here and elsewhere; man falling on his face before it proclaims man's fallen state as a result of the Fall in the Garden of Eden.

The phrase, "Son of man, stand upon your feet," reflects the "born-again" experience, and the lifting up of man from his fallen state.)

2 And the Spirit *(Holy Spirit)* entered into me when He spoke unto me, and set me upon my feet, that I heard Him Who spoke unto me. *(The phrase, "And the Spirit entered into me," refers to Ezekiel being given the Holy Spirit in order to perform a particular service. It is not the same as the Baptism with the Holy Spirit, which could be entered into after the Cross of Christ [Jn. 14:17].)*

3 And He said unto me, Son of man, I send you to the children of Israel, to a rebellious nation that has rebelled against Me: they and their fathers have transgressed against Me, even unto this very day. *(Ezekiel, in this Book, is addressed as "Son of man," and not as a Son of Abraham, for Israel was now Lo-Ammi [Hos. 1:9]. Jesus was "The Son of Man." This was His title in rejection; hence He forbade His Disciples to announce Him as the Messiah, for He, as "The Son of Man," was to suffer [Lk., Chpt. 9].*

The phrase, "I send you to the Children of Israel," refers to Ezekiel's first Commission. Actually, this great Prophet began His Ministry

some five or six years before the destruction of Jerusalem in 586 B.C.)

4 For they are impudent children and stiffhearted. I do send you unto them; and you shall say unto them, Thus saith the Lord GOD. *(The words which Ezekiel were to speak were to be the words of Adonai Jehovah. God was their Author. In the Hebrew, the Name "Lord GOD" is "Adonai Jehovah." As such, it is characteristic of Ezekiel's Prophecies. It occurs 214 times.)*

5 And they, whether they will hear, or whether they will forbear, (for they are a rebellious house,) yet shall know that there has been a Prophet among them. *(For the first time, the Lord designates the calling of "Prophet" to Ezekiel! The Lord is speaking primarily of the Exiles.)*

6 And you, son of man, be not afraid of them, neither be afraid of their words, though briers and thorns be with you, and you do dwell among scorpions: be not afraid of their words, nor be dismayed at their looks, though they be a rebellious house. *(Their rebellion was against God, and despite the miracles, Law, Patriarchs, and Prophets. They simply would not obey the Bible.)*

7 And you shall speak My Words unto them, whether they will hear, or whether they will forbear; for they are most rebellious. *(The phrase, "And you shall speak My Words unto them," is encouraging in that the Words conveyed would be those given by Jehovah. At the same time, there is a warning against the intermingling of lower thoughts and self-originated message, which is the bane of the modern Church. As Jehovah spoke thus to Ezekiel of old, He speaks the same today! Only God's Words are to be given to the people.)*

8 But you, son of man, hear what I say unto you; Be not thou rebellious like that rebellious house: open your mouth, and eat that I give you. *(The phrase, "Be not thou rebellious like that rebellious house," is a warning against the Prophet's natural weakness. The phrase, "Open your mouth, and eat that I give you," concerns the Lord giving him the Words he was to say.)*

9 And when I looked, behold, an hand was sent unto me; and, lo, a roll of a Book was therein *(the "books" of that day were actually several skins sewn together to make a long piece which was rolled up from each end. The phrase, "An hand was sent unto me," seems to imply that even though it came from the One on the Throne, still, it was separate from Him or the*

Living Creatures. It seemed to appear mysteriously by itself, as in the history of Belshazzar's feast [Dan. 5:5]. In one sense of the word, as it wrote the doom of Belshazzar's kingdom years later, it was now writing the doom of God's Own people, Judah and Jerusalem!);

10 And He spread it before me; and it was written within and without: and there was written therein lamentations, and mourning, and woe. *(As the Lord "spread it before him," he finds that it is no message of glad tidings, but instead of "lamentations, and mourning, and woe.")*

CHAPTER 3
(595 B.C.)
EZEKIEL EATS THE ROLL

MOREOVER He said unto me, Son of man, eat that you find; eat this roll, and go speak unto the House of Israel. *(The phrase, "Eat that you find," is a reminder that the True Prophet does not choose his message [Acts 4:20], but delivers what is given unto him by the Lord. As well, the word "eat" signifies that he was to be thoroughly acquainted with its contents in order to deliver this message to "Israel.")*

2 So I opened my mouth, and He caused me to eat that roll. *(This implies that the Lord helped Ezekiel to understand what was written. Actually, he did not literally eat a Book or Roll, as all of this is given in a Vision [1:1].)*

3 And He said unto me, Son of man, cause your belly to eat, and fill your bowels with this roll that I give you. Then did I eat it; and it was in my mouth as honey for sweetness. *(The Word of God is ever sweet to a spiritual palate; however, it is bitter to the flesh [3:14]; for the Word of the Lord judges the nature and activities of the flesh, and announces the Wrath of God which is coming upon it.)*

HIS SECOND COMMISSION: TO SPEAK GOD'S MESSAGES TO ISRAEL

4 And He said unto me, Son of man, go, get thee unto the House of Israel, and speak with My words unto them. *(Ezekiel's Ministry begins here. Its character should be compared with that of Jeremiah's. His Ministry was begun at least while God was still in relationship with Israel, and while He yet spoke of them as "My People.")*

5 For you are not sent to a people of a strange speech and of an hard language, but

to the House of Israel (*as Ezekiel was sent to "Israel," likewise, Christ was sent to Israel. As Israel would not hear him, Israel would not hear Christ! In both cases, they went to their doom!*);

6 Not to many people of a strange speech and of an hard language, whose words you can not understand. Surely, had I sent you to them, they would have hearkened unto you. (*The Divine statement, "Surely they would hearken unto you," throws a shaft of light across the darkness of the heathen world, and actually, in shadow, proclaims the coming Gentile Church.*)

7 But the House of Israel will not hearken unto you; for they will not hearken unto Me: for all the House of Israel are impudent and hardhearted. (*The word "impudent" means to be contemptuous, and in this sense holding the Word of God in contempt and exhibiting a cocky boldness. The word "hardhearted" means "unfeeling and pitiless."*)

8 Behold, I have made your face strong against their faces, and your forehead strong against their foreheads. (*As the rebellion is deep, the Lord gives Ezekiel a powerful anointing that he may be able to continue to minister despite their obstinacy.*)

9 As an adamant harder than flint have I made your forehead: fear them not, neither be dismayed at their looks, though they be a rebellious house. (*The word "adamant" could be translated "diamond," which is the hardest substance known to man. The phrase, "Neither be dismayed at their looks," proclaims the fact that the Prophet had a natural tendency to shrink back from their threats, revilings, and their scowls of hatred. Irrespective, he was to deliver the Message, even "though they be a rebellious house."*)

10 Moreover He said unto me, Son of man, all My words that I shall speak unto you receive in your heart, and hear with your ears. (*The stress is laid on the word "all." The Prophet was not to pick and choose out of the Message, but was to deliver "all the counsel of God" [Acts 20:27].*)

11 And go, get thee to them of the captivity, unto the children of your people, and speak unto them, and tell them, Thus saith the Lord GOD; whether they will hear, or whether they will forbear. (*The phrase, "And go, get thee to them of the captivity," refers to his Message being directed to this group. Due to the Northern Kingdom having been taken captive well over a hundred years previous, and some from the Southern Kingdom now being taken captive, the total*

number in captivity would have been quite large.

Ezekiel's responsibility was to deliver the Message, rather than their response to it.*)

EZEKIEL VISITS THE EXILES BY THE RIVER CHEBAR

12 Then the Spirit took me up, and I heard behind me a voice of a great rushing, saying, Blessed be the Glory of the LORD from His place. (*The exclamation, "Blessed be the Glory of the LORD from His place," probably means that the Glory awakens Praise wherever it goes, and so could make even Babylonia "God's place."*

The phrase, "Then the Spirit took me up," refers to the Holy Spirit, Who energized the Cherubims and the wheels, and then took hold of Ezekiel to energize him.)

13 I heard also the noise of the wings of the Living Creatures that touched one another, and the noise of the wheels over against them, and a noise of a great rushing. (*All of this which Ezekiel has been observing, such as the Cherubims, etc., he now becomes a part of!*)

14 So the Spirit lifted me up, and took me away, and I went in bitterness in the heat of my spirit; but the hand of the LORD was strong upon me. (*The phrase, "And I went in bitterness in the heat of my spirit," refers to the wrath or anger of the Prophet respecting the sins of the people and their opposition and rebellion against God.*)

15 Then I came to them of the captivity at Tel-abib, who dwelt by the river of Chebar, and I sat where they sat, and remained there astonished among them seven days. (*All that is known of "Tel-abib" is said here. It is by the "river of Chebar." The phrase, "And I sat where they sat," refers to Ezekiel beginning his Ministry in silence.*)

16 And it came to pass at the end of seven days, that the Word of the LORD came unto me, saying (*Ezekiel did not move until the Lord said so!*),

COMMISSIONED TO BE A WATCHMAN TO ISRAEL

17 Son of man, I have made you a watchman unto the House of Israel: therefore hear the word at My mouth, and give them warning from Me. (*In the ancient world, watchmen walked the walls in order to spot any hostile action against the city. They were also there to give word to the king of any person approaching*

the city wall [II Sam. 18:24-27; II Ki. 9:17-20].
Ezekiel was to be a "watchman.")

18 When I say unto the wicked, You shall surely die; and you give him not warning, nor speak to warn the wicked from his wicked way, to save his life; the same wicked man shall die in his iniquity; but his blood will I require at your hand. *(This Passage tells us that ignorance of the Gospel does not save one. As well, the Preacher is to warn the wicked, and in no uncertain terms. If the wicked aren't warned, meaning that the Preacher preaches a false message, while the wicked person will die in his sin, still, his blood will be required at the hand of the false preacher.*

In fact, every single Preacher in the world should read this Text every day.)

19 Yet if you warn the wicked, and he turn not from his wickedness, nor from his wicked way, he shall die in his iniquity; but you have delivered your soul. *(The phrase, "But you have delivered your soul," means that the judgment passed on the Prophet does not depend on the results of his Ministry, whether men will hear or whether they will forbear, but rather that he has "delivered his soul," i.e., "has done his duty as a watchman." Therefore, the implication is that the Prophet will lose his soul if he does not faithfully deliver the Word of God.)*

20 Again, When a righteous man does turn from his righteousness, and commit iniquity, and I lay a stumblingblock before him, he shall die: because you have not given him warning, he shall die in his sin, and his righteousness which he has done shall not be remembered; but his blood will I require at your hand. *(This Passage lays to rest the unscriptural doctrine of Unconditional Eternal Security. As well, the Preacher is not only to preach to the lost, but he is to also warn the righteous who turns from his righteousness. If the Preacher doesn't do so, once again, even though that person will be lost, the Lord says, "I will require at your hand" that individual's blood.*

How many modern Preachers are faithfully warning the wicked? the righteous?)

21 Nevertheless if you warn the righteous man, that the righteous sin not, and he does not sin, he shall surely live, because he is warned; also you have delivered your soul. *(This tells us that the righteous must be constantly warned, or else many, if not most, righteous will be turned aside. This puts a tremendous responsibility on the Preacher of the Gospel. God help us if we fail in that responsibility!)*

GOD'S HAND ON EZEKIEL; VISION OF GOD'S GLORY

22 And the hand of the LORD was there upon me; and He said unto me, Arise, go forth into the plain, and I will there talk with you. *(To hear the Word from His Mouth, the servant of the Lord must be willing to withdraw into the "plain" or "low place," for it is there that the Master speaks with the servant and afresh reveals Himself in His Glory to him, and where he receives a fresh enduement of Spiritual Power. [In the Hebrew, the expression, "the plain," means "a low place reached with difficulty through obstacles."]*

23 Then I arose, and went forth into the plain: and, behold, the glory of the LORD stood there, as the glory which I saw by the river of Chebar: and I fell on my face. *(The phrase, "And I fell on my face," is spoken of Ezekiel six times [Vs. 23; 1:28; 9:8; 11:13; 43:3; 44:4]. Once again, this tells us that it is Scriptural for people to be "slain in the Spirit.")*

24 Then the Spirit entered into me, and set me upon my feet, and spoke with me, and said unto me, Go, shut yourself within your house. *(The phrase, "Then the Spirit entered into me," refers to the Holy Spirit, Who will lead us into all Truth [Jn. 16:7-15].)*

25 But thou, O son of man, behold, they shall put bands upon you, and shall bind you with them, and you shall not go out among them *(when under the control of the Holy Spirit [a control which indeed must be freely given], the lips are taught when to be dumb and when to speak)*:

26 And I will make your tongue cleave to the roof of your mouth, that you shall be dumb, and shall not be to them a reprover: for they are a rebellious house. *(The phrase, "For they are a rebellious house," implied that his subjects were far more "rebellious" than he realized, and he must have the absolute leading of the Spirit in all action of Ministry. As well, the Lord had other things He wanted to do with the Prophet before he began his preaching Ministry, as the next two Chapters will affirm.)*

27 But when I speak with you, I will open your mouth, and you shall say unto them, Thus saith the Lord GOD; He who hears, let him hear; and he who forbears, let him forbear: for they are a rebellious house. *(These Passages proclaim the manner of operation regarding the imparting of the Word to the hearer by the Holy Spirit. It is done by the messenger*

proclaiming the Message, and the subject hearing what is proclaimed [Rom. 10:17].)

CHAPTER 4
(595 B.C.)
SYMBOLS OF THE SIEGE: THE TILE

THOU also, son of man, take thee a tile, and lay it before you, and pourtray upon it the city, even Jerusalem *(the "tile" was the manner in which records were kept in ancient times. They were all sizes, which the average being about two feet long and one foot wide. They were covered with very small writing, at least in most cases, and, at times, pictorial representation.*

The symbolism of the "tile" is the first the Lord will use through Ezekiel, all to portray His Message. A portrayal of the outline of the city of Jerusalem was to be put on the tile):

2 And lay siege against it, and build a fort against it, and cast a mount against it; set the camp also against it, and set battering rams against it round about. *(This was taking place in Babylonia approximately four years before Jerusalem would be destroyed by Nebuchadnezzar; therefore, the time of destruction is drawing near, which the Lord desires to portray to the Exiles.*

The Prophet was to exhibit this "tile" portraying the outline of Jerusalem, and to make of wood or dirt all the necessary articles of destruction against the city, describing a "siege."

This was probably left in a conspicuous place for quite some time, and no doubt studied minutely by many of the Exiles, who very easily discerned its message.)

THE IRON PAN, A SIGN

3 Moreover take thou unto you an iron pan, and set it for a wall of iron between you and the city: and set your face against it, and it shall be besieged, and you shall lay siege against it. This shall be a sign to the House of Israel. *(The "iron pan" signified a "wall of iron" surrounding the city in question, or at least from the side of the siege, portraying the power of the army of the Babylonians.)*

THE LENGTH OF GOD'S PUNISHMENT: THE SIGN OF LYING 390 DAYS ON THE LEFT SIDE — PUNISHMENT OF ISRAEL

4 Lie thou also upon your left side, and lay the iniquity of the House of Israel upon it:

according to the number of the days that you shall lie upon it you shall bear their iniquity. *(The Lord will now use another type of symbolism, that of Ezekiel physically lying on his left side 390 days, and then on his right side for 40 days. This was to be done for a few minutes each day.*

The symbolism was to portray both the Northern Kingdom of "Israel" and the Southern Kingdom of "Judah." It was meant to portray these two kingdoms crushed to the ground.)

5 For I have laid upon you the years of their iniquity, according to the number of the days, three hundred and ninety days: so shall you bear the iniquity of the House of Israel. *(The "390 days" was to represent the "390 years of their iniquity," counting both the Northern and the Southern Kingdoms. The Lord showed extreme displeasure with the Northern Kingdom as a result of their splitting the nation and going into idol worship [I Ki. 12:16-20, 28-30].)*

THE SIGN OF LYING ON THE RIGHT SIDE 40 DAYS — PUNISHMENT OF JUDAH

6 And when you have accomplished them, lie again on your right side, and you shall bear the iniquity of the House of Judah forty days: I have appointed you each day for a year. *(As the Northern Kingdom had been symbolized, likewise, the Southern Kingdom of Judah would be symbolized by the "40 days" of Ezekiel lying on his "right side." This was not to be 40 days added to the 390 days, but rather that the 40 was to be simultaneous with the 390, with both periods ending with the fall of Judah and Jerusalem.)*

THE SIGN OF THE BARE ARM BOUND — JERUSALEM HELPLESS TO AVERT HER DOOM

7 Therefore you shall set your face toward the siege of Jerusalem, and your arm shall be uncovered, and you shall prophesy against it. *(Ezekiel lying on his left side and then on his right side was possibly immediately before the symbolism of the "tile." He was to "face" this model of the siege, with one arm "uncovered." This was meant to denote the fact that both Judah and Israel, because of sin, were naked to the judgment of God.)*

8 And, behold, I will lay bands upon you, and you shall not turn yourself from one side to another, till you have ended the days of your siege.

THE FAMINE DURING THE SIEGE

9 Take thou also unto you wheat, and barley, and beans, and lentiles, and millet, and fitches, and put them in one vessel, and make thee bread thereof, according to the number of the days that you shall lie upon your side, three hundred and ninety days shall you eat thereof. *(The "390 days" did not mean that the siege would last for this period of time; in fact, it lasted about 2 years. Rather, it was meant to imply that the destruction of Jerusalem and Judah pertained to the entire time of the iniquity, which was 390 years, at least for the Northern Kingdom, and which included the Southern Kingdom of Judah.)*

10 And your meat which you shall eat shall be by weight, twenty shekels a day: from time to time shall you eat it. *(The "twenty shekels a day" would buy about ten ounces, which was to be consumed each day. As Ezekiel went through this regimen each day, the sameness of the procedure could not help but have a lasting effect on the Exiles, as it portrayed by Prophetic symbolism that which was coming shortly to Jerusalem.)*

11 You shall drink also water by measure, the sixth part of an hin: from time to time shall you drink. *("The sixth part of an hin" would be about a half pint. This was, as the food, to be doled out once a day. To "drink also water by measure" showed that water would be at a premium, as food, in the coming siege.)*

12 And you shall eat it as barley cakes, and you shall bake it with dung that comes out of man, in their sight. *(The implication of the Lord is that fuel to heat the stoves would be in such short supply that the population would be forced to use the dried contents of the cesspools of Jerusalem for fuel in order to try to cook their food, such as it was.)*

13 And the LORD said, Even thus shall the children of Israel eat their defiled bread among the Gentiles, whither I will drive them. *(Under the ceremonial Law of Moses, bread cooked by the fuel of human dung was "defiled." This was to serve as a symbolism of the banishment of the Jews among the Gentiles, whom the Jews called unclean. As such, they considered themselves defiled and ceremonially unclean, and constantly!)*

14 Then said I, Ah Lord GOD! behold, my soul has not been polluted; for from my youth up even till now have I not eaten of that which dies of itself, or is torn in pieces; neither came there abominable flesh into my mouth.

(Ezekiel, as a Priest, had faithfully followed the Law of Moses, and had done his best to keep himself from any kind of defilement. That of which he speaks is noted in Ex. 22:31 and Lev. 7:24, 11:39-40, and 17:15.)

15 Then He said unto me, Lo, I have given you cow's dung for man's dung and you shall prepare your bread therewith. *(In response to the plea of the Prophet, the Lord would allow Ezekiel to use "cow's dung" rather than "man's dung." However, this also was more than likely ceremonially unclean, but at least not as repugnant in Ezekiel's sight. Without going into explanation, these were ceremonial and not moral laws, which means there was no actual sin involved either way.)*

16 Moreover He said unto me, Son of man, behold, I will break the staff of bread in Jerusalem: and they shall eat bread by weight, and with care; and they shall drink water by measure, and with astonishment *(this pertained to the terrible famine which ensued as a result of the siege of Jerusalem, and which was also described by Jeremiah upon its fulfillment [Lam. 4:8-10])*:

17 That they may want bread and water, and be astonied one with another, and consume away for their iniquity. *(To the horror of the famine and its physical privation, there was to be added the consciousness that it was caused by their own sins.)*

CHAPTER 5
(594 B.C.)
SIGNS OF JERUSALEM'S FATE: RAZOR, KNIFE, AND FIRE

AND you, son of man, take thee a sharp knife, take thee a barber's razor, and cause it to pass upon your head and upon your beard: then take thee balances to weigh, and divide the hair. *(Again, the Lord uses symbolism to portray the desired Message. It is the symbol of the "barber's razor." In Old Testament times, the head and beard being shaved represented shame, and was symbolic of the leper who was required to shave his head and beard. Therefore, Judah and Jerusalem were classified by the Lord as "spiritual lepers.")*

2 You shall burn with fire a third part in the midst of the city, when the days of the siege are fulfilled: and you shall take a third part, and smite about it with a knife: and a third part you shall scatter in the wind; and I will draw out a sword after them. *(The symbolic*

action predicted that the fire, i.e., the Wrath of God [in pestilence and famine], should destroy approximately one-third of the nation, with war destroying a second part, and the Exiles representing the third part, which would be "scattered in the wind." Many of these also were to perish by sword and famine. In short, the carnage, when it did take place, was terrible, to say the least!)

3 You shall also take thereof a few in number, and bind them in your skirts. *(This "number" represented the "few" who would not fall into the categories of Verse 2. In a population of several million, such would be normal! The next Verse tells what will happen to them.)*

4 Then take of them again, and cast them into the midst of the fire, and burn them in the fire; for thereof shall a fire come forth into all the House of Israel. *(The judgment is to be so complete that even those who thought they had escaped, by whatever means, would find the "fire" of judgment chasing them, of which they could not escape.)*

JUDGMENT COMING BECAUSE OF SINS

5 Thus saith the Lord GOD; This is Jerusalem: I have set it in the midst of the nations and countries that are round about her. *(The phrase, "This is Jerusalem," is strong indeed! She, as representing the all of Israel, was placed in the center of the nations in order to shed upon them the light of the Gospel. But she rebelled against Truth more than the heathen, multiplied idols, and sank morally lower than her neighbors.)*

6 And she has changed My Judgments into wickedness more than the nations, and My Statutes more than the countries that are round about her: for they *(the Jews)* have refused My Judgments and My Statutes, they have not walked in them. *(The phrase, "She has changed My Judgments into wickedness," refers to the Law of Moses, which was not only ignored, but was twisted and "changed" to mean something else entirely!)*

7 Therefore thus saith the Lord GOD; Because you multiplied more than the nations that are round about you, and have not walked in My Statutes; neither have kept My Judgments, neither have done according to the judgments of the nations that are round about you *(the idea of this Verse is that the heathen nations were at least true to the gods whom*

they worshipped, while Jerusalem had rebelled against Jehovah);

8 Therefore thus saith the Lord GOD; Behold, I, even I, am against you, and will execute Judgments in the midst of you in the sight of the nations. *(The phrase, "I, even I," emphasizes the certitude of the Wrath of God, just as Isa. 43:25 emphasizes the certitude of the pardoning Love of God; and it rebukes the unbelief of the natural heart which denies both these activities of the Divine Essence.)*

9 And I will do in you that which I have not done, and whereunto I will not do any more the like, because of all your abominations. *(The phrase, "And I will do in you that which I have not done," refers to the soon destruction of Jerusalem. The phrase, "I will not do any more the like," has reference to the present and to the future. It held both Promise and Judgment!)*

10 Therefore the fathers shall eat the sons in the midst of you, and the sons shall eat their fathers; and I will execute Judgments in you, and the whole remnant of you will I scatter into all the winds. *(This was literally fulfilled during the siege of the city by the Chaldeans, as it had occurred years before in the siege of Samaria [II Ki. 6:28-29], and was to occur afterwards, in connection with the siege by the Romans in A.D. 70.)*

11 Wherefore, as I live, saith the Lord GOD, surely, because you have defiled My Sanctuary with all your detestable things, and with all your abominations, therefore will I also diminish you; neither shall My eye spare, neither will I have any pity. *(The righteous Judgments, consequent upon the abominations of this Verse, which are detailed in Verses 8 through 17, are still in operation, and will reach a crisis under the reign of the Antichrist, when the "indignation" against Israel will be consummated [Dan. 11:36; 12:1].)*

12 A third part of you shall die with the pestilence, and with famine shall they be consumed in the midst of you: and a third part shall fall by the sword round about you; and I will scatter a third part into all the winds, and I will draw out a sword after them. *(Ezekiel draws this Passage, no doubt, from Lev. 26:33. Verse 12 describes the manner in which the judgment will fall.)*

13 Thus shall My anger be accomplished, and I will cause My fury to rest upon them, and I will be comforted: and they shall know that I the LORD have spoken it in My zeal,

when I have accomplished My fury in them. *(Righteousness must, from its nature, be restless till evil is judged. Then it is comforted. Such was the effect of the judgment of sin at Calvary; and those who recognize this Gospel fact and take refuge in the great God and Saviour, the Lord Jesus Christ, Who was the Participant in it, taste the sweetness of the Divine comfort.)*

14 Moreover I will make you waste, and a reproach among the nations that are round about you, in the sight of all who pass by. *(Of all the suffering experienced by Judah, perhaps the worst of all was the "reproach among the nations," and "in the sight of all who pass by.")*

15 So it shall be a reproach and a taunt, an instruction and an astonishment unto the nations that are round about you, when I shall execute judgments in you in anger and in fury and in furious rebukes. I the LORD have spoken it. *(This is drawn perhaps from Deut. 28:37. The phrase, "So it shall be a reproach and a taunt," refers to Jerusalem, which is to be the great object lesson in God's education of mankind. The idea was that if Jehovah would do this to His Own City and People, He would do at least as much to the heathen. This He did, and this He does! He calls it "furious rebukes.")*

16 When I shall send upon them the evil arrows of famine, which shall be for their destruction, and which I will send to destroy you: and I will increase the famine upon you, and will break your staff of bread. *(As an arrow shot by an expert marksman goes true to its target, so will these "arrows" unleashed by the Lord. They will be "arrows" of "famine" and "destruction." They are of necessity called "evil arrows."*

The phrase, "And will break your staff of bread," refers to the fact that Judah always reaped abundant harvests, and consequently felt that "famine" was impossible. Nevertheless, the Lord warns them that not only is such possible, but most surely will come, which it did!)

17 So will I send upon you famine and evil beasts, and they shall bereave you: and pestilence and blood shall pass through you; and I will bring the sword upon you. I the LORD have spoken it. *(The "evil beasts" speak of the Babylonian horde! The Chapter ends with the words, "I the LORD have spoken it," which is the final stroke of all, guaranteeing that even though the words came from Ezekiel, they, of necessity, belong to the Lord. As such, they were guaranteed of fulfillment.)*

CHAPTER 6
(594 B.C.)
PROPHECY AGAINST THE MOUNTAINS OF ISRAEL

AND the Word of the LORD came unto me, saying,

2 Son of man, set your face toward the mountains of Israel, and prophesy against them *(while the prior Message attacked idolatry in the city of Jerusalem, this Message attacks it in the Land of Judah. The "mountains of Israel" are especially pointed out because of idol temples, which usually were erected on mountains and hills, and by water courses, and in valleys. These were, as should be obvious, an insult to Jehovah. Despite repeated admonitions, they had not been removed. Now they would be removed by force)*,

3 And say, You mountains of Israel, hear the Word of the Lord GOD; Thus saith the Lord GOD to the mountains, and to the hills, to the rivers, and to the valleys; Behold, I, even I, will bring a sword upon you, and I will destroy your high places. *(Just as the Prophet [I Ki. 13:2] disdained to speak to the king and addressed himself to the idolatrous altar, so here Ezekiel addresses the idolatrous centers of worship.)*

4 And your altars shall be desolate, and your images shall be broken: and I will cast down your slain men before your idols. *(The phrase, "And your altars shall be desolate," refers to the fact that these "altars" were theirs and not God's. The Lord had only one Altar, which represented Calvary and the Sacrifice of His Only Son, which would take place in the future. Every other altar represented a false way of Salvation.)*

5 And I will lay the dead carcases of the Children of Israel before their idols, and I will scatter your bones round about your altars. *(The idea of this Verse is that God will not tolerate any other "altar" than His Sacred Altar of Calvary. As it was true then, it is most definitely true now!)*

6 In all your dwellingplaces the cities shall be laid waste, and the high places shall be desolate; that your Altars may be laid waste and made desolate, and your idols may be broken and cease, and your images may be cut down, and your works may be abolished. *(This Verse illustrates the expression, "abomination of desolation," which is the desolation brought on by the moral and material result of idolatry. This*

*fundamental moral principle, i.e., that deso-
lation is produced by idolatry, may be verified
in modern as well as ancient times, for today
vast portions of the richest districts in the world
are now desert because of idolatry. In the case
of multitudes, a sad personal experience demonstrates this fact, as well! If the heart is governed by an "idol," and religious idols are the
worst of all, there is inward desolation, with
spiritual fruit, wealth, and beauty virtually
unknown [Rev. 3:17].)*

7 And the slain shall fall in the midst of
you, and you shall know that I am the LORD.
*(God can be known in Grace or in Wrath, in
Salvation or in Judgment. Israel proved Him by
experience to be a Saviour when He redeemed
them out of Egypt [Ex. 10:2]; likewise, they
proved Him by experience to be a Judge when He
abandoned them to exile because of idolatry, as
it evidenced in this Verse.)*

A REMNANT WILL BE SAVED

8 Yet will I leave a remnant, that you may
have some who shall escape the sword among
the nations, when you shall be scattered
through the countries. *(The phrase, "When
you shall be scattered through the countries,"
occurred in Ezekiel's day, but occurred in earnest in A.D. 70, when Titus destroyed Jerusalem, with over one million Jews dying in that
horror, and with well over one million being
sold into slavery.)*

9 And they who escape of you shall remember Me among the nations whither they shall
be carried captives, because I am broken with
their whorish heart, which has departed from
Me, and with their eyes, which go a whoring
after their idols: and they shall loathe themselves for the evils which they have committed in all their abominations. *(The phrase,
"Because I am broken with their whorish heart,"
could be translated to mean that God's heart
was broken because of Israel's determined idolatry. The phrase, "And they shall loathe themselves for the evils which they have committed,"
will not actually be fulfilled until the Second
Coming [Zech. 12:10].)*

10 And they shall know that I am the
LORD, and that I have not said in vain that I
would do this evil unto them. *(Someone has
said that the greatest thing one can do regarding the Lord is to simply believe His Word.
Regrettably, most did not then, and most do
not now!)*

THE LAND WILL BE MADE DESOLATE

11 Thus saith the Lord GOD; Smite with your
hand, and stamp with your foot, and say, Alas
for all the evil abominations of the House of
Israel! for they shall fall by the sword, by the
famine, and by the pestilence.

12 He who is far off shall die of the pestilence; and he who is near shall fall by the sword;
and he who remains and is besieged shall die
by the famine: thus will I accomplish My fury
upon them. *(It is amazing when one considers
the continued Prophecies of Jeremiah and Ezekiel
proclaiming coming doom, and yet unheeded!)*

13 Then shall you know that I am the LORD,
when their slain men shall be among their
idols round about their Altars, upon every
high hill, in all the tops of the mountains,
and under every green tree, and under every
thick oak, the place where they did offer sweet
savour to all their idols. *(The phrase, "Then
shall you know that I am the LORD," implies
that Judah little believed the predictions of
the Prophet.)*

14 So will I stretch out My hand upon them,
and make the land desolate, yea, more desolate than the wilderness toward Diblath, in all
their habitations: and they shall know that I
am the LORD. *(The Holy Spirit through the
Prophet would not continue making the statement, "And they shall know that I am the LORD,"
if the unbelief of Judah, Jerusalem, and the exiles had not been so pronounced!)*

CHAPTER 7
(594 B.C.)
JUDGMENT ON THE LAND OF ISRAEL

MOREOVER the Word of the LORD came
unto me, saying,

2 Also, thou son of man, thus saith the Lord
GOD unto the land of Israel; An end, the end
is come upon the four corners of the land. *(The
"end" of the pleadings through Jeremiah and
Ezekiel for Judah and Jerusalem to repent have
come! They have refused to repent and therefore, the judgment will fall!)*

3 Now is the end come upon you, and I
will send My anger upon you, and will judge
you according to your ways, and will recompense upon you all your abominations. *(This
Verse proclaims a side of the Lord mostly denied,
the side of Judgment. However, if Mercy is
rejected, whether then or now, ultimately Judgment must come.)*

4 And My eye shall not spare you, neither will I have pity: but I will recompense your ways upon you, and your abominations shall be in the midst of you: and you shall know that I am the LORD. *(If men will not repent, the Lord cannot "spare" or "have pity.")*

5 Thus saith the Lord GOD; An evil, an only evil, behold, is come. *(This "evil" refers to the soon to come Babylonian invasion. The phrase, "Only evil," pertains to it being all judgment, with no mercy or pity. In other words, there will be no respite!*

The phrase, "Behold, is come," refers to the Truth that if the people repented, even though their souls would be saved, the City, the Temple, and the Land would not now be spared. Repentance at an earlier time would have avoided this, but it is now too late to save the City and the Temple.)

6 An end is come, the end is come: it watches for you; behold, it is come. *(The repetition guarantees the certitude of fulfillment.)*

7 The morning is come unto you, O you who dwell in the land: the time is come, the day of trouble is near, and not the sounding again of the mountains. *(The Verse means: as the day begins, Judgment is beginning. The Prophet says, "the time is come.")*

8 Now will I shortly pour out My fury upon you, and accomplish My anger upon you: and I will judge you according to your ways, and will recompense you for all your abominations. *(This Verse is very similar to Verse 3. Its repetition, as given by the Holy Spirit, only increases its severity.)*

9 And My eye shall not spare, neither will I have pity: I will recompense you according to your ways and your abominations that are in the midst of you; and you shall know that I am the LORD Who smites. *(The Lord either touches to heal, as was evidenced in Christ, Who came not to condemn, but to save, but if rejected, will "smite," exactly as Jerusalem was smitten in A.D. 70.)*

10 Behold the day, behold, it is come: the morning is gone forth; the rod has blossomed, pride has budded. *(The phrase, "The rod has blossomed," refers to Nebuchadnezzar, who was ready to strike. The phrase, "Pride has budded," pertains to Israel's determined sin which demanded the rod, and is unique here. It means "proud luxuriance." In other words, the Blessing of God had been turned into license.)*

11 Violence is risen up into a rod of wickedness: none of them shall remain, nor of their multitude, nor of any of theirs: neither shall there be wailing for them. *(The "violence" goes with the "pride" of Verse 10. Wherever there is "pride," there will be "violence," as self-righteous men demand to have their way! The phrase, "Violence is risen up into a rod of wickedness," refers to the fact that by violent injustice they destroyed and impoverished each other. As the Nobles of Judah practiced this "rod of wickedness" on the weak and the helpless, the Lord then practiced it on them!)*

12 The time is come, the day draws near: let not the buyer rejoice, nor the seller mourn: for wrath is upon all the multitude thereof. *(The idea is: the conduct of business, which had become all-important to Judah, was soon to come to an end. This, within itself, was only the tip of the iceberg concerning the judgment that was coming.)*

13 For the seller shall not return to that which is sold, although they were yet alive: for the vision is touching the whole multitude thereof, which shall not return; neither shall any strengthen himself in the iniquity of his life. *(The phrase, "For the seller shall not return to that which is sold," refers to the false prophecies claiming the immediate restoration of the Exiles. The "sellers" would not see their estates again, even though their children might! They were to be in Babylonia for some 70 years, at least from the time of the first deportation, which had about 50 years to run.)*

THE DEATH AND SUFFERING OF THE PEOPLE

14 They have blown the trumpet, even to make all ready; but none goes to the battle: for My wrath is upon all the multitude thereof. *(The phrase, "They have blown the trumpet," refers to the Year of Jubilee, when lands that had been sold reverted to their original owners [Lev., Chpt. 25]. The prediction here was that none of these sellers and buyers would live to see the next Jubilee. In fact, the "trumpet" would be blown, but it would not be for Jubilee, but rather for "battle.")*

15 The sword is without, and the pestilence and famine within: he who is in the field shall die with the sword; and he who is in the city, famine and pestilence shall devour him. *(The idea is that one cannot escape from the coming Judgment.)*

16 But they who escape of them shall escape,

and shall be on the mountains like doves of the valleys, all of them mourning, every one for his iniquity. *(It is a Law of God that if one does not "mourn" for their sin, they will "mourn" because of their sin [Gal. 6:7-8]. All true Repentance is born of a sense of sin against God.)*

17 All hands shall be feeble, and all knees shall be weak as water. *(All of this for fear of the Babylonians.)*

18 They shall also gird themselves with sackcloth, and horror shall cover them; and shame shall be upon all faces, and baldness upon all their heads. *(The phrase, "Gird themselves with sackcloth," speaks of a last minute effort to repent. But it will be too late!)*

19 They shall cast their silver in the streets, and their gold shall be removed: their silver and their gold shall not be able to deliver them in the day of the wrath of the LORD: they shall not satisfy their souls, neither fill their bowels: because it is the stumblingblock of their iniquity. *(The "stumblingblock of their iniquity" was their sin of making idols out of silver and gold, and the subsequent idolatry. They had traded Jehovah for a stupid looking idol made of metal or wood. Consequently, they became like the idol they worshipped — dumb, stupid, senseless, and without spiritual intelligence. Such characterizes almost all the present world.)*

20 As for the beauty of His ornament, He set it in majesty: but they made the images of their abominations and of their detestable things therein: therefore have I set it far from them. *(The phrase, "As for the beauty of His ornament, He set it in majesty," refers to the Temple in Jerusalem. The phrase, "And of their detestable things therein," refers to the Hebrew idolaters who set up the idols in the Temple.)*

21 And I will give it into the hands of the strangers for a prey, and to the wicked of the Earth for a spoil; and they shall pollute it. *(This refers to the Temple and all of its ornaments being given to the Chaldeans, who were "strangers" to God.)*

22 My face will I turn also from them, and they shall pollute My secret place: for the robbers shall enter into it, and defile it. *("My secret place" pertained to the "Holy of Holies," where resided the Ark of the Covenant, the Mercy Seat, and the Cherubim, and where God also resided. When Jerusalem fell, heathen Babylonians would come into this "Holy of Holies.")*

THE SIGN OF A CHAIN SIGNIFYING CAPTIVITY AND JUDGMENT

23 Make a chain: for the land is full of bloody crimes, and the city is full of violence. *(The words, "Make a chain," are a symbolic prediction of the captivity, just as the "rod of wickedness" foretold the invasion of Verse 11.)*

24 Wherefore I will bring the worst of the heathen, and they shall possess their houses: I will also make the pomp of the strong to cease; and their holy places shall be defiled. *(The "worst of the heathen" referred to the coming Babylonians. It is as if the Holy Spirit is saying of the religious leaders of Jerusalem, "You desire to practice evil; therefore, I will bring upon you those who are experts in this practice.")*

25 Destruction comes; and they shall seek peace, and there shall be none. *(The phrase, "And they shall seek peace, and there shall be none," refers to overtures made to the Babylonian Generals, which were rejected!)*

26 Mischief shall come upon mischief, and rumour shall be upon rumour; then shall they seek a vision of the Prophet; but the Law shall perish from the Priest, and counsel from the ancients. *(On the very eve of destruction, the people of Jerusalem would turn to the "Prophet, Priest, and Elders." But, alas, these were corrupt. Consequently, no help would come from this source.)*

27 The king shall mourn, and the prince shall be clothed with desolation, and the hands of the people of the land shall be troubled: I will do unto them after their way, and according to their deserts will I judge them; and they shall know that I am the LORD. *(The phrase, "The king shall mourn," probably refers to Zedekiah. He rightly had something to mourn about, but he also was a weak individual, which would have exacerbated his mental state. The phrase, "And the hands of the people of the land shall be troubled," refers to all commerce, political life, and business — down even to the day laborers. Everything would come to a grinding halt.)*

CHAPTER 8
(594 B.C.)

A VISION OF THE ABOMINATIONS IN JERUSALEM

AND it came to pass in the sixth year, in the sixth month, in the fifth day of the month, as I sat in my house, and the elders of Judah sat

before me, that the hand of the Lord GOD fell there upon me. *(This is Ezekiel's second vision, or rather series of visions, and would take place "in the sixth year," referring to his sixth year of captivity, which was approximately five years before the destruction of Judah and Jerusalem. This Prophecy closes at Chapter 11.)*

2 Then I beheld, and lo a likeness as the appearance of fire: from the appearance of His loins even downward, fire; and from His loins even upward, as the appearance of brightness, as the colour of amber. *(The fiery appearance that Ezekiel saw had the likeness of a man. He was the God of Israel and was accompanied by the Glory. And He it was Who spoke in vision to the Prophet.)*

3 And He put forth the form of an hand, and took me by a lock of my head; and the Spirit lifted me up between the Earth and the Heaven, and brought me in the visions of God to Jerusalem, to the door of the inner gate that looks toward the north; where was the seat of the image of jealousy, which provokes to jealousy. *(All of this was in a vision. The phrase, "The image of jealousy," was probably the "Asherah," which was set up close to the "Brazen Altar." This idol was upon a pedestal, wounding with jealousy the Love that shone forth in the Glory of God.*

The phrase, "Provokes to jealousy," pertains to Ex. 34:12-14.)

4 And, behold, the glory of the God of Israel was there, according to the vision that I saw in the plain. *(The Holy Spirit is careful to emphasize that it is "the Glory of the God of Israel" which they had forsaken for this stone idol!)*

THE WORSHIP OF IDOLS AND IMAGES

5 Then said He unto me, Son of man, lift up your eyes now the way toward the north. So I lifted up my eyes the way toward the north, and behold northward at the gate of the Altar this image of jealousy in the entry. *(Some of the religious leaders of Judah had placed this idol "at the gate of the Altar." This was the Brazen Altar, where the Temple Sacrifices were supposed to be offered for the sins of the people, typifying Calvary. How many "idols" presently have we added to the Cross? Humanistic psychology is definitely one. And any way other than "Jesus Christ and Him Crucified" must also be construed as an idol.)*

6 He said furthermore unto me, Son of man, do you see what they do? even the great

abominations that the House of Israel committed here, that I should go far off from My Sanctuary? but you turn yet again, and you shall see greater abominations. *(The phrase, "That I should go far off from My Sanctuary," refers to the Lord leaving the Temple as Ezekiel will shortly outline. This was now a "God-deserted" place. His visitation now would be one of Judgment, and as a Destroyer.)*

7 And He brought me to the door of the court; and when I looked, behold a hole in the wall. *(The "door," in whatever capacity in the Temple, spoke of Christ. This "door," it seems, was boarded up with "a wall.")*

8 Then said He unto me, Son of man, dig now in the wall: and when I had digged in the wall, behold a door. *(The Prophet was demanded to "dig now in the wall," i.e., "break down the wall," so that the door will be made plainly visible.)*

9 And He said unto me, Go in, and behold the wicked abominations that they do here. *(These "wicked abominations" were being conducted and carried out in the very Temple of God, which was His residing Place [I Tim. 3:16].)*

10 So I went in and saw; and behold every form of creeping things, and abominable beasts, and all the idols of the House of Israel, pourtrayed upon the wall round about. *(This was during the time of the reign of Zedekiah, when he was endeavoring to bring about an alliance between himself and Pharaoh. To impress the Egyptians, he had allowed their worship to be brought into the Temple, which is described by the Holy Spirit as "creeping things and abominable beasts.")*

11 And there stood before them seventy men of the ancients of the House of Israel, and in the midst of them stood Jaazaniah the son of Shaphan, with every man his censer in his hand; and a thick cloud of incense went up. *(In this chamber of Egyptian idolatry, in the very Temple itself, stood all the seventy members of the Hebrew Synod worshipping the loathsome reptiles portrayed on the walls. The deep pain of this scene is sharpened by the presence of Jaazaniah. His father, Shaphan, had taken part in the Godly reformation of Josiah [II Ki., Chpt. 22], and two of his brothers were friendly to Jeremiah [Jer. 26:24; 36:10, 25].)*

12 Then said He unto me, Son of man, have you seen what the ancients of the House of Israel do in the dark, every man in the chambers of his imagery? for they say, the LORD seeth us not; the LORD has forsaken the Earth.

(Men deny a future Judgment, and claim that God, if He exists at all, takes no active part in the affairs of man. They are terribly wrong on both counts, as was Judah of old!)

13 He said also unto me, Turn thee yet again and you shall see greater abominations that they do. *(The degree of evil will now increase, as all evil must increase unless rooted out by Christ.)*

WOMEN WEEPING FOR THEIR GOD, TAMMUZ

14 Then He brought me to the door of the gate of the LORD's House which was toward the north; and, behold, there sat women weeping for Tammuz. *("Tammuz" was a Phoenician deity. It was in July when the ceremonies concerning this supposed deity were to be conducted. The women were to pour themselves out in lamentations over the waxen image of a beautiful dead young man who had perished in his prime. As well, they were to engage in orgiastic joy over his return to life, which brought on the rainy season and the consequent revival of nature.)*

15 Then said He unto me, Have you seen this, O son of man? turn thee yet again, and you shall see greater abominations than these. *(The only power in Heaven or Earth that can break the deadly cycle of sin is Faith in Christ and what He did for us at Calvary. That Alone sets the captive free!*

The Catholic worship of the Virgin Mary, although with a change of names, is derived from the worship of Tammuz, which the Lord portrayed to Ezekiel as an abomination!)

THE WORSHIP OF THE SUN

16 And He brought me into the inner court of the LORD's House, and, behold, at the door of the Temple of the LORD, between the porch and the Altar, were about five and twenty men, with their backs toward the Temple of the LORD, and their faces toward the east; and they worshipped the sun toward the east. *(The final and most appalling form of idolatrous abomination was that of the High Priest and the Chiefs of the twenty-four courses of Aaron standing in the Holy Place in the Temple, with their backs to the Most Holy Place, worshipping the sun!*

The sun-worship here is to have had a Persian character, as being offered to the sun itself as a solar god. Of such worship, traces are found in

Deut. 4:19 and 17:3, Job 31:26, and II Ki. 23:5, 11; it was expressly forbidden.)

JUDGMENT FOR THESE SINS

17 Then He said unto me, Have you seen this, O son of man? Is it a light thing to the House of Judah that they commit the abominations which they commit here? for they have filled the land with violence, and have returned to provoke Me to anger: and, lo, they put the branch to their nose. *(Four times in the Hebrew Scriptures, the Holy Spirit addresses the Messiah as "the Branch," that is, as the Author of Life. Satan's parody of this was the "Asherah" — the Greek Phallus [a man's reproductive organ]. The ancients, in their efforts to reach back to the origin of life and worship it as a god, arrived at the lowest depth of moral and intellectual degradation by the institution of Phallic worship.*

That this was the deepest depth of abomination is affirmed by the words of burning indignation: "Lo, they put the branch to My nose!" Or freely translated: "Look at them; they are thrusting the branch into My face!")

18 Therefore will I also deal in fury: My eye shall not spare, neither will I have pity: and though they cry in My ears with a loud voice, yet will I not hear them. *(Idolatry blinds! The God of Glory was actually present in His Temple [Vs. 4], but the Priests and Elders declared He was not there. This blindness is affirmed again in the following Chapter [Vss. 3, 9].*

Such blindness exists today. The heart that is governed by any form of idolatry, whether material, scientific, or philosophic, is insensible to fellowship with God, and cannot see His Glory as revealed in the Face of Jesus Christ [II Cor. 4:6].)

CHAPTER 9
(594 B.C.)
JUDGMENT COMMANDED; THE RIGHTEOUS MARKED FOR DELIVERANCE

HE cried also in my ears with a loud voice, saying, Cause them who have charge over the city to draw near, even every man with his destroying weapon in his hand. *(One should consider the "loud voice" of Verse 18 of Chapter 8 with the "loud voice" in Verse 1 of this Chapter. The former "loud voice" represents an unrepentant heart which demands*

mercy, with the latter "loud voice" guaranteeing judgment.

The phrase, "Cause them who have charge over the city to draw near," refers to the seven supernatural beings who will mark each individual person for death or life, depending on their relationship with Christ. This gives us a view into the spirit world of the action of God concerning events.)

2 And, behold, six men came from the way of the higher gate, which lies toward the north, and every man a slaughter weapon in his hand; and one Man among them was clothed with linen, with a writer's inkhorn by his side: and they went in, and stood beside the brasen altar. *(These seven beings were evidently supernatural. Even though Ezekiel spoke of them as men, they were, in reality, Angels. Six were ministers of wrath and one of Grace. The phrase, "And one Man among them was clothed with linen," seems to imply that He was part of the six. However, the original Hebrew sets Him apart from the six, making a total of seven. Because He was "clothed in linen," which symbolizes Righteousness, and because His Ministry was to set a Divine mark upon all who judged and bewailed the abominations that were practiced in the City and Temple, this white-robed Minister pictures Israel's True and Great High Priest, the Lord Jesus Christ [Rev., Chpts. 7, 14].)*

3 And the Glory of the God of Israel was gone up from the Cherub, whereupon He was, to the threshold of the house. And He called to the Man clothed with linen, which had the writer's inkhorn by His side *(the One doing the calling seems to be God the Father, while the One to Whom He called is God the Son);*

4 And the LORD said unto Him, Go through the midst of the city, through the midst of Jerusalem, and set a mark upon the foreheads of the men who sigh and who cry for all the abominations that be done in the midst thereof. *(This refers to the entire righteous population which was small.)*

THE DEATH OF THE GUILTY

5 And to the others He said in my hearing, Go ye after Him through the city, and smite: let not your eye spare, neither have ye pity *(the "others" refer to the "six" who were slated to mark for Judgment, as the "One" was slated to mark for Salvation and Protection):*

6 Slay utterly old and young, both maids, and little children, and women: but come not near any man upon whom is the mark; and begin at My Sanctuary. Then they began at the ancient men which were before the house. *(These Angels did not actually kill these people, but only marked them for destruction; this action was unseen and unfelt by the individuals involved. The few who were marked for righteousness were to be spared.*

The phrase, "Begin at My Sanctuary," proclaims the fact that "Judgment begins at the House of God" [I Pet. 4:17]. There is a throb of anguished love in the words, "My Sanctuary.")

7 And He said unto them, Defile the house, and fill the courts with the slain: go ye forth. And they went forth, and slew in the city. *(As stated, the Judgment would begin at the House of God.)*

8 And it came to pass, while they were slaying them, and I was left, that I fell upon my face, and cried, and said, Ah Lord GOD! will You destroy all the residue of Israel in Your pouring out of Your fury upon Jerusalem? *(The phrase, "And I was left," refers to all the Priests marked for death except himself. As is obvious here, almost all the people, including the Priests, were marked for destruction.)*

9 Then said He unto me, The iniquity of the House of Israel and Judah is exceeding great, and the land is full of blood, and the city full of perverseness: for they say, the LORD has forsaken the Earth, and the LORD sees not. *(While it is true that the Lord does not see the sins which are washed in the Blood of the Lamb, still, He most definitely sees the sins of the Believer which are unconfessed and for which there is no Repentance [Jn. 1:6-10].)*

10 And as for Me also, My eye shall not spare, neither will I have pity, but I will recompense their way upon their head. *(Three times it is declared that "pity" will not be shown [8:18; 9:5, 10]; but this is not the triple language of pleasure, but of agony. It is Love compelled to keep reminding itself of the sad necessity of Judgment.)*

11 And, behold, the Man clothed with linen, which had the inkhorn by His side, reported the matter, saying, I have done as You have commanded Me. *(As stated, "The Man clothed with linen" was most probably a pre-incarnate appearance of Christ [II Tim. 4:1]. "The inkhorn by His side" proclaims the names of the redeemed written in the "Lamb's Book of Life" [Rev. 20:15].)*

CHAPTER 10
(594 B.C.)

GOD'S GLORY DEPARTS FROM THE TEMPLE; DESCRIPTION OF THE CHERUBIM

THEN l looked, and, behold, in the firmament that was above the head of the Cherubims there appeared over them as it were a sapphire stone, as the appearance of the likeness of a throne. *(The departure of the Glory of God from the Temple is the Vision of this Chapter. It retires unwillingly. Its Throne was the Most Holy Place. This Chapter plus the next will show the God of Israel in lingering Love forsaking His City and Temple, not to return until 43:4, which yet lies in the future.*

We also learn here that the "Living Creatures" are "Cherubims.")

2 And He spoke unto the Man clothed with linen, and said, Go in between the wheels, even under the Cherub, and fill Your hand with coals of fire from between the Cherubims, and scatter them over the city. And He went in in my sight. *(Righteousness is the foundation of Divine action, whether in Redemption or Judgment. He Who in Grace set the mark upon the redeemed also casts the burning fire upon the rebels. The Righteousness of God in His Judgment of sin at Calvary and in His Faithfulness in fulfilling His Promises to the Believer is the foundation of the Christian's assurance of Salvation. And it is the Righteousness of God which assures eternal condemnation to the rejecter of Christ.*

The "Coals of fire from between the Cherubims" are the same as 1:13. They signify God's Judgment against sin.)

3 Now the Cherubims stood on the right side of the house, when the Man went in; and the cloud filled the inner court. *(The phrase, "And the cloud filled the inner court," was the same cloud that filled the house over 400 years before when Solomon dedicated the Temple [II Chron. 5:14]. Then it was coming, now it is going. The Reader must sense the great sadness that filled the heart of the Prophet as he observes this scene.)*

4 Then the glory of the LORD went up from the Cherub, and stood over the threshold of the house; and the house of was filled with the cloud, and the court was full of the brightness of the LORD's glory. *(As He leaves the Temple, the "Glory of the Lord" pauses "over the threshold of the house," which is its entrance. It is as*

if He does not want to go, but has no choice but to leave, because He is no longer wanted. One can literally feel the pathos of the heart of God in this description.)

5 And the sound of the Cherubims' wings was heard even to the outer court, as the voice of the Almighty God when He speaks. *(It is beautiful and yet amazing that the Holy Spirit uses the Name "Almighty God" respecting this event. In the Hebrew, it says "El Shaddai," which means "The Breasted One," or "The All-Sufficient One." But yet, Judah took no advantage at all of this One Who can meet every need.)*

6 And it came to pass, that when He had commanded the Man clothed with linen, saying, Take fire from between the wheels, from between the Cherubims; then He went in, and stood beside the wheels.

7 And one Cherub stretched forth his hand from between the Cherubims unto the fire that was between the Cherubims, and took thereof, and put it into the hands of Him Who was clothed with linen: Who took it, and went out. *(This is similar to what John saw when he spoke of the "Angel, who took a censer and filled it with the fire of the Altar, and cast it into the Earth" [Rev. 8:5].)*

8 And there appeared in the Cherubims the form of a man's hand under their wings. *(The detailed statement of Verses 8 through 22 is not a meaningless repetition of Chapter 1. What the Holy Spirit repeats claims the deeper attention of the Believer. Much instruction is suggested here. The God of Glory Who appeared to the obedient captives by the River Chebar in blessing was the very same God of Glory Who appeared in Judgment to the rebels at Jerusalem. This was quite opposed to the religious thinking of the citizens of that guilty city. They thought themselves blessed and the captives cursed.)*

9 And when I looked, behold the four wheels by the Cherubims, one wheel by one Cherub, and another wheel by another Cherub: and the appearance of the wheels was as the colour of a beryl stone. *(The indication is that the "wheels" have to do with direction because of the "eyes" [Vs. 12].)*

10 And as for their appearances, they four had one likeness, as if a wheel had been in the midst of a wheel. *(The "wheel in the middle of a wheel" simulates constant activity, referring to sure and certain direction.)*

11 When they went, they went upon their four sides; they turned not as they went, but to the place whither the head looked they

followed it; they turned not as they went. *("Wheels" normally turn, but these do not: "they turned not as they went." The phrase, "But to the place whither the head looked they followed it," refers to the "chief" or "principal" wheel, which it seems determined the course of the others.*

All of this is beyond the comprehension of man. Even though it was given in vision to Ezekiel, still, the Lord did not explain any of these things concerning the Throne of God. So, Ezekiel just reported what he saw, without any explanation.)

12 And their whole body, and their backs, and their hands, and their wings, and the wheels, were full of eyes round about, even the wheels that they four had. *(In 1:18, Ezekiel said that the "rings" or "rims" of the wheels were "full of eyes round about them four." However, in this Passage, he adds to it, saying that the "whole body" of the Cherubims, even including their "backs," "hands," and "wings," were "full of eyes round about.")*

13 As for the wheels, it was cried unto them in my hearing, O wheel. *(The phrase, "O wheel," should read, "As for the wheels, it was cried unto each one of them, 'Move!'" That is, each wheel was commanded to move in order to execute the Divine purpose.)*

14 And every one had four faces: the first face was the face of a cherub, and the second face was the face of a man, and the third the face of a lion, and the fourth the face of an eagle. *(This description is slightly different from the first, inasmuch as the "Cherub" was substituted for the "ox" [1:10]. Here, it is first in order instead of being, as there, the third. It is as though, in this second Vision, he recognizes that this was emphatically the Cherubic form. In other words, the face of the "ox," because of the Glory of the Lord, was made to look Cherubic.)*

15 And the Cherubims were lifted up. This is the Living Creature that I saw by the river of Chebar.

16 And when the Cherubims went, the wheels went by them: and when the Cherubims lifted up their wings to mount up from the Earth, the same wheels also turned not from beside them. *(The "wheels" and the "wings" of the Cherubims all move as by one harmonious impulse.)*

17 When they stood, these stood; and when they were lifted up, these lifted up themselves also: for the Spirit of the Living Creature was in them. *(The phrase, "For the Spirit of the Living Creature was in them," implies the Holy Spirit, as it does in 1:20.)*

18 Then the glory of the LORD departed from off the threshold of the house, and stood over the Cherubims. *(This portrays the Holy Spirit leaving the Temple in Jerusalem. One is reminded of the wife of Phinehas, who, shortly before she died, "named the child Ichabod, saying, The Glory is departed from Israel" [I Sam. 4:21].)*

19 And the Cherubims lifted up their wings, and mounted up from the Earth in my sight: when they went out, the wheels also were beside them, and every one stood at the door of the east gate of the LORD's house; and the glory of the God of Israel was over them above. *(This describes the place of departure of the "Glory of the Lord" and also of its return, as described in 43:4, which has not yet happened, but most surely will, when the Temple is restored after the Second Coming of Christ.)*

20 This is the Living Creature that I saw under the God of Israel by the river of Chebar; and I knew that they were the Cherubims. *(The phrase, "This is the Living Creature that I saw under the God of Israel," refers to the Cherubims being a part of the Throne of God, which is borne out by John the Beloved [Rev. 4:6-11].)*

21 Every one had four faces apiece, and every one four wings; and the likeness of the hands of a man was under their wings. *(The difference in John's description and Ezekiel's is that John's has six wings, whereas Ezekiel's has four wings [Rev. 4:8].)*

22 And the likeness of their faces was the same faces which I saw by the river of Chebar, their appearances and themselves: they went every one straight forward. *(The phrase, "They went every one straight forward," signifies that with "the Father of Lights there is no variableness, neither shadow of turning" [James 1:17].)*

CHAPTER 11

(594 B.C.)

EVIL PRINCES REBUKED

MOREOVER the Spirit lifted me up, and brought me unto the east gate of the LORD's house, which looks eastward: and behold at the door of the gate five and twenty men; among whom I saw Jaazaniah the son of Azur, and Pelatiah the son of Benaiah, princes of the people. *(The phrase, "Moreover the Spirit lifted me up," refers to the Holy Spirit. Three times it says the Spirit lifted up the Prophet [3:14; 8:3; 11;1]. It also says that it carried him [37:1]. The "five and twenty men" could have been those mentioned in 8:16. However,*

those were probably Priests, and at least two of these are named as "princes of the people." Irrespective of who they were, they represented rebellion against God.)

2 Then said He unto me, Son of man, these are the men who devise mischief, and give wicked counsel in this city *(the phrase, "And given wicked counsel in this city," referred to any counsel which contradicted the Prophecies of Jeremiah and Ezekiel, but mostly referred to Jeremiah, because he was the one prophesying in Jerusalem. These men denied any coming invasion by the Babylonians, and that their city would be destroyed, along with the Temple):*

3 Which say, It is not near; let us build houses: this city is the caldron, and we be the flesh. *(The phrase, "This city is the caldron, and we be the flesh," refers to the claims by these false prophets that the inhabitants of Jerusalem were as secure as if surrounded by iron.)*

JUDGMENT ANNOUNCED

4 Therefore prophesy against them, prophesy, O son of man. *(The Holy Spirit tells the Prophet to strongly oppose the false message of these false prophets. So much for those who claim that such Preaching should not be brought forth.)*

5 And the Spirit of the LORD fell upon me, and said unto me, Speak; Thus saith the LORD; Thus have you said, O House of Israel: for I know the things that come into your mind, every one of them. *(The Omniscience of the Lord is brought forth in this statement, "For I know the things that come into your mind, every one of them." This is in response to Judah's statement, "The Lord has forsaken the Earth, and the Lord sees not" [9:9].)*

6 You have multiplied your slain in this city, and you have filled the streets thereof with the slain. *(The idea of this Verse is that the terrible destruction coming upon Jerusalem is not the fault of God, but the fault of the spiritual leaders in their rebellion against God. Therefore, the Lord lays the blame at their feet.)*

7 Therefore thus saith the Lord GOD; Your slain whom you have laid in the midst of it, they are the flesh, and this city is the caldron: but I will bring you forth out of the midst of it. *(The princes declared this city to have a ring of iron around it, i.e., they claimed it was what one might call impregnable. It was instead to be a boiling pot, i.e., "cauldron," and the people in it as boiling "flesh." As a result, the "slain" would be many.*

The phrase, "But I will bring you forth out of the midst of it," concerns some of the princes, if not all, who would be taken captive to Riblah and there put to death.)

8 You have feared the sword; and I will bring a sword upon you, saith the Lord GOD. *(Observing the Babylonian Empire seeking to extend its borders, and having already suffered two deportations, the Nobles of Judah and Jerusalem, despite their bluster and bravado, feared the oncoming horde. They were well aware of the ferociousness of the Babylonians, and rightly "feared the sword.")*

9 And I will bring you out of the midst thereof, and deliver you into the hands of strangers, and will execute judgments among you. *(The phrase, "And I will bring you out of the midst thereof," refers back to the words of Moses. He said, "That the land spue not you out also, when you defile it, as it spued out the nations that were before you" [Lev. 18:28].)*

10 You shall fall by the sword; I will judge you in the border of Israel; and you shall know that I am the LORD. *(The phrase, "I will judge you in the border of Israel," refers to the princes being carried to Riblah and there put to death.)*

11 This city shall not be your caldron *(fortress)*, neither shall you be the flesh in the midst thereof *(protected in the fortress)*; but I will judge you in the border of Israel *(the Lord was not speaking here of the majority of the population of the city, but of the king and many of the nobles who thought they may escape):*

12 And you shall know that I am the LORD: for you have not walked in My Statutes, neither executed My Judgments, but have done after the manners of the heathen who are round about you. *(The Believer is "in" the world, but he is not to be "of" the world.!)*

THE PROMISE OF RESTORATION AND RENEWAL

13 And it came to pass, when I prophesied, that Pelatiah the son of Benaiah died. Then fell I down upon my face, and cried with a loud voice, and said, Ah Lord GOD! will You make a full end of the remnant of Israel? *(Pelatiah, evidently, was one of the leaders of those who "gave wicked counsel in Jerusalem" [Vss. 1-2]. The emphasis is that his death was a judgment from God.)*

14 Again the word of the LORD came unto me, saying,

15 Son of man, your brethren, even your

brethren, the men of your kindred, and all the House of Israel wholly, are they unto whom the inhabitants of Jerusalem have said, Get you far from the LORD: unto us is this land given in possession. *(Ezekiel is comforted by the Message that his real brethren and kindred were the captives in Babylon, at least those who truly served the Lord, and not the Priests in Jerusalem, who had proudly said to the Exiles, "You are far from the Lord, for this land is given unto us in possession!")*

16 Therefore say, Thus saith the Lord GOD; Although I have cast them far off among the heathen, and although I have scattered them among the countries, yet will I be to them as a little Sanctuary in the countries where they shall come. *(The comfort the Lord gave Ezekiel was deepened by the Prophecy that though the captives had no material Temple, yet God Himself would be to them a Sanctuary for the "little while" their exile was to last, i.e., the predicted seventy years.*

The idea is: it is "The Presence of Jehovah" that makes the Sanctuary, and not the Sanctuary that secures the Presence.)

17 Therefore say, Thus saith the Lord GOD; I will even gather you from the people, and assemble you out of the countries where you have been scattered, and I will give you the land of Israel. *(This was fulfilled partially upon the return of the Exiles some seventy years after the first deportation; however, its total fulfillment yet speaks of a future time, which will actually take place in the coming Kingdom Age.)*

18 And they shall come thither, and they shall take away all the detestable things thereof and all the abominations thereof from thence. *(Once again, this Prophecy will be fulfilled totally after the Second Coming of Christ.)*

19 And I will give them one heart, and I will put a new spirit within you; and I will take the stony heart out of their flesh, and will give them an heart of flesh *(this will be fulfilled at Christ's Second Coming and the acceptance of Him as their Saviour)*:

20 That they may walk in My Statutes, and keep My Ordinances, and do them: and they shall be My people, and I will be their God.

21 But as for them whose heart walks after the heart of their detestable things and their abominations, I will recompense their way upon their own heads, saith the Lord GOD. *(This Verse now returns to the present and Israel's rebellion against the Lord.)*

22 Then did the Cherubims lift up their wings, and the wheels beside them; and the Glory of the God of Israel was over them above. *("The Glory of the God of Israel" was the strength of this Land, City, Temple, and people, and yet they little knew or understood it. They are now about to lose it.)*

23 And the Glory of the LORD went up from the midst of the city, and stood upon the mountain which is on the east side of the city. *("The mountain which is on the east side of the city" is the Mount of Olivet. The phrase, " And the Glory of the LORD went up from the midst of the city," denotes a reluctance to leave. However, the Holy Spirit is no longer wanted or desired; therefore, He has no choice but to leave.*

Having reluctantly left the Temple, the Glory then forsook the city, lingering for a while with sorrowing Love upon this Mountain. But the Glory returned to that Mount, veiled in the sinless flesh of the Messiah; once more Love looked upon the Beloved but rebellious City and wept over it [Lk. 19:41].

A few weeks later, Christ ascended from that same Mountain; and yet, in a future day, in the Glory of His Second Advent, His Feet shall stand, once again, upon it [Zech. 14:4]. Then shall Israel have one heart and a new spirit.)

24 Afterwards the Spirit took me up, and brought me in a Vision by the Spirit of God into Chaldea, to them of the captivity. So the Vision that I had seen went up from me. *(The phrase, "And brought me in a Vision," denotes the fact that Ezekiel did not go to Jerusalem literally, but only in a "Vision.")*

25 Then I spoke unto them of the captivity all the things that the LORD had shown me. *(As Ezekiel related to his compatriots what the Lord had shown him, they were no doubt very much comforted with the wonderful revelation that Israel's God of Glory was in their midst as a Sanctuary, a True and Pure Temple; that He would continue to be so for the entire period of the captivity; that He shared their Exile with them; and that He would certainly restore them to the homeland.)*

CHAPTER 12
(594 B.C.)
SIGNS AND SYMBOLS — PROPHECIES OF BABYLONIAN CAPTIVITY

THE Word of the LORD also came unto me, saying,

2 Son of man, you dwell in the midst of a rebellious house, which have eyes to see, and

see not; they have ears to hear, and hear not: for they are a rebellious house. *(The idea, as given by the Holy Spirit, is that they had "spiritual eyes," but refused to see, and "spiritual ears," but refused to hear.)*

3 Therefore, thou son of man, prepare thee stuff for removing, and remove by day in their sight; and you shall remove from your place to another place in their sight: it may be they will consider, though they be a rebellious house. *(The teaching by Vision ceases, and now that of direct message or symbolic acts are resumed. In this object lesson, the Prophet predicted the attempted escape and capture of king Zedekiah. The Prophecy preceded the event by about five years.*

Ezekiel was commanded to make a bundle as for a journey, which was to portray the futile attempt of king Zedekiah to escape. There is every reason to believe that Zedekiah received this Message from Ezekiel, but, sadly, refused it.)

4 Then shall you bring forth your stuff by day in their sight, as stuff for removing: and you shall go forth at evening in their sight, as they who go forth into captivity. *(The "stuff" represented the baggage of Zedekiah, which would be gathered for the escape attempt.)*

5 Dig thou through the wall in their sight, and carry out thereby. *(The Prophet, in his object lesson, was not to take the "stuff" through the door of the house, but instead "dig through the wall," thus illustrating Zedekiah's escape attempt by going through a broken part of the wall of Jerusalem.)*

6 In their sight shall you bear it upon your shoulders, and carry it forth in the twilight: you shall cover your face, that you see not the ground: for I have set you for a sign unto the House of Israel. *(What must have been Zedekiah's response when he read these predictions from Ezekiel, as he, at the same time, heard the similar Prophecies of Jeremiah?)*

7 And I did so as I was commanded: I brought forth my stuff by day, as stuff for captivity, and in the evening I dug through the wall with my hand; I brought it forth in the twilight, and I bore it upon my shoulder in their sight. *(I wonder how many of the people took this lesson seriously, and how many ridiculed the "sensationalism" of the Prophet?)*

8 And in the morning came the word of the LORD unto me, saying,

9 Son of man, has not the House of Israel, the rebellious house, said unto you, What doest thou? *(Even though the Prophet carried out what the Lord told him to do, still, it seems that at this passage of time, he little knew what it represented; therefore, he had to tell them that he would wait and see what the Lord told him, which was soon coming, actually the next "morning.")*

10 Say thou unto them, Thus saith the Lord GOD; This burden concerns the prince in Jerusalem, and all the House of Israel that are among them. *(The phrase, "This burden concerns the prince in Jerusalem," referred to Zedekiah. The word "prince" [instead of "king"] was used by the Holy Spirit because, at least in the Mind of God, Zedekiah was not the true king of Judah, only one who served as a stopgap measure. In the Mind of God, Jehoiachin was the last king, at least in the line of David — the line which was absolutely necessary to sit on the Throne. Actually, Zedekiah was Jehoiachin's uncle, with the word "brother," at least in this account, meaning "next of kin" [II Chron. 36:10].)*

11 Say, I am your sign: like as I have done, so shall it be done unto them: they shall remove and go into captivity. *(The phrase, "Say, I am your sign," referred to Ezekiel and the captives, who were a "sign" to the people in Judah and Jerusalem, meaning that as they had been brought into captivity, "so shall it be done unto them," i.e., Jerusalem will be taken captive.)*

12 And the prince who is among them shall bear upon his shoulder in the twilight, and shall go forth: they shall dig through the wall to carry out thereby: he shall cover his face, that he see not the ground with his eyes. *(The minute detail in which this was given to Ezekiel is startling indeed! However, it should be quickly stated that it was done out of Love by God for the king in Jerusalem, but still unheeded.)*

13 My net also will I spread upon him, and he shall be taken in My snare: and I will bring him to Babylon to the land of the Chaldeans; yet shall he not see it, though he shall die there. *(All, as fore-pictured, came to pass [II Ki., Chpt. 25; Jer., Chpt. 39]. Zedekiah, disguised so as not to be recognized, and with a few articles for the journey, forsook the city by night through a hole made in the city wall, and fled to the plains of Jericho. But God, using the Chaldean army as a net, captured him and brought him to Riblah; they put out his eyes and transported him to Babylon, where he died.*

Josephus said that this Prophecy was sent to Zedekiah. But he declared that Jeremiah contradicted Verse 13 of this Chapter, because it

stated that he should not see Babylon, and Jeremiah predicted he would be carried there. He, therefore, concluded to believe neither [Jer. 24:8-9].)

14 And I will scatter toward every wind all who are about him to help him, and all his bands; and I will draw out the sword after them. *(Thus, the false expectations of the captives that they would be immediately restored to their native land and the equally false expectations of the people of Jerusalem that they would never be conquered by the Babylonians were all destroyed by the symbolic Prophesy of these Verses.*

Just as did Zedekiah, Ahab, many years before, tried, but in vain, to outwit God. Their actions were the more wicked because God, in His Love and pity, told them beforehand their fate if they persisted in their folly. He did not want them to perish.)

15 And they shall know that I am the LORD, when I shall scatter them among the nations, and disperse them in the countries. *(All who refused to flee from the Wrath to come must get to know God in Judgment. Those who obeyed the Commands shall get to know Him in Grace, as the next Verse implies.)*

A REMNANT SAVED

16 But I will leave a few men of them from the sword, from the famine, and from the pestilence; that they may declare all their abominations among the heathen whither they come; and they shall know that I am the LORD. *(The few reserved from destruction were spared that they might vindicate God's action by informing the nations of the abominations which justified it. Dan. 9:5-14 illustrates this prediction.)*

EATING AND DRINKING IN DESPAIR

17 Moreover the word of the LORD came to me, saying,

18 Son of man, eat your bread with quaking, and drink your water with trembling and with carefulness *(all of this was in order to symbolize the coming judgment upon Judah and Jerusalem)*;

19 And say unto the people of the land, Thus saith the Lord GOD of the inhabitants of Jerusalem, and of the land of Israel; They shall eat their bread with carefulness, and drink their water with astonishment, that her land may be desolate from all that is therein, because of the violence of all them who dwell therein. *(The phrase, "Because of the violence of all them who dwell therein," refers to the reason for the Judgment. When the Lord is denied, Mercy and Grace are no more, with men's attitudes, actions, and efforts then becoming "violent.")*

20 And the cities that are inhabited shall be laid waste, and the land shall be desolate; and you shall know that I am the LORD. *("Waste" and "desolation" are the two words describing that which is soon to come.)*

GOD WILL EXECUTE SPEEDY JUDGMENT

21 And the word of the LORD came unto me, saying,

22 Son of man, what is that proverb that you have in the land of Israel, saying, The days are prolonged, and every vision fails? *(So corrupt and unbelieving is man that he turns the patience and longsuffering of God into a mocking proverb.)*

23 Tell them therefore, Thus saith the Lord GOD; I will make this proverb to cease, and they shall no more use it as a proverb in Israel; but say unto them, The days are at hand, and the effect of every vision. *(The Lord tells the Prophet to institute a new proverb: "The days are at hand when the true vision will be fulfilled." In other words, the true vision will not fail; it is at hand; every word will be fulfilled in total reality.)*

24 For there shall be no more any vain vision nor flattering divination within the House of Israel. *(The "vain vision" and "flattering divination" pertain to the messages of the false prophets. The Holy Spirit is saying that soon their messages will be shown to be what they really are: lies.)*

25 For I am the LORD: I will speak, and the word that I shall speak shall come to pass; it shall be no more prolonged: for in your days, O rebellious house, will I say the word, and will perform it, saith the Lord GOD. *(God's Word is looked at even above His Name. It has the guarantee of His Power behind it in order that it be fulfilled [Ps. 138:2].)*

26 Again the word of the LORD came to me, saying,

27 Son of man, behold, they of the House of Israel say, The vision that he sees is for many days to come, and he prophesies of the times that are far off. *(Those in exile with Ezekiel did not call him a false prophet, but instead said that his Prophecies little concerned the present,*

but rather pertained to the distant future. In other words, they desired to believe the false prophets who proclaimed that the Exiles would be restored to Judah within a matter of months.)

28 Therefore say unto them, Thus saith the Lord GOD; There shall none of My words be prolonged any more, but the word which I have spoken shall be done, saith the Lord GOD. *(This statement insinuates that the fulfillment of the Prophecies of Judgment had in fact been "prolonged" in order that Judah and Jerusalem may repent, but to no avail! Now, the Holy Spirit says, "The prolonging has ended.")*

CHAPTER 13
(594 B.C.)
FALSE PROPHETS CONDEMNED

AND the Word of the LORD came unto me, saying,

2 Son of man, prophesy against the prophets of Israel who prophesy, and say thou unto them who prophesy out of their own hearts, Hear ye the Word of the LORD *(as there were false prophets and prophetesses in Jerusalem, there were such among the Exiles, as well! The Holy Spirit will now direct His attention to them in no uncertain terms!);*

3 Thus saith the Lord GOD, Woe unto the foolish prophets, who follow their own spirit, and have seen nothing! *(The phrase, "Who follow their own spirit," means that they did not follow the Holy Spirit. They preached what the people wished to hear, in this case a speedy restoration to the Land of Judah.)*

4 O Israel, your prophets are like the foxes in the deserts. *(Foxes made their homes in the desert among ruins. The false prophets likewise made financial profit out of the ruin of Israel, and, in effect, made that ruin worse.)*

5 You have not gone up into the gaps, neither made up the hedge for the House of Israel to stand in the battle in the day of the LORD. *(These "foolish prophets" made merchandise of the time by telling the people a lie instead of the truth. They made them feel comfortable in their sins, and further told them that peace and prosperity were just around the corner. This slandered the Prophecies of Jeremiah and Ezekiel, and in effect also slandered God.)*

6 They have seen vanity and lying divination, saying, The LORD saith: and the LORD has not sent them: and they have made others to hope that they would confirm the word. *(The phrase, "They have seen vanity and lying*

divination," means that they have believed their own lies and have tried to confirm their own predictions. They did so by claiming, "The LORD saith," when in fact "the LORD has not sent them," and had not said anything to them.)

7 Have you not seen a vain vision, and have you not spoken a lying divination, whereas you say, The LORD said it; albeit I have not spoken? *(The Lord called the utterances of these false prophets "a vain vision" and "lying divinations." Regrettably, it is the same presently in the modern Church. False prophets abound!)*

8 Therefore thus saith the Lord GOD; Because you have spoken vanity, and seen lies, therefore, behold, I am against you, saith the Lord GOD. *(The word "vanity" means "empty nothings," which constituted the messages of these individuals. As well, they "saw lies," because they did not see the Word of God.)*

9 And My hand shall be upon the prophets who see vanity, and who divine lies: they shall not be in the assembly of My people, neither shall they be written in the writing of the House of Israel, neither shall they enter into the Land of Israel; and you shall know that I am the Lord GOD. *(The Judgment denounced against these prophets was that on the restoration of Israel, which would ultimately come to pass, they shall be excluded from the Church and people and the Land of Israel, so their names should be blotted out of the Book of Life. In other words, they lost their souls!)*

10 Because, even because they have seduced My people, saying, Peace; and there was no peace; and one built up a wall, and, lo, others daubed it with untempered morter *(there is a seduction about false doctrine, because it tells the people what they want to hear instead of what they need to hear):*

11 Say unto them which daub it with untempered morter, that it shall fall: there shall be an overflowing shower; and you, O great hailstones, shall fall; and a stormy wind shall rend it. *(Christ said that the storms are coming, and only the house that is built on the Rock will stand. Quite possibly, Christ had this very Passage in mind when He uttered His Words in Mat., Chpt. 7.)*

12 Lo, when the wall is fallen, shall it not be said unto you, Where is the daubing wherewith you have daubed it? *(The false message of peace given by the false prophets was likened to a wall that was built with "untempered mortar," which has to do with mortar that will not hold the stones together; it is, in fact, only mud*

which quickly dries, losing its holding ability. When this wall falls, symbolically speaking, the people who had been seduced by the false message will then question the false prophet, but it's too late. They should have questioned what they heard in the beginning.)

13 Therefore thus saith the Lord GOD; I will even rend it with a stormy wind in My fury; and there shall be an overflowing shower in My anger, and great hailstones in My fury to consume it. *(The thoughts of the Lord regarding these false prophets can be summed up in the word used twice in this Verse: "fury"!)*

14 So will I break down the wall that you have daubed with untempered morter, and bring it down to the ground, so that the foundation thereof shall be discovered, and it shall fall, and you shall be consumed in the midst thereof: and you shall know that I am the LORD. *(The mud-house then and the mud-house now are both built by those who do not desire to obey God or His Word; they are being "whitened," falsely so, by "modern Preachers.")*

15 Thus will I accomplish My wrath upon the wall, and upon them who have daubed it with untempered morter, and will say unto you, The wall is no more, neither they who daubed it *(the phrase, "Thus will I accomplish My wrath upon the wall," refers to God's Anger against all that is false);*

16 To wit, the prophets of Israel which prophesy concerning Jerusalem, and which see visions of peace for her, and there is no peace, saith the Lord GOD. *(As far as is known, at least at this time, Jeremiah and Ezekiel were the only two Prophets being used of God concerning the fate of Judah and Jerusalem. Daniel was being used mightily at this time, but in another capacity. However, the "prophets" spoken of here seem to have been many, even as the false prophets abound presently.)*

THE SINS OF THE PROPHETESSES

17 Likewise, thou son of man, set your face against the daughters of your people, which prophesy out of their own heart; and prophesy thou against them. *(In addition to the false prophets, there were false prophetesses. Ezekiel was told, "Prophesy against them." In the modern Church that is a "no-no." But according to the Word of God, somebody has to stand up and say, "That's right," or "That's wrong"!)*

18 And say, Thus saith the Lord GOD; Woe to the women who sew pillows to all armholes, and make kerchiefs upon the head of every stature to hunt souls! Will you hunt the souls of My people, and will you save the souls alive who come unto you? *(The "wall" of Verses 10 through 15 was not literal; it was instead meant to symbolize false teaching. Likewise, the "pillows" and "kerchiefs" of this Verse are symbolic, as well. The implication is that the men prophets built the house, and the women prophets furnished it. The "pillows" symbolize the teaching which gave a false rest, and which the people wished to hear. The ornamental coverings for the head picture attractive and pleasing doctrines which obscure the facts of death and the judgment to come.)*

19 And will you pollute Me among My people for handfuls of barley and for pieces of bread, to slay the souls who should not die, and to save the souls alive who should not live, by your lying to My people who hear your lies? *(The idea of this Verse is that false prophetesses were selling out cheap, i.e., "handfuls of barley and pieces of bread." However, irrespective of the amount of money, fame, or popularity received for the false divination, still, the idea of selling their lies in the Name of the Lord would bring a judicial judgment upon their heads.)*

THEIR JUDGMENT

20 Wherefore thus saith the Lord GOD; Behold, I am against your pillows, wherewith you there hunt the souls to make them fly, and I will tear them from your arms, and will let the souls go, even the souls that you hunt to make them fly. *(The phrase, "To make them fly," refers to making their hearers fly into their nets of bondage so that they might plunder them. The phrase, "And I will tear them from your arms, and will let the souls go," refers to the people being "delivered out of the snare of the fowler" [Ps. 91:3; 124:7]. These people would no longer be in the power of those who traded on their credulity.)*

21 Your kerchiefs also will I tear, and deliver My people out of your hand, and they shall be no more in your hand to be hunted; and you shall know that I am the LORD. *(The idea of this Verse is that even though the people have been deceived by these false prophets and prophetesses, yet the Lord has promised to so move and "deliver My people out of your hand." As well, there is to be absolutely no doubt as to Who has done this. "You shall know that I am*

the LORD.")

22 Because with lies you have made the heart of the righteous sad, whom I have not made sad; and strengthened the hands of the wicked, that he should not return from his wicked way, by promising him life *(the heart of Ezekiel was saddened greatly by the false message of these individuals who "strengthened the hands of the wicked" by promising them eternal life without them having to forsake their evil way. As well, such characterizes most modern Churches. It should sadden "the heart of the righteous"):*

23 Therefore you shall see no more vanity, nor divine divinations: for I will deliver My people out of your hand: and you shall know that I am the LORD. *(This was certainly accomplished by the few who were delivered when Judah and Jerusalem were destroyed. Still, its total fulfillment awaits a future date.)*

CHAPTER 14
(594 B.C.)
THE HYPOCRISY AND IDOLATRY
OF THE ELDERS

THEN came certain of the elders of Israel unto me, and sat before me. *(The "Elders of Israel" concerned those among the captives.)*

2 And the Word of the LORD came unto me, saying,

3 Son of man, these men have set up their idols in their heart, and put the stumblingblock of their iniquity before their face: should I be enquired of at all by them? *(The phrase, "These men have set up their idols in their heart," goes to the very seat of the problem. The statement means that these Elders were hankering after the old false worship in which they had once taken part. They had left Egypt, so to speak, but Egypt was still in them. In fact, this one Verse characterizes so much of modern Christianity. The "idol" in the heart was just as real as if they had been falling down to false gods as did the heathen.)*

4 Therefore speak unto them, and say unto them, Thus saith the Lord GOD; Every man of the House of Israel who sets up his idols in his heart, and puts the stumblingblock of his iniquity before his face, and comes to the Prophet; I the LORD will answer him who comes according to the multitude of his idols *(God can have no fellowship with evil. He, therefore, not only refuses to answer such prayers, but He replies to them with just judgments. Let me quickly state: Any object of faith other than*

"Christ and Him Crucified" is constituted by the Lord as an "idol" [I Jn. 5:21]);

5 That I may take the House of Israel in their own heart, because they are all estranged from Me through their idols. *(However fair the outward profession of faith in God may be, the Holy Spirit can unmask the evil lodged within the heart.)*

6 Therefore say unto the House of Israel, Thus saith the Lord GOD; Repent, and turn yourselves from your idols; and turn away your faces from all your abominations. *(God loved and pitied these hypocrites and the fact of this Love added to the certitude and horror of the just doom that was impending over them. He cried to them to repent, no longer to keep far from Him, and He would receive and acknowledge them as "My people.")*

7 For every one of the House of Israel, or of the stranger who sojourns in Israel, which separates himself from Me, and sets up his idols in his heart, and puts the stumblingblock of his iniquity before his face, and comes to a prophet to enquire of him concerning me; I the LORD will answer him by Myself *(the idea is: these particular individuals wanted help from God, but did not want to rid themselves of their sins. The phrase, "I the LORD will answer him by Myself," is found in the next Verse; however, it means that one cannot hold to God with one hand while holding to the world with the other):*

JUDGMENT ON THE IDOLATERS

8 And I will set My face against that man, and will make him a sign and a proverb, and I will cut him off from the midst of My people; and you shall know that I am the LORD. *(The threatenings in this Prophecy are, in substance and language, all found in Leviticus and Deuteronomy. This Passage, as so many others, completely refutes the unscriptural doctrine of "Unconditional Eternal Security." The phrase, "I will cut him off from the midst of My people," says, at the same time, that for one to be "cut off," one has to first of all be attached.)*

JUDGMENT ON THE FALSE PROPHETS

9 And if the prophet be deceived when he has spoken a thing, I the LORD have deceived that prophet, and I will stretch out My hand upon him, and will destroy him from the midst of My people Israel. *(The phrase, "I the LORD have deceived that prophet," actually means that*

the Lord permitted that prophet to be deceived, and actually aided the process, because this is what the prophet wanted. It is most just that God should cause one who deceives others to himself be deceived. The history of Jacob illustrates this moral principle.)

10 And they shall bear the punishment of their iniquity: the punishment of the prophet shall be even as the punishment of him who seeks unto him (both the false prophet and his hearers can expect judgment. This is a clear condemnation, not only to the false prophet, but also to those who entertain and support his false message);

11 That the House of Israel may go no more astray from Me, neither be polluted any more with all their transgressions; but that they may be My people, and I may be their God, saith the Lord GOD. (The heart of God beats in this Verse. It is the cry of the Holy Spirit that all "transgressions" be put away, and that these people "may be My people, and I may be their God." This will eventually be realized in the New Earth [Rev. 21:3-7; 22:3].)

JUDGMENTS ON JERUSALEM

12 The word of the LORD came again to me, saying (here, a new section of Prophecy begins. What follows is strikingly similar to Jer. 15:1-2),

13 Son of man, when the land sins against Me by trespassing grievously, then will I stretch out My hand upon it, and will break the staff of the bread thereof, and will send famine upon it, and will cut off man and beast from it (we find from this Verse that the prosperity of a nation is directly linked to the spiritual prosperity of its people):

14 Though these three men, Noah, Daniel, and Job, were in it, they should deliver but their own souls, by their righteousness, saith the Lord GOD. (In Jer. 15:1, Jerusalem was told that the Intercession of Moses and Samuel [Ex. 32:11-14; Num. 14:13-20; I Sam. 7:8-12] would fail to revert her coming doom. In this Chapter it is added that the presence of Noah, Daniel, and Job would also fail to preserve it from destruction. From this, we learn that sinners cannot be saved by the righteousness of others.)

15 If I cause noisome beasts to pass through the land, and they spoil it, so that it be desolate, that no man may pass through because of the beasts (the four sore judgments mentioned in this Chapter are: famine [Vs. 13], wild beasts

[Vs. 15], war [Vs. 17], and pestilence [Vs. 19]):

16 Though these three men were in it, as I live, saith the Lord GOD, they shall deliver neither sons nor daughters; they only shall be delivered, but the land shall be desolate. (Once again, let us state: the righteousness of others cannot save the sinner. He must personally come to the Lord and be Born-Again [Jn. 3:3].)

17 Or if I bring a sword upon that land, and say, Sword, go through the land; so that I cut off man and beast from it (anytime war comes to a people or a nation, this Passage plus others tell us that the Lord allows such because of the wickedness of the people. As well, it proclaims that the Godly, by their Godly lives and Intercession, can at times hold off such. However, the wickedness of a people can become so great that even the righteous cannot hold back the judgment):

18 Though these three men were in it, as I live, saith the Lord GOD, they shall deliver neither sons nor daughters, but they only shall be delivered themselves. (Four times the Holy Spirit repeats this phraseology [Vss. 14, 16, 18, 20]. Such repetition is meant to impress upon all the severity of the situation.)

19 Or if I send a pestilence into that land, and pour out My fury upon it in blood, to cut off from it man and beast. (In the Hebrew, the word "blood" expresses every kind of unnatural death.)

20 Though Noah, Daniel, and Job, were in it, as I live, saith the Lord GOD, they shall deliver neither son nor daughter; they shall but deliver their own souls by their righteousness. (The Lord testifies here to the Righteousness of Noah, Daniel, and Job. Of the three, Daniel was still alive.)

21 For thus saith the Lord GOD; How much more when I send my four sore judgments upon Jerusalem, the sword and the famine, and the noisome beast, and the pestilence, to cut off from it man and beast? (The argument of this Verse is that if these three men could not turn aside one judgment, how could they turn aside four sore ones?)

22 Yet, behold, therein shall be left a remnant that shall be brought forth, both sons and daughters: behold, they shall come forth unto you, and you shall see their way and their doings: and you shall be comforted concerning the evil that I have brought upon Jerusalem, even concerning all that I have brought upon it. (The "remnant" addressed here concerns the few who would be saved from the judgments of Verse 21 and brought as captives to Babylonia.

This means that the nation will be spared. And so it has been!)

23 And they shall comfort you, when you see their ways and their doings: and you shall know that I have not done without cause all that I have done in it, saith the Lord GOD. *(No doubt many of the faithful captives had very near and dear relatives who were still living in Jerusalem. That the Wrath of God should fall on these must have perplexed and deeply agitated the Exiles. But when they were told of the evil and wickedness of Jerusalem, even among its spiritual leaders, they were comforted concerning the evil that God would bring upon them.)*

CHAPTER 15
(594 B.C.)
JERUSALEM LIKE A USELESS VINE: CONSUMED, SIGNIFYING JUDGMENT

AND the Word of the LORD came unto me, saying,

2 Son of man, What is the vine tree more than any tree, or than a branch which is among the trees of the forest? *(In the Scriptures, Israel is symbolized as a "Vine," as an "Olive," and as a "Fig Tree." The "Vine" symbolized spiritual privilege. The one and only business of the Vine is to bear grapes. Otherwise it is worthless, except as fire wood [Jn. 15:6]. Israel was the Vine brought out of Egypt, whose one duty and privilege was to bear moral fruit unto God [Mat. 21:33-46].*

The question, "What is the Vine Tree more than any tree?", refers to the truth that if the Vine does not bring forth fruit, it is not even as valuable as any other tree in the forest. Its sole function is to bear fruit.)

3 Shall wood be taken thereof to do any work? Or will men take a pin of it to hang any vessel thereon? *(The analogy drawn by the Holy Spirit is that the Vine can be used for nothing except to bear fruit. It is useless and valueless even as timber, and actually not fit to even make simple pegs "on which to hang a vessel.")*

4 Behold, it is cast into the fire for fuel; the fire devours both the ends of it, and the midst of it is burned. Is it meet for any work? *(The phrase, "Behold, it is cast into the fire for fuel," refers to the judgment that was coming to this "Vine" because of sin. The phrase, "And the midst of it is burned," refers to Jerusalem, which was then on the eve of being burned by the Chaldeans.*

The question, "Is it meet for any work?", refers to the Work of God, and is answered in the next Verse.)

5 Behold, when it was whole, it was meet for no work: how much less shall it be meet yet for any work, when the fire has devoured it, and it is burned? *(Before Jerusalem was burned, it was useless as a moral agent; therefore, it was wholly useless when burned. Its total purpose was to be a reflector of the Light of Christ. With the reflector marred because of sin, Israel was of no more use.)*

6 Therefore thus saith the Lord GOD; As the vine tree among the trees of the forest, which I have given to the fire for fuel, so will I give the inhabitants of Jerusalem. *(II Ki. 25:9 records the fulfillment of this prediction.)*

7 And I will set My face against them; they shall go out from one fire, and another fire shall devour them; and you shall know that I am the LORD, when I set My face against them. *(The phrase, "They shall go out from one fire," referred to the destruction of Jerusalem, when multitudes perished. The phrase, "And another fire shall devour them," referred to the captivity, during which much of the residue perished.)*

8 And I will make the land desolate, because they have committed a trespass, saith the Lord GOD. *(The cause of their doom is declared in this Verse. They perversely fell into determined rebellion. In other words, they sinned against Light. Consequently, they were not merely sinners, as the surrounding nations; they were worse, for they were apostates, transgressors, and rebels. They sinned against Light, for to them alone had been given the Law, i.e., "the Bible.")*

CHAPTER 16
(594 B.C.)
THE SIGN OF A CHILD; JERUSALEM, A FOUNDLING

AGAIN the Word of the LORD came unto me, saying,

2 Son of man, cause Jerusalem to know her abominations *("Jerusalem" is the subject, because she, as the capital and where the Temple was located, answers for the entirety of Judah),*

3 And say, Thus saith the Lord GOD unto Jerusalem; Your birth and your nativity is of the land of Canaan; your father was an Amorite, and your mother an Hittite. *(The phrase, "Your birth and your nativity," refers to her origin, which was not heavenly, but earthly. Such is said because religious pride had so filled Jerusalem, as she held herself spiritually far*

above other cities and nations, that she no longer saw herself for what she really was. With a piercing blow, the Holy Spirit through the Prophet strikes at her pride, saying, "your birth is of the land of Canaan.")

4 And as for your nativity, in the day you were born your navel was not cut, neither were you washed in water to supple you; you were not salted at all, nor swaddled at all. *(The interpretation of this Prophecy belongs to that city and nation, but in application truly describes the moral condition of all men by natural birth; for these Verses give a true picture of man's essential corruption.)*

5 No eye pitied you, to do any of these unto you, to have compassion upon you; but you were cast out in the open field, to the loathing of your person, in the day that you were born. *(The phrase, "No eye pitied you," refers to all the surrounding nations, from then until now.")*

6 And when I passed by you, and saw you polluted in your own blood, I said unto you when you were in your blood, Live; yea, I said unto you when you were in your blood, Live. *(The Grace of the Redeemer, in loving such a foul being, in making her His Bride, and in giving her such a priceless trousseau, surpasses all human experience.)*

7 I have caused you to multiply as the bud of the field, and you have increased and waxed great, and you are come to excellent ornaments: your breasts are fashioned, and your hair is grown, whereas you were naked and bare. *(Israel really never became a nation until the advent of David as king. Under Saul, who was man's choice [as David was God's choice], Israel little came together as a unified people. Only under David, of which these Passages speak, did Israel become a cohesive unity.*

The phrase, "And you are come to excellent ornaments," refers to the Ark of the Covenant, and ultimately the Temple, where God dwelt. No other nation in the world was blessed with such "excellent ornaments," which also inspired the enmity of the nations.

The phrase, "Your breasts are fashioned," referred to her spiritual maturity, in that she was to nurture the nations of the world in the knowledge of God. Sadly, in this she failed!)

GOD RESCUES HER

8 Now when I passed by you, and looked upon you, behold, your time was the time of love; and I spread My skirt over you, and covered your nakedness: yea, I swore unto you, and entered into a covenant with you, saith the Lord GOD, and you became Mine. *(The phrase, "And I spread My skirt over you, and covered your nakedness," is illustrated by Ruth lying at the feet of Boaz [Ruth 3:9]. The "Covenant" into which the Lord entered with Israel was actually the Covenant of Ex. 24:7-8. All of this is also spelled out in Deut., Chpt. 28. There, the positives and negatives of the Covenant are given. The Lord never broke the Covenant, but Israel did, and repeatedly! God's fidelity to the Covenant is enjoined in the words, "I swore unto you, and entered into a Covenant with you.")*

9 Then washed I you with water; yea, I thoroughly washed away your blood from you, and I anointed you with oil. *(The "water" refers to the Word of God, and the "oil" refers to the Holy Spirit, which Israel alone of the nations had.)*

10 I clothed you also with broidered work, and shod you with badgers' skin, and I girded you about with fine linen, and I covered you with silk. *(This Passage speaks of the following:*

A. "I clothed you with broidered work": speaks of the "Garment of Praise" [Isa. 61:3];

B. "I shod you with badgers' skin": a type of the Incarnation of Christ;

C. "I girded you about with fine linen": speaks of Righteousness;

D. "I covered you with silk": prosperity!)

11 I decked you also with ornaments, and I put bracelets upon your hands, and a chain on your neck. *(More gifts:*

E. "I decked you also with ornaments": this consisted of the holy utensils used in the Temple for the worship of Jehovah;

F. "And I put bracelets upon your hands": this speaks of the Blessings of God;

G. "And a chain upon your neck": this typifies the umbilical cord to Christ.)

12 And I put a jewel on your forehead, and earrings in your ears, and a beautiful crown upon your head. *(Gifts continue:*

H. "And I put a jewel in your forehead": this speaks of possession, and means that Israel belonged solely to the Lord;

I. "And earrings in your ears": this signifies that they were to hear only His Voice;

J. "And a beautiful crown upon your head": as such, they were signified as the head of all nations.)

13 Thus were you decked with gold and silver; and your raiment was of fine linen, and

silk, and broidered work; you did eat fine flour, and honey, and oil: and you were exceeding beautiful, and you did prosper into a kingdom. *(The blessings continue:*

K. "Thus were you decked with gold and silver": the gold spoke of Deity, and the silver spoke of Redemption. Jehovah was their Head and He had redeemed them;

L. "You did eat fine flour": such portrays the Incarnation of the spotless Son of God;

M. "And honey": typified the sweet "Word of God" [Ps. 119:103];

N. "And oil": as would be obvious, typifies the Holy Spirit, which is the second time He is typified, denoting great help [Vs. 9];

O. "And you were exceeding beautiful": they were the nation of nations; however, all of their blessing and beauty came totally and solely from the Lord;

P. "And you did prosper into a kingdom": under David and Solomon they became the most powerful nation in the world.)

14 And your renown went forth among the heathen for your beauty: for it was perfect through My comeliness, which I had put upon you, saith the Lord GOD. *(That a mighty Prince should make of an abandoned infant His Queen is amazing. But what adds to the wonder of it all is that this Divine Prince knew beforehand that His Bride would forsake Him and ultimately betray Him and crucify Him.*

Such affection is impossible among men, for when a man adopts a child, he hopes for a recompense in the love of the child; but who would adopt a child knowing beforehand that the child would hate and murder its benefactor?

The Love that provided such a marriage, as described in Verses 10 through 14, is a Love that passes knowledge.)

THE FOUNDLING BECOMES A PROSTITUTE: THE SINS OF JUDAH

15 But you did trust in your own beauty, and played the harlot because of your renown, and poured out your fornications on every one who passed by; his it was. *(The two especially horrible features of the impure and cruel forms of idolatry to which Jerusalem madly gave herself are described in Verses 15 through 34. They were impure; for in her frenzied rage for idol worship, she especially adopted the idolatries of Egypt and Chaldea, both characterized by obscenity. The cruelty of her favored form*

of worship was the burning alive of little children in honor of the idol god, Moloch.)

16 And of your garments you did take, and decked your high places with divers colours, and played the harlot thereupon: the like things shall not come, neither shall it be so. *(The phrase, "The like things shall not come, neither shall it be so," refers to a frenzied fervor of debauchery that has never been witnessed before, at least to this degree, and shall never again be witnessed!)*

17 You have also taken your fair jewels of My gold and of My silver, which I had given you, and made to yourself images of men, and did commit whoredom with them *(the phrase, "And made to yourself images of men, and did commit whoredom with them," is thought to intimate phallus worship, i.e., the Asherah — the male reproductive organ),*

18 And took your broidered garments, and covered them: and you have set My oil and My incense before them. *(The phrase, "And you have set My oil and My incense before them," refers to this filthy idol possibly being placed even in the very Holy of Holies beside the Ark of the Covenant, or at least in the Holy Place beside the Altar of Worship. It is thought by some that Manasseh did this [II Chron. 33:3-7].)*

19 My meat also which I gave you, fine flour, and oil, and honey, wherewith I fed you, you have even set it before them for a sweet savour: and thus it was, saith the Lord GOD. *(The phrase, "And thus it was, saith the Lord GOD," means "I saw it; it is really true, saith Adonai-Jehovah." The sense here is: How could such a shameful object of worship, made of wood, stone, or metal, give "rest" to either heart or conscience?)*

20 Moreover you have taken your sons and your daughters, whom you have borne unto Me, and these have you sacrificed unto them to be devoured. Is this of your whoredoms a small matter,

21 That you have slain My children, and delivered them to cause them to pass through the fire for them? *(The throbbing agony of these two Verses can be felt by the Reader. Divine indignation and anguish combined in crying out to this faithless wife, "Bad as was your conduct in forsaking Me for vile and worthless lovers, yet greater is your guilt and cruelty in putting My children to so horrible a death.")*

22 And in all your abominations and your whoredoms you have not remembered the days of your youth, when you were naked and

bare, and were polluted in your blood. *(Israel forgot that the Lord raised her up from nothing, and even less than nothing, if possible!)*

23 And it came to pass after all your wickedness, (woe, woe unto you! Saith the LORD GOD *[the phrase, "Woe, woe unto you!" refers to the coming judgment upon Judah and Jerusalem by the Chaldeans: it is because of "all your wickedness]*;)

24 That you have also built unto you an eminent place, and have made you an high place in every street. *(This "high place" or "eminent place" referred to these religious ceremonies of idol worship.)*

25 You have built your high place at every head of the way, and have made your beauty to be abhorred, and have opened your feet to every one who passed by, and multiplied your whoredoms. *(The phrase, "You have built . . .," proclaims the industry of Judah and Jerusalem in the increase of their sin.)*

26 You have also committed fornication with the Egyptians your neighbors, great of flesh; and have increased your whoredoms, to provoke Me to anger. *(The phrase, "You have also committed fornication with the Egyptians," points to the political and commercial alliances in themselves as whoredom [Isa. 23:17; Nah. 3:4].*

Please note the terms of "fornication" and "whoredoms," which had to do in essence with "spiritual adultery." The Apostle Paul used virtually the same terminology concerning Christians, who are married to Christ but yet look to things other than the Cross for victory [Rom. 7:1-4].)

27 Behold, therefore I have stretched out My hand over you, and have diminished your ordinary food, and delivered you unto the will of them who hate you, the daughters of the Philistines, which are ashamed of your lewd way. *(The phrase, "The daughters of the Philistines, which are ashamed of your lewd way," is striking indeed! Israel had sunk lower even than these heathen people. And then the judgment begins, with the Lord trying to bring Israel back to her rightful place.)*

28 You have played the whore also with the Assyrians, because you were unsatiable; yea, you have played the harlot with them, and yet could not be satisfied. *(The phrase, "You have played the whore also with the Assyrians," includes political alliances like that of Ahaz with Tiglath-Pileser [II Ki. 26:7], as well as the adoption of idolatrous worship.*

The word "unsatiable" referred to one being incapable of being satisfied, in this case, desiring to sin more and more!)*

29 You have moreover multiplied your fornication in the land of Canaan unto Chaldea; and yet you were not satisfied herewith. *(The Holy Land became morally "the land of Canaan" because of its adoption of the foul and ancient religion of Canaan. The phrase, "And yet you were not satisfied herewith," once again reinforces the truth that lust is never satisfied. The more one sins, the more one must sin.)*

30 How weak is your heart, saith the LORD GOD, seeing you do all these things, the work of an imperious whorish woman *(the phrase, "How weak is your heart," refers to Israel, spiritually speaking, giving herself to anyone and everyone)*;

31 In that you build your eminent place in the head of every way, and make your high place in every street; and have not been as an harlot, in that you scorn hire *(the phrase, "And have not been as an harlot, in that you scorn hire," refers to the fact that a harlot was paid for her services, but Israel was so eager to commit spiritual adultery that she gave herself away to any and all for the asking; if they didn't ask, it was freely offered)*;

32 But as a wife who commits adultery, which takes strangers instead of her husband! *(God considered Israel as His Covenant wife. She was unfaithful to Him, in that she gave worship and adoration to "strangers instead of her husband," i.e., Jehovah.)*

33 They give gifts to all whores: but you give your gifts to all your lovers, and hire them, that they may come unto you on every side for your whoredom. *(The phrase, "That they may come unto you on every side for your whoredom," points to Judah and Jerusalem actively soliciting alliances with the heathen and eagerly desiring to worship their false gods.)*

34 And the contrary is in you from other women in your whoredoms: whereas none follows you to commit whoredoms, and in that you give a reward, and no reward is given unto you, therefore you are contrary. *(The phrase, "And the contrary is in you from other women in your whoredoms," refers to other nations which remained true to their gods, and did not take upon themselves the worship of the gods of other countries. But Judah forsook the worship of Jehovah, engaging in the worship of foreign gods. In this, they were contrary to other nations.*

The phrase, "Whereas none follows you to commit whoredoms," meant that Judah, at least

among the nations, was alone in committing this foul sin.)

JUDGMENT ON JERUSALEM

35 Wherefore, O harlot, hear the word of the LORD *(the Holy Spirit through the Prophet addresses Judah as "O harlot"! Is the Lord saying the same thing about the modern Church? Inasmuch as the modern Church has left Christ, and, in fact, serves "another Jesus," which means that it's a Jesus without the Cross [II Cor. 11:4], then the modern Church must be judged the same as Judah of old!):*

36 Thus saith the Lord GOD; Because your filthiness was poured out, and your nakedness discovered through your whoredoms with your lovers, and with all the idols of your abominations, and by the blood of your children, which you did give unto them *(the word translated "filthiness" actually should have been translated "brass." It probably referred to the money spent by Jerusalem on the establishment and maintenance of idol worship. Silver figured clean money and spoke of Redemption, while brass figured the unclean.*

The phrase, "And by the blood of your children," which you did give unto them," refers to Judah going into idol worship to such an extent, and seeking to please these foreign countries, that she actually offered up her own children in sacrifice to heathen gods);

37 Behold, therefore I will gather all your lovers, with whom you have taken pleasure, and all them that you have loved, with all them that you have hated; I will even gather them round about against you, and will discover your nakedness unto them, that they may see all your nakedness. *(The phrase, "Your lovers," refers to the Assyrians, Egyptians, and the Chaldeans. The phrase, "All them that you have hated," refers to the Moabites, Ammonites, and the Philistines. The phrase, "And will discover your nakedness unto them," pertains to her coming defeat which will expose her to those she thought were her friends, but in reality were her enemies. It also refers to those who had always been jealous of her and who would now gloat over her defeat.)*

38 And I will judge you, as women who break wedlock and shed blood are judged; and I will give you blood in fury and jealousy. *(The Holy Spirit, in this Passage, is referring to Lev. 20:10 and Deut. 22:22. Joining Verse 38 with Rom. 7:1-4, we learn that God*

judges as a "spiritual adulterer" any person who allows the object of their faith to be other than the Cross of Christ.)

39 And I will also give you into their hand, and they shall throw down your eminent place, and shall break down your high places: they shall strip you also of your clothes, and shall take your fair jewels, and leave you naked and bare. *(This Verse proclaims the fact that not only would these places of idol worship be destroyed by the coming conquerors, but the true glory of Judah and Jerusalem would also be destroyed.)*

40 They shall also bring up a company against you, and they shall stone you with stones, and thrust you through with their swords. *(The phrase, "Stone you with stones," probably refers to the great engines of war employed by the Chaldeans, which hurled great stones against the walls of the city, and even into the city.)*

41 And they shall burn your houses with fire, and execute judgments upon you in the sight of many women: and I will cause you to cease from playing the harlot, and you also shall give no hire any more. *(This refers to the city being sacked and burned and, therefore, no longer able to finance idolatrous worship, or even to engage in it, except in their hearts. The phrase, "In the sight of many women," refers to the surrounding nations, which were also likened by the Holy Spirit to harlots [Vs. 34], which would observe with glee the defeat and destruction of Jerusalem.)*

42 So will I make My fury toward you to rest, and My jealousy shall depart from you, and I will be quiet, and will be no more angry. *(From the Word of God, we learn that the Wrath of God is a reality; the language and teaching of Scripture are calculated to impress upon us the severity by which it is characterized.)*

43 Because you have not remembered the days of your youth, but have fretted Me in all these things; behold, therefore I also will recompense your way upon your head, saith the Lord GOD: and you shall not commit this lewdness above all your abominations. *(The phrase, "Because you have not remembered the days of your youth," presents a more tender tone than the previous statements, hence mixing Mercy with Wrath, thus sparing a Remnant.)*

44 Behold, every one who uses proverbs shall use this proverb against you, saying, As is the mother, so is her daughter. *(Because Jerusalem adopted the loathsome form of idolatry*

practiced by the Canaanites, she, therefore, morally became their daughter.)

45 You are your mother's daughter, who loathes her husband and her children; and you are the sister of your sisters, which loathed their husbands and their children: your mother was an Hittite, and your father an Amorite. *(This Verse proclaims Judah conducting herself not as belonging to the Lord of Glory, but rather belonging to the heathen nations surrounding her, because she had adopted all of their ways.)*

46 And your elder sister is Samaria, she and her daughters who dwell at your left hand: and your younger sister, who dwells at your right hand, is Sodom and her daughters. *(Historically, Sodom, as the oldest representative of evil, seemed to claim precedence. However, Samaria influenced Judah far more regarding evil, and was, therefore, called the elder sister, primarily because Sodom had been destroyed even before Israel became a nation. Nevertheless, empires which did greatly influence Judah for evil, such as Assyria and the Chaldeans, had been greatly influenced by the evil of Sodom, as had the entire world of that day, hence the phrase, "Sodom and her daughters.")*

47 Yet have you not walked after their ways, nor done after their abominations: but, as if that were a very little thing, you were corrupted more than they in all your ways. *(The idea of this Verse is: Judah was not only as bad as the heathen nations, but actually became much worse!)*

48 As I live, saith the Lord GOD, Sodom your sister has not done, she nor her daughters, as you have done, you and your daughters. *(When Judah was placed beside Sodom, she was found wanting! Such is almost beyond imagination. And yet Christ would say the same thing concerning the Israel of His day [Mat. 11:24].)*

49 Behold, this was the iniquity of your sister Sodom, pride, fullness of bread, and abundance of idleness was in her and in her daughters, neither did she strengthen the hand of the poor and needy. *(Four sins, as given here, characterized Sodom, but "pride" headed the list.)*

50 And they were haughty, and committed abomination before Me: therefore I took them away as I saw good. *(The "abomination" they committed was the sin of homosexuality, i.e., "sodomy.")*

51 Neither has Samaria committed half of your sins; but you have multiplied your abominations more than they, and have justified your sisters in all your abominations which you have done. *(The idea is: all the heathen nations, including Sodom, were made to appear innocent by comparison with the guilt of Jerusalem — not positively, but relatively [II Ki. 21:9].)*

52 You also, which have judged your sisters, bear your own shame for your sins that you have committed more abominable than they: they are more righteous than you: yea, be thou confounded also, and bear your shame, in that you have justified your sisters. *(The Lord called Judah "more abominable than they." To make the case even more ironclad, He turned it around and said: "they are more righteous than you.")*

REGATHERING OF ISRAEL

53 When I shall bring again their captivity, the captivity of Sodom and her daughters, and the captivity of Samaria and her daughters, then will I bring again the captivity of your captives in the midst of them *(the future Restoration of Jerusalem together with Samaria and Sodom is predicted in Verses 53 through 63. This will take place in the coming Kingdom Age.*

The amazing nature of the Grace that will perform this regeneration is preceded by the argument of Verses 53 through 59, which appears to be that Jerusalem had no more claim to forgiveness and Restoration than either Sodom or Samaria. Therefore, her recovery was as eternally hopeless as theirs.

However, the principle of Grace now appears as Paul outlines in Rom. 11:34. But a Grace rich enough to forgive Jerusalem must, in its nature, be rich enough to forgive her less guilty companions, for there is no difference — all have sinned):

54 That you may bear your own shame, and may be confounded in all that you have done, in that you are a comfort unto them. *(The fact of pardon being granted to Jerusalem brings "comfort" to Samaria and Sodom. As stated, this will take place in the coming Kingdom Age!)*

55 When your sisters, Sodom and her daughters, shall return to their former estate, and Samaria and her daughters shall return to their former estate, then you and your daughters shall return to your former estate. *(It is humbling to religious pride to be compelled to seek Mercy in the company of the most degraded and fallen, and of those formerly despised.)*

SINS OF JUDAH

56 For your sister Sodom was not mentioned by your mouth in the day of your pride *(the name of Sodom was not even uttered by Judah in the days of her prosperity. It was too vile for utterance except as a byword of reproach. Isaiah had in vain reminded her that she had made herself like them [Isa. 1:9-10]. Such is self-righteousness!)*,

57 Before your wickedness was discovered, as at the time of your reproach of the daughters of Syria, and all that are round about her, the daughters of the Philistines, which despise you round about. *(The phrase, "Before your wickedness was discovered," refers to Judah being humbled as those she had despised.)*

58 You have borne your lewdness and your abominations, saith the LORD. *(This Scripture presents the reason that Judah sank to the spiritual level, or even below, of their surrounding heathen neighbors, i.e., "lewdness" and "abominations.")*

59 For thus saith the Lord GOD; I will even deal with you as you have done, which have despised the oath in breaking the Covenant. *(The "Oath" and "Covenant" formed the marriage bond of Sinai, which was the Law. Jerusalem was unfaithful to that bond; but not so her Heavenly Husband, as the next Verse will declare.)*

GOD'S COVENANT: RESTORATION
OF ISRAEL

60 Nevertheless I will remember My covenant with you in the days of your youth, and I will establish unto you an Everlasting Covenant. *(Even though Judah did not keep the Covenant, the Lord did. And as such, He has made an everlasting marriage bond with her. This is yet future, in that she will be fully restored, which will take place at the Second Coming, when Israel will repent and finally accept Christ as her Saviour, Messiah, and Lord.*

The phrase, "I will remember My Covenant with you in the days of your youth," refers to the Promises made to Abraham, the Patriarchs, and the Prophets. Despite Israel's wickedness, and because of her Repentance, each of these Promises will be kept in full. The "Everlasting Covenant" refers to the New Covenant of Grace already given, which Israel would not accept, but now shall in totality [Heb. 13:20].)

61 Then you shall remember your ways, and be ashamed, when you shall receive your sisters, your elder and your younger: and I will give them unto you for daughters, but not by your covenant. *(At the time this New Covenant is ratified with Israel, and upon her acceptance of Christ as her Lord and Saviour, He will, at the same time, give her, as bridesmaids, so to speak, her sisters, Sodom and Samaria. This will take place shortly after the Second Coming [Zech. 13:1].)*

62 And I will establish My covenant with you; and you shall know that I am the LORD *(the "Covenant" of which the Lord now speaks is not the Law of Moses, but rather the "New Covenant" perfected by Christ by Him giving His Life on the Cross of Calvary, and doing so for the entirety of the world, Israel included!):*

63 That you may remember, and be confounded, and never open your mouth any more because of your shame, when I am pacified toward you for all that you have done, saith the Lord GOD. *(The phrase, "When I am pacified toward you," means that Israel is forgiven. The Lord has accepted a propitiation for Israel. This propitiation was consummated at Calvary. It provides the righteous ground upon which God may meet and forgive the vilest sinners without injury to the Righteousness which is the establishment of His Throne. For if God were to forgive sins unrighteously, He would wreck His Throne and cease to be God.)*

CHAPTER 17
(594 B.C.)

PARABLE OF A GREAT EAGLE:
NEBUCHADNEZZAR

AND the Word of the LORD came unto me, saying,

2 Son of man, put forth a riddle and speak a parable unto the house of Israel *(the phrase, "Put forth a riddle," speaks of an enigma — a dark saying. It was also a parable, that is, the comparison of one thing to another);*

3 And say, Thus saith the Lord GOD; A great eagle with great wings, longwinged, full of feathers, which had divers colours, came unto Lebanon, and took the highest branch of the cedar *(the phrase, "A great eagle with great wings," speaks of Nebuchadnezzar. The phrase, "Came unto Lebanon," actually speaks of Jerusalem; the houses therein were built of cedar from Lebanon. The phrase, "And took the highest branch of the cedar," speaks of Jehoiachin being taken captive after serving only three months as king of Judah [II Ki. 24:8, 15-16]):*

4 He cropped off the top of his young twigs, and carried it into a land of traffick; he set it in a city of merchants. *(This speaks of the more eminent citizens of Jerusalem also being taken captive along with Jehoiachin.)*

5 He took also of the seed of the land, and planted it in a fruitful field; he placed it by great waters, and set it as a willow tree. *(The phrase, "He took also of the seed of the land," refers to Nebuchadnezzar making Zedekiah king of Judah. The phrase, "And planted it in a fruitful field," refers to the possibility of Zedekiah's reign being fruitful, with the land of Judah enjoying prosperity, that is, if he had only submitted himself to Nebuchadnezzar, as the Lord had directed. However, this he did not do.)*

6 And it grew, and became a spreading vine of low stature whose branches turned toward him, and the roots thereof were under him: so it became a vine, and brought forth branches, and shot forth sprigs. *(The phrase, "And it grew," refers to prosperity under Zedekiah, at least for a short time.)*

THE SECOND GREAT EAGLE: PHARAOH

7 There was also another great eagle with great wings and many feathers: and, behold, this vine did bend her roots toward him, and shot forth her branches toward him, that he might water it by the furrows of her plantation. *(The one referred to as "another great eagle with great wings and many feathers" was Pharaoh-Hophra, king of Egypt.)*

8 It was planted in a good soil by great waters, that it might bring forth branches, and that it might bear fruit, that it might be a goodly vine. *(The idea of this Verse is that if Zedekiah had obeyed the Prophet of the Lord, placing himself and Judah under the domain of Nebuchadnezzar, then Judah would have had a fair measure of prosperity. The vine might have borne fruit.)*

ZEDEKIAH'S REBELLION

9 Say thou, Thus saith the Lord GOD; Shall it prosper? Shall he not pull up the roots thereof, and cut off the fruit thereof, that it wither? It shall wither in all the leaves of her spring, even without great power or many people to pluck it up by the roots thereof. *(The question, "Thus saith the Lord GOD; Shall it prosper?", refers to this alliance between Zedekiah and Pharaoh. The answer is: "No." For he,*

Nebuchadnezzar, would uproot Zedekiah and destroy his kingdom.)

10 Yea, behold, being planted, shall it prosper? Shall it not utterly wither, when the east wind touches it? It shall wither in the furrows where it grew. *(The phrase, "It shall wither in the furrows where it grew," means that this alliance with Egypt will die aborning, and will infuriate Nebuchadnezzar, with awful results.)*

JEHOIACHIN'S CAPTIVITY

11 Moreover the word of the LORD came unto me, saying,

12 Say now to the rebellious house, Know ye not what these things mean? Tell them, Behold, the king of Babylon is come to Jerusalem, and has taken the king thereof, and the princes thereof, and led them with him to Babylon. *(This is the same as Verses 3 and 4, which speak of Nebuchadnezzar taking Jehoiachin and the princes to Babylon.)*

13 And has taken of the king's seed, and made a covenant with him, and has taken an oath of him: he has also taken the mighty of the land *(the "king's seed" was Zedekiah, whom he made king of Judah. The phrase, "And made a Covenant with him, and has taken an oath of him," refers to the fact that Zedekiah did this in the Name of Jehovah, and the Lord expected him to keep it):*

14 That the kingdom might be base, that it might not lift itself up, but that by keeping of his covenant it might stand. *(The phrase, "It might stand," refers to God's loving purpose, which was the peace and prosperity of His People in subjection to the Gentiles, at least at this time; and that they should be a witness for Him. So should they have been His recognized People and a Light to lighten the Gentiles. But their rebellion lost this prosperity and that glory.)*

ZEDEKIAH'S REBELLION AND
HIS TRUST IN EGYPT

15 But he rebelled against him in sending his ambassadors into Egypt, that they might give him horses and much people. Shall he prosper? Shall he escape who does such things? or shall he break the covenant, and be delivered? *(This refers to Zedekiah actively seeking an alliance with the Egyptians, which was totally opposed to the Will of God, and which would bring ruin to Judah.)*

16 As I live, saith the Lord GOD, surely in the place where the king dwells who made him king, whose oath he despised, and whose covenant he broke, even with him in the midst of Babylon he shall die. *(Zedekiah was taken captive by Nebuchadnezzar, blinded, and then sent to Babylon, where he died. So much for the alliance with Egypt. This Prophecy was probably written when the hopes of Zedekiah and his counselors were at their highest point, when the Chaldeans had in fact raised the siege of Jerusalem in anticipation of the arrival of the Egyptian army [Jer. 37:5-11]. Ezekiel, like Jeremiah, declared that the relief would be but temporary. And so it was!)*

17 Neither shall Pharaoh with his mighty army and great company make for him in the war, by casting up mounts, and building forts, to cut off many persons *(Pharaoh coming against Nebuchadnezzar proved to be more blow and bluster than anything else. Egypt was quickly neutralized)*:

18 Seeing he despised the oath by breaking the covenant, when, lo, he had given his hand, and has done all these things, he shall not escape. *(As stated, when Zedekiah broke the Covenant with Nebuchadnezzar, it was the same as breaking it with the Lord.)*

19 Therefore thus saith the Lord GOD; As I live, surely My oath that he has despised, and My covenant that he has broken, even it will I recompense upon his own head. *(Zedekiah freely agreed by covenant to rule Judah under Nebuchadnezzar. He took an oath to obey him, but rebelled after serving for several years. He turned to Egypt for help. For this, God cursed him.)*

20 And I will spread My net upon him, and he shall be taken in My snare, and I will bring him to Babylon, and will plead with him there for his trespass that he has trespassed against Me. *(The words, "And will plead with him there," along with Jer. 32:5 and 34:4-5, suggest that in his Earthly prison and physical blindness, Grace gave Zedekiah inward eyesight and spiritual freedom. In other words, it seems that he finally made his peace with God, even after long years of rebellion.)*

21 And all his fugitives with all his bands shall fall by the sword, and they who remain shall be scattered toward all winds: and you shall know that I the LORD have spoken it. *(This Passage refers to the terrible carnage which developed when Jerusalem fell to the Babylonians.)*

RESTORATION OF THE DAVIDIC KINGDOM UNDER THE MESSIAH

22 Thus saith the Lord GOD; I will also take of the highest branch of the high cedar, and will set it; I will crop off from the top of his young twigs a tender one, and will plant it upon an high mountain and eminent *(the Kingdom predicted in Verses 22 through 24 is that of the Messiah. It will take place in the coming Kingdom Age)*:

23 In the mountain of the height of Israel will I plant it: and it shall bring forth boughs, and bear fruit, and be a goodly cedar: and under it shall dwell all fowl of every wing; in the shadow of the branches thereof shall they dwell. *(The Kingdom of the Messiah will have no end. At that time, all the nations of the world will look to Christ for all prosperity. They will not be disappointed!)*

24 And all the trees of the field shall know that I the LORD have brought down the high tree, have exalted the low tree, have dried up the green tree, and have made the dry tree to flourish: I the LORD have spoken and have done it. *(The phrases, "High tree" and "Green tree," both refer to man's proud dominion, which will be brought down and dried up. The "Low tree" and "Dry tree" refer to Israel, which will then be made to flourish, becoming the most powerful nation in the world. As stated, this will be in the coming Kingdom Age.)*

CHAPTER 18
(594 B.C.)
THE SINNER SHALL DIE

THE Word of the LORD came unto me again, saying,

2 What mean ye, that you use this proverb concerning the land of Israel, saying, The fathers have eaten sour grapes, and the children's teeth are set on edge? *(The miseries suffered by the people in Jerusalem because of the Babylonian war were declared by them to be due to their fathers' sins, for they themselves, or so they claimed, were righteous. Hence, their proverb of Verse 2, repeated in Verse 19, was insisted upon in Verses 25 and 29. That is, they charged God with injustice, for man always throws the blame upon God, as did Adam [Gen. 3:12; Ex. 20:5].)*

3 As I live, saith the Lord GOD, you shall not have occasion any more to use this proverb

in Israel. *(Actually, this proverb declared, even in a round about way, that there was unrighteousness with God. They were taking a proverb which had a measure of truth in it and distorting it into a falsehood.)*

4 Behold, all souls are Mine; as the soul of the father, so also the soul of the son is Mine: the soul that sins, it shall die. *(Emphatically, the Lord through the Prophet declares that these people are suffering for their own sins, not the sins of their fathers. The phrase, "The soul that sins, it shall die," proclaims the truth that God judges each person upon his own actions, not upon the actions of others.)*

THE RIGHTEOUS SHALL LIVE

5 But if man be just, and do that which is lawful and right *(the righteous principle upon which God acts in pardoning original sin and personal sins is revealed in Rom. 3:21-26),*

6 And has not eaten upon the mountains, neither has lifted up his eyes to the idols of the House of Israel, neither has defiled his neighbor's wife, neither has come near to a menstruous woman. *(The idea of this and the following Verses is not the promotion of Salvation by works, but instead that if a person has truly repented and is attempting to do "that which is lawful and right," such action will portray itself in a definite way in his life, thereby, showing True Repentance.)*

7 And has not oppressed any, but has restored to the debtor his pledge, has spoiled none by violence, has given his bread to the hungry, and has covered the naked with a garment *(true Faith, Faith in Christ and the Cross, always produces good works; however, good works can never produce true Faith);*

8 He who has not given forth upon usury, neither has taken any increase, who has withdrawn his hand from iniquity, has executed true judgment between man and man *(traits of the righteous!).*

9 Has walked in My statutes and has kept My judgments, to deal truly; he is just, he shall surely live, saith the Lord GOD. *(Once again, we state: true Faith will always result, in one way or the other, in true works.)*

THE WICKED SON OF A RIGHTEOUS MAN SHALL DIE

10 If he *(the righteous man)* beget a son who is a robber, a shedder of blood, and who

does the like to any one of these things *(Verses 10 through 13 portray the wicked son of a righteous father, in which the righteousness of the father does not atone for the wickedness of the son),*

11 And who does not any of those duties, but even has eaten upon the mountains, and defiled his neighbour's wife *(once again, the truth is conveyed that unrighteous individuals produce unrighteous acts),*

12 Has oppressed the poor and needy, has spoiled by violence, has not restored the pledge, and has lifted up his eyes to the idols, has committed abomination *(as the righteous is ever upward, the unrighteous is ever downward),*

13 Has given forth upon usury, and has taken increase: shall he then live? He shall not live: he has done all these abominations; he shall surely die; his blood shall be upon him. *(The phrase, "He shall surely die," means that he will lose his soul, that is, if he continues in such a lifestyle.)*

THE RIGHTEOUS SON OF A WICKED FATHER SHALL LIVE

14 Now, lo, if he beget a son, who sees all his father's sins which he has done, and considers, and does not such like *(this son is the exact opposite of the son of Verse 10; he will be treated accordingly, which the Holy Spirit brings out),*

15 Who has not eaten upon the mountains, neither has lifted up his eyes to the idols of the House of Israel, has not defiled his neighbor's wife *(the Holy Spirit goes to all lengths to place responsibility upon the individual involved, meaning that each person will give account, irrespective as to the disposition of his father, whether righteous or unrighteous),*

16 Neither has oppressed any, has not withheld the pledge, neither has spoiled by violence, but has given his bread to the hungry, and has covered the naked with a garment *(Christianity that shows no love for one's fellow man, despite the loud profession, has no love for God),*

17 Who has taken off his hand from the poor, who has not received usury nor increase, has executed My Judgments, has walked in My Statutes; he shall not die for the iniquity of his father, he shall surely live. *(The phrase, "He shall not die for the iniquity of his father, he shall surely live," places the responsibility upon the individual involved. The father is not responsible, spiritually speaking, for the sins of*

his son, as the son is not responsible for the sins of the father. Each person, in the Eyes of God, is responsible for his own sins.)

THE WICKED FATHER SHALL DIE
FOR HIS SINS

18 As for his father, because he cruelly oppressed, spoiled his brother by violence, and did that which is not good among his people, lo, even he shall die in his iniquity. *(The Holy Spirit again and again proclaims the truth that the ungodly father is not saved as a result of the Godly son, as the ungodly son is not saved as a result of a Godly father.)*

INDIVIDUAL RESPONSIBILITY;
THE WAYS OF GOD ARE JUST

19 Yet you say, Why? Does not the son bear the iniquity of the father? When the son has done that which is lawful and right, and has kept all My Statutes, and has done them, he shall surely live.

20 The soul that sins, it shall die. The son shall not bear the iniquity of the father, neither shall the father bear the iniquity of the son: the righteousness of the righteous shall be upon him, and the wickedness of the wicked shall be upon him. *(This proclaims in no uncertain terms that Salvation in entirely a personal matter.)*

21 But if the wicked will turn from all his sins that he has committed, and keep all My Statutes, and do that which is lawful and right, he shall surely live, he shall not die. *(So far from God punishing a man for the sins of others, He will not even punish him for his own sins, if he repents and avails himself of God's Salvation, which is Christ. As well, this Promise is given to any and all, with none excluded!)*

22 All his transgressions that he has committed, they shall not be mentioned unto him: in his righteousness that he has done he shall live. *(Actually, this Passage, although in a veiled way, speaks of Justification by Faith.)*

23 Have I any pleasure at all that the wicked should die? saith the Lord GOD: and not that he should return from his ways, and live? *(The question of this Verse is answered in Verse 32. The Lord has no pleasure in the death of the wicked. Actually, for every wicked person who dies without God, the terrible death of Christ on Calvary was in vain.)*

24 But when the righteous turns away from his righteousness, and commits iniquity, and does according to all the abominations that the wicked man does, shall he live? All his righteousness that he has done shall not be mentioned: in his trespass that he has trespassed, and in his sin that he has sinned, in them shall he die. *(As all sins are blotted out upon one's Repentance, likewise, all righteousness is blotted out if one ceases to have faith in Christ and what He has done at the Cross. This, thereby, completely refutes the unscriptural doctrine of Unconditional Eternal Security [Heb. 6:4-6; 10:26-29].)*

25 Yet you say, The way of the LORD is not equal. Hear now, O House of Israel; Is not My way equal? Are not your ways unequal? *(Self-righteous men object to God's justice, however plainly manifested, because they do not wish to recognize it. They want God to condone sin. That, however, if He is to be true to His Nature, He cannot do!)*

26 When a righteous man turns away from his righteousness, and commits iniquity, and dies in them; for his iniquity that he has done shall he die. *(The phrase, "When a righteous man," actually means "any righteous man," and denotes that God is no respecter of persons. All come under the same rules, whether wicked or righteous, which is for the benefit of all.)*

27 Again, when the wicked man turns away from his wickedness that he has committed, and does that which is lawful and right, he shall save his soul alive. *(The word, "Again," refers to the Holy Spirit going to the trouble of repeating the same thing He has said in Verse 21. Once again, the offer is given for all past transgressions to be blotted out and new life to be given to the individual. It is mankind's greatest offer! The Holy Spirit emphatically states, "He shall save his soul alive." The manner in which this is done is for the individual to accept Christ and what Christ has done for us at the Cross [Jn. 3:16].)*

28 Because he considers, and turns away from all his transgressions that he has committed, he shall surely live, he shall not die. *(The phrase, "He shall not die," refers to spiritual death, not physical death.)*

29 Yet saith the House of Israel, The way of the LORD is not equal. O House of Israel, are not My ways equal? Are not your ways unequal? *(God's Ways are always equal, because He demands the same of all, irrespective of their status, position, gender, or the period of time in which they live. Man's ways are grossly unequal,*

because unrighteous judges can be bought off. Legislatures make laws which favor some and abuse others, with prejudice, racial and religious bias playing their insidious parts relative to mankind.

To be frank, the ways of man are so unequal as to be preposterous! And as unequal as man's ways are, as equal are God's Ways!)

SINNERS ARE ENCOURAGED TO REPENT AND LIVE

30 Therefore I will judge you, O House of Israel, every one according to his ways, saith the Lord GOD. Repent, and turn yourselves from all your transgressions; so iniquity shall not be your ruin. *(The Holy Spirit through the Prophet now gives an Altar Call. It is one of the clearest, most impassioned pleas found in the entirety of the Bible.)*

31 Cast away from you all your transgression, whereby you have transgressed; and make you a new heart and a new spirit: for why will you die, O House of Israel? *(Conversion and Regeneration can only be effected by the Holy Spirit. But the sinner is responsible to repent and to seek this new moral nature. Directly he tries to provide himself with these, he discovers his helplessness. Broken in spirit and casting himself on God for Salvation, the Holy Spirit reveals Christ to him and, thus, works the mighty miracle of the New Birth.)*

32 For I have no pleasure in the death of him who dies, saith the Lord GOD: wherefore turn yourselves, and live ye. *(Twice the Holy Spirit emphasizes the truth that the Lord has no pleasure in the death of the wicked. The repetition is not by accident.)*

CHAPTER 19
(594 B.C.)
LAMENTATION FOR THE PRINCES OF ISRAEL; JEHOAHAZ

M OREOVER take thou up a lamentation for the princes of Israel *(the word "lamentation" is used referring to the woe upon the nation of Judah by the ungodly action of two of its kings, Jehoahaz and Jehoiakim. The mourner is Immanuel),*

2 And say, What is your mother? A lioness: she lay down among lions, she nourished her whelps among young lions. *(The question, "What is your mother?", refers to Jerusalem as the great lion, and in a good sense [Isa. 29:1].*

The phrase, "She lay down among lions," refers to the surrounding heathen nations, which she was supposed to lead to God, but she was instead led astray herself! She adopted their cruelty and ferocity, thereby losing the Glory of God.

The phrase, "She nourished her whelps among young lions," refers to Jehoahaz and Jehoiakim taking the cue from the "young lions," i.e., "kings of the surrounding nations," rather than from the Lord.)

3 And she brought up one of her whelps: it became a young lion, and it learned to catch the prey; it devoured men. *(The phrase, "One of her whelps," points to Jehoahaz, who became like the heathen princes in the surrounding countries.)*

4 The nations also heard of him; he was taken in their pit, and they brought him with chains unto the land of Egypt. *(Jehoahaz was taken prisoner by Pharaoh-Necho and brought in chains to Egypt.)*

JEHOIAKIM

5 Now when she saw that she had waited, and her hope was lost, then she took another of her whelps, and made him a young lion. *(This relates to Jehoiakim, who reigned eleven years and was made king in the place of his brother, Jehoahaz.)*

6 And he went up and down among the lions, he became a young lion, and learned to catch the prey, and devoured men. *(The phrase, "And he went up and down among the lions," refers to him associating with the heathen nations, exactly as did his brother, Jehoahaz. Josephus, the Jewish Historian, says: "He was unjust and wicked by nature, and was neither reverent toward God nor kind to man.")*

7 And he knew their desolate palaces, and he laid waste their cities; and the land was desolate, and the fullness thereof, by the noise of his roaring. *(The phrase, "And he knew their desolate palaces," means that he plundered the nation in order to pay Egypt and to build his costly edifices. The phrase, "And the fullness thereof, by the noise of his roaring," refers to his violent nature in imposing his will upon Judah.)*

8 Then the nations set against him on every side from the provinces, and spread their net over him: he was taken in their pit. *(In this dallying with Egypt, he angered the Babylonians, and they "set against him on every side.")*

9 And they put him in ward in chains, and brought him to the king of Babylon: they brought him into holds, that his voice should

no more be heard upon the mountains of Israel. *(The phrase, "And brought him to the king of Babylon," does not mean that he was taken to Babylon, but that he was taken before Nebuchadnezzar. Even though the Scripture does not say how he died, it is believed that he died on the way to Babylon, drawn and cast forth and unburied. He was 36 years old when he died, without God and unlamented!)*

ZEDEKIAH

10 Your mother is like a vine in your blood, planted by the waters: she was fruitful and full of branches by reason of many waters. *(The phrase, "Your mother is like a vine," is referred to in 17:6, and refers to Judah as a Vine. The phrase, "She was fruitful and full of branches by reason of many waters," refers to the Blessings of God given unto her, which made her the envy of the nations.)*

11 And she had strong rods for the scepters of them who bore rule, and her stature was exalted among the thick branches, and she appeared in her height with the multitude of her branches. *(The phrase, "And she had strong rods for the scepters of them who bore rule," refers to the kingly line of David, which was God-appointed, and thereby blessed, actually becoming the greatest among nations.)*

12 But she was plucked up in fury, she was cast down to the ground, and the east wind dried up her fruit: her strong rods were broken and withered; the fire consumed them. *(The phrase, "But she was plucked up in fury," refers to the Judgment of God which came upon her because of her great sin. The Judgment was not light, but did come in stages.)*

13 And now she is planted in the wilderness, in a dry and thirsty ground. *(Whereas she had once been "planted by the waters," i.e., the Blessings of God, now she is "in a dry and thirsty ground," i.e., with no spiritual sustenance whatsoever, because of her rebellion against the Lord.)*

14 And fire is gone out of a rod of her branches, which has devoured her fruit, so that she has no strong rod to be a sceptre to rule. This is a lamentation, and shall be for a lamentation. *(The phrase, "And fire is gone out of a rod of her branches," refers to the evil capacity of her kings after Josiah, and the Judgment of God which was swiftly coming upon them. As such, all the glory described in Verses 10 and 11 is now gone, and sin "has devoured her fruit."*

The phrase, "And shall be for a Lamentation,"

refers to Zedekiah, whose doom was still future at the time that this Lament was given by the Spirit to the Prophet.)*

CHAPTER 20
(593 B.C.)
THE ELDERS' ENQUIRY

A ND it came to pass in the seventh year, in the fifth month, the tenth day of the month, that certain of the elders of Israel came to enquire of the LORD, and sat before me. *(This is a new Prophecy; it begins with this Verse and follows through the conclusion of Chapter 23. The "seventh year" pertains to the length of the Prophet's captivity up to this time.*

The Elders came before Ezekiel because the false prophets among the Exiles were at this time predicting a speedy restoration to Judah [Jer. 28:11]. These Elders desired Ezekiel to preach the same comfortable message, but he refused to do so. On the contrary, he exposed the deep-seated idolatry of their hearts and announced an accession of the Wrath of God upon them.)

GOD'S ANSWER: ISRAEL'S REBELLION AND DEFILEMENT WITH EGYPTIAN GODS

2 Then came the word of the LORD unto me, saying,

3 Son of man, speak unto the elders of Israel, and say unto them, Thus saith the Lord GOD; Are you come to enquire of Me? As I live, saith the Lord GOD, I will not be enquired of by you. *(The last phrase is a startling statement indeed! The Lord will not accede to their request and will not hear their prayers. These men outwardly professed the worship of God, but inwardly they loved idolatry.)*

4 Will you judge them, son of man, will you judge them? Cause them to know the abominations of their fathers *(the Holy Spirit, by "causing them to know the abominations of their fathers," will in no uncertain terms proclaim the justness of God's actions; furthermore, He will relate their own culpability)*:

5 And say unto them, Thus saith the Lord GOD; In the day when I chose Israel, and lifted up My hand unto the seed of the House of Jacob, and made Myself known unto them in the land of Egypt, when I lifted up My hand unto them, saying, I am the LORD your God *(the phrase, "In the day when I chose Israel," reverts back to Chapter 16, portraying the truth*

that the Lord did not choose them because they were great or grandiose, but instead because He loved them);

6 In the day that I lifted up My hand unto them, to bring them forth of the land of Egypt into a land that I had espied for them, flowing with milk and honey, which is the glory of all lands *(The phrase, "Flowing with milk and honey," appears first in Ex. 3:8, and became proverbial. This entire Verse is also a portrayal of the great Plan of Redemption affording God's Salvation. The Lord not only delivers the believing sinner from bondage, but also delivers them to Blessing, all through Christ, and by the means of the Cross):*

7 Then said I unto them, Cast ye away every man the abominations of his eyes, and defile not yourselves with the idols of Egypt: I am the LORD your God. *(This Verse portrays the fact that they were idol worshippers in Egypt, and the Lord demanded their disengagement from such abominations.)*

8 But they rebelled against Me, and would not hearken unto Me: they did not every man cast away the abominations of their eyes, neither did they forsake the idols of Egypt: then I said, I will pour out My fury upon them, to accomplish My anger against them in the midst of the land of Egypt. *(The phrase, "To accomplish My anger against them in the midst of the land of Egypt," portrays Israel's wrongdoing, even in the midst of being delivered. This is not so pointedly outlined in the Book of Exodus, as that account concerns itself more so with their deliverance than with their obedience; nevertheless, this portrays the truth that God was almost as angry with His Own as He was with the Egyptians. This Passage tells us that there was little, if any, difference in the two peoples.)*

ISRAEL'S REBELLION IN THE WILDERNESS

9 But I wrought for My Name's sake, that it should not be polluted before the heathen, among whom they were, in whose sight I made Myself known unto them, in bringing them forth out of the land of Egypt. *(The phrase, "But I wrought for My Name's sake," refers to the truth that the only reason they were spared was not their holiness, but His Holiness and "Name's sake.")*

10 Wherefore I caused them to go forth out of the land of Egypt, and brought them into his wilderness.

11 And I gave them My Statutes, and showed them My Judgments, which if a man do, he shall even live in them. *(The "Statutes" and "Judgments" spoken of here pertain to the Law of Moses given to the Children of Israel on Mount Sinai. They were to "live" by these Laws.)*

12 Moreover also I gave them My Sabbaths, to be a sign between Me and them, that they might know that I am the LORD Who sanctifies them. *(The "Sabbaths" were typical of the "rest" which could be found only in Christ. Serving Christ today constitutes "keeping the Sabbath"; that particular day is no longer in force, because the One it typified, the Lord Jesus Christ, has come.*

The Divine Title "Jehovah-Mekaddishkem" [Lev. 20:8] is repeated here in the words, "I am the LORD Who sanctifies them." This portrays the fact that Israel could not sanctify themselves, and neither can any modern Believer.

Presently, all Believers are sanctified, and remain that way, simply by constantly looking to Christ and what He has done for us at the Cross. Then the Holy Spirit can effect Sanctification within our lives, and on a constant basis [Rom. 8:1-2, 11].)

13 But the House of Israel rebelled against Me in the wilderness: they walked not in My Statutes, and they despised My Judgments, which if a man do, he shall even live in them; and My Sabbaths they greatly polluted: then I said, I would pour out My fury upon them in the wilderness, to consume them. *(When fathers are hardened in sin, as Verses 13 through 17 will portray, hope has recourse in their children; but then, as now, these are found to possess the same corrupt nature as their parents, and consequently to love the same sins, as Verses 18 through 21 will also proclaim!)*

14 But I wrought for My Name's sake, that it should not be polluted before the heathen, in whose sight I brought them out. *(This, as Verse 9, portrays God's reason for not destroying the Children of Israel.)*

15 Yet also I lifted up My hand unto them in the wilderness, that I would not bring them into the land which I had given them, flowing with milk and honey, which is the glory of all lands *(from this Passage, we learn how absolutely close that Israel came to being totally exterminated in the wilderness. It was only the Intercession of Moses which caused them, after a fashion, to be spared [Num. 14:11-35]);*

16 Because they despised My Judgments, and walked not in My Statutes, but polluted My Sabbaths: for their heart went after their

idols. *(This Passage portrays to us the truth that Laws, even if they do originate with the Lord, cannot change an individual. Only a work effected in the "heart" can bring about this change. It is called the "New Birth" [Jn. 3:3].)*

17 Nevertheless My eye spared them from destroying them, neither did I make an end of them in the wilderness. *(His "eye spared them" for His Name's sake.)*

18 But I said unto their children in the wilderness, Walk ye not in the statutes of your fathers, neither observe their judgments, nor defile yourselves with their idols *(the phrase, "But I said unto their children in the wilderness," refers to the generation who followed those who died off in the wilderness because of their rebellion):*

19 I am the LORD your God; walk in My Statutes, and keep My Judgments, and do them;

20 And hallow My Sabbaths; and they shall be a sign between Me and you, that you may know that I am the LORD your God. *(Once again, the keeping of a particular day called the "Sabbath" is not imposed upon Christians. The Sabbath of the Old Covenant was a day of "rest." It typified Christ, Who would give perfect rest to those who would believe Him [Mat. 11:28-30]. Serving Christ now constitutes keeping the Sabbath.)*

21 Notwithstanding the children rebelled against Me: they walked not in My Statutes, neither kept My Judgments to do them, which if a man do, he shall even live in them; they polluted My Sabbaths: then I said, I would pour out My fury upon them, to accomplish My anger against them in the wilderness. *(As they did in Egypt, as described in Verse 8, and as the fathers did in the wilderness, the children had the same corrupt nature as their parents. Consequently, they loved the same sins.)*

22 Nevertheless I withdrew My hand, and wrought for My Name's sake, that it should not be polluted in the sight of the heathen, in whose sight I brought them forth. *("For His Name's sake" the Lord allowed the second generation to go into the Promised Land. He did it so the heathen would not be able to mock His Name by claiming that He had brought them into the wilderness and could not deliver them.)*

23 I lifted up My hand unto them also in the wilderness, that I would scatter them among the heathen, and disperse them through the **countries** *(they were not to think that because He had allowed them to go into the Land, that this was a sign of His approval);*

24 Because they had not executed My Judgments, but had despised My Statutes, and had polluted My Sabbaths, and their eyes were after their fathers' idols. *(As the fathers had sinned, so did the children! As their fathers were judged, so were they!)*

25 Wherefore I gave them also statutes that were not good, and judgments whereby they should not live *(the phrase, "Wherefore I gave them," means that He permitted them to pollute themselves);*

26 And I polluted them in their own gifts, in that they caused to pass through the fire all that opens the womb, that I might make them desolate, to the end that they might know that I am the LORD. *(God commanded that their children should be passed over to Him and live. Idolatry commanded that they should pass through to Moloch and die.)*

ISRAEL'S IDOLATRY IN THE LAND OF PROMISE

27 Therefore son of man, speak unto the House of Israel, and say unto them, Thus saith the Lord GOD; Yet in this your fathers have blasphemed Me, in that they have committed a trespass against Me. *(It actually says, "They trespassed a trespass." That is, they were guilty of a supreme trespass, i.e., they associated idols with God.)*

28 For when I had brought them into the land, for the which I lifted up My hand to give it to them, then they saw every high hill, and all the thick trees, and they offered there their sacrifices, and there they presented the provocation of their offering: there also they made their sweet savour, and poured out there their drink offerings. *(The fourfold repetition of the word "there," stipulating the places of idol worship, is employed to emphasize the contrast with the one Divinely appointed place of acceptance, i.e., Calvary, as foreshadowed by Mount Moriah.*

Access to God, forgiveness, and righteousness, as Abel proved, can only be enjoyed through Christ's Atonement; for He is, as He Himself said, the One and Only Way to God [Jn. 14:6].)

29 Then I said unto them, What is the high place whereunto you go? And the name thereof is called Bamah unto this day. *(The word "Bamah" means "high place." This word became a by-word expressing the displeasure of God upon such places — a memorial of the guilt of the people. In fact, the very name, "high place," convicted these worshippers of rebellion, and not*

of ignorance [Deut. 12:1-5].)

30 Wherefore say unto the House of Israel, Thus saith the Lord GOD; Are you polluted after the manner of your fathers? And commit ye whoredom after their abominations? *(This period of Israel's idolatrous history is the subject of Verses 30 through 32. It pertains to the Exiles. Every evidence points to the fact that they polluted themselves with idolatry after the manner of their fathers. For the words, "ye" and "you," of these Verses are emphatic, and the interrogative form is adopted here to express strong affirmation.)*

31 For when you offer your gifts, when you make your sons to pass through the fire, you pollute yourselves with all your idols, even unto this day: and shall I be enquired of by you, O House of Israel? As I live, saith the Lord GOD, I will not be enquired of by you. *(Ezekiel, by Inspiration, refused to pray for his visitors. They must have been very angry with him, for, instead of preaching to them the comfortable messages which the other prophets announced, he exposed their idolatries and hypocrisies and predicted their eternal ruin, as is stated in Verse 38.*

The expression, "As I live," and as used by the Lord, was to emphasize the absolute Truth of what was being spoken.)

32 And that which comes into your mind shall not be at all, that you say, We will be as the heathen, as the families of the countries, to serve wood and stone. *(If the Temple were to be destroyed, as Jeremiah and Ezekiel were prophesying, this would mean, at least in their minds, that they could no longer worship Jehovah, and would be free to "be as the heathen," to serve "wood and stone"! In their thinking, if Jehovah did not intend for them to do this, then there would be no destruction of the Temple, and no dispersion among the nations.*

They could not be more wrong!)

FUTURE REGATHERING AND JUDGMENT

33 As I live, saith the Lord GOD, surely with a mighty hand, and with a stretched out arm, and with fury poured out will I rule over you *(the Lord now answers the thoughts of their minds in stating to them that they could not abrogate their high position; they would remain under the burden of its responsibilities):*

34 And I will bring you out from the people, and will gather you out of the countries wherein you are scattered, with a mighty hand, and with a stretched out arm, and with fury poured out.

(These baseless enquiries by the Elders of Judah in exile will occasion the Holy Spirit giving these profound Prophecies concerning Israel's future Salvation. This Scripture will not be fulfilled until the Second Coming and the beginning of the Kingdom Age, which are yet future.)

35 And I will bring you into the wilderness of the people, and there will I plead with you face to face. *(This Passage pertains to the time when the Antichrist will actually invade Israel and defeat her, with a million or more escaping to the "wilderness," i.e., "Petra," which is in modern Jordan. Then Israel will realize what a fool she has been in thinking that the Antichrist was the Messiah. At that time, the Lord will really begin to deal with them [Isa. 16:1-5; 42:11-13; Hos. 2:14-23; Rev. 12:6, 13-16].)*

36 Like as I pleaded with your fathers in the wilderness of the land of Egypt, so will I plead with you, saith the Lord GOD. *(During this time of "pleading," they will be brought "face-to-face" with their failures, rebellion, and iniquities.)*

37 And I will cause you to pass under the rod, and I will bring you into the bond of the covenant *(the phrase, "And I will cause you to pass under the rod," refers primarily to the rod of chastisement. It concerns itself with the latter half [3 1/2 years] of the Great Tribulation, when Israel will come close to extinction. Jesus said it will be the worst time ever [Mat. 24:21]):*

38 And I will purge out from among you the rebels, and them who transgress against Me: I will bring them forth out of the country where they sojourn, and they shall not enter into the land of Israel: and you shall know that I am the LORD. *(The purging will take place during the last three and a half years of the Great Tribulation, and will have to do with the two-thirds who will be destroyed during that time, and especially during the Battle of Armageddon.)*

39 As for you, O House of Israel, thus saith the Lord GOD; Go ye, serve ye every one his idols, and hereafter also if you will not hearken unto Me: but pollute ye My holy name no more with your gifts, and with your idols. *(The Holy Spirit through the Prophet now brings the Prophecy away from the future back to the present. The Elders are addressed.*

The Lord tells them: "Go ye, serve ye every one his idols," but do not make the sin worse by the hypocrisy of unreal worship, by mixing the Name of Jehovah with the ritual of Moloch. By their double worship of Him and idols, they were "polluting His Holy Name.")

FUTURE RESTORATION

40 For in My holy mountain, in the mountain of the height of Israel, saith the Lord GOD, there shall all the House of Israel, all of them in the land, serve Me: there will I accept them, and there will I require your offerings, and the firstfruits of your oblations, with all your holy things. *(Now the Holy Spirit reverts back to Prophecies concerning the future. Redeemed Israel, in the happy day of her future glory, will recognize and confess that all her happiness is due to the worthfulness of the Name of Jesus, and not to any moral value in herself, for her "ways" were evil and her "doings" were corrupt.*

This Passage pertains to the coming Millennial Reign, when Christ will Personally reign supreme from Jerusalem. Then the contesting of the Land will end.)

41 I will accept you with your sweet savour, when I bring you out from the people, and gather you out of the countries wherein you have been scattered; and I will be sanctified in you before the heathen. *(The acceptance of the worshipper is the result of the value of the victim offered in Sacrifice for sin. Hence, Believers are engraced in the Beloved One [Eph. 1:6], Christ; for we have no Grace in ourselves.)*

42 And you shall know that I am the LORD, when I shall bring you into the land of Israel, into the country for the which I lifted up My hand to give it to your fathers. *(This refers to the tremendous Prophecies which seem so impossible to the natural mind, and yet which the Lord declares that He is able to bring to pass, and which He did!)*

43 And there shall you remember your ways, and all your doings, wherein you have been defiled; and you shall loathe yourselves in your own sight for all your evils that you have committed. *(This concerns Israel's acceptance of Christ at the Second Coming, when they realize Who He is, and especially how they crucified Him and brought upon themselves such judgment and sorrow.)*

44 And you shall know that I am the LORD when I have wrought with you for My Name's sake, not according to your wicked ways, nor according to your corrupt doings, O ye House of Israel, saith the Lord GOD. *(Israel will know in that day that their Salvation and Restoration are not brought about because of their holiness; in fact, their ways were "wicked" and their doings were "corrupt." Their Restoration will be for His Name's sake.)*

THE PROPHECY AGAINST THE SOUTH: DESTRUCTION OF JUDAH AND JERUSALEM

45 Moreover the word of the LORD came unto me, saying *(the balance of this Chapter speaks of the near judgment upon Judah and Jerusalem. As is by now obvious, rebellion against God ensconced in their idol worship was basically the cause),*

46 Son of man, set your face toward the south, and drop your word toward the south, and prophesy against the forest of the south field *(this Prophecy forms an introduction to Chapters 21 through 32. The phrase, "Set your face," determines direction and certitude of accomplishment. The fourfold repetition of the word "south" made absolute Judah as the scene of the approaching judgment);*

47 And say to the forest of the south, Hear the Word of the LORD; Thus saith the Lord GOD; Behold, I will kindle a fire in you, and it shall devour every green tree in you, and every dry tree: the flaming flame shall not be quenched, and all faces from the south to the north shall be burned therein. *(The "green tree" symbolizes the righteous, while the "dry tree" symbolizes the wicked. The inclusion of the righteous with the wicked in national and universal judgments is one of the principles of God's moral government. It is important to recognize this principle. He does not promise exemption to His People from the suffering which justly follows national sin; but He makes this great distinction: that the wicked perish under such suffering, while the righteous are sustained in it, and finally, in Resurrection, delivered from it [Heb. 11:35].)*

48 And all flesh shall see that I the LORD have kindled it: it shall not be quenched. *(The accomplishment of the prediction proves the Divine origin of the Prophecy.)*

49 Then said I, Ah Lord GOD! they say of me, Does he not speak parables? *(The ridicule of unbelief is often more painful than the anger of unbelief!)*

CHAPTER 21
(593 B.C.)

THE SIGN OF THE DRAWN SWORD: COMPLETE DESTRUCTION

AND the Word of the LORD came unto me, saying *(this is a part of the Prophecy of the previous Chapter, which continues without*

interruption),

2 Son of man, set your face toward Jerusalem; and drop your word toward the Holy Places, and prophesy against the land of Israel *(this Verse is very similar to Verse 46 of the previous Chapter, with the words, "Jerusalem" and "Holy Places," replacing the word "south" in that Verse. The words, "Holy Places," refer to the Temple in Jerusalem),*

3 And say to the land of Israel, Thus saith the LORD; Behold, I am against you, and will draw forth My sword out of his sheath, and will cut off from you the righteous and the wicked. *(As in the previous Verse, the words, "the righteous and the wicked," replace "the green tree and the dry tree" of Verse 47 in the previous Chapter. The phrase, "Thus saith the LORD; Behold I am against you," records Judah's doom, as nothing else!)*

4 Seeing then that I will cut off from you the righteous and the wicked, therefore shall My sword go forth out of his sheath against all flesh from the south to the north *(the phrase, "Against all flesh from the south to the north," refers to total destruction of the country, leaving no part untouched, and having no mercy on the old, or even on little children):*

5 That all flesh may know that I the LORD have drawn forth My sword out of his sheath: it shall not return any more. *("My sword" proclaims the fact of God's independent action.)*

CONVULSIVE SIGHING, A SIGN OF SUFFERING

6 Sigh therefore, thou son of man, with the breaking of your loins; and with bitterness sigh before their eyes. *(The phrase, "Sigh therefore, thou son of man," refers to Ezekiel being so burdened with the portent of this coming disaster that it "breaks his loins," i.e., breaks his heart.)*

7 And it shall be, when they say unto you, Wherefore sighest thou? That you shall answer, For the tidings; because it comes: and every heart shall melt, and all hands shall be feeble, and every spirit shall faint, and all knees shall be weak as water: behold, it comes, and shall be brought to pass, saith the Lord GOD. *(That which Ezekiel now experiences will be exactly what will happen to the entirety of the Exiles some four years later, when word was received of the fall and destruction of Jerusalem. This is emphasized in the words, "For the tidings." These tidings will be awful indeed!)*

THE SHARPENED SWORD: FOR JUDGMENT

8 Again the word of the LORD came unto me, saying *(the Holy Spirit will now go into great detail regarding the coming carnage, which is meant to portray to the people the severity of the judgment, and hopefully to instigate Repentance; however, the Repentance never materialized!),*

9 Son of man, prophesy, and say, Thus saith the LORD; Say, A sword, a sword is sharpened, and also furbished. *(This Verse speaks of the Divine mission of the Chaldean sword, i.e., the Babylonian army, and its success against Judah and against Ammon. This Prophecy preceded the destruction of Judah by some four or five years, and of Ammon, by ten years.*

The minuteness of detail in these predictions, years before they actually became history, is one of the striking facts of Inspiration.)

10 It is sharpened to make a sore slaughter; it is furbished that it may glitter; should we then make mirth? It contemns the rod of My son, as every tree. *(The phrase, "It is sharpened to make a sore slaughter," refers to the Lord handing the sharpened sword to the Chaldean slayer in order that it may be used against the Judean wrongdoer.)*

11 And He has given it to be furbished, that it may be handled: this sword is sharpened, and it is furbished, to give it into the hand of the slayer. *(The Babylonian Monarch no doubt thought himself to be a free agent. But long before his campaign against Judah, his victory over Zedekiah, his recourse to divination at the parting of the high roads in northern Israel, and his victory over the Ammonites, all were foretold here.)*

12 Cry and howl, son of man: for it shall be upon My people, it shall be upon all the princes of Israel: terrors by reason of the sword shall be upon My people: smite therefore upon your thigh. *(In Verse 10, the Holy Spirit uses the phrase, "My son," as He uses it in this Verse, "My people." The Grace and Love that recognizes here idolatrous Judah in this capacity awaken wonder and worship in the heart.)*

13 Because it is a trial, and what if the sword contemn even the rod? It shall be no more, saith the Lord GOD. *(The meaning of this Passage is that a test of strength between Nebuchadnezzar and Zedekiah will soon commence; the latter will be defeated, his scepter forever broken.)*

14 Thou therefore, son of man, prophesy, and smite your hands together, and let the sword be doubled the third time, the sword of the slain: it is the sword of the great men who are slain, which enters into their privy chambers. *(The phrase, "And let the sword be doubled the third time," predicts the third and final campaign against Jerusalem. The first invasion took place in 605 B.C., the second happened in 597 B.C., and the last occurred in 586 B.C., which was some four or five years in the future.)*

15 I have set the point of the sword against all their gates, that their heart may faint, and their ruins be multiplied: ah! it is made bright, it is wrapped up for the slaughter. *(Judah had many opportunities to repent, but instead they hardened their hearts. Each time they refused the admonishment of Jeremiah and Ezekiel, they "multiplied" the judgment that was coming, thereby "multiplying the ruins.")*

16 Go thee one way or other, either on the right hand, or on the left, whithersoever your face is set. *(The idea of this Verse is that the sword is promised success here in whatever direction it turns. Such is demanded by the Lord.)*

17 I will also smite My hands together, and I will cause My fury to rest: I the LORD have said it. *(The phrase, "And I will cause My fury to rest," refers to the truth that His fury will not rest until every single prediction is fulfilled concerning the destruction of Judah and Jerusalem. To emphasize the certitude of this action, the Holy Spirit says, "I the LORD have said it.")*

GOD USES BABYLON AS A SWORD OF JUDGMENT

18 The word of the LORD came unto me again, saying *(Ezekiel sees, as in a Vision, Nebuchadnezzar and his army on the march),*

19 Also, thou son of man, appoint thee two ways, that the sword of the king of Babylon may come: both twain shall come forth out of one land: and choose you a place, choose it at the head of the way to the city. *(The phrase, "Appoint thee two ways," refers to two different roads. When Nebuchadnezzar reached Damascus [or somewhere nearby], there was an intersection; one road led to Rabbath, the capital of the Ammonites [Deut. 3:11; II Sam. 11:1], and the other road led to Jerusalem.*

The Exiles and the people of Judah thought that Rabbath would be Nebuchadnezzar's destination and, therefore, Judah would be spared. It was not to be that way!)

20 Appoint a way, that the sword may come to Rabbath of the Ammonites, and to Judah in Jerusalem the defenced. *(The balance of this Passage actually speaks of the sword coming to both cities, but now the decision is to be made as to which city comes first!)*

21 For the king of Babylon stood at the parting of the way, at the head of the two ways, to use divination: he made his arrows bright, he consulted with images, he looked in the liver. *(Two arrows, one marked "Ammon" and the other marked "Jerusalem.," were placed in a quiver by Nebuchadnezzar. Whichever one the king drew was accepted as an omen. As well, the liver of a beast or a fowl offered in sacrifice was also examined; its healthy or unhealthy condition accepted as favorable or unfavorable.*

However, and unknown to Nebuchadnezzar, the Lord would make the choice.)

22 At his right hand was the divination for Jerusalem, to appoint captains, to open the mouth in the slaughter, to lift up the voice with shouting, to appoint battering rams against the gates, to cast a mount, and to build a fort. *(Nebuchadnezzar placed his hand into the quiver to pull out one of the arrows; he looked at it; he saw that it signified Jerusalem.*

The phrase, "To appoint captains," referred to orders and instructions being given for the siege of Jerusalem.)

23 And it shall be unto them as a false divination in their sight, to them who have sworn oaths: but He will call to remembrance the iniquity, that they may be taken. *(The phrase, "And it shall be unto them as a false divination in their sight," refers to the false prophets in Jerusalem, who still continued to preach peace and prosperity, causing the king and the people to believe that Nebuchadnezzar was not going to come to Jerusalem.*

The phrase, "To them who have sworn oaths," referred to Zedekiah, who had sworn an oath to Nebuchadnezzar but had dallied with the Egyptian faction, conspiring to throw off their subjugation. In fact, Zedekiah went to Babylon in 593 B.C., possibly to allay suspicion concerning his involvement in the plot [Jer. 51:59].)

JUDGMENT ON JUDAH

24 Therefore thus saith the Lord GOD; Because you have made your iniquity to be remembered, in that your transgressions are discovered, so that in all your doings your sins do appear; because, I say, that you are come to

remembrance, you shall be taken with the hand. *(This Verse further emphasizes the treachery of Zedekiah. The iniquity, the transgression, and the sin was this breach of the oath of allegiance taken in the Name of Jehovah. The plural of majesty is used here to emphasize that great transgression and that great sin.)*

25 And you, profane wicked prince of Israel, whose day is come, when iniquity shall have an end *(the Holy Spirit calls Zedekiah a "wicked prince of Israel"),*

26 Thus saith the Lord GOD; Remove the diadem, and take off the crown: this shall not be the same: exalt him who is low, and abase him who is high. *(The phrase, "Remove the diadem," refers to the Mitre of the High Priest, who would no longer have a Temple nor an avenue for his services. The phrase, "And take off the crown," refers to the Throne of Judah being abolished by Nebuchadnezzar. The Mitre and the Crown shall alike pass away — taken from their unworthy wearers.)*

27 I will overturn, overturn, overturn, it: and it shall be no more, until He come Whose right it is; and I will give it Him. *(The phrase, "I will overturn, overturn, overturn, it," refers to Judah being destroyed as a nation, and especially its supreme authority and its Throne never again being established, at least not "until He come Whose right it is." This is the despised Jesus of Nazareth, Who will return. To Him shall the diadem be given, "Whose right it is." Meanwhile, God overturns all efforts to give that Crown to another.)*

JUDGMENT ON THE AMMONITES

28 And thou, son of man, prophesy and say, Thus saith the Lord GOD concerning the Ammonites, and concerning their reproach; even say thou, The sword, the sword is drawn: for the slaughter it is furbished, to consume because of the glittering *(the phrase, "Thus saith the Lord GOD concerning the Ammonites," refers to these ancient enemies of Israel. When Nebuchadnezzar took the road to Jerusalem instead of coming to Rabbath, the Ammonites thought surely they had escaped the judgment. This Prophecy proclaims differently!*

The phrase, "And concerning their reproach," concerns their rejoicing at the destruction of Jerusalem. However, some five years after the fall of Jerusalem, the Chaldeans invaded Ammon; they destroyed it so effectually that it ceased to exist as a nation):

29 While they see vanity unto you, while they divine a lie unto you, to bring you upon the necks of them who are slain, of the wicked, whose day is come, when their iniquity shall have an end. *(The phrase, "While they see vanity unto you," refers to the pride of Ammon. The phrase, "While they divine a lie unto you," refers to the soothsayers among them who divined that Nebuchadnezzar would not attack them as he would Jerusalem, but that they would be spared. The Holy Spirit called their divination "a lie.")*

30 Shall I cause it to return into his sheath? I will judge you in the place where you were created, in the land of your nativity. *(The phrase, "I will judge you in the place where you were created," refers to Nebuchadnezzar bringing his army directly into the land, and so destroying Ammon that she would no more exist.)*

31 And I will pour out My indignation upon you, I will blow against you in the fire of My wrath, and deliver you into the hand of brutish men, and skilful to destroy. *(No mercy would be shown by the Babylonians to Ammon. This was because of their gloating over the fall of Judah and Jerusalem.)*

32 You shall be for fuel to the fire; your blood shall be in the midst of the land; you shall be no more remembered: for I the LORD have spoken it. *(The phrase, "You shall be no more remembered," refers to all hope of restoration being dashed. Therefore, it seems that God judged them more severely even than He did Sodom [Ezek. 16:53]. The Prophecy spelled their eternal doom.*

However, their destruction was not instantaneous. They survived into the Second Century B.C., which was about 300 years after this Prophecy. Today there are no more Ammonites and there will never be again.)

CHAPTER 22
(593 B.C.)
THE SINS OF JERUSALEM

MOREOVER the Word of the Lord came unto me, saying,

2 Now, thou son of man, will you judge, will you judge the bloody city? Yea, you shall show her all her abominations. *(As the previous Prophecy concerned itself with the land of Judah as a whole, this Prophecy concerns itself with the city of Jerusalem. Concerning the city, and coupled with the review of Israel's moral history in Chapter 20, and with the entire Book*

of Jeremiah, there should be extraordinary interest because these things mark the transference of the government of the world from Israel to the Gentiles.)

3 Then say thou, Thus saith the Lord GOD, the city sheds blood in the midst of it, that her time may come, and makes idols against herself to defile herself. *(The blood shed in the city was that of children sacrificed to Moloch, and of people murdered for the sake of gain [Vss. 6, 9, 12-13].)*

4 You are become guilty in your blood that you have shed; and have defiled yourself in your idols which you have made; and you have caused your days to draw near, and are come even unto your years: therefore have I made you a reproach unto the heathen, and a mocking to all countries. *(The phrase, "And you have caused your days to draw near," refers to the soon-to-come judgment.)*

5 Those who be near, and those who be far from you, shall mock you, which are infamous and much vexed. *(The phrase, "And much vexed," refers to Jerusalem in a state of moral tumult and disorder as the consequence of its guilt.)*

6 Behold, the princes of Israel, every one was in you to their power to shed blood. *(The kings of Israel used their power for violence, injustice, and murder, and not for protection, peace, and righteousness.*

The phrase, "Every one was in you to their power to shed blood," refers to the fact that there was no restraint upon the doer of evil other than the limitation of his capacity.)

7 In you have they set light by father and mother: in the midst of you have they dealt by oppression with the stranger: in you have they vexed the fatherless and the widow. *(The phrase, "In you," refers to Jerusalem, which should have provided the leadership for the entire nation, and in fact the world; however, they did the very opposite!)*

8 You have despised My holy things, and have profaned My Sabbaths. *(The phrase, "My holy things," refers to the entirety of the Law and the Divine Ordinances. They not only forsook them, but they "despised" them, proving that sin never remains static, but always involves itself in its increase.)*

9 In you are men who carry tales to shed blood: and in you they eat upon the mountains: in the midst of you they commit lewdness. *(The phrase, "In you are men who carry tales to shed blood," pertains to the Lord knowing*

and seeing through every plot, irrespective of how much men may think their sins are hidden.)

10 In you have they discovered their fathers' nakedness: in you have they humbled her who was set apart for pollution. *(The phrase, "In you have they discovered their fathers' nakedness," speaks of incest between a son and his mother, which constituted the vilest of vile sins, and seems, horribly so, to have been quite common.*

The phrase, "In you have they humbled her who was set apart for pollution," refers to women being forced to commit the sex act even during the time of their monthly period. This was forbidden by the Lord, because the monthly period of the woman, which discharged impurities from her physical body, was meant by the Lord to portray as such the Fall of man and the subsequent spiritual condition of all babies born thereafter. As a result of this serving as such a symbol, the Lord forbade intercourse during this particular time each month. By ignoring this Command of the Lord, at least at this time, the guilty party was in effect refuting the lostness of man and the need for a Saviour.)

11 And one has committed abomination with his neighbour's wife; and another has lewdly defiled his daughter-in-law; and another in thee has humbled his sister; his father's daughter. *(This Passage, as well, speaks of adultery and incest.)*

12 In you have they taken gifts to shed blood; you have taken usury and increase, and you have greedily gained of your neighbours by extortion, and have forgotten Me, saith the Lord GOD. *(Added to the sexual immorality was the immorality of murder and greed.)*

JUDGMENT; THE DROSS A SIGN OF PUNISHMENT FOR SIN

13 Behold, therefore I have smitten My hand at your dishonest gain which you have made, and at your blood which has been in the midst of you. *(The Lord will no longer tolerate such actions, and the gesture signifies a soon conclusion with the coming of great judgment. The idea is: the Lord will stop the evil, and use whatever means necessary to do so!)*

14 Can your heart endure, or can your hands be strong, in the days that I shall deal with you? I the LORD have spoken it, and will do it. *(The question of this Verse implies an answer in the negative.)*

15 And I will scatter you among the heathen,

and disperse you in the countries, and will consume your filthiness out of you. *(The actions threatened in Verse 14 are described in Verses 15 and 16. The Divine purpose was that Israel should be apart from and enthroned as Queen above the nations of the Earth; but her own conduct caused her to lose that supremacy, and thus, she profaned herself by making herself a common nation.)*

16 And you shall take your inheritance in yourself in the sight of the heathen, and you shall know that I am the LORD. *(Her inheritance was squandered by trying to become as the "heathen.")*

17 And the word of the LORD came unto me, saying,

18 Son of man, the House of Israel is to Me become dross; all they are brass, and tin, and iron, and lead, in the midst of the furnace; they are even the dross of silver. *(This Passage refers to the unholy mixture of idol worship with the worship of the True God. Silver is used by the Holy Spirit as a symbol of Redemption and Righteousness. The baser metals were used as symbols of unrighteousness.)*

19 Therefore thus saith the Lord GOD; Because you are all become dross, behold, therefore I will gather you into the midst of Jerusalem. *(The phrase, "Because you are all become dross," speaks of so few righteous being in the city that it could not be spared.)*

20 As they gather silver, and brass, and iron, and lead, and tin, into the midst of the furnace, to blow the fire upon it, to melt it; so will I gather you in My anger and in My fury, and I will leave you there, and melt you. *(The Lord appeals for Repentance; if such is forthcoming, it is always met with approval and resultant blessing. If such is not forthcoming, judgment is the only other recourse, and is always done in "My anger and in My fury.")*

21 Yea, I will gather you, and blow upon you in the fire of My wrath, and you shall be melted in the midst thereof. *(This refers to the bellows which blew upon the fire in the crucible, supplying more oxygen and, thereby, greater heat. The Lord here says that He will serve as those bellows.)*

22 As silver is melted in the midst of the furnace, so shall you be melted in the midst thereof; and you shall know that I the LORD have poured out My fury upon you. *(The phrase, "And you shall know," proclaims the truth that even though they did not previously believe, there would come an hour, and shortly, that they would* believe, but it would be too late!)*

PROPHECY AGAINST ISRAEL; THE EXTENT OF THE APOSTASY

23 And the word of the LORD came unto me, saying *(a third Prophecy now opens, with the Prophet addressing himself not to Jerusalem only, but to the entire Land of Judah),*

24 Son of man, say unto her, You are the land that is not cleansed, nor rained upon in the day of indignation. *(The conscience that is not cleansed by the Precious Blood of Christ and the heart that is not fertilized by the rain of the Holy Spirit are necessarily unclean, however adorned with religious ceremonies the outward life may be.)*

25 There is a conspiracy of her prophets in the midst thereof, like a roaring lion ravening the prey; they have devoured souls; they have taken the treasure and precious things; they have made her many widows in the midst thereof. *(The phrase, "There is a conspiracy of her prophets in the midst thereof," refers to false prophets who conspire against Jeremiah and Ezekiel, but more particularly against Jeremiah, because he prophesied in Jerusalem. They determined by collusion to fill the land with their false prophecies and, thereby, counteract his true Prophecies.)*

26 Her Priests have violated My Law, and have profaned My holy things: they have put no difference between the holy and profane, neither have they showed difference between the unclean and the clean, and have hid their eyes from My Sabbaths, and I am profaned among them. *(The phrase, "Her Priests have violated My Law," did not mean that the Priests suppressed the Bible, of which they were the custodians, but that they violated it. For example, they denied its Inspiration and Authority; they profaned it teachings, that is, they lowered the Book to the common level of other books; they thrust aside its teaching as to separation from evil; and by making the Sabbath as under the Law similar to rest of the days of the week, they degraded its Author to a position in the common multitude of gods, and thus profaned Him.)*

27 Her princes in the midst thereof are like wolves ravening the prey, to shed blood, and to destroy souls, to get dishonest gain. *(The Holy Spirit referred to the leaders of Judah as "wolves ravening the prey.")*

28 And her prophets have daubed them with untempered morter, seeing vanity, and

divining lies unto them, saying, Thus saith the Lord GOD, when the LORD has not spoken. *(The princes and their popular Preachers had one main object in view — the amassing of wealth by fair means or foul.)*

29 The people of the land have used oppression, and exercised robbery, and have vexed the poor and needy: yea, they have oppressed the stranger wrongfully. *(Not only were the leaders and the prophets corrupt, but the common people of the land fell into the same category; they took their cue from the leaders and the prophets.)*

30 And I sought for a man among them, who should make up the hedge, and stand in the gap before Me for the land, that I should not destroy it: but I found none. *(The phrase, "And I sought for a man among them," portrays Judah and Jerusalem in dire straits indeed! Jeremiah, it is true, was there; but he had been taken out by God from among them and forbidden to pray for them [Jer. 11:14]. Among the citizens, none were found able or willing to attempt a reformation or call the nation to prayer.)*

31 Therefore have I poured out My indignation upon them; I have consumed them with the fire of My wrath: their own way have I recompensed upon their heads, saith the Lord GOD. *(Neither a reformer ["the hedge"] nor an Intercessor ["the gap"] was found in the guilty city to save it from destruction. "Therefore have I poured out My indignation upon them.")*

CHAPTER 23
(593 B.C.)
PARABLE OF TWO SISTERS;
AHOLAH (SAMARIA) AND
AHOLIBAH (JERUSALEM)

THE Word of the LORD came again unto me, saying *(this Chapter clearly and graphically illustrates the sin and wickedness of both the Northern and the Southern Kingdoms of Samaria and Judah)*,

2 Son of man, there were two women, the daughters of one mother *(pictures both Kingdoms, Samaria and Judah. The phrase, "The daughters of one mother," refers to Sarah, who gave birth to Isaac, who sired Jacob, from whom sprang the twelve sons representing the Twelve Tribes of Israel)*:

3 And they committed whoredoms in Egypt; they committed whoredoms in their youth: there were their breasts pressed, and there they bruised the teats of their virginity.

(This Chapter reviews their conduct from Egypt to the final destruction of their city and the nation. Thus, under this lengthened test of about 1,100 years was demonstrated the incurable idolatry of man's fallen nature. Idolatry continues today in the realm of Believers making something other than the Cross of Christ the object of their faith.)

4 And the names of them were Aholah the elder, and Aholibah her sister: and they were mine, and they bore sons and daughters. Thus were their names; Samaria is Aholah, and Jerusalem Aholibah. *("Aholibah" in the Hebrew means "Shalibah," and refers to Jerusalem and means "My tent is in her." The phrase, "The elder," referring to "Aholah" [Samaria], probably would have been better translated "the greater," because, at least at the beginning, the power of the Northern Kingdom of the Ten Tribes was greater, because they greatly outnumbered the population of the Two Tribes of Judah.)*

AHOLAH'S IDOLATRY
AND PROSTITUTION

5 And Aholah played the harlot when she was Mine; and she doted on her lovers, on the Assyrians her neighbours *(the phrase, "And Aholah played the harlot," refers to her adopting the gods of the "Assyrians." This was probably the worship of Ishtar [Ashtoreth] as the Queen of Heaven. The phrase, "When she was Mine," refers to the whole of Israel belonging to the Lord by the Mosaic Covenant, which the Lord had made with them, and caused them to become His wife by Covenant relationship [Isa. 54:5])*,

6 Which were clothed with blue, captains and rulers, all of them desirable young men, horsemen riding upon horses. *(This Passage brings before us the magnificent array of the Assyrian Cavalry — a force in which Israel, throughout its history, was deficient [Judg. 5:10; Zech. 9:9; Isa. 36:8].)*

7 Thus she committed her whoredoms with them, with all them who were the chosen men of Assyria, and with all on whom she doted: with all their idols she defiled herself. *(This refers to the Northern Kingdom of Samaria being enamored by the power and pomp of the Assyrians. The phrase, "With all their idols she defiled herself," proclaims her attempting to gain the plaudits of "these chosen men of Assyria" by accepting their idols.)*

8 Neither left she her whoredoms brought from Egypt: for in her youth they lay with her,

and they bruised the breasts of her virginity, and poured their whoredom upon her. *(This tells us that the worship of Egyptian idols was never completely expunged from Samaria. As well, the presence of this wickedness made it much easier to accept the Assyrian idols.)*

9 Wherefore I have delivered her into the hand of her lovers, into the hand of the Assyrians, upon whom she doted. *(What Believers want, if they insist upon it, the Lord will ultimately allow them to have, whether good or bad.)*

10 These discovered her nakedness: they took her sons and her daughters, and slew her with the sword: and she became famous among women; for they had executed judgment upon her. *(To be "naked" meant to be open to the Judgment of God, which would allow heathen nations to have their way, as with Assyria. The phrase, "She became famous among women," actually means that she became infamous, because of the Judgment of God upon her, among the surrounding nations.)*

JUDAH'S GREATER SINS WITH ASSYRIA AND BABYLON

11 And when her sister Aholibah saw this, she was more corrupt in her inordinate love than she, and in her whoredoms more than her sister in her whoredoms. *(Judgment, having already destroyed Samaria in sweeping its people into captivity, now a similar doom is impending over Jerusalem. She, far from taking warning from the fate of her northern sister, plunged deeper into the abominations of idolatry.*

There was no moral difference between these sisters. The same conduct showed the same nature. The heart at the close was the same as at the beginning. They both were idolaters.)

12 She doted upon the Assyrians her neighbours, captains and rulers clothed most gorgeously, horsemen riding upon horses, all of them desirable young men. *(Jerusalem, as her northern sister, courted the alliance of the kings of Assyria, as in the case of Ahaz [II Ki. 16:7-10] and Tiglath-Pileser. Even Hezekiah followed in the same line, though his trust was in Egypt — and afterwards rebelled. Manasseh too paid tribute and made Jerusalem the scene of a confluent idolatry, which included that of Assyria.)*

13 Then I saw that she was defiled, that they took both one way *(this refers to the way of disobedience rather than God's Way)*,

14 And that she increased her whoredoms: for when she saw men pourtrayed upon the wall, the images of the Chaldeans pourtrayed with vermilion *(this pertains to pictures of gods, which were painted on the walls in various government buildings in Babylon)*,

15 Girded with girdles upon their loins, exceeding in dyed attire upon their heads, all of them princes to look to, after the manner of the Babylonians of Chaldea, the land of their nativity *(when Judah began to lose her way, because of pulling farther and farther away from Jehovah, they lost the Presence of God, and then the glitter of other nations became very enticing)*:

16 And as soon as she saw them with her eyes, she doted upon them, and sent messengers unto them into Chaldea. *(This refers to Judah actively seeking alliances with the Babylonians, which was not at all pleasing to the Lord. The idea is: the Believer must put total and complete trust and faith in the Lord, and for all things. If we look to man, we get what man can supply, which is nothing. If we look to God, we get what God can supply, which is everything!)*

17 And the Babylonians came to her into the bed of love, and they defiled her with their whoredom, and she was polluted with them, and her mind was alienated from them. *(All of these terms, such as "whoredom," etc., pertained to Judah being unfaithful to the Lord, and doing so by worshipping idols. The phrase, "And her mind was alienated from them," is a strange statement! It means that what she thought she was getting, she did not receive. Impure love usually ends in open hatred. So Israel, in the end, hated the Egyptians, the Assyrians, and the Babylonians, and they hated her.)*

18 So she discovered her whoredoms, and discovered her nakedness: then My mind was alienated from her, like as My mind was alienated from her sister. *(Because of her sin, the "Mind" of the Lord was alienated from Judah. Whether Judah or a lone Believer, the end result of such disposition on the part of God is catastrophic.)*

19 Yet she multiplied her whoredoms, in calling to remembrance the days of her youth, wherein she had played the harlot in the land of Egypt. *(Recalling old sins frequently leads to a resumption of them.)*

20 For she doted upon their paramours, whose flesh is as the flesh of asses, and whose issue is like the issue of horses. *(The phrase, "For she doted upon their paramours," refers to*

the Egyptian princes, whose favor Judah courted. She threw herself into the idolatrous ritual of Egypt with an almost orgiastic passion.

The last phrase is likened to a wife who, in her unfaithfulness, not only commits adultery with a man, but has sexual relations with an animal. He uses such as an example to portray Judah leaving His Presence for the presence of the idol worshipping heathen.)

21 Thus you called to remembrance the lewdness of your youth, in bruising your teats by the Egyptians for the paps of your youth. *(The harlot nation returned, as it were, to her first love and renewed the whoredoms of her youth, actually, the very whoredoms from which she was delivered [II Pet. 2:20-22].)*

BABYLON, GOD'S INSTRUMENT OF WRATH AGAINST JERUSALEM (AHOLIBAH)

22 Therefore, O Aholibah, thus saith the Lord GOD; Behold, I will raise up your lovers against you, from whom your mind is alienated, and I will bring them against you on every side *(the Passage refers to the Babylonians and others, which would turn against Judah. In other words, the very safety and protection she thought she was securing would turn out to be the very opposite!);*

23 The Babylonians, and all the Chaldeans, Pekod, and Shoa, and Koa, and all the Assyrians with them: all of them desirable young men, captains and rulers, great lords and renowned, all of them riding upon horses. *("Pekod, Shoa, and Koa" were eastern nations. They are all named in the Babylonian inscriptions. The phrase, "Riding upon horses," refers to something which once greatly impressed Judah; but now they ride over her in destruction.)*

24 And they shall come against you with chariots, wagons, and wheels, and with an assembly of people, which shall set against you buckler and shield and helmet round about: and I will set judgment before them, and they shall judge you according to their judgments. *(The Passage refers to the fact that no pity will be shown whatsoever to hapless Judah.)*

25 And I will set My jealousy against you, and they shall deal furiously with you: they shall take away your nose and your ears; and your remnant shall fall by the sword: they shall take your sons and your daughters; and your residue shall be devoured by the fire. *(The phrase, "They shall take away your nose*

and your ears," refers to the manner in which the Babylonians mutilated their prisoners by cutting off their nose and ears. They slaughtered others, or even burned them alive. Others, they stripped of their property and clothes, making them slaves.)

26 They shall also strip you out of your clothes, and take away your fair jewels.

27 Thus will I make your lewdness to cease from you, and your whoredom brought from the land of Egypt: so that you shall not lift up your eyes unto them, nor remember Egypt any more. *(The fact that Israel was an idolater in Egypt is again recalled, because she had never fully overcome the propensity toward this evil.)*

28 For thus saith the Lord GOD; Behold, I will deliver you into the hand of them whom you hate, into the hand of them from whom your mind is alienated *(refers to a former love for Babylon that had now passed into loathing. They will now receive with disgust their fill of that for which they had once so ardently sought):*

29 And they shall deal with you hatefully, and shall take away all your labour, and shall leave you naked and bare: and the nakedness of your whoredoms shall be discovered, both your lewdness and your whoredoms. *(All of this speaks of them forsaking Jehovah and resorting to idols.)*

30 I will do these things unto you, because you have gone a whoring after the heathen, and because you are polluted with their idols. *(The phrase, "And because you are polluted with their idols," refers to what always happens to the Child of God concerning involvement with the world. It always brings "spiritual pollution.")*

31 You have walked in the way of your sister; therefore will I give her cup into your hand. *(This refers to the Northern Kingdom of Samaria, with her way referring to idol worship and, above all, the way of the world instead of the Way of God.)*

32 Thus saith the Lord GOD; You shall drink of your sister's cup deep and large: you shall be laughed to scorn and had in derision; it contains much. *(The phrase, "You shall drink of your sister's cup deep and large," pertains to the judgment being far more severe than anyone contemplated.*

The phrase, "You shall be laughed to scorn and had in derision," refers to them laughing at the Prophecies of Jeremiah and Ezekiel, who had been sent by the Lord. Now, in turn, the surrounding nations will do the same to Judah upon her fall.

The phrase, "It contains much," refers to them answering the Prophets by saying that it contained little!)

33 You shall be filled with drunkenness and sorrow, with the cup of astonishment and desolation, with the cup of your sister Samaria. *(The "drunkenness" of the first phrase does not refer to alcohol inebriation, but instead the drunkenness of anguish — an anguish so great as to cause the captives to beat their bosoms in despair.)*

34 You shall even drink it and suck it out, and you shall break the sherds thereof, and pluck off your own breasts: for I have spoken it, saith the Lord GOD. *(The phrase, "You shall even drink it and suck it out," refers to not only the entire cup being drunk, but the bitter dregs at the bottom being consumed, as well. The mutilation of "your own breasts" refers to the anguish being so severe that many would take a "shard," a fragment of brittle substance, and cut themselves with it.)*

35 Therefore thus saith the Lord GOD; Because you have forgotten Me, and cast Me behind your back, therefore bear thou also your lewdness and your whoredoms. *(The first phrase pertains to Judah forsaking the Word of God and, thereby, forsaking God. The latter phrase refers to idol worship with all its attendant demon spirits.)*

GOD'S JUDGMENT ON AHOLAH (SAMARIA) AND AHOLIBAH (JERUSALEM)

36 The LORD said moreover unto me; Son of man, will you judge Aholah and Aholibah? yea, declare unto them their abominations *(the phrase, "Yea, declare unto them their abominations," pertains to the sins being named, which they were);*

37 That they have committed adultery, and blood is in their hands, and with their idols have they committed adultery, and have also caused their sons, whom they bore unto Me, to pass for them through the fire, to devour them. *(The phrase, "They have committed adultery," refers to idol worship, because the Lord looks at Judah as His wife and He, her husband [Isa. 54:5]. The phrase, "To pass for them through the fire, to devour them," had to do with Judah offering up her sons in human sacrifice to the hideous god, Molech.)*

38 Moreover this they have done unto Me: they have defiled My Sanctuary in the same day, and have profaned My Sabbaths. *(The phrase, "Moreover this they have done unto Me," proclaims the truth that the deepest depth of evil is the association of idolatry with God, which these Judaites did!)*

39 For when they had slain their children to their idols, then they came the same day into My Sanctuary to profane it; and, lo, thus have they done in the midst of My House. *(In other words, they would offer up their children as sacrifice in the morning [which is horrible beyond contemplation], and then they would take a lamb to the Temple that afternoon and offer it up in Sacrifice.)*

40 And furthermore, that you have sent for men to come from far, unto whom a messenger was sent; and, lo, they came: for whom you did wash yourself, painted your eyes, and decked yourself with ornaments. *(This refers to ambassadors which had been sent from time to time by both Samaria and Jerusalem to Egypt, Assyria, and Babylon, seeking alliances. To secure those alliances, they embraced the idol worship of each respective country.)*

41 And sat upon a stately bed, and a table prepared before it, whereupon you have set My incense and My oil. *(The phrase, "And sat upon a stately bed," has reference to the Altar, or "Table" of worship," which sat before the Veil immediately in front of the Holy of Holies. There the Priests would offer up Incense after partaking of idol worship.)*

42 And a voice of a multitude being at ease was with her: and with the men of the common sort were brought Sabeans from the wilderness, which put bracelets upon their hands, and beautiful crowns upon their heads. *(The phrase, "And a voice of a multitude [tumult] being at ease was with her," refers to the fact that Jerusalem had strayed so far from God that now the heathen were "at ease with her." The reason: Judah's religion was no different than theirs!)*

43 Then said I unto her who was old in adulteries, Will they now commit whoredoms with her, and she with them? *(This pertains to the heathen nations which Judah courted, and which had been long in debauchery — actually all of their existence.)*

44 Yet they went in unto her, as they go in unto a woman who plays the harlot: so went they in unto Aholah and unto Aholibah, the lewd women. *(Here the Lord calls Samaria and Jerusalem, "the lewd women.")*

45 And the righteous men, they shall judge them after the manner of adulteresses, and

after the manner of women who shed blood; because they are adulteresses, and blood is in their hands. *(The idea of Verses 45 through 49 is that inasmuch as Jerusalem is both a murderess and an adulteress, she shall suffer the punishment of stoning, which the Law commanded for such [Lev. 20:10; Deut. 22:22, 24]. It refers to a sentence of death, which the Babylonians carried out!)*

46 For thus saith the Lord GOD; I will bring up a company upon them, and will give them to be removed and spoiled. *(The phrase, "And will give them to be removed and spoiled," refers to the people being removed from the Promised Land.)*

47 And the company shall stone them with stones, and dispatch them with their swords; they shall slay their sons and their daughters, and burn up their houses with fire. *(As stated, the sentence was "death"!)*

48 Thus will I cause lewdness to cease out of the land, that all women may be taught not to do after your lewdness. *(The "lewdness" refers to idolatry, which would be made "to cease out of the land." And that's exactly what ultimately happened!*

The phrase, "That all women may be taught not to do after your lewdness," refers to the heathen nations who were supposed to have been taught about the Lord by Judah, but instead were taught otherwise. Therefore, at least in part, they abrogated their very reason for existing.)

49 And they shall recompense your lewdness upon you, and you shall bear the sins of your idols: and you shall know that I am the Lord GOD. *(Jerusalem suffered the just doom of an adulteress; her walls were beaten down with stones, her houses burned with fire, and her children slain with the sword. This fearful doom was occasioned by their own conduct; it could not be ascribed to Divine injustice.*

The phrase, "And they shall recompense your lewdness upon you," refers to her receiving the very opposite of what she thought she would receive by her alliances with these heathen nations.)

CHAPTER 24
(590 B.C.)
PARABLE OF THE BOILING POT

AGAIN in the ninth year, in the tenth month, in the tenth day of the month, the Word of the LORD came unto me, saying *(the phrase, "Again in the ninth year, in the tenth month, in the tenth day of the month," refers to the very*

day that Nebuchadnezzar came against Jerusalem to destroy it completely. The siege lasted about 18 months before the fall of the city),

2 Son of man, write thee the name of the day, even of this same day: the king of Babylon set himself against Jerusalem this same day. *(For some 38 years, Jeremiah had been prophesying of this time, and Ezekiel about 4 years. Tragically, even with Nebuchadnezzar at their door, and no one allowed to go in or come out of the city, the people still would not repent. Their hopes were on Egypt to come to their rescue, and not the Lord. Such shows the incurable disposition of their wicked hearts, in that they would rebel against the Lord unto the very last.)*

3 And utter a parable unto the rebellious house, and say unto them, Thus saith the Lord GOD; Set on a pot, set it on, and also pour water into it *(Jerusalem was the pot, and the fire under it represented the Babylonians, who were besieging the city):*

4 Gather the pieces thereof into it, even every good piece, the thigh, and the shoulder; fill it with the choice bones. *(The expressions, "every good piece" and "choice bones," represented the Nobles and chief men of the people. The intent of the statement is that these would suffer the same fate as the common people.)*

5 Take the choice of the flock, and burn also the bones under it, and make it boil well, and let them seethe the bones of it therein. *(The phrase, "And make it boil well," refers to the agony of this time not being short, but instead protracted and exceedingly painful.)*

6 Wherefore thus saith the Lord GOD; Woe to the bloody city, to the pot whose scum is therein, and whose scum is not gone out of it! Bring it out piece by piece; let no lot fall upon it. *(The phrase, "And whose scum is not gone out of it," refers to the entirety of the pot being "scum," which is how the Lord characterized Jerusalem.)*

7 For her blood is in the midst of her; she set it upon the top of a rock; she poured it not upon the ground, to cover it with dust *(this refers to the Law as commanded in Lev. 17:13. It stated that blood should be hidden in the earth. Jerusalem's guilt was visible and open, and cried as loudly for judgment as blood exposed on the top of a rock. God, therefore, dealt with her as a blood-stained city);*

8 That it might cause fury to come up to take vengeance; I have set her blood upon the top of a rock, that it should not be covered. *(The phrase, "I have set her blood upon the top*

of a rock, that it should not be covered," in its simplest form means that if they would not allow Christ to cover their sins, their sins and the resultant judgment would be open to all.)

9 Therefore thus saith the Lord GOD; Woe to the bloody city! I will even make the pile for fire great. *(Once again, and about Jerusalem, we have the words which Nahum had used of Nineveh, and because of its terrible cruelty.)*

10 Heap on wood, kindle the fire, consume the flesh, and spice it well, and let the bones be burned. *(This Verse expresses the severity of the judgment that has already begun.)*

11 Then set it empty upon the coals thereof, that the brass of it may be hot, and may burn, and that the filthiness of it may be molten in it, that the scum of it may be consumed. *("Scum" pictures idolatry, as the people had become like that which they worshipped; they were, therefore, to be "consumed.")*

12 She has wearied herself with lies, and her great scum went not forth out of her: her scum shall be in the fire. *(The phrase, "She has wearied herself with lies," refers to all that which was not the Word of God. Jerusalem chose to believe the lie instead of believing the truth.)*

13 In your filthiness is lewdness: because I have purged you, and you were not purged, you shall not be purged from your filthiness any more, till I have caused My fury to rest upon you. *("Filthiness" must be purged by Calvary, or else it will be purged by judgment, but purged it shall be!)*

14 I the LORD have spoken it: it shall come to pass, and I will do it; I will not go back, neither will I spare, neither will I repent; according to your ways, and according to your doings, shall they judge you, saith the Lord GOD. *(The gist of this Verse is that Judah had gone so far down the road of wickedness that even Repentance would not spare the nation, although it would save their souls.)*

THE DEATH OF EZEKIEL'S WIFE;
A SIGN — NO MOURNING,
SIGNIFYING JUDGMENT

15 Also the word of the LORD came unto me, saying,

16 Son of man, behold, I take away from you the desire of your eyes with a stroke: yet neither shall you mourn nor weep, neither shall your tears run down. *(By the words, "The desire of your eyes," we know that the relationship of this husband and wife was very close.*

His love for her was excelled only by his love for God. The death of the Prophet's wife was to be a sign to the Exiles.)

17 Forbear to cry, make no mourning for the dead, bind the tire of your head upon you, and put on your shoes upon your feet, and cover not your lips, and eat not the bread of men. *(A son of Aaron, as Ezekiel was, was permitted to remove his turban as a sign of grief [Lev. 10:6; 13:45; 21:10]. Ezekiel was denied this privilege. He was to show no sign of mourning whatsoever!)*

18 So I spoke unto the people in the morning: and at evening my wife died; and I did in the morning as I was commanded. *(Ezekiel, knowing that his wife had but hours left to live, yet obeyed the Lord in conducting a service "in the morning." The Text simply says: "And at evening my wife died." When she expired, he no doubt was by her side. His hand must have held hers and caressed her so tenderly and gently, but then the deadly "stroke" came, and she was gone.)*

19 And the people said unto me, Will you not tell us what these things are to us, that you do so? *(There is no way that one can know the sorrow that filled Ezekiel's heart that eventful night. And yet, his strange demeanor, which the Lord demanded of him, had the effect it was meant to have. It aroused these Exiles to ask questions.)*

20 Then I answered them, The word of the LORD came unto me, saying *(it seems that the Lord had given Ezekiel little reason as to why his wife was to be taken. But now, almost immediately after her death, the explanation will be given),*

21 Speak unto the House of Israel, Thus saith the Lord GOD; Behold, I will profane My Sanctuary, the excellency of your strength, the desire of your eyes, and that which your soul pities; and your sons and your daughters whom you have left shall fall by the sword. *(Ezekiel's wife was a symbol of the Temple, the desire of the eyes of Israel. As his wife died, so the Temple would die. And there is no way that one could properly explain what the loss of the Temple meant to Israel, and for the entirety of the world, for that matter! This was where God dwelt, between the Mercy Seat and the Cherubim. It was His building, and in fact the only building on Earth that had been designed and occupied by Him, at least at that time. From there He governed His People, with His Presence constantly hovering over them.)*

22 And you shall do as I have done: you

shall not cover your lips, nor eat the bread of men. *(As a sign to these hapless Exiles, Ezekiel had not been allowed by the Lord to weep or mourn over the passing of his wife. Likewise, the Exiles were not to weep over the plight of their loved ones back home.)*

23 And your tires shall be upon your heads, and your shoes upon your feet: you shall not mourn nor weep; but you shall pine away for your iniquities, and mourn one toward another. *(The idea, as presented by the Lord, is that national calamity is going to be so severe that personal grief would be swallowed up in that sorrow. As well, the people were to understand that this calamity had come upon them because of "your iniquities.")*

24 Thus Ezekiel is unto you a sign: according to all that he has done shall you do: and when this comes, you shall know that I am the Lord GOD. *(The phrase, "And when this comes," refers to the destruction of Jerusalem being yet future, but only months away.)*

25 Also, thou son of man, shall it not be in the day when I take from them their strength, the joy of their glory, the desire of their eyes, and that whereupon they set their minds, their sons and their daughters. *(The phrase, "When I take from them their strength," refers to the Temple, which will be destroyed, and which is their strength. In fact, they had ceased to understand what the Temple really represented.)*

26 That he who escapes in that day shall come unto you, to cause you to hear it with your ears? *(All that Jeremiah and Ezekiel had prophesied, which the people had refused to believe, now they would "hear it with their ears.")*

27 In that day shall your mouth be opened to him which is escaped, and you shall speak, and be no more dumb: and you shall be a sign unto them; and they shall know that I am the LORD. *(After this message, it seems that the Prophet was to speak no more to his people, but was instead to "be dumb" until the arrival some months later of the messengers announcing the fall of Jerusalem and the destruction of the Temple.)*

CHAPTER 25
(590 B.C.)
THE PROPHECY AGAINST
THE AMMONITES

THE Word of the LORD came again unto me, saying,

2 Son of man, set your face against the Ammonites, and prophesy against them *(the country of Ammon, with Rabbah as its chief city, bordered Israel on the east [modern day Jordan]. The Holy Spirit tells Ezekiel: "Prophesy against them")*;

3 And say unto the Ammonites, Hear the word of the Lord GOD; Thus saith the Lord GOD; Because you said, Aha, against My Sanctuary, when it was profaned; and against the Land of Israel when it was desolate; and against the House of Judah, when they went into captivity *(the Ammonites rejoiced when Judah and Jerusalem fell. We must learn from this that we should not rejoice when God punishes guilty men, for that will bring His Anger upon those who do so. Psalm 83, the Prophecy of Obadiah, Psalm 137, Amos 1:11, and Lamentations, Chapter 4 should be read in connection with this Prophecy)*;

4 Behold, therefore I will deliver you to the men of the east for a possession, and they shall set their palaces in you, and make their dwellings in you: they shall eat your fruit, and they shall drink your milk. *(The "men of the east" referred to Babylon. About five years after the destruction of Jerusalem, the Babylonians took Ammon.)*

5 And I will make Rabbah a stable for camels, and the Ammonites a couching place for flocks: and you shall know that I am the LORD. *(As Ammon had humiliated Judah, now they would be humiliated.)*

6 For thus saith the Lord GOD; Because you have clapped your hands, and stamped with the feet, and rejoiced in heart with all your despite against the land of Israel *(the phrase, "Stamped with the feet," means that they danced with joy when the Temple was burned and Jerusalem was destroyed)*;

7 Behold, therefore I will stretch out My hand upon you, and will deliver you for a spoil to the heathen; and I will cut you off from the people, and I will cause you to perish out of the countries: I will destroy you; and you shall know that I am the LORD. *(Exactly as predicted, the Babylonians destroyed Ammon, and the country actually ceased to exist about 300 years later.)*

PROPHECY AGAINST MOAB

8 Thus saith the Lord GOD; Because that Moab and Seir do say, Behold, the House of Judah is like unto all the heathen *(the sin of "Moab" and "Seir" was like that of Ammon in*

that they exulted in the fall of Jerusalem);

9 Therefore, behold, I will open the side of Moab from the cities, from his cities which are on his frontiers, the glory of the country, Beth-jeshimoth, Baal-meon, and Kiriathaim *(Moab and Seir bordered Israel on the east and lay immediately south of Ammon),*

10 Unto the men of the east with the Ammonites, and will give them in possession, that the Ammonites may not be remembered among the nations. *(This is the second time that the Lord says that Ammon will be no more. This is not idle repetition, but to denote the certitude of the promised action.)*

11 And I will execute judgments upon Moab; and they shall know that I am the LORD. *(As Ammon, the Lord says, "So will be Moab.")*

PROPHECY AGAINST EDOM

12 Thus saith the Lord GOD; Because that Edom has dealt against the House of Judah by taking vengeance, and has greatly offended, and revenged himself upon them *(judgment is pronounced upon Edom likewise, and for the same sin of rejoicing in the fall of Judah and Jerusalem);*

13 Therefore thus saith the Lord GOD; I will also stretch out My hand upon Edom, and will cut off man and beast from it; and I will make it desolate from Teman; and they of Dedan shall fall by the sword. *(The judgment upon Edom is demanded by Gen. 25:23.)*

14 And I will lay My vengeance upon Edom by the hand of My people Israel: and they shall do in Edom according to My anger and according to My fury; and they shall know My vengeance, saith the Lord GOD. *(Edom took vengeance upon Judah [Vs. 12], and now the Lord will take vengeance upon them.)*

PROPHECY AGAINST THE PHILISTINES

15 Thus saith the Lord GOD; Because the Philistines have dealt by revenge, and have taken vengeance, with a despiteful heart, to destroy it for the old hatred. *(The phrase, "Old hatred," proclaims the fact that the Philistines and Israel had been enemies for centuries. It is from their name that the modern name "Palestine" is derived. However, the modern Palestinians are not descendants of the Philistines, but rather they are Egyptians, Syrians, Jordanians, etc.)*

16 Therefore thus saith the Lord GOD; Behold, I will stretch out My hand upon the Philistines, and I will cut off the Cherethims, and destroy the remnant of the sea coast. *(The "Cherethims" are probably the same as the "Cherethites" [II Sam. 8:18; 15:18]. They also would be destroyed. All of this proclaims the Lord's dominion over all Gentile powers, in fact, the entirety of the world.)*

17 And I will execute great vengeance upon them with furious rebukes; and they shall know that I am the LORD, when I shall lay My vengeance upon them. *(Thus, these four nations [Vss. 5, 11, 14, 17] would get to know to their sorrow that the God of Israel exists, and that He judges sin.)*

CHAPTER 26
(588 B.C.)
PROPHECIES AGAINST TYRUS

AND it came to pass in the eleventh year, in the first day of the month, that the word of the LORD came unto me, saying *(the Holy Spirit devotes Chapters 26, 27, and 28 to Tyre. We will find out the reason as we proceed),*

2 Son of man, because that Tyrus has said against Jerusalem, Aha, she is broken that was the gates of the people: she is turned unto Me: I shall be replenished, now she is laid waste *(according to Herodotus, Tyre was founded in 2700 B.C. The city became prosperous and became the principal Phoenician port controlling the Phoenician coast. It was on the border of Israel to the north. The phrase, "The gates of the people," referring to Jerusalem, proclaimed the fact of Jerusalem's supremacy. Tyre also rejoiced over her fall):*

NEBUCHADNEZZAR WILL BE GOD'S INSTRUMENT OF DESTRUCTION

3 Therefore thus saith the Lord GOD; Behold, I am against you, O Tyrus, and will cause many nations to come up against you, as the sea causes his waves to come up. *(The phrase, "As the sea causes his waves to come up," refers to the first great wave of the Babylonians against Tyre, and the last, the Greeks; for the Prophecy of this Chapter embraces both destructions.)*

4 And they shall destroy the walls of Tyrus, and break down her towers: I will also scrape her dust from her, and make her like the top of a rock. *(The "walls" refer to the first destruction by Nebuchadnezzar, with the phrase, "I will also scrape her dust from her," referring to Alexander the Great, who built a causeway to*

attack the new Tyre. History records that his soldiers, in order to complete the causeway, gathered the dust of old Tyre in baskets and emptied them into the waters, fulfilling this Prophecy.)

5 It shall be a place for the spreading of nets in the midst of the sea: for I have spoken it, saith the Lord GOD: and it shall become a spoil to the nations. *(All of this was fulfilled in entirety.)*

6 And her daughters which are in the field shall be slain by the sword; and they shall know that I am the LORD. *(The "daughters" refer to the neighboring towns which were dependent upon Tyre.)*

7 For thus saith the Lord GOD; Behold, I will bring upon Tyrus Nebuchadnezzar king of Babylon, a king of kings, from the north, with horses, and with chariots, and with horsemen, and companies, and much people. *(The phrase, "Behold, I will bring upon Tyrus . . . ," refers to the Lordship of Christ as Sovereign Ruler over all. One may notice that the title, "a king of kings," is given to Nebuchadnezzar by the Holy Spirit. This was so, for many other kings submitted to him. However, Christ is "The King of kings," and is the only One Who will ever serve in this capacity.)*

8 He shall slay with the sword your daughters in the field: and he shall make a fort against you, and cast a mount against you, and lift up the buckler against you. *(This Verse proclaims the nature of the siege that Nebuchadnezzar would lay against Tyre. The siege lasted thirteen years before Tyre eventually fell.)*

9 And he shall set engines of war against your walls, and with his axes he shall break down your towers. *(The "engines of war" consisted of huge catapults designed to hurl great stones at the walls in order to make a breach in them.)*

10 By reason of the abundance of his horses their dust shall cover you: your walls shall shake at the noise of the horsemen, and of the wheels, and of the chariots, when he shall enter into your gates, as men enter into a city wherein is made a breach. *(When the walls were finally breached by Nebuchadnezzar, the might and power of his army and cavalry quickly overran the city.)*

11 With the hoofs of his horses shall he tread down all your streets: he shall slay your people by the sword, and your strong garrisons shall go down to the ground. *(The "he" and "his" of Verses 9 through 11 proclaim Nebuchadnezzar; the "they" of Verse 12, the soldiers of Alexander. The two invasions were separated by about 150 years.)*

12 And they shall make a spoil of your riches, and make a prey of your merchandise; and they shall break down your walls, and destroy your pleasant houses: and they shall lay your stones and your timber and your dust in the midst of the water. *(As stated, the last phrase of this Verse, concerning the "dust in the midst of the water," refers to Alexander's invasion.)*

13 And I will cause the noise of your songs to cease; and the sound of your harps shall be no more heard. *(Tyre was eminent no less for its culture than for its commerce.)*

14 And I will make you like the top of a rock: you shall be a place to spread nets upon; you shall be built no more: for I the LORD have spoken it, saith the Lord GOD. *(The phrase, "You shall be built no more," speaks of this "rock" where old Tyre was located. Today, as for centuries past, the sight of the ancient city, as described here, is a bare rock upon which fishermen dry their nets. However, a short time before World War II, a new Tyre was built somewhat inland, but stretching to the sea. It presently has a population of 10,000 – 20,000.)*

THE LAMENT OF THE SEAPORT RULERS OVER TYRUS

15 Thus saith the Lord GOD to Tyrus; Shall not the isles shake at the sound of your fall, when the wounded cry, when the slaughter is made in the midst of you? *(That which happened to Jerusalem would ultimately happen to Tyre.)*

16 Then all the princes of the sea shall come down from their thrones, and lay away their robes, and put off their broidered garments: they shall clothe themselves with trembling; they shall sit upon the ground, and shall tremble at every moment, and be astonished at you. *(The phrase, "Princes of the sea," referred to the merchant princes who had made Tyre one of the greatest centers of commerce in the world. Now they are astonished at the fall of Tyre, which they thought could not happen.)*

17 And they shall take up a lamentation for you, and say to you, How are you destroyed, that was inhabited of seafaring men, the renowned city, which was strong in the sea, she and her inhabitants, which cause their terror to be on all who haunt it! *(Due to the riches and power of Tyre, the surrounding countries did not think she would fall, and especially considering that it took Nebuchadnezzar 13 years to subdue the city.)*

18 Now shall the isles tremble in the day of your fall; yea, the isles that are in the sea shall be troubled at your departure. *(The troubling of the surrounding countries is due to the commerce of Tyre, which had contributed to their prosperity, but would now be lost.)*

19 For thus saith the Lord GOD; When I shall make you a desolate city, like the cities that are not inhabited; when I shall bring up the deep upon you, and great waters shall cover you *(the city that had been so rich and prosperous now will be made "desolate");*

20 When I shall bring you down with them who descend into the pit, with the people of old time, and shall set you in the low parts of the Earth, in places desolate of old, with them who go down to the pit, that you be not inhabited; and I shall set Glory in the Land of the Living *(the phrase, "When I shall bring you down with them who descend into the pit," is actually a portrayal of Hell itself, and her shut up with the antediluvians, i.e., "with the people of old time." The phrase, "And I shall set Glory in the Land of the Living," refers to the Messiah ultimately reigning in Glory in the Land of the Living, at Jerusalem, in the midst of the redeemed sons of Israel, which will take place in the coming Kingdom Age);*

21 I will make you a terror, and you shall be no more: though you be sought for, yet shall you never be found again, saith the Lord GOD. *(This Passage and all the information given about Tyre [which represents the system of this world] portray the fact that this system is going to ultimately perish, and Jesus Christ will reign supreme. In fact, that time is nearer now than ever!)*

CHAPTER 27
(588 B.C.)
THE LAMENTATION OVER TYRUS; HER SPLENDOR AND WEALTH

THE Word of the LORD came again unto me, saying *(the reason the Holy Spirit gives such detail concerning Tyrus is because this city is a symbol of Satan's efforts to build an earthly kingdom and, thereby, meet the needs of man without God. As such, Tyre serves in the Old Testament as a symbol of the world's corrupt system, as a rebuilt Babylon will serve in the New Testament. As the Lord destroyed the former, He likewise will destroy the latter!),*

2 Now, thou son of man, take up a lamentation for Tyrus *(the "lamentation" for Tyrus is* given by the Holy Spirit because this city and its commerce was helped greatly by Satan, and was, thereby, used as a spiritual projection of his gospel of deception);*

3 And say unto Tyrus, O thou that are situate at the entry of the sea, which are a merchant of the people for many isles, Thus saith the Lord GOD; O Tyrus, you have said, I am of perfect beauty. *(The phrase, "O Tyrus, you have said, I am of perfect beauty," refers to the pride of that city, which Chapter 28 will address more thoroughly. In fact, the same phrase is used of Satan [28:12].)*

4 Your borders are in the midst of the seas, your builders have perfected your beauty. *(The phrase, "Your builders have perfected your beauty," refers to the merchants of this great commercial activity, in effect, being helped by Satan regarding the prosperity of the city.)*

5 They have made all your ship boards of fir trees of Senir: they have taken cedars from Lebanon to make masts for you. *(Many years before, these "cedars" had been used to build the Temple, the dwellingplace of Jehovah under the old economy of God.)*

6 Of the oaks of Bashan have they made your oars; the company of the Ashurites have made your benches of ivory, brought out of the Isles of Chittim. *(The use of ivory in ship- or house-building seems to have been one of the arts for which Tyre was famous.)*

7 Fine linen with broidered work from Egypt was that which you spread forth to be your sail; blue and purple from the Isles of Elishah was that which covered you. *(This refers to some of the fine, broidered sails that graced some of the ships of Tyre, relative to the common sails of most ships.)*

8 The inhabitants of Zidon and Arvad were your mariners: your wise men, O Tyrus, who were in you, were your pilots. *(The intent of this Verse is to proclaim the fact that the common sailors came from Zidon and Arvad, while Tyre furnished the officers. Thus, Tyre is held as a cut above the others, even as Satan intended! [Zidon, sometimes spelled "Sidon," was about 30 miles north of Tyre.])*

9 The ancients of Gebal and the wise men thereof were in you your calkers: all the ships of the sea with their mariners were in you to occupy your merchandise. *(This refers to the constant business activity of the merchant ships in continuing, and without fail, to increase the riches of Tyre.)*

TYRUS' MILITARY MIGHT

10 They of Persia and of Lud and of Phut were in your army, your men of war: they hanged the shield and helmet in you; they set forth your comeliness. *(The phrase, "They set forth your comeliness," means they guarded the riches.)*

11 The men of Arvad with your army were upon your walls round about, and the Gammadims were in your towers: they hanged their shields upon your walls round about; they have made your beauty perfect. *(This Scripture proclaims the military might of Tyre; consequently, she was so strong that had not the Lord helped Nebuchadnezzar, he would never have been able to take the city.)*

THE MERCHANTS OF TYRUS

12 Tarshish was your merchant by reason of the multitude of all kind of riches; with silver, iron, tin, and lead, they traded in your fairs. *(The phrase, "Tarshish was your merchant," refers to Spain, where Jonah had attempted to go [Jonah 1:3].)*

13 Javan, Tubal, and Meshech, they were your merchants: they traded the persons of men and vessels of brass in your market. *(The phrase, "They traded the persons of men and vessels of brass in your market," referred to the buying and selling of slaves, as well as merchandise.)*

14 They of the house of Togarmah traded in your fairs with horses and horsemen and mules. *("Togarmah" was Armenia. The area was famous for its "horses and horsemen and mules.")*

15 The men of Dedan were your merchants; many isles were the merchandise of your hand: they brought you for a present horns of ivory and ebony. *("Ebony" is a rock-hard heavy wood, yielded by various old world tropical dicotyledonous trees. It was very valuable and used to make fine furniture, etc.)*

16 Syria was your merchant by reason of the multitude of the wares of your making: they occupied in your fairs with emeralds, purple, and broidered work, and fine linen, and coral, and agate. *(As is obvious in these Passages, Tyre was the trading point of the world. Therefore, her wealth must have been extensive, to say the least!)*

17 Judah, and the land of Israel, they were your merchants: they traded in your market wheat of Minnith, and Pannag, and honey, and oil, and balm. *(When "Judah" and the "Land of Israel" are mentioned, even though the Holy Spirit does not highlight their mention, still, there is a quickening of the Spirit.)*

18 Damascus was your merchant in the multitude of the wares of your making, for the multitude of all riches; in the wine of Helbon, and white wool.

19 Dan also and Javan going to and fro occupied in your fairs: bright iron, cassia, and calamus, were in your market. *(The "Dan" spoken of here is not the Tribe of Dan, but instead a place in Arabia known for its steel used for sword-blades, for which Yemen was famous, hence, "bright iron.")*

20 Dedan was your merchant in precious clothes for chariots. *(This probably referred to a type of colorful carpet used as saddle-clothes. As well, the material was used to ritually decorate expensive chariots.)*

21 Arabia, and all the princes of Kedar, they occupied with you in lambs, and rams, and goats: in these were they your merchants. *("Dedan" and "Kedar" both were in Arabia.)*

22 The merchants of Sheba and Raamah, they were your merchants: they occupied in your fairs with chief of all spices, and with all precious stones, and gold. *(It is readily observable that every single thing in the world of that day was traded, with Tyre being the center of all such activity.)*

23 Haran, and Canneh, and Eden, the merchants of Sheba, Asshur, and Chilmad, were your merchants. *("Haran" was the same city where Abraham lived for a while before going on into the Land of Canaan. It was about 300 miles north of Damascus.)*

24 These were your merchants in all sorts of things, in blue clothes, and broidered work, and in chest of rich apparel, bound with cords, and made of cedar, among your merchandise.

25 The ships of Tarshish did sing of you in your market: and you were replenished, and made very glorious in the midst of the seas. *("Tarshish" was in Spain, showing the distance to which the trade extended. The phrase, "And made very glorious in the midst of the seas," refers to vessels from all over the world of that day, signifying the port of Tyre as their destination.)*

THE TOTAL DESTRUCTION OF TYRUS

26 Your rowers have brought you into great waters: the east wind has broken you in the midst of the seas. *(Beginning with this Verse and through the remainder of the Chapter, all*

the glory and glamour of Tyre is predicted to be brought to ruin, and meant to serve as a symbol of Satan and his kingdom of darkness ultimately being brought to destruction.)

27 Your riches and your fairs, your merchandise, your mariners, and your pilots, your calkers, and the occupiers of your merchandise, and all your men of war, who are in you, and in all your company which is in the midst of you, shall fall into the midst of the seas in the day of your ruin. *(As stated, as the Lord destroyed the Tyrus of the Old World, He will also destroy the Tyrus of the New World [Babylon], both symbols of the efforts of Satan to rebuild the Garden of Eden without the benefit of the Tree of Life, Who is the Lord Jesus Christ. In fact, Rev., Chpt. 18, corresponds with Verses 27 through 36 of this 27th Chapter of Ezekiel.)*

28 The suburbs shall shake at the sound of the cry of your pilots. *(The fall of Tyre, which came about 15 years later, and which the city thought impossible, would result in a "shaking" of all the sister cities and countries which depended on her.)*

29 And all who handle the oar, the mariners, and all the pilots of the sea, shall come down from their ships, they shall stand upon the land *(as stated, this has a similarity to the coming destruction of Babylon, which is yet future [Rev. 18:18-19]);*

30 And shall cause their voice to be heard against you, and shall cry bitterly, and shall cast up dust upon their heads, they shall wallow themselves in the ashes:

31 And they shall make themselves utterly bald for you, and gird themselves with sackcloth, and they shall weep for you with bitterness of heart and bitter wailing. *(Riches were their god, and now that the riches are lost, they have nothing! Such are all who place their confidence in anything other than the Lord. Not only do they lose their souls, but they also lose the very thing for which they sold their souls!)*

32 And in their wailing they shall take up a lamentation for you, and lament over you, saying, What city is like Tyrus, like the destroyed in the midst of the sea?

33 When your wares went forth out of the seas; you filled many people; you did enrich the kings of the Earth with the multitude of your riches and of your merchandise. *(Considering the riches of Tyre, why did Nebuchadnezzar desire to destroy her? Whatever his personal reasons were, the overriding factor was that the Lord had chosen him as an instrument*

for the destruction of this city. Likewise, many nations of the world cannot presently understand why the leaders of the former Soviet Union, which outwardly looked so monolithic, allowed it to destruct before the eyes of the world! But yet, it was done because God commanded that it be done.)

34 In the time when you shall be broken by the seas in the depths of the waters your merchandise and all your company in the midst of you shall fall. *(As stated, because the Lord deemed it so!)*

35 All the inhabitants of the isles shall be astonished at you, and their kings shall be sore afraid, they shall be troubled in their countenance. *(The entire Verse indicates that world leaders were shaken as a result of Tyre's destruction.)*

36 The merchants among the people shall hiss at you; you shall be a terror, and never shall be any more. *(With her destruction by Nebuchadnezzar, and again about 150 years later by Alexander the Great, the greatness and glory of Tyre died, never to rise again. This is the Old Testament portrayal of that which will happen in a coming day, when rebuilt Babylon will likewise be destroyed, signifying the end of a system that has brought only death, destruction, and darkness. To be sure, as Tyre was destroyed, likewise Babylon and all of its system also will be destroyed. This will happen immediately before the Second Coming [Rev., Chpts. 17-18].)*

CHAPTER 28
(588 B.C.)
JUDGMENT ON THE PRINCE OF TYRUS

THE Word of the LORD came again unto me, saying *(regarding the spirit world, this Chapter is one of the most remarkable in the Bible. As the Holy Spirit through Ezekiel had concerned Himself with the city, He now concerns Himself with its ruler, who is symbolic of Satan. In fact, this Chapter, in combination with Isa., Chpt. 14, gives us great insight into the ruler of darkness, Lucifer),*

2 Son of man, say unto the prince of Tyrus, Thus saith the Lord GOD; Because your heart is lifted up, and you have said, I am a god, I sit in the seat of God, in the midst of the seas; yet you are a man, and not God, though you set your heart as the heart of God *(it is noticeable that Paul's description of the "man of sin" [II Thess. 2:4] presents the same picture in nearly the same words. Even though this Passage speaks*

of the Earthly "Prince of Tyrus," nevertheless it is Satan himself who energizes his victim. The characterization of this earthly prince is "pride," which denotes the foundation sin of all sin):

3 Behold, you are wiser than Daniel; there is no secret that they can hide from you (he was not really wiser than Daniel, only wiser in his own eyes):

4 With your wisdom and with your understanding you have gotten yourself riches, and have gotten gold and silver into your treasures (Daniel's wisdom was used to carry out the Will of God, while this man's wisdom was used to gain riches, as most of the wisdom of this world is used):

5 By your great wisdom and by your traffick have you increased your riches, and your heart is lifted up because of your riches (if successful, and even in the things of the Lord, men quickly become lifted up in themselves):

6 Therefore thus saith the Lord GOD; Because you have set your heart as the heart of God (this is the great sin of mankind, fueled by pride. Satan wants to be God, and all who follow Satan have the same spirit);

7 Behold, therefore I will bring strangers upon you, the terrible of the nations: and they shall draw their swords against the beauty of your wisdom, and they shall defile your brightness. (This refers to the army of Babylon, which will soon come against this rich city and its king. Men rule, but God overrules!)

8 They shall bring you down to the pit, and you shall die the deaths of them who are slain in the midst of the seas. (The phrase, "They shall bring you down to the pit," refers to Hell itself. The phrase, "And you shall die the deaths of them who are slain in the midst of the seas," means that he would not be given a royal funeral, but that his body would be thrown into the waters, as are all who die on ships.

It is not known from secular history as to exactly what did happen to Ithobal, King of Tyre. Nebuchadnezzar, as stated, laid siege to the city for thirteen years. After his conquest, judges were appointed, and these ruled for periods of several months each. All this indicates a period of confusion and anarchy — the consequence of a great catastrophe.

Unless a specific date is given, it must be remembered that most Prophecies germinate over a period of time. This means that what the Prophet saw in vision, as wrought out in a moment of time, was actually the outcome, at least in many cases, of the slow decay of centuries, and of catastrophes separated from each other by long intervals of dwindling history. Sometimes, the main facts of that history may be briefly stated, with the totality of the Prophecy covering many years, even centuries, but ultimately being brought to pass.)

9 Will you yet say before him who slays thee, I am God? but you shall be a man, and no God, in the hand of him who slays you. (Up beside Nebuchadnezzar, the Tyrian Monarch will prove to be no match, because Nebuchadnezzar was God's instrument.)

10 You shall die the deaths of the uncircumcised by the hand of strangers: for I have spoken it, saith the Lord GOD. (This Scripture refers to the Tyrian Monarch dying lost.)

LAMENTATION FOR THE ANGELIC KING OF TYRUS: SATAN

11 Moreover, the word of the LORD came unto me, saying (the tenor of this Chapter will now change from the earthly Monarch, the "Prince of Tyre," to his sponsor, Satan, of which the earthly king was a symbol),

12 Son of man, take up a lamentation upon the king of Tyrus, and say unto him, Thus saith the Lord GOD; You seal up the sum, full of wisdom, and perfect in beauty. (As is obvious, even though the king of Tyrus is used as a symbol, the statements made could not refer to any mere mortal. In fact, they refer to Satan.

The phrase, "You seal up the sum," means that Lucifer, when originally created by God, was the perfection of wisdom and beauty. In fact, the phrase intimates that Lucifer was the wisest and most beautiful Angel created by God, and served the Lord in Holiness and Righteousness for a given period of time.

The phrase, "Perfect in beauty," means that he was the most beautiful of God's Angelic creation. The Holy Spirit even labeled his beauty as "perfect.")

13 You have been in Eden the Garden of God; every precious stone was your covering, the sardius, topaz, and the diamond, the beryl, the onyx, and the jasper, the sapphire, the emerald, and the carbuncle, and gold: the workmanship of your tabrets and of your pipes was prepared in you in the day that you were created. (The phrase, "You have been in Eden the Garden of God," does not actually refer to the "Eden" of Gen., Chpt. 3, but rather to the "Eden" which existed on this planet before Adam and Eve, which evidently was ruled by Lucifer

before his rebellion.

The phrase, "Every precious stone was your covering," presents itself as very similar to the dress of the High Priest of Israel [Ex. 28:19].

The phrase, "The workmanship of your tabrets and of your pipes," has to do with music. There is every indication that Lucifer's leadership had something to do with the worship of God. As well, he is called, "O Lucifer, son of the morning" [Isa. 14:12]. When the Earth was originally created, the Scripture says, "The morning stars sang together, and all the sons of God shouted for joy" [Job 38:4-7]. So, if the idiom, "son of the morning," can be linked to the "morning stars," these Passages tell us that Lucifer, at least before his fall, was greatly used in leading the Worship of God.

In fact, this is the reason that Satan has done everything within his power to corrupt the music of the world, and to corrupt the music of the Church above all. Inasmuch as the Book of Psalms is the longest Book in the Bible, we learn from this that music and singing are among the highest forms of worship of the Lord.)

14 You are the anointed Cherub who covers; and I have set you so: you were upon the Holy Mountain of God; you have walked up and down in the midst of the stones of fire. (The phrase, "You are the anointed Cherub who covers," means that Lucifer was chosen and "anointed" by God for a particular task and service. This probably was the "worship" to which we have just alluded.

The phrase, "You were upon the Holy Mountain of God," speaks of his place and position relative to the Throne [Rev. 4:2-11]. The phrase, "You have walked up and down in the midst of the stones of fire," has reference to his nearness to the Throne [1:26-27]. As well, the phrase, "Walked up and down," seems to imply that not just any Angel would have been given such latitude.)

15 You were perfect in your ways from the day that you were created, till iniquity was found in you (pride was the form of this iniquity [Lk. 10:17-18]. The rebellion of Lucifer against God probably caused the catastrophe which occurred between the First and Second Verses of Gen., Chpt. 1),

16 By the multitude of your merchandise they have filled the midst of you with violence, and you have sinned; therefore I will cast you as profane out of the Mountain of God: and I will destroy you, O covering Cherub, from the midst of the stones of fire. ("Violence" has

been the earmark of Satan's rule and reign in the world of darkness [Jn. 10:10]. Lucifer being "cast out" of the "Mountain of God" refers to him losing his place and position, which he had held with God since his creation. It was because "he had sinned," which spoke of pride that caused him to lift himself up against God.)

17 Your heart was lifted up because of your beauty, you have corrupted your wisdom by reason of your brightness: I will cast you to the ground, I will lay you before kings, that they may behold you. (The phrase, "Your heart was lifted up because of your beauty," tells us the reason for his fall. As stated, it was pride. He took his eyes off of Christ, noticing his own beauty as it grew more and more glorious in his eyes. At some point in time, his "heart" was changed from Christ to himself. As far as we know, this was the origin of evil in all of God's creation.

The phrase, "You have corrupted your wisdom by reason of your brightness," does not refer to the loss of wisdom, but instead refers to wisdom corrupted, hence the insidious design practiced upon the human family [Jn. 10:10].

The phrase, "I will cast you to the ground," refers to his ultimate defeat [Rev. 12:7-12]. The phrase, "I will lay you before kings, that they may behold you," refers to him ultimately being cast into the Lake of Fire, where all the kings of the Earth who have died lost will behold him in his humiliation [Mat. 25:41; Rev. 20:10].)

18 You have defiled your sanctuaries by the multitude of your iniquities, by the iniquity of your traffick; therefore will I bring forth a fire from the midst of you, it shall devour you, and I will bring you to ashes upon the Earth in the sight of all them who behold you. (When Satan at long last will be thrown into the Lake of Fire [Rev. 20:10], all the billions he has duped, who also are in Hell because of him, will hate him with a passion that words cannot begin to express, and a hatred which will last forever and forever.)

19 All they who know you among the people shall be astonished at you: you shall be a terror, and never shall you be any more. (Then the prayer of Christ, "Your Will be done in Earth, as it is in Heaven," will finally be answered and brought to pass [Mat. 6:9-10].)

THE PROPHECY AGAINST ZIDON

20 Again the word of the LORD came unto me, saying,

21 Son of man, set your face against Zidon,

and prophesy against it *(Zidon [Sidon] was about 30 miles north of Tyre. Tyre and Zidon were sister cities, but yet Tyre served as the chief city)*,

22 And say, Thus saith the Lord GOD; Behold, I am against you, O Zidon; and I will be glorified in the midst of you: and they shall know that I am the LORD, when I shall have executed judgments in her, and shall be sanctified in her. *(Suffering, but not extinction, was the judgment of Zidon. She exists today, but her history has been one of pestilence and blood. The phrase, "Shall be sanctified in her," refers to the truth that the Lord will be sanctified either by righteous living on the part of His subjects or righteous judgment on those who rebel against Him.)*

23 For I will send into her pestilence, and blood into her streets; and the wounded shall be judged in the midst of her by the sword upon her on every side; and they shall know that I am the LORD. *(The "pestilence" and "blood into her streets" have to do with the terrible invasions she suffered from this time forward.)*

24 And there shall be no more a pricking brier unto the House of Israel, nor any grieving thorn of all who are round about them, who despised them; and they shall know that I am the Lord GOD. *(They — the Zidonians — shall get to know [to their sorrow] that I am Adonai-Jehovah. They will "prick" Israel no more!)*

RESTORATION OF ISRAEL

25 Thus saith the Lord GOD; When I shall have gathered the House of Israel from the people among whom they are scattered, and shall be sanctified in them in the sight of the heathen, then shall they dwell in their land that I have given to My servant Jacob. *(The gathering of Israel, as stated here, will take place in the coming Kingdom Age. The phrase, "Then shall they dwell in their land that I have given to My servant Jacob," refers to the longest conflict that has engaged this planet, speaking of the conflict over the Land of Israel. In this Passage and many others, the Lord proclaims that He has given this Land to His People; He also specifies exactly where this Land should be [Gen. 15:18]. When He uses the phrase, "My servant Jacob," He, at the same time, is saying that He did not give it to Esau, i.e., the Arabs. The Palestinians, as well as the entirety of the world, should read this Verse.)*

26 And they shall dwell safely therein, and shall built houses, and plant vineyards; yea, they shall dwell with confidence, when I have executed judgments upon all those who despise them round about them; and they shall know that I am the LORD their God. *(The return of the Hebrews to the Land of Israel is foretold in many Prophecies [Deut. 30:3-4; Isa. 11:11-13; 27:12-13; Jer. 31:8-10; 32:37; Ezek. 34:13; 37:21; Amos 9:14-15; Rom., Chpt. 11].)*

CHAPTER 29
(589 B.C.)
PROPHECIES AGAINST EGYPT; JUDGMENT

I N the tenth year, in the tenth month, in the twelfth day of the month, the Word of the LORD came unto me, saying, *(this Prophecy was given about six months before Jerusalem fell. They cover the period from 587-572 B.C.; they appear in moral, and not in chronological order. In fact, each of these Prophecies [or else a portion of the Prophecy] was called forth by the political events of the time, and should be studied in connection with them.)*

2 Son of man, set your face against Pharaoh king of Egypt, and prophesy against him, and against all Egypt *(Egypt is the last world-kingdom addressed by Ezekiel. It is first addressed by Jeremiah [Chpt. 46], while Babylon is the last [Chpt. 50])*:

3 Speak, and say, Thus saith the Lord GOD; Behold, I am against you, Pharaoh king of Egypt, the great dragon who lies in the midst of his rivers, who has said, My river is my own, and I have made it for myself. *(This Verse begins a pronounced judgment against Egypt, which would ensure its denigration, at least until the Second Coming of the Lord. Pharaoh considered himself to be god, and thus, the creator, which caused him to say of himself: "My river is my own, and I have made it for myself.")*

4 But, I will put hooks in your jaws, and I will cause the fish of your rivers to stick unto your scales, and I will bring you up out of the midst of your rivers, and all the fish of your rivers shall stick unto your scales. *("The fish of your rivers" refer to Pharaoh's adherents. The idea is, Pharaoh and the entire land of Egypt will be destroyed. Tragically, this man, Pharaoh-Hophra, was the one Zedekiah relied upon for deliverance from Nebuchadnezzar.)*

5 And I will leave you thrown into the wilderness, you and all the fish of your rivers: you shall fall upon the open fields; you shall not be brought together, nor gathered: I have given you for meat to the beasts of the field

and to the fowls of the Heaven. *(It is said that Pharaoh attacked Tyre and Zidon and then failed in an enterprise against Cyrene. He was then deposed by Amasis in 596 B.C. It was probably this expedition against Cyrene which led to the revolt of Amasis against Pharaoh-Hophra, which resulted in his defeat, of which this Scripture and others refer!)*

CAUSE OF JUDGMENT ON EGYPT

6 And all the inhabitants of Egypt shall know that I am the LORD, because they have been a staff of reed to the House of Israel. *(At least one of the causes of God's great Anger outlined against Egypt is because of her betrayal of Judah. Even though it was God's Will that Babylon serve as the chastiser of Judah, still, His Anger at Egypt for promising what they could not deliver, which at least in some fashion added to Judah's plight, would now cause Judgment to be brought on them.)*

7 When they took hold of you by your hand, you did break, and rend all their shoulder: and when they leaned upon you, you broke, and made all their loins to be at a stand. *(As a result of Egypt's promises that they would deliver Judah, Zedekiah held out against Nebuchadnezzar. This greatly incensed the Babylonian Monarch and caused him to wreak terrible vengeance when his army finally breached the walls of Jerusalem. Egypt was partly responsible for this; this is that of which the Lord speaks here.)*

8 Therefore thus saith the Lord GOD; Behold, I will bring a sword upon you, and cut off man and beast out of you. *(This refers to what the Babylonians would do to them; and it was designed by the Lord.)*

9 And the land of Egypt shall be desolate and waste; and they shall know that I am the LORD: because he *(Pharaoh)* has said, The river is mine, and I have made it. *(The Holy Spirit through the Prophet refers back to the boastful pride of Pharaoh by the phrase which the Egyptian Monarch used: "The river is mine, and I have made it." The idea is: if Pharaoh created the river, surely he can stop the "desolation and waste." But, of course, Pharaoh is helpless to do this, because, despite his bluster, he is just a man, and as such is helpless in the Face of God.)*

DESOLATION FOR FORTY YEARS; EGYPT'S FUTURE LOWLY ESTATE

10 Behold, therefore I am against you, and against your rivers, and I will make the land of Egypt utterly waste and desolate, from the tower of Syene even unto the border of Ethiopia. *(It should read, "from Migdol to Syene, even unto the border of Ethiopia." Migdol represented the northern extremity of Egypt, as Syene represented the southern; therefore, the entirety of Egypt is included in the statement.)*

11 No foot of man shall pass through it, nor foot of beast shall pass through it, neither shall it be inhabited forty years. *(The idea is that no "man" or "beast" shall pass through Egypt regarding the prosperity of the nation. There would certainly be men and beasts there, but they would be subject to foreign rulers, which actually lasted for "forty years.")*

12 And I will make the land of Egypt desolate in the midst of the countries that are desolate, and her cities among the cities that are laid waste shall be desolate forty years: and I will scatter the Egyptians among the nations, and will disperse them through the countries. *(Even though there is no historical records of the fulfillment of these particular Passages, still, knowing that Nebuchadnezzar invaded Egypt after the destruction of Jerusalem, we may assume, with little risk of doubt, that he "scattered the Egyptians among the nations." Such was the practice of invaders, in order that it would be deprived of its elite and, therefore, incapable of insurrection.)*

13 Yet thus saith the LORD GOD; At the end of forty years will I gather the Egyptians from the people whither they were scattered *(at approximately the time that Israel was allowed by Cyrus to go back to the Promised Land, likewise, Egypt was then allowed a measure of statehood):*

14 And I will bring again the captivity of Egypt, and will cause them to return into the land of Pathros, into the land of their habitation; and they shall be there a base kingdom. *(The phrase, "A base kingdom," means one that is a subordinate kingdom, which Egypt has been from then until now. In other words, her greatness of the past was never again duplicated.)*

15 It shall be the basest of the kingdoms; neither shall it exalt itself any more above the nations: for I will diminish them, that they shall no more rule over the nations. *(It came to pass exactly as the Lord said. Today, Egypt is basically little more than a shabby sextant of ancient tombs; however, in the coming Kingdom Age, Egypt will be restored and blessed [Isa., Chpt. 19].)*

16 And it shall be no more the confidence of the House of Israel, which brings their iniquity to remembrance, when they shall look after them: but they shall know that I am the Lord GOD. *(Israel "looked after" the Egyptians instead of "after" Jehovah; by so doing, they kept bringing their iniquity [unbelief] to God's remembrance. The phrase, "And it shall be no more the confidence of the House of Israel," refers to the Biblical Truth that the Lord desires His People, whether Israel of old or the modern Church, to trust solely in Him instead of the world. As this was Israel's great temptation, it is the great temptation of the modern Church also!)*

EGYPT TO BE GIVEN TO NEBUCHADNEZZAR FOR HIS WAGES

17 And it came to pass in the seven and twentieth year, in the first month, in the first day of the month, the word of the LORD came unto me, saying *(adding Verses 1 and 17 together, we find that the Prophecy of Verses 17 through 21 was given seventeen years after the Prophecy of Verses 1 through 17. They were introduced here to secure the unity of the subject)*,

18 Son of man, Nebuchadnezzar king of Babylon caused his army to serve a great service against Tyrus: every head was made bald, and every shoulder was peeled: yet had he no wages, nor his army, for Tyrus, for the service that he had served against it *(as stated, the siege of Tyre lasted 13 years. The Babylonian king undertook it at God's Command [Jer. 25:9]. He captured the city, but secured no treasure, for the Tyrians had removed it and most of the citizens to other cities by sea)*:

19 Therefore thus saith the Lord GOD; Behold, I will give the land of Egypt unto Nebuchadnezzar king of Babylon; and he shall take her multitude, and take her spoil, and take her prey; and it shall be the wages for his army. *(Of course, Nebuchadnezzar had no knowledge of what the Lord was doing; nevertheless, the Babylonian Monarch carried out the Will of God, whether he realized it or not!)*

20 I have given him the land of Egypt for his labour wherewith he served against it, because they wrought for Me, saith the Lord GOD.

A PROMISE TO ISRAEL

21 In that day will I cause the horn of the House of Israel to bud forth, and I will give you the opening of the mouth in the midst of them; and they shall know that I am the LORD. *(The words, "In that day," refer to the coming restoration of Israel at the beginning of the Kingdom Age. Israel will be the central nation in the midst of all the nations of the world, because then Christ will be her ultimate King, even "The King of kings," meaning that He will be the Lord of the entirety of the Earth.)*

CHAPTER 30
(572 B.C.)
EGYPT'S APPROACHING DOOM

THE Word of the LORD came again unto me, saying *(Williams says, "The natural heart quickly wearies of these repeated threatenings of judgment, hence the Book of Jeremiah and Ezekiel are by and large unpopular in Christendom, and largely unread. But these repetitions reveal God's Heart and man's heart — the one so loving, the other so evil. Love sought continually to save; rebellion refused continually to listen")*,

2 Son of man, prophesy and say, Thus saith the Lord GOD; Howl ye, Woe worth the day! *(This Chapter is basically divided into two sections. Verses 1 through 9 have to do with the coming Great Tribulation, while Verses 10 through 26 have to do with the judgment that Egypt was facing from Babylon in Ezekiel's day.*

The phrase, "Woe worth the day," actually says, "Woe be to the day." It refers, as stated, to the coming Great Tribulation. It actually will be a time when the entirety of the world will "howl.")

3 For the day is near, even the day of the LORD is near, a cloudy day; it shall be the time of the heathen. *(The phrase, "The day of the LORD," refers to the Second Advent of Christ and continues through the Millennium. The Holy Spirit through the Prophet is saying that the Great Tribulation means that the Second Coming "is near."*

The phrase, "A cloudy day," speaks of the judgments just referred to, which will encompass the whole of humanity. This "cloudy day" will last for seven years, called "Daniel's seventieth Week" [Dan. 9:27].)

4 And the sword shall come upon Egypt, and great pain shall be in Ethiopia, when the slain shall fall in Egypt, and they shall take away her multitude, and her foundations shall be broken down.

5 Ethiopia, and Libya, and Lydia, and all

the mingled people, and Chub, and the men of the land that is in league, shall fall with them by the sword. *(These two Verses have to do with the opening of the "second seal" in the coming Great Tribulation, when power will be given to the Antichrist to "take peace from the Earth" [Rev. 6:4]. Even though the Tribulation will be worldwide, its greatest concentration will be, according to the Bible, in the area around the Mediterranean and Northern Africa.)*

6 Thus saith the LORD; They also who uphold Egypt shall fall; and the pride of her power shall come: down from the tower of Syene shall they fall in it by the sword, saith the Lord GOD. *(The description furnished in this Passage pertains to "one end of Egypt to the other.")*

7 And they shall be desolate in the midst of the countries that are desolate, and her cities shall be in the midst of the cities that are wasted. *(The desolation that is referred to in this Verse will have its fulfillment in the "third seal." There it says, "Come and see. And I beheld, and lo a black horse; and he who sat on him had a pair of balances in his hand" [Rev. 6:5]. This speaks of terrible famine, resulting in terrible desolation, which will grip Egypt when that nation is destroyed by the Antichrist.)*

8 And they shall know that I am the LORD, when I have set a fire in Egypt, and when all her helpers shall be destroyed. *(Even though the Antichrist will attack Egypt, making his bid for world dominion, of which Egypt will be the first, still, the Lord is the One setting the parameters for the Antichrist, and actually for all else.)*

9 In that day shall messengers go forth from Me in ships to make the careless Ethiopians afraid, and great pain shall come upon them, as in the day of Egypt: for lo, it comes. *(The phrase, "For lo, it comes," proclaims the certitude of the Prophecies. There is no way that man can avoid it, but with one exception! I speak of the Rapture of the Church [I Thess. 4:13-18; 5:9].)*

IMMEDIATE JUDGMENT BY BABYLON

10 Thus saith the Lord GOD; I will also make the multitude of Egypt to cease by the hand of Nebuchadnezzar king of Babylon. *(As is often done with Bible Prophecy, the thrust of direction will automatically change, and without warning [Isa. 61:1-3; Lk. 4:18-19]. Now, the Holy Spirit through the Prophet is speaking of the soon-to-come destruction of Egypt by Nebuchadnezzar.)*

11 He and his people with him, the terrible of the nations, shall be brought to destroy the land: and they shall draw their swords against Egypt, and fill the land with the slain. *(The phrase, "The terrible of the nations," refers to the power of the Babylonians as those who were to execute the Divine Judgments.)*

12 And I will make the rivers dry, and sell the land into the hand of the wicked: and I will make the land waste, and all who are therein, by the hand of strangers: I the LORD have spoken it.

13 Thus saith the Lord GOD; I will also destroy the idols, and I will cause their images to cease out of Noph; and there shall be no more a prince of the land of Egypt: and I will put a fear in the land of Egypt. *("Noph" was the Greek Memphis, the capital of lower Egypt and the chief center of the worship of the god "Phthah." These were destroyed by the invading Babylonians.*

The phrase, "And there shall be no more a prince of the land of Egypt," had an immediate fulfillment, for from the days of the Persians through Roman rule, which lasted for about 1,500 years, the kings of Egypt were not Egyptians by race. Due to their subjugation and subsequent decline, thus always being under the hand of conquerors, there was a perpetual "fear in the land of Egypt.")

14 And I will make Pathros desolate, and will set fire in Zoan, and will execute judgments in No. *(These were all major cities in Egypt; each was the location of concentrated idol worship.)*

15 And I will pour My fury upon Sin, the strength of Egypt; and I will cut off the multitude of No. *("Sin" was a major Egyptian city in the Egyptian Delta. It stood on the eastern branch of the Nile, surrounded by swamps, and its position made it, in modern terminology, the "key" of Egypt. Ezekiel, describing it as "the strength of Egypt," proclaims its strategic location.*

"No" was another major Egyptian city, situated on the Tanitic branch of the Nile Delta. It was the sacred name of the Egyptian Thebes.)

16 And I will set fire in Egypt: Sin shall have great pain, and No shall be rent asunder, and Noph shall have distresses daily. *(The Babylonians were so sure of their victory that they gave little respect to Egyptian defenses, as prophesied by Ezekiel.)*

17 The young men of Aven and of Pi-beseth shall fall by the sword: and these cities shall go into captivity. *(These two cities, "Aven" and "Pi-beseth," are Heliopolis and Bubastis, where*

a famous temple to the Sun was situated. Bubastis was located on what is now the Suez Canal; it derived its name from the cat-headed goddess "Pasht"; it was the chief seat of the gnome which was named after it.

Special judgments seemed to be tendered toward these cities steeped in heathenistic idolatry!)

18 At Tehaphnehes also the day shall be darkened, when I shall break there the yokes of Egypt: and the pomp of her strength shall cease in her: as for her, a cloud shall cover her, and her daughters shall go into captivity. ("Tehaphnehes" was the "Tehaphnehes" of Jer. 43:7. It was located on the Syrian frontier of Egypt. The phrase, "When I shall break there the yokes of Egypt," pertains to the oppressive rule imposed by Egypt on other nations. The phrase, "As for her, a cloud shall cover her," addresses itself to the predictions given by the Lord concerning her becoming "a base kingdom" [29:14].

The phrase concerning her "daughters" has reference not only to the women being led into captivity, but also to her idols, i.e., "daughters," which were taken by Nebuchadnezzar to Babylon, where he would have ensconced them in the temple of the god Bel.)

19 Thus will I execute judgments in Egypt: and they shall know that I am the LORD. (The phrase, "And they shall know that I am the LORD," is used repeatedly by the Holy Spirit through Ezekiel. The statement is made in order to counter the boastful, prideful, arrogant attitudes of not only Egypt, but every other nation, as well!)

GOD WILL BREAK THE ARMS
OF PHARAOH

20 And it came to pass in the eleventh year, in the first month, in the seventh day of the month, that the word of the LORD came unto me, saying (This was about three months before the destruction of Jerusalem [II Ki. 25:2-3]. As well, it was about 16 years before Nebuchadnezzar invaded Egypt. Verses 20 through 26 seem to have been written at about the time of the abortive attempt of Pharaoh-Hophra to come to the relief of Jerusalem),

21 Son of man, I have broken the arm of Pharaoh king of Egypt; and, lo, it shall not be bound up to be healed, to put a roller to bind it, to make it strong to hold the sword. (This Verse pertains to the destruction of Egypt by Nebuchadnezzar, and it never rising again as a world power.)

22 Therefore thus saith the Lord GOD; Behold, I am against Pharaoh king of Egypt, and will break his arms, the strong, and that which was broken; and I will cause the sword to fall out of his hand. (The phrase, "And will break his arms," actually has reference to two distinct engagements. The first arm was broken at Carchemish by Nebuchadnezzar, as prophesied by Jeremiah [46:2]. The other arm also was broken by Nebuchadnezzar when he invaded Egypt a few years later.)

23 And I will scatter the Egyptians among the nations, and will disperse them through the countries. (This, Nebuchadnezzar did!)

24 And I will strengthen the arms of the king of Babylon, and put My sword in his hand: but I will break Pharaoh's arms, and he shall groan before him with the groanings of a deadly wounded man.

25 But I will strengthen the arms of the king of Babylon, and the arms of Pharaoh shall fall down; and they shall know that I am the LORD, when I shall put my sword into the hand of the king of Babylon, and he shall stretch it out upon the land of Egypt. (The facts were: the Lord would "strengthen" the "king of Babylon," while He would "weaken" the "arms of Pharaoh." As a result, his arms would "fall down.")

26 And I will scatter the Egyptians among the nations, and disperse them among the countries; and they shall know that I am the LORD. (After the scattering, they will see that they have been fighting against God. So the Prophet ends this Chapter with the ever-recurring formula, "they shall know that I am the LORD.")

CHAPTER 31
(588 B.C.)

PROPHECIES AGAINST PHARAOH

AND it came to pass in the eleventh year, in the third month, in the first day of the month, that the word of the LORD came unto me, saying (this Chapter was written about two or three months before the fall of Jerusalem. It deals with the ruin of two mighty empires, Egypt and Assyria [the latter had fallen years before], and their banishment to eternal Hell. The language is striking, and leaves nothing to the imagination),

2 Son of man, speak unto Pharaoh king of Egypt, and to his multitude; Whom are you like in your greatness? (The question, "Whom are you like in your greatness?", is speaking of Sardana-Palus, the last king of Assyria, who was

conquered by Nebuchadnezzar. Possibly, Pha-
raoh looked up to this now dead despot; how-
ever, his end will be as his, defeated and lost!)

3 Behold, the Assyrian was a cedar in Lebanon with fair branches, and with a shadowing
shroud, and of an high stature; and his top was
among the thick boughs. *(The Prophet likens*
empires to great trees, and their kings to the
highest branches. The Prophecy penetrates the
world of the dead, and reveals the disembodied
spirits of deceased kings as no longer royal per-
sonages, but members of the general multitude
of the dead and the damned. Thus, this Chapter
is one of the few which unveils the mysterious
spirit world.)

4 The waters made him great, the deep set
him up on high with her rivers running round
about his plants, and sent out her little rivers
unto all the trees of the field. *(The waters, the*
deep, and the rivers pictured the nations that
contributed to the wealth of the empire; and
the trees of the fields symbolized the subordi-
nate kings. Such is portrayed to proclaim the
splendor of the Assyrian kingdom, and how it
was thought to be impossible to be brought to
destruction.)

5 Therefore his height was exalted above
all the trees of the field, and his boughs were
multiplied, and his branches became long because of the multitude of waters, when he
shot forth. *(The "exaltation" was enjoyed be-*
cause of the supremacy of the Assyrian empire;
however, this supremacy was gained by brute
terror and force.)

6 All the fowls of Heaven made their nest
in his boughs, and under his branches did all
the beasts of the field bring forth their young,
and under his shadow dwelt all great nations.
(The phrase, "And under his shadow dwelt all
great nations," imposes the fact that much of
the riches and greatness of the Assyrian empire
was derived from heavy taxation levied on those
subjugated nations.)

7 Thus was he fair in his greatness, in the
length of his branches: for his root was by
great waters. *(The Holy Spirit uses the word*
"greatness" in describing the Assyrian empire,
but yet it was a "greatness" in the eyes of man,
and not God.)

8 The cedars in the Garden of God could
not hide him: the fir trees were not like his
boughs, and the chestnut trees were not like
his branches; nor any tree in the Garden of
God was like unto him in his beauty. *(The*
phrase, "In the Garden of God," represents the

Sovereignty of the Lord over these nations, even
though they did not know Him, nor even recog-
nize Him, but were rather idol worshippers.)

9 I have made him fair by the multitude of
his branches: so that all the trees of Eden, that
were in the Garden of God, envied him. *(The*
phrase, "Envied him," not only pertains to Pha-
raoh, but also to the other nations of the world.
Tragically, even Israel, the Northern Kingdom,
which was supposed to be the people of God, and
consequently looking to Jehovah, instead "en-
vied him," i.e., "Assyria.")

10 Therefore thus saith the Lord GOD; Because you have lifted up yourself in height,
and he has shot up his top among the thick
boughs, and his heart is lifted up in his height
(the phrase, "Because you have lifted up yourself
in height," reveals the reason for the destruction
of Assyria. It was great pride!);

11 I have therefore delivered him into the
hand of the mighty one of the heathen; he shall
surely deal with him: I have driven him out
for his wickedness. *("The mighty one of the*
heathen" refers to Nebuchadnezzar, who would
subjugate the mighty Assyrian empire, because
the Lord deemed it necessary.)

12 And strangers, the terrible of the nations,
have cut him off, and have left him: upon the
mountains and in all the valleys his branches
are fallen, and his boughs are broken by all the
rivers of the land; and all the people of the
Earth are gone down from his shadow, and have
left him. *(The idea of the Holy Spirit is to im-*
press upon Pharaoh the cause of the destruction
upon the proud empire of the Assyrians, and that
the Egyptians were facing the same ruin, because
they were traveling in the same wicked direction.)

13 Upon his ruin shall the fowls of the
Heaven remain, and all the beasts of the field
shall be upon his branches. *(The idea of this*
Verse is that once this tree stood tall and proud,
but now it is no more, and the vultures and
jackals hover and creep over the carcass of the
dead, decaying trunk.)

14 To the end that none of all the trees by
the waters exalt themselves for their height,
neither shoot up their top among the thick
boughs, neither their trees stand up in their
height, all that drink water: for they are all
delivered unto death, to the nether parts of
the Earth, in the midst of the children of men,
with them who go down to the pit. *(The*
phraseology in this Verse suggests that Hell [or
Sheol] is situated in the center of the Earth. In
that "pit," the greatest monarchs rank with the

disembodied spirits of the generality of men. The mightiest and the greatest are "in the midst of the children of men, with them who go down to the pit."

What a warning to the whole of humanity! But, it is largely ignored!)

15 Thus saith the Lord GOD; In the day when he went down to the grave I caused a mourning: I covered the deep for him, and I restrained the floods thereof, and the great waters were stayed: and I caused Lebanon to mourn for him, and all the trees of the field fainted for him. *(The phrase, "In the day when he went down to the grave," does not refer to the burying of a body in a grave, as the word is commonly used, but rather refers to "Sheol." This is the place of departed spirits who are in Hell, and who have full consciousness. Jesus said so [Lk. 16:19-31].)*

16 I made the nations to shake at the sound of his fall, when I cast him down to Hell with them who descend into the pit: and all the trees of Eden, the choice and best of Lebanon, all who drink water, shall be comforted in the nether parts of the Earth. *(The phrase, "When I cast him down to Hell with them who descend into the pit," pertains to the Lord casting the last king of the Assyrian empire, Sardana-Palus, down into Sheol, i.e., Hell.*

The phrase, "Shall be comforted in the nether parts of the Earth," refers to the mighty empire and nations, already fallen and in Hell. They are "comforted" with the thought that yet another kingdom mightier than they has fallen as they fell.)

17 They also went down into Hell with him unto them that be slain with the sword; and they who were his arm, who dwelt under his shadow in the midst of the heathen. *(Sadly and regrettably, almost all of mankind has died eternally lost, which means they went to Hell. Jesus said so [Mat. 7:13-15].)*

18 To whom are you thus like in glory and in greatness among the trees of Eden? yet shall you be brought down with the trees of Eden unto the nether parts of the Earth: you shall lie in the midst of the uncircumcised with them that be slain by the sword. This is Pharaoh and all his multitude, saith the Lord GOD. *(The question, "To whom are you. . . ?" is repeated as it was given in Verse 2. The answer here is that Pharaoh was only comparable to ordinary monarchs, and that his death would be without honor. And so it fell out, for he was strangled. So the Prophet exclaims, pointing to him: "This is Pharaoh.")*

CHAPTER 32
(587 B.C.)
A LAMENTATION OVER PHARAOH

AND it came to pass in the twelfth year, in the twelfth month, in the first day of the month, that the Word of the LORD came unto me, saying *(this Prophecy was uttered over a year after the destruction of Jerusalem),*

2 Son of man, take up a lamentation for Pharaoh king of Egypt, and say unto him, You are like a young lion of the nations, and you are as a whale in the seas: and you came forth with your rivers, and troubled the waters with your feet, and fouled their rivers. *(The first Prophecy of this Chapter [Vss. 1-16] links the Divine Judgments on Egypt at the time of the Exodus [Vss. 6-7] with those about to be executed, and with the future Judgments of the Antichrist and his kingdom, of which Pharaoh and Egypt are symbols.)*

THE SWORD OF BABYLON WILL FALL ON EGYPT; JUDGMENT

3 Thus saith the Lord GOD; I will therefore spread out My net over you with a company of many people; and they shall bring you up in My net. *(It is an apt illustration, "My net," signifying the Babylonians appointed by the Lord to take Egypt down, which they did.)*

4 Then will I leave you upon the land, I will cast you forth upon the open field, and will cause all the fowls of the Heaven to remain upon you, and I will fill the beasts of the whole Earth with you.

5 And I will lay your flesh upon the mountains, and fill the valleys with your height. *(As Pharaoh surveyed his troops, and no doubt admired their supposed power, he little realized that their destiny had already been decided, and that those of which he thought so highly would soon be rotting corpses.)*

6 I will also water with your blood the land wherein you swim, even to the mountains; and the rivers shall be full of you. *(The Nile Valley is formed by the Eastern and Western Mountains. As the waters were turned into blood in the days of Moses, so the land would be drenched with blood in the days of Nebuchadnezzar.)*

7 And when I shall put you out, I will cover the Heaven, and make the stars thereof dark; I will cover the sun with a cloud, and the moon shall not give her light. *(This Verse leads back to the plague of darkness that gripped Egypt*

during the time of Moses [Ex. 10:21]. Then it was literal; now it is poetical, and intending the overthrow of the imperial and executive governments. As such, their light would go out and they would be no more.)

8 All the bright lights of Heaven will I make dark over you, and set darkness upon your land, saith the Lord GOD. *(This Verse, although obscure and little thought of [as its surrounding Passages], has to do greatly with the rise and fall of nations. The degree of their Judgment has to do with the Light once given, and rejected.)*

9 I will also vex the hearts of many people, when I shall bring your destruction among the nations, into the countries which you have not known. *(The idea is: concerning the "vexing of hearts," if Egypt could not stand against the mighty Babylonians, where did that leave smaller and weaker nations?)*

10 Yea, I will make many people amazed at you, and their kings shall be horribly afraid for you, when I shall brandish my sword before them; and they shall tremble at every moment, every man for his own life, in the day of your fall. *(The idea of this Verse proclaims the helplessness of those who have boasted of their invincibility, hence, "tremble at every moment." Men can easily boast of their power, but when God begins to make His Power felt, the mighty efforts of even the strongest men quickly are shown to be insignificant.)*

11 For thus saith the Lord GOD; The sword of the king of Babylon shall come upon you. *(Very plainly, the Prophet proclaims the coming destruction of Egypt by the Babylonians, and even several years before it actually happened, but with no favorable response from Pharaoh. Pharaoh did not believe Jehovah, so why should he believe His Prophet?)*

12 By the swords of the mighty will I cause your multitude to fall, the terrible of the nations, all of them: and they shall spoil the pomp of Egypt, and all the multitude thereof shall be destroyed. *(The phrase, "And they shall spoil the pomp of Egypt," refers to Egypt's pride, which was boasting itself through Pharaoh-Hophra; however, this "pomp" would be destroyed, as he was strangled to death by his own men.)*

13 I will destroy also all the beasts thereof from beside the great waters; neither shall the foot of man trouble them any more, nor the hoofs of beasts trouble them. *(The phrase, "The foot of man," pertained to individuals who peddled an apparatus designed to lift water from the Nile in order to irrigate the land. The invasion by Nebuchadnezzar would cause the cattle to be killed or taken as a war prize, with all irrigation stopped, which means the crops would be nonexistent that year.)*

14 Then will I make their waters deep, and cause their rivers to run like oil, saith the Lord GOD.

15 When I shall make the land of Egypt desolate, and the country shall be destitute of that whereof it was full, when I shall smite all them who dwell therein, then shall they know that I am the LORD. *(The idea is: the heathen did not believe the Prophecies, the Prophets, or Jehovah Who sent them; however, their unbelief would have no effect whatsoever on the carrying out of these Prophecies. They would know that Jehovah was "Lord GOD," in contrast to their gods, which had no power against the Most High.)*

16 This is the lamentation wherewith they shall lament her: the daughters of the nations shall lament her: they shall lament for her, even for Egypt, and for all her multitude, saith the Lord GOD. *(In the minds of these heathen, the contest was always between gods. Therefore, before the fact, the idea of Jehovah, Who had already suffered defeat by the Babylonians [at least in their thinking], being stronger than their gods was laughable. And then, when the destruction came, their "lamentation" was great, not only for the destruction of Egypt, but for the testing of her gods by Jehovah, which put them in jeopardy, as well!)*

EGYPT WILL JOIN OTHER NATIONS IN HELL

17 It came to pass also in the twelfth year, in the fifteenth day of the month, that the word of the LORD came unto me, saying *(these Passages are some of the few which permit a momentary glance into the dreadful mystery of the spirit world)*,

18 Son of man, wail for the multitude of Egypt, and cast them down, even her, and the daughters of the famous nations, unto the nether parts of the Earth, with them who go down into the pit. *(The phrases, "Nether parts of the Earth" and "The pit," refer to "Hell." This, as stated, is in the center of the Earth.*

The loss of their nation was dreadful to say the least, but the loss of their souls even worse! Hence the Holy Spirit records this fact.)

19 Whom do you pass in beauty? go down,

and be thou laid with the uncircumcised. *(The words, "uncircumcised," occurs some ten times in this Prophecy. It expresses non-relationship to God and corresponds to the modern word "unconverted.")*

20 They shall fall in the midst of them who are slain by the sword: she is delivered to the sword: draw her and all her multitudes. *(The phrase, "Slain by the sword," is repeated twelve times in this Prophecy. It signifies Divine Judgment.)*

21 The strong among the mighty shall speak to him out of the midst of Hell with them who help him: they are gone down, they lie uncircumcised, slain by the sword. *(The "strong" refers to the other Pharaohs and other mighty kings, such as the Assyrians, who had already gone to Hell and would "speak to him," i.e., Pharaoh. That which they will speak will not be words of encouragement, respect, or appreciation, but instead words of scorn.)*

22 Asshur is there and all her company: his graves are about him: all of them slain, fallen by the sword *(the word, "graves," at least in this instance, refers to the tomb or sepulcher, the place of the body, not the place of the soul. It merely means that they died, with the next Verses telling the eternal abode of their souls and spirit)*:

23 Whose graves are set in the sides of the pit, and her company is round about her grave: all of them slain, fallen by the sword, which caused terror in the land of the living. *(The idea is: the mightiest of the mighty on Earth, when in Hell, will have no more sway or influence that the lowliest of the low.)*

24 There is Elam and all her multitude round about her grave, all of them slain, fallen by the sword, which are gone down uncircumcised into the nether parts of the Earth, which caused their terror in the land of the living; yet have they borne their shame with them who go down to the pit. *(The phrase, "Their shame," refers to the fact that on Earth they were robed with honor, while in Sheol, they are "clothed with shame.")*

25 They have set her a bed in the midst of the slain with all her multitude: her graves are round about him: all of them uncircumcised, slain by the sword: though their terror was caused in the land of the living, yet have they borne their shame with them who go down to the pit: he is put in the midst of them that be slain. *(The pronoun "they" refers to Assyria and Elam. The pronoun "her" refers to

Egypt; the pronoun "him" refers to Pharaoh.)*

26 There is Meshech, Tubal, and all her multitude: her graves are found about him: all of them uncircumcised, slain by the sword, though they caused their terror in the land of the living. *(The pronoun "him" refers once again to Pharaoh. He is in the midst of these other fallen and slain: "Meshech, Tubal," and the others mentioned.)*

27 And they shall not lie with the mighty who are fallen of the uncircumcised, which are gone down to Hell with their weapons of war: and they have laid their swords under their heads, but their iniquities shall be upon their bones, though they were the terror of the mighty in the land of the living. *(The idea of the Verse is that "Meshech" and "Tubal" have a lower place in Hell, if such is possible. The phrase, "Which are gone down to Hell with their weapons of war," does not mean that such items are taken down to Hell with the lost soul, but that there was no honor at all in their death, and they were buried without the honor of war. In other words, their swords were not placed beneath their heads at the burial.)*

28 Yea, you shall be broken in the midst of the uncircumcised, and shall lie with them that are slain with the sword.

29 There is Edom, her kings, and all her princes, which with their might are laid by them who were slain by the sword: they shall lie with the uncircumcised, and with them who go down to the pit. *(The phrase, "There is Edom," is used by the Holy Spirit as an exclamation! It is said in this manner because the exultation which the Edomites had shown over the fall of Jerusalem [Ps. 137:7] had exacerbated their already perilous spiritual condition. As such, this would guarantee their destruction.)*

30 There be the princes of the north, all of them, and all the Zidonians, which are gone down with the slain; with their terror they are ashamed of their might; and they lie uncircumcised with them that be slain by the sword, and bear their shame with them who go down to the pit. *(Inasmuch as the Holy Spirit through the Prophet names the "Zidonians" and the "princes of the north," it suggests the direction of Northern Syria, including cities like Damascus, Hamath, Arpad, and others. These too went to Hell!)*

31 Pharaoh shall see them, and shall be comforted over all his multitude, even Pharaoh and all his army slain by the sword, saith the Lord GOD. *(As other nations were glad that*

Pharaoh would join them in Hell and likewise share their misery, now Pharaoh is glad to see others come to share his misery. All are sharers alike in the fiend-like temper which exults in the miseries of others.)

32 For I have caused my terror in the land of the living: and he shall be laid in the midst of the uncircumcised with them that are slain with the sword, even Pharaoh and all his multitude, saith the Lord GOD. *(The election of Nebuchadnezzar as God's "sword" and "terror" is one of the great facts of Scripture. The sword humbled Egypt, in whom Israel trusted. It also humbled all the neighboring nations, and thus destroyed many snares which entrapped the sons of Israel. All these judgments reached forward to a future day, and will be followed by the establishment in Grace of the redeemed nations in union with the New Israel [Isa. Chpt. 19], so forming the one flock of Jn. 10:16 in the Shepherd-care of the Messiah.)*

CHAPTER 33
(587 B.C.)
THE WATCHMAN'S DUTIES

AGAIN the Word of the LORD came unto me, saying,

2 Son of man, speak to the children of your people, and say unto them, When I bring the sword upon a land, if the people of the land take a man of their coasts, and set him for their watchman *(a great part of this Chapter will deal with the Ministry of the "watchman," to which Ezekiel is appointed by the Lord. In 24:15-27, the Prophet had been committed to silence, at least regarding Israel, but is now permitted to resume his ministry to the Exiles):*

3 If when he sees the sword come upon the land, he blow the trumpet, and warn the people *(the responsibility of the "watchman" is to correctly "see" and "warn." He was to "warn" by "blowing the trumpet." The modern Preacher is to do the same thing by correctly preaching the True Gospel [I Cor. 1:17]);*

4 Then whosoever hears the sound of the trumpet, and takes not warning; if the sword come, and take him away, his blood shall be upon his own head. *(If one is to notice, there is a demand by the Holy Spirit that the people be allowed to "hear" that which is Truth. What they do with it is then "upon his own head.")*

5 He heard the sound of the trumpet, and took not warning; his blood shall be upon him. But he who takes warning shall deliver his

soul. *(The opportunity to accept or reject is demanded by the Holy Spirit. Therefore, it is incumbent upon the True Preacher of the Gospel to blow a certain and sure sound. The responsibility is then with the hearer. If he "takes not warning," the loss of his soul will be his own responsibility.)*

6 But if the watchman see the sword come, and blow not the trumpet, and the people be not warned; if the sword come, and take any person from among them, he is taken away in his iniquity; but his blood will I require at the watchman's hand. *(Two types of warnings are given in this Passage: the "warning" that should be given to the people by faithful watchmen; and the "warning" that should be given by the Holy Spirit to unfaithful watchmen.)*

7 So thou, O son of man, I have set you a watchman unto the House of Israel; therefore you shall hear the word at My mouth, and warn them from Me. *(The commission of Ezekiel is once again enjoined. He is called, "O son of man," which is the same designation that will be given to "The Son of Man," the Lord Jesus Christ [Mat. 13:37; Lk. 9:44, 56].)*

8 When I say unto the wicked, O wicked man, you shall surely die; if you do not speak to warn the wicked from his way, that wicked man shall die in his iniquity; but his blood will I require at your hand. *(This Chapter is similar in many ways and to a great degree to Chapter 3. The repetition, due to the extreme seriousness of the matter, is by design.)*

9 Nevertheless, if you warn the wicked of his way to turn from it; if he do not turn from his way, he shall die in his iniquity; but you have delivered your soul. *(The True Preacher is not responsible for the response of the individual to the Message, but the True Preacher most definitely is responsible that the right Message be delivered.)*

GOD'S DEALINGS ARE JUST

10 Therefore, O thou son of man, speak unto the House of Israel; Thus you speak, saying, If our transgressions and our sins be upon us, and we pine away in them, how should we then live? *(This Scripture addressed itself to the scorn, incredulity, and derision heaped upon the Prophet, when he told of the coming judgment. The people trusted in the promises of the false prophets [13:6]. Now they stand face-to-face with the fulfillment of the Prophet's words. The question, "How should we then live?",*

proclaims the hopelessness of the people, inasmuch as they now realize the seriousness of their sin.)

11 Say unto them, As I live, saith the Lord GOD, I have no pleasure in the death of the wicked; but that the wicked turn from his way and live: turn ye, turn ye from your evil ways; for why will you die, O House of Israel? *(This is a plea for Repentance, without which these individuals will be lost!)*

12 Therefore, thou son of man, say unto the children of your people, The righteousness of the righteous shall not deliver him in the day of his transgression: as for the wickedness of the wicked, he shall not fall thereby in the day that he turns from his wickedness; neither shall the righteous be able to live for his righteousness in the day that he sins. *(This Passage and many others are a plain and clear rebuke to those who teach the unscriptural doctrine of unconditional eternal security. If the Believer turns from his righteousness and begins to live a life of sinning, and refuses to repent, he will die lost. Conversely, if the wicked individual quits his wickedness by turning to the Lord, his wickedness will not be remembered against him.)*

13 When I shall say to the righteous, that he shall surely live; if he trust to his own righteousness, and commit iniquity, all his righteousnesses shall not be remembered; but for his iniquity that he has committed, he shall die for it. *(The idea of this Verse is: if an individual thinks he can trust his past righteousness to save him when he has committed sin and continues therein, refusing to repent, his past "righteousness shall not be remembered." Again, this completely refutes the unscriptural doctrine of unconditional eternal security.)*

14 Again, when I say unto the wicked, You shall surely die; if he turn from his sin, and do that which is lawful and right;

15 If the wicked restore the pledge, give again that he had robbed, walk in the statutes of life, without committing iniquity; he shall surely live, he shall not die. *(The phrase, "Give again that he had robbed," illustrates the power of the new life in Christ to fulfill the requirements of the Moral Law as it was evidenced in the conversion of Zacchaeus [Lk. 19:1-10].)*

16 None of his sins that he has committed shall be mentioned unto him: he has done that which is lawful and right; he shall surely live. *(The first part of this Verse constitutes Justification by Faith. These sins are not mentioned any more because in the Mind of God they*

do not exist and in fact they have never existed.

The phrase, "He shall surely live," constitutes Salvation, i.e., "the born again experience," which negates spiritual death [Jn. 3:3]. This constitutes the greatest thing that can happen to any human heart and life.)

17 Yet the children of your people say, The way of the Lord is not equal: but as for them, their way is not equal. *(Israel, as most, was claiming that their righteousness and unrighteousness should be balanced one against the other. They construed the Ways of the Lord as unequal, inasmuch as He did not judge in that manner. In fact, it was not God's Ways which were unequal, but their ways.*

Even in the practical application of life, that which they were contending, the balancing of one against the other, does not hold true. For instance, if a man lives 1,000 days without taking poison and then on the 1,001 day takes poison, all the previous days free of poison will not assuage the results.)

18 When the righteous turns from his righteousness, and commits iniquity; he shall even die thereby. *(The Holy Spirit is emphatic in that the present condition is what counts with God; it is also that which should count with man.)*

19 But if the wicked turn from his wickedness, and do that which is lawful and right, he shall live thereby. *(As well, the Lord judges the "wicked" exactly as He does the "righteous," all according to their present status. If the wicked man repents, the Lord will instantly save, wiping out all past wickedness.)*

20 Yet you say, The way of the Lord is not equal. O ye House of Israel, I will judge you every one after his ways. *(Perfect love beams in Verse 11; perfect justice, in Verse 20. The judgment is just, equal, fair, and right in that "every one is judged after his ways," which shows no partiality.)*

THE NEWS OF JERUSALEM'S FALL

21 And it came to pass in the twelfth year of our captivity, in the tenth month, in the fifth day of the month, that one who had escaped out of Jerusalem came unto Me saying, The city is smitten. *(The phrase, "The city is smitten," even though said by the messenger [whoever he was], is given as a sob by the Holy Spirit. How so unnecessary this was! But yet, it was done only after the Lord had exhausted every means to bring the people to Repentance, but to no avail!)*

22 Now the hand of the LORD was upon me in the evening, afore he that was escaped came; and had opened my mouth, until he came to me in the morning; and my mouth was opened, and I was no more dumb. *(The phrase, "And my mouth was opened, and I was no more dumb," refers back to 24:26-27. It is not exactly known how long he was not permitted to prophesy regarding Judah. But now he is to prophesy again.)*

PROPHECY TO THE REMNANT; THEIR SINS AND JUDGMENT

23 Then the word of the LORD came unto me, saying,

24 Son of man, they who inhabit those wastes of the land of Israel speak, saying, Abraham was one, and he inherited the land: but we are many; the land is given us for inheritance. *(The argument of this ungodly remnant was that if a mighty nation was born of one man, Abraham, how much more powerful a nation could spring out of the many sons of Abraham who had been left in Judah by the Babylonian king! In fact, the faith that said, "the land is given us for inheritance," was a proud and carnal faith and would not be honored by God. Judgment upon their iniquities, not blessings snatched by presumption, would be the result of their carnal and ungodly thinking.)*

25 Wherefore say unto them, Thus saith the Lord GOD; You eat with the blood, and lift up your eyes toward your idols, and shed blood: and shall you possess the land? *(To "eat with the blood" violated Lev. 19:26 and was done in honor of an idol. Consequently, this was a double sin against the Law. Though they claimed to be children of Abraham [therefore, Children of God], they were idolatrous, self-confident, violent, and impure.)*

26 You stand upon your sword, you work abomination, and you defile every one his neighbour's wife: and shall you possess the land? *(The Holy Spirit through the Prophet, even though many hundreds of miles away from destroyed Judah, still, speaks the same thing as the Prophet Jeremiah had prophesied. Despite the judgment, this "remnant" in Judah continued to be idol worshippers, rebels against God, and dependent upon their own feeble military preparation; this actually bordered on idiocy, inasmuch as they were a defeated people.)*

27 Say thou thus unto them, Thus saith the Lord GOD; As I live, surely they who are in the wastes shall fall by the sword, and him who is in the open field will I give to the beasts to be devoured, and they who be in the forts and in the caves shall die of the pestilence. *(Concerning the ungodly remnant in Judah, Ezekiel prophesies, exactly as Jeremiah had prophesied, that there was no escape for them from the judging Hand of God, and rightly so, because of their rebellion.)*

28 For I will lay the land most desolate, and the pomp of her strength shall cease; and the mountains of Israel shall be desolate, that none shall pass through. *(Concerning Judah, the phrase, "And the pomp of her strength shall cease," was brought to pass in stark reality, undeniable by all!)*

29 Then shall they know that I am the LORD, when I have laid the land most desolate because of all their abominations which they have committed. *(At any time along the way, if Repentance had been engaged for these "abominations," they would have been instantly forgiven and put away, with Mercy and Grace extended. Inasmuch as there was no Repentance, their sins, i.e., "abominations," brought about the desolation, as such will bring about desolation in any nation, heart, or life!)*

EZEKIEL WILL BE VINDICATED

30 Also, thou son of man, the children of your people still are talking against you by the walls and in the doors of the houses, and speak one to another, every one to his brother, saying, Come, I pray you, and hear what is the word that comes forth from the LORD. *(It seems that the word "against" would have been better translated "of." If so, it would mean that the Exiles were proud of their Prophet Ezekiel, admiring his preaching and crowding to hear him, but did not for a moment intend any change of conduct. Similar features present themselves today in the professing Christian Church.)*

31 And they come unto you as the people comes, and they sit before you as My people, and they hear your words, but they will not do them: for with their mouth they show much love, but their heart goes after their covetousness. *(The words, "As My People," mean "professing to be My People." The phrase, "Their covetousness," refers to money-getting and all forms of self-pleasing. The phrase, "They show much love," means that they profess love, but in truth have no love of God, or for God.)*

32 And, lo, you are unto them as a very lovely song of one who has a pleasant voice,

and can play well on an instrument, for they hear your words, but they do them not. *(The phrase, "A very lovely song," refers to the people coming to hear the Prophet as they would to hear a hired singer at a banquet. The Prophet's words passed over them and left no lasting impression.)*

33 And when this comes to pass, (lo, it will come,) then shall they know that a Prophet has been among them. *(The Revelation of the rebellious corruption of the listeners' hearts saved the Prophet from the self-complacent corruption of his own heart, which his popularity as a Preacher would naturally excite.*

The phrase, "And when this comes to pass," refers back to Verses 10 through 20 and demands Repentance. It means that unless they repent, they will "surely die." The Holy Spirit emphasizes the statement by saying, "lo, it will come," meaning the time of eternal destiny.

When this time would come, they would "know that a Prophet has been among them," and that they had been listening, not to a hireling singer, but to a Prophet of Jehovah.)

CHAPTER 34
(587 B.C.)
PROPHECY AGAINST THE SHEPHERDS (LEADERS) OF ISRAEL; THEIR SINS

AND the Word of the LORD came unto me, saying,

2 Son of man, prophesy against the shepherds of Israel, prophesy, and say unto them, Thus saith the Lord GOD unto the shepherds; Woe be to the shepherds of Israel who do feed themselves! should not the shepherds feed the flocks? *("Shepherds" in this Chapter refer to rulers, more specifically, the four last kings of Judah; however, the general meaning definitely includes spiritual leaders of any stripe.)*

3 You eat the fat, and you clothe yourself with the wool, you kill them that are fed: but you feed not the flock. *(The only motive of these false shepherds is to get, instead of to give.)*

4 The diseased have you not strengthened, neither have you healed that which was sick, neither have you bound up that which was broken, neither have you brought again that which was driven away, neither have you sought that which was lost; but with force and with cruelty have you ruled them. *(The "diseased" refers to weak sheep, while the "sick" refers to those who are suffering from more definite maladies. The "broken" are those which have fallen from a rock, or from some such precipice and thus, maimed*

themselves. *Each case required the appropriate treatment.*

As well, the fourfold "neither" should be noticed. The idea is: the Holy Spirit notes each particular need and the required care for that need by true shepherds, which these were not!)

5 And they were scattered, because there is no shepherd, and they became meat to all the beasts of the field, when they were scattered. *(They had no true shepherd to protect them [Mat. 9:36].)*

6 My sheep wandered through all the mountains, and upon every high hill: yea, My flock was scattered upon all the face of the Earth, and none did search or seek after them. *(Of the Northern Kingdom of Israel, not a single shepherd, i.e., king, was Godly. Thankfully, several in Judah were Godly, but the last four, as stated, were anything but Godly. These four were: Jehoahaz, Jehoiakim, Jehoiachin, and Zedekiah.)*

THEIR JUDGMENT

7 Therefore, you shepherds, hear the word of the LORD *(Ezekiel had been told to "hear the Word at My Mouth and warn them from Me" [33:7], and now that warning will come, as delivered faithfully by the Prophet)*;

8 As I live, saith the Lord GOD, surely because My flock became a prey, and My flock became meat to every beast of the field, because there was no shepherd, neither did My shepherds search for My flock, but the shepherds fed themselves, and fed not My flock *(the phrase, "As I live, saith the Lord GOD," is strong indeed! It is actually an oath taken by the Lord that the shepherds would be destroyed, inasmuch as they destroyed the sheep. The modern "money gospel" fits this description!)*;

9 Therefore, O ye shepherds, hear the word of the LORD;

10 Thus saith the Lord GOD; Behold, I am against the shepherds; and I will require My flock at their hand, and cause them to cease from feeding the flock; neither shall the shepherds feed themselves any more; for I will deliver My flock from their mouth, that they may not be meat for them. *(This will not come to pass until the coming Kingdom Age, when Israel will finally accept the Great Shepherd, the Lord Jesus Christ [Zech. 13:1].)*

RESTORATION OF THE FLOCK

11 For thus saith the Lord GOD; Behold, I,

even I, will both search My sheep, and seek them out. *(The action, the love, and the unselfishness of the True Shepherd are set out in Verses 11 through 16.)*

12 As a shepherd seeks out his flock in the day that he is among his sheep that are scattered; so will I seek out My sheep, and will deliver them out of all places where they have been scattered in the cloudy and dark day. *(The "cloudy and dark day" refers to the coming Great Tribulation, when Israel will come close to annihilation. Zechariah said that two-thirds of the people will be destroyed [Zech. 13:8].)*

13 And I will bring them out from the people, and gather them from the countries, and will bring them to their own land, and feed them upon the mountains of Israel by the rivers, and in all the inhabited places of the country. *(The phrase, "To their own land," refers to the country promised to Abraham, Isaac, and Jacob; and this is to be theirs forever — the Land of Israel.)*

14 I will feed them in a good pasture, and upon the high mountains of Israel shall their fold be: there shall they lie in a good fold, and in a fat pasture shall they feed upon the mountains of Israel. *(The repetition given in Verses 13 and 14 is done by design. The Holy Spirit seeks to bring out the truth of sincerity, peace, satisfaction, fulfillment, and acceptance. All this is finally done because of a right relationship with Christ. This will take place, as stated, during the coming Kingdom Age.)*

15 I will feed My flock, and I will cause them to lie down, saith the Lord GOD. *(The phrase, "I will feed My flock," refers to the tender care of the Shepherd watching with an individualizing care over each sheep that has been brought back. Every broken limb will be bound up. Every sickness will be treated with its appropriate means of healing.*

The phrase, "And I will cause them to lie down," refers to total serenity, peace, safety, protection, dependence, trust, and reliance upon the Lord, the Great Shepherd.)

16 I will seek that which was lost, and bring again that which was driven away, and will bind up that which was broken, and will strengthen that which was sick: but I will destroy the fat and the strong; I will feed them with judgment. *(In this Verse, "The fat and the strong" are contrasted with the "broken" and the "sick." The idea is this: When He comes, the Great Shepherd, the Lord Jesus Christ, will "destroy the fat and the strong," which refers to*

the nations of the world which threw in their lot with the Antichrist, attempting to destroy Israel. They will "be fed with judgment," and given no more place and position regarding supremacy.)*

THE LORD'S CARE FOR HIS FLOCK; FALSE LEADERS SEPARATED FROM THE FLOCK

17 And as for you, O My flock, thus saith the Lord GOD; Behold, I judge between cattle and cattle, between the rams and the he goats. *(This Passage actually has to do with the judgment of the nations, which will take place immediately after the Second Coming of Christ [Mat. 25:31-33].)*

18 Does it seem a small thing unto you to have eaten up the good pasture, but you must tread down with your feet the residue of your pastures? and to have drunk of the deep waters, but you must foul the residue with your feet? *(This pertains to the nations of the world which, during the time of the Great Tribulation, tried to harm Israel.)*

19 And as for My flock, they eat that which you have trodden with your feet; and they drink that which you have fouled with your feet. *(In other words, the Jews, at least in the minds of many, were looked at like refuse.)*

20 Therefore thus saith the Lord GOD unto them; Behold, I, even I, will judge between the fat cattle and between the lean cattle. *(At the beginning of the Kingdom Age, the Lord will judge all nations, and the judgment will be according to how they treated Israel.)*

21 Because you have thrust with side and with shoulder, and pushed all the diseased with your horns, till you have scattered them abroad *(whether nations which lorded it over the Jews, or even the false shepherds of Israel, all will answer!);*

22 Therefore will I save My flock, and they shall no more be a prey; and I will judge between cattle and cattle. *(The phrase, "Between cattle and cattle," probably would have been better translated, "between sheep and sheep."*

In the coming Kingdom Age, and after Israel has accepted Christ, they will no longer be at the mercy of the world, as they in fact have been for so many centuries.)

RESTORATION; DAVIDIC KINGDOM SET UP

23 And I will set up one shepherd over them, and he shall feed them, even My servant David;

he shall feed them, and he shall be their shepherd. *(The Hebrew Text reads, "A Shepherd, One," that is, One Preeminent and Unique Shepherd — the Only One of His Kind, to Whom none other is comparable. The word "David" here means "The Beloved One," i.e., the True David, the Messiah [Isa. 55:3-4; Jer. 30:9; Hos. 3:5].*

However, as it refers to the "Son of David," it also refers to "David," the same David who was chosen by God and anointed by Samuel. He will rule Israel under Christ!)

24 And I the LORD will be their God, and My servant David a prince among them; I the LORD have spoken it. *(The phrase, "And My servant David a prince among them," fulfills the Promise made to David by the Lord, as recorded in II Sam. 7:8-29.)*

25 And I will make with them a covenant of peace, and will cause the evil beasts to cease out of the land: and they shall dwell safely in the wilderness, and sleep in the woods. *(The phrase, "And I will make with them a covenant of peace," will be carried out, and can be carried out, because of Israel's acceptance of Christ.*

The phrase, "And will cause the evil beast to cease out of the land," is a euphemism referring to demon spirits as "beasts.")

26 And I will make them and the places round about My hill a blessing; and I will cause the shower to come down in his season; there shall be showers of blessing. *(The phrase, "There shall be showers of blessing," first of all refers to spiritual blessings which will generate economic, physical, and domestic blessings, as well!)*

27 And the tree of the field shall yield her fruit, and the Earth shall yield her increase, and they shall be safe in their land, and shall know that I am the LORD, when I have broken the bands of their yoke, and delivered them out of the hand of those who served themselves of them. *(There are two particulars that are noted in this Scripture: the first is, "fruit, increase, and safety"; the second is, "broken bands and deliverance." The former is the result of the latter.)*

28 And they shall no more be a prey to the heathen, neither shall the beast of the land devour them; but they shall dwell safely, and none shall make them afraid. *(At long last, Israel will be what the Lord intended all along. As stated, it will be during the coming Kingdom Age!)*

29 And I will raise up for them a plant of renown, and they shall be no more consumed with hunger in the land, neither bear the shame of the heathen any more. *(The "Plant of Renown" is none other than Jesus Christ, Whom they rejected, but will now accept. That "Plant" will be so rich with nourishment that they who feed upon it shall be no more pinched with hunger, and their happy condition will secure Renown for the Plant and not for themselves. However, in securing it for "Him," they, at the same time, will secure it for themselves.)*

30 Thus shall they know that I the LORD their God am with them, and that they, even the House of Israel are My people, saith the Lord GOD. *(Even though they are the people of God, still, they forsook the Lord; consequently, He has not been with them, except from afar, for some 2,000 years. Now, upon their acceptance of Him, the Lord Jesus Christ, this "Plant of Renown," this "Branch" [Isa. 4:2; 11:1; Jer. 23:5; 33:15], they will know that He is "with them." Then the Lord can truly say of them, "They are My People.")*

31 And you My flock, the flock of My pasture, are men, and I am your God, saith the Lord GOD. *(The idea of this Verse is that even though the word "sheep" was used as a metaphor, still, the Lord is speaking of "men," and not merely just "sheep." But there is here also a deeper meaning. Helpless, sinful "men" could never do such marvels, only the God Who is Adonai-Jehovah.)*

CHAPTER 35
(587 B.C.)

PROPHECY AGAINST MOUNT SEIR (EDOM): JUDGMENT

MOREOVER the Word of the LORD came unto me, saying,

2 Son of man, set your face against Mount Seir, and prophesy against it *(this Prophecy concerns Edom; therefore, it leaves the glorious future and returns to the destitute present. One of the great reasons for God's Anger against Edom is this country's hatred of Israel, which was not only regarded as personal, but was also expressive of man's enmity against the people of God in every age)*,

3 And say unto it, Thus saith the Lord GOD; Behold, O Mount Seir, I am against you, and I will stretch out My hand against you, and I will make you most desolate. *(To have one nation pitted against another nation is one thing, but to have God pitted against a nation is something else altogether!)*

4 I will lay your cities waste, and you shall be desolate, and you shall know that I am the LORD. *(Ezekiel formerly prophesied against Edom [25:12-14], but that Prophecy was several years before the fall of Jerusalem. This Prophecy is after the fall of the city and concerns itself with Edom's disposition at that time, along with their previous sins against God's People.)*

5 Because you have had a perpetual hatred, and have shed the blood of the Children of Israel by the force of the sword in the time of their calamity, in the time that their iniquity had an end *(Edom had been Israel's hereditary foe from the days of Esau and Jacob [Gen. 25:22; 27:37]; however, that which brought all of this to a head was that Edom rejoiced at the fall of Jerusalem, and they actually helped the Babylonians to kill Israelites. When they did that, they crossed the line!)*:

6 Therefore, as I live, saith the Lord GOD, I will prepare you unto blood, and blood shall pursue you: since you have not hated blood, even blood shall pursue you. *(In that Edom did not "hate" or detest the shedding of the "blood" of the people of Judah and Jerusalem, the Holy Spirit emphasizes the fact that "blood" would be their destiny — their blood.)*

7 Thus will I make Mount Seir most desolate, and cut off from it him who passes out and him who returns. *(The Lord decides here the controversy between Edom and Israel. To the one He adjudges perpetual desolation; to the other, ever-enduring prosperity. This is the last message to Esau, so to speak!)*

8 And I will fill his mountains with his slain men: in your hills, and in your valleys, and in all your rivers, shall they fall who are slain with the sword. *(Some may take exception to the terminology given here. However, no one would fault a surgeon for removing a malignancy. Likewise, no one should fault the Lord for doing the same!)*

9 I will make you perpetual desolations, and your cities shall not return: and you shall know that I am the LORD. *(The use of the phrase, "You shall know that I am the LORD," means that Edom would note, to her sorrow, Jehovah's power to punish.)*

10 Because you have said, These two nations and these two countries shall be mine, and we will possess it; whereas the LORD was there *(the words, "two nations," refer to Ephraim, the Northern Kingdom, and Judah, the Southern Kingdom. Edom coveted this Land. She would have done much better to have coveted*

any land in the world except this Land. The Palestinians and the Arabs should read this Passage, as well!):

11 Therefore, as I live, saith the Lord GOD, I will even do according to your anger, and according to your envy which you have used out of your hatred against them; and I will make Myself known among them, when I have judged you. *(The phrase, "When I have judged you," sums up the Verse. The suffering which people desire for others sometimes falls upon themselves. Far from Edom securing Israel, she would ultimately be deprived of her own land, and would in fact perish forever as a nation.)*

12 And you shall know that I am the LORD, and that I have heard all your blasphemies which you have spoken against the mountains of Israel, saying, They are laid desolate, they are given us to consume. *(To persecute those who are God's is to persecute God. Likewise, to slander one of God's is to slander God.)*

13 Thus with your mouth you have boasted against Me, and have multiplied your words against Me: I have heard them. *(These Passages should be a solemn lesson to all! "Bitter words against God's People are accounted by God as spoken against Himself." The phrase is emphatic, "I have heard them.")*

14 Thus saith the Lord GOD; When the whole Earth rejoices, I will make you desolate. *(The idea is: when the sons of the Kingdom enter into joy, their haters shall descend into the gloom.)*

15 As you did rejoice at the inheritance of the House of Israel, because it was desolate, so will I do unto you: you shall be desolate, O Mount Seir, and all Idumea, even all of it: and they shall know that I am the LORD. *(The phrase, "You shall be desolate, O Mount Seir," sums up the Verse. That's exactly what happened!)*

CHAPTER 36
(587 B.C.)
GOD WILL JUDGE ISRAEL'S ENEMIES

ALSO, thou son of man, prophesy unto the mountains of Israel, and say, You mountains of Israel, hear the Word of the LORD *(this Prophecy is divided into two parts, with Verses 1 through 15 connecting with the previous Chapter, and the second part beginning with Verse 16 and closing at 37:14. The subject of the first part is Israel's restoration)*:

2 Thus saith the Lord GOD; Because the enemy has said against you, Aha, even the ancient high places are ours in possession *(this*

"enemy" was Edom):

3 Therefore prophesy and say, Thus saith the Lord GOD; Because they have made you desolate, and swallowed you up on every side, that you might be a possession unto the residue of the heathen, and you are taken up in the lips of talkers, and are an infamy of the people *(the sense of Verse 3 is that the heathen charged Jehovah with inability to protect His Land):*

THE FUTURE RESTORATION OF ISRAEL

4 Therefore, you mountains of Israel, hear the word of the Lord GOD; Thus saith the Lord GOD to the mountains, and to the hills, to the rivers, and to the valleys, to the desolate wastes, and to the cities that are forsaken, which became a prey and derision to the residue of the heathen who are round about *(God chastens His People, as this Verse proclaims, but destroys their enemies);*

5 Therefore thus saith the Lord GOD; Surely in the fire of My jealousy have I spoken against the residue of the heathen, and against all Idumea, which have appointed My land into their possession with the joy of all their heart, with despiteful minds, to cast it out for a prey. *(Edom not only proposed to take "My Land," but to do so with a "gleeful joy," and with "despiteful minds," i.e., "with contempt of soul," meaning that Edom held Judah and Judah's God Jehovah in contempt.)*

6 Prophesy therefore concerning the land of Israel, and say unto the mountains, and to the hills, to the rivers, and to the valleys, Thus saith the Lord GOD; Behold, I have spoken in My jealousy and in My fury, because you have borne the shame of the heathen *(the key to this Verse is the phrase, "You have borne the shame of the heathen," which means that the shame of God's People is temporary, while that of their enemies is perpetual. The Law of Retribution is demanded by the absolute Righteousness of God. The judicial visitations of God cannot possibly be one-sided. That which has been meted out to Israel for their sin will be meted out to Edom, as well as all other opposing nations):*

7 Therefore thus saith the Lord GOD; I have lifted up My hand, Surely the heathen who are about you, they shall bear their shame. *(The certitude is found in the phrase, "I have lifted up My hand," which refers to God taking an oath that what He has stated about the heathen and their punishment will come to pass.)*

8 But ye, O mountains of Israel, you shall shoot forth your branches, and yield your fruit to My people of Israel; for they are at hand to come. *(The phrases, "O mountains of Israel" and "The everlasting hills" of Gen. 49:26, are terms expressive of the moral elevation of Israel over the physical elevation of Edom.)*

9 For, behold, I am for you, and I will turn unto you, and you shall be tilled and sown *(as the Lord said that He was "against Edom" [35:3], He, conversely, says of Israel, "I am for you"):*

10 And I will multiply men upon you, all the House of Israel, even all of it: and the cities shall be inhabited, and the wastes shall be built *(as the Lord outlined the destruction of Edom and other nations, He here outlines the coming blessing and prosperity of "the House of Israel"):*

11 And I will multiply upon you man and beast; and they shall increase and bring fruit: and I will settle you after your old estates, and will do better unto you than at your beginnings: and you shall know that I am the LORD. *(This pertains to the coming Kingdom Age.)*

12 Yea, I will cause men to walk upon you, even My people Israel; and they shall possess you, and you shall be their inheritance, and you shall no more henceforth bereave them of men. *(Edom said they would possess the Land. They are indicative of the modern Palestinians. The Lord says, "My people Israel shall possess you," i.e., the Land.)*

13 Thus saith the Lord GOD; Because they say unto you, Your land devours up men, and has bereaved your nations *(concerning Israel, the heathen spread the evil report that the Land of Israel had devoured its inhabitants and was, therefore, cursed!):*

14 Therefore you shall devour men no more, neither bereave your nations any more, saith the Lord GOD. *(The idea of the Verse is this: the great spiritual conflict between light and darkness has brought about the terrible contest for the Land of Israel, which began immediately upon its inception, and which has continued throughout its history.*

Upon the return of Christ, the cause of this conflict will be removed; hence, it will "devour men no more, neither bereave the nations.")

15 Neither will I cause men to hear in you the shame of the heathen any more, neither shall you bear the reproach of the people any more, neither shall you cause your nations to fall any more, saith the Lord GOD. *(This was not fulfilled, not even in the slightest, upon the return of the Exiles from their bondage, but will*

be fulfilled totally in the coming Kingdom Age.)

ISRAEL'S PAST SINS AND JUDGMENTS

16 Moreover the word of the LORD came unto me, saying,

17 Son of man, when the House of Israel dwelt in their own land, they defiled it by their own way and by their doings: their way was before Me as the uncleanness of a removed woman. *(The "uncleanness" pictures the vileness of the sinner in God's sight. The first statement of Verse 29 declares the ability of the Saviour to fully cleanse the sinner.*

The phrase, "As the uncleanness of a removed woman," refers to a woman's monthly period, and was used as an example of Israel's uncleanness.)

18 Wherefore I poured My fury upon them for the blood that they had shed upon the land, and for their idols wherewith they had polluted it *(this Verse proclaims that the idol worshipped produced the shedding of blood and the offering up of little children in human sacrifices. Because of this, the anger of the Lord knew no bounds):*

19 And I scattered them among the heathen, and they were dispersed through the countries: according to their way and according to their doings I judged them. *(This not only concerned Ezekiel's day, but also concerned itself with A.D. 70, when Titus destroyed Jerusalem. This was done because they had shed "the Blood of Christ.")*

20 And when they entered unto the heathen, whither they went, they profaned My holy name, when they said to them, These are the people of the LORD, and are gone forth out of His land. *(The phrase, "These are the people of the LORD," is the key phrase to this Verse. Their being defeated caused the heathen to conclude that Jehovah had either behaved capriciously toward His People and cast them off, or had proved unequal to the task of protecting them. In either case, the honor of Jehovah had been lessened in the mind and tarnished by the words of the heathen. This had been brought about by Israel's sin.)*

21 But I had pity for My holy name, which the House of Israel had profaned among the heathen, whither they went. *(The idea is: the Lord will restore Israel, but not because of any good in them, but because of good in Himself.)*

THE RE-GATHERING AND RESTORATION OF ISRAEL

22 Therefore say unto the House of Israel, thus saith the Lord GOD; I do not this for your sakes, O House of Israel, but for My holy name's sake, which you have profaned among the heathen, whither you went. *(This Scripture further reinforces the statement regarding Verse 21, in that the Lord is not doing what He is doing for Israel's sake, but instead "for His Holy Name's sake.")*

23 And I will sanctify My great name, which was profaned among the heathen, which you have profaned in the midst of them; and the heathen shall know that I am the LORD, saith the Lord GOD, when I shall be sanctified in you before their eyes. *(God's acts of Grace toward guilty men — solely because of His Name as Saviour and not because of any moral excellence in them — are shown in Verses 21 through 23 and 32. The sinner's only claim for Life and Righteousness is the admitting of his sinfulness and not his righteousness, of which he has none.)*

24 For I will take you from among the heathen, and gather you out of all countries, and will bring you into your own land. *(This Passage was not fulfilled when the Children of Israel came back from Babylonian captivity, and has not even been fulfilled as of yet! It will be fulfilled immediately after the Second Coming of Christ.)*

25 Then will I sprinkle clean water upon you, and you shall be clean: from all your filthiness, and from all your idols, will I cleanse you. *(The word "then" marks the time for the fulfillment of these Prophecies. Israel, as a nation, will not be won to Christ until the Antichrist is defeated by the Second Coming of Christ. Israel "then" will accept Christ as Saviour, Lord, and Messiah.)*

26 A new heart also will I give you, and a new spirit will I put within you: and I will take away the stony heart out of your flesh, and I will give you an heart of flesh. *(This speaks of the New Birth, and totally refutes the claims of those who say that modern Israel will not be restored, and that they have no part or parcel in the Gospel program, presently or in the future.)*

27 And I will put My Spirit within you, and cause you to walk in My statutes, and you shall keep My judgments, and do them. *(The phrase, "And I will put My Spirit within you," refers both to regeneration, as carried out by the Holy Spirit at the time of one being Born-Again, and also to the Baptism with the Holy Spirit, which was first evidenced on the Day of Pentecost [Acts 2:1-4]. The entrance of the Holy Spirit is made possible solely by the Cross of Christ [Jn. 14:17],*

and the "Statutes" and "Judgments" fall into the same category. In other words, one can keep those only by and through the Power of the Holy Spirit, Who works exclusively within the framework of the Finished Work of Christ, which demands the constant Faith of the Believer [Rom. 6:3-5; 8:1-2, 11; Lk. 9:23-24].)

28 And you shall dwell in the land that I gave to your fathers; and you shall be My people, and I will be your God. (The conflict regarding the Land of Israel will be solved only when Christ comes back. All hinges on Christ, as all always hinges on Christ.)

29 I will also save you from all your uncleannesses: and I will call for the corn, and will increase it, and lay no famine upon you. (Regeneration, not reformation – a new heart, and not a changed heart – is essential to Salvation.)

30 And I will multiply the fruit of the tree, and the increase of the field, that you shall receive no more reproach of famine among the heathen.

31 Then shall you remember your own evil ways, and your doings that were not good, and shall loathe yourselves in your own sight for your iniquities and for your abominations. (The effect of Grace is self-judgment, which will then make possible the Blessing of Verse 30.)

32 Not for your sakes do I this, saith the Lord GOD, be it known unto you: be ashamed and confounded for your own ways, O House of Israel. (All that is done for the Child of God is done "for Christ's sake" [Eph. 4:32; 1 Jn. 2:12].)

33 Thus saith the Lord GOD; In the day that I shall have cleansed you from all your iniquities I will also cause you to dwell in the cities, and the wastes shall be built. (Israel's conversion to Christ will precipitate their Blessing. Only when all iniquities have been "cleansed" can the individual then "dwell" in the inheritance, with the "wastes" then being reclaimed, i.e., "built.")

34 And the desolate land shall be tilled, whereas it lay desolate in the sight of all who passed by. (For nearly 2,000 years, the Land of Israel lay "desolate." This was the Promised Land, and yet there was little semblance of that which originally was. It is now beginning to be restored, but will not fully be made right until the Coming of the Lord.)

35 And they shall say, This land that was desolate is become like the Garden of Eden; and the waste and desolate and ruined cities are become fenced, and are inhabited. (Tyre and Assyria claimed to be like the Garden of Eden. But this similitude belongs only to Israel [Ezek. 28:13; 31:8-9; Isa. 51:3].)

36 Then the heathen who are left round about you shall know that I the LORD build the ruined places, and plant that that was desolate: I the LORD have spoken it, and I will do it. (All that the Lord says He will do in this Verse is predicated on Israel's acceptance of Him as Lord and Saviour.)

37 Thus saith the Lord GOD; I will yet for this be enquired of by the House of Israel, to do it for them; I will increase them with men like a flock. (The phrase, "I will yet for this be enquired of by the House of the Israel," refers to the coming Great Tribulation of the future, which will bring them to utter desolation and threatened annihilation, which will precipitate their crying to Him for Deliverance. This will bring Israel to a full Repentance and dependence upon God [Isa. Chpt. 64; Zech. 12:10; 13:1; Mat. 23:37-39; Rom. 11:25-29].)

38 As the holy flock, as the flock of Jerusalem in her solemn Feasts; so shall the waste cities be filled with flocks of men: and they shall know that I am the LORD. (The theme of these Chapters is the relationship between Jehovah and His People. Hence, there are no details given respecting the First Advent. The Chapters present a general picture of the Last Days, of the rebirth of Israel, and of her enjoyment of Earthly Glory and Blessing, which will take place in the coming Kingdom Age.)

CHAPTER 37

(587 B.C.)

VISION OF THE VALLEY OF DRY BONES

THE hand of the LORD was upon me, and carried me out in the Spirit of the LORD, and set me down in the midst of the valley which was full of bones (as the last Chapter graphically spoke of Israel's coming Restoration, Chapter 37 graphically portrays the spiritual manner of that Restoration),

2 And caused me to pass by them round about: and, behold, there were very many in the open valley; and, lo, they were very dry. (The repetition of "behold" fastens the attention upon the two facts — that the bones were very many and very dry. The phrase, "Very dry," speaks of a total absence of spirituality.)

3 And He said unto me, Son of man, can these bones live? And I answered, O Lord GOD, You know. (Ezekiel's answer to the question of the Lord, "O Lord GOD, You know,"

signifies that within the realm of human endeavor the task was impossible!)

PROPHECY AND THE RESULTS

4 Again He said unto me, Prophesy upon these bones, and say unto them, O ye dry bones, hear the word of the LORD. *(The Prophet is told to "Prophesy upon these bones," meaning that the Lord will give a "Word" which will guarantee their Restoration and Revival; however, such could only be done according to the "Word of the LORD.")*

5 Thus saith the Lord GOD unto these bones; Behold, I will cause breath to enter into you, and you shall live *(the "breath" spoken of is the same breath as when God "breathed into his nostrils the breath of life," respecting Adam, and he "became a living soul" [Gen. 2:7]. The life that is spoken of in this Passage is national life and spiritual life. National life of the nation has already begun, having its beginning in 1948 and continuing. However, spiritual life will begin in the coming Great Tribulation, when 144,000 Jews will accept Christ as their Saviour. But the fullness of Spiritual Life will not come until the Second Coming [Zech. 13:1, 9]):*

6 And I will lay sinews upon you, and will bring up flesh upon you, and cover you with skin, and put breath in you, and you shall live; and you shall know that I am the LORD. *("You shall live," i.e., "you shall come to life again, so shall you get to know that I am Jehovah." God demonstrates His Existence and Power by raising the dead [Jn. 5:21; Rom. 1:3; 4:17; II Cor. 1:9].)*

7 So I prophesied as I was commanded: and as I prophesied, there was a noise, and behold a shaking, and the bones came together, bone to his bone. *(The phrase, "There was a noise," in the Hebrew actually says, "a voice.")*

8 And when I beheld, lo, the sinews and the flesh came up upon them, and the skin covered them above: but there was no breath in them. *(As stated, national Israel began in 1948; however, the phrase, "But there was no breath in them," signifies the fact that national Israel presently has no spiritual life.)*

9 Then said He unto me, Prophesy unto the wind, prophesy, son of man, and say to the wind, Thus saith the Lord GOD; Come from the four winds, O breath, and breath upon these slain, that they may live. *(The phrase, "Prophesy unto the wind," actually says in the Hebrew, "Prophesy unto the Spirit." The phrase, "Come from the four winds," actually says in*

the Hebrew, *"Come from the four breaths." The number "four" is symbolic of "fourfold," denoting an absolute, total, and complete Restoration.)*

10 So I prophesied as He commanded me, and the breath came into them, and they lived, and stood up upon their feet, an exceeding great army. *(As the preceding Verses spoke of Israel's national identity, now this Verse speaks of Israel's spiritual identity, signifying their spiritual revival, which will take place at the Second Coming.*

The phrase, "And stood upon their feet," speaks of Spiritual Life enabling such. For a long time, even over 2,000 years, Israel has not "stood upon their feet" spiritually. But in that coming Glad Day, they shall! Then they shall be an "exceeding great army," but an "exceeding great army" for the Lord.)

THE WHOLE HOUSE OF ISRAEL
TO BE RE-GATHERED

11 Then He said unto me, Son of man, these bones are the whole House of Israel: behold, they say, Our bones are dried, and our hope is lost: we are cut off for our parts. *(The phrase, "The whole House of Israel," speaks of the entirety of the thirteen Tribes. The latter part of this Verse, "behold, they say," refers to the latter half of the coming Great Tribulation. At that time, it will look like the entirety of their nation will be totally destroyed, with "hope lost" and "cut off for our parts." This has reference to Zechariah's Prophecy, when he said, "two parts therein shall be cut off and die" [Zech. 13:8].)*

12 Therefore prophesy and say unto them, Thus saith the Lord GOD; Behold, O My people, I will open your graves, and cause you to come up out of your graves, and bring you into the land of Israel. *(As Prophecy sometimes does, the previous Verse spoke of the last few months or even weeks before the Coming of the Lord and, therefore, the relief of Israel, whereas this Verse goes back even to World War II and forward.)*

13 And you shall know that I am the LORD, when I have opened your graves, O My people, and brought you up out of your graves *(the phrase, "And brought you up out of your graves," has reference in totality to the fact that Israel, and for all practical purposes, in the Battle of Armageddon is all but totally destroyed; actually, there is no Earthly way they can be salvaged. However, there is a Heavenly Way! And that Heavenly Way is Christ),*

14 And shall put My Spirit in you, and you shall live, and I shall place you in your own land: then shall you know that I the LORD have spoken it, and performed it, saith the LORD. *(This Passage signals the great Revival that will take place in Israel at the Coming of the Lord. Zechariah gave in greater detail the happening of this great moving of the Holy Spirit [Zech. 12:10-14; 13:1, 9].)*

THE SIGN OF TWO STICKS: ISRAEL AND JUDAH REJOINED

15 The word of the LORD came again unto me, saying *(now begins the second Prophesy predicting the unity of the nation, and its happy settlement under the government of the Messiah),*

16 Moreover, thou son of man, take thee one stick, and write upon it, For Judah, and for the Children of Israel his companions: they take another stick, and write upon it, For Joseph, the stick of Ephraim and for all the House of Israel his companions *(the "two sticks" represent the two Houses of Israel, the Northern Confederation of Israel, sometimes called Ephraim or Samaria, and the Southern Kingdom known as Judah. The phrase, "His companions," refers to Benjamin and Levi, and also possibly Simeon, being joined with Judah. The other Tribes pertained to Ephraim):*

17 And join them one to another into one stick; and they shall become one in your hand. *(This Verse predicts that both Kingdoms will now become one Kingdom, signifying one people, which can only be brought about by the "Hand of the Lord," which means that they will never again be divided.)*

18 And when the children of your people shall speak unto you, saying, Will you not show us what you mean by these? *(This Prophecy, which incorporates the balance of the Chapter, predicts the future union of the Tribes, their Restoration to the Land of Israel, and their settlement there under One Shepherd, and teaches that a Divinely wrought union is real and enduring, and brings its subjects into fellowship with God, and disposes them around a Divine center.)*

RESTORATION OF ISRAEL AND JUDAH UNDER MESSIAH AND DAVID

19 Say unto them, Thus saith the Lord GOD; Behold, I will take the stick of Joseph, which is in the hand of Ephraim, and the Tribes of Israel his fellows, and will put them with him, even with the stick of Judah, and make them one stick, and they shall be one in My hand. *(When God takes groups of His servants and unites them, they actually become one in His Hand. This means that not only is the old division gone, but the cause of division has also been erased.)*

20 And the sticks whereon you write shall be in your hand before their eyes. *(It is amazing that the Lord would take something that simple, such as "sticks," to express and portray something of such vital consequence [I Cor. 1:27].)*

21 And say unto them, Thus saith the Lord GOD; Behold, I will take the Children of Israel from among the heathen, whither they be gone, and will gather them on every side, and bring them into their own land *(the total fulfillment of this will take place in the coming Kingdom Age):*

22 And I will make them one nation in the land upon the mountains of Israel; and one King shall be King to them all: and they shall be no more two nations, neither shall they be divided into two kingdoms any more at all. *(The phrase, "In the Land," refers to the Land of Israel, as promised to Abraham [Gen. 12:7]. Its boundary on the west is the Mediterranean; on the south, the Suez Canal, which includes the Arabian Peninsula; on the east, the Euphrates River; on the north, Lebanon.)*

23 Neither shall they defile themselves any more with their idols, nor with their detestable things, nor with any of their transgressions: but I will save them out of all their dwellingplaces, wherein they have sinned, and will cleanse them: so shall they be My people, and I will be their God. *(This will take place almost immediately after the Second Coming of Christ.)*

24 And David My servant shall be king over them; and they all shall have One Shepherd: they shall also walk in My Judgments, and observe My Statutes, and do them. *(David was ever looked at as the example for all the kings of Israel, and will consequently serve in this capacity under Christ forever.)*

25 And they shall dwell in the land that I have given unto Jacob My servant, wherein your fathers have dwelt; and they shall dwell therein, even they, and their children, and their children's children for ever: and My servant David shall be their prince for ever. *(This Passage goes back to the Messianic Promise of II Sam. 7:12-16. Some have concluded that the name "David" refers to the Messiah; however, the Holy*

Spirit uses the phrase, "My servant David," but never once is Christ called "My servant David." So it is obvious that King David is the one predicted here to be "their prince forever.")

A NEW AND EVERLASTING COVENANT

26 Moreover I will make a covenant of peace with them; it shall be an Everlasting Covenant with them: and I will place them, and multiply them, and will set My Sanctuary in the midst of them for evermore. *(The setting of the "Divine Sanctuary" in Jerusalem will cause the heathen to know that God has especially chosen Israel for His peculiar treasure. This Sanctuary is described in Chapters 40 through 48.)*

27 My Tabernacle also shall be with them: yea, I will be their God, and they shall be My people. *(This "Tabernacle" refers to an ozone type of covering, much greater than presently, which will be during the Millennium, when the light of the Sun will be increased sevenfold and the light of the moon will be as the present light of the Sun [Isa. 4:5].)*

28 And the heathen shall know that I the LORD do sanctify Israel, when My Sanctuary shall be in the midst of them for evermore. *(God's Presence with Israel is the sign that He is with them and that the world must, and in fact will, recognize this approval.)*

CHAPTER 38
(587 B.C.)
PROPHECY AGAINST GENTILE POWERS
AT ARMAGEDDON;
GOD TO BE REPULSED

AND the Word of the LORD came unto me, saying,

2 Son of man, set your face against Gog, the land of Magog, the chief prince of Meshech and Tubal, and prophesy against him *("Gog" is another name for the Antichrist),*

3 And say, Thus saith the Lord GOD; Behold, I am against you, O Gog, the chief prince of Meshech and Tubal *(for many years, Bible teachers have thought that these Passages referred to Russia, but a closer investigation of the statements prove otherwise; therefore, the phrase, "Behold, I am against you, O Gog," is not referring to Russia, but instead to the Antichrist):*

4 And I will turn you back, and put hooks into your jaws, and I will bring you forth, and all your army, horses and horsemen, all of them clothed with all sorts of armour, even a great company with bucklers and shields, all of them handling swords *(this Prophecy refers to the Battle of Armageddon, which will be the second invasion by the Antichrist of Israel, in which he will be totally destroyed. The first invasion will take place in the midst of the Great Tribulation, when the Antichrist will then show his true colors):*

5 Persia, Ethiopia, and Libya with them; all of them with shield and helmet:

6 Gomer, and all his bands; the house of Togarmah of the north quarters, and all his bands: and many people with you. *(These Passages merely reinforce the statements previously made, that the army of the Antichrist will consist of people from many countries, including Russia.)*

7 Be thou prepared, and prepare for yourself, you, and all your company that are assembled unto you, and be thou a guard unto them. *(The phrase, "Be thou prepared," merely refers to a taunt given by the Holy Spirit to the Antichrist. In other words, "Prepare yourself to the very best of your ability, and still it will avail you nothing, as you will be totally defeated.")*

GOG TO INVADE ISRAEL
IN THE LAST DAYS

8 After many days you shall be visited: in the latter years you shall come into the land that is brought back from the sword, and is gathered out of many people, against the mountains of Israel, which have been always waste: but it is brought forth out of the nations, and they shall dwell safely all of them. *(The two phrases, "After many days" and "In the latter years," refer to this present time and the immediate future; therefore, any claims that this Chapter has already been fulfilled are spurious.*

The phrase, "The land that is brought back from the sword," refers to the many conflicts Israel has had since becoming a nation in 1948.

The phrase, "And is gathered out of many people," refers to the various nations, such as Egypt, Syria, Iraq, etc., which did not desire Israel to become a nation, and which, therefore, greatly opposed her.

The phrase, "But it is brought forth out of the nations," pertains to the United Nations voting that Israel would become a State, with even Russia voting her approval.

The phrase, "And they shall dwell safely all of them," refers to the terrible horror of the Holocaust in World War II, with some 6,000,000

Jews being slaughtered by Hitler, and Israel then demanding a homeland instead of being scattered all over the world. Their feeling was that if this could be obtained, then they would be "safe.")

9 You shall ascend and come like a storm, you shall be like a cloud to cover the land, you, and all your bands, and many people with you. *(As stated, this is the Battle of Armageddon.)*

10 Thus saith the Lord GOD; It shall also come to pass, that at the same time shall things come into your mind, and you shall think an evil thought *(the "evil thought" will consist of the plans of the Antichrist, inspired of Satan, to destroy Israel and the Jews. That plan is the Battle of Armageddon!)*:

11 And you shall say, I will go up to the land of unwalled villages; I will go to them who are at rest, who dwell safely, all of them dwelling without walls, and having neither bars nor gates *(the phrases, "The land of unwalled villages," "Dwelling without walls," and "Having neither bars nor gates," refer to Israel's efforts at mobilization to be rather weak, at least in the mind of the Antichrist)*,

12 To take a spoil, and to take a prey; to turn your hand upon the desolate places that are now inhabited, and upon the people that are gathered out of the nations, which have gotten cattle and goods, who dwell in the midst of the land. *(This is the invasion of Israel by the Antichrist, called the "Battle of Armageddon," which will precipitate the Second Coming of the Lord.)*

13 Sheba, and Dedan, and the merchants of Tarshish, with all the young lions thereof, shall say unto you, Are you come to take a spoil? have you gathered your company to take a prey? to carry away silver and gold, to take away cattle and goods, to take a great spoil? *(The questions asked by these particular nations are not meant to proclaim an adversarial position; in fact, they will probably throw in their lot with the Antichrist, hoping to get a part of the "great spoil.")*

GOG'S ATTACK AGAINST GOD'S LAND

14 Therefore, son of man, prophesy and say unto Gog, Thus saith the Lord GOD; In that day when My people of Israel dwell safely, shall you not know it? *(The idea of this Verse is: despite the Antichrist invading Israel and defeating her at the midpoint of the Great Tribulation, thereby breaking his seven-year pact, still, due to him having pressing business elsewhere [Dan. 11:44], Israel will then filter back into*

the land, reoccupying it, and seemingly will dwell safely. This will no doubt infuriate the "man of sin," and he will set about to handle the situation once and for all!)

15 And you shall come from your place out of the north parts, you, and many people with you, all of them riding upon horses, a great company, and a mighty army *(the "north parts" do not refer to Russia, as some think, but rather to Syria. In fact, the Antichrist [Gog] will come from Syria; however, the Syria of Daniel's Prophecies, of which this speaks, included modern Syria, Iraq, and Iran)*:

16 And you shall come up against My people of Israel, as a cloud to cover the land; it shall be in the latter days, and I will bring you against My land, that the heathen may know Me, when I shall be sanctified in you, O Gog, before their eyes. *(The phrase, "In the latter days," refers to the last of the last days, which pertain to the present and near future. In other words, these Prophecies have already begun to come to pass, and, with each passing day, will accelerate their fulfillment.)*

MANY PROPHECIES TO BE FULFILLED

17 Thus saith the Lord GOD; Are you he of whom I have spoken in old time by My servants the Prophets of Israel, which prophesied in those days many years that I would bring you against them? *(The Lord is actually speaking here of the Prophecies given to Ezekiel, of which this is one, as well as those of Isaiah, Daniel, Zechariah, and others!)*

GOG TO BE DESTROYED AT
ARMAGEDDON

18 And it shall come to pass at the same time when Gog shall come against the land of Israel, saith the Lord GOD, that My fury shall come up in My face. *(Once again, this is the Battle of Armageddon. The phrase, "My fury shall come up in My Face," corresponds to the statement of Zechariah [Zech. 14:3].)*

19 For in My jealousy and in the fire of My wrath have I spoken, Surely in that day there shall be a great shaking in the land of Israel *(the "great shaking in the Land of Israel" can only transpire in the Battle of Armageddon, and only by the Hand of the Lord)*;

20 So that the fishes of the sea, and the fowls of the Heaven, and the beasts of the field, and all creeping things that creep upon the Earth,

and all the men who are upon the face of the Earth, shall shake at My presence, and the mountains shall be thrown down, and the steep places shall fall, and every wall shall fall to the ground. *(This Verse pertains to the Second Coming, which will be the most cataclysmic event in human history.)*

21 And I will call for a sword against him throughout all My mountains, saith the Lord GOD: every man's sword shall be against his brother. *(This portrays the fact that the Lord has control over all things!)*

22 And I will plead against him with pestilence and with blood; and I will rain upon him, and upon his bands, and upon the many people who are with him, an overflowing rain, and great hailstones, fire, and brimstone. *(This Verse proclaims the fact that the Lord will use the elements, over which neither the Antichrist nor any other man has any control.)*

23 Thus will I magnify Myself, and sanctify Myself; and I will be known in the eyes of many nations, and they shall know that I am the LORD. *(The phrase, "Thus will I magnify Myself," has reference to anger held in check for a long time, and then exploding with a fury that defies description.)*

CHAPTER 39
(587 B.C.)
THE PROPHECY AGAINST GOG: THE SLAUGHTER OF GOG'S ARMY

THEREFORE, thou son of man, prophesy against Gog, and say, Thus saith the Lord GOD; Behold, I am against you, O Gog, the chief prince of Meshech and Tubal *(this Chapter proclaims Gog's defeat by the Lord Jesus Christ. As stated, it is the Battle of Armageddon, as described in Rev. 16:16)*:

2 And I will turn you back, and leave but the sixth part of you, and will cause you to come up from the north parts, and will bring you upon the mountains of Israel *(five-sixths of the army of the Antichrist will be killed by the Second Coming of the Lord. The phrase, "And will cause you to come up from the north parts," does not, as previously stated, refer to Russia. It instead refers to the invasion route being the same as it was for the Assyrians, Babylonians, Grecians, and others in the past)*:

3 And I will smite your bow out of your left hand, and will cause your arrows to fall out of your right hand. *(The Antichrist, called "Gog," will think he is fighting Israel only, when,*

in Truth, he is fighting the Lord, a battle he cannot hope to win.)

4 You shall fall upon the mountains of Israel, you, and all your bands, and the people that is with you: I will give you unto the ravenous birds of every sort, and to the beasts of the field to be devoured. *(The idea is that the defeat of the Antichrist and his armies will be so severe that vultures and beasts will feed upon the multitudes of dead bodies littering the "mountains of Israel."*

The phrase, "You shall fall," signifies not only the defeat of the "man of sin," but also the collapse of corrupt human society, which includes corrupt human government.)

5 You shall fall upon the open field: for I have spoken it, saith the Lord GOD. *(The phrase, "Open field," refers to the time of the defeat of the Antichrist. It will be in the very midst of the Battle, with the Antichrist bearing down on Jerusalem, thinking that victory is within his grasp [Zech. 14:1-3].)*

6 And I will send a fire on Magog, and among them who dwell carelessly in the isles: and they shall know that I am the LORD. *(The phrase, "Send a fire on Magog," simply means that the Lord will personally use the elements of the heavens to destroy the vast Gentile armies following the Antichrist.*

The phrase, "And among them who dwell carelessly in the isles," pertains to other nations of the world, which, in their minds, are neutral and are simply turning a blind eye to this wholesale slaughter against Israel by the Antichrist.)

7 So will I make My Holy Name known in the midst of My people Israel; and I will not let them pollute My Holy Name any more: and the heathen shall know that I am the LORD, the Holy One in Israel. *(This Verse captures all the Promises made by the Lord to the Patriarchs and Prophets of old!)*

8 Behold, it is come, and it is done, saith the Lord GOD; this is the day whereof I have spoken. *(This Verse pertains to the coming Great Tribulation, and more especially to these events at the very conclusion of that particular time, including the Battle of Armageddon [Zech. 14:7].)*

9 And they who dwell in the cities of Israel shall go forth, and shall set on fire and burn the weapons, both the shields and the bucklers, the bows and the arrows, and the handstaves, and the spears, and they shall burn them with fire seven years *(to think of something being burned "with fire seven years"*

allows us to know the extent of the destruction):

10 So that they shall take no wood out of the field, neither cut down any out of the forests; for they shall burn the weapons with fire: and they shall spoil those who spoiled them, and rob those who robbed them, saith the Lord GOD.

SEVEN MONTHS TO BURY THE DEAD OF GOG'S ARMY AFTER ARMAGEDDON

11 And it shall come to pass in that day, that I will give unto Gog a place there of graves in Israel, the valley of the passengers on the east of the sea: and it shall stop the noses of the passengers: and there shall they bury Gog and all his multitude: and they shall call it The valley of Hamon-gog. *(No doubt, several millions of men are going to be killed in that which is known as "the Battle of Armageddon." Even employing modern equipment to hasten the burial of so many human bodies, still, the stench will "stop the noses of the passengers.")*

12 And seven months shall the House of Israel be burying of them, that they may cleanse the land.

13 Yea, all the people of the land shall bury them; and it shall be to them a renown the day that I shall be glorified, saith the Lord GOD. *(The Lord links this spectacle to the sanctifying of His Name.)*

14 And they shall sever out men of continual employment, passing through the land to bury with the passengers those who remain upon the face of the earth, to cleanse it: after the end of seven months shall they search. *(The Executive Government of Israel will employ and pay the men described in this Verse to collect the human bones, wherever found, and bury them in the huge trench or area of Verse 11. This project, as stated, will require seven months.)*

15 And the passengers who pass through the land, when any sees a man's bone, then shall he set up a sign by it, till the buriers have buried it in the valley of Hamon-gog. *(It seems that all the bones will be collected and taken to "the valley of Hamon-gog," and there buried. If this is the case, it will be done for a reason, the portraying of such as a monument to Satan's defeat, and the victory, even the great victory, of the Lord Jesus Christ.)*

16 And also the name of the city shall be Hamonah. Thus shall they cleanse the land. *(The name "Hamonah" means "multitude." No doubt, it will be a "city" of graves, housing the silent dead, and not a city of the living.)*

THE BIRDS AND ANIMALS GATHERED FOR A SACRIFICIAL FEAST

17 And, thou son of man, thus saith the Lord GOD; Speak unto every feathered fowl, and to every beast of the field, Assemble yourselves, and come; gather yourselves on every side to My sacrifice that I do sacrifice for you, even a great sacrifice upon the mountains of Israel, that you may eat flesh, and drink blood. *(This is the same command as Rev. 19:17-18, 20.)*

18 You shall eat the flesh of the mighty, and drink the blood of the princes of the Earth, of rams, of lambs, and of goats, of bullocks, all of them fatlings of Bashan. *(The words, "The mighty" and "princes," signify the military and political elite of the army of the Antichrist. As well, the "rams, lambs, goats, and bullocks" signify the same!)*

19 And you shall eat fat till you be full, and drink blood till you be drunken, of My sacrifice which I have sacrificed for you. *(The idea is that if they would not accept the Sacrifice of Christ at Calvary, then they would be made a sacrifice, which they were, but which would not save their souls, but would serve as a part of the salvation of the world.)*

20 Thus you shall be filled at My table with horses and chariots, with mighty men, and with all men of war, saith the Lord GOD. *(The Antichrist will think to set a "table" portraying the defeat of Israel, but instead he and his army will be the "table," i.e., "My table," i.e., the Table of the Lord.)*

THE PURPOSE OF GOD

21 And I will set My glory among the heathen, and all the heathen shall see My judgment that I have executed, and My hand that I have laid upon them. *(The Bible regards as "the heathen" all who do not accept the Lord Jesus Christ as their Saviour. Therefore, that includes almost all the world.)*

22 So the House of Israel shall know that I am the LORD their God from that day and forward. *(Along with "the heathen" seeing this glorious spectacle, likewise, "the House of Israel" will now "know" exactly Who the Messiah is. They will know that the One they rejected and crucified is actually "the LORD their God." They will know it "from that very day and forward.")*

23 And the heathen shall know that the House of Israel went into captivity for their iniquity: because they trespassed against Me, therefore hid I My face from them, and gave them into the hand of their enemies: so fell they all by the sword. *(The dispersions under the Assyrians and the Romans having been effected by the sword, as well as all who have been exiled through the centuries, and more particularly the terrible Holocaust of World War II, it can justly be stated: "they all fell by the sword."*

The phrase, "They trespassed against Me," refers to Israel's rebellion from the very beginning, which finally necessitated their destruction and dispersion; however, the crowning "trespass" of all was their rejection of Christ and His Crucifixion. As a result, they were given over "into the hand of their enemies," where they remained for nearly 2,000 years.)

24 According to their uncleanness and according to their transgressions have I done unto them, and hid My face from them. *(As they did not desire Him, He "hid His Face from them." This was all He could do! Regrettably, this scenario has not yet ended. Continuing to reject Him, Israel will instead accept "another" as their Messiah [Jn. 5:43]. This will happen in the very near future, and will bring Israel yet another Holocaust! [Mat. 24:21-22].*

However, and finally, Israel will come out of the darkness into the light, and will accept Christ as their Saviour and Messiah. The next Passages tell us how!)

ISRAEL TO BE RE-GATHERED AND CONVERTED

25 Therefore thus saith the Lord GOD; Now will I bring again the captivity of Jacob, and have mercy upon the whole House of Israel, and will be jealous for My Holy Name *(He will have "Mercy" because of their Repentance, which will take place at the Second Coming. The phrase, "And will be jealous for My Holy Name," is a fearsome statement. "His Holy Name" stands behind His Word. He is "Jealous" that His Honor be protected and that every single Prophecy be fulfilled);*

26 After that they have borne their shame, and all their trespasses whereby they have trespassed against Me, when they dwelt safely in their land, and none made them afraid. *(The idea of this and succeeding Verses is the explanation of the word "now" in the previous Verse. The "shame" resulting from the "trespasses" is*
now over. "Now" they can "dwell safely in their land, and none shall make them afraid.")*

27 When I have brought them again from the people, and gathered them out of their enemies' lands, and am sanctified in them in the sight of many nations *(this great gathering will take place after the Second Coming of Christ, and will include every Jew from every country in the world, who will be brought, and gladly, to Israel. The phrase, "And am sanctified in them in the sight of many nations," refers to His Plan for them finally being realized);*

28 Then shall they know that I am the LORD their God, which caused them to be led into captivity among the heathen: but I have gathered them unto their own land, and have left none of them any more there. *(So certain is the future Restoration of Israel that the past tense is used here in predicting it.)*

29 Neither will I hide My face any more from them: for I have poured out My Spirit upon the House of Israel, saith the Lord GOD. *(This Passage and many others emphatically state that Israel will never again go astray because of the "poured out Spirit of God" upon them. This Vision opens and closes with a valley of dry bones. The first Vision saw the resurrection of those bones [Chpt. 37]; in the second part of the Vision, nothing but bones will remain, signifying the catastrophic end of the armies of the Antichrist.*

So these two valleys contrast the one with the other — the one, a testimony to God's faithfulness and love; the other, to His fidelity and judgment.)

CHAPTER 40
(574 B.C.)

EZEKIEL'S VISION OF THE TEMPLE (THE MILLENNIAL SANCTUARY)

IN the five and twentieth year of our captivity, in the beginning of the year, in the tenth day of the month, in the fourteenth year after that the city was smitten, in the selfsame day the hand of the LORD was upon me, and brought me thither. *(The phrase, "In the five and twentieth year of our captivity," concerns itself with the first invasion of Jerusalem by Babylon, which occurred in 605 B.C. During this invasion, the city was partly destroyed and many of the people were carried away captive. The city was further devastated in 597 B.C. and finally burned and desolated in 586 B.C.)*

2 In the Visions of God brought He me into the land of Israel, and set me upon a very high

mountain, by which was as the frame of a city on the south. *(The events of Chapters 40 through 48 concern things in the Kingdom Age, when Christ will Personally rule from Jerusalem. This will immediately follow the Battle of Armageddon and the Second Coming of the Lord.)*

3 And He brought me thither, and, behold, there was a Man, Whose appearance was like the appearance of brass, with a line of flax in His hand, and a measuring reed; and He stood in the gate. *(If we compare the descriptions given in Ezek. 1:26-27, Dan. 10:6, and Rev. 1:15, the "Man Whose appearance was like the appearance of brass" is Christ. Personally, He will give the Prophet the information regarding the coming Glory and Grandeur of restored Jerusalem and the Temple.*

The phrase, "With a line of flax in His Hand, and a measuring reed," speaks of Righteousness.)

THE EASTERN WALL AND GATE

4 And the Man said unto me, Son of man, behold with your eyes, and hear with your ears, and set your heart upon all that I shall show you; for to the intent that I might show them unto you are you brought hither: declare all that you see to the House of Israel. *(The phrase, "Son of man, behold with your eyes, and hear with your ears," portrays the Truth that all given concerning dimensions, portrayals, and specifications have a spiritual reference, with all pertaining to Christ.*

The carnal heart will see little blessing in these tedious statements and measurements, and consequently will reap little! However, the spiritual heart will dig and probe that these nuggets of spiritual gold may be brought to the surface [Col. 2:3].)

5 And behold a wall on the outside of the house round about, and in the Man's hand a measuring reed of six cubits long by the cubit and an hand breadth: so He measured the breadth of the building, one reed; and the height, one reed. *(A "reed" represents nine feet. It is interesting that the Tabernacle had no wall, nor did the Temple, or at least no wall that was an essential part of the Sacred Structure. Here, however, the wall constitutes an integral portion of the whole, and was designed "to make a separation between the Sanctuary and the profane place." This "wall" encloses the square in which will stand the Sacred Palace.)*

6 Then came He unto the gate which looks toward the east, and went up the stairs thereof, and measured the threshold of the gate, which was one reed broad; and the other threshold of the gate, which was one reed broad. *(In the construction of these three Places of Worship, nothing is left to man's taste or imagination. Everything, even in the matter of measurements, was commanded by God, and, as stated, holds great spiritual meaning.*

For instance, the phrase, "And went up the stairs thereof," pertains to God's Plan of Salvation. Even though the number of steps is not given here, they are mentioned in Verses 22 and 26 concerning the Northern and Southern Gates as being "seven."

"Seven" is God's number, implying perfection, completion, and totality. Such is God's Salvation, afforded by Christ Jesus and offered freely to man.)

7 And every little chamber was one reed long, and one reed broad; and between the little chambers were five cubits; and the threshold of the gate by the porch of the gate within was one reed. *(These are actually guard-chambers intended for the Levite sentinels who stood guard over the House. It is not that guards are needed; they are for decorative purposes only! Nevertheless, the spiritual application is appropriate. The Child of God is ordered to "watch" and to "pray" [Mk. 13:33].)*

8 He measured also the porch of the gate within, one reed.

9 Then measured He the porch of the gate, eight cubits; and the posts thereof, two cubits; and the porch of the gate was inward. *(Christ is the One Who measures; as the Lord of Glory, He is Perfect in His design.)*

10 And the little chambers of the gate eastward were three on this side, and three on that side; they three were of one measure: and the posts had one measure on this side and on that side.

11 And He measured the breadth of the entry of the gate, ten cubits; and the length of the gate, thirteen cubits. *(This is the Eastern Gate to the Temple; it is nearly twenty feet high.)*

12 The space also before the little chambers was one cubit on this side, and the space was one cubit on that side: and the little chambers were six cubits on this side, and six cubits on that side. *(This area or "space" immediately before the "little chambers" most likely was to enable the guardsman, by stepping beyond his cell, to observe the happenings in the Gate without interrupting those coming and going. Spiritually speaking, what kind of guard do we have*

which observes what goes in and what comes out? Nothing should be allowed to enter that stains, corrupts, pollutes, or spoils.)

13 He measured then the gate from the roof of one little chamber to the roof of another: the breadth was five and twenty cubits, door against door. *(If the Guard Chambers are scrutinized this closely, as to measurement and direction, then the significance should not be lost upon us. To guard our mind, which is the doorway to our spirit, in order that defilement not enter, can be done only as the Believer places his Faith in Christ and what Christ has done for us at the Cross. In essence, Christ must not be separated from the Cross, and we speak of its benefits [Rom. 6:3-5; 8:1-2, 11; I Cor. 1:17-18, 23; 2:2; Gal. 6:14].)*

14 He made also posts of threescore cubits, even unto the post of the court round about the gate. *(These "posts" are ninety feet high, and are different than the little short posts mentioned in Verse 10. I think the Holy Spirit does not desire this "post" of ninety feet height to be contrasted with the little "post" of only three feet height [Vs. 9]. To serve in any capacity in the Kingdom of God is of utmost significance. As one is needed, the other is also needed!)*

15 And from the face of the gate of the entrance unto the face of the porch of the inner gate were fifty cubits. *(The "fifty cubits" are seventy-five feet. This comprised the whole length of the Eastern Gate, from the outer entrance to the inner exit.)*

16 And there were narrow windows to the little chambers, and to their posts within the gate round about, and likewise to the arches: and windows were round about inward: and upon each post were palm trees. *(Similar windows existed in the Temple of Solomon [I Ki. 6:4]. It is notable that the only type of trees mentioned as being a part of the decoration of the Millennial Temple is the "palm tree." This tree symbolizes "rest.")*

OUTER COURT

17 Then brought He me into the outward court, and, lo, there were chambers, and a pavement made for the court round about: thirty chambers were upon the pavement.

18 And the pavement by the side of the gates over against the length of the gates was the lower pavement.

19 Then He measured the breadth from the forefront of the lower gate unto the forefront of the inner court without, an hundred cubits eastward and northward. *(The Hebrew word for "pavement" suggests ornamental pavement. The pavement of the Outer Court was called "the lower pavement" to distinguish it from that laid in the Inner Court, which stood at a higher elevation.)*

THE NORTHERN GATE OF THE OUTER COURT

20 And the gate of the outward court that looked toward the north, He measured the length thereof, and the breadth thereof.

21 And the little chambers thereof were three on this side and three on that side; and the posts thereof and the arches thereof were after the measure of the first gate: the length thereof was fifty cubits, and the breadth five and twenty cubits.

22 And their windows, and their arches, and their palm trees, were after the measure of the gate that looks toward the east; and they went up unto it by seven steps; and the arches thereof were before them. *(There will be no West Gate, for the Messiah, when seated on His Throne within the Temple, will face the East; the worshippers will enter by the North and South Gates and stand before Him; behind Him will, perhaps, stand the Cherubims of Glory.*

The "seven steps," as we have explained, denote perfection, totality, completion, and universality; "seven" is God's number and applies to Christ Himself.)

23 And the gate of the Inner Court was over against the gate toward the north, and toward the east; and He measured from gate to gate an hundred cubits. *(The distance is identical from the north, east, and south: 150 feet.)*

THE SOUTHERN GATE OF THE OUTER COURT

24 After that He brought me toward the south, and behold a gate toward the south: and He measured the posts thereof and the arches thereof according to these measures.

25 And there were windows in it and in the arches thereof round about, like those windows: the length was fifty cubits, and the breadth five and twenty cubits.

26 And there were seven steps to go up to it, and the arches thereof were before them: and it had palm trees, one on this side, and another on that side, upon the posts thereof. *(All

three gates, east, north, and south, have "seven steps" leading up from the outside of the outer wall. Actually, the design of the Temple area is very simple, forming a square, with the dimensions identical from all entrances. This portrays the exactness, perfection, and harmony of God's Salvation Plan, exemplified in Christ, Who is Perfect from every side. In fact, any way one looks at Christ, one sees nothing but perfection. If one comes through the South Gate, it is identical to that which leads through the North Gate; therefore, whichever one enters, there is no confusion. What a beautiful picture of true Bible Christianity!)

THE INNER COURT GATES AND WALLS

27 And there was a gate in the inner court toward the south: and He measured from gate to gate toward the south an hundred cubits.

28 And He brought me to the inner court by the south gate: and He measured the south gate according to these measures;

29 And the little chambers thereof, and the posts thereof, and the arches thereof, according to these measures: and there were windows in it and in the arches thereof round about: it was fifty cubits long, and five and twenty cubits broad.

30 And the arches round about were five and twenty cubits long, and five cubits broad.

31 And the arches thereof were toward the utter court; and palm trees were upon the posts thereof: and the going up to it had eight steps. *(There were "eight steps" that led to the South Inner Gate, whereas there were "seven" that led to the North Outer Gate. God's number, which is "seven," cannot be improved upon, and is not meant to be improved upon; therefore, the number "eight," respecting the steps that lead to the "Inner Court," should be added to the seven, totaling fifteen.*

This corresponds to the Pilgrim Psalms, or "Songs of Degrees" or "Ascents," which were fifteen. They are Psalms 120 through 134. They were supposed to have been sung, one upon each step, by the choir of Levites, as they ascended first into the Outer and then the Inner Court of Solomon's Temple.

These "Songs of Degrees" symbolize the spiritual journey of every Believer. The first Psalm of each group speaks of distress and trouble [Ps. 120, 123, 126, 129, 132]; the second Psalm of each group speaks of trust and deliverance by God [Ps. 121, 124, 127, 130, 133]; the third

Psalm of each group speaks of Blessing and Triumph upon Zion [Ps. 122, 125, 128, 131, 134].)

32 And He brought me into the inner court toward the east: and He measured the gate according to these measures.

33 And the little chambers thereof, and the posts thereof, and the arches thereof, were according to these measures: and there were windows therein and in the arches thereof round about: it was fifty cubits long, and five and twenty cubits broad.

34 And the arches thereof were toward the outward court; and palm trees were upon the posts thereof, on this side, and on that side: and the going up to it had eight steps.

35 And He brought me to the north gate, and measured it according to these measures;

36 The little chambers thereof, the posts thereof, and the arches thereof, and the windows to it round about: the length was fifty cubits, and the breadth five and twenty cubits.

37 And the posts thereof were toward the utter court; and palm trees were upon the posts thereof, on this side, and on that side: and the going up to it had eight steps. *(The same minute specifications are again repeated, as if to show that all parts in this Divinely-fashioned edifice are of equal moment and, therefore, symbolize Christ.)*

38 And the chambers and the entries thereof were by the posts of the gates, where they washed the burnt offering. *(The Sacrifices included the "Whole Burnt Offering," which spoke of Christ giving His all.)*

TABLES FOR PREPARING THE SACRIFICES

39 And in the porch of the gate were two tables on this side, and two tables on that side, to slay thereon the Burnt Offering and the Sin Offering and the Trespass Offering.

40 And at the side without, as one goes up to the entry of the north gate, were two tables; and on the other side, which was at the porch of the gate, were two tables.

41 Four tables were on this side, and four tables on that side, by the side of the gate; eight tables, whereupon they slew their Sacrifices.

42 And the four tables were of hewn stone for the Burnt Offering, of a cubit and an half long, and a cubit and an half broad, and one cubit high: whereupon also they laid the instruments wherewith they slew the Burnt Offering and the Sacrifice.

43 And within were hooks, an hand broad,

fastened round about: and upon the tables was the flesh of the offering. *(Actually, three types of Offerings would be offered here, the "Burnt Offering," the "Sin Offering," and "Trespass Offering." There were twelve tables in all, eight on which the Sacrifices were placed, and four for placing the instruments employed in killing the animals.*

Although reinstituted, as under the Old Covenant, the Sacrifices do not now take away sin any more than they did then [Heb. 10:4]. The Sacrifices are merely symbolic, and are meant to portray the Great Sacrifice made by Christ at Calvary. This is to never be forgotten; the daily offering of the Sacrifices will be a constant ritual, so that the entire world will never forget.

That which saved man, the shed Blood of Jesus Christ at Calvary, did not come cheaply or easily; therefore, it is thought of so highly in the Mind of God, and rightly so, that the never-ending repetition of Sacrifices will constantly be offered as an ongoing reminder.)

CHAMBERS OF THE SINGERS

44 And without the inner gate were the chambers of the singers in the inner court, which was at the side of the north gate; and their prospect was toward the south: one at the side of the east gate having the prospect toward the north. *(The "singers," whose worship will accompany the Sacrifices, portray the Truth that the great price paid at Calvary brought eternal joy to the human heart, and is ever to be expressed accordingly. Therefore, the Truth is evident here that if the Church goes further than Calvary, it loses its way with God. As well, if Calvary is ever lifted up as the focal point of man's Redemption and Sanctification, which it most certainly is, then great joy always accompanies this great Truth [Rom. 6:3-14].)*

BUILDING FOR THE PRIESTS

45 And He said unto me, This chamber, whose prospect is toward the south, is for the Priests, the keepers of the charge of the house. *(The indication is that this Chamber is exclusively for the "Priests.")*

46 And the chamber whose prospect is toward the north is for the Priests, the keepers of the charge of the Altar: these are the sons of Zadok among the sons of Levi, which come near to the LORD to minister unto Him. *(The two Chambers mentioned in Verses 45 and 46*

both pertain to the Priests. Those in Verse 45 face toward the south and are for those in charge of the Temple. The one facing north is for those having charge of the Altar.)

THE PORCH OF THE HOUSE

47 So He measured the court, an hundred cubits long, and an hundred cubits broad, foursquare; and the Altar that was before the house. *(The "cubit" was about 18 inches long. The Great Altar was situated in the very center of the four squares, and is 18 feet square. The Revelation of all of this testifies to the interest of God in His People. He will rebuild His Sanctuary among them; and He has informed them of this fact, and of its details, as a testimony of His faithful love, and as a Message to their hearts and consciences. Therefore, the Prophet was commanded to show these things to the House of Israel [Vs. 4].)*

48 And He brought me to the porch of the house, and measured each post of the porch, five cubits on this side, and five cubits on that side: and the breadth of the gate was three cubits on this side, and three cubits on that side.

49 The length of the porch was twenty cubits, and the breadth eleven cubits; and He brought me by the steps whereby they went up to it: and there were pillars by the posts, one on this side, and another on that side. *(The "Most Holy Place," specified in Verse 4 of the next Chapter, is larger than the "porch of the House," or entrance, thus signifying that God's Grace is far greater than anything that could be brought to it. Consequently, this fact illustrates a great spiritual Truth. In this building and its dependencies, the measurements of "foundations" and the "posts" have great importance; for the one word expresses stability, the other, permanence.*

In the Bible, the "posts" of the door mean the whole house as an erect structure, and they figure its strength. This is imitated in the massive stone door-posts of the Egyptian Temples. If, therefore, the posts of the door shake, the whole house shakes.

In this House of Jehovah, all the foundations will be of like measure, signifying its Great Strength, which is Christ.)

CHAPTER 41
(574 B.C.)

THE MEASURING OF THE TEMPLE

AFTERWARD He brought me to the temple, and measured the posts, six cubits broad

on the one side, and six cubits broad on the other side, which was the breadth of the Tabernacle. *(The massiveness and loftiness of the "posts" or "pillars" proclaim the strength and magnificence of the Temple. "Six" is used for a reason, because it denotes the number of man, and corresponds with the Words of Christ [Rev. 3:12].)*

2 And the breadth of the Door was ten cubits; and the sides of the door were five cubits on the one side, and five cubits on the other side: and He measured the length thereof, forty cubits: and the breadth, twenty cubits. *(The phrase, "And the breadth of the Door was ten cubits," refers to the "Door" that led into the Holy Place, which was fifteen feet wide. This corresponds again to Jesus as "the Door" [Jn. 10:7]. The Holy Place was sixty feet long and thirty feet wide. This was the same dimensions as Solomon's Temple.)*

3 Then went He inward, and measured the post of the Door, two cubits; and the Door, six cubits; and the breadth of the Door, seven cubits. *(The phrase, "Then went He inward," speaks of the Most Holy Place, which was situated immediately behind the Holy Place. No one but the High Priest could go into the "Most Holy Place," and that only once a year; therefore, Christ, it seems, went in Alone, leaving Ezekiel outside.*

The height of the Door is "six cubits"; this refers to Christ as the Door to Salvation, i.e., man's approach to God, since "six" is man's number; the width of the Door is "seven cubits," which portrays God's Perfect Salvation in Christ, God's number being "seven," which speaks of perfection.)

4 So He measured the length thereof, twenty cubits; and the breadth, twenty cubits, before the Temple: and He said unto me, This is the Most Holy Place. *(The "Most Holy Place" was the place where the Ark of the Covenant was kept in the Tabernacle and in Solomon's Temple. Actually, the dimensions were the same as Solomon's Temple: thirty feet long and thirty feet wide.*

At Solomon's Temple, the "Altar" was thirty feet long and thirty feet wide, the same size as the "Most Holy Place." However, in the Millennial Temple, the "Altar" will be smaller than the Most Holy Place, only eighteen feet square.

Solomon's Altar was larger because it represented a price yet to be paid, while the "Altar" in the Millennial Temple is smaller, thereby representing a price already paid [II Chron. 4:1; Ezek. 43:16].)

5 After He measured the wall of the house, six cubits; and the breadth of every side chamber, four cubits, round about the house on every side. *(The wall of this "House" will be "six cubits," or nine feet, thick. The massive thickness of the "wall" will no doubt serve as a symbol of strength and indestructibility concerning Christ as the True Temple. In other words, this House is secure, whereas the house built by man fell!)*

6 And the side chambers were three, one over another, and thirty in order; and they entered into the wall which was of the house for the side chambers round about, that they might have hold, but they had not hold in the wall of the house.

7 And there was an enlarging, and a winding about still upward to the side chambers: for the winding about of the house went still upward round about the house: therefore the breadth of the house was still upward, and so increased from the lowest chamber to the highest by the midst. *(The width of the wall for the first story was 7 1/2 feet, whereas this was diminished to 6 feet for the second story, and to 4 1/2 feet for the third story.)*

8 I saw also the height of the house round about: the foundations of the side chambers were a full reed of six great cubits. *(The "foundations" of these Chambers were 9 feet thick, constituting a "firm foundation.")*

9 The thickness of the wall, which was for the side chamber without, was five cubits: and that which was left was the place of the side chambers that were within. *(The symbolism is here intended to convey the spiritual message desired: in this case, the firm foundation of our spiritual experience in Christ, along with the firm walls denoting the structure of Salvation and the reign of Christ as being absolutely secure and eternal in its consequence.)*

10 And between the chambers was the wideness of twenty cubits round about the house on every side.

11 And the doors of the side chambers were toward the place that was left, one door toward the north, and another door toward the south: and the breadth of the place that was left was five cubits round about.

12 Now the building that was before the separate place at the end toward the west was seventy cubits broad; and the wall of the building was five cubits thick round about, and the length thereof ninety cubits. *(This building was a separate place, or structure, which was*

built behind the Temple on the west, which was marked off from the rest of the ground on which the Temple, with its Courts and Chambers, stood; it was most likely devoted to less sacred purposes. Actually, behind Solomon's Temple lay a similar space [II Ki. 23:11; I Chron. 26:18].)

13 So He measured the house, an hundred cubits long; and the separate place, and the building, with the walls thereof, an hundred cubits long;

14 Also the breadth of the face of the house, and of the separate place toward the east, an hundred cubits. *(That which is instituted, even though it would contain some of the trappings of the Mosaic Law, still, is carried forth mostly as a symbol or memorial that men never forget what Christ did at Calvary for the human family in order than men may be saved.)*

15 And He measured the length of the building over against the separate place which was behind it, and the galleries thereof on the one side and on the other side, an hundred cubits, with the inner temple, and the porches of the court;

DETAILS ABOUT THE INTERIOR OF THE TEMPLE

16 The door posts, and the narrow windows, and the galleries round about on their three stories, over against the door, ceiled with wood round about, and from the ground up to the windows, and the windows were covered;

17 To that above the door, even unto the inner house, and without, and by all the wall round about within and without, by measure. *(These three-storied houses, as the Palace itself, will be finished off with wooden wainscotting ornamented with Cherubims and Palm Trees. The wood no doubt typified the Incarnation of Christ, when God became Man in order to become the Last Adam, and to redeem humanity.)*

18 And it was made with cherubims and palm trees, so that a palm tree was between a cherub and a cherub; and every cherub had two faces *(as in Solomon's Temple [I Ki. 6:29], the wainscotting was adorned with artistic coverings of Cherubims and Palm Trees, a Palm Tree and a Cherub standing alternately. As the wood denoted Christ's humanity, likewise, the "Cherubims" denote His Holiness. The "Palm Trees" denote the lifting of the curse from the Earth and from man, with harmony now prevailing, typifying "rest");*

19 So that the face of a man was toward the palm tree on the one side, and the face of a young lion toward the palm tree on the other side: it was made through all the house round about. *(The phrase, "So that the face of a man was toward the palm tree on the one side," refers to God becoming Man, "The Man Christ Jesus," in order to redeem man and lift the curse.*

The phrase, "And the face of a young lion toward the Palm Tree on the other side," refers to Christ coming "as a Lion from the Tribe of Judah" [Rev. 5:5].)

20 From the ground unto above the door were cherubims and palm trees made, and on the wall of the Temple. *(Throughout the Temple, "even unto the Inner House" [Vs. 17], the Holy of Holies will be the symbols.)*

21 The posts of the Temple were squared, and the face of the Sanctuary; the appearance of the one as the appearance of the other. *(They were "squared," which signified the fourfold Gospel of Jesus Christ: Salvation by the Blood, the Baptism with the Holy Spirit, Divine Healing, and the Second Coming of Christ. All now, in the Kingdom Age, are reality, hence the appearance of the one as the appearance of the other.)*

22 The Altar of wood was three cubits high, and the length thereof two cubits; and the corners thereof, and the length thereof, and the walls thereof, were of wood: and He said unto me, This is the table that is before the LORD. *(This is not the Altar of Sacrifice, which sat in the center of the 100-cubit square and in front of the Temple, but instead the "Altar of Incense." It is in the Holy Place, immediately in front of the Holy of Holies, exactly where it sat in the Tabernacle and in Solomon's Temple.)*

23 And the Temple and the Sanctuary had two doors. *(These "doors" led to the "Holy Place" and the "Most Holy Place.")*

24 And the doors had two leaves apiece, two turning leaves; two leaves for the one door, and two leaves for the other door.

25 And there were made on them, on the doors of the Temple, cherubims and palm trees, like as were made upon the walls; and there were thick planks upon the face of the porch without. *(As Solomon's Temple also represented the coming Kingdom Age, likewise, this Temple, which is the Kingdom Age, has the same symbols. They stand for Holiness and Harmony.)*

26 And there were narrow windows and palm trees on the one side and on the other side, on the sides of the porch, and upon the side chambers of the house, and thick planks.

(Solomon's Temple was heavily ornamented with gold, whereas such is not present in the Kingdom Temple, because Christ, which the gold represented, is now present; therefore, the gold is no longer necessary. The implication is this: the abundance of gold made Solomon's Temple beautiful; however, Christ will so far eclipse the luster of mere gold that even if gold were present, it would not be noticed for the Glory of the Lord.)

CHAPTER 42

(574 B.C.)

THE NORTH OUTER COURT

T HEN He brought me forth into the utter court, the way toward the north: and He brought me into the chamber that was over against the separate place, and which was before the building toward the north. *(The Utter Court actually refers to "Outer Court." The survey of the Temple has now been completed, and Ezekiel is taken outside by Christ into the "Outer Court.")*

2 Before the length of an hundred cubits was the north door, and the breadth was fifty cubits. *(The length is 150 feet; the width is 75 feet. This building contains the Priests' Chambers.)*

3 Over against the twenty cubits which were for the inner court, and over against the pavement which was for the utter court, was gallery against gallery in three stories. *(This building is three stories high, with a "gallery" or "porch" running the length of the building on all three stories.)*

4 And before the chambers was a walk to ten cubits breadth inward, a way of one cubit; and their doors toward the north.

5 Now the upper chambers were shorter: for the galleries were higher than these, than the lower, and than the middlemost of the building. *(The Verse seems to mean that the "Upper Chambers," or the second and third stories, were smaller than the bottom floor.)*

6 For they were in three stories, but had not pillars as the pillars of the courts: therefore the building was straitened more than the lowest and the middlemost from the ground. *(The bottom floors being smaller suggests, in the spiritual sense, an enlarged vision enjoyed in communion; the upper stories being smaller suggests a humbling experience gained in service.*

In communion with the Lord, and sensing His

Great Presence, the recipient of this Presence, and for the moment, thinks himself capable of miraculous events. However, the actual service quickly demonstrates the inabilities of the flesh, and humbles the participant.)*

7 And the wall that was without over against the chambers, toward the utter court on the forepart of the chambers, the length thereof was fifty cubits.

8 For the length of the chambers that were in the utter court was fifty cubits: and, lo, before the temple were an hundred cubits.

EAST ENTRANCE — OUTER COURT

9 And from under these chambers was the entry on the east side, as one goes into them from the utter court. *(Quite possibly, the elevation of this building, regarding ground level, will be higher than the Outer Court, but lower than the Temple area. Consequently, the "entry" is represented as lying under the Chambers.)*

10 The chambers were in the thickness of the wall of the court toward the east, over against the separate place, and over against the building.

11 And the way before them was like the appearance of the chambers which were toward the north, as long as they, and as broad as they: and all their goings out were both according to their fashions, and according to their doors.

12 And according to the doors of the chambers that were toward the south was a door in the head of the way, even the way directly before the wall toward the east, as one enters into them.

CHAMBERS OF THE PRIESTS

13 Then said He unto me, The north chambers and the south chambers, which are before the separate place, they be holy chambers, where the Priests who approach unto the LORD shall eat the most holy things: there shall they lay the most holy things, and the Meat Offering, and the Sin Offering, and the Trespass Offering, for the place is holy.

14 When the Priests enter therein, then shall they not go out of the holy place into the utter court, but there they shall lay their garments wherein they minister; for they are holy; and shall put on other garments, and shall approach to those things which are for the people. *(The regulation as to the Priestly*

garments of the sons of Zadok reveals a feature of the spiritual life peculiar to the modern Christian, that there are affections, energies, and ministries which belong exclusively to the life of communion and intercession, and must, therefore, be reserved expressly for the Lord. Refreshed and enabled by this inner communion, the Christian can then go out to minister to the world.

Observing Christ as the King of kings and Lord of lords, despite the nail-prints in His Hands, resplendent in beauty and glory, one is apt to forget what He did to redeem humanity. These repetitive sacrificial rituals will be a constant reminder.)

THE MEASUREMENTS OF
THE TEMPLE AREA

15 Now when He had made an end of measuring the inner house, He brought me forth toward the gate whose prospect is toward the east, and measured it round about. *(As the Lord measures the dimensions for the Kingdom Temple, likewise, He measures the government, operation, and service of His Church. As His dimensions are exact for the coming Temple, likewise, they are exact for His Church.)*

16 He measured the east side with the measuring reed, five hundred reeds, with the measuring reed round about.

17 He measured the north side, five hundred reeds, with the measuring reed round about.

18 He measured the south side, five hundred reeds, with the measuring reed.

19 He turned about to the west side, and measured five hundred reeds with the measuring reed. *(This is called the "Most Outer Court" or the "Profane Place," which could be used by the people coming to the Sanctuary itself.)*

20 He measured it by the four sides: it had a wall round about, five hundred reeds long, and five hundred broad, to make a separation between the Sanctuary and the profane place. *(The Sanctuaries given by Inspiration to Moses and to David were built, and thus set visibly before the eyes of Israel. The Sanctuary given in Vision to Ezekiel is yet to be built. But its details are revealed in writing [43:11] as a testimony and instruction to Israel.*

These details make real God's interest in His ancient People, and gives substance to His Promise to establish His home among them. Thus, this Vision is a perpetual call to Repentance [43:10-11].)

CHAPTER 43
(574 B.C.)
THE GLORY OF THE LORD
FILLS THE TEMPLE

AFTERWARD He brought me to the gate, even the gate that looks toward the east *(this Chapter is glorious indeed, inasmuch as it heralds the return of the Holy Spirit to the Millennial Temple and, therefore, to Israel. Ezekiel saw Him leave [11:23] and now he sees Him return. Atonement, as the eternal foundation of God's relationship with man, is the keynote of this Chapter, which will occasion the Coming of the Spirit. As stated, this will be at the beginning of the Kingdom Age):*

2 And, behold, the glory of the God of Israel came from the way of the east: and His voice was like a noise of many waters: and the Earth shined with His glory. *(Israel rejected Him and so He left! Now Israel has been washed and cleansed by the Blood of the Lamb and, therefore, He returns.)*

3 And it was according to the appearance of the Vision which I saw, even according to the Vision that I saw when I came to destroy the city: and the Visions were like the Vision that I saw by the river Chebar: and I fell upon my face. *(Taking the latter phrase first, "And I fell upon my face," one is left with the proper position in the Presence of the Lord of Glory. The phrase, "That I saw when I came to destroy the city," does not mean that Ezekiel personally destroyed it, but that he was the announcer of this tragic event!*

The idea of Ezekiel's terminology is that as God, in the past, had shown Himself as One of Justice and Judgment by overturning and destroying the old, likewise, He will now exhibit Himself as a God of Grace and Mercy by condescending to establish His abode in the new. Consequently, Ezekiel saw the destruction and the restoration, and in a manner unlike any other Prophet before or since!)

4 And the glory of the LORD came into the house by the way of the gate whose prospect is toward the east *(comes into the newly built Millennial Temple).*

5 So the Spirit took me up, and brought me into the inner court; and, behold, the Glory of the LORD filled the house. *(The Lord is now entering into and taking possession of the "House," as formerly He had entered into and taken possession of the Tabernacle and the Temple of old [Ex. 40:34-35; I Ki. 8:10-11].)*

6 And I heard Him speaking unto me out of the house; and the Man stood by me. *(It is the Holy Spirit Who is speaking to Ezekiel. As well, the "Man" standing by Ezekiel is none other than the Lord Jesus Christ, Who has conducted Ezekiel through the entirety of this manifestation [40:3-4].)*

7 And He said unto me, Son of man, the place of My Throne, and the place of the soles of My feet, where I will dwell in the midst of the Children of Israel for ever, and My Holy Name, shall the House of Israel no more defile, neither they, nor their kings, by their whoredom, nor by the carcases of their kings in their high places. *(The words, "This is," are to be supplied before "the Place of My Throne." The phrase, "Where I will dwell in the midst of the Children of Israel forever," goes beyond anything that had been spoken concerning either the Tabernacle of Moses or the Temple of Solomon.)*

EXHORTATION TO ISRAEL

8 In their setting of their threshold by My thresholds, and their post by My posts, and the wall between Me and them, they have even defiled My Holy Name by their abominations that they have committed: wherefore I have consumed them in My anger. *(The wording of "their threshold," "My thresholds," "their post," and "My posts" refers to their idol Temple erected by the side of God's Holy House, which of course occasioned their destruction.)*

9 Now let them put away their whoredom, and the carcases of their kings, far from Me, and I will dwell in the midst of them for ever. *(The theology here presented harmonizes with that of the Old and New Testament writers, who invariably proclaimed purity of heart and life as a necessary condition of God's abiding in the heart, while asserting such Divine indwelling in the heart as the only certain Creator of such purity; for one cannot create such himself [Isa. 1:16, 25; 26:12; Jn. 14:23; II Cor. 6:17; James 4:8]. The idea of this Verse is not that such sin dwelt in Israel at this particular time [the time of the Millennium], but that God's attitude toward sin never changes. In fact, such sin will never again happen in Israel!)*

10 Thou son of man, show the house to the house of Israel, that they may be ashamed of their iniquities: and let them measure the pattern. *(This refers to iniquities of the past, and not of the present. But yet they are to be ashamed of their past, as we should be ashamed*

of all sin, especially personal sin.

The phrase, "And let them measure the pattern," concerns itself with the Great Sanctuary, which will be the dwelling-place of the Lord. Comparing this glorious Palace with the pagan and Papal Temples of idolatrous worship, the people will be ashamed of shrines, both ancient and modern, of which they are now so proud.

Similarly, a comparison between the Way of Salvation and Holiness patterned in the Scriptures and those invented by man fill the contrite heart with self-condemnation.)

11 And if they be ashamed of all that they have done, show them the form of the house, and the fashion thereof, and the goings out thereof, and the comings in thereof, and all the forms thereof, and all the ordinances thereof, and all the forms thereof, and all the laws thereof: and write it in their sight, that they may keep the whole form thereof, and all the ordinances thereof, and do them. *(The idea of this Verse is that God will not dwell in anything except that which He Himself has made. Only that which is of God, all of God and only of God, can be accepted. And this has been the problem with religious man from the beginning until now. He seeks to insert that of his own making into that which is of God, which the Lord will never tolerate. The Message always has been, and always will be, "Jesus Christ and Him Crucified" [I Cor. 1:23].)*

12 This is the Law of the House; Upon the top of the mountain the whole limit thereof round about shall be most holy. Behold, this is the law of the house. *(As the Holy of Holies, the Tabernacle, and the Temple of old were "most holy," likewise, the entirety of that which pertains to this Sanctuary is to be considered as a "Holy of Holies." In fact, the entire summit of this mountain is to be reserved for Immanuel.)*

MEASUREMENTS OF THE ALTAR

13 And these are the measures of the Altar after the cubits: The cubit is a cubit and an hand breadth; even the bottom shall be a cubit, and the breadth a cubit, and the border thereof by the edge thereof round about shall be a span: and this shall be the higher place of the Altar. *(As stated at the beginning of this Chapter, Atonement is the eternal foundation of God's relationship with man, of which the "Altar" is symbolic. Such symbolizes Calvary, and will forever serve as a reminder and a memorial of what Christ did in order that humanity*

be redeemed.)

14 And from the bottom upon the ground even to the lower settle shall be two cubits, and the breadth one cubit; and from the lesser settle even to the greater settle shall be four cubits, and the breadth one cubit. *(The "cubit" is approximately 18 inches long.)*

15 So the Altar shall be four cubits; and from the Altar and upward shall be four horns.

16 And the Altar shall be twelve cubits long, twelve broad, square in the four squares thereof.

17 And the settle shall be fourteen cubits long and fourteen broad in the four squares thereof; and the border about it shall be half a cubit; and the bottom thereof shall be a cubit about; and his stairs shall look toward the east. *(This Altar was 18 feet long and 18 feet wide. It is approximately 10 1/2 feet high.)*

ORDINANCES OF THE ALTAR

18 And He said unto me, Son of man, thus saith the Lord GOD; These are the ordinances of the altar in the day when they shall make it, to offer Burnt Offerings thereon, and to sprinkle blood thereon. *(The "Ordinances of the Altar," as given here, do not pertain to the regulations for the Sacrificial worship to be afterwards performed upon this Altar, for the rites to be observed at this time were for its consecration only. In other words, it was to be dedicated by a special ceremony before being brought into ordinary use. The same was done for the Tabernacle and Solomon's Temple [Ex. 29:1-46; Lev. 8:11-33; I Ki. 8:63-66; II Chron. 7:4-10].)*

19 And you shall give to the Priests the Levites that be of the seed of Zadok, which approach unto Me, to minister unto Me, saith the Lord GOD, a young bullock for a Sin Offering. *(The "Priests" who would participate in this dedication and cleaning were to be "of the seed of Zadok," David's faithful High Priest. Hence, by the choosing of these "sons of Zadok," the Holy Spirit proclaims to us the value of faithfully adhering to the Will of God, instead of the will of man.)*

20 And you shall take of the blood thereof, and put it on the four horns of it, and on the four corners of the settle, and upon the border round about: thus shall you cleanse and purge it. *(The "blood" formed an integral part of every expiatory offering. It was to be placed on the "four horns" of the Altar, which pointed in every direction, signifying that Redemption was the same the world over. It was also to be smeared on the "four corners of the settle," which formed a part of the base or foundation of the Altar. It also was to be smeared on the "border," with the implication being that the blood was smeared around the entire border. Thus was the "Altar" cleansed and purged.*

Consequently, when Christ died on Calvary, His Blood, which stained the Cross and the Earth beneath it, purged and cleansed this most vile form of death.)

21 You shall take the bullock also of the Sin Offering, and he shall burn it in the appointed place of the house, without the Sanctuary. *(The idea is: the skin and dung of the bullock should be burned without the camp [Ex. 29:14; Lev. 4:12, 21; 9:11, 15].)*

22 And on the second day you shall offer a kid of the goats without blemish for a Sin Offering; and they shall cleanse the Altar, as they did cleanse it with the bullock. *(The Reader must wonder as to the need for different animals, or another animal at all? Actually, there were five Levitical Offerings given in the Law of Moses, with all typifying what Christ would do at Calvary. In other words, it took five Offerings to wholly portray His One Sacrificial Offering on the Cross. They were: the Whole Burnt Offering, the Peace Offering, the Sin Offering, the Trespass Offering, and the Meat [Meal] Offering.)*

23 When you have made an end of cleansing it, you shall offer a young bullock without blemish, and a ram out of the flock without blemish.

24 And you shall offer them before the LORD, and the Priests shall cast salt upon them, and they shall offer them up for a Burnt Offering unto the LORD. *(A comparison here with Leviticus is instructive. There, the Burnt Offering preceded the Sin Offering; here, it follows. Then Faith praised in looking forward to the Sin Offering of Calvary; in the future day, Faith will praise looking back to Calvary. Thus the great Sin Offering of the Lamb of God stands in the midst of the ages, and is preceded and followed by praise.*

Actually, there will be no Day of Atonement in Millennial Worship; for the Sacrifices then will recall the One All-Sufficing Atonement perfected at Golgotha.

The "salt" placed on the Offerings typifies the fact that all of this is according to the Word of God.)

25 Seven days shall you prepare every day a goat for a Sin Offering: they shall also

prepare a young bullock, and a ram out of the flock, without blemish. *(The perfection of the Atonement appears in the seven days of its action. "Seven," as God's number, denotes perfection, completion, fulfillment, totality, and universality.)*

26 Seven days shall they purge the Altar and purify it; and they shall consecrate themselves. *(Likewise, as this consecrated the Priests, it consecrates all who believe in the vicarious, atoning Offering of Christ at Calvary.)*

27 And when these days are expired, it shall be, that upon the eighth day, and so forward, the Priests shall make your Burnt Offerings upon the Altar, and your Peace Offerings; and I will accept you, saith the Lord GOD. *(As a result of Calvary, this House shall stand, whereas every other house has fallen. God can accept mankind only on the basis of the Sacrifice of Calvary, and our Faith in that Finished Work. By any way other than the Cross, acceptance is denied [Eph. 2:13-18].)*

CHAPTER 44
(574 B.C.)
THE GATE OF THE PRINCE

THEN He brought me back the way of the gate of the outward Sanctuary which looks toward the east; and it was shut. *(Inasmuch as the Messiah has entered His Palace, the Inner Gate of the eastern entry shall be shut, thus giving a memorial of the fact, and an assurance that He never again will forsake His Temple.)*

2 Then said the LORD unto me; This gate shall be shut, it shall not be opened, and no man shall enter in by it; because the LORD, the God of Israel, has entered in by it, therefore it shall be shut. *(Jehovah, the God of Israel, is the Messiah. The North and South Gates will be the principal entry points of worshippers day and night, who no doubt will come from all over the world, and continually.)*

3 It is for the prince; the prince, he shall sit in it to eat bread before the LORD; he shall enter by the way of the porch of that gate, and shall go out by the way of the same. *(Exactly who this "Prince" is, is not known! However, he is probably the High Priest.)*

4 Then brought He me the way of the north gate before the house: and I looked, and, behold, the Glory of the LORD filled the house of the LORD: and I fell upon my face. *(The result of the "Glory of the Lord" filling the house was Ezekiel falling on his face. Thus is man humbled!)*

5 And the LORD said unto me, Son of man, mark well, and behold with your eyes, and hear with your ears all that I say unto you concerning all the ordinances of the house of the LORD, and all the laws thereof; and mark well the entering in of the house, with every going forth of the Sanctuary. *(The phrase, "Mark well," means "sit the heart upon." The heart, the eyes, and the ears are all to be engaged with Jehovah's House and its Ordinances, Laws, and Statutes. On entering God's Presence, it is of the utmost importance that the heart should be deeply affected; it also should be deeply exercised when going forth from the Divine Presence.)*

6 And you shall say to the rebellious, even to the House of Israel, Thus saith the Lord GOD; O ye house of Israel, let it suffice you of all your abominations *(actually, the Lord takes the Prophet back to the original happenings at the North Gate, for this was the scene of the "abominations," which, at least in part, caused the original destruction of Judah and Jerusalem [8:5]. Consequently, a stern reminder and warning is given that the nations should now be preserved from lapsing into similar transgression. Thankfully, there will be no repeating by Israel of these "abominations"),*

7 In that you have brought into My Sanctuary strangers, uncircumcised in heart, and uncircumcised in flesh, to be in My Sanctuary, to pollute it, even My house, when you offer My bread, the fat and the blood, and they have broken My covenant because of all your abominations. *(Those who do not know the Lord profane a true temple of worship by professing to be what they are not.)*

8 And you have not kept the charge of My holy things: but you have set keepers of My charge in My Sanctuary for yourselves. *(The implication is: in the Old Economy of God, the Levites, who were supposed to attend to the duties of the Temple, grew weary of this service, and engaged others, even Gentiles [uncircumcised in the flesh or heart], to discharge the services [Neh. 13:3-9].)*

INSTRUCTIONS FOR THE PRIESTS

9 Thus saith the Lord GOD; No stranger, uncircumcised in heart, nor uncircumcised in flesh, shall enter into My Sanctuary, or any stranger who is among the Children of Israel. *(It seems from this Verse that in the coming Kingdom Age that the Lord intends for Israel only to serve in the capacity of the Temple, and even*

certain ones in Israel, "the sons of Zadok," with the "Levites" in lesser positions. Israel is to be what the Lord intended for them to be at the very beginning, "a Kingdom of Priests" [Ex. 19:6].)

10 And the Levites who are gone away far from Me, when Israel went astray, which went astray from Me after their idols; they shall even bear their iniquity. *(Due to the transgressions of the past, of which the Levites were some of the leaders, they now cannot take part in the sacred ministry of the Millennial Temple. However, they will be used, but in a lower type of service.)*

11 Yet they shall be ministers in My sanctuary, having charge at the gates of the house, and ministering to the house: they shall slay the Burnt Offering and the sacrifice for the people, and they shall stand before them to minister unto them.

12 Because they ministered unto them before their idols, and caused the House of Israel to fall into iniquity; therefore have I lifted up My hand against them, saith the Lord GOD, and they shall bear their iniquity. *(The Levites appointed to teach the Law turned from that Holy Book and taught man's way of salvation. In this, they have many modern imitators.)*

13 And they shall not come near unto Me, to do the office of a Priest unto Me, nor to come near to any of My holy things, in the Most Holy Place: but they shall bear their shame, and their abominations which they have committed. *(The Levites will be confined to the Court of the Priests and not permitted to enter the Temple itself. Such will be their punishment all through the Millennial Age.)*

14 But I will make them keepers of the charge of the house, for all the service thereof, and for all that shall be done therein. *(Some may think it cruel that sentence be imposed on these Levites, who had nothing to do with the sins committed by their fathers many, many centuries in the past; however, the Lord is not holding them responsible personally, but only the Order of Levites itself! Actually, it is Grace fueled by Love that affords them even this privilege. As a Jew, to have the privilege to serve in the Sanctuary in any capacity, irrespective of how small it may seem to be, is a privilege indeed!)*

15 But the Priests the Levites, the sons of Zadok, who kept the charge of My sanctuary when the children of Israel went astray from Me, they shall come near to Me, to minister unto Me, and they shall stand before Me to offer unto Me the fat and the blood, saith the Lord GOD. *(Those "sons of Zadok" who had*

remained true to the Southern Kingdom will have charge of the most holy services in the Millennial Temple.)

16 They shall enter into My sanctuary, and they shall come near to My table, to minister unto Me, and they shall keep My charge. *(Once again, these are the sons of Zadok [I Ki. 2:35].)*

17 And it shall come to pass, that when they enter it at the gates of the inner court, they shall be clothed with linen garments; and no wool shall come upon them, whiles they minister in the gates of the inner court, and within. *(The phrase, "They shall be clothed with linen garments," suggests the Righteousness of Christ, of which they were symbols. The phrase, "And no wool shall come upon them, while they minister," pertains to that which would cause sweat, symbolizing one's own efforts. Salvation is not of works; it is the Gift of God [Eph. 2:8-9].)*

18 They shall have linen bonnets upon their heads, and shall have linen breeches upon their loins; they shall not gird themselves with any thing that causes sweat. *(The phrase, "Linen bonnets upon their heads," implies that they are to understand, and understand fully, that their Righteousness is of Christ, and not of themselves. As well, the "linen breeches" symbolize the Truth that all that is done for Christ is due to His Righteousness freely imputed to us who believe, and not to our own abilities.)*

19 And when they go forth into the utter court, even into the utter court to the people, they shall put off their garments wherein they ministered, and lay them in the holy chambers, and they shall put on other garments; and they shall not sanctify the people with their garments. *(Not sanctifying the people with their garments is meant to make a statement. Man is unholy, while Christ is holy! As well, there is nothing that man can do within himself to obtain holiness, except freely admit that he is unholy, and then look exclusively to Christ and the Cross; upon Faith, Christ will then freely impute Holiness and Righteousness to such a Believer.)*

20 Neither shall they shave their heads, nor suffer their locks to grow long; they shall only poll their heads. *(Egyptian priests and Roman monks shaved the head and those of the Greek Church wear their hair long. God's Priests will follow neither fashion.)*

21 Neither shall any Priest drink wine, when they enter into the inner court. *(The drinking of intoxicating beverages caused the deaths of Nadab and Abihu, the sons of Aaron. They offered strange fire before the Lord [Lev. 10:1-2, 9].)*

22 Neither shall they take for their wives a widow, nor her who is put away *(divorced)*: but they shall take maidens of the seed of the house of Israel, or a widow who had a Priest before. *(Consequently, celibacy is not advised or sanctioned, except in certain cases; hence, the celibacy of the Roman Catholic Priests has occasioned untold problems for the Catholic Church, in that it is unnatural and unscriptural!)*

23 And they shall teach My people the difference between the holy and profane, and cause them to discern between the unclean and the clean. *(This has always been the duty of the God-called Preacher of the Gospel, whether as Priests under the Old Economy or Preachers under the New Covenant [II Tim. 4:1-2].)*

24 And in controversy they shall stand in judgment; and they shall judge it according to My Judgments: and they shall keep My Laws and My Statutes in all My assemblies; and they shall hallow My Sabbaths. *(This simply means that everything is to be "judged" according to the Word of God.)*

25 And they shall come at no dead person to defile themselves: but for father, or for mother, or for son, or for daughter, for brother, or for sister who has had no husband, they may defile themselves. *(The Priests will not be allowed to touch any dead person, with the exception of very close relatives. Death is symbolic of the fruit of sin and, therefore, the prohibition [Rom. 6:23].)*

26 And after he is cleansed, they shall reckon unto him seven days. *(Even in touching the dead body of a close relative, the Priest would have to go through a cleansing ceremony for seven days.)*

27 And in the day that he goes into the Sanctuary, unto the inner court, to minister in the Sanctuary, he shall offer his Sin Offering, saith the Lord GOD. *(Along with going through the seven days of ceremonial cleansing, such a Priest would also be required to offer up a "Sin Offering." This did not mean that he had personally sinned, but that in his required duties, which pertained to the touching of a dead body, such spoke of the awful effect of sin.)*

28 And it shall be unto them for an inheritance: I am their inheritance: and you shall give them no possession in Israel: I am their possession. *(This Passage declares that during the Millennial Reign all Priests should have Jehovah as their possession, and not any territorial or tribal tract such as should be assigned to the other Tribes [Chpt. 48].)*

29 They shall eat the Meat Offering, and the Sin Offering, and the Trespass Offering: and every dedicated thing in Israel shall be theirs. *(All of their sustenance will come from the Temple and its many services.)*

30 And the first of all the firstfruits of all things, and every oblation of all, of every sort of your oblations, shall be the Priest's: you shall also give unto the Priest that first of your dough, that he may cause the blessing to rest in your house. *(The firstfruits, probably one-tenth, of all the Tithes which will go to the Temple belong to the Priests. The phrase, "That he may cause the Blessing to rest in your house," implies that if the people do not obey, the Blessing will cease; this principle will automatically ensure obedience.)*

31 The Priests shall not eat of any thing that is dead of itself, or torn, whether it be fowl or beast. *(The idea is: The animals brought for Sacrifice must not be animals that have died of natural causes or been killed by beasts, but instead the healthiest of the healthy. Calvary, of which all of this was a Type, will be shown to be the Divine Center of God's Purposes of Grace and Wrath.)*

CHAPTER 45
(574 B.C.)
A PORTION OF THE LAND TO BE AN OBLATION TO THE LORD

MOREOVER, when you shall divide by lot the land for inheritance, you shall offer an oblation unto the LORD, an holy portion of the land: the length shall be the length of five and twenty thousand reeds, and the breadth shall be ten thousand. This shall be holy in all the borders thereof round about. *(Verses 1 through 8 portray the portions of land in Israel which are to be allotted to the Sanctuary, the City, and the Prince. The length of this Holy Oblation [area of land] is about 42 miles. The width is roughly 17 miles. The phrase, "When you shall divide by lot the land for inheritance," probably means that it is the area already allotted by the Holy Spirit.)*

2 Of this there shall be for the Sanctuary five hundred in length, with five hundred in breadth, square round about; and fifty cubits round about for the suburbs thereof. *(This is probably referring to the Outer Court, which is 750 feet square. This area includes not only the Outer Court, but the Inner Court, as well as the Temple and Altar area. All of it is looked at*

primarily as the "Sanctuary."

God's Love for man and His hatred of injustice appear in Him making His dwelling-place among them, and in His Laws respecting land [Vs. 8], Courts of Justice, excessive taxation, evictions [Vs. 9], and commercial property [Vss. 10-12]. Thus, the poor and defenseless will be cared for by Him.)

3 And of this measure shall you measure the length of five and twenty thousand, and the breadth of ten thousand: and in it shall be the Sanctuary and the Most Holy Place. *(In this area, some 42 miles long and 17 miles wide, the "Sanctuary" and "Most Holy Place" will be situated.)*

4 The holy portion of the land shall be for the Priests the ministers of the Sanctuary, which shall come near to minister unto the LORD: and it shall be a place for their houses, and an holy place for the Sanctuary. *(This area will be occupied not only by the "Sanctuary," but also by the "houses" of the Priests.)*

5 And the five and twenty thousand of length, and the ten thousand of breadth shall also the Levites, the ministers of the house, have for themselves, for a possession for twenty chambers. *(The portion of the Levites, forty-two miles long and seventeen miles wide, will be the same as the portion of the Priests. All Priests were Levites, but all Levites were not Priests.)*

6 And you shall appoint the possession of the city five thousand broad, and five and twenty thousand long, over against the oblation of the holy portion: it shall be for the whole house of Israel. *(This Passage represents a third tract of territory exclusively for Jerusalem itself. It is about forty-two miles long and about eight and a half miles wide, which constitutes a rather large city.)*

THE PRINCE AND THE LAND

7 And a portion shall be for the prince on the one side and on the other side of the oblation of the holy portion, and of the possession of the city, before the oblation of the holy portion, and before the possession of the city, from the west side westward, and from the east side eastward: and the length shall be over against one of the portions, from the west border unto the east border. *(From the description, it seems like the "portion for the Prince" will lie on both sides of the Holy Portion, or the portions of the Priests and the Levites. Even though the Scripture is not exactly clear as to the size of these "portions," still, some think it will be quite large, even about four miles square. This we do know:*

the Prince will be in charge of all the Millennial Worship [Vss. 16-17].)

8 In the land shall be his possession in Israel: and My princes shall no more oppress My people; and the rest of the land shall they give to the house of Israel according to their Tribes. *(This Scripture should read, "As touching the Land, this shall be his possession in Israel," i.e., the Prince shall have no Land other than these two portions.)*

9 Thus saith the Lord GOD; Let it suffice you, O princes of Israel: remove violence and spoil, and execute judgment and justice, take away your exactions from My people, saith the Lord GOD. *(The "Prince" is to set the example for the entirety of the world, which he will do under Christ. And for the first time, the entirety of the world will know fairness, honesty, and integrity in government.)*

VARIOUS OTHER REGULATIONS:
HONEST WEIGHTS

10 You shall have just balances, and a just ephah, and a just bath.

11 The ephah and the bath shall be of one measure that the bath may contain the tenth part of an homer, and the ephah the tenth part of an homer: the measure thereof shall be after the homer.

12 And the shekel shall be twenty gerahs: twenty shekels, five and twenty shekels, fifteen shekels, shall be your maneh. *(The idea of these Passages is to portray a justice system which cannot be bought, bribed, or set aside. In other words, there will be no favoritism! The "ephah" and "bath" are the same, being about one bushel. A "homer" or a "cor" is about ten bushels. The "shekel," as it is here portrayed, would be worth about ten dollars in 2004 currency. However, it is very difficult to equate the purchasing power of Bible money with that of present times.)*

OFFERINGS

13 This is the oblation that you shall offer; the sixth part of an ephah of an homer of wheat, and you shall give the sixth part of an ephah of an homer of barley:

14 Concerning the ordinance of oil, the bath of oil, you shall offer the tenth part of a bath out of the cor, which is an homer of ten baths; for ten baths are an homer.

15 And one lamb out of the flock, out of two hundred, out of the fat pastures of Israel; for a

Meat Offering, and for a Burnt Offering, and for Peace Offerings, to make reconciliation for them, saith the Lord GOD. *(The word "Oblation" means that which is offered as a Sacrifice or Gift to the Lord. The amounts here represented, or the equivalency in money, were to be given to the Sanctuary by all Israelites in order to support the rulers of Israel.)*

SUMMARY OF MILLENNIAL AND ETERNAL WORSHIP

16 All the people of the land shall give this oblation for the prince in Israel. *(These Offerings will be incumbent upon all!)*

17 And it shall be the prince's part to give Burnt Offerings, and Meat Offerings, and Drink Offerings, in the Feasts, and in the new moons, and in the Sabbaths, in all solemnities of the house of Israel: he shall prepare the Sin Offering, and the Meat Offering, and the Burnt Offering, and the Peace Offerings, to make reconciliation for the House of Israel. *(The phrase, "To make reconciliation for the House of Israel," refers to Atonement; however, it is to be ever understood that it is only symbolic, as Christ has already made Atonement, thereby, reconciling Israel and all the world to God by His death at Calvary.)*

OFFERINGS ON CERTAIN HOLY DAYS

18 Thus saith the Lord GOD; In the first month, in the first day of the month, you shall take a young bullock without blemish, and cleanse the Sanctuary. *(The contrast between the legislation of Verses 18 through 25 and that of Leviticus emphasizes the difference between Mosaic and Millennial Worship. Here the year begins with a demonstration of accomplished Redemption and the provision of a pure ground of worship. Thus, shall Atonement be made for the house on the first day, and for the worshippers on the seventh day. The year will, therefore, begin with the memorial of a perfected Atonement for sin. In Leviticus the year closed with an Atonement pointing forward to a cleansing yet to be accomplished.)*

19 And the Priest shall take of the blood of the Sin Offering, and put it upon the posts of the house, and upon the four corners of the settle of the Altar, and upon the posts of the gate of the inner court. *(As the "young bullock" of Verse 18 typified Christ, Who died in the prime of His Manhood, this Verse typifies*

His shed Blood, on which the foundation of Salvation is based. Inasmuch as these Sacrifices will be carried on forever, and strictly as a memorial of what Christ did at Calvary, this should, by all means, portray to us the value placed here by the Lord on the Finished Work of Calvary.)

20 And so you shall do the seventh day of the month for every one who errs, and for him who is simple: so shall you reconcile the house. *(The phrase, "Every one who errs," refers to those who have drifted from the straight path through ignorance or foolishness. The "simple" pertains to the one who, for whatever reason, does not fully understand the ramifications of his actions.*

These Passages portray to us the absolute abhorrence of sin by the Lord and, therefore, the absolute perfection demanded. Inasmuch as such is not possible even for redeemed man [not yet in the Glorified State], provision is here made.)

21 In the first month, in the fourteenth day of the month, you shall have the Passover, a Feast of seven days; unleavened bread shall be eaten. *(The two Feasts of Passover and Tabernacles will be marked by sevenfold Offerings in contrast to the twofold ones of Leviticus. And this because these Offerings will testify to the perfection of the cleansing for sin fulfilled at Calvary.*

The character of worship in that future day and the sense of the sufficiency of Christ's Sacrifice of Himself as the Sin Offering and the Burnt Offering will be perfect. Thus, these two Feasts will celebrate the perfection and sufficiency of the Atoning Work of Christ. Together with the Feasts of the Sabbath and the New Moon, they testify to the fulfillment of God's Promises to Israel in bringing them into rest and making them to be a light to the Gentiles [Isa., Chpts. 60, 66].)

22 And upon that day shall the prince prepare for himself and for all the people of the land a bullock for a Sin Offering. *(The "Passover," as conducted here, will continue forever, fulfilling Ex. 12:14].)*

23 And seven days of the Feast he shall prepare a Burnt Offering to the LORD, seven bullocks and seven rams without blemish daily the seven days; and a kid of the goats daily for a Sin Offering.

24 And he shall prepare a Meat Offering of an ephah for a bullock, and an ephah for a ram, and an hin of oil for an ephah. *(The "Prince" will be in charge of the Sacrifices, which is the work of the High Priest.)*

25 In the seventh month, in the fifteenth day

of the month, shall he do the like in the Feast of the seven days, according to this Sin Offering, according to the Burnt Offering, and according to the Meat Offering, and according to the oil. *(Whereas the Passover was celebrated in the first month, this Feast is celebrated in the seventh month, thereby representing the Feast of Tabernacles. As stated, these two Feasts, Passover and Tabernacles, will be celebrated forever.)*

CHAPTER 46
(574 B.C.)
SABBATH AND NEW MOON OFFERINGS; DUTIES OF THE PRINCE

THUS saith the Lord GOD; The gate of the inner court that looks toward the east shall be shut the six working days; but on the Sabbath it shall be opened, and in the day of the new moon it shall be opened. *(This Chapter opens with "Thus saith the Lord GOD," emphasizing the seriousness of these Commands inasmuch as obeying them guarantees the prosperity, both spiritually and economically, of the entirety of the world [Isa. 60:3].)*

2 And the prince shall enter by the way of the porch of that gate without, and shall stand by the post of the gate, and the Priests shall prepare his Burnt Offering and his Peace Offerings, and he shall worship at the threshold of the gate: then he shall go forth; but the gate shall not be shut until the evening. *(The Prince will provide the Offerings and the Priests will present them. The Offerings of the Sabbath will number seven, denoting the Perfection of Christ, but there will be no wine. In Leviticus, they numbered four, and with wine.)*

3 Likewise the people of the land shall worship at the door of this gate before the LORD in the Sabbaths and in the new moons. *(The reason the Prince has greater access, even unto the porch, is because he is a Type of Christ. However, even he cannot go beyond the inner door. The "Sabbath" signifies the "rest" afforded only in Christ, which Israel will truly have in the coming Kingdom Age. The "New Moon" signifies the perpetuity of this "rest," guaranteeing its existence forever.)*

4 And the Burnt Offering that the prince shall offer unto the LORD in the Sabbath day shall be six lambs without blemish, and a ram without blemish.

5 And the Meat Offering shall be an ephah for a ram, and the Meat Offering for the lambs as he shall be able to give, and an hin of oil to an ephah. *(The Divine foundation being laid — the blood and the oil — the heart is given freedom to express its joy and its communion in the Meal Offering, i.e., fellowship with God in the enjoyment of Christ as the Bread that came down, and comes down, from Heaven, whereof if a man eat, he shall never die [Jn. 6:50-51].)*

6 And in the day of the new moon it shall be a young bullock without blemish, and six lambs, and a ram: they shall be without blemish.

7 And he shall prepare a Meat Offering, an ephah for a bullock, and an ephah for a ram, and for the lambs according as his hand shall attain unto, and an hin of oil to an ephah. *(The Offerings of the Feasts of the New Moon number nine without wine; this stands in contrast with the nineteen of Leviticus with wine.)*

8 And when the prince shall enter, he shall go in by the way of the porch of that gate, and he shall go forth by the way thereof. *(The "Prince" is the High Priest, and, as a Type of Christ, shall enter the Sanctuary by the way of the Eastern Gate.)*

9 But when the people of the land shall come before the LORD in the solemn Feasts, he who enters in by the way of the north gate to worship shall go out by the way of the south gate; and he who enters by the way of the south gate shall go forth by the way of the north gate: he shall not return by the way of the gate whereby he came in, but shall go forth over against it. *(The idea is, one must partake of all of Christ and not just part of Christ. To go all the way through, irrespective of what side one came in, signifies the partaking of all [Jn. 6:53].)*

10 And the prince in the midst of them, when they go in, shall go in; and when they go forth, shall go forth. *(This Verse seems to imply that in such times of worship, the Prince will stand on a level with the people, and both enter and retire by the same door. This signifies Christ, Who became One with the people in the Incarnation. However, He did not become one with them in their sin; this is represented here by the "Prince" associating with the worship of the people only on a certain level, and at certain times.)*

RULES GOVERNING OFFERINGS

11 And in the Feast and in the solemnities the Meat Offering shall be an ephah to a bullock, and an ephah to a ram, and to the lambs as he is able to give, and an hin of oil to an ephah. *(The amounts stipulated here differ from the Law of Moses in that they are increased*

[Num. 15:1-9]. Such typifies the fulfillment of the Promise, whereas the Law of Moses typified the Promise of the fulfillment.)

12 Now when the prince shall prepare a voluntary Burnt Offering or Peace Offerings voluntarily unto the LORD, one shall then open him the gate that looks toward the east, and he shall prepare his Burnt Offering and his Peace Offerings, as he did on the Sabbath day: then he shall go forth; and after his going forth one shall shut the gate. *(As repeatedly stated, all the Offerings typify Christ, and will be done as a memorial of what He did at Calvary. Thus, this momentous occasion, which happened so long ago, will never lose its significance and meaning among the people, and will continue to portray the reason for our deliverance and blessing.)*

13 You shall daily prepare a Burnt Offering unto the LORD of a lamb of the first year without blemish: you shall prepare it every morning.

14 And you shall prepare a Meat *(Meal)* Offering for it every morning, the sixth part of an ephah, and the third part of an hin of oil, to temper with the fine flour; a Meat Offering continually by a perpetual ordinance unto the LORD.

15 Thus shall they prepare the lamb, and the Meat Offering, and the oil, every morning for a continual Burnt Offering. *(Under the Law of Moses, there was the Morning and Evening Sacrifice, but under perfected Righteousness, which characterizes the Millennium, there will be only the Morning Lamb; for to that Day there will be no evening.)*

RULES CONCERNING INHERITANCES

16 Thus saith the Lord GOD, If the prince give a gift unto any of his sons, the inheritance thereof shall be his sons'; it shall be their possession by inheritance.

17 But if he give a gift of his inheritance to one of his servants, then it shall be his to the year of liberty; after it shall return to the prince: but his inheritance shall be his sons' for them. *(Unlike gifts to his sons, which are forever, that given to servants will be theirs only until "the Year of Liberty," i.e., "Year of Jubilee," which comes every 50 years. At this time, the "Gift" will be returned to the Prince.)*

18 Moreover the prince shall not take of the people's inheritance by oppression, to thrust them out of their possession; but he shall give his sons inheritance out of his own possession: that My people be not scattered every man from his possession. *(God's hatred of robbery, oppression, and injustice appears in the legislation of Verses 16 through 18; and His loving care for the physical needs of His servants is shown in Verses 19 through 24.)*

PLACE FOR PREPARING THE OFFERINGS

19 After he brought me through the entry, which was at the side of the gate, into the holy chambers of the Priests, which looked toward the north: and, behold, there was a place on the two sides westward.

20 Then said He unto me, This is the place where the Priests shall boil the Trespass Offering and the Sin Offering, where they shall bake the Meat Offering; that they bear them not out into the utter court, to sanctify the people. *(There is a Ministry to God only, typified in this Verse, whereas there is a ministry to man, as is typified in Verse 24. In service for the Lord, this distinction must be observed; and the richer will be the ministry to man if that to God be given first place.*

The idea of this Verse is: Such Offerings as specified here were for the Priests only, and thereby, typified their personal worship of the Lord. This also typified that even though they were God's chosen, and even Priests, still, they were sinners and, therefore, desperately needing a Saviour.)

21 Then He brought me forth into the utter court, and caused me to pass by the four corners of the court; and, behold, in every corner of the court there was a court. *(This Verse signifies that in all four corners of the Outer Court these places were located in order that the Priests may prepare Sacrifices for themselves.)*

22 In the four corners of the court there were courts joined of forty cubits long and thirty broad: there four corners were of one measure.

23 And there was a row of building round about in them, round about them four, and it was made with boiling places under the rows round about.

24 Then said He unto me, these are the places of them who boil, where the ministers of the house shall boil the sacrifice of the people. *(The Sacrifices were to be prepared in a certain way, and these places were designated for that preparation.)*

CHAPTER 47
(574 B.C.)
THE RIVER FLOWING FROM THE TEMPLE

AFTERWARD He brought me again unto the door of the house; and, behold, waters issued out from under the threshold of the house eastward: for the forefront of the house stood toward the east, and the waters came down from under from the right side of the house, at the south side of the Altar. *(The first twelve Verses portray the River of the Sanctuary, with the remainder portraying the Borders of the Land. "The Door of the House" speaks of the Sanctuary from which the waters will flow. As well, the "Door" is Christ [Jn. 14:6]. The phrase, "And, behold, waters issued out," signifies the Holy Spirit, Who issues forth from Christ. It is not "water" but "waters." It literally issues from the "House," with its Source being the Throne of Jehovah [Jn. 7:37-39].*

The phrase, "From under the threshold of the House eastward," shows that the waters shall grow of themselves, and not, as in nature, by accession from side streams. The "threshold" speaks of the floor, and, in the spiritual sense, denotes humility.

The phrase, "At the south side of the Altar," denotes the channel, or course, of the River. It is the Altar of Jehovah, i.e., Calvary.)

2 Then brought He me out of the way of the gate northward, and led me about the way without unto the utter gate by the way that looks eastward; and, behold, there ran out waters on the right side. *(The phrase, "Then brought He me out of the way of the gate northward," simply means that the East Inner Gate was shut, and the East Outer Gate was shut as well; therefore, the Lord led him outside of the Inner and the Outer Courts by the North Gate.*

There is a spiritual meaning in this seemingly obscure Passage. Many hunger for the Lord, but do not know exactly how to receive Him. Admittedly, the course, although direct, is not reached in a direct way. However, all will receive who persist, because all are invited to come [Rev. 22:17].)

3 And when the Man Who had the line in His Hand went forth eastward, He measured a thousand cubits, and He brought me through the waters; the waters were to the ankles. *(The "Man" is Christ! As the waters issue out from under the threshold of the Sanctuary, and as they flow eastward, the channel begins to widen. At this first stage, it is about 1,500 feet wide, and*

is still very shallow, only "to the ankles." The "ankles" represent the entrance into the River, thereby portraying Salvation.)*

4 Again He measured a thousand, and brought me through the waters, the waters were to the knees. Again, He measured a thousand, and brought me through; the waters were to the loins. *("Knees" signify prayer and a total dependence on the Lord, those things being done by the Power of the Holy Spirit instead of the flesh. So, the "knees" also portray the Baptism with the Holy Spirit [Acts 2:4].*

The implication in these Passages is that the "Man with the line in His Hand" be followed, as that is what He intends!

The "loins" represent the procreative part of man, which points to the miracle-working Power of God, which should be prevalent with all Spirit-Baptized people.)

5 Afterward He measured a thousand; and it was a River that I could not pass over: for the waters were risen, waters to swim in, a River that could not be passed over. *(The stream has widened, until it is now "a River that could not be passed over." This "River" represents the last progression, with itself open-ended, which symbolizes the whole Gospel for the whole man. In a sense, the "River" is a physical type of the Holy Spirit, and His Work within our lives.)*

6 And He said unto me, Son of man, have you seen this? Then He brought me, and caused me to return to the brink of the River. *(Christ will now turn the attention of Ezekiel from the "Course" of the River to the "Force" of the River. Therefore, in this scenario, one has the "Source," which is the Sanctuary, the "Course," which is by the Altar, and now the "Force," which will portray that which the River does.)*

7 Now when I had returned, behold, at the bank of the River were very many trees on the one side and on the other. *("Very many trees" signify "much fruit" [Jn. 15:5]. The "trees" grow on both sides of the River.)*

8 Then said He unto me, These waters issue out toward the east country, and go down into the desert, and go into the sea: which being brought forth into the sea, the waters shall be healed. *(The idea of the River is to bring life to the "desert," as the Holy Spirit Alone through Christ can bring life to unregenerate man, who is dead in trespasses and sins. Literally, this speaks of the Dead Sea, which contains no life whatsoever. The "Dead Sea" will then be healed, symbolic of what the Lord can do through the Holy Spirit in a person's life [Jn. 7:37-39].)*

9 And it shall come to pass, that every thing that lives, which moves, whithersoever the Rivers shall come, shall live: and there shall be a very great multitude of fish, because these waters shall come thither: for they shall be healed; and every thing shall live whither the River comes. *(The word "Rivers" signifies two great Rivers. As this River flows eastward out from the Sanctuary, it will then turn south toward the Dead Sea. At some point on the southern journey, it will split, with one side continuing on to the Dead Sea, with the other going to the Mediterranean [Zech. 14:8]. As a result, and by whatever means, whereas the Dead Sea formerly contained no life, now "there shall be a very great multitude of fish," signifying an abundance of life. Once again, this portrays what Christ can do in the heart and life of any individual.*

The phrase, "And every thing shall live whither the River comes," portrays the result of the Born-Again, Spirit-filled life.)

10 And it shall come to pass, that the fishers shall stand upon it from En-gedi even unto En-eglaim; they shall be a place to spread forth nets; their fish shall be according to their kinds, as the fish of the great sea, exceeding many. *(This is speaking of the Dead Sea, which is no longer dead, but teeming with life. It speaks of many different kinds of fish, "exceeding many." This speaks of the harvest, in which the Holy Spirit has always engaged.)*

11 But the miry places thereof and the marishes thereof shall not be healed; they shall be given to salt. *(The reason these places aren't healed is because imperfection will continue to exist during the Millennium, for man will still be under trial. He will have freedom of choice. If he accepts the rule of the Messiah, he will enjoy the Blessings pictured in Verses 1 through 10 and Verse 12. But if he rejects that government, he, like Lot's wife, will be turned into salt, for Grace despised involves bitterness and death. [This speaks of natural people and not Glorified Saints.]*

Millennium Blessing will be powerful and abiding. It will greatly surmount and almost efface evil, but not entirely. For only in the New heaven and New Earth will there be perfection.)

12 And by the River upon the bank thereof, on this side and on that side, shall grow all trees for meat, whose leaf shall not fade, neither shall the fruit thereof be consumed: it shall bring forth new fruit according to his months, because their waters they issued out of the Sanctuary: and the fruit thereof shall be for meat, and the leaf thereof for medicine.

(Now Ezekiel is shown the purpose of these miracle Trees which grow on either side of these Rivers. These "Trees" shall perpetually bring forth new fruit because they are nourished by waters issuing from the Sanctuary. The fruit will heal as well as nourish. Such is the character of a Life and Ministry based upon Calvary, and energized by the Holy Spirit.

In fact, the population of the world [which will include all, with the exception of the Glorified Saints] will continue to live perpetually by the means of the "fruit" and the "leaf" of these Trees. In other words, the aging process will be halted. [Glorified Saints will not need such.])

BORDERS OF THE LAND AND INSTRUCTIONS FOR DIVIDING IT

13 Thus saith the Lord GOD; This shall be the border, whereby you shall inherit the land according to the twelve Tribes of Israel: Joseph shall have two portions. *(In Joshua, the Land was divided from south to north. In the coming day of Restoration, it will be apportioned from north to south. The phrase, "Joseph shall have two portions," is because he personally received none, but instead it went to his two sons, Manasseh and Ephraim.)*

14 And you shall inherit it, one as well as another: concerning the which I lifted up My hand to give it unto your fathers: and this land shall fall unto you for inheritance. *(The phrase, "And you shall inherit it, one as well as another," refers to each Tribe, irrespective of their size, receiving equal portions. The latter phrase proclaims the certitude of this action.)*

15 And this shall be the border of the land toward the north side, from the great sea, the way of Hethlon, as men go to Zedad;

16 Hamath, Berothah, Sibraim, which is between the border of Damascus and the border of Hamath; Hazar-hatticon, which is by the coast of Haruan.

17 And the border from the sea shall be Hazar-enan, the border of Damascus, and the north, northward, and the border of Hamath. And this is the north side. *(The Northern Border of the Promised Land, at least in that day, will begin on the Mediterranean Sea and go to the other side of Damascus, which will take in all of modern Syria.)*

18 And the east side you shall measure from Hauran and from Damascus, and from Gilead, and from the land of Israel by Jordan, from

the border unto the east sea. And this is the east side. *(The Eastern Border of the Promised Land in that day will take in all of modern Jordan, for "Gilead" is that area. The "East Sea" probably speaks of the Persian Gulf.)*

19 And the south side southward, from Tamar even to the waters of strife in Kadesh, the river to the great sea. And this is the south side southward. *(The Southern Border will extend down into the Sinai, for this is where Kadesh is located. Actually, this does not include the whole South of the Promised Land; that will take in all the Arabian Peninsula, when Gen. 15:18-21 and Isa. 11:13-16 and 19:17-25 are fulfilled.*

As well, the Eastern Border, as given in Verse 18, will extend to the Euphrates River, which means that at least a part of Iraq will be included.)

20 The west side also shall be the great sea from the border, till a man come over against Hamath. This is the west side. *(The Western Border is easily defined: the Mediterranean Sea.)*

21 So shall you divide this land unto you according to the Tribes of Israel.

22 And it shall come to pass, that you shall divide it by lot for an inheritance unto you, and to the strangers who sojourn among you, which shall beget children among you: and they shall be unto you as born in the country among the children of Israel; they shall have inheritance with you among the Tribes of Israel.

23 And it shall come to pass, that in what Tribe the stranger sojourns, there shall you give him his inheritance, saith the Lord GOD. *(The word "strangers" refers to Gentiles. Inheritance to the Gentiles was forbidden under Law; but, in the Millennium, it will be fully granted. Then will God's original purpose be effected — Israel will first be possessed, and then the greater territory promised to Abraham secured.)*

CHAPTER 48
(574 B.C.)
THE DIVISION OF THE LAND

NOW these are the names of the Tribes. From the north end to the coast of the way of Hethlon, as one goes to Hamath, Hazar-enan, the border of Damascus northward, to the coast of Hamath; for these are his sides east and west; a portion for Dan. *(The phrase, "A portion for Dan," portrays this Tribe mentioned first. As is obvious, it is the Holy Spirit Who draws off the "portions." None are decided by men, all by the Lord.)*

2 And by the border of Dan, from the east side unto the west side, a portion for Asher.

3 And by the border of Asher, from the east side even unto the west side, a portion for Naphtali.

4 And by the border of Naphtali, from the east side unto the west side, a portion for Manasseh.

5 And by the border of Manasseh, from the east side unto the west side, a portion for Ephraim.

6 And by the border of Ephraim, from the east side even unto the west side, a portion for Reuben.

7 And by the border of Reuben, from the east side unto the west side, a portion for Judah. *(Seven Tribes will have their possession north of the Oblation, and five Tribes, south of the Oblation, i.e., "Sacrifices.")*

THE LAND FOR THE PRIESTS AND LEVITES

8 And by the border of Judah, from the east side unto the west side, shall be the Offering which you shall offer of five and twenty thousand reeds in breadth, and in length as one of the other parts, from the east side unto the west side: and the Sanctuary shall be in the midst of it. *(This portion is approximately 42 miles long and 42 miles wide. It seems to be out of proportion compared to the allotment to the other Tribes. However, it is thought by some that quite possibly the portions concerning the Priests, Levites, and the City are included in this portion.*

This much is clear: The totality of the Promised Land in the coming Kingdom Age will be approximately 100 times larger than it is presently.)

9 The oblation that you shall offer unto the LORD shall be of five and twenty thousand in length, and of ten thousand in breadth.

10 And for them, even for the Priests, shall be this holy oblation; toward the north five and twenty thousand in length, and toward the west ten thousand in breadth, and toward the east ten thousand in breadth, and toward the south five and twenty thousand in length: and the sanctuary of the LORD shall be in the midst thereof. *(As all the Tribes were proportioned around the Tabernacle in the wilderness [Num., Chpts. 1-3], they are likewise proportioned here, although not in the same order. And yet, as everything was in proportion to the Tabernacle then, everything is in proportion to the Sanctuary now!*

The reason is simple, it is where the Lord dwells!

This is the crowning Truth portrayed by the Holy Spirit in these directions and instructions.)

11 It shall be for the Priests who are sanctified of the sons of Zadok; which have kept My charge, which went not astray when the Children of Israel went astray, as the Levites went astray.

12 And this oblation of the land that is offered shall be unto them a thing most holy by the border of the Levites. *(The faithfulness of "Zadok" [I Ki. 1:8] is ever called to account, as faithfulness will ever be remembered!*

The area in Verse 12 called "most holy" is the area of the "Sanctuary.")

13 And over against the border of the Priests the Levites shall have five and twenty thousand in length, and ten thousand in breadth: all the length shall be five and twenty thousand, and the breadth ten thousand.

14 And they shall not sell of it, neither exchange, nor alienate the firstfruits of the land: for it is holy unto the LORD. *(The portion here described is that reserved for the Levites, who will have a part in Sanctuary duties, but not the Sacrifices. That will be attended to solely by the "sons of Zadok." Their portion will be about 42 miles long and 17 miles wide. They will not be able to "sell, neither exchange, nor alienate" this portion. It is holy.*

The "firstfruits" of the land, i.e., the first crop the land produces, is not to be sold, but instead given to the Lord as an offering. This typifies our inheritance in Christ!)

A PORTION FOR THE CITY
FOR GENERAL USE

15 And the five thousand, that are left in the breadth over against the five and twenty thousand, shall be a profane place for the city, for dwelling, and for suburbs: and the city shall be in the midst thereof. *(The term, "profane place," simply means that it is not dedicated to sacred use in the same sense as the Sanctuary. The area will be about 42 miles long and 8 miles wide.*

The phrase, "The city shall be in the midst thereof," concerns a city unlike any the world has ever seen or known. It will be a city totally free from crime, poverty, hunger, hate, war, greed, etc. Even though every other city in the world at that time will fall into the same category, still, none will have the Glory of God as this "city" [Isa. 62:2-3].)

16 And these shall be the measures thereof;

the north side four thousand and five hundred, and the south side four thousand and five hundred, and on the east side four thousand and five hundred, and the west side four thousand and five hundred. *(These dimensions speak of the city proper, pertaining to business, etc. It will be about five miles square. The measurement is given for each side of the city in repetition in order that it may be known that this city is just as grand on one side as on the other.)*

17 And the suburbs of the city shall be toward the north two hundred and fifty, and toward the south two hundred and fifty, and toward the east two hundred and fifty, and toward the west two hundred and fifty. *(There will be about a half mile laid out on each side of the city called "the suburbs," which will probably be left as a garden or park.)*

18 And the residue in length over against the oblation of the holy portion shall be ten thousand eastward, and ten thousand westward: and it shall be over against the oblation of the holy portion; and the increase thereof shall be for food unto them who serve the city.

19 And they who serve the city shall serve it out of all the Tribes of Israel. *(These Scriptures portray the fact that two sections of land will be set aside, reserved for farming, on either side of the city. Each side will measure approximately 17 miles long and 8 miles wide. This will be ample land to support the city with food, plus the Sanctuary area. Inasmuch as the curse will be lifted, the abundance produced will be more than enough.*

The phrase, "They who serve the city," will probably be representatives from all the Tribes of Israel; therefore, there will be no partiality shown, nor favoritism.)

20 All the oblation shall be five and twenty thousand by five and twenty thousand: you shall offer the holy oblation foursquare, with the possession of the city. *(The entirety of the area, including city, suburbs, farming land, and the place of the Sanctuary, will measure about 42 miles long and 42 miles wide. It will be, as stated, "foursquare," thereby, signifying the totality of the Gospel of Jesus Christ as the whole Gospel for the whole man.*

Of all the world, this area will be the most important on Earth, because Christ is there.)

A LAND FOR THE PRINCE

21 And the residue shall be for the prince, on the one side and on the other of the holy

oblation, and of the possession of the city, over against the five and twenty thousand of the oblation toward the east border, and westward over against the five and twenty thousand toward the west border, over against the portions for the prince: and it shall be the holy oblation; and the Sanctuary of the house shall be in the midst thereof. *(The land East and West of the Holy Oblation will be for the Prince of Israel. This area on both sides is called "the residue." It seems these portions given to him will be about 8 1/2 miles long and 8 1/2 miles wide. They will be on the East and West corners, respectively. Therefore, he will have access to whatever he needs from either side.*

Once again, the Holy Spirit by design repeats the phrase, "And the Sanctuary of the House shall be in the midst thereof." It is meant to impress upon the Believer that all Blessing flows from this Sanctuary and, therefore, from Christ.)

22 Moreover from the possession of the Levites, and from the possession of the city, being in the midst of that which is the prince's, between the border of Judah and the border of Benjamin, shall be for the prince. *(One portion for the Prince [High Priest] will border the Tribe of "Judah," while the other portion will border the Tribe of "Benjamin." These were the two Tribes that remained true to the Temple and the Worship of God when the nation of Israel was divided upon the death of Solomon. Therefore, their faithfulness is not forgotten, but will ever portray their allegiance to the Lord of Glory and His Word.)*

PORTIONS FOR OTHER TRIBES

23 As for the rest of the Tribes, from the east side unto the west side, Benjamin shall have a portion.

24 And by the border of Benjamin, from the east side unto the west side, Simeon shall have a portion.

25 And by the border of Simeon, from the east side unto the west side, Issachar a portion.

26 And by the border of Issachar, from the east side unto the west side, Zebulun a portion.

27 And by the border of Zebulun, from the east side unto the west side, Gad a portion.

28 And by the border of Gad, at the south side southward, the border shall be even from Tamar unto the waters of strife in Kadesh, and to the river toward the great sea.

29 This is the land which you shall divide by lot unto the Tribes of Israel for inheritance, and these are their portions, saith the Lord GOD. *(The phrase, "Divide by lot," originally referred to the Urim and the Thummim, which were held by the High Priest and used to discern the Mind of God [Josh. 13:7; 15:1; 16:1; 17:1]. Therefore, the statement, as recorded here, simply means that each possession and its boundaries have been decided by the Holy Spirit.*

The phrase, "These are their portions, saith the Lord GOD," proclaims the fact that the portions will never again be changed or taken by an enemy.)

THE CITY OF JERUSALEM TO BE FOURSQUARE, PATTERNED AFTER THE HEAVENLY JERUSALEM

30 And these are the goings out of the city on the north side, four thousand and five hundred measures. *(This final portion is dedicated to the gates, dimensions, and name of the city. The phrase, "And these are the goings out of the city," refers to the walls around the city and its measurement, which will be about 7 1/2 miles on each side.)*

31 And the gates of the city shall be after the names of the Tribes of Israel: three gates northward; one gate of Reuben, one gate of Judah, one gate of Levi. *(This city will be foursquare, with three Gates to each side, totaling twelve Gates; the "names of the Tribes of Israel" will be on the twelve Gates.)*

32 And at the east side four thousand and five hundred: and three gates; and one gate of Joseph, one gate of Benjamin, one gate of Dan.

33 And at the south side four thousand and five hundred measures: and three gates; one gate of Simeon, one gate of Issachar, one gate of Zebulun.

34 At the west side four thousand and five hundred, with their three gates; one gate of Gad, one gate of Asher, one gate of Naphtali.

35 It was round about eighteen thousand measures: and the name of the city from that day shall be, The LORD is there. *(The city will be about 30 miles in circumference at its perimeter. Even though this Glorious Name, "The LORD is there," is given here, this is only one of a number of new names for the Earthly Jerusalem.*

The phrase, "The LORD is there," means in Hebrew, "Adonai-Shammah" or "Jehovah-Shammah," meaning literally what it says. For the Messiah will be there reigning visibly and eternally in Israel [Isa. 9:6-7; Lk. 1:32-33; Rev. 11:15; 20:4-10].)

THE BOOK OF
DANIEL

CHAPTER 1
(607 B.C.)
THE FIRST DEPORTATION TO BABYLON

IN the third year of the reign of Jehoiakim king of Judah came Nebuchadnezzar king of Babylon unto Jerusalem, and besieged it. *(The phrase, "In the third year of the reign of Jehoiakim," seems to be a contradiction in that Jeremiah records this siege of Jerusalem as occurring in the fourth year of king Jehoiakim [Jer. 24:1]. However, in this there is no discrepancy, for Daniel points to the setting out of the Babylonian Monarch toward Jerusalem, while Jeremiah relates his arrival the following year.)*

2 And the Lord gave Jehoiakim king of Judah into his hand, with part of the vessels of the House of God: which he carried into the land of Shinar to the house of his god; and he brought the vessels into the treasure house of his god. *(The phrase, "And the Lord gave Jehoiakim king of Judah into his hand," refers to the Lord being totally the Disposer of events. The phrase, "With part of the vessels of the House of God," tells us of the plunder of a part of the Temple. Exactly which Vessels were plundered is not stated.*

Nebuchadnezzar's placing of these Vessels in the "house of his god" proclaims the fact that the heathen Monarch erroneously thought his god Nebo was greater than Jehovah of Israel.)

DANIEL AND HIS FRIENDS CHOSEN
FOR THE KING'S SERVICE

3 And the king spoke unto Ashpenaz the master of his eunuchs, that he should bring certain of the Children of Israel, and of the king's seed, and of the princes *(the boys chosen belonged to the royal family and, therefore, to nobility; they were most probably in their teens. Daniel and the three Hebrew children were included. The word "eunuchs" has as its primary meaning "court officer." In some cases, these individuals were castrated; however, this does not seem to be the case with Daniel and his companions, for they were "without blemish");*

4 Children in whom was no blemish, but well favoured, and skilful in all wisdom, and cunning in knowledge, and understanding science, and such as had ability in them to stand in the king's palace, and whom they might teach the learning and the tongue of the Chaldeans. *(The phrase, "The tongue of the Chaldeans," probably referred to the learning of the Aramaic language and the cuneiform style of writing employed by ancient Babylon.)*

5 And the king appointed them a daily provision of the king's meat, and of the wine which he drank: so nourishing them three years, that at the end thereof they might stand before the king. *(The "three year" period had to do with their education and their physical well-being. The type of "wine" used here had to do with the gods worshipped by Nebuchadnezzar. In fact, it was wine which had been offered to idols. The thinking of the Babylonians was that the drinking of this particular "wine" would enhance the intelligence of Daniel and the others.)*

6 Now among these were of the children of Judah, Daniel, Hananiah, Mishael, and Azariah *(no doubt, there were many, possibly hundreds, who were set apart, groomed to serve as wise men of the Babylonian Empire. Daniel and the Hebrew children were only "among these"):*

THEIR NAMES CHANGED

7 Unto whom the prince of the eunuchs gave names: for he gave unto Daniel the name of Belteshazzar; and to Hananiah, of Shadrach; and to Mishael, of Meshach; and to Azariah, of Abed-nego. *(By giving these men new names, Nebuchadnezzar was trying to blot out the name and memory of Jehovah, the God of the Hebrews.)*

DANIEL'S PURPOSE

8 But Daniel purposed in his heart that he would not defile himself with the portion of the king's meat, nor with the wine which he drank: therefore he requested of the prince of the eunuchs that he might not defile himself. *(The phrase, "But Daniel purposed in his heart," means that he was resolutely determined, whatever the price that would have to be paid. In other words, he stood ready to give up his life before he would disobey the Lord, if that's what*

was demanded.)

9 Now God had brought Daniel into favour and tender love with the prince of the eunuchs. *(Men rule, but God overrules!)*

10 And the prince of the eunuchs said unto Daniel, I fear my lord the king, who has appointed your meat and your drink: for why should he see your faces worse liking than the children which are of your sort? then shall you make me endanger my head to the king. *(What Daniel was demanding was a very serious thing. To not partake of the "meat" and "wine" was an insult to the king. However, the Lord would give Daniel wisdom as to the disposition of this problem.)*

11 Then said Daniel to Melzar, whom the prince of the eunuchs had set over Daniel, Hananiah, Mishael, and Azariah. *("Melzar" was the steward, or butler, who had charge of the king's meat and wine. He answered to the "prince of the eunuchs.")*

THE TEN-DAY TEST

12 Prove your servants, I beseech you, ten days; and let them give us pulse to eat, and water to drink. *(Daniel proposed a test of "ten days" during which they would be given only vegetables to eat and water to drink. This didn't mean that Daniel and the others were vegetarians, but rather that the meat provided by the Babylonians was unlawful to eat because of being unclean, or else it was not properly prepared!)*

13 Then let our countenances be looked upon before you, and the countenance of the children who eat of the portion of the king's meat: and as you see, deal with your servants.

14 So he consented to them in this matter, and proved them ten days. *(Evidently, the Lord told Daniel to do this. The Lord also helped Daniel, because otherwise ten days would not be enough time to show much either way.)*

15 And at the end of ten days their countenances appeared fairer and fatter in flesh than all the children which did eat the portion of the king's meat.

16 Thus Melzar took away the portion of their meat, and the wine that they should drink; and gave them pulse. *(It is evident that the Lord took a hand in the proceedings.)*

GOD'S BLESSINGS; THEIR SUPERIORITY TO OTHERS

17 As for these four children, God gave them knowledge and skill in all learning and wisdom: and Daniel had understanding in all visions and dreams. *(The phrase, "God gave," refers to the proclamation by the Holy Spirit that the three years of their training in all the sciences and arts of Babylonian learning did them no good whatsoever. It was the Lord Who gave them what they needed.)*

18 Now at the end of the days that the king had said he should bring them in, then the prince of the eunuchs brought them in before Nebuchadnezzar. *(When these young men stood before Nebuchadnezzar, the ruler of the world, little did the Monarch realize how prominently four of them, and especially Daniel, would figure in the remainder of his life.)*

19 And the king communed with them; and among them all was found none like Daniel, Hananiah, Mishael, and Azariah: therefore stood they before the king. *(The king found "these four children" were far superior to all others.)*

20 And in all matters of wisdom and understanding, that the king enquired of them, he found them ten times better than all the magicians and astrologers who were in all his realm. *(This is astounding, considering that these four were still only boys, probably still in their teen years, or in their early twenties at the most.)*

21 And Daniel continued even unto the first year of king Cyrus. *(The word "continued" means that he continued in office until the first year of King Cyrus. He actually lived two or three years longer. He witnessed the commencement and the ending of the seventy-year captivity.)*

CHAPTER 2
(603 B.C.)
NEBUCHADNEZZAR'S DREAM; HIS WISE MEN CALLED

AND in the second year of the reign of Nebuchadnezzar Nebuchadnezzar dreamed dreams wherewith his spirit was troubled, and his sleep broke from him. *(The "second year" of this Verse concerns his reign as sole king. Actually, he had reigned as co-regent with his father for several years, in which some or all of the three-year time period took place. The "dream" which "troubled" him was sent by the Lord.)*

2 Then the king commanded to call the magicians, and the astrologers, and the sorcerers, and the Chaldeans, for to shew the king his dreams. So they came and stood before

the king. *(The king's action in consulting priests and mediums is one of the many proofs of the accuracy of this history, for in their difficulties unconverted men seek help in every direction other than from the Lord.)*

3 And the king said unto them, I have dreamed a dream, and my spirit was troubled to know the dream.

NEBUCHADNEZZAR'S DEMAND

4 Then spoke the Chaldeans to the king in Syriack, O king, live for ever: tell your servants the dream, and we will shew the interpretation. *(Had the dream been told unto them, the "interpretation" they would have given would have been something made up out of their own minds, and would not have been the true interpretation.)*

5 The king answered and said to the Chaldeans, The thing is gone from me: if you will not make known unto me the dream, with the interpretation thereof, you shall be cut in pieces, and your houses shall be made a dunghill. *(The Lord directed this scenario that Nebuchadnezzar couldn't even remember his dream, much less its meaning.)*

6 But if you show the dream, and the interpretation thereof, you shall receive of me gifts and rewards and great honour: therefore shew me the dream, and the interpretation thereof. *(As Nebuchadnezzar had threatened these magicians and astrologers with death upon their lack of ability, now he promises them great riches if they will but only live up to their advertisement.)*

7 They answered again and said, Let the king tell his servants the dream, and we will show the interpretation of it.

8 The king answered and said, I know of certainty that you would gain the time, because you see the thing is gone from me. *(Their answer to him has the very opposite effect than they had hoped.)*

9 But if you will not make known unto me the dream, there is but one decree for you: for you have prepared lying and corrupt words to speak before me, till the time be changed: therefore tell me the dream, and I shall know that you can show me the interpretation thereof. *(The king now knows that their silence was due to their inability to answer.)*

INABILITY OF THE WISE MEN

10 The Chaldeans answered before the king, and said, There is not a man upon the Earth who can shew the king's matter: therefore there is no king, lord, nor ruler, who asked such things at any magician, or astrologer, or Chaldean. *(They were wrong! There was at least one man who could, but only because he knew the Lord. His name was Daniel.)*

11 And it is a rare thing that the king requires, and there is none other that can show it before the king, except the gods, whose dwelling is not with flesh. *(The king was wrong in using the word "gods." There were no "gods," only One God, Jehovah. The king would soon learn about Jehovah!)*

NEBUCHADNEZZAR'S DECREE

12 For this cause the king was angry and very furious, and commanded to destroy all the wise men of Babylon. *(The idea is: he had lost faith, at least to some degree, in his gods, Nebo and Bel, whom his wise men represented.)*

13 And the decree went forth that the wise men should be slain; and they sought Daniel and his fellows to be slain.

DANIEL'S OFFER TO INTERPRET THE DREAM AND HIS PRAYER FOR HELP

14 Then Daniel answered with counsel and wisdom to Arioch the captain of the king's guard, which was gone forth to slay the wise men of Babylon:

15 He answered and said to Arioch the king's captain, Why is the decree so hasty from the king? Then Arioch made the thing known to Daniel. *(This proclaims "Arioch," who is spoken of favorably by the Holy Spirit, seeking to find a way out of this dilemma.)*

16 Then Daniel went in, and desired of the king that he would give him time, and that he would shew the king the interpretation. *(The phrase, "And that he would show the king the interpretation," shows an assurance on Daniel's part that the Lord would reveal such to him. God's Plan was being brought about exactly as designed by the Holy Spirit!)*

17 Then Daniel went to his house, and made the thing known to Hananiah, Mishael, and Azariah, his companions:

18 That they would desire mercies of the God of Heaven concerning this secret; that Daniel and his fellows should not perish with the rest of the wise men of Babylon. *(They called a prayer meeting!)*

THE DREAM REVEALED TO DANIEL

19 Then was the secret revealed unto Daniel in a night vision. Then Daniel blessed the God of Heaven. *(This Passage means that the same dream that was given to Nebuchadnezzar was now given to Daniel, and no doubt that very night.)*

20 Daniel answered and said, Blessed be the name of God for ever and ever: for wisdom and might are His *(in this and the following Passages, we are given an account of the total and absolute rulership and control by the Lord of all His Creation)*:

21 And He changes the times and the seasons: He removes kings, and sets up kings: He gives wisdom unto the wise, and knowledge to them who know understanding *(the phrase, "He changes the times and the seasons," has reference to the successive Empires, as allowed by the Lord and seen by Daniel in the vision of the night)*:

22 He reveals the deep and secret things: He knows what is in the darkness, and the light dwells with him. *(God is not only the God of nature, of providence, and of man, but also of Revelation. He can make known to man what otherwise man could never know. He is the very Source of all light and enlightenment [I Tim. 6:16].)*

23 I thank You, and praise You, O Thou God of my fathers, Who has given me wisdom and might, and has made known unto me now what we desired of You: for You have now made known unto us the king's matter. *(Daniel now particularizes his reasons for praise and thanksgiving. He addresses God as the God of his fathers. He appeals to Him as the Covenant God of Israel, Who had led their fathers through the wilderness.)*

DANIEL BEFORE NEBUCHADNEZZAR; GLORIFIES GOD; TELLS THE KING THE DREAM

24 Therefore Daniel went in unto Arioch, whom the king had ordained to destroy the wise men of Babylon: he went and said thus unto him; Destroy not the wise men of Babylon: bring me in before the king, and I will show unto the king the interpretation.

25 Then Arioch brought in Daniel before the king in haste, and said thus unto him, I have found a man of the captives of Judah, who will make known unto the king the interpretation.

(How much that Daniel had revealed unto Arioch, if anything, we aren't told.)

26 The king answered and said to Daniel, whose name was Belteshazzar, Are you able to make known unto me the dream which I have seen, and the interpretation thereof?

27 Daniel answered in the presence of the king, and said, The secret which the king has demanded cannot the wise men, the astrologers, the magicians, the soothsayers, shew unto the king *(there is a shade of rebuke to the king implied in Daniel's answer. He asks this question, no doubt, at the instigation of the Holy Spirit)*;

28 But there is a God in Heaven Who reveals secrets, and makes known to the king Nebuchadnezzar what shall be in the latter days. Your dream, and the visions of your head upon your bed, are these *(the phrase, "What shall be in the latter days," is revealing indeed! Those who claim that Daniel's Prophecies have no reference to the last days, but instead were fulfilled at the time of Christ, evidently have not read this Verse)*;

29 As for you, O king, your thoughts came into your mind upon your bed, what should come to pass hereafter: and He Who reveals secrets makes known to you what shall come to pass. *(The idea of Daniel's statement is to let the king know that this dream and its interpretation is of tremendous import, hence, the reason for the king being so troubled as to know what it was and its meaning.)*

30 But as for me, this secret is not revealed to me for any wisdom that I have more than any living, but for their sakes who shall make known the interpretation to the king, and that you might know the thoughts of your heart. *(Daniel gave all glory to the Lord! As well, in all of this the Lord took pity on these heathen sages! Such is God, and such is His Mercy!*

The phrase, "And that you might know the thoughts of your heart," presents the beginning of the appeal of the Holy Spirit to this heathen Monarch, which quite possibly ultimately resulted in his Salvation.)

31 Thou, O king, saw, and behold a great image. This great image, whose brightness was excellent, stood before you; and the form thereof was terrible. *(The two words, "excellent" and "terrible," both characterize the history of Gentile powers from the days of Nebuchadnezzar and continuing on to the coming of Christ with His Saints. Excellent and terrible things often exist side by side. When Christ sets*

up His Millennial Kingdom, only that which is excellent will exist.

The "great image" would portray all the World Empires for the future, at least as they related to Israel.)

32 This image's head was of fine gold, his breast and his arms of silver, his belly and his thighs of brass.

33 His legs of iron, his feet part of iron and part of clay. (The Holy Spirit outlines the successive kingdoms by a representation of precious metals, iron, and clay.)

34 You saw till that a Stone was cut out without hands, which smote the image upon his feet that were of iron and clay, and broke them to pieces. (The "Stone" is the Lord Jesus Christ, and symbolizes His Second Coming. The phrase, "Without hands," is an expression emphasizing the absence of all human instrumentality and the act of God alone. This destroys the popular belief that Christianity will take over the world, with the Gospel gradually conquering all of mankind.

Actually, Bible Christianity ultimately will cover the entirety of the Earth, but only after the Second Coming, even as this Verse proclaims.)

35 Then was the iron, the clay, the brass, the silver, and the gold, broken to pieces together, and became like the chaff of the summer threshingfloors; and the wind carried them away, that no place was found for them: and the Stone that smote the image became a great mountain, and filled the whole Earth. (This portrays the Second Coming of the Lord and the destruction of all Gentile powers, meaning that never again will Gentile power hold sway, for that time is forever ended.

After the Second Coming, Christ will set up His Kingdom of Righteousness, with Israel then being the predominant nation in the world, and remaining that way forever. Hence, the promises made to the Patriarchs and Prophets of old will be fulfilled in totality.)

THE INTERPRETATION: HEAD OF GOLD IS BABYLON

36 This is the dream; and we will tell the interpretation thereof before the king.

37 Thou, O king, are a king of kings: for the God of Heaven has given you a kingdom, power, and strength, and glory. (This confirms the statement of Daniel in Verse 21, "He removes kings, and sets up kings.")

38 And wheresoever the children of men dwell, the beasts of the field and the fowls of

the heaven has He given into your hand, and has made you ruler over them all. You are this head of gold. ("This head of gold" represented the Babylonian Empire, which was the grandest of all, at least as far as splendor and glory were concerned.)

BREAST AND ARMS OF SILVER: MEDO-PERSIA; BELLY AND THIGHS OF BRASS: GRECIA

39 And after you shall arise another kingdom inferior to you, and another third kingdom of brass, which shall bear rule over all the earth. (The first kingdom [after Babylon] is the "Medo-Persian Empire," which would replace the Babylonian Empire, and which would come up in a few years. It would be "inferior" only in grandness and glory, not in strength. The "third kingdom" mentioned here is the Grecian Empire, which will proclaim the rise of Alexander the Great. It would come about in a little over two hundred years from this time.)

LEGS OF IRON: ROME

40 And the fourth kingdom shall be strong as iron: forasmuch as iron breaks in pieces and subdues all things: and as iron that breaks all these, shall it break in pieces and bruise. (This "fourth kingdom" is the Roman Empire, and is represented by the "legs of iron." It would be the strongest of all!)

FEET OF IRON AND CLAY: REVISED ROMAN EMPIRE

41 And whereas you saw the feet and toes, part of the potters' clay, and part of iron, the kingdom shall be divided; but there shall be in it of the strength of the iron, forasmuch as you saw the iron mixed with miry clay. (All that we have previously studied represents Empires that have come and gone; however, the "feet" and "toes" of this statue of iron and clay represent that which is yet to come.)

42 And as the toes of the feet were part of iron, and part of clay, so the kingdom shall be partly strong, and partly broken. (This Verse represents the ten-nation confederation, with the "toes of the feet" symbolic of this confederation, which will greatly oppose Israel in the very near future.)

43 And whereas you saw iron mixed with miry clay, they shall mingle themselves with

the seed of men: but they shall not cleave one to another, even as iron is not mixed with clay. *(Their confederation will not succeed, because of the "miry clay," which expresses that some of the kingdoms are weak. As stated, this will take place in the near future.)*

THE STONE: THE KINGDOM OF HEAVEN ON EARTH UNDER THE MESSIAH

44 And in the days of these kings shall the God of Heaven set up a kingdom, which shall never be destroyed: and the kingdom shall not be left to other people, but it shall break in pieces and consume all these kingdoms, and it shall stand for ever. *(This Verse is basically the same as Verses 34 and 35. It portrays the Coming of the Lord, and the Millennial Kingdom which He will bring about.)*

45 Forasmuch as you saw that the Stone was cut out of the mountain without hands, and that it broke in pieces the iron, the brass, the clay, the silver, and the gold, the great God has made known to the king what shall come to pass hereafter: and the dream is certain, and the interpretation thereof sure. *(Inasmuch as the king has seen all of this in his dream, he consequently now has no excuse to continue worshipping his dead idols; he should rather worship the "Great God" Who "has made known to the king what shall come to pass hereafter.")*

DANIEL PROMOTED

46 Then the king Nebuchadnezzar fell upon his face, and worshipped Daniel, and commanded that they should offer an oblation and sweet odours unto him. *(There is no indication that Daniel accepted this worship.)*

47 The king answered unto Daniel, and said, Of a truth it is, that your God is a God of gods, and a Lord of kings, and a revealer of secrets, seeing you could reveal this secret. *(The word "answered" supports the conviction that Daniel refused Divine honors and directed the king away from himself to God. In his statement, Nebuchadnezzar concedes that Jehovah is the greatest, at least as it regards the "revealing of secrets.")*

48 Then the king made Daniel a great man, and gave him many great gifts, and made him ruler over the whole province of Babylon, and chief of the governors over all the wise men of Babylon. *(Therefore, next to the king, Daniel was the most powerful man in the world. He was also looked at as the wisest man in the world,*

and rightly so!)

49 Then Daniel requested of the king, and he set Shadrach, Meshach, and Abed-nego, over the affairs of the province of Babylon: but Daniel sat in the gate of the king. *(The phrase, "But Daniel sat in the gate of the king," means he was appointed Prime Minister, the most powerful position in the world of that day other than the king himself. The "gate" means "the door" to the king.)*

CHAPTER 3
(580 B.C.)
THE IMAGE OF GOLD AND THE COMMAND TO WORSHIP IT

NEBUCHADNEZZAR the king made an image of gold, whose height was threescore cubits, and the breadth thereof six cubits: he set it up in the plain of Dura, in the province of Babylon. *(According to the Septuagint, Nebuchadnezzar built the image of gold in the 18th year of his reign, about a year before he burned Jerusalem [586 B.C.]. Daniel and his friends had been in Babylon now for nearly 20 years. The erection of this image was approximately 15 years after the events of the dream and its interpretation. This illustrates the darkness and incurable rebellion of the natural heart. It proves that, apart from a new spiritual birth, no circumstances, however powerful, can teach man to know and worship God.)*

2 Then Nebuchadnezzar the king sent to gather together the princes, the governors, and the captains, the judges, the treasurers, the counselors, the sheriffs, and all the rulers of the provinces, to come to the dedication of the image which Nebuchadnezzar the king had set up.

3 Then the princes, the governors, and captains, the judges, the treasurers, the counselors, the sheriffs, and all the rulers of the provinces, were gathered together unto the dedication of the image that Nebuchadnezzar the king had set up; and they stood before the image that Nebuchadnezzar had set up. *(There is some indication that this group of notables also included all of the conquered nations. However, it is only an indication and by no means certain from the original text.)*

4 Then an herald cried aloud, To you it is commanded, O people, nations, and languages,

5 That at what time you hear the sound of the cornet, flute, harp, sackbut, psaltery, dulcimer, and all kinds of musick, you fall down

and worship the golden image that Nebuchadnezzar the king has set up:

6 And whoso falls not down and worships shall the same hour be cast into the midst of a burning fiery furnace. *(Satan not only demands worship, and in many and varied ways, but also attaches a penalty to all those who will not obey. Actually, only a tiny few refuse to obey!)*

7 Therefore at that time, when all the people heard the sound of the cornet, flute, harp, sackbut, psaltery, and all kinds of musick, all the people, the nations, and the languages, fell down and worshipped the golden image that Nebuchadnezzar the king had set up. *(This Passage indicates that all of the leaders from the conquered nations from all over the Babylonian Empire were brought in.)*

SHADRACH, MESHACH, AND ABED-NEGO ON TRIAL FOR DISOBEDIENCE

8 Wherefore at that time certain Chaldeans came near, and accused the Jews. *(The phrase, "Accused the Jews," was pointed more particularly at "Shadrach, Meshach, and Abed-nego," but actually pertained to all Jews.)*

9 They spoke and said to the king Nebuchadnezzar, O king, live for ever.

10 Thou, O king, have made a decree, that every man that shall hear the sound of the cornet, flute, harp, sackbut, psaltery, and dulcimer, and all kinds of musick, shall fall down and worship the golden image:

11 And whoso falls not down and worships, that he should be cast into the midst of a burning fiery furnace.

12 There are certain Jews whom you have set over the affairs of the province of Babylon, Shadrach, Meshach, and Abed-nego; these men, O king, have not regarded you: they serve not your gods, nor worship the golden image which you have set up. *(Upon reading this narrative, one may think that these proceedings only related to the swollen ego of this Monarch. While this no doubt strongly entered into the proceedings, still, this entire scenario pertained to the supremacy of Babylon and the worship of its gods.)*

13 Then Nebuchadnezzar in his rage and fury commanded to bring Shadrach, Meshach, and Abed-nego. Then they brought these men before the king. *(Quite possibly, along with their disobedience, the jealousy of the Babylonian officials showed itself regarding these "certain Jews." These, under Daniel, had been elevated to high positions of power in the Empire; therefore, with*

great joy, the accusers will point a finger of accusation at "these men," as they are called, demanding that Nebuchadnezzar take steps.)*

14 Nebuchadnezzar spoke and said unto them, Is it true, O Shadrach, Meshach, and Abed-nego, do not you serve my gods, nor worship the golden image which I have set up? *(The question, "Is it true?" concerning their refusal to bow, is actually asked of every single person in one form or the other. The answer has no middle ground; it is either an unequivocal "yes" or "no"!)*

15 Now if you be ready that at what time you hear the sound of the cornet, flute, harp, sackbut, psaltery, and dulcimer, and all kinds of musick, you fall down and worship the image which I have made; well: but if you worship not, you shall be cast the same hour into the midst of a burning fiery furnace; and who is that God Who shall deliver you out of my hands? *(The king was to quickly find out as to Who exactly "that God" was!)*

16 Shadrach, Meshach, and Abed-nego, answered and said to the king, O Nebuchadnezzar, we are not careful to answer you in this matter. *(The phrase, "We are not careful to answer you in this matter," is somewhat clumsy in the English translation. It actually means that it is not something they have to think about or give careful consideration to, as the matter is not open to discussion. It is a decision they made a long time ago, and the consequences are of no concern.)*

17 If it be so, our God Whom we serve is able to deliver us from the burning fiery furnace, and He will deliver us out of your hand, O king. *(At this stage, they have no assurance that they will be delivered, only that the Lord is able to deliver.)*

18 But if not, be it known unto you, O king, that we will not serve your gods, nor worship the golden image which you have set up. *(The words, "but if not," do not show a lack of Faith, but only that they are not functioning in the realm of presumption, as do so many Believers.)*

NEBUCHADNEZZAR SENTENCES THEM TO THE FIERY FURNACE

19 Then was Nebuchadnezzar full of fury, and the form of his visage was changed against Shadrach, Meshach, and Abed-nego: therefore he spoke, and commanded that they should heat the furnace one seven times more than it was wont to be heated. *(To express his wrath and to appease the gods, he will order the furnace to*

be heated sevenfold hotter. *The Babylonians rec-*
ognized seven planets and seven gods of the plan-
ets, one for each. Therefore, the number "seven"
may have been used to appease these "gods.")

20 And he commanded the most mighty
men who were in his army to bind Shadrach,
Meshach, and Abed-nego, and to cast them into
the burning fiery furnace. *(These "mighty men"*
were no doubt chosen for a particular reason.
The king might be ready to admit that no accu-
mulation of human power could equal Divine
power, yet it is obvious that these men of might
were chosen for the purpose that, despite Divine
power [at least if such should manifest itself],
the royal sentence might still be carried out.)

21 Then these men were bound in their
coats, their hosen, and their hats, and their
other garments, and were cast into the midst
of the burning fiery furnace. *(This was no*
doubt done because the king thought that these
items of clothing, being of inflammable mate-
rial, would hasten their deaths. Conversely, it
did the very opposite, proving the miracle-work-
ing Power of God.)

22 Therefore because the king's commandment was urgent, and the furnace exceeding
hot, the flame of the fire slew those men who
took up Shadrach, Meshach, and Abed-nego.

23 And these three men, Shadrach, Meshach,
and Abed-nego, fell down bound into the midst
of the burning fiery furnace. *(The furnace was*
so hot that the "mighty men" employed by Nebu-
chadnezzar were killed by the excruciating heat.)

GOD'S SUPERNATURAL DELIVERANCE;
THE KING AMAZED

24 Then Nebuchadnezzar the king was
astonied, and rose up in haste, and spoke, and
said unto his counselors, Did not we cast three
men bound into the midst of the fire? They
answered and said unto the king, True, O king.
(The word "astonied" means "terrified." What
the king saw terrified him!)

25 He answered and said, Lo, I see four men
loose, walking in the midst of the fire, and
they have no hurt; and the form of the fourth
is like the Son of God. *(The original language*
reads: "a son of God.")

26 Then Nebuchadnezzar came near to the
mouth of the burning fiery furnace, and spoke
and said, Shadrach, Meshach, and Abed-nego,
you servants of the Most High God, come forth,
and come hither. Then Shadrach, Meshach,
and Abed-nego, came forth of the midst of the

fire. *(The constant repetition of the names,*
"Shadrach, Meshach, and Abed-nego," is not due
to poor sentence structure on the part of the
Holy Spirit, but is instead by design. The Holy
Spirit desires the world to know that it was the
same three men who went into the fire who also
came out of the fire.)

27 And the princes, governors, and captains,
and the king's counselors, being gathered together, saw these men, upon whose bodies the
fire had no power, nor was an hair of their
head singed, neither were their coats changed,
nor the smell of fire had passed on them. *(The*
Babylonian god of fire was "Iz-bar." Conse-
quently, this event was all the more important
to the Babylonians. The God of Israel was thus
manifested as so much higher than this "Iz-bar,"
inasmuch that He could deliver His servants even
when in the very element in which "Iz-bar" sup-
posedly had his power.)

28 Then Nebuchadnezzar spoke, and said,
Blessed be the God of Shadrach, Meshach, and
Abed-nego, Who has sent His Angel, and delivered His servants who trusted in Him, and
have changed the king's word, and yielded
their bodies, that they might not serve nor
worship any god, except their own God. *(There*
is no evidence, even regarding the statements
made by the Monarch, that he accepted the Lord
at this time. Actually, all evidence is that he did
not! This would come at a later date. But still,
before all he acknowledges the supremacy of Je-
hovah in comparison to his national deities.)

NEBUCHADNEZZAR'S DECREE

29 Therefore I make a decree, That every
people, nation, and language, which speak any
thing amiss against the God of Shadrach,
Meshach, and Abed-nego, shall be cut in pieces,
and their houses shall be made a dunghill:
because there is no other God Who can deliver
after this sort. *(The idea expressed in this Verse*
is that words spoken against Jehovah might ex-
cite His Wrath and bring down damage on the
Empire. Therefore, Nebuchadnezzar was not
necessarily jealous for the honor of Jehovah, but
rather for the safety of the Babylonian supremacy.
In this, he at least had more sense than most
modern political leaders.)

30 Then the king promoted Shadrach,
Meshach, and Abed-nego, in the province
of Babylon. *(A few minutes before, the king*
was commanding their deaths, and now he is
commanding their promotion. Such is the Lord!)

CHAPTER 4
(570 B.C.)
THE KING'S PROCLAMATION

NEBUCHADNEZZAR the king, unto all people, nations, and languages, who dwell in all the Earth; Peace be multiplied unto you. *(The salutation is actually the benediction. The king begins this account of a terrible seven-year period of insanity by giving Glory to God. He begins after the fact, showing that all was unnecessary and was brought on by his pride and stubbornness before God. He now recognizes that and begins the Chapter by praising the Lord, which shows Repentance on his part.*

The phrase, "In all the Earth," must be understood as all the Earth under Nebuchadnezzar — not elsewhere.)

2 I thought it good to show the signs and wonders that the High God has wrought toward me.

3 How great are His signs! And how mighty are His wonders! His Kingdom is an everlasting kingdom, and His Dominion is from generation to generation. *(The phrase, "The signs and wonders that the High God has wrought toward me," is all because of Daniel and the three Hebrew Children. How fortunate was this king to have had such in his Empire, and, above that, that he had the foresight to recognize it, and ultimately to be blessed.)*

NEBUCHADNEZZAR'S VISION OF A TREE

4 I Nebuchadnezzar was at rest in my house, and flourishing in my palace:

5 I saw a dream which made me afraid, and the thoughts upon my bed and the visions of my head troubled me. *(Now the king will begin to give his account of what happened to him, which brought him to the place evidenced in Verses 1 through 3. This was the 18th year of his reign, which would have been about 15 years after the dream of the image and the interpretation. It was about a year before the capture of Jerusalem, which, according to Jer. 52:12, happened in the 19th year of Nebuchadnezzar. Therefore, he burned Jerusalem almost immediately before his insanity.)*

6 Therefore made I a decree to bring in all the wise men of Babylon before me, that they might make known unto me the interpretation of the dream.

7 Then came in the magicians, the astrologers, the Chaldeans, and the soothsayers: and I told the dream before them; but they did not make known unto me the interpretation thereof. *(Quite possibly, they gave him some type of "interpretation" which he knew in his spirit was wrong. Therefore, he sent for Daniel.)*

8 But at the last Daniel came in before me, whose name was Belteshazzar, according to the name of my god, and in whom is the spirit of the holy gods: and before him I told the dream, saying *(the phrase, "Whose name was Belteshazzar, according to the name of my god," reflects him still leaning toward these fake Babylonian deities. The great miracle he had seen years before, regarding the Revelation of the dream and the interpretation, and the recent miracle of the fiery furnace were tremendously impressive and gave the king serious pause; but they did not involve him personally, at least in a negative way, and consequently, they did not bring him to surrender.*

The phrase, "And in whom is the spirit of the holy gods," portrays him putting the God of Daniel in a superior position, but still clinging to the old gods),

9 O Belteshazzar, master of the magicians, because I know that the spirit of the holy gods is in you, and no secret troubles you, tell me the visions of my dream that I have seen, and the interpretation thereof. *(The manner in which Nebuchadnezzar referred to Daniel did not mean that he was a part of the magicians, etc., but rather that he was recognized as having more wisdom that all the so-called wise men of the Babylonian Empire.)*

10 Thus were the visions of my head in my bed; I saw, and behold a tree in the midst of the Earth, and the height thereof was great. *(Actually, the Assyrians, whom the Babylonians had defeated, had a sacred tree, the symbol of life, which was perpetually introduced into the sculptures of Nineveh, and seen also in some Babylonian cylinders, especially in connection with royal acts of worship.)*

11 The tree grew, and was strong, and the height thereof reached unto heaven, and the sight thereof to the end of all the Earth:

12 The leaves thereof were fair, and the fruit thereof much, and in it was meat for all: the beasts of the field had shadow under it, and the fowls of the heaven dwelt in the boughs thereof, and all flesh was fed of it. *(As this tree is symbolic of the Babylonian Empire, its description is apt. From the Persian Gulf to the Mediterranean Sea, it stretched, in all probability, from the Cataracts of the Nile into Asia Minor.)*

13 I saw in the visions of my head upon my bed, and, behold, a Watcher and an Holy One came down from Heaven *(the word "Watcher" occurs only in this Chapter in the Bible; however, it is used a score of times in the Book of Enoch, which was supposed to have been written about 130 B.C. That Book, as is obvious, is not included in the Canon of Scripture)*;

14 He cried aloud, and said thus, Hew down the tree, and cut off his branches, shake off his leaves, and scatter his fruit: let the beasts get away from under it, and the fowls from his branches *(the "Watcher" gives instructions as to what is to be done with the tree)*:

15 Nevertheless leave the stump of his roots in the Earth, even with a band of iron and brass, in the tender grass of the field; and let it be wet with the dew of heaven, and let his portion be with the beasts in the grass of the Earth *(the "tree" is not to be destroyed, but only cut down; it will, therefore, sprout again. Actually, the "band of iron and brass" symbolizes the mental darkness Nebuchadnezzar will be under, with him bound, at least to some extent, with fetters)*:

16 Let his heart be changed from man's, and let a beast's heart be given unto him; and let seven times pass over him. *(This Verse leaves absolutely no doubt that the Holy Spirit is speaking here of a man. "Seven times" represents seven years.)*

17 This matter is by the decree of the Watchers, and the demand by the word of the Holy Ones: to the intent that the living may know that the Most High rules in the kingdom of men, and gives it to whomsoever He will, and sets up over it the basest of men. *(In other words, in one way or the other, God controls all!)*

18 This dream I king Nebuchadnezzar have seen. Now you, O Belteshazzar, declare the interpretation thereof, forasmuch as all the wise men of my kingdom are not able to make known unto me the interpretation: but you are able; for the spirit of the holy gods is in you. *(This would be totally unlike the dream of years before, when Daniel exclaimed to him, "You are this head of gold" [2:38]. Now this "head of gold" will be reduced to a "stump.")*

DANIEL INTERPRETS THE KING'S DREAM

19 Then Daniel, whose name was Belteshazzar, was astonied for one hour, and his thoughts troubled him. The king spoke, and said, Belteshazzar, let not the dream, or the interpretation thereof, trouble you. Belteshazzar answered and said, My lord, the dream be to them who hate you, and the interpretation thereof to your enemies. *(When Daniel heard the king's dream, the interpretation which the Lord gave to him literally terrified him, even so much that his countenance was changed.)*

20 The tree that you saw, which grew, and was strong, whose height reached unto the heaven, and the sight thereof to all the Earth;

21 Whose leaves were fair, and the fruit thereof much, and in it was meat for all; under which the beasts of the field dwelt, and upon whose branches the fowls of the heaven had their habitation:

22 It is you, O king, who are grown and become strong: for your greatness is grown, and reaches unto heaven, and your dominion to the end of the Earth. *(These statements proclaim the fact that the Monarch's dominion was vast, but it had been given to him by the Lord. This he did not recognize, and hence the Judgment that came upon him!)*

23 And whereas the king saw a Watcher and an Holy One coming down from Heaven, and saying, Hew the tree down, and destroy it; yet leave the stump of the roots thereof in the Earth, even with a band of iron and brass, in the tender grass of the field; and let it be wet with the dew of heaven, and let his portion be with the beasts of the field, till seven times pass over him *(the phrase, "Hew the tree down, and destroy it," refers to Nebuchadnezzar being cut down from his place of position and authority by the reason of insanity. The phrase, "Yet leave the stump of the roots thereof in the Earth," refers to his life being spared, with a restoration intended for the future. The phrase, "And let it be wet with the dew of heaven," refers to the type of insanity, which caused him to seek habitation in the open as an animal. Some think his form of insanity was a disease known as "lycanthropy," in which a man imagines himself to be some form of animal)*;

24 This is the interpretation, O king, and this is the decree of The Most High, which is come upon my lord the king *(the phrase, "The Most High," is an appellative denoting supremacy of supremacy. This is the One Who has the final say! This is the One Who everyone will answer to ultimately!)*:

25 That they shall drive you from men, and your dwelling shall be with the beasts of the field, and they shall make you to eat grass as oxen, and they shall wet you with the dew of

heaven, and seven times shall pass over you, till you know that The Most High rules in the kingdom of men, and gives it to whomsoever He will. *(Despite all that Nebuchadnezzar had seen, still, pride and ego were the culprits of his rebellion against God. He considered himself to be the master of his own fate and the ruler of his own kingdom. He would not recognize that he had been placed in this position by "The Most High," but gave himself credit, making himself a god. However, the Lord loved him enough to resort to drastic measures in order to bring him to his senses.)*

26 And whereas they commanded to leave the stump of the tree roots; your kingdom shall be sure unto you, after that you shall have known that the heavens do rule. *(Once again, the Holy Spirit repeats the cause and reason for this act of God: "After that you shall have known that the heavens do rule.")*

ADVICE GIVEN TO THE KING; THE ADVICE REJECTED

27 Wherefore, O king, let my counsel be acceptable unto you, and break off your sins by righteousness, and your iniquities by shewing mercy to the poor; if it may be a lengthening of your tranquility. *(An offer of Repentance is extended, which, if accepted, will negate this judgment. Regrettably, it was not accepted.)*

28 All this came upon the King Nebuchadnezzar. *(It came upon him, because he rejected the Word of the Lord. He was given twelve months respite in order that he may repent, but to no avail!)*

29 At the end of the twelve months he walked in the palace of the kingdom of Babylon. *(The phrase, "He walked in the palace of the kingdom of Babylon," denotes a prideful attitude, filled with pomp, majesty, a sense of wellbeing and, in his case, the master of the world, or so he thought! He was his own man, captain of his own fate and, therefore, subservient to none! Was not this "palace" and the city itself proof of such?)*

30 The king spoke and said, Is not this great Babylon, that I have built for the house of the kingdom by the might of my power, and for the honour of my majesty? *(He now gives his answer to the appeal of the Holy Spirit. It will be a pompous answer, as is most of the world. To be sure, as he was called to account, all will ultimately be called to account.)*

THE DREAM FULFILLED

31 While the word was in the king's mouth, there fell a voice from Heaven, saying, O King Nebuchadnezzar, to you it is spoken; The kingdom is departed from you. *(The phrase, "The kingdom is departed from you," is a stupefying statement indeed! All this which he claimed for his own and made by his own hand instead would be proved otherwise. It could be said, concerning the Bible and all its warnings and pleadings to the whole of humanity, "to you it is spoken!")*

32 And they shall drive you from men, and your dwelling shall be with the beasts of the field: they shall make you to eat grass as oxen, and seven times shall pass over you, until you know that The Most High rules in the kingdom of men, and gives it to whomsoever He will. *(The actual stipulation of the Judgment is repeated here almost identically with the original verdict of Verse 25, no doubt because the king, during the twelve-month period of respite, had discounted this dire prediction, thinking that such a strange thing could never come to pass.)*

33 The same hour was the thing fulfilled upon Nebuchadnezzar: and he was driven from men, and did eat grass as oxen, and his body was wet with the dew of heaven, till his hairs were grown like eagles' feathers, and his nails like birds' claws. *(The phrase, "The same hour was the thing fulfilled upon Nebuchadnezzar," means that his mind snapped almost immediately after the voice was heard from Heaven.)*

NEBUCHADNEZZAR RESTORED; PRAISES GOD

34 And at the end of the days I Nebuchadnezzar lifted up my eyes unto Heaven, and my understanding returned unto me, and I blessed The Most High, and I praised and honoured Him Who lives for ever, Whose dominion is an everlasting dominion, and His kingdom is from generation to generation *(exactly as the Holy Spirit through Daniel had stated, upon the completion of the "seven years," his sanity returned as quickly as it had left. The phrase, "I Nebuchadnezzar lifted up my eyes unto Heaven," signifies that, upon his return to sanity, he repented and gave Glory to God):*

35 And all the inhabitants of the Earth are reputed as nothing: and He does according to His will in the army of Heaven, and among the inhabitants of the Earth: and none can stay His hand, or say unto Him, What doest Thou?

(The phrase, "And all the inhabitants of the Earth are reputed as nothing," has reference to Nebuchadnezzar and all who would think their place or position signifies their importance. The idea is: no man has ever reigned quite as did Nebuchadnezzar; consequently, no man has ever been brought lower than Nebuchadnezzar, portraying the supremacy of Jehovah.)

36 At the same time my reason returned unto me; and for the glory of my kingdom, my honour and brightness returned unto me; and my counsellors and my lords sought unto me; and I was established in my kingdom, and excellent majesty was added unto me. *(As the kingdom was taken away, it is now restored. Actually, one of the functions of the Holy Spirit is Restoration.)*

37 Now I Nebuchadnezzar praise and extol and honour the King of Heaven, all Whose works are truth, and His ways judgment: and those who walk in pride He is able to abase. *(The Verse begins with the word "Now." It is after he has been humbled, chastened, and restored. Before his insanity, he did not "praise and extol and honor the King of Heaven" at all! "Now" that is all he does!)*

CHAPTER 5

(538 B.C.)
BELSHAZZAR'S FEAST

BELSHAZZAR the king made a great feast to a thousand of his lords, and drank wine before the thousand. *(Timewise, this Chapter follows Chapter 8. Daniel did this possibly because he wanted the prophetical sections to be uninterrupted. Belshazzar and the companions of his orgy drank wine out of the Sacred Vessels of the Temple of God.)*

2 Belshazzar, while he tasted the wine, commanded to bring the golden and silver vessels which his father Nebuchadnezzar had taken out of the Temple which was in Jerusalem; that the king, and his princes, his wives, and his concubines, might drink therein. *(The contempt shown by this man was double: A. To use these Sacred Vessels at all; and, B. To use them as a sacrifice to heathen gods.)*

3 Then they brought the golden vessels that were taken out of the Temple of the House of God which was at Jerusalem; and the king, and his princes, his wives, and his concubines, drank in them. *(The bringing of the "golden vessels" was by design. Inasmuch as Bel had given them the victory over the Judeans, or so*

they thought, this would afford an occasion for praising Bel, who surely would give them the victory over the Medes and the Persians, or so they thought!)

4 They drank wine, and praised the gods of gold, and of silver, of brass, of iron, of wood, and of stone. *(These "gods" which they praised were more than likely the gods of the nations which they had conquered. Therefore, they insulted Jehovah and praised these monstrosities.)*

THE HANDWRITING ON THE WALL

5 In the same hour came forth fingers of a man's hand, and wrote over against the candlestick upon the plaister of the wall of the king's palace: and the king saw the part of the hand that wrote. *(This is the same "hand" which inscribed the Ten Commandments on two tables of stone, and which wrote on the ground concerning a poor, accused woman [Jn. 8:6, 8].)*

6 Then the king's countenance was changed, and his thoughts troubled him, so that the joints of his loins were loosed, and his knees smote one against another. *(The phrase, "And his knees smote one against another," shows him now to be dead sober, but stricken with fear.)*

7 The king cried aloud to bring in the astrologers, the Chaldeans, and the soothsayers. And the king spoke, and said to the wise men of Babylon, Whosoever shall read this writing, and show me the interpretation thereof, shall be clothed with scarlet, and have a chain of gold about his neck, and shall be the third ruler in the kingdom. *(The phrase, "Third ruler in the kingdom," means that Belshazzar was only the second ruler in the kingdom, with Nabonidus, his father, being first.)*

8 Then came in all the king's wise men: but they could not read the writing, nor make known to the king the interpretation thereof. *(These "Astrologers, Chaldeans, and soothsayers" will do him no more good than they had done his grandfather, Nebuchadnezzar. The phrase, "Whosoever shall read this writing," seems to prove that the language was not Chaldee or even Hebrew. There is no indication as to what language it was!)*

9 Then was king Belshazzar greatly troubled, and his countenance was changed in him, and his lords were astonied. *(The word "astonied" refers to tremendous fear, resulting in uncontrolled trembling of the body, with possibly even the loss of bodily functions.)*

THE QUEEN'S ADVICE

10 Now the queen by reason of the words of the king and his lords came into the banquet house: and the queen spoke and said, O king, live for ever: let not your thoughts trouble you, nor let your countenance be changed (*it seems that the "Queen" was not present during the revelry, but only came into the "banquet house" upon hearing of this strange phenomenon*):

11 There is a man in your kingdom, in whom is the spirit of the holy gods; and in the days of your father light and understanding and wisdom, like the wisdom of the gods, was found in him; whom the King Nebuchadnezzar your father, the king, I say, your father, made master of the magicians, astrologers, Chaldeans, and soothsayers (*this signifies that the Queen, Belshazzar's mother, knew Daniel; however, it seems that Belshazzar did not know him, only having "heard of" him. At this time, Daniel was probably between seventy and eighty years old*):

12 Forasmuch as an excellent spirit, and knowledge, and understanding, interpreting of dreams, and showing of hard sentences, and dissolving of doubts, were found in the same Daniel, whom the king named Belteshazzar: now let Daniel be called, and he will show the interpretation. (*The phrase, "Forasmuch as an excellent spirit," proves that she possibly had spent considerable time being taught by Daniel, and had been greatly impressed by the Christlike Spirit radiating from him. She had no faith in the "astrologers, Chaldeans, and soothsayers," but she had faith in Daniel!*)

BELSHAZZAR CALLS FOR DANIEL

13 Then was Daniel brought in before the king, And the king spoke and said unto Daniel, Are you that Daniel, which are of the children of the captivity of Judah, whom the king my father brought out of Jewry? (*The phrase, "Then was Daniel brought in," shows the king, true to fallen man's unchanging action, seeking help from God as a last resource, and not as the first. But even then the great big pompous fool condescendingly says, "I have even heard of you" [Vs. 14]. Furthermore, he does not add that "the Spirit of the Holy God is in you," as the Queen Mother had said, but rather that "the spirit of the gods" is in you.*)

14 I have even heard of you, that the spirit of the gods is in you, and that light and understanding and excellent wisdom is found in you.

(*And yet, he had never consulted him!*)

15 And now the wise men, the astrologers, have been brought in before me, that they should read this writing, and make known unto me the interpretation thereof: but they could not show the interpretation of the thing (*no, they would not "show the interpretation of the thing," and neither can the modern prognosticators! Actually, the "handwriting on the wall" is presently obvious and apparent in all the world, but few now, as then, can "show the interpretation of the thing"*):

16 And I have heard of you, that you can make interpretations, and dissolve doubts: now if you can read the writing, and make known to me the interpretation thereof, you shall be clothed with scarlet, and have a chain of gold about your neck, and shall be the third ruler in the kingdom. (*It is sad, but the modern Church, as Belshazzar, is promising the same thing.*)

DANIEL REBUKES THE KING

17 Then Daniel answered and said before the king, Let your gifts be to yourself, and give your rewards to another; yet I will read the writing unto the king, and make known to him the interpretation.

18 O thou king, The Most High God gave Nebuchadnezzar your father a kingdom, and majesty, and glory, and honour:

19 And for the majesty that He gave him, all people, nations, and languages, trembled and feared before him: whom he would he slew; and whom he would he kept alive; and whom he would he set up; and whom he would he put down. (*Daniel emphatically states that the might, majesty, splendor, glory, and greatness of the Babylonian Empire were all because of "The Most High God," and not these foolish idols.*)

20 But when his heart was lifted up, and his mind hardened in pride, he was deposed from his kingly throne, and they took his glory from him (*Daniel is telling this king that his grandfather's pride caused him to "be deposed from his kingly throne" and, likewise, the same is about to happen to Belshazzar. However, Nebuchadnezzar repented and was restored, whereas his grandson showed no inclination whatsoever toward Repentance and, therefore, was not restored*):

21 And he was driven from the sons of men; and his heart was made like the beasts, and his dwelling was with the wild asses: they fed him with grass like oxen, and his body was wet

with the dew of heaven; till he knew that The Most High God ruled in the kingdom of men, and that He appoints over it whomsoever He will. *(Daniel, with words of burning power, thrust the Sword of the Spirit into the king's heart and conscience.)*

22 And you his son, O Belshazzar, have not humbled your heart, though you knew all this *(due to the peculiarity of the Chaldee, the phrase, "his son," is literally "his grandson")*;

23 But have lifted up yourself against the Lord of Heaven; and they have brought the vessels of His house before you, and you, and your lords, your wives, and your concubines, have drunk wine in them; and you have praised the gods of silver, and gold, of brass, iron, wood, and stone, which see not, nor hear, nor know: and the God in Whose hand your breath is, and Whose are all your ways, have you not glorified *(all the sins of Belshazzar and his lords and ladies could be summed up in the last line of this Verse, concerning the Lord of Glory, of Whom it was said, "have you not glorified")*:

24 Then was the part of the hand sent from him; and this writing was written. *(It seems that the fingers of a hand were still on the wall, poised in mid-air, which would have been a fearful sight. The phrase, "And this writing was written," signifies such that cannot be changed! It is from Jehovah, therefore, unalterable.)*

25 And this is the writing that was written, MENE, MENE, TEKEL, UPHAR-SIN. *(The repetition of the word "MENE" announced the immediateness of the doom.)*

DANIEL INTERPRETS THE WRITING ON THE WALL

26 This is the interpretation of the thing: MENE; God has numbered your kingdom, and finished it. *(Actually, the word "MENE" being repeated twice means "numbered, numbered"; the repetition was for the sake of emphasis and to declare, as stated, the immediate fulfillment, which did occur!)*

27 TEKEL; You are weighed in the balances, and are found wanting. *(The word "TEKEL" means "weighed.")*

28 PERES; Your kingdom is divided, and given to the Medes and Persians. *(There is no contradiction in the Scripture. The word "UPHAR-SIN" or "PHARSIN" is the plural of "PERES," meaning division. So it means that the great Babylonian Empire will be split up and given to the Medes and Persians.*

The Septuagint says, "Numbered is the time of your kingdom; ceases your kingdom; cut short and ended has been your kingdom; to the Medes and the Persians has it been given.")

29 Then commanded Belshazzar, and they clothed Daniel with scarlet, and put a chain of gold about his neck, and made a proclamation concerning him, that he should be the third ruler in the kingdom. *(Even though Belshazzar did treat Daniel with kindness and respect, there is no evidence that he repented, even in the face of impending doom.)*

THE WRITING FULFILLED

30 In that night was Belshazzar the king of the Chaldeans slain. *(The phrase, "In that night," refers to the very night of the drunken feast and the "handwriting on the wall.")*

31 And Darius the Median took the kingdom, being about threescore and two years old *(62 years old).*

CHAPTER 6
(538 B.C.)
THE PLOT AGAINST DANIEL

IT pleased Darius to set over the kingdom an hundred and twenty princes, which should be over the whole kingdom *(the number of princes fluctuated according to need. A short time before, it was 127 [Esther 1:1]);*

2 And over these three presidents; of whom Daniel was first: that the princes might give accounts unto them, and the king should have no damage. *(This portrays the fact that Daniel was the most powerful man in the world after Darius.)*

3 Then this Daniel was preferred above the presidents and princes, because an excellent spirit was in him; and the king thought to set him over the whole realm. *(This also gives the reason for the jealousy exhibited in Verses 4 and 5.)*

4 Then the presidents and princes sought to find occasion against Daniel concerning the kingdom; but they could find none occasion nor fault; forasmuch as he was faithful, neither was there any error or fault found in him. *(At this time, Daniel was upwards of eighty years of age. He was just as faithful to Truth in his old age as when he was a young man. His enemies no doubt hated him because of his determined opposition to bribery and corruption, and most of all because of his attachment to the Word of God.)*

5 Then said these men, We shall not find any occasion against this Daniel, except we find it against him concerning the Law of his God. *(Even his enemies could not find any occasion of fault in him. What a testimony!)*

6 Then these presidents and princes assembled together to the king, and said thus unto him, King Darius, live for ever. *(The phrase, "These presidents," refers to those other than Daniel, i.e., the ones plotting against him. In fact, the entire conspiracy is the work of Daniel's co-presidents.)*

7 All the presidents of the kingdom, the governors, and the princes, the counsellors, and the captains, have consulted together to establish a royal statute, and to make a firm decree, that whosoever shall ask a petition of any God or man for thirty days, save of you, O king, he shall be cast into the den of lions. *(Their plot was well conceived.)*

8 Now, O king, establish the decree, and sign the writing, that it be not changed, according to the law of the Medes and Persians, which alters not. *(The king, no doubt, was perfectly agreeable with this, especially considering that religion was so much a part of national life and was the secret of his success, or so he thought. In his mind, the proper gods of the Medes and the Persians would be suitably worshipped, and the foreign deities would be put in their proper place of submission. Therefore, he willingly signed the "decree.")*

9 Wherefore king Darius signed the writing and the decree. *(The king would have signed this, giving little, if any, thought to Daniel whatsoever. He probably reasoned that inasmuch as the Temple in Jerusalem was in ruins and that Daniel did not pray to idols, that he could make no objection to this order. So the king signed it.)*

THE STEADFASTNESS OF DANIEL

10 Now when Daniel knew that the writing was signed, he went into his house; and his windows being open in his chamber toward Jerusalem, he kneeled upon his knees three times a day, and prayed, and gave thanks before his God, as he did aforetime. *(The phrase, "And his windows being opened in his chamber toward Jerusalem," implied that he prayed toward Jerusalem constantly. There was a reason for this, which has nothing to do with the New Covenant. It is obvious that Daniel was a man of prayer — "three times a day.")*

11 Then these men assembled, and found Daniel praying and making supplication before his God. *(In fact, Daniel was the very reason for the plot.)*

12 Then they came near, and spoke before the king concerning the king's decree; Have you not signed a decree, that every man who shall ask a petition of any God or man within thirty days, save of you, O king, shall be cast into the den of lions? The king answered and said, The thing is true, according to the law of the Medes and Persians, which alters not. *(The law of the Medes and the Persians, once enacted, was supposed to be unalterable.)*

13 Then answered they and said before the king, That Daniel, which is of the children of the captivity of Judah, regards not you, O king, nor the decree that you have signed, but makes his petition three times a day. *(Now they lie about Daniel, claiming that he has no regard for the king.)*

THE KING'S EFFORTS

14 Then the king, when he heard these words, was sore displeased with himself, and set his heart on Daniel to deliver him: and he laboured till the going down of the sun to deliver him. *(His efforts were directed to find some way out of the constitutional dilemma into which he had been entrapped. He probably now full well realizes the extent of this trap set for Daniel and his own unwitting complicity.)*

15 Then these men assembled unto the king, and said unto the king, Know, O king, that the law of the Medes and Persians is, That no decree nor statute which the king establishes may be changed. *(While it was true that the king could not save Daniel, still, the Lord could and did!)*

DANIEL IN THE LIONS' DEN

16 Then the king commanded, and they brought Daniel, and cast him into the den of lions. Now the king spoke and said unto Daniel, Your God Whom you serve continually, He will deliver you. *(There are some who believe that this "Darius" was Astyages, who, some years before, married Esther, choosing her as his Queen. If that in fact was the case, Darius would have had some knowledge about God.)*

17 And a stone was brought, and laid upon the mouth of the den; and the king sealed it with his own signet, and with the signet of his

lords; that the purpose might not be changed concerning Daniel. *(The king sealing the "stone" with his "own signet" would serve the purpose of God. When Daniel was delivered, none could say a trick had been played and Daniel escaped accordingly!)*

DANIEL DELIVERED BY GOD

18 Then the king went to his palace, and passed the night fasting: neither were instruments of music brought before him: and his sleep went from him. *(As the night descends, the king realizes what a foolhardy thing he has allowed himself to be led into.)*

19 Then the king arose very early in the morning, and went in haste unto the den of lions. *(The actions of the king portray graphically so his regard and love for Daniel.)*

20 And when he came to the den, he cried with a lamentable voice unto Daniel: and the king spoke and said to Daniel, O Daniel, servant of the living God, is your God, Whom you serve continually able to deliver you from the lions? *(There is some indication that the king took with him these "presidents" and others who had maneuvered him into signing this decree. Thus, they all stand before the lions' den in the early morning hour.)*

21 Then said Daniel unto the king, O king, live for ever. *(The trap is now sprung, but it is not on Daniel, but rather on his enemies.)*

22 My God has sent His Angel, and has shut the lions' mouths, that they have not hurt me: forasmuch as before Him innocency was found in me; and also before you, O king, have I done no hurt. *(The phrase, "My God has sent His Angel," insinuates that Daniel saw the Angel sent to him.)*

DANIEL'S ENEMIES DESTROYED

23 Then was the king exceedingly glad for him, and commanded that they should take Daniel up out of the den. So Daniel was taken up out of the den, and no manner of hurt was found upon him, because he believed in his God. *(The phrase, "Because he believed in his God," is referred to in Heb. 11:33.)*

24 And the king commanded, and they brought those men which had accused Daniel, and they cast them into the den of lions, them, their children, and their wives; and the lions had the mastery of them, and broke all their bones in pieces or ever they came at the bottom of the den. *(Daniel had no more say regarding the king's command to cast these men and their families into the lions' den than he had had over his own situation.)*

THE DECREE BY DARIUS

25 Then king Darius wrote unto all people, nations, and languages, that dwell in all the Earth; Peace be multiplied unto you. *(The Septuagint says: "Then Darius wrote to all nations and tongues and countries dwelling in all his land, saying, 'Let all men who are in my kingdom stand and worship, and serve the God of Daniel, for He Alone abides, and lives to generation of generations forever. I, Darius, will worship and serve Him all my days, for none of the idols that are made with hands are able to deliver as the God of Daniel did Daniel.'")*

26 I make a decree, That in every dominion of my kingdom men tremble and fear before the God of Daniel: for He is the Living God, and stedfast for ever, and His kingdom that which shall not be destroyed, and His dominion shall be even unto the end. *(His statement concerning "His Kingdom" and "His Dominion" and their eternal consequence portrays a knowledge which could only be acquired by careful observation.)*

27 He delivers and rescues, and He works signs and wonders in Heaven and in Earth, Who has delivered Daniel from the power of the lions. *(Despite the unbelief of religious dignitaries and the disavowal of much of the Word of God, God still "delivers" and "rescues"; and He will do it for any and all who will dare to believe Him.)*

28 So this Daniel prospered in the reign of Darius, and in the reign of Cyrus the Persian. *(There is every evidence that "Cyrus the Persian" was the son of Darius and Esther, and was brought up in Jewish training and taught about God and His Word.)*

CHAPTER 7
(555 B.C.)
DANIEL'S VISION OF THE FOUR WINDS AND THE FOUR BEASTS

IN the first year of Belshazzar King of Babylon Daniel had a dream and visions of his head upon his bed: then he wrote the dream, and told the sum of the matters. *(Chapters 7 through 12, sometimes called The Second Book of Daniel, is mainly occupied with the predictions*

of the "fourth beast," which pertain to the Endtime.)

2 Daniel spoke and said, I saw in my vision by night, and, behold, the four winds of the heaven strove upon the great sea. *(The phrase, "The four winds of the heaven," refers to wars, strife, and judgments from God [Jer. 25:32-33; Rev. 7:1-3]. The phrase, "Strove upon the great sea," refers to large numbers of people [Rev. 13:1; 17:1, 15].)*

3 And four great beasts came up from the sea, diverse one from another. *("Beasts" in symbolic Passages represent kingdoms [Rev. 17:8-11] and their rulers, and more than all the fallen angels behind these kingdoms [Rev. 11:7; 13:18; 17:8]. As stated, "the sea" has reference to great numbers of people, i.e., "came up from the people.")*

THE FIRST BEAST, A LION: BABYLON

4 The first was like a lion, and had eagle's wings: I beheld till the wings thereof were plucked, and it was lifted up from the Earth, and made stand upon the feet as a man, and a man's heart was given to it. *(The phrase, "The first was like a lion," refers to the Babylonian Empire. The "eagle's wings" symbolize the rapid pace with which the Babylonian Empire conquered its enemies and gained its ascendancy. The phrase, "I beheld till the wings thereof were plucked," pertains to the rapid expansion of this Empire, until Nebuchadnezzar went insane as a result of pride [4:25-26].)*

THE SECOND BEAST, A BEAR: MEDO-PERSIA

5 And behold another beast, a second, like to a bear, and it raised up itself on one side, and it had three ribs in the mouth of it between the teeth of it: and they said thus unto it, Arise, devour much flesh. *(On the statue of Chapter 2, the Medo-Persian Empire was represented by a breastplate of silver. The statue as seen in Nebuchadnezzar's dream represented these kingdoms as man sees them. The dream given to Daniel represents these kingdoms as God sees them, i.e., "ferocious."*

The term, "Raised up itself on one side," simply means that the strength of the Persians ultimately was greater than the Medes. The three ribs in the mouth of it between the teeth refer to the bear devouring much flesh. It symbolized the conquest of Babylon, Lydia, and Egypt.)

THE THIRD BEAST, A LEOPARD: GRECIA

6 After this I beheld, and lo another, like a leopard, which had upon the back of it four wings of a fowl; the beast had also four heads; and dominion was given to it. *(This short description defines the Grecian Empire under Alexander the Great as a "leopard." This Empire would come to the fore about 200 years from Daniel's day. The "four wings of a fowl" symbolized swiftness out of proportion to normal conquests.*

The "four heads" symbolized the breakup of this Empire after the death of Alexander at 32 years of age. Heads always symbolize kingdoms in Bible Prophecy. Those four divisions were: Greece, Thrace, Syria, and Egypt.)

THE FOURTH BEAST, NON-DESCRIPT: ROMAN EMPIRE

7 After this I saw in the night visions, and behold a fourth beast, dreadful and terrible, and strong exceedingly; and it had great iron teeth: it devoured and broke in pieces, and stamped the residue with the feet of it; and it was diverse from all the beasts that were before it; and it had ten horns. *(This beast represents the Roman Empire, which was the strongest and most powerful of all. It lasted for nearly a thousand years.*

The phrase, "And it had ten horns," speaks of that which was a part of this beast, and for a particular reason. But it had nothing to do with the conquests of the original Roman Empire. These "ten horns" portray ten kingdoms which will arise in the latter days, in fact, in the very near future. These ten nations will persecute Israel.)

THE TEN HORNS AND THE "LITTLE HORN": REVISED ROME AND REVIVED GRECIA

8 I considered the horns, and, behold, there came up among them another little horn, before whom there were three of the first horns plucked up by the roots: and, behold, in this horn were eyes like the eyes of a man, and a mouth speaking great things. *(At first, Daniel did not understand the horns. Even though the Roman Empire has come and gone, still, the "ten horns" have not yet risen to power; however, the breakup of the former Soviet*

Union is the beginning of the fulfillment of this Passage. If one is to notice, the "ten horns" were a part of the non-descript beast, which has to do with the territory which the old Roman Empire controlled.

The phrase, "There came up among them another little horn," means this one came up after the "ten horns" were fully grown. The "little horn" is the Antichrist.

Three of the horns will be plucked by the "little horn," meaning that he will defeat these countries in battle, with the others then submitting to him. This will take place in the first half of the Great Tribulation.)

THE JUDGMENT

9 I beheld till the thrones were cast down, and the Ancient of days did sit, Whose garment was white as snow, and the hair of His head like the pure wool: His throne was like the fiery flame, and His wheels as burning fire. *(The phrase, "I beheld till the thrones were cast down," speaks of all the Empires, even from Babylon straight through to the Antichrist. All of them have already been "cast down" with the exception of the "ten horns" and the "little horn." However, as surely as the others were cast down, these two kingdoms also will be cast down.*

The phrase, "And the Ancient of days did sit," refers to God the Father and His Dominion. His Kingdom will remain!)

10 A fiery stream issued and came forth from before Him: thousand thousands ministered unto Him, and ten thousand times ten thousand stood before Him: the judgment was set, and the books were opened. *(In the Hebrew, the number is "chiliads of chiliads." It is a Hebraism meaning "countless numbers." The phrase, "The judgment was set, and the books were opened," has to do with the judgment of the nations, which will take place at the beginning of the Millennial Reign.)*

THE "LITTLE HORN" DESTROYED

11 I beheld then because of the voice of the great words which the horn spoke: I beheld even till the beast was slain, and his body destroyed, and given to the burning flame. *("The great words which the horn spoke" speak of great opposition against God. At the Second Coming of Christ, the Antichrist will be killed and cast into Hell.)*

THE BEASTS PRECEDING THE RULE OF THE "LITTLE HORN"

12 As concerning the rest of the beasts, they had their dominion taken away: yet their lives were prolonged for a season and time. *(The phrase, "As concerning the rest of the beasts," refers to the kingdoms preceding the little horn, beginning back with the Babylonian Empire. Even though these Empires have long since passed away, still, Gentiles rule the world; this is referred to as the "Times of the Gentiles" [Lk. 21:24]. The "prolonging" will continue until the Second Coming.)*

THE SECOND ADVENT OF THE MESSIAH

13 I saw in the night visions, and, behold, One like the Son of Man came with the clouds of Heaven, and came to the Ancient of days, and they brought Him near before Him. *(This "One like the Son of Man" is "The Lord Jesus Christ." We have here the Trinity represented: God the Father, i.e., "the Ancient of Days," "The Son of Man," Who, as stated, is Jesus Christ, and the Holy Spirit, Who inspired this.)*

14 And there was a given Him dominion, and glory, and a kingdom, that all people, nations, and languages, should serve Him: His dominion is an everlasting dominion, which shall not pass away, and His kingdom that which shall not be destroyed. *(This Verse corresponds with 2:35. This Kingdom of Righteousness will begin immediately after the Second Coming, with Christ as its Supreme and Eternal Head.)*

THE INTERPRETATION OF THE VISION

15 I Daniel was grieved in my spirit in the midst of my body, and the visions of my head troubled me.

16 I came near unto one of them who stood by, and asked him the truth of all this. So he told me, and made me know the interpretation of the things. *(The phrase, "One of them who stood by," refers to the countless numbers who are standing before the Throne of God. Quite possibly, this was Gabriel; however, we have no proof.)*

17 These great beasts, which are four, are four kings, which shall arise out of the Earth. *(The "four kings" are, as stated, Babylon, Medo-Persia, Greece, and Rome. The phrase, "Which shall arise out of the Earth," simply means that they*

are of the people, of man, and, therefore, not of God. *The Kingdom of Verse 14 is of God and from God, and consequently will last forever.)*

18 But the Saints of the most High shall take the kingdom, and possess the kingdom for ever, even for ever and ever. *("The Saints" in this Passage refer to Israel, which will be restored and become the leading nation in the world under Christ.)*

19 Then I would know the truth of the fourth beast, which was diverse from all the others, exceeding dreadful, whose teeth were of iron, and his nails of brass; which devoured, broke in pieces, and stamped the residue with his feet *(the "fourth beast," as stated, is a symbol of the old Roman Empire, the fourth of four kingdoms in succession. It is mentioned by name only in the New Testament [Jn. 11:48; Acts 2:10; 16:21].*

The phrase, "And his nails of brass," presents something added, which is not mentioned in the description given in Verses 7 and 8. They symbolize the Grecian Empire element of the image of 2:39, 45.

This means that the Antichrist will have characteristics of both the Roman Empire and the ancient Grecian Empire);

20 And of the ten horns that were in his head, and of the other which came up, and before whom three fell; even of that horn that had eyes, and a mouth that spoke very great things, whose look was more stout than his fellows. *(The "other which came up" is the same as the "little horn" of Verse 8, and is the Antichrist, who will come on the world scene shortly after Rapture of the Church [II Thess. 2:7-8].)*

21 I beheld, and the same horn made war with the Saints, and prevailed against them *(the "Saints" mentioned here are not the Church, but rather Israel. The "war" spoken of here concerns the Antichrist signing a seven-year non-aggression pact with Israel, and then breaking it at approximately the midpoint, then declaring war on Israel);*

22 Until the Ancient of days came, and judgment was given to the Saints of the Most High; and the time came that the Saints possessed the kingdom. *(The phrase, "Until the Ancient of days came," refers back to Verses 9, 13 and 14. It does not actually mean that God the Father will come to planet Earth at this time, but instead that He will direct the proceedings from His Throne.*

The phrase, "And the time came that the Saints possessed the kingdom," refers to the Second Coming of the Lord, when Israel will then accept Christ as Saviour, Lord, and Messiah, and will be restored and brought back to her rightful place and position.*

23 Thus he said, The fourth beast shall be the fourth kingdom upon Earth, which shall be diverse from all kingdoms, and shall devour the whole Earth, and shall tread it down, and break it in pieces. *(The Angel Gabriel speaks in Verses 17 and 18 in answer to Daniel's request; then Daniel asks more questions in Verses 19 through 22. Gabriel now picks up the dialogue and continues with the explanation through Verse 27.*

The phrase, "And shall devour the whole Earth, and shall tread it down, and break it in pieces," refers to the ferocity and the total power of the Roman Empire. It ruled the world not too much short of a thousand years.)

24 And the ten horns out of this kingdom are ten kings that shall arise: and another shall rise after them; and he shall be diverse from the first, and he shall subdue three kings. *(Some teach that the ten toes and ten horns of Daniel, Chapters 2 and 7, are ten barbarous tribes which overran the old Roman Empire between A.D. 351-474. However, this is error because of the following:*

The God of Heaven is to set up a Kingdom on Earth "in the days of these kings" [2:44-45; Rev. 19:11-20:7]. It should be obvious to all that the Lord did not set up such a Kingdom in A.D. 351-474. In fact, He has not yet done so; therefore, it is obvious that the "ten horns" representing ten nations are yet future.)

25 And he shall speak great words against the Most High, and shall wear out the Saints of the Most High, and think to change times and laws: and they shall be given into his hand until a time and times and the dividing of time. *(The phrase, "And he shall speak great words against the Most High," is used several times by the Holy Spirit in various ways, drawing our attention to the blasphemy of the Antichrist.*

The phrase, "And they shall be given into his hand until a time and times and the dividing of time," refers to Israel being defeated and being greatly persecuted for a period of three and a half years.)

26 But the judgment shall sit, and they shall take away his dominion, to consume and to destroy it unto the end. *(The Angel refers back to Verse 10. The phrase, "But the Judgment shall sit," refers to the Throne of God and the Judgment passed upon the Antichrist by that Heavenly Court.)*

27 And the kingdom and dominion, and the greatness of the kingdom under the whole heaven, shall be given to the people of the Saints of the Most High, Whose Kingdom is an Everlasting Kingdom, and all dominions shall serve and obey Him. *(The phrase, "The greatness of the kingdom under the whole heaven," refers to the entirety of the Earth, with Christ Jesus reigning supreme.)*

28 Hitherto is the end of the matter. As for me Daniel, my cogitations much troubled me, and my countenance changed in me: but I kept the matter in my heart. *(This Verse indicates that Daniel, despite the interpretation of the Angel, still did not fully comprehend the extent of his vision.)*

CHAPTER 8
(553 B.C.)
DANIEL'S VISION OF THE RAM AND HE GOAT: THE TIME OF THE VISION

IN the third year of the reign of king Belshazzar a vision appeared unto me, even unto me Daniel, after that which appeared unto me at the first. *(The phrase, "In the third year of the reign of king Belshazzar," means that this Vision was given some two years after the Vision of Chapter 7. Consequently, this was not long before the overthrow of the Babylonian Empire, as described in Chapter 5. So, chronologically, both Chapters 7 and 8 preceded Chapter 6.)*

2 And I saw in a vision; and it came to pass, when I saw, that I was at Shushan in the palace, which is in the province of Elam; and I saw in a Vision, and I was by the river of Ulai. *("Shushan" was the chief city of Persia.)*

THE RAM: MEDO-PERSIA

3 Then I lifted up my eyes, and saw, and, behold, there stood before the river a ram which had two horns: and the two horns were high; but one was higher than the other, and the higher came up last. *(The phrase, "A ram which had two horns," symbolized the Medo-Persian Empire, ruled by two kings, Darius of the Medes and Cyrus of Persia. The phrase, "And the two horns were high," spoke of their power, which was great enough to overthrow the mighty Babylonian Empire, to which they had been subject for many years. The phrase, "But one was higher than the other, and the higher came up last," pertains to Persia developing after the*

Median Empire, but ultimately growing into the stronger of the two.)

4 I saw the ram pushing westward, and northward, and southward; so that no beasts might stand before him, neither was there any that could deliver out of his hand; but he did according to his will, and became great. *(The "ram" is used here by the Holy Spirit as symbolic of the Empire of the Medes and the Persians. The phrase, "I saw the ram pushing westward," refers to an event of the recent past, the taking of Babylon. The phrase, "And northward," refers to Lydia, while "southward" refers to Egypt.)*

THE HE-GOAT: GRECIA

5 And as I was considering, behold, an he goat came from the west on the face of the whole Earth, and touched not the ground: and the goat had a notable horn between his eyes. *(In Nebuchadnezzar's dream, the Grecian Empire is represented by the "belly and thighs of brass." In Daniel's first Vision in Chapter 7, a "leopard with four wings and also four heads" symbolized this Empire. In this Vision, it is symbolized by an "he goat."*

The phrase, "And touched not the ground," refers to the speed of Alexander's conquests, which were symbolized in the first Vision by a leopard with four wings. In thirteen years, he conquered the whole known world. The "notable horn" refers to its first king, Alexander the Great.)

WAR: MEDO-PERSIA AND GRECIA

6 And he came to the ram that had two horns, which I had seen standing before the river, and ran unto him in the fury of his power. *(The phrase, "The fury of his power," portrays the speed of his conquests and the ferociousness of his attack, plus military strategy that completely overwhelmed the much larger force of the Medes and the Persians.)*

7 And I saw him come close unto the ram, and he was moved with choler against him, and smote the ram, and broke his two horns: and there was no power in the ram to stand before him, but he cast him down to the ground, and stamped upon him: and there was none who could deliver the ram out of his hand. *(As Daniel sees this, of course, it is yet future. The word "choler" means that Alexander was greatly angry at the Medo-Persians.)*

THE FOUR HORNS

8 Therefore the he goat waxed very great: and when he was strong, the great horn was broken; and for it came up four notable ones toward the four winds of heaven. *(The phrase, "And when he was strong, the great horn was broken," refers to the untimely death of Alexander the Great in 323 B.C., when he was at the apex of his strength. He was 32 years old when he died.*

The phrase, "And for it came up four notable ones toward the four winds of heaven," is referring to his kingdom being split into four parts upon his death.)

THE "LITTLE HORN": ANTICHRIST

9 And out of one of them came forth a little horn, which waxed exceeding great, toward the south, and toward the east, and toward the pleasant land. *(The phrase, "And out of one of them came forth a little horn," refers to the future Antichrist coming out of one of these four divisions of the old Grecian Empire. "Toward the south" refers to Egypt; "toward the east" refers to Syria, Iraq, and Iran; "toward the pleasant land" refers to Israel. From this area, the Antichrist will make his bid for world dominion.)*

10 And it waxed great, even to the host of heaven; and it cast down some of the host and of the stars to the ground, and stamped upon them. *(The phrase, "And it waxed great, even to the host of heaven," refers to the "little horn" [Antichrist] breaking his seven-year Covenant with Israel, which Daniel speaks of in a future Vision [9:27], actually declaring war on Israel at that time, seeking to destroy her. This is symbolized by the phrase, "And it [little horn[cast down some of the host and of the stars to the ground, and stamped upon them," referring to Israel being defeated at that time, which is yet future.)*

11 Yea, he magnified himself even to the prince of the host, and by him the daily sacrifice was taken away, and the place of his sanctuary was cast down. *(The phrase, "Yea, he magnified himself even to the prince of the host," refers to the Antichrist usurping authority over the High Priest of Israel. These Verses actually speak of the war which will be instituted by the Antichrist when he breaks his seven-year Covenant with Israel and other countries, actually invading the "pleasant land." He will defeat Israel and stop the daily sacrifices, which will have been re-instituted by Israel after a lapse of approximately 2,000 years. This tells us that the*

Jewish Temple is going to be rebuilt.)

12 And an host was given him against the daily sacrifice by reason of transgression, and it cast down the truth to the ground; and it practised, and prospered. *(The phrase, "By reason of transgression," refers to the Antichrist breaking his seven-year covenant with Israel, therefore, committing "transgression." As stated, he will then stop the "daily sacrifice." The phrase, "And it practiced, and prospered," refers to the fact that much of the world will applaud him in these actions.)*

13 Then I heard one Saint speaking, and another Saint said unto that certain Saint which spoke, How long shall be the vision concerning the daily sacrifice, and the transgression of desolation, to give both the Sanctuary and the host to be trodden under foot? *(These are "Saints" in Heaven; Daniel overheard their conversation, but had no identification as to who they were. The "Sanctuary" spoken of here is the rebuilt Temple. The "Host to be trodden under foot," refers to the worshippers, with their worship stopped, as well as the High Priest and associating Priests abruptly stopping their duties, if not being killed. This is when the Antichrist invades Israel in the middle of the seven-year tribulation period [9:27].)*

14 And he said unto me, Unto two thousand and three hundred days; then shall the Sanctuary be cleansed. *(This Verse makes reference to 2,300 evenings and mornings [Vss. 11-13, 26], as there are two sacrifices a day. Cutting that in half, which has reference to the number of days, the number is 1,150 [in Daniel's day, the years were counted as 360 days long, instead of our present method of using 365 days]. Hence, the three years, two months, and ten days are the whole and actual length of the doing away of the daily sacrifices in the Temple before they are offered again by the Jews when the Sanctuary is cleansed of the abomination of desolation. Jesus mentioned this [Mat. 24:15-16].)*

THE INTERPRETATION; ANGELIC INTERPRETERS

15 And it came to pass, when I, even I Daniel, had seen the Vision, and sought for the meaning, then, behold, there stood before me as the appearance of a man. *(This is actually the mighty Angel, "Gabriel," who stands in the Presence of God [Lk. 1:19].)*

16 And I heard a man's voice between the banks of Ulai, which called, and said, Gabriel,

make this man to understand the vision. *(It is not known whether the "man's voice" spoken of here refers to an Angel or a redeemed man. At any rate, he will inform "Gabriel" that he is to "make Daniel to understand the Vision.")*

TIME OF FULFILLMENT

17 So he came near where I stood: and when he came, I was afraid, and fell upon my face: but he said unto me, Understand, O son of man: for at the time of the end shall be the vision. *(The phrase, "For at the time of the end shall be the vision," refers to the Endtime, namely the very days in which we now live, extending into the immediate future.)*

18 Now as he was speaking with me, I was in a deep sleep on my face toward the ground: but he touched me, and set me upright. *(The phrase, "My face toward the ground," is not by accident! Daniel senses his tremendous unworthiness, especially in such Presence.)*

19 And he said, Behold, I will make you know what shall be in the last end of the indignation: for at the time appointed the end shall be. *(The phrase, "What shall be in the last end of the indignation," concerns God's past, present, and future indignation against Israel. To that indignation, He has set an appointed limit. However, the far greater part of the "indignation" spoken of here concerns the "last end," i.e., the last days, the Great Tribulation.)*

THE RAM: MEDO-PERSIA

20 The ram which you saw having two horns are the kings of Media and Persia. *(Daniel served in this Empire for a number of years before his death.)*

THE HE-GOAT: GRECIA

21 And the rough goat is the king of Grecia: and the great horn that is between his eyes is the first king. *(The "great horn" is Alexander the Great.)*

THE FOUR HORNS: GREECE, TURKEY, SYRIA, AND EGYPT

22 Now that being broken, whereas four stood up for it, four kingdoms shall stand up out of the nation, but not in his power. *(The phrase, "That being broken," refers to the "great horn," symbolizing the death of Alexander the*

Great. The phrase, "Whereas four stood up for it," refers to four generals who took the Empire after the death of Alexander, dividing it up among themselves. The phrase, "But not in his power," means that Alexander did not designate these kingdoms to them, because he was dead.)*

THE "LITTLE HORN"

23 And in the latter time of their kingdom, when the transgressors are come to the full, a king of fierce countenance, and understanding dark sentences, shall stand up. *(The phrase, "And in the latter time of their kingdom," pertains to the coming of the Antichrist. The phrase, "When the transgressors are come to the full," refers to the nation of Israel reaching the climax of her guilt by accepting the Antichrist instead of Christ, as predicted by the Lord Himself [Jn. 5:43]. The phrase, "A king of fierce countenance, and understanding dark sentences, shall stand up," proclaims the Antichrist having a majestic presence and superhuman knowledge, which is actually inspired of Satan.)*

THE "LITTLE HORN'S" POWER AND WAR ON THE SAINTS

24 And his power shall be mighty, but not by his own power: and he shall destroy wonderfully, and shall prosper, and practise, and shall destroy the mighty and the holy people. *(The phrase, "And he shall destroy wonderfully," refers to Rev. 6:4-8. The phrase, "And shall prosper, and practice," means that his efforts will be extremely successful. The phrase, "And shall destroy the mighty and the holy people," refers to Israel.)*

HIS EXALTATION AND WAR WITH THE MESSIAH

25 And through his policy also he shall cause craft to prosper in his hand; and he shall magnify himself in his heart, and by peace shall destroy many: he shall also stand up against the Prince of princes; but he shall be broken without hand. *(The word "craft" in the Hebrew is "mirmah," meaning "deceit." The Antichrist will be the greatest deceiver of all [II Thess. 2:8-12; Rev. 13:14; 19:20]. The last phrase, "He shall stand up against the Prince of princes," refers to his war against Christ, which will culminate with the Battle of Armageddon [Joel, Chpt. 3; Zech., Chpt. 14; Rev. 16:13-16; 19:11-21].)*

THE TIME OF THE VISION

26 And the Vision of the evening and the morning which was told is true: wherefore shut thou up the Vision; for it shall be for many days. *(The phrase, "For it shall be for many days," signifies that the Vision from Daniel's day would be a long time in coming to fulfillment. Actually, it has not yet been fulfilled, but it most definitely shall be in the near future.)*

27 And I Daniel fainted, and was sick certain days; afterward I rose up, and did the king's business; and I was astonished at the vision, but none understood it. *(The phrase, "But none understood it," refers to the fact that the comprehension of events in the distant future was difficult. Presently, in the light of the history of many of these things, especially considering that they are beginning now to come to pass, our understanding of those things which the Angel Gabriel intended is being enlightened!)*

CHAPTER 9
(538 B.C.)
DANIEL'S VISION OF SEVENTY WEEKS OF YEARS; HIS CONFESSION AND PRAYER FOR HIMSELF AND ISRAEL

IN the first year of Darius the son of Ahasuerus, of the seed of the Medes, which was made king over the realm of the Chaldeans *(this Vision was seen about a year after the one in Dan., Chpt. 8. The unique glory of this Chapter and of this Prophecy is that this alone foretold the time of the Messiah's appearing and the very year of His Crucifixion.*

This Chapter will detail Daniel's third Vision: the seventy weeks of years [490 years] and their application to Israel);

2 In the first year of his reign I Daniel understood by books the number of the years, whereof the word of the LORD came to Jeremiah the Prophet, that He would accomplish seventy years in the desolations of Jerusalem. *(This "seventy years" has nothing to do with the seventy weeks of years which Daniel will see in the Vision in the latter part of the Chapter [Vss. 24-27]. The information of this Verse did not come about through Visions, but through the Scriptures which God had already given to Jeremiah. Daniel read the revelations of Jeremiah; by thoroughly studying this Prophecy, he understood the number of years of the exile. The information of seventy years of captivity followed by a restoration is recorded in Jeremiah*

[Jer. 25:11-12; 29:1, 5-10; II Chron. 36:21].)

3 And I set my face unto the LORD GOD, to seek by prayer and supplications, with fasting, and sackcloth, and ashes *(Daniel was seeking God for the deliverance of Israel from this seventy-year captivity as was promised by the Lord. His prayer was based upon the "Books," i.e., the Bible [Lev., Chpt. 26; II Chron., Chpt. 36; Jer., Chpts. 25 and 29]):*

4 And I prayed unto the LORD my God, and made my confession, and said, O Lord, the great and dreadful God, keeping the covenant and mercy to them who love Him, and to them that keep His Commandments *(there is a reference here to Deut. 7:9, from which the latter clause is quoted verbatim. This particular Chapter in Deuteronomy exhibits God's love for Israel, and hence, as that love is his plea, Daniel appeals to it. As well, one should note the evidence of careful acquaintance with preceding Scripture);*

5 We have sinned, and have committed iniquity, and have done wickedly, and have rebelled, even by departing from Your Precepts and from Your Judgments *(Daniel includes himself in this confession of wrongdoing. The phrase, "Even by departing from Your Precepts and from Your Judgments," defines what sin is. It is a departing from the Word of God. As it was then, so it is now! It is summed up in the word "rebellion"):*

6 Neither have we hearkened unto Your servants the Prophets, which spoke in Your name to our kings, our princes, and our fathers, and to all the people of the land. *(Judah had suffered seventy years of captivity because she would not listen to the one true Prophet, Jeremiah, who was raised up by the Lord; they rather heeded the false prophets.)*

7 O LORD, righteousness belongs unto You, but unto us confusion of faces, as at this day; to the men of Judah, and to the inhabitants of Jerusalem, and unto all Israel, that are near, and that are far off, through all the countries whither You have driven them, because of their trespass that they have trespassed against You. *(The phrase, "But unto us confusion of faces," refers to shame. Sin always brings shame, and only God can take it away.)*

8 O Lord, to us belongs confusion of face, to our kings, to our princes, and to our fathers, because we have sinned against You. *(The Lord will only accept from the truly repentant heart, i.e., "we have sinned against You," because all sin, in one way or the other, is directed against God.)*

9 To the Lord our God belong mercies and forgivenesses; though we have rebelled against Him (*Mercy will always be shown and forgiveness will always be tendered if the individual, irrespective as to what has been done, will only humble himself before God*);

10 Neither have we obeyed the voice of the LORD our God, to walk in His Laws, which He set before us by His servants the Prophets. (*Once again, the Word of God is held up as the guideline for all living. It is called "the Voice of the LORD our God."*)

11 Yea, all Israel have transgressed Your Law, even by departing, that they might not obey Your voice; therefore the curse is poured upon us, and the oath that is written in the Law of Moses the servant of God, because we have sinned against Him. (*When a curse is promised for certain action, it will be done according to God's Word, just as a reward is granted for obedience.*)

12 And He has confirmed His words, which He spoke against us, and against our judges who judged us, by bringing upon us a great evil: for under the whole heaven has not been done as has been done upon Jerusalem. (*God will always confirm His Word and curse those who sin and bless those who obey [Gal. 6:7-8]. His attitude in this respect does not change from the Old Covenant to the New. That we are presently under Grace and God does not look at sin as He once did is a facetious idea indeed! God's attitude toward sin has never changed and in fact cannot change.*)

13 As it is written in the Law of Moses, all this evil is come upon us: yet made we not our prayer before the LORD our God, that we might turn from our iniquities, and understand Your Truth. (*The idea of this Verse is: Judah would not repent although repeatedly warned before the judgment; they also would not repent after the judgment.*

The phrase, "And understand Your Truth," means that the Truth here is extended to its fullest meaning, "God's Supreme Reality." God, being God, implies necessarily that every Word of Promise or Threatening He utters is true; veracity and faithfulness are equally involved in Jehovah being God.)

14 Therefore has the LORD watched upon the evil, and brought it upon us: for the LORD our God is righteous in all His works which He does: for we obeyed not His voice. (*The idea is: what the Lord has done is the right thing to have done, and His Righteousness is vindicated in judgment on sin that refuses to be repented of.*)

15 And now, O Lord our God, Who has brought Your people forth out of the land of Egypt with a mighty hand, and have gotten You renown, as at this day; we have sinned, we have done wickedly. (*The phrase, "And have gotten You renown, as at this day," is an exact quotation from Jer. 32:20, as in the original Text. The short phrase, "Your people," tells us that Israel, even in apostasy and dispersion, was considered the chosen People of God. In the sense of the Promises made to the Patriarchs and Prophets of old, they still fit this category. However, this designation has to do only with the Promises and Covenants, and in no way specifies Salvation.*)

16 O LORD, according to all Your righteousness, I beseech You, let Your anger and Your fury be turned away from Your city Jerusalem, Your holy mountain: because for our sins, and for the iniquities of our fathers, Jerusalem and Your people are become a reproach to all who are about us. (*In effect, Daniel is asking that the "anger" of the Lord, which has been poured out for the last seventy years on "Jerusalem" and "Your people," be abated. The appeal is made to God's Righteousness, because now the seventy years were nearing their end, and God's Righteousness is involved in the time not being exceeded.*)

17 Now therefore, O our God, hear the prayer of Your servant, and his supplications, and cause Your face to shine upon Your sanctuary that is desolate, for the Lord's sake. (*Daniel is calling the Lord to the petition of the Psalmist, where Asaph said, "Turn us again, O God, and cause Your Face to shine; and we shall be saved" [Ps. 80:3]. This has reference to the Blessings of God.*)

18 O my God, incline Your ear, and hear; open Your eyes, and behold our desolations, and the city which is called by Your name: for we do not present our supplications before You for our righteousnesses, but for Your great mercies. (*God's Blessings are not given because we deserve them, because, in fact, we do not.*)

19 O Lord, hear; O Lord, forgive; O Lord, hearken and do; defer not, for Your Own sake, O my God: for Your city and Your people are called by Your Name. (*Daniel repeatedly uses the title, "Adonai," in saying, "O Lord, hear." The short sentences give a feeling of intensity to the prayer suitable to the circumstances.*)

GABRIEL'S INTERPRETATION OF THE VISION OF THE SEVENTY WEEKS

20 And while I was speaking, and praying, and confessing my sin and the sin of my people Israel, and presenting my supplication before the LORD my God for the holy mountain of my God *(Daniel declared that Jerusalem has been called by God's Name, and has been chosen by God. Actually, it will be the capital of His Eternal Kingdom on Earth [Ps. 2:6; 48:2; 87:2; 102:16; 132:13; Isa. 2:2-4; Ezek., Chpt. 48; Zech., Chpt. 14]);*

21 Yea, while I was speaking in prayer, even the man Gabriel, whom I had seen in the Vision at the beginning, being caused to fly swiftly, touched me about the time of the evening oblation. *(Once again, "Gabriel" is sent to Daniel's side. The phrase, "About the time of the evening Oblation," referred to 3 p.m., which was the time of the evening Sacrifice; however, this does not imply that those Offerings were made in Babylon, but simply that, through the nearly seventy years that had intervened since the fall of Jerusalem, the sacred hour had been kept in remembrance, and possibly as one consecrated to prayer.)*

22 And he informed me, and talked with me, and said, O Daniel, I am now come forth to give you skill and understanding. *(The phrase, "To give you skill and understanding," refers to the future of Israel and last-day events.)*

23 At the beginning of your supplications the commandment came forth, and I am come to show you; for you are greatly beloved: therefore understand the matter, and consider the Vision. *(The study of Bible Prophecy was not for Daniel a mere intellectual entertainment, but moral and spiritual nourishment.)*

24 Seventy weeks are determined upon your people and upon your holy city, to finish the transgression, and to make an end of sins, and to make reconciliation for iniquity, and to bring in everlasting righteousness, and to seal up the Vision and Prophecy, and to anoint the Most Holy. *(The phrase, "Seventy weeks are determined upon your people," actually means seventy sevens, which translates into 490 years. This period of time has to do with "your people" and "your holy city," referring to the Jews and Jerusalem. The Second Coming of Christ and their acceptance of Him will "finish the transgression."*

The phrase, "To make reconciliation [atonement] for iniquity," refers to the fact that Israel will not only accept Christ at the Second Coming

but will also accept what He did for us at Calvary. One can well imagine this moment, for they are the ones who crucified Christ.

The phrase, "To anoint the Most Holy," has to do with the building of the Millennial Temple, even as described by Ezekiel in Chapters 40-48 of his Book.)

25 Know therefore and understand, that from the going forth of the Commandment to restore and to build Jerusalem unto the Messiah the Prince shall be seven weeks, and threescore and two weeks: the street shall be built again, and the wall, even in troublous times. *(If one is to notice in this Scripture, the "seventy weeks" of years is broken up into two periods. One "shall be seven weeks" [49 years] and the other will be "threescore and two weeks" [434 years], totaling 483 years. The phrase, "That from the going forth of the Commandment to restore and rebuild Jerusalem," is the beginning of this 490-year period. However, from that time until it was actually finished was some 141 years. Actually, the clock stopped and started several times in this 141-year period, totaling some 49 years when work was truly in progress, comprising the first seven weeks of years [49 years].*

The second block of time started at the end of the 49 years and ended with the Crucifixion of the Lord Jesus Christ, which was 434 years. Combining, as stated, the 49 years with the 434 years brings the total to 483 years.

The third block of time, which we will study in the last Verse, will be the last week of years, totaling seven years, which will make up the Great Tribulation period, concluding Daniel's Prophecy of seventy weeks of years.

Again, it must be remembered that these 490 years did not run consecutively. There were stoppages, as stated, in the first 49 years; then there has been a huge halt of nearly 2,000 years from the time that Christ was crucified, which has not concluded yet. In other words, the last week of years [seven years] is yet to come.)

26 And after threescore and two weeks shall Messiah be cut off, but not for himself: and the people of the prince who shall come shall destroy the city and the sanctuary; and the end thereof shall be with a flood, and unto the end of the war desolations are determined. *(The phrase, "And after threescore and two weeks shall Messiah be cut off," gives us the exact time, even the very year, that the Messiah would be crucified. The words, "cut off," refer to His Crucifixion.*

The phrase, "But not for Himself," refers to

Jesus dying for mankind and taking upon Himself the penalty for mankind. In other words, He did not die for crimes He had committed, but rather for the crimes mankind had committed.

The phrase, "And the people of the prince who shall come shall destroy the City and the Sanctuary," refers to the Romans, who fulfilled this Prophecy in A.D. 70. However, the "prince," as used here, actually refers to the Antichrist, who has not yet come, but will come from among the ten kingdoms yet to be formed inside the old Roman Empire territory. The next Verse proves this.)

27 And he shall confirm the covenant with many for one week: and in the midst of the week he shall cause the sacrifice and the oblation to cease, and for the overspreading of abominations he shall make it desolate, even until the consummation, and that determined shall be poured upon the desolate. (The phrase, "And he shall confirm," refers to the Antichrist. The phrase, "And in the midst of the week," refers to three and a half years, at which time the Antichrist will show his true colors and stop the Sacrifices in the newly-built Temple. At that time, he will actually invade Israel, with her suffering her first defeat since her formation as a nation in 1948.

The phrase, "Even until the consummation," means until the end of the seven-year Great Tribulation period. The phrase, "And that determined shall be poured upon the desolate," refers to all the Prophecies being fulfilled regarding the great suffering that Israel will go through the last three and a half years of the Great Tribulation [Mat. 24:21-22].)

CHAPTER 10

(534 B.C.)

DANIEL'S FOURTH VISION: ISRAEL IN THE LAST DAYS UNDER THE ANTICHRIST: TIME AND PLACE

I N the third year of Cyrus king of Persia a thing was revealed unto Daniel, whose name was called Belteshazzar; and the thing was true, but the time appointed was long: and he understood the thing, and had understanding of the Vision. (The phrase, "And the thing was true, but the time appointed was long," has reference to the fulfillment of this Vision being in the far distant future, at least from Daniel's day. In fact, it will be fulfilled shortly!)

2 In those days I Daniel was mourning three full weeks. (It is thought that this Vision was given about five years after the Vision of the seventy weeks of the previous Chapter.)

3 I ate no pleasant bread, neither came flesh nor wine in my mouth, neither did I anoint myself at all, till three whole weeks were fulfilled. (There are some who argue that Daniel was on a total fast, in other words, abstaining from any food whatsoever; however, the phrase, "No pleasant bread," seems to indicate otherwise, meaning that he was on a partial fast, with his diet being vegetables, which is the same thing he ate in Chapter 1 when presented to Melzar [1:5, 8, 12-16].)

4 And in the four and twentieth day of the first month, as I was by the side of the great river, which is Hiddekel (the "Hiddekel" is the modern Tigris River);

VISION OF THE MESSIAH

5 Then I lifted up my eyes, and looked, and behold a certain man clothed in linen, whose loins were girded with fine gold of Uphaz (the similarity of the apparition in Verses 5 and 6 and in Rev. 1:13, 16 suggests that it was Immanuel Himself Who appeared to Daniel):

6 His body also was like the beryl, and His face as the appearance of lightning, and His eyes as lamps of fire, and His arms and His feet like in colour to polished brass, and the voice of His words like the voice of a multitude. (I think there is no doubt that this is a pre-incarnate appearance of Christ.)

THE EFFECT OF THE VISION

7 And I Daniel alone saw the Vision: for the men who were with me saw not the Vision; but a great quaking fell upon them, so that they fled to hide themselves. (Even though these companions "saw not the Vision," still they greatly felt the Power of the Presence, for "a great quaking fell upon them." This means they were terrified!)

8 Therefore I was left alone, and saw this great Vision, and there remained no strength in me: for my comeliness was turned in me into corruption, and I retained no strength. (The phrase, "For my comeliness was turned in me into corruption," underlies the true meaning of this Passage. When our Righteousness is compared with that of Christ's, there truly is no comparison.)

9 Yet heard I the voice of His words: and when I heard the voice of His words, then was I in a deep sleep on my face, and my face toward

the ground. *(This is the same reaction that Daniel had upon the appearance of Gabriel, concerning the Vision of Chapter 8. The experience of Peter, James, and John on the Mount of Transfiguration was similar.)*

10 And, behold, an hand touched me, which set me upon my knees and upon the palms of my hands. *(Even though the Scripture is unclear, it seems that the "hand" that "touched" Daniel was not necessarily the Hand of Christ, of Verses 5 and 6. Every implication is that it is Gabriel's.)*

11 And he said unto me, O Daniel, a man greatly beloved, understand the words that I speak unto you, and stand upright: for unto you am I now sent. And when he had spoken this word unto me, I stood trembling. *(The message that Gabriel is about to give Daniel will be the concluding "Vision," and will actually tie all the other Visions together.)*

ANGELIC INTERPRETER; GABRIEL DETAINED BY SATAN'S FORCES OVER PERSIA

12 Then said he unto me, Fear not, Daniel: for from the first day that you did set your heart to understand, and to chasten yourself before your God, your words were heard, and I am come for your words. *(The phrase, "For from the first day," speaks of his petition to God and his effort to understand God's purpose concerning His People. Then God commissioned Gabriel to come to him.)*

13 But the prince of the kingdom of Persia withstood me one and twenty days: but, lo, Michael, one of the Chief Princes, came to help me; and I remained there with the kings of Persia. *(The phrase, "The prince of the kingdom of Persia," refers to an evil angel appointed by Satan to control the Persian Government, which, of course, was done without the knowledge of its earthly king. This Passage appears to reveal that Satan places an agent in charge of every nation [fallen angel]; and, if so, this may explain national hatreds and national movements.*

Similarly, God has His Angelic Agents operating in opposition to Satan's. The conflict of Eph., Chpt. 6 and the Battle of Rev., Chpt. 12 harmonize with this supposition.)

OBJECT AND SUBJECT OF THE VISION: EFFECT ON DANIEL

14 Now I am come to make you understand what shall befall your people in the latter days: for yet the Vision is for many days. *(The phrase, "What shall befall your people," refers solely to the Jews [9:24; 12:1]. Therefore, the Gentile nations are included, but only as they affect Israel, and only as Israel is ensconced in her land and offering Sacrifices in the Temple; in fact, this Temple will soon be built.)*

15 And when he had spoken such words unto me, I set my face toward the ground, and I became dumb. *(Quite possibly, the many times mentioned concerning the Vision being fulfilled in the "latter days" is because Daniel may have thought that these things would happen shortly, with Israel ultimately being restored to her place and position of power and supremacy.)*

16 And, behold, one like the similitude of the sons of men touched my lips: then I opened my mouth, and spoke, and said unto Him Who stood before me, O my Lord, by the Vision my sorrows are turned upon me, and I have retained no strength. *(Quite possibly, this was Christ, because Daniel addressed Him as "O my Lord!")*

17 For how can the servant of this my Lord talk with this my Lord? for as for me, straightway there remained no strength in me, neither is there breath left in me. *(The implication is that it is not the Vision alone causing the physical weakness, but rather the very Presence of Christ.)*

18 Then there came again and touched me one like the appearance of a man, and he strengthened me,

19 And said, O man greatly beloved, fear not: peace be unto you, be strong, yea, be strong. And when He had spoken unto me, I was strengthened, and said, Let my Lord speak; for You have strengthened me. *(It seems that this is the Lord, in a pre-incarnate appearance, actually speaking to Daniel.)*

THE PRINCE OF GRECIA

20 Then said He, Knowest thou wherefore I come unto you? and now will I return to fight with the prince of Persia: and when I am gone forth, lo, the prince of Grecia shall come. *(It seems that now Gabriel once again picks up the conversation. The phrase, "And now will I return to fight with the prince of Persia," did not mean that he would leave immediately, but, when the Vision was completed, he would resume the conflict with this Satanic prince.*

The phrase, "And when I am gone forth, lo,

the prince of Grecia shall come," refers to Gabriel ultimately being successful in this conflict, allowing the Satanic prince to bring in the Grecian Empire. This would take place less than 200 years in the future.

The "prince of Grecia" is not an earthly prince, but instead a fallen angel working under the direct instructions of Satan, who would control the Grecian Empire when it did come into being. It was this evil prince which helped Alexander the Great conquer the known world of that day, although without his knowledge. This "prince" is now confined to the underworld, but will be released in the last days in order to help the Antichrist [Rev. 17:8-14].

It is the same presently, with fallen angels controlling entire nations [Eph. 6:12].)

MICHAEL AND GABRIEL

21 But I will show you that which is noted in the Scripture of Truth: and there is none who holds with me in these things, but Michael your prince. ("The Scripture of Truth" refers to the dream originally given to Nebuchadnezzar [2:39], which showed these Empires, as well as the two Visions already given to Daniel, as noted in 7:5-6 and 8:3-8. The phrase, "And there is none who holds with me in these things, but Michael your prince," denotes the Truth that as these fallen angels reigned supreme over certain empires, Michael served in the same position over Israel, and in fact still does!)

CHAPTER 11
(534 B.C.)
THE INTERPRETATION OF DANIEL'S VISION: FROM THE PERSIAN EMPIRE TO ALEXANDER'S DEATH

ALSO I in the first year of Darius the Mede, even I, stood to confirm and to strengthen him. (The phrase, "I stood to confirm and to strengthen him," refers to Michael the Archangel helping Gabriel as it regards the conflict in question. We see from all this that force has to be used to remove certain Satanic rulers [fallen angels] regarding particular nations, so that another fallen angel can take their place, even as it was with the Grecian Empire taking over the Medo-Persian Empire. All of this happens in the spirit world and is unseen with the natural eye; however, the effects can definitely be felt.

All of this tells us that there is always conflict in Satan's kingdom, which is here made obvious.)

2 And now will I show you the truth. Behold, there shall stand up yet three kings in Persia; and the fourth shall be far richer than they all: and by his strength through his riches he shall stir up all against the realm of Grecia. (These three Persian kings were Cyrus, Cambyses, and Darius I. The fourth was Xerxes, who fulfilled this Verse according to riches. Actually there were six Persian kings after the four mentioned in this Verse; however, the conflict against Greece began with Xerxes, who Gabriel said would "stir up all against the realm of Grecia.")

3 And a mighty king shall stand up, who shall rule with great dominion, and do according to his will. (This pertains to Alexander the Great, who gained the throne when he was only 19 years old.)

4 And when he shall stand up, his kingdom shall be broken, and shall be divided toward the four winds of heaven; and not to his posterity, nor according to his dominion which he ruled: for his kingdom shall be plucked up, even for others beside those. (The phrase, "And when he shall stand up," means when he was at the height of his power, and refers to Alexander the Great. The phrase, "His kingdom shall be broken," has to do with his sudden death at 32 years old, and to the breaking up of the Grecian Empire into four divisions, which were taken over by four of his Generals. The phrase, "And not to his posterity, nor according to his dominion which he ruled," speaks of his son, who should have gotten the throne, but did not. It must be remembered that these Prophecies were given by Daniel nearly 200 years before they actually came to pass.)

WARS BETWEEN THE PTOLEMIES AND SELEUCIDS

5 And the king of the south shall be strong, and one of his princes; and he shall be strong above him, and have dominion; his dominion shall be a great dominion. (The phrase, "And one of his princes; and he shall be strong above him, and have dominion," refers to Seleucus I, called Nicator, the Conqueror. He founded the Seleucid Empire, 312-280 B.C. To the unspiritual mind, this Chapter is without interest; to the skeptical and critical mind, untruthful; for it is contended that these pretended Prophecies were written after the events took place. But students of history know that these Prophecies were written before they began to come to pass, and that their most important predictions yet

await fulfillment [Vss. 35-45].

Further, the heart that is in fellowship with God takes an intense interest in all this history, both past and future, because it concerns God's dearly-loved People and His pleasant Land.)

6 And in the end of years they shall join themselves together; for the king's daughter of the south shall come to the king of the north to make an agreement: but she shall not retain the power of the arm; neither shall he stand, nor his arm: but she shall be given up, and they who brought her, and he who begat her, and he who strengthened her in these times. *(The phrase, "For the king's daughter of the south shall come to the king of the north to make an agreement," refers to Ptolemy II, the king of the south, and Antiochus, the king of the north. "The king's daughter" was Berenice, daughter of Ptolemy. The "agreement" pertains to Syria and Egypt agreeing to terminate their differences; however, the agreement was based on the marriage of Berenice to Antiochus II, king of Syria. It didn't work out, inasmuch as she and her son were murdered.)*

7 But out of a branch of her roots shall one stand up in his estate, which shall come with an army, and shall enter into the fortress of the king of the north, and shall deal against them, and shall prevail *(the brother of Berenice, who had just been murdered, was Ptolemy III, who had just succeeded to the Egyptian throne. The "king of the north" was Seleucus II. Ptolemy invaded Syria and defeated Seleucus)*:

8 And shall also carry captives into Egypt their gods, with their princes, and with their precious vessels of silver and of gold; and he shall continue more years than the king of the north. *(The phrase, "And shall also carry captives into Egypt their gods," referred to Ptolemy carrying back to Egypt the gods which Cambyses, king of Persia, had taken from Egypt nearly 300 years before, along with much booty.)*

9 So the king of the south shall come into his kingdom, and shall return into his own land. *(Even though he won many victories elsewhere, Ptolemy was having problems back in Egypt, his home base.)*

10 But his sons shall be stirred up, and shall assemble a multitude of great forces: and one shall certainly come, and overflow, and pass through: then shall he return, and be stirred up, even to his fortress. *(The phrase, "But his sons shall be stirred up," refers to the sons of Seleucus II. They were determined to recover their father's dominion, which had been taken*

by Ptolemy III, king of the south, Egypt.

Antiochus III was the only one who did actually war against Egypt, with his brother Seleucus III poisoned by two of own generals.)

11 And the king of the south shall be moved with choler, and shall come forth and fight with him, even with the king of the north: and he shall set forth a great multitude; but the multitude shall be given into his hand. *("The king of the south" was Ptolemy Philopater, and he defeated Antiochus, "the king of the north," thereby fulfilling the Prophecy, "but the multitude shall be given into his hand.")*

12 And when he has taken away the multitude, his heart shall be lifted up; and he shall cast down many ten thousands: but he shall not be strengthened by it. *(The pronoun "he" refers to "the king of the south," Ptolemy Philopater. He was greatly lifted up by his victory and oppressed many in his own land, especially the Jews; irrespective, his kingdom suffered a steady decline.)*

13 For the king of the north shall return, and shall set forth a multitude greater than the former, and shall certainly come after certain years with a great army and with much riches. *(The "king of the north" is Antiochus III, called "the great." He ruled from 223-187 B.C. The phrase, "Shall return, and shall set forth a multitude greater than the former," pertains to him returning some 14 years later to fight the Egyptians, and with a greater army than ever before. He would win!)*

14 And in those times there shall many stand up against the king of the south: also the robbers of your people shall exalt themselves to establish the vision; but they shall fall. *(The first phrase refers to Antiochus the Great and Philip of Macedonia uniting in order to conquer Egypt. He won; however, Rome stepped in and forced him to surrender his conquest. The phrase, "Also the robbers of your people shall exalt themselves to establish the vision," refers to the Jews who thought by helping Antiochus they would bring about the fulfillment of Prophecy and, therefore, the independence of Judah. But the results were that they all perished at the hand of the Egyptians, fulfilling the Prophecy, "but they shall fall."*

Had they read the Prophecy correctly to begin with, they would not have suffered this defeat.)

15 So the king of the north shall come, and cast up a mount, and take the most fenced cities: and the arms of the south shall not withstand, neither his chosen people, neither shall

there be any strength to withstand. *(Egypt would be defeated by the "king of the north," i.e., Syria.)*

16 But he who comes against him shall do according to his own will, and none shall stand before him: and he shall stand in the glorious land, which by his hand shall be consumed. *(The phrase, "And he shall stand in the glorious land," refers to Judea, and the Jews attempting to help Antiochus the Great defeat Ptolemy, which he did. Even though Antiochus showed the Jews great favor, still, Israel's dependence was not on the Lord, but instead on man; consequently, Judea was greatly reduced to poverty through the long wars, fulfilling the phrase, "which by his hand shall be consumed.")*

17 He shall also set his face to enter with the strength of his whole kingdom, and upright ones with him; thus shall he do: and he shall give him the daughter of women, corrupting her: but she shall not stand on his side, neither be for him. *(This Verse speaks of Antiochus the Great making a treaty with Ptolemy V, that is, a treaty of peace, fulfilling the phrase, "And upright ones with him." The conditions were that Antiochus' daughter, Cleopatra, aged 11, should marry Ptolemy. The Holy Spirit here describes her as "the daughter of women," denoting great beauty.*

The phrase, "Corrupting her," means that her father, Antiochus the Great, ordered her to be a spy in the Egyptian Court in his interests, but she ultimately sided with her husband, and defeated her father's plans by inviting the protection of the Romans, fulfilling the Prophecy, "but she shall not stand on his side, neither be for him.")

18 After this shall he turn his face unto the isles, and shall take many: but a prince for his own behalf shall cause the reproach offered by him to cease; without his own reproach he shall cause it to turn upon him. *(Antiochus attacked Asia Minor and Greece, but the Roman General, Lucius Scipio, defeated him and restored the prestige of the Roman name, which had suffered "reproach" because the Roman Senate had failed to protect Egypt and Greece.*

Scipio turned the "reproach" from the Romans onto Antiochus by offering him great conditions of peace.)

19 Then he shall turn his face toward the fort of his own land: but he shall stumble and fall, and not be found. *(In trying to raise the money demanded by Rome, he plundered a popular temple; the enraged worshippers then killed him, fulfilling the Prophecy, "but he shall stumble and fall, and not be found.")*

20 Then shall stand up in his estate a raiser of taxes in the glory of the kingdom: but within few days he shall be destroyed, neither in anger, nor in battle. *(The phrase, "Raiser of taxes," referred to Seleucus IV mainly engaged in raising money to satisfy the Roman tribute. Concerning "the glory of the kingdom," this speaks of him sending Heliodorus into Judah to plunder the temple. On his return Heliodorus poisoned him, and thus he died "neither in anger nor in battle," fulfilling that Prophecy.)*

PERSECUTION OF ISRAEL BY ANTIOCHUS EPIPHANES

21 And in his estate shall stand up a vile person, to whom they shall not give the honour of the kingdom: but he shall come in peaceably, and obtain the kingdom by flatteries. *(The phrase, "In his estate," refers to the kingdom of Syria, including the ancient Assyria, and even the modern Armenia. The "vile person" refers to Antiochus IV, called Epiphanes, the Illustrious. Verses 21 through 34 refer to him. Antiochus Epiphanes, in his character, actions, and cruelties illustrates the closing predictions of this Chapter, but does not fulfill them. Despite the claims of some, Antiochus Epiphanes was not the Antichrist.)*

22 And with the arms of a flood shall they be overflown from before him, and shall be broken; yea, also the prince of the covenant. *(The pronoun "they" refers to his opponents, who were overthrown in their attempt to take the throne. The phrase, "Also the prince of the covenant," concerns the High Priest of Israel, who was deposed, with Antiochus installing Jason in his place [Judah was a small part of his kingdom].)*

23 And after the league made with him he shall work deceitfully: for he shall come up, and shall become strong with a small people. *(The phrase, "He shall work deceitfully," refers to the fact that the league was broken with Jason, when he put wicked Menelaus in the office of High Priest. Menelaus offered him more money than had Jason.)*

24 He shall enter peaceably even upon the fattest places of the province; and he shall do that which his fathers have not done, nor his fathers' fathers; he shall scatter among them the prey, and spoil, and riches: yea, and he shall forecast his devices against the strong holds, even for a time.

25 And he shall stir up his power and his courage against the king of the south with a great army; and the king of the south shall be stirred up to battle with a very great and mighty army; but he shall not stand: for they shall forecast devices against him. *(The phrase, "And he shall stir up his power and his courage against the king of the south," refers to his making war on Egypt and being victorious. He had himself crowned king of Egypt.)*

26 Yea, they who feed of the portion of his meat shall destroy him, and his army shall overflow: and many shall fall down slain. *(The amazing detail of these Prophecies actually staggers the imagination! Only God could forecast, and in such detail, the actual events, which would take place concerning great nations, kings, and mighty armies, with every detail coming to pass exactly as predicted.)*

27 And both of these kings' hearts shall be to do mischief, and they shall speak lies at one table; but it shall not prosper: for yet the end shall be at the time appointed. *(The two kings spoken of here are Antiochus Epiphanes of Syria and Ptolemy Philometor of Egypt. The phrase, "For yet the end shall be at the time appointed," means that it was not God's Will that Antiochus Epiphanes take Egypt at this time. That would come later, at least after a fashion.)*

28 Then shall he return into his land with great riches; and his heart shall be against the Holy Covenant; and he shall do exploits, and return to his own land. *(The phrase, "And his heart shall be against the Holy Covenant," pertains to him turning against the Jews, because he heard there had been rejoicing in Jerusalem, because they thought he had been killed. This angered him greatly and he made the decision to break his Covenant with Judah.)*

29 At the time appointed he shall return, and come toward the south; but it shall not be as the former, or as the latter. *(The phrase, "At the time appointed he shall return," has to do with the latter portion of Verse 27, which now has come of time. He will take a second expedition into Egypt, but will not be as successful as before!)*

30 For the ships of Chittim shall come against him: therefore he shall be grieved, and return, and have indignation against the Holy Covenant: so shall he do; he shall even return, and have intelligence with them who forsake the Holy Covenant. *(The phrase, "For the ships of Chittim shall come against him," refers to the coming of the Romans demanding*

his discontinuance of his war on Egypt. The phrase, "Therefore he shall be grieved, and return," specifies the reason for the grief, as he was within seven miles of Alexandria, the great city of Egypt. He then turned against Jerusalem, killing some 40,000 Jews and selling many as slaves.*

The phrase, "And have intelligence with them who forsake the Holy Covenant," refers to the apostate Jews who helped him pollute the Temple and place within it "the abomination of desolation," which was a sow on the Temple Altar, as well as doing away with Temple Sacrifices.)

31 And arms shall stand on his part, and they shall pollute the Sanctuary of strength, and shall take away the daily sacrifice, and they shall place the abomination that makes desolate. *(The phrase, "And arms shall stand on his part," refers to him having military power to take Jerusalem and to carry out his will. The phrase, "And shall take away the daily sacrifice, and they shall place the abomination that makes desolate," refers to the offering up of a sow, as mentioned, on the Altar, thereby greatly polluting it, as would be obvious.)*

32 And such as do wickedly against the Covenant shall he corrupt by flatteries: but the people that do know their God shall be strong, and do exploits. *(The phrase, "And such as do wickedly against the Covenant shall he corrupt by flatteries," refers to his old method of deceit, and some Jews being led into apostasy, thereby helping him because he flattered them. The latter phrase refers to the Jews under the Maccabees.)*

33 And they who understand among the people shall instruct many: yet they shall fall by the sword, and by flame, by captivity and by spoil, many days. *(This proclaims the constant struggle by God's People from Daniel's day forward to the birth of Christ. As we have attempted to outline, especially the activity of the Maccabees, their situation, at times, was perilous.*

The phrase, "And they who understand among the people shall instruct many," refers to a terrible spiritual drought from Malachi's time to John the Baptist, when Israel, for some 400 years, would not hear the voice of a Prophet. However, there would be some, although not of prophetical status, who would labor faithfully, attempting to get the people to obey the Law of Moses.)

34 Now when they shall fall, they shall be holpen with a little help: but many shall cleave to them with flatteries. *(The phrase, "Now when they shall fall," refers to many Jews falling by the sword in the many conflicts that took place.*

The phrase, "But many shall cleave to them with flatteries," refers to an inducement to apostatize regarding the Jews who faithfully followed the Lord. Satan has two weapons against faithfulness to Truth; one is violence, the other is flattery.)

WARS BETWEEN SYRIA AND EGYPT IN THE LAST DAYS

35 And some of them of understanding shall fall, to try them, and to purge, and to make them white, even to the time of the end: because it is yet for a time appointed. (With this Verse begins the account of the Endtime, which will continue through the Twelfth Chapter. Therefore, the entirety of the time, now totaling nearly 2,000 years, is omitted in Scripture, which includes the entirety of the Church Age, because Gabriel told Daniel, "These Prophecies only pertain to 'your people,' and more particularly, 'in the latter days'" [10:14].)

36 And the king shall do according to his will; and he shall exalt himself, and magnify himself above every god, and shall speak marvellous things against the God of gods, and shall prosper till the indignation be accomplished: for that that is determined shall be done. (The phrase, "And the king shall do according to his will," refers to the Antichrist, who will pretty much have his way until the Second Advent of Christ. The phrase, "And magnify himself above every god," actually refers to him deifying himself [II Thess. 2:4]. At this time, and according to 9:27, he will take over the newly-built Temple in Jerusalem, do away with the Jewish Sacrifices which have not long since begun, and will set up an image of himself [Rev. 13:15].

The phrase, "And shall speak marvelous things against the God of gods," means that he will literally declare war on Christ. His campaign of declaring himself "god" will, of necessity, demand that he blaspheme the True God as no one has ever blasphemed.

The phrase, "And shall prosper till the indignation be accomplished," means that much of the world will accept his claims, joining with him in their hatred of the God of the Bible.)

37 Neither shall he regard the God of his fathers, nor the desire of women, nor regard any god: for he shall magnify himself above all. (The phrase, "Neither shall he regard the God of his fathers," no doubt refers to him being a Jew. He will not regard the God of "Abraham, Isaac, and Jacob."

The phrase, "Nor the desire of women," probably refers to him turning against the Catholic Church and, thereby, the Virgin Mary.

The phrase, "Nor regard any god: for he shall magnify himself above all," refers to all the religions of the world, all of which will be outlawed, at least where he has control, demanding that worship be centered up on him.)

38 But in his estate shall he honour the god of forces; and a god whom his fathers knew not shall he honour with gold, and silver, and with precious stones, and pleasant things. (The phrase, "And a god whom his fathers knew not shall he honor," refers to a "strange god" mentioned in the next Verse, who is actually the Fallen Angel who empowered Alexander the Great. He is called "the Prince of Grecia," which does not refer to a mortal, but instead a Fallen Angel [10:20]. This "god," his fathers, Abraham, Isaac, and Jacob did not know.)

39 Thus shall he do in the most strong holds with a strange god, whom he shall acknowledge and increase with glory: and he shall cause them to rule over many, and shall divide the land for gain. (The phrase, "Thus shall he do in the most strong holds," refers to the great financial centers of the world, which will be characterized by rebuilt Babylon. This "strange god," as stated, is a Fallen Angel; therefore, he will probably think he is giving praise and glory to himself, when in reality he is actually honoring this "Fallen Angel."

The phrase, "And he shall cause them to rule over many," refers to the many nations he will conquer because of the great power given to him by this Fallen Angel, instigated by Satan.)

THE KING OF THE NORTH (SYRIA) ANTICHRIST VICTORIOUS OVER KING OF THE SOUTH (EGYPT); THE EIGHTH EMPIRE, REVIVED GREECE, FORMED IN MIDDLE OF DANIEL'S SEVENTIETH WEEK

40 And at the time of the end shall the king of the south (Egypt) push at him: and the king of the north (the Antichrist, Syria) shall come against him like a whirlwind, with chariots, and with horsemen, and with many ships; and he shall enter into the countries, and shall overflow and pass over. (The phrase, "And at the time of the end," refers to the time of the fulfillment of these Prophecies, which in fact is just ahead. It is known that "the king of the south" refers to Egypt, because that's who is referred to

at the beginning of this Chapter, which spoke of the breakup of the Grecian Empire. As well, "the king of the north" proves that the Antichrist will come from the Syrian division of the breakup of the Grecian Empire. So the Antichrist will more than likely be a Syrian Jew.)

41 He shall enter also into the glorious land *(into Israel),* **and many countries shall be overthrown** *(those in the Middle East):* **but these shall escape out of his hand, even Edom, and Moab, and the chief of the children of Ammon.** *(Edom, Moab, and Ammon comprise modern Jordan. His entering into the "glorious land" refers to his invasion of Israel at the midpoint of his seven-year nonaggression pact with them, therefore, breaking his Covenant [9:27].*

The countries listed comprise modern Jordan, where ancient Petra is located, to which Israel will flee upon the Antichrist "entering into the Glorious Land" [Rev. 12:6].)

42 He shall stretch forth his hand also upon the countries: and the land of Egypt shall not escape. *("Egypt" refers to "the king of the south" of Verse 40, as stated.)*

43 But he shall have power over the treasures of gold and of silver, and over all the precious things of Egypt: and the Libyans and the Ethiopians shall be at his steps. *(The "precious things of Egypt" no doubt refer to the ancient mysteries of Egypt, regarding the tombs, the pyramids, etc. He will no doubt claim to unlock many of these mysteries; he very well could do so, regarding the supernatural power given to him by the powers of darkness.)*

ADVERSARIES TO THE NORTH AND EAST

44 But tidings of the east and out of the north shall trouble him: therefore he shall go forth with great fury to destroy, and utterly to make away many. *(After the Antichrist breaks his covenant with Israel, actually "entering into the Glorious Land," he will be prevented from further destroying her by the "tidings of the east and out of the north" that "shall trouble him." No doubt, these will be nations, probably led by Russia [north], Japan, and China [east], forming a union against him, but which will have no success.)*

KING OF THE NORTH (SYRIA)
ANTICHRIST SETS HIS THRONE
IN THE TEMPLE IN JERUSALEM

45 And he shall plant the tabernacles of his palace between the seas in the glorious holy mountain; yet he shall come to his end, and none shall help him. *(The phrase, "And he shall plant the tabernacles of his palace," refers to his taking over the newly-built Temple and stopping the Sacrifices, as prophesied in 8:9-12.*

The phrase, "Between the seas in the Glorious Holy Mountain," refers to the Dead Sea and the Mediterranean Sea. The "Glorious Holy Mountain" is Mount Moriah, where the Temple is located.

The phrase, "Yet he shall come to his end, and none shall help him," is tied to the first part of this Verse, which speaks of him desecrating the Temple. This ensures his destruction by the Lord, which will take place at the Second Coming.)

CHAPTER 12
(534 B.C.)
THE GREAT TRIBULATION

AND at that time shall Michael stand up, the great prince which stands for the children of your people: and there shall be a time of trouble, such as never was since there was a nation even to that same time: and at that time your people shall be delivered, every one who shall be found written in the Book.** *("Michael" is the great "Archangel"; he is also referred to as "The Great Prince." He is the Lord Protector of Israel, "which stands for the children of your people." If not for him, Israel would no doubt be annihilated at this time.*

The phrase, "A time of trouble, such as never was since there was a nation even to that same time," is the same thing Jesus would say, and concerns the last three and a half years of the Great Tribulation [Mat. 24:21].

The phrase, "And at that time your people shall be delivered, every one who shall be found written in the Book," refers to the translation of the 144,000 Jews at approximately the middle of the Great Tribulation. This is the "man child" of Rev. 12:5.

Exactly how these 144,000 Jews will find Christ as their Saviour, especially during the first half of the Great Tribulation when Israel in fact will think the Antichrist is the Messiah, is unknown at present; however, if the Bible says it will happen [which it definitely does], then it will happen!

There is no mention here of the Church except possibly in Verse 3. The reason is simple: these Prophecies have to do with "your people" [10:14].

The "Book" spoken of is the Book of Life [Rev. 22:18-19].)

THE RESURRECTIONS

2 And many of them who sleep in the dust of the Earth shall awake, some to everlasting life, and some to shame and everlasting contempt. *(There are two Resurrections pointed to in this Verse. These are separated by a long period of a thousand years [Rev. 20:3, 5-6; Jn. 5:28]. Those who will be resurrected to "Everlasting Life" speak of the First Resurrection, which pertains to every Believer who has ever lived from the time of Abel forward. This is when the Church, so to speak, will be raptured [I Thess. 4:13-18].*

The Second Resurrection, which is the Resurrection of Damnation, will take place at approximately a thousand years after the First Resurrection, actually at the end of the Millennium. It will include all the wicked who have died from the very beginning. This will be the time of the Great White Throne Judgment [Rev. 20:4-6, 11-15].)

REWARDS FOR THE RIGHTEOUS

3 And they that be wise shall shine as the brightness of the firmament; and they that turn many to righteousness as the stars for ever and ever. *(The "wise" are they who live for God and do everything they can to take the Gospel to others.)*

SEALING THE PROPHECIES FOR FUTURE FULFILLMENT

4 But thou, O Daniel, shut up the words, and seal the Book even to the time of the end: many shall run to and fro, and knowledge shall be increased. *(The phrase, "But thou, O Daniel, shut up the words, and seal the Book," means that Daniel has been given the entire blueprint concerning the fate of Israel, and nothing else is to be said. The phrase, "Even to the time of the end," has reference to the fact that the Prophecies recently given by Daniel have reference to the Endtime.*

The phrase, "Many shall run to and fro, and knowledge shall be increased," refers to the tremendous increase in technology, which made its great debut at the beginning of the Twentieth Century. It also refers to knowledge of the Word of God being greatly increased in these last days, especially knowledge concerning Bible Prophecy.)

5 Then I Daniel looked, and, behold, there stood other two, the one on this side of the bank of the river, and the other on that side of the bank of the river. *(Daniel is speaking of the River "Hiddekel," i.e. the Tigris, which is close to the Euphrates. The "other two" spoken of here probably refer to Angels, with no identification given.)*

6 And one said to the Man clothed in linen, Who was upon the waters of the river, How long shall it be to the end of these wonders? *(The phrase, "The Man clothed in linen," no doubt refers to the same One described in 10:5-6. He is Christ. The phrase, "Who was upon the waters of the river," actually says, "Who was above the waters of the river," meaning that Christ, seemingly, was suspended in mid-air, immediately above the river.)*

7 And I heard the Man clothed in linen, Who was upon the waters of the river, when He held up His right hand and His left hand unto Heaven, and swore by Him Who lives for ever that it shall be for a time, times, and an half; and when he *(the Antichrist)* **shall have accomplished to scatter the power of the holy people, all these things shall be finished.** *(The "swearing" of this "Man" proves Him to be a Divine Person, for not one time in Scripture does an ordinary Angel make an oath to God or man.*

The phrase, "That it shall be for a time, times, and an half," refers to three and a half years. This is the last half of the Great Tribulation, when tremendous persecution will be brought to bear upon Israel by the Antichrist. Therefore, the Lord Himself gives the time that these things will happen.

The phrase, "And when he shall have accomplished to scatter the power of the holy people," refers to the Antichrist attempting to destroy Israel, but in fact only scattering them.)

8 And I heard, but I understood not, then said I, O my Lord, what shall be the end of these things?

9 And He said, Go your way, Daniel: for the words are closed up and sealed till the time of the end. *(This Verse declares that these Prophecies belong to the future. However, "the time of the end" is now very close!*

The word "end" does not mean the end of the world, but instead "the end of these things," i.e., the Prophecies concerning Israel and the last days.)

10 Many shall be purified, and made white, and tried; but the wicked shall do wickedly: and none of the wicked shall understand; but the wise shall understand. *(The phrase, "Many shall be purified, and made white, and tried,"*

could refer to the Church, but could also refer to the 144,000 Jews who will come to Christ during the first half of the Great Tribulation.

The phrase, "None of the wicked shall understand," refers to the world not at all understanding the Vision or even caring about it.

The phrase, "But the wise shall understand," refers to the few who truly know the Lord and who avidly search the Scriptures, believing them to be the very Word of God.)

11 And from the time that the daily sacrifice shall be taken away *(at the midpoint of the Great Tribulation)*, and the abomination that makes desolate set up *(refers back to 8:9-12)*, there shall be a thousand two hundred and ninety days.

12 Blessed is he who waits, and comes to the thousand three hundred and five and thirty days. *(This is forty-five days more than the number of days given in Verse 11, and seventy-five more days than given in Verse 7. Why the extra forty-five days over Verse 11? First, we know that those who come to this time will be "blessed." This has to do with the beginning of the Kingdom Age and the events carried out to establish the beginning of the Kingdom.)*

13 But go thou your way till the end be: for you shall rest, and stand in your lot at the end of the days. *(The phrase, "But go thou your way till the end be," refers to Daniel dying and then being a part of the First Resurrection of Life. Until that time, Christ said, "you shall rest."*

The phrase, "And stand in your lot at the end of the days," refers to Daniel having a part in the glorious things that will take place after the Second Coming.)

HOSEA

CHAPTER 1
(785 B.C.)
INTRODUCTION: AUTHOR
AND BACKGROUND

THE Word of the LORD that came unto Hosea, the son of Beeri, in the days of Uzziah, Jotham, Ahaz, and Hezekiah, kings of Judah, and in the days of Jeroboam the son of Joash, king of Israel. *(The name "Hosea" means "Salvation." He was a contemporary of Isaiah. The phrase, "In the days . . .," refers to four kings of Judah, "Uzziah, Jotham, Ahaz, and Hezekiah." One "king of Israel," the Northern Kingdom, is mentioned, "Jeroboam." Hosea's ministry began when he was a young man, while "Uzziah" was on the Throne of Judah and "Jeroboam II" was on the Throne of Israel.)*

HOSEA'S MARRIAGE WITH GOMER, A PROSTITUTE; BIRTH OF JEZREEL: MEANING

2 The beginning of the Word of the LORD by Hosea. And the LORD said to Hosea, Go, take unto you a wife of whoredoms and children of whoredoms: for the land has committed great whoredom, departing from the LORD. *(The phrase, "Go, take unto you a wife of whoredoms and children of whoredoms," actually means "children of idolatry." The nation of Israel, constituting the Northern Kingdom, is appealed to under the figure of an unfaithful wife, because of its devotion to idols and forsaking of Jehovah.)*

3 So he went and took Gomer the daughter of Diblaim; which conceived, and bore him a son. *(There is some evidence that "Gomer" was the name of a harlot well known at that particular time. If so, the shame heaped upon Hosea would have been multi-fold.)*

4 And the LORD said unto him, Call his name Jezreel; for yet a little while, and I will avenge the blood of Jezreel upon the house of Jehu, and will cause to cease the kingdom of the house of Israel. *(The name "Jezreel" means, "God will scatter or sow." This was Hosea's first son.*

The phrase, "And I will avenge the blood of Jezreel upon the house of Jehu," has reference to the commission given to Jehu by the Lord, in carrying out God's Judgment upon the house of Ahab. However, Jehu carried this commission too far, exacting greater Judgment than the Lord intended. And then, above all, he went into the same sins for which the Lord had judged Ahab [II Ki. 10:31-36].

The phrase, "And will cause to cease the kingdom of the house of Israel," signals the beginning of the end for the Northern Kingdom of Israel, even though it would take some seventy years for it to be brought to a total consummation.)

5 And it shall come to pass at that day, that I will break the bow of Israel, in the valley of Jezreel. *(The sign of the coming fall of this kingdom was the breaking of the "bow," because the Northern Kingdom of Israel was famous for its use of the bow.)*

THE BIRTH OF LO-RUHAMAH: MEANING

6 And she conceived again, and bore a daughter. And God said unto him, Call her name Lo-ruhamah: for I will no more have mercy upon the house of Israel; but I will utterly take them away. *("Lo-ruhamah" means "not pitied." Because of Israel going into total idolatry and refusing to repent, even though great Prophets were sent unto them, the Northern Kingdom would be destroyed as a nation, never to rise again, at least in that capacity.)*

7 But I will have mercy upon the house of Judah, and will save them by the LORD their God, and will not save them by bow, nor by sword, nor by battle, by horses, nor by horsemen. *(About 200 years before, ten Tribes had broken away and continued to refer to themselves as "Israel." The larger Tribe of Judah remained, and referred to itself as "Judah," with the Tribe of Benjamin throwing in their lot with Judah [II Chron. 10:12-19]. Even though the Lord here pronounces judgment upon the Northern Kingdom of Israel, He says here that the Southern Kingdom of Judah will be spared.*

He is referring here to the deliverance from Sennacherib in the days of Hezekiah, when in one night the Angel of the Lord smote 185,000 of the flower of the Assyrian host [II Ki., Chpt. 19; Isa., Chpt. 37]. Still, its total fulfillment

belongs to the future [II Thess., Chpt. 2].)

THE BIRTH OF LO-AMMI: MEANING

8 Now when she had weaned Lo-ruhamah, she conceived and bore a son. *(Even though it would be about 70 years before the fall of Israel, still, the children are born in quick succession, proclaiming the finality of the Judgment of God.*

As the three deportations would in later years be a warning to Judah, likewise, the births of these three children are warnings to Israel; however, whereas the deportations were some years apart, the births of these children were in quick succession, denoting the absence of any spiritual quality.)

9 Then said God, Call his name Lo-ammi: for you are not My people, and I will not be your God. *("Lo-ammi" means "not My people." As stated, the Prophet's children symbolized, step by step, Israel's fast coming calamity. There will be no reprieve, because there will be no Repentance.)*

FUTURE REGATHERING OF ISRAEL

10 Yet the number of the Children of Israel shall be as the sand of the sea, which cannot be measured nor numbered; and it shall come to pass, that in the place where it was said unto them, You are not My people, there it shall be said unto them, You are the sons of the Living God. *(There is no contradiction between Verses 9 and 10. Even though the Northern Kingdom of Israel was totally destroyed as a nation, and in fact will never, as such, rise again, still, "the Children of Israel" were not destroyed, and, in truth, will be, in a future happy day, completely restored. Consequently, this Passage and Verse 11 have to do with the coming Kingdom Age.)*

11 Then shall the Children of Judah and the Children of Israel be gathered together, and appoint themselves one head, and they shall come up out of the land: for great shall be the day of Jezreel. *(The restoration under Zerubbabel did not satisfy the prediction of Verses 10 or 11, for it was very small, and did not secure national independence. However, the future will satisfy the Prophecy, for then will God "sow" the Hebrew people unto Himself in Righteousness. As stated, it will be in the coming Kingdom Age, when, at the beginning of it, Israel will accept Christ.)*

CHAPTER 2
(785 B.C.)

GOMER, A PICTURE OF ISRAEL; GOD'S LOVE FOR HIS UNFAITHFUL PEOPLE

S AY ye unto your brethren, Ammi; and to your sisters, Ruhamah. *(These words are addressed to a small company of true Believers, which was then ensconced in backslidden Israel, and which the Lord has in all ages, and which is here distinguished by the affectionate titles of "My people" [Ammi] and "the engraced" [Ruhamah].)*

2 Plead with your mother, plead: for she is not my wife, neither am I her husband: let her therefore put away her whoredoms out of her sight, and her adulteries from between her breasts *(the phrase, "Plead with your mother, plead," speaks of the whole people of Israel taken together as a national unit. The "pleading" to Israel is to be done by those who still love and serve their Lord. In effect, they were to act as Evangelists.*

The phrase, "For she is not my wife, neither am I her husband," in its strict sense, refers to Gomer, who had left Hosea, even after bearing him three children, going back out into the world of sin and iniquity. As Gomer left Hosea for whoredoms, likewise, Israel had left God for whoredoms. So the marriage in both cases was dissolved);

3 Lest I strip her naked, and set her as in the day that she was born, and make her as a wilderness, and set her like a dry land, and slay her with thirst. *(The first phrase refers to the fact that Gomer, rather than gaining prosperity, was instead reduced to abject poverty, as future Verses will portray.)*

4 And I will not have mercy upon her children; for they be the children of whoredoms. *(The nation as a whole with its body politic is spoken of as the parent. Its citizenry is spoken of as the "children." The children proved themselves to be no better than the mother who bore them; they were the worthless progeny of a worthless parent.)*

5 For their mother has played the harlot: she who conceived them has done shamefully: for she said, I will go after my lovers, who give me my bread and my water, my wool and my flax, my oil and my drink. *(Likewise, Israel, of which Gomer was a symbol, ran after her "lovers," who were the Assyrians and the Egyptians. As a result, Israel worshipped the idols of these heathen nations, and also ascribed her blessings*

as not from Jehovah, but from these idol gods.)

6 Therefore, behold, I will hedge up your way with thorns, and make a wall, that she shall not find her paths. *(Both Gomer and Israel had avowed their determination to pursue their evil course shamefully and sinfully, as if in despite and defiance of the Almighty; consequently, the Lord affirms His determination to thwart their course of sin and shame.)*

7 And she shall follow after her lovers, but she shall not overtake them; and she shall seek them, but shall not find them: then shall she say, I will go and return to my first husband; for then was it better with me than now. *(Partially so, regarding Israel, of which Gomer was a type, this Scripture was fulfilled about 200 years later, with some of Israel returning with Judah from Babylonian captivity; however, it was only a partial fulfillment. The total fulfillment awaits the Second Coming of the Lord.)*

8 For she did not know that I gave her corn, and wine, and oil, and multiplied her silver and gold, which they prepared for Baal. *(The phrase, "For she did not know that I gave . . .," portrays an unnecessary spiritual ignorance. Israel forgot that the great blessings she was showered with came from Jehovah. She claimed them as hers, and as having been given to her by her idols. But God said that He gave them to her, that they were His, and that He would now take them back.)*

9 Therefore will I return, and take away My corn in the time thereof, and My wine in the season thereof, and will recover My wool and My flax given to cover her nakedness. *(The action here is one of chastisement and, therefore, of love, for the Lord "chastises those He loves" [Heb. 12:5-11].)*

10 And now will I discover her lewdness in the sight of her lovers, and none shall deliver her out of My hand. *(Israel would find that none of her idols could deliver her from the Assyrians, which would take her captive.)*

11 I will also cause all her mirth to cease, her feast days, her new moons, and her sabbaths, and all her solemn feasts. *(As Israel had said by her actions that she did not desire these things, which in truth were the cause of her blessings, the Lord in turn would remove her to where there would be no opportunity to partake of these Ordinances.)*

12 And I will destroy her vines and her fig trees, whereof she has said, These are my rewards that my lovers have given me: and I will make them a forest, and the beasts of the field shall eat them. *(As Israel had forgotten Who truly was the Source of her prosperity, even attributing such to idols, the Lord would take away their prosperity. Then she would be made to see as to exactly Who had been her Benefactor. It definitely was not her idols.)*

13 And I will visit upon her the days of Baalim, wherein she burned incense to them, and she decked herself with her earrings and her jewels, and she went after her lovers, and forgot Me, saith the LORD. *(The phrase, "And I will visit upon her the days of Baalim," simply means "I will punish them for serving Baal." The name of "Baal" came to be used generally as the designation of any idol or false god; consequently, the "days of Baal" were the days consecrated to Baal, and on which the worship of the true God was transferred to that idol.)*

ISRAEL IS RESTORED

14 Therefore, behold, I will allure her, and bring her into the wilderness, and speak comfortably unto her. *(The balance of the Verses of this Chapter predict the restoration of Israel under the Covenant of Grace as opposed to that of Law. The nation is pictured as a faithless and debauched wife betrothed as a spotless bride to Immanuel. This impossibility will be effected by the miracle of the New Birth. The old impure Israel will die and a pure virgin will appear as the new nation. As stated, this will take place at the beginning of the coming Kingdom Age.)*

15 And I will give her her vineyards from thence, and the valley of Achor for a door of hope: and she shall sing there, as in the days of her youth, and as in the day when she came up out of the land of Egypt. *(The phrase, "And I will give her her vineyards from thence," signifies that the way to the "vineyards" is through the wilderness. Spiritual discipline precedes blessing and fits it for joy. Hence, the words "from thence."*

The phrase, "And the valley of Achor for a door of hope," signals back to a vale of horror as described in Josh. 7:24, but which is to become for Israel "a door of hope."

The truth is presented here by the Holy Spirit that where the Wrath of God justly fell, the Grace of God is to brightly shine. The valley of horror becomes the vale of hope. Such was Calvary — a place of horror to the Suffering Saviour under the Wrath of God, but a door of hope to the redeemed sinner under the Grace of God.

Thus, this "valley of Achor" proclaims to the

Believer who has suffered defeat that the very area of such defeat can become their area of victory.)

16 And it shall be at that day, saith the LORD, that you shall call Me Ishi; and shall call Me no more Baali. *(The word "Ishi" means "my Husband," while the word "Baali" means "my Lord." In other words, Israel will no more refer to Baal as her Lord, but will rightly serve Jehovah.)*

17 For I will take away the names of Baalim out of her mouth, and they shall no more be remembered by their name. *(The names of Baal shall become so abhorrent to blood-washed Israel that they shall pass away at once from their mouths and from their memories, never more to be mentioned and never more to be remembered.)*

18 And in that day will I make a covenant for them with the beasts of the field, and with the fowls of Heaven, and with the creeping things of the ground: and I will break the bow and the sword and the battle out of the Earth, and will make them to lie down safely. *(The phrase, "And in that day will I make a Covenant for them," refers to the New Covenant, which Israel will accept immediately after the Second Coming. At that time, there will be no more war, which speaks to the universal safety of not only Israel, but of the entirety of the world.)*

19 And I will betroth you unto Me for ever; yea, I will betroth you unto Me in righteousness, and in judgment, and in lovingkindness, and in mercies. *(This betrothal between the Lord and Israel will take place immediately after the Second Coming of Christ. Israel will then accept Him, not only as Saviour, but also as Messiah and Lord.)*

20 I will even betroth you unto Me in faithfulness: and you shall know the LORD. *(The phrase, "You shall know the LORD," means that all evils come from not knowing Him [Isa. 1:3; Lk. 19:42, 44].)*

21 And it shall come to pass in that day, I will hear, saith the LORD, I will hear the Heavens, and they shall hear the Earth *(this speaks of the "Earth that shall be full of the knowledge of the LORD, as the waters cover the sea" [Isa. 11:9]);*

22 And the Earth shall hear the corn, and the wine, and the oil; and they shall hear Jezreel. *(Whereas the name "Jezreel" pertained to judgment when originally given, now it refers to the very opposite. Whereas the Lord scattered and sowed Israel in heathen lands, now He scatters and sows them in the Land of Israel*

proper, and in prosperity. In other words, the blessing of Israel will be the blessing of the entirety of the world, and the world will also realize that!)

23 And I will sow her unto Me in the Earth; and I will have mercy upon her that had not obtained mercy; and I will say to them which were not My people, You are My people; and they shall say, You are my God. *(Israel was Lo-ruhamah and Lo-ammi, meaning "no more mercy" and "not My people." Now, Israel will become "Ruhamah," i.e., "pitied one," and "Ammi," i.e., "My people."*

The phrase, "And I will say to them which were not My people, You are My people," is quoted in Rom. 9:25. It refers in that case to the Gentiles, as an illustration of what may be true in their case as well as in Israel's.)

CHAPTER 3
(785 B.C.)

HOSEA AND THE ADULTERESS

THEN said the LORD unto me, Go yet, love a woman beloved of her friend, yet an adulteress, according to the love of the LORD toward the children of Israel, who look to other gods, and love flagons of wine. *(The phrase, "Then said the LORD unto me," signals another step that is to be taken by the Prophet, this one perhaps even more severe than the first. The short phrase, "Go yet," means that the Lord is not through with His object lesson concerning Israel. That which will now be portrayed, even though painfully executed, will nevertheless portray the Love of God in a fashion that nothing else could.*

The Command of the Lord to Hosea is to "love a woman beloved of her friend, yet an adulteress." The idea of the entirety of this scenario is that Gomer, who was an adulteress, and which symbolized the idolatry of Israel, proved faithless to the Prophet and fell into degraded bondage. Nevertheless, Hosea was commanded still to love her, to redeem her from slavery, to remain faithful to her for a lengthened period, and then to fully restore her.

The phrase, "Beloved of her friend," is striking indeed! It means that Gomer was loved by Hosea, but she had forfeited by her misconduct the right to use the honorable words of "wife" and "husband." Therefore, the word "friend" instead would be used, because she was "yet an adulteress.")

2 So I bought her to me for fifteen pieces of

silver, and for an homer of barley, and an half homer of barley (*the redemption price of a slave was thirty pieces of silver [Ex. 21:32] and so much barley. Fifteen pieces of silver and so little barley marked the worthlessness of this slave. No one can fully understand the pain and suffering evidenced in the words, "So I bought her to me for fifteen pieces of silver." Gomer was now used up, therefore, wanted and desired by no one!*

One can only guess at the hurt that filled Hosea's heart as he stood before Gomer. She was no doubt dressed in rags and had been reduced by abuse to less than a slave. She must have reasoned, "How could he love me after all this?"

He could do so, because, about 800 years later, One would hang on a Cross, Who had also been sold for thirty pieces of silver, the price of a slave. That One took her place of suffering that she might take His place of Glory.

And thus it is with us all!):

3 And I said unto her, You shall abide for me many days; you shall not play the harlot, and you shall not be for another man: so will I also be for you. (*The idea is: Gomer had left Hosea for "many days" and had now come back to him, even though in a deplorable condition; now she would be his wife again. This symbolizes Israel, who will come to Christ at the Second Coming. She will then call Him "Ishi," i.e., "my Husband"; and she will never again "play the harlot."*)

4 For the Children of Israel shall abide many days without a King, and without a Prince, and without a Sacrifice, and without an Image, and without an Ephod, and without Teraphim (*Gomer leaving Hosea and going back into whoredoms typify Israel leaving the Lord, which has now lasted for nearly 2,000 years, i.e., "many days"*):

ISRAEL TO BE RESTORED
UNDER THE MESSIAH

5 Afterward shall the Children of Israel return, and seek the LORD their God, and David their king; and shall fear the LORD and His goodness in the latter days. (*While Verse 4 is in the state of fulfillment, Verse 5 remains to be fulfilled. The words, "His Goodness," should be translated "His Gracious One," that is, the Messiah [14:2; Eph. 1:6].*

The phrase, "Latter days," refers to the coming Kingdom Age.)

CHAPTER 4
(780 B.C.)
GOD'S INDICTMENT OF ISRAEL

HEAR the Word of the LORD, you Children of Israel: for the LORD has a controversy with the inhabitants of the land, because there is no truth, nor mercy, nor knowledge of God in the land. (*All of this Chapter, except Verse 15, is addressed to the Ten Tribes; and yet Grace calls them "My people" [Vss. 6, 8]. The phrase, "For the LORD has a controversy with the inhabitants of the land," is a strong statement indeed! It refers to a judicial inquiry and cause.*)

2 By swearing, and lying, and killing, and stealing, and committing adultery, they break out, and blood touches blood. (*The phrase, "They break out," speaks of the terrible sins mentioned and presents the allusion of water overflowing its banks and spreading in all directions. It means to "break through the wall."*)

JUDGMENT ON ISRAEL

3 Therefore shall the land mourn, and every one who dwells therein shall languish, with the beasts of the field, and with the fowls of Heaven; yea, the fishes of the sea also shall be taken away. (*The phrase, "Therefore shall the land mourn," is the result of the sins of Verse 2, for the evils detailed result from not knowing God. The phrases concerning the "Beasts of the field," "Fowls of Heaven," and "Fishes of the sea" specify that all of creation, animate and inanimate, suffer as a result of man's sin [Rom. 8:22].*)

4 Yet let no man strive, nor reprove another: for your people are as they who strive with the Priest. (*This refers back to the true position of the High Priest in Israel, whose word was Law; consequently, there was no point in striving with him. Consequently, it is also useless concerning the coming Judgment.*

The phrase, "Nor reprove another," refers to further admonishment as being hopeless!)

5 Therefore shall you fall in the day, and the prophet also shall fall with you in the night, and I will destroy your mother. (*The first part of this Verse has to do with both "people" and "prophet," which actually refers to false prophets, and that all would fall alike, whether day or night. The destruction of the "mother" has to do with the entirety of the nation. As a nation, they would exist no more.*)

6 My people are destroyed for lack of knowledge: because you have rejected knowledge, I will also reject you, that you shall be no Priest to Me: seeing you have forgotten the Law of your God, I will also forget your children. *(The phrase, "My people are destroyed for lack of knowledge," is the cause of all the problems in the Church, and the world, for that matter! The "knowledge" spoken of is the Bible. This "lack of knowledge" was not ignorance, but rather a willful rejection of the Law of God. They didn't know, but it was because they didn't want to know!)*

7 As they were increased, so they sinned against Me: therefore will I change their glory into shame. *(The "increase" speaks both numerically and economically. The phrase, "Therefore will I change their glory into shame," may also read: "My glory have they changed into shame"; that is, they substituted an idol for God.)*

8 They eat up the sin of My people, and they set their heart on their iniquity. *(The phrase, "They eat up the sin of My people," actually meant that the Priests ate the Sin Offering instead of offering it as a "Burnt Offering," as they were supposed to do.)*

9 And there shall be, like people, like Priest: and I will punish them for their ways, and reward them their doings. *("Like people, like Priests," they were one in guilt and, therefore, justly one in punishment. The word "reward" is generally used in the positive sense, but here it is used in the negative!)*

10 For they shall eat, and not have enough: they shall commit whoredom, and shall not increase: because they have left off to take heed to the LORD. *(The phrase, "They shall commit whoredom, and shall not increase," means that because of "whoredom," i.e., idolatry, the Lord will stop the numerical increase of the nation. A large population was then desired, because it represented strength. It was "because they have left off to take heed to the LORD.")*

11 Whoredom and wine and new wine take away the heart. *(Idol worship and its licentious rites destroy the understanding and make men insensible to their own good.)*

ISRAEL'S IDOLATRY; JUDGMENT

12 My people ask counsel at their stocks, and their staff declares unto them: for the spirit of whoredoms has caused them to err, and they have gone a whoring from under their God. *(The phrase, "Their stocks," refers to wooden idols. "Their staff" refers to divination rods [Ezek. 21:21-22].)*

13 They sacrifice upon the tops of the mountains, and burn incense upon the hills, under oaks and poplars and elms, because the shadow thereof is good: therefore your daughters shall commit whoredom, and your spouses shall commit adultery.

14 I will not punish your daughters when they commit whoredom, nor your spouses when they commit adultery: for themselves are separated with whores, and they sacrifice with harlots: therefore the people who do not understand shall fall. *(The tops of mountains, of hills, and of houses were chosen for the worship of idols because they were nearer to the sun, moon, and stars. The wives and daughters were guilty of actual adultery, because their husbands and fathers had volunteered them to temple prostitution; consequently, the Lord, impatient with the recital of such shameful licentiousness and indignant at such presumptuous sinning, closes abruptly with the declaration of the ruin of all such offenders with the words, "the people who do not understand shall fall."*

In other words, anyone who would have no more spiritual sense than this, especially those who belong to God, can expect coming Judgment.)

WARNING TO JUDAH

15 Though you, Israel, play the harlot, yet let not Judah offend; and come not ye unto Gilgal, neither go ye up to Beth-aven, nor swear, The LORD lives. *(The phrase, "Though you, Israel, play the harlot, yet let not Judah offend," means that Israel had passed the point of no return. Judah is advised to not follow suit. The phrase, "Nor swear, the LORD lives," refers to idol worship which associated God with idols.)*

16 For Israel slides back as a backsliding heifer: now the LORD will feed them as a lamb in a large place. *(This Verse could read, "Israel is refractory as a refractory heifer," that is, one who throws the yoke off its neck. The phrase, "Now the LORD will feed them as a lamb in a large place," means that He will scatter them in Exile throughout the whole world of that day. They will resemble a lamb taken into a wilderness and left to range the wild and live at large, but without provision and without protection. Consequently, untended by the shepherd's watchful care, unguarded from ravening wolves or other beasts of prey, such a lamb is in a lost and perishing condition.)*

17 Ephraim is joined to idols; let him alone. *(Ephraim, being the dominant Tribe, gave its name, along with Israel, to the Northern Kingdom. The phrase, "Joined to idols," means that he is mated or united to his idols and will not get a divorce from them.*

The phrase, "Let him alone," refers to the Lord ceasing any and all effort to salvage the situation; consequently, Jehovah says to the Prophet, "cease to reprove, for it is of no use.")

18 Their drink is sour: they have committed whoredom continually: her rulers with shame do love, Give ye. *(The phrase, "Committed whoredom continually," shows that idolatry was the cause of their spiritual condition, which would result in their destruction. The phrase, "Her rulers with shame do love, Give ye," pertains to the leaders of the nation, who were supposed to lead the people to Jehovah, but instead led them toward idol worship, encouraging them in this direction, with the words, "Give ye," i.e., "Give ye devotion to idols!")*

19 The wind has bound her up in her wings, and they shall be ashamed because of their sacrifices. *("The wind," i.e., the spirit of idolatry [Vs. 12], carries its devotees into bondage and the result of their sacrifices is that they are put to shame. As a result, the "wind" will become a strong storm of Divine Wrath, which will seize on Ephraim, wrapping her up with its wings, and will carry her away.*

While the time would come that she would be "ashamed because of these heathen sacrifices," still, it would be too late, for the nation by then would have been completely destroyed.)

CHAPTER 5
(780 B.C.)
GOD'S DISPLEASURE WITH ISRAEL AND JUDAH

HEAR ye this, O Priests; and hearken, you house of Israel; and give ye ear, O house of the king; for judgment is toward you, because you have been a snare on Mizpah, and a net spread upon Tabor. *(Neither the kings nor priests of the Northern Kingdom were legitimate, but they claimed to be kings and priests, and God met them on their own ground, and in Grace warned them of the judgment about to fall upon them because of the idolatry established at Mizpah and Tabor.*

Instead of being safeguards of the people, as they were supposed to be, these priests and kings of the Northern Kingdom had been a snare to them.)

2 And the revolters are profound to make slaughter, though I have been a rebuker of them all. *(This Verse may be better translated, "And the apostates are deeply resolved to slaughter victims in sacrifice, but I will be a rebuker of them all." The idea of the Verse is that despite the "rebukes" of the Lord, which should have been a cause of warning, but which instead were ignored, they continued with this terrible sin of human sacrifice. God calls them "revolters"; to Him, they are "revolting.")*

3 I know Ephraim, and Israel is not hid from Me: for now, O Ephraim, you commit whoredom, and Israel is defiled. *("Ephraim" was the largest Tribe; consequently, the entirety of the Northern Kingdom went by that name. Similarly, Judah became the name of the Southern Kingdom, because of it being the ruling Tribe.*

"Ephraim," being the largest, led the other Tribes of the Northern Kingdom into idolatry, and hence, defiled the entirety of the nation.)

4 They will not frame their doings to turn unto their God: for the spirit of whoredoms is in the midst of them, and they have not known the LORD. *(In these Prophecies, the term, "to know the LORD," means in Hebrew to know experientially rather than from a mere intellectual stance.*

In this Verse, the evil doings are traced to an "evil spirit of whoredoms," i.e., of idolatries, which impels them blindly to not resist evil; and, at the same time, it expels the knowledge of God.

The phrase, "And they have not known the LORD," means that this generation had not known Him at all. They were actually heathen at heart.)

5 And the pride of Israel does testify to His face: therefore shall Israel and Ephraim fall in their iniquity; Judah also shall fall with them. *(The phrase, "And the pride of Israel does testify to His Face," means that this pride, as all pride, was in the very Face of God, and consequently was an unending stench in His Nostrils. Now, Hosea mentions Judah, and in a negative sense.)*

6 They shall go with their flocks and with their herds to seek the LORD; but they shall not find Him; He has withdrawn Himself from them. *(The idea of this Verse is that in the not-too-distant future, Israel would see the calamity of Assyria coming upon them, and would then try to bargain with God, but too late.*

The "flocks" and "herds" speak of Sacrifice, but not with sincerity.

The phrase, "But they shall not find Him,"

refers to Ephraim seeking after the Lord in all the wrong ways, as so many do presently.

The phrase, "He has withdrawn Himself from them," proclaims such being done simply because the Lord had no other choice. He could not tolerate a "marriage of convenience," so to speak!)

7 They have dealt treacherously against the LORD; for they have begotten strange children: now shall a month devour them with their portions. *(The phrase, "They have dealt treacherously against the LORD," presents the reason their sacrifices were not accepted. The phrase, "For they have begotten strange children," refers to those who were not really serving God, but rather bound to their idols. The phrase, "Now shall a month devour them with their portions," probably refers to Shallum reigning for only a month [II Ki. 15:13]. The "portions" refer to idols [Deut. 32:9; Isa. 57:6].)*

8 Blow ye the cornet in Gibeah, and the trumpet in Ramah: cry aloud at Beth-aven, after you, O Benjamin. *(These areas seem to be the line of march of the Assyrians coming into the Northern Kingdom. Even though it would be some 50-60 years into the future, still, the Holy Spirit outlines it as if it has already happened. The Tribe of "Benjamin" is mentioned because these areas are near Israel's borders; consequently, they would be affected by this excursion.)*

9 Ephraim shall be desolate in the day of rebuke: among the Tribes of Israel have I made known that which shall surely be. *(The first phrase refers to Ephraim's present prosperity but that which shall surely end. The phrase, "Among the Tribes of Israel have I made known that which shall surely be," proclaims the fact that the Lord was constantly warning Israel before Judgment came, so they are without excuse.)*

10 The princes of Judah were like them who remove the bound: therefore I will pour out My wrath upon them like water. *(The Princes of Judah, like those of Israel, removed "the bound," i.e., broke away from the Bible [Deut. 19:14; 27:17], just as the professing Churches do today.*

The pronoun "them" actually refers to both Ephraim and Judah. Ahaz, the king of Judah, set aside the Bible and the Altar [II Ki. 16:10-18]. To forsake the Bible is to ultimately incur the Wrath of God, whether then or now!)

11 Ephraim is oppressed and broken in judgment, because he willingly walked after the commandment *(walked after the commandment of men rather than after the Commandment of the Lord).*

12 Therefore will I be unto Ephraim as a moth, and to the house of Judah as rottenness. *(If the Ways of the Lord are followed, it means blessing; however, if the Ways of the Lord are rejected, it means judgment.)*

13 When Ephraim saw his sickness, and Judah saw his wound, then went Ephraim to the Assyrian, and sent to king Jareb: yet could he not heal you, nor cure you of your wound. *(The word "Judah" should be supplied before "sent to king Jareb." Jareb was king of Assyria and his name numerically spells "666." Concerning this Verse, Calvin says, "Here God declares that whatever the Israelites might seek would be in vain. 'You think,' He says, 'that you can escape My Hand by these remedies; but your folly will at length betray itself, for he will avail you nothing; that is, King Jareb will not heal you.'")*

14 For I will be unto Ephraim as a lion, and as a young lion to the house of Judah: I, even I, will tear and go away; I will take away, and none shall rescue him. *(If no Repentance was forthcoming, which it was not, then the pressure would become fierce, as it did!)*

15 I will go and return to My place, till they acknowledge their offence, and seek My face: in their affliction they will seek Me early. *(The phrase, "I will go and return to My place," refers to the Lord having carried out His Purpose and Design; He now withdraws His Presence and Spirit from the offending people.*

The phrase, "In their affliction they will seek Me early," refers to the fact of chastisement, but does not guarantee Repentance. However, if Repentance is forthcoming, it will be because of "affliction.")

CHAPTER 6

(780 B.C.)

REPENTANCE OF ISRAEL PROPHESIED FOR THE LAST DAYS

COME, and let us return unto the LORD: for He has torn, and He will heal us; He has smitten, and He will bind us up. *(This speaks of Israel, in the last half of the Great Tribulation, under great persecution finally turning back to the Lord. And how do we know that? We know it because Israel as a nation has never come to the Lord in the fashion represented here, but which they will do immediately before and after the Second Coming [Zech. 13:1].)*

2 After two days will He revive us: in the third day He will raise us up, and we shall live

in His sight. *(This Verse could very well apply prophetically to the period of Israel's subjection, affliction, and Restoration. Her subjection has lasted 2,000 years, or nearly so [two days], and her Millennial Reign will last for 1,000 years [the third day].*

The word "day" normally refers to a twenty-four hour period of time. However, it can be, and often is, used figuratively for a specified or unspecified period of time.

The phrase, "In the third day He will raise us up," refers to the Second Coming of Christ, when He will deliver Israel from the Antichrist.)

3 Then shall we know, if we follow on to know the LORD: His going forth is prepared as the morning; and He shall come unto us as the rain, as the latter and former rain unto the Earth. *(The phrase, "His going forth is prepared as the morning," signals that His Second Coming is fixed as surely as the morning is eternally fixed to come at a certain time daily.*

The "Latter and former rain" actually refer to two outpourings of the Spirit, the "former" pertaining to the Early Church, with the "latter" pertaining to the present time, stretching into the Millennium [Acts 2:17-21]. The "latter" is mentioned here before the "former" because Christ was rejected at His First Advent, but will be accepted by Israel at the Second Advent.)

GOD'S CASE AGAINST ISRAEL

4 O Ephraim, what shall I do unto you? O Judah, what shall I do unto you? for your goodness is as a morning cloud, and as the early dew it goes away. *(The question, "What shall I do unto you?", refers to the Lord using every possible method to turn both kingdoms around, but to no avail. The phrase, "For your goodness is as a morning cloud, and as the early dew it goes away," refers to a superficial religious effort, which had no substance and quickly dissipated [Mat. 13:5-6].)*

5 Therefore have I hewed them by the Prophets; I have slain them by the words of My mouth: and your judgments are as the light that goes forth. *(The phrase, "Therefore have I hewed them by the Prophets," is a figurative statement borrowed from the hewing of hard wood and shaping it so as to assume the required form. Despite the powerful statements by the "Prophets," which were given by the Lord, Israel was unmoved.*

The phrase, "I have slain them by the words of My Mouth," refers to an Anointing so powerful upon the "Prophets" that it was enough to make anyone listen, but still, to no avail!

The phrase, "And your judgments are as the light that goes forth," proclaims that Faith can always take refuge in God, Whose "Judgments" are perfect!)

6 For I desire mercy, and not sacrifice; and the knowledge of God more than Burnt Offerings. *(This Passage was quoted in part by Christ [Mat. 9:13; 12:7]. Israel tried to replace "Mercy" and "the knowledge of God" with mere ritual!)*

7 But they like men have transgressed the Covenant: there have they dealt treacherously against Me. *(The word "men" in the Hebrew is "Adam" and should have been translated accordingly. "The Covenant" spoken of concerns the prohibition respecting the forbidden fruit. Adam's children, like their father, perpetually transgressed and dealt treacherously. Loss of fellowship with God and expulsion from Eden were the penal consequences that immediately followed upon Adam's transgression; likewise, the expulsion of Israel from the Promised Land.)*

8 Gilead is a city of them who work iniquity, and is polluted with blood. *(The area of "Gilead" consists of the east side of the Jordan. In the New Testament, it is spoken of under the name of Perea. Jeremiah would say, "Is there no balm in Gilead. . . ?" [Jer. 8:22].)*

9 And as troops of robbers wait for a man, so the company of priests murder in the way by consent: for they commit lewdness. *("Gilead" was also known as "Ramoth Gilead." It had been originally chosen by the Lord as a City of Refuge. Now it was a city of workers of iniquity and the road to it was tracked with blood.*

The phrase, "By consent," should have been translated "Shechem," for it also was a City of Refuge. Likewise, its priests, instead of saving men, "murdered" them by making them idolaters, for they taught them to commit lewdness, i.e., to practice idol worship.)

10 I have seen an horrible thing in the house of Israel: there is the whoredom of Ephraim, Israel is defiled. *(The "whoredom of Ephraim" was idol worship. God calls it "an horrible thing.")*

11 Also, O Judah, He has set an harvest for you, when I returned the captivity of My people. *(The idea of this Verse spans a length of time all the way to the coming Great Tribulation. That will be the "harvest of wrath," which will come upon Judah at that time. The phrase, "When I return the captivity of My people," refers to Israel ultimately making her way back to God,*

which will take place at the Second Coming.)

CHAPTER 7
(780 B.C.)
ISRAEL HAS REBELLED AGAINST GOD

WHEN I would have healed Israel, then the iniquity of Ephraim was discovered, and the wickedness of Samaria: for they commit falsehood; and the thief comes in, and the troop of robbers spoils without. *(The first seven Verses of this Chapter declare the inherent evil of man's heart, and the remaining Verses the weakness, folly, and rebellion which are its fruit. The phrase, "When I would have healed Israel," refers to the fact that the Lord not only wanted and desired to heal "Israel," but eagerly searched for a way to do so! However, because of their great sin, there was no way to make this rotten apple whole.*

The sense of this Verse is: "When I wished to blot out the old sins of My people on account of ancient idolatry, Ephraim and Samaria discovered new idols.")

2 And they consider not in their hearts that I remember all their wickedness: now their own doings have beset them about; they are before My face. *(Evil conceived in the heart produces manifest fruits which are seen by both God and man. The phrase, "And they consider not in their hearts that I remember all their wickedness," proclaims these people as placing God in a position of less than Deity. This is far more serious than meets the eye.)*

3 They make the king glad with their wickedness, and the princes with their lies. *(Wicked kings and princes welcome religious teachers who assure them that there is no Wrath to come or Lake of Fire. These lies make glad the hearers.)*

4 They are all adulterers, as an oven heated by the baker, who ceases from raising after he has kneaded the dough, until it be leavened. *(The phrase, "They are all adulterers," speaks of idol worship, i.e., "spiritual adultery." This Verse in essence says, "Sin, if left unchecked, will, as leaven, corrupt the whole.")*

5 In the day of our king the princes have made him sick with bottles of wine; he stretched out his hand with scorners. *(The idea is: the corruption and spiritual rot permeated the whole of Israel from the Throne to the hovel. All were leavened.)*

6 For they have made ready their heart like an oven, while they lie in wait: their baker sleeps all the night; in the morning it burns as

a flaming fire. *(The idea of this Verse is that the heart of the people is compared to an oven, but with this difference: no baker was needed to sit up all night to keep up its temperature, for it was so enflamed with wickedness that it burned in the morning as a flaming fire. Thus, this Verse stands in relation to Verse 4.)*

7 They are all hot as an oven, and have devoured their judges; all their kings are fallen: there is none among them who calls unto Me. *(The phrase, "There is none among them who calls unto Me," means that amid the horrid scenes of blood and violence, of disorder and anarchy, there were none of these kings who realized the calamities of the times or recognized the cause. Consequently, there was no one to discover the remedy and apply it to the true and only Source of relief, which was the Lord.)*

TRUSTING IN OTHER NATIONS

8 Ephraim, he has mixed himself among the people, Ephraim is a cake not turned. *(The phrase, "Ephraim, he has mixed himself among the people," refers to them adopting the idolatries of the neighboring nations in addition to their own semi-idolatry of the calves. The phrase, "Ephraim is a cake not turned," has reference to the first phrase in that it is burned on one side and raw on the other. It has insinuation of being partly a Jew and partly a Gentile, at least in actions.)*

9 Strangers have devoured his strength, and he knows it not: yea, gray hairs are here and there upon him, yet he knows not. *(The "gray hairs" signal the end of life and the approach of death. Yet, Israel "knows it not.")*

10 And the pride of Israel testifies to his face: and they do not return to the LORD their God, nor seek Him for all this. *(The phrase, "And they do not return to the LORD their God, nor seek Him for all this," emphasizes their obstinate blindness and perverseness.)*

11 Ephraim also is like a silly dove without heart: they call to Egypt, they go to Assyria. *(In effect, the Lord calls "silly" all those who refuse to seek Him, or else do so improperly.)*

12 When they shall go, I will spread My net upon them; I will bring them down as the fowls of the Heaven; I will chastise them, as their congregation has heard. *(The warnings in the Law and those given by the Prophets repeatedly declared that Judgments would fall upon the disobedient and rebellious [Lev. 26:14-39; Deut. 28:15-68; 32:15-35].)*

13 Woe unto them! for they have fled from Me: destruction unto them! because they have transgressed against Me: though I have redeemed them, yet they have spoken lies against Me. *(Spiritual declension is further marked by: 1. Turning away from the Lord; 2. Transgressing against Him; 3. Speaking lies respecting Him; and, 4. Rebellion against Him.)*

14 And they have not cried unto Me with their heart, when they howled upon their beds: they assemble themselves for corn and wine, and they rebel against Me. *(They cried with a voice but not with the heart. It was not the soft sobbing of Repentance, but the howling with pain of a hurt beast; in other words, a ritual, or an act, if you please!)*

15 Though I have bound and strengthened their arms, yet do they imagine mischief against Me. *(The Lord helped Jeroboam II to win all his victories; yet his response and that of his subjects was to imagine mischief against that Gracious God, that is, they planned and kept on practicing idolatry [II Ki. 14:24].)*

16 They return, but not to the Most High: they are like a deceitful bow: their princes shall fall by the sword for the rage of their tongue: this shall be their derision in the land of Egypt. *(The phrase, "They return, but not to the Most High," concerns them seeking help from other sources. The phrase, "They are like a deceitful bow," refers to a bow that warps so that to shoot straight is impossible. In Egypt they trusted, and by Egypt they were ridiculed because of their Fall.)*

CHAPTER 8
(780 B.C.)
IDOLATRY OF ISRAEL

SET the trumpet to your mouth. He shall come as an eagle against the house of the LORD, because they have transgressed My covenant, and trespassed against My Law. *(The one king trusted the Assyrians; the other, a "defenced city." Neither sought help from God. Thus, there is no difference between the "flesh" of an idolater and the "flesh" of a nominal Christian.*

The phrase, "He shall come as an eagle against the House of the LORD," refers to the Assyrian Monarch. The cause of this, as the last phrase implies, was disobedience to the Bible.)

2 Israel shall cry unto Me. My God, we know You. *(Their profession of the knowledge of God and of attachment to Him was false*

[Mat. 7:22; Jn. 8:54-55].)*

3 Israel has cast off the thing that is good: the enemy shall pursue him. *(The "good" which Israel rejected is God, the One Good; Jehovah, the Greatest Good; the Law, which was good; and also all the goodness which the Lord bestowed on such as keep His Covenant.)*

4 They have set up kings, but not by Me: they have made princes, and I knew it not: of their silver and their gold have they made them idols, that they may be cut off. *(The phrase, "Not by Me," means that these kings were not sanctioned by the Lord. As well, they took their prosperity, i.e., "the silver and the gold," and made "idols" with it.)*

5 Your calf, O Samaria, has cast you off; My anger is kindled against them: how long will it be ere they attain to innocency? *(The actual meaning of this Verse is that idol worship had been the cause of their rejection. The question, "How long will it be ere they attain to innocency?", only shows their hypocrisy.)*

6 For from Israel was it also: the workman made it; therefore it is not God: but the calf of Samaria shall be broken in pieces. *(The phrase, "For from Israel was it also," refers to the people inventing the calf. It was broken in pieces by the Assyrians, and thus was demonstrated its impotency to save. Regrettably, concerning most of that presently which goes under the guise of Christianity, one also would have to say, "the workman made it," meaning, "therefore, it is not of God.")*

DISPERSION OF ISRAEL; JUDGMENT

7 For they have sown the wind, and they shall reap the whirlwind: it has no stalk: the bud shall yield no meal: if so be it yield, the strangers shall swallow it up. *(The analogy drawn by the Holy Spirit is of a man attempting to sow seed in the face of a strong wind. Obviously, the seed will be blown away, with the harvest reaping only that which the "whirlwind" gives.)*

8 Israel is swallowed up: now shall they be among the Gentiles as a vessel wherein is no pleasure. *(The Assyrian "swallowed up" the Ten Tribes, and they have been thrown aside as a despised vessel ever since.)*

HARLOTRY AND IDOLATRY

9 For they are gone up to Assyria, a wild ass alone by himself: Ephraim has hired

lovers. *(The phrase, "For they are gone up to Assyria," portrays them seeking help from the very ones who would destroy them. The phrase, "A wild ass alone by himself," portrays the nature of such an animal who stands alone by itself, even as stupid and stubborn as that animal is, which does so to secure its independence.*

The phrase, "Ephraim has hired lovers," portrays her as not even having as much sense as a stupid, wild ass. What an indictment!)

10 Yea, though they have hired among the nations, now will I gather them, and they shall sorrow a little for the burden of the king of princes. *(Assyria would demand great tribute, throwing a tremendous hardship on the people. Excavations at about the turn of the Twentieth Century at Nineveh show Menaham's name [King of Israel] as a vassal in the inscriptions.)*

11 Because Ephraim has made many altars to sin, altars shall be unto him to sin. *(The idea is: to him who wills to sin, God wills further sin!)*

12 I have written to him the great things of My law, but they were counted as a strange thing. *(The "strange thing" was a matter with which they had no concern, speaking of the Bible. As then, so now! The Bible today is accounted as outside of and unconnected with personal, family, and political life.)*

13 They sacrifice flesh for the sacrifices of My offerings, and eat it; but the LORD accepts them not; now will He remember their iniquity, and visit their sins: they shall return to Egypt. *(The phrase, "They shall return to Egypt," did not mean a literal return to Egypt, but that their captivity in Assyria would be, in its nature, as the Egyptian bondage.)*

14 For Israel has forgotten his Maker, and built temples; and Judah has multiplied fenced cities: but I will send a fire upon his cities, and it shall devour the palaces thereof. *(The phrase, "For Israel has forgotten his Maker, and built Temples," refers to Israel building shrines to idol gods on high places. As well, the phrase, "Judah has multiplied fenced cities," portrays her trusting in these "fenced cities" and not in Jehovah. The consequences would be disastrous!)*

CHAPTER 9
(760 B.C.)
CAPTIVITY TO EGYPT AND ASSYRIA

REJOICE not, O Israel, for joy, as other people: for you have gone a whoring from your God, you have loved a reward upon every cornfloor. *(Evil Menaham, now king of the Northern Kingdom, had probably made a treaty with the Assyrians, which occasioned this "joy." The Lord's admonishment, "Rejoice not, O Israel, for joy, as other people," proclaims Him being extremely agitated at this act. The phrase, "As other people," proclaims Israel attempting to be like the other nations, which the Lord pointedly tells them they are not! The phrase, "For you have gone a whoring from your God," is what God calls this treaty!*

The phrase, "You have loved a reward upon every cornfloor," is a reference to them giving honor to their idol gods for the blessings of the harvest, and for their treaty with Assyria. Loss of fellowship with God and loss of fruitfulness for God result from the association of idols with God. When the world, which is idolatry, is permitted to share the heart with Christ, fellowship and fruit cease [Jn. 15:1-11].)

2 The floor and the winepress shall not feed them, and the new wine shall fail in her. *(Treaties were made in order to secure the future. In essence, the Lord is saying that instead of Israel making her future secure by making this treaty, she actually has guaranteed the insecurity of her future. To be sure, all such compromises, whether then or now, lead to the same conclusion. The bountiful harvest expected from their idols failed of realization.)*

3 They shall not dwell in the LORD's land; but Ephraim shall return to Egypt, and they shall eat unclean things in Assyria. *(The phrase, "They shall not dwell in the LORD's land," is emphatic! In other words, this alliance, which they had made to secure the land of Israel, would now be the occasion of casting them out of the land. The effect of the Verse is that they should have made an alliance with the Lord instead.*

The phrase, "But Ephraim shall return to Egypt," did not refer to an actual sojourn into Egypt, but that, spiritually speaking, Israel had returned to the bondage of Egypt [II Pet. 2:22]. The phrase, "And they shall eat unclean things in Assyria," implies the coming captivity to Assyria [II Ki., Chpt. 17; Ezek. 4:13].)

4 They shall not offer wine offerings to the LORD, neither shall they be pleasing unto Him: their sacrifices shall be unto them as the bread of mourners; all who eat thereof shall be polluted: for their bread for their soul shall not come into the house of the LORD. *(Worship in imitation of the Levitical model was observed, but was disowned by God and declared by Him to be polluted.)*

5 What will you do in the solemn day, and in the day of the feast of the LORD? *(The idea of this Verse is: the time would shortly come, which it did, that they, held captive in a strange land, would strongly desire to keep the "Feasts of the LORD," but such would be impossible to do! Away in a distant foreign land, without Temple and without ritual, they would bewail the loss of their annual celebrations, their national festivals, and religious solemnities.)*

6 For, lo, they are gone because of destruction: Egypt shall gather them up, Memphis shall bury them: the pleasant places for their silver, nettles shall possess them: thorns shall be in their Tabernacles. *(The answer to the question in Verse 5 is found in this Verse. It means that religious festivals would be impossible because the Land of Israel would be denuded of its inhabitants. This is evidenced in the phrase, "For, lo, they are gone because of destruction.")*

7 The days of visitation are come, the days of recompence are come; Israel shall know it: the prophet is a fool, the spiritual man is mad, for the multitude of your iniquity, and the great hatred. *(The phrase, "The days of visitation are come," refers to the Wrath of God. In this Verse, the Lord calls the false prophets "fools." As well, the Lord declares "mad," i.e., spiritually insane, those who claim spirituality while at the same time worshipping idols.)*

CORRUPTION OF ISRAEL

8 The watchman of Ephraim was with my God: but the prophet is a snare of a fowler in all his ways, and hatred in the house of his God. *(The phrase, "The watchman of Ephraim was with my God," refers to what Ephraim [Israel] had been, but had now changed! In the days of Joshua, Israel was a true watchman in fellowship with Hosea's God, but she had now become a false prophet, a provocation in the house of her false god — and hence, a moral snare, with the result that she sank to the horrid depths of Gibeah in vileness, as recorded in Judg., Chpt. 19.)*

9 They have deeply corrupted themselves, as in the days of Gibeah: therefore he will remember their iniquity, he will visit their sins. *(This reference to the "days of Gibeah" shows that at this time the Book of Judges was well known to all the people. The historical event here alluded to was the abominable and infamous treatment of the Levite's concubine by the* men of Gibeah. This was the foulest blot on Israel's history during all the rule of the Judges.)*

10 I found Israel like grapes in the wilderness; I saw your fathers as the firstripe in the fig tree at her first time: but they went to Baal-peor, and separated themselves unto that shame; and their abominations were according as they loved. *(Grapes in the wilderness and first-ripe figs are most refreshing and delicious to the traveler. Such was Israel to God at the first; but they went away from Him and served Baal-peor [Num., Chpt. 25; Deut., Chpt. 4] and consecrated themselves unto that shameful worship, prostitution being its highest religious action. Its moral result was that the worshippers became as abominable as the object of their worship.)*

CALAMITY OF EPHRAIM

11 As for Ephraim, their glory shall fly away like a bird, from the birth, and from the womb, and from the conception. *(This Verse predicts the complete destruction of Ephraim and their dispersion among the nations.)*

12 Though they bring up their children, yet will I bereave them, that there shall not be a man left: yea, woe also to them when I depart from them! *(The thrust of this Verse is that God would continue to deal with Israel, even in Judgment, attempting to bring them back to Himself; however, the day would come that upon continued rebellion, He would be forced to say to them, according to the name of Hosea's third child, "Lo-ammi," i.e., "not My people.")*

13 Ephraim, as I saw Tyrus, is planted in a pleasant place: but Ephraim shall bring forth his children to the murderer. *("Tyre" was also beautifully situated, as was Ephraim at the beginning; but now her fruitful birth-rate only provided victims for the murderer, i.e., Assyria.)*

14 Give them, O LORD: what will you give? give them a miscarrying womb and dry breasts. *(The prayer of this Verse is a prayer of compassion. Of two evils, the Prophet chooses the lesser. Better to be childless than to provide children for the murderer.)*

15 All their wickedness is in Gilgal: for there I hated them: for the wickedness of their doings I will drive them out of My house, I will love them no more: all their princes are revolters. *("In Gilgal" they dethroned Immanuel [I Sam. 8:7; 11:14-15], and later they enthroned the golden calf under Jeroboam. Hence, the expression, "all their wickedness," i.e., their chief*

guilt, was found there. The phrase, "For the wickedness of their doings I will drive them out of My house," portrays an outraged husband who has entered into divorce and has put his guilty wife outside the house. God is Love, and He must of necessity hate evil and judge it. His Righteousness demands no less!

The phrase, "I will love them no more," does not mean that He doesn't love them now, but that if they continue on their present course, His Love and Protection will be withdrawn. The actual meaning is that love cannot be forever expressed to someone who will not return the love.)

16 Ephraim is smitten, their root is dried up, they shall bear no fruit: yea, though they bring forth, yet will I slay even the beloved fruit of their womb. (Without the Love of God, "Ephraim is smitten." Even though they did not know it, their sustenance, blessing, glory, strength, and power existed totally in Jehovah. Without Him, "their root is dried up, they shall bear no fruit.")

17 My God will cast them away, because they did not hearken unto Him: and they shall be wanderers among the nations. (The phrase, "My God will cast them away," refutes the unscriptural doctrine of Unconditional Eternal Security. History records the fulfillment of the prediction, "and they shall be wanderers among the nations." In 1948, after nearly 2,000 years of "wanderings," Israel once again became a nation, which again strains toward the fulfillment of Prophecy regarding their Restoration, which will take place at the Second Coming.)

CHAPTER 10
(740 B.C.)
ISRAEL'S IDOL ALTARS WILL CRUMBLE

ISRAEL is an empty vine, he brings forth fruit unto himself: according to the multitude of his fruit he has increased the altars; according to the goodness of his land they have made goodly images. (The phrase, "Israel is an empty vine," meant that it was abundant in leaves, but had no "fruit." And what little "fruit" that was brought forth was not unto God, but "unto himself." The fruit that was brought forth was not used for the Lord, but only to "increase the altars," i.e., altars to idol gods.)

2 Their heart is divided; now shall they be found faulty: he shall break down their altars, he shall spoil their images. (The phrase, "Their heart is divided," proclaims the fact that this was the source of their evil. Their heart was divided, so they halted between two opinions — between the worship of Jehovah and the worship of idolatry.)

3 For now they shall say, We have no king, because we feared not the LORD; what then should a king do to us? (The natural heart, due to the Fall, is opposed to God. It sets up in self-will a king, declaring him to be a necessity, but, when God removes him in Wrath, they at once say, "We can do very well without him; what use is he?"

In sin, all Israel had asked for a king, when the Lord was their King; in sin, Ephraim had made Jeroboam king; in sin, their subsequent kings were made without the counsel and advice of God; now, at the close of all, they reflect how fruitless it all was.)

4 They have spoken words, swearing falsely in making a covenant: thus judgment springs up as hemlock in the furrows of the field. (Israel swore allegiance to the Assyrian Monarch and, at the same time, made a treaty with the king of Egypt. Therefore, Divine Wrath would cover the whole Land as the common weeds springing up in the furrow.)

5 The inhabitants of Samaria shall fear because of the calves of Beth-aven: for the people thereof shall mourn over it, and the priests thereof who rejoiced on it, for the glory thereof, because it is departed from it. ("The calves of Beth-aven refer to the golden calf of Bethel. The phrase, "The people therefore shall mourn over it," refers to the people of Israel now being called the people of the calf, as they once had been called the People of Jehovah. They had chosen the calf for their god. Now they mourn for their idol, which can neither help itself nor them.)

6 It shall be also carried unto Assyria for a present to king Jareb: Ephraim shall receive shame, and Israel shall be ashamed of his own counsel. ("King Jareb" is Shalmaneser. The phrase, "It shall be also carried unto Assyria for a present," refers to the calf, the national god of Israel.

The phrase, "His own counsel," refers back approximately 175 years to the first king of the Northern Kingdom, Jeroboam, who set up the golden calf [I Ki. 12:28]. He thought this was a very clever stroke of policy, which would keep the people of Israel from going down to Jerusalem to worship at the true Temple of the Lord. His "counsel" led to the destruction of Israel.)

7 As for Samaria, her king is cut off as the foam upon the water. (Such was the king of

Samaria, sometimes called Israel and sometimes called Ephraim, because the position was not God-ordained, but was rather a position that was man-made.)

8 The high places also of Aven, the sin of Israel, shall be destroyed: the thorn and the thistle shall come up on their altars; and they shall say to the mountains, Cover us; and to the hills, Fall on us. *(The phrase, "The high places also of Aven," pertains to Bethel. Aven means "emptiness" or "vanity." What was the House of God — Bethel — became the house of vanity, the sin of Israel. Such is corrupt Christendom at the present.*

This Verse speaks of the coming day when Israel will be destroyed, which it was by the Assyrians. Consequently, thorns and thistles grew up around these heathen altars.)

ISRAEL'S FORTS WILL FALL

9 O Israel, you have sinned from the days of Gibeah: there they stood: the battle in Gibeah against the children of iniquity did not overtake them. *(The Holy Spirit uses the incident at Gibeah, which took place nearly 500 years before, and pertained to the shameful outrage committed on the Levite's concubine by the men of Gibeah. In the battle that followed over this incident, the Tribe of Benjamin was all but exterminated, with only about 600 men left alive [Judg., Chpt. 19]. Thus, the Holy Spirit is drawing a comparison in that the Ten Tribes will come close to extinction.)*

10 It is in My desire that I should chastise them; and the people shall be gathered against them, when they shall bind themselves in their two furrows. *(That is: both Judah and Israel would be carried into captivity and made to toil like oxen, each in his own furrow. Judah would fall about 133 years after the fall of Israel. The phraseology of this Verse expresses God's determination to punish sin and vindicate His Justice as the infinitely Holy One.)*

11 And Ephraim is as an heifer that is taught, and loves to tread out the corn; but I passed over upon her fair neck: I will make Ephraim to ride; Judah shall plow, and Jacob shall break his clods *(the sense of this Verse is that inasmuch as both kingdoms [Israel and Judah] were unwilling to bear the easy yoke of their Divine Ruler, they would, therefore, be subjected to the tyrant mastery of man. Sadly, these Prophecies, as given by Hosea to both the Northern and Southern Kingdoms, would go unheeded):*

12 Sow to yourselves in righteousness, reap in mercy; break up your fallow ground: for it is time to seek the LORD, till He come and rain righteousness upon you. *(In the midst of the dire warnings, Grace sends a message of Mercy, which, had it been accepted, would have saved them; however, it was not accepted.*

The command, "Break up your fallow ground," denotes effort that must be expended on the part of the individual. That effort is summed in the invitation to "seek the LORD"!)

JUDGMENT INEVITABLE

13 You have plowed wickedness, you have reaped iniquity; you have eaten the fruit of lies: because you did trust in your way, in the multitude of your mighty men. *(Tragically, they did not "sow righteousness," but rather sowed wickedness; therefore, they reaped "iniquity" and "lies." Their inward trust was "their way," i.e., their false religion, and their outward confidence was their standing army. Both these saviours would fail them and Samaria would perish at the hand of Shalmaneser.)*

14 Therefore shall a tumult arise among your people, and all your fortresses shall be spoiled, as Shalman spoiled Beth-arbel in the day of battle: the mother was dashed in pieces upon her children. *(The phrase, "And all your fortresses shall be spoiled," refers to the invasion by Shalmaneser, king of Assyria, which would come in the near future. It is referred to in II Ki., Chpt. 17.*

The phrase, "As Shalman spoiled Beth-arbel in the day of battle," pertains to one of the previous invasions of Israel by Assyria. Actually, there were several invasions, of which the last saw their total captivity and destruction.

The phrase, "The mother was dashed in pieces upon her children," portrays the ferocity of the former invasions, which should have been a warning of what would ultimately happen!)

15 So shall Beth-el do unto you because of your great wickedness: in a morning shall the king of Israel utterly be cut off. *(The phrase, "So shall Beth-el do unto you because of your great wickedness," refers to their idolatry, and to where it had brought them, and that the cruelties to be suffered by them were not to be chargeable to God, but rather to themselves.*

The "king of Israel" was Hoshea [II Ki., Chpt. 17]. The phrase, "cut off," refers to the nation literally ceasing to be.)

CHAPTER 11
(740 B.C.)
PERSISTENT REBELLION

WHEN Israel was a child, then I loved him, and called My son out of Egypt. *(This Passage was quoted concerning Christ in Mat. 2:15. It properly explains how Prophecy can have a double fulfillment.*

First of all, it pertains to Israel being delivered from Egyptian bondage. And then it also pertains to Christ, as a baby, being taken to Egypt by Joseph and Mary in order to escape the murderous intent of Herod. When King Herod died, which evidently was brought about shortly, an Angel then told Joseph that it would now be safe to leave Egypt and go back to Israel, which they did [Mat. 2:13-21].)

2 As they called them, so they went from them: they sacrificed unto Baalim, and burned incense to graven images. *(The phrase, "As they called them," refers to the Prophets calling Israel to Repentance. The phrase, "So they went from them," pertains to Israel turning a deaf ear to those who were their truest friends and best advisors. They continued to offer sacrifices to Baal, and "burn incense to graven images.")*

3 I taught Ephraim also to go, taking them by their arms; but they knew not that I healed them. *(The first phrase is a picture of God's guiding and guarding care over His People, and that despite their waywardness. The phrase, "They knew not that I healed them," pertains to their going astray, suffering its consequences, and then being picked up by the Lord, Who handled them tenderly and gently, healing their hurts and misdirection. However, they did not apprehend or appreciate God's gracious design and dealings with them. To use an old adage, they "bit the hand that fed them.")*

4 I drew them with cords of a man, with bands of love: and I was to them as they who take off the yoke on their jaws, and I laid meat unto them. *(The idea of the Verse is that the Lord was abundantly good to Israel, and in every way, but they still had no desire for Him.)*

5 He shall not return into the land of Egypt, but the Assyrian shall be his king, because they refused to return. *(The phrase, "He shall not return into the land of Egypt," refers to Ephraim's expectation of help from the king of Egypt, as found in II Ki. 17:4. However, that help was not forthcoming, because the Lord had decreed,* "but the Assyrian shall be his king."

All of this happened because they refused to repent and "return to the Lord.")

6 And the sword shall abide on his cities, and shall consume his branches, and devour them, because of their own counsels. *(The phrase, "Because of their own counsels," refers to their clever plan of playing off the king of Assyria against the king of Egypt. However, those "counsels" would lead to their destruction.)*

7 And My people are bent to backsliding from Me: though they called them to the Most High, none at all would exalt Him. *(The first phrase of this Verse is extremely expressive, with almost every word having an emphasis of its own. With all their sinfulness and shortcomings, Israel was still the People of God — "My people." Moreover, the "backsliding" was not an occasional lapse, but was their habit, their tendency.*

The phrase, "Though they called them to the Most High," refers to the Prophets calling Israel from their idols to Jehovah, but all to no avail. The phrase, "None at all will exalt Him," refers to them refusing to abandon their idols and give allegiance to the "Most High.")

GOD STILL LOVES ISRAEL

8 How shall I give you up, Ephraim? how shall I deliver you, Israel? how shall I make you as Admah? how shall I set you as Zeboim? My heart is turned within Me, My repentings are kindled together. *(The agony of the love which pulsates in this Verse touches the heart. Admah And Zeboim were the companion cities of Sodom and Gomorrah and suffered like destruction [Gen. 14:2, 8]. Ephraim had become so sinful that there was nothing left to do but destroy — hence the pleadings of God for the nation to seek Him and do that which was right in His Sight.*

The word "repentings," as it refers to God, which it does in this case, implies no change of purpose on the side of God, but only a change of procedure consistent with His Purpose of Everlasting Love.)

9 I will not execute the fierceness of My anger, I will not return to destroy Ephraim: for I am God, and not man; the Holy One in the midst of you: and I will not enter into the city. *(Verses 9 through 11 proclaim the Second Advent of Christ, when the Lord will come from Heaven, with all the Saints, and will set up the*

Kingdom Age. The phrase, "I will not return to destroy Ephraim," refers to the Lord's Second Coming, which will not be to destroy Ephraim, but instead to save Ephraim.

The phrase, "For I am God, and not man," refers to Him being able to see the end from the beginning.

The phrase, "The Holy One in the midst of you," pertains to Israel's stupidity in not accepting such a One, Who is able to lead them, guide them, and give them protection from all their enemies. Even though He was "in the midst" of them, and not in other nations, still, they would not serve Him, heed Him, or obey Him.)

GOD WILL RESTORE ISRAEL

10 They shall walk after the LORD: He shall roar like a lion: when He shall roar, then the children shall tremble from the west. *(The word "west" is interesting! Of the approximate 12,000,000 Jews in the world, approximately 5,000,000 are in Israel proper, and approximately 5,000,000 are in the United States, which is "west" of Israel. These will gladly leave America in order to reside with Christ, Whom they will then recognize as their Messiah.*

The word "tremble" is also interesting, in that Israel, although delirious with joy because of their great Deliverance from the Antichrist, still, will realize that the One Who has saved them is the One Whom they crucified so long ago.)

11 They shall tremble as a bird out of Egypt, and as a dove out of the land of Assyria: and I will place them in their houses, saith the LORD. *(The phrase, "And I will place them in their houses, saith the LORD," refers to all the Jews, and from all over the world, being restored to the Land of Israel, and made safe and secure, i.e., "in their houses.")*

SINS OF ISRAEL

12 Ephraim compasses Me about with lies, and the house of Israel with deceit: but Judah yet rules with God, and is faithful with the Saints. *(This Prophecy contrasts Ephraim and Jacob — the former, self-reliant and trusting the kings of Assyria and Egypt; the latter [Judah], weak, dependent, and trusting Jehovah, the God of his father Isaac. So the lesson is here once more taught that God cannot give victories to the flesh, and that Jehovah's servant, Judah, is strong when he is weak [II Cor. 12:10].)*

CHAPTER 12
(725 B.C.)
ISRAEL'S CAPTIVITY TO ASSYRIA COMING

EPHRAIM feeds on wind, and follows after the east wind: he daily increases lies and desolation; and they do make a covenant with the Assyrians, and oil is carried into Egypt. *(The first phrase refers to the treaties with the Assyrians and with the Egyptians. "Wind" is employed figuratively to denote what is empty, vain, and of no real worth or practical benefit. The phrase, "He daily increases lies and desolation," refers to Israel's dependence on these foreign powers, which was based on "lies," and which resulted in "desolation."*

The last phrase refers to the abundance of olive oil in the Land of Israel and the object of sending it to Egypt as a present to secure their interest and help against Assyria.)

GOD'S CASE AGAINST JUDAH (JACOB)

2 The LORD has also a controversy with Judah, and will punish Jacob according to his ways; according to his doings will He recompense him. *(While most of these Prophecies pertain to the Northern Kingdom of Israel, still, "Judah," the Southern Kingdom, was not without sin.*

What was this controversy with Judah? It was little different than with Israel except, at least at this time, Judah had not abandoned themselves totally to sin and wickedness as their northern sister, Israel.)

3 He took his brother by the heel in the womb, and by his strength he had power with God *(the phrase, "He took his brother by the heel in the womb," refers to Jacob's birth. It is recorded in Gen. 25:26. The phrase, "And by his strength he had power with God," refers to his wrestling with the Angel [Gen. 32:24-32].*

Prevention and humiliation are both Divine instruments. Jacob was prevented by the Lord from achieving what he desired through the flesh, and was humiliated by his weakness in the coming confrontation with his brother Esau, which drove him to the Lord):

4 Yea, he had power over the Angel, and prevailed: he wept, and made supplication unto Him: He found him *(found Jacob)* in Beth-el, and there He spoke with us *(the phrase, "Yea, he had power over the Angel, and prevailed," actually refers to Jacob wrestling with the Lord; for the Angel was God.*

The short phrase, "He wept," shows broken-ness and humbling before the Lord, the place to which Jehovah had been seeking to bring him all along.

The phrase, "And made supplication unto Him," refers to Jacob's statement, "I will not let You go, except You bless me" [Gen. 32:26].

The phrase, "He found him in Beth-el, and there He spoke with us," refers to the fact that Beth-el, now a seat of idolatry [I Ki. 12:28-33], can be made into "Beth-el," a "House of God," i.e., that is, if Israel will only repent. As Jacob found God in Beth-el, likewise, Israel can find God in Beth-el, but not in these idols!);

5 Even the LORD God of Hosts; the LORD is his memorial. *("Even the LORD God of Hosts" is declared to be the hope of Israel, as He was of Jacob. The Holy Spirit pleads with Israel, that if they will allow the Lord to be their "Memorial," as He was with Jacob, instead of foreign powers or idol gods, they too can reap the benefits given to Jacob.)*

APPLICATION TO ISRAEL;
HER SINS RESTATED

6 Therefore turn thou to your God: keep mercy and judgment and wait on your God continually. *(The argument of this Verse is: imitate Jacob, turn to Jehovah, live uprightly, and keep trusting Him.)*

7 He is a merchant, the balances of deceit are in his hand: he loves to oppress. *(The Hebrew word for "merchant" and "Canaanite" is the same word. With holy contempt, the Spirit of God calls here Ephraim a "Canaanite." Self-reliant and clever, he defrauded ["oppressed"], and boastfully declared that "they," i.e., the Prophets, should find nothing wrong in his business activities, for his commercial prosperity demonstrated his honest dealing. The idea of the Verse is that Jacob was once the "deceiver" and the "oppressor," but was changed by the Power of God. Israel can be changed, as well, if only they will turn to the Lord!)*

8 And Ephraim said, Yet I am become rich, I have found me out substance, in all my labours they shall find none iniquity in me that were sin. *(The phrase, "And Ephraim said," shows a haughtiness on Ephraim's part. The very phraseology speaks of pride, hardness, and dependence on self. Ephraim equated financial prosperity with the favor of God, exactly as the modern Church. They were to find, to their dismay, that they did not have the favor of God.)*

9 And I that am the LORD your God from the land of Egypt will yet make you to dwell in tabernacles, as in the days of the solemn feast. *(The thrust of this Verse is yet future. As 11:9-11 spoke of the coming Kingdom Age, likewise, this Verse also does!)*

10 I have also spoken by the Prophets, and I have multiplied visions, and used similitudes, by the ministry of the Prophets. *(The three modes of Divine Communication referred to here are: "prediction [Prophets], vision, and similitude." "Similitudes" refer to illustrations, such as Hosea's marriage to Gomer and the birth of their three children, etc. Thus, God left no means of admonishing them untried.)*

11 Is there iniquity in Gilead? surely they are vanity: they sacrifice bullocks in Gilgal; yea, their altars are as heaps in the furrows of the fields. *(Gilead and Gilgal had become wholly idolatrous, and the idol altars were as numerous as the heaps of stones and the furrows of the fields. In stony agricultural countries, such heaps are numberless.)*

12 And Jacob fled into the country of Syria, and Israel served for a wife, and for a wife he kept sheep. *(The lowest form of servitude in the east is that of a shepherd. This is the fourth reference to Jacob and completes the argument that weakness wins victories. As an infant, his feeble hand won the Birthright; as a penniless vagabond, he won the Kingdom; as a slave, he won Rachel; and as a cripple, he won a Title.*

The Divine Jacob, i.e., Immanuel, is the Great Antitype; for, by weakness, He won the Birthright, the Throne, the Kingdom, and the Bride.)

13 And by a Prophet the LORD brought Israel out of Egypt, and by a Prophet was he preserved. *(The Text says, "by a Prophet," i.e., Moses — not a soldier, but a Prophet. Nations are saved by Prophets such as Whitfield, Wesley, and Moody, and not by military generals.)*

14 Ephraim provoked him to anger most bitterly: therefore shall he leave his blood upon him, and his reproach shall his LORD return unto him. *(Ephraim refused to listen to the Prophets and provoked Immanuel most bitterly. It is only love that can be thus provoked.)*

CHAPTER 13
(725 B.C.)
ISRAEL'S JUDGMENT AND
DOOM IMPENDING

WHEN Ephraim spoke trembling, he exalted himself in Israel; but when he

offended in Baal, he died. *(The thrust of this Verse speaks of Ephraim, who once walked with God, as in the days of Joshua, and spoke with authority to which the people trembled. He had position of dignity and power. But he turned to idolatry and died spiritually, as Adam did when he sinned.*

The Christian has moral power and dignity so long as his heart is wholly governed by Christ and is free from idolatry.)

2 And now they sin more and more, and have made them molten images of their silver, and idols according to their own understanding, all of it the work of the craftsmen: they say of them, Let the men who sacrifice kiss the calves. *(The phrase, "Their own understanding," refers to a self-will worship [Col. 2:23], which is the principle of idolatry. And its ritual, as at the present day, necessitates the labor of many craftsmen, and I speak of anything in which faith is placed other than the Cross of Christ.*

The phrase, "Let the men who sacrifice kill the calves," was an expression of adoration. The kissing of images, statues, and so-called sacred pictures and icons is a prominent feature of modern idolatrous worship.)

3 Therefore they shall be as the morning cloud, and as the early dew that passes away, as the chaff that is driven with the whirlwind out of the floor, and as the smoke out of the chimney. *(Israel is likened here to four figures: "the morning cloud, the early dew, the chaff, and the smoke." All express brevity and worthlessness.)*

4 Yet I am the LORD your God from the land of Egypt, and you shall know no god but Me: for there is no saviour beside Me. *(Israel's greatest glory was that Jehovah was her God and Shepherd. The two titles, "God" and "Saviour," present the Lord not only as Deity, but also as Deity Who will save. The phrase, "Yet I am the LORD your God from the land of Egypt," does not mean that He was not their God before this time, for actually He was, beginning with Abraham; but never before had the evidence of His Power and Love to His People been so signal and conspicuous as at the period of the Exodus and onward.*

The phrase, "And you shall know no god but Me," should be studied carefully by modern Christians, as Israel of old! To worship Christ minus the Cross constitutes "another Jesus" [II Cor. 11:4], and is the bane of the modern Church.)

5 I did know you in the wilderness, in the land of great drought. *(The phrase, "I did know you," refers to the Lord knowing them as a shepherd knows his sheep [Jn. 10:27]. The phrase, "The wilderness, in the land of great drought," refers to the fact that there was absolutely no means of sustenance or livelihood in this howling waste except for Him. In fact, spiritually speaking, it is the same presently with this world. In Christ Alone, there is sustenance.)*

6 According to their pasture, so were they filled; they were filled, and their heart was exalted; therefore have they forgotten Me. *(The phrase, "According to their pasture, so were they filled," sadly refers to the fact that Israel did not know that it was the Lord Who was blessing them. The phrase, "They were filled, and their heart was exalted," means that in proportion as God prospered them, so did they forget Him. In Verse 2, they associated an idol with Him; in this corresponding Verse, they forgot Him. Such is ever the moral action of the natural heart. It associates idols with God and then forgets Him; it degrades Him and then suppresses Him.)*

7 Therefore I will be unto them as a lion: as a leopard by the way will I observe them:

8 I will meet them as a bear that is bereaved of her whelps, and will rend the caul of their heart, and there will I devour them like a lion: the wild beast shall tear them. *(The four wild beasts of these two Verses predict the military monarchies of Babylon [the lion], Persia [the bear], Greece [the leopard], and Rome [the wild beast]. Forsaking the Lord, Israel was at the mercy of the Gentile powers.)*

FINAL RESTORATION OF ISRAEL; PRESENT JUDGMENTS; REDEMPTION PROMISED

9 O Israel, you have destroyed yourself; but in Me is your help. *(The argument of this Verse is: in turning away from her True Helper, Israel brought all her calamities upon herself.)*

10 I will be your King: where is any other who may save you in all your cities? and your judges of whom you said, Give me a king and princes? *(In answer to the question, "Where is your king?", the reply to be supplied is, "In prison," for it was there that Shalmaneser put Hoshea. As well, this Passage has reference to the coming Antichrist, who in effect would be their king. Of all their sad choices of the past, this will be the saddest of all [Jn. 5:43].)*

11 I gave you a king in My anger, and took him away in My wrath. *(The king given in anger was Jeroboam I, and the king taken away*

in wrath was Hoshea. Jeroboam was Ephraim's first king and Hoshea was her last king. However, its future fulfillment concerns the Antichrist, whom the Lord, in "His [God's] anger," will allow Israel to have.

In the Battle of Armageddon, the Lord will "take him away in My Wrath," referring to the Antichrist being destroyed by the Lord at the time of the Second Coming [Rev. 19:19-20].)

12 The iniquity of Ephraim is bound up; his sin is hid. *(The idea of this Verse is that the day of reckoning would certainly come for Ephraim, because their sin was neither forgotten nor blotted out, because they would not repent.)*

13 The sorrows of a travailing woman shall come upon him: he is an unwise son; for he should not stay long in the place of the breaking forth of children. *(The Holy Spirit through the Prophet likens this Verse to a woman who cannot escape the anguish of childbirth — she is helpless. As well, a son who lingers where there is an abundance of men and a scarcity of work is foolish, for he does not look ahead and recognize the certain prospect of poverty.*

The idea is: a prudent man foresees the evil, but the senseless sinner lives for the moment and takes no steps to escape approaching calamity.)

14 I will ransom them from the power of the grave; I will redeem them from death: O death, I will be your plagues; O grave, I will be your destruction: repentance shall be hid from My eyes. *(The phrase, "I will ransom them from the power of the grave," looks ahead to Israel's coming Redemption, which will take place at the beginning of the Kingdom Age. In effect, Mercy rejoices against Judgment, and so Grace bursts out with a cry: "Guilty, sinful, and foolish though they be, yet will I ransom them" [I Cor. 15:55].*

The phrase, "Repentance shall be hid from My eyes," has reference to that coming future day when Israel's "Repentance" will be "hid," which means "bound up" and noted carefully by God, exactly as her sins had once been "hid" or "bound up." Now sins are replaced by Repentance. As a result, this "Repentance" causes the sins to be washed away and, therefore, "hidden from God's Eyes." It is called "Justification by Faith.")

COMPLETE DESOLATION FIRST

15 Though he be fruitful among his brethren, an east wind shall come, the wind of the LORD shall come up from the wilderness, and his spring shall become dry, and his fountain

shall be dried up: he shall spoil the treasure of all pleasant vessels. *(As quickly as the Prophet switched from pronounced Judgment to coming Restoration, he as quickly switches back to Judgment.*

The phrase, "An east wind shall come, the wind of the LORD shall come up from the wilderness," refers to the Assyrians. It was a wind, not coming by chance, but commissioned by Jehovah as a minister of vengeance to execute His Wrath. As a result, this "flourishing tree of Ephraim" will dry up.

The phrase, "He shall spoil the treasure of all pleasant vessels," refers to Shalmaneser, the Assyrian Monarch, as God's unwitting instrument.)

16 Samaria shall become desolate; for she has rebelled against her God: they shall fall by the sword: their infants shall be dashed in pieces, and their women with child shall be ripped up. *(This Verse proclaims the Truth that the coming Judgment will not be tepid, but instead flaming hot — in other words, "awful"!)*

CHAPTER 14

(725 B.C.)

ISRAEL INTREATED TO RETURN TO GOD

O Israel, return unto the LORD your God; for you have fallen by your iniquity. *(This Chapter is the presentation of a glorious Altar Call. In fact, it also tells of Israel's Restoration is a coming Glad Day, but which could have taken place in Hosea's time or any time forward, if Israel had only repented. The Lord is always ready to receive all who come to Him. He will always do so, gladly, kindly, and with open arms. He offers no condemnation, only acceptance.)*

2 Take with you words, and turn to the LORD: say unto Him, Take away all iniquity, and receive us graciously: so will we render the calves of our lips. *(Divine Love provides the fitting words for the truly repentant tongue. The phrase, "Take with you words," in essence says, "Not sacraments, not ceremonies, but 'words.'"*

The phrase, "Turn to the LORD," proclaims the fact that these "words" are not to be taken to men, but rather to the Lord.

The phrase, "Say unto Him, Take away all iniquity," presents what these "words" ought to be.

The phrase, "And receive us graciously," refers to the fact that we are saved by Grace through Faith, it is the Gift of God [Eph. 2:8-9]. Grace is simply the goodness of God extended to

undeserving people. It is received, whether by the sinner or the Saint, by Faith evidenced in Christ and what He did for us at the Cross. In fact, the Cross is what makes the Grace of God [the goodness of God] available to all.

The phrase, "So will we render the calves of our lips," refers to Sacrifice, and, in reality, the Sacrifice of the Cross. In essence, we are to thank the Lord for saving us, and that it was made possible by and through the Cross.)

3 Asshur shall not save us; we will not ride upon horses: neither will we say any more to the work of our hands, You are our gods: for in You the fatherless find mercy. (The phrase, "Asshur shall not save us," pertains to the fact that man cannot save man. The phrase, "We will not ride upon horses," means that we will not trust in what man can do. The phrase, "For in You the fatherless find mercy," refers to Israel as "Lo-ruhamah" [no more mercy] and "Lo-ammi" [not My people]. Despite these facts, the Lord says that if Israel [or anyone, for that matter] will truly turn to Him, He will receive and accept them [Eph. 2:13-18].)

RESTORATION; THE PROMISE OF GOD'S BLESSING

4 I will heal their backsliding, I will love them freely: for My anger is turned away from him. (The Divine response of Verses 4 through 8 exhibits the moral result of true conversion.)

5 I will be as the dew unto Israel: he shall grow as the lily, and cast forth his roots as Lebanon. (The "dew" speaks of the Holy Spirit, the "lily" speaks of Righteousness, and the "roots of Lebanon" speak of one's place and position in Christ. All of this awaits the believing sinner!)

6 His branches shall spread, and his beauty shall be as the olive tree, and his smell as Lebanon. (The phrase, "His branches shall spread," speaks of spiritual growth. The phrase, "And his beauty shall be as the olive tree," speaks of "fruit." The phrase, "And his smell as Lebanon," proclaims the fact that certain types of trees emit aromas which repel all insects and reptiles. Spiritually, it speaks of protection from the powers of darkness by Faith in Christ and His Cross [Rom. 6:3-5].)

7 They who dwell under His shadow shall return; they shall revive as the corn, and grow as the vine: the scent thereof shall be as the wine of Lebanon. (This Verse speaks of Israel restored and now reigning supreme in the coming Kingdom Age.)

8 Ephraim shall say, What have I to do any more with idols? I have heard him, and observed him: I am like a green fir tree. From Me in your fruit found. (This Verse may be thus displayed:

Ephraim, "What have I to do any more with idols?"

Immanuel, "I have heard him and observed him."

Ephraim, "I am like a green fir tree."

Immanuel, "Yes, but remember that from Me is your fruit found."

The question concerning Ephraim, "What have I to do any more with idols?", is a full, final, and forever renunciation of idolatry.)

9 Who is wise, and he shall understand these things? prudent, and he shall know them? for the ways of the LORD are right, and the just shall walk in them: but the transgressors shall fall therein. (This Verse forms the epilogue to the whole Prophecy. God's Way of Salvation is a stepping stone to the Believer, but a stumbling stone to the unbeliever. Christ is a Rock of defense to the one, but a Rock of offense to the other [I Cor. 1:23].)

THE BOOK OF
JOEL

CHAPTER 1
(800 B.C.)

THE DEVASTATION WROUGHT
BY THE LOCUSTS

THE Word of the LORD that came to Joel the son of Pethuel. *(This signifies that the Prophecy was not originated by Joel; God composed it and gave it to him, as to all the Prophets [Lk. 1:7]. As well, the Prophecy of Joel is undated, for it is general. It covers the period of "the times of the Gentiles," that is, from Nebuchadnezzar to the Antichrist. Hence, it speaks of the Temple and its Levitical worship, but makes no mention of a king.*

The name "Joel" means "Jehovah is God."

Even though the exact time of Joel's Ministry is not known, it is believed that he ministered shortly before Jeremiah.)

2 Hear this, ye old men, and give ear, all ye inhabitants of the land. Has this been in your days, or even in the days of your fathers? *(The idea of this Scripture is that the judgments to come would be so exceptional as to be without previous experience.)*

3 Tell ye your children of it, and let your children tell their children, and their children another generation. *(The manner in which this solemn announcement is given, i.e., using the phraseology in the Second Verse, "Hear this" and "give ear," is meant to impress upon the hearers the significance of the Message delivered. The coming Judgment is proclaimed, along with the sin that caused it, together with a plea for Repentance, and is meant to speak to every generation, etc.)*

4 That which the palmerworm has left has the locust eaten; and that which the locust has left has the cankerworm eaten; and that which the cankerworm has left has the caterpiller eaten. *(At the time this Prophecy was given by God to Joel, quite possibly Judah was utterly devastated and ruined by a plague of locusts; this fact was used to illustrate the Divine Judgments that were about to be inflicted upon the land, which would have their climax in the dread "Day of the Lord" at the close of Judah's history. These Judgments, as previously stated, would be so exceptional as to be without previous experience, and all because of sin!)*

CALL TO AWAKE

5 Awake, ye drunkards, and weep; and howl, all ye drinkers of wine, because of the new wine; for it is cut off from your mouth. *(The phrase, "Awake, ye drunkards, and weep," has to do with the spiritual state of Judah. Instead of crying to God from a position of spiritual strength, they were, instead, faced with the problem of awakening the "drunkards" from their stupefaction. In other words, there was no spiritual base upon which to build.*

The phrase, "Because of the new wine; for it is cut off from your mouth," is meant to impress upon the "drunkards" that shortly the enemy was going to come into their country, with all vineyards being destroyed, with them either killed or taken captive; consequently, there would be no more "wine.")

6 For a nation is come up upon My land, strong, and without number, whose teeth are the teeth of a lion, and he has the cheek teeth of a great lion. *(The phrase, "For a nation is come up upon My land," has a twofold meaning: First of all, it refers to the soon-to-come Babylonian invasion of Judah. Actually, Babylon is symbolized by a "lion" [Dan. 7:4]. Second, the phrase, "And he has the cheek teeth of a great lion," refers to the coming Antichrist, who will come from Syria and Babylon [Ezek., Chpts. 38-39; Dan. 11:41-45; II Thess. 2:3-4; Rev. 13:2; 16:13-16; 19:11-21].)*

7 He has laid My vine waste, and barked My fig tree: he has made it clean bare, and cast it away; the branches thereof are made white. *(The destruction of the "vine" and "fig tree" denotes the devastation of the Land of Judah, which would take place upon the advent of the Babylonian invasion.)*

THE LOCUSTS, A SIGN OF COMING
JUDGMENT BY THE ASSYRIANS
AND CHALDEANS

8 Lament like a virgin girded with sackcloth for the husband of her youth. *(The idea*

of this Verse concerns a young lady about to be married. But tragically, her sweetheart is killed before the wedding can take place. As she would "lament" for him, and rightly so, Judah is admonished to weep and cry for the destruction that is soon to come upon the land. Tragically, Judah would not heed!

It is believed, as stated, that Joel was prophesying to Judah a few years before Jeremiah.)

9 The Meat Offering and the Drink Offering is cut off from the house of the LORD; the Priests, the LORD's ministers, mourn. (This Verse proclaims the coming destruction of the Temple.)

10 The field is wasted, the land mourns; for the corn is wasted: the new wine is dried up, the oil languishes. (This Verse proclaims the devastation and desolation of the land upon the invasion of Nebuchadnezzar.)

11 Be ye ashamed, O ye husbandmen; howl, O ye vinedressers, for the wheat and for the barley; because the harvest of the field is perished. (The idea of this Passage is "shame." There was no excuse for Judah's plight. Sin was the cause of their ruin, but could have been repented of at any time, thereby ensuring the commencement of the Blessings of God. But Judah would not repent!)

12 The vine is dried up, and the fig tree languishes; the pomegranate tree, the palm tree also, and the apple tree, even all the trees of the field, are withered: because joy is withered away from the sons of men. (This Verse shows a definite link of economic depression, which always follows spiritual depression.)

13 Gird yourselves, and lament, you Priests: howl, you ministers of the Altar: come, lie all night in sackcloth, you ministers of my God: for the Meat Offering and the Drink Offering is withheld from the house of your God. (The idea is: unless Repentance is enjoined, the Sacrifices will be no more, because the Temple will be no more. As well, the "Priests" were to take the lead if the nation was to follow suit.)

14 Sanctify ye a fast, call a solemn assembly, gather the elders and all the inhabitants of the land into the house of the LORD your God, and cry unto the LORD. (Step by step, the Holy Spirit through the Prophet Joel tells Judah what she must do, which, if done, would avoid destruction. But sadly, it was to no avail.)

DESTRUCTION IN THE DAY OF THE LORD

15 Alas for the day! for the day of the LORD is at hand, and as a destruction from the Almighty shall it come. (This Prophecy leaps forward to the coming Great Tribulation, which has not even yet come to pass, but will shortly [Rev. 6:17].)

16 Is not the meat cut off before our eyes, yea, joy and gladness from the house of our God? (If it was true that locusts had already denuded the land, then the Prophecy concerns something already at least partially fulfilled; however, it also refers to the coming Great Tribulation, when Israel will experience suffering as never before [Mat. 24:21].)

17 The seed is rotten under their clods, the garners are laid desolate, the barns are broken down; for the corn is withered. (All of this took place in the Babylonian invasion, but the greater fulfillment concerns the coming Great Tribulation.)

18 How do the beasts groan! the herds of cattle are perplexed, because they have no pasture; yea, the flocks of sheep are made desolate. (It is obvious from this Passage and many others in the Bible that animals suffer much because of the sins of man.)

19 O LORD, to You will I cry: for the fire has devoured the pastures of the wilderness, and the flame has burned all the trees of the field. (The words, "O LORD, to You will I cry," pertain to Faith, which hides herself in the very God Who executes the Judgment. Such is the reason for the Judgment, in that the people would realize their sin and cry to the Lord.)

20 The beasts of the field cry also unto You: for the rivers of waters are dried up, and the fire has devoured the pastures of the wilderness. (As this happened not too many years from Joel's day, even more so it will happen in the coming Great Tribulation.)

CHAPTER 2
(800 B.C.)
CALL TO ALARM

BLOW ye the trumpet in Zion, and sound an alarm in My holy mountain: let all the inhabitants of the land tremble: for the day of the LORD comes, for it is near at hand (the terms, "Zion," "My Holy Mountain," and "The Land," define Israel and Jerusalem as the scene of these future events. The phrase, "Let all the inhabitants of the land tremble," refers to Israel, where the Battle of Armageddon will take place. The phrase, "For the Day of the LORD comes, for it is near at hand," refers to

the period in the future when the Messiah will interfere on behalf of His ancient People and deliver and restore them. Its details are predicted in the Book of Revelation.

As well, modern Preachers must "sound an alarm" at the condition of the modern Church, for these events of which Joel speaks are near at hand. This also means that the Rapture of the Church, which will precede these events, is very near [I Thess. 4:13-18; II Thess. 2:7-12]);

THE ARMIES OF GOD AT ARMAGEDDON DESCRIBED

2 A day of darkness and of gloominess, a day of clouds and of thick darkness, as the morning spread upon the mountains: a great people and a strong; there has not been ever the like, neither shall be any more after it, even to the years of many generations. *(The phrase, "A day of darkness and of gloominess, a day of clouds and of thick darkness," refers to the beginning days of the Battle of Armageddon, when the Antichrist "shall ascend and come like a storm, and [he] shall be like a cloud to cover the land" [Ezek. 38:9].*

The phrase, "Neither shall be any more after it, even to the years of many generations," describes the Coming of the Lord with His mighty Army, which the world has never seen before and will not see again until the end of the Millennium, when Satan and his angels and demons will appear on Earth in an effort to once again take it over, at which time God will send His Army of Heaven against them for the second time [Isa. 24:22; Rev. 20:7-10].

This is what the "many generations" refer to, which concerns a time span of about a thousand years between the Second Coming and the end of the Millennium.)

3 A fire devours before them; and behind them a flame burns: the land is as the Garden of Eden before them, and behind them a desolate wilderness; yea, and nothing shall escape them. *(This Verse corresponds with Ezek. 38:22, "and great hailstones, fire, and brimstone," which refers to the Second Coming of the Lord, which will take place in the Battle of Armageddon [Zech. 14:3].)*

4 The appearance of them is as the appearance of horses; and as horsemen, so shall they run. *(The pronoun "them" refers to all the Saints who will be with the Lord at the Second Coming, which corresponds with Rev. 19:14. All the Saints of God who have ever lived will then come*

back with the Lord, and will be riding on "white horses." These, of course, will be spirit horses.)

5 Like the noise of chariots on the tops of mountains shall they leap, like the noise of a flame of fire that devours the stubble, as a strong people set in battle array. *(This Verse tells us that the Second Coming will not only be glorious, but its power will express itself in a manner which the world has never known before. The phrase, "As a strong people set in battle array," will be in answer to the boasts and taunts of the Antichrist, which will fill the world the last three and a half years of the Great Tribulation.)*

6 Before their face the people shall be much pained: all faces shall gather blackness. *(The Antichrist, seeing this tremendous power arrayed against him, "shall be much pained.")*

7 They shall run like mighty men; they shall climb the wall like men of war; and they shall march every one on his ways, and they shall not break their ranks *(the initial thrust of this Verse is that the Second Coming of the Lord will not, at least in its initial stages, be for the blessing of the world, but instead for the destruction of evil. Hence, they are called "men of war." As well, "they shall not break their ranks" until this job of defeating the Antichrist and his armies is completed; and, completed it will be!):*

8 Neither shall one thrust another; they shall walk every one in his path: and when they fall upon the sword, they shall not be wounded. *(The phrase, "And when they fall upon the sword, they shall not be wounded," shows that the Glorified Saints, the army of the Lord, will have Glorified Bodies, which are impervious to harm. In other words, they cannot be killed.)*

9 They shall run to and fro in the city; they shall run upon the wall, they shall climb up upon the houses; they shall enter in at the windows like a thief. *(The idea of this Verse is that no place will be inaccessible to this army of the Lord.)*

10 The Earth shall quake before them; the heavens shall tremble: the sun and the moon shall be dark, and the stars shall withdraw their shining *(the sense of this Verse is that the coming of the Son of God will be so resplendent with Glory, with the very heavens lit up to such a degree that they will literally "tremble"; moreover, the "sun," the "moon," and the "stars" will be so outshone that it will seem as if they have no light. Jesus mentioned this [Mat. 24:27-30]):*

11 And the LORD shall utter His Voice

before His army: for His camp is very great: for He is strong Who executes His Word: for the day of the LORD is great and very terrible; and who can abide it? *(The phrase, "And the LORD shall utter His Voice before His Army," speaks of all the happenings of Verses 2 through 11. The phrase, "For He is strong Who executes His Word," proclaims the Lord having the Power to back up His Word, and that all these predictions shall come to pass exactly as stated. All of this speaks of the Second Coming!)*

CALL TO REPENTANCE AND FASTING

12 Therefore also now, saith the LORD, turn ye even to Me with all your heart, and with fasting, and with weeping, and with mourning *(as Verses 2 through 11 spoke of the Second Coming, Verses 12 through 17 portray the call to Repentance for Israel, which will take place at the Second Coming, and will guarantee her future Restoration. It also speaks to the Judah of Joel's day, but more so to the Second Coming and what will then happen.)*

13 And rend your heart, and not your garments, and turn unto the LORD your God: for He is gracious and merciful, slow to anger, and of great kindness, and repents Him of the evil. *(This is a description of what will take place in Israel at the Second Coming, as it regards Israel's Repentance.)*

14 Who knows if he will return and repent, and leave a blessing behind him; even a Meat Offering and a Drink Offering unto the LORD your God? *(As the Righteousness of God demands Judgment upon unconfessed sin, likewise, the same Righteousness demands Blessing when sin is repented of and turned from.)*

15 Blow the trumpet in Zion, sanctify a fast, call a solemn assembly *(in essence, this speaks of the events in Israel immediately after the Second Coming. Even though Israel at that time will not be able to literally blow a trumpet, just the same, the image is sufficient. As well, even though none of this pertains to the Church, the example could also well apply!):*

16 Gather the people, sanctify the congregation, assemble the Elders, gather the children, and those who suck the breasts: let the bridegroom go forth of his chamber, and the bride out of her closet. *(As stated, all of this will take place immediately after the Second Coming, when Israel finally repents.)*

17 Let the Priests, the Ministers of the LORD, weep between the porch and the Altar, and let them say, Spare Your people, O LORD, and give not Your heritage to reproach, that the heathen should rule over them: wherefore should they say among the people, Where is their God? *(The idea of this Repentance in that coming day pertains, in effect, to Israel's rejection of Christ and their crucifying Him. They will now learn that the One Whom they crucified is, in fact, their Messiah; hence, the religious leaders of Israel at that time will lead in this contrition before the Lord.)*

THE FORGIVENESS OF GOD AND RESTORATION

18 Then will the LORD be jealous for His land, and pity His people. *(Upon Israel's Repentance, the phrase, "Be jealous for His Land," proclaims the fact that as the Lord sought once to destroy it because of sin, now He will be quick to bless the Land and all that is in it. The phrase, "And pity His People," means that the Lord will accept Israel's Repentance and restore them to their rightful place and position in the world.)*

19 Yea, the LORD will answer and say unto His people, Behold, I will send you corn, and wine, and oil, and you shall be satisfied therewith: and I will no more make you a reproach among the heathen *(now, because Israel has properly repented before the Lord, the "reproach" is finally gone and prosperity now begins!):*

DESTRUCTION OF ENEMIES

20 But I will remove far off from you the northern army, and will drive him into a land barren and desolate, with his face toward the east sea, and his hinder part toward the utmost sea, and his stink shall come up, and his ill savour shall come up, because he has done great things. *(The total fulfillment of this Prophecy speaks of the coming Antichrist, who will be defeated in the Battle of Armageddon [Ezek. 38:15].*

The "east sea" is the Dead Sea and the "utmost sea" is probably the Mediterranean. Therefore, the defeat of the Antichrist will be total!

The phrase, "And his stink shall come up, and his ill savor shall come up," refers to the great number of the soldiers of the Antichrist being killed, as prophesied in Ezek. 39:11-16.

The phrase, "Because he has done great things," refers to the Antichrist magnifying himself to do great things; for he will propose to attack and defeat Immanuel Himself [Rev. 19:19]. The

"great things" of the Antichrist will prove to be nothing, while the "great things" of the next Verse, as accomplished by the Lord, will be magnificent.)

RESTORATION OF THE LAND AND PEOPLE

21 Fear not, O land; be glad and rejoice: for the LORD will do great things. *(All of the following pertains to what the Lord will do for Israel at the beginning of the Kingdom Age, which is immediately after His Return and Israel's Repentance.)*

22 Be not afraid, ye beasts of the field: for the pastures of the wilderness do spring, for the tree bears her fruit, the fig tree and the vine do yield their strength. *(This portrays the coming Kingdom Age, when the wild, carnivorous nature of the animal kingdom will be changed, because the curse has been lifted.*

The phrase, "For the pastures of the wilderness do spring," refers to the deserts blossoming as the rose [Isa. 35:1]. The phrase, "For the tree bears her fruit, the fig tree and the vine do yield their strength," refers, as stated, to the curse being lifted, with the land all over the world producing that which was originally intended. In other words, it will be a time of such plenty and prosperity as the world has never known.)

23 Be glad then, you children of Zion, and rejoice in the LORD your God: for He has given you the former rain moderately, and He will cause to come down for you the rain, the former rain, and the latter rain in the first month. *(The phrase, "Be glad then, you children of Zion," refers to Israel now restored as the premier nation of the world, which is her rightful place. In other words, the world cannot be properly blessed until Israel is in her rightful place, which she will be not long after the Second Coming.*

The "former rain" and the "latter rain" refer to the two rainy seasons in Israel. The first, or "former," coming in October, promoted the germination and growth of the seed previously sown; the "latter," coming in April, matured the crops and got them ready for harvest. Spiritually speaking, the "former rain" speaks of the outpouring of the Holy Spirit on the Early Church. The "latter rain" speaks of the outpouring of the Spirit which began at approximately the turn of the Twentieth Century and which will continue on through the Millennial Reign [James 5:7].)

24 And the floors shall be full of wheat, and the vats shall overflow with wine and oil. *(This speaks of the harvest of prosperity which will be gathered in the coming Kingdom Age.)*

25 And I will restore to you the years that the locust has eaten, the cankerworm, and the caterpiller, and the palmerworm, My great army which I sent among you. *(The phrase, "And I will restore to you the years," refers to that period of time which began with Nebuchadnezzar and which now has lasted for about 2,500 years. The mention of the "locusts," etc., is meant to be symbolic of the years lost to the "times of the Gentiles." The phrase, "My great army which I sent among you," speaks of the great empires which ruled Israel because of Israel's sin and refusal to repent.)*

26 And you shall eat in plenty, and be satisfied, and praise the name of the LORD your God, Who has dealt wondrously with you: and My people shall never be ashamed. *(Now, Israel will function as she should; as a result, they will "eat in plenty, and be satisfied." As well, never again will God's People "be ashamed.")*

27 And you shall know that I am in the midst of Israel, and that I am the LORD your God, and none else: and My people shall never be ashamed. *(Once again, the Holy Spirit through the Prophet uses the phrase, "And My people shall never be ashamed," because Israel in fact has lived in "shame" for over 2,500 years.)*

THE OUTPOURING OF GOD'S SPIRIT

28 And it shall come to pass afterward, that I will pour out My Spirit upon all flesh; and your sons and your daughters shall prophesy, your old men shall dream dreams, your young men shall see visions *(the word "afterward" refers to the occurrences predicted in Verses 30 through 32. This Promise of the Spirit is placed out of chronological order in order to couple it with the material blessings of Verses 21 through 27 and to provide for Acts, Chpt. 2. In fact, the phrase, "And it shall come to pass afterward, that I will pour out My Spirit upon all flesh," even though beginning on the Day of Pentecost, still, will not be totally fulfilled until the coming Kingdom Age.*

The phrase, "And your sons and your daughters shall prophesy," refers to the Gifts of the Spirit, which accompanied the outpouring of the Holy Spirit during the time of the Early Church, and which continues to this hour [I Cor. 12:7-11]; however, and as stated, this will have a complete fulfillment in the coming Kingdom Age.

As well, the outpouring of the Spirit is for all — old and young, men and women):

29 And also upon the servants and upon the handmaids in those days will I pour out My Spirit. *(Even though the words, "In those days," actually refer to the coming Kingdom Age, still, and according to what was said by the Apostle Peter, that which happened on the Day of Pentecost was the beginning of the "pouring out of My Spirit," which continues unto this day, and as stated, will be fully realized in the coming Kingdom Age.)*

SIGNS PRECEDING THE SECOND COMING OF CHRIST AND THE DAY OF THE LORD

30 And I will show wonders in the Heavens and in the Earth, blood, and fire, and pillars of smoke. *(This pertains to the Great Tribulation, which will immediately precede the Second Coming.)*

31 The sun shall be turned into darkness, and the moon into blood, before the great and terrible day of the LORD come. *(This is fulfilled in Rev. 6:12 under the "sixth seal.")*

32 And it shall come to pass, that whosoever shall call on the name of the LORD shall be delivered: for in Mount Zion and in Jerusalem shall be deliverance, as the LORD has said, and in the remnant whom the LORD shall call. *(The entirety of these Passages proclaim three great outpourings of the Holy Spirit:*

1. On the Day of Pentecost, which continues unto this hour [Acts 2:1-28:31];

2. During the future Great Tribulation [Acts 2:16-21]; and,

3. During the Millennium [Isa. 32:15; 44:3; Ezek. 36:26-27; 39:29; Zech. 12:10].)

CHAPTER 3
(800 B.C.)
JUDAH AND JERUSALEM RESTORED

FOR behold, in those days, and in that time, when I shall bring again the captivity of Judah and Jerusalem *(this Chapter follows the preceding one without a break; in it, the Spirit describes: the future Deliverance of Israel; the Judgment of the nations that oppressed her; the ascension of Immanuel upon the Throne of Jehovah at Jerusalem; His vindication of His ancient People; the destruction of the army of the Antichrist; the moral glory of Jerusalem; its appointment as a center of blessing to the Earth;*

and the future amazing fertility of the Land of Israel.

The phrase, "When I shall bring again the captivity of Judah and Jerusalem," is a Hebrew idiom for Restoration),

JUDGMENT ON HER ENEMIES

2 I will also gather all nations, and will bring them down into the valley of Jehoshaphat, and will plead with them there for My people and for My heritage Israel, whom they have scattered among the nations, and parted My land. *(The phrase, "I will also gather all nations," refers to soldiers from many nations of the world aiding and abetting the Antichrist in his efforts to destroy Israel. Whatever the plans of these people, it will be the Lord Who is doing the gathering.*

The phrase, "And will bring them down into the valley of Jehoshaphat," pertains to the valley of Megiddo. The name "Jehoshaphat" means "Jehovah has judged."

The words, "And will plead with them there for My people and for My heritage Israel," refers to the Second Coming of the Lord, when He will fight as He once fought in the day of battle [Zech. 14:1-3].)

3 And they have cast lots for My people; and have given a boy for an harlot, and sold a girl for wine, that they might drink. *(The idea of this Verse speaks for all time. Even though the statements pointedly concern the coming Antichrist, and consequently the Battle of Armageddon, still, the Holy Spirit is referring to all ages and times. In other words, He is saying that such treatment of Israel is over.)*

4 Yea, and what have you to do with Me, O Tyre, and Zidon, and all the coasts of Palestine? will you render Me a recompence? and if you recompense Me, swiftly and speedily will I return your recompence upon your own head *(even though these people, the Jews, are presently far away from God, still, the Promise the Lord made to Abraham ever holds true. He said, "And I will bless them who bless you, and curse him who curses you" [Gen. 12:3])*;

5 Because you have taken My silver and My gold, and have carried into your temples My goodly pleasant things *(in other words, when people or nations touched Israel in a negative way, they touched God!)*:

6 The children also of Judah and the children of Jerusalem have you sold unto the Grecians, that you might remove them far from

their border. *(The "Grecians" have reference to the Antichrist, who will come from the Syrian division of the old Grecian Empire.)*

7 Behold, I will raise them out of the place whither you have sold them, and will return your recompence upon your own head *(the words, "sold them," do not necessarily refer to selling them as slaves, at least in this case, but actually refers to the dire straits to which they have been forced as a result of the actions of the Antichrist. The phrase, "Out of the place," no doubt pertains to Petra, where Israel will be forced to flee in the Great Tribulation, when the Antichrist declares war on her [Rev., Chpt. 12]. The last phrase says that the Antichrist is now going to be called to account)*:

8 And I will sell your sons and your daughters into the hand of the children of Judah, and they shall sell them to the Sabeans, to a people far off: for the LORD has spoken it. *(The phrase, "And I will sell your sons and your daughters into the hand of the children of Judah," refers to the defeat of the Antichrist in the Battle of Armageddon, when all Gentile powers will then come under the domain of Israel, including the Arabs, symbolized by the "Sabeans.")*

MOBILIZATION FOR WAR

9 Proclaim ye this among the Gentiles; Prepare war, wake up the mighty men, let all the men of war draw near; let them come up *(Verses 9 through 11 picture the assembling of the mighty army which the Antichrist will lead against Jerusalem)*:

10 Beat your plowshares into swords, and your pruninghooks into spears: let the weak say, I am strong. *(This proclaims the nations of the world under the domain of the Antichrist preparing for war against Israel, who is now recovering herself somewhat since her defeat by the Antichrist some three and a half years before.)*

11 Assemble yourselves, and come, all ye heathen, and gather yourselves together round about: thither cause your mighty ones to come down, O LORD. *(This Scripture refers to Rev. 16:16.)*

12 Let the heathen be wakened, and come up to the valley of Jehoshaphat: for there will I sit to judge all the heathen round about. *(This Passage pertains to the Battle of Armageddon, when the Lord will judge the nations of the world; it will not be a pretty picture [Ezek., Chpts. 38-39].)*

DESTRUCTION OF ANTICHRIST AND HIS ARMIES AT ARMAGEDDON

13 Put ye in the sickle, for the harvest is ripe: come, get you down; for the press is full, the fats overflow; for their wickedness is great. *(This Verse has to do with Rev. 14:16, 20.)*

14 Multitudes, multitudes in the valley of decision: for the day of the LORD is near in the valley of decision. *(This "Valley of Jehoshaphat," where the Battle of Armageddon, at least partially, shall be fought, is called here "the valley of decision." It means that the Lord has made the "decision" to there meet Satan and his man, the Antichrist, which will instigate the Second Coming.)*

15 The sun and the moon shall be darkened, and the stars shall withdraw their shining. *(This will be a literal happening at the Second Advent of Christ [Mat. 24:19-31].)*

16 The LORD also shall roar out of Zion, and utter His voice from Jerusalem; and the Heavens and the Earth shall shake: but the LORD will be the hope of His people, and the strength of the children of Israel. *(All of this refers to the Almighty Power of the Lord Jesus Christ, which will be used to defend Israel, which refers to the defeat of the Antichrist.)*

FUTURE RESTORATION OF ISRAEL FOLLOWING THE BATTLE OF ARMAGEDDON: THE LORD REIGNING IN ZION

17 So shall you know that I am the LORD your God dwelling in Zion, My holy mountain: then shall Jerusalem be holy, and there shall no strangers pass through her any more. *(The first phrase refers to the fulfillment of Ezekiel's Vision of the building of the Millennial Temple, and actually the city itself [Ezek., Chpts. 40-48]. The phrase, "And there shall no strangers pass through her any more," means "to pass through in order to destroy"!)*

MATERIAL BLESSINGS FOR ISRAEL

18 And it shall come to pass in that day, that the mountains shall drop down new wine, and the hills shall flow with milk, and all the rivers of Judah shall flow with waters, and a fountain shall come forth out of the house of the LORD, and shall water the valley of Shittim. *(This Verse pertains to the great prosperity that will come to Israel in the Kingdom Age, which*

will bless the entirety of the world. The phrase, "And a fountain shall come forth out of the House of the LORD," pertains to the river that will come from the Temple in Jerusalem, as seen by the Prophet Ezekiel [Ezek. 47:1-12]. This will be a literal river coming out from under a literal Temple in Jerusalem, which will take place in the Kingdom Age.

The phrase, "And shall water the valley of Shittim," refers to the Dead Sea valley, which will now be productive.)

ISRAEL'S ENEMIES DESOLATE

19 Egypt shall be a desolation, and Edom shall be a desolate wilderness, for the violence against the children of Judah, because they have shed innocent blood in their land. *(There is no contradiction concerning Egypt between Verse 19 and Isa., Chpt. 19. The Judgment here predicted is past; the Promise there [Isaiah] is future.)*

JUDAH AN ETERNAL PEOPLE

20 But Judah shall dwell for ever, and Jerusalem from generation to generation. *(In that day, Judah will include all the Children of Israel from all the Tribes, for all will be there [Ezek. 48:1-29]. The Promise of God is that this Land, "Judah," and this city, "Jerusalem," will last forever. It will be occupied by Jews, and not by Muslims!)*

21 For I will cleanse their blood that I have not cleansed: for the LORD dwells in Zion. *(The word "cleanse" means "to avenge" This Prophecy ends, like that of Ezekiel, with the fact of God living visibly on the Earth with men.)*

AMOS

CHAPTER 1

(787 B.C.)

PROPHECIES OF JUDGMENT ON ISRAEL'S NEIGHBOURS

THE words of Amos, who was among the herdmen of Tekoa, which he saw concerning Israel in the days of Uzziah king of Judah, and in the days of Jeroboam the son of Joash king of Israel, two years before the earthquake. *(The phrase, "The words of Amos, who was among the herdmen of Tekoa," specifies him as a shepherd. The phrase, "Which he saw concerning Israel," could very well have been a vision. Man's words cannot be "seen," only God's Words.*

The phrase, "In the days of Uzziah king of Judah, and in the days of Jeroboam the son of Joash king of Israel," concerns the time of the moving of the Holy Spirit upon Amos, and the delivering of his Prophecy. Incidentally, this was Jeroboam II. The phrase, "Two years before the earthquake," is said by Josephus, the Jewish historian, to be attributed to God's displeasure at Uzziah's usurpation of the Priest's office [II Chron. 26:16].)

2 And he said, The LORD will roar from Zion, and utter His voice from Jerusalem; and the habitations of the shepherds shall mourn, and the top of Carmel shall wither. *(The phrase, "The LORD will roar from Zion," portrays Jerusalem. Here was Jehovah's Throne. The kings of the nations uttered their feeble voices from their governmental centers, but Jehovah roared as a lion from out of Zion.*

The phrase, "And the habitations of the shepherds shall mourn," refers to the coming Judgment of the Lord to be so severe that it would affect every part of Israel, even the peaceful pastures of the shepherds, even to "the top of Carmel.")

THE JUDGMENT AGAINST DAMASCUS

3 Thus saith the LORD; For three transgressions of Damascus, and for four, I will not turn away the punishment thereof; because they have threshed Gilead with threshing instruments of iron *(the phrase, "For three transgressions of Damascus, and for four," portrays an*

abrupt change by the Holy Spirit from His pronouncement of Judgment on Israel to the proclamation of punishment on neighboring heathen nations for their injurious treatment of His Own People):

4 But I will send a fire into the house of Hazael, which shall devour the palaces of Benhadad. *(This probably referred to "Ben-hadad III," the son of Hazael, who was a Monarch of small ability; under his sway, Syria sank into insignificance [II Ki., Chpt. 13]. Incidentally, "Benhadad" is a title corresponding to Pharaoh, Caesar, etc.)*

5 I will break also the bar of Damascus, and cut off the inhabitant from the plain of Aven, and him who holds the sceptre from the house of Eden: and the people of Syria shall go into captivity unto Kir, saith the LORD. *(The phrase, "And the people of Syria shall go into captivity unto Kir, saith the LORD," no doubt pertains to the invasion some 50 years later of the Assyrian, Tiglath-Pileser, who killed Rezon and sacked Damascus, as well as leading multiple thousands of Syrians "into captivity unto Kir," exactly as prophesied.)*

THE JUDGMENT AGAINST GAZA (PHILISTIA)

6 Thus saith the LORD; For three transgressions of Gaza, and for four, I will not turn away the punishment thereof; because they carried away captive the whole captivity, to deliver them up to Edom *(the phrase, "Three transgressions . . . and for four," is a Hebrew idiom expressive of "many." The phrase, "To deliver them up to Edom," speaks of the Philistines handing over the captive Israelites to their bitterest enemies, the Edomites, as slaves. God's anger, as is obvious here, burns against such treachery and slavery, hence, the judgment on Gaza):*

7 But I will send a fire on the wall of Gaza, which shall devour the palaces thereof *("Gaza" is used here as the representative of the five cities of the Philistines):*

8 And I will cut off the inhabitant from Ashdod, and him who holds the sceptre from Ashkelon, and I will turn My hand against

Ekron: and the remnant of the Philistines shall perish, saith the Lord GOD. *(Exactly as prophesied, there is no trace of "Philistines" left at this time, with part of this area presently occupied by the modern Palestinians, who are Egyptians, Syrians, Jordanians, etc.)*

THE JUDGMENT AGAINST TYRUS

9 Thus saith the LORD; For three transgressions of Tyrus, and for four, I will not turn away the punishment thereof; because they delivered up the whole captivity to Edom, and remembered not the brotherly covenant *(evidently, to warrant this judgment, Tyre, in some way, had gotten its hands on some Israelitish prisoners, whom they delivered over to the Edomites. This cruel conduct was quite unprovoked, as no Jewish king had ever made war against Phoenicia or its capital.*

The phrase, "And remembered not the brotherly covenant," refers to the original covenant made with Tyre by David and Solomon [II Sam. 5:11; I Ki. 5:1, 7-11; 9:11-14; II Chron. 2:11]):

10 But I will send a fire on the wall of Tyrus, which shall devour the palaces thereof. *(The punishments by Sargon of Assyria, and later by Nebuchadnezzar, who besieged the city for thirteen years, as well as its capture and destruction by Alexander the Great, are well-known.)*

THE JUDGMENT AGAINST EDOM

11 Thus saith the LORD; For three transgressions of Edom, and for four, I will not turn away the punishment thereof; because he did pursue his brother with the sword, and did cast off all pity, and his anger did tear perpetually, and he kept his wrath for ever *(now, the Prophet commences his denouncements against the three nations that were more kindred to Israel: Edom, Ammon, and Moab. The phrase, "And he kept his wrath forever," refers to Edom's relentless persecution, inhumanity, savage fury, and persistent anger against Israel. Edom sprang from Esau, and, in effect, is a brother of Israel, i.e., "Jacob"):*

12 But I will send a fire upon Teman, which shall devour the palaces of Bozrah.

THE JUDGMENT AGAINST AMMON

13 Thus saith the LORD; For three transgressions of the children of Ammon, and for four, I will not turn away the punishment thereof; because they have ripped up the women with child of Gilead, that they might enlarge their border *("Ammon" was connected with Israel by being an offspring of Lot, which "Moab" was, as well! The phrase, "That they might enlarge their border," concerns their greed for more territory, especially in later years when they seized the possessions of the Tribe of Gad — a proceeding which brought upon them the denunciation of Jeremiah [Jer. 49:2-6]):*

14 But I will kindle a fire in the wall of Rabbah, and it shall devour the palaces thereof, with shouting in the day of battle, with a tempest in the day of the whirlwind *("Rabbah" was the capital of Ammon, about 25 miles northeast of the Dead Sea, and is the same as present-day Ammon, Jordan):*

15 And their king shall go into the captivity, he and his princes together, saith the LORD. *(All these judgments were occasioned by the persecution inflicted by these heathen nations on God's People, Israel.)*

CHAPTER 2
(787 B.C.)

THE JUDGMENT AGAINST MOAB

THUS saith the LORD; For three transgressions of Moab, and for four, I will not turn away the punishment thereof; because he burned the bones of the king of Edom into lime *(Amos now denounces Moab, also connected by ties of blood with Israel. The phrase, "Because he burned the bones of the king of Edom into lime," shows that God's Anger burns against unnatural and cruel crimes, even though their victims be as cruel and wicked as was the king of Edom):*

2 But I will send a fire upon Moab, and it shall devour the palaces of Kirioth: and Moab shall die with tumult, with shouting, and with the sound of the trumpet *(the phrase, "And Moab shall die with tumult," refers to her destruction beginning with Nebuchadnezzar. In fulfillment of this Passage, the Moabites ultimately ceased to have independent existence as a nation):*

3 And I will cut off the judge from the midst thereof, and will slay all the princes thereof with him, saith the LORD. *(These six nations, "Syria, Philistia, Tyre, Edom, Ammon, and Moab," defiled Immanuel's land, for they lived within its original boundaries; judgment, therefore, expelled them.)*

PROPHECIES AGAINST GOD'S COVENANT NATIONS: AGAINST JUDAH BY BABYLON

4 Thus saith the LORD; For three transgressions of Judah, and for four, I will not turn away the punishment thereof; because they have despised the Law of the LORD, and have not kept His Commandments, and their lies caused them to err, after the which their fathers have walked *(as God pronounced judgments upon heathen nations, which Judah and Israel no doubt thought were amply deserved, likewise, the thrust is now turned toward Judah, even the people who retained the Temple and its worship. This amply portrays that God cannot abide sin in His Own any more than He can those who are not His private possession)*:

5 But I will send a fire upon Judah, and it shall devour the palaces of Jerusalem. *(And that's exactly what happened! Not too many years later, the nation and city were completely destroyed by the Babylonians.)*

AGAINST ISRAEL BY ASSYRIA

6 Thus saith the LORD; For three transgressions of Israel, and for four, I will not turn away the punishment thereof; because they sold the righteous for silver, and the poor for a pair of shoes *(as the Northern Kingdom of Israel sank lower and lower into sin and depravity, all justice flew out the window. They sold the "righteous" and the "poor" into slavery, and for a pittance)*;

7 That pant after the dust of the Earth on the head of the poor, and turn aside the way of the meek: and a man and his father will go in unto the same maid, to profane My holy name *(these Passages portray the fact that Israel had laid aside the Word of God for their own inventions. In other words, they had made up their own laws and concocted their own salvation. Now, they were progressive, liberal, and unrestricted by the old-fashioned ideas of the Bible; however, the Lord was carefully observing all they did; upon refusal to repent, they would face judgment, and terrible judgment at that!)*:

8 And they lay themselves down upon clothes laid to pledge by every altar, and they drink the wine of the condemned in the house of their god. *(As is obvious here, the Lord observed all that was being done.)*

9 Yet destroyed I the Amorite before them, whose height was like the height of the cedars, and he was strong as the oaks; yet I destroyed his fruit from above, and his roots

from beneath. *(The name "Amorite" [Josh. 24:18] is meant to serve as a representative of the seven nations of Canaan, who were dispossessed by the Israelites [Gen. 15:16; Ex. 23:27; 24:11].)*

10 Also I brought you up from the land of Egypt, and led you forty years through the wilderness, to possess the land of the Amorite. *(The Lord not only defeated the "Amorite," but also gave their land to Israel as an inheritance. The phrase, "And led you forty years through the wilderness," is meant to bring to mind that terrible odyssey, which, by all rights, should have forfeited the Blessings, but instead the Grace of God gave them everything.)*

11 And I raised up of your sons for Prophets, and of your young men for Nazarites. Is it not even thus, O ye children of Israel? saith the LORD. *("Nazarites" were those who took a special vow, whether temporary or lifelong. Of perpetual Nazarites, we have as instances Samson, Samuel, and John the Baptist.*

The question, "Is it not even thus, O ye children of Israel? saith the LORD," is meant to specify that these things stated are undeniable, thereby signaling favor from God, making Israel separate from other nations, and binding them to be a holy people.)

12 But you gave the Nazarites wine to drink; and commanded the Prophets, saying, Prophesy not. *(The idea of the Verse is: this ungrateful nation systematically tried to silence the voices which were a standing rebuke to them.)*

13 Behold, I am pressed under you, as a cart is pressed that is full of sheaves. *(The sense of this Verse is that God is burdened and wearied with their sins.)*

14 Therefore the flight shall perish from the swift, and the strong shall not strengthen his force, neither shall the mighty deliver himself *(upon hearing the Message of Amos, the people seemingly made light of his Prophecy, as Verse 12 outlines. Their attitude was that such could not happen; and, if such a preposterous thing somehow actually did happen, they certainly would be able to properly defend themselves.*

The Holy Spirit, knowing their thoughts, addresses them forthwith by implying that He will fight for the enemy, and against them):

15 Neither shall he stand who handles the bow; and he who is swift of foot shall not deliver himself: neither shall he who rides the horse deliver himself. *(By their sins and rebellion, the people of Israel no longer desired God's Deliverance, but claimed they could deliver themselves; however, the Holy Spirit says otherwise!)*

16 And he who is courageous among the mighty shall flee away naked in that day, saith the LORD. *(The word "naked" means to be "weaponless." When he runs away, a soldier throws aside his armor and weapons in order to more easily escape; this would be the plight of Israel — so says the Lord!)*

CHAPTER 3
(787 B.C.)
THE LION ROARS

HEAR this Word that the LORD has spoken against you, O children of Israel, against the whole family which I brought up from the land of Egypt, saying *(having addressed several nations dwelling near the Promised Land, God now addresses the whole family of Israel redeemed from the land of Egypt. This family alone He recognized "known" as His; for this reason, He would punish them for their iniquities),*

2 You only have I known of all the families of the Earth: therefore I will punish you for all your iniquities. *(Of all the nations in the world, Israel alone belonged to the Lord. The phrase, "You only have I known," means loved, acknowledged, and chosen. The phrase, "Therefore I will punish you for all your iniquities," means that they must not presume upon their privileges. Their retention of God's favor depended upon obedience to His Word [Ex. 19:5]. The nearer they were brought to God, the greater their guilt if they fell from God.)*

3 Can two walk together, except they be agreed? *(Companionship with God can only be enjoyed upon the basis of separation from evil.)*

4 Will a lion roar in the forest, when he has no prey? will a young lion cry out of his den, if he have taken nothing? *(As the lion roars when it has found its prey, God, therefore, makes the Prophet utter his voice because He is ready to execute vengeance.)*

5 Can a bird fall in a snare upon the Earth, where no gin is for him? shall one take up a snare from the Earth, and have taken nothing at all? *(The idea is: the bird is caught because it is too close to the trap. The trap which the sinner sets for himself is sin.)*

6 Shall a trumpet be blown in the city, and the people not be afraid? shall there be evil in a city, and the LORD has not done it? *(Two great principles — one of Law, the other of Grace — appear in Verses 6 through 8. First: God will judge evil. Second: He forewarns those whom He is about to judge. There is just cause when He should judge evil, but love intervenes with her warning.)*

7 Surely the Lord GOD will do nothing, but He reveals His secret unto His servants the Prophets. *(Consequently, this is the Grace spoken of here. The Lord forewarned those whom He is about to judge. Such is done to provoke Repentance, that is, if possible, that the judgment be halted.)*

8 The lion has roared, who will not fear? the Lord GOD has spoken, who can but prophesy? *(The idea is: as the lion's roar causes fear, likewise, when the Lord speaks, the Prophet must be fearful not to prophesy.)*

ISRAEL'S SINS

9 Publish in the palaces at Ashdod, and in the palaces in the land of Egypt, and say, Assemble yourselves upon the mountains of Samaria, and behold the great tumults in the midst thereof, and the oppressed in the midst thereof. *(The Philistines and the Egyptians are invited to behold the great evils and oppressions in the midst of Samaria [Israel] and to recognize the justice of God in sending them. This principle appears frequently in the Scriptures: the heathen are oftentimes righteous judges of the professing People of God. The implication is: it was the eternal disgrace of Israel that there were doings in her cities which the very heathen would condemn.)*

10 For they know not to do right, saith the LORD, who store up violence and robbery in their palaces. *(Persistence in the evil of covetousness and the love of money deadens moral consciousness.)*

CAPTIVITY TO ASSYRIA

11 Therefore thus saith the Lord GOD; An adversary there shall be even round about the land; and he shall bring down your strength from you, and your palaces shall be spoiled. *(The phrase, "An adversary there shall be," at least in this case, refers to Sennacherib, the Assyrian king; he emptied the palaces in Israel filled with the spoils robbed from the poor, etc.)*

12 Thus saith the LORD; As the shepherd takes out of the mouth of the lion two legs, or a piece of an ear; so will the children of Israel be taken out who dwell in Samaria in the corner of a bed, and in Damascus in a couch. *(So thorough would be the action of Sennacherib that the few people left alive would only be comparable to a piece of an ear of a sheep taken out*

of the mouth of a lion to prove to the owner that it was killed. The phrase, "In Samaria in the corner of a bed, and in Damascus in a couch," denotes the luxurious rich; but Israel would find that such riches would not save them.)

13 Hear ye, and testify in the house of Jacob, saith the Lord GOD, the God of Hosts (to the insults and denials of these individuals in Samaria, Amos claims, and rightly so, that his words are really the Words of the "Lord GOD," the "Almighty God"),

14 That in the day that I shall visit the transgressions of Israel upon him I will also visit the altars of Beth-el: and the horns of the altar shall be cut off, and fall to the ground. (The word "altars" is plural of magnitude, for the great altar erected at Beth-el by Jeroboam I for the worship of the golden calf. The phrase, "And the horns of the altar shall be cut off, and fall to the ground," referred to the altar of the golden calf. The "horns" represented the most sacred of this heathen altar; the prediction is that when judgment comes, these "horns" will be broken off, signifying God's rejection of this man-made altar as an atonement for sin.

Be it known: Just as in this prediction, the "horns" of every man-made altar [which attempts to take the place of Calvary] shall ultimately be cut off and "fall to the ground.")

15 And I will smite the winter house with the summer house; and the houses of ivory shall perish, and the great houses shall have an end, saith the LORD. (This Passage speaks of the obvious prosperity of Samaria, where luxury, ease, and comfort, among other things, had sapped all spiritual strength from God's People. The phrase, "And the great houses shall have an end, saith the LORD," refers to every house in this world which is built on sand. They will ultimately fall [Mat. 7:26].)

CHAPTER 4
(787 B.C.)
THE DEPRAVITY OF ISRAEL

HEAR this word, you kine of Bashan, that are in the mountain of Samaria, which oppress the poor, which crush the needy, which say to their masters, Bring, and let us drink. (The phrase, "Hear this word, you kine of Bashan," pertains to the rich pastureland east of Jordan, where cattle there fed became strong and fat. The Nobles of Samaria are compared to them here.

The phrase, "Which oppress the poor, which crush the needy," registers God's Love for the poor and His indignation against oppression, which is a feature of the Book of Amos.

The phrase, "Which say to their masters, Bring, and let us drink," refers to the Nobles appealing to Jeroboam II to provide them with luxurious banquets furnished by money robbed from the poor.)

2 The Lord GOD has sworn by His holiness, that, lo, the days shall come upon you, that he will take you away with hooks, and your posterity with fishhooks. (This Scripture addresses the Assyrian Monarch, who, upon subjugating an enemy, passed hooks through the lower lips of their captives and thus led them away to slavery. This would happen to Israel!)

3 And you shall go out at the breaches, every cow at that which is before her; and you shall cast them into the palace, saith the LORD. (They will be led forth, not through the gates of the city of Samaria, but through its broken walls; they will go quietly and in a straight line so as to mitigate the pain of their tortured lips. The last phrase could be better said, "You shall be cast as slaves into the palace of Sennacherib." In other words, the luxury of Samaria would be reduced to slavery.)

ISRAEL'S FAILURE TO REPENT

4 Come to Beth-el, and transgress; at Gilgal multiply transgression; and bring your sacrifices every morning, and your tithes after three years:

5 And offer a sacrifice of thanksgiving with leaven, and proclaim and publish the free offerings: for this liketh you, O ye children of Israel, saith the Lord GOD. (The invitation of Verses 4 and 5 is meant to portray irony. "Go to Beth-el — but not to worship Me — to transgress against Me!" Israel professed to be God's worshippers, but they adored Him under the similitude of the golden calf — as multitudes do today under the similitude of man-made directions other than the Cross of Calvary. God denounces as "idolatry" all worship that is not based on the atoning work of Calvary.)

6 And I also have given you cleanness of teeth in all your cities, and want of bread in all your places: yet have you not returned unto Me, saith the LORD. (In this and the following Verses, the Holy Spirit through the Prophet sets forth instances of judgment which He had sent at various times to correct Israel. The phrase, "Yet have you not returned unto Me, saith the

LORD," proclaims God's unwearied love, which had not conquered their rebellion.)

7 And also I have withheld the rain from you, when there were yet three months to the harvest: and I caused it to rain upon one city, and caused it not to rain upon another city: one piece was rained upon, and the piece whereupon it rained not withered. (All of this proclaims the Lord having total control, as should be obvious!)

8 So two or three cities wandered unto one city, to drink water; but they were not satisfied: yet have you not returned unto Me, saith the LORD. (The phrase used again, "Yet have you not returned unto Me, saith the LORD," has reference to the fact that while they were staggering from one city to another in order to find water, still, their hearts were so hard that their acute circumstances were not enough to bring them to Repentance.)

9 I have smitten you with blasting and mildew: when your gardens and your vineyards and your fig trees and your olive trees increased, the palmerworm devoured them: yet have you not returned unto Me, saith the LORD. (The Lord dealt with Israel with famine, drought, and now blight, but to no avail!)

10 I have sent among you the pestilence after the manner of Egypt: your young men have I slain with the sword, and have taken away your horses; and I have made the stink of your camps to come up unto your nostrils: yet have you not returned unto Me, saith the LORD. (The phrase, "I have sent among you the pestilence after the manner of Egypt," has no reference to the plague of Ex. 9:3, etc., but was an allusion to the plague which was reckoned to be epidemic in Egypt and other loathsome diseases for which that country was notorious. No judgments seemed to be enough to bring Israel back to the Lord!)

11 I have overthrown some of you, as God overthrew Sodom and Gomorrah and you were as a firebrand plucked out of the burning: yet have you not returned unto Me, saith the LORD. (The phrase, "And you were as a firebrand plucked out of the burning," refers to the fact that it was only the Mercy of God which stopped the destruction short of total; but impenitence was the unchanging response of each stroke — "yet have you not returned unto Me.")

12 Therefore thus will I do unto you, O Israel: and because I will do this unto you, prepare to meet your God, O Israel. (As a consequence, they are now warned of a Supreme Judgment —

that is, to meet God Himself. The phrase, "Prepare to meet your God, O Israel," means to make ready to meet God in Judgment, turning to Him with changed heart, praying that He will forgive and withdraw His heavy Hand.)

13 For, lo, He Who forms the mountains, and creates the wind, and declares unto man what is his thought, Who makes the morning darkness, and treads upon the high places of the Earth, The LORD, The God of Hosts, is His name. (The Majesty of God is set forth in this Scripture. The mountains may be seen; the wind, unseen; man's thought, unread; day and night, unchangeable; and the revolution of the Earth in its orbit, invariable: but all was in the power of this dread Judge — "Jehovah Elohim Sabaioth" is His Name!)

CHAPTER 5
(787 B.C.)
A SONG OF LAMENT AND GRIEF OVER ISRAEL

HEAR ye this word which I take up against you, even a lamentation, O house of Israel. (The phrase, "Hear ye this word which I take up against you," refers to the certitude of the coming judgment because Israel would not repent, because they saw no need to repent. The phrase, "Even a lamentation, O house of Israel," is the same as a funeral dirge.)

2 The virgin of Israel is fallen; she shall no more rise: she is forsaken upon her land; there is none to raise her up. (The Northern Kingdom is here compared to a virgin, because never hitherto conquered. The phrase, "She shall no more rise," means that she will never again be restored as a separate nationality.)

3 For thus saith the Lord GOD; The city that went out by a thousand shall leave an hundred, and that which went forth by an hundred shall leave ten, to the house of Israel. (So great would be the destruction of her armies in the battles with the Assyrians that battalions a thousand strong, or companies a hundred strong, that marched away from the cities to the war would only have a hundred, or ten, survivors, respectively.)

GOD'S CALL FOR ISRAEL TO REPENT AND AVERT JUDGMENT; "SEEK ME AND YOU SHALL LIVE".

4 For thus saith the LORD unto the house of Israel, Seek ye me and ye shall live (this is

a pure and plain offer to repent, which would avoid the Judgment, but sadly, all to no avail!):

5 But seek not Beth-el, nor enter into Gilgal, and pass not to Beer-sheba: for Gilgal shall surely go into captivity, and Beth-el shall come to nought. *(Beth-el was the great center of the worship of God under the similitude of a calf. But that idol could not quench the fire that broke out in the house of Joseph. Gilgal, Beer-sheba, and Beth-el are in Judah. The idea is: those from the Northern Kingdom who tried to escape to the Southern Kingdom, that is, when judgment came, would not succeed. Whatever their plans were, they "shall surely go into captivity.")*

6 Seek the LORD, and you shall live; lest He break out like fire in the house of Joseph, and devour it, and there be none to quench it in Beth-el. *(The idea is: "Turn to the Lord, or suffer the fire of judgment!")*

7 Ye who turn judgment to wormwood, and leave off righteousness in the Earth *(God can have no fellowship either with falsehood in doctrine [Vs. 5] or evil-doing in conduct, as is described in this Verse. This latter denounces bribery and injustice. Justice was cast to the ground and perverted to most bitter wrong),*

8 Seek Him Who makes the seven stars and Orion, and turns the shadow of death into the morning, and makes the day dark with night: Who calls for the waters of the sea, and pours them out upon the face of the Earth: the LORD is His name *(the "seven stars" refer to the "Pleiades." "Orion" is the constellation commonly known as "the Giant." The space in the sword of the Giant alone is estimated to be 2,200,000,000,000,000,000 [two quintillion, two hundred quadrillion] times larger than the sun. Therefore, what is here discussed, referring to God's Creation, is so large that it beggars description.*

The entirety of the phrase, "The shadow of death into the morning," pertains to the coming Resurrection of Life. As well, the phrase, "And makes the day dark with night," refers to the coming Resurrection of Damnation):

9 Who strengthens the spoiled against the strong, so that the spoiled shall come against the fortress. *(The idea is that God can smite the strongest; no fortress is a refuge from Him.)*

10 They hate him who rebukes in the gate, and they abhor him who speaks uprightly. *(The pronoun "they" refers to the Judges of Israel. The pronoun "him" refers to Amos, who was hated because he "spoke uprightly." He no doubt*

stood in the "gate of the city" and rebuked the worshippers who were coming to Beth-el. If so, this would have been extremely annoying to the religious leaders!)

11 Forasmuch therefore as your treading is upon the poor, and you take from him burdens of wheat: you have built houses of hewn stone, but you shall not dwell in them; you have planted pleasant vineyards, but you shall not drink wine of them. *(God's Anger burns against exactions ["burdens"] upon the poor; the luxury obtained by such oppression is short-lived; He knows the multitude and magnitude of such cruel deeds.)*

12 For I know your manifold transgressions and your mighty sins: they afflict the just, they take a bribe, and they turn aside the poor in the gate from their right.

13 Therefore the prudent shall keep silence in that time; for it is an evil time. *(The pronoun "they" refers to evil Judges. "Turn aside" addresses the perversion of justice. Consequently, prudent men suffered wrong in silence and did not prosecute those who injured them, knowing it to be useless, because of the corruption of the courts of law.)*

14 Seek good, and not evil, that you may live: and so the LORD, the God of Hosts, shall be with you, as you have spoken.

15 Hate the evil, and love the good, and establish judgment in the gate: it may be that the LORD God of Hosts will be gracious unto the remnant of Joseph. *(The prescription for the avoidance of these terrible judgments is given here. In effect, the Holy Spirit condescends to give another Altar Call by saying, "Seek good, and not evil, that you may live.")*

REASON FOR LAMENTATION

16 Therefore the LORD, the God of Hosts, the LORD, saith thus; Wailing shall be in all streets; and they shall say in all the highways, Alas! alas! and they shall call the husbandman to mourning, and such as are skilful of lamentation to wailing.

17 And in all vineyards shall be wailing: for I will pass through you, saith the LORD. *(The phrase, "Wailing shall be in all streets," refers to the coming invasion of the Assyrians, because Israel refused to seek the Lord. Such speaks of terrible suffering. The phrase, "And in all vineyards shall be wailing," portrayed the fact that the carnage would be not only in the cities, but the countryside, as well!)*

18 Woe unto you who desire the day of the LORD! to what end is it for you? the day of the LORD is darkness, and not light. *(A double "Woe" is the burden of this Message. The first was pronounced upon false profession [Vss. 18-27]; the second, upon false peace [Chpt. 6]. The phrase, "Woe unto you who desire the day of the LORD!" professes Israel's claim of readiness to welcome the establishment of Messiah's Kingdom, which would commence with the Coming of the Lord.*

The idea of the Verse, and which precipitated their audacious reply concerning the "Day of the LORD," is in answer to Amos' demand, "prepare to meet your God, O Israel" [4:12].)

19 As if a man did flee from a lion, and a bear met him; or went into the house, and leaned his hand on the wall, and a serpent bit him. *(The idea of this Verse is: Israel, because of refusal to repent, is destined for death. It cannot be avoided!)*

20 Shall not the day of the LORD be darkness, and not light? even very dark, and no brightness in it? *(Amos further appeals to them, by asking the question, "Do you not feel in your inmost hearts that, in the case of such guilt as yours, the Lord can visit but to punish?")*

GOD HATES HYPOCRISY

21 I hate, I despise your feast days, and I will not smell in your solemn assemblies. *(Regarding their man-made religion, even though it closely resembled God's True Way of Salvation, still, the Lord's response is, "This I hate." Let it be understood: God "hates" every proposed form of "atonement" other than the Cross of Christ [Gal. 5:2].*

The phrase, "And I will not smell in your solemn assemblies," pertains to the "sweet savor" which ascended to the Lord upon proper "Burnt Offerings" being offered unto Him [Ex. 29:18]. He is saying that no sweet savor ascends to God from such sacrifices. So the phrase is equivalent to "I will not accept" and "I will take no delight in" [Gen. 8:21; Ex. 29:18; Lev. 26:31].)

22 Though you offer Me burnt offerings and your meat offerings, I will not accept them: neither will I regard the peace offerings of your fat beasts. *(This Passage proclaims the fact that they maintained the formal ritual of the Mosaic worship in their idolatry. It is the same presently as it regards "Christ and the Cross." Such are mentioned by the modern Church; however, as Israel of old, the object of faith is something else entirely.)*

23 Take thou away from Me the noise of your songs; for I will not hear the melody of your viols. *(The idea is: while the sacrifices were being offered before the golden calf, Psalms and Hymns of praise were being offered to God, accompanied by exquisite sacred music. But the Lord would have none of this! Why? The object of their faith was in the ritual, and not at all in what the sacrifices were supposed to represent, namely, the Coming Redeemer, Who would give His Life on the Cross!)*

24 But let judgment run down as waters, and righteousness as a mighty stream. *(Improper faith always results in improper justice. Proper faith, which is Faith in Christ and what He has done for us at the Cross, always results in "righteousness" [Gal. 2:20-21].)*

THEIR IDOLATRY AND JUDGMENT

25 Have you offered unto Me sacrifices and offerings in the wilderness forty years, O house of Israel? *(Verses 25 through 27 reveal that the evil of associating idols with God had been their rule from the beginning, and now re-appeared in the calf of Beth-el — it was the resurrection of the Golden Calf. In other words, they were without excuse!)*

26 But you have borne the tabernacle of your Moloch and Chiun your images, the star of your god, which you made to yourselves. *(God did not question the fact that they did offer sacrifices in the wilderness. His objection was that the sacrifices were not always to Him. The "unto Me" is emphatic. If God is not served Alone, and with the whole heart, He is not served at all. If the Offering is accepted, then the offeror is accepted. If the offering is rejected, then the offeror also is rejected. Israel's offering was rejected! [Gen., Chpt. 4].)*

27 Therefore will I cause you to go into captivity beyond Damascus, saith the LORD, Whose Name is The God of Hosts. *(Enemies of Inspiration affirm that Stephen erred in saying, "Babylon" and not "Damascus" [Acts 7:43]. However, there are two replies to this:*

First, Babylon is beyond Damascus. Second, Stephen did not say, "As it is written in the Book of the Prophet," but rather, "in the Book of the Prophets," i.e., the Scriptures. The Prophets more than once predicted a captivity beyond Babylon. And so it fell out. The Ten Tribes were carried beyond Damascus and the two Tribes beyond Babylon.)

CHAPTER 6

(787 B.C.)

WOE TO THOSE WHO ARE AT EASE IN ZION AND TRUST IN MEN

WOE to them who are at ease in Zion, and trust in the mountain of Samaria, which are named chief of the nations, to whom the house of Israel came! *(The phrase, "Woe to them who are at ease in Zion," is the second "Woe" pronounced, and it denounces a false peace. The first "Woe," found in 5:18, addresses itself to the insulting sarcasm of Israel's self-righteousness.)*

2 Pass ye unto Calneh, and see; and from thence go ye to Hamath the great: then go down to Gath of the Philistines: be they better than these kingdoms? or their border greater than your border? *(The cities mentioned in this Verse were great and prosperous at this particular time. But yet, both Judah and Israel are invited by the Holy Spirit to go and compare their condition with that of other countries, from the furthest east to the north and to their own neighbors, and they will see that God has done so much more for them than for these others. Israel is bidden to remember that she is much more favored than all these.)*

3 Ye who put far away the evil day, and cause the seat of violence to come near *(the phrase, "Ye who put far away the evil day," addresses the approaching day of God's Wrath. The "seat of violence" refers to the corrupt Court of Justice. Upon hearing Amos' stern words, the religious leaders of Samaria assigned a distant date to the time of punishment and calamity, that is, if it should come at all!);*

4 Who lie upon beds of ivory, and stretch themselves upon their couches, and eat the lambs out of the flock, and the calves out of the midst of the stall *(the phrase, "Who lie upon beds of ivory," is meant to portray their spiritual insensibility, somewhat a result of their prosperity; however, their gain was ill-gotten.)*

5 Who chant to the sound of the viol, and invent to themselves instruments of music, like David *(as is obvious, prosperity, producing ease and luxury, was coupled with entertainment; this is not so much different than the modern Church);*

6 Who drink wine in bowls, and anoint themselves with the chief ointments: but they are not grieved for the affliction of Joseph. *(The phrase, "Who drink wine in bowls," actually referred to the sacrificial bowls, which were used in libations of wine and in the sprinkling of blood, regarding the sacrifices. The phrase, "And anoint themselves with the chief ointments," could very well have referred to the "holy ointment," as described in the Law of Moses, which was to be used only to anoint "the Ark," "the Table," "the Candlestick," etc. It was definitely not to be put on one's flesh [Ex. 30:32-33].)*

CAPTIVITY TO ASSYRIA

7 Therefore now shall they go captive with the first who go captive, and the banquet of them who stretched themselves shall be removed. *(The phrase, "Therefore now shall they go captive with the first who go captive," speaks of Israel falling to the Assyrians about 133 years before the Southern Kingdom of Judah fell to the Babylonians. The last phrase refers to the Nobles of Israel being "removed," which is a gross understatement, to say the least! They would be "removed" as slaves, at least the ones who were not killed.)*

8 The Lord GOD has sworn by Himself, saith the LORD the God of Hosts, I abhor the excellency of Jacob, and hate his palaces: therefore will I deliver up the city with all that is therein. *(The phrase, "The Lord GOD has sworn by Himself," speaks of the threat proceeding directly from Him; it is, therefore, immutable. The balance of this Scripture does not mean that God hates prosperity, but that He hates prosperity that is not gained by His Hand.)*

9 And it shall come to pass, if there remain ten men in one house, that they shall die. *(Pestilence would accompany captivity, or follow it, so deadly that even a large family of ten persons should have but one survivor, if that!)*

10 And a man's uncle shall take him up, and he who burns him, to bring out the bones out of the house, and shall say unto him who is by the sides of the house, Is there yet any with you? and he shall say, No. Then shall he say, Hold your tongue: for we may not make mention of the name of the LORD. *(The phrase, "For we may not make mention of the Name of the LORD," refers to the fact that so conscious would be the survivors that it was a Divine Judgment, they would feel that they dare not use the ordinary language of spiritual consolation uttered at funerals.)*

11 For, behold, the LORD commands, and He will smite the great house with breaches, and the little house with clefts. *(The "great house" pertains to the Ten Tribes of the Northern*

Kingdom, while the "little house" refers to the Two Tribes of the Southern Kingdom.)

12 Shall horses run upon the rock? will one plow there with oxen? for you have turned judgment into gall, and the fruit of righteousness into hemlock (the phrase, "For we have turned judgment into gall, and the fruit of righteousness into hemlock," refers to Israel turning the Word of God, and all that it promised, against themselves instead of for themselves. Obedience brings blessing, while disobedience brings the opposite!):

13 You which rejoice in a thing of nought, which say, Have we not taken to us horns by our own strength? (The phrase, "You which rejoice in a thing of naught," pertains to Israel trusting idols. The question, "Have we not taken to us horns by our own strength?", refers to military strength and Israel's belief that they were impregnable. Their boast was a consequence of the successful wars with the Syrians [II Ki. 14:25-28]. The Prophet proceeds to demolish their proud vaunt.)

14 But, behold, I will raise up against you a nation, O house of Israel, saith the LORD the God of Hosts; and they shall afflict you from the entering in of Hemath unto the river of the wilderness. (The first phrase refers to the Assyrians. The latter phrase predicts the entirety of Israel being wrecked by the Assyrians.)

CHAPTER 7
(787 B.C.)
PROPHECIES (SIGNS) OF DESTRUCTION: GRASSHOPPERS

THUS has the Lord GOD showed unto me; and, behold, He formed grasshoppers in the beginning of the shooting up of the latter growth; and, lo, it was the latter growth after the king's mowings. (The revelation of the first nine Verses is: persistence in evil, after repeated forgiveness, will meet with eternal judgment. The first phrase refers to locusts coming upon the harvest. The latter phrase refers to the king taking the first crop of hay and the locusts taking the second, with nothing remaining for the unhappy people. The entirety of this Passage points to the moral Government of God, Who uses Nature to work His Purposes.)

2 And it came to pass, that when they had made an end of eating the grass of the land, then I said, O Lord GOD, forgive, I beseech You: by whom shall Jacob arise? for he is small. (When praying for personal pardon, sin should be magnified; when pleading for the pardon of a neighbor, sins should be minimized.

The first phrase refers to the exhaustion of all sustenance, with no one to help them but the Lord. And sadly, they had no right to ask Him for anything, because they had sinned greatly against Him. The last phrase records Amos acting as an Intercessor on behalf of this hapless people, which the Lord graciously answered.)

3 The LORD repented for this: It shall not be, saith the LORD. (The first phrase literally means that God changed His Direction. The use of the word "repent," at least as it refers to the Lord, infers no wrongdoing whatsoever on His part. It merely means that He wills a change, without changing His Will; for that He cannot do.

The phrase, "It shall not be, saith the LORD," concerns this particular destruction, in this particular way, but not the overall thrust of the judgment, barring the people's repentance.)

THE FIRE

4 Thus has the Lord GOD showed unto me: and, behold, the Lord GOD called to contend by fire, and it devoured the great deep, and did eat up a part. (The phrase, "Thus has the Lord GOD showed unto me," refers to a further judgment that had been decided in the high counsels of Heaven against Israel. It was a "judgment by fire," and was to be so great that it would "devour the great deep," which means to drink up the very ocean itself.

As bad as this seems, due to the prayer of Amos, it appears that this judgment was lessened in its intensity dramatically so; therefore, the people were given more time to repent, which, sadly, they did not.)

5 Then said I, O Lord GOD, cease, I beseech You: by whom shall Jacob arise? for he is small. (This petition is the same as in Verse 2, except Jacob says here, "cease," instead of "forgive." Actually, the word "cease" fits perfectly, in that the second invasion of Tiglath-Pileser II was cut short, no doubt in answer to this prayer.)

6 The LORD repented for this: This also shall not be, saith the Lord GOD. (Once again, Amos importunes, and once again, the Lord answers. It is similar to that which Abraham asked of the Lord concerning Sodom and Gomorrah [Gen., Chpt. 18].)

THE VISION OF THE PLUMBLINE:
NO MORE MERCY

7 Thus He showed me: and, behold, the

LORD stood upon a wall made by a plumbline, with a plumbline in His hand. *(Every evidence is that Amos actually saw the Lord in a vision. The phrase, "And, behold, the LORD stood upon a wall made by a plumbline," actually speaks of the "wall" as the Kingdom of Israel, once carefully built up, solidly constructed, and accurately arranged.*

In effect, the Lord is saying that Israel, from henceforth, will have to measure up to the "plumbline," and that all the mercy that could be shown to Israel, due to the petitions of Amos, had been shown, and could not be extended.)

8 And the LORD said unto me, Amos, what seest thou? And I said, A plumbline. Then said the LORD, Behold, I will set a plumbline in the midst of My people Israel: I will not again pass by them any more *(the first phrase portrays the intimacy of the fellowship between Immanuel and the Prophet, and appears with peculiar sweetness in the Prophet being addressed as "Amos" [Jn. 10:3]. The phrase, "I will not again pass by them any more," means He would not spare or forgive any more, and the Prophet is thereby instructed to intercede no more. The judgment is irremediable, with the final conquest by Shalmaneser typified here):*

9 And the high places of Isaac shall be desolate, and the sanctuaries of Israel shall be laid waste; and I will rise against the house of Jeroboam with the sword. *(The first phrase refers to the entirety of Israel. The latter phrase was fulfilled, as recorded in II Ki. 15:10.)*

AMOS AND AMAZIAH

10 Then Amaziah the priest of Beth-el sent to Jeroboam king of Israel, saying, Amos has conspired against you in the midst of the house of Israel: the land is not able to bear all his words. *(The first phrase portrays the fact that the type of preaching done by Amos was out of place in the Royal Chapel. A State Religion negates any civil and religious liberty. If it is of human origination, it cannot endure the testimony of Truth.*

Not to be a member of the State Church is to be, in a degree, a rebel. The king, being the head of the Church, no religious teaching could be permitted which was displeasing to him and to the priests whom he appointed [I Ki. 12:31; 13:1-4]. Amaziah was one of these man-made priests. He was not of the house of Aaron. His charge that Amos predicted the death of the king was a falsehood. Amos predicted the doom of

the "house of Jeroboam."

The middle phrase means that at least some few of the Israelites had been convinced by the Prophet's words and had joined ranks with him. Hence, Amaziah speaks of a "conspiracy" against the king.

The phrase, "The land is not able to bear all his words," reveals the effect the Ministry of Amos had on Israel. God give us more today as Amos!)

11 For thus Amos said, Jeroboam shall die by the sword, and Israel shall surely be led away captive out of their own land. *(As stated, the first phrase pertains to the false accusation by Amaziah that Amos had predicted the death of the king. The latter phrase was correct in that it predicted the captivity of Israel. Such is the most hurtful lie of all, in that it contains some truth!)*

12 Also Amaziah said unto Amos, O thou Seer, go, flee thee away into the land of Judah, and there eat bread, and prophesy there *(in other words, you are not wanted here! There is no record that Jeroboam took any steps in consequence of this accusation, either deeming the words of Amos to be unworthy of serious consideration or, like Herod [Mat. 14:5], fearing the people, who had been impressed by the Prophet's words and bold bearing. Consequently, Amaziah seeks by his own authority to make Amos leave the country. He evidently thought that Amos, like himself, preached for money):*

13 But prophesy not again any more at Beth-el: for it is the king's chapel, and it is the king's court. *(This heathen priest, as he speaks of the "king's chapel" and the "king's court," acts as if human authority is everything, and the Lord, of Himself, had no claims on the land or the place.)*

14 Then answered Amos, and said to Amaziah, I was no Prophet, neither was I a Prophet's son; but I was an herdman, and a gatherer of sycomore fruit *(the first phrase proclaims the fact that Amos was not a Preacher of his own will, nor of the will of others. He was not meaning that he was not a "Prophet," but that his calling was not of human origin, but of God):*

15 And the LORD took me as I followed the flock, and the LORD said unto me, Go, prophesy unto My people Israel. *(The first phrase proclaims the fact that Prophets are not born such, nor are they self-made, nor made by others. The phrase, "Go, prophesy unto My people Israel," specifies that the Lord gave Amos a direct Message for Israel, which was not to be*

added to or taken from!)

16 Now therefore hear thou the word of the LORD: You say, Prophesy not against Israel, and drop not your word against the house of Isaac. *(God had not renounced His Rights as the God of Israel. He called them "My people Israel," and, therefore, pronounced this judgment upon Amaziah. The phrase, "Now therefore hear thou the Word of the LORD," refers to a Prophecy being directed to this heathen priest personally. The pronoun "thou" emphasizes this.)*

17 Therefore thus saith the LORD; Your wife shall be an harlot in the city, and your sons and your daughters shall fall by the sword, and your land shall be divided by line; and you shall die in a polluted land: and Israel shall surely go into captivity forth of his land. *(If, in Amos, we have an example of a faithful Prophet, in Amaziah, we have an example of an unfaithful priest. The fate predicted for Amaziah was indeed terrible; but we discern in its appointment, not the malice of a human foe, but the justice of a Divine Ruler.*

Concerning the demand of Amaziah, "you shall not prophesy," Amos' keen retort was, "Thus saith the LORD." Such will always be the case with the True Prophet of God.)

CHAPTER 8

(787 B.C.)

THE VISION OF THE BASKET OF RIPE FRUIT: ISRAEL SOON TO PERISH

THUS has the Lord GOD showed unto me: and behold a basket of summer fruit. *(The gathering of fruit was the last harvest of the year, and was done in October. As it was the last harvest of the year, it also fitly typified the final warning to Israel.)*

2 And He said, Amos, what do you see? And I said, A basket of summer fruit. Then said the LORD unto me, The end is come upon My people of Israel; I will not again pass by them any more. *(The last phrase means that the Lord will not forgive them any more, nor show any more Mercy, because of their refusal to repent.)*

3 And the songs of the temple shall be howlings in that day, saith the Lord GOD: there shall be many dead bodies in every place; they shall cast them forth with silence. *("Howlings" portray the coming disposition of Israel changed from its present occupation of revelry, luxury, and entertainment to one of judgment, desolation, destitution, and stark horror. The Lord is represented here as casting dead bodies to the*

ground so that death is everywhere, with the interjection, "Hush!" as an admonition to bend beneath the hand of an avenging God.)

SINS OF ISRAEL

4 Hear this, O ye who swallow up the needy, even to make the poor of the land to fail *(God's love for the poor and His burning Anger against their oppressors once more appear)*,

5 Saying, When will the new moon be gone, that we may sell corn? and the sabbath, that we may set forth wheat, making the ephah small, and the shekel great, and falsifying the balances by deceit? *(By reducing the size of the ephah, by overcharging, and by falsifying the scales, they robbed the defenseless; plunging them into debt, they sold them into slavery for a trifle, in defiance of Lev. 25:39.*

The phrase, "Saying, When will the new moon be gone, that we may sell corn?", refers to the first day of the month on which all trade was supposed to be suspended. Num. 28:18 proclaims this. These greedy individuals kept the festivals, but they grudged the time given to them, and considered them as wasted. In other words, they had no time for the Lord!)

6 That we may buy the poor for silver, and the needy for a pair of shoes; yea, and sell the refuse of the wheat? *(The idea of this Verse is that the poor, because of the dishonesty of much of the upper class, kept getting poorer, and they were compelled to pay their debt by selling themselves into slavery. The phrase, "And the needy for a pair of shoes," means that they dealt harshly even for the smallest debt.*

The phrase, "Yea, and sell the refuse of the wheat," referred to a type of scale, which, when the grain was poured into it for weighing, had openings in the bottom, not visible to the seller, which caused as much as 10-20 percent of the grain to sift into an unseen container, giving a short weight. They would then sell that which was called "refuse," which had actually been stolen, adding more dishonest gain to their already dishonest gain.)

JUDGMENT AND WANDERINGS

7 The LORD has sworn by the excellency of Jacob, Surely I will never forget any of their works. *(The phrase, "The excellency of Jacob," speaks of God Himself. In Verse 2, He says, "I will not forgive"; now He says, "I will never forget," expressing His pity for the oppressed and*

His eternal Anger against the oppressors.)

8 Shall not the land tremble for this, and every one mourn who dwells therein? and it shall rise up wholly as a flood; and it shall be cast out and drowned, as by the flood of Egypt. *(The idea is that coming judgment shall flood the land.)*

9 And it shall come to pass in that day, saith the Lord GOD, that I will cause the sun to go down at noon, and I will darken the Earth in the clear day *(this speaks of an eclipse of the sun. At exactly what time the Holy Spirit is speaking of in this particular Passage is not known)*:

10 And I will turn your feasts into mourning, and all your songs into lamentation; and I will bring up sackcloth upon all loins, and baldness upon every head; and I will make it as the mourning of an only son, and the end thereof as a bitter day. *(The last phrase, "And the end thereof as a bitter day," sums up the entirety of this Passage. It speaks of the attack by the Assyrians and the shock of its brutal force finally registering upon Israel.)*

11 Behold, the days come, saith the Lord GOD, that I will send a famine in the land, not a famine of bread, nor a thirst for water, but of hearing the words of the LORD *(what the leaders of Israel had demanded of Amos, they will now get! They will be carted away to captivity, at least those who were left, with the results being that there would be no more "hearing the words of the LORD." What Israel wanted, Israel got; however, what she got did not turn out to be what she thought she wanted!)*:

12 And they shall wander from sea to sea, and from the north even to the east, they shall run to and fro to seek the word of the LORD, and shall not find it. *(Then the word of the Lord would be eagerly desired, but not realized; sought, but not found; called for, but not answered! And it must be quickly added, nothing could be worse! On all counts, the prosperity of a people and a nation is "the Word of the LORD." Deprived of that, the people are left aimless and without direction.)*

13 In that day shall the fair virgins and young men faint for thirst. *(The "thirst" spoken of here concerns spiritual thirst, which can only be satisfied by the "Word of the LORD.")*

14 They who swear by the sin of Samaria, and say, Your god, O Dan, lives; and, The manner of Beer-sheba lives; even they shall fall, and never rise up again. *(Samaria, Dan, Beth-el, Gilgal, and Beer-sheba were centers of idolatry in Israel [Hos. 4:15; 9:15; 12:11; I Ki.*

12:26-30]. This truth is demonstrated by the fate of the Jews who will not receive Christ as the promised Messiah and consequently have fallen to "never rise up again." And so shall it be for all who reject Christ as their eternal Saviour!)

CHAPTER 9
STRIKING THE LINTEL; GOD'S JUDGMENTS ARE INESCAPABLE

I saw the LORD standing upon the Altar: and He said, Smite the lintel of the door, that the posts may shake: and cut them in the head, all of them; and I will slay the last of them with the sword: he who flees of them shall not flee away, and he who escapes of them shall not be delivered. *(The first phrase refers to Amos actually and literally seeing the Lord, as He stood upon the "Brazen Altar" in front of the Temple in Jerusalem. Even though the pronouncement of judgment is more pointedly against the Northern Kingdom, still, the whole of both kingdoms is meant, because the restoration of both kingdoms is referred to in Verses 11 through 15.*

The phrase, "And He said, Smite the lintel of the door, that the posts may shake," refers to the destruction of the Temple, which would take place a little over 150 years from Amos' time. The implication is: total destruction from summit to base.)

2 Though they dig into Hell, thence shall My hand take them; though they climb up to heaven, thence will I bring them down *(the Holy Spirit, upon reading the minds of the people as they heard the words of Amos, proclaims to them the folly of their thoughts of escape. Men presently, and for all time, have "dug into Hell," i.e., delved into witchcraft, but found that demon spirits could not protect them from the Hand of God. As well, they have "climbed up to heaven," the exploration of near space; but, despite the Russian Cosmonauts declaring that they nowhere saw God, still, "He brought them down," i.e., destroyed the Soviet Union)*:

3 And though they hide themselves in the top of Carmel, I will search and take them out thence; and though they be hid from My sight in the bottom of the sea, thence will I command the serpent, and he shall bite them *(the idea is: there will be no escaping this coming judgment!)*:

4 And though they go into captivity before their enemies, thence will I command the

sword, and it shall slay them: and I will set My eyes upon them for evil, and not for good. *(For the Lord to do such a thing means that countless opportunities for Repentance have been spurned, with every plea by the Holy Spirit rejected.)*

FINAL PROPHECY OF DISPERSION

5 And the Lord GOD of Hosts is He Who touches the land, and it shall melt, and all who dwell therein shall mourn: and it shall rise up wholly like a flood; and shall be drowned, as by the flood of Egypt. *(The title, "Lord GOD of Hosts," in the Hebrew is "Jehovah Elohim Zebaoth," and represents God not only as ruler of the heavenly bodies, but as the Monarch of a multitude of Heavenly spirits, who execute His Will, worship Him in His abiding-place, and are attendants and witnesses of His Glory.*

As the Nile River in Egypt floods at times and covers the land, likewise, the Judgment of God will cover Israel.)

6 It is He Who builds His stories in the Heaven, and has founded His troop in the Earth; He Who calls for the waters of the sea, and pours them out upon the face of the Earth: The LORD is His name. *(The phrase, "It is He Who builds His stories in the Heaven," refers to God's headquarters on planet Heaven. The phrase, "And has founded His troop in the Earth," seems, in the original language, to have the idea of making the arch of the heavens above the Earth, that is, the immediate heaven surrounding the Earth, i.e., the expanse, clouds, atmosphere, etc.*

The phrase, "The LORD is His Name," refers to God as Creator of all things, and not mindless evolution.)

7 Are ye not as children of the Ethiopians unto me, O children of Israel? saith the LORD. Have not I brought up Israel out of the land of Egypt? and the Philistines from Caphtor, and the Syrians from Kir? *(The proud boast of the Israelites, namely, that they were God's peculiar People and that their Redemption from Egypt demonstrated that they were His favorites, was a fleshly boast, and is combatted by this Verse.*

Spiritually, they were "as Ethiopians" [Jer. 13:23]; historically, they could only rank as the Philistines and the Syrians, whom God, in His providence, had also delivered from captivity and probably had also brought out of Egypt originally. Consequently, as Israel of old, election by God cannot, and in fact does not, guarantee Salvation when the conduct does not correspond with God's Word.)

8 Behold, the eyes of the Lord GOD are upon the sinful kingdom, and I will destroy it from off the face of the Earth; saving that I will not utterly destroy the house of Jacob, saith the LORD. *(The phrase, "And I will destroy it from off the face of the Earth," refers to both Israel and ultimately Judah ceasing as independent nations. The Ten-Tribe Kingdom was destroyed by the Assyrians a few years after the time of Amos, never to rise again. About 133 years after their destruction, Judah also fell!*

After the dispersion, elements of all the Tribes came back to the Promised Land, although as a vassal state to a foreign power until their destruction in A.D. 70. For nearly 2,000 years, they ceased to be a nation, but did remain as a people. Only since 1948 have they enjoyed Statehood, but they are to see some very difficult days not too far into the future.)

9 For, lo, I will command, and I will sift the house of Israel among all nations, like as corn is sifted in a sieve, yet shall not the least grain fall upon the Earth. *(In Verses 8 and 9, the Lord says, "I will destroy," "I will command," "I will sift." God Himself promises to be the Principal. Even though it sounds extremely negative, still, this is all lovely and consoling to Faith. It secures the absolute Salvation of the Remnant. The smallest grain is as sure of eternal safety as the largest, hence the phrase, "Yet shall not the least grain fall upon the Earth.")*

10 All the sinners of My people shall die by the sword, which say, The evil shall not overtake nor prevent us. *(Even though the Lord calls them "My people," still, He also calls them "sinners"; barring Repentance, these "sinners" will "die by the sword." As well, they will lose their souls!)*

RESTORATION OF DAVID'S KINGDOM UNDER THE MESSIAH

11 In that day will I raise up the Tabernacle of David that is fallen, and close up the breaches thereof; and I will raise up his ruins, and I will build it as in the days of old *(the phrase, "In that day," refers to the future day of Restoration, which will follow the present night of desolation. As well, it is the "Tabernacle of David" which is to be raised up, and not of Jeroboam, nor of Jehu, etc. The phrase, "And I will build it as in the days of old," is also quoted in Acts 15:14-18. It refers to the fact that this will be fulfilled only after the Church Age, actually in the Kingdom Age)*:

12 That they may possess the remnant of Edom, and of all the heathen, which are called by My name, saith the LORD Who does this. *(The phrase, "That they may possess the remnant of Edom, and of all the heathen," actually refers to "Adam," that is, all of mankind. The new-born Israel, after the Second Coming of the Lord, will take possession of all nations and bring them to Immanuel, thus totally fulfilling the Commission of Mat. 28:19. As well, these nations will come willingly and gladly, realizing that Israel is the source of all blessings.)*

13 Behold, the days come, saith the LORD, that the plowman shall overtake the reaper, and the treader of grapes him who sows seed; and the mountains shall drop sweet wine, and all the hills shall melt. *(The phrase, "Behold, the days come, saith the LORD," pertains to the certitude of this action. As the day of Judgment was sure to come, likewise, the day of Blessing is sure to come, as well!*

This speaks of the coming Kingdom Age, when Israel will truly be a Land flowing with "milk and honey," which will bless the entirety of the Earth.)

14 And I will bring again the captivity of My people of Israel, and they shall build the waste cities, and inhabit them; and they shall plant vineyards, and drink the wine thereof; they shall also make gardens, and eat the fruit of them. *(Verses 13 through 15 concern the coming Restoration of Israel, which will take place immediately following the Second Coming. The phrase, "And I will bring again the captivity of My people of Israel," concerns a length of time that has now lasted for nearly 2,000 years; if we count the time they were a vassal state, it is some 2,500 years.*

The tone and intent of the Verse also claim that the contesting of the Land of Israel will be forever ended. This signifies that Satan's day is done!)

15 And I will plant them upon their land, and they shall no more be pulled up out of their land which I have given them, saith the LORD your God. *(Thus, Amos closes his great Book with the words, "saith the LORD your God," which seal the Predictions and Promises.)*

OBADIAH

EDOM'S FALL PREDICTED
(587 B.C.)

THE vision of Obadiah. Thus saith the Lord GOD concerning Edom; We have heard a rumour from the LORD, and an ambassador is sent among the heathen, Arise ye, and let us rise up against her in battle. *("The vision of Obadiah" is actually the title of the Book, that is, if this short Prophecy could be declared as such. The word "vision" concerns the manner in which the Holy Spirit gave this Word to Obadiah.*

The meaning of the word "Edom" is "red" or "rosy," the same as Adam. Hence, Edom typifies the first Adam, who failed and, therefore, the flesh, while Israel typified the Last Adam, Christ, Who succeeded by the Power of the Holy Spirit.

The last phrase refers to the Lord guiding these particular nations respecting opposition to Edom, portraying His minute involvement, not only in the affairs of individuals, but even entire nations.)

2 Behold, I have made you small among the heathen: you are greatly despised. *(The Edomites boasted of their strength, the impregnability of their country, and their wisdom. Actually, the Edomites at this time were a powerful nation, and possessed an almost impregnable seat at Petra. But yet, the words of Verse 1, "Let us rise up," refer to the nations coming against her, with little fear of her boasts.)*

3 The pride of your heart has deceived you, you who dwell in the clefts of the rock, whose habitation is high; who says in his heart, Who shall bring me down to the ground? *(The phrase, "The pride of your heart has deceived you," refers to the reason for God's opposition to these people. The phrase, "You who dwell in the clefts of the rock, whose habitation is high," refers to the capital city of Petra. Consequently, not only were they "high" respecting topography, but "high" in their own hearts, as evidenced in this Scripture.*

Their question, "Who shall bring me down to the ground?", was directed at Israel's God as much as at any nation. They considered themselves superior to Israel and their god superior to Jehovah.)

4 Though you exalt yourself as the eagle, and though you set your nest among the stars, thence will I bring you down, saith the LORD. *(Even though such is spoken to Edom, the thrust of the Message is directed at Edom's sponsor, Satan [Isa. 14:13-15].)*

5 If thieves came to you, if robbers by night, (how are you cut off!) would they not have stolen till they had enough? if the grapegatherers came to you, would they not leave some grapes? *(The idea is: foreign powers would heavily tax the country, thereby representing the "thieves," while ultimately Edom would be invaded, signifying violence. The Prophet then exclaims, "How are you cut off!" signifying a total desolation, which is exactly what happened down through the centuries, until there are no Edomites left.)*

THE REASON FOR JUDGMENT
EXPLAINED: SIN

6 How are the things of Esau searched out! how are his hidden things sought up! *(Edom sprang from Esau, Jacob's brother; it is believed that Esau may have founded the city of Petra. Considering that this city was a great emporium of trade between Arabia and Syria and that in it great treasures were stored, this Verse predicts that these "hidden things" will be "sought up" and pilfered!)*

7 All the men of your confederacy have brought you even to the border: the men who were at peace with you have deceived you, and prevailed against you; they who eat your bread have laid a wound under you: there is none understanding in him. *(The first phrase probably refers to Moab, Ammon, Tyre, and Zidon, who joined together to resist Nebuchadnezzar and were smitten by him [Jer. 27:3]. Edom sent ambassadors to these allies, asking help, but the messengers were conducted back to their borders with their request not granted, because the allies were unwilling to entangle themselves in the fate of Edom.*

The middle phrase refers to these nations mentioned of their confederacy, but which would not give Edom the help promised. As well, no amount of argument could persuade them to change their political stance, hence fulfilling the Passage,

"and prevailed against you."

The next to the last phrase implies the closest friendship being violated by deception and treachery.

The last phrase, "There is none understanding in him," portrays the shock of this defection of allies, to where they [Edom] did not know where to turn or what to do.)

8 Shall I not in that day, saith the LORD, even destroy the wise men out of Edom, and understanding out of the Mount of Esau? (The first phrase refers to the Lord Himself Personally intervening in the thinking processes of the individuals involved, so that they should not any more be able to offer prudent counsel or suggest plans of safety. The conclusion of the question, "And understanding out of the Mount of Esau?" is not thus designated by chance. It is meant to infer that all human wisdom, irrespective of its brilliance and sagacity, will ultimately be brought to extinction.

The entirety, therefore, of the prediction, even though applying to "Edom" of old, nevertheless points to the entirety of the human family and the cause of all problems and its destruction.)

9 And your mighty men, O Teman, shall be dismayed, to the end that every one of the mount of Esau may be cut off by slaughter. (The phrase, "To the end," concerns a judicial blindness inflicted that all may perish, and by the Lord at that! The last phrase tells us that they do not go quietly into that dark night.)

10 For your violence against your brother Jacob shame shall cover you, and you shall be cut off for ever. (The first phrase refers to the ruin and captivity of the children of Judah and Jerusalem, which caused great jubilation among the sons of Esau. As well, her opposition included far more than jubilation over Israel's troubles, but instead included hostile action.

Their conduct was aggravated by the fact that the victim was their "brother Jacob," who was commanded not to hate the Edomites [Deut. 23:7]. As stated, they were descendants of Esau, Jacob's brother, which, in a sense, made them brothers to Israel. Nevertheless, the Edomites had always been actively hostile to Israel.)

11 In the day that you stood on the other side, in the day that the strangers carried away captive his forces, and foreigners entered into his gates, and cast lots upon Jerusalem, even you were as one of them. (In this Verse, it is not likely that Obadiah was speaking of the sack of Jerusalem and Nebuchadnezzar, because every evidence is that his Prophecy was given before that time. So the reference is probably to the Philistines and Arabians [II Chron. 21:16].

The phrase, "Even you were as one of them," places Edom, even though a blood relative of Israel, in the same category as the "strangers" and "foreigners," meaning they were such to the God of Israel.)

12 But you should not have looked on the day of your brother in the day that he became a stranger; neither should you have rejoiced over the Children of Judah in the day of their destruction; neither should you have spoken proudly in the day of distress. (As the previous Verse spoke of past offenses, this Verse speaks of future offenses. Consequently, it should have been translated, "Do not look," "Do not rejoice," etc. Obadiah, knowing their past behavior, knowing that Jerusalem will suffer another and more fatal conquest, warns the Edomites against repeating this malicious conduct.

They first looked, and now they rejoiced, but they never dreamed that God is observing all of their actions. In fact, they didn't even believe in Jehovah.)

13 You should not have entered into the gate of My people in the day of their calamity; yea, you should not have looked on their affliction in the day of their calamity, nor have laid hands on their substance in the day of their calamity (Three times the Holy Spirit uses the phrase, "In the day of their calamity," referring to Israel, in order to make certain of the time of which He speaks. Such insinuates their helplessness, and the anger expressed by the Lord at Edom taking advantage of that helplessness. It didn't sit well, not at all, with the Lord!);

14 Neither should you have stood in the crossway, to cut off those of His who did escape; neither should you have delivered up those of His who did remain in the day of distress. (Even though Judah had greatly sinned and was suffering the judgment of God, still, the Lord looked with jaundiced eye at those who would seek to further hinder them, as did Edom.)

EDOM IN THE DAY OF THE LORD; THEIR FATE

15 For the day of the LORD is near upon all the heathen: as you have done, it shall be done unto you: your reward shall return upon your own head. (The phrase, "The day of the LORD," points to the far off future day of God's Wrath, at least "far off" from Obadiah's day. At this point, the Prophecy passes on to the future and

predicts an annihilation of all the nations, as nations, that seek to injure God's ancient People.

The phrase, "As you have done, it shall be done unto you," was, in effect, quoted by Christ [Mat. 7:2].)

16 For as you have drunk upon My holy mountain, so shall all the heathen drink continually, yea, they shall drink and they shall swallow down, and they shall be as though they had not been. *(The phrase, "For as you have drunk upon My Holy Mountain," is to be taken literally. It quite possibly refers to the destruction of Jerusalem by Nebuchadnezzar, with the Edomites gloating over the Fall of the city and the destruction of the Temple, with them also indulging in unseemly revelry and then profaning with their idolatrous festival the mountain which had been hallowed by God's Presence. The "drinking" here, as stated, is literal, while, in the following phrase, it is figurative.*

The phrase, "So shall all the heathen drink continually," does not refer to them drinking wine, but to drinking the Wrath of God [Jer. 25:15].

Even though this judgment will take into consideration all the many centuries past, still, the heavier weight will fall on the activity during the Great Tribulation. Then the Antichrist will make his debut, not only to take over the entirety of the world; but, as Hitler, he will also seek to totally annihilate the Jews!)

ISRAEL'S ULTIMATE TRIUMPH AND RESTORATION

17 But upon Mount Zion shall be deliverance, and there shall be holiness; and the house of Jacob shall possess their possessions. *(The restoration and age-enduring prosperity of the house of Jacob are the themes of Verses 17 through 21. The entire land from the Euphrates to the river of Egypt, promised to Abraham, shall become the possession of his children. All of this will take place in the coming Kingdom Age!)*

18 And the house of Jacob shall be a fire, and the house of Joseph a flame, and the house of Esau for stubble, and they shall kindle in them, and devour them; and there shall not be any remaining of the house of Esau: for the LORD has spoken it. *(About 2,500 years ago, this prediction was written. Today no Edomite can be found. But the symbolic Edom persists and will persist up to the Day of the Lord [Isa. 63:1-6]. In the spiritual sense, and as we have stated, "Edom," or "this house of Esau," represents all who oppose God and His Plan. Of this, the Scripture plainly says, "And there shall not be any remaining of the house of Esau; for the Lord has spoken it.")*

19 And they of the south shall possess the mount of Esau; and they of the plain the Philistines: and they shall possess the fields of Ephraim, and the fields of Samaria: and Benjamin shall possess Gilead. *(The idea of this Verse is that Israel will finally possess the entirety of her land, with it never to be contested any more. This will be done by the Power of God; in fact, Israel, at that time, the Kingdom Age, will be the most powerful nation in the world.)*

20 And the captivity of this host of the children of Israel shall possess that of the Canaanites, even unto Zarephath; and the captivity of Jerusalem, which is in Sepharad, shall possess the cities of the south. *(The phrase, "And the captivity of this host of the children of Israel," concerns all the Jews in the world, who will then come back to Israel, and gladly so!)*

21 And saviours shall come up on Mount Zion to judge the Mount of Esau; and the kingdom shall be the LORD's. *(The phrase, "And saviours shall come up on Mount Zion to judge the Mount of Esau," refers to the coming of the Lord, together with all His Glorified Saints, and all the Angels [Isa. 63:1-6; Zech. 14:1-5, 14; II Thess. 1:7-10; Jude 14-15; Rev. 19:11-21].*

The phrase, "And the kingdom shall be the LORD's," refers to the Kingdom which will never end, and which was seen by Nebuchadnezzar in his dream of the statue, which was interpreted by Daniel [Dan. 2:44-45].)

JONAH

CHAPTER 1
(862 B.C.)

GOD COMMISSIONS JONAH

NOW the Word of the LORD came unto Jonah the son of Amittai, saying (*it is thought that the Book of Jonah was written about 800 B.C., or possibly a little later. Jonah means "a dove," while Amittai means "true." The phrase, "The Word of the LORD," is a decisive statement, which claims and demonstrates the truthfulness of the entire Book. The same statement is used some seven times in the entirety of the Book, with the number "seven" exclaiming the totality and perfection of the statement [1:1; 2:10; 3:1,3; 4:4, 9, 10].*

The phrase, "Unto Jonah the son of Amittai, saying," specifies the Prophet and that he is to deliver the Message, and no one else),

2 Arise, go to Nineveh, that great city, and cry against it; for their wickedness is come up before Me. (*"Nineveh" was the capital of the mighty Assyrian Empire, which was the dominant force in the world of that day. The Message given to Jonah by the Holy Spirit, "Arise, go to Nineveh," must have been a shock to the Prophet, to say the least! No Prophet had ever been sent, as such, to the Gentiles, and especially to those as cruel as the Ninevites.*

As well, the command given by the Lord, "Cry against it," certainly was not a word that would endear him to the people of that city. To warn men of their sins and to tell them of judgment to come, whether near or far, is seldom met with approbation. It is normally met with hostility and censure; consequently, many Prophets were killed.)

JONAH REFUSES AND FLEES FROM GOD

3 But Jonah rose up to flee unto Tarshish from the presence of the LORD, and went down to Joppa; and he found a ship going to Tarshish: so he paid the fare thereof, and went down into it, to go with them unto Tarshish from the presence of the LORD. (*"Tarshish" was located on the south coast of Spain; it was in the opposite direction to Nineveh. Jonah was sent to the far east, while he fled to the distant west. The phrase, "From the Presence of the Lord," is repeated twice by the Holy Spirit, which is not by accident, but by design.*)

THE LORD SENDS A STORM

4 But the LORD sent out a great wind into the sea, and there was a mighty tempest in the sea, so that the ship was like to be broken. (*The phrase, "But the LORD sent out a great wind into the sea," is but the first of several phases of this nature, where the Lord took a direct hand in guiding the affairs of the Prophet.*)

THE MARINERS' PRAYERS

5 Then the mariners were afraid, and cried every man unto his god, and cast forth the wares that were in the ship into the sea, to lighten it of them. But Jonah was gone down into the sides of the ship; and he lay, and was fast asleep. (*There is no conscience so insensible as that of a disobedient Believer. The sailors were praying, but Jonah was sleeping. He first went down to Joppa, then down into the ship, and then down into the sides of the ship.*

The storm was powerful, and the sailors onboard tried to do everything possible to save their ship. But the problem wasn't their goods; it was Jonah!)

JONAH TOLD TO PRAY

6 So the shipmaster came to him, and said unto him, What meanest thou, O sleeper? arise, call upon your God, if so be that God will think upon us, that we perish not. (*Here the Prophet's stupor is rebuked by the heathen's faith. The phrase, "arise, call upon your God," petitions Jonah to pray to Jehovah. The phrase, "if so be that God will think upon us, that we perish not," is interesting indeed! Even though these mariners worshipped many gods, they here use the word "God" with the article, "Ha Elohim" ["the God"], as if they have a dim notion of One Supreme Deity, which no doubt they did!*)

CASTING LOTS; JONAH CHOSEN

7 And they said every one to his fellow,

Come, and let us cast lots, that we may know for whose cause this evil is upon us. So they cast lots, and the lot fell upon Jonah. *(The "lot" they cast did not tell them the problem, but only of the person who could point out the problem. That person was "Jonah.")*

JONAH'S CONFESSION

8 Then said they unto him, Tell us, we pray you, for whose cause this evil is upon us; What is your occupation? and from where do you come? what is your country? and of what people are you? *(Considering how they probed Jonah, the questions asked by these heathen hit at the very heart of the Plan of God, not only for Israel, but for the entirety of the human family, and for all time!)*

9 And he said unto them, I am an Hebrew; and I fear the LORD, the God of Heaven, which has made the sea and the dry land. *(The last phrase means, at least to the ears of these heathen, that Jehovah was not a local deity like the false gods whom they worshipped, but the Creator of Heaven and Earth, the Maker and Ruler of sea and dry land. By his statement, they perfectly understood of Whom he was speaking; the next Verse proclaims their response.)*

10 Then were the men exceedingly afraid, and said unto him, Why have you done this? For the men knew that he fled from the presence of the LORD, because he had told them. *(The phrase, "Then were the men exceedingly afraid," proclaims their understanding of the greatness of Jehovah and the terrible risk incurred by one who offends Him. The last phrase proclaims their amazement that one who worshipped the Almighty Creator should disobey His Command. To them, this seemed outrageous and even criminal, which it was!)*

11 Then said they unto him, What shall we do unto you, that the sea may be calm unto us? for the sea wrought, and was tempestuous. *(By now, they are very cognizant of the fact that their plight is not ordinary, that they are facing power far beyond anything they have ever known, and that this man Jonah is the pivot point. The last phrase tells us that the storm was growing more intense even by the moment.)*

12 And he said unto them, Take me up, and cast me forth into the sea; so shall the sea be calm unto you: for I know that for my sake this great tempest is upon you. *(There is a note of resignation in this statement given by Jonah, portraying that he had come to the place of*

recognition regarding his disobedience, and that it would do no good to resist further. He was willing to suffer the fate that was due him because of his disobedience, which he thought was death!)*

13 Nevertheless the men rowed hard to bring it to the land; but they could not: for the sea wrought, and was tempestuous against them. *(The first phrase proclaims the fact that even though they were sure about him being the cause, still, they were not certain as to what his God would do to them, inasmuch as throwing him overboard would mean his certain death. The storm was now raging, and they knew that Jehovah was the cause of such; whatever they did, they did not want to further offend the Lord.*

The phrase, "For the sea wrought, and was tempestuous against them," refers to the Lord bringing the waves against them to just an extent that it would stop their progress but not destroy their ship.)

14 Wherefore they cried unto the LORD, and said, We beseech You, O LORD, we beseech You, let us not perish for this man's life, and lay not upon us innocent blood: for You, O LORD, have done as it pleased You. *(This prayer is remarkable, considering that they neither knew nor served Jehovah!)*

JONAH CAST OVERBOARD

15 So they took up Jonah, and cast him forth into the sea: and the sea ceased from her raging. *(The phrase, "So they took up Jonah," means "with reverence." The phrase, "And cast him forth into the sea," means they did so with great regret, thinking they were certainly sending him to his doom.*

Immediately this was done, the sea ceased from her raging, showing it had been sent on Jonah's account, and that they had not sinned or committed any type of wrongdoing by executing this sentence upon him.)

16 Then the men feared the LORD exceedingly, and offered a sacrifice unto the LORD, and made vows. *(There is evidence here that they accepted Jehovah because of what they had seen. The phrase, "Then the men feared the LORD exceedingly," has reference to the Truth that they feared God even more than Jonah did, at least up to this point.*

The phrase, "And offered a Sacrifice unto the LORD," probably means that they offered up an animal immediately, which the original Text implies. Quite possibly, there was a lamb or a small calf on board, which was used for this purpose.

The short phrase, "And made vows," means

that they promised themselves to continue to offer Sacrifices unto Jehovah. Thus, their actions portray their belief in God, the renouncing of idol worship, and their conversion to Judaism.)

17 Now the LORD had prepared a great fish to swallow up Jonah. And Jonah was in the belly of the fish three days and three nights. *(The phrase, "Now the LORD had prepared a great fish," does not mean that the fish was created then and there, but that the Lord ordered it to be at a certain place and at a certain time in order to swallow Jonah.*

Frank Bullen, a famous writer of the early 1900's, states in his books that he often saw in the stomach of whales whole fish, ten to twelve times the size of a man.

The phrase, "And Jonah was in the belly of the fish three days and three nights," refers to at least 72 hours, because it spoke of three literal days and three literal nights.

The historical nature of this occurrence is even more so substantiated by Christ's reference to it as a figure of His Own Burial and Resurrection.)

CHAPTER 2
(862 B.C.)
JONAH'S PRAYER, REPENTANCE, AND DELIVERANCE

THEN Jonah prayed unto the LORD his God out of the fish's belly *(the three short words, "Then Jonah prayed," pertain to the place to which the Holy Spirit had been attempting to bring the Prophet all along)*,

2 And said, I cried by reason of my affliction unto the LORD, and He heard me; out of the belly of Hell cried I, and You heard my voice. *(In Verses 2 through 9, the Prophet quotes from eight Psalms — 120, 43, 31, 69, 18, 116, 3, 142.*

The phrase, "Out of the belly of Hell cried I, and You heard my voice," does not mean that Jonah actually went to the burning side of Hell, or even to Paradise [which, in fact, is a part of Hell]. He is using a metaphor, or a symbolism, concerning the terrible ordeal which he experienced.

As well, from the Text, there is no evidence that he literally died and was resurrected, as some teach. It basically refers to destitution and a situation so terrible, from which only the Lord could deliver.

Consequently, and with great joy, he once again says, "And You heard my voice.")

3 For You had cast me into the deep, in the midst of the seas; and the floods compassed me about: all Your billows and Your waves passed over me. *(The phrase, "For You had cast*

me into the deep, in the midst of the seas," refers to the sailors, as the agents of Divine Will, carrying out this unsavory task.

The phrase, "And the floods compassed me about: all Your billows and Your waves passed over me," pertains to the time between when he was thrown into the sea and when he was swallowed up by the "great fish." During this time, he thought he was going to drown!

No doubt, his praying commenced at that moment; however, the "belly of Hell" of Verse 2 is actually speaking of the belly of the "great fish.")

4 Then I said, I am cast out of Your sight; yet I will look again toward Your Holy Temple. *(The first phrase refers to his despair when cast overboard. His words are similar to Ps. 31:22.*

The phrase, "Yet I will look again toward Your Holy Temple," refers to him praying to the Lord and importuning Him for Mercy.)

5 The waters compassed me about, even to the soul: the depth closed me round about, the weeds were wrapped about my head. *(There is evidence that the ship in which Jonah was sailing was not very far offshore when the storm broke, because the mariners attempted to row back to shore to put Jonah back on land [Vs. 13]. Consequently, the possibility exists that the waters were not so deep at this particular place, and that he could have gone to the bottom, or nearly so, when he was thrown overboard, resulting in "weeds being wrapped about his head." The phrase, "The waters compassed me about, even to the soul," refers to Jonah nearly drowning.)*

6 I went down to the bottoms of the mountains; the Earth with her bars was about me for ever; yet have You brought up my life from corruption, O LORD my God. *(The phrase, "I went down to the bottoms of the mountains, the Earth with her bars was about me forever," expresses Jonah's near-drowning experience. The phrase, "Yet have You brought up my life from corruption," has reference to him being saved from drowning and from the "corruption" of the past few days, referring to his running from God.*

He gives the Lord all the Praise and Glory for this great act of Mercy, with the statement, "O LORD my God." The phrase shows that Jonah is now back in fellowship with the Lord!)

7 When my soul fainted within me I remembered the LORD: and my prayer came in unto You, into Your Holy Temple. *(The first phrase refers to desperation! The last phrase refers to that desperation causing him to cry unto the Lord!)*

8 They who observe lying vanities forsake their own mercy. *(The fact that suffering and*

self-ruin result from self-will and the negation of God had now become a matter of personal experience to the Prophet, for he had forsaken God and united in travel with idolaters.

The phrase, "Forsake their own mercy," is interesting indeed! It means that God is ready, able, and willing to show "Mercy" to any and all who will dare to believe Him. To forsake that is to forsake everything!)

9 But I will sacrifice unto You with the voice of thanksgiving; I will pay that that I have vowed. Salvation is of the LORD. (The phrase, "Salvation is of the LORD," presents the last lesson that proud man consents to learn; for it teaches him that he cannot contribute to his own Salvation — for what could Jonah do inside the great fish — and so, if man is to be saved, the Salvation must be wholly Divine.

The phrase, "But I will sacrifice unto You with the voice of thanksgiving," refers to the "Peace Offering," which Jonah hoped to offer when possible [Lev. 7:11-12].)

10 And the LORD spoke unto the fish, and it vomited out Jonah upon the dry land. (The phrase, "And the LORD spoke unto the fish," once again portrays the Lord in total control over all His Creation. The "fish" quickly obeyed the Lord, while Jonah did not come to this position so easily.)

CHAPTER 3
(862 B.C.)
JONAH'S SECOND COMMISSION; HIS OBEDIENCE

AND the Word of the LORD came unto Jonah the second time, saying (Chapter 1 is the story of Jonah's call and rebellion, while Chapter 2 portrays his Repentance and Salvation from what looked like certain death. Chapter 3 proclaims Jonah's preaching in Nineveh and the Repentance of that city.

The phrase, "The second time," seems to imply that Jonah earnestly sought the Lord regarding his continued commission; fearful he would do something the Lord did not desire, he waited until there was a definite re-commission. Such does not show a reticence on his part, but rather a compelling desire to please God),

2 Arise, go unto Nineveh, that great city, and preach unto it the preaching that I bid you. (The commission given here is basically the same as that given in Verse 2 of Chapter 1. There the Holy Spirit said, "Cry against it," where here He says, "Preach unto it."

The phrase, "And preach unto it the preaching that I bid you," refers to the Lord being the Author of all that Jonah was to say.)

3 So Jonah arose, and went unto Nineveh, according to the Word of the LORD. Now Nineveh was an exceeding great city of three days' journey. (The phrase, "Now Nineveh was an exceeding great city of three days' journey," concerns the size of the city and not the distance of Jonah's travel. The city was about 64 miles around, which would take a man about three days' walking to get around the city.)

4 And Jonah began to enter into the city a day's journey, and he cried, and said, Yet forty days, and Nineveh shall be overthrown. (The first phrase probably means that Jonah came into the city about 12 miles distance. The phrase, "And he cried," proclaims him standing possibly in some marketplace or at a busy intersection, lifting up his voice, loudly shouting the Message the Lord had given him. His Message was as follows: "Yet forty days, and Nineveh shall be overthrown."

As recorded in Mat. 16:1-4 and Lk. 11:30, Jonah was a "sign" to the Ninevites; that is, he was a personal illustration of the Wrath and Grace of God.)

NINEVEH REPENTED; GRANTED MERCY

5 So the people of Nineveh believed God, and proclaimed a fast, and put on sackcloth, from the greatest of them even to the least of them. (We have here one of the few times in history where people, even heathen, actually believed the Prophet sent by the Lord. As such, they repented, "from the greatest of them even to the least of them," i.e., from the king down to lowest servant.)

6 For word came unto the king of Nineveh, and he arose from his throne, and he laid his robe from him, and covered him with sackcloth, and sat in ashes. (The phrase, "For word came unto the king of Nineveh," proclaims the fact that the tokens of penitence mentioned in Verse 5 were not exhibited in obedience to any royal command; rather, as the impression made by the Prophet spread among the people, and as they adopted these modes of showing their sorrow, the news of this movement reached the king, and he put himself at the head of it.

The reigning Monarch was probably either Shalmaneser III or one of the two who succeeded him, Asshur-Danil or Asshur-Nirari.

The phrase, "And he arose from his throne," proclaims a heartfelt disposition which abdicated his lofty position as the leading Monarch of the

world in favor of Jehovah. In other words, he was saying, "Lord, You are King, and not I."

The phrase, "And he laid his robe from him," also signifies a total commitment to the commands of the Lord.

7 And he caused it to be proclaimed and published through Nineveh by the decree of the king and his nobles, saying, Let neither man nor beast, herd nor flock taste any thing: let them not feed, nor drink water *(to be sure, the "decree of the king and his nobles" in no way caused the Repentance, but was rather a result of what was already happening. Repentance cannot be legislated, and Salvation cannot be legislated. Such action always must be a "result of" rather than a "cause of"):*

8 But let man and beast be covered with sackcloth, and cry mightily unto God: yea, let them turn every one from his evil way, and from the violence that is in their hands. *(True Repentance always involves separation from evil. The phrase, "And cry mightily unto God," refers to all people, from the least to the greatest, admitting their sin before God and that they deserve destruction, but were pleading for mercy.*

The phrase, "Yea, let them turn every one from his evil way," is, as we have said, the very ingredient of Repentance. The idea is to turn from the "evil way" to "God's Way." God does not save "in sin," but instead "from sin." Therefore, the idea that the Blood of Jesus Christ is the only difference between the saved and the unsaved is facetious indeed!

The phrase, "And from the violence that is in their hands," refers to the "acts of violence" that their hands had committed. This was, in fact, the special sin of the Assyrians — always grasping after empires, oppressing other nations, and doing so with great violence. They were an extremely cruel people!)

9 Who can tell if God will turn and repent, and turn away from His fierce anger, that we perish not? *(His terminology, in the form of a question, "Who can tell if God will . . .?", proclaims an understanding of God that is of far greater dimension than most. Even though the Scripture is silent, still, it seems that Jonah may have had a personal audience with the king, for Verse 6 says, "For word came unto the king of Nineveh." It is unlikely that he would have had merely by hearsay a firm grasp of spiritual matters, which it seems he did have.*

The phrase, "That we perish not," concerns the Monarch truly believing the Word of the Lord, which is not the case with most presently!)

10 And God saw their works, that they turned from their evil way; and God repented of the evil, that He had said that He would do unto them; and He did it not. *(Fear and a sense of guilt cause a man to repent; love and a sense of pity, God; for He reserves liberty of action to Himself. With God, Repentance means a change of purpose or action and never wrongdoing on His part. With man, Repentance also means a change of purpose or action, but always refers to wrongdoing on his part.*

The phrase, "And God saw their works," does not refer to Salvation being of works, but that their faith had works, which was Repentance [James 2:26].)

CHAPTER 4
(862 B.C.)
JONAH'S DISPLEASURE, ANGER, AND COMPLAINT

BUT it displeased Jonah exceedingly, and he was very angry. *(Man's moral consciousness demands punishment for evil, and a fleshly orthodoxy requires suppression of mercy and compassion. Jonah was religiously indignant that the crimes and cruelties of Nineveh should be lightly regarded by God in this fashion and forgiven, just as a moral man is shocked at the idea that God will forgive, cleanse, and pardon in a moment's time, even the vilest of sin, upon proper confession and admission to Him [I Jn. 1:9].)*

2 And he prayed unto the LORD, and said, I pray You, O LORD, was not this my saying, when I was yet in my country? Therefore I fled before unto Tarshish: for I knew that You are a gracious God, and merciful, slow to anger, and of great kindness, and You repent of the evil. *(In this Verse, Jonah quotes Ex. 34:6 and Num. 14:18. He no doubt reasoned that a total destruction of Nineveh, manifestly Divine, would advantage his own nation spiritually and politically. It would remove her oppressor and, at the same time, convince his countrymen of the wickedness and folly of idolatry.*

As well, God's Plan was to teach Israel by the example of Nineveh how inexcusable was their own impenitence and how inevitable their ruin.

There is every evidence from his question, "Was not this my saying, when I was yet in my country?", that the Lord had already told him that Nineveh would repent, if the Message was properly delivered. Jonah did not desire this, so, at first, he refused to go.

His statement, "Therefore I fled before unto

Tarshish," tells us that he did not desire Nineveh to be spared. Such an attitude is unthinkable, but yet such attitude continues to plague the modern Church.)

3 Therefore now, O LORD, take, I beseech You, my life from me; for it is better for me to die than to live. *(First of all, Jonah probably thought that his fellow countrymen would not be happy at all with the turn of events regarding Nineveh; and of that, he was probably right. However, what others think is of little consequence; it's what God knows that counts!)*

GOD'S LESSON TO JONAH

4 Then said the LORD, Do you well to be angry? *(Irrespective of Jonah's attitude, the Lord's handling of the Prophet, as always, was with gentleness. The Lord bids him to consider whether his anger is reasonable?)*

5 So Jonah went out of the city, and sat on the east side of the city, and there made him a booth, and sat under it in the shadow, till he might see what would become of the city. *(The phrase, "So Jonah went out of the city," respects the view that he thought there still may be a possibility that God would destroy Nineveh. We see him leaving this Move of God because he took no joy in seeing the conversion of these people.)*

6 And the LORD God prepared a gourd, and made it to come up over Jonah, that it might be a shadow over his head, to deliver him from his grief. So Jonah was exceeding glad of the gourd. *(The phrase, "And the LORD God prepared a gourd," proclaims the same action as the "Lord preparing the great fish," and later "preparing the worm," and the "east wind." So, Jonah pouts, while the Lord positions.)*

7 But God prepared a worm when the morning rose the next day, and it smote the gourd that it withered. *(Religious emotions which are personal and not of the Holy Spirit can be easily affected by the provision or loss of material comforts, because such actually are not Faith. So now, the Lord will prepare a worm to smite the gourd. The Lord is teaching the Prophet that He can give and He can take away!)*

8 And it came to pass, when the sun did arise, that God prepared a vehement east wind; and the sun beat upon the head of Jonah, that he fainted, and wished in himself to die, and said, It is better for me to die than to live. *(He could have been in Nineveh rejoicing with the people at the mercy of God, but instead he is sitting out in the desert wishing to die! Self-will*

is Satanic; therefore, the Holy Spirit will go to all lengths to rid us of this malady. Someone has well said: The Lord died on Calvary not only to save us from sin, but also to save us from self.)*

9 And God said to Jonah, Do you well to be angry for the gourd? and he said, I do well to be angry, even unto death. *(It is very striking when one begins to notice the variety of names used of the Lord in these Passages [Vss. 6-9]. The production of the gourd is attributed to "Jehovah-Elohim" [Vs. 6], which is a composite name, which serves to mark the transition from "Jehovah" in Verse 4 to "Elohim" in Verses 7 and 8.*

"Jehovah" Who replies to the Prophet's complaint [Vs. 4] prepares the plant as "Elohim," the Creator, and the worm as "Ha Elohim," the Personal God.

Likewise, "Elohim," the Ruler of nature, sends the east wind to correct the Prophet's impatience. In Verse 10, "Jehovah" sums up the history and teaches the lesson to be learned from it.

Despite the Prophet's attitude, the Lord continued to be patient with him! What a wonderful Lord we serve!)

10 Then said the LORD, You have had pity on the gourd, for the which you have not laboured, neither made it grow; which came up in a night, and perished in a night *(the phrase, "For the which you have not labored, neither made it grow," refers to the Prophet having no investment whatsoever in the plant, but yet being grieved at its loss, because it represented a loss to him personally)*:

11 And should not I spare Nineveh, that great city, wherein are more than sixscore thousand *(120,000)* persons who cannot discern between their right hand and their left hand; and also much cattle? *(Many have misunderstood this Scripture, thinking that Nineveh contained only 120,000 people. However, the phrase, "Who cannot discern," is speaking only of infants. Therefore, the population of the city must have been somewhere around 500,000 or more!*

The Book ends abruptly, but its object has been accomplished. Jonah is silenced; he can make no reply; he can only confess that he is entirely wrong, and that God is righteous — hence, the reason for the Book.

Jonah learned the lesson that God would have all men to be saved, and that anything which would stand in the way of this all-important task is extremely displeasing to Him and alien to His Design.

How long Nineveh remained true to the Lord, we aren't told.)

MICAH

CHAPTER 1

(750 B.C.)

INTRODUCTION

THE Word of the LORD that came to Micah the Morasthite in the days of Jotham, Ahaz, and Hezekiah, kings of Judah, which he saw concerning Samaria and Jerusalem. *(Micah ministered at the same time as Isaiah, which was about 750 years before Christ. Of the kings mentioned here, "Jotham" was righteous, while "Ahaz" was wicked. And yet, "Hezekiah," the son of Ahaz, was one of the Godliest kings to grace the Throne [II Ki. 18:5; II Chron. 29:2].)*

SECOND ADVENT OF MESSIAH

2 Hear, all ye people; hearken, O Earth, and all that therein is: and let the Lord GOD be witness against you, the LORD from His Holy Temple. *(This Verse may read, "Adonai Jehovah shall be a witness against you." The Lord, knowing men's hearts and acquainted with every action of our lives, is truly a most powerful witness.)*

3 For, behold, the LORD comes forth out of His place, and will come down, and tread upon the high places of the Earth. *(This Verse implies God's absolute sovereignty over the universe, which He created.)*

4 And the mountains shall be molten under Him, and the valleys shall be cleft, as wax before the fire, and as the waters that are poured down a steep place. *(The language is figurative and describes the Second Coming, with the Antichrist and all his armies destroyed by the mighty Power of God. The Holy Spirit likens His Power as so Almighty that "mountains shall be molten [melted] under Him.")*

THE SINS OF JUDAH AND ISRAEL

5 For the transgression of Jacob is all this, and for the sins of the house of Israel. What is the transgression of Jacob? is it not Samaria? and what are the high places of Judah? are they not Jerusalem? *(The transgression of Jacob was the idol worship set up at Samaria; and the sins of the high places of Judah, the idolatrous*

altar set up in Jerusalem. The Prophecy suddenly shifts from a portrayal of the Second Coming, which has not even yet happened, back to the sins of Judah and Israel.)*

ISRAEL'S CAPTIVITY BY ASSYRIA

6 Therefore I will make Samaria as an heap of the field, and as plantings of a vineyard: and I will pour down the stones thereof into the valley, and I will discover the foundations thereof. *(The terminology of this Passage tells us that this Prophecy was delivered before the destruction of Samaria in the fourth year of Hezekiah.)*

7 And all the graven images thereof shall be beaten to pieces, and all the hires thereof shall be burned with the fire, and all the idols thereof will I lay desolate: for she gathered it of the hire of an harlot, and they shall return to the hire of an harlot. *(The words, "The hires thereof," refer to the costly vessels donated to the idol temples. The phrase, "For she gathered it," speaks of the wealth gained by idolatry, which would be carried off by the Assyrian idolaters.)*

LAMENTATION FOR ISRAEL

8 Therefore I will wail and howl, I will go stripped and naked: I will make a wailing like the dragons, and mourning as the owls. *(The idea of Verses 8 through 16 refers to the lamentation for Israel. At this time, Samaria was rich, prosperous, and strong! Therefore, the notion that the time was shortly coming that this city and its people would "wail and howl," denoting tremendous suffering and pain, was strange to the ears of the people.*

The phrase, "Go stripped and naked," denotes captivity; therefore, the destruction would be total!)

9 For her wound is incurable; for it is come unto Judah; he is come unto the gate of My people, even to Jerusalem. *(The phrase, "For her wound is incurable," pertains to the terrible sin of Samaria, which was so deep that even Repentance at this late hour, although saving the soul, could not save the nation.*

The phrase, "He is come unto the gate of My

people, even to Jerusalem," predicts that Sennacherib will come to the gate of Jerusalem, but no further; for the city was delivered in answer to Hezekiah's prayer, thereby fulfilling the Prophecy of Micah [II Chron., Chpt. 32; Isa., Chpt. 37].)

10 Declare ye it not at Gath, weep ye not at all: in the house of Aphrah roll yourself in the dust. *(The destructive and triumphant march of the Assyrian host upon Jerusalem is poetically described in Verses 10 through 16, and a corresponding description appears in Isa. 10:28-32. The towns would call to each other for help, and Jerusalem would appeal to them all for assistance, but in vain.)*

11 Pass ye away, you inhabitant of Saphir, having your shame naked: the inhabitant of Zaanan came not forth in the mourning of Bethezel; he shall receive of you his standing. *(The idea of this Verse is: if the Lord had not delivered Jerusalem from the Assyrians, it could not have been delivered!)*

12 For the inhabitant of Maroth waited carefully for good: but evil came down from the LORD unto the gate of Jerusalem. *(This refers, as stated, to the proposed invasion of Jerusalem by Sennacherib, and it being stopped at the very "gate of Jerusalem." Even though the army of the Assyrians did not come this far, still, Rabshakeh, who headed up the Assyrian expedition, did stand before the gate at Jerusalem to deliver his haughty message, as described by Isaiah [Isa., Chpt 36].)*

13 O thou inhabitant of Lachish, bind the chariot to the swift beast: she is the beginning of the sin to the daughter of Zion: for the transgressions of Israel were found in you. *(In a short time, the Northern Kingdom of Samaria [Israel] would fall; however, it would be about 10 years before Sennacherib would make his foray against Jerusalem.*

"Lachish" was about 30 miles southwest of Jerusalem. It was taken by Sennacherib, as well as most all of Judah, with the exception of Jerusalem, as predicted here by the Prophet.)

14 Therefore shall you give presents to Moresheth-gath: the houses of Achzib shall be a lie to the kings of Israel. *(Lachish had introduced Samaria's idolatry to Zion; the Lord, accordingly, gave Lachish to Sennacherib.)*

15 Yet will I bring an heir unto you, O inhabitant of Mareshah: he shall come unto Adullam the glory of Israel. *(The first phrase refers to Sennacherib, whom God appointed as heir to the inhabitants of the city of Mareshah. The phrase, "He shall come unto Adullam the*

glory of Israel," means that when Sennacherib would lay siege to these cities, some of its richest nobility would flee to the cave of Adullam.)

16 Make you bald, and poll you for your delicate children; enlarge your baldness as the eagle; for they are gone into captivity from you. *(The phrase, "For they are gone into captivity from you," actually has reference to the Fall of Jerusalem some 133 years after the Fall of the Northern Kingdom of Samaria.*

Very few captives were taken by Sennacherib in his expedition into Judah. His plan certainly was terminated by the visitation of the Angel who killed 185,000 Assyrian soldiers in one night [II Ki. 19:35]. Therefore, the prediction would leap ahead to the Babylonian captivity, when Jerusalem would be completely destroyed, with the Temple razed to the ground and with tens of thousands taken captive to Babylonia.)

CHAPTER 2
(730 B.C.)
THE SINS OF ISRAEL

WOE to them who devise iniquity, and work evil upon their beds! when the morning is light, they practise it, because it is in the power of their hand. *(The first phrase pertains to men planning iniquity, to whom, in turn, the Lord will plan calamity. The phrase, "Because it is in the power of their hand," means that they had the ability to do so; therefore, in their eyes, their might makes right.*

As well, the Hebrew has the idea of this translation, "Because it is in the power of their hand, which is their god.")

2 And they covet fields, and take them by violence; and houses, and take them away: so they oppress a man and his house, even a man and his heritage. *(The Commandment against coveting [Ex. 20:17] taught the Jews that God regards sins of thought as well as of action.)*

JUDGMENT ON ALL ISRAEL

3 Therefore thus saith the LORD; Behold, against this family do I devise an evil, from which you shall not remove your necks; neither shall you go haughtily: for this time is evil. *(The first phrase proclaims the fact that as they devised evil, God devised a penalty. The phrase, "From which you shall not remove your necks," means that even though some may escape man's vengeance, none will escape God's!*

The phrase, "Neither shall you go haughtily,"

means with head erect. In other words, their pride would be brought low. The short phrase, "For this time is evil," refers to that which is planned for them, which speaks of the coming Assyrian invasion.)

LAMENTATION FOR ISRAEL

4 In that day shall one take up a parable against you, and lament with a doleful lamentation, and say, We be utterly spoiled: he has changed the portion of My people: how has He removed it from me! turning away He has divided our fields. *(Man generally blames God as the Author of the evils which his own sins cause. God has not "changed" or broken His Covenant, as Verses 12 and 13 prove; but, in a just anger, He divided the fields of Israel to the invader.*

The words, "Turning away He has divided our fields," means that "to an apostate He divided our fields." The apostate is the king of Assyria, and then later Chaldea.)

5 Therefore you shall have none who shall cast a cord by lot in the congregation of the LORD. *(The phrase, "[To] cast a cord," means to measure a farm. They had abused the privilege of owning the land, as is described in Verse 3, and now they would suffer its loss.*

As a result, there would be no one else going into the Temple, i.e., "the congregation of the LORD," checking these various boundaries, as originally designed by the Holy Spirit through Joshua, as they had done for centuries. The land would no longer belong to them, but would be confiscated by the heathen.)

SINS AND JUDGMENT ON THE HOUSE OF JACOB

6 Prophesy ye not, say they to them who prophesy: they shall not prophesy to them, that they shall not take shame. *(Israel refused the testimony of Truth; by a just judgment, it was replaced by a spirit of falsehood. If men will not listen to the Holy Spirit, they will be condemned to listen to the unholy one.*

The phrase, "Prophesy ye not," was directed at Micah by the false prophets, and also by the people who took the side of the false prophets.)

7 O you who are named the house of Jacob, is the Spirit of the LORD straitened? are these His doings? do not My Words do good to him who walks uprightly? *(The first question of the Verse should have been translated, "Is the Spirit*

of the LORD shortened?", meaning, "Does He not know what He is saying, and to whom He is saying it?" In effect, Micah is saying that when they criticized him, they were criticizing the Lord, and, more so, the Spirit of God.

The second question of the Verse holds the key. God's "Words" toward people will be a blessing only if they will "walk uprightly," i.e., "abide by the Word of God.")

8 Even of late My people is risen up as an enemy: you pull of the robe with the garment from them who pass by securely as men averse from war. *(The phrase, "Even of late My People is risen up as an enemy," implies recent action — and repeated. These were not old offenses of which the Lord was speaking, but sins of recent and daily occurrence.*

The last phrase has to do with the poorest of the poor in the land being treated as badly as prisoners of war.)

9 The women of My people have you cast out from their pleasant houses; from their children have you taken away My glory for ever. *(The first phrase refers to the widows, who ought to have been protected and cared for. The phrase, "Have you cast out," refers to violent expulsion, which saw them literally thrown on the street without any means of support. The last phrase refers to the setting aside of the Law of Moses, which is called here "My Glory," and which the children, the coming generation, would not be privileged to have.*

Such was totally true, for in a few years the Northern Kingdom of Israel was totally destroyed by Assyria, with tens, if not hundreds, of thousands of people being led away into slavery, where they would never again have the privilege of living according to the Law of Moses.)

10 Arise ye, and depart; for this is not your rest: because it is polluted, it shall destroy you, even with a sore destruction. *(The phrase, "Arise ye, and depart," concerns the Lord taking action on these heartless oppressors by promising them that they would be banished from their homes and land, even as they had torn others from their homes. What they measured would be measured unto them again [Mat. 7:2].*

The phrase, "For this is not your rest," refers to Canaan as a resting place for Israel, actually, their own Promised Land [Deut. 12:9-10; Josh. 1:13]. However, this land is about to be taken from them and given to oppressors [the Assyrians], with the people being sold as slaves.

The reason? "Because it is polluted," which refers to the land being polluted by the sins of

its inhabitants. Consequently, "it shall destroy you, even with a sore destruction," which speaks of the land vomiting the people out.)

11 If a man walking in the spirit and falsehood do lie, saying, I will prophesy unto you of wine and of strong drink; he shall even be the prophet of this people. *(The phrase, "If a man walking in the spirit [evil spirit] and falsehood do lie," speaks of false prophets, who prophesied by a lying spirit of falsehood and deceit. The phrase, "I will prophesy unto you of wine and of strong drink," does not necessarily refer to literal "wine" and "strong drink," but rather to "temporal blessings." In other words, they dwelt on God's Promises of material prosperity. As such, they were identical to the modern false prophets of the "Greed Gospel."*

The phrase, "He shall even be the prophet of this people," pertains to the ones who were popular, i.e., those preaching the "Greed Gospel," namely, the ones to whom the people would listen.)

SECOND ADVENT OF THE MESSIAH

12 I will surely assemble, O Jacob, all of you; I will surely gather the remnant of Israel; I will put them together as the sheep of Bozrah, as the flock in the midst of their fold: they shall make great noise by reason of the multitude of men. *(To the unknowing eye and ear, it may seem as if the Twelfth Verse is totally unconnected to the Eleventh. However, such is not the case!*

In Verse 11, Micah was pointing out the false prophets who were promising peace and prosperity now. In Verse 12, he tells the people that it is certainly true that peace and prosperity is coming. Still, it would be a long way off. At present, it has been about 2,700 years, and this Prophecy is still not fulfilled; but it most certainly shall be in the future.

The phrase, "I will surely assemble, O Jacob, all of you," actually refers to the Second Coming of Christ. This is known because such has never happened in the past and will only happen at that Coming Glad Day.

The phrase, "I will surely gather the remnant of Israel," refers to sure Repentance on Israel's part and them gladly gathering at the Banner of Christ, with Him now being their Shepherd, even as He always wanted to be [Mat. 23:37].)

13 The breaker is come up before them: they have broken up, and have passed through the gate, and are gone out by it: and their king shall pass before them, and the LORD on the head of them. *("The breaker" is the Antichrist, the one making a breach. The last phrase has to do with the triumphant entry of Christ, which will take place immediately after the Second Coming, which this Verse portrays; at this time, Christ will then be accepted, not only as "Lord," but also as Messiah.)*

CHAPTER 3
(710 B.C.)
THE SINS OF THE RULERS OF ISRAEL

A ND I said, Hear, I pray you, O heads of Jacob, and you princes of the house of Israel; Is it not for you to know judgment? *(This Scripture is addressed to the Magistrates. The question, "Is it not for you to know judgment?", refers to the fact that they, of all men, should know and practice what is just and fair.)*

2 Who hate the good, and love the evil; who pluck off their skin from off them, and their flesh from off their bones *(the first phrase proclaims these Magistrates as hating the Bible and loving their own laws and ways, which were "evil." The last phrase speaks of greatly oppressing the poor, charging exorbitant rates of interest, and being bribed in order to circumvent the law, etc.);*

3 Who also eat the flesh of My people, and flay their skin from off them; and they break their bones, and chop them in pieces, as for the pot, and as flesh within the caldron. *(The idea is: the people are treated as animals, such as cattle or sheep, etc., chopped and broken up as meat for the cook-pot. Once the Word of God, as here, is violated, cruelty becomes the norm.)*

JUDGMENT ON ISRAEL'S LEADERS

4 Then shall they cry unto the LORD, but He will not hear them: He will even hide His face from them at that time, as they have behaved themselves ill in their doings. *(The pronoun "they" refers to the Magistrates. The phrase, "But He will not hear them," is fearsome indeed, in that their only hope of help is now cut off. The phrase, "He will even hide His Face from them at that time," refers to the time of the coming Assyrian invasion. It refers back to 2:3. The last phrase, "As they have behaved themselves ill in their doings," means that men cannot do ill and fare well.)*

JUDGMENT ON THE PROPHETS

5 Thus saith the LORD concerning the

prophets who make My people err, who bite with their teeth, and cry, Peace; and he who puts not into their mouths, they even prepare war against Him. *(The first phrase refers to the lying prophets of whom Jeremiah also complained [Lam. 2:14]. The phrase, "Who bite with their teeth," refers to an abundance of food, and is another way of expressing the "peace and prosperity" proclaimed by these false prophets.*

The phrase, "And cry, Peace," refers to the fashionable preacher proclaiming "Peace," i.e., that there is no future Wrath of God, no Lake of Fire, and no Judgment to come. The True Preacher, as in Verse 8, denounces sin and announces Judgment. The phrase, "And he who puts not into their mouths," pertains to these preachers who preach for large salaries; they, therefore, trim their message according to what they are paid.

The phrase, "They even prepare war against him," pertains to the false prophets being at war with the True Prophets.)

6 Therefore night shall be unto you, that you shall not have a vision; and it shall be dark unto you, that you shall not divine; and the sun shall go down over the prophets, and the day shall be dark over them. *(The gist of this Verse is: at the time of this coming judgment, all the false preachers shall be confounded. They shall cover their lips, i.e., be compelled to silence, for they shall have no answer from God.)*

7 Then shall the seers be ashamed, and the diviners confounded: yea, they shall all cover their lips; for there is no answer of God. *(The phrase, "Then shall the seers be ashamed," refers to the false prophets, who prognosticated peace and prosperity, but instead saw the very opposite. They will be "ashamed" because their oracles are proved to be delusive.*

The phrase, "And the diviner confounded," pertains to the fact that everything they said was utterly wrong. The phrase, "For there is no answer of God," means that what the false prophets said was not from God, even though they claimed it was. It was instead out of their own minds.)

MICAH, A TRUE PROPHET

8 But truly I am full of power by the Spirit of the LORD, and of Judgment, and of Might, to declare unto Jacob his transgression, and to Israel his sin. *(In contrast to the false prophets, Micah says the very opposite; actually, he claims three things in the Text, and the Holy Spirit says it is so:*

1. Full of Power by the Spirit.

2. A Correct Judgment of the Word of God.

3. And of Might, which refers to the Anointing of the Holy Spirit, Who helped him to deliver the Message.)

SINS OF THE LEADERS

9 Hear this, I pray you, ye heads of the house of Jacob, and princes of the house of Israel, who abhor judgment, and pervert all equity. *(Micah, after projecting what the future will be for these false prophets and their followers, now reverts back to the present. He plainly and bluntly advises the spiritual leadership of both Israel and Judah to "hear this." As usual, it would not be a Message they desired to hear, but instead one which angered them greatly!)*

10 They build up Zion with blood, and Jerusalem with iniquity. *(The idea is: great palaces were built with money gained by extortion, rape, and judicial murders, like that of Naboth [I Ki., Chpt. 21]. The phrase, "And Jerusalem with iniquity," refers to gain, but by unlawful means.)*

11 The heads thereof judge for reward, and the priests thereof teach for hire, and the prophets thereof divine for money: yet will they lean upon the LORD, and say, Is not the LORD among us? none evil can come upon us. *(The phrase, "The heads thereof judge for reward," means that they took bribes. The "priests" taught what the people wanted to hear instead of what they needed to hear. They were thereby paid well. Also, the false prophets sold their revelations, pretending they came from God. They "divine for money"!*

In all of this, they claimed they were doing the Will of the Lord and that "no evil can come upon us." They claimed God as the Author of their prosperity, and that Micah's predictions of coming judgment were facetious.)

DESTRUCTION OF JERUSALEM
AND THE TEMPLE

12 Therefore shall Zion for your sake be plowed as a field, and Jerusalem shall become heaps, and the mountain of the house as the high places of the forest. *(This is the Prophecy quoted by the elders to King Jehoiakim [Jer. 26:18]. The phrase, "Therefore shall Zion for your sake be plowed as a field," was not fulfilled when Nebuchadnezzar later took the city, but was fulfilled with its destruction by Titus in*

A.D. 70. At that time, the Temple was completely razed, with plows actually run over the very ground on which it sat.

The destruction on Samaria [1:6] and that on Jerusalem were similar — both a heap of stones — but the causes, dissimilar. Doctrine doomed Samaria; conduct, Jerusalem.)

CHAPTER 4
(710 B.C.)

MILLENNIAL RESTORATION; MESSIAH'S KINGDOM

BUT in the last days it shall come to pass, that the mountain of the House of the LORD shall be established in the top of the mountains, and it shall be exalted above the hills; and people shall flow unto it. (Verses 1 through 3 are quoted virtually verbatim in Isa. 2:1-4; however, which Prophet gave them first is not actually known. Micah also prophesied during the time of Isaiah, at least in Isaiah's early years. This Verse speaks of the coming Kingdom Age!)

2 And many nations shall come, and say, Come, and let us go up to the mountain of the LORD, and to the House of the God of Jacob; and he will teach us of His ways, and we will walk in His paths: for the Law shall go forth of Zion, and the Word of the LORD from Jerusalem. (The phrase, "And many nations shall come, and say, Come," presents the new revelation of Righteousness, which shall be so conspicuous and so attractive that all men shall hear and desire to become partakers of it.

The phrase, "And let us go up to the mountain of the LORD, and to the House of the God of Jacob," presents the Gentiles coming to the Temple from all over the world. Then they will do what the Lord intended for them to do all along [Mk. 11:17].

The phrase, "For the Law shall go forth of Zion, and the Word of the LORD from Jerusalem," does not really pertain to the Mosaic Law, but instead a rule for life [Prov. 6:23]. This is the reason given by the Prophet for the eagerness of the nations to resort to Christ in Jerusalem.)

UNIVERSAL PEACE

3 And He shall judge among many people, and rebuke strong nations afar off; and they shall beat their swords into plowshares, and their spears into pruninghooks: nation shall not lift up a sword against nation, neither shall they learn war any more. (The phrase, "And He shall judge among many people," means to "arbitrate between." The result of His arbitration and reproving will be the abolition of war and the establishment of universal peace and prosperity.

The phrase, "And rebuke strong nations afar off," actually means to "act as umpire for" disputes and differences. The arbitration of the sword shall no more be used.

The last three phrases of the Verse speak of the fact that the economy of the world, which, to a certain degree, has always been geared for war, will now be geared for peace.)

UNIVERSAL PROSPERITY

4 But they shall sit every man under his vine and under his fig tree; and none shall make them afraid; for the mouth of the LORD of Hosts has spoken it. (The phrase taken from the midst of this Verse, "And none shall make them afraid," is undoubtedly one of the greatest statements ever made. Fear will be a thing of the past, because that which brings about fear is now gone, "for the mouth of the LORD of Hosts has spoken it.")

SPIRITUAL COMMITMENT

5 For all people will walk every one in the name of his god, and we will walk in the name of the LORD our God for ever and ever. (The first phrase, "For all people will walk every one in the name of his god," has reference to the time in which Micah lived, as well as before and after. It refers to idol worship by the nations, or their rejection of the Lord of Glory, etc., as most have done for all these many centuries.

However, Micah says, "And we will walk in the name of the LORD our God forever and ever," meaning that Israel's God is the only True God; despite Israel's failings, this must never be lost.

The idea is: Israel's God, "The LORD our God," will ultimately lead the nations of the world out of idolatry into true worship. This will be during the coming Kingdom Age!)

RESTORATION OF ISRAEL: AN ETERNAL NATION UNDER THE MESSIAH

6 In that day, saith the LORD, will I assemble her who halts, and I will gather her who is driven out, and her whom I have afflicted (the first phrase refers to "Jacob," who

did not become "Israel" till he was maimed. So, "Jacob," as a nation, will not be restored and blessed until she is spiritually maimed by affliction, hence fulfilling the last phrase, "And her whom I have afflicted." This Verse speaks of Israel's restoration. Israel, which was driven out, will now be brought back);

7 And I will make her who halted a remnant, and her who was cast far off a strong nation: and the LORD shall reign over them in mount Zion from henceforth, even for ever. *(The phrase, "And I will make her who halted a remnant," refers to the portion of Israel which will come out of the Great Tribulation [Zech. 13:8]. The phrase, "And her who was cast far off a strong nation," refers to them being "cast far off" after their Crucifixion of Christ, but now being regathered. As well, of this small remnant, the Lord will make a "strong nation." The last phrase proclaims the certitude of these Prophecies.)*

8 And you, O tower of the flock, the strong hold of the daughter of Zion, unto you shall it come, even the first dominion; the kingdom shall come to the daughter of Jerusalem. *(The phrase, "And you, O tower of the flock," refers to Jerusalem. The phrase, "The stronghold of the daughter of Zion, unto you shall it come," is wrapped up in the phrase, "Even the first dominion," which speaks of the former dominion under Solomon.*

To assure the doubting heart, the Spirit adds: "The Kingdom shall come to the daughter of Jerusalem," i.e., the second dominion, which is not named, but implied, referring to the coming restoration. Hence it is called "the daughter of. . . ." Micah is predicting the restoration of that Kingdom, which will take place in the Kingdom Age.)

BABYLONIAN CAPTIVITY FIRST

9 Now why do you cry out aloud? is there no king in you? is your counsellor perished? for pangs have taken you as a woman in travail. *(The "Now" of Verses 9, 11, and 5:1 should instead read, "Meanwhile." That is, during the long period preceding restoration, the Hebrew people shall suffer extreme affliction. That affliction has now lasted for about 2,500 years.)*

10 Be in pain, and labour to bring forth, O daughter of Zion, like a woman in travail: for now shall you go forth out of the city, and you shall dwell in the field, and you shall go even to Babylon; there shall you be delivered;

there the LORD shall redeem you from the hand of your enemies. *(The first phrase was partially fulfilled with Babylonian captivity, but will be totally fulfilled in the coming Great Tribulation. The phrase, "And you shall go even to Babylon," was fulfilled approximately 150 years from the time of this Prophecy. The phrase, "There shall you be delivered," refers to the conclusion of their seventy years of captivity, with a remnant being brought back to Judah and Jerusalem.)*

ISRAEL TO BE REESTABLISHED; THE KINGDOM TO BE SET UP

11 Now also many nations are gathered against you, that say, Let her be defiled, and let our eye look upon Zion. *(The Holy Spirit now jumps from the coming servitude to Babylon to the distant Great Tribulation and the Battle of Armageddon, which is described in the phrase, "Now also many nations are gathered against you" [Zech. 14:14-15].)*

12 But they know not the thoughts of the LORD, neither understand they His counsel: for He shall gather them as the sheaves into the floor. *(The nations of the world at that time will not understand that it is the Lord Who is gathering them to the Battle of Armageddon [Rev. 16:14-16]. The phrase, "Neither understand they His counsel," refers to His employing Israel as His instrument to judge them there, as is outlined in the next Verse.)*

13 Arise and thresh, O daughter of Zion: for I will make your horn iron, and I will make your hoofs brass: and you shall beat in pieces many people: and I will consecrate their gain unto the LORD, and their substance unto the Lord of the whole Earth. *(The phrase, "Arise and thresh, O daughter of Zion," refers to Israel being given supernatural strength and ability at the Second Coming. As such, she will throw off the Antichrist and his armies, but with the help of the Lord. At that time, the wealth of the nations will be gathered from the battlefield of Armageddon and divided in the midst of victorious Judah.)*

CHAPTER 5
(710 B.C.)

THE FIRST ADVENT OF THE MESSIAH; HIS REDEMPTIVE WORK

NOW gather yourself in troops, O daughter of troops: he has laid siege against us:

they shall smite the judge of Israel with a rod upon the cheek. *(Verses 1 and 2 have to do with the First Advent of the Messiah and His Redemptive Work. The phrase, "Now gather yourself in troops, O daughter of troops," refers to Judah. The word "troops" is used because of the coming invasion of Titus, the Roman General.*

The phrase, "They shall smite the Judge of Israel with a rod upon the cheek," speaks of the mockers and persecutors of the Messiah, both Jews and Romans [Mat. 26:68; 27:30]. To "smite upon the cheek" is the grossest insult, and was done repeatedly to Christ.

It is interesting that the Holy Spirit refers to Christ as "the Judge!" To be sure, that He certainly is, but not only the Judge of Israel, but of all men [Mat. 25:31-46; Acts 17:31].)

2 But you, Beth-lehem Ephratah, though you be little among the thousands of Judah, yet out of you shall He come forth unto Me Who is to be Ruler in Israel; Whose goings forth have been from of old, from everlasting. *(The question could be asked as to why the Holy Spirit would give these Prophecies in this fashion, having little or no chronological order? The answer probably falls into the same category as to why the Lord, in His earthly Ministry, mostly spoke in Parables [Lk. 8:10].*

The phrase, "But you, Bethlehem Ephratah," speaks of the birthplace of Christ. The phrase, "Though you be little among the thousands of Judah," signifies a small place, though the birthplace of David, as well! The phrase, "Yet out of you shall He come forth unto Me, Who is to be Ruler in Israel," speaks of Christ coming from the Tribe of Judah. This was prophesied by Jacob long before [Gen. 49:10].

The phrase, "Whose goings forth have been from of old, from everlasting," is meant to portray to any and all that this is not just any person, but rather, as Isaiah prophesied, "Immanuel, God with us" [Isa. 7:14].)

ISRAEL GIVEN UP UNTIL HER REPENTANCE

3 Therefore will He give them up, until the time that she which travails has brought forth: then the remnant of His brethren shall return unto the children of Israel. *(The phrase, "Therefore will He give them up," refers to their rejection of the Judge of Israel at His First Advent and their consequent destruction at the hands of Titus in A.D. 70. The phrase, "Until the time that she which travails has brought forth," has*

already been about 2,000 years; however, the time of Israel's great "travail" has not yet come, but will take place in the latter half of the coming Great Tribulation [I Thess. 5:3].

The phrase, "Then the remnant of His brethren shall return unto the children of Israel," refers to Israel's conversion to Christ at the Second Coming [Isa. 66:7-8; Zech. 10:12-13:1; Rom. 11:25-29].)

ISRAEL TO BE DELIVERED FROM THE ANTICHRIST AT THE MESSIAH'S SECOND ADVENT

4 And He shall stand and feed in the strength of the LORD, in the majesty of the name of the LORD His God; and they shall abide: for now shall He be great unto the ends of the Earth. *(The phrase, "And He shall stand and feed in the strength of the LORD," refers to the "Ruler" or "Shepherd," i.e., the Messiah. The word "feed" concerns the Lord feeding His flock, with them allowing Him to feed them, which they would not do upon His First Advent.*

The phrase, "And they shall abide," refers to His sheep [Israel] dwelling in permanent security. The phrase, "For now shall He be great unto the ends of the Earth," speaks to His "Strength" and "Majesty" being great, not only in Israel, but all over the world.

In effect, at that time, there will be a one-world government, with Christ as its Head [Isa. 9:6].)

5 And this Man shall be the Peace, when the Assyrian shall come into our land: and when he shall tread in our palaces, then shall we raise against him seven shepherds, and eight principal men. *(The phrase, "And this Man shall be the Peace," refers to Christ, Who will come at the time of the Battle of Armageddon, defeating the Antichrist and restoring Israel. The phrase, "When the Assyrian shall come into our land," refers to the Antichrist. The phrase, "And when he shall tread in our palaces," concerns the time that the Antichrist will break his seven-year covenant with Israel and take over the future Jewish Temple at Jerusalem [Dan. 9:27; 11:44-45; Mat. 24:15; II Thess. 2:3-4; Rev. 11:1-2].*

The phrase, "Then shall we raise against him seven shepherds, and eight principal men," leaves no clue as to who these are. Possibly the meaning is in the numbers. "Seven" refers to God's perfect number, denoting completion, totality, and perfection, which could refer to a total victory.

"Eight" pertains to God's Resurrection number, and could denote the resurrection of Israel.)

6 And they shall waste the land of Assyria with the sword, and the land of Nimrod in the entrances thereof: thus shall He deliver us from the Assyrian, when He comes into our land, and when He treads within our borders. *(The first phrase speaks of the supernatural strength which will be given to the army of Israel at the Coming of the Lord. The phrase, "And the land of Nimrod in the entrances thereof," refers to Babylon; from this description, therefore, it seems that the Battle of Armageddon will cover not only the Land of Israel but also the entirety of the Middle East.*

The phrase, "Thus shall He deliver us from the Assyrian," proclaims Christ defeating the Antichrist, which will be at the Battle of Armageddon [Ezek., Chpts. 38-39]. The last phrase concerns the Antichrist invading Israel and the anger of God aroused because of the audacity of this man.)

ISRAEL WILL BE RESTORED WHEN THE MESSIAH RETURNS

7 And the remnant of Jacob shall be in the midst of many people as a dew from the LORD, as the showers upon the grass, that tarries not for man, nor waits for the sons of men. *(In that great day of Restoration, the nation of Israel will be to the world as "Dew" and as a "Lion" [Vs. 8]; that is, they will be the channel of Divine Grace toward the obedient and the instrument of Divine Wrath upon the rebels. Both energies are independent of human cooperation.*

The phrase, "And the remnant of Jacob," means that the number will be few — but, O so mighty! The last phrase tells us that in that day, i.e., at the beginning of the Kingdom Age, Israel's supernatural strength and ability will be wholly from God and not dependent whatsoever upon man.)

8 And the remnant of Jacob shall be among the Gentiles in the midst of many people as a lion among the beasts of the forest, as a young lion among the flocks of sheep: who, if he go through, both treads down, and tears in pieces, and none can deliver. *(It is interesting that the Holy Spirit would continue to use the phrase, "And the remnant of Jacob," denoting its small numbers, but yet expressing its tremendous Might. That Might is Christ. This portrays Israel as a terrible power among the nations and invincible in strength.*

The phrase, "Shall be among the Gentiles," refers to every nation in the world. Furthermore, she will be "in the midst of many people as a lion among the beasts of the forest," meaning that she is the king of the forest [nations] as a "Lion" is king of the beasts. She is that because Jesus is the "Lion of the Tribe of Judah" [Rev. 5:5].

The phrase, "As a young lion among the flocks of sheep," portrays the fact that all other nations of the world will be in comparison to Him, and also to Israel, as a lamb is to a lion.

The last phrase refers perhaps to some few, who, at the outset, may seek to test His Power. They will be quickly dispatched, because "none can deliver" out of His Hand! As Jesus is the True Man, the True Church, He is also the "True Israel.")

9 Your hand shall be lifted up upon your adversaries, and all your enemies shall be cut off. *(In that day, the Kingdom Age, there will be no such thing as Buddhism, Islam, Mormonism, Hinduism, etc. All "enemies shall be cut off.")*

10 And it shall come to pass in that day, saith the LORD, that I will cut off your horses out of the midst of you, and I will destroy your chariots *(this simply means that the nations of the world will disarm [Isa. 2:4])*:

11 And I will cut off the cities of your land, and throw down all your strong holds *(the "cities" and "strongholds" mentioned here refer to centers of idolatry, etc. Consequently, Rome, as the seat of Catholicism, will be totally changed. Bangkok, as the center of Buddhism, will also be changed! Mecca, in Saudi Arabia, will be changed, and totally. Every vestige of demon worship, which centers up in these false religions, will be totally eliminated; therefore, Salt Lake City, as the center of Mormonism, will be no more, at least in that capacity)*:

12 And I will cut off witchcrafts out of your hand; and you shall have no more soothsayers *(in fact, at that time, and we speak of the Kingdom Age, every demon spirit, every fallen angel, and Satan will be in the bottomless pit [Rev. 20:1-3])*:

13 Your graven images also will I cut off, and your standing images out of the midst of you; and you shall no more worship the work of your hands. *(Every vestige of religion will be eliminated. A part of the reason why Cain's sacrifice was rejected was because it was a "work of his hands," and not a "Work of God's Hands." Only the true worship of Christ will remain, and that speaks of the Crucified Christ [Zech. 13:6].)*

14 And I will pluck up your groves out of the midst of you: so will I destroy your cities. *(These Verses constitute the remaking of this planet, which includes all of its civilizations and societies, with every evil way eliminated.)*

15 And I will execute vengeance in anger and fury upon the heathen, such as they have not heard. *(The phrase, "Such as they have not heard," actually means "which have not hearkened." In other words, all who are disobedient will not be allowed to continue in this rebellion, but will quickly experience the "anger and fury" of the Lord. That which has caused the pain and suffering of the past will not be allowed to take root in the coming Kingdom Age.*

The phrase, "And I will execute vengeance," speaks of a swift retribution on those who will try the metal of Christ, so to speak!)

CHAPTER 6
(710 B.C.)
THE LORD'S CONTENTION WITH ISRAEL

H EAR ye now what the LORD says; Arise, contend thou before the mountains, and let the hills hear your voice. *(In view of the tremendous Prophecies given through Micah by the Holy Spirit concerning Israel, the Prophet will now make a strident appeal to the people in order that some of them, hopefully, will repent.*

The phrase, "Arise, contend thou," has reference to the fact that Micah's task will not be easy. In effect, he is contending with a rebellious, stiff-necked, hard-hearted people!)

2 Hear ye, O mountains, the LORD'S controversy, and ye strong foundations of the Earth: for the LORD has a controversy with His people, and He will plead with Israel. *(The phrase, "Hear ye, O mountains, the LORD's controversy," is strong indeed! Once again, the creation of nature is called upon as a witness. The phrase, "For the LORD has a controversy with His People," makes the "controversy" extremely personal. He calls them "His People," even though they are no longer living for Him, and they are actually heading rapidly toward an eternal doom.)*

3 O My people, what have I done unto you? and wherein have I wearied you? testify against Me. *(In the entirety of the Bible, no "pleading" is done so graphically and tenderly as is here brought out. The phrase, "Testify against Me," is the same as a Court of Law. The Lord is bringing forth His case and He demands that Israel bring forth her case. It must be quickly said that throughout the entirety of the* Earth, and for all time, no person can stand and honestly *"testify against God"* that He has wronged them in any way.)*

4 For I brought you up out of the land of Egypt, and redeemed you out of the house of servants; and I sent before you Moses, Aaron, and Miriam. *(The Lord reminds Israel that He is their Saviour. As well, He gave them great leadership in Moses, Aaron, and Miriam.)*

5 O My people, remember now what Balak king of Moab consulted, and what Balaam the son of Beor answered him from Shittim unto Gilgal; that you may know the righteousness of the LORD. *(A period should follow the word "him" and the word "remember" should be repeated before "from Shittim unto Gilgal." The idea of this Verse is as follows: After Israel experienced the great deliverance from Egyptian bondage, they now faced the sorcery of "Balak king of Moab." The word "consulted" refers to the manner in which the snare against Israel would be laid. "Balak" would employ "Balaam the son of Beor," seeking to ensnare Israel. It is recorded in Num., Chpts. 23-24.*

The phrase, "Remember from Shittim unto Gilgal," speaks of "Shittim" as the Israelite's last station before crossing the Jordan, and "Gilgal," the first in the land of Canaan. God bids them "remember" all that happened to them between those places — their sin in Shittim and the mercy then shown them [Num., Chpt. 25], the miraculous passage of the Jordan, and the renewal of the Covenant at Gilgal [Josh. 5:9].)

THE REQUIREMENTS OF THE LORD

6 Wherewith shall I come before the LORD, and bow myself before the High God? shall I come before Him with Burnt Offerings, with calves of a year old? *(Even though the tone changes slightly, still, this is the Lord continuing to speak to Israel, in effect, telling Israel what she must do. Israel now held the idea that the ritual of Sacrifices offered Salvation, which it did not! [Heb. 10:4])*

7 Will the LORD be pleased with thousands of rams, or with ten thousands of rivers of oil? shall I give my firstborn for my transgression, the fruit of my body for the sin of my soul? *(The question, "Will the LORD be pleased with thousands of rams?", insinuates that the people came to the place where they thought quantity enhanced the value, etc. In this Verse, the Lord is plainly saying that none of these things, even the offering up one's son or daughter, "the fruit*

of my body," can atone for "the sin of my soul." *Consequently, He cuts through all the false ideas and false doctrine that permeated the society of His People. It permeates it no less today!)*

8 He has shown you, O man, what is good; and what does the LORD require of you, but to do justly, and to love mercy, and to walk humbly with your God? *(The Revelation given here is found in Deut. 10:12; consequently, there was no excuse! In this Verse, the Lord proclaims not so much the Way of Salvation, but instead the results of true Salvation. The phrase, "He has showed you, O man, what is good," draws Israel back to the Bible. The answer to the question, "And what does the Lord require of you?", is here given:*

1. Honesty!

2. Mercy!

3. Humility!)

9 The LORD's voice cries unto the city, and the man of wisdom shall see your name: hear ye the rod, and Who has appointed it. *(The phrase, "The LORD's voice cries unto the city," refers to Jerusalem. The phrase, "And the man of wisdom shall see your name," refers to true wisdom recognizing the just action of judging the city because of its evil. The phrase, "Hear ye the rod," in effect says, "Hear, O Jerusalem, what punishment awaits you, and from Whom.")*

10 Are there yet the treasures of wickedness in the house of the wicked, and the scant measure that is abominable? *(The words, "Are there yet. . . .?", describe the practice of abominations of fraud, falsehood, and robbing of the poor. The entirety of the question, "Are there yet the treasures of wickedness in the house of the wicked?", means that all these sacrifices brought by these individuals to the Temple were treasures obtained by wrongdoing.)*

11 Shall I count them pure with the wicked balances, and with the bag of deceitful weights? *(The idea is: the people thought their religious activity atoned for their crimes. In effect, the Lord is saying that these sacrifices offered up to Him were looked at in His sight as "deceitful" and as "wicked balances." Consequently, they turned the Temple into a "house of the wicked" instead of a "House of God."*

Due to the Cross presently being ignored in most Churches, this means that they are "houses of wickedness" instead of "houses of Righteousness.")

12 For the rich men thereof are full of violence, and the inhabitants thereof have spoken lies, and their tongue is deceitful in their mouth. *(This is sad that God's People were violent, liars, and deceitful!)*

13 Therefore also will I make you sick in smiting you, in making you desolate because of your sins. *(The idea is: the Judgment will be awful and certain! As the sin, so the Judgment.)*

14 You shall eat, but not be satisfied; and your casting down shall be in the midst of you; and you shall take hold, but shall not deliver; and that which you deliver will I give up to the sword. *(Money will not satisfy. The phrase, "Your casting down shall be in the midst of you," means that Jerusalem would fall because of internal distress rather than outward attack. Even though Nebuchadnezzar would be the instrument used by God, still, it was not his might and power that brought about the Fall of the city, but instead Jerusalem's sin.*

The phrase, "And you shall take hold, but shall not deliver," refers to their money-bags filled by fraud and their attempting to escape and carry them away, but being unable to do so. In fact, some few would escape, but they too would fall into the hands of the enemy, thereby being stricken by the sword. Man is foolish to think he can outwit God!)

15 You shall sow, but you shall not reap; you shall tread the olives, but you shall not anoint yourself with oil; and sweet wine, but shall not drink wine. *(All of this means that others would reap the harvest for which the Hebrews had labored. These Verses proclaim God's Anger instead of His Blessing.)*

16 For the statutes of Omri are kept, and all the work of the house of Ahab, and you walk in their counsels; that I should make you a desolation, and the inhabitants thereof an hissing: therefore you shall bear the reproach of My people. *(All of this proclaims that Judah was immersed in idolatry; and because of such, the Lord would "make you a desolation." This means that the punishment was connected with the sin.)*

CHAPTER 7
(710 B.C.)
ISRAEL DESOLATE OF RIGHTEOUSNESS

WOE is me! for I am as when they have gathered the summer fruits, as the grapegleanings of the vintage: there is no cluster to eat: my soul desired the firstripe fruit. *(The exclamation, "Woe is me!" presents Micah representing repentant Israel by confessing its corruption and lamenting the necessity*

of punishment. *The phrase, "For I am as when they have gathered the summer fruits," means that there is no fruit left, even though one searches diligently. Israel has borne no good fruit for the Lord!)*

2 The good man is perished out of the Earth: and there is none upright among men: they all lie in wait for blood; they hunt every man his brother with a net. *(The idea is: the entirety of the fabric of the nation of Judah was so spoiled, with corruption and vileness beginning at the top and filtering down, that there was nothing good that could be said!)*

3 That they may do evil with both hands earnestly, the prince asks, and the judge asks for a reward; and the great man, he utters his mischievous desire: so they wrap it up. *(The first phrase proclaims that the people were ready enough to do evil; the next phrase says they can be bribed to do anything. The phrase, "And the great man, he utters his mischievous desire," means that the rich man communicates to the judge the evil he proposes against the poor, and "they," i.e., the rich man and the judge, concoct the matter between them, i.e., "they wrap it up.")*

4 The best of them is as a brier: the most upright is sharper than a thorn hedge: the day of your watchmen and your visitation comes; now shall be their perplexity. *(The first phrase, In referring to their best, lets us know just how vile were their worst. The phrase, "The day of your watchmen and your visitation comes," refers to the Prophets of old who predicted this coming wrath. The phrase, "Now shall be their perplexity," proclaims "a problem without a solution," which characterizes all those who disregard the warnings of the Lord.)*

5 Trust ye not in a friend, put ye not confidence in a guide: keep the doors of your mouth from her who lies in your bosom. *(Verses 5 and 6 portray the low level to which Israel and Judah had sunk, showing that selfishness reigned everywhere, and not even the closest relations could be trusted.)*

6 For the son dishonours the father, the daughter rises up against her mother, the daughter-in-law against her mother-in-law; a man's enemies are the men of his own house. *(The Lord [Mat. 10:35-36] quotes this Verse to prove that Gospel Grace, when rejected, arouses the iniquity of the heart; further, the entrance and nearness of Perfect Love, i.e., Christ, exasperate into activity its hatred. The idea is: light rejected becomes darkness deepened.)*

RESTORATION OF ISRAEL; HER REPENTANCE IN THE LAST DAYS

7 Therefore I will look unto the LORD; I will wait for the God of my salvation: my God will hear me. *(With most of the Prophets, the Holy Spirit, even after announcing severe judgment, would leap ahead and portray the glorious future which Israel will ultimately see, thereby fulfilling the Promises made to the Patriarchs and Prophets of old! In fact, Verses 7 through 9 portray Israel's repentance in the last days [Zech. 12:10]. Such is evidenced by the phrase, "Therefore I will look unto the LORD.")*

8 Rejoice not against me, O my enemy: when I fall, I shall arise; when I sit in darkness, the LORD shall be a light unto me. *(The phrase, "Rejoice not against me, O my enemy," refers to all those who had written Israel off. The phrase, "When I sit in darkness, the LORD shall be a light unto me," refers to the darkness that has lasted now for nearly 2,000 years, and which will even deepen during the first half of the Great Tribulation, when Israel will think the Antichrist is the Messiah. But during the coming Battle of Armageddon, Israel will call on the Lord; at that time, He "shall be a light unto me.")*

9 I will bear the indignation of the LORD, because I have sinned against Him, until He plead my cause, and execute judgment for me: He will bring me forth to the light, and I shall behold His righteousness. *(The Prophet, energized as was Daniel [Dan., Chpt. 9] by the Spirit of Intercession proper to the High Priest of Israel's confession [Heb. 3:1], confesses that nation's sins as his own; accepts the Wrath of God as just; and confidently awaits a future vindication. This is a most touching feature of the prophetic office. "If," said Jeremiah, "he be a Prophet, let him make intercession to Jehovah" [Jer. 27:18].*

The phrase, "And I shall behold His Righteousness," pertains to the Lord's Second Coming, with the Antichrist destroyed, and more perfect their acceptance of His Salvation.)

ISRAEL'S ENEMIES HUMBLED

10 Then she that is my enemy shall see it, and shame shall cover her which said unto me, Where is the LORD your God? my eyes shall behold her: now shall she be trodden down as the mire of the streets. *(The question, "Where is the LORD your God?", pertains to the boasts of Sennacherib [II Chron. 32:17] and*

the future Assyrian, who will likewise taunt Israel accordingly. The phrase, "My eyes shall behold her," means that Jerusalem beheld the destruction of the Assyrian host and will likewise behold the destruction of the Antichrist.)

The phrase, "Now shall she be trodden down as the mire of the streets," refers to the Angel who was sent against the Assyrians and the Lord Jesus Christ, Who will come against the Antichrist.)

ISRAEL REGATHERED

11 In the day that your walls are to be built, in that day shall the decree be far removed. (The first phrase describes Zion as a vineyard where the fence had been destroyed but which now has been rebuilt. It speaks of the coming restoration at the beginning of the Kingdom Age. The phrase, "In that day shall the decree be far removed," concerns Israel's captivity, which was decreed because of her sin and rejection of Christ, but which has now been removed. It has been removed because Israel now accepts Christ, which will take place immediately after the Second Coming.)

12 In that day also he shall come even to you from Assyria, and from the fortified cities, and from the fortress even to the river, and from sea to sea, and from mountain to mountain. (The first phrase continues to refer to the restoration, which will begin the Kingdom Age, with "Assyria" used as a type of the greatest enemy of God. The phrase, "And from the fortified cities," pertains to Egypt, which symbolizes the world. The phrase, "And from the fortress even to the river," actually concerns itself, and symbolically so, from Egypt to the Euphrates. This part of the world presently, and in the past, has been Israel's greatest nemesis. The last phrase refers to every nation in the world giving up the dispersed of Israel, who all will return home to Israel proper.)

13 Notwithstanding the land shall be desolate because of them who dwell therein, for the fruit of their doings. (The word "Notwithstanding" actually means "but before this" shall be desolation! This desolation lasted for nearly 2,000 years before Israel finally became a State again in 1948.

The phrase, "For the fruit of their doings," proclaims the reason for Israel's past state and their near-future judgment at the hands of the man of sin.)

14 Feed your people with your rod, the flock of your heritage, which dwell solitarily in the wood, in the midst of Carmel: let them feed in Bashan and Gilead, as in the days of old. (The prayer of this Verse is addressed to the Messiah, the Great Shepherd of His People. This rod will comfort them and not smite them. His People will dwell solitarily; that is, they shall enjoy distinct nationality [Num. 23:9] in absolute security [the wood] and with abounding prosperity. Once again, this is the Kingdom Age!)

JUDGMENT ON ISRAEL'S ENEMIES

15 According to the days of your coming out of the land of Egypt will I show unto him marvellous things. (Verses 15 through 17 give the Great Shepherd's prompt reply to the prayer of Micah. The phrase, "Will I show unto him marvelous things," records the Lord doing great things for Israel, which will commence with the Second Coming.)

16 The nations shall see and be confounded at all their might: they shall lay their hand upon their mouth, their ears shall be deaf. (Without Christ, Israel is nothing! With Christ, Israel, in the Kingdom Age, will be the greatest nation on the face of the Earth. In fact, all prosperity for the entirety of the world will be because Israel now occupies her rightful place and position.)

17 They shall lick the dust like a serpent, they shall move out of their holes like worms of the Earth: they shall be afraid of the LORD our God, and shall fear because of you. (The phrase, "They shall lick the dust like a serpent," is a figure of complete defeat. This is the Battle of Armageddon and the immediate aftermath. The phrase, "They shall be afraid of the LORD our God," means that the armies of the Antichrist and the nations of the world shall be driven by terror to acknowledge the God of Israel because of the demonstration of the Lord's Almighty Power.)

ISRAEL'S CONFIDENCE IN GOD

18 Who is a God like unto You, Who pardons iniquity, and passes by the transgression of the remnant of His heritage? He retains not His anger for ever, because He delights in mercy. (Upon the revelation of this tremendous coming restoration, Micah exclaims, "Who is a God like unto You?" The Lord "pardons," He "forgives," "His righteous anger quickly cools," and "He delights in mercy." There is no one like Him, as there can be no one like Him!)

19 He will turn again, He will have compassion upon us; He will subdue our iniquities; and you will cast all their sins into the depths of the sea. *(The phrase, "He will turn again," means that as He has had compassion before, and many times, He will do so again. The phrase, "He will subdue our iniquities," actually means that He will literally tread under foot "our iniquities," consequently totally rescuing us from their grasp.*

The phrase, "And you will cast all their sins into the depths of the sea," is the nearest to the oft-quoted statement about "casting sins into the sea of forgetfulness to be remembered no more." *Thus, the Prophecy, like the Epistle to the Romans, begins with God's Wrath against sin and closes with God's forgiveness of sin.)*

20 You will perform the truth to Jacob, and the mercy to Abraham, which You have sworn unto our fathers from the days of old. *(The general meaning of this Verse is that God will absolutely perform the Promises made to the forefathers. The two words, "have sworn," are the certitude of this coming action. In other words, the fulfillment of these Promises is guaranteed!)*

NAHUM

CHAPTER 1

(713 B.C.)

ATTRIBUTES OF GOD

THE burden of Nineveh. The Book of the vision of Nahum the Elkoshite. *(It seems that Nahum was from the village of Capernaum, which means "village of Nahum." The Book of Jonah records the repentance of Nineveh, while Nahum predicts its destruction. Nahum prophesied about 100 years after Jonah, with the city being destroyed about 100 years after that.*

While the Book is undated, it seems that Nahum was a contemporary of Isaiah and Hezekiah.

The phrase, "The burden of Nineveh," concerns the weight of the Message that the Lord had laid on the Prophet's heart concerning that city.)

2 God is jealous, and the LORD revenges; the LORD revenges, and is furious; the LORD will take vengeance on His adversaries, and He reserves wrath for His enemies. *(The phrase, "God is jealous," means that He has a jealous love for His People and will allow no one to injure them, though He may employ nations as instruments to chastise them. Actually, one of the names of Jehovah is "Jealous" [Ex. 34:14].*

The phrase, "And the LORD revenges," means rather "avenges." He avenges His People on their adversaries and possesses wrath for their enemies.)

3 The LORD is slow to anger, and great in power, and will not at all acquit the wicked: the LORD has His way in the whirlwind and in the storm, and the clouds are the dust of His feet. *(The Lord's longsuffering is not due to impotency, for He is great in Power. The phrase, "And will not at all acquit the wicked," means that a passage of time in no way, at least in the Mind of God, lessens the guilt. The phrase, "And the clouds are the dust of His Feet," probably refers to the scientific discovery that clouds owe their beauty and even their very existence to the presence of dust-particles in the atmosphere; this undoubtedly was completely unknown to Nahum. The vapor, it is said, condenses on these particles, which then become visible as clouds, hence the scientific accuracy of Nahum's statement.)*

4 He rebukes the sea, and makes it dry, and dries up all the rivers: Bashan languishes, and Carmel, and the flower of Lebanon languishes. *(The great physical changes and convulsions in the world are tokens of God's Wrath on sinful nations. The phrase, "He rebukes the sea, and makes it dry," refers to the Red Sea, when it was pushed back to allow the passage of the Children of Israel [Ex. 14:21]. The phrase, "And dries up all the rivers," refers to the Jordan [Josh. 3:17; II Ki. 2:8, 14].*

The areas of "Bashan," "Carmel," and "Lebanon" were known as being remarkable for their fertility. Even so, they are used here proverbially to express the Truth that God can cause the most luxuriant region to wither at His Word.)

5 The mountains quake at Him, and the hills melt, and the Earth is burned at His presence, yea, the world, and all that dwell therein. *(This Verse is meant to portray that not only does the Lord have total latitude in respect to His People, Israel, but also the entirety of "the world, and all that dwell therein." Nature, whether animate or inanimate, is represented as being actuated by the terror of conscious guilt.)*

6 Who can stand before His indignation? and who can abide in the fierceness of His anger? His fury is poured out like fire, and the rocks are thrown down by Him. *(The Holy Spirit takes the opportunity to show that the Lord is perfectly capable of destroying the mighty Assyrian Empire; He also is able to bring to heel the entirety of the world, which He soon shall do!*

The question, "Who can stand before His indignation?", has to do with the coming Great Tribulation [Rev. 6:17; 14:10]. The last phrase of the Verse refers to the sixth Seal of Rev. 6:12-17.)

7 The LORD is good, a strong hold in the day of trouble; and He knows them who trust in Him. *(Pure and simple, "The LORD is good!" The phrase, "A stronghold in the day of trouble," was proved by Hezekiah, when he took refuge in the Lord and was delivered and the Assyrians destroyed.*

The phrase, "And He knows them who trust in Him," concerns the delight the Lord takes in those who place their trust in Him and His Word, and not on the frail arm of man. The two words, "He knows," are a consolation to all who totally trust Him; their trust, though maligned by the world and by most of the Church, is rather recognized and blessed by Him.)

8 But with an overrunning flood He will make an utter end of the place thereof, and darkness shall pursue His enemies. *(The phrase, "But with an overrunning flood," was literally fulfilled! An usually heavy and long-continued flood of the River Tigris carried away a large section of the huge ramparts surrounding the city. Through this gap, the Babylonians forced their way within the walls and captured the place.*

The phrase, "He will make an utter end of the place thereof," was literally fulfilled, as well! When the city fell, it was plundered by the Medes, and was left to fall into a heap of desolate ruin, which it is today. This happened [it is believed] in August 612 B.C., approximately 100 years after Nahum's Prophecy.)

NINEVEH'S JUDGMENT: DESTRUCTION

9 What do you imagine against the LORD? He will make an utter end: affliction shall not rise up the second time. *(The question, "What do you imagine against the LORD?", pertains to the Assyrians attempting to take Jerusalem. The phrase, "He will make an utter end," refers to the Assyrian Empire being destroyed, and by the Lord at that! The phrase, "Affliction shall not rise up the second time," means that as Assyria had in fact subdued the Northern Kingdom and had greatly threatened Judah and Jerusalem, they would never have the power to do so again.)*

10 For while they be folden together as thorns, and while they are drunken as drunkards, they shall be devoured as stubble fully dry. *(Continuing to speak of the Assyrians, the Lord says that even though they be "folden together," i.e., militarily equipped as an overwhelming army, impregnable as the folded thorns of the east, and drunk with pride and strength, yet should they "be devoured as stubble, fully dry." The idea of the Verse addresses itself to the boasts of the Assyrians and their slurs against Jehovah.*

The phrase, "And while they are drunken as drunkards," has as its primary meaning, "drunk with power.")

11 There is one come out of you, who imagines evil against the LORD, a wicked counsellor. *(Sennacherib, or possibly Rabshakeh, is intended here; but, as well, to the future Antichrist, Nahum points.)*

JUDAH'S DELIVERANCE

12 Thus saith the LORD; Though they be quiet, and likewise many, yet thus shall they be cut down, when He shall pass through. Though I have afflicted you, I will afflict you no more. *(The great boasts of Sennacherib, through Rabshakeh, were made in Verse 11; consequently, the Lord now answers and says what will actually happen. The phrase, "Though they be quiet, and likewise many," means that the Assyrians will feel secure, because of their tremendous numbers. In their thinking, Jerusalem is ripe for the plucking, and they are quick to say so.*

The phrase, "Yet thus shall they be cut down, when He shall pass through," refers to the Lord passing through the Assyrian host in judgment and killing 185,000 of them, just as He "passed through" the land of Egypt and killed the firstborn.

The phrase, "Though I have afflicted you, I will afflict you no more," refers not to the Assyrians, but to Israel. They were afflicted, but only in measure; the Assyrians, eternally.)

13 For now will I break his yoke from off you, and will burst your bonds in sunder. *(Thus was the Assyrian yoke broken from off Hezekiah! The phrase, "And will burst your bonds in sunder," concerns an instant deliverance and not a protracted one. And that's exactly what happened, with the Angel killing 185,000 of their choice leaders and soldiers; as a result, Sennacherib canceled all plans for the subjection of Jerusalem and straggled back to his own country [II Ki. 19:35].)*

14 And the LORD has given a commandment concerning you, that no more of your name be sown: out of the house of your gods will I cut off the graven image and the molten image: I will make your grave; for you are vile. *(Such speaks of Sennacherib and his boasts! As Sennacherib had made his boasts concerning the Lord, now "the Lord has given a Commandment concerning you." Whereas the Assyrian was incapable of carrying out his boasts, the word "Commandment" guarantees that God's prediction will be carried out, which it was!*

The phrase, "That no more of your name be sown," pronounces the finality of Assyrian power, which would come to an end in a little over 100 years.

The phrase, "Out of the house of your gods will I cut off the graven image and the molten image," pertains to the fact that as the Assyrians destroyed the images of the gods worshipped by conquered nations [II Ki. 19:18], likewise, the Lord would do such to their gods.

The phrase, "I will make your grave," proclaims the death of Sennacherib; he was killed

in the temple of his idol, slain by his own sons. The reason? "For you are vile." The word "vile" in the Hebrew is also translated "light," and means "weighed in the balances and found wanting," as in Dan. 5:27.)

HER MISSIONARY PROGRAM IN THE MILLENNIUM

15 Behold upon the mountains the feet of him who brings good tidings, who publishes peace! O Judah, keep your solemn feasts, perform your vows: for the wicked shall no more pass through you; he is utterly cut off. *(Upon the visitation of the Angel and the destruction of 185,000 Assyrian soldiers in one night, the excited messengers hastened over the mountains to Jerusalem with these glad tidings. Actually, the 126th Psalm was written [probably by Hezekiah] respecting this great deliverance.*

The phrase, "for the wicked shall no more pass through you," in effect refers to the coming Antichrist and the greatest victory of all regarding Israel, which will actually occasion the Second Coming.)

CHAPTER 2
(713 B.C.)
JUDAH ENCOURAGED AGAINST THE ASSYRIAN INVADER

H E who dashes in pieces is come up before your face: keep the munition, watch the way, make your loins strong, fortify your power mightily. *(This Verse has to do with the coming destruction of Nineveh, which is predicted and described here. It would be carried out by the Babylonians under Nabopolassar, father of Nebuchadnezzar. Such is Bible Prophecy! Over 100 years before the actual siege and destruction would take place, the mode of its capture is minutely foretold.*

The phrase, "He who dashes in pieces is come up before your face," speaks of the army of the Medes, which, at the time of the Prophecy, didn't even exist, but which would humble Nineveh on that coming day.

The phrase, "Make your loins strong, fortify your power mightily," speaks of preparation, but says, in effect, that whatever is done, irrespective of the warning given here, Nineveh will fall!)

2 For the LORD has turned away the excellency of Jacob, as the excellency of Israel: for the emptiers have emptied them out, and marred their vine branches. *(The first phrase*

has to do with the Lord humbling the Ten Tribes, using the Assyrian as His instrument; they "emptied out" the whole land of the Northern Kingdom of Israel. The phrase, "And marred their vine branches," refers to the Fall and destruction of Israel, as well as the effort to subdue Judah; the latter did not succeed!)

NINEVEH TO EXPERIENCE JUDGMENT: BATTLE IN HER STREETS

3 The shield of his mighty men is made red, the valiant men are in scarlet: the chariots shall be with flaming torches in the day of his preparation, and the fir trees shall be terribly shaken. *(This Verse describes the Babylonian Host, which would come against Nineveh a little over 100 years into the future.)*

4 The chariots shall rage in the streets, they shall justle one against another in the broad ways: they shall seem like torches, they shall run like the lightnings. *(The language of these Verses vividly describes an ancient army marching into battle. The phrase, "The chariots shall rage in the streets," refers to the tremendous number of these instruments of war owned by Nabopolassar, the Babylonian king.*

Incidentally, this Verse does not apply to the modern automobile, as some claim. It refers rather to the invasion by the Medes.)

5 He shall recount his worthies: they shall stumble in their walk; they shall make haste to the wall thereof, and the defence shall be prepared. *(This Verse pictures the vain effort of the king of Nineveh and his troops to defend the city. The preparation of their defenses, even though extensive, was fruitless, simply because the Lord was fighting against them. As such, they could not hope to win.)*

6 The gates of the rivers shall be opened, and the palace shall be dissolved. *(This explains the flood of 1:8 that made the Fall of the city possible. The Hebrew verb here translated "dissolved" may be better read as "become molten," which describes the king of Nineveh, Sardanapalus, collecting his wives and his treasures into the palace and setting it on fire, with all perishing in the flames. Thus remarkably and minutely does the Prophet describe the capture and fate of Sardanapalus some 50 years before he was born!)*

NINEVEH'S CAPTIVITY

7 And Huzzab shall be led away captive,

she shall be brought up, and her maids shall lead her as with the voice of doves, tabering upon their breasts. *("Huzzab" was probably the queen who escaped the burning of the palace and was led away captive.)*

8 But Nineveh is of old like a pool of water: yet they shall flee away. Stand, stand, shall they cry; but none shall look back. *(The first phrase refers to the multiple thousands of traders and merchants who flocked to the city as water flows into a pool. The phrase, "Yet they shall flee away," pertains to the siege of the city and its ultimate Fall, which saw all of these people running away, concerned only for their own safety, despite the captains saying, "Stand, stand." Irrespective, they fled and "none shall look back.")*

NINEVEH SPOILED

9 Take ye the spoil of silver, take the spoil of gold: for there is none end of the store and glory out of all the pleasant furniture. *(This Verse is addressed to the invading Babylonians. The word "glory" here signifies abundance and costliness. Many valuables have been found in the ruins of Nineveh, but no gold or silver, showing how completely the Babylonians responded to this injunction. The last phrase pertains, as well, to its riches. Sardanapalus is said to have placed 150 golden beds and as many tables of the same metal on his funeral pyre, plus gold and silver vases and ornaments in enormous quantities, along with costly raiment.)*

HER UTTER RUIN

10 She is empty, and void, and waste: and the heart melts, and the knees smite together, and much pain is in all loins, and the faces of them all gather blackness. *("She is empty, and void, and waste" portrays three Hebrew words, all similar in sound, each having more syllables than its predecessor, thus expressing the solemnity and finality of the city's doom. The Hebrew words for "empty," "void," and "waste" are "bukah," "bukahum," and "um'bulakah.")*

11 Where is the dwelling of the lions, and the feedingplace of the young lions, where the lion, even the old lion, walked, and the lion's whelp, and none made them afraid? *(The Hebrew word "where" expresses wonder and awe. The question, "Where is the dwelling of the lions?", pictures Nineveh as a lion's den, but secure and well fed. The phrase, "Even the old*

lion, walked," refers to its original builder, Nimrod [Gen. 10:11]. From the construction of the Hebrew Text, it seems that Asshur may have built Nineveh, but under the guidance and direction of Nimrod.*

The phrase, "The old lion," could have referred to the age of Nineveh, which was nearly 2,000 years old when it was destroyed. The phrase, "And none made them afraid," referred to her tremendous strength, which caused her to stand for so many years.)

12 The lion did tear in pieces enough for his whelps, and strangled for his lionesses, and filled his holes with prey, and his dens with ravin. *(The "lion" was the symbol of Assyria; "Nergal," its war god, was portrayed as a winged lion with a man's face. The phrase, "The lion did tear in pieces enough for his whelps," refers to the expansion of the Assyrian Empire and their plundering of other nations, fulfilling the phrase, "And filled his holes with prey, and his dens with ravin.")*

GOD IS HER DESTROYER

13 Behold, I am against you, saith the LORD of Hosts, and I will burn her chariots in the smoke, and the sword shall devour your young lions: and I will cut off your prey from the Earth, and the voice of your messengers shall no more be heard. *(After denoting the tremendous strength of the Assyrian Empire, noted by its capital city, Nineveh, the Prophet says, "Behold, I am against you, saith the LORD of Hosts." The phrase, "And I will cut off your prey from the Earth," means that the Lord would stop once and for all the pillage of other countries by the Assyrians. The phrase, "And the voice of your messengers shall no more be heard," signifies its end, with the same being said of the former Soviet Union.)*

CHAPTER 3
(713 B.C.)
NINEVEH'S CRIMES AND WARS:
THE REASON FOR HER DOOM

WOE to the bloody city! it is all full of lies and robbery; the prey departs not *(Nineveh is described here by the Holy Spirit in three words, "bloodshed, deceit, and violence");*

2 The noise of a whip, and the noise of the rattling of the wheels, and of the pransing horses, and of the jumping chariots. *(Verses 2 and 3 describe the Babylonian army advancing*

to the attack upon Nineveh, with the cracking of the whips urging on the chariot horses, and with the noise of the chariot wheels.)

3 The horseman lifts up both the bright sword and the glittering spear: and there is a multitude of slain, and a great number of carcases; and there is none end of their corpses; they stumble upon their corpses *(the number of the dead was so great that the invaders themselves are impeded by the heaps of dead bodies which they have to climb over, fulfilling the Passage, "they stumble upon their corpses"):*

4 Because of the multitude of the whoredoms of the wellfavoured harlot, the mistress of witchcrafts, that sells nations through her whoredoms, and families through her witchcrafts. *(The word "whoredoms" actually refers to "idolatries." The "well-favored harlot" refers to being "idolatrous." Idolatry and its accompaniments of oppression and violence caused the ruin of Nineveh.*

The phrase, "The mistress of witchcrafts," pertained to the Assyrians conquering nations and then erecting symbols of their [Assyrian] deities and compelling conquered nations to receive them and pay them divine honor. The phrase, "That sells nations through her whoredoms," literally means that nations were bought and sold by idolatry.)

JUDGMENT FROM GOD

5 Behold, I am against you, saith the LORD of Hosts; and I will discover your skirts upon your face, and I will show the nations your nakedness, and the kingdoms your shame. *(The phrase, "Behold, I am against you, saith the LORD of Hosts," places the Assyrian Empire, for all its might, in an untenable position. The phrase, "And I will discover your skirts upon your face," pertains to her being unable to defend herself as the mighty Babylonian army approached. The phrase, "And I will show the nations your nakedness, and the kingdoms your shame," spoke of her utter defeat, with her great city being ransacked, her leaders killed, and her gods destroyed as helpless!)*

6 And I will cast abominable filth upon you, and make you vile, and will set you as a gazingstock. *(The custom of the ancients was to strip a debauched woman, exposing her to the public, and then to spatter her with all kinds of filth. Nineveh's character and doom are here so pictured.)*

7 And it shall come to pass, that all they who look upon you shall flee from you, and say, Nineveh is laid waste: who will bemoan her? whence shall I seek comforters for you? *(The idea of Assyria being defeated, especially at this particular time, was preposterous, at least in the minds of the wise men of the world. As well, to be defeated to this degree, "that all they who look upon you shall flee from you," was unthinkable!*

The phrase, "Nineveh is laid waste," was a statement which not a single person in the world believed, except those who believed God. The last phrase concerns the world of that day being pleased that this empire of great cruelty had now received her just dues.)

THE RIGHTNESS OF DIVINE JUDGMENT

8 Are you better than populous No, that was situate among the rivers, that had the waters round about it, whose rampart was the sea, and her wall was from the sea? *("Populous No" means No-Ammon, i.e., "Thebes." This great city, like Nineveh, was so fortified by the Nile and its canals as to be deemed impregnable; yet was it captured by the Assyrians. Its stupendous ruins excite even today the astonishment of the world.*

The Prophet here asks Nineveh, "Are you 'better' or more strongly situated than Thebes, Egypt?")

9 Ethiopia and Egypt were her strength, and it was infinite; Put and Lubim were your helpers. *(The phrase, "And it was infinite," concerning the "strength" of Ethiopia and Egypt, respects them as being thought to be so strong that they were impregnable. But yet, and as the Holy Spirit calls to attention, Assyria defeated these mighty empires.)*

10 Yet was she carried away, she went into captivity: her young children also were dashed in pieces at the top of all the streets: and they cast lots for her honourable men, and all her great men were bound in chains. *(The phrase, "Yet was she carried away," refers to the destruction of Thebes [No], despite her strong position and infinite resources. Likewise, Nineveh would fare no better!)*

11 You also shall be drunk: you shall be hid, you also shall seek strength because of the enemy. *(The word "drunk" means to be drunk with the cup of God's Wrath. The phrase, "You shall be hid," means to be covered up with the sands of the desert, which she was after her terrible defeat by the Babylonians. In fact, she was so effectually "hidden" that her very site was*

discovered only in the last 100 or so years.

The phrase, "You also shall seek strength be-cause of the enemy," actually means that they would seek to leave the city and find another stronghold of defense; however, history records that the effort to retreat from Nineveh during the siege was unsuccessful.)

12 All your strong holds shall be like fig trees with the firstripe figs: if they be shaken, they shall even fall into the mouth of the eater. *(The Holy Spirit forecasts here, about 100 years before it happened, the actual thoughts that would come into the minds of the defenders of Nineveh, of endeavoring to retreat to a second line of de-fense. He is telling them here through the Prophet that such would be useless.)*

13 Behold, your people in the midst of you are women: the gates of your land shall be set wide open unto your enemies: the fire shall devour your bars. *(The phrase, "Behold, your people in the midst of you are women," denotes the fighting ability of the Assyrians being so di-minished that they were incapable of defense. The phrase, "The gates of your land shall be set wide open unto your enemies," refers to the part of the wall that was swept away by the flood, leaving gaping holes. The phrase, "The fire shall devour your bars," actually pertains to the gates of the city that were set on fire after the Baby-lonians had gained access to the city because of the flood.)*

14 Draw thee waters for the siege, fortify your strong holds: go into clay, and tread the morter, make strong the brickkiln. *(In effect, the Lord is saying that irrespective of what is done, Assyria is going to go down, and nothing can stop it.)*

15 There shall the fire devour you; the sword shall cut you off, it shall eat you up like the cankerworm: make yourself many as the can-kerworm, make yourself many as the locusts. *(The argument of Verses 15 through 17 is: though the soldiers of Nineveh were as countless as the locusts, and her merchants more in number than*

the stars, yet should they perish as the locusts that flee from the rising sun.)

16 You have multiplied your merchants above the stars of Heaven: the cankerworm spoils, and flees away. *(The first phrase per-tains to the extensive trading carried on by Nineveh, which was really, at that time, the hub of commerce for much of the world. The last phrase has to do with the city spreading herself everywhere, and now is gone, as if disappeared.)*

17 Your crowned are as the locusts, and your captains as the great grasshoppers, which camp in the hedges in the cold day, but when the sun arises they flee away, and their place is not known where they are. *(This Verse pro-claims the fabric of this vast number of world leaders and empire builders coming apart like rotten cloth.)*

18 Your shepherds slumber, O king of Assyria: your nobles shall dwell in the dust: your people is scattered upon the mountains, and no man gathers them. *(The phrase, "Your shepherds slumber, O king of Assyria," refers to their military generals sleeping the sleep of death. The phrase, "Your people is scattered upon the mountains," concerns their terrible defeat at the hands of the Babylonians, with the people being leaderless as a result of the decapitation of its leadership. The phrase, "No man gathers them," means that there will be no leaders left to rally them, hence the empire would go into oblivion.)*

19 There is no healing of your bruise; your wound is grievous: all who hear the bruit of you shall clap the hands over you: for upon whom has not your wickedness passed con-tinually? *(The phrase, "There is no healing of your bruise," means that there was no remedy for the coming destruction. "Your wound is grievous" points to the fact that the leaders of Assyria had passed the point of no return. The phrase, "All who hear the bruit of you shall clap the hands over you," concerns the nations of the world who hear the tidings [bruit] of Assyria's defeat and rejoice greatly!)*

HABAKKUK

CHAPTER 1
(626 B.C.)
WHY DOES GOD PERMIT INJUSTICE AND ALLOW OPPRESSION?

THE burden which Habakkuk the Prophet did see. *(This "burden" concerned an oracle of judgment upon Judah, which was to be destroyed and taken captive by the Chaldeans. This Prophecy was given only about 40-50 years before Nebuchadnezzar's first incursion into Jerusalem in 605 B.C. Jeremiah's prophetic Ministry began about 627 B.C., not long after Habakkuk's; therefore, the earlier Prophet's Ministry would have served as a staging area for Jeremiah.*

Considering that Babylon had not yet come into power, and considering that Habakkuk spoke of the coming Chaldeans, such would have aroused more curiosity than fear; nevertheless, it would come to pass exactly as the Holy Spirit predicted.)

2 O LORD, how long shall I cry, and You will not hear! even cry out unto You of violence, and You will not save! *(The phrase, "O LORD, how long shall I cry, and You will not hear!", proclaims the Prophet's heart, jealous for God and the Law, asking why God is silent and inactive in view of the cruelties ["iniquities"], oppression ["grievance"], robbery, violence, strife, and contention practiced by the rich in Zion against the poor, owing to the slackness of law and the corrupt administration of justice.*

The exclamation, "O LORD, how long shall I cry, and You will not hear!", implies that the Prophet had long been complaining of the moral depravity of Judah and calling for help against it. He was discouraged that the Lord did not seem to answer his petition.

The last phrase pertains to the Prophet frustrated in the knowledge that God has the power to do something about these things, but seemingly does nothing. The implication is: the helpless and poor of the land had appealed to Habakkuk to cry to the Lord on their behalf regarding their oppression by the ruling aristocracy, who no longer cared for the things of God but rather their own enrichment.

They are crying in the Prophet's ears; therefore, he cries into God's ears, but with what looks like little result.)

3 Why do You show me iniquity, and cause me to behold grievance? for spoiling and violence are before me: and there are who raise up strife and contention. *(The question, "Why do You show me iniquity, and cause me to behold grievance?", has reference to the Prophet's frustration.)*

4 Therefore the Law is slacked, and judgment does never go forth: for the wicked does compass about the righteous; therefore wrong judgment proceeds. *(The phrase, "Therefore the Law is slacked," means that the Law of Moses was ignored, or even set aside, by the ruling aristocracy of Judah. Where the Bible does not rule, injustice does!*

The phrase, "And judgment does never go forth," means a lack of fair and equitable judgment for all.)

GOD'S USE OF THE CHALDEANS (THE BABYLONIAN CAPTIVITY)

5 Behold ye among the heathen, and regard, and wonder marvelously: for I will work a work in your days, which ye will not believe, though it be told you. *(The Apostle Paul, in Acts 13:41, quotes this Verse. His argument was: just as the Hebrews would not believe Habakkuk foretelling the destruction of Jerusalem by the Chaldeans, and the Salvation offered to Israel, so the Jews did not believe Paul foretelling the destruction that then impended at the hands of the Romans, and the Salvation proclaimed through Christ.*

The phrase, "Behold ye among the heathen," is meant to point to Babylon, which shall be the instrument used by Jehovah to punish Judah. This was something that Habakkuk did not understand, in that God would use those more wicked than Judah to punish Judah. Therefore, he would "regard" and "wonder marvelously."

The phrase, "For I will work a work in your days," is actually part of the answer to Habakkuk's inquiry. The words, "In your days," meant that some of those now living would see this coming chastisement; therefore, Judah was beginning the countdown, a countdown which would ultimately lead to her destruction.

The phrase, "I will work," signifies that the

Lord will "work" to bring destruction, upon an absence of Repentance, just as He "works" to bring blessing upon obedience. The phrase, "Which you will not believe, though it be told you," was fulfilled in totality. The people did not believe Habakkuk, and they did not believe Jeremiah, even when on the very eve of destruction.)

6 For, lo, I raise up the Chaldeans, that bitter and hasty nation, which shall march through the breadth of the land, to possess the dwellingplaces that are not theirs. *(The phrase, "For, lo, I raise up the Chaldeans," would have presented a somewhat puzzling spectrum to the people of Judah. At this time, Babylon did not even exist as an empire. In fact, at least at this time, such a thought was preposterous. However, the short phrase, "I raise up," portrays the Lord as able to do what He says that He will do. The Babylonians will take the land of Judah!)*

7 They are terrible and dreadful: their judgment and their dignity shall proceed of themselves. *(The phrase, "They are terrible and dreadful," is meant to emphasize not only what the Babylonians will be but also the entirety of Gentile dominion. This Gentile dominion was carried out by the Babylonians, by the Medes and Persians, by the Greeks, and by the Romans. It will also continue under the coming Antichrist.*

The phrase, "Their judgment and their dignity shall proceed of themselves," means that the Babylonians would be led not at all by God, but their own selfish desires — in reality, by Satan.)

8 Their horses also are swifter than the leopards, and are more fierce than the evening wolves: and their horsemen shall spread themselves, and their horsemen shall come from far; they shall fly as the eagle that hastes to eat. *(These "horsemen," although beginning with the Babylonians, would also pertain to the Medes and the Persians, the Greeks, the Romans, the Barbarians, the Turks, the Arabs, the Spanish, etc., and the Germans. Tragically, it has not ended even yet; it will culminate with the Antichrist. It pertains to the "times of the Gentiles" [Lk. 21:24].)*

9 They shall come all for violence: their faces shall sup up as the east wind, and they shall gather the captivity as the sand. *(The phrase, "They shall come all for violence," concerns the manner of operation of the Babylonians, as well as all who would follow thereafter.)*

10 And they shall scoff at the kings, and the princes shall be a scorn unto them: they shall deride every strong hold; for they shall heap dust, and take it. *(The first phrase pertains to*

the fact that no mercy will be shown even to the Potentates. The phrase, "They shall deride every stronghold," means that Judah's strongest defense would be as nothing to them.)

11 Then shall his mind change, and he shall pass over, and offend, imputing this his power unto his god. *(The phrase, "Then shall his mind change," refers to the arrogance of Nebuchadnezzar, when he became lifted up in pride. The phrase, "Imputing this his power unto his god," means that he defied the Lord and made his might his god.)*

GOD'S CHARACTER; WHY SHOULD HE USE THE WICKED TO PUNISH THE LESS WICKED?

12 Are you not from everlasting, O LORD my God, my Holy One? we shall not die. O LORD, You have ordained them for judgment; and, O mighty God, You have established them for correction. *(In the balance of this Chapter, the Prophet complains of the Divine action in employing for chastisement a people more wicked than the Jews, whom they were commissioned by God to punish. This perplexed Habakkuk. The phrase, "And, O mighty God, You have established them for correction," means that the Lord has set in motion a series of events, which will establish the Babylonians in power that they may bring about these corrective measures to Judah.)*

13 You are of purer eyes than to behold evil, and cannot not look on iniquity: wherefore look Thou upon them who deal treacherously, and hold Your tongue when the wicked devours the man who is more righteous than he? *(The phrase, "You are of purer eyes than to behold evil, and cannot look on iniquity," means that God cannot look with complacency on evil. And yet the Lord proposes to permit evil men, called the "Chaldeans," to afflict the Holy Seed. This is the Prophet's perplexity, which he lays before the Lord.*

The question, "And hold Your tongue when the wicked devours the man who is more righteous than he?", is a question that has perplexed more than Habakkuk.)

14 And make men as the fishes of the sea, as the creeping things, who have no ruler over them? *(The Verse refers to the Babylonians showing no restraint, because God did not rule them. They were ruled by men, and evil men at that, who had no respect for decency, compassion, or mercy.)*

15 They take up all of them with the angle,

they catch them in their net, and gather them in their drag: therefore they rejoice and are glad. *(In this Scripture, Habakkuk refers to the people as fish [all of them] and the "net" as the army of the Babylonians.)*

16 Therefore they sacrifice unto their net, and burn incense unto their drag; because by them their portion is fat, and their meat plenteous. *(The phrase, "Therefore they sacrifice unto their net," means that they gave their idol gods the credit for their vast success, little understanding that Jehovah had allowed their place and privilege.)*

17 Shall they therefore empty their net, and not spare continually to slay the nations? *(Habakkuk now realizes that the Lord is the Author of this which is coming.)*

CHAPTER 2
(626 B.C.)
GOD'S ANSWER: HE WILL PUNISH
THE CHALDEANS LATER;
THEY ARE ROBBERS

I will stand upon my watch, and set me upon the tower, and will watch to see what He will say unto me, and what I shall answer when I am reproved. *(The phrase, "I will stand upon my watch, and set me upon the tower," pertains to a watchtower that is speaking symbolically [Ezek. 3:17; 33:2, 6; Mic. 7:4]. The phrase, "And will watch to see what He will say unto me," means that Habakkuk, totally unlike the modern prophets, believed that a man could pray and the Lord would answer.*

The phrase, "And what I shall answer when I am reproved," seems to imply that Habakkuk felt that his questions addressed to the Lord may not be proper. He expects "reproof," but instead will be given an in-depth answer by the Lord.)

2 And the LORD answered me, and said, Write the vision, and make it plain upon tables, that he may run who reads it. *(The phrase, "Write the vision, and make it plain upon tables," was carried out to the letter by Habakkuk, in the form of the Book that bears his name; consequently, the Lord wanted not only Habakkuk to hear the answer, but all men, and for all time. The phrase, "That he may run who reads it," speaks of those who are charged with a Divine Message, who were to use all dispatch in making it known.)*

3 For the vision is yet for an appointed time, but at the end it shall speak, and not lie: though it tarry, wait for it; because it will surely come,

it will not tarry. *(The phrase, "For the Vision is yet for an appointed time," actually speaks of the Second Coming of Christ, as proved in Heb. 10:37; however, it could also pertain to something promised personally by the Lord to an individual, but long delayed! Even though delayed, it is not forgotten, but is actually for an "appointed time."*

The phrase, "But at the end it shall speak," actually says in the original, "at the end it shall breathe," meaning that it breathes and pants or hastes toward the end. The phrase, "And not lie," expresses the certitude of this coming action.

The phrase, "Though it tarry, wait for it," means that it is not going to happen at the moment; consequently, faith is to wait with confidence for that which the Vision promises. In doing so, the heart oppressed by feelings to which Faith itself gives birth is sustained and comforted. God, Who values Faith, will certainly intervene and not tarry.)

4 Behold, his soul which is lifted up is not upright in him: but the just shall live by his faith. *(The first phrase of this Verse speaks of one who is proud, presumptuous, thinking much of himself, despising others, and who is not straightforward and upright before God. As such, he carries in himself the seeds of destruction. The phrase, "But the just shall live by his Faith," implies a loving trust in God, confident in His Promises, resulting in due performance of His Will.*

This Passage can be translated, "As to the just, through his Faith, he shall live." This is the great Passage used by the Apostle Paul on the basis of his great argument of Faith versus works [Rom. 1:17].)

5 Yea also, because he transgresses by wine, he is a proud man, neither keeps at home, who enlarges his desire as Hell, and is as death, and cannot be satisfied, but gathers unto him all nations, and heaps unto him all people *(Habakkuk now begins to express the results of the individual who trusts in his own resources and not God, and speaks of the person proclaimed at the beginning of Verse 4.*

The phrase, "Yea also, because he transgresses by wine," is meant to express the ways of the world, more so than literal inebriation. The phrase, "Neither keeps at home," refers to the unfettered sexual appetites, unfaithfulness, as well as ever attempting to conquer new horizons, even at the expense of family and home.

The phrase, "Who enlarges his desire as Hell," means that as Hell is never satisfied with the

number of people who enter its confines, neither is the worldling satisfied, irrespective of his attainments or accomplishments. The phrase, "And is as death, and cannot be satisfied," proclaims the lustful desire of the human family which does not know God.

The phrase, "But gathers unto him all nations," signifies the Babylonians overrunning one nation after the other, but still not satisfied. The phrase, "And heaps unto him all people," refers to the Babylonians, as all conquerors, putting more and more people under subjection to them [Mat. 20:25-26]):

6 Shall not all these take up a parable against him, and a taunting proverb against him, and say, Woe to him who increases that which is not his! how long? and to him that lades himself with thick clay! (The question in the form of an exclamation concerns itself with this spirit made evident in the previous Verse, which has characterized humanity for all time. Sooner or later, oppressed people rise up against their oppressors, exactly as was done in the former Soviet Union, and has been done through the ages. The idea is: as all these oppressors, wherever they may be, oppress the people by ruinous taxation or levies, likewise, the oppressor is piling up debt to Almighty God, Who cares for the oppressed [Jer. 17:11].)

7 Shall they not rise up suddenly who shall bite you, and awake who shall vex you, and you shall be for booties unto them? (The question, "Shall they not rise up suddenly who shall bite you . . .?", actually refers to the Persians, who destroyed the Babylonian power as quickly and as unexpectedly as it had arisen. As well, it applies even to the individual who oppresses others, that ultimately the oppressor will be "bitten."

The phrase, "And you shall be for booties unto them," concludes this question asked by the Lord. As the Babylonians looted their conquered peoples, likewise, they shall be looted!)

8 Because you have spoiled many nations, all the remnant of the people shall spoil you; because of men's blood, and for the violence of the land, of the city, and of all who dwell therein. (Even though Nebuchadnezzar was an instrument of God in punishing Judah and Jerusalem, still, he took his commission too far, as is described here by the Lord. He laid a heavy hand of "violence" on God's People, and likewise the Babylonian Empire would suffer the same injustice. The idea is that God's People, whether Jews or Gentiles, are to be treated only as the Lord dictates.)

THE CHALDEANS ARE COVETOUS: WOE TO THEM

9 Woe to him who covets an evil covetousness to his house, that he may set his nest on high, that he may be delivered from the power of evil! (As the first "Woe" concerned oppression, this "Woe" concerns covetousness. The idea of this Verse pertains to rich men gathering wealth in order to establish their families in assured affluence; but they, in reality, devise shame to their children and ruin to their own souls because of the injury done to others.

The phrase, "Woe to him who covets an evil covetousness to his house," actually refers to the leadership of Babylon, which would conclude in Belshazzar, who thought to secure its stability and permanence by amassing godless gain.)

10 You have consulted shame to your house by cutting off many people, and have sinned against your soul. (This Passage refers to the very means the Empire took to secure its power, but proved to be its ruin.)

11 For the stone shall cry out of the wall, and the beam out of the timber shall answer it. (This is evidenced by the great palace in Babylon, as well as the other great buildings, which were built by the enforced labor of miserable captors and adorned with the fruits of fraud and pillage.)

12 Woe to him who builds a town with blood, and stablishes a city by iniquity! (This is the third "Woe" mentioned; it concerns violence and cruelty. The other two are found in Verses 6 and 9. The phrase, "Woe to him who builds a town with blood," concerns mighty Babylon, or any city for that matter, built by riches gained by the murder of conquered nations. The phrase, "And stablishes a city by iniquity!" refers to a city, or anything, built as the result of sin.)

13 Behold, is it not of the LORD of Hosts that the people shall labour in the very fire, and the people shall weary themselves for very vanity? (God has ordained for the "fire" the great and strong cities and palaces which the nations weary themselves in building.)

GOD'S ULTIMATE PURPOSE IN THE EARTH

14 For the Earth shall be filled with the knowledge of the Glory of the LORD, as the waters cover the sea. (This Passage is very similar to what Isaiah said in 11:9 of his Book. As the Lord answers Habakkuk, His statements,

although alluding to coming Babylon, rather uses Babylon to symbolize the world as a whole without God. However, the Holy Spirit proclaims: "For the Earth shall be filled," not with injustice, murder, greed, avarice, hate, or oppression, but instead "with the knowledge of the Glory of the LORD." This will take place in the coming Millennium, beginning immediately after the Second Coming of Christ.)

WOE TO DRUNKARDS

15 Woe unto him who gives his neighbour drink, who puts your bottle to him, and makes him drunk also, that you may look on their nakedness! *(This "Woe" speaks of drunkenness. The phrase, "Woe unto him who gives his neighbor drink," refers, first of all, to the deepened idol worship and debauchery to which the conquered nations were exposed upon their defeat by the Babylonians. All sense of nationhood was taken away from these conquered peoples, with them virtually reduced to slaves; consequently, they were reduced to constant inebriation in order to try to stand the pain, etc.*

As well, even though in a secondary position, it pertains to all those who make and distribute alcoholic beverage. The Lord has pronounced a "Woe" of "violence" on all who participate in this scourge of debilitation to one's fellow man.

The phrase, "That you may look on their nakedness!" refers to the total debilitation of the individual. "Nakedness" refers to the person having no covering or protection, being exposed to the mercy of others, of which there is precious little.)

16 You are filled with shame for glory: drink thou also, and let your foreskin be uncovered: the cup of the LORD's right hand shall be turned unto you, and shameful spewing shall be on your glory. *(The phrase, "You are filled with shame for glory," proclaims the very opposite type of glory to that in the Promise of the "knowledge of the Glory of the LORD." That "Glory" is wonderful to behold, while this "glory" is "shame."*

The phrase, "Drink thou also, and let your foreskin be uncovered," refers to the uncircumcised. To be uncircumcised meant that the person was not in Covenant relationship with the Lord and was consequently judged as a heathen.

The idea of the phrase is: the Babylonians, i.e., the world, have no relationship or Covenant with God. Consequently, "the cup of the LORD's right hand shall be turned unto you," which

means that judgment will surely come, and figures not only the destruction of the Babylon of ancient times, but the entirety of spiritual Babylon, the world's system.

The phrase, "And shameful spewing shall be on your glory," refers to the "cup" of the Wrath of God, which will be poured out upon her.)

17 For the violence of Lebanon shall cover you, and the spoil of beasts, which made them afraid, because of men's blood, and for the violence of the land, of the city, and of all who dwell therein. *(The phrase, "For the violence of Lebanon shall cover you," pertains to violence against Jerusalem and the Temple — called here "Lebanon," because it was built with cedars brought from thence. The phrase, "And the spoil of beasts, which made them afraid," here pictures the nations as wild beasts, which would rend the Chaldean Monarchy. This was effected by the Medes and Persians.*

The last phrase refers to Judah and Jerusalem. When Nebuchadnezzar took the city, the slaughter was terrible, with the Lord promising vengeance because of the "violence." And yet, this Prophecy is given before the Babylonians even came to power or Nebuchadnezzar was even born!)

WOE TO IDOLATERS

18 What profits the graven image that the maker thereof has graven it; the molten image, and a teacher of lies, that the maker of his work trusts therein, to make dumb idols? *(The question, "What profits the graven image that the maker thereof has graven it?", goes to the heart of Babylonian thought. They would attribute all their success to their gods. The phrase, "The molten image," further reinforces the fact that the thing is made, designed, and fashioned by man and, therefore, worthless.*

The phrase, "And a teacher of lies," refers to the customs and culture built around this idol, which encouraged its worshippers in lying delusions, which is an entire contrast to Jehovah, Who is Truth.)

19 Woe unto him who says to the wood, Awake; to the dumb stone, Arise, it shall teach! Behold, it is laid over with gold and silver, and there is no breath at all in the midst of it. *(This is the fifth and final "Woe," and speaks to idolaters. The phrase, "Woe unto him who says to the wood, Awake; to the dumb stone, Arise, it shall teach!", actually means, in the Hebrew, "shall this teach?" — an emphatic question expressing astonishment.*

The phrase, "Behold, it is laid over with gold and silver," implies that in the mind of the "maker" the precious metal denotes some type of special worth. While the precious metal may be valuable, still, that was true before it was placed on that idol.

The phrase, "There is not breath at all in the midst of it," presents the fact that despite the accoutrements, it is still a dead, lifeless object!)

20 But the LORD is in His holy temple: let all the Earth keep silence before Him. (The first phrase refers to Heaven itself and means that man should consult Him, not these dumb idols. He is a Living God, whereas these other things "have no breath in them." As such, He will demonstrate this fact so effectually that all the Earth will stand hushed in silence before Him. In idolatry the idol is silent and its worshippers eloquent.)

CHAPTER 3
(626 B.C.)
A PRAYER OF HABAKKUK:
ASKS FOR MERCY

A prayer of Habakkuk the Prophet upon Shigionoth. (The word "Shigionoth" is the plural of "Shiggaion," and means "a crying aloud.")

2 O LORD, I have heard Your speech, and was afraid: O LORD, revive Your work in the midst of the years, in the midst of the years make known; in wrath remember mercy. (This Verse may be thus paraphrased: "O Jehovah, I have heard Your fame, and I bowed in reverent worship. O Jehovah, repeat Your doings of old in the midst of these years of affliction; in the midst of these years of sorrow, demonstrate Your power; in wrath, remember Mercy.")

GOD SAVES THE RIGHTEOUS; THE
WICKED ARE CONDEMNED

3 God came from Teman, and the Holy One from Mount Paran. Selah. His glory covered the Heavens, and the Earth was full of His praise. (This phrase, "God came from Teman," refers to Sinai. It refers to the Lord leading the Children of Israel out of Egypt through this barren wasteland. The phrase, "And the Holy One from Mount Paran," refers to Mount Sinai proper, where the Law was given.

The one word "Selah" pronounces the entirety of this Chapter, especially considering the last line in Verse 19, as a song or ode, given by the

Lord to Habakkuk, and him reciting or singing it with the worship choir in the Temple.)

4 And His brightness was as the light; He had horns coming out of His hand: and there was the hiding of His power. (The phrase, "And His brightness was as the light," refers to the Glory of God, which is of such magnitude that mere mortals, especially in the unconverted state, could not stand it. The phrase, "He had horns coming out of His Hand," has the idea of beaming rays of glory and power coming out of His Hands for healing and miracles [Lk. 4:4]. The phrase, "And there was the hiding of His Power," has reference to His full Power, which was hidden in His Being.)

5 Before Him went the pestilence, and burning coals went forth at His feet. (The idea of the Verse concerns judgment on sin and rebellion. Even though He has evidenced such in the past, still, the greatest portrayal of this judgment concerning the "pestilence," etc. will be brought to bear in the coming Great Tribulation.)

6 He stood, and measured the Earth: He beheld, and drove asunder the nations; and the everlasting mountains were scattered, the perpetual hills did bow: His Ways are everlasting. (The phrase, "He stood, and measured the Earth," has to do with measuring it for judgment, and more particularly, the land of Egypt in the deliverance of the Children of Israel. He will measure it again in the coming Great Tribulation [Rev. 11:1-2].

The phrase, "He beheld, and drove asunder the nations," has to do with the nations that occupied Israel, which were defeated by God's Power as Joshua and the armies of Israel took the land of Canaan.

The phrase, "And the everlasting mountains were scattered, the perpetual hills did bow," has to do with creation obeying Him explicitly, while man doesn't!

The phrase, "His Ways are everlasting," has reference to His unchangeability. What He was yesterday, He is now, and will ever be. As such, man can trust His Word, because it proclaims His unchangeable "Ways.")

7 I saw the tents of Cushan in affliction: and the curtains of the land of Midian did tremble. (The phrase, "I saw the tents of Cushan in affliction," refers to Egypt at the death of the firstborn. The phrase, "And the curtains of the land of Midian did tremble," refers to the country between Egypt and Canaan. The idea is: God took stringent measures upon the enemies of His People when He was delivering them from

Egyptian bondage. So, Habakkuk's song or ode recounts the great victories given to Israel by the Lord against her enemies, the enemies, therefore, of God.)

8 Was the LORD displeased against the rivers? was Your anger against the rivers? was Your wrath against the sea, that You did ride upon Your horses and Your chariots of salvation? *(The question, "Was the LORD displeased against the rivers?", uses the plural of majesty for the great river, the Nile, when turned by Moses into blood. "The sea" concerns the Red Sea, when it was divided and a passage was made for the Children of Israel who were leaving Egypt.*

The idea is: the Lord was not angry with His Creation, but with the manner in which Egypt had made a god out of the Nile and thought to use the Red Sea to trap the Israelites. In other words, they were trying to use God's Creation against God. Consequently, He used His Creation to serve His Purpose, showing them exactly Who God is!

The last phrase speaks of the Lord as the Leader of a mighty Host, which came with chariots and horses to defend the Israelites and to crush their foes.)

9 Your bow was made quite naked, according to the oaths of the Tribes, even Your Word. Selah. You did cleave the Earth with rivers. *(The phrase, "Your bow was made quite naked," refers to God's Word. The phrase, "According to the oaths of the Tribes, even Your Word," refers to a plural of excellence for the great Promise, confirmed with an oath, made to Abraham and to the Tribes, for they were then in his loins. The phrase, "You did cleave the Earth with rivers," refers to the Lord bringing forth water out of the rock to quench the thirst of Israel [Ex. 17:6].)*

10 The mountains saw You, and they trembled: the overflowing of the water passed by: the deep uttered his voice, and lifted up his hands on high. *(The first phrase concerns the earthquake that shook Sinai at the Presence of the Lord, when the Law was given [Ex. 19:18]. The phrase, "The overflowing of the water passed by," refers to the opening of the Jordan for Israel under Joshua to pass through. The last phrase is a poetic figure picturing the Jordan lifting up its voice and hands in worship to God.)*

11 The sun and moon stood still in their habitation: at the light of Your arrows they went, and at the shining of Your glittering spear. *(The first phrase concerns the miracle*

given to Joshua when he faced the combined forces of the enemy at Gibeon. There "the sun stood still, and the moon stayed" [Josh. 10:13-14]. The phrase, "At the light of Your arrows they went," has to do with the Lord " casting down great stones from Heaven" upon the enemy in this great victory given to Joshua [Josh. 10:11].)

12 You did march through the land in indignation, You did thresh the heathen in anger. *("The land" speaks of Canaan; "the heathen" refers to the inhabitants who possessed it, who were to be driven out. The Lord was "indignant" against them because of their idol worship and deep sin.)*

13 You went forth for the salvation of Your people, even for salvation with Your anointed: You wounded the head out of the house of the wicked, by discovering the foundation unto the neck. Selah. *(The first phrase refers to the Lord as being the General directing the activities of Joshua in the taking of the land of Canaan. The phrase, "Even for Salvation with Your Anointed," pertains to Joshua and God's People Israel, but more perfectly to the Heavenly Joshua, the Lord Jesus Christ. The Hebrew name for Jesus is "Joshua."*

The phrase, "You wounded the head out of the house of the wicked," refers to the five kings of the Amorites, who were defeated by Joshua and executed [Josh. 10:5. 26]. The last phrase concerns Joshua telling his captains to put their feet upon the necks of these kings, thereby proclaiming total victory over them [Josh. 10:24].)

14 You did strike through with his staves the head of his villages: they came out as a whirlwind to scatter Me: their rejoicing was as to devour the poor secretly. *(The first phrase continues respecting the great victory given by the Lord to Joshua concerning the defeat of the five kings. The phrase, "They came out as a whirlwind to scatter Me," refers to the confederation of the five kings determined to overwhelm Joshua and the army of Israel. The last phrase pertains to the plans of the five kings to destroy Israel, looking at them as "poor," i.e., without modern weapons, at least modern for that time. The word "secretly" addresses their secret plans, which, of course, were not secret to God.)*

15 You did walk through the sea with Your horses, through the heap of great waters. *(The first phrase refers to the seven nations of Canaan. The words, "with Your horses," refer back to Verse 8 and the Lord fighting for Joshua, undoubtedly encircling the enemy with these unseen*

"horses and chariots of Salvation." The phrase, "Through the heap of great waters," pertains to the confederacy of the enemy, as mentioned, and the Lord defeating them greatly.)

DESPITE ADVERSITY, HABAKKUK HAS FAITH

16 When I heard, my belly trembled; my lips quivered at the voice: rottenness entered into my bones, and I trembled in myself, that I might rest in the day of trouble: when he come up unto the people, he will invade them with his troops. *(The first phrase addresses the effect of the entirety of that given to him by the Lord, as denoted in this short Book. He "trembles," realizing that God has shown him a picture, not only of Judah at present, but also of the coming Gentile world powers and the Power of the Lord to deliver, which He ultimately will.*

The phrase, "Rottenness entered into my bones, and I trembled in myself," refers to the coming Babylonians, and the grief they would cause for Judah. The phrase, "That I might rest in the day of trouble," concerns this coming invasion by the Chaldeans, and his plea to the Lord that it may be far enough into the future that he will have lived out his lifespan and would not see this terrible thing. Every indication is that his request was granted.

The last phrase refers to the Chaldeans invading the People of God and overcoming them.)

17 Although the fig tree shall not blossom, neither shall fruit be in the vines; the labour of the olive shall fail, and the fields shall yield no meat; the flock shall be cut off from the fold, and there shall be no herd in the stalls *(in effect, the Prophet is asking the Lord to grant his request that the invasion be held off until his demise. But if he is fated to witness the devastation of the country, he will still rejoice in the Lord, Who, as his strength, will enable him morally to walk above the trials and sorrows of the times, just as a deer walks securely upon the edge of the giddiest precipice):*

18 Yet I will rejoice in the LORD, I will joy in the God of my salvation. *(Such is the triumph of Faith! It trusts God in the darkest hours and sharpest trials; it awaits His vindication of His Actions and looks forward with conviction to the sure dawning of the promised Day of Glory.)*

19 The LORD God is my strength, and He will make my feet like hinds' feet, and He will make me to walk upon my high places. To the chief singer on my stringed instruments. *(The reason the Prophet could rejoice, irrespective of what happened in the future, was because "the LORD God [was his] strength." The phrase, "To the chief singer on my stringed instruments," implies that this last Chapter was used as a musical composition or ode for worship in the Temple. It was adapted for the public service to the accompaniment of stringed instruments. As well, from the statement, "my stringed instruments," it could be inferred that Habakkuk was a Levite and, therefore, had a right to take part in the Temple services. Also, part of the Verse could be translated, "He makes me to mount upon the high places, that I may conquer by His song," thus by Faith singing a song of triumph as Deborah of old [Judg., Chpt. 5].)*

ZEPHANIAH

CHAPTER 1
(630 B.C.)
GOD'S JUDGMENT ON JUDAH AND JERUSALEM: BABYLONIAN CAPTIVITY

THE Word of the LORD which came unto Zephaniah the son of Cushi, the son of Gedaliah, the son of Amariah, the son of Hizkiah, in the days of Josiah the son of Amon, king of Judah. *(It is believed that Zephaniah began his Prophetic Ministry immediately before the Prophet Jeremiah, or in the beginning days of Jeremiah's Ministry. Josiah was the last Godly King to grace the Throne of Judah, and Zephaniah may well have had some Godly influence on the king, which propelled him in the right direction. In fact, Zephaniah was a great-grandson of Hezekiah, and also a distant relative of King Josiah.)*

2 I will utterly consume all things from off the land, saith the LORD. *(The Gospel in Zephaniah, as in the Epistle to the Romans [Rom. 1:18], begins with the Wrath of God; consequently, any other so-called gospel is false! In the original Hebrew, the warning given here is so strong that it actually has the same connotation of the awful warning of the judgment of the Flood.*

The phrase, "All things from off the land," actually says, "from the face of the Earth," not the land of Judah alone. This pertains to the Truth that, due to the fact that Judah alone knew Jehovah, her state and position affected the entire Earth of that day.)

3 I will consume man and beast; I will consume the fowls of the Heaven, and the fishes of the sea, and the stumblingblocks with the wicked: and I will cut off man from off the land, saith the LORD. *(The phrase, "I will consume man and beast," is not mere hyperbole, but instead expresses the terrible blight of sin as a result of the Fall, which affects not only man, but even the lower creation. Even material nature suffers from man's sin [Gen. 3:17; Rom. 8:22].)*

4 I will also stretch out My hand upon Judah, and upon all the inhabitants of Jerusalem; and I will cut off the remnant of Baal from this place, and the name of the Chemarims with the Priests *(the phrase, "Stretching out the hand," is an expression used when God is about to do great things or inflict notable punishment [Ex. 3:20; Deut. 4:34; Isa. 5:25].*

The phrase, "And I will cut off the remnant of Baal from this place," speaks of the sin of God's chosen People being more severe than that of the heathen. The heathen did not know better, while Judah did know better! They ought to have abhorred idolatry and maintained the True Faith.

The phrase, "And the name of the Chemarims with the Priests," referred to the black-robed priests of Baal here found in fellowship with the Priests of Jehovah);

5 And them who worship the host of Heaven upon the housetops; and them who worship and who swear by the LORD, and who swear by Malcham *(the first phrase addresses the sin of idolatry which characterized much of the ancient world, and even the present world. Planetary bodies were believed to guide the destiny and fortune of events; consequently, the flat roofs of the houses in that part of the world were used as places to erect altars for family worship of the heavenly bodies. Here they burned incense [Jer. 19:13] and offered animal sacrifices [II Ki. 23:12].*

The phrase, "And them who worship and who swear by the LORD," did not actually mean that they worshipped the Lord, but rather that they claimed to worship Him; in reality, they worshipped "Malcham." "Malcham" actually was "Moloch," to whom was offered human sacrifices and other forms of worship);

6 And them who are turned back from the LORD; and those who have not sought the LORD, nor enquired for Him. *(Four companies appear in Verses 5 and 6: idolaters, uniters of Jehovah and idols, backsliders, and agnostics. The Wrath of God does not distinguish between these.*

At that day, as today, it was fashionable to profess and practice the fundamental unity of all religions, and so to make the Salvation of the Bible complementary to the great religions of the east, etc. But there are only two ways of worship in existence; they are antagonistic, and the one will destroy the other. These ways are: man's religion and God's Salvation.)

THE DAY OF THE LORD: PUNISHMENT

7 Hold your peace at the presence of the Lord GOD: for the Day of the LORD is at hand: for the LORD has prepared a sacrifice, He has bid His guests. *(This Verse holds a double meaning: first of all, the "sacrifice" mentioned here speaks of the coming Babylonian invasion, which would take place about 50 or 60 years in the future; however, its plenary fulfillment will take place at the Second Advent of Christ, and we speak of the Battle of Armageddon.*

The phrase, "He has bid His guests," refers to the beasts and fowls that will eat the dead bodies of the slain of Nebuchadnezzar's invasion; but, most of all, it pertains to the multitudes which will be slain at the Battle of Armageddon [Isa. 34:6; Jer. 46:10; Mat. 24:27-28; Lk. 17:34-37].)

8 And it shall come to pass in the day of the LORD's sacrifice, that I will punish the princes, and the king's children, and all such as are clothed with strange apparel. *(This Verse can be summed up in the phrase, "And all such as are clothed with strange apparel": the word "strange" implies foreign apparel; it also implies foreign manners and habits. Israel even had a special way to dress, which was designed by the Lord, because they were a peculiar people, consecrated to God's service [Num. 15:37-39; Deut. 22:12]; however, Judah forsook the design of the Lord and assumed the dress of the Egyptians and the Babylonians.)*

9 In the same day also will I punish all those who leap on the threshold, which fill their masters' houses with violence and deceit. *(The phrase, "Leap on the threshold," was a common term then for burglary and stealing with violence. The idea is: many of the Nobles of Judah employed thieves to steal and plunder.)*

10 And it shall come to pass in that day, saith the LORD, that there shall be the noise of a cry from the fish gate, and an howling from the second, and a great crashing from the hills. *(Verses 10 and 11 describe the arrival of the Chaldean army at Jerusalem and its victorious penetration of the city from the northern fish gate to Maktesh, where the wealthy merchants had their palaces. The phrase, "And an howling from the second," pertains to the second district or the lower city upon the hill Acra, which was north of Zion.)*

11 Howl, you inhabitants of Maktesh, for all the merchant people are cut down; all they who bear silver are cut off. *(The phrase, "Howl, you inhabitants of Maktesh," pertains, as stated, to the places where the wealthy merchants had their homes in Jerusalem.)*

12 And it shall come to pass at that time, that I will search Jerusalem with candles, and punish the men who are settled on their lees: who say in their heart, The LORD will not do good, neither will He do evil. *(The phrase, "And punish the men who are settled on their lees," pertains to those who are hardened in their evil habits. The phrase, "Who say in the heart, the LORD will not do good, neither will He do evil," proclaims these individuals as "fools," who denied God's moral government of the world. In other words, they did not deny that there was a God and did not openly ridicule Him, but instead ignored Him; and by that action, they made themselves god.)*

13 Therefore their goods shall become a booty, and their houses a desolation: they shall also build houses, but not inhabit them; and they shall plant vineyards, but not drink the wine thereof. *(Verses 13 through 18 give a vivid picture of the coming sack of Jerusalem, and in fact the ruin of the whole country.)*

THE NEARNESS OF THE DAY

14 The great day of the LORD is near, it is near, and hastens greatly, even the voice of the day of the LORD: the mighty man shall cry there bitterly. *(Verses 14 through 18, in effect, have a double meaning. They refer, first of all, to the near destruction of Jerusalem, which would be about 50 years in the future. As well, they speak of the coming Great Tribulation and the Battle of Armageddon, which is even yet to come to pass.)*

15 That day is a day of wrath, a day of trouble and distress, a day of wasteness and desolation, a day of darkness and gloominess, a day of clouds and thick darkness *(Joel, who prophesied about 100 years before Zephaniah, basically used the same terminology of this Verse, "a day of darkness and of gloominess, a day of clouds and of black darkness" [Joel 2:2]. As stated, the Verse speaks of the near destruction of Jerusalem and then the coming day of the Antichrist.),*

16 A day of the trumpet and alarm against the fenced cities, and against the high towers.

17 And I will bring distress upon men, that they shall walk like blind men, because they have sinned against the LORD: and their blood shall be poured out as dust, and their flesh as the dung. *(Jerusalem would experience this shortly; however, its greatest fulfillment will be when blood will flow to the horses' bridles in the*

Battle of Armageddon [Rev. 14:20]. No doubt, this will be blood mixed with water because of the overflowing rain, as prophesied by Ezekiel [Ezek. 38:22].)

18 Neither their silver nor their gold shall be able to deliver them in the day of the LORD's wrath; but the whole land shall be devoured by the fire of His jealousy: for He shall make even a speedy riddance of all them who dwell in the land. (All of man's security is nothing without the Lord.)

CHAPTER 2
(630 B.C.)
AN ADMONITION TO JUDAH

GATHER yourselves together, yea, gather together, O nation not desired (the first three Verses of this Chapter are an appeal to Israel to repent, but, sadly, to no avail! Man's problem is sin, and the only solution to that problem, even as it always has been, is "Jesus Christ and Him Crucified" [I Cor. 1:23]);

2 Before the decree bring forth, before the day pass as the chaff, before the fierce anger of the LORD come upon you, before the day of the LORD'S anger come upon you. (If one is to notice, the word "before" is used four times in this one Verse. It is another graphic plea by the Holy Spirit through the Prophet for Judah to repent.)

3 Seek ye the LORD, all you meek of the Earth, which have wrought His judgment; seek righteousness, seek meekness: it may be you shall be hid in the day of the LORD'S anger. (This Third Verse is not only addressed to the people, but even more importantly, to King Josiah and his supporters, who wrought God's judgment upon the idols [I Ki. 13:2; II Ki. 23:17]. They were admonished to keep on seeking the Lord, and seeking righteousness and meekness, so escape might be possible for them.

In fact, Josiah was a Godly king, actually one of the Godliest to ever grace the Throne of Judah. He was a true son of David. And yet, despite his qualitative leadership, and even though Judah reformed outwardly, still, in their hearts they continued to worship idols and to rebel against Jehovah.)

GOD'S JUDGMENT ON SURROUNDING
NATIONS: AGAINST GAZA
AND THE PHILISTINES

4 For Gaza shall be forsaken, and Ashkelon a desolation: they shall drive out Ashdod at the noon day, and Ekron shall be rooted up. (Without a break in stride, the remainder of this Chapter predicts the fierce anger of God upon the Philistines on the west, the Moabites and Ammonites on the east, the Egyptians on the south, and the Assyrians on the north.

Why would the Holy Spirit, without breaking stride or changing the subject, suddenly cease the denunciation of Judah and immediately pronounce judgment on the Gentiles? It speaks of the fact that Israel will one day be restored and that the "Times of the Gentiles" will come to an end, which is even yet future [Lk. 21:24], which will happen at the Second Coming of the Lord.)

5 Woe unto the inhabitants of the sea coast, the nation of the Cherethites! the word of the LORD is against you; O Canaan, the land of the Philistines, I will even destroy you, that there shall be no inhabitant. (This Passage was fulfilled some years later; however, its plenary fulfillment yet awaits! The phrase, "Woe unto the inhabitants of the sea coast," as well, pertains to the modern Palestinians, who presently occupy this area, and which, according to modern treaty, have established, at least in theory, a Palestinian State.

The phrase, "The Word of the LORD is against you," signifies the impossibility of their success, despite every effort made on their behalf. True, the Palestinian question will not be solved until the Second Coming, but then, most definitely, it will be solved!)

6 And the sea coast shall be dwellings and cottages for shepherds, and folds for flocks. (This area, the Gaza Strip in Israel, that is now so hotly contested and which will be even more contested in the future, will ultimately, however, be as the Lord intends for it to be — docile, peaceful, and serene. The Word of the Lord shall bring it to pass.)

7 And the coast shall be for the remnant of the house of Judah; they shall feed thereupon: in the houses of Ashkelon shall they lie down in the evening: for the LORD their God shall visit them, and turn away their captivity. (This was partially fulfilled on the return of the Jews from Babylonian exile; however, its total fulfillment awaits the Second Coming!)

MOAB AND AMMON JUDGED

8 I have heard the reproach of Moab, and the revilings of the children of Ammon, whereby they have reproached My people, and

magnified themselves against their border. *(As Verses 4 through 7 spoke of the Philistines and their inhabiting the sea coasts next to the Mediterranean, Verses 8 through 11 speak to Moab and Ammon on the eastern side of Israel. The phrase, "And magnified themselves against their border," speaks of Israel's border. God had Himself assigned these boundaries to Israel; therefore, to invade these was, and is, an offense against Him.)*

9 Therefore as I live, saith the LORD of Hosts, the God of Israel, Surely Moab shall be as Sodom, and the children of Ammon as Gomorrah, even the breeding of nettles, and saltpits, and a perpetual desolation: the residue of My people shall spoil them, and the remnant of My people shall possess them. *(The phrase, "Therefore as I live, saith the LORD of Hosts," pledges God's determination to the Truth of His declaration [Deut. 32:40; Isa. 49:18]. By using the phrase, "LORD of Hosts," He is signifying that He is able to carry out that which He speaks.*

"Moab" and "Ammon" are no more, exactly as the Lord said; the area is now occupied by modern Jordan. However, in the coming Kingdom Age, Israel will occupy the entirety of that area, plus much, much more.)

10 This shall they have for their pride, because they have reproached and magnified themselves against the people of the Lord of Hosts. *(It is remarkable that the Lord would pronounce coming judgment on Judah, and then turn around and also pronounce judgment on those who have "reproached and magnified themselves against the people of the Lord of Hosts." This should let all and sundry know that the Lord looks at all persecution of His Children with a jaundiced eye. In other words, every Believer must be treated kindly — not so much because of who they are, but to Whom they belong!)*

11 The LORD will be terrible unto them: for He will famish all the gods of the Earth; and men shall worship Him, every one from his place, even all the isles of the heathen. *(The phrase, "For He will famish all the gods of the Earth," means He will deprive the idols of their worshippers. The phrase, "And men shall worship Him," refers to the coming day when all the inhabitants of the Earth will worship the Lord, which will be in the coming Kingdom Age.)*

ETHIOPIA AND ASSYRIA JUDGED

12 Ye Ethiopians also, you shall be slain by My sword. *(But yet the judgment of extinction was not pronounced on them; therefore, they survive unto this hour!)*

13 And He will stretch out His hand against the north, and destroy Assyria; and will make Nineveh a desolation, and dry like a wilderness. *(The phrase, "And He will stretch out His hand against the north, and destroy Assyria," would have sounded strange to the hearers. At that time, the Assyrian power was total. The idea that such could come was preposterous to the carnal mind. However, the Lord said it would come; and come it did, even in about 20-25 years.*

After its destruction by the Babylonians, Nineveh was not rebuilt and became exactly as prophesied: "a desolation, and dry like a wilderness.")

14 And flocks shall lie down in the midst of her, all the beasts of the nations: both the cormorant and the bittern shall lodge in the upper lintels of it; their voice shall sing in the windows; desolation shall be in the thresholds; for he shall uncover the cedar work. *(The phrase, "For he [Nebuchadnezzar] shall uncover the cedar work," respects the destruction of the great and beautiful palaces of the Assyrians. The entirety of the Verse speaks of total destruction, which came about exactly as prophesied.)*

15 This is the rejoicing city that dwelt carelessly, that said in her heart, I am, and there is none beside me: how is she become a desolation, a place for beasts to lie down in! every one who passes by her shall hiss, and wag his hand. *(The phrase, "That said in her heart, I am, and there is none beside me," has Nineveh, in effect, claiming for herself the attributes of Almighty God. However, the Lord has promised, and for all world powers who have defied him, that they will "become a desolation, a place for beasts to lie down in!")*

CHAPTER 3
(630 B.C.)

WOE TO SINFUL JUDAH

WOE to her that is filthy and polluted, to the oppressing city! *("Woe to her" is now pronounced against Jerusalem. The phrase, "That is filthy and polluted," has to do with idol worship and all its attendant filth, i.e., both male and female prostitution. Such polluted the city.)*

2 She obeyed not the voice; she received not correction; she trusted not in the LORD; she drew not near to her God. *(The love that throbs in these words, "her God," is pathetic.*

Proud and polluted as Jerusalem was, yet God said she was His, and that He was "her God." The following are the charges:

1. *She obeyed not the voice;*
2. *She received not correction;*
3. *She trusted not in the Lord; and,*
4. *She did not draw near to her God.)*

3 Her princes within her are roaring lions; her judges are evening wolves; they gnaw not the bones till the morrow. *(Princes, judges, Preachers, and Priests were workers of iniquity and teachers of falsehood. "They gnaw not" would be better translated: "They defer not till tomorrow to gnaw the bones." Ravenous wolves gnaw the bones, immediately they have devoured the flesh.)*

4 Her prophets are light and treacherous persons: her priests have polluted the Sanctuary, they have done violence to the Law. *(The phrase, "Her prophets are light and treacherous persons," referred to false prophets, who had no true mission from God. The word "light" means that they were "frivolous and empty boasters."*

The phrase, "Her priests have polluted the Sanctuary," actually means they polluted what was holy. The phrase, "They have done violence to the Law," means that they abrogated the Law of Moses by distorting its meaning, neither observing it themselves nor teaching others to keep it.)

5 The just LORD is in the midst thereof; He will not do iniquity: every morning does He bring His judgment to light, He fails not; but the unjust knows no shame. *(Jehovah, as the Just Judge, is here contrasted with the unjust judges of Verse 3.)*

6 I have cut off the nations: their towers are desolate; I made their streets waste, that none passes by: their cities are destroyed, so that there is no man, that there is none inhabitant. *(The phrase, "I have cut off the nations," respects all the many nations that God defeated in the past relative to protecting Israel. This was well known to all the people of Judah, and should have served as a dire warning to the people. However, Judah felt themselves above the heathen and would not believe the True Prophets, even though the Lord repeatedly spoke through them respecting coming judgment. In other words, they felt they were in a class unto themselves, and that the Lord would not require of them what He required of the heathen.)*

7 I said, Surely you will fear Me, you will receive instruction; so their dwelling should not be cut off, howsoever I punished them: but they rose early, and corrupted all their doings. *(The phrase, "So their dwelling should not be cut off," respected the Lord not desiring at all to bring judgment. In fact, He made every effort to bring the people to Repentance, but to no avail! The phrase, "Howsoever I punished them," speaks of chastisements which were ignored.*

The phrase, "But they rose early, and corrupted all their doings," means that they hardened their hearts and ignored the warnings of the Prophets. Consequently, the Lord was left with no choice, because the light within them had been turned to darkness.)

THE LAST DAYS: ARMAGEDDON

8 Therefore wait ye upon Me, saith the LORD, until the day that I rise up to the prey: for My determination is to gather the nations, that I may assemble the kingdoms, to pour upon them My indignation, even all My fierce anger: for all the Earth shall be devoured with the fire of My jealousy. *(This Passage actually has to do with the coming Battle of Armageddon, which will precipitate the Second Coming [Rev. 16:13-17].)*

CONVERSION OF ALL NATIONS

9 For then will I turn to the people a pure language, that they may all call upon the name of the LORD, to serve Him with one consent. *(The Hebrew for "pure language" is "barar sepheth," which means "cleansed or purged lips or speech in contrast with unclean lips" [Isa. 6:5]. The phrase, "That they may all call upon the Name of the LORD," refers to the entirety of the world calling upon God in the Name of Jesus, with all other religions, idols, and false ways of worship done away with.*

The phrase, "To serve Him with one consent," constitutes the fulfillment of what is referred to as the Lord's Prayer [Mat. 6:10].)

10 From beyond the rivers of Ethiopia My suppliants, even the daughter of My dispersed, shall bring My offering. *(The idea of the Verse is: respecting the particular nations in which the Jews are ensconced, the Gentiles will help get them to Israel, and gladly so. This will be at the outset of the Kingdom Age.)*

JUDAH PURGED OF REBELS

11 In that day shall you not be ashamed for all your doings, wherein you have transgressed against Me: for then I will take away out of the

midst of you them who rejoice in your pride, and you shall no more be haughty because of My holy mountain. *(The phrase, "In that day," refers to the beginning of the Kingdom Age, when Christ will reign supreme over the entirety of the world, and do so from Jerusalem. At that time, Israel will be the supreme nation on the face of the Earth. Then, the haughty spirit of Israel will be broken, because Israel will have accepted Christ as Saviour, Lord, and Messiah.)*

12 I will also leave in the midst of you an afflicted and poor people, and they shall trust in the name of the LORD. *(The "afflicted and poor people" spoken of in this Passage portrays the Jews who have come through the fire of the Great Tribulation, and who have allowed it to refine them and make them "poor in spirit." It means their self-confidence has been abolished, with trust being placed solely in the Lord.)*

13 The remnant of Israel shall not do iniquity, nor speak lies; neither shall a deceitful tongue be found in their mouth: for they shall feed and lie down, and none shall make them afraid. *(The phrase, "The remnant of Israel shall not do iniquity, nor speak lies," actually addresses false prophets, who will no longer be in the land. Zechariah also mentions this [Zech. 13:2]. The last phrase, "For they shall feed and lie down, and none shall make them afraid," proclaims the total security of Israel in that coming Glad Day, when the Lord will be their Shepherd. This, they could have had all along, if they had only obeyed, because it was promised to them in the Law [Lev. 26:5-6].)*

MESSIAH REIGNING IN ZION

14 Sing, O daughter of Zion; shout, O Israel; be glad and rejoice with all the heart, O daughter of Jerusalem. *(Beginning with Verse 8 through the remainder of the Chapter, the Restoration of Israel is promised. It was a Restoration they could have had at the First Advent of Christ, but brutally refused by murdering their Messiah. When they finally do accept Christ, which will be immediately after the Second Coming, there will be "great joy" in Israel.)*

15 The LORD has taken away your judgments, He has cast out your enemy: the king of Israel, even the LORD, is in the midst of you: you shall not see evil any more. *(The phrase, "The LORD has taken away your judgments," refers to Divine chastisements being halted. This will be in the Kingdom Age, when Israel will have accepted Christ. The last phrase, "You shall not see evil any more," refers to the*

terrible judgments that came upon Israel in the past, which now will never happen again, because the Lord resides in the midst of her, with her gladly serving Him.)*

16 In that day it shall be said to Jerusalem, Fear thou not: and to Zion, Let not your hands be slack. *(For nearly 2,000 years now, the Jews have lived in "fear." Considering the terrible persecution over many centuries, they have had just cause to fear. In the coming Kingdom Age, "Jerusalem" will be, in essence, the capital city of the world. One might well call it, "Jerusalem, D.C.," i.e., "David's Capital."*

The phrase, "And to Zion, Let not your hands be slack," means that they must make up for all the time that has been lost. This they shall do, and more, because Christ reigns among them.)

17 The LORD your God in the midst of you is mighty; He will save, He will rejoice over you with joy; He will rest in His love, He will joy over you with singing. *(Verse 17 contrasts with Verse 5; the latter is past; the former, future. In Verse 5, He was in the midst of rebellious Jerusalem offering Himself as a Righteous Judge able to correct its evil; in Verse 17, He will reside in redeemed Jerusalem mightily to prevent any evil.)*

RESTORATION OF ISRAEL

18 I will gather them who are sorrowful for the solemn assembly, who are of you, to whom the reproach of it was a burden. *(The corruption of Israel and the consequent reproach leveled at it by the heathen were, and are, burdens upon the hearts that lived in fellowship with God. The "reproach" in that coming day will be ended!)*

19 Behold, at that time I will undo all who afflict you: and I will save her who halts, and gather her that was driven out; and I will get them praise and fame in every land where they have been put to shame. *(After Israel accepts Christ, she will be restored to her rightful place as the leading nation of the world; then, the "shame" will be forever ended!)*

20 At that time will I bring you again, even in the time that I gather you: for I will make you a name and a praise among all people of the Earth, when I turn back your captivity before your eyes, saith the LORD. *(Concerning Israel, this is one of the greatest Promises of all! In the Prophet's eye, the restoration from captivity and the times of the Messiah are synchronous. The former is so closely connected in idea with the latter that he speaks of both under one set of terms, applying the same imagery to both.)*

HAGGAI

CHAPTER 1

(520 B.C.)

THE PEOPLE ENCOURAGED TO REBUILD GOD'S TEMPLE; GOD'S ANSWER TO THE OBJECTORS

I N the second year of Darius the king, in the sixth month, in the first day of the month, came the Word of the LORD by Haggai the Prophet unto Zerubbabel the son of Shealtiel, governor of Judah, and to Joshua the son of Josedech, the High Priest, saying *(the Ministry of Haggai was separated from the Prophet Zephaniah by approximately 100 years. The exiles returned to the Holy Land from Babylon in 536 B.C., fulfilling the seventy-year period of captivity prophesied by Jeremiah [Jer. 25:11; 29:10].*

At that time, Zerubbabel, a descendant of David and of the Royal House of Judah, led the first group of nearly 50,000 people from Babylonia to the Holy Land. Almost immediately, the foundation of the Temple was laid; however, the work was greatly hindered and actually stopped until 520 B.C., when a fresh beginning was made. This fresh beginning was inspired by the prophesying of both Haggai and Zechariah, which saw the Temple completed.

The Book of Haggai records the unwillingness of the returned exiles to build, their shame over the inferiority of the new House, and their fear of the Persian Government because they built without special permission [Ezra, Chpts. 4-6]. Haggai probably wrote his Book in about 530 B.C.

The phrase, "In the second year of Darius the king," probably refers to Darius Hystapes Ahasuerus Artaxerxes the Persian. He reigned about 15 years after the Cyrus who commanded the building of the city and the laying of the foundation of the Temple, and who was thought to have been the son of Esther [Ezra, Chpt. 1; Isa. 45:13].

Haggai was the first Prophet after the captivities to Babylon),

2 Thus speaks the LORD of Hosts, saying, This people say, The time is not come, the time that the LORD's house should be built. *(Unbelief never fails of arguments, but always has this capital defect of leaving God out. The religious argument at that time was: the time, i.e., the seventy years of captivity, was not yet*

expired; therefore, the building of the Temple should wait. As another excuse, they said that they did not have the king's permission [Ezra, Chpt. 4].)

3 Then came the Word of the LORD by Haggai the Prophet, saying *(the phrase, "Then came the Word of the LORD," is repetition by the Holy Spirit, and by design. It is meant to impress upon the people the severity of the situation and the depth of their sin),*

4 Is it time for you, O ye, to dwell in your cieled houses, and this house lie waste? *(The question, "Is it time for you . . . ?", has the emphasis placed on the pronoun "you." It is used in derision, as the phrase "This people" is used in Verse 2 instead of "My people." The phrase, "O ye, to dwell in your cieled houses," has the Holy Spirit comparing their houses with His House. The comparison is not very favorable toward the people.)*

5 Now therefore thus saith the LORD of Hosts; Consider your ways. *(The word "consider" actually means "set your heart upon.")*

6 You have sown much, and bring in little; you eat, but you have not enough; you drink, but you are not filled with drink; you clothe yourselves, but there is none warm; and he who earns wages earns wages to put it into a bag with holes. *(Seldom does the Holy Spirit so clearly and plainly delineate the cause of lack of progress as He does in this particular Verse. Among other things, He shows us that to divert money from God's Work to personal use causes poverty of soul and oftentimes of pocket. Though they did have fine houses to dwell in, it seems that they had been visited with scanty harvest and weak bodily health. In these statements, given by the Holy Spirit through the Prophet, one is made to realize what God can do and what He will not do.)*

7 Thus saith the LORD of Hosts; Consider your ways. *(The Holy Spirit prefaced Verse 5 with the same admonition. Now, for effect, He repeats it. It is done by design.)*

8 Go up to the mountain, and bring wood, and build the house; and I will take pleasure in it, and I will be glorified, saith the Lord. *(The Holy Spirit quietly reminds them that the materials for doing the job were just a short distance*

away. The implication is: no costly offerings were required, only a willingness to work.)

9 You looked for much, and, lo, it came to little; and when you brought it home, I did blow upon it. Why? saith the LORD of Hosts. Because of My house that is waste, and you run every man unto his own house. *(God first is the secret of spiritual and temporal prosperity. The phrase, "You looked for much, and, lo, it came to little," is one step further than the first phrase of Verse 6. There they sowed much and brought in little; here, they expect much and get little.*

The phrase, "And when you brought it home, I did blow upon it," signifies that what little harvest they did get was cursed by the Lord, because they were not attending to His Work. Please understand: this was for all the people, not just the Priests, etc.)

10 Therefore the Heaven over you is stayed from dew, and the Earth is stayed from her fruit. *(No doubt, the people ascribe the meagerness of their crops to natural causes; they would not see the judicial nature of their infliction. The phrase, "And the Earth is stayed from her fruit," is an actual portrayal of the problems of the planet, even unto this day!)*

11 And I called for a drought upon the land, and upon the mountains, and upon the corn, and upon the new wine, and upon the oil, and upon that which the ground brings forth, and upon men, and upon cattle, and upon all the labour of the hands. *(This Verse portrays the Truth that every single thing in Judah of that particular time, including "the labor of the hands," was cursed by God; consequently, and irrespective of the amount of labor, ingenuity, ability, and investment, the people could not hope to prosper.*

There was a tremendous urgency by the Holy Spirit for the Temple to be completed, as is evident in this Book. Consequently, the opposition by the Samaritans and the demand to cease construction by the Persian king were not recognized by the Lord. In fact, absolutely no excuse should ever be allowed to hinder work that should be done for the Lord.)

THE PEOPLE ARE MOVED TO REBUILD

12 Then Zerubbabel the son of Shealtiel, and Joshua the son of Josedech, the High Priest, with all the remnant of the people, obeyed the voice of the LORD their God, and the words of Haggai the Prophet, as the LORD their God had sent him, and the people did fear before

the LORD. *("Zerubbabel" was the "Governor of Judah," no doubt appointed by the King of Persia. Thankfully, the leadership of the nation, headed up by Zerubbabel and Joshua the High Priest, led the way regarding obedience. The last phrase, "And the people did fear before the LORD," proclaims their reaction upon hearing the Message, and rightly so!)*

13 Then spoke Haggai the LORD's messenger in the LORD's message unto the people, saying, I am with you, saith the LORD. *(The obedient heart of Verse 12 always is rewarded with the "I am with you" of this Verse. There could be no greater blessing than for the Lord to be with a person — any person!)*

14 And the LORD stirred up the spirit of Zerubbabel the son of Shealtiel, governor of Judah, and the spirit of Joshua the son of Josedech, the High Priest, and the spirit of all the remnant of the people; and they came and did work in the house of the LORD of Hosts, their God *(this is one of the few recorded instances of all rulers and people stirred to obedience),*

15 In the four and twentieth day of the sixth month, in the second year of Darius the king. *(It seems that the Prophetic Message was delivered on the first of the sixth month [Vs. 1] and obeyed on the 24th of the same month. Thankfully, they did obey; however, such portrays the slowness of the heart to accept and obey the Word of the Lord.*

The phrase, "In the second year of Darius the king," recognizes the supremacy of the Gentiles and the sin of Judah which resulted in this supremacy. They would not have the Lord as their King; therefore, the Lord gave them a Gentile king.

Worse still, about 550 years later, the leaders of Israel would say, concerning the Kingship of Christ, "We have no king but Caesar" [Jn. 19:15]. They have found, to their terrible dismay, that Caesar has been a hard taskmaster.)

CHAPTER 2
(520 B.C.)
MESSAGE ON THE TEMPLES:
CONCERNING SOLOMON'S TEMPLE

IN the seventh month, in the one and twentieth day of the month, came the Word of the LORD by the Prophet Haggai, saying *(as Haggai's first Prophecy filled the entirety of Chapter 1, his second Prophecy spans Verses 1 through 9 of this Chapter. The 21st day of this*

particular month was the last and great day of the Feast of Tabernacles [Lev. 23:34]),

2 Speak now to Zerubbabel the son of Shealtiel, governor of Judah, and to Joshua the son of Josedech, the High Priest, and to the residue of the people, saying *(Haggai is instructed by the Lord, first of all, to direct his Message to the Civil and Spiritual Leaders, and then to the people. This, of course, is the order as it should be; but, if the Leaders will not comply, it is doubtful that many of the people will comply. Thankfully, Judah, at this particular time, had Godly Leaders),*

3 Who is left among you who saw this house in her first glory? and how do you see it now? is it not in your eyes in comparison of it as nothing? *(The question as asked by the Lord, "Who is left among you who saw this house in her first glory?", is addressed to some who had seen Solomon's Temple. Some have even thought that Haggai may have been in that number.*

Solomon's Temple was destroyed by Nebuchadnezzar in 586 B.C. As it is now 520 B.C., sixty-six years had elapsed since the Temple's destruction. Some of these old men who were present that day had undoubtedly, as young boys, seen the original Temple in all of its splendor and glory.

The second question, "And how to you see it now?", is meant to express the thoughts of their hearts, which tended toward faithlessness because of what greeted their eyes. The Holy Spirit, in reading their minds, answers the question for them by saying, "is it not in your eyes in comparison of it as nothing?"

At all times, the Child of God must "see" with the eye of Faith rather than surrounding circumstances.)

4 Yet now be strong, O Zerubbabel, saith the LORD; and be strong, O Joshua, son of Josedech, the High Priest; and be strong, all you people of the land, saith the LORD, and work: for I am with you, saith the LORD of Hosts *(the "strength" mentioned here comes about only by and through Faith in the Lord and His Word. Faith having Christ and the Cross as its object can always be assured of the Presence of the Holy Spirit; hence the Promise, "for I am with you, saith the LORD of Hosts"):*

5 According to the word that I covenanted with you when you came out of Egypt, so My Spirit remains among you: fear ye not. *(The phrase, "According to the Word that I covenanted with you when you came out of Egypt," actually speaks of the Law of Moses [Ex. 19:5-6; 29:45-46;*

Deut. 7:6; Jer. 7:23]. The phrase, "So My Spirit remains among you," refers to the Holy Spirit speaking by the Prophets and blessing all who would follow the Lord, according to God's Word.

When we do what the Lord desires that we do, we need have no "fear.")

RENOVATION OF HEAVEN AND EARTH

6 For thus saith the LORD of Hosts; Yet once, it is a little while, and I will shake the heavens, and the Earth, and the sea, and the dry land *(The first phrase could be translated, "Once again within a little time." The Holy Spirit through the Prophet desires to show the people the far larger picture than their Temple they are presently building; consequently, He launches from that present time even into the coming glorious future, when He will "fill this House with Glory," and thereby the entirety of the world.*

The phrase, "And I will shake the Heavens, and the Earth, and the sea, and the dry land," has a double meaning:

1. The coming Great Tribulation outlined in the Book of Rev., Chpts. 6-19;

2. The future renovation of the heavens and Earth by fire, when certain things will be removed and others will remain [Rev. 21:1].

The idea is: the building of this Temple, as unimpressive as it may have seemed to be, was linked to all of these great things which are even yet to come to pass. This is meant to show us how important the Work of God is in every capacity, no matter how small it may seem to be at the present. We must always remember: it is linked to something far larger, meaning we must not fail in our task);

MESSIAH'S SECOND ADVENT;
THE MILLENNIAL TEMPLE

7 And I will shake all nations, and the desire of all nations shall come, and I will fill this House with Glory, saith the LORD of Hosts. *(The phrase, "And I will shake all nations," refers to the coming Great Tribulation and, more specifically, the Battle of Armageddon, which Christ will interrupt by His Second Coming. The phrase, "And the desire of all nations shall come," actually means the "object of the desire," which does not refer to things, but instead to Christ Alone, Who can and will satisfy the desire of all nations. The phrase, "And I will fill this House with Glory, saith the LORD of Hosts,"*

speaks of the coming Kingdom Age.)

8 The silver is Mine, and the gold is Mine, saith the LORD of Hosts. *(The reason for this Passage interspersed between Verses 7 and 9 is because the people were thinking of what this present Temple would be by comparison to Solomon's Temple. Whereas the former had much silver and gold, Zerubbabel's Temple would have little or none. They were grieved over this. However, the Lord through the Prophet tells them that the Glory of the Temple is not in "silver" or "gold," but instead in His Spirit.*

As well, the Lord informs the people that all the "silver" and "gold" are His; if He were so minded, He could fill the House with such ornamentation. So, the lack was by design. He wanted the people's eyes to be not on the ostentatiousness of this building, but on the Spirit of God. In fact, silver and gold are never the end result of the great Plan of God, but instead that the Spirit of God may be with us and, in Truth, in us, and functioning mightily [Eph. 2:22].)

9 The Glory of this latter House shall be greater than of the former, saith the LORD of Hosts: and in this place will I give peace, saith the LORD of Hosts. *(The first phrase addresses itself to the future Millennial Temple, which will be built in Jerusalem, described by Ezekiel in Chapters 40 through 48 of his Book. Even though all the Temples are looked at basically as one, still, this "latter House" will be "Greater" than all, simply because of the Presence in that day of the "Prince of Peace," the Lord Jesus Christ.*

The phrase, "And in this place will I give peace," proclaims the fact that in that coming day all war will cease. The name of the first builder of the Temple was Solomon, which means "peaceful." This latter Temple will be glorified by the Presence of the "Peace-Bringer" [Gen. 49:10].)

REASONS WHY THEY WERE NOT BLESSED

10 In the four and twentieth day of the ninth month, in the second year of Darius, came the Word of the LORD by Haggai the Prophet, saying *(this is Haggai's third Prophecy, and occupies Verses 10 through 19. It was given about two months after the second Prophecy. As an aside, between the second and third Prophecies, Zechariah's first Prophecy was uttered [Zech. 1:2-6]. The phrase, "In the second year of Darius," once again is given by the Holy Spirit in order that all may know that the Gentiles now rule God's chosen People because of the rejection of the Lord as her King by Judah),*

11 Thus saith the LORD of Hosts; Ask now the Priests concerning the Law, saying *(the phrase "Ask now the Priests concerning the Law, saying," is meant to direct the Priests, who were to carry out the ritual and spiritual duties, back to the Bible),*

12 If one bear holy flesh in the skirt of his garment, and with his skirt do touch bread, or pottage, or wine, or oil, or any meat, shall it be holy? And the Priests answered and said, No. *(Verses 12 through 14 proclaim the Truth that Sacrifices, however holy in themselves, cannot sanctify disobedience and self-will. That which is holy cannot sanctify what is profane; but that which is unclean defiles that which is holy. The presence of evil destroys Holiness, but the Presence of God excludes evil. And when He is acknowledged, the Power of His Presence banishes defilement and brings blessing. The legislation of Verse 12 and 13 is found in Lev. 6:27 and 10:10-11.*

The phrase, "If one bear holy flesh in the skirt of his garment," speaks of the Sacrifice [meat] being borne by the Priests. As well, the Priests who carried this Sacrifice were, according to the Commandments of the Lord, to be holy.

In Truth, anything that touched the flesh of the Sacrifice was to be holy; therefore, unholy things, such as the "wine," "oil," etc., were not allowed to touch the Sacrifices. If such did happen, it would necessitate ceremonial cleansing before the Priestly work could be carried on again. Consequently, the answer, "No," by the Priests to Haggai's question was what it should have been.)

13 Then said Haggai, If one who is unclean by a dead body touch any of these, shall it be unclean? And the Priests answered and said, It shall be unclean. *(The entirety of this Text is found in Num. 6:6, 11. The implication is: death was caused by sin and came upon man as a result of the Fall; consequently, the touching of a dead body by anyone made one ceremonially unclean. To become clean again, one would have to go through the ceremony of the "Law of the red heifer," as found in Num. 19:22. Therefore, in respect to the touching of a dead body, the Priests answered and said, "It shall be unclean.")*

14 Then answered Haggai, and said, So is this people, and so is this nation before Me, saith the LORD; and so is every work of their hands; and that which they offer there is unclean. *(The indictment, as given by the Lord, is severe! If one is to notice, the Lord says "this*

people" instead of "My people," because, by their acts, they had disowned God [1:2]. The phrase, "And so is every work of their hands," means that as they were unclean, likewise, so was their labor. Therefore, an unholy vessel cannot produce a holy result.

The phrase, "And that which they offer there is unclean," refers to their Sacrifices, which, in effect, were not accepted by the Lord. Part, if not most, of the problem was that they thought the Sacrifices within themselves were enough, and that the other duties carried on in the Temple [when there was a Temple] were of little consequence. Therefore, by their actions, they had determined, reckoning the Plan of God, what was necessary and what was not necessary, thereby making up their own salvation.

How many Preachers and people today are pronounced "unclean" by the Lord because they have neglected, ignored, or flatly disbelieved part of His Word?")

15 And now, I pray you, consider from this day and upward, from before a stone was laid upon a stone in the Temple of the LORD (the phrase, "And now, I pray you, consider from this day and upward," demands a spiritual inventory to be presently taken. The phrase, "From before a stone was laid upon a stone in the Temple of the LORD," goes back some 16 years to the time the foundation was laid. Through the Prophet, the Holy Spirit is going to show the people exactly where they are, where they have been, and the reason for their difficulties):

16 Since those days were, when one came to an heap of twenty measures, there were but ten; when one came to the pressfat for to draw out fifty vessels out of the press, there were but twenty. (The phrase, "Since those days were," concerns the entirety of the past 16 years. It was a long time to be out of the Will of God, for to be out of His Will is to be out of His Blessing. The idea of the Verse is: when they expected a certain amount from their harvests, they actually only received about half that much.)

17 I smote you with blasting and with mildew and with hail in all the labours of your hands; yet you turned not to Me, saith the LORD. (The phrase, "I smote you . . . ," plainly spells out the Lord's judicial actions regarding His People. These judgments were sent upon them in order that they may hopefully turn to the Lord. However, the Scripture says, "yet you turned not to Me, saith the LORD.")

18 Consider now from this day and upward, from the four and twentieth day of the ninth month, even from the day that the foundation of the LORD's Temple was laid, consider it. (The idea of this Verse is that the Lord wanted them to "consider now this day." He is speaking of the "twenty-fourth day of the ninth month," which is the very day and moment that this Prophecy was being given. The Lord is actually telling them that they are to consider these years of loss; then, beginning this very day, they are to watch Him as He blesses them as they obey Him, which they will now begin to see.)

19 Is the seed yet in the barn? yea, as yet the vine, and the fig tree, and the pomegranate, and the olive tree, have not brought forth: from this day will I bless you. (At this particular time, the early part of the season, there was no way they could yet tell exactly what the harvest would be. However, the Lord through the Prophet is saying that, irrespective as to how the "vine," "fig tree," "pomegranate," and "olive tree" presently look, He will see to it that the harvest will be abundant. He says, "from this day will I bless you."

That day, as stated, was to be the "twenty-fourth day of the ninth month." In other words, because of their obedience, they could point back to this day as the beginning of God's Blessings.

Incidentally, the word "Blessing" means "to endue with power for success, prosperity, longevity, etc." In essence, one who is blessed is given a rich and abundant life.

Can this great Promise, "from this day will I bless you," be pulled over to this present time? Without a doubt it can, if proper obedience is rendered to the Lord.)

THE LORDS' PROMISE TO ZERUBBABEL: GOD WILL TRIUMPH; GENTILE NATIONS OVERTHROWN AT MESSIAH'S SECOND ADVENT

20 And again the Word of the LORD came unto Haggai in the four and twentieth day of the month, saying (even though this was the fourth Prophecy given by Haggai, still, it was given on the same day as the third Prophecy. It spans Verses 21 through 23),

21 Speak to Zerubbabel, Governor of Judah, saying, I will shake the heavens and the Earth (Verse 6 of this Chapter is here repeated. The phrase, "I will shake the heavens and the Earth," is letting this Godly dispossessed king [Zerubbabel] know that Israel's captive state will not remain this way forever. There is coming a day

when the Lord will change the order of events; this change will be so cataclysmic that it will literally "shake the heavens and the Earth." He is speaking of the Battle of Armageddon and the Second Coming of the Lord, which will bring Israel back to her rightful place);

22 And I will overthrow the throne of kingdoms, and I will destroy the strength of the kingdoms of the heathen; and I will overthrow the chariots, and those who ride in them; and the horses and their riders shall come down, every one by the sword of his brother. *(This awaits fulfillment in the coming Great Tribulation, and, more particularly, the Battle of Armageddon. This will be at the Second Advent of Christ, when He takes over the kingdoms of this world [Isa. 63:1-5; Ezek., Chpts. 38-39; Zech. 14:1-21; Lk. 1:32-33; Rev. 11:15; 19:11-21].)*

23 In that day, saith the LORD of Hosts, will I take you, O Zerubbabel, My servant, the son of Shealtiel, saith the LORD, and will make you as a signet: for I have chosen you, saith the LORD of Hosts. *(Even though addressed to Zerubbabel, because he was in the lineage of David, still, it actually concerns Him of Whom Zerubbabel was a type, the Messiah, God's Chosen One.*

The phrase, "And will make you as a signet," refers to the Signet Ring on the Hand that is to overthrow all thrones. The Prophecy teaches us that war and fratricidal slaughter will continue up to the Advent of the Great King of Israel.

The phrase, "For I have chosen you, saith the LORD of Hosts," was not actually a personal assurance only to Zerubbabel, because, as stated, neither he nor his natural seed reigned in Jerusalem, at least as king, but instead must be looked at for fulfillment in Christ [Lk. 1:26, 32-33].)

ZECHARIAH

CHAPTER 1
(520 B.C.)
GOD'S CALL FOR REPENTANCE

IN the eighth month, in the second year of Darius, came the Word of the LORD unto Zechariah, the son of Berechiah, the son of Iddo the Prophet, saying *(the Book of Zechariah was written by the Prophet, probably at about the same time as the Book of Haggai, which was about 530 B.C. His and Haggai's Prophetic Ministries would be the last, with the exception of Malachi, who would follow approximately 100 years later, after which Israel would plunge into a night of prophetic silence lasting about 400 years. The advent of John the Baptist, the forerunner of Christ, would break that silence.*

As well, it is believed that Zechariah was the one Jesus spoke of [Mat. 23:35], who was murdered by the sons of Israel. If, in fact, that was the case, counting Christ, Israel murdered two of the last four Prophets sent to them.

Zechariah began his Ministry some two months after Haggai began to prophesy [Hag. 1:1]),

2 The LORD has been sore displeased with your fathers. *(Their present disposition and the past captivity are obvious evidence of this sad truth.)*

3 Therefore say thou unto them, Thus saith the LORD of Hosts; Turn ye unto Me, saith the LORD of Hosts, and I will turn unto you, saith the LORD of Hosts. *(The phrase, "Thus saith the LORD of Hosts," is used some three times in this one Verse, which signifies the Authorship of the Message. The words, "Turn ye," speak of Repentance, meaning sincerely and from the heart, and not only outwardly, in the renunciation of idolatry, as described in Verse 4.)*

4 Be ye not as your fathers, unto whom the former Prophets have cried, saying, Thus saith the LORD of Hosts; Turn ye now from your evil ways, and from your evil doings: but they did not hear, nor hearken unto Me, saith the LORD. *(The first phrase refers to the Prophets previous to the captivity. This would have included Isaiah, Jeremiah, Hosea, Joel, Amos, etc. The phrase, "But they did not hear, nor hearken unto Me, saith the LORD," marks, sadly, the attitude of most. Men hearken unto other men*

readily, but little to the Lord.

The phrase, "Turn ye now from your evil ways, and from your evil doings," characterizes the result of True Repentance. Otherwise, it is not true!)

5 Your fathers, where are they? and the Prophets, do they live for ever? *(The argument of the Verse is that both Preachers and hearers have died, but the Message of the True Prophets, being Divine, was not dead; therefore, the judgment predicted overtook Jerusalem and she was carried into captivity.*

The question, "Your fathers, where are they?", is meant to portray the sad conclusion of those who did not heed the Word of the Lord.)

6 But My Words and My Statutes, which I commanded My servants the Prophets, did they not take hold of your fathers? and they returned and said, Like as the LORD of Hosts thought to do unto us, according to our ways, and according to our doings, so has He dealt with us. *(The phrase, "But My Words and My Statutes," spoke of the Law of Moses and the Word of the Prophets, as given by the Lord. The question, "Did they not take hold of your fathers?", rather means, "did not the threatened chastisements, however long delayed, reach your fathers in the end?"*

The phrase in the middle of the Verse, "And they returned and said," means only that the Jews to whom Zechariah was ministering turned so far as to acknowledge that the threats had been fully accomplished and carried out. It does not mean that, in their acknowledgment, they sought to do the Will of the Lord, which they obviously didn't in their long delay in rebuilding the Temple.)

VISION OF A MAN ON A RED HORSE AMONG MYRTLE TREES

7 Upon the four and twentieth day of the eleventh month, which is the month Sebat, in the second year of Darius, came the Word of the LORD unto Zechariah, the son of Berechiah, the son of Iddo the Prophet, saying *(this Message is given about three months after the Message recorded in Verse 1. The phrase, "Which is the month Sebat," refers to parts of*

our January and February. This was about five months since the building of the Temple, which, upon the Prophecies of Haggai, had been resumed. It seems that Haggai had finished his Prophecies by now, and Zechariah carries on the Revelation.

The first of his Visions will now commence and will show what is the nature of the restored theocracy, and what shall befall it),

8 I saw by night, and behold a Man riding upon a red horse, and he stood among the myrtle trees that were in the bottom; and behind him were there red horses, speckled, and white. (The phrase, "I saw by night," simply means that the Vision came at night, and while Zechariah was awake. In other words, it was not a Dream, but a Vision. The phrase, "And behold a Man riding upon a red horse," is to be taken literally. The "Man" was probably a pre-incarnate appearance of Christ. These "horses" were "spirit horses.")

9 Then said I, O my Lord, what are these? And the Angel Who talked with me said unto me, I will show you what these be. (The question, "Then said I, O my Lord, what are these?", refers to Zechariah referring to the appearance of this Being as "Lord," proving Him to be Christ. The name or designation "Angel," as used in the Bible, can refer to either the Lord, man, or Angels [as we think of Angels]. The proper understanding, as here, must be derived from the context.)

10 And the Man Who stood among the myrtle trees answered and said, These are they whom the LORD has sent to walk to and fro through the Earth. (The phrase, "These are they whom the LORD has sent to walk to and fro through the Earth," pertains to Angels, who were riding the other spirit horses, and who were sent forth as instruments to execute God's Wrath upon the oppressors to whom He had committed the government of the world, but who, at ease themselves, were indifferent to the misery and ruin of God's People. Even though the word "Earth" is used, it does not actually speak of the entirety of the Earth, but only the part that had to do with Israel.)

11 And they answered the Angel of the LORD Who stood among the myrtle trees, and said, We have walked to and fro through the Earth, and, behold, all the Earth sits still, and is at rest. (The first phrase seems to imply that the One speaking to Zechariah, Who is the Lord of Glory, had not previously been with the others, but now joins them, in respect to information that will be given to the Prophet. As well, the designation, "Angel of the LORD," Who was "the Man riding upon the red horse" [Vs. 8], further confirms this One as Deity. It is a term usually held to denote a manifestation of the Logos, the Second Person of the Holy Trinity, namely, a pre-incarnate appearance of Christ.

The phrase, "And, behold, all the Earth sits still, and is at rest," probably means that the leadership of the Medo-Persian Empire, which then ruled the world of that day, little regarded the plight of the Jews in Jerusalem, but now would be stirred to action, which they were.)

JUDGMENT OF JUDAH'S ENEMIES

12 Then the Angel of the LORD answered and said, O LORD of Hosts, how long will You not have mercy on Jerusalem and on the cities of Judah, against which You have had indignation these threescore and ten years? (The phrase, "Then the Angel of the LORD answered," seems to refer to a different Angel than the One mentioned in Verse 11. That "Angel" is Jehovah, while this Angel is one of the attending Angels on one of the other spirit horses.

The question, "O LORD of Hosts, how long will You not have mercy on Jerusalem and on the cities of Judah?", is asked that Zechariah may be given more information and that Judah would be comforted. The last phrase signifies that the Lord strongly desires to have Mercy; He was wanting the time period of some seventy years of chastisement to end, even more so than the people to whom it was intended, His People, the Jews. However, at times, the Lord can little show Mercy simply because of the apathy of Believers, even as is evidenced here.)

13 And the LORD answered the Angel who talked with me with good words and comfortable words. (The answer of "the LORD" is in regard to the question asked by the Angel of Verse 12. Due to the people favorably responding to the prophesying of Haggai and Zechariah, at least at this time, the answer of the Lord will be "good words and comfortable words," which the Lord desires to give to all, if Believers will only obey Him.)

14 So the Angel who communed with me said unto me, Cry thou, saying. Thus saith the LORD of Hosts; I am jealous for Jerusalem and for Zion with a great jealousy. (The first phrase seems to present an Angel other than Jehovah, who will convey the Message of the Lord to the Prophet. The phrase, "Cry thou, saying,

Thus saith the LORD of Hosts," proclaims a Message of great blessing and prosperity. It is in two parts, with the second part found in the next Verse.

First of all, He says, "I am jealous for Jerusalem and for Zion with a great jealousy": this means that however humiliated the present position of His People, still, He loves them supremely. As well, the term implies ardent love, which cannot bear itself to be slighted, or the object of its affection to be injured, hence the term "with a great jealousy.")

15 And I am very sore displeased with the heathen who are at ease: for I was but a little displeased, and they helped forward the affliction. *(The first phrase pertains to the present leader of Medo-Persia, who some time back had stopped work on the Temple. With this, the Lord was "very sore displeased." The phrase, "For I was but a little displeased," is not speaking of the Persians, as the first phrase did, but instead of Israel. God had been angry with His People, but only in measure, chastising them and not destroying them.*

The phrase, "And they helped forward the affliction," once again refers to "the heathen," in this case, the Babylonians, who were used as instruments of God to bring about the chastisement. Therefore, "they [the Babylonians] helped forward the affliction.")

JUDAH YET TO BE RESTORED

16 Therefore thus saith the LORD; I am returned to Jerusalem with mercies: My house shall be built in it, saith the LORD of Hosts, and a line shall be stretched forth upon Jerusalem. *(The first two phrases proclaim the fact that the Lord will now have "mercies" upon the city of Jerusalem. The phrase, "My house shall be built in it, saith the LORD of Hosts," pertains to the Temple, which will be finished shortly; then Temple duties shall begin, which will restore Fellowship and Communion of the Lord with His People. Regrettably, the people, it seems, had not been too concerned about this.*

The phrase, "And a line shall be stretched forth upon Jerusalem," pertains to the ultimate destiny of Jerusalem, which actually speaks of the Headquarters of the Messiah, which will take place in the coming Kingdom Age. In other words, the Lord is addressing Himself to this city and to its present ruined condition, telling the people to look beyond the present and into the prophetic future. What they now see

is not good, but what they then see will be glory beyond compare.

The "stretching of the line" refers to the certitude of this coming action.)

17 Cry yet, saying, Thus saith the LORD of Hosts; My cities through prosperity shall yet be spread abroad; and the LORD shall yet comfort Zion, and shall yet choose Jerusalem. *(This prediction concerns the immediate future from Zechariah's day, but, more importantly, speaks of the coming Kingdom Age. In fact, Josephus tells us that in later times Jerusalem outgrew its walls and once again became a thriving metropolis.)*

THE HORNS AND THE CARPENTERS

18 Then lifted I up my eyes, and saw, and behold four horns. *(Horns are symbols of strength and power.)*

19 And I said unto the Angel who talked with me, What be these? And he answered me, These are the horns which have scattered Judah, Israel, and Jerusalem. *(The phrase, "These are the horns which have scattered . . .", speaks in the past tense, even though, at that time, at least two were yet future — Rome and the Antichrist. In fact, one is still future — the coming Antichrist. However, it is spoken in this way because, in the Mind of God, it is already a settled fact, and is decreed to surely happen. Therefore, it is spoken accordingly:*

1. The first "horn" was the Assyrians, which scattered the Northern Kingdom of Israel;

2. The Babylonians destroyed Judah and Jerusalem in 586 B.C.;

3. The Romans destroyed Jerusalem in A.D. 70, which, of course, was then future from Zechariah's day;

4. The Antichrist is the one who will scatter Israel who is yet to come. After that their scattering will be over!)

20 And the LORD showed me four carpenters. *(These "four carpenters" represent four Divine instruments or agencies raised up by God to overthrow these Empires, which will all be symbolized in the coming Antichrist. As to exactly who these "four carpenters" actually are, we aren't told. They could be Heavenly Angels [Mat. 24:31; II Thess. 1:7-10], the Resurrected Saints [Zech. 14:5; Jude 14-15; Rev. 19:14], or Israel [Zech. 14:14]. However, the greatest Carpenter of all will be "Christ," Who is the Head of all [Mat. 24:29-31; Rev. 19:11-21].)*

21 Then said I, What come these to do? And

he spoke, saying, These are the horns which scattered Judah, so that no man did lift up his head: but these are come to fray them, to cast out the horns of the Gentiles, which lifted up their horn over the land of Judah to scatter it. *(The phrase, "So that no man did lift up his head," refers to the helplessness of Israel as it regards these Empires, especially considering that they had cast away the Lord as their King, instead accepting Gentile dominion. Consequently, it was a sorry trade, with Israel suffering terribly so, even unto today.*

The phrase, "But these are come to fray them," pertains to these "four carpenters," who will defeat the Antichrist, who represents all of these Empires, at the Battle of Armageddon. The phrase, "To cast out the horns of the Gentiles," means the end of Gentile dominion; Jesus referred to it as "the Times of the Gentiles" [Lk. 21:24].

All of this will happen at the Second Coming, when the "carpenters" will "cast out the horns of the Gentiles." Then Israel will be restored as the Lord intended at the very beginning.)

CHAPTER 2
(519 B.C.)
THE MAN WITH THE MEASURING LINE

I lifted up my eyes again, and looked, and behold a man with a measuring line in his hand. *(Three Visions were given to Zechariah in Chapter 1 and concerned Israel's outward prosperity. Three more Visions are given in Chapters 2 and 3 and concern Israel's inward purity. Nations as well as individuals must be cleansed from their sins and endowed with a new moral nature or else prosperity will be a hindrance instead of a help to them. Beautifying a pump will not purify the foul water that is in the well.*

The phrase, "I lifted up my eyes again, and looked," concerns the fourth Vision that is about to be given to the Prophet. The phrase, "And behold a man with a measuring line in his hand," does not portray Christ, as some have claimed, but instead one of the Angels riding the spirit horses spoken of in Chapter 1.

The "measuring" is meant to portray the future Jerusalem as it shall be under the Messiah in the coming Kingdom Age, when He will rule in splendor and glory. The measuring is meant to encourage the small remnant in Jerusalem, as they observe the present ruined city, by pointing to the future and, thereby, exclaiming what that day will bring forth.)

2 Then said I, Whither goest thou? And he said unto me, To measure Jerusalem, to see what is the breadth thereof, and what is the length thereof. *(The "measuring" of Jerusalem, concerning its breadth and length, more so concerns its purity and prosperity than its actual size. As well, that particular measurement, because it is of Christ, knows no "breadth and length," because Christ is inexhaustible, as the next Verses proclaim. This will all take place in the coming Kingdom Age.)*

3 And, behold, the Angel who talked with me went forth, and another Angel went out to meet him. *(Now another "Angel" joins the first one, who was proceeding toward the measuring.)*

JERUSALEM UNDER THE MESSIAH

4 And said unto him, Run, speak to this young man, saying, Jerusalem shall be inhabited as towns without walls for the multitude of men and cattle therein *(the phrase, "Towns without walls," as stated, speaks of the coming Kingdom Age and the fact that Jerusalem will then be at peace and will not need any protection such as walls. In fact, at that coming day, that will be the first "peace" that Jerusalem will have seen, at least for any period of time):*

5 For I, saith the LORD, will be unto her a wall of fire round about, and will be the glory in the midst of her. *(The ancient Arabs built watch-fires for protection around their camps, but the Messiah will be a wall of fire to Jerusalem and a canopy of "glory in the midst of her.")*

ISRAEL REGATHERED

6 Ho, ho, come forth, and flee from the land of the north, saith the LORD: for I have spread you abroad as the four winds of the heaven, saith the LORD. *(The first phrase speaks of the millions of Jews scattered all over the world, who will, in the coming Kingdom Age, all come to Judah and Jerusalem. The phrase, "For I have spread you abroad as the four winds of the heaven, saith the LORD," concerns their "scattering" being carried out by the Lord, and done so many centuries ago, because of their rebellion.)*

7 Deliver yourself, O Zion, who dwells with the daughter of Babylon. *(This was partially fulfilled with the return of the Exiles to the Holy Land, which was carried out immediately after the dispersion. However, its plenary fulfillment awaits the coming day when Israel will be delivered from "spiritual Babylon" [Rev., Chpt. 17].)*

8 For thus saith the LORD of Hosts; After the glory has he sent me unto the nations which spoiled you: for he who touches you touches the apple of His Eye. (The "nations which spoiled" Israel did so under the guidance of the Lord, even though they were not aware of such. As well, and as stated here, Dan., Chpt. 10, proclaims the Lord sending Angels, even Michael and Gabriel, into the Medo-Persian Empire to ultimately bring about its downfall and to usher in the Grecian Empire. In other words, the Lord's Hand was in all of these proceedings, ever what they might have been, and we speak of the proceedings which involved Israel.

The phrase, "For he who touches you touches the apple of His Eye," speaks of God's Eye. It is meant to portray God's constant love for His People [Gen. 12:3].)

9 For, behold, I will shake My hand upon them, and they shall be a spoil to their servants: and you shall know that the LORD of Hosts has sent Me. (The phrase, "For, behold, I will shake My hand upon them," for instance, was amply illustrated by the "handwriting on the wall," which overthrew the mighty Chaldean Empire, making it possible for Israel to come back to the Holy Land [Dan. 5:5-6]. The phrase, "And they [Israel] shall be a spoil to their servants," implies that the roles will ultimately be reversed. In other words, Israel will one day be the dominant nation of the world and will, in turn, rule the Gentiles, with the Gentiles then being servants. That will be in the coming Kingdom Age.

The phrase, "And you shall know that the LORD of Hosts has sent Me," refers to the Deity and Humanity of the Messiah asserted here, Who will bring all of this to pass. For He is the Sender in the one case and the Sent in the other.

This overthrow of ancient Babylon and Restoration of Zion but feebly pictures the future Deliverance of Jerusalem. For, in that day, whole nations will be converted to God and shall become one with Israel, with all loving and serving the Saviour. But the special Promises of Supremacy and Priesthood to Israel will be fulfilled, for Zion shall be the Lord's Throne, with Judah as His Portion and Israel as His Land.)

MESSIAH REIGNING IN ZION

10 Sing and rejoice, O daughter of Zion: for, lo, I come, and I will dwell in the midst of you, saith the LORD. (The first phrase speaks of the coming Kingdom Age, when Israel will have accepted Christ, not only as her Saviour but also as her Messiah. The phrase, "For, lo, I come," speaks of the Second Coming of the Lord Jesus Christ. The last phrase pertains to Christ, upon His Second Coming, dwelling in Jerusalem, actually in the Holy Temple [Ezek. 43:7; 48:35; Dan. 7:13-14; Zech., Chpt. 14; Lk. 1:32-33; Rev. 11:1-5; 20:1-10].)

ALL NATIONS CONVERTED

11 And many nations shall be joined to the LORD in that day, and shall be My people: and I will dwell in the midst of you, and you shall know that the LORD of Hosts has sent Me unto you. (The first phrase refers to the many Gentile nations which will accept the Lord as Saviour at the outset of the Kingdom Age. They will be looked at as God's People, exactly as Israel. However, this doesn't necessarily mean that every person in these nations will accept the Lord, for some won't. They will, however, be forced to serve the Lord, whether they accept Him or not!

The last phrase, "You shall know that the LORD of Hosts has sent Me unto you," refers to the fact that Israel, at the Second Coming, will then know, beyond the shadow of a doubt, that the Christ they crucified was, and is, their Messiah [13:6].)

12 And the LORD shall inherit Judah His portion in the Holy Land, and shall choose Jerusalem again. (The first phrase actually includes the entirety of the Thirteen Tribes, as is evident in Ezek., Chpt. 48.

The phrase, "And shall choose Jerusalem again," actually speaks of Jerusalem being chosen the first time as the capital of Israel and the site of the Temple; however, at the First Advent of Christ, Jerusalem, which included the Jewish religious leadership, rejected Christ and crucified Him. At that time, the Lord forsook Jerusalem, because Jerusalem had forsaken Him. As a result, it was totally destroyed by the Romans in A.D. 70.

At the Second Coming, the Lord "shall choose Jerusalem again.")

13 Be silent, O all flesh, before the LORD: for He is raised up out of His holy habitation. (During this present period of His indignation against Israel, which has lasted now for about 2,000 years, the Lord is silent. The mouths of the nations have been, and are, filled with proud boasting. But the day is coming when He will come forth from His present retirement, hence "raised up out of His Holy Habitation," and will come back to this Earth to claim His Own.)

CHAPTER 3
(519 B.C.)
JOSHUA, THE HIGH PRIEST

AND He showed me Joshua the High Priest standing before the Angel of the LORD, and Satan standing at his right hand to resist him. *(At about this time, the Lord had spoken through the Prophet Haggai, "from this day will I bless you" [Hag. 2:19]. Consequently, this Blessing, which will be both material and spiritual, now commences, with the material part promised to Haggai and the spiritual part given to Zechariah.*

The first phrase speaks of the first High Priest, "Joshua," after the captivity, succeeding his father Josedech, who died in Babylon. Joshua, as the High Priest, was representative of the entirety of the Priesthood, and also of Israel. The "Angel of the LORD," at least in this instance, is Jehovah, as proved in the next Verse. Zechariah is seeing all of this in a Vision, which gives us a glimpse into the spirit world.

The phrase, "And Satan standing at his right hand to resist him," is the same personality described in Job 1:6-12 and 2:1. As well, Joshua the High Priest didn't see the Vision, only Zechariah. Satan resisting Joshua the High Priest, in effect, is resisting all of Israel, with an effort to stop these Prophecies from being fulfilled.)

2 And the LORD said unto Satan, The LORD rebuke you, O Satan; even the LORD Who has chosen Jerusalem rebuke you: is not this a brand plucked out of the fire? *(The first phrase contains the Lord's answer to Satan's accusation of Joshua the High Priest and, in effect, all of Israel. The Lord's rebuke paralyzed the hostile power. The phrase, "Even the LORD Who has chosen Jerusalem rebuke you," portrays the second rebuke by the Lord of Satan, and is done so by design. It is not that the second rebuke is needed, at least as far as Satan is concerned, but that the certitude of God's action is not lost on any, and especially the Believer. In other words, the Lord is saying that these predictions concerning the Restoration of Israel are most definitely going to come to pass. Satan will not be able to stop this.)*

3 Now Joshua was clothed with filthy garments, and stood before the Angel. *(At stated, Joshua was a representative of the entirety of Israel. The truth, as evidenced here, was: Israel, in fact, had no moral worth, to which Satan points, thereby claiming his right to hinder.)*

4 And He *(the Lord)* answered and spoke unto those who stood before him, saying, Take away the filthy garments from him. And unto him He said, Behold, I have caused your iniquity to pass from you, and I will clothe you with change of raiment. *(The idea of this Verse is: the Lord is going to cleanse filthy Israel, which will take place at the Second Coming, but only when Israel properly repents, which she most definitely will do, thereby accepting as her Saviour, Lord, and Messiah the One Whom she crucified, the Lord Jesus Christ. The "filthy garments" cannot be taken "from him," i.e., "Israel," until this Repentance is enjoined.)*

5 And I said, Let them set a fair mitre upon his head. So they set a fair mitre upon his head, and clothed him with garments. And the Angel of the LORD stood by. *(The phrase, "And I said, Let them set a fair mitre upon his head," proclaims a request of Zechariah. The "fair mitre" stood for the official headdress of Aaron, which was to be worn by all High Priests, and which bore upon its front the golden plate inscribed: "Holiness unto the Lord" [Ex. 28:36-38].*

This proclaims the fact that, at the Second Coming, Israel will be restored and will in fact become a nation of Priests for the entire world. The phrase, "So they set a fair mitre upon his head, and clothed him with garments," proclaims the Priestly garments, which now are pure and clean.)

CHARGE TO JOSHUA

6 And the Angel of the LORD protested unto Joshua, saying *(the word "protested" here means "to solemnly and earnestly admonish," meaning that even though all of this would happen in the distant future, still, Joshua, who was the type, must also serve as an example of Righteousness),*

7 Thus saith the LORD of Hosts; If you will walk in My ways, and if you will keep My charge, then you shall also judge My house, and shall also keep My courts, and I will give you places to walk among these who stand by. *(Five things are said in this Verse; since "five" is the number of Grace, we know that it is only enabling Grace which can help the High Priest to obey the charge and reap the benefits.)*

VISION OF GOD'S SERVANT: THE BRANCH; HIS ANOINTING

8 Hear now, O Joshua the High Priest, you, and your fellows who sit before you: for they

are men wondered at: for, behold, I will bring forth My servant the BRANCH. *(The first phrase proclaims the fact that Joshua and all who are with him are to give all of their attention to this very important announcement that is about to be made. Even though Joshua was not privileged to see the Vision as Zechariah, no doubt Zechariah related it to him word for word. The two words, "your fellows," refer to his fellow Priests, who aided him in his ministerial duties, and who took their orders from him and sat with him in counsel.*

The phrase, "For they are men wondered at," implies that they are a foreshadow of future events, which actually spoke of good things. The phrase, "For, behold, I will bring forth My servant the BRANCH," speaks of Christ, Who Alone will be able to bring all of this to pass. He will do so by going to the Cross, which Israel eventually must, and will, accept!)

9 For behold the Stone that I have laid before Joshua; upon one Stone shall be seven eyes: behold, I will engrave the graving thereof, saith the LORD of Hosts, and I will remove the iniquity of that Land in one day. *(The phrase, "For behold the Stone that I have laid before Joshua," is symbolic of the Messiah, called "The BRANCH" [Isa. 28:16; Ps. 118:22; Mat. 21:42; Acts 4:11; Eph. 2:20-21; I Pet. 2:4-7]. The phrase, "Upon one Stone shall be seven eyes," signifies the Holy Spirit upon Christ, with the number "seven" implying a perfect union. John saw the same Vision, but enlarged [Rev. 5:6].*

John also saw "seven horns," which Zechariah did not see, which pertain to total dominion. This was because Christ had already gone to the Cross, thereby guaranteeing this dominion, which had not yet taken place at the time of Zechariah. Whereas the "seven eyes" speak of perfect illumination, likewise, and as stated, the "seven horns" speak of perfect dominion, all made possible by what Christ did at the Cross.

The phrase, "Behold, I will engrave the graving there, saith the LORD of Hosts," has to do with the Incarnation. Christ, as The BRANCH, supplies life and food to His People, who rest beneath its shadow. As the Stone, He is to them an imperishable foundation.

The phrase, "And I will remove the iniquity of that Land in one day," refers to the day of Christ's visible return to Earth, when all Israel shall be saved and ungodliness turned from Jacob [Zech. 12:10-13:1; Rom. 11:25-29]. Israel will mourn and repent for three days; on the third day, they will live [Hos. 6:2].)

UNIVERSAL PROSPERITY

10 In that day, saith the LORD of Hosts, shall you call every man his neighbour under the vine and under the fig tree. *(The phrase, "In that day," has to do with the coming Kingdom Age, when the Lord will Personally reign supreme from Jerusalem, and over the entirety of the world. There will then be universal peace and prosperity, of which this last phrase is a symbol [Mic. 4:4].)*

CHAPTER 4
(519 B.C.)
THE GOLDEN CANDLESTICK AND THE OLIVE TREES

AND the Angel Who talked with me came again, and waked me, as a man who is wakened out of his sleep. *(The "Angel" is Jehovah and is the same One in this Vision as in the previous. It is not known how long it was between the previous Vision and this Vision. The phrase, "Wakened out of his sleep," shows that this was not a Dream, but rather a "Vision.")*

2 And said unto me, What seest thou? And I said, I have looked, and behold a candlestick all of gold, with a bowl upon the top of it, and His seven lamps thereon, and seven pipes to the seven lamps, which are upon the top thereof *(the Vision consists of a "Candlestick" with its "Seven Lamps" fed to two "Olive Trees"; the Prophet is told to describe it. The "Candlestick all of gold" describes Christ, with "gold" symbolizing His Deity, even though He will be "Incarnate." In other words, even though He became "Very Man," He never, even for a moment, ceased to be "Very God." He was 100% Man and 100% God [Phil. 2:8].*

The phrase, "With a bowl upon the top of it," signifies the Holy Spirit. In other words, Christ and what He would do at the Cross would make it possible for there to be an uninterrupted supply of the Holy Spirit to the Believer [Jn. 14:16-17; 16:7-15].

The phrase, "And His Seven Lamps thereon," pertains to perfect illumination, which the Holy Spirit Alone can give. This is meant to illuminate the Word to God's People, which most definitely will be done, that is, if Believers will humble themselves and tremble at God's Word [Isa. 11:1-2; 66:2].

The phrase, "And Seven Pipes to the Seven Lamps, which are upon the top thereof," pertains to a total supply of the Holy Spirit to the Spirit-filled Believer, symbolized by the number

"seven," all made possible by the Cross [I Cor. 1:17-18, 23; 2:2]):

3 And two olive trees by it, one upon the right side of the bowl, and the other upon the left side thereof. *(The phrase, "And two Olive Trees by it," picture, at least in this instance, Zerubbabel and Joshua in the work of restoring the Temple and the nation of Judah after the Babylonian activity. However, the Vision reaches on to Rev., Chpt. 11, for two other representatives appear, but with this difference: they themselves are "Lampstands" and "Olive Trees."*

These "two Olive Trees," as representative of all, are, in effect, told to carefully observe God's method of the supply of spiritual energy, for this is what it represents. It is so easy for man to get his eyes on other than that which is the True Source, Who is Christ, and by the Power of the Holy Spirit, with all made possible by the Cross.

As one was on either side of the Candlestick, the idea is: just as the Holy Spirit was the Source of Power for Israel of old, likewise, He is for the modern Church, as well. God has not changed His Methods.)

4 So I answered and spoke to the Angel Who talked with me, saying, What are these, my Lord? *(The question, "What are these, my Lord?", is meant to speak of the entirety of the Vision. Even though he plainly observed it, he was not sure if he understood what it all meant. In reply to his question, the answer is forthcoming.)*

ZERUBBABEL ANOINTED WITH THE SPIRIT AND POWER

5 Then the Angel Who talked with me answered and said unto me, Knowest thou not what these be? and I said, No, my Lord. *(The reply of the Lord in the form of a question was not meant to point out the Prophet's slowness of comprehension, but instead to call attention to the answer that is about to be given.)*

6 Then He answered and spoke unto me, saying, This is the Word of the LORD unto Zerubbabel, saying, Not by might, nor by power, but by My Spirit, saith the LORD of Hosts. *(The Message of the Vision to Zerubbabel and also to all others, at least according to the need, was: not by military might, nor by political power, but by spiritual energy, he would certainly complete the building of the Temple.*

The phrase, "Not by [human] might, nor by [human] power, but by My Spirit," presents God's Method of accomplishing His Work. Everything that has ever been done on this Earth, as it regards the Godhead, has been done by the Holy Spirit, with the exception of Christ and His Crucifixion; however, the Holy Spirit even superintended that from beginning to end [Lk. 4:18-19].

If it is claimed to be for the Lord, whatever is being done must be done by the Moving, Operation, Power, and Person of the Holy Spirit through Believers. Otherwise, it will not be recognized by God; in fact, it will be constituted as a "work of the flesh" [Rom. 8:1].

The phrase, "Saith the LORD of Hosts," presents God's Supreme Personal Power over everything in the material and spiritual universe. All is organized under His Command. As well, the word "Hosts," as used here, is associated with warfare and relates to the word "armies." In other words, He is the "LORD of Armies.")

7 Who are you O great mountain? before Zerubbabel you shall become a plain: and he shall bring forth the headstone thereof with shoutings, crying, Grace, grace unto it. *(The question, "Who are you O great mountain?", is meant to refer to Hystapes, king of the mighty Medo-Persian Empire, who made a decree that the work on the Temple should cease [Ezra, Chpt. 4]. Cyrus, who in fact was Esther's son, had, some 16 years earlier, made the decree that the Temple should be rebuilt. This was in 536 B.C. [Ezra 1:1-2]. He reigned for nine years; his son, Cambyses, reigned seven years; and then Hystapes followed him. He is the one who gave the order that no Temple was to be built in Jerusalem, countermanding, in effect, the order given by Cyrus.*

The question, "Who are you O great mountain?", is asked in sarcasm by the Holy Spirit. In other words, the Holy Spirit is saying, "Who do you think you are, attempting to stop the Work of God?"

The phrase, "Before Zerubbabel you shall become a plain," means that the Lord will shave the face of this empire, with this king being totally removed. In fact, this was fulfilled in totality; this man was executed by Darius I. He was, in fact, removed because of his efforts to hinder the Work of God.

The phrase, "And he [Zerubbabel] shall bring forth the headstone thereof with shoutings, crying, Grace, grace unto it," refers to the Ministry of Christ, which would ultimately come, in which all of this played its part [Jn. 1:17].)

THE RESTORATION OF THE TEMPLE TO BE FINISHED BY ZERUBBABEL

8 Moreover the Word of the LORD came

unto me, saying,

9 The hands of Zerubbabel have laid the foundation of this house; his hands shall also finish it; and you shall know that the LORD of Hosts has sent me unto you. *(The first phrase refers back to the beginning of the foundation of the Temple some 16 years earlier, and now he's finishing it, even in the face of tremendous opposition. However, the greater meaning pertains to Christ; the Lord laid the foundation of the House, and the Lord will finish it. Paul said, "Jesus Christ Himself being the Chief Cornerstone" [Eph. 2:20-21].*

The pronoun "me" refers to the Prophet Zechariah being sent by the Lord with this all-important Message.)

10 For who has despised the day of small things? for they shall rejoice, and shall see the plummet in the hand of Zerubbabel with those seven; they are the eyes of the LORD, which run to and fro through the whole Earth. *(The question, "For who has despised the day of small things?", has to do with the leaders of returned Israel, who had little regard for this new Temple, at least in comparison to the Temple of old. It was humble, with no costly ornamentation, and seemed, at least in their eyes, unworthy of the Lord. However, the Lord was to give them several assurances respecting the situation.*

The phrase, "For they shall rejoice, and shall see the plummet in the hand of Zerubbabel," signifies that the Temple will be completed. The short phrase, "With those seven," speaks of the "eyes of the Lord, which run to and fro through the whole Earth." This refers to the absolute and perfect knowledge and illumination of the Lord. Those Eyes being all-seeing and all-understanding, they could well provide for and defend Zerubbabel.)

EXPLANATION OF THE OLIVE TREES

11 Then answered I, and said unto Him, What are these two Olive Trees upon the right side of the Candlestick and upon the left side thereof?

12 And I answered again, and said unto Him, What be these two olive branches which through the two golden pipes empty the golden oil out of themselves? *(As the Lord had two witnesses, Zerubbabel and Joshua, after the restoration from Babylon, He will likewise have His two witnesses in the future Restoration of Israel. They are comparable now, and will be comparable then, to Olive Trees and Lampstands.)*

13 And He answered me and said, Knowest thou not what these be? And I said, No, my Lord. *(In fact, there was no way that Zechariah could know what all of this meant without a proper explanation from the Lord, which is now given.)*

14 Then said He, These are the two anointed ones, who stand by the LORD of the whole Earth. *(Israel was designed to be, and will yet be, a Golden Lampstand — gold representing Divine relationship — which will enlighten the whole world — Christ, as King and Priest, ministering the Holy Spirit as the Oil to nourish the Light. This will happen in the coming Kingdom Age.*

The "two anointed ones" will be Elijah and Enoch, who will come on the scene for the last three and a half years of the coming Great Tribulation. These two men have never died, but rather were translated. They will contend with the Antichrist and do great things for three and a half years. Then the Lord will allow them to be killed [Rev. 11:3-12]; and then they will be shortly resurrected.)

CHAPTER 5

(519 B.C.)

THE FLYING ROLL

THEN I turned, and lifted up my eyes, and looked, and behold a flying roll. *(This signifies a new Vision. The "roll" was actually a "scroll." Inasmuch as this "roll" was "flying," it denotes the speedy arrival of judgment, which will characterize the coming Great Tribulation, with which this Vision is concerned.)*

2 And He said unto me, What do you see? And I answered, I see a flying roll; the length thereof is twenty cubits, and the breadth thereof ten cubits. *(This "flying roll" was thirty feet long and fifteen feet wide.)*

THIS IS THE CURSE

3 Then said He unto me, This is the curse that goes forth over the face of the whole Earth: for every one who steals shall be cut off as on this side according to it; and every one who swears shall be cut off as on that side according to it. *(The first phrase refers to the "curse of the Law," which pronounced death upon Lawbreakers. This is its function, hence the word "curse," which means "sentence of death" [Rom. 5:12; Gal. 3:10]. Inasmuch as it covered "the whole Earth," escape was impossible. The last*

three words of this Scripture, "according to it," mean that the word of the roll was to be the judge, not man's religious opinions.

The two sins of "stealing" and "swearing" stand for all offenses against the Ten Commandments, which form the core of the moral law.)

4 I will bring it forth, saith the LORD of Hosts, and it shall enter into the house of the thief, and into the house of him who swears falsely by My name: and it shall remain in the midst of his house, and shall consume it with the timber thereof and the stones thereof. (This Passage basically speaks of the coming Great Tribulation, when the Wrath of God will be poured out on a world that has forgotten God days without number. The phrase, "And it shall enter into the house of the thief . . .," simply has reference to the entirety of the world answering to God in a collective, yet personal, way.

The phrase, "And into the house of him who swears falsely by My name," speaks of all the false religions of the world, especially the part of Christianity which is apostate. The phrase, "And it shall remain in the midst of his house," refers to the evil of the Antichrist, and his sudden and cataclysmic defeat in the Battle of Armageddon by the Coming of the Lord, which will finish him and all such evil.

The phrase, "And shall consume it with the timber thereof and the stones thereof," refers to Christ bringing judgment on the entirety of the world and all that man has built, with the "Times of the Gentiles" being brought to a sudden and cataclysmic end. This pictures the Stone coming from Heaven and smashing the feet of the statue, as seen by Nebuchadnezzar and interpreted by Daniel [Dan. 2:34-35].)

THE VISION OF AN EPHAH

5 Then the Angel Who talked with me went forth, and said unto me, Lift up now your eyes, and see what is this that goes forth.

6 And I said, What is it? And He said, This is an ephah that goes forth. He said moreover, This is their resemblance through all the Earth. (The "ephah" is a dry measure containing about six gallons. "Six" is the number of man, therefore, of imperfection and incompleteness; this tells us, consequently, that all idolatrous systems are similar. In fact, this addresses Rev. 17:7.

The phrase, "He said moreover, This is their resemblance through all the Earth," has reference to all the religions of the world. Irrespective of what they look like or proclaim, if they

are not according to the Bible, they are evil and wicked. They all have the same father, Satan.

The word "resemblance" actually means "their eye," i.e., their evil purpose, that is, the aim to corrupt everything, which religion does!)

7 And, behold, there was lifted up a talent of lead: and this is a woman who sits in the midst of the ephah. (This woman is used figuratively in an evil sense; she represents wickedness, fallacy, uncleanness, and unfaithfulness. She represents all false religion [Ezek. 16:15, 22, 26, 28-59; 23:1-49; 36:17; Hos. 1:2; 2:2-17; 3:1; Rev., Chpt. 17].)

8 And He said, This is wickedness. And He cast it into the midst of the ephah; and He cast the weight of lead upon the mouth thereof. (The phrase, "And He said, This is wickedness," plainly tells us what all of this represents. It is the culmination of all evil headed up under the Antichrist in the coming Great Tribulation. It is marked by all the false religions of the world, which represent man's rebellion against God and His Son, the Lord Jesus Christ.

The phrase, "And He cast it into the midst of the ephah," refers to the woman attempting to get out, with the Angel casting the lid of lead back onto the ephah and closing its mouth. All of this proclaims the efforts of the Antichrist in the coming Great Tribulation to take over the world, to do so by declaring himself to be God, and then to declare total war on Israel, hoping to abrogate all the many Prophecies of her Restoration and the setting up the Kingdom Age under Christ. He would succeed but for the Coming of the Lord, evidenced by the "casting of the weight of lead on the mouth thereof," which speaks of the Antichrist being totally defeated, with Satan locked away [Rev. 20:1-3].)

9 Then lifted I up my eyes, and looked, and, behold, there came out two women, and the wind was in their wings; for they had wings like the wings of a stork: and they lifted up the ephah between the Earth and the heaven. (The "two women" here represent evil; in fact, they portray the false prophet and the Antichrist. The phrase, "And the wind was in their wings," has to do with the speed of the Antichrist and his coming march of world conquest [Rev. 13:2]. The phrase, "For they had wings like the wings of a stork," makes reference to an unclean bird [Lev. 11:19; Deut. 14:18]. This symbolizes what Daniel saw, as well [Dan. 7:6]. The phrase, "And they lifted up the ephah between the Earth and the Heaven," represents the coming bold thrust of the Antichrist in his efforts to take over

the entirety of the world.

The ephah being "between the Earth and the heaven" symbolizes that the Antichrist's efforts are as much religious as they are military and political.)

10 Then said I to the Angel Who talked with me, Where do these bear the ephah? *(Even though the efforts of the Antichrist will be to take over the entirety of the world, still, his beginning thrusts will be from the Middle East; consequently, this Passage tells us where the foment of this coming time will begin, hence all the problems in the Middle East at present, which will not get better but will rather worsen.)*

11 And He said unto me, To build it an house in the land of Shinar: and it shall be established, and set there upon her own base. *("Shinar" is Babylon. This re-built city, whether a system or the city proper, and no doubt both, will be the center and headquarters of the commercial enterprises and religious activity of the Antichrist. In other words, it all began there, and it all will end there. The excursion of the United States into Iraq has great significance, in that all of this is being prepared for the fulfillment of Bible Prophecy concerning Endtime events. This should tell us how close we are to the Coming of the Lord.*

The phrase, "And it shall be established, and set there upon her own base," specifies this area as the headquarters of the Antichrist. As to exactly how the Lord will bring this about, we aren't told. However, it is possible that the United States might overcome Muslim terrorism in Iraq, with the area then becoming a great commercial center. In fact, Iraq has one of the greatest deposits of oil in the world, which will undoubtedly help fuel the economic enterprises of the Antichrist, when that time does come.)

CHAPTER 6
(519 B.C.)
THE FOUR CHARIOTS

AND I turned, and lifted up my eyes, and looked, and, behold, there came four chariots out from between two mountains; and the mountains were mountains of brass. *(This portrays yet another Vision! The phrase, "And, behold, there came four chariots from between two mountains," denotes emissaries from the Lord; they are, in fact, very similar to the ones described in 1:8. The entirety of the Earth, it seems, is sectioned off between the Angelic occupants of these four chariots; perhaps, at times,*

they all cover a given area. As this was true then, it is undoubtedly true presently!

The phrase, "And the mountains were mountains of brass," must symbolize the Judgment of God, inasmuch as "brass" [copper] was the metal which covered the wood of the Brazen Altar, which itself symbolized judgment upon sin.)

2 In the first chariot were red horses; and in the second chariot black horses;

3 And in the third chariot white horses; and in the fourth chariot grisled and bay horses. *(It is generally agreed that the colors of these horses are significant in their meaning, simply because the Holy Spirit is so careful to delineate such. These portray the symbolic horses of Rev., Chpt. 6, which portray the beginning of the Great Tribulation and the Judgment of God, which, at that time, will cover this Earth.*

We are given here a glimpse into the spirit world. Evil men think they are the shakers and movers; however, they can only do, as described here, what the Lord allows them to do.)

GOD'S JUDGMENT

4 Then I answered and said unto the Angel Who talked with me, What are these, my Lord?

5 And the Angel answered and said unto me, These are the four spirits of the heavens, which go forth from standing before the LORD of all the Earth. *(The phrase, "And the Angel answered and said unto me," is probably the same Angel as previous, in reality, a pre-incarnate appearance of Christ.*

The phrase, "These are the four spirits of the heavens," indicates, from other descriptions, that they are spirits of judgment delegated by the Lord to various places of the Earth. The phrase, "Which go forth from standing before the LORD of all the Earth," indicates that their instructions come strictly from Him.)

6 The black horses which are therein go forth into the north country; and the white go forth after them; and the grisled go forth toward the south country. *(If one is to notice, the "red horses" are not mentioned here, possibly because they were not in function at that time, due to the absence of war.*

The phrase, "The black horses which are therein go forth into the north country," refers to north of Israel, as this Land is always the focal point. All of this has to do with the situation of the world during Zechariah's day, concerning the overthrow of the Babylonian Empire and the rise of the Medo-Persians. Men thought they were

running the show, but we are told here that the Lord was guiding it all.)

7 And the bay went forth, and sought to go that they might walk to and fro through the Earth: and He said, Get you hence, walk to and fro through the Earth. So they walked to and fro through the Earth. *(The thrice-repeated phase, "Walk to and fro," heightens the sense of the wholehearted energy of these mighty executors of Divine Justice.*

All of this represents judgment upon the Earth in Zerubbabel's time. Many who do not understand God or His Ways consider these actions as cruel, especially when the judgment is severe. What they fail to realize is that there is such wickedness, corruption, and evil in the world that, if certain measures were not taken, the wickedness and evil would only be intensified. Even though the surgery may be painful, still, the disease is far worse. If surgery [judgment] was not performed, the disease [sin] would destroy the patient [the world].)

8 Then cried He upon me, and spoke unto me, saying, Behold, these who go toward the north country have quieted My spirit in the north country. *(This probably refers to the defeat of the Babylonians by the Medes and the Persians, with the consequent rise to power of Cyrus, who gave the decree that the Temple was to be rebuilt in Jerusalem [Ezra 1:1-3]. The building project was interrupted for a time, but it was ultimately brought to fruition, which "quieted [God's] Spirit.")*

JOSHUA CROWNED: A SIGN OF
ENCOURAGEMENT FOR
RESTORED JUDAH

9 And the Word of the LORD came unto me, saying,

10 Take of them of the captivity, even of Heldai, of Tobijah, and of Jedaiah, which are come from Babylon, and come thou the same day, and go into the house of Josiah the son of Zephaniah *(through the Prophecy of Zechariah, the men here named are given a task, which, as we see, is very important);*

11 Then take silver and gold, and make crowns, and set them upon the head of Joshua the son of Josedech, the High Priest. *("Joshua" symbolizes the Messiah with His double crown of Kingship and Priesthood. Heldai, of the previous Verse, and his companions foreshadow the future Exiles of Zion, who will return thither bringing their wealth with them, and who will*

become builders of the Temple, of which the Messiah will be the Master-Builder.

The plural "crowns" is used, but not necessarily denoting more crowns than one. In Rev. 19:12, Christ is said to have upon His Head many crowns, by which is meant a diadem composed of several circles. In fact, the Mitre of the High Priest is never called a "crown"; consequently, that which was placed upon the head of Joshua was a royal crown, a token of royal dignity, not his own, but His Whom he represents — Christ, the Eternal Priest, the Universal King.)

JOSHUA, A SYMBOL OF THE PRIEST-KING,
THE MESSIAH, WHO WILL BUILD THE
MILLENNIAL TEMPLE

12 And speak unto him, saying, Thus speaks the LORD of Hosts, saying, Behold the Man Whose name is The BRANCH; and He shall grow up out of His place, and He shall build the Temple of the LORD *(the phrase, "And speak unto him, saying," refers to Zechariah speaking to Joshua, the High Priest. The phrase, "Behold the Man Whose name is The BRANCH," literally says in the Hebrew, "Behold the Man, BRANCH is His Name." Christ is called "The Man" in both Testaments — in this Verse and in I Tim. 2:5.*

The name "BRANCH" has reference to the Son or "Shoot" of David; consequently, it is speaking of the Incarnation, i.e., God becoming Man [Isa. 7:14].

The phrase, "And He shall grow up out of His place, and He shall build the Temple of the LORD," actually, even in the same Passage, refers to both the First and the Second Advents. "Growing up out of His place" speaks of Christ being born of the Virgin Mary and of the Tribe of Judah. "Building the Temple of the LORD" speaks of His Second Advent, when He will come with Power and Glory and will set up His Eternal Kingdom):

13 Even He shall build the Temple of the LORD; and He shall bear the glory, and shall sit and rule upon His Throne; and He shall be a Priest upon His Throne: and the counsel of peace shall be between Them Both. *(The phrase, "And He shall bear the Glory," refers to the "Glory" that Christ should have received, but did not, at His First Advent, but now certainly shall. The phrase, "And He shall be a Priest upon His Throne," proclaims the Eternal Priesthood of Christ, with Him serving as an Intercessor on behalf of all Believers [Heb. 7:26-8:2].*

The phrase, "And the counsel of peace shall be between Them Both," presents the two offices of King and Priest combined in One Person, the Lord Jesus Christ. Neither office is exalted higher than the other; consequently, there will be no enmity between the two offices as there is when two men fill them.)

14 And the crowns shall be to Helem, and to Tobijah, and to Jedaiah, and to Hen the son of Zephaniah, for a memorial in the Temple of the LORD. (The great "Crown" ["Crowns" — plural of excellency] was made with the silver and gold brought by Exiles as a gift to the Temple then being built. It was deposited in the Temple as a memorial of the faith and love of these Believers and of their hopes. It also was a memorial pledging the fulfillment of the promised appearance and glorious reign and Priesthood of the Man Whose Name is The BRANCH.

Even though the "Crown" would certainly speak of the First Advent of Christ, more perfectly it speaks of His Second Advent, when He will truly realize His proper place and position.)

MANY WILL COME AND HELP BUILD

15 And they who are far off shall come and build in the Temple of the LORD, and you shall know that the LORD of Hosts has sent me unto you. And this shall come to pass, if you will diligently obey the voice of the LORD your God. (The "Temple of the LORD" spoken of in this Verse is of far greater import than the Temple being built by Zerubbabel. Even though that was implied, still, the greater meaning had to do with Christ and the building of His Church [Mat. 16:18], and the privilege of His Body in the helping of this building [Eph. 4:11-12].)

CHAPTER 7
(518 B.C.)
THE QUESTION ABOUT EXTRA FASTS

AND it came to pass in the fourth year of king Darius, that the Word of the LORD came unto Zechariah in the fourth day of the ninth month, even in Chisleu (this "Word of the LORD" came about two years after the beginning of Zechariah's Ministry. The year was probably 518 B.C. In some two years, the Temple will be finished [Ezra 6:15], and, at this time, the work was no doubt proceeding rapidly. "Chisleu" refers to part of our November and December);

2 When they had sent unto the house of God Sherezer and Regem-melech, and their men, to pray before the LORD,

3 And to speak unto the Priests which were in the house of the LORD of Hosts, and to the Prophets, saying, Should I weep in the fifth month, separating myself, as I have done these so many years? (These inquirers asked the Priests if they were bound to keep commemorating the fasts of the fifth and seventh months observed during the captivity. These fasts commemorated, respectively, the destruction of Jerusalem and the murder of Gedaliah [Jer., Chpt. 41].

It is not recorded what reply the Priests made, but this first Message records the reply that God interposed. The only fast day enjoined by the Law of Moses, therefore given by the Lord and held inviolable, was the Great Day of Atonement, which was on the tenth day of the seventh month of the year [Lev. 23:26]. However, the Jews added several others, and, by the time of Christ, the total fast days had risen to at least 104 each year, all of them man-designed.)

GOD'S ANSWER: THE DECEITFULNESS
OF THEIR FASTS

4 Then came the Word of the LORD of Hosts unto me, saying,

5 Speak unto all the people of the land, and to the Priests, saying, When you fasted and mourned in the fifth and seventh month, even those seventy years, did you at all fast unto Me, even to Me? (Men are quite ready, from time to time, to separate themselves from their occupations and associations, which usually tire them, in order to observe what they call a retreat. But they are little willing to separate from their sins, which they like.

The question, "Did you at all fast unto Me, even to Me?", proclaims that these fasts were not God's Command and, therefore, they did Him no honor.)

6 And when you did eat, and when you did drink, did not you eat for yourselves, and drink for yourselves? (The idea from the latter part of Verse 5 and all of Verse 6 is that whatever they did, "fasting" or "eating," it was "for themselves," not unto God. In effect, it is "self" that is concerned.)

7 Should you not hear the Words which the LORD has cried by the former Prophets, when Jerusalem was inhabited and in prosperity, and the cities thereof round about her, when men inhabited the south and the plain? (The Lord directs Israel back to the years

immediately before the captivity. At that time, had they obeyed the Word of the Lord given through the Prophets, i.e., Jeremiah, etc., there would have been no captivities, and consequently no reasons for instituting these fasts.

The question, "Should you not hear the Words which the LORD has cried by the former Prophets. . . ?", directs the people to the Word of God. It had been a common cry of the Prophets from early times that men must not put their trust in the observance of outward ceremonies, but instead attend to the cultivation of moral obedience and purity.

The balance of the Scripture speaks of Israel before the captivity, when they were then prosperous; they could have remained that way, had they only obeyed the Lord.)

WHY THEIR PRAYERS WERE UNANSWERED AND JUDGMENTS HAD COME

8 And the Word of the LORD came unto Zechariah, saying *(this is the second Message given to the Prophet; it states that God requires moral conduct rather than self-invented religious ceremonies),*

9 Thus speaks the LORD of Hosts, saying, Execute true judgment, and show mercy and compassions every man to his brother *(the phrase, "Thus speaks the LORD of Hosts," uses, in the Hebrew, a forceful verb which means "past, present, and future." In other words, what He said then was right, what He says now is right, and what He will say in the future is right!*

All their religious ceremony should have translated itself into action toward others; however, religious ceremony never does that, but only inflates the self-righteousness of the participant):

10 And oppress not the widow, nor the fatherless, the stranger, nor the poor; and let none of you imagine evil against his brother in your heart. *(We are shown here that the only real way that a person can truly say they love God is that they love their fellowman. To claim the former while omitting the latter portrays hypocrisy [I Jn. 3:17].)*

11 But they refused to hearken, and pulled away the shoulder, and stopped their ears, that they should not hear. *(The Lord is speaking of Judah just before the captivity and also of any and all who fit the category, which number untold millions.)*

12 Yea, they made their hearts as an adamant stone, lest they should hear the Law, and the Words which the LORD of Hosts hast sent in His Spirit by the former Prophets: therefore came a great wrath from the LORD of Hosts. *(The phrase, "Therefore came a great wrath from the LORD of Hosts," refers, at least in this case, to the seventy-year captivity.)*

13 Therefore it is come to pass, that as He cried, and they would not hear; so they cried, and I would not hear, saith the LORD of Hosts *(the statement is that He will hear our cry only if we hear His cry!):*

14 But I scattered them with a whirlwind among all the nations whom they knew not. Thus the land was desolate after them, that no man passed through nor returned: for they laid the pleasant land desolate. *(Thus, God ordained then, and since the Roman overthrow, that Israel would remain practically uninhabited and uncultivated, which it was, until 1948, when the Jews finally returned after some 1,900 years wandering all over the world.)*

CHAPTER 8
(518 B.C.)
GOD PROMISES TO RESTORE HIS PEOPLE (ISRAEL)

AGAIN the Word of the LORD of Hosts came to me, saying,

2 Thus saith the LORD of Hosts; I was jealous for Zion with great jealousy, and I was jealous for her with great fury. *(The phrase, "Thus saith the LORD of Hosts," occurs ten times in this Chapter and proclaims the certitude of the coming action. The phrase, "I was jealous for Zion with great jealousy," carries, in its verb, the force of: "I was, I am, and I will be jealous."*

The entirety of this Passage portrays God's great love for Israel and that love being shown in the punishment of her enemies.)

3 Thus saith the LORD; I am returned unto Zion, and will dwell in the midst of Jerusalem: and Jerusalem shall be called a city of Truth; and the mountain of the LORD of Hosts the holy mountain. *(The phrase, "I am returned unto Zion, and will dwell in the midst of Jerusalem," only had a limited fulfillment with the restoration of Israel from Babylon. Its greater fulfillment awaits a Coming Day, when Jesus Christ will Personally return to this Earth. It will be the coming Kingdom Age.*

The phrase, "And Jerusalem shall be called a city of Truth," means that it will be a "faithful city" [Isa. 1:26], in which all that is true and real shall flourish. The phrase, "And the

mountain of the LORD of Hosts the Holy Mountain," refers to the Temple site, which is outlined in Ezek., Chpts. 40-48.)

4 Thus saith the LORD of Hosts; There shall yet old men and old women dwell in the streets of Jerusalem, and every man with his staff in his hand for very age. *(Even though this had a partial fulfillment at the time of Zechariah and thereafter, still, its complete and future glorious fulfillment awaits the coming Kingdom Age. Consequently, this Passage does not speak of those who are decrepit in years, but instead of vitality and zest of life, despite being "old" or "for very age.")*

5 And the streets of the city shall be full of boys and girls playing in the streets thereof. *(This Passage continues to speak of the coming Kingdom Age and notes a city free of crime, which also speaks of the entirety of the world of that day.*

Incidentally, marrying and having children does not include those who are a part of the First Resurrection, who, consequently, have Glorified Bodies. They [we] will be like Christ [Mat. 22:30; I Jn. 3:2].)

6 Thus saith the LORD of Hosts; If it be marvellous in the eyes of the remnant of this people in these days, should it also be marvellous in My eyes? saith the LORD of Hosts. *(If the restoration from Babylon was wonderful, how much more wonderful will be Israel's future Restoration! The former was marvelous in men's eyes; should the latter be marvelous in God's Eyes?)*

7 Thus saith the LORD of Hosts; Behold, I will save My people from the east country, and from the west country *(to some degree, this Passage began to be fulfilled in 1948, when Israel, and for the first time in 1,900 years, became a sovereign State. From that time, Jews have continued to be gathered to Israel, with the latest incursion being from the former Soviet Union. Nevertheless, the plenary fulfillment of this Passage awaits the beginning of the Kingdom Age, when every single Jew on the face of the Earth will then gladly return to Israel.*

The phrase, "Behold, I will save My People," proclaims the greatest Salvation the world has ever known, which will take place immediately after the Second Coming [13:1]);

8 And I will bring them, and they shall dwell in the midst of Jerusalem: and they shall be My people, and I will be their God, in truth and in righteousness. *(The phrase, "And I will bring them," denotes the certitude of the action,*

because it is performed by Jehovah Himself. The phrase, "And they shall dwell in the midst of Jerusalem," will, once and for all, proclaim the ownership of this city. It does not belong to the Arabs, as presently claimed, but to these ancient people, the Jews, the seed of Abraham, the seed of Isaac, and, above all, "thy Seed, which is Christ" [Gal. 3:16].

The phrase, "And I will be their God, in Truth and in Righteousness," means that as He deals truly and righteously with them, they, and for the first time, will deal truly and righteously with Him. In actuality, God cannot deal with anyone, except in "Truth and Righteousness," which is the very essence of His Nature. Then these twin attributes will prevail in the world, whereas presently the lie and unrighteousness prevail!)

RESTORED JUDAH WILL BE BLESSED IF THE CONDITIONS ARE MET

9 Thus saith the LORD of Hosts; Let your hands be strong, ye who hear in these days these words by the mouth of the Prophets, which were in the day that the foundation of the house of the LORD of Hosts was laid, that the Temple might be built. *(The phrase, "Thus saith the LORD of Hosts; Let your hands be strong," simply means to believe God and to not allow hindrances to deter one from carrying out their duly appointed mission.)*

10 For before these days there was no hire for man, nor any hire for beast; neither was there any peace to him who went out or came in because of the affliction: for I set all men every one against his neighbour. *(The idea of this Verse is that the state of affairs during the cessation of the work on the Temple was sad indeed! Due to the people not obeying God by not forging ahead with what He had told them to do, which was the construction of the Temple, the Lord allowed certain detriments to take place.*

Neglect of their duty caused the three judgments of this Verse, with its obedience securing the four blessings of Verse 12.)

11 But now I will not be unto the residue of this people as in the former days, saith the LORD of Hosts. *(The phrase, speaking of the Lord, "But now I will not be . . . ," refers to the Lord's attitude changing for the better toward the people, because of their obedience.)*

12 For the seed shall be prosperous; the vine shall give her fruit, and the ground shall give her increase, and the heavens shall give their dew; and I will cause the remnant of this people

to possess all these things. *(He said, "I will cause . . . ," referring to Him manipulating the ground, the heavens, the enemies, etc. He does no less presently, at least for those who will believe and obey Him!)*

13 And it shall come to pass, that as you were a curse among the heathen, O House of Judah, and House of Israel; so will I save you, and you shall be a blessing: fear not, but let your hands be strong. *(God's People in harmony with Him are a blessing to all! God's People out of harmony with Him are a curse to all!)*

14 For thus saith the LORD of Hosts; As I thought to punish you, when your fathers provoked Me to wrath, saith the LORD of Hosts, and I repented not *(this Verse portrays the past disobedience of Israel, with the words, "I repented not," speaking of the Lord not altering His Purpose, but actually banishing Israel for seventy years. With equal fixity of purpose, He will now do them good and restore them, even as the next verse proclaims. Disobedience was the cause of the judgment, while obedience is the cause of the Blessing)*:

15 So again have I thought in these days to do well unto Jerusalem and to the House of Judah: fear ye not. *(Even though Israel had been disobedient in the past 16 years in not finishing the Temple, still, upon proper heartfelt Repentance, the Lord turns His Attitude toward Israel from mild judgment to blessing. Consequently, He tells them, "fear ye not.")*

16 These are the things that you shall do; Speak ye every man the truth to his neighbour; execute the judgment of truth and peace in your gates *(very clearly the Holy Spirit says, "These are the things that you shall do." Consequently, as the Prophet spells it out, the people have no excuse. They know exactly what is expected of them)*:

17 And let none of you imagine evil in your hearts against his neighbour; and love no false oath: for all these are things that I hate, saith the LORD. *(This shows that the prevalent sins of this time were not idolatry but rather cheating, lying, and injustice, vices which they may have learned in exile, when they turned their energies to the traffic of commerce instead of serving the Lord. In other words, the ways of Babylon had become their ways.)*

GOD'S ANSWER CONCERNING FASTS (7:1-3)

18 And the Word of the LORD of Hosts came unto me, saying,

19 Thus saith the LORD of Hosts; The fast of the fourth month, and the fast of the fifth, and the fast of the seventh, and the fast of the tenth, shall be to the House of Judah joy and gladness, and cheerful feasts; therefore love the truth and peace. *(Religious men, bent on self-will, invent fasts, which only exacerbate their self-righteousness; God appoints feasts, which are the very opposite! These feasts might then, and ever since, have been enjoyed, had the Commands of Verses 16 and 17 been obeyed. They were not obeyed, though man's fasts and traditions were rigidly observed.*

As a result, the Lord tells them to cease their fasts on these particular days, and, in turn, convert these days into times of "joy and gladness, and cheerful feasts.")

JERUSALEM TO BE THE SPIRITUAL CENTER OF THE EARTH

20 Thus saith the LORD of Hosts; It shall yet come to pass, that there shall come people, and the inhabitants of many cities *(this pertains to the coming Kingdom Age, because it has not happened in the past, at least in this capacity, which is a capacity of peace of prosperity)*:

21 And the inhabitants of one city shall go to another, saying, Let us go speedily to pray before the LORD, and to seek the LORD of Hosts: I will go also. *(During the Kingdom Age, Israel will then eagerly seek the Lord, because they have accepted the Lord. The phrase, "I will go also," refers to the Gentiles and their eagerness to also worship the Lord, exactly as the Jews.)*

22 Yea, many people and strong nations, shall come to seek the LORD of Hosts in Jerusalem, and to pray before the LORD. *(At this time, the coming Kingdom Age, the greatest nations in the world will constantly be sending emissaries to Jerusalem in order " to seek the LORD of Hosts" and "to pray before the LORD.")*

JEWS WILL EVANGELIZE OTHER NATIONS

23 Thus saith the LORD of Hosts; In those days it shall come to pass, that ten men shall take hold out of all languages of the nations, even shall take hold of the skirt of him who is a Jew, saying, We will go with you: for we have heard that God is with you. *(Whereas for centuries men have spoken of the Jew as being cursed, then they will speak of the Jew as being blessed, and will strongly desire to be associated.)*

CHAPTER 9
(487 B.C.)
ISRAEL DELIVERED FROM HER ENEMIES

THE burden of the Word of the LORD in the land of Hadrach, and Damascus shall be the rest thereof: when the eyes of man, as of all the Tribes of Israel, shall be toward the LORD. *(The last section of this Book, beginning here, contains two "burdens" [9:1; 12:1]. These concern: first, the oppressor [Chpts. 9-11], and second, the oppressed [Chpts. 12-14]. Judgment having begun at the House of God [Chpts. 7-9], it now passes on to the enemies of that House — first, the enemies within Immanuel's Land [Vss. 1-8], and then the enemies exterior to that Land [Vss. 10-15].*

Verses 1 through 8 pertain somewhat to the approximately 500 years from Zechariah's time to Christ, but will have its greater fulfillment at the Second Coming of the Lord. The first phrase concerns the defeat of the Antichrist at the Battle of Armageddon, with the Lord bringing total victory to Israel. Then, for the first time, Syria, represented by "Hadrach and Damascus," which has always opposed Israel almost from her beginning, shall now be "at rest."

This is proclaimed in the Passage, "When the eyes of man, as of all the Tribes of Israel, shall be toward the LORD." This has not happened in the past; therefore, it remains to happen in the future.)

2 And Hamath also shall border thereby; Tyrus, and Zidon, though it be very wise. *(The phrase, "Though it be very wise," has to do with Ezek., Chpt. 28, where the leader of Tyre claimed to be "wiser than Daniel" [Ezek. 28:3]. However, their wisdom will not be able to help them either in that near future or in the coming day.)*

3 And Tyrus did build herself a strong hold, and heaped up silver as the dust, and fine gold as the mire of the streets. *(This concerns the "Tyrus" of Zechariah's day and following.)*

4 Behold, the LORD will cast her out, and He will smite her power in the sea; and she shall be devoured with fire. *(This took place with the siege of Alexander the Great.)*

5 Ashkelon shall see it, and fear; Gaza also shall see it, and be very sorrowful, and Ekron; for her expectation shall be ashamed; and the king shall perish from Gaza, and Ashkelon shall not be inhabited. *(The order of this Chapter is that judgment by Alexander the Great would first of all come upon the nations bordering the Promised Land.)*

6 And a bastard shall dwell in Ashdod, and I will cut off the pride of the Philistines. *(The word "bastard" would probably have been better translated "mongrel race." The phrase, "And I will cut off the pride of the Philistines," refers to their nationality being totally lost. Incidentally, the modern Palestinians, who now occupy a part of Israel, are not descendants of these people, but are rather Jordanians, Egyptians, Syrians, etc.)*

7 And I will take away his blood out of his mouth, and his abominations from between his teeth: but he who remains, even he, shall be for our God, and he shall be as a governor in Judah, in Ekron as a Jebusite. *(As the previous Verses spoke of destruction that followed about 200 years after Zechariah, with the invasion of Alexander the Great, Verse 7 leaps ahead to the coming Kingdom Age, further proving that the plenary fulfillment of these Passages lies yet in the future.*

The phrase, "And I will take away his blood out of his mouth," has to do with the practice of drinking the blood of sacrifices as an act of worship. The phrase, "And his abominations from between his teeth," addresses the eating of those sacrifices.

The phrase, "But he who remains, even he, shall be for our God," pertains to the fact that whoever occupies this area in the coming Kingdom Age will serve the Lord Jesus Christ.)

8 And I will encamp about My house because of the army, because of him who passes by, and because of him who returns: and no oppressor shall pass through them any more: for now have I seen with My eyes. *(The phrase, "And I will encamp about My house because of the army," refers to the Lord defending Jerusalem in the coming Battle of Armageddon. That Battle is described by the phrase, "Because of him who passes by, and because of him who returns," with the pronoun "him" referring to the Antichrist and his invasion of Israel.*

The phrase, "And no oppressor shall pass through them any more," pertains to the many conflicts seen by Judah and Jerusalem, with this one, the invasion of the Antichrist, being the last. The phrase, "For now have I seen with My eyes," pertains to the Second Coming, when Christ, in Person, will look at the armies of the Antichrist and even the son of perdition himself, measuring them for total defeat!)

MESSIAH'S FIRST ADVENT

9 Rejoice greatly, O daughter of Zion;

shout, O daughter of Jerusalem: behold, your King comes unto you: He is just, and having salvation; lowly, and riding upon an ass, and upon a colt the foal of an ass. *(This Scripture pertains to the First Advent of Christ, and is a definite prediction that the Messiah would be the King of the Jews. It is said that in this Verse the four Gospels appear:*

As portrayed in Matthew, He is "your King"; in Mark, He is "lowly," hence, a Servant; in Luke, He is "just," hence, the Man; in John, He is God, therefore, "having Salvation." He thus appears as the Prince of Peace in His First Advent — not as in His Second Advent, mounted on a war-horse as the Mighty Conqueror [Rev., Chpt. 19].

The phrase, "Behold, your King comes unto you," refers to Jesus riding into Jerusalem on "the foal of an ass" on the first day of the week in which He was crucified.)

MESSIAH'S SECOND ADVENT

10 And I will cut off the chariot from Ephraim, and the horse from Jerusalem and the battle bow shall be cut off: and He shall speak peace unto the heathen: and His dominion shall be from sea even to sea, and from the river even to the ends of the Earth. *(As Verse 9 refers to the First Advent, Verse 10 refers to the Second Advent. At His First Advent, He came in peace; at His Second Advent, He will come in war. Between these two Verses, over 1,900 years have already passed; this period has been filled by the Church, which is not here mentioned, because this Passage pertains only to Israel.*

The phrase, "And I will cut off the chariot from Ephraim," refers to the Battle of Armageddon. The phrase, "And He shall speak peace to the heathen," means that Christ will extend the peace He brings to the entirety of the world, teaching the heathen to receive His spiritual rule and, in effect, to accept Him as Lord and Saviour, which many, if not most, will do!

The last phrase refers to His total dominion of the entirety of the world [Gen. 12:3].)

11 As for you also, by the blood of your covenant I have sent forth your prisoners out of the pit wherein is no water. *(Taking the latter phrase first, "I have sent forth your prisoners out of the pit wherein is no water," refers to Israel's miserable condition and the even worse condition at the Second Coming. The phrase, "As for you also, by the Blood of your Covenant," refers to God's Covenant to Zion made with Abraham*

and secured by the Precious Blood of Calvary, as foreshadowed by the death of the Covenant victim of Gen. 15:17-18. In effect, it will be the "New Covenant," of which the "Old Covenant" was a shadow [Mat. 26:28; Heb. 8:6; 9:15].)*

GOD IS JUDAH'S DEFENSE AGAINST THE ANTICHRIST (AND THE REVIVED GRECIAN EMPIRE) AT ARMAGEDDON

12 Turn you to the strong hold, you prisoners of hope: even to day do I declare that I will render double unto you *(the phrase, "Your prisoners of hope," is beautiful indeed, because it portrays Israel as a "prisoner" of their own rebellion, but yet with "hope," which pertains to these Prophecies. The phrase, "Even today do I declare that I will render double unto you," is identical to Job, with the Lord making his latter end doubly as prosperous as his beginning);*

13 When I have bent Judah for Me, filled the bow with Ephraim, and raised up your sons, O Zion, against your sons, O Greece, and made you as the sword of a mighty man. *(The phrase, "And raised up your sons, O Zion, against your sons, O Greece," presents a Passage, among others, which predicts the revival of the Grecian Empire under the Antichrist to fight against Israel in the Battle of Armageddon. As it involved the "revived Grecian Empire," it is speaking only of that which is in the realm of the spirit world. In fact, the same fallen angel who helped Alexander the Great will help the Antichrist [Rev. 13:2; 17:8].*

The phrase, "And made you as the sword of a mighty man," pertains to the prowess of Israel during that time, even though poorly armed. The Lord will, in fact, give them superhuman strength.)

14 And the LORD shall be seen over them, and His arrow shall go forth as the lightning: and the LORD God shall blow the trumpet, and shall go with whirlwinds of the south. *(The phrase, "And the LORD shall be seen over them," refers to the Battle of Armageddon and the Second Coming.)*

15 The LORD of Hosts shall defend them; and they shall devour, and subdue with sling stones; and they shall drink, and make a noise as through wine; and they shall be filled like bowls, and as the corners of the Altar. *(The phrase, "And they shall devour, and subdue with sling stones," refers to the resurgence of the tiny army of Israel, which, upon the Advent of Christ, will suddenly be endued with Power from on*

High. The phrase, "And they shall be filled like bowls, and as the corners of the Altar," speaks of the blood that filled the sacrificial vessels upon the sacrifice of the lambs. In fact, so great will be the bloodshed in the Battle of Armageddon, of which this is a description! [Rev. 14:20])

16 And the LORD their God shall save them in that day as the flock of His people: for they shall be as the stones of a crown, lifted up as an ensign upon His land. (The first phrase has a far greater meaning beyond the mere deliverance from their enemies. It speaks of God's glorious Salvation given to Israel, as they are "saved by Grace" [Eph. 2:8-9]. As well, the phrase, "The flock of His People," has to do with the Twenty-third Psalm, which will then be fulfilled in totality in the coming Kingdom Age.

The phrase, "Lifted up as an ensign upon His Land," pertains to Restored, Redeemed Israel finally occupying the Land as was originally intended. In other words, the Lord will look at them as precious stones beautifying the Land.)

17 For how great is His goodness, and how great is His beauty! corn shall make the young men cheerful, and new wine the maids. (The Text should read, "How great shall be their beauty and how great shall be their prosperity!" For it speaks entirely of Israel.)

CHAPTER 10
(487 B.C.)
NATURAL AND SPIRITUAL RAIN

ASK ye of the LORD rain in the time of the latter rain; so the LORD shall make bright clouds, and give them showers of rain, to every one grass in the field. (Even though this Chapter has some reference to the Prophet's time, and even before, still, its basic and plenary fulfillment awaits the future. The phrase, "Ask ye of the Lord rain in the time of the latter rain," seems to be a strange thing — asking rain in the time of rain. The idea is this:

Because of Israel's spiritual condition during the time of Jeremiah, the promised "Latter Rain" was withheld and the harvests were, therefore, sparse. Consequently, the Holy Spirit is saying that, had Israel not turned aside to idols, they would have received the early rain and the latter rain and would not have been carried away into captivity.

The phrase, "So the LORD shall make bright clouds, and give them showers of rain," speaks of the Lord as totally controlling the climatic conditions which either helped or hindered Israel's harvests.

The phrase, "To every one grass in the field," speaks of a bountiful harvest, which, in its totality, will take place in the coming Kingdom Age.)

2 For the idols have spoken vanity, and the diviners have seen a lie, and have told false dreams; they comfort in vain: therefore they went their way as a flock, they were troubled, because there was no shepherd. (The phrase, "For the idols have spoken vanity," takes Israel back to the cause of her captivity — idols. The word "vanity" means "empty nothings." The phrase, "And the diviners have seen a lie," is the second superstition, and speaks of soothsayers, i.e., persons who pretended to predict the future.

The phrase, "And have told false dreams," speaks of a third group, which claims to have dreamed certain things, which speaks of direction, but is actually deceit.

The Scripture bluntly states: "They comfort in vain!" In other words, the poor dupes who believed this foolishness experienced a little comfort, but it proved to be short-lived.

The phrase, "Therefore they went their way as a flock, they were troubled," refers to being led away into captivity. It was all because they trusted in vain superstitions instead of the Lord.

The Holy Spirit bluntly states: "because there was no shepherd," i.e., no one to distinguish between right and wrong, no "righteous shepherd.")

JUDAH STRENGTHENED TO FIGHT AT ARMAGEDDON

3 My anger was kindled against the shepherds, and I punished the goats: for the LORD of Hosts has visited His flock the House of Judah, and has made them as His goodly horse in the battle. (The phrase, "My anger was kindled against the shepherds," has to do with the latter part of Verse 2. This speaks of Judah's last four kings. It was said of the last three of them, "he did that which was evil in the sight of the Lord" [II Chron. 36:6, 9, 12].

The phrase, "And I punished the goats," refers to the other countries which overstepped their commission in the punishment of Israel.

The phrase, "For the LORD of Hosts has visited His flock the House of Judah," refers to their coming Restoration; in fact, the first stages have already begun. The last phrase refers to the Lord giving Israel super strength in the Battle of Armageddon, as they oppose the Antichrist.)

4 Out of Him came forth the corner, out of Him the nail, out of Him the battle bow, out of

Him every oppressor together. *(The Messiah is described here. He is the "Cornerstone," He is the "Tent Pole," He is the "Battle Bow," and He is the "Ruler." The phrase, "Out of Him every oppressor together," could have been better translated, "from Him every expeller of oppression.")*

5 And they shall be as mighty men, which tread down their enemies in the mire of the streets in the battle: and they shall fight, because the LORD is with them, and the riders on horses shall be confounded. *(The entire Scripture refers to great "might" given to Israel by the Lord during the Battle of Armageddon.)*

JOSEPH AND JUDAH REGATHERED

6 And I will strengthen the House of Judah, and I will save the House of Joseph, and I will bring them again to place them; for I have mercy upon them: and they shall be as though I had not cast them off: for I am the LORD their God, and will hear them. *(The introduction of "Joseph" in this Verse and "Ephraim" in Verse 7, for they both mean the same and refer to the Northern Kingdom of Israel, decide the futurity of this Prophecy; for they had no existence, as such, in Zechariah's day, nor have they at the present.*

The first phrase of the Verse refers to both the Northern and Southern Kingdoms being once again joined and never again separated. This will take place in the coming Kingdom Age.)

7 And they of Ephraim shall be like a mighty man, and their heart shall rejoice as through wine: yea, their children shall see it, and be glad; their heart shall rejoice in the LORD. *(This speaks of the time that Israel will accept Christ as Saviour, Lord, and Messiah. It will be almost immediately after the Second Coming [13:1].)*

8 I will hiss for them, and gather them; for I have redeemed them: and they shall increase as they have increased. *(The phrase, "I will hiss for them, and gather them," actually means that the Lord summons them. The phrase, "And they shall increase as they have increased," refers to an explosive increase in population; again, this will take place in the Kingdom Age.)*

THE DISPERSING AND
REGATHERING OF ISRAEL

9 And I will sow them among the people: and they shall remember Me in far countries; and they shall live with their children, and turn again. *(The phrase, "And I will sow them among the people," refers to Jews increasing among the nations of the world where they were to be scattered. This scattering took place first of all in the Babylonian Empire, and then, some 500 years later, by Rome.*

This one phrase, "I will sow," proclaims the Lord's watchful eye over them all of these centuries, even though they were out of Covenant. The phrase, "And they shall remember Me in far countries," means that they will attempt to maintain the Jewish way of worship wherever they may be.

The phrase, "And they shall live with their children," simply means that despite all the efforts of Satan to exterminate these ancient people, the Promise is given here that Satan will not be successful. The three words, "And turn again," have to do with their ultimate return to the Land of Israel, which, of course, began in 1948 [Isa. 35:10].)

10 I will bring them again also out of the land of Egypt, and gather them out of Assyria; and I will bring them into the land of Gilead and Lebanon; and place shall not be found for them. *(Egypt and Assyria here represent all of Israel's foes; for Egypt was the first and the Assyrian, i.e., Antichrist, will be the last. The phrase, "And place shall not be found for them," simply refers to the large number which will return to Israel in that coming Glad Day.)*

11 And He shall pass through the sea with affliction, and shall smite the waves in the sea, and all the deeps of the river shall dry up: and the pride of Assyria shall be brought down, and the sceptre of Egypt shall depart away. *(The idea of this Verse is: "He [Messiah] shall pass through the sea of affliction." As Captain of His People's Deliverance, He will accompany them through their future affliction, as He led them through the Red Sea and through the Jordan.*

The phrase, "And the pride of Assyria shall be brought down," refers to the Antichrist and his defeat at the Battle of Armageddon. The phrase, "And the scepter of Egypt shall depart away," concerns the "Times of the Gentiles" coming to an end, expressed in this manner.)

12 And I will strengthen them in the LORD; and they shall walk up and down in His Name, saith the LORD. *(To be strengthened in the Lord is the greatest strength of all! The phrase, "They shall walk up and down in His Name," means "in God's Beloved Son," and in safety, with dignity, as conquerors.)*

CHAPTER 11
(487 B.C.)

THE FIRST ADVENT OF THE MESSIAH:
THE SHEPHERD KING REJECTED

O PEN your doors, O Lebanon, that the fire may devour your cedars. *(This Chapter proclaims the First Advent of Christ and His rejection, with the last three Verses proclaiming the coming Antichrist. The phrase, "Open your doors, O Lebanon," speaks of the coming destruction of Israel by the Romans. The way the word "Lebanon" is used here, it does not refer to the country itself, which borders Israel on the north, but instead refers to the houses in Jerusalem, which were largely built of cedar from Lebanon [Hab. 2:17].)*

2 Howl, fir tree; for the cedar is fallen; because the mighty are spoiled: howl, O ye oaks of Bashan; for the forest of the vintage is come down. *(The trees of this Verse symbolize the cities destroyed by the Romans as they marched through Israel onto Jerusalem. The argument is: some of these cities were strong, and they were still unable to stand; so, how much more sure was the Fall of Jerusalem?!*

The phrase, "For the forest of the vintage is come down," refers to Jerusalem fortifying itself, but to no avail because the Holy Spirit says, "It will come down." And so it did, with over one million Jews being killed, with hundreds of thousands of others being sold as slaves all over the world.)

3 There is a voice of the howling of the shepherds; for their glory is spoiled: a voice of the roaring of young lions; for the pride of Jordan is spoiled. *(The phrase, "There is a voice of the howling of the shepherds," refers to the Priests, who were lamenting the destruction of the Temple. The phrase, "A voice of the roaring of young lions," refers to the Nobles of Jerusalem. The phrase, "For the pride of Jordan is spoiled," proclaims Joshua crossing the Jordan about 1,500 years earlier, and his taking of the Land of Israel, with Jerusalem under David ultimately being made its Capital. Now the "pride" of that conquest, Jerusalem, is spoiled.)*

4 Thus saith the LORD my God; Feed the flock of the slaughter *(the phrase, "Feed the flock of the slaughter," is an admonition given to Zechariah, and yet Israel ultimately will not accept what is fed them; they will, therefore, be "slaughtered."*

Even though it is addressed to Zechariah and, as stated, to all who are in places of spiritual leadership, still, it really refers to Christ, Who will "feed this flock" as they have never before been fed, but yet that which they will not accept!);

5 Whose possessors slay them, and hold themselves not guilty: and they who sell them say, Blessed be the LORD; for I am rich: and their own shepherds pity them not. *(The phrase, "Whose possessors slay them, and hold themselves not guilty," refers to the spiritual leadership of Israel at the time of Christ. The "possessors" were the Pharisees, Sadducees, and Herodians. They, as most religious professors, were deceived by their own deception; consequently, they did not "hold themselves guilty" and would, therefore, not repent.*

The two words, "Slay them," concern the people being killed spiritually by unbelief and the "traditions of men" [Mk. 7:13]. The phrase, "And they who sell them say, Blessed be the LORD," means that they cloaked their entire ungodly procedure with religion. It further means that they rejected and crucified Christ in the "Name of the Lord."

The four words, "For I am rich," hold the idea that their wealth, even though ill-gotten, meant, in their minds, that God had blessed them. The phrase, "And their own shepherds pity them not," meant, in effect, that they had no True Shepherds [Mat. 9:36].)

6 For I will no more pity the inhabitants of the land, saith the LORD: but, lo, I will deliver the men every one into his neighbour's hand, and into the hand of his king: and they shall smite the land, and out of their hand I will not deliver them. *(The first phrase pertains to Israel being turned over to "slaughter" because of their rejection and crucifixion of God's only Son and their Messiah, the Lord Jesus Christ. The phrase, "But, lo, I will deliver the men every one into his neighbor's hand," refers to the Romans, who ruled Israel during the time of Christ.*

The phrase, "And they shall smite the land," refers to Titus and the Roman Tenth Legion laying siege to Jerusalem and totally destroying it in A.D. 70. The phrase, "And out of their hand I will not deliver them," means that inasmuch as Israel rejected the True King, now they would have to accept what the false king would do unto them.)

BEAUTY AND BANDS

7 And I will feed the flock of slaughter, even you, O poor of the flock. And I took unto me two staves; the one I called Beauty,

and the other I called Bands; and I fed the flock. *(The phrase, "And I will feed the flock of slaughter," refers back to Verse 4. He would feed them, i.e., give them Christ, but they would not accept Christ. Hence, they were destined for "slaughter." The phrase, "Even you, O poor of the flock," refers to the Disciples and others who received Him, and who consequently formed the nucleus of what would be called "the Church" [Mat. 16:18].*

The phrase, "The one I called Beauty, and the other I called Bands," pertains to "graciousness" [beauty] and "union" [bands]. These two staves, which were found with all shepherds, intimate the manifold character of God for His flock from the earliest times and the two Blessings which He designed to bestow, as the names of the staves proclaim.

First of all, He dealt with them with "Grace," which means the favor of God. Second, He meant for them all to be one, hence the word "Bands," or "the Union" of all the members of the flock, especially that between Israel and Judah. This made one flock under one Shepherd.

The phrase, "And I fed the flock," refers to God's care all through the history of Israel by giving them Prophets — and ultimately the greatest Gift of all, the Lord Jesus Christ.)

8 Three shepherds also I cut off in one month; and My soul loathed them, and their soul also abhorred Me. *(These three shepherds are unnamed, but probably refer to the "Pharisees, Sadducees, and Herodians." The words, "cut off," mean "to be destroyed," which they all were with the Fall of Jerusalem in A.D. 70.)*

9 Then said I, I will not feed you: that that die, let it die; and that that is to be cut off, let it be cut off; and let the rest eat every one the flesh of another. *(Due to the fact that Israel rejected her Messiah, crucifying Him, they were "cut off." Consequently, in this one Verse is predicted a horror upon Jerusalem and Judah to such an extent as they had never before known. They wanted Caesar, so they got Caesar! It would prove to be a sorry trade [Jn. 19:15].)*

GOD'S GRACIOUSNESS (BEAUTY) CUT OFF: NO MORE MERCY ON ISRAEL UNTIL MESSIAH'S SECOND ADVENT

10 And I took My staff, even Beauty, and cut it asunder, that I might break My covenant which I had made with all the people. *(The first phrase means that the Lord withdrew His Grace from Israel, in effect leaving them to the*

mercy of their foes. The last phrase speaks of the breaking or abolishment of the Old Covenant made with Moses and all the people about 1,500 years before.*

Scripture is very clear that the Law of Moses was fulfilled by Christ on the Cross [II Cor. 3:6-15; Gal. 3:13-25; Col. 2:14-17]. It literally came to an end and was broken in one day, the day of the Crucifixion of Christ, even as the next Verse proclaims.)

11 And it was broken in that day: and so the poor of the flock who waited upon Me knew that it was the Word of the LORD. *(The phrase, "And so the poor of the flock . . .," refers to the few, among them His Disciples, who paid respect to His Words and, therefore, believed Him. However, the bulk of the nation took no heed, learned no lesson and, therefore, suffered the horrible consequence.*

The phrase, "Who waited upon Me knew that it was the Word of the LORD," means that only the few who knew their Bibles understood His Mission. However, even these were slow to understand, as is born out in the Gospels.)

MESSIAH SOLD BY THE PEOPLE (THE FLOCK)

12 And I said unto them, If you think good, give Me My price; and if not, forbear. So they weighed for My price thirty pieces of silver. *(The first phrase refers to the Lord speaking, even though He uses the Prophet as His instrument. The Lord is speaking in the Person of the Great Shepherd. He asks His hire of the flock, because the flock represents men.*

The phrase, "And if not, forbear," means "I leave it to you to decide." The phrase, "So they weighed for My price thirty pieces of silver," proclaims what Israel thought of their Messiah and His care through all the many centuries. They valued Him at thirty shekels, the price of an injured slave [Ex. 21:32].

It is amazing that the Pharisees, who claimed to be such sticklers for the Law, would read these words, especially after the act had been performed, and still not relate it to themselves. Such is the marvel of unbelief!)

13 And the LORD said unto me, Cast it unto the potter: a goodly price that I was prised at of them. And I took the thirty pieces of silver, and cast them to the potter in the House of the LORD. *(The phrase, "And the LORD said unto me," now refers to His Response to their actions. This was all prophesied about 500 years*

before it would actually take place. The phrase, "Cast it unto the potter," implies the contemptuous rejection of the paltry sum; at the same time, it intimates the ultimate destination, i.e., a field in which to bury the penniless [Mat. 27:3-10]. This was fulfilled to the letter by the action of Judas Iscariot.

The phrase, "A goodly price that I was prised at of them," is used as sarcasm. Such was the "price" that they valued Him. The pronoun "them" is used strongly by the Holy Spirit, and of contempt; it speaks of the leadership of Israel at that time!

The phrase, "And I took the thirty pieces of silver . . .," is quoted in Mat. 27:9. The phrase, "And cast them to the potter in the House of the LORD," represents that all of this took place in the Temple.)

THE BANDS (UNION) CUT OFF: ISRAEL DISPERSED

14 Then I cut asunder My other staff, even Bands, that I might break the brotherhood between Judah and Israel. *(The first phrase concerns the union of the Twelve Tribes being broken by the destruction of the Romans in A.D. 70. When Grace was taken away [Vs. 10], then the union could not help but be destroyed.*

The phrase, "That I might break the brotherhood between Judah and Israel," pertains to it being so completely broken that most Jews now have no idea to which Tribe they originally belonged. As the breaking of the first staff [Vs. 10] indicated the withdrawing of God's Care, the breaking of this staff, called "Bands," signified the utter dissolution of all the bonds that held the nation together. They rejected Him and now He rejects them.

As He was their total protection, whenever He rejected them, there was nothing left but anarchy, confusion, and ruin.)

A WORTHLESS SHEPHERD TAKES THE GOOD SHEPHERD'S PLACE: AFTER ANTICHRIST, ISRAEL WILL APPRECIATE THE GOOD SHEPHERD

15 And the LORD said unto me, Take unto you yet the instruments of a foolish shepherd. *(In this Verse, the "foolish shepherd," the future Antichrist, is described.)*

16 For, lo, I will raise up a shepherd in the land, which shall not visit those that be cut off, neither shall seek the young one, nor heal that that is broken, nor feed that that stands still: but he shall eat the flesh of the fat, and tear their claws in pieces. *(The contrast is given here between the True Shepherd, the Lord Jesus Christ, Who was rejected by Israel, and the "false shepherd," the Antichrist, who will deceive and seek to destroy them. They would not accept Christ, so He would see to it that a false shepherd would be given to them, hence the words, "For, lo, I will raise up. . . .")*

17 Woe to the idol shepherd who leaves the flock! the sword shall be upon his arm, and upon his right eye: his arm shall be clean dried up, and his right eye shall be utterly darkened. *(The phrase, "Woe to the idol shepherd," has reference to the Antichrist, who will claim to be God and who also will demand worship [II Thess. 2:3-4; Rev. 13:16-18]. The phrase, "Who leaves the flock," pertains to the Antichrist breaking his seven-year Covenant with Israel and then attacking her, when she will suffer her first military defeat since becoming a nation in 1948 [Dan. 9:27]. This will happen at the midpoint of the coming Great Tribulation.*

The Antichrist will set out with the "sword" to destroy Israel, but, in turn, will be destroyed. This will be at the Second Coming and will also signal the Restoration of Israel.)

CHAPTER 12
(487 B.C.)
BURDEN FOR ISRAEL: SIEGE OF JERUSALEM BY THE ANTICHRIST

THE burden of the Word of the LORD for Israel, saith the LORD, which stretches forth the heavens, and lays the foundation of the Earth, and forms the spirit of man within him. *(The "burden" of the first phrase concerns wholly the future, as the first "burden" [9:1] concerned both the present and future. As well, it foretells Israel's deliverance by Him Whom they rejected and pierced, their consequent conversion, and Zion's resultant glory.*

The phrase, "Which stretches forth and lays the foundation of the Earth," portrays the force of three Hebrew verbs as both past and present. Immanuel made and maintains all things [Col. 1:16]. His Power as Creator and Sustainer assures the fulfillment of His Promises; consequently, the Holy Spirit opens this section proclaiming the certitude of the coming action.

The phrase, "And forms the spirit of man within him," proclaims one of two Hebrew words translated "spirit" in the Bible. The one is "spirit"

as common to man and the animal creation; the other is an emanation from God possessed only by man, and ever existing, i.e., the Holy Spirit.

The "spirit of man within him," and thus "formed" by God, proclaims man's spirit as higher than the spirit of animals. In fact, man is in a class by himself, i.e., in the Image of God [Gen. 1:26].)

2 Behold, I will make Jerusalem a cup of trembling unto all the people round about, when they shall be in the siege both against Judah and against Jerusalem. *(The Holy Spirit uses the word "Israel" in Verse 1, while using the word "Judah" in this Verse. Both are interchangeable and mean the same thing.*

The first phrase pictures this city, Jerusalem, as the focal point of the nations of the world. This will take place in the coming Great Tribulation. The phrase, "When they shall be in the siege both against Judah and against Jerusalem," concerns the Battle of Armageddon.)

3 And in that day will I make Jerusalem a burdensome stone for all people: all who burden themselves with it shall be cut in pieces, though all the people of the Earth be gathered together against it. *(The first phrase refers to a "stone" which is difficult to lift or to move. The efforts of the Antichrist to displace it will cause his own destruction, for the Stone of Daniel, Chapter 2, will fall upon him from Heaven.*

The phrase, "All who burden themselves with it shall be cut in pieces," concerns any and all nations of the world which join with the Antichrist in his efforts to destroy Jerusalem and Judah at the Battle of Armageddon.)

MESSIAH'S SECOND ADVENT; JUDAH AT ARMAGEDDON

4 In that day, saith the LORD, I will smite every horse with astonishment, and his rider with madness: and I will open My eyes upon the house of Judah, and will smite every horse of the people with blindness. *(The phrase, "In that day, saith the LORD," refers to the Battle of Armageddon. The phrase, "I will smite every horse with astonishment, and his rider with madness," pertains to a frenzy inspired by terror. In fact, the last phrase is the same as the first, but repeated to emphasize its certitude.)*

5 And the governors of Judah shall say in their heart, The inhabitants of Jerusalem shall be my strength in the LORD of Hosts their God. *(This Verse portrays, possibly, the very first collective faith of the leaders and people*

of Israel in the Lord their God since the days of Josiah, if even then. This will no doubt be at the instant of the Lord's return, with Israel in the process of repenting at that very time.)

6 In that day will I make the governors of Judah like an hearth of fire among the wood, and like a torch of fire in a sheaf; and they shall devour all the people round about, on the right hand and on the left: and Jerusalem shall be inhabited again in her own place, even in Jerusalem. *(Concerning the first phrase, the idea is: the Lord, upon His return, will give the "governors of Judah" wisdom and strength respecting the closing hours of the battle to a degree that possibly man has never known. The phrase, "And Jerusalem shall be inhabited again in her own place, even in Jerusalem," refers to the city being saved from the onslaught of the man of sin. It being "inhabited again" concerns the rebuilding by the Messiah. It will, no doubt, be the most beautiful city on the face of the Earth.)*

7 The LORD also shall save the tents of Judah first, that the glory of the house of David and the glory of the inhabitants of Jerusalem do not magnify themselves against Judah. *(The idea of this Verse is: Judah recognizes and confesses as a source of strength the Faith of Jerusalem; the Messiah will reward this humility by rescuing Judah first; thus will there be equality of glory to both. "Judah" refers to the entirety of the area given to the Tribe of Judah during the time of Joshua. The reason for this is because Jesus came from the Tribe of Judah [Gen. 49:10].)*

8 In that day shall the LORD defend the inhabitants of Jerusalem; and he who is feeble among them at that day shall be as David; and the house of David shall be as God, as the Angel of the LORD before them. *(This refers to the coming Battle of Armageddon. The phrase, "And he who is feeble among them at that day shall be as David," refers back to Verse 6. David was Israel's greatest warrior and was that because of the anointing of the Holy Spirit upon him for this purpose. Likewise, the Holy Spirit tells us here that, at that coming day, the most "feeble among them" will have the strength of a "mighty David."*

The phrase, "And the house of David shall be as God," has to do with the Tribe of Judah. The phrase, "As the Angel of the LORD before them," pertains to Jehovah, Who led Israel through the wilderness after their Deliverance from Egypt.)

9 And it shall come to pass in that day, that

I will seek to destroy all the nations that come against Jerusalem. *(Once again, this is the Battle of Armageddon.)*

MESSIAH REVEALED TO ISRAEL

10 And I will pour upon the house of David and upon the inhabitants of Jerusalem, the Spirit of grace and of supplications: and they shall look upon Me Whom they have pierced, and they shall mourn for Him, as one mourns for his only son, and shall be in bitterness for Him, as one that is in bitterness for his first-born. *(The phrase, "And I will pour . . . ," refers to the Lord pouring out fire upon Zion's adversaries, but the Holy Spirit upon her inhabitants [II Thess., Chpt. 1]. If one is to notice, the Messiah Himself is speaking in the entirety of this Chapter as far as the word "pierced"; then the Holy Spirit points to the moral effect produced by the revelation. The phrase, "Upon the House of David," proclaims the Promise originally given to David concerning his seed upon the Throne of Israel [II Sam. 7:12-16].*

The phrase, "I will pour upon them the Spirit of Grace," concerns the goodness of God and means they are no longer trusting in their Law, but instead the "Grace of God," which is found only in the Lord Jesus Christ. The phrase, "And I will pour upon them the Spirit of Supplications," speaks of Israel supplicating the Lord and the Lord supplicating the Father on their behalf. The word means "to ask humbly and earnestly."

The phrase, "And they shall look upon Me Whom they have pierced," identifies who and what they are and Who He is. The phrase, "And they shall mourn for Him, as one mourns for his only son," now proclaims the moral effect produced by this Revelation, as given by the Holy Spirit. They will then make their supplications to Him for Mercy and Forgiveness. The phrase, "And shall be in bitterness for Him," means "a sense of intense shame." It speaks of True Repentance.

The last phrase, "As one who is in bitterness for his firstborn," refers to the loss of an only son, the firstborn. In effect, they killed their own son, and the firstborn at that, which meant that the family line could not continue; it was, in fact, destroyed, at least as far as the Covenant was concerned; however, this "Son," or "First-born," rose from the dead. Even though they would not accept it then, they will accept it now — and because He lives, they shall live also!)

ISRAEL'S REPENTANCE

11 In that day shall there be a great mourning in Jerusalem, as the mourning of Hadad-rimmon in the valley of Megiddon. *(As Verse 10 proclaims, there is personal "mourning," with national "mourning" in Verse 11, and domestic "mourning" in Verses 12 through 14. Every man will feel himself guilty of piercing Immanuel, which is the way they should feel.*

The last phrase refers to King Josiah being killed in this place [II Chron. 35:22-25]. His reign was the one gleam of light in the gloom that covered the nation from Manasseh to the captivity. Consequently, there was great "mourning" respecting his death.)

12 And the land shall mourn, every family apart; the family of the house of David apart, and their wives apart; the family of the house of Nathan apart, and their wives apart;

13 The family of the house of Levi apart, and their wives apart; the family of Shimei apart, and their wives apart *(the house of David and Nathan speaks of the princely line of Israel, while the family of Levi and Shimei speaks of the Priests. Consequently, these two Verses proclaim a personal and general Repentance on the part of both the civil and spiritual leadership);*

14 All the families that remain, every family apart, and their wives apart. *(The phrase, "All the families that remain," speaks now of the balance of Israel. Judah's repentance and conversion will not be motivated by fear of punishment, but by the overwhelming sense of guilt affecting the heart, when they recognize that their Deliverer is Jesus Whom they crucified, and that all along, despite their hatred and their conduct, He kept on loving them!)*

CHAPTER 13
(487 B.C.)
THE FOUNTAIN OF CLEANSING
FOR ISRAEL

IN that day there shall be a fountain opened to the house of David and to the inhabitants of Jerusalem for sin and for uncleanness. *(The phrase, "In that day," occurs eighteen times from 9:16 through 14:21. This shows how precious "that day" is to the Messiah's heart. In that day, His victory over the enemies of His People will be great, but greater will be His moral victory over His People themselves.*

The Christian's true triumphs are God's triumphs over him, and God's triumphs over His

People are their only victories. Such was Jacob of old, who represented Israel in that coming Glad Day. The conversion of the Apostle Paul illustrates the future conversion of Israel. He hated Jesus, but on the Damascus Road, he looked upon Him Whom he had pierced, mourned, and wept.

The phrase, "In that day there shall be a fountain opened," does not mean that it is first opened there, but that Israel will only begin to partake of it "in that day," i.e., the beginning of the Kingdom Age. This fountain was historically opened at Calvary, but will be consciously opened to repentant Jews in the future day of her Repentance. For the fact and function of that fountain only becomes conscious to the awakened sinner.

A true sense of sin and guilt in relationship to God awakens the sense of the need of cleansing, and so the shed and cleansing Blood of the Lamb of God becomes precious to convicted conscience. As well, the ever-living efficacy of Christ's Atoning Work, with its power to cleanse the conscience and the life, is justly comparable to a fountain and not to a font. The sense of the Hebrew Text is that this Fountain shall be opened and shall remain open.

The phrase, "To the house of David and to the inhabitants of Jerusalem for sin and for uncleanness," portrays the possibility that, of all sinners, the Jerusalem sinners may be accounted the greatest. It was Jerusalem that stoned the Prophets and crucified the Messiah; therefore, great sinners may hope for pardon and cleansing in this Fountain opened for the House of David.

The entrance of Christ judges sin, unmasks its true character, and arouses a moral consciousness which approves that judgment. That entrance dominates, adjusts, disciplines, instructs, and cleanses man's affections, relationships, and desires. All of this must be cleansed, not only in Israel of a future day, but also in any and all of who come to Christ. That Fountain is open to all!)

2 And it shall come to pass in that day, saith the LORD of Hosts, that I will cut off the names of the idols out of the land, and they shall no more be remembered: and also I will cause the prophets and the unclean spirit to pass out of the land. (Through sin, man has so degraded his emotions that God must cleanse and adjust them. When this is done, the effect is that man's moral consciousness is so harmonized with God's nature that man will not only abolish idolatry, but he will put to death his own child who tries to support it, as the next Verse proclaims.

Israel's problems of the past had much to do with literal "idols." Such will be so utterly abolished that their very names will perish. As well, "false prophets," which once abounded in Israel, will be no more.

The phrase, "And the unclean spirit to pass out of the land," is, among other things, the lying spirit which works in false prophets [I Ki. 22:19-23]. In fact, Satan, along with all demon spirits and fallen angels, will be consigned to the "bottomless pit" [Rev. 20:1-3].)

FALSE PROPHETS EXECUTED

3 And it shall come to pass, that when any shall yet prophesy (prophesy falsely), then his father and his mother who begat him shall say unto him, You shall not live; for you speak lies in the name of the LORD: and his father and his mother who begat him shall thrust him through when he prophesies. (The most dangerous form of idolatry is that which speaks lies in the Name of the Lord. Such is the part of Christendom that is corrupt.

This Verse does not mean that there actually will be false prophets in Israel during the time of the Kingdom Age, for there will not. The idea is: so zealous will be Israel for the Lord in that coming hour that even if a son would begin to prophesy falsely, he would be properly restrained by his parents, even to the place of execution, if necessary.

The Holy Spirit is impressing upon the Reader how different Israel will be in that coming Glad Day after their conversion.)

4 And it shall come to pass in that day, that the prophets shall be ashamed every one of his vision, when he has prophesied; neither shall they wear a rough garment to deceive (the idea of this Verse is: in the coming Kingdom Age, so knowledgeable will most people be in the Word of God that those who are false will not dare attempt to propagate "his false vision"):

5 But he shall say, I am no prophet, I am an husbandman; for man taught me to keep cattle from my youth. (In essence, this Verse proclaims that most preachers ought to simply quit, because they have not been called by God in the first place. The Truth is: "they are no prophet," but instead "an husbandman," i.e., a follower of secular employment.)

THE CRUCIFIED MESSIAH REVEALED

6 And one shall say unto Him, What are

these wounds in Your Hands? Then He shall answer, Those with which I was wounded in the house of My friends. *(In these Passages, the false prophets are placed beside the True Prophet, the Lord Jesus Christ. They, before the Coming of the Lord, too oftentimes were rewarded, while He, as each True Prophet, was greatly opposed, even crucified. The false prophets thrust themselves forward and claimed reverence and position; He Himself, the greatest of the Prophets, did not claim to be a professional Prophet — that was not His Mission in coming to Earth — but became a Bond-servant and a Shepherd; made and appointed such in the Divine Purpose of Redemption. For man having sold himself into slavery, it was necessary that Christ should take that position in order to redeem him.*

The phrase, "And one shall say unto Him," refers to the moment of recognition, as outlined in 12:10, where it says, "And they shall look upon Me Whom they have pierced, and they shall mourn for Him." This will be immediately after the Second Coming, with the Antichrist now defeated and Christ standing before Israel. They will then know, beyond the shadow of a doubt, that He is the Messiah; then will they ask, "What are these wounds in Your Hands?"

These wounds, which He will ever carry, will be an instant and constant reminder of Who He is and what was done to Him, which presents Him as the Sin-Bearer of the world. Even though He was the Redeemer of all mankind, still, this shows how He was treated by man, especially by His Own.

The phrase, "Then He shall answer," will be an answer that will cause their terrible "mourning" of 12:10-14. It will also be the cause of the "Fountain opened to the House of David and to the inhabitants of Jerusalem for sin and for uncleanness" [13:1].

The phrase, "Those with which I was wounded in the house of My friends," proclaims His Crucifixion and those who did it to Him. The words, "My friends," are said in irony.)

ISRAEL'S REDEMPTION THROUGH THE SUFFERING OF THE MESSIAH

7 Awake, O sword, against My shepherd, and against the Man Who is My fellow, saith the LORD of Hosts: smite the Shepherd, and the sheep shall be scattered: and I will turn My hand upon the little ones. *(The phrase, "Awake, O sword, against My Shepherd," concerns the Crucifixion of Christ, because Christ was the*

"Good Shepherd" [Jn. 10:11], in effect, "God's Shepherd." The phrase, "And against the Man Who is My fellow, saith the LORD of Hosts," refers to Christ as the "Fellow" of Jehovah.*

The phrase, "Smite the Shepherd," pertains to the fact that not only was sin upon the sinless Substitute at Calvary, but the Substitute Himself, Jehovah's equal. He Himself must die in order that man might live; for the curse that rested upon man was the doom of death [separation from God] because of sin. Christ's Death was, therefore, necessary to satisfy that claim and to vindicate and magnify Divine Righteousness.

The phrase, "And the sheep shall be scattered," pertains to them "scattered" as a nation, but not finally lost, for His Hand, pierced by the flock, shall cause the "little ones" to return to Zion, which these Passages and many others proclaim! The phrase, "And I will turn My Hand upon the little ones," pertains to the Coming of the Lord and the Restoration of Israel, which will bring "the little ones" back.

In astronomy, a near planet and a distant fixed star may appear side-by-side in the heavens, though the one is millions of miles more distant than the others; so, in the Scriptures, often two Prophecies may be side-by-side in the Text but, as here, be separated by many hundreds, sometimes thousands, of years.)

ISRAEL PURGED AND PURIFIED DURING THE TRIBULATION

8 And it shall come to pass, that in all the land, saith the LORD, two parts therein shall be cut off and die; but the third shall be left therein. *(This Verse pertains to the Great Tribulation, more particularly, the last half of that dreadful time. Zechariah predicts that two-thirds of the population of Israel will die during those last three and a half years, leaving one-third to fight the Antichrist at Armageddon and to make up the nation that will be brought into being at the Second Coming of Christ [Rom. 11:25-29].*

There are approximately five million Jews in Israel presently. If there are six million at that time, this means that some four million will be killed. Very few times in history has such a large percentage of the population of a nation been destroyed, if ever!)

9 And I will bring the third part through the fire, and will refine them as silver is refined, and will try them as gold is tried: they shall call on My name, and I will hear them: I will say, It is My people: and they shall say,

The LORD is my God. *(The phrase, "And I will bring the third part through the fire," refers to those who are left alive after the Battle of Armageddon, who will look upon Him Whom they pierced and repent [12:10-14]. The "fire" is the Great Tribulation, which Jesus mentioned [Mat. 24:21].*

The phrase, "And will refine them as silver is refined, and will try them as gold is tried," proclaims the purpose of the coming Great Tribulation. The phrase, "They shall call on My Name, and I will hear them," refers to proper relationship being restored.

The phrase, "I will say, It is My people: and they shall say, The LORD is my God," pertains to the remnant who has been "refined" as silver and "tried" as gold. These will repent; as a result, they will once again be owned by the Lord, as He says, "It is My People." He will do so because they shall say, "The LORD is my God," i.e., Jesus Christ is Lord!

At that time, the Prophecy of Hosea will be fulfilled: "You shall call Me Ishi; and shall call me no more Baali" [Hos. 2:16]. "Ishi" means "My Husband.")

CHAPTER 14
(487 B.C.)
THE DAY OF THE LORD: BEGINNING AT ARMAGEDDON

BEHOLD, the day of the LORD comes, and your spoil shall be divided in the midst of you. *(The phrase, "Behold, the day of the LORD comes," presents this day as beginning with the Second Coming and lasting until the end of the Millennium. At that time, the end of the Millennium, the "Day of God" begins and will continue through eternity [I Cor. 15:24-28; Eph. 1:10; II Pet. 3:10-13].*

The phrase, "and your spoil shall be divided in the midst of you," concerns the Antichrist coming against Israel [Ezek. 38:11-12].)

2 For I will gather all nations against Jerusalem to battle; and the city shall be taken, and the houses rifled, and the women ravished; and half of the city shall go forth into captivity, and the residue of the people shall not be cut off from the city. *(The first phrase refers to the mobilization of the nations to Armageddon [Ezek., Chpts. 38-39; Joel, Chpt. 3; Rev. 16:13-16; 19:11-21]. The phrase, "And the city shall be taken," actually means that the Antichrist will prepare to take Jerusalem, with actually half of it being taken. The phrase, "And the houses rifled, and*

the women ravished," expresses extreme cruelty practiced by the army of the Antichrist.

The phrase, "And half of the city shall go forth into captivity," means that half of Jerusalem will fall to the advances of the Antichrist, with the other half fighting furiously to save themselves, but with futility, other than the Coming of the Lord. Actually, the phrasing of the sentence structure portrays Israel fighting with a ferocity that knows no bounds, but yet not able to stand against the powerful onslaught of the combined armies of the man of sin.

The phrase, "And the residue of the people shall not be cut off from the city," refers to the army of Israel already cut to pieces, but determined to defend the city, even house to house, and, if necessary, to die to the last man.)

3 Then shall the LORD go forth, and fight against those nations, as when He fought in the day of battle. *("Then" is the key word!*

1. "Then": when Israel will begin to cry to God for Deliverance, knowing that He is their only hope.

2. "Then": when half of Jerusalem has fallen and it looks like the other half is about to fall.

3. "Then": when it looks like every Jew will be annihilated, with two-thirds already killed.

4. "Then": when it looks like the Promises of God made to the Patriarchs and Prophets of old will fall down.

5. "Then": when it looks like the Antichrist will win this conflict, which will make Satan the lord of the earth.

The phrase, "Then shall the LORD go forth," refers to the Second Coming, which will be the most cataclysmic event that the world has ever known. The phrase, "And fight against those nations," pertains to the nations under the banner of the Antichrist, which have set out to destroy Israel, and actually with annihilation in mind.

The phrase, "As when He fought in the day of battle," probably refers to the time when the Lord led the Children of Israel out of Egypt by way of the Red Sea [Ex. 14:14; 15:3]. This was Israel's first battle when Jehovah Messiah "went forth" and fought for them. Israel then passed through a valley between mountains of water; in this, their last battle, they will escape through a valley between mountains of rock, which the next Verse proclaims.)

MESSIAH'S SECOND ADVENT: CHANGES IN PALESTINE

4 And His feet shall stand in that day upon

the Mount of Olives, which is before Jerusalem on the east, and the Mount of Olives shall cleave in the midst thereof toward the east and toward the west, and there shall be a very great valley; and half of the mountain shall remove toward the north, and half of it toward the south. *(The first phrase refers to Christ literally standing on the Mount of Olives, which will be His landing point at the Second Coming, fulfilling the prediction of the two Angels at His Ascension [Acts 1:10-11]. The phrase, "And the Mount of Olives shall cleave in the midst thereof toward the east and toward the west," actually speaks of a great topographical change, which Israel will use at that hour as a way of escape from the Antichrist. With every road blocked, the Lord will open a way through the very center of the mountain, as He opened a path through the Red Sea.*

The phrase, "And there shall be a very great valley," refers to the escape route of Israel. The phrase, "And half of the mountain shall remove toward the north, and half of it toward the south," refers to the wall of rock on either side of escaping Israel, which makes it similar to the wall of water on either side when Israel escaped Egypt.)

5 And you shall flee to the valley of the mountains; for the valley of the mountains shall reach unto Azal: yea, you shall flee, like as you fled from before the earthquake in the days of Uzziah king of Judah: and the LORD my God shall come, and all the Saints with you. *(The phrase, "And you shall flee to the valley of the mountains," should read "through the valley." As stated, this will be Israel's escape route from the Antichrist. The phrase, "For the valley of the mountains shall reach unto Azal," probably refers to Beth-ezel, mentioned in Micah 1:11 as a village on the east of Olivet.*

The phrase, "Yea, you shall flee," is that the people might not be involved in the judgments which shall fall upon the enemy. The phrase, "Like as you fled from before the earthquake in the days of Uzziah king of Judah," also pertains to an earthquake which the Lord will use to produce this phenomenon.

The phrase, "And the Lord my God shall come, and all the Saints with you," pertains to the Lord coming at this particular time, which will have caused the cataclysmic events in the first place. The Passage, "All the Saints with you," refers to every Saint of God who has ever lived being with the Lord at the Second Coming [Rev. 19:14].)

6 And it shall come to pass in that day, that the light shall not be clear, nor dark *(the phrase,*

"And it shall come to pass in that day," refers to the very day that Christ appears on Earth, during the Battle of Armageddon. At that time, the day will be extended, thereby giving the Antichrist no respite):

7 But it shall be one day which shall be known to the LORD, not day, nor night: but it shall come to pass, that at evening time it shall be light. *(The entirety of the Battle of Armageddon will last many days; however, the "day" mentioned here will probably be extended to last approximately 24 hours.)*

THE RIVER FROM UNDER
THE SANCTUARY

8 And it shall be in that day, that Living Waters shall go out from Jerusalem; half of them toward the former sea, and half of them toward the hinder sea: in summer and in winter shall it be. *(The Prophecy now jumps from the Battle of Armageddon to the finished Sanctuary in Jerusalem. From under that Sanctuary will flow a river, prophesied by Ezekiel [Ezek. 47:1-12], with the river parting after a distance, with one part going to the Dead Sea, called "the former sea," making it teem alive with fish, with the other part going to the Mediterranean, termed "the hinder sea."*

The words, "Living Waters," are used in this Verse because of the river's life-giving properties, totally unlike any other river the world has ever known. In fact, Ezekiel said, "And everything shall live whither the river cometh" [Ezek. 47:9]. No doubt, these "Living Waters" will be responsible for the trees which will grow on both sides of this river, which will "bring forth new fruit according to his month," and "the leaves thereof for medicine." The "fruit" and "leaves" will no doubt be transported all over the world. The "fruit" will probably guarantee unending life, while the "leaves" serve as "medicine" for any and all sickness, which will be more preventive than anything else [Ezek. 47:12].

The phrase, "In summer and in winter shall it be," proclaims the continuance of the seasons.)

THE EXTENT OF MESSIAH'S REIGN

9 And the LORD shall be King over all the Earth: in that day shall there be one LORD, and His Name One. *(The first phrase refers to the Lord Jesus Christ and his total dominion over all nations. The phrase, "In that day shall there be one LORD," rather says, "Jehovah shall be One."*

He shall be universally acknowledged as "the blessed and only Potentate" [I Tim. 6:15].)

CHANGES IN ISRAEL

10 All the land shall be turned as a plain from Geba to Rimmon south of Jerusalem: and it shall be lifted up, and inhabited in her place, from Benjamin's gate unto the place of the first gate, unto the corner gate, and from the tower of Hananeel unto the king's winepresses. *(This Verse proclaims that there will be a tremendous topographical change in the Jerusalem area, where a great plain will be formed; upon that mighty platform, the future city and palace of Jehovah Messiah will be built. This great platform will be the "Holy Oblation" of Ezek. 45:1-5. Through it will pass the broad and noble "Living Waters," which will connect the Dead Sea with the Mediterranean.*

As well, the phrase, "From Geba to Rimmon south of Jerusalem," refers to almost all, if not all, of the original territory of the Tribe of Judah.)

JERUSALEM RESTORED

11 And men shall dwell in it, and there shall be no more utter destruction; but Jerusalem shall be safely inhabited. *(The phrase, "And men shall dwell in it," refers to unending peace and safety. The phrase, "And there shall be no more utter destruction," literally says, "there shall be no more anathema," or curse! The phrase, "But Jerusalem shall be safely inhabited," pertains to the Lord dwelling there as the Supreme Authority Who will guarantee these Promises.)*

DESTRUCTION OF THE ARMIES AT ARMAGEDDON

12 And this shall be the plague wherewith the LORD will smite all the people who have fought against Jerusalem; Their flesh shall consume away while they stand upon their feet, and their eyes shall consume away in their holes, and their tongue shall consume away in their mouth. *(The Prophecy now reverts back to the Battle of Armageddon. The mighty power of the Lord will be used at the Second Coming to destroy the Antichrist and his armies, a power which the world has never previously seen, at least in this fashion!)*

13 And it shall come to pass in that day, that a great tumult from the LORD shall be among them; and they shall lay hold every one on the hand of his neighbour, and his hand shall rise up against the hand of his neighbour. *(At this time, the weaponry used by the Lord will also cause a mental discomfiture, bringing about that predicted.)*

JUDAH'S PART OF THE SPOILS OF WAR AT ARMAGEDDON

14 And Judah also shall fight at Jerusalem; and the wealth of all the heathen round about shall be gathered together, gold, and silver, and apparel, in great abundance. *(The phrase, "And Judah also shall fight at Jerusalem," refers to the army of Israel that has escaped Jerusalem as a result of the "very great valley" formed, due to the Coming of the Lord, as outlined in Verse 4. After having made their escape, they will then turn around and attack the remainder of the vast armies of the Antichrist, now surrounded in Jerusalem.*

The phrase, "And the wealth of all the heathen round about shall be gathered together," refers to the tremendous spoil which will be taken from the defeated massive armies of the Antichrist. The Antichrist went against Israel to "take a spoil," but instead will be himself "spoiled" [Ezek. 38:11-13].)

PLAGUE ON THE ANIMALS

15 And so shall be the plague of the horse, of the mule, of the camel, and of the ass, and of all the beasts that shall be in these tents, as this plague. *(This Verse speaks of "the plague," which will not only befall men at the Battle of Armageddon, as spoken in Verses 12 and 13, but also on the animals! Inasmuch as modern warfare little includes such animals, the reference is actually to the airplanes, tanks, artillery, and mechanized equipment of the armies of the Antichrist. "As this plague" destroys men, it will also make ineffective the mechanical mechanisms of machinery, and we speak of that which belongs to the Antichrist.)*

WORSHIP AT JERUSALEM

16 And it shall come to pass, that every one who is left of all the nations which came against Jerusalem shall even go up from year to year to worship the King, the LORD of Hosts, and to keep the Feast of Tabernacles. *(This "Feast of Tabernacles" was a delightful week of holiday in the month of October at the close of the year's*

toil, and was kept, at least it was supposed to be kept, all during the time of the Mosaic Law [Ex. 23:16; Lev. 23:33-43; Deut. 16:13]. This "Feast" will be re-instituted in the Kingdom Age, which will be kept not only by Israel, but also by all the other nations of the world.)

THE NATIONS CONQUERED AND ISRAEL SACRED TO THE LORD

17 And it shall be, that whoso will not come up of all the families of the Earth unto Jerusalem to worship the King, the LORD of Hosts, even upon them shall be no rain. *(This Scripture tells us that even though Jesus Christ is "King" and "LORD of Hosts," still, there will be some in the Earth, despite all the tremendous blessings and prosperity, who will not accept Him as Saviour and Lord, who, therefore, will not properly serve Him. To be sure, they will not be allowed to foment rebellion, wickedness, or evil, but will be forced to subscribe to the letter of the Law, if not the spirit. In other words, they will not be allowed to entertain the evil thoughts of their hearts. Also, all of this proclaims the Truth that the coming Kingdom Age will not be ruled by force, but rather by love; and yet force will be used where it is absolutely necessary.*

The phrase, "Even upon them shall be no rain," speaks of these recalcitrant leaders of nations who will not desire to be subservient to the "King," i.e., the Lord Jesus Christ. The Lord will then take care of the situation by stopping the rain, which will hinder the harvests, which will be felt by the people. The people will then take active measures to see to it that their appointed leaders from henceforth obey the Law of the Lord.)

18 And if the family of Egypt go not up, and come not, who have no rain; there shall be the plague, wherewith the LORD will smite the heathen who come not up to keep the Feast of Tabernacles. *(This speaks of the nations of the world which did not depend on rain, as "Egypt," being dealt with in another fashion. As to exactly what this "plague" will be, we aren't told!)*

19 This shall be the punishment of Egypt, and the punishment of all nations that come not up to keep the Feast of Tabernacles. *(The certitude of its affliction is especially repeated in this Verse. In other words, this Law will not be abrogated, despite who the people are, as it is so often presently. As well, inasmuch as it is the Lord Who makes the decisions in these cases,*

one can be certain that the judgment, if needed, will be fair and equitable.)

20 In that day shall there be upon the bells of the horses, HOLINESS UNTO THE LORD; and the pots in the LORD'S house shall be like the bowls before the Altar. *(The idea of this Verse and the following is that, in this coming day in Israel, even the most common things used by men shall be signified as holy, whether used in work, profit, or ornament. All shall be consecrated to God's service.*

The phrase, "In that day shall there be upon the bells of the horses, HOLINESS UNTO THE LORD," signifies the same inscription used upon the golden plate of the mitre [hat] of the High Priest [Ex. 28:36]. Then, only the High Priest, Who was a Type of Christ, carried this inscription, whereas now, even the lowliest things, as "bells of the horses," will be signified as such! Such is meant to portray the atmosphere which will guarantee the action of the preceding Verses. It is "HOLINESS UNTO THE LORD"; and the Lord will not allow it to be changed by the evil hearts of wicked men.

The phrase, "Shall be like the bowls before the Altar," concerns the Vessels which held the blood of the victims in Old Testament times for sprinkling upon the Altar, and were considered of superior sanctity. The Prophet announces that now all shall be holy, the lowest equal to the highest.)

21 Yea, every pot in Jerusalem and in Judah shall be holiness unto the LORD of Hosts: and all they who sacrifice shall come and take of them, and seethe therein: and in that day there shall be no more the Canaanite in the house of the LORD of Hosts. *(These two Verses speak of the entirety of the Land of Israel being holy unto the Lord, and not just a designated part, as the Temple of old! As is obvious here, the "Sacrificial System" will be re-instituted; but, as of old, it will not save. It will be strictly for a memorial [6:14].*

The phrase, "And in that day there shall be no more the Canaanite in the House of the LORD of Hosts," means that there will be no more a trafficker in the House of the LORD [Jn. 2:14-16]. In other words, the Sacred Ministry will cease to be adopted because of salaried profession or other secular interests.

The word "Holy" [or "Holiness"] simply means to be set apart for sacred use. It is removed from the realm of the common and moved to the sphere of the sacred.)

MALACHI

CHAPTER 1
(397 B.C.)
GOD'S LOVE FOR JACOB (ISRAEL)

THE burden of the Word of the LORD to Israel by Malachi. *(Malachi was one of the three Prophets after the Exile, the others being Haggai and Zechariah; however, he ministered about 100 years later than Haggai and Zechariah. In fact, the greater bulk of his Ministry was during the time of Nehemiah's second visit to Jerusalem, of which we have only the barest and most summary account [Neh. 13:7-31].*

Malachi's Book proves, as history affirms, that reformations and revivals are short-lived. It also demonstrates the corruption of the natural heart; for although God preferred Israel to Edom [1:2-5], had just delivered them from captivity, and blessed their land with abundance [Hag. 2:19], yet they questioned His Love, treated with contempt His worship, and put aside the Book of the Law.

After Malachi, there was no Prophet until John the Baptist, claiming an interval of prophetic darkness for about 400 years.)

2 I have loved you, saith the LORD. Yet you say, Wherein have You loved us? Was not Esau Jacob's brother? saith the LORD: yet I loved Jacob *(the phrase, "I have loved you, saith the LORD," is meant to proclaim to the people God's Love and its past action, in contrast to their ingratitude for that Love. The question, "Yet you say, Wherein have You loved us?", provides the unjust complaints of the people. They doubted God's Love and Faithfulness, because events had not turned out as they expected.*

The question, "Was not Esau Jacob's brother?", was meant to draw Israel's attention to the miserable condition of the Edomites, who were descendants of Esau, in comparison to the fortunate and blessed condition of the Israelites, who were descendants of Jacob, despite their spiritual declension! The phrase, "Saith the LORD: yet I loved Jacob," does not refer to an arbitrary choice. The Lord loved Jacob because Jacob loved Him),

3 And I hated Esau, and laid his mountains and his heritage waste for the dragons of the wilderness. *(The phrase, "And I hated Esau," is used here as an idiom of preference*

[Lk. 14:25-27]. It does not express personal malice as we think of such presently. In fact, if Esau, as Jacob, would have honestly sought the Lord in Repentance, he would have been treated with the same kindness, love, and help that his brother, Jacob, received.

The phrase, "And laid his mountains and his heritage waste for the dragons of the wilderness," refers to the ultimate destruction of Edom, which sprang from the loins of Esau. By comparison, Israel was greatly blessed.)

4 Whereas Edom says, We are impoverished, but we will return and build the desolate places; thus saith the LORD of Hosts, They shall build, but I will throw down; and they shall call them, The border of wickedness, and, The people against whom the LORD has indignation for ever. *(The phrase, "Whereas Edom says," presents this country in defiance of God. Edom boasted that she would be restored; however, Edom never actually recovered its power. It became the prey of the Persians and others, with the Mohammedan conquests finally effecting its utter ruin.*

The phrase, "And they shall call them, The border of wickedness," means "the territory of iniquity." The phrase, "The people against whom the LORD has indignation forever," is a statement spelling the doom, not only of this people, but also of any and all against whom it is uttered.

While the Lord is angry with the wicked every day [Ps. 7:11], the indignation spoken of here concerns an added infraction, which in Edom's case was their gloating over Judah's fall to the Babylonians.)

5 And your eyes shall see, and you shall say, The LORD will be magnified from the border of Israel. *(The phrase, "And your eyes shall see, and you shall say," portrays the very opposite concerning Israel, relative to Edom. The last phrase means that Israel will yet become as the Garden of Eden; and its beauty and fertility will magnify Jehovah-Messiah. This will transpire in the coming Kingdom Age.)*

ISRAEL'S DISOBEDIENCE:
SINS OF THE PRIESTS

6 A son honors his father, and a servant

his master: if then I be a Father, where is My honour? and if I be a Master, where is My fear? saith the LORD of Hosts unto you, O Priests, who despite My name. And you say, Wherein have we despised Your name? (*The Priests and the people despised the ineffable name by agreeing that anything was good enough for God. They showed Him no respect, gratitude, or acceptable service. The Lord was the Father of Israel, and consequently, they were His Children. As such, they were to honor Him as any child, at least one who is trying to do right, would honor his Earthly father. However, they did not do such.*)

7 You offer polluted bread upon My Altar; and you say, Wherein have we polluted You? In that you say, The Table of the LORD is contemptible. (*The phrase, "You have offered bread upon My Altar," is a covering term for all Sacrifices. The word "pollution" spoke of imperfect Sacrifices, which is outlined in the next Verse.*

The question, "And you say, Wherein have we polluted You?", means that they did not acknowledge the Truth that when the Sacraments were violated, He Himself, Whose Sacraments they were, was violated. It is ironical that they considered the ritual itself as containing Salvation, and yet they would offer improper Sacrifices!]

The phrase, "In that you say, The Table of the LORD is contemptible," refers to the Brazen Altar. Even though they probably did not actually say the words, still, their actions did say it, and loudly!)

8 And if you offer the blind for sacrifice, is it not evil? and if you offer the lame and sick, is it not evil? offer it now unto your Governor; will he be pleased with you, or accept your person? saith the LORD of Hosts. (*The question, "And if you offer the blind for sacrifice, is it not evil?", has reference to the Law of Moses, which ordered that the victims [lambs] should be perfect and without blemish [Lev. 22:19-25]. The question, "Offer it now unto your Governor, will he be pleased with you, or accept your person?", is speaking of the rulers set over Judah by the Persian King. The Lord is actually saying, "Would you dare offer such things to your Governor?", irrespective as to who the Governor was!*)

9 And now, I pray you, beseech God that He will be gracious unto us: this has been by your means: will He regard your persons? saith the LORD of Hosts. (*The first phrase is not actually an earnest, sincere appeal of repentance, but rather irony. In other words, the Prophet is saying, "Will you come and beseech the Lord with these polluted sacrifices?" The phrase, "This has been by your means," refers to the Priests, who were responsible for this disobedience to God's Word, for they were appointed to teach that Word [2:7].*

The question, "Will He regard your persons? saith the LORD of Hosts," actually has reference to the Priests acting as mediators, which they were called to do. The Lord is actually saying that He would not accept them as mediators between God and the people, simply because of their sinful actions.)

10 Who is there even among you who would shut the doors for nought? neither do you kindle fire on My Altar for nought. I have no pleasure in you, saith the LORD of Hosts, neither will I accept an offering at your hand. (*The idea of this Verse is: it would be morally better to close the Temple than to continue such hypocritical services; actually, the Priests had come to the place that they would not perform the smallest function without pay. The phrase, "I have no pleasure in you, saith the LORD of Hosts," is a striking term indeed! It points to God's displeasure and places the blame at the doorstep of religious leadership.*

The phrase, "Neither will I accept an offering at your hand," refers to any type of Offering, even the "Meal Offerings," which were naturally pure and unpolluted. Presently, it strikes at motive of the heart for God not to accept what we give. Paul said that we give to the Lord "to prove the sincerity of our love" [II Cor. 8:8].)

GOD'S PLAN FOR THE MILLENNIUM: PURE WORSHIP UNIVERSAL

11 For from the rising of the sun even unto the going down of the same My name shall be great among the Gentiles; and in every place incense shall be offered unto My name, and a pure offering: for My name shall be great among the heathen, saith the LORD of Hosts. (*The first phrase presents a prediction and was fulfilled when the Gospel went to the Gentiles [Acts, Chpt. 10]. Actually, this prediction has come to pass exactly as the Lord promised, with the Church made up mostly of "Gentiles." The phrase, "And in every place incense shall be offered unto My Name, and a pure offering," refers to prayer and praise based on the Offering of Calvary [Heb. 9:14; 10:10], and presented by the Great High Priest, the Lord Jesus Christ [Heb. 13:15].*)

THEIR HYPOCRISY AND CORRUPT OFFERINGS TO GOD

12 But you have profaned it, in that you say, The Table of the LORD is polluted; and the fruit thereof, even His meat, is contemptible. *(The phrase, "But you have profaned it," refers to the fact that the Work of God can be profaned; tragically so, it is profaned most of the time! The phrase, "In that you say, The Table of the LORD is polluted," refers to the Priests saying that it was polluted, but not for the same purpose and reason as spoken by the Lord.*

The phrase, "And the fruit thereof, even His meat, is contemptible," is a complaint offered by the Priests of the sickly animals brought for Sacrifice, which provided them sustenance, because it was, as the next Verse proclaims, "torn, lame, and sick."

Of most of the Sacrifices offered, the Priests were to receive a portion of it for their own use, which provided a part of their living and sustenance for them and their families. However, the Sacrifices were so "contemptible" that there was nothing for the Priests. In other words, the people were bringing as Sacrifice their sickly animals instead of the best; this is what the Lord is addressing.

The Priests didn't care about the Lord being insulted — only that they didn't get what they wanted.)

13 You said also, Behold, what a weariness is it! and you have snuffed at it, saith the LORD of Hosts; and you brought that which was torn, and the lame, and the sick; thus you brought an offering: should I accept this of your hand? saith the LORD. *(The first phrase portrays the Priests complaining because the service and worship of God was a drudgery. Such proclaims those who do not have a proper relationship with the Lord. The phrase, "And you have snuffed it, saith the LORD of Hosts," means that the people complained by sniveling at this service for God.*

The phrase, "And you brought that which was torn, and the lame, and the sick," means they gave to the Lord that which was of no service to them. In other words, they could not sell it or even give it away, so, in their minds, and inasmuch as the offerings were to be burned on the Brazen Altar, why not bring these "torn, lame, and sick"?

They completely misunderstood the meaning of the Sacrifices. It had degenerated until it was a mere ritual. They did not understand anymore that these Sacrifices represented the Coming Redeemer, the Lord Jesus Christ, and, as such, were to be "without blemish."

The phrase, "Thus you brought an Offering," is said with contempt! The answer of the Lord is: "Should I accept this of your hand? saith the LORD." The idea is: He did not accept it!)

14 But cursed be the deceiver, which has in his flock a male, and vows, and sacrifices unto the LORD a corrupt thing: for I am a great King, saith the LORD of Hosts, and My Name is dreadful among the heathen. *(The phrase, "But cursed be the deceiver," concerned those who offered a female of "his flock," claiming that he had no male lamb, when such was not true. The phrase, "And vows, sacrifices unto the Lord a corrupt thing," concerns a vow made to the Lord and then paying it by presenting a blemished animal [Lev. 3:1, 6].*

The phrase, "For I am a great King, saith the LORD of Hosts," is meant to portray the seriousness of the matter, in that God should be given our very best. A "Great King" deserves a "Great Sacrifice." The phrase, "And My Name is dreadful among the heathen," refers to the tremendous miracles God has performed, of which the heathen were aware, and yet even though they held Him in high regard, His Own People showed Him nothing but disrespect.)

CHAPTER 2
(397 B.C.)

GOD REBUKES HIS PRIESTS, WARNS THEM OF JUDGMENT

AND now, O ye Priests, this Commandment is for you. *(This reveals a pointed direction by the Holy Spirit and leaves absolutely no doubt as to who or what is intended. The first nine Verses of this Chapter form a special Message to the Priests; the remaining Verses, a special Message to the people. It is also a "Commandment" and not a suggestion!)*

2 If you will not hear, and if you will not lay it to heart, to give glory unto My Name, saith the LORD of Hosts, I will even send a curse upon you, and I will curse your blessings: yea, I have cursed them already, because you do not lay it to heart. *(The phrase, "If you will not hear," concerns the free moral agency of man. They can "hear" or refuse to "hear"! The phrase, "And if you will not lay it to heart," speaks of the manner in which man responds to the Lord. It is not merely to be an intellectual response, but rather a "heart" response!*

The phrase, "I will even send a curse upon

you," pertains to a blight upon all the efforts of the people. The phrase, "And I will curse your blessings," actually means to stop the blessings, and has to do with the first fourteen verses of Deut., Chpt. 28. In these verses, blessing after blessing is intoned; however, in Verses 15 through 68 of the same Chapter, curses are listed which, in the event of disobedience, will cancel out the blessings; therefore, the blessings were cursed because of sin!

The last phrase proclaims the fact that the curse had already begun to work with these Israelites.)

3 Behold, I will corrupt your seed, and spread dung upon your faces, even the dung of your solemn feasts; and one shall take you away with it. (The idea of this Verse is: if they considered anything good enough for God, then anything was good enough for them. In effect, because they offered to Him in Sacrifice the "torn, lame, and sick," the Lord is saying they have offered no more than "dung." I wonder how the Lord looks at our offerings presently?)

4 And you shall know that I have sent this Commandment unto you, that My Covenant might be with Levi, saith the LORD of Hosts. (The first phrase proclaims the fact that the Lord's threats are not being made in vain. In other words, God says what He means, and means what He says! The last phrase presents the Lord as saying that He desired to have a body of Priests who would keep their vows and maintain the true Priestly character.)

5 My Covenant was with him of life and peace; and I gave them to him for the fear wherewith he feared Me, and was afraid before My Name. (The phrase, "My Covenant was with him of life and peace," refers to that which God promised to these Levites, which pertained to the blessings of life, abundance, prosperity, and also the privilege of serving as a Type of Christ, which, within itself, brought untold blessings.

The Lord is referring to the blessing pronounced on Phinehas for his conduct in the matter of Zimri [Num. 25:12-13]. That day, because of the faith of Phinehas, the Tribe of Levi won the Priesthood; a "Covenant" went with it, which conferred certain privileges and also involved certain duties.

The phrase, "And I gave them to him for the fear wherewith he feared Me," simply means: "I gave him the fear of Me." This expresses man's part in the Covenant. In other words, the blessings would come on the condition that he feared, reverenced, worshipped, and obeyed the Lord.

The phrase, "And was afraid before My Name," means that Phinehas, with whom this original Covenant was made, and who was the High Priest of the Tribe of Levi, faithfully kept the Covenant before the Lord [Ex. 32:26-29; Num. 25:10-13]. Phinehas lived about a thousand years before, but is still used as an example.)

6 The law of truth was in his mouth, and iniquity was not found in his lips: he walked with Me in peace and equity, and did turn many away from iniquity. (The life and service of Phinehas, which all Priests who followed were to emulate, turned many to God, which is always to be the case, and proves that competent spiritual leadership brings about the same in the people, i.e., "truth, peace, and equity.")

7 For the Priest's lips should keep knowledge, and they should seek the Law at His mouth: for he is the messenger of the LORD of Hosts. (Priests were to know the Word of God, should give that Word to the people, and do so in undiluted form, serving actually as "the messenger of the LORD of Hosts.")

8 But you are departed out of the way; you have caused many to stumble at the Law; you have corrupted the Covenant of Levi, saith the LORD of Hosts. (The Priests of Malachi's day made void this Covenant, causing many to stumble in the Law by superimposing their traditions [Mat. 15:3-6] and having respect of persons in administering the Law, which the next Verse proclaims. The phrase, "But you are departed out of the way," means that the Priests of Malachi's time had departed from "the Law of Truth," thereby substituting something else to take its place.

The phrase, "You have caused many to stumble at the Law," means that they did not properly teach the Law, which caused spiritual weakness in the people [Ezek. 3:20]. The phrase, "You have corrupted the Covenant of Levi, saith the LORD of Hosts," pertains to the broken Covenant; therefore, Jehovah held Himself no longer bound by it; consequently, the "blessings" would be cursed.)

9 Therefore have I also made you contemptible and base before all the people, according as you have not kept My ways, but have been partial in the Law. (Thus, these nine Verses record the corruption of Truth by the sons of Levi; and the following seven Verses, the violation of the institution of marriage by the people. Both violations resulted in disobedience to the Word of God. The phrase, "Therefore have I also made you contemptible and base before all the people,"

means that as the Priests no longer honored Him, He no longer honored them.

The phrase, "But have been partial in the Law," means that some people were given preferential treatment. As an example, when some brought sick animals to be used for Sacrifice, they were sorely reprimanded, while others were allowed to do so without rebuke!)

THE TREACHERY OF JUDAH; JUDGMENT FOR TREACHERY

10 Have we not all one father? has not one God created us? why do we deal treacherously every man against his brother, by profaning the Covenant of our fathers? (The question, "Have we not all one father?", actually has a double reference. It speaks of Abraham and of God. The question, "Has not one God created us?", is not actually meant to portray the Lord as Creator of each person, but instead the Creator of Israel as a nation. So, in effect, they were saying that by simply being born a Jew, this meant they were saved!

The last phrase proclaims the Truth that when men began to break their Covenant with God, they then began to "deal treacherously" against their fellowman; even more specifically, against their "brother," i.e., in the Lord. The two, "violation of the Covenant" and "dealing treacherously," go hand in hand!)

11 Judah has dealt treacherously, and an abomination is committed in Israel and in Jerusalem; for Judah has profaned the Holiness of the LORD which He loved, and has married the daughter of a strange god. (The phrase, "Judah has dealt treacherously," here has to do with Judah's dealings with the Lord, in that there were mixed marriages with heathen women. This was against the Law of God [Ex. 34:16; Deut. 7:3; Josh. 23:12-13]. The phrase, "And an abomination is committed in Israel and in Jerusalem," is meant, by the mention of the two names of "Judah" and "Jerusalem," to mark the seriousness of this sin. The mention of these names marks God's Covenant with these people — the Mosaic Law.

The phrase, "For Judah has profaned the Holiness of the LORD which He loved," portrays the result of this sin [intermarriage with foreign women] and of any sin. In other words, all sin is designed by Satan and carried out by the perpetrator, whether realized or not, as an affront against the "Holiness of the LORD."

The phrase, "And has married the daughter of a strange god," referred to women who were idolatresses, i.e., they adhered to a foreign deity.)

12 The LORD will cut off the man who does this, the master and the scholar, out of the tabernacles of Jacob, and him who offers an offering unto the LORD of Hosts. (The phrase, "The LORD will cut off the man who does this," refers to the sins of Verse 11. The words, "cut off," mean "to lose one's soul"! The phrase, "And him who offers an offering unto the LORD of Hosts," concerned all the people who came to offer Sacrifices at the Temple.)

13 And this have you done again, covering the Altar of the LORD with tears, with weeping, and with crying out, insomuch that He regards not the offering any more, or receives it with good will at your hand. (The phrase, "And this have you done again," refers to Ezra, nearly 100 years before, who had effected a reform in this same matter, but with the people now lapsing again into this same sin [Ezra, Chpt. 10]. We speak of Jews marrying "strange women," i.e., foreign women who worshipped "strange gods." Satan, once again, attempts to pull Israel back into idolatry.

The phrase, "Covering the Altar of the LORD with tears, with weeping, and with crying out," does not pertain to hypocrisy, as some have thought, but instead to divorced wives and children who had been wronged, taking their case to the Lord. To be sure, as recorded here, the Lord saw their "tears" and heard their "crying."

The phrase, "Insomuch that He regards not the offering any more, or receives it with good will at your hand," means that the wrongdoers [in this case, the husbands] could not assuage their sin with sacrifices. For the sin to be assuaged and the sacrifices to be effective, the problem had to be correctly addressed!)

14 Yet you say, Wherefore? Because the LORD has been witness between you and the wife of your youth, against whom you have dealt treacherously: yet is she your companion, and the wife of your covenant. (The question, "Yet you say, Wherefore?", proclaims the Holy Spirit through the Prophet mimicking the people in their asking the Prophet just exactly why the Lord would not accept their sacrifices! They, as most, would not acknowledge their guilt. This question, "Wherefore?", shows they were as insensible to natural affection as to Divine affection. The latter insensibility quickly occasions the former.

The phrase, "Because the Lord has been witness between you and the wife of your youth,"

signifies the Lord seeing all and not being fooled whatsoever by the sacrifices, as He is not fooled presently! The phrase, "Yet is she your companion, and the wife of your Covenant," refers to the solemn vow made when the ceremony of marriage was engaged. In effect, it was "till death do us part."

One sin leads to another still deeper. The restored Exiles [Neh. 13:23], contrary to the Bible [Deut. 7:3], married heathen wives. To this evil they now added the deeper one of divorcing their Hebrew wives in order to marry a foreign woman.)

15 And did not He make one? Yet had He the residue of the Spirit. And wherefore one? that He might seek a Godly seed. Therefore take heed to your spirit, and let none deal treacherously against the wife of his youth. *(The question, "And did not He make one?", means that God made only one wife for Adam. This condemns polygamy [being married to several wives at the same time] and divorce! The phrase, "Yet had He the residue of the Spirit," means that God, being the Author of life, could have given Adam, if He so desired, many wives and so have instituted polygamy. Therefore, what God originally did and intended must not be changed.*

The question, "And wherefore one?", has reference to Abraham, to whom God gave one wife and a Godly seed by her [Isaac]. Malachi's critics objected that Abraham had two wives, referring to Sarah and Hagar, and that they might also, to which Malachi had a double reply: 1. Abraham took a second wife, not to gratify passion, but to procure an heir; and, 2. That in so acting, he grieved God and brought suffering upon himself and others. God's appointment of monogamy is here stated in order to produce holy children [I Chron. 7:14].

The phrase, "Therefore take heed to your spirit," has to do with the corruption of one's own spirit, which leads to all types of sin, i.e., making one dead to the conviction of the Holy Spirit. The phrase, "And let none deal treacherously against the wife of his youth," has some inference to the beauty fading with the passing years, with the youth of the foreign women becoming more attractive, and even possibly more accessible. At any rate, it was a wicked direction these men were taking.)

16 For the LORD, the God of Israel says that He hates putting away: for one covers violence with his garment, saith the LORD of Hosts: therefore take heed to your spirit, that

you deal not treacherously. (The phrase, "For the LORD, the God of Israel," in its structure, portrays the tremendous significance of the statement about to be made. The phrase, "Says that He hates putting away," means that God hates divorce. The reasons should be obvious.

Divorce is contrary to God's original institution and, in effect, constitutes a direct attack on the sacredness of the home and family unit, which was originally prescribed by God in the Garden of Eden. There are two Scriptural conditions given for divorce and remarriage.

They are:

1. Fornication is committed by one partner [Mat. 5:32];

2. Desertion by one partner, and because of the Gospel; in other words, an unequal yoke [I Cor. 7:1-16].

The phrase, "For one covers violence with his garment, saith the LORD of Hosts," is actually a negative term. The "garment" is used in the sense of the bridegroom casting the skirt of his garment over her who is betrothed to him [Ruth 3:9]. So the idea is: when one engages in divorce and remarriage without Scriptural grounds, one is throwing his "garment" over "violence," for such will be the end result of this action.

In view of these dire predictions, which most certainly are true because they are uttered by the Lord, divorce and remarriage should not even be considered unless there is absolutely no other alternative.)

17 You have wearied the LORD with your words. Yet you say, Wherein have we wearied Him? When you say, Every one who does evil is good in the sight of the LORD, and He delights in them; or, Where is the God of judgment? *(The phrase, "You have wearied the LORD with your words," concerns the very things these backslidden Jews were saying. This should cause us to realize and understand that God hears what we say, and He is either offended or gladdened by our statements.*

The Jews were claiming that it really didn't matter too much what one did, inasmuch as some of the nations around them were idolatrous and wicked, and yet were prosperous, which seemed to mean, at least in their minds, that God approved of wickedness. The question, "Where is the God of judgment?", is a challenge to Malachi by these malcontents, that, in effect, said: "Produce proofs that God judges evil!" The answers to their accusations and questions are found in the first six Verses of Chapter 3.)

CHAPTER 3
(397 B.C.)
MESSIAH'S FIRST ADVENT

BEHOLD, I will send My messenger, and he shall prepare the way before Me: and the LORD, Whom you seek, shall suddenly come to His temple, even the Messenger of the Covenant, Whom you delight in: behold, He shall come, saith the LORD of Hosts. *(The phrase, "Behold, I will send My messenger, and he shall prepare the way before Me," predicts the First Advent of Christ, with 4:4-6 predicting the Second Advent. But the moral facts of the First cover both. Now Israel's question of 2:17 is answered. The "Messenger" is John the Baptist [Mat. 2:3; 11:10; Mk. 1:2-3; Lk. 1:76; 3:4; 7:26-27; Jn. 1:23].*

The phrase, "And he shall prepare the way before Me," means to remove moral obstacles and bring one to contrition of heart. This would happen some 400 years after being predicted by Malachi, speaking of John the Baptist preparing the way for Christ.

The phrase, "And the LORD, Whom you seek, shall suddenly come to His Temple," actually means: "in Whom you delight." The Jews eagerly desired the coming of a conquering Prince who would set them at the head of the nations and endow them with wealth and glory. In effect, they had a totally erroneous conception of Who and What the Messiah would be! Israel did not desire a Judge Who would expose their sins.

The phrase, "Even the Messenger of the Covenant, Whom you delight in," proclaims Christ as the Messenger not only of the First Covenant [Ex. 3:2-6; Acts 7:38], but also the Messenger of the Second. This "Messenger" is Christ and not the "messenger" of the first phrase, who is John the Baptist.

The phrase, "Behold, He shall come, saith the LORD of Hosts," proclaims the certitude of this action. In other words, this is not a conditional Prophecy, but rather an unconditional Prophecy, meaning that whatever happens, at the appointed time, Christ would come. And so He did!)

MESSIAH'S SECOND ADVENT

2 But who may abide the day of His coming? and who shall stand when He appears? for He is like a refiner's fire, and like fullers' soap *(Verses 2 and 3 are another instance of the First and Second Comings of Christ being referred to in the same Passage.*

The question, "But who may abide the day of His coming?", addresses the accusation of the Jews to Malachi, "Where is the God of judgment?" As well, this phrase speaks of His Second Coming rather than His First.

The question, "And who shall stand when He appears?", concerns Him coming with Power, Glory, and with vengeance on the Antichrist and on all who are associated with this evil despot. At that time, Christ will judge the nations [Mat. 25:31-23]. Israel, at that time, will be judged as well! Then, the question, "Where is the God of judgment?", will be answered.

The phrase, "For He is like a refiner's fire, and like fullers' soap," defines the manner in which He will judge all. The "refiner's fire" separates the precious metal from the refuse. "Fullers' soap" speaks of cleansing [Zech. 13:1]):

3 And He shall sit as a Refiner and Purifier of silver: and He shall purify the sons of Levi, and purge them as gold and silver, that they may offer unto the LORD an offering in Righteousness. *(The phrase, "And He shall sit as a Refiner and Purifier of silver," refers to the purifier who sits watching the silver and maintaining the temperature; directly he sees his face reflected in the metal, he stops the process. In other words, when the Lord sees Himself sufficiently in Israel, He will then say, "It is enough," and the dire process of "refining" and "purifying" will be ended. In essence, the time of "Jacob's Trouble" will be forever ended [Jer. 30:7].*

The phrase, "And He shall purify the sons of Levi, and purge them as gold and silver," refers to Judgment beginning at the House of God. The phrase, "That they may offer unto the LORD an offering in Righteousness," speaks of True Repentance, in which these "sons of Levi" will, at long last, engage; they will, in turn, receive the true "Righteousness," which only Christ can give.)

ISRAEL RESTORED

4 Then shall the offering of Judah and Jerusalem be pleasant unto the LORD, as in the days of old, and as in former years. *(The word "Then" refers to the Second Advent of Christ, when He shall come back to judge and purify men. After Israel's True Repentance, "Then shall the offering of Judah and Jerusalem be pleasant unto the LORD." The phrase, "As in the days of old, and as in former years," refers to the times when the Sacrifices were offered in the right attitude and spirit, pointing to the One Who was to come, namely Christ.*

To be sure, as the Book of Ezekiel bears out, the Sacrifices will be maintained in the coming Kingdom Age as a memorial.)

JUSTICE WILL BE METED OUT

5 And I will come near to you to judgment; and I will be a swift witness against the sorcerers, and against the adulterers, and against false swearers, and against those who oppress the hireling in his wages, the widow, and the fatherless, and that turn aside the stranger from his right, and fear not Me, saith the LORD of Hosts. *(They had asked the question in 2:17, "Where is the God of judgment?" He now tells them, and in no uncertain terms, "I will come near to you in judgment." Witchcraft, immorality, false prophets, and those who practice injustice will be judged.*

The phrase, "And that turn aside the stranger from his right," refers to Israel forgetting that they were "strangers" in Egypt, and that they should ever remember this by treating all "strangers" kindly! The phrase, "And fear not Me, saith the LORD of Hosts," proclaims the reason for practicing these sins. There is no fear of God!)

6 For I am the LORD, I change not; therefore you sons of Jacob are not consumed. *(The phrase, "For I am the LORD, I change not," refers to the nature and character of God, which cannot change. The phrase, "Therefore you sons of Jacob are not consumed," pertains to the Lord having made Covenants with the Patriarchs, and those Covenants being kept by Him [Gen. 12:1-3, Chpt. 15; Hag. 2:20-23; Zeph. 3:18-20, etc.].*

The reason why the Hebrews were not as totally destroyed as the Philistines and other nations was because of the unchangeableness of God's electing Love and Promises. To be sure, these Promises were not secured by Israel's unchangeable love to God, but by His unchangeable Love to them.)

7 Even from the days of your fathers you are gone away from My ordinances, and have not kept them. Return unto Me, and I will return unto Me, and I will return unto you, saith the LORD of Hosts. But you said, Wherein shall we return? *(The first phrase pertains to the displacement of the Holy Scriptures as the authority and rule of life. Such originated declension and corruption. The phrase, "And have not kept them," refers to the Holy Spirit through the Prophet bluntly telling them that despite what they say, they have not adhered to the Word of God.*

The phrase, "Return unto Me, and I will return

unto you," is a plea for Repentance and is as simple as the language enjoined. The question, "But you said, Wherein shall we return?", proclaims Israel so spiritually deadened that they did not even know their true spiritual condition.)

8 Will a man rob God? Yet you have robbed Me. But you say, Wherein have we robbed You? In tithes and offerings. *(The question, "Will a man rob God?", is blunt and to the point; it instantly portrayed Israel's present condition, in that they had, in fact, robbed God! The phrase, "Yet you have robbed Me!" proclaims unequivocally that they had robbed God, which is a serious charge indeed!*

The question, "But you say, Wherein have we robbed You?", brings back the quick answer through the Prophet, "In tithes and offerings." Some claim that "tithes" are a part of the old Mosaic system and are not applicable under the New Covenant! However, paying tithes was practiced long before the Law [Gen. 14:20; 28:22]; it was also commanded under Grace in the New Testament [Mat. 23:23; Rom. 2:22; I Cor. 9:7-14; 16:2; Gal. 6:6; Heb. 7:1-10].

Abraham, a type of all Believers, paid tithes to Melchizedek, a Type of Christ [Gen. 14:20], which sets the standard; inasmuch as we are children of Abraham, we are to continue to pay tithes to the Work of God, which, in effect, is the propagation of the Message of Christ and Him Crucified [Gal. 3:6-7; I Cor. 1:23].)

9 You are cursed with a curse: for you have robbed Me, even this whole nation. *(The phrase, "You are cursed with a curse," is dire indeed! The effect of this curse was scarcity and barrenness, as we see from Verses 10 through 12. Robbing God of tithes and offerings brings a curse. These belong to God by virtue of Covenant agreements with man; to use them for personal gain is robbery of that which rightly belongs to Him.*

The phrase, "For you have robbed Me, even this whole nation," proclaims the reason for the poverty, among other things, of the nations of the world.)

10 Bring ye all the tithes into the storehouse, that there may be meat in My house, and prove Me now herewith, saith the LORD of Hosts, if I will not open you the windows of Heaven, and pour you out a blessing, that there shall not be room enough to receive it. *(The phrase, "Bring ye all the tithes into the storehouse," referred to the Temple and cities of the Levites under the Old Covenant. Under the New Covenant, it refers to the place where one's soul is fed, wherever that might be. Some have claimed*

that the local Church is the "storehouse" where all giving is to be brought; however, that is incorrect, inasmuch as those who propose such fail to understand what "Church" actually is! "Church" is made up of all members of the Body of Christ, irrespective of who they are or where they are. It has nothing to do with the building, organization, or religious institution. It is the "Message" which must be supported — not an institution.

The phrase, "That there may be meat in My house," has reference to the support of the Priesthood in the Temple of old. The Lord has no such "house" at present, because Jesus fulfilled all that the ancient Temple represented, with Him now residing through the agency of the Holy Spirit in the hearts and lives of all Believers [I Cor. 3:16].

The phrase, "And prove Me now herewith, saith the LORD of Hosts," presents a challenge presented by the Lord for men to prove Him regarding the rewards of tithing. The phrase, "If I will not open you the windows of Heaven, and pour you out a blessing, that there shall not be room enough to receive it," speaks of a superabundant amount. The same phrase, "Windows of Heaven," is used in Gen. 7:11 regarding the flood; therefore, we are speaking of blessings unparalleled!)

11 And I will rebuke the devourer for your sakes, and he shall not destroy the fruits of your ground; neither shall your vine cast her fruit before the time in the field, saith the LORD of Hosts. (In the first phrase, the Holy Spirit uses the word "devourer"; then, He uses the pronoun "he," symbolizing a personality behind the destruction, i.e., Satan. As well, the word "rebuke" means "to turn back" or "keep down."

So, if we fail to give to God, the Lord proclaims that He will not turn back the "devourer." This will result in the "fruits" of our efforts being destroyed. To give to God means the opposite. Crops will be abundant, with efforts resulting in prosperity.

The last phrase simply speaks of the harvest being gathered, and abundantly so, and not being lost.)

12 And all nations shall call you blessed: for you shall be a delightsome land, saith the LORD of Hosts. (The first phrase speaks of the blessings of the Lord as being so abundant that other nations will enquire as to the reason.)

13 Your words have been stout against Me, saith the LORD. Yet you say, What have we spoken so much against You? (The manner in which the Lord used Malachi is different than any other Prophet. The accusation by the Lord

is given, with the remonstrance of the people also given. Such left absolutely no room for doubt as to what was being said.

The phrase, "Your words have been stout against Me," portrays their deeds having been exposed, their words are now recalled. They were "words" against God! The question, "Yet you say, What have we spoken so much against You?", has to do with what they said in their conversations one with another. Now, He will tell them exactly what they have said and the reason they said it!)

14 You have said, It is vain to serve God: and what profit is it that we have kept His ordinance, and that we have walked mournfully before the LORD of Hosts? (The phrase, "You have said, It is vain to serve God," once again harks back to 2:17. The word "vain" means "empty nothings," and claims them saying that serving God brought no acknowledgement or reward.

The question, "And what profit is it that we have kept His ordinance?", has to do with His Commandments and Laws. In effect, they had not "kept His ordinances," willfully deceiving themselves and others by pretending obedience they never really did.

The question, "And that we have walked mournfully before the LORD of Hosts?", concerned their fasts that they had entered into, of which the Lord had already spoken years before through Zechariah, "Did you at all fast unto Me, even to Me?" [Zech. 7:5]. These "fasts" were merely religious observances and were not out of reverence and awe to Jehovah.)

15 And now we call the proud happy; yea, they who work wickedness are set up; yea, they who tempt God are even delivered. (The first phrase proclaims Israel as considering the "happy ones" to be those who scoffed at God, who seemingly were prosperous. They fell into the same trap as Asaph of old, as is recorded in Psalm 73.

The phrase, "Yea, they who work wickedness are set up," means that these wicked have wealth and families and leave a name behind them; their not serving God seemed to have brought them no ill consequences. The phrase, "Yea, they who tempt God are even delivered," means that they, whoever they may have been, provoked God by their sin and rebellion and yet escaped punishment. In other words, they resist God and are yet safe.

Let it, however, ever be known: The "tempting of God" may, for a time, evoke only silence from Jehovah; but ultimately, there will be a

reckoning day.)

16 Then they who feared the LORD spoke often one to another: and the LORD hearkened, and heard it, and a book of remembrance was written before Him for them who feared the LORD, and who thought upon His Name. *(Irrespective of the majority in Israel, the Lord had then, as now, those who loved and feared Him. The phrase, "Then they who feared the LORD spoke often one to another," proclaims the necessity of united worship, even though it may be only "two or three" [Mat. 18:20]. As well, the word "often" should proclaim the necessary frequency.*

The phrase, "And the LORD hearkened, and heard it," means that He attends every service, even as He said in Mat. 18:20. The last phrase portrays Heaven lovingly recording the worship of little groups of believing people whom Earth despises. What intense interest these records will excite when published in the coming Millennial Day!)

17 And they shall be Mine, saith the LORD of Hosts, in that day when I make up My jewels; and I will spare them, as a man spares his own son who serves him. *(The phrase, "And they shall be Mine, saith the LORD of Hosts," has reference to these precious ones as being His peculiar treasure. They lived for Him, served Him, and were faithful to Him, when most did the very opposite. The phrase, "In that day when I make up My jewels," has reference to the jewels on the Breastplate of the High Priest; likewise, the Lord considers each Believer as a "jewel." The last phrase refers to the fact that these "jewels" will never be judged in a negative sense.)*

18 Then shall you return, and discern between the righteous and the wicked, between him who serves God and him who serves Him not. *(The phrase, "Then shall you return," refers to the proud skeptics and oppressors of Verses 7 and 15. These denied any distinction on the part of God between a righteous man and a wicked man; but the day appointed by God will compel them to turn from their skepticism, and to recognize and confess that God does distinguish between His servants and His enemies [3:17; 4:1, 3].*

The "Then" of Verse 18 is to be contrasted with the "Then" of Verse 16. The latter is the Believer's present day of affliction; the former, the unbeliever's future day of doom. The phrase, "And discern between the righteous and the wicked," means that the day is coming when there will be absolutely no doubt as to God's direction.

The phrase, "Between him who serves God and

him who serves Him not," is actually what everything boils down to. Men are either serving Him or they are not serving Him. There is no in-between!)

CHAPTER 4
(397 B.C.)
DESTRUCTION OF THE UNGODLY

FOR, behold, the day comes, that shall burn as an oven; and all the proud, yea, and all who do wickedly, shall be stubble: and the day that comes shall burn them up, saith the LORD of Hosts, that it shall leave them neither root nor branch.** *(The phrase, "For, behold, the day comes," has a double meaning: 1. It refers to the coming Battle of Armageddon, which will precipitate the Coming of the Lord, Who will come with flaming fire; and, 2. It refers to the "Great White Throne Judgment," which will take place after the Millennial Reign [Rev. 20:11-15].*

The latter phrase refers to the coming day when the entirety of the Earth shall be cleansed by fire. It pertains to the coming New heavens and New Earth [II Pet. 3:12-13]. The phrase, "Neither root nor branch," means that not one vestige of sin or rebellion against God will remain anywhere in the universe. Peter likened it to a "New Earth wherein dwells Righteousness.")

SALVATION FOR THE RIGHTEOUS

2 But unto you who fear My Name shall the Sun of Righteousness arise with healing in His wings; and you shall go forth, and grow up as calves of the stall. *(The phrase, "But unto you who fear My Name," refers to the small remnant of 3:16. It refers to all who, from the very beginning, have truly lived for God. The phrase, "Shall the Sun of Righteousness arise with healing in His wings," pertains to the Second Advent of Christ, when He will come back, bringing healing to every person on Earth, not only for physical sickness, but for spiritual sickness, as well!*

Here, Christ is compared to the "Sun," with its healing rays of light coming over the Earth [Isa. 30:26]. As well, the word "wings" does not refer, at least in this case, as wings would normally be understood, but actually refers to something that is overspreading. The Hebrew word is "kanaph," which means "an edge or extremity." When Christ comes back in what is referred to as the "Second Coming," healing rays will be coming from Him in a way that can

only be compared with the "Sun."

The last phrase is a symbolism expressing great joy. When calves are released from the stall into a sunny field, they skip for joy.)

THE WICKED TRODDEN DOWN BY THE RIGHTEOUS AT ARMAGEDDON

3 And you shall tread down the wicked; for they shall be ashes under the soles of your feet in the day that I shall do this, saith the LORD of Hosts. *(The proud now treat as dirt beneath their feet the confessors of Messiah's Name. In the future, that position will be reversed. The phrase, "In the day that I shall do this, saith the LORD of Hosts," pertains to the coming Kingdom Age, when Righteousness shall prevail, with Christ ruling supremely over the entirety of the Earth. Now, and sadly so, unrighteousness prevails. But, in the coming Glad Day, Righteousness will be the order of all mankind.)*

THE COMMAND TO OBEY GOD'S LAWS

4 Remember ye the Law of Moses My servant, which I commanded unto him in Horeb for all Israel, with the Statutes and Judgments. *(The phrase, "Remember ye the Law of Moses My servant," addresses the last command in the Old Testament, for Malachi would be the last Prophet before John the Baptist, a time frame of some 400-plus years. When Christ came, the Law of Moses would be abolished and annulled on the Cross [II Cor., Chpt. 3; Gal., 3:19-25; 4:21-31; Col. 2:14-17; Heb., Chpts. 7-10]. Consequently, the remembering of the Law of Moses, with its "Statutes" and "Judgments," was a requirement for the period before Christ, but does not apply to the time of the New Covenant.*

Of course, that which applied to moral particulars was carried over into the New Testament and is certainly to be "remembered" and adhered to. However, the moral law is kept perfectly when one places one's Faith entirely in Christ and what He did for us at the Cross [Rom. 8:1-2].)

THE LAST PROPHECY TO JUDAH BEFORE MESSIAH'S FIRST ADVENT; THE COMING OF ELIJAH BEFORE MESSIAH'S SECOND ADVENT

5 Behold, I will send you Elijah the Prophet before the coming of the great and dreadful day of the LORD *(the phrase, "Behold, I will send you Elijah the Prophet," does not refer to the coming of John the Baptist, who only came in the spirit of Elijah. It actually refers to "Elijah the Prophet," who was translated about 500 years before the time of Malachi, and who will be sent back to the Earth by the Lord in the midst of the coming Great Tribulation.*

At that time, he and Enoch of Rev. 11:3 will be used of God mightily as they prophesy in Jerusalem. Their Ministry will last for the entirety of the last three and a half years of the Great Tribulation. Both will be killed by the Antichrist at the end of the Great Tribulation, "when they shall have finished their testimony." However, after three and a half days, they will be resurrected and raptured [Rev. 11:11-12].

As John the Baptist prepared the way for the First Advent of Christ, these two, Elijah and Enoch, will prepare the way for the Second Coming of Christ. The phrase, "Before the coming of the great and dreadful day of the LORD," addresses the coming Great Tribulation, and, more specifically, the Second Coming. It will be a "great day" for God's People and a "dreadful day" for His enemies!):

6 And he shall turn the heart of the fathers to the children, and the heart of the children to their fathers, lest I come and smite the Earth with a curse. *(The first phrase proclaims "Elijah" and "Enoch" beginning the process, in the latter half of the Great Tribulation, of "turning the hearts of the fathers to the children, and the hearts of the children to their fathers." The "fathers" speak of the Patriarchs and Prophets of old. The phrase, "Lest I come and smite the Earth with a curse," proclaims the obvious fact that there is no word following "curse" in this last Verse of the Old Covenant, meaning there is more to follow. Thank God!*

In contrast, the word "Amen" follows the last words of the Book of Revelation, closing out the Canon of Scripture, because after "Grace," which is the theme of the Ministry of Christ, there is nothing left to be said but "Amen." Thank God! The world was not left with the "curse," but Jesus Christ came and "redeemed us from the curse of the Law, being made a curse for us" [Gal. 3:13].

Hallelujah!)

BETWEEN THE TESTAMENTS

From Malachi, the last prophet of the Old Testament, until the time of Christ was approximately four hundred years. This time span is sometimes called the *"silent"* years, but there was much activity. For example, when the Old Testament period closed, Judea was a Persian province.

After the time of the kings in Jewish history ending with Solomon (c. 931 B.C.), the twelve tribes of Israel divided into two kingdoms. The Northern Kingdom was called Israel; the Southern Kingdom, Judah. Due to sin, wickedness, and idolatry, both kingdoms fell. The Northern Kingdom (Israel) was captured by Assyria, with the final fall of Samaria being in 722 B.C. The kingdom of Judah (the Southern Kingdom) was the better and stronger one, and it continued until the final fall of Jerusalem to Babylon in 586 B.C.

Babylon supremacy ended in 538 B.C. when the Medes and the Persians overran Babylon. As a result, the Jews were liberated from captivity. They were able to return home to Jerusalem and rebuild the walls and the temple. Haggai, Zechariah, and Malachi prophesied to the Jews after their return from captivity. The people needed exhortation to finish building the temple, and Malachi dealt with their faithlessness, their mixed marriages and divorces, along with their skepticism and indifference. The promised blessings enunciated by Haggai and Zechariah had not materialized, and the people became lax in their commitment to God. They were exhorted to renew their dedication to God, and reminded of the promise that one *"Elijah"* would come. Between that time (c. 430 B.C.) and its fulfillment when John the Baptist came announcing the coming of the Messiah, was a period of a little over four hundred years.

At the close of the Old Testament period, the Persians were the dominant political power. Their control continued until the Greek period, which began in 332 B.C., when the Greeks under Alexander the Great became the great world power. When Alexander the Great died at the age of thirty-two years and eight months, his kingdom was divided (when four of his generals split the kingdom among themselves). Ptolemy took the area of Egypt, Palestine, and Arabia. Cassander took Macedonia and Greece. Lysimachus took the area of Thrace and Bithynia. Seleucus I took Syria (Assyria). Today their territory would cover Greece, Turkey, Syria, Egypt, and several other smaller territories. The Jews were under the Ptolemies for a time. But there was conflict between the descendants of Ptolemy and the descendants of Seleucus, so that when Ptolemy IV died, Antiochus III (the Great) took Palestine in 198 B.C. Later Antiochus IV, called Epiphanes, ruled the area of Palestine. During this period, some severe actions were taken against the Jews. Many of them were killed, while others faced severe persecution. Antiochus Epiphanes desecrated the temple in Jerusalem by boiling a pig and sprinkling the liquid around the temple. He tried to destroy the worship of Jehovah.

The Maccabean Revolt: The Jews were being severely oppressed. An officer of Antiochus Epiphanes came to the village of Modin, which is located about fifteen miles west of Jerusalem. The officer demanded Mattathias, a priest, to come forward and make a sacrifice to a pagan idol. Mattathias firmly refused, setting a good example for his people. But a weak Jew went to the altar to make the pagan sacrifice. This so enraged Mattathias that he killed the apostate Jew and the emissary of Antiochus Epiphanes. Mattathias, with the help of his five sons — John, Simon, Judas, Eleazar, and Jonathan — destroyed the heathen altar and then they fled to the hills.

The orthodox Jews refused to fight, or do anything else, on the Sabbath. The Syrians would take advantage of this, and they murdered many of the Jews who would not defend themselves. Mattathias decided that it would be right for them to fight in self-defense on the Sabbath. Soon after the revolt began, Mattathias died. His son Judas was selected to take his place. He was known as *"the Maccabee,"*

BETWEEN THE TESTAMENTS

which meant *"the hammer."* Thus, the followers of Judas came to be called the Maccabees. The Jews rallied behind Judas to defeat the Syrians against seemingly impossible odds. They reconquered Jerusalem, removed the pagan altars, and cleansed the temple which Antiochus Epiphanes had desecrated. The temple was rededicated and cleansed in 165 B.C. They celebrated an eight-day feast for this dedication, known as Hanukkah, the Festival of Lights. There were other battles and difficulties, but they primarily had a period of independence from 167-163 B.C.

Judas, the military genius, was killed in 160 B.C. Following the death of Judas, his brother Jonathan took over and ruled from 161-144 B.C. He was called the *"cunning."* Through diplomatic means and strategy, he accomplished many goals. The condition of the Syrian throne continued to be unsettled, and Jonathan died at the hands of the Assyrian ruler.

He was followed by Simon who ruled from 144-135 B.C. Simon had great prudence and administrative ability, and was absolutely sovereign over the kingdom. Even though he was really the first to fully rule the kingdom, he wasn't permitted to be called king. He was assassinated in 135 B.C. by his son-in-law, Ptolemy. Following the murder of Simon *"The Just,"* John Hyrcanus ruled from 135-106 B.C.

Under Roman Control: Following this, Aristobulus and his sons ruled until Rome took over. After a period of independence under the Maccabees, Palestine came under Roman control in 63 B.C. under Pompey. He besieged Jerusalem for three months and reportedly killed twelve thousand Jews after he took the city.

The Romans entered the temple and the Holy of Holies, but they did not take the costly furnishings. They allowed the temple worship to continue. However, Jerusalem and Judea were made tributaries to the Romans, thus ending the independence for the Jews. A yearly tribute had to be paid to the Romans, which some of the Jews detested doing.

Antipater, an Idumean (an Edomite, descendant of Esau), was appointed to rule Judea. Antipater was succeeded by his son, Herod the Great, who was king of Judah from about 37 B.C. to 4 B.C. He sought to obtain the favor of the Jews by rebuilding the temple with great splendor. He was ruler of Judah when Jesus was born and, being a brutal and cruel man,

slew the children of Bethlehem in an attempt to destroy the *"King of the Jews."*

Political Parties and Religious Groups: There were several sects and groups present in Palestine. The Herodians favored the rule and control of Herod. They were purely political in their interest and support of the Herods. On the opposite end of the political spectrum were the Zealots; patriots who resisted Rome at all costs. It was their fanaticism that resulted in war with Rome in A.D. 70 when the army of Titus destroyed Jerusalem and its temple.

One of the outstanding groups in Jesus' day was the Pharisees, which means *"separated ones."* While the idea of separation and distinction for the Jews may have begun much further back, this group may have developed in the 3rd Century B.C. under the Greek domination. They wanted to separate themselves from the corrupting and evil influence of Hellenism (Greek culture). They had a great zeal for biblical law, and the Pharisees observed meticulously all the laws regarding ceremonial purity. They developed a system of traditions and sought to apply the law to every circumstance. Their commentaries on the law were ultimately raised to the level of the law itself. They became extremely legalistic and ultimately in conflict with Christ.

Another sect that originated about the time of the Pharisees was the Sadducees. The Sadducees were more of the wealthy aristocratic class. They made peace with political rulers and attained positions of wealth and influence. They held themselves aloof from the masses, and were not popular with the people. The Sadducees did not believe in the resurrection, in spirits, or in angels. They were mostly negative in their emphasis. The Pharisees and Sadducees had very little in common except for their antagonism of Jesus.

The scribes are often referred to in the Scriptures. Because they copied the Scriptures and in the process became very familiar with them, they were considered authorities. Not only did they study and interpret the Scriptures, but also they were recognized as authorities of both the written law and the oral law which contained their traditions that had developed over the years.

Preparations for Christ's Advent: Jesus' birth in Bethlehem and life in Nazareth were not simply by chance. His coming was ordained

by God, and was achieved when all the preparations had been made. Paul declares in Galatians 4:4 that in the fullness of time God sent forth His Son. World conditions were precisely ready for God's supreme revelation in history. Social, economic, moral, religious, and other factors had all converged to provide the proper setting for the manifestation of the Son of God. The study of world conditions at the time of the birth of Christ has some practical value, which lies in the discovery of the modern conditions which parallel the return of Christ.

Political Preparation: Political preparation was one such condition. The known world had been unified under Caesar's achievement, and that entire area was under Roman domination. Frontiers between all the countries were open, resulting in great roads and good travel. Travel on the high seas was also possible. These were some of the factors involved in the political preparation that would enhance the spread of the Gospel once Jesus came. The language of the people was another factor relating to the political preparation and world unity at the time Jesus came. There was no language barrier because all the people knew Greek. Each province had its own tongue or dialect, but Greek, the common language, was a marvelous vehicle of expression. (The New Testament was written in Greek.)

Economic Preparation: Not only in the fullness of time was the political preparation accomplished, but also the economic preparation. Great luxury and magnificence abounded on one hand, with unrest and poverty on the other. Two out of every three people on the streets of Rome were slaves, considered no more than property or chattel. Many of them rebelled and desired to go free. The majority of the people lived under much difficulty in economic depression. The coming of Christ into human history made straight a way through the desert and a highway for God. So many were at their extremity and needing God's opportunity. There was a breakdown of all human resources, and many were prepared to listen to Christ to find hope and eternal life.

Moral Preparation: The world was also ready morally, for the Roman world had sunk to a state of utter moral hopelessness. It would take the Spirit of Christ to change the moral fiber of men and nations. This is also true in today's world. The moral fibers of society are fast degenerating and wickedness is becoming greater and greater. The hearts of many people long for the return of Christ and for the establishment (fully and completely) of the kingdom of God and the millennial reign.

Religious Preparation: When Jesus came the first time, it was to the fullness of religious need. The old gods of Rome were meaningless. There were mystery religions and idols of various kinds. Also, the worship of Caesar, the emperor himself, was accorded divine honors. But all of these had failed. The hearts of the people were hungry and their souls stabbed with the remorse of sin. The Jews themselves had been looking for centuries for their Messiah. The great mass of their literature during the period between the Old Testament and New Testament was full of the hope of a coming Messiah. When John the Baptist began to preach and his voice rang out across the land, they seriously questioned, *"Is this the Messiah?"* There was great expectation. Certainly the fullness of time had come.

The Redeemer came in a time ordained by God; a time that had been prepared in many ways; and a time needing the Redeemer.

THE
NEW TESTAMENT

of Our Lord and Saviour

Jesus Christ

Translated out of the original Greek
and with the former translations diligently
compared and revised.

THE GOSPEL ACCORDING TO
MATTHEW

CHAPTER 1
(A.D. 1)
THE GENEALOGY OF JESUS CHRIST

THE Book *(account)* of the generation *(lineage)* of Jesus Christ *(Saviour, Messiah)*, the Son of David, the Son of Abraham *(the Incarnation, God becoming man [Isa. 7:14; II Sam. 7:16, 19; Gen. 12:1-3; 17:7; Gal. 3:16])*.

2 Abraham begat *(fathered)* Isaac; and Isaac begat Jacob; and Jacob begat Judas and his brethren;

3 And Judas begat Phares and Zara of Thamar; and Phares begat Esrom; and Esrom begat Aram;

4 And Aram begat Aminadab; and Aminadab begat Naasson; and Naasson begat Salmon;

5 And Salmon begat Boaz of Rahab *(Rahab was not the actual mother of Boaz, but his mother several times removed)*; and Boaz begat Obed of Ruth; and Obed begat Jesse;

6 And Jesse begat David the king; and David the king begat Solomon of her *who had been the wife* of Uriah;

7 And Solomon begat Rehoboam; and Rehoboam begat Abia; and Abia begat Asa;

8 And Asa begat Jehoshaphat; and Jehoshaphat begat Joram; and Joram begat Ozias;

9 And Ozias begat Joatham; and Joatham begat Achaz; and Achaz begat Ezekias;

10 And Ezekias begat Manasses; and Manasses begat Amon; and Amon begat Josias;

11 And Josias begat Jechonias and his brethren, about the time they were carried away to Babylon *(about 593 B.C.)*:

12 And after they were brought to Babylon, Jechonias begat Salathiel; and Salathiel begat Zerubbabel;

13 And Zerubbabel begat Abiud; and Abiud begat Eliakim; and Eliakim begat Azor;

14 And Azor begat Sadoc; and Sadoc begat Achim; and Achim begat Eliud;

15 And Eliud begat Eleazar; and Eleazar begat Matthan; and Matthan begat Jacob;

16 And Jacob begat Joseph the husband of Mary, of whom was born Jesus *(Saviour)*, Who is called Christ *(the Anointed, the Messiah)*.

17 So all the generations from Abraham to David *are* fourteen generations; and from David until the carrying away into Babylon *are* fourteen generations; and from the carrying away into Babylon unto Christ *are* fourteen generations.

THE BIRTH OF JESUS CHRIST

18 Now the Birth of Jesus Christ was on this wise: When as His Mother Mary was espoused *(engaged)* to Joseph, before they came together *(before they were married)*, she was found with Child of the Holy Spirit *(by decree of the Holy Spirit)*.

19 Then Joseph her husband, being a just *man*, not willing to make her a public example, was minded to put her away privily *(to quietly break the engagement)*.

20 But while he thought on these things, behold, the Angel of the Lord appeared unto him in a dream, saying, Joseph, thou son of David, fear not to take unto you Mary your wife; for that which is conceived in her is of the Holy Spirit.

21 And she shall bring forth a Son, and you shall call His Name JESUS *(Saviour)*: for He shall save His people from their sins.

22 Now all this was done, that it might be fulfilled which was spoken of the Lord by the Prophet, saying,

23 Behold, a Virgin shall be with Child, and shall bring forth a Son, and they shall call His Name Emmanuel, which being interpreted is, God with us *(Isa. 7:14)*.

24 Then Joseph being raised from sleep did as the Angel of the Lord had bidden him, and took unto him his wife *(immediately went ahead with the wedding ceremony)*:

25 And knew her not *(had no sexual relations with her)* till she had brought forth her First-born Son: and he called His Name JESUS *(meaning Saviour; after the Birth of Christ, Joseph did have relations with Mary, with four other boys being born, and several sisters [Mat. 13:55-56])*.

CHAPTER 2
(A.D. 1)
THE VISIT OF THE MAGI FROM THE EAST

NOW when Jesus was born in Bethlehem of Judaea *(Mic. 5:2)* in the days of Herod

the king, behold, there came Wise men from the east to Jerusalem,

2 Saying, Where is He Who is born King of the Jews? for we have seen His Star in the east, and are come to worship Him.

3 When Herod the king had heard *these things*, he was troubled, and all Jerusalem with him.

4 And when he had gathered all the Chief Priests and Scribes of the people together, he demanded of them where Christ should be born.

5 And they said unto him, In Bethlehem of Judaea: for thus it is written by the Prophet,

6 And thou Bethlehem, *in* the Land of Judah, are not the least among the princes of Judah: for out of you shall come a Governor, Who shall rule My people Israel *(Mic. 5:2)*.

7 Then Herod, when he had privily *(privately)* called the Wise men, inquired of them diligently what time the star appeared.

8 And he sent them to Bethlehem, and said, Go and search diligently for the young child; and when you have found *Him*, bring me word again, that I may come and worship Him also.

9 When they had heard the king, they departed; and, lo, the star, which they saw in the east, went before them, till it came and stood over where the young Child was *(not Bethlehem, but some other place, maybe Nazareth)*.

10 When they saw the star *(where the star stopped)*, they rejoiced with exceeding great joy.

11 And when they were come into the house *(not the stable where He was born in Bethlehem)*, they saw the young Child with Mary His Mother, and fell down, and worshipped Him: and when they had opened their treasures, they presented unto Him gifts; gold, and frankincense, and myrrh.

12 And being warned of God in a dream that they should not return to Herod, they departed into their own country another way.

THE FLIGHT INTO EGYPT

13 And when they were departed, behold, the Angel of the Lord appeared to Joseph in a dream, saying, Arise, and take the young Child and His Mother, and flee into Egypt, and stay there until I bring you word: for Herod will seek the young Child to destroy Him.

14 When he arose, he took the young Child and His Mother by night, and departed into Egypt:

15 And was there until the death of Herod: that it might be fulfilled which was spoken of the Lord by the Prophet, saying, Out of Egypt have I called My Son *(Hos. 11:1)*.

SLAUGHTER OF THE CHILDREN IN BETHLEHEM

16 Then Herod, when he saw that he was mocked of the Wise men *(they ignored his demand that when they found the Child, they were to come back and report to him)*, was exceeding wroth, and sent forth, and killed all the children who were in Bethlehem, and in all the coasts thereof, from two years old and under, according to the time which he had diligently inquired of the Wise men *(these words decide that two years, or nearly so, had elapsed since Herod had seen the Wise men)*.

17 Then was fulfilled that which was spoken by Jeremiah the Prophet, saying,

18 In Rama was there a voice heard, lamentation, and weeping, and great mourning, Rachel weeping *for* her children, and would not be comforted, because they are not *(Jer. 31:15)*.

THE RETURN FROM EGYPT TO NAZARETH

19 But when Herod was dead, behold, an Angel of the Lord appeared in a dream to Joseph in Egypt *(this is the third of four dreams given to Joseph by the Lord)*,

20 Saying, Arise, and take the young Child and His Mother, and go into the Land of Israel: for they are dead which sought the young Child's life.

21 And he arose, and took the young Child and His Mother, and came into the Land of Israel.

22 But when he heard that Archelaus did reign in Judaea in the room of his father Herod, he was afraid to go thither: notwithstanding, being warned of God in a dream, he turned aside into the parts of Galilee *(the fourth and final dream recorded as given by the Lord to Joseph)*:

23 And he came and dwelt in a city called Nazareth: that it might be fulfilled which was spoken by the Prophets, He shall be called a Nazarene *(the word "Nazarene" is meant to portray the action instead of the location; He would be despised, as Nazareth was despised [Jn. 1:46])*.

CHAPTER 3
(A.D. 29)
THE PREACHING OF JOHN THE BAPTIST

IN those days *(immediately preceding the introduction of Christ)* came John the Baptist, preaching in the wilderness of Judaea *(the area near Jericho)*;

2 And saying, Repent you *(recognize one's wrong direction)*: for the Kingdom of Heaven *(Kingdom from the Heavens, headed up by Jesus Christ)* is at hand *(was being offered to Israel)*.

3 For this is he *(John the Baptist)* who was spoken of by the Prophet Isaiah, saying, The voice of one crying in the wilderness, Prepare you the Way of the LORD, make His paths straight *(Isa. 40:3)*.

4 And the same John had his raiment of camel's hair, and a leather girdle about his loins; and his meat was locusts and wild honey.

5 Then went out to him Jerusalem, and all Judaea, and all the region round about Jordan *(the Jordan River)*,

6 And were baptized of him in Jordan *(dipped completely under)*, confessing their sins.

7 But when he saw many of the Pharisees and Sadducees *(two sects of self-righteous and zealous Jews)* come to his baptism *(Water Baptism)*, he said unto them, O generation of vipers *(snakes)*, who has warned you to flee from the wrath to come?

8 Bring forth therefore fruits *(evidence)* meet for *(befitting)* Repentance:

9 And think not to say within yourselves, We have Abraham to *our* father *(pride)*: for I say unto you, that God is able of these stones to raise up children unto Abraham *(the Lord has raised up the Gentiles as children unto Abraham [Gal. 3:7, 14])*.

10 And now also the axe is laid unto the root of the trees: therefore every tree which brings not forth good fruit is hewn down, and cast into the fire *(Israel was cut down because of unbelief [Rom. 11:20])*.

11 I indeed baptize you with water unto Repentance *(Water Baptism was an outward act of an inward work already carried out)*: but He *(Christ)* Who comes after me is mightier than I, Whose Shoes I am not worthy to bear: He shall Baptize you with the Holy Spirit, and *with* fire *(to burn out the sinful dross [Acts 2:2-4])*:

12 Whose fan *is* in His Hand *(the ancient method for winnowing grain)*, and He will thoroughly purge His Floor *("purging it, that it may bring forth more fruit" [Jn. 15:2])*, and

gather His Wheat into the garner *(the end product as developed by the Spirit)*; but He will burn up the chaff with unquenchable fire *(the wheat is symbolic of the Work of the Spirit, while the chaff is symbolic of the work of the flesh)*.

JOHN'S BAPTISM OF JESUS

13 Then came Jesus from Galilee to Jordan unto John, to be baptized of him *(signifying the greatest moment in human history thus far; the earthly Ministry of Christ would now begin)*.

14 But John forbad Him, saying, I have need to be Baptized of You, and come You to me?

15 And Jesus answering said unto him, Suffer *it to be so* now *(permit Me to be baptized)*: for thus it becomes us to fulfill all Righteousness *(Water Baptism is a type of the death, burial, and Resurrection of Christ [Rom. 6:3-5])*. Then he suffered Him.

16 And Jesus, when He was baptized *(this was the beginning of His earthly Ministry)*, went up straightway *(immediately)* out of the water *(refers to Baptism by immersion and not by sprinkling)*: and, lo, the Heavens were opened unto Him *(the only One, the Lord Jesus Christ, to Whom the Heavens would be opened)*, and he saw the Spirit of God *(Holy Spirit)* descending like a dove, and lighting upon Him *(John saw a visible form that reminded him of a dove)*:

17 And lo a Voice from Heaven, saying *(the Voice of God the Father)*, This is My Beloved Son, in Whom I am well pleased *(the Trinity appears here: the Father speaks, the Spirit descends, and the Son prays [Lk. 3:21])*.

CHAPTER 4
(A.D. 29)
THE TEMPTATION OF JESUS IN THE WILDERNESS

THEN *(immediately after the descent of the Holy Spirit upon Him)* was Jesus led up *(urgently led)* of the Spirit *(Holy Spirit)* into the wilderness *(probably close to Jericho)* to be tempted of the Devil *(as the Last Adam, He would be tempted in all points like as we are [Heb. 4:15; I Cor. 15:21-22, 45, 47])*.

2 And when He had fasted forty days and forty nights, He was afterward hungry *(other than Christ, three men in the Bible fasted forty days and forty nights: Moses [Deut. 9:9, 18, 25; 10:10], Joshua [Ex. 24:13-18; 32:15-17], and Elijah [I Ki. 19:7-8])*.

3 And when the tempter *(Satan)* came to

Him, he said, If You be the Son of God (since You are the Son of God), command that these stones be made bread (Christ was tempted to use His Power for His Own benefit, which He was to never do).

4 But He answered and said, It is written, Man shall not live by bread alone, but by every Word that proceeds out of the Mouth of God ([Deut. 8:3]; man is a spiritual being as well as a physical being; therefore, dependent on God).

5 Then the Devil took Him up (a powerful force) into the Holy City (Jerusalem), and set Him on a pinnacle of the Temple (its highest point, which Josephus stated, was about 700 feet from the ravine below),

6 And said unto Him, If You be the Son of God (since You are the Son of God), cast Yourself down (literally spoken): for it is written, He shall give His Angels charge concerning You: and in their hands they shall bear You up, lest at any time You dash Your foot against a stone (derived from Psalms 91:11-12).

7 Jesus said unto him, It is written again, you shall not tempt the Lord your God ([Deut. 6:16]; to tempt God is to question His Word, which casts doubt on His ability to do what He has promised).

8 Again (the third temptation), the Devil took Him up into an exceeding high mountain (not definitely known, but probably Nebo), and showed Him all the kingdoms of the world, and the glory of them (showed them to Him, not in a physical sense, but rather in a spiritual sense);

9 And said unto Him, All these things will I give You, if You will fall down and worship me (the temptation was that Christ abrogate the Cross, through which He would regain all things).

10 Then said Jesus unto him, Get thee hence, Satan (presents Christ for the first time Personally addressing Satan): for it is written, you shall worship the Lord your God, and Him only shall you serve (Satan desires that mankind worship and serve him; we are to worship and serve the Lord Alone).

11 Then the Devil left Him ("departed from Him for a season," meaning that there would be other temptations [Lk. 4:13]), and, behold, Angels came and ministered unto Him (in what manner they ministered, we aren't told).

JESUS BEGINS HIS MINISTRY; REJECTED IN NAZARETH — MOVES TO CAPERNAUM

12 Now when Jesus had heard that John was cast into prison (John's Ministry was now finished; he had properly introduced Christ), He (Jesus) departed into Galilee (where would be the central core of His Ministry);

13 And leaving Nazareth (refers to His rejection there [Lk. 4:16-30]), He came and dwelt in Capernaum (made this city His Headquarters), which is upon the sea coast (refers to the Sea of Galilee), in the borders of Zabulon and Nephthalim (refers to these two Tribes bordering the Sea of Galilee):

14 That it might be fulfilled which was spoken by Isaiah the Prophet, saying (Isaiah prophesied of Christ more than any other Prophet),

15 The land of Zabulon, and the land of Nephthalim, by the way of the sea (Sea of Galilee), beyond Jordan, Galilee of the Gentiles (the great Roman Road ran near the Sea of Galilee from Damascus; almost all Gentiles traveling in this direction did so on this road; the Headquarters of Christ was within the confines of the Tribe of Naphtali);

16 The people which sat in darkness (implies a settled acceptance of this darkness; the moral darkness was even greater than the national misery) saw great Light (Christ is the Light of the world, and the only True Light); and to them which sat in the region and shadow of death (spiritual death is the result of this spiritual darkness) light (spiritual illumination in Christ) is sprung up.

17 From that time (the move to Capernaum) Jesus began to preach (the major method of the proclamation of the Gospel), and to say, Repent (beginning His Ministry, the first word used by Christ, as recorded by Matthew, was "Repent"): for the Kingdom of Heaven is at hand (the Kingdom from Heaven, headed up by Christ, for the purpose of reestablishing the Kingdom of God over the Earth; the Kingdom was rejected by Israel).

JESUS CALLS FOUR FISHERMEN

18 And Jesus, walking by the Sea of Galilee, saw two Brethren, Simon called Peter, and Andrew his brother, casting a net into the sea: for they were fishermen.

19 And He said unto them, Follow Me (the Messiah's advent was signaled by three great words: "Repent," "Follow," and "Blessed" [Mat. 5:3]), and I will make you fishers of men (the greatest call of all).

20 And they straightway (immediately) left their nets (their fishing business), and followed Him.

21 And going on from thence, He saw other two Brethren, James *the son* of Zebedee, and John his brother, in a ship with Zebedee their father, mending their nets; and He called them *(the first three called, Peter, James, and John, were the closest to Christ)*.

22 And they immediately left the ship and their father, and followed Him *(He called them to a higher fishing, as He called David to a higher feeding [Ps. 78:70-72])*.

SECOND TOUR OF GALILEE;
JESUS' FAME SPREADS

23 And Jesus went about all Galilee, teaching in their Synagogues, and preaching *(Preaching proclaims the Gospel, while Teaching explains it)* the Gospel of the Kingdom *(the good news of the establishment upon Earth of the perfect Government of Heaven; as stated, it was rejected)*, and healing all manner of sickness and all manner of disease among the people *(Jesus is not only the Saviour; He as well is the Healer)*.

24 And His fame went throughout all Syria *(the account of what He did went beyond the borders of Israel)*: and they brought unto Him all sick people who were taken with divers *(different kinds)* diseases and torments, and those which were possessed with devils *(demons)*, and those which were lunatic *(insane, whether by demon possession, or physical disabilities)*, and those who had the palsy, and He healed them *(He turned no one away)*.

25 And there followed Him great multitudes of people from Galilee, and *from* Decapolis *(the eastern side of the Jordan River)*, and *from* Jerusalem, and *from* Judaea, and *from* beyond Jordan.

CHAPTER 5
(A.D. 31)
SERMON ON THE MOUNT:
INTRODUCTION

A ND seeing the multitudes, He went up into a mountain *(unknown, but probably was a small mountain near the Sea of Galilee; two sermons, both delivered on mountains, opened and closed the Lord's public Ministry; the last was upon Olivet near Jerusalem [Mat., Chpt. 24])*: and when He was set *(He sat down in order to Teach, which was the custom at that time)*, His disciples came unto Him *(referring not to the Twelve, but to any and all who closely followed Him at that time)*:

2 And He opened His Mouth *(signifying a carefully thought out Message of purpose and will)*, and taught them, saying *(begins the greatest moment of spiritual and Scriptural instruction that had ever been given in the history of mankind)*,

THE BEATITUDES

3 Blessed *(happy) are* the poor in spirit *(conscious of moral poverty)*: for theirs is the Kingdom of Heaven *(the moral characteristics of the citizens of the Kingdom of the heavens; and so it is apparent that the New Birth is an absolute necessity for entrance into that Kingdom [Jn. 3:3]; this Kingdom is now present spiritually, but not yet physically)*.

4 Blessed *are* they who mourn *(grieved because of personal sinfulness)*: for they shall be comforted *(what the Holy Spirit will do for those who properly evaluate their spiritual poverty)*.

5 Blessed *are* the meek *(the opposite of the self-righteous; the first two Beatitudes guarantee the "meekness")*: for they shall inherit the earth *(speaks of the coming Kingdom Age, when the "Kingdom of Heaven" will be brought down to Earth, when the Saints will rule, with Christ as its Supreme Lord)*.

6 Blessed *are* they which do hunger and thirst *(intense desire)* after Righteousness *(God's Righteousness, imputed by Christ, upon Faith in His Finished Work)*: for they shall be filled *(but first of all must be truly empty of all self-worth)*.

7 Blessed *are* the merciful *(shows itself in action which goes beyond the thought)*: for they shall obtain mercy *(to obtain mercy from God, we must show mercy to others)*.

8 Blessed *are* the pure in heart *(those who have received a new moral nature in regeneration)*: for they shall see God *(will see Him manifest Himself in one's life)*.

9 Blessed *are* the peacemakers *(pertains to peace with God, which comes with Salvation, and all who proclaim such are called "peacemakers")*: for they shall be called the Children of God *(expresses the "peacemaker" and the one who has received the "peace")*.

10 Blessed *are* they which are persecuted for Righteousness' sake *(means that those who operate from the realm of self-righteousness will persecute those who trust in God's "Righteousness")*: for theirs is the Kingdom of Heaven *(having God's Righteousness, which is solely in*

Christ, such have the Kingdom of Heaven).

11 Blessed *are* **you, when** *men* **shall revile you, and persecute** *you*, **and shall say all manner of evil against you falsely, for My sake** *(only Christ could say, "For My sake," for He is God; there is an offence to the Cross [Gal. 5:11]).*

12 Rejoice *(the present inner result of one who is "blessed"),* **and be exceeding glad** *(self-righteousness persecuting Righteousness is the guarantee of the possession of Righteousness, and the occasion for great joy):* **for great** *is* **your reward in Heaven** *(meaning it will not necessarily come while on Earth):* **for so persecuted they the Prophets which were before you** *(presents the fact that "God's Way" will bring "persecution," severely so, at times by both the world and the Church).*

BELIEVERS ARE AS SALT AND LIGHT

13 You are the salt *(preservative)* **of the earth: but if the salt have lost his savour, wherewith shall it be salted? it is thenceforth good for nothing, but to be cast out, and to be trodden under foot of men** *("Salt" is a Type of the Word of God; the professing Believer who no longer holds to the Word is of no use to God or man).*

14 You are the Light of the world *(we are a reflector of the light which comes from Christ).* **A city that is set on an hill cannot be hid** *(proper light will not, and in fact, cannot be hid).*

15 Neither do men light a candle, and put it under a bushel, but on a candlestick *(the light is not to be hid);* **and it gives light unto all who are in the house** *(that is the purpose of the light).*

16 Let your light so shine before men, that they may see your good works *(proper Faith will always produce proper works, but proper works will never produce proper Faith),* **and glorify your Father which is in Heaven** *(proper works will glorify our Heavenly Father, while improper works glorify man).*

CHRIST AND THE LAW

17 Think not that I am come to destroy the Law *(this was the Law of Moses),* **or the Prophets** *(the predictions of the Prophets of the Old Testament):* **I am not come to destroy, but to fulfill** *(Jesus fulfilled the Law by meeting its just demands with a Perfect Life, and satisfying its curse by dying on the Cross [Gal. 3:13]).*

18 For verily I say unto you *(proclaims the ultimate authority!),* **Till Heaven and Earth pass** *(means to be changed, or pass from one condition to another, which will take place in the coming Perfect Age [Rev., Chpts. 21-22]),* **one jot** *(smallest letter in the Hebrew alphabet)* **or one tittle** *(a minute ornamental finish to ancient Hebrew letters)* **shall in no wise pass from the Law, till all be fulfilled** *(the Law was meant to be fulfilled in Christ, and was in fact, totally fulfilled by Christ, in His Life, Death, and Resurrection, with a New Testament or New Covenant being brought about [Acts 15:5-29; Rom. 10:4; II Cor. 3:6-15; Gal. 3:19-25; 4:21-31; 5:1-5, 18; Eph. 2:15; Col. 2:14-17]).*

19 Whosoever therefore shall break one of these least Commandments, and shall teach men so, he shall be called the least in the Kingdom of Heaven *(those who are disloyal to the authority of the Word of God shall be judged; "He shall be called the least," means that he will not be in the Kingdom at all):* **but whosoever shall do and teach** *them*, **the same shall be called great in the Kingdom of Heaven** *(the Lord sets the Bible as the Standard of all Righteousness, and He recognizes no other).*

20 For I say unto you, That except your righteousness shall exceed *the righteousness* **of the Scribes and Pharisees** *(which was self-righteousness)*, **you shall in no case enter into the Kingdom of Heaven** *(the absolute necessity of the New Birth is declared here as imperative in every case).*

JESUS AND ANGER

21 You have heard that it was said by them of old time *(referring back to the Law of Moses)*, **Thou shall not kill** *(should have been translated, You shall not murder);* **and whosoever shall kill** *(murder)* **shall be in danger of the judgment** *(Ex. 20:13; Lev. 24:21; Num., Chpt. 35; Deut. 5:17; 19:12);*

22 But I say unto you *(Christ gives the true interpretation of the Bible, with in fact, the Bible and Christ, in essence, being one and the same),* **That whosoever is angry with his brother without a cause** *(places unjust anger in the same category as murder, i.e., "springs from an evil heart")* **shall be in danger of the judgment** *(certain of judgment):* **and whosoever shall say to his brother, Raca** *(the words "Raca" and "thou fool" were Hebrew expressions of murderous anger)*, **shall be in danger of the Council** *(Sanhedrin):* **but whosoever shall say, Thou fool, shall be in danger of hell fire** *(men may beat justice in a human court of law, but will never do such in God's Court of Law).*

ON RESTITUTION AND PRAYER

23 Therefore if you bring your gift to the Altar *(referring to the Brazen Altar as used in the offering of Sacrifices in the Law of Moses)*, and there remember that your brother has ought against you *(is meant to describe our relationship with our fellowman)*;

24 Leave there your gift before the Altar *(the intimation is that the Lord will not accept our "gift" unless we do all within our power to make things right with the offended party)*, and go your way *(make every effort to bring about reconciliation, if at all possible)*; first be reconciled to your brother, and then come and offer your gift *(worship will not be accepted by the Lord, if we have wronged our brother, and have not done all within our power to make amends)*.

CHRISTIAN RELATIONSHIPS

25 Agree with your adversary quickly, while you are in the way with him *(if we offend our brother and do not make amends, the Lord becomes our adversary, or opponent, which places one in a serious situation indeed)*; lest at any time the adversary deliver you to the judge, and the judge deliver you to the officer, and you be cast into prison *(regarding a Believer who offends a fellow Christian, and will not make amends, God becomes that person's Adversary, and thereby is Judge instead of his Saviour, and spiritually speaking, puts such a person in a spiritual prison)*.

26 Verily I say unto you *(the absolute solemnity of this statement)*, You shall by no means come out thence *(come out of this spiritual prison)*, till you have paid the uttermost farthing *(the Lord's method of teaching was symbolic and figurative; if the Believer doesn't make amends with his fellowman who he has wronged, he will suffer one reverse after the other; God will see to it)*.

JESUS' TEACHING ON ADULTERY

27 You have heard that it was said by them of old time *(the Mosaic Law)*, You shall not commit adultery *(the Seventh Commandment [Ex. 20:14])*.

28 But I say unto you *(the phrase does not deny the Law of Moses, but rather takes it to its conclusion, which could only be done by Christ; the Old Covenant pointed the way to the New Covenant, which came with Christ)*, That whosoever

looks on a woman to lust after her *(to look with intense sexual desire)* has committed adultery with her already in his heart *(the Lord addresses the root of sin, which is an evil heart; the Cross is the only answer)*.

29 And if your right eye offend you, pluck it out, and cast *it* from you *(as stated, the Lord's method of teaching was symbolic and figurative)*: for it is profitable for you that one of your members should perish, and not *that* your whole body should be cast into Hell *(the Lord does not intend for His statement to be taken literally, as He has already explained that the offence is not in the "eye" or "hand," but, instead, the heart!; in effect, a blind man can lust)*.

30 And if your right hand offend you, cut it off, and cast *it* from you: for it is profitable for you that one of your members should perish, and not *that* your whole body should be cast into Hell *(showing the fact that if such action is not stopped, the person will lose their soul; as stated, the Cross is the only means by which evil passions can be subdued [Rom. 6:3-5, 11, 14])*.

ON DIVORCE AND REMARRIAGE

31 It has been said *(Deut. 24:1-4)*, Whosoever shall put away his wife *(refers to divorce proceedings)*, let him give her a writing of divorcement *(the Jews had perverted the Law, greatly weakening the sanctity of marriage)*:

32 But I say unto you *(the Lord now gives the true meaning of the Law)*, That whosoever shall put away his wife *(divorce her)*, saving for the cause of fornication *(cohabiting with others, thereby breaking the marriage vows)*, causes her to commit adultery *(if she marries someone else, but the intimation is that the fault is not hers)*: and whosoever shall marry her who is divorced commits adultery *(the man who marries the woman who is divorced unscripturally, even though it's not her fault, commits adultery as well; we should learn here the sanctity of marriage, with divorce and remarriage allowed only on the grounds of fornication and spiritual desertion [I Cor. 7:10-11])*.

THE SIGNIFICANCE OF WORDS

33 Again, you have heard that it has been said by them of old time *(such phraseology means that the Word of God had been twisted to mean something it did not say)*, You shall not forswear yourself, but shall perform unto the Lord your oaths *(Vss. 33-37 have to do*

with the Third Commandment, "You shall not take the Name of the Lord your God in vain" [Ex. 20:7]):

34 But I say unto you *(proclaiming the true meaning of the Law)*, Swear not at all; neither by Heaven; for it is God's Throne *(this has nothing to do with profanity, but rather of flippantly using God's Name)*:

35 Nor by the earth; for it is His footstool: neither by Jerusalem; for it is the city of the great King *(not only must the Name of God not be flippantly used, but as well, His Creation is off limits also)*.

36 Neither shall you swear by your head, because you cannot make one hair white or black *(man is God's highest creation)*.

37 But let your communication be *(verbal communication with others)*, Yes, yes; No, no: for whatsoever is more than these comes of evil *(the followers of Christ must stand out by their truthfulness, honesty, and integrity; subterfuge and doubletalk are out)*.

RETALIATION

38 You have heard that it has been said, An eye for an eye, and a tooth for a tooth *([Ex. 21:24; Lev. 24:20; Deut. 19:21]; the letter of the Law was that which God would carry out in His Own way [Mat. 7:2] man was not to resort to such, even as Jesus will now say)*:

39 But I say unto you, That you resist not evil *(do not reward evil with evil)*: but whosoever shall smite you on the right cheek, turn to him the other also *(once again, the language is figurative, for the Lord when smitten on the cheek [Jn. 18:22-23] did not turn the other cheek but with dignity rebuked the assailant)*.

40 And if any man will sue you at the law, and take away your coat, let him have *your* cloak also *(this does not refer to righteous action, which is sometimes necessary, but rather to a contentious spirit, which demands one's rights, down to the minute detail)*.

41 And whosoever shall compel you to go a mile, go with him two *(the entirety of the idea has to do with the heart of man, not so much his outward actions, but which most surely would guide his actions accordingly)*.

42 Give to him who asks of you, and from him who would borrow of you turn not you away *(this pertains to those truly in need, and not those who are lazy and will not work [II Thess. 3:10])*.

THE LAW OF LOVE

43 You have heard that it has been said, You shall love your neighbor, and hate your enemy *(once again, Christ is correcting the perversion of Scripture; the "hating of the enemy" was probably derived from Deut. 7:1-6; but nowhere in that Passage does it say to hate the enemy; while we are to hate the sin, we are not to hate the sinner [Jn. 3:16])*.

44 But I say unto you, Love your enemies, bless them who curse you, do good to them who hate you, and pray for them which despitefully use you, and persecute you *(the actions of the enemies of goodness and of righteousness are to be "hated" with a holy hatred; but personal hatred is to be met by love)*;

45 That you may be the Children of your Father which is in Heaven: for He makes His sun to rise on the evil and on the good, and sends rain on the just and on the unjust *(we are to imitate our Heavenly Father)*.

46 For if you love them which love you, what reward have you? do not even the publicans the same? *(Only those who have the true Love of God in their hearts can love those who do not love them.)*

47 And if you salute your Brethren only, what do you more *than others*? do not even the publicans so? *(If our love is of no greater definition than that of the world, then our claims are empty.)*

48 Be you therefore perfect, even as your Father which is in Heaven is perfect *(Jesus is not teaching sinless perfection, for the Bible does not teach such; He is teaching that our imitation of our Heavenly Father must be as perfect as possible; the Holy Spirit Alone can help us do these things, which He does according to our Faith in Christ and the Cross [Rom. 8:1-2, 11])*.

CHAPTER 6
(A.D. 31)
JESUS' TEACHING ON GIVING

TAKE heed *(a serious matter)* that you do not your alms *(Righteousness)* before men, to be seen of them *(what is the reason for our giving?)*: otherwise you have no reward of your Father which is in Heaven.

2 Therefore when you do *your* alms *(in this case, giving, and portrays the necessity of giving)*, do not sound a trumpet before you *(do not make a show)*, as the hypocrites do in the Synagogues and in the streets, that they may

have glory of men *(be seen of men)*. Verily I say unto you, They have their reward *(God will not reward such, whether on Earth or in Heaven)*.

3 But when you do alms *(Righteousness, and once again, proclaims the necessity of giving)*, let not your left hand know what your right hand does *(not meant to be taken literally, but rather to point to the intent of the heart)*:

4 That your alms may be in secret *(simply means that from the heart it is done as unto the Lord, and not for the praise of men)*: and your Father *(Heavenly Father)* which sees in secret Himself shall reward you openly *(both on Earth and when you get to Heaven)*.

JESUS' TEACHING ON PRAYER

5 And when you pray *(the necessity of prayer)*, you shall not be as the hypocrites *are*: for they love to pray standing in the Synagogues and in the corners of the streets, that they may be seen of men *(they do it for show)*. Verily I say unto you, They have their reward *(meaning that there will be no reward from God in any capacity)*.

6 But you *(sincere Believer)*, when you pray, enter into your closet, and when you have shut your door, pray to your Father which is in secret; and your Father which sees in secret shall reward you openly *(the word "closet" is not to be taken literally, but means that our praying must not be done for show; if we make God's interests our own, we are assured that He will make our interest His Own)*.

7 But when you pray, use not vain repetitions, as the heathen *do (repeating certain phrases over and over, even hundreds of times)*: for they think that they shall be heard for their much speaking *(they will not be heard by God)*.

8 Be not you therefore like unto them: for your Father *(Heavenly Father)* knows what things you have need of, before you ask Him *(He is omniscient, meaning that He knows all things, past, present, and future)*.

THE MODEL PRAYER

9 After this manner therefore pray you *(is meant to be in total contrast to the heathen practice; as well, it is to be prayed in full confidence, that the Heavenly Father will hear and answer according to His Will)*: Our Father *(our prayer should be directed toward our Heavenly Father, and not Christ or the Holy Spirit)* Who is in Heaven, Hallowed be Your Name *(we reverence His Name)*.

10 Your Kingdom come *(this will definitely happen at the Second Coming)*, Your Will be done in Earth, as *it is* in Heaven *(the Will of God is all-important; it will be carried out on Earth, beginning with the Kingdom Age)*.

11 Give us this day our daily bread *(we are to look to the Lord for sustenance, both natural and spiritual)*.

12 And forgive us our debts, as we forgive our debtors *(the word "debts" here refers to "trespasses" and "sins"; His forgiveness on our part is predicated on our forgiving others)*.

13 And lead *(because of self-confidence)* us not into temptation *(help us not to be led into testing — the idea is, in my self-confidence, which stems from the flesh and not the Spirit, please do not allow me to be led into temptation, for I will surely fail!)*, but deliver us *(the trap is more powerful than man can handle; only God can deliver; He does so through the Power of the Holy Spirit, according to our Faith in Christ and the Cross [Rom. 8:1-2, 11])* from evil *(the Evil One, Satan himself)*: For Yours is the kingdom *(this Earth belongs to the Lord and not Satan; he is an usurper)*, and the power *(God has the Power to deliver, which He does, as stated, through the Cross)*, and the glory *(the Glory belongs to God, and not Satan)*, forever *(none of this will ever change)*. Amen *(this Word expresses a solemn ratification; in the Mind of God, the defeat and destruction of Satan and, therefore, all evil in the world, is a foregone conclusion)*.

14 For if you forgive men *(it must be the God kind of forgiveness)* their trespasses *(large sins)*, your Heavenly Father will also forgive you *(forgiveness rests totally on the Atoning Work of Christ; it is an act of sheer Grace)*:

15 But if you forgive not men their trespasses, neither will your Father forgive your trespasses *(if we want God to forgive us, we must at the same time forgive others; if not, His forgiveness for us is withheld; consequently, such a person is in jeopardy of losing their soul)*.

JESUS' TEACHING ON FASTING

16 Moreover when you fast *(no set time)*, be not, as the hypocrites, of a sad countenance: for they disfigure their faces, that they may appear unto men to fast. Verily I say unto you, They have their reward *(so much in the religious realm falls into this category; it is done for "show" whether it be fasting or giving, etc.;*

the Lord will never reward such).

17 But you *(referring to those who are truly God's Children),* when you fast, anoint your head, and wash your face *(the "anointing" and the "washing" were actually symbols of joy; this was the opposite of the sad countenance);*

18 That you appear not unto men to fast *(there is to be no appearance of fasting),* but unto your Father *(Heavenly Father)* which is in secret: and your Father, which sees in secret, shall reward *(bless)* you openly *(the implication is God was not the "Father" of the Pharisees, and will not be the "Father" of any who follow in their train).*

TREASURES IN HEAVEN

19 Lay not up for yourselves treasures upon earth *(everything on the Earth is temporal),* where moth and rust does corrupt, and where thieves break through and steal *(if the eye be set upon treasures on Earth, the life and character of the Believer will be shrouded in moral darkness):*

20 But lay up for yourselves treasures in Heaven, where neither moth nor rust does corrupt, and where thieves do not break through nor steal:

21 For where your treasure is, there will your heart be also *(a man's aim determines his character; if that aim be not simple and Heavenward but earthward and double, all the faculties and principles of his nature will become a mass of darkness; it is impossible to give a divided allegiance).*

THE LIGHT

22 The light of the body is the eye *(a figure of speech; He is, in effect, saying that the light of the soul is the spirit):* if therefore your eye be single *(the spirit of man should have but one purpose, and that is to Glorify God),* your whole body shall be full of Light *(if the spirit of man is single in its devotion to God [meaning not divided] then all the soul will be full of light).*

23 But if your eye be evil, your whole body shall be full of darkness *(if the spirit be evil, the entirety of the soul will be full of darkness).* If therefore the light that is in you be darkness *(the light is not acted upon, but rather perverted),* how great *is* that darkness *(the latter state is worse than if there had been no light at all)!*

24 No man can serve two masters: for either he will hate the one, and love the other; or else he will hold to the one, and despise the other. You cannot serve God and mammon *(this is flat out, stated as, an impossibility; it is total devotion to God, or ultimately it will be total devotion to the world; the word, "mammon" is derived from the Babylonian "Mimma," which means "anything at all").*

AGAINST WORRY AND ANXIETY

25 Therefore I say unto you, Take no thought for your life, what you shall eat, or what you shall drink; nor yet for your body, what you shall put on *(don't worry about these things).* Is not the life more than meat, and the body than raiment? *(Life is more than things, and the physical body is more than the clothes we wear.)*

26 Behold the fowls of the air: for they sow not, neither do they reap, nor gather into barns; yet your Heavenly Father feeds them. Are you not much better than they? *(The fowls of the air are a smaller part of God's great Creation. If the Lord has provided for them, most assuredly, He has provided for His Children.)*

27 Which of you by taking thought *(worrying and fretting)* can add one cubit unto his stature? *(Whatever is going to happen cannot be stopped by worry; and if it doesn't happen, there is nothing to worry about. For His Children, the Lord always fills in the bottom line.)*

28 And why do you take thought *(worry)* for *(about)* raiment *(clothes)*? Consider the lilies of the field, how they grow; they toil not, neither do they spin *(the man grows the flax [toil] the woman weaves it [spins]; the statement is meant to proclaim the fact that the beauty of the lily has nothing to do with its effort, but is given completely by the Creator):*

29 And yet I say unto you, That even Solomon in all his glory was not arrayed like one of these *(it is said that the lilies of Israel had brilliant coloring, and especially the purple and white Huleh Lily found in Nazareth).*

30 Wherefore, if *(since)* God so clothed the grass of the field *(is meant to portray God's guarantee),* which today is, and tomorrow is cast into the oven *(portrays how inconsequential is this part of His Creation, and yet, how much care He expends on it),* shall *He* not much more *clothe* you, O you of little faith? *(We are told here the reason for our lack; it is "little faith"; because God is Faithful, He can be trusted fully to completely carry out His commitments*

to us in Christ [I Cor. 1:9; 10:13; II Cor. 1:18; I Thess. 5:24; II Thess. 3:3; etc.].)

31 Therefore take no thought (don't worry), **saying, What shall we eat? or, What shall we drink? or, Wherewithal shall we be clothed?** (The Greek Text actually means that even one anxious thought is forbidden. Such shows a distrust of the Lord.)

32 (For after all these things do the Gentiles seek:) (Gentiles had no part in God's Covenant with Israel; consequently, they had no part in God's economy, and, basically, had to fend for themselves) **for your Heavenly Father knows that you have need of all these things** (the phrase is meant to express the contrast between those who do not know the Lord and those who do; if we live for Him, ever seeking His Will, we have the guarantee of His Word, which He will provide for us; is God's Word good enough? I think it is!).

33 But seek you first the Kingdom of God, and His Righteousness (this gives the "condition" for God's Blessings; His interests are to be "first"); **and all these things shall be added unto you** (this is the "guarantee" of God's Provision).

34 Take therefore no thought for the morrow (don't worry about the future): **for the morrow shall take thought for the things of itself** (this is meant to refer back to Verse 27). **Sufficient unto the day is the evil thereof** (this means that we should handle daily difficulties in Faith, and have Faith for the future that the present difficulties will not grow into larger ones; we have God's assurance that they won't, that is, if we will sufficiently believe Him).

CHAPTER 7
(A.D. 31)
JUDGING OTHERS

JUDGE not, that you be not judged (this statement by Christ harks back to Verses 25 through 34 of the previous Chapter; the idea is, God may permit poverty to test His Child, but fellow Believers are not to err, as Job's friends did, and believe the trial to be a judgment for secret sin; as well, the word, "judging," as used here, covers every aspect of dealing with our fellowman).

2 For with what judgment you judge, you shall be judged (whatever motive we ascribe to others, such motive will ultimately be ascribed to us): **and with what measure you mete, it shall be measured to you again** (a double emphasis is given here in order to proclaim the seriousness of the Words of our Lord; when we judge others, we are judging ourselves).

3 And why do you behold the mote that is in your brother's eye (the Believer is not to be looking for fault or wrongdoing in the lives of fellow Believers), **but consider not the beam that is in your own eye?** (We have plenty in our own lives which need eliminating, without looking for faults in others. The "mote" and "beam" are contrasted! The constant judging of others portrays the fact that we are much worse off than the one we are judging.)

4 Or how will you say to your brother, Let me pull out the mote out of your eye (the seriousness of setting ourselves up as judge, jury, and executioner); **and, behold, a beam is in your own eye?** (Once again draws attention to the fact that the person doing the judging is in far worse spiritual condition than the one being judged.)

5 You hypocrite (aptly describes such a person), **first cast out the beam out of your own eye; and then you shall see clearly to cast out the mote out of your brother's eye** (the very fact that we do not address ourselves, but rather others, portrays the truth that our personal situation is worse; when we properly analyze ourselves, then, and only then, can we "see clearly"; this is speaking of character assassination and not the correction of doctrine).

6 Give not that which is holy unto the dogs, neither cast you your pearls before swine (there may be problems in the Church, as Verses 1 through 5 proclaim, but still, the Church is never to reach out into the world, i.e., "dogs," for help in order to solve its internal disputes), **lest they trample them under their feet, and turn again and rend you** (no help will be coming from the world, but rather destruction.; we are to take our problems to the Lord, obeying His Word, concerning disputes [Mat. 18:15-17]).

GETTING THINGS FROM GOD

7 Ask, and it shall be given you (if we ask for wisdom as it regards the settling of disputes, or for anything, it shall be given); **seek, and you shall find** (the answer may not be forthcoming immediately; therefore, we should "seek" to know the reason why); **knock, and it shall be opened unto you** (we must make sure that it is His door on which we are knocking; if it is, it definitely will be opened to us):

8 For every one who asks receives; and he who seeks finds; and to him who knocks it shall be opened (assumes that the person's heart

is sincere before the Lord).

9 Or what man is there of you, whom if his son ask bread, will he give him a stone? *(Even a human being will not do such, much less God!)*

10 Or if he asks a fish, will he give him a serpent? *(If, in fact, what we are asking for is not God's Will, and would turn out to be a "stone," or "serpent," He will guard us from receiving such, and during the time of waiting and consecration, will show us what we truly need.)*

11 If you then, being evil *(refers to parents sometimes giving their children things which are not good for them, as well as things which are good)*, know how to give good gifts unto your children, how much more shall your Father which is in Heaven give good things to them who ask Him? *(The Lord gives only good things.)*

THE GOLDEN RULE

12 Therefore all things whatsoever you would that men should do to you, do you even so to them; for this is the Law and the Prophets *(this rule does not authorize capricious benevolent action, but only what is reasonable and morally helpful, and controlled by Divine imitation [Mat. 5:48]; this principle of action and mode of life is, in fact, the sum of all Bible teaching).*

THE NARROW WAY AND THE BROAD WAY

13 Enter you in at the strait gate *(this is the Door, Who is Jesus [Jn. 10:1])*: for wide *is* the gate, and broad *is* the way, that leads to destruction, and many there be which go in thereat *(proclaims the fact of many and varied religions of the world, which are false, and lead to eternal hellfire)*:

14 Because strait *is* the gate, and narrow *is* the way, which leads unto life, and few there be that find it *(every contrite heart earnestly desires to be among the "few"; the requirements are greater than most are willing to accept).*

FALSE PROPHETS AND DECEPTIONS

15 Beware of false prophets, which come to you in sheep's clothing, but inwardly they are ravening wolves *("beware of false prophets" is said in the sternest of measures! there will be and are false prophets, and are some of Satan's greatest weapons).*

16 You shall know them by their fruits *(this is the test as given by Christ as it regards*

identification of false prophets and false apostles). Do men gather grapes of thorns, or figs of thistles? *(It is impossible for false doctrine, generated by false prophets, to bring forth good fruit.)*

17 Even so every good tree brings forth good fruit; but a corrupt tree brings forth evil fruit *(the good fruit is Christlikeness, while the evil fruit is self-likeness).*

18 A good tree cannot bring forth evil fruit, neither *can* a corrupt tree bring forth good fruit *(the "good tree" is the Cross, while the "corrupt tree" pertains to all of that which is other than the Cross).*

19 Every tree that brings not forth good fruit is hewn down, and cast into the fire *(Judgment will ultimately come on all so-called gospel, other than the Cross [Rom. 1:18]).*

20 Wherefore by their fruits you shall know them *(the acid test).*

AGAINST MERE PROFESSION

21 Not every one who says unto Me, Lord, Lord, shall enter into the Kingdom of Heaven *(the repetition of the word "Lord" expresses astonishment, as if to say: "Are we to be disowned?")*; but he who does the Will of My Father which is in Heaven *(what is the Will of the Father? Verse 24 tells us).*

22 Many will say to Me in that day, Lord, Lord, have we not Prophesied in Your Name? and in Your Name have cast out devils? and in Your Name done many wonderful works? *(These things are not the criteria, but rather Faith in Christ and what Christ has done for us at the Cross [Eph. 2:8-9, 13-18]. The Word of God alone is to be the judge of doctrine.)*

23 And then will I profess unto them, I never knew you *(again we say, the criteria alone is Christ and Him Crucified [I Cor. 1:23])*: depart from Me, you who work iniquity *(we have access to God only through Christ, and access to Christ only through the Cross, and access to the Cross only through a denial of self [Lk. 9:23]; any other Message is Judged by God as "iniquity," and cannot be a part of Christ [I Cor. 1:17]).*

THE TWO BUILDERS: A WISE MAN AND A FOOLISH MAN

24 Therefore whosoever hears these sayings of Mine, and does them, I will liken him unto a wise man, which built his house upon a rock *(the "Rock" is Christ Jesus, and the Foundation is the Cross [Gal. 1:8-9]):*

25 And the rain descended, and the floods came, and the winds blew, and beat upon that house; and it fell not; for it was founded upon a rock *(the Foundation of our belief system must be Christ and Him Crucified [Gal. 6:14])*.

26 And every one who hears these sayings of Mine, and does them not, shall be likened unto a foolish man, which built his house upon the sand *(but for the foundation, this house looked the same as the house that was built upon the rock)*:

27 And the rain descended, and the floods came, and the winds blew, and beat upon that house; and it fell: and great was the fall of it *(while the sun shines, both houses look good; but, when adversity comes and come it shall, Faith, which is alone in Christ and Him Crucified will stand [I Cor. 1:18])*.

28 And it came to pass, when Jesus had ended these sayings *(ended the Sermon on the Mount)*, the people were astonished at His Doctrine *(this Message proclaimed the True intent of the Law of Moses, and, above all, laid the Foundation for the New Covenant)*:

29 For He taught them as *one* having authority *(refers to Divine Authority, which He had by the Power of the Holy Spirit; this Sermon and that of Lk., Chpt. 6 are probably one and the same; the Holy Spirit lays the emphasis here on the heart, while in Luke, emphasis is laid on actions produced by the heart; consequently, the distinction between "standing" and "state" is apparent)*, and not as the Scribes *(those who claimed to be expert in the Law of Moses)*.

CHAPTER 8
(A.D. 31)
JESUS HEALS A LEPER

WHEN He was come down from the mountain *(this particular Message is now finished)*, great multitudes followed Him *(this is the result of the "authority" with which He taught)*.

2 And, behold, there came a leper *(leprosy was then considered a symbol of sin)* and worshipped Him *(did so as Lord, recognizing Him as the Messiah)*, saying, Lord, if You will, You can make me clean *(Christ Alone can cleanse from sin, of which leprosy was a type)*.

3 And Jesus put forth *His* Hand, and touched him, saying, I will; be you clean *(this statement forever settles the Will of God as it regards Salvation and Healing; His touch did not cleanse him, but rather His Word; according to the*

Greek, *by the time His Hand touched the man he was already clean; so, Jesus did not break the Law by touching a leper)*. And immediately his leprosy was cleansed *(immediately upon the word "I will" being spoken)*.

4 And Jesus said unto him, See that you tell no man *(the Mission of our Lord in His First Advent was to deal with sin and suffer its judgment at Calvary; He suppressed anything that would hinder that purpose of Grace, and so forbade the man to publish the fact of his healing)*; but go your way, show yourself to the Priest, and offer the gift that Moses Commanded, for a Testimony unto them *(the Law of the Cleansing of the leper is found in Lev., Chpts. 13 and 14)*.

HEALING OF THE CAPTAIN'S SERVANT

5 And when Jesus was entered into Capernaum *(His Headquarters)*, there came unto Him a Centurion *(a Roman Captain over 100 men)*, beseeching Him *(strongly requesting of Him, begging Him; Jesus came not only to cleanse Israel, but to liberate the Gentile as well, and, accordingly, the servant of the Roman officer was set free from his malady)*,

6 And saying, Lord *(the leprous Jew had called Jesus, "Lord," and now, the Gentile Centurion calls Him "Lord," proclaiming Him Lord of All)*, my servant lies at home sick of the palsy, grievously tormented *(this disease was a paralysis with contraction of the joints, accompanied with intense suffering; the man's life was threatened)*.

7 And Jesus said unto him, I will come and heal him *(the emphasis is not on the coming, but, instead, on the One Who is coming, Namely Christ; the "I" is emphatic, meaning, "I can, and I will!" once again, the "I will" settles the question regarding Divine Healing)*.

8 The Centurion answered and said, Lord, I am not worthy that You should come under my roof *(probably his referral to being a Gentile)*: but speak the Word only, and my servant shall be healed *(the Word of Christ was all that was needed, and the soldier knew that)*.

9 For I am a man under authority, having soldiers under me: and I say to this *man*, Go, and he goes; and to another, Come, and he comes; and to my servant, Do this, and he does it *(the intelligence of this Centurion was remarkable; he argued that the soldiers had to obey him because in his person resided the authority of the Emperor, and, similarly, disease obeyed*

Jesus because in Him was the Authority of God).

10 When Jesus heard *it*, He marveled *(records one of the only two times He marveled; the "faith" of this Gentile, and the "unbelief" of the Jews [Mk. 6:6]),* and said to them that followed, Verily I say unto you, I have not found so great faith, no, not in Israel *(this is a portrayal of the fact that the Gentiles would accept Christ, while Israel would not).*

11 And I say unto you *(proclaims the acceptance of Christ by the Gentiles, and His rejection by the Jews),* That many *(Gentiles)* shall come from the east and west, and shall sit down with Abraham, and Isaac, and Jacob, in the Kingdom of Heaven *(would come into the Abrahamic Covenant [Gen. 12:1-3; Gal. 3:14]).*

12 But the children of the Kingdom *(Israel)* shall be cast out into outer darkness: there shall be weeping and gnashing of teeth *(would die without God, thereby going to Hell, because of rejecting Christ).*

13 And Jesus said unto the Centurion, Go your way; and as you have believed *(believe, not doing),* *so* be it done unto you. And his servant was healed in the selfsame hour.

PETER'S MOTHER-IN-LAW HEALED

14 And when Jesus was come into Peter's house *(in Capernaum),* He *(Jesus)* saw his wife's mother laid *(Peter's mother-in-law),* and sick of a fever.

15 And He *(Jesus)* touched her hand, and the fever left her *(immediately)*: and she arose, and ministered unto them *(prepared a meal).*

DEMONS CAST OUT; MANY HEALED

16 When the evening was come *(when the Sabbath ended at sunset),* they brought unto Him *(Jesus)* many who were possessed with devils *(demons)*: and He cast out the spirits with *His* Word, and healed all who were sick:

17 That it might be fulfilled which was spoken by the Prophet Isaiah *(Isa. 53:4),* saying, Himself took our infirmities, and bear *our* sicknesses *(took our sin penalty and sicknesses).*

TESTS OF DISCIPLESHIP

18 Now when Jesus saw great multitudes about Him, He gave commandment *(instructions)* to depart unto the other side *(the eastern side of the Sea of Galilee).*

19 And a certain Scribe *(expert in the Law of*

Moses) came, and said unto Him, Master, I will follow You wherever You go.

20 And Jesus said unto him, The foxes have holes, and the birds of the air *have* nests; but the Son of Man has nowhere to lay *His* head *(the Earth had room for foxes and birds, but not Christ; "Son of Man" refers to the fact that He will take back dominion, which was done at the Cross).*

21 And another of His Disciples *(not one of the Twelve)* said unto Him, Lord, suffer me first to go and bury my father *(take care of my father until he dies).*

22 But Jesus said unto him *(tone of censure),* Follow Me *(nothing must stand in the way)*; and let the dead bury their dead *(let the spiritually dead bury their physically dead).*

JESUS STILLS THE STORM

23 And when He was entered into a ship, His Disciples followed Him,

24 And, behold, there arose a great tempest in the sea *(great storm),* insomuch that the ship was covered with the waves: but He was asleep.

25 And His Disciples came to *Him*, and awoke Him, saying, Lord, save us: we perish *(He Alone can save us).*

26 And He said unto them *(the reason for their dilemma),* Why are you fearful, O you of little faith *(misplaced faith)*? Then He arose, and rebuked the winds and the sea *(great power)*; and there was a great calm *("O you of little faith" occurs four times [care, Mat. 6:30; fear, Mat. 8:26; doubt, Mat. 14:31; reasoning, Mat. 16:8]).*

27 But the men marveled *(were astonished),* saying, What manner of man is this, that even the winds and the sea obey Him! *(He is man, but as well He is God.)*

THE GERGESENE DEMONIACS

28 And when He was come to the other side *(eastern side of Galilee)* into the country of the Gergesenes, there met Him two possessed with devils *(demons),* coming out of the tombs *(where they lived),* exceeding fierce *(maniacs),* so that no man might pass by that way.

29 And, behold, they cried out *(speaking to Christ),* saying, What have we to do with You, Jesus, Thou Son of God? *(The demons had more intelligence than do the disciples of modern thought.)* *Are You* come here to torment us before the time? *(Judgment [Rev. 20:1-3].)*

30 And there was a good way off from them an herd of many swine (hogs) feeding.

31 So the devils (demons) besought Him, saying, If You cast us out (since You are casting us out), suffer us to go away into the herd of swine (leave the men and inhabit the hogs).

32 And He said unto them, Go (proclaims His approval). And when they were come out, they went into the herd of swine: and, behold, the whole herd of swine ran violently down a steep place into the sea (the Sea of Galilee), and perished in the waters.

33 And they that kept them fled (quickly), and went their ways into the city, and told every thing, and what was befallen to the possessed of the devils (his complete deliverance).

34 And, behold, the whole city came out to meet Jesus: and when they saw Him (took a little while to find Him), they besought Him that he would depart out of their coasts (borders).

CHAPTER 9
(A.D. 31)
JESUS HEALS A PARALYZED MAN

AND He entered into a ship, and passed over and came into His Own city (Capernaum).

2 And, behold, they brought to him a man sick of the palsy (paralyzed), lying on a bed: and Jesus seeing their faith (the action of faith) said unto the sick of the palsy; Son, be of good cheer; your sins be forgiven you (the sickness was caused by sin).

3 And, behold, certain of the Scribes (experts in the Law of Moses) said within themselves (murmured among themselves), This man blasphemes (they did not recognize Him as Lord).

4 And Jesus knowing their thoughts said (revealed to Him by the Spirit), Why do you think evil in your hearts? (Unbelief!)

5 For whether is easier, to say, Your sins be forgiven you; or to say, Arise, and walk? (Original sin and its corresponding result, sickness.)

6 But that you may know that the Son of Man has power on earth to forgive sins (proclaims His Deity), (then said He to the sick of the palsy,) Arise, take up your bed, and go unto your house (power to forgive sins and heal).

7 And he arose (the physical action of a spiritual result), and departed to his house.

8 But when the multitudes saw it (healing of the man), they marvelled, and glorified God, which had given such power unto men (the multitudes still didn't understand that He was the Messiah).

THE CALLING OF MATTHEW

9 And as Jesus passed forth from thence, He saw a man, named Matthew (the Spirit directed Him), sitting at the receipt of custom (Matthew was a tax collector — a publican): and He (Jesus) said unto him (Mathew), Follow Me (the call to be one of the Twelve). And he arose (immediately), and followed Him.

10 And it came to pass (after a few days), as Jesus sat at meat (a meal) in the house (Matthew's house), behold, many Publicans (tax collectors) and sinners came and sat down with Him and His Disciples (on His terms, and not on theirs).

11 And when the Pharisees saw it (heard of it a little later), they said unto His Disciples, Why does your Master eat with Publicans and sinners (self-righteousness)?

12 But when Jesus heard that (a short time later), He said unto them (His Disciples), They who be whole need not a physician, but they who are sick (He came for sinners, which includes all).

13 But go you and learn what that means, I will have mercy, and not sacrifice (the keeping of rituals, i.e., sacrifices, won't save; asking for mercy will): for I am not come to call the Righteous (self-righteous), but sinners to Repentance.

FASTING

14 Then came to Him the Disciples of John (John was now in prison), saying, Why do we and the Pharisees fast often, but Your Disciples fast not? (They fasted twice a week.)

15 And Jesus said unto them (introduction of the New Covenant), Can the children of the bridechamber mourn, as long as the bridegroom is with them? (Jesus is the Bridegroom, so it was not the time to fast) but the days will come, when the Bridegroom shall be taken from them (Death, Resurrection, and Ascension of Christ), and then shall they fast (fasting pictures something wrong that needs remedying, which the Coming of Christ will address).

16 No man puts a piece of new cloth (New Covenant) onto an old garment (Old Covenant), for that which is put in to fill it up takes from the garment (a patch), and the rent is made worse (to revert to Law is to worsen the situation; the Cross is the New Covenant).

17 Neither do men put new wine *(New Covenant)* into old bottles *(skins)*: else the bottles break *(new wine splits the wineskin)*, and the wine runs out *(reverting to Law frustrates Grace [Gal. 2:21])*, and the bottles *(skins)* perish *(Law destroys Grace)*: but they put new wine into new bottles *(new skins)*, and both are preserved *(the New Covenant can only function by Faith [new skins] and not law)*.

MIRACLES

18 While He spoke these things unto them *(subject matter of previous Verse)*, behold, there came a certain Ruler *(Jarius)*, and worshipped Him *(as Lord and Messiah)*, saying, My daughter is even now dead *(is dying)*: but come and lay Your hand upon her, and she shall live.

19 And Jesus arose, and followed him *(immediately)*, and *so did* His Disciples.

20 And, behold *(an interruption)*, a woman, which was diseased with an issue of blood *(physically and ceremonially unclean [Lev. 15:25] probably from a female disorder)* twelve years, came behind *Him*, and touched the hem *(border)* of His garment *(a blue and white tassel worn at the four corners of the upper garment [Num. 15:37-41])*:

21 For she said within herself *(inasmuch as she could not get a private audience)*, If I may but touch His garment, I shall be whole *(her faith)*.

22 But Jesus turned Him about *(in response to her touch)*, and when He saw her *(took a moment to find her)*, He said, Daughter *(a change of relationship from "woman" to "daughter")*, be of good comfort *(don't fear)*; your Faith has made you whole *(if He doesn't touch you, you can touch Him)*. And the woman was made whole from that hour *(tradition says her name was Veronica)*.

23 And when Jesus came into the Ruler's house *(Jarius, ruler of the Synagogue)*, and saw the minstrels *(paid mourners, which was the custom then; by now the child had died)* and the people making a noise *(making lamentation over the death of the child)*,

24 He said unto them, Give place *(leave the room where the child was)*: for the maid is not dead, but asleep *(will not remain dead)*. And they laughed Him to scorn *(they knew the child was dead, and surmised that He could do nothing)*.

25 But when the people were put forth *(they didn't go quietly)*, He went in *(He wouldn't go in until the skeptics left)*, and took her by the hand, and the maid arose *(He raised her from the dead; life touched death; no one died or stayed dead in His Presence)*.

26 And the fame hereof went abroad into all that land *(all over Israel and beyond)*.

THE BLIND HEALED

27 And when Jesus departed thence *(left the home of Jarius)*, two blind men followed Him, crying, and saying, *Thou* Son of David *(the Messianic title)*, have mercy on us *(a cry to which He always responds)*.

28 And when He was come into the house *(probably the house of Peter)*, the blind men came to Him *(they no doubt heard He had raised the dead)*: and Jesus said unto them, Do you believe that I am able to do this? *(He only required Faith.)* They said unto Him, Yes, Lord.

29 Then touched He their eyes *(light touched darkness)*, saying, According to your Faith be it unto you *(the Law of Faith)*.

30 And their eyes were opened *(instantly)*; and Jesus straitly *(strongly)* charged them, saying, See *that* no man know *it* *(His fame was already such that Israel would shortly clamor to make Him king, but for all the wrong reasons)*.

31 But they, when they were departed, spread abroad His fame in all that country *(at least they spread His fame and not theirs)*.

DUMB MAN HEALED

32 As they went out *(from the house, probably Peter's)*, behold, they brought to him a dumb man possessed with a devil *(a demon spirit had caused the dumbness)*.

33 And when the devil *(demon)* was cast out, the dumb spoke: and the multitudes marvelled, saying, It was never so seen in Israel *(demon spirits are the cause of many things)*.

34 But the Pharisees said *(strongest religious group in Israel, and were bitterly opposed to Christ)*, He casts out devils *(demons)* through the prince of the devils *(by the power of Satan)*.

35 And Jesus went about all the cities and villages, teaching *(explaining truth)* in their Synagogues, and preaching *(proclaiming truth)* the Gospel of the Kingdom *(good news)*, and healing every sickness and every disease

among the people (*preaching, teaching, and healing are the Gospel program*).

LABOURERS NEEDED

36 But when He saw the multitudes, He was moved with compassion on them (*had great pity and sympathy*), because they fainted, and were scattered abroad, as sheep having no shepherd (*no spiritual leadership*).

37 Then said He unto His Disciples, The harvest (*souls to be saved*) truly *is* plenteous, but the labourers *are* few (*not many Preachers of Righteousness*);

38 Pray you (*intercede*) therefore the Lord of the Harvest (*Christ is the Lord*), that He will send forth labourers into His Harvest (*the harvest of souls is His, and must be gathered in His way*).

CHAPTER 10
(A.D. 31)
THE TWELVE

AND when He had called unto *Him* His Twelve Disciples (*for instruction and a special mission*), He gave them power *against* unclean spirits, to cast them out, and to heal all manner of sickness and all manner of disease (*all such power comes from God*).

2 Now the names of the Twelve Apostles are these; The first, Simon, who is called Peter, and Andrew his brother; James *the son* of Zebedee, and John his brother (*none of the twelve were of the aristocracy of Israel*);

3 Philip, and Bartholomew; Thomas, and Matthew the publican (*tax collector*); James *the son* of Alphaeus, and Lebbaeus whose surname (*last name*) was Thaddaeus;

4 Simon the Canaanite (*the zealot*), and Judas Iscariot, who also betrayed him (*eleven were Galileans; one, Judas Iscariot, was a Judaean*).

THE MISSION

5 These Twelve Jesus sent forth, and Commanded them, saying, Go not into the way of the Gentiles, and into *any* city of the Samaritans enter you not (*Israel must be addressed first; after the Cross, Resurrection, and Ascension, the Command would be to go into all the world [Mk. 16:15]*):

6 But go rather to the lost sheep of the House of Israel (*notice the "lost sheep," which refutes unconditional eternal security*.

7 And as you go, preach, saying, The Kingdom of Heaven is at hand (*the Kingdom was rejected by Israel*).

8 Heal the sick, cleanse the lepers, raise the dead, cast out devils (*demons*): freely you have received, freely give (*a monetary charge is never to be made*).

9 Provide neither gold, nor silver, nor brass in your purses (*the Lord is to be depended upon for everything*),

10 Nor scrip for *your* journey, neither two coats, neither shoes, nor yet staves: for the workman is worthy of his meat (*it is criminal to receive the fruit of the labor, without labor*).

11 And into whatsoever city or town you shall enter, enquire who in it is worthy (*of like faith*); and there abide till you go thence (*work with them*).

12 And when you come into an house, salute it (*bestow peace*).

13 And if the house be worthy (*of like faith*), let your peace (*blessing*) come upon it: but if it be not worthy (*proves not to be of like faith*), let your peace return to you (*don't bless it*).

14 And whosoever shall not receive you, nor hear your words, when you depart out of that house or city, shake off the dust of your feet (*a curse is now upon such*).

15 Verily I say unto you (*extremely important announcement*), It shall be more tolerable (*degrees of punishment*) for the land of Sodom and Gomorrha in the Day of Judgment (*Great White Throne Judgment, Rev., Chpt. 20*), than for that city.

PERSECUTION

16 Behold, I send you forth (*Christ does the sending*) as sheep in the midst of wolves (*most wolves are in the Church*): be you therefore wise as serpents, and harmless as doves.

17 But beware of men (*religious apostates*): for they will deliver you up to the Councils, and they will scourge you in their Synagogues (*the religious world is opposed to Christ and the Cross*);

ENMITY

18 And you shall be brought before Governors and Kings (*persecution by the Church is often followed by that of the State*) for My sake (*animosity against Christ*), for a testimony against them (*take the opportunity to witness to them*) and the Gentiles (*a prediction of the soon*

to come Church).

19 But when they deliver you up *(not "if" but "when")*, take no thought how or what you shall speak *(defense is left up to the Lord)*: for it shall be given you in that same hour what you shall speak *(unction of the Spirit)*.

20 For it is not you who speaks, but the Spirit of your Father *(Holy Spirit)* which speaks in you *("in you," Baptism with the Spirit [Acts 2:4])*.

21 And the brother shall deliver up the brother to death, and the father the child: and the children shall rise up against *their* parents, and cause them to be put to death *(animosity against Christ and the Cross is greater than love for loved ones)*.

22 And you shall be hated of all *men* for My Name's sake *(the offense of the Cross)*: but he who endures to the end shall be saved *(persecution will continue until the Second Coming)*.

23 But when they persecute you in this city *(the certainty of opposition)*, flee you into another *(keep evangelizing)*: for verily I say unto you *(remember this)*, You shall not have gone over the cities of Israel *(due to persecution, which was the case)*, till the Son of Man be come *(boldly announcing the Second Coming)*.

INSTRUCTION

24 The disciple is not above *his* master *(as they persecuted Christ, they will persecute His followers)*, nor the servant above his lord *(said in two ways to emphasize certitude of fulfillment)*.

25 It is enough for the disciple that he be as his master, and the servant as his lord *(the Believer must experience the same opposition as his Lord)*. If they have called the master of the house Beelzebub *(of the Devil)*, how much more *shall they call* them of his household?

26 Fear them not therefore *(fear must not guide the Message)*: for there is nothing covered, that shall not be revealed; and hid, that shall not be known *(a reckoning is coming)*.

27 What I tell you in darkness *(in prayer)*, *that* speak you in light *(openly)*: and what you hear in the ear *(what the Spirit reveals)*, *that* preach you upon the housetops *(publicly)*.

28 And fear not them which kill the body, but are not able to kill the soul *(don't fear men)*: but rather fear Him *(God)* which is able to destroy both soul and body in hell.

29 Are not two sparrows sold for a farthing *(cheap)*? and one of them shall not fall on the ground without your Father *(without His Knowledge or Will)*.

30 But the very hairs of your head are all numbered *(seek to please God Who knows all things, and can do all things)*.

31 Fear you not therefore *(what do we have to fear, serving One Who is all-knowing, and all-powerful?)*, you are of more value than many sparrows *(if God takes care of them, and He does, will He not take care of you?)*.

32 Whosoever therefore shall confess Me before men *(to tie man to God)*, him will I confess also before My Father which is in Heaven *(upon one's confession of Christ, a corresponding confession is made by Christ)*.

33 But whosoever shall deny Me before men *(Christ Alone is the focal point)*, him will I also deny before my Father which is in Heaven.

OPPOSITION

34 Think not that I am come to send peace on earth *(the entrance of Christ into the world manifests the evil of the heart)*: I came not to send peace, but a sword *(the sword against the Righteous will be the response of religious reprobates)*.

35 For I am come to set a man at variance *(odds)* against his father, and the daughter against her mother, and the daughter-in-law against her mother-in-law.

36 And a man's foes *shall be* they of his own household *(speaks not only of immediate family, but at times, of one's Church family)*.

DISCIPLESHIP

37 He who loves father or mother more than Me is not worthy of Me *(Christ must come first in all things)*: and he who loves son or daughter more than Me is not worthy of Me *(worthy to receive what I did for him at the Cross)*.

38 And he who takes not his cross *(total "Faith" in the Cross to the exclusion of everything else)*, and follows after Me *(we can only follow Him by the "Way" of the Cross)*, is not worthy of Me *(not worthy of the blessings afforded by the "victory" of the Cross)*.

39 He who finds his life shall lose it *(he who refuses the Cross loses his life)*: and he who loses his life for My sake shall find it *(places his life into Christ, which is done by the Cross [Rom. 6:3-5])*.

REWARDS

40 He who receives you receives Me *(he who*

receives *My Messenger receives Me*), and he who receives Me receives Him *(God the Father)* Who sent Me.

41 He who receives a Prophet in the name of a Prophet *(because he is a true Prophet)* shall receive a Prophet's reward; and he who receives a Righteous man in the name of a Righteous man *(because he is a Righteous man)* shall receive a Righteous man's reward *(one on a Righteous Mission)*.

42 And whosoever shall give to drink unto one of these little ones *(newest Believer)* a cup of cold *water* only in the name of a Disciple *(because he is a follower of Christ)*, verily I say unto you, he shall in no wise lose his reward *(a reward is guaranteed)*.

CHAPTER 11
(A.D. 31)
JOHN THE BAPTIST

AND it came to pass, when Jesus had made an end of commanding His Twelve Disciples *(refers to the teaching of the previous Chapter; He commanded, which is different than suggesting)*, He departed thence to teach and to preach *(to explain and to proclaim)* in their cities.

2 Now when John had heard in the prison the works of Christ *(John is now imprisoned, and discouraged)*, he sent two of his disciples *(sent them to Jesus)*,

3 And said unto Him, Are You He Who should come, or do we look for another? *(Doubt is the nemesis of Faith, and plagues every Christian at one time or the other.)*

JESUS' ANSWER TO JOHN THE BAPTIST

4 Jesus answered and said unto them *(if we ask, we will receive [Mat. 7:8])*, Go and shew John again those things which you do hear and see *(the Divine answer referred him to Isaiah 35:5-6; 61:1-2)*:

5 The blind receive their sight, and the lame walk, the lepers are cleansed, and the deaf hear, the dead are raised up, and the poor have the Gospel preached to them *(Jesus called John's attention away from the political scene — restoring at that time the Kingdom to Israel — to the true purpose of His Mission, the restoration of the individual)*.

6 And blessed is *he*, whosoever shall not be offended in Me *(the Lord adds another Beatitude to those given in Chapter 5)*.

JESUS' TESTIMONY OF JOHN THE BAPTIST

7 And as they departed *(the two disciples of John the Baptist)*, Jesus began to say unto the multitudes concerning John, What went you out into the wilderness to see? A reed shaken with the wind? *(Despite appearances — John being in prison — Jesus proclaims what John really is.)*

8 But what went you out for to see? A man clothed in soft raiment? behold, they who wear soft *clothing* are in kings' houses *(if Herod's gold could have bought John, he would not now be in prison)*.

9 But what went you out for to see? *(The third time this question is posed.)* A Prophet? yes, I say unto you, and more than a Prophet *(more than all Prophets before him)*.

10 For this is *he*, of whom it is written *(proclaims John as the last of the Old Testament Prophets)*, Behold, I send My messenger before Your face *(John was that messenger)*, which shall prepare Your way before You *(John prepared the way for Christ)*.

11 Verily I say unto you, Among them who are born of women there has not risen a greater than John the Baptist *(places John at the forefront of the Prophets)*: notwithstanding he who is least in the Kingdom of Heaven is greater than he *(speaks of the New Covenant [Heb. 8:6])*.

12 And from the days of John the Baptist *(John introduced "the Kingdom of Heaven")* until now *(speaks of Christ Who would bring in the New Covenant)* the Kingdom of Heaven suffers violence *(the Crucifixion, the price that Christ paid [Gen. 3:15])*, and the violent take it by force *(speaks of Christ taking the dominion away from Satan, who had taken it from Adam [Col. 2:14-15])*.

13 For all the Prophets and the Law prophesied until John *(the Prophets and the Law testified of the coming Christ, and John was the last of those Prophets)*.

14 And if you will receive *it (if you will receive the Kingdom of Heaven)*, this is Elijah, which was for to come *(had the nation received John, he would have represented Elijah to them, and would have been reckoned by God as Elijah [Mal. 4:5-6])*.

15 He who has ears to hear, let him hear *(Israel would not hear)*.

16 But whereunto shall I liken this generation? *(That generation most privileged, rejected Christ.)* It is like unto children sitting in the

markets, and calling unto their fellows,

17 And saying, We have piped unto you, and ye have not danced; we have mourned unto you, and ye have not lamented (*Israel refused to mourn with the Baptist when he demanded Repentance, or to rejoice with Christ*).

18 For John came neither eating nor drinking, and they say, He has a devil (*demon — what the religious said; John had no social life*).

19 The Son of Man came eating and drinking, and they say, Behold a man gluttonous, and a winebibber, a friend of Publicans and sinners (*this is what Christ's enemies said of Him, and not what was actually true*). But wisdom is justified of her children (*wisdom justified both courses, that of John and Christ. Israel rejected both*).

JUDGMENT

20 Then began He to upbraid the cities wherein most of His mighty works were done, because they repented not (*He is speaking mostly of the religious leaders of these places*):

21 Woe unto you, Chorazin! woe unto thee, Bethsaida! for if the mighty works, which were done in you, had been done in Tyre and Sidon, they would have repented long ago in sackcloth and ashes (*what a condemnation of Israel!*).

22 But I say unto you, It shall be more tolerable (*different degrees of punishment*) for Tyre and Sidon at the day of judgment (*Great White Throne Judgment*), than for you (*the pronoun "you" is emphatic; in the Mind of God, the "Judgment" has already been pronounced*).

23 And you, Capernaum (*"you" again emphatic, reserving this city for the worst judgment of all*), which are exalted unto Heaven (*exalted not because of Christ, but rather because of its economic prosperity*), shall be brought down to hell (*most of its inhabitants went to Hell*): for if the mighty works, which had been done in you, had been done in Sodom, it would have remained until this day (*what an indictment on Capernaum!*).

24 But I say unto you, That it shall be more tolerable for the land of Sodom, in the day of judgment, than for you (*the Christ-rejecter is morally lower than the idolaters of Tyre and Sidon, or the citizens of Sodom, and will be punished accordingly*).

REJOICING OVER DIVINE REVELATION

25 At that time Jesus answered and said, I thank you, O Father, Lord of Heaven and Earth, because You have hid these things from the wise and prudent (*a judicial judgment on the Religious Leaders of Israel*), and have revealed them unto babes (*to other than the religious leaders*).

26 Even so, Father (*His Own Personal Father*): for so it seemed good in Your sight (*the Gospel is hidden to those who reject Christ and the Cross whomever they might be, and revealed to those who accept Christ and the Cross; this is "good" in God's sight [Jn. 3:16]*).

27 All things are delivered unto Me of My Father (*"All things" mean that Christ is both Saviour and Judge*): and no man knows the Son, but the Father (*Christ is an eternal Member of the Godhead*); neither knows any man the Father, save the Son (*the only way to God the Father is through Christ [Jn. 14:6]*), and *he* to whomsoever the Son will reveal *Him* (*Salvation is never a matter of education but of Revelation*).

THE GREAT INVITATION

28 Come unto Me (*is meant by Jesus to reveal Himself as the Giver of Salvation*), all *you* who labor and are heavy laden (*trying to earn Salvation by works*), and I will give you rest (*this "rest" can only be found by placing one's Faith in Christ and what He has done for us at the Cross [Gal. 5:1-6]*).

29 Take My yoke upon you (*the "yoke" of the "Cross" [Lk. 9:23]*), and learn of Me (*learn of His Sacrifice [Rom. 6:3-5]*); for I am meek and lowly in heart (*the only thing that our Lord Personally said of Himself*): and ye shall find rest unto your souls (*the soul can find rest only in the Cross*).

30 For My yoke *is* easy, and My burden is light (*what He requires of us is very little, just to have Faith in Him, and His Sacrificial Atoning work*).

CHAPTER 12
(A.D. 31)
JESUS IS LORD OF THE SABBATH

AT that time Jesus went on the Sabbath day through the corn (*either wheat or barley*); and His Disciples were hungry, and began to pluck the ears of corn, and to eat (*to pluck the sheaf's of wheat or barley*).

2 But when the Pharisees saw *it*, they said unto Him (*these religious leaders, by now, were*

watching every move made by Christ and His Disciples; they were trying to find fault), Behold, Your Disciples do that which is not lawful to do upon the Sabbath day (*this was a law they had made up themselves; the Law of Moses permitted them to do what they were doing [Deut. 23:25]*).

3 But He said unto *them* (*His defense was not the Law of Moses, although He could have referred to that, but rather, if David the King when rejected ate the Showbread, the Son of David, when in a similar case might enjoy a similar privilege*), Have you not read what David did, when he was hungry, and they who were with him;

4 How He entered into the House of God (*the Tabernacle*), and did eat the showbread, which was not lawful for him to eat, neither for them which were with him, but only for the Priests (*Sam. 21:6*)?

5 Or have you not read in the Law, how that on the Sabbath days the Priests in the Temple profane the Sabbath, and are blameless? (*The Priests did as much work, if not more, on the Sabbath Day in their preparing the Sacrifices, plus other duties, than possibly any other day! and yet they were not accused of breaking the Law.*)

6 But I say unto you (*meant to portray the Truth of the Word of God*), That in this place is *One* greater than the Temple (*He was speaking of Himself; He was a greater Prophet than Moses, and a greater King than David*).

7 But if you had known what *this* means, I will have mercy, and not sacrifice (*sacrifice was the means, mercy the end; sacrifice the road, mercy the goal; Israel had lost sight of what the sacrifices actually meant*), you would not have condemned the guiltless (*He and His Disciples were guiltless, and all who trust Him are likewise guiltless*).

8 For the Son of Man is Lord even of the Sabbath day (*rejected by the nation as Messiah the King, He now presented Himself to them as Elohim the Creator of the Sabbath*).

HEALING ON THE SABBATH

9 And when He was departed thence (*refers to the following taking place some days later*), He went into their Synagogue (*probably happened during the first two and one-half years of His Ministry, as He was banned from most Synagogues the last year*):

10 And, behold, there was a man which had *his* hand withered (*the "withered hand" was a portrayal of the spiritual condition of Israel and, as well, of all mankind*). And they asked Him, saying, Is it lawful to heal on the Sabbath days? that they might accuse Him (*the Pharisees were completely devoid of the understanding and purpose of Christ or the Sabbath*).

11 And He said unto them (*He always answered their questions*), What man shall there be among you, who shall have one sheep, and if it fall into a pit on the Sabbath Day, will he not lay hold on it, and lift *it* out? (*The answer to the question was obvious!*)

12 How much then is a man better than a sheep? (*The answer should have shamed them! However, the hardened heart has no shame.*) Wherefore it is lawful to do well on the Sabbath Days (*His question and His answer showed that the religious leaders of Israel thought more of sheep than they did of men; regrettably, that spirit persists still!*).

13 Then said He to the man (*He did not ask their permission, and because they could not control Him, they hated Him*), Stretch forth your hand (*spiritually, Christ is still saying the same thing to all men*). And He stretched *it* forth; and it was restored whole, like as the other.

14 Then the Pharisees went out, and held a council against Him, how they might destroy Him (*His love only excited their hatred*).

MULTITUDES HEALED

15 But when Jesus knew *it* (*refers to the plotting of the Pharisees and Herodians against Him*), *He* withdrew Himself from thence (*went to another town*): and great multitudes followed Him, and He healed them all (*"all" is emphatic, meaning that not one single person left without healing*);

16 And charged them that they should not make Him known (*He would not allow the fame of His miracles to hinder His purpose of offering up Himself as a sacrifice for sin; the latter was His real mission*):

17 That it might be fulfilled which was spoken by Isaiah the Prophet, saying (*Isaiah is quoted in the Gospels more than any other Prophet*),

18 Behold My Servant (*He was the Father's Servant*), Whom I have chosen (*chosen by God and not man, hence rejected by man*); My Beloved, in Whom My soul is well pleased (*to please God and not man, should be the goal of every Believer*): I will put My Spirit upon Him (*Holy Spirit*), and He shall show judgment to

the Gentiles (*speaks of the coming Church, which is made up virtually of Gentiles*).

19 He shall not strive, nor cry (*will not demand His rights*); neither shall any man hear His voice in the streets (*He never promoted Himself*).

20 A bruised reed shall He not break, and smoking flax shall He not quench (*even though they rejected Him, He will not give up on Israel*), till He send forth judgment unto victory (*Israel will accept Him at the Second Coming*).

21 And in His Name shall the Gentiles trust (*His Name means "Saviour," and even though the Jews rejected Him, the Gentiles accepted Him*).

BLIND AND DUMB MAN HEALED

22 Then was brought unto Him one possessed with a devil (*Demon*), blind, and dumb (*the man represented Israel, and in fact, all of mankind*): and He healed him, insomuch that the blind and the dumb both spoke and saw (*those who are "born-again" can now spiritually speak and spiritually see*).

23 And all the people were amazed, and said, Is not this the son of David? (*Had their religious leaders properly led them, the people of Israel would have accepted Christ.*)

BLASPHEMING THE HOLY SPIRIT

24 But when the Pharisees heard it (*heard what the people were saying about Jesus being the Son of David, which He was*), they said, This *fellow* (*the Pharisees never referred to Him even one time by His Name*) does not cast out devils (*demons*), but by Beelzebub the prince of the devils (*they didn't deny His Power, but claimed that it was of Satan*).

25 And Jesus knew their thoughts (*revealed to Him by the Holy Spirit*), and said unto them, Every kingdom divided against itself is brought to desolation; and every city or house divided against itself shall not stand (*the idea of the statement is that Satan does not oppose himself! He does not possess one with an evil spirit and then cast out that spirit*):

26 And if Satan cast out Satan, he is divided against himself; how shall then his kingdom stand? (*Jesus admits here that Satan has a kingdom, which is the kingdom of darkness.*)

27 And if I by Beelzebub cast out devils (*demons*), by whom do your children cast *them* out? (*The Pharisees and their disciples claimed to cast out demons, but in reality they didn't; because they were as well of Satan.*) therefore they shall be your judges (*the word "children" refers to the disciples of the Pharisees; Jesus by posing this question did not deny or affirm that they, in fact, actually did cast out demons; He was using the statement only as argument to prove His point*).

28 But if I cast out devils (*demons*) by the Spirit of God (*Jesus did not cast out demons because He was God, but as a man filled with the Spirit*), then the Kingdom of God is come unto you (*this placed the Pharisees in an untenable position; if the Spirit of God was actually helping Him and He had already made it clear that such could not be done without the Spirit of God, then they must admit that He is the Messiah; their accusation backfired on them!*).

29 Or else how can one enter into a strong man's house (*Satan is pictured here as strong — stronger than men*), and spoil his goods (*which Jesus did at the Cross*), except he first bind the strong man? (*Only Jesus could bind this strong man.*) and then he will spoil his house (*at Calvary Satan was totally defeated [Col. 2:14-15]*).

30 He who is not with Me is against Me (*it is impossible to take a neutral position regarding Christ; the word "against" denotes intense opposition*); and he who gathers not with Me scatters abroad (*refers to the Truth that one cannot be with "Christ" and "against" His true servants; the presence of Immanuel tests everything and everybody*).

31 Wherefore I say unto you (*addressing the most fearsome statement*), All manner of sin and blasphemy shall be forgiven unto men (*that is if they properly confess the sin to the Lord [I Jn. 1:9]*): but the blasphemy *against* the *Holy* Spirit shall not be forgiven unto men (*when they accused Him of casting out demons by the power of Satan, when in reality He was doing so by the Power of the Holy Spirit, they blasphemed the Spirit of God; blaspheming the Holy Spirit can only be committed by someone who professes to know the Lord, as the Pharisees of old, or else has once known Him, and then turned against Him; the unredeemed, who have never known the Lord, cannot blaspheme the Holy Spirit simply because they have no true knowledge of the Spirit*).

32 And whosoever speaks a word against the Son of Man, it shall be forgiven him (*once again, if forgiveness is sought*): but whosoever speaks against the Holy Spirit, it shall not be

forgiven him, neither in this world, neither in the *world* to come (*such a person is doomed! however, the statements do not mean that a backslider cannot come back to the Lord; but they do mean that one who has actually blasphemed the Holy Spirit, will have no desire to come to the Lord, but in fact, will continue to oppose Him; anyone who desires to come to the Lord, which desire is placed there by the Holy Spirit, can do so [Rev. 22:17]*).

GOOD AND CORRUPT FRUIT

33 Either make the tree good, and his fruit good; or else make the tree corrupt, and his fruit corrupt: for the tree is known by *his* fruit (*a single tree cannot bring forth both good fruit and corrupt fruit; either the Pharisees were right, or He was right; both could not be right! His fruit was good, inasmuch as it produced changed lives; their fruit produced nothing but corruption*).

34 O generation of vipers (*Jesus called the Pharisees snakes, and did so to their face*), how can you, being evil, speak good things? (*Due to being evil, they could not produce good fruit.*) for out of the abundance of the heart the mouth speaks (*men's words reveal their thoughts and character*).

35 A good man out of the good treasure of the heart brings forth good things (*the "good man" of this Verse is the same as the "good tree" of Verse 33; as the "good tree" will bring forth good fruit, likewise, the "good man" will bring forth "good treasure" out of his heart*): and an evil man out of the evil treasure brings forth evil things (*an evil heart cannot do otherwise*).

36 But I say unto you, That every idle word that men shall speak (*concerns claims of righteousness which did not exist*), they shall give account thereof in the day of judgment (*the Great White Throne Judgment [Rev. 20:11-15]*).

37 For by your words you shall be justified (*a confession of Christ and the price that He paid on the Cross, justifies any person [Rom. 5:1-2]*), and by your words you shall be condemned (*a confession of anything other than Christ and the Cross will condemn, i.e., "eternally lost"*).

THE SIGN OF JONAH

38 Then certain of the Scribes and of the Pharisees (*the Scribes were a part of the Pharisees, because they shared the same doctrine*)

answered, saying, Master (*teacher*), we would see a sign from *You* (*there were signs galore! for instance, they had just seen the man blind, dumb, and demon possessed instantly delivered, and healed; the sign, however, which they actually wanted, was not Deliverance from sin and its effects, but rather from Rome*).

39 But He answered and said unto them, An evil and adulterous generation seeks after a sign (*"adulterous" spoke of Israel's spiritual unfaithfulness to God; they were committing spiritual adultery, which means that they were worshiping something other than God; had they been worshiping God, they would have accepted Christ*); and there shall no sign be given to it, but the sign of the Prophet *Jonah* (*He was speaking of His Death and Resurrection*):

40 For as Jonah was three days and three nights in the whale's belly; so shall the Son of Man be three days and three nights in the heart of the Earth (*Christ would be dead three days and three nights; during this time, He would be in Paradise, and would preach to the spirits in prison who were fallen angels [Lk. 23:43; I Pet. 3:19-20] there is no scriptural record that Jesus was in the burning side of Hell, as some teach*).

41 The men of Nineveh shall rise in judgment with this generation, and shall condemn it (*Jesus proclaims here the Gentiles of Nineveh as far more righteous than the Pharisees, for they repented, while the Pharisees wouldn't; this infuriated these religious leaders*): because they repented at the preaching of Jonah; and, behold, a greater than Jonah *is* here (*"this generation" of Israel, was visited by no less than the Son of God, whereas Nineveh was privileged to hear only the Prophet Jonah; as well, Christ performed the greatest miracles ever known, while Jonah performed none; Israel was left with no excuse*).

42 The queen of the south (*Queen of Sheba, another Gentile*) shall rise up in the judgment with this generation, and shall condemn it: for she came from the uttermost parts of the earth to hear the wisdom of Solomon; and, behold, a greater than Solomon *is* here (*this woman marks a higher stage of inquiry and faith, inasmuch as she traveled a great distance to hear the wisdom of Solomon; by contrast, Jesus came directly to Israel, but still they wouldn't receive Him, even though He was far greater than Solomon in both wisdom and power; what an indictment!*).

THE RETURN OF UNCLEAN SPIRITS

43 When the unclean spirit is gone out of a

man *(regarding Israel, unclean spirits would retreat before Christ)*, he *(the unclean spirit)* walks through dry places, seeking rest, and finding none *(these spirits of darkness were not actually cast out of Israel, but only retreated before Christ, because He was the stronger Man).*

44 Then he *(the unclean spirit)* says, I will return into my house from whence I came out *(which happened when Israel rejected Christ)*; and when he *(the evil spirit)* is come, he finds it *(Israel)* empty, *(empty of the Spirit of God)* swept *(clean of the things of God, meaning there was nothing of God left)*, and garnished *(filled with religious ritual).*

45 Then goes he *(the evil spirit)*, and takes with himself seven other spirits more wicked than himself, and they enter in and dwell there *(which is what happened when Israel rejected Christ)*: and the last *state* of that man is worse than the first. Even so shall it be also unto this wicked generation *(having rejected Christ, Israel was now far worse than she was before He came; it is the same with the modern Church, which hears the Message of the Cross, and then rejects it).*

JESUS' TRUE FAMILY

46 While He *(Christ)* yet talked to the people *(concerns the terrible Word He has just delivered concerning Israel's present and future state)*, behold, *His* mother and His brethren stood without, desiring to speak with Him *(Jesus was probably in a particular house, with it being filled with people, with no more room for others to come in, hence His family not able to get to Him; their desire to speak with Him was not in a positive sense).*

47 Then one said unto Him, Behold, Your mother and Your brethren stand without, desiring to speak with You *(they had things to say to Him, but they little desired to hear what He had to say to them; thankfully, that would change after His Death and Resurrection).*

48 But He answered and said unto him who told Him, Who is My mother? and who are My brethren? *(This totally refutes the claims later made by the Catholic Church.)*

49 And He stretched forth His Hand toward His Disciples *(refers to the original Twelve, but is not limited to them, as it refers to any and all who follow Him, as the next Passage proclaims)*, and said, Behold My mother and My brethren!

50 For whosoever *(increases the dimensions of His family to include all who follow Him)* shall do the will of My Father which is in Heaven *(proclaims the qualifications for being a part of the Family of God)*, the same is My brother, and sister, and mother *(places no significance on physical birth, but everything on spiritual birth).*

CHAPTER 13
(A.D. 31)
THE PARABLE OF THE SOWER

THE same day *(the day the teaching was given as recorded in the previous Chapter)* went Jesus out of the house *(probably Peter's house)*, and sat by the sea side *(Sea of Galilee).*

2 And great multitudes were gathered together unto Him *(they wanted Him to teach them, which He did)*, so that He went into a ship, and sat *(which was the custom then regarding sitting while one taught)*; and the whole multitude stood on the shore.

3 And He spoke many things unto them in Parables *(a comparison illustration, used in order to explain a truth)*, saying, Behold, a sower went forth to sow *(concerns an illustration with which all would have been familiar);*

4 And when he sowed, some *seeds* (Word of God) fell by the way side, and the fowls *(demon spirits)* came and devoured them up:

5 Some *(seed)* fell upon stony places, for they had not much earth: and forthwith they sprung up, because they had no deepness of earth *(no depth):*

6 And when the sun was up, they were scorched; and because they had no root, they withered away *(because of having no depth, persecutions soon caused them to fall by the wayside; all of this pertains to the presentation of the Gospel, and as obvious, completely refutes the unscriptural doctrine of unconditional eternal security).*

7 And some *(seed)* fell among thorns; and the thorns sprung up, and choked them *(other things were allowed to come in and hinder the growth of the Word in the heart):*

8 But other *(seed)* fell into good ground *(receptive ground)*, and brought forth fruit, some an hundredfold, some sixtyfold, some thirtyfold *(Jn. 15:1-8).*

9 Who hath ears to hear, let him hear *(whoever hears is responsible to hear, i.e., to obey, and will be so judged; the secret of this first Parable is that only about one-fourth of the expended efforts succeed, and three-fourths fail; subsequent history demonstrates the accuracy of this Prophecy).*

JESUS EXPLAINS THE PURPOSE OF SPEAKING IN PARABLES

10 And the Disciples came, and said unto Him *(seems to pertain to a later time when they were alone)*, **Why do You speak to them in Parables?** *(This portrays consternation on their part!)*

11 He answered and said unto them *(concerns the Lord's method of dealing with two different classes of people, those who really wanted to know God's Ways and those who were merely curious)*, **Because it is given unto you to know the mysteries of the Kingdom of Heaven, but to them it is not given** *(two categories are presented here; in which category are you?)*.

12 **For whosoever has** *(and wants more)*, **to him shall be given, and he shall have more abundance** *(if one wills Righteousness, the Lord wills more Righteousness to them)*: **but whosoever has not** *(no interest for more)*, **from him shall be taken away even that he has** *(he not only loses what he could have had, but even that which he has; to those who accept the Cross, they will have even more, and to those who reject the Cross, they will lose everything, even that which they previously had)*.

13 **Therefore speak I to them in Parables** *(in order to separate those who hunger and thirst for Righteousness from those who don't)*: **because they seeing see not; and hearing they hear not, neither do they understand** *(that is, they do not wish to see or hear or understand; and hence by a just judgment they lose this triple moral ability)*.

14 **And in them** *(those who reject the Cross [I Cor. 1:23])* **is fulfilled the Prophecy of Isaiah, which says, By hearing ye shall hear, and shall not understand; and seeing ye shall see, and shall not perceive** *(a willful deafness, a willful blindness, and a willful dullness; this Passage is quoted in one form or the other some seven times in the New Testament [Mat. 13:14-15; Mk. 4:12; Lk. 8:10; Jn. 12:39-40; Acts 28:26-27; Rom. 11:8])*:

15 **For this people's heart is waxed gross** *(this is the reason for their spiritual dullness and, therefore, rejection of Christ; Spiritual rejection or acceptance begins in the heart)*, **and their ears are dull of hearing** *(they have heard, and heard, and little acted on what they heard, and the Holy Spirit pulls back until they lose even that which they had)*, **and their eyes they have closed** *(deliberately did so, even in the face of irrefutable proof)*; **lest at any time they should see with** *their* **eyes, and hear with** *their* **ears, and should understand with** *their* **heart, and should be converted, and I should heal them** *(they would not turn to Him; had they done so He would most certainly have healed them morally, and spiritually; this speaks of those who have accepted the Lord, but for various reasons will fall by the wayside; as stated, this completely refutes the unscriptural doctrine of unconditional eternal security)*.

16 **But blessed** *are* **your eyes, for they see: and your ears, for they hear** *(this is the group who desires to know the Lord in an even greater way)*.

17 **For verily I say unto you** *(signals a very important statement)*, **That many Prophets and righteous** *men* **have desired to see** *those things* **which ye see** *(that which Christ presented to Israel, but which were rejected)*, **and have not seen** *them*; **and to hear** *those things* **which you hear, and have not heard** *them* *(contrasted were the many, who "desired" to see, hear, and to understand)*.

PARABLE OF THE SOWER EXPLAINED

18 **Hear ye therefore the Parable of the sower** *(Christ will now explain it)*.

19 **When any one hears the Word of the Kingdom** *(refers to the Word of God; it speaks of God's Way vs. Satan's way)*, **and understands it not** *(does not refer to one who is incapable of understanding, but instead, to one who has no desire to understand)*, **then cometh the wicked one** *(Jesus compares Satan to a vulture)*, **and catches away that which was sown in his heart** *(refers to Satan being allowed to do such a thing by the individual involved; the initiative does not lie with the Lord or with Satan, but with the person)*. **This is he which receives seed by the way side** *(the word "way side" refers to the fact that the individual doesn't give it credence, i.e., "unbelief")*.

20 **But he who receives the seed** *(Word of God)* **into stony places** *(refers to the second group)*, **the same is he who hears the Word, and anon** *(immediately)* **with joy receives it** *(they make a good start, but then fall by the wayside)*;

21 **Yet has he not root in himself** *(refers to the "stony places")*, **but endures for a while** *(he hears the Word of God, believes it, and accepts Christ; it is all done with joy; but then something else happens)*: **for when tribulation or persecution arises because of the Word** *(which it definitely will)*, **by and by** *(immediately)* **he is**

offended (the offense of the Cross [Gal. 5:11]).

22 He also who received seed (the Word of God) among the thorns is he who hears the Word (he receives the Word; the soil is fertile and good with plenty depth); and the care of this world (ways of this world), and the deceitfulness of riches (deceitful, simply because the acquiring of such makes a person believe erroneous things), choke the Word (stops its growth), and he becomes unfruitful (such a one is ultimately lost [Jn. 15:2, 6]).

23 But he who receives seed into the good ground (prepared ground — ground plowed up by the Spirit of conviction because of sin) is he who hears the Word (does so with eagerness), and understands it (he wanted to understand, and the Lord rewards such by giving more understanding); which also bears fruit (Christian growth), and brings forth, some an hundredfold, some sixty, some thirty (the idea is one hundredfold; the Holy Spirit strives to bring the thirty fold and the sixty fold up to a hundred fold [Jn. 15:1-8]).

THE PARABLE OF THE WHEAT AND TARES

24 Another Parable put He forth unto them, saying (presents the second Parable), The Kingdom of Heaven is likened unto a Man (Christ) which sowed good seed (the Word of God) in his field (the world):

25 But while men slept (the Church is often asleep), His (Christ's) enemy came (Satan) and sowed tares (apostates) among the wheat (true Christians), and went his way (Satan works mostly through professed Believers).

26 But when the blade was sprung up (refers to the good seed taking root, growing, and having a healthy start), and brought forth fruit (refers to its intended purpose), then appeared the tares also (the Church has both the true and the false).

27 So the servants of the householder came and said unto him (refers to those who had helped sow the "good seed"), Sir, did not you sow good seed in your field? from whence then has it tares? (No tares were sowed, so why are they there?)

28 He said unto them, An enemy has done this (refers to Satan and his ministers [II Cor. 11:13-15]). The servants said unto him, Will you then that we go and gather them up? (Rid the field of the tares?)

29 But he said, No; lest while you gather up the tares, ye root up also the wheat with them

(while the tares [false doctrine] were to be pointed out, no force was to be used to take them out of the field; to do so, would be to destroy some wheat).

30 Let both grow together until the harvest (refers to the First Resurrection of Life): and in the time of the harvest I will say to the reapers (refers to the Lord performing this all-important task, because only He has the Wisdom and Ability to do), Gather ye together first the tares, and bind them in bundles to burn them (the tares will be eternally lost): but gather the wheat into my barn (refers to those who will be in the First Resurrection [I Thess. 4:13-18]).

THE PARABLE OF THE MUSTARD SEED

31 Another Parable put He forth unto them, saying (the third Parable), The Kingdom of Heaven is like to a grain of mustard seed (Word of God), which a man took (Christ), and sowed in his field (the world):

32 Which indeed is the least of all seeds (concerns the small beginnings of the Gospel of Jesus Christ): but when it is grown (which it now is), it is the greatest among herbs (Christianity is the largest faith on Earth, with approximately two billion adherents), and becomes a tree (a mustard bush that becomes a tree is abnormal), so that the birds of the air (all kind of birds, representing all kinds of doctrine) come and lodge in the branches thereof (thus in conduct and in doctrine the failure of what is called Christianity is revealed here beforehand).

THE PARABLE OF THE LEAVEN

33 Another Parable spoke He unto them (the fourth); The Kingdom of Heaven is like unto leaven (invariably presented in Scripture as a symbol of evil), which a woman took (frequently in Scripture the woman as well is presented as an agent of idolatry), and hid in three measures of meal (the meal is the Word of God), till the whole was leavened (more tares than wheat).

JESUS' USE OF PARABLES

34 All these things spoke Jesus unto the multitude in Parables (relates only to this segment of His Teaching); and without a Parable spoke He not unto them:

35 That it might be fulfilled which was spoken by the Prophet (Asaph [Ps. 78:2]), saying, I will open My Mouth in Parables; I will utter things which have been kept secret from the

foundation of the world *(refers to Truths which have never before been revealed, but are now given, albeit in shadow; as an example, the Gentiles being brought in)*.

THE PARABLE OF THE WHEAT AND
THE TARES EXPLAINED

36 Then Jesus sent the multitude away, and went into the house *(He had been teaching by the seaside, and now goes into Peter's home)*: and His Disciples came unto Him, saying, Declare unto us the Parable of the tares of the field *(a private audience)*.

37 He answered and said unto them, He who sows the good seed *(Word of God)* is the Son of Man *(Christ is the Lord of the Harvest)*;

38 The field is the world *(not just the Jews, which in effect, speaks of the coming Church)*; the good seed are the children of the Kingdom *(refers to true Believers of the Word of God)*; but the tares are the children of the wicked *one (they profess to be children of the Kingdom, but in effect, were Satan's ministers in one way or the other [II Cor. 11:13-15])*;

39 The enemy that sowed them *(bad seed)* is the devil; the harvest is the end of the world *(end of the age; the Judgment)*; and the reapers are the Angels *(the Angels which will come back with Christ, and all redeemed Saints, at the Second Coming [Rev., Chpt. 19])*.

40 As therefore the tares *(bad seed)* are gathered and burned in the fire *(Great White Throne Judgment [Rev. 20:11-15])*; so shall it be in the end of this world *(end of this age)*.

41 The Son of Man shall send forth His Angels, and they shall gather out of His Kingdom *(separate the tares from the wheat)* all things that offend, and them which do iniquity *(Great White Throne Judgment)*;

42 And shall cast them into a furnace of fire: there shall be wailing and gnashing of teeth *(the Second Resurrection of Damnation, i.e., "the Second Death" [Rev. 20:11-15])*.

43 Then *(the beginning of the Kingdom Age)* shall the Righteous shine forth as the sun in the Kingdom of their Father *(the perfect age to come [Rev., Chpts. 21-22])*. Who has ears to hear, let him hear *(proclaims the certitude of such action)*.

THE PARABLE OF THE
HIDDEN TREASURE

44 Again *(the fifth Parable)*, the Kingdom of Heaven is like unto treasure *(the New Covenant)* hid in a field *(the world)*; the which when a man has found *(the treasure is Christ)*, he hides it, and for joy thereof goes and sells all that he has, and buys that field *(the moral is, Christ is worth more than everything else, and by far)*.

THE PARABLE OF THE PEARL
OF GREAT PRICE

45 Again *(the sixth Parable)*, the Kingdom of Heaven is like unto a merchant man, seeking goodly pearls *(this man is rich, but yet not satisfied, and rightly so; "Pearls" are the only substance which cannot be improved by man; this Pearl represents Christ)*:

46 Who, when he had found one pearl of great price *(this one pearl among many pearls, which was greater than all, i.e., "Christ")*, went and sold all that he had, and bought it *(this Pearl is worth everything, and everything is what it will take to obtain it)*.

THE PARABLE OF THE NET

47 Again *(the seventh Parable)*, the Kingdom of Heaven is like unto a net, that was cast into the sea, and gathered of every kind *(all type of Believers come into the Church)*:

48 Which, when it was full *(when the dispensation of the Church runs its course; it is almost over)*, they drew to shore, and sat down, and gathered the good into vessels, but cast the bad away *(the separation of the tares and the wheat)*.

49 So shall it be at the end of the world *(at the end of the age)*: the Angels shall come forth, and sever the wicked from among the just *(the "just" are those who trust in Christ and the Cross)*,

50 And shall cast them *(the wicked)* into the furnace of fire *(Great White Throne Judgment [Rev. 20:11-15])*: there shall be wailing and gnashing of teeth.

THE HOUSEHOLDER

51 Jesus said unto them, Have you understood all these things? They say unto Him, Yes, Lord.

52 Then said He unto them, Therefore every Scribe *(all Believers are likened here as Scribes, which means they diligently search the Word of God)* **which** is instructed *(versed in the*

Word, which should be all Believers) unto the Kingdom of Heaven is like unto a man *who is* an householder *(possesses the keys to the Kingdom)*, which brings forth out of his treasure *things* new and old *(can enrich others out of his store of Divine Truth; that Truth as to time is old, i.e., eternal, as to experience, power, and character perpetually new)*.

JESUS REJECTED AT NAZARETH

53 And it came to pass, *that* when Jesus had finished these Parables, He departed thence.

54 And when He was come into His own country *(Nazareth)*, He taught them in their Synagogue *(Lk. 4:16-30)*, insomuch that they were astonished *(rendered speechless)*, and said, Whence has this *Man* this wisdom, and *these* mighty works? *(Meant to cast aspersions on Christ.)*

55 Is not this the carpenter's son? *(This was a denial of His claim regarding Messiahship.)* is not his mother called Mary? and His brethren, James, and Joses, and Simon, and Judas? *(They were denying as well, His Virgin Birth.)*

56 And His sisters, are they not all with us? Whence then has this *Man* all these things? *(If all of these things were so, they were saying, His family, by now, would have mentioned it.)*

57 And they were offended in Him *(Luke said they were "filled with wrath," and would have killed Him had they been able to do so [Lk. 4:28-30])*. But Jesus said unto them, A Prophet is not without honour, save in his own country, and in his own house *(the last phrase "in his own" is revealing; it proclaims the fact that His own family didn't believe in Him [Jn. 7:5])*.

58 And He did not many mighty works there *(in Nazareth)* because of their unbelief *(they would not bring the sick and afflicted to Him; unbelief was the reason)*.

CHAPTER 14
(A.D. 32)
JOHN THE BAPTIST BEHEADED

A T that time Herod the Tetrarch *(the son of Herod who slew the infants of Bethlehem)* heard of the fame of Jesus *(it speaks of the miracles Christ performed, even to the raising of the dead)*,

2 And he said unto his servants, This is John the Baptist *(a guilty conscience)*; he is risen from the dead; and therefore mighty works do shew forth themselves in him.

3 For Herod had laid hold on John, and bound him, and put *him* in prison *(the Castle of Machaerus on the shores of the Dead Sea)* for Herodias' sake, his brother Philip's wife *(refers to the reason John had been arrested by Herod and placed in prison)*.

4 For John said unto him, It is not lawful for you to have her *(Herodias was his niece and the wife of his brother Phillip)*.

5 And when he would have put him to death, he feared the multitude, because they counted him as a prophet.

6 But when Herod's birthday was kept, the daughter of Herodias danced before them, and pleased Herod.

7 Whereupon he promised with an oath to give her whatsoever she would ask.

8 And she, being before instructed of her mother, said, Give me here John Baptist's head in a charger *(the mother of Salome, Herodias, was one of the most wicked women who ever lived)*.

9 And the king was sorry: nevertheless for the oath's sake, and them which sat with him at meat *(a meal)*, he commanded *it* to be given her *(to save face)*.

10 And he sent, and beheaded John in the prison.

11 And his head was brought in a charger, and given to the damsel: and she brought *it* to her mother.

12 And his disciples came, and took up the body, and buried it, and went and told Jesus *(the mission of John the Baptist was to introduce Jesus; that he did!)*.

JESUS FEEDS THE FIVE THOUSAND

13 When Jesus heard *of it*, He departed thence by ship into a desert place apart *(He was grieved over the death of John, His beloved fore-runner; He could have stopped the execution; however, it was not the Will of God to do so)*: and when the people had heard *thereof*, they followed Him on foot out of the cities.

14 And Jesus went forth, and saw a great multitude, and was moved with compassion toward them, and He healed their sick.

15 And when it was evening, His Disciples came to Him, saying, This is a desert place, and the time is now past *(the people had been without food all day, and if they were going to find food, they would need to leave now)*; send the multitude away, that they may go into the villages, and buy themselves victuals.

16 But Jesus said unto them, They need not depart; give ye them to eat *(He was speaking*

then of the physical sense, but His words carried a higher spiritual cogitation; the Body of Christ is to be fed regarding the Word of God).

17 And they say unto Him, We have here but five loaves, and two fishes (little is much if God be in it!).

18 He said, Bring them hither to Me (the secret is Christ! we are to bring what little we have to Him).

19 And He commanded the multitude to sit down on the grass (this presents order and a method by which the distribution was made), and took the five loaves, and the two fishes, and looking up to Heaven, He blessed, and brake, and gave the loaves to His Disciples, and the Disciples to the multitude (He took, He Blessed, He did break, and He gave; that is His order with Believers as well).

20 And they did all eat, and were filled: and they took up of the fragments that remained twelve baskets full (an astounding miracle!).

21 And they who had eaten were about five thousand men, beside women and children (possibly as many as fifteen thousand people).

JESUS WALKS ON THE WATER

22 And straightway Jesus constrained (firmly demanded) His Disciples to get into a ship, and to go before Him unto the other side (back to Capernaum), while He sent the multitudes away (but He sent them away, filled both physically and spiritually).

23 And when He had sent the multitudes away (implying that they did not want to leave), He went up into a mountain apart to pray (expresses what He often did [Mat. 26:36; Mk. 6:46; 14:32; Lk. 6:12; 9:28; Jn. 17:9-20]): and when the evening was come, He was there alone.

24 But the ship was now in the midst of the sea (concerns not only the Sea of Galilee, but as well, the Sea of Life), tossed with waves (turbulence): for the wind was contrary (difficulties, as well, facing mankind as a result of the Fall).

25 And in the fourth watch of the night (between 3 a.m. and 6 a.m.) Jesus went unto them (the Holy Spirit revealed to Him, that they were in trouble), walking on the sea (even though the waters were very turbulent, where He walked, it became calm).

26 And when the Disciples saw Him walking on the sea, they were troubled (it was more than they could grasp), saying, It is a spirit (they did not actually think it was Jesus); and they cried out for fear (they thought they were about to die).

27 But straightway (immediately) Jesus spoke unto them (once they saw Him), saying, Be of good cheer; it is I; be not afraid (we are to face adverse circumstances with cheer, knowing the Lord will handle the situation).

28 And Peter answered Him and said, Lord, if it be You (better translated, "since it is You"), bid Me come unto You on the water.

29 And He (Jesus) said, Come (the Master's response to Faith). And when Peter was come down out of the ship, he walked on the water, to go to Jesus.

30 But when he saw the wind boisterous, he was afraid (he now sees the wind instead of Jesus); and beginning to sink, he cried, saying, Lord, save me (a prayer the Lord will always answer).

31 And immediately Jesus stretched forth His hand, and caught him (this prevented him from sinking further), and said unto him, O you of little faith, wherefore did you doubt? (We must not allow circumstances to bring about doubt.)

32 And when they were come into the ship (every evidence is, after Jesus caught him, Peter walked on the water the second time), the wind ceased (the Power of Christ over the elements).

33 Then they who were in the ship came and worshipped Him (as God), saying, Of a truth You are the Son of God (recognized Him as the Messiah).

JESUS HEALS THE SICK

34 And when they were gone over (came back to Capernaum), they came into the land of Gennesaret (on the western side of the Sea of Galilee, somewhat inward).

35 And when the men of that place had knowledge of Him (knowledge of His Presence in their vicinity), they sent out into all that country round about, and brought unto Him all who were diseased;

36 And besought Him that they might only touch the hem of His garment: and as many as touched were made perfectly whole (if the Hem of His garment is so rich with Blessing, how rich must be His Hand and Heart!).

CHAPTER 15
(A.D. 32)

JESUS REBUKES THE SCRIBES AND PHARISEES

THEN came to Jesus Scribes and Pharisees, which were of Jerusalem, saying (almost

all of the opposition to Christ came from religious leaders),

2 Why do your Disciples transgress the tradition of the elders? *(Their confidence was in their man-made rules rather then the Word of God.)* **for they wash not their hands when they eat bread** *(had no sanitary meaning; this tradition taught that an evil spirit could sit on the hands of people, and when the hands were washed, the evil spirit would be removed).*

3 But He answered and said unto them *(proclaims Christ drawing them back to the Word of God),* **Why do you also transgress the Commandment of God by your tradition?** *(He ignored their tradition because it was not Scriptural. He then tells them that their traditions were causing them to transgress the Commandment of God.)*

4 For God commanded, saying, Honour your father and mother: and, He who curses father or mother, let him die the death *(Ex. 20:12; 21:17).*

5 But you say *(in direct contradiction to what God commanded),* **Whosoever shall say to** *his* **father or** *his* **mother,** *It is* **a gift** *(dedicate their estate to the Temple so that they wouldn't have to take care of their aged parents, and a crooked Priest would then give it back to them, after taking a percentage),* **by whatsoever you might be profited by Me** *(making an illegal profit off of God, which compounded their sin);*

6 And honour not his father or his mother, *he shall be free (free from responsibility).* **Thus have you made the Commandment of God of none effect by your tradition.**

7 You *(was said to their faces)* **hypocrites, well did Isaiah prophesy of you, saying,**

8 This people draw near unto Me with their mouth, and honor Me with *their* **lips; but their heart is far from Me** *(this defines the hypocrite).*

9 But in vain they do worship Me *(worship that was not accepted by God indicative of much of the modern Church as well!),* **teaching** *for* **doctrines the commandments of men** *(anything that adds to or takes away from the Word of God).*

THE THINGS THAT DEFILE

10 And He called the multitude, and said unto them *(did so in front of the Scribes and Pharisees),* **Hear, and understand** *(what He will now say, will be the opposite said by the Scribes and Pharisees):*

11 Not that which goes into the mouth defiles a man; but that which comes out of the mouth, **this defiles a man** *(Christ draws the minds of the people away from externals to the true condition of the heart).*

12 Then came His Disciples, and said unto Him *(concerns a time of private contemplation regarding the things said by Christ),* **Do you not know that the Pharisees were offended** *(scandalized),* **after they heard this saying?** *(As one divine of old said, "if offence arises from the statement of the Truth, it is more expedient that offence be permitted to arise than that the Truth should be abandoned.")*

13 But He answered and said *(He did not remain silent, but further proclaimed His position),* **Every plant, which My Heavenly Father has not planted, shall be rooted up** *(means that the doctrine of the Pharisees was not of divine origin, but of earthly origin; the day is coming when the tares will be removed from among the wheat).*

14 Let them alone *(does not mean to not address their error, but means that them being offended is not to be a deterrent to preaching the Truth):* **they be blind leaders of the blind** *(a designation applied to all who were not following the Word of God).* **And if the blind lead the blind, both shall fall into the ditch** *(a guaranteed ultimate conclusion).*

15 Then answered Peter and said unto him, Declare unto us this parable *(give us more explanation).*

16 And Jesus said, Are you also yet without understanding? *(The great reason for the need to be filled with the Spirit, and led by the Spirit [Rom. 8:14].)*

17 Do you not yet understand, that whatsoever enters in at the mouth goes into the belly, and is cast out into the draught? *(Proclaims the fact that the eating of food has nothing to do with the spiritual side of man.)*

18 But those things which proceed out of the mouth come forth from the heart; and they defile the man *(not everything that comes out of the mouth of a man is defiling, but only that which proceeds from an evil heart).*

19 For out of the heart proceed evil thoughts, murders, adulteries, fornications, thefts, false witness, blasphemies *(this proclaims the depravity of the unconverted human heart, which was the condition of the Pharisees, despite their religiosity):*

20 These are *the things* **which defile a man: but to eat with unwashed hands defile not a man** *(Satan is a master at placing the emphasis on the insignificant, instead of the real problem).*

THE HEALING OF THE DAUGHTER
OF THE CANAANITE

21 Then Jesus went thence *(left Capernaum)*, and departed into the coasts *(borders)* of Tyre and Sidon.

22 And, behold, a woman of Canaan *(a Gentile)* came out of the same coasts *(borders)*, and cried unto Him *(the woman was desperate)*, saying, Have mercy on me, O Lord, *Thou* Son of David; my daughter is grievously vexed with a devil *(demon)*.

23 But He answered her not a word *(being a Gentile, her petition was wrong, addressing Him as "Son of David"; only the Jews were then privileged to use that term)*. And His Disciples came and besought Him, saying, Send her away; for she crieth after us *(better translated, "do something for her")*.

24 But He answered and said, I am not sent but unto the lost sheep of the house of Israel *(His Mission, at least in His First Advent, was exclusively to the Jews)*.

25 Then came she and worshipped Him, saying, Lord, help me *(her position is now beginning to change!)*.

26 But He answered and said, It is not meet *(appropriate)* to take the children's bread *(that which belonged to the Jews)*, and to cast *it* to dogs *(Gentiles were looked at as "dogs," so in effect, He was testing her faith)*.

27 And she said, Truth, Lord: yet the dogs eat of the crumbs which fall from their masters' table *(when she took the place of a "dog," thus admitting that she had no claim, throwing herself on His Grace as Lord, He at once responded, just as He will presently)*.

28 Then Jesus answered and said unto her, O woman, great *is* your faith: be it unto you even as you will. And her daughter was made whole from that very hour *(the Lord always responds to faith; only two people are spoken of as having "great Faith"; the first was the Gentile Centurion [Mat. 8:5-10], and now this Gentile woman)*.

JESUS HEALS THE SICK

29 And Jesus departed from thence, and came near unto the Sea of Galilee; and went up into a mountain, and sat down there *(probably on the northeast side of the Sea of Galilee)*.

30 And great multitudes came unto Him *(could have been several thousands of people)*, having with them *those who were* lame, blind, dumb, maimed, and many others, and cast them down at Jesus' feet; and he healed them *(He healed them all)*:

31 Insomuch that the multitude wondered, when they saw the dumb to speak, the maimed to be whole, the lame to walk, and the blind to see: and they glorified the God of Israel.

JESUS FEEDS FOUR THOUSAND

32 Then Jesus called *His Disciples unto Him*, and said, I have compassion on the multitude, because they continue with Me now three days, and have nothing to eat: and I will not send them away fasting, lest they faint in the way *(probably ten thousand or more, had had very little to eat in the last three days and nights)*.

33 And His Disciples say unto Him, Where should we get so much bread in the wilderness, as to fill so great a multitude? *(Did they not remember the great Miracle He performed a short time before of this same nature? How so quick we are to forget as well!)*

34 And Jesus said unto them, How many loaves have you? And they said, Seven, and a few little fishes.

35 And He commanded the multitude to sit down on the ground.

36 And He took the seven loaves and the fishes, and gave thanks, and broke *them*, and gave to His Disciples, and the Disciples to the multitude *(the Disciples had to keep coming to Jesus for fresh supplies for the need of the multitude; they had no resources of their own; they were dependent totally upon Him; this is what He is teaching us)*.

37 And they did all eat, and were filled *(satisfied)*: and they took up of the broken *meat* that was left seven baskets full.

38 And they who did eat were four thousand men, beside women and children *(probably near ten thousand people)*.

39 And He sent away the multitude *(but sent them away filled physically, and spiritually)*, and took ship, and came into the coasts of Magdala *(a small town located about ten miles south of Capernaum)*.

CHAPTER 16
(A.D. 32)
JESUS REBUKES THE PHARISEES

THE Pharisees also with the Sadducees came *(proclaims the joining of these two groups who were normally antagonistic to each other)*,

and tempting desired Him that He would show them a sign from Heaven *(they wanted Him to call fire down from Heaven, as did Elijah; but they would not accept the recent feeding of the thousands with seven loaves and a few fish)*.

2 He answered and said unto them *(His answer to them shows the hostility of the natural heart)*, When it is evening, you say, *It will be* fair weather: for the sky is red.

3 And in the morning, *It will be* foul weather to day: for the sky is red and lowring. O *ye* hypocrites, you can discern the face of the sky; but can you not *discern* the signs of the times?

4 A wicked and adulterous generation seeks after a sign *(regrettably, this characterizes this present generation as well)*; and there shall no sign be given unto it, but the sign of the Prophet Jonah *(Jesus was sent from Heaven, but they would not accept Him; He was the greatest sign of all)*. And He left them, and departed *(He departed both physically and spiritually)*.

5 And when His Disciples were come to the other side *(from the western shore of the Sea of Galilee, to the northeastern shore)*, they had forgotten to take bread.

THE LEAVEN

6 Then Jesus said unto them, Take heed and beware of the leaven *(false doctrine)* of the Pharisees and of the Sadducees.

7 And they reasoned among themselves *(shows an appalling lack of Scriptural and Spiritual knowledge)*, saying, *It is* because we have taken no bread.

8 *Which* when Jesus perceived, He said unto them *(the Holy Spirit told Him what they were "reasoning")*, O you of little faith *(Faith in Christ and the Cross is the one necessary ingredient)*, why reason you among yourselves, because you have brought no bread?

9 Do you not yet understand *(the insensibility of the Disciples to the Lord's Actions and to His Teaching, is a humiliating proof of the darkness of man's heart to moral realities)*, neither remember the five loaves of the five thousand, and how many baskets you took up?

10 Neither the seven loaves of the four thousand, and how many baskets you took up?

11 How is it that you do not understand that I spoke *it* not to you concerning bread *(bread that one can eat)*, that you should beware of the leaven of the Pharisees and of the Sadducees? *(Is meant to censure their want of*

spiritual discernment.)*

12 Then understood they how that He bade *them* not beware of the leaven of bread, but of the doctrine of the Pharisees and of the Sadducees.

PETER'S CONFESSION

13 When Jesus came into the coasts *(borders)* of Caesarea Philippi *(about thirty miles north of the Sea of Galilee)*, He asked His Disciples, saying, Whom do men say that I the Son of Man am? *(The third form of unbelief manifested itself in popular indifference, indolence, or mere curiosity respecting the Messiah Himself. Upon the answer to this all-important question, hinges the Salvation of man.)*

14 And they said, Some *say that you are* John the Baptist: some, Elijah; and others, Jeremiah, or one of the Prophets *(this form of unbelief manifests itself in the frivolity of the natural heart)*.

15 He said unto them, But whom say you that I am? *(Addressed personally to the Twelve.)*

16 And Simon Peter answered and said, You are the Christ, the Son of the Living God *(the Great Confession)*.

17 And Jesus answered and said unto him, Blessed are you, Simon Bar–jona *(Peter is the son of Jonah, as Jesus is the Son of God)*: for flesh and blood have not revealed *it* unto you *(mere human ingenuity)*, but My Father which is in Heaven *(all spiritual knowledge must be by Revelation)*.

18 And I say also unto you, That you are Peter *(the Lord changed his name from Simon to Peter, which means "a fragment of a rock")*, and upon this rock *(immovable mass; Jesus is the Living Rock on which the Redeemed as living stones are built; for other foundation can no man lay [I Cor. 3:11])* I will build My Church *(the Church belongs to Christ, and He is the Head [Col. 1:18])*; and the gates of Hell shall not prevail against it *(the power of death caused by sin, shall not prevail against it, which victory was won at the Cross [Vss. 21, 24])*.

19 And I will give unto you *("you" refers to all Believers)* the keys of the Kingdom of Heaven *(refers to symbols of authority, the privilege of preaching or proclaiming the Gospel, which is the privilege of every Believer)*: and whatsoever you shall bind on earth shall be bound in Heaven *(Christ has given the authority and power to every Believer to bind Satan and his minions of darkness, and to do so by using the*

Name of Jesus [Mk. 16:17-18; Lk. 10:19]): and whatsoever you shall loose on earth shall be loosed in Heaven (looses the Power of God according to the usage of the Name of Jesus; this is the authority of the Believer).

20 Then charged He (Commanded) His Disciples that they should tell no man that He was Jesus the Christ (the Name as used here, is a proclamation of Messiahship; by this time, it is painfully obvious that Israel has rejected her Messiah and, therefore, any further proclamation is pointless!).

JESUS FORETELLS HIS DEATH AND RESURRECTION

21 From that time forth began Jesus to show unto His Disciples, how that He must go unto Jerusalem, and suffer many things of the Elders and Chief Priests and Scribes, and be killed, and be raised again the third day (His sufferings, and the glories that should follow are always associated in Scripture [I Pet. 1:11; 4:13]; the Cross was ever His destination, the very reason He came; the Resurrection was never in doubt).

22 Then Peter took Him, and began to rebuke Him (Peter chides Jesus for speaking of suffering and death; regrettably, many Preachers continue to do the same, as they reject the Cross), saying, Be it far from You, Lord: this shall not be unto You (at that time Peter, nor any of the Disciples, understood the Cross as it regarded its necessity).

23 But He turned, and said unto Peter (respects strong action; would be the sternest of rebukes), Get thee behind Me, Satan (Jesus used nearly the same words in rebuking Peter, and the other Disciples that He had used to the Devil, and His temptation [4:10]; all denial of the Cross in any form, is of Satan): you are an offence unto Me (speaks directly to Peter, because he is now being used by Satan): for you savor not the things that be of God, but those that be of men (if it's not the Cross, then it's of men, which means it is of Satan).

24 Then said Jesus unto His Disciples, If any man will come after Me, let him deny himself (not asceticism, but rather the denial of one's own strength and ability), and take up his cross (the benefits of the Cross, what Jesus did there [Col. 2:14-15]), and follow Me (if Christ is not followed by the means of the Cross, He cannot be followed at all).

25 For whosoever will save his life shall lose it (tries to live his life outside of Christ and the Cross; it can only be lived in Christ through the Cross): and whosoever will lose his life for My sake shall find it (lose his life to Christ, which means to give his life to Christ, which can only be done through the Cross; he then finds "newness of life" [Rom. 6:3-5]).

26 For what is a man profited, if he shall gain the whole world, and lose his own soul? (Christ refers here to "gain" and "loss.") or what shall a man give in exchange for his soul? (Nothing is more important than the soul, because it is eternal.)

27 For the Son of Man shall come in the Glory of His Father with His Angels (while the Son must suffer, nevertheless, Glory will follow; He speaks here of the Second Coming); and then He shall reward every man according to his works ("every man" refers first of all to the Saints and the Judgment Seat of Christ, where rewards will be handed out, and to the unredeemed at the Great White Throne Judgment, where eternal damnation will be meted out [Rev. 20:11-15]).

28 Verily I say unto you, There be some standing here, which shall not taste of death, till they see the Son of Man coming in His Kingdom (refers to the Transfiguration of Christ, which would take place in a few hours, and would be observed by Peter, James, and John).

CHAPTER 17
(A.D. 32)
THE TRANSFIGURATION

AND after six days (in the Hebrew language is exclusive, meaning, that all the days and time are not included; Luke said, "about eight days," but in the Hebrew is inclusive, meaning that everything is included) Jesus took Peter, James, and John his brother, and brought them up into an high mountain apart (does not tell us which mountain; "apart" from the other Disciples),

2 And was transfigured before them (means that the Glory did not shine upon Jesus, but instead, shone out from Him through His raiment): and His Face did shine as the sun (Rev. 1:16), and His Raiment was white as the light (the light made it white).

3 And, behold, there appeared unto them Moses and Elijah talking with Him (Moses and Elijah represented the Law and the Prophets, the dead, and raptured Saints; they spoke with Him of His Atoning Death [Lk. 9:31]; this

doctrine is the great theme of Heaven [Rev. 1:5; 5:6, 9; 7:14]).

4 Then answered Peter, and said unto Jesus, Lord, it is good for us to be here: if you will, let us make here three Tabernacles; one for You, and one for Moses, and one for Elijah (God will not have even the greatest Saints associated with His Beloved Son in worship or teaching).

5 While He yet spoke, behold, a bright cloud overshadowed them (this was a demonstration of the Shechinah, a token of the presence of the Most High, which had appeared over the Tabernacle in the wilderness): and behold a Voice out of the cloud (the "cloud" overshadowing them was a fore-view of the Work of the Holy Spirit after the Day of Pentecost in glorifying Christ [Jn. 16:14]), which said, This is My Beloved Son, in Whom I am well pleased (we have here the Trinity, the Voice out of the cloud, which was the Father, Jesus, standing in a radiant light, and the Holy Spirit present with the overshadowing cloud); hear ye Him (Hear Him Alone; everything comes through Christ, and what Christ did at the Cross; the Holy Spirit works accordingly [Rom. 8:2]).

6 And when the Disciples heard it, they fell on their face, and were sore afraid (the words, "sore afraid," meant that they were fearful that they would die).

7 And Jesus came and touched them, and said, Arise, and be not afraid (ever the Voice of the Saviour to those who are truly sincere, but yet wrong).

8 And when they had lifted up their eyes (proclaims them earnestly surveying the locality), they saw no man, save Jesus only (everything hinges on Jesus, and what He did at the Cross).

9 And as they came down from the mountain, Jesus charged them (Commanded them), saying, Tell the Vision to no man, until the Son of Man be risen again from the dead (as stated, due to the Victory of the Cross, the Resurrection was never in doubt).

JOHN THE BAPTIST AND ELIJAH

10 And His Disciples asked Him, saying, Why then say the Scribes that Elijah must first come? (They were referring to Mal. 4:5. As well, they were confusing the First and the Second Comings.)

11 And Jesus answered and said unto them, Elijah truly shall first come, and restore all things (Christ speaks here of Elijah who will

come in the middle of the Great Tribulation, heralding the Second Coming [Rev., Chpt. 11]).

12 But I say unto you, That Elijah is come already, and they knew him not, but have done unto him whatsoever they listed (had Israel received John the Baptist, they would have received Christ, and John would have been Elijah to Jerusalem at that time, because he came in the spirit and power of Elijah [Lk. 1:17]). Likewise shall also the Son of Man suffer of them (Jesus once again predicts the Cross; nine passages in this Gospel foretell the Crucifixion [16:21; 17:12, 22; 20:17-19, 28; 26:20, 28, 31, 45]).

13 Then the Disciples understood that He spoke unto them of John the Baptist.

THE DISCIPLES' LACK OF POWER

14 And when they were come to the multitude (to the foot of the mountain), there came to Him a certain man, kneeling down to Him, and saying,

15 Lord, have mercy on my son: for he is lunatick, and sore vexed: for ofttimes he falls into the fire, and often into the water (caused by a demon spirit).

16 And I brought him to Your Disciples, and they could not cure him (the inadequacy of man, even believing man).

17 Then Jesus answered and said, O faithless and perverse generation (wrong direction), how long shall I be with you? how long shall I suffer you? (Perturbed at the lack of faith on the part of His Disciples.) bring him hither to Me.

18 And Jesus rebuked the devil (demon); and he departed out of him: and the child was cured from that very hour (the Word of Christ is such that demons must obey).

PRAYER AND FASTING

19 Then came the Disciples to Jesus apart (privately), and said, Why could not we cast him out?

20 And Jesus said unto them, Because of your unbelief (improper understanding regarding Christ and the Cross): for verily I say unto you, If you have faith as a grain of mustard seed (symbolism), you shall say unto this mountain, Remove hence to yonder place; and it shall remove (the impossible made possible); and nothing shall be impossible unto you (that which is the Will of God).

21 Howbeit this kind goes not out but by prayer and fasting (the fasted life [Lk. 9:23-24]).

AGAIN FORETELLS DEATH AND RESURRECTION

22 And while they abode in Galilee, Jesus said unto them *(lends credence to the thought that it was Mount Tabor, which was in Galilee, where the Transfiguration took place)*, The Son of Man shall be betrayed into the hands of men *(draws the Disciples back to the Mission at hand; that Mission was the Redemption of humanity, which would require the offering of the perfect Sacrifice, which was His Body)*:

23 And they shall kill Him *(but only because He allowed such [Jn. 10:17-18])*, and the third day He shall be raised again *(Resurrection)*. And they were exceeding sorry *(but still without understanding)*.

MIRACULOUS PROVISION

24 And when they were come to Capernaum, they that received tribute *money* came to Peter, and said, Does not your master pay tribute? *(Temple tax, of about a half shekel per person, required of every Jew yearly [Ex. 30:13].)*

25 He *(Peter)* said, Yes. And when he was come into the house, Jesus prevented *(confronted)* him, saying, What do you think, Simon? *(Revealed by the Spirit, Jesus questions Peter even before Peter broaches the subject.)* of whom do the kings of the earth take custom or tribute? of their own children, or of strangers? *(Assumes the answer.)*

26 Peter said unto him, Of strangers *(the correct answer)*. Jesus said unto him, Then are the children free *(Jesus was Lord of the Temple, therefore, did not owe the tax, nor His Disciples)*.

27 Notwithstanding, lest we should offend them *(proclaims Him paying the tax, even though not owed, in order that His enemies not have any occasion against Him)*, go thou to the sea *(Galilee)*, and cast an hook, and take up the fish that first comes up; and when you have opened his mouth, you shall find a piece of money: that take, and give unto them from Me and you *(it was a shekel, which was enough to pay the tax for both Peter and Christ)*.

CHAPTER 18
(A.D. 32)
JESUS EXPLAINS GREATNESS

AT the same time came the Disciples unto Jesus *(probably in the home of Peter)*, saying, Who is the greatest in the Kingdom of Heaven? *(Jesus addresses wrong attitudes.)*

2 And Jesus called a little child unto Him, and set him in the midst of them *(the single greatest lesson taught by Christ)*,

3 And He said, Verily I say unto you, Except you be converted *(born-again)*, and become as little children *(a child is totally dependent on its parents, and Believers must be as dependent on Christ)*, you shall not enter into the Kingdom of Heaven *(failure of total dependence on Christ and the Cross, will pull one into unbelief, and, thereby, a lost condition)*.

4 Whosoever *(no exceptions to this rule)* therefore shall humble himself as this little child *(requirement for greatness)*, the same is greatest in the Kingdom of Heaven *(direct opposite of the standard of the world)*.

5 And whoso shall receive one such little child in My Name receives Me *(Believers who depend on self, will not accept the Cross, for this is what this means and, therefore, will not receive such a one who does [Lk. 9:27-28])*.

THE SERIOUSNESS OF OFFENCES

6 But whoso shall offend one of these little ones which believe in Me *(doesn't refer to weak Christians as some believe, but rather to those who trust Christ and the Cross exclusively)*, it were better for him that a millstone were hanged about his neck, and *that* he were drowned in the depth of the sea *(Christ again uses symbolism)*.

7 Woe unto the world because of offences! *(Offences against true Believers.)* for it must needs be that offences come *(due to the Fall)*; but woe to that man by whom the offence cometh! *(All who touch true Believers touch Christ.)*

8 Wherefore if your hand or your foot offend you, cut them off, and cast *them* from you *(symbolism)*: it is better for you to enter into life halt or maimed, rather than having two hands or two feet to be cast into everlasting fire *(while not offending true Believers will not save one, offending them will definitely bring about the most serious degree of punishment in eternity)*.

9 And if your eye offend you, pluck it out, and cast *it* from you: it is better for you to enter into life with one eye, rather than having two eyes to be cast into hell fire *(Christ continues to use symbolism)*.

10 Take heed that you despise not one of these little ones *(one who trusts in Christ and the Cross)*; for I say unto you, That in Heaven

their Angels do always behold the Face of My Father which is in Heaven *(every true Believer is assigned an Angel, who reports to the Heavenly Father, any and all things pertaining to that Believer)*.

THE LOST SHEEP

11 For the Son of Man is come to save that which was lost *(Salvation was paid for at great price; therefore, all who accept that Salvation become the property of God the Father [I Cor. 6:20])*.

12 How do you think? if a man has an hundred sheep, and one of them be gone astray, does he not leave the ninety and nine, and go into the mountains *(proclaims the extensive efforts of the Lord to find the lost one)*, and seeks that which is gone astray? *(Proves that Believers can go astray and, therefore, refutes the unscriptural doctrine of unconditional eternal security.)*

13 And if so be that he find it *(proclaims the fact, that it is possible, that the sheep be not found)*, verily I say unto you, he rejoices more of that *sheep*, than of the ninety and nine which went not astray *(is not meant to place any approval on the straying, but instead, on being found; such proclaims a great victory over Satan)*.

14 Even so it is not the will of your Father which is in Heaven, that one of these little ones should perish *(proclaims the fact that a Believer can cease to believe and, therefore, become an unbeliever; if so, such a one will be lost; this shows the preciousness of the soul)*.

DISPUTES AMONG BELIEVERS

15 Moreover if your brother *(brother in the Lord)* shall trespass against you *(sin against you)*, go and tell him his fault between you and him alone: if he shall hear you, you have gained your brother *(the way to settle disputes)*.

16 But if he will not hear *you*, *then* take with you one or two more, that in the mouth of two or three witnesses every word may be established *(in the hearing of impartial witnesses)*.

17 And if he shall neglect to hear them, tell *it* unto the Church *(Elders of the Church)*: but if he neglect to hear the Church, let him be unto you as an heathen man and a publican *(there can be no fellowship)*.

THE POWER OF BELIEVERS

18 Verily I say unto you, Whatsoever you shall bind on Earth shall be bound in Heaven: and whatsoever you shall loose on Earth shall be loosed in Heaven *(if the Believer conducts himself Scripturally, the decision reached will be honored and ratified in Heaven)*.

THE POWER OF UNITED PRAYER

19 Again I say unto you, That if two of you shall agree on earth as touching any thing that they shall ask, it shall be done for them of My Father which is in Heaven *("anything" is conditional on it being the Will of God; God will never allow His Word to be used against Himself)*.

20 For where two or three are gathered together in My Name, there am I in the midst of them *(the requirement is to meet in His Name; doing such by even two or three, in the Eyes of God, constitute a "Church")*.

FORGIVENESS

21 Then came Peter to Him, and said, Lord, how often shall my brother sin against me, and I forgive him? till seven times? *(One of the most important questions asked by any Disciple.)*

22 Jesus said unto him, I say not unto you, Until seven times: but, Until seventy times seven *(there must be unlimited forgiveness [Lk. 17:4])*.

23 Therefore is the Kingdom of Heaven likened unto a certain king, which would take account of his servants *(a Parable illustrating the principle of forgiveness)*.

24 And when he had begun to reckon *(to check the books)*, one was brought unto him, which owed him ten thousand talents *(if in gold, it represented approximately four billion dollars; if silver, it represented approximately eighty million dollars; a tremendous sum to say the least!)*.

25 But forasmuch as he couldn't pay, his lord commanded him to be sold, and his wife, and children, and all that he had, and payment to be made *(this represents the sinner who cannot hope to pay such a staggering amount, no matter what he does!)*.

26 The servant therefore fell down, and worshipped him, saying, Lord, have patience with me, and I will pay you all *(he couldn't pay such a vast debt, and neither can we, which is meant to illustrate that which we owe to God)*.

27 Then the lord of that servant was moved with compassion, and loosed him, and forgave him the debt *(to forgive one, is at the same time, to loose him)*.

28 But the same servant went out, and found one of his fellow-servants, which owed him an hundred pence (*represents about three hundred dollars*): and he laid hands on him, and took *him* by the throat, saying, Pay me that you owe (*he did not show the compassion that had been shown him; it becomes more heinous when one considers the difference in the debt*).

29 And his fellow-servant fell down at his feet, and besought him, saying, Have patience with me, and I will pay you all (*basically says the same thing, as the first debtor had said*).

30 And he would not (*would not forgive him the three hundred dollars*): but went and cast him into prison, till he should pay the debt (*which means that him being in prison makes it virtually impossible for him to pay the debt; so he will likely stay there until he dies*).

31 So when his fellow-servants saw what was done, they were very sorry, and came and told unto their lord all that was done (*to be sure, the Lord always knows what was done*).

32 Then his lord (*Christ is Lord of all*), after that he had called him (*the one he had forgiven the ten thousand talents*), said unto him, O you wicked servant, I forgave you all that debt, because you desired it of me (*unforgiveness of others is wicked, and puts one in the category of a "wicked servant"*):

33 Should not you also have had compassion on your fellow-servant, even as I had pity on you? (*We must never forget how much the Lord has forgiven us, and likewise, show the same spirit toward others, who owe us much less than we owe the Lord.*)

34 And his lord was wroth (*angry*), and delivered him to the tormentors, till he should pay all that was due unto him (*lack of forgiveness of others revokes the forgiveness of God to us; a sobering thought!*).

35 So likewise shall My Heavenly Father do also unto you, if you from your hearts forgive not every one his brother their trespasses (*true forgiveness comes from the heart, and God knows when it is true*).

CHAPTER 19
(A.D. 33)
JESUS SPEAKS CONCERNING DIVORCE

AND it came to pass, *that* when Jesus had finished these sayings, He departed from Galilee, and came into the coasts (*borders*) of Judaea beyond Jordan (*He would not come back; it was His farewell to the scene of most of His Miracles and Ministry*);

2 And great multitudes followed Him; and He healed them there (*the multitudes trusted Him; the Pharisees tempted Him*).

3 The Pharisees also came unto Him, tempting Him (*trying to trap Him*), and saying unto Him, Is it lawful for a man to put away his wife for every cause? (*The question of divorce and remarriage was the overriding question in Israel of that particular time.*)

4 And He answered and said unto them, Have you not read, that He (*God*) which made *them* at the beginning made them male and female (*destroys the theory of evolution; Jesus was actually the Creator [Jn. 1:1-3]*),

5 And said, For this cause shall a man leave father and mother, and shall cleave to his wife: and they twain shall be one flesh? (*Proclaims God as the founder of marriage, which makes it a Divine institution.*)

6 Wherefore they are no more twain (*two*), but one flesh (*God looks at a man and his wife not as two, but instead "one"*). What therefore God has joined together, let not man put asunder (*the Will of the Lord is to be sought regarding marriage; however, God recognizes the institution of marriage whether His Will or not*).

7 They say unto Him, Why did Moses then command to give a writing of divorcement, and to put her away (*Deut. 24:1-2*)?

8 He said unto them, Moses because of the hardness of your hearts suffered you to put away your wives: but from the beginning it was not so (*divorce is not the Will of God; regarding a Christian husband and wife, there are no true grounds for divorce — if both conduct themselves Scripturally, there will never be a need for divorce*).

9 And I say unto you, Whosoever shall put away his wife, except *it be* for fornication (*an adulterous lifestyle*), and shall marry another, commits adultery: and whoso marries her which is put away doth commit adultery (*if the marriage is dissolved for Scriptural grounds — fornication or desertion [I Cor. 7:15], remarriage is Scripturally allowed*).

10 His Disciples say unto Him, If the case of the man be so with *his* wife, it is not good to marry (*their thinking was wrong [Prov. 18:22]*).

11 But He said unto them, All *men* cannot receive this saying, save *they* to whom it is given (*in effect, Christ is saying that all should marry, save the few who are called of God to do otherwise; the next Verse tells us what that is*).

12 For there are some eunuchs, which were

so born from *their* mother's womb *(accident of birth — no sex drive whatsoever)*: and there are some eunuchs, which were made eunuchs of men *(castrated, in order to serve the State, which was a custom then)*: and there be eunuchs, which have made themselves eunuchs for the Kingdom of Heaven's sake *(personal resolve, were not castrated, as the Apostle Paul)*. He who is able to receive *it*, let him receive *it* *(refers to the last group, and speaks of those called of the Lord for such a task, which would be few)*.

JESUS BLESSES LITTLE CHILDREN

13 Then were there brought unto Him little children, that He should put *His* hands on them, and pray: and the Disciples rebuked them *(a number of women, hearing the teaching on the sanctity of marriage as given by Christ, brought their children to Jesus for Him to Bless them; their intelligence was higher than that of the Disciples, who tried to prevent this action)*.

14 But Jesus said, Suffer little children, and forbid them not, to come unto Me: for of such is the Kingdom of Heaven *(children are dependent on parents; Believers are to be totally dependent on Christ, of which children are an example)*.

15 And he laid *His* hands on them, and departed thence.

THE RICH YOUNG RULER

16 And, behold, one came and said unto Him, Good Master *(addressed Him merely as a teacher)*, what good thing shall I do, that I may have eternal life? *("Doing" is not the answer, but rather, "believing" [Jn. 3:16].)*

17 And He said unto him, Why do you call Me good? *(You don't recognize Me as God.)* *there* is none good but One, *that is*, God *(Jesus wasn't saying that He wasn't good; in fact, He definitely was good, because He is God)*: but if you will enter into life, keep the Commandments *(is meant to answer the man on the same grounds which he has asked — the grounds of good works! He will show him that he, in fact, cannot attain to eternal life by "keeping Commandments," i.e., "good works")*.

18 He said unto him, Which? *(A ridiculous question!)* Jesus said, you shall not commit murder, you shall not commit adultery, you shall not steal, you shall not bear false witness *(Jesus didn't say keep one Commandment, but rather all of them, which the man had not done, nor*

any other man for that matter — except Christ),

19 Honour your father and *your* mother: and, you shall love your neighbour as yourself *(this latter Commandment is taken from Lev. 19:18; it was not a part of the original Ten, but actually summed up all the Commandments, which dealt with one's fellowman)*.

20 The young man said unto Him, All these things have I kept from my youth up *(he was mistaken; he had not)*: what lack I yet? *(This question proclaims the fact that something was wrong.)*

21 Jesus said unto him, If you will be perfect, go *and* sell that you have, and give to the poor, and you shall have treasure in Heaven: and come *and* follow Me *(Jesus put His finger on the two great Commandments of the Law and said: "If you love your neighbor as yourself, then share your wealth with him; and if you love Jehovah your God with all your heart, then follow Me, for one only is good, that is God, and I am He")*.

22 But when the young man heard that saying, he went away sorrowful: for he had great possessions *(the Gospel makes mad, sad, or glad; Naaman went away in a rage; the rich ruler went away sorrowful; but Zacchaeus received Christ joyfully)*.

A WARNING TO THE RICH

23 Then said Jesus unto His Disciples, Verily I say unto you, That a rich man shall hardly enter into the Kingdom of Heaven *(this was contrary to Jewish doctrine, for they taught that riches signified God's approval)*.

24 And again I say unto you, It is easier for a camel to go through the eye of a needle, than for a rich man to enter into the Kingdom of God *(it is impossible for a camel to go through the eye of a needle, and it is equally impossible for the most deeply religious man to enter Heaven on the principle of merit)*.

25 When His Disciples heard *it*, they were exceedingly amazed, saying, Who then can be saved? *(Entrance into the Kingdom of God by man as man, however cultivated and moral, is here declared by the Infallible Judge to be impossible.)*

26 But Jesus beheld *them*, and said unto them, With men this is impossible; but with God all things are possible *(so then what cannot be obtained by merit may be received by gift; for the Gift of God is eternal life [Rom. 6:23])*.

REWARDS FOR CONSECRATION

27 Then answered Peter and said unto Him,

Behold, we have forsaken all, and followed you; what shall we have therefore? *(This proclaims the fact that it is just as hard for the poor man to leave his little house as it is for the rich noble to forsake his great palace.)*

28 And Jesus said unto them, Verily I say unto you, That you which have followed Me, in the regeneration *(the Millennium)* when the Son of Man shall sit in the throne of His glory *(during the coming Kingdom Age Jesus will reign Personally from Jerusalem and, in effect, govern the entirety of the world)*, you also shall sit upon twelve thrones, judging the twelve tribes of Israel *(this graphically answers the question posed by Peter; they had exchanged a little fishing boat for a Kingdom; it pays to live for God)*.

29 And every one who has forsaken houses, or brethren, or sisters, or father, or mother, or wife, or children, or lands, for My Name's sake, shall receive an hundredfold *(Mark added, "now in this time" [Mk. 10:30] Christ meant exactly what He said, but we must take everything into account)*, and shall inherit everlasting life *(this is freely given on acceptance of Christ [Rom. 6:23])*.

30 But many *who are* first shall be last; and the last *shall be* first *(Israel was "first" and the "Church" is last in relation to time, but in respect to position the last shall be first)*.

CHAPTER 20
(A.D. 33)
THE PARABLE OF THE LABORERS

FOR the Kingdom of Heaven is like unto a man *who is* an householder, which went out early in the morning to hire labourers into his vineyard *(a Parable — in effect, Jesus is answering Peter's question, "what shall we have therefore?", the primary lesson that we will learn is that reward of the Kingdom is not of debt, but of Grace)*.

2 And when he had agreed with the labourers for a penny a day *(about forty dollars a day in our present money)*, he sent them into his vineyard.

3 And he went out about the third hour *(9 a.m. in the morning)*, and saw others standing idle in the marketplace,

4 And said unto them; Go ye also into the vineyard, and whatsoever is right I will give you. And they went their way *(they left the amount of payment up to the householder)*.

5 Again he went out about the sixth and ninth hour *(12 o'clock noon and 3 p.m. in the afternoon)*, and did likewise.

6 And about the eleventh hour *(5 o'clock in the afternoon)* he went out, and found others standing idle, and said unto them, Why stand you here all the day idle?

7 They say unto him, Because no man has hired us. He said unto them, Go ye also into the vineyard; and whatsoever is right, *that* shall ye receive *(they as well, took him at his word)*.

8 So when evening was come *(about 6 p.m.)*, the lord of the vineyard said unto his steward, Call the labourers, and give them *their* hire, beginning from the last unto the first *(the ones hired last were to be paid first, with the ones hired first being paid last)*.

9 And when they came who *were hired* about the eleventh hour, they received every man a penny *(about forty dollars for the one hour's work)*.

10 But when the first came *(the first ones hired)*, they supposed that they should have received more; and they likewise received every man a penny *(forty dollars)*.

11 And when they had received *it*, they murmured against the goodman of the house,

12 Saying, These last have wrought *(worked)* but one hour, and you have made them equal unto us, which have borne the burden and heat of the day.

13 But he answered one of them, and said, Friend, I do you no wrong: did not you agree with me for a penny?

14 Take *that* which *is* yours, and go your way: I will give unto this last, even as unto you *(our Lord is teaching Grace here, which means that we do not obtain Salvation from Him by merit, but as well, it speaks of Israel and the Church; the Church although last, will receive just as much as Israel, who was first)*.

15 Is it not lawful for me to do what I will with mine own? Is your eye evil, because I am good? *(No man has the right to make a claim on God because of merit. It must all be by Faith in Christ and the Cross [Rom. 3:20-31].)*

16 So the last shall be first, and the first last *(the Church was chosen last, but will be first, because Israel which was chosen first, rejected the Lord)*: for many be called, but few chosen *(many are called, but only a few choose to heed the call)*.

JESUS AGAIN FORETELLS HIS DEATH
AND RESURRECTION

17 And Jesus going up to Jerusalem *(when*

and where He would be Crucified) took the twelve Disciples apart in the way (privately), and said unto them,

18 Behold, we go up to Jerusalem; and the Son of Man shall be betrayed unto the Chief Priests and unto the Scribes, and they shall condemn Him to death,

19 And shall deliver Him to the Gentiles (the Romans) to mock, and to scourge (to beat Him), and to crucify Him: and the third day He shall rise again (both the Jews and the Gentiles condemned Christ).

THE MOTHER OF JAMES AND JOHN

20 Then came to Him the mother of Zebedee's children (Salome) with her sons (James and John), worshipping Him, and desiring a certain thing of Him (the fourth prediction of the Crucifixion failed like that of 17:22-23 to displace in the hearts of the Disciples self-interest and self-importance).

21 And He said unto her, What do you want? She said unto Him, Grant that these my two sons (James and John) may sit, the one on your right hand, and the other on the left, in Your Kingdom (we see here the first signs of politics in the Church).

22 But Jesus answered and said, You know not what you ask (unless the Holy Spirit enlightens the heart, the clearest spiritual teaching has neither meaning nor power; this fact humbles man's pride). Are you able to drink of the cup that I shall drink of (the cup of suffering), and to be baptized with the baptism that I am baptized with? (This is the baptism that's of suffering. The Cross will illicit opposition from both the Church and the world, but more so from the Church.) They say unto Him, We are able (they did not know what they were saying; they were thinking of thrones in glory, and definitely not of suffering).

23 And He said unto them, you shall drink indeed of My cup, and be baptized with the baptism that I am baptized with (every true Christian will suffer the indignities of the Cross; if not, they aren't living and preaching the Cross, which means they are not living and preaching the Gospel): but to sit on My right hand, and on My left, is not Mine to give, but it shall be given to them for whom it is prepared of My Father (positions in the Kingdom of the Son were planned by the Father, and the Son, and the Unity of the Godhead, would only give such positions to those to whom the Father had determined to

grant them).

24 And when the ten (remaining Disciples) heard it (heard what was requested by Salome), they were moved with indignation (they wanted the positions themselves) against the two brethren (James and John).

25 But Jesus called them (all twelve) unto Him, and said, you know that the princes of the Gentiles exercise dominion over them, and they who are great exercise authority upon them (worldly greatness, which is the opposite of spiritual greatness).

26 But it shall not be so among you (the Believer is not to aspire to worldly greatness): but whosoever will be great among you, let him be your minister (servant);

27 And whosoever will be chief among you, let him be your servant (one giving himself wholly to another's will, at least that which is scriptural):

28 Even as the Son of Man came not to be ministered unto (not to have servants wait on him), but to minister (to serve others), and to give His life a ransom for many (which He did on the Cross).

JESUS HEALS TWO BLIND MEN

29 And as they departed from Jericho (the only time He went to Jericho of which we are aware), a great multitude followed Him (Jesus is on His way to Jerusalem).

30 And, behold, two blind men sitting by the way side, when they heard that Jesus passed by, cried out, saying, Have mercy on us, O Lord, Thou Son of David (Bartimaeus was one of these men; both were healed).

31 And the multitude rebuked them, because they should hold their peace (demanded that they be quiet): but they cried the more, saying, Have mercy on us, O Lord, Thou Son of David (this designation recognized Christ as the Messiah).

32 And Jesus stood still, and called them, and said, What will you that I shall do unto you?

33 They say unto Him, Lord, that our eyes may be opened.

34 So Jesus had compassion on them, and touched their eyes: and immediately their eyes received sight, and they followed Him (two blind men are mentioned by Matthew in keeping with his Gospel; they represent the Hebrew nation in its two divisions of Israel and Judah; and their receiving sight illustrates and predicts the light that will shine upon the nation in the

future day, when the Son of David will make His grand entrance into Jerusalem at the Second Coming).

CHAPTER 21
(A.D. 33)
THE TRIUMPHAL ENTRY
INTO JERUSALEM

AND when they drew nigh unto Jerusalem (the last six days of the Lord's earthly life began here), and were come to Bethphage (very near Jerusalem), unto the Mount of Olives, then sent Jesus two Disciples (tradition says that it was Peter and John),

2 Saying unto them, Go into the village over against you (probably refers to Bethphage), and straightway (immediately) you shall find an ass tied, and a colt with her: loose them, and bring them unto Me.

3 And if any man say ought (anything) unto you, you shall say, The Lord has need of them; and straightway (immediately) he will send them.

4 All this was done, that it might be fulfilled which was spoken by the prophet, saying,

5 Tell ye the daughter of Sion, Behold, your King comes unto you, meek, and sitting upon an ass, and a colt the foal of an ass (Zech. 9:9).

6 And the Disciples went, and did as Jesus commanded them,

7 And brought the ass, and the colt, and put on them their clothes (a saddle of sorts), and they set Him thereon (He rode the colt, with the other one, its mother, following with its back also prepared for a rider, nevertheless absent, which served as a symbol of Israel which rejected Christ).

8 And a very great multitude spread their garments in the way (concerned the thousands who were coming into Jerusalem to celebrate the three great Feast's, "The Passover, Unleavened Bread, and First-fruits"; Christ would fulfill all three); others cut down branches from the trees, and strawed (scattered) them in the way (probably referred to palm fronds and branches from olive trees).

9 And the multitudes that went before, and that followed (represents Israel before and the Church which followed), cried, saying, Hosanna to the Son of David (this was a Feast of Tabernacles expression, but premature): Blessed is He Who comes in the Name of the Lord; Hosanna in the highest (all of this was terminology by the people recognizing Him as the Messiah; but

He was not recognized as such by the religious leaders of Israel).

10 And when He was come into Jerusalem, all the city was moved, saying, Who is this? ("Was moved" refers to "quake" as in an earthquake; thousands before and behind Him, were making the city ring with the great Salutation, "Hosanna in the Highest".)

11 And the multitude said, This is Jesus the Prophet of Nazareth of Galilee (this is the title that was most understandable to the people. On this day, the 69th week [483 years] of Daniel's prediction was completed [Dan. 9:27]).

THE CLEANSING OF THE TEMPLE

12 And Jesus went into the Temple of God, and cast out all them who sold and bought in the Temple, and overthrew the tables of the moneychangers, and the seats of them who sold doves (this was in the Court of the Gentiles; it was a different incident than that narrated in Jn. 2:13; the first commenced the beginning of His Ministry, this last one, its close),

13 And said unto them, It is written, My house shall be called the house of prayer; but you have made it a den of thieves (Isa. 56:7).

14 And the blind and the lame came to Him in the Temple; and He healed them (Heaven condemned the wrong use of the Temple, He now showed them the right use of it).

15 And when the Chief Priests and Scribes saw the wonderful things that He did, and the children crying in the Temple, and saying, Hosanna to the Son of David; they were sore displeased (most of the modern Church world is "sore displeased" as well, at any demonstration of the Holy Spirit),

16 And said unto Him, do You hear what these say? And Jesus said unto them, Yes; have you never read, Out of the mouth of babes and sucklings (little children) You have perfected praise? (The strength of the weak is praise, and worship of Christ is strength [Ps. 8:2].)

THE BARREN FIG TREE CURSED

17 And He left them (the religious leaders), and went out of the city (Jerusalem) into Bethany (home of Lazarus, Mary, and Martha); and He lodged there (probably out in the open; there was no room for Him when He began His Life, and no room for Him at the end of His Life).

18 Now in the morning as He returned into the city (Jerusalem), He hungered (suggests that

He did not spend the night with Lazarus, Mary, and Martha, but rather in the open).

19 And when He saw a fig tree in the way, He came to it, and found nothing thereon, but leaves only *(symbolic of Israel; all leaves and no fruit)*, and said unto it, Let no fruit grow on you henceforward for ever *(during the whole of time unto Israel's present position).* And presently the fig tree withered away *(immediately began to wither; Israel, upon her rejection of Christ, immediately began to whither).*

20 And when the Disciples saw *it*, they marvelled, saying, How soon is the fig tree withered away! *(This was the next day. They saw the miracle, but did not know what the miracle was intended to teach.)*

21 Jesus answered and said unto them *(He deals with them on their level, not on the level the miracle was intended to convey)*, Verily I say unto you, If you have faith, and doubt not, you shall not only do this *which is done* to the fig tree, but also if you shall say unto this mountain, Be thou removed, and be thou cast into the sea; it shall be done *(symbolic terminology respecting the power of true Faith; all Faith must rest in Christ and Him Crucified, meaning that its correct object is always the Cross; the Will of God will then be carried out, and mountains of difficulties removed).*

22 And all things, whatsoever you shall ask in prayer, believing, you shall receive *("all things" according to the Will of God; "Believing" pertains to the correct object of Faith, which must always be the Cross [I Cor. 1:17-18,23; 2:2]).*

JESUS ESTABLISHES HIS AUTHORITY

23 And when He was come into the Temple *(early in the morning)*, the Chief Priests and the Elders of the people *(religious leaders)* came unto Him as He was teaching *(interrupted His teaching)*, and said, By what authority do You do these things? and who gave You this authority? *(If He claimed that God gave Him this authority that would have been admittance that He was the Messiah. This they wanted Him to do, in order to accuse Him of blasphemy.)*

24 And Jesus answered and said unto them, I also will ask you one thing, which if you tell Me, I likewise will tell you by what authority I do these things *(in effect, by the question He will pose, will be the answer).*

25 The Baptism of John *(of repentance)*, from where was it? from Heaven, or of men? And they reasoned with themselves, saying, If we shall say, From Heaven; He will say unto us, Why did you not then believe him? *(John introduced Christ as the Messiah.)*

26 But if we shall say, Of men; we fear the people; for all hold John as a Prophet *(whichever way they answered, put them in a dilemma; if they admitted that John was the predicted forerunner of Christ, then they were bound to receive Jesus as the Messiah).*

27 And they answered Jesus, and said, We cannot tell *(this was untrue; they were the religious leaders of Israel and were supposed to know right from wrong).* And He said unto them, Neither tell I you by what authority I do these things *(Jesus showed that they knew and were unwilling to answer.; in effect He said, "If you will not be honest with Me and the people, it is pointless to continue this conversation").*

THE PARABLE OF THE TWO SONS

28 But what think you? *(This Parable and the next are directed to these religious leaders, as well as the people.)* A *certain* man had two sons; and he came to the first, and said, Son, go work today in my vineyard *(the "certain Man" represents the Lord; the "two sons" represent the unredeemed, who made no pretense at Salvation, while the second represented the Pharisees and their followers, who made every pretense of religion).*

29 He answered and said, I will not: but afterward he repented, and went *(this represents the first son, who at the outset made no pretense of Salvation, but later repented).*

30 And he came to the second, and said likewise. And he answered and said, I *go*, sir: and he went not *(this represents the Pharisees and their followers, who claimed much, but had nothing).*

31 Which of the two did the will of *his* father? They say unto Him, The first *(this proclaims the only answer that could be given; they little realized in their self-righteous piety that the Parable was directed at them; they were the ones who proclaimed their allegiance to God and His Word, but in reality, had no allegiance at all!).* Jesus said unto them, Verily I say unto you, That the publicans and the harlots go into the Kingdom of God before you *(He said this to their faces, and before the people; He could not have insulted them more, putting them beneath publicans, whom they considered to be traitors, and harlots).*

32 For John *(John the Baptist)* came unto you in the way of righteousness, and you believed

him not (speaking to the religious leaders): but the publicans and the harlots believed him: and you, when you had seen it, repented not afterward, that you might believe him (they saw the changed lives as a result of John's Gospel, but still wouldn't believe).

THE WICKED HUSBANDMAN

33 Hear another Parable: There was a certain householder (represents God the Father), which planted a vineyard (the vineyard illustrated the Kingdom of Heaven, which was entrusted to Israel), and hedged it round about (the Lord protected it), and dug a winepress in it (represents Blessings), and built a tower (represents the position of watchmen who were to serve as protectors of the vineyard), and let it out to husbandmen (at the time of Christ, the husbandmen represent the Scribes and the Pharisees), and went into a far country (left the vineyard in their care):

34 And when the time of the fruit drew near (the time when Israel was to extend the Kingdom among other nations), he sent his servants to the husbandmen (the Prophets were sent to Israel), that they might receive the fruits of it.

35 And the husbandmen (religious leaders) took his servants (the Prophets), and beat one, and killed another, and stoned another (Mat. 23:37).

36 Again, he sent other servants (Prophets) more than the first: and they did unto them likewise.

37 But last of all he sent unto them his son (the Lord Jesus Christ), saying, They will reverence my son (this Parable also asserts the Doctrine of the Trinity).

38 But when the husbandmen saw the son, they said among themselves, This is the heir (the religious leaders of Israel knew that Jesus was the Son of God and, therefore, the Messiah of Israel); come, let us kill Him (the religious leaders of Israel were murderers), and let us seize on His inheritance (they imagined that if they could destroy Christ, they could continue in their position of the inheritance; they killed that they might possess, but killing was the road to their sure destruction).

39 And they caught Him (that which would take place a few hours later), and cast Him out of the vineyard (excommunicated Him, in effect, claiming to Israel that He was an imposter), and slew Him (was done only after they had pronounced their curses upon Him, which

in their minds legitimized their hideous action of murder).

40 When the lord therefore of the vineyard comes, what will he do unto those husbandmen? (The religious leaders are not quite sure where Jesus is going with this, and consequently, will continue to bite until they hang themselves.)

41 They say unto Him, He will miserably destroy those wicked men (they little realized that they were speaking of themselves), and will let out His vineyard unto other husbandmen (is exactly what happened! the Lord turned from the Jews to the Gentiles [Acts 18:6]), which shall render him the fruits in their seasons (after a fashion, the Church has done that).

42 Jesus said unto them, Did you never read in the Scriptures (Jesus directs them to the Word of God), The Stone (Christ) which the builders rejected (Israel rejected Christ [Ps. 118:22-23]), the same is become the Head of the corner (everything hinged on Christ): this is the Lord's doing (the Plan of God), and it is marvellous in our eyes? (In the eyes of those who accept Christ.)

43 Therefore I say unto you, The Kingdom of God shall be taken from you (taken from the religious leaders and the people of Israel, which it was in 70 A.D., when Titus, the Roman General destroyed Jerusalem; in "saving their lives they lost them" [Mat. 16:25]), and given to a nation bringing forth the fruits thereof (refers to the Gentiles, of which most of the Church consists, who took the place of the Jews in the Plan of God [Acts 13:46-49; 15:13-18; Rom. 10:19; 11:26]).

44 And whosoever shall fall on this stone shall be broken (refers to Judgment and not Blessing, as some claim): but on whomsoever it shall fall, it will grind him to powder (refers to those who put themselves in active opposition to Christ and His Kingdom; they will ultimately be destroyed, and without hope of recovery, which includes every religion of the world).

45 And when the Chief Priests and Pharisees had heard His Parables, they perceived that He spoke of them (speaks of the very leading religious leaders, who had conveyed to them that which Jesus had said).

46 But when they sought to lay hands on Him (proclaims the wickedness of their evil hearts), they feared the multitude (their only restraint), because they took Him for a Prophet (the last "they" speak of the multitude, and not the Pharisees and Chief Priests, etc.).

CHAPTER 22
(A.D. 33)
THE PARABLE OF THE MARRIAGE FEAST

AND Jesus answered and spoke unto them again by Parables, and said (*Jesus is still in the Temple, and continuing with His Message; "them" refers to the religious leaders of Israel*),

2 The Kingdom of Heaven is like unto a certain king (*God the Father*), which made a marriage for his son (*the Lord Jesus Christ*),

3 And sent forth his servants (*the Prophets*) to call them (*Israel*) who were bidden to the wedding: and they would not come (*they rejected the Prophets and even their Messiah; the phrase proclaims a studied and deliberate rejection*).

4 Again, he sent forth other servants (*which could well refer to His personal Disciples, and the Apostle Paul, and those in the Early Church, whose Ministry was yet future*), saying, Tell them which are bidden (*this is an invitation directed personally to the people of Israel; the first few Chapters of the Book of Acts will bear this out*), Behold, I have prepared my dinner: my oxen and *my* fatlings *are* killed, and all things *are* ready (*a strong sense of urgency, for time is running out*): come unto the marriage (*respects the last invitation given to the Jews that could well have been given by the Apostle Paul [Acts, Chpt. 23]*).

5 But they made light of *it* (*Israel's response to the Gospel*), and went their ways (*their ways instead of God's Ways*), one to his farm, another to his merchandise (*Israel had no interest in the Gospel; they were more interested in money; how much does this characterize the modern Church!*):

6 And the remnant (*those of Israel who didn't want the Gospel, which included the religious leaders*) took his servants (*the Apostles*), and entreated *them* spitefully, and slew *them* (*the time of the Early Church was glorious, but as well, a time of intense persecution*).

7 But when the king (*the Heavenly Father*) heard *thereof*, he was wroth (*extremely angry*): and he sent forth his armies, and destroyed those murderers, and burned up their city (*exactly what happened in A.D. 70, when Titus destroyed Jerusalem*).

8 Then said he to his servants (*the Plan of God is not halted, only its direction*), The wedding is ready (*will go as planned, but with a change of guests*), but they which were bidden were not worthy (*concerns Israel who would not accept the worthiness of Christ*).

9 Go ye therefore into the highways (*the balance of the world*), and as many as you shall find (*love invites "the many"*), bid to the marriage (*give an invitation to the Gentiles, which was the Lord's Plan all along, but not in this fashion*).

10 So those servants (*Apostles and Prophets*) went out into the highways (*world evangelism, actually begun by the Apostle Paul*), and gathered together all as many as they found (*the Gospel invitation given to everyone; none are excluded*), both bad and good (*proclaims the fact that the "good" need Salvation, as well as the "bad"*): and the wedding was furnished with guests (*respects the redeemed who will be made up of both Jews and Gentiles*).

11 And when the king (*God the Father*) came in to see the guests (*it was customary for the host to come and see their guests after they were assembled*), he saw there a man which had not on a wedding garment (*a wedding garment supplied by the King, which was the custom in those days*):

12 And he said unto him, Friend (*used in a negative way*), how did you think you could come in hither not having a wedding garment? (*You have on your own garment, which is self-righteousness, and have refused my garment, which is the Righteousness of Christ.*) And he was speechless (*this man deemed his own garment of self-righteousness good enough for the feast; and it suited him very well until the king came in, and then he was exposed, and cast out*).

13 Then said the king (*God the Father*) to the servants (*Angels, in this case*), Bind him hand and foot, and take him away (*also refers to true Preachers who proclaim Salvation to Christ-acceptors, and doom to those who are Christ-rejecters*), and cast *him* into outer darkness; there shall be weeping and gnashing of teeth (*Hell is the end result of all self-righteousness*).

14 For many are called (*includes the whole world, which are many — and called by God*), but few *are* chosen (*few respond favorably to the call*).

TRIBUTE MONEY TO CAESAR

15 Then went the Pharisees (*the self-righteous hypocrites to whom Christ was speaking*), and took counsel (*with the Herodians and Sadducees*) how they might entangle Him in His talk (*trap Him so they could arrest Him; how foolish they were!*).

16 And they sent out unto Him their Disciples *(Disciples of the Pharisees)* with the Herodians *(those who claimed Herod to be the Messiah)*, saying, Master *(teacher)*, we know that You *are* true, and teach the way of God in truth, neither carest Thou for any *man:* for You regard not the person of men *(flattery, which they did not at all believe, but was a part of their clever trap; they were foolish to try and match wits with Him, but in their stupidity they kept trying).*

17 Tell us therefore, What do you think? Is it lawful *(the Law of Moses)* to give tribute *(pay taxes)* unto Caesar, or not? *(This question raged in Israel at that time. In their thinking, either way He answered would trap Him. If He said it was not lawful, this would have put Him in opposition to the Roman government. Had He said it was lawful, He would have denied His claim as Messiah, the King of Israel.)*

18 But Jesus perceived their wickedness *(pertains to the hypocrisy which prompted their question)*, and said, Why tempt you Me *(He saw through their craftiness)*, you hypocrites? *(He said this to their faces.)*

19 Show Me the tribute money *(the type of coin used to pay the tax)*. And they brought unto Him a penny *(the coin)*.

20 And He said unto them, Whose *is* this image and superscription? *(Was probably the image of Tiberius on the coin.)*

21 They say unto Him, Caesar's. Then said He unto them, Render therefore unto Caesar the things which are Caesar's; and unto God the things that are God's *(lawful government is here recognized, and support for government approved; if done correctly, support for government and support for God will not clash).*

22 When they had heard *these words (in this short statement, a new sphere of government was introduced, the two spheres of Church and State to be distinct and not joined)*, they marveled *(were left speechless)*, and left Him, and went their way *(they were silenced, but their evil hearts were not changed).*

THE RESURRECTION

23 The same day came to Him the Sadducees *(the third party in Israel which tried to trap Him)*, which say that there is no Resurrection *(they did not believe in a future life of the soul, or the Resurrection of the body)*, and asked Him,

24 Saying, Master *(teacher)*, Moses said *(they studied the Bible, but not for it to mold their life)*, If a man die, having no children, his brother shall marry his wife, and raise up seed unto his brother *([Deut. 25:5-10] this was only under the Old Covenant, and was not carried over into the New Covenant).*

25 Now there were with us seven brethren *(a hypothetical case)*: and the first, when he had married a wife, deceased *(died)*, and, having no issue *(no children)*, left his wife unto his brother:

26 Likewise the second also, and the third, unto the seventh.

27 And last of all the woman died also.

28 Therefore in the Resurrection whose wife shall she be of the seven? for they all had her *(they now spring their trap).*

29 Jesus answered and said unto them *(that which seemed to be unanswerable to others, was simple for Him)*, You do err, not knowing the Scriptures *(once again, He takes them to the Word of God)*, nor the power of God *(addresses itself to the denial by the Sadducees of the supernatural).*

30 For in the Resurrection *(this proclaims by Christ the validity of the Doctrine of the Resurrection)* they *(all who are saved)* neither marry, nor are given in marriage, but are as the Angels of God in Heaven *(do not die; as well, Christ proclaims existence of Angels, which the Sadducees also denied).*

31 But as touching the Resurrection of the dead *(guarantees their Resurrection and as well, life after death)*, have you not read that which was spoken unto you by God, saying *(Ex. 3:6, 16)*,

32 I am the God of Abraham, and the God of Isaac, and the God of Jacob? God is not the God of the dead, but of the living *(portrays the fallacy of the great Plan of God being built and predicated on that which is nonexistent; the Lord is saying that these men of whom He spoke, and all others who had died in the Faith were then alive, and will be ever alive; in this, Christ teaches the immortality of the soul and that God is the God of all departed souls; also, the great investment that Christ would make at the Cross, was definitely not to be made for all the Sainted dead who will have no existence).*

33 And when the multitude heard *this*, they were astonished at His doctrine *(at the simplicity of what He said concerning the Resurrection, by using examples from the Word of God).*

THE GREAT COMMANDMENT

34 But when the Pharisees had heard that He had put the Sadducees to silence, they were gathered together *(they normally hated each other)*.

35 Then one of them, *which was* a lawyer *(Scribe)*, asked *Him a question*, tempting Him, and saying,

36 Master *(teacher)*, which *is* the great Commandment of the law? *(The Law of Moses.)*

37 Jesus said unto him, You shall love the Lord your God with all your heart, and with all your soul, and with all your mind *(this is the foundation of all the Law, and as well, applies to the present Day of Grace)*.

38 This is the first and great Commandment *(Love of God must be "first" before anything else can be claimed)*.

39 And the second *is* like unto it, You shall love your neighbour as yourself *(as one loves their neighbor, accordingly, one loves God)*.

40 On these two Commandments hang all the Law and the Prophets *(this includes the New Testament, as well!)*.

DAVID'S SON

41 While the Pharisees were gathered together *(refers to Jesus speaking to the great crowd in the Temple, which contained many Pharisees)*, Jesus asked them *(concerns the most important question they will ever be asked, because it pertains to the Person of Christ, the Messiah)*,

42 Saying, What do you think of Christ? *(What were their thoughts concerning the Messiah?)* whose Son is He? *(He will now bring them face-to-face with His identity.)* They say unto him, *The Son* of David *(this is the correct answer as outlined in II Sam., Chpt. 7)*.

43 He said unto them, How then does David in spirit call Him Lord, saying *(the Messiah was David's Son — in his lineage — and as well, David's Lord; this was revealed to David by the Holy Spirit, and brings together Christ's Humanity and Deity)*,

44 The LORD said unto My Lord *([Ps. 110:1] this refers to God the Father speaking to God the Son)*, Sit Thou on My Right Hand *(refers to Christ being exalted to the highest position in Heaven, which immediately followed the ascension [Phil. 2:9-11])*, till I make Your enemies Your footstool? *(Refers to all enemies being put down during the Millennium and at its conclusion [I Cor. 15:24-28; Eph. 1:10].)*

45 If David then call Him, Lord, how is He his Son? *(He is David's Lord because He is God; He is David's Son because He became man through Mary of the House of David [Lk. 1:34-35; 3:23-38] this one question presents to them the truth of His Incarnation — God becoming Man.)*

46 And no man was able to answer Him a word *(they could not refute His argument)*, neither does any *man* from that day forth ask Him any more *questions (portrays the fact that His Spiritual and Scriptural intelligence far exceeded anything they had ever seen or known)*.

CHAPTER 23
(A.D. 33)

THE SINS OF THE SCRIBES
AND PHARISEES

THEN spoke Jesus to the multitude, and to His Disciples *(this is not the Jesus of the modern Church or fashionable pulpit)*,

2 Saying, The Scribes and the Pharisees sit in Moses' seat *(the "Scribes" proclaimed to be interpreters of the Law of Moses for the people)*:

3 All therefore whatsoever they bid you observe, *that* observe and do *(concerned a correct interpretation of the Scriptures, and not their glosses)*; but do not ye after their works: for they say, and do not *(they do not practice what they preach; remember, Jesus is saying this, in the Temple, before the Pharisees and the people)*.

4 For they bind heavy burdens and grievous to be borne, and lay *them* on men's shoulders *(concerns the glosses and additions that had been made to the law by these hypocrites)*; but they *themselves* will not move them with one of their fingers *(they do not themselves do what they demand of others)*.

5 But all their works they do for to be seen of men *(self-righteousness)*: they make broad their phylacteries *(a small box worn on the arm or forehead, and containing Scriptures)*, and enlarge the borders of their garments *(tassels composed of white and blue threads, intended to remind the wearers of the Commandments of the Lord; they made these overly large to draw attention to themselves)*,

6 And love the uppermost rooms at feasts *(the most honored place at the table)*, and the chief seats in the synagogues *(seats of honor)*,

7 And greetings in the markets *(flowery salutations)*, and to be called of men, Rabbi, Rabbi *("teacher," a favorite title claimed by the Pharisees)*.

8 But you are not to be called Rabbi *(it

concerned the greedy ambition which loved the empty title, and took any means to obtain it): **for One is your Master** (Teacher, Leader, Guide), **even Christ** (the Lord Jesus Christ); **and all you are brethren** (no one Believer is higher than another, and neither can have from Christ any authority over other Believers [I Pet. 5:1-8]).

9 **And call no man your father upon the earth** (eminent teachers to whom the people were taught to look to rather than God): **for one is your Father, which is in Heaven** (all true Bible teachers must cause men to look to God, and not to themselves as the source of power and truth).

10 **Neither be ye called masters** (means that Preachers are not to be called spiritual leaders): **for one is your Master, even Christ** (actually means that God and Christ are the only One's Who have any right to these titles).

11 **But he who is greatest among you shall be your servant** (the definition of Christian greatness, i.e., "the servant principle").

12 **And whosoever shall exalt himself shall be abased** (pride and vanity); **and he who shall humble himself shall be exalted** (is the universal Law of God's dealings with men).

WOES UPON THE SCRIBES AND PHARISEES

13 **But woe unto you, Scribes and Pharisees, hypocrites!** (The first of eight woes, and said to their faces. There could be no greater insult to them than being called "hypocrites"!) **for you shut up the Kingdom of Heaven against men** (is the first scheme of Satan, and is carried out through religion): **for you neither go in yourselves, neither suffer ye them who are entering to go in** (they refuse to accept Christ, and stood in the door to bar access to any and all who would attempt to come in).

14 **Woe unto you, Scribes and Pharisees, hypocrites! for you devour widows' houses, and for a pretence make long prayer** (projects a false piety which deceives people, and the most helpless at that): **therefore you shall receive the greater damnation** (this tells us that religious wickedness is the greatest wickedness of all).

15 **Woe unto you, Scribes and Pharisees, hypocrites! for you compass sea and land to make one proselyte** (working zealously to draw people to themselves, instead of the Lord), **and when he is made, you make him twofold more the child of hell than yourselves** (religious people are the hardest of all to bring to the Lord).

16 **Woe unto you, you blind guides** (these religious leaders were spiritually blind, but yet they were serving as spiritual guides for the people, which guaranteed the people's spiritual destruction; is it any different presently?), **which say, Whosoever shall swear by the Temple, it is nothing** (an oath that need not be kept); **but whosoever shall swear by the gold of the Temple, he is a debtor!** (If one does such, he is bound to hold to his oath.)

17 **You fools and blind** (proclaims Christ adding to the epithets of hypocrites and blind, the word "fools!"): **for whether is greater, the gold, or the Temple that sanctifieth the gold?** (The answer of Christ was not meant to place a seal of approval on swearing oaths, but instead, the foolishness of such a position. The "gold" didn't sanctify the "Temple" but rather, the opposite!)

18 **And, Whosoever shall swear by the Altar, it is nothing** (an oath that doesn't need to be kept); **but whosoever sweareth by the gift** (Sacrifice) **that is upon it, he is guilty** (if one swears an oath by the Sacrifice on the Altar, he's bound to keep such an oath, or so they said).

19 **You fools and blind: for whether is greater, the gift** (Sacrifice), **or the Altar that sanctifieth the gift?** (The religious leaders of Israel had a wrong conception of the entirety of the Plan of God.)

20 **Whoso therefore shall swear by the Altar, sweareth by it, and by all things thereon** (all were equally important).

21 **And whoso shall swear by the Temple, sweareth by it, and by Him Who dwells therein** (their sin was the sin of making God a part of their evil; it is the same presently with many modern Preachers).

22 **And he who shall swear by Heaven swears by the Throne of God, and by Him Who sits thereon** (Christ says here that to swear by "Heaven" includes God and His Throne whether realized or not).

23 **Woe unto you, Scribes and Pharisees, hypocrites! for you pay tithe of mint and anise and cummin** (small plants used for seasoning), **and have omitted the weightier matters of the Law, Judgment, Mercy, and Faith** (they were meticulous about these insignificant things, but gave little or no heed at all, to those things which really mattered): **these ought you to have done** (pertaining to Scriptural Judgment, Mercy, and Faith), **and not to leave the other undone** (make sure, as well, that you pay tithe on all that you have; all of the Word of God is to be obeyed, not just part).

24 **You blind guides, which strain at a gnat,**

and swallow a camel *(this is self-righteousness taken to an ultra extreme)*.

25 Woe unto you, Scribes and Pharisees, hypocrites! for you make clean the outside of the cup and of the platter *(outward show)*, but within they are full of extortion and excess *(the heart)*.

26 You blind Pharisee, cleanse first that *which is* within the cup and platter *(the heart)*, that the outside of them may be clean also *(has to do with moral purity which comes from within, and if such is the case, the outside will be clean as well)*.

27 Woe unto you, Scribes and Pharisees, hypocrites! for you are like unto whited sepulchres, which indeed appear beautiful outward *(once a year, the Jews white washed the tombs in order to make them conspicuous that men may not contract ceremonial defilement by touching or walking over them [Num. 19:16])*, but are within full of dead *men's* bones, and of all uncleanness *(this symbolized the Pharisees)*.

28 Even so you also outwardly appear righteous unto men, but within you are full of hypocrisy and iniquity.

29 Woe unto you, Scribes and Pharisees, hypocrites! *(Presents the eighth and final "woe"!)*, because you build the tombs of the Prophets, and garnish the sepulchres of the righteous *(speaks of the honors paid to departed Saints, while at the same time, planning to murder living Saints, even Christ!)*,

30 And say, If we had been in the days of our fathers, we would not have been partakers with them in the blood of the Prophets *(all the time they were plotting to murder Christ)*.

31 Wherefore you be witnesses unto yourselves *(be honest with yourself)*, that you are the children of them which killed the Prophets *(you have the same murderous hearts as those you condemn)*.

32 Fill ye up then the measure of your fathers *(their wickedness was about to bring judgment, which it did!)*.

33 You serpents, you generation of vipers *(He likens them to that old serpent, their father, the Devil [Jn. 8:44; Rev. 12:9; 20:2])*, how can you escape the damnation of Hell? *(Eternal destiny of these religious leaders would be Hell. What an indictment!)*

34 Wherefore, behold, I send unto you Prophets, and wise men, and Scribes *(pertains to those of the Early Church)*: and *some* of them you shall kill and crucify; and *some* of them shall you scourge in your Synagogues, and persecute *them* from city to city *(the Book of Acts records all of this, exactly as stated by Christ)*:

35 That upon you may come all the righteous blood shed upon the earth *(speaks of the cup of iniquity being filled; Judgment was about to come, which it did!)*, from the blood of righteous Abel *(Gen., Chpt. 4)* unto the blood of Zechariah, son of Barachias, whom you killed between the Temple and the Altar *(more than likely, Zechariah the Prophet [Zech. 1:1])*.

36 Verily I say unto you, All these things shall come upon this generation *(and it did! about thirty-seven years later, in 70 A.D., Jerusalem was totally destroyed by Titus, the Roman General)*.

JESUS WEEPS OVER JERUSALEM

37 O Jerusalem, Jerusalem *(presents Jesus standing in the Temple when He gave this sorrowing account)*, *you* who kill the Prophets, and stone them which are sent unto you *(presents the terrible animosity tendered toward these Messengers of God)*, how often would I have gathered your children together, even as a hen gathers her chickens under *her* wings, and you would not! *(Proclaims every effort made by the Lord, and made "often," to bring Israel back to her senses.)*

38 Behold, your house *(the Temple or Jerusalem, are no longer God's habitation)* is left unto you desolate *(without God, which means they were at the mercy of Satan)*.

39 For I say unto you, you shall not see Me henceforth, till you shall say, Blessed *is* He Who comes in the Name of the Lord *(the Second Coming)*.

CHAPTER 24
(A.D. 33)
DESTRUCTION OF THE TEMPLE PREDICTED

AND Jesus went out, and departed from the Temple *(when He left, God left)*: and His Disciples came to *Him* for to show Him the buildings of the Temple *(this structure was one of the most beautiful in the world of that day)*.

2 And Jesus said unto them, Do you not see all these things? *(Is asked by Christ in response to the remarks made by His Disciples concerning the beauty of the Temple.)* verily I say unto you, There shall not be left here one stone upon another, that shall not be thrown down *(was fulfilled in total exactness; it took place in 70 A.D.)*.

SIGNS OF THE ENDTIME

3 And as He sat upon the Mount of Olives (*the coming siege of Jerusalem by the Romans some thirty-seven years later, began at this exact spot where Christ was sitting*), the Disciples came unto Him privately (*out of earshot of the many Pilgrims in the city for the Passover*), saying, Tell us, when shall these things be? (*Has to do here with the utterance He had just given concerning the destruction of the Temple.*) and what *shall be* the sign of Your coming (*refers to the Second Coming*), and of the end of the world? (*Should have been translated "age."*)

4 And Jesus answered and said unto them (*will now give the future of Israel, and how it will effect the entirety of the world*), Take heed that no man deceive you (*places deception as Satan's greatest weapon*).

5 For many shall come in My Name (*concerns itself primarily with the time immediately before the coming Great Tribulation, and especially its first half*), saying, I am Christ; and shall deceive many (*the greatest of these will be the Antichrist, who will claim to be the Messiah*).

6 And you shall hear of wars and rumours of wars (*has abounded from the beginning, but will accelerate during the first half of the Great Tribulation*): see that you be not troubled (*concerns true Believers*): for all *these things* must come to pass (*we are very near presently to the beginning of fulfillment of what Jesus said*), but the end is not yet (*the end will be at the Second Coming*).

7 For nation shall rise against nation, and Kingdom against Kingdom: and there shall be famines, and pestilences, and earthquakes, in divers places (*few places in the world, if any, will be exempt from these judgments*).

8 All these *are* the beginning of sorrows (*first half of the Great Tribulation*).

9 Then shall they deliver you up to be afflicted, and shall kill you (*pertains to the mid-point of the Great Tribulation when the Antichrist, whom Israel thought was the Messiah, will show his true colors*): and you shall be hated of all nations for My Name's sake (*no nation will come to her rescue; Israel hates Christ, but Christ is the reason that the world hates Israel*).

10 And then shall many be offended (*some Jews will accept Christ, which will be an offence to others*), and shall betray one another, and shall hate one another (*the Jews who accept Christ, will be the brunt of this animosity*).

11 And many false prophets shall rise, and shall deceive many (*they will help the Antichrist*).

12 And because iniquity shall abound (*the Antichrist called "the man of sin" [II Thess. 2:3]*), the love of many shall wax cold (*some who accept Christ, will turn their backs on Him*).

13 But he who shall endure unto the end (*refers to the end of the Great Tribulation*), the same shall be saved (*speaks of survival, and not the Salvation of the Soul*).

14 And this Gospel of the Kingdom (*refers to the same type of Gospel preached by Christ and Paul*) shall be preached in all the world for a witness unto all nations (*not every person, but to all nations; this is close presently to being fulfilled*); and then shall the end come (*the Second Coming*).

THE ABOMINATION OF DESOLATION

15 When you therefore shall see the abomination of desolation, spoken of by Daniel the Prophet, stand in the Holy Place (*speaks of the Antichrist invading Israel, and taking over the Temple*), (whoso reads, let him understand:) (*Reads it in the Word of God [Dan. 8:9-14; 9:27; 11:45; 12:1, 7, 11].*)

16 Then let them which be in Judaea flee into the mountains (*when the Antichrist invades Israel at the mid-point of the Great Tribulation*):

17 Let him which is on the housetop not come down to take any thing out of his house (*houses are flat on top in that part of the world; during the summer, people often sleep on top of the house; speaks of the necessity of haste*):

18 Neither let him which is in the field return back to take his clothes.

19 And woe unto them who are with child, and to them who give suck in those days! (*The necessity of fleeing will be so urgent, that it will be difficult for pregnant women, and mothers with little babies.*)

20 But pray ye that your flight be not in the winter (*bad weather*), neither on the Sabbath Day (*concerns the strict religious observance of the Sabbath, doesn't permit travel*):

GREAT TRIBULATION

21 For then shall be great tribulation (*the last three and one half years*), such as was not since the beginning of the world to this time, no, nor ever shall be (*the worst the world has ever known, and will be so bad that it will never be repeated*).

22 And except those days should be shortened, there should no flesh be saved *(refers to Israel coming close to extinction)*: but for the elect's *(Israel's)* sake those days shall be shortened *(by the Second Coming)*.

23 Then if any man shall say unto you, Lo, here is Christ, or there; believe *it* not *(don't be deceived)*.

24 For there shall arise false Christs, and false prophets *(the Antichrist and the false prophet [Rev., Chpt. 13])*, and shall show great signs and wonders *(which will be offered as proof)*; insomuch that, if *it were* possible, they shall deceive the very elect *(will attempt to deceive Israel)*.

25 Behold, I have told you before *(is meant to emphasize the seriousness of the matter)*.

26 Wherefore if they shall say unto you, Behold, he is in the desert; go not forth: behold, *he is* in the secret chambers; believe *it* not *(the next Verse will tell the manner of His Coming, which will eclipse all pretenders)*.

THE COMING OF THE SON OF MAN

27 For as the lightning cometh out of the east, and shineth even unto the west *(is meant to proclaim the most cataclysmic event the world has ever known)*; so shall also the coming of the Son of Man be *(no one will have to ask, is this really Christ; it will be overly obvious!)*.

28 For wheresoever the carcase is *(speaks of the Battle of Armageddon)*, there will the eagles be gathered together *(should have been translated, "there will the vultures be gathered together" [refers to Ezek. 39:17])*.

29 Immediately after the tribulation of those days *(speaks of the time immediately preceding the Second Coming)* shall the sun be darkened, and the moon shall not give her light *(the light of these orbs will be dim by comparison to the light of the Son of God)*, and the stars shall fall from Heaven *(a display of Heavenly fireworks at the Second Coming)*, and the powers of the Heavens shall be shaken *(will work with the Son of God against the Antichrist, at the Second Coming)*:

30 And then shall appear the sign of the Son of Man in Heaven *(pertains to the Second Coming, which will take place in the midst of these Earth and Heaven shaking events)*: and then shall all the tribes of the Earth mourn *(concerns all the nations of the world which possibly will see this phenomenon by Television)*, and they shall see the Son of Man *(denotes Christ and His human, Glorified Body)* coming in the clouds of Heaven with power and great glory *(lends credence to the thought that much of the world will see Him by Television as He makes His dissent)*.

31 And He shall send His Angels *(they will be visible)* with a great sound of a trumpet *(announcing the gathering of Israel)*, and they shall gather together His elect *(Israel)* from the four winds, from one end of Heaven to the other *(Jews will be gathered from all over the world, and brought to Israel)*.

THE PARABLE OF THE FIG TREE

32 Now learn a Parable of the fig tree *(the Bible presents three trees, the fig, the olive, and the vine, as representing the nation of Israel, nationally, spiritually, and dispensationally)*; When his branch is yet tender, and putteth forth leaves *(is meant to serve as the illustration of Israel nationally)*, ye know that summer *is* near *(refers to Israel as the greatest Prophetic Sign of all, telling us that we are now living in the last of the last days)*:

33 So likewise ye *(points to the modern Church)*, when you shall see all these things *(which we are now seeing as it regards Israel)*, know that it is near, *even* at the doors *(the fulfillment of Endtime Prophecies)*.

34 Verily I say unto you, This generation shall not pass *(the generation of Jews which will be alive at the beginning of the Great Tribulation; as well, it was a prediction by Christ, that irrespective of the problems that Israel would face, even from His day, they would survive)*, till all these things be fulfilled *(there is no doubt, they will be fulfilled)*.

35 Heaven and earth shall pass away *(doesn't refer to annihilation, but rather a change from one condition or state to another)*, but My Words shall not pass away *(what the Word of God says, will be!)*.

36 But of that day and hour knows no *man*, no, not the Angels of Heaven, but My Father only.

DESTRUCTION OF THE WICKED

37 But as the days of Noah *were*, so shall also the coming of the Son of Man be *(the men of Noah's day were insensible to the Prophecies predicting the coming flood, and so will men be blind to these Prophecies announcing the coming of the Son of Man)*.

38 For as in the days that were before the flood they were eating and drinking, marrying and giving in marriage *(refers to an absolute lack of concern respecting Noah's Message of a coming flood)*, until the day that Noah entered into the Ark *(means they watched him build the Ark, and heard him preach Righteousness for many years, but took no heed)*,

39 And knew not until the flood came *(didn't believe the Message until the water began its precipitous rise)*, and took them all away *(they were all drowned, and consequently, eternally lost)*; so shall also the coming of the Son of Man be *(the similarity with Noah's time)*.

40 Then shall two be in the field; the one shall be taken, and the other left *(does not refer to the Rapture as many believe, but rather to the terrible loss of life during the Great Tribulation)*.

41 Two *women shall be* grinding at the mill; the one shall be taken, and the other left.

42 Watch therefore *(a warning to Israel to be prepared)*: for you know not what hour your Lord does come *(present Believers know that the Second Coming will take place during the Battle of Armageddon [Zech., Chpt. 12] but unredeemed Israel will not know)*.

43 But know this, that if the goodman of the house had known in what watch the thief would come, he would have watched, and would not have suffered his house to be broken up *(as unexpected as this, will likewise be the Coming of the Lord)*.

44 Therefore be ye also ready: for in such an hour as you think not the Son of Man cometh *(when Israel, during the Battle of Armageddon, will have given up hope, Jesus will come!)*.

PARABLE OF THE FAITHFUL AND UNFAITHFUL SERVANT

45 Who then is a faithful and wise servant *(refers to all Believers for all time)*, whom his Lord has made ruler over His household *(in this case, the Church)*, to give them meat in due season? *(God-called Preachers are responsible for properly feeding the flock.)*

46 Blessed *is* that servant, whom his Lord when He comes shall find so doing *(refers to faithfulness till the Rapture)*.

47 Verily I say unto you, That He shall make him ruler over all his goods *(refers to the Resurrected Saints being made "rulers" in the coming Kingdom Age, and the faithful of Israel being placed in the same capacity as the premiere nation in the world)*.

48 But and if that evil servant shall say in his heart, My Lord delays His coming *(exactly what many in the modern Church are now saying)*;

49 And shall begin to smite *his* fellowservants, and to eat and drink with the drunken *(not only to be in the world, but to be as well, of the world)*;

50 The Lord of that servant shall come in a day when he looks not for *Him*, and in an hour that he is not aware of *(not ready for the Rapture; most of the modern Church, sadly, falls into this category)*,

51 And shall cut him asunder, and appoint *him* his portion with the hypocrites *(despite his profession)*: there shall be weeping and gnashing of teeth *(will lose his soul, and go to an eternal Hell; most in the modern Church, sadly and regrettably, fall into this category; they are religious but lost!)*.

CHAPTER 25
(A.D. 33)
THE PARABLE OF THE TEN VIRGINS

THEN shall the Kingdom of Heaven be likened unto ten *(the number "10" in the Bible speaks of perfection)* virgins *(represents those who belong to the Lord)*, which took their lamps *(represents the light of Christ in all Believers)*, and went forth to meet the bridegroom *(Christ)*.

2 And five of them were wise, and five *were* foolish *(indicative of modern Christianity)*.

3 They who *were* foolish took their lamps, and took no oil with them *(began to live outside the domain of the Holy Spirit)*:

4 But the wise took oil in their vessels with their lamps *(a constant flow of the Spirit within their hearts and lives, which can only come about and be maintained, by one's Faith in Christ and the Cross [Rom. 8:1-2, 11])*.

5 While the bridegroom tarried, they all slumbered and slept *(does not imply by this that they were doing something wrong)*.

6 And at midnight there was a cry made, Behold, the bridegroom cometh; go ye out to meet him *(the Rapture of the Church)*.

7 Then all those virgins arose, and trimmed their lamps *(but without the oil, the trimming was useless; it is religious activity without the Holy Spirit)*.

8 And the foolish said unto the wise, Give us of your oil; for our lamps are gone out *(it's too late now!)*.

9 But the wise answered, saying, *Not so*;

lest there be not enough for us and you: but go you rather to them who sell, and buy for yourselves *(proclaims the truth that spiritual energy cannot be derived from others)*.

10 And while they went to buy, the bridegroom came; and they who were ready went in with him to the marriage: and the door was shut *(there will come a time, when it's too late; today is the day . . . [Heb. 3:15])*.

11 Afterward came also the other virgins, saying, Lord, Lord, open to us *(because they were religious, they thought they were saved)*.

12 But He answered and said, Verily I say unto you, I know you not *(millions presently are in the Church, but not in Christ)*.

13 Watch therefore, for you know neither the day nor the hour wherein the Son of Man cometh *(our lives are to be lived as if Jesus would come today)*.

THE PARABLE OF THE TALENTS

14 For *the Kingdom of Heaven is* as a man travelling into a far country, *who* called his own servants, and delivered unto them his goods *(represents Christ at His first Advent)*.

15 And unto one he gave five talents, to another two, and to another one; to every man according to his several ability; and straightway *(immediately)* took his journey *(every single Believer, none excluded, is given a proper Ministry)*.

16 Then he who had received the five talents went and traded with the same, and made *them* other five talents *(the talents were awarded according to faithfulness)*.

17 And likewise he who *had received* two, he also gained other two *(he was faithful with what he had)*.

18 But he who had received one went and digged in the earth, and hid his lord's money *(he wasn't faithful)*.

19 After a long time the lord of those servants cometh, and reckoneth with them *(service for the Lord ends at death; however, the reckoning is reserved for the Rapture)*.

20 And so he who had received five talents came and brought other five talents, saying, Lord, you delivered unto me five talents: behold, I have gained beside them five talents more *(this will take place at the Judgment Seat of Christ)*.

21 His lord said unto him, Well done, *thou* good and faithful servant: you have been faithful over a few things, I will make you ruler over many things: enter thou into the joy of your Lord *(as is obvious, it is faithfulness here that is being rewarded; contrary to popular thought, God hasn't called us to be successful, but rather to be faithful)*.

22 He also who had received two talents came and said, Lord, you delivered unto me two talents: behold, I have gained two other talents beside them *(faithfulness as well!)*.

23 His Lord said unto him, Well done, good and faithful servant; you have been faithful over a few things, I will make you ruler over many things: enter thou into the joy of your Lord *(if it is to be noticed, both received equal rewards; as stated, the criterion is faithfulness and not other things)*.

24 Then he which had received the one talent came and said, Lord, I know you and that you are an hard man, reaping where you have not sown, and gathering where you have not planted *(pure and simple, his statements constitute a lie)*:

25 And I was afraid, and went and hid your talent in the earth: lo, *there* you have *that* which is Yours *(the purpose of the "talent" was not preservation, but rather, multiplication; his action proclaims not only indolence, but as well, insolence; untold numbers, who claim to be Christians, fall into this category)*.

26 His Lord answered and said unto him, *You* wicked and slothful servant, you knew that I reap where I sowed not, and gather where I have not planted *(if you really believed that, you would not have done what you did)*:

27 You ought therefore to have put My money to the exchangers, and *then* at My coming I should have received mine own with usury *(regrettably, the majority of professors of religion, fall into this category)*.

28 Take therefore the talent from him, and give *it* unto him which has ten talents *(this is the law of the faithful; light rejected, is light taken, and given to the one who already has an abundance of light)*.

29 For unto every one who has shall be given, and he shall have abundance: but from him who has not shall be taken away even that which he has *(in fact, this happens unnumbered times, every single day; observe religious denominations, which have rejected light!)*.

30 And cast ye the unprofitable servant into outer darkness: there shall be weeping and gnashing of teeth *(these individuals do not merely lose reward, but rather their souls; all of this, as should be overly obvious, completely*

refutes the unscriptural doctrine of uncondi-
tional eternal security).

JUDGMENT ON THE NATIONS

31 When the Son of Man shall come in His glory, and all the Holy Angels with Him, then shall He sit upon the Throne of His glory *(the Second Coming)*:

32 And before Him shall be gathered all nations: and He shall separate them one from another, as a shepherd divides *his* sheep from the goats *(this is called the "judgment of the nations," which will commence at the outset of the Kingdom Age)*:

33 And He shall set the sheep on His right hand *(refers to nations which would not cooperate with the Antichrist)*, but the goats on the left *(nations which cooperated with the Antichrist)*.

34 Then shall the King say unto them on His right hand, Come, you blessed of My Father, inherit the Kingdom prepared for you from the foundation of the world *(has nothing to do with Salvation, but rather these particular nations being allowed to enter into the Kingdom Age)*:

35 For I was hungry, and you gave Me meat: I was thirsty, and you gave Me drink: I was a stranger, and you took Me in *(although the adage proves true for all time, Christ is basically speaking here of Israel and her treatment by various nations during the Great Tribulation)*:

36 Naked, and you clothed Me: I was sick, and you visited Me: I was in prison, and you came unto Me.

37 Then shall the righteous answer Him, saying, Lord, when did we see you hungry, and fed *You?* or thirsty, and gave *You* drink? *(The word, "righteous," does not pertain to the Righteousness of Christ given to Believers at Salvation, but instead, righteous dealings with Israel by these nations.)*

38 When saw we You a stranger, and took You in? or naked, and clothed *You?*

39 Or when did we see You sick, or in prison, and came unto You?

40 And the King shall answer and say unto them, Verily I say unto you, Inasmuch as you have done *it* unto one of the least of these My brethren, you have done *it* unto Me *(as stated, the adage holds true for all time, but Christ is primarily speaking here of Israel, and the help given her by certain nations during the Great Tribulation)*.

41 Then shall He say also unto them on the left hand *(the goat nations)*, Depart from Me, you cursed, into everlasting fire, prepared for the devil and his angels *(nations that hindered or tried to harm Israel during the Great Tribulation)*:

42 For I was hungry, and you gave Me no meat: I was thirsty, and you gave Me no drink:

43 I was a stranger, and you took Me not in: naked, and you clothed Me not: sick, and in prison, and you visited Me not.

44 Then shall they also answer Him, saying, Lord, when did we see You hungry, or thirsty, or a stranger, or naked, or sick, or in prison, and did not minister unto You?

45 Then shall He answer them, saying, Verily I say unto you, Inasmuch as you did *it* not to one of the least of these, you did *it* not to Me *(to bless one who belongs to God, is to bless God; to harm one who belongs to God, is to harm God; we see here the results of such action)*.

46 And these shall go away into everlasting punishment: but the righteous into life eternal *(all of this will happen soon after the Second Coming; the leaders of the nations who tried to help the Antichrist against Israel, during the Great Tribulation, will evidently be executed, and consequently will die eternally lost; conversely, the leaders of the nations who tried to help Israel at that time, will be given an opportunity to accept Christ as Saviour, which they no doubt will, and will thereby be given "life eternal")*.

CHAPTER 26
(A.D. 33)

THE PLOT TO KILL JESUS

AND it came to pass, when Jesus had finished all these sayings, He said unto His Disciples *(this concluded His public teaching, even though other discourses were given to the Disciples only [Jn. 13:31; 17:26])*,

2 You know that after two days is *the Feast* of the *Passover*, and the Son of Man is betrayed to be Crucified *(the Holy Spirit revealed to Christ the fact that Judas would betray Him)*.

3 Then assembled together the Chief Priests, and the Scribes, and the Elders of the people *(possibly other members of the Sanhedrin)*, unto the palace of the High Priest, who was called Caiaphas *(these men plotted to kill Christ, as they would kill a wild beast; Caiaphas committed suicide about two years later)*,

4 And consulted *(the topic of their conversation was the most diabolical crime ever conceived in the hearts of wicked men)* that they might take Jesus by subtilty *(they couldn't do it*

openly, so they plotted to do it undercover), **and kill** *Him (their actions would result in the destruction of their nation, and in such a bloody way as to defy description!).*

5 **But they said, Not on the feast** *day (should have been translated, "not during the Feast"),* **lest there be an uproar among the people** *(many of the people loved Christ).*

MARY OF BETHANY ANOINTS JESUS

6 **Now when Jesus was in Bethany, in the house of Simon the leper** *(it is believed by some that Martha was the wife of Simon the leper, Lazarus and Mary being, consequently, brother-in-law and sister-in-law to Simon),*

7 **There came unto Him a woman** *(Mary [Jn. 12:3])* **having an alabaster box of very precious ointment** *(worth about twelve thousand dollars in 2003 money),* **and poured it on His head, as He sat** *at meat (anointing Him while He was alive, proved that she believed in His Resurrection; seemingly, she was the only one who did; there was only one anointing).*

8 **But when His Disciples saw** *it,* **they had indignation** *(Judas originated this complaint [Jn. 12:4]),* **saying, To what purpose** *is* **this waste?**

9 **For this ointment might have been sold for much, and given to the poor** *(Judas said this [Jn. 12:4] his motives were probably to steal the money [Jn. 12:6]).*

10 **When Jesus understood** *it,* **He said unto them, Why do you trouble the woman? for she has wrought a good work upon Me** *(it concerned His Death at Calvary).*

11 **For you have the poor always with you; but Me you have not always** *(He spoke of His human body being removed from the touch and sight of men, and is even now in Heaven).*

12 **For in that she has poured this ointment on My body, she did** *it* **for My burial** *(this was normally done after death, but Mary believed that He would rise from the dead).*

13 **Verily I say unto you, Wheresoever this Gospel shall be preached in the whole world,** *there* **shall also this, that this woman has done, be told for a memorial of her** *(opponents of inspiration deny the fact of prediction; but they cannot deny the fact of this Prophecy; it was made nearly two thousand years ago, and has been fulfilled untold times).*

THE BETRAYAL

14 **Then one of the twelve, called Judas**

Iscariot, went unto the Chief Priests,

15 **And said** *unto them,* **What will you give me, and I will deliver Him unto you? And they covenanted with him for thirty pieces of silver** *(this was the price of a slave [Ex. 21:32]; as well, it was prophesied hundreds of years before, that Jesus would be sold for thirty pieces of silver [Zech. 11:13]).*

16 **And from that time he sought opportunity to betray Him.**

PREPARATION FOR THE PASSOVER

17 **Now the first** *day* **of the** *Feast of* **Unleavened Bread** *(it meant the day was approaching, which was Thursday; the day the following question was asked was Tuesday)* **the Disciples came to Jesus, saying unto Him, Where will You that we prepare for You to eat the Passover?** *(Jesus would eat the Passover a day early. In fact, He was the Passover, with His Death fulfilling some fifteen hundred years of this ritual.)*

18 **And He said, Go into the city** *(He went into Jerusalem, for He was presently at Bethany)* **to such a man** *(who the man was is not known; some think he was the father of John Mark, who wrote the Gospel of Mark),* **and say unto him, The Master says, My time is at hand** *(the statement that carries with it the meaning of the ages);* **I will keep the Passover at your house with My Disciples** *(what an honor for that family and that house).*

19 **And the Disciples did as Jesus had appointed them; and they made ready the Passover** *(speaks of the last Passover that would ever be offered, at least that God would recognize!).*

THE LAST PASSOVER

20 **Now when the evening was come, He sat down with the twelve** *(it was probably about 6 p.m. Tuesday night; but by Jewish reckoning at that time, it would have been the first hour of the new day of Wednesday; their new day always started at sunset, instead of midnight as it now does for us).*

21 **And as they did eat, He said, Verily I say unto you, that one of you shall betray Me** *(presents Christ giving Judas a last chance of Repentance before the final act; in fact, Christ made several such like efforts regarding Judas).*

22 **And they** *(all the Disciples)* **were exceeding sorrowful, and began every one of them to say unto Him, Lord, is it I?** *(They realized the import of these words, but it seems that none, at*

least at this time, suspected Judas.)

23 And He answered and said, He who dips *his* hand with Me in the dish, the same shall betray Me *(this was spoken to all the Disciples, inasmuch as all had dipped into the dish; consequently, the information was not too revealing)*.

24 The Son of Man goeth as it is written of Him *(refers to all that the Prophets had said concerning this time)*: but woe unto that man by whom the Son of Man is betrayed! it had been good for that man if he had not been born *(proclaims the eternal consequence of Judas' action, as well as all others who refuse Christ)*.

25 Then Judas, which betrayed Him, answered and said, Master, is it I? He said unto him, You have said *(the Lord's reply was evidently so quiet that the others did not hear)*.

THE LORD'S SUPPER INSTITUTED

26 And as they were eating, Jesus took bread, and blessed *it*, and broke *it*, and gave *it* to the Disciples, and said, Take, eat; this is My body *(this was the symbol of that which He would do, and become; He was the "bread" and consequently, "blessed," likewise, His Body was "broken" at Calvary; as well, He "gave" the results of this action at Calvary to the world, for all who would believe [Jn. 3:16])*.

27 And He took the cup, and gave thanks, and gave *it* to them, saying, Drink ye all of it *(the cup is meant to serve as a symbol of His shed Blood at Calvary)*;

28 For this is My Blood of the New Testament *(New Covenant)*, which is shed for many for the remission of sins *(His Death at Calvary would settle forever the sin debt, and for all of humanity, at least for all who will believe [Jn. 1:29]; as is obvious, the Lord's Supper ever directs the Believer to the Cross)*.

29 But I say unto you, I will not drink henceforth of this fruit of the vine, until that day when I drink it new with you in my Father's Kingdom *(refers to the coming Kingdom Age)*.

30 And when they had sung an hymn, they went out into the Mount of Olives *(refers to Psalms 115 and 118)*.

JESUS FORETELLS PETER'S DENIAL

31 Then said Jesus unto them, All you shall be offended because of Me this night *(all of them would forsake Him, but He would never forsake them)*: for it is written, I will smite the shepherd, and the sheep of the flock shall be scattered abroad *(Zech. 13:7)*.

32 But after I am risen again, I will go before you into Galilee *(it seemed that none believed what He said)*.

33 Peter answered and said unto Him, Though all *men* shall be offended because of you, *yet* will I never be offended *(boastful pride!)*.

34 Jesus said unto him, Verily I say unto you, That this night, before the rooster crows, you shall deny Me thrice.

35 Peter said unto Him, Though I should die with You, yet will I not deny You. Likewise also said all the Disciples *(all made boastful claims)*.

JESUS IN THE GARDEN

36 Then cometh Jesus with them unto a place called Gethsemane *(just across the Kidron Valley from Jerusalem, about two hundred yards from the city wall)*, and said unto the Disciples, Sit you here, while I go and pray yonder.

37 And He took with him Peter and the two sons of Zebedee *(James and John)*, and began to be sorrowful and very heavy *(tremendous stress and pressure)*.

38 Then said He unto them, My soul is exceeding sorrowful, even unto death *(means that He, as a Man, could not have endured it but for added Angelic strength [Lk. 22:43-44])*: tarry ye here, and watch with Me *(He needed their presence, even though it would prove to be of little solace)*.

39 And he went a little farther *(more than physical, the distance He went in agony and prayer at this time, no human being could follow)*, and fell on His face, and prayed *(He did so repeatedly, meaning that He would fall to the ground, struggle to get up, and then fall again)*, saying, O My Father, if it be possible, let this cup pass from Me *(this "cup" was threefold: bearing the sin penalty of humanity, separation from the Father, and death)*: nevertheless not as I will, but as You will *(proclaims the Divine Will as the expression of Divine Righteousness and Love, which limits the exercise of Divine Power and, therefore, supplies the necessary check to the expectations which might otherwise arise from the belief in Omnipotence)*.

40 And He came unto the Disciples, and finding them asleep *(portraying the fact that they did not realize the acute danger for which they were ill-prepared)*, and said unto Peter *(evidently awaking him)*, What, could you not watch

with Me one hour?

41 Watch and pray, that you enter not into temptation (*a warning of the temptation that was about to come upon them — the temptation to forsake Him*): the spirit (*spirit of man*) indeed *is* willing, but the flesh *is* weak (*this battle can be won only by our Faith being placed exclusively in Christ and His Cross, which then gives the Holy Spirit latitude to work within our lives [Rom. 6:3-14; 8:1-2,11]*).

42 He went away again the second time, and prayed, saying, O My Father, if this cup may not pass away from Me, except I drink it, Your will be done (*a total acquiescence to God's Will*).

43 And He came and found them asleep again: for their eyes were heavy (*Love is always ready to excuse weakness, for example, the lateness of the hour, and the fact that they were sleeping for sorrow [Lk. 22:45]*).

44 And He left them, and went away again, and prayed the third time, saying the same words (*sometimes we must pray the same words again, and again*).

45 Then cometh He to His Disciples, and said unto them, Sleep on now, and take *your* rest (*may be translated, "do you sleep on now, continuing to take your rest"?*): behold, the hour is at hand, and the Son of Man is betrayed into the hands of sinners (*refers to Judas, who is even now entering the Garden with the Temple guard and others in order to arrest Christ*).

46 Rise, let us be going: behold, he is at hand who does betray Me (*the Holy Spirit had told Him exactly what was happening, and when it would happen*).

THE BETRAYAL AND ARREST OF JESUS

47 And while He yet spake, lo, Judas, one of the twelve, came (*is given in this fashion by the Holy Spirit in order to enhance his guilt. Never in human history has so perfidious an act been carried out against One Who was so good, kind, and gracious*), and with him a great multitude with swords and staves (*the Temple guard, and some Roman soldiers*), from the Chief Priests and Elders of the people (*the Church has ever killed the Lord, in the Name of the Lord*).

48 Now he who betrayed Him gave them a sign, saying, Whomsoever I shall kiss, that same is He: hold Him fast (*speaks of the most despicable, treacherous moment in human history*).

49 And forthwith he came to Jesus, and said, Hail, Master; and kissed Him (*Ps. 55:21*).

50 And Jesus said unto him, Friend (*said in kindness and not sarcasm*), wherefore are you come? (*Could be translated, "do that for which you are come."*) Then came they, and laid hands on Jesus, and took Him (*presents the beginning of the action of the murderous hearts of the religious leaders of Israel; they hated Christ, and would have done this much sooner, had the opportunity presented itself*).

51 And, behold, one of them which were with Jesus stretched out *his* hand, and drew his sword, and struck a servant of the High Priest's, and smote off his ear (*John said this was Simon Peter; as well, the name of the servant is Malthus; incidentally, Jesus healed the man's ear, which was His last miracle before His Death*).

52 Then said Jesus unto him (*unto Peter*), Put up again your sword into his place (*the Magistrate to whom God gives a sword, is responsible to use it against evil-doers; that is "his place" [Rom. 13:4]*): for all they who take the sword shall perish with the sword (*the sword has no place in the propagation of the Gospel*).

53 Thinkest thou that I cannot now pray to My Father, and He shall presently give Me more than twelve legions of Angels? (*Seventy-two thousand Angels.*)

54 But how then shall the Scriptures be fulfilled, that thus it must be? (*The word "must" affirms the Divine Inspiration of the Scriptures; for had they been composed by men there would have been no necessity compelling their fulfillment.*)

55 In that same hour said Jesus to the multitudes (*believed to have been approximately six hundred men*), Are you come out as against a thief with swords and staves for to take Me? I sat daily with you teaching in the Temple, and you laid no hold on Me (*Jesus pointing out the fact that they didn't arrest Him in the Temple, because they feared the people*).

56 But all this was done (*could have been translated, "all this has come to pass"*), that the Scriptures of the Prophets might be fulfilled (*through foreknowledge, the Holy Spirit predicted this many centuries in advance [Gen. 3:15; 49:10; Isa. 7:14; Chpt. 53; Zech. 11:12] the Scriptures were ever the foundation of all that was done, and had better be the same presently*). Then all the Disciples forsook Him, and fled (*fulfilled that which was written [Zech. 13:7]*).

THE TRIAL

57 And they that had laid hold on Jesus led *Him* away to Caiaphas the High Priest

(Matthew omits the account of Jesus being led first before Annas, the former High Priest, as recorded in Jn. 18:13, 19-24), where the Scribes and the Elders were assembled *(pertains to the palace or court of the High Priest)*.

58 But Peter followed Him afar off *(presents the Apostle turning back toward Christ from Whom he had fled at first; no doubt, he is ashamed of his actions, and now in a quandary, timidly follows the route taking Jesus to the Palace)* unto the High Priest's palace, and went in, and sat with the servants, to see the end.

59 Now the Chief Priests, and Elders, and all the council, sought false witness *(they didn't care if the witness was true or false)* against Jesus, to put Him to death *(these were the religious leaders of Israel)*;

60 But found none *(found none who would collaborate each other)*: yes, though many false witnesses came, *yet* found they none. At the last came two false witnesses *(these seized upon a statement made by Christ, and twisted it out of context)*,

61 And said, This *("fellow" was inserted by the translators, and was not in the original Text; the accuser might have pointed a finger at Christ, referring to Him contemptuously, as "This!")* *fellow* said, I am able to destroy the Temple of God, and to build it in three days *(this is a distortion of what He actually said; Jesus had actually said, "destroy this Temple [speaking of His physical body], and in three days I will raise it up" [Jn. 2:19])*.

62 And the High Priest *(Caiaphas)* arose, and said unto Him, Answerest thou nothing? *(Presents Christ answering His accusers not at all.)* what *is it which* these witness against You?

63 But Jesus held His peace *(fulfilled the Scripture, "He was oppressed, and He was afflicted, yet He opened not His Mouth [Isa. 53:7])*. And the High Priest answered and said unto Him, I adjure You by the Living God, that You tell us whether You be the Christ, the Son of God.

64 Jesus said unto him, You have said *(presents Christ giving a direct affirmation, with Mark saying it even clearer, "I am" [Mk. 14:62])*: nevertheless I say unto you *(would have been better translated, "but moreover I say unto you")*, Hereafter shall you see the Son of Man *(speaking of Himself)* sitting on the right hand of power *(actually speaks of the Great White Throne Judgment; they are now judging Him; He will then judge them)*, and coming in the clouds of Heaven *(Second Coming)*.

65 Then the High Priest rent his clothes *(ripped the shawl thrown across His shoulder, signifying his supposed horror of Jesus referring to Himself as the Son of God)*, saying, He hath spoken blasphemy *(meaning He had made Himself One with God)*; what further need have we of witnesses? *(Means they can dispense with all the liars.)* behold, now you have heard His blasphemy *(the entire Sanhedrin had heard His statement; but He did not blaspheme; He spoke the truth)*.

66 What do you think? *(Was spoken by Caiaphas to the Sanhedrin, which was composed of seventy-one members, if all were present.)* They answered and said, He is guilty of death *(when they sentenced Him to death, they sentenced themselves as well!)*.

67 Then *(refers in the modern vernacular to "fair game")* did they spit in His face *(considered to be the greatest insult to a person)*, and buffeted Him *(hit Him with their fist, probably done by the Temple guards, but was undoubtedly done as well by some members of the Sanhedran)*; and others smote *Him* with the palms of their hands *(should have been translated, "smote Him with rods"; the Prophet had said, "as many as were astonished at You; His visage was so marred more than any man, and His form more than the sons of men" [Isa. 52:14])*,

68 Saying, Prophesy unto us *(Jesus had just done this [Vs. 64])*, Thou Christ *(the words were spoken contemptuously! Christ means "the Anointed," and spoke of the Messiah; they were making fun of His claims, and consequently, ridiculing the Anointing of the Holy Spirit upon Him; they were doing what they had accused Him of doing — blaspheming)*, Who is he who smote you? *(Mark and Luke said they blindfolded Him [14:65; 22:64].)*

PETER'S DENIAL

69 Now Peter sat without in the palace *(the way the Court was constructed, Peter could see Christ, and Christ could see Peter [Lk. 22:61])*: and a damsel came unto him *(probably referred to the lady who kept the door, which gave entrance into the court yard)*, saying, You also *were* with Jesus of Galilee *(with sarcasm)*.

70 But he denied before *them* all *(first denial, spoken before a number of people standing with the girl)*, saying, I know not what you say.

71 And when he was gone out into the porch *(referred to him seemingly trying to remove*

himself from those who had just fingered him), another *maid* saw him, and said unto them who were there, This *fellow* was also with Jesus of Nazareth *(as well, with sarcasm)*.

72 And again he denied with an oath *(what the oath was, we do not know)*, I do not know the man *(He claims not even to know His Name)*.

73 And after a while *(represents according to Lk. 22:59, about an hour of time)* came unto *him* they that stood by, and said to Peter, Surely you also are *one* of them; for your speech betrays you *(he was a Galilean, as were all the Disciples, with the exception of Judas)*.

74 Then began he to curse and to swear *(not profanity, but rather to take a solemn oath such as men do in a Court of Justice, and then to call upon God to curse him if the oath was false; it was a sin of appalling magnitude and depth)*, *saying*, I know not the man *(meaning that he swore by the name of God that he did not know Christ)*. And immediately the cock *(rooster)* *crowed.*

75 And Peter remembered the word of Jesus, which said unto him, Before the rooster crows, you shall deny Me thrice *(Vs. 34)*. And he went out, and wept bitterly *(tradition says that for the rest of his life, Peter could not hear a rooster crow without falling upon his knees and weeping)*.

CHAPTER 27
(A.D. 33)
JESUS SENT TO PILATE

WHEN the morning was come *(referred to Wednesday morning; Jesus would be crucified in a matter of hours; He was not crucified on Good Friday as many claim!)*, all the Chief Priests and Elders of the people took counsel against Jesus to put him to death *(the morning session was that of the entire Sanhedrin; it followed the unofficial meeting in the High Priest's house [26:57])*:

2 And when they had bound Him, they led *Him* away *(refers to His Hands being tied behind His back with a rope)*, and delivered Him to Pontius Pilate the governor *(he held this office for some ten years, at the end of which time he was removed for cruelty and extortion, and banished to Vienne in Gaul, where he committed suicide)*.

JUDAS KILLS HIMSELF

3 Then Judas, which had betrayed Him, when he saw that He was condemned *(refers to what the religious leaders had done to Jesus and*

their brutal treatment of Him; in fact, he probably saw Jesus, and was sickened by what he saw)*, and repented himself *(in the Greek, means to have a deep remorse at the consequence of sin, but not deep regret at the cause of it; the word is never used of genuine Repentance to God)*, and brought again the thirty pieces of silver *(the price he had been given)* to the Chief Priests and Elders *(concerns the blood money, and the religious leaders with blood on their hands)*,

4 Saying, I have sinned *(presents him confessing this sin to man, an evil man at that, but not to God)* in that I have betrayed the innocent blood *("the" emphasizes that the Blood of Christ was the only truly innocent blood that has ever been)*. And they said, What *is that* to us? see thou *to that* *(they knew that Jesus was innocent, but did not care!)*.

5 And he cast down the pieces of silver in the Temple *(presents him flinging the shekels onto the marble floor)*, and departed, and went and hanged himself *(he probably hanged himself with his own sash, which was wound around his waist; tradition says that the limb broke from the tree to which the sash was tied, and he fell heavily to the rocks below, where a passing wagon, unable to stop, crushed and disemboweled him)*.

6 And the Chief Priests took the silver pieces *(represents the blood money now in their hands where it rightfully belonged all the time!)*, and said, It is not lawful for to put them into the treasury, because it is the price of blood *(it is ironic! they were gagging at a gnat and swallowing a camel)*.

7 And they *(the Sanhedrin)* took counsel *(institutionalized religion opposed Christ from the very beginning; it still does!)*, and bought with them *(the thirty pieces of silver)* the potter's field, to bury strangers in *(Gentiles — a place on the south of Jerusalem, across the valley of Hinnom)*.

8 Wherefore that field was called, The field of blood, unto this day *(was not the name given it by the religious leaders of Israel, but others! up to the mid 1800's, it was still being used for this purpose, the burying of the unhonored dead of Jerusalem)*.

9 Then was fulfilled that which was spoken by Jeremiah the Prophet *(although the Scriptures do not say, this was probably originally spoken by Jeremiah, and done so by the Holy Spirit, but not written down; it was then repeated and recorded by that same Spirit in Zech. 11:12-13 or else a copyist made a mistake in copying it from the original text; no original text remains)*, saying, And they took the thirty

pieces of silver, the price of Him that was valued, Whom they of the Children of Israel did value *(this was the price of a slave; it is given in this manner by the Holy Spirit in order to emphasize the fact that this was the price or worth that Israel placed upon her Messiah)*;

10 And gave them *(thirty pieces of silver)* for the potter's field, as the Lord appointed Me *(appointed the Messiah; did not the religious leaders of Israel know about this Prophecy?)*.

JESUS BEFORE PILATE

11 And Jesus stood before the governor *(speaks of Pontius Pilate)*: and the governor asked Him, saying, are You the King of the Jews? *(In reality, Jehoiachin, who reigned some six hundred years before, was the last King recognized by God, to sit on the Throne of Judah [II Chron. 36:9-10].)* And Jesus said unto him, Thou sayest *(in effect, says, "I am the King of the Jews"; as far as is recorded, this is the first time Jesus had made such a claim; John added more of the answer of Christ, with Jesus saying, "My Kingdom is not of this world" [Jn. 18:36]; consequently, Pilate knew that His claims were spiritual and, therefore, not of this world)*.

12 And when He was accused of the Chief Priests and Elders, He answered nothing *(He would not defend Himself before people who cared nothing for the truth)*.

13 Then said Pilate unto Him, Do You not hear how many things they witness against You? *(Pilate was somewhat confused as to why Jesus did not defend Himself against these accusations.)*

14 And He answered him to never a word *(fulfilling Isaiah 53:7)*; insomuch that the governor marvelled greatly *(Pilate was astonished that Jesus defended Himself not at all against these accusations, seeing that they could lead to His Death)*.

JESUS CONDEMNED;
BARABBAS RELEASED

15 Now at *that* feast *(the Passover)* the governor was wont *(accustomed)* to release unto the people a prisoner, whom they would *(in other words, the people could choose, and the one chosen would be released; Pilate thought he had found a way out of his dilemma; he knew that Jesus was innocent)*.

16 And they had then a notable prisoner *(should have been translated "notorious")*, called Barabbas *(Mark said that Barabbas was a*

murderer, and had led an insurrection against Roman authority [Mk. 15:7])*.

17 Therefore when they were gathered together *(Pilate and Jesus standing on the porch of the hall, before the people below)*, Pilate said unto them, Whom will you that I release unto you? Barabbas, or Jesus which is called Christ? *(In some manuscripts, Barabbas is referred to as "Jesus Barabbas." So the people were faced with a choice, "Jesus Barabbas, the murderer," or "Jesus Christ, the Giver of Eternal Life.")*

18 For He knew that for envy they had delivered Him *(they envied the respect given Him by the people, and His Miracles)*.

19 When he was sat down on the judgment seat *(a chair on a raised platform in front of the praetorian)*, his wife sent unto him, saying, Have thou nothing to do with that just Man: for I have suffered many things this day in a dream because of Him *(her name was Claudia — another name Procula; tradition says that she ultimately became a Christian; what her dream was, the record does not say; however, in all of the account of the sufferings of Christ this last week before His Death, she, a Gentile is the only one, it seems, who gave Him a kind word)*.

20 But the Chief Priests and Elders persuaded the multitude that they should ask Barabbas *(asked for the release of Barabbas the murderer; consequently, murderers have ruled them from then until now, even unto this hour, considering the bombings in Israel)*, and destroy *(kill)* Jesus.

21 The governor answered and said unto them, Whether of the two will you that I release unto you? *(Presents no alternative but Jesus or Barabbas.)* They said, Barabbas.

22 Pilate saith unto them, What shall I do then with Jesus which is called Christ? *(The greatest question ever asked. The answer to it decides the eternal destiny of the human soul.) They* all say unto him, Let Him be crucified *(they specified "crucifixion," because such a death would cause all the people, they thought, to turn against him; the Law of Moses condemned anyone hanged upon a tree as being cursed by God [Deut. 21:23])*.

23 And the governor said, Why, what evil has He done? *(He had done no evil. He was perfect! He had never sinned.)* But they cried out the more, saying, Let Him be crucified *(proclaims them offering no answer to the question of Pilate, because they had no answer; as the morning sun begins to break over Olivet, it will dawn on a day of infamy such as the world has*

never seen before or since).

24 When Pilate saw that he could prevail nothing, but *that* rather a tumult was made *(he feared that if he did not give in to their demands, a riot might occur, with him then being accused before Rome of refusing to punish a pretender to the Jewish Throne)*, he took water, and washed *his* hands before the multitude *(by this act, he attempted to clear himself of guilt, and to cast the guilt upon the people, as if the administration of Justice lay with them and not with him)*, saying, I am innocent of the blood of this just person: see you *to it (him saying it here, did not make it so! he didn't have the courage to do what was right; one cannot take a neutral position as it regards Christ).*

25 Then answered all the people, and said, His blood *be* on us, and on our children *(the malediction they invoked upon themselves and upon their children rests upon them still, and was, and is, a malediction of appalling horror and suffering).*

26 Then released he Barabbas unto them *(proclaims the choice of the people)*: and when he *(Pilate)* had scourged Jesus *(a punishment so horrible, that sometimes it killed the victim before the act of crucifixion could be employed [Isa. 50:6])*, he delivered Him to be crucified *(Isa., Chpt. 53).*

JESUS CROWNED WITH THORNS

27 Then the soldiers *(Roman soldiers)* of the governor took Jesus into the common hall, and gathered unto Him the whole band *of soldiers (about two hundred men, which was the third part a "cohort").*

28 And they stripped Him *(referred to His Robe, not the inner garments)*, and put on *Him* a scarlet robe *(either a worn-out officer's cloak or else a cast-off garment from the wardrobe of Herod).*

29 And when they had platted a crown of thorns *(called "victor's thorns" and which grew up to six inches in length)*, they put *it* upon His head *(the Greek word for "crown" is "stephanos," and means "a victory crown"; even though they meant it for shame and mockery, by this crown of thorns, the Lord portrayed the Victory of the Cross and its certitude, even before Jesus actually died)*, and a reed in His right hand: and they bowed the knee before Him, and mocked Him, saying, Hail, King of the Jews! *(At the coming Great White Throne Judgment, these same soldiers will once again stand before Christ,*

and once again bow the knee to Him. But this time, it will not be in mocking tone.)

30 And they spit upon Him, and took the reed, and smote Him on the head *(driving the thorns deeper, which no doubt caused His head to swell).*

31 And after that they had mocked Him, they took the robe off from Him, and put His own raiment on Him, and led Him away to crucify *Him (Crucifixion is supposed to have been invented by Semiramis, Queen of Nimrod, who founded the Babylonian system of mysteries).*

32 And as they came out *(on the way to Calvary)*, they found a man of Cyrene, Simon by name *(Alexander and Rufus were the sons of Simon [Mk. 15:21; Rom. 16:13])*: him they compelled to bear His cross *(it was not the entire Cross, but probably the "patibulum," or the cross bar; it would have weighed not much short of a hundred pounds; in His weakened condition, Jesus could not bear that load).*

THE CRUCIFIXION

33 And when they were come unto a place called Golgotha, that is to say, a place of a skull *(tradition says that Adam was buried here, and that his skull was found here),*

34 They gave Him vinegar to drink mingled with gall: and when He had tasted *thereof*, He would not drink *(this was a stupefying potion, given to help alleviate sufferings; Christ refused it).*

35 And they crucified Him, and parted His garments *(this was their "extra pay" for serving this ghastly duty)*, casting lots *(they drew straws, so to speak)*: that it might be fulfilled which was spoken by the Prophet, They parted My garments among them, and upon My vesture did they cast lots *(Ps. 22:18).*

36 And sitting down they watched Him there *(made sure that friends didn't come and take the condemned One down, before He died)*;

37 And set up over His head His accusation written *(this pertained to the crime for which the accused was condemned)*, THIS IS JESUS THE KING OF THE JEWS *(it is said that this was written in three languages, Hebrew, Greek, and Latin; they printed this in mockery, but no words were ever more true).*

38 Then were there two thieves crucified with Him *(Isa. 53:12)*, one on the right hand, and another on the left.

39 And they who passed by reviled Him, wagging their heads *(for the most part, these were the religious leaders of Israel [Ps. 109:25]),*

40 And saying, You who will destroy the Temple, and build *it* in three days *(Jesus never said that! He did say, that His physical Body would be destroyed, and in three days He would raise it up, which is exactly what happened),* save Yourself *(He didn't come to save Himself, but rather others).* If You be the Son of God, come down from the Cross *(had He come down from the Cross, no one would've ever been saved, and those in the prison of Paradise, would have remained there forever).*

41 Likewise also the Chief Priests mocking *Him,* with the Scribes and Elders, said *(this is religion at work!),*

42 He saved others *(that He did, but the "others" did not include these religious leaders, because they would not accept Him);* Himself He cannot save *(the actual truth, Himself He will not save).* If He be the King of Israel, let Him now come down from the Cross, and we will believe Him *(blasphemers are also liars!).*

43 He trusted in God *(Ps. 22:8);* let Him deliver Him now, if He will have Him *(they wouldn't have Him, but God would):* for He said, I am the Son of God *(represents exactly what He said!).*

44 The thieves also, which were crucified with Him, cast the same in His teeth *(they both did at first, but a little later, one repented, recorded by Luke 23:42).*

THE DEATH OF JESUS

45 Now from the sixth hour *(12 Noon)* there was darkness over all the land unto the ninth hour *(3 p.m. — for these three hours, God would literally hide His Face from His Son; during this time, Jesus did bear the sin penalty of mankind [II Cor. 5:21]. "This darkness" was not the result of an eclipse, for then the moon was full; it was brought on by God in that He could not look upon His Son, as He did bear the sin penalty of the world).*

46 And about the ninth hour Jesus cried with a loud voice *(showing He didn't die from weakness, but rather laid down His Own Life [Jn. 10:17-18]),* saying, Eli, Eli, lama sabachthani? that is to say, My God, my God, why have You forsaken Me? *(The question as to why God had forsaken Him was not asked in a sense of not knowing, but in a sense of acknowledging the act. God didn't deliver Him, even as He always had, because, to have done such, would have forfeited Redemption for mankind. Incidentally, Jesus spoke in Aramaic, which was commonly used by the Lord.)*

47 Some of them who stood there, when they heard *that,* said, This *man* calls for Elijah *(this would have referred to Jews, because Romans would have known nothing about Elijah).*

48 And straightway *(immediately)* one of them ran, and took a spunge, and filled *it* with vinegar, and put *it* on a reed, and gave Him to drink *(the evidence is, it touched His lips, and He died; it had nothing to do with His Life or Death).*

49 The rest said, Let be, let us see whether Elijah will come to save Him *(said in mockery!).*

50 Jesus, when He had cried again with a loud voice, yielded up the ghost *(He freely laid down His Life, meaning that He didn't die from His wounds; as well, He didn't die until the Holy Spirit told him to do so [Heb. 9:14]).*

51 And, behold, the Veil of the Temple *(that which hid the Holy of Holies; Josephus said it was sixty feet high from the ceiling to the floor, four inches thick, and was so strong, that four yoke of oxen could not pull it apart)* was rent in twain from the top to the bottom *(meaning that God alone could have done such a thing; it also signified, that the price was paid completely on the Cross; signified by the rent Veil; regrettably, some say, the Cross — didn't finish the task with other things required; this Verse says differently);* and the earth did quake, and the rocks rent *(represented an earthquake, but had nothing to do with the renting of the Veil, which took place immediately before this phenomenon);*

52 And the graves were opened; and many bodies of the Saints which slept arose *(does not teach "soul sleep" as some claim, but rather that the bodies of the Sainted dead do sleep; not the soul and the spirit, which then went to Paradise, but since the Cross, at death, now go to be with Christ [Phil. 1:23]),*

53 And came out of the graves after His resurrection, and went into the holy city *(Jerusalem),* and appeared unto many *(while all were delivered out of Paradise, and taken to Heaven, some, even many, stopped over in Jerusalem for a short period of time, "and appeared unto many"; how many there were, we aren't told, and to whom they appeared, we aren't told; Matthew alone gives this account).*

54 Now when the centurion, and they who were with him, watching Jesus, saw the earthquake, and those things that were done, they feared greatly, saying, Truly this was the Son of God *(he was the first Gentile to render this testimony of Faith; tradition affirms that the*

Centurion's name was Longinus, and that he became a devoted follower of Christ, preached the Faith, and died a martyr's death).

55 And many women were there beholding afar off, which followed Jesus from Galilee, ministering unto Him *(concerns those who came from Galilee, and were with Him unto the end):*

56 Among which was Mary Magdalene *(Jesus had delivered her [Mk. 16:9; Lk. 8:2]),* and Mary the mother of James and Joseph *(probably the wife of Cleophas [Jn. 19:25]),* and the mother of Zebedee's children *(Salome [Mk. 15:40] the mother of James and John).*

THE BURIAL OF JESUS

57 When the evening was come *(referred to a period of time between 3 p.m. until sunset, the Passover Sabbath — not the weekly Sabbath),* there came a rich man of Arimathaea, named Joseph *(he was a member of the Sanhedrin, but was no doubt, not present at the so-called trial of Jesus),* who also himself was Jesus' Disciple *(he was a follower of Christ, which means that he had accepted him as Lord):*

58 He went to Pilate *(proves that he had access to the governor),* and begged the body of Jesus *(it seems that his devotion to Christ had previously been "in secret for fear of the Jews" [Jn. 19:38]).* Then Pilate commanded the body to be delivered *(proclaims the Roman Governor as the only one who could give such an order).*

59 And when Joseph had taken the body *(had taken it down from the Cross),* he wrapped it in a clean linen cloth *(this was the physical body, prepared by God, to be used as a Sacrifice, which it was, in order to redeem Adam's fallen race [Heb. 10:5]),*

60 And laid it in his own new tomb *(which had never been used),* which he had hewn out in the rock *(it was cut out of solid rock):* and he rolled a great stone to the door of the sepulchre, and departed *(this is the same "great stone" that the Angel rolled away [28:2]).*

61 And there was Mary Magdalene, and the other Mary *(the wife of Cleophas, and the sister of Mary, the Mother of Jesus),* sitting over against the sepulcher *(all of this shows that none of them actually had any faith that Jesus would come from the dead; it seems that only Mary of Bethany actually believed such [26:6-13]).*

THE TOMB SEALED AND GUARDED

62 Now the next day, that followed the day of the preparation *(refers to the High Sabbath and the Chief Day of the Passover Festival),* the Chief Priests and Pharisees came together unto Pilate *(referred to the day after the Crucifixion),*

63 Saying, Sir, we remember that that deceiver said, while He was yet alive, After three days I will rise again *(their testimony here confirms that Jesus died and did not merely swoon as some modern unbelievers claim).*

64 Command therefore that the sepulchre be made sure until the third day *(insures three days and three nights in the Tomb),* lest His Disciples come by night, and steal Him away, and say unto the people, He is risen from the dead *(by their actions, they will make the proof of His Resurrection irrefutable):* so the last error shall be worse than the first *(their claiming that the people's belief in Him had been an "error," and if they in any way thought He had risen from the dead, this would be an even greater "error").*

65 Pilate said unto them, You have a watch *(referred to a guard of four soldiers which was changed every three hours, meaning that it was continuous):* go your way, make *it* as sure as ye can *(they not only had the soldiers at their command, but were free to do whatever else they saw fit to guarantee the security of the Tomb).*

66 So they went, and made the sepulchre sure, sealing the stone *(they passed a cord around the stone that closed the mouth of the sepulcher to the two sides of the entrance; this was sealed with wax or prepared clay in the center and at the ends, so that the stone could not be removed without breaking the seals or the cord),* and setting a watch *(the four soldiers took up their position at the mouth of the Tomb and in front of the Stone; His enemies made the proof of His Resurrection incontrovertible).*

CHAPTER 28
(A.D. 33)
THE RESURRECTION OF CHRIST

IN the end of the Sabbath *(the regular weekly Sabbath, which was every Saturday),* as it began to dawn toward the first *day* of the week *(this was just before daylight on Sunday morning; Jesus rose from the dead some time after sunset on Saturday evening; the Jews began the new day at sunset, instead of midnight, as we do presently),* came Mary Magdalene and the other Mary to see the sepulcher *(they wanted to put spices on the body of Christ).*

2 And, behold, there was a great earthquake

(presents the second earthquake, with the first taking place, when Christ died [27:51]): **for the Angel of the Lord descended from Heaven** *(was probably observed by the Roman soldiers, who alone witnessed it and gave the account)*, **and came and rolled back the stone from the door** *(Christ had already risen from the dead and had left the Tomb when the stone was rolled away; His glorified Body was not restricted by obstacles)*, **and sat upon it** *(this was done as a show of triumph; in other words, death was vanquished!)*.

3 His countenance was like lightning, and his raiment white as snow *(there is no evidence that any of the women or Disciples saw this glorious coming of the Angel; however, the next Verse tells us that the Roman guards did see it, and were terrified!)*:

4 And for fear of Him *(the Angel)* **the keepers** *(guards)* **did shake, and became as dead men** *(inasmuch as this happened at night, the situation was even more frightful)*.

5 And the Angel answered and said unto the women *(this was just before dawn, and after the soldiers had run away)*, **Do not fear: for I know that you seek Jesus, which was crucified** *(the Angel now uses this word, "Crucified," in a most glorious manner; it is now "the Power of God and the Wisdom of God" [I Cor. 1:23-24])*.

6 He is not here *(is the beginning of the most glorious statement that could ever fall upon the ears of mere mortals)*: **for he is risen** *(a dead and risen Saviour is the life and substance of the Gospel [I Cor. 15:1-4])*, **as He said** *(the Angel brought to the attention of the women, the fact that Christ had stated several times that He would be crucified and would rise from the dead)*. **Come, see the place where the Lord lay** *(they were looking for a corpse, but instead, would find a risen Lord; they were looking for a Tomb containing a corpse, but instead, would find it empty)*.

7 And go quickly, and tell His Disciples that He is risen from the dead *(the Disciples should have been the ones telling others, but because of unbelief, the women will tell them; this is the greatest Message that humanity has ever received)*; **and, behold, He goes before you into Galilee; there shall ye see Him** *(He would reveal Himself to whom and to where He so desired)*: **lo, I have told you** *(guarantees the certitude of this action)*.

THE TESTIMONY OF THE WOMEN

8 And they departed quickly from the sepulcher *(they had actually gone into the burial chamber, and had seen with their own eyes that Jesus was not there [Lk. 24:3])* **with fear and great joy** *(this was a "healthy fear," which every Believer ought to have; and as is understandable, there was "great joy")*; **and did run to bring His Disciples word** *("they did run" because they had a Message to tell, and what a Message it was! this would be the greatest "word" the Disciples would ever hear)*.

9 And as they went to tell His Disciples, behold, Jesus met them *(this was not the first appearance of Jesus, that being to Mary Magdalene [Mk. 16:9])*, **saying, All hail** *(actually meant, "all joy"!)*. **And they came and held Him by the feet, and worshipped Him** *(they would find that they were touching a human body of flesh and bone, and that it was not an apparition or ghostly figure; they knew He had been raised from the dead; still, they were not at all certain as to what was meant by that; His appearance to them, with them touching Him, removed all doubts as to what the Resurrection meant)*.

10 Then said Jesus unto them, Be not afraid *(it definitely is understandable that they were afraid)*: **go tell My brethren that they go into Galilee, and there shall they see Me** *(means more than merely an appearance; actually, He would also appear to them in Jerusalem, even proclaiming great Truths [Jn. 20:19-23]; John in the last Chapter of his Book gives the appearance in Galilee in detail)*.

THE REPORT OF THE SOLDIERS

11 Now when they were going *(referring to the women after seeing Jesus, going to the Disciples)*, **behold, some of the watch** *(soldiers)* **came into the city, and showed unto the Chief Priests all the things that were done** *(speaks of the four soldiers who had actually seen the coming of the Angel — him rolling the stone away from the mouth of the Tomb)*.

12 And when they *(Chief Priests)* **were assembled with the Elders** *(the Sanhedrin)*, **and had taken counsel** *(how they could counteract what had happened)*, **they gave large money unto the soldiers** *(all now knew, and beyond the shadow of a doubt that Jesus was Who He had said He was; they knew they had Crucified the Son of God; they knew these Roman soldiers were not making up this story; for them to desert their post was a capital offence; in other words, they could be executed for such an act, but still, they did not repent! such is the hardened heart)*,

13 Saying, you say, His Disciples came by night, and stole Him *away* while we slept *(what an absurd story, but yet, many Jews believe it unto this hour)*.

14 And if this come to the Governor's ears, we will persuade him, and secure you *(meaning that the Sanhedrin would take full responsibility for this action; no harm ever came to the soldiers; evidently Pilate believed that Jesus had risen from the dead; it is said in one of the Chronicles, of that time, that Pilate sent an account of this matter to Tiberius, who, in consequence, we are told, endeavored to make the Roman Senate pass a decree enrolling Jesus in the list of Roman gods; Tertullian attests this fact)*.

15 So they took the money, and did as they were taught *(means that the matter was rehearsed over, and over again by the Sanhedrin until all had the same story)*: and this saying is commonly reported among the Jews until this day *(it is said that the Jews at that time sent emissaries in all directions to spread this false report)*.

THE TESTIMONY OF THE DISCIPLES

16 Then the eleven Disciples went away into Galilee *(the sequence seems to indicate that it took place at least a week after the Resurrection [Jn. 20:26; 21:1]; the number "11" is specifically mentioned, in that the Holy Spirit desires that the betrayal not be forgotten)*, into a mountain where Jesus had appointed them *(gives no evidence as to exactly where this mountain was; the word, "appointed," specifies that this was a designated meeting, which would have insured a definite place)*.

17 And when they saw Him *(seems to indicate that there were more present than the eleven)*, they worshipped Him *(and rightly so!)*: but some doubted *(not the eleven! who they were, we do not know; why they doubted,* we do not know; however, it seems the doubts soon faded*)*.

THE GREAT COMMISSION

18 And Jesus came and spoke unto them *(the same meeting on the mountain, and constitutes the Great Commission)*, saying, All power is given unto Me in Heaven and in Earth *(this is not given to Him as Son of God; for, as God nothing can be added to Him or taken from Him; it is rather a power, which He has merited by His Incarnation and His death at Calvary on the Cross [Phil. 2:8-10]; this authority extends not only over men, so that He governs and protects the Church, disposes human events, controls hearts and opinions; but the forces of Heaven also are at His Command; the Holy Spirit is bestowed by Him, and the Angels are in His employ as ministering to the members of His Body. When He said, "all power," He meant, "all power!")*.

19 Go ye therefore *(applies to any and all who follow Christ, and in all ages)*, and teach all nations *(should have been translated, "and preach to all nations", for the word "teach" here refers to a proclamation of truth)*, baptizing them in the Name of the Father, and of the Son, and of the Holy Spirit *(presents the only formula for Water Baptism given in the Word of God)*:

20 Teaching them *(means to give instruction)* to observe all things *(the whole Gospel for the whole man)* whatsoever I have commanded you *(not a suggestion)*: and, lo, I am with you always *(It is I, Myself, God, and Man, Who am — not "will be" — hence, forever present among you, and with you as Companion, Friend, Guide, Saviour, God)*, *even* unto the end of the world *(should have been translated "age")*. Amen *(it is the guarantee of My Promise)*.

THE GOSPEL ACCORDING TO
MARK

CHAPTER 1
(A.D. 26)

THE MINISTRY OF JOHN THE BAPTIST

THE beginning of the Gospel of Jesus Christ, the Son of God (*could read, "the beginning of the Good News concerning Jesus, the Messiah, the Son of God"; the Holy Spirit begins this Book by testifying to the Kingship and Deity of Christ before setting out His Perfection as a Servant; the actual beginning of this Gospel is the Ministry of John the Baptist*);

2 As it is written in the Prophets (*proclaims the Old Testament as the Word of God*), Behold, I send My Messenger (*John the Baptist*) before Your Face (*Christ*), which shall prepare Your Way before You (*preparation for the introduction of the Messiah [Mal. 3:1]*).

3 The voice of one crying (*the preaching of John the Baptist was full of emotion and feeling*) in the wilderness (*typical of Israel's spiritual condition*), Prepare ye the Way of the Lord (*the sense of a military command*), make His paths straight (*rightly discern the Word, and obey it*).

4 John did baptize in the wilderness (*Water Baptism in this fashion was unique*), and preach the baptism of repentance (*Repentance of the individual*) for the remission of sins (*should have been translated, "because of the remission of sins"; the people were being baptized because they had already repented in their hearts; there is no Salvation in the ceremony of Water Baptism*).

5 And there went out unto Him all the land of Judaea, and they of Jerusalem, and were all baptized of him in the river of Jordan, confessing their sins (*meaning that the confessing of sins and the act of Water Baptism, were at times, simultaneous*).

6 And John was clothed with camel's hair (*characteristic of the doctrine which John taught, namely penitence and contempt of the world*), and with a girdle of a skin about his loins (*a sash*); and he did eat locusts and wild honey (*the locust were dried to a crispness in the sun and eaten with honey, not uncommon in those days*);

7 And preached (*deep emotion*), saying, There comes One (*not merely "one," but rather "The One"*) mightier than I (*"The Almighty One"*) after me (*I will prepare the way*), the latchet of Whose shoes I am not worthy to stoop down and unloose (*the difference being, the former was a created being, while the Latter is the Creator*).

8 I indeed have baptized you with water: but He shall baptize you with the Holy Spirit (*due to the Cross, the Holy Spirit can now come into the heart and life of the Believer to abide permanently [Jn. 14:16-17]*).

THE BAPTISM OF JESUS

9 And it came to pass in those days (*the close of the Ministry of John the Baptist*), that Jesus came from Nazareth of Galilee (*respects the beginning of the Ministry of Christ*), and was baptized of John in Jordan.

10 And straightway (*immediately*) coming up out of the water (*Water Baptism is by immersion, which alone can satisfy the type, not by sprinkling*), he (*John*) saw the Heavens opened (*saw the Heavens rent asunder, whatever that might mean*), and the Spirit like a dove descending upon Him (*Luke said, "in a bodily shape like a dove" [Lk. 3:22] exactly what he saw, we don't know, but he definitely did see something*):

11 And there came a Voice from Heaven (*The Voice came from the rent or opened heavens, no form was seen, but a "voice" was heard*), saying, You are My Beloved Son (*in contradistinction to all others*), in Whom I am well pleased (*this means that God is pleased with us, only as long as we are in Christ; we have here the Trinity, the Voice from Heaven, God the Father, the Holy Spirit being sent, and the Son on Whom He is sent*).

THE TEMPTATIONS OF JESUS

12 And immediately (*the first act of the Spirit on Christ*) the Spirit (*Holy Spirit*) driveth Him (*strongly moved upon Him*) into the wilderness (*believed to be near Jericho*).

13 And He was there in the wilderness forty days (*probationary period*), tempted of Satan (*tempted constantly during the forty days and*

nights); **and was with the wild beasts** (*the last Adam had an entirely different setting than the first Adam, which was Paradise*); **and the Angels ministered unto Him** (*as to exactly how, we aren't told*).

THE CALL

14 Now after that John was put in prison, Jesus came into Galilee, Preaching the Gospel (*Good News*) **of the Kingdom of God** (*a realm in which a King, namely Christ exercises His Power to act and control*),

15 And saying, The time is fulfilled (*as predicted by the Prophets, Christ has now come*), **and the Kingdom of God is at hand** (*is available*): **repent ye, and believe the Gospel** (*"repent and believe" may be regarded as a summary of the method of Salvation. This means that Repentance and Faith are the conditions of admission into this Kingdom, i.e., "the New Covenant"*).

16 Now as He walked by the sea of Galilee, He saw Simon (*Peter*) **and Andrew his brother casting a net into the sea: for they were fishers.**

17 And Jesus said unto them, Come ye after Me, and I will make you to become fishers of men.

18 And straightway (*immediately*) **they forsook their nets, and followed Him.**

19 And when He had gone a little farther thence, He saw James the son of Zebedee, and John his brother, who also were in the ship mending their nets.

20 And straightway He called them (*the Ministry is a "call" not a career*): **and they left their father Zebedee in the ship with the hired servants, and went after Him** (*it seems they had the blessings of their father*).

AUTHORITY OVER DEMON SPIRITS

21 And they went into Capernaum (*where Jesus made His Headquarters*); **and straightway** (*immediately*) **on the Sabbath Day He entered into the Synagogue, and taught.**

22 And they were astonished at His doctrine (*what He taught, and the way He taught it; His Doctrine was the Word of God, while the Scribes basically taught tradition*): **for He taught them as One Who had authority, and not as the Scribes** (*a group supposed to be expert in the Law of Moses*).

23 And there was in their Synagogue a man with an unclean spirit (*the word, "unclean"*

runs the gamut of all the activity of Satan from immorality to deceptive, lying, religious spirits [Rev. 16:13-16]); **and he cried out,**

24 Saying, Let *us* **alone** (*the lead demon cried out, but there were more demons than one in this man*); **what have we to do with You, Thou Jesus of Nazareth?** (*They resented the intrusion of Christ into their domain.*) *Are You* **come to destroy us?** (*They knew that He had the power to do whatever needed to be done.*) **I know You Who You are, the Holy One of God** (*demon spirits knew Who He was, but the religious leaders of Israel didn't know, or rather refused to know*).

25 And Jesus rebuked him (*the lead demon*), **saying, Hold your peace, and come out of him** (*in effect, He said, "shut up, and come out of him"*).

26 And when the unclean spirit had torn him (*hastily, trying to come out*), **and cried with a loud voice** (*represents a screech of fear — fear of Christ, and fear not to obey Christ immediately*), **he came out of him** (*there was no delay*).

27 And they were all amazed (*speechless*), **insomuch that they questioned among themselves** (*the Scribes animated, prolonged discussion*), **saying, What thing is this?** (*In effect, "Who is this Man," referring to the possibility, and their thinking, that He might be the Messiah.*) **what new doctrine** *is* **this?** (*Doesn't refer to "new" in respect to time, but instead, in comparison to the dry as dust droning of the Scribes.*) **for with authority commands He even the unclean spirits, and they do obey Him** (*this is absolute power over Satan and all demon spirits, and with obedience carried out immediately*).

28 And immediately His fame spread abroad throughout all the region round about Galilee (*when it would spread to Jerusalem, it would infuriate the religious leaders*).

HEALING

29 And forthwith, when they were come out of the Synagogue, they entered into the house of Simon (*Peter*) **and Andrew** (*Peter's brother*), **with James and John** (*these four were probably the only Disciples He had at that time, which was the early part of His Ministry*).

30 But Simon's wife's mother lay sick of a fever (*bedridden*), **and anon** (*immediately*) **they tell Him of her** (*there is no mention of the wife of Peter by name in the New Testament; according to the testimony of Clement of Alexandria, and Eusebiu, she suffered martyrdom, and was led away to death in the sight of her husband,*

whose last words to her were, "remember thou the Lord").

31 And He *(Jesus)* came and took her by the hand, and lifted her up; and immediately the fever left her *(healed immediately)*, and she ministered unto them *(probably helped prepare a meal).*

DEMONS CAST OUT; MANY HEALED

32 And at evening, when the sun did set *(when the Sabbath ended)*, they brought unto Him all who were diseased, and them who were possessed with devils *(demons).*

33 And all the city was gathered together at the door *(all the sick and afflicted).*

34 And He healed many who were sick of divers diseases *(many and varied types of diseases, and of every kind)*, and cast out many devils *(demons)*; and suffered not the devils to speak, because they knew Him *(means they knew Him to be the Messiah).*

A PREACHING TOUR

35 And in the morning, rising up a great while before day *(was between 3 a.m. and 6 a.m.)*, He went out, and departed into a solitary place, and there prayed *(the example of a strong prayer life, was a habit with Him, and provides an example for us [Mat. 14: 23; Mk. 1:35; 6:46; Lk. 6:12; 9:28; 11:1]).*

36 And Simon and they who were with Him followed after Him *(sought to find Him).*

37 And when they had found Him, they said unto Him, All *men* seek for You *(the pronoun, "You" is emphatic, meaning that those who sought Jesus would not be satisfied with seeing His Disciples).*

38 And He said unto them, Let us go into the next towns *(while in prayer, He had heard from Heaven, and had been given direction respecting what to do and where to go)*, that I may preach there also: for therefore came I forth *(He was to cover the majority of the land of Israel).*

39 And He preached in their Synagogues throughout all Galilee, and cast out devils *(healing and Deliverance, as important as they were, were secondary to the "preaching" of the Word).*

JESUS HEALS A LEPER

40 And there came a leper to Him, beseeching Him *(begging Him)*, and kneeling down to

Him *(this was not merely a rendering of honor to an earthly being; it was a rendering of reverence to a Divine Being)*, and saying unto Him, If You will, You can make me clean *(leprosy was so loathsome, that the leper didn't know if Jesus would heal him or not, even though he knew, that Jesus had the Power).*

41 And Jesus, moved with compassion *(is a portrayal of the Heart of God)*, put forth *His* hand, and touched him, and said unto him, I will; be thou clean *(according to the Greek, His Word healed the man, and not His touch; when He touched him, the healing had already been effected, and the man was "clean"; the words "I will" forever settled the question of the Will of God to heal the sick).*

42 And as soon as He had spoken, immediately the leprosy departed from him *(proclaiming the spoken Word to be enough)*, and he was cleansed.

43 And He *(Jesus)* straitly charged him *(strongly demanded of him)*, and forthwith sent him away *(sent him to the Priest, as the Law demanded [Lev. 14:2]);*

44 And said unto him, See thou say nothing to any man *(not at the present time)*: but go your way *(first)*, show yourself to the Priest, and offer for your cleansing those things which Moses commanded, for a testimony unto them *(this pertained to the Law of the cleansing of the Leper, which was a complicated affair [Lev. 14:1-32]).*

45 But he went out, and began to publish *it* much, and to blaze abroad the matter, insomuch that Jesus could no more openly enter into the city *(was Capernaum)*, but was without in desert places *(because of the press of the great crowds)*: and they came to Him from every quarter *(the man not obeying what Jesus told him to do, gave occasion for the enemies of Christ to accuse Him; in other words, they would say that He had ignored the Law, which of course He hadn't, but the man did, and despite the admonition).*

CHAPTER 2
(A.D. 31)
JESUS HEALS A PALSIED MAN

AND again He entered into Capernaum after *some* days *(maybe several weeks)*; and it was noised that He was in the house *(Peter's house).*

2 And straightway *(immediately)* many were gathered together, insomuch that there was no room to receive *them*, no, not so much as about

the door: and He preached the Word unto them *(preaching and teaching always came first)*.

3 And they come unto Him, bringing one sick of the palsy *(paralysis)*, which was borne *(carried)* of four.

4 And when they could not come near unto Him for the press *(the great crowd)*, they uncovered the roof where He was *(houses have flat roofs in that part of the world, usually with steps on the outside leading to the top)*: and when they had broken *it* up *(there were usually one or more trap doors in the roof, and it was one of these, which they probably enlarged)*, they let down the bed wherein the sick of the palsy lay.

5 When Jesus saw their faith *(faith without works is dead)*, He said unto the sick of the palsy, Son, your sins be forgiven you *(the wretched physical condition of the sick man was due to his sinful life, therefore, Jesus first of all, addressed the real cause; no condemnation, just forgiveness and healing)*.

6 But there were certain of the Scribes sitting there, and reasoning in their hearts *(represents a hostile spirit on their part, which could be felt by Christ)*,

7 Why does this *man* thus speak blasphemies? *(Would have been correct had Christ been only a man. Inasmuch as He was God manifested in the flesh, they were totally incorrect. They will now come face-to-face with the Deity of Christ.)* who can forgive sins but God only? *(Proclaims a truth, but yet, Jesus was God.)*

8 And immediately when Jesus perceived in His spirit that they so reasoned within themselves *(the Holy Spirit revealed their thinking to Him)*, He said unto them, Why reason ye these things in your hearts? *(This must have been startling to them. They had not spoken these things aloud, had only thought them in their hearts.)*

9 Whether is it easier to say to the sick of the palsy, *Your* sins be forgiven you; or to say, Arise, and take up your bed, and walk? *(God Alone can forgive sins, and God Alone can heal. Therefore, to heal validates the power to forgive sins. As stated, they were now coming face-to-face with His Deity.)*

10 But that you may know that the Son of Man has power on earth to forgive sins, (He said to the sick of the palsy,) *(He did all of this in full view of everyone, even the skeptics, and especially the skeptics!)*,

11 I say unto you, Arise, and take up your bed, and go your way into your house *(all there*

knew, including the skeptics that this man could not take up his bed and carry it, unless he was truly healed; whether they admitted it or not, they also knew that only the Power of God could accomplish this).

12 And immediately he arose *(the Word of Christ healed him)*, took up the bed, and went forth before them all *(including the skeptics)*; insomuch that they were all amazed *(there was no doubt about the healing)*, and glorified God, saying, We never saw it on this fashion *(whether this included the skeptics or not, we aren't told!)*.

JESUS CALLS MATTHEW

13 And He went forth again by the sea side *(Sea of Galilee)*; and all the multitude resorted unto Him, and He taught them.

14 And as He passed by, He saw Levi *(Matthew)* the *son* of Alphaeus sitting at the receipt of custom *(he was a tax collector, an abomination in the eyes of Israel)*, and said unto him, Follow Me *(it was not a request, but a Command)*. And he arose and followed Him *(he did so instantly, responding to the Master's Command)*.

JESUS EATS WITH SINNERS

15 And it came to pass, that, as Jesus sat at meat in his house *(the house of Matthew)*, many publicans and sinners sat also together with Jesus and His Disciples *(expresses a gathering called by Matthew, evidently to celebrate him being Called by Christ; he was giving up the tax-collecting business)*: for there were many, and they followed Him *(the indication is, they accepted Him as Lord and Master of their lives)*.

16 And when the Scribes and Pharisees saw Him eat with publicans and sinners, they said unto His Disciples *(it seems that many of the Scribes and Pharisees had heard of the Call of Matthew, and this resulted in their gathering, and had come, although uninvited, to see what was taking place)*, How is it that He eats and drinks with publicans and sinners? *(Poses the idea that they thought that He was committing a great sin by associating with these people. This was their self-righteousness in action.)*

17 When Jesus heard *it*, He said unto them, They who are whole have no need of the physician, but they who are sick *(explains fully as to the "why" of His Presence)*: I came not to call the Righteous, but sinners to repentance *(Christ was and is the Physician of sinners, not their companion)*.

FASTING

18 And the disciples of John and of the Pharisees used to fast: and they come and say unto Him *(unto Jesus)*, Why do the disciples of John *(John the Baptist, who was now in prison)* and of the Pharisees fast, but Your Disciples fast not? *(Any ordinance or ritual given in the Bible, such as fasting, must never be looked at as holy within itself, but rather as to what it represents.)*

19 And Jesus said unto them, Can the children of the bridechamber fast, while the bridegroom is with them? as long as they have the bridegroom with them, they cannot fast *(Jesus is the Bridegroom)*.

20 But the days will come, when the bridegroom shall be taken away from them *(which took place at the Ascension)*, and then shall they fast in those days *(while fasting helps the Believer in many ways, the greatest way of all is what it symbolizes; in essence, fasting states that things aren't right, and will not be right until Jesus comes back; so fasting, at least in part, is a plea for Him to come quickly).*

21 No man also sews a piece of new cloth on an old garment: else the new piece that filled it up takes away from the old, and the rent is made worse *(the "new cloth" symbolizes the New Covenant which Christ would bring in; it would not be a part of the Old Covenant that being done away, but would be completely new; to try to mix the two, as He states, will not work; regrettably, most modern Christians, whether they realize it or not, are in fact, attempting to mix the two).*

22 And no man puts new wine into old bottles: else the new wine does burst the bottles, and the wine is spilled, and the bottles will be marred: but new wine must be put into new bottles *(same principle as the "new cloth," given in a different way to emphasize this Truth).*

THE SABBATH

23 And it came to pass, that He went through the corn fields *(should have been translated barley or wheat fields, because there was no corn in the Middle East, or Europe, as we think of such presently, at that time)* on the Sabbath Day; and His Disciples began, as they went, to pluck the ears of corn *(stalks of barley or wheat).*

24 And the Pharisees said unto Him *(means in the Greek that they kept on badgering Him about the matter)*, Behold, why do they *(the Disciples)* on the Sabbath Day that which is not lawful? *(They claimed the Disciples were breaking the Law of Moses by plucking and eating the grain on the Sabbath; Deut. 23:24-25 said, otherwise.)*

25 And He said unto them *(He could have taken them to Deuteronomy, but instead, he took them to I Sam., Chpt. 21; He would take them at their own game)*, Have you never read what David did, when he had need, and was hungry, he, and they who were with him? *(He was showing them the futility of religion and ceremony, when there was no change in the heart.)*

26 How He went into the House of God in the days of Abiathar the High Priest, and did eat the shewbread, which is not lawful to eat but for the Priests, and gave also to them which were with him? *(David was not a Priest, so by the Law, could not eat one of these special loaves in the Tabernacle; however, he wisely judged that a positive law forbidding the laity to eat this bread, which it did, ought to yield to a Law of necessity and of nature, which it did!)*

27 And He said unto them *(its original construction contains the idea that He said these things over, and over; it took some talking to get the idea across to their minds, which were warped with a warped theology)*, The Sabbath was made for man, and not man for the Sabbath *(the force of the argument is this: the Sabbath was made on account of man, not man on account of the Sabbath; the Sabbath was a day of rest; it was meant to point to the "spiritual rest" which would come in Christ)*:

28 Therefore the Son of Man is Lord also of the Sabbath *(in this statement, Christ was saying, "I am the Messiah," and these religious leaders knew what He was saying!).*

CHAPTER 3
(A.D. 31)
JESUS HEALS ON THE SABBATH

AND He entered again into the Synagogue *(on the Sabbath Day, and probably in Capernaum)*; and there was a man there which had a withered hand *(a symbol of withered, undone humanity, as a result of the Fall).*

2 And they watched Him, whether He would heal him on the Sabbath Day; that they might accuse Him *(religion really doesn't care for people, only its rules and regulations).*

3 And He said unto the man which had the withered hand, Stand forth *(whatever He did, was done openly; in other words, He threw this challenge to the Pharisees and into their teeth).*

4 And He said unto them *(speaks pointedly to the Pharisees, and in front of everyone present)*, **Is it lawful to do good on the Sabbath Days, or to do evil? to save life, or to kill?** *(He was telling them that living for God was not a question of keeping rules and regulations, but a question of "doing good or evil!" To have the power to set this man free and not do so was "evil".)* **But they held their peace** *(Wuest says, "theirs was a painful, embarrassing silence")*.

5 And when He had looked round about on them with anger *(proves that "anger" is not necessarily a manifestation of sin and Satan; only its wrong use falls into that category)*, being grieved for the hardness of their hearts *(there is no hardness of the heart like religious hardness; He knew that this would lead the Pharisees and Israel to destruction)*, **He said unto the man, Stretch forth your hand** *(once again, being done in full view of all)*. **And he stretched** *it* **out: and his hand was restored whole as the other** *(pictures what Christ can do with the human heart)*.

6 And the Pharisees went forth *(they were angry; they had no concern for the man who had been miraculously healed)*, **and straightway** *(immediately)* **took counsel with the Herodians** *(a group who believed that Herod was the Messiah, and whom the Pharisees normally hated)* **against Him, how they might destroy Him** *(this was the condition of the religions leaders of Israel)*.

MANY HEALED

7 But Jesus withdrew Himself with His Disciples to the sea: and a great multitude from Galilee followed Him, and from Judaea,

8 And from Jerusalem *(the religious leadership of Israel resided in this city)*, **and from Idumaea** *(this was south of the Dead Sea, and about one hundred miles from the Sea of Galilee, a long way in those days)*, **and** *from* **beyond Jordan** *(east of the Jordan River, which would have included Paneas and the Decapolis)*; **and they about Tyre and Sidon** *(about fifty miles north of the Sea of Galilee, mostly inhabited by Gentiles)*, **a great multitude, when they had heard what great things He did, came unto Him** *(this will be repeated in the coming Kingdom Age, but on a far grander scale)*.

9 And He spoke to His Disciples, that a small ship should wait on Him because of the multitude, lest they should throng Him *(this*

would have been a small boat, pushed out a little distance from the shore, with Him teaching the people from this particular platform)*.

10 For He had healed many; insomuch that they pressed upon Him for to touch Him, as many as had plagues *(all were healed and He never turned one away)*.

11 And unclean spirits, when they saw Him, fell down before Him, and cried, saying, **You are the Son of God** *(they kept falling down before Him, and kept constantly crying; they knew He was the Son of God, even though the religious leaders of Israel didn't)*.

12 And He straitly charged them *(a military command)* **that they should not make Him known** *(He wanted no advertisement from this sort)*.

THE TWELVE CHOSEN AND ORDAINED

13 And He goeth up into a mountain, and called *unto Him* whom He would: and they came unto Him *(there could have been as many as forty or fifty people personally selected, and maybe even near a hundred)*.

14 And He ordained *(appointed)* **Twelve** *(the Biblical number for Government)*, **that they should be with Him** *(the secret of all power)*, **and that He might send them forth to preach,**

15 And to have power *(delegated authority, all from Christ)* **to heal sicknesses, and to cast out devils** *(demons)*:

16 And Simon He surnamed Peter *(a stone)*;

17 And James the *son* of Zebedee, and John the brother of James; and He surnamed them Boanerges, which is, The sons of thunder *(the names suggested their impetuosity and zeal, which characterized both the brothers)*:

18 And Andrew, and Philip, and Bartholomew, and Matthew, and Thomas, and James the *son* of Alphaeus, and Thaddaeus, and Simon the Canaanite *(Simon the Zealot)*,

19 And Judas Iscariot, which also betrayed Him *(the only one of the Disciples who was of the Tribe of Judah; Christ was from that Tribe as well!)*: **and they went into an house** *(probably referred to Peter's house in Capernaum)*.

20 And the multitude came together again *(when they heard He was present)*, so that they could not so much as eat bread.

21 And when His friends heard *of it* *(His immediate relatives, as Verse 31 proclaims)*, **they went out to lay hold on Him** *(means they intended to stop Him, even by using force and against His Will, if necessary!)*: **for they said,**

He is beside Himself *(means, they actually believed He was insane; His open opposition to the Pharisees and the religious leaders of Israel, would have occasioned this, with them knowing that it was ultimately going to bring severe trouble; however, His brothers, at that time, did not actually believe that He was the Son of God [Jn. 7:5]).*

THE PHARISEES BLASPHEME THE HOLY SPIRIT

22 And the Scribes which came down from Jerusalem said *(evidently sent by the Sanhedrin in order to find something in which they could undermine His influence)*, He has Beelzebub, and by the prince of the devils casteth He out devils *(they blasphemed the Holy Spirit when they accused Christ of casting out devils by the power of Satan).*

23 And He called them *unto Him (the Scribes)*, and said unto them in Parables, How can Satan cast out Satan? *(Why would Satan undo what he had done?)*

24 And if a kingdom be divided against itself, that kingdom cannot stand.

25 And if a house be divided against itself, that house cannot stand *(internal fighting respecting a family will ultimately lead to the destruction of that family).*

26 And if Satan rise up against himself, and be divided, he cannot stand, but has an end *(would wreck his kingdom of darkness).*

27 No man can enter into a strong man's house *(in this case the house of Satan)*, and spoil his goods, except he will first bind the strong man *(Jesus overthrew Satan)*; and then he will spoil his house *(Christ defeated Satan at the Cross, by atoning for all sin [Col. 2:14-15]).*

THE UNPARDONABLE SIN

28 Verily I say unto you *(speaking to all, but more directly to the Scribes)*, All sins shall be forgiven unto the sons of men, and blasphemies wherewith soever they shall blaspheme *(providing forgiveness is asked of the Lord; this is a wonderful promise, and has been upheld in the hearts and lives of untold millions)*:

29 But he who shall blaspheme against the Holy Spirit hath never forgiveness *(only a Believer who has ceased to believe, in other words, ceases to evidence Faith in Christ, and a professor of religion, such as these Pharisees, etc., can blaspheme the Holy Spirit; an unsaved person,* who has made no profession of faith, cannot blaspheme the Spirit; and when one does blaspheme the Holy Spirit, there will not be any desire to serve Christ, as there was no desire by the Pharisees, etc., to serve Christ)*, **but is in danger of eternal damnation** *(refers to those who would attribute the Power of God to Satan, as the Pharisees had done; to label anything which is actually of God, as being of Satan is a serious offense indeed!)*:

30 Because they said, He has an unclean spirit *(most serious).*

JESUS' TRUE KIN

31 There came then His brethren *(He had four brothers [Mat. 13:55], and several sisters)* and his mother, and, standing without *(outside of the house)*, sent unto Him, calling Him *(they sent Him word by way of the crowd that they desired to see Him).*

32 And the multitude sat about Him, and they said unto Him, Behold, Your mother and Your brethren without seek for You.

33 And He answered them, saying, Who is My mother, or My brethren? *(He meant to place this relationship in its proper setting.)*

34 And He looked round about on them which sat about Him *(presents a look that is serious, but yet not critical)*, and said, Behold My mother and My brethren! *(He gestures toward those who hungrily desired to hear His Words, and answered His Own question.)*

35 For whosoever shall do the Will of God *(proclaims the qualifications for the high and lofty position of being in His family)*, the same is My brother, and My sister, and mother *(places all Born-Again Believers in a status even greater than flesh-and-blood relationships, while never for a moment demeaning those relationships).*

CHAPTER 4
(A.D. 31)

THE PARABLE OF THE SOWER

AND He began again to teach by the sea side: and there was gathered unto Him a great multitude, so that He entered into a ship, and sat in the sea *(sat in the ship on the Sea of Galilee)*; and the whole multitude was by the sea on the land.

2 And He taught them many things by Parables, and said unto them in His Doctrine *(had He stayed upon the shore the diseased could have touched Him and been healed; but His*

business as a Servant was to deal with sin rather than with its effects),

3 Hearken *(be listening)*; Behold, there went out a sower to sow *(this Parable is given in Mat., Chpt. 13, and repeated in Lk., Chpt. 8, but worded somewhat different; these were illustrations taken from everyday life and living, which people understood. But yet, they seldom understood His Parables)*:

4 And it came to pass, as He sowed, some fell by the way side, and the fowls of the air came and devoured it up *(the "seed sowed" is the Gospel; the "fowls of the air" represent Satan and his demon powers)*.

5 And some fell on stony ground, where it had not much earth; and immediately it sprang up, because it had no depth of earth:

6 But when the sun was up, it was scorched; and because it had no root, it withered away *(many start out for Christ, but don't last long; all of this completely refutes the unscriptural doctrine of unconditional eternal security)*.

7 And some *(seed)* fell among thorns, and the thorns grew up, and choked it *(cares of this life, etc.)*, and it yielded no fruit.

8 And other fell on good ground, and did yield fruit that sprang up and increased; and brought forth, some thirty, and some sixty, and some an hundred *(an hundredfold, etc.)*.

9 And He said unto them, He who has ears to hear, let him hear *(those who would properly "hear," would attend to these Words of Christ, pondering them, until somehow the Truth was eventually revealed; the Gospel is designed this way purposely by the Holy Spirit, in order to ferret out the insincere)*.

THE PURPOSE OF PARABLES

10 And when He was alone, they who were about Him with the Twelve *(possibly as many as forty or fifty)* asked of Him the Parable *(what it meant)*.

11 And He said unto them, Unto you it is given to know the mystery of the Kingdom of God *(those who truly want to know)*: but unto them who are without *(who have no desire to know)*, all *these* things are done in Parables *(Parables were used to reject the merely curious, and to pull in the sincerely desirous)*:

12 That seeing they may see, and not perceive; and hearing they may hear, and not understand; lest at any time they should be converted, and *their* sins should be forgiven them *(Judicial blindness and deafness justly befall*

those who do not wish to see and hear; the emphasis is on the person and not on God. He desires that all see and hear)*.

13 And He said unto them, Know ye not this Parable? *(Contains a gentle reproach. The question as given by the Lord, indicates that they should have known.)* and how then will you know all Parables? *(The Parable of the Sower lays down the principle of all Parables concerning the understanding thereof.)*

PARABLE OF THE SOWER

14 The sower sows the Word *(the Word of God. This "seed" must be sowed to the entirety of the world [Mk. 16:15])*.

15 And these *(the ones who merely hear but do not receive)* are they by the way side, where the Word is sown; but when they have heard, Satan comes immediately, and takes away the Word that was sown in their hearts *(the structure of the sentence is these individuals do not have to allow Satan to take away the Word)*.

16 And these *(those who hear and receive, but have no durability)* are they likewise which are sown on stony ground; who, when they have heard the Word, immediately receive it with gladness *(millions fall into this category)*;

17 And have no root in themselves *(once again, it is the fault of the individual)*, and so endure but for a time *(meaning that they truly were Born-Again)*: afterward, when affliction or persecution ariseth for the Word's sake *(as surely it will)*, immediately they are offended *(can't stand the opposition, because they have no root, meaning that the ground was not sufficiently prepared)*.

18 And these *(make a great start, and even endure for a while, but they allow the world to stop them)* are they which are sown among thorns; such as hear the Word,

19 And the cares of this world, and the deceitfulness of riches, and the lusts of other things entering in, choke the Word, and it becomes unfruitful *(means that they did bear fruit for a while, but allowed the things of the world to choke it off, until they became totally unfruitful, and lost their way; the Parable of the sower completely refutes the unscriptural doctrine of unconditional eternal security, as should be obvious here)*.

20 And these *(those who hear, receive, bring forth fruit, and continue to bring forth fruit forever; they allow nothing to stop them)* are they which are sown on good ground *(the individual determines whether the ground is good*

or not); such as hear the Word, and receive *it*, and bring forth fruit, some thirtyfold, some sixty, and some an hundred.

THE GOSPEL

21 And He said unto them, Is a candle brought to be put under a bushel, or under a bed? and not to be set on a candlestick? *(The Gospel is not to be merely enjoyed privately, but rather imparted as a lamp imparts its light.)*

22 For there is nothing hid, which shall not be manifested; neither was any thing kept secret, but that it should come abroad *(the Gospel is not meant to be hid, or kept secret, but is to be spread abroad, throughout the world).*

23 If any man have ears to hear, let him hear *(the Lord will make the Gospel known to all Nations, and all will be held responsible who hear it).*

24 And He said unto them, Take heed what you hear *(there is no excuse for Believers not hearing correctly)*: with what measure you mete, it shall be measured to you: and unto you who hear shall more be given *(in proportion to the diligence given to Bible Study, so will spiritual intelligence be measured to the student).*

25 For he who has, to him shall be given: and he who has not, from him shall be taken even that which he has *(spiritual gifts, if exercised, will be developed; if not, they will be lost).*

THE PARABLE OF THE SEED

26 And He said, So is the Kingdom of God, as if a man should cast seed into the ground *(responsibility of Believers to spread the Gospel)*;

27 And should sleep, and rise night and day, and the seed should spring and grow up, he knows not how *(the Word if properly sown, will without fail, have its proper effect).*

28 For the earth brings forth fruit of herself; first the blade, then the ear, after that the full corn in the ear *(this is the Law of the Gospel in "sowing and reaping").*

29 But when the fruit is brought forth, immediately he puts in the sickle, because the harvest is come *(has reference to the end of the age, when the Church will be called to account).*

THE PARABLE OF THE MUSTARD SEED

30 And He said, Whereunto shall we liken the Kingdom of God? or with what comparison shall we compare it? *(Is meant to proclaim the manner in which Satan will endeavor to corrupt the Word of God.)*

31 *It is* like a grain of mustard seed, which, when it is sown in the earth, is less than all the seeds that be in the earth *(the Church began very small)*:

32 But when it is sown, it grows up, and becomes greater than all herbs, and shoots out great branches *(Christianity is presently the largest religion on Earth, claiming nearly two billion adherents, in one form or the other)*; so that the fowls of the air may lodge under the shadow of it *(refers to most of Christianity being corrupted by Satanic Powers as explained in Mat. 13:19 and Lk. 8:12).*

33 And with many such Parables spoke He the Word unto them, as they were able to hear it *(able to understand).*

34 But without a Parable spoke He not unto them: and when they were alone, He expounded all things to His Disciples *(gave them extended instruction).*

JESUS STILLS THE STORM

35 And the same day, when the evening was come *(refers to the same day that He had been teaching the people through Parables)*, He said unto them *(the Twelve)*, Let us pass over unto the other side *(presents itself as a microcosm of this present life; the storms come, and it is only with Christ, that we can make it to the other shore).*

36 And when they had sent away the multitude, they took Him even as He was in the ship *(meaning that He was very tired, even to the point of physical exhaustion; as a man, He grew tired, just as we do).* And there were also with Him other little ships *(referred to those who wanted to be near Him, and understandably so!).*

37 And there arose a great storm of wind, and the waves beat into the ship, so that it was now full *(represents in the spiritual sense, the storms of life, which come to every person).*

38 And He was in the hinder part of the ship, asleep on a pillow: and they awake Him, and say unto Him, Master, carest Thou not that we perish? *(The Lord had said, "let us pass over unto the other side." This means that despite the storm, or anything else for that matter, they would reach the other shore. The people of God are in the same boat with Christ, and we cannot perish because He cannot perish. But we must expect storms of opposition for they are sure to come [Ps. 93].)*

39 And He arose, and rebuked the wind, and

said unto the sea, Peace, be still (the Greek intimates, "Silence! Hush!"). And the wind ceased, and there was a great calm (instantly).

40 And He said unto them, Why are you so fearful? (This type of fear, shows improper love [I Jn. 4:18].) How is it that ye have no faith? (The Disciples had accepted His Messiahship, but had a most inadequate view of what that office carried with it.)

41 And they feared exceedingly (means that their fear of Him, was greater even then their fear had been of the storm), and said one to another, What manner of man is this, that even the wind and the sea obey Him? (The Disciples were right! The wind and sea did obey Him, and so does everything else. So why should we fear?)

CHAPTER 5

(A.D. 31)

THE DEMONIAC DELIVERED

AND they came over unto the other side of the sea (refers to the eastern shore of Galilee), into the country of the Gadarenes (the area of the town of Gadara, which was three miles from the Sea of Galilee).

2 And when He was come out of the ship, immediately there met Him out of the tombs a man with an unclean spirit (symbolizes the great mission for which Christ came to the world; He had calmed the storm on the sea, and now He would calm the storm in a man's soul),

3 Who had his dwelling among the tombs (the wages of sin is death); and no man could bind him, no, not with chains (sin and the powers of darkness will yield only to Christ, and what He did at the Cross on our behalf; this rules out humanistic psychology, and anything else instituted by man in order to address this problem):

4 Because that he had been often bound with fetters and chains, and the chains had been plucked asunder by him, and the fetters broken in pieces (superhuman strength given to him by the unclean spirit): neither could any man tame him (once again, reinforces the great Truth that Christ and the Cross alone, are the only answer).

5 And always, night and day (there is no peace for those who do not know the Lord), he was in the mountains, and in the tombs, crying, and cutting himself with stones (a symbolic picture, which takes place with all unredeemed in the spiritual).

6 But when he saw Jesus afar off, he ran

and worshipped Him (the demon spirit worshiped Him; all demon spirits and Satan himself are made to pay homage to God the Son; Satan and all of his minions were defeated at the Cross [Col. 2:14-15]),

7 And cried with a loud voice, and said, What have I to do with You, Jesus, Thou Son of the Most High God? (Refers to this evil spirit knowing exactly as to who Jesus was!) I adjure Thee by God, that You torment me not (a certain time has been appointed by God to which these spirits will be confined to the pit [Rev. 20:1-3]).

8 For He said unto him, Come out of the man, you unclean spirit (constitutes a direct order, which the unclean spirit must obey).

9 And He (Christ) asked him, What is your name? (Why did Jesus ask this question? He did so, because He knew that other spirits inhabited this man also.) And he answered, saying, My name is Legion: for we are many (the unclean spirit was the head demon, but many more were there as well).

10 And he besought him (besought Christ) much that He would not send them away out of the country (this area was full of Hellenistic apostate Jews, and evidently was loved by demon spirits; we learn here that demon spirits enjoy places that have little or no mention of Christ).

11 Now there was there near unto the mountains a great herd of swine feeding (they were, no doubt, owned by Jews, even though Jews were forbidden by the Law to eat pork).

12 And all the devils (demons) besought Him, saying, Send us into the swine, that we may enter into them (they could not enter into these hogs without the express permission of Christ, so how much less could they enter into "the sheep of His pasture!").

13 And forthwith Jesus gave them leave (means that He did not command them to do this, but instead, gave them permission). And the unclean spirits went out, and entered into the swine: and the herd ran violently down a steep place into the sea, (they were about two thousand;) and were choked in the sea (many have questioned the right of Christ to do this, which destroyed other people's property; however, even though the Holy Spirit through Mark didn't explain it, we know that everything the Lord does is right; it's not merely right because He does it, but because it actually is right).

14 And they who fed the swine fled, and told it in the city, and in the country. And they went out to see what it was that was done (a great multitude).

15 And they come to Jesus *(the loss of the animals would have been nothing in comparison to what they would have received upon their acceptance of Christ, at least, had they done so, which they didn't)*, and see him who was possessed with the devil *(had been possessed with demons)*, and had the legion, sitting, and clothed *(clothing, no doubt, given to him by the Disciples)*, and in his right mind *(irrespective as to how much education a person may have, until they come to Christ, they aren't completely in their right mind)*: and they were afraid *(regrettably, they did not allow this fear to bring them to Christ)*.

16 And they who saw *it* told them how it befell to him who was possessed with the devil, and *also* concerning the swine *(lends credence to the thought that the swine-herders had witnessed the entire episode, concerning the action of Christ in delivering the demoniac, and allowing the demons to go into the hogs)*.

17 And they began to pray Him *(Jesus)* to depart out of their coasts *(it is remarkable!; they thought more of the swine than they did of the eternal life that Christ could have given them; and so it is with most of the world)*.

18 And when He *(Jesus)* was come into the ship, he who had been possessed with the devil prayed Him that he might be with Him *(he wanted to go with Jesus and the Disciples, and no wonder!)*.

19 Howbeit Jesus suffered him not, but said unto him, Go home to your friends, and tell them how great things the Lord has done for you, and has had compassion on you *(A. Go tell; B. Great things which the Lord has done; and, C. Tell of the compassion)*.

20 And he departed, and began to publish in Decapolis *(a region east of the Jordan River, containing a number of towns and cities)* how great things Jesus had done for him *(he became an Evangelist)*: and all *men* did marvel *(evidently, many had known him before, and now see what the Lord has done for him; this is the story of untold millions)*.

HEALINGS AND MIRACLES

21 And when Jesus was passed over again by ship unto the other side *(back to Capernaum, on the west side)*, much people gathered unto Him: and He was near unto the sea *(means that hundreds, if not thousands, were waiting on the shore for Him to come back to Capernaum)*.

22 And, behold, there cometh one of the rulers of the Synagogue, Jairus by name *(each Synagogue had several rulers)*; and when he saw Him *(Jesus)*, he fell at His feet *(a posture of worship)*,

23 And besought Him greatly *(an impassioned plea)*, saying, My little daughter lies at the point of death *(actually, she probably died about the time that Jairus was importuning Christ)*: I *pray You*, come and lay Your hands on her, that she may be healed; and she shall live *(the Greek actually says, "to save her from death")*.

24 And *Jesus* went with him; and much people followed Him *(Jesus)*, and thronged Him.

25 And a certain woman *(tradition says her name was Veronica)*, which had an issue of blood twelve years *(speaks of a constant hemorrhage for that period of time. A female disorder)*,

26 And had suffered many things of many physicians *(means that she had suffered extreme pain at the hands of these doctors)*, and had spent all that she had *(many of these physicians had treated her merely for the money, knowing all the time they could not help her)*, and was nothing bettered, but rather grew worse *(had not helped her at all, but had worsened the situation)*,

27 When she had heard of Jesus *(the Greek actually says, "the Jesus" distinguishing Him from all others)*, came in the press behind *(the great crowd of people)*, and touched His garment *(probably referred to the touching of the hem of the shawl thrown over His shoulder, which contained a blue fringe, which the Jews were required to wear, to remind them they were God's People [Num. 15:38-41; Deut. 22:12])*.

28 For she said *(means she kept saying it over and over to herself, or even possibly to others near by)*, If I may touch but His clothes, I shall be whole *(concerns her level of faith)*.

29 And straightway *(immediately)* the fountain of her blood was dried up; and she felt in *her* body that she was healed of that plague *(she knew she was healed)*.

30 And Jesus, immediately knowing in Himself that virtue *(power)* had gone out of Him, turned Him about in the press *(crowd)*, and said, Who touched My clothes? *(The Holy Spirit had not seen fit to reveal to Him who had touched Him.)*

31 And His Disciples said unto Him, You see the multitude thronging You, and You say, Who touched Me?

32 And He looked round about to see her who had done this thing.

33 But the woman fearing and trembling,

knowing what was done in her, came and fell down before Him, and told Him all the truth (*proclaims her now seeking mercy as she had previously sought healing; it would be granted as well!*).

34 And He said unto her, Daughter (*in the Twenty-fifth Verse, she was addressed merely as "a certain woman," now she is called "daughter," which refers to relationship; He, in effect, had made her a member of the Family of God*), your faith has made you whole (*if He doesn't touch us, we can touch Him*); go in peace (*gain Salvation as well as healing*), and be whole of your plague (*meaning that the malady would never return*).

35 While He yet spoke (*was speaking to the woman*), there came from the ruler of the Synagogue's *house certain* (*a certain one*) which said, Your daughter is dead: why troublest thou the Master any further? (*The faith of this certain one wasn't high enough to believe that Jesus could raise the dead.*)

36 As soon as Jesus heard the word that was spoken (*He overheard what was being said*), He said unto the ruler of the Synagogue, Be not afraid, only believe (*in effect, Jesus said, "stop fearing, and be believing"*).

37 And He suffered no man to follow Him, save Peter, and James, and John the brother of James (*He took these three with Him to the home of Jairus*).

38 And He came to the house of the Ruler of the Synagogue, and seeing the tumult, and them who wept and wailed greatly (*hired mourners which was the custom in those days*).

39 And when He was come in (*into the home of Jairus*), He said unto them, Why *do you* make this ado, and weep? (*Jesus was not in sympathy with this custom and practice*) the damsel is not dead, but sleeps (*did not mean that she was actually not dead, but that the child was not dead to stay dead; as well, the word, "sleepeth," brings us to the fact of the Resurrection; in the Scriptures, the dead are constantly referred to as "sleeping"; however, it is only the body which sleeps, with the soul and the spirit at death, instantly going to be with Christ that is, if the person is saved*).

40 And they (*the paid mourners*) laughed Him to scorn (*meaning that they ridiculed Him; what simpletons!*). But when He had put them all out (*demanded that they leave*), He took the father and the mother of the damsel, and them who were with Him (*Peter, James, and John*), and entered in where the damsel was lying

(*the word, "entereth," actually refers to a person going on a journey; even though only a few feet, at least in this instance, it conveyed the idea of distance; in effect, it pointed forward to the coming Resurrection*).

41 And He took the damsel by the hand (*refers to a strong grip*), and said unto her, Talitha cumi; which is, being interpreted, Damsel, I say unto you, arise (*this was spoken in Aramic, the same tongue used concerning our Lord's Words on the Cross, "My God, My God why have You forsaken Me?"; as the original language was reported in these two cases, quite possibly they relate to each other; as Jesus defeated death at the home of Jairus, likewise, and for the whole world, He defeated death at Calvary*).

42 And straightway (*immediately*) the damsel arose, and walked; for she was *of the age* of twelve years. And they were astonished with a great astonishment (*the Scriptures only record three people being raised from the dead by Christ, but Augustine says that He raised many more*).

43 And He charged them straitly (*commanded them*) that no man should know it (*they must not relate the account of this miracle; there were reasons for this, the least not being the furor which religious leaders would cause; but it is certain that such news could not be kept*); and commanded that something should be given her to eat (*due to her illness, which actually killed her, she probably had not eaten for days*).

CHAPTER 6
(A.D. 31)
UNBELIEF IN NAZARETH

AND He went out from thence (*from Capernaum*), and came into His own country (*Nazareth*); and His Disciples follow Him.

2 And when the Sabbath Day was come, He began to teach in the Synagogue: and many hearing *Him* were astonished, saying, From whence hath this *Man* these things? and what wisdom *is* this which is given unto Him, that even such mighty works are wrought by *His Hands*? (*They did not question the wisdom or the works, but rather His right to do such things. In their thoughts, He wasn't worthy!*)

3 Is not this the carpenter (*Chrysostom said, that He made ploughs and yokes for oxen; in the minds of His critics, this disqualified Him as a great teacher*), the Son of Mary, the brother of James, and Joseph, and of Juda, and Simon? and are not His sisters here with us? (*This disproves the claims by the Catholic Church that*

Jesus had no brothers or sisters.) And they were offended at Him (He did not meet their approval).

4 But Jesus said unto them (represents His answer to their unbelief), A Prophet is not without honour (to show deference and reverence), but in his own country, and among his own kin, and in his own house (I don't think that Mary was a part of this unbelief, but it definitely included the balance of the family, with Joseph by now, probably having passed on).

5 And He could there do no mighty work (actually means, not even one; it was not that He couldn't, but they wouldn't bring the sick and the diseased to Him; they would rather see their loved ones sick, than to see Christ heal them!), save that He laid His Hands upon a few sick folk (a few sickly ones), and healed them.

6 And He marveled because of their unbelief (expresses the view of His Humanity; the Holy Spirit mentions Him marveling twice, once at the faith of a Gentile, and at the unbelief of His Own [Mat. 8:10]). And He went round about the villages, teaching.

THE TWELVE SENT OUT

7 And He called unto Him the Twelve (speaks of their first Mission where they were sent without Him), and began to send them forth by two and two; and gave them power over unclean spirits;

8 And commanded them that they should take nothing for their journey (is not a suggestion, but a Command), save a staff only (a wooden staff for walking); no scrip (a leather pouch for food), no bread, no money in their purse (means they were not to store up these things before they went, but were to rather trust the Lord);

9 But be shod with sandals (spoke of association with the common people who wore such); and not put on two coats (the most simple of quality and quantity were sufficient).

10 And He said unto them, In what place soever you enter into an house, (they accept you) there abide till you depart from that place (don't flit from place to place).

11 And whosoever shall not receive you, nor hear you (basically refers to the area, even the city, and not the house in which they were invited), when you depart thence (meant to express the significance of the visit), shake off the dust under your feet for a testimony against them (a symbolic gesture). Verily I say unto you, It shall be more tolerable for Sodom and

Gomorrha in the day of judgment, than for that city (has reference to the fact that Sodom and Gomorrha had no Gospel witness, while these places did).

12 And they went out, and preached that men should repent (the Message didn't change, and shouldn't change now).

13 And they cast out many devils (demons), and anointed with oil many who were sick, and healed them (oil is symbolic of the Holy Spirit, it has nothing to do with medicine [Ex. 27:20; 30:25; Num. 6:15; I Sam. 16:1,13; Ps. 45:7]).

JOHN THE BAPTIST BEHEADED

14 And king Herod (Antipas) heard of Him (Jesus); (for His name was spread abroad:) and he said, That John the Baptist was risen from the dead, and therefore mighty works do show forth themselves in him (proclaims a troubled and guilty conscience for putting John the Baptist to death).

15 Others said (refers to the Court of Herod, as well as many in Israel), That it is Elijah. And others said, That it is a Prophet, or as one of the Prophets (it seems that Israel would admit to anything except the Truth that He was the Messiah, the Son of the Living God).

16 But when Herod heard thereof, he said, It is John, whom I beheaded: he is risen from the dead (means he kept saying it over and over, in response to the prediction of others as to Who Christ was!).

17 For Herod himself had sent forth and laid hold upon John, and bound him in prison (the Holy Spirit wanted to make certain that no one misunderstood that it was Herod who had done this dastardly thing) for Herodias' sake, his brother Philip's wife (John had been in prison because Herod's wife Herodias, had demanded it): for he (Herod) had married her.

18 For John had said unto Herod, It is not lawful for you to have your brother's wife (means that he said it more than once, to both Herod and the people).

19 Therefore Herodias had a quarrel against him (she never let up on her fury toward the Baptist for daring to denounce her private relations with Herod, and waited her time for revenge), and would have killed him; but she could not (means that she did not lack the will, only the way; she would find the way):

20 For Herod feared John, knowing that he was a just man and an holy (means that he was in a continual state of fear respecting the Prophet),

and observed him *(means he watched over John to keep him safe from the evil plots of Herodias)*; and when he heard him, he did many things, and heard him gladly *(he kept going back to the dank prison cell over, and over again to speak with the Prophet; in other words, the Holy Spirit was dealing with Herod's soul)*.

21 And when a convenient day was come *(refers to a convenient time for Herodias to kill John the Baptist)*, that Herod on his birthday made a supper to his lords, high captains, and chief *estates* of Galilee *(Herodias would find her time for revenge at this gathering)*;

22 And when the daughter of the said Herodias came in, and danced, and pleased Herod and them who sat with him *(she degraded herself in a licentious dance)*, the king said unto the damsel, Ask of me whatsoever you will, and I will give *it* to you *(they were probably drunk, or nearly so. Herodias would now spring her trap)*.

23 And he sware unto her *(puts himself under oath)*, Whatsoever you shall ask of me, I will give *it* to you, unto the half of my kingdom *(he doesn't want to lose face in front of his guests)*.

24 And she went forth, and said unto her mother *(implies her knowledge of at least a part of the plan of revenge)*, What shall I ask? And she said, The head of John the Baptist.

25 And she *(the daughter of Herodias)* came in straightway *(immediately)* with haste unto the king *(presents her immediately making her demand, so the king will have no opportunity to renege on his promise)*, and asked, saying, I will that you give me by and by *(immediately)* in a charger *(on a platter)* the head of John the Baptist.

26 And the king was exceeding sorry; *yet* for his oath's sake, and for their sakes which sat with him *(he would save face)*, he would not reject her *(the life of the greatest Prophet who ever lived, had boiled down to the worth of a lewd dance, at least to these men)*.

27 And immediately the king sent an executioner, and commanded his head to be brought: and he went and beheaded him in the prison *(the prison was actually connected to the palace where the celebration was being held)*,

28 And brought his head in a charger, and gave it to the damsel: and the damsel gave it to her mother *(proclaims Herodias, according to Jerome thrusting the tongue through with a long pen; because she could not bear to hear the truth, therefore, she would puncture the tongue that* had spoken the truth; both Herodias and Herod, a short time later, were banished by a decree of the Roman Senate to Lyons where they both perished miserably; Salome, the daughter who danced, died shortly thereafter, by having her head nearly cut off by the sharp edges of broken ice; "Vengeance is Mine; I will repay saith the Lord" [Rom. 12:19]).*

29 And when his disciples heard *of it (the disciples of John the Baptist)*, they came and took up his corpse *(Josephus says that after the beheading, the mutilated remains were cast out of the prison and left neglected)*, and laid it in a tomb *(and so concludes the life and Ministry of the greatest Prophet who ever lived)*.

JESUS FEEDS FIVE THOUSAND

30 And the Apostles gathered themselves together unto Jesus *(relates back to Verse 7 where the Twelve had been sent forth "two and two"; they now come back to report to Christ)*, and told Him all things, both what they had done, and what they had taught.

31 And He said unto them, Come ye yourselves apart into a desert place, and rest a while: for there were many coming and going, and they had no leisure so much as to eat.

32 And they departed into a desert place by ship privately *(probably one of the vessels belonging to Zebedee)*.

33 And the people saw them departing, and many knew Him, and ran afoot thither out of all cities, and outwent them *(presents them waiting for Him whenever the boat docked in this desert place)*, and came together unto Him.

34 And Jesus, when He came out, saw much people, and was moved with compassion toward them, because they were as sheep not having a shepherd *(the nation was more religious than ever before, but with few true shepherds)*: and He began to teach them many things *(presents the only true Gospel that many of them had ever heard)*.

35 And when the day was now far spent, His Disciples came unto Him, and said, This is a desert place, and now the time *is* far passed *(growing late in the day)*:

36 Send them away, that they may go into the country round about, and into the villages, and buy themselves bread: for they have nothing to eat.

37 He answered and said unto them, Give ye them to eat *(He was speaking in both the physical and the spiritual sense)*. And they say

unto Him, Shall we go and buy two hundred pennyworth of bread, and give them to eat? *(Probably equal to seven or eight thousand dollars presently)*.

38 He said unto them, How many loaves have you? *(They were thinking of thousands of loaves.)* go and see. And when they knew, they say, Five, and two fishes *(according to Andrew, this small collection belonged to a boy [Jn. 6:8-9]; little is much if God be in it)*.

39 And He Commanded them to make all sit down by companies upon the green grass *(considering that the grass was green, it was probably about April)*.

40 And they sat down in ranks, by hundreds, and by fifties.

41 And when He had taken the five loaves and the two fishes *(signifies the beginning of the Miracle, and because it was in His Hands)*, He looked up to Heaven *(it is from God from whence all Blessings come)*, and blessed *(His Blessing guarantees everything)*, and broke the loaves, and gave *them* to His Disciples to set before them; and the two fishes divided He among them all *(the Miracle took place between the breaking and the giving; each Disciple soon exhausted his supply and so had to return to Jesus for more, and was never disappointed)*.

42 And they did all eat, and were filled *(Jehovah of Psalm 132 revealed Himself here)*.

43 And they took up twelve baskets full of the fragments, and of the fish.

44 And they who did eat of the loaves were about five thousand men *(possibly as many as 10,000 to 15,000 total, including women and children)*.

JESUS WALKS ON THE SEA

45 And straightway *(immediately)* He constrained His Disciples to get into the ship *(they were reluctant to do so)*, and to go to the other side before unto Bethsaida, while He sent away the people *(but He sent them away healed, fed, and filled)*.

46 And when He had sent them away, He departed into a mountain to pray *(prayer establishes relationship)*.

47 And when evening was come, the ship was in the midst of the sea, and He alone on the land.

48 And He saw them toiling in rowing; for the wind was contrary unto them *(inasmuch as it was night, He could not have seen them physically, so the Holy Spirit must have revealed this*

to Him): and about the fourth watch of the night He cometh unto them *(between 3 a.m. and 6 a.m.)*, walking upon the sea *(the inference is that the sandals of our Lord actually had contact with the water; He walked on the surface of the sea as we walk on a hard pavement)*, and would have passed by them *(should have been translated, "and came near to them")*.

49 But when they saw Him walking upon the sea *(couldn't believe their eyes)*, they supposed it had been a spirit, and cried out *(they thought it was an apparition)*:

50 For they all saw Him, and were troubled *(all Twelve saw Him)*. And immediately He talked with them, and said unto them, Be of good cheer: it is I; be not afraid *(He evidently was very near when He said this to them)*.

51 And He went up unto them into the ship *(Mark omits Peter walking on the water, as recorded by Matthew)*; and the wind ceased *(emphasizes the fact that such was done solely because He was now in the ship)*: and they were sore amazed in themselves beyond measure, and wondered *(they had witnessed something beyond the power of their comprehension)*.

52 For they considered not *the miracle* of the loaves: for their heart was hardened *(the desire to make Jesus King as John mentioned, was paramount, in the minds of His Disciples; consequently, the true mission of Christ was lost on them, at least at this time; and deviation from the true Will of God always "hardens the heart"; nothing dulls spiritually like the religious enthusiasm of the carnal nature acting in fellowship with the religious world)*.

JESUS HEALS MANY SICK PEOPLE

53 And when they had passed over *(the ship had begun without Jesus, but concludes with Him; what a Miracle!)*, they came into the land of Gennesaret, and drew to the shore *(was a fertile plain on the north shore of Galilee and west of the Jordan River)*.

54 And when they were come out of the ship *(insinuates a ship of some size; probably one of the larger fishing vessels of Zebedee)*, straightway *(immediately)* they knew Him,

55 And ran through that whole region round about *(proclaims runners going from village to village announcing that Jesus was in the vicinity)*, and began to carry about in beds those who were sick, where they heard He was *(this was a pathetic, yet understandable sight!)*.

56 And whithersoever He entered, into

villages, or cities, or country, they laid the sick in the streets, and besought Him that they might touch if it were but the border of His garment: and as many as touched Him were made whole *(this had to have been a situation astounding to behold!; what a sight it must have been!; it will be this way when He comes back the second time, and even greater).*

CHAPTER 7
(A.D. 32)
JESUS REBUKES THE SCRIBES AND PHARISEES

T HEN came together unto Him the Pharisees, and certain of the Scribes, which came from Jerusalem *(the religious leaders were becoming alarmed at the tremendous popularity of Jesus).*

2 And when they saw *(means they were earnestly seeking some fault, by which they might accuse Him)* some of His Disciples eat bread with defiled, that is to say, with unwashed, hands, they found fault *(had nothing to do with sanitary cleanliness; the Pharisees taught that demons, unseen, could sit on the hands of anyone, and consequently, if the hands were not washed, the demons could be ingested).*

3 For the Pharisees, and all the Jews, except they wash *their* hands often, eat not *(ceremonial religion)*, holding the tradition of the Elders *(this tradition was only of man, and not at all of God, as are many traditions in the modern Church).*

4 And *when they come* from the market, except they wash, they eat not *(spending an inordinate amount of time engaging in this foolishness)*. And many other things there be, which they have received to hold, *as* the washing of cups, and pots, brasen vessels, and of tables *(they had a certain religious way to wash these things, all which amounted to nothing).*

5 Then the Pharisees and Scribes asked Him *(means they kept on asking Him, demanding an answer)*, Why walk not Your Disciples according to the tradition of the Elders, but eat bread with unwashed hands? *(All of this was outward show only, and brought Christ into direct conflict with these religious leaders.)*

6 He answered and said unto them *(runs through Verse 13, and constitutes a startling answer, which pull no punches and minced no words)*, Well has Isaiah prophesied of you hypocrites *(said this to their faces. "You hypocrites" actually says in the Greek, "You, the hypocrites,"*

which means the outstanding ones of all time)*, as it is written, This people honor Me with *their* lips, but their heart is far from Me *(hits at the very heart of what true Salvation is and isn't [Isa. 29:13]).*

7 Howbeit in vain *(means empty nothings, no profit)* do they worship Me, teaching *for* doctrines the commandments of men *(the state [Herod] put to death the Preacher of Righteousness [Mat. 14:10], and the Church [the Scribes], corrupted the Word of Righteousness).*

8 For laying aside the Commandment of God, you hold the tradition of men, *as* the washing of pots and cups: and many other such like things you do *(said with sarcasm; they washed cups and pots but not their hearts; the ceremonial washing of their hands could not remove the guilt that stained them).*

9 And He said unto them, Full well you reject the Commandment of God, that you may keep your own tradition *(it was a studied and deliberate rejection).*

10 For Moses said *(drew their attention back to the Word of God)*, Honor your father and your mother; and, Whoso curses father or mother, let him die the death *(is deserving of death)*:

11 But you say *(presents a stark contrast to the Word of God)*, If a man shall say to his father or mother, *It is* Corban, that is to say, a gift, by whatsoever you might be profited by Me; *he shall be free (the Pharisees had made it a practice of claiming they were giving their material possessions to the Temple, which absolved them of responsibility toward their parents, with a crooked Priest then giving it back to them for a small percentage).*

12 And you suffer him no more to do ought for his father or his mother *(to such extremities did these covetous Scribes and Pharisees drive their victims who, were their aged parents, with no way to care for themselves);*

13 Making the Word of God of none effect through your tradition *(Jesus had just nailed them with the Fifth Commandment)*, which you have delivered *(meaning that their glosses of the Word had come from men and not from God)*: and many such like things do you *(this which Christ had given as an example, was only the tip of the proverbial iceberg).*

JESUS EXPLAINS WHAT DEFILES

14 And when He had called all the people *unto Him (He called the people closer so they could hear exactly what He was saying)*, He said

unto them, Hearken unto Me every one *of you,* and understand *(the people have a choice, they can hear Him or these hypocritical Pharisees and Scribes; it is the same presently)*:

15 There is nothing from without a man, that entereth into him can defile him *(refers to food, not intoxicating drinks, narcotics, poisons, or tobacco, etc.)*: but the things which come out of him, those are they that defile the man *(it is evident that what comes out of the heart must exist in the heart)*.

16 If any man have ears to hear, let him hear *(the Lord is telling the people that they have a choice; they can hear him or the Pharisees, but not both!)*.

17 And when He was entered into the house *(probably Peter's house)* from the people *(from teaching the people)*, His Disciples asked Him concerning the Parable *(regarding that which enters into a man, and that which comes from his heart)*.

18 And He said unto them, Are you so without understanding also? *(Shows some disappointment on the part of Christ respecting His Disciples.)* Do you not perceive, that whatsoever thing from without enters into the man, *it* cannot defile him *(presents the exact opposite of what the Pharisees, and Scribes taught)*;

19 Because it enters not into his heart *(food is not spiritual)*, but into the belly, and goes out into the draught, purging all meats? *(Refers to the digestive and elimination system of the human body.)*

20 And He said, That which comes out of the man, that defiles the man *(an evil heart produces evil actions)*.

21 For from within, out of the heart of men, proceed evil thoughts, adulteries, fornications, murders *(the necessity of the creation of a new heart, i.e., "a new man," is here declared)*,

22 Thefts, covetousness, wickedness, deceit, lasciviousness, an evil eye, blasphemy, pride, foolishness *(this statement by Christ, destroys the belief that the natural heart is good, and makes foolish modern efforts to improve human nature)*:

23 All these evil things come from within, and defile the man *(proclaims the result of the Fall, and the absolute necessity of the new birth)*.

HEALING, THE CHILDREN'S BREAD

24 And from thence He arose, and went into the borders of Tyre and Sidon *(has the idea from the Greek Text that He did not merely cross over the border into Gentile territory, but instead,*

went deep into the heart of that country)*, and entered into an house, and would have no man know *it,* but He could not be hid.

25 For a *certain* woman *(this is the reason He came)*, whose young daughter had an unclean spirit, heard of Him, and came and fell at His feet:

26 The woman was a Greek, a Syrophenician by nation *(a Gentile)*; and she besought Him that he would cast forth the devil *(demon)* out of her daughter.

27 But Jesus said unto her *(begins the odyssey which will proclaim one of the greatest displays of faith ever!)*, Let the children first be filled *(has reference to Israel)*: for it is not meet *(proper)* to take the children's bread, and to cast *it* unto the dogs *(Jesus used the Word for "little pet dogs")*.

28 And she answered and said unto Him *(proclaims a level of faith which should be a lesson to all Believers)*, Yes, Lord *(the word, "Lord," in the Greek Text, as used by the woman, does not refer to Deity or of Jesus being the Jewish Messiah; she would have had scant knowledge of this; she, instead, uses the word, "Lord," in the sense of Jesus being an important Person, etc.)*: yet the dogs under the table eat of the children's crumbs *(now places her in the position of faith, a position which enables her to receive)*.

29 And He said unto her, For this saying *(because you have taken a position of humility)* go your way; the devil *(demon)* is gone out of your daughter *(means that it is out, and will stay out; it is a permanent cure)*.

30 And when she was come to her house, she found the devil gone out, and her daughter laid upon the bed *(refers to a restful repose, which indicated that previously she had not been easily restrained)*.

JESUS HEALS A DEAF AND DUMB MAN

31 And again, departing from the coasts *(borders)* of Tyre and Sidon, He came unto the Sea of Galilee, through the midst of the coasts *(borders)* of Decapolis *(He was now on the eastern side of the Sea of Galilee)*.

32 And they bring unto Him one who was deaf, and had an impediment in his speech *(proclaims the usual difficulties of the deaf)*; and they *(friends of the deaf man)* beseech Him to put His hand upon him.

33 And He took him aside from the multitude *(there was a purpose for this)*, and put His fingers into his ears, and He spit, and touched his tongue *(He probably spat on His Finger first,*

touched the man's tongue, and then put both index fingers in the man's ears; the "spittle" represented His Perfect Life);

34 And looking up to Heaven *(all help comes from above),* He sighed *(speaks of the terrible dilemma, due to the Fall, in which man now finds himself),* and said unto him, Ephphatha, that is, Be opened *(expresses the command).*

35 And straightway *(immediately)* his ears were opened, and the string of his tongue was loosed, and he spoke plain *(symbolizes in the physical that which takes place in the spiritual, as it regards the Salvation of the Soul).*

36 And He charged *(commanded)* them that they should tell no man: but the more He charged them, so much the more a great deal they published *it;*

37 And were beyond measure astonished *(what Jesus had done, was beyond their comprehension),* saying, He has done all things well *(means in the Greek that they said this, and continued to say it over, and over):* He makes both the deaf to hear, and the dumb to speak *(His whole life on Earth was one connected, continued manifestation of lovingkindness).*

CHAPTER 8
(A.D. 32)
JESUS FEEDS FOUR THOUSAND

IN those days the multitude being very great *(numbering thousands)* and having nothing to eat *(outside of Christ, the world "has nothing to eat"),* Jesus called His Disciples *unto Him,* and said unto them,

2 I have compassion on the multitude *(portrays the Love of God; it would be the same as saying, "My heart goes out to them"),* because they have now been with Me three days, and have nothing to eat *(they wanted so much to be in His Presence that they slept where they could, and ate what little they had, if anything, with that long since having run out):*

3 And if I send them away fasting to their own houses, they will faint by the way: for divers *(many)* of them came from far.

4 And His Disciples answered Him, From whence can a man satisfy these *men* with bread here in the wilderness? *(The insensibility of the natural heart appears in this Verse. The Disciples apparently learned nothing from the previous feeding of the multitude [Chpt. 6].)*

5 And He asked them, How many loaves have you? And they said, Seven *(before they had "five" loaves, which is God's number of*

Grace, while now they have "seven," which is God's Perfect number of completion).

6 And He commanded the people to sit down on the ground: and He took the seven loaves *(in the Disciples' hands they were nothing, in His Hands they are everything!; the action is not in the loaves, but rather in Him),* and gave thanks, and break, and gave to His Disciples to set before *them (proclaims the actual time of the multiplication; the giving was a continual act, until all were filled);* and they did set *them* before the people.

7 And they had a few small fishes *(did not give the number):* and He blessed, and commanded to set them also before *them.*

8 So they did eat, and were filled: and they took up of the broken *meat (bread)* that was left seven baskets.

9 And they who had eaten were about four thousand *(probably didn't include women and children, which would have increased it by several thousands):* and He sent them away *(but only after they were healed and filled).*

THE DEMAND FOR A SIGN

10 And straightway *(immediately)* He entered into a ship with His Disciples, and came into the parts of Dalmanutha *(on the western shore of Galilee).*

11 And the Pharisees came forth *(Matthew said the Sadducees were present as well [Mat. 16:1]),* and began to question with Him *(they were standing before the Creator of the Ages, Who had the answer to all things, but yet, they are so spiritually stupid, that they will ply Him only with silly questions),* seeking of Him a sign from Heaven, tempting Him *(and these were the religious leaders of Israel!).*

12 And He sighed deeply in His Spirit *(meaning, He groaned in His Spirit),* and said, Why does this generation seek after a sign? *(It is useless to give evidence to unbelief.)* verily I say unto you, There shall no sign be given unto this generation *(no more signs than what had already been given, which were astounding to say the least, regarding healings and miracles, etc.).*

13 And He left them *(spiritually speaking, He left them to their doom),* and entering into the ship again departed to the other side *(the northeastern shore).*

THE LEAVEN

14 Now *the Disciples* had forgotten to take

bread, neither had they in the ship with them more than one loaf (*the short trip would take several hours*).

15 And He charged them (*in the Greek Text, means that He kept on speaking to them, making certain they understood that of which He was speaking*), saying, Take heed, beware of the leaven of the Pharisees (*false doctrine*), and *of* the leaven of Herod (*the claim by some Jews that this despot was the Messiah, which they did for financial prosperity*).

16 And they reasoned among themselves, saying, *It is* because we have no bread (*they had not the slightest idea of what He was speaking*).

17 And when Jesus knew *it*, He said unto them (*the Holy Spirit revealed to Him their confusion*), Why reason you, because you have no bread? (*In other words, I'm not talking about physical bread.*) perceive ye not yet, neither understand? have ye your heart yet hardened? (*They were looking too much in the physical, and not at all in the spiritual.*)

18 Having eyes, see ye not? (*Pertains to spiritual eyes they were not using.*) and having ears, hear ye not? (*They were not hearing correctly, they were not hearing spiritually.*) and do you not remember? (*We should remember what the Lord has done for us in the past, and learn a lesson.*)

19 When I broke the five loaves among five thousand, how many baskets full of fragments took ye up? They say unto Him, Twelve.

20 And when the seven among four thousand, how many baskets full of fragments took ye up? And they said, Seven.

21 And He said unto them, How is it that you do not understand? (*The question would have been better translated, "do you yet not understand?"; there is a hint in the Greek Text that, in fact, they finally did begin to understand; actually, Matthew tells us this was the case [Mat. 16:12].*)

JESUS HEALS A BLIND MAN

22 And He comes to Bethsaida (*probably refers to Bethsaida Julias situated on the northeast shore of the Sea of Galilee*): and they bring a blind man unto Him, and besought Him to touch him.

23 And He took the blind man by the hand, and led him out of the town (*Jesus had already placed a curse on this city because of their refusal to repent; consequently, He would not perform another miracle in its confines [Mat. 11:21]*);

and when He had spit on his eyes (*pertains to the second time such was done [7:33]; He probably put spittle on His Finger and touched the man's eyes*), and put His hands upon him, He asked him if he saw ought (*has in the Greek Text that He kept on asking him*).

24 And he looked up, and said, I see men as trees, walking (*the Greek Text actually says, "I see men; for I behold them as trees, walking"; the word, "walking," refers to the men and not to the trees"; there seemed to be a mist of sorts over his eyes, which disfigured things*).

25 After that He put *His* hands again upon his eyes, and made him look up: and he was restored, and saw every man clearly (*the only incident in the four Gospels, of Jesus dealing with someone the second time in this fashion; why did Jesus have to lay His Hands on him a second time?; the next Verse possibly tells us*).

26 And He sent him away to his house (*implies that he was not a native of Bethsaida Julias*), saying, Neither go into the town, nor tell *it* to any in the town (*refers to the fact, as stated, that Jesus had placed a curse on this town for their refusal to repent [Mat. 11:21]; due to this, Christ seemed unwilling to give Bethsaida any more evidence of the visitation of God; this could well be the reason why Jesus had to lay His Hands on the man a second time; the curse had been pronounced and the die cast, consequently, it was as if the door was shut*).

PETER'S CONFESSION

27 And Jesus went out, and His Disciples, into the towns of Caesarea Philippi (*places Him about forty miles north of the Sea of Galilee, and about forty miles south of Damascus*): and by the way He asked His Disciples, saying unto them, Whom do men say that I am? (*Constitutes Who He really was, and the drawing out of the Disciples, as to Who they thought He was. The Greek Text says, "He kept on asking," meaning that the question so startled them that at first they did not answer.*)

28 And they answered, John the Baptist: but some *say*, Elijah; and others, One of the Prophets (*their answers were strange, but yet reflected the thinking of much of Israel at that particular time*).

29 And He said unto them, But whom say you that I am? (*Concerns the greatest question that could ever be asked. It is a question that all must ultimately answer.*) And Peter answered and said unto Him, You are the Christ (*Peter*

actually said, "You are the Messiah," because that's what the Word "Christ" actually means; it was the Great Confession).

30 And He charged them (commanded them) that they should tell no man of Him (relates the fact that it was now obvious that Israel had rejected Him, and consequently, there was no further point in projecting the issue).

JESUS FORETELLS HIS DEATH AND RESURRECTION

31 And He began to teach them (proclaims an explanation as to what was to happen, despite the fact that He was the Messiah), that the Son of Man must suffer many things (proclaimed the fact, that they believed otherwise!), and be rejected of the Elders, and of the Chief Priests, and Scribes ("rejected" means that the religious leaders of Israel put Jesus to the test; however, He did not meet their specifications; He was not the kind of a Messiah the Jews wanted; they wanted a military leader who would liberate them from the yoke of Rome, not a Saviour who would free them from their bondage of sin), and be killed (the Crucifixion), and after three days rise again (the Resurrection was never in doubt, due to the victorious success of the Cross in atoning for all sin).

32 And He spoke that saying openly (means that He kept saying it). And Peter took Him (probably put His hands on the shoulders of Christ), and began to rebuke Him (means that He spoke with force, denying what Jesus had said).

33 But when He had turned about and looked on His Disciples, He rebuked Peter (He did not at all take lightly what Peter had said; and now, He made sure that His Disciples understood His reaction), saying, Get thee behind Me, Satan (presents Jesus speaking directly to Satan, and not Peter; however, the Words of our Lord, brands Peter's words as Satanic; the words, "behind Me," in effect, say, "get out of My Face!"): for you (now speaks to Peter) savor not the things that be of God, but the things that be of men (unredeemed man doesn't want what God wants).

34 And when He had called the people unto Him with His Disciples also, He said unto them (speaks of an interval of some period of time between His rebuke of Peter and this present statement), Whosoever will come after Me, let him deny himself (deny his own strength, ability, talent, power, and carnal intellect), and take up his cross (not suffering as many suppose, but rather the benefits of the Cross), and follow Me (implying that Jesus cannot be followed, unless it's by the way of the Cross).

35 For whosoever will save his life shall lose it (if one refuses to place his life in Christ); but whosoever shall lose his life for My sake and the Gospel's, the same shall save it (to place one's life entirely in Christ, which can only be done by way of the Cross, and in doing so, saves one's life, and does so forever).

36 For what shall it profit a man, if he shall gain the whole world, and lose his own soul? (The simple equation of profit and loss, which states that one's soul, is worth more than the whole world.)

37 Or what shall a man give in exchange for his soul? (The soul is eternal, therefore, worth more than anything.)

38 Whosoever therefore shall be ashamed of Me and of My Words (the present conduct of the individual now determines Christ's future conduct with reference to that person) in this adulterous and sinful generation (pertains to the character of Israel at the time of Christ, and as well, to every generation which has followed); of him also shall the Son of Man be ashamed (means that such attitude will be reciprocated in like kind), when He comes in the Glory of his Father with the Holy Angels (the Second Coming).

CHAPTER 9
(A.D. 32)

THE TRANSFIGURATION

AND He (Jesus) said unto them (the twelve), Verily I say unto you, That there be some of them who stand here (in this case, Peter, James, and John), which shall not taste of death (did not mean they would not ultimately die, but that before they died, they would see beyond the veil into the Kingdom), till they have seen the Kingdom of God come with power (this was an anticipatory picture of the coming Millennium).

2 And after six days (Luke says "eight days" [Lk. 9:28]; there is no discrepancy; in Luke the Greek phrase is inclusive, meaning that all the time was addressed, while in Mark it is exclusive, meaning that all the days and time were not included) Jesus took with Him Peter, and James, and John (the second experience in which they were included, but not the other Disciples; the raising of the daughter of Jairus from the dead was the first), and leadeth them up into an high

mountain apart by themselves *(we aren't told which mountain)*: and He *(Jesus)* was transfigured before them *(refers to the act of giving outward expression of one's inner character)*.

3 And His raiment became shining, exceeding white as snow; so as no fuller on earth can white them *(the radiance of glory shining from within Him)*.

4 And there appeared unto them Elijah with Moses *(their appearance had to do with the coming Kingdom Age)*: and they were talking with Jesus *(the Greek Text indicates that the conversation was a protracted one)*.

5 And Peter answered and said to Jesus, Master, it is good for us to be here: and let us make three Tabernacles; one for You, and one for Moses, and one for Elijah *(Peter compounds His error by placing Moses and Elijah in the same category as Jesus)*.

6 For he wist not what to say; for they were sore afraid *(terrified)*.

7 And there was a cloud that overshadowed them *(was the Shekinah Glory Cloud which guided Israel out of Egypt, and which rested above the Mercy Seat in the Holy of Holies in the Tabernacle)*: and a voice came out of the cloud *(proclaims the actual Voice of God)*, saying, This is My Beloved Son *(in the Greek Text, "this is My Son, The Beloved One,")*: hear Him *(the phrase, "Hear Him," refers to Christ; in other words, Moses and Elijah are not to be placed on the same par with Christ; the phrase actually means, "be constantly hearing Him"; it as well refers to obeying what is heard)*.

8 And suddenly *(proclaims a sudden change)*, when they had looked round about, they saw no man any more, save Jesus only with themselves *(they had just witnessed something which no other human beings had ever seen)*.

9 And as they came down from the mountain, He charged them that they should tell no man what things they had seen, till the Son of Man were risen from the dead.

10 And they kept that saying with themselves *(meaning that they obeyed the Command of the Lord)*, questioning one with another what the rising from the dead should mean *(they still did not understand the purpose and reason for His coming to this world, which was to redeem man, which would necessitate His going to the Cross; in other words, the Cross was ever His destination)*.

11 And they asked Him, saying, Why say the Scribes that Elijah must first come? *(They were referring to Mal. 4:5.)*

12 And He answered and told them *(but with them still lacking in understanding)*, Elijah verily cometh first, and restoreth all things *(refers to this Prophet coming as one of the two witnesses not long before the Second Advent [Rev. 11:3-12])*; and how it is written of the Son of Man, that He must suffer many things, and be set at nought *(as predicted by the Prophet Isaiah, Chpt. 53)*.

13 But I say unto you, That Elijah is indeed come *(refers to John the Baptist who came in the spirit and power of Elijah [Lk. 1:17])*, and they have done unto him whatsoever they listed, as it is written of Him *(refers to John's execution by Herod)*.

LACK OF POWER

14 And when He came to *His Disciples (joined the other nine at the foot of the mountain after the Transfiguration)*, He saw a great multitude about them, and the Scribes questioning with them *(actually, taunting them)*.

15 And straightway *(immediately)* all the people, when they beheld Him, were greatly amazed, and running to *Him* saluted Him *(greeted Him with great warmth and admiration)*.

16 And He asked the Scribes *(supposed experts in the Law of Moses)*, What question ye with them? *(In effect, what is the problem?)*

17 And one of the multitude answered and said, Master, I have brought unto You my son, which has a dumb spirit *(a correct analysis of the situation; a demon spirit had bound the boy's tongue and vocal organs, plus as well, had tried to kill him several times)*;

18 And wheresoever he *(the demon spirit)* takes him, he tears him: and he foams, and gnasheth with his teeth, and pines away: and I spoke to Your Disciples that they should cast him out; and they could not *(the idea is, they tried repeatedly, but without success; hence, the taunts of the Scribes)*.

19 He answered him, and said, O faithless generation *(rather, a misplaced faith; Gal., Chpt. 5 will explain it)*, how long shall I be with you? *(Will My short time be enough?)* how long shall I suffer you? *(Is it possible for even the Twelve who are constantly with Me, to understand?)* bring him unto Me *(implies that the boy was not immediately with the father, but was being held by others a short distance away)*.

20 And they brought him unto Him: and when he *(the demon spirit)* saw Him *(Jesus)*, straightway *(immediately)* the spirit *(demon*

spirit) *tore* him *(the boy)*; and he fell on the ground, and wallowed foaming.

21 And He *(Jesus)* asked his father, How long is it ago since this came unto him? And he said, Of a child *(the incident tells us that children can be oppressed or even possessed by demon spirits)*.

22 And ofttimes it has cast him into the fire, and into the waters, to destroy him *(reflects suicidal tendencies, as promoted by this spirit)*: but if You can do any thing, have compassion on us, and help us *(his faith was weak, due to the failure of the Disciples)*.

23 Jesus said unto him, If you can believe, all things *are* possible to him who believes *(if He has promised it, and you can believe it, you can have it)*.

24 And straightway *(immediately)* the father of the child cried out *(speaks of a loud cry that comes from the very depths of the man's soul)*, and said with tears, Lord, I believe *(proclaims belief, but yet imperfect belief!; the "tears" proclaimed the consternation of the battle that is raging in the man's soul)*; help Thou mine unbelief *(proclaims the deficiency of his faith; it is a prayer the Lord will always answer)*.

25 When Jesus saw that the people came running together *(He evidently was standing a little ways from the people, as He spoke with the man, with the Disciples holding the people back; but they can hold them no longer)*, He rebuked the foul spirit, saying unto him, *You* dumb and deaf spirit, I charge you, come out of him, and enter no more into him *(he was to come out, which he did, and was never to come back again)*.

26 And *the spirit (demon spirit)* cried, and rent him sore, and came out of him *(it seems that he attempted to kill the boy as he came out)*: and he was as one dead; insomuch that many said, He is dead *(the boy lay motionless and pallid as a corpse)*.

27 But Jesus took him by the hand, and lifted him up; and he arose *(concerned more than just a helping hand; healing power flooded the boy's body, healing that which the demon had damaged)*.

28 And when He was come into the house *(doesn't say which house)*, His Disciples asked Him privately, Why could not we cast him out? *(They had been successful at other times, so why not now? There is evidence that this demon was more powerful than any that Jesus had addressed.)*

29 And He said unto them, This kind *(demon spirits of this power)* can come forth by nothing, but by prayer and fasting *("fasting" includes not only, doing without food, but as well, denying one's own strength and ability, and looking exclusively to the Cross [I Cor. 1:17-18])*.

HIS DEATH AND RESURRECTION

30 And they departed thence, and passed through Galilee; and He would not that any man should know *it (by now there was terrible opposition against Him from the religious leaders of the area; in fact, this would get progressively worse)*.

31 For He taught His Disciples, and said unto them, The Son of Man is delivered into the hands of men *(means that His betrayal in the heart of Judas had already begun)*, and they shall kill Him *(the Crucifixion)*; and after that He is killed, He shall rise the third day *(the Resurrection was never in doubt)*.

32 But they understood not that saying, and were afraid to ask Him *(stemmed back to Peter rebuking Him when He had previously made this announcement and His response, which had been strong indeed!)*.

WHO IS GREATEST?

33 And He came to Capernaum: and being in the house *(Peter's house)* He asked them, What was it that you disputed among yourselves by the way? *(Concerned a very serious problem in their lives.)*

34 But they held their peace *(means they were ashamed to relate to Him what they had been, in fact, discussing)*: for by the way they had disputed among themselves, who *should be* the greatest *(it is not unlikely that the preference given by our Lord to Peter, James, and John, may have given occasion for this contention)*.

35 And He sat down, and called the Twelve, and said unto them, If any man desire to be first *(in response to their question as to whom should be the greatest)*, *the same* shall be last of all, and servant of all *(means to think of one's self last, with all others first, to minister to others, which is the very opposite of the world)*.

36 And He took a child, and set him in the midst of them: and when He had taken him in His arms, He said unto them *(will use the child as an example)*,

37 Whosoever shall receive one of such children in My Name, receives Me *(in effect, says that if the person doesn't have a childlike spirit, he should not be received)*: and whosoever shall receive Me, receives not Me, but Him Who sent

Me *(the way to Christ is through a childlike spirit, and the way to the father is through Christ [Jn. 14:6])*.

38 And John answered Him, saying, Master, we saw one casting out devils in Your Name, and he followeth not us: and we forbad him, because he followeth not us *(portrays the sectarianism that is beginning to creep in)*.

39 But Jesus said, Forbid him not *(Jesus did not say, "receive him," for the man's motive did not appear; however, he does say that the attitude toward such a one should at least be neutral)*: for there is no man which shall do a miracle in My Name, that can lightly speak evil of Me *(providing it truly is a miracle)*.

40 For he who is not against us is on our part *(the marks of false teachers are numerous in Scripture, so that no mistake need be made in detecting them [Mat. 7:15-20; 23:1-33; Acts 8:9; 13:8; Rom. 1:18-32; 16:17; I Cor. 1:18-31; I Tim. 4:1-8; II Tim. 3:1-13; 4:3-4; II Pet., Chpt. 2; III Jn., Vss. 9-10; Jude, Vss. 4-19; Rev. 2:14, 20])*.

41 For whosoever shall give you a cup of water to drink in My Name, because you belong to Christ, verily I say unto you, He shall not lose His reward *(refers to helping take the Gospel to others; all help respecting this will be rewarded, no matter how small that help might be)*.

CONCERNING OFFENCES

42 And whosoever shall offend one of *these* little ones who believe in Me, it is better for him that a millstone were hanged about his neck, and he were cast into the sea *(as the smallest help will be rewarded, likewise, the smallest offense will be likewise addressed; these admonitions had better be taken seriously)*.

43 And if your hand offend you, cut it off *([symbolic], do not allow yourself to be placed in the position of opposing those who truly are of God)*: it is better for you to enter into life maimed, than having two hands to go into hell, into the fire that never shall be quenched *(proves the reality of Hell, and of it being the destiny of those who oppose true Believers, who are truly doing the Work of God)*:

44 Where their worm dies not, and the fire is not quenched *(Christ is proclaiming what one faces who opposes true Believers; the punishment is eternal)*.

45 And if your foot offend you, cut it off: it is better for you to enter halt into life, than having two feet to be cast into hell, into the fire that never shall be quenched:

46 Where their worm dies not, and the fire is not quenched.

47 And if your eye offend you, pluck it out: it is better for you to enter into the Kingdom of God with one eye, than having two eyes to be cast into hell fire:

48 Where their worm dies not, and the fire is not quenched *(when Christ gives an illustration of this magnitude, it is of extreme importance; when He doubles it, as He does here, it becomes extremely important; but when He triples it, as He definitely does, then its significance is of such magnitude as to defy description; most of the opposition against true Believers, and especially against those called of God for specific work, comes from the religious sector; to oppose that apostatized religious sector, may generate harm to one's person; but it is better to endure that harm, than to lose one's soul)*.

49 For every one shall be salted with fire *(whether tested to offend, or tested by the offender)*, and every sacrifice shall be salted with salt *(salt is a type of the Word of God; if the Sacrifice is to be true, it will be centered up in the Cross)*.

50 Salt *is* good *(the Word of God which acts as a preservative)*: but if the salt have lost his saltness *(the Word of God has been diluted)*, wherewith will you season it? *(The preservation is now gone.)* Have salt in yourselves *(abide according to the Word of God)*, and have peace one with another *(abiding by the Word, will guarantee peace)*.

CHAPTER 10
(A.D. 33)

CONCERNING MARRIAGE AND DIVORCE

AND He arose from thence *(from Capernaum)*, and cometh into the coasts *(borders)* of Judaea by the farther side of Jordan *(the east side of the Jordan River; He will not come back to this region, but will be crucified in Jerusalem)*: and the people resort unto Him again *(it was the time of Passover and many people were on their way to Jerusalem)*; and, as He was wont *(accustomed to doing)*, He taught them again *(they so much needed His Teaching, but it was His Death that would set them free)*.

2 And the Pharisees came to Him *(there were Pharisees in the crowd, going to Jerusalem)*, and asked Him, Is it lawful for a man to put away *his* wife? *(The question of divorce and*

remarriage was the great controversy at that time in Israel.) tempting Him.

3 And He answered and said unto them, What did Moses command you? *(Took them to the Word, but not as they thought — not to the Law of Moses.)*

4 And they said, Moses suffered to write a bill of divorcement, and to put *her* away *([Deut. 24:1], but they misinterpreted Moses, even as many do).*

5 And Jesus answered and said unto them, For the hardness of your heart he wrote you this precept *(the Lord does not deny that Moses permitted divorce; commanded he did not; consequently, for the Pharisees to shelter themselves under the temporary recognition of a necessary evil, was to confess that they had not outgrown the moral stature of their fathers).*

6 But from the beginning of the creation God made them male and female *(not from the beginning of Creation per se, but rather, from the beginning of the creation of humankind).*

7 For this cause *(has to do with the way man and woman were created and, therefore, meant to live)* shall a man leave his father and mother, and cleave to his wife *(completely debunks the homosexual lifestyle)*;

8 And they twain *(two)* shall be one flesh *(one of the reasons that adultery and fornication are so wicked)*: so then they are no more twain, but one flesh *(the Will of God carried out to its logical and beautiful conclusion).*

9 What therefore God has joined together *(places the seal of God's approval on the marriage union; and we speak of the nuclear family of husband, wife, and children)*, let not man put asunder *(there are only two Scriptural grounds for divorce and remarriage: A. Fornication [Mat. 5:32]; and, B. Desertion on spiritual grounds [I Cor. 7:14-15]).*

10 And in the house *(where evidently they had stopped for the night on the way to Jerusalem)* His Disciples asked Him again of the same matter *(the matter of divorce and remarriage).*

11 And He said unto them *(concerns marriage after divorce)*, Whosoever shall put away his wife *(refers to divorce)*, and marry another, commits adultery against her *(refers to having no Scriptural grounds; in doing such, he commits sin not only against God, but also against his wife).*

12 And if a woman shall put away her husband *(divorce)*, and be married to another, she commits adultery *(again, has no Scriptural grounds; such constitutes the sin of adultery).*

JESUS BLESSES LITTLE CHILDREN

13 And they brought young children to Him, that He should touch them *(this custom finds its symbolism in Gen. 48:14-15)*: and *His* Disciples rebuked those who brought *them (presents a paradox; the Disciples were strongly rebuking the people for bringing their children to Jesus, while Jesus was strongly blessing those brought to Him).*

14 But when Jesus saw *it (saw what the Disciples were doing)*, He was much displeased *(was moved with strong indignation)*, and said unto them, Suffer the little children to come unto Me, and forbid them not: for of such is the Kingdom of God *(to start a child out right, is to insure its Salvation [Prov. 22:6]).*

15 Verily I say unto you, Whosoever shall not receive the Kingdom of God as a little child *(the simplicity of the little child is the model and the rule for everyone who desires, by the Grace of Christ, to obtain the Kingdom of Heaven)*, he shall not enter therein *(presents a double negative in the Greek, and consequently, presents an emphatic denial).*

16 And He took them up in His arms, put *His* hands upon them, and blessed them *(He blessed them fervently).*

THE RICH YOUNG RULER

17 And when He was gone forth into the way *(refers to Him the next morning leaving the house, and going toward Jerusalem)*, there came one running, and kneeled to Him *(he is not asking for physical help, but rather for spiritual help)*, and asked Him, Good Master, what shall I do that I may inherit eternal life? *(In the first place, one cannot inherit eternal life. It is a free gift, which comes with the acceptance of Christ [Rom. 10:9-10, 13].)*

18 And Jesus said unto him, Why do you call Me good? *there is* none good but one, *Who is*, God *(is not meant to state that Christ Himself wasn't good, but rather that the word "good" be placed in its proper perspective; Christ is God!).*

19 You know the Commandments *(draws the young man to the Word of God, in both a positive and negative sense; positive, because the Word alone holds the answer; and negative, because it will show him as a mirror where he is wrong)*, Do not commit adultery, Do not kill, Do not steal, Do not bear false witness, Defraud not, Honour your father and mother.

20 And he answered and said unto Him,

Master, all these have I observed from my youth *(there is no eternal life in the keeping of the Commandments, as wonderful as that is; had there been, he would not be seeking the satisfaction of the conscience).*

21 Then Jesus beholding him loved him, and said unto him *(loved him despite the fact that he really had not kept the Commandments, as he was claiming; and of course, Jesus knew that!),* One thing you lack: go your way, sell whatsoever you have, and give to the poor, and you shall have treasure in Heaven *(puts the finger directly on the man's problem):* and come, take up the Cross, and follow Me *(without explanation, Christ tells the young man here, and all others for that matter, that Salvation is in the Cross alone; and it is only by and through the Cross, that we can truly follow Christ).*

22 And he was sad at that saying *(concerns the attitude of multiple millions; they, as he, desire Salvation, but on their own terms!),* and went away grieved: for he had great possessions *(the only possession that really matters is Eternal Life).*

WARNING TO THE RICH

23 And Jesus looked round about, and said unto His Disciples *(He looks searchingly at His Disciples),* How hardly shall they who have riches enter into the Kingdom of God! *(It's not the riches which constitute the sin, but the attitude toward them.)*

24 And the Disciples were astonished at His words *(the Jews of that time considered riches to be the approval of God; at the same time, they considered poverty to be His disapproval).* But Jesus answered again, and said unto them, Children *(using this word, He now takes them back to His dissertation concerning receiving the Kingdom of God as a little child; a child does not grasp after things),* how hard is it for them who trust in riches to enter into the Kingdom of God! *(As stated, it is the trust in riches, which constitutes the sin.)*

25 It is easier for a camel to go through the eye of a needle, than for a rich man to enter into the Kingdom of God *(the word that Jesus uses here for "needle," doesn't refer to a small hole in the wall as some think, but rather the type of needle used with thread).*

26 And they were astonished out of measure, saying among themselves, Who then can be saved? *(Presents their theology being completely turned over.)*

27 And Jesus looking upon them said *(knew that His statement would produce this type of reaction),* With men *it is* impossible *(whether rich or poor, it is impossible to be saved without God),* but not with God: for with God all things are possible *(only through God, is the Salvation process possible).*

THE REWARDS OF CONSECRATION

28 Then Peter began to say unto Him, Lo, we have left all, and have followed You *(by this statement, Peter shows that they are still thinking in terms of material rather than spiritual riches).*

29 And Jesus answered and said, Verily I say unto you *(concerns all Believers, not just the Twelve),* There is no man who has left house, or brethren, or sisters, or father, or mother, or wife, or children, or lands, for My sake, and the Gospel's *(to many, Jesus is just a means to an end, in other words, to get what they want in the realm of material things; He completely debunks that here; contrary to that, He says here that everything must be placed secondary to Christ),*

30 But he shall receive an hundredfold now in this time *(refers to this present life),* houses, and brethren, and sisters, and mothers, and children, and lands *(we have the use of these things, and of that alone, we are to be concerned),* with persecutions *(regrettably, most of the persecution will come from the Church);* and in the world to come eternal life *(the world to come is eternal, and one must have eternal life to enter into that world. That alone is what counts!).*

31 But many *who are* first shall be last; and the last first *(Israel, although first, will be last, because of rejection of Christ; the Church, although last, will be first because of acceptance of Christ).*

JESUS AGAIN SPEAKS OF HIS COMING DEATH AND RESURRECTION

32 And they were in the way going up to Jerusalem; and Jesus went before them *(presents Christ walking ahead of His Disciples, and for a purpose and reason):* and they were amazed *(there was something about Him that was now different — a great sadness);* and as they followed, they were afraid *(speaks not only of the Disciples, but as well, of all who were near Him).* And He took again the twelve *(apart from the others),* and began to tell them what

things should happen unto Him *(He had already told them this several times, but still they didn't understand)*,

33 *Saying*, Behold, we go up to Jerusalem *(they had gone to Jerusalem several times in the past, but this time would be different)*; and the Son of Man shall be delivered unto the Chief Priests, and unto the Scribes *(betrayed by Judas)*; and they shall condemn Him to death *(the Sanhedrin would pass sentence upon Him)*, and shall deliver Him to the Gentiles *(to the Romans)*:

34 And they shall mock Him, and shall scourge Him, and shall spit upon Him *(both Jews and Gentiles would do such)*, and shall kill Him *(the Crucifixion)*: and the third day He shall rise again *(predicts His Resurrection, even as He had already done several times before; but they actually didn't believe it)*.

THE REQUEST OF JAMES AND JOHN

35 And James and John, the sons of Zebedee, come unto Him *(Matthew claims Salome, their mother, evidently traveling with them, as making the request [Mat. 20:20], the sons prompted her to do such)*, saying, Master, we would that You should do for us whatsoever we shall desire *(constitutes a most selfish request; how often do we approach Him in the same manner?)*.

36 And He said unto them, What would you that I should do for you? *(In effect, He is asking every Believer the same question!)*

37 They said unto Him, Grant unto us that we may sit, one on Your right hand, and the other on Your left hand, in Your glory *(concerned the most coveted positions; they were speaking of "glory," while He was speaking of "death")*.

38 But Jesus said unto them, You know not what you ask *(characterizes so many petitions made by Believers)*: can you drink of the cup that I drink of? and be baptized with the baptism that I am baptized with? *(Both of these questions signify the Cross!)*

39 And they said unto Him, We can *(a mere profession of moral courage, not a claim to spiritual power; they really didn't know what they were saying)*. And Jesus said unto them, You shall indeed drink of the cup that I drink of; and with the baptism that I am baptized withal shall you be baptized *(concerns not only the Twelve, but all who follow Christ, and for all time — the Cross demands this)*:

40 But to sit on My right hand and on My left hand is not Mine to give *(positions in the Kingdom are determined solely by the Will of God)*;

but *it shall be given to them* for whom it is prepared *(Jerome said, "our Lord does not say, 'you shall not sit,' lest He put to shame these two; neither does He say, 'you shall sit,' lest the others should be envious; but by holding out the prize to all, He animates all to contend for it")*.

41 And when the ten heard *it*, they began to be much displeased with James and John *(the sons of Zebedee want to be first, and the ten were unwilling to be last!; such was the energy of the carnal nature in all Twelve)*.

42 But Jesus called them *to Him*, and said unto them, You know that they which are accounted to rule over the Gentiles exercise lordship over them *(the way of the world)*; and their great ones exercise authority upon them *(in the world, the greater the position, the greater the authority)*.

43 But so shall it not be among you *(the way of the world, is not the way of the Lord)*: but whosoever will be great among you, shall be your minister *(servant)*:

44 And whosoever of you will be the chiefest *(hold the greater position)*, shall be servant of all *(in the Kingdom of God the greatness of the individual comes from the lowly place he takes as a servant of all)*.

45 For even the Son of Man came not to be ministered unto *(proclaims Christ as the example)*, but to minister *(be a servant)*, and to give His life a ransom for many *(He is Very God of Very God, but became incarnate in human flesh and a Servant to mankind; what a rebuke to His Disciples, and to us!)*.

THE HEALING OF BLIND BARTIMAEUS

46 And they came to Jericho *(this is the only record of Him being in Jericho; it was to be a red-letter day for some)*: and as He went out of Jericho with His Disciples and a great number of people, blind Bartimaeus, the son of Timaeus *(suggests the possibility of Bartimaeus coming from a family of some note)*, sat by the highway side begging *(symbolic of all the sons of Adam's fallen race)*.

47 And when he heard that it was Jesus of Nazareth *(he had, no doubt, long since prayed for this moment)*, he began to cry out *(means in the Greek that he kept crying over, and over to Jesus)*, and say, Jesus, *Thou* Son of David *(a title that referred to the Messiah; this blind beggar knew He was the Messiah, but the religious leaders of Israel didn't)*, have mercy on me *(he pled the right kind of petition)*.

48 And many charged him that he should hold his peace *(the word "charged" is strong, meaning to "censure severely"; in other words, they were telling him, and in no uncertain terms, to "shut up")*: but he cried the more a great deal *(proclaims their demand as having the opposite effect on him)*, **Thou** Son of David, have mercy on me.

49 And Jesus stood still *(faith caused Christ to stop; it will do the same presently!)*, and commanded him to be called *(constitutes the greatest moment in the life of this blind beggar)*. And they call the blind man, saying unto him, Be of good comfort, rise; He calls you *(should be the message of every single Believer to every single lost soul)*.

50 And he, casting away his garment *(this was a garment just for beggars; during the day he would spread it out, for people to throw coins on it, and would use it as a blanket at night; he knew he would never need it again)*, rose, and came to Jesus *(if the whole world came to Jesus, they would receive even more than Bartimaeus [spiritual sight])*.

51 And Jesus answered and said unto him, What will you that I should do unto you? *(That's the question asked of all Believers. Our answer reveals our spiritual condition.)* The blind man said unto Him, Lord, that I might receive my sight.

52 And Jesus said unto him, Go your way; your faith has made you whole *("whole" in the Greek is "sozo," it means, "to save"; it is used either as a physical healing or of spiritual Salvation; consequently, the implication is that Bartimaeus was not only healed, but saved as well!)*. And immediately he received his sight, and followed Jesus in the way *(tradition says that he followed Jesus to Jerusalem, and became an ardent Disciple in the Early Church)*.

CHAPTER 11
(A.D. 33)
THE TRIUMPHAL ENTRY
INTO JERUSALEM

AND when they came near to Jerusalem, unto Bethphage and Bethany, at the Mount of Olives *(concerned two villages, suburbs of Jerusalem east of the city)*, He sent forth two of His Disciples *(tradition says Peter and John)*,

2 And said unto them, Go your way into the village over against you *(probably Bethphage, because it was nearer)*: and as soon as you be entered into it, you shall find a colt tied, whereon never man sat *(no one had ever ridden the colt)*; loose him, and bring *him.*

3 And if any man say unto you, Why do you this? *(Implying that this would be the case, and so it was.)* say you that the Lord has need of him *(as God, the Lord needs nothing; as the Son of Man, He did need certain things)*; and straightway *(immediately)* he will send him hither *(will give permission to use the colt, all of this revealed to Christ by the Holy Spirit)*.

4 And they went their way, and found the colt tied by the door without in a place where two ways met; and they loose him *("their way" was "His Way")*.

5 And certain of them who stood there said unto them, What are you doing, loosing the colt? *(Represents that no prior arrangements had been made.)*

6 And they said unto them even as Jesus had commanded *(the Lord has need of him)*: and they let them go *(an instant obedience; what a privilege these men had to lend their colt to Christ)*.

7 And they brought the colt to Jesus, and cast their garments on him; and He sat upon him *(proclaims the beginning of the Triumphal Entry; this was a fulfillment of the Prophecy given by Zechariah [Zech. 9:9])*.

8 And many spread their garments in the way *(this was His formal presentation of Himself as the Messiah; as is obvious, it would be rejected)*: and others cut down branches off the trees, and strawed *them* in the way *(probably palm fronds)*.

9 And they who went before, and they who followed *(represents crowds both behind Christ and in front of Christ, as He went into Jerusalem)*, cried, saying, Hosanna; Blessed *is* He Who comes in the Name of the Lord *(taken from Psalms 118:25-26; this acclamation was given at the "Feast of Tabernacles," as the Priests marched once daily for seven days around the Altar with palm branches in their hands; on the eighth day they marched seven times, which was the "Great Hosanna"; the people believed that Jesus was now about to take the Throne; they felt the great Kingdom Age was now beginning; the truth is, it could have, but the religious leadership of Israel rejected Him)*:

10 Blessed *be* the Kingdom of our father David *(should have been translated, "Blessed be the Kingdom that comes, the Kingdom of our Father David")*, that comes in the Name of the Lord *(should have been translated, "Who comes in the Name of the Lord"; Jesus was that*

Person!): **Hosanna in the Highest** *(meant that He was the Highest One; consequently, the Only One Who could save them).*

11 And Jesus entered into Jerusalem, and into the Temple: and when He had looked round about upon all things *(He observed all the haggling, bartering, arguing, over prices, which probably was in the Court of the Gentiles; He would come back the next day, and cleanse the place),* **and now the eventide was come, He went out unto Bethany with the Twelve** *(it was probably Sunday, and if so, one week later Jesus would rise from the dead; consequently, the intervening week would be one of such magnitude of sorrow as to defy description).*

JESUS PLACES A CURSE ON A BARREN FIG TREE

12 And on the morrow *(suggests it was Monday; Matthew says it was early, probably before 6 a.m., with the Disciples, He has probably spent the night in the open),* **when they were come from Bethany, He was hungry:**

13 And seeing a fig tree afar off having leaves, He came, if haply He might find any thing thereon *(according to all appearances, there should have been figs):* **and when He came to it, He found nothing but leaves** *(no fruit);* **for the time of figs was not *yet*** *(means that despite its appearance, which suggested fruit, and which there should have been fruit, it was barren).*

14 And Jesus answered and said unto it *(proclaims the Lord forgetting His natural hunger and the thought of a spiritual figure which the sight of this tree began to present to His mind),* **No man eat fruit of you hereafter forever** *(symbolic of the Jewish nation; a curse was placed on the fig tree, not necessarily for being barren, but for being false; as well, the word "forever," should have been translated "for the age," that is, until the times of the Gentiles be fulfilled; this will be at the Second Coming).* **And His Disciples heard *it*** *(they will learn a lesson from this, even as we shall see!).*

JESUS CLEANSES THE TEMPLE

15 And they come to Jerusalem: and Jesus went into the Temple *(refers to the fact that its condition, spiritually speaking, had been on His mind all night; He was probably in the Court of the Gentiles),* **and began to cast out them who sold and bought in the Temple, and overthrew the tables of the moneychangers, and the seats**

of them who sold doves;

16 And would not suffer that any man should carry *any* vessel through the Temple *(He would have the whole of His Father's House regarded as sacred).*

17 And He taught, saying unto them *(no doubt to a large crowd of people who had gathered, watching, as it seems, with open-mouth astonishment!),* **Is it not written** *(took the people and His actions to the Word of God),* **My House shall be called of all nations the House of Prayer?** *(Signifying, as stated, that He was in the Court of the Gentiles, which had been turned into a market place. His statement is derived from Isa. 65:7 and Jer. 7:11.)* **but you have made it a den of thieves** *(should have been translated "robbers," for the Greek word signifies operations on a large and systematic scale).*

18 And the Scribes and Chief Priests heard it *(they were the "robbers," because they were in charge of what was taking place there, and actually profited personally from what was being done),* **and sought how they might destroy Him** *(meant to not only kill Him, but to utterly destroy His influence as a great spiritual energy in the world):* **for they feared Him** *(feared that He would use His Power to upset their corrupted place and position),* **because all the people was astonished at His Doctrine** *(a "Doctrine" which was so different than their doctrine).*

19 And when evening was come, He went out of the city *(there is no indication that Jesus ever spent the night in Jerusalem, with the exception of the night that He was on trial).*

THE LESSON FROM THE WITHERED FIG TREE

20 And in the morning *(probably refers to Tuesday),* **as they passed by, they saw the fig tree dried up from the roots** *(means that it was completely withered away; Israel in a short time would do the same, actually ceasing to be a nation).*

21 And Peter calling to remembrance said unto Him, Master, behold, the fig tree which You cursed is withered away *(Jesus could have done the same thing with His enemies, had He so desired; but He never used His Power, except in the way that the Heavenly Father told Him to use it).*

22 And Jesus answering said unto them *(indicates Jesus dealing with what happened, rather than why it happened; they were not able yet to grasp the fig tree as a symbol of Israel; that*

would come later!), **Have faith in God** *(literally says, "Have the Faith of God"; such a faith judges profession [the fig tree] removes difficulties [the mountain] forgives injuries).*

23 **For verily I say unto you, That whosoever shall say unto this mountain, Be thou removed, and be thou cast into the sea; and shall not doubt in his heart, but shall believe that those things which he says shall come to pass; he shall have whatsoever he says** *(the "mountain" is used as a symbol, i.e., "mountain of difficulties," etc.; God is a Miracle working God, and will do so for any of His Children, "whosoever"; however, every petition must be predicated as well on the Will of God).*

24 **Therefore I say unto you, What things soever you desire** *(one seeking to do the Will of God, will want only what God desires)*, **when you pray** *(the value of prayer, without which these things cannot be done)*, **believe** *(have faith)* **that you receive** *them*, **and you shall have** *them* *(as is obvious here, the receiving of these things, whatever they might be, requires relationship, and that is the key).*

25 **And when you stand praying, forgive, if you have ought against any** *(implying, that the above Promises will not be honored, if we harbor unforgiveness)*: **that your Father also which is in Heaven may forgive you your trespasses** *(forgiveness from the Lord on our part, is predicated on us forgiving others).*

26 **But if you do not forgive, neither will your Father which is in Heaven forgive your trespasses** *(implies, unforgiveness breaks down relationship, which destroys the whole program of God; in such a case, our sins are not forgiven, and neither can we expect God to answer prayer; these are extremely serious implications).*

JESUS' AUTHORITY QUESTIONED

27 **And they come again to Jerusalem: and as He was walking in the Temple** *(represents the third day in which He visits this edifice)*, **there come to Him the Chief Priests, and the Scribes, and the Elders** *(these were the religious leaders of Israel),*

28 **And say unto Him, By what authority do You do these things? and who gave You this authority to do these things?** *(They were the custodians of the Temple. Our Lord, by forcibly ejecting those who were engaged in business in the Temple, was claiming a superior jurisdiction.)*

29 **And Jesus answered and said unto them, I will also ask of you one question** *(His question*

and the answer, will greatly simplify the issue), **and answer Me, and I will tell you by what authority I do these things** *(actually means that the correct response to His question will provide the answer to their questions).*

30 **The baptism of John, was** *it* **from Heaven, or of men? answer Me** *(John had introduced Christ as the Messiah; if they claimed the Prophet to be of God, then they would have to acknowledge the One he had introduced; they had tried to put Jesus on the spot, and now they are instead on the spot).*

31 **And they reasoned with themselves, saying, If we shall say, From Heaven; He will say, Why then did you not believe Him?** *(Refers to believing what John said about Jesus.)*

32 **But if we shall say, Of men; they feared the people: for all** *men* **counted John, that he was a Prophet indeed** *(the respect for John by the people had even deepened since his martyrdom; they feared if they denied John's calling, the people might stone them then and there).*

33 **And they answered and said unto Jesus, We cannot tell** *(their answer was ridiculous to say the least!; they were the very ones who were supposed to know).* **And Jesus answering said unto them, Neither do I tell you by what authority I do these things** *(in effect, "I will not answer you, because your answer to My question is the answer to your own"; Jerome says, "He thus shows that they knew, but would not answer; they saved themselves from this dilemma by professing ignorance").*

CHAPTER 12
(A.D. 33)
THE PARABLE OF THE WICKED HUSBANDMEN

AND **He began to speak unto them by Parables** *(represents the first time He had used this method in Jerusalem, although it had been used plentifully in Galilee).* **A** *certain* **man planted a vineyard** *(constitutes no other than God Himself)*, **and set an hedge about** *it* *(the Power of God about the nation)*, **and digged** *a place for* **the winefat** *(better translation, "wine-vat"; speaks of the product of the vineyard)*, **and built a tower** *(would contain a watchman, which was to guard the vineyard from plunderers; it spoke of the spiritual leaders of Israel)*, **and let it out to husbandmen** *(left it in the hands of the people)*, **and went into a far country** *(refers to God's residence being in Heaven).*

2 **And at the season** *(harvest season)* **he sent**

to the husbandmen a servant *(speaks of Old Testament Prophets)*, that he might receive from the husbandmen of the fruit of the vineyard *(respects that which was rightly his)*.

3 And they caught *him*, and beat him, and sent *him* away empty *(the failure to receive fruit points to the failure of Israel to heed the preaching of the Prophets)*.

4 And again he sent unto them another servant; and at him they cast stones, and wounded *him* in the head, and sent *him* away shamefully handled.

5 And again he sent another; and him they killed, and many others; beating some, and killing some *(proclaims an increase in the rebellion and its obvious results; barring Repentance, sin never slows, but instead, increases)*.

6 Having yet therefore one son, his wellbeloved, he sent him also last unto them, saying, They will reverence my son *(refers to the Lord Jesus Christ)*.

7 But those husbandmen said among themselves *(in this case, the Sanhedrin)*, This is the heir *(it means that the religious leaders of Israel knew that Jesus was the Messiah)*; come, let us kill him, and the inheritance shall be ours *(constitutes the plan of Satan from the very beginning; he wants that which belongs to God, and will usually work through organized religion to further his purpose)*.

8 And they took him, and killed *him*, and cast *him* out of the vineyard *(this was the last effort of Divine Mercy — the sending of the incarnate God, whom the Jews put to death without the city)*.

9 What shall therefore the lord of the vineyard do? *(The Lord had the Power to do whatever He desired; yet, they treated Him as if He had no power at all!)* *He* will come and destroy the husbandmen *(this is exactly what happened in A.D. 70)*, and will give the vineyard unto others *(speaks of the Church, made up mostly of Gentiles, and this being the channel through which God is operating temporarily while Israel is in dispersion, and until Israel will be regathered at the Second Advent, and restored to fellowship and usefulness to God)*.

10 And have you not read this Scripture *(refers to Psalms 118:22-23)*; The Stone which the builders *(the spiritual leaders of Israel)* rejected *(He was not the type of Messiah they wanted)* is become the Head of the Corner *(the "Corner" represents the Corner Stone which is the pivot point for the structure; Christ is the Head of the Church, and of the Work of God, due to what*

He did at the Cross [Zech. 4:7])*:

11 This was the Lord's doing *(refers to the Great Plan of God, which necessitated God becoming flesh and dwelling among men, in order to bring about the Redemption of man)*, and it is marvellous in our eyes? *(It wasn't marvelous in the eyes of Israel of Jesus' day, and the results were awful. As the Church, we should take a lesson, in what He has done. It had better be marvelous in our eyes.)*

12 And they sought to lay hold on Him *(they were growing even more incensed at Him)*, but feared the people *(whatever they did, would have to be done in secret)*: for they knew that He had spoken the Parable against them *(He predicted that they would kill Him and, as well, what would happen to them; God would destroy them!; but still they wouldn't turn around)*: and they left Him, and went their way *(they definitely didn't go His Way)*.

TRIBUTE TO CAESAR

13 And they send unto Him certain of the Pharisees and of the Herodians *(these two parties normally hated each other)*, to catch Him in His words *(something for which they could incriminate Him)*.

14 And when they were come, they say unto Him *(these were the most brilliant minds of the Pharisees and the Herodians)*, Master *([teacher] the word was not used without design)*, we know that You are true, and care for no man: for You regard not the person of men, but teach the Way of God in truth *(they didn't believe any of this, but they were baiting their trap)*: Is it lawful to give tribute to Caesar, or not? *(This question raged in Israel at that time. The Jews were not necessarily discussing the legality of paying a poll tax to Caesar, but whether a Jew should do so in view of his theocratic relationship to God.)*

15 Shall we give, or shall we not give? *(This placed the situation in strictly a "yes" or "no" mode, or so they thought! They would trap Him either way He answered.)* But He, knowing their hypocrisy, said unto them *(He knew they had no desire for the true answer, but only were attempting to embarrass Him before the crowd, or to have something in order to accuse Him to Rome)*, Why tempt you Me? *(This told them that He knew what they were doing.)* bring Me a penny, that I may see *it (refers to the Roman Denarius, the coin with which the tax was to be paid)*.

16 And they brought *it (there was no coin like this in the Temple, as such was not allowed,*

so one had to be brought in). And He said unto them, Whose *is* this image and superscription? *(Speaking of the image on the coin.)* And they said unto Him, Caesar's *(referred to the image of Tiberius Caesar, the then reigning Roman Emperor; consequently, the coin of the country proved the subjection of the country to him whose image was upon it, in this case, Caesar).*

17 And Jesus answering said unto them *(in a sense, Jesus placed His Approval by His Answer on the separation of Church and State, which did not exist in Israel),* Render to Caesar the things that are Caesar's, and to God the things that are God's. And they marvelled at Him *(the Jewish leaders had used the "give" respecting tribute or taxes paid to Caesar, while Jesus used the word, "render," which speaks of paying something as a debt; in other words, He was saying that Israel owed Rome certain obligations, such as taxes, etc.; it also means that Believers are obligated to pay taxes, and as well, to submit to Civil Government in every respect, providing its demands do not abrogate the Word of God).*

THE RESURRECTION

18 Then come unto Him the Sadducees *(another party in Israel),* which say there is no Resurrection *(this denial was their major platform; it was a denial of the possibility of such a thing as a Resurrection from the dead);* and they asked Him, saying,

19 Master *(their use of this title was purely formal; they in no way considered Jesus to be a great teacher),* Moses wrote unto us *(proclaims them quoting the Scripture, but attempting as many, to subvert it),* If a man's brother die, and leave *his* wife *behind him,* and leave no children, that his brother should take his wife, and raise up seed unto his brother *(quoted from Deut. 25:5-6; this law was given, to prevent the family inheritance from being broken up, among other things).*

20 Now there were seven Brethren: and the first took a wife, and dying left no seed.

21 And the second took her, and died, neither left he any seed *(children):* and the third likewise.

22 And the seven had her, and left no seed: last of all the woman died also *(none of the above Text is in the Law of Moses; it is all a made-up story in order to prove, they think, their argument against the Resurrection; these skeptics will have a good laugh at Jesus' expense).*

23 In the Resurrection therefore, when they shall rise, whose wife shall she be of them? for the seven had her to wife *(this is the pivot point of their trap).*

24 And Jesus answering said unto them *(proclaims an answer they had never yet received, even though having argued about this matter with the Pharisees for many years),* Do you not therefore err, because you know not the Scriptures *(points to their ignorance which was inexcusable, seeing that most Sadducees were members of the Priesthood),* neither the Power of God? *(They assumed either that God could not raise the dead, or that He could raise them only to a life, which would be a counterpart of the present. Their failure to know "the Power of God" stems from unbelief.)*

25 For when they shall rise from the dead *(proclaims the guarantee by Christ of the coming Resurrection),* they neither marry, nor are given in marriage *(marriage was instituted by God to bring forth and perpetuate the human race; due to having glorified bodies in Heaven, which will take place in the Resurrection, there will be no death and, therefore, no need to perpetuate the race, therefore, no need for marriage);* but are as the Angels which are in Heaven *(only in the sense of which He speaks).*

26 And as touching the dead, that they rise *(refers to dead bodies, and not the soul and spirit, which are already with the Lord, that is, if the person was saved when they died):* have you not read in the Book of Moses, how in the bush God spoke unto him *(Ex. 3:5-6),* saying, I *am* the God of Abraham, and the God of Isaac, and the God of Jacob? *(God did not say, "I was the God of Abraham . . ." referring to someone who was dead, out of existence, and was no more. He instead said, "I am the God of Abraham . . ." meaning that these individuals continued to be alive at the time of Moses, even though their bodies were dead.)*

27 He is not the God of the dead *(meaning that God is not the God of something which no longer exists),* but the God of the Living *(meaning that no individual goes out of existence at death, but actually lives forever, whether redeemed or in a fallen state; the soul and the spirit of man are eternal):* you therefore do greatly err *(not merely "err," but rather "greatly err").*

THE GREAT COMMANDMENT

28 And one of the Scribes came *(probably a Pharisee),* and having heard them reasoning

together, and perceiving that He had answered them well, asked Him, Which is the first Commandment of all? *(Was not asked in sarcasm, but sincerely. He is one of the few who took advantage of the Perfect Knowledge of Christ. He was not really referring to the single most important Commandment of the Ten, but rather, which was the most important, the ritual or the ethical?)*

29 And Jesus answered him, The first of all the Commandments *is*, Hear, O Israel; The Lord our God is one Lord *(the word, "one" in the Hebrew is "echad," and means "to be united as one, one in number")*:

30 And you shall love the Lord your God with all your heart, and with all your soul, and with all your mind, and with all your strength: this *is* the First Commandment *(this is the type of "love" which the world doesn't have, and in fact, cannot have, which only a Believer can have, and which can only be given by the Lord).*

31 And the second *is* like, *namely* this, You shall love your neighbour as yourself. There is none other Commandment greater than these *(if we truly love God, we will as well, "love our neighbor"; this is the answer to all war, prejudice, hate, bias, racism, etc.).*

32 And the Scribe said unto him, Well, Master, You have said the truth *(refers to a Pharisee, who for a change, spoke kindly to and of Jesus)*: for there is one God; and there is none other but He:

33 And to love Him with all the heart and with all the understanding, and with all the soul, and with all the strength, and to love *his* neighbour as himself, is more than all whole Burnt Offerings and Sacrifices *(proclaims the fact that this Pharisee understood what the Sacrifices actually were all about; in other words, they were not mere rituals).*

34 And when Jesus saw that he answered discreetly, He said unto him *(means that this man had a mind of his own, which means he did not blindly follow the religious leaders of his day)*, You are not far from the Kingdom of God *(not there yet, but close!; the distance from the "Kingdom of God" is measured neither by miles, nor by ceremonial standards, but by spiritual conditions; however, being close is not enough; regrettably, millions fall into this category).* And no man after that does ask Him *any question (none were able to match wits with Christ!; it is tragic that they approach Christ in this fashion, and not in worship and adoration; but how many, approach Christ presently in the same fashion?!).*

DAVID'S SON

35 And Jesus answered and said, while He taught in the Temple *(is presented by Matthew as Jesus talking with the Pharisees [Mat. 22:41-42])*, How say the Scribes that Christ is the Son of David? *(This concerns the Incarnation, i.e., God becoming man, and dwelling among men.)*

36 For David himself said by the Holy Spirit *(affirms by Christ that David wrote Psalm 110; as well, it proclaims the fact that it was inspired by the Holy Spirit)*, The LORD said to my Lord *(the first "LORD" is the august title of God in the Hebrew Old Testament, i.e., "Jehovah"; so the first "LORD" refers to God the Father with the second "Lord" referring to God the Son; in effect, the entirety of the Trinity is addressed here; the Holy Spirit makes up the Third Person, the One Who inspired what was said)*, Sit thou on My Right Hand, till I make Your enemies Your footstool *(refers to the time after the Cross, when Christ is exalted, which speaks of the present time [Heb. 1:3]; in essence, all enemies were defeated at the Cross [Col. 2:14-15], but will be defeated in a practical sense by the end of the Kingdom Age [Rev. 20; 1 Cor. 15:24-28]).*

37 David therefore himself calls Him Lord *(recognizes Christ as Deity, actually, the Jehovah of the Old Testament)*; and whence is He *(Christ)* **then** his son? *(David's Son, which speaks of the Incarnation, God becoming man. Jesus is God, and at the same time, He is David's Son.)* And the common people heard Him gladly *(means that the common people believed Him respecting His claim as Messiah, but the religious leaders did not; with this statement about David, He brings them face-to-face with His claim as Messiah, a claim they could not deny; so they said nothing [Mat. 22:46]).*

38 And He said unto them in His Doctrine *(specifies that His Doctrine was totally different than that of the Pharisees and the religious leaders)*, Beware of the Scribes *(those who claim to be expert in the Law of Moses)*, which love to go in long clothing *(priestly or royal robes)*, and *love* salutations in the marketplaces *(to be called "Rabbi," or "Doctor"; He was not condemning these titles, but only the greedy grasping after them)*,

39 And the chief seats in the Synagogues *(seats reserved for officials and persons of distinction)* and the uppermost rooms at feasts *(the place for the most honored guest at a feast)*:

40 Which devour widows' houses *(for money)*, and for a pretence make long prayers *(praying*

long and loud for these widows and in their presence, hoping they would make out a will in favor of the Scribes): these shall receive greater damnation (teaches degrees of punishment in the coming Judgment).

THE WIDOW'S MITE

41 And Jesus sat over against the treasury (He did so for a purpose), and beheld how the people cast money into the treasury (not the amount that they cast in, but rather "how" it was cast in): and many who were rich cast in much (made an ostentatious display of their gift, in order that all may know how much it was).

42 And there came a certain poor widow (proclaims her being noticed not at all, except by the Lord; the word, "poor," in the Greek Text is "ptochos," and is used to designate a pauper rather than a mere peasant; the woman was destitute), and she threw in two mites, which make a farthing (it was referred to as a "lepton," which was the smallest Greek copper coin, with both of them being presently worth about a dollar, if that, in 2003 currency).

43 And He called unto Him His Disciples, and said unto them, Verily I say unto you, That this poor widow has cast more in, than all they which have cast into the treasury:

44 For all they did cast in of their abundance; but she of her want did cast in all that she had, even all her living (God judges our gift, not only by the amount, but how much we have left, and our motives).

CHAPTER 13
(A.D. 33)
DESTRUCTION OF THE TEMPLE FORETOLD

A ND as He went out of the Temple (He went out spiritually as well as physically, which guaranteed its doom), one of His Disciples said unto Him (concerns a conversation no doubt held on the Mount of Olives, as Jesus and the Disciples overlooked the Temple and surrounding area), Master, see what manner of stones and what buildings are here! (Josephus said that this building was one of the wonders of the world.)

2 And Jesus answering said unto him, Seest thou these great buildings? (This included the entire Temple enclosure, pertaining to several buildings.) there shall not be left one stone upon another, that shall not be thrown down (this was fulfilled in exact totality, in 70 A.D., by the Roman General Titus).

SIGNS OF THE ENDTIME

3 And as He sat upon the Mount of Olives over against the Temple, Peter and James and John and Andrew asked Him privately (it was extremely dangerous to speak of the destruction of the Temple, or anything that resembled such, for fear of the Scribes and Pharisees; so they would "ask Him privately"),

4 Tell us, when shall these things be? and what shall be the sign when all these things shall be fulfilled? (They were speaking more than likely of the near future. His answer would incorporate the future of Israel, in essence, forever.)

5 And Jesus answering them began to say (there is a possibility that one or more of them was taking notes), Take heed lest any man deceive you (Jesus begins His discourse with a warning of deception; this is Satan's greatest weapon):

6 For many shall come in My Name (after the Ascension of Christ, a number of Jews appeared on the scene, claiming to be the Messiah, who would lead Israel out from under the dominion of the Romans; those false Messiahs led Israel to her destruction in A.D. 70), saying, I am Christ (carries the meaning as well, of saying "I am of Christ"); and shall deceive many.

7 And when you shall hear of wars and rumours of wars, be ye not troubled (has to do with the mission at hand of Evangelizing the world; our Lord exhorts the Disciples and all who would follow, not to permit political and national upheavals to distract them from their work of Evangelism): for such things must needs be (due to Israel rejecting Christ, the world was and is subjected to all of these problems); but the end shall not be yet (means that the "end" will not be brought about until the Second Coming).

8 For nation shall rise against nation, and kingdom against kingdom (two thousand years of education, culture, and experience have not ameliorated the problem): and there shall be earthquakes in divers places (proclaims disturbance at the very foundation of the Earth [Rom. 8:22]), and there shall be famines and troubles (the natural product of the course taken by the human family and their rejection of Jesus Christ; and this problem will not be made right until Israel accepts Christ, which she will at the Second Coming): these are the beginnings of sorrows (not short-lived, but of duration; as well, it speaks of the greatest "sorrow" of all, the coming Great Tribulation).

9 But take heed to yourselves *(leaves the national scope, and addresses all Believers on a personal basis)*: for they shall deliver you up to councils; and in the Synagogues you shall be beaten *(the Early Church records this)*: and you shall be brought before rulers and kings for My sake *(such has happened all over the world, from then until now)*, for a testimony against them *(should have been translated, "For a testimony to them")*.

10 And the Gospel must first be published among all nations *(it didn't say every person, but it did say "all nations"; to a great degree this has been done, and is being done, but yet there is so much more to be done)*.

11 But when they shall lead *you*, and deliver you up *(refers to persecution)*, take no thought beforehand what you shall speak, neither do you premeditate *(the Lord does not mean that we are not to premeditate a prudent and wise answer, seeking His Face for guidance, but that we are not to be anxious about it; He is speaking of fear, and that it is not to beset us)*: but whatsoever shall be given you in that hour, you speak that: for it is not you who speaks, but the Holy Spirit *(this concerns His constant leading, guidance, companionship, and counsel)*.

12 Now the brother shall betray the brother to death, and the father the son; and children shall rise up against *their* parents, and shall cause them to be put to death *(beginning with Verse 11, even though the admonition holds true for other times, it mostly speaks of the coming Great Tribulation; during that time, some Jews will come to Christ, and many of them will lose their lives, betrayed by even their close loved ones)*.

13 And you shall be hated of all *men* for My Name's sake *(while Israel has been hated for so very long, that hatred will intensify in the coming Great Tribulation; all because of Christ; it is ironic, Israel proper hates the Name of Jesus, and they are hated for His Name's sake!)*: but he who shall endure unto the end, the same shall be saved *(concerns the Jews during the coming Great Tribulation who accept Christ, which some few shall, and that they must be "faithful unto death"; if so, the Lord has said, "I will give you a Crown of Life" [Rev. 2:10])*.

THE ABOMINATION OF DESOLATION

14 But when you shall see the abomination of desolation, spoken of by Daniel the Prophet *(speaks of the Antichrist taking over Jerusalem and the Temple, actually declaring war on Israel [Dan. 9:27])*, standing where it ought not *(refers to this abomination, the image of the Antichrist, being set up in the Holy of Holies in the Temple)*, (let him who reads understand,) *(means there is no reason to misunderstand, because Daniel has plainly foretold this happening)* then let them who be in Judaea flee to the mountains *(as stated, this refers to the time that the Antichrist will show his true colors, and invade Israel, in which she will be defeated for the first time since becoming a nation again in 1948)*:

15 And let him who is on the housetop *(in Israel, the tops of the houses are flat; during the summer time, people sleep, at times, in these areas)* not go down into the house, neither enter *therein*, to take any thing out of his house *(make haste)*:

16 And let him who is in the field not turn back again for to take up his garment.

17 But woe to them who are with child *(pregnant women)*, and to them who give suck in those days! *(Who have little babes in arms.)*

18 And pray you that your flight be not in the winter *(bad weather)*.

THE GREAT TRIBULATION

19 For *in* those days *(the last three and one half years of the Great Tribulation)* shall be affliction, such as was not from the beginning of the creation which God created unto this time, neither shall be *(the last half of the Great Tribulation will be worse than the Earth has ever seen, and so bad in fact, that such will never be seen again)*.

20 And except that the Lord had shortened those days, no flesh should be saved *(meaning that every Jew would be killed, and that could apply to the majority of the world)*: but for the elect's sake *(Israel's sake, not the Church, for the Church is now with the Lord)*, whom He has chosen *(the Lord chose these people, actually raising them up from the loins of Abraham and the womb of Sarah)*, He hath shortened the days *(by how much, we aren't told)*.

21 And then if any man shall say to you *(the word "then" refers to the last half of the Great Tribulation, a time period of some three and one half years)*, Lo, here is Christ *(Messiah)*; or, lo, *He is* there; believe *him* not *(the Lord is actually speaking here of the Antichrist who will make great claims)*:

22 For false Christs and false prophets shall rise, and shall show signs and wonders, to

seduce, if *it were* possible, even the elect *(the word "elect" refers to the Jews, but as it is used here, to those who have accepted Christ).*

23 But take ye heed *(repeated four times in this Chapter [Verses 5, 9, 23, 33]; "ye" is emphatic, specifically meaning that each individual must take heed):* behold, I have foretold you all things *(this leaves no one with an excuse).*

THE SECOND COMING

24 But in those days *(the Second Coming),* after that tribulation, the sun shall be darkened, and the moon shall not give her light *(pertains to the fifth time the planets will be affected in part, or in whole, during Daniel's 70th week),*

25 And the stars of Heaven shall fall *(pertains to meteorites, but as well, can definitely pertain to spirit beings of the spirit world of darkness),* and the powers that are in Heaven shall be shaken *(refers to the Satanic hosts that now rule the air [Eph. 2:1-3; 6:12]).*

26 And then shall they see *(it is quite possible that Television will portray the Second Coming and do so to the whole world)* the Son of Man coming *(the Second Coming)* in the clouds *(doesn't speak of clouds as we think of such, but rather, a great multitude of people who will be with Him, namely all the Saints who have ever lived)* with great power and glory *(in other words, when Christ truly comes back, no one will have to ask the question, is this really Him?; it will be overly obvious that it is).*

27 And then shall He send His Angels, and shall gather together His elect from the four winds, from the uttermost part of the earth to the uttermost part of Heaven *(all the Jews then alive on Earth, will be brought to the land of Israel; they will gladly come, even helped by Angels, simply because, they have finally accepted their Messiah, the Lord Jesus Christ, Whom they rejected so long ago).*

THE PARABLE OF THE FIG TREE

28 Now learn a Parable of the fig tree *(symbolic of Israel and the Second Coming);* When her branch is yet tender, and putteth forth leaves *(refers to the rebirth of Israel as it began in 1948; for about nineteen hundred years this "fig tree" produced nothing, now this tree, taking life from the roots, is beginning to "put forth leaves"),* you know that summer is near *(Israel is God's prophetic time clock; looking at Israel,* we now know that summer is near, i.e., "the Endtime Prophecies are about to be fulfilled"):

29 So you in like manner, when you shall see these things come to pass *(the beginning of these things predicted by Christ, has already begun),* know that it is near, *even* at the doors *(should have been translated, "He is near," because it refers to Christ).*

30 Verily I say unto you, that this generation shall not pass *(concerns the generation in existence at the time of these happenings, which will be the time of the Great Tribulation),* till all these things be done *(speaks of the events proclaimed in Rev., Chpts. 6-19).*

31 Heaven and Earth shall pass away *(better translated, "Heaven and Earth shall pass from one condition to another"):* but My Words shall not pass away *(what Christ is saying will come to pass, and without fail!).*

THE DAY OF CHRIST'S COMING UNKNOWN

32 But of that day and *that* hour knows no man, no, not the Angels which are in Heaven, neither the Son, but the Father *(the Son of Man under the self-imposed limitations of the Incarnation, says that even He Himself did not at that time know the hour of the Second Advent, and of the time of the fulfillment of these other things grouped around that event; without a doubt, He now knows, and I'm sure the Angels now know as well; but then they didn't!).*

33 Take ye heed, watch and pray *(the idea is a state of watchfulness, which is seasoned by prayer):* for you know not when the time is *(the "time" itself is not that important, but "watchfulness" is!).*

34 *For the Son of Man is* as a man taking a far journey *(Christ is speaking of Himself, when He would go back to Heaven, which He did),* Who left His house *(refers to the Work He established on Earth, constituted as the "Church" [Mat. 16:18]),* and gave authority to his servants *(pertains to every Believer),* and to every man his work *(every Believer is called by God for a particular task, no exceptions),* and commanded the porter to watch *(conveys the idea of wakefulness).*

35 Watch ye therefore: for you know not when the Master of the house cometh, at even, or at midnight, or at the cockcrowing, or in the morning *(Christ is not speaking here of the Rapture of the Church, but specifically to Israel; but yet, the admonition can definitely apply*

to modern Believers, and should apply as it regards the Rapture):

36 Lest coming suddenly He find you sleeping *(regrettably most of the modern Church is spiritually asleep; most little know and realize the lateness of the hour)*.

37 And what I say unto you *(the Disciples and Israel)* I say unto all *(includes the Church)*, Watch *(the last Word of Christ respecting this dissertation; we should take it very seriously)*.

CHAPTER 14
(A.D. 33)
THE PLOT

AFTER two days was *the Feast of* the Passover *(the greatest Feast of the Jewish year, celebrating the deliverance from Egypt; it lasted one day)*, and of Unleavened Bread *(the Second Feast, which began on the day of the Passover, and continued for seven days; during that time no leaven was to be placed in bread or anything else; the "Passover" symbolized the price that Christ would pay on Calvary's Cross, and "Unleavened Bread" symbolized His Perfect Life and Perfect Body, which would be offered in Sacrifice)*: and the Chief Priests and the Scribes sought how they might take Him by craft *(deceit)*, and put *Him* to death *(in doing such, they would destroy themselves as well)*.

2 But they said, Not on the Feast *Day (Passover)*, lest there be an uproar of the people.

JESUS ANOINTED AT BETHANY

3 And being in Bethany *(a small village, actually a suburb of Jerusalem, to the east of the city)* in the house of Simon the leper *(a man whom Jesus had healed)*, as He sat at meat, there came a woman *(probably refers to Mary, the sister of Lazarus [Jn. 11:1-2])* having an alabaster box of ointment of spikenard very precious *(the Greek word, "pistikos," is used, meaning that it was genuine, not imitation or adulterated; it was very costly.)*; and she broke the box, and poured *it* on His head *(she broke the seal that kept the fragrance preserved; the pouring upon Him, spoke of her anointing Him for His burial; anointing Him now, which was generally done after death, testified to her belief in the Resurrection; she seems to have been the only one who did believe in His Resurrection before the fact)*.

4 And there were some who had indignation within themselves *(pertained to some, if not all, of the Disciples but with Judas Iscariot taking the lead)*, and said, Why was this waste of the ointment made? *(It is believed by some that this ointment would have been worth about $10,000 in 2003 currency. The truth is, nothing given to Christ is wasted, while much of the world's resources used otherwise are, in fact, wasted.)*

5 For it might have been sold for more than three hundred pence, and have been given to the poor *(originated with Judas [Jn. 12:4-6]; he probably had other things in mind, such as stealing it)*. And they murmured against her *(no case of murmuring has ever been justified or sanctioned by God in Scripture regardless of how right the cause; and to make matters worse, this cause wasn't right)*.

6 And Jesus said, Let her alone *(it appears from Jn. 12:7 that Jesus addressed Himself here pointedly to Judas)*; why trouble ye her? *(Concerns the murmuring.)* she has wrought a good work on Me *(even though they didn't understand it, her action showed her Faith in His Resurrection)*.

7 For you have the poor with you always *(regrettably, portrays a condition resulting from the Fall in the Garden of Eden)*, and whensoever you will you may do them good *(the two, Himself and the poor, are equivalent in His Sight [Mat. 25:40-45])*: but Me you have not always *(speaking of His present position, which was soon to change)*.

8 She has done what she could *(she had been moved by the Holy Spirit to do this)*: she is come aforehand to anoint My Body to the burying *(His Body had been prepared by God for Sacrifice [Heb. 10:5])*.

9 Verily I say unto you, Wheresoever this Gospel shall be preached throughout the whole world *(a prediction that it would go throughout the whole world, which it has)*, this also that she has done shall be spoken of for a memorial of her *(this act is connected with her and will never be forgotten)*.

THE BETRAYAL

10 And Judas Iscariot, one of the Twelve *(is noted by design by the Holy Spirit, in that all will know that it is Judas who did this, and that he forfeited one of the most important offices ever given to a human being in the history of mankind)*, went unto the Chief Priests, to betray Him unto them.

11 And when they heard *it (the religious leaders of Israel)*, they were glad, and promised to

give him money (that amount was "thirty pieces of silver" [Mat. 26:15]). And he sought how he might conveniently betray Him (the word, "conveniently," refers to the fact that he would attempt to carry it out in a manner in which his part and activity would be concealed; however, it was not to be!).

PREPARATION FOR THE PASSOVER

12 And the first day of Unleavened Bread, when they killed the Passover (the lamb was killed), His Disciples said unto Him, Where will You that we go and prepare that You may eat the Passover? (A place had to be prepared.)

13 And He sent forth two of His Disciples (refers to Peter and John [Lk. 22:8]), and said unto them, Go ye into the city (Jerusalem), and there shall meet you a man bearing a pitcher of water (this was seldom done by men): follow him (in a spiritual sense, this man was a Type of the Holy Spirit).

14 And wheresoever he shall go in, say ye to the goodman of the house (believed to have been owned by John Mark, or his family, who wrote the Gospel according to Mark), The Master says, Where is the guestchamber, where I shall eat the Passover with My Disciples? (Actually says, "My guestchamber.")

15 And He (the owner of the house) will show you a large upper room furnished and prepared (was in a state of readiness): there make ready for us (has to do with the preparation of the Passover ingredients).

16 And His Disciples went forth, and came into the city, and found as He had said unto them: and they made ready the Passover (meant that Peter and John took the Paschal Lamb to the Temple where it was there killed, with the Priests officiating, with the blood poured out at the base of the Brazen Altar; the carcass of the lamb would have then been brought back to this house, where it would have been roasted and prepared by the Disciples).

THE LAST PASSOVER

17 And in the evening He cometh with the Twelve (He would be arrested that night, after He had eaten the Passover).

18 And as they sat and did eat (on the first Passover in Egypt, they were to eat standing, because they had not yet been delivered; now in the Promise Land, their inheritance, they were to eat "sitting," signifying that the work had been done), Jesus said, Verily I say unto you, One of you which eats with Me shall betray Me (the words, "eat with Me," are not merely to point to the individual who would betray Christ, but to the enormity of the offense).

19 And they began to be sorrowful, and to say unto Him one by one, Is it I? and another said, Is it I?

20 And He answered and said unto them, It is one of the Twelve, who dips with Me in the dish (all were dipping with Him in the dish, so that statement really did not tell them very much).

21 The Son of Man indeed goeth, as it is written of Him ([Ps. 22; Isa., Chpt. 51; Gen. 3:15], actually, the tenor of the entirety of the Old Testament points to Christ giving His Life as a ransom for many, even to which all the Sacrifices pointed): but woe to that man by whom the Son of Man is betrayed! (This predestined purpose of God did not make the guilt any the less of those who brought the Saviour to His Cross. The "woe" is not of vindictiveness, or even in the nature of a curse, but rather, "reveals a misery which love itself could not prevent.") good were it for that man if he had never been born (obedient to the Divine Purpose, Christ must die as a Sacrifice for sin, but that necessity did not excuse the free agent who brought it about).

THE LORD'S SUPPER

22 And as they did eat, Jesus took bread, and blessed, and broke it, and gave to them (this is typical of what the Lord has to do with us; He takes us, blesses us, and then breaks us, and only then can we be given to others), and said, Take, eat: this is My Body (the word "is" means "represents").

23 And He took the cup, and when He had given thanks, He gave it to them: and they all drank of it (signifies the shedding of the Saviour's Blood at Calvary, and that which it afforded, Eternal Life, at least to those who will take Christ as Saviour).

24 And He said unto them, This is (represents) My blood of the New Testament (New Covenant), which is shed for many (for the whole world [Jn. 3:16]).

25 Verily I say unto you, I will drink no more of the fruit of the vine, until that day that I drink it new in the Kingdom of God (the coming Kingdom Age).

26 And when they had sung an hymn (Ps. 118), they went out into the Mount of Olives (where He would be betrayed).

PETER'S DENIAL FORETOLD

27 And Jesus said unto them, All you shall be offended because of Me this night *(referred to His betrayal, and subsequent arrest by the Romans; "offended" means to, "find occasion of stumbling")*: for it is written, I will smite the Shepherd, and the sheep shall be scattered *([Zech. 13:7], all the Disciples would flee)*.

28 But after that I am risen *(Resurrection again foretold, but still they didn't believe)*, I will go before you into Galilee *(after the Resurrection, and two appearances in Jerusalem)*.

29 But Peter said unto Him, Although all shall be offended, yet *will* not I *(constitutes presumption on his part, and an insult toward the others)*.

30 And Jesus said unto him, Verily I say unto you, That this day, *even* in this night *(means that Peter would not even have the strength to last out the night)*, before the cock crow twice, you shall deny Me thrice *(three times)*.

31 But he spoke the more vehemently *(he kept on speaking, disavowing that he would ever fail Christ)*, If I should die with You, I will not deny You in any wise *(Peter was so carried away by the fervor of his zeal and love for Christ that he regarded neither the weakness of his own flesh, nor the truth of his Master's Word)*. Likewise also said they all.

THE GARDEN OF GETHSEMANE

32 And they came to a place which was named Gethsemane *(a garden at the foot of the Mount of Olives; "Gethsemane" means, "the place of the Olive-press")*: and He said to His Disciples, Sit ye here, while I shall pray *(if Jesus had to pray, what about us?)*.

33 And He took with Him Peter and James and John *(the third time such a thing was done, in reference to the other Disciples)*, and began to be sore amazed, and to be very heavy *(Swet says: "The Lord was overwhelmed with sorrow, but His first feeling was one of terrified surprise; His foreseeing the passion was one thing, but when it came clearly into view, its terrors exceeded His anticipations" [Heb. 5:7-8])*;

34 And said unto them *(to Peter, James, and John)*, My Soul is exceeding sorrowful unto death *(means that grief, so overwhelmed Him that He was close to dying; in fact, Satan definitely tried to kill Him at this time!)*: tarry you here, and watch *(regrettably, they didn't watch very well, but rather went to sleep, but probably from spiritual and physical exhaustion, more than anything else)*.

35 And He went forward a little, and fell on the ground *(actually means that He fell on the ground repeatedly; it portrays the desperation of the struggle)*, and prayed that, if it were possible, the hour might pass from Him *(continued to put forth the same petition, saying it over and over; the "hour" spoken of here pertains to the Cross, and His terrible Death in this fashion, which pertained to the bearing of the sin penalty of the world)*.

36 And He said, Abba, Father *(is actually the expression of two languages; He thus in His agony cried to God in the name of the whole human family, the Jew first, and also the Gentile)*, all things *are* possible unto You *(tells us that God could have affected the Salvation and Redemption of humanity in another way; such was possible!; but such was not His Will!)*; take away this cup from Me *(if He had not offered this petition, He would not have been Who and What He was)*: nevertheless not what I will, but what You will *(proclaims the principle of Faith for all Believers; His Will was subject to the Will of the Father as our wills must be subject)*.

37 And He comes, and finds them sleeping, and said unto Peter, Simon *(addressing him by his old name)*, sleepest thou? *(All of this was a part of the problem of Peter depending on self.)* could not you watch one hour? *(Pertains to the struggle between the flesh and the spirit.)*

38 Watch ye and pray, lest you enter into temptation *(this is not a suggestion, but actually, a Command!; prayer is imperative, if proper relationship is to be established)*. The Spirit truly is ready *(the human spirit)*, but the flesh *is* weak *(the "flesh" pertains to our own personal strength, ability, and will power; these things within themselves are insufficient for the task; unless the Believer properly understands the Cross; as it regards Sanctification, he will inevitably fall back on the flesh)*.

39 And again He went away, and prayed, and spoke the same words *(many times we have to pray the same thing over and over; this is not a sign of lack of faith, but rather of great Faith)*.

40 And when He returned, He found them asleep again, (for their eyes were heavy,) *(in the Greek Text means literally they were "weighed down"; their sleep was not deliberate, but the result of an oppressive sorrow)* neither wist they what to answer Him *(they couldn't account for their condition, so they said nothing)*.

41 And He cometh the third time, and said

unto them, Sleep on now, and take *your* rest *(said in irony)*: it is enough, the hour is come *(this is the "hour" which had been planned even before the foundation of the world [Rev. 13:8])*; behold, the Son of Man is betrayed into the hands of sinners *(the word "sinners," expresses not only Judas, but the religious leaders as well)*.

42 Rise up, let us go *(this was His hour and He was there to meet it)*; lo, he who betrays Me is at hand.

THE ARREST OF JESUS

43 And immediately, while He yet spoke, cometh Judas, one of the Twelve *(speaks of their arrival, even while Jesus was speaking)*, and with Him a great multitude with swords and staves, from the Chief Priests and the Scribes and the Elders *(sadly this was the "Church" of that day!)*.

44 And he who betrayed Him had given them a token *(proclaims the scheme perpetrated by Judas and the religious leaders)*, saying, Whomsoever I shall kiss, that same is He; take Him, and lead *Him* away safely *(proclaims the most perfidious act in human history; Judas had told his co-conspirators that the one he kissed would be Jesus [Ps. 109:5-20])*.

45 And as soon as He was come, he went straightway to Him, and said, Master, Master; and kissed Him.

46 And they *(the religious leaders)* laid their hands on Him, and took Him *(they only could do so, because He allowed them to do so [Jn. 10:17-18])*.

47 And one of them who stood by *(Simon Peter)* drew a sword, and smote a servant of the High Priest, and cut off his ear *(the servant's name was "Malchus"; Luke is the only one who mentions the healing of the wound by our Lord [Lk. 22:51])*.

48 And Jesus answered and said unto them, Are you come out, as against a thief, with swords and *with* staves to take Me? *(The Lord protests the manner in which this act is carried out. He was not a thief, so why were they treating Him as one?)*

49 I was daily with you in the Temple teaching, and you took Me not *(they did not take Him then, because they did not have any legitimate charge to bring against Him; as well, they feared the people)*: but the Scriptures must be fulfilled *(the Holy Spirit through foreknowledge saw what would happen [Isa., Chpt. 53; Zech. 11:13; 13:7])*.

50 And they all forsook Him, and fled *(refers to the Eleven Disciples; not being allowed to fight, they fled; the flesh will fight or flee, but it will not "trust")*.

51 And there followed Him a certain young man *(even though it is not known for sure, most think that this "young man" was Mark, who wrote this Gospel)*, having a linen cloth cast about *his* naked *body (the "linen cloth" was not that which people of poor circumstances could have owned; therefore, he belonged to a family of means)*; and the young men laid hold on him *(means the soldiers were setting about to arrest him)*:

52 And he left the linen cloth *(in the struggle, his garment was pulled from him)*, and fled from them naked *(probably means that he only had undergarments; there is no evidence that they pursued him)*.

THE TRIAL

53 And they led Jesus away to the High Priest *(refers to Caiaphas; however, we learn from Jn. 18:13 that Jesus was first brought before Annas, the father-in-law of Caiaphas)*: and with him *(Caiaphas)* were assembled all the Chief Priests and the Elders and the Scribes *(proclaims the religious hierarchy of Israel)*.

54 And Peter followed Him afar off *(the Holy Spirit delineates the "afar off"; the idea is meant to call our attention to the boasts of Peter, which this following at a distance occasioned)*, even into the palace of the High Priest *(refers to the court of the palace where the guards and servants were assembled)*: and he sat with the servants, and warmed himself at the fire.

55 And the Chief Priests and all the Council *(the Sanhedrin, the ruling body of Israel)* sought for witness against Jesus to put Him to death *(they were attempting to legalize their vile action)*; and found none *(refers to the emptiness of their accusations)*.

56 For many bear false witness against Him, but their witness agreed not together *(proclaims such being contrary to the Law of Moses, which required a trial to begin with those things which would acquit the accused, instead of condemning Him)*.

57 And there arose certain *(speaks of two men, as given in Mat. 26:60)*, and bear false witness against Him, saying *(proclaims the Sanhedrin as thinking they finally had a proper accusation against Him; however, they were to see that this was false as well!)*,

58 We heard Him say, I will destroy this

Temple that is made with hands, and within three days I will build another made without hands *(they had added the words, "that is made with hands, and I will build another made without hands"; they tried to make it seem as if Jesus was talking about the Jerusalem Temple, when actually what He did say, was speaking of His physical body; He really said: "destroy this Temple," and speaking of His Own body, "and in three days I will raise it up").*

59 But neither so did their witness agree together *(the idea in the Greek Text is that they made repeated attempts to bring testimony that would warrant conviction, but without success).*

60 And the High Priest stood up in the midst *(this man had become exasperated by their inability to bring forth a credible witness, and sought to make up by bluster, the lack of evidence),* and asked Jesus, saying, Answerest Thou nothing? *(He didn't answer, because they had no desire to hear the Truth.)* what *is it which* these witness against You? *(He demanded an answer from Christ concerning the accusations, but Jesus said nothing, at least to that charge.)*

61 But He held His peace, and answered nothing *(He kept on maintaining His silence).* Again the High Priest asked Him, and said unto Him, Are You the Christ, the Son of the Blessed? *(Actually means, "are You the Messiah?", namely, "The Anointed of God.")*

62 And Jesus said, I am *(constitutes a bold declaration of who He was; the pronoun "I" is used for emphasis; it is, "as for myself, in contradistinction to all others"; His answer left absolutely no doubt):* and you shall see *(proclaims the fact, that the entirety of the Jewish Sanhedrin, would ultimately "see" that what Jesus had said was absolutely true)* the Son of Man sitting on the Right Hand of Power, and coming in the clouds of Heaven *(refers to the Great White Throne Judgment, and the Second Coming, the latter happening first).*

63 Then the High Priest rent His clothes *(this was a sign that he considered what Jesus said to have been blasphemy),* and said, What need we any further witnesses? *(In their minds this was the sought for evidence. The prisoner had incriminated himself.)*

64 You have heard the blasphemy *(proclaims the High Priest rendering his conclusion even before testing the claims of Jesus; consequently, it becomes more and more obvious that this farce of a trial was not convened to seek for Truth, but instead, to find any way to condemn Christ):* what do you think? *(Actually, this is the question of* the ages, and a question, that every person must answer.)* And they all condemned Him to be guilty of death *(Joseph of Arimathaea, and Nicodemus, although members of the Sanhedrin, were not present; so the "all" pertained to those present, and not those absent).*

65 And some began to spit on Him, and to cover His face, and to buffet Him *(the "some" included members of the Sanhedrin, as well as the Temple guards and soldiers. Actually, the evidence is that the latter did not join in these indignities until they observed the members of the Sanhedrin engaging in these vile acts),* and to say unto Him, Prophesy *(they now add spiritual abuse to the physical abuse):* and the servants did strike Him with the palms of their hands *(Isaiah, some eight hundred years before, had prophesied, "His visage was so marred more than any man" [Isa. 52:14]).*

PETER DENIES JESUS

66 And as Peter was beneath in the palace *(speaks of the porch of the palace; the trial of Jesus was held in an upper story),* there cometh one of the maids of the High Priest:

67 And when she saw Peter warming himself, she looked upon him, and said, And you also was with Jesus of Nazareth *(the very fact that Peter was there, shows that he did not want to desert Jesus; however, his actions will show that he will not desire to stand up for Him either!).*

68 But he denied, saying, I know not, neither understand I what you say. And he went out into the porch; and the rooster crowed *(Peter's test came in an unexpected form, and discovered a weak point — his lack of moral courage).*

69 And a maid saw him again, and began to say to them who stood by, This is *one* of them *(this is a different maid).*

70 And he denied it again. And a little after, they who stood by said again to Peter, Surely you are *one* of them: for you are a Galilaean, and your speech agrees *thereto.*

71 But he began to curse and to swear, *saying,* I know not this man of whom you speak *(this does not refer to profanity but rather "to declare anathema or cursed"; Peter thus declares himself subject to the Divine curse if he is not telling the truth when he disclaims all acquaintance with Jesus; in fact, what he did was much worse than the use of profanity).*

72 And the second time the rooster crowed. And Peter called to mind the word that Jesus said unto him, Before the rooster crowed twice,

you shall deny Me thrice. And when he thought thereon, he wept (the word "wept" refers to racking sobs, which came from the depths of his being; in fact, this was the time of Peter's Repentance, which is portrayed by "a broken and a contrite heart" [Ps. 51:17]).

CHAPTER 15
(A.D. 33)
JESUS BEFORE PILATE

AND straightway (immediately) in the morning the Chief Priests held a consultation with the Elders and Scribes and the whole Council, and bound Jesus, and carried Him away, and delivered Him to Pilate (sentences of condemnation might not be legally pronounced on the day of trial; yet our Lord was tried, condemned, and crucified on the same day; as they took Him to Pilate, they continued to strike and beat Him).

2 And Pilate asked Him, Are You the King of the Jews? (To him, this was a political question. He had no regard or concern for the religious controversy.) And He answering said unto him, You say it (Jesus answered in the affirmative; in effect, He said, "You say that which is true").

3 And the Chief Priests accused Him of many things: but He answered nothing (He knew that to refute their erroneous and false charges, was a waste of time).

4 And Pilate asked Him again, saying, Answerest Thou nothing? behold how many things they witness against You (Pilate had never seen a man, who would not defend himself; he didn't understand Christ!).

5 But Jesus yet answered nothing; so that Pilate marveled (the silence of a blameless life pleads more powerfully than any defense, however elaborate).

6 Now at that feast (Passover) he (Pilate) released unto them (Israel) one prisoner, whomsoever they desired (immediately before the situation concerning Barabbas, Pilate sent Jesus to Herod, which is omitted by Mark [in Lk., Chpt. 23]; the custom of releasing a prisoner regarding its origin is anyone's guess).

JESUS SENTENCED TO DIE

7 And there was one named Barabbas (this man had been arrested for homicidal political terrorism; there is some evidence that he was referred to as "Jesus Barabbas"; if so, the Jews had the choice of "Jesus Barabbas" or "Jesus Christ"), which lay bound with them who had made insurrection with him, who had committed murder in the insurrection.

8 And the multitude crying aloud began to desire him (Pilate) to do as he had ever done unto them (concerned the releasing of a particular prisoner).

9 But Pilate answered them, saying, Will you that I release unto you the King of the Jews? (Referred to Jesus, in that which Pilate hoped this crowd would do. He used the title "King of the Jews," in sarcasm.)

10 For he knew that the Chief Priests had delivered Him for envy (inasmuch as the "envy" was so obvious that even this pagan could see it, tells us exactly to what level these religious leaders had sunk).

11 But the Chief Priests moved the people, that he should rather release Barabbas unto them.

12 And Pilate answered and said again unto them, What will you then that I shall do unto Him whom you call the King of the Jews?

13 And they cried out again, Crucify Him (they wanted Him crucified, because they thought this would prove to the people that He was not of God).

14 Then Pilate said unto them, Why, what evil has He done? (It was not for "evil" that they wanted to Crucify Him, but because of His "good.") And they cried out the more exceedingly, Crucify Him (Luke says they repeated the cry again, and again [Lk. 23:23]).

15 And so Pilate, willing to content the people (he was willing to content the people, but not willing to content God; untold thousands of preachers do the same every week), released Barabbas unto them (presents a study in irony!; they accused Christ of being an insurrectionist, which He was not, and yet demanded Barabbas be released, who had actually made insurrection!; such is evil!), and delivered Jesus, when he had scourged Him, to be crucified (the scourging was so severe, that many who experienced this ordeal didn't survive it).

JESUS CROWNED WITH THORNS

16 And the soldiers led Him away into the hall, called Praetorium (this was actually the barracks of the soldiers, which could have numbered as many as six hundred); and they call together the whole band (they would now mock Him).

17 And they clothed Him with purple (they

were mocking Him as King), and platted a crown of thorns, and put it about His *Head (the Greek word for "crown" as used here, is "stephanos," and means the "the victor's crown"; in the Mind of God, the victory had already been won, because He knew that Calvary would pay the total price)*,

18 And began to salute Him, Hail, King of the Jews! *(He was the King of the Jews, even though they didn't know it, but as well, He was the King of the whole world, which the world will recognize in the coming Kingdom Age.)*

19 And they smote Him on the head with a reed *(this was a stiff object which would have driven the thorns deep within His Scalp)*, and did spit upon Him, and bowing *their* knees worshipped Him *(but in mockery)*.

20 And when they had mocked Him, they took off the purple from Him, and put His own clothes on Him, and led Him out to Crucify Him.

21 And they compel one Simon a Cyrenian *(due to the beatings, Jesus could no longer physically carry the Cross, so they pressed this particular man to carry it for Him)*, who passed by, coming out of the country *(means that he was not a part in any way to these insidious proceedings, but just happened to be standing near when Jesus came by)*, the father of Alexander and Rufus, to bear His Cross *(speaks of the sons of Simon who would give their hearts to Christ, becoming well-known Disciples, and all because of what happened here this day)*.

THE CRUCIFIXION

22 And they bring Him unto the place Golgotha, which is, being interpreted, The place of a skull *(two meanings: A. Some claim this is the place where Adam was buried, and his skull later found; however, there is no evidence whatsoever of this tradition; and, B. Others think the interpretation simply means that the rock face of the hill resembles a skull, which is probably the correct interpretation)*.

23 And they gave Him to drink wine mingled with myrrh *(referred to a strong narcotic made of sour wine and mingled with bitter herbs; it was supposed to dull the sense of pain; some think that Christ was offered the drink twice, but there is some indication that it was offered three times)*: but He received *it* not *(He would not seek alleviation of the agonies of the Crucifixion by any drug potion which might render Him insensible; He would bear the full burden consciously)*.

24 And when they had crucified Him *(referred to them nailing Him to the Cross)*, they parted His garments, casting lots upon them, what every man should take *(His garments, with the exception of the seamless Robe, were divided among the soldiers; not wanting to tear the seamless Robe apart, they cast lots with the winner taking ownership of the garment [Ps. 22:18])*.

25 And it was the third hour *(9 a.m. in the morning, the time of the morning Sacrifice)*, and they crucified Him.

26 And the superscription of His accusation was written over *(over the Cross)*, THE KING OF THE JEWS *(out of anger, no doubt toward the Jews, Pilate wrote the title himself [Jn. 19:19]; the Chief Priests were visibly angry over this, and strongly requested that it be changed to read, "He said, I am King of the Jews"; Pilate answered by saying, "what I have written I have written" [Jn. 19:21-22]; so, Who, and What Jesus really was, were fitly placed over His Head on the Cross)*.

27 And with Him they crucify two thieves *(robbers)*; the one on His right hand, and the other on His left.

28 And the Scripture was fulfilled, which said, And He was numbered with the transgressors *([Isa. 53:12], He took the place of the transgressors; so His Death, its manner, and with whom He died, were fitting!)*.

29 And they who passed by railed on Him *([Ps. 22:7-8], "they," referred to the religious leaders of Israel)*, wagging their heads, and saying, Ah, You Who destroyed the Temple, and build *it* in three days *(they were referring to the statement He did make, recorded in [Jn. 2:19-21], which referred to His Body the Temple, its Death, and Resurrection in three days; He wasn't talking about the Temple in Jerusalem)*,

30 Save Yourself, and come down from the Cross *(this jest was the harder to endure since it appealed to a consciousness of power held back only by the self-restraint of a Sacrificed Will; had He saved Himself, no one else could have been saved)*.

31 Likewise also the Chief Priests mocking said among themselves with the Scribes, He saved others; Himself He cannot save *(they could not deny the fact that He saved others, but they attempted to turn that fact against Him, by alleging that He performed these miracles by the power of Satan, rather than by the Power of God)*.

32 Let Christ the King of Israel descend now from the Cross *(said in mockery)*, that we may

see and believe *(they lied!; He rose from the dead after the third day, and they still didn't believe).* **And they who were crucified with Him reviled Him** *(while both did revile Him, one shortly thereafter repented and was saved, which Mark did not mention).*

THE DEATH OF JESUS

33 **And when the sixth hour was come** *(12 noon)*, **there was darkness over the whole land until the ninth hour** *(until 3 p.m.; as it was now the Passover time the moon was full, so that it could not have been caused by an eclipse; for when the moon is full it cannot intervene between the Earth and the sun; how far this darkness extended, we aren't told; we do know that it went as far as Egypt toward the south, and as far as Bithynia toward the north; it was at this time that He became the Burnt-offering, and the Sin-offering of Lev. 1:4).*

34 **And at the ninth hour** *(3 p.m.)* **Jesus cried with a loud voice** *(proving that He did not die from physical weakness, but that He purposely, laid down His Own life [Jn. 10:17-18]),* **saying, Eloi, Eloi, lama sabachthani? which is, being interpreted, My God, My God, why have You forsaken Me?** *(During this three hour period when darkness covered that part of the world, if not the whole Earth, He bore the sin penalty of mankind, on which the Heavenly Father could not look [Hab. 1:13; I Pet. 2:24].)*

35 **And some of them who stood by** *(refers to the Roman soldiers, even some of the religious leaders of Israel),* **when they heard** *it,* **said, Behold, He calls Elijah** *(mockingly said by the religious leaders of Israel).*

36 **And one ran and filled a spunge full of vinegar** *(according to John, this was placed on hyssop [Jn. 19:29] which fulfilled [Ex. 12:22]),* **and put** *it* **on a reed, and gave Him to drink** *(there is no record that He drank it),* **saying, Let alone; let us see whether Elijah will come to take Him down** *(sarcasm!).*

37 **And Jesus cried with a loud voice** *(once again, proving that His Death was not brought about by physical weakness),* **and gave up the ghost** *(should have been translated, "breathed out His Life"; in fact, He didn't die, until the Holy Spirit told Him to die [Heb. 9:14]).*

38 **And the Veil of the Temple was rent in twain from the top to the bottom** *(this signified that the price had been paid, with all sin atoned; now, the way to the Holy of Holies was opened up that man might come, for the Veil hid the Holy of Holies).*

39 **And when the centurion** *(he was the first Gentile to render this testimony of Faith; tradition affirms that his name was Longinus, and that he became a devoted follower of Christ, preached the Faith, and died a martyr's death),* **which stood over against Him** *(beside Christ),* **saw that He so cried out, and gave up the ghost, he said, Truly this man was the Son of God** *(in effect, he was saying, many have claimed to be God, but this One is God).*

40 **There were also women looking on afar off** *(speaks of women from Galilee, and not women from Jerusalem):* **among whom was Mary Magdalene, and Mary the mother of James the less and of Joseph, and Salome** *(there is no record that Mary the Mother of Jesus was there; no doubt, the strain was more than she could bear, and John undoubtedly took her away);*

41 **(Who also, when He was in Galilee, followed Him, and ministered unto Him;)** *(did what they could to help)* **and many other women which came up with Him unto Jerusalem** *(who they were, we aren't told).*

THE BURIAL OF JESUS

42 **And now when the evening was come** *(soon to come. It was now approximately 3 p.m. — the evening would be at about 6 p.m. so they had about three hours to work),* **because it was the preparation** *(to prepare for the Passover, for it would begin at 6 p.m. that evening),* **that is, the day before the Sabbath** *(this was the High Sabbath of the Passover Feast, which was Thursday, and not the ordinary weekly Sabbath, which was Saturday [Lev. 23:6-7]; Jesus was crucified on a Wednesday, and not on Friday, as many think, spending three full days and nights in the Tomb, and rose on the first day of the week, even as He had said He would do [Mat. 12:40]),*

43 **Joseph of Arimathaea, an honourable counselor** *(he was a member of the Grand Council of Jerusalem, the Sanhedrin),* **which also waited for the Kingdom of God** *(spoke of his spiritual hunger, which was fulfilled in Jesus),* **came, and went in boldly unto Pilate** *(means that such was not commonly done),* **and craved the body of Jesus** *(he strongly requested that he be given the remains).*

44 **And Pilate marvelled if He** *(Jesus)* **were already dead** *(it normally took several days for one to die on the cross; Jesus had only been on the cross for six hours, so Pilate was skeptical):* **and calling** *unto him* **the centurion, he asked**

him whether he had been any while dead *(how long he had been dead)*.

45 And when he knew *it* of the centurion *(it was affirmed by the Roman soldier)*, he gave the body to Joseph *(the word "body" in the Greek is "ptoma," and means "a corpse")*.

46 And he *(Joseph)* bought fine linen *(a piece of expensive cloth used to wrap around the body of Jesus)*, and took Him down *(took Him down from the Cross)*, and wrapped Him in the linen, and laid Him in a sepulchre which was hewn out of a rock *(the tomb was in the garden adjacent to the place of Crucifixion, most certainly the property of Joseph)*, and rolled a stone unto the door of the sepulcher *(proving that the tomb had never before been used)*.

47 And Mary Magdalene and Mary *the mother* of Joseph beheld where He was laid.

CHAPTER 16
(A.D. 33)
THE TESTIMONY OF THE ANGEL

AND when the Sabbath was past *(the regular weekly Sabbath of Saturday)*, Mary Magdalene, and Mary the *mother* of James, and Salome, had bought sweet spices, that they might come and anoint Him *(proving that they really did not believe that He would rise from the dead; if so, it would have been pointless to have wasted money on the purchase of these expensive items)*.

2 And very early in the morning the first *day* of the week *(Sunday morning)*, they came unto the sepulchre at the rising of the sun.

3 And they said among themselves *(means in the Greek Text that "they kept on saying among themselves")*, Who shall roll us away the stone from the door of the sepulchre? *(The stone would have to be rolled away, so they could apply the spices to the corpse.)*

4 And when they looked, they saw that the stone was rolled away: for it was very great.

5 And entering into the sepulchre, they saw a young man sitting on the right side *(sitting on the raised projection, which had contained the body of Jesus; Him "sitting" portrayed far more than posture; it meant that the work of the Resurrection was completed, and death had been defeated)*, clothed in a long white garment *(the "young man" was an Angel; Expositors remarked that no such robe was worn by young men on Earth)*; and they were affrighted *(no wonder, Matthew said, "his countenance was like lightning" [Mat. 28:3])*.

6 And he said unto them, Be not affrighted *(fear not)*: You seek Jesus of Nazareth, Who was crucified: He is risen *(without a doubt, the greatest statement ever made in the annals of human history)*; He is not here *(speaks of victory over death, Hell, and the grave)*: behold the place where they laid Him *(signifies the empty tomb; in other words, He definitely was dead, but is now definitely alive!)*.

7 But go your way, tell His Disciples and Peter *(no censor or reprimand concerning their unbelief; as well, "Peter" is added to let him know that he is included, despite his denial of Christ, because Peter had repented)* that He goes before you into Galilee: there shall you see Him, as He said unto you *(there were several appearances of Christ to the Disciples in Jerusalem before the Galilee appearance, but it was only during the latter appearance that He recommissioned them [Jn., Chpt. 21])*.

THE TESTIMONY OF THE WOMEN

8 And they went out quickly, and fled from the sepulchre; for they trembled and were amazed *(proclaims them seeing more than they could comprehend, digest, or even accept for the moment)*: neither said they any thing to any *man*; for they were afraid *(they were fearful that they would be accused of stealing the body)*.

9 Now when *Jesus* was risen early the first *day* of the week *(referred to some time after sundown Saturday, which would have been the beginning of the Jewish Sunday, the first day of the week)*, He appeared first to Mary Magdalene *(He appeared to her even before appearing to His Disciples)*, out of whom He had cast seven devils *(gives us at least a hint as to the cause of her love and devotion)*.

10 *And* she went and told them who had been with Him *(referred to His Disciples)*, as they mourned and wept *(as stated, they had not believed that He would rise from the dead, despite the fact that He had plainly told them so [Mat. 12:40])*.

11 And they, when they had heard that He was alive, and had been seen of her, believed not *(they flatly rejected her testimony; Luke said that it seemed to them "as idle tales" [Lk. 24:11]; the repeated unbelief of the Apostles concerning the Resurrection, destroys the theory that they invented the Resurrection)*.

THE TESTIMONY OF THE DISCIPLES

12 After that He appeared in another form

unto two of them (*"another form," in the Greek Text literally says, "In a different outward expression or appearance"; this is given in detail in Lk. 24:13-35*), as they walked, and went into the country (*outside of Jerusalem toward Emmaus; it is believed that the two were Cleophas and Luke*).

13 And they went and told *it* unto the residue (*to the Disciples*): neither believed they them (*places them at the position of disbelieving two different and distinct sources*).

14 Afterward He appeared unto the Eleven as they sat at meat (*could have been His Appearance to them by the Sea of Galilee [Jn. 21:4-23]*), and upbraided them with their unbelief and hardness of heart, because they believed not them which had seen Him after He was risen (*He rebuked them, and did so sharply*).

THE GREAT COMMISSION

15 And He said unto them, Go ye into all the world (*the Gospel of Christ is not merely a western Gospel, as some claim, but is for the entirety of the world*), and preach the Gospel to every creature (*"preaching" is God's method, as is here plainly obvious; as well, it is imperative that every single person have the opportunity to hear; this is the responsibility of every Believer*).

16 He who believes (*believes in Christ and what He did for us at the Cross*) and is baptized (*baptized into Christ [Rom. 6:3-5] not water baptism*) shall be saved; but he who believes not shall be damned (*Jn. 3:16*).

17 And these signs shall follow them who believe (*not these "sins" shall follow them who believe*); In My Name shall they cast out devils (*demons — Jesus defeated Satan, fallen angels,*

and all demon spirits at the Cross [Col. 2:14-15]*); they shall speak with new tongues (*baptism with the Holy Spirit with the evidence of speaking with other tongues [Acts 2:4]*);

18 They shall take up serpents (*put away demon spirits [Lk. 10:19] has nothing to do with reptiles*); and if they drink any deadly thing, it shall not hurt them (*speaks of protection; in no way does it speak of purposely drinking poison, etc., in order to prove one's faith; the word, "if," speaks of accidental ingestion*); they shall lay hands on the sick, and they shall recover (*means to do so "in the Name of Jesus" [Acts 5:12; 13:3; 14:3; 19:11; 28:8; I Tim. 4:14; II Tim. 1:6; Heb. 6:2; James 5:14]*).

THE ASCENSION

19 So then after the Lord had spoken unto them, He was received up into Heaven (*the Ascension*), and sat on the right Hand of God (*[Heb. 1:3] signifying that the work of Redemption, was total and complete, i.e., "a finished work"*).

THE EARLY CHURCH

20 And they went forth (*refers to the entirety of the Early Church, and not just the Twelve Apostles*), and preached everywhere (*at the end of the First Century, the Gospel of Christ had been taken to the greater majority of the Roman Empire*), the Lord working with *them* (*He will "work" if His Commands are followed*), and confirming the Word (*the Word of God, what He had said*) with signs following (*if the "signs" are not "following," the Gospel is not being preached, but rather something else*). Amen (*Truth*).

THE GOSPEL ACCORDING TO
LUKE

CHAPTER 1
(A.D. 1)
INTRODUCTION

FORASMUCH as many have taken in hand to set forth in order a declaration (*means many were attempting at that time to write accounts of the Life and Ministry of Christ, which proved to have no inspiration of the Holy Spirit, and consequently, were unreliable*) of those things which are most surely believed among us (*proclaims the Gospel as a narrative concerning facts fully established*),

2 Even as they delivered them unto us (*concerns those who were there, and actually observed what took place*), which from the beginning were eyewitnesses, and ministers of the Word (*probably concerned members of the "Twelve" and the "Seventy," as well as others*);

3 It seemed good to me also (*moved upon by the Holy Spirit to do such*), having had perfect understanding of all things from the very first (*means that he made absolutely certain of the reliability of these "eyewitness accounts"*), to write unto you in order (*refers to an orderly design, not necessarily in chronological order*), most excellent Theophilus (*it is not known exactly as to who this man was; he was evidently a Gentile of high rank in the Roman world of that day, who had accepted Christ as his Saviour*),

4 That you might know the certainty of those things (*means that he could rely on what Luke told him*), wherein you have been instructed (*he will now be able to sort the facts from the fiction; Luke writing this Gospel to Theophilus has helped millions to "know" the "certainty of these things"*).

JOHN THE BAPTIST

5 There was in the days of Herod, the king of Judaea (*Herod the Great; the event concerning the birth of John the Baptist took place towards the end of his reign*), a certain Priest named Zacharias (*should be pronounced, "Zechariah"; it means "remembered of Jehovah"*), of the course of Abia (*pertains to the twenty-four courses for Temple service; each of the twenty-four courses lasted for one week [I Chron. 24:1]; Zacharias was especially distinguished by belonging to the first of the twenty-four courses or families*): and his wife *was* of the daughters of Aaron, and her name *was* Elisabeth (*meaning that both the husband and the wife traced their lineage back to Aaron, the first High Priest — a coveted distinction in Israel*).

6 And they were both Righteous before God (*tells us that at this time, there were precious few who were actually Righteous before God*), walking in all the Commandments and Ordinances of the Lord blameless (*proclaims a lifestyle of Righteousness which not many had; what an honor to be called by the Holy Spirit, "blameless!"*).

7 And they had no child (*they desperately wanted children*), because that Elisabeth was barren (*placed her in the same category as Sarah*), and they both were *now* well stricken in years (*Elisabeth was now beyond the age of child bearing; consequently, John's birth was just as miraculous as that of Isaac [Rom. 4:17-21; Heb. 11:11]*).

8 And it came to pass, that while he (*Zacharias*) executed the Priest's office before God in the order of his course (*some think this was the month of July, if so, Jesus was conceived six months later [Lk. 1:26], which would have been in January, consequently, being born nine months later in October*),

9 According to the custom of the Priest's office, his lot was to burn Incense when he went into the Temple of the Lord (*this was done by coals of fire taken from the Brazen Altar, a Type of Christ and His Crucifixion, and taken to the Altar of Incense, with coals placed on the Altar, with Incense poured over the coals; this was done twice a day at the time of the morning and evening Sacrifices*).

10 And the whole multitude of the people were praying without at the time of Incense.

11 And there appeared unto him an Angel of the Lord (*Gabriel*) standing on the right side of the Altar of Incense (*the right side is the side of propitiation, which in effect, means that God accepts the Sacrifice [Heb. 1:3]*).

12 And when Zacharias saw *him*, he was troubled, and fear fell upon him.

13 But the Angel said unto him, Fear not, Zacharias: for your prayer is heard *(the Greek translation should read, "was heard," implying that it was no longer offered because of their age; but every prayer prayed in the Will of God is always heard by the Lord, and will be answered in His due time)*; and your wife Elisabeth shall bear you a son, and you shall call his name John *(John means, "Jehovah shows favor or grace"; it was an apt description of the one who would introduce the Lord of Glory)*.

14 And you shall have joy and gladness; and many shall rejoice at his birth *(the rejoicing would be because he would introduce the Messiah)*.

15 For he shall be great in the sight of the Lord *(his greatness would come because of his introduction of Christ)*, and shall drink neither wine nor strong drink *(meant that he was a "Nazarite" [Num., Chpt. 6])*; and he shall be filled with the Holy Spirit, even from his mother's womb *(has no reference to the Acts 2:4 experience, which had not yet come to pass; he would have unusual help from the Holy Spirit due to his mission, which was to introduce Christ)*.

16 And many of the children of Israel shall he turn to the Lord their God *(he would be the first Prophet since Malachi, a time span of about four hundred years; there would be a great move of the Spirit under his Ministry)*.

RIGHTEOUSNESS

17 And he shall go before Him *(Christ)* in the spirit and power of Elijah *(John could have been Elijah to the people, thereby ushering in the Kingdom Age, if Israel had only accepted Christ)*, to turn the hearts of the fathers to the children *(that the Israel of John's day might have the Righteousness of the Godly Patriarchs of the past)*, and the disobedient to the wisdom of the just *(God and His Word)*; to make ready a people prepared for the Lord *(preparation for the coming Messiah, Whom John would introduce)*.

18 And Zacharias said unto the Angel, Whereby shall I know this? for I am an old man, and my wife well stricken in years *(a posture of unbelief)*.

19 And the Angel answering said unto him, I am Gabriel *(the same Angel who had come to Daniel [Dan. 8:16; 9:21], and shortly would be sent to Mary [Lk. 1:26])*, who stands in the Presence of God *(may well represent the highest rank of all among Angels)*; and am sent to speak unto you, and to show you these glad tidings *(sent from the throne of God)*.

20 And, behold, you shall be dumb *(there is some indication in the Greek Text that he would be both deaf, and dumb)*, and not able to speak, until the day that these things shall be performed *(he had asked for a sign and had been given one most painful)*, because you believed not my words *(unbelief is a sin)*, which shall be fulfilled in their season *(irrespective of your unbelief, it shall happen)*.

21 And the people waited for Zacharias *(pertained to the usual custom of the Priest finishing his duties, then coming out and pronouncing a blessing upon the people)*, and marvelled that he tarried so long in the Temple *("marveled" does not show impatience, but rather anticipation; they were not to be disappointed!)*.

22 And when he came out, he could not speak unto them *(the "sign" had already begun)*: and they perceived that he had seen a vision in the Temple *(probably referred to a possible glow on his countenance)*: for he beckoned unto them, and remained speechless.

23 And it came to pass, that, as soon as the days of his ministration were accomplished *(it was about a week)*, he departed to his own house.

24 And after those days his wife Elisabeth conceived *(we aren't told how old she was, just "well-stricken in years" [Vs. 7])*, and hid herself five months, saying *(she hid herself in order to seek the Lord regarding how this child was to be raised, and how he should be trained)*,

25 Thus hath the Lord dealt with me in the days wherein he looked on *me*, to take away my reproach among men *(she would no longer be childless, but in fact would give birth to the greatest Prophet who ever lived)*.

MARY

26 And in the sixth month *(refers to six months after Elisabeth had conceived; consequently, John was six months older than Jesus)* the Angel Gabriel was sent from God unto a city of Galilee, named Nazareth *(strangely enough, Nazareth was held in scorn by Israel at that time)*,

27 To a virgin *(in the Greek Text is "parthenos," which refers to a pure virgin who has never known a man, and never experienced a marriage relationship; in the Hebrew, the word is "Ha-alma," which means, "the Virgin — the only one who ever was, or ever will be a mother in this way")* espoused *(engaged)* to a man whose name was

Joseph, of the house of David *(he was in the direct lineage of David through Solomon)*; and the Virgin's name *was* Mary *(Mary went back to David through another of David's sons, Nathan; so their lineage was perfect as it regards the Prophecies that the Messiah would come from the House of David [II Sam., Chpt. 7]).*

28 And the Angel came in unto her, and said *(presents the greatest moment in human history, the announcement of the coming birth of the Lord of Glory in the Incarnation, i.e., "God becoming man"),* Hail, *you that are* highly favoured *(means "much engraced," not "full of grace," as the Catholic Church teaches, but one who, herself meritless, had received signal Grace from God),* the Lord *is* with you *(signals her position of humility)*: blessed *are* you among women *(does not say "above women," as the Catholics teach; however, she definitely was much blessed).*

29 And when she saw *him*, she was troubled at his saying *(a total disturbance; not a partial, or light agitation),* and cast in her mind what manner of salutation this should be *(she in no way understood the reason that he addressed her as he did).*

30 And the Angel said unto her, Fear not, Mary: for you have found favour with God *(should have been translated, "you have received Grace from God").*

31 And, behold, you shall conceive in your womb *(should have been translated, "You shall forthwith conceive in your womb," meaning immediately),* and bring forth a Son *(proclaims the Incarnation, "God manifest in the flesh, God with us, Immanuel" [Isa. 7:14; 9:6]),* and shall call His name JESUS *(the Greek version of the Hebrew, "Joshua"; it means "Saviour," or "The Salvation of Jehovah").*

32 He shall be great, and shall be called the Son of the Highest *(actually means "The Most High," and refers to "Jehovah")*: and the Lord God shall give unto Him the throne of His father David *(II Sam., Chpt. 7)*:

33 And He shall reign over the house of Jacob for ever; and of His Kingdom there shall be no end *(this will begin at the Second Coming, and will last forever; it could have begun at the beginning of His Ministry, but He was rejected by Israel; but at the Second Coming, they will accept Him as their Saviour, Messiah, and King [Zech., Chpts. 12-14]).*

34 Then said Mary unto the Angel, How shall this be, seeing I know not a man? *(She was probably in her late teens.)*

35 And the Angel answered and said unto her, The Holy Spirit shall come upon you *(has the same connotation as, "the Spirit of God moved upon the face of the waters" [Gen. 1:2]),* and the power of the Highest shall overshadow you *(has the same reference as, "And God said, let there be light: and there was light" [Gen. 1:3]):* therefore also that holy thing which shall be born of you shall be called the Son of God *(constitutes the Incarnation, "God becoming Man"; He would be Very God and Very Man).*

36 And, behold, your cousin Elisabeth *(the word, "cousin," in the Greek Text is "suggenes," which means "countryman," and not necessarily a cousin in the sense of a blood relative; however, Mary definitely could have been personally kin to Elisabeth),* she has also conceived a son in her old age: and this is the sixth month with her, who was called barren.

37 For with God nothing shall be impossible *(what is impossible with man is very much possible with God).*

38 And Mary said, Behold the handmaid of the Lord *(beautifully portrays the humility of this young lady; I think she would be greatly grieved at the unscriptural manner in which Catholicism has elevated her — even to the place of Deity);* be it unto me according to your word *(she gives this consent in a word that was simple and sublime, which involved the most extraordinary act of Faith that a woman ever consented to accomplish).* And the Angel departed from her.

MARY VISITS ELISABETH

39 And Mary arose in those days *(concerned the time immediately after the appearance of the Angel Gabriel),* and went into the hill country with haste, into a city of Judah *(tradition places this at Hebron);*

40 And entered into the house of Zacharias, and saluted Elisabeth *(she was welcomed wholeheartedly).*

41 And it came to pass, that, when Elisabeth heard the salutation of Mary *(the account that the Angel Gabriel had given to Mary concerning the birth of Jesus),* the babe *(the one who would be known as John the Baptist)* leaped in her womb *(at the mention of Jesus, the Holy Spirit moved upon this unborn child and it responded; it doesn't mean that the unborn child had comprehension);* and Elisabeth was filled with the Holy Spirit *("filled" in the Greek Text is "pletho," and means to "imbue, influence or supply"; it does not have the meaning of that which*

happened on the day of Pentecost, referring to Acts 2:4):

42 And she *(Elisabeth)* spake out with a loud voice and said, Blessed *are* you *(Mary)* among women *(not above women as the Catholics claim; however, Mary was truly blessed, as would be obvious),* and blessed *is* the fruit of your womb *(Jesus Christ was that "fruit!").*

43 And whence *is* this to me *(why am I honored in this way?),* that the mother of my Lord should come to me? *(She used the word "Lord" in its highest sense; great as her own child was to be in the sight of the Lord, here was the mother of One yet greater, even the Lord Himself.)*

44 For, lo, as soon as the voice of your salutation sounded in my ears, the babe leaped in my womb for joy *(as stated, this was a manifestation of the Holy Spirit Who produced this response).*

45 And blessed *is* she who believed *(refers to Mary and her faith):* for there shall be a performance of those things which were told her from the Lord *(the words "shall be" are a certitude of action).*

THE MAGNIFICAT

46 And Mary said *(the following actually constitutes a song, and is in the tradition of the "song of Deborah" [Judg. 5:1-31]),* My soul doth magnify the Lord *(she "magnified the Lord," while the Catholic Church erroneously magnifies her),*

47 And my spirit has rejoiced in God my Saviour *(disproves the theory of the "Immaculate Conception," or the total absence of original sin in Mary; God was her Saviour, so she must have been a sinner, in order to be saved; the Scripture says, "all have sinned" [Rom. 3:23]).*

48 For He has regarded the low estate of His handmaiden *(humility):* for, behold, from henceforth all generations shall call me blessed *(the word "blessed" is a single syllable here, and simply means "a recipient of Grace").*

49 For He Who is mighty has done to me great things; and Holy *is* His Name *("Holy" is the essence of His Being, and speaks of God the Father).*

50 And His Mercy *is* on them who fear Him from generation to generation *(mercy is extended to those who truly revere, i.e., "respect Him").*

51 He has showed strength with His arm *(proclaims the Power of God in the manner in which it is used);* He has scattered the proud in the imagination of their hearts *(proclaims the*

Messianic reversal of man's conception of what is great and little).

52 He has put down the mighty from *their* seats, and exalted them of low degree *(the Lord ignored the proud self-exaltation of the religious elite of Israel, and showered His Attention on a little "handmaiden").*

53 He has filled the hungry with good things *(concerns they who hunger and thirst after righteousness [Mat. 5:6]);* and the rich He has sent empty away *(refers to those who claim to be rich and increased with goods, and have need of nothing [Rev. 3:17]).*

54 He has helped His servant Israel, in remembrance of *His* mercy *(regrettably, Israel didn't want His help, or His Mercy);*

55 As He spoke to our fathers, to Abraham, and to his seed for ever *(Mary's song opens with "magnifying the Lord," and closes with the "Promises of God being remembered forever").*

56 And Mary abode with her *(Elisabeth)* about three months, and returned to her own house *(every indication is Joseph and Mary were married almost immediately after the appearance of the Angel Gabriel [Mat. 1:18-25]).*

THE BIRTH OF JOHN THE BAPTIST

57 Now Elisabeth's full time came that she should be delivered; and she brought forth a son.

58 And her neighbours and her cousins heard how the Lord had shown great mercy upon her; and they rejoiced with her.

59 And it came to pass, that on the eighth day they came to circumcise the child *(this was the Command originally given to Abraham by the Lord [Gen. 17:10-12]);* and they called him Zacharias, after the name of his father *("they" referred to friends and relatives, not Zacharias and Elisabeth).*

60 And his mother answered and said, Not so; but he shall be called John *(in obedience to what Gabriel had demanded).*

61 And they said unto her, There is none of your kindred who is called by this name.

62 And they made signs to his father, how he would have him called *(shows that he could not hear or speak).*

63 And he asked for a writing table, and wrote, saying, His name is John. And they marvelled all *(upon obedience, as the next verse proclaims, Zacharias could now hear and speak, and possibly related to them the account of the appearance of Gabriel).*

64 And his mouth was opened immediately, and his tongue *loosed*, and he spoke, and praised God.

65 And fear came on all who dwelt round about them: and all these sayings were noised abroad throughout all the hill country of Judaea *(God was moving again in Israel; the four hundred year prophetic drought was being broken; once again, they would hear, "Thus saith the Lord . . . .").*

66 And all they who heard *them* *(the predictions of Gabriel as related by Zacharias and Elisabeth)* laid *them* up in their hearts, saying, What manner of child shall this be! And the hand of the Lord was with him *(this is Luke's way of expressing all that would happen to John the Baptist through the entirety of his life).*

ZECHARIAH'S PROPHECY

67 And his father Zacharias was filled with the Holy Spirit *(pertains to the Holy Spirit helping him)*, and prophesied, saying *(concerned what John the Baptist would do and be in his Ministry)*,

68 Blessed *be* the Lord God of Israel; for He has visited and redeemed His people *(the word "Blessed," as used here, is a double syllable, "Bless-ed," and means that God is full of Grace, and actually the dispenser of Grace; the great Redemption had long been a promise; now it is to be a reality!)*,

69 And has raised up an Horn of Salvation for us in the house of His servant David *("an Horn of Salvation" is another name given to Christ by the Holy Spirit)*;

70 As He spoke by the mouth of his Holy Prophets, which have been since the world began *(this began with Gen. 3:15)*:

71 That we should be saved from our enemies, and from the hand of all who hate us *(proclaims Salvation by Grace, but as well to Israel, and will be fulfilled at the Second Coming)*;

72 To perform the mercy *promised* to our fathers, and to remember His Holy Covenant *(Jesus is the bearer of that "Mercy," actually He is Mercy!)*;

73 The oath which He swore to our father Abraham *(this "Oath" is found in Gen. 12:3; 17:4; 22:16-17)*,

74 That He would grant unto us, that we being delivered out of the hand of our enemies might serve Him without fear *(pertains to Salvation, and as well to the coming Kingdom Age)*,

75 In Holiness and Righteousness before Him, all the days of our life *(will totally be fulfilled in the coming Kingdom Age)*.

76 And you, child *(John the Baptist)*, shall be called the Prophet of the Highest: for you shall go before the Face of the Lord to prepare His ways *(John the Baptist would be the forerunner of the King about Whom the Prophets had written)*;

77 To give knowledge of Salvation unto His people by the remission of their sins *(which would be done by Jesus going to the Cross)*,

78 Through the tender Mercy of our God; whereby the Dayspring from on high has visited us *(another name for Christ, "The Dayspring from on High")*,

79 To give light to them who sit in darkness and *in* the shadow of death, to guide our feet into the way of peace *(Jesus is the Light of the world)*.

80 And the child grew, and waxed strong in spirit *(in the ways of the Lord)*, and was in the deserts till the day of his showing unto Israel *(he remained there until he was thirty years of age, before beginning his Ministry, which was the fulfilling of the Law [Num. 4:3])*.

CHAPTER 2
(A.D. 1)
THE BIRTH OF JESUS CHRIST

AND it came to pass in those days, that there went out a decree from Caesar Augustus *(Caius Octavius, the adopted son and successor of Julius Caesar; he reigned 29 B.C. to 14 B.C.)* that all the world should be taxed *(a figure of speech; a whole is put for a part; it was only the part of the world of which it spoke)*.

2 (*And* this taxing was first made when Cyrenius was governor of Syria.) *(This Verse should have been translated, "This census was before Cyrenius was Governor of Syria.")*

3 And all went to be taxed, every one into his own city.

4 And Joseph also went up from Galilee, out of the city of Nazareth, into Judaea, unto the city of David, which is called Bethlehem; (because he was of the house and lineage of David:) *(It was a distance of about 80 miles.)*

5 To be taxed with Mary his espoused wife, being great with child *(the trip must have been very difficult for her)*.

6 And so it was, that, while they were there, the days were accomplished that she should be delivered *(this concerned the most important delivery of a baby in human history; God*

would become flesh, and offer up Himself on the Cross as a Perfect Sacrifice in order to deliver humanity).

7 And she brought forth her Firstborn Son (this is meant to emphasize the fact that there were no other children up to this time; as well, it refutes the error of the Catholic Church, which claims that Mary, thereafter, had no other children, and remained a Virgin throughout her life; actually, Jesus had four brothers, "James, Joseph, Simon, and Jude," as well as two or three sisters [Mat. 13:55-56]), **and wrapped Him in swaddling clothes, and laid Him in a manger** (spoke of a feeding place for animals); **because there was no room for them in the inn** (the Inn of Bethlehem was of ancient duration, being mentioned in Jer. 41:17; this type of "Inn" was for the poorest of the poor, and offered little more than the shelter of its walls and roof).

THE ANGELIC ANNOUNCEMENT

8 And there were in the same country (referred to the area around Bethlehem) **shepherds abiding in the field** (pertained to the lowest caste in society at that time), **keeping watch over their flock by night** (gives indication that December 25th was not the day on which Jesus was born; it was the custom to send flocks out after the Passover, which was in April, to stay until the first rain in October or November).

9 And, lo, the Angel of the Lord came upon them (proclaims the fact that the Birth of the Lord was not announced to the notables of Israel, but rather to obscure shepherds), **and the glory of the Lord shone round about them: and they were sore afraid** (this was the visible token of the presence of the Eternal, which appeared first in the bush before Moses, and then in the pillar of fire and cloud, which guided the desert wanderings, and then in the Tabernacle and the Temple).

10 And the Angel said unto them, Fear not: for, behold, I bring you good tidings of great joy, which shall be to all people (includes all races).

11 For unto you is born this day in the city of David a Saviour, which is Christ the Lord (this Baby was not to become a King and a Saviour — He was born both).

12 And this *shall be* **a sign unto you; You shall find the baby wrapped in swaddling clothes, lying in a manger.**

13 And suddenly there was with the Angel a multitude of the Heavenly Host praising God, and saying (many other Angels had been with the Angel who spoke to the shepherds, but now the shepherds can see them as well; this presents sinless Angels praising God for sending the Redeemer; if they did so, certainly we should as well),

14 Glory to God in the highest, and on earth peace, good will toward men (Jesus is that "peace"; during His approximate 33 years of life on this Earth, the Roman Empire was relatively at peace; it was because the Prince of Peace was here; peace will not return until Jesus returns).

THE SHEPHERDS

15 And it came to pass, as the Angels were gone away from them into Heaven, the Shepherds said one to another, Let us now go even unto Bethlehem, and see this thing which is come to pass, which the Lord has made known unto us (proclaims one of the greatest honors in the whole of human history; the Lord would dispatch Angels only to these lowly shepherds in exclusion of all others).

16 And they came with haste, and found Mary, and Joseph (means they had to do a small amount of searching), **and the baby lying in a manger.**

17 And when they had seen *it* (should have been translated, "and when they had seen Him"; theirs were the first human eyes to see Jesus after His Birth, other than His foster Father and His Mother), **they made known abroad the saying which was told them concerning this Child** (they were the first Preachers to proclaim His Birth, as Mary Magdalene was the first to proclaim His Resurrection).

18 And all they who heard *it* **wondered at those things which were told them by the shepherds.**

19 But Mary kept all these things, and pondered *them* **in her heart** (means that she thought about them almost constantly, and no wonder!).

20 And the shepherds returned (to their flocks), **glorifying and praising God for all the things that they had heard and seen, as it was told unto them** (this proclaims the fact that these men truly knew the Lord, hence at least one of the reasons that the Angels appeared to them).

THE NAMING OF JESUS

21 And when eight days were accomplished for the circumcising of the Child (this was according to the Law of Moses; it is said that the

blood did not properly coagulate in the little baby boy until he was eight days old), His Name was called JESUS *(meaning Saviour)*, which was so named of the Angel before He was conceived in the womb.

THE PRESENTATION

22 And when the days of her purification according to the Law of Moses were accomplished *(speaks of forty days after the Birth of Jesus; it was eighty days in the case of a daughter [Lev. 12:1-6])*, they brought Him to Jerusalem, to present *Him* to the Lord *(all the firstborn of the boy babies belonged to the Lord, and were to be presented to Him as a token of His rightful claim to them [Num. 3:44; 18:15])*;

23 (As it is written in the Law of the Lord, Every male that opens the womb shall be called Holy to the Lord;) *(refers to the firstborn only)*.

24 And to offer a sacrifice according to that which is said in the Law of the Lord *(Lev. 12:8)*, A pair of turtledoves, or two young pigeons *(proclaimed that which could be offered in place of a "Lamb," providing the offerer could not afford the Lamb; this tells us that Mary and Joseph were poor, at least as far as this world's goods were concerned; it also tells us that Mary was not sinless, as claimed by the Catholic Church; if so, she would not have had to offer these Sacrifices for her impurity)*.

THE PROPHECY OF SIMEON

25 And, behold, there was a man in Jerusalem, whose name *was* Simeon; and the same man *was* just and devout, waiting for the consolation of Israel *(is a term describing the Coming and Ministry of the Messiah)*: and the Holy Spirit was upon him *(he was being led by the Spirit)*.

26 And it was revealed unto him by the Holy Spirit, that he should not see death, before he had seen the Lord's Christ *(consequently, each day he was anticipating this great event)*.

27 And he came by the Spirit into the Temple *(the Spirit of the Lord had pressed upon him strongly that at this particular time he was to go to the Temple)*: and when the parents *(Joseph and Mary)* brought in the Child Jesus, to do for Him after the custom of the Law *(Jesus was made of woman under the Law [Gal. 4:4]; the Law is mentioned five times in this Chapter, and so confirms the statement in Galatians; to save man justly doomed to death by the Law, it*

was necessary that Christ should be born under the Law),

28 Then took he Him up in his arms, and blessed God, and said *(proclaims Simeon the first on record to have "handled the Word of Life," other than Mary and Joseph)*,

29 Lord, now let Thou Thy servant depart in peace, according to Your Word *(indicates that it had been a number of years since the Lord had revealed to Simeon that He would actually see "the Lord's Christ")*:

30 For my eyes have seen Your Salvation *(Simeon didn't have to ask Mary Who the Child was; he recognized Him at once by inspiration as Jehovah's Anointed; Jesus is Salvation, and Salvation is Jesus)*,

31 Which You have prepared before the face of all people *(opens the door of Salvation to every human being on the face of the Earth, regardless of color, nationality, or country)*;

32 A light to lighten the Gentiles *(once again, the Holy Spirit includes all people)*, and the glory of Your people Israel *(regrettably, Israel would not accept Him)*.

33 And Joseph and His Mother marvelled at those things which were spoken of Him *(if it is to be noticed, the Holy Spirit through Luke wrote "Joseph and His Mother," and not "His Father and Mother"; the reason is obvious! Joseph was only His foster Father, so to speak)*.

34 And Simeon blessed them *(refers only to Joseph and Mary, and not Jesus; while Christ blesses all, none are qualified to bless Christ; sometimes the word, "blessed," is used in the sense of "praise," which then becomes not only acceptable, but desirable)*, and said unto Mary His mother, Behold, this *Child is* set for the fall and rising again of many in Israel *(according to the acceptance or rejection of Christ)*; and for a sign which shall be spoken against *(men who have agreed in nothing else have agreed in hating Christ)*;

35 (Yes, a sword shall pierce through your own soul also,) *(pertained to the rejection of Jesus' Ministry by the religious leaders of Israel, and ultimately His Crucifixion on the Cross)* that the thoughts of many hearts may be revealed *(presents the purpose of the Gospel of Christ; Mary's own heart, being carnal as all others, had to come under the rays of this great light, and her soul had to feel the piercing of the Divine Sword of the Word of God; she was indeed blessed as the chosen Vessel of the Incarnation, but all women who follow Jesus are as blessed [Lk. 11:27])*.

THE ADORATION OF ANNA

36 And there was one Anna, a Prophetess, the daughter of Phanuel (*presents this dear lady as a Preacher of the Gospel; in the Bible the first woman to Prophesy was Rachel, even though she is not called a Prophetess [Gen. 30:24]*), of the Tribe of Aser (*refers to the Tribe of Asher*): she was of a great age, and had lived with an husband seven years from her virginity (*means that her husband died seven years after they were married, and she never remarried*);

37 And she *was* a widow of about fourscore and four years (*it had been eighty-four years since her husband had died; consequently, she was well over one hundred years old*), which departed not from the Temple (*she had literally lived in the Temple, probably being provided a small room or chamber, and was assigned some small tasks*), but served *God* with fastings and prayers night and day (*notes her wonderful consecration to the Lord*).

38 And she coming in that instant gave thanks likewise unto the Lord (*proclaims the fact that the Holy Spirit revealed unto her that this Child was indeed the Messiah*), and spoke of Him to all them who looked for redemption in Jerusalem (*she related to all her experience at seeing the Child, and the Lord had revealed to her that He was the Messiah; they both, Simeon and Anna, loved the Courts of Jehovah's House, and He met them there*).

39 And when they had performed all things according to the Law of the Lord (*referred to the Law of Moses*), they returned into Galilee, to their own city Nazareth (*Luke does not mention the visit of the Wise men, or the flight into Egypt as Matthew does not mention the shepherds*).

40 And the Child grew, and waxed strong in spirit (*Jesus did not have a sin nature, so this means that He was never sick, and neither did He ever sin*), filled with wisdom (*there is every evidence that Jesus began studying the Bible from the time He learned to read*): and the Grace of God was upon Him (*the Goodness of God*).

JESUS AS A BOY

41 Now His parents went to Jerusalem every year at the Feast of the Passover (*the word, "went" means that they were accustomed to going, for they were Godly people*).

42 And when He (*Jesus*) was twelve years old (*refers to the age at which every Jewish boy became "a son of the Law"*), they went up to Jerusalem after the custom of the Feast (*Jerusalem was where the Feast was held, and in fact, must be held*).

43 And when they had fulfilled the days (*pertained to seven days, which actually incorporated three Feasts: The Feast of Passover, the Feast of Unleavened Bread, and the Feast of Firstfruits*), as they returned (*were leaving Jerusalem to go to Nazareth*), the Child Jesus tarried behind in Jerusalem (*at twelve years of age, every Jewish boy from henceforth was treated as an Adult, which meant that there was now much less supervision than had previously been*); and Joseph and His mother knew not *of it* (*Joseph and Mary were not being lax in their supervision; they were treating Jesus as an adult, which the custom then demanded, and felt that He would join up with them at a given point*).

44 But they, supposing Him to have been in the company (*with another group going to Nazareth*), went a day's journey (*again, this was the custom in those days, with all groups headed to a certain destination, meeting at a particular point, and then going together*); and they sought Him among *their* kinsfolk and acquaintance.

45 And when they found Him not, they turned back again to Jerusalem, seeking Him (*refers to a diligent search; it also speaks of concern and anxiety*).

46 And it came to pass, that after three days they found Him in the Temple (*probably refers to the third day after originally leaving Jerusalem; they spent the first day traveling from Jerusalem to the designated meeting point; upon not finding Jesus, they then journeyed back to Jerusalem the next day; on the third day, they found Him in the Temple*), sitting in the midst of the doctors (*included the most famous Bible Scholars of that day*), both hearing them, and asking them questions (*what a sight this must have been, these most famous doctors of the Mosaic Law with this twelve-year-old Boy sitting in their midst, and with most of the attention directed toward Him; it is believed that Nicodemus was in this group*).

47 And all who heard Him were astonished at His understanding and answers (*the word, "astonished" in the Greek Text refers to amazement to such an extent that one is beside oneself; in truth, His "understanding and answers" were far beyond that of these learned Doctors*).

48 And when they saw Him, they were amazed (*referring to His parents*): and His mother said unto Him, Son, why have you

thus dealt with us? *(The possibility does exist that the Holy Spirit had Jesus to do this purposely, in order to awaken Mary and Joseph to His true Mission and Purpose, even though it would not truly begin until He was thirty years of age.)* behold, Your Father and I have sought You sorrowing *(Mary used the phrase, "Your Father," and Jesus gently reminded her in the next Verse Who His Father actually was; legally, Joseph was His Father, but only in the foster sense).*

49 And He said unto them, How is it that you sought Me? *(He gently reminded them that they should have known Who He was, and His Mission.)* wist you not that I must be about My Father's business? *(This was His first recorded utterance; with the words, "It is finished," His last recorded utterance before His Crucifixion [Jn. 19:30], which means He Finished the Father's Business.)*

50 And they understood not the saying which He spoke unto them *(they should have understood!).*

51 And He went down with them, and came to Nazareth, and was subject unto them *(concerns the next eighteen years)*: but His mother kept all these sayings in her heart *(refers to all that pertained to Jesus).*

52 And Jesus increased in wisdom and stature, and in favour with God and man *(this means that He perfectly kept the Law of God, and did perfectly the Will of God).*

CHAPTER 3
(A.D. 26)
JOHN THE BAPTIST

NOW in the fifteenth year of the reign of Tiberius Caesar *(the stepson of the Emperor Augustus, whom he succeeded; he reigned from 14 B.C. to A.D. 37, consequently covering the entire span of Jesus' Life and Ministry)*, Pontius Pilate being Governor of Judaea, and Herod being Tetrarch of Galilee *(he was known as "Antipas"; he was a son of Herod the Great, and reigned for more than forty years)*, and his brother Philip Tetrarch of Ituraea and of the region of Trachonitis *(the area northeast of the Sea of Galilee, which included Caesarea Philippi, which was actually built by him)*, and Lysanias the Tetrarch of Abilene *(referred to the district now known as southern Lebanon; the title "Tetrarch" meant "ruler of a fourth part," but actually came to be used of all Governors).*

2 Annas and Caiaphas being the High Priests *(the High Priests were supposed to be descendants of Aaron; however, the office was now controlled by Rome, with both men now serving somewhat in this capacity)*, the Word of God came unto John the son of Zacharias in the wilderness *(it was now time for John to begin his Ministry).*

3 And he came into all the country about Jordan *(the location of his Ministry centered around the Jordan River)*, preaching the baptism of repentance for the remission of sins *(he was preaching personal Repentance which guaranteed remission of sins, which was to be followed by Water Baptism)*;

4 As it is written in the Book of the words of Isaiah the Prophet *(Isa. 40:3-5)*, saying, The voice of one crying in the wilderness *(John's Ministry was predicted by Isaiah some 800 years before)*, Prepare you the Way of the Lord, make His paths straight *(Israel must come in line with the Word of God, inasmuch as the Messiah is about to be introduced).*

5 Every valley shall be filled, and every mountain and hill shall be brought low; and the crooked shall be made straight, and the rough ways *shall be* made smooth *(concerns a proper interpretation of the Word of God, which produces proper lives)*;

6 And all flesh shall see the Salvation of God *(all Israel would see the Lord Jesus Christ, their Messiah, Who is the "Salvation of God").*

7 Then said he to the multitude who came forth to be baptized of him *(Water Baptism in this fashion, was new to Israel)*, O generation of vipers *(this is what the Holy Spirit through John said of the Israel of that time)*, who has warned you to flee from the wrath to come? *(Wrath is guaranteed to come on all Christ rejecters; this means that one can flee that wrath only by accepting Christ.)*

8 Bring forth therefore fruits worthy of repentance *(in effect, says that Water Baptism would do them no good unless there had first been Repentance, and if there was true Repentance, fruits would be evident)*, and begin not to say within yourselves, We have Abraham to *our* father *(there is no such thing as a national salvation)*: for I say unto you, That God is able of these stones to raise up children unto Abraham *(proclaims John striking boldly at the very root of Jewish pride).*

9 And now also the axe is laid unto the root of the trees *(the "trees" spoke of Israel, and the "axe" spoke of the Judgment of God; it did not say that the axe was then severing the roots, but that it was poised to do so, that is if*

Repentance was not forthcoming): **every tree therefore which brings not forth good fruit is hewn down, and cast into the fire** *(this is a Law of God that applies to every individual person).*

10 **And the people asked him, saying, What shall we do then?** *(We come again, as will be obvious, to the Fruits of Repentance.)*

11 **He answered and said unto them, He who has two coats, let him impart to him who has none; and he who has meat, let him do likewise** *(John's answer has no reference to the doing of these things as the cause of Salvation, but rather the result).*

12 **Then came also publicans to be baptized, and said unto him, Master, what shall we do?** *(Publicans were tax-collectors, in a sense employees of Rome and, thereby, looked at as traitors by Israel as a whole; most didn't even believe that publicans could be saved.)*

13 **And he said unto them, Exact no more than that which is appointed you** *(we find here that John treated the publicans no different than he did the Pharisees, who claimed to be so religious; the message was the same to all).*

14 **And the soldiers likewise demanded of him, saying, And what shall we do?** *(Israel had no army, so these could very well have been Gentiles.)* **And he said unto them, Do violence to no man, neither accuse** *any* **falsely; and be content with your wages** *(these men, both publicans and soldiers, are not bidden by the inspired Prophet of the Highest to change their way of life, but only its manner).*

JOHN'S PREDICTION OF JESUS

15 **And as the people were in expectation** *(proclaims the fact that all of Israel at that time were looking for the Messiah),* **and all men mused in their hearts of John, whether he were the Christ, or not** *(had they known the Word, they would have known better)*;

16 **John answered, saying unto** *them* **all, I indeed baptize you with water** *(the best that mortal man can do, even one as holy as John the Baptist)*; **but One mightier than I comes** *(only the Almighty can set men free),* **the latchet of Whose shoes I am not worthy to unloose** *(presents the humility of John, and the humility demanded of all)*: **He shall baptize you with the Holy Spirit and with fire** *(this was made possible by the Cross, and was fulfilled according to Acts 2:4, with untold millions having received this experience)*:

17 **Whose fan** *is* **in His hand** *(the fan used to*

blow the chaff away from the wheat), **and He will thoroughly purge His floor** *(will separate the chaff from the wheat, which is a violent process),* **and will gather the wheat into His garner** *(the wheat alone is accepted)*; **but the chaff He will burn with fire unquenchable** *(all that's not of God will be consigned to Hell).*

18 **And many other things in his exhortation preached he unto the people** *(preaching was God's Way then, and preaching is God's Way now).*

19 **But Herod the Tetrarch, being reproved by him** *(by John the Baptist)* **for Herodias his brother Philip's wife** *(Herod had taken Philip's wife for himself),* **and for all the evils which Herod had done** *(an evil depraved man),*

20 **Added yet this above all, that he shut up John in prison** *(the Holy Spirit says that this was the worst thing Herod did; he put his hand on the Lord's anointed).*

JOHN BAPTIZES JESUS

21 **Now when all the people were baptized** *(were being baptized),* **it came to pass, that Jesus also being baptized** *(this was to testify of His Death, Burial, and Resurrection, of which Water Baptism is a Type),* **and praying** *(as He came up out of the water, He came up praying),* **the Heaven was opened** *(Heaven had been closed to man since the Fall; through Jesus it would now open),*

22 **And the Holy Spirit descended in a bodily shape like a Dove upon Him** *(the Holy Spirit is a Person, the Third Person of the Godhead, separate from the Father and the Son),* **and a voice came from Heaven, which said** *(the voice of God the Father),* **You are My Beloved Son** *(literally, "as for You," in contradistinction to all others)*; **in You I am well pleased** *(God is pleased with us, only as long as we are in Christ).*

THE GENEALOGY OF JESUS

23 **And Jesus Himself began to be about thirty years of age** *(at this age a Priest entered into his Office [Num. 4:3]; Jesus is our Great High Priest),* **being (as was supposed)** *(should have been translated, "being by legal adoption")* **the son of Joseph, which was** *the son* **of Heli** *(Joseph was the son of Jacob [Mat. 1:16] by birth and the son of Heli by marriage; it was ordained in Num., Chpt. 36 that the man who married the daughter of a father having no son became the son of that father and inherited his property),*

24 Which was *the son* of Matthat, which was *the son* of Levi, which was *the son* of Melchi, which was *the son* of Janna, which was *the son* of Joseph,

25 Which was *the son* of Mattathias, which was *the son* of Amos, which was *the son* of Naum, which was *the son* of Esli, which was *the son* of Nagge,

26 Which was *the son* of Maath, which was *the son* of Mattathias, which was *the son* of Semei, which was *the son* of Joseph, which was *the son* of Juda,

27 Which was *the son* of Joanna, which was *the son* of Rhesa, which was *the son* of Zorobabel, which was *the son* of Salathiel, which was *the son* of Neri,

28 Which was *the son* of Melchi, which was *the son* of Addi, which was *the son* of Cosam, which was *the son* of Elmodam, which was *the son* of Er,

29 Which was *the son* of Jose, which was *the son* of Eliezer, which was *the son* of Jorim, which was *the son* of Matthat, which was *the son* of Levi,

30 Which was *the son* of Simeon, which was *the son* of Juda, which was *the son* of Joseph, which was *the son* of Jonan, which was *the son* of Eliakim,

31 Which was *the son* of Melea, which was *the son* of Menan, which was *the son* of Mattatha, which was *the son* of Nathan, which was *the son* of David,

32 Which was *the son* of Jesse, which was *the son* of Obed, which was *the son* of Booz *(Boaz)*, which was *the son* of Salmon, which was *the son* of Naasson,

33 Which was *the son* of Aminadab, which was *the son* of Aram, which was *the son* of Esrom, which was *the son* of Phares, which was *the son* of Juda,

34 Which was *the son* of Jacob, which was *the son* of Isaac, which was *the son* of Abraham, which was *the son* of Thara, which was *the son* of Nachor,

35 Which was *the son* of Saruch, which was *the son* of Ragau, which was *the son* of Phalec, which was *the son* of Heber, which was *the son* of Sala,

36 Which was *the son* of Cainan, which was *the son* of Arphaxad, which was *the son* of Sem *(Shem)*, which was *the son* of Noe *(Noah)*, which was *the son* of Lamech,

37 Which was *the son* of Mathusala *(Methuselah)*, which was *the son* of Enoch, which was *the son* of Jared, which was *the son* of Maleleel, which was *the son* of Cainan,

38 Which was *the son* of Enos, which was *the son* of Seth, which was *the son* of Adam, which was *the Son* of God *(was a son of God by creation, and not by the Born-Again experience; it was the intention of God that humanity bring sons and daughters of God into the world, which they could do by procreation; however, due to the Fall, children cannot be born in the likeness of God, but rather in the likeness of Adam, i.e., the sinful nature; as wonderful as being in the genealogy of Christ was, some, if not many, of these individuals were not saved; and in fact, some of them were ungodly; this proves that Salvation does not come by inheritance or genealogy; it comes only by accepting Christ as one's Saviour [Jn. 3:16]).*

CHAPTER 4
(A.D. 27)
THE TEMPTATION OF JESUS

AND Jesus being full of the Holy Spirit *(in Christ's case, He received the Spirit without measure [Jn. 3:34; Acts 10:38])* returned from Jordan *(His Water Baptism)*, and was led by the Spirit into the wilderness *(speaks of great urgency by the Spirit)*,

2 Being forty days tempted of the devil *(refers to being tempted for the entirety of this time; "forty" is God's number for probation).* And in those days He did eat nothing *(speaks of Him fasting for forty days and nights)*: and when they were ended, He afterward hungered *(some claim that God suspended hunger during this forty days and nights regarding Christ, but that is not so; Jesus suffered hunger exactly as we do).*

3 And the devil said unto Him *(Satan is a fallen Angel, who led a revolution against God in eternity past; he is at least one of the most powerful Angels ever created by God, and served God in righteousness and holiness for an undetermined period of time before his Fall [Isa., Chpt. 14; Ezek., Chpt. 28])*, If You be the Son of God *(should have been translated, "since You are the Son of God")*, command this stone that it be made bread *(the temptation was that Jesus use His Power for personal gratification, which was outside the Will of God).*

4 And Jesus answered him, saying, It is written, That man shall not live by bread alone, but by every Word of God *([Deut. 8:3], Jesus answered Satan's temptation with the Word; merely quoting it will not garner the same*

results; Jesus also said, "you shall know the Truth, and the Truth shall make you free" [Jn. 8:32]).

5 And the devil, taking Him up into an high mountain *(constitutes that which was literally done, at least as it regards the mountain),* **showed unto Him all the Kingdoms of the world in a moment of time** *(this was not literally, but rather was done by suggestion).*

6 And the devil said unto Him, All this power will I give You, and the glory of them *(proclaims Satan's method of operation; he has captured many by the offer of a part of the glory of earthly dominion)*: **for that is delivered unto me** *(referred back to the Garden of Eden when Satan gained such authority because of the default of Adam and Eve)*; **and to whomsoever I will I give it** *(makes Satan the pseudo-ruler of this world [Jn. 12:31; II Cor. 4:4; Eph. 2:1-3; Rev. 13:2, 7]; however, even then his authority is limited, with the Lord actually having the final say in everything).*

7 If You therefore will worship me, all shall be Yours *(was a lie; but yet, the world has fallen for this lie from the beginning of time; Satan was attempting to have Christ gain the world without going through the Cross; He is still proposing the same, and mostly going through the Church to do such; every Believer is an "heir of the world," but only through the Cross [Rom. 4:13]).*

8 And Jesus answered and said unto him, Get thee behind Me, Satan: for it is written, You shall worship the Lord your God, and Him only shall you serve *([Deut. 6:13; 10:20], the answer given by Christ addresses itself to worship, as the first addressed itself to desire; men desire the wrong thing, the opposite of the Word of God, and worship the wrong thing, that proposed by Satan).*

9 And he *(Satan)* **brought Him** *(Jesus)* **to Jerusalem, and set Him on a pinnacle of the Temple** *(seems to have been literally done, meaning that it was not a vision),* **and said unto Him, If You be the Son of God** *(since You are the Son of God),* **cast Yourself down from hence:**

10 For it is written, He shall give His Angels charge over You, to keep You *(a misquote from Psalms 91:11-12; the correct quotation is, "to keep you in all Your ways," which refers to the "Ways of God"; protection is guaranteed under those circumstances, but not as Satan said):*

11 And in *their* **hands they shall bear You up, lest at any time You dash Your foot against a stone** *(Satan again misquoted the Text by adding the words "at any time," which changes the*

meaning altogether; this tells us that Satan knows the Word very well, and to his own advantage subtly changes it to make it say something it originally did not say; as well, if one is to notice, Satan didn't quote the Thirteenth Verse in the 91st Psalm, for it predicts his destruction by the Lord Jesus Christ).

12 And Jesus answering said unto him, It is said, You shall not tempt the Lord your God *(expresses the sin of presumption; presumption is an attitude or belief dictated by probability; in other words, God's Word is not probable, but certain).*

13 And when the devil had ended all the temptation, he departed from Him for a season *(means that he would return, which he no doubt did again and again; the implication is that Jesus was tempted by Satan throughout His Ministry).*

14 And Jesus returned in the Power of the Spirit into Galilee *(there is no power without the Holy Spirit)*: **and there went out a fame of Him through all the region round about** *(concerned all the miracles being performed, which actually began with the changing of the water to wine at Cana [Jn. 2:1-11]).*

NAZARETH

15 And He taught in their Synagogues, being glorified of all *(this was the beginning; it would soon change).*

16 And He came to Nazareth, where He had been brought up *(makes vivid the fact that Jesus was Very Man, even as He was Very God)*: **and, as His custom was** *(in our language presently He was faithful to Church),* **He went into the Synagogue on the Sabbath day, and stood up for to read** *(it was common to ask visitors to expound on the Word).*

17 And there was delivered unto Him the Book *(Scroll)* **of the Prophet Isaiah. And when He had opened the Book, He found the place where it was written** *(Isa. 61:1),*

18 The Spirit of the Lord *is* **upon Me** *(we learn here of the absolute necessity of the Person and Work of the Holy Spirit within our lives),* **because He has anointed Me** *(Jesus is the ultimate Anointed One; consequently, the Anointing of the Holy Spirit actually belongs to Christ, and the Anointing we have actually comes by His Authority [Jn. 16:14])* **to Preach the Gospel to the poor** *(the poor in spirit)*; **He has sent Me to heal the brokenhearted** *(sin breaks the heart, or else is responsible for it being broken; only*

Jesus can heal this malady), to Preach deliverance to the captives *(if it is to be noticed, He didn't say to "deliver the captives," but rather "Preach deliverance," which refers to the Cross [Jn. 8:32])*, and recovering of sight to the blind *(the Gospel opens the eyes of those who are spiritually blind)*, to set at liberty them who are bruised *(the vicissitudes of life at times place a person in a mental or spiritual prison; the Lord Alone, and through what He did at the Cross, can open this prison door)*,

19 To Preach the acceptable Year of the Lord *(it is believed that the day, on which Jesus delivered this Message was the first day of the year of Jubilee)*.

20 And He closed the book, and He gave *it* again to the Minister, and sat down *(portrays the custom of that time)*. And the eyes of all them who were in the Synagogue were fastened on Him *(even though most there would fail to see it, this represented a moment far exceeding anything these people had ever known)*.

21 And He began to say unto them, This day is this Scripture fulfilled in your ears *(in effect, He is saying, "I am the Messiah," the fulfillment of these Scriptures)*.

22 And all bear Him witness *(all understood exactly what He said, but all did not believe Him)*, and wondered at the gracious words which proceeded out of His mouth *(means that we are given only a small portion of the things He actually said)*. And they said, Is not this Joseph's Son? *(This refers to the fact that they could not equate these "gracious words" with the carpenter they had known for about thirty years.)*

23 And He said unto them, You will surely say unto Me this Proverb, Physician, heal Yourself *(how could this carpenter be the Messiah?)*: whatsoever we have heard done in Capernaum, do also here in your country *(perform the same miracles; but they would give him no opportunity to do so)*.

24 And He said, Verily I say unto you, No Prophet is accepted in his own country *(He predicts their unbelief)*.

25 But I tell you of a truth *(will proclaim in no uncertain terms Israel's problem of self-righteousness resulting from pride)*, many widows were in Israel in the days of Elijah, when the Heaven was shut up three years and six months, when great famine was throughout all the land *(proclaims the time of Ahab, and the great wickedness concerning the northern kingdom of Israel)*;

26 But unto none of them was Elijah sent, save unto Sarepta, *a city* of Sidon, unto a woman *who was* a widow *(she was a Gentile as well)*.

27 And many lepers were in Israel in the time of Elisha the Prophet; and none of them was cleansed, saving Naaman the Syrian *(another Gentile)*.

28 And all they in the Synagogue, when they heard these words, were filled with wrath *(incensed that He would hold up two Gentiles as examples of receiving from the Lord, while the Jews were shut out; He, in effect, was telling them that this is what would happen to Israel; the Gentiles would receive Him but Israel would refuse Him; "wrath" is generally the response of unbelief)*,

29 And rose up, and thrust Him out of the city *(means that they bodily seized Him, taking Him by force out of the Synagogue and out of the city; this was their response to their own Messiah, God's only Son, and their only Saviour)*, and led Him unto the brow of the hill whereon their city was built, that they might cast Him down headlong *(presents Nazareth, His Own village, as the first to seek His Death)*.

30 But He passing through the midst of them went His way *(did so by the Power of God, and left never to return)*,

HEALINGS AND DELIVERANCE

31 And came down to Capernaum, a city of Galilee *(this would be His Home and Headquarters for the entirety of His Ministry of some three and one half years)*, and taught them on the Sabbath days *(in their Synagogues)*.

32 And they were astonished at His doctrine *(had to do with the manner in which He explained the Scriptures)*: for His Word was with power *(pertained to the Anointing of the Holy Spirit, which they had never experienced before)*.

33 And in the Synagogue there was a man, which had a spirit of an unclean devil *(demon)*, and cried out with a loud voice *(the voice of this demon spirit using the vocal cords of the man)*,

34 Saying, Let *us* alone *(refers to the fact that Jesus Alone has power over these spirits of darkness)*; what have we to do with You, *Thou* Jesus of Nazareth? *(This portrays the total separation of the spirit world of Light from the spirit world of darkness.)* Are You come to destroy us? I know You Who You are; the Holy One of God *(knowing Who He was, they also knew that He had come to destroy their kingdom of darkness)*.

35 And Jesus rebuked him *(rebuked the evil spirit in the man)*, saying, Hold your peace

(shut up), and come out of him *(a command that had to be obeyed)*. And when the devil had thrown him in the midst *(threw him down)*, he came out of him, and hurt him not *(meaning that he was commanded by the Lord to do no damage upon his exit)*.

36 And they were all amazed, and spoke among themselves, saying, What a word *is* this! *(presents that which they had never before seen)* for with authority and power He Commands the unclean spirits, and they come out *(they recognized His "Authority" and "Power")*.

37 And the fame of Him went out into every place of the country round about.

PETER'S MOTHER-IN-LAW

38 And He arose out of the Synagogue, and entered into Simon's house *(this was His headquarters during the three and one half years of His public Ministry)*. And Simon's wife's mother was taken with a great fever *(was life threatening)*; and they besought Him for her *(asked Him to heal her)*.

39 And He stood over her, and rebuked the fever *(indicates that this was an evil spirit causing the fever)*; and it left her *(the spirit left along with the sickness)*: and immediately she arose and ministered unto them *(speaks of an instant recovery, with her probably helping to prepare an evening meal)*.

CASTING OUT DEMONS

40 Now when the sun was setting *(meaning the Sabbath was ending; each new day in Jewish reckoning at that time began at the setting of the sun, where ours begin at midnight)*, all they who had any sick with divers diseases brought them unto Him; and He laid His hands on every one of them, and healed them.

41 And devils *(demons)* also came out of many, crying out *(speaks of deliverances other than healings)*, and saying, You are Christ the Son of God *(speaks of these spirits having personalities and intelligence; they knew who He was, even though the religious leaders of Israel didn't)*. And He rebuking *them* suffered them not to speak: for they knew that He was Christ *(He wanted no testimony from them)*.

42 And when it was day *(insinuates that He Ministered all night long)*, He departed and went into a desert place *(He desired a place of solitude for privacy)*: and the people sought Him, and came unto Him, and stayed Him,

that He should not depart from them *(they desired that He spend all His Time in Capernaum and not go elsewhere)*.

43 And He said unto them, I must Preach the Kingdom of God to other cities also: for therefore Am I sent *(modern thought belittles Preaching and exalts ceremony; the Eternal Son of God was wholly a Preacher; this fact, and the opposition of Satan to Preaching, demonstrates its importance)*.

44 And He Preached in the Synagogues of Galilee.

CHAPTER 5
(A.D. 31)
A BORROWED SHIP

AND it came to pass, that, as the people pressed upon Him to hear the Word of God, He stood by the lake of Gennesaret *(the Sea of Galilee)*,

2 And saw two ships standing by the lake *(two among the many)*: but the fishermen were gone out of them, and were washing *their* nets *(Peter, Andrew, James, and John had fished all night and caught nothing)*.

3 And he entered into one of the ships, which was Simon's *(proclaims Him borrowing this vessel to serve as a platform or pulpit)*, and prayed him that he would thrust out a little from the land. And He sat down *(the custom then)*, and taught the people out of the ship.

THE MIRACLE

4 Now when He had left speaking *(had finished preaching and teaching)*, He said unto Simon, Launch out into the deep, and let down your nets for a draught *(came as a surprise to these fishermen; they had fished all night and caught nothing, so they must have wondered as to what He was doing; in effect, He will pay for the use of the boat; God will owe man nothing)*.

5 And Simon answering said unto Him, Master, we have toiled all the night, and have taken nothing: nevertheless at Your Word I will let down the net *(the idea is that Peter would not have bothered himself to have let down the net on the word of anyone else other than Jesus)*.

6 And when they had this done, they inclosed a great multitude of fishes: and their net broke *(so many fish that it broke the net)*.

7 And they beckoned unto *their* partners *(Peter and Andrew beckoned to James and John)*, which were in the other ship, that they should

come and help them. And they came, and filled both the ships, so that they began to sink (*Christ had the same power over the fish of the sea as He had over the frogs, lice, and locusts of Egypt*).

8 When Simon Peter saw *it* (*proclaims the effect of this lesson is not to give Simon high thoughts of himself, but low thoughts; such is ever the effect of a manifestation of Divine Power and Grace upon the conscience of fallen man*), he fell down at Jesus' knees, saying, Depart from me; for I am a sinful man, O Lord (*proclaims this miracle revealing the hidden unbelief of Simon's heart, for without a doubt, when casting the nets he said to himself: "we shall catch nothing"*).

9 For he was astonished, and all who were with him, at the draught of the fishes which they had taken:

10 And so *was* also James, and John, the sons of Zebedee, which were partners with Simon. And Jesus said unto Simon, Fear not; from henceforth you shall catch men (*the first recorded instance of Jesus using the words, "fear not," with His Disciples; His statement elevated them to being fishers of men, and constituted their call to Discipleship, and as Apostles*).

11 And when they had brought their ships to land, they forsook all, and followed Him (*means they immediately did so*).

JESUS HEALS A LEPER

12 And it came to pass, when He was in a certain city, behold a man full of leprosy (*the man was in the last stages of leprosy, actually close to death*): who seeing Jesus fell on *his* face, and besought Him, saying, Lord, if You will, You can make me clean (*he expressed doubt about the willingness of Jesus, rather than His Power; many Jews at that time, knowing that leprosy was a type of sin, didn't even believe that a leper could be saved; hence the statement of this leper concerning the willingness of Christ to cleanse Him*).

13 And He put forth *His* hand, and touched him, saying, I will: be thou clean (*His answer and action forever settled the question of God's Will regarding the healing of the sick*). And immediately the leprosy departed from him (*the Greek structure of the sentence proclaims the fact that it was Jesus' Word which healed the man, so when He touched him, healing had already been effected*).

14 And he charged him to tell no man: but go, and show yourself to the Priest, and offer for your cleansing, according as Moses commanded, for a testimony unto them (*this concerned the Law of the cleansing of the Leper* [*Lev., Chpt. 14*]).

15 But so much the more went there a fame abroad of Him: and great multitudes came together to hear, and to be healed by Him of their infirmities.

16 And He withdrew Himself into the wilderness, and prayed (*if Jesus had to pray, what about us?!*).

HEALING AND FORGIVENESS

17 And it came to pass on a certain day, as He was teaching, that there were Pharisees and Doctors of the Law sitting by, which were come out of every town of Galilee, and Judaea, and Jerusalem (*now the great opposition will begin*): and the power of the Lord was *present* to heal them (*the implication is that sick people were being healed without Jesus even addressing their sicknesses or infirmities; the Spirit of God emanating from Him overwhelmed the sicknesses and diseases; in other words, His mere Presence brought healing*).

18 And, behold, men brought in a bed a man which was taken with a palsy (*four men as Mark testified; the man had a type of "paralysis"*): and they sought *means* to bring him in, and to lay *him* before Him (*the place was so thronged with people that they could not get into the house*).

19 And when they could not find by what *way* they might bring him in because of the multitude, they went upon the housetop (*houses are normally flat on top in that part of the world*), and let him down through the tiling with *his* couch into the midst before Jesus (*they probably enlarged a trap door that was in the ceiling*).

20 And when He saw their faith (*true Faith always has action*), He said unto him, Man, your sins are forgiven you (*indicates that the wretched physical condition of the sick man was due to his sinful life; yet, Jesus treated him with the utmost of kindness*).

21 And the Scribes and the Pharisees began to reason, saying, Who is this which speaks blasphemies? Who can forgive sins, but God alone? (*There was a hostile atmosphere in the room, and our Lord sensed it. What they thought in their hearts was expressed on their faces, and in their actions, and very personalities.*)

22 But when Jesus perceived their thoughts (*the Holy Spirit revealed to Him what they were thinking*), He answering said unto them, What reason ye in your hearts? (*He not only could*

forgive sins, but He could read the minds of individuals as the Holy Spirit revealed it to Him, proving that He was also God.)

23 Whether is easier, to say, Your sins be forgiven you; or to say, Rise up and walk? (The idea of the question as posed by Christ is that God Alone could do both, "forgive and heal.")

24 But that you may know that the Son of Man has power upon earth to forgive sins (to prove that power), (He said unto the sick of the palsy,) I say unto you, Arise, and take up Your couch, and go into your house.

25 And immediately he rose up before them (implying that he could not do so previously), and took up that whereon he lay (carried his own bed), and departed to his own house, Glorifying God (he had come sick, unable to walk, and left healed and well; no wonder he Glorified God).

26 And they were all amazed (the Truth was incontestable), and they Glorified God (insinuating that even the Scribes and Pharisees did so), and were filled with fear, saying, We have seen strange things today (in fact, they had seen what no human beings had ever before seen).

JESUS CALLS MATTHEW

27 And after these things He went forth, and saw a Publican (a tax-collector), named Levi (Matthew), sitting at the receipt of custom (this was a lucrative occupation, but one despised by the Jews; in other words, they hated tax-collectors because they represented Rome; the task was so odious that most Publicans hired others to physically collect the taxes; but it seemed that Matthew little cared what people thought of him): and He (Jesus) said unto him (Matthew), Follow Me (it was not in Indian-file nature, with one following another, but a side-by-side walk down the same road).

28 And he left all, rose up, and followed Him (he left his tax-collector's position, and did so immediately).

29 And Levi made Him (Jesus) a great feast in his own house (speaks of the fact that Matthew was a person of consideration and position): and there was a great company of Publicans and of others who sat down with them (speaks of a group of people who were probably not even allowed in the Synagogues).

THE PHARISEES

30 But their Scribes (were supposed to be expert in the Law of Moses) and Pharisees (the fundamentalist religious party in Israel) murmured against His Disciples, saying, Why do ye eat and drink with Publicans and sinners? (They would not have even remotely considered having a meal with any of these people, much less treating them in a friendly fashion.)

31 And Jesus answering said unto them, They who are whole need not a physician; but they who are sick (the association with "Publicans and sinners" was not the Pharisees' problem, but rather their black hearts, which were more wicked in the sight of God even than the ones whom they were condemning).

32 I came not to call the righteous, but sinners to repentance (in other words, the very reason I have come is for these people you are condemning).

FASTING

33 And they said unto Him, Why do the disciples of John fast often, and make prayers, and likewise the disciples of the Pharisees (this question was probably asked by the disciples of John the Baptist); but yours eat and drink? (This referred to the Disciples of Jesus in comparison to the disciples of John.)

34 And He said unto them, Can you make the children of the bridechamber fast, while the bridegroom is with them? (The object of all that is done by the Believer, whether it be fasting or feasting, is Jesus. He Alone is the focal point of all. The fasting done previously under the Old Covenant was in relationship to His Coming, which speaks of the First Advent because, as is obvious, He was not with them at that time. He is now with them, so there is no need for fasting, at least at that particular time.)

35 But the days will come, when the bridegroom (Christ) shall be taken away from them (Believers), and then shall they fast in those days (it refers to the period of time of the Church Age, which has lasted now for about 2,000 years; while the reasons for fasting are varied and many, the main reason of all pertains to Him not being here, which involves many things; when He comes back, joy, prosperity, and feasting will then be the order of the entirety of the world).

36 And He spoke also a Parable unto them; No man puts a piece of a new garment upon an old; if otherwise, then both the new makes a rent, and the piece that was taken out of the new agrees not with the old (the New Covenant is to be complete within itself, and not a part of

the Old; in other words, the New Covenant cannot be patched onto the Old Covenant).

37 And no man puts new wine into old bottles *(wineskins)*; else the new wine will burst the bottles, and be spilled, and the bottles shall perish *(to try to attach the New Covenant to the Old would destroy both Covenants)*.

38 But new wine *(New Covenant)* must be put into new bottles *(new skins)*; and both are preserved *(the "new wine" is the New Covenant; the "new bottles" constitute the Church; this means that Judaism will have no place whatsoever in Christianity, even though the roots of Christianity are definitely in Judaism)*.

39 No man also having drunk old *wine* straightway *(immediately)* desires new: for he says, The old is better *(the Old Covenant had to be done away with completely, or else the New would not have been accepted; Why? "Works" are always more appealing to men than "Faith"; Why? "Works" appeals to pride, while "Faith" appeals to the Cross)*.

CHAPTER 6

(A.D. 31)
THE SABBATH

AND it came to pass on the second Sabbath after the first *(refers to the regular Saturday Sabbath that followed the special Sabbath, which began the Feast regardless of what day of the week on which it fell)*, that He went through the corn fields *(barley or wheat)*; and His Disciples plucked the ears of corn *(grain)*, and did eat, rubbing *them* in *their* hands *(they did this to shed the husks, and then would eat the grain raw, which was quite common at that time)*.

2 And certain of the Pharisees said unto them, Why do you that which is not lawful to do on the Sabbath Days? *(This means from the Greek Text that the Pharisees kept prodding Jesus and the Disciples by asking the question over and over again, until Jesus finally responded; in fact, there was nothing in the Law of Moses restricting this, the restriction being of their own making.)*

3 And Jesus answering them said, Have you not read so much as this, what David did, when himself was hungry, and they which were with him *(He took them to I Sam. 21:3-6)*;

4 How he went into the House of God *(refers to the Tabernacle at Nob, which was only a short distance from Jerusalem)*, and did take and eat the showbread, and gave also to them who were with him *(pertained to the hallowed bread which, since it had evidently just been*

baked, meant it was the Sabbath)*; which it is not lawful to eat but for the Priests alone? *(Our Lord proclaims the fact here that necessity overrode rulings, even though they were the legitimate Law of Moses; however, that which the Disciples did, which the Pharisees condemned, was not of the Law of Moses, but rather a law made up by the Pharisees.)*

5 And He said unto them, That the Son of Man is Lord also of the Sabbath *(this statement by Christ, in effect, declares Him to be God, and to be sure, the Pharisees plainly understood His meaning)*.

HEALING ON THE SABBATH

6 And it came to pass also on another Sabbath, that He entered into the Synagogue and taught: and there was a man whose right hand was withered.

7 And the Scribes and Pharisees watched Him *(means they kept watching, so as to find something for which they could accuse Him, such is religion!)*, whether He would heal on the Sabbath Day; that they might find an accusation against Him *(if one is to notice, Jesus paid no attention whatsoever to the silly rules made up by men)*.

8 But He knew their thoughts *(the Holy Spirit told Him what they were thinking)*, and said to the man which had the withered hand, Rise up, and stand forth in the midst *(means that what was done was carried out for all to see)*. And he arose and stood forth *(it is said that this man's exact petition to Christ was preserved in the Early Church; it is as follows, as he stood before Jesus: "I was a stonemason earning my livelihood with my own hands; I pray Thee, Jesus, restore me to health, in order that I may not with shame beg my bread")*.

9 Then said Jesus unto them, I will ask you one thing; Is it lawful on the Sabbath Days to do good, or to do evil? to save life, or to destroy *it*? *(To have the power to "do good," and not do it, is consequently "to do evil.")*

10 And looking round about upon them all *(with an astute gaze; Mark said, "with anger, being grieved for the hardness of their hearts" [Mk. 3:5])*, He said unto the man, Stretch forth your hand *(the withered hand)*. And he did so: and his hand was restored whole as the other *(before their very eyes, a miraculous healing took place)*.

11 And they *(Scribes and Pharisees)* were filled with madness *(constitutes their reaction*

to this great miracle; they had no regard whatsoever for the plight of this poor man, only for their petty rules; "madness" speaks of "folly"); **and communed one with another what they might do to Jesus** *(speaks of their hearts being filled with murder; they would kill Him simply because He had healed a man on the Sabbath; such is religion).*

TWELVE DISCIPLES

12 And it came to pass in those days, that He went out into a mountain to pray, and continued all night in prayer to God *(the record shows that Jesus prayed constantly; among other things, He was seeking the Will of His Father, as it regards the choice of the Twelve Disciples; many were following Him at that time).*

13 And when it was day, He called *unto Him* His Disciples *(could have been as many as a hundred or more)*: **and of them He chose Twelve** *(the number of God's Government)*, **whom also He named Apostles** *(one sent with a special Message, which will always be according to the Word of God, and will set the standard for the Church)*;

14 Simon, (whom he also named Peter,) *(his name means, "fragment of rock," which designates how that Christ would take this man who was weak within himself, and make of him a pillar of faith; such would characterize all of His Disciples in one way or the other, and in fact, all Believers)* **and Andrew his brother, James and John, Philip and Bartholomew,**

15 Matthew and Thomas, James the *son* of Alphaeus, and Simon called Zelotes *(the Zealot)*,

16 And Judas *the brother* of James *(he was also called "Lebbaeus" and "Thaddaeus")*, **and Judas Iscariot, which also was the traitor** *(this man leaves the Gospel story "a doomed and damned man" because he chose it so, and God confirmed him in that dreadful choice).*

HEALINGS

17 And He *(Jesus)* **came down with them, and stood in the plain** *(as He had delivered the Sermon on the Mount, He will now deliver the Sermon in the Plain)*, **and the company of His Disciples** *(as Jesus traveled from place to place, there were no doubt as many as fifty to a hundred people who traveled with Him most of the time)*, **and a great multitude of people out of all Judaea and Jerusalem, and from the sea coast of Tyre and Sidon, which came to hear Him, and to be healed of their diseases;**

18 And they who were vexed with unclean spirits *("vexed" means "to harass"; these things caused particular types of sicknesses among the people, and no doubt do so presently)*: **and they were healed.**

19 And the whole multitude sought to touch Him: for there went virtue *(power)* **out of Him, and healed *them* all** *(it was a sight and a scene that the world had never experienced in all of its history).*

SERMON ON THE PLAIN

20 And He lifted up His eyes on His Disciples, and said *(could have been Luke's account of the Sermon on the Mount, and could have been another Message altogether; Jesus no doubt repeated Himself many times, in order that the Message not be lost)*, **Blessed *be the* poor** *(poor in spirit, denoting humility)*: **for yours is the Kingdom of God** *(the Kingdom of God and the Kingdom of Heaven are basically the same).*

21 Blessed *are you who* hunger now *(hunger and thirst after Righteousness)*: **for you shall be filled** *(the Lord always rewards spiritual hunger)*. **Blessed *are you who* weep now** *(mourn, because of spiritual weakness)*: **for you shall laugh** *(defeat will be turned to victory).*

22 Blessed are you *(happy are you)*, **when men shall hate you, and when they shall separate you *from their company*, and shall reproach *you*, and cast out your name as evil, for the Son of Man's sake** *(those who subscribe to the Cross will be treated accordingly).*

23 Rejoice ye in that day, and leap for joy *(the rejection by the religious world is a great sign that one is on the right track, which gives occasion for great joy)*: **for, behold, your reward *is* great in Heaven** *(means the greater reward awaits your arriving there)*: **for in the like manner did their fathers unto the Prophets** *(if the religious establishment did such unto the Prophets, and they definitely did, then we can expect no less; the Cross is the great dividing line for the Church, and in fact has always been; to accept the Cross as the answer is to reject all of man's ways, which doesn't set well with religion [Gal: 6:14]).*

FOUR WOES

24 But woe unto you who are rich! *(Rich and increased with goods, and claim to have need of nothing [Rev. 3:17].)* **for you have received your consolation** *(you have traded the*

Spirit of God for "things," and that is what you will have).

25 Woe unto you who are full! *(Things of the world.)* for you shall hunger *(they will not satisfy).* Woe unto you who laugh now! *(Do not see your spiritual failure.)* for you shall mourn and weep *(mourn now over spiritual weakness, which all have, or mourn later over lost opportunity).*

26 Woe unto you, when all men shall speak well of you! for so did their fathers to the false prophets *(such have always had men singing their praises, and do so no less today; however, it is because they are telling men what they want to hear instead of what God wants them to hear).*

LOVE FOR ENEMIES

27 But I say unto you which hear *(refers to the fact that many refuse to hear)*, Love your enemies, do good to them which hate you *(begins the most revolutionary lifestyle ever known in the history of man; no religion in the world can remotely compare with this; for instance, compare this with the religion of Islam)*,

28 Bless them who curse you *(speak well of)*, and pray for them which despitefully use you *(pray that they will see God's Way).*

29 And unto him who smites you on the *one* cheek offer also the other *(is meant to serve as a principle and not to be taken literally; for example: the Lord, Himself, did not offer Himself to be stricken again [Jn. 18:22-23], but firmly, though with courtesy, rebuked the one who struck Him; the principle is that one should not seek retaliation)*; and him who takes away your cloak forbid not *to take your* coat also *(if one demands his rights too loudly, the loss could even be greater than the cloak and coat).*

30 Give to every man who asks of you *(speaks of those truly in need; it is not meant to reward slothfulness)*; and of him who takes away your goods ask *them* not again *(portrays unselfishness, which ought to characterize every Believer).*

THE GOLDEN RULE

31 And as you would that men should do to you, do ye also to them likewise *(this is the Verse referred to as the "Golden Rule"; it is also a teaching of the Law [Lev. 19:18]).*

32 For if you love them which love you, what thank have you? *(The idea is Jesus loved us when we were unlovable [Rom. 5:8], and we are to do the same for them who are unlovable.)* for sinners also love those that love them *(to love*

those who do not love us portrays Godliness).

33 And if you do good to them which do good to you, what thank have you? for sinners also do even the same *(the rule of man is to return good for good and evil for evil; then beneath this there is the returning of evil for good, which is devilish; while above it there is the returning of good for evil, which is Divine — that commanded of the followers of Christ).*

34 And if you lend *to them* of whom you hope to receive, what thank have you? for sinners also lend to sinners, to receive as much again.

35 But love ye your enemies, and do good, and lend, hoping for nothing again *(how can we call it "lending," if it is not to be repaid? Solomon gave the answer: "He who has pity upon the poor lends unto the LORD; and that which he has given will He pay him again" [Prov. 19:17])*; and your reward shall be great *(the idea is the Lord will repay, and He does so abundantly)*, and you shall be the children of the Highest *(means that we will be like our Heavenly Father)*: for He is kind unto the unthankful and *to* the evil *(what we should do as well).*

36 Be ye therefore merciful, as your Father also is merciful *(as He has been merciful to us, we are to be merciful to others; everything we do is to be based on what He has done for us).*

JUDGING OTHERS

37 Judge not *(do not judge one's motives)*, and you shall not be judged *(implying that you will be judged by the Lord, if you do not obey this admonition)*: condemn not *(do not pass sentence)*, and you shall not be condemned *(meaning conversely, that if you pass sentence on others, the Lord will ultimately pass sentence on you)*: forgive, and you shall be forgiven *(implying that if you do not forgive, God will not forgive you, which puts a person in a terrible dilemma)*:

38 Give, and it shall be given unto you *(God's economy; it refers not only to the giving of money, but as well to mercy, grace, love, help, etc.)*; good measure, pressed down, and shaken together, and running over, shall men give into your bosom *(constitutes a remarkable Promise).* For with the same measure that you mete withal it shall be measured to you again *(is a Law of God which everyone should take very seriously, for Christ means exactly what He says).*

39 And He spoke a Parable unto them, Can the blind lead the blind? shall they not both fall into the ditch? *(These are false religious teachers.)*

40 The disciple is not above his master *(those who listen to false teachers will become as perfectly deluded as their masters, for pupils cannot see more clearly than their teachers; hence the disciples of Romanism, Mormonism, etc., become as wholly deluded as their teachers)*: but every one who is perfect shall be as his master *(would have been better translated, "but every one who has been perfected," i.e., "embraced this false doctrine," shall be as his teacher)*.

41 And why behold thou the mote that is in your brother's eye *(don't look for faults in others)*, but perceive not the beam that is in your own eye? *(If you want to inspect, inspect yourself. You have plenty there to inspect, which desperately needs improvement.)*

42 Either how can you say to your brother, Brother, let me pull out the mote that is in your eye, when you yourself behold not the beam that is in your own eye? *(This does not pertain to doctrine, which must be judged constantly [Mat. 7:15-20], but rather one's person and character. Once again, we have enough about ourselves that needs improving, rather than condemning others.)* Thou hypocrite, cast out first the beam out of your own eye, and then shall you see clearly to pull out the mote that is in your brother's eye *(if we deal with ourselves as we should, then we will then be able to "see clearly," which means we'll have no desire to find fault with others)*.

THE FRUIT

43 For a good tree brings not forth corrupt fruit *(is the method delineated by Jesus for separating the good from the bad)*; neither does a corrupt tree bring forth good fruit *(the manner in which we are to judge false doctrine)*.

44 For every tree is known by his own fruit *(for example, look at the fruit of Islam, or even the part of Christianity which is corrupt)*. For of thorns men do not gather figs, nor of a bramble bush gather they grapes *(it's impossible to get good fruit from a corrupt tree)*.

45 A good man out of the good treasure of his heart brings forth that which is good *(refers to the fact that all of this, whether good or evil, begins in the heart)*; and an evil man out of the evil treasure of his heart brings forth that which is evil *(no matter the claims, what is in the heart is going to ultimately come forth)*: for of the abundance of the heart his mouth speaks *(there can be an imitation of the fruit of the Spirit, as a paper rose may be so like a real*

one as to be indistinguishable; but a bee will make no mistake!)*.

46 And why do you call Me, Lord, Lord, and do not the things which I say? *(Both the True Prophet and the false prophet will freely use the title "Lord," but Christ is "Lord" only to those who obey His Word.)*

TWO FOUNDATIONS

47 Whosoever comes to Me *(truly accepts Christ)*, and hears My sayings *(the Word of God)*, and does them *(the hearing must culminate in the doing)*, I will show you to whom he is like *(the end result)*:

48 He is like a man which built an house *(we ought to grow in grace and knowledge)*, and digged deep *(deep into the Word)*, and laid the foundation on a rock *(that "Rock" is Christ and Him Crucified [I Cor. 1:23])*: and when the flood arose *(problems will arise)*, the stream beat vehemently upon that house *(Satan will try to destroy the house)*, and could not shake it: for it was founded upon a rock *(once again, "that Rock" is "Jesus Christ and Him Crucified," which must ever be the object of our Faith)*.

49 But he who hears, and does not *(doesn't obey the Word)*, is like a man that without a foundation *(the object of his faith is not the Cross of Christ)* built an house upon the earth *(outwardly this one looked identical to the one built on the rock)*; against which the stream did beat vehemently, and immediately it fell; and the ruin of that house was great *(if our Faith is not in the Cross of Christ, things may go well for awhile, but sooner or later the storm will come, and Satan will win the day)*.

CHAPTER 7
(A.D. 31)
THE SPOKEN WORD

NOW when He had ended all His sayings in the audience of the people, He entered into Capernaum.

2 And a certain centurion's *(an officer in the Roman army, a Gentile)* servant, who was dear unto him, was sick, and ready to die.

3 And when he heard of Jesus *(better translated, "and when he had heard about Jesus")*, he sent unto Him the Elders of the Jews *(he evidently thought that they would have more sway on Christ than he would as a Gentile)*, beseeching Him that He would come and heal his servant.

4 And when they came to Jesus, they *(the Elders of the Jews)* besought Him instantly, saying, That he *(the centurion)* was worthy for whom He should do this *(portrays the basis on which most people expect an answer; but prayer is never answered on this basis)*:

5 For he loves our nation, and he has built us a Synagogue *(evidently this Gentile was sick of the pagan ways of Rome, and had become very interested in the God of Abraham, Isaac, and Jacob)*.

6 Then Jesus went with them. And when He was now not far from the house, the centurion sent friends to Him *(Matthew says the centurion came personally; Luke states here that he came by deputation; both statements are true; for his messengers represented him, and also the word "him" as is given in Verse 9 supports the belief that the centurion followed his messengers and, in his anxiety for his servant, repeated the message he had given them to deliver)*, saying unto him, Lord, trouble not yourself: for I am not worthy that You should enter under my roof *(not knowing exactly what the Jews had told the Lord, he wanted Christ to know exactly who he was, a Gentile, which carried with it many connotations)*:

7 Wherefore neither thought I myself worthy to come unto You *(seems to be the stage that the centurion now approaches Christ personally)*: but say in a word, and my servant shall be healed *(proclaims a level of faith seldom, if ever, equaled by anyone in the Bible, at least of this nature)*.

8 For I also am a man set under authority, having under me soldiers *(proclaims the meaning of spiritual authority, and from a Gentile at that!)*, and I say unto one, Go, and he goes; and to another, Come, and he comes; and to my servant, Do this, and he does *it* *(the authority of this centurion came from Caesar; likewise, all authority possessed by Believers comes from the Lord; also, unlike the centurion, authority held by Believers is never to be exercised over other people, but rather over spirits of darkness [Lk. 10:19])*.

9 When Jesus heard these things, He marvelled at him *(records one of the two instances when Jesus marveled, the other being at unbelief [Mk. 6:6])*, and turned him about *(will use him as an example)*, and said unto the people that followed Him *(who followed Jesus)*, I say unto you, I have not found so great faith, no, not in Israel *(all of this tells us that only "unbelief" or "faith," with all their attendant results both negative and positive, are the occasion in the Eyes of God for astonishment)*.

10 And they who were sent *(the friends of Verse 6)*, returning to the house, found the servant whole who had been sick.

RAISING THE DEAD

11 And it came to pass the day after *(after the healing of the centurion's servant)*, that He went into a city called Nain; and many of His Disciples went with Him, and much people *(recorded only by Luke)*.

12 Now when He came nigh to the gate of the city *(about to enter the city)*, behold, there was a dead man carried out, the only son of his mother, and she was a widow: and much people of the city was with her.

13 And when the Lord saw her, He had compassion on her, and said unto her, Weep not.

14 And He came and touched the bier *(refers to a wooden frame on which the dead were laid, wrapped in folds of linen, with the entire apparatus carried on the shoulders of four men; it was against the Mosaic Law to touch anything pertaining to death; however, this didn't apply to Jesus, for His touching the bier portrayed His touching and defeating death itself, which He would do on the Cross of Calvary)*: and they who bear *him* stood still *(in His Presence, everything must stop, including death)*. And he said, Young man, I say unto you *(presents His Deity)*, Arise *(speaks of His Resurrection Power, which will be used shortly to raise all of the Sainted dead [I Cor. 15:51-55])*.

15 And he who was dead sat up, and began to speak *(what a scene that must have been)*. And He delivered him to his mother *(she could now dry her tears; as well, this represents the great meeting that will one day take place in Heaven between loved ones)*.

16 And there came a fear on all *(such power was incomprehensible)*: and they Glorified God *(everything that Jesus did brought Glory to God)*, saying, That a great Prophet is risen up among us *(in that, they were correct, but only partially so; He was God and, therefore, their Messiah, but that they could not understand)*; and, That God has visited his people *(proclaims a Truth, but in far greater degree than they imagined)*.

17 And this rumour of Him went forth throughout all Judaea, and throughout all the region round about *(pertained to the debate as to Who He actually was; in other words, was this the Messiah?)*.

18 And the disciples of John showed him of all these things *(they told John all about Christ).*

JOHN THE BAPTIST

19 And John calling *unto him* two of his disciples sent *them* to Jesus, saying, Are You He Who should come? or look we for another? *(At times, Faith waivers, even in the strongest, as evidenced here by John. It is only the Master Who never turns aside from the path of right. Quite possibly, John the Baptist was puzzled. If Jesus was truly the Messiah, why didn't he deliver Him from prison?)*

20 When the men were come unto Him *(unto Jesus),* they said, John Baptist has sent us unto You, saying, Are You He Who should come? or look we for another? *(Even though John may have temporarily doubted, no criticism is in order, as the answer of Christ projects!)*

JESUS' ANSWER

21 And in that same hour *(when the disciples of John the Baptist came to Him)* He cured many of *their* infirmities and plagues, and of evil spirits; and unto many *who were* blind He gave sight *(miracles, as miracles, did not accredit Jesus to be the Promised Messiah; what did accredit Him was that He worked those predicted of Him in the Scriptures [Isa. 29:18; 35:4-6; 61:1-3]; the false prophet will also work amazing miracles [Rev. 13:13]).*

22 Then Jesus answering said unto them *(proclaims Him not answering their question until everyone around Him had received their healing or deliverance),* Go your way, and tell John what things you have seen and heard *(were things never "seen and heard" by any previous generation);* how that the blind see, the lame walk, the lepers are cleansed, the deaf hear, the dead are raised, to the poor the Gospel is preached.

23 And blessed is *he (begins this mild rebuke regarding John's questions, and is actually given in the form of a Beatitude),* whosoever shall not be offended in Me *(would not find an occasion of stumbling in the manner in which Christ had actually come).*

JESUS SPEAKS OF JOHN THE BAPTIST

24 And when the messengers of John were departed, He began to speak unto the people concerning John *(Jesus did not want the people to think less of John because of these questions),* What went you out into the wilderness for to see? A reed shaken with the wind? *(Christ will now build up John as no other man, and that despite his temporal doubting.)*

25 But what went you out for to see? A man clothed in soft raiment? *(John was clothed with Camel's hair, a crude garment.)* Behold, they which are gorgeously apparelled, and live delicately, are in kings' courts *(if John had compromised his Message, he would have been Herod's preacher; instead, he was Herod's prisoner).*

26 But what went you out for to see? A Prophet? Yes, I say unto you, and much more than a Prophet *(this one statement places John in a category all to himself; at that moment, the people may have thought less of him, but not God!)*

27 This is *he,* of whom it is written *(Jesus always took people to the Word),* Behold, I send My messenger before Your face *(before the face of Christ),* which shall prepare Your way before You *(John the Baptist prepared the way for the Lord to be introduced).*

28 For I say unto you, Among those who are born of women there is not a greater Prophet than John the Baptist *(all the Prophets before said that Jesus was coming; John said, "Behold, He is here" [Jn. 1:29]; he introduced Christ, which made him greater):* but he who is least in the Kingdom of God is greater than he *(since the Cross, the New Covenant affords us far greater privileges than those had under the Old Covenant, of which John was a part [Heb. 8:6]).*

29 And all the people who heard *Him,* and the Publicans *(tax-collectors),* justified God *(proclaimed the fact that God had done a glorious thing by sending John to precede Christ, and prepare the way for Christ),* being baptized with the baptism of John *(the Baptism of Repentance; proclaims the fact that Jesus recognized the fact of the Salvation of those baptized by John because they truly had repented).*

30 But the Pharisees and lawyers *(those who argued the Law of Moses)* rejected the counsel of God against themselves, being not baptized of him *(they refused to admit they needed to repent).*

31 And the Lord said, Where unto then shall I liken the men of this generation? *(This was the generation of Jesus' day, which had rejected both the Ministry of John and Ministry of Christ.)* and to what are they like? *(The Lord will answer His Own Question in the following Verses.)*

32 They *(the religious leaders of Israel)* are like unto children sitting in the marketplace,

and calling one to another, and saying, We have piped unto you, and you have not danced; we have mourned to you, and you have not wept (*proclaims the two methods used by the Lord to reach Israel, His Ministry and the Ministry of John the Baptist, both to no avail*).

33 For John the Baptist came neither eating bread nor drinking wine (*refers to John's austere lifestyle spent in the desert*); and you say, He has a devil (*presents the response of the religious leaders of Israel to the Message of John demanding Repentance*).

34 The Son of Man is come eating and drinking (*refers to the lifestyle of Jesus as being totally opposite to that of John*); and you say, Behold a gluttonous man, and a winebibber (*this was not what Jesus was, but what they said He was; they also claimed that He performed His Miracles by the power of Satan*), a friend of Publicans and sinners! (*For a change, they now proclaim something truthful of Jesus. He was a friend to these groups; however, being their "friend" did not mean that He partook of their lifestyles, or even condoned them.*)

35 But wisdom is justified of all her children (*the children of wisdom in this case are the two methods used by the Holy Spirit, i.e., "wisdom," to reach Israel; we speak of the Ministry of John the Baptist and of Christ; both were rejected by Israel, and Israel went to her doom*).

JESUS AND THE WOMAN

36 And one of the Pharisees desired Him that He would eat with him (*constitutes the enemy of the "wisdom" mentioned in Verse 35; this incident is peculiar to Luke*). And He went into the Pharisee's house, and sat down to meat (*implies that Jesus was given no prominent place at the table and, as stated, had to find seating for Himself, which was an insult!*).

37 And, behold, a woman in the city (*probably was Nain*), which was a sinner (*we are given no further information*), when she knew that *Jesus* sat at meat in the Pharisee's house (*she evidently was determined to see Him*), brought an alabaster box of ointment (*very expensive, so she must have been a woman of means; however, her riches did not satisfy the hunger and thirst of her heart*),

38 And stood at His feet behind *Him* weeping (*signified Repentance; she had possibly witnessed Him raising the young man from the dead, and maybe heard His Message to the Pharisees and the lawyers; His Words had found a place in her heart*), and began to wash His feet with tears (*these were tears of sorrow and of joy — sorrow because of her sins, and joy because this was the One Who could forgive those sins, and in fact did!*), and did wipe *them* with the hairs of her head, and kissed His feet (*this was then a custom among the Jews, Greeks, and Romans; it was a mark of affection and reverence*), and anointed *them* with the ointment (*spoke of His Feet; as a sinner washed and anointed His Feet, likewise sinners gave Him the only crown He wore — a crown of thorns*).

39 Now when the Pharisee which had bidden Him saw *it*, He spoke within Himself (*not out loud*), saying, This Man, if He were a Prophet, would have known who and what manner of woman *this is* who touches Him: for she is a sinner (*"this man" judged both Jesus and the woman; he was wrong on both counts; while she was a sinner, the Pharisee was in fact a greater sinner*).

40 And Jesus answering said unto him, Simon, I have somewhat to say unto you (*the Holy Spirit told the Saviour what this man was thinking*). And he said, Master, say on (*is laced with sarcasm; therefore, he little expects the words of wisdom he will receive; he has already revealed the unbelief of his heart by using the words, "this man, if he were a Prophet . . ."*).

THE PARABLE

41 There was a certain creditor (*a moneylender*) which had two debtors (*individuals to whom money had been loaned*): the one owed five hundred pence (*about twenty thousand dollars in 2003 currency*), and the other fifty (*about two thousand dollars*).

42 And when they had nothing to pay, he frankly forgave them both (*refers to the moneylender writing off the debts*). Tell me therefore, which of them will love him most? (*Now comes the point illustrated by the Parable.*)

43 Simon answered and said, I suppose that *he*, to whom he forgave most. And He said unto him, You have rightly judged (*Jesus was appealing to this man on his own level*).

44 And He turned to the woman (*records the first instance of Jesus acknowledging the woman in any way*), and said unto Simon, Do you see this woman? (*The Lord speaks of her as a trophy of Grace!*) I entered into your house, you gave Me no water for My feet (*proclaims the studied insult now being noted*): but she has washed My feet with tears, and wiped *them* with the

hairs of her head.

45 You gave Me no kiss *(was a custom in those days)*: **but this woman since the time I came in has not ceased to kiss my feet** *(Simon would not kiss the Face of Jesus, which denoted His Kingship; however, the Holy Spirit had the woman to kiss the "feet" of Jesus, denoting His Authority, Power, and Rule).*

46 My head with oil you did not anoint *(presents another custom of that day)*: **but this woman has anointed my feet with ointment** *(this act, brought about by the Holy Spirit, signified Jesus as the Messiah [Lk. 4:18]).*

47 Wherefore I say unto you, Her sins, which are many, are forgiven *(Jesus is performing that which only the Messiah could actually do, and which Simon had denied, and Jesus now declares)*; **for she loved much** *(what is wanting in order to love much is not sin, but the knowledge of it)*: **but to whom little is forgiven,** *the same* **loves little** *(every Believer must realize that he has been forgiven much; consequently, he will love much).*

48 And He said unto her, Your sins are forgiven *(the guiltiest who believe upon Christ shall enjoy assurance of Salvation and the conscious forgiveness of sin).*

49 And they who sat at meat with Him began to say within themselves, Who is this Who forgives sins also? *(His act of forgiving this woman, should have told them, and in fact did tell them that He was the Messiah.)*

50 And He said to the woman, Your faith has saved you *(Jesus did not say to the woman, "your love has saved you" or "your tears have saved you," but, "your faith has saved you")*; **go in peace** *(should have been translated, "go into peace"; this was justifying peace, meaning this woman was justified before God because of her Faith in Christ).*

CHAPTER 8
(A.D. 31)
THE GOSPEL

AND it came to pass afterward *(refers to the events of the previous Chapter)*, **that He went throughout every city and village** *(His Love unchilled by unbelief and hatred, He visited every city and village with the glad tidings of the Gospel)*, **preaching** *(man magnifies sacraments and ceremonies, and belittles preaching; God magnifies preaching)* **and showing the glad tidings** *(Good News)* **of the Kingdom of God** *(the "Kingdom of God" is the Gospel of*

Jehovah's King, the Lord Jesus Christ; it is a dispensational term and refers to Messiah's Kingdom on Earth; it was offered by both John and Jesus, but was rejected and thus postponed until Christ comes the Second Time [Rev., Chpt. 19]): **and the Twelve** *were* **with Him** *(means that the Twelve remained with Him constantly),*

2 And certain women *(women are prominent and honorably mentioned in Luke; it was not a woman who sold the Lord for thirty pieces of silver; it was not women who forsook Him and fled, etc.; it was women who were the first to visit His Tomb on the Resurrection morning)*, **which had been healed of evil spirits and infirmities** *(healed of that which had been caused by evil spirits)*, **Mary called Magdalene, out of whom went seven devils** *(she was from Magdala, a little town near Tiberias; she loved much because she had been forgiven much; there is no proof that she is the woman who anointed His Feet with the ointment of Lk. 7:37-38),*

3 And Joanna the wife of Chuza Herod's steward *(is believed to be the family whose dying son was healed by Jesus [Jn. 4:46])*, **and Susanna, and many others, which ministered unto Him of their substance** *(some of these women were wealthy, and they used their money to minister to the Lord's necessities; He could with a few loaves feed thousands, but He did not feed Himself; thus, He proved that He was a man like His fellowmen; true disciples now as then minister to Him; mere professors do not).*

THE PARABLE OF THE SOWER

4 And when much people were gathered together, and were come to Him out of every city, He spoke by a Parable *(Parables had a tendency to confuse His opposers, and to enlighten those who were truly His followers)*:

5 A sower *(in this case, the Evangelist)* **went out to sow his seed** *(the Word of God)*: **and as he sowed, some fell by the way side** *(referred to an area which had not been prepared for the seed)*; **and it was trodden down, and the fowls of the air devoured it** *(demon spirits).*

6 And some *(seed)* **fell upon a rock** *(covered by a very shallow layer of soil)*; **and as soon as it was sprung up, it withered away, because it lacked moisture** *(due to the rock, the roots could not go down into the soil where the moisture was).*

7 And some *(seed)* **fell among thorns** *(pertains to good ground, but yet the competition of the thorns would prove to be a debilitating*

factor); and the thorns sprang up with it, and choked it.

8 And other fell on good ground (means ground that was not full of rocks or thorns), and sprang up (refers to bountiful growth), and bear fruit an hundredfold (presents a tremendous harvest). And when He had said these things, He cried, He who has ears to hear, let him hear (many did not have "ears to hear" because their hearts were hardened; some few did, and they changed the world!).

9 And His Disciples asked Him, saying, What might this Parable be? (This proclaims the story being understood perfectly well, but not its meaning.)

10 And He said, Unto you (all who sincerely seek to know the Lord, and have a deeper understanding of His Word) it is given to know the mysteries (the word implies knowledge withheld; however, Jesus is saying that the Scriptural significance to these mysteries is about to be revealed, at least to those who hunger and thirst after Righteousness) of the Kingdom of God: but to others in Parables (the Divine story would be veiled to the careless and indifferent); that seeing they might not see, and hearing they might not understand (pertained to a willful blindness and a willful lack of comprehension; they had no desire to know).

11 Now the Parable is this: The seed is the Word of God.

12 Those by the way side are they who hear; then comes the devil, and takes away the Word out of their hearts (he is able to do this simply because they have little regard for the Word), lest they should believe and be saved (a willful blindness resulted in a judicial blindness).

13 They on the rock are they, which, when they hear, receive the Word with joy; and these have no root, which for a while believe, and in time of temptation fall away (completely refutes the unscriptural doctrine of unconditional eternal security).

14 And that which fell among thorns are they, which, when they have heard, go forth, and are choked with cares and riches and pleasures of this life, and bring no fruit to perfection (actually means that there is a beginning of fruit, but it is not allowed to ripen and is, therefore, unusable; they believe for a while and then fall away; there are many like this).

15 But that on the good ground (constitutes the fourth group which will bring forth "fruit to perfection," i.e., "fruit to maturity") are they, which in an honest and good heart (tells us

that the problem is with the heart and not with circumstances), having heard the Word, keep it, and bring forth fruit with patience (merely hearing the Word is not enough; one must "keep it" as well).

THE CANDLE

16 No man, when he has lit a candle, covers it with a vessel, or puts it under a bed (means that Christ using Parables is not meant to hide Truth from sincere, inquiring hearts, but rather the very opposite); but sets it on a candlestick, that they which enter in may see the light (the teaching of Christ was designed to appeal to the honest, seeking heart; He wants men to "see the light").

17 For nothing is secret, that shall not be made manifest (addresses itself to the mysteries of the Gospel); neither any thing hid, that shall not be known and come abroad (it would all be made known in the New Covenant).

18 Take heed therefore how you hear (refers to not only what is heard, but how it is heard): for whosoever has, to him shall be given (constitutes a Divine Law that whosoever accepts Truth will be given Truth); and whosoever has not, from him shall be taken even that which he seems to have (light rejected is light withdrawn).

TRUE RELATIVES

19 Then came to Him His mother and His brethren (refers to those of His immediate family), and could not come at Him for the press (the crowd was so large that they simply could not get to Him).

20 And it was told Him by certain which said, Your mother and Your brethren stand without, desiring to see You.

21 And He answered and said unto them (presents a principle which places God first in all things), My mother and My brethren are these which hear the Word of God, and do it (plainly proclaims allegiance to God, is even more solemn than family ties; Jesus here refutes the Catholic contention that Mary is above all).

THE STORM

22 Now it came to pass on a certain day, that He went into a ship with His Disciples: and He said unto them, Let us go over unto the other side of the lake (from the western shore of Galilee to the eastern shore). And they

launched forth.

23 But as they sailed He fell asleep *(physical exhaustion from healing and delivering, as well as teaching; this portrayed His Humanity)*: and there came down a storm of wind on the lake *(from the Greek Text a "furious storm or hurricane")*; and they were filled *with water*, and were in jeopardy *(they were actually in danger of sinking, and of even losing their lives)*.

24 And they came to Him, and awoke Him *(refers to them not doing so until the danger was acute)*, saying, Master, Master, we perish *(He Alone can stop the soul from perishing)*. Then He arose, and rebuked the wind and the raging of the water *(refers to an evil spirit behind the storm attempting to kill the Disciples; Satan knew that Jesus could not be killed, but he also knew the Disciples to be very mortal)*: and they ceased, and there was a calm *(the change was instant; no power on Earth can even begin to approach such Authority; as well, He can instantly calm the storm in a man's soul)*.

25 And He said unto them, Where is your faith? *(Christ is the answer concerning all the storms of life.)* And they being afraid wondered *(the Disciples had accepted His Messiahship, but had a most inadequate view of the same)*, saying one to another, What manner of man is this! *(They evidently did not recognize all the implications, which His Office carried with it.)* for He commands even the winds and water, and they obey Him *(proclaims His total control not only over demon spirits, sickness, and death, but as well, the elements)*.

DELIVERANCE

26 And they arrived at the country of the Gadarenes *(was on the eastern side of the Sea of Galilee)*, which is over against Galilee *(refers to the part of Decapolis which bordered the Sea of Galilee on the southern tip and the eastern side)*.

27 And when He went forth to land *(when they beached the boat)*, there met Him out of the city a certain man *(he was from the nearby city, but no longer lived there)*, which had devils *(demons)* long time *(had long been possessed)*, and wore no clothes *(a type of man in the spiritual who is naked to the Judgment of God because of being in rebellion against God)*, neither abode in *any* house, but in the tombs *(death is the end result of sin)*.

28 When he saw Jesus *(the spirit world of darkness is subservient to the Lord Jesus Christ)*,

he cried out *(for fear)*, and fell down before Him *(an acknowledgment of Him as Lord and Master)*, and with a loud voice said, What have I to do with You, Jesus, *You* Son of God most High? *(Even though most of mankind professes not to know, demon spirits know Who Jesus is.)* I beseech You, torment me not *(proclaims them knowing and realizing that Jesus has the Power to do with them whatsoever He desires; proper Faith in Christ and the Cross will put us in the position of tormenting demons, instead of them tormenting us)*.

29 (For He had commanded the unclean spirit to come out of the man *(speaks of the head spirit or demon who was the leader of all the others, a great host, as we shall see)*. For oftentimes it had caught him *(refers to this spirit or spirits taking control of this man and giving him, as we shall see, super human strength)*: and he was kept bound with chains and in fetters *(restraint was attempted, but to no avail)*; and he broke the bands, and was driven of the devil into the wilderness.) *(He was totally taken over by demons and had no choice but to do what they desired.)*

30 And Jesus asked him, saying, What is your name? *(This proclaims these demons as personalities.)* And he said, Legion *(could refer to as many as 6,000; that this many demons could inhabit one human being is startling to say the least)*: because many devils *(demons)* were entered into him.

31 And they besought Him that He would not command them to go out into the deep *(refers to the "bottomless pit" [Rev. 20:1-3])*.

32 And there was there an herd of many swine feeding on the mountain *(is recorded as being "about 2,000" [Mk. 5:13])*: and they besought Him that He would suffer *(permit)* them to enter into them. And He suffered them *(if demons have to ask permission from the Lord to enter swine, surely it should be understood that He wouldn't allow them to enter the Sheep of His Pasture)*.

33 Then went the devils *(demons)* out of the man, and entered into the swine *(refers to these demons doing exactly what the Lord told them to do)*: and the herd ran violently down a steep place into the lake, and were choked *(drowned)*.

34 When they who fed *them* saw what was done, they fled, and went and told *it* in the city and in the country *(means they told not only the owners, but any and all who would hear them)*.

35 Then they *(the owners and others)* went out to see what was done; and came to Jesus, and found the man, out of whom the devils *(demons)* were departed *(no doubt, as they had never witnessed him before)*, sitting at the feet of Jesus *(our Lord was teaching him)*, clothed *(no doubt the Disciples had loaned him some clothes, and he was also clothed with Salvation)*, and in his right mind *(perfectly sound of mind)*: and they were afraid *(they couldn't understand such power)*.

36 They also which saw *it* told them by what means he who was possessed of the devils was healed *(they gave a blow-by-blow account to the owners of the hogs, plus others)*.

37 Then the whole multitude of the country of the Gadarenes round about besought Him to depart from them *(presents one of the saddest episodes in the Gospels; they felt they could not keep both the Saviour and their swine, of the two they preferred the swine! What an indictment on the human race, for this mirrors most of humanity)*; for they were taken with great fear *(constituted fear, which should have brought them to the Lord, but instead they responded in the opposite manner)*: and He went up into the ship, and returned back again *(to the western side of the lake)*.

38 Now the man out of whom the devils *(demons)* were departed besought Him that he might be with Him *(proclaims the very opposite of his countrymen, which is quickly noted by the Holy Spirit)*: but Jesus sent him away, saying *(constitutes a denial regarding his request, but yet with a mission to perform; He carried it out to great distinction)*,

39 Return to your own house, and show how great things God has done unto you *(constitutes a commission for this man, and for all Believers; for all Believers, the Lord has done "great things")*. And he went his way, and published throughout the whole city how great things Jesus had done unto him *(doesn't tell us exactly which city, but does proclaim this man's success; the day before, he was a demon-crazed maniac, totally insane; twenty-four hours later or less, he is an Evangelist for the Lord Jesus Christ)*.

HEALINGS AND MIRACLES

40 And it came to pass, that, when Jesus was returned *(to Capernaum)*, the people *gladly* received Him: for they were all waiting for Him.

41 And, behold, there came a man named Jairus, and he was a ruler of the Synagogue *(this man was a fair representative of the wealthy and highly orthodox Jew)*: and he fell down at Jesus' feet, and besought Him that He would come into his house:

42 For he had one only daughter, about twelve years of age, and she lay a dying *(proclaims the acuteness of the situation)*. But as He *(Jesus)* went *(to the house of Jairus)* the people thronged Him.

43 And a woman having an issue of blood twelve years *(probably referred to a female disorder)*, which had spent all her living upon physicians, neither could be healed of any *(there was no earthly remedy for her sickness, as there is no earthly remedy for sin; but there is a remedy, as we soon shall see!)*,

44 Came behind *Him*, and touched the border of His garment *(pertained to one of the four tassels, which formed part of the Jewish mantle; the blue of the tassel, which was worn by most men, reminded Israel that their help came from above, and of their duty to keep the Law [Num. 15:28-41; Deut. 22:12])*: and immediately her issue of blood stanched *(her cure was permanent, and she would never be troubled with this problem again)*.

45 And Jesus said, Who touched Me? *(In fact, many were touching Jesus, but none with the Faith this woman had.)* When all denied, Peter and they who were with him said, Master, the multitude throng You and press *You*, and You say, Who touched Me? *(This is actually as much an exclamation as it is a question.)*

46 And Jesus said, Somebody has touched Me: for I perceive that virtue *(Power)* is gone out of Me *(Jesus didn't touch the woman, she touched Him; this tells us that if the Lord doesn't touch us, we still can touch Him, and receive that which we need)*.

47 And when the woman saw that she was not hid *(means that she evidently was trying to hide)*, she came trembling *(it startled her that Jesus would stop, in essence, calling for her, especially considering the great throng of people)*, and falling down before Him, she declared unto Him before all the people for what cause she had touched Him *(she withheld nothing, telling all)* and how she was healed immediately.

48 And He said unto her, Daughter *(at first she was referred to as "a woman," and now she is referred to as "Daughter"; this speaks of relationship, pertaining to both Salvation and healing)*, be of good comfort *(addresses itself to her fear concerning her previous uncleanliness; she need have no fear that anyone would judge her*

unclean now): **your faith has made you whole** (*Faith is the only requirement*); **go in peace** (*Justifying Peace; she was now "just" in the sight of God because she had trusted Christ, Who Alone can bring about our Justification; tradition says her name was Veronica, and she lived at Caesarea Philippi*).

49 **While He yet spoke, there came one from the ruler of the Synagogue's** *house,* **saying to him** (*to Jairus*), **Your daughter is dead; trouble not the Master** (*while sufferers and their friends, and even the Lord's Disciples in countless instances, asked Him to heal, etc., no one ever asked Him to raise the dead to life; to the last, despite what they had seen, none could persuade themselves that He was indeed the Lord of death as well as of life, until after the Resurrection*).

50 **But when Jesus heard** *it,* **He answered him, saying, Fear not** (*in essence saying, "despite death," everything is going to be alright*): **believe only, and she shall be made whole** (*the only requirement is Faith in Christ*).

51 **And when He came into the house** (*refers to the home of Jairus*), **He suffered no man to go in, save Peter, and James, and John, and the father and the mother of the maiden** (*represents the first time these three Disciples had been singled out; they would be singled out a total of three times [Lk. 9:28; Mat. 26:37]*).

52 **And all wept, and bewailed her** (*represents paid mourners, which was then the custom*): **but He said, Weep not; she is not dead, but asleep** (*in fact, she was physically dead, but to Jesus she was only "asleep"*).

53 **And they laughed Him to scorn** (*the paid mourners*), **knowing that she was dead.**

54 **And He put them all out** (*the Greek Text proclaims the fact that it must have been very close to a forceful ejection, as in the case of the cleansing of the Temple*), **and took her by the hand** (*a firm grip*), **and called, saying, Maid, arise** (*continues the exhibition of His Authority*).

55 **And her spirit came again** (*demonstrates the separate existence of the spirit as independent of the body; her spirit and soul were once again reunited with her body, with the body instantly coming alive*), **and she arose straightway** (*immediately*): **and He commanded to give her meat** (*food*).

56 **And her parents were astonished** (*they were transfixed to the spot, actually barely able to move, if at all*): **but He charged them that they should tell no man what was done** (*Jesus sought neither publicity nor admiration*).

CHAPTER 9
(A.D. 31)
THE TWELVE

THEN **He called His Twelve Disciples together** (*a Divine call*), **and gave them power and authority over all devils** (*demons*), **and to cure diseases** (*Spiritual Authority is never exercised over people, but always over the spirit world of darkness only [Lk. 10:19]*).

2 **And He sent them to preach** (*the great business of the true man of God is preaching*) **the Kingdom of God** (*they were then to preach that the Kingdom was now available, because the King was present; the King, regrettably, was rejected; the Message now is "Jesus Christ and Him Crucified," which will ultimately usher in the Kingdom on Earth that will come about at the Second Coming [I Cor. 1:21, 23]*), **and to heal the sick** (*constituted a part of these missions, and continued all the days of the Early Church and unto the present; anyone under the New Covenant is allowed to pray for the sick and expect healing [Mk. 16:17]*).

3 **And He said unto them, Take nothing for** *your* **journey** (*referring to the Call of Ministry*), **neither staves, nor scrip** (*a small bag for carrying things*), **neither bread, neither money; neither have two coats apiece** (*instead of waiting until those things can be afforded, carry out the Work of the Lord, and trust the Lord to provide*).

4 **And whatsoever house you enter into, there abide, and thence depart** (*don't be gadding about from house to house; the idea of your business is the Preaching of the Gospel, not socializing*).

5 **And whosoever will not receive you** (*be it a single house, or the entirety of a city*), **when ye go out of that city, shake off the very dust from your feet for a testimony against them** (*the Gospel refused always heralds judgment in one form or another, whether for a single person or the entirety of an area*).

6 **And they departed** (*the Twelve*), **and went through the towns, preaching the Gospel, and healing everywhere** (*anything less is not the True Gospel*).

JOHN THE BAPTIST

7 **Now Herod the Tetrarch** (*Herod Antipas*) **heard of all that was done by Him** (*pertained to Jesus*): **and he was perplexed, because that it was said of some, that John was risen from the**

dead *(presented a terrifying spectacle to the hurting conscience of Herod who had murdered John)*;

8 And of some *(some were saying)*, that Elijah had appeared *(in other words that Jesus was Elijah)*; and of others, that one of the old Prophets was risen again *(all of this portrayed a graphic ignorance of the Word)*.

9 And Herod said, John have I beheaded *(is not said of bravado or scorn, but rather of fear)*: but who is this, of whom I hear such things? *(The "such things" brought great joy to many, but fear to Herod because of a guilty conscience.)* And he desired to see Him *(this desire would be gratified, but not at the present; he did see Him on the day of the Crucifixion when Pilate sent Christ to Herod for judgment)*.

FIVE THOUSAND FED

10 And the Apostles, when they were returned *(from their preaching mission of Verse 1)*, told Him all that they had done. And He took them, and went aside privately into a desert place belonging to the city called Bethsaida *(this refers to Bethsaida, Julias situated on the northeastern shore of the Sea of Galilee; it was only a short distance from Capernaum)*.

11 And the people, when they knew *it (knew where He had gone)*, followed Him *(went to where He was)*: and He received them, and spoke unto them of the Kingdom of God, and healed them who had need of healing.

12 And when the day began to wear away, then came the Twelve, and said unto Him, Send the multitude away, that they may go into the towns and country round about, and lodge, and get victuals *(food)*: for we are here in a desert place *(the world is a desert place, but where Jesus is, the need can be met)*.

13 But He said unto them, Give ye them to eat *(proclaims that which within themselves they could not do)*. And they said, We have no more but five loaves and two fishes; except we should go and buy meat for all this people *(they were thinking in material terms, when He was thinking in spiritual terms; our thinking shouldn't be what can we do, but rather what can He do)*.

14 For they were about five thousand men *(counting the women and children, it could easily have been ten thousand or more)*. And He said to His Disciples, Make them sit down by fifties in a company *(this way they could all be fed, whereas otherwise it would have been bedlam; God always functions from the position of order)*.

15 And they did so, and made them all sit down.

16 Then He took the five loaves and the two fishes *(in their hands, it was nothing; in His hands, they were everything)*, and looking up to Heaven *(when will we learn that our help comes from above?)*, He blessed them *(that which He takes, He blesses)*, and broke *(unfortunately there's a lot of self-will left in all of us, which requires a "breaking" that is not pleasant to say the least)*, and gave to the Disciples to set before the multitude *(before we can properly be given to the multitude, we must first be blessed, then broken; far too many try to ignore the "breaking," depending only on the "blessing"; such can never be honored by the Lord)*.

17 And they did eat, and were all filled *(that which the Lord provides always satisfies)*: and there was taken up of fragments that remained to them twelve baskets *(what man does subtracts; what God does adds)*.

PETER'S CONFESSION

18 And it came to pass, as He was alone praying *(some eight times Luke alludes to Jesus praying, which should serve as a lesson to us; while He definitely was God, and never ceased to be God, He functioned on this Earth as "Man"; as such, He had to pray)*, His Disciples were with Him: and He asked them, saying, Whom say the people that I am? *(The answer to this question held grave consequences.)*

19 They answering said, John the Baptist; but some *say*, Elijah; and others *say*, that one of the old Prophets is risen again *(the Bible does not teach reincarnation, neither does it teach transmigration of one's spirit to another)*.

20 He said unto them, But whom say you that I am? *(He was looked at by the Disciples as the Master of Masters, and a Mystery over and above.)* Peter answering said, The Christ of God *(proclaims the correct answer; "Christ" is actually a title, and means "anointed," or more perfectly, "The Anointed," meaning "Messiah")*.

HIS DEATH AND RESURRECTION

21 And He straitly charged them, and commanded *them* to tell no man that thing *(why? the religious leaders of Israel had already rejected Him, and for the Disciples to herald it far and wide Who He really was would have only brought about great problems)*;

22 Saying, The Son of Man must suffer many things *(is mentioned apart from the glory that follows the sufferings)*, and be rejected of the Elders and Chief Priests and Scribes *(concerned the entirety of the religious leadership of Israel)*, and be slain *(refers to the Crucifixion of Christ; the religious leaders would be guilty of His Death)*, and be raised the third day *(the Resurrection, which was never in doubt; the purpose of God becoming man was to go to the Cross because this is the only way sin could be addressed, and sin is the problem)*.

DISCIPLESHIP

23 And He said to *them* all, If any *man* will come after Me *(the criteria for Discipleship)*, let him deny himself *(not asceticism as many think, but rather that one denies one's own willpower, self-will, strength, and ability, depending totally on Christ)*, and take up his cross *(the benefits of the Cross, looking exclusively to what Jesus did there to meet our every need)* daily *(this is so important, our looking to the Cross; that we must renew our Faith in what Christ has done for us, even on a daily basis, for Satan will ever try to move us away from the Cross as the object of our Faith, which always spells disaster)*, and follow Me *(Christ can be followed only by the Believer looking to the Cross, understanding what it accomplished, and by that means alone [Rom. 6:3-5, 11, 14; 8:1-2, 11; I Cor. 1:17-18, 21, 23; 2:2; Gal. 6:14; Eph. 2:13-18; Col. 2:14-15])*.

24 For whosoever will save his life shall lose it *(try to live one's life outside of Christ and the Cross)*: but whosoever will lose his life for My sake, the same shall save it *(when we place our Faith entirely in Christ and the Cross, looking exclusively to Him, we have just found "more abundant life" [Jn. 10:10])*.

25 For what is a man advantaged, if he gain the whole world, and lose himself, or be cast away? *(One cannot have both Christ and the world. One or the other must go. And if one gains the whole world and loses his soul, what has it profited him?)*

26 For whosoever shall be ashamed of Me *(ashamed of the Cross of Christ)* and of My Words *(a demand for the denial of self and the taking up of the Cross daily)*, of him shall the Son of Man be ashamed *(a denial of Christ and the Cross is a denial of Salvation)*, when He shall come in His Own Glory *(those who accept Christ and the Cross will be with Him when He comes, otherwise they will be "cast away")*, and in his Father's *(the Glory of the Father)*, and of the Holy Angels *(if one wants to be on the side of Christ, the Heavenly Father, and the Holy Angels, one must accept Christ and the Cross, which automatically denies perfidious ways)*.

27 But I tell you of a truth, there be some standing here, which shall not taste of death, till they see the Kingdom of God *(speaking of the transfiguration which would shortly take place)*.

THE TRANSFIGURATION

28 And it came to pass about an eight days after these sayings *(Mark says "six days" [Mk. 9:2]; there is no discrepancy; Mark's statement is exclusive, which means all the days and time are not included in the statement; Luke's statement is inclusive)*, He took Peter and John and James, and went up into a mountain to pray *(the first time these three were singled out was the raising of the daughter of Jairus from the dead)*.

29 And as He prayed, the fashion of His countenance was altered *(means that it took on a glow that was obvious to all; as well, the Glory He was now experiencing did not come from without, but from within)*, and His raiment *was* white *and* glistering *(this inward Glory turned those homespun, peasant garments into a thing of such beauty that it was absolutely indescribable)*.

30 And, behold, there talked with Him two men, which were Moses and Elijah *(Moses had been dead for about 1,500 years, and Elijah had been translated, and in fact had never died, but had been in Heaven or Paradise for about 900 years; all of this puts to rest the erroneous doctrine of "soul sleep," which teaches that the soul and the spirit sleep at death and will so until the Resurrection)*:

31 Who appeared in glory *(their "glory" is that which came from without, actually from God the Father, while the "Glory" of Christ came from within Him because He is God, the Second Person of the Godhead)*, and spoke of His decease which He should accomplish at Jerusalem *(the "Cross" was the topic of this conversation, and should be the topic of ours as well)*.

32 But Peter and they who were with Him were heavy with sleep: and when they were awake, they saw His Glory, and the two men that stood with Him *(this portrays to us how the Child of God will die, simply going to sleep in Jesus and awakening in Heaven in His Presence)*.

33 And it came to pass, as they departed

from Him *(pertains to Moses and Elijah disappearing from the scene)*, Peter said unto Jesus, Master, it is good for us to be here: and let us make three tabernacles; one for You, and one for Moses, and one for Elijah: not knowing what He said *(proclaims Peter placing these two on the same par with Christ, which was not looked at favorably by God)*.

34 While He thus spoke, there came a cloud *(the same as that which accompanied the Lord leading the Children of Israel in their wilderness wanderings, and as well that which rested over the Tabernacle, i.e., "the Glory of God")*, and overshadowed them: and they feared as they entered into the cloud *(Christ didn't fear, but rather the three Disciples)*.

35 And there came a voice out of the cloud *(the Voice of God the Father)*, saying, This is My Beloved Son: hear Him *(actually says, "be constantly hearing Him," as well meaning that no mortal must be put on the same par with Christ; the Catholics should note that He didn't say, "hear Mary," but rather, "hear Him")*.

36 And when the voice was past, Jesus was found alone *(proclaims the fact that the Voice did not come from a physical body)*. And they kept *it* close, and told no man in those days any of those things which they had seen *(meaning that they did not relate the account of this incident until after the Resurrection)*.

LESSONS

37 And it came to pass, that on the next day, when they were come down from the hill, much people met Him *(implies they were waiting for Him)*.

38 And, behold, a man of the company cried out *(a man in the crowd)*, saying, Master, I beseech You, look upon my son: for he is mine only child *(peculiar to Luke; he is the only one who mentions that this poor tormented boy was an only child)*.

39 And, lo, a spirit *(evil spirit)* takes him, and he suddenly cries out *(speaks of the demon spirit taking control of the boy)*; and it tears him that he foams again, and bruising him hardly departing from him *(constant occurrences)*.

40 And I besought Your Disciples to cast him out; and they could not *(Mark says that Jesus said that the reason was the "prayerlessness" of the Disciples; in fact, the emphasis in the Greek Text is on their "prayerlessness," rather than their "lack of fasting" [Mk. 9:29])*.

41 And Jesus answering said, O faithless and perverse generation *(was spoken to the whole of Israel)*, how long shall I be with you, and suffer you? *(This portrays a human exasperation on the part of Jesus.)* Bring your son hither *(indicates that the boy was being restrained a short distance away)*.

42 And as he was yet a coming, the devil threw him down, and tore *him (represents this demon's last effort to hurt this child)*. And Jesus rebuked the unclean spirit, and healed the child, and delivered him again to his father *(Jesus cast the demon out, and healed that which the demon had damaged regarding the child's physical body)*.

43 And they were all amazed at the mighty power of God. But while they wondered every one at all things which Jesus did, He said unto His Disciples *(portrays the idea coming up once again, as recorded in the next Verse, of Him being the Triumphant Messiah and, therefore, being made King)*,

44 Let these sayings sink down into your ears *(concerned that which they did not want to hear)*: for the Son of Man shall be delivered into the hands of men *(presents that which He had already said to them, but which they did not understand)*.

45 But they understood not this saying, and it was hid from them, that they perceived it not *(it was not purposely hidden from them, but was rather hidden because of their unbelief)*: and they feared to ask Him of that saying *(means that what He had said did not line up with their thinking)*.

46 Then there arose a reasoning among them, which of them should be greatest *(the spirit of self-will, which was the cause of them not understanding)*.

47 And Jesus, perceiving the thought of their heart *(refers to the Holy Spirit revealing to Him this which the Apostles were discussing)*, took a child, and set him by Him *(is thought to be Peter's child)*,

48 And said unto them, Whosoever shall receive this child in My Name receives Me *(carries the idea of service to others, which addresses the argument of the Disciples as to who will be the greatest; to bless a child, one must do so strictly out of Love, because a child cannot return the favor)*: and whosoever shall receive Me receives him Who sent Me *(unless one comes as a little child, one cannot receive Christ; and when one receives Christ, one has received at the same time God the Father; everything is through Christ)*: for he who is least among you all, the

same shall be great *(the work for which Christ's Gospel came into the world was no less than to put down the mighty from their seat, and to exalt the humble and the meek)*.

49 And John answered and said, Master, we saw one casting out devils *(demons)* in Your Name; and we forbad him, because he followeth not with us *(this is the sin of sectarianism, which in essence means, "the exclusion of all others, outside of a particular group")*.

50 And Jesus said unto him, Forbid *him* not: for he who is not against us is for us *(forbids all sectarianism)*.

51 And it came to pass, when the time was come that He should be received up *(this particular "time" had been planned by the Godhead since before the foundation of the world [I Pet. 1:20; Rev. 13:8])*, He stedfastly set His face to go to Jerusalem *(this is where the terrible deed must be carried out)*,

52 And sent messengers before His face *(referred to Disciples or others who went to make preparation for them to spend some time, at least one night, in this particular village)*: and they went, and entered into a village of the Samaritans, to make ready for Him *(descendants of the pagans who settled in this particular part of Israel at the time of the captivities; they intermarried with a few Jews who remained in the land [II Ki. 17:24-34])*.

53 And they did not receive Him *(presents the greatest mistake they ever made, and regrettably the great mistake made by most)*, because His face was as though He would go to Jerusalem *(had to do with the ongoing argument between the Jews and the Samaritans; in other words, they allowed their religion to cause them to miss the greatest moment in their history, and their religion probably took them to Hell)*.

54 And when His Disciples James and John saw *this (probably proclaims the two sent to the village by Jesus seeking accommodations)*, they said, Lord, will You that we command fire to come down from heaven, and consume them, even as Elijah did? *(Zeal without knowledge and failure to rightly divide the Word of Truth cause well-meaning men to greatly err.)*

55 But He turned, and rebuked them *(is the same Word used by Jesus when He rebuked evil spirits [Mat. 17:18]; the spirit of the Disciples at that time and demon spirits were all the same, hence they were both rebuked accordingly)*, and said, you know not what manner of spirit you are of *(portrays them operating in the spirit of the Evil One; how many modern Christians do the same?)*.

56 For the Son of Man is not come to destroy men's lives, but to save *them (proclaims the true mission of Christ)*. And they went to another village *(constituted the greatest moment the "other village" would ever know)*.

DISCIPLESHIP

57 And it came to pass, that, as they went in the way *(continuing the next morning their trip toward Jerusalem)*, a certain *man* said unto him, Lord, I will follow You whithersoever You go *(proclaimed this man, according to Matthew, as being a Scribe [Mat. 8:19])*.

58 And Jesus said unto him, Foxes have holes, and birds of the air *have* nests; but the Son of Man has not where to lay *His* head *(the implication regarding the Scribe is that he had not counted the cost, and when revealed, did not desire to pay the price)*.

59 And He said unto another, Follow Me *(to this man, Christ extends an invitation)*. But he said, Lord, suffer me first to go and bury my father *(proclaims the "cares of this life" robbing him of preeminence with Christ)*.

60 Jesus said unto him, Let the dead bury their dead *(was not meant to show disrespect for the dead, or of shirking of responsibility; it wasn't the idea of burying his father, but rather of placing such things first; Christ must come first in all things)*: but go thou and preach the Kingdom of God *(there were plenty of people to perform the other tasks, but precious few to preach the Word of God)*.

61 And another also said, Lord, I will follow You; but let me first go bid them farewell, which are at home at my house *(the Holy Spirit is here portraying to us the single-minded purpose which must be paramount in the life of every Believer, that is, if they are to follow Christ as they should)*.

62 And Jesus said unto him, No man, having put his hand to the plough, and looking back, is fit for the Kingdom of God *(attachment to Christ and to His Service must be unconditional)*

CHAPTER 10
(A.D. 32)
THE SEVENTY

AFTER these things *(the things of the previous Chapter)*, the Lord appointed other seventy also *(other than the Twelve; this was done toward the close of His Ministry; as well, it*

was the Lord Who appointed, and pertains to that which man cannot do; Why seventy? It is God's number representing His Spirit-Anointed Ministry), **and sent them two and two before His face into every city and place, whither He Himself would come** (when the Lord sends Preachers to certain places, it is because He desires to come there; the people must not forget this).

2 Therefore said He unto them, The harvest truly is **great, but the labourers** are **few** (this tells us that the Salvation of souls is a priority with the Lord; in fact, for everyone who doesn't have the privilege to hear, as far as that person is concerned, Jesus died in vain; there are many engaged in the fishing business, but very few who are actually fishing): **pray ye therefore the Lord of the harvest** (prayer must be the foundation on which the harvest is gathered; as well, we must remember that it is Jesus Christ Who is the Lord of the harvest), **that He would send forth labourers into His harvest** (if there are no "labourers," the harvest cannot be gathered).

3 Go your ways (respects those whom the Lord has called, and concerns where they are sent): **behold, I send you forth as lambs among wolves** (no shepherd deliberately sends his sheep among wolves, but this Shepherd can because He is almighty to save [Ps., Chpt. 23]).

4 Carry neither purse, nor scrip, nor shoes (God will provide): **and salute no man by the way** (do not be deterred from the mission at hand).

5 And into whatsoever house you enter, first say, Peace be **to this house** (proclaims a Blessing promised by the Lord to any who aid and abet those He has called, providing they are carrying out the Great Commission).

6 And if the son of peace be there (refers to one who desires the Blessings of the Lord, attempting to serve in any capacity possible), **your peace shall rest upon it** (the Blessing will be given): **if not, it shall turn to you again** (any hindrance to this all-important task stops the Blessings of God).

7 And in the same house remain, eating and drinking such things as they give (pertains not only to a single house, but the field of ministry assigned by the Lord): **for the labourer is worthy of his hire** (this is the only quotation in the Epistles from the Gospel [I Tim. 5:18]). **Go not from house to house** (in modern times, it refers to Preachers seeking better Churches simply because they pay more money; money is never to be the object, but rather the Call of God and wherever that leads).

8 And into whatsoever city you enter, and

they receive you (implies that some will not receive the Gospel), **eat such things as are set before you** (and don't complain):

9 And heal the sick who are therein (pertains to both physical and spiritual, a Part of the Blessing), **and say unto them, The Kingdom of God is come nigh unto you** (the greatest thing that could ever happen to any family or place).

10 But into whatsoever city you enter (to where the Lord has sent you), **and they receive you not** (implying that this will be the case at times), **go your ways out into the streets of the same, and say** (that which is not desired is not to be given),

11 Even the very dust of your city, which cleaves on us, we do wipe off against you (the idea is the Lord keeps a careful record): **notwithstanding be ye sure of this, that the Kingdom of God is come nigh unto you** (it is imperative that all have the opportunity to hear, but woe be unto those who reject Christ; the Great White Throne Judgment will record the rejection [Rev. 20:11-15]).

12 But I say unto you, that it shall be more tolerable in that day (the Great White Throne Judgment) **for Sodom, than for that city** (the cities of which Jesus speaks have heard the Gospel; Sodom did not have that opportunity).

13 Woe unto You, Chorazin! woe unto You, Bethsaida! for if the mighty works had been done in Tyre and Sidon, which have been done in you, they had a great while ago repented, sitting in sackcloth and ashes (these are two cities where Jesus had performed mighty works — the greatest works in the history of mankind; men will be judged not only for what they have done or failed to do, but their opportunities, their circumstances, their chances in life, will be strictly taken into account before they are judged).

14 But it shall be more tolerable for Tyre and Sidon at the judgment, than for you (these twin cities did not see the Power of God as did those spoken of by Christ; cities and places which have had little opportunity will not be spared, but will not be judged as harshly).

15 And You, Capernaum, which are exalted to Heaven (chosen by the Holy Spirit as the headquarters of Christ during His earthly Ministry), **shall be thrust down to hell** (constitutes the most severe pronounced punishment).

16 He who hears you hears Me (proclaims Spiritual Authority given to the Messenger of the Lord); **and He who despises you despises Me** (fearsome indeed!); **and he who despises Me despises Him Who sent Me** (God the Father;

these are most serious statements; in fact, some of the most serious ever uttered by Christ).

THE SEVENTY RETURN

17 And the seventy returned again with joy, saying, Lord, even the devils *(demons)* are subject unto us through Your Name *(demons are subject to us only through His Name).*

18 And He said unto them, I beheld Satan as lightning fall from Heaven *(by the Power of the Holy Spirit, Jesus saw into the future, observing Satan as he will be cast out of Heaven at the approximate mid-point of the coming Great Tribulation [Rev. 12:9]).*

19 Behold, I give unto you power to tread on serpents and scorpions, and over all the power of the enemy: and nothing shall by any means hurt you *(this is the domain of Spiritual Authority; it is only over spirit beings, and not at all over humans).*

20 Notwithstanding in this rejoice not, that the spirits are subject unto you *(this should not be the occasion of our joy)*; but rather rejoice, because your names are written in Heaven *(tells us that the Salvation of the soul must always be the occasion for rejoicing; when the Church rejoices more over other things than people being saved, something is wrong).*

21 In that hour Jesus rejoiced in spirit *(actually means in the Greek Text that Jesus greatly exulted in the Holy Spirit, which spoke of a great joy like a fountain springing up that came from the depths of His Soul; as the previous Verses proclaim, He saw the total and complete victory that would come about as a result of the Cross)*, and said, I thank You, O Father, Lord of Heaven and Earth *(Satan is not the Lord of either place, but rather God the Father)*, that You have hid these things from the wise and prudent, and have revealed them unto babes *(the religious hierarchy never saw this of which Jesus spoke, but these fishermen chosen by Christ did)*: even so, Father; for so it seemed good in Your sight *(unfortunately, far too much of the modern Church labels things "good" that God labels otherwise).*

22 All things are delivered to Me of My Father *(refers to Jesus being given the responsibility by the Father for defeating Satan and putting down his evil revolution, which would be done at the Cross)*: and no man knows Who the Son is, but the Father *(means that Jesus is of the Father, and not of man)*; and Who the Father is, but the Son *(no man can reach the "Father," or*

even know Who the "Father" is, except through the "Son," i.e., the Lord Jesus Christ; Jesus Alone is the Door [Jn. 10:9])*, and *he* to whom the Son will reveal *Him* *(Salvation is not a matter of education, but of Revelation).*

23 And He turned Him unto *His* Disciples, and said privately *(refers to not only the "Twelve," but the "Seventy" also)*, Blessed *are* the eyes which see the things that you see *(He is speaking of seeing "with the eye of faith," and believing what is seen)*:

24 For I tell you, that many Prophets and Kings have desired to see those things which you see, and have not seen *them*; and to hear those things which you hear, and have not heard *them* *(He is speaking here of all the Old Testament greats who pointed to His Coming, but of course, did not live to see such; but they believed just the same! as well, tens of thousands during Jesus' public Ministry did see and hear, but still would not believe; this shows that faith is not in the senses, but rather in the heart).*

THE GOOD SAMARITAN

25 And, behold, a certain lawyer stood up *(one who was supposed to be expert in the Mosaic Law)*, and tempted Him *(means that he would test the Lord's knowledge of the Law; he did not know that Jesus was the Law)*, saying, Master, what shall I do to inherit eternal life? *(This so-called expert in the Law was evidently not much of an expert at all, or He would have used the word "merit" and not "inherit"; inheritance is by birth; eternal life is man's greatest interest, and no more tremendous question could be asked than that of this Verse.)*

26 He said unto him, What is written in the Law? *(This presents Jesus immediately pointing to the Bible as the infallible authority.)* how readest thou? *(Jesus was speaking not only of knowing the Word, but properly understanding it as well.)*

27 And He answering said, You shall love the Lord Your God with all your heart, and with all your soul, and with all your strength, and with all your mind; and your neighbour as yourself *(this is quoted from Deut. 6:5 and Lev. 19:18).*

28 And He *(Jesus)* said unto him, You have answered right *(proclaims Christ, in effect, saying, "you know it, but you are not doing it")*: this do, and you shall live *(means that he was not doing what he knew to do; in fact, it wasn't possible for him, or anyone else for that matter,*

to fully obey the Law; so there was no Salvation in this direction).

29 But he, willing to justify himself, said to Jesus, And who is my neighbour? *(This statement discovers the character of the lawyer. He was self-righteous. He was determined to win Heaven by religious self-efforts.)*

30 And Jesus answering said, A certain *man* went down from Jerusalem to Jericho, and fell among thieves, which stripped him of his raiment, and wounded *him*, and departed, leaving *him* half dead.

31 And by chance there came down a certain Priest that way: and when he saw him, he passed by on the other side *(selfishness is the commanding force in human nature).*

32 And likewise a Levite *(spoke of those who were of the tribe of Levi),* when he was at the place, came and looked *on him,* and passed by on the other side *(proclaims this man at least looking on, while the Priest did not even bother with that).*

33 But a certain Samaritan *(the Samaritans and the Jews normally were enemies),* as he journeyed, came where he was *(where the wounded Israelite was):* and when he saw him, he had compassion *on him,*

34 And went to *him,* and bound up his wounds, pouring in oil and wine *(in those days, a wound was cleansed with grape-juice with oil then applied, which aided healing),* and set him on his own beast, and brought him to an inn, and took care of him *(tells us that this wounded traveler was not rich and, therefore, could not possibly repay the kindness extended to him).*

35 And on the morrow when he *(the good Samaritan)* departed, he took out two pence, and gave *them* to the host, and said unto him, Take care of him; and whatsoever you spend more, when I come again, I will repay you.

36 Which now of these three *(the three men who came in contact with the wounded traveler),* do you think, was neighbour unto him who fell among the thieves?

37 And he said, He who showed mercy on him. Then said Jesus unto him, Go, and do thou likewise *(another lesson taught in this Parable is that some need to be placed in the position of the wounded traveler in order that they be willing to receive help from anyone, even the hated Samaritan).*

MARY AND MARTHA

38 Now it came to pass, as they went, that

He entered into a certain village *(speaks of Bethany [Jn. 11:1; 12:1-3], a suburb of Jerusalem):* and a certain woman named Martha received Him into her house.

39 And she had a sister called Mary, which also sat at Jesus' feet, and heard His Word *(sitting at Jesus' feet is a safe refuge from assaults upon the authority and inspiration of the Scriptures).*

40 But Martha was cumbered about much serving, and came to Him, and said, Lord, do You not care that my sister has left me to serve alone? bid her therefore that she help me *(had Martha fully realized that Jesus was Jehovah, she never would have spoken so petulantly to Him).*

41 And Jesus answered and said unto her, Martha, Martha *(is said in pitying love),* you are careful and troubled about many things *(concerned things which were important, but not the most important!):*

42 But one thing is needful *(proclaims to us the Mind of God, and tells us where is all victory):* and Mary has chosen that good part *(means that this is a "choice"),* which shall not be taken away from her *(the greatest thing is communion with Christ).*

CHAPTER 11
(A.D. 33)
PRAYER

AND it came to pass, that, as He was praying in a certain place *(Jesus here does what He had admonished Martha to do — have fellowship with the Father, which Mary did),* when He ceased, one of His Disciples said unto Him *(they evidently noted the ease with which He prayed),* Lord, teach us to pray, as John also taught his disciples *(the answer to their request as given by Christ forms the basis for all prayer).*

2 And He said unto them, When you pray *(meaning that there should be a set time for prayer each day),* say, Our Father *(this speaks of relationship, and that He Alone can supply our every need)* which art in Heaven *(help comes from Heaven; none comes from this Earth),* Hallowed be Your Name *(open with praise).* Your Kingdom come *(the Believer is to pray for this Kingdom to come, and for all the obvious reasons).* Your will be done, as in Heaven, so in Earth *(the "Will of God," and not our Will, should be the supreme goal of every Believer; the Will of God is not being presently done on Earth, but it will be when the Kingdom comes; then war, sickness, and suffering will end).*

3 Give us day by day our daily bread

(physical sustenance and spiritual sustenance, which the Lord Alone can give).

4 And forgive us our sins *(this proclaims the fact that there are no perfect Believers, only a Perfect God; the best of us, whomever that may be, still live in a house of flawed flesh; consequently, we must constantly look to Christ);* for we also forgive every one who is indebted to us *(the Lord forgiving us is predicated as well on our forgiving others).* And lead us not into temptation *(in effect states help me in my weakness not to be led into temptation);* but deliver us from evil *(there is only One Deliverer, that is the Lord; man cannot deliver man, despite the claims of humanistic psychology; and God delivers through what Jesus did at the Cross, and our Faith in that Finished Work).*

5 And He said unto them *(a continuance of the explanation regarding prayer),* Which of you shall have a friend, and shall go unto him at midnight, and say unto him, Friend, lend me three loaves *(a meager request);*

6 For a friend of mine in his journey is come to me, and I have nothing to set before him? *(We as Believers must give the Message of Eternal Life to all of mankind, but the truth is, within ourselves, we have nothing to give.)*

7 And he from within shall answer and say, Trouble me not: the door is now shut, and my children are with me in bed; I cannot rise and give to you *(an obvious denial).*

8 I say unto you, Though he will not rise and give him, because he is his friend, yet because of his importunity he will rise and give him as many as he needs *(the argument of this Parable is that if a sufficiency for daily need can, by importunity, i.e., "persistence," be obtained from an unwilling source, how much more from a willing Giver, Which and Who is the Lord).*

9 And I say unto you *(telling us how to approach the Lord for whatever we need),* Ask, and it shall be given you; seek, and you shall find; knock, and it shall be opened unto you *(all of this speaks of persistence and guarantees a positive answer, at least if it's in the Will of God).*

10 For every one who asks receives; and he who seeks finds; and to him who knocks it shall be opened *(he says "everyone," and that includes you!).*

11 If a son shall ask bread of any of you who is a father, will he give him a stone? or if *he ask* a fish, will he for a fish give him a serpent?

12 Or if he shall ask an egg, will he offer him *(an egg containing)* a scorpion?

13 If you then, being evil, know how to give good gifts unto your children *(means that an earthly parent certainly would not give a child a stone who has asked for bread, etc.):* how much more shall *your* Heavenly Father give the Holy Spirit to them who ask Him? *(This refers to God's Goodness, and the fact that everything from the Godhead comes to us through the Person and Agency of the Holy Spirit; and all that He does for us is based upon the Cross of Christ, and our Faith in that Finished Work.)*

BLASPHEMY

14 And He was casting out a devil *(demon),* and it was dumb *(the Greek Text implies a mute silence, which was a form of insanity).* And it came to pass, when the devil *(demon)* was gone out, the dumb spoke; and the people wondered *(in a moment's time, the man was completely delivered and healed).*

15 But some of them said *(some of the religious leaders in Israel),* He casts out devils *(demons)* through Beelzebub the chief of the devils *(concerns a startling accusation, which constituted the terrible sin of blaspheming the Holy Spirit, for which there is no forgiveness; "Beelzebub" was the Philistine god of flies [II Ki. 1:2]; it meant "the dung god," or "lord of the dung hill"; a most contemptuous and vile idol).*

16 And others, tempting *Him (attempting to ensnare Christ in His speech or actions),* sought of Him a sign from Heaven *(strange, considering that they had just witnessed a sign of unprecedented proportions; they actually demanded a stunt, such as calling fire down from Heaven; what these foolish men didn't realize was, if He had done such, the fire would have fallen on them; but they were so spiritually insensitive, they couldn't see the danger they were in).*

17 But He, knowing their thoughts *(presents the Holy Spirit informing Him of what they were thinking, which means that they had not been saying these things so that the crowd of people could hear),* said unto them, Every Kingdom divided against itself is brought to desolation; and a house *divided* against a house falls *(division based on dissension is the sure destroyer of all).*

18 If Satan also be divided against himself, how shall his kingdom stand? *(This tells us unequivocally of the existence of such a kingdom of evil, all armed and thoroughly organized to carry out its dread purposes.)* because you say that I cast out devils *(demons)* through Beelzebub *(presents the absurdity of such an accusation).*

19 And if I by Beelzebub cast out devils *(demons)*, by whom do your sons cast *them* out? *(This means that by condemning Him, accordingly they were condemning themselves.)* **therefore shall they be your judges** *(the crowd knew that they had never heard of anyone casting out demons by the power of Satan).*

20 But if I with the Finger of God *(Power of God)* **cast out devils** *(demons)* *(they could not question the Healings, Miracles or Deliverances)*, **no doubt the Kingdom of God is come upon you** *(every evidence said that He was of God; His Power was undeniable!).*

21 When a strong man *(Satan)* **armed keeps his palace** *(the world)*, **his goods are in peace** *(represents freedom from hostile action, which Satan enjoyed until the First Advent of Christ):*

22 But when a stronger than he *(Jesus Christ is stronger)* **shall come upon him, and overcome him** *(referred to what Jesus did at the Cross [Col. 2:14-15]),* **He takes from him all his armour wherein he trusted** *(Jesus Christ defeated Satan totally and completely at the Cross, where He atoned for all sin),* **and divides his spoils** *(means that multiple millions have been Redeemed from Satan's clutches, and instead of being captives of Satan they are now captives of Jesus Christ [Eph. 4:8-9]).*

23 He who is not with Me is against Me *(presents the fact that there is no neutrality with Christ):* **and he who gathers not with Me scatters** *(everything is either of the Devil or of Christ; there is no middle ground).*

24 When the unclean spirit is gone out of a man *(concerns the efforts of man, whatever they may be, to save himself other than by Christ and Him Crucified),* **he walks through dry places, seeking rest** *(concerns the "unclean spirit" which has gone out);* **and finding none, he says, I will return unto my house whence I came out** *(unless Christ affects the work, whatever it might be, it is not truly affected).*

25 And when he *(the evil spirit)* **comes, he finds it swept and garnished** *(means that it was filled with that other than Christ).*

26 Then goes he, and takes *to him* seven other spirits more wicked than himself *(concerns the reoccupation by demon spirits);* **and they enter in, and dwell there** *(proving that most of the world is controlled by demon spirits):* **and the last** *state* **of that man is worse than the first** *(this was the state of Israel after they had rejected Christ, which ultimately led to their total destruction).*

27 And it came to pass, as He spoke these things, a certain woman of the company lifted up her voice, and said unto Him *(the Lord was teaching the most solemn truths about the terrors of the spirit world of darkness, and this woman rudely interrupted with her carnal thoughts),* **Blessed** *is* **the womb that bear you, and the paps which you have sucked** *(it was true what the woman said, but out of place at this time).*

28 But He said, Yea rather, blessed *are* they who hear the Word of God, and keep it *(the Lord gently reproved her, pointing out that the natural man and natural relationships cannot be recognized in the kingdom of spiritual realities).*

JONAH

29 And when the people were gathered thick together, He began to say, This is an evil generation *(proclaims the unbelief of Israel; they were extremely religious, and yet did not know God Whom they spoke of constantly):* **they seek a sign; and there shall no sign be given it, but the sign of Jonah the Prophet** *(the sign of which Jesus spoke was the resurrection of Jonah from the belly of the whale; likewise, Jesus would be Resurrected from the dead, but regrettably, Israel did not believe that sign).*

30 For as Jonah was a sign unto the Ninevites *(they must have heard of his deliverance from the great fish; he was entombed in this monster for three days and three nights; and so was a Type of Him Who was three days and three nights in the heart of the Earth),* **so shall also the Son of Man be to this generation** *(Nineveh was given forty days in which to repent; Jerusalem was given forty years; Repentance in the one case averted the judgment; unbelief in the other determined the destruction).*

31 The queen of the south shall rise up in the judgment with the men of this generation, and condemn them: for she came from the utmost parts of the earth to hear the wisdom of Solomon; and, behold, a greater than Solomon *is* here.

32 The men of Nineveh shall rise up in the judgment with this generation, and shall condemn it: for they repented at the preaching of Jonah; and, behold, a greater than Jonah *is* here *(in Verses 29 through 32; the Lord Jesus testifies to the truthfulness of the Scriptures respecting the Queen of the South, plus Jonah and the men of Nineveh; and further, He affirms the fact of the Resurrection and the judgment to come, declaring that all those persons will rise from the dead; this supplemental statement establishes the*

historic truth of the Book of Jonah).

THE LIGHT

33 No man, when he has lit a candle, puts *it* in a secret place, neither under a bushel, but on a candlestick, that they which come in may see the light *(Christ is the Light of the world; He did not hide that light, it shone fully on every man; but few accepted it, for the majority were so willfully blind that they remained unilluminated).*

34 The light of the body is the eye *(what a lamp is to a room, the eye is to the body)*: therefore when your eye is single, your whole body also is full of light *(the emphasis is on the word "single"; it means singleness of purpose, which keeps us from the snare of having a double treasure and consequently a divided heart);* but when *your eye* is evil, your body also *is* full of darkness *(Jesus is the Light; if the "eye" does not see Him fully, moral and spiritual darkness prevails).*

35 Take heed therefore that the light which is in You be not darkness *(this speaks of deception; the Verse could be translated, "take heed therefore that the light that is in you be not artificial light and, therefore, darkness").*

36 If your whole body therefore *be* full of light, having no part dark, the whole shall be full of light, as when the bright shining of a candle does give you light *(the problem with the Church is "part dark" and "part light").*

PHARISEES

37 And as He spoke, a certain Pharisee besought Him to dine with him: and He went in, and sat down to meat.

38 And when the Pharisee saw *it*, he marvelled that He *(Jesus)* had not first washed before dinner *(the "washing" spoken of here had nothing to do with sanitation; the Pharisees taught that a demon sat on unwashed hands, and unless a certain ritual was performed, the demon could be ingested while eating).*

39 And the Lord said unto him, Now do you Pharisees make clean the outside of the cup and the platter *(outward show)*; but your inward part is full of ravening and wickedness *(presents a scathing denunciation).*

40 You fools *(what an indictment! and He said this to the man's face)*, did not He *(God)* Who made that which is without make that which is within also? *(The inward man must be changed as well, and can only be changed by the*

Power of God.)

41 But rather give alms of such things as you have; and, behold, all things are clean unto you *(the Greek here reads: "But rather the things that are within, that is the heart, the will, the affections, then all other actions proceeding from a heart truly given to God, will be acceptable to Him; otherwise such actions will be 'dead works'; thus, the Lord perpetually taught the necessity of the New Birth").*

42 But woe unto you, Pharisees! *(Once again, this is a scathing denunciation.)* for you tithe mint and rue *(leaves of certain plants)* and all manner of herbs *(meaning that they were meticulous to pay their tithes)*, and pass over judgment and the Love of God *(the giving of money will not take the place of righteous living)*: these ought you to have done *(you ought to pay your tithes)*, and not to leave the other undone.

43 Woe unto you, Pharisees! for you love the uppermost seats in the Synagogues *(position of importance)*, and greetings in the markets *(to be greeted as a superior).*

44 Woe unto you, Scribes *(supposed to be experts in the Law of Moses)* and Pharisees *(supposed to be the religious leaders of Israel)*, hypocrites! *(You aren't what you claim to be.)* for you are as graves which appear not, and the men who walk over *them* are not aware *of them (according to the Mosaic Law, it was wrong to touch anything that pertained to death because it represented sin; Jesus was saying that these religious leaders of Israel were like covered-over graves, with men walking over them and being defiled, and not aware of it; in other words, the religious leaders of Israel were sin and, therefore, death and a defilement to Israel).*

45 Then answered one of the lawyers *(supposed to be experts in the Law of Moses)*, and said unto Him, Master, thus saying You reproach us also *(insult us).*

46 And He *(Jesus)* said, Woe unto you also, *you* lawyers! for you laden men with burdens grievous to be borne *(kept adding things to the original Law of Moses)*, and you yourselves touch not the burdens with one of your fingers *(they did not themselves live up at all to that which they demanded of the people; such is religion!).*

47 Woe unto you! for you build the sepulchres of the Prophets, and your fathers killed them *(they built gorgeous tombs for the Prophets of Old who had long since died, but in truth their hearts were just as murderous as their fathers of the past who killed the Prophets).*

48 Truly you bear witness that you allow

the deeds of your fathers *(means they were following in the same vein)*: for they indeed killed them, and you build their sepulchres *(it is far easier to admire dead Saints than to identify one's self with living ones)*.

49 Therefore also said the Wisdom of God *(Christ [I Cor. 1:24])*, I will send them Prophets and Apostles, and *some* of them they shall slay and persecute *("I" is emphatic, and speaks of the Divine self-consciousness of Jesus; in other words, the Redeemer identifies Himself with God, and actually as God"; "they" refers to the religious leaders of Israel who killed the Prophets and the Apostles)*:

50 That the blood of all the Prophets, which was shed from the foundation of the world, may be required of this generation *(the "generation" of which Jesus spoke was the generation of His day; the reason such judgment was called down upon their heads, which was fulfilled in A.D. 70, was that they rejected the One Whom the Prophets had predicted would come, namely Christ)*;

51 From the blood of Abel unto the blood of Zachariah, which perished between the Altar and the Temple *(God keeps an account of every injustice, no matter how large or small)*: verily I say unto you, It shall be required of this generation.

52 Woe unto you, lawyers! for you have taken away the key of knowledge *(they took the Word of God from the people, substituting their own glosses; such characterizes much of the modern Ministry as well!)*: you entered not in yourselves *(you are not even saved yourselves)*, and them who were entering in you hindered *(by teaching error, they kept the True Word of God from the people, thereby hindering them; once again, it is the same presently!)*.

53 And as He said these things unto them, the Scribes and the Pharisees began to urge *Him* vehemently *(trying to get Him to say something by which they could accuse Him)*, and to provoke Him to speak of many things:

54 Laying wait for Him, and seeking to catch something out of His mouth, that they might accuse Him *(speaks of all types of verbal traps they laid for Him, but all to no avail!)*.

CHAPTER 12
(A.D. 33)
THE LEAVEN

IN the mean time, when there were gathered together an innumerable multitude of people, insomuch that they trode one upon another, He began to say unto His Disciples first of all *(rejected by the religious leaders of Israel, He confines His Words to His Disciples, at least at this time)*, Beware ye of the leaven of the Pharisees, which is hypocrisy *("leaven" was the interpretations and traditions of men, which they substituted for the Word of God; Jesus labels this as hypocrisy, which is the acting out of the part of a character, or being something other than what one really is; in fact, all religion is hypocrisy, for the rules of men, which is religion, cannot change the heart)*.

2 For there is nothing covered, that shall not be revealed; neither hid, that shall not be known *(what is right or wrong will ultimately be revealed)*.

3 Therefore whatsoever you have spoken in darkness shall be heard in the light *(wrong doctrine, which is darkness, will ultimately be revealed as to what it actually is by the light of the Word of God)*; and that which you have spoken in the ear in closets shall be proclaimed upon the housetops *(the Pharisees plotted in secret to kill Christ; their secrets are now known all over the world; and so shall all ungodliness be ultimately found out)*.

4 And I say unto you My friends, Be not afraid of them who kill the body, and after that have no more that they can do *(Believers are not to fear men)*.

5 But I will forewarn you whom you shall fear: Fear Him *(God)*, which after He has killed *(life and death are in the Hands of God Alone)* has power to cast into hell *(the greater fear of God would banish the lesser fear of man; for man can only touch the body, but God can reach the soul and cast it into Hell)*; yea, I say unto you, Fear Him *(presents the second time this is stated and is, therefore, meant to be clearly understood)*.

6 Are not five sparrows sold for two farthings *(an insignificant transaction)*, and not one of them is forgotten before God? *(Every incident and transaction, no matter how small or seemingly insignificant, is known and recorded by God.)*

7 But even the very hairs of your head are all numbered *(presents a degree of knowledge which is beyond the ability of any human being to comprehend)*. Fear not therefore: you are of more value than many sparrows *(for those who truly follow the Lord, these words should greatly comfort all Believers; our every action is known by Him, and He will superintend every action,*

if we will allow Him to do so).

8 Also I say unto you, Whosoever shall confess Me before men, him shall the Son of Man also confess before the Angels of God *(if we confess Him before men, however painful that testimony might be, He will confess us before Angels):*

9 But he who denies Me before men shall be denied before the Angels of God *(if we disown Him before men, He will disown us before Angels; these Passages declare to all that Jesus Christ, the poor Galilee Rabbi is in Truth King of kings and Lord of lords!).*

THE UNPARDONABLE SIN

10 And whosoever shall speak a word against the Son of Man, it shall be forgiven him *(that is, if forgiveness is sought [I Jn. 1:9]):* but unto him who blasphemes against the Holy Spirit it shall not be forgiven *(this "blasphemy" cannot be committed by those who make no profession of the Lord; this means that only professors of religion commit this sin; there is no forgiveness for this sin, and in fact, the perpetrators will not even seek forgiveness).*

OPPOSITION

11 And when they bring you unto the Synagogues, and *unto* magistrates, and powers *(officials),* take you no thought how or what thing you shall answer, or what you shall say *(simply means not to be full of anxiety; it does not mean that no preparation should be made, but only that trust must be placed in the Lord to provide the suitable answers):*

12 For the Holy Spirit shall teach you in the same hour what you ought to say *(the Believer should always look to the Holy Spirit for leading and guidance).*

COVETOUSNESS

13 And one of the company said unto Him, Master, speak to my brother, that he divide the inheritance with me *(the insensibility and rudeness of the natural heart is here exhibited; this man interrupted the Lord, making a ridiculous request).*

14 And He said unto him, Man, who made Me a judge or a divider over you? *(Had the Lord interfered in Civil Government, He would have placed Himself in the power of His enemies; that was not His place. He dealt with souls, and directed men's attention to another life that lies beyond the grave.)*

15 And He said unto them, Take heed, and beware of covetousness *(the desire of wrong things, or attempting to obtain right things in the wrong way):* for a man's life consisteth not in the abundance of the things which he possesseth *(most of the world tries to find life in possessions; however, there is no "life" in these things; "Life" is found only in Christ [Jn. 14:6]).*

THE RICH FOOL

16 And He spoke a Parable unto them, saying, The ground of a certain rich man brought forth plentifully *(riches, if rightly acquired, should be thought of as blessings from God, and treated accordingly):*

17 And he thought within himself, saying, What shall I do, because I have no room where to bestow my fruits? *(The "fruits" had been given to him by God, and should be used accordingly. But instead he will heap them up unto himself, which regrettably, is what most do.)*

18 And he said, This will I do: I will pull down my barns, and build greater; and there will I bestow all my fruits and my goods *(he was meant to use these "fruits" for the Glory of God, which was to take the Gospel to the world, but instead he did the opposite).*

19 And I will say to my soul, Soul, you have much goods laid up for many years; take your ease, eat, drink, *and* be merry *(the truth was his soul had nothing; in fact, he had provided for the flesh, but he hadn't provided for the soul; how many rich Christians, regrettably, fall into this same category?).*

20 But God said unto him *(what is God saying to me and you?),* *You* fool *(the Lord is saying the same to all who follow in the train of covetousness),* this night your soul shall be required of you *(sooner or later, "this night" will come):* then whose shall those things be, which you have provided? *(He didn't give them to God, and now "these things" are to be squandered.)*

21 So *is* he who lays up treasure for himself, and is not rich toward God *(if riches come, they can either be used for self or God; which are they?).*

WORRY

22 And He said unto His Disciples, Therefore I say unto you, Take no thought for your life, what you shall eat; neither for the body, what you shall put on *(don't worry about these things).*

23 The life is more than meat, and the body *is more* than raiment *(in other words, take care of the spiritual, and the Lord will take care of the material and the physical)*.

24 Consider the ravens *(an unclean fowl)*: for they neither sow nor reap; which neither have storehouse nor barn; and God feeds them *(no matter how lowly they are)*: how much more are you better than the fowls? *(If the Lord feeds buzzards, don't you think that He will feed us, that is, if we truly trust Him!)*

25 And which of you with taking thought *(by worry)* can add to his stature one cubit? *(Of all creation, man alone is given to worry, fear, rebellion, sin, and unbelief.)*

26 If you then be not able to do that thing which is least *(if we cannot change by worry even the smallest things)*, why take you thought for the rest?

27 Consider the lilies how they grow: they toil not, they spin not *(whirling around in a state of mental confusion)*; and yet I say unto you, that Solomon in all his glory was not arrayed like one of these *(the lily abides by God's Creation, and if the Believer will do the same, he will enjoy the provision of that Creation)*.

28 If then God so clothe the grass, which is to day in the field, and tomorrow is cast into the oven *(assures us of the fact that God even provides for that which is of short duration)*; how much more *will He clothe* you, O ye of little faith? *(Speaks of Believers being eternal, and consequently, of untold value; to observe God's glorious Creation and how He Cares for it, and then to doubt His Care for us is an insult to the Lord of the highest magnitude.)*

29 And seek not ye what you shall eat, or what you shall drink *(trust the Lord for these things)*, neither be ye of doubtful mind *(a distracted state of mind, wavering between hope and fear)*.

30 For all these things do the nations of the world seek after *(speaks of the world's economy, and not God's Economy)*: and your Father knows that you have need of these things *(means that we are now in His Kingdom; therefore, we are in His creative Care)*.

31 But rather seek ye the Kingdom of God *(tells us what we are to truly seek)*; and all these things shall be added unto you *(when we come to Christ, we leave the world's economy and enter into God's Economy, which the latter is a never failing economy)*.

32 Fear not *(not a suggestion, but rather a Command)*, little flock *expressing the Great Shepherd's tender care for His Sheep)*; for it is your Father's good pleasure to give you the Kingdom *(this is the Kingdom of God, thereby, far greater than the kingdoms of this world)*.

RICHES

33 Sell that you have, and give alms *(the idea is not to hoard and covet such as the world does; as God blesses us, we should give liberally and generously to His Work; however, we must make certain that it is His Work to which we are giving)*; provide yourselves bags which wax not old, a treasure in the Heavens that fails not, where no thief approaches, neither moth corrupts *(lay up treasures in Heaven)*.

34 For where your treasure is, there will your heart be also *(treasure here will fail because of thieves and corruption; however, treasure there, referring to Heaven, will never fail; the "heart" is one's very being; the implication is that if there is no treasure in Heaven, the person will not go there when he dies; no matter his profession, his heart is where his treasure is)*.

WATCHING SERVANTS

35 Let your loins be girded about, and *your* lights burning *(working and waiting should characterize the Christian)*;

36 And you yourselves like unto men who wait for their Lord *(refers to the Rapture of the Church)*, when He will return from the wedding *(in essence, means to "return from preparations for the wedding")*; that when He comes and knocks, they may open unto him immediately *(speaks of readiness at all times)*.

37 Blessed *are* those servants, whom the Lord when He comes shall find watching *(proclaims those ready for the Rapture)*: verily I say unto you, that He *(the Lord)* shall gird Himself, and make them to sit down to meat, and will come forth and serve them *(speaks of the Marriage Supper of the Lamb, with Jesus as the Host)*.

38 And if He shall come in the second watch *(9 p.m. to 12 midnight)*, or come in the third watch *(12 midnight till 3 a.m.)*, and find *them* so, blessed are those servants *(the idea is that we are to be ready for His Coming at all times)*.

THE GOODMAN OF THE HOUSE

39 And this know, that if the goodman of the house had known what hour the thief would come, he would have watched, and not

have suffered his house to be broken through *(if one is truly watching for the Lord, then at the same time He will be watching as it respects Satan that the evil one not destroy his "house").*

40 Be you therefore ready also: for the Son of Man comes at an hour when you think not *(regrettably, most of the modern Church doesn't think the Rapture will take place; this means that it will definitely take place, and very soon!).*

THE UNFAITHFUL SERVANT

41 Then Peter said unto Him, Lord, do you speak this Parable unto us, or even to all? *(Peter is thinking of an earthly kingdom about to begin, with the Twelve paramount in that Kingdom; in fact, Jesus is speaking to all.)*

42 And the Lord said, Who then is that faithful and wise steward *(some have claimed that the "steward" refers to Ministers only; however, the very nature of the word pertains not to position, but to responsibility, which applies to all),* whom *His* lord shall make ruler over His household, to give *them their* portion of meat in due season? *(It is the steward who is "faithful and wise.")*

43 Blessed *is* that servant *(stewards and servants are the same),* whom his Lord when He comes shall find so doing *(being faithful in what the Lord has called us to do, proclaiming the fact that such are also wise).*

44 Of a truth I say unto you, that He will make him ruler over all that He has *(a ruler in the Kingdom of God, which is yet to come, is the reward which the "faithful and wise" will seek, and not things of this world).*

45 But and if that servant say in his heart, My Lord delays His coming *(regrettably, most of the modern Church falls into this category);* and shall begin to beat the menservants and maidens *(to not properly love God is to not properly love our neighbor as ourselves),* and to eat and drink, and to be drunken *(proclaims Believers who have ceased to believe and have, thereby, lost their way, which will ultimately conclude in the loss of their souls; as well, this completely refutes the Unscriptural Doctrine of Unconditional Eternal Security);*

46 The lord of that servant will come in a day when he looks not for *Him,* and at an hour when he is not aware, and will cut him in sunder, and will appoint him his portion with the unbelievers *(this clearly points to former Believers who have ceased to believe and will, thereby, die eternally lost [Heb. 6:4-6; 10:23-29]).*

47 And that servant *(one who had formerly been saved),* which knew his Lord's will, and prepared not *himself,* neither did according to His *(God's)* will, shall be beaten with many *stripes (degrees of punishment; people who have known God, but have turned from Him, will suffer greater punishment in eternity than will those who had little opportunity, if any, to know the Lord).*

48 But he who knew not *(did not know the way of the Lord),* and did commit things worthy of stripes, shall be beaten with few *stripes (fewer stripes than his counterpart who had every opportunity).* For unto whomsoever much is given, of him shall be much required: and to whom men have committed much, of him they will ask the more *(from these Scriptures, Catholics claim the doctrine of purgatory; but purgatory is said to be purgative and not punitive; hence, these verses do not apply).*

OPPOSITION

49 I am come to send fire on the earth *(the Work of the Lord will bring about persecution; regrettably, most of it will come from that which refers to itself as the "Church");* and what will I, if it be already kindled? *(This speaks of the terrible opposition of the Pharisees and Scribes against Him, which would mark the position of the apostate Church, even as it continues unto this hour.)*

50 But I have a baptism to be baptized with *(speaks of the baptism of suffering, which would lead to the Cross);* and how am I straitened *(pressed)* till it be accomplished!

51 Suppose ye that I am come to give peace on earth? I tell you, No; but rather division *(His object was to bring peace, but the effect was fire and sword; this effect was caused through the corruption of man's nature, for the presence of Christ brought to the surface the evil of the human heart; the depth of that evil and the hatred of the heart for God were manifested in the Cross; regarding "division," Christ is not the cause of division, but the occasion of it; division is caused by the rebellion of men against the Gospel [II Cor. 2:14-17]):*

52 For from henceforth there shall be five in one house divided, three against two, and two against three *(because of Christ, the "division" in families has been obvious from that time until the present).*

53 The father shall be divided against the son, and the son against the father; the mother against the daughter, and the daughter against the mother; the mother-in-law against her daughter-in-law, and the daughter-in-law

against her mother-in-law (blood ties are not strong enough to assuage this hatred; it may be addressed toward the individual, but it is actually toward Christ).

THE PHARISEES

54 And He said also to the people (all the previous instruction had been given solely to His Disciples), When you see a cloud rise out of the west, straightway you say, There comes a shower; and so it is.

55 And when *you see* the south wind blow, you say, There will be heat; and it comes to pass.

56 You hypocrites, you can discern the face of the sky and of the earth; but how is it that you do not discern this time? (In these statements, the Lord warns the people of Israel of approaching judgment. He bases this warning upon two factors, signs and their own moral consciousness.)

57 Yea, and why even of yourselves judge you not what is right? (He accuses them of willful blindness to the Prophecies of Daniel, which define the actual appearing of the Messiah. This blindness was more inexcusable because of their intelligence in observing the weather. They could observe that, but they could not observe Him, and He was much more obvious than the weather.)

58 When you go with your adversary to the Magistrate (in this case, the Holy Spirit), *as you are* in the way, give diligence that you may be delivered from Him (in other words, get right with God); lest He (the Holy Spirit) hale you to the Judge (God the Father), and the Judge deliver you to the officer (the Angels), and the officer cast you into prison (into Hell).

59 I tell you, you shall not depart thence, till you have paid the very last mite (the condition of release laid down in this Verse is impossible to the sinner, for he could never discharge his indebtedness of a perfect obedience to God's Law; the only answer is Jesus; He paid all the price that we may go free; simple trust in Him discharges all our spiritual debt; but Israel refused Him, even as most of the world refuses Him; consequently, if He is not allowed to pay the debt, then the individual must pay the debt, which is eternal Hell, and in fact, can never be paid).

CHAPTER 13
(A.D. 33)
REPENTANCE

THERE were present at that season (probably referred to the previous Passover when this event took place) some who told Him of the Galilaeans, whose blood Pilate had mingled with their sacrifices (something happened at the Temple, which is not explained here, with Pilate dispatching soldiers to quell the disturbance; whatever it was, some had been killed while they were offering up Sacrifices at the great Altar immediately in front of the Temple; as a result, their "blood" had mingled with the blood of the Sacrifices).

2 And Jesus answering said unto them, Do you suppose that these Galilaeans were sinners above all the Galilaeans, because they suffered such things? (This is exactly what the religious leaders thought.)

3 I tell you, No: but, except you repent, you shall all likewise perish (this is a Message of somber note; evidently, they had assumed in their minds that the judgments suffered by these people was because of their great sins; they reasoned that they themselves were much more righteous, and would not suffer such — Jesus tells them differently).

4 Or those eighteen, upon whom the tower in Siloam fell, and slew them, think ye that they were sinners above all men who dwelt in Jerusalem? (It is said that the Jews looked on the catastrophe as a judgment on the workmen who perished because Pilate paid them out of Temple money. It had to do with the pool of Siloam located in Jerusalem.)

5 I tell you, No: but, except you repent, you shall all likewise perish (if Christ says something one time, it is of extreme significance; if it is said twice, as here, then it takes on a consequence of unprecedented proportions; the tragedy is in A.D. 70; they did perish when Titus, the Roman General, completely destroyed Jerusalem).

THE BARREN FIG TREE

6 He spoke also this Parable (refers to it being said immediately after the demand for Repentance); A certain *man* had a fig tree planted in his vineyard (the "fig tree" is symbolic of Israel); and he came and sought fruit thereon, and found none (Israel had brought forth no fruit for the Lord at all, despite all their religiosity; this should be a lesson for the modern Church).

7 Then said He unto the Dresser of His Vineyard (portrays the "owner" as God, and the "Dresser" as Jesus; the "Vineyard," i.e., "belonged to God"; as well, the Church also belongs to Him [Mat. 16:18]), Behold, these three years I come seeking fruit on this fig tree, and

find none *(illustrates the three years of the Lord's Ministry up to now; despite the greatest miracles the world had ever seen, and by far, Israel remained spiritually blind and dumb; there was no fruit)*: cut it down; why cumbereth it the ground? *(This was a warning to Israel that if no fruit was forthcoming, judgment was imminent. But still, they did not heed or listen.)*

8 And He *(the Lord Jesus)* answering said unto Him *(God the Father)*, Lord, let it alone this year also, till I shall dig about it, and dung it *(represents the last months of the last year of the Master's Ministry, for it is thought that His Ministry lasted for about three and a half years; this portrays the fact that Christ had pleaded with the Father for a little more time)*:

9 And if it bear fruit, *well:* and if not, *then* after that You shall cut it down *(in fact, the last few months of His public Ministry were opposed more than ever; Israel did not bear any fruit, and in A.D. 70 they were "cut down").*

THE SABBATH

10 And He was teaching in one of the Synagogues on the Sabbath *(by now, most Synagogues were closed to Him; this evidently was one of the few which still allowed Him to Minister)*.

11 And, behold, there was a woman which had a spirit of infirmity eighteen years *(means that a demon spirit had caused this sickness, which no doubt is the cause of much sickness presently, as well)*, and was bowed together, and could in no wise lift up *herself (constituted, some think, a curvature of the spine; she was an example of what Satan has done to the whole of humanity; mankind in general, at least in one way or the other, has "a spirit of infirmity" brought on by Satan, and is "bound together"; as well, man in no wise, can "lift up himself")*.

12 And when Jesus saw her, He called *her to Him (means that this miracle, like that of Nain, was unsolicited)*, and said unto her, Woman, you are loosed from your infirmity *(a declaration of deliverance, needed by the entirety of the human race)*.

13 And He laid *His* hands on her: and immediately she was made straight, and glorified God *(this portrays the fact that this woman knew the Lord, which means that she was right with God, but yet was bound by this "spirit of infirmity," proving to us that such can happen, even now, and no doubt does; this doesn't mean the woman was demon possessed, for she wasn't; it does mean that she was "oppressed by demon spirits," which* can happen to any Believer [Acts 10:38]).

14 And the ruler of the Synagogue answered with indignation, because that Jesus had healed on the Sabbath Day *(there was nothing in the Law of Moses that said a person could not be healed on the Sabbath Day; this was an invention purely of man)*, and said unto the people, There are six days in which men ought to work: in them therefore come and be healed, and not on the Sabbath Day *(proclaims this self-righteous bigot rebuking Christ; religious evil is the highest form of evil!)*.

15 The Lord then answered him, and said, *You* hypocrite *(proclaims righteous indignation, and rightly so! and let it be understood that Christ said this out loud in front of all the people)*, does not each one of you on the Sabbath loose his ox or *his* ass from the stall, and lead *him* away to watering? *(He vividly draws a contrast between animals and human beings, and made these Pharisees look like fools, which they were!)*

16 And ought not this woman, being a daughter of Abraham *(proclaims Covenant relationship)*, whom Satan has bound, lo, these eighteen years *(Satan is the cause of all bondage, be it physical, mental, financial, or spiritual)*, be loosed from this bond on the Sabbath Day? *(This proclaims the Deliverance of this woman as more important than keeping some silly man-made rule.)*

17 And when He had said these things, all His adversaries were ashamed *(they were ashamed, but not changed, for they would not repent)*: and all the people rejoiced for all the glorious things that were done by Him *(but this incensed these hypocrites even more!)*.

THE MUSTARD SEED

18 Then said He, Unto what is the Kingdom of God like? *(This is meant to portray what Satan and religious men have done to the Great Plan of God as given to Abraham and Moses, as well as the Prophets. It would apply presently to the Church as well!)* and whereunto shall I resemble it? *(This presents God Himself revealing His Judgment about that which professed to be His Kingdom.)*

19 It is like a grain of mustard seed, which a man took, and cast into his garden *(has to do with the humble beginnings of the Kingdom of God on Earth, going as far back as Abel; in fact, its beginnings were so small that the Bible only records two conversions up to Noah, a period of some 1600 years)*; and it grew, and waxed

a great tree (*speaks of the nation of Israel growing into millions of people*); and the fowls of the air lodged in the branches of it (*proclaims demon spirits making their home in this Kingdom; hence, this explains the spiritual attitude of the Ruler of the Synagogue where Jesus healed the woman, as well as the entirety of the religious leadership of Israel*).

THE LEAVEN

20 And again He said, Whereunto shall I liken the Kingdom of God?

21 It is like leaven (*meant to portray rot and corruption*), which a woman took (*the word "woman" as used here represents wickedness, fallacy, uncleanness, unfaithfulness, and false religion*) and hid in three measures of meal (*meal symbolizes the Word of God*), till the whole was leavened (*portrays Israel during the time of Christ as being thoroughly corrupted, and as well, refers to the modern Church*).

MERE PROFESSION

22 And He went through the cities and villages, teaching, and journeying toward Jerusalem (*infers that He was no longer welcome in any Synagogue; these were the last few months, or even weeks, of the Master's Ministry*).

23 Then said one unto Him, Lord, are there few that be saved? (*This question was asked, no doubt, because of the statements just made by Christ concerning the "mustard tree" and the "three measures of meal."*) And He said unto them,

24 Strive to enter in at the strait gate (*automatically narrows the opening for admittance to Salvation; it is not that God refuses people, but people refuse God, or at least God's Way*): for many, I say unto you, will seek to enter in, and shall not be able (*proclaims the fact of many trying to enter in by a way other than the Cross, which is impossible!*).

25 When once the master of the house is risen up, and has shut to the door (*pertains to death*), and you begin to stand without (*refers to great multitudes, who thought they were within, but in reality, were "without"; there is nothing worse than a false way of Salvation*), and to knock at the door, saying, Lord, Lord, open unto us (*a prayer that could have been answered at any time before death, but cannot be answered after death*); and He shall answer and say unto you, I know you not whence ye are (*Christ will say to all who have rejected the Cross, "I know

you not"; there could be no more chilling announcement*):

26 Then shall you begin to say, We have eaten and drunk in Your presence, and You have taught in our streets (*pertains to the Israel of Jesus' day, who were so familiar with Christ, but rejected Him; it pertains now, to the vast multitudes, who are religious but lost*).

27 But He shall say, I tell you, I know you not whence you are (*proclaims Jesus Christ Alone as the Judge*); depart from Me, all *ye* workers of iniquity (*anyone who rejects the Cross, is a "worker of iniquity," whether they understand such or not; rejecting the Cross puts one in a state of rebellion*).

28 There shall be weeping and gnashing of teeth (*places the professors of religion on the same par as the atheist and Christ-rejecters*), when you shall see Abraham, and Isaac, and Jacob, and all the Prophets, in the Kingdom of God (*presents these as being with the Lord*), and you *yourselves* thrust out (*to be shut out from Heaven is to be shut into Hell*).

29 And they shall come from the east, and *from* the west, and from the north, and *from* the south (*proclaims an end of any type of exclusivity of the Gospel as practiced by the Jews in Jesus' day; it will go to the world, which it did*), and shall sit down in the Kingdom of God (*predicts the Gentile Church having the same rights as the Jews, at least the Jews who are saved [Eph. 2:13-18]*).

30 And, behold, there are last which shall be first (*refers basically to the Church which is "last," i.e., after Israel, but will come in "first," because of being the first to accept Christ*), and there are first which shall be last (*refers to Israel which was first in line to receive Christ, but instead rejected Him, and will consequently, be the "last" to accept Him, which they will do at the Second Coming*).

HEROD

31 The same day there came certain of the Pharisees, saying unto Him, Get Thee out, and depart hence: for Herod will kill You (*proclaims a pretense on their part at friendliness and concern, when their only true objective was to stop Christ in His Work and silence His Preaching; this was the same Herod who murdered John the Baptist*).

32 And He said unto them, You go, and tell that fox (*literally reads in the Greek Text, "she-fox," which was the most contemptuous name ever

given anyone by Jesus), **Behold, I cast out devils** *(demons)*, **and I do cures today and tomorrow** *(speaks of His Personal Ministry, i.e., "today," and this Ministry that would continue through His followers, i.e., "tomorrow"; in this statement, He is actually declaring Herod to be of the devil, and that the day is coming, when such as he, will no longer rule among the sons of men; this awaits the Second Coming, but is closer now than ever)*, **and the third** *day* **I shall be perfected** *(predicts His Death, Resurrection, Ascension, and Exaltation).*

33 Nevertheless I must walk today, and tomorrow, and the *day* **following** *(simply meant that He was on His way to Jerusalem, which would take some three days)*: **for it cannot be that a Prophet perish out of Jerusalem** *(a terrible indictment on that city! Satan has contested this city as no other, because the Lord chose Jerusalem wherein His Name would be placed [II Chron. 6:6]; at the Second Coming there will finally be peace).*

JERUSALEM

34 O Jerusalem, Jerusalem *(said as a cry of anguish and of love, but yet with a deep foreboding!)*, **which kills the Prophets, and stones them who are sent unto you** *(this affected not only Israel, but the entirety of the world; the rejection of Christ by His Own People, caused the "times of the Gentiles" to be continued, with the Government of God concerning this planet delayed)*; **how often would I have gathered thy children together, as a hen** *does gather* **her brood under** *her* **wings, and you would not!** *(Proclaims the countless opportunities given for Repentance, but to no avail.)*

35 Behold, your house is left unto you desolate *(in effect speaks of the Temple, which with the rejection of Him, will now be rejected by God)*: **and verily I say unto you, You shall not see Me** *(having rejected Christ, they would see "Caesar," which would prove to be a catastrophic choice)*, **until** *the time* **come when you shall say, Blessed** *is* **He Who comes in the Name of the Lord** *(quoted from Psalms 118:26; it speaks of the coming Kingdom Age, which will begin with the Second Coming; at that time Israel will then accept Christ as Lord, Saviour, and Messiah).*

CHAPTER 14
(A.D. 33)
SABBATH

AND it came to pass, as He went into the house of one of the chief Pharisees to eat

bread on the Sabbath Day *(concerns a very influential Rabbi, or even possibly a member of the vaunted Sanhedrin)*, **that they watched Him** *(suggests that this man was not a guest, but was brought there purposely by the Pharisees in order to accuse Jesus of Sabbath-breaking if He healed him).*

2 And, behold, there was a certain man before Him which had the dropsy *(has reference to a disease causing swelling due to excess water).*

3 And Jesus answering spoke unto the Lawyers and Pharisees, saying *(proclaims Jesus instantly recognizing the situation, and immediately judging the hypocrisy, which broke the Sabbath when their own interests were involved)*, **Is it lawful to heal on the Sabbath Day?** *(He turns the trap on their own heads.)*

4 And they held their peace *(means they did not know what to say).* **And He** *(Jesus)* **took** *him* *(means that He zeroed in on the man, so there would be absolutely no doubt what was being done)*, **and healed him, and let him go** *(means that his healing was instantaneous, and easily observable by all; in other words, even miraculously, the excess fluid in the man's body disappeared; He did not "let him go" until the effects of this healing were obvious to all)*;

5 And answered them, saying, Which of you shall have an ass or an ox fallen into a pit, and will not straightway *(immediately)* **pull him out on the Sabbath Day?** *(The Lord was not criticizing them for doing such a thing, but rather their hypocrisy in condemning Him for a greater and nobler act.)*

6 And they could not answer Him again to these things *(their silence was the better part of wisdom; to have answered it at all would have shown them up even worse than they already looked).*

HUMILITY

7 And He put forth a Parable to those which were bidden *(refers to the invited guests of this feast, which is obvious were the wealthy class)*, **when He marked how they chose out the chief rooms** *(after the healing of the man was completed, the invited guests were called to be seated for the banquet; evidently, there was an obvious scurrying for the "chief seats")*; **saying unto them,**

8 When you are bidden of any *man* **to a wedding, sit not down in the highest room** *(actually strikes at the very heart of these hypocrites, which was a love of praise as well as place*

and position); **lest a more honourable man than you be bidden of him** *(positions the Believer in God's Hands, instead of the hands of self-seeking);*

9 And He who bade you and him come and say to you, Give this man place; and you begin with shame to take the lowest room *(the one who seeks self-willed position will ultimately be forsaken by the Lord, or put down by the Lord; this is a "shame" that can be avoided by letting the Lord do the doing; in other words, the Believer is to refrain from self-promotion).*

10 But when you are bidden, go and sit down in the lowest room *(is the place and position that the truly God-called will always take; to do so lets the Lord chart the course);* **that when He who bade you comes, He may say unto you, Friend, go up higher** *(places the Lord in the position of Leader and Guide):* **then shall you have worship in the presence of them who sit at meat with you** *(the idea in all of this is many do not advance because they do not allow the Lord to do the advancing, but seek to do such themselves).*

11 For whosoever exalteth himself shall be abased *(this speaks of self-exaltation, which the Lord cannot tolerate; its end result will always be "abasement");* **and he who humbles himself shall be exalted** *(humility, which can only come by a proper understanding of the Cross, is the requirement for advancement by the Lord).*

THE WEDDING FEAST

12 Then said He also to him who bade Him *(who invited Him to the Feast; the previous Parable had been spoken to the guests, while this is spoken to the host),* **When you make a dinner or a supper, call not your friends, nor your brethren, neither your kinsmen, nor** *your* **rich neighbours; lest they also bid you again, and a recompence be made to you** *(it is not the activity that is condemned, but rather its purpose).*

13 But when you make a feast, call the poor, the maimed, the lame, the blind *(that is, if you really want to do something good for people):*

14 And you shall be blessed *(is a single promise given by God, with His Word standing as surety);* **for they cannot recompense you** *(the idea is if we really want to be blessed by the Lord, we are to do good things for people who, in turn, cannot do good things for us; that is Christlike, because He has done so much for us when we in turn could not do anything for Him):* **for you shall be recompensed at the resurrection of**

the just *(proclaims the fact that God keeps the account of all things, and to be sure, every good thing, at least that which He labels as "good," will be rewarded at the Resurrection, i.e., "the Judgment Seat of Christ").*

15 And when one of them who sat at meat with Him heard these things, he said unto Him *(proclaims a total lack of knowledge about what the Lord was saying),* **Blessed** *is* **he who shall eat bread in the Kingdom of God** *(by using the word "blessed," and directing it toward himself, this Pharisee loudly trumpets his self-righteousness; the Lord's answer will be very revealing, as we shall see).*

THE GREAT SUPPER

16 Then said He unto him, A certain man made a great supper, and bade many:

17 And sent his servant at supper time to say to them who were bidden, Come; for all things are now ready *(was the Message of both John the Baptist and Christ concerning entrance into the Kingdom of God).*

18 And they all with one *consent* **began to make excuse** *(proclaimed Israel then, and regrettably most of the Church now!).* **The first said unto Him, I have bought a piece of ground, and I must needs go and see it: I pray you have me excused** *(the purchase of the ground wasn't wrong, but the self-interest was wrong).*

19 And another said, I have bought five yoke of oxen, and I go to prove them: I pray you have me excused *(as the previous was self-interest, this one was that of self-will).*

20 And another said, I have married a wife, and therefore I cannot come *(this spoke of self-love).*

21 So that servant came, and showed his Lord these things *(Jesus is the "servant," and the "Lord" is the Heavenly Father).* **Then the Master of the house being angry said to His servant** *(proclaims the Just anger of God over the rejection by Israel to the great invitation to enter the Kingdom of God),* **Go out quickly into the streets and lanes of the city, and bring in hither the poor, and the maimed, and the halt, and the blind** *(this is an apt description of the Gentile world, spiritually speaking! but out of this came the Church).*

22 And the servant said, Lord, it is done as You have commanded, and yet there is room *(proclaims the vastness of the Gospel Message; what Jesus did at Calvary was sufficient to cleanse the stain of every sin, of every human*

being in the entirety of the world, and for all time, at least for those who will come; "yet, there is room").

23 And the Lord said unto the servant *(proclaims Jesus as being the Light of the World),* **Go out into the highways and hedges** *(the Gospel must be taken to the entirety of the world),* **and compel** *them* **to come in** *(there is a compelling force about the Gospel when it is preached under the Anointing of the Spirit),* **that My house may be filled** *(irrespective of the fall of Israel, the Plan of God will not be thwarted; His House will be filled!).*

24 For I say unto you, That none of those men which were bidden *(and wouldn't come)* **shall taste of My supper** *(this is the answer of Christ to the statement of the man of Verse 15).*

DISCIPLESHIP

25 And there went great multitudes with Him *(proclaims Him having left the home of this Pharisee, and now continuing His journey toward Jerusalem):* **and He turned, and said unto them** *(He was anxious now, at the end, clearly to make it known to all these multitudes what serving Him really signified),*

26 If any *man* **come to Me** *(no exceptions),* **and hate** *(prefer)* **not his father, and mother, and wife, and children, and brethren, and sisters, yea, and his own life also** *(no affection, however strong, must be permitted to compete with or displace Christ),* **he cannot be My Disciple** *(once again, no exceptions!).*

27 And whosoever does not bear his Cross *(this doesn't speak of suffering as most think, but rather ever making the Cross of Christ the object of our Faith; we are saved and we are victorious not by suffering, although that sometimes will happen, or any other similar things, but rather by our Faith, but always with the Cross of Christ as the object of that Faith),* **and come after Me** *(one can follow Christ only by Faith in what He has done for us at the Cross; He recognizes nothing else),* **cannot be My Disciple** *(the statement is emphatic! if it's not Faith in the Cross of Christ, then it's faith that God will not recognize, which means that such people are refused [I Cor. 1:17-18, 21, 23; 2:2; Rom. 6:3-14; 8:1-2, 11, 13; Gal. 6:14; Eph. 2:13-18; Col. 2:14-15]).*

COUNTING THE COST

28 For which of you, intending to build a tower *(is the example that Jesus will use in order to explain the Cross-bearing, Christ-following life),* **sits not down first, and counts the cost** *(this is not meant that we can earn Salvation, but rather that there will be a price to pay for the acceptance of Christ and the Cross; sadly, most of the opposition will come from the Church, exactly as it came from Israel in Jesus' day),* **whether he have** *sufficient* **to finish** *it?* *(This proclaims that the race must be finished, before it can be said to have been run. This completely refutes the Unscriptural Doctrine of Unconditional Eternal Security.)*

29 Lest haply, after he has laid the foundation, and is not able to finish *it,* *(regrettably, millions do not finish this race, i.e., "tower")* **all who behold** *it* **begin to mock Him** *(in the spiritual sense which Jesus intends here, the far greater degree of mocking will come from Satan himself and his evil spirits),*

30 Saying, This man began to build, and was not able to finish *(not only does the Lord monitor our progress constantly, but Satan and his cohorts do as well).*

31 Or what king, going to make war against another king *(Jesus continues to use illustrations from everyday life which are familiar to all),* **sits not down first, and consults whether he be able with ten thousand to meet him who comes against him with twenty thousand?** *(This type of invitation is a far cry from the majority of the invitations given today regarding the acceptance of Christ. Presently it is, "come to Christ and get rich!" But the Message of Jesus was and is, "come to Christ, and face the opposition of the world and of organized religion.")*

32 Or else, while the other is yet a great way off, he sends an ambassador, and desires conditions of peace *(unfortunately, the modern Church has made peace with Satan; this means they have forsaken Christ and the Cross; however, the "peace" they have is a false peace).*

33 So likewise, whosoever he be of you who forsakes not all that he has, he cannot be My Disciple *(the key to victory regarding the world is the gathering of great resources to oneself; however, the key to this spiritual conflict is the very opposite, the "forsaking of all that one has"; this refers to a denial of dependence on self, and total trust being placed in Christ and what He has done for us at the Cross).*

34 Salt *is* **good** *(salt seasons and preserves, and so does the true Believer):* **but if the salt have lost his savour** *(refers to salt no longer being salty, and consequently, good for nothing),*

wherewith shall it be seasoned? *(This means that there is no alternative to Christ. He and the Word are the saltiness of the salt. If that be removed from Israel, which it was, then Israel was of no more use. It is the same presently with individuals.)*

35 It is neither fit for the land *(means that it can no longer serve its intended purpose, because it no longer has that which gives it purpose)*, nor yet for the dunghill; but men cast it out *(many things, if not used for their intended purpose, can be used elsewhere; however, the savorless Christian does not fall into that category, actually becoming totally worthless)*. He who has ears to hear, let him hear *(meaning that only those who have spiritual ears will hear what He is saying and, thereby, understand it).*

CHAPTER 15
(A.D. 33)
MURMURING

THEN drew near unto Him all the Publicans and sinners for to hear Him *(Publicans were tax-collectors, and looked at as traitors by the religious hierarchy of Israel; consequently, they were afforded no opportunity for Salvation whatsoever; they were classified with the "sinners"; but these desired to hear Jesus, and rightly so!).*

2 And the Pharisees and Scribes murmured *(presents them conducting themselves exactly as their Fathers in the wilderness, which brought plagues then and will bring the greatest plague of all now, the destruction of themselves and their country [Ex. 16:7-12; Num. 14:27; 17:5-10])*, saying, This man receives sinners, and eats with them *(if it is to be noticed, Jesus gave the Pharisees and Scribes no place or position at all, and for the obvious reasons; He did give place and position to the Publicans and sinners, and for the purpose of saving their souls).*

THE LOST SHEEP

3 And He spoke this Parable unto them, saying,

4 What man of you, having an hundred sheep, if he lose one of them *(proclaims the value the Lord places on just one soul)*, does not leave the ninety and nine in the wilderness, but go after that which is lost, until he find it? *(This does not mean the ninety-nine are left alone, but rather that every effort is to be made to retrieve the one that is lost.)*

5 And when he has found *it*, he lays *it* on his shoulders, rejoicing *(the Parable of the lost sheep is also found in Mat. 18:12; there it expresses the love that seeks; here, the joy that finds).*

6 And when he comes home, he calls together *his* friends and neighbours *(should have been the religious leaders of Israel)*, saying unto them, Rejoice with me *(is really the only occasion of rejoicing in Heaven other than rejoicing over the Work and Person of the Lord Jesus Christ [Rev. 5:11-14])*; for I have found my sheep which was lost *(according to Heaven, the greatest statement that could ever be made).*

7 I say unto you, that likewise joy shall be in Heaven over one sinner who repents *(while other things are certainly important, still, nothing can match a soul being saved)*, more than over ninety and nine just persons, which need no repentance *(this must properly be understood; the ninety-nine were rejoiced over when they were saved, exactly as this sinner is now rejoiced over).*

THE LOST COIN

8 Either what woman having ten pieces of silver, if she lose one piece *(points to something of value; the one sheep was valuable, and the coin as well is valuable; both are like unto a lost soul)*, does not light a candle, and sweep the house, and seek diligently till she find *it*? *(The "Light" of the Gospel, which is Jesus Christ and Him Crucified, can alone find the lost soul. Let it be understood, we didn't find Christ, He found us!)*

9 And when she has found *it*, she calls *her* friends and *her* neighbours together, saying, Rejoice with me; for I have found the piece which I had lost.

10 Likewise, I say unto you, there is joy in the presence of the Angels of God over one sinner who repents *(this Verse is very similar to Verse 7, but there is an addition; this takes us to the very Throne of God, placing even more emphasis on the significance of the Salvation of a lost soul).*

THE PRODIGAL SON

11 And he said, A certain man had two sons *(it is possible that the one sheep and the coin represent the Gentiles who were eagerly sought after because they were helpless; the Prodigal represents the Jew who was not so much sought after, but had to come of his own accord, as will happen at the Second Coming):*

12 And the younger of them said to *his* Father *(will be treated as the Jewish people even though it definitely can apply to any and all)*, Father, give me the portion of goods that falls *to me* *(was typical of Roman Law at that time)*. And he divided unto them *his* living *(by the use of the pronoun "them," it seems that a certain amount was guaranteed by law to each; the younger one took his and left)*.

13 And not many days after the younger son gathered all together *(concerned an inheritance that he really had not earned, but that had been freely given to him because of his relationship with his Father)*, **and took his journey into a far country** *(the son fell while yet in the Father's house; he fell at the moment he desired the Father's goods without the Father's company; and it only needed a few days to find him in the far country; backsliding begins in the heart, and very soon places the feet with the swine; sin will take you further than you want to go, and cost you more than you can afford to pay)*, **and there wasted his substance with riotous living** *(this characterizes the world)*.

14 And when he had spent all *(Satan does not replenish; he only uses and abuses)*, **there arose a mighty famine in that land** *(ultimately the "famine" will come to the wayward Believer)*; **and he began to be in want** *(represents the first time in his life he had ever experienced such a malady; he always had plenty at his Father's house, but now the "want" will only increase)*.

15 And he went and joined himself to a citizen of that country *(the word "joined" translates into forcing himself upon an unwilling employer; in short, he was reduced to begging)*; **and he sent him into his fields to feed swine** *(represented the most degrading occupation in which any Jew could ever engage)*.

16 And he would fain have filled his belly with the husks that the swine did eat *(means that he not only fed the swine, but was forced to eat their swill as well! from so high, he had fallen so low!)*: **and no man gave unto him** *(in the Devil's country nothing is given, everything must be bought; and bought at a terrible price)*.

17 And when he came to himself *(fully admitted to what he was and where he was)*, **he said, How many hired servants of my Father's have bread enough and to spare** *(many have bought Satan's lie that living for God deprives one of so many good things; nothing could be further from the truth)*, **and I perish with hunger!** *(Even though the illustration is addressing itself to the physical sense, the spiritual lesson it*

conveys pertains to the soul of man, which hungers for the Lord and can only be satisfied by the Lord, and never by worldly things.)*

18 I will arise and go to my Father *(the first step for the penitent soul; until that step is taken, the realization of need, nothing can be done; the word "arise" tells us that the journey to God is always upward, while that with Satan is always downward)*, **and will say unto him, Father, I have sinned against Heaven, and before you** *(the young man did not plead extenuating circumstances, lay the blame on others, or plead wrongs done to him; he placed the blame squarely where it belonged, upon himself; confession of wrong-doing is always demanded by God [I Jn. 1:9])*,

19 And am no more worthy to be called your son *(this presents the second requirement — admitted unworthiness)*: **make me as one of your hired servants** *(presents the position of humility, which is necessary; however, God has never received one as such; in other words, He will never make a "hired servant" out of a "son")*.

20 And he arose, and came to his Father *(anyone can do this if he so desires [Rev. 22:17])*. **But when he was yet a great way off, his Father saw him,** *(the Father was earnestly looking for him)*, **and had compassion** *(the Lord always has compassion)*, **and ran** *(the only occasion given in the Bible of God running, and that is to welcome home a lost soul)*, **and fell on his neck, and kissed him** *(this is what awaits every sinner who comes to the Lord)*.

21 And the son said unto him, Father, I have sinned against Heaven, and in Your sight, and am no more worthy to be called Your son *(this is as far as the young man got; he had intended to continue as Verse 19 proclaims, "make me as one of Your hired servants"; but the Father interrupted him)*.

22 But the Father said to his servants, Bring forth the best robe, and put *it* on him *(Grace ran to kiss the Prodigal in his rags, and Righteousness hasted to dress him in its robes; the robe was that of II Cor. 5:21)*; **and put a ring on his hand** *(the "ring" addressed here was a seal or signet ring, which was much the same as a modern credit card; the ring bore the crest of his Father's house)*, **and shoes on *his* feet** *(this denotes ownership, for slaves did not wear shoes; all these things were provided for him and declared his sonship; servants were not thus arrayed and feasted)*:

23 And bring hither the fatted calf, and kill *it*; and let us eat, and be merry *(signifies that the young man is now back in Covenant and*

celebrated by feasting; the true "merriment" is never in alcoholic beverage or other things, but only in Christ):

24 For this my son was dead, and is alive again; he was lost, and is found *(so beautifully portrays the Salvation experience)*. **And they began to be merry** *(once again, Christ proclaims the joy of a lost soul coming home)*.

25 Now his elder son was in the field *(inasmuch as the Father did not bring the elder son in for the celebration, tells us that he knew the heart of the elder son; so he left him "in the field")*: **and as he came and drew near to the house, he heard musick and dancing** *(signifies the celebration then taking place respecting the return of the Prodigal)*.

26 And he called one of the servants *(proclaims the servant knowing more about the Father's business than even he, the elder son, knew)*, **and asked what these things meant** *(proclaims him not knowing that which was dearest to the Father's heart)*.

27 And he *(the servant)* **said unto him, Your brother is come** *(it is astounding that an event of this magnitude was happening and he knew nothing of it; the reason will be obvious shortly)*; **and your father has killed the fatted calf, because he has received him safe and sound** *(proclaims the celebration that takes place in Heaven upon the Salvation of souls, and should as well take place on Earth among Believers; however, much of the time, the joy and the energy are spent on other pursuits)*.

28 And he was angry *(shows the true nature of the heart, and why he didn't know what was going on; the elder brother portrayed the Pharisee; he neither understood nor shared in the Father's joy)*, **and would not go in** *(proclaims rebellion! Jesus said of the Scribes and Pharisees that they would not go in themselves, and would try to stop all others from going in [Mat. 23:13])*: **therefore came his father out, and intreated him** *(proclaims Jesus making every appeal to the Scribes and Pharisees, but as here, to no avail; the patience He had shown with the Prodigal, He shows with the rebellious as well; such is our Heavenly Father!)*.

29 And he answering said to *his* **father** *(will be an answer totally different than that given by his younger brother)*, **Lo, these many years do I serve you** *(is said in the realm of merit; he thought this way because he had no relationship with the Father; consequently, it was just a job to him; he "served" for all the wrong reasons)*, **neither transgressed I at any time Your**

Commandment *(self-righteous, he claimed to have given a perfect obedience)*: **and yet you never gave me a kid, that I might make merry with my friends** *(he wanted "merriment" for all the wrong reasons; this shows that morally he was as much lost to his Father as his younger brother had been)*:

30 But as soon as this your son was come *(now portrays him disowning any relationship with his younger brother; self-righteousness always feels this way!)*, **which has devoured your living with harlots** *(the two phrases, "You never gave me a kid (a lamb,) for a celebration," and "Your son, who has devoured your living with harlots," showed the hatred of his heart to his Father and to his brother)*, **you have killed for him the fatted calf** *(is a proclamation of self-righteousness, which cannot conceive of such a thing; instead of "making merry," the younger brother should be punished, and severely, or so the elder brother thought; not understanding Grace, this is the attitude, regrettably, of most modern Christians)*.

31 And he said unto him, Son, you are ever with me, and all that I have is yours *(in effect says that he really had not partaken of these riches, even though they were his for the asking; he had tried to earn them, which was unnecessary, and actually unacceptable; he missed the entirety of the point of what Salvation really was)*.

32 It was meet *(necessary)* **that we should make merry, and be glad: for this your brother was dead** *(dead in trespasses and sins)*, **and is alive again** *(has come to Christ)*; **and was lost, and is found** *(the death of the sinless calf was a necessity ere the feast could be enjoyed; had the Prodigal refused this raiment and claimed the right to enter the Father's house in his rags and nakedness, he, like Cain, would have been rejected; but his was true Repentance, and so it accepted these gifts assuring purity, perpetuity, position, and provision)*.

CHAPTER 16
(A.D. 33)
THE UNJUST STEWARD

AND **He said also unto His Disciples** *(someone has said that Chapter 15 was addressed to the Pharisees in the hearing of the Disciples; Chapter 16 to the Disciples in the hearing of the Pharisees)*, **There was a certain rich man, which had a steward** *(the moral of the Parable seems to be found in Verse 8)*; **and the same was**

accused unto him that he had wasted his goods *(the man had wasted his employer's goods)*.

2 And He called him, and said unto him, How is it that I hear this of You? *(That you have wasted my goods.)* give an account of your stewardship *(will be the very words or similar which will be spoken to every Believer at the Judgment Seat of Christ)*; for you may be no longer steward *(how many Believers are wasting that which the Lord has placed into their hands; in other words, they are not attending very well to the Lord's business)*.

3 Then the steward said within himself, What shall I do? *(This proclaims him beginning to make plans.)* for my lord takes away from me the stewardship: I cannot dig *(has reference to digging out stores of goods from stockpiles to replace what was lost; the idea is the goods which he was charged with have been wasted, and there is no more stockpile)*; to beg I am ashamed *(many Believers will be ashamed at the Judgment Seat of Christ)*.

4 I am resolved what to do *(the beginning of a plan or scheme to provide for himself)*, that, when I am put out of the stewardship, they may receive me into their houses *(he will ingratiate himself to those who owe money to his former Master)*.

5 So he called every one of his lord's debtors *unto him* *(the beginning of his scheme)*, and said unto the first, How much do you owe unto my lord? *(It is typical in one way or the other of that which is happening all over the world, each and every day, and millions of times over. The scheming and planning are the ordinary course of events in the world, and as Paul said, "They do it to obtain a corruptible crown" [I Cor. 9:25].)*

6 And he said, An hundred measures of oil *(this "steward" actually had the right, as given to him by his employer, to set the price of certain commodities; however, as we see here, he misused that right in order to ingratiate himself with these debtors)*. And he said unto him, Take your bill, and sit down quickly, and write fifty *(he was wiping out half of their debt)*.

7 Then said he to another, And how much do you owe? And he said, An hundred measures of wheat. And he said unto him, Take your bill, and write fourscore *(he reduced his by twenty measures)*.

8 And the lord *(not the Lord of Glory, but rather his employer)* commended the unjust steward, because he had done wisely *(exclaimed as to his cleverness, inasmuch as his dishonesty could not now be proven)*: for the children of this world are in their generation wiser than the children of light *(this closing statement is the entirety of the moral of this Parable as given by Christ; the "children of the world" are "wiser" because the diligence given, crooked or otherwise, is the very best effort they have; but all too often, the "children of light," even though possessing that which is far and away more important than anything the world has, still, most of the time pay precious little attention or diligence to the all-important task of living for God)*.

GOD AND MAMMON

9 And I say unto you, Make to yourselves friends of the mammon of unrighteousness *(simply means that Believers must learn to be faithful with money regarding others and the Work of God; money is here called the "mammon of unrighteousness" simply because the love of such is the root of all forms of evil [I Tim. 6:10])*; that, when ye fail *(when you die)*, they *(the Angels)* may receive you into everlasting habitations *(Heaven)*.

10 He who is faithful in that which is least is faithful also in much *(implies that if a Believer is faithful with the money that God gives him, he will more than likely be faithful in all other aspects of his Christian endeavor)*: and he who is unjust in the least is unjust also in much *(if the Believer will not allow the Lord to have first place respecting money, he will be unjust as well in spiritual matters)*.

11 If therefore you have not been faithful in the unrighteous mammon *(this tells us that the Lord judges the faithfulness of a Believer, at least in part, as to how he handles money, which our Lord refers to as "the mammon of unrighteousness")*, who will commit to your trust the true *riches*? *(If you can't handle the "least" money, than how can you handle the "much" — spiritual riches?)*

12 And if ye have not been faithful in that which is another man's *(strikes at our practical everyday living)*, who shall give you that which is your own? *(This tells us that the Lord will not bless anyone who does not discharge their responsibilities as they should.)*

13 No servant can serve two masters *(we cannot serve the Lord and ourselves)*: for either he will hate the one, and love the other; or else he will hold to the one, and despise the other *(mostly Jesus dealt with the Pharisees; here, He addresses the Publicans; they, plus every Believer,*

must be very careful about money, or anything for that matter that's not truly of the Lord). Ye cannot serve God and mammon *(places God and money side by side, for this is what "mammon" means, at least in this case; money is not demeaned here by Christ; but the manner in which we hold or handle it; neither is the amount in question, but rather our faithfulness).*

14 And the Pharisees also *(His statements applied to the Pharisees, as well as the Publicans),* who were covetous, heard all these things: and they derided Him *(Israel had come to believe that riches equaled Godliness, and poverty equaled the curse of God; so they sneered at Christ, actually making fun of Him).*

15 And He said unto them, You are they which justify yourselves before men *(means they tried to do things to make themselves look Holy in the sight of men);* but God knows your hearts *(that's a powerful phrase, "God knows," and to be sure He does!):* for that which is highly esteemed among men is abomination in the sight of God *(religious works are highly esteemed among men, hence the adulation of the Catholic Nun called "Mother Teresa"; if men attempt to justify themselves with works, instead of by Faith in Christ and the Cross, God refers to it as "abomination").*

16 The Law and the Prophets *were* until John *(actually means, "as far as John," which included that Prophet; in other words, John ministered unto the Law, but was the last Prophet of that era):* since that time the *Kingdom* of God is preached *(the "Kingdom of God" is obtained by being "born-again," which comes about by Faith in Christ, and what Christ has done at the Cross),* and every man presses into it *("every man" is welcome into the New Covenant).*

17 And it is easier for Heaven and earth to pass, than one tittle of the Law to fail *(Jesus would fulfill the Law, and in every capacity, and in fact would be the only One Who ever did because He was the only One Who could).*

18 Whosoever puts away his wife, and marries another, commits adultery *(Jesus addresses the subject here, even though it seems out of place, because the Pharisees treated divorce lightly and were secretly covetous and immoral; this is why, when exposed by the Lord, they derided Him):* and whosoever marries her that is put away from *her* husband commits adultery *(the Pharisees taught that if one was divorced, irrespective that they had no Scripture as grounds to do so, that they were then free to marry or to be married to such; Jesus refutes this, and does so pointedly).*

19 There was a certain rich man, which was clothed in purple and fine linen, and fared sumptuously every day *(the Jews of Jesus' day concluded that riches were the favor of God, and poverty was the curse of God; therefore, this illustration given by Christ ripped to shreds their false doctrine):*

20 And there was a certain beggar named Lazarus *(many claim this is a Parable not to be taken literally; however, as it is to be noticed, Jesus uses names in this illustration, meaning that it's not a Parable but actually, something that really happened; consequently, it is chilling indeed!),* which was laid at his gate, full of sores *(the rich man saw Lazarus constantly, but offered no help whatsoever; as stated, such concluded ones like Lazarus to be cursed of God, and to help such would be thwarting the Plan of God; how so much the Word of God is twisted by so many),*

21 And desiring to be fed with the crumbs which fell from the rich man's table *(probably means that this rich man felt very good with himself in even allowing "crumbs" to be given to this beggar):* moreover the dogs came and licked his sores *(proclaims the fact that this man was not only poverty stricken, but as well was sick; he would not fit the mold of the modern prosperity gospel, which in fact is no Gospel at all; but he definitely did fit God's mold; we should consider all of this very carefully).*

22 And it came to pass, that the beggar died *(more than likely, no one cared, but the Lord cared, as we shall see),* and was carried by the Angels into Abraham's bosom *(Paradise; where all Believers went before the Cross; as well, Jesus also tells us here that whenever a Believer dies, his soul and spirit are escorted by Angels into the Presence of God):* the rich man also died, and was buried *(no Angels carried him away, for he died eternally lost; him being rich did not carry any weight as it regards his soul's Salvation);*

23 And in hell he lift up his eyes *(Jesus here plainly proclaims the doctrine of eternal Hell; as well, He also proclaims the fact that the soul and the spirit immediately go to Heaven or Hell at the time of death, and that the soul and the spirit are totally conscious),* being in torments *(to say the least, Hell is not a pleasant place, and as stated, it is eternal),* and seeth Abraham afar off, and Lazarus in his bosom *(all Believers before the Cross expressed faith in the Revelation given to Abraham by God as it regards Redemption, and in a sense, it is the same presently [Rom. 4:16]).*

24 And he cried and said, Father Abraham, have mercy on me *(there are no unbelievers in Hell, nor is there any Salvation there; the rich man repented, but too late)*, and send Lazarus *(he had no concern for Lazarus back on Earth, but his conscience now recalls many things, but too late)*, that he may dip the tip of his finger in water *(evidently there is no water there)*, and cool my tongue; for I am tormented in this flame *(the Bible teaches that the fires of Hell are literal; Jesus said so!)*.

25 But Abraham said, Son, remember that you in your lifetime received your good things *(in no way does it mean that this was the cause of him being lost; it merely means that he was treated very well, but showed no thankfulness for his blessings)*, and likewise Lazarus evil things *(the rich man didn't allow his blessings to bring him to the Lord, and Lazarus didn't allow his poverty to keep him from the Lord)*: but now he is comforted *(because he had accepted the Lord)*, and you are tormented *(the word "now" is that which is all-important; it speaks of the time after death; will it be one of "comfort" or "torment"?)*.

26 And beside all this, between us and you there is a great gulf fixed *(this is in the heart of the Earth [Mat. 12:40]; before the Cross, even though all who went to Paradise were comforted, they were still captives of Satan, with him hoping that ultimately he would get them over into the burning pit [Eph. 4:8-9]; this means that when Believers died before the Cross, due to the fact that the blood of bulls and goats could not take away sins, the sin debt remained, and Satan still had a claim on them; so all those in Paradise were awaiting the Cross, which would deliver them)*: so that they which would pass from hence to you cannot *(proclaims the fact that all opportunities for Salvation are on this side of the grave; this means that the Catholic doctrine of Purgatory is a "fool's hope"; there is no such place)*; neither can they pass to us, that *would come* from thence *(but yet it was possible for those in Hell to look over and see those in Paradise, and it seems to speak to them; that place, due to the Cross, is now empty, with all liberated by Christ after the price was paid [Eph. 4:8-9])*.

27 Then he said, I pray thee therefore, father, that you would send him *(send Lazarus)* to my father's house *(this is the only example of praying to a dead Saint in Scripture; let those who do so remember that prayer to all other dead Saints will avail just as much as this prayer did — nothing)*:

28 For I have five brethren; that he may testify unto them *(these statements proclaim the fact that this man had a working knowledge of God and more than likely even professed Salvation before his death; but he wasn't saved!)*, lest they also come into this place of torment *(he did not ask this grace for himself, for he knew that he was eternally entombed; it is easy to step into Hell, but impossible to step out)*.

29 Abraham said unto him, They have Moses and the Prophets; let them hear them *(doesn't mean that this event happened during the time of Moses, but that Abraham is referring to the Word of God; this tells us that at least a part of the Old Testament had then been written)*.

30 And he said, Nay, father Abraham: but if one went unto them from the dead, they will repent *(the Scriptures contain all that is necessary to Salvation; a returned spirit could add nothing to them; and a man who will not listen to the Bible would not listen to a multitude, if raised from the dead; in fact, a few days later, the Lord did raise a man named Lazarus from the grave, and the Pharisees went about to put Him to death)*.

31 And he said unto him, If they hear not Moses and the *Prophets*, neither will they be persuaded, though one rose from the dead *(this illustration as given by Christ, actually happened and in fact presents a startling portrayal of life after death; we learn from this, and in stark reality, that the only thing that really matters in life is being right with God; there is a Heaven and there is a Hell, and every soul who has ever lived has gone or is going to one or the other; the only way to make Heaven one's eternal Home is to accept Christ; He Alone is the Door; everything else leads one to Hell, exactly as the rich man found out, and to his eternal dismay)*.

CHAPTER 17
(A.D. 33)
FORGIVENESS AND FAITH

THEN said He unto the Disciples *(presents the teaching given here by Christ as immediately following the illustration given concerning the rich man in Hell)*, It is impossible but that offences will come *(refers to the fact of opposition against the Child of God, and from whom it will mostly come)*: but woe *unto him*, through whom they come! *(Strangely enough, most opposition will come from the religious sector! There is an offence to the Cross! And those who reject the Cross, which are the far*

greater majority, will oppose those who accept the Cross. To reject the Cross is to reject Christ! Judgment is guaranteed to follow such action.)

2 It were better for him that a millstone were hanged about his neck, and he cast into the sea *(pronounces the judgment which awaits Christ-rejecters)*, than that he should offend one of these little ones *("little ones" mentioned here have nothing to do with children, but rather Believers who are clothed with humility, consequently allowing the Lord to defend them; they are "little" in their own eyes, judged to be the same by the offenders, but held very dear by the Lord and watched over minutely by Him).*

3 Take heed to yourselves *(speaking directly to His Disciples, warning them that this spirit of offence can come on anyone unless they are careful)*: If your brother trespass against you, rebuke him *(has to do with Mat. 18:15-17)*; and if he repent, forgive him.

4 And if he trespass against you seven times in a day, and seven times in a day turn again to you, saying, I repent; you shall forgive him *(while the untiring, fearless rebukers of all sin, at the same time, we must never tire of exercising forgiveness the moment the offender is sorry).*

5 And the Apostles said unto the Lord, Increase our faith *(this is the request of many; however, the answer the Lord will give is extremely interesting).*

6 And the Lord said, If you had faith as a grain of mustard seed *(a very small seed, telling us in effect that it's not really the amount of faith, but rather the correct object of Faith; the correct object is the Cross [I Cor. 1:18])*, you might say unto this sycamine tree, Be thou plucked up by the root, and be thou planted in the sea; and it should obey you *(the removal of trees and mountains were proverbial figures of speech among the Jews at that time, expressing the overcoming of great difficulties).*

THE FAITHFUL SERVANT

7 But which of you, having a servant plowing or feeding cattle, will say unto him by and by *(immediately)*, when he is come from the field, Go and sit down to meat?

8 And will not rather say unto him, Make ready wherewith I may sup, and gird yourself, and serve me, till I have eaten and drank; and afterward you shall eat and drink? *(A faithful servant will attend to his duties first, and himself second.)*

9 Does he thank that servant because he did the things that were commanded him? I trow not *(I think not!).*

10 So likewise, when you shall have done all those things which are commanded you, say, We are unprofitable servants: we have done that which was our duty to do *(the Lord, in essence, says that having fulfilled all these conditions, which were their duty to do, they would be no better than unprofitable servants; this is a fatal blow to the doctrine of Salvation by works; the Disciple is to say, "I am an unprofitable servant"; the Master will then say, "well done, good and faithful servant" [Mat. 25:21]).*

THE LEPERS

11 And it came to pass, as He went to Jerusalem, that He passed through the midst of *(between)* Samaria and Galilee *(the Lord was traveling eastward to the Jordan, which He would cross, and travel south toward Jerusalem on the eastward side, which was the longer route).*

12 And as He entered into a certain village, there met Him ten men who were lepers, which stood afar off *(Levitical Law stated that they had to remain approximately one hundred feet or so from other people [Lev. 13:21, 45-46; 14:2]):*

13 And they lifted up *their* voices *(they were not allowed to come closer to Christ, or anyone else for that matter, so they had to shout to make themselves heard)*, and said, Jesus, Master, have mercy on us *(they had no doubt heard many wonderful things about Jesus, and now, miracle of miracles, he was standing not too far from them).*

14 And when He saw *them*, He said unto them *(they got His attention)*, Go show yourselves unto the Priests *(this command assured cleansing; for only a cleansed leper was to show himself to the Priests).* And it came to pass, that, as they went, they were cleansed *(they knew they were unclean; but they believed Christ's Word, went away with the conviction that it was true, and were immediately healed on the way).*

15 And one of them, when He saw that He was healed *(concerned the Samaritan)*, turned back, and with a loud voice glorified God *(every Believer should praise the Lord continually),*

16 And fell down on *his* face at His feet, giving Him thanks: and he was a Samaritan *(what Jesus did for him destroyed his national faith in Mount Gerizim, and rightly so, and pulled him into the right way [Jn. 4:22]).*

17 And Jesus answering said, Were there not ten cleansed? but where *are* the nine? *(The "nine" were indicative of most of Israel of that*

particular time, unthankful!)

18 There are not found who returned to give Glory to God, save this stranger *(as well, the "stranger" who had been healed would be indicative of the Gentile Church, which was shortly to be brought about).*

19 And He said unto him, Arise, go your way *(Jesus lifts people up)*: your faith has made you whole *(proclaims the fact that not only was he healed, but saved as well; all of them showed Faith by asking Christ for healing, which they received; however, only one, it seems, was given eternal life because He Glorified God).*

THE KINGDOM OF GOD

20 And when He was demanded of the Pharisees, when the Kingdom of God should come *(the Lord, in effect, answered that the Kingdom of God was at that moment in their midst, for He was the Kingdom of God)*, He answered them and said, The Kingdom of God cometh not with observation *(the Jews claimed that when the Messiah came, He would overthrow Rome, etc.; Jesus is telling them that their "observations" are wrong):*

21 Neither shall they say, Lo here! or, lo there! *(He is saying that all these outward signs they were talking about are not Scriptural, and really have no bearing on the Kingdom of God.)* for, behold, the Kingdom of God is within you *(would have been better translated, "the Kingdom of God is within your midst," for the Kingdom is Jesus, but Israel would not recognize Him; the "born-again" experience brings Christ into the heart and, thereby, places the "Kingdom of God within the person").*

SECOND COMING

22 And He said unto the Disciples, The days will come, when you shall desire to see one of the days of the Son of Man, and you shall not see *It (after the Day of Pentecost, all the followers of Christ, and especially the Disciples, would have a far greater understanding of all the things that Jesus said and did, and would love to have the opportunity to relive those former days).*

23 And they shall say to you, See here; or, see there: go not after *them*, nor follow *them (He is speaking of the Second Coming).*

24 For as the lightning, that lighteneth out of the one *part* under Heaven, shineth unto the other *part* under Heaven; so shall also the Son of Man be in His day *(in other words, He is saying that when He really does come back, there will be such a display of Heavenly Glory that no one will have to ask the question, "is it really Him?"; it will be overly obvious to all that it is He).*

25 But first must He suffer many things, and be rejected of this generation *(the Glories of that coming day will have a relation to and will be the result of His Atoning Sufferings at Calvary).*

WARNINGS

26 And as it was in the days of Noah, so shall it be also in the days of the Son of Man *(means that the world, at the time of the Second Coming, will be as indifferent and corrupt as in the days of Noah and Lot for that matter).*

27 They did eat, they drank, they married wives, they were given in marriage *(proclaims business as usual; in other words, as the world did not expect the predictions of Noah to come to pass respecting the flood, neither will the world expect the Second Coming, which is proclaimed in the Bible)*, until the day that Noah entered into the ark *(means that up to that very moment they laughed at his predictions; they saw him enter the ark, and it was met with derision)*, and the flood came, and destroyed them all *(their negative response in no way altered the judgment that soon came).*

28 Likewise also as it was in the days of Lot; they did eat, they drank, they bought, they sold, they planted, they built *(pertains to the destruction of Sodom and Gomorrah);*

29 But the same day that Lot went out of Sodom it rained fire and brimstone from Heaven, and destroyed *them* all *(the Judgment did not come, however, until the Righteous concerning both Noah and Lot had been taken out; even though all of this pertains to the Second Coming, it could also pertain to the Rapture of the Church, which will take out the Believers and usher in tremendous Judgment as recorded in Rev., Chpts. 6-19).*

30 Even thus shall it be in the day when the Son of Man is revealed *(this is the Second Coming).*

31 In that day *(this definitely refers to the Second Coming, and not the Rapture)*, he which shall be upon the housetop, and his stuff in the house, let him not come down to take it away *(in the Middle East, almost all of the houses have flat roofs, and in Jesus' day, especially during the summer months, many would sleep on*

top of the house, even as some still do presently): and he who is in the field, let him likewise not return back (these particular statements have nothing to do with the Rapture, inasmuch as that will be sudden, "in the twinkling of an eye"; Verses 31 through 37 pertain to the mobilization of Israel against the Antichrist; Ezekiel describes it in Chapters 38 and 39; that mobilization will be hurried).

32 Remember Lot's wife (the emphasis is if Israel hesitates at that particular time, they will be destroyed exactly as was Lot's wife; incidentally, in this one Passage, Jesus proclaims the historical fact of Lot's wife being turned to salt [Gen. 19:26]).

33 Whosoever shall seek to save his life shall lose it (refers to the Jews at that time who will think fleeing in other directions will preserve them, but in reality it will have the opposite effect); and whosoever shall lose his life shall preserve it (refers to those who go forward to the battle (Battle of Armageddon), and as a result, will have the protection of the Lord [Zech. 12:8]).

34 I tell you, in that night there shall be two men in one bed; the one shall be taken, and the other shall be left.

35 Two women shall be grinding together (grinding at the mill); the one shall be taken, and the other left.

36 Two men shall be in the field; the one shall be taken, and the other left (once again, all of this speaks of the mobilization of Israel at the Battle of Armageddon; it does not speak of the Rapture as many have been led to believe).

37 And they answered and said unto Him, Where, Lord? (They did not know where or what the Lord was talking about, at least at that time.) And He said unto them, Wheresoever the body is, thither will the eagles be gathered together (it refers directly to the Battle of Armageddon, and once again not the Rapture as some think! [Ezek. 39:17]).

CHAPTER 18
(A.D. 33)
PERSEVERING PRAYER

AND He spoke a Parable unto them to this end, that men ought always to pray (without a proper prayer life, Faith cannot be truly exercised, irrespective to how much it is claimed) and not to faint (don't lose heart; believe and keep praying);

2 Saying, There was in a city a judge, which feared not God, neither regarded man (but yet a poor widow woman, without influence, was able to bend him to her will):

3 And there was a widow in that city; and she came unto him, saying, Avenge me of my adversary (do me justice).

4 And he would not for a while (at the beginning, he paid her no mind): but afterward he said within himself, Though I fear not God, nor regard man;

5 Yet because this widow troubles me, I will avenge her, lest by her continual coming she weary me (means that every time the judge looked up she was there, and he gave her that for which she asked!).

6 And the Lord said, Hear what the unjust judge says (if such a judge will in the end listen to the petition of a supplicant for whom he cares nothing, will not God surely listen to the repeated prayer of someone whom He loves with a deep, enduring love?).

7 And shall not God avenge His Own elect (especially considering that God is not unjust, as was that judge), which cry day and night unto Him (keep on praying), though He bear long with them? (Even though the judge delayed for selfish indifference, God at times delays for an all-wise purpose, depending on what is asked, or whether one has Faith or not.)

8 I tell you that He will avenge them speedily (is the assurance that God will answer prayer, and in comparison to man, He will answer "speedily"). Nevertheless when the Son of Man comes, shall He find faith on the Earth? (Considering that the Church has been taken out of the world, at the Second Coming there won't be very much Faith in the world; nevertheless, this will not stop or hinder the Second Coming.)

THE PHARISEE AND THE PUBLICAN

9 And He spoke this Parable unto certain which trusted in themselves (self-righteousness) that they were righteous, and despised others (the twin curse of self-righteousness):

10 Two men went up into the Temple to pray (only one would be heard by God, who would probably be the very opposite of the one most men would choose); the one a Pharisee (a fundamentalist, who claimed to believe all the Bible), and the other a Publican (a tax-collector, referred to by Israel as traitors and, thereby, beyond Salvation).

11 The Pharisee stood and prayed thus with himself (meaning that his Prayer got no further

than himself; even though it was directed toward God, it was not heard by God), God, I thank You, that I am not as other men *are*, extortioners, unjust, adulterers, or even as this Publican (*he put himself on a much higher plane than the Publican; he actually asked the Lord for nothing, and that's exactly what he received; as far as he was concerned, he had everything, "have need of nothing" [Rev. 3:17]*).

12 I fast twice in the week, I give tithes of all that I possess (*Verse 11 portrays relative righteousness and this Verse portrays works righteousness, both rejected by the Lord*).

13 And the Publican, standing afar off (*means he did not feel free to come close to the Temple appointments as had the Pharisee*), would not lift up so much as *his* eyes unto Heaven (*refers to him realizing and admitting just how unclean he actually was*), but smote upon his breast, saying, God be merciful to me a sinner (*brought instant results because the plea was based upon Atonement and not on self-righteousness; every afternoon at 3 o'clock the evening Lamb was offered up as a propitiation for the sins of that day; the Publican pleaded forgiveness and acceptance because of the merit of that atoning blood; it foreshadowed the Atoning death of the Lamb of God, Who was Himself the propitiation, i.e., the "Mercy-Seat"*).

14 I tell you, this man went down to his house justified (*declared a righteous man; there are no degrees in justification; one is either justified totally, or not justified at all!*) *rather* than the other (*the Pharisee who depended on his self-righteousness was not justified and, therefore, lost*): for every one who exalts himself shall be abased (*rejected*); and he who humbles himself shall be exalted (*proclaims the basis for acceptance by God*).

LITTLE CHILDREN

15 And they brought unto Him also infants, that He would touch them: but when *His* Disciples saw *it*, they rebuked them (*erroneously thinking that Jesus should not be bothered with such*).

16 But Jesus called them *unto Him* (*called the parents with their infants*), and said, Suffer little children to come unto Me, and forbid them not: for of such is the Kingdom of God (*Jesus is presenting an object lesson; a little child is completely dependent on its parents or guardians; likewise, we are to be totally dependent in the same manner on the Lord*).

17 Verily I say unto you, Whosoever shall not receive the Kingdom of God as a little child shall in no wise enter therein (*the greatest hindrance to entering the "Kingdom of God" is the refusal of many to humble themselves before God; it is the pride factor, which is the opposite of little children*).

THE RICH YOUNG RULER

18 And a certain ruler asked Him, saying, Good Master, what shall I do to inherit eternal life? (*Inasmuch as this is detailed three times [Mat. 19:16; Mk. 10:17; Lk. 18:18] tells us that the Holy Spirit strongly desires that the message be heeded. In the first place, eternal life cannot be inherited, it being a free gift from God upon Faith in Christ and His Atoning Work.*)

19 And Jesus said unto him, Why do you call Me good? (*He really did not conclude Jesus to be the Messiah, which is what the word "good" denotes.*) none *is* good, save One, *that is*, God (*this destroyed the entire myth of his belief; actually he thought of himself as "good"*).

20 You know the Commandments, Do not commit adultery, Do not kill, Do not steal, Do not bear false witness, Honour your father and your mother (*why did Jesus take this tact, knowing that no one could keep all the Commandments all the time? only Christ did that! Jesus addressed Him in this fashion in order to show him that his ground for Salvation was faulty; if these things had saved him, why was he still unsure?*).

21 And he said, All these have I kept from my youth up (*he was serving as his own judge, which is always a sure sign of self-righteousness; and yet, Jesus, as recorded by Mark, "loved him," denoting a feeling beyond the normal love that God has for all men*).

22 Now when Jesus heard these things, He said unto him, Yet you lack one thing (*Jesus will now hit at the heart of the matter*): sell all that you have, and distribute unto the poor, and you shall have treasure in Heaven: and come, follow Me (*this statement by Christ is not meant to institute a charity program for the poor; as needful as they may be, they are not the subjects of this conversation; this man's material possessions stood in-between him and obeying the Lord; consequently they proved a hindrance, and whatever they may have been had to be laid aside; that is, if he was to have eternal life*).

23 And when he heard this, he was very sorrowful: for he was very rich (*proclaims the heart

attitude of multiple millions; they want the Lord, but they do not desire to pay the price the Lord demands; that price is the forsaking of all else in favor of Christ).

WARNING

24 And when Jesus saw that he was very sorrowful, he said, How hardly shall they who have riches enter into the Kingdom of God! *(This was a shock to His Disciples, because the Jews of Jesus' day thought that riches signified the favor of God.)*

25 For *it* is easier for a camel to go through a needle's eye *(means a literal needle)*, than for a rich man to enter into the Kingdom of God *(riches aren't necessarily wrong; it's the dependence on these things that constitutes the wrong).*

26 And they who heard *it* said, Who then can be saved? *(This question proclaims the fact that their idea of Salvation was totally confused, even as it is presently.)*

27 And He said, The things which are impossible with men are possible with God *(Salvation in any case is impossible with man; however, it is possible with God, and Jesus is that Salvation).*

CONSECRATION

28 Then Peter said, Lo, we have left all, and followed You *(the statement as given by Peter seems to indicate that when they first set out to follow Christ, they thought it would lead to great earthly riches; they are now seeing that they misunderstood many things).*

29 And He said unto them, Verily I say unto you, There is no man who has left house, or parents, or brethren, or wife, or children, for the Kingdom of God's sake *(God will owe no man anything),*

30 Who shall not receive manifold more *(many times more)* in this present time *(before Heaven)*, and in the world to come life everlasting *(serving God is the greatest thing a person could ever do).*

DEATH AND RESURRECTION

31 Then He took *unto Him* the Twelve, and said unto them, Behold, we go up to Jerusalem *(which will bring Him to the end of His earthly Ministry)*, and all things that are written by the Prophets concerning the Son of Man shall be accomplished *(pertaining to many*

things, but mostly the Crucifixion).

32 For He shall be delivered unto the Gentiles *(that which would be done would have to be done by Rome, since the Jews had no authority to crucify anyone)*, and shall be mocked, and spitefully entreated, and spit on *(how is it possible that they could hate Him?):*

33 And they shall scourge *Him (beat Him)*, and put Him to death *(the Crucifixion):* and the third day He shall rise again *(His Resurrection).*

34 And they understood none of these things *(His Words fell upon deaf ears):* and this saying was hid from them, neither knew they the things which were spoken *(the reason for this was that they had a Plan of God worked out in their minds, which was contrary to the Word of God).*

A BLIND BEGGAR

35 And it came to pass, that as He was come near unto Jericho *(Matthew and Mark speak of Jesus going out of Jericho when this healing took place; however, there is no discrepancy or contradiction; Luke is simply saying that as Jesus was coming into Jericho, at that particular time a blind man was sitting by the side of the highway begging, on the other side of Jericho)*, a certain blind man sat by the way side begging *(Jesus will eventually get to him):*

36 And hearing the multitude pass by, he asked what it meant *(refers to a later time after Jesus had already entered the city, and was now actually departing).*

37 And they told him, that Jesus of Nazareth passes by *(this would be the greatest news that had ever fallen upon his ears).*

38 And he cried, saying *(points to his desperation and determination)*, Jesus, *Thou* Son of David *(is a Messianic salutation, which means that irrespective as to what others might have said, Bartimaeus believed Jesus Christ was the Messiah)*, have mercy on me *(seems to be a request he had studiously thought out; if Jesus did come his way, this is what he would say; in fact, this is the first recorded occasion of Jesus going to Jericho).*

39 And they which went before rebuked him, that he should hold his peace *(in other words, they told him to "shut up")*: but he cried so much the more *(he doubled his efforts), Thou* Son of David, have mercy on me *(it was a request that Christ would not deny).*

40 And Jesus stood *(stood still)*, and commanded him to be brought unto Him *(proclaims*

Jesus answering Faith): **and when he was come near, He asked him,**

41 Saying, What will you that I shall do unto you? *(What a question!)* **And he said, Lord, that I may receive my sight** *(one of the versions says, "That our eyes might be opened and we might see you," for Matthew said there were two blind men [Mat. 20:29-34]).*

42 And Jesus said unto him, Receive your sight: your faith has saved you *(means that he was not only healed, but saved as well).*

43 And immediately he received his sight, and followed Him, glorifying God *(tradition says that He followed Christ to Jerusalem, and was a staunch Believer in the Early Church; and no wonder!):* **and all the people, when they saw** *it,* **gave praise unto God** *(incidentally, this man was not only saved and healed, he was no longer a beggar, but rather a Child of God).*

CHAPTER 19
(A.D. 33)
ZACCHAEUS

AND *Jesus* **entered and passed through Jericho** *(He always left a place better than when He found it).*

2 And, behold, *there was* **a man named Zacchaeus, which was the chief among the Publicans** *(tax-collectors),* **and he was rich** *(we find that the blind beggar is here preferred, for he was healed first before the rich tax-collector; he is last but is put first; he was told to "rise," but Zacchaeus to "come down"; thus rich and poor meet on the one level as sinners before God).*

3 And he sought to see Jesus who He was *(as Bartimaeus he sought to see Jesus; also as Bartimaeus, he was lacking because money never satisfies the spiritual thirst of the human heart);* **and could not for the press** *(the great multitude of people),* **because he was little of stature** *(evidently means that he was head and shoulders shorter than most other men).*

4 And he ran before *(he ascertained the direction Jesus was going, and sought to find a vantage point, which he did),* **and climbed up into a sycomore tree to see Him: for He was to pass that** *way (a statement of monumental proportions).*

5 And when Jesus came to the place, He looked up, and saw him *(all were orchestrated by the Holy Spirit; a hungry, seeking, heart will always find the Lord),* **and said unto him, Zacchaeus, make haste, and come down; for to day I must abide at your house** *(proclaims the*

Deity and Kingship of Jesus, although little used; He did not ask for lodging, but as King commanded such; the Salvation of Zacchaeus is one of the most striking in the Gospels; it was personal: "Zacchaeus"; it was pressing: "make haste"; it was humbling: "come down"; it was immediate: "today"; it was abiding: "I must abide"; it was social: "at thy house").

6 And he made haste, and came down, and received Him joyfully *(the moral effect of the conversion was seen in Zacchaeus taking his stand along with Jesus in public).*

7 And when they saw it *(the multitude),* **they all murmured** *(murmuring is always a sin),* **saying, That He was gone to be guest with a man who is a sinner** *(Jesus never catered whatsoever to public whim, prevailing opinion, or conventional wisdom).*

8 And Zacchaeus stood, and said unto the Lord; Behold, Lord, the half of my goods I give to the poor *(unlike the rich young ruler, he immediately volunteers such);* **and if I have taken any thing from any man by false accusation, I restore** *him* **fourfold** *(Roman law required a fourfold restitution, but Levitical Law only demanded the principle and one-fifth part added [Num. 5:7]; but he imposed upon himself the severe measure of Ex. 22:1; thus, he judged himself, and true Repentance acts as he did).*

9 And Jesus said unto him, This day is Salvation come to this house *(Jesus is the answer to all problems),* **forsomuch as he also is a son of Abraham** *(Jesus is saying that Zacchaeus has as much right to Salvation as any other person in Israel; because he was a tax-collector, the religious leadership may have shut him out, but the Lord didn't; we should think about that statement very carefully).*

10 For the Son of Man is come to seek and to save that which was lost *(the "seeking of the lost," at least on the part of God, involves far more than a mere quest, but rather an extremely active participation; so much so in fact, that it took Christ to the Cross).*

THE TEN POUNDS

11 And as they heard these things, He added and spoke a Parable, because He was near to Jerusalem, because they thought that the Kingdom of God should immediately appear *(His going to Jerusalem, and the recent happenings with Bartimaeus and Zacchaeus, probably exacerbated the feelings of the people; they didn't realize that He was on His Way to be crucified;*

they thought He was about to take the Throne).

12 He said therefore, A certain Nobleman went into a far country to receive for himself a Kingdom, and to return *(this was Jesus Himself!).*

13 And He called His ten servants *(the number "ten" in Jewish ideology pertains to an indefinite number and, therefore, includes all who would follow Him),* and delivered them ten pounds *(about $5,000 in 2003 currency),* and said unto them, Occupy till I come *(refers to the discharge of that responsibility on the part of each, until the Lord returns).*

14 But His citizens hated Him *(refers to the Jews at His First Coming),* and sent a message after Him, saying, We will not have this *Man* to reign over us.

15 And it came to pass, that when He was returned *(speaks of the Second Coming),* having received the kingdom *(Rev. 11:15),* then He commanded these servants to be called unto Him, to whom He had given the money, that He might know how much every man had gained by trading *(pertains to the Judgment Seat of Christ, which will take place immediately before the Second Coming; but the action of that Judgment will not be carried out until the Kingdom Age, which will commence with the Second Coming).*

16 Then came the first, saying, Lord, Your pound has gained ten pounds *(about $50,000 in 2003 currency).*

17 And He said unto him, Well, thou good servant: because you have been faithful in a very little *("faithfulness," or the lack thereof, constitutes the basis of all judgment),* have thou authority over ten cities *(some have claimed this pertains to the coming Kingdom Age, with Believers given rulership over particular cities; however, considering all Believers, there aren't that many cities in the world; so the statement merely has to do with the degree of reward).*

18 And the second came, saying, Lord, Your pound has gained five pounds.

19 And He said likewise to him, Be thou also over five cities.

20 And another came, saying, Lord, behold, *here is* Your pound, which I have kept laid up in a napkin *(represents the one who did nothing):*

21 For I feared You, because You are an austere man *(untrue):* You take up that You laid not down, and reap that which You did not sow *(all of this is untrue).*

22 And He *(Jesus)* said unto him, Out of your own mouth will I judge you, *you* wicked servant *(doesn't seem to have been involved in* gross sin, but seems to have been guilty of spiritual apathy, which characterizes so many Christians). You knew that I was an austere man *(in other words, if you really believe that),* taking up that I laid not down, and reaping that I did not sow:

23 Wherefore then gave not you My money into the bank, that at My coming I might have received My Own with usury? *(With interest.)*

24 And He said unto them who stood by, Take from him the pound, and give *it* to him who has ten pounds *(he was judged not so much because of what he did, but because of what he failed to do).*

25 (And they said unto Him, Lord, he has ten pounds.) *(The people said this because they were aghast that the pound taken from the man would be given to the one who already had ten pounds.)*

26 For I say unto you, That unto every one which has shall be given; and from him who has not, even that he has shall be taken away from him *(this is the "Law of Diminishing Returns"; light given and then rejected causes the person not only to lose what they could have had, but even what they presently have; this means that if the Message of the Cross is heard and rejected, not only will those particular individuals lose what they could have had, but they will lose what little they have previously had, which translates into spiritual wreckage).*

27 But those My enemies, which would not that I should reign over them, bring hither, and slay *them* before Me *(pertains to all who fall into this category, including the entirety of the Earth, and for all time; this will take place at the "Great White Throne Judgment" [Rev. 20:11-15]).*

THE TRIUMPHANT ENTRY

28 And when He had thus spoken, He went before, ascending up to Jerusalem *(is literally correct, for Jerusalem is approximately 3,500 feet higher in elevation than Jericho).*

29 And it came to pass, when He was come nigh to Bethphage and Bethany, at the Mount called *the Mount* of Olives *(the suburbs of Jerusalem),* He sent two of His Disciples *(the identity of the two is not known exactly, but was believed to have been Peter and John),*

30 Saying, Go ye into the village over against *you (was either Bethany or Bethphage);* in the which at your entering you shall find a colt tied, whereon yet never man sat: loose him,

and bring *him hither* *(proclaims that the triumphant entry would begin now, as predicted by the Prophet Zechariah [Zech. 9:9]).*

31 And if any man ask you, Why do ye loose *him? (This portrays that no previous preparation had been made for the borrowing of the animal. Why? Jesus as King, for this was what He represented at that time, does not, and in fact, must not ask permission. He is Sovereign.)* thus shall you say unto him, Because the Lord has need of him.

32 And they who were sent went their way, and found even as He had said unto them *(this will always be the case!).*

33 And as they were loosing the colt, the owners thereof said unto them, Why loose ye the colt?

34 And they said, The Lord has need of him *(evidently the owners immediately acquiesced; what a privilege it was for them to supply the animal — there were actually two animals — used by the Lord at this time).*

35 And they brought him *(the animal)* to Jesus: and they cast their garments upon the colt *(making a saddle of sorts)*, and they set Jesus thereon.

36 And as He went, they spread their clothes in the way *(concerned the vast number of pilgrims who had come from all over Israel for the Passover; this road would have been filled with people).*

37 And when He was come near, even now at the descent of the Mount of Olives, the whole multitude of the Disciples *(all the followers of Christ, not merely the Twelve)* began to rejoice and praise God with a loud voice for all the mighty works that they had seen;

38 Saying, Blessed *be* the King Who comes in the Name of the Lord *(the Prophecy of Zechariah demanded this public presentation of Jesus as the King of Israel, even though He would be rejected)*: peace in Heaven, and glory in the highest *(these phrases are of great magnitude; Jesus was to suffer and die in a few hours; this would bring peace to Heaven as well as Earth; He completely defeated Satan, making it possible for all things to be reconciled in Heaven and Earth; this is not yet done, but because of the Cross, it most assuredly will be done [Col. 2:14-17; Heb. 2:14-15]).*

39 And some of the Pharisees from among the multitude said unto Him, Master, rebuke Your Disciples *(Satan will do all within his power to stop people from praising the Lord, and will mostly use the Church to carry out his* devious designs).

40 And He answered and said unto them, I tell you that, if these should hold their peace, the stones would immediately cry out *(God demands praise, and true Christians will definitely praise Him; this proclaims to the spirit world that God's Plan will succeed and Satan will be overthrown).*

JERUSALEM

41 And when He was come near, He beheld the city *(Jerusalem, at that time, was a city of unparalleled beauty; the Temple was gleaming white, and one of the most beautiful buildings in the world)*, and wept over it *(refers to loud crying, lamentations, even wailing; what must have been the reaction of people as they saw Him do this?),*

42 Saying, If you had known, even you, at least in this your day, the things *which belong* unto your peace! *(The things that Israel could have had, had they only obeyed the Word of God.)* but now they are hid from your eyes *(refers to willful blindness, which resulted in judicial blindness; Leadership will be given now unto the Gentiles).*

43 For the days shall come upon you, that your enemies shall cast a trench about you *(was fulfilled in totality in A.D. 70)*, and compass you round, and keep you in on every side *(the Romans surrounded Jerusalem with a stone wall, making escape impossible),*

44 And shall lay you even with the ground *(the Roman General Titus, with the Tenth Legion, reduced the city to rubble)*, and your children within you *(concerning the siege, over one million were killed, with hundreds of thousands of others sold as slaves)*; and they shall not leave in you one stone upon another *(this concerned the Temple, and was fulfilled in totality; every stone was removed and a plough run over the place where it had stood, fulfilling Micah 3:12)*; because you knew not the time of your visitation *(refers to the life and Ministry of Jesus, which constituted the greatest visitation ever experienced by any people).*

THE TEMPLE

45 And He went into the Temple *(actually refers to the next day)*, and began to cast out them who sold therein, and them who bought *(probably took place in the Court of the Gentiles)*;

46 Saying unto them, It is written *(Isa. 56:7),*

My house is the house of prayer: but you have made it a den of thieves (Satan had done this by and through religious leaders).

47 And He taught daily in the Temple (pertained to the approximate five days before His arrest and trial on the sixth day). But the Chief Priests and the Scribes and the Chief of the people sought to destroy Him (concerns, as is obvious, the religious hierarchy of Israel; but no matter how powerful that hierarchy might be, to oppose God is a fight that cannot be won; they only succeeded in destroying themselves),

48 And could not find what they might do (couldn't find a way to destroy Him): for all the people were very attentive to hear Him (so whatever they would do could not be done in the open, but had to be done in secret, which it was).

CHAPTER 20
(A.D. 33)
AUTHORITY

AND it came to pass, that on one of those days (probably was Monday; He was arrested Wednesday night, for the new day began at the going down of the sun rather than midnight as we now reckon time), as He taught the people in the Temple, and preached the Gospel ("preaching" and "teaching" are still God's Way of proclaiming the Word), the Chief Priests and the Scribes came upon Him with the Elders (they were very angry with Him for several reasons, but the greatest reason of all was that they were full of the Devil),

2 And spoke unto Him, saying, Tell us, by what authority do You these things? (This is a trap designed to force Him to openly claim a Divine Commission.) or who is he who gave You this authority? (They knew He claimed God as His sole Authority, but they wanted Him to say it publicly in the Temple. Of course, they did not believe His Source was God. Yet it was very difficult for them to explain away the miracles; therefore, they attributed these to Satan, which in fact was Blasphemy of the Holy Spirit [Mat. 12:24-32].)

3 And He answered and said unto them, I will also ask you one thing; and answer Me (in demanding an answer from them, the Lord was claiming an answer from authorized teachers, which they claimed to be; so the tables were now turned, with Him putting them on the spot):

4 The baptism of John, was it from Heaven, or of men? (His question was not a trick question as theirs had been, but rather a legitimate question, with a legitimate and obvious answer pointing to the Source of His Authority.)

5 And they reasoned with themselves (they went into a huddle; they were on the horns of a dilemma!), saying, If we shall say, From Heaven; He will say, Why then believed you him not? (If they acknowledged that John was a true Prophet of God, then they would have to acknowledge his Message, and more importantly the One he introduced, the Lord Jesus Christ.)

6 But and if we say, Of men; all the people will stone us: for they be persuaded that John was a Prophet (concerns the people being far ahead of their spiritual leaders).

7 And they answered, that they could not tell whence it was (in fact, they were the very ones who were supposed to be able to answer such a question; their lame answer showed that they had no spirituality at all; what a cop-out!).

8 And Jesus said unto them, Neither tell I you by what authority I do these things.

THE WICKED HUSBANDMEN

9 Then began He to speak to the people this Parable (will outline in graphic detail the answer to the question these religious leaders had asked); A certain man (God) planted a Vineyard (Israel), and let it forth to husbandmen (referred to the religious leaders of Israel, whomever they were, and for the entire time of the nation), and went into a far country for a long time (pertains from the time of Abraham up to Christ).

10 And at the season He sent a servant to the husbandmen (speaks of the Prophets who were sent at intervals), that they should give Him of the fruit of the vineyard: but the husbandmen beat him, and sent him away empty (concerns the treatment of the Prophets).

11 And again He sent another servant (another Prophet): and they beat him also, and entreated him shamefully, and sent him away empty.

12 And again He sent a third: and they wounded him also, and cast him out.

13 Then said the Lord of the Vineyard, What shall I do? (The question does not lack knowledge on the part of God as to what He will do, but, in effect, actually states what will be done.) I will send My Beloved Son (the Lord Jesus Christ): it may be they will reverence Him when they see Him (the Son was the Heir, therefore, the Vineyard belonged to Him).

14 But when the husbandmen saw Him, they reasoned among themselves (exactly as

the religious leaders did), **saying, This is the Heir** *(proclaims in no uncertain terms that the Scribes and Pharisees knew exactly Who Jesus really was):* **come, let us kill Him** *(even though they knew Who He was, their response to Him was one of murder),* **that the inheritance may be ours** *(untold millions have said the same thing; they do not want the Plan of God for this world and for their lives; they desire to chart their own course, which always leads to destruction; they have done nothing but wreck the inheritance).*

15 So they cast Him out of the Vineyard, and killed *Him (says in no uncertain terms exactly what they would do, and in fact, did do!).* **What therefore shall the Lord of the Vineyard do unto them?** *(Even though they are warned, even as the next Verse proclaims, they would not listen.)*

16 He shall come and destroy these husbandmen *(it happened some thirty-seven years later, exactly as He said it would, as Rome destroyed Jerusalem and did so completely),* **and shall give the Vineyard to others** *(has reference to the Gentile Church).* **And when they heard** *it,* **they said, God forbid** *(proclaims that they knew exactly what Jesus was saying, and exactly what He meant; their answer was "God forbid," meaning, "God will not allow such!"; their answer should have been, "God have mercy on us").*

17 And He beheld them, and said, What is this then that is written *(Ps. 118:22),* **The Stone which the builders rejected** *(that "Stone" is Christ),* **the same is become the Head of the Corner?** *(Israel's rejection of Christ did not abrogate His position as "Cornerstone." He is that to the Church, and will ultimately be that to Israel.)*

18 Whosoever shall fall upon that Stone shall be broken *(speaks of Israel, and any nation or people or a person for that matter who sets out to destroy Christ, i.e., "set Him aside"; instead, they are broken themselves; this is a battle that no one can win, for Jesus is God!);* **but on whomsoever it shall fall, it will grind him to powder** *(speaks of Christ ultimately smashing the Kingdoms of this world, which He will do at the Second Coming, making them His Own [Dan. 2:35]; Jesus presents Himself here as the principal figure of the entirety of humanity and the world, and proclaims their rise or fall based on their acceptance or rejection of Him).*

TRIBUTE MONEY

19 And the Chief Priests and the Scribes the same hour sought to lay hands on Him *(they were incensed at the Parable He had just related to them, and especially Him speaking of Himself as the "Stone," i.e., "Cornerstone");* **and they feared the people: for they perceived that He had spoken this Parable against them** *(so what they did was not at all in ignorance, but rather from the position of rebellion).*

20 And they watched *Him (refers to the fact that they were trying to catch Him in His Words in order to level a charge of treason against Him),* **and sent forth spies, which should feign themselves just men, that they might take hold of His words** *(how foolish they were),* **that so they might deliver Him unto the power and authority of the Governor** *(Pilate).*

21 And they asked Him, saying, Master, we know that You say and teach rightly, neither do You accept the person *of any,* **but teach the Way of God truly** *(all of this was true, but they didn't believe it, only saying these words in order to attempt to snare Him):*

22 Is it lawful for us to give tribute unto Caesar, or no? *(This "tribute" was tax levied by Rome on every person in Israel at a Denarius a head. If He said "yes," He would be labeled a traitor by Israel, because they abhorred this tax inasmuch as it proclaimed them a subject of Rome. If He said "no," He could be branded an insurrectionist by Rome. So in their minds, either way He answered would incriminate Him.)*

23 But He perceived their craftiness *(He instantly recognized their treachery and trickery),* **and said unto them, Why do you tempt Me?** *(He lets them know that He knows exactly what they're doing, and their hypocrisy.)*

24 Show Me a penny *(the Roman Denarius; such was not normally brought into the Temple because there was an inscription of Caesar on its face).* **Whose image and superscription has it? They answered and said, Caesar's.**

25 And He said unto them, Render therefore unto Caesar the things which be Caesar's, and unto God the things which be God's *(Jesus is saying that debts to man and debts to God are both to be discharged, and the two spheres of duty are at once distinct and reconcilable; in effect, Jesus was teaching here in its beginning forms the separation of Church and State).*

26 And they could not take hold of His words before the people *(His answer was so perfect that they had no rebuttal):* **and they marvelled at His answer, and held their peace** *(in their trickery, they were positive that His Answer would incriminate Him in one way or*

the other, but to their amazement, it served no purpose at all for their evil designs).

THE RESURRECTION

27 Then came to *Him* **certain of the Sadducees** *(the Modernists of Israel of that day, and who mostly controlled the High Priesthood and the Sanhedrin),* **which deny that there is any Resurrection** *(their false interpretation of the Word of God ruled out an after-life, consequently reducing the Plan of God to mere window dressing);* **and they asked Him,**

28 Saying, Master, Moses wrote unto us, If any man's brother die, having a wife, and he die without children, that his brother should take his wife, and raise up seed unto his brother *([Deut. 25:5], they claimed to believe Genesis through Deuteronomy, but placed no credence in the balance of the Bible of that day, which was Joshua through Malachi).*

29 There were therefore seven brethren: and the first took a wife, and died without children.

30 And the second took her to wife, and he died childless.

31 And the third took her; and in like manner the seven also: and they left no children, and died.

32 Last of all the woman died also.

33 Therefore in the Resurrection whose wife of them is she? for seven had her to wife *(Deuteronomy does not contain this illustration, at least in this fashion; this is a hypothetical situation conjured up by the Sadducees, which they thought sealed their argument that there was no such thing as a Resurrection).*

34 And Jesus answering said unto them, The children of this world *(this life before death)* **marry, and are given in marriage** *(this places the institution of marriage solely in this present world, and not in the world to come):*

35 But they which shall be accounted worthy to obtain that world *(eternal life, brought about by the "born-again" experience),* **and the Resurrection from the dead** *(proclaims unequivocally that there will be a "Resurrection"),* **neither marry, nor are given in marriage** *(this pertains to those who have part in the First Resurrection, which will include every Believer who has ever lived up unto the conclusion of the Great Tribulation):*

36 Neither can they die any more *(at that time, all Saints of God will have Glorified bodies; there will be no more death among them):*

for they are equal unto the Angels *(speaking only of immortality);* **and are the Children of God, being the Children of the Resurrection** *(all Believers will be "Children of the Resurrection," simply because they are "Children of God" through the Born-Again experience [Jn. 3:3]).*

37 Now that the dead are raised, even Moses showed at the bush *(takes the Sadducees to the very part of the Bible they claim to believe),* **when he called the Lord the God of Abraham, and the God of Isaac, and the God of Jacob** *(presents a solid truth concerning life after death, which the next Verse will explain).*

38 For He is not a God of the dead *(meaning that there is life after death, whether in Heaven or Hell),* **but of the living** *(in effect, Moses was saying that Abraham, Isaac, and Jacob were even then alive, even though they had physically died many years before; it is the same with all Believers):* **for all live unto Him** *(He is not a God of dead beings, but of living beings; God cannot be the God of a being who does not exist).*

THE INCARNATION

39 Then certain of the Scribes answering said, Master, You have well said *(the Scribes were Pharisees, and did believe in the Resurrection).*

40 And after that they do not ask Him any *question at all (both Pharisees and Sadducees gave up this method of attack).*

41 And He said unto them, How say they that Christ is David's son? *("Christ" means Anointed One" or "Messiah." This question, posed by Christ, had to do with the Incarnation.)*

42 And David himself said in the Book of Psalms, The LORD said unto My Lord, Sit Thou on My right hand *([Ps. 110:1] this statement proclaims Deity on the part of the Messiah, which struck at the heart of the false belief of the Jews concerning Jesus, who expected their Messiah to be merely a "beloved man"; in essence, "God the Father says to God the Son . . . ."),*

43 Till I make your enemies your footstool *(Jesus did this through the Cross [Col. 2:14-15]).*

44 David therefore called Him Lord, how is He then His Son? *(With this question, Jesus placed the Incarnation, God becoming man, squarely before the Pharisees. Jesus is David's Lord because He is God. He is David's Son, in respect to His Humanity, God becoming man.)*

45 Then in the audience of all the people He said unto His Disciples *(said the following in the hearing of all the people),*

46 Beware of the Scribes, which desire to

walk in long robes, and love greetings in the markets, and the highest seats in the Synagogues, and the chief rooms at feasts (their religion was a "show," and contained no substance; but yet, they were the Pastors of the people);

47 Which devour widows' houses, and for a show make long prayers (prayed these prayers in the presence of these particular women in order to get their money): the same shall receive greater damnation (refers to judgment; Hell will be the hottest for this type, who are mere professors, but do not actually possess).

CHAPTER 21

(A.D. 33)

THE TWO MITES

AND He looked up (our Lord was in the covered colonnade of that part of the Temple which was open to the Jewish women; here was the treasury with its thirteen boxes on the wall, where the people could give offerings), and saw the rich men casting their gifts into the treasury (implying that they were making a show of their gifts, desiring to impress the people by the amount, etc.).

2 And He saw also a certain poor widow casting in thither two mites (was probably worth something less than a dollar in 2003 purchasing power).

3 And He said, Of a truth I say unto you (presents a new concept of giving), that this poor widow has cast in more than they all (the term "poor widow" means that she worked very hard for what little she received):

4 For all these have of their abundance cast in unto the offerings of God (means that they had much left, constituting very little given, at least in the Eyes of God): but she of her penury (poverty) has cast in all the living that she had (spoke of her gift, as small as it was, being larger than all others combined because she gave all; God judges our giving by many factors; motive plays very heavily into the account).

THE TEMPLE

5 And as some spoke of the Temple (was said on the Mount of Olivet, as Jesus and His Disciples left the city), how it was adorned with goodly stones and gifts (this building was one of the most beautiful in the world), He said,

6 As for these things which you behold (referred to the beauty of the Temple, which the Disciples were even then admiring), the days

will come, in the which there shall not be left one stone upon another, that shall not be thrown down (this is exactly what happened in A.D. 70, when Titus destroyed the Temple and the city).

7 And they asked Him, saying, Master, but when shall these things be? (While Mat., Chpt. 24 deals primarily with the Second Coming, Luke addressed himself to the Words of Christ, which concerned the coming destruction by Titus the Roman General.) and what sign will there be when these things shall come to pass? (This is somewhat different than the question recorded by Matthew, "what shall be the sign of Your Coming and of the end of the world?")

SIGNS OF THE ENDTIME

8 And He said (for the next four Verses, Luke deals with the signs of the times as it regards the Second Coming), Take heed that you be not deceived (presents the exact manner in which Matthew begins his account — the warning of deception; it is mainly in the realm of religion): for many shall come in My Name, saying, I am Christ (of Christ); and the time draws near (the Rapture of the Church): go ye not therefore after them (be very careful as to whom you follow).

9 But when you shall hear of wars and commotions, be not terrified (when Israel rejected Christ, this subjected the world to some 2,000 more years of terror): for these things must first come to pass (which in effect have characterized the world from then until now); but the end is not by and by (means that the end is not immediate).

10 Then said He unto them, Nation shall rise against nation, and kingdom against kingdom (refers to the time immediately preceding the Great Tribulation, and on into that particular time period):

11 And great earthquakes shall be in divers places, and famines, and pestilences; and fearful sights and great signs shall there be from Heaven (these things will take place on this particular scale during the Great Tribulation Period).

JERUSALEM

12 But before all these (speaking of the time very soon after He made these statements), they shall lay their hands on you, and persecute you, delivering you up to the Synagogues,

and into prisons, being brought before kings and rulers for My Name's sake *(the Book of Acts records these events, and history records that which followed the Book of Acts).*

13 And it shall turn to you for a Testimony *(Believers must not allow their "Testimony" to be hindered by persecution, but rather make it the cause of being strengthened).*

14 Settle *it* therefore in your hearts, not to meditate before what you shall answer *(does not condemn careful thought, but encourages total trust in the Lord without fear):*

15 For I will give you a mouth and wisdom *(speaks of the unction of the Holy Spirit in the heart and life of the Believer, giving the help that is needed),* which all your adversaries shall not be able to gainsay nor resist.

16 And you shall be betrayed both by parents, and brethren, and kinsfolks, and friends *(this portrays the power of demon religions and their control of their victims);* and *some* of you shall they cause to be put to death *(some will not be delivered, but will rather die for their Testimony).*

17 And you shall be hated of all *men* for My Name's sake *(this one Verse is ample proof of the validity of Christianity, in that anything which could survive such opposition, and even grow — until it is now the largest in the world — proves the integrity of its Founder, the Lord Jesus Christ, and the sincerity of its converts).*

18 But there shall not an hair of your head perish *(our Lord is speaking now of the coming destruction of Jerusalem in A.D. 70; in that carnage, which resulted in over one million Jews being killed, not a single Christian lost his life because they read these very Verses, and did exactly what Jesus said to do).*

19 In your patience possess ye your souls *(if the situation does not seem to improve, the Believer is to be "patient," knowing that God has all things under control, and everything that He does is for the benefit of the Believer and not His hurt).*

20 And when you shall see Jerusalem compassed with armies *(speaks of the invasion by Titus in A.D. 70),* then know that the desolation thereof is near *(speaks of the moment that Titus would begin to surround Jerusalem, which would be the signal that Christians were to leave, which they did!).*

21 Then let them which are in Judaea flee to the mountains *(spoke of all those who believed this Word, which all Christians did);* and let them which are in the midst of it depart out *(means that no part of Judaea would be safe from the Roman armies);* and let not them who are in the countries enter thereinto *(speaks of Christians who lived in surrounding countries, who at this time were not to come into Judaea).*

22 For these be the days of vengeance *(refers to judgment; Israel had rejected Christ; now they must pay),* that all things which are written may be fulfilled *(concerning the fulfillment of these very Words as given by Christ, as well as all prophecies; to be sure, every single Word of God will come to pass, exactly as predicted).*

23 But woe unto them who are with child, and to them who give suck, in those days! for there shall be great distress in the land, and wrath upon this people *(once again speaks of the terrible days which were to come on Jerusalem, and which did come in A.D. 70).*

24 And they shall fall by the edge of the sword, and shall be led away captive into all nations *(hundreds of thousands of Jews after the carnage of A.D. 70 were sold as slaves all over the world of that day; as well, the Jewish people as a whole were scattered all over the world, fulfilling exactly what Jesus said would happen):* and Jerusalem shall be trodden down of the Gentiles, until the times of the Gentiles be fulfilled *(has actually proved the case since Jerusalem was destroyed by the Babylonians some six hundred years before Christ; in fact, it has continued unto this hour, and will for all practical purposes continue until the Second Coming; then the "times of the Gentiles will be fulfilled," with Israel once again becoming the premiere nation of the world, which they will do under Christ).*

25 And there shall be signs in the sun, and in the moon, and in the stars *(proclaims the Lord now returning to His former subject of signs concerning His Second Coming, which was first broached in Verses 8 through 11);* and upon the Earth distress of nations, with perplexity *(refers to problems without a solution, which will prevail in the coming Great Tribulation);* the sea and the waves roaring *(does not pertain to bodies of water, but rather to nations roaring in discontent, anger, rebellion, and war [Rev. 17:15]);*

26 Men's hearts failing them for fear *(has nothing to do with heart disease, but rather men losing heart, i.e., having no more courage to continue),* and for looking after those things which are coming on the Earth *(Rev., Chpts. 6-19 give*

us in graphic detail an account of that which will happen): **for the powers of Heaven shall be shaken** (proclaims the Judgment of God that will fall upon unbelieving Israel and the Gentile nations, which will have no precedent in all past history, and will have no counterpart in all succeeding history [Mat. 24:21]).

27 And then (refers to the conclusion of the Great Tribulation) **shall they see the Son of Man coming** (refers to the Second Coming, and may very well be televised by News Agencies covering the Battle of Armageddon, raging at that time, which will portray this Coming all over the world) **in a cloud** (does not speak of the clouds of the heavens, but rather clouds of Saints and Angels, which will be coming back with the Lord at that Coming) **with power and great glory** (as stated, when He comes the second time, the world will not have to ask if it is really Him; it will be overly obvious!).

28 And when these things begin to come to pass (refers to the "signs" of Verses 8 through 11, as well as Verses 25 and 26), **then look up, and lift up your heads; for your Redemption draws nigh** (does not refer to the Rapture, for that will have already happened years before, but rather the deliverance of Israel at the Second Coming when Christ comes with Raptured Saints [Isa. 11:10-12; 66:7-8; Zech., Chpt. 14; Mat. 24:29-31; Rom. 11:25-29; Rev., Chpt. 19]).

THE FIG TREE

29 And He spoke to them a Parable; Behold the fig tree, and all the trees (Jesus is using a simple illustration which is meant to point to the Second Coming);

30 When they now shoot forth, you see and know of your own selves that summer is now nigh at hand (the season of Spring tells us that the season of Summer is about to begin).

31 So likewise ye, when you see these things come to pass (once again speaks of the happenings of Verses 8 through 11, as well as Verses 25 and 26), **know ye that the Kingdom of God is near at hand** (points to the Second Coming, which will usher in the Kingdom Age).

32 Verily I say unto you, This generation shall not pass away, till all be fulfilled (the generation that will be alive at the time of these happenings).

33 Heaven and earth shall pass away (will pass from one condition to another): **but My Words shall not pass away** (the Word of God is more sure of fulfillment even than the stability of Heaven and Earth).

WATCH AND PRAY

34 And take heed to yourselves (begins a portion of teaching that applies to the entirety of the body of Christ, and for all times), **lest at any time your hearts be overcharged** (weighed down) **with surfeiting** (debauchery), **and drunkenness, and cares of this life** (things which are not spiritual), **and so that day come upon you unawares** (actually points to the Second Coming, but can point as well to the Rapture and Death).

35 For as a snare shall it come on all them who dwell on the face of the whole earth (in other words, things will not turn out as man thinks they will, for the Second Coming will change everything).

36 Watch ye therefore, and pray always (watch events which transpire, and equate them in whatever capacity with the Word, asking the Lord to give discernment), **that you may be accounted worthy to escape all these things that shall come to pass** (it speaks of the Rapture of the Church; the "worthiness" spoken of here by Jesus has nothing to do with self-righteousness, but rather the righteousness which is freely given to anyone who expresses Faith in Christ and the Cross; that and that alone is the key), **and to stand before the Son of Man** (refers to being taken to be with the Lord before the Coming Great Tribulation [I Thess. 4:13-18]).

37 And in the daytime He was teaching in the Temple (concerned His last hours before the Crucifixion); **and at night He went out, and abode in the Mount that is called the Mount of Olives** (we have here the Son of God, the Creator of all things, the Maker of Heaven and Earth, Who would actually have no place to lay His Head, with the exception of a rock; the humiliation He suffered has no comparison in the annals of human history).

38 And all the people came early in the morning to Him in the Temple (concerns the many thousands who filled Jerusalem, for it was the time of the Passover), **for to hear Him** (to hear the "Giver of Life," present the "Words of Life").

CHAPTER 22
(A.D. 33)
THE PLOT

NOW the Feast of Unleavened Bread drew nigh, which is called the Passover (it

began on April 14th; there were three Feasts held at this particular time, "Passover, Unleavened Bread, and First Fruits").

2 And the Chief Priests and Scribes sought how they might kill Him (represented the religious hierarchy of Israel; it is ironic; the world did not crucify Him so much as did the Church, i.e., "Israel"); for they feared the people (they should have feared God!).

JUDAS ISCARIOT

3 Then entered Satan into Judas surnamed Iscariot (pertained to the present time, even though Satan had been working on Judas for quite some time), being of the number of the Twelve (the Holy Spirit wanted all to know what an opportunity this man had, but threw it all away).

4 And he (Judas) went his way (it was not God's Way), and communed with the Chief Priests and Captains, how he might betray Him unto them (proclaims the most evil deed ever carried out by a human being).

5 And they were glad (portrays evil beyond belief; it is more tragic still when one realizes that this was the "Church" of Jesus' day; however, it hasn't changed; were Christ here now, institutionalized religion would do the same thing as was done then), and covenanted to give him money (thirty pieces of silver, the price of a slave).

6 And he promised, and sought opportunity to betray Him unto them in the absence of the multitude (they had to carry out this act when He was Alone, or at least in the presence of His Disciples only; Judas promised to provide this opportunity).

THE PASSOVER

7 Then came the day of Unleavened Bread, when the Passover must be killed (Jesus, God's Passover, must be killed because the Scriptures predicted it; only His Atoning Death could expiate man's sin; all four Gospels record at great length His Death, while only two briefly record His Birth).

8 And He sent Peter and John, saying (had to do with the preparation of the Passover, which constituted the Last Supper), Go and prepare us the Passover, that we may eat (means that Peter and John, representing the Apostolic band, took a lamb to the Temple where it was killed).

9 And they said unto Him, Where will You

that we prepare? (At this time, they did not know where it would be eaten. In fact, Jesus would eat the Passover a day early.)

10 And He said unto them, Behold, when you are entered into the city, there shall a man meet you, bearing a pitcher of water (in those days, men seldom carried pitchers of water, that being reserved for women; consequently, such would be easy to spot); follow him into the house where he enters in (would be the place where the Passover would be eaten; some think this was the home of John Mark, who wrote the Gospel that bears his name).

11 And you shall say unto the goodman of the house, The Master says unto you, Where is the guestchamber, where I shall eat the Passover with My Disciples? (If it is to be noticed, Jesus does not ask permission; for Kings tell instead of ask.)

12 And he shall show you a large upper room furnished (prepared): there make ready (this could well be the same "upper room" from Acts 1:13, as it most probably was).

13 And they went, and found as He had said unto them (will always be the case regarding anything He has spoken unto us): and they made ready the Passover (means that they prepared the Lamb for roasting, along with the making of the Unleavened Bread, etc.).

THE LORD'S SUPPER

14 And when the hour was come (was a little after sundown, which was Wednesday, at least as Israel then reckoned time), He sat down, and the Twelve Apostles with Him (including Judas as is obvious).

15 And He said unto them, With desire I have desired to eat this Passover with you before I suffer (it would be symbolic of the New Covenant, brought about by what He would suffer through the Cross):

16 For I say unto you, I will not any more eat thereof (this would be the last Passover, at least which God would recognize, because Jesus, Who was in reality the Passover, would meet its requirements on the Cross), until it be fulfilled in the Kingdom of God (even though the total price was paid at Calvary, still, all that Redemption affords has not yet been received, but will be received at the Resurrection of Life [I Cor. 15:49-58]).

17 And He took the cup, and gave thanks (evidently a large cup), and said, Take this, and divide it among yourselves (a small portion

was poured for each one):

18 For I say unto you, I will not drink of the fruit of the vine, until the Kingdom of God shall come (same as Verse 16).

19 And He took bread, and gave thanks, and broke it, and gave unto them, saying, This is My Body which is given for you (His Body was prepared by God, in order that it be a Perfect Sacrifice [Heb. 10:5]): this do in remembrance of Me (in remembrance of His Death on the Cross of Calvary that purchased our Redemption, which we celebrate in that referred to as "the Lord's Supper").

20 Likewise also the cup after supper, saying, This cup is the New Testament (New Covenant) in My blood (the terminology is symbolic and figurative, not literal; Lev. 3:17 and Lev. 7:26 forbade the eating of blood), which is shed for you (which was done on the Cross of Calvary).

THE BETRAYAL FORETOLD

21 But, behold, the hand of him who betrays Me is with Me on the table (it doesn't tell us much because the hands of all of the Apostles were on the table).

22 And truly the Son of Man goes, as it was determined (God's foreknowledge does not abrogate man's responsibility; God wills in the sense of permission, but not necessarily): but woe unto that man by whom He is betrayed! (This tells us that it was not predetermined who the man would be, even though it was predetermined that some man would do such a thing.)

23 And they began to enquire among themselves, which of them it was that should do this thing (at this time, none of the Disciples knew of the disposition of Judas).

STRIFE

24 And there was also a strife among them (took place almost immediately after Supper; "Strife" in this instance means "contention"), which of them should be accounted the greatest (Christ was about to die, and His Disciples were arguing over place and position; they still did not have a clue as to what was about to happen to Him).

25 And He said unto them, The kings of the Gentiles exercise lordship over them (proclaims the way of the world, which the Believer is not to emulate); and they that exercise authority upon them are called benefactors (presents the means by which these dictators justify themselves; they claim to give all types of good things to the people, but most give nothing).

26 But ye shall not be so (the "lordship spirit" is the way of the world, and is not to be adopted by the Church): but he who is greatest among you, let him be as the younger; and he who is chief, as he who does serve (all Believers, and especially those who will be greatly used by the Lord, must know and live as the "servant").

27 For whether is greater, he who sits at meat, or he who serves? (This is meant to point out the total contrast between the ways of the world and the Ways of God.) is not he who sits at meat? (The world looks at the one who is being served as the Greatest, but now Jesus shows us true Greatness.) but I am among you as He who serves (as is obvious, Jesus lived by the servant principle, which as stated is the opposite of the world; and we must do the same).

28 You are they which have continued with Me in My temptations (He was the Man of Sorrows; His whole Life was a series of trials, griefs, hatreds, and sufferings).

29 And I appoint unto you a Kingdom (though He foreknew that they would all forsake Him, yet in His most wonderful and tender Love, He praised their fidelity and courage and promised them a recompense out of all proportion to their service), as My Father has appointed unto Me (we become a joint heir with Christ [Rom. 8:17]);

30 That you may eat and drink at My Table in My Kingdom (has reference to the coming Kingdom Age, mentioned in Verse 18), and sit on thrones judging the Twelve Tribes of Israel (is a privilege to be enjoyed only by the Twelve Apostles, with Matthias taking the place of Judas).

PETER

31 And the Lord said, Simon, Simon, behold, Satan has desired to have you (portrays to us a glimpse into the spirit world, which was very similar to the same request made by Satan concerning Job), that he may sift you as wheat (Satan tempts in order to bring out the bad, while God tests in order to bring out the good; the simple truth is God, at times using Satan as His instrument in addressing character, causes men to seek God's Holiness rather than their own):

32 But I have prayed for you, that your faith fail not (Satan's attack is always delivered against Faith, for if that fails all fail): and when you are converted, strengthen your brethren (does

not refer to being saved again, but rather coming to the right path of trust and dependence on the Lord, instead of on self; that lesson learned, one is then able to strengthen the brethren).

33 And he *(Peter)* said unto Him, Lord, I am ready to go with You, both into prison, and to death *(most probably Peter's true feelings, but his confidence was in self, and self cannot perform the task).*

34 And He said, I tell you, Peter *(Jesus seldom addressed Peter by this name; it means "a rock"; so by Him referring to Peter in this fashion, in essence, told him that, despite the terrible denial which was coming, Peter would survive the onslaught),* the cock shall not crow this day, before that you shall thrice deny that you know Me *(pinpoints the time, and exactly the number of times this would happen).*

35 And He said unto them, When I sent you without purse, and scrip, and shoes, lacked you any thing? And they said, Nothing *(speaks of every need being met and abundantly so).*

36 Then said He unto them, But now, he who has a purse, let him take *it,* and likewise *his* scrip *(a bag for carrying things, placed over the shoulder or around the waist; He is telling them that while the needs will always be met, it will not be nearly so easy as it had been in the past):* and he who has no sword, let him sell his garment, and buy one *(all of these terms are symbolic; the "sword" has reference to the fact that Believers are to accept the protection of an ordered Government).*

37 For I say unto you, that this that is written must yet be accomplished in Me *(refers to Isa., Chpt. 53, and is the first time the Lord refers to that Text),* And He was reckoned among the transgressors *(does not mean that He was actually a transgressor, but that Israel considered Him one even though they could find no wrongdoing for which He could be charged):* for the things concerning Me have an end *(He had come to fulfill all the Prophecies of the past, and this He would do shortly).*

38 And they said, Lord, behold, here *are* two swords *(proclaims that they did not understand that to which He referred concerning the purchasing of a sword; they took it literally, whereas He was speaking symbolically respecting the authority of Gentile nations).* And He said unto them, It is enough *(proclaims Him making no attempt to correct their false assumption in this securing of two swords, knowing that the meaning would become abundantly clear after the Day of Pentecost).*

GETHSEMANE

39 And He came out, and went, as He was wont *(accustomed),* to the Mount of Olives *(constitutes the beginning of the agony in the Garden);* and His Disciples also followed Him *(proclaims, it seems, that they did not quite know what He was going to do, and what the occasion would present).*

40 And when He was at the place *(Gethsemane, the place of surrender),* He said unto them, Pray that you enter not into temptation *(the temptation of subverting the Will of God).*

41 And He was withdrawn from them about a stone's cast, and kneeled down, and prayed *(His Prayer Life was exceptional, and ours should be as well!),*

42 Saying, Father, if You be willing, remove this cup from Me *(speaks of that which He would have to drink in the spiritual sense):* nevertheless not My will, but Thine, be done *(this is the price of surrender).*

43 And there appeared an Angel unto Him from Heaven, strengthening Him *(this was the peace of surrender; as a human being, He suffered now as possibly no other has suffered, thereby desperately needing the help of the Angel).*

44 And being in an agony He prayed more earnestly *(Heb. 5:7 shows that the wrath of God was to judge Him as if He, and He Alone, were the only sinner who ever existed, even though He was no sinner at all; this caused that agony; so His Death was not just a great example of resignation and self-sacrifice, as multitudes vainly think):* and His sweat was as it were great drops of blood falling down to the ground *(portrays a recognized fact that under extreme mental pressure, the pores may become so dilated that blood may issue from them in the form of bloody sweat).*

45 And when He rose up from prayer, and was come to His Disciples *(signals the victory won, at least in this great struggle concerning the Will of God),* He found them sleeping for sorrow *(the agony upon Him also affected His Disciples),*

46 And said unto them, Why sleep ye? *(This presents the moment He awakened them. He does not expect an answer.)* rise and pray, lest you enter into temptation *(would have been better translated, "lest you succumb to temptation").*

THE ARREST

47 And while He yet spoke, behold a

multitude *(pertains to the group coming to arrest Jesus, consisting of Roman Legionnaires and of Levitical guards belonging to the Temple)*, and he who was called Judas, one of the Twelve, went before them *(proclaims the Holy Spirit purposely explaining who Judas was, so as not to confuse him with others of the same name)*, and drew near unto Jesus to kiss Him *(the prearranged design)*.

48 But Jesus said unto him, Judas, you betrayest thou the Son of Man with a kiss? *(This was the most infamous "kiss" in history.)*

49 When they which were about Him saw what would follow *(saw that He was about to be arrested)*, they said unto Him, Lord, shall we smite with the sword? *(This presents the very opposite of what He wanted them to do.)*

50 And one of them smote the servant of the High Priest *(this was Simon Peter; as well, John gives the servant's name as Malchus)*, and cut off his right ear *(evidently, Peter was trying to kill him!)*.

51 And Jesus answered and said, Suffer you thus far *(probably means, although it has been debated, "bear with My Disciples")*. And He touched his ear, and healed him *(presents the last miracle of healing He performed before the Crucifixion)*.

52 Then Jesus said unto the Chief Priests, and Captains of the Temple, and the Elders, which were come to Him *(represented the religious hierarchy of Israel, the very ones who should have welcomed Him instead)*, Be ye come out, as against a thief, with swords and staves? *(This presents two thoughts: 1. If I wanted to use My Power against you, your swords and staves would do you no good at all; and, 2. I am not a thief, as should be obvious, so why do you treat Me as one?)*

53 When I was daily with you in the Temple, you stretched forth no hands against Me *(presents the truth of His Position, and the fallacy of theirs)*: but this is your hour *(refers to God allowing the religious leaders of Israel to do this dastardly thing)*, and the power of darkness *(means that the energy by which they were doing this thing was the energy of the "power of darkness," i.e., Satan himself!)*.

THE DENIAL

54 Then took they Him, and led *Him*, and brought Him into the High Priest's house *(the High Priest at this time was Caiaphas, son-in-law to Annas, who was the legal High Priest, but*

who had been deposed by the Romans some time before)*. And Peter followed afar off *(does not record the reason for Peter's failure, as some believe; his problem, as with us all, was self-will)*.

55 And when they had kindled a fire in the midst of the hall, and were set down together *(speaks of those who had arrested Jesus, bringing Him to the house of the High Priest)*, Peter sat down among them *(proclaims him arriving at the Palace with John who was able to procure admission for the both of them, due to John being known to the High Priest)*.

56 But a certain maid beheld him as he sat by the fire, and earnestly looked upon him *(provides the first occasion for the terrible denial)*, and said, This man was also with Him *(probably came as a surprise to Peter)*.

57 And he denied Him, saying, Woman, I know Him not *(the first of three denials)*.

58 And after a little while another saw him, and said, You are also of them. And Peter said, Man, I am not *(the second denial)*.

59 And about the space of one hour after another confidently affirmed, saying, Of a truth this *fellow* also was with Him: for he is a Galilaean *(represents the occasion for the third and final denial)*.

60 And Peter said, Man, I know not what you say. And immediately, while he yet spoke, the rooster crowed *(the third denial, and exactly the number that Jesus predicted)*.

61 And the Lord turned, and looked upon Peter *(probably refers to the moment that Jesus was being led from the interrogation before Caiaphas, to be examined before the Sanhedrin)*. And Peter remembered the Word of the Lord, how He had said unto him, Before the rooster crows, you shall deny Me three times *(presents this coming back to Peter in full force, with all its attendant implications)*.

62 And Peter went out, and wept bitterly *(this type of "weeping" signals Repentance [Ps. 51:17])*.

THE TRIAL

63 And the men who held Jesus mocked Him *(referred to them goading Jesus that He use His Power to stop them; that is, if He had any power)*, and smote Him *(fulfilled the Prophecies of Isaiah [Isa. 52:14])*.

64 And when they had blindfolded Him, they struck Him on the face *(many struck Him, no doubt causing His Face to swell)*, and asked Him, saying, Prophesy, who is it who smote You? *(These mockers will one day stand before*

God, with each name being called out and exactly the number of blows that they delivered to the Face of Jesus.)

65 And many other things blasphemously spoke they against Him.

66 And as soon as it was day (*the trial which had been conducted that night was actually illegal; so now the Sanhedrin will meet again during the day, to try to legitimize what they had already done*), the Elders of the people and the Chief Priests and the Scribes came together, and led Him into their council, saying (*was to constitute His trial they thought, but in reality it was their trial*),

67 Are You the Christ? (*Evidently, all who were present were aware that Jesus had admitted to this while before Caiaphas, which Luke incidentally passes over, but is recounted by both Matthew and Mark.*) tell us (*said with anger and determination*). And He said unto them, If I tell you, you will not believe (*constitutes an answer far broader than they had asked*):

68 And if I also ask *you* (*refers to questions that, if properly answered, would have proved His Messiahship*), you will not answer Me (*refers to the fact that they were not looking for Truth*), nor let *Me* go (*this meant that the trial was a farce*).

69 Hereafter shall the Son of Man (*presents the last time Jesus will refer to Himself as such; in effect, this answers their question*) sit on the right hand of the Power of God (*refers to the Great White Throne Judgment, in effect saying, "you are judging Me today, but tomorrow I will judge you"*).

70 Then said they all, Are you then the Son of God? (*This was said with sarcasm!*) And He said unto them, You say that I am (*even though not resident in the Greek, in the Hebrew denotes a strong affirmation; in other words, in the clearest possible language He said, "I am!"*).

71 And they said, What need we any further witness? (*This proclaims exactly what they wanted.*) for we ourselves have heard of His Own mouth (*means they would all witness against Him to Pilate that He had made this claim*).

CHAPTER 23
(A.D. 33)
JESUS BEFORE PILATE

AND the whole multitude of them arose (*included the entirety of the seventy members of the Sanhedrin, with the possible exception of Joseph of Arimathaea and Nicodemus,* who were also members but loved Christ) and led Him unto Pilate (*presents the second step which must be carried out if, in fact, they were to rid themselves of Jesus once and for all, or so they thought!*).

2 And they began to accuse Him (*presents their response to Christ, and from the very beginning of His Ministry*), saying, We found this *fellow* perverting the nation (*claiming that Christ was attempting to agitate the nation of Israel to enter into rebellion against Caesar; this was a total fabrication, with Him doing the very opposite*), and forbidding to give tribute to Caesar (*constituted their second accusation, which was also a lie!*), saying that He Himself is Christ a King (*they were claiming He was telling Israel that He was King instead of Caesar, which was another lie*).

3 And Pilate asked Him, saying, Are You the King of the Jews? (*This presents Pilate completely ignoring the first two accusations, seeing clearly that they were baseless.*) And He answered him and said, You say *it* (*in effect, He answered in the affirmative*).

4 Then said Pilate to the Chief Priests and *to* the people, I find no fault in this Man (*and neither has any other human being ever truly found any "fault" in Him*).

5 And they were the more fierce (*proclaims the fact that Pilate's position came somewhat as a surprise to these fanatics*), saying, He stirs up the people (*the Greek word "stirs" is somewhat like inciting a mob to riot; of course, what they were saying was basely false*), teaching throughout all Jewry, beginning from Galilee to this place.

HEROD

6 When Pilate heard of Galilee, he asked whether the man were a Galilaean.

7 And as soon as he knew that He belonged unto Herod's jurisdiction, he sent Him to Herod (*proclaims him thinking he could wash his hands of this affair*), who himself also was at Jerusalem at that time (*constituted the Passover Season, which brought Herod to the city; his usual residence was Capernaum, which had been the headquarters of Jesus, but yet seemingly without much impact upon this murderer*).

8 And when Herod saw Jesus, he was exceeding glad (*constitutes a gladness for all the wrong reasons*): for he was desirous to see Him of a long *season*, because he had heard many things of Him (*had to do somewhat with both of*

them headquartered at Capernaum); and he hoped to have seen some miracle done by Him *(Jesus was to Herod Antipas, the slayer of John the Baptist, as a juggler is to a sated court — an object of curiosity; it seems he had very little interest in Him otherwise!).*

9 Then he questioned with Him in many words; but He answered him nothing *(tells us that the questions were trivial; this pompous egomaniac did not for a moment realize that the Lord of Glory, the Creator of all things, was standing before him).*

10 And the Chief Priests and Scribes stood and vehemently accused Him *(they all evidently followed in order to accuse Jesus before Herod; we have here before us secular devils and religious devils; as bad as the secular devils might be, the religious devils are worse!).*

11 And Herod with his men of war set Him at nought, and mocked *Him (records the attitude and thinking of this despot),* and arrayed Him in a gorgeous robe, and sent Him again to Pilate *(means, as well, that Herod found no cause for death in Him; consequently, we have a second record and public attestation of His innocence).*

12 And the same day Pilate and Herod were made friends together: for before they were at enmity between themselves *(worldly men with differences meet together, when opportunity offers itself for wounding Christ).*

BARABBAS

13 And Pilate, when he had called together the Chief Priests and the Rulers and the people *(once again at Pilate's judgment hall),*

14 Said unto them, You have brought this man unto me, as one who perverts the people: and, behold, I, having examined *Him* before you, have found no fault in this man touching those things whereof you accuse Him *(presents the second public confession of Pilate, who also publicly acknowledged that the civil rulers of Galilee had found no fault in Him as well!):*

15 No, nor yet Herod: for I sent you to Him *(refers to the Sanhedrin being sent to Herod, along with Jesus);* and, lo, nothing worthy of death is done unto Him *(should have been translated "by Him").*

16 I will therefore chastise Him *(scourge Him; he would subject a Man Whom he had pronounced innocent to the horrible punishment of scourging just to satisfy the clamor of the Sanhedrists, because he was fearful of what they*

might accuse him of at Rome, where he knew he had enemies), and release *Him (was said concerning the release of one prisoner each year at the Passover).*

17 (For of necessity he must release one unto them at the feast.) *(This custom was probably introduced at Jerusalem by the Roman power. There is no evidence of such in Levitical Law.)*

18 And they cried out all at once *(proclaims their strong opposition to his decision to release Jesus),* saying, Away with this *Man,* and release unto us Barabbas *(this is exactly what they got, and have had ever since; they preferred a "robber," as John styled him, to the Son of God; so they got the robber, and they've had robbers ever since; the nations of the world have robbed them of their dignity, pride, and lives for nearly 2,000 years):*

19 (Who for a certain sedition made in the city *(tried to stir up insurrection against Rome),* and for murder, was cast into prison.) *(It was bad enough to prefer a "robber" over Jesus, but to prefer a "murderer" was a horror, which would be perpetrated upon them from that day forward. History is replete with the accounts!)*

20 Pilate therefore, willing to release Jesus, spoke again to them *(presents the Governor attempting to release Jesus for the fourth time as recorded by Luke, but to no avail!).*

21 But they cried, saying, Crucify *Him,* crucify Him *(presents the type of execution they demanded; Why? the Levitical Law said that one who was hung upon a tree for gross crimes was cursed by God; consequently, Him being Crucified would prove to the people, or so they thought, that He was not of God; were He of God, they reasoned, God would not allow such [Deut. 21:22-23]).*

22 And he said unto them the third time *(refers to the times he had attempted to free Jesus on the premise of the custom of releasing at the Passover each year; actually, this was about the fifth time he had made such an attempt over all),* Why, what evil has He done? *(He had done no evil, and Pilate knew the accusations of the religious hierarchy against Him to be false.)* I have found no cause of death in Him *(little did the Governor know that of which He spoke; had there been a cause of death in Jesus, He could not have served as the Sacrifice for sin):* I will therefore chastise Him, and let *Him* go *(sounds a note of desperation).*

23 And they were instant with loud voices, requiring that He might be crucified *(many have said that the same crowd who was crying,*

"Hosanna to the Highest" at the Triumphant Entry was now crying, "Crucify Him!"; that is incorrect; the rabble that joined the religious leaders that early morning hour was, for the most part, the night people, or lackeys of the Sanhedrin). **And the voices of them and of the Chief Priests prevailed** (presents their success, but a success they would ever rue; their prevailing sealed their own doom).

24 And Pilate gave sentence that it should be as they required (would prove to be the worst day of his life, but could have been the best).

25 And he released unto them him who for sedition and murder was cast into prison, whom they had desired (they got exactly that for which they asked, which has followed them unto this hour); **but he delivered Jesus to their will** (was the worst thing that Pilate would ever do in all his life).

26 And as they led Him away (presents the horrifying trip to the place of Crucifixion, Golgotha, with Jesus carrying the Cross), **they laid hold upon one Simon, a Cyrenian, coming out of the country** (as Mark tells us, this was the father of "Alexander, and Rufus," notable persons in the Early Church [Mk. 15:21]), **and on him they laid the cross, that he might bear** it **after Jesus** (probably means that Jesus, due to being beaten so severely, which no doubt resulted in a great loss of blood, ultimately became too weak to bear the weight of the Cross; so Simon was compelled; what an honor to carry it for Jesus).

THE WOMEN

27 And there followed Him a great company of people (there were many, no doubt, in the crowd whom He had healed), **and of women, which also bewailed and lamented Him** (no woman is mentioned in the Gospels as having spoken against the Lord, or as having a share in His Death).

28 But Jesus turning unto them said (represents the first time He spoke since His last interrogation before Pilate), **Daughters of Jerusalem** (a fixture of the "Song of Solomon"), **weep not for Me, but weep for yourselves, and for your children** (proclaims His rejection by the religious leaders of Israel, and the subsequent judgment which will follow).

29 For, behold, the days are coming (would actually see fulfillment about thirty-seven years from this time), **in the which they shall say, Blessed** are **the barren, and the wombs that**

never bear, and the paps which never gave suck (presents a strange Beatitude; He was speaking of the horror that was coming, which would be so bad that the dead would be blessed, along with the children never born).

30 Then shall they begin to say to the mountains, Fall on us; and to the hills, Cover us (this Prophecy speaks of the destruction of Jerusalem in A.D. 70).

31 For if they do these things in a green tree (He was the "Green Tree"), **what shall be done in the dry?** (When He would be gone! Concerns the great Tribulation, even yet to come.)

THE CRUCIFIXION

32 And there were also two others, malefactors (criminals; some think these were companions of Barabbas, who had just been released), **led with Him to be put to death.**

33 And when they were come to the place, which is called Calvary, where they crucified Him (the Cross, which was the most horrifying instrument of torture the world had ever known, became an emblem of beauty because of what Jesus did on that Cross), **and the malefactors** (the two criminals), **one on the right hand, and the other on the left** (may not have been the only ones crucified that day, but were the only ones in this particular position).

34 Then said Jesus, Father, forgive them; for they know not what they do (presents the only prayer ever prayed by Jesus, which was not answered; if men will not seek forgiveness, even Christ praying for them will not avail!). **And they parted His raiment** (divided up His Garments), **and cast lots** (His robe was without seam, so rather than cutting it up, they would draw straws).

35 And the people stood beholding (who made up this crowd is not known). **And the Rulers also with them derided** Him (means that they "mocked Him"), **saying, He saved others; let Him save Himself, if He be Christ, the Chosen of God** (if He had saved His Life, which He certainly could have done, He could not have saved others; in fact, the Cross had been planned from before the foundation of the world [I Pet. 1:18-20]).

36 And the soldiers also mocked Him (was probably carried out by these heathen simply because they heard the religious leaders mocking Him), **coming to Him, and offering Him vinegar** (was in response to His plea for water

[Jn. 19:28]),

37 And saying, If You be the King of the Jews, save Yourself (*what they did not know was that He was not only the "King of the Jews," but the Creator of the Heavens and Earth, the Maker of all things*).

38 And a superscription also was written over Him in letters of Greek, and Latin, and Hebrew (*constituted that written by Pilate; he probably did it to mock the religious leaders of Israel*), THIS IS THE KING OF THE JEWS.

THE PENITENT THIEF

39 And one of the malefactors which were hanged railed on Him, saying, If You be Christ, save Yourself and us (*is reported by Matthew and Mark as both doing this in the beginning; however, at a point, one, which we will read about momentarily, changed completely*).

40 But the other answering rebuked Him, saying (*proclaims the spirit of true Repentance*), Do not You fear God, seeing you are in the same condemnation? (*This means that he is owning up to his guilt, which is the first requirement of Repentance.*)

41 And we indeed justly; for we receive the due reward of our deeds (*proclaims him making no excuses, admitting to his sin, holding no enmity toward his executors, which presents a powerful truth*): but this Man has done nothing amiss (*presents the only kind word uttered about Christ at this time, other than that spoken by the Centurion*).

42 And He said unto Jesus (*speaks of recognition as to Who Jesus really was*), Lord, remember me when You come into Your Kingdom (*presents the simple prayer of Repentance; it is one of the most remarkable conversions recorded in the Bible*).

43 And Jesus said unto him, Verily I say unto you, Today shall you be with Me in Paradise (*a statement of fact, and not a question, as some claim; however, his stay in Paradise would be very short; some three days later, he would accompany Christ to Heaven, along with every other person in Paradise, which included all the Old Testament Saints*).

THE DEATH OF JESUS

44 And it was about the sixth hour (*12 noon*), and there was a darkness over all the Earth until the ninth hour (*3 p.m., this was the time that Jesus bore the penalty of sin for the entirety*

of mankind, and for all time).

45 And the sun was darkened (*means that the darkness was so deep that it literally blotted out the light of the sun; what He experienced during this 3-hour period, no one will ever know [Ps. 22:1-21]*), and the Veil of the Temple was rent in the midst (*probably referred to the approximate time He died, about 3 p.m.; this "Veil" separated the Holy Place in the Temple from the Holy of Holies, where God was supposed to dwell; the Veil being torn apart, in effect, stated that God had accepted the Sacrifice, and now the way was open for sinful man to come to God and be cleansed; but he would have to come by the Way of Christ and the Cross; there is no other way of Salvation [Jn. 14:6]*).

46 And when Jesus had cried with a loud voice (*proclaims the fact that He did not die from weakness; actually, they did not take His Life, He gave it up freely [Jn. 10:17-18]*), He said, Father, into Your hands I commend My Spirit (*proclaims the last words He uttered*): and having said thus, He gave up the ghost (*He didn't die until the Holy Spirit told Him He could die [Heb. 9:14]*).

47 Now when the Centurion saw what was done, he glorified God (*this hard-bitten Roman Centurion knew that Jesus was the Son of God, but the religious leaders of Israel didn't!*), saying, Certainly this was a Righteous Man (*tradition says that his name was Longinus, and that he became an avid follower of Christ, and died a martyr to the cause*).

48 And all the people who came together to that sight, beholding the things which were done (*seems to indicate that quite a few were there when He died, standing in the darkness, hearing His last Words and, thereby, experiencing the earthquake; but yet, due to the darkness, they really did not see Him die; in fact, no one did!*), smote their breasts, and returned (*speaks of an agony of heart, knowing that something horrible has happened, and that a great wrong has been done*).

49 And all His acquaintance (*concerned His chosen Disciples and some chosen followers*), and the women who followed Him from Galilee, stood afar off, beholding these things (*seems to indicate that they stood near the Cross for a time [Jn. 19:25-27], and then retired for whatever reason to a further distance [Mat. 27:55-56]*).

THE BURIAL OF JESUS

50 And, behold, *there was* a man named

Joseph, a Counsellor *(this was Joseph of Arimathaea, a member of the Sanhedrin and a person of high distinction in Jerusalem and evidently of great wealth);* **and he was** a good man, and a just:

51 (The same had not consented to the counsel and deed of them;) *(speaks of the illegal and unjust decision of the Sanhedrin, of which he was a part)* **he was** of Arimathaea, a city of the Jews *(the home of the Prophet Samuel; however, he now lived in Jerusalem due to the fact of being a member of the Sanhedrin):* who also himself waited for the Kingdom of God *(he would be shown that Kingdom, and would enter that Kingdom).*

52 This **man** went unto Pilate *(it seems that the Centurion who had testified at the Death of Jesus accompanied Joseph to an audience with Pilate),* and begged the body of Jesus *(there is an urgency about this because the High Sabbath of the Passover would begin at sundown Thursday; if Jesus was not taken down from the Cross before then and placed in a tomb, they would have to allow Him to remain on the Cross for another twenty-four hours).*

53 And he took it down *(refers to the Body of Jesus, which says so very much, while saying so very little),* and wrapped it in linen *(pertained to a part of the burial process, which was done very hurriedly because the High Sabbath of the Passover would begin at sundown, necessitating that all work must stop),* and laid it in a sepulchre that was hewn in stone, wherein never man before was laid *(the tomb belonged to Joseph, and was the very kind predicted by Isaiah [Isa. 53:9]).*

54 And that day was the preparation *(spoke of the preparation of the Passover, which was to be eaten the next day, Thursday),* and the Sabbath drew on *(is not speaking of the regular weekly Sabbath of Saturday, but rather the High Sabbath of the Passover, which would commence at sundown).*

55 And the women also, which came with Him from Galilee *(Matthew records that there were "many women who were there"),* followed after, and beheld the sepulchre, and how His body was laid *(does not exactly say that they participated in this which was done by Joseph and Nicodemus, but possibly they did!).*

56 And they returned, and prepared spices and ointments *(means that they returned to the places where they were staying while in Jerusalem, and would have made these preparations on Friday);* and rested the Sabbath day according to the Commandment *(the next day, Thursday, was the High Sabbath of the Passover, and so they could not prepare these things that day; they would have prepared them on Friday; and then resting again on the weekly Sabbath of Saturday as required, would have come early on Sunday morning to apply the ingredients, but would be greatly surprised at what they found).*

CHAPTER 24
(A.D. 33)
THE RESURRECTION

NOW upon the first *day* of the week *(Sunday),* very early in the morning *(before the rising of the sun),* they came unto the sepulchre *(speaks of the women of Verse 55 of the previous Chapter),* bringing the spices which they had prepared *(proclaims that none of these women, or the Disciples, or anyone for that matter, believed that Jesus would rise from the dead; had they believed, they would not have been coming to the tomb with spices for the corpse),* and certain *others* with them *(who they were, we aren't told).*

2 And they found the stone rolled away from the sepulchre *(this "stone" weighed several hundred pounds, thereby requiring at least several men to roll it away from the door where it had been placed; so, the stone being rolled away was no doubt very strange to them).*

3 And they entered in *(entered the tomb),* and found not the body of the Lord Jesus *(His Resurrection Title is, "Lord Jesus").*

4 And it came to pass, as they were much perplexed thereabout *(they did not know what to make of the situation),* behold, two men stood by them in shining garments *(these were Angels, and their "shining garments" were literally unlike anything these women had ever seen, regarding glory):*

5 And as they were afraid, and bowed down *their* faces to the earth *(implying that the appearance of these Angels was so dazzling that it blinded their eyes, causing them to look downward),* they said unto them *(the Angels spoke to the women),* Why seek ye the living among the dead? *(Notes a mild rebuke, with a touch of sarcasm.)*

6 He is not here, but is risen *(this phrase, or a derivative, became the watchword of the Early Church; "He is Risen"):* remember how He spoke unto you when He was yet in Galilee *(proclaims the Angels drawing these women back to the Words of Christ, when He had related to*

them and the Disciples how He would be killed in Jerusalem, and would rise from the dead; He had even told them how long He would be in the tomb [Mat. 12:40]),

7 Saying, The Son of Man must be delivered into the hands of sinful men, and be crucified, and the third day rise again ([Lk. 18:32-33] the Angels referred to the religious leaders of Israel and the Romans as "sinful men").

8 And they remembered His words (recollection is more important than information),

THE TESTIMONY

9 And returned from the sepulchre, and told all these things unto the Eleven, and to all the rest (records the fact that women were the first Preachers of the Resurrection).

10 It was Mary Magdalene, and Joanna (the wife of Chuza, Herod's steward [Lk. 8:3]), and Mary the mother of James (James and John), and other women who were with them, which told these things unto the Apostles.

11 And their words seemed to them as idle tales (means in the Greek, "silly nonsense"), and they believed them not (the reason for their unbelief, resulting in their demeanor, was a departure from the Word of God; every wrongdoing and wrong direction are always, and without exception, a departure from the Word; the persistence of the Apostles in Preaching the Resurrection everywhere after Pentecost proves that the Resurrection was a fact; for if not a fact, how could they confidently affirm to be true that which they had steadfastly refused to believe?).

12 Then arose Peter, and ran unto the sepulchre (he was accompanied by John [Jn. 20:3]); and stooping down, he beheld the linen clothes laid by themselves (this proved that His Body had not been stolen; if such had been the case, the thief certainly would not have stopped to take all the time to unwrap the linen from around the corpse; as well, this linen wrapping was neatly folded and laid to the side, which no thieves would have done), and departed, wondering in himself at that which was come to pass (presents the beginning of Faith, but yet very weak).

THE TWO DISCIPLES

13 And, behold, two of them (one was Cleopas, the father of James the Less and husband of Mary, the sister of the Mother of Jesus [Jn. 19:25]; we are not told who the other man was; many

ancient scholars hold that it was Luke himself, and they further say that he was one of the seventy, and the reason he did not mention himself was that he was the writer of this account) went that same day to a village called Emmaus, which was from Jerusalem about threescore furlongs (about seven miles).

14 And they talked together of all these things which had happened (pertaining to the Crucifixion and as well to the testimonies of the women concerning the appearance of Angels, etc.).

15 And it came to pass, that, while they communed together and reasoned (they were deep in thought), Jesus himself drew near, and went with them (this would not of itself have occasioned surprise; the roads in those days were heavily trafficked with pedestrians, and someone doing this would not have been out of the ordinary).

16 But their eyes were holden that they should not know Him (was done purposely by the Lord so they would not recognize Him; He would not reveal Himself to these two Disciples until He had brought them into a fitting condition of soul).

17 And He said unto them, What manner of communications are these that you have one to another, as you walk, and are sad? (Many modern Christians are uselessly sad, even as here, because of unbelief!)

18 And the one of them, whose name was Cleopas, answering said unto Him (had He known this was Jesus, He would have conducted himself quite differently), Are You only a stranger in Jerusalem, and have not known the things which are come to pass therein these days? (This is asked with some sarcasm!)

19 And He said unto them, What things? (The question is asked solely for the purpose of drawing them out.) And they said unto Him, Concerning Jesus of Nazareth, which was a Prophet mighty in deed and word before God and all the people (if it is to be noticed, Cleopas did not mention Jesus being the Messiah; while they had once believed this, their faith was now shaken):

20 And how the Chief Priests and our Rulers delivered Him to be condemned to death, and have crucified Him (organized religion did this!).

21 But we trusted that it had been He which should have redeemed Israel (they had confined their Bible study to that which the Scriptures promised respecting the Messiah's glory and Kingdom, but they had been blind to the

multitude of types and Prophecies foretelling His Sufferings as an Atoning Saviour): **and beside all this, today is the third day since these things were done** *(they dwelt on the third day, and rightly so).*

22 Yea, and certain women also of our company made us astonished, which were early at the sepulchre *(speaks of their testimony of the tomb being empty)*;

23 And when they found not His body, they came, saying, that they had also seen a vision of Angels, which said that He was alive.

24 And certain of them which were with us went to the sepulchre *(Peter and John)*, **and found** *it* **even so as the women had said: but Him they saw not** *(the last phrase carries an element of doubt).*

25 Then He said unto them, O fools *(should have been translated, "foolish men!")*, **and slow of heart to believe all that the Prophets have spoken** *(proclaims the fact that the Lord concludes as very "foolish" those who do not make His Word as the basis for all actions and decisions; He pulls them back to the Bible; It alone is the criteria for all things)*:

26 Ought not Christ to have suffered these things *(means the Bible predicted His Sufferings, which should have been obvious to His followers and would have been had they only devoted time and attention to the Word of God)*, **and to enter into His glory?** *(Proclaims that the Bible does outline the coming Kingdom of Glory, hence the "Triumphant Messiah;" however, it must be preceded by the mission of the "Suffering Messiah.")*

27 And beginning at Moses and all the Prophets *(the Lord here makes two declarations respecting the Bible: 1. It is the supreme authority as to Faith and Doctrine because it is inspired; and, 2. Its subject are the sufferings and glories of Christ — His Sufferings as sin-bearer and His glories as sin-purger [Phil. 2:5-11; Heb. 1:3])*, **He expounded unto them in all the Scriptures the things concerning Himself** *(it may truly be said that Christ went into death Bible in hand, and that He came out from among the dead Bible in hand; He insisted that it predicted His Death and Resurrection in relation to sin and its judgment).*

28 And they drew nigh unto the village, whither they went *(Emmaus)*: **and He made as though He would have gone further** *(how many are there to whom He has drawn near, but with whom He has not tarried because they have allowed Him to "go away").*

29 But they constrained Him, saying, Abide with us *(they insisted, and strongly!)*: **for it is toward evening, and the day is far spent. And He went in to tarry with them** *(He will tarry with any and all who sincerely desire Him to do so).*

30 And it came to pass, as He sat at meat with them, He took bread, and blessed *it*, **and break, and gave to them** *(symbolic of what He does with us; He "takes us," and then "blesses us," and then "breaks us," for the flesh must ultimately be broken, and then "gives us" to the Church; if this pattern is not followed, we will be of no blessing whatsoever).*

31 And their eyes were opened *(He now allowed them to truly see)*, **and they knew Him** *(what joy must have filled their hearts; Jesus is alive!)*; **and He vanished out of their sight** *(but only after He had revealed Himself to them).*

32 And they said one to another, Did not our heart burn within us, while He talked with us by the way, and while He opened to us the Scriptures? *(The business of Christ, through the Holy Spirit, is to help us understand the Word of God.)*

33 And they rose up the same hour, and returned to Jerusalem *(presents a joy they could not contain, and no wonder)*, **and found the Eleven gathered together, and them who were with them** *(presents a meeting that will quickly change from despair to great joy; admittedly, they had to arrive at this place by stages, but were on their way; praise God!)*,

34 Saying, The Lord is risen indeed *(presents a conversation of victory, in fact the greatest victory ever recorded in human history)*, **and has appeared to Simon** *(the Scripture does not give us the account of this appearance, but the likelihood is that Peter was the first man to see Jesus after His Resurrection).*

35 And they told what things *were done* **in the way** *(an excited presentation)*, **and how He was known of them in breaking of bread.**

JESUS APPEARS

36 And as they thus spoke, Jesus Himself stood in the midst of them *(refers to an instant appearance and Revelation; John added that "the doors were shut")*, **and said unto them, Peace** *be* **unto you** *(presents His first words to them as a group after the Resurrection).*

37 But they were terrified and affrighted *(speaks to the suddenness of the event, and the manner in which it was done; one moment He*

is not there, and the next moment He is!), **and supposed that they had seen a spirit** *(this shows that they still didn't understand the Resurrection; they did not doubt the appearances, but did not really recognize these appearances for what they actually were).*

38 And He said unto them, Why are you troubled? *(Being troubled robs us of peace.)* **and why do thoughts arise in your hearts?** *(This pertains to fear, doubt, discouragement, and even despair, all brought on by lack of Faith in God's Word. We should, as well, take the questions to heart.)*

39 Behold My hands and My feet, that it is I Myself: handle Me, and see *(they will now understand what His Resurrection really was);* **for a spirit has not flesh and bones, as You see Me have** *(in other words, Jesus was telling them that He was not a disembodied spirit; He, in fact, had a physical body of flesh and bones; no blood is mentioned because the Glorified Body has no blood; whereas now the life of the flesh is in the blood, then, when our bodies are glorified, the life will be in the Spirit, i.e., "Holy Spirit").*

40 And when He had thus spoken, He showed them *His* hands and *His* feet *(John also adds that He had invited them as well to see the wound in His Side; in fact, He will retain these wounds forever [Zech. 13:6; Rev. 5:6]).*

41 And while they yet believed not for joy, and wondered *(indicates that their faith was still weak; we have a tendency to correct them, but would we have done any better?),* **He said unto them, Have you here any meat?** *(This is meant to further portray to them the fact that He still retained a human body, albeit Glorified, and that as such He could partake of food. A "spirit" does not have flesh and bones, and likewise does not eat.)*

42 And they gave Him a piece of a broiled fish, and of an honeycomb *(it is speculated that this was in the home of John Mark, who wrote the Book of Mark).*

43 And He took *it*, and did eat before them *(if it is to be noticed, Jesus did not ask His Disciples to believe anything that was contrary to their senses).*

44 And He said unto them, These *are* the words which I spoke unto you, while I was yet with you, that all things must be fulfilled, which were written in the Law of Moses, and *in* the Prophets, and *in* the Psalms, concerning Me *(the Jews divided the Old Testament into three parts — the Law of Moses, the Prophets, and the Psalms, which consisted of the Wisdom Books;*

the entire story of the Old Testament is the story of Jesus and the Cross, and what the Cross affords; in fact, if we do not understand that, we cannot fully understand the Word of God; as is made plainly obvious here, "Christ and Him Crucified" is the key to all understanding).*

45 Then opened He their understanding, that they might understand the Scriptures *(he who doesn't understand the Scriptures, understands little or nothing; let us say it again: "Jesus Christ and Him Crucified," is the Story of the Bible; every Doctrine must be built upon that Foundation, which constitutes the house built upon the Rock; otherwise, it's a house built upon sand),*

THE GREAT COMMISSION

46 And said unto them, Thus it is written *(proves what I have just stated concerning Christ and the Cross),* **and thus it behoved Christ to suffer, and to rise from the dead the third day** *(let us say it again, this is the story of the Bible):*

47 And that repentance and remission of sins should be preached in His Name *(presents God's method of proclaiming His Word, and carrying out His Work; any other method is unscriptural)* **among all nations, beginning at Jerusalem** *(God's Plan of Salvation is identical for all regarding race, color, or culture; it is for the whole world).*

48 And you are witnesses of these things *(Christianity was not begun as the result of an enlightened philosophy, as with all religions; it was begun by men and women who literally witnessed the incarnate Son of God in all His earthly Ministry, as well as His Death and Resurrection; consequently, they could say, "we have seen, and do testify").*

49 And, behold, I send the Promise of My Father upon you *(the Baptism with the Holy Spirit, which would come on the Day of Pentecost [Acts 1:4-5]):* **but tarry ye in the city of Jerusalem** *(this was where the Temple was located, and where the Day of Pentecost was always celebrated, which would occasion the outpouring of the Spirit; this was only for the initial outpouring; since then, Jesus Baptizes with the Holy Spirit wherever the person might be [Acts, Chpts. 8-10, 19]),* **until you be endued with power from on high** *(this is the Baptism with the Holy Spirit, which is always accompanied by the speaking with other tongues [Acts 2:4]; without being thus endued, the Believer and the Church are of little worth to the Kingdom of God).*

THE ASCENSION

50 And He led them out as far as to Bethany *(this little village was located on the far side of the Mount of Olives, and is actually a suburb of Jerusalem; it was the home of Jesus' beloved friends, Mary, Martha, and Lazarus)*, **and He lifted up His hands, and blessed them** *(proclaims Him as Israel's High Priest, having made Atonement, consequently lifting up His Hands and blessing the people, which the High Priests of Israel had done for nearly 1,600 years; all is a type of what He would ultimately do; but let it be understood that His Blessing is for all, and not merely the Jews).*

51 And it came to pass, while He blessed them *(implies continued blessing, which means that it continues even unto this hour, and will in fact continue forever)*, **He was parted from them, and carried up into Heaven** *(pertains to the Ascension; He hastened to the Cross in order to Atone for His People's sins, but He did not hasten to Glory, for He was reluctant to leave His Beloved sheep).*

52 And they worshipped Him *(means His Presence was still with them, even though He had already ascended)*, **and returned to Jerusalem with great joy** *(signaled a different group of people, at least regarding faith, spirit, and emotions, than at the Crucifixion; then all was darkness; now all is light):*

53 And were continually in the Temple, praising and blessing God *(due to the Promise of the Father being made real in our hearts, we now are the Temple [I Cor. 3:16] and should praise the Lord continually).* **Amen** *(all of the four Gospels close with the word "Amen," which means "Truth").*

THE GOSPEL ACCORDING TO
JOHN

CHAPTER 1
(A.D. 26)

THE DEITY OF CHRIST

IN the beginning (*does not infer that Christ as God had a beginning, because as God He had no beginning, but rather refers to the time of Creation [Gen. 1:1]*) **was the Word** (*the Holy Spirit through John describes Jesus as "the Eternal Logos"*), **and the Word was with God** (*"was in relationship with God," and expresses the idea of the Trinity*), **and the Word was God** (*meaning that He did not cease to be God during the Incarnation; He "was" and "is" God from eternity past to eternity future*).

2 **The same was in the beginning with God** (*this very Person was in eternity with God; there's only one God, but manifested in three Persons — God the Father, God the Son, God the Holy Spirit*).

3 **All things were made by Him** (*all things came into being through Him; it refers to every item of Creation one by one, rather than all things regarded in totality*); **and without Him was not any thing made that was made** (*nothing, not even one single thing, was made independently of His cooperation and volition*).

4 **In Him was Life** (*presents Jesus, the Eternal Logos, as the first cause*); **and the Life was the Light of men** (*He Alone is the Life Source of Light; if one doesn't know Christ, one is in darkness*).

5 **And the Light shines in darkness** (*speaks of the Incarnation of Christ, and His coming into this world; His "Light," because it is derived from His Life, drives out "darkness"*); **and the darkness comprehended it not** (*should have been translated, "apprehended it not"; it means that Satan, even though he tried with all his might, could not stop "the Light"; today it shines all over the world, and one day soon, there will be nothing left but that "Light"*).

JOHN THE BAPTIST

6 **There was a man sent from God, whose name *was* John.**

7 **The same came for a witness** (*speaks of the Mission of the Prophet*), **to bear witness of the Light** (*spoke of Jesus and only Jesus*), **that all *men* through Him might believe** (*presents that Jesus is not only for Israel, but also for the entirety of the world*).

8 **He was not that Light** (*John the Baptist was not the Light*), **but *was sent* to bear witness of that Light** (*presents the sum total that man can do*).

THE INCARNATION

9 ***That* was the true Light** (*there are many false lights; Jesus is the only True Light*), **which lighteth every man who comes into the world** (*if man is to find Light, it will be only in Christ, and it is for "every man"*).

10 **He was in the world** (*the Eternal Logos, the "Creator"*), **and the world was made by Him** (*as it was originally created before the fall of Lucifer and the Fall of man*), **and the world knew Him not** (*the world cannot know Christ by wisdom, but only by Revelation*).

11 **He came unto His Own** (*the world in general, but more specifically to the Jews*), **and His Own received Him not** (*He came as the Heir unto His Own Possessions [Mat. 21:38], but His Own servants did not receive Him; on the contrary, they killed Him*).

12 **But as many as received Him** (*some did receive Him, and some do receive Him*), **to them gave He power to become the sons of God** (*constitutes one of the greatest Promises in the Word of God*), ***even* to them who believe on His Name** (*Faith in Christ and in what He has done for us at the Cross alone can make a person a "son or daughter of God"*):

13 **Which were born, not of blood** (*means that men become God's Children not by natural birth*), **nor of the will of the flesh** (*man cannot earn Salvation, it is a free gift, received upon Faith*), **nor of the will of man** (*refers to man's religious efforts*), **but of God** (*Salvation is not at all of man, but altogether of God*).

14 **And the Word was made flesh** (*refers to the Incarnation, "God becoming man"*), **and dwelt among us** (*refers to Jesus, although Perfect, not holding Himself aloft from all others, but rather lived as all men, even a peasant*), **(and we beheld His Glory, the Glory as of**

the Only Begotten of the Father,) *(speaks of His Deity, although hidden from the eyes of the merely curious; while Christ laid aside the expression of His Deity, He never lost the possession of His Deity)* full of Grace and Truth *(as "flesh," proclaimed His Humanity, "Grace and Truth" His Deity).*

THE TESTIMONY

15 John bear witness of Him *(John was raised up for this very purpose)*, and cried, saying, This was He of Whom I spoke *(concerns the Ministry of John regarding the Person of Jesus)*, He who comes after me is preferred before me *(should have been translated, "existed before me")*: for He was before me *(once again, a testimony to the Deity of Christ; as God, He has always been).*

16 And of His fulness have all we received *(John has told us Who Jesus is, now he tells us what He does)*, and Grace for Grace *(should have been translated, "Grace upon Grace;" this is the provision of His Love heaped one upon another in this supply of His People's needs).*

17 For the Law was given by Moses, *but* Grace and Truth came by Jesus Christ *(proclaims Him as the Representative Law-keeper for all humanity, i.e., to all who will believe; the Law manifested man [full of wickedness]; the Son manifested God [full of goodness]).*

18 No man has seen God at any time *(better translated, "No man has ever comprehended or experienced God at any time in all His fullness")*; the Only Begotten Son *(Jesus Christ and the Incarnation, Who Alone could perfectly declare the Father)*, which is in the bosom of the Father *(proclaims the most intimate and loving fellowship with the Father)*, He has declared *Him (in essence, God the Father and God the Son are One).*

19 And this is the record of John, when the Jews sent Priests and Levites from Jerusalem to ask him, Who are you? *(At the time, some thought that John the Baptist was the Messiah.)*

20 And he confessed *(there was absolutely no hesitation in his confession regarding who he actually was, and above all, his mission)*, and denied not *(he did not deny that some were calling him "Christ," however, to not even the slightest degree did he encourage this and, in fact, grandly repudiates the rumor)*; but confessed, I am not the Christ *(in the Greek actually says, "I, for my part, am not the Christ," and is said with emphasis)*

21 And they asked him, What then? Are you Elijah? *(Malachi had predicted the coming again from Heaven of Elijah the Prophet [Mal. 4:5].)* And he said, I am not *(presents a categorical negative; some of the Jews were insinuating that He was the actual reincarnation of Elijah).* Are you that Prophet? *(This spoke of the Prophet mentioned by Moses in Deut. 18:15-18. This was the Messiah. So again, they asked him if he was the Messiah?)* And he answered, No.

22 Then said they unto him, Who are you? that we may give an answer to them who sent us *(they were not really seeking proper information, or the Truth about the matter, but rather desired that he claim something of which they could accuse him).* What say you of yourself? *(His answer is extremely revealing!)*

23 He said, I *am* the voice of one crying in the wilderness *(is taken from Isa. 40:3)*, Make straight the Way of the Lord, as said the Prophet Isaiah *(proclaims his mission as the first phrase proclaims his identity).*

24 And they which were sent were of the Pharisees *(the Holy Spirit is careful to delineate the source of these questions; the opposition now begins).*

25 And they asked him, and said unto him, Why do you baptize then, if you be not that Christ, nor Elijah, neither that Prophet? *(They were indignant that John not only baptized without ecclesiastical authority, but baptized contrary to the practice of the Pharisees. In other words, he had not asked nor sought their permission, nor did it seem that he cared whether they agreed or not!)*

26 John answered them, saying, I baptize with water *(meaning that it was but a temporary symbol of the true, abiding, and effectual baptism of the One Who would baptize with the Holy Spirit)*: but there stands One among you, Whom you know not *(points to their spiritual ignorance; Christ was in their very midst, and they did not know!)*;

27 He it is *(the Messiah is already here, even though you do not know Him, and He, as stated, is not me)*, Who coming after me is preferred before me *(Who existed before me, in fact, has existed eternally)*, Whose shoe's latchet I am not worthy to unloose *(by comparison to Christ, the greatest Prophet born of woman labels himself, and rightly so!).*

28 These things were done in Bethabara beyond Jordan, where John was baptizing *(probably not far from Jericho).*

29 The next day *(refers to the day after John*

had been questioned by the emissaries from the Sanhedrin) **John sees Jesus coming unto him** (is no doubt after the baptism of Jesus, and the temptation in the wilderness), **and said, Behold the Lamb of God** (proclaims Jesus as the Sacrifice for sin, in fact the Sin-Offering, Whom all the multiple millions of offered lambs had represented), **which takes away the sin of the world** (animal blood could only cover sin, it could not take it away; but Jesus offering Himself as the Perfect Sacrifice took away the sin of the world; He not only cleansed acts of sin, but as well, addressed the root cause [Col. 2:14-15]).

30 This is He of Whom I said (proclaims John making a positive identification; it is the One Who "takes away the sin of the world"), **After me comes a Man which is preferred before me** (affirms His essential Humanity): **for He was before me** (affirms His essential Deity).

31 And I knew Him not (doesn't mean that he was not acquainted with Christ, but that he was not to introduce Christ until the Holy Spirit said so): **but that He should be made manifest to Israel** (means that at a certain time, and not before, Jesus was to be introduced to Israel as the Messiah, which John carried out exactly as led), **therefore am I come baptizing with water** (proclaims that which the Holy Spirit told him to do).

32 And John bear record (means that this is exactly what the Holy Spirit said would happen, concerning the identity of Jesus as the Messiah), **saying, I saw the Spirit descending from Heaven like a dove** (we must come to the conclusion that John saw something, which was the Holy Spirit; Luke recorded, "descending in a bodily shape like a Dove upon Him," [Lk. 3:22]; we must conclude from these statements that the Holy Spirit has a Spirit Body of some nature), **and it abode upon Him** (the Spirit coming upon Him signaled the beginning of His Ministry).

33 And I knew Him not (is used the second time by John, and with purpose; the Holy Spirit wants all to know that John's introduction of Jesus as the Messiah was not according to the flesh, i.e., personal knowledge, circumstances, etc., but rather by Revelation from on High; no one can really know Jesus, unless revealed by the Holy Spirit): **but He Who sent me to baptize with water** (telling us that Water Baptism as instituted by John was not that Prophet's idea at all, but rather was given to him by Revelation from God), **the same said unto me, Upon Whom you shall see the Spirit descending, and remaining on Him** (was to be the Revelation from God, which John was to heed, and he did), **the same is He which baptizes with the Holy Spirit** (proclaims what Jesus would do after His Death and Resurrection; the Cross would make this possible!).

34 And I saw, and bear record that this is the Son of God (John the Baptist had followed his instructions to the letter, and according to the Revelation, he knew without doubt that Jesus was the Son of God).

THE FIRST DISCIPLES

35 Again the next day after John stood (the day after he made the previous statements), **and two of his disciples** (was Andrew and no doubt John, who at that time were Disciples of the Baptist);

36 And looking upon Jesus as He walked (takes us back to Verse 29, for both Verses speak of the same incident), **he said, Behold the Lamb of God!** (This phrase is used here again, in order to develop the time frame for the account about to be given.)

37 And the two disciples heard Him speak, and they followed Jesus (in essence, this was the beginning of their becoming Disciples of Christ).

38 Then Jesus turned, and saw them following, and said unto them, What do you seek? (It was a penetrating question that had eternal consequences.) **They said unto Him, Rabbi, (which is to say, being interpreted, Master,) where do You dwell?** (They were speaking of an earthly abode, while the full answer to that question incorporated a dimension that was beyond the comprehension of any mere mortal. His actual dwelling place was the Throne of God.)

39 He said unto them, Come and see (the journey they began that day has not stopped, even unto this hour, and in fact never will!). **They came and saw where He dwelt, and abode with Him that day: for it was about the tenth hour** (it has been debated for centuries as to whether John the Beloved was using Jewish time or Roman time; Jewish time would have been 4 p.m., while Roman time would have been 10 a.m.).

40 One of the two which heard John speak, **and followed him, was Andrew, Simon Peter's brother** (the manner in which "Andrew" is addressed, as the brother of "Simon Peter," tells us that Peter's name was now recognized to a greater degree than any of the other Apostles).

41 He (Andrew) **first found his own brother Simon, and said unto him, We have found the Messiah, which is, being interpreted, the Christ**

(was entirely the cause of Andrew's eagerness and excitement).

42 And he brought him to Jesus. And when Jesus beheld him *(Jesus was enabled by the Holy Spirit to look into the very soul of Peter),* He said, You are Simon the son of Jonah *("Simon" means "hearing"; Peter was named after "Simeon," the second son of Jacob and Leah [Gen. 29:32-33]):* you shall be called Cephas, which is by interpretation, A stone *(proclaims the ability of Christ to change men fundamentally and characteristically — or rather to re-create men).*

43 The day following Jesus would go forth into Galilee *(seems to insinuate that His journey from the place of His Water Baptism and Wilderness Temptation, the latter which John does not mention, toward Galilee will now commence),* and found Philip, and said unto him, Follow Me *(doesn't exactly tell us where this happened; however, there is some small indication that it was in Galilee).*

44 Now Philip was of Bethsaida, the city of Andrew and Peter *(this town was located on the northern shore of the Sea of Galilee; it had been the home of these men before they moved to Capernaum, about six miles distant).*

45 Philip found Nathanael *(Nathanael is also called "Bartholomew"),* and said unto him, We have found Him, of Whom Moses in the Law, and the Prophets, did write *(in Philip's mind, Jesus met the criteria of the Word of God),* Jesus of Nazareth, the son of Joseph *(Jesus was really not the Son of Joseph, due to the Virgin Birth, but was referred to in this manner for the obvious reasons).*

46 And Nathanael said unto him, Can there any good thing come out of Nazareth? *(The town of Nazareth was not held by Israel as a distinguished place, but rather the opposite.)* Philip said unto him, Come and see *(proclaims within itself the basic thrust of Christianity).*

47 Jesus saw Nathanael coming to Him, and said of him, Behold an Israelite indeed, in whom is no guile! *(Jesus did not say that this man was sinless, but "guileless," which means, "to be without deceit.")*

48 Nathanael said unto Him, From where do You know me? *(This proclaims the potential Disciple as being startled.)* Jesus answered and said unto him, Before that Philip called you, when you were under the fig tree, I saw you *(the Holy Spirit revealed this to Him).*

49 Nathanael answered and said unto Him, Rabbi, You are the Son of God; You are the King of Israel *(Nathanael's faith will never possess more than it embraces at this moment).*

50 Jesus answered and said unto him, Because I said unto you, I saw you under the fig tree, causes you to believe? You shall see greater things than these *(to be sure, he certainly did!).*

51 And He said unto him, Verily, verily, I say unto you, Hereafter you shall see Heaven open, and the Angels of God ascending and descending upon the Son of Man *(has to do with Jacob's dream [Gen. 28:11-13]; it was fulfilled in Jesus; He Alone could open Heaven, because He Alone is the way to God).*

CHAPTER 2

(A.D. 30)

THE FIRST MIRACLE

AND the third day *(speaks of the amount of time which had lapsed since Jesus left the Wilderness Temptation to begin His public Ministry)* there was a marriage in Cana of Galilee *(occasions the site of His very First Miracle);* and the mother of Jesus was there *(indicates that she was already there when Jesus came):*

2 And both Jesus was called, and His Disciples, to the marriage *(He may have only had some five Disciples this early in His Ministry).*

3 And when they wanted wine *(they had run out of wine; the Greek word for wine, as used here, is "oinos"; it means either fermented or unfermented, according to how it is used; every indication is it was unfermented, i.e., "grape juice"),* the mother of Jesus *(Mary)* said unto Him, They have no wine *(there was an indication in her spirit, placed there by the Holy Spirit, that she should appeal to her Son).*

4 Jesus said unto her, Woman, what have I to do with you? *(The term "Woman," as then used, was basically the same as our present use of "Madam." The language implies that the period of subjection to Mary [it is believed that Joseph was now dead] was now at an end.)* My hour is not yet come *(He is meaning that if this is the hour when He is to begin His Miracle Ministry, such direction would have to come from God, and God Alone! in other words, as it regards spiritual things, He was not there to do what His Mother wanted, but rather what God wanted; the Catholic Church should note this).*

5 His mother said unto the servants *(indicates a Revelation to her by the Holy Spirit),* Whatsoever He says unto you, do it *(represents the last recorded words of Mary; with this word*

she stepped aside, in effect, telling the servants to turn from her to Him).

6 And there were set there six waterpots of stone, after the manner of the purifying of the Jews *("six" represents the number of man, and always falls short of perfection represented by the number "7," called "God's number"),* **containing two or three firkins apiece** *(referred to 18 to 27 gallons each, depending on the size; as is obvious, they were quite large).*

7 Jesus said unto them, Fill the waterpots with water *(means that His hour had come, and He had been given instructions from His Heavenly Father as to what He should do).* **And they filled them up to the brim** *(presented all that man could do; the balance was left up to our Lord).*

8 And He said unto them, Draw out now, and bear unto the Governor of the feast *(that was all that was said and done).* **And they bear** *it.*

9 When the Ruler of the feast had tasted the water that was made wine, and knew not whence it was *(evidently, this scenario had taken place only in the presence of a few people):* **(but the servants which drew the water knew;) the Governor of the feast called the bridegroom,**

10 And said unto him, Every man at the beginning does set forth good wine; and when men have well drunk *(doesn't mean that they were intoxicated, as some suppose, but that they had already consumed a lot),* **then that which is worse:** *but* **you have kept the good wine until now** *(the best was saved until the last, but not intentionally!).*

11 This beginning of miracles did Jesus in Cana of Galilee *(this was the First Miracle He performed; there would be many more!),* **and manifested forth His Glory** *(this type of miracle was performed first in order to show that He could change things, and do so miraculously);* **and His Disciples believed on Him** *(their faith increased due to the manifestation of His Glory in the changing of the water to wine).*

12 After this He went down to Capernaum *(we aren't told why, but quite possibly He was thinking now of making it His headquarters),* **He, and His mother, and His brethren** *(it seems that His brothers were not now opposed to Him, as they would later be; at least two of them, despite their former opposition, would become leaders in the Church; I speak of James and Jude; Joseph is not mentioned here, so he was possibly dead by now; as well, His sisters aren't mentioned, so they were probably married, and at*

their own respective houses), **and His Disciples** *(as stated, exactly how many He had at this time is not known):* **and they continued there not many days** *(has reference to the "Passover," which was to commence shortly in Jerusalem).*

THE TEMPLE

13 And the Jews' Passover was at hand *(it had been Jehovah's Passover, but corruption had permeated it and now it was "The Jew's Passover"),* **and Jesus went up to Jerusalem** *(proclaims Him making this trip, although as events will relate, not with enthusiasm),*

14 And found in the Temple those who sold oxen and sheep and doves, and the changers of money sitting *(probably refers to the Court of the Gentiles; it was not the selling of the animals to which Jesus objected, but where they were being sold; the same would go for the moneychangers):*

15 And when He had made a scourge of small cords *(represents the Lord's first cleansing of the Temple; the second and last cleansing was that of Mat. 21:12),* **He drove them all out of the Temple, and the sheep, and the oxen; and poured out the changers' money, and overthrew the tables** *(what He did was Scriptural [Ps. 69:9]; spiritually, I suspect the modern Church is guilty of the same sin);*

16 And said unto them who sold doves, Take these things hence *(tradition says that He opened the cages, letting the doves loose, with them flying over the heads of the people, etc.);* **make not My Father's House an house of merchandise** *(His statement in essence says that He is the "Son of God Most High").*

17 And His Disciples remembered that it was written, The zeal of Your House has eaten Me up *(this is a foreshadowing of the reproach and agony which will befall the Righteous Servant of God in His Passion for God's Honor).*

A SIGN

18 Then answered the Jews and said unto Him *(concerns itself with the opposition, which would only grow in intensity),* **What sign do You show us, seeing that You do these things?** *(The proper translation is, "what sign do You show unto us that You are the Messiah, seeing that You do these things?")*

19 Jesus answered and said unto them, Destroy this Temple *(referred to His physical Body, not the structure built by Herod),* **and in three days I will raise it up** *(speaks of His Resurrection*

and exactly when it would be, three days after His Death).

20 Then said the Jews, Forty and six years was this Temple in building, and will you rear it up in three days? *(The last statement is spoken in sarcasm.)*

21 But He spoke of the Temple of His Body *(this is said after the fact; however, when He originally made the statement, more than likely He pointed to His Body, but still they would have not understood His meaning).*

22 When therefore He was risen from the dead, His Disciples remembered that He had said this unto them *(realizing that it referred to His Death and Resurrection, and not the Temple built by Herod)*; and they believed the Scripture, and the Word which Jesus had said *(perhaps they were referring here to Ps. 16:10; a Divine Faith is always based upon the Scriptures).*

23 Now when He was in Jerusalem at the Passover, on the Feast *Day (speaks of the same time in which He had cleansed the Temple),* many believed in His Name, when they saw the Miracles which He did.

24 But Jesus did not commit Himself unto them *(means that He paid little attention to their praises, which were occasioned by the miracles; their faith was a shallow faith, and was rooted not necessarily in the Scriptures, but rather in outward observances),* because He knew all *men (refers to the fickleness of man, especially those whose faith is as misplaced as these),*

25 And needed not that any should testify of man *(means that He Alone properly discerned the true nature of man)*: for He knew what was in man *(total depravity).*

CHAPTER 3
(A.D. 30)
NICODEMUS

THERE was a man of the Pharisees, named Nicodemus *(said to have been one of the three richest men in Jerusalem),* a Ruler of the Jews *(a member of the Sanhedrin, the Ruling body of Israel)*:

2 The same came to Jesus by night *(it is not known exactly as to why he came by night),* and said unto Him, Rabbi, we know that You are a Teacher come from God *(the pronoun "we" could indicate that Nicodemus represented several members of the Sanhedrin; Nicodemus addresses Christ here as a man, and not as God; the Cross would change Him)*: for no man can do these miracles that You do, except God be

with Him *(in this, he is correct!).*

3 Jesus answered and said unto him *(presents an answer totally different from that which he expected),* Verily, verily, I say unto you, Except a man be born again *(the term, "born again," means that man has already had a natural birth, but now must have a Spiritual Birth, which comes by Faith in Christ, and what He has done for us at the Cross, and is available to all),* he cannot see the Kingdom of God *(actually means that without the New Birth, one cannot understand or comprehend the "Kingdom of God").*

4 Nicodemus said unto Him, How can a man be born when he is old? *(This proclaims this spiritual leader of Israel as having no knowledge at all of what Jesus is saying. Had he truly been "born-again," he would have understood these terms.)* can he enter the second time into his mother's womb, and be born? *(It seems he did not know the language of the Prophets concerning circumcision of the heart [Deut. 30:6; Jer. 4:4], and concerning a hard heart and right spirit [Ps. 51:10; Ezek. 36:26-27].)*

5 Jesus answered, Verily, verily, I say unto you, Except a man be born of water and *of* the Spirit *(the phrase, "Born of water," speaks of the natural birth, which Jesus says in the next Verse, and pertains to a baby being born; being "Born of the Spirit" speaks of a Spiritual Birth, which is brought about by God Alone; and neither does it speak of Water Baptism),* he cannot enter into the Kingdom of God.

6 That which is born of the flesh is flesh *(has to do with the natural birth, and is illustrated, as stated, by the phrase, "Born of Water")*; and that which is born of the Spirit is spirit *(has to do with that which is solely of God; the one [flesh] has no relationship to the other [Spirit] and cannot be joined).*

7 Marvel not that I said unto you, You must be born again *(evidently addresses itself to the surprise, which must have been registered on the countenance of Nicodemus).*

8 The wind blows where it listeth, and you hear the sound thereof, but cannot tell from where it comes, and whither it goes *(presents the way in which Jesus explains the "born-again" experience; He likens it to the wind which comes and goes, but is impossible to tell exactly how)*: so is every one who is born of the Spirit *(it is a spiritual birth, so it cannot be explained intellectually).*

9 Nicodemus answered and said unto Him, How can these things be? *(Not being*

"born-again" at this particular time, and despite his vast intelligence in other areas, he has no understanding of this great Truth; he is religious but lost!)

10 Jesus answered and said unto him, Are you a Master of Israel *(was held in very high regard as one of the spiritual leaders of Israel),* and knowest not these things? *(As a spiritual leader, he should have known the way of Salvation, but the sad fact was he didn't.)*

11 Verily, verily, I say unto you, We speak that we do know *(Jesus was speaking of the Triune Godhead, and as well of all the "Apostles and Prophets"; in essence, He is speaking of the Word of God, and is directing Nicodemus to that Source instead of tradition),* and testify that we have seen *(means that one can actually "see" the fruit or benefits of this "Testimony," i.e., "The Word of God");* and you receive not our witness *(has to do with the Jewish Sanhedrin).*

12 If I have told you earthly things, and you believe not *(refers to the earthly type and events in the Bible, such as the Sacrifices and Feast Days, etc., which Nicodemus no doubt read many times, but was so blind that he did not see nor believe their lessons),* how shall you believe, if I tell you *of* Heavenly things? *(In effect, this tells us that if we are to know Jesus as God [Heavenly things], we must first know Jesus and the Incarnation [earthly things]. Nicodemus had addressed Jesus as merely a "Teacher." So until he understands God becoming flesh and dwelling among men, he will not understand Heavenly things.)*

13 And no man has ascended up to Heaven, but He who came down from Heaven *(He came down from Heaven and became Man, and approximately three and a half years later will ascend up to Heaven, when His Mission is complete),* **even** the Son of Man which is in Heaven *(better translated, "which is from Heaven").*

14 And as Moses lifted up the serpent in the wilderness *(refers to Num. 21:5-9; the "serpent" represents Satan who is the originator of sin),* even so must the Son of Man be lifted up *(refers to Christ being lifted up on the Cross, which alone could defeat Satan and sin):*

15 That whosoever *(destroys the erroneous hyper-Calvinistic explanation of predestination that some are predestined to be saved, while all others are predestined to be lost; the word "whosoever" means that none are excluded from being lost, and none are excluded from being saved)* **believes** in Him *(believes in Christ and what He did at the Cross; otherwise, one would perish)*

should not perish, but have Eternal Life *(the Life of God, the Ever-Living One, Who has life in Himself, and Alone has immortality).*

16 For God so loved the world *(presents the God kind of love),* that He gave His Only Begotten Son *(gave Him up to the Cross, for that's what it took to redeem humanity),* that whosoever believes in Him should not perish, but have Everlasting Life.

17 For God sent not His Son into the world to condemn the world *(means that the object of Christ's Mission was to save, but the issue to those who reject Him must and can only be condemnation);* but that the world through Him might be saved *(Jesus Christ is the only Salvation for the world; there is no other! as well, He is Salvation only through the Cross; consequently, the Cross must ever be the object of our Faith).*

18 He who believes on Him is not condemned *(is not condemned to be eternally lost in the Lake of Fire forever and forever [Rev. 20:11-15]):* but he who believes not is condemned already, because he has not believed in the Name of the Only Begotten Son of God *(all of this refers to Christ and what He did at the Cross in order to redeem humanity; Salvation is never by works, but rather by Grace through Faith, with the Cross ever the Object of that Faith).*

19 And this is the condemnation, that Light is come into the world *(refers to Jesus as the "Light;" there is no other!),* and men loved darkness rather than light, because their deeds were evil *(proclaims the fact that the great penalty of sin is sinful desire; the love of darkness is the consequence of man's wicked ways; the rejection of Jesus Christ is not the occasion of man's lostness, but rather the result of it).*

20 For every one who does evil hates the Light *(presents a striking rebuke to Nicodemus with a keen thrust of the sharp sword, saying to him that evil-doers choose the darkness, so why did this Pharisee come by night?),* neither cometh to the Light, lest his deeds should be reproved *(to truly come to Jesus means the Revelation and condemnation of every evil way, which is totally unlike the religions of the world which reveal nothing; the "Light" automatically reveals what is hidden by the darkness).*

21 But he who does truth comes to the Light *(the desire for truth must be placed in the heart of man by the Holy Spirit, by the means of the revealed Word of God; if the person sincerely wants to "do truth," he must come to Christ, for Christ is the only "Light"),* that his deeds may

be made manifest, that they are wrought in God (*proclaims the great change that takes place in the Believing sinner's life upon coming to Christ; the evil deeds are forever gone, with righteous deeds taking their place*).

22 After these things came Jesus and His Disciples into this land of Judaea (*means that Jesus and His Disciples left the metropolis of Jerusalem, where hostility was already beginning to mount, especially considering His cleansing of the Temple; they went to other parts of Judaea*); and there He tarried with them, and baptized (*He actually did not do any baptizing Himself; it was done by His Disciples, but no doubt under His Direction; the Scripture seems to indicate that this practice wasn't carried forth too very long; no doubt it was done by Christ to further validate the Ministry of John the Baptist, whose great emphasis was Water Baptism*).

JOHN THE BAPTIST

23 And John also was baptizing in Aenon near to Salim, because there was much water there (*is believed to have been located about fifty miles north of Jerusalem in Samaria*): and they came, and were baptized (*means the crowds kept coming, but were actually diminishing by this time*).

24 For John was not yet cast into prison (*the Holy Spirit is telling us here that the Ministry of John the Baptist is about to conclude*).

25 Then there arose a question between *some* of John's disciples and the Jews about purifying (*it was a very angry debate! the debate was over the many laws and rituals which had been fabricated by the Pharisees; in other words, a great ado about nothing!*).

26 And they came unto John, and said unto him, Rabbi, He Who was with You beyond Jordan, to Whom you bear witness (*Jesus*), behold, the same baptizeth, and all *men* come to Him (*they were trying to instigate a rivalry between Christ and John, and more particularly to demean John*).

27 John answered and said, A man can receive nothing, except it be given him from Heaven (*John's Ministry was from God and, therefore, from Heaven; and the Ministry of Christ was from God and, therefore, from Heaven; consequently, they complimented each other; there was no rivalry!*).

28 You yourselves bear me witness, that I said, I am not the Christ (*means that he is subservient and submissive to the One Who is*

actually the Christ*), but that I am sent before Him (*proclaims the fact that John is under the authority of Christ, and not the authority of the Pharisees, or any part of the religious hierarchy of Israel*).

29 He who has the bride is the bridegroom (*he is saying that all the souls he has won in reality belong to Jesus, and not him, because Jesus is the "Bridegroom"; consequently, he takes no umbrage at the great crowds now going to Jesus, which had originally come to him*): but the friend of the bridegroom (*that which John concludes himself to be*), which stands and hears Him (*refers to the Ministry of Christ, which exceeds all that John could ever have surmised*), rejoices greatly because of the bridegroom's voice (*refers to the Ministry of Christ*): this my joy therefore is fulfilled (*John had not only "fulfilled" his mission, but he was "fulfilled"*).

30 He must increase (*He must ever "increase," not men, denominations, religious offices, the Virgin Mary, Apostles, etc.*), but I *must* decrease (*the Ministers of the New Covenant must all take note of Divine Praise and self-depletion, as we prepare the way of the Lord to human hearts; we must hide ourselves behind the greater Glory of our Lord; we are successful, only as we succeed in doing this*).

31 He who comes from above is above all (*refers to the fact that Christ was a man, but above all that He was more than man, in fact, God*): he who is of the Earth is earthly, and speaks of the Earth (*refers to all men, even the great Prophets, which are of necessity limited*): He who comes from Heaven is above all (*places Christ in a category above all men, even as He ever shall be!*).

32 And what He has seen and heard, that He testifies (*refers to that which Jesus received from the Father, which testified of Him and He of it*); and no man receives His Testimony (*means that no man contributed to His Testimony, but that it was all from God*).

33 He who has received His Testimony (*refers to all who have believed on His Name and accepted Him as Lord and Saviour*) has set to His seal that God is true (*has to do with man receiving the witness of the Son as the Giver of Eternal Life; as the witness of Jesus is true in every respect, such portrays that God is true to His Word*).

34 For He Whom God has sent speaks the Words of God (*refers to Christ Who always spoke the Mind of God and, thereby, the Word of God*): for God gives not the Spirit by measure *unto*

Him (refers to the fact that all others, whomever they may have been and even the very greatest, while having the Holy Spirit, did so by "measure," which was not so with Jesus; He had the Spirit in totality, hence the constant healings and miracles).

35 The Father loves the Son (refers to the Incarnation, and what Christ would do to redeem humanity), and has given all things into His hand (refers to the great Plan of Redemption and it being carried out by the Lord Jesus Christ).

36 He who believes on the Son has Everlasting Life (proclaims to one and all the simple Plan of Salvation; the consequences are eternal): and he who believes not the Son shall not see life (this means that there is only one way to be saved, and that is by trusting Christ and what He has done for us at the Cross); but the wrath of God abides on him (the only way to be cleansed from sin is by the Precious Blood of Christ, and our Faith in that Finished Work; to not do that means that sin remains, and the Wrath of God must evermore be opposed to sin, and those who allow it to remain in their lives).

CHAPTER 4
(A.D. 30)
SYCHAR

WHEN therefore the Lord knew how the Pharisees had heard that Jesus made and baptized more disciples than John (Him hearing this information portrays His Humanity; even though He was God, and never ceased to be God, He never used His Power of Personal Deity, but rather was led and guided by the Holy Spirit exactly as we are, or should be),

2 (Though Jesus Himself baptized not, but His Disciples,) (His Baptism then was the same as that of John, the "Baptism of Repentance," which was carried out by His Disciples).

3 He left Judaea, and departed again into Galilee (He did so at the behest of the Holy Spirit).

4 And He must needs go through Samaria (this direction as well was instigated by the Holy Spirit; normally, Jews coming from Judaea up to Galilee went around Samaria, because they were not particularly enamored with Samaritans).

5 Then comes He to a city of Samaria, which is called Sychar (is said by some to refer to the ancient city of Shechem), near to the parcel of ground that Jacob gave to his son Joseph (proclaims, as is obvious, this spot having a long Bible history).

6 Now Jacob's well was there (in fact, this well is still there, nearly four thousand years after Jacob). Jesus therefore, being wearied with His journey, sat thus on the well (proclaims His Humanity; hence, John impresses upon us the full humanity, the definite human existence of Jesus; even as He was "the Only Begotten Son of the Father", He was "The Word made flesh"): and it was about the sixth hour (if using Jewish time, it would have been 12 o'clock noon).

7 There comes a woman of Samaria to draw water (would prove to be the greatest moment of her life): Jesus said unto her, Give Me to drink (this must have startled the woman, because most Jews, as she knew Jesus to be, would not even speak to a Samaritan, much less ask a favor).

8 (For His Disciples were gone away unto the city to buy meat.) (Some feel that John was the one Disciple who remained behind; it was his custom not to mention himself when relating these experiences, even though he was present.)

9 Then said the woman of Samaria unto Him (proclaims these two isolated hearts meeting — His isolated by Holiness, for He was separate from sinners, hers by sin, for she was separate from society), How is it that You, being a Jew, askest drink of me, which am a woman of Samaria? (She was perplexed that He would address her at all, much less ask of her a favor!) for the Jews have no dealings with the Samaritans (referred to hospitality, for ordinary buying and selling were in fact carried on; however, Jesus didn't have this animosity!).

10 Jesus answered and said unto her, If you knew the Gift of God (proclaims Jesus as that Gift, and the Salvation He Alone affords), and Who it is Who says to you, Give me to drink (proclaims her so close to Eternal Life, but yet at this moment, so far!); you would have asked of Him, and He would have given you Living Water (proclaims Him asking her for water to slake His physical thirst, while in turn He will give her "Living Water," which refers to Salvation that will forever slake her spiritual thirst).

11 The woman said unto Him, Sir, You have nothing to draw with, and the well is deep (she was right, the well was very deep, but we speak of the spiritual well!): from where do You get this Living Water? (She finds the phrase, "Living Water," to be intriguing!)

12 Are You greater than our father Jacob, which gave us the well, and drank thereof himself, and his children, and his cattle? (Her emphasis had always been on Jacob, as was the emphasis of most Samaritans; Jesus will have to draw her away from that, without denigrating Jacob.)

13 Jesus answered and said unto her, Whosoever drinks of this water shall thirst again *(presents one of the most simple, common, yet at the same time, profound statements ever uttered; the things of the world can never satisfy the human heart and life, irrespective as to how much is acquired):*

14 But whosoever drinks of the water that I shall give him shall never thirst *("Whosoever" means exactly what it says! Christ accepted is spiritual thirst forever slaked!);* but the water that I shall give him shall be in him a well of water springing up into Everlasting Life *(everything that the world or religion gives pertains to the externals; but this which Jesus gives deals with the very core of one's being, and is a perennial fountain).*

15 The woman said unto Him, Sir, give me this water *(proclaims that she now has some understanding, although faint, of what Jesus is saying; she senses that it is not literal water of which He speaks, but rather something else altogether),* that I thirst not, neither come hither to draw *(she knows now that the water of which He speaks cannot be drawn from Jacob's well).*

16 Jesus said unto her, Go, call your husband, and come hither *(a profession of Faith in Christ that ignores the question of sin, the Holiness of God, the spirituality of worship as distinct from sacerdotal ceremonies, the need of pardon, and the condition of trust in an Atoning and Revealed Saviour — such a profession is worthless).*

17 The woman answered and said, I have no husband *(presents a truth, but only partially so!).* Jesus said unto her, You have well said, I have no husband *(bores to the very heart of her problem; it speaks to her domestic and spiritual life, and points out her problem and the solution):*

18 For you have had five husbands *(must have come as a shock to her, especially considering that she knew He did not know her; as well, the Samaritans worship five gods, so He will show her that her worship of five heathen gods has a great deal to do with her domestic problems of having had five husbands);* and he whom you now have is not your husband: in that said you truly *(the man she was now living with was not her husband, i.e., "not one of the five").*

19 The woman said unto Him, Sir, I perceive that You are a Prophet *(had to do with the belief of the Samaritans and their interpretation of Whom the Messiah would be).*

20 Our fathers worshipped in this mountain *(speaks of Mount Gerizim, which was about fifty miles north of Jerusalem; in a sense, they worshipped "this mountain");* and You say, that in Jerusalem is the place where men ought to worship *(she admitted that Jesus fit the profile of the Great Prophet Who would come as Moses had predicted, but she was perplexed because He was a Jew and worshipped in Jerusalem, which the Samaritans believed were false).*

21 Jesus said unto her, Woman, believe Me *(He is telling her to hear carefully what He is saying, and then to believe it),* the hour comes, when you shall neither in this mountain, nor yet at Jerusalem, worship the Father *(Calvary, which did away with the entire Jewish system, would introduce a new way of Worship).*

22 You worship you know not what *(He minced no words, telling her plainly that the Samaritan way of worship held no validity with God; regrettably it is the same with most presently):* we know what we worship: for Salvation is of the Jews *(meaning that through the Jewish people, came the Word of God, and as well the Son of God, Who Alone brought Salvation, and did so by going to the Cross).*

23 But the hour comes, and now is, when the true worshippers shall worship the Father in spirit and in truth *(God is not looking for Holy Worship; He is looking for Holy Worshippers; as stated, Calvary would make possible an entirely different type of worship, which did not require ceremonies or rituals, etc.):* for the Father seeketh such to worship Him *(means that by the word "seeketh" such are not easily found).*

24 God *is* a Spirit *(simply means that "God is a Spirit Being"):* and they who worship Him must worship *Him* in spirit and in truth *(man worships the Lord through and by his personal spirit, which is moved upon by the Holy Spirit; otherwise it is not worship which God will accept).*

25 The woman said unto him, I know that Messiah comes, which is called Christ *(the Samaritans had adopted the Hebrew word of "Messiah," and they were looking for Him to come; "Christ" means the Anointed One"):* when He is come, He will tell us all things *(constituted Truth, but not in the way this woman suspected).*

26 Jesus said unto her, I Who speak unto you am *He* *(it is nothing short of amazing that Jesus little revealed Himself to Nicodemus, except in a veiled way, but plainly and clearly reveals Himself to this woman — a Samaritan at that! and to the seeking soul . . .).*

27 And upon this came His Disciples, and

marvelled that He talked with the woman *(as stated, there were no dealings normally between Jews and Samaritans, and even above that, Rabbis did not converse with women in public or instruct them in the Law)*: yet no man said, What do You seek? or, Why do You talk with her? *(This means that they kept their astonishment at Jesus' actions to themselves.)*

28 The woman then left her waterpot, and went her way into the city *(so a woman became the first Preacher of the Gospel to the Gentile nations, and so effective was her preaching that it caused a Revival)*, and said to the men *(refers to the fact that she went directly to the leaders of the particular Samaritan religion)*,

29 Come, see a Man, which told me all things that ever I did *(Christianity is not a philosophy nor a religion; it is really, as stated, a "Man," the Man Christ Jesus)*: is not this the Christ? *(Her question presupposes that, as stated, her fellow Samaritans were looking for a Messiah.)*

30 Then they went out of the city, and came unto Him *(the Holy Spirit knew there were hungry hearts in this place, and so would have Christ go through Samaria)*.

31 In the mean while His Disciples prayed Him, saying, Master, eat *(they urged Him to eat, out of concern for His Health)*.

32 But He said unto them, I have meat to eat that you know not of *(the insensibility of the Disciples to spiritual realities is again evidenced in Verses 31 through 38; and His "meat" and "harvest" were the Samaritans, who at the moment were leaving the city and coming to Him, and believing on Him)*.

33 Therefore said the Disciples one to another, Has any man brought Him *ought* to eat? *(At this stage, the Disciples could only think in carnal terms, whereas Jesus spoke almost exclusively in spiritual terms.)*

34 Jesus said unto them, My meat is to do the will of Him Who sent Me *(this statement, although brief, constitutes the whole duty of man [Eccl. 12:13-14])*, and to finish His work *(the work is His, and not ours!)*.

35 Say not ye, There are yet four months, and *then* cometh harvest? *(The harvest is now!)* behold, I say unto you, Lift up your eyes, and look on the fields *(simply means that we don't have to go very far to see the need)*; for they are white already to harvest.

36 And He who reaps receives wages *(the wages are souls)*, and gathers fruit unto life eternal *(the Salvation of a soul will bring forth fruit forever, and will be marked to the credit of the Sowers and Reapers; what an investment!)*: that both he who sows and he who reaps may rejoice together *(this speaks of all who play their parts, and do so without failure)*.

37 And herein is that saying true, One sows, and another reaps *(God has a special Ministry for each individual; the "Sowers" are those who make it possible for the "reapers" to reap; the Preacher can only reap what has been sowed!)*.

38 I sent you to reap that whereon you bestowed no labour *(whatever is done for Christ is brought to fruition as a result of much labor on the part of many different people)*: other men laboured, and you have entered into their labours *(He is actually speaking here of the Prophets of Old; in Christ, their Prophecies are now coming to pass, and the Apostles will reap what they sowed down through the many centuries; it is the same with us presently, as it regards both the Prophets and the Apostles, etc.)*.

SALVATION

39 And many of the Samaritans of that city believed on Him for the saying of the woman, which testified *(this is a perfect example of true Christianity in action)*, He told me all that ever I did *(while Jesus did expose her sin, as the Gospel always does, it was not done in a negative, condemnatory fashion, but rather to deliver her from sin; He then gave her Eternal Life)*.

40 So when the Samaritans were come unto Him *(bespoke hearts ready to receive from God)*, they besought Him that He would tarry with them *(presents a request that was not denied, and in fact, a request that will never be denied)*: and He abode there two days *(the greatest two days they would ever see and know)*.

41 And many more believed because of His Own Word *(this is what happened during the two days)*;

42 And said unto the woman, Now we believe, not because of your saying *(should have been translated, "not only because of your saying," because her saying was the testimony which originally brought them to Christ)*: for we have heard *Him* ourselves, and know that this is indeed the Christ, the Saviour of the world *(proclaims one of the most profound statements ever made, which occurs only one other time in the Bible [I Jn. 4:14]; it fell from the lips of Samaritans; regrettably, toward the end of His Ministry, there were some Samaritans who would not receive Him [Lk. 9:51-56])*.

GALILEE

43 Now after two days He departed thence, and went into Galilee.

44 For Jesus Himself testified, that a Prophet has no honour in His Own country (*He would later extend this statement to say, "and among His Own kin, and in His Own house" [Mat. 13:57; Mk. 6:4]*).

45 Then when He was come into Galilee, the Galilaeans received Him (*Faith based on outward observances is at best feeble; but as feeble as their Faith might be, He, obedient to His Father's Will, acted in Grace and Power whenever He met with Faith, however poor*), having seen all the things that He did at Jerusalem at the Feast: for they also went unto the Feast (*they needed the miracles to believe, with the evidence being that the Samaritans needed only His Word, for they had the greater Faith*).

THE NOBLEMAN'S SON

46 So Jesus came again into Cana of Galilee, where He made the water wine (*His First Miracle*). And there was a certain nobleman, whose son was sick at Capernaum (*pertains to one who was an officer of Herod Antipas, Tetrarch of Galilee*).

47 When he heard that Jesus was come out of Judaea into Galilee, he went unto Him (*the news had spread to Capernaum that Jesus was back in Galilee, even at Cana, only about twenty miles distant*), and besought Him that He would come down, and heal his son: for he was at the point of death (*contains, buried within the text, the faint idea that due to his place and position in the political structure of Galilee that Jesus would be impressed by who he was, an officer in Herod's Court; at any rate, he was desperate!*).

48 Then said Jesus unto him, Except you see signs and wonders, you will not believe (*proclaims Jesus knowing this man's heart and its unbelief, so He will draw him out; He will pull him to the highest Faith, taking Christ at His Word!*).

49 The nobleman said unto Him, Sir, come down ere my child die (*one can feel the pathos in this man's plea, with the mild rebuke preparing for what Jesus is about to say*).

50 Jesus said unto him, Go your way; your son lives (*presents a startling statement, and one which must have taken this man by surprise; his Faith is now being tested, and he will rise to

the challenge*). And the man believed the Word that Jesus had spoken unto him, and he went his way (*back to Capernaum*).

51 And as he was now going down, his servants met him, and told *him*, saying, Your son lives (*the very words that Jesus had used*).

52 Then enquired he of them the hour when he began to amend (*portrays him putting the times together when Jesus had spoken the Word and when the boy was healed*). And they said unto him, Yesterday at the seventh hour the fever left him (*if Roman time, 7 p.m. the day before*).

53 So the father knew that *it was* at the same hour, in the which Jesus said unto him, Your son lives (*his Faith, ever how weak it had previously been, was greatly rewarded*): and himself believed, and his whole house (*all became converts to Christ*).

54 This *is* again the second miracle *that* Jesus did (*was speaking only of Galilee; actually, He had performed quite a number of miracles in the last few days in Jerusalem [Jn. 2:23]*), when He was come out of Judaea into Galilee (*proclaims that everywhere He went, miracles followed, plus the changing of lives; such was Jesus then, and such is Jesus now!*).

CHAPTER 5

(A.D. 31)

THE POOL OF BETHESDA

AFTER this there was a Feast of the Jews (*even though the Scriptures don't say, most think this was Passover; if correct, Jesus would have been little over a year into His public Ministry*); and Jesus went up to Jerusalem (*speaks of the express purpose of keeping this "Feast"*).

2 Now there is at Jerusalem by the sheep *market* a pool (*should have been translated, "by the sheep gate"*), which is called in the Hebrew tongue Bethesda, having five porches (*means, "house of grace and mercy"; it was somewhat like a public infirmary*).

3 In these lay a great multitude of impotent folk, of blind, halt, withered (*presents a perfect description of humanity; due to the Fall, man is "impotent," helpless to save himself*), waiting for the moving of the water.

4 For an Angel went down at a certain season into the pool, and troubled the water (*not given by John as folklore, but rather as a fact*): whosoever then first after the troubling of the water stepped in was made whole of whatsoever disease he had (*earthly princes on entering

a city resort to the houses of the great and rich, but the feet of the Prince of princes immediately turned to the abode of misery and suffering, the fruits of sin).

5 And a certain man was there *(the healing of the impotent man contrasts the quickening Power of Christ with the powerlessness of the Law; it demanded strength on the part of the sinner in order to obtain the life it promised; but man is without strength [Rom. 5:6]),* **which had an infirmity thirty and eight years** *(a perfect type of Israel, which because of her sin was helpless, shut up in the desert for thirty-eight years; the similarity is not coincidental).*

6 When Jesus saw him lie *(presents a picture of Israel of Jesus' day, but as well, of all humanity),* **and knew that he had been now a long time** *in that case (once again speaks of Israel),* **He said unto him, Will you be made whole?** *(This must, beyond a doubt, be the greatest question of all time! Man is not "whole," and in fact cannot be "whole" without Jesus. This is where the great contention is.)*

7 The impotent man answered Him, Sir, I have no man, when the water is troubled, to put me into the pool *(proclaims his dependence on man, which has brought nothing but disappointment):* **but while I am coming, another steps down before me** *(Love, no doubt, selected this man as being the most miserable, needy, and helpless in all that sad company; and wisdom chose him as a vessel of instruction to the nation).*

8 Jesus said unto him, Rise, take up your bed, and walk *(a single word from Christ sufficed).*

9 And immediately the man was made whole, and took up his bed, and walked *(strength was given, that fact demonstrated by the man carrying his bed):* **and on the same day was the Sabbath** *(and what a Sabbath of rest, relief, and joy for this man!).*

10 The Jews therefore said unto him who was cured *(proclaims, as we shall see, no joy over his healing and deliverance, but rather the opposite, as religion always does),* **It is the Sabbath Day: it is not lawful for you to carry** *your* **bed** *(pointed only to man's laws, and not God's Laws; Jesus paid absolutely no attention to the man-made laws, as numerous as they were).*

11 He answered them, He Who made me whole *(proclaims the man using Jesus as his authority, which is what he should have done),* **the Same said unto me, Take up your bed, and walk** *(Sabbath or no Sabbath, it was a command that he eagerly obeyed; it meant the Healing*

and Salvation of his physical body).

12 Then answered they him, What man is that which said unto you, Take up your bed, and walk?

13 And he who was healed knew not who it was *(it seems that after the healing, Jesus left instantly, so as not to create a scene; consequently, the man really did not know Who it was that had healed him):* **for Jesus had conveyed Himself away, a multitude being in** *that* **place** *(He did so because He knew the hatred of the leaders and the result of His breaking their man-made laws; this is perhaps the reason He did not stay to heal others; at any rate, it was the Holy Spirit Who told Him what to do).*

14 Afterward Jesus finds him *(the man He had healed)* **in the Temple, and said unto him** *(proclaims Jesus seeking him out, and for a purpose),* **Behold, you are made whole** *(refers to the Salvation experience, as well as physical healing):* **sin no more, lest a worse thing come unto you** *(this tells us first of all that his sickness of thirty-eight years had been brought up on him because of sin; as well, it tells us that disobedience to the Lord can open the door for "worse things").*

15 The man departed, and told the Jews that it was Jesus, which had made him whole *(some have claimed that this man was ungrateful; however, he had no way of knowing of the animosity of the religious leaders against Jesus, so he probably thought he was doing the right thing).*

16 And therefore did the Jews persecute Jesus *(the opposition from the religious hierarchy will do nothing but increase from now forward),* **and sought to kill Him, because He had done these things on the Sabbath day** *(this is ironical; the religious leaders of Israel wanted to kill the Lord in the Name of the Lord; this is how blind they were!).*

EQUALITY WITH GOD

17 But Jesus answered them *(proclaims that this was a face-to-face confrontation),* **My Father worketh hitherto, and I work** *(this says two things: 1. He claims equality with God, and that He was God; and, 2. The very "Work" of the Father and the Son was to deliver mankind, whether physically or spiritually, or both, which brought the true Sabbath to the soul of man, for which it was originally intended).*

18 Therefore the Jews sought the more to kill Him *(means that He not only did not seek any type of accommodations with these hypocrites, but rather reinforced His position to such*

an extent that no one had absolutely any doubt as to what He was saying or doing), **because He not only had broken the Sabbath** *(He had not really broken the Sabbath, but only one of their silly man-made rules)*, **but said also that God was His Father, making Himself equal with God** *(presents a charge not disclaimed by Jesus, because He did make Himself equal with God, and rightly so)*.

19 **Then answered Jesus and said unto them, Verily, verily, I say unto you, The Son can do nothing of Himself** *(proclaims the humanity of Christ, with Him freely giving up the expression of His Deity while never losing its possession)*, **but what He sees the Father do** *(proclaims His total subservience to the Father, which as a Man He was to do and did do)*: **for what things soever He does, these also do the Son likewise** *(setting an example of humility and dependence, which the human family seriously lacked)*.

20 **For the Father loves the Son** *(the obedience of the Son is based on the love the Father has for the Son)*, **and shows Him all things that Himself does** *(plainly says that everything Jesus did is that which the Father told Him to do)*: **and He will show Him greater works than these, that you may marvel** *(has to do with Verses 28 and 29, which speak of the coming Resurrection)*.

21 **For as the Father raises up the dead, and quickens** *them* *(proclaims as a fact the Truth of the coming Resurrection of Life)*; **even so the Son quickens** *(makes spiritually alive)* **whom He will** *(portrays the truth that Salvation is not of him who wills [in the sense of willing Salvation by works, etc.], but of God Who shows Mercy)*.

22 **For the Father judges no man** *(judges no one who has come to Christ, for all sin has been settled in Christ)*, **but has committed all judgment unto the Son** *(Christ is the Saviour today, but will be the Judge tomorrow)*:

23 **That all** *men* **should honour the Son, even as they honour the Father** *(claims equality with God in honor [Heb. 2:7-9])*. **He who honors not the Son honors not the Father which has sent Him** *(proclaims in no uncertain terms that if Jesus is dishonored, the Father is dishonored as well!)*.

24 **Verily, verily, I say unto you, He who hears My Word** *(the Word of the Cross [Jn. 3:14-15])*, **and believes on Him Who sent Me** *(if one doesn't believe in Jesus, they cannot believe in God; to have the Son is to have the Father)*, **has Everlasting Life** *(outside of Christ, there is no spiritual life)*, **and shall not come into condemnation** *(Christ took the condemnation at the Cross)*; **but is passed from death unto life** *(Born-Again)*.

25 **Verily, verily, I say unto you** *(always signals a statement of the highest authority, and proclaims Jesus as that authority)*, **The hour is coming, and now is, when the dead shall hear the voice of the Son of God: and they who hear shall live** *(has a double meaning: 1. It refers to people being saved, thereby, coming from spiritual death to Spiritual Life; and, 2. It refers to the coming Resurrection of Life, when all Saints will be Resurrected)*.

26 **For as the Father has Life in Himself** *(refers to God as the Eternal Fountain of Life, the Source Ultimate)*; **so has He given to the Son to have Life in Himself** *(Jesus saying that He is not merely a participator in this "Life," but in fact is, as well, the Source of Life and, in Truth, the Ultimate Source exactly as the Father; consequently, He again claims Deity)*;

27 **And has given Him authority to execute judgment also** *(this speaks of "The Judgment Seat of Christ," which will be for all Believers, and as well, the "Great White Throne Judgment," which will be for all the unsaved)*, **because He is the Son of Man** *(refers to Him paying the price on Calvary's Cross, and by the merit of such, He will also be the "Judge")*.

28 **Marvel not at this** *(these statements, as given by Christ, left the religious leaders of Israel speechless)*: **for the hour is coming, in the which all who are in the graves shall hear His voice** *(speaks of the Resurrection of Life and the Resurrection of Damnation; again, these statements proclaim Christ as the Lord of both life and death)*,

29 **And shall come forth** *(portrays both Resurrections as we shall see, and according to His "voice")*; **they who have done good, unto the Resurrection of Life** *(pertains to the First Resurrection, or as commonly referred, "The Rapture" [I Thess. 4:13-18])*; **and they who have done evil, unto the Resurrection of Damnation** *(this last Resurrection will take place approximately a thousand years after the First Resurrection of Life [Dan. 12:2; Rev., Chpt. 20])*.

30 **I can of Mine Own Self do nothing** *(in His Humanity, He derived all authority from the Father)*: **as I hear, I judge** *(the Judgment He pronounced was that which He heard in His Ear, as given by the Father [Isa. 50:4])*: **and My judgment is just** *(it is perfect, because it comes from the Throne of God)*; **because I seek not Mine**

Own Will, but the Will of the Father which has sent Me (*proclaims the fact that the human consciousness of the Son becomes the basis for the Father's Judgment, which is uttered absolutely and finally through human lips of the Son of God; He sought only the Will of the Father, and we must seek only the Will of the Father, which is given in His Word*).

31 If I bear witness of Myself (*as to Who and What I am*), My witness is not true (*if I Alone bear witness; but as we shall see, there are also other witnesses*).

32 There is another Who bears witness of Me (*speaks of John the Baptist*); and I know that the witness which he witnesses of Me is true (*John's witness of Christ carried all the authority of the Word of God*).

33 You sent unto John (*refers to the happenings of Jn. 1:19-27*), and he bear witness unto the truth (*proclaims the things that John told them when they asked if he was the Messiah*).

34 But I receive not testimony from man (*in effect, says, "even though John's testimony is true, I will not use a testimony from any man"*): but these things I say, that you might be saved (*in effect, Jesus is telling the religious leaders of Israel that they are unsaved*).

35 He was a burning and a shining light (*John the Baptist was "a light," but he wasn't "the Light," Who Alone is Christ*): and you were willing for a season to rejoice in his light (*the religious leaders of Israel were willing for a brief period to listen to John, but when they saw that the major thrust of his Ministry was to introduce Jesus as the Son of God and Lamb of God, they turned away*).

36 But I have greater witness than *that* of John (*does not in any way demean the witness of John*): for the works which the Father has given Me to finish (*the miracles and Calvary*), the same works that I do, bear witness of Me, that the Father has sent Me (*all the healings and miracles, which could not be refuted*).

37 And the Father Himself, which has sent Me, has borne witness of Me (*it is the Father, Who through the Holy Spirit gave Christ the Power to do these things [Lk. 4:18-19]*). You have neither heard His voice at any time, nor seen His shape (*in essence, Jesus is saying that these Jews to whom He was speaking believed that God existed, even though they had never heard His Voice or seen His Shape; therefore, why should they not believe the One sent by the Father, which the miracles and deliverances have proved?*).

38 And you have not His Word abiding in you (*if they truly knew God as they claimed, they would have His Word abiding in them, and would, therefore, believe the Son, for the Word spoke of the Son*): for Whom He has sent, Him you believe not (*the rejection of Christ by the religious leaders of Israel demonstrated not only ignorance of God, but hostility to Him*).

THE SCRIPTURES

39 Search the Scriptures (*proclaims an imperative command, not a mere suggestion*); for in them you think you have Eternal Life (*should have been translated, "You claim to believe the Scriptures, so believe what they say about Me"*): and they are they which testify of Me (*the entire story of the Bible is "Christ and Him Crucified"*).

40 And You will not come to Me, that you might have Life (*all Life is in Christ; to have that Life, one must accept what Christ has done at the Cross*).

41 I receive not honour from men (*He sought honor from God Alone; that must be our criteria as well!*).

42 But I know you, that you have not the Love of God in you (*if one is truly saved, one will truly have the Love of God*).

43 I am come in My Father's Name, and you receive Me not (*proclaims that the real reason they did not receive Him is because they did not know the Father, despite their claims*): if another shall come in his own name, him you will receive (*actually speaks of the coming Antichrist, as well as all other false Messiahs; shortly after the Rapture of the Church, Israel will receive a false Messiah, claiming that he is the one for whom they have long looked; they will find, to their dismay, how wrong they are!*).

UNBELIEF

44 How can you believe, which receive honour one of another (*proclaims that God does not minister to the pride of man, nor modify truth so as to please it and feed it*), and seek not the honour that *comes* from God only? (*To seek and receive such honor, which portrays itself in the Moving and Operation of the Holy Spirit, most of the time will incur the wrath of the religious establishment; consequently, most Preachers seek the honor that comes from men.*)

45 Do not think that I will accuse you to the Father (*means that they are already accused*):

there is *one* who accuses you, *even* Moses, in whom ye trust *(they were claiming to abide by the Law of Moses, but in reality they were not)*.

46 For had you believed Moses, you would have believed Me *(despite their claims, they did not keep the Law; for if they did they would believe Christ)*: for he *(Moses)* wrote of Me *(Gen. 3:15; 17:18; 49:10; Deut. 18:5-18; Lk. 24:27, 44, etc.)*.

47 But if ye believe not his writings *(bluntly tells them to their faces that despite their claims to the contrary, they were, in fact, unbelievers; all the religious machinery was but a show! at heart they did not believe the Bible any more than the heathen)*, how shall you believe My words? *(This question proclaims the unity of Christ and the Scriptures.)*

CHAPTER 6
(A.D. 32)
JESUS FEEDS FIVE THOUSAND

AFTER these things *(refers to the recent trip to Jerusalem where the tremendous exchange took place between Jesus and the religious leaders of Israel)* Jesus went over the Sea of Galilee, which is *the Sea* of Tiberias *(it was referred to by several names)*.

2 And a great multitude followed Him *(there were at least 5,000 men, besides the women and children)*, because they saw His miracles which He did on them who were diseased *(and He turned none of them away, but healed all who came to Him despite their spiritual condition, because He is the "Bearer of Grace")*.

3 And Jesus went up into a mountain, and there He sat with His Disciples *(contemplates a time of teaching and instruction)*.

4 And the Passover, a Feast of the Jews, was near *(the Ministry of Christ had now passed the milestone of its second year)*.

5 When Jesus then lifted up *His* eyes, and saw a great company come unto Him *(represented this great multitude who had followed Him)*, He said unto Philip, Where shall we buy bread, that these may eat? *(According to Matthew, Mark, and Luke, this had been preceded by a period of time given over to teaching and healing. This was not recorded by John.)*

6 And this He said to prove him *(carries the idea in the Greek of testing or examining Him; He would test the Faith of Philip)*: for He Himself knew what He would do *(even though we do not know at times, He always knows; consequently, we must ever seek His Face for leading and guidance)*.

7 Philip answered Him *(presents carnal thinking, as all of us far too often do)*, Two hundred pennyworth of bread is not sufficient for them, that every one of them may take a little *(this is the way the world plans, but it is not the way that the Child of God should plan)*.

8 One of His Disciples, Andrew, Simon Peter's brother, said unto Him *(at least Andrew included Jesus in his thinking)*,

9 There is a lad here, which has five barley loaves, and two small fishes *(some scholars believe that this boy traveled with the company of Christ for the purpose of bearing their food, considering that at times they were in places which were secluded, even as here)*: but what are they among so many? *(In the boy's hands, they were nothing; but in the Hands of Christ, they were everything.)*

10 And Jesus said, Make the men sit down *(Mark adds, "by hundreds, and by fifties" [Mk. 6:40])*. Now there was much grass in the place *(being the Passover season, this was spring, the month of April)*. So the men sat down, in number about five thousand *(counting the women and children, the crowd probably totaled about ten to fifteen thousand)*.

11 And Jesus took the loaves *(little is much if God be in it)*; and when He had given thanks *(this He always did, and so must we!)*, He distributed to the Disciples, and the Disciples to them who were set down; and likewise of the fish as much as they would *(exactly how this miracle happened, we aren't told; however, at some point, it began to multiply, which obviously was a miracle of astounding proportions)*.

12 When they were filled *(all ate as much as they desired)*, He said unto His Disciples, Gather up the fragments that remain, that nothing be lost *(this bread in a sense represented Christ and the Gospel; none of it, therefore, must be wasted)*.

13 Therefore they gathered *them* together, and filled twelve baskets with the fragments of the five barley loaves, which remained over and above unto them who had eaten *(presents a Law that is known only to God, of which man has no understanding; everything that man does depletes; everything that God does multiplies; the numbers "7" and "12" are brought to bear here; "7" [five loaves and two fish] speaks of perfection, while "12" speaks of God's Government; if we have His Government, we have His Perfection)*.

14 Then those men, when they had seen the miracle that Jesus did, said *(presents a picture*

of Israel desiring to use Jesus for their own purposes, instead of realizing the true purpose for which He came), **This is of a truth that Prophet Who should come into the world** *(refers to Deut. 18:15; these people recognize Jesus as the Messiah, but for all the wrong reasons)*.

15 When Jesus therefore perceived that they would come and take Him by force, to make Him a king *(represented the type of King that Israel did not need)*, **He departed again into a mountain Himself Alone** *(refers to Him having already sent the Disciples away, actually back to Capernaum)*.

WALKING ON THE WATER

16 And when evening was *now* **come, His Disciples went down unto the sea** *(that which happened before He went up into the mountain Alone)*,

17 And entered into a ship, and went over the sea toward Capernaum *(where Jesus told them to go)*. **And it was now dark, and Jesus was not come to them** *(John sets the stage for that which will now appear)*.

18 And the sea arose by reason of a great wind that blew *(the Scripture does not say it was a storm, but that the wind was adverse; in other words, it was blowing against them to where they could not make any headway)*.

19 So when they had rowed about five and twenty or thirty furlongs *(represents approximately four miles, and portrays them being pushed out into the middle of the lake)*, **they see Jesus walking on the sea, and drawing near unto the ship: and they were afraid** *(and no wonder!)*.

20 But He said unto them, It is I; be not afraid *(the literal translation is, "I am; be not afraid"; in effect, He was telling them that He was the "I am" of the Old Testament, i.e., "Jehovah!")*.

21 Then they willingly received Him into the ship *(without Jesus in the ship, their progress was difficult, if not impossible; with Him in the ship, all things change, and immediately!)*: **and immediately the ship was at the land where they went** *(at Capernaum, a distance of about four miles; this means that one second the ship was about a distance of four miles from the land, and the next second it was at the land)*.

THE BREAD OF LIFE

22 The day following, when the people which stood on the other side of the sea saw that there was none other boat there, save that one whereinto His Disciples were entered *(no other boat from Capernaum)*, **and that Jesus went not with His Disciples into the boat, but** *that* **His Disciples were gone away alone** *(they saw that the boat left without Jesus)*;

23 (Howbeit there came other boats from Tiberias near unto the place where they did eat bread, after that the Lord had given thanks:) *(These particular boats were from Tiberias, not Capernaum.)*

24 When the people therefore saw that Jesus was not there, neither His Disciples *(despite the fact that Jesus did not go with His Disciples in the boat, the people could not find Him)*, **they also took shipping, and came to Capernaum** *(implies that some of them possibly hired some of the boats from Tiberias)*, **seeking for Jesus** *(regrettably, they were seeking Him, as the Text will portray, for all the wrong reasons)*.

25 And when they had found Him on the other side of the sea *(in Capernaum)*, **they said unto Him, Rabbi, when did You come here?** *(The people, knowing the Disciples had left without Jesus, were puzzled as to how the Lord now came to be in Capernaum; Jesus little answered their question, for His Mission was a moral one, rather than an intellectual or material one.)*

26 Jesus answered them and said, Verily, verily, I say unto you *(presents an answer that is so startling as to defy all description)*, **You seek Me, not because you saw the miracles** *(would have been better translated, "you seek Me, not because you properly understood the miracles")*, **but because you did eat of the loaves, and were filled** *(reads perfectly their true motives; the modern "Word of Faith" message falls into the same category)*.

27 Labour not for the meat which perishes *(regrettably, this is where much of the modern Church is presently [Rev. 3:17])*, **but for that meat which endures unto Everlasting Life** *(the idea is that our efforts must rest in things which are eternal, rather than things which are temporal)*, **which the Son of Man shall give unto you** *("Son of Man" refers to what Christ would do at the Cross, and the manner in which men will receive Eternal Life)*: **for Him has God the Father sealed** *(refers to the One, and the only One Who can fill, and in fact has filled, this role; all other claimants are spurious)*.

28 Then said they unto Him, What shall we do, that we might work the works of God? *(They wanted to do the Works of God, when in reality most of them did not even know God.*

This was because of erroneous leadership.)

29 Jesus answered and said unto them, This is the Work of God, that you believe on Him Whom He has sent *(it offends the self-righteous to tell them that, without Faith, it is impossible to please God [Heb. 11:6]; the Great work that God requires is Faith in His Beloved Son Whom He has sent; otherwise, works, however pious, are "dead works").*

30 They said therefore unto Him, What sign do You then show *(presents these people ignoring what Jesus has just said concerning "Believing on Him," and at once demanding a "sign"),* that we may see, and believe You? *(Many of them had just seen the miracle of the loaves and the fish, but seemingly to no avail!)* what do You work? *(The gross ignorance of the people was astounding to say the least! But is it any better presently?)*

31 Our fathers did eat Manna in the desert; as it is written, He gave them bread from Heaven to eat *(they were implying that the bread Jesus had multiplied didn't come from Heaven, as did the Manna)*

32 Then Jesus said unto them, Verily, verily, I say unto you, Moses gave you not that bread from Heaven *(setting the people straight that it was not Moses who sent the Manna from Heaven, but rather God the Father);* but My Father gives you the true bread from Heaven *(He was pulling their attention from the meat which perishes to the True Bread, which and Who is Himself, the Lord Jesus Christ).*

33 For the Bread of God is He which comes down from Heaven *(once again presents Himself as the Messiah, the True Lord of Israel),* and gives life unto the world *(the meat that perishes will not give Eternal Life; Christ Alone, gives such Life).*

34 Then said they unto Him, Lord, evermore give us this Bread *(strangely enough, when they find out that the Bread is Jesus, and the requirement for obtaining this Bread, many would leave Him, which follows through unto this very hour).*

35 And Jesus said unto them, I am the Bread of Life *(proclaims Him dropping all disguise, and gathering up into one burning Word all the previous teaching which they might have fathomed, but did not):* He who comes to Me shall never hunger *(pertains to spiritual hunger);* and he who believes on Me shall never thirst *(pertains to spiritual thirst; Christ satisfies all spiritual desire).*

36 But I said unto you, That you also have seen Me, and believe not *(despite overwhelming evidence!).*

37 All who the Father gives Me shall come to Me *(refers to all, whomever they may be, whether Israelites, Gentiles, Pharisees, Scoffers, Harlots, or even the very Castaways of the Devil);* and him who comes to Me I will in no wise cast out *(proclaims to all a promise of unparalleled proportion; no one has ever been turned away, and no one will ever be turned away).*

38 For I came down from Heaven *(proclaims God becoming Man, thereby, the "Incarnation"),* not to do My Own Will, but the Will of Him Who sent Me *(He is telling the Jews that Jehovah, Whom they claim to know and serve, is the Very One Who sent Him; and what He does and says is the Will of God, and to ignore it or reject it is to violate that Will).*

39 And this is the Father's will which has sent Me *(pertains to the ultimate Blessing of Redemption),* that of all which He has given Me I should lose nothing *(what He came to do would be done),* but should raise it up again at the last day *(speaks of the coming Resurrection, when all Believers will have all the benefits of the Cross).*

40 And this is the Will of Him Who sent Me *(speaks of the Father's desires),* that every one which sees the Son, and believes on Him, may have Everlasting Life *(one must "see" or comprehend the Lord Jesus Christ, which refers to what He did at the Cross, and believe on Him; it is never doing, but rather "Believing"):* and I will raise Him up at the last day *(a guaranteed Resurrection).*

THE BREAD OF LIFE

41 The Jews then murmured at Him *(murmuring was one of the great sins of Israel, which denotes rebellious feelings against God [Ex. 16:7-9; Num. 11:1; 14:27]),* because He said, I am the Bread which came down from Heaven *(this means that the Jews did not misunderstand His meaning; they understood it perfectly and rebelled against it).*

42 And they said, Is not this Jesus, the son of Joseph, whose father and mother we know? *(They did not believe the Incarnation, despite the fact that Jesus met every single criteria.)* how is it then that He says, I came down from Heaven? *(Unbelief questions everything, and cannot comprehend Truth.)*

43 Jesus therefore answered and said unto them, Murmur not among yourselves *(their*

"murmuring" showed their disapproval and rejection).

44 No man can come to Me, except the Father which has sent Me draw him (*the idea is that all initiative toward Salvation is on the part of God toward the sinner and not from the sinner himself; without this "drawing of the Father," which is done by the Holy Spirit, no one could come to God, or even have any desire to come to God*): **and I will raise him up at the last day** (*for the third time in this Chapter alone, Jesus addresses the Resurrection*).

45 It is written in the Prophets, And they shall be all taught of God (*this is found in Isa. 54:13; God draws sinners to Christ by a spiritual operation consonant to their moral nature and enlightening their rational conviction, and He effects through the Scriptures as written in the Prophets*). **Every man therefore who has heard, and has learned of the Father, comes unto Me** (*our Lord is telling the Jews that if they really knew the Father, they would accept Christ*).

46 Not that any man has seen the Father (*"seen" in the Greek is "horao," and means "to fully comprehend and understand with the mind; to see Truth fully"*), **save He which is of God, He has seen the Father** (*the pronoun "He" refers to Christ; He Alone fully understands and comprehends the Father; so all that is learned about God, must be learned through Jesus Christ, which will be according to the Word*).

47 Verily, verily, I say unto you, He who believes on Me has Everlasting Life (*this is obtained immediately upon "Believing"; it is not something the Believer shall have, but something the Believer presently has*).

48 I am that Bread of Life (*as the Bread of Life, Christ gives Life to the Believer, and He sustains that Life; by using the words "I am," Jesus plainly identifies Himself as the Jehovah of the Old Testament [Ex. 3:14]*).

49 Your fathers did eat Manna in the wilderness, and are dead (*the Manna which God gave in the wilderness was a Type of Christ; however, "types" had no life within themselves and, therefore, could not effect Salvation; Jesus was speaking of Spiritual Life and physical life*).

50 This is the Bread which comes down from Heaven (*quite possibly when Jesus said this, He was pointing to Himself; in essence, He would have been speaking of His physical body, which was to be given in Sacrifice for the purchase of lost humanity*), **that a man may eat thereof, and not die** (*speaks of that which is spiritual, and means that man is restored to union with*

God, when previously he had been alienated; once again, our Lord is speaking of Spiritual Life).

51 I am the Living Bread which came down from Heaven (*now proclaims Jesus presenting Himself as God ["I am"], while in the previous Verse He presented Himself as Man; and so He is the God-Man Jesus Christ*): **if any man eat of this Bread, he shall live forever** (*says the same thing as in the previous Verse, but in a different way; there He said, "and not die," now He says, "shall live forever"; the latter adds to the former*): **and the Bread that I will give is My flesh, which I will give for the life of the world** (*this speaks of Him giving Himself on the Cross as a Sacrifice, which would guarantee Salvation for all who would Believe*).

52 The Jews therefore strove among themselves (*presents the inevitable results of unbelief*), **saying, How can this man give us** *His* **flesh to eat?** (*This presents them thinking in the physical, while He is speaking in the Spiritual. Unredeemed man, despite all his intellectual loftiness, cannot think as God thinks, despite education and self-improvement; for all that. He thinks little above the level of a beast.*)

53 Then Jesus said unto them, Verily, verily, I say unto you (*instead of softening or modifying this seemingly harsh Doctrine, He instead intensified it by declaring it indispensable to Salvation*), **Except you eat the flesh of the Son of Man, and drink His Blood, you have no life in you** (*this terminology addresses the Cross; Christ would give Himself on the Cross for the Salvation of mankind; to fully believe in Him and what He did for us is what He means here; however, this Verse tells us the degree of believing that is required; it refers to the Cross being the total object of one's belief; failing that, there is no Life in you*).

54 Whoso eats My flesh, and drinks My Blood, has Eternal Life (*once again, Christ reiterates the fact that if the Cross is the total object of one's Faith, such a person has "Eternal Life"*); **and I will raise him up at the last day** (*constitutes the fourth time this is spoken by Christ; consequently, the Believer has a fourfold assurance of the Resurrection*).

55 For My flesh is meat indeed, and My Blood is drink indeed (*the idea is that one must continue eating and drinking even on a daily basis, which speaks of bearing the Cross daily [Lk. 9:23]*).

56 He who eats My flesh, and drinks My Blood, dwells in Me, and I in him (*the only way that one can dwell in Christ and Christ in him,*

which guarantees a victorious, overcoming life, is for the Cross to ever be the object of Faith and, as stated, on a daily basis).

57 As the Living Father has sent Me *("Life-giving Father")*, and I live by the Father *(speaks of the Incarnation)*: so he who eats Me, even he shall Live by Me *(proclaims the Truth that as Jesus did not live an independent life apart from the Father, so the Believer does not, and in fact cannot, live an independent life apart from Christ; we obtain and maintain this "Life" by ever looking to the Cross; the Believer never departs from the Cross; to do so is to invite spiritual wreckage [Gal. 2:20]).*

58 This is that Bread which came down from Heaven *(once again points to Himself, and extols the outsized superiority over the Law, etc.)*: not as your fathers did eat Manna, and are dead *(makes the comparison between that bread, a mere symbol of the True Bread which was to come, and the True Bread which now has come)*: he who eats of this Bread shall live for ever *(He Alone, as the True Bread of Life, could give Eternal Life, but one had to "eat of this Bread" in order to have this Life, which means to accept Him as for Who He is and What He would do, which speaks of Calvary).*

59 These things said He in the Synagogue, as He taught in Capernaum.

60 Many therefore of His Disciples, when they had heard *this (spoke of those other than the Twelve)*, said, This is an hard saying; who can hear it? *(They were unwilling to accept the bloody death of their Messiah, or to entrust themselves to a Divine Personality Whose most distinctive act would be His Sacrifice of Himself. This was the gross and terrible offence which made the Cross a stumblingblock to the Jews [Mat. 16:21; I Cor. 1:23; Gal. 5:11].)*

61 When Jesus knew in Himself that His Disciples murmured at it *(registered unbelief)*, He said unto them, Does this offend you? *(In fact, the Cross is an offence to the entirety of the world, and regrettably even most of the Church [Gal. 5:11].)*

62 *What* and if you shall see the Son of Man ascend up where He was before? *(Jesus points out that if His Death were a stumblingblock to them, how much more would be His Resurrection? But would not that prove the reality and value of His Death, and the depth of their unbelief?)*

63 It is the Spirit Who quickens *(the Holy Spirit)*; the flesh profits nothing *(in effect, says, "If you could literally eat My Flesh, and drink My Blood, it would not save your souls"; the word "flesh" as it is used here speaks of man's efforts, whatever they might be, apart from Christ and the Cross)*: the words that I speak unto you, *they* are spirit, and *they* are Life *(of the Holy Spirit, Who gives Life by and through the Finished Work of Christ).*

64 But there are some of you who believe not *(they did not believe what He said about Himself, which referred to the Cross; millions presently in the Church fall into the same category).* For Jesus knew from the beginning who they were who believed not *(not the individuals per se, but rather that which would occasion their unbelief)*, and who should betray Him *(it is speaking here of Judas Iscariot and the occasion of His betrayal, which was the Cross).*

65 And He said, Therefore said I unto you, that no man can come unto Me, except it were given unto him of My Father *(the invitation is to "whosoever will"; however, if the person rejects the Cross, the Father Commands the Holy Spirit to bar all entrance [Eph. 2:18]).*

66 From that *time* many of His Disciples went back, and walked no more with Him *(the claims of Christ were so profoundly different from what they anticipated that they now refused to accept Him at all!).*

PETER'S CONFESSION

67 Then said Jesus unto the Twelve, Will you also go away? *(The defection of these former Disciples must have deeply pained the Lord's Heart. His question to the original Twelve abrogates the Doctrine of Unconditional Eternal Security. In fact, Judas did go away.)*

68 Then Simon Peter answered Him, Lord, to whom shall we go? *(This presents the Apostle for the second time confessing Who Jesus is, but in more emphatic language.)* You have the words of Eternal Life *(other than Judas, they believed what He said).*

69 And we believe and are sure that You are that Christ, the Son of the Living God *(we have believed, and have got to know [have learned by experience] that you are the Messiah, the Son of the Living God).*

70 Jesus answered them, Have not I chosen you Twelve *(proclaims far more than random selection, but rather specific direction as given to Him by the Father)*, and one of you is a devil? *(Jesus chose Judas, and Judas as well at first chose Christ; however, Judas' choice was turned by unbelief as it has been with millions.)*

71 He spoke of Judas Iscariot *the son* of Simon (*means that he was "a man of Kerioth," a place in Judah [Josh. 15:25]; as far as is known, he was the only one of the Twelve who came from Judah, the Tribe of Jesus*): for he it was who should betray Him, being one of the Twelve (*it is said in this manner because the Holy Spirit will have all know what Judas threw away; it seems that with this Message as delivered by Christ, the Message of the Cross, rebellion began in Judas' heart*).

CHAPTER 7
(A.D. 32)
THE FEAST OF TABERNACLES

AFTER these things Jesus walked in Galilee (*covers a span of approximately six months, from the Passover in April to the Feast of Tabernacles in October*): for He would not walk in Jewry, because the Jews sought to kill Him (*spoke of Jerusalem and Judaea; these were the religious leaders of the nation, and are to be distinguished from the multitude of the people*).

2 Now the Jews' Feast of Tabernacles was at hand.

3 His brethren therefore said unto Him (*refers to James, Joseph, Simon, and Jude [Mat. 13:55]*), Depart hence, and go into Judaea, that Your Disciples also may see the works that You do (*a proclamation of sarcasm; by the use of the Word, "Your Disciples," they were saying that they [His Brothers] are not His Disciples, and want all to know that they have no association with His group*).

4 For *there is* no man *who* does any thing in secret, and he himself seeks to be known openly (*they knew full well the animosity of the religious leaders against Jesus; so they cannot help but know that He would be greatly exposing Himself if He went there at this time*). If You do these things, show yourself to the world (*very similar to the temptations offered by Satan in the wilderness [Mat. 4:1-11]*).

5 For neither did His brethren believe in Him (*had His mother, brothers, and sisters presented themselves as moral lepers for cleansing from their sins, they would have learned Who and What He was, for knowledge of spiritual realities only reaches the soul through a sin-convicted heart, not through a religious intellect*).

6 Then Jesus said unto them, My time is not yet come (*He was speaking of the time of His Crucifixion, which would take place in about six months; they did not understand this, and neither did His closest Disciples*): but your time is always ready (*His statement proclaims that their ideas were akin to the world, and hence the Devil*).

7 The world cannot hate you (*their thinking at that time was in line with the thinking of the world, which was of Satan*); but Me it hates (*the world of religion*), because I testify of it, that the works thereof are evil (*pertains mostly to anything in the religious sense which is not Scriptural*).

8 Go ye up unto this Feast (*pertains to the fact that most of the people who attended this Feast little understood its true spiritual meaning*): I go not up yet unto this Feast; for My time is not yet full come (*His time for fulfilling what this Feast represented had not yet come, and will not come until the Millennium*).

9 When He had said these words unto them, He abode *still* in Galilee (*waited there two or three days before He finally went to Jerusalem*).

10 But when His brethren were gone up, then went He also up unto the Feast (*insinuates that Jesus did not want to travel with His brethren, considering their hostility, even though His other reasons for delay were far weightier*), not openly, but as it were in secret (*proclaimed such being done for particular reasons*).

11 Then the Jews sought Him at the Feast, and said, Where is He? (*This speaks of the religious hierarchy of Israel. To be sure, they were not seeking Him for the right reasons.*)

12 And there was much murmuring among the people concerning Him (*pertained to both negative and positive remarks*): for some said, He is a good man: others said, No; but He deceives the people (*the latter group no doubt was attempting to curry favor with the religious leaders of Israel, whom they knew were in opposition to Christ*).

13 Howbeit no man spoke openly of Him (*spoke favorably*) for fear of the Jews.

THE TEMPLE

14 Now about the midst of the Feast Jesus went up into the Temple, and taught.

15 And the Jews marveled (*spoke of the ruling and learned class*), saying, How knows this man letters, having never learned? (*This spoke of the great theological schools in Jerusalem. In spite of their opposition to Him, the immediate effect of His Message was great astonishment. Despite themselves, they were moved by what He said and how He said it.*)

16 Jesus answered them, and said, My Doctrine is not Mine, but His who sent Me *(presents a far greater claim than any of the Prophets of Old; in other words, His Doctrine is of God).*

17 If any man will do His Will *(is willing to do God's Will),* he shall know of the Doctrine, whether it be of God, or *whether* I speak of Myself *(if you truly know God, and are striving to do His Will, you will instantly recognize My Words as Truth, thereby knowing them to be from God).*

18 He who speaks of himself seeks his own glory *(refers to those who speak words of man's origin, whether of themselves or others)*: but he who seeks His glory Who sent him *(seeks to bring glory to God),* the same is true, and no unrighteousness is in Him *(Christ is saying that He is True and Righteous because He seeks that all Glory go to God).*

19 Did not Moses give you the Law, and *yet* none of you keep the Law? *(The idea is that they claimed they did keep the Law, and Jesus in effect is calling them liars to their faces.)* Why go you about to kill Me? *(This was in itself an indictment against their claims of Law-keeping, inasmuch as the Law forbade murder.)*

20 The people answered and said, You have a devil *(these were the people, and not the religious leaders)*: who goes about to kill You? *(They were ignorant of the plot, and so were astonished at His statement.)*

21 Jesus answered and said unto them, I have done one work, and you all marvel *(He was speaking of a healing of a man on the Sabbath, which was done about a year and a half previous; more than likely, the religious leaders had brought up the subject).*

22 Moses therefore gave unto you Circumcision *(means that the Lord told Moses to include Circumcision in the Law)*; (not because it is of Moses, but of the fathers;) *(means that it actually had its beginning with Abraham [Gen. 17:9-14])* and you on the Sabbath Day circumcise a man *(Jesus is pointing out that if Circumcision was lawful on the Sabbath Day, how much more lawful is an action which benefited a person greatly, such as healing).*

23 If a man on the Sabbath Day receive Circumcision, that the Law of Moses should not be broken; are you angry at Me, because I have made a man every whit whole on the Sabbath Day? *(The question meant that Jesus, Who was actually the fulfillment of these Laws, and to Whom they originally pointed, had done the very things these Laws symbolized, but could not perform.)*

24 Judge not according to the appearance *(in effect, says, "if you think you have not violated the Sabbath in Circumcision, then how can you think I broke the Sabbath when I healed one of you who had been helpless for thirty-eight years?"),* but judge righteous judgment *(says that Judgment must be rendered according to the whole Word of God, and not merely by taking a part and perverting it to one's own satisfaction).*

25 Then said some of them of Jerusalem *(concerned natives of that city),* Is not this He, Whom they seek to kill? *(This means that the plot to kill Jesus by the religious authorities was not a complete secret, at least to those in Jerusalem.)*

26 But, lo, He speaks boldly, and they say nothing unto Him *(Christ didn't pull any punches, and the rulers at this time said nothing to Him simply because of the massive crowds listening to Him).* Do the rulers know indeed that this is the very Christ? *(This proclaims how widespread and how detailed the idea of the Coming Christ was.)*

27 Howbeit we know this man whence He is *(this is said in a negative sense; they are meaning that they knew His parentage, the place of His early life, etc.; they gave Him no respect)*: but when Christ comes, no man knows whence He is *(proclaims a common error of that time concerning the Messiah; the Bible taught the very opposite).*

28 Then cried Jesus in the Temple as He taught, saying, You both know Me, and you know whence I am *(in effect says, "you think you know Me, and where I come from, but you actually do not")*: and I am not come of Myself, but He Who sent Me is true *(in effect says, "you know Me as Jesus of Nazareth; and yet you do not know Me, for you do not know Him Who sent Me; but I am from Him and He did send Me"),* Whom you know not *(despite all their claims and great display of religion, He plainly tells them that they do not know God).*

29 But I know Him *(They were of the same essence)*: for I am from Him, and He has sent Me *(means that He is from the Father in a unique way and position, as were no Prophets or Angels).*

30 Then they sought to take Him *(these were the religious leaders of Israel, and they were so incensed, so angry, and so empowered by Satan that they hated Him)*: but no man laid hands on Him, because His hour was not yet come *(the Holy Spirit orchestrated events in holding back these jackals; it was not yet the time that*

Jesus should be Crucified, that coming about six months later).

31 And many of the people believed on Him *(did not refer at all to the religious authorities, but instead to the crowds gathered for the Feast of Tabernacles, who had come from all over Israel and even other parts of the Roman Empire),* and said, When Christ comes, will He do more miracles than these which this *Man* has done? *(The evidence of the Power of God in delivering people was obvious to all. Consequently, the religious leaders are now on the horns of a dilemma.)*

32 The Pharisees heard that the people murmured such things concerning Him *(constituted a different group than the rulers, but equally opposed to Him)*; and the Pharisees and the Chief Priests sent officers to take Him *(proclaims these two groups as joining forces against Him).*

33 Then said Jesus unto them, Yet a little while am I with you *(in effect, Jesus is saying that in about six months, which would actually be at the next Passover, He would become the Passover Lamb for all men),* and *then* I go unto Him Who sent Me *(back to God the Father, which He did do!).*

34 You shall seek Me, and shall not find *Me (refers to the time when they would desperately need Him, which would be about thirty-seven years in the future when Titus would destroy their city and the very Temple in which they now stand)*: and where I am, *there* you cannot come *(actually means that they can come now, but they will not do so because of their unbelief and rebellion).*

35 Then said the Jews among themselves, Where will He go, that we shall not find Him? *(This presents minds that are darkened by unbelief and are, therefore, putting ironical and confusing meanings into His Words, in order to pour an air of contempt over His reply.)* will He go unto the dispersed among the Gentiles, and teach the Gentiles? *(Their question constituted the utter scorn of the Jewish mind for a pseudo Messiah Who, failing with His Own People and here in the Courts of the Lord's House, would instead turn to the Gentiles. However, even though they meant it as the insult of all insults, still they were far closer to the Truth than they ever would dare realize.)*

36 What *manner of* saying is this that He said, You shall seek Me, and shall not find *Me:* and where I am, *there* you cannot come? *(By the very tenor of its construction, their sarcasm*

proclaims the spiritual meaning to be completely lost on them.)

THE FEAST

37 In the last day, that great *day* of the Feast *(spoke of the eighth day of the Feast of Tabernacles),* Jesus stood and cried, saying, If any man thirst, let him come unto Me, and drink *(presents the greatest invitation ever given to mortal man).*

38 He who believes on Me *(it is "not doing," but rather, "believing"),* as the Scripture has said *(refers to the Word of God being the story of Christ and Him Crucified; all the Sacrifices pointed to Christ and what He would do at the Cross, as well as the entirety of the Tabernacle and Temple and all their appointments),* out of his belly *(innermost being)* shall flow rivers of Living Water *(speaks of Christ directly, and Believers indirectly).*

39 (But this spoke He of the Spirit *(Holy Spirit),* which they who believe on Him should receive *(it would begin on the Day of Pentecost)*: for the Holy Spirit was not yet *given (He has now been given)*; because that Jesus was not yet glorified.) *(The time of which John wrote was shortly before the Crucifixion. When Jesus died on the Cross and was Resurrected three days later, He was raised with a Glorified Body, which was one of the signs that all sin had been atoned, now making it possible for the Holy Spirit to come in a new dimension.)*

DIVISION

40 Many of the people therefore, when they heard this saying, said *(as the Temple Mount was thronged with people at that time, many hundreds heard what Jesus said, and as well felt the power of what He said),* Of a truth this is the Prophet *(probably refers to Deut. 18:15).*

41 Others said, This is the Christ *(this means "The Anointed," which alone, at least in this fashion, spoke of the Messiah).* But some said, Shall Christ come out of Galilee? *(This proclaims that they did not Scripturally connect Galilee with the Messiah. They evidently were overlooking the remarkable prediction in Isa. 9:1.)*

42 Has not the Scripture said, That Christ comes of the Seed of David, and out of the town of Bethlehem, where David was? *(Christ was of the Seed of David, and was born in Bethlehem. However, it seems that they somewhat misunderstood Micah's prediction, thinking that*

the Messiah would make this little village his home. The Prophet Micah did not say that!)

43 So there was a division among the people because of Him (the "division" was caused by a lack of understanding of the Scriptures, plus a desire on the part of some to win the approval of the religious leaders [Jn. 7:48]).

44 And some of them would have taken Him (would have arrested Him); but no man laid hands on Him (evidently they were stopped in some manner by the Holy Spirit).

45 Then came the officers to the Chief Priests and Pharisees (the officers who had been sent to arrest Him, as outlined in Verse 32); and they said unto them (said to the officers), Why have you not brought Him? (This means that they had firmly intended that He be arrested.)

46 The officers answered, Never man spoke like this Man (it was the Holy Spirit they were feeling and sensing, although they little understood that, if at all!).

47 Then answered them the Pharisees (seems to indicate that these men were the leading spirits in this assault upon Jesus), Are you also deceived? (Even though this was directed to these officers, it was in reality their problem.)

48 Have any of the rulers or of the Pharisees believed on Him? (The Pharisees asked this question of these officers.)

49 But this people who know not the Law are cursed (should have been translated, "but this ignorant rabble, in speaking of the people, unlearned in the Law, are a cursed set"; this is what the religious leaders thought of the people!).

50 Nicodemus said unto them (presents this vaunted member of the Sanhedrin, who incidentally greatly outranked the Pharisees, now speaking up for Jesus), (he who came to Jesus by night, being one of them,) (This refers back some three years earlier. He was one of the rulers.)

51 Does our Law judge any man, before it hear him, and know what he does? (Although feeble and timid as was the plea of Nicodemus, yet was it precious to the Lord, and so is honorably recorded here by the Holy Spirit.)

52 They answered and said unto him (to Nicodemus), Are you also of Galilee? Search, and look: for out of Galilee arises no Prophet (they failed to check out the facts; Jesus was born in Bethlehem, not Galilee; also, had they searched the Scriptures, they would have found that Jonah, Hosea, Elijah, Elisha, and others were from the Northern Kingdom and not from Judaea).

53 And every man went unto his own house (even though these men had houses to which

they could retire, Jesus had no place to lay His Head; so the next Verse says that He "went unto the Mount of Olives").

CHAPTER 8
(A.D. 32)
ADULTERY

JESUS went unto the Mount of Olives (there, out in the open, He spent the night).

2 And early in the morning He came again into the Temple (speaks of daybreak), and all the people came unto Him; and He sat down, and taught them (proclaims Him revealing Himself as the "Word of God," the "Light of the World," and "Eternal Life"; this Chapter, plus those following will record His rejection in all these relationships).

3 And the Scribes and Pharisees brought unto him a woman taken in adultery (in the Greek, it means that she was "dragged by main force"); and when they had set her in the midst (proclaims the results of self-righteousness; they would subject her to great shame, caring not at all about her feelings),

4 They say unto Him, Master (was not meant at all as a term of endearment; they were merely referring to Him as a "teacher"), this woman was taken in adultery, in the very act (why wasn't the man brought as well?).

5 Now Moses in the Law commanded us, that such should be stoned (was true, but for both the man and the woman [Lev. 20:10]): but what do You say? (In fact, His answer alone matters, and will always be according to the Word; therefore, how did He obey the Law, and at the same time, let her go free?)

6 This they said, tempting Him, that they might have to accuse Him (it was a trap!). But Jesus stooped down, and with His finger wrote on the ground, as though He heard them not (actually meant that He wrote in the dust on the stone, for the Temple Court was paved; what did He write? had the Holy Spirit desired that we know, He would have told us; He may have written what He momentarily said to them).

7 So when they continued asking Him (means they pressed the issue, demanding an answer), He lifted up Himself, and said unto them, He who is without sin among you, let him first cast a stone at her (now turns the tables from her, and Him for that matter, onto the accusers; they didn't expect this!).

8 And again He stooped down, and wrote on the ground (once again, we aren't told what

He wrote).

9 And they which heard *it*, being convicted by *their own* conscience (*tells us that their position was so spiritually and morally untenable that they could only vacate the premises*), went out one by one, beginning at the eldest, *even* unto the last (*portrays them one by one dropping the stones held in their hands, and quietly retiring away from this Awful Presence*): and Jesus was left alone, and the woman standing in the midst (*probably presented her continuing to cower in shame and mortal fear*).

10 When Jesus had lifted up Himself, and saw none but the woman, He said unto her (*the accusers were gone, with the great multitude continuing to observe the proceedings*), Woman, where are those your accusers? has no man condemned you? (*This actually means that none are qualified to "accuse."*)

11 She said, No man, Lord (*by her calling Him "Lord," she had made Him her Salvation*). And Jesus said unto her, Neither do I condemn you: go, and sin no more (*records the sweetest words she had ever heard in all her life; He kept the Law perfectly by dying in her place, exactly as He did with all of us; that's how He could let her go free, as well as you and me*).

THE LIGHT OF THE WORLD

12 Then spoke Jesus again unto them, saying, I am the Light of the world (*He is the Light of the World, because He is the Source of its Life*): he who follows Me shall not walk in darkness, but shall have the Light of Life (*in effect, says that all who do not follow Jesus, walk in darkness*).

13 The Pharisees therefore said unto Him, You bear record of Yourself; Your record is not true (*brings up the same argument used in Chapter 5*).

14 Jesus answered and said unto them, Though I bear record of Myself, *yet* My record is true (*as He now nears the end of His Ministry, He no longer placates the Pharisees as He did in Chapter 5, but rather uses Himself as a Witness; He did not do this in Chapter 5, but He was certainly entitled to have done so*): for I know from where I came, and where I go (*proclaims His Deity*); but you cannot tell from where I come, and where I go (*is freighted with meaning respecting their unbelief*).

15 You judge after the flesh (*has reference to His Incarnation; they were of the flesh, which means that they did not understand spiritual things, and so they judged everything after the flesh*); I judge no man (*simply means that He did not come to Judge, but rather to Save*).

16 And yet if I judge, My judgment is true (*means that His previous statement of "judging no man" is not in any way meant to abrogate His position as the ultimate Judge of all men, but simply that this was not His Mission at present!*): for I am not alone, but I and the Father Who sent Me (*places an entirely different perspective on the claims of Christ; in effect, He is saying that any judgment rendered does not rest on mere human consciousness, but rather on the infallible decisions of God the Father*).

17 It is also written in your Law, that the testimony of two men is true (*is derived from Deut. 17:6; 19:15; Jesus is merely saying that upon the common principles of jurisprudence as laid down in the Law of Moses, He is willing to rest His claim*).

18 I am One who bears witness of Myself (*reflects His Own Divine self-consciousness*), and the Father Who sent Me bears witness of Me (*did so through the miracles and healings, etc.*).

19 Then said they unto Him, Where is Your Father? (*They did not ask: "Who is He?" or "What is He?" Rather, "Where is He?" is asked with acute sarcasm!*) Jesus answered, You neither know Me, nor My Father (*bluntly He tells them that they are without God, and consequently without hope!*): if you had known Me, You should have known My Father also (*another utterance, implying the most intimate relation between Himself and the Father*).

20 These words spoke Jesus in the treasury, as He taught in the Temple (*where He stood teaching were two colossal golden Lampstands on which hung a multitude of lamps that were lit during the Feast of Tabernacles, and around which the people danced with great rejoicing; as He stands in the midst of these lamps, He declares Himself the "Light of Life," as proclaimed in Verse 12*): and no man laid hands on Him; for His hour was not yet come (*no one had any power over Him in any capacity, save only that which was given them by the Father*).

21 Then said Jesus again unto them, I go My way, and you shall seek Me (*refers to the fact that they had rejected Him, and would consequently continue to look for a Messiah, but obviously in vain!*), and shall die in your sins (*one of the most sobering statements ever made by our Lord; from then until now, they have died in their sins, because they rejected Him*): Where I go, you cannot come (*proclaims His*

departure to the Father by a blood-stained pathway by means of a violent death, but a death which would liberate mankind, at least those who will believe).

22 Then said the Jews, Will He kill Himself? (This query was one of harsh mockery, and its hurtful intent can hardly be exaggerated.) Because He said, Where I go, you cannot come (they had no spiritual understanding, so they did not comprehend what He said in the least).

23 And He said unto them, you are from beneath (meaning that they were of Satan); I am from above (speaks of Heaven): you are of this world; I am not of this world (in effect, says that they are lost without God, because they would not accept Him Who Alone could save them).

24 I said therefore unto you, that you shall die in your sins (to be sure, this type of preaching arouses great animosity and even hatred on the part of those to whom such words are delivered): for if you believe not that I am *He*, you shall die in your sins (states the reason, and in no uncertain terms, for their spiritual depravity).

25 Then said they unto Him, Who are You? (This, in effect, says, "Who are You to deal out threats to us like this?") And Jesus said unto them, Even *the same* that I said unto you from the beginning (the beginning of this Message, referring to Verse 12).

26 I have many things to say and to judge of you (even though they dismissed His Words as inconsequential, the bitter consequences would be reaped nonetheless; their treatment of Him and Him Alone decided their destiny, as it does every man): but He Who sent Me is true (as God is true, so is Christ); and I speak to the world those things which I have heard of Him (he who accepts Christ accepts God the Father, and He Who rejects Christ rejects God the Father).

27 They understood not that He spoke to them of the Father (not knowing the Son, speaks loudly that they did not know the Father as well).

28 Then said Jesus unto them, When you have lifted up the Son of Man (speaks of the Cross), then shall you know that I am *He* (that time has not even yet arrived, but will take place at the Second Coming when they look upon Him Whom they have pierced [Zech. 12:10; Rev. 1:7]), and *that* I do nothing of Myself (Christ was led totally by the Holy Spirit); but as My Father has taught Me, I speak these things (even though He was God, still He was also Man, and functioned totally as a Man while on this Earth;

as such, He had to learn exactly as we do).

29 And He Who sent Me is with Me (speaks of a union that is beyond comprehension to mere mortals; He and the Father were indivisible; they were of the same essence): the Father has not left Me alone (the Holy Spirit was constantly with Christ); for I do always those things that please Him (Christ pleased the Father without fail, which no other human being can say).

ABRAHAM

30 As He spoke these words, many believed on Him (their Faith, as we shall see, was misplaced and unacceptable!).

31 Then said Jesus to those Jews which believed on Him (now presents a part of the Message upon which their Faith will falter; thus resides millions!), If you continue in My word, *then* are you My Disciples indeed (simply means that one has to believe all the Word, not just part, and then continue in that believing; regrettably, as the Parable of the Sower points out, many do not continue to believe; consequently, this refutes the Unscriptural Doctrine of Unconditional Eternal Security);

32 And you shall know the Truth, and the Truth shall make you free (this is the secret of all abundant Life in Christ; the "Truth" is "Jesus Christ and Him Crucified," which alone is the answer to the problems of Man).

33 They answered Him, We be Abraham's seed, and were never in bondage to any man (proclaims an ironical statement, inasmuch as they had been in bondage to the Egyptians, the Assyrians, the Babylonians, the Persians, the Greeks, and were even now in bondage to the Romans): why do You say, you shall be made free? (This proclaims them not seeing nor admitting their true spiritual condition, which Jesus will now readily address.)

34 Jesus answered them, Verily, verily, I say unto you, Whosoever commits sin is the servant of sin (and whosoever is the servant of sin is not free; there's only one way for the Believer to overcome sin, and that is the Cross of Christ ever being the object of our Faith [Gal. 6:14]).

35 And the servant abides not in the house for ever (the servant of sin will ultimately be cast out of the house, i.e., "out of the Kingdom of God"): *but* the Son abideth ever (whosoever abides in the Son, will abide in the house; otherwise, he will be cast out).

36 If the Son therefore shall make you free (Christ Alone can make one free, and He does so

through and by what He did at the Cross, and our Faith in that Finished Work), **you shall be free indeed** *(a freedom which the world cannot give, and in fact doesn't even understand)*.

37 I know that you are Abraham's seed *(in effect, Jesus is saying that being "Abraham's Seed" by physical birth contains no Salvation)*; **but you seek to kill Me** *(this completely negated their spiritual claims)*, **because My Word has no place in you** *(signifies the reason for their murderous hearts, despite their claims)*.

38 I speak that which I have seen with My Father *(again and again Christ reiterates the fact that He did only the Father's Will)*: **and you do that which you have seen with your father** *(signifying that their father was the Devil, despite their religious claims)*.

39 They answered and said unto Him, Abraham is our father *(was true according to the flesh, but not true spiritually)*. **Jesus said unto them, If you were Abraham's children** *(spiritual children)*, **you would do the works of Abraham** *(means that Abraham loved God, had Faith in God, and longingly looked for God's Son, Who would ultimately come)*.

40 But now you seek to kill Me *(that He could know their hearts should have told them Who He actually was)*, **a Man Who has told you the truth** *(presents the first and only time that Jesus referred to Himself in this fashion; He did so to mark the contrast between Himself and the "man-slayer" of Jn. 8:44; "murderer" is "man-slayer" in the Greek Text; Jesus is a "Man-saver," while Satan is a "man-slayer")*, **which I have heard of God** *(the very highest representation of the very conception of a Divine Commission, and a Divine Message)*: **this did not Abraham** *(proclaims the fact that while they may be Abraham's "seed," they were not his children, and he in this sense could not be their "father")*.

41 You do the deeds of your father *(while claiming to be Abraham's seed, they were not doing the deeds of Abraham, but rather the Devil)*. **Then said they to Him, We be not born of fornication** *(has reference to the false worship and idolatry that so often characterized Israel of old; as well, they may, at the same time, have been accusing Jesus of having been thusly born)*; **we have one Father, even God** *(presents the proud claim made still by those who are morally the children of Satan, even as untold millions do presently)*.

42 Jesus said unto them, If God were your Father, you would love Me *(Jesus Alone is the yard stick)*: **for I proceeded forth and came from God** *(He Alone has done this, with no other able to say such a thing)*; **neither came I of Myself, but He sent Me** *(places the entirety of the Godhead in unison respecting the Redemption of mankind, and concerning that which Jesus would do)*.

43 Why do ye not understand My speech? *(The unconverted man cannot understand the Word of the Lord [I Cor. 3:14].)* **even because you cannot hear My Word** *(they heard it physically, but did not hear it spiritually because they did not know the Lord)*.

44 You are of your father the Devil, and the lusts of your father you will do *(presents the Lord repudiating in terrible language the spiritual claims made by these Jews respecting their association with Jehovah; this is the cause of all the problems in the world)*. **He was a murderer from the beginning** *(refers to the fact that Satan originated sin, and sin brings forth death)*, **and abode not in the truth** *(it means he was actually in truth, for a time, until he rebelled against God)*, **because there is no truth in him** *(no truth in him since his rebellion)*. **When he speaks a lie, he speaks of his own: for he is a liar, and the father of it** *(Satan is the originator of the "lie"; consequently, his entire kingdom of darkness, in totality, is built on the "lie")*.

45 And because I tell you the truth, you believe Me not *(truth can only be believed and accepted by one's Faith being exclusively in Christ, and the price He paid on the Cross)*.

46 Which of you convinces Me of sin? *(They could not point to any sin that He had committed, so that alone should have told them Who He was.)* **And if I say the truth, why do you not believe Me?** *(They didn't believe Him because they were not of God. This clearly and plainly showed them up for what they really were.)*

47 He who is of God hears God's Words *(could be said, "the closer to God one is, the more one hears and abides by the Word of God")*: **you therefore hear them not, because you are not of God** *(this is the reason for so much error in the modern Church; most aren't of God!)*.

DECLARATION

48 Then answered the Jews, and said unto Him, Say we not well that You are a Samaritan, and have a devil? *(Calling Him a "Samaritan" was the grossest insult they could level at anyone. So, they were saying that His Doctrine was as the Samaritans — false, corrupt, and in effect, a lie.)*

49 Jesus answered, I have not a devil *(presents Him making a simple denial, and taking no notice of the charge of being a Samaritan)*; but I honour My Father, and you do dishonour Me *(in effect, says that by dishonoring Him, they were dishonoring the Father as well, Whom they claimed to serve).*

50 And I seek not My Own glory *(in effect, says that He didn't come to this Earth for "Glory," but rather to Redeem mankind)*: there is One who seeks and judges *(actually means that God sought Glory for Jesus, and Judged Him worthy of Glory).*

51 Verily, verily, I say unto you, If a man keep My saying, he shall never see death *(means that he shall not see spiritual or eternal death).*

52 Then said the Jews unto Him, Now we know that You have a devil *(they were denying Him Who Alone could give Life!)*. Abraham is dead, and the Prophets *(portrays a total lack of understanding of what He had said; while these men were dead physically, they were very much alive spiritually, and actually in Paradise at that very moment)*; and You say, If a man keep My saying, he shall never taste of death *(they changed what He said by inserting the word "taste" in place of the word "see"; they had reduced His statement from the spiritual to the physical).*

53 Are You greater than our father Abraham, which is dead? and the Prophets are dead *(yes, He is greater than all of these!)*: what do You make Yourself? *(He didn't make anything of Himself as the Man Christ Jesus! God made Him what He was.)*

54 Jesus answered, If I honour Myself, My honour is nothing *(He now addresses Himself to their question)*: it is My Father Who honors Me *(His answer should have given them room for pause)*; of Whom you say, that He is your God *(He has repeatedly stated in every way possible that if they truly knew God, they would know Him)*:

55 Yet you have not known Him *(is blunt, and speaks exactly the Truth)*; but I know Him *(as no one has ever known Him)*: and if I should say, I know Him not, I shall be a liar like unto you *(as is painfully obvious, Jesus pulled no punches)*: but I know Him, and keep His saying *(which is in contrast to these religious leaders).*

56 Your father Abraham rejoiced to see My day: and he saw *it*, and was glad *(in the great Revelation of Justification by Faith given to Abraham by God, he was made to understand that this great Redemption Plan was wrapped up, not in a philosophy, but rather a Man, the Man Christ Jesus, and what He would do at the Cross; the Patriarch rejoiced in that).*

57 Then said the Jews unto Him, You are not yet fifty years old *(the Jews at that time believed that a man did not reach full maturity, regarding wisdom and intellect, until fifty years old)*, and have You seen Abraham? *(They were either misinterpreting His Words, or they in fact did understand what He said, but did not believe Him, consequently answering sarcastically.)*

58 Jesus said unto them, Verily, verily, I say unto you, Before Abraham was, I am *(in essence He said, "Before Abraham was brought into being, I was eternally existent"; He also said, "Abraham was," "I am").*

59 Then took they up stones to cast at Him *(presents their response to their Messiah)*: but Jesus hid Himself, and went out of the Temple, going through the midst of them, and so passed by *(means that He slowly walked through them and went on His way, with them doing nothing; thus was the response of the religious leaders of Israel to their Messiah!).*

CHAPTER 9
(A.D. 32)
BORN BLIND

AND as *Jesus* passed by, He saw a man which was blind from *his* birth *(proclaims the only instance of such a healing being recorded; this is a picture of humanity born in sin, consequently spiritually blind from birth).*

2 And His Disciples asked Him, saying, Master, who did sin, this man, or his parents, that he was born blind? *(Many believed, as evidenced by the question of the Disciples, that every peculiar disaster pointed to some special or particular sin. It seems they had not learned much from the Book of Job, which repudiates this type of thinking.)*

3 Jesus answered, Neither has this man sinned, nor his parents *(does not mean that our Lord asserts these people are sinless, but rather severs the supposed link between their conduct and the specific affliction before us)*: but that the Works of God should be made manifest in Him *(means that Jesus did not come to the Earth to condemn men for their fallen condition because in fact they are already condemned; He came to set man free by the Power of God).*

4 I must work the Works of Him Who sent Me *("We" should be substituted for "I," simply because these works are meant to be continued

by all who follow Christ), while it is day *(this life span)*: the night comes, when no man can work *(refers to the end of this life span).*

5 As long as I am in the world *(the span of His earthly Ministry)*, I am the Light of the world *(proclaims Jesus as sublimely conscious of His Power to do for the moral world what the Sun was doing for the physical world).*

6 When He had thus spoken, He spat on the ground, and made clay of the spittle *(is meant to express to the morally blind eyes of men Christ in a body of lowly clay, animated by Divine Breath; the clay symbolized His Humanity, and the moisture of His Lips the life that animated it)*, and He anointed the eyes of the blind man with the clay *(was meant to serve as a symbol of the human Body of Christ serving as the Perfect Sacrifice for sin)*,

7 And said unto him, Go, wash in the pool of Siloam *(symbolizing the shed Blood of Christ, which cleanses from all sin)*, (which is by interpretation, Sent.) *(This refers to Jesus being sent from God for the Salvation of the world.)* He went his way therefore, and washed, and came seeing *(spiritually refers to all who are washed in the precious shed Blood of the Lord Jesus Christ; only then can we "see").*

8 The neighbours therefore, and they which before had seen him who was blind, said *(proclaims those who personally knew Him, witnessing the miraculous change which had taken place)*, Is not this he who sat and begged? *(He would beg no more.)*

9 Some said, This is he: others *said*, He is like him: *but* he said, I am *he (he wants everyone to know who he is, and Who performed this miracle; despite the religious leaders, he is not ashamed of Christ, neither does he fear them).*

10 Therefore said they unto him, How were your eyes opened?

11 He answered and said, A man Who is called Jesus made clay, and anointed my eyes, and said unto me, Go to the pool of Siloam, and wash *(proclaims this man repeating almost exactly what Jesus had told him to do; He began where all Disciples must, with the man, i.e., a "Man called Jesus")*: and I went and washed, and I received sight *(think of this! this man, born blind, had never seen anything, and now he can see).*

12 Then said they unto him, Where is He? *(This seems to be asked with some sarcasm.)* He said, I know not *(seems to be said with the thought in mind that even though he did not then know, he was determined to find out).*

THE PHARISEES

13 They *(seems to be those who are trying to cause trouble)* brought to the Pharisees him who aforetime was blind.

14 And it was the Sabbath Day when Jesus made the clay, and opened his eyes *(we now come to another confrontation over religious rules, which has plagued humanity almost from the beginning).*

15 Then again the Pharisees also asked him how he had received his sight. He said unto them, He put clay upon my eyes, and I washed, and do see *(it seems that this man is beginning to suspect that some charge is being trumped up against Jesus; therefore, he shrewdly omits the "saliva" and the "making of the clay," as well as the place where he had been sent to wash, which things the Pharisees claimed were the breaking of the Law of Moses).*

16 Therefore said some of the Pharisees, This man is not of God, because he keeps not the Sabbath Day *(as given in the Greek, it is especially contemptuous)*. Others said, How can a man who is a sinner do such miracles? *(This provides a dilemma for the Pharisees because the truth is that a sinner could not do such Miracles.)* And there was a division among them *(proclaims the obvious!).*

17 They say unto the blind man again, What do you say of Him, Who has opened your eyes? *(This portrays the idea as presented by the Pharisees that Jesus might have performed this miracle through the agency of demon spirits.)* He said, He is a Prophet *(having scant knowledge of Jesus, he calls Him a "Prophet" because that is the highest title he can now apply).*

18 But the Jews did not believe concerning him, that he had been blind, and received his sight *(not only do the Pharisees deny Christ, they now deny what has been obviously done, claiming they need more proof)*, until they called the parents of him who had received his sight.

19 And they asked them, saying, Is this your son, who you say was born blind? *(The question implies that they even somewhat doubted the testimony of the parents.)* how then does he now see? *(What a stupid question!)*

20 His parents answered them and said, We know that this is our son, and that he was born blind:

21 But by what means he now sees, we know not *(true, in that they only knew what their son had told them)*; or who has opened his eyes, we know not *(does not quite present all the truth;*

surely they knew it was Jesus, but experiencing the obvious animosity, they will not confess Christ): he is of age; ask him: he shall speak for himself (actually presents them distancing themselves from the Miracle and, in a sense, from their own son).

22 These *words* spoke his parents, because they feared the Jews (proclaims the man-fear which Jesus had earlier addressed): for the Jews had agreed already, that if any man did confess that He was Christ, He should be put out of the Synagogue (excommunication, which cut them off from family, from social ties, from employment, literally everything).

23 Therefore said his parents, He is of age; ask him (the Holy Spirit brings this out twice in order to highlight the position taken by the parents).

24 Then again called they the man who was blind, and said unto him, Give God the praise (implies that they want the man to repudiate Jesus; in this type of instance, to give God praise was the equivalent of swearing to tell the truth [Josh. 7:19]): we know that this man is a sinner (their blasphemy and threats did not sway the former blind man in the least!).

25 He answered and said, Whether He be a sinner *or no*, I know not (even though the translation seems to leave doubt, in the original Greek Text there is no hint of such; in effect, "you assert it, but the facts of my experience are altogether of a different kind"): one thing I know, that, whereas I was blind, now I see (pulls the attention back to the great Miracle which had been performed by Jesus; they had an argument, while he had an experience!).

26 Then said they to him again, What did He to you? (This represents the third time they have asked him how he was healed.) how opened He your eyes? (Once again, the implication is that it was done by the power of demon spirits. In effect, these religious leaders were blaspheming the Holy Spirit.)

27 He answered them, I have told you already, and you did not hear (presents a courage that few in Israel had at that time): wherefore would ye hear *it* again? (This actually says, "What is the point of telling you again?") will ye also be His Disciples? (The former blind man now uses sarcasm, and rightly so!)

28 Then they reviled him (means to vilify, to rail at, and to abuse by words), and said, You are His Disciple (presents them telling the Truth for a change); but we are Moses' disciples (despite their claims, they were no more the Disciples of

Moses than they were of Christ).

29 We know that God spoke unto Moses (that is true, but they did not at all obey what God spoke to Moses): as *for* this *fellow*, we know not from whence He is (had they truly known Moses, they would have known Christ).

30 The man answered and said unto them, Why herein is a marvellous thing, that ye know not from whence He is, and *yet* He has opened mine eyes (in effect, says, "even you ought to know that only God can open blinded eyes!").

31 Now we know that God hears not sinners (in effect, says, "we know God does not listen to the cry of sinners, when, as sinners, they ask from the ground of their sin to secure their own sinful purpose): but if any man be a worshipper of God, and does His Will, him He hears (proclaims the deepest Truth of the Divine Revelation about the conditions of acceptable prayer; it is obvious that this man had a knowledge of God that few people in Israel possessed at that time).

32 Since the world began was it not heard that any man opened the eyes of one who was born blind (portrays the magnitude of this miracle).

33 If this Man were not of God, He could do nothing (thus, the Pharisees are compelled for a few moments to hear from one known as a street beggar, words of teaching along the finest lines of a deep experience).

34 They answered and said unto him, You were altogether born in sins, and do you teach us? (The question presents them unable to answer his Scriptural charge, so they have no other weapon to use but invectiveness and persecution.) And they cast him out (means they excommunicated him from the Synagogue).

JESUS

35 Jesus heard that they had cast him out; and when He had found him, He said unto him, Do you believe on the Son of God? (Jesus is introducing Himself to this former beggar as the Messiah of Israel.)

36 He answered and said, Who is He, Lord, that I might believe on Him? (This question is asked with the idea that he already suspects Jesus is speaking of Himself!)

37 And Jesus said unto him, You have both seen Him (saw Him physically and spiritually), and it is He Who talks with you (proclaims the greatest Revelation that could ever be given to any person at any time!).

38 And he said, Lord, I believe (what did he

believe? he believed that Jesus was and is the "Son of God," the Saviour of mankind, the Redeemer of the world, the Messiah of Israel). **And he worshipped Him** (both for the great Miracle of Healing that he received, and as well the Great Salvation he has now received, which was the greatest of all).

39 **And Jesus said, For judgment I am come into this world** (what men think of Christ is the question that decides in every age their moral condition before God), **that they which see not might see** (pertains mostly to the Gentile world); **and that they which see might be made blind** (could be translated, "they which think they see, but in reality do not, and with the presentation of the Gospel, refuse to accept it, thinking they have no need of such").

40 **And** some **of the Pharisees which were with Him heard these words, and said unto Him, Are we blind also?** (This seems to have been asked in sarcasm.)

41 **Jesus said unto them, If ye were blind, ye should have no sin** (doesn't mean that the absence of light abrogates their condition as sinners; all men are sinners [Rom. 3:9-18]; Jesus is saying that if they admitted they were spiritually blind, which they were, then this particular sin of rejecting the Light would not be attributed to them): **but now you say, We see; therefore your sin remains** (therefore, they were guilty of the terrible sin of refusing the True Light, which meant that the Light they did have would be taken away, with them being left totally "blind" in the spiritual sense).

CHAPTER 10
(A.D. 32)
THE GOOD SHEPHERD

VERILY, verily, I say unto you, He who enters not by the door into the sheepfold (proclaims to us that there is a "door," and in fact only one "door!"), **but climbs up some other way, the same is a thief and a robber** (using a "way" other than Christ; He Alone is the Door).

2 **But he who enters in by the Door** (Way) **is the Shepherd of the sheep** (Jesus Alone is the True Shepherd).

3 **To Him the porter opens** (means that the Law, the Doorkeeper, immediately admitted Him because He had perfectly kept the Law, and actually was the only One Who had done such a thing); **and the sheep hear His voice** (means that True sheep hear the Voice of the True Shepherd): **and He calls His Own sheep by name**

(this speaks of relationship which Salvation automatically brings), **and leads them out** (speaks of finding suitable pasture; the one who truly wants to know the Word of God will be led into all Truth [Jn. 16:13]).

4 **And when He puts forth His Own sheep** (He is Owner as well as Shepherd of the sheep, and has, therefore, so to speak, a double love for us), **He goes before them** (He has planned everything), **and the sheep follow Him: for they know His voice** (the true heart will know His Voice, and the false heart will follow others).

5 **And a stranger will they not follow, but will flee from him** (refers to "thieves and robbers, and false prophets" [Mat. 7:15-20]): **for they know not the voice of strangers** (true sheep cannot be deceived).

6 **This Parable spoke Jesus unto them: but they understood not what things they were which He spoke unto them** (the Pharisees did not understand because they were not true sheep).

EXPLANATION

7 **Then said Jesus unto them again, Verily, verily, I say unto you, I am the Door of the sheep** ("I am," exclusive of all others! there is only "One Door," and that "Door" is Christ).

8 **All who ever came before Me are thieves and robbers** (pertains to any and all before or after Christ, who claim to have the way of Salvation without Christ!): **but the sheep did not hear them** (true sheep cannot be deceived).

9 **I am the Door** (presents an emphatic statement; the Church is not the door to Christ, as the Catholics teach, but Christ is the Door to the Church): **by Me if any man enter in, he shall be saved** (as the "Door," Jesus is the "Saviour"), **and shall go in and out, and find pasture** (they went in for safety and went out for pasture).

10 **The thief comes not, but for to steal, and to kill, and to destroy** (speaks of Satan and his emissaries who peddle a false way of Salvation): **I am come that they might have life, and that they might have** it **more abundantly** (the Source of this "Life" is Christ; all true Believers have such; however, all true Believers enjoy such only by constant Faith in Christ and the Cross).

11 **I am the good Shepherd** (speaks of Jesus dying for the sheep; the "Good Shepherd" dies for the sheep, the "Great Shepherd" lives for the sheep [Heb. 13:20], and the "Chief Shepherd" comes for the sheep [I Pet. 5:4]): **the good**

Shepherd gives His life for the sheep *(the Cross: His "Life," if given for the sheep, would guarantee "Eternal Life"; the "Cross" is ever the Central point of Christianity).*

12 But he who is an hireling, and not the shepherd *(presents the one who poses as a shepherd, but really is not)*, whose own the sheep are not *(true sheep do not belong to false shepherds)*, sees the wolf coming, and leaves the sheep, and flees *(the purpose of the "hireling" is to fleece the sheep, not protect the sheep)*: and the wolf catches them, and scatters the sheep *(destruction awaits those who follow false shepherds).*

13 The hireling flees, because he is an hireling, and cares not for the sheep *(false apostles have no real concern for the sheep, but only for other things, mostly money).*

14 I am the good Shepherd, and know My sheep *(the Lord approves those who are His because they have trusted Him for Salvation)*, and am known of Mine *(I know My sheep, and they know Me).*

15 As the Father knows Me, even so know I the Father *(in effect, Jesus is claiming omniscience exactly as God, for He is God!)*: and I lay down My life for the sheep *(once again speaks of the Crucifixion).*

16 And other sheep I have, which are not of this fold *(speaks of the Gentile Church)*: them also I must bring, and they shall hear My voice *(the Apostle Paul was used by the Lord to help plant the Gentile Church)*; and there shall be one fold *(one flock, made up of both Jews and Gentiles)*, *and* one Shepherd *(the Lord Jesus Christ).*

17 Therefore does My Father love Me *(proclaims that what Christ was to do held a special value in God's Heart)*, because I lay down My Life *(the entirety of the idea of the Incarnation was to purposely "lay down His Life")*, that I might take it again *(the Resurrection).*

18 No man takes it from Me, but I lay it down of Myself *(His Death was not an execution nor an assassination, it was a Sacrifice; the idea is that He allowed His Death to take place)*. I have power to lay it down, and I have power to take it again *(proclaims that what He did, He did voluntarily; He did not step out of the path of obedience, for He died as commanded)*. **This Commandment have I received of My Father** *(this means that God the Father gave Him the latitude to do what He desired, and His desire was to do the Will of God; so He purposely laid down His Life).*

DIVISION

19 There was a division therefore again among the Jews for these sayings *(this tells us of the fact of the division, while the cause of the division lay with the religious leadership of Israel).*

20 And many of them said, He has a devil *(proclaims the policy of the Pharisees and Scribes who claim that Jesus cast out demons by the power of Satan)*, and is mad *(claiming He was insane)*; why hear you Him? *(This portrays the Pharisees seeking to dissuade the people from paying attention to Christ.)*

21 Others said, These are not the words of Him Who has a devil *(demon)*. Can a devil open the eyes of the blind? *(The answer is an obvious "no.")*

MESSIAH

22 And it was at Jerusalem the Feast of the Dedication, and it was winter *(this particular Feast was appointed by Judas Maccabaeus to commemorate the purification of the Temple, after Antiochus Epiphanes had defiled it; it took place in December, and actually was not a Biblical Feast).*

23 And Jesus walked in the Temple in Solomon's porch.

24 Then came the Jews round about Him *(portrays them doing such in a threatening manner, demanding an immediate answer)*, and said unto Him, How long do You make us to doubt? *(It was not Christ Who made them doubt, but rather their own unbelief.)* If You are the Christ, tell us plainly *(actually, He had already told them in every conceivable way possible).*

25 Jesus answered them, I told you, and you believed not *(refers to their expectations of a type of Messiah, which role Jesus would not fill)*: the works that I do in My Father's Name, they bear witness of Me *(this "witness" was Scriptural and, therefore, pointed Israel to the Bible [Isa. 61:1]).*

26 But you believe not, because you are not of My sheep, as I said unto you *(they were not His sheep because they did not desire to be His sheep; the decision was theirs, and reached because of unbelief).*

27 My sheep hear My voice *(Christ is the head of the Church, not men)*, and I know them *(refers to perfect and absolute knowledge, even on an individual basis)*, and they follow Me *(proclaims what True Sheep will do):*

28 And I give unto them Eternal Life *(carries with it a promise that cannot be matched elsewhere under any circumstances)*; and they shall never perish *(means that no Believer need ever fear that God will change His Mind respecting their Salvation)*, neither shall any *man* pluck them out of My hand *(refers to any and all outside forces; however, if one so desires, one can take one's self out of His Hand, which regrettably millions have done)*.

29 My Father, which gave *them* to Me, is greater than all *(proclaims the Power of God that is able to keep any and all, which He does through the Spirit by what Christ did at the Cross, and our Faith in that Finished Work)*; and no *man* is able to pluck *them* out of My Father's hand *(when one has Christ, one at the same time has the Father, and the protection of the Father)*.

30 I and *My* Father are One *(the Greek Text says, "We are One"; these simple words destroy the teaching of those who deny the distinction of persons in the Godhead, and those who question the Deity of Christ)*.

THE JEWS

31 Then the Jews took up stones again to stone Him *(thus was the answer of "God's chosen people" to "God's chosen Gift," the Lord Jesus Christ!)*.

32 Jesus answered them, Many good works have I showed you from My Father *(speaks of healing the sick, casting out demons, cleansing lepers, etc.)*; for which of those works do you stone Me? *(This is a good question indeed!)*

33 The Jews answered Him, saying, For a good work we stone You not *(at the same time meant the Jews had no regard for His "Good Works," and in reality would have stopped them had they the power)*; but for blasphemy *(the truth is they were the blasphemers, not Christ)*; and because that You, being a man, make Yourself God *(it was true that He was a Man, but at the same time He was God!)*.

DEITY

34 Jesus answered them, Is it not written in your Law *(presents the Lord taking up one illustration from among many in the Scriptures that the union between man and God lay at the heart of their Law; by Jesus using the word "your," He was not implying that the Law was not His; actually there's not a shadow of disrespect cast on* the Law by the pronoun, but it is used in such a sense that His hearers may identify with it)*, I said, you are gods? *(This is taken from Ps. 82:6; the word "gods" is used here in the sense of magistrates and Prophets appointed and energized by the Word of God. In this case, it did not refer to Deity.)*

35 If he called them gods, unto whom the Word of God came *(once again, "gods" as used here refer to "Magistrates and Judges," etc.)*, and the Scripture cannot be broken *(proclaims to one and all the standard to which our Lord held the Scripture)*;

36 Say ye of Him, Whom the Father has Sanctified, and sent into the world *(for the purpose of the Redemption of mankind)*, You blaspheme *(presents a most serious charge indeed!)*; because I said, I am the Son of God? *(This portrays Him presenting Himself in a far greater dignity than even they had aspired the Messiah would be.)*

37 If I do not the Works of My Father, believe Me not *(He tells them to judge Him on the basis of the Miracles He has performed, in effect, telling them that everything He did was commanded Him by God)*.

38 But if I do *(refers to the carrying out of these Mighty Works)*, though you believe not Me, believe the Works *(actually says they are without excuse)*: that you may know, and believe, that the Father *is* in Me, and I in Him *(further explains Verse 30, "I and My Father are One")*.

JESUS

39 Therefore they sought again to take Him *(speaks of their efforts, but without success)*: but He escaped out of their hand *(Reynolds said, "His escape was facilitated by the strange moral power He could exert to render their physical assaults upon Him in vain. They stretched out hands which dropped harmlessly at their side, verifying the solemn statement of Verse 18.")*,

40 And went away again beyond Jordan into the place where John at first baptized; and there He abode *(our Lord had about three and a half months of Ministry remaining before the Crucifixion)*.

41 And many resorted unto Him *(indicates that they did so in the right way)*, and said, John did no miracle: but all things that John spoke of this Man were true *(they accepted Him as Lord and Saviour)*.

42 And many believed on Him there *(these*

recognized the fact of sin and the need of pardon, which no doubt evidenced a True Faith that was different from the carnality of Jn. 2:23 and 8:30).

CHAPTER 11
(A.D. 33)
LAZARUS

NOW a certain *man* was sick, *named* Lazarus *(was not the same Lazarus of Lk., Chpt. 16, who had died sometime before now)*, of Bethany *(a small village about two miles from Jerusalem, situated on the eastern slope of the Mount of Olives)*, the town of Mary and her sister Martha *(the sisters of Lazarus)*.

2 (It was *that* Mary which anointed the Lord with ointment, and wiped His feet with her hair *(the "anointing" took place very shortly before the Crucifixion, and after the event of Lazarus being raised from the dead)*, whose brother Lazarus was sick.)

3 Therefore his sisters sent unto Him, saying, Lord, behold, he whom You love is sick *(refers to more than a mere malady, but a life-threatening affliction, which, in fact, did take his life, at least at the time)*.

4 When Jesus heard *that*, He said, This sickness is not unto death *(the Greek Text actually says, "he shall not fall prey to death," which is the way it should have been translated)*, but for the Glory of God, that the Son of God might be glorified thereby *(this tells us that even though the Lord does not receive glory from sin or sickness, He definitely does receive glory in delivering men from sin, and from healing the sick)*.

5 Now Jesus loved Martha, and her sister, and Lazarus *(the result of a long acquaintance)*.

6 When He had heard therefore that he *(Lazarus)* was sick *(seems to indicate that a messenger was sent before Lazarus died, with Lazarus dying shortly after he had left, but the messenger did not know this when he approached Christ)*, He abode two days still in the same place where He was *(He did so on instructions from the Holy Spirit; in fact, the Spirit told Him that Lazarus had died)*.

JUDAEA

7 Then after that said He to *His* Disciples, Let us go into Judaea again *(Reynolds said, "The use of the word 'again' points forcibly back to the last visit, when He told both friends and foes that the Good Shepherd would snatch His sheep*

from the jaws of death, even though He lay down His own Life in the doing of it")*.

8 *His* Disciples said unto him, Master, the Jews of late sought to stone You; and You are going there again? *(How different this language is from that of His Own brothers [Jn. 7:3-5].)*

9 Jesus answered, Are there not twelve hours in the day? *(Our Lord is using this terminology as an analogy.)* If any man walk in the day, he stumbles not, because he sees the light of this world *(refers to the sun shining according to the rotation of the Earth)*.

10 But if a man walk in the night, he stumbles *(using a natural expression to express a spiritual Truth)*, because there is no light in him *(destroys the doctrine of the "inner light" as claimed by man in natural birth; in truth, man within himself has no spiritual light)*.

11 These things said He: and after that He said unto them, Our friend Lazarus sleeps *(Jesus is not teaching "soul sleep" here; at death, it is only the body of the Believer that sleeps, not the soul and the spirit, which immediately go to be with Christ; actually, the soul and spirit of Lazarus went down into Paradise at this time, because Jesus had not yet been glorified)*; but I go, that I may awake him out of sleep *(refers to the fact that the Holy Spirit had told Jesus to raise this man from the dead)*.

12 Then said His Disciples, Lord, if he sleep, he shall do well *(they did not know what Jesus was actually saying)*.

13 Howbeit Jesus spoke of His death *(this proclaims the fact that John, who wrote this account, does not hide the fact of the spiritual dullness of the Disciples)*: but they thought that He had spoken of taking of rest in sleep *(they put a carnal interpretation on His statements)*.

14 Then said Jesus unto them plainly, Lazarus is dead.

15 And I am glad for your sakes that I was not there *(portrays the fact that if Jesus had been there, Lazarus would not have died; Jesus would have healed him)*, to the intent you may believe *(has reference to the fact that the Holy Spirit instructed Jesus to perform the Miracle of raising Lazarus from the dead for a variety of reasons; among them, to teach the Disciples the fact of the coming Resurrection)*; nevertheless let us go unto him.

16 Then said Thomas, which is called Didymus, unto his fellow-Disciples, Let us also go, that we may die with him *(this statement, as given by Thomas, proclaims the fact that the Disciples had given up hope of a Messianic*

Kingdom, which they had thought would come immediately).

THE RESURRECTION

17 Then when Jesus came, He found that he (Lazarus) had *lain* in the grave four days already (on the fourth day of death, decomposition begins to set in; so there was no doubt about the death of this man).

18 Now Bethany was near unto Jerusalem, about fifteen furlongs off (about two miles from Jerusalem):

19 And many of the Jews came to Martha and Mary, to comfort them concerning their brother (this shows that the family could well have been one of some wealth, position, and importance).

20 Then Martha, as soon as she heard that Jesus was coming, went and met Him (implies that Jesus, upon coming close to Bethany, stopped short of coming into the town; knowing the animosity against Him, He did not desire to attract any undue disturbance, especially at this time; evidently He had sent someone to their home to inform them He had arrived, with information as to where He was): but Mary sat *still* in the house (someone had to be in the house to meet the people who came to pay their respects).

21 Then said Martha unto Jesus, Lord, if You had been here, my brother had not died (evidently she does not seem to think of Jesus as raising her brother from the dead).

22 But I know, that even now, whatsoever You will ask of God, God will give it You (the terminology used by Martha shows it was still unclear to her exactly Who Jesus was).

23 Jesus said unto her, Your brother shall rise again (very plainly, Jesus tells her what is about to happen; but in her doubt, she misunderstands).

24 Martha said unto Him, I know that he shall rise again in the Resurrection at the last day (proclaims what she had probably learned at the feet of Jesus [Dan. 12:2,13; Jn. 6:39-40, 44, 54; 12:48]).

25 Jesus said unto her, I am the Resurrection, and the Life (in effect, He is saying, "Martha, look at Me, you are looking at the Resurrection and the Life"; this shows that "Resurrection" and "Life" are not mere doctrines, but in reality a Person, the Lord Jesus Christ): he who believes in Me, though he were dead, yet shall he live (speaks of the coming Resurrection of Life, when all the Sainted dead will rise [I Thess. 4:13-18]):

26 And whosoever lives and believes in Me shall never die ("whoever believes in Me will live Eternally"). Do you believe this? (The Resurrection is the end of death; consequently death has no more to do with the Redeemed; it has done all it can do; it is finished! the Redeemed live in the imparted life that put an end to it; for them, the old life, its death and judgment no longer exist.)

27 She said unto Him, Yes, Lord: I believe that You are the Christ, the Son of God, which should come into the world (proclaims her belief in the Lord in a different light than she had known Him previously; she now believes that Jesus is God!).

JESUS AND MARY

28 And when she had so said, she went her way, and called Mary her sister secretly (she relates to her sister what Jesus had just said), saying, The Master is come, and calls for you (has to be one of the most beautiful statements found in the entirety of the Word of God).

29 As soon as she heard *that*, she arose quickly, and came unto Him (she did such with a great spirit of anticipation).

30 Now Jesus was not yet come into the town, but was in that place where Martha met Him (probably a very short distance from the home of the sisters).

31 The Jews then which were with her in the house, and comforted her, when they saw Mary, that she rose up hastily and went out, followed her, saying, She goes unto the grave to weep there (they little knew what was about to happen!).

32 Then when Mary was come where Jesus was, and saw Him, she fell down at His feet (represents, in a sense, her anticipation), saying unto Him, Lord, if You had been here, my brother had not died (the same words as uttered by her sister Martha; they believed, but I think it was still very difficult for them to grasp the fact that He would raise their brother from the dead, even though he had been dead for some four days).

COMPASSION

33 When Jesus therefore saw her weeping, and the Jews also weeping which came with her, he groaned in the spirit, and was troubled (Reynolds said, "At that time, there flashed upon His Spirit all the terrible moral consequences of which death was the ghastly symbol."),

34 And said, Where have you laid him? They said unto Him, Lord, come and see *(they would lead Him to the tomb)*.

35 Jesus wept *(tears of sorrow because of the terrible specter of death, brought on the human race by sin)*.

36 Then said the Jews, Behold how He loved him! *(However, His tears had to do with a far greater degree of misery than was evident here.)*

37 And some of them said, Could not this Man, which opened the eyes of the blind, have caused that even this man should not have died? *(This seems to have been said by some of the onlookers with some sarcasm.)*

38 Jesus therefore again groaning in Himself comes to the grave *(if there is anything which symbolizes all the pain and hurt resulting from the Fall of man, the "grave" or "tomb" is that example; Death is such an enemy!)*. It was a cave, and a stone lay upon it *(presents the striking end of all men, for it is "appointed unto men once to die")*.

39 Jesus said, Take ye away the stone *(presents one of the most poignant moments in human history)*. Martha, the sister of him who was dead, said unto Him, Lord, by this time he stinks: for he has been *dead* four days *(her Faith seems to wane and weaken when she stands before the cold reality of this tomb)*.

40 Jesus said unto her, Said I not unto you, that, if you would believe, you should see the glory of God? *(Corruption, whether physical or moral, is no obstacle to Him Who is the Resurrection and the Life.)*

PRAYER

41 Then they took away the stone *from the place* where the dead was laid. And Jesus lifted up *His* eyes, and said, Father, I thank You that You have heard Me *(proclaims this as a thanksgiving for that which had already been prayed and heard)*.

42 And I knew that You hear Me always *(this speaks of relationship beyond our comprehension)*: but because of the people which stand by I said *it*, that they may believe that You have sent Me *(the people heard Him pray to the Father, and now they will see the Father answer His prayer; consequently, the proof of Who He is will be undeniable)*.

LAZARUS

43 And when He thus had spoken, He cried with a loud voice, Lazarus, come forth *(constitutes a Command, and from the Creator of the Ages; considering that He is the Resurrection and the Life, had He not called Lazarus by name all the other Sainted dead would have come forth as well!)*.

44 And he who was dead came forth *(constitutes the greatest Miracle in human history)*, bound hand and foot with graveclothes *(his legs were no doubt bound separately with him able to walk, but with some difficulty)*: and his face was bound about with a napkin *(concerns a cloth which had been tied over his face, but which he had probably partially removed)*. Jesus said unto them, Loose him, and let him go *(refers, as is obvious, to this burial shroud being taken off his body; Lazarus had been called up from Paradise where he had been for the past four days; one can only surmise as to what happened when the Voice of Jesus rang out in that place concerning Lazarus)*.

45 Then many of the Jews which came to Mary, and had seen the things which Jesus did, believed on Him *(Jesus would later say, "blessed are they who have not seen, and yet have believed" [Jn. 20:29])*.

46 But some of them went their ways to the Pharisees, and told them what things Jesus had done *(how is it that individuals could observe the type of Miracle just witnessed, and still oppose Christ?)*.

PHARISEES

47 Then gathered the Chief Priests and the Pharisees a Council, and said, What do we? *(This presents both the Pharisees and Sadducees joining in their denunciation of Jesus, even though they were normally bitter enemies between themselves.)* for this Man does many Miracles *(presents not all of them denying the Miracles, but some actually admitting to their veracity)*.

48 If we let Him thus alone, all *men* will believe on Him: and the Romans shall come and take away both our place and nation *(in fact, the Romans did exactly that; their rejection of Christ brought it all about; how spiritually blind they were!)*.

49 And one of them, *named* Caiaphas, being the High Priest that same year *(presents the political spectrum of this high office)*, said unto them, you know nothing at all *(could be translated, "you do not understand the dangers we face!")*,

50 Nor consider that it is expedient for us,

that one man should die for the people, and that the whole nation perish not (Williams said, "the death of Jesus, proposed and commanded by the High Priest, was resolved upon that fearful moment; for the raising of Lazarus, had brought their malignity to a head.").

51 And this spoke he not of himself (actually means that their condemning Jesus to death, even though evil and wicked for which they would pay dearly, would be used of God for the Redemption of mankind): but being High Priest that year, he prophesied that Jesus should die for that nation (once again fell out to that which was ordained by God, but which in no way absolved these of blame);

52 And not for that nation only (refers to the fact that when Jesus died, He died for the entirety of the world, not for Israel only), but that also He should gather together in one (one body consisting of both Jews and Gentiles) the Children of God who were scattered abroad (the Apostle Paul would be given the meaning of the New Covenant, which was the meaning of the Cross that would establish the Church).

53 Then from that day forth they took counsel together for to put Him to death (if men reject Christ, the next step is to kill Him, i.e., repudiate Him for Who and What He is).

54 Jesus therefore walked no more openly among the Jews (the raising of Lazarus from the dead was the great Miracle that brought all of this to a climax); but went thence unto a country near to the wilderness, into a city called Ephraim, and there continued with His Disciples (seems to represent a place in connection with Bethel [II Chron. 13:19]; it was probably about fifteen miles north of the Jerusalem of that day).

55 And the Jews' Passover was nigh at hand (He was the True Passover, and would fulfill the type by dying on Calvary): and many went out of the country up to Jerusalem before the Passover, to purify themselves (pertained to going through a Levitical, ceremonial cleansing from touching the dead and other unclean things [Num. 9:6-10]).

56 Then sought they for Jesus (seems to present the authorities seeking Him in order that He be arrested), and spoke among themselves, as they stood in the Temple, What think ye, that He will not come to the Feast? (In almost every place, hundreds, if not thousands, of people seeking to hear Him or be healed by Him surrounded him; so, their task of arresting Him would not be easy!)

57 Now both the Chief Priests and the Pharisees had given a commandment, that, if any man knew where He were, he should show it, that they might take Him (they had determined that He must be stopped, and at all costs; the truth is that it cost them everything, both life and soul).

CHAPTER 12
(A.D. 33)

MARY ANOINTS JESUS

THEN Jesus six days before the Passover came to Bethany (represents the closing days of His Ministry and Work), where Lazarus was which had been dead, whom He raised from the dead (He went to where He was welcome; He was not welcome in the Temple, even though it was His House; His Presence there would be looked at as an intrusion in a short time, as it is in most Churches presently).

2 There they made Him a supper (probably in the house of Simon the Leper [Mat. 26:6; Mk. 14:3]); and Martha served: but Lazarus was one of them who sat at the table with Him (possibly Simon the Leper was there as well! if so, there would have been seated at the table two transcendent proofs of the Power of Jesus to save not only from the semblance of death as was Simon the Leper, but from the reality of death by the Resurrection of Lazarus).

3 Then took Mary a pound of ointment of spikenard, very costly (probably worth about ten thousand dollars in 2003 currency), and anointed the feet of Jesus, and wiped His feet with her hair (harmonious with the purpose of this Gospel and setting forth the Deity of the Lord Jesus, only the Anointing of His feet is recorded): and the house was filled with the odour of the ointment (it was testimony to His coming Resurrection, and she knew she would have no other opportunity; incidentally, Mary was not found at the empty Tomb; she was too spiritually intelligent to be there).

4 Then said one of His Disciples, Judas Iscariot, Simon's son, which should betray Him (was not Simon the Leper in whose house this supper was prepared),

5 Why was not this ointment sold for three hundred pence, and given to the poor? (Reynolds said, "sinful motive often hides itself under the mask of reverence for another virtue.")

6 This he said, not that he cared for the poor (this was not his real reason); but because he was a thief, and had the bag, and bear what

was put therein *(had the ointment been sold and the money given to Christ, Judas would have stolen it; unfortunately, most of the money presently given for that which is supposed to be the Work of God is "stolen," i.e., "used for the wrong purposes")*.

7 Then said Jesus, Let her alone *(Jesus places His seal of approval on what she is doing)*: against the day of My burying has she kept this *(indicating she had this ointment for quite some time)*.

8 For the poor always you have with you *(presents that which is regrettable, but true!)*; but Me you have not always *(Jesus would not be with them in the flesh very much longer)*.

THE PLOT

9 Much people of the Jews therefore knew that He was there *(at the home of Lazarus)*: and they came not for Jesus' sake only, but that they might see Lazarus also, whom He had raised from the dead *(no doubt there were many and varied questions that people had concerning death, which they desired to ask Lazarus; and yet, the Scripture is silent on this subject)*.

10 But the Chief Priests consulted that they might put Lazarus also to death *(it had been about two months since Jesus had performed this greatest of Miracles; these religious leaders were not speaking of a judicial execution, but rather how they could hire some brigand to murder Lazarus in cold blood; religious evil is the worst evil of all!)*;

11 Because that by reason of Him many of the Jews went away, and believed on Jesus *(one cannot be in sympathy with Christ and at the same time remain in league with the evil of this religious hierarchy; one or the other must go!)*.

THE TRIUMPHANT ENTRY

12 On the next day much people who were come to the Feast *(the Passover)*, when they heard that Jesus was coming to Jerusalem *(their excitement is understandable)*,

13 Took branches of palm trees, and went forth to meet Him *(as was the custom; presents them waving these palm fronds in token of the approach of a conqueror)*, and cried, Hosanna *(in the Hebrew means, "saved we pray")*: Blessed is the King of Israel Who comes in the Name of the Lord *(is taken from Ps. 118:25-26; while the people at that moment were proclaiming Jesus as King, the religious leaders were plotting His Death)*.

14 And Jesus, when He had found a young ass, sat thereon; as it is written *(presents an animal that had never before been ridden; Matthew tells us that the foal was accompanied by its mother, and both animals satisfied the prediction of Zech., Chpt. 9, and Isa 62:11)*,

15 Fear not, daughter of Sion: behold, The King comes, sitting on an ass's colt *(is recorded by John from Zech. 9:9)*.

16 These things understood not His Disciples at the first *(refers to His Disciples being a part of this great celebration, but yet not knowing or realizing that they were fulfilling Prophecy)*: but when Jesus was glorified *(refers to the glorified Body of Jesus after His Resurrection)*, then remembered they that these things were written of Him *(speaks of the time after the Day of Pentecost when they were Baptized with the Holy Spirit, and He began to explain things to them)*, and *that* they had done these things unto Him *(the Scriptures portrayed what was to be done, and in fact what was done)*.

17 The people therefore who was with Him when He called Lazarus out of his grave, and raised him from the dead, bear record *(they had been giving the testimony of what they had seen and heard from the moment it happened, with, no doubt ready ears to listen)*.

18 For this cause the people also met Him, for that they heard that He had done this Miracle *(proclaims the raising of Lazarus as the catalyst which instigated the Triumphant Entry)*.

19 The Pharisees therefore said among themselves, Perceive ye how you prevail nothing? behold, the world is gone after Him *(John portrays the anger of the Pharisees as no other writer; this public entrance associated with the supreme Miracle of the raising of Lazarus compelled Priests and people to a decision; while the people were praising Him, the Priests decided to Crucify Him, but they could have "prevailed nothing" had He not voluntarily surrendered Himself)*.

GREEKS

20 And there were certain Greeks among them who came up to worship at the Feast *(pertained to a large group of Gentiles)*:

21 The same came therefore to Philip, which was of Bethsaida of Galilee *(one of the Twelve Apostles)*, and desired Him, saying, Sir, we would see Jesus *(they were ready to plead with Him to go among them and offer His Message to the Gentiles!)*.

22 Philip comes and tells Andrew: and again Andrew and Philip tell Jesus *(may present more, much more, than the passing on of information; but the time was wrong, which Jesus will now address)*.

THE PREDICTION

23 And Jesus answered them *(answered the Greeks as well as His Disciples)*, **saying, The hour is come** *(the Crucifixion, which would pay the price for Adam's fallen race)*, **that the Son of Man should be glorified** *(this statement guarantees the Resurrection, because Jesus could not be Glorified unless He was Resurrected)*.

24 Verily, verily, I say unto you *(the pronoun "you" is emphatic toward the Disciples that their idea of circumventing His Death was a violation of the Word of God, and a hindrance to the very purpose and reason for which He came)*, Except a corn of wheat fall into the ground and die, it abideth alone *(says that His Atoning Death was a necessity)*: **but if it die, it brings forth much fruit** *(proclaims the very purpose for His Death was to bring forth Life)*.

DISCIPLESHIP

25 He who loves his life shall lose it *(hits at the very heart of man's problem; it could be paraphrased, "He who loves self shall not see fulfillment")*; **and he who hates his life in this world shall keep it unto Life Eternal** *(refers to putting self last, and Christ first in all things)*.

26 If any man serve Me, let him follow Me *(follow Christ exclusively)*; **and where I am, there shall also My servant be** *(actually means to be "Crucified together" [Rom. 6:3-5], "Glorified together" [Rom. 8:17])*: **if any man serve Me, him will *My* Father honour** *(this is the true honor which comes from God)*.

JESUS PRAYS

27 Now is My soul troubled *(proclaims Him facing that which would come about in a very short time)*; **and what shall I say? Father, save Me from this hour** *(could be translated, "should I pray to the Father that He save Me from this hour?")*: **but for this cause came I unto this hour** *(could be translated, "No, for this cause came I unto this hour")*.

28 Father, glorify Your Name *(proclaims that which Jesus always sought to do)*. **Then came there a Voice from Heaven, *saying*, I have both** glorified *it*, and will glorify *it* again *(it was glorified at the raising of Lazarus, and it will be glorified again with the Resurrection of Christ)*.

29 The people therefore, who stood by, and heard *it*, said that it thundered *(does not mean that it was unintelligible, but that the Voice sounded with such Power that it was like thunder)*: **others said, An Angel spoke to Him** *(proclaims the fact that they did hear what was said, and did at least understand the words, even though they did not understand the meaning)*.

30 Jesus answered and said, This voice came not because of Me *(proclaims in no uncertain terms that Jesus was not in doubt as to Who and What He was)*, **but for your sakes** *(refers to God making this statement, and in an audible voice that all who were there may hear and know)*.

31 Now is the judgment of this world *(pertains to that which Jesus would do at Calvary; He would suffer the wrath of God instead of the world)*: **now shall the prince of this world be cast out** *(Jesus would defeat Satan by atoning for all sin; sin is the legal means by which Satan keeps men in captivity; that means being removed, which it was by Christ, leaves the evil one with no legal right, unless men freely give him that right; acceptance of Christ and the Cross defeats Satan and breaks his bondage)*.

32 And I, if I be lifted up from the earth *(refers to His Death at Calvary; He was "lifted up" on the Cross; the "Cross" is the foundation of all victory)*, **will draw all *men* unto Me** *(refers to the Salvation of all who come to Him, believing what He did, and trusting in its atoning work)*.

33 This He said, signifying what death He should die *(Reynolds says, "In these Words, we learn that the attraction of the Cross of Christ will prove to be the mightiest, and most sovereign motive ever brought to bear on the human will, and, when wielded by the Holy Spirit as a Revelation of the matchless Love of God, will involve the most sweeping judicial sentence that can be pronounced upon the world and its prince.")*.

34 The people answered Him *(proclaims an unsatisfactory answer, actually an answer of unbelief!)*, **We have heard out of the Law that Christ abides forever** *(refers to several passages out of the Old Testament being taken out of context)*: **and how do You say, The Son of Man must be lifted up?** *(This presents these people attempting to excuse their unwillingness to obey moral appeal to the conscience by raising some Bible difficulty.)* **who is this Son of Man?** *(If they did not now know, there is nothing that could be*

done that would ever help them to know.)

35 Then Jesus said unto them, Yet a little while is the Light with you *(the warning is clearly given that their day was nearly gone, and the eternal darkness was coming).* **Walk while you have the Light, lest darkness come upon you** *(presents a choice!)*: **for he who walks in darkness knows not where he goes** *(proclaims the majority of the world at present, and in fact, since the beginning of time).*

36 While you have the Light *(Jesus is the Light),* **believe in the Light** *(make Christ the central focus of your life and living),* **that you may be the Children of Light** *(which at the same time means they were not the children of light).* **These things spoke Jesus, and departed, and did hide Himself from them** *(this was the last public Word of Jesus; if the Word of God is rejected, ultimately the Lord will hide Himself, fulfilling Prov. 1:24-30).*

REJECTION

37 But though He had done so many Miracles before them *(seems to be proclaimed with a sigh by the Holy Spirit),* **yet they believed not on Him** *(if people will not believe the Word of God, they will little believe Miracles, irrespective as to how powerful they may be)*:

38 That the saying of Isaiah the Prophet might be fulfilled, which he spoke *(Isa., Chpt. 53),* **Lord, who has believed our report?** *(This doesn't mean no one believed, but it does mean that the number was few.)* **and to whom has the arm of the Lord been revealed?** *(This speaks of the Messiah being revealed to Israel, but they would not accept Him!)*

39 Therefore they could not believe *(means that Israel willfully shut their eyes to the Message of the Miracles),* **because that Isaiah said again** *(refers to where their unbelief led them),*

40 He has blinded their eyes, and hardened their heart *(God set in motion the "Law of Unbelief," which, in effect, is the "Law of Sowing and Reaping");* **that they should not see with** *their* **eyes, nor understand with** *their* **heart, and be converted, and I should heal them** *(because they willfully refused to believe, God willed a judicial blindness and hardness accordingly).*

41 These things said Isaiah, when he saw His glory, and spoke of Him *(in this Passage, John proclaims that the vision Isaiah had of the Lord [Isa. 6:1-2] was actually of the pre-Incarnate Christ; so we are told here that the Jehovah of the Old Testament was Jesus).*

42 Nevertheless among the Chief Rulers also many believed on Him *(does not relate exactly who they were, with the exception of Nicodemus and Joseph of Arimathea);* **but because of the Pharisees they did not confess** *Him,* **lest they be put out of the Synagogue** *(proclaims not only their excuses, but the excuses of many millions the world over)*:

43 For they loved the praise of men more than the praise of God *(this means that they counted God as less than men; what an indictment!).*

TEACHING

44 Jesus cried and said, He who believes on Me *(claims the absolute necessity of believing on Christ as God manifest in the flesh and, therefore, the Saviour of mankind, which He was through the Cross),* **believes not on Me** *(believes not on Me Alone),* **but on Him Who sent Me** *(to have the Son is to have the Father; to refuse the Son is to refuse the Father).*

45 And he who sees Me sees Him Who sent Me *(had to be done by Faith, because Christ in His human form offered no expression of Deity).*

46 I am come a Light into the world *(reveals all understanding, all purifying, all gracious influence which are shed on human affairs, nature, and destiny),* **that whosoever believes on Me should not abide in darkness** *(the only way out of darkness is through Christ; He Alone is the Light!).*

47 And if any man hear My words, and believe not, I judge him not *(means that He is not pronouncing sentence now; He has come as Saviour)*: **for I came not to judge the world, but to save the world** *(proclaims His present Mission, which has lasted now for nearly 2,000 years).*

48 He who rejects Me, and receives not My Words, has One Who Judges him *(presents a Truth that the Church desperately needs to hear and understand, and the entirety of the world for that matter)*: **the Word that I have spoken, the same shall judge him in the last day** *(speaks of the "Judgment Seat of Christ" for Believers, and the "Great White Throne Judgment" for unbelievers).*

49 For I have not spoken of Myself *(His Words are not simply His Own, but rather from the Father, i.e., in effect, the entirety of the Godhead);* **but the Father which sent Me** *(He was sent by the Father for a distinct purpose and mission),* **He gave Me a Commandment, what I should say, and what I should speak** *(in effect, says, "in rejecting Me and My Words, men reject*

and insult the Father; His Word that they dare to renounce is as solemn and unalterable as the Word spoken on Sinai").

50 And I know that His Commandment is Life Everlasting (as well says that Life Everlasting is found in the words of no one else): whatsoever I speak therefore, even as the Father said unto Me, so I speak (His Doctrine, its Substance, and the very words used in its proclamation are all of Divine origin).

CHAPTER 13
(A.D. 33)
THE LAST PASSOVER

NOW before the Feast of the Passover (refers to the preparation day of the Passover, our Tuesday sunset to Wednesday sunset, with Wednesday being the day of the Crucifixion), when Jesus knew that His hour was come (refers to the Crucifixion, which was the purpose for which He came) that He should depart out of this world unto the Father (refers to the Resurrection and the Ascension), having loved His Own which were in the world, He loved them unto the end (presents not so much an expression of time as of degree).

2 And supper being ended (actually refers to the preparation for the Supper being ended, not the Supper itself; it was just beginning), the devil having now put into the heart of Judas Iscariot, Simon's son, to betray Him (a short time before Satan did this thing);

HUMILITY

3 Jesus knowing that the Father had given all things into His Hands (portrays two things in His heart as He girded Himself, His conscious Deity and the heartless conduct of Judas), and that He was come from God, and went to God (was something that He knew, at least from the time that He was twelve years old);

4 He rose from supper (He rose from the table when the preparation had been completed), and laid aside His garments (physically, His outer robe; spiritually, He laid aside the expression of His Deity, while never losing the possession of His Deity); and took a towel (refers to the action of the lowliest slave or servant in a household; it represents the servant spirit possessed by Christ), and girded Himself (wrapped Himself in the towel; spiritually speaking, it refers to His Human Body provided for Him by the Father [Heb. 10:5] in order to serve as a Sacrifice on the Cross for sin).

5 After that He poured water into a basin (spiritually, it referred to the Holy Spirit, which would pour from Him like a River [7:38-39]), and began to wash the Disciples' feet (presenting the servant principle which we are to follow, but even more particularly the cleansing guaranteed by the Holy Spirit concerning our daily walk, which comes about according to our Faith in Christ and what He did for us at the Cross), and to wipe them with the towel wherewith He was girded (refers to the Incarnation, which made possible His Death on Calvary that atoned for all sin and made cleansing possible for the human race).

PETER'S RESPONSE

6 Then cometh He to Simon Peter (seems to indicate it was Peter to whom He first approached): and Peter said unto him, Lord, do you wash my feet? ("The flesh" cannot understand spiritual realities; it is too backward or too forward, too courageous or too cowardly; it is incapable of ever being right, and it is impossible to improve, consequently, it must "die.")

7 Jesus answered and said unto him, What I do you know not now; but you shall know hereafter (when Peter was filled with the Spirit, which he was on the Day of Pentecost).

8 Peter said unto Him, You shall never wash my feet (the Greek Text actually says, "Not while eternity lasts"; Calvin said, "With God, obedience is better than worship"). Jesus answered him, If I wash you not, you have no part with Me (the statement as rendered by Christ speaks to the constant cleansing needed regarding our everyday walk before the Lord, which the washing of the feet [our walk], at least in part, represented).

9 Simon Peter said unto Him, Lord, not my feet only, but also my hands and my head (Chrysostom said, "In his deprecation he was vehement, and his yielding more vehement, but both came from his love").

10 Jesus said to Him, He who is washed needs not save to wash His feet (as stated, pertains to our daily walk before God, which means that the Believer doesn't have to get saved over and over again; the "head" refers to our Salvation, meaning that we do not have to be repeatedly saved, while the "hands" refer to our "doing," signifying that this doesn't need to be washed because Christ has already done what needs to be done; all of this is in the spiritual

sense), **but is clean every whit** (*refers to Salvation, and pertains to the Precious Blood of Jesus that cleanses from all sin; the infinite Sacrifice needs no repetition*): **and you are clean, but not all** (*refers to all the Disciples being saved with one exception, which was Judas*).

11 For He knew who should betray Him (*portrays Him knowing this quite some time earlier*); **therefore said He, You are not all clean** (*actually presents Jesus making another appeal to Judas*).

12 So after He had washed their feet, and had taken His garments, and was set down again (*now He is their Teacher and Lord*), **He said unto them, Do you know what I have done to you?** (*Reynolds said, "There was no affectation [pretense] of humility about it; the purpose of the Lord was distinctly practical and ethical."*)

13 Ye call Me Master and Lord (*presents a double title which was not given except to the most accredited teachers*): **and you say well; for so I am** (*He is also telling them that, even though He has washed their feet, in no way does this diminish His position as the Lord God of Glory; we will not be diminished by such activity either, but rather exalted*).

14 If I then, your Lord and Master, have washed your feet (*speaks of and proclaims the example set*); **you also ought to wash one another's feet** (*is not meant to be taken literally, but is to serve as an example of the Servant Principle*).

15 For I have given you an example (*meaning that "foot washing" is not meant to be a Church Ordinance, such as the Lord's Supper, etc.*), **that you should do as I have done to you** (*were it mere ceremony, they would have instantly known what He was doing*).

16 Verily, verily, I say unto you, The servant is not greater than his Lord (*Jesus, Who is Lord, has set the example that we must follow*); **neither he who is sent greater than he who sends him** (*He must ever increase, as we must ever decrease*).

17 If ye know these things, happy are you if you do them (*knowing and doing are often perilously divorced*).

JUDAS

18 I speak not of you all (*we are about to be presented with another attempt to bring Judas back from the crumbling edge, but sadly without success*): **I know whom I have chosen** (*the Holy Spirit told Him whom to choose as His*

Personal Disciples): **but that the Scripture may be fulfilled, He who eats bread with Me has lifted up his heel against Me** (*in effect, He is saying, "I am the person spoken of in Ps. 41:9"*).

19 Now I tell you before it come (*proclaims Him knowing exactly what is going to happen, at least according to what the Scripture has foretold*), **that, when it is come to pass, you may believe that I am He** (*once again, proclaims Himself as being the One spoken of in Ps. 41:9*).

20 Verily, verily, I say unto you, He who receives whomsoever I send receives Me (*in effect, says that we might be hated and betrayed as He the Master was, yet like Him our mission is Divine*); **and he who receives Me receives Him Who sent Me** (*proclaims the fact that acceptance or rejection reaches all the way to the Throne of God*).

21 When Jesus had thus said, He was troubled in spirit (*proclaims a strong expression used of the sorrows of Christ*), **and testified, and said, Verily, verily, I say unto you, that one of you shall betray Me** (*proclaims Jesus saying plainly that which He had previously hinted*).

22 Then the Disciples looked one on another, doubting of whom He spoke (*Judas was not suspected, showing that his actions of the past had not been those of treachery*).

23 Now there was leaning on Jesus' bosom one of His Disciples (*presents the manner in which they then reclined when dining; meals were then much more formal than now*), **whom Jesus loved** (*pertains to John the Beloved who wrote this Gospel*).

24 Simon Peter therefore beckoned to him (*to John*), **that he should ask who it should be of whom He spoke** (*refers to Peter sitting far enough away from Jesus that he could not whisper to Him personally, so that others would not hear and would, therefore, ask John to do so for him*).

25 He then lying on Jesus' breast said unto Him, Lord, who is it? (*This proclaims none suspecting Judas.*)

26 Jesus answered, He it is, to whom I shall give a sop, when I have dipped it (*in its normal sense, this was a mark of honor for the guest who received it; it was another appeal to Judas*). **And when He had dipped the sop, He gave it to Judas Iscariot, the son of Simon** (*Verse 21 records Jesus appealing to the conscience of Judas, and now appealing to his heart, all to no avail!*).

27 And after the sop Satan entered into him (*he yielded to Satan*). **Then said Jesus unto**

him, That you do, do quickly *(it was quickly done, but the results were not quickly done, as such results are never quickly done).*

28 Now no man at the table knew for what intent He spoke this unto him *(the remaining Eleven little knew, it seems, what was actually happening).*

29 For some *of them* thought, because Judas had the bag *(Judas was the treasurer of the group),* that Jesus had said unto him, Buy *those things* that we have need of against the Feast; or, that he should give something to the poor *(it seems they gave to the poor quite regularly).*

30 He then having received the sop went immediately out *(this means that Judas was not present when Jesus gave His discourse as given in the next four Chapters, which immediately followed the Supper):* and it was night *(dark as was the night upon Judas' head, there was a blacker night in his heart; all was darkness in his soul).*

A NEW COMMANDMENT

31 Therefore, when he was gone out *(refers to the fact that Jesus could not give His discourse to the Disciples, which now follows, until the traitor had left),* Jesus said, Now is the Son of Man glorified, and God is glorified in Him *(Christ glorified God in Death, and God glorified Him in Resurrection).*

32 If God be glorified in Him *(refers to the perfect obedience of Jesus Christ as the "Second Man," i.e., "Last Adam"),* God shall also glorify Him in Himself, and shall straightway *(immediately)* glorify Him *(the Son of Man was glorified on the Cross in a much more admirable way than He will be by the Millennial Glories attaching to that title; for on the Cross as the Son of Man, He displayed all the Moral Glory of God).*

33 Little children, yet a little while I am with you *(He would only be with them for about another forty-four days before the Ascension).* You shall seek Me *(simply made reference to the fact that He would be gone):* and as I said unto the Jews, Where I go, you cannot come *(referring to Heaven, at least at that particular moment);* so now I say to you *(presents an entirely different statement than that given to the faithless Jews).*

34 A new Commandment I give unto you, That you love one another *(is beyond the Old Commandment in Lev. 19:18, "you shall love your neighbor as yourself");* as I have loved you,

that you also love one another *(in effect, He is saying, "I have loved each of you unto death; and in loving one another you are loving Me; you are loving an object of My tender Love").*

35 By this shall all *men* know that you are My Disciples *(not only proclaims this "Love" as the foundation of the New Covenant, but as well, proclaims it as the basis for recognition that one is truly in the New Covenant),* if you have love one to another *(this type of Love is the "God-Kind of Love," and is impossible for anyone to have without accepting Christ as one's Saviour; as well, "Love" and the "Cross" are indivisible).*

DENIAL

36 Simon Peter said unto Him, Lord, where are you going? *(As stated, the Disciples had no idea as to what Jesus was saying regarding His departure.)* Jesus answered him, Where I go, you cannot follow Me now; but you shall follow Me afterwards *(He assures them that where He is going, they would follow later, which they did!).*

37 Peter said unto Him, Lord, why cannot I follow You now? *(Their immaturity was so obvious at this time, but would change after the Day of Pentecost.)* I will lay down My Life for your sake *(Peter thought himself ready to die for His Lord, before His Lord had died for him).*

38 Jesus answered him, Will you lay down your life for My sake? *(This is a question that does not really expect an answer, because the answer was already known.)* Verily, verily, I say unto you, The rooster shall not crow, till you have denied Me thrice *(proclaims a coming terrible moment in the life of Peter, and one which was the very opposite of what he was claiming).*

CHAPTER 14
(A.D. 33)
COMFORT AND PROMISE

LET not your heart be troubled *(is said by Christ immediately after predicting Peter's shameful denial):* you believe in God, believe also in Me *(means simply to have Faith in Him, as they had Faith in God; this is His Highest and most complete Revelation of Himself as God).*

2 In My Father's house are many mansions *(proclaims Heaven as a large place; a place so large actually, that its possibilities transcend one's imagination and exceed our comprehension):* if it were not *so,* I would have told you *(has reference to the fact that He is speaking from firsthand*

knowledge). **I go to prepare a place for you** (*refers to Him Personally superintending this extra building project in Heaven*).

3 **And if I go and prepare a place for you, I will come again, and receive you unto Myself** (*proclaims the first mention of the Rapture of the Church [I Thess. 4:13-18]*); **that where I am,** *there* **you may be also** (*refers to Heaven, where the Saints of God will go at the Resurrection*).

4 **And where I go you know** (*He had just told them*), **and the way you know** (*actually spoke of Himself, for He is the "Way"*).

5 **Thomas said unto Him, Lord, we know not where You go** (*presents this Disciple striving after Truth and reality through intellectualism, and not Faith*); **and how can we know the way?** (*Christ will answer immediately!*)

JESUS

6 **Jesus said unto Him, I am the Way, the Truth, and the Life** (*proclaims in no uncertain terms exactly Who and What Jesus is*): **no man comes unto the Father, but by Me** (*He declares positively that this idea of God as Father, this approach to God for every man is through Him — through what He is and what He has done*).

7 **If you had known Me, you should have known My Father also** (*means "If you had learned to know me spiritually and experientially, you should have known that I and the Father are One," i.e., One in essence and unity, and not in number*): **and from Henceforth you know Him, and have seen Him** (*when one truly sees Jesus, one truly sees the Father; as stated, they are "One" in essence*).

8 **Philip said unto Him, Lord, show us the Father, and it suffices us** (*like Philip, all, at least for the most part, want to see God, but the far greater majority reject the only manner and way to see Him, which is through Jesus*).

9 **Jesus said unto Him, Have I been so long with you, and yet have you not known Me, Philip?** (*Reynolds says, "There is no right understanding of Jesus Christ until the Father is actually seen in Him."*) **He who has seen Me has seen the Father** (*presents the very embodiment of Who and What the Messiah would be; if we want to know what God is like, we need only look at the Son*); **and how do you say** *then,* **Show us the Father?**

10 **Do you believe not that I am in the Father, and the Father in Me?** (*The key is "believing."*) **the words that I speak unto you I speak not of Myself** (*the words which came out of the mouth of the Master are, in fact, those of the Heavenly Father*): **but the Father who dwells in Me, He does the works** (*the Father does such through the Holy Spirit*).

11 **Believe Me that I** *am* **in the Father, and the Father in Me** (*once again places Faith as the vehicle and Jesus as the Object*): **or else believe Me for the very works' sake** (*presents a level which should be obvious to all, and includes present observation as well*).

POWER

12 **Verily, verily, I say unto you, He who believes on Me, the Works that I do shall he do also** (*believing on Christ gives one access to the Father, Who does the Works*); **and greater** *Works* **than these shall He do; because I go unto My Father** (*it respects quantity rather than quality; the Works of Christ were confined to greater Israel, while the works of Believers cover the entirety of the world*).

13 **And whatsoever you shall ask in My Name, that will I do** (*the Christian is given the Power of Attorney to use the Name of Christ; but if one is to notice, all the usage of His Name is confined to the spirit world; Believers are never given authority over other Believers*), **that the Father may be glorified in the Son** (*is accomplished through the great Work of Christ being extended through all Believers*).

14 **If you shall ask any thing in My Name, I will do** *it* (*refers to that which is in harmony with His Character and Will*).

THE HELPER

15 **If you love Me, keep My Commandments** (*His Commandments can be kept only in one way; the Believer must ever make Christ and the Cross the Object of his Faith, which will then give the Holy Spirit latitude to work within our lives and help us do these things which we must do*).

16 **And I will pray the Father, and He shall give you another Comforter** (*"Parakletos," which means "One called to the side of another to help"*), **that He may abide with you forever** (*before the Cross, the Holy Spirit could only help a few individuals, and then only for a period of time; since the Cross, He lives in the hearts and lives of Believers, and does so forever*);

17 *Even* **the Spirit of Truth** (*the Greek says, "The Spirit of the Truth," which refers to the Word of God; actually, He does far more than*

merely superintend the attribute of Truth, as Christ "is Truth" [I Jn. 5:6]); **Whom the world cannot receive** *(the Holy Spirit cannot come into the heart of the unbeliever until that person makes Christ his or her Saviour; then He comes in),* **because it sees Him not, neither knows Him** *(refers to the fact that only Born-Again Believers can understand the Holy Spirit and know Him):* **but you know Him** *(would have been better translated, "But you shall get to know Him");* **for He dwells with you** *(before the Cross),* **and shall be in you** *(which would take place on the Day of Pentecost and forward, because the sin debt has been forever paid by Christ on the Cross, changing the disposition of everything).*

18 I will not leave you comfortless *(helpless):* **I will come to you** *(through the Person of the Holy Spirit).*

19 Yet a little while, and the world sees Me no more *(in a few days He would be taken back to Glory);* **but you see Me** *(after the Day of Pentecost, we will see Christ in the Person of the Holy Spirit):* **because I live, you shall live also** *(refers to His coming Resurrection, which guarantees the Work of the Cross).*

20 At that day *(after the Resurrection, and the coming of the Holy Spirit on the Day of Pentecost)* **you shall know that I** *am* **in My Father** *(speaks of Deity; Jesus is God!),* **and you in Me** *(has to do with our Salvation by Faith),* **and I in you** *(enables us to live a victorious life [Gal. 2:20]).*

21 He who has My Commandments, and keeps them, he it is who loves Me *(as stated, we can keep His Commandments only by allowing the Holy Spirit to work within our lives, which He does based on our Faith expressed in Christ and the Cross):* **and he who loves Me shall be loved of My Father** *(provides the criteria of approval by the Father),* **and I will love him, and will manifest Myself to him** *(means to fully disclose His Person, Nature, and Goodness to the Believer).*

22 Judas said unto Him, not Iscariot, Lord, how is it that You will manifest Yourself unto us, and not unto the world? *(Also known as Lebbaeus or Thaddaeus. He was the brother of James the Less. His questions have implications of Israel being restored to her place of glory and grandeur.)*

23 Jesus answered and said unto him, If a man love Me, he will keep My Words *(presents this of which Jesus speaks as based on Love, which is the exact opposite of what the Apostles were*

speaking, which was force; they wanted Jesus to use His Power to force Rome and other people of the world to recognize Israel as the Premier Nation): **and My Father will love him, and We will come unto him** *(all through the Holy Spirit),* **and make Our abode with him** *(Jesus explained that His manifestation of Himself was to the heart; it was inward and spiritual, so that the heart would consciously enjoy His abiding in it).*

24 He who loves Me not keeps not My sayings *(millions claim to love Jesus, but such is an empty claim if His "sayings" are ignored):* **and the Word which you Hear is not Mine, but the Father's which sent Me** *(Reynolds said, "Love involves obedience, and obedience involves Love. Consequently, obedience is the great proof of Love, and if Love is absent, this means that obedience of the Word is absent as well.").*

25 These things have I spoken unto you, being *yet* **present with you** *(tells us that His time is short in this capacity).*

26 But the Comforter *(Helper),* **which is** **the Holy Spirit** *(proclaims the Third Person of the Godhead),* **Whom the Father will send in My Name** *(because Jesus paid the price on the Cross, enabling the Holy Spirit to come in a completely new dimension),* **He shall teach you all things, and bring all things** *(proclaims the Holy Spirit as the Great Teacher of the Word of God, which is the only way one can learn the Word)* **to your remembrance, whatsoever I have said unto you** *(refers to the Holy Spirit helping the Apostles remember what Jesus had said, and as well to understand what He had said).*

PEACE

27 Peace I leave with you *(Sanctifying Peace),* **My Peace I give unto you** *(there is a vast difference in "Peace with God," which all Believers have, and "The Peace of God" of which Jesus speaks here):* **not as the world gives, give I unto you** *(the peace of the world is but surface; that given by Christ is in the heart).* **Let not your heart be troubled, neither let it be afraid** *("The Peace of God" heals the troubled heart, and takes away fear).*

28 You have heard how I said unto you, I go away, and come *again* **unto you** *(He is speaking of sending the Holy Spirit, which He did!).* **If you loved Me, you would rejoice, because I said, I go unto the Father** *(Christ going to the Father proclaimed the fact that His Great Sacrifice on the Cross had been accepted, and*

Righteousness could now be imputed to men, all carried out by the Holy Spirit): **for My Father is greater than I** *(speaks of Christ as it regards His Incarnation).*

29 And now I have told you before it come to pass *(refers to all the things He would do, which pertained to the Crucifixion, the Resurrection, and the Ascension; as well, it spoke of Him sending back the Holy Spirit, Who in effect would take His place),* **that, when it is come to pass, you might believe** *(has reference to the fact that the fulfillment would be very soon, actually beginning the next day).*

30 Hereafter I will not talk much with you *(could be translated, "Hereafter I will not have much more time to talk with you")*: **for the prince of this world comes** *(speaks of Satan),* **and has nothing in Me** *(Satan had no hold over Jesus, no claim on Jesus, no sin in Jesus, nothing of evil about Jesus; He was totally Holy, completely, absolutely, and irrevocably above sin and Satan).*

31 But that the world may know that I love the Father *(presents Himself in the same mode which He demanded of His Disciples)*; **and as the Father gave Me Commandment, even so I do** *(proclaims His Perfect Example; we are to follow accordingly!).* **Arise, let us go Hence** *(it expressed haste to accomplish the Father's Will).*

CHAPTER 15
(A.D. 33)
THE TRUE VINE

I **Am the True Vine** *(the True Israel, as He is the True Church, and the True Man; more specifically, He Alone is the Source of Life),* **and My Father is the Husbandman** *(refers to God the Father not simply as the Vinedresser, but also the Owner so to speak).*

2 Every branch *(Believer)* **in Me** *(to have Salvation, we must be "in Christ" which refers to trusting in what He did at the Cross)* **that beareth not fruit** *(the Holy Spirit Alone can bring forth fruit within our lives, and He does such through the Finished Work of Christ, which demands that the Cross ever be the Object of our Faith)* **He takes away** *(if the Believer refuses the Cross, ultimately, he will be taken out of the Body of Christ)*: **and every** *branch* **that bears fruit** *(has some understanding of Christ and the Cross),* **He purges it** *(uses whatever means necessary to make the Cross the total Object of one's Faith),* **that it may bring forth more fruit** *(only when the Cross becomes the total Object of one's Faith*

can the Holy Spirit perform His Work of bringing forth proper fruit [Rom. 8:1-2, 11]).

3 Now you are clean through the Word which I have spoken unto you *(the answer, as always, is found in the Word of God; the story of the Bible is "Jesus Christ and Him Crucified").*

4 Abide in Me *(look to Him exclusively, and what He has done for us at the Cross),* **and I in you** *(if we properly abide in Him, which we can only do by ever making the Cross the Object of our Faith, then He will abide in us without fail).* **As the branch** *(Believer)* **cannot bear fruit of itself** *(one cannot Sanctify one's self! it is impossible!),* **except it abide in the Vine** *(abiding in Him refers to the fact that we understand that every solution we seek, for whatever the need might be, is found only in Christ and the Cross; we must never separate Christ from the Cross [I Cor. 1:23; 2:2]);* **no more can you, except you abide in Me.**

5 I am the Vine *(not the Church, not a particular Preacher, not even a particular Doctrine, but Christ Alone),* **you** *are* **the branches** *(Believers)*: **He who abides in Me, and I in him, the same brings forth much fruit** *(let us say it again; the Believer must understand that everything we receive from God comes to us exclusively through Christ and the Cross; that being the case, the Cross must ever be the Object of our Faith; then the Holy Spirit can develop fruit within our lives; it can be done no other way!)*: **for without Me** *(what He did for us at the Cross)* *you* **can do nothing** *(the Believer should read that phrase over and over).*

6 If a man abide not in Me *(refuses to accept the Cross, which means he is serving "another Jesus" [II Cor. 11:4]),* **he is cast forth as a branch** *(is removed from the Source of Life),* **and is withered** *(without proper Faith in Christ and the Cross, the Believer ultimately withers)*; **and men gather them, and cast** *them* **into the fire, and they are burned** *(the implication is striking! if proper Faith in Christ and the Cross is not maintained, the ultimate result is eternal hell).*

7 If you abide in Me *(keep your Faith anchored in Christ and the Cross),* **and My Words abide in you** *(in fact, the entirety of the Word of God is the story of "Christ and the Cross"),* **you shall ask what you will, and it shall be done unto you** *(proper Faith in Christ and the Cross desires only the Will of God, which Will is guaranteed now to be carried forth).*

8 Herein is My Father Glorified *(that Believers totally and completely place their Faith exclusively in Christ and the Cross),* **that you**

bear much fruit *(meaning that Jesus did not die in vain, but that His Death on the Cross will result in "much fruit")*; **so shall you be My Disciples** *(Lk. 9:23-24)*.

9 **As the Father has loved Me** *(the Heavenly Father loves us accordingly, as we abide in Christ)*, **so have I loved you** *(the Good Shepherd gives His Life for the sheep)*: **continue ye in My Love** *(we can continue in His Love, only as we continue in our Faith, which must ever have the Cross as its Object)*.

10 **If you keep My Commandments** *(this can be done only by the Holy Spirit working within us, which He does according to our Faith in Christ and the Cross)*, **You shall abide in My Love** *(this can be done* only *in the manner stated)*; **even as I have kept My Father's Commandments, and abide in His Love** *(the Father's Commandment regarding Christ was that He was to go to the Cross [Mat. 16:21-24]; His Commandment to us is that we ever make Christ and the Cross Alone the Object of our Faith [Jn. 6:53])*.

11 **These things have I spoken unto you, that My joy might remain in you** *(His joy remains in us, only as our Faith is properly placed in Him and the Cross)*, **and** *that* **your joy might be full** *(the Christian cannot know "full joy" until He properly understands the Cross, which means that he then properly understands Christ)*.

12 **This is My Commandment, That you love one another** *(we can only do so through a proper understanding of the Cross)*, **as I have loved you** *(He loved us enough to give His Life for us)*.

13 **Greater love has no man than this** *(the epitome of love)*, **that a man lay down his life for his friends** *(this portrays the Cross, as is obvious)*.

14 **You are My friends** *(consequently, I lay down My Life for you)*, **if ye do whatsoever I Command you** *(as stated, we can only do what He Commands, as we allow the Holy Spirit latitude within our lives, which is done by ever making the Cross the Object of our Faith)*.

15 **Henceforth I call you not servants** *(Faith in Christ and the Cross Alone can lift the Believer to a new status)*; **for the servant knows not what his lord does** *(with faith improperly placed, the Lord cannot confide in us)*: **but I have called you friends; for all things that I have heard of My Father I have made known unto you** *(therefore, we have no excuse!)*.

16 **You have not chosen Me, but I have chosen you** *(it is not really that we find the Lord; the truth is, He finds us)*, **and ordained you** *(has chosen us for a purpose)*, **that you should**

go **and bring forth fruit** *(as stated, we can only do this by ever looking to the Cross [Gal. 6:14])*, **and** *that* **your fruit should remain** *(as our Faith remains in the Cross, the fruit will remain)*: **that whatsoever you shall ask of the Father in My Name** *(using His Name always refers to the victory He won at the Cross)*, **He may give it you.**

17 **These things I Command you, that you love one another** *(if Faith is improperly placed, there is no love, even as there can be no love)*.

HATRED

18 **If the world hate you** *(as it definitely will, if you make Christ and the Cross the Object of your Faith)*, **you know that it hated Me before** *it hated* **you.** *(Why? The world refuses to admit it is so evil that God would have to become man and die on a Cross in order that men might be saved. Therefore, Christ bears the brunt of that animosity.)*

19 **If you were of the world** *(looking to a way other than Christ and the Cross)*, **the world would love his own** *(the world loves its own, and its own love the world)*: **but because you are not of the world** *(refuse to accept the proposed solutions presented by the world)*, **but I have chosen you out of the world** *(brought us out of the system of the world, into the way of the Lord)*, **therefore the world hates you** *(the world hates us because we deny its proposed solutions, and claim that Christ is the only answer; this impacts the pride of man)*.

20 **Remember the word that I said unto you, The servant is not greater than his Lord** *([Jn. 13:16], there it was used concerning humility; here it is used respecting opposition)*. **If they have persecuted Me** *(and they definitely did)*, **they will also persecute you** *(most of the persecution will come from the world of religion)*; **if they have kept My saying** *(they didn't)*, **they will keep yours also** *(meaning that the world, as the world, will not accept our solution of Christ and Him Crucified)*.

21 **But all these things will they do unto you for My Name's sake** *(the Name that is held with more love, and at the same time more contention, is the Name of Jesus)*, **because they know not Him Who sent Me** *(despite the claims of the religions of the world, if they reject Christ, it means they do not know God)*.

22 **If I had not come and spoken unto them, they had not had sin** *(the sin of rejecting Christ, which is the greatest sin of all)*: **but now they have no cloak for their sin** *(means that since*

the Cross, the world is without excuse).

23 He who hates Me hates My Father also *(in every way possible, Jesus repeatedly stated that it was impossible to separate Him from the Father or the Father from Him).*

24 If I had not done among them the Works which none other man did, they had not had sin *(proclaims that His Preaching, Teaching, and Miracles all plainly revealed Who He was)*: but now have they Both seen and hated Both Me and My Father *(the most awful condemnation that can be pronounced on mortal beings).*

25 But *this comes to pass,* that the Word might be fulfilled that is written in their Law *(doesn't mean that they were forced to do this thing, but that it was predicted they would),* They hated Me without a cause *(Ps. 35:19; 69:4).*

26 But when the Comforter *(Helper)* is come *(the Holy Spirit),* Whom I will send unto you from the Father *(presents Jesus as the Baptizer with the Holy Spirit [Mat. 3:11; Jn. 1:31-33]),* **even** the Spirit of Truth *(concerns the veracity of the Word of God; the Holy Spirit superintended its writing all the way from Moses, who began with Genesis, to the closing as given to John on the Isle of Patmos),* which proceeds from the Father *(proclaims the Father sending the Holy Spirit in the Name of Jesus and by the Authority of Jesus),* He shall testify of Me *(Who Christ is [God] and What Christ has done — the Cross):*

27 And you also shall bear witness *(the Apostles),* because you have been with Me from the beginning *(speaks of them observing all He did and all He said [Eph. 2:20]).*

CHAPTER 16
(A.D. 33)
PERSECUTION

THESE things have I spoken unto you, that you should not be offended *(concerns all the warnings of the coming persecution).*

2 They shall put you out of the Synagogues *(religion, which refers to that which man has devised, will not accept Christ and the Cross):* yes, the time comes, that whosoever kills you will think that he does God service *(speaks of terrible religious deception [I Tim. 4:1]).*

3 And these things will they do unto you *(in one way or the other),* because they have not known the Father, nor Me *(despite their claims!).*

THE HOLY SPIRIT

4 But these things have I told you, that

when the time shall come, you may remember that I told you of them *(if the world loves us, something is wrong with our testimony).* And these things I said not unto you at the beginning *(the beginning of His Ministry was not the time to reveal these things),* because I was with you *(but now He is about to leave them, so He reveals what is going to happen).*

5 But now I go My way to Him Who sent Me *(back to the Father in Heaven);* and none of you asks Me, Where do You go? *(They are not asking now, simply because it seems they are beginning to understand what He is saying, at least about leaving.)*

6 But because I have said these things unto you, sorrow has filled your heart *(they somewhat understood Him going back to the Father, but still they didn't understand the coming Resurrection).*

7 Nevertheless I tell you the truth; It is expedient for you that I go away *(the Mission and Ministry of the Holy Spirit to the Body of Christ depended upon the return of Christ to the Father):* for if I go not away, the Comforter *(Holy Spirit)* will not come unto you *(concerns the respective Office Work of Both Jesus and the Holy Spirit — Jesus as the Saviour of men, and the Holy Spirit as the Power of the Church);* but if I depart, I will send Him unto you *(a Finished Work on the Cross was demanded of Christ, before the Holy Spirit could be sent).*

8 And when He *(the Holy Spirit)* is come, He will reprove *(convict)* the world of sin *(the supreme sin of rejecting Christ),* and of Righteousness *(Jesus is Righteousness, and declared so by the Resurrection),* and of judgment *(Satan was judged at Calvary, and all who follow him are likewise judged):*

9 Of sin, because they believe not on Me *(to reject Christ and the Cross is to reject Salvation);*

10 Of Righteousness, because I go to My Father *(Jesus presented a spotless Righteousness to the Father, namely Himself, which pertained to His Sacrifice at Calvary, that was accepted by God; consequently, that Righteousness is imputed to all who will believe in Him and His Work on the Cross),* and you see me no more *(meaning that His Work was Finished);*

11 Of judgment, because the prince of this world is judged *(Satan was completely defeated at Calvary and, thereby, judged as eternally condemned; all who follow him will suffer his fate, the Lake of Fire, and that fate will be forever and forever [Rev. 20:12-15]).*

12 I have yet many things to say unto you

(pertained to the entirety of the New Covenant that would be given to the Apostle Paul, and which foundation had already been laid by Christ), but ye cannot bear them now.

13 Howbeit when He, the Spirit of Truth, is come *(which He did on the Day of Pentecost)*, He will guide you into all Truth *(if our Faith is properly placed in Christ and the Cross, the Holy Spirit can then bring forth Truth to us; He doesn't guide into some truth, but rather "all Truth")*: for He shall not speak of Himself *(tells us not only What He does, but Whom He represents)*; but whatsoever He shall hear, *that* shall He speak *(doesn't refer to lack of knowledge, for the Holy Spirit is God, but rather He will proclaim the Work of Christ only)*: and He will show you things to come *(pertains to the New Covenant, which would shortly be given)*.

14 He shall glorify Me *(will portray Christ and what Christ did at the Cross for dying humanity)*: for He shall receive of Mine *(the benefits of the Cross)*, and shall show *it* unto you *(which He did, when He gave these great Truths to the Apostle Paul [Rom., Chpts. 6-8, etc.])*.

15 All things that the Father has are Mine *(has always been the case; however, due to the Cross, all these things can now be given to the Believer as well)*: therefore said I, that He shall take of Mine, and shall show *it* unto you *(the foundation of all the Holy Spirit reveals to the Church is what Christ did at the Cross [Rom. 6:3-14; 8:1-2, 11; I Cor. 1:17-18, 21, 23; 2:2; Gal., Chpt. 5, etc.])*.

16 A little while, and you shall not see Me *(refers to His Ascension, which would take place in a few days)*: and again, a little while, and you shall see Me *(refers to the coming of the Holy Spirit, Who would be sent back by Christ)*, because I go to the Father *(means that the great Plan of Redemption is completed)*.

17 Then said *some* of His Disciples among themselves, What is this that He said unto us, A little while, and you shall not see Me: and again, a little while, and you shall see Me: and, Because I go to the Father?

18 They said therefore, What is this that He said, A little while? we cannot tell what He says.

19 Now Jesus knew that they were desirous to ask Him, and said unto them, Do you inquire among yourselves of that I said *(evidently the Holy Spirit informed Him of that which they were whispering among themselves)*, A little while, and you shall not see Me: and again, a little while, and you shall see Me?

20 Verily, verily, I say unto you, That you shall weep and lament *(regarding His Crucifixion)*, but the world shall rejoice *(the religious leaders of Israel would rejoice, because they were of the world and not of God)*: and you shall be sorrowful, but your sorrow shall be turned into joy *(the Resurrection and the sending of the Holy Spirit)*.

21 A woman when she is in travail has sorrow, because her hour is come *(speaks of the pain which accompanies the birth of a child)*: but as soon as she is delivered of the child, she remembers no more the anguish, for joy that a man is born into the world *(the sorrow of the Cross will vanish away in the hearts of His followers, when they see what the Cross has accomplished)*.

22 And you now therefore have sorrow: but I will see you again *(speaks of the Resurrection)*, and your heart shall rejoice, and your joy no man takes from you *(because you now know the Truth)*.

PRAYER

23 And in that day *(after the Day of Pentecost)* you shall ask Me nothing *(will not ask Me Personally, as you now do)*. Verily, verily, I say unto you, Whatsoever you shall ask the Father in My Name *(according to what He did at the Cross, and our Faith in that Finished Work)*, He will give *it* you *(He places us in direct relationship with the Father, enjoying the same access as He Himself enjoys)*.

24 Hitherto have you asked nothing in My Name *(while He was with them, the Work on the Cross had not been accomplished; so His Name could not be used then as it can be used now)*: ask, and you shall receive *(ask in His Name, which refers to the fact that we understand that all things are given unto us through and by what Christ did at the Cross)*, that your joy may be full *(it can only be full when we properly understand the Cross)*.

25 These things have I spoken unto you in Proverbs *(concerns the Parables, and as well His portraying Truths to them in a veiled way, and for purpose)*: but the time comes, when I shall no more speak unto you in Proverbs, but I shall show you plainly of the Father *(this could not be done until the Cross was a Finished Work; then the Holy Spirit could reveal things plainly, but only if one properly understands the Cross)*.

26 At that day *(after the Day of Pentecost)* you shall ask in My Name *(in a sense, we are*

given the power of attorney): **and I say not unto you, that I will pray the Father for you** *(His very Presence before the Father guarantees that the Sacrifice of the Cross was accepted; therefore, all who truly follow Christ are instantly accepted as well; if Jesus had to pray to the Father for us, that would mean the Cross was not a Finished Work)*:

DEPARTURE

27 For the Father Himself Loves you, because you have loved Me *(acceptance of Christ is acceptance by the Father)*, **and have believed that I came out from God** *(concerns the Faith of the Believer as it is registered in Christ)*.

28 I came forth from the Father *(speaks of His Deity, and the Mission for which He was sent)*, **and am come into the world** *(but for one purpose, that was to go to the Cross that man might be Redeemed [I Pet. 1:18-20])*: **again, I leave the world, and go to the Father** *(the Mission is complete)*.

29 His Disciples said unto Him, Lo, now You are speaking plainly, and speak no Proverb *(however, they still only understood in a partial sense)*.

30 Now are we sure that You know all things *(they now strongly sense that nothing in their hearts was hidden from Him)*, **and need not that any man should ask You** *(means that before they could ask particular questions, He, already discerning their thoughts, would begin to answer their proposed inquiry)*: **by this we believe that You came forth from God** *(but still their Faith was imperfect, even as we shall see)*.

31 Jesus answered them, Do you now believe? *(He will now tell them just how imperfect their Faith is.)*

32 Behold, the hour comes, yes, is now come *(the Crucifixion was just hours away)*, **that you shall be scattered, every man to his own** *(proclaims their Faith weakening as to its power, but not its essential quality)*, **and shall leave Me Alone** *(proclaims exactly what it says, at the end He was alone!)*: **and yet I am not alone, because the Father is with Me** *(the Father would be with Him every moment, with the exception of the three hours between 12 noon, and 3 p.m. when He was on the Cross, bearing the penalty of sin)*.

33 These things I have spoken unto you, that in Me you might have peace *(in effect, says to them, "Things may look dark, however, despite how they look, everything is under control; trust*

what I have said and believe Me!"). **In the world you shall have tribulation** *(concerns the fundamental condition of Divine Life in this world; the world is totally opposed because its system is solely of Satan)*: **but be of good cheer; I have overcome the world** *(He did this through the Cross [Col. 2:14-15], so may we overcome the world)*.

CHAPTER 17
(A.D. 33)
INTERCESSION

THESE **words spoke Jesus, and lifted up His eyes to Heaven, and said** *(portrays in the following the longest of the Lord's Prayers in the four Gospels; as well, it is the only one stated to have been prayed with the Disciples)*, **Father, the hour is come** *(the time for the Redemption of man, which would be accomplished at the Cross, and which had been planned from eternity past [I Pet. 1:18-20])*; **glorify Your Son** *(the Cross, as horrible as it was, would glorify Christ because it would effect the Redemption of untold millions)*, **that Your Son also may glorify You** *(refers to Him taking upon Himself all the burden of human sorrow, and as well exhausting the poison of the sting of death, which He would do at the Cross and would Glorify God)*:

2 As You have given Him power over all flesh *(presents Christ as the Channel through which Eternal Life may be given)*, **that He should give Eternal Life to as many as You have given Him** *(refers to those who meet the conditions laid down in Scripture concerning Faith [Jn. 3:16; I Tim. 2:4; II Pet. 3:9; Rev. 22:17])*.

3 And this is Life Eternal *(proclaims the true kernel of what Eternal Life actually is)*, **that they might know You the only True God, and Jesus Christ, Whom You have sent** *(the Cross would make all of this possible!)*.

4 I have glorified You on the earth *(proclaims Christ carrying out the Will of God in all things)*: **I have finished the Work which You gave Me to do** *(that Work was the Cross of Calvary; He was so much committed to that Work that He could call it done, even though its conclusion was a few hours in the future)*.

5 And now, O Father, Glorify Thou Me with Thine Own Self *(proclaims that all True Glory exists only in God; when Christ as God became Man, He divested Himself of that Glory)* **with the Glory which I had with You before the world was** *(a request that He would be glorified as Man with the Glory which is Eternally His as*

God; this prayer was answered at the Resurrection, when He came forth with a Glorified Body).

HIS DISCIPLES

6 I have manifested Your Name unto the men which You gave Me out of the world (proclaims the fact that the Name of God was but partially and imperfectly understood before): Yours they were, and You gave them to Me (proclaims a precondition; it means that God had ordained them for this task long before they heard Jesus say, "follow Me," and no doubt long before they were even born; the Omniscience of God can do this, without affecting the free moral agency of man); and they have kept Your Word (doesn't mean that they were perfect, but does mean that they were true to the Light).

7 Now they have known that all things whatsoever You have given Me are of You (actually the Disciples, insensible and full of faults, and yet the Grace that loved them spoke of them in the admiring words of Verses 6 through 8).

8 For I have given unto them the Words which You gave Me (over and over again, Jesus proclaims that He was led by the Father in all that He did, even to the very Words He spoke); and they have received them (does not necessarily mean that they understood them, at least at the time, but they did believe them, and later come to understand them), and have known surely that I came out from You (portrays the bedrock of their Faith), and they have believed that You did send Me (proclaims a core belief not only in His Person, but as well regarding His Mission, even though that knowledge at this time was imperfect).

UNITY

9 I pray for them (concerns His Intercession on their behalf, and is assured of an answer): I pray not for the world (only speaks of this moment, as He, no doubt, prayed much for the world in days past; actually, His entire Ministry was the expression of the Father's Love to the whole world [Jn. 3:16]), but for them which You have given Me (presents Grace which reveals these desires as wonderful, and the privileges that flow from His Care for His Own); for they are Thine (presents all that Jesus had and did as First belonging to the Father).

10 And all Mine are Thine (proclaims total consecration in that they were the Father's before they were His), and Thine are Mine (a man can say, "all mine are Thine," but only Jesus could say, "all Thine are Mine"; this is a claim of perfect equality with the Father); and I am Glorified in them (the Lord is Glorified in Eternal Souls, and not in things).

11 And now I am no more in the world (speaks of His Mission being finished, with Him returning to the Father shortly), but these are in the world (speaks of a hostile environment, with God Alone able to keep them), and I come to You (the Ascension). Holy Father, keep through Your Own Name those whom You have given Me (this would be done by the means of the Cross, and our Faith in that Finished Work), that they may be one, as We are (one in love and unity).

12 While I was with them in the world, I kept them in Your Name (all who truly follow, referring to Faith anchored in the Cross, will be kept): those who You gave Me I have kept, and none of them is lost, but the son of perdition (it refers to the fact that Satan tried to destroy all the Disciples, as would be obvious); that the Scripture might be fulfilled (Judas was not lost that Prophecy might come to pass, but Prophecy foretold the fact of his willful sin and lost state [Ps. 41:9; 69:25-29; 109:8; Acts 1:20-25]).

13 And now come I to You (He set the example relative to prayer; we are meant to follow suit); and these things I speak in the world (He is praying this prayer in a hostile environment, and believes that the Father's Care will protect them in this hostile environment), that they might have My joy fulfilled in themselves (this would be answered on the Day of Pentecost).

14 I have given them Your Word (speaks of a permanent endowment; we must live by the Word); and the world has hated them, because they are not of the world, even as I am not of the world (the spirit of the world is ruled by Satan, the Prince of Darkness, so it is greatly antagonistic toward the Lord).

KEPT FROM EVIL

15 I pray not that You should take them out of the world (in fact, we should be Light in the face of the darkness of this world), but that You should keep them from the evil (this is done through the Cross, and our Faith in that Finished Work).

16 They are not of the world (the calling and election of all Saints have nothing to do with the world or its systems), even as I am not of the world (reflects that the servants should be like

their Lord).

17 Sanctify them through Your Truth *(refers to the Word of God; it alone must ever be the criteria for all things)*: **Your Word is Truth** *(means that the Bible does not merely contain Truth, but "is Truth")*.

18 As You have sent Me into the world *(refers to a Commission which He carried out on the Cross)*, **even so have I also sent them into the world** *(to preach and live the Cross [I Cor. 1:18, 23; 2:2])*.

19 And for their sakes I Sanctify Myself *(I separate Myself unto God in order to do His Will)*, **that they also might be Sanctified through the Truth** *(no one can Sanctify oneself; this is a Work of the Holy Spirit, which is carried out as the Believer evidences Faith in the Cross of Christ [Rom. 8:1-2, 11])*.

BELIEVERS

20 Neither pray I for these alone *(Jesus is speaking not only of His present Disciples, but the multitudes in all ages who would believe their Testimony)*, **but for them also which should believe on Me through their Word** *(has reference to the fact that all must take the Word to others)*;

21 That they all may be One *(again He prays for unity among Believers, which can only be brought about by Love)*; **as You, Father, *are* in Me** *(unity and "Communion")*, **and I in You** *(unity and "Purpose")*, **that they also may be One in Us** *(the pronoun "Us" proclaims the Trinity)*: **that the world may believe that You have sent Me** *(proclaims the Father sending the Son into the world to save the world, and the Son sending His Disciples into the world for the same purpose)*.

22 And the glory which You gave Me I have given them *(unity and "Glory")*; **that they may be one, even as We are One** *(one in "Communion," "Purpose," and "Glory")*:

23 I in them, and You in Me *(spoken distinctly by Christ; Jesus is the mediating link of relation between the Father and Believers)*, **that they may be made perfect in one** *(all of this can be done only through the Cross)*; **and that the world may know that You have sent Me** *(proclaims what this unity brings about)*, **and have loved them, as You have Loved Me** *(that God loves His People will draw more people to Christ than anything else)*.

24 Father, I will that they also, whom You have given Me, be with Me where I am *(one with the Father)*; **that they may behold My Glory, which You have given Me** *(pertains to the exaltation that He will receive at His Resurrection, which was only hours away)*: **for You Loved Me before the foundation of the world** *(Jesus proclaims His preexistence with the Father and, therefore, His Deity)*.

25 O Righteous Father, the world has not known You *(the reason: due to the Fall, it is spiritually dead)*: **but I have known You** *(pertains to far more than mere acquaintance; it speaks of relationship beyond the pale of human comprehension)*, **and these have known that You have sent Me** *(refers to His Mission of Redeeming the world)*.

26 And I have declared unto them Your Name, and will declare *it* *(they do now know, but they have more to learn, much more, which the Spirit will teach them)*: **that the Love wherewith You have Loved Me may be in them, and I in them** *("Love" is the Foundation of all which Christ speaks)*.

CHAPTER 18
(A.D. 33)
THE BETRAYAL

WHEN Jesus had spoken these Words *(probably refers to everything said in Chapters 14 through 17)*, **He went forth with His Disciples over the brook Cedron** *(the brook Cedron [Kedron] runs in a deep valley between the Mount of Olivet and the City of Jerusalem)*, **where was a garden, into the which He entered, and His Disciples** *(spoke of "Gethsemane")*.

2 And Judas also, which betrayed Him, knew the place: for Jesus ofttimes resorted thither with His Disciples *(seems to be where He spent most nights while in the City of Jerusalem)*.

3 Judas then, having received a band *of* men and officers from the Chief Priests and Pharisees *(proclaims John completely omitting the Passion of Christ in the Garden, and cutting straight through to His arrest)*, **coming thither with lanterns and torches and weapons** *(being Passover, it was a full moon; but treachery and hatred distrusted its pure and gentle light; therefore, His enemies brought torches and lanterns)*.

4 Jesus therefore, knowing all things that should come upon Him *(speaks of being perfectly led by the Father and through the Ministry of the Holy Spirit)*, **went forth, and said unto them, Whom seek ye?** *(This speaks of His arrest as He is met by the soldiers and Temple guards; such is evil; and above all, such is religious evil.)*

5 They answered Him, Jesus of Nazareth

(proclaims them speaking the Greatest Name in the annals of human history). **Jesus said unto them, I am** He (should have been translated, "I am," for the pronoun "He" was added by the translators; as such, He was saying the same thing He said to Moses some 1600 years earlier [Ex. 3:14]). **And Judas also, which betrayed Him, stood with them** (Judas had a choice to make; he could stand with Jesus or with the religious hierarchy; he could not stand with both!).

6 **As soon then as He had said unto them, I am** He (describes that Power and Force were in these Words), **they went backward, and fell to the ground** (there could have been a hundred or more men present; His Answer and their response fulfilled the prediction by David concerning this moment [Ps. 27:2]).

7 **Then asked He them again, Whom seek ye?** (He asked this question again, because with this demonstration of Power He wants them to fully understand what they are doing, and exactly Whom they are arresting.) **And they said, Jesus of Nazareth** (it would seem that His display of Power would have spoken to them, and given them pause; however, the human heart, in its hardness, does not easily give way to Righteousness).

8 **Jesus answered, I have told you that I am** He: **if therefore you seek Me, let these go their way** (speaking of His Disciples, and presents a request which they dared not disobey):

9 **That the saying might be fulfilled, which He spoke** (is an insertion into the Narrative given by John), **Of them which You gave Me have I lost none** ([Jn. 17:12], the Lord is speaking of this moment concerning His arrest).

10 **Then Simon Peter having a sword drew it, and smote the High Priest's servant, and cut off his right ear** (presents Peter, I think, attempting to cleave the man's skull; the Holy Spirit no doubt turned aside his aim, with the sword severing the ear only). **The servant's name was Malchus** (the servant's name was given by John only; however, John does not mention the healing of the man's ear as did Luke [Lk. 22:51]).

11 **Then said Jesus unto Peter, Put up your sword into the sheath** (in one sentence, Jesus is proclaiming to the Church that the Gospel is not to be spread by the sword and, in fact, cannot be!): **the cup which My Father has given Me, shall I not drink it?** (This proclaims that which must be done.)

CAIAPHAS

12 **Then the band and the captain and officers** of the Jews took Jesus, and bound Him (this was a part of their procedure for all who were arrested),

13 **And led Him away to Annas first** (he was perhaps the head of the Sanhedrin, the ruling body of Israel); **for he was father-in-law to Caiaphas, which was the High Priest that same year** (this office was now by appointment of Roman authorities).

14 **Now Caiaphas was he, which gave counsel to the Jews, that it was expedient that one man should die for the people** (this "counsel" would destroy their nation!).

PETER

15 **And Simon Peter followed Jesus, and** so did **another Disciple** (refers to John the beloved, who wrote this account): **that Disciple was known unto the High Priest, and went in with Jesus into the palace of the High Priest** (how well John knew Caiaphas is not known).

16 **But Peter stood at the door without** (which probably meant that even though John had permission to enter, Peter did not). **Then went out that other Disciple, which was known unto the High Priest, and spoke unto her who kept the door, and brought in Peter.**

17 **Then said the damsel that kept the door unto Peter, Are you not also** one **of this Man's Disciples?** (This now begins the scenario that will be so hurtful to Peter and to Jesus.) **He said, I am not** (this was a terrible sin; and as sin does, the failure would become increasingly worse).

18 **And the servants and officers stood there, who had made a fire of coals; for it was cold: and they warmed themselves: and Peter stood with them, and warmed himself** (pictures Peter taking up position with the enemies of the Lord).

THE TRIAL

19 **The High Priest then asked Jesus of His Disciples** (refers to all followers of Christ), **and of His Doctrine** (pertained to the things He taught).

20 **Jesus answered him, I spoke openly to the world** (means that He had said nothing in secret); **I ever taught in the Synagogue, and in the Temple, whither the Jews always resort** (in essence says, "if you are claiming that I preached or taught something wrong, why did you not arrest Me in one of the Synagogues, or in the Temple? Why did you not accuse Me before the

people?"); and in secret have I said nothing *(there was no sedition)*.

21 Why do you ask Me? *(In effect, this punches through their hypocrisy.)* ask them which heard Me, what I have said unto them: behold, they know what I said *(the spirit of Darkness in them fought against the Spirit of Light in Him; admittedly they were religious, but in truth, they were religious devils, which in one form or the other characterizes all religion)*.

22 And when He had thus spoken, one of the officers which stood by struck Jesus with the palm of his hand *(probably did this in order to curry favor with the High Priest)*, **saying, Answerest Thou the High Priest so?** *(This answers the fact that they were looking for a reason to strike Him.)*

23 Jesus answered him, If I have spoken evil, bear witness of the evil *(in essence says, "if I have spoken or committed some type of evil, tell Me what it is!)*: but if well, why do you smite Me? *(What have I said or done to deserve this?)*

24 Now Annas had sent Him bound unto Caiaphas the High Priest *(spoken in the past tense and, therefore, speaks of Jesus being sent from Annas to whom He had been sent first)*.

PETER

25 And Simon Peter stood and warmed himself *(now picks up the account of Peter as it ended in Verse 18)*. They said therefore unto him, Are you not also *one* of His Disciples? *(This presents others taking up the accusation, along with the damsel of Verse 17.)* He denied *it*, and said, I am not *(presents the second denial)*.

26 One of the servants of the High Priest, being *his* kinsman whose ear Peter cut off, said, Did not I see you in the garden with Him? *(This presents the occasion for the third denial.)*

27 Peter then denied again: and immediately the rooster crowed *(proclaims the fulfillment of the prediction of Jesus [Lk. 22:34])*.

PILATE

28 Then led they Jesus from Caiaphas unto the hall of judgment *(speaks of Pilate's judgment hall)*: and it was early *(represented the fourth watch of the night, which was between 3 a.m. and 6 a.m. in the morning, but closer to 6 a.m.)*; and they themselves went not into the judgment hall, lest they should be defiled *(ironical! they could murder the Lord of Glory, but their religion forbade them to enter the*

house of a Gentile; such is self-righteousness!)*; but that they might eat the Passover *(has reference to the idea that cleansing from such defilement would take a period of time, and, therefore, they would not be able to partake of the Passover that day; they did not even remotely realize that they were killing the True Passover)*.

29 Pilate then went out unto them, and said, What accusation bring you against this Man?

30 They answered and said unto him, If He were not a malefactor, we would not have delivered Him up to you *(actually records no answer at all, simply because they did not have a case against Him)*.

31 Then said Pilate unto them, Take you Him, and judge Him according to your Law *(proclaims him desiring to rid himself of this matter)*. The Jews therefore said unto him, It is not lawful for us to put any man to death *(they had already condemned Him in their hearts; they wanted Him dead!)*:

32 That the saying of Jesus might be fulfilled, which He spoke, signifying what death He should die *(Jesus had foretold this in Jn. 3:14; 8:28; 12:32; the Mind of God had long since settled this question [I Pet. 1:18-20])*.

33 Then Pilate entered into the judgment hall again, and called Jesus *(refers to him calling Jesus to his side, out of hearing of the crowd)*, and said unto him, Are You the King of the Jews? *(He expected a negative reply; should He answer in the affirmative, it might easily suggest to Pilate that He must be under some futile hallucination.)*

34 Jesus answered him, Do you say this thing of yourself, or did others tell it to you of Me? *(This question, as asked by Jesus, is meant to take the Governor beyond the hurled accusations of those who were thirsty for blood.)*

35 Pilate answered, Am I a Jew? *(The question is asked with some sarcasm, and is actually more of a statement than a question.)* Your Own nation and the Chief Priests have delivered You unto me *(in effect, says, "I am not making the charge, they are!")*: what have you done? *(This is as much asked of himself as it is of Jesus.)*

36 Jesus answered, My Kingdom is not of this world *(in no way denies His Kingship, but does claim that the origin of His Kingdom and Kingship are not of this world)*: if My Kingdom were of this world, then would My servants fight, that I should not be delivered to the Jews *(in essence says that if He was what the Jews claimed Him to be, a usurper over Rome, His followers would have long since been incited to*

use force): **but now is My Kingdom not from hence** (now it's not of this world, but in the future it will be [Hab. 2:14; Rev., Chpt. 19]).

37 **Pilate therefore said unto Him, Are You a King then?** (This question is not exactly asked in sarcasm or sincerity; quite probably, there is a little of both!) **Jesus answered, You say that I am a King** (is the same as saying "yes, it is so!"). **To this end was I born** (addresses the Incarnation, God becoming Man [Isa. 7:14]), **and for this cause came I into the world** (He is to be King in the hearts of all who believe Him), **that I should bear witness unto the Truth** (carries in its statement the entirety of the embodiment of the Ways of God). **Every one who is of the Truth hears My Voice** (only those who sincerely desire Truth will know Christ, i.e., "hear His Voice").

BARABBAS

38 **Pilate said unto Him, What is Truth?** (Pilate shows himself by his question to be a cynic.) **And when he had said this, he went out again unto the Jews, and said unto them** (is done so in the midst of tumult), **I find in Him no fault** at all (Pilate knew that Jesus was not guilty of treason against Rome, or any other type of infraction).

39 **But you have a custom, that I should release unto you one at the Passover** (seems to have taken place immediately upon Jesus being returned to him from Herod): **will you therefore that I release unto you the King of the Jews?** (This is said with some sarcasm, but yet as an appeal to the absurdity of these charges.)

40 **Then cried they all again, saying, Not this man, but Barabbas** (Pilate thought maybe he could get off the hook, thinking surely they would not prefer a robber over Jesus! he was to be sadly disappointed!). **Now Barabbas was a robber** (they chose a robber, and they have been mercilessly robbed ever since).

CHAPTER 19
(A.D. 33)
CROWN OF THORNS

THEN **Pilate therefore took Jesus, and scourged** Him (Pilate seemed to hope that the scourging would satisfy their blood lust! he was again to be disappointed).

2 **And the soldiers platted a crown of thorns** (Victor's thorns), **and put** it **on His head, and they put on Him a purple robe** (probably the

one placed on Him by Herod),

3 **And said, Hail, King of the Jews!** (This was meant to insult not only Christ, but the nation of Israel as well!) **and they smote Him with their hands** (means that they continued hitting Him in the face with their open palms or doubled-up fists).

CRUCIFY HIM

4 **Pilate therefore went forth again, and said unto them, Behold, I bring Him forth to you, that you may know that I find no fault in Him** (proclaims another fruitless appeal to the perverted humanity and justice of the maddened mob).

5 **Then came Jesus forth, wearing the crown of thorns** (again, the Governor hoped to mitigate their ferocity), **and the purple robe. And** Pilate **said unto them, Behold the Man!** (His appeal was in vain; not a voice in Jesus' favor broke the silence.)

6 **When the Chief Priests therefore and officers saw Him** (this Pagan, who knows not God, is moved to pity by this sight, but the religious leadership of Israel showed no pity at all; such is religion!), **they cried out, saying, Crucify** Him, **crucify** Him (registers the most hideous words that ever came out of the mouths of any human beings at any time). **Pilate said unto them, Take ye Him, and crucify** Him: **for I find no fault in Him** (proclaims the Governor once again attempting to absolve himself of blame).

7 **The Jews answered him, We have a law, and by our law He ought to die** (spoke of the Jewish Sanhedrin, the Ruling Body of Israel, both Civil and Religious), **because He made Himself the Son of God** (He did not make Himself the Son of God, but in fact was the Son of God).

PILATE

8 **When Pilate therefore heard that saying, He was the more afraid** (in the Greek, it means to be "exceedingly afraid");

9 **And went again into the judgment hall** (he will question Jesus further), **and said unto Jesus, Who are You?** (Pilate was asking Jesus if He was God.) **But Jesus gave him no answer** (this fulfilled Isa. 53:7).

10 **Then said Pilate unto Him, Do You refuse to speak unto Me?** (The Governor was irritated that Jesus did not answer him.) **Do You** not **know that I have power to crucify You, and have power to release You?**

11 **Jesus answered, You could have no power**

at all against Me, except it were given you from above *(tells us the degree of control exercised by God)*: therefore he who delivered Me unto you has the greater sin *(we learn from this that some sins are worse than others, thereby we learn that the Jews were held by God as more culpable than the Romans).*

12 And from thenceforth Pilate sought to release Him *(he has just said that he has the power to do so, but he is a spineless man)*: but the Jews cried out, saying, If you let this man go, you are not Caesar's friend *(ironical! they hated Caesar; however, they hated their own Messiah more!)*: whosoever makes himself a king speaks against Caesar *(hits at Pilate's weakest spot; the slightest hint of disloyalty to the Emperor would bring serious consequences).*

FINAL REJECTION

13 When Pilate therefore heard that saying, he brought Jesus forth *(presents Jesus brought out of the Judgment Hall to stand before the mob)*, and sat down in the judgment seat in a place that is called the Pavement, but in the Hebrew, Gabbatha *(was a stone platform in the open Court in front of the praetorium, the place of final sentence).*

14 And it was the preparation of the Passover *(was actually a Wednesday instead of Friday, as supposed by most)*, and about the sixth hour *(6 a.m.)*: and he said unto the Jews, Behold your King! *(This sounds like resignation on the part of Pilate, recognizing his tepid efforts to save Christ will not be realized.)*

15 But they cried out, Away with *Him*, away with *Him*, crucify Him *(only Rome could crucify! they want Jesus crucified, hoping this would disprove that He was actually the Son of God; they were taking their cue from Deut. 21:22-23)*. Pilate said unto them, Shall I crucify your King? *(This was exactly what they wanted.)* The Chief Priests answered, We have no king but Caesar *(they elected Caesar to be their king; by Caesar they were destroyed).*

THE CRUCIFIXION

16 Then delivered he Him therefore unto them to be crucified *(he acquiesced to their wishes)*. And they took Jesus, and led *Him* away *(proclaims that which they wanted and they got).*

17 And He bearing His cross *(this is the answer of humanity to the only good Man Who ever lived)* went forth into a place called *the*

place of a skull, which is called in the Hebrew Golgotha *(undoubtedly speaks of that which is referred to presently as "Gordon's Calvary," named for the British General who discovered the place of Crucifixion and the Tomb)*:

18 Where they crucified Him *(Crucifixion was one of the most hideous forms of death that the tortured mind of man could ever begin to conceive)*, and two other with Him, on either side one, and Jesus in the midst *(proclaims such being designed purposely, placing Him between two criminals; however, in this His enemies fulfilled Isa. 53:9).*

19 And Pilate wrote a title, and put *it* on the cross *(it was done by Pilate, despite the Jews)*. And the writing was, JESUS OF NAZARETH THE KING OF THE JEWS *(although intended as sarcasm, nevertheless it was the Truth, and so was engineered by the Holy Spirit).*

20 This title then read many of the Jews *(served its purpose exactly as Pilate hoped it would)*: for the place where Jesus was crucified was nigh to the city *(means it was immediately outside the city limits and alongside a major highway)*: and it was written in Hebrew, *and* Greek, *and* Latin.

21 Then said the Chief Priests of the Jews to Pilate, Write not, The King of the Jews; but that He said, I am King of the Jews.

22 Pilate answered, What I have written I have written *(in effect, He was saying, "You have falsely charged Him with rebelling against Caesar, and you know that you have lied to my face").*

23 Then the soldiers, when they had crucified Jesus *(pertains to the gruesome work being completed of nailing Him to the Cross)*, took His garments, and made four parts, to every soldier a part *(means that four soldiers were employed in the Crucifixion; this was their extra pay for so gruesome a detail)*; and also *His* coat: now the coat was without seam, woven from the top throughout *(the value of this particular garment was that it was without seam, meaning it was all one piece of cloth).*

24 They said therefore among themselves, Let us not rend it, but cast lots for it, whose it shall be *(presents that which John evidently saw and heard with his own eyes and ears; actually it seems he was the only Disciple to stand near the Cross at this time)*: that the Scripture might be fulfilled, which said, They parted My raiment among them, and for My vesture they did cast lots *(Ps. 22:18)*. These things therefore the soldiers did *(little did they realize they were fulfilling Scripture).*

25 Now there stood by the Cross of Jesus His Mother *(the suffering she must have endured as she watched this spectacle is, no doubt, beyond comprehension!)*, and His Mother's sister, Mary *(Maria)* the *wife* of Cleophas, and Mary Magdalene.

26 When Jesus therefore saw His Mother, and the Disciple standing by, whom He loved *(John, the author of this Gospel)*, He said unto His Mother, Woman, behold your son! *(Due to His Own half-brothers not believing in Him, Jesus would place the care of Mary into the hands of John the Beloved; however, the Resurrection would cure this.)*

27 Then said He to the Disciple, Behold your mother! *(Jesus told John that from that moment on, he was to look at Mary exactly as his own Mother.)* And from that hour that Disciple took her unto his own *home (proclaims John speaking of himself in the third person; tradition says that John carried out the Master's Command in totality)*.

DEATH

28 After this, Jesus knowing that all things were now accomplished *(speaks of the last minutes before His Death)*, that the Scripture might be fulfilled, said, I thirst *(Ps. 69:21)*.

29 Now there was set a vessel full of vinegar *(presents a type of wine, which was not an intoxicant)*: and they filled a spunge with vinegar, and put *it* upon hyssop, and put *it* to His mouth *(it was "hyssop," which was also used to put the blood on the doorpost in Egypt at the First Passover; in a sense, it is symbolic of the humanity of Christ)*.

30 When Jesus therefore had received the vinegar *(pertained to the moistening of the lips and tongue, which had dried up because of the loss of body fluid; most probably He asked for this in order that He might speak the last words)*, He said, It is finished *(proclaims the greatest Words, albeit at great price, that any sinner could ever hear; in effect, the world's debt was paid; every iota of the Law had been fulfilled)*: and He bowed His head, and gave up the ghost *(Jesus did not die from His wounds; He freely gave up His Life, in fact dying when the Holy Spirit told Him to die [Heb. 9:14])*.

31 The Jews therefore, because it was the preparation *(concerned the preparation of the Passover meal, carried out the day before the actual Passover)*, that the bodies should not remain upon the Cross on the Sabbath Day, (for that Sabbath Day was an high day,) *(does not speak of the regular Jewish Sabbath of Saturday, but rather the "High Day" of the Passover, also called a Sabbath, which took place on a Thursday)* besought Pilate that their legs might be broken, and *that* they might be taken away *(the shock of the broken legs would kill the victims on the Cross, in order that they might be taken down, thereby not being left on the Cross on the Sabbath)*.

32 Then came the soldiers, and broke the legs of the first, and of the other which was crucified with Him *(speaking of the two thieves)*.

33 But when they came to Jesus, and saw that He was dead already *(presents something unusual, because the victims usually hung on the Cross for days before expiring)*, they broke not His legs:

34 But one of the soldiers with a spear pierced His side *(along with the remainder of the Verses of this Chapter, is fundamentally valuable as affirming beyond controversy the actual Death of Jesus Christ)*, and forthwith came there out blood and water *(is proclaimed by some to be the result of a broken or ruptured heart)*.

35 And He that saw *it* bear record, and His record is true: and He knows what He says is true, that you might believe *(refers to John speaking of himself as an eyewitness)*.

36 For these things were done, that the Scripture should be fulfilled, A bone of Him shall not be broken *(Ex. 12:46; Num. 9:12; Ps. 34:20; at this moment, the Jews were hurrying to eat their Paschal Lamb, not a bone of which could be legally broken, which was a Type of Christ)*.

37 And again another Scripture said, They shall look on Him Whom they pierced *(Ps. 22:16-17; Zech. 12:10; Rev. 1:7)*.

THE BURIAL

38 And after this Joseph of Arimathaea *(he was a member of the Jewish Sanhedrin, along with Nicodemus)*, being a Disciple of Jesus *(a follower of Christ)*, but secretly for fear of the Jews *(speaks of fear of what others would say, and what they would do — the problem with millions presently)*, besought Pilate that he might take away the Body of Jesus *(it took the Cross to bring Joseph of Arimathaea to the place that he would now boldly and openly take a stand for Christ)*: and Pilate gave *him* leave *(allowed him to do so)*. He came therefore, and took the Body of Jesus *(foiled the plans of the Jews to*

remove the corpse to the Valley of Hinnom, which in reality was a garbage dump).

39 And there came also Nicodemus, which at the first came to Jesus by night *(as well, the Cross changed him)*, and brought a mixture of myrrh and aloes, about an hundred pound *weight (this pertained to the embalming process as it was then done by wealthy Jews; this would have been very costly! at the same time, it shows that they did not at all expect Jesus to be raised from the dead).*

40 Then took they the Body of Jesus, and wound it in linen clothes with the spices, as the manner of the Jews is to bury *(whatever their thoughts concerning the Resurrection, both Joseph and Nicodemus were making the statement by their actions that they were friends of Christ).*

41 Now in the place where He was Crucified there was a garden *(John alone mentions the "garden")*; and in the garden a new sepulchre, wherein was never man yet laid *(among other things, this prevented the possibility of any confusion or the Lord's Sacred Body coming into contact with corruption).*

42 There laid they Jesus therefore because of the Jews' preparation *day (spoke of the Passover, which would commence at sundown)*; for the sepulchre was near at hand *(was close to the place of Crucifixion).*

CHAPTER 20
(A.D. 33)
THE RESURRECTION

THE first *day* of the week *(Sunday)* comes Mary Magdalene early, when it was yet dark, unto the sepulchre *(probably about 5 o'clock in the morning)*, and sees the stone taken away from the sepulchre *(proclaims that which she did not expect to find).*

2 Then she ran, and came to Simon Peter, and to the other Disciple, whom Jesus loved *(John the Beloved)*, and said unto them, They have taken away the Lord out of the sepulchre, and we know not where they have laid Him *(all of this shows that the women and the Disciples did not believe He would be Resurrected; maybe they thought Joseph and Nicodemus had moved the Body of Jesus to some other place).*

3 Peter therefore went forth, and that other Disciple *(John)*, and came to the sepulchre *(had they really believed He would rise from the dead, they would have never left the sepulchre).*

4 So they ran both together: and the other Disciple *(John)* did outrun Peter, and came first to the sepulchre *(John arrived first).*

5 And he *(John)* stooping down, *and looking in*, saw the linen clothes lying *(referred to the "linen cloth" of Jn. 19:40; if someone had stolen His Body, they would not have bothered to take the linen from the remains)*; yet went he not in.

6 Then came Simon Peter following him *(John)*, and went into the sepulchre, and saw the linen clothes lie *(the "lie" indicates that this material was neatly folded)*,

7 And the napkin, that was about His head, not lying with the linen clothes *(presents that which is extremely interesting, considering that Jesus' Head and Face had been so maltreated He was hardly recognizable)*, but wrapped together in a place by itself *(none of these actions speak of haste, which would have accompanied the moving or stealing of a body, but rather something done deliberately and with precision; this shouted "Resurrection!").*

8 Then went in also that other Disciple, which came first to the sepulchre *(speaks of John also entering the Tomb now with Peter)*, and he saw, and believed *(refers to what Mary Magdalene reported, and not that Jesus had risen from the dead, as the next Scripture reveals).*

9 For as yet they knew not the Scripture, that He must rise again from the dead *(evidently refers to Ps. 16:10-11).*

10 Then the Disciples went away again unto their own home *(the place where they were temporarily residing, respecting their coming to Jerusalem to keep the Passover).*

MARY MAGDALENE

11 But Mary stood without at the sepulchre weeping *(presents her staying after Peter and John had gone; evidently, she came back not long after them)*: and as she wept, she stooped down, *and looked* into the sepulchre *(evidently represents the second time she had done this [Mat. 28:1-7; Mk. 16:1-7; Lk. 24:1-11])*,

12 And saw two Angels in white sitting *(apparently represents the second appearance of Angels)*, the one at the head, and the other at the feet, where the Body of Jesus had lain *(in a sense, this represents the true Mercy-Seat, with the Angels representing the Cherubim; the Angels sat, but the Cherubim stood, for Redemption was now accomplished [Ex. 25:19]; obviously, these Angels were Princes, for the dignity and importance of the Resurrection demanded the Ministry of the highest Angels [Dan. 9:21;*

10:21; 12:1; Lk. 1:19,26] — Williams).

13 And they say unto her, Woman, why do you weep? *(The truth is that soon she will be shouting!)* She said unto them, Because they have taken away my Lord, and I know not where they have laid Him *(in essence says, "wherever He is, even though it is only a dead Body, there I want to be")*.

14 And when she had thus said, she turned herself back *(would have been better translated, "she was caused to turn back"; perhaps she noticed the Angels looking past her at someone else; Williams said, "to a wounded heart seeking Christ Himself, Angels, however glorious, have no interest")*, and saw Jesus standing, and knew not that it was Jesus *(regarding our Lord's appearances after the Resurrection, there seem to have been two reasons He was not easily recognizable; the first was unbelief, and the second was that His Appearance was changed, at least to a small degree; but unbelief was the biggest problem!)*.

15 Jesus said unto her, Woman, why do you weep? *(This is identical to that asked by the Angels. By virtue of His Death and Resurrection, He for all practical purposes had removed the cause of weeping.)* Whom do you seek? *(This presents the second question asked by Jesus, and really gets to the heart of the matter.)* She, supposing Him to be the gardener *(evidently means she thought this man worked for Joseph of Arimathaea, who owned this garden; still, there is no thought of Resurrection!)*, said unto Him, Sir, if you have borne Him hence, tell me where you have laid Him *(in her mind, the Sacred Body was to be embalmed with the precious spices, which quite possibly she had spent her all to buy; she probably knew that the Jews desired to take His Body and place it in the garbage dump, so she was concerned)*, and I will take Him away *(simply means that if they will allow her, she will give Him a proper burial)*.

16 Jesus said unto her, Mary *(the first expression of "woman" makes her the representative of the whole of suffering humanity; the second expression of "Mary" proclaims the individuality of the Gospel and the manner in which our Lord deals with all who come to Him)*. She turned herself *(refers to her recognizing His Voice)*, and said unto Him, Rabboni; which is to say, Master *(the Greek Text says, "My Master!"; in this Fourth Gospel, the Holy Spirit records four appearances of the Lord after He rose from the dead, and these appearances banished four great enemies of the human heart — "sorrow, fear, doubt, and care")*.

17 Jesus said unto her, Touch Me not *(in effect, says, "Do not hold onto Me, do not try to detain Me")*; for I am not yet ascended to My Father *(Reynolds said, "He, Who is Father of Christ and Father of men, is so in different ways. He is Father of Christ by nature, and of men by Grace." [Forty days later, He would ascend])*: but go to My brethren, and say unto them *(speaks not of those who were his half-brothers in the flesh, but rather His Chosen Disciples, minus Judas who was now dead)*, I ascend unto My Father, and your Father; and *to* My God, and your God *(this statement as given by Christ, portrays a great relationship between the Believer and the Heavenly Father; actually, the very purpose of Calvary and the Resurrection was to establish this relationship through Redemption, which it did!)*.

18 Mary Magdalene came and told the Disciples that she had seen the Lord, and *that* He had spoken these things unto her *(He appeared first of all to her! regrettably, her account was met with unbelief [Mk.16: 9-11])*.

THE TEN DISCIPLES

19 Then the same day at evening, being the first *day* of the week *(proclaims the first gathering on a Sunday)*, when the doors were shut where the Disciples were assembled for fear of the Jews *(the "fear" expressed here pertained to the idea or thought that the religious authorities having now murdered Jesus, may very well seek to do the same to His closest followers; the Day of Pentecost would remove this "fear")*, came Jesus and stood in the midst *(gives us no information as to how this was done; He just seems to have suddenly appeared)*, and said unto them, Peace *be* unto you *(presents a common salutation, but coming from Him, and especially at this time, it spoke Volumes)*.

20 And when He had so said, He showed unto them *His* hands and His side *(had to do with His Wounds, which proved He was not a spirit)*. Then were the Disciples glad, when they saw the Lord *(means that the "Peace which they had not had, they now have"; Jesus is Alive!)*.

21 Then said Jesus to them again, Peace *be* unto you *(is said again by design; the first "Peace" gave to all who were assembled a new Revelation; the second "Peace," a summons to service as we shall see)*: as *My* Father has sent Me, even so send I you *(pertains to the Great Commission of taking the Gospel of Jesus Christ to the world)*.

22 And when He had said this, He breathed on *them* (*presents the same act performed in Gen. 2:7; and to Adam He had breathed the Breath of Life, and now upon our Lord's sons and daughters He breathed the Holy Spirit*), and said unto them, Receive ye the Holy Spirit (*in essence, Jesus is saying to them that what He did at Calvary will now make it possible for them and all Believers to "receive" or to be Baptized with the Holy Spirit [Jn. 7:39; Acts 2:4]*):

23 Whose soever sins you remit, they are remitted unto them (*in its simplest form means that when the Gospel of Jesus Christ is preached and accepted by sinners, the Preacher of the Gospel, or any Believer for that matter, can announce unequivocally to the new Believer that all his sins are "remitted," i.e., forgiven*); *and* whose soever sins you retain, they are retained (*is the same as the former, but exactly opposite; if the Gospel is refused, the Believer has the obligation to inform the Christ-rejecter that, despite whatever else he might do, he is still in his sins, and barring Repentance will suffer the consequences*).

24 But Thomas, one of the Twelve, called Didymus (*Judas had long since been replaced by Matthias by the time John wrote this Gospel*), was not with them when Jesus came (*this should be a lesson to us all! I'm sure it was a lesson to Thomas that he ever again be present*).

25 The other Disciples therefore said unto him, We have seen the Lord (*was the greatest announcement they had ever made, at least since their conversion*). But he said unto them, Except I shall see in His hands the print of the nails, and put my finger into the print of the nails, and thrust my hand into His side, I will not believe (*unbelief ever takes us lower and lower; the problem with untold millions is that "they will not Believe"*).

THE ELEVEN DISCIPLES

26 And after eight days again His Disciples were within, and Thomas with them (*presents Jesus meeting with them again on Sunday, the First Day of the week, the Day of His Resurrection*): then came Jesus, the doors being shut, and stood in the midst (*proclaims His entrance exactly as eight days earlier*), and said, Peace *be* unto you (*all of these times, He is speaking of Sanctifying Peace*).

27 Then said He to Thomas, Reach hither your finger, and behold My Hands; and reach hither your hand, and thrust *it* into My Side (*presents Jesus, at least in the latter phrase, using*

the same words that Thomas had used, showing that He knew exactly what Thomas had said): and be not faithless, but believing (*simply means, "have faith!"; every evidence is that Thomas did exactly that!*).

28 And Thomas answered and said unto Him, My Lord and My God (*there is no evidence that Thomas touched the wounds of the Master; however, he was the first to give this title to Jesus, other than the Prophets in predicting these events [Isa. 9:6-7; Ps. 45:6-7]*).

29 Jesus said unto Him, Thomas, because you have seen Me, you have believed (*presents the lowest form of Faith*): blessed *are* they who have not seen, and *yet* have believed (*concerns the entirety of the Church, and through all ages; they [we] believe even though we haven't personally seen Him; but one day we will!*).

THIS GOSPEL

30 And many other signs truly did Jesus in the presence of His Disciples (*refers to the entirety of His Ministry*), which are not written in this Book (*refers to the Gospel of John*):

31 But these are written, that you might believe that Jesus is the Christ, the Son of God (*pertains to the fact that John did not feel led of the Spirit to record great numbers of Miracles, but rather in his Book is to make prominent the Eternal Life that all who believe in Him, apart from Miracles and material vision, receive*); and that believing you might have Life through His Name (*proclaims that the Holy Spirit desires that Faith accept the Testimony of the Scripture that Jesus of Nazareth is the Messiah officially, and the Son of God essentially; and that whosoever believes in Him shall Live Eternally in ever-enduring bliss*).

CHAPTER 21
(A.D. 33)
JESUS

AFTER these things Jesus showed himself again to the Disciples (*proclaims the fact that Jesus only appeared, it seems, to those who were His followers; Believers in Him were those alone who could see His Spiritual Body*) at the Sea of Tiberias (*Sea of Galilee*); and on this wise showed He *Himself* (*represents the fourth appearance of the Lord, at least in the context of His great victories over various life problems*).

2 There were together Simon Peter, and Thomas called Didymus, and Nathanael of

Cana in Galilee, and the *sons* of Zebedee, and two other of His Disciples.

3 Simon Peter said unto them, I go a fishing *(even though the Scripture is not clear, it seems this fishing expedition was not for pleasure, but rather the necessity of making a living for their families; however, a Ministry which originates in the energy of the carnal will is fruitless; but when under the Governance of the Head of the Church, it brings forth rich fruit).* They say unto him, We also go with you *(represents the other six Disciples present; we aren't told where the remaining four were at this time).* They went forth, and entered into a ship immediately *(probably referred to one of the vessels formerly used by Peter and the sons of Zebedee in their former fishing business)*; and that night they caught nothing *(points to the fact that they were doing this for income, not for pleasure).*

THE MIRACLE

4 But when the morning was now come *(they had fished all night, but without success),* Jesus stood on the shore *(presents the beginning of a most valuable lesson)*: but the Disciples knew not that it was Jesus *(once again portrays the same experience as had by others).*

5 Then Jesus said unto them, Children, have you any meat? *(This question was meant to draw them out, because their concern at the time was making a living for their families.)* They answered Him, No *(showed their lack of success for a night's work).*

6 And He said unto them, Cast the net on the right side of the ship, and you shall find *(what must have been their thoughts concerning the admonition of this stranger!).* They cast therefore *(seems to suggest that John may have suspected this was the Lord),* and now they were not able to draw it for the multitude of fishes *(this appearance of Christ addressed the life problem of "care").*

7 Therefore that Disciple whom Jesus loved *(John)* said unto Peter, It is the Lord *(without a doubt, it would be one of the greatest moments of their lives).* Now when Simon Peter heard that it was the Lord, he girded *his* fisher's coat *unto him,* (for he was naked,) *(does not refer to a total lack of clothing, but rather that he had laid aside his outer garment in order that it not be soiled),* and did cast himself into the sea *(presents such being done not to attend the overburdened net, but rather to come quickly to Jesus).*

8 And the other Disciples came in a little ship *(different than the main vessel);* (for they were not far from land, but as it were two hundred cubits,) *(approximately one hundred yards)* dragging the net with fish *(represents a tremendous catch which took only a few minutes, versus their night-long efforts which had produced only an empty net; such is the effort with Christ, and such is the effort without Christ!).*

9 As soon then as they were come to land, they saw a fire of coals there, and fish laid thereon, and bread *(where did Jesus get these provisions? I personally believe He miraculously supplied them).*

10 Jesus said unto them, Bring of the fish which you have now caught *(this portrays the fact that the fish Jesus had cooked didn't come from this particular supply).*

11 Simon Peter went up, and drew the net to land full of great fish *(insinuating that each fish was larger than normal),* an hundred and fifty and three *(the exact number is given by the Holy Spirit for purpose and reason; the Disciples were to be fishers of men, not of fish per se; consequently, the number given of the fish portrays the fact that each soul is precious in the sight of God, and numbered accordingly)*: and for all there were so many, yet was not the net broken *(presents a contrast with the miraculous catch given in Lk. 5:6, where the net did break; symbolically speaking, the net broke then because the Holy Spirit had not yet come; with the Holy Spirit, the net won't break).*

12 Jesus said unto them, Come *and* dine *(presents Him functioning as a Servant as usual, even in His Glorified State).* And none of the Disciples did ask Him, Who are You? knowing that it was the Lord *(regrettably, many today are asking, concerning certain religious phenomenon, "Who are You?"; meaning that the earmarks of the True Gospel are little present).*

13 Jesus then comes, and takes bread, and gives them, and fish likewise *(the "bread" was symbolic of Himself, with the fish, i.e., "meat," being symbolic of His Word).*

14 This is now the third time that Jesus showed Himself to His Disciples, after that He was risen from the dead *(third time to His Disciples; there is some discrepancy as to how many times He appeared, but the fact is He did appear to many after His Resurrection, before His Ascension).*

THE COMMISSION

15 So when they had dined, Jesus said to

Simon Peter, Simon, *son* of Jonah, do you love Me more than these? *(This question is referring to Peter's boasts immediately before the Crucifixion that He loved Jesus more than the other Disciples [Mat. 26:31-35; Mk. 14:29].)* He said unto him, Yes, Lord; You know that I love You *(Jesus used the Greek verb "Agapao" for love, which means "Ardent, Supreme, and Perfect," while Peter used the Greek verb "Phileo," which means "to be fond of, to feel friendship for another").* He said unto him, Feed My lambs *(refers to the newest converts, which need special attention, and who will be entrusted to Peter).*

16 He said to him again the second time, Simon, *son* of Jonah, do you love Me? *(The question presents Jesus leaving off the words, "more than these"; however, He does continue to use the strong Greek word "Agapao" for love; by leaving off these words, Jesus will draw Peter away from a boastful attitude.)* He said unto him, Yes, Lord; You know that I love You *(presents Peter continuing to use the same Greek verb "Phileo" for Love as He did the first time; this is not a negative, but rather a positive; he is finally seeing that he cannot trust the flesh).* He said unto him, Feed My sheep *(by Christ using the word "Sheep," He now is speaking of strong, mature Believers).*

17 He said unto him the third time, Simon, *son* of Jonah, Do you love Me? *(Jesus now uses the weaker word "Phileo" for Love, as Peter had used.)* Peter was grieved because he said unto him the third time, Do you Love Me? *(Peter very well understands that Jesus has Himself now used the lesser word for Love, which says something to the Apostle.)* And he said unto Him, Lord, You know all things *(the Apostle now knows that Jesus knows all things about him — that which he did, thought, and felt; he also knows that the Lord has wounded his heart in order to train and fit him for the high honor of shepherding that which was most precious to Himself, i.e., the Sheep of Jn., Chpt. 10);* You know that I love You *(and Jesus, of course, did know).* Jesus said unto him, Feed My sheep *(expresses total and complete confidence).*

PROPHECY

18 Verily, verily, I say unto you, When you were young, you girded yourself, and walked where you would *(refers to his prime of life):* but when you shall be old, you shall stretch forth your hands, and another shall gird you *(predicted Peter's faithfulness unto death, which*

undoubtedly comforted and strengthened his pierced heart, and as well prevented the other Disciples from scornfully reminding him of his former cowardice),* and carry *you* where you would not *(refers to the time and distant day when Peter would die).*

19 This spoke He, signifying by what death he should glorify God *(Tertullain and Eusebius said that the Apostle, upon facing death, preferred Crucifixion with his head downwards on the plea that to be Crucified as His Master was too great an honor for one who had denied his Lord).* And when He had spoken this, He said unto him *(said to Peter),* Follow Me *(with one word, the Lord now corrects every one of Peter's failings, and institutes him into His sublime Mission).*

JOHN

20 Then Peter, turning about, seeing the Disciple whom Jesus loved following *(spoke of John, and once more, even this soon, presents Peter's extraordinary characteristic to guide rather than to follow; old habits die hard!);* which also leaned on His breast at supper, and said, Lord, which is he who betrays You? *(This question presents John speaking of himself, and taking us back to the Last Supper.)*

21 Peter seeing Him said to Jesus, Lord, and what *shall* this man *do*? *(This presents Peter asking something for which He will be rebuked.)*

22 Jesus said unto him, If I will that he tarry till I come, what *is that* to you? *(In effect, Jesus is proclaiming to Peter that it is none of his business as to what the Will of God is for John.) You* follow Me *(the pronoun "you" is emphatic; the lesson we should learn from this is not the glory of any Church, but the Personal Glory of the Lord Jesus; we are to follow Him, which means we follow nothing else; that alone will keep us occupied to the extent that, if done properly, we will not try to attend to the business of others).*

23 Then went this saying abroad among the brethren, that that Disciple should not die *(proclaims the manner in which Scripture can be misinterpreted):* yet Jesus said not unto him, He shall not die *(refers to John setting the record straight as to what Jesus had actually said to him);* but, If I will that he tarry till I come, what *is that* to you? *(This presents Jesus in the words, "If I will," as the absolute disposer of human life and, as well, reveals His Godhead. Jesus did come to him on the Isle of Patmos and gave him the great Revelation, which closed out the Canon of Scripture.)*

TESTIMONY

24 This is the Disciple which testifies of these things *(presents John as an eye-witness of all he relates)*, **and wrote these things** *(verifies John as the author of this Gospel)*: **and we know that his testimony is true** *(verifies the Inspiration of the Holy Spirit upon these accounts in that which we refer to as "The Gospel according to John")*.

25 And there are also many other things which Jesus did *(speaks, no doubt, of the many Miracles He performed, some which are not recorded in any of the four Gospels)*, **the which, if they should be written every one** *(lends credence to the idea that there were far more Miracles performed by Jesus and not recorded, than those which were recorded)*, **I suppose that even the world itself could not contain the books that should be written. Amen** *(Christ is infinite, the Earth finite; hence, the supposition of the Verse is most reasonable)*.

THE
ACTS OF THE APOSTLES

CHAPTER 1
(A.D. 33)
POST-RESURRECTION

THE former treatise have I made *(refers to the Gospel of Luke, which was probably finished a year or so before the writing of this account called, "The Acts of the Apostles")*, O Theophilus *(the same person addressed by Luke in that Gospel)*, of all that Jesus began both to do and teach *(is the Standard, the Principal, and the Foundation of the Gospel)*,

2 Until the day in which He was taken up *(the Resurrection)*, after that He through the Holy Spirit *(refers to the fact that the Spirit of God is the Speaker and Actor in this Book)* had given Commandments unto the Apostles whom He had chosen *(refers to our Lord's Ministry of some three and a half years, which the Apostles witnessed)*:

3 To whom also He showed Himself alive after His passion by many infallible proofs *(many people saw Him after His Resurrection, and before His Ascension)*, being seen of them forty days *(from the time of the Resurrection to the time of His Ascension)*, and speaking of the things pertaining to the Kingdom of God *(it seems that much teaching was included during this period of time)*:

HOLY SPIRIT

4 And, being assembled together with *them* *(speaks of the time He ascended back to the Father; this was probably the time of the "above five hundred" [I Cor. 15:6])*, Commanded them *(not a suggestion)* that they should not depart from Jerusalem *(the site of the Temple where the Holy Spirit would descend)*, but wait for the Promise of the Father *(spoke of the Holy Spirit which had been promised by the Father [Lk. 24:49; Joel, Chpt. 2])*, which, said *He*, you have heard of Me *(you have also heard Me say these things [Jn. 7:37-39; 14:12-17, 26; 15:26; 16:7-15])*.

PROPHECY

5 For John truly baptized with water *(merely symbolized the very best Baptism Believers could receive before the Day of Pentecost)*; but you shall be baptized with the Holy Spirit not many days hence *(spoke of the coming Day of Pentecost, although Jesus did not use that term at that time)*.

6 When they therefore were come together, they asked of Him, saying *(seemingly presents the last meeting before the Ascension)*, Lord, will You at this time restore again the Kingdom to Israel? *(He would later answer this question through the Apostle Paul [II Thess., Chpt. 2].)*

7 And He said unto them, It is not for you to know the times or the seasons, which the Father has put in His Own power *(the Master is saying that it is not the business of the followers of Christ to know this information, but rather to "occupy till I come" [Lk. 19:13])*.

POWER

8 But you shall receive power *(Miracle-working Power)*, after that the Holy Spirit is come upon you *(specifically states that this "Power" is inherent in the Holy Spirit, and solely in His Domain)*: and you shall be witnesses *(doesn't mean witnessing to souls, but rather to one giving one's all in every capacity for Christ, even to the laying down of one's life)* unto Me *(without the Baptism with the Holy Spirit, one cannot really know Jesus as one should)* both in Jerusalem, and in all Judaea, and in Samaria, and unto the uttermost part of the Earth *(proclaims the Work of God as being worldwide)*.

THE ASCENSION

9 And when He had spoken these things *(refers to His last instructions to His followers)*, while they beheld, He was taken up *(refers to Him ascending before their very eyes)*; and a cloud received Him out of their sight *(represents the Shekinah Glory of God, which enveloped Christ as He ascended)*.

SECOND ADVENT

10 And while they looked stedfastly toward Heaven as He went up *(these statements are*

important because they affirm His actual Ascension testified to by eyewitnesses), behold, two men stood by them in white apparel (these two "men" were actually Angels);

11 Which also said, You men of Galilee, why do you stand gazing up into Heaven? (This does not mean that it was only men who were present, but rather that this was a common term used for both men and women.) this same Jesus, which is taken up from you into Heaven (refers to the same Human Body with the nail prints in His Hands and Feet, etc.), shall so come in like manner as you have seen Him go into Heaven (refers to the same place, which is the Mount of Olivet).

THE UPPER ROOM

12 Then returned they unto Jerusalem from the Mount called Olivet (represents, as stated, the place of His Ascent, which will also be the place of His Descent), which is from Jerusalem a Sabbath Day's journey (represents a little over half a mile).

13 And when they were come in, they went up into an upper room (was probably the same room where they had eaten the Passover with Christ [Lk. 22:12]), where abode both Peter, and James, and John, and Andrew, Philip, and Thomas, Bartholomew, and Matthew, James the son of Alphaeus, and Simon Zelotes, and Judas the brother of James (this Judas is also called "Lebbaeus" and "Thaddaeus" [Mat. 10:3; Mk. 3:18]).

14 These all continued with one accord in prayer and supplication (proclaims the manner in which these meetings were conducted), with the women, and Mary the Mother of Jesus (concerns the women who followed Christ from Galilee [Mat. 27:55-56]), and with His Brethren.

THE SUCCESSOR TO JUDAS ISCARIOT

15 And in those days Peter stood up in the midst of the Disciples (represents Peter taking the lead), and said, (the number of names together were about an hundred and twenty,) (in essence forms the beginning of the "Church").

16 Men and brethren, this Scripture must needs have been fulfilled, which the Holy Spirit by the mouth of David spoke before concerning Judas, which was guide to them who took Jesus (is derived from Ps. 69:25-28).

17 For He was numbered with us, and had obtained part of this Ministry (means He was one of the Apostles, and chosen by the Lord).

18 Now this man purchased a field with the reward of iniquity (refers to Pharisees taking the blood money from Judas, and buying his burying place [Mat. 27:6-8]); and falling headlong, he burst asunder in the midst, and all his bowels gushed out (he committed suicide [Mat. 27:3-8]).

19 And it was known unto all the dwellers at Jerusalem (actually means that it "became known"); insomuch as that field is called in their proper tongue, Aceldama, that is to say, The field of blood (was also known as the "Potter's Field").

20 For it is written in the Book of Psalms, Let his habitation be desolate, and let no man dwell therein (the indication is that the name of Judas had been in the Book of Life, but had been blotted out because of his sin): and His bishoprick let another take (refers to his Apostleship).

21 Wherefore of these men which have companied with us all the time that the Lord Jesus went in and out among us (probably spoke of the seventy [Lk. 10:17]),

22 Beginning from the Baptism of John, unto that same day that He was taken up from us (spans the entirety of the three and one half years of the Ministry of Christ), must one be ordained to be a witness with us of His Resurrection (we learn from this that the Resurrection of Christ from the dead is a Cardinal Doctrine of the Gospel).

23 And they appointed two, Joseph called Barsabas, who was surnamed Justus, and Matthias (they would present these two to the Lord for His choice).

24 And they prayed (shows their utter dependence on the Lord for leading and guidance), and said, You, Lord, which knows the hearts of all men (tells us where alone the Truth can be found), show whether of these two You have chosen (proclaims their desire for God's Choice, and His Choice Alone),

25 That he may take part of this Ministry and Apostleship (the Foundation of the Church), from which Judas by transgression fell (tells us plainly that Judas once knew the Lord, for how can one fall from something to which one has never attained), that he might go to his own place (self-will will take one to eternal hell, even as it did Judas).

26 And they gave forth their lots (was similar to the Urrim and Thummim with which the Disciples would have been familiar and the Lord,

in Old Testament times, gave leading to His People [Deut. 33:8-10; Num. 27:21]); **and the lot fell upon Matthias** (*probably means that the names of the two men were placed on two stones, pieces of parchment, or wood, and then placed into an urn, with one lot drawn out [Lev. 16:8-9; Josh. 14:2]*); **and he was numbered with the Eleven Apostles** (*indicates that he was God's Choice*).

CHAPTER 2
(A.D. 33)
PENTECOST

AND when the Day of Pentecost was fully come (*the Feast of Pentecost, one of the seven great Feasts ordained by God and practiced by Israel yearly; it took place fifty days after Passover*), **they were all with one accord in one place** (*not the Upper Room where they had been previously meeting, but rather the Temple [Lk. 24:53; Acts 2:46]*).

2 **And suddenly there came a sound from Heaven as of a rushing mighty wind** (*portrays the coming of the Holy Spirit in a new dimension, all made possible by the Cross*), **and it filled all the house** (*the Temple*) **where they were sitting** (*they were probably in the Court of the Gentiles*).

3 **And there appeared unto them cloven tongues like as of fire** (*the only record of such in the New Testament, and was the fulfillment of the Prophecy of John the Baptist concerning Jesus [Mat. 3:11]*), **and it sat upon each of them** (*refers to all who were there, not just the Twelve Apostles; the exact number is not known*).

4 **And they were all filled with the Holy Spirit** (*all were filled, not just the Apostles; due to the Cross, the Holy Spirit could now come into the hearts and lives of all Believers to abide permanently [Jn. 14:16]*), **and began to speak with other tongues** (*the initial physical evidence that one has been Baptized with the Spirit, and was predicted by the Prophet Isaiah [Isa. 28:9-12], and by Christ [Mk. 16:17; Jn. 15:26; 16:13]*), **as the Spirit gave them utterance** (*meaning they did not initiate this themselves, but that it was initiated by the Spirit; as we shall see, these were languages known somewhere in the world, but not by the speaker*).

5 **And there were dwelling at Jerusalem Jews, devout men, out of every nation under Heaven** (*Jews were then scattered all over the Roman World, with thousands coming in from every nation to keep the Feast*).

6 **Now when this was noised abroad** (*multitudes who were in the Temple heard and saw the proceedings, and as well, began to tell others*), **the multitude came together** (*what was happening attracted a multitude*), **and was confounded, because that every man heard them speak in his own language** (*means that these on-looking Jews heard these people speaking in many different languages, in fact languages of the nation's of their residence, wherever that might have been, proving that this was not gibberish or babble as some claim*).

7 **And they were all amazed and marveled** (*mostly centered upon this speaking with other tongues*), **saying one to another, Behold, are not all these which speak Galilaeans?** (*This means that the Galilaean accent was peculiar and well-known [Mk. 14:70; Lk. 22:59].*)

8 **And how hear we every man in our own tongue, wherein we were born?** (*This proves once again that this was not babble, mere chatter, or gibberish, but rather a language known somewhere in the world, but not by the speaker.*)

9 **Parthians, and Medes, and Elamites, and the dwellers in Mesopotamia, and in Judaea, and Cappadocia, in Pontus, and Asia,**

10 **Phrygia, and Pamphylia, in Egypt, and in the parts of Libya about Cyrene, and strangers of Rome, Jews and proselytes,**

11 **Cretes and Arabians, we do hear them speak in our tongues the wonderful Works of God** (*this tells us what speaking in tongues actually is, a recitation of the "Wonderful Works of God"*).

12 **And they were all amazed, and were in doubt** (*should have been translated, "and were perplexed;" they had no rational answer to their perplexity*), **saying one to another, What does this mean?** (*This was asking more in wonder than demanding an answer.*)

13 **Others mocking said** (*they scoffed; whether by gesture or word, they jeered at the Testimony of this given by the Holy Spirit*), **These men are full of new wine** (*was actually an accusation that they were drunk, i.e., "intoxicated"; some were amazed and some "mocked," which continues to be done even unto this hour*).

PETER

14 **But Peter, standing up with the Eleven, lifted up his voice, and said unto them** (*Peter will now preach the inaugural Message of the Church on that Day of Pentecost*), **You men of Judaea, and all you who dwell at Jerusalem, be this known unto you, and hearken to my**

words (*the Message was probably delivered on Solomon's Porch, a part of the Court of the Gentiles; it was where debates and such like were commonly conducted*):

15 For these are not drunken, as you suppose (*in effect, says they are drunk, but not in the common manner*), seeing it is *but* the third hour of the day (*9 a.m.*).

16 But this is that which was spoken by the Prophet Joel (*please notice that Peter did not say, "this fulfills that spoken by the Prophet Joel," but rather, "this is that . . ." meaning that it will continue*);

17 And it shall come to pass in the last days, saith God (*proclaims these "last days" as beginning on the Day of Pentecost, and continuing through the coming Great Tribulation*), I will pour out of My Spirit upon all flesh (*speaks of all people everywhere and, therefore, not limited to some particular geographical location; as well, it is not limited respecting race, color, or creed*): and your sons and your daughters shall Prophesy (*includes both genders*), and your young men shall see visions, and your old men shall dream dreams (*all given by the Holy Spirit; the Hebrew language insinuates, "both your young men and old men shall see visions, and both your old men and young men shall dream dreams"; it applies to both genders as well*):

18 And on My servants and on My handmaidens I will pour out in those days of My Spirit (*is meant purposely to address two classes of people who had been given very little status in the past, slaves and women*); and they shall Prophesy (*pertains to one of the "Gifts of the Spirit" [I Cor. 12:8-10]*):

19 And I will show wonders in Heaven above, and signs in the earth beneath; blood, and fire, and vapour of smoke (*pertains to the fact that these "days of My Spirit" will cover the entirety of the Church Age, even into the coming Great Tribulation; that time limit has now been nearly two thousand years*):

20 The sun shall be turned into darkness, and the moon into blood (*not meant to be literal, but rather that the moon will look blood red because of atmospheric conditions*), before that great and notable Day of the Lord come (*the Second Coming*):

21 And it shall come to pass, *that* whosoever shall call on the Name of the Lord shall be saved (*Joel 2:30-32; presents one of the most glorious statements ever made; it includes both Jews and Gentiles equally*).

22 You men of Israel, hear these words (*the inaugural Message of the Church*); Jesus of Nazareth, a Man approved of God among you (*Jesus must ever be the theme of our Message; He was approved of God, but not of men*) by miracles and wonders and signs, which God did by Him in the midst of you (*what Peter knew firsthand, because he was there*), as you yourselves also know (*so many of these things were done that there was absolutely no excuse for them not to know*):

23 Him, being delivered by the determinate counsel and foreknowledge of God (*it was the Plan of God that Jesus would die on the Cross; however, it was not the Plan of God for the religious leaders of Israel to do this thing; that was of their own making and choice*), you have taken, and by wicked hands have crucified and slain (*presents a charge so serious it absolutely defies description! but yet, if they will seek mercy and forgiveness, God will forgive them, even as we shall see*):

24 Whom God has raised up (*concerns the Resurrection*), having loosed the pains of death (*death could not hold Him because He atoned for all sin, which occasions death [Rom. 6:23]*): because it was not possible that He should be held by it (*death would liked to have held Him in its grip, but it could not because He had taken away its legal right; as stated, He atoned for all sin, which defeated death, Satan, and all principalities and powers [Col. 2:14-15]*).

25 For David speaks concerning Him (*Ps. 16:8-11*), I foresaw the Lord always before My face, for He is on My Right Hand, that I should not be moved (*through the Cross, Christ would gain this position at the Father's Right Hand, which speaks of power and authority, all on our behalf [Heb. 1:3]*):

26 Therefore did My heart rejoice (*concerns Christ rejoicing over His Father's guarantee and protection regarding His descent into the death world; He knew that the Father would bring Him out*), and My tongue was glad (*refers to the things He said regarding His Resurrection [Mat. 16:21; 17:23; 20:17-19; Mk. 8:31]*); moreover also My flesh shall rest in hope (*refers to resting on the Promises of God relating to the Resurrection*):

27 Because You will not leave My soul in hell (*it was not the burning part of Hell [Lk. 16:19-31], neither will You (God the Father) suffer Your Holy One to see corruption (*His physical body, being sinless, saw no corruption, which normally accompanies death; in fact, it

was glorified and raised from the dead).

28 You have made known unto Me the ways of Life *(presents Christ as the Pattern, and as well presents the Resurrection not only of Himself, but all Believers);* You shall make Me full of joy with Your countenance *(God's Face did shine upon Christ, and it shines upon us as well, as we are "in Christ").*

29 Men *and* Brethren, let me freely speak unto you of the Patriarch David *(presents the only time David is referred to in Scripture as a "Patriarch"),* that he is both dead and buried, and his sepulchre is with us unto this day *(is given here to dispel the erroneous notions held by the Pharisees and religious leaders of Israel concerning the Messiah).*

30 Therefore being a Prophet *(concerns the many Prophecies given by David in the Psalms regarding Christ),* and knowing that God had sworn with an oath to him, that of the fruit of his loins, according to the flesh *(II Sam. 7:11-16),* He *(God)* would raise up Christ to sit on his throne *(to sit on David's Throne, which has not yet happened, but most surely will in the coming Kingdom Age; all of this portrays the Incarnation, God becoming Man and doing so through the lineage of David);*

31 He *(David)* seeing this before spoke of the Resurrection of Christ *(tells the religious leaders of Israel David plainly Prophesied that Jesus would be raised from the dead [Ps. 16:8-11]),* that His soul was not left in Hell *(as stated, He did not go to the burning side of Hell, but rather into Paradise [Lk. 16], and as well to some particular prisons in that infernal region [I Pet. 3:19-20]),* neither did His flesh see corruption *(He was not tormented in Hell as some teach, neither was there any decay in His physical Body; rather it was Glorified).*

32 This Jesus *(the One you Crucified)* has God raised up *(speaks of the physical Jesus and not some spirit),* whereof we all are witnesses *(Peter is telling them that despite what they say, all of Israel knows that Jesus was raised from the dead).*

33 Therefore being by the Right Hand of God exalted *(Christ is now exalted, not only as Creator, but as well as Saviour, the latter made possible by the Cross),* and having received of the Father the Promise of the Holy Spirit *(proves that Jesus was accepted by the Father because the Holy Spirit was sent back, even as Promised [Jn. 16:7]),* He has shed forth this, which you now see and hear *(they saw the people, and they heard them speak with tongues).*

34 For David is not ascended into the Heavens *(given by Peter to prove that these Prophecies were not given to David concerning himself, but rather the One Who was to come, namely the Lord Jesus Christ; evidently, some of the religious leaders of Israel were claiming that these Prophecies pertained to David, and had nothing to do with Jesus, which Peter repudiates here):* but he *(David)* said himself, The LORD said unto My Lord *(God the Father said to God the Son),* Sit Thou on My Right Hand *([Ps. 110:1] this is where Jesus now abides [Heb. 1:3]),*

35 Until I make Your foes Your footstool *(all made possible by the Cross [Col. 2:14-15], but will not be fully realized until the conclusion of the Kingdom Age [Rev., Chpt. 20; I Cor. 15:24-25]).*

36 Therefore let all the house of Israel know assuredly *(is leveled by Peter directly toward the religious leadership of Israel, and is inspired by the Holy Spirit),* that God has made that same Jesus, Whom you have Crucified, both Lord and Christ *(Jesus was and is "Jehovah," and as well, Israel's "Messiah").*

THE EFFECT

37 Now when they heard *this*, they were pricked in their heart *(the convicting Power of the Holy Spirit),* and said unto Peter and to the rest of the Apostles, Men *and* Brethren, what shall we do? *(This proclaims these people, whomever they may have been, desiring to get right with God.)*

38 Then Peter said unto them, Repent *(admit that God is right, and we are wrong),* and be baptized every one of you in the Name of Jesus Christ *(by the authority of that Name; there is no baptismal formula given in the Book of Acts; the only formula given was given by Christ in Mat. 28:19)* for the remission of sins *(should have been translated, "because of remission of sins"; one is Baptized in Water because one's sins have already been remitted due to Faith in Christ, and not that sins should be remitted),* and you shall receive the Gift of the Holy Spirit *(Repentance guarantees Salvation, which makes the Believer ready to be Baptized with the Holy Spirit; one is not Baptized with the Spirit automatically at conversion; it is an experience that follows Salvation, and is always accompanied by speaking with other tongues [Acts 2:4; 10:44-46; 19:1-7]).*

39 For the Promise *(of the Baptism with the Holy Spirit)* is unto you *(directed toward the*

many Jews standing in the Temple listening to Peter that day), **and to your children** (*means that this great outpouring did not stop with the initial outpouring, but continues on*), **and to all who are afar off** (*meaning that it's not only for those in Jerusalem, but the entirety of the world as well*), *even* **as many as the Lord our God shall call** (*that "Call" is "whosoever will" [Jn. 7:37-39; Rev. 22:17]*).

40 **And with many other words did he testify and exhort** (*tells us that we only have a part of Peter's Message here*), **saying, Save yourselves from this untoward generation** (*it is a call to Repentance*).

41 **Then they who gladly received his word were baptized** (*some believed what Peter said, gave their hearts to God, and repented of their sins; they were then Baptized in Water*): **and the same day there were added** *unto them* **about three thousand souls** (*on the first Day of Pentecost, the Day the Law was given, some three thousand men died [Ex. 32:28]; on this Day of Pentecost, due to the Cross, some three thousand people were saved*).

THE EARLY CHURCH

42 **And they continued stedfastly in the Apostles' Doctrine** (*that Doctrine is found in Verse 38*) **and fellowship, and in breaking of bread** (*had to do with the celebration of the Lord's Supper, which was probably a much more informal setting than presently*), **and in prayers** (*simply meant it was a praying Church*).

43 **And fear came upon every soul** (*speaks of the Moving and Operation of the Holy Spirit; seeing the things that the Spirit was doing, all had a sense of awe, wonder, and fear*): **and many wonders and signs were done by the Apostles** (*the Holy Spirit did this in order to give the Church a great start; it continued, even as it is meant to continue, but on a more limited basis, as the latter part of the Book of Acts bears out*).

44 **And all who believed were together** (*due to the great animosity of the Jews against the followers of Christ, Believers had to band together*), **and had all things common** (*due to thousands losing their jobs because of persecution, those who had material goods shared with those who didn't*);

45 **And sold their possessions and goods** (*they sold things they did not absolutely need, in order that they may be able to help those who were in great need*), **and parted them to all** **men,** **as every man had need** (*proclaimed a*

Christlike community because of the great persecution at hand).

46 **And they, continuing daily with one accord in the Temple** (*in a sense, the Temple had been turned into a Church, which must have been extremely irritating to the religious authorities*), **and breaking bread from house to house** (*means that the Church per se was actually ensconced in houses all over Jerusalem*), **did eat their meat with gladness and singleness of heart** (*they had a joy that persecution could not hinder*),

47 **Praising God, and having favour with all the people** (*Jerusalem as a whole was favorably impressed by what they saw respecting these followers of Christ*). **And the Lord added to the Church daily such as should be saved** (*many were coming to the Lord*).

CHAPTER 3
(A.D. 33)

HEALING

NOW **Peter and John went up together into the Temple at the hour of prayer,** *being* **the ninth** *hour* (*3 o'clock in the afternoon*).

2 **And a certain man lame from his mother's womb was carried, whom they laid daily** (*seemed to be a daily occurrence which had taken place in one way or the other since the man was a child; little did he realize that this would be the greatest day of his life*) **at the gate of the Temple which is called Beautiful** (*according to Josephus, it was made of costly Corinthian brass; it was said to be about 62 feet wide and 31 feet high*), **to ask alms of them who entered into the Temple** (*he was a beggar*);

3 **Who seeing Peter and John about to go into the Temple asked an alms.**

4 **And Peter, fastening his eyes upon him with John** (*indicates they were moved upon by the Holy Spirit to do this thing*), **said, Look on us** (*Peter wanted him to hear what he was about to say*).

5 **And he gave heed unto them, expecting to receive something of them** (*expecting to receive money*).

6 **Then Peter said, Silver and gold have I none** (*I wonder how this statement as given by Peter concerning silver and gold relates to the modern greed message?*); **but such as I have give I thee** (*presently, the modern Church has silver and gold, but doesn't have the Power of God*): **In the Name of Jesus Christ of Nazareth rise up and walk** (*it is not in the name of Mohammed,*

or Confucius, etc.).

7 And he took him by the right hand, and lifted *him* up *(was not presumption, but rather Faith in action)*: and immediately his feet and ankle bones received strength *(this was a Miracle)*.

8 And he leaping up stood, and walked, and entered with them into the Temple, walking, and leaping, and praising God.

9 And all the people saw him walking and praising God *(constantly praising God)*:

10 And they knew that it was he which sat for alms at the Beautiful Gate of the Temple *(he had been coming there, no doubt, for years)*: and they were filled with wonder and amazement at that which had happened unto him *(his healing was indisputable)*.

11 And as the lame man which was healed held Peter and John *(he didn't want to let Peter and John out of his sight; it was as if his malady would return when they left, or so he thought)*, all the people ran together unto them in the porch that is called Solomon's, greatly wondering *(it drew a crowd, which the Holy Spirit intended)*.

THE SERMON

12 And when Peter saw *it (the crowd gathering)*, he answered unto the people, You men of Israel, why do you marvel at this? *(In essence, he is saying that Jesus is alive, and His Work is continuing.)* or why look you so earnestly on us, as though by our own power or holiness we have made this man to walk? *(He turns the attention from himself and John to the Lord Jesus Christ.)*

13 The God of Abraham, and of Isaac, and of Jacob, the God of our fathers, has glorified His Son Jesus *(Chrysostom said, "He thrust himself upon the Fathers of old, lest he should appear to be introducing a new doctrine.")*; Whom you delivered up *(pertains to the Chief Priest delivering Jesus to Pilate to be Crucified)*, and denied Him in the presence of Pilate, when he was determined to let *Him* go *(the Holy Spirit puts most of the blame on the religious leaders of Israel)*.

14 But you denied the Holy One and the Just *(proclaims the terrible sin of Israel, and the terrible sin of most of humanity as well, and for all time)*, and desired a murderer to be granted unto you *(speaks of Barabbas [Mat. 27:15-26], and murderers have ruled them ever since!)*;

15 And killed the Prince of Life *(Peter minced no words, not at all softening his Message)*, Whom God has raised from the dead *(the Resurrection, as would be obvious, ratified what was done at the Cross)*; whereof we are witnesses *(means that they had personally seen the Resurrected Christ; there is no greater witness than an eye-witness)*.

16 And His Name through Faith in His Name has made this man strong *(presents the key to all things!)*, whom you see and know *(there was no denying the Miracle)*: yes, the Faith which is by Him *(Jesus)* has given him *(the crippled man)* this perfect soundness in the presence of you all *(no partial healing, but a total healing, which is the way the Lord does things)*.

17 And now, brethren, I reckon that through ignorance you did *it*, as *did* also your Rulers *(while they were ignorant, regrettably it was a willful ignorance; in other words, they had no desire to know the Truth about Jesus)*.

18 But those things, which God before had showed by the mouth of all His Prophets *(in other words, had they known the Bible, which they certainly should have known, they would have known about Jesus)*, that Christ should suffer *(the entirety of the story of the Bible is "Jesus Christ and Him Crucified")*, He has so fulfilled *(proclaims that His Death was predestined, but not who would commit the deed)*.

19 Repent ye therefore, and be converted *(Repentance is an admittance that God is right, and we are wrong; he was speaking to the Rulers as well as to the people)*, that your sins may be blotted out *(speaks of Justification by Faith)*, when the times of refreshing shall come from the Presence of the Lord *(should have been translated, "In order that the times of refreshing shall come from the Presence of the Lord")*;

20 And He shall send Jesus Christ *(pertains to the Second Coming [Rev., Chpt. 19])*, which before was preached unto you *(through the Prophets, and as well the public Ministry of Christ to Israel for some three and a half years)*:

21 Whom the Heaven must receive until the times of restitution of all things *(refers to Jesus remaining in Heaven until this Dispensation of Grace has run its course, after which He will return to this Earth)*, which God has spoken by the mouth of all His Holy Prophets since the world began *(once again, had they known the Word of God, which then consisted of Genesis through Malachi, they would have known all these things)*.

22 For Moses truly said unto the Fathers

(Deut. 18:15-19), A Prophet shall the Lord your God raise up unto you of your brethren, like unto me (the Promise of the Messiah); Him shall you hear in all things whatsoever He shall say unto you (could not be clearer).

23 And it shall come to pass, that every soul, which will not hear that Prophet (refers to the entirety of the world), shall be destroyed from among the people (will be eternally lost!).

24 Yes, and all the Prophets from Samuel (even though there were Prophets before Samuel, he was the first one to stand in the Office of the Prophet), and those who follow after, as many as have spoken, have likewise foretold of these days (speaks of all the Prophets, at least in one way or another, pointing to the coming Redeemer, Who would be the Lord Jesus Christ).

25 You are the children of the Prophets (means that they should have known what the Prophets had said), and of the Covenant which God made with our Fathers (refers to the Abrahamic Covenant [Gen. 12:1-3]), saying unto Abraham, And in your seed shall all the kindreds of the earth be blessed (speaks of Jesus Christ as that "Seed").

26 Unto you first (refers to the offer of Salvation being made first to the Jews [Lk. 24:47; Rom. 1:16; 2:10]) God, having raised up His Son Jesus (refers to the Resurrection), sent Him to bless you, in turning away every one of you from his (your) iniquities (only Jesus could do this, which He did by His atoning Work at the Cross [Eph. 2:13-18]).

CHAPTER 4
(A.D. 33)
PERSECUTION

AND as they spoke unto the people, the Priests, and the captain of the Temple, and the Sadducees, came upon them (the "Sadducees" almost completely controlled the High Priesthood, and actually most of the Priestly duties of the Temple),

2 Being grieved that they taught the people (worried), and preached through Jesus the resurrection from the dead (they were angry that Jesus and the Resurrection were being preached, which Doctrine the Sadducees denied [Lk. 20:27]).

3 And they laid hands on them (arrested them), and put them in hold unto the next day (a small prison in the confines of the Temple): for it was now evening.

4 Howbeit many of them which heard the Word believed (they believed on Christ, thereby accepting Him as the Messiah of Israel and the Saviour of men); and the number of the men was about five thousand (seems to speak only of men, so including women and children, it could have numbered ten thousand or more).

5 And it came to pass on the morrow, that their Rulers, and Elders, and Scribes,

6 And Annas the High Priest, and Caiaphas, and John (probably was Johanan Ben Zakkai, a famous Rabbi of that time), and Alexander (probably was Alexander Lysimachus, one of the richest Jews of his time who contributed very generously to the Temple), and as many as were of the kindred of the High Priest (possibly all five sons of Annas were present), were gathered together at Jerusalem (some of them probably didn't live in Jerusalem, but happened to be there at that time).

7 And when they had set them in the midst (Peter and John), they asked, By what power, or by what name, have you done this? (By the crippled man being healed, they already knew the answer.)

8 Then Peter, filled with the Holy Spirit, said unto them (the Holy Spirit is mentioned in one way or the other in the Book of Acts over fifty times), You Rulers of the people, and Elders of Israel (the Holy Spirit, through Peter, is pointing out the responsibility these religious leaders hold as the spiritual guides of the people),

9 If we this day be examined of the good deed done to the impotent man (proclaims Peter, in effect, asking as to how or why a good deed such as this should be questioned at all?!), by what means he is made whole (presents the cause of the attitude and action of the ruling body of Israel);

10 Be it known unto you all, and to all the people of Israel (once again, Peter will not mince words), that by the Name of Jesus Christ of Nazareth (he desired that there be no mistake as it regards the One of Whom He was speaking; since the Baptism with the Holy Spirit, Peter is not the same man he was when he denied Christ even before a young maiden; he will now boldly stand up for Christ in front of the entirety of the ruling body of Israel), Whom you Crucified (places the emphasis on the word "you," thereby pointedly and directly fastening the terrible sin of Crucifying their Messiah squarely on their shoulders; as stated, he pulled no punches), Whom God raised from the dead (proclaims words they certainly didn't want to hear), even by Him does this man stand here before you

whole *(the man was evidently brought with Peter and John before the Council; in essence, Peter is saying that a dead man could not produce these results).*

11 This is the Stone which was set at nought of you builders *(Jesus is the Stone [Ps. 118:22-23])*, which is become the Head of the Corner *(Israel rejected Him, but it did not stop the Plan of God; Israel only succeeded in destroying themselves).*

12 Neither is there Salvation in any other *(proclaims unequivocally that Jesus Alone holds the key to Salvation, and in fact is Salvation):* for there is none other name under Heaven given among men, whereby we must be saved *(says it all!).*

RELEASE

13 Now when they saw the boldness of Peter and John *(pertains not only to what was spoken, but to the power with which it was spoken as well)*, and perceived that they were unlearned and ignorant men, they marveled *(means they had not studied in the Rabbinical Schools; in fact, they were not "unlearned and ignorant," but rather the very opposite!)*; and they took knowledge of them, that they had been with Jesus *(this explained it all)*.

14 And beholding the man which was healed standing with them *(presents a beautiful picture!)*, they could say nothing against it *(proclaims the proof which was obvious to all!)*.

15 But when they had commanded them to go aside out of the Council *(proclaims the fact that God had left this Council a long time ago)*, they conferred among themselves *(but not with the Scriptures)*,

16 Saying, What shall we do to these men? *(Why would they want to do anything negative to these men?)* for that indeed a notable miracle has been done by them *is* manifest to all them who dwell in Jerusalem; and we cannot deny *it (infers that the news of this man's Miraculous Healing had spread far and wide, even in the last few hours).*

17 But that it spread no further among the people *(seems to present their greatest fear)*, let us straitly threaten them, that they speak henceforth to no man in this Name *(automatically places the situation into a posture which cannot be obeyed).*

18 And they called them, and commanded them not to speak at all nor teach in the Name of Jesus.

19 But Peter and John answered and said unto them, Whether it be right in the Sight of God to hearken unto you more than unto God, judge ye *(in effect, Peter and John are saying that these religious leaders are not of God, are not doing the Work of God and, consequently, do not have the Mind of God, irrespective of their claims).*

20 For we cannot but speak the things which we have seen and heard *(there are two groups of Christians, those who "cannot speak" and those who "cannot but speak").*

21 So when they had further threatened them, they let them go, finding nothing how they might punish them *(what had they done that warranted punishment?)*, because of the people *(they feared an uprising):* for all *men* Glorified God for that which was done *(and rightly so!).*

22 For the man was above forty years old *(carries the idea that this man was mature, responsible, and, therefore, could be believed)*, on whom this Miracle of Healing was showed.

PRAISE AND PRAYER

23 And being let go *(Peter and John were no longer under arrest)*, they went to their own company *(probably the other Apostles and others, perhaps many others)*, and reported all that the Chief Priests and Elders had said unto them *(presents the first account of opposition against the Early Church; it was not long in coming).*

24 And when they heard that *(heard the account)*, they lifted up their voice to God with one accord, and said *(all were praying in one way or the other)*, Lord, You *are* God, which has made Heaven, and Earth, and the sea, and all that in them is *(a compendium of what was said):*

25 Who by the mouth of Your servant David has said *(refers to the Second Psalm)*, Why did the heathen rage, and the people imagine vain things? *(This is used by the Holy Spirit to refer to these religious leaders concerning Jesus. This proclaims the fact that the Messiah is the Person spoken of in the Second Psalm.)*

26 The Kings of the earth stood up, and the Rulers were gathered together against the Lord, and against His Christ *(this Psalm speaks of all the opposition against Christ from the very beginning, but more particularly speaks of the coming Antichrist).*

27 For of a truth against Your Holy Child Jesus, Whom You have anointed *(proclaims*

Jesus as the fulfillment of all the Prophecies, the Son of God, the Incarnate One, the Saviour of Men), **both Herod, and Pontius Pilate, with the Gentiles** *(the Romans)*, **and the people of Israel, were gathered together** *(they were "gathered together" for the express purpose of Crucifying Christ)*,

28 For to do whatsoever Your Hand and Your Counsel determined before to be done *(speaks of predestination concerning Christ, His Death on Calvary's Cross, and His Resurrection from the dead; but again we state that those who were to Crucify Him were not determined by God; they did this cruel deed by their own choice)*.

29 And now, Lord, behold their threatenings *(proclaims those praying turning over these rulers and others to the Lord, in order that He may handle the situation)*: **and grant unto Your servants, that with all boldness they may speak Your Word** *(proclaims the very opposite of that demanded by the religious leaders of Israel)*,

30 By stretching forth Your Hand to heal *(proclaims the request for more Healings and Miracles)*; **and that signs and wonders may be done by the Name of Your Holy Child Jesus** *(all speak of the Power of God, but in the "Name of Jesus")*.

31 And when they had prayed, the place was shaken where they were assembled together *(this literally happened; the assembly place shook, and did so by the Power of God)*; **and they were all filled with the Holy Spirit** *(it means the Holy Spirit was leading and guiding them)*, **and they spoke the Word of God with boldness** *(the Lord answered their prayer by giving them more boldness, and they did not hesitate to speak accordingly; this is something the modern Church desperately needs as well, and would have if the Holy Spirit were prevalent and present)*.

BELIEVERS

32 And the multitude of them who believed were of one heart and of one soul *(speaks of unity which can only be brought about by the Holy Spirit; man's efforts to do such always fall short)*: **neither said any** *of them* **that ought of the things which he possessed was his own; but they had all things common** *(once again, this refers to the great persecution suffered by the Believers in Jerusalem at that time; many who came to Christ lost their jobs because they were excommunicated from the Synagogue; many were put out of their apartments, etc.; so, others who did not suffer such losses had to share, which*

they gladly did).

33 And with great power gave the Apostles witness of the Resurrection of the Lord Jesus *(this was done by the Holy Spirit greatly anointing the Apostles to attest to the Resurrection of Christ, and by signs and wonders being performed as well)*: **and great Grace was upon them all** *(is a portrayal of the beginning of the great dispensation of Grace, which actually began on the Day of Pentecost)*.

34 Neither was there any among them who lacked *(those who lost their employment, etc., had their needs met)*: **for as many as were possessors of lands or houses sold them, and brought the prices of the things that were sold** *(refers to extra possessions, etc.)*,

35 And laid *them* **down at the Apostles' feet** *(they were entrusted with this largesse)*: **and distribution was made unto every man according as he had need** *(no hint of communism here, as some have suggested)*.

36 And Joseph, who by the Apostles was surnamed Barnabas *(Barnabas became a Prophet and an Apostle [Acts 13:1; 14:14]*, **(which is, being interpreted, The son of consolation,) a Levite,** *and* **of the country of Cyprus** *(he was a Jew who had been born in Cyprus and lived there for a considerable period of time, as likely his father had done before him; being a Levite, he was of the Priestly class, although not a Priest)*,

37 Having land, sold *it*, **and brought the money, and laid** *it* **at the Apostles' feet** *(probably refers to property in Cyprus)*.

CHAPTER 5
(A.D. 33)
ANANIAS AND SAPPHIRA

BUT **a certain man named Ananias, with Sapphira his wife, sold a possession** *(the story of this man and his wife was placed here in graphic detail by the Holy Spirit as a warning)*,

2 And kept back *part* **of the price, his wife also being privy** *to it* *(instantly proclaims the conception of this great sin and its deception in being carried out)*, **and brought a certain part, and laid** *it* **at the Apostles' feet** *(a detailed plan with a very wide application; it was done with a certain purpose in mind)*.

3 But Peter said, Ananias, why has Satan filled Your heart to lie to the Holy Spirit *(presents two Gifts of the Spirit in operation: "Discerning of Spirits," and "A Word of Knowledge"; how many millions of professing Christians are presently lying to the Holy Spirit?)*, **and to keep**

back *part* of the price of the land? *(This details their insidious plan.)*

4 While it remained, was it not your own? and after it was sold, was it not in your own power? *(This means simply that God did not require of them to sell the land, or to give all the money received to the Work of the Lord.)* why have you conceived this thing in your heart? *(This proclaims to us where sin originates.)* you have not lied unto men, but unto God *(actually portrays the object of all sin; it is against God!).*

5 And Ananias hearing these words fell down, and gave up the ghost *(he was stricken dead on the spot)*: and great fear came on all them who heard these things *(this is the type of healthy fear of God that all men should have).*

6 And the young men arose, wound him up, and carried *him* out, and buried *him* *(prepared him for burial).*

7 And it was about the space of three hours after, when his wife, not knowing what was done, came in.

8 And Peter answered unto her, Tell me whether you sold the land for so much? And she said, Yes, for so much *(all of this seems to indicate that these were not strangers among the thousands who had gotten saved, but were fairly well known; she had an opportunity to tell the truth, but didn't!).*

9 Then Peter said unto her, How is it that you have agreed together to tempt the Spirit of the Lord? *(Peter's question concerning the tempting of the Holy Spirit seems to imply that the Spirit of God dealt with them greatly so, but to no avail. They pushed aside His Warnings.)* behold, the feet of them which have buried your husband *are* at the door, and shall carry you out *(seems to imply that the Lord had already told Peter what her reaction would be, and that the same young men who had attended her husband were waiting to do the same with her).*

10 Then fell she down straightway at his feet, and yielded up the ghost *(presents the Judgment of God striking her exactly as it had stricken her husband)*: and the young men came in, and found her dead, and, carrying *her* forth, buried *her* by her husband *(prepared her for burial).*

11 And great fear came upon all the Church, and upon as many as heard these things *(inasmuch as the Holy Spirit again makes the same statement as He had made in Verse 5, we are made to realize that God is to be feared as well as praised; also, if it is to be known, the same Judgment is happening presently, but not so dramatic; the Holy Spirit is the same, so the results have to be the same).*

POWER

12 And by the hands of the Apostles were many signs and wonders wrought among the people *(the Church was founded on the Power of God, and is meant to continue by the Power of God)*; (and they were all with one accord in Solomon's porch *(portrays a roofed colonnade bearing Solomon's name, which ran along the eastern wall in the Court of the Gentiles of Herod's Temple).*

13 And of the rest does no man join himself to them *(to the Apostles)*: but the people magnified them *(they knew the Apostles were of the Lord and that the Lord was greatly using them, so they found no fault with them).*

14 And Believers were the more added to the Lord, multitudes both of men and women.) *(It could have been as many as forty or fifty thousand, or even more.)*

15 Insomuch that they brought forth the sick into the streets, and laid *them* on beds and couches *(evidently refers to two or three different streets on which Peter and the Apostles came to the Temple each day; the crowds were so large they could not all get into the Temple Court),* that at the least the shadow of Peter passing by might overshadow some of them *(implying that when this happened, healing resulted).*

16 There came also a multitude *out* of the cities round about unto Jerusalem, bringing sick folks *(proclaims the extent to which this Move of God had reached)*, and them which were vexed with unclean spirits *(probably implying that much of the sickness was caused by demon spirits)*: and they were healed every one *(delivered and healed).*

PERSECUTION

17 Then the High Priest rose up *(either speaks of Annas or Caiaphas, which one is not clear)*, and all they who were with him, (which is the sect of the Sadducees,) and were filled with indignation *(refers here to "envy" or "jealousy")*,

18 And laid their hands on the Apostles *(refers to all Twelve)*, and put them in the common prison.

DELIVERANCE

19 But the Angel of the Lord by night opened the prison doors *(should have been translated,*

"an Angel"; it was one of the many Angels who serve as Ministering Spirits to Believers [Heb. 1:14], and brought them forth, and said (brought them out of the prison),

20 Go, stand and speak in the Temple to the people all the words of this life (presents instructions directly opposite of those the religious leaders had given; these were "Words" announcing Eternal Life to dying men).

21 And when they heard that, they entered into the Temple early in the morning, and taught (proclaims it was the night before that they were released by the Angel). But the High Priest came, and they who were with Him, and called the Council together, and all the senate of the children of Israel (the entirety of the Jewish Sanhedrin, the ruling body of Israel), and sent to the prison to have them brought (they were in for quite a surprise).

22 But when the officers came, and found them not in the prison, they returned, and told (presents a scenario which is absolutely unbelievable, but yet totally true!),

23 Saying, The prison truly found we shut with all safety (presents the fact that nothing seemed unusual, and that the locks had not been tampered with), and the keepers standing without before the doors (presents the fact that the guards had no idea what had happened): but when we had opened, we found no man within (what must these jailers have thought?).

24 Now when the High Priest and the Captain of the Temple and the Chief Priests heard these things (imagine their surprise!), they doubted of them whereunto this would grow (they were thoroughly perplexed; no one could explain what had happened or where it would stop!).

ON TRIAL

25 Then came one and told them, saying, Behold, the men whom you put in prison are standing in the Temple, and teaching the people (they obeyed exactly what the Angel had said do).

26 Then went the Captain with the officers, and brought them without violence (means they did not bind them, but simply asked that they follow): for they feared the people, lest they should have been stoned (they feared the people, but they did not fear Him Who manifested His Power in opening the prison, for their hearts and consciences were hardened with hatred against Him and His followers).

27 And when they had brought them, they set them before the Council (implies the full Sanhedrin of seventy-one members, plus onlookers): and the High Priest asked them,

28 Saying, Did not we straitly Command you that you should not teach in this Name? and, behold, You have filled Jerusalem with your doctrine (proclaims the success of their Preaching and Teaching), and intend to bring this Man's blood upon us (seems to now seek to avoid their own imprecation, having previously prayed that "His Blood might be on them and on their children" [Mat. 27: 25]).

29 Then Peter and the other Apostles answered and said (represents their answer being instant and unequivocally clear), We ought to obey God rather than men (in this brave reply there was neither pride nor self-will; there was faithfulness, subjection to Truth, and intelligence in the Scriptures; Hervey said, "The rule is a golden one for all men, all circumstances, and all time").

30 The God of our fathers raised up Jesus (Peter links Jesus with the Patriarchs and Prophets of old, as well with God), Whom you slew and hanged on a tree (places the responsibility of the murder of Christ squarely on the shoulders of the Sanhedrin).

31 Him has God exalted with his Right Hand (refers to the fact that the Power of God not only raised Jesus from the dead, but as well has seated Him at His Own Right Hand in the Heavenlies [Rom. 8:34; Eph. 1:20]) to be a Prince and a Saviour (as "Prince," He is the Titular Leader of Israel and the Church; as "Saviour," He is the "Deliverer," and there is no other), for to give repentance to Israel, and forgiveness of sins (tells us that not only is the Lord Jesus the Medium of Forgiveness and Life, but He is the Dispenser of both; as well, He "Gives," not sells!").

32 And we are His witnesses of these things (in effect, says that their Doctrine was not a mere philosophy, but rather eyewitness accounts); and so is also the Holy Spirit, Whom God has given to them who obey Him (the witness of the Holy Spirit in the hearts and lives of Believers guarantees the veracity of all that Christ has done at the Cross).

33 When they heard that, they were cut to the heart (Peter's words were said with powerful conviction), and took counsel to slay them (is the reaction which normally comes from the world of religion).

GAMALIEL

34 Then stood there up one in the Council, a

Pharisee, named Gamaliel, a Doctor of the Law, had in reputation among all the people *(constitutes one of the most celebrated and honored Jewish Rabbis; He was Grandson of Hillel and succeeded as President of the Sanhedrin on the death of His Father, Rabbi Simeon, son of Hillel)*, and commanded to put the Apostles forth a little space *(in order that his word of wisdom may be given to the members of the Sanhedrin)*;

35 And said unto them, You men of Israel, take heed to yourselves what you intend to do as touching these men *(evidently, the Holy Spirit moved upon him to take this position)*.

36 For before these days rose up Theudas, boasting himself to be somebody *(evidently concerns a particular insurrection led by this man, which had recently taken place)*; to whom a number of men, about four hundred, joined themselves: who was slain; and all, as many as obeyed him, were scattered, and brought to nought *(refers to those who were dupes of this self-pronounced Messiah, or some such)*.

37 After this man rose up Judas of Galilee in the days of the taxing, and drew away much people after him *(another insurrectionist)*: he also perished; and all, *even* as many as obeyed him, were dispersed *(proclaims these as coming to the same end as those under Theudas)*.

38 And now I say unto you, Refrain from these men, and let them alone *(in effect, Gamaliel was saying, "let them alone, Rome will handle the problem")*: for if this counsel or this work be of men, it will come to nought *(in this case, such advice was correct)*:

39 But if it be of God, you cannot overthrow it *(presents a great Truth as given by Gamaliel)*; lest haply you be found even to fight against God *(presents the very worst position in which anyone can find themselves)*.

PERSECUTION

40 And to him they agreed *(at least about not killing them)*: and when they had called the Apostles, and beaten *them (presents a cruel and brutal punishment which was cowardly and unjust)*, they commanded that they should not speak in the Name of Jesus, and let them go *(presents the second command not to Preach in this Name [Acts 4:17-18])*.

REJOICING

41 And they departed from the presence of the Council *(proclaims that from which the Lord had long since departed)*, rejoicing that they were counted worthy to suffer shame for His Name *(presents the first sharp stroke of persecution; it was bitter and painful to the flesh, but caused rejoicing in the spirit; shame is Glory if suffered for the Name)*.

42 And daily in the Temple *(presents them boldly and properly disregarding their illegal Judges, as they kept on preaching that Jesus was the Promised Messiah)*, and in every house, they ceased not to teach and preach Jesus Christ *(tells us that the Churches then were in houses for the most part, if not altogether)*.

CHAPTER 6
(A.D. 33)
THE FIRST DEACONS

AND in those days, when the number of the Disciples was multiplied *(the followers of Christ were multiplying)*, there arose a murmuring of the Grecians against the Hebrews *(refers to Jews who spoke Greek as a result of having once lived in various countries where Greek was spoken)*, because their widows were neglected in the daily ministration *(speaks of relief in the form of food and money given to "widows" in the Church in Jerusalem who had no way to provide for themselves)*.

2 Then the Twelve *(Twelve Apostles)* called the multitude of the Disciples *unto them*, and said *(constitutes probably the very first business meeting in the Early Church)*, It is not reason that we should leave the Word of God, and serve tables *(refers to the voluminous administrative duties which accompanied the great growth of the Early Church in Jerusalem)*.

3 Wherefore, brethren, look ye out among you seven men of honest report, full of the Holy Spirit and wisdom *(is thought by some to represent the first Deacons, even though they are not called that in this Chapter)*, whom we may appoint over this business *(the Holy Spirit told the "Twelve" what to do, the number to choose, and how they were to be chosen)*.

4 But we will give ourselves continually to prayer, and to the Ministry of the Word *(tells us that "Prayer" is mentioned first, and is more important than "Preaching"; without a proper Prayer Life, there can be no proper Ministry)*.

5 And the saying pleased the whole multitude *(proclaims wisdom the people could not fault, for it was wisdom from above)*: and they chose Stephen, a man full of Faith and of the Holy Spirit, and Philip, and Prochorus, and

Nicanor, and Timon, and Parmenas, and Nicolas a proselyte of Antioch (presents the seven men):

6 Whom they set before the Apostles (now presented for acceptance and confirmation): and when they had prayed (sought the Lord's approval of these men, which evidently they received), they laid their hands on them (the laying on of hands was to designate them for an office, work, or Ministry, as Moses did Joshua [Num. 27:18-23]).

7 And the Word of God increased (means that more and more men were Preaching the Gospel of Jesus); and the number of the Disciples multiplied in Jerusalem greatly (could have been as many as one hundred thousand people who had accepted the Lord); and a great company of the Priests were obedient to the Faith (presents one of the greatest Testimonies to date of the Power of God).

STEPHEN

8 And Stephen, full of faith and power (speaks of a great knowledge of the Word of God, and of the Holy Spirit controlling this man, and, thereby, using him), did great wonders and miracles among the people (these things were Divinely done).

9 Then there arose certain of the Synagogue, which is called the Synagogue of the Libertines (speaks of Jews who had been taken as slaves to Rome or elsewhere in the Roman Empire, but now had been set free, consequently coming back to Jerusalem; they had a Synagogue in Jerusalem, and perhaps several), and Cyrenians, and Alexandrians, and of them of Cilicia and of Asia (pertains to each one of these groups of Jews who had a Synagogue in Jerusalem), disputing with Stephen (it is thought by some that Paul, then known as Saul, was the leading disputer against Stephen; he could have been associated with the Synagogue that pertained to Cilicia, as Tarsus, the hometown of Paul, was in that region).

10 And they were not able to resist the wisdom and the spirit by which he spoke (if it was Paul who led the dispute against Stephen, it would have been most interesting, considering that Paul was the hope of the Pharisees at that time and, therefore, reputed to have great knowledge of the Law; the difference is that the Holy Spirit anointed Stephen!).

11 Then they suborned men (they planned and formed a scheme together, which held no validity or truth), which said, We have heard him speak blasphemous words against Moses, and against God (concerns their concocted scheme).

12 And they stirred up the people, and the Elders, and the Scribes (refers to the lies they told and kept telling respecting Stephen), and came upon him, and caught him, and brought him to the Council (refers to them getting permission from the Sanhedrin to arrest Stephen, which they did),

13 And set up false witnesses, which said (proclaims the similarity of Stephen's trial with that of our Lord), This man ceases not to speak blasphemous words against this holy place, and the Law (this was their charge, which was false):

14 For we have heard him say (represents a distortion of what Stephen had probably said; they probably based their accusation upon some semblance of Truth, but totally distorted its meaning), that this Jesus of Nazareth (said in such a way as to be most contemptuous) shall destroy this place (probably referred to the Words said by Jesus in the Olivet discourse [Mat. 24:2]), and shall change the customs which Moses delivered us (it is true that the customs were to be changed as a result of the New Covenant, and in fact were meant to be changed).

15 And all that sat in the Council (Sanhedrin), looking stedfastly on him (gazed intently, and for purpose and reason), saw his face as it had been the face of an Angel (pertains to the Glory of the Lord shinning on the face of Stephen).

CHAPTER 7

(A.D. 33)

STEPHEN'S DEFENSE

THEN said the High Priest, Are these things so? (This was asked concerning the charges!)

2 And he said (Stephen), Men, brethren, and fathers, hearken (addresses and is meant to address the religious hierarchy of Israel); The God of Glory appeared unto our father Abraham, when he was in Mesopotamia, before he dwelt in Charran (doesn't tell us exactly what this appearance was, whether visible or that the Lord may have used someone else to deliver the Message; the exact place in that land was Ur of the Chaldees [Gen. 15:7]),

3 And said unto him, Get thee out of your country (pertained to a land of idol worship), and from your kindred (in effect, says they were idol-worshippers as well), and come into the

land which I shall show you *(refers to the land of Canaan)*.

4 Then came he out of the land of the Chaldaeans, and dwelt in Charran *(about 700 miles north of Ur of the Chaldees; he stayed there approximately two or three years)*: and from thence, when his father was dead, he removed him into this land, wherein you now dwell *(the Land of Canaan)*.

5 And He *(God)* gave him none inheritance in it, no, not *so much as* to set his foot on *(means that Abraham personally never owned any of the Land of Canaan, except the "Cave of Machpelah," which was used for a burial place for he and Sarah [Gen. 23])*: yet he promised that he would give it to him for a possession, and to his seed after him *(refers to the seed of Isaac, not Ishmael [Gen. 17:19])*, when *as yet* he had no child *(for all of this to be done, Abraham and Sarah must have an heir, which they ultimately did have in Isaac)*.

6 And God spoke on this wise *(concerns the Prophecy given to Abraham by the Lord respecting the future of his seed)*, That his seed should sojourn in a strange land *(Egypt)*; and that they should bring them into bondage, and entreat *them* evil four hundred years *(the whole length of the Dispensation of Promise [Abraham to Moses] was 430 years [Ex. 12:40; Gal. 3:14-17]; the 400 years of Gen. 15:13 and Acts 7:6 are to be reckoned from the confirmation of Isaac as the seed when Ishmael was cast out [Gen. 21:12; Gal. 4:30]; this was five years after the birth of Isaac)*.

7 And the nation to whom they shall be in bondage will I judge, said God *(speaks of Egypt [Ex. 1:1-14; 31])*: and after that shall they come forth, and serve Me in this place *(the Children of Israel were delivered from Egyptian bondage and given the Promised Land, which Stephen refers to as "this place")*.

8 And He *(God)* gave him *(Abraham)* the Covenant of Circumcision *(refers to the Abrahamic Covenant of Gen. 12:1-3; 17:9-27, and not the Mosaic Covenant which continued Circumcision, but did not originate it)*: and so *Abraham* begat Isaac, and circumcised him the eighth day; and Isaac *begat* Jacob; and Jacob *begat* the Twelve Patriarchs *(speaks of his sons as the Twelve Heads of the Tribes of Israel, and who came under the same Covenant of Circumcision)*.

9 And the Patriarchs, moved with envy, sold Joseph into Egypt *(they were jealous of him, in that he was chosen by his father Jacob to inherit the Birthright [I Chron. 5:1-2])*: but God was with him *(men rule, but God overrules!)*,

10 And delivered him out of all his afflictions *(does not say there were no afflictions, but that the Lord delivered Joseph out of every snare set for him by Satan)*, and gave him favour and wisdom in the sight of Pharaoh king of Egypt; and he made him Governor over Egypt and all his house *(portrays, for a change, a wise ruler!)*.

11 Now there came a dearth over all the land of Egypt and Canaan *(refers to the seven year famine)*, and great affliction: and our fathers found no sustenance *(all of this was orchestrated purposely by the Lord, in order that His Plan be carried out respecting the nation of Israel)*.

12 But when Jacob heard that there was corn in Egypt, he sent out our fathers first *(he sent his sons)*.

13 And at the second *time* Joseph was made known to his brethren *(refers to their second trip to Egypt with Joseph testing them [Gen. 45:1-28])*; and Joseph's kindred was made known unto Pharaoh *(they were introduced to Pharaoh, with Joseph seeking permission for his family to come into Egypt)*.

14 Then sent Joseph, and called his father Jacob to *him* *(this is symbolic of the Second Coming, when Israel will finally come to Jesus)*, and all his kindred, threescore and fifteen souls *(seventy-five souls; Stephen was including the five sons of Manasseh and Ephraim; Gen. 46:27 and Deut. 10:22 mention seventy people who went into Egypt, but did not include these five)*.

15 So Jacob went down into Egypt, and died, he, and our fathers *(while his life and Ministry were in Egypt, his heart was in Canaan)*,

16 And were carried over into Sychem, and laid in the sepulchre that Abraham bought for a sum of money of the sons of Emmor *the father* of Sychem *(refers to "Shechem" [Gen. 23:6-20; 33:19; 47:30; 49:29; 50:5; Ex. 13; 19; Josh. 24:32]; this was in Canaan)*.

17 But when the time of the Promise drew near *(God's timing is just as important as His Promise)*, which God had sworn to Abraham *(the Promise of God concerned the Land of Canaan being given to the Children of Israel)*, the people *(Israelites)* grew and multiplied in Egypt,

18 Till another king arose *(another Pharaoh)*, which knew not Joseph *(means that this new Pharaoh had no regard for Egypt's past respecting Joseph, and consequently had no regard for Joseph's people, the Israelites!)*.

19 The same dealt subtilly with our kindred,

and evil entreated our fathers *(proclaimed such being allowed by the Lord, and for purpose and reason; had they been treated kindly by this Pharaoh, they would not have desired to leave Egypt)*, so that they cast out their young children, to the end they might not live *(speaks of the demand ordered by Pharaoh that all the boy babies of the Israelites be killed when they were born)*.

20 In which time Moses was born *(presents another step in the Plan of God for Israel's deliverance)*, and was exceeding fair *(describes the appearance of the child)*, and nourished up in his father's house three months *(pertained to the time he was hidden by his parents, in order that he not be killed as was demanded by Pharaoh of all newly-born baby boys)*:

21 And when he was cast out *(speaks of the time when he could not be hidden any longer)*, Pharaoh's daughter took him up, and nourished him for her own son *(again, this was orchestrated by the Lord)*.

22 And Moses was learned in all the wisdom of the Egyptians *(highly educated)*, and was mighty in words and in deeds *(Josephus says that Moses ultimately became a General in the Egyptian Army, and defeated the Ethiopians)*.

23 And when he was full forty years old *(pertains to the years Moses spent in Pharaoh's Court)*, it came into his heart to visit his brethren the Children of Israel *(before now it seems that he had not been too occupied with the plight of "his brethren")*.

24 And seeing one *of them* suffer wrong, he defended *him* *(the Holy Spirit begins to move Moses in this direction)*, and avenged him who was oppressed, and smote the Egyptian *(Moses had the right motive, but this was the wrong way)*:

25 For he supposed his brethren would have understood how that God by his hand would deliver them *(the sentence structure here tells us that the Lord was definitely dealing with Moses about the deliverance of the Children of Israel; however, the people were not ready and neither was Moses!)*: but they understood not.

26 And the next day he showed himself unto them as they strove, and would have set them at one again *(these two Israelites were angry with each other)*, saying, Sirs, you are brethren; why do ye wrong one to another? *(This will bring forth an answer he was not anticipating.)*

27 But he who did his neighbour wrong thrust him *(Moses)* away *(plainly proclaims the man rejecting the leadership of Moses)*, saying, Who made you a ruler and a judge over us? *(As stated, neither Moses nor the people were yet*

ready for deliverance.)*

28 Will you kill me, as you did the Egyptian yesterday? *(Evidently, Moses did not realize that his killing of the Egyptian was known; however, he had been seen!)*

29 Then fled Moses at that saying *(Moses was soon to find out that Pharaoh also knew and was angry, so he fled Egypt [Ex. 2:14-15])*, and was a stranger in the land of Madian, where he begat two sons *(their names were Gershom and Eliezer [Ex. 2:22; 18:3-4])*.

30 And when forty years were expired *(it only took a very short time to get Moses out of Egypt, but forty years to get Egypt out of Moses; the flesh dies hard!)*, there appeared to him in the wilderness of Mount Sina an Angel of the Lord in a flame of fire in a bush *(this was actually God Himself appearing to Moses [Ex. 3:2; 4:17])*.

31 When Moses saw *it* *(the burning bush)*, he wondered at the sight: and as he drew near to behold *it*, the Voice of the Lord came unto him *(after forty years, the Lord now speaks)*,

32 *Saying*, I *am* the God of your fathers, the God of Abraham, and the God of Isaac, and the God of Jacob *(in essence says that He was the same One Who had spoken to them; it also means they were alive at that very time, actually in Paradise)*. Then Moses trembled, and turned his face away *(Ex. 3:6)*.

33 Then said the Lord to him *(begins a scenario that would only end some forty years later)*, Put off your shoes from your feet: for the place where you stand is Holy Ground *(the pulling off of the shoes signified that Moses was relinquishing ownership to everything; slaves do not wear shoes, and he, in effect, would be a slave of Christ, exactly as Paul)*.

34 I have seen, I have seen the affliction of My people which is in Egypt *(God sees all and knows all)*, and I have heard their groaning *(groaning under the burden imposed by the Egyptian taskmasters, who were types of Satan)*, and am come down to deliver them *(He delivered them by the means of the slain lamb and the blood applied to the doorposts, in essence the Cross; the Cross is still the only manner of Deliverance [Ex. 12:13])*. And now come, I will send you into Egypt *(presents one of the most appalling commissions ever given to any man)*.

35 This Moses whom they refused, saying, Who made you a ruler and a judge? *(This is meant by the Holy Spirit through Stephen to show that the Jesus they had rejected and crucified was their only Present and Eternal Saviour.)*

the same did God send *to be* a ruler and a deliverer by the hand of the Angel which appeared to him in the bush *(the Sanhedrin were overly familiar with this; however, they surely understood the implication)*.

36 He brought them out *(speaks of Egypt, but is meant to convey as well the Deliverance effected regarding every believing sinner upon coming to Christ)*, after that he had showed wonders and signs in the land of Egypt *(he manifested His great Power to Egypt, so that the Egyptians were without excuse)*, and in the Red Sea *(speaks of the greatest Miracle that had ever been performed up to that time)*, and in the wilderness forty years *(presents the Divine protection of God for this length of time, even though it was His Will that they only be there about two years, if that!)*.

37 This is that Moses, which said unto the Children of Israel *(portrays Stephen now presenting the fact of Christianity, even though it was not even called such then)*, A Prophet shall the Lord your God raise up unto you of your brethren, like unto me; Him shall you hear *(points directly to Jesus as the fulfillment of that Prophecy given by Moses so long before)*.

38 This is he *(Moses)*, who was in the Church in the wilderness with the Angel which spoke to him in the Mount Sina *(actually refers to God Himself, Who gave Moses the Law)*, and *with* our fathers *(refers to the fact that the Elders of Israel, were to help Moses, but rather, did the opposite!)*: who received the lively oracles to give unto us *(refers to the Law of Moses)*:

39 To whom our fathers would not obey *(marks the history of Israel, which ultimately led to their destruction)*, but thrust *him* from them *(had God not intervened, at least several times, they would have killed Moses)*, and in their hearts turned back again into Egypt *(puts the finger right square on the problem; their "hearts" were still in Egypt, just like the hearts of many Believers presently are still in the world)*,

40 Saying unto Aaron, Make us gods to go before us *(proclaims the sin which ultimately destroyed Israel)*: for *as for* this Moses, which brought us out of the land of Egypt, we know not what is become of him *(while God was preparing great things for them, they were preparing to worship idols!)*.

41 And they made a calf in those days *(this was their idol)*, and offered sacrifice unto the idol *(probably represented a Lamb, but in times to come would include human sacrifice)*, and rejoiced in the works of their own hands *(it is still the problem presently, with the Church little*

desiring to lean solely on Christ and what He has done at the Cross; many prefer a Salvation "of their own hands")*.

42 Then God turned, and gave them up to worship the host of Heaven *(refers to the sun, moon, and stars)*; as it is written in the Book of the Prophets, O ye house of Israel, have you offered to Me slain beasts and sacrifices *by the space of* forty years in the wilderness? *(While Israel did offer up Sacrifices, they were not always to God. "To Me" is emphatic!)*

43 Yes, you took up the tabernacle of Moloch *(refers to the name of the main Ammonite Deity to whom children were offered by fire [Lev. 18:21; 20:2; Deut. 18:10; II Ki. 16:3; 26:6; 23:10; Jer. 19:5; 32:35])*, and the star of your god Remphan, figures which you made to worship them *(this was the star-god of Babylon)*: and I will carry you away beyond Babylon *(Stephen quotes from Amos 5:25-27; however, he used the name "Babylon" while Amos used the name "Damascus"; both were correct)*.

44 Our fathers had the tabernacle of witness in the wilderness, as he had appointed *(means that God gave them the "Tabernacle" plus the articles of Sacred Vessels, in order that His People may have a way to worship Him)*, speaking unto Moses, that he should make it according to the fashion that he had seen *(presents the design exclusively by the Lord, which means that Moses was not to deviate from that design)*.

45 Which also our fathers who came after brought in with Jesus *(Joshua)* into the possession of the Gentiles *(refers to the Land of Canaan)*, whom God drove out before the face of our fathers, unto the days of David *(refers to a time span of approximately five hundred years; during that time, victories were sparse)*;

46 Who found favour before God *(referring to David)*, and desired to find a Tabernacle for the God of Jacob *(speaks of the Ark of the Covenant being brought into Jerusalem, after being untended for approximately seventy years [II Sam. 6:12; Ps. 132:6])*.

47 But Solomon built Him *(God)* an house *(the plans were given to David, but it is Solomon, his son, who built the house)*.

48 Howbeit the most High dwells not in Temples made with hands *(speaks of the prayer offered by Solomon at the dedication of the Temple [I Ki. 8:27])*; as said the Prophet *(this phrase should have been in the next Verse, because it speaks of Isaiah)*,

49 Heaven *is* My Throne, and earth *is* My Footstool *(God is bigger and greater than anything)*:

what house will you build Me? says the Lord *(the Temple was to be merely a stop-gap measure until Christ would come)*: or what *is* the place of My rest? *(Israel had come to the place where they believed the Temple was all in all. They didn't see it as a step toward an ultimate goal. The "rest" is found only in Christ [Mat. 11:28-30].)*

50 Has not My Hand made all these things? *(He has made the heavens and the Earth and all that is therein, so why would He want to confine Himself totally to one small building on Earth?)*

51 You stiffnecked and uncircumcised in heart and ears *(presents Stephen using the same language as Moses when he conveyed God's rebuke to Israel [Deut. 10:16])*, you do always resist the Holy Spirit: as your fathers *did*, so *do* you *(everything carried out by God on Earth is through the Person and Office of the Holy Spirit; to resist Him is to resist God, for He is God; they resisted Him by resisting the Plan of God, Who and What was Jesus Christ).*

52 Which of the Prophets have not your fathers persecuted? *(This is very similar to that stated by Christ [Mat. 5:12; 23:30-31, 34-37; Lk. 13:33-34].)* and they have slain them which showed before of the coming of the Just One *(they killed the Prophets who pointed to the One Who was to come, Namely Jesus)*; of Whom you have been now the betrayers and murderers *(is about as strong as anything that could be said; how different this is from most of the modern Preaching!)*:

53 Who *(Israel)* have received the Law *(Law of Moses)* by the disposition of Angels *(speaks of the myriads of Angels who were present and were used to help give the Law of Moses to Israel [Ps. 68:17])*, and have not kept *it (contradicted their claims!).*

THEIR ANSWER

54 When they heard these things, they were cut to the heart *(refers to the depth to which the Holy Spirit took Stephen's words, which, in effect, were the "Words of the Lord")*, and they gnashed on him with *their* teeth *(proclaims their answer to Stephen and the Holy Spirit).*

55 But he, being full of the Holy Spirit *(the second time this is said of him [Acts 6:5])*, looked up stedfastly into Heaven *(means that Stephen saw something in Heaven which immediately seized his attention)*, and saw the Glory of God *(he saw the Throne of God)*, and Jesus standing on the Right Hand of God *(Christ is usually presented as sitting at the Right Hand of God*

[Heb. 1:3], but here He is seen standing, as rising to welcome His Faithful martyr and to place on his head the Crown of Life),

56 And said, Behold, I see the Heavens opened *(proclaims Jesus in His Glory as God, just as the Heavens had opened to see Jesus in His humiliation on Earth as Man [Jn. 1:51])*, and the Son of Man standing on the Right Hand of God *(proclaims His rightful place by virtue of His achievements and exaltation to original Glory [Jn. 17:5; Eph. 1:20-23; Phil. 2:9-11; Heb. 1:3-4]).*

57 Then they *(members of the Sanhedrin)* cried out with a loud voice *(had they cried out in Repentance, the future of Israel could have been drastically changed for the better)*, and stopped their ears *(means that they no longer desired to hear anything he desired to say)*, and ran upon him with one accord *(all of the religious leadership of Israel were guilty)*,

58 And cast *him* out of the city, and stoned *him (this was their answer to the plea of God for their souls)*: and the witnesses laid down their clothes at a young man's feet *(they took off their outer garments so as to be free to hurl the stones at their victim with greater force)*, whose name was Saul *(presents the first mention of this man who would have a greater positive impact on Christianity than any other human being who has ever lived; the death of Stephen, no doubt, played a part in the later conversion of Paul).*

59 And they stoned Stephen, calling upon *God (presents a monstrous offense on the part of his murderers; we must remember, he was murdered by the religious leaders of Israel)*, and saying, Lord Jesus, receive my spirit *(presents Stephen rendering Divine Worship to Jesus Christ in the most sublime form, and in the most solemn moment of his life).*

60 And he kneeled down, and cried with a loud voice, Lord, lay not this sin to their charge *(presents him dying on his knees, without malice toward his murderers).* And when he had said this, he fell asleep *(portrays the body falling asleep, while his soul and spirit instantly went to be with Jesus; due to what Jesus did at the Cross; death is now looked at as merely going to sleep).*

CHAPTER 8
(A.D. 34)
SAUL

A ND Saul *(Paul)* was consenting unto his death *(means that he expressed hearty*

approval of the stoning of Stephen). And at that time there was a great persecution against the Church which was at Jerusalem (the Church, as far as we know, was then confined to Jerusalem); and they were all scattered abroad throughout the regions of Judaea and Samaria (the persecution helped take the Gospel to these particular regions; so Satan's plan backfired), except the Apostles (they stayed in Jerusalem, no doubt at the behest of the Holy Spirit; for the Apostles to leave at that time could have destroyed the infant Church).

2 And devout men carried Stephen to his burial (proclaims the high esteem with which they held this man, and rightly so!), and made great lamentation over him (what a difference between his death and that of Ananias and Sapphira).

3 As for Saul, he made havock of the Church (it seems he was the leader of this persecution), entering into every house (referring to those houses he knew contained followers of Christ), and haling men and women committed them to prison (he spared no age or gender, but forced them all before magistrates).

4 Therefore they who were scattered abroad (refers to a result of the persecution) went every where preaching the Word (as stated, the persecution backfired; instead of stopping the "Word" it rather scattered the "Word!"; Satan dreads the preaching of the Gospel by the Anointing of the Holy Spirit, but has no controversy with either ritualism or philanthropy).

PHILIP

5 Then Philip went down to the city of Samaria (should have been translated, "a city of Samaria," which was probably "Sychem;" this was the Philip of Acts 6:5), and preached Christ unto them (refers to him proclaiming Jesus as the Messiah, God manifest in the flesh, and being raised from the dead; He would not have understood much about the Cross at this particular time; that awaiting the conversion of Paul).

6 And the people with one accord gave heed unto those things which Philip spoke (proclaims a great acceptance of the Gospel), hearing and seeing the miracles which he did (verified the Message he preached).

7 For unclean spirits, crying with loud voice, came out of many who were possessed with them (the Name of Jesus was used to cast out demons): and many taken with palsies, and who were lame, were healed.

8 And there was great joy in that city (when the Message of Christ is accepted, it always brings "great joy").

THE SORCERER

9 But there was a certain man, called Simon, which beforetime in the same city used sorcery (pertained to the practice of the rites of the art of the Magi; it is of Satan), and bewitched the people of Samaria, giving out that himself was some great one (it seemed they believed his claims):

10 To whom they all gave heed, from the least to the greatest (proclaims that all were duped by his sorceries), saying, This man is the great power of God (they attributed his magic and stunts to being done by the Power of God, when in reality it was of Satan; much in the modern Church which claims to be the Power of God falls into the same category).

11 And to him they had regard, because that of long time he had bewitched them with sorceries (the word "bewitched" refers to the fact that the person or persons are deprived of the ability to think or order their thoughts correctly).

12 But when they believed Philip preaching the things concerning the Kingdom of God (they now encountered a Power which was greater than the powers of darkness), and the Name of Jesus Christ (Salvation is in that Name and what it refers to, which speaks of the Cross; the very Name "Jesus" means "Saviour"), they were baptized, both men and women (they were baptized in water after they were saved, not baptized in order to be saved).

13 Then Simon himself believed also (every evidence is that Simon truly gave his heart and life to the Lord Jesus; the word "believed" is used here exactly as it was in the previous Verse, which signifies Salvation [Jn. 3:16; Rom. 10:9-13]): and when he was baptized (plainly informs us that Philip saw enough evidence of Repentance and Faith in Christ that he baptized Simon exactly as he did the others), he continued with Philip, and wondered, beholding the miracles and signs which were done (he watched carefully what Philip was doing, and noted that there was no trickery involved).

THE HOLY SPIRIT

14 Now when the Apostles which were at Jerusalem heard that Samaria had received the Word of God (many had been saved), they sent

unto them Peter and John *(for a reason which we will see)*:

15 Who, when they were come down, prayed for them, that they might receive the Holy Spirit *(this was their purpose for coming, and this is how important it is for Believers to be Baptized with the Spirit)*:

16 (For as yet He *(the Holy Spirit)* was fallen upon none of them *(evidently Philip had strongly preached Salvation, but had not preached the Baptism with the Holy Spirit)*: only they were baptized in the Name of the Lord Jesus.) *(This is meant to infer that they had been baptized in water, but not the Baptism with the Spirit.)*

17 Then laid they *their* hands on them *(presents one of the ways Believers can be Baptized with the Spirit, but this is not necessary in order to be filled [Acts 2:4; 10:44-48])*, and they received the Holy Spirit *(doesn't give any more information, but we know from Acts 2:4; 10:44-48; 19:1-7 that they also spoke with tongues)*.

THE SINFUL PROPOSAL

18 And when Simon saw that through laying on of the Apostles' hands the Holy Spirit was given *(what did he see? he saw and heard them speak with tongues)*, he offered them money *(he would not have offered money for the mere laying on of hands)*,

19 Saying, Give me also this power, that on whomsoever I lay hands, he may receive the Holy Spirit *(money cannot purchase these Gifts, or anything else of God for that matter)*.

20 But Peter said unto him, Your money perish with you, because you have thought that the Gift of God may be purchased with money *(every Preacher must be extra careful that money not be made a part of the equation; God has nothing for sale; everything He has is a "Gift" [Jn. 3:16])*.

21 You have neither part nor lot in this matter *(the word "matter" in the Greek, as it is used here, is "Logos," and means "a word or speech"; Peter is referring to these Believers speaking with other tongues)*: for your heart is not right in the Sight of God *(self-will is the cause of the evil heart)*.

22 Repent therefore of this your wickedness *(proclaims just how bad the sin was, but yet that hope is offered)*, and pray God, if perhaps the thought of your heart may be forgiven you *(tells us that God Alone could remedy this situation, and He always will upon proper Repentance, which says that He is right and I am wrong)*.

23 For I perceive *(refers to the Holy Spirit informing Peter of the exact cause, and not mere symptoms)* that you are in the gall of bitterness *(condition of extreme wickedness)*, and *in* the bond of iniquity *(a bondage of greed for money, power, and control over other men)*.

24 Then answered Simon, and said, Pray ye to the Lord for me *(suggests a right attitude on the part of Simon)*, that none of these things which you have spoken come upon me *(has reference to him potentially perishing, that is if he remained on that particular course)*.

25 And they, when they had testified and preached the Word of the Lord *(they, no doubt, saw a Church established there)*, returned to Jerusalem, and preached the Gospel in many villages of the Samaritans *(on their way to Jerusalem, they preached in many towns and villages, probably taking several weeks to do so)*.

PHILIP

26 And the Angel of the Lord spoke unto Philip *(proclaims another mission entirely for Philip, rather than going back to Jerusalem with Peter and John)*, saying, Arise, and go toward the south unto the way that goes down from Jerusalem unto Gaza, which is desert *(probably referred to the road that led to the Old Testament Gaza, which was destroyed in 93 B.C.)*.

27 And he arose and went *(a distance of approximately one hundred miles; He immediately obeyed)*: and, behold, a man of Ethiopia, an Eunuch of great authority under Candace Queen of the Ethiopians *(evidently presents a Gentile who was proselyte to the Covenant of Israel)*, who had the charge of all her treasure *(he was the treasurer of that African country)*, and had come to Jerusalem for to worship *(could refer to the Feast of Tabernacles, which was held in October; Eusebius says, "He was the very first Gentile to convert to Christ, at least in the Early Church.")*,

28 Was returning *(returning to Ethiopia)*, and sitting in his chariot read Isaiah the Prophet *(more than likely spoke of a translation into Greek)*.

29 Then the Spirit *(Holy Spirit)* said unto Philip *(the Holy Spirit will lead and guide all who desire such a relationship)*, Go near, and join yourself to this chariot.

30 And Philip ran thither to *him (the driver had probably stopped to water the horses)*, and heard him read the Prophet Isaiah *(means that he was reading aloud)*, and said, Do you

understand what you are reading? *(This was perhaps asked because the Holy Spirit told him to ask such a question.)*

31 And he said, How can I, except some man should guide me? *(This is the reason the God-called Preacher is so very important!)* And he desired Philip that he would come up and sit with him *(he wanted Philip to explain the Scripture to him)*.

32 The place of the Scripture which he read was this *(as well presents an orchestration carried out by the Holy Spirit)*, He was led as a sheep to the slaughter; and like a lamb dumb before his shearer, so opened He not His mouth *(this refers to the Cross and the manner of approach by our Lord to this Sacrifice)*:

33 In His humiliation His judgment was taken away *(means that all justice was suspended concerning the trial and Crucifixion of Christ)*: and who shall declare His generation? *(This means that the Jewish Sanhedrin had tried to blot out His Memory, but with no success at all.)* for His life is taken from the earth *(despite their evil intentions, the Plan of God was carried out to total fulfillment)*.

34 And the Eunuch answered Philip, and said, I pray thee, of whom speaks the Prophet this? *(This presents, as will become obvious, a heart hungry for God.)* of himself, or of some other man? *(This presents the correct question, which Philip will answer.)*

35 Then Philip opened his mouth, and began at the same Scripture, and preached unto him Jesus *(refers to Isa. 53:7-8; He explains to the Ethiopian that the Prophet Isaiah is speaking of Jesus)*.

36 And as they went on *their* way, they came unto a certain water *(as they journeyed a little ways, with Philip explaining to him all of this time, they come to a place where there was water; evidently, Philip had explained to him that Water Baptism was the outward sign that Jesus had been accepted in the heart)*: and the Eunuch said, See, here is water; what does hinder me to be baptized? *(He had accepted Christ, and was now eager to follow the Lord in Water Baptism.)*

37 And Philip said, If you believe with all your heart, you may *(presents the only Scriptural requirement for Salvation)*. And he answered and said, I believe that Jesus Christ is the Son of God *(this shows that Philip had explained the Gospel Program to this man very well!)*.

38 And he *(the Ethiopian)* commanded the chariot to stand still: and they went down both into the water, both Philip and the Eunuch

(this tells us that Water Baptism is by immersion, and not by mere sprinkling as taught by some); and he *(Philip)* baptized him.

39 And when they were come up out of the water, the Spirit of the Lord caught away Philip *(means exactly what it says)*, that the Eunuch saw him no more *(this would have been quite an experience)*: and he *(the Ethiopian)* went on his way rejoicing *(his trip had been well worthwhile)*.

40 But Philip was found at Azotus *(this was the old Ashdod, situated on the Mediterranean)*: and passing through he preached in all the cities, till he came to Caesarea *(about sixty miles north of Azotus)*.

CHAPTER 9
(A.D. 35)
SAUL

AND Saul, yet breathing out threatenings and slaughter against the Disciples of the Lord *(presents Paul as the Leader of the persecution against the Early Church)*, went unto the High Priest *(if it was A.D. 35, Caiaphas was the High Priest; once again, we see the evil of religion)*,

2 And desired of him letters to Damascus to the Synagogues *(proclaims the persecution led by Paul branching out to other cities)*, that if he found any of this way *(portrays the description of the Early Church [Jn. 14:6; Acts 18:25-26; 19:9, 23; 22:4; 24:14, 22])*, whether they were men or women, he might bring them bound unto Jerusalem *(refers to them appearing before the Sanhedrin, the same group that Crucified Christ)*.

3 And as he journeyed, he came near Damascus *(approximately 175 miles from Jerusalem)*: and suddenly there shined round about him a light from Heaven *(proclaims the appearance of Christ in His Glory)*:

4 And he fell to the earth *(implies that the Power of God knocked him down)*, and heard a voice saying unto him, Saul, Saul, why do you persecute Me? *(To touch one who belongs to the Lord in a negative way is to touch the Lord!)*

5 And he said, Who are You, Lord? *(Paul uses this in the realm of Deity, not merely as respect as some have claimed.)* And the Lord said, I am Jesus Whom you persecute *(presents the Lord using the Name that Paul hated)*: it is hard for you to kick against the pricks *(has reverence to sharp goads, which were placed immediately behind the oxen and were attached*

to the plow; to kick against it, would cause sharp pain).

6 And he trembling and astonished said *(he was stupefied and astounded)*, **Lord, what will You have me to do?** *(This constitutes the moment that Paul was saved.)* **And the Lord** *said* **unto him, Arise, and go into the city, and it shall be told you what you must do** *(pertains to the Plan of God for Paul, which, in effect, would change the world).*

7 **And the men which journeyed with him stood speechless** *(they were very much aware that something had happened, but they did not know exactly what)*, **hearing a voice, but seeing no man** *(but Paul saw the man, and that man was Christ).*

SAUL BLINDED

8 **And Saul arose from the earth; and when his eyes were opened, he saw no man** *(it seems that his eyes had been blinded by the Glory of the Lord)*: **but they led him by the hand, and brought** *him* **into Damascus** *(Paul, the champion of the persecutors, is now led like the blind man he temporarily is).*

9 **And he was three days without sight** *(speaks only of the physical sense; in fact, for the very first time he was now able to see)*, **and neither did eat nor drink** *(presents him fasting three days and nights).*

ANANIAS

10 **And there was a certain Disciple at Damascus, named Ananias** *(the word "Disciple," as used without exception in the Book of Acts, refers to followers of Christ)*; **and to him said the Lord in a vision, Ananias** *(he actually saw the Lord, but in Vision form)*. **And he said, Behold, I** *am here,* **Lord** *(proclaims an extensive familiarity with the Lord, far beyond the normal).*

11 **And the Lord** *said* **unto him, Arise, and go into the street which is called Straight** *(proclaims the street, which still exists even after nearly two thousand years)*, **and enquire in the house of Judas for** *one* **called Saul of Tarsus** *(expresses the name of the man who was the most notorious scourge of the followers of Christ in the world of that time)*: **for, behold, he prays** *(Paul had much to pray about),*

12 **And has seen in a vision a man named Ananias coming in** *(proclaims the second Vision that Paul had in a very short period of time)*, **and putting** *his* **hand on him, that he might receive his sight.**

13 **Then Ananias answered, Lord, I have heard by many of this man** *(how empty our fears often are! how ignorant we are of where our chief good lies hid! but God knows; let us trust Him)*, **how much evil he has done to Your Saints at Jerusalem** *(but yet, the Lord has changed this man, and he will become the greatest blessing to the Saints of anyone in history)*:

14 **And here he has authority from the Chief Priests to bind all who call on Your Name** *(Paul's evil intentions had preceded him; but the Lord invaded those intentions, completely changing them).*

15 **But the Lord said unto him, Go your way** *(presents an urgency which demands instant obedience by Ananias)*: **for he is a chosen vessel unto Me** *(it means, "Divine Selection")*, **to bear My Name before the Gentiles, and Kings, and the Children of Israel** *("Gentiles" are placed first; that was Paul's principal calling)*:

16 **For I will show him how great things he must suffer for My Name's sake** *(this is altogether different from much of the modern Gospel, which, in fact, is no Gospel at all!).*

THE HOLY SPIRIT

17 **And Ananias went his way, and entered into the house** *(he obeyed the Command of the Lord)*; **and putting his hands on him** *(on Paul)* **said, Brother Saul** *(he addressed Paul in this manner because Paul was already saved, and had been so for the last three days and nights)*, **the Lord,** *even* **Jesus, Who appeared unto you in the way as you came, has sent me, that you might receive your sight, and be filled with the Holy Spirit** *(this proclaims the fact that one is not Baptized with the Holy Spirit at conversion, as many teach; in fact, the Baptism with the Holy Spirit is a separate work of Grace, which takes place after conversion [Acts 2:4; 8:14-17; 19:1-7]).*

18 **And immediately there fell from his eyes as it had been scales: and he received sight forthwith, and arose, and was baptized** *(was baptized with water, after he was Baptized with the Holy Spirit).*

PREACHING CHRIST

19 **And when he had received meat, he was strengthened** *(refers to him ending his three-day fast).* **Then was Saul certain days with the Disciples which were at Damascus** *(probably means that Ananias introduced him to these*

followers of Christ; he had come to arrest them, and now he joins them; what a mighty God we serve!).

20 And straightway *(immediately)* he preached Christ in the Synagogues *(these were the very Synagogues to which letters of the High Priest were addressed, empowering Paul to arrest any Jewish Believers who called upon the Name of Jesus),* that He is the Son of God *(the first time in Acts that Jesus is referred to by this title).*

21 But all who heard *him* were amazed, and said; Is not this he who destroyed them which called on this Name in Jerusalem, and came hither for that intent, that he might bring them bound unto the Chief Priests? *(This means that those in the Synagogues had been expecting him, but not what he is now saying.)*

22 But Saul increased the more in strength *(refers to his greater understanding of the Word of God as the days wore on; in fact, for the first time, he understands the Word),* and confounded the Jews which dwelt at Damascus, proving that this is very Christ *(proving from the Word of God that, Jesus, was the Messiah).*

JEWISH LEADERS

23 And after that many days were fulfilled, the Jews took counsel to kill him *(the persecutor is now persecuted):*

24 But their laying await was known of Saul *(presents Believers informing him of the proposed action of the Jews).* And they watched the gates day and night to kill him *(which he was informed of as well; therefore, he will escape by a different route).*

25 Then the Disciples *(followers of Christ)* took him by night, and let *him* down by the wall in a basket.

JERUSALEM

26 And when Saul was come to Jerusalem *(presents his first visit there after his conversion),* he assayed to join himself to the Disciples: but they were all afraid of him, and believed not that he was a Disciple *(they thought it was a ploy!).*

27 But Barnabas took him *(presents the same one mentioned in Acts 4:36),* and brought *him* to the Apostles *(actually only refers to Peter and James, the Lord's brother [Gal. 1:19]),* and declared unto them how he *(Paul)* had seen the Lord in the way *(the Vision on the road to Damascus),* and that He *(Jesus)* had spoken to

him, and how he had preached boldly at Damascus in the Name of Jesus *(Barnabas had heard this report, and now testifies to its veracity).*

28 And he *(Paul)* was with them *(the Apostles)* coming in and going out at Jerusalem *(probably refers to the approximate fifteen days he spent there, most of it with Simon Peter [Gal. 1:18]).*

29 And he spoke boldly in the Name of the Lord Jesus *(he did this, as is obvious, in the very center or core of Jesus hate),* and disputed against the Grecians *(he disputed with the Grecian Jews, probably preaching in the very Synagogues in which he had heard Stephen, and maybe even had debated him):* but they went about to kill him *(presents the same spirit now against him that he had presented against Stephen).*

30 *Which* when the brethren knew *(knew about the efforts to kill him),* they brought him down to Caesarea, and sent him forth to Tarsus *(speaks of his home; as a result, we hear no more of Paul until Acts 11:25).*

31 Then had the Churches rest throughout all Judaea and Galilee and Samaria *(the attention of the Jews was diverted at this time from the Believers to other things, thereby giving the Churches rest from persecution, at least for a while),* and were edified *(without interruption, the Lord now builds His house)*; and walking in the fear of the Lord, and in the comfort of the Holy Spirit, were multiplied *(many people were saved).*

PETER'S MINISTRY

32 And it came to pass, as Peter passed throughout all *quarters (now shifts the attention to this Apostle, and for a reason),* he came down also to the Saints which dwelt at Lydda *(refers to a town about thirty miles west of Jerusalem).*

33 And there he found a certain man named Aeneas, which had kept his bed eight years, and was sick of the palsy *(portrays, as is obvious, his helplessness).*

34 And Peter said unto him, Aeneas, Jesus Christ makes you whole *(refers to Peter staunchly giving Christ the credit for these Miracles):* arise, and make your bed *(as a token of his Miraculous Cure).* And he arose immediately *(he was healed instantly, and healed completely).*

35 And all who dwelt at Lydda and Saron saw him, and turned to the Lord *(the word "all," as it is given in the original Greek, does not necessarily mean every single person in these areas, but rather to those who "saw him," which no*

doubt numbered many).

TABITHA

36 Now there was at Joppa a certain Disciple named Tabitha, which by interpretation is called Dorcas (it was "Tabitha" in Syrian and "Dorcas" in the Greek; both names mean "a gazelle"): this woman was full of good works and almsdeeds which she did (she was a lady of fine reputation and love for God).

37 And it came to pass in those days, that she was sick, and died (refers to the days in which Peter was at Lydda; her death was unexpected): whom when they had washed, they laid her in an upper chamber (it means that they laid her out for viewing).

38 And forasmuch as Lydda was near to Joppa, and the Disciples (followers of Christ) had heard that Peter was there (tells us that there was a Church in Joppa), they sent unto him two men, desiring him that he would not delay to come to them (it seems that they were expecting a Miracle, irrespective that the woman was dead).

39 Then Peter arose and went with them (indicates that he was led by the Lord to do so). When he was come, they brought him into the upper chamber: and all the widows stood by him weeping, and showing the coats and garments which Dorcas made, while she was with them (seems to indicate that Dorcas was a widow as well!).

40 But Peter put them all forth, and kneeled down, and prayed; and turning him to the body said, Tabitha, arise (exactly the same as that said by Jesus when He raised the daughter of Jairus from the dead [Mk. 5:41]). And she opened her eyes: and when she saw Peter, she sat up (presents the first person being raised from the dead in the Early Church).

41 And he gave her his hand, and lifted her up (a common courtesy), and when he had called the Saints and widows, presented her alive (she is one of few in human history who has actually died, and then come back to tell the story; all who did so were connected with the Lord).

42 And it was known throughout all Joppa (one can well imagine the impact this Miracle had); and many believed in the Lord.

43 And it came to pass, that he tarried many days in Joppa with one Simon a tanner (probably referred to several months; about eight years had passed now since Pentecost, during which time the Gospel had been preached only to the Jews; that is about to change).

CHAPTER 10
(A.D. 41)
CORNELIUS

THERE was a certain man in Caesarea called Cornelius (presents the beginning of one of the great turning points of history), a centurion of the band called the Italian band (in charge of about a hundred men),

2 A devout man (but unsaved!), and one who feared God with all his house (but unsaved!), which gave much alms to the people (but unsaved!), and prayed to God always (but unsaved! all of these things were wonderful, and certainly noticed by the Lord; but they did not save the man, even as they do not save anyone now; being religious does not constitute Salvation; there must be an acceptance of Christ and His Finished Work, if one is to be saved [Jn. 3:16; Rom. 10:9-10, 13]).

3 He saw in a vision evidently about the ninth hour of the day (but which did not save him) an Angel of God coming in to him (this as well did not save him!), and saying unto him, Cornelius (the Angel knowing his name did not save him!).

4 And when he (Cornelius) looked on him (the Angel), he was afraid, and said, What is it, Lord? (The title "Lord," in the manner in which Cornelius used it, does not refer to Deity, but rather refers to respect or honor.) And he (the Angel) said unto him, Your prayers and your alms are come up for a memorial before God (a seeking heart will find the Lord).

5 And now send men to Joppa (proclaims the Angel telling Cornelius what to do in order to hear the Gospel, but not presenting the Gospel himself; that privilege is given to man and not to Angels), and call for one Simon, whose surname is Peter (through Peter, the Lord will open the door to the Gentile world, for whom Christ died):

6 He lodges with one Simon a tanner, whose house is by the sea side (presents, as should be obvious, the Lord knowing at all times exactly where His People are): he shall tell you what you ought to do (all he had previously done, as commendable as it was, did not save him).

7 And when the Angel which spoke unto Cornelius was departed (signals the beginning of this scenario which will shake the world), he called two of his household servants, and a devout soldier of them who waited on him continually (concerns the three who would go to fetch Peter; it was about thirty-five miles from

Caesarea to Joppa);

8 And when he had declared all *these* things unto them (*no doubt referred to the visitation by the Angel, and what the Angel had said*), he sent them to Joppa.

THE VISION

9 On the morrow, as they went on their journey, and drew near unto the city (*probably means that they left Caesarea very shortly after being given instructions by Cornelius the day before*), Peter went up on the housetop to pray about the sixth hour (*12 noon*):

10 And he became very hungry, and would have eaten (*proclaims that he was about to quit praying and have lunch*): but while they made ready, he fell into a trance (*a state in which one ceases to be aware of surroundings, but sees only what is portrayed to him*),

11 And saw Heaven opened (*before Jesus, Heaven had been closed; due to the Cross, it is now open!*), and a certain vessel descending unto him, as it had been a great sheet knit at the four corners, and let down to the Earth (*an object lesson*):

12 Wherein were all manner of fourfooted beasts of the Earth, and wild beasts, and creeping things, and fowls of the air (*they all seemed to be unclean animals and fowls as listed in Lev., Chpt. 11*).

13 And there came a Voice to him (*proclaims the Lord now speaking to Peter*), Rise, Peter; kill, and eat (*literally says in the Greek Text, "sacrifice and eat"*).

14 But Peter said, Not so, Lord (*Peter will now have to be taught a lesson*); for I have never eaten any thing that is common or unclean (*refers to that which is defiled and forbidden by the Law of Moses [Lev. 11; Deut. 14; Mk. 7:2]*).

15 And the voice *spoke* unto him again the second time (*proclaims a correction tended toward Peter by the Lord*), What God has cleansed, *that* call not thou common (*struck at the very heart of present Jewish beliefs; as stated, the Lord is giving Peter an object lesson, proclaiming the fact that what He did on the Cross was for the Gentile world as well as the Jewish world, with Gentiles being symbolized by the unclean animals*).

16 This was done thrice (*meant to impress the significance of what is being said*): and the vessel was received up again into Heaven (*the Vision ended*).

17 Now while Peter doubted in himself what this vision which he had seen should mean (*proclaims that, at this stage, Peter did not actually know what the Lord was telling him*), behold, the men which were sent from Cornelius had made enquiry for Simon's house, and stood before the gate (*he will soon know what the Vision meant, and will understand perfectly what the Lord is telling him*),

18 And called, and asked whether Simon, which was surnamed Peter, were lodged there (*specifies emphatically, so that only Peter would do!*).

19 While Peter thought on the Vision (*trying to understand what the Lord had told him*), the Spirit (*Holy Spirit*) said unto him, Behold, three men seek you.

20 Arise therefore, and get thee down (*pertains to Peter being on the housetop, which in those days, as now, in that area are flat*), and go with them, doubting nothing (*do not waver or hesitate to obey*): for I have sent them (*now he will begin to understand what the Lord was telling him*).

21 Then Peter went down to the men which were sent unto him from Cornelius; and said, Behold, I am he whom you seek: what *is* the cause wherefore you are come? (*The Holy Spirit didn't tell Peter what they wanted or the reason for their coming. He just told Peter to go with them, "doubting nothing."*)

22 And they said, Cornelius the Centurion (*portrays to Peter immediately that this man is a Gentile*), a just man, and one who fears God, and of good report among all the Nation of the Jews, was warned from God by an Holy Angel to send for you into his house, and to hear words of you (*what Cornelius must hear in order to be saved; Peter had been chosen to deliver to those "Words," and now it was up to Cornelius to "hear them"*).

23 Then called he them in, and lodged *them* (*tells us that Peter now knows what the Vision meant, or at least has a good idea*). And on the morrow Peter went away with them, and certain brethren from Joppa accompanied him (*six Jewish brethren accompanied him [Acts 11:1-18; 15:7]*).

PETER

24 And the morrow after they entered into Caesarea (*they probably had spent the night at Apollonia, which was about halfway along on the coast road*). And Cornelius waited for

them, and had called together his kinsmen and near friends *(probably was quite a crowd)*.

25 And as Peter was coming in, Cornelius met him *(this meeting probably took place outside the house, at the gate)*, and fell down at his feet, and worshipped *him (does not necessarily mean that Cornelius was worshipping Peter, but was merely worshipping, inasmuch as the pronoun "him" was added by the translators)*.

26 But Peter took him up *(better translated, "but Peter raised him up")*, saying, Stand up; I myself also am a man *(he is not to be bowed before or worshipped)*.

27 And as he *(Peter)* talked with him *(portrays Peter putting himself on the same level as Cornelius)*, he went in, and found many who were come together *(implies that they were awestruck when they saw him)*.

28 And he said unto them, You know how that it is an unlawful thing for a man who is a Jew to keep company, or come unto one of another nation *(proclaims him relating something that was quite well-known by all Gentiles who had resided in Israel for any length of time)*; but God has showed me that I should not call any man common or unclean *(tells us that Peter now fully understands what the Vision was all about, concerning the sheet let down from Heaven)*.

29 Therefore came I *unto you* without gainsaying, as soon as I was sent for *(means he questioned nothing, but obeyed as the Holy Spirit had told him to)*: I ask therefore for what intent you have sent for me? *(This actually pertains to that which he already knew, but wanted to hear from Cornelius.)*

30 And Cornelius said, Four days ago I was fasting until this hour; and at the ninth hour I prayed in my house *(3 p.m.)*, and, behold, a man stood before me in bright clothing *(the Angel who radiated with the Presence of God)*,

31 And said, Cornelius, your prayer is heard, and your alms are had in remembrance in the sight of God *(God remembers both the bad and the good; in His Time, He rewards both accordingly!)*.

32 Send therefore to Joppa, and call hither Simon, whose surname is Peter *(second time related, which tells us how important all of this is)*; he is lodged in the house of *one* Simon a tanner by the sea side: who, when he comes, shall speak unto you *(refers to the Way of Salvation made clear by Peter; this signifies that God uses men in this capacity, and not Angels)*.

33 Immediately therefore I sent to you

(implies that such was done within the hour); and you have well done that you are come *(means that they are so very pleased that Peter has come, and that he came as soon as possible)*. Now therefore are we all here present before God, to hear all things that are Commanded you of God *(they were ready!)*.

THE GENTILES

34 Then Peter opened *his* mouth, and said *(proclaims a profound truth, as simple as it was; the Gospel will now break the bounds of Judaism, despite the efforts of man to do otherwise)*, Of a truth I perceive that God is no respecter of persons *(not meant to be implied by Peter that this Truth is new, for it is not [II Sam. 14:14], but up to this time Peter had applied it to Jews only, not Gentiles)*:

35 But in every Nation *(the Gospel is for all)* he who fears Him, and works righteousness, is accepted with Him *(the pronoun "Him" refers to Christ; God accepted the Sacrifice of Christ on the Cross, and all who accept Christ and the Cross are accepted with "Him")*.

36 The Word which *God* sent unto the Children of Israel, preaching peace by Jesus Christ *(this is justifying Peace, which comes instantly upon the acceptance of Christ)*: (He is Lord of all:) *(Jesus Christ is Lord because He has made Salvation possible for all who will believe [Phil. 2:11])*.

37 That word, *I say*, you know *(refers to the Life, Ministry, Death, Resurrection, and Ascension of Christ)*, which was published throughout all Judaea, and began from Galilee, after the Baptism which John preached *(John introduced Christ)*;

38 How God anointed Jesus of Nazareth with the Holy Spirit and with Power *(as a Man, Christ needed the Holy Spirit, as we certainly do as well! in fact, everything He did was by the Power of the Spirit)*: who went about doing good *(everything He did was good)*, and healing all who were oppressed of the devil *(only Christ could do this, and Believers can do such only as Christ empowers them by the Spirit)*; for God was with Him *(God is with us only as we are "with Him")*.

39 And we *(the Apostles and others)* are witnesses of all things which He did both in the land of the Jews, and in Jerusalem *(Jerusalem is inferred because it was the center of religious authority; so they were without excuse)*; Whom they slew and hanged on a tree *("they"*

referred to "the Sanhedrin," the religious leaders of Israel):

40 Him God raised up the third day *(Peter is affirming the Resurrection of Christ)*, **and showed Him openly** *(Jesus revealed Himself after the Resurrection to quite a number of people)*;

41 Not to all the people *(not to all of Israel)*, **but unto witnesses chosen before of God** *(refers to those who had Faith in Him and Believed)*, *even* **to us, who did eat and drink with Him after He rose from the dead** *(proclaims that Jesus was not a spirit, or mere apparition, but rather real, physical, and alive)*.

42 And He Commanded us to preach unto the people *(presents God's Way of spreading the Gospel)*, **and to testify that it is He which was ordained of God** *to be* **the Judge of the quick** *(living)* **and dead** *(today Jesus is the Saviour, tomorrow He will be the Judge)*.

43 To Him give all the Prophets witness *(means that He fulfilled all of the Prophecies)*, **that through His Name** *(His Name Alone)* **whosoever** *(anyone in the world)* **believes in Him** *(Believes in Who and What He has done, referring to the Cross)* **shall receive remission of sins** *(freedom, deliverance, forgiveness)*.

THE HOLY SPIRIT

44 While Peter yet spoke these words *(concerning Believing in Him)*, **the Holy Spirit fell on all them which heard the Word** *(even though we are given very little information here, this is the moment when Cornelius and his household accepted Christ, and were saved)*.

45 And they of the Circumcision *(Jews)* **which believed** *(Believed in Christ)* **were astonished** *(at what they saw the Lord doing, which could not be denied)*, **as many as came with Peter, because that on the Gentiles also was poured out the Gift of the Holy Spirit** *(Cornelius and his household were saved, and then moments later Baptized with the Holy Spirit; it was quite a meeting!)*.

46 For they heard them speak with tongues *(this is the initial, physical evidence that one has been Baptized with the Holy Spirit; it always and without exception accompanies the Spirit Baptism)*, **and magnify God** *(means that some of them would stop speaking in tongues momentarily, and then begin to praise God in their natural language, magnifying His Name)*. **Then answered Peter** *(presents the Apostle about to take another step)*,

47 Can any man forbid water, that these should not be baptized *(they had accepted Christ and had been Baptized with the Spirit, so now they should be Baptized in Water, which they were)*, **which have received the Holy Spirit as well as we?** *(Multiple millions of Gentiles since that day have been Baptized with the Holy Spirit.)*

48 And he Commanded them to be baptized in the Name of the Lord *(simply means, "by the Authority of the Lord")*. **Then prayed they him to tarry certain days** *(which he possibly did!)*.

CHAPTER 11
(A.D. 41)

THE GENTILE QUESTION

AND the Apostles and brethren who were in Judaea *(refers to the Eleven other than Peter, as well as others)* **heard that the Gentiles had also received the Word of God** *(this type of news travels fast)*.

2 And when Peter was come up to Jerusalem *(presents a time of great significance)*, **they who were of the Circumcision** *(Jewish Believers)* **contended with him** *(it means, at least at the outset, that they were not accepting Peter's explanation, feeling he had made himself unclean by associating with Gentiles)*,

3 Saying, you went in to men uncircumcised *(Gentiles)*, **and did eat with them** *(there is nothing in the Law of Moses which forbids eating with Gentiles; this was an addition made by men, not God)*.

PETER'S DEFENSE

4 But Peter rehearsed *the matter* from the beginning *(proclaims the Apostle being very patient, and for cause; if it is to be remembered, the Lord had been patient with him)*, **and expounded** *it* **by order unto them, saying** *(portrays him taking the entire episode step-by-step)*,

5 I was in the city of Joppa praying: and in a trance I saw a Vision, A certain vessel descending, as it had been a great sheet, let down from Heaven by four corners; and it came even to me *(proclaims what he saw, and that he knew it was meant for him)*:

6 Upon the which when I had fastened my eyes, I considered, and saw fourfooted beasts of the earth, and wild beasts, and creeping things, and fowls of the air.

7 And I heard a Voice saying unto me, Arise, Peter; kill and eat *(this was not a suggestion,*

but rather a Command; therefore, intended to be obeyed).

8 But I said, Not so, Lord: for nothing common or unclean has at any time entered into my mouth.

9 But the Voice answered me again from Heaven *(he didn't see a form, but only heard a Voice)*, What God has cleansed, *that* call not thou common.

10 And this was done three times: and all were drawn up again into Heaven.

GENTILES AND THE GOSPEL

11 And, behold, immediately there were three men already come unto the house where I was, sent from Caesarea unto me.

12 And the Spirit *(Holy Spirit)* bade me go with them, nothing doubting. Moreover these six brethren accompanied me *(he now tells how many went with him)*, and we entered into the man's house *(the house of Cornelius)*:

13 And he showed us how he had seen an Angel in his house, which stood and said unto him, Send men to Joppa, and call for Simon, whose surname is Peter *(all of this proclaims that God works through men)*;

14 Who shall tell you words, whereby you and all your house shall be saved *(proclaims unequivocally that they were not saved before Peter came and preached the Gospel, even though Cornelius had done many good things)*.

15 And as I began to speak *(had gotten a little way into the Message)*, the Holy Spirit fell on them, as on us at the beginning *(speaks of Cornelius and his household being Baptized with the Spirit, exactly as the Apostles and others had been on the Day of Pentecost)*.

16 Then remembered I the Word of the Lord, how that He said *(pertains to something that Peter had not mentioned in the actual happening)*, John indeed baptized with water; but you shall be Baptized with the Holy Spirit *(Acts 1:5; Mat. 3:11)*.

17 Forasmuch then as God gave them *(the Gentiles)* the like Gift *(Salvation and the Holy Spirit Baptism)* as *He did* unto us, who believed on the Lord Jesus Christ *(the requirement)*; what was I, that I could withstand God? *(To not go would be to disobey God.)*

18 When they heard these things, they held their peace, and glorified God *(they not only stifled their own thoughts of opposition, but glorified God as well for what had been done)*, saying, Then has God also to the Gentiles granted

Repentance unto Life *(proclaims in no uncertain terms that they were given such "Life" strictly on Faith, which included none of the rituals and Ceremonies of Judaism)*.

ANTIOCH

19 Now they which were scattered abroad upon the persecution that arose about Stephen *(concerns that which happened in Acts, Chpt. 8, about six or seven years before)* travelled as far as Phenice *(Lebanon)*, and Cyprus, and Antioch *(a city of Syria)*, preaching the Word to none but unto the Jews only *(pertained basically to proclaiming Jesus as the Messiah of Israel and the Saviour of the world, and that He had risen from the dead)*.

20 And some of them were men of Cyprus and Cyrene *(implies that they were latecomers to Antioch)*, which, when they were come to Antioch, spoke unto the Grecians *(pertains to Gentiles, not Greek-speaking Jews as some claim)*, preaching the Lord Jesus *(indicates that Jews who preached to them were not demanding that they also keep the Law of Moses)*.

21 And the Hand of the Lord was with them *(signifies that God was pleased with the Gospel being preached to these Gentiles)*: and a great number believed, and turned unto the Lord *(they gave their hearts and lives to the Lord Jesus Christ)*.

22 Then tidings of these things came unto the ears of the Church which was in Jerusalem *(which was then the headquarters Church; these "tidings" spoke of good news)*: and they sent forth Barnabas, that he should go as far as Antioch *(Barnabas was the right man!; therefore, they were led by the Spirit in sending him)*.

23 Who, when he came, and had seen the Grace of God *(refers to the fact that Barnabas saw the changed lives of these Gentiles)*, was glad, and exhorted them all, that with purpose of heart they would cleave unto the Lord *(be led by the Holy Spirit)*.

24 For he was a good man *(this is what the Holy Spirit said)*, and full of the Holy Spirit and of Faith *(describes Barnabas in the same manner as Stephen [Acts 6:5])*: and much people was added unto the Lord *(many Jews and Gentiles were coming to Christ)*.

25 Then departed Barnabas to Tarsus, for to seek Saul *(this is one of the single most important Verses in the entirety of the Word of God; the Holy Spirit led him to do this; as well, the Text implies that he had some difficulty in finding

Paul; this was around the year A.D. 43, about ten years after the Crucifixion):

26 And when he had found him, he brought him unto Antioch. And it came to pass, that a whole year they assembled themselves with the Church, and taught much people *(could well signal the beginning of teaching of the New Covenant as it had been given to Paul by Christ)*. And the Disciples were called Christians first in Antioch *(they received the name of "Christians," as followers of Christ, from the outside world and accepted it [Acts 26:28; I Pet. 4:16])*.

27 And in these days came Prophets from Jerusalem unto Antioch *(probably refers to near the conclusion of the year spent by Paul and Barnabas in Antioch at that time)*.

28 And there stood up one of them named Agabus *(proclaims Agabus giving forth a Prophetic Utterance, as he did in Acts 21:10 as well)*, and signified by the Spirit that there should be great drought throughout all the world *(the known world of that day)*: which came to pass in the days of Claudius Caesar *(the Holy Spirit informed them of this for a reason, as we shall see)*.

29 Then the Disciples, every man according to his ability, determined to send relief unto the Brethren which dwelt in Judaea *(there was already great hardship in Jerusalem due to multiple thousands of Believers being excommunicated from the Synagogue, and now this drought added extra strain, as would be obvious)*:

30 Which also they did, and sent it to the Elders by the hands of Barnabas and Saul *(they took the offering to Jerusalem)*.

CHAPTER 12
(A.D. 44)
PERSECUTION

NOW about that time *(pertains to the time Paul and Barnabas went to Jerusalem)* Herod the king *(speaks of Herod Agrippa, the son of Aristobulus, grandson of Herod the Great, who murdered the babies of Bethlehem)* stretched forth *his* hands to vex certain of the Church *(was probably done to ingratiate himself with the Jewish Leadership)*.

2 And he killed James the brother of John with the sword *(the first of the Apostles to die; no successor for James was ever chosen; in fact, with the exception of Judas who was replaced by Mathias, no others ever followed any of the Twelve in Office; in other words, there is no such thing as Apostolic Succession, as taught by some)*.

PETER

3 And because he saw it pleased the Jews, he proceeded further to take Peter also. (Then were the days of Unleavened Bread.) *(It was the time of the Passover, i.e., April.)*

4 And when he had apprehended him, he put *him* in prison *(represents the third time Peter was arrested [Acts 4:3; 5:18-19])*, and delivered *him* to four quaternions of soldiers to keep him *(represented sixteen soldiers, four to the watch)*; intending after Easter to bring him forth to the people *(should have been translated, "Intending after Passover . . .")*.

5 Peter therefore was kept in prison: but prayer was made without ceasing of the Church unto God for him *(presents the greatest weapon at the Church's disposal)*.

6 And when Herod would have brought him forth *(Herod had probably spread the word all over Jerusalem that he was going to put on a show, which would be the death of the great Apostle Peter)*, the same night Peter was sleeping between two soldiers, bound with two chains: and the keepers before the door kept the prison *(Peter was sleeping, even though he was supposed to die the next day; he wasn't worried because the Lord had told him that he would not die young, but old [Jn. 21:18])*.

THE ANGEL

7 And, behold, the Angel of the Lord came upon *him* *(should have been translated, "An Angel of the Lord")*, and a light shined in the prison *(meaning there was no doubt this being was "from the Lord")*: and he smote Peter on the side, and raised him up, saying, Arise up quickly *(simply means that the Angel awakened him)*. And his chains fell off from *his* hands *(great power!)*.

8 And the Angel said unto him, Gird yourself, and bind on your sandals. And so he did. And he said unto him, Cast your garment about you, and follow me *(speaks of the outer garment, with Peter now being fully dressed)*.

9 And he went out, and followed him *(presents Peter doing something, which at the moment he is not certain is real)*; and wist not that it was true which was done by the Angel; but thought he saw a Vision *(he had difficulty making the transition to the supernatural; he kept thinking that he was seeing a Vision)*.

10 When they were past the first and the second ward *(probably means that Herod had*

placed Peter in the inner prison; as well, they went through the doors and passed the guards without them knowing what was happening; in some way, the Angel made all of this invisible to these individuals), they came unto the iron gate that leads unto the city *(pertained to the gate of the Prison);* which opened to them of his own accord *(means that it opened automatically):* and they went out, and passed on through one street; and forthwith the Angel departed from him *(so Miraculous that it actually defies description).*

11 And when Peter was come to himself *(meaning he now knows that this had not been a vision or a dream, but that he had been truly delivered by an Angel),* he said, Now I know of a surety, that the Lord has sent His Angel, and has delivered me out of the hand of Herod *(proclaims Peter giving God all the Glory),* and *from* all the expectation of the people of the Jews *(Herod would be deprived of his show, and all who were expecting to see the blood-letting).*

PETER'S ACCOUNT

12 And when he had considered *the thing,* he came to the house of Mary the mother of John, whose surname was Mark *(the John Mark mentioned here is the one who wrote the Gospel which bears his name);* where many were gathered together praying *(proclaims they were praying for Peter around the clock; most think that Peter was rescued between 3 a.m. and 6 a.m.).*

13 And as Peter knocked at the door of the gate *(not the door to the house, but the gate at the fence that surrounded the house, which was normally kept locked),* a damsel came to hearken, named Rhoda *(pertains to this lady who was a servant in this house, with a part of her duties being to welcome guests).*

14 And when she knew Peter's voice *(tells us that the wall and gate were tall, with her unable to see who was knocking),* she opened not the gate for gladness, but ran in, and told how Peter stood before the gate *(presents her message as being so astounding, as to be unbelievable!).*

15 And they said unto her, You are mad *(in other words, they not only did not believe her, but concluded that she was losing touch with reality).* But she constantly affirmed that it was even so *(pertains to her claim being made with more and more conviction).* Then said they, It is his Angel *(proclaims a belief in that day that all Jews had a Guardian Angel).*

16 But Peter continued knocking *(refers to Peter knocking ever harder):* and when they had opened *the door,* and saw him, they were astonished *(they were speechless, even to the extent of putting them in a daze).*

17 But he, beckoning unto them with the hand to hold their peace *(they were all speaking to him at one time),* declared unto them how the Lord had brought him out of the prison. And he said, Go show these things unto James, and to the Brethren *(referred to the Lord's half-brother and the Elders of the Church in Jerusalem, plus any other of the Twelve who may have been in Jerusalem at that time).* And he departed, and went into another place *(evidently he didn't tell anyone where he was going).*

HEROD

18 Now as soon as it was day, there was no small stir among the soldiers, what was become of Peter *(losing their prisoner meant certain death for them).*

19 And when Herod had sought for him, and found him not, he examined the keepers *(means that he did not believe their story; it was, in fact, quite a story!),* and commanded that *they* should be put to death. And he went down from Judaea to Caesarea, and *there* abode *(has reference to the fact that he had been embarrassed before the people, not being able to put forth his spectacle concerning Peter; so he left Jerusalem).*

JUDGMENT

20 And Herod was highly displeased with them of Tyre and Sidon *(gives us no clue for the reason of this displeasure):* but they came with one accord to him, and, having made Blastus the king's chamberlain their friend, desired peace *(they tried to make peace with Herod because of some disruption, which history failed to mention);* because their country was nourished by the king's *country (pertains to trade agreements regarding food, etc.).*

21 And upon a set day Herod, arrayed in royal apparel, sat upon his throne *(all of this was done with great fanfare and ceremony),* and made an oration unto them *(concerns him speaking with great pride about the agreement he had just made with Tyre and Sidon; he made it appear that he was the saviour of these cities).*

22 And the people gave a shout *(means that whatever he was saying greatly pleased them),*

saying, *It is* the voice of a god, and not of a man (*means they kept shouting this over and over!*).

23 And immediately the Angel of the Lord smote him (*may have been the same Angel who delivered Peter*), because he gave not God the glory (*in other words, he accepted the acclamations of the people that he was a "little god"*): and he was eaten of worms (*Josephus said that he lingered for five days with agonizing pains in his stomach*), and gave up the ghost (*he died; this took place A.D. 44*).

24 But the Word of God grew and multiplied (*didn't say the "Church grew," but rather "the Word of God grew . . ."*).

25 And Barnabas and Saul returned from Jerusalem (*proclaims such happening, but does not tell us exactly when*), when they had fulfilled *their* Ministry (*speaks of the offerings brought to Jerusalem from the Saints in Antioch, and possibly elsewhere as well*), and took with them John, whose surname was Mark (*Mark would join with them on the very first Missionary Journey*).

CHAPTER 13
(A.D. 45)
FIRST MISSIONARY JOURNEY

NOW there were in the Church that was at Antioch certain Prophets and Teachers (*the Holy Spirit, as we shall see, shifts the emphasis from Jerusalem to this Syrian city*); as Barnabas, and Simeon who was called Niger, and Lucius of Cyrene, and Manaen, which had been brought up with Herod the Tetrarch, and Saul.

2 As they ministered to the Lord, and fasted (*refers to worship*), the Holy Spirit said (*the Holy Spirit still speaks, at least to all who have the right type of relationship, and anyone can who so desires*), Separate me Barnabas and Saul for the work whereunto I have called them (*expresses a strong Command; in other words, it is not a suggestion; the Lord does the calling, not man*).

CYPRUS

3 And when they had fasted and prayed (*the Early Church was a praying Church; it is a shame that the same cannot be said for the modern Church*), and laid *their* hands on them (*it signified the Blessings of the Church upon Paul and Barnabas*), they sent *them* away (*represents, as far as is known, the very first Missionary trip to new places for the expressed purpose of planting new Churches*).

4 So they, being sent forth by the Holy Spirit (*presents the Spirit not only calling them, but sending them as well; due to the Cross, the Holy Spirit now has far greater latitude to work within our lives*), departing unto Seleucia; and from thence they sailed to Cyprus (*represented a journey of approximately one hundred miles; as well, Cyprus was the boyhood home of Barnabas, where he no doubt still had many friends [Acts 4:36]*).

5 And when they were at Salamis (*one of the principal cities on the Island of Cyprus*), they preached the Word of God in the Synagogues of the Jews (*upon arriving in a new city, Paul would normally first go to the Synagogue and minister; it was the Jew first, and then the Gentile*): and they had also John to *their* minister (*speaks of John Mark, who wrote one of the Four Gospels which bears his name; he was their helper*).

6 And when they had gone through the isle unto Paphos (*the Capitol of Cyprus*), they found a certain sorcerer, a false prophet, a Jew, whose name was Bar-jesus (*this man claimed to be of God, but in reality was of Satan*):

7 Which was with the deputy of the country, Sergius Paulus, a prudent man (*he had this sorcerer with him; being a pagan, he did not know the difference between sorcery and that which was legitimately of God*); who called for Barnabas and Saul, and desired to hear the Word of God (*the news of these men had got around*).

8 But Elymas the sorcerer (for so is his name by interpretation) withstood them (*he saw a threat in Paul and Barnabas*), seeking to turn away the deputy from the faith (*means that the Governor was believing the Message of Jesus Christ, as presented by Paul and Barnabas*).

9 Then Saul, (who also *is called* Paul,) (*presents here the change of name; he will be referred to as Paul from now on; "Paul" is the Roman derivative of the Hebrew "Saul"*), filled with the Holy Spirit (*not only speaks of an ongoing state, but seems to imply a special new Anointing*), set his eyes on him (*did so according to the leading of the Holy Spirit*),

10 And said, O full of all subtilty and all mischief, *you* child of the devil, *you* enemy of all Righteousness (*this was the Gift of "Discerning of spirits" [I Cor. 12:10]*), will you not cease to pervert the Right Ways of the Lord? (*This glaringly proclaims that this sorcerer who claimed to be of God was not of God at all, but*

11 And now, behold, the Hand of the Lord *is* upon you *(would have been better translated, "is against you")*, and you shall be blind, not seeing the sun for a season *(there is indication that there was opportunity for Repentance; in other words, it was a remedial chastisement)*. And immediately there fell on him a mist and a darkness *(was used by the Holy Spirit to teach this man that his message was "darkness")*; and he went about seeking some to lead him by the hand *(indicates that he now has no followers due to the fact that he has been shown up for what he truly is, an imposter!)*.

12 Then the deputy, when he saw what was done, believed *(he accepted the Lord Jesus Christ as his Saviour)*, being astonished at the Doctrine of the Lord *(speaks to the fact that this "Doctrine" was not mere rhetoric, but was accompanied by Power as well)*.

13 Now when Paul and his company loosed from Paphos, they came to Perga in Pamphylia *(presents them going back to the mainland from the Island of Cyprus)*: and John departing from them returned to Jerusalem *(speaks of Mark who wrote the Gospel which bears his name; even though the Holy Spirit is silent regarding why Mark did this, we do know that his departure caused hardship on this Missionary Team [Acts 15:37-39])*.

PISIDIA

14 But when they departed from Perga, they came to Antioch in Pisidia *(proclaims an Antioch other than the Antioch of Syria, where the home Church was located [Acts 13:1])*, and went into the Synagogue on the Sabbath Day, and sat down *(has reference to special seats, thus intimating that they were willing to speak if invited, as was the custom in the Synagogue)*.

15 And after the reading of the Law and the Prophets the Rulers of the Synagogue sent unto them *(proclaims the custom)*, saying, *You* men *and* Brethren, if you have any word of exhortation for the people, say on *(as stated, this was generally the manner in which Paul began his Evangelism in any given area; he would first go to the Jewish Synagogue, and then to the Gentiles)*.

SALVATION BY FAITH

16 Then Paul stood up, and beckoning with *his* hand said, Men of Israel, and you who fear God *(Gentiles who attended Jewish Synagogues were given a particular place to sit, and were called "God-fearers")*, give audience *(the gist of Paul's Message is given here, but doesn't go into much detail in the record of later sermons)*.

17 The God of this people of Israel chose our Fathers *(presents Paul beginning his Message much as Steven had years before)*, and exalted the people when they dwelt as strangers in the land of Egypt, and with an high arm brought He them out of it.

18 And about the time of forty years suffered He their manners in the wilderness *(bad manners)*.

19 And when He had destroyed seven nations in the land of Canaan *(referred to the Canaanites, Hittites, Girgashites, Amorites, Havites, Perizzites, and Jebusites)*, He divided their land to them by lot *(speaks of the Urim and Thummim; gave different portions to different Tribes)*.

20 And after that He gave *unto them* judges about the space of four hundred and fifty years, until Samuel the Prophet *(Samuel was the last Judge, and the first man to stand in the Office of the Prophet)*.

21 And afterward they desired a king: and God gave unto them Saul the son of Cis, a man of the Tribe of Benjamin, by the space of forty years *(meaning that he ruled for forty years)*.

22 And when He *(God)* had removed him *(removed Saul)*, He raised up unto them David to be their king *(David was meant to be the first king of Israel, but the people jumped the gun, so to speak; they demanded a king and got Saul, which proved to be a disaster)*; to whom also He gave testimony, and said, I have found David the *son* of Jesse, a man after Mine own heart, which shall fulfil all My Will.

23 Of this man's seed *(David's seed)* has God according to *His* Promise raised unto Israel a Saviour, Jesus *(proclaims the Apostle now introducing the One Who is the Cause and Reason for everything; He is the only "Saviour")*:

24 When John had first preached before His coming the Baptism of Repentance to all the people of Israel *(the Ministry of John the Baptist)*.

25 And as John fulfilled his course, he said, Whom think ye that I am? I am not *He*. But, behold, there comes One after me, Whose shoes of *His* feet I am not worthy to loose *(John bluntly announces the fact that he is not the Messiah, but rather Jesus)*.

26 Men *and* Brethren, children of the stock

of Abraham *(the Jews)*, and whosoever among you fear God *(the Gentiles)*, to you is the word of this Salvation sent *(presents Paul, without apology, including the Gentiles in this great Plan of Salvation)*.

27 For they who dwell at Jerusalem, and their Rulers *(pinpoints the murderers of Christ)*, because they knew Him not *(implies a willful ignorance that brought about a willful blindness)*, nor yet the voices of the Prophets which are read every Sabbath Day *(the Prophets told them of Christ, but they would not believe)*, they have fulfilled *them* in condemning *Him (Isa., Chpt. 53)*.

28 And though they found no cause of death *in Him (they opposed Him from the very beginning; they heard Him with closed minds, and as a result closed their ears)*, yet desired they Pilate that He should be slain.

29 And when they had fulfilled all that was written of Him *(pertained to that which the Prophets had predicted)*, they took *Him* down from the tree *(speaks of the Cross; if it is to be noticed, both Paul and Peter used the term "tree" regarding the Cross; it is derived from Deut. 21:23)*, and laid *Him* in a sepulchre.

30 But God raised Him from the dead *(as Paul proclaimed the Crucifixion of Jesus, he now proclaims His Resurrection)*:

31 And He was seen many days of them which came up with Him from Galilee to Jerusalem *(concerns a number of appearances over a time span of some forty days)*, who are His witnesses unto the people *(Paul is making the case that there were too many appearances for His Resurrection to be denied)*.

32 And we declare unto you Glad Tidings *(speaks of the Good News of the Gospel, all wrapped up in Christ)*, how that the Promise which was made unto the Fathers *(had its beginnings in Gen. 3:15, and spanned the entirety of Old Testament history)*,

33 God has fulfilled the same unto us their children *(means simply that the Lord did exactly what He had Promised)*, in that He has raised up Jesus again *(the Resurrection)*; as it is also written in the Second Psalm, You are My Son, this day have I begotten You *(refers to the Incarnation when the Second Person of the Divine Trinity took a perfect human body, in order that it would be offered up as Sacrifice to Redeem humanity [Isa. 7:14; 9:6; Phil. 2:5-11])*.

34 And as concerning that He raised Him up from the dead, *now* no more to return to corruption *(this phrase proclaims the fact that Jesus was raised from the dead in greater form than when He went into the abode of death; He died with a regular, although Perfect, human Body, but was raised with a Glorified Body)*, He said on this wise, I will give You the sure mercies of David *(actually refers to the Lord Jesus Christ, Who embodies all of these great "Mercies" [Isa. 55:3])*.

35 Wherefore He said also in another *Psalm,* You shall not suffer Your Holy One to see corruption *(refers to Ps. 16:10; this passage, as many others, shoots down the "Jesus died Spiritually Doctrine"; if Jesus had gone to the burning side of Hell when He died, and suffered there for three days and nights as some claim, He would definitely have seen corruption; but this He did not do)*.

36 For David, after he had served his own generation by the Will of God, fell on sleep *(refers to David's death)*, and was laid unto his Fathers, and saw corruption *(this shows that the great Davidic Covenant pertained to the greater son of David, and not David himself)*:

37 But He, Whom God raised again, saw no corruption *(Paul's Message here is very similar to that of Peter in Acts, Chpt. 2)*.

38 Be it known unto you therefore, men *and* Brethren, that through this Man is preached unto you the forgiveness of sins *(presents Jesus as having paid the price for man's Redemption, and through Him Alone can be "forgiveness of sins")*:

39 And by Him *(what He did at the Cross)* all who believe *(place our Faith in what He did at the Cross)* are justified from all things *(the Scripture here plainly says, "all things," not just some things)*, from which you could not be justified by the Law of Moses *(dogmatically and without apology sets aside the Law of Moses as being empty of any ability to justify one with God)*.

40 Beware therefore, lest that come upon you, which is spoken of in the Prophets *(speaks of the Judgment of God, and plainly says that it will come upon rejecters of Truth)*;

41 Behold, you despisers, and wonder, and perish *([Hab. 1:5] spoke of Israel which rejected Christ, and holds true for all Christ Rejecters, whomever and wherever they might be)*: for I work a work in your days, a work which you shall in no wise believe, though a man declare it unto you *(predicts the unbelief of mankind respecting Jesus Christ as the source of all Salvation)*.

42 And when the Jews were gone out of the

Synagogue *(indicates that some had got angry at Paul's statements)*, **the Gentiles besought that these words might be preached to them the next Sabbath** *(speaks of those Gentiles referred to as "God-fearers," who were in the Synagogue and heard Paul's Message)*.

43 Now when the congregation was broken up, many of the Jews and religious proselytes *(Gentiles who had accepted Judaism)* **followed Paul and Barnabas** *(wanted to hear more)*: **who, speaking to them, persuaded them to continue in the Grace of God** *(not only must they accept Christ, they must also continue in Christ)*.

OPPOSITION

44 And the next Sabbath Day came almost the whole city together to hear the Word of God *(during the intervening week, it seems the new converts quickly spread the Message of Grace through Jesus Christ; consequently, there is a great crowd on this particular Sabbath Day to hear the Gospel)*.

45 But when the Jews saw the multitudes, they were filled with envy *(they did not expect this large a crowd)*, **and spoke against those things which were spoken by Paul, contradicting and blaspheming** *(the Synagogue leaders were trying to contradict Paul, and blaspheming Christ as well)*.

46 Then Paul and Barnabas waxed bold *(this boldness was given to them by the Holy Spirit)*, **and said, It was necessary that the Word of God should first have been spoken to you** *(should be first given to the Jews)*: **but seeing you put it from you, and judge yourselves unworthy of Everlasting Life, lo, we turn to the Gentiles** *(proclaims a statement of far-reaching magnitude; one might say this was the beginning of Western Civilization)*.

47 For so has the Lord Commanded us *(speaks not only of His Personal Call, but of the Prophecy given by Isaiah as well)*, **saying, I have set you to be a Light of the Gentiles** *(is taken from Isa. 49:6, and refers to the Messiah)*, **that you should be for Salvation unto the ends of the earth** *(the Salvation afforded by Christ is intended for the entirety of the world)*.

48 And when the Gentiles heard this, they were glad, and glorified the Word of the Lord *(they knew this meant them, and it brought great joy, even as it should)*: **and as many as were ordained to Eternal Life believed** *(means that God has appointed and provided Eternal Life for all who will believe [Jn. 3:15-20; Rom. 1:16;*

10:9-10; I Tim. 2:4; II Pet. 3:9; Rev. 22:17]).

49 And the Word of the Lord was published throughout all the region *(it didn't say the Church, or some religious institution, etc., but "the Word of the Lord"; this shows us where the emphasis must be)*.

50 But the Jews *(those who opposed the Gospel)* **stirred up the devout and Honourable women** *(seems to indicate female Gentile Proselytes)*, **and the Chief men of the city, and raised persecution against Paul and Barnabas** *(means that these individuals believed the lies they were told about these two)*, **and expelled them out of their coasts** *(they were not merely requested to leave, but forcibly ejected; there is no evidence of physical violence, but definite evidence that physical violence was threatened)*.

51 But they shook off the dust of their feet against them *(presents that which Jesus Commanded His Disciples to do under these circumstances [Mat. 10:14; Mk. 6:11; Lk. 9:5; 10:11])*, **and came unto Iconium** *(a city in the southern part of the Roman Province of Galatia)*.

52 And the Disciples were filled with joy *(proclaims the fact that the Holy Spirit informed them that the problem in Antioch was not their fault; this brings them great joy)*, **and with the Holy Spirit** *(means that the Spirit of God was the Author of this "joy")*.

CHAPTER 14
(A.D. 45)
ICONIUM

AND it came to pass in Iconium, that they **went both together** *(Paul and Barnabas)* **into the Synagogue of the Jews, and so spoke** *(presents them continuing with their custom of going to the Jews first)*, **that a great multitude both of the Jews and also of the Greeks believed** *(they accepted Christ)*.

2 But the unbelieving Jews *(as obvious, some of the Jews didn't believe)* **stirred up the Gentiles** *(means that these Gentiles were not of the ruling class)*, **and made their minds evil affected against the brethren** *(the unbelieving Jews used any lie they could tell)*.

3 Long time therefore abode they speaking boldly in the Lord *(the unbelieving Gentiles who were stirred up by the unbelieving Jews did not have immediate sway, as those Gentiles in the previous city; so Paul and Barnabas were able to minister there for some weeks)*, **which gave testimony unto the Word of His Grace** *(this "Grace" speaks of God's unmerited favor*

in sending Jesus to save us from our sins), and granted signs and wonders to be done by their hands (healings, miracles, and deliverances).

4 But the multitude of the city was divided (though Grace be its keynote, the Message causes dissension and disrupts families, communities and nations): and part held with the Jews, and part with the Apostles (proclaims the extent of this division).

5 And when there was an assault made both of the Gentiles, and also of the Jews with their rulers, to use them despitefully, and to stone them (constitutes their plan, but with Paul and Barnabas leaving before it was put into motion),

LYSTRA

6 They were ware (made aware) of it, and fled unto Lystra and Derbe, cities of Lycaonia, and unto the region that lies round about (doesn't mean that Paul and Barnabas were afraid, but that these were the instructions of the Lord):

7 And there (Lystra and Derbe) they preached the Gospel (preaching is the method chosen by God to reach people, irrespective of their locality or circumstances).

8 And there sat a certain man at Lystra, impotent in his feet, being a cripple from his mother's womb, who never had walked:

9 The same heard Paul speak (seems that Paul was preaching in the town square): who stedfastly beholding him, and perceiving that he had faith to be healed (presents Paul being drawn to this man by the Holy Spirit, because the man apparently believed what he heard Paul saying about Christ; evidently Paul referred to Christ in his Message, not only as the Saviour, but the Healer as well),

10 Said with a loud voice (Paul spoke loudly), Stand upright on your feet (this was no doubt in front of a great crowd). And he leaped and walked (proclaims him being healed immediately).

11 And when the people saw what Paul had done, they lifted up their voices, saying in the speech of Lycaonia (presents their native language), The gods are come down to us in the likeness of men (Greek Mythology pointed to many gods, and their coming down to Earth in human form).

12 And they called Barnabas, Jupiter; and Paul, Mercurius (presents their two principal gods), because he (Paul) was the chief speaker.

13 Then the priest of Jupiter, which was before their city (speaks of the temple of Jupiter, which was constructed just outside the gates), brought oxen and garlands unto the gates, and would have done sacrifice with the people (spoke of offering up the animals and actually worshiping Paul and Barnabas).

14 Which when the apostles, Barnabas and Paul, heard of (probably means the people were speaking in their native language, so the Apostles at first did not know what was happening), they rent their clothes, and ran in among the people, crying out (this was to show their disapproval of what was happening),

15 And saying, Sirs, why do you these things? (Why do people in India bathe in the filth of the Ganges River, thinking that such will guarantee them some type of eternal life? Why do many in Africa smear cow dung over their bodies, working themselves into a frenzy as someone beats a drum?) We also are men of like passions with you (Paul and Barnabas disavowed the ridiculous claims of these people that they are gods), and preach unto you that you should turn from these vanities unto the living God (other than the Living God Who can only be found through Jesus Christ, all is vanity), which made Heaven, and Earth, and the sea, and all things that are therein:

16 Who in times past (before the Cross) suffered all nations to walk in their own ways (means that He did not destroy them despite their evil ways, as abominable as they were).

17 Nevertheless He left not Himself without witness, in that He did good, and gave us rain from Heaven, and fruitful seasons, filling our hearts with food and gladness (however powerful Creation may be as a "witness," it is not a Saviour; while it could point men toward God, it within itself could not save men; despite that "witness", they died eternally lost).

18 And with these sayings scarce restrained they the people (the people were still somewhat fearful of not heeding Paul and Barnabas), that they had not done sacrifice unto them (the people were restrained at the last moment).

PERSECUTION

19 And there came thither certain Jews from Antioch and Iconium, who persuaded the people (this evidently took place some days after the situation concerning the proposed Sacrifice; these Jews persuaded the people to turn against Paul and Barnabas), and, having stoned Paul, drew him out of the city, supposing he

had been dead *(they considered Paul to be the leader, with Barnabas, it seems, being spared from the stoning; Paul was near death)*.

20 Howbeit, as the Disciples stood round about him *(speaks of those who had come to Christ in the last few days or weeks)*, he rose up *(indicates that however serious the situation was, he was instantly healed)*, and came into the city *(means that Paul's detractors had now left, thinking he was dead)*: and the next day he departed with Barnabas to Derbe *(presents a distance of about forty miles)*.

21 And when they had preached the Gospel to that city *(proclaims their Evangelism not slowing at all despite the persecution)*, and had taught many *(preaching had brought them to Christ, and now they needed to be taught)*, they returned again to Lystra, and *to* Iconium, and Antioch *(they were led by the Holy Spirit to go back to these places of their persecution; as such, Satan would not be able to kill them)*,

22 Confirming the souls of the Disciples *(pertained to the new converts in these areas)*, *and* exhorting them to continue in the Faith *(it is not he who begins, but he who finishes)*, and that we must through much tribulation enter into the Kingdom of God *(quite a different Message than that being presently proposed)*.

23 And when they had ordained them Elders *(Preachers)* in every Church *(by the help of the Holy Spirit, a Pastor from the local congregation was selected to lead the local flock)*, and had prayed with fasting *(means that Paul, Barnabas, and others sought the Lord earnestly as to His Will in these matters)*, they commended them to the Lord *(seeking the Lord's Blessings on them after the appointment)*, on Whom they believed *(believing that He would lead and guide them, which He did!)*.

THE HOME CHURCH

24 And after they had passed throughout Pisidia, they came to Pamphylia *(Pamphylia is southwest of Pisidia)*.

25 And when they had preached the Word in Perga, they went down into Attalia *(there is no record that they ministered in Attalia)*:

26 And thence sailed to Antioch *(the home Church)*, from whence they had been recommended to the Grace of God for the work which they fulfilled *(the Holy Spirit says here that Paul and Barnabas did exactly what the Lord wanted them to do regarding this Missionary journey)*.

THE REPORT

27 And when they were come, and had gathered the Church together *(at Antioch)*, they rehearsed all that God had done with them *(related it all to the congregation)*, and how He had opened the door of Faith unto the Gentiles *(how receptive the Gentiles were)*.

28 And there *(Antioch, Syria)* they abode long time with the Disciples *(with the congregation, possibly as long as two years)*.

CHAPTER 15
(A.D. 51)
THE COUNCIL

AND certain men which came down from Judaea taught the Brethren *(presents the greatest crisis of the Early Church)*, *and said*, Except you be circumcised after the manner of Moses, you cannot be saved *(they were attempting to refute Paul's Message of Grace through faith; in other words, they were attempting to circumvent the Cross, trying to add the Law of Moses to the Gospel of Grace)*.

2 When therefore Paul and Barnabas had no small dissension and disputation with them *(seems to indicate that these men came to Antioch not long after Paul and Barnabas had returned from their first Missions tour)*, they *(the Elders of the Church at Antioch)* determined that Paul and Barnabas, and certain other of them, should go up to Jerusalem unto the Apostles and Elders about this question *(no doubt refers to the trip mentioned by Paul in Gal. 2:1-10)*.

3 And being brought on their way by the Church *(means that the Church at Antioch paid the expenses of the Brethren respecting this trip)*, they passed through Phenice and Samaria, declaring the conversion of the Gentiles *(indicates that they stopped to visit Churches all along the way)*: and they caused great joy unto all the Brethren *(seems to indicate that the Judaizers had not brought their false doctrine to these Churches)*.

4 And when they had come to Jerusalem, they were received of the Church *(indicates they were received with open arms)*, and *of* the Apostles *(refers to the Twelve, minus James the brother of John who had been martyred)* and Elders *(other Preachers)*, and they declared all things that God had done with them *(gave a report of their recent Missions trip)*.

5 But there rose up certain of the sect of

the Pharisees which believed *(refers to them as having accepted Christ as their Saviour; they were in the Church at Jerusalem)*, saying, That it was needful to circumcise them, and to command *them* to keep the Law of Moses *(speaking of new converts; this was the great controversy; even though this was a different group, it was the same erroneous message)*.

6 And the Apostles and Elders came together for to consider of this matter *(this was not a closed meeting, but was rather played out before many Believers)*.

PETER

7 And when there had been much disputing *(much questioning and discussion)*, Peter rose up, and said unto them *(portrays the Apostle, at least now and at this particular meeting, in the position of Leadership)*, Men *and* Brethren, you know how that a good while ago God made choice among us, that the Gentiles by my mouth should hear the Word of the Gospel, and believe *(harks back some ten to twelve years earlier to Peter's experience with Cornelius [Acts, Chpt. 10])*.

8 And God, which knows the hearts *(speaks of this action concerning Cornelius being of the Lord and not of Peter)*, bear them witness *(witnessed to the validity of their conversion)*, giving them the Holy Spirit, even as *he did* unto us *(all of this without Circumcision and Law-keeping)*;

9 And put no difference between us and them *(in other words, these Gentiles were just as saved as Jews, and without all of the Laws of the Jews)*, purifying their hearts by Faith *(Faith in Christ and Faith in Christ alone, not by Law-keeping)*.

10 Now therefore why do you tempt God *(calls into question that which God has done)*, to put a yoke upon the neck of the Disciples *(followers of Christ)*, which neither our Fathers nor we were able to bear? *(Peter was not speaking disparagingly of the Law of Moses, but stating that its demands were beyond the ability of human beings to meet because of man's fallen condition.)*

11 But we *(the Apostles)* believe that through the Grace of the Lord Jesus Christ we shall be Saved *(without Law-keeping)*, even as they *(even as the Gentiles)*.

THE GENTILES

12 Then all the multitude kept silence *(refers to the introduction of both "Barnabas and Paul" to the audience)*, and gave audience to Barnabas and Paul *(Barnabas is listed first because he was known to the Church at Jerusalem; he probably spoke first)*, declaring what miracles and wonders God had wrought among the Gentiles by them *(they simply gave an account, which refers to the fact that Paul and Barnabas preached Grace and Faith to the Gentiles, and didn't preach the Law at all; God honored it by giving them signs and wonders, which would not have been the case had He been displeased)*.

13 And after they had held their peace *(concluding their remarks)*, James answered, saying, Men *and* Brethren, hearken unto me *(presents the Lord's Brother as the presiding Elder of the Church in Jerusalem)*:

14 Simeon has *(Peter)* declared how God at the first did visit the Gentiles *(refers to the conversion of Cornelius and his household)*, to take out of them a people for His Name *(presents this as the Plan of God, which it surely was!)*.

15 And to this agree the words of the Prophets *(James now appeals directly to the Word of God, which verifies all that has been said)*; as it is written *(Amos 9:11)*,

16 After this I will return *(speaks of the Church Age and the Second Coming of the Lord)*, and will build again the Tabernacle of David, which is fallen down; and I will build again the ruins thereof, and I will set it up *(speaks of the restoration of Israel and the coming Kingdom Age, in which all the Prophets declare [Isa. 9:6-7; Dan. 7:13-14; Hos. 3:4-5; Lk. 1:32-33; Rom., Chpts. 9-11; Rev. 11:15; 20:1-10; 22:4-5])*:

17 That the residue of men might seek after the Lord, and all the Gentiles *(a worldwide harvest of souls during the Kingdom Age)*, upon whom My Name is called, saith the Lord *(refers to the Gentile world which has been favorable toward the Lord to a degree)*, Who does all these things *(refers to the Power of God in performing all of this)*.

18 Known unto God are all His works from the beginning of the world *(the Plan of God regarding the human family was known from "the beginning of the world" [Gen., Chpt. 4])*.

19 Wherefore my sentence is *(would have been better translated, "I think it good")*, that we trouble not them, which from among the Gentiles are turned to God *(carries the idea that it does not make any sense to demand certain other things of them, claiming such things are needed in order to be saved, when in fact the people are already saved!)*:

20 But that we write unto them, that they abstain from pollutions of idols (*this was common in the heathen world of that day*), and *from* fornication (*all forms of immorality*), and *from* things strangled (*which refers to the blood not being properly drained from the flesh*), and *from* blood (*not to eat blood, which was somewhat common among the heathen during those days; in any case, blood was not to be imbibed, but this did not refer to transfusion; man is saved by the shed Blood of Christ, so blood must be treated accordingly*).

21 For Moses of old time has in every city them who preach him, being read in the Synagogues every Sabbath Day (*the idea is that Gentiles who desire to know more about the Law of Moses need only to go to one of the Synagogues on the Sabbath, which was every Saturday*).

THE DECISION

22 Then pleased it the Apostles and Elders, with the whole Church, to send chosen men of their own company to Antioch with Paul and Barnabas (*proclaims the fact that all of the Church at Jerusalem, or at least the greater majority, totally agreed with what James had said respecting Gentiles and the Law of Moses*); namely, Judas surnamed Barsabas, and Silas, Chief men among the Brethren (*Silas was to play a very important part regarding his help to Paul with respect to future Evangelism*):

23 And they wrote *letters* by them after this manner; The Apostles and Elders and Brethren *send* greeting unto the Brethren which are of the Gentiles in Antioch and Syria and Cilicia:

24 Forasmuch as we have heard, that certain which went out from us have troubled you with words, subverting your souls (*evidently speaks of those mentioned in Verse 1*), saying, *You must* be circumcised, and keep the Law: to whom we gave no *such* Commandment (*specifies exactly what the error was; these individuals, whomever they may have been, were not sent by the Church in Jerusalem, nor were they given any Commandment to teach any type of false doctrine*):

25 It seemed good unto us, being assembled with one accord (*proclaims the unity of the Brethren in Jerusalem*), to send chosen men unto you with our beloved Barnabas and Paul (*places a gracious and kind endearment toward Paul and Barnabas, which spoke volumes as well*),

26 Men who have hazarded their lives for the Name of our Lord Jesus Christ (*tells us for Whom it was done!*).

27 We have sent therefore Judas and Silas, who shall also tell *you* the same things by mouth (*with these two men accompanying this letter, and verifying its contents, no false prophet could claim that the letter was forged, etc.*).

28 For it seemed good to the Holy Spirit, and to us (*proclaims without a doubt that the Holy Spirit led and guided these proceedings*), to lay upon you no greater burden than these necessary things (*when men leave the Word of God, they get into a lot of "unnecessary things"*);

29 That you abstain from meats offered to idols, and from blood, and from things strangled, and from fornication: from which if you keep yourselves, you shall do well. Fare ye well.

30 So when they (*possibly six or seven Brethren*) were dismissed (*sent away with great love*), they came to Antioch: and when they had gathered the multitude together, they delivered the Epistle (*we aren't told how large the Church was in Antioch; however, it could have numbered several hundred; that being the case, they would have met outdoors for this Epistle to be read to them*):

31 *Which* when they had read, they rejoiced for the consolation (*tells us that the Law/Grace issue had been very serious; now this settles the dispute, at least for the time being*).

32 And Judas and Silas, being Prophets also themselves (*means that they stood in the Office of the Prophet [Eph. 4:11]*), exhorted the Brethren with many words, and confirmed *them* (*they addressed the multitude with words of great encouragement*).

33 And after they (*Judas and Silas*) had tarried *there* a space, they were let go in peace from the Brethren unto the Apostles (*refers to Judas returning to Jerusalem, but not Silas*).

34 Notwithstanding it pleased Silas to abide there still (*it was the Holy Spirit Who moved on him to remain in Antioch*).

SECOND MISSIONARY JOURNEY

35 Paul also and Barnabas continued in Antioch, teaching and preaching the Word of the Lord, with many others also (*this Church was blessed, to say the least!*).

36 And some days after (*could have been as much as a year*) Paul said unto Barnabas, Let us go again and visit our Brethren in every city where we have preached the Word of the Lord, *and see* how they do (*refers to the Churches they*

had planted on the first Missionary Journey).

37 And Barnabas determined to take with them John, whose surname was Mark *(the word "determined" implies a "deliberate action," which means that Barnabas was adamant on the subject).*

38 But Paul thought not good to take him with them, who departed from them from Pamphylia *(suggests a rupture)*, and went not with them to the work *(he did not go with them to the work to which God called them, as he ought to have done).*

39 And the contention was so sharp between them *(means to dispute to the point of anger)*, that they departed asunder one from the other *(it created an abrupt and severe rupture; it is my feeling that Barnabas should have acquiesced to Paul; the Holy Spirit had said "separate Me Barnabas and Paul for the work whereunto I have called them"; the Holy Spirit didn't mention Mark)*: and so Barnabas took Mark, and sailed unto Cyprus *(Barnabas will not be mentioned again in the great Book of Acts, and yet we dare not take away from the Godliness of this man);*

PAUL AND SILAS

40 And Paul chose Silas, and departed *(proclaims the beginning of the Second Missionary Journey; this is the reason the Holy Spirit had Silas remain behind in Antioch)*, being recommended by the Brethren unto the Grace of God *(he wholeheartedly approved of the great Covenant of Grace, which was absolutely necessary if he was to be of help to Paul).*

41 And he *(Paul)* went through Syria and Cilicia, confirming the Churches *(teaching in each Church, which obviously was so very much needed).*

CHAPTER 16
(A.D. 53)
TIMOTHY

THEN came he *(Paul)* to Derbe and Lystra *(the Second Missionary Journey will have a greater effect on civilization than anything that has ever happened, other than the First Advent of Christ)*: and, behold, a certain Disciple was there, named Timothy, the son of a certain woman, which was a Jewess, and believed *(speaks of Timothy and his Mother as being followers of Christ)*; but his Father *was* a Greek *(it seems he was not a Believer):*

2 Which was well reported of by the Brethren Who were at Lystra and Iconium *(Timothy's consecration is obvious here).*

3 Him would Paul have to go forth with him *(which was undoubtedly a leading of the Spirit)*; and took and circumcised him because of the Jews which were in those quarters *(this was wisdom on Paul's part, which he felt led by the Holy Spirit to do)*: for they knew all that his Father was a Greek *(Paul would do all he could to appease people, but not at the expense of compromising the Gospel).*

4 And as they went through the cities, they delivered them the decrees for to keep, that were ordained of the Apostles and Elders which were at Jerusalem *(pertained to copies of the decision concerning the Law/Grace issue, which came out of the Council at Jerusalem).*

5 And so were the Churches established in the Faith *(Jesus Christ and Him Crucified)*, and increased in number daily *(many were being saved).*

6 Now when they had gone throughout Phrygia and the region of Galatia *(implies a time frame of probably several months)*, and were forbidden of the Holy Spirit to preach the Word in Asia *(refers to the area now known as northwestern Turkey; while the Holy Spirit definitely wanted the Gospel to go to this area, there was another place He desired first),*

7 After they were come to Mysia, they assayed to go into Bithynia *(represented an area east of the Ephesus area)*: but the Spirit suffered them not *(proclaims the door being closed to this area as well!).*

8 And they passing by Mysia came down to Troas *(this area would be closed for the time being also).*

THE MACEDONIAN CALL

9 And a Vision appeared to Paul in the night *(proclaims the Holy Spirit now telling the Apostle exactly where He wanted him to go)*; there stood a man of Macedonia *(the northern part of modern Greece, from the Adriatic to the Hebrus River)*, and prayed him, saying, Come over into Macedonia, and help us *(thus was ushered in the most momentous event in the history of the world, the going forth of Paul to take the Gospel to the nations of the West).*

10 And after he had seen the Vision, immediately we endeavored to go into Macedonia *(by the use of the pronoun "we," we know that Luke, the writer of this Book of Acts, now joins*

Paul here at Troas), **assuredly gathering that the Lord had called us for to preach the Gospel unto them** *(they knew they now had the Mind of the Lord)*.

PHILIPPI

11 Therefore loosing from Troas, we came with a straight course to Samothracia, and the next *day* **to Neapolis** *(this would be the very first presentation of the Gospel on European soil, which would have such a bearing on what is presently referred to as "Western Civilization");*

12 And from thence to Philippi, which is the chief city of that part of Macedonia *(Paul's destination)*, *and* **a colony** *(was a colony of Rome)*: **and we were in that city abiding certain days** *(represents tremendous hardships, but a Church was established here)*.

FIRST CONVERT

13 And on the Sabbath we went out of the city by a river side, where prayer was wont to be made *(evidently meant there was no Synagogue in the city; what few Jews were there met by the Riverside)*; **and we sat down, and spoke unto the women which resorted** *thither* *(seems to tell us that no men were present other than Paul and his party)*.

14 And a certain woman named Lydia, a seller of purple, of the city of Thyatira *(she was a businesswoman)*, **which worshipped God** *(proclaims her as a Gentile who had probably begun visiting a Jewish Synagogue in Thyatira)*, **heard** *us* *(Paul evidently was asked to speak to these women, thus proclaiming the story of Jesus Christ and His Redemption afforded by the Cross of Calvary)*: **whose heart the Lord opened** *(presents her hungry for God)*, **that she attended unto the things which were spoken of Paul** *(she gave her heart to Christ, and was, thereby, the first convert on European soil)*.

15 And when she was baptized *(evidently took place some days later)*, **and her household** *(refers to the fact that all of those with her accepted the Lord as well, and were baptized)*, **she besought** *us*, **saying, If you have judged me to be faithful to the Lord, come into my house, and abide** *there* *(as well, her house was probably the first Church on European soil)*. **And she constrained us** *(means they did not acquiesce at first, feeling perhaps that it may be an imposition on her; but she would not take no for an answer)*.

DELIVERANCE

16 And it came to pass, as we went to prayer *(does not tell us exactly where this was, but does specify that it was a certain place, more than likely the home of Lydia)*, **a certain damsel possessed with a spirit of divination met us** *(speaks of the girl being demon possessed)*, **which brought her masters much gain by soothsaying** *(claiming to give advice and counsel from the spirit world, which brought quite a sum of money to her owners)*:

17 The same followed Paul and us, and cried, saying *(implies that this went on for some time, possibly several days)*, **These men are the servants of the Most High God, which show unto us the way of Salvation** *(should have been translated, "a way of Salvation," because that's the way it is in the original Text)*.

18 And this did she many days *(for some reason, the Holy Spirit didn't give Paul latitude to pray for the girl until now)*. **But Paul, being grieved, turned and said to the spirit** *(addressed himself to the evil spirit, and not directly to the girl)*, **I Command you in the Name of Jesus Christ to come out of her. And he** *(the evil spirit)* **came out the same hour** *(means that the spirit came out instantly)*.

19 And when her masters saw that the hope of their gains was gone *(meaning that the girl could no longer function as she had previously done)*, **they caught Paul and Silas, and drew** *them* **into the marketplace unto the Rulers** *(these men evidently had some sway with these Rulers)*,

20 And brought them to the Magistrates *(pertained to Romans appointed by Rome)*, **saying, These men, being Jews, do exceedingly trouble our city** *(the manner in which the word "Jews" is used implies contempt)*,

21 And teach customs, which are not lawful for us to receive, neither to observe *(a gross untruth! actually, Judaism was a legal religion in the Roman Empire; even though Paul and Silas were not actually teaching Judaism, but rather proclaiming Jesus, still the Romans would not have been able to distinguish the difference)*, **being Romans** *(implying superiority)*.

22 And the multitude rose up together against them *(presents a stacked audience against Paul and Silas)*: **and the Magistrates rent off their clothes** *(took off Paul and Silas' clothes, at least to the waist)*, **and commanded to beat** *them* *(Paul recalls this in I Thess. 2:2; scourging under Roman Law was a most brutal and cruel punishment)*.

23 And when they had laid many stripes upon them *(the lictors were egged on by the mob, with the Apostles being beaten almost to death)*, they cast *them* into prison *(prisons then were far worse than anything we can now imagine)*, charging the jailor to keep them safely *(contains the implication that Paul and Silas were desperados)*:

24 Who, having received such a charge *(means that he could punish them even more if he so desired, which he did)*, thrust them into the inner prison *(reserved for the most violent of criminals)*, and made their feet fast in the stocks *(the legs were pulled wide apart, with the individual laying on their back on the floor; after a short time, the muscles in the legs would begin to constrict, causing severe pain)*.

THE CONVERSION

25 And at midnight Paul and Silas prayed *(doesn't mean they began to pray at midnight, but rather that they were still praying at midnight having begun some time earlier)*, and sang praises unto God *(the Greek Text suggests that bursts of song broke out from time to time as they prayed; their song was probably one of the Psalms)*: and the prisoners heard them *(means they prayed and sang so loud that other prisoners heard them)*.

26 And suddenly there was a great earthquake *(this was no ordinary earthquake)*, so that the foundations of the prison were shaken *(presents the Lord as the Instigator of this upheaval, not a normal force of nature)*: and immediately all the doors were opened, and every one's bands were loosed *(this implies no normal earthquake, but rather something supernatural)*.

27 And the keeper of the prison awaking out of his sleep, and seeing the prison doors open *(automatically causes him to assume that all the prisoners had fled)*, he drew out his sword, and would have killed himself, supposing that the prisoners had been fled *(meaning that under the penalty of death, he was responsible for the prisoners)*.

28 But Paul cried with a loud voice *(Paul sees what the jailer is about to do to himself)*, saying, Do yourself no harm: for we are all here *(tells us that none of the prisoners, ever how many there were, took the opportunity to escape; this also tells us that quite possibly some, if not all, had given their hearts to the Lord)*.

29 Then he called for a light, and sprang in, and came trembling *(proclaims that something powerful was happening to this man, over and above the shock of the earthquake and his thoughts of suicide)*, and fell down before Paul and Silas *(the jailer treated Paul with great brutality, but Paul treated him with great humanity)*,

30 And brought them out *(brought Paul and Silas out of the prison)*, and said, Sirs, what must I do to be saved? *(This presents terminology that shows some familiarity with the Gospel; quite possibly before the arrest of the Apostle, the jailer had heard him preach)*

31 And they said, Believe on the Lord Jesus Christ, and you shall be saved *(presents the most beautiful explanation of Salvation that could ever be given)*, and your house *(means that Salvation is not limited merely to the jailer, but is available to the entirety of his family as well, that is if they will meet the conditions of Faith in Christ required of them)*.

32 And they spoke unto him the Word of the Lord *(pertained to a fleshing out of the answer given in the previous Verse, explaining what believing in Christ really meant)*, and to all that were in his house *(presents this service being conducted sometime after midnight, which resulted in all of his family giving their hearts to Christ; what a beautiful night it turned out to be!)*.

33 And he *(the jailer)* took them *(Paul and Silas)* the same hour of the night, and washed *their* stripes *(speaks of the terrible beating they had suffered a short time before)*; and was baptized, he and all his, straightway *(immediately)*.

34 And when he had brought them into his house, he set meat before them *(proclaims, as obvious, a meal prepared for them)*, and rejoiced, believing in God with all his house *(a night of misery turned into a night of great joy, and joy which would last forever for this jailer and his family)*.

THE MAGISTRATES

35 And when it was day, the Magistrates sent the serjeants *(probably refers to the same men who had administered the beating to Paul and Silas)*, saying, Let those men go *(the Codex Bezae says that the Magistrates came into Court that morning feeling that their treatment of Paul and Silas had brought on the earthquake; they were right!)*.

36 And the keeper of the prison told this saying to Paul, The Magistrates have sent to let you go: now therefore depart, and go in peace.

37 But Paul said unto them, They have beaten us openly uncondemned, being Romans *(presents a scenario which puts an entirely different complexion on the matter; it was against Roman Law for Romans to be beaten; so, in beating them, the Magistrates had broken the law, evidently not realizing they were Romans)*, and have cast *us* into prison; and now do they thrust us out privily? *(They were treated as common criminals.)* No verily; but let them come themselves and fetch us out *(in this way, the city of Philippi would know that the charges were false)*.

38 And the serjeants told these words unto the Magistrates: and they feared, when they heard that they were Romans *(if Paul and Silas so desired, they could have brought charges against these individuals, which could have resulted in severe consequences)*.

39 And they came and besought them, and brought *them* out *(refers to the fact that the "Magistrates" now came to Paul and Silas)*, and desired *them* to depart out of the city *(has reference to the fact that they were pleading with the Apostles not to bring charges against them, but rather depart in peace)*.

40 And they went out of the prison, and entered into *the house of* Lydia *(they were somewhat the worse for wear in the physical sense, but greatly encouraged in the spiritual sense)*: and when they had seen the Brethren, they comforted them, and departed *(these were new converts in the Philippian Church)*.

CHAPTER 17
(A.D. 53)
THESSALONICA

NOW when they had passed through Amphipolis and Apollonia, they came to Thessalonica *(presents Paul's destination evidently directed here by the Holy Spirit)*, where was a Synagogue of the Jews *(presents Paul once again taking the Gospel first of all to the Jews)*:

2 And Paul, as his manner was, went in unto them *(should have been translated, "as his custom was")*, and three Sabbath Days reasoned with them out of the Scriptures *(the Old Testament, and concerning Christ)*,

3 Opening and alleging *(to expound and present)*, that Christ must needs have suffered *(had to go to the Cross in order that all sin might be atoned [Gen. 3:15; Ex. 12:13; Isa., Chpt. 53])*, and risen again from the dead *(Lev. 14:1-7; Ps. 16:10)*; and that this Jesus, whom I preach unto you, is Christ *(is the Messiah, the One pointed to in the Scriptures)*.

4 And some of them believed *(some Jews)*, and consorted with Paul and Silas *(wanted to hear more about Jesus)*; and of the devout Greeks a great multitude *(many Gentiles were saved)*, and of the Chief women not a few *(could have referred to the wives of some of the Civil Rulers in the city, or at least wives of influential men)*.

5 But the Jews which believed not, moved with envy *(presents a perfect example of religious people who refuse the Light of the Gospel, and then set about to stop the propagation of that Light)*, took unto them certain lewd fellows of the baser sort, and gathered a company, and set all the city on an uproar *(presents these Jews as being unable to Scripturally counter Paul's Message, so they now resort to other measures)*, and assaulted the house of Jason, and sought to bring them out to the people *(evidently refers to where Paul and his associates were staying)*.

6 And when they found them not *(evidently Paul and Silas were not there at the time)*, they drew Jason and certain Brethren unto the Rulers of the city *(proclaims the mob determined to take their anger out on someone, if not Paul!)*, crying, These who have turned the world upside down are come hither also *(tells us that the Jews had prepped certain people in this mob thoroughly)*;

7 Whom Jason has received *(charges Jason as being a part of the alleged conspiracy)*: and these all do contrary to the decrees of Caesar, saying that there is another King, *One* Jesus *(presents that which is blatantly false, and the Jews knew it was false)*.

8 And they troubled the people and the Rulers of the city, when they heard these things *(by their lies, they created a commotion)*.

9 And when they had taken security of Jason *(probably means that Jason put up a security bond of some sorts)*, and of the other *(probably refers to a guarantee on the part of Jason and others that Paul and his party would leave the city, even though they were not to blame)*, they let them go *(implies that the authorities were now satisfied)*.

BEREA

10 And the Brethren immediately sent away Paul and Silas by night unto Berea *(this town is about fifty miles from Thessalonica; they*

left by night, because to remain longer could have caused more problems): **who coming** *thither* **went into the Synagogue of the Jews** *(presents, as stated, Paul's custom, but which this time will turn out better, for a change).*

11 These were more noble than those in Thessalonica *(we now learn God's definition of "noble"),* **in that they received the Word with all readiness of mind** *(this is the meaning of the word "noble"),* **and searched the Scriptures daily, whether those things were so** *(tells us why they so eagerly accepted the Message of Jesus Christ).*

12 Therefore many of them believed *(speaks of Jews who accepted Christ as Saviour);* **also of Honourable women which were Greeks, and of men, not a few** *(speaks of Gentiles who had been attending the Jewish Synagogue and, as well, accepted Christ).*

13 But when the Jews of Thessalonica had knowledge that the Word of God was preached of Paul at Berea *(these Jews in Thessalonica, not content with what they had done in their city, now attempt to stop that which is happening in Berea),* **they came thither also, and stirred up the people** *(shows how effective a lie can be).*

14 And then immediately the Brethren sent away Paul to go as it were to the Sea *(speaks of the Aegean, which was about seventeen miles from Berea):* **but Silas and Timotheus abode there still** *(remained in Berea).*

15 And they who conducted Paul brought him unto Athens *(presents the chief city of Greece, famed for its learning):* **and receiving a commandment unto Silas and Timotheus for to come to him with all speed, they departed** *(Paul sends the Message back with these men that Silas and Timothy are to come to Athens as soon as possible).*

ATHENS

16 Now while Paul waited for them at Athens, his spirit was stirred in him, when he saw the city wholly given to idolatry *(means it was full of idols).*

17 Therefore disputed he in the Synagogue with the Jews *(from the Scriptures, he would preach Jesus; the Scriptures then, at least as far as the Jews were concerned, were the Old Testament),* **and with the devout persons** *(singles out the Jews who really seemed to be devoted to the Scriptures),* **and in the market daily with them that met with him** *(this was a place in Athens, where speakers generally gave forth).*

18 Then certain philosophers of the Epicureans *(those who claimed that gratification of the appetites and pleasure were the only end in life),* **and of the Stoics** *(they taught that man was not to be moved by either joy or grief),* **encountered him** *(challenged his statements about Christ).* **And some said, What will this babbler say?** *(This presents the highest insult of which they could think.)* **other some, He seems to be a setter forth of strange gods** *(in their minds, anything outside of Greek philosophy was of no consequence):* **because he preached unto them Jesus, and the Resurrection** *(they didn't want a Resurrection, simply because they did not desire the idea of living this life over again; this shows they totally misunderstood what Paul said).*

19 And they took him, and brought him unto Areopagus *(refers to Mars Hill which faces the Acropolis; this was the Supreme Court of Athens),* **saying, May we know what this new doctrine, whereof you speak,** *is?* *(This presents Paul facing this Supreme Court Justices' of Athens.)*

20 For you bring certain strange things to our ears *(it's strange that those who brought Paul to this place labeled what he said as mere babblings, but yet think it important enough to be taken to the highest Court in Athens):* **we would know therefore what these things mean** *(presents a noble request to Paul, and an unparalleled opportunity).*

21 (For all the Athenians and strangers which were there spent their time in nothing else, but either to tell, or to hear some new thing.) *(With the great Philosophers now dead, Athens was attempting to live off the glory of former times.)*

MARS' HILL

22 Then Paul stood in the midst of Mars' hill, and said, *You* **men of Athens, I perceive that in all things you are too superstitious** *(in this one sentence, he debunks all of their philosophies; they are guided by superstition, which is no way to live).*

23 For as I passed by, and beheld your devotions *(has reference to their objects of worship),* **I found an Altar with this inscription, TO THE UNKNOWN GOD** *(by addressing the situation in this way, he could not be accused of preaching a foreign god to them).* **Whom therefore you ignorantly worship, Him declare I unto you** *(refers to them acknowledging that maybe they did not have the last word on gods! actually,*

they did not have any word at all).

24 God Who made the world and all things therein *(presents God as the Creator)*, seeing that he is Lord of Heaven and Earth *(proclaims Him not only as Creator, but the constant Manager of all that He has created as well)*, dwells not in Temples made with hands *(He is bigger than that!)*;

25 Neither is worshipped with men's hands *(the Second Commandment forbids the making of any graven image of God, or the worship of any type of statue, etc.)*, as though He needed any thing *(God needs nothing!)*, seeing He gives to all life, and breath, and all things *(presents His Creation needing what He provides, which is provided by no other source)*;

26 And has made of one blood all nations of men for to dwell on all the face of the earth *(proclaims all having their origin in Adam)*, and has determined the times before appointed, and the bounds of their habitation *(pertains to particular parts of the world, and those who occupy these areas; however, the statement, "one blood all nations of men," eliminates any type of racial superiority)*;

27 That they should seek the Lord *(presents the chief end of all God's dealings with men [I Pet. 2:24; II Pet. 3:9; Jn. 3:15-20; Rev. 22:17])*, if haply they might feel after Him, and find Him *(Paul is appealing to the action of logic and common sense in trying to address these Pagans)*, though He be not far from every one of us *(speaks of the Creator being very close to His Creation)*:

28 For in Him we live, and move, and have our being *(proclaims God as the source of all life [Heb. 1:3])*; as certain also of your own poets have said, For we are also His offspring *(presents a direct quote from Aratus of Tarsus, Paul's own country)*.

29 Forasmuch then as we are the offspring of God *(is offered by Paul in the sense of Creation; it does not mean the "Fatherhood of God, and the Brotherhood of Man," as many contend)*, we ought not to think that the Godhead is like unto gold, or silver, or stone, graven by art and man's device *(Paul is saying that God is not a device of man, as all the Greek gods in fact were)*.

30 And the times of this ignorance God winked at *(does not reflect that such ignorance was Salvation, for it was not! before the Cross, there was very little Light in the world, so God withheld Judgment)*; but now commands all men every where to repent *(but since the Cross,*

the "Way" is open to all; it's up to us Believers to make that "Way" known to all men):

31 Because He has appointed a day *(refers to the coming of the Great White Throne Judgment [Rev. 20:11-15])*, in the which He will Judge the world in Righteousness by *that* Man Whom He has ordained *(this Righteousness is exclusively in Christ Jesus and what He has done for us at the Cross, and can be gained only by Faith in Him [Eph. 2:8-9; Rom. 10:9-10,13; Rev. 22:17])*; *whereof* He has given assurance unto all *men*, in that He has raised Him from the dead *(refers to the Resurrection ratifying that which was done at Calvary, and is applicable to all men, at least all who will believe!)*.

32 And when they heard of the Resurrection of the Dead, some mocked *(the "mocking" was caused by sheer unbelief)*: and others said, We will hear you again of this *matter (many were touched by Paul's Message, but regrettably procrastinated)*.

33 So Paul departed from among them *(they ascertained that he had broken none of their laws, so he was free to go, which he did!)*.

34 Howbeit certain men clave unto him, and believed *(these believed wholeheartedly, recognizing in Paul the true Words of Life)*: among the which *was* Dionysius the Areopagite *(he was a member of the Great Court of Athens; tradition says that he became the Pastor of the Church in Athens)*, and a woman named Damaris *(a person of prominence)*, and others with them.

CHAPTER 18
(A.D. 54)
CORINTH

AFTER these things Paul departed from Athens *(seems to imply that he departed alone, with Silas and Timothy joining him later at Corinth)*, and came to Corinth *(one of the great cities of the Roman Empire)*;

2 And found a certain Jew named Aquila, born in Pontus, lately come from Italy, with his wife Priscilla *(pertains to a husband and wife who became very close friends to Paul)*; (because that Claudius had commanded all Jews to depart from Rome:) *(believed to have occurred in about A.D. 49 or 50)* and came unto them *(Paul came to them)*.

3 And because he was of the same craft, he abode with them, and wrought *(evidently means that Paul had inquired concerning those involved in this occupation)*: for by their occupation

they were tentmakers *(tentmakers wove the black cloth of goat or camel's hair with which tents were made).*

4 And he reasoned in the Synagogue every Sabbath *(preached Christ from the Old Testament),* and persuaded the Jews and the Greeks *(his argument was ironclad).*

SILAS AND TIMOTHY

5 And when Silas and Timothy were come from Macedonia *(probably means that Silas had come from Berea, with Timothy coming from Thessalonica; Macedonia was a Province which included both places),* Paul was pressed in the spirit, and testified to the Jews *that* Jesus *was* Christ *(the Holy Spirit told him to bear down even harder!).*

6 And when they opposed themselves, and blasphemed *(proclaims the response of some of these Jews to Paul's claim that Christ was the Messiah),* he shook *his* raiment, and said unto them, Your blood *be* upon your own heads; I *am* clean *(in other words, he had delivered his soul)*: from henceforth I will go unto the Gentiles *(does not mean that he would no longer minister to Jews if given the opportunity, which he did do at Ephesus [Acts 19:8], but that the thrust would be toward the Gentiles).*

THE HOUSE

7 And he departed thence *(out of the Synagogue),* and entered into a certain *man's* house *(a meeting place for Church),* named Justus, *one* who worshipped God, whose house joined hard to the Synagogue *(evidently points to Justus in the recent past as having accepted Christ under Paul's Ministry).*

8 And Crispus, the Chief Ruler of the Synagogue, believed on the Lord with all his house *(this must have been galling to the Jews to have their Chief Ruler of the Synagogue converted to Christ)*; and many of the Corinthians hearing believed, and were baptized *(speaks of many Gentiles now being saved).*

9 Then spoke the Lord to Paul in the night by a Vision *(does not clarify whether Paul saw the Lord, or only heard Him speak? it being a "Vision" implies that he was awake),* Be not afraid, but speak, and hold not your peace *(there evidently was fear in Paul's heart regarding the tremendous opposition against him; he was told by the Lord to speak with boldness)*:

10 For I am with you, and no man shall set on you to hurt you *(speaks to the idea that Paul had threats on his life, threats which were not empty, but rather deadly serious)*: for I have much people in this city *(concerns the great Church which will be raised up at Corinth).*

11 And he continued *there* a year and six months, teaching the Word of God among them *(records the longest time that Paul spent in any place other than Ephesus, where he spent some three years).*

12 And when Gallio was the deputy of Achaia *(it is believed that he was Proconsul in A.D. 52-53),* the Jews made insurrection with one accord against Paul, and brought him to the judgment seat *(Jews had no power to punish any person in a Roman Province, so they were obliged to bring Paul before the Roman Governor),*

13 Saying, This *fellow* persuades men to worship God contrary to the Law *(does not pertain to Roman Law as some claim, but rather the Law of Moses).*

14 And when Paul was now about to open *his* mouth *(refers to him waiting for his accusers to cease their tirade against him),* Gallio said unto the Jews *(proclaims the Proconsul interrupting Paul),* If it were a matter of wrong or wicked lewdness, O *you* Jews, reason would that I should bear with you *(proclaims the Governor putting everything in its proper perspective immediately!)*:

15 But if it be a question of words and names, and *of* your Law, look ye *to it (in effect, tells them to settle this thing themselves because it had no place in a Roman Court)*; for I will be no judge of such *matters (in essence says, "you will not use a Roman Court to carry forth your personal schemes!").*

16 And he drove them from the judgment seat *(implies the humiliating dismissal of the case, without even being tried or further heard).*

17 Then all the Greeks took Sosthenes, the Chief Ruler of the Synagogue *(presents the man who took the place of Crispus, with the latter having given his heart to the Lord),* and beat *him* before the judgment seat *(gives us little clue as to why this was done, unless they had refused to dissemble).* And Gallio cared for none of those things *(means that he considered the whole matter outside his jurisdiction).*

EPHESUS

18 And Paul *after this* tarried *there* yet a good while *(could have referred to several months),* and then took his leave of the Brethren *(was*

done strictly according to the timing of the Lord), and sailed thence into Syria, and with him Priscilla and Aquila *(they had now become fast friends of Paul);* having shorn *his* head in Cenchrea: for he had a vow *(Cenchrea was the Port of Corinth; there was a Church there as well; we aren't told what this "vow" was).*

19 And he came to Ephesus *(Ephesus was the most important city in the Roman Province of Asia),* and left them there *(has to do with Priscilla and Acquila remaining in Ephesus when Paul left some days later):* but he himself entered into the Synagogue, and reasoned with the Jews *(has no reference to the previous phrase; no doubt, Priscilla and Acquila were with him during this meeting).*

20 When they *(the Jews in the Synagogue)* desired *him* to tarry longer time with them, he consented not *(Paul left, but Priscilla and Acquila remained and, no doubt, continued teaching these Jews about Christ);*

ANTIOCH

21 But bade them farewell *(speaks of Priscilla and Acquila, and possibly some few Jews who had accepted Christ),* saying, I must by all means keep this Feast that comes in Jerusalem *(probably was the Passover):* but I will return again unto you, if God will *(portrays the manner in which all Believers should conduct everything).* And he sailed from Ephesus *(places him on his way to Jerusalem).*

22 And when he had landed at Caesarea *(puts him about sixty-five miles northwest of Jerusalem),* and gone up, and saluted the Church *(refers to the Mother Church at Jerusalem),* he went down to Antioch *(refers to Antioch, Syria).*

THIRD MISSIONARY JOURNEY

23 And after he had spent some time *there,* he departed *(portrays the beginning of his Third Missionary Journey),* and went over *all* the country of Galatia and Phrygia in order, strengthening all the Disciples *(probably lasted about six months; it is believed that Timothy, Erastus, Gaius, and Aristarchus may have been traveling with Paul at this time; Titus may have been included as well).*

APOLLOS

24 And a certain Jew named Apollos, born at Alexandria, an eloquent man, *and* mighty in the Scriptures, came to Ephesus *(introduces a man whom Paul came to hold in high esteem).*

25 This man was instructed in the Way of the Lord *(however, his knowledge was greatly limited respecting Grace and the Baptism with the Holy Spirit);* and being fervent in the spirit *(spoke of his own spirit and not the Holy Spirit),* he spoke and taught diligently the things of the Lord, knowing only the Baptism of John *(speaks of Repentance and Water Baptism).*

26 And he began to speak boldly in the Synagogue: whom when Aquila and Priscilla had heard *(presents that which was all in the providence of God),* they took him unto *them,* and expounded unto him the Way of God more perfectly *(no doubt pertained to the full complement of Salvation by the Grace of God exclusively, correct Water Baptism, and the Baptism with the Holy Spirit with the evidence of speaking with other Tongues).*

27 And when he *(Apollos)* was disposed to pass into Achaia *(refers to Greece, across the Aegean Sea, and Corinth in particular),* the Brethren wrote, exhorting the Disciples to receive him: who, when he was come, helped them much which had believed through Grace *(he is now proficient in this most excellent Message of the Grace of God that comes through the Cross):*

28 For he mightily convinced the Jews, *and that* publickly, showing by the Scriptures that Jesus was Christ *(had reference more than likely to ministering in their Synagogue).*

CHAPTER 19
(A.D. 58)
EPHESUS

AND it came to pass, that, while Apollos was at Corinth *(pertains to Acts 18:27),* Paul having passed through the upper coasts came to Ephesus *(refers back to Acts 18:23):* and finding certain Disciples *(they were followers of Christ, but deficient in their understanding),*

2 He said unto them, Have you received the Holy Spirit since you believed? *(In the Greek, this is literally, "having believed, did you receive?" We know these men were already saved because every time the word "Disciples" is used in the Book of Acts, it refers to individuals who have accepted Christ. Paul could tell that these individuals, although saved, had not yet been Baptized with the Holy Spirit.)* And they said unto him, We have not so much as heard whether there be any Holy Spirit *(doesn't mean*

that they didn't know of the existence of the Holy Spirit, but they were not aware that the age of the Spirit had come, and that Believers could literally be Baptized with Him; at Salvation, the Holy Spirit Baptizes Believing sinners into Christ; at the Spirit Baptism, Jesus Baptizes Believers into the Holy Spirit [Mat. 3:11]).

3 And he said unto them, Unto what then were you baptized? *(After asking about the Holy Spirit Baptism, Paul was met with a blank stare, so to speak.)* And they said, Unto John's Baptism *(this was the Baptism of Repentance).*

4 Then said Paul, John verily baptized with the Baptism of Repentance *(which, in effect, was all that could be done at that particular time),* saying unto the people, that they should believe on Him which should come after him, that is, on Christ Jesus *(proclaims John the Baptist lifting up Jesus as the Saviour of mankind).*

5 When they heard *this (no doubt, Paul said much more; however, the evidence is they instantly believed and accepted what Paul said, and they then desired what he said),* they were baptized in the name of the Lord Jesus *(means, "by the authority of the Lord Jesus"; the only Baptismal formula in the Word of God is Mat. 28:19).*

6 And when Paul had laid *his* hands upon them *(constitutes a Biblical principle [Acts 8:17; 9:17-18]),* the Holy Spirit came on them *(refers to them being Baptized with the Holy Spirit);* and they spoke with tongues, and prophesied *(proclaims Tongues as the initial physical evidence that one has been Baptized with the Holy Spirit; sometimes there is Prophesying at that time, and sometimes not [Acts 8:17; 9:17; 10:46]).*

7 And all the men were about twelve *(it seems that no women were involved at this particular time).*

THE SYNAGOGUE

8 And he *(Paul)* went into the Synagogue, and spoke boldly for the space of three months *(it seems that he lasted longer here than he had in most Synagogues),* disputing and persuading the things concerning the Kingdom of God *(he would have brought reasonable proofs from the Old Testament Scriptures to show that the Kingdom [ruled authority] of God is revealed in Jesus, Who is now Ascended to the Right Hand of the Father and seated at the Father's Throne [Acts 2:30-33]).*

THE CHURCH

9 But when divers were hardened, and believed not, but spoke evil of that way before the multitude *(they rebelled against the Gospel of Christ),* he departed from them, and separated the Disciples *(proclaims the break with the Synagogue),* disputing daily in the school of one Tyrannus *(is thought to be the Lecture Hall of a Greek Philosopher).*

10 And this continued by the space of two years *(probably referred to most every night and, at times, during the day as well; he spent a total of three years in Ephesus [Acts 20:31]);* so that all they which dwelt in Asia heard the Word of the Lord Jesus, both Jews and Greeks *(does not refer to every single person, but rather to people from all walks of life, and from all surrounding areas).*

MIRACLES

11 And God wrought special Miracles by the hands of Paul *(the Lord did these things, not Paul):*

12 So that from his body were brought unto the sick handkerchiefs or aprons *(there is no indication in the Text that he purposely sent these things out, although he definitely may have, but rather that people on their own simply picked them up; they took them to the diseased or demon-possessed, evidently placing the cloth on the person, with them receiving healing and/or deliverance),* and the diseases departed from them, and the evil spirits went out of them *(it was not the pieces of cloth which did this, but rather the Power of God using these cloths as a point of contact regarding Faith).*

13 Then certain of the vagabond Jews, exorcists *(speaks of individuals who practiced divination, and who were not of God, but rather of Satan),* took upon them to call over them which had evil spirits the name of the Lord Jesus *(apparently these people had heard Paul minister and observed him praying for the sick and casting out demons; they evidently noted that he used "The Name of Jesus," which had a powerful effect),* saying, We adjure you by Jesus Whom Paul preaches *(seems to be their own formula or incantation they cooked up by observing Paul).*

14 And there were seven sons of *one* Sceva, a Jew, *and* Chief of the Priests, which did so *(infers that this man may have been a member of the Jewish Council at Ephesus).*

15 And the evil spirit answered and said *(points to a man who was demon-possessed, and that some or all of these seven sons had been hired to exorcise this spirit)*, **Jesus I know, and Paul I know; but who are you?** *(This represents two different and distinct Greek verbs regarding the word "know." Referring to Jesus, it implied fear! Referring to Paul, there was much less action.)*

16 And the man in whom the evil spirit was leaped on them, and overcame them, and prevailed against them *(probably involved all seven sons being soundly whipped by the demon-possessed man)*, so that they fled out of that house naked and wounded *(the Greek Text indicates that they suffered wounds severe enough to effect them for a while)*.

17 And this was known to all the Jews and Greeks also dwelling at Ephesus *("all" does not mean every single person, but rather quite a number)*; and fear fell on them all *(they now knew not to trifle with the Name of Jesus)*, and the Name of the Lord Jesus was magnified *(presents the constant idea of the Holy Spirit that Jesus will always be Glorified [Jn. 16:14])*.

18 And many who believed came *(speaks of those who had trusted the Lord for Salvation, but as of yet had not given up particular sins)*, and confessed, and showed their deeds *(concerns the Holy Spirit now leading these Believers to Holiness and Righteousness, even as He had led them to Salvation previously)*.

19 Many of them also which used curious arts brought their books together, and burned them before all *men* *("curious arts" refers to the practicing of magic; so the Holy Spirit was mightily working in people's lives, just as He desires to do always; if we will allow Him, He will clean us up; He does it through our Faith in Christ and the Cross [Rom. 8:2])*: and they counted the price of them, and found *it* fifty thousand *pieces* of silver *(it must have been many, many books, etc., for the amount in 2003 dollars would be approximately $2,000,000)*.

20 So mightily grew the Word of God and prevailed *(it doesn't say that the Church grew mightily, but rather the "Word of God . . .")*.

21 After these things were ended, Paul purposed in the Spirit *(refers to the Holy Spirit)*, when he had passed through Macedonia and Achaia, to go to Jerusalem *(he wanted to be there for the Feast of Pentecost [Acts 20:16])*, saying, After I have been there, I must also see Rome *(the Greek Text indicates a Divine Hand laid upon Paul)*.

22 So he sent into Macedonia two of them who ministered unto him, Timothy and Erastus *(concerned preparations they would make in the Churches for Paul's visit a short time later)*; but he himself stayed in Asia for a season *(stayed in Ephesus a little longer, maybe two or three months)*.

EPHESUS

23 And the same time there arose no small stir about that Way *("that Way" is the "Pentecostal Way," which characterizes the entirety of the Book of Acts)*.

24 For a certain *man* named Demetrius, a silversmith *(he was probably the guild-master of the silversmith guild or trade union)*, which made silver shrines for Diana *(speaks of miniatures of the Temple of Diana with the goddess in the middle of the Temple background)*, brought no small gain unto the craftsmen *(speaks of those who made their living by this particular craft)*;

25 Whom he called together with the workmen of like occupation *(whom Demetrius called together)*, and said, Sirs, you know that by this craft we have our wealth *(tells us that their chief concern was not really the worship or the honor of this goddess, but their own prosperity)*.

26 Moreover you see and hear, that not alone at Ephesus, but almost throughout all Asia *(presents a powerful Testimony, from an enemy no less, to the power and effectiveness of Paul's labors and his Message)*, this Paul has persuaded and turned away much people, saying that they be no gods, which are made with hands *(proclaims that which Paul had preached, and which many people had come to believe, and rightly so)*:

27 So that not only this our craft is in danger to be set at nought *(follows the idea that it would fall in disrepute)*; but also that the Temple of the great goddess Diana should be despised, and her magnificence should be destroyed, whom all Asia and the world worships *(there was quite a bit of exaggeration here)*.

28 And when they heard *these sayings*, they were full of wrath *(the accusations of Demetrius had the desired effect)*, and cried out, saying, Great *is* Diana of the Ephesians *(actually, the great wealth and prominence of the city of Ephesus were largely due to its great Temple of Diana, but it was basically localized to that city)*.

29 And the whole city was filled with confusion *(the mob is forming)*: and having caught Gaius and Aristarchus, men of Macedonia, Paul's companions in travel, they rushed with

one accord into the theatre *(recognizing these two men as Paul's associates, they dragged them into the amphitheater).*

30 And when Paul would have entered in unto the people *(Paul was determined to go into the theater and address the mob),* the Disciples suffered him not *(these were the Believers who were a part of the Church at Ephesus, and who knew the danger that awaited Paul).*

31 And certain of the chief of Asia, which were his friends *(these were men of high rank and great wealth, which presents another striking proof of the enormous influence of Paul's preaching in Asia),* sent unto him, desiring *him* that he would not adventure himself into the theatre *(seems to me that they sent Paul word, but did not come to him in person).*

32 Some therefore cried one thing, and some another *(presents the actions and mannerisms of a mob):* for the assembly was confused; and the more part knew not wherefore they were come together *(means that a few were agitating the many).*

33 And they drew Alexander out of the multitude, the Jews putting him forward *(exactly as to who this Alexander was is not clear).* And Alexander beckoned with the hand, and would have made his defence unto the people *(presents that which is to no avail).*

34 But when they knew that he was a Jew *(proclaims the reason for their outburst which followed),* all with one voice about the space of two hours cried out, Great *is* Diana of the Ephesians *(despite all of this, history records that the Gospel, which Paul preached, had such an effect that the worshipers of the goddess Diana came in ever fewer numbers, while the Church in Ephesus continued to flourish).*

35 And when the townclerk had appeased the people *(presents an office of influence),* he said, *You* men of Ephesus, what man is there who knows not how that the city of the Ephesians is a worshipper of the great goddess Diana, and of the *image* which fell down from Jupiter? *(The idea is that Ephesus is the proud possessor of this goddess, of which no other city in the world could boast.)*

36 Seeing then that these things cannot be spoken against *(appeals to the pride of these individuals, as to Diana being so great),* you ought to be quiet, and to do nothing rashly *(represents good advice, although coming from a heathen).*

37 For you have brought hither these men *(speaking of Gaius and Aristarchus),* which are neither robbers of Churches, nor yet blasphemers of your goddess *(means that Paul had not directed attention to this particular idol, but had, no doubt, referred to idols made by men's hands [Vs. 26]).*

38 Wherefore if Demetrius, and the craftsmen which are with him, have a matter against any man, the law is open *(reflects the common sense of the town clerk),* and there are deputies: let them implead one another *(he was saying that if Demetrius really had a case against Paul and those with him, he should pursue it in open Court).*

39 But if you inquire any thing concerning other matters *(in effect, is saying, if there are other complaints against Paul than that mentioned, it should be addressed correctly, and not by mob action),* it shall be determined in a lawful assembly *(open Court).*

40 For we are in danger to be called in question for this day's uproar *(refers to Roman peace being disturbed for no good reason),* there being no cause whereby we may give an account of this concourse *(proclaims the town clerk wondering how this mob action could be explained to Roman authorities, if called to account).*

41 And when he had thus spoken, he dismissed the assembly *(common sense prevailed, and Gaius and Aristarchus were released forthwith).*

CHAPTER 20
(A.D. 60)
MACEDONIA AND GREECE

AND after the uproar was ceased *(the mob had dispersed),* Paul called unto *him* the Disciples, and embraced *them (speaks of some of the Believers of the Church in Ephesus),* and departed for to go into Macedonia *(pertained to his care for the Churches in that region).*

2 And when he had gone over those parts *(no doubt included Philippi, Thessalonica, and Berea),* and had given them much exhortation *(refers to the teaching of the Word of God, as is obvious),* he came into Greece *(probably refers to a repeat visit to Athens, Corinth, and Cenchrea, as well as other places),*

3 And *there* abode three months *(he probably spent most of this time at Corinth [I Cor. 16:6]).* And when the Jews laid wait for him, as he was about to sail into Syria *(these were most probably Jews from the Synagogue at Corinth, who planned to kill him),* he purposed to return through Macedonia *(basically presents the opposite direction, actually to Philippi, from where*

he would then turn toward Syria).

4 And there accompanied him into Asia Sopater of Berea; and of the Thessalonians, Aristarchus and Secundus; and Gaius of Derbe, and Timothy; and of Asia, Tychicus and Trophimus *(some expositors believe that some of these men where chosen by various Churches to travel with Paul, and take their offerings for the poor in Jerusalem [Acts 19:29; 27:2; Rom. 15:25-28; I Cor. 16:3; II Cor. 8:19-23]).*

5 These going before tarried for us at Troas *(by the use of the pronoun "us," Luke indicates that he has once again joined Paul and his party).*

PAUL AT TROAS

6 And we sailed away from Philippi after the days of unleavened bread *(speaks of the Passover Week),* and came unto them to Troas in five days *(evidently portrays the length of time it took to make the voyage by ship);* where we abode seven days.

7 And upon the first *day* of the week *(Sunday),* when the Disciples came together to break bread *(Sunday had become the main day of worship),* Paul preached unto them, ready to depart on the morrow; and continued his speech until midnight *(proclaims him preaching possibly for several hours).*

8 And there were many lights in the upper chamber *(evidently spoke of a third story room, which would seat two or three hundred people),* where they were gathered together *(this was the meeting place or Church in Troas).*

9 And there sat in a window a certain young man named Eutychus, being fallen into a deep sleep: and as Paul was long preaching, he sunk down with sleep, and fell down from the third loft, and was taken up dead *(the Greek Text declares that he was a lifeless corpse; the fall had killed him).*

10 And Paul went down, and fell on him, and embracing *him* said *(presents the example of Elijah in this, which is probably what Paul intended [I Ki. 17:17-21]),* Trouble not yourselves; for his life is in him *(does not mean, as some claim, that the boy had merely been knocked unconscious, but rather that he had been dead, and that the Lord had infused life back into him; he was raised from the dead!).*

11 When he *(Paul)* therefore was come up again, and had broken bread, and eaten, and talked a long while, even till break of day *(this all night Message was interrupted only by the raising of the boy from the dead; he had much to tell them, and there was much they needed to hear),* so he departed.

12 And they brought the young man alive, and were not a little comforted *(what a night it had been!).*

PAUL

13 And we went before to ship *(refers to Luke and the men of Verse 4, but not Paul, at least at this time),* and sailed unto Assos *(a short distance of about forty miles around Cape Electum),* there intending to take in Paul: for so had he appointed, minding himself to go afoot *(by land it was about twenty miles; he would walk this distance alone, no doubt desiring to be alone with the Lord in prayer).*

14 And when he met with us at Assos, we took him in, and came to Mitylene *(presented another approximate forty miles by ship).*

15 And we sailed thence, and came the next *day* over against Chios *(presents another Island about the size of Lesbos; it lay due west of both Smyrna and Ephesus, about a hundred miles in distance);* and the next *day* we arrived at Samos, and tarried at Trogyllium; and the next *day* we came to Miletus.

16 For Paul had determined to sail by Ephesus *(not stop there),* because he would not spend the time in Asia *(tells us, I think, he did not want to tarry, having settled this thing with the Lord respecting this eventful trip):* for he hasted, if it were possible for him, to be at Jerusalem the Day of Pentecost *(the Holy Spirit has warned him of the coming difficulties he will face on this trip, and it is almost as if he must haste, lest he draw back because of these coming difficulties).*

EPHESIAN ELDERS

17 And from Miletus he sent to Ephesus, and called the Elders of the Church *(it was about thirty miles to Ephesus; he wanted the Elders to come meet him at Melitus before he left).*

18 And when they were come to him *(probably represents two or three days from the time the Messenger was originally sent),* he said unto them, You know, from the first day that I came into Asia *(takes them back to the very beginning of the Church at Ephesus),* after what manner I have been with you at all seasons *(indicates him nurturing them with the Gospel of Jesus Christ),*

19 Serving the Lord with all humility of

mind (*presents that which was the very opposite of the Judaizers and other false teachers, who were attempting to draw a following after themselves*), **and with many tears** (*Paul's emotions ran deep*), **and temptations** (*a provocation to deal with a situation outside the Ways of the Lord*), **which befell me by the lying in wait of the Jews** (*the constant plots against Paul by the Jews were never ceasing*):

20 *And* **how I kept back nothing that was profitable** *unto you* (*he did not allow anything to silence his voice respecting the great Doctrine of Jesus Christ and Him Crucified*), **but have showed you** (*explained the Scriptures*), **and have taught you publickly, and from house to house** (*most Churches were then in houses*),

21 **Testifying both to the Jews, and also to the Greeks** (*the Gospel is the same for all*), **repentance toward God, and Faith toward our Lord Jesus Christ** (*presents the Gospel in the proverbial nutshell; Faith in Christ pertains to Faith in what He did at the Cross*).

22 **And now, behold, I go bound in the spirit unto Jerusalem** (*speaks of the Holy Spirit, and the desire of the Spirit that Paul take this trip, irrespective of the coming difficulties*), **not knowing the things that shall befall me there** (*the Holy Spirit tells him to go to Jerusalem and that there will be great problems, but doesn't tell him exactly what they will be*):

23 **Save that the Holy Spirit witnesses in every city** (*tells us that such happened, but gave no information about the actual events*), **saying that bonds and afflictions abide me** (*the Holy Spirit didn't tell Paul exactly how these things would come about*).

24 **But none of these things move me** (*proclaims Paul putting himself entirely in the hands of the Lord*), **neither count I my life dear unto myself** (*his life belonged to the Lord, and the Lord could do with it as He so desired*), **so that I might finish my course with joy** (*and that he ultimately did*), **and the ministry, which I have received of the Lord Jesus, to testify the Gospel of the Grace of God** (*proclaims basically what this "course" actually is; his Message was Jesus Christ and Him Crucified*).

25 **And now, behold, I know that you all, among whom I have gone preaching the Kingdom of God** (*he had faithfully preached the Message to these Ephesians*), **shall see my face no more** (*he knew this would be the last time he would see them, and therefore, the reason he had sent for them*).

26 **Wherefore I take you to record this day** (*the Heavenly record will show*), **that I** *am* **pure from the blood of all** *men* (*means that he had delivered the Gospel to everyone who heard him preach, exactly as it was given to him by the Lord*).

27 **For I have not shunned to declare unto you** (*refers to the fact that the temptation was always there to trim the Message*) **all the Counsel of God** (*all the Word of God, holding back nothing*).

28 **Take heed therefore unto yourselves, and to all the Flock** (*this word is directed to the Pastors who had come from Ephesus to meet him*), **over the which the Holy Spirit has made you overseers** (*Elders, Bishops, Overseers, Shepherds, and Presbyters all mean the same thing, "Pastor"*), **to feed the Church of God** (*to tend as a Shepherd*), **which He has purchased with His Own Blood** (*Christ bought us at a great price*).

29 **For I know this, that after my departing shall grievous wolves enter in among you, not sparing the flock** (*presents a perfect description of those who merchandise the Body of Christ, and in whatever way*).

30 **Also of your own selves shall men arise** (*will not come from the outside, but from the inside*), **speaking perverse things, to draw away Disciples after them** (*not to Christ, but to themselves*).

31 **Therefore watch** (*be spiritually vigilant*), **and remember, that by the space of three years I ceased not to warn every one night and day with tears** (*Paul not only preached the Truth of the Word, but warned of and pointed out false doctrine and false apostles as well*).

32 **And now, Brethren, I commend you to God** (*he has planted enough of the Gospel in them that they will not turn from the Lord*), **and to the Word of His Grace** (*that "Word" is "the Cross"*), **which is able to build you up** (*the Gospel of Grace alone can build one up*), **and to give you an inheritance among all them which are Sanctified** (*the Believer is Sanctified only by making the Cross the Object of His Faith, which gives the Holy Spirit the latitude to carry out this work within our hearts and lives; the Believer cannot Sanctify himself*).

33 **I have coveted no man's silver, or gold, or apparel** (*he was not after their money as were these grievous wolves of Verse 29*).

34 **Yes, you yourselves know, that these hands have ministered unto my necessities, and to them who were with me** (*refers to Paul repairing tents to support himself [Acts 18:3]*).

35 **I have showed you all things** (*means that this particular aspect of unselfishness is to serve*

as an example), how that so labouring you ought to support the weak (everything the Believer does is to set a spiritual example), and to remember the Words of the Lord Jesus, how He said, It is more blessed to give than to receive (these words are not recorded in the Gospels; however, we know that only a tiny part of what He said and did is recorded; Peter, or one of the other Apostles who were with Jesus, evidently related this to Paul).

36 And when he had thus spoken (represented the last time they would ever hear him speak to them), he kneeled down, and prayed with them all (as well, concerns the last time he will pray with them, even though he will continue to pray for them).

37 And they all wept sore (concerns their great love for the Apostle), and fell on Paul's neck, and kissed him (his Message had brought them from death to life),

38 Sorrowing most of all for the words which he spoke, that they should see his face no more (so far as is known, these Ephesians never saw the Apostle again until they saw him in Glory). And they accompanied him unto the ship (this was at the port of Melitus).

CHAPTER 21
(A.D. 60)
TYRE

AND it came to pass, that after we (Luke is with the party) were gotten from them, and had launched (left the Elders from Ephesus), we came with a straight course unto Coos, and the day following unto Rhodes, and from thence unto Patara (located on the West Coast of Lucia and Pamphylia):

2 And finding a ship sailing over unto Phenicia, we went aboard, and set forth (they changed ships at Patara).

3 Now when we had discovered Cyprus, we left it on the left hand (means they did not stop at this Island), and sailed into Syria, and landed at Tyre: for there the ship was to unlade her burden.

4 And finding Disciples (followers of Christ), we tarried there seven days (during this time, his teaching was invaluable to them): who said to Paul through the Spirit, that he should not go up to Jerusalem (would have been better translated, "who said to Paul in consequence of the Spirit"; the idea is that due to what the Spirit of God was portraying to these Believers concerning the coming problems in Jerusalem, the individuals themselves were voicing their own feelings that he should not go; it was not the Holy Spirit saying, "don't go"; the Spirit was actually constraining him to go [Acts 20:22]).

CAESAREA

5 And when we had accomplished those days (the past seven days), we departed and went our way; and they all brought us on our way, with wives and children, till we were out of the city (shows the love and affection Paul continued to gain in these last few days, even from the children): and we kneeled down on the shore, and prayed (I think the strength of Paul's prayer life is now obvious).

6 And when we had taken our leave one of another, we took ship; and they returned home again (these Believers at Tyre returned to their homes, but with a full heart and an exercised soul).

7 And when we had finished our course from Tyre, we came to Ptolemais (about thirty miles from Tyre; proclaims the end of Paul's voyage by ship), and saluted the Brethren, and abode with them one day.

8 And the next day we who were of Paul's company departed, and came unto Caesarea (approximately sixty miles; they evidently walked this distance; the "company" could have been as many as nine): and we entered into the house of Philip the Evangelist (presents the same Philip of Acts 8:40), which was one of the seven (Acts 6:5); and abode with him (his house was evidently quite large).

9 And the same man had four daughters, virgins (insinuates they had given themselves over to perpetual virginity, meaning they would not marry, but would give their lives totally in serving the Lord), which did Prophesy (the idea is that they were Evangelists exactly as their father, which strikes down the idea that women cannot preach).

10 And as we tarried there many days (waiting for the Day of Pentecost), there came down from Judaea a certain Prophet (the same Brother mentioned in Acts 11:28), named Agabus.

11 And when he was come unto us, he took Paul's girdle (a sash worn around the waist like a belt), and bound his own hands and feet (presents that which the Holy Spirit told him to do as an object lesson), and said, Thus saith the Holy Spirit, So shall the Jews at Jerusalem bind the man who owns this girdle, and shall deliver him into the hands of the Gentiles (this

was designed by the Holy Spirit to test Paul's resolution to obey the inward voice which bound him to go, even as Elijah tested Elisha).

12 And when we heard these things, both we, and they of that place, besought him not to go up to Jerusalem *(but Paul must listen to the Holy Spirit, not men).*

13 Then Paul answered, What mean you to weep and to break mine heart? *(They kept trying to persuade him, becoming emotionally distraught with some of them weeping.)* for I am ready not to be bound only, but also to die at Jerusalem for the Name of the Lord Jesus *(proclaims the consecration already settled in Paul's heart and mind respecting these coming events).*

14 And when he would not be persuaded, we ceased, saying, The Will of the Lord be done *(means that all had now come to the place where they realized what Paul was doing and the direction he was going were indeed the Will of God; Paul was a chosen vessel to offer the Kingdom to Israel, as well as to proclaim it among the Gentiles; the final offer he would shortly give to Israel was a Divine necessity; but as we shall see, they rejected that offer and went to their doom).*

JERUSALEM

15 And after those days we took up our carriages *(referred to their baggage, whatever that may have been),* and went up to Jerusalem *(it was approximately sixty miles, and they probably walked).*

16 There went with us also *certain* of the Disciples of Caesarea *(meant that the party is now quite large, possibly numbering fifteen to twenty people, or even more),* and brought with them one Mnason of Cyprus *(he was originally from Cyprus, but now lived in Jerusalem, or nearby),* an old Disciple *(does not necessarily mean old in age, but thought by some to have been one of the original group Baptized with the Holy Spirit on the Day of Pentecost),* with whom we should lodge *(Mnason had invited Paul and his party to stay at his home while in Jerusalem).*

17 And when we were come to Jerusalem, the Brethren received us gladly *(indicates some of the Saints in Jerusalem, but not necessarily the leaders of the Church at this particular time; that would come the next day).*

GENTILES

18 And the *day* following Paul went in with us unto James *(refers to James, the Lord's Brother, who was the Senior Pastor of the Church in Jerusalem);* and all the Elders were present *(refers to the many Pastors who served with James concerning the Church in Jerusalem; the Church was quite large, perhaps numbering as many as thirty thousand members or more).*

19 And when he *(Paul)* had saluted them *(greeted them),* he declared particularly what things God had wrought among the Gentiles by his Ministry *(gave an account of his second and third Missionary Journeys with the planting of many Churches).*

20 And when they heard *it,* they glorified the Lord *(praised the Lord for what had been done),* and said unto him, you see, brother, how many thousands of Jews there are which believe *(probably spoken by James, and referring to the Church in Jerusalem, made up almost exclusively of Jews);* and they are all zealous of the Law *(meaning their new-found Faith in Christ stirred them up to serve the Lord with a new zeal, which they channeled in the direction of attempting to obey the Law of Moses to an even greater degree than ever):*

21 And they are informed of you *(concerned itself with charges against Paul relative to what he was teaching concerning the Law/Grace issue),* that you teach all the Jews which are among the Gentiles to forsake Moses *(was not correct, at least in the manner in which it was being said; in fact, Paul preached almost exclusively from the Old Testament, holding up all that it stated as pointing to Christ),* saying that they ought not to Circumcise *their* children, neither to walk after the customs *(once again, this was not exactly what Paul was saying; he taught that Circumcision did not save the soul, and that no flesh shall be justified by the deeds of the Law [Rom. 3:24-31; 4:21; Gal. 3:19-25]).*

22 What is it therefore? *(I think this illustrates that James himself was not settled on the matter, respecting Paul.)* the multitude must needs come together: for they will hear that you are come *(we aren't told anything about this particular meeting of which James spoke).*

23 Do therefore this that we say to you *(proclaims a plan James, it seems, thought might defuse the situation):* We have four men which have a vow on them *(pertained to the Nazarite Vow [Num. 6:14-20]);*

24 Them take, and purify yourself with them, and be at charges with them, that they may shave *their* heads *(proclaims the fact that Paul was to pay for all of these sacrifices out of his*

own pocket, which in 2003 money amounted to several thousands of dollars): **and all may know that those things, whereof they were informed concerning you, are nothing** (the thought here is that if Paul was as opposed to the Law as it was claimed, he certainly would not be in the Temple carrying out a Nazarite Vow, which was a part of the Mosaic Law); **but that you yourself also walk orderly, and keep the Law** (no answer from Paul is recorded; we know that Paul didn't keep the Law as it regarded all of its rituals and ceremonies; in fact, all of that was fulfilled in Christ; the only answer we can give concerning Paul's action in doing what James said is that he was trying to prevent a split in the Church; it is my opinion that James didn't understand the Message of Grace as he should, and was still trying to hold to the Law; about ten years later, the Lord made it impossible for the Law to be kept anymore, in that the Temple was totally destroyed by the Roman Army).

25 As touching the Gentiles which believe, we have written and concluded that they observe no such thing (releases Gentiles from obligation to the Mosaic Law; it is obvious here, however, that James didn't include the Jews in this freedom, which presented a dichotomy and caused great problems in the Early Church), **save only that they keep themselves from things offered to idols, and from blood, and from strangled, and from fornication** (this was right; but as stated, James didn't include the Jews, which made that part wrong).

PERSECUTION

26 Then Paul took the men (the four men of Verse 23), **and the next day purifying himself with them entered into the Temple, to signify the accomplishment of the days of purification** (presents something which Paul had, no doubt, done at times in the past), **until that an offering should be offered for every one of them** (speaks of the Sacrifices to be offered at the conclusion of the seven days).

27 And when the seven days were almost ended (seven days of purification), **the Jews which were of Asia** (Jews came from all over the Roman Empire to keep the various Feasts; Ephesus was in Asia, so these Jews knew Paul and were not happy with him at all), **when they saw him in the Temple, stirred up all the people, and laid hands on him** (they bodily seized him),

28 Crying out, Men of Israel, help (Paul was in the innermost Court with other men): **This is the man, who teaches all men every where against the people, and the Law, and this place** (once again portrays one of Satan's favorite tactics of twisting what has actually been said to make it mean something else entirely): **and further brought Greeks also into the Temple, and has polluted this Holy Place** (was an entirely false accusation; the four men with Paul were Jews).

29 (**For they had seen before with him in the city Trophimus an Ephesian, whom they supposed that Paul had brought into the Temple.**) (They jumped to conclusions!)

30 And all the city was moved (the claim that Paul had brought a Gentile into the Innermost Court spread like wildfire), **and the people ran together: and they took Paul, and drew him out of the Temple** (actually means they dragged him out, beating him as they went; he was dragged into the Court of the Gentiles, which was the Outer Court): **and forthwith the doors were shut** (referred to the doors of the Court of the Gentiles, and the Court of Women).

31 And as they went about to kill him (such is religion!), **tidings came unto the Chief Captain of the band, that all Jerusalem was in an uproar** (pertained to the Roman Tribune who commanded a cohort of approximately a thousand soldiers).

32 Who immediately took soldiers and centurions, and ran down unto them (probably represented about two hundred men): **and when they saw the Chief Captain and the soldiers, they left beating of Paul** (which, no doubt, saved Paul's life).

ARRESTED

33 Then the Chief captain came near, and took him, and commanded him to be bound with two chains (refers to him being bound to a soldier on each side); **and demanded who he was, and what he had done** (speaking to the Jews).

34 And some cried one thing, some another, among the multitude (generally proclaims the conduct of a mob, for this is what the crowd now was!): **and when he could not know the certainty for the tumult, he commanded him to be carried into the castle** (he gave instructions for Paul to be taken into the Fortress, or Tower of Antonia).

35 And when he came upon the stairs, so it was, that he was borne of the soldiers for the violence of the people (in order to protect him the soldiers were forced to lift him up, possibly

even above their heads).

36 For the multitude of the people *(the Jews)* followed after, crying, Away with him *(presents the cry of those who had also thirsted for the Blood of Jesus Christ [Lk. 23:18]).*

PAUL

37 And as Paul was to be led into the castle, he said unto the Chief Captain, May I speak unto you? *(This presents Paul speaking to the Captain in the Greek language, which was actually the major language of the Roman Empire.)* Who said, Can you speak Greek? *(The next Verse explains the reason for this question.)*

38 Are not you that Egyptian, which before these days made an uproar, and led out into the wilderness four thousand men who were murderers? *(This question portrays how this Captain was mistaken about Paul's identity.)*

39 But Paul said, I am a man *which am* a Jew of Tarsus, *a city* in Cilicia, a citizen of no mean city *(presents an entirely different scenario to this Roman Captain, inasmuch as Tarsus was famous for philosophy and learning)*: and, I beseech you, suffer me to speak unto the people *(Paul was, no doubt, impressed by the Holy Spirit to do this).*

40 And when he *(the Roman Captain)* had given him licence *(told him he could address the crowd)*, Paul stood on the stairs, and beckoned with the hand unto the people *(presents the last time the Holy Spirit will appeal to Israel as a Nation, at least as far as is recorded).* And when there was made a great silence, he spoke unto *them* in the Hebrew tongue, saying *(it is possible that Paul was speaking in the ancient Biblical Hebrew, which was read every week in the Synagogues; as stated, it was the last appeal by the Spirit),*

CHAPTER 22
(A.D. 60)
PAUL'S DEFENSE

MEN, Brethren, and Fathers *(presents the beginning of Paul's final address to Israel, at least which is recorded, which will culminate the next day with the Sanhedrin)*, hear you my defence *which I make* now unto you *(presents some of the greatest words they will ever hear; Paul was the instrument, but the Holy Spirit was the Speaker).*

2 (And when they heard that he spoke in the Hebrew tongue to them, they kept the more silence: and he said,)

3 I am verily a man *which am* a Jew, born in Tarsus, *a city* in Cilicia, yet brought up in this city at the feet of Gamaliel *(automatically gave Paul credibility)*, *and* taught according to the perfect manner of the Law of the Fathers, and was zealous toward God, as you all are this day *(all of this means Paul was a Scholar in the Mosaic Law).*

4 And I persecuted this Way *(the Way of the Lord Jesus Christ)* unto the death *(his persecution of Believers had resulted in the death of some)*, binding and delivering into prisons both men and women *(proclaims that he showed no mercy).*

5 As also the High Priest does bear me witness, and all the estate of the Elders *(even though this happened some twenty-five years before, there, no doubt, were some Jewish Leaders present who knew what he was talking about)*: from whom also I received letters unto the Brethren *(Acts 9:1-2)*, and went to Damascus, to bring them which were there *(followers of Christ)* bound unto Jerusalem, for to be punished.

CONVERSION

6 And it came to pass, that, as I made my journey, and was come near unto Damascus about noon *(a day Paul would never forget)*, suddenly there shone from Heaven a great light round about me *(would later be described by him as brighter than the noonday Sun [Acts 26:13]).*

7 And I fell unto the ground *(knocked down by the Power of God)*, and heard a Voice saying unto me, Saul, Saul, why do you persecute Me? *(When we oppose those who truly belong to the Lord, and I speak of opposing their Righteousness, we are at the same time opposing God.)*

8 And I answered, Who are You, Lord? *(Paul knew that it was Deity to Whom he was speaking.)* And He said unto me, I am Jesus of Nazareth, Whom you persecute *(describes the Lord using the very Name so hated by Paul).*

9 And they who were with me saw indeed the light, and were afraid *(tells us that all of Paul's Testimony could be confirmed by witnesses)*; but they heard not the Voice of Him Who spoke to me *(should have been translated, "they did not hear what the Voice said, they only heard the sound").*

10 And I said, What shall I do, Lord? *(At this moment, Paul accepted Christ as his Lord and Saviour.)* And the Lord said unto me, Arise, and go into Damascus; and there it shall be

told you of all things which are appointed for you to do *(proclaims the Plan of God for Paul's life and Ministry)*.

11 And when I could not see for the Glory of that Light *(the Light shining from Christ was so bright that it blinded Paul)*, being led by the hand of them who were with me, I came into Damascus *(presents Paul coming into the city in an entirely different posture than he had heretofore reckoned)*.

12 And one Ananias, a devout man according to the Law, having a good report of all the Jews which dwelt *there* *(he was a follower of Christ, but still was loved and respected by the Jews who were not friendly to Christ)*,

13 Came unto me, and stood, and said unto me, Brother Saul *(referred to him in this manner because Paul was already saved)*, receive your sight *(he was healed immediately, and it seems at that moment Baptized with the Holy Spirit, with the evidence of speaking with other Tongues [Acts 9:17])*. And the same hour I looked up upon him *(Acts 9:18 says, "there fell from his eyes as it had been scales")*.

14 And he said, The God of our Fathers has chosen you *(Paul was chosen by the Lord for a particular task)*, that you should know His Will *(what the Lord wanted, not what Paul wanted)*, and see that Just One *(Jesus Christ was to be the focal point of all things)*, and should hear the Voice of His Mouth *(this made Paul a witness to His Resurrection on the same level as those who saw Him alive before His Ascension)*.

15 For you shall be His witness unto all men of what you have seen and heard *(this speaks of his Great Commission to take the Gospel to the world of that day)*.

16 And now why do you tarry? *(In essence, this presents Ananias telling Paul that it is time to begin.)* arise, and be Baptized, and wash away your sins *(refers to a present action being done because of a past action; he was being Baptized in water because his sins had already been washed away by the Blood of Jesus)*, calling on the Name of the Lord *(your sins were washed when you called on the Name of the Lord)*.

THE GENTILES

17 And it came to pass, that, when I was come again to Jerusalem *(pertains to Acts 9:26)*, even while I prayed in the Temple, I was in a trance *(speaks of his high regard for the Temple, and at the same time refutes the accusation by some of the Jews that he would pollute the Temple)*;

18 And saw Him *(Jesus)* saying unto Me, Make haste, and get thee quickly out of Jerusalem *(presents the Lord once more indicting this city, His city, but now in total rebellion against Him)*: for they will not receive your testimony concerning Me *(they not only have rejected the Message of Christ, but would kill Paul as well, if given the opportunity)*.

19 And I said, Lord, they know that I imprisoned and beat in every Synagogue them who believed on You:

20 And when the blood of your martyr Stephen was shed *(presents this event which undoubtedly had a lasting effect on Paul)*, I also was standing by, and consenting unto his death, and kept the raiment of them who killed him *(this made Paul a party to the death of this man)*.

21 And he *(Jesus)* said unto me, Depart: for I will send you far hence unto the Gentiles *(this was the particular calling of Paul, even as he had been told by Ananias at the time of his conversion [Acts 9:15])*.

22 And they gave him audience unto this word *(speaks of the word "Gentiles")*, and *then* lifted up their voices, and said, Away with such a *fellow* from the earth: for it is not fit that he should live *(presents these people claiming they are Scriptural in their demand for Paul's life)*.

23 And as they cried out, and cast off *their* clothes, and threw dust into the air *(portrayed their anger)*,

24 The Chief Captain commanded him to be brought into the castle, and bade that he should be examined by scourging *(a most terrible form of torture)*; that he might know wherefore they cried so against him *(considering that Paul was speaking in Hebrew, the Roman Captain little knew what was taking place)*.

A ROMAN CITIZEN

25 And as they bound him with thongs *(getting him ready for the beating that would now be inflicted)*, Paul said unto the centurion who stood by, Is it lawful for you to scourge a man who is a Roman, and uncondemned? *(Paul did not shrink from torture when it was directly connected with the Name of Jesus, but he quietly and with much dignity avoided it when ordered by official ignorance.)*

26 When the centurion heard *that*, he went and told the Chief Captain, saying, Take heed what you do: for this man is a Roman *(the rights of Roman citizens were guarded as something*

sacred by Rome).

27 Then the Chief Captain came, and said unto him, Tell me, are you a Roman? He said, Yes *(in fact, the Chief Captain had broken the Law even by binding Paul)*.

28 And the Chief Captain answered, With a great sum obtained I this freedom *(proclaims one of the ways Roman citizenship could be gained)*. And Paul said, But I was *free* born *(Paul was born a Roman citizen, either through some service performed for Rome by his family, or else because of living in the city of Tarsus)*.

29 Then straightway *(immediately)* they departed from him which should have examined him *(refers to those who were going to scourge Paul quickly retiring)*: and the Chief Captain also was afraid, after he knew that he was a Roman, and because he had bound him.

30 On the morrow, because he would have known the certainty wherefore he was accused of the Jews, he loosed him from *his* bands *(he was no longer restricted, but at the same time held in custody that the Captain may hopefully gain some information)*, and commanded the Chief Priests and all their Council to appear *(the Jewish Sanhedrin, the highest Jewish Council, and ruling Civil and Religious body)*, and brought Paul down, and set him before them.

CHAPTER 23
(A.D. 60)
THE SANHEDRIN

AND Paul, earnestly beholding the Council *(evidently speaks of all seventy-one members of the Sanhedrin, with the High Priest Ananias serving as its President)*, said, Men *and* Brethren, I have lived in all good conscience before God until this day *(means that whatever he had been doing, he had thought it right at the time, whether true or not)*.

2 And the High Priest Ananias commanded them who stood by him to smite him on the mouth *(this man would have hated Paul; history records he was appointed about nine years before this through political influence; he ruled like a tyrant in Jerusalem, and was a glutton according to the Jewish Talmud; Zealots assassinated him in A.D. 66 for his pro-Roman sympathies)*.

3 Then said Paul unto him, God shall smite you, *you* whited wall *(in effect, says, "you whitewashed wall," meaning that the whitewash covered a black heart)*: for you sit to judge me after the Law, and command me to be smitten contrary to the Law? *(This presents Paul knowing*

the Law of Moses to a far greater degree than any of these members of the Sanhedrin.)

4 And they who stood by said, Do you revile God's High Priest? *(Paul did not know this man was the High Priest.)*

5 Then said Paul, I did not know, Brethren, that he was the High Priest *(it was very difficult at that time for a visitor to Jerusalem, as Paul was, to know who was High Priest; the Romans made and unmade them at their pleasure, in addition to those made and unmade by the Sanhedrin; in other words, the High Priest was no longer a son of Aaron, as Scripturally they should have been)*: for it is written, You shall not speak evil of the Ruler of your people *(Ex. 22:28)*.

6 But when Paul perceived that the one part were Sadducees, and the other Pharisees *(we aren't told how he came about this information)*, he cried out in the Council, Men *and* Brethren, I am a Pharisee, the son of a Pharisee *(expresses the party with which Paul had been associated before his conversion, and his Father having been the same)*: of the hope and resurrection of the dead I am called in question *(the whole Christian Faith is built around Christ, His Death on the Cross, and His Bodily Resurrection; without Faith in both, men are lost)*.

7 And when he had so said, there arose a dissension between the Pharisees and the Sadducees: and the multitude was divided *(speaks of the Sanhedrin itself, but typifies the majority of the Church world presently)*.

8 For the Sadducees say that there is no Resurrection, neither Angel, nor spirit *(they were the modernists of that present time)*: but the Pharisees confess both *(they were the fundamentalists of that time, which means to profess belief in all the Bible)*.

9 And there arose a great cry: and the Scribes *who were* of the Pharisees' part arose, and strove, saying, We find no evil in this man *(proclaims the situation being decided on the basis of Doctrine, and not on Paul personally)*: but if a spirit or an Angel has spoken to him, let us not fight against God.

10 And when there arose a great dissension, the Chief Captain, fearing lest Paul should have been pulled in pieces of them, commanded the soldiers to go down, and to take him by force from among them, and to bring *him* into the castle *(portrays the fact that the situation had gotten completely out of hand)*.

11 And the night following the Lord stood by him, and said *(presents another appearance*

by Jesus Christ to Paul [Acts 22:8, 14, 18; I Cor. 9:1; 15:8; II Cor. 12:1-4]), Be of good cheer, Paul (evidently, Paul was greatly discouraged at this time, hence the needed admonition given by Christ): for as you have testified of Me in Jerusalem, so must you bear witness also at Rome (this meant that despite the hatred and great efforts of his enemies, the Jews in Jerusalem would not be able to take his life, which they didn't).

THE JEWS

12 And when it was day, certain of the Jews banded together, and bound themselves under a curse (their "curse" was a religious curse, which sought to put God in a position where He would have to do their will; their thinking was ridiculous!), saying that they would neither eat nor drink till they had killed Paul (such is religion!).

13 And they were more than forty which had made this conspiracy.

14 And they came to the Chief Priests and Elders, and said, We have bound ourselves under a great curse, that we will eat nothing until we have killed Paul (they now seek to make their efforts official).

15 Now therefore you with the Council signify to the Chief Captain that he bring him down unto you tomorrow, as though you would enquire something more perfectly concerning him: and we, or ever he come near, are ready to kill him (proclaims the depth of infamy to which the religion of the carnal heart can sink cultured and religious people).

THE PLOT DISCOVERED

16 And when Paul's sister's son heard of their lying in wait (presents Paul's Nephew and all we know of his family other than references in Rom. 16:7, 11, 21), he went and entered into the castle, and told Paul (we aren't told how he came by this knowledge).

17 Then Paul called one of the Centurions unto him, and said, Bring this young man unto the Chief Captain: for he has a certain thing to tell him.

18 So he (the Centurion) took him (Paul's Nephew), and brought him to the Chief Captain, and said, Paul the prisoner called me unto him, and prayed me to bring this young man unto you, who has something to say unto you.

19 Then the Chief Captain took him by the hand, and went with him aside privately, and asked him, What is that you have to tell me? (This portrays an honest effort on the Chief Captain's part to obtain the Truth in all these matters.)

20 And he said, The Jews have agreed to desire you that you would bring down Paul tomorrow into the Council, as though they would enquire something of him more perfectly.

21 But do not thou yield unto them: for there lie in wait for him of them more than forty men, which have bound themselves with an oath, that they will neither eat nor drink till they have killed him: and now are they ready, looking for a promise from you (a plot to which the Tribune would probably have innocently agreed had the young man not warned him; in fact, what the Jews were doing was totally against Roman Law).

22 So the Chief Captain then let the young man depart, and charged him, See you tell no man that you have showed these things to me (it is believed, although not stated, that the young man went and related to Paul his ready acceptance by the Tribune, which no doubt encouraged Paul greatly).

CAESAREA

23 And he called unto him two Centurions, saying, Make ready two hundred soldiers to go to Caesarea, and horsemen threescore and ten (seventy), and spearmen two hundred, at the third hour of the night (9 p.m.);

24 And provide them beasts, that they may set Paul on (probably placed the Apostle next to one of the Centurions in the very midst of the force), and bring him safe unto Felix the Governor (not exactly a man of kind disposition to whom Paul must answer).

25 And he wrote a letter after this manner:

26 Claudius Lysias (the Roman Tribune) unto the most Excellent Governor Felix sends greeting.

27 This man was taken of the Jews, and should have been killed of them: then came I with an army, and rescued him, having understood that he was a Roman.

28 And when I would have known the cause wherefore they accused him, I brought him forth into their Council (Sanhedrin):

29 Whom I perceived to be accused of questions of their Law (Law of Moses), but to have nothing laid to his charge worthy of death or of bonds.

30 And when it was told me how that the Jews laid wait for the man, I sent straightway *(immediately)* to you, and gave commandment to his accusers also to say before you what *they had* against him. Farewell.

31 Then the soldiers, as it was commanded them, took Paul, and brought *him* by night to Antipatris *(about forty miles from Jerusalem, with about twenty miles left to Caesarea; the soldiers must have marched without stopping for about fifteen hours).*

32 On the morrow they left the horsemen to go with him *(the infantry of about four hundred Soldiers returned to Jerusalem, while the Calvary, consisting of some seventy horsemen, took Paul the balance of the way to Caesarea),* and returned to the castle:

33 Who, when they came to Caesarea, and delivered the epistle to the Governor *(the letter written by the Roman Tribune),* presented Paul also before him.

34 And when the Governor had read *the letter,* he asked of what province he was *(the home of Paul).* And when he understood that *he was* of Cilicia *(this automatically gave the Governor jurisdiction; the fact that Paul was a Roman citizen from this important Province, meant that Felix could not ignore him);*

35 I will hear you *(he speaks to Paul),* said he, when your accusers are also come *(pertained to members or representatives of the Sanhedrin).* And he commanded him to be kept in Herod's Judgment Hall *(a part of the lavish Palace built by Herod the Great; it served as the Capitol Building as well as the official residence of the Roman Governors; it evidently had some prison cells within its confines).*

CHAPTER 24
(A.D. 60)
PAUL BEFORE FELIX

A ND after five days Ananias the High Priest descended with the Elders *(represented members of the Sanhedrin who were Sadducees),* and *with* a certain orator *named* Tertullus, who informed the Governor against Paul *(he served as the prosecutor for the Jews).*

2 And when he was called forth, Tertullus began to accuse *him,* saying, Seeing that by you *(Felix)* we enjoy great quietness, and that very worthy deeds are done unto this nation by your providence *(Josephus said that even though Felix did suppress some of the robbers and murderers in Judaea, he was himself "more hurtful than them all"),*

3 We accept *it* always, and in all places, most noble Felix, with all thankfulness.

4 Notwithstanding, that I be not further tedious unto you, I pray you that you would hear us of your clemency a few words *(Felix was not a man of clemency).*

5 For we have found this man a pestilent *fellow,* and a mover of sedition among all the Jews throughout the world, and a ringleader of the sect of the Nazarenes *(presents the name for followers of Christ coined by the Jews):*

6 Who also has gone about to profane the Temple *(Paul didn't profane the Temple in any manner):* whom we took, and would have judged according to our Law *(presents another outright lie; they had no intention of giving him a trial as the word "judge" implies, but rather were attempting to beat him to death before he was rescued by the Tribune).*

7 But the Chief Captain Lysias came *upon us,* and with great violence took *him* away out of our hands *(is meant to throw the Roman Tribune in a bad light; it was a bad mistake on the part of Tertullus; no doubt, the Holy Spirit had him go in this direction),*

8 Commanding his accusers to come unto you: by examining of whom yourself may take knowledge of all these things, whereof we accuse him *(refers to the fact that the situation is now in the Court of the Governor, even though the Jews do not think it should be here; for all their plotting, they have not helped their cause).*

9 And the Jews also assented, saying that these things were so *(refers to the High Priest and those with him who joined Tertullus with their voices of approval respecting their hired prosecutor's statements; as stated, it was a mistake on their part).*

PAUL'S DEFENSE

10 Then Paul, after that the Governor had beckoned unto him to speak, answered *(presents that which the Holy Spirit had said that Paul would do, "to bear My Name before the Gentiles, and Kings, and the Children of Israel" [Acts 9:15]),* Forasmuch as I know that you have been of many years a judge unto this nation, I do the more cheerfully answer for myself *(there was no one in the world at that time who knew Mosaic Law any better than Paul; as well, being a Roman citizen, he was also quite knowledgeable of Roman Law):*

11 Because that you may understand, that

there are yet but twelve days since I went up to Jerusalem for to worship *(in essence, Paul is stating that what they were accusing him of was impossible, considering the short period of time).*

12 And they neither found me in the Temple disputing with any man, neither raising up the people, neither in the Synagogues, nor in the city *(refers to the fact that absolutely nothing had been done that could be misconstrued in any way, referring to these charges):*

13 Neither can they prove the things whereof they now accuse me *(they couldn't prove their charge because they never happened).*

14 But this I confess unto you, that after the way which they call heresy *(following Christ),* so worship I the God of my Fathers *(places Christianity as the fulfillment of the great Promises and Predictions given to the "Fathers," i.e., all the Old Testament Worthies),* believing all things which are written in the Law and in the Prophets *(the entirety of the Old Testament):*

15 And have hope toward God *(in essence, states that the Law and the Prophets were not complete within themselves, only pointing to the One Who was to come),* which they themselves also allow *(even his enemies among the Jews believed in the coming Messiah, but not that He was Jesus),* that there shall be a resurrection of the dead, both of the just and unjust *(proclaims, as is obvious, two Resurrections).*

16 And herein do I exercise myself *(diligence constantly practiced by Paul so that his life and conduct please the Lord in all things),* to have always a conscience void of offence toward God, and *toward* men *(Mat. 22:37-40).*

17 Now after many years I came to bring alms to my nation, and offerings *(probably refers to the six or seven years Paul had been away from Jerusalem).*

18 Whereupon certain Jews from Asia found me purified in the Temple, neither with multitude, nor with tumult *(refers to the fact that absolutely nothing was going on at that time which could have given any type of credence to these accusations).*

19 Who ought to have been here before you, and object, if they had ought against me *(the ones who accused him were not present here; the High Priest and the members of the Sanhedrin who were present had not witnessed any of these so-called infractions).*

20 Or else let these same *here* say *(now puts the High Priest and those with him on the spot),* if they have found any evil doing in me, while I stood before the Council *(shifts the attention away from those not present to those who are),*

21 Except it be for this one voice, that I cried standing among them, Touching the resurrection of the dead I am called in question by you this day *(this had to do with Jewish Law, which interested the Romans not at all).*

22 And when Felix heard these things, having more perfect knowledge of *that* way *(Felix had greater knowledge of Christianity than Tertullus, and the Jews present at that trial were willing to give him credit),* he deferred them, and said *(means simply that he refused to give a verdict at this time),* When Lysias the Chief Captain shall come down, I will know the uttermost of your matter *(he was trying to delay the matter, hoping it would defuse the situation; moreover, there is no record he ever sent for Lysias).*

23 And he commanded a Centurion to keep Paul, and to let *him* have liberty *(tells us that Felix considered Paul someone above the ordinary; he was under house arrest, but basically had the run of the place),* and that he should forbid none of his acquaintance to minister or come unto him *(he could have as many visitors as he liked, with no restraint on such activity).*

24 And after certain days, when Felix came with his wife Drusilla, which was a Jewess *(his wife was the young daughter of Herod Agrippa I, the Herod who killed James [the Brother of John] with a sword [Acts 12:1-2]),* he sent for Paul, and heard him concerning the Faith in Christ *(it seems to imply that his interest was sincere).*

25 And as he *(Paul)* reasoned of Righteousness *(Righteousness can only come through Christ),* temperance *(the bondages and vices which affect humanity),* and judgment to come *(all must one day stand before God),* Felix trembled, and answered *(proclaims tremendous Holy Spirit conviction),* Go your way for this time; when I have a convenient season, I will call for you *(presents the sinner's excuse when under conviction and refusing to surrender).*

26 He hoped also that money should have been given him of Paul, that he might loose him *(the love of money was probably one of the reasons he would not give his heart to the Lord):* wherefore he sent for him the oftener, and communed with him *(there is no record that he ever came to Christ; so close, but so far off!).*

SILENCE

27 But after two years *(gives us no hint as to what took place during this particular time)*

Porcius Festus came into Felix' room *(means that Festus now replaced Felix as Governor)*: and Felix, willing to show the Jews a pleasure, left Paul bound *(presents a terrible travesty of Justice)*.

CHAPTER 25
(A.D. 62)
PAUL BEFORE FESTUS

NOW when Festus was come into the Province *(refers to him taking the position of Governor at Caesarea)*, after three days he ascended from Caesarea to Jerusalem *(according to topography, he ascended; but according to geography, he descended; Jerusalem is about 2,500 feet above sea level, while Caesarea, situated on the coast, is just a few feet above the level of measurement)*.

2 Then the High Priest and the Chief of the Jews informed him against Paul, and besought him *(they began to besiege Festus with repeated accusations against Paul)*,

3 And desired favour against him, that he would send for him to Jerusalem, laying wait in the way to kill him *(proclaims the idea, as thought by some, that this was to be done by the same forty men who had originally made the vow to kill Paul [Acts 23:16])*.

4 But Festus answered, that Paul should be kept at Caesarea, and that he himself would depart shortly *thither (seems to imply that the Governor had about had his fill of the hatred and hypocrisy of these Jews)*.

5 Let them therefore, said he, which among you are able, go down with *me*, and accuse this man, if there be any wickedness in him *(in effect, he is saying Paul is a Roman citizen and must be treated as such)*.

6 And when he had tarried among them more than ten days, he went down unto Caesarea; and the next day sitting on the judgment seat commanded Paul to be brought *(this meant the Governor was calling for a new official trial; Festus could do this because Felix had never officially handed down a decision)*.

7 And when he was come, the Jews which came down from Jerusalem stood round about *(evidently some Jews from Jerusalem had immediately come to Caesarea in order to testify against Paul)*, and laid many and grievous complaints against Paul, which they could not prove *(undoubtedly proclaims the same complaints they had registered some two years before; they charged that Paul had indeed violated*

Roman Law in some manner at which in the next Verse hints, but which Luke did not specify).

8 While he answered for himself, Neither against the Law of the Jews, neither against the Temple, nor yet against Caesar, have I offended any thing at all *(it seems they were claiming that Paul had instigated a new religion, which, if true, would have been against Roman Law)*.

9 But Festus, willing to do the Jews a pleasure, answered Paul, and said *(Festus feared these Jewish leaders, knowing that if they were willing to bring these types of false charges against Paul, they would not hesitate to do the same against him to Rome)*, Will you go up to Jerusalem, and there be judged of these things before me? *(This presents the compromise of the Governor.)*

CAESAR

10 Then said Paul, I stand at Caesar's judgment seat, where I ought to be judged *(proclaims the Apostle seeing through this ploy, knowing that if he went to Jerusalem the Jews would find some way to kill him)*: to the Jews have I done no wrong, as you very well know *(proclaims that which is true, and which Paul hammers home, and rightly so!)*.

11 For if I be an offender, or have committed any thing worthy of death, I refuse not to die *(in effect, Paul is attempting not so much to save his life, but rather to declare his innocence)*: but if there be none of these things whereof these accuse me, no man may deliver me unto them. I appeal unto Caesar *(means it is the Will of God for him to stand before Caesar, not the Jews)*.

12 Then Festus, when he had conferred with the Council, answered *(refers to the legal advisory Council of the Governor, which evidently advised Festus that he acquiesce to Paul because of Roman Law)*, Have you appealed unto Caesar? unto Caesar shall you go.

AGRIPPA AND FESTUS

13 And after certain days king Agrippa *(pertains to the second son of Herod Agrippa who is mentioned in Acts 12:1)* and Bernice *(she was Agrippa's sister)* came unto Caesarea to salute Festus *(to pay their respects to the new Governor)*.

14 And when they had been there many days, Festus declared Paul's cause unto the king, saying *(Festus thought Herod had a better*

understanding of Jewish Law than he did, which was true), There is a certain man left in bonds by Felix *(speaks of Paul):*

15 About whom, when I was at Jerusalem, the Chief Priests and the Elders of the Jews informed *me*, desiring *to have* judgment against him *(means that the Jews did not really want another trial for Paul, but rather that Festus accept their accusations at face value and pronounce the death sentence on Paul without any further trial or investigation).*

16 To whom I answered, It is not the manner of the Romans to deliver any man to die, before that he which is accused have the accusers face to face *(presents this heathen as having a better sense of justice than the Religious Jews who, of all people, should have known better),* and have licence to answer for himself concerning the crime laid against him *(portrays the justice of the heathen Government of Rome, with Israel, who was supposed to be God's chosen, having no justice whatsoever).*

17 Therefore, when they were come hither, without any delay on the morrow I sat on the judgment seat *(proclaims, as is obvious, the recounting of this episode to King Agrippa by Festus),* and commanded the man to be brought forth.

18 Against whom when the accusers stood up, they brought none accusation of such things as I supposed *(he really didn't understand their accusations):*

19 But had certain questions against him of their own superstition *(he was actually saying, "against him of their own religion"),* and of One Jesus *(shows that Paul, in his defense, readily preached Jesus to the Governor and these Jewish Leaders; in this account as given by Luke, we only have a capsule sketch),* which was dead, Whom Paul affirmed to be alive *(proclaims the Resurrection which, in its manner, was the most astounding Miracle the world had ever known; Jesus had been Crucified; the Roman records could show this, and Festus could check if he so desired; as well, Roman soldiers made the Tomb secure; all of this, as stated, was a matter of record).*

20 And because I doubted of such manner of questions *(he was at a loss as to how to decide such questions),* I asked *him* whether he would go to Jerusalem, and there be judged of these matters.

21 But when Paul had appealed to be reserved unto the hearing of Augustus *(Nero),* I commanded him to be kept till I might send him to Caesar.

22 Then Agrippa said unto Festus, I would also hear the man myself. To morrow, said he *(Festus),* you shall hear him.

23 And on the morrow, when Agrippa was come, and Bernice, with great pomp, and was entered into the place of hearing, with the Chief Captains, and principal men of the city *(the King and his sister took this opportunity to let the city of Caesarea see their glory),* at Festus' commandment Paul was brought forth *(it is suggested that Luke was in attendance this particular day as well, and was a witness of all the proceedings).*

24 And Festus said, King Agrippa, and all men which are here present with us, you see this man, about whom all the multitude of the Jews have dealt with me, both at Jerusalem, and *also* here, crying that he ought not to live any longer.

25 But when I found that he had committed nothing worthy of death, and that he himself has appealed to Augustus, I have determined to send him.

26 Of whom I have no certain thing to write unto my lord *(once again refers to Nero; the Governor is complaining that he is going to send a man to Caesar for a trial, but he has no idea what to tell the Emperor he has done).* Wherefore I have brought him forth before you, and especially before you, O king Agrippa, that, after examination had, I might have somewhat to write *(he hopes the King, being a Jew, might be able to define the charges a little better).*

27 For it seems to me unreasonable to send a prisoner, and not withal to signify the crimes *laid* against him *(the Roman world found no fault in Paul, even as Pilate found no fault in Jesus; but the world of religion did, as the world of religion always does!).*

CHAPTER 26
(A.D. 62)
PAUL'S DEFENSE

THEN Agrippa said unto Paul, You are permitted to speak for yourself. Then Paul stretched forth the hand, and answered for himself:

2 I think myself happy, king Agrippa, because I shall answer for myself this day before you touching all the things whereof I am accused of the Jews:

3 Especially *because I know* you to be expert in all customs and questions which are

among the Jews *(this was not offered as flattery; in fact, Agrippa's Father, King Agrippa I, was zealous for the Jewish Law up to almost the end of his life)*: wherefore I beseech you to hear me patiently.

4 My manner of life from my youth, which was at the first among mine own nation at Jerusalem, know all the Jews *(concerns Paul being immersed in Jewish Ritual and Law from the time he was old enough to begin his advanced studies, which was probably about twelve years of age)*;

5 Which knew me from the beginning *(means simply that what he is saying can be easily proven)*, if they would testify, that after the most straitest sect of our religion I lived a Pharisee *(pertains to this group being the most strict in Doctrines and moral practices)*.

6 And now I stand and am judged for the hope of the promise made of God unto our Fathers *(this "hope" was the Messiah, the Lord Jesus Christ Whom the Jews rejected)*:

7 Unto which *promise* our Twelve Tribes, instantly serving God day and night, hope to come. For which hope's sake, king Agrippa, I am accused of the Jews *(many of the Jews were looking forward to the fulfillment of the Prophecies regarding the coming Messiah; the great dissension was over Jesus)*.

8 Why should it be thought a thing incredible with you, that God should raise the dead? *(Israel's history was one of Miracles, so the dead being raised, as extraordinary as it is, should not come as a surprise.)*

9 I verily thought with myself, that I ought to do many things contrary to the Name of Jesus of Nazareth *(presents Paul taking himself back to his dreadful time of unbelief)*.

10 Which thing I also did in Jerusalem: and many of the saints did I shut up in prison, having received authority from the Chief Priests; and when they were put to death, I gave my voice against *them* *(we know of Stephen; however, there may have been more)*.

11 And I punished them oft in every Synagogue, and compelled *them* to blaspheme *(should have been translated, "and attempted to compel them to blaspheme," because the Greek Text implies that he was not successful in this effort)*; and being exceedingly mad against them, I persecuted *them* even unto strange cities *(indicates that Damascus was not the only city, other than Jerusalem, where Paul was practicing his deadly wares)*.

12 Whereupon as I went to Damascus with authority and commission from the Chief Priests *(intending to continue his persecution in that city)*,

HIS CONVERSION

13 At midday, O king, I saw in the way a Light from Heaven *(proclaims one of, if not, the most dramatic conversions the world has ever known)*, above the brightness of the Sun, shining round about me and them which journeyed with me *(this was the Glory of Jesus Christ)*.

14 And when we were all fallen to the earth *(the Power of God was so strong that Paul and all his associates with him fell to the ground)*, I heard a Voice speaking unto me, and saying in the Hebrew tongue *(actually speaks of all hearing the Voice, but only Paul knowing what was said [Acts 9:7])*, Saul, Saul *(his Hebrew name)*, why do you persecute Me? *(This proclaims the fact that when we persecute those who belong to the Lord we, in fact, persecute the Lord.)* it is hard for you to kick against the pricks *(proclaims a common idiom of that day and even now; in other words, you will only succeed in hurting yourself; you will not stop the Plan of God)*.

15 And I said, Who are you, Lord? *(This proclaims the fact that Paul knew he was speaking to Deity.)* And He said, I am Jesus Whom you persecute *(proclaims the Lord using the Name Paul hated the most — Jesus)*.

16 But rise, and stand upon your feet *(very similar to what the Lord had said to Job many years before [Job 38:3])*: for I have appeared unto you for this purpose *(specifies that the Lord has a very important work for Paul to do)*, to make you a Minister and a witness both of these things which you have seen, and of those things in the which I will appear unto you *(in fact, it would be to Paul that the Lord would give the meaning of the New Covenant, which, in effect, was the meaning of the Cross [II Cor. 12:1-12])*;

17 Delivering you from the people *(refers to the Jews)*, and *from* the Gentiles, unto whom now I send you *(the Lord would not allow the death of the Apostle until he had finished his Mission; his primary Mission was to take the Gospel to the Gentiles, which he did)*,

18 To open their eyes, *and* to turn *them* from darkness to light, and *from* the power of Satan unto God, that they may receive forgiveness of sins, and inheritance among them which are Sanctified by Faith that is in Me *(the Apostle pointed out that man is blind, enslaved,*

impure, immoral, poverty-stricken, and unholy, but he can receive sight, liberty, forgiveness, true wealth and holiness upon the Principle of Faith in Christ and what Christ has done at the Cross).

LIGHT

19 Whereupon, O king Agrippa, I was not disobedient unto the Heavenly Vision *(Paul had faithfully carried out that which the Lord had called him to do)*:

20 But showed first unto them of Damascus *(he preached Christ in Damascus immediately after being saved)*, **and at Jerusalem, and throughout all the coasts of Judaea** *(pertains to Paul going to Jerusalem immediately after Damascus, and then later to other areas of Judaea)*, **and** *then* **to the Gentiles** *(speaks of the far greater majority of his Ministry, even up to this particular time)*, **that they should repent and turn to God, and do works meet for repentance** *(turn from the heathen idols to God)*.

21 For these causes the Jews caught me in the Temple, and went about to kill *me* *(Paul is saying that the Jews do not hate him because of their stated reasons, but rather because of his preaching Jesus)*.

22 Having therefore obtained help of God, I continue unto this day, witnessing both to small and great *(proclaims the fact that God has sustained him through some very difficult times)*, **saying none other things than those which the Prophets and Moses did say should come** *(Paul claims total Scripturality for his Message, which it certainly was)*:

23 That Christ *(the Messiah)* **should suffer** *(means that he would die; in other words that was the reason He came [Isa., Chpt. 53])*, **and that he should be the first who should rise from the dead** *(Jesus is the "Firstfruits" of the Resurrection and, therefore, the guarantee of the Resurrection of all Believers [I Cor. 15:1-23; Rev. 1:5])*, **and should show light unto the people, and to the Gentiles** *(refers to the Lord Jesus Christ as being the only "Light," and for all people)*.

FESTUS

24 And as he thus spoke for himself, Festus said with a loud voice, Paul, you are beside yourself; much learning does make you mad *(as a heathen, Festus could not understand as Agrippa could the great argument that the Atoning Death and Resurrection of the Messiah* fulfilled the predictions of the Prophets, and were necessary in order to effect the Salvation of sinful men).

25 But he said, I am not mad *(insane)*, **most noble Festus; but speak forth the Words of Truth and soberness** *(presents the only "Truth" the Governor and others present had ever heard)*.

26 For the King *(Agrippa)* **knows of these things, before whom also I speak freely: for I am persuaded that none of these things are hidden from him; for this thing was not done in a corner** *(King Agrippa most certainly knew of Jesus; it would have been impossible for him not to have known)*.

ALMOST PERSUADED

27 King Agrippa, do you believe the Prophets? *(This presents an Altar Call being given to this King and his Sister, which drilled straight to the heart of this profligate Jew.)* **I know that you believe** *(presents the Apostle answering for the King, which saved him from embarrassment)*.

28 Then Agrippa said unto Paul, Almost thou persuadest me to be a Christian *(the Greek Text does not give any more indication of what the King actually said; it is not known if he was really moved and then said sincerely, "you almost persuade me to be a Christian!" or "do you think you can easily make me a Christian?!")*.

29 And Paul said, I would to God, that not only you, but also all who hear me this day, were both almost, and altogether such as I am *(the Apostle, through and by the Gospel of Jesus Christ, proclaims the position of the Believer in Christ as being above any other office or position in the world)*, **except these bonds** *(this must have been a dramatic moment when, coupled with the majesty of his words, Paul lifts up his manacled hands forming a picture of arresting grandeur)*.

30 And when he had thus spoken, the King rose up, and the Governor, and Bernice, and they who sat with them *(they did not want to hear anymore, so they rose and thus closed the audience, and their opportunity for Eternal Life)*:

31 And when they were gone aside, they talked between themselves, saying, This man does nothing worthy of death or of bonds *(they had been brought face-to-face with themselves, and above all with God; as such, they would never be the same again, even though they had rejected the appeal and the plea)*.

32 Then said Agrippa unto Festus, This man might have been set at liberty, if he had not

appealed unto Caesar *(implies that the appeal had already been registered, and now must be carried out; behind it all, the Lord wanted the Apostle to go to Rome)*.

CHAPTER 27
(A.D. 62)
PAUL SAILS FOR ROME

A ND when it was determined that we *(Luke is still with Paul)* should sail into Italy *(the time has now arrived when Paul will now go to Rome)*, they delivered Paul and certain other prisoners unto *one* named Julius, a centurion of Augustus' band *(this was an elite "band" directly responsible to the Emperor)*.

2 And entering into a ship of Adramyttium, we launched, meaning to sail by the coasts of Asia; *one* Aristarchus, a Macedonian of Thessalonica, being with us *(proclaims another of Paul's converts being with him along with Luke; consequently, Festus allowed Paul two traveling associates [Acts 20:4])*.

3 And the next *day* we touched at Sidon *(a port about seventy miles north of Caesarea)*. And Julius courteously entreated Paul, and gave *him* liberty to go unto his friends to refresh himself *(Paul and his associates were allowed to stay with these people in Sidon until the ship sailed; this shows how much trust the Centurion placed in Paul)*.

4 And when we had launched from thence *(from Sidon)*, we sailed under Cyprus, because the winds were contrary.

5 And when we had sailed over the sea of Cilicia and Pamphylia, we came to Myra, *a city* of Lycia.

6 And there the centurion found a ship of Alexandria sailing into Italy; and he put us therein *(they changed ships)*.

7 And when we had sailed slowly many days, and scarce were come over against Cnidus, the wind not suffering us, we sailed under Crete, over against Salmone *(the winds were not favorable, so they were not making good time)*;

8 And, hardly passing it, came unto a place which is called The fair havens; near whereunto was the city *of* Lasea *(there was no town at Fair Havens for them to replenish their stores, with Lasea being about five miles distant)*.

9 Now when much time was spent *(spoke of several days with still no favorable winds)*, and when sailing was now dangerous *(pertained to any time after September 14th)*, because the

fast was now already past, Paul admonished *them* *(pertained to the Great Day of Atonement, and was actually a one day fast which Paul and his two associates no doubt kept)*,

10 And said unto them, Sirs, I perceive that this voyage will be with hurt and much damage, not only of the lading *(cargo)* and ship, but also of our lives *(presents that which the Lord had evidently already related to Paul)*.

11 Nevertheless the Centurion believed the master and the owner of the ship, more than those things which were spoken by Paul *(they would find to their chagrin that they had chosen wrong)*.

12 And because the haven *(Fair Havens)* was not commodious to winter in, the more part advised to depart thence also, if by any means they might attain to Phenice, *and there* to winter; *which is* an haven of Crete, and lies toward the southwest and northwest *(pertains to a harbor which, in fact, was commodious, and where some imperial grain ships actually did tie up for the winter; it was about fifty miles west of Fair Havens)*.

13 And when the south wind blew softly, supposing that they had obtained *their* purpose, loosing *thence*, they sailed close by Crete *(pertains to a wind direction for which they had been waiting)*.

THE STORM

14 But not long after there arose against it a tempestuous wind, called Euroclydon *(this was a hurricane)*.

15 And when the ship was caught, and could not bear up into the wind, we let *her* drive *(means that the helmsman simply could not hold the wheel for the force of the wind; so he could do nothing but let the ship drive toward whatever the direction the wind wanted it to go)*.

16 And running under a certain island which is called Clauda, we had much work to come by the boat *(the "boat" of which Luke speaks was a little skiff they were pulling, which was the custom then and remained so for many centuries; due to the storm, they had great difficulty getting this small boat on-board)*:

17 Which when they had taken up, they used helps, undergirding the ship *(these were large ropes which were pulled under the ship and made sure, helping to hold the vessel together in the storm)*; and, fearing lest they should fall into the quicksands, strake sail, and so were driven *(this way they would be driven by the wind, but*

with few or no sails stretched at all; hopefully the wind would change before they were driven onto the rocks).

18 And we being exceedingly tossed with a tempest, the next *day* they lightened the ship *(they had to throw certain things overboard);*

19 And the third *day* we cast out with our own hands the tackling of the ship *(pertains to the third day after leaving Clauda; they now threw overboard ship equipment, even that which was desperately needed).*

20 And when neither sun nor stars in many days appeared, and no small tempest lay on *us,* all hope that we should be saved was then taken away *(now all on-board knew that they should have listened to Paul).*

THE VISION

21 But after long abstinence *(does not refer to a "fast" as some claim, but rather that they hadn't had a prepared meal for some days)* Paul stood forth in the midst of them, and said, Sirs, you should have hearkened unto me, and not have loosed from Crete, and to have gained this harm and loss *(is not really meant as a reprimand by the Apostle, but rather to give foundation to what he is about to say).*

22 And now I exhort you to be of good cheer: for there shall be no loss of *any man's* life among you, but of the ship *(plainly tells us that the ship will be lost with its cargo of wheat, but not a person will lose their life).*

23 For there stood by me this night the Angel of God, Whose I am, and Whom I serve *(the statements "Whose I am," "Whom I serve," and "I believe God" [Vs. 25] form a noble confession of Faith),*

24 Saying, Fear not, Paul *(said in this manner because there had been fear in Paul's heart, as well as everyone else on-board);* you must be brought before Caesar *(not because of Paul's appeal to Caesar, or because of the charges brought against him by the Jews, but rather because of the Divine Plan):* and, lo, God has given you all them who sail with you *(every Saint had better know as to what Preacher he is "with").*

25 Wherefore, sirs, be of good cheer: for I believe God, that it shall be even as it was told me *(insinuates that possibly some did not believe what Paul was saying).*

26 Howbeit we must be cast upon a certain island *(the Angel evidently did not tell Paul what Island!).*

THE SHIPWRECK

27 But when the fourteenth night was come *(pertained to the length of time after leaving Fair Havens; so the storm had lasted now for about two weeks),* as we were driven up and down in Adria, about midnight the shipmen deemed that they drew near to some country *(they could hear waves breaking on the beach, or rocks, at some distance);*

28 And sounded, and found *it* twenty fathoms *(a depth of about 120 feet):* and when they had gone a little further, they sounded again, and found *it* fifteen fathoms.

29 Then fearing lest we should have fallen upon rocks, they cast four anchors out of the stern, and wished for the day *(were anxious for the night to be over, so they could see where they were).*

30 And as the shipmen were about to flee out of the ship, when they had let down the boat into the sea *(portrays some, if not all, of the ship's crew about to take the only small boat they had and attempt to escape to shore, in effect, deserting the ship),* under cover as though they would have cast anchors out of the foreship *(presents their deception, but Paul was watching),*

31 Paul said to the Centurion and to the soldiers, Except these abide in the ship, you cannot be saved *(to obtain God's Promises, we must abide by His Conditions).*

32 Then the soldiers cut off the ropes of the boat, and let her fall off *(the Centurion now believes Paul).*

33 And while the day was coming on, Paul besought *them* all to take meat, saying, This day is the fourteenth day that you have tarried and continued fasting, having taken nothing *("nothing!" the Greek word used here means they had eaten no regular meal).*

34 Wherefore I pray you to take *some* meat: for this is for your health *(they should attempt to force at least some food down, irrespective of their seasickness, which, no doubt, some of them still had):* for there shall not an hair fall from the head of any of you *(that is, if you will do what I say).*

35 And when he had thus spoken, he took bread, and gave thanks to God in presence of them all *(which every Believer should do at every meal, as well):* and when he had broken *it,* he began to eat.

36 Then were they all of good cheer, and they also took *some* meat *(some food).*

37 And we were in all in the ship two hundred

threescore and sixteen souls (276 people on-board, which meant the ship was quite large).

38 And when they had eaten enough, they lightened the ship, and cast out the wheat into the sea (what was left of the cargo still on-board).

39 And when it was day, they knew not the land (they did not know where they were): but they discovered a certain creek with a shore, into the which they were minded, if it were possible, to thrust in the ship (they wanted to take the ship as close to the shore as possible).

40 And when they had taken up the anchors, they committed themselves unto the sea, and loosed the rudder bands, and hoisted up the mainsail to the wind, and made toward shore (once again, trying to get as close as possible!).

41 And falling into a place where two seas met, they ran the ship aground; and the forepart stuck fast, and remained unmoveable, but the hinder part was broken with the violence of the waves (they had not gotten in as close as they desired).

42 And the soldiers' counsel was to kill the prisoners, lest any of them should swim out, and escape (the reason for this is that Roman Law condemned guards to death if prisoners escaped under their watch).

43 But the Centurion, willing to save Paul, kept them from their purpose (presents this man now knowing Paul was not just another prisoner); and commanded that they which could swim should cast themselves first into the sea, and get to land:

44 And the rest, some on boards, and some on broken pieces of the ship. And so it came to pass, that they escaped all safe to land (fulfilled exactly that which the Angel had conveyed to Paul).

CHAPTER 28
(A.D. 62)
MELITA

AND when they were escaped, then they knew that the island was called Melita (it is now called Malta, and is about fifty miles south of Sicily in the Mediterranean).

2 And the barbarous people showed us no little kindness (is not meant by Luke to be an insult; it just referred to people who were not influenced by Greek culture): for they kindled a fire, and received us every one, because of the present rain, and because of the cold.

THE MIRACLE

3 And when Paul had gathered a bundle of sticks, and laid them on the fire, there came a viper out of the heat, and fastened on his hand (presents Satan, having been unsuccessful in killing Paul with a storm, now trying another tactic).

4 And when the barbarians saw the venomous beast hang on his hand, they said among themselves, No doubt this man is a murderer, whom, though he has escaped the sea, yet vengeance suffers not to live (they knew that the poison of this particular type of viper would kill any man).

5 And he shook off the beast into the fire, and felt no harm (doesn't mean that he did not feel the pain of the bite, but rather did not begin to swell, as instantly was the case normally!).

6 Howbeit they looked when he should have swollen, or fallen down dead suddenly (they had personally seen the snake bite Paul, even hanging on his hand; so, they knew the reptile had bitten full force): but after they had looked a great while, and saw no harm come to him, they changed their minds, and said that he was a god (probably referred to Hercules; he was one of the gods of the Phoenicians and was worshiped on Malta under the title of "dispeller of evil").

7 In the same quarters were possessions of the Chief man of the island, whose name was Publius (this man had a Roman name, so it probably means he was the Roman official on this Island); who received us, and lodged us three days courteously.

HEALING

8 And it came to pass, that the father of Publius lay sick of a fever and of a bloody flux (presents a medical term which Luke would have used, being a Physician; the man had a reoccurring fever and dysentery): to whom Paul entered in, and prayed, and laid his hands on him, and healed him (the Lord is still the Healer).

9 So when this was done, others also, which had diseases in the island, came, and were healed:

10 Who also honoured us with many honours (evidently indicates material things such as clothing, food, and even gifts of money, etc.); and when we departed, they laded us with such things as were necessary (no doubt, refers to the entirety of the 276 people who had been shipwrecked).

11 And after three months we departed in a ship of Alexandria, which had wintered in the isle, whose sign was Castor and Pollux *(evidently portrayed another grain ship from the same city where the wrecked ship had been based [Acts 27:6]; the two signs mentioned here were the favorite divinities of Mediterranean seamen at that time; it was the custom to have their images, whatever they were, on the head and stern of their ships)*.

12 And landing at Syracuse, we tarried *there* three days *(Syracuse was the capitol of Sicily, about eighty miles north of Malta)*.

13 And from thence we fetched a compass *(took a heading)*, and came to Rhegium: and after one day the south wind blew, and we came the next day to Puteoli *(Puteoli was the chief port on the Bay of Naples)*:

14 Where we found Brethren *(those who were followers of Christ)*, and were desired to tarry with them seven days *(the Centurion allowed Paul to remain with these Brethren and, no doubt, preach the Gospel to them for this length of time)*: and so we went toward Rome *(finds them finishing this perilous journey on foot)*.

15 And from thence, when the Brethren *(from Rome)* heard of us, they came to meet us as far as Appii forum, and The Three Taverns *(a runner evidently went to the Capitol informing the Brethren that Paul was coming; consequently, it seems a group went to meet Paul)*: whom when Paul saw, he thanked God, and took courage *(refers to the fellowship the Apostle and those with him greatly enjoyed)*.

ROME

16 And when we came to Rome, the Centurion delivered the prisoners to the Captain of the Guard *(pertained to the Commander of Nero's Praetorian Guard)*: but Paul was suffered to dwell by himself with a soldier who kept him *(obviously means Paul was treated differently from the other prisoners; he was evidently granted special favors)*.

17 And it came to pass, that after three days Paul called the Chief of the Jews together *(not only refers to the main Jewish Leader in Rome, but the other leaders as well)*: and when they were come together, he said unto them, Men *and* Brethren *(the following account seems to indicate that the Brethren of Verse 15 had no connection with these Jewish Leaders)*, though I have committed nothing against the people, or customs of our Fathers, yet was I delivered prisoner from Jerusalem into the hands of the Romans *(proclaims the Apostle relating the situation exactly as it had happened)*.

18 Who, when they had examined me, would have let *me* go, because there was no cause of death in me *(pertained to the Romans, not the Jews, as the next Verse explains)*.

19 But when the Jews spoke against *it*, I was constrained to appeal unto Caesar *(proclaims the Apostle having done this in order to save his life)*; not that I had ought to accuse my nation of *(he was in no way in Rome to bring charges against the Jews or to cause them problems in any manner)*.

20 For this cause therefore have I called for you, to see *you*, and to speak with *you:* because that for the hope of Israel I am bound with this chain *(in effect, he is saying that all of this is because of his proclamation of Christ as the Messiah of Israel, and the Saviour of the world)*.

PAUL

21 And they said unto him, We neither received letters out of Judaea concerning you, neither any of the Brethren who came showed or spoke any harm of you *(probably pertained to the fact that Roman Law punished unsuccessful prosecutors of Roman citizens; it is difficult to comprehend that these Jewish Leaders in Rome had never heard of Paul, but it seems somewhat that this was the case, or else their knowledge of him was scant)*.

22 But we desire to hear of you what you think *(proclaims a great opportunity now presented to Paul)*: for as concerning this sect *(Christianity)*, we know that everywhere it is spoken against *(true Bible Christianity continues to be "everywhere spoken against")*.

23 And when they had appointed him a day, there came many to him into *his* lodging *(it is believed that he was allowed to rent a house, and there abide during his stay in Rome)*; to whom he expounded and testified the Kingdom of God, persuading them concerning Jesus, both out of the Law of Moses, and *out of* the Prophets, from morning till evening *(they heard the "Word" as they had never heard the "Word" before; above all, they heard about Jesus, to Whom the Word pointed)*.

24 And some believed the things which were spoken, and some believed not *(some embraced Christ as Lord, Messiah, and Saviour, and some did not)*.

THE JEWS

25 And when they agreed not among themselves, they departed, after that Paul had spoken one word, Well spoke the Holy Spirit by Isaiah the Prophet unto our Fathers *(proclaims the instrument as Isaiah, but the Speaker as the Holy Spirit)*,

26 Saying, Go unto this people, and say, Hearing you shall hear, and shall not understand; and seeing you shall see, and not perceive *(Isa. 6:9-10; presents the sixth of seven times this is recorded by the Holy Spirit [Isa. 6:9; Mat. 13:14; Mk. 4:12; Lk. 8:10; Jn. 12:40; Acts 28:26; Rom. 11:8])*:

27 For the heart of this people is waxed gross, and their ears are dull of hearing, and their eyes have they closed; lest they should see with *their* eyes, and hear with *their* ears, and understand with *their* heart, and should be converted, and I should heal them *(this is a willful rejection of Truth, which brings about a willful judgment of the hardening of the heart)*.

28 Be it known therefore unto you, that the Salvation of God is sent unto the Gentiles, and *that* they will hear it *(presents Paul's last statement to the Jewish leadership of Rome that day; in effect, he says that the "Salvation of God" is found only in Jesus)*.

29 And when he had said these words, the Jews departed, and had great reasoning among themselves *(discussing greatly what he had said)*.

ROME

30 And Paul dwelt two whole years in his own hired house *(rented house)*, and received all who came in unto him *(no doubt, strengthened the Church mightily in Rome)*,

31 Preaching the Kingdom of God *(refers to the Rule of God in the human heart and life)*, and teaching those things which concern the Lord Jesus Christ, with all confidence, no man forbidding him *(it is said that even some from Caesar's household were converted [Phil. 4:22])*.

THE EPISTLE OF PAUL THE APOSTLE TO THE
ROMANS

CHAPTER 1
(A.D. 60)
INTRODUCTION

PAUL *(the only Bible writer who discarded his Jewish name [Saul] for his Gentile name [Paul]),* **a servant** *(a voluntary Bondslave)* **of Jesus Christ, called** *to be* **an Apostle** *(he puts "Bondslave" ahead of Apostle),* **separated unto the Gospel of God** *(means that Paul was separated by God from all mankind for his Apostleship),*

2 (Which He *(God)* had promised afore by His Prophets in the Holy Scriptures,) *(He promised the Redeemer, Who would be the Lord Jesus Christ.)*

3 Concerning his Son Jesus Christ our Lord *(speaks of Jesus being the Core Message of the Old Testament),* which was made *(signifies entrance into a new condition)* of the seed of David *(through the family of David)* according to the flesh *(the Incarnation, God becoming man);*

4 And declared *to be* the Son of God with power *(he was the Son of David regarding His Humanity, and the Son of God regarding His Deity),* according to the Spirit of Holiness *(presents another Name for the Holy Spirit),* by the Resurrection from the dead *(the Jews Crucified Jesus because He claimed to be the Son of God; God Resurrected Him because He was the Son of God):*

5 By Whom *(by God)* we have received Grace *(unmerited favor)* and Apostleship *(the Call),* for obedience to the Faith *(Jesus Christ and Him Crucified)* among all nations *(one Gospel for the entirety of the world),* for His Name *(He is the One Who has purchased our Redemption, by and through the Cross of Calvary);*

6 Among whom *(all Believers)* are you also the called of Jesus Christ *(every person who is saved has been called of the Lord from something to something):*

7 To all who be in Rome, Beloved of God, called *to be* Saints *("to be" was improperly supplied by the Translators; every person who is saved is a Saint, and made so by Jesus Christ and what He did at the Cross):* Grace to you *(which comes through the Cross)* and peace *(Sanctifying Peace)* from God our Father, and the Lord Jesus Christ *(presents the Trinity, with the Holy Spirit inspiring these words to be written).*

THANKSGIVING

8 First, I thank my God through Jesus Christ for you all, that your faith is spoken of throughout the whole world *(speaks of the Roman Empire).*

9 For God is my witness, whom I serve with my spirit *(his human spirit)* in the Gospel of His Son *(Jesus Christ and Him Crucified),* that without ceasing I make mention of you always in my prayers *(Paul had a strong prayer life);*

10 Making request *(has to do with seeking the Lord about a certain thing, in this case the privilege of ministering to the Church at Rome),* if by any means now at length I might have a prosperous journey by the Will of God to come unto you *(Acts, Chpts. 27 and 28, record that journey; it was very prosperous spiritually, but not prosperous in other ways).*

11 For I long to see you, that I may impart unto you some spiritual gift *(does not mean, as some think, that Paul could impart one or more of the nine Gifts of the Spirit, but rather speaks of explaining to them more perfectly the Word of God),* to the end you may be established *(spiritual Gifts, as valuable as they are, do not establish anyone; it is the Truth of the Word which establishes, and that alone [Jn. 8:32]);*

12 That is, that I may be comforted together with you by the mutual faith both of you and me *(carries the idea of a mutual strengthening brought about by his Ministry among them, and their Love shown to him).*

13 Now I would not have you ignorant, Brethren *(a phrase often used by Paul),* that oftentimes I purposed to come unto you, (but was let hitherto,) *(something hindered)* that I might have some fruit among you also, even as among other Gentiles *(he knew that his teaching concerning the Cross would help them to grow in Grace).*

14 I am debtor *(true of every Believer)* both to the Greeks, and to the Barbarians; both to the wise, and to the unwise *(to all people, whomever they might be, and wherever they might be).*

15 So, as much as in me is, I am ready to preach the Gospel to you who are at Rome also.

THE POWER

16 For I am not ashamed of the Gospel of Christ *(is said in reference to the Cross)*: for it is the Power of God unto Salvation to every one who believes; to the Jew first, and also to the Greek *(through the Cross, and the Cross alone, man is reconciled unto God)*.

17 For therein *(through the Cross)* is the Righteousness of God *(Right with God)* revealed from faith to faith *("from Faith" relates to God as the Provider and "to Faith" relates to man as the receiver)*: as it is written, The just shall live by Faith *(proclaims Paul showing that Righteousness by Faith is no new idea, but found in the Prophets [Hab. 2:4])*.

GUILT

18 For the Wrath of God *(God's Personal emotion with regard to sin)* is revealed from Heaven *(this anger originates with God)* against all ungodliness and unrighteousness of men *(God must unalterably be opposed to sin)*, who hold the truth in unrighteousness *(who refuse to recognize Who God is, and What God is)*;

19 Because that which may be known of God is manifest in them *(speaks of the universal objective knowledge of God as the Creator, which is more or less in all men)*; for God has showed *it* unto them *(means that His Signature is in Creation)*.

20 For the invisible things of Him from the creation of the world are clearly seen *(explains Verse 19)*, being understood by the things that are made *(Creation demands a Creator)*, *even* His Eternal Power and Godhead; so that they are without excuse *(the Creation tells us of the Eternal Power of God, and is obvious to all)*:

APOSTASY

21 Because that, when they knew God, they glorified *Him* not as God *(if men do not understand God in the realm of Creation, they will not understand Him in anything else)*, neither were thankful *(refusing to honor Him resulted in a lack of gratitude for His Gifts)*; but became vain in their imaginations *(presents the only direction that fallen man can go, considering he has rejected God)*, and their foolish heart was darkened *(speaks of the rejection of Light)*.

22 Professing themselves to be wise, they became fools *(lays waste to all so-called wisdom which is not of God)*,

23 And changed the glory of the uncorruptible God *(presents the sin of the ages, and points not only to the heathen of old, but also much of modern Christendom)* into an image made like to corruptible man, and to birds, and four-footed beasts, and creeping things *(proclaims the degeneration of man, which is the opposite of evolution)*.

RESULTS OF APOSTASY

24 Wherefore God also gave them up to uncleanness through the lusts of their own hearts *(not merely permissive, but God judicially delivered them over)*, to dishonour their own bodies between themselves *(speaks of every type of immorality)*:

25 Who changed the Truth of God into a lie *(refers back to Verse 23, which speaks of spiritual and sexual uncleanness)*, and worshipped and served the creature more than the Creator *(this refers to man worshiping the creation of his own hands, which means that he is worshiping something less than himself)*, who is blessed forever. Amen *(should have been translated "Bless-ed" [two syllables], because it refers to the One doing the blessing, in this case the Lord)*.

26 For this cause God gave them up unto vile affections *(the Lord removed His restraints and, therefore, gave them unimpeded access to their desires)*: for even their women did change the natural use into that which is against nature *(in short speaks of Lesbianism)*:

27 And likewise also the men *(homosexuality)*, leaving the natural use of the woman *(speaks of the sex act which is performed between the man and his wife)*, burned in their lust one toward another *(raging lust)*; men with men working that which is unseemly *(specifies its direction, which is total perversion)*, and receiving in themselves that recompence of their error which was meet *(refers to the penalty attached to wrongdoing)*.

28 And even as they did not like to retain God in *their* knowledge *(carries the idea of the human race putting God to the test for the purpose of approving or disapproving Him)*, God gave them over to a reprobate mind *(Light rejected is Light withdrawn)*, to do those things which are not convenient *(which are not fitting)*;

APOSTATES

29 Being filled with all unrighteousness, fornication, wickedness, covetousness,

maliciousness; full of envy, murder, debate, deceit, malignity; whisperers,

30 Backbiters, haters of God, despiteful, proud, boasters, inventors of evil things, disobedient to parents,

31 Without understanding, covenant breakers, without natural affection, implacable, unmerciful (these things listed are the end results of forsaking God, which is the reason for all the strife in the world):

32 Who knowing the judgment of God (in essence saying, "do Your worst, and it will not stop us"), that they which commit such things are worthy of death (Divine Judgment is implied), not only do the same, but have pleasure in them who do them (proclaims the result of the "reprobate mind").

CHAPTER 2
(A.D. 60)
CRITICS

THEREFORE you are inexcusable, O man, whosoever you are who judges (presents this segment as directed to the Jews): for wherein you judge another, you condemn yourself (in effect, says that God judges one who judges another in the same manner in which he himself has judged, hence, "condemning himself" [Mat. 7:1-2]); for you who judge do the same things (in effect, says that the Jews were no better than the Gentiles, whom they constantly berated).

GOD'S JUDGMENT

2 But we are sure that the Judgment of God is according to Truth (proclaims that which is never of presumption) against them which commit such things (proclaims a perfect Judgment, because it comes from Truth).

3 And do you think this, O man, who judges them which do such things, and do the same (you, the Jew), that you shall escape the Judgment of God? (Many Jews thought the privilege of birth as a Jew would of itself insure his entrance into the Kingdom [Mat. 3:8-9].)

4 Or despise you the riches of his goodness and forbearance and longsuffering (presents the Jew as holding these things in contempt, thinking that they were worthy of such); not knowing that the goodness of God leads you (trying to lead you) to Repentance?

5 But after your hardness and impenitent heart (speaks of a hardness toward God, with a refusal to repent) treasured up unto yourself

wrath against the day of wrath and revelation of the Righteous Judgment of God (Judgment was building up, and ultimately exploded over the Jews; we speak of A.D. 70);

6 Who will render to every man according to his deeds (we reap what we sow!):

7 To them who by patient continuance in well doing (portrays those who are not trusting in place or position for their Salvation, but rather in Christ) seek for glory and honour and immortality, Eternal Life (this speaks of that which comes exclusively from God):

8 But unto them who are contentious (carries the idea of contending with God), and do not obey the Truth (attempt to devise a way other than Christ and Him Crucified), but obey unrighteousness, indignation and wrath (the opposite of Truth),

9 Tribulation and anguish, upon every soul of man who does evil (presents the natural results of the unnatural act of sin), of the Jew first (held more responsible), and also of the Gentile (will answer as well!);

NO RESPECTER OF PERSONS

10 But glory, honour, and peace, to every man who works good (presents God's logic, which proclaims if certain things are done, certain things will follow), to the Jew first, and also to the Gentile (is given again to show the place of prominence respecting the Jew, but which they forfeited):

11 For there is no respect of persons with God (literally translated, the Verse reads, "for there is not a receiving of face in the Presence of God"; it means that God doesn't receive or accept anyone's face, irrespective as to whom they might be).

12 For as many as have sinned without Law shall also perish without Law (while the Lord will not hold the Gentiles accountable to the Law of Moses regarding Old Testament times, this in no way means that He will not hold them accountable for their sin; the fact of sin is not abrogated in any case respecting ignorance): and as many as have sinned in the Law shall be judged by the Law (in effect, places the Jew in a more responsible and even fearful situation);

13 (For not the hearers of the Law are just before God (the mere having of the Law, or even hearing the Law, saves no one), but the doers of the Law shall be justified (is used by Paul in this manner to make a point; he is not meaning that the keeping of the Law of Moses

could actually bring Justification; in fact, due to man's fallen condition, he could not keep the Law).

14 For when the Gentiles, which have not the Law *(Law of Moses)*, do by nature the things contained in the Law *(their conscience told them some semblance of right and wrong)*, these, having not the Law, are a Law unto themselves *(at the Great White Throne Judgment, God will Judge the Gentile world which existed before the Law according to that which they did know; once again, this has nothing to do with Salvation; ignorance has never brought Salvation)*:

15 Which show the work of the Law written in their hearts *(means that no one, whomever they might be and wherever they might be, is absent of all Light)*, their conscience also bearing witness *(but which can be seared)*, and *their* thoughts the mean while accusing or else excusing one another *(conscience does not prove a reliable guide, as is proclaimed here);)*

16 In the day when God shall Judge the secrets of men by Jesus Christ *(lays to rest any idea that Judgment will be on any other basis; while many other things, such as conscience, may be a witness, still Jesus Alone is the criteria)* according to my Gospel *(Jesus Christ and Him crucified)*.

GUILT

17 Behold, you are called a Jew *(implying special favor from God)*, and rest in the Law *(presents the picture of a blind and mechanical reliance on the Mosaic Law which could not save, and had never been meant to save)*, and make your boast of God *(glorying in who they were)*,

18 And know *His* Will *(Israel had the literal Word of God, which no other Nation in the world had at that time)*, and approve the things that are more excellent *(they had proved the Word over and over)*, being instructed out of the Law *(in essence means that they were instructed by the very Mouth of God)*;

19 And are confident that you yourself are a guide of the blind *(the Jews were meant by God to be the guides of the Gentiles, to lead them to the Lord)*, a light of them which are in darkness *(it was always God's Will that His Word, Will, and Way, be given to the entirety of mankind)*,

20 An instructor of the foolish *(the Gentile world was foolish in their worship of their gods of human invention)*, a teacher of babes *(presents the Holy Spirit looking at Greek Philosophers as*

no more than infants), which have the form of knowledge and of the truth of the Law *(the Jews had the Word of God, which put them light years ahead of the balance of mankind)*.

21 You therefore which teach another, do you not teach yourself? *(The Jews made fun of the Gentile world, but little applied themselves to the Law, at least as they should have.)* you who preach a man should not steal, do you steal? *(Most of them did!)*

22 You who say a man should not commit adultery, do you commit adultery? *(Many did!)* you who abhor idols, do you commit sacrilege? *(In a sense, the Holy Spirit through Paul is placing Israel in the same state as the Gentile world.)*

23 You who make your boast of the Law, through breaking the Law you dishonor God? *(In other words, due to having the Law and not keeping the Law, they were dishonoring God, even more than the Gentiles were.)*

24 For the Name of God is blasphemed among the Gentiles through you *(proclaims the Jews bringing reproach upon the Lord by living in open contradiction to their own profession)*, as it is written *(Isa. 52:5)*.

25 For Circumcision verily profits, if you keep the Law *(in other words, Circumcision profited nothing if they were breaking the Law of God)*: but if you be a breaker of the Law, your Circumcision is made uncircumcision *(proclaims the fact that religious rites, no matter how much God-given, contain no properties of Salvation)*.

26 Therefore if the uncircumcision *(Gentiles)* keep the Righteousness of the Law *(through Jesus Christ)*, shall not his uncircumcision be counted for Circumcision? *(This proclaims that one's trust in Jesus satisfies the demands of the Law and, thereby, secures the "Righteousness of the Law," which, in fact, is the only way it can be secured.)*

27 And shall not uncircumcision which is by nature, if it fulfil the Law, judge you *(proclaims the obvious results of the changed life upon Faith in Christ)*, who by the letter and Circumcision do transgress the Law? *(This speaks of the Jews who, outside of Christ, try to keep the letter of the Law by engaging in all of its Rituals, but continue to transgress the Law. In other words, what they are doing doesn't change their lives.)*

DEFINITION

28 For he is not a Jew, which is one outwardly

(completely destroys national Salvation); neither is that Circumcision, which is outward in the flesh (the mere Ritual is no true Circumcision at all, and spiritually affords nothing):

29 But he is a Jew, which is one inwardly (it is only the work carried out by Christ inwardly which constitutes Salvation); and Circumcision is that of the heart, in the spirit (refers to the "heart" of the individual being changed, which is done in one's spirit and speaks of being "Born-Again"), and not in the letter (refers to the rules and regulations of the Law of Moses, or even such in the Church); whose praise is not of men, but of God (keeping religious Rituals garners the praise of men, but not of God; men can truly praise God only when they truly accept Christ, which means to truly trust Christ and not men's religious Rituals).

CHAPTER 3
(A.D. 60)
THE JEW

WHAT advantage then has the Jew? (This proclaims the Apostle asking such after he has shown that the mere possession of the Law does not exempt the Jew from Judgment.) or what profit is there of Circumcision? (The rite of Circumcision symbolizes the entirety of the Law.)

2 Much every way (proclaims tremendous advantages, but none which could save their souls, other than simple Faith in Christ and the Cross, which all the Sacrifices of the Law symbolized): chiefly, because that unto them were committed the Oracles of God (presents the title for the Old Testament as given by the Holy Spirit).

3 For what if some did not believe? (This proclaims the unbelief which rejected the Bible, but by no means nullified its Truthfulness.) shall their unbelief make the Faith of God without effect? (The unbelief of Israel in no way affected the Great Plan that God has provided for humanity, which is built on the premise of Faith.)

4 God forbid (proclaims Paul's answer to the questions of Verse 3): yes, let God be true, but every man a liar (shows us that the problem is always of man, never of God); as it is written, That you might be justified in your sayings, and might overcome when you are judged ([Ps. 51:4] this statement is from David's Repentance regarding the matter of Uriah, in which David absolves God from all blame and takes the blame on himself; this is a pattern for True Repentance).

5 But if our unrighteousness commend the Righteousness of God, what shall we say? (In no way does this mean that God places an approval upon sin of any nature.) Is God unrighteous Who takes vengeance? (The answer is "No!") (I speak as a man) (This is meant apologetically in that only a foolish man would ask such a question.)

6 God forbid (once again serves as Paul's answer to the preposterous question of the previous Verse): for then how shall God Judge the world? (This is the Great White Throne Judgment [Rev. 20:11-15]. The fact that this Judgment cannot be avoided means the hypothesis of man is foolish indeed.)

7 For if the Truth of God has more abounded through my lie unto His Glory (is meant to be answered in the negative, for such a thing cannot be done); why yet am I also judged as a sinner? (This is meant to portray the foolishness of such thinking.)

8 And not rather, (as we be slanderously reported, and as some affirm that we say,) Let us do evil, that good may come? (This presents the reason Paul is addressing this subject. Because of his strong teaching on Grace, his detractors were slandering him by claiming he was teaching something he wasn't.) whose damnation is just (proclaims the Apostle saying that those who report such slander are liable to a just damnation).

GUILT

9 What then? are we better than they? (Are Jews better than Gentiles?) No, in no wise: for we have before proved both Jews and Gentiles, that they are all under sin (points to the supposed claim of the Jews of superiority, which is refuted);

10 As it is written (Ps. 14:1-3), There is none righteous, no, not one (addresses the complaint of the Jews and clinches the argument with the Scriptures, which the Jews could not deny):

11 There is none who understands (proclaims total depravity), there is none who seek after God (man left on his own will not seek God and, in fact, cannot seek God; he is spiritually dead).

12 They are all gone out of the Way (speaks of the lost condition of all men; the "Way" is God's Way), they are together become unprofitable (refers to the terrible loss in every capacity

of wayward man); there is none who does good, no, not one *(the Greek Text says, "useless!").*

13 Their throat *is* an open sepulcher *(the idea is of an open grave, with the rotting remains sending forth a putrid stench);* with their tongues they have used deceit *(speaks of guile, deception, hypocrisy, etc.);* the poison of asps *is* under their lips *(man cannot be trusted in anything he says):*

14 Whose mouth *is* full of cursing *(wishing someone evil or hurt)* and bitterness *(bitter and reproachful language):*

15 Their feet *are* swift to shed blood *(the world is filled with murder, killing, and violence):*

16 Destruction and misery *are* in their ways *(all brought about by sin):*

17 And the way of peace have they not known *(and cannot know until Christ returns):*

18 There is no fear of God before their eyes *(there is no fear of God, because unbelieving man does not know God).*

19 Now we know that what things soever the Law says, it says to them who are under the Law *(is meant first of all to inform the Jews that Verses 10 through 18 apply to them as well as the Gentiles):* that every mouth may be stopped *(the Gentiles were claiming ignorance, while the Jews were claiming exception from Judgment),* and all the world may become guilty before God *(states the case exactly as it is, meaning all need a Saviour).*

20 Therefore by the deeds of the Law there shall no flesh be justified in His sight *(should read, "by works of the Law"):* for by the Law *is* the knowledge of sin *(the Law in itself was only meant to define sin, it in no way delivered from sin, nor was it designed to do so!).*

THE REMEDY

21 But now the Righteousness of God without the Law is manifested *(should read, "apart from Law", i.e., "from works of merit"),* being witnessed by the Law and the Prophets *(Testimony of the Law to the Divine Principle of Justification by Faith is found in Gen. 15:6; the Testimony of the Prophets in Hab. 2:4);*

22 Even the Righteousness of God *which is* by Faith of Jesus Christ *(concerns Imputed Righteousness, and tells how it is obtained)* unto all and upon all them who believe *(the criteria is believing, and believing in Christ and Him Crucified):* for there is no difference *(Salvation is by Faith, whether the person is a Jew or a Gentile):*

23 For all have sinned *(presents all men placed in the same category),* and come short of the Glory of God *(the Greek Text infers that even the most Righteous among us continue to come short of the Glory of God on a continuing basis);*

24 Being justified freely by His Grace *(made possible by the Cross)* through the Redemption that is in Christ Jesus *(carried out at the Cross):*

25 Whom God has set forth *to be* a propitiation *(Atonement or Reconciliation)* through Faith in His Blood *(again, all of this is made possible by the Cross),* to declare His Righteousness for the remission of sins that are past *(refers to all who trusted Christ before He actually came, which covers the entirety of the time from the Garden of Eden to the moment Jesus died on the Cross),* through the forbearance *(tolerance)* of God *(meaning that God tolerated the situation before Calvary, knowing the debt would be fully paid at that time);*

26 To declare, *I say,* at this time His Righteousness *(refers to God's Righteousness which must be satisfied at all time, and is in Christ and only Christ):* that He *(God)* might be just *(not overlooking sin in any manner),* and the Justifier of him which believes in Jesus *(God can justify a believing [although guilty] sinner, and His Holiness not be impacted, providing the sinner's Faith is exclusively in Christ; only in this manner can God be "just" and at the same time "Justify" the sinner).*

27 Where *is* boasting then? *(This refers primarily to the Jews boasting of themselves as a result of the Law of God given to them, but the principle is true for modern Christians as well!)* It is excluded *(not only means that God will not accept such boasting [outside of Christ], but that it actually serves to keep one from Salvation).* By what Law? of works? *(In a sense, this tells us where and how the boasting, God will not accept, originates).* No: but by the Law of Faith *(refers to trust exclusively in Christ and what He did at the Cross; Faith in Christ and Him Crucified is more than a principle; it is a Law, meaning that God will not deviate at all from this proclamation).*

28 Therefore we conclude that a man is justified by Faith *(and only by Faith, with the Cross ever being the Object of such Faith)* without the deeds of the Law *(faith in works is out).*

29 *Is He* the God of the Jews only? *is He* not also of the Gentiles? Yes, of the Gentiles also *(it is one Salvation for all, and all gain this Salvation by Faith):*

30 Seeing *it is* One God, which shall justify

the Circumcision by Faith *(places the Jew on the same level as the Gentile)*, and uncircumcision through faith *(Jews and Gentiles are all saved alike, through Faith in Christ and what Christ has done at the Cross).*

31 Do we then make void the Law *(Law of Moses)* through faith? God forbid: yes, we establish the Law *(the Law ever pointed to Faith in Christ).*

CHAPTER 4
(A.D. 60)
ABRAHAM

WHAT shall we say then that Abraham our father, as pertaining to the flesh, has found? *(Having stated that the Old Testament teaches that God justifies the sinner on the Faith principle as opposed to the merit principle, the Holy Spirit now brings forward Abraham.)*

2 For if Abraham were justified by works *(which he wasn't)*, he has *whereof* to glory; but not before God *(the boasting of Salvation by works, which God will not accept).*

3 For what says the Scripture? Abraham believed God, and it was counted unto him for Righteousness *([Gen. 15:6] if one properly understands this Verse, he properly understands the Bible; Abraham gained Righteousness by simple Faith in God, Who would send a Redeemer into the world [Jn. 8:56]).*

4 Now to him who works *(tries to earn Salvation)* is the reward *(Righteousness)* not reckoned of Grace *(the Grace of God)*, but of debt *(claiming that God owes us something, which He doesn't!).*

5 But to him who works not *(doesn't trust in works for Salvation)*, but believes on Him Who Justifies the ungodly *(through Christ and the Cross)*, his faith is counted for Righteousness *(God awards Righteousness only on the basis of Faith in Christ and His Finished Work).*

6 Even as David *(both Abraham and David were progenitors of the Promised Messiah, and as such they held a unique place in the Faith and veneration of the Work of God)* also describes the blessedness of the man *(a blessed man)*, unto whom God imputes Righteousness without works *(works will never gain the Righteousness of God)*,

7 *Saying*, Blessed *are* they whose iniquities are forgiven *([Ps. 32:1-2] iniquities can only be forgiven by Faith in Christ)*, and whose sins are covered *(the Cross made this possible).*

8 Blessed *is* the man to whom the Lord will

not impute sin *(the Lord will not impute sin to the person who places his Faith solely in Christ and what Christ did at the Cross).*

9 *Comes* this blessedness then upon the Circumcision *only*, or upon the uncircumcision also? *(It comes on all alike!)* for we say that Faith was reckoned to Abraham for Righteousness *(presents Faith alone as the ingredient).*

10 How was it then reckoned? *(This may be the greatest question of all time.)* when he was in Circumcision, or in uncircumcision? Not in Circumcision, but in uncircumcision *(because of his Faith, Abraham was declared Righteous by God before the Covenant of Circumcision [Gen. 15:6]).*

11 And he received the sign of Circumcision *(Gen. 17:9-14)*, a seal of the Righteousness of the Faith which *he had yet* being uncircumcised *(plainly states that his Righteousness was by Faith, and was received long before Circumcision)*: that he might be the father of all them who believe *(Jews and Gentiles)*, though they be not Circumcised *(places the ground or Foundation of Salvation squarely on Faith instead of works)*; that Righteousness might be imputed unto them also *(Righteousness has never been imputed on the ground of works, but always on the ground of Faith)*:

12 And the father of Circumcision to them who are not of the Circumcision only *(presents Abraham as being the father of all Believers, whether Jews or Gentiles)*, but who also walk in the steps of that Faith of our father Abraham *(refers to him simply believing God, and God accounting his Faith to him for Righteousness [Gen. 15:6])*, which *he had* being *yet* uncircumcised *(clinches the argument and opens up Salvation to all who come by Faith in Christ, irrespective as to whom they may be).*

THE PROMISE

13 For the Promise, that he should be the heir of the world, *was* not to Abraham, or to his seed, through the Law *(the Law of Moses, which had not even been given during the time of Abraham)*, but through the Righteousness of Faith *(when Paul uses the word "Faith," without exception, he is speaking of Faith in Christ and what Christ did at the Cross; in fact, Christ must never be separated from the Cross, as it regards His Redemptive Work).*

14 For if they which are of the Law *be* heirs *(only those in the Law)*, faith is made void *(Salvation cannot exist in both works and Faith;*

either one cancels out the other), **and the Promise made of none effect** (faith in works cancels out Christ and all that He has done for us):

15 Because the Law works wrath (Law has a penalty, so it must work wrath): **for where no Law is,** *there is* **no transgression** (Christ has satisfied the Law, thereby, taking away all transgression).

16 Therefore *it is* **of Faith, that** *it might be* **by Grace** (Grace functions only on Faith, and we speak of Faith in Christ; otherwise, Grace stops); **to the end the Promise might be sure to all the seed** (refers to the whole of humanity, at least those who will believe); **not to that only which is of the Law** (Jews), **but to that also which is of the faith of Abraham** (everything is by Faith); **who is the father of us all** (proclaims the Patriarch being used as an example of Faith [Gen. 15:6]),

JUSTIFICATION

17 (**As it is written, I have made you a father of many nations** [Gen. 12:1-3; 17:4-5],) **before Him Whom he believed,** *even* **God** (refers to Abraham believing God), **who quickens the dead** (makes spiritually alive those who are spiritually dead), **and calls those things which be not as though they were** (if God has said it to us personally, we can call it; otherwise, it is presumption).

18 Who against hope believed in hope (a description of Abraham's Faith, as it regarded the birth of Isaac), **that he might become the father of many nations; according to that which was spoken** (the Promise of God), **So shall your seed be** (Gen. 15:5).

19 And being not weak in faith (strong Faith), **he considered not his own body now dead, when he was about an hundred years old** (no longer able to have children), **neither yet the deadness of Sarah's womb** (placed her in the same situation as her husband):

20 He staggered not at the Promise of God through unbelief (he did not allow difficulties to deter him from the intended conclusion); **but was strong in Faith, giving Glory to God** (his Faith came from the Word of God);

21 And being fully persuaded (no turning back) **that, what He** (God) **had Promised, He was able also to perform** (whatever it was, God could do it!).

22 And therefore it was imputed to him for Righteousness (simple Faith in God brought Abraham a spotless Righteousness).

23 Now it was not written for his sake alone (his struggle of Faith was meant to serve as an example), **that it was imputed to him** (serves as the example of how we receive from God, whether it be Salvation or anything else);

24 But for us also, to whom it shall be imputed (we can have that which Abraham had, a perfect Righteousness), **if we believe on Him Who raised up Jesus our Lord from the dead** (proclaims the condition for Salvation);

25 Who was delivered for our offences (had to do with Jesus dying on the Cross for our sins; He had no sins), **and was raised again for our Justification** (we were raised with Him in newness of life [Rom. 6:4-5]).

CHAPTER 5
(A.D. 60)
JUSTIFICATION BY FAITH

THEREFORE being Justified by Faith (this is the only way one can be justified; refers to Faith in Christ and what He did at the Cross), **we have peace with God** (justifying peace) **through our Lord Jesus Christ** (what He did at the Cross):

2 By Whom also we have access by Faith into this Grace (we have access to the Goodness of God by Faith in Christ) **wherein we stand** (wherein alone we can stand), **and rejoice in hope** (a hope that is guaranteed) **of the Glory of God** (our Faith in Christ always brings Glory to God; anything else brings glory to self, which God can never accept).

3 And not only *so,* **but we glory in tribulations also** (in the fact that tribulations do not hurt us): **knowing that tribulation works patience** (points to the characteristic of a man who is unswerved from his deliberate purpose and his loyalty to Faith, even by the greatest trials and sufferings);

4 And patience, experience (points to an end result); **and experience, hope** (presents the natural product of an approved experience).

5 And hope makes not ashamed (in effect, tells us that this is not a false hope); **because the Love of God is shed abroad in our hearts** (God's Love brings all of this about) **by the Holy Spirit which is given unto us** (all of this is wholly a work of the Holy Spirit).

6 For when we were yet without strength (before we were saved), **in due time** (at the appointed time) **Christ died for the ungodly** (the entirety of humanity fell into this category).

7 For scarcely for a Righteous man will one

die (not many would do such): yet peradventure for a good man some would even dare to die (some few might).

8 But God Commendeth His Love toward us (Christ dying for the ungodly is a proof of Love immeasurable), in that, while we were yet sinners, Christ died for us (Jesus died for those who bitterly hate Him).

9 Much more then (if Christ died for us while we were yet sinners, how much more will He do for us now that we are Redeemed and, thereby, reconciled to Him!), being now Justified by His Blood (we are justified now, and the Blood of Christ stands as the guarantee for that Justification), we shall be saved from wrath through Him (the Wrath of God, which is always manifested against sin).

10 For if, when we were enemies, we were reconciled to God by the Death of His Son (the only way we could be reconciled; this Verse shoots down the "Jesus died spiritually doctrine"), much more, being reconciled, we shall be saved by His life (does not speak of His Perfect Life, but rather the pouring out of His Life's Blood at Calvary).

11 And not only so, but we also joy in God through our Lord Jesus Christ (we are to boast of our Reconciliation to God, for it is a true confidence [I Cor. 1:31; II Cor. 10:17]), by Whom we have now received the Atonement (Reconciliation).

ADAM

12 Wherefore, as by one man sin entered into the world (by Adam), and death by sin (both spiritual and physical death); and so death passed upon all men (for all were in Adam), for that all have sinned (all are born in sin, because of Adam's transgression):

13 (For until the Law (Law of Moses) sin was in the world (caused by Adam's Fall): but sin is not imputed when there is no Law (before the Law was given, sin and its immediate Judgment were not imputed to the account of those who were then alive; but by the fact of Adam's Fall, they were still sinners).

14 Nevertheless death reigned from Adam to Moses (because of the sin nature that was in all men due to Adam's Fall), even over them who had not sinned after the similitude of Adam's transgression (irrespective that all did not in essence commit high treason against God, as did Adam, they were still sinners), who is the figure of Him Who was to come (Adam

was the fountainhead of all sin and death, while Christ is the Fountainhead of all Redemption and Life).

CONTRASTS

15 But not as the offence, so also is the free gift (would have probably been better translated, "as the offence, much more the Free Gift"; the "Free Gift" refers to Christ and what He did at the Cross, which addressed all that was lost at the Fall). For if through the offence of one (Adam) many be dead, much more the Grace of God (proclaims the inexhaustible Power of this attribute), and the Gift by Grace (presents Jesus as that "Gift"), which is by One Man, Jesus Christ (what He did at the Cross), has abounded unto many (this "One Man," the Lord Jesus Christ, nullified the offence of the "One Man" Adam).

16 And not as it was by one who sinned, so is the Gift (so much greater is the Gift): for the judgment was by one to condemnation (by Adam), but the Free Gift is of many offences unto Justification (cleanses from all sin).

17 For if by one man's offence death reigned by one (Adam's Fall); much more they which receive abundance of Grace (not just "Grace," but "Abundance of Grace"; all made possible by the Cross) and of the Gift of Righteousness (Righteousness is a Gift from God which comes solely through Jesus Christ, and is received by Faith) shall reign in life by One, Jesus Christ.) (This proclaims the Believer "reigning," even as death had reigned, but from a position of much greater power than that of death.)

18 Therefore as by the offence of one judgment came upon all men to condemnation (Judged by God to be lost); even so by the Righteousness of One (Christ) the Free Gift came upon all men unto Justification of life (received by simply believing in Christ and what He did at the Cross, which is the only answer for sin).

19 For as by one man's disobedience many were made sinners (the "many" referred to all), so by the obedience of One (obedient unto death, even the death of the Cross [Phil. 2:8]) shall many be made Righteous ("many" refers to all who will believe).

20 Moreover the Law entered, that the offence might abound (the Law of Moses, that the offence might be identified). But where sin abounded, Grace did much more abound (where sin increased, Grace super-abounded, and then some on top of that):

21 That as sin has reigned unto death *(sin reigns as an absolute monarch in the being of the unredeemed)*, **even so might Grace reign through Righteousness unto Eternal Life by Jesus Christ our Lord** *(Grace reigns unto Life, but it reigns "through Righteousness," i.e., because of God's Righteous Judgment of sin at Calvary executed in the Person of His Son Jesus Christ)*.

CHAPTER 6
(A.D. 60)
THE CROSS

WHAT **shall we say then?** *(This is meant to direct attention to Rom. 5:20.)* **Shall we continue in sin, that Grace may abound?** *(Just because Grace is greater than sin doesn't mean that the Believer has a license to sin.)*

2 **God forbid** *(presents Paul's answer to the question, "Away with the thought, let not such a thing occur")*. **How shall we, who are dead to sin** *(dead to the sin nature)*, **live any longer therein?** *(This portrays what the Believer is now in Christ.)*

3 **Know you not, that so many of us as were baptized into Jesus Christ** *(plainly says that this Baptism is into Christ and not water [I Cor. 1:17; 12:13; Gal. 3:27; Eph. 4:5; Col. 2:11-13])* **were baptized into His Death?** *(When Christ died on the Cross, in the Mind of God, we died with Him; in other words, He became our Substitute, and our identification with Him in His Death gives us all the benefits for which He died; the idea is that He did it all for us!)*

4 **Therefore we are buried with Him by baptism into death** *(not only did we die with Him, but we were buried with Him as well, which means that all the sin and transgression of the past were buried; when they put Him in the Tomb, they put all of our sins into that Tomb as well)*: **that like as Christ was raised up from the dead by the Glory of the Father, even so we also should walk in newness of life** *(we died with Him, we were buried with Him, and His Resurrection was our Resurrection to a "Newness of Life")*.

5 **For if we have been planted together** *(with Christ)* **in the likeness of His Death** *(Paul proclaims the Cross as the instrument through which all Blessings come; consequently, the Cross must ever be the Object of our Faith, which gives the Holy Spirit latitude to work within our lives)*, **we shall be also** *in the likeness* **of His Resurrection** *(we can have the "likeness of His Resurrection," i.e., "live this Resurrection Life," only as*

long *as we understand the "likeness of His Death," which refers to the Cross as the means by which all of this is done)*:

6 **Knowing this, that our old man is Crucified with** *Him* *(all that we were before conversion)*, **that the body of sin might be destroyed** *(the power of sin broken)*, **that henceforth we should not serve sin** *(the guilt of sin is removed at conversion, because the sin nature no longer rules within our hearts and lives)*.

7 **For he who is dead** *(He was our Substitute, and in the Mind of God, we died with Him upon Believing Faith)* **is freed from sin** *(set free from the bondage of the sin nature)*.

8 **Now if we be dead with Christ** *(once again pertains to the Cross, and our being Baptized into His Death)*, **we believe that we shall also live with Him** *(have Resurrection Life, which is more Abundant Life [Jn. 10:10])*:

9 **Knowing that Christ being raised from the dead dies no more** *(means that His Work was a Finished Work, and will require nothing else)*; **death has no more dominion over Him** *(because all sin has been Atoned; inasmuch as Christ is our Substitute, if death has no more dominion over Him, it has no more dominion over us; this means that the power of the sin nature is broken)*.

10 **For in that He died, He died unto sin** *(the sin nature)* **once** *(actually means, "He died unto the sin nature, once, for all")*: **but in that He lives** *(the Resurrection)*, **He lives unto God** *(refers to the fact that all life comes from God, and that we receive that life by virtue of the Cross and our Faith in that Finished Work)*.

11 **Likewise reckon** *(account)* **you also yourselves to be dead indeed unto** *(the)* **sin** *(while the sin nature is not dead, we are dead unto the sin nature by virtue of the Cross and our Faith in that Sacrifice, but only as long as our Faith continues in the Cross)*, **but alive unto God** *(living the Resurrection Life)* **through Jesus Christ our Lord** *(refers to what He did at the Cross, which is the means of this Resurrection Life)*.

SANCTIFICATION

12 **Let not sin** *(the sin nature)* **therefore reign** *(rule)* **in your mortal body** *(showing that the sin nature can once again rule in the heart and life of the Believer, if the Believer doesn't constantly look to Christ and the Cross; the "mortal body" is neutral, which means it can be used for Righteousness or unrighteousness)*, **that you should obey it in the lusts thereof** *(ungodly lusts*

are carried out through the mortal body, if Faith is not maintained in the Cross [I Cor. 1:17-18]).

13 Neither yield you your members *(of your mortal body)* as instruments of unrighteousness unto sin *(the sin nature)*: but yield yourselves unto God *(we are to yield ourselves to Christ and the Cross; that alone guarantees victory over the sin nature)*, as those who are alive from the dead *(we have been raised with Christ in "Newness of Life")*, and your members *as* instruments of Righteousness unto God *(this can be done only by virtue of the Cross and our Faith in that Finished Work, and Faith which continues in that Finished Work from day-to-day [Lk. 9:23-24])*.

14 For sin shall not have dominion over you *(the sin nature will not have dominion over us if we as Believers continue to exercise Faith in the Cross of Christ; otherwise, the sin nature most definitely will have dominion over the Believer)*: for you are not under the Law *(means that if we try to live this life by any type of law, no matter how good that law might be in its own right, we will conclude by the sin nature having dominion over us)*, but under Grace *(the Grace of God flows to the Believer on an unending basis only as long as the Believer exercises Faith in Christ and what He did at the Cross; Grace is merely the Goodness of God exercised by and through the Holy Spirit, and given to undeserving Saints)*.

15 What then? *(This presents Paul going back to the first question he asked in this Chapter.)* shall we sin, because we are not under the Law, but under Grace? *(If we think such a thing, then we're completely misunderstanding Grace. The Grace of God gives us the liberty to live a Holy life, which we do through Faith in Christ and the Cross, and not license to sin as some think.)* God forbid *(every true Believer hates sin; so the idea of living under its dominion is abhorrent to say the least!)*.

16 Know you not, that to whom you yield yourselves servants to obey, his servants you are to whom you obey *(the Believer is either a slave to Christ, for that's what the word "servant" means, or else a slave to sin, which he will be if he doesn't keep his Faith in Christ and the Cross)*; whether of sin unto death *(once again allow us to state the fact that if the Believer attempts to live for God by any method other than Faith in the Finished Work of Christ, the Believer will fail, no matter how hard he otherwise tries)*, or of obedience unto Righteousness? *(The Believer is required to obey the Word of the Lord. He cannot do that within his own strength, but only by understanding that he receives all things through what Christ did at the Cross and his continued Faith in that Finished Work, even on a daily basis. Then the Holy Spirit, Who Alone can make us what we ought to be, can accomplish His work within our lives.)*

17 But God be thanked, that you were the servants of sin *(slaves to the sin nature, what we were before we were saved)*, but you have obeyed from the heart that form of Doctrine *(Jesus Christ and Him Crucified; understanding that all things come to the Believer from God by the means of the Cross)* which was delivered you *(the Lord gave this "form of Doctrine" to Paul, and he gave it to us in his Epistles)*.

18 Being then made free from sin *(being made free from the sin nature; it has no more power over the Believer, but only as we continue to look to the Cross)*, you became the servants of Righteousness *(whereas you were formerly a slave to the sin nature, you are now a slave to Righteousness; if Faith is maintained in the Cross, there is a constant pull of the Believer toward Righteousness)*.

19 I speak after the manner of men because of the infirmity of your flesh *("the manner of men" pertains to the Fall, which has made the flesh weak; this speaks of our own personal strength and ability)*: for as you have yielded your members servants to uncleanness *(which the Believer will do, if the object of his Faith is anything but the Cross)* and to iniquity unto iniquity *(without constant Faith in the Cross, the Believer's situation regarding sin will get worse and worse)*; even so now yield your members servants to Righteousness unto Holiness *(which, as repeatedly stated, can only be done through constant Faith in the Cross; understanding that it is by and through the Cross that we receive all things, and that the Holy Spirit, Who Alone can develop Righteousness and Holiness in our lives, works exclusively through the Cross)*.

20 For when you were the servants of sin *(slaves to sin)*, you were free from Righteousness *(speaking of our lives before conversion to Christ)*.

21 What fruit had you then in those things whereof you are now ashamed? *(This means that absolutely nothing of any value can come out of the sinful experience. It is impossible for there to be any good fruit.)* for the end of those things *is* death *(if the Believer refuses to look to the Cross, but rather looks to something else regarding his Sanctification, domination by the*

sin nature is going to be the result, and spiritual death will be the conclusion; the Cross is the only answer for sin!).

22 But now *(since coming to Christ)* **being made free from sin** *(set free from the sin nature)*, **and become servants** *(slaves)* **to God** *(but this yoke is a light yoke [Mat. 11:28-30])*, **you have your fruit unto Holiness** *(which the Holy Spirit will bring about, providing the Cross is ever the Object of our Faith)*, **and the end Everlasting Life** *(so the Believer has the choice of "death," which is the end result of trusting something other than Christ and the Cross, or "Everlasting Life," which is the result of trusting Christ and the Cross)*.

23 For the wages of sin *is* **death** *(speaks of spiritual death, which is separation from God)*; **but the Gift of God** *is* **Eternal Life through Jesus Christ our Lord** *(as stated, all of this, without exception, comes to us by the means of what Christ did at the Cross, which demands that the Cross ever be the Object of our Faith, thus giving the Holy Spirit latitude to work within our lives and bring forth His Fruit)*.

CHAPTER 7
(A.D. 60)
THE LAW AND SIN

KNOW ye not, Brethren *(Paul is speaking to Believers)*, **(for I speak to them who know the Law,)** *(he is speaking of the Law of Moses, but it could refer to any type of religious Law)* **how that the Law has dominion over a man as long as he lives?** *(The Law has dominion as long as he tries to live by Law. Regrettably, not understanding the Cross regarding Sanctification, virtually the entirety of the Church is presently trying to live for God by means of the Law. Let the Believer understand that there are only two places he can be, Grace or Law. If he doesn't understand the Cross as it refers to Sanctification, which is the only means of victory, he will automatically be under Law, which guarantees failure.)*

2 For the woman which has an husband is bound by the Law to *her* **husband so long as he lives** *(presents Paul using the analogy of the marriage bond)*; **but if the husband be dead, she is loosed from the Law of** *her* **husband** *(meaning that she is free to marry again)*.

3 So then if, while *her* **husband lives, she be married to another man, she shall be called an adulteress** *(in effect, the woman now has two husbands, at least in the Eyes of God; following*

this analogy, the Holy Spirit through Paul will give us a great truth; many Christians are living a life of spiritual adultery; they are married to Christ, but they are, in effect, serving another husband, "the Law"; it is quite an analogy!)*: **but if her husband be dead** *(the Law is dead by virtue of Christ having fulfilled the Law in every respect)*, **she is free from that Law** *(if the husband dies, the woman is free to marry and serve another; the Law of Moses, being satisfied in Christ, is now dead to the Believer and the Believer is free to serve Christ without the Law having any part or parcel in his life or living)*; **so that she is no adulteress, though she be married to another man** *(presents the Believer as now married to Christ, and no longer under obligation to the Law)*.

4 Wherefore, my Brethren, you also are become dead to the Law *(the Law is not dead per se, but we are dead to the Law because we are dead to its effects; this means that we are not to try to live for God by means of "Law," whether the Law of Moses, or Laws made up by other men or of ourselves; we are to be dead to all Law)* **by the body of Christ** *(this refers to the Crucifixion of Christ, which satisfied the demands of the broken Law we could not satisfy; but Christ did it for us; having fulfilled the Law in every respect, the Christian is not obligated to Law in any fashion, only to Christ and what He did at the Cross)*; **that you should be married to another** *(speaking of Christ)*, *even* **to Him Who is raised from the dead** *(we are raised with Him in newness of life, and we should ever understand that Christ has met, does meet, and shall meet our every need; we look to Him exclusively, referring to what He did for us at the Cross)*, **that we should bring forth fruit unto God** *(proper fruit can only be brought forth by the Believer constantly looking to the Cross; in fact, Christ must never be separated from the Work of the Cross; to do so is to produce "another Jesus" [II Cor. 11:4])*.

5 For when we were in the flesh *(can refer to the unsaved state or to the Believer who is attempting to overcome the powers of sin by his own efforts, i.e., "the flesh")*, **the motions of sins** *(denotes being under the power of the sin nature, and refers to the "passions of the sin nature")*, **which were by the Law** *(the effect of the Law is to reveal sin, which Law is designed to do whether it's the Law of God or Laws made up of ourselves; that doesn't mean its evil, for it isn't; it just means that there is no victory in the Law, only the Revelation of sin and its penalty)*,

did work in our members to bring forth fruit unto death *(when the Believer attempts to live for the Lord by means of Law, which regrettably most of the modern Church does, the end result is going to be sin and failure; in fact, it can be no other way; let us say it again! if the Believer doesn't understand the Cross, as it refers to Sanctification, then the Believer is going to try to live for God by means of Law; the sadness is that most of the modern Church thinks it is under Grace, when in reality it is living under Law because of not understanding the Cross).*

6 But now we are delivered from the Law *(delivered from its just demands, meaning that Christ has paid its penalty),* that being dead *(dead to the Law by virtue of having died with Christ on the Cross)* wherein we were held *(we were once held down by the sin nature);* that we should serve in newness of Spirit *(refers to the Holy Spirit and not man's spirit; the Believer has a completely new way of living, which is Faith in Christ and what He did at the Cross on our behalf; this guarantees perpetual victory),* and not *in* the oldness of the letter *(this refers to the Law of Moses; most modern Believers would argue that they aren't living after the Law of Moses; but, as we have stated, the truth is if they do not understand the Cross as it refers to Sanctification, then in some way they're still living under that old Law).*

THE STRUGGLE AGAINST SIN

7 What shall we say then? *(In Verses 1 through 6 of this Chapter, Paul has shown that the Believer is no longer under Law; in the remainder of the Chapter, he shows that a Believer putting himself under Law, thus failing to avail himself of the resources of Grace, is a defeated Christian.) Is* the Law sin? God forbid *(man's condition is not caused by the Law of God, for the Law is Holy; rather it is exposed).* No, I had not known sin, but by the Law *(means that the Law of Moses defined what sin actually is, but gave no power to overcome sin):* for I had not known lust, except the Law had said, You shall not covet *(tells us that the desire for what is forbidden is the first conscious form of sin; this is the sin nature at work!).*

8 But sin *(the sin nature),* taking occasion by the Commandment, wrought in me all manner of concupiscence *("concupiscence" is "evil desire," meaning, if the Believer attempts to live for God by means other than the Cross, he will be ruled by "evil desires"; and no matter* how dedicated he might be otherwise, he will not be able to stop the process in that manner, with it getting worse and worse).* For without the Law sin *was* dead *(means that the Law of Moses fully exposed what was already in man's heart; that's one of the reasons God gave the Law).*

9 For I was alive without the Law once *(Paul is referring to himself personally and his conversion to Christ; the Law, he states, had nothing to do with that conversion; neither did it have anything to do with his life in Christ):* but when the Commandment came *(having just been saved, and not understanding the Cross of Christ, he tried to live for God by keeping the Commandments through his own strength and power; in his defense, no one else at that time understood the Cross; in fact, the meaning of the Cross, which is actually the meaning of the New Covenant, would be given to Paul),* sin revived *(the sin nature will always, without exception, revive under such circumstances, which results in failure),* and I died *(he was not meaning that he physically died, as would be obvious, but that he died to the Commandment; in other words, he failed to obey no matter how hard he tried; let all Believers understand that if the Apostle Paul couldn't live for God in this manner, neither can you!).*

10 And the Commandment, which *was* ordained to life *(refers to the Ten Commandments),* I found *to be* unto death *(means that the Law revealed the sin, as it always does, and its wages which are death; in other words, there is no victory in trying to live by Law; we are to live by Faith, referring to Faith in Christ and the Cross).*

11 For sin *(the sin nature),* taking occasion by the Commandment *(in no way blames the Commandment, but that the Commandment actually did agitate the sin nature, and brought it to the fore, which it was designed to do),* deceived me *(Paul thought, now that he had accepted Christ, by that mere fact alone he could certainly obey the Lord in every respect; but he found he couldn't, and neither can you, at least in that fashion),* and by it slew *me (despite all of his efforts to live for the Lord by means of Law-keeping, he failed; and again, I say, so will you!).*

12 Wherefore the Law *is* Holy *(points to the fact that it is God's Revelation of Himself; the problem is not in the Law of God, the problem is in us),* and the Commandment Holy, and just, and good *(the Law is like a mirror which shows man what he is, but contains no power to change him).*

13 Was then that which is good made death unto me? God forbid (once again, it is not the Law that is at fault, but rather the sin in man which is opposed to the Law). But sin (the sin nature), that it might appear sin (proclaims the Divine intention of the Law, namely that sin might show its true colors), working death in me by that which is good (the Law was good, and is good, but if one attempts to keep its moral precepts by means other than constant Faith in the Cross, the end result will be the "working of death" instead of life; all of this can be done, but only by Faith in Christ and the Cross); that sin (the sin nature) by the Commandment might become exceeding sinful (this greatly confuses the Believer; he is trying to live for God, and trying with all of his strength and might, but continually fails; he doesn't understand why! the truth is that no one can live for God in this fashion; it is not God's prescribed order; that order is the Cross).

14 For we know that the Law is spiritual (refers to the fact that the Law is totally of God and from God): but I am carnal, sold under sin (refers to Adam's Fall, which has affected all of mankind and for all time; this means that no one, even Spirit-filled Believers, can keep the Law of God if they attempt to do so outside of Faith in the Cross; in other words, it is all in Christ).

15 For that which I do (the failure) I allow not (should have been translated, "I understand not"; these are not the words of an unsaved man, as some claim, but rather a Believer who is trying and failing): for what I would, that do I not (refers to the obedience he wants to render to Christ, but rather fails; why? as Paul explained, the Believer is married to Christ, but is being unfaithful to Christ by spiritually cohabiting with the Law, which frustrates the Grace of God; that means the Holy Spirit will not help such a person, which guarantees failure [Gal. 2:21]); but what I hate, that do I (refers to sin in his life which he doesn't want to do, and in fact hates, but finds himself unable to stop; unfortunately, due to the fact of not understanding the Cross as it refers to Sanctification, this is the plight of most modern Christians).

16 If then I do that which I would not (presents Paul doing something against his will; he doesn't want to do it, and is trying not to do it, whatever it might be, but finds himself doing it anyway), I consent unto the Law that it is good (simply means that the Law of God is working as it is supposed to work; it defines sin, portraying the fact that the sin nature will rule in man's heart if not addressed properly).

17 Now then it is no more I that do it (this has been misconstrued by many! it means, "I may be failing, but it's not what I want to do"; no true Christian wants to sin because now the Divine Nature is in his life and it is supposed to rule, not the sin nature [II Pet. 1:4]), but sin (the sin nature) that dwells in me (despite the fact that some Preachers claim the sin nature is gone from the Christian, Paul here plainly says that the sin nature is still in the Christian; however, if our Faith remains constant in the Cross, the sin nature will be dormant, causing us no problem; otherwise, it will cause great problems; while the sin nature "dwells" in us, it is not to "rule" in us).

18 For I know that in me (that is, in my flesh,) dwells no good thing (speaks of man's own ability, or rather the lack thereof in comparison to the Holy Spirit, at least when it comes to spiritual things): for to will is present with me (Paul is speaking here of his willpower; regrettably, most modern Christians are trying to live for God by means of willpower, thinking falsely that since they have come to Christ, they are now free to say "no" to sin; that is the wrong way to look at the situation; the Believer cannot live for God by the strength of willpower; while the will is definitely important, it alone is not enough; the Believer must exercise Faith in Christ and the Cross, and do so constantly; then he will have the ability and strength to say "yes" to Christ, which automatically says, "no" to the things of the world); but how to perform that which is good I find not (outside of the Cross, it is impossible to find a way to do good).

19 For the good that I would I do not (if I depend on self, and not the Cross): but the evil which I would not (don't want to do), that I do (which is exactly what every Believer will do no matter how hard he tries to do otherwise, if he tries to live this life outside of the Cross [Gal. 2:20-21]).

20 Now if I do that I would not (which is exactly what will happen if the Believer tries to live this life outside of God's Prescribed Order), it is no more I that do it, but sin (the sin nature) that dwells in me (this emphatically states that the Believer has a sin nature; in the original Greek Text, if it contains the definite article before the word "sin" which originally did read "the sin," it is not speaking of acts of sin, but rather the sin nature or the evil nature; the idea is not getting rid of the sin nature, which actually

cannot be done, but rather controlling it, which the Apostle has told us how to do in Rom., Chpts. 6 and 8; when the Trump sounds, we shall be changed and there will be no more sin nature [Rom. 8:23]).

21 I find then a Law *(does not refer in this case to the Law of Moses, but rather to the "Law of sin and death" [Rom. 8:2]),* **that, when I would do good, evil** *(the evil nature)* **is present with me** *(the idea is that the sin nature is always going to be with the Believer; there is no hint in the Greek that its stay is temporary, at least until the Trump sounds; we can successfully address the sin nature in only one way, and that is by Faith in Christ and the Cross, which Paul will detail in the next Chapter).*

22 For I delight in the Law of God *(refers to the moral Law of God ensconced in the Ten Commandments)* **after the inward man** *(refers to the spirit and soul of man which has now been regenerated):*

23 But I see another Law in my members *(the Law of sin and death desiring to use my physical body as an instrument of unrighteousness),* **warring against the Law of my mind** *(this is the Law of desire and willpower),* **and bringing me into captivity to the Law of sin** *(the Law of sin and death)* **which is in my members** *(which will function through my members, and make me a slave to the Law of sin and death; this will happen to the most consecrated Christian if that Christian doesn't constantly exercise Faith in Christ and the Cross, understanding that it is through the Cross that all powers of darkness were defeated [Col. 2:14-15]).*

24 O wretched man that I am! *(Any Believer who attempts to live for God outside of God's Prescribed Order, which is "Jesus Christ and Him Crucified," will in fact live a wretched and miserable existence. This life can only be lived in one way, and that way is the Cross.)* **Who shall deliver me from the body of this death?** *(The minute he cries "Who," he finds the path to Victory, for he is now calling upon a Person for help, and that Person is Christ; actually, the Greek Text is masculine, indicating a Person).*

25 I thank God through Jesus Christ our Lord *(presents Paul revealing the answer to his own question; Deliverance comes through Jesus Christ and Christ Alone, and more particularly what Jesus did at Calvary and the Resurrection).* **So then with the mind I myself serve the Law of God** *(the "will" is the trigger, but it within itself can do nothing unless the gun is loaded with explosive power; that Power is the Cross);*

but with the flesh the Law of sin *(if the Believer resorts to the "flesh," [i.e., "self-will, self-effort, religious effort"] which refers to his own ability outside of Christ and the Cross, he will not serve the Law of God, but rather the Law of sin).*

CHAPTER 8
(A.D. 60)
LIFE IN THE SPIRIT

*T*HERE **is therefore now no condemnation** *(guilt)* **to them which are in Christ Jesus** *(refers back to Rom. 6:3-5 and our being Baptized into His Death, which speaks of the Crucifixion),* **who walk not after the flesh** *(depending on one's personal strength and ability or great religious efforts in order to overcome sin),* **but after the Spirit** *(the Holy Spirit works exclusively within the legal confines of the Finished Work of Christ; our Faith in that Finished Work, i.e., "the Cross," guarantees the help of the Holy Spirit, which guarantees Victory).*

2 For the Law *(that which we are about to give is a Law of God, devised by the Godhead in eternity past [I Pet. 1:18-20]; this Law, in fact, is "God's Prescribed Order of Victory")* **of the Spirit** *(Holy Spirit, i.e., "the way the Spirit works")* **of Life** *(all life comes from Christ, but through the Holy Spirit [Jn. 16:13-14])* **in Christ Jesus** *(any time Paul uses this term or one of its derivatives, he is, without fail, referring to what Christ did at the Cross, which makes this "life" possible)* **has made me free** *(given me total Victory)* **from the Law of Sin and Death** *(these are the two most powerful Laws in the Universe; the "Law of the Spirit of Life in Christ Jesus" alone is stronger than the "Law of Sin and Death"; this means that if the Believer attempts to live for God by any manner other than Faith in Christ and the Cross, he is doomed to failure).*

3 For what the Law could not do, in that it was weak through the flesh *(those under Law had only their willpower, which is woefully insufficient; so despite how hard they tried, they were unable to keep the Law then, and the same inability persists presently; any person who tries to live for God by a system of laws is doomed to failure, because the Holy Spirit will not function in that capacity),* **God sending his own Son** *(refers to man's helpless condition, unable to save himself and unable to keep even a simple Law and, therefore, in dire need of a Saviour)* **in the likeness of sinful flesh** *(this means that Christ was really human, conformed in*

appearance to flesh which is characterized by sin, but yet sinless), **and for sin** *(to atone for sin, to destroy its power, and to save and Sanctify its victims)*, **condemned sin in the flesh** *(destroyed the power of sin by giving His Perfect Body as a Sacrifice for sin, which made it possible for sin to be defeated in our flesh; it was all through the Cross)*:

4 That the Righteousness of the Law might be fulfilled in us *(the Law finding its full accomplishment in us can only be done by Faith in Christ, and what Christ has done for us at the Cross)*, **who walk not after the flesh** *(not after our own strength and ability)*, **but after the Spirit** *(the word "walk" refers to the manner in which we order our life; when we place our Faith in Christ and the Cross, understanding that all things come from God to us by means of the Cross, ever making it the Object of our Faith, the Holy Spirit can then work mightily within us, bringing about the Fruit of the Spirit; that is what "walking after the Spirit" actually means!)*.

5 For they who are after the flesh do mind the things of the flesh *(refers to Believers trying to live for the Lord by means other than Faith in the Cross of Christ)*; **but they who are after the Spirit the things of the Spirit** *(those who place their Faith in Christ and the Cross, do so exclusively; they are doing what the Spirit desires, which alone can bring Victory)*.

CONTRAST

6 For to be carnally minded is death *(this doesn't refer to watching too much Television, as some think, but rather to trying to live for God outside of His Prescribed Order; the results will be sin and separation from God)*; **but to be Spiritually minded is life and peace** *(God's Prescribed Order is the Cross; this demands our constant Faith in that Finished Work, which is the Way of the Holy Spirit)*.

7 Because the carnal mind is enmity against God *(once again, this refers to attempting to live for God by means other than the Cross, which places one "against God")*: **for it is not subject to the Law of God, neither indeed can be** *(in its simplest form means that what is being done, whatever it may be, is not in God's prescribed order, which is the Cross)*.

8 So then they that are in the flesh cannot please God *(refers to the Believer attempting to live his Christian Life by means other than Faith in Christ and the Cross)*.

9 But you are not in the flesh *(in one sense of the word is asking the question, "since you are now a Believer and no longer depending on the flesh, why are you resorting to the flesh?")*, **but in the Spirit** *(as a Believer, you now have the privilege of being led and empowered by the Holy Spirit; however, He will do such for us only on the premise of our Faith in the Finished Work of Christ)*, **if so be that the Spirit of God dwell in you** *(if you are truly saved)*. **Now if any man have not the Spirit of Christ, he is none of His** *(Paul is saying that the work of the Spirit in our lives is made possible by what Christ did at Calvary, and the Resurrection)*.

10 And if Christ be in you *(He is in you through the Power and Person of the Spirit [Gal. 2:20])*, **the body is dead because of sin** *(means that the physical body has been rendered helpless because of the Fall; consequently, the Believer trying to overcome by willpower presents a fruitless task)*; **but the Spirit is life because of Righteousness** *(only the Holy Spirit can make us what we ought to be, which means we cannot do it ourselves; once again, He performs all that He does within the confines of the Finished Work of Christ)*.

11 But if the Spirit *(Holy Spirit)* **of Him** *(from God)* **who raised up Jesus from the dead dwell in you** *(and He definitely does)*, **He who raised up Christ from the dead shall also quicken your mortal bodies** *(give us power in our mortal bodies that we might live a victorious life)* **by His Spirit Who dwells in you** *(we have the same power in us, through the Spirit, that raised Christ from the dead, and is available to us only on the premise of the Cross and our Faith in that Sacrifice)*.

12 Therefore, Brethren *(means that Paul is addressing Believers)*, **we are debtors** *(refers to what we owe Jesus Christ for what He has done for us on the Cross)*, **not to the flesh** *(we do not owe anything to our own ability, meaning that such cannot save us or give us victory)*, **to live after the flesh** *("living after the flesh" pertains to our works, which God can never accept, and which can never bring us victory, but rather defeat)*.

13 For if ye live after the flesh *(after your own strength and ability, which is outside of God's Prescribed Order)*, **you shall die** *(you will not be able to live a victorious, Christian life)*: **but if you through the Spirit** *(by the Power of the Holy Spirit)* **do mortify the deeds of the body** *(which the Holy Spirit Alone can do)*, **you shall live** *(shall walk in victory; but once again, even at the risk of being overly repetitive, we*

must never forget that the Spirit works totally and completely within the confines of the Cross of Christ; this means that we must ever make the Cross the Object of our Faith, giving Him latitude to work).

DELIVERANCE

14 For as many as are led by the Spirit of God *(the Spirit will always lead us to the Cross)*, they are the sons of God *(we live as sons of God, which refers to total victory within every respect of our lives; if the sin nature is dominating a person, he certainly isn't living as a son of God).*

15 For you have not received the spirit of bondage *(to try to live after a system of works and laws will only succeed in placing one in "bondage")* again to fear *(such living creates a perpetual climate of fear in the heart of such a Believer)*; but you have received the Spirit of Adoption *(the Holy Spirit has adopted us into the Family of God)*, whereby we cry, Abba, Father *(the Holy Spirit enables the Child of God to call God "Father," which is done so because of Jesus Christ).*

16 The Spirit itself *(Himself)* bears witness with our spirit *(means that He is constantly speaking and witnessing certain things to us)*, that we are the Children of God *(meaning that we are such now, and should enjoy all the privileges of such; we can do so if we will understand that all these privileges come to us from God, by the means of the Cross)*:

17 And if children *(Children of God)*, then heirs *(a privilege)*; heirs of God *(the highest enrichment of all)*, and joint-heirs with Christ *(everything that belongs to Christ belongs to us through the Cross, which was done for us)*; if so be that we suffer with *Him (doesn't pertain to mere suffering, but rather suffering "with Him," referring to His suffering at the Cross which brought us total victory)*, that we may be also glorified together *(He has been glorified, and we shall be glorified; all made possible by the Cross).*

18 For I reckon that the sufferings of this present time *(speaks of the world and its condition because of the Fall)* are not worthy *to be compared* with the glory *(the glory of the coming future time will bear no relation to the misery of this present time)* which shall be revealed in us *(our glory will be a reflective glory, coming from Christ).*

19 For the earnest expectation of the creature *(should have been translated, "for the earnest expectation of the Creation")* waits for the manifestation of the sons of God *(pertains to the coming Resurrection of Life).*

20 For the creature *(Creation)* was made subject to vanity *(Adam's Fall signaled the fall of Creation)*, not willingly *(the Creation did not sin, even as such cannot sin, but became subject to the result of sin which is death)*, but by reason of Him Who has subjected *the same* in Hope *(speaks of God as the One Who passed sentence because of Adam's Fall, but at the same time gave us a "Hope"; that "Hope" is Christ, Who will rectify all things),*

21 Because the creature *(Creation)* itself also shall be delivered *(presents this "Hope" as effecting that Deliverance, which He did by the Cross)* from the bondage of corruption *(speaks of mortality, i.e., "death")* into the glorious liberty of the Children of God *(when man fell, Creation fell! when man shall be delivered, Creation will be delivered as well, and is expressed in the word "also").*

22 For we know that the whole Creation *(everything has been affected by Satan's rebellion and Adam's Fall)* groans and travails in pain together until now *(refers to the common longing of the elements of the Creation to be brought back to their original perfection).*

23 And not only *they (the Creation, and all it entails)*, but ourselves also *(refers to Believers)*, which have the Firstfruits of the Spirit *(even though Jesus addressed every single thing lost in the Fall at the Cross, we only have a part of that possession now, with the balance coming at the Resurrection)*, even we ourselves groan within ourselves *(proclaims the obvious fact that all Jesus paid for in the Atonement has not yet been fully realized)*, waiting for the Adoption *(should be translated, "waiting for the fulfillment of the process, which Adoption into the Family of God guarantees")*, *to wit*, the Redemption of our body *(the glorifying of our physical body that will take place at the Resurrection).*

24 For we are saved by hope *(means that the greater part of our Salvation is yet future)*: but hope that is seen is not hope *(proclaims in another way the great Truth that all Salvation affords is not yet given unto the Believer)*: for what a man sees, why does he yet hope for? *(In effect, this bluntly tells us that what is coming is so far beyond that which is here at the present, as to be no comparison.)*

25 But if we hope for that we see not *(plainly*

tells us that more, much more, is coming), **then do we with patience wait for** *it (proclaims the certitude of its coming, because the Holy Spirit has promised it would).*

26 Likewise the Spirit *(Holy Spirit)* **also helps our infirmities** *(the help given to us by the Holy Spirit is made possible in its entirety by and through what Jesus did at the Cross):* **for we know not what we should pray for as we ought** *(signals the significance of prayer, but also that without the Holy Spirit, all is to no avail):* **but the Spirit itself** *(Himself)* **makes intercession for us** *(He petitions or intercedes on our behalf)* **with groanings which cannot be uttered** *(not groanings on the part of the Holy Spirit, but rather on our part, which pertains to that which comes from the heart and cannot properly be put into words).*

27 And He Who searches the hearts *(God the Father)* **knows what** *is* **the Mind of the Spirit** *(what the Spirit wants done, and not what we want done),* **because He** *(Holy Spirit)* **makes intercession for the Saints according to** *the Will of* **God** *(the overriding goal of the Spirit is to carry out the Will of God in our lives, not our personal wills; in other words, the Spirit is not a glorified bellhop).*

CONQUERORS

28 And we know that all things work together for good *(but only if certain conditions are met)* **to them who love God** *(the first condition),* **to them who are the called according to** *His* **purpose** *(this means it's "His Purpose, and not ours," which is the second condition; otherwise, all things will not work together for our good).*

29 For whom He *(God)* **did foreknow** *(God's foreknowledge),* **He also did predestinate** *to be* **conformed to the Image of His Son** *(it is never the person that is predestined, but rather the Plan),* **that He** *(Jesus)* **might be the First-born among many Brethren** *(doesn't mean that Jesus was Born-Again as a sinner, as some teach, but rather that He is the Father of the Salvation Plan, having paid the price on the Cross, which made it all possible).*

30 Moreover whom He *(God)* **did predestinate** *(to be conformed to the Image of His Son),* **them He also called** *(without that "Call," man cannot be saved; sadly, many refuse the "Call" [Prov. 1:24-33]):* **and whom He called, them He also justified** *(those who responded faithfully to the Call):* **and whom He justified, them**

He also glorified *(shall glorify at the Resurrection; Justification guarantees it will be done).*

31 What shall we then say to these things? *(This refers to the suffering presently endured [Vss. 17-18] in comparison to "the Glory which shall be revealed in us.")* **If God** *be* **for us** *(should have been translated, "since God is for us"),* **who** *can be* **against us?** *(It is who can be against us that will really matter.)*

32 He Who spared not His Own Son *(concerns the Great Gift of God, i.e., the Lord Jesus Christ),* **but delivered Him up for us all** *(the Cross),* **how shall He not with Him also freely give us all things?** *(We can have all things that pertain to Life and Godliness, which Jesus paid for at the Cross, providing our Faith is ever in Christ and the Cross [II Pet. 1:3-7].)*

33 Who shall lay any thing to the charge of God's elect? *(In effect, means, "Who shall pronounce those guilty whom God pronounces Righteous?")* **It is God who justifies** *(it is God Who sets the rules for Justification, not man).*

34 Who is he who condemns? *(No man has the right to condemn God's Justification Plan.)* **It** *is* **Christ Who died** *(if one condemns a Believer who is trusting Christ solely for Justification and Sanctification, he is at the same time condemning Christ and His Death on the Cross),* **yea rather, Who is risen again** *(the Resurrection ratified the fact that Jesus was the Perfect Sacrifice, and that God accepted Him as such),* **Who is even at the Right Hand of God** *(refers to the exaltation of Christ),* **Who also makes intercession for us** *(at the Right Hand of God, showing that His Sacrifice has been accepted, which guarantees intercession for us).*

35 Who shall separate us from the Love of Christ? *(This speaks of the Love of Christ for the Believer, instead of the Believer's Love for Christ.)* *shall* **tribulation, or distress, or persecution, or famine, or nakedness, or peril, or sword?** *(We are protected against all outside influence, but not from ourselves. If a person so desires, he can separate himself from the Love of Christ by rejecting the Cross.)*

36 As it is written *(Ps. 44:22),* **For Your sake we are killed all the day long** *(the world has always been opposed to Christ and what He did at the Cross; regrettably, so is most of the Church);* **we are accounted as sheep for the slaughter** *(the way the world looks at us; in their eyes, we are fit only for slaughter).*

37 Nay, in all these things we are more than conquerors *(it is a Holy arrogance of Victory and the Might of Christ)* **through Him Who**

loved us (*He loved us enough to give His Life on the Cross, which alone makes us "more than conquerors"*).

38 For I am persuaded (*the Apostle has faced the things of which He now speaks*), that neither death, nor life, nor Angels, nor principalities, nor powers, nor things present, nor things to come,

39 Nor height, nor depth, nor any other creature, shall be able to separate us from the Love of God, which is in Christ Jesus our Lord (*this Love of God extended to us is made possible solely by Christ, and what He has done for us at the Cross; once again, this is God's Love for us, which never wavers because we are "in Christ Jesus"*).

CHAPTER 9
(A.D. 60)
REJECTION

I say the Truth in Christ, I lie not (*Paul refutes the accusation in preaching to the Gentiles; he is not animated by hostility to the Jews*), my conscience also bearing me witness in the Holy Spirit (*his own spirit is exactly in tune with the Holy Spirit*),

2 That I have great heaviness and continual sorrow in my heart (*grieving over the plight of the Israel of his day; they were in this state because they rejected Christ and the Cross; regrettably, the Church, with some exceptions, is doing the same*).

3 For I could wish that myself were accursed from Christ for my Brethren (*presents a moot point, for such is impossible*), my kinsmen according to the flesh (*Jews*):

4 Who are Israelites (*God's chosen People, yet who rejected the Lord*); to whom *pertains* the Adoption (*refers to the selection of Israel to be God's peculiar People [Ex. 19:5]*), and the glory (*refers to the Divine Presence which was always with them, at least until they rejected God [Ex. 16:7, 10; 24:16-17; Lev. 9:6; Num. 14:10, 21; Deut. 5:24]*), and the Covenants (*various Covenants God made with Israel, such as the Abrahamic, first of all promising Salvation by Faith [Gen. 15:6]*), and the giving of the Law (*the Mosaic Law*), and the service *of* God (*Tabernacle, offerings, Priesthood, etc.*), and the Promises (*the Messianic Promises*);

5 Whose *are* the fathers (*refers basically to Abraham, Isaac, and Jacob*), and of whom as concerning the flesh Christ *came* (*through the Jews*), Who is over all (*the very purpose of Israel*

was to bring the Redeemer into the world*), God blessed forever (*Jesus is the Redeemer, Who is God*). Amen (*Truth*).

6 Not as though the Word of God has taken none effect (*even though Israel failed, the Word of God didn't fail; the Redeemer came*). For they *are* not all Israel, which are of Israel (*is meant to denounce national Salvation; in other words, one is not saved just because he is an Israelite*):

7 Neither, because they are the seed of Abraham, *are they* all children (*further debunks the nationalistic Salvation theory*): but, In Isaac shall your seed be called (*Ishmael was not included, even though a son of Abraham; this means that all works of the flesh are rejected*).

THE DISTINCTION

8 That is, They which are the children of the flesh, these *are* not the Children of God (*are not Children of God merely because they are Jews*): but the Children of the Promise are counted for the seed (*those who believe in "the Promise," Who is Christ*).

9 For this *is* the Word of Promise (*pertains to Faith, not works*), At this time will I come, and Sarah shall have a son (*Abraham is not the principle figure, neither is Sarah or Isaac for that matter; only the "Promise," which would ultimately figure into Christ*).

10 And not only *this* (*he will now give another example*); but when Rebecca also had conceived by one, *even* by our father Isaac (*Paul further shoots down the idea of nationalistic Salvation, as we shall see*);

11 (For *the children* being not yet born, neither having done any good or evil (*refers to Esau and Jacob, who were twins*), that the purpose of God according to election might stand (*speaks of God's foreknowledge*), not of works, but of Him Who calls;) (*This pronounces the entire basis of God's dealings with men and His manner of operation.*)

12 It was said unto her (*refers to the Lord speaking to Rebecca, found in Gen. 25:23*), The Elder shall serve the younger (*in the spiritual analysis, the Sin Nature, which is the oldest in the Believer because the Believer is born with such, will serve the Divine Nature, which is younger; that is, if the Believer properly follows Christ*).

13 As it is written (*Mal. 1:2-3*), Jacob have I loved, but Esau have I hated (*was not done capriciously; God did not indiscriminately love Jacob, nor did He indiscriminately hate Esau;*

both passions, love and hate, were based on the attitudes of both men toward God).

14 What shall we say then? *(This is meant to counter the claim that God was unfair in His Disposition toward Jacob and Esau.)* **Is there unrighteousness with God? God forbid** *(there is no unrighteousness with God, Who, through foreknowledge, sees the attitude of both these boys and judges accordingly).*

15 For He said to Moses, I will have Mercy on whom I will have Mercy, and I will have Compassion on whom I will have Compassion *([Ex. 33:19] God has Mercy and Compassion on those who meet His Conditions).*

16 So then it is not of him who wills, nor of him who runs *(Mercy and Compassion cannot be earned or merited by the sinner; consequently, this completely rules out a "works" Salvation),* **but of God Who shows Mercy** *(God shows Mercy on the basis of man's acceptance of Christ and the Cross; otherwise, there is no Mercy).*

17 For the Scripture said unto Pharaoh *(Ex. 9:16),* **Even for this same purpose have I raised you up** *(presents the Lord using what is available, but not forcing the issue; in other words, God did not predestine Pharaoh to take a position of rebellion, leaving him having no choice in the matter),* **that I might show My Power in you, and that My Name might be declared throughout all the earth** *(as stated, God used the stubbornness of Pharaoh, which was Pharaoh's own choice, to glorify His Name — God's Name).*

18 Therefore has He Mercy on whom He will *have Mercy (God will always have Mercy on those who meet His Conditions),* **and whom He will He hardens** *(stubbornness towards God will be met with God forcing the issue by providing the setting which will make the heart even harder; in other words, if one wants hardness, one will get hardness).*

JUSTICE AND MERCY

19 You will say then unto me *(Paul knows the argument of the Jews),* **Why does He yet find fault?** *(Why does God find fault with man?)* **For who has resisted His Will?** *(Untold numbers have resisted His Will, but never with success!)*

20 No but, O man, who are you who replies against God? *(Man finds fault with God!)* **Shall the thing formed say to Him Who formed it, Why have you made me thus?** *(Man wants to blame God for his predicament!)*

21 Has not the potter power over the clay *(God is likened to a "Potter"),* **of the same lump to make one vessel unto honour, and another unto dishonour?** *(He has the power to make it possible for man to choose honor or dishonor. The fault is never with God, but always with man. God is not to blame simply because He gives man the power of choice, and man chooses the way of dishonor!)*

22 What if God, willing to show his wrath, and to make His power known *(in effect, is saying, inasmuch as there are vessels of dishonor; there is a Divine necessity that God should demonstrate the Power of His Wrath, as well as the riches of His Mercy),* **endured with much long-suffering the vessels of wrath fitted to destruction** *(those who choose dishonor will ultimately be destroyed, but God in His longsuffering will bear long with them, even though He knows beforehand their fate):*

23 And that He might make known the riches of His Glory on the Vessels of Mercy *(pertains to those, whether Jews or Gentiles, who accept the "riches of His Glory" unto Salvation),* **which He had afore prepared unto Glory** *(doesn't mean that God predestined these for Salvation, but does mean that those who accepted His Mercy and Grace would be "prepared unto Glory"),*

24 Even us, whom He has called *(God initiates the Call, but regrettably many, if not most, refuse),* **not of the Jews only, but also of the Gentiles?** *(The Lord had always intended that the Gentiles be included as well.)*

25 As He said also in Hosea *(Hos. 2:23),* **I will call them My people, which were not My people; and her beloved, which was not beloved** *(is used by Paul in the context of the Gentiles, even though it was originally meant for the Jews).*

26 And it shall come to pass, that in the place where it was said unto them *(Hos. 1:9-10),* **You are not My people; there shall they be called the Children of the Living God** *(once again, the Apostle is taking a Passage that was given exclusively to Israel, and broadening it in order that it cover the Gentiles).*

27 Isaiah also cried concerning Israel *(Isa. 10:22),* **Though the number of the Children of Israel be as the sand of the sea, a remnant shall be saved** *(despite the vast number of Israelites down through the many centuries, only a small number were actually saved; it is the same in the modern Church):*

28 For He will finish the work *(which He did at the Cross),* **and cut it short in Righteousness**

(God's Righteousness demands such! however, what is short to Him is not necessarily short to mankind): because a short work will the Lord make upon the earth (by comparison to Eternity, the six thousand years we have now seen constitute a short time).

29 And as Isaiah said before (Isa. 1:9), Except the Lord of Sabaoth (the Lord of Hosts) had left us a seed (the Remnant), we had been as Sodom, and been made like unto Gomorrha (completely destroyed).

30 What shall we say then? (Paul wants to say something good about the spiritual condition of the Jews, but finds there is nothing good to say.) That the Gentiles, which followed not after Righteousness (has reference to the fact that these Pagans did not pursue after God or Righteousness, of which their history is replete; they were idol worshippers), have attained to Righteousness (because they accepted Christ), even the Righteousness which is of Faith (Faith in Christ and what He did at the Cross, which Israel rejected).

31 But Israel, which followed after the Law of Righteousness (presents Israel following in the wrong way, by works), has not attained to the Law of Righteousness (couldn't attain to Righteousness by works; it can only be attained by trusting in Christ and the Cross).

32 Wherefore? (Why?) Because they sought it not by faith (proper Faith can only be exercised by accepting Christ and the Cross, which Israel rejected), but as it were by the works of the Law (by their performance, which can never measure up). For they stumbled at that stumblingstone (presents the necessity of Faith in the Lord Jesus Christ, the One Whom all the Sacrifices had symbolized);

33 As it is written (Isa. 8:14), Behold, I lay in Sion (Israel) a stumblingstone and rock of offence (refers to Jesus Christ; He was not the type of Saviour they wanted; they needed Salvation from sin, but they wanted something else): and whosoever believes on Him shall not be ashamed (portrays that Salvation is open to all, not a select predestined few, as many teach).

CHAPTER 10
(A.D. 60)
ISRAEL

BRETHREN, my heart's desire and prayer to God for Israel is, that they might be saved (Israel, as a nation, wasn't saved, despite their history; what an indictment!).

2 For I bear them record that they have a zeal of God (should read, "for God"; they had a zeal which had to do with God as its object), but not according to knowledge (pertains to the right kind of knowledge).

3 For they being ignorant of God's Righteousness (spells the story not only of ancient Israel, but almost the entirety of the world, and for all time; "God's Righteousness" is that which is afforded by Christ, and received by exercising Faith in Him and what He did at the Cross, all on our behalf; Israel's ignorance was willful!), and going about to establish their own righteousness (the case of anyone who attempts to establish Righteousness by any method other than Faith in Christ and the Cross), have not submitted themselves unto the Righteousness of God (God's Righteousness is ensconced in Christ and what He did at the Cross).

4 For Christ is the end of the Law for Righteousness (Christ fulfilled the totality of the Law) to everyone who believes (Faith in Christ guarantees the Righteousness which the Law had, but could not give).

RIGHTEOUSNESS

5 For Moses described the Righteousness which is of the Law (tells us plainly that the Law did contain Righteousness, but Righteousness to which man could not attain due to his fallen condition), That the man which does these things shall live by them (Paul is saying that no matter how hard a person tries to render perfect obedience, he will not be able to).

6 But the Righteousness which is of Faith speaks on this wise (will proclaim the wonderful and beautiful simplicity found only in Christ), Say not in your heart, Who shall ascend into Heaven? (that is, to bring Christ down from above:) (For one to be saved, one does not have to perform some great task such as bring Christ down in Person from Heaven. As we shall see, God's Word is enough.)

7 Or, Who shall descend into the deep? (That is, to bring up Christ again from the dead.) (Christ does not need to be brought down from Heaven or up from the abyss to impart to the sinner forgiveness and Holiness. The Christian Message contains no impossibilities.)

8 But what does it say? (In other words, it says how to be saved!) The Word is near you (the Word of God), even in your mouth (speaks of the confession which must come from the mouth in order for one to be saved, even as Paul

will say in the next Verse), **and in your heart** *(proclaims the part of man in which Faith begins):* **that is, the Word of Faith, which we preach** *(presents the declaration by Paul that Justification is on the Faith-Principle, as opposed to the Works-Principle; it speaks of Faith in Christ and what He did at the Cross; in other words, every Preacher should "Preach Christ and Him Crucified");*

HOW TO RECEIVE

9 **That if you shall confess with your mouth the Lord Jesus** *(confess that Jesus is the Lord of Glory, and the Saviour of men, and that He died on the Cross that we might be saved),* **and shall believe in your heart that God has raised Him from the dead** *(pertains to the Bodily Resurrection of Christ, as is obvious),* **you shall be saved** *(it is that simple!).*

10 **For with the heart man believes unto Righteousness** *(presents the word "believing" in a mode of "thinking," not of feeling; the "believing" has to do with believing Christ, and that His Sacrifice of Himself Atoned for all sin);* **and with the mouth confession is made unto Salvation** *(when Faith comes forth from its silence to announce itself and proclaim the Glory and the Grace of the Lord, its voice "is confession").*

11 **For the Scripture says** *(combining parts of Isa. 28:16 with 49:23),* **Whosoever believes on Him** *(proclaims the fact that Salvation is reachable by all)* **shall not be ashamed** *(in essence says, "shall not be put to shame," but rather will receive what is promised).*

12 **For there is no difference between the Jew and the Greek** *(should read, "between the Jew and the Gentile"; all must come the same way, which is by and through Christ and what He did at the Cross on our behalf):* **for the same Lord over all is rich unto all who call upon Him** *(the riches of Grace will be given to all who truly call upon the Lord).*

13 **For whosoever** *(anyone, anywhere)* **shall call upon the Name of the Lord shall be saved** *(speaks of the sinner coming to Christ, but can refer to any Believer and with whatever need; the Cross is the means by which all of this is done).*

14 **How then shall they call on Him in Whom they have not believed?** *(The great sin of mankind is the sin of "unbelief.")* **and how shall they believe in Him of Whom they have not heard?** *(Ignorance is not Salvation. It is the business of the Church to take the Gospel to the world.)* **and how shall they hear without a Preacher?** *(This reveals God's Method of proclaiming His Message.)*

15 **And how shall they Preach, except they be sent?** *(Those who send the Preacher are just as important as the Preacher.)* **as it is written** *(Isa. 52:7),* **How beautiful are the feet of them who Preach the Gospel of Peace** *(presents the Message which, if accepted, will make things right between the sinner and God),* **and bring glad tidings** *(Good News)* **of good things!** *(It's all made possible by the Cross.)*

16 **But they have not all obeyed the Gospel** *(all who hear the Gospel will not heed the Gospel).* **For Isaiah said, Lord, who has believed our report?** *([Isa. 53:1] despite the fact of Who Christ was and what He did, only a few accepted Him as the Messiah.)*

17 **So then Faith** *comes* **by hearing** *(it is the publication of the Gospel which produces Faith in it),* **and hearing by the Word of God** *(Faith does not come simply hearing just anything, but rather by hearing God's Word, and believing that Word).*

NO EXCUSE

18 **But I say, Have they not heard?** *(This proclaims Paul bringing the subject matter back to the Jews.)* **Yes verily, their sound went into all the earth, and their words unto the ends of the world** *(plainly proclaims the fact that Israel knew about Christ, and rejected Him anyway).*

19 **But I say, Did not Israel know?** *(There was no excuse for Israel not to know. They had the Word of God for their guide.)* **First Moses said** *(Deut. 32:21),* **I will provoke you to jealousy by** *them who are* **no people,** *and* **by a foolish nation I will anger you** *(some 1,600 years before Paul's day, Moses Prophesied the acceptance of the Gospel by the Gentiles).*

20 **But Isaiah is very bold, and said** *(Isa. 65:1-2),* **I was found of them who sought Me not; I was made manifest unto them who asked not after Me** *(as Moses, the Prophet Isaiah predicted that the Gentiles would hear and receive the Gospel).*

21 **But to Israel He said, All day long I have stretched forth My hands unto a disobedient and gainsaying people** *(by their rejection of Christ and the Cross, the majority of Israel fashioned themselves into vessels of wrath through their self-will and unbelief; is the Church presently doing the same?)*

CHAPTER 11
(A.D. 60)
GOD'S PURPOSE

I say then, Has God cast away His people? *(This is phrased in the Greek Text so that it requires a negative answer.)* God forbid. For I also am an Israelite, of the seed of Abraham, *of* the Tribe of Benjamin *("Israelite" is the most august title of the three names).*

2 God has not cast away His people which He foreknew *(refers to Israel as a Nation, and the many Promises made respecting the future of these ancient people).* Do you not know what the Scripture says of Elijah? *(I Ki. 19:10, 14)* how he makes intercession to God against Israel, saying *(carries the thought that the Prophet should have pleaded for Israel, not against Israel),*

3 Lord, they have killed your Prophets, and dug down your Altars *(the true worship of God at that time was forsaken, and in its place idols were substituted [I Ki. 12:28-33]);* and I am left alone, and they seek my life *(in fact, Elijah was not alone, even as we shall see).*

4 But what was the answer of God unto him? I have reserved to myself seven thousand men, who have not bowed the knee to *the image of* Baal *(this tells us that True Faith always has the attachment of spiritual action).*

A REMNANT

5 Even so then at this present time *(Paul's day)* also there is a Remnant according to the election of Grace *(definitely speaks of Predestination, but not as many think; it is the "Remnant" that is elected or predestined, not who will be in the Remnant).*

6 And if by Grace *(the Goodness of God, all made possible by the Cross),* then *is it* no more of works *(no one can point to their works as grounds for Salvation):* otherwise Grace is no more Grace *(if works are mixed with Grace, they nullify Grace).* But if *it be* of works, then is it no more Grace *(works can never produce Grace):* otherwise work is no more work *(for example, Water Baptism, if acted upon wrongly, nullifies its true meaning; this holds true as well for all other great Ordinances of the Lord).*

REBELLION AND UNBELIEF

7 What then? *(This was asked regarding Israel, but can also apply to the Church as well!)* Israel has not obtained that for which he seeks *(emphatically states that Salvation cannot be obtained in any manner or way other than God's Way, which is the Cross);* but the election has obtained it *(refers to the Jews who did not attempt to claim Salvation by Merit, but rather by Grace),* and the rest were blinded *(refers to a judicial blindness).*

8 (According as it is written *(Isa. 29:10),* God has given them the spirit of slumber *(that's what they wanted, so that's what they got!),* eyes that they should not see, and ears that they should not hear;) *(This refers to not being able to "see" even though the evidence is plainly visible, or to "hear" even though the words are plainly spoken.)* unto this day *(refers to a condition that will not correct itself, but will actually grow worse).*

9 And David said *(Ps. 69:22),* Let their table be made a snare *(refers to their prosperity),* and a trap *(pertains to the end result of the "snare"),* and a stumblingblock *(Israel stumbled over the very blessings which were intended for her betterment),* and a recompence unto them *(a negative end result):*

10 Let their eyes be darkened, that they may not see *(they didn't want to "see," so the Lord gave them what they wanted),* and bow down their back always *(refers to them coming under the burden of captivity, which is exactly what happened).*

GENTILES

11 I say then, Have they stumbled that they should fall? *(Never to rise again?)* God forbid: but *rather* through their fall Salvation *is come* unto the Gentiles *(is another manner of expressing the formation or building of the Church),* for to provoke them to jealousy *(harks back to the Prophecy of Noah after the flood, "God shall enlarge Japheth [Gentiles], and he shall dwell in the tents of Shem," i.e., "Israel"; Japheth will receive the blessings intended for Shem, which is exactly what has happened [Gen. 9:26-27]).*

12 Now if the fall of them *be* the riches of the world *(the idea is that their Fall did not stop the Gospel from coming to the world; the manner of the translation makes it seem as if the world has been greatly enriched by the Fall of Israel; however, that is not the case!),* and the diminishing of them the riches of the Gentiles *(the Blessings that were supposed to go to Israel came to the Gentiles, and we speak of the Church,*

i.e., "The True Church"); how much more their fulness? *(In this one question, Paul implies Israel's rightful place in the Kingdom of God yet to come, which will then bring everything into line, with Israel being the great Blessing that God always intended.)*

13 For I speak to you Gentiles *(it speaks of nations which are distinct from Israel),* inasmuch as I am the Apostle of the Gentiles *(speaks of Paul's special Calling by the Lord),* I magnify my office *(the Office of the Apostle, which refers to the Message of Grace that would affect every Believer):*

14 If by any means I may provoke to emulation *them which are* my flesh, and might save some of them *(Paul hoped Israel might see the Blessings of the Lord on the Gentiles, and, desiring those Blessings, accept Christ and, thereby, be saved).*

15 For if the casting away of them *be the* reconciling of the world *(refers to the Act of God in setting Israel aside temporarily as a channel through which to bring the Good News of Salvation to the world, and in their place the substitution of the Church),* what *shall* the receiving *of them be,* but life from the dead? *(All of this is with a view to bringing Israel back into fellowship with Himself and service in the coming Millennium. Their conversion is likened to a Resurrection.)*

16 For if the Firstfruit *be* Holy *(refers to the Patriarchs of Israel, who were Abraham, Isaac, and Jacob),* the lump *is* also *Holy (does not refer to personal attributes, but simply that Israel has been Called of God, and set apart by God for a special task which will ultimately be performed):* and if the root *be* Holy, so *are* the branches *(this pertains to their work, their reason for being; they are even <u>now</u> in the beginning stages of being brought back "from the dead").*

17 And if some of the branches be broken off *(not all the branches, but some; referring to the fact that Israel will ultimately be brought back),* and you *(refers to the Church, i.e., "the Gentiles"),* being a wild olive tree *(inferior),* were grafted in among them *(presents the inferior being grafted into the superior, which is totally against nature),* and with them partake of the root and fatness of the olive tree *(means that the Church derives its life from the common Root that was originally given to Israel of long ago);*

18 Boast not against the branches *(the Church has not replaced Israel in the Plan of God, even though the Church is included in the Plan of God due to Israel's rejection of Christ).* But if you boast, you bear not the root, but the root you *(as stated, the Church was grafted in, and is built upon the Promises originally given to Israel, which still apply to Israel and one day will be fulfilled).*

19 You will say then, The branches were broken off, that I might be grafted in *(the Church must ever know and understand that it was and is second choice).*

20 Well; because of unbelief they *(Israel)* were broken off *(unbelief respecting Christ and the Cross),* and you stand by Faith *(proclaims that the Church was brought in because of Faith and not merit, and stands in its present position by Faith and not merit).* Be not highminded, but fear *(the reason is given in the next Verse):*

21 For if God spared not the natural branches *(Israel),* *take heed* lest He also spare not you *(again refers to the Church, as is obvious).*

22 Behold therefore the goodness and severity of God *(don't mistake the Goodness of God for license):* on them which fell, severity *(speaks of Judgment which came on Israel, God's chosen People);* but toward you, goodness, if you continue in *His* Goodness *(proclaims the condition; the continuing of that "Goodness" pertains to continued Faith in Christ and the Cross):* otherwise you also shall be cut off *(is the modern Church on the edge of that even now? Rev. 3:15-22 tells us this is the case!).*

23 And they also *(Israel),* if they abide not still in unbelief, shall be grafted in *(Israel's unbelief will end at the Second Coming):* for God is able to graft them in again *(and that He will do!).*

24 For if you were cut out of the olive tree which is wild by nature *(refers to the Gentile world, and in this case the Church),* and were grafted contrary to nature into a good olive tree *(the inferior into the superior):* how much more shall these, which be the natural *branches,* be grafted into their own olive tree? *(Israel failed, but the Plan did not fail. Israel will ultimately be brought back and will Evangelize the world as originally planned. This will take place in the coming Kingdom Age [Isa. 66:19].)*

RESTORATION

25 For I would not, Brethren, that you should be ignorant of this mystery *(what has happened to Israel),* lest you should be wise in your own conceits *(the Gentiles were not pulled in because of any merit or Righteousness on their part, but strictly because of the Grace of God);*

that blindness in part is happened to Israel *(is the "mystery" of which Paul speaks)*, until the fulness of the Gentiles be come in *(refers to the Church; in fact, the Church Age is even now coming to a close)*.

26 And so all Israel shall be saved *(when the Church Age ends, and the Second Coming commences; then Israel will accept Christ and be saved)*: as it is written *(Isa. 27:9; 59:20-21)*, There shall come out of Sion the Deliverer *(Jesus Christ will be the Deliverer)*, and shall turn away ungodliness from Jacob *(Christ will deliver Israel from the Antichrist, and more importantly will deliver them from their sins)*:

27 For this *is* my Covenant unto them *(a Promise)*, when I shall take away their sins *(as stated, it will be done at the Second Coming [Zech. 13:1])*.

28 As concerning the Gospel, *they are* enemies for your sakes *(refers to the Gospel of Jesus Christ)*: but as touching the election, *they are* beloved for the fathers' sakes *(speaks of their Calling)*.

29 For the Gifts and Calling of God *are* without Repentance *(the Gifts and Calling of God are not subject to a change of mind on God's Part)*.

30 For as you in times past have not believed God *(concerns the Gentile world which lived outside of the Promises of God for about 4,000 years)*, yet have now obtained Mercy through their unbelief *(refers to the unbelief of Israel, but their unbelief did not stop Mercy being granted to the Gentiles, which God had planned all along)*:

31 Even so have these also now not believed *(pertains once again to Israel, and the fact that even though they are now in unbelief; this will ultimately change)*, that through your Mercy *(the Church)* they also may obtain Mercy *(the Mercy which was extended to the Gentiles will ultimately bring Israel back as well, with the entirety of the Plan of God now coming full circle)*.

32 For God has concluded them all in unbelief *(both Jews and Gentiles; the Jews were loathe to accept this conclusion)*, that He might have Mercy upon all *(proclaims God's condition of dealing with the entirety of the human family, both Jew and Gentile)*.

GREATNESS OF GOD

33 O the depth of the riches both of the wisdom and knowledge of God! *(This depth is beyond our comprehension.)* how unsearchable *are* His Judgments, and His Ways past finding out! *(They cannot be found out by the intellect, only by Revelation which comes by the Spirit.)*

34 For who has known the Mind of the Lord? *(As stated, the only way the Mind of the Lord can be known is for it to be revealed by the Holy Spirit.)* or who has been His counsellor? *(It would have to be, "no one.")*

35 Or who has first given to Him *(Job 41:11)*, and it shall be recompensed unto him again? *(What we sow, we reap!)*

36 For of Him *(refers to Creation)*, and through Him *(refers to His Perfect Knowledge)*, and to Him *(His Presence is everywhere)*, are all things *(He Alone is the First Cause)*: to Whom be Glory forever *(He Alone deserves the Glory)*. Amen *(Truth)*.

CHAPTER 12
(A.D. 60)
CONSECRATION

I beseech you therefore, Brethren *(I beg of you please)*, by the Mercies of God *(all is given to the Believer, not because of merit on the Believer's part, but strictly because of the "Mercy of God")*, that you present your bodies a Living Sacrifice *(the word "Sacrifice" speaks of the Sacrifice of Christ, and means that we cannot do this which the Holy Spirit demands unless our Faith is placed strictly in Christ and the Cross, which then gives the Holy Spirit latitude to carry out this great work within our lives)*, holy *(that which the Holy Spirit Alone can do)*, acceptable unto God *(actually means that a holy physical body, i.e., "temple," is all that He will accept)*, **which is** your reasonable service *(reasonable if we look to Christ and the Cross; otherwise impossible!)*.

2 And be not conformed to this world *(the ways of the world)*: but be ye transformed by the renewing of your mind *(we must start thinking spiritually, which refers to the fact that everything is furnished to us through the Cross, and is obtained by Faith and not works)*, that you may prove what *is* that good *(is put to the test and finds that the thing tested meets the specifications laid down)*, and acceptable, and perfect, Will of God *(presents that which the Holy Spirit is attempting to bring about within our lives, and can only be obtained by ever making the Cross the Object of our Faith)*.

SPIRITUAL GIFTS

3 For I say, through the grace given unto

me *(refers to Paul's Apostleship given by the Grace of God [Eph. 3:8]),* to every man who is among you, not to think *of himself* more highly than he ought to think *(Israel had fallen, and the reason at least in part was because of this very thing — a prideful, unscriptural evaluation of themselves);* but to think soberly *(don't be high-minded),* according as God has dealt to every man the measure of Faith *(this is given by the Holy Spirit at conversion).*

4 For as we have many members in one body *(refers to every person who is in the Body of Christ),* and all members have not the same office *(a mode of acting or function):*

5 So we, *being* many, are one body in Christ *(speaks of the unity which ought to be prevalent within the Body),* and every one members one of another *(in effect, says that whatever is true according to one is also true according to the other; this does not speak of "offices," but rather being a member of the Body).*

6 Having then gifts differing according to the grace that is given to us *(speaks of different "Gifts" or "Offices"),* whether Prophecy, *let us Prophesy* according to the proportion of Faith *(has to do with "the measure of Faith");*

7 Or Ministry *(one who serves),* let us wait on *our* Ministering *(would have been better translated, "let us Minister according to the proportion of Faith"):* or he who teaches, on teaching *(carries the same idea; it is a wise man who stays within the sphere of service for which God, the Holy Spirit, has fitted him, and does not invade some other field of service for which he is not fitted);*

8 Or he who exhorts, on exhortation: he who gives, *let him do it* with simplicity *(proclaims "giving" as a "Gift" or "Office");* he who rules, with diligence *(a position of authority);* he who shows mercy, with cheerfulness *(the Holy Spirit says that this is a "Gift" as well).*

COMMANDS

9 *Let* love be without dissimulation *(real, not feigned or hypocritical).* Abhor that which is evil *(the Christian is to express his hatred of evil by a withdrawal from it and a loathing of it);* cleave to that which is good *(fasten, and firmly).*

10 *Be* kindly affectioned one to another with brotherly love *(speaks of the Brotherhood of Believers, which is even closer than the blood ties of relatives who aren't saved);* in honour preferring one another *(the respect shown another, which is measured by one's evaluation of another);*

11 Not slothful in business *(must be done with fervency, diligence, and attention to detail, with responsibility);* fervent in Spirit *(should have been translated, "fervent in the Holy Spirit"; looking to the Spirit constantly for leading and guidance);* serving the Lord *(serving Him in everything we do);*

12 Rejoicing in hope *(constantly rejoicing in the sphere of hope, always believing God);* patient in tribulation *(to remain under the test in a God-honoring manner; not seeking to escape it, but eager to learn the lessons it was sent to teach);* continuing instant in prayer *(the idea is that we pray about everything continually, and be quick to do so);*

13 Distributing to the necessity of Saints *(pertains to concern and generosity);* given to hospitality *(kindness toward all, even strangers).*

14 Bless them which persecute you *(speak well of such a one):* bless, and curse not *(the Christian is to only bless, and not pronounce judgment on others, even our most strident enemies; we must leave judgment to the Lord).*

15 Rejoice with them who do rejoice *(speaks of the Believer being sincerely glad for the Blessings of others),* and weep with them who weep *(expresses the Believer being sincerely sorry for and with those who experience tribulation and sorrow).*

16 *Be* of the same mind one toward another *(have the same mind toward all, whether great or small, rich or poor).* Mind not high things, but condescend to men of low estate *(the manner in which a Believer treats a person who occupies the lowest station of life [whatever that might be] when no one else is seeing or hearing shows what you are).* Be not wise in your own conceits *(proclaims the antipathy felt by the Apostle to every sort of spiritual aristocracy, and to every caste-distinction within the Church).*

CONDUCT

17 Recompense to no man evil for evil *(we are not to repay evil in like kind, but rather with the very opposite).* Provide things honest in the sight of all men *(the Christian is exhorted to take careful forethought that his manner of life and his outward expression conforms to, and is honestly representative of, what he is, a Child of God).*

18 If it be possible, as much as lieth in you, live peaceably with all men *(the Believer has*

no control over the conduct of another, but the idea is that the initiative in disturbing the peace is never to lie with the Christian).

19 Dearly beloved, avenge not yourselves (*proclaims action respecting fellow human beings*), but *rather* give place unto wrath (*speaks of God's Wrath, and means to leave room for it and not take God's proper Work out of His Hands*): for it is written, Vengeance *is* Mine; I will repay, saith the Lord (*[Lev. 19:18] the righting of wrong is to be committed to the Lord*).

20 Therefore if your enemy hunger, feed him; if he thirst, give him drink (*we should treat our enemies with goodness*): for in so doing you shall heap coals of fire on his head (*coals of fire were taken from the Brazen Altar, a Type of the Cross, and placed on the Altar of Incense; the Cross diverted judgment to intercession, of which the Altar of Incense was a type; by showing kindness to an enemy, we are diverting judgment, and showing mercy which God has shown us*).

21 Be not overcome of evil (*don't meet evil with evil, which only breeds more evil*), but overcome evil with good (*the initiative has changed from evil to good*).

CHAPTER 13
(A.D. 60)
HONOR AUTHORITY

LET every soul be subject unto the higher powers (*refers to Human Government*). For there is no power but of God (*refers to the fact that God has ordained Government*): the powers that be are ordained of God (*refers to Human Government being a permanent institution, brought into being by God for the regulation of human affairs*).

2 Whosoever therefore resists the power, resists the Ordinance of God (*anarchy is not of God*): and they who resist shall receive to themselves damnation (*the Law of the Land is always to be obeyed, providing it does not offend our conscience or the Word of God; the "damnation" mentioned here does not necessarily refer to such coming from God, but rather from men*).

3 For rulers are not a terror to good works, but to the evil (*concerns the Divine right of Government to oppose crime and to protect its citizens*). Will you then not be afraid of the power? (*This means that Civil Government should be respected, and all should fear breaking the Law.*) do that which is good, and you shall have praise of the same (*refers to obeying the Law, as all Christians ought to do; as well, it assumes that the Laws are right and just*):

4 For he (*the Civil Magistrate*) is the minister of God to you for good (*proclaims Government as a Divine Institution*). But if you do that which is evil, be afraid; for he bears not the sword in vain (*the sword is the symbol of the right of the State to inflict Capital punishment for Capital crimes*): for he is the minister of God (*not a Preacher of the Gospel, but a servant of the State*), a revenger to *execute* wrath upon him who does evil (*proclaims the right of the State, as ordained by God, to use whatever force is necessary to stop "evil," i.e., crime*).

5 Wherefore *you* must needs be subject (*plainly tells us that Christians are subject to the Law of the Land; that is, if it does not violate the Word of God*), not only for wrath, but also for conscience sake (*refers to the fact that the Believer has a higher principle than that of the unbeliever*).

6 For for this cause pay ye tribute also (*refers to the paying of taxes*): for they are God's ministers, attending continually upon this very thing (*refers to public servants*).

7 Render therefore to all their dues (*means that it is proper and right for all people to pay taxes, Christians as well!*): tribute to whom tribute *is due* (*refers to that which is owed, and should be paid*); custom to whom custom (*addresses hidden taxes, which we should pay as well*); fear to whom fear; honour to whom honour (*Government is an Institution to be respected, extending to all Civil servants from the lowest to the highest*).

PUBLIC RELATIONSHIPS

8 Owe no man any thing (*carries the idea that Christians do not "owe" their Brethren in the Lord the same obedience that is owed Civil Rulers*), but to love one another (*proclaims the only requirement between Believers*): for he who loves another has fulfilled the Law (*pertains to what the Law of Moses intended, but wasn't able to bring about; it can be done under Christ, and Christ Alone*).

9 For this, You shall not commit adultery (*sex in any form outside of marriage is unlawful [Gen. 2:23-24]*), You shall not kill (*should have been translated, "murder"*), You shall not steal (*don't take what's not yours*), You shall not bear false witness (*don't lie*), You shall not covet (*do not try to unlawfully take that which belongs to another*); and if *there be* any other

Commandment, it is briefly comprehended in this saying, namely, You shall love your neighbour as yourself (*Divine Love produced by the Holy Spirit is self-sacrificial in its nature*).

10 Love works no ill to his neighbour (*will not hurt his neighbor*): therefore love *is* the fulfilling of the Law (*proclaims the fact that this is all the Law formally requires, but can only be done in Christ*).

11 And that, knowing the time (*the Believer is to do everything with the Judgment Seat of Christ in view*), and now *it is* high time to awake out of sleep (*spiritual apathy and lethargy must be shaken off*): for now *is* our Salvation nearer than when we believed (*actually speaks of the coming Rapture of the Church, and the Believer at that time being Glorified*).

12 The night is far spent, the day is at hand (*refers to everything up until the coming Resurrection as "night"; all after the Resurrection is referred to as "day," with both day and night used as symbols*): let us therefore cast off the works of darkness (*could be translated, "let us therefore cast off the clothes of darkness"; former bad habits of life are here, as elsewhere, regarded as clothing once worn, but now to be put off*), and let us put on the armour of light (*could be translated, "and let us put on the clothes of Light"*).

13 Let us walk honestly, as in the day (*we should conduct ourselves in a manner befitting our high station in life as Saints of the Most High God*); not in rioting and drunkenness (*the ways of the world*), not in chambering and wantonness (*speaks of sexual immorality of every nature*), not in strife and envying (*speaks of constant manipulation and exploitation to best others regarding business, place, or position*).

14 But put ye on the Lord Jesus Christ (*avail yourself of all that Christ has accomplished at the Cross, which is available to all Believers*), and make not provision for the flesh, to *fulfil* the lusts *thereof* (*Faith in the Cross will give the Holy Spirit latitude within our lives, which alone gives us victory over the flesh*).

CHAPTER 14
(A.D. 60)
DOUBTFUL THINGS

HIM who is weak in the faith receive ye (*refers to the Believer not understanding the Cross as he should*), *but* not to doubtful disputations (*is directed toward the strong Believers and those "weak in the Faith"; it means that the strong, who welcome those of weak Faith into the fellowship of the Church, are to do so unreservedly and not with the purpose of judging and attempting to rule their minds*).

2 For one believes that he may eat all things (*pertains to the strength of one's Faith, based on a proper understanding of what Jesus did for us at the Cross*): another, who is weak, eats herbs (*this latter group doesn't properly understand the Finished Work of Calvary, and think that eating or not eating certain things gauge their Sanctification and Holiness, etc.*).

3 Let not him who eats despise him who eats not (*speaks of the spirit of spiritual superiority*); and let not him which eats not judge him who eats (*is the same thing in reverse; spiritual superiority or spiritual pride is no respecter of persons; it can fasten itself to either group with equal tenacity*): for God has received him (*speaks of the individuals in either case, strong or weak*).

4 Who are you who judges another man's servant? (*This actually says, "As for you, who are you to judge God's Servant?"*) to his own master he stands or falls (*the Lord Alone is to be the judge*). Yes, he shall be held up: for God is able to make him stand (*has reference to the fact that God Alone can hold us up, and He is able to do so; the idea is that brow beating an individual will never help the person!*).

5 One man esteems one day above another (*is actually referring back to the Jewish Sabbaths*): another esteems every day *alike* (*subject every day to scrutiny; this is the proper course*). Let every man be fully persuaded in his own mind (*the Apostle is not speaking of things here that are morally wrong and which the Word of God has already condemned; he is speaking of Rituals only*).

6 He who regards the day, regards *it* unto the Lord (*whatever Ritual someone may be attempting to keep, he is supposed to be doing it unto the Lord, and not for some personal satisfaction*); and he who regards not the day, to the Lord he does not regard *it* (*the interests of the Lord should be in view in either case*). He who eats, eats to the Lord, for he gives God thanks (*his Faith is sufficient and whatever the food might be is of no consequence*); and he who eats not, to the Lord he eats not, and gives God thanks (*has the same end in view, or at least it should, to please the Lord*).

7 For none of us lives to himself, and no man dies to himself (*no Christian is his own end in life; what is always present in his mind

as a rule of his conduct is the will and interest of his Lord).

8 For whether we live, we live unto the Lord; and whether we die, we die unto the Lord *(everything in our lives is to be, "unto the Lord"):* **whether we live therefore, or die, we are the Lord's** *(reflects the Lord having total control over our lives and deaths, which we must desire He use to the fullest).*

9 For to this end *(refers to the fact of Christ's absolute ownership of the Believer, spirit, soul, and body)* **Christ both died, and rose, and revived** *(a price was paid for us of such magnitude that it absolutely defies description),* **that He might be Lord both of the dead and living** *(refers to the Lordship of Christ over all Saints, whether alive or having passed on).*

10 But why do you judge your brother? *(Is any Believer qualified to judge another Believer? "Your Brother" is another reason for not judging. It is inconsistent with the recognition of the Brotherhood of Believers.)* **or why do you set at nought your brother?** *(There is only one reason for refusing fellowship, and that reason is unconfessed, unrepentant, habitual sin in a person's life [I Cor., Chpt. 5].)* **for we shall all stand before the Judgment Seat of Christ** *(we will be judged there, not for our sins, those having been handled at the Cross, but as it regards our stewardship and our motives, etc.; gain or loss of reward will be the result).*

11 For it is written *(Isa. 45:23),* **As I live, saith the Lord** *(God cannot die),* **every knee shall bow to me, and every tongue shall confess to God** *(to make a confession of God's Honor, and as well, to praise Him).*

12 So then every one of us shall give account of himself to God *(each is responsible, meaning that the blame cannot be shifted elsewhere).*

RESPONSIBILITY

13 Let us not therefore judge one another any more *(can be translated, "let us no longer have the habit of criticizing one another"):* **but judge this rather, that no man put a stumbling-block or an occasion to fall in** *his* **brother's way** *(tells us what is, in fact, permissible to judge; as Believers, we are to judge every Brother and Sister and situation which surrounds them, irrespective what it might be, as to how we can help them, instead of harming them).*

14 I know, and am persuaded by the Lord Jesus *(means that this declaration is of the Lord, not merely of Paul's reasoning power),* **that** *there*

is nothing unclean of itself *(speaks of ceremonial impurity, not of actual immorality; in the manner in which everything was originally created by the Lord and intended to be used, there is nothing unclean):* **but to him who esteems any thing to be unclean, to him** *it is* **unclean** *(is this way because of Faith placed in things other than the Cross).*

15 But if your brother be grieved with *your* **meat, now walkest thou not charitably** *(do not take that as an occasion to be uncharitable toward him).* **Destroy not him with your meat, for whom Christ died** *(our actions should always be motivated by the fact that Jesus died for this person, and this person belongs to Christ; we should treat him accordingly!).*

16 Let not then your good be evil spoken of *(our "good" must be exercised with a gracious spirit, always considering others):*

17 For the Kingdom of God is not meat and drink *(actually refers to rules, regulations, ceremonies, or rituals, etc.);* **but Righteousness, and Peace, and Joy in the Holy Spirit** *(a right spirit, which refers to a spirit that is controlled by the Holy Spirit, will always produce Righteousness, Peace, and Joy, not argument, etc.).*

18 For he who in these things serves Christ is acceptable to God *(Righteousness, Peace, and Joy are acceptable to the Lord; but not contention, quarreling, and fighting in the Church),* **and approved of men** *(Righteousness, Peace, and Joy alone will bring men together).*

19 Let us therefore follow after the things which make for Peace *(following that which is of God, and not that devised by men),* **and things wherewith one may edify another** *(refers to that which is produced by the Holy Spirit, and not by man).*

20 For meat destroy not the Work of God *(let's not fight over incidental things, which are what most Church fights are all about).* **All things indeed** *are* **pure** *(refers to that which is created by God, and used for its intended purpose);* **but** *it is* **evil for that man who eats with offence** *(refers to the man who is "weak in Faith").*

21 *It is* **good neither to eat flesh, nor to drink wine, nor** *any thing* **whereby your brother stumbles, or is offended, or is made weak** *(the idea is that love is to be the ruling guide, not our freedom of liberties).*

22 Have you faith? *(This is addressed to the strong.)* **have** *it* **to yourself before God** *(don't run the risk of injuring a Brother's conscience merely for the sake of exercising in a special way the spiritual freedom we have the happiness to*

possess). **Happy** *is* he who condemns not himself in that thing which he allows *(refers to this being joy enough, without us taking our liberty further and, thereby, hindering a weaker Brother or Sister).*

23 And he who doubts is damned if he eat, because *he eats* **not of faith** *(Faith, that is proper Faith, is the criteria for all things)*: **for whatsoever** *is* **not of faith is sin** *(the type of Faith addressed here is Faith in "Jesus Christ and Him Crucified"; any other type of faith is "sin").*

CHAPTER 15
(A.D. 60)
UNITY IN CHRIST

WE then who are strong ought to bear the infirmities of the weak *(has the end result in mind of these weaker Brethren also becoming strong in Faith and knowledge of the Lord)*, **and not to please ourselves** *(pleasing self ruins our Christian fellowship).*

2 Let every one of us please *his* **neighbour for** *his* **good to edification** *(refers to the Believer foregoing a legitimate act because a weaker Christian thinks it to be wrong).*

3 For even Christ pleased not Himself *(the entirety of the Life and Ministry of Christ was to do the Will of the Father)*; **but, as it is written** *(Ps. 69:9)*, **The reproaches of them who reproached You fell on Me** *(Christ suffered this reproach for our sakes, and surely not to please Himself; this should be our example).*

4 For whatsoever things were written aforetime were written for our learning *(refers to the whole of Old Testament Scriptures)*, **that we through patience and comfort of the Scriptures might have hope** *(the Word of God must always be our criteria, and not our own self-will).*

5 Now the God of Patience and Consolation grant you to be likeminded one toward another *(presents God as the Author of the Patience and Consolation lodged in the Scriptures, which nourish the Hope of Believers)* **according to Christ Jesus** *(once again, if we place our Faith exclusively in Christ and the Cross, these admonitions will not be difficult to obey):*

6 That you may with one mind *and* **one mouth glorify God** *(proclaims the Christlikeness of the previous Verse as the only manner in which differences can be correctly settled)*, **even the Father of our Lord Jesus Christ** *(contains the rendering of Christ pleasing the Father, Whom we must desire to please accordingly).*

7 Wherefore receive ye one another *(to take into friendship and fellowship)*, **as Christ also received us to the Glory of God** *("Us" covers all parties in the Church, however they may be distinguished; if Christ receives both, we are bound to receive each other).*

ONE IN CHRIST

8 Now I say that Jesus Christ was a Minister of the Circumcision for the Truth of God *(proclaims the fact that Jesus was obligated first of all to the Jews, and for particular reasons)*, **to confirm the Promises** *made* **unto the Fathers** *(proclaims the fulfillment of the Messianic Promises to Israel):*

9 And that the Gentiles might Glorify God for *His* **Mercy** *(we Gentiles are grafted in, not because of any merit on our part, but strictly because of "Mercy" on His Part)*; **as it is written** *(Ps. 18:49)*, **For this cause I will confess to You** *(to God)* **among the Gentiles, and sing unto Your Name** *(Christ is assumed here to be the Speaker, even as He is in all the Psalms; He gives thanks to God among the Gentiles, when the Gentiles give thanks to God through Him [Heb. 2:12]).*

10 And again He says, Rejoice, you Gentiles, with His people *(by joining "Gentiles" with Israel, "His People," Moses predicts the grafting of the "wild olive tree" into the "good olive tree" [Rom. 11:17-24]).*

11 And again *(Ps. 117:1)*, **Praise the Lord, all you Gentiles; and laud Him, all you people** *(this predicted the day about a thousand years in the future that the Gentiles would Praise the Lord and "Laud Him," meaning to extol His Grace and Virtue).*

12 And again *(Isa. 11:1)*, **Isaiah said, There shall be a root of Jesse** *(concerns Jesus coming from the family of David, regarding the Incarnation)*, **and He Who shall rise to reign over the Gentiles** *(this Passage predicts that Jesus will ultimately "reign" as King over the entirety of the Earth)*; **in Him shall the Gentiles trust** *(the Church is almost entirely made up of Gentiles).*

MINISTRY

13 Now the God of Hope fill you with all Joy and Peace in believing *(that which the Lord imparts to Believers rests on Faith)*, **that you may abound in Hope, through the Power of the Holy Spirit** *(the Holy Spirit will help us*

have all these things if we place our Faith exclusively in Christ and the Cross [I Cor. 1:18]).

14 And I myself also am persuaded of you, my Brethren *(has faith in these Believers)*, that you also are full of goodness *(means that they had such because of Christ)*, filled with all knowledge *(knowledge of the Word)*, able also to admonish one another *(they could correct each other if need be, because of their knowledge of the Word).*

15 Nevertheless, Brethren, I have written the more boldly unto you in some sort *(with greater confidence than otherwise)*, as putting you in mind, because of the Grace that is given to me of God *(his peculiar Mission as Apostle to the Gentiles gave him the right to admonish them)*,

16 That I should be the Minister of Jesus Christ to the Gentiles *(Paul presents his Calling as an Apostle to the Church)*, Ministering the Gospel of God *(the word "Ministering" is used in the sense of the Priests and Levites of old, who were busied with the Sacred Rites in the Tabernacle and Temple)*, that the offering up of the Gentiles might be acceptable *(presents Paul perceiving himself as presenting to God the Gentile Church as an "Offering")*, being Sanctified by the Holy Spirit *(the Holy Spirit, through Paul, pictures the Apostle offering up the Gentiles as a pure Sacrifice acceptable to God, because they were washed in the Blood and Sanctified by the Holy Spirit).*

17 I have therefore whereof I may glory through Jesus Christ *(everything is through Christ, and what Christ has done at the Cross)* in those things which pertain to God *(the idea is that all of Paul's Ministry, and in whatever capacity, is ordered and directed by the Holy Spirit, signifying the Divine Order).*

18 For I will not dare to speak of any of those things which Christ has not wrought by me *(as the Apostle, in fact, the first Apostle, to the Gentiles, he is here claiming inspiration in the writing of this Epistle, and rightly so)*, to make the Gentiles obedient, by word and deed *(it is not on his own impulse that he write this Epistle, but in Christ that He does it; the Romans as Gentiles, lie within this sphere in which Christ works through him),*

19 Through mighty signs and wonders, by the Power of the Spirit of God *(proclaims the Mighty Power of God in operation)*; so that from Jerusalem, and round about unto Illyricum, I have fully Preached the Gospel of Christ *(he preached all the Gospel, compromising it not at all).*

20 Yes, so have I strived to Preach the Gospel *(speaks of his earnest zeal)*, not where Christ was named *(means that Paul never sought to Evangelize where Christianity was already established)*, lest I should build upon another man's foundation *(Jesus, as the Head of the Church, gives direction through and by the Holy Spirit to particular workers; that "direction," must not be impugned by others):*

21 But as it is written *(Isa. 52:15)*, To whom He was not spoken of, they shall see: and they who have not heard shall understand *(refers to the Message of Redemption going to the Gentiles, as is obvious).*

ROME

22 For which cause also *(refers to Paul preaching these number of years in areas that did not have the Gospel)* I have been much hindered from coming to you *(his desire to minister in Rome was not born out of personal ambition, but was directed by the Holy Spirit concerning his Apostleship).*

23 But now having no more place in these parts *(meaning he had finished his work in the places mentioned)*, and having a great desire these many years to come unto you *(proclaims that which had been strong within his heart, and placed there by the Holy Spirit);*

24 Whensoever I take my journey into Spain, I will come to you *(there is no record in Scripture or history that Paul ever fulfilled this proposed journey to Spain)*: for I trust to see you in my journey, and to be brought on my way thitherward by you *(implies that he hoped to take a select number from the Church in Rome to Spain with him)*, if first I be somewhat filled with your *company (refers to his proposed stop in the Imperial City on his way to Spain).*

25 But now I go unto Jerusalem to Minister unto the Saints *(to take offerings from the Gentile Churches to Jerusalem to minister to many Saints who were in dire need).*

26 For it has pleased them of Macedonia and Achaia to make a certain contribution for the poor Saints which are at Jerusalem *(had to do with the persecution leveled at the Church in Jerusalem by the Jewish Sanhedrin).*

27 It has pleased them verily; and their debtors they are *(refers to the Jews of Antiquity being the bearers of Salvation, which was a great Blessing to the Gentile world).* For if the Gentiles have been made partakers of their spiritual things, their duty is also to minister unto

them in carnal things (*this goes for the entirety of the Gospel, and for all time; if we are ministered to spiritually, we should in turn minister back in material things*).

28 When therefore I have performed this (*to take the Offerings to Jerusalem*), and have sealed to them this fruit (*everything the Believer does for the Lord is looked at by the Holy Spirit as "fruit"*), I will come by you into Spain (*there is a tradition that Paul did ultimately go to Spain; but as stated, there is no historical or Scriptural proof*).

29 And I am sure that, when I come unto you, I shall come in the fulness of the Blessing of the Gospel of Christ (*proclaims the fact of great Truths held by Paul, actually given to him by Christ [Gal. 1:11-12], which he wished to give to the Roman Church*).

PRAYER

30 Now I beseech you, Brethren, for the Lord Jesus Christ's sake (*refers to the Work of God; even though the Lord has paid the price on the Cross for man's Redemption, it is up to us to take the Message to the world*), and for the Love of the Spirit (*that he would always be led by the Spirit*), that you strive together with me in *your* prayers to God for me (*proclaims the humility of this man, and the Power of Prayer*);

31 That I may be delivered from them who do not believe in Judaea (*the Nation of Israel, which had rejected Christ*); and that my service which I *have* for Jerusalem may be accepted of the Saints (*concerns the Offering for the poor Saints in Jerusalem who were in desperate need*);

32 That I may come unto you with joy by the Will of God (*refers to the fact that it definitely was the Will of God for Paul to go to Rome*), and may with you be refreshed (*reveals that Paul had many friends in Rome, hence, the warmness of his statements*).

33 Now the God of Peace *be* with you all. Amen.

CHAPTER 16
(A.D. 60)
COMMENDATIONS

I commend unto you Phebe our sister, which is a servant of the Church which is at Cenchrea (*the word "servant" in the Greek is "diakonos," with our words "Deacon" and "Deaconess" derived from it; this shows that it is Scriptural for a woman to serve in this capacity as*

well as a man; Cenchrea was the Port of Corinth, about nine miles from that city):

2 That you receive her in the Lord, as becometh Saints (*refers to receiving her into companionship and fellowship; in fact, she delivered the Epistle to the Romans to the Church in Rome; of this, Renan says: "Phoebe carried under the folds of her robe the whole future of Christian Theology*), and that you assist her in whatsoever business she has need of you (*suggests that she may have had business in Rome of a legal nature*): for she has been a succourer of many, and of myself also (*Phoebe was a great Blessing to the Work of God*).

PERSONAL GREETINGS

3 Greet Priscilla and Aquila my helpers in Christ Jesus (*Paul first met them at Corinth, but evidently they had now gone back to Rome*):

4 Who have for my life laid down their own necks (*means they risked their lives for Paul; exactly where and how aren't known*): unto whom not only I give thanks, but also all the Churches of the Gentiles (*all the Churches of the Gentiles thanked Priscilla and Aquila as well*).

5 Likewise *greet* the Church that is in their house (*evidently, they had one of the house Churches in Rome*). Salute my well-beloved Epaenetus, who is the Firstfruits of Achaia unto Christ (*this man was among the first in Corinth to give his heart to Christ*).

6 Greet Mary, who bestowed much labour on us (*other than this statement, no information is given concerning this dear lady*).

7 Salute Andronicus and Junia, my kinsmen (*probably refers to fellow Jews, and not blood relatives*), and my fellow-prisoners (*implies that these two had been, like himself, imprisoned at some time for the Faith*), who are of note among the Apostles (*doesn't mean they were Apostles themselves, but that they were well-known to the original Twelve*), who also were in Christ before me (*their conversion predated his*).

8 Greet Amplias my beloved in the Lord.

9 Salute Urbane, our helper in Christ, and Stachys my beloved (*it seems these men had been Paul's helpers in earlier times*).

10 Salute Apelles approved in Christ. Salute them which are of Aristobulus' *household* (*probably refers to slaves who had once belonged to this man*).

11 Salute Herodion my kinsman (*another

Jew). Greet them who be of the *household* of Narcissus, which are in the Lord *(does not refer to Narcissus personally, but to slaves of his household, at least those who were followers of the Lord).*

12 Salute Tryphena and Tryphosa, who labour in the Lord *(presents two more slaves, for theirs are slave names).* Salute the beloved Persis, which laboured much in the Lord *(refers to a woman).*

13 Salute Rufus chosen in the Lord, and his mother and mine *(he was probably the son of Simon of Cyrene who helped Jesus bear the Cross).*

14 Salute Asyncritus, Phlegon, Hermas, Patrobas, Hermes, and the Brethren which are with them.

15 Salute *(greet)* Philologus, and Julia, Nereus, and his sister, and Olympas, and all the Saints which are with them.

16 Salute one another with an holy kiss *(presents that which was the custom of all Oriental people at that time, not only Christians).* The Churches of Christ salute you *(refers to the Churches planted by Paul who in turn were greeting the Church in Rome).*

ADMONITION

17 Now I beseech you, Brethren, mark them which cause divisions and offences contrary to the doctrine which you have learned *(refers to the fact that false teachers are to be identified);* and avoid them *(turn away from and shun these).*

18 For they who are such serve not our Lord Jesus Christ, but their own belly *(the satisfaction of creature needs, and not the Work of God);* and by good words and fair speeches deceive the hearts of the simple *(refers to those who have little true understanding of the Word of God).*

OBEDIENCE

19 For your obedience is come abroad unto all *men (refers to Paul not linking the Saints in the Church in Rome with these false teachers, whomever they may have been).* I am glad therefore on your behalf *(expresses his joy at their maturity in the Lord):* but yet I would have you wise unto that which is good, and simple concerning evil *(he wanted them to be so grounded in the Word that they would instantly know false doctrine when it came their way).*

20 And the God of Peace shall bruise Satan under your feet shortly *(all who trust Christ and what He has done at the Cross are guaranteed victory, and in every capacity).* The grace of our Lord Jesus Christ *be* with you. Amen *(presents the standard Benediction of Paul, which he uses in one form or the other in all of his Epistles, even Hebrews).*

GREETINGS

21 Timothy my workfellow *(refers to Paul's young understudy and fellow worker),* and Lucius, and Jason, and Sosipater, my kinsmen *(fellow Jews),* salute you.

22 I Tertius, who wrote *this* Epistle, salute you in the Lord *(he was Paul's Scribe to whom he dictated the letter to the Romans).*

23 Gaius my host, and of the whole Church, salutes you *(probably means that Paul was staying in this man's home in Corinth).* Erastus the chamberlain of the city salutes you *(probably the one mentioned in II Tim. 4:20 and Acts 19:22),* and Quartus a brother.

24 The Grace of our Lord Jesus Christ *be* with you all. Amen.

BENEDICTION

25 Now to Him Who is of power to stablish you according to my Gospel *(Paul's Gospel was, "Jesus Christ and Him Crucified"),* and the Preaching of Jesus Christ *(Paul Preached the Cross [I Cor. 1:23; 2:2]),* according to the Revelation of the Mystery, which was kept secret since the world began *(proclaims that which is now revealed in his Gospel, the story of Redemption),*

26 But now is made manifest *(the actual Greek reads, "but now has been made known through Prophetic writings"),* and by the Scriptures of the Prophets *(refers to the Old Testament, which Scriptures constantly pointed to the coming of Christ),* according to the Commandment of the Everlasting God *(actually means that, according to the appointment of God, the "Mystery" should now at last be made known),* made known to all nations for the Obedience of Faith *(it must be Preached to the whole world):*

27 To God only wise, *be* Glory through Jesus Christ forever. Amen *(the Great Price Jesus paid by giving himself in Sacrifice will forever bring Glory to God, in that it has brought about the Salvation of untold numbers of souls).*

THE FIRST EPISTLE OF PAUL THE APOSTLE TO THE
CORINTHIANS

CHAPTER 1
(A.D. 59)
INTRODUCTION

PAUL, called *to be* an Apostle *(this Calling presents the titular leader of the Church, and pertains to the Message; in other words, every God-called Apostle has been given a special emphasis by the Holy Spirit regarding his Message)* of Jesus Christ through the Will of God *(by God's Own Appointment and Will)*, and Sosthenes *our* brother *(Acts 18:17)*,

2 Unto the Church of God which is at Corinth *(this form of address shows the absence of any fixed Ecclesiastical Government)*, to them who are Sanctified in Christ Jesus *(set apart unto Christ)*, called *to be* Saints *(means that everyone who is "in Christ" is a "Saint")*, with all who in every place call upon the Name of Jesus Christ our Lord *(pertains to the fact that this Epistle is meant not only for the Church at Corinth, but for all other Churches and for all time)*, both theirs and ours *(deals a death blow to Christians who claim a monopoly on Christ for themselves and their own sects, etc.)*:

3 Grace *be* unto you, and Peace *(Grace is the beginning of all Blessings, while Peace is the end of all Blessings; all are made possible by the Cross)*, from God our Father, and *from* the Lord Jesus Christ *(places the "Father" first; in this paternal role, He is the Source of every good gift and every perfect gift, but does so through Jesus Christ and what He did at the Cross).*

THANKSGIVING

4 I thank my God always on your behalf *(the natural overflow of a full heart)*, for the Grace of God which is given you by Jesus Christ *(as stated, all Grace, which is the Goodness of God, is made possible by the Cross, and the Cross alone!)*;

5 That in every thing you are enriched by Him *(meant to exclaim the Source of "every good thing," Who is Christ Jesus)*, in all utterance *(is not speaking of the Gift of Tongues as some think, but rather all the Promises of God which He has uttered or given since the beginning of time)*, and *in* all knowledge;

6 Even as the Testimony of Christ was confirmed in you *(what Christ did at the Cross had played out in the lives of some of these Corinthians)*:

7 So that you come behind in no Gift *(is not limited to the nine Gifts of the Spirit, but rather every single thing given by the Lord, which He paid for at the Cross)*; waiting for the Coming of our Lord Jesus Christ *(pertains here to the Rapture of the Church [I Thess. 4:13-18])*:

8 Who shall also confirm you unto the end *(refers to the keeping power of "our Lord Jesus Christ," which is done by the Holy Spirit as the Believer ever makes the Cross the Object of his Faith)*, *that you may be* blameless in the day of our Lord Jesus Christ *(once again, such a life can only be attained by constant Faith in the Cross of Christ).*

9 God *is* Faithful *(was a favorite expression of the integrity of God among Jews [II Cor. 1:18; I Thess. 5:24; II Thess. 3:3])*, by Whom you were called unto the fellowship of His Son Jesus Christ our Lord *("called" refers to Predestination, but of the Plan and not the person).*

DIVISIONS

10 Now *(implies the transition from thanksgiving to reproof)* I beseech you *(I beg you)*, Brethren, by the Name of our Lord Jesus Christ *(proclaims the Lord as the Head of the Church)*, that you all speak the same thing *(demands unity with respect to the Person of Christ, and what He has done to Redeem us through the Cross)*, and *that* there be no divisions among you *(as it regards Christ and the Cross)*; but *that* you be perfectly joined together in the same mind and in the same judgment *(presents that which can only be done by the Cross ever being the Object of one's Faith, which then gives the Holy Spirit the latitude to bring about these things in our lives).*

11 For it has been declared unto me of you, my Brethren, by them *which are of the House of Chloe (Paul wisely and kindly mentions his authority for these reports)*, that there are contentions among you. *(We will see that these contentions centered on disagreements concerning the Cross.)*

12 Now this I say, that every one of you says *(refers to a self-assertive manner)*, I am of Paul; and I of Apollos; and I of Cephas *(Simon Peter)*; and I of Christ. *(In effect, this latter group was saying they didn't need any Preachers at all, which is wrong.)*

13 Is Christ divided? *(Is there a Baptist Christ, a Pentecostal Christ, or a Holiness Christ? The answer is a solid "No.")* was Paul crucified for you? *(The Apostle rebukes the partisanship, which attached itself to his own name.)* or were you baptized in the name of Paul? *(This proclaims the idea that he had never attempted to draw away Disciples after himself, but rather to Christ.)*

14 I thank God that I baptized none of you, but Crispus and Gaius *(if Water Baptism were essential to Salvation, as some claim, I hardly think Paul would have blatantly announced that he had only baptized these few, as he did here)*;

15 Lest any should say that I had baptized in mine own name *(nothing must be done to draw away allegiance from Christ)*.

16 And I baptized also the household of Stephanas: besides, I know not whether I baptized any other *(informs us that the inspiration of the Apostles in writing the Scriptures involved none of the mechanical infallibility ascribed to them by popular dogma)*.

17 For Christ sent me not to baptize *(presents to us a Cardinal Truth)*, but to Preach the Gospel *(the manner in which one may be saved from sin)*: not with wisdom of words *(intellectualism is not the Gospel)*, lest the Cross of Christ should be made of none effect. *(This tells us in no uncertain terms that the Cross of Christ must always be the emphasis of the Message.)*

WISDOM

18 For the Preaching *(Word)* of the Cross is to them who perish foolishness *(Spiritual things cannot be discerned by unredeemed people, but that doesn't matter; the Cross must be Preached just the same, even as we shall see)*; but unto us which are saved it is the Power of God. *(The Cross is the Power of God simply because it was there that the total sin debt was paid, giving the Holy Spirit, in Whom the Power resides, latitude to work mightily within our lives.)*

19 For it is written *(Isa. 29:14)*, I will destroy the wisdom of the wise, and will bring to nothing the understanding of the prudent *(speaks to those who are wise in their own eyes, in effect, having forsaken the Ways of the Lord)*.

20 Where *is* the wise? *(This presents the first of three classes of learned people who lived in that day.)* where *is* the Scribe? *(This pertained to the Jewish Theologians of that day.)* where *is* the disputer of this world? *(This speaks of the Greeks, who were seekers of mystical and metaphysical interpretations.)* has not God made foolish the wisdom of this world? *(This pertains to what God did in sending His Son to Redeem humanity, which He did by the Cross. All the wisdom of the world couldn't do this!)*

21 For after that in the Wisdom of God the world by wisdom knew not God *(man's puny wisdom, even the best he has to offer, cannot come to know God in any manner)*, it pleased God by the foolishness of Preaching *(Preaching the Cross)* to save them who believe. *(Paul is not dealing with the art of preaching here, but with what is preached.)*

22 For the Jews require a sign *(the sign of the Messiah taking the Throne and making Israel a great Nation once again)*, and the Greeks seek after wisdom *(they thought that such solved the human problem; however, if it did, why were they ever seeking after more wisdom?)*:

23 But we Preach Christ Crucified *(this is the Foundation of the Word of God and, thereby, of Salvation)*, unto the Jews a stumblingblock *(the Cross was the stumblingblock)*, and unto the Greeks foolishness *(both found it difficult to accept as God a dead Man hanging on a Cross, for such Christ was to them)*;

24 But unto them which are called *(refers to those who accept the Call, for the entirety of mankind is invited [Jn. 3:16; Rev. 22:17])*, both Jews and Greeks *(actually stands for both "Jews and Gentiles")*, Christ the Power of God *(what He did at the Cross Atoned for all sin, thereby, making it possible for the Holy Spirit to exhibit His Power within our lives)*, and the Wisdom of God. *(This Wisdom devised a Plan of Salvation which pardoned guilty men and at the same time vindicated and glorified the Justice of God, which stands out as the wisest and most remarkable Plan of all time.)*

25 Because the foolishness of God is wiser than men *(God achieves the mightiest ends by the humblest means)*; and the weakness of God is stronger than men *(refers to that which men take to be weak, but actually is not — the Cross)*.

26 For you see your calling, Brethren *(refers to the nature and method of their Heavenly Calling)*, how that not many wise men after the flesh, not many mighty, not many noble, *are* Called *(are Called and accept)*:

27 But God has chosen the foolish things of the world to confound the wise (the Preaching of the Cross confounds the wise because it falls out to changed lives, which nothing man has can do); and God has chosen the weak things of the world to confound the things which are mighty (the Cross is looked at as weakness, but it brings about great strength and power, regarding those who accept the Finished Work of Christ);

28 And base things of the world, and things which are despised, has God chosen (it is God working in the base things and the despised things which brings about miraculous things), yes, and things which are not, to bring to nought things that are (God can use that which is nothing within itself, but with Him all things become possible):

29 That no flesh (human effort) should glory in His Presence.

30 But of Him are you in Christ Jesus (pertains to this great Plan of God which is far beyond all wisdom of the world; we are "in Christ Jesus," by virtue of the Cross — what He did there), Who of God is made unto us Wisdom, and Righteousness, and Sanctification, and Redemption (we have all of this by the Holy Spirit, through Christ and what He did at the Cross; this means the Cross must ever be the Object of our Faith):

31 That, according as it is written (Jer. 9:23), He who glories, let him glory in the Lord. (He who boasts, let him boast in the Lord, and not in particular Preachers.)

CHAPTER 2
(A.D. 59)
TRUE WISDOM

AND I, Brethren, when I came to you, came not with excellency of speech or of wisdom (means that he depended not on oratorical abilities, nor did he delve into philosophy, which was all the rage of that particular day), declaring unto you the Testimony of God (which is Christ and Him Crucified).

2 For I determined not to know any thing among you (with purpose and design, Paul did not resort to the knowledge or philosophy of the world regarding the Preaching of the Gospel), save Jesus Christ, and Him Crucified (that and that alone is the Message which will save the sinner, set the captive free, and give the Believer perpetual victory).

3 And I was with you in (personal) weakness (an expression of utter dependence on God), and in fear (fear that he might not properly Preach the Cross), and in much trembling. (He realized the significance of what he was Preaching, and his inadequacy regarding his own person.)

4 And my speech and my Preaching was not with enticing words of man's wisdom (he knew that would not set anyone free; the modern Church should take a lesson from this), but in demonstration of the Spirit and of power (which speaks of what the Holy Spirit can do in the hearts and lives of Believers, if the Cross is properly Preached):

5 That your Faith should not stand in the wisdom of men (speaks of any proposed way other than the Cross), but in the Power of God (made possible only by the Cross).

6 Howbeit we speak wisdom among them who are perfect (only the spiritually mature can understand the Wisdom of God, which is the Cross): yet not the wisdom of this world (the Wisdom of God pertaining to Salvation has absolutely no relationship whatsoever to the "wisdom of this world"), nor of the princes of this world, that come to nought (the great Sages and Philosophers of the world contributed nothing to Paul, nor do they to us as well):

7 But we speak the Wisdom of God in a mystery, even the hidden wisdom (God's Wisdom leads sinful men to the great Sacrifice of history, the offering up of Jesus on the Cross of Calvary, which paid the terrible sin debt of man, at least for all who will believe), which God ordained before the world unto our glory (in the Mind of God, Christ was offered up on the Cross even before the foundation of the world [I Pet. 1:18-20]):

8 Which none of the princes of this world knew (pertains to their ignorance being a willful ignorance, which was their judgment for rejecting Christ [Acts 3:17; 13:27]): for had they known it (had they desired to know), they would not have Crucified the Lord of Glory. (These words bring in juxtaposition the lowest humiliation and the most splendid exaltation.)

THE HOLY SPIRIT

9 But as it is written (Isa. 64:4), Eye has not seen, nor ear heard, neither have entered into the heart of man (the purpose is to show that we cannot come to a knowledge of God through these normal ways of learning), the things which God has prepared for them who love Him.

10 But God has revealed them unto us by

His Spirit *(tells us the manner of impartation of spiritual knowledge, which is Revelation)*: for the Spirit searches all things, yes, the deep things of God. *(The Holy Spirit is the only One amply qualified to reveal God because He is God, and He is the member of the Godhead Who deals directly with man.)*

11 For what man knows the things of a man, save the spirit of man which is in him? *(The spirit of a man can know some things about another man, but within itself cannot know anything about God.)* even so the things of God knows no man, but the Spirit of God. *(Men cannot learn about God through scientific investigation or human reasoning, but only as the Spirit of God reveals such to the Believer.)*

12 Now we have received, not the spirit of the world *(which is of Satan)*, but the Spirit which is of God *(upon conversion, the Believer receives the Spirit of God)*; that we might know the things that are freely given to us of God *(the only way we can truly know)*.

13 Which things also we speak, not in the words which man's wisdom teaches *(corrupted wisdom)*, but which the Holy Spirit teaches *(which is an understanding of the Word of God)*; comparing spiritual things with spiritual *(communicating spiritual Truths to spiritual men by the Spirit)*.

14 But the natural man receives not the things of the Spirit of God *(speaks of the individual who is not Born-Again)*: for they are foolishness unto him *(a lack of understanding)*: neither can he know *them* *(fallen man cannot understand spiritual Truths)*, because they are spiritually discerned *(only the Regenerated spirit of man can understand the things of the Spirit)*.

15 But he who is spiritual judges all things *(portrays only the spiritual person as capable of proper judgment)*, yet he himself is judged of no man *(refers to judgment which God will accept)*.

16 For who has known the Mind of the Lord, that he may instruct him? *(The answer is no one! [Isa. 40:14].)* But we have the Mind of Christ. *(They who have the Mind of Christ see things as God sees them.)*

CHAPTER 3
(A.D. 59)
THE CARNAL STATE

AND I, Brethren, could not speak unto you as unto spiritual, but as unto carnal *(a solemn rebuke; they were carnal because they had shifted their Faith from the Cross to other things)*, *even* as unto babes in Christ. *(Ironically enough, this is spoken to people who considered themselves to be spiritual giants.)*

2 I have fed you with milk, and not with meat *(because of their carnality)*: for hitherto you were not able *to bear it*, neither yet now are you able. *(They were still functioning in spiritual immaturity. Their spiritual growth had stopped.)*

3 For you are yet carnal *(in the short version, carnality is the placing of one's faith in that other than the Cross; in other words, such a one makes the Cross of Christ of none effect [1:17])*: for whereas *there is* among you envying, and strife, and divisions, are you not carnal, and walk as men? *(They acted and spoke in the same way men of the world act and speak; in other words, as the unconverted.)*

4 For while one said, I am of Paul; and another, I *am* of Apollos; are you not carnal? *(This is the party spirit, which has wrecked so many Churches.)*

LABORERS

5 Who then is Paul, and who *is* Apollos *(the idea is these men, though used greatly by God, were still mere men)*, but Ministers by whom you believed *(better translated, "Though whom you believed")*, even as the Lord gave to every man? *(Whatever Gifts each Preacher had came from the Lord, and was not due to their own, abilities or merit.)*

6 I have planted *(refers to Paul being the founder of the Church per se under Christ)*, Apollos watered *(the strengthening of the Faith of wavering Churches)*; but God gave the increase *(pertains to souls and their Spiritual Growth)*.

7 So then neither is he who plants any thing, neither he who waters *(the Planter and the Waterer are nothing by comparison to the Lord)*; but God Who gives the increase. *(Man by his own ability cannot bring about the increase, no matter how much he plants or waters, spiritually speaking.)*

8 Now he who plants and he who waters are one *(literally means in the Greek, "one thing")*: and every man shall receive his own reward according to his own labour. *(Paul did not say, "according to his own success," but rather "labor." God hasn't called us to be successful, but He has called us to be Faithful.)*

9 For we are labourers together with God *(pertains to Labor in the harvest)*: **you are God's husbandry** *(God's field, God's tilled land)*, *you are* **God's building** *(Vineyard).*

10 According to the Grace of God which is given unto me, as a wise masterbuilder *(in essence, Paul, under Christ, founded the Church)*, **I have laid the foundation** *(Jesus Christ and Him Crucified)*, **and another builds thereon** *(speaks of all Preachers who followed thereafter, even unto this very moment, and have built upon this Foundation).* **But let every man take heed how he builds thereupon.** *(All must Preach the same Doctrine Paul Preached, in essence, "Jesus Christ and Him Crucified.")*

FOUNDATION

11 For other foundation can no man lay than that is laid *(anything other than the Cross is another foundation and, therefore, unacceptable to the Lord)*, **which is Jesus Christ** *(Who He is, God manifest in the flesh, and What He did, Redemption through the Cross).*

12 Now if any man build upon this foundation gold, silver, precious stones *(presents Paul using symbols; the first three are materials which will stand the test of fire, symbolic of the Word of God which is the Standard)*, **wood, hay, stubble** *(will not stand the test of fire)*;

13 Every man's work shall be made manifest *(at the Judgment Seat of Christ)*: **for the day shall declare it** *(the time of the Judgment Seat of Christ)*, **because it shall be revealed by fire** *(the fire of God's Word)*; **and the fire shall try every man's work of what sort it is.** *("Fire" in the Greek is "puri," and speaks of the ability of Christ, Who will be the Judge and Who sees through everything we do [Rev. 2:18]. He Alone knows our very motives!)*

14 If any man's work abide which he has built thereupon *(assuming it to be true)*, **he shall receive a reward** *(pertains to that which will be eternal, although we aren't told what it will be).*

15 If any man's work shall be burned, he shall suffer loss *(refers to the loss of reward, but not Salvation)*: **but he himself shall be saved; yet so as by fire.** *(Actually, this means the person is saved "despite the fire." While the fire of the Word of God will definitely burn up improper works, it will not touch our Salvation, that being in Christ and the Cross.)*

THE TEMPLE

16 Know you not that you are the Temple of God *(where the Holy Spirit abides)*, **and** *that* **the Spirit of God dwells in you?** *(That makes the Born-Again Believer His permanent home.)*

17 If any man defile the Temple of God *(our physical bodies must be a living Sacrifice, which means that we stay Holy by ever making the Cross the Object of our Faith [Rom. 12:1])*, **him shall God destroy** *(to fail to function in God's Prescribed Order [the Cross], opens the Believer up to Satan, which will ultimately result in destruction)*; **for the Temple of God is Holy, which** *Temple* **you are.** *(We are "Holy" by virtue of being "in Christ." We remain Holy by the Work of the Holy Spirit, Who demands that our Faith ever be in the Cross, which has made all of this possible.)*

18 Let no man deceive himself *(proclaims that which is possible, or the admonition would not have been given).* **If any man among you seems to be wise in this world** *(is not meant to denigrate education, but rather to portray the Truth that neither God nor His Ways can be found through the wisdom of this world, i.e., higher education, etc.)*, **let him become a fool** *(let the person accept the Lord as his Saviour, and then go to the Word of God to learn about the Lord, which the world thinks is foolish)*, **that he may be wise** *(concerns itself with True wisdom).*

19 For the wisdom of this world is foolishness with God *(because it's all wrong).* **For it is written** *(Job 5:13)*, **He takes the wise in their own craftiness.** *(God will see to it that such people are caught in the traps they set for other people.)*

20 And again *(Ps. 94:11)*, **The Lord knows the thoughts of the wise** *(the worldly wise)*, **that they are vain** *(empty nothings).*

21 Therefore let no man glory in men *(but rather the Lord).* **For all things are yours** *(everything given by God is available to every single Believer, providing it is the Will of God; God does not play favorites)*;

22 Whether Paul, or Apollos, or Cephas, or the world, or life, or death, or things present, or things to come *(the Lord Rules all things)*; **all are yours** *(nothing can happen to us, but that the Lord directs the action)*;

23 And you are Christ's *(we are bought with a price, the Cross)*; **and Christ** *is* **God's** *(refers to what Christ has done to Redeem humanity by*

means of the Cross, which was the Plan of God [I Pet. 1:18-20]).

CHAPTER 4
(A.D. 59)
JUDGMENT

LET a man so account of us, as of the Ministers of Christ *(Christians should form some estimate of the position of Ministers of the Gospel, and Paul tells us what that estimate should be)*, and Stewards *(literally a house-manager)* of the Mysteries of God. *(These are Truths once hidden, but now revealed.)*

2 Moreover it is required in Stewards, that a man be found Faithful *(as stated, God doesn't demand success, but He does demand Faithfulness).*

3 But with me it is a very small thing that I should be judged of you *(judged regarding his motives)*, or of man's judgment *(refers to any man judging him regarding motives)*: yes, I judge not mine own self. *(In effect, this says a Believer is not actually even qualified to properly judge himself, much less others.)*

4 For I know nothing by myself *(in effect, "the verdict of my own conscience acquits me of all intentional unfaithfulness"; but this is insufficient, because God sees with clearer eyes than ours)*; yet am I not hereby justified *(I know of nothing in my life or Ministry that is contrary to the Lord, still it is not my judgment that counts in this case, but rather that of the Lord)*: but He who judges me is the Lord *(refers to the Lord as the final Command, in fact the only True Judge).*

5 Therefore judge nothing before the time, until the Lord come *(refers to the coming "Judgment Seat of Christ")*, Who both will bring to light the hidden things of darkness, and will make manifest the counsels of the hearts *(at that time, the Lord will reveal the true motives behind the actions of His People)*: and then shall every man have praise of God *(actually means "such praise as he deserves").*

HUMILITY

6 And these things, Brethren, I have in a figure transferred to myself and *to* Apollos for your sakes *(he has used himself and Apollos as examples)*; that you might learn in us not to think *of men* above that which is written *(refers to the Scriptures)*, that no one of you be puffed up for one against another *(an inflation of pride).*

7 For who makes you to differ *from another?* *(All are on the same level, in desperate need of God.)* and what have you that you did not receive? *(Whatever we have is a Gift, not a merit.)* now if you did receive *it*, why do you glory, as if you had not received *it*? *(This presents a fake boast!)*

8 Now you are full, now you are rich *(presents the Apostle using irony)*, you have reigned as kings without us *(you are acting as if you do not need our Ministry)*: and I would to God you did reign, that we also might reign with you *(in effect, says he wished they were actually in the Millennium).*

9 For I think that God has set forth us the Apostles last, as it were appointed to death *(gladiators in the arena, appointed to die)*: for we are made a spectacle unto the world, and to Angels, and to men. *(God-called men and women are exhibited as a spectacle in a theatre to the world of men and to Angels.)*

10 We *are* fools for Christ's sake *(continuing to be the spectacle)*, but you *are* wise in Christ *(telling the Corinthians, and all others for that matter, that if they truly walk close to Christ, they will meet with the same contempt and hatred men showed to Christ)*; we *are* weak *(all Believers are weak, at least as far as the flesh is concerned)*, but you *are* strong *(these Corinthians were busy telling everyone just how strong they were in the Lord)*; you *are* honourable, but we *are* despised. *(The more popular the Church is, the further away from God it is. True Believers are despised!)*

11 Even unto this present hour *(speaks of the moment in which he was writing this particular Epistle)* we both hunger, and thirst, and are naked, and are buffeted, and have no certain dwellingplace *(perhaps this homelessness was among the severest of all trials)*;

12 And labour, working with our own hands *(spoke of his tentmaking, which he did in order to meet his needs in places where he was attempting to plant a Church)*: being reviled, we bless *(presents the correct spiritual stance for the Child of God)*; being persecuted, we suffer it *(put it in the Hands of the Lord)*:

13 Being defamed, we intreat *(irrespective as to how evil the response to the Message was, the Apostle would not allow his spirit to be affected by the opposition)*: we are made as the filth of the world *(could be translated, "we are treated as the filth of the world")*, *and are* the offscouring of all things unto this day *(shoots down popularity).*

COUNSEL

14 I write not these things to shame you (*carries the idea that he is not merely venting his spleen, so to speak; there is a lesson the Holy Spirit desires that he teach*), but as my beloved sons I warn *you*. (*These four Chapters are not merely presenting the hurt feelings of a Preacher who has been rejected, but rather proclaiming that these Corinthians were completely getting off track, which would fall out to their hurt if continued.*)

15 For though you have ten thousand instructors in Christ (*refers to Teachers*), yet *have you* not many fathers (*speaks of one who has brought the Gospel to the sinner so that he might be saved*): for in Christ Jesus I have begotten you through the Gospel. (*This presents far more than merely preaching. It actually speaks of the entirety of the Call of God on a man's life, resulting in souls.*)

16 Wherefore I beseech you (*I beg you*), be ye followers of me (*should have been translated, "be ye imitators of me"; Paul preached the Cross, lived the Cross, and knew if victory was to be had by anyone, it would have to be by the Cross; unfortunately, all Preachers then, as now, were not Preaching the Cross; hence the admonition of the Apostle*).

17 For this cause have I sent unto you Timothy (*Paul knew that the letter would arrive before Timothy*), who is my beloved son, and Faithful in the Lord (*his son in the Lord; Paul had won him to Christ some years before*), who shall bring you into remembrance of my ways which be in Christ, as I teach every where in every Church. (*Timothy would Preach the Cross, exactly as did Paul [I Cor. 1:17-18, 23; 2:2].*)

18 Now some are puffed up (*prideful attitudes*), as though I would not come to you (*should have been translated, "as though they would not eventually have to face me in person"*).

19 But I will come to you shortly, if the Lord will (*expresses a humble spirit of dependence*), and will know, not the speech of them which are puffed up, but the power. (*He addresses these remarks to those who actually thought their spirituality was greater than his.*)

20 For the Kingdom of God *is* not in word, but in power. (*The Message of the Cross changes lives, and does so by the Power of God.*)

21 What will you? (*This actually comes from the Holy Spirit, and delivers an ultimatum.*) shall I come unto you with a rod, or in love, and *in* the spirit of meekness? (*If the Cross is rejected, trouble ultimately is in the offing. Accepted? The opposite!*)

CHAPTER 5
(A.D. 59)
MORAL STANDARDS

IT is reported commonly *that there is* fornication among you (*fornication speaks of all types of immorality; it seemed to have been more widespread than just a case or two*), and such fornication as is not so much as named among the Gentiles (*meaning this type was not common among the Gentiles*), that one should have his father's wife (*refers to the man's step-mother; it also seems the Father was alive [II Cor. 7:12]*).

2 And you are puffed up (*it seems that some were attempting to say such was allowed under the guise of Christian liberty*), and have not rather mourned (*presents that which should have been the norm, but seemingly was not*), that he who has done this deed might be taken away from among you (*the idea is the individual repent, thereby ceasing such activity or be disfellowshiped*).

JUDGMENT OF SIN

3 For I verily, as absent in body, but present in spirit (*means that even though he is not present personally in Corinth, the direction he will now give is still to be taken just as seriously as if he were there personally*), have judged already, as though I were present, *concerning* him who has so done this deed. (*Does not, as some think, contradict Jesus' instructions to not judge [Mat. 7:1-5]. Paul is judging an action here, as all Believers are called upon to do, i.e., "Fruit" [Mat. 7:15-20].*)

4 In the Name of our Lord Jesus Christ (*refers to Christ as the Head of the Church*), when you are gathered together (*presents the authority of the local Church*), and my spirit (*refers to Paul being there in spirit, even though he could not be there in the flesh*), with the power of our Lord Jesus Christ. (*The authority is in the "Name," and the "Power" is in the Person of Christ. This recognizes Him totally as the Head of the Church.*)

5 To deliver such an one (*the one committing the sin of incest*) unto Satan for the destruction of the flesh (*it refers to ceasing all prayer for such an individual, and can be done by the local Body, providing the Church is correct*

in its position; God will no more honor wrong committed by the Church than He will by an individual), that the spirit may be saved in the day of the Lord Jesus (it is hoped that such action will cause the person to repent).

LEAVEN

6 Your glorying *is* not good (these people had taken liberty into license). Do you not know that a little leaven leaveneth the whole lump? (Leaven is figurative of such that is minuscule in quantity, but extremely pervasive in its penetrating force.)

7 Purge out therefore the old leaven (spoken in Old Covenant terminology, but with the same meaning carried over in the hearts and lives of New Testament Believers), that you may be a new lump (start acting like what your are, "a new creation"), as you are unleavened (speaks of the position that one has in Christ; that is our "standing"; it is the business of the Spirit to bring our "state" up to our "standing"). For even Christ our Passover is Sacrificed for us (the Believer can have victory over all sin by placing his Faith exclusively in the Cross of Christ, which Sacrifice addressed all sin):

8 Therefore let us keep the feast (is meant to serve as a symbol of the Jewish Passover, when all leaven was purged from the household), not with old leaven (old sins committed before conversion), neither with the leaven of malice and wickedness (refers to the ways of the world from which the Child of God has been delivered); but with the unleavened *bread* of sincerity and truth (can only be attained by one's Faith being anchored solely in the Sacrifice of Christ).

SOCIAL RELATIONS

9 I wrote unto you in an Epistle (refers to a previous letter written to the Church of Corinth, which has been lost) not to company with fornicators (actually means, "not to be mingled up among"):

10 Yet not altogether with the fornicators of this world (places a difference between those in the world and those in the Church), or with the covetous, or extortioners, or with idolaters; for then must you needs go out of the world (refers to normal commerce and activity with those who are unsaved, which is different than those who profess Christ).

11 But now I have written unto you not to keep company (Believers must not condone such immoral activity in other Christians, considering that they refuse to repent), if any man who is called a brother be a fornicator, or covetous, or an idolater, or a railer, or a drunkard, or an extortioner (plainly tells us that many will call themselves "Christian" or "Brother," who practice these type of sins); with such an one no not to eat (speaks more so of the Lord's Supper than anything else).

12 For what have I to do to judge them also who are without? (The idea is that we have no right to apply these standards to people who have not professed Christ as Saviour.) do not you judge them who are within? (As Believers, we have enough on our plate without having to call unbelievers to task. That is not our obligation.)

13 But them who are without (unsaved) God judges (so let's leave the unredeemed to Him). Therefore put away from among yourselves that wicked person (If the Believer will not repent of obvious wrongdoing, and we speak of scandalous sins, then that person must be disfellowshiped).

CHAPTER 6
(A.D. 59)
CIVIL LAW

DARE any of you, having a matter against another, go to Law before the unjust (this situation had evidently been brought to Paul's attention by the House of Chloe [1:11]), and not before the Saints? (This portrays what our Lord proclaimed as He laid down the rule for "Believers" to settle quarrels among themselves [Mat. 18:15-17].)

2 Do you not know that the Saints shall judge the world? (This refers to the Millennial and Eternal Reigns of Jesus Christ and His Saints.) and if the world shall be judged by you, are you unworthy to judge the smallest matters? (This presents a fitting rebuke.)

3 Know you not that we shall judge Angels? (This only pertains to those Angels who fell with Lucifer [II Pet. 2:4; Jude, Vs. 6; Rev. 20:10].) how much more things that pertain to this life? (The statement regards this present life as being elementary in comparison to that life to come.)

4 If then you have judgments of things pertaining to this life (seems like there were many quarrels in the Church at Corinth), set them to judge who are least esteemed in the Church (presents Paul again using irony).

5 I speak to your shame (I shouldn't have to

say these things). Is it so, that there is not a wise man among you? *(The question drips with sarcasm.)* No, not one who shall be able to judge between his Brethren? *(This is asked in the Greek in a manner which demands an affirmative answer. "Of course there is!")*

6 But brother goes to Law with brother, and that before the unbelievers *(a bad example!).*

7 Now therefore there is utterly a fault among you, because you go to Law one with another *(should not be among Christians).* Why do you not rather take wrong? *(This portrays the perfect example of uncrucified self.)* why do ye not rather *suffer yourselves* to be defrauded? *(It is better to suffer material loss, than to suffer spiritual loss.)*

8 No, you do wrong, and defraud, and that *your* Brethren *(to defraud anyone is bad enough, but to defraud a fellow Brother in the Lord is worse still!).*

PURITY

9 Do you not know that the unrighteous shall not inherit the Kingdom of God? *(This shoots down the unscriptural Doctrine of Unconditional Eternal Security.)* Be not deceived *(presents the same words of our Lord, "let no man deceive you" [Mk. 13:5]):* neither fornicators, nor idolaters, nor adulterers, nor effeminate, nor abusers of themselves with mankind *(the proof of true Christianity is the changed life),*

10 Nor thieves, nor covetous, nor drunkards, nor revilers, nor extortioners, shall inherit the Kingdom of God *(refers to those who call themselves "Believers," but yet continue to practice the sins mentioned, whom the Holy Spirit says are not saved, irrespective of their claims).*

11 And such were some of you *(before conversion):* but you are washed *(refers to the Blood of Jesus cleansing from all sin),* but you are Sanctified *(one's position in Christ),* but you are Justified *(declared not guilty)* in the Name of the Lord Jesus *(refers to Christ and what He did at the Cross, in order that we might be saved),* and by the Spirit of our God *(proclaims the Third Person of the Triune Godhead as the Mechanic in this great Work of Grace).*

12 All things are Lawful unto me *(refers to the fact that Christianity is not a religion which consists of rules, etc.),* but all things are not expedient *(not profitable):* all things are Lawful for me, but I will not be brought under the power of any *(Grace does not give a license to*

sin, but rather liberty to live a Holy Life).

13 Meats for the belly, and the belly for meats *(food contains no spiritual application):* but God shall destroy both it and them *(don't make a god out of your belly; it won't set well with the Lord).* Now the body *is* not for fornication, but for the Lord *(our physical bodies are Temples of the Holy Spirit [3:16]);* and the Lord for the body *(if we keep the Temple pure, which we can only do by His Grace, He will keep it well).*

14 And God has both raised up the Lord *(the Resurrection of our Lord),* and will also raise up us by His Own Power *(carries the idea that the human body belongs to God, not just the soul and spirit, because it will also participate in the physical Resurrection of Believers).*

15 Do you not know that your bodies are the members of Christ? *(When a person is saved, they are saved holistically, meaning spirit, soul, and body. We become a member of Christ as a unity, with the Holy Spirit looking at the triune being of man as "one.")* shall I then take the members of Christ, and make *them* the members of an harlot? *(This constitutes every part of the physical body, including the sex organs, as belonging to Christ.)* God forbid *("may it never be!").*

16 What? *(How could anyone, especially a Believer, think the Holy Spirit would sanction the terrible sin of fornication!)* do you not know that he which is joined to an harlot is one body? *(Involves an argument against this sin which is the most original and impressive that could have been used.)* for two, said He, shall be one flesh *([Gen. 2:24] this means that no type of sexual intercourse between the sexes is free from sin, except under the sanction of marriage).*

17 But he who is joined unto the Lord *(indicates the closest possible union, symbolized by the sexual union of a Christian husband and wife)* is one spirit *(reflects the same union with Christ, albeit in a spiritual sense, as a husband and wife have in a physical sense).*

18 Flee fornication *(is not a suggestion, but a Command; fornication, as an abbreviated definition, pertains to any type of immorality).* Every sin that a man does is without the body *(speaks of all sins other than fornication; gluttony, drunkenness, or drug addiction, etc., while effecting the body in a negative way, originate from without; with fornication, the source of uncleanness is in the heart);* but he who commits fornication sins against his own body

(presents in the physical sense a type of the spiritual union of man with devils; that's the reason God referred to Israel worshiping idols as "spiritual adultery or fornication" [Jer. 3:1-9; Ezek. 23:1-45; Hos., Chpt. 4]).

19 What? *(By this time, you should know!)* do you not know that your body is the Temple of the Holy Spirit *which is* in you *(actually refers to the human body of the Born-Again Believer as being a Sanctuary of the Holy Spirit),* which you have of God *(means that it's all of God and must be treated accordingly),* and you are not your own? *(We belong to the Lord.)*

20 For you are bought with a price *(the price was the shed Blood of Christ at Calvary):* therefore Glorify God in your body *(the house of the Spirit),* and in your spirit *(the use of the house),* which are God's *(because we were created by God, and have been purchased at great price).*

CHAPTER 7
(A.D. 59)
UNMARRIED CHRISTIANS

NOW concerning the things whereof you wrote unto me *(the Apostle will now address things he was asked in a letter; the previous Chapters addressed things he had been told):* *It is* good for a man not to touch a woman *(it is not wrong for a man not to marry, providing the Lord desires this for the man's personal life).*

2 Nevertheless, *to avoid* fornication, let every man have his own wife, and let every woman have her own husband *(this is a rule, not merely permission).*

MARRIED CHRISTIANS

3 Let the husband render unto the wife due benevolence *(it refers to the husband respecting the sexual needs of his wife, and to meet them accordingly; of course, we speak of legitimate needs):* and likewise also the wife unto the husband *(proclaims the same duty imposed upon the wife regarding the husband).*

4 The wife has not power of her own body, but the husband: and likewise also the husband has not power of his own body, but the wife *(refers to the fact that the husband and wife belong to each other, meaning neither has the right to refuse normal demands).*

5 Defraud you not one the other *(it seems that some married couples in that day were refraining from sexual activity, which they erroneously thought enabled them to live more spiritual*

lives; man seems to go from one extreme to the other!), except *it be* with consent for a time, that ye may give yourselves to fasting and prayer *(not mandatory, but given as a suggestion);* and come together again, that Satan tempt you not for your incontinency *(the idea is that the Believer not unnecessarily place himself or herself into a self-tormenting repression beyond what God demands).*

6 But I speak this by permission, *and* not of Commandment. *(The Holy Spirit, through Paul, leaves the details of lives, whether celibate or married, to the individual consciences, though with large-hearted wisdom and charity. He would emancipate them from human and unauthorized restrictions.)*

THE UNMARRIED

7 For I would that all men were even as I myself *(is not said by Paul to denigrate marriage as some have claimed; in effect, he is saying that he wished for the Coming Resurrection, when all would be as he was then).* But every man has his proper Gift of God, one after this manner, and another after that *(speaks of different types of Ministry).*

8 I say therefore to the unmarried and widows *(advice evidently given in response to a question),* It is good for them if they abide even as I *(is explained in Verse 26, where he says, "for the present distress," speaking of the hostility of Rome).*

9 But if they cannot contain, let them marry *(refers to the sex drive):* for it is better to marry than to burn *(refers to burning with passion).*

REGULATIONS

10 And unto the married I command, *yet* not I, but the Lord *(means that this is not mere permission as in Verse 6, but rather a Commandment),* Let not the wife depart from *her* husband *(pertains to departing on grounds which were not Scriptural; in other words, the husband being unsaved did not give the wife the right to divorce him on those grounds):*

11 But and if she depart, let her remain unmarried, or be reconciled to *her* husband *(refers to her getting a divorce or else Paul would not have restricted her to remain single, not remarrying unless it was to her former husband):* and let not the husband put away *his* wife *(places the same restriction on the husband as it*

does the wife; the Holy Spirit, through the Apostle, gives women the same rights as men).

12 But to the rest speak I, not the Lord *(doesn't mean this is not inspired! the Apostle is merely saying that Jesus did not teach anything about what to do with mixed marriages, i.e., "Believers and unbelievers")*: If any brother has a wife who believes not *(not a Christian)*, and she be pleased to dwell with him, let him not put her away *(such a situation does not provide grounds for divorce)*.

13 And the woman which has an husband who believes not, and if he be pleased to dwell with her, let her not leave him *(same as the previous Verse)*.

14 For the unbelieving husband is Sanctified by the wife, and the unbelieving wife is Sanctified by the husband *(means that the Believer, by virtue of being one flesh with his or her unbelieving spouse, is not considered living in an unlawful relationship; "Sanctified" means that God looks at the home as a Christian home and marriage, even though one or the other partner is unsaved)*: else were your children unclean; but now are they holy *(looked at by the Lord as being born in a Christian home, despite the fact that either the Mother or Dad is unsaved)*.

15 But if the unbelieving depart, let him depart *(speaks of desertion, and desertion for the sole purpose of the Cause of Christ)*. A brother or a sister is not under bondage in such *cases (means there is nothing the Believer could have done to stop the unbelieving spouse from departing, and in that case, the Believer is free to remarry)*: but God has called us to peace. *(An unbelieving husband or wife who doesn't want to keep the marriage together destroys all peace, which creates an untenable situation.)*

16 For what knowest thou, O wife, whether you shall save *your* husband? or how knowest thou, O man, whether you shall save *your* wife? *(Everything should be done to keep the marriage together, believing that eventually the unsaved spouse will come to the Lord, which may be their only opportunity.)*

17 But as God has distributed to every man *(refers to the rule that the circumstances of our lives are regulated by the Providence of God, and must not be arbitrarily altered on our own caprice)*, as the Lord has called every one, so let him walk *(the Lord allocates our way, so don't try to change the position unless it is obviously wrong, or there's nothing you can do about the change)*. And so ordain I in all Churches *(the instructions given are applicable to all Believers everywhere and for all time)*.

18 Is any man called being Circumcised? *(Jews)* let him not become uncircumcised. Is any called in uncircumcision? *(Gentiles)* let him not be Circumcised.

19 Circumcision is nothing, and uncircumcision is nothing *(Paul is saying that Christ has fulfilled all the old Levitical Law, so it is no longer binding)*, but the keeping of the Commandments of God. *(Those Commandments are found in Mat. 22:36-40. They can only be kept by the Believer understanding that all power and strength come through the Cross, which must ever be the Object of our Faith. That gives the Holy Spirit latitude to work in our lives, helping us to do that which needs to be done.)*

20 Let every man abide in the same calling wherein he was called. *(The idea pertains to the state or position one is in when one comes to Christ, respecting positions or particular jobs that are honorable.)*

21 Are you called *being* a servant? care not for it *(actually refers to a slave; the Holy Spirit can make His Home in the heart of a slave just as well as He can anyone else)*: but if you may be made free, use *it* rather *(refers to freedom as a preference, if such can be obtained; otherwise, serve God as a slave; slaves were the majority of the population in those days)*.

22 For he who is called in the Lord, *being* a servant *(slave)*, is the Lord's freeman *(in the Lord such a one is free, despite their station in life; that's all that really matters)*: likewise also he who is called, *being* free, is Christ's servant *(means that a person who is not a slave becomes a Bond Slave of Christ)*.

23 You are bought with a price *(refers to the ransom price which was the Precious Shed Blood of Jesus at Calvary's Cross)*; be not ye the servants of men. *(Liberation by Jesus Christ not only frees us from sin, but also from the fear of man and what man can do to us.)*

24 Brethren, let every man, wherein he is called, therein abide with God. *(The third time Paul says this [Vss. 17, 20]; the Holy Spirit places everybody in Christendom on the same level.)*

VIRGINS

25 Now concerning virgins I have no Commandment of the Lord *(meaning that the Old Testament or the Lord in His earthly Ministry did not say anything about this question; yet what He will now say is definitely inspired of*

God): yet I give my judgment, as one who has obtained mercy of the Lord to be faithful. (Paul seems to imply here that he had been celibate all his life, and the Lord had given him Grace as it regards the sex drive.)

26 I suppose therefore that this is good for the present distress (persecution by Rome), I say, that it is good for a man so to be. (He is speaking primarily of Preachers and the hardships they would encounter regarding a family concerning the "present distress.")

27 Are you bound unto a wife? seek not to be loosed (as stated, he is primarily speaking to Preachers). Are you loosed from a wife? seek not a wife. (In other words, if you aren't married, it might be best that you stay that way. But understand that Paul was speaking only of that particular time, which as well would have bearing on certain future times.)

28 But and if you marry, you have not sinned (speaks of the men whose wives had deserted them because of accepting Christ and Preaching the Gospel; it is not a sin for that man [or woman] to remarry); and if a virgin marry, she has not sinned (refers to young ladies who had thought to remain so for the balance of their lives, but found they were in love with a young man, etc.). Nevertheless such shall have trouble in the flesh (refers to the "present distress," i.e., "persecution"): but I spare you (wants to spare them some problems if he can!).

MARRIED CHRISTIANS

29 But this I say, Brethren, the time is short (we must make the most of the time we have and not unnecessarily burden ourselves, thereby, hindering our life for the Lord): it remains, that both they who have wives be as though they had none (Christians should sit loose to earthly interest; the Lord is to come first in all things);

30 And they who weep, as though they wept not (all earthly things are transient; we must remember that!); and they who rejoice, as though they rejoiced not; and they who buy, as though they possessed not;

31 And they who use this world, as not abusing It (we are just passing through): for the fashion of this world passes away (it is like a melting vapor, therefore, Christians shouldn't anchor in it).

RESPONSIBILITIES

32 But I would have you without carefulness (we are not to be burdened down with care). He who is unmarried cares for the things that belong to the Lord, how he may please the Lord (refers once again to Preachers of the Gospel, and especially considering the "present distress"):

33 But he who is married cares for the things that are of the world, how he may please his wife. (Once again, the "present distress" concerned what Nero was about to do, which would result in many Christians losing their lives.)

34 There is difference also between a wife and a virgin (concerns only the manner of availability for the Lord). The unmarried woman cares for the things of the Lord, that she may be Holy both in body and in spirit (Paul is not speaking to all Christian women, only those who are called to Ministry, and more specifically only those for which this would be the Will of God): but she who is married cares for the things of the world, how she may please her husband (actually means that her interest is divided between the Lord and her husband, whereas that of an unmarried woman is only of the Lord, or at least it is supposed to be!).

35 And this I speak for your own profit; not that I may cast a snare upon you (means that his words are not binding, but are meant to serve as advice and counsel; each individual is to seek the Lord respecting his own life and Ministry), but for that which is comely, and that you may attend upon the Lord without distraction (whatever the Will of the Lord might be in each individual case).

36 But if any man think that he behaves himself uncomely toward his virgin (does not speak of a sweetheart as it seems here, but rather the Father of this young lady), if she pass the flower of her age (was considered to be twenty years old at that time; as such, she must now be allowed to make her own decision concerning marriage, etc.), and need so require, let him do what he will, he sins not (due to the daughter now being an adult, she is free to make her own decisions, with the Father no longer responsible): let them marry.

37 Nevertheless he who stands stedfast in his heart, having no necessity (the daughter doesn't desire to marry; therefore, the Father could continue with his dedication respecting her), but has power over his own will, and has so decreed in his heart that he will keep his virgin, does well (concerns his dedication of her to the Lord, which is her desire as well, with the understanding that he will bear the expense of

caring for her all of his life).

38 So then he who gives *her* in marriage does well *(if that is what she wants)*; but he who gives *her* not in marriage does better *(is not meant to state that it is better morally, but rather "better relative to the Work of God").*

CHRISTIAN WIDOWS

39 The wife is bound by the law as long as her husband lives; but if her husband be dead, she is at liberty to be married to whom she will; only in the Lord *(to marry another Christian).*

40 But she is happier if she so abide, after my judgment *(remain single)*: and I think also that I have the Spirit of God *(places Paul's advice out of the realm of mere human judgment and into the realm of the Divine).*

CHAPTER 8
(A.D. 59)
FOOD SACRIFICED TO IDOLS

NOW as touching things offered unto idols *(lambs and oxen were offered up and Sacrificed to idols, with part of the meat then offered for sale in the market place)*, we know that we all have knowledge *(but our consecration must not stop there).* Knowledge puffs up *(knowledge without love)*, but charity *(love)* edifies *(builds up).*

2 And if any man think that he knows anything *(refers to the fact that we never know as much about the Word of God as we think we know)*, he knows nothing yet as he ought to know *(we ought to know much more).*

3 But if any man love God, the same is known of him. *(We all should have knowledge of the Word, but the emphasis must be on Love.)*

4 As concerning therefore the eating of those things that are offered in Sacrifice unto idols, we know that an idol *is* nothing in the world *(in effect, Paul is saying that the eating of such meat contains no offense to the Lord or His Word)*, and that *there is* none other God but one. *(The gods the heathen worshiped actually didn't exist.)*

5 For though there be that are called gods, whether in Heaven or in earth, (as there be gods many, and lords many,)

6 But to us *there is but* one God *("One" in unity and not "One" in number; it can refer to either)*, the Father *(speaks of relationship)*, of whom *are* all things *(refers to God as the Creator of all things)*, and we in Him *(which we are by virtue of Christ and the Cross)*; and one Lord Jesus Christ *(our Saviour)*, by whom *are* all things *(what He did at the Cross made it all possible)*, and we by Him. *(Everything we have from God comes to us from Christ, with the Cross being the means by which it is done.)*

7 Howbeit *there is* not in every man that knowledge *(the knowledge of the Cross was deficient, even as Paul said in I Cor. 1:17)*: for some with conscience of the idol unto this hour eat *it* as a thing offered unto an idol *(means some could not dismiss from their minds the painful sense that, by eating the idol-sacrifice, they are participating in idol-worship)*; and their conscience being weak is defiled *(refers to these Gentiles who until recently had been idolaters).*

8 But meat commendeth us not to God: for neither, if we eat, are we the better; neither, if we eat not, are we the worse *(has nothing to do with spirituality).*

CHRISTIAN FREEDOM

9 But take heed lest by any means this liberty of yours become a stumblingblock to them who are weak. *(We make men worse if, by our example, we teach them to act in contradiction to their conscience.)*

10 For if any man see you which has knowledge sit at meat in the idol's temple *(speaks of those who knew and understood true Christian Liberty, but yet lacked wisdom)*, shall not the conscience of him which is weak be emboldened to eat those things which are offered to idols *(contains the idea that such action on the part of the "strong" could very well fall out to the spiritual destruction of the one who is "weak")*;

11 And through your knowledge shall the weak brother perish, for whom Christ died? *(Paul could use no word that would more effectually point his warning.)*

12 But when you sin so against the Brethren, and wound their weak conscience, you sin against Christ *(to sin against a brother in any capacity is to sin against Christ).*

13 Wherefore, if meat make my brother to offend, I will eat no flesh while the world stands, lest I make my brother to offend. *(Everything we do must be done always with the idea of how it affects others.)*

CHAPTER 9
(A.D. 59)
PAUL'S APOSTLESHIP

AM I not an Apostle? *(The idea is not so much to defend his Apostleship, as it is to show how he has abnegated his own rights in order to be a proper example to others.)* am I not free? *(Being free, he has liberty, but he did not use that liberty in every case, even as he will further discuss.)* have I not seen Jesus Christ our Lord? *(This refers to the Vision on the Road to Damascus [Acts 9:3, 17; 22:7-8].)* are not you my work in the Lord? *(The Fruit was abundant!)*

2 If I be not an Apostle unto others *(meaning that some in the Early Church did not regard Paul's Apostleship)*, yet doubtless I am to you *(the Corinthians knew, or at least should have known, he was an Apostle)*: for the seal of my Apostleship are you in the Lord *(presents Paul using an example which was undeniable)*.

A NORMAL LIFE

3 My answer to them who do examine me is this *(those who question his Ministry)*,

4 Have we not power to eat and to drink? *(He could have asked them for financial help. He had every right to do so, but didn't, even though others who had no right did.)*

5 Have we not power to lead about a sister, a wife, as well as other Apostles, and *as* the Brethren of the Lord, and Cephas? *(The Churches, it seems, helped other Apostles with expenses, but Paul asked for none.)*

6 Or I only and Barnabas *(presents Paul mentioning Barnabas after the quarrel [Acts, Chpt. 15], which shows the Apostle regarded him with love and esteem)*, have not we power to forbear working? *(This means to give up the manual labor by which he maintained himself.)*

7 Who goeth a warfare any time at his own charges? *(The idea is if a soldier would expect to receive rations and wages from the Government he is serving, a Minister of the Gospel should expect the same.)* who plants a vineyard, and eats not of the fruit thereof? or who feeds a flock, and eats not of the milk of the flock?

8 Say I these things as a man? *(This presents Paul making the case that his statements are not merely his own thoughts, but are rather of God.)* or saith not the Law the same also? *(This refers to the Law of Moses, and is given in the next Verse.)*

SUPPORT

9 For it is written in the Law of Moses *(Deut. 25:4)*, you shall not muzzle the mouth of the ox that treads out the corn *(presents basically what Jesus said in Lk. 10:7)*. Does God take care for oxen? *(If the Lord cares for a lowly beast, and He certainly does, would He not do much more for those who are taking His Gospel to the world?!)*

10 Or said He *it* altogether for our sakes? For our sakes, no doubt, *this* is written: that he who plows should plow in hope; and that he who threshes in hope should be partaker of his hope.

11 If we have sown unto you spiritual things, *is it* a great thing if we shall reap your carnal things? *(The pronoun "we" proclaims the fact that the argument applies not only to Paul's own case, but as well to all Preachers of the Gospel.)*

12 If others be partakers of *this* power over you, *are* not we rather? *(It seems these other Teachers, whomever they may have been, were well paid, while Paul received nothing.)* Nevertheless we have not used this power *(this privilege)*; but suffer all things, lest we should hinder the Gospel of Christ *(that which should ever be foremost in the heart and mind of every Preacher of the Gospel)*.

13 Do you not know that they which Minister about Holy things live *of the things* of the Temple? *(This pertains to the Old Economy of God, which Paul is using as an example.)* and they which wait at the Altar are partakers with the Altar? *(This pertained to certain portions of the Sacrifices given to the Priests [Num. 18:8-13; Deut. 18:1].)*

14 Even so has the Lord ordained that they which Preach the Gospel should live of the Gospel. *(The idea, as is obvious, is that those who Minister in spiritual things should be supported financially by those to whom they Minister.)*

15 But I have used none of these things *(he had the right to be supported financially, but he never exercised that right, except in a limited way)*: neither have I written these things, that it should be so done unto me *(as well, he's not making these statements in order to spur the people to send him offerings)*: for *it were* better for me to die, than that any man should make my glorying void. *(In essence, this says he would rather die than stoop to such a level as that. To do such a thing would be manipulation, which the Lord can never bless.)*

16 For though I Preach the Gospel, I have

nothing to glory of *(within himself; even though he is an Apostle, boasting of these gifts is out)*: for necessity is laid upon me *(the Preaching of the Gospel is not merely a choice on his part, but rather a Command from the Lord)*; yes, woe is unto me, if I Preach not the Gospel! *(This proclaims an overwhelming moral compulsion.)*

17 For if I do this thing willingly, I have a reward *(the reward comes from the Lord)*: but if against my will, a dispensation *of the Gospel* is committed unto me. *(The word "dispensation" means "administration or stewardship." It actually refers back to the "Parable of the Talents" [Mat. 25:14-30]. In other words, the Preaching of the Gospel must never be looked at in any manner except that we give it our very best. Otherwise, we will lose the reward.)*

18 What is my reward then? *(This is different than the reward of Verse 17.)* **Verily** that, when I Preach the Gospel, I may make the Gospel of Christ without charge *(a price must never be put on the Gospel)*, **that I abuse not my power in the Gospel.** *(The Preacher must make double certain that he does not exploit the people, but rather that he edify the people.)*

PAUL'S POLICY

19 For though I be free from all *men (Christ is Lord and Master, not man)*, **yet have I made myself servant unto all** *(a voluntary submission, which is the Way of the Spirit)*, **that I might gain the more.** *(This is God's Way. Men rule, but the Lord serves! We must emulate our Lord.)*

20 And unto the Jews I became as a Jew, that I might gain the Jews *(Paul describes here the innocent concessions which arise from the harmless and generous condescension of a loving spirit)*; to them who are under the Law, as under the Law, that I might gain them who are under the Law *(him having Timothy to be Circumcised is a perfect example [Acts 16:3])*;

21 To them who are without Law *(Gentiles)*, as without Law, (being not without Law to God, but under the Law to Christ,) *(being "under the Law to Christ" satisfies every Law of God; it is simple Faith in Christ and what He has done for us at the Cross)* that I might gain them who are without Law *(gain the Gentiles)*.

22 To the weak became I as weak, that I might gain the weak *(refers to Paul not availing himself of some of his Christian Liberties simply because of the possibility of causing weak Christians to stumble)*: I am made all things to all *men*, that I might by all means save some.

(As stated, he is speaking of innocent concessions, never of compromising the Gospel.)

23 And this I do for the Gospel's sake *(the Gospel of Christ being the only means of Salvation, it must take first place in all things)*, **that I might be partaker thereof with *you*.** *(This is the love every Preacher ought to show.)*

CONDITIONS

24 Know ye not that they which run in a race run all, but one receives the prize? So run, that you may obtain. *(In athletic events, only one receives the prize. However, all who run for Christ, spiritually speaking, win the Crown. There are no losers!)*

25 And every man who strives for the mastery is temperate in all things. *(The Apostle is saying we should let the athlete striving and training to win a temporary crown be a lesson to us Christians regarding diligence.)* **Now they** *do it* **to obtain a corruptible crown; but we an incorruptible.** *(If they will do such for the "corruptible," how much more should we do the same for the "incorruptible"?)*

26 I therefore so run, not as uncertainly *(all Believers who run and continue to run, spiritually speaking, are certain of winning)*; **so fight I, not as one who beats the air** *(the Apostle now switches from the metaphor of running a race to boxing; he is not fighting uselessly, but rather the good fight of Faith, which speaks of Faith anchored exclusively in the Cross; regrettably, far too many Christians in this Christian endeavor are simply "beating the air")*:

27 But I keep under my body, and bring *it* into subjection *(which he does by understanding that all victory is in the Cross)*: **lest that by any means, when I have Preached to others, I myself should be a castaway.** *(This means that even if a man is a Preacher of the Gospel, if he doesn't look to Christ and the Cross, and ever make the Cross the emphasis, he will conclude as a castaway, i.e., "disapproved." The Lord has one way of victory, which is the same for both Preachers and the laity. It is "Jesus Christ and Him Crucified.")*

CHAPTER 10
(A.D. 59)
ISRAEL

MOREOVER, Brethren, I would not that you should be ignorant *(this means the Holy Spirit doesn't want us to be ignorant about*

these Truths), **how that all our fathers were under the cloud** (*the Presence of God, which led Israel*), **and all passed through the Sea** (*the Red Sea, typifying passing from death to life*);

2 And were all baptized unto Moses (*the Law-giver was a Type of Christ*) **in the cloud** (*a Type of the Presence of the Lord*) **and in the sea** (*a type of Water Baptism*);

3 And did all eat the same spiritual meat (*speaking of the Manna as a type of the "Lord's Supper"*);

4 And did all drink the same spiritual drink (*refers to the Smitten Rock [Ex. 17:6; Num. 20:11; Ps. 78:15]*): **for they drank** (*says literally, "they were drinking," implying a continuous gift*) **of that spiritual Rock that followed them** (*there is a Jewish legend that says the original Smitten Rock at Rephidim [Ex. 17:6] followed them throughout their entire Wilderness Journey and supplied water for them; every evidence is that it was true*): **and that Rock was Christ** (*the Rock typified Christ*).

5 But with many of them God was not well pleased (*should have been translated, "most of them"*): **for they were overthrown in the wilderness.** (*This actually refers to God purposely designing their destruction because of their rebellion.*)

6 Now these things were our examples (*we are to learn from them, and not make the same mistakes*), **to the intent we should not lust after evil things, as they also lusted** (*proclaims the same results of destruction for modern Christians as for the Israelites of old, that is if modern Believers insist upon living in sin*).

7 Neither be ye idolaters, as *were* **some of them** (*religion is the greatest idolatry of all*); **as it is written** (*Ex. 32:6*), **The people sat down to eat and drink, and rose up to play.** (*I am afraid much of the modern Church is "playing," exactly as Israel of Old.*)

8 Neither let us commit fornication, as some of them committed, and fell in one day three and twenty thousand (*a warning against immorality [Num. 25:1-9]*).

9 Neither let us tempt Christ, as some of them also tempted (*refers to questioning the Word of God*), **and were destroyed of serpents** (*Num. 21:5-9*).

10 Neither murmur ye, as some of them also murmured (*refers to finding fault with the way God is doing things*), **and were destroyed of the destroyer.** (*God is the ultimate Destroyer, even though He may use many other things as His instrument.*)

11 Now all these things happened unto them for ensamples (*as a warning; we had best heed those warnings*): **and they are written for our admonition, upon whom the ends of the world are come** (*should have been translated, "to whom the fulfillment of the ages has arrived," i.e., "the Church Age"*).

WARNING

12 Wherefore let him who thinks he stands (*is addressed to all Believers*) **take heed lest he fall.** (*This means to not merely fall from fellowship as some teach, but to fall from Eternal Salvation. This won't happen if the Cross is ever in view.*)

13 There has no temptation taken you but such as is common to man (*refers to the limitations God has placed upon Satan respecting that which he can or cannot do*): **but God** *is* **faithful, who will not suffer you to be tempted above that you are able** (*we have His Promise; all temptation is overcome by our Faith remaining constant in Christ and the Cross, which gives the Power of the Holy Spirit to help us [Rom. 8:2]*); **but will with the temptation also make a way to escape, that you may be able to bear** *it*. (*As stated, the "way of escape" is always the Cross [Eph. 6:10-18].*)

14 Wherefore, my dearly beloved, flee from idolatry. (*Anything in which we place our Faith, other than the Cross of Christ, becomes an idol.*)

15 I speak as to wise men (*whether they were or not, this is what they should have been*); **judge ye what I say** (*meaning in this case, "what I am about to say"*).

16 The Cup of Blessing which we bless, is it not the Communion of the Blood of Christ? (*The Lord's Supper is a Blessing, if it is understood properly.*) **The bread which we break, is it not the Communion of the Body of Christ?** (*The "Blood" and the "Body" refer to the price Christ paid on the Cross.*)

17 For we *being* **many are one bread,** *and* **one body** (*Christ is the "Bread," and the only "Bread" which produces one Body, i.e., "the Church"*): **for we are all partakers of that one Bread.** (*This speaks of Jesus Christ as being the only "Bread of Life." There is no other!*)

18 Behold Israel after the flesh (*the Law of Moses*): **are not they which eat of the Sacrifices partakers of the Altar?** (*This would probably have been better translated, "have they not Communion with the Altar?" It has reference to the next Verse.*)

19 What say I then? *(What am I saying?)* that the idol is anything, or that which is offered in Sacrifice to idols is anything? *(As a strict point, the idol is nothing, nor is the Sacrifice offered to idols anything.)*

20 But *I say*, that the things which the Gentiles Sacrifice, they Sacrifice to devils, and not to God *(proclaims in blunt terms the powers of darkness behind these idols)*: and I would not that you should have fellowship with devils. *(In effect, he is saying, "I do not want you to be sharers or partakers in demons." The same could be said for most modern movies, plus most modern entertainment.)*

21 You cannot drink the Cup of the Lord, and the cup of devils *(if we are going to associate with demons, the Lord will not remain)*: you cannot be partakers of the Lord's table *(the Lord's Supper)*, and of the table of devils *(that which the world offers)*.

22 Do we provoke the Lord to jealousy? *(He is definitely jealous of anything in our lives which competes with Him, as ought to be obvious [James 4:5].)* are we stronger than He? *(This proclaims the warning that God's "jealousy" cannot be challenged with impunity.)*

THE GLORY OF GOD

23 All things are Lawful for me, but all things are not expedient *(addresses Christian Liberty, and, as well, the manner in which it should be attended)*: all things are Lawful for me, but all things edify not. *(This addressed the contention of some of the Corinthians who claimed their Christian "rights" gave them the freedom to act as they saw fit.)*

24 Let no man seek his own, but every man another's *wealth*. *(This should have been translated, "every man another's good," meaning we should think of others regarding all things that we do. Freedom doesn't mean to seek my own good, but rather the good of others.)*

25 Whatsoever is sold in the shambles *(refers to the market place or the meat market)*, *that* eat, asking no question for conscience sake *(don't bother to inquire whether or not it was originally offered to idols)*:

26 For the earth *is* the Lord's, and the fulness thereof. *(Paul uses this Text to justify eating all foods, providing they are desired [Ps. 24:1].)*

27 If any of them who believe not *(unsaved)* bid you *to a feast*, and you be disposed to go *(pertains to the homes of these individuals, not to idol Temples)*; whatsoever is set before you, eat, asking no question for conscience sake *(don't investigate, just eat it and be thankful for it)*.

28 But if any man say unto you, This is offered in Sacrifice unto idols, eat not for his sake who showed it, and for conscience sake *(this stand is to be taken only if the information is revealed by the host)*: for the earth *is* the Lord's, and the fulness thereof *(meaning that this fullness, speaking of meat offered to idols, is not being used in the way the Lord intends)*:

29 Conscience, I say, not your own, but of the other *(refers to the fact that we must always be conscious of others)*: for why is my liberty judged of another *man's* conscience? *(Meaning all that we do must be done with the thought in mind of how it will affect others.)*

30 For if I by Grace be a partaker, why am I evil spoken of for that for which I give thanks? *(The Apostle is saying we cannot please everyone. Some will find fault irrespective what we do.)*

31 Whether therefore you eat, or drink, or whatsoever you do, do all to the Glory of God. *(With anything and everything we do, we should always ask ourselves the question: "does this bring Glory to God?")*

32 Give none offence, neither to the Jews, nor to the Gentiles, nor to the Church of God:

33 Even as I please all *men* in all *things*, not seeking my own profit *("seek to please all men in all things")*, but the *profit* of many, that they may be saved *(always with the view in mind of the Salvation of souls)*.

CHAPTER 11
(A.D. 59)
ADMONITION

BE ye followers *(imitators)* of me, even as I also *am* of Christ. *(Those who imitate Christ have a right to call upon others to imitate them.)*

2 Now I praise you, Brethren, that you remember me in all things *(Paul is thanking the Corinthians for seeking his Counsel)*, and keep the Ordinances, as I delivered *them* to you *(refers to the whole Body of Truth of the Gospel)*.

3 But I would have you know, that the Head of every man is Christ *(refers to authority)*; and the Head of the woman *is* the man *(pertains to the creation model)*; and the Head of Christ *is* God *(speaks here of two separate and distinct Persons [I Tim. 2:5])*.

REGULATIONS

4 Every man praying or Prophesying (refers either to the Gift of Prophecy or Preaching [I Cor. 12:10]), having *his* head covered, dishonors his Head (*dishonors Christ; such portrays a covering other than Christ*).

5 But every woman who prays or Prophesies (*tells us that women did pray and Preach in the Church, or wherever*) with *her* head uncovered dishonors her Head (*portrays the fact that, due to the Creation model, the woman should have long hair, at least longer than that of the man*): for that is even all one as if she were shaven. (*Refers to the fact that some women in those days had their heads shaved as a punishment for whoredom or adultery. The Apostle is saying that Christian women should not insist upon their rights so much that they begin to look like the worst of the world.*)

6 For if the woman be not covered, let her also be shorn (*in effect, says, "if the woman wants to wear her hair short like a man, why not go all the way and be shorn"*): but if it be a shame for a woman to be shorn or shaven, let her be covered. (*This refers to the fact that if she does not want to look like an adulteress, let her be covered, i.e., "have long hair."*)

7 For a man indeed ought not to cover *his* head (*while praying or Preaching*), forasmuch as he is the Image and Glory of God: but the woman is the Glory of the man. (*This refers to the fact that Eve was not "God's Image and Glory" in the same sense as Adam.*)

8 For the man is not of the woman (*Adam was not in any way derived from woman*); but the woman of the man. (*In fact, the woman was derived from man by the Power of God.*)

9 Neither was the man created for the woman; but the woman for the man. (*This probably would have been better translated, "for also man was not created on account of the woman; on the contrary, woman on account of the man."*)

10 For this cause (*refers again to the creation model that "the woman is for the man"*) ought the woman to have power on *her* head (*long hair, i.e., "authority"*) because of the Angels. (*This has to do with her submission to God's Plan as a constant reminder to the fallen Angels, who rebelled against God's Plan and the Revolution led by Lucifer, which took place long before Adam.*)

11 Nevertheless neither is the man without the woman (*needs the woman*), neither the woman without the man (*the woman also needs the man*), in the Lord. (*This refers to the fact that this is the manner in which the Lord created the original model, and demands that it continue.*)

12 For as the woman *is* of the man (*refers to the fact that Eve was originally created from Adam [Gen. 2:21-22]*), even so *is* the man also by the woman (*by or through the medium of natural birth*); but all things of God. (*This puts everything on an even keel, meaning that men are no more important than women, or women than men.*)

13 Judge in yourselves (*refers to common sense*): is it comely that a woman pray unto God uncovered? (*This doesn't refer to a hat nearly so much as it refers to long hair, or at least hair that's longer than that of a man.*)

14 Does not even nature itself teach you, that, if a man have long hair, it is a shame unto him? (*A man wearing long hair is really not in accord with the nature of a man.*)

15 But if a woman have long hair, it is a glory to her (*is a way of saying that such manifests woman's voluntary submission to God's Will*): for *her* hair is given her for a covering. (*This points to the idea that man is the head or covering of the woman under Christ.*)

16 But if any man seem to be contentious (*refers to both men and women, who were insisting on conducting themselves wrongly*), we have no such custom (*we have no custom other than what I have said*), neither the Churches of God. (*What I have said is being done in all the other Churches.*)

DIVISIONS

17 Now in this that I declare *unto you* I praise *you* not (*what he is about to say*), that you come together not for the better, but for the worse. (*This refers to the Church Services. They were being conducted in a manner which did not bring Glory to God.*)

18 For first of all, when you come together in the Church, I hear that there be divisions among you (*these "divisions" did not come about over Doctrine, at least at this time, but rather along sociological lines*); and I partly believe it. (*He is loathe to believe the worst, even on Testimony that is good.*)

19 For there must be also heresies among you (*a departure from the Word of God*), that they which are approved may be made manifest among you. (*Contains the idea that those*

who were prosperous, were claiming that they were "the approved ones." Sounds familiar doesn't it?)

THE LORD'S SUPPER

20 When you come together therefore into one place *(refers to the Assembly of Believers)*, *this* is not to eat the Lord's Supper. *(This has reference to the fact that they may have called it such, but the way it was being done was not recognized as such by the Holy Spirit.)*

21 For in eating every one takes before *other* his own supper *(some brought lavish meals)*: and one is hungry *(some were slaves, and had nothing to bring)*, and another is drunken *(means intoxicated)*.

22 What? *(This shows the indignation of the Apostle.)* have ye not houses to eat and to drink in? *(This is directed toward the wealthy.)* or despise you the Church of God, and shame them who have not? *(The very poor were shamed by their lack in the midst of such plenty, of which they were offered little or nothing at all.)* What shall I say to you? shall I praise you in this? I praise *you* not. *(He seems to ask himself; "do these people really realize what they are doing?")*

23 For I have received of the Lord that which also I delivered unto you *(refers to the instructions he is about to give concerning the Lord's Supper)*, That the Lord Jesus the *same* night in which He was betrayed took bread *(recalls the sacred occasion)*:

24 And when He had given thanks, He broke it, and said, Take, eat *(the remarkable thing about this is the interpretation our Lord gives)*: this is My Body, which is broken for you *(is meant to symbolize the Death of Christ on the Cross)*: this do in remembrance of Me. *(This pertains to the Believer actually partaking of that Sacrifice by Faith. In brief, this is the meaning of the New Covenant.)*

25 After the same manner also *He took* the cup, when He had supped, saying, This cup is the New Testament in My Blood *(the New Covenant would be ratified by the shedding of Jesus' Own Blood, which forever satisfied the sin debt)*: this do you, as oft as ye drink *it*, in remembrance of Me *(never forgetting what He has done for us, speaking of the Cross)*.

26 For as often as you eat this bread, and drink this cup *(symbolic gestures)*, you do show the Lord's death till He come. *(This is meant to proclaim not only the Atoning Sacrifice necessary* for our Salvation, but as well as an ongoing cause of our continued victory in life.)*

27 Wherefore whosoever shall eat this bread, and drink *this* cup of the Lord, unworthily *(tells us emphatically that this can be done, and is done constantly, I'm afraid)*, shall be guilty of the Body and Blood of the Lord *(in danger of Judgment, subject to Judgment)*.

28 But let a man examine himself *(examine his Faith as to what is its real object)*, and so let him eat of *that* bread, and drink of *that* cup *(after careful examination)*.

29 For he who eats and drinks unworthily, eats and drinks damnation to himself *(does not necessarily mean the loss of one's soul, but rather temporal penalties, which can become much more serious)*, not discerning the Lord's Body. *(Not properly discerning the Cross refers to a lack of understanding regarding the Cross. All of this tells us that every single thing we have from the Lord, comes to us exclusively by means of the Cross of Christ. If we do not understand that, we are not properly "discerning the Lord's Body.")*

30 For this cause *(not properly discerning the Lord's Body)* many *(a considerable number)* are weak and sickly among you *(the cause of much sickness among Christians)*, and many sleep. *(This means that many Christians die prematurely. They don't lose their souls, but they do cut their lives short. This shows us, I seriously think, how important properly understanding the Cross is.)*.

31 For if we would judge ourselves *(we should examine ourselves constantly, as to whether our Faith is properly placed in the Cross of Christ)*, we should not be judged *(with sickness, and even premature death)*.

32 But when we are judged *(by the Lord, because we refuse to judge ourselves)*, we are chastened of the Lord *(Divine discipline)*, that we should not be condemned with the world *(lose our soul)*.

33 Wherefore, my Brethren, when you come together to eat, tarry one for another. *(This proclaims the idea that all must share, and share alike.)*

34 And if any man hunger, let him eat at home *(the wealthy should prepare their sumptuous meals at home, but not in the context of the gathered assembly where some "have nothing")*; that you come not together unto condemnation. *(This refers to this "love feast" turning into a detriment instead of a Blessing. I would certainly think Paul's admonition would*

be heeded *after the warning given.)* **And the rest will I set in order when I come** *(probably other instructions which needed to be given).*

CHAPTER 12
(A.D. 59)
SPIRITUAL GIFTS

NOW concerning Spiritual *Gifts*, **Brethren** *(in this case, this has to do with the nine Gifts of the Spirit outlined in Verses 8 through 10),* **I would not have you ignorant** *(proclaims the Spirit of God, through Paul, saying He wanted the entirety of the Church to know about these Gifts).*

2 You know that you were Gentiles *(meaning that, before their conversion, they had no knowledge of God),* **carried away unto these dumb idols, even as you were led.** *(They were primarily led by superstition and witchcraft.)*

3 Wherefore I give you to understand, that no man speaking by the Spirit of God calls Jesus accursed *(the True Spirit of God would never do such a thing; so those who did such, were not of God):* **and** *that* **no man can say that Jesus is the Lord, but by the Holy Spirit.** *(Any other manner will be incorrect. It is the Holy Spirit Alone, Who reveals the Lordship of Christ to the Believer.)*

DIVERSITIES

4 Now there are diversities of Gifts *(different types of Gifts),* **but the same Spirit** *(all of this means the Holy Spirit never contradicts Himself).*

5 And there are differences of Administrations *(different Services, Ministries, Offices),* **but the same Lord.** *(Christ is the One Who assigns the different Ministries, with the Holy Spirit then carrying out the function. As well, Christ never contradicts Himself.)*

6 And there are diversities of Operations *(different ways the Gifts work),* **but it is the same God which works all in all** *(has reference to the fact it is God the Father Who energizes all things and all ways).*

PURPOSE

7 But the manifestation of the Spirit *(pertains to that which the Gifts make manifest or reveal)* **is given to every man to profit withal.** *(If the Gifts are allowed to function properly, which they definitely will if the Holy Spirit has* *His Way, all will profit.)*

NINE GIFTS

8 For to one is given by the Spirit *(proclaims the Holy Spirit as being the One Who carries out the instructions of Christ, relative to who gets what)* **the Word of Wisdom** *(pertains to information concerning the future, whether of people, places, or things);* **to another the Word of Knowledge** *(concerns the past or the present, relative to persons, places, or things; it is to be noted that it's "the Word of," which means a small amount)* **by the same Spirit** *(it is the Holy Spirit Who functions in all of these Gifts);*

9 To another Faith *(special Faith)* **by the same Spirit; to another the Gifts of Healing** *(prayer for the sick)* **by the same Spirit;**

10 To another the working of Miracles *(extraordinary things);* **to another Prophecy** *(this is for "edification, exhortation, and comfort [I Cor. 14:3]"; this has nothing to do with the Office of the Prophet);* **to another discerning of spirits** *(whether the Spirit of God, human spirits, or evil spirits);* **to another** *divers* **kinds of tongues** *(meant to be interpreted);* **to another the interpretation of tongues:**

DISTRIBUTION

11 But all these work that one and the selfsame Spirit *(refers to the fact that all the abilities and powers of the Gifts are produced and operated by the energy of the Spirit),* **dividing to every man severally as He** *(the Holy Spirit)* **will.** *(All the distribution is within the discretion of the Holy Spirit, which means that men or women cannot impart Gifts to other individuals. That is the domain of the Spirit Alone!)*

ONE BODY

12 For as the Body *(Church)* **is one, and has many members, and all the members of that one Body, being many, are one Body** *(refers to the Church as being the "Body of Christ"):* **so also** *is* **Christ** *(presents the Saviour as oneness in multiplicity, as is the Church).*

13 For by one Spirit *(the Holy Spirit Alone does this)* **are we all baptized into one Body** *(at Salvation, the Holy Spirit Baptizes the Believing sinner into the Body of Christ, which is the Born-Again experience; it doesn't refer to Water Baptism),* **whether** *we be* **Jews or Gentiles, whether** *we be* **bond or free** *(all must come in the same*

manner, "by and through Jesus Christ and what He did for us at the Cross"); and have been all made to drink into one Spirit. *(The Holy Spirit is the agent Who affects the work of Redemption carried out in our lives, which is made possible by the Death, Burial, Resurrection, Ascension, and Exaltation of Christ.)*

14 For the body *(human body)* is not one member, but many.

15 If the foot shall say, Because I am not the hand, I am not of the body; is it therefore not of the body?

16 And if the ear shall say, Because I am not the eye, I am not of the body; is it therefore not of the body? *(Just because these various organs are different in their functions does not make them any less necessary for the successful working of the entirety of the human body.)*

17 If the whole body *were* an eye, where *were* the hearing? If the whole *were* hearing, where *were* the smelling? *(For a human body to be whole, it has to have the various different organs.)*

18 But now has God set the members every one of them in the body *(human body)*, as it has pleased Him.

19 And if they were all one member, where *were* the body? *(If the human body were one great eye or one large ear, etc., it would no longer be a body, but rather a monstrosity.)*

20 But now *are they* many members, yet but one body.

21 And the eye cannot say unto the hand, I have no need of you: nor again the head to the feet, I have no need of you *(proclaims a mutual interdependence in the human body, which beautifully typifies the interdependence in the Body of Christ).*

22 No, much more those members of the body, which seem to be more feeble, are necessary *(all play their important part, without which there would be serious repercussion):*

23 And those *members* of the body, which we think to be less honourable, upon these we bestow more abundant honour *(probably speaks of the internal organs)*; and our uncomely *parts* have more abundant comeliness *(in reference to covering and dress).*

24 For our comely *parts* have no need *(being "comely," they do not need the same attention as others):* but God has tempered the body together *(giving dignity to all, but special dignity to the inferior parts)*, having given more abundant honour to that *part* which lacked:

25 That there should be no schism in the body *(refers to disunion and disruption)*; but *that* the members should have the same care one for another *(refers to the fact that all should be treated alike).*

26 And whether one member suffer, all the members suffer with it *(presents it the way it ought to be)*; or one member be honoured, all the members rejoice with it.

27 Now you are the Body of Christ *(refers to the Church)*, and members in particular. *(This refers to every single individual in the Church who is truly Born-Again.)*

28 And God has set some in the Church *(man or religious denominations cannot do the "setting," that being God's domain in its entirety)*, first Apostles *(God-called Apostles set the tone for the Church because of the special Message God has given them)*, secondarily Prophets *(is meant to include Evangelists as well, even as Teachers are meant to include Pastors; Prophets have the same function under the New Covenant as the Old, with one exception; Apostles have taken their place in the realm of Leadership; as well, this is the Office of the Prophet)*, thirdly Teachers *(those who explain the Word)*, after that Miracles *(pertains to this particular Gift of the Spirit)*, then Gifts of Healings *(examples of Gifts of the Spirit which should operate in the Ministry)*, Helps *(refers to every kind of help God sets in the Church, whatever it might be)*, Governments *(those who endeavor to hold the Church strictly in the Government of God, with all its many functions)*, Diversities *(many different languages, but unknown by the speaker and normally unknown by the hearer)* of Tongues *(the Gift which requires interpretation).*

29 *Are* all Apostles? *are* all Prophets? *are* all Teachers? *are* all workers of Miracles? *(There are different Offices and Gifts, but all are needed, as all organs of the physical body are needed.)*

30 Have all the Gifts of Healing? *(The answer is obviously, "no.")* do all speak with tongues? *(Paul is not addressing himself here to the initial Baptism with the Spirit, which is always and without exception accompanied by speaking with other Tongues, but rather is addressing the Gift of Tongues, which all do not have, although Baptized with the Spirit.)* do all Interpret? *(Again, the answer is "no," but some do!)*

31 But covet earnestly the best Gifts *(in essence, speaks of that which the Holy Spirit wants a particular Believer to have):* and yet show I unto you a more excellent way. *(This refers to the Foundation of Love that must undergird all we have and do in the Lord, which the Apostle*

addresses in the next Chapter.)

CHAPTER 13
(A.D. 59)
LOVE

THOUGH I speak with the tongues of men and of Angels *(actually says in the Greek, "If it were possible to speak with the tongues of men and of Angels"; as well, Paul is not denigrating speaking with Tongues, as some have claimed [I Cor. 14:18])*, **and have not charity** *(love)*, **I am become** *as* **sounding brass, or a tinkling cymbal** *(does not refer to our modern musical instrument which we call by that name, but that which made no more than a clattering sound)*.

2 **And though I have** *the Gift of* **Prophecy, and understand all mysteries, and all knowledge; and though I have all Faith, so that I could remove mountains** *(tells us that the Gifts of the Spirit can be had by less than perfect people, as should be obvious)*, **and have not charity** *(love)*, **I am nothing.** *(We now see the basis on which everything must be built — it is love. If not, we are nothing!)*

3 **And though I bestow all my goods to feed** *the poor*, **and though I give my body to be burned** *(shifts from Gifts to "Works")*, **and have not charity** *(love)*, **it profits me nothing.** *(As commendable as the acts may be, they bring a grade of zero unless God's Love motivates them.)*

CHARACTERISTICS

4 **Charity** *(love)* **suffers long** *(refers to patience)*, *and* **is kind** *(represents the second side of the Divine attitude toward human kind)*; **charity** *(the God kind of Love)* **envies not** *(does not want that which belongs to others)*; **Love vaunts not itself** *(is never a braggart)*, **is not puffed up** *(is not prideful)*,

5 **Does not behave itself unseemly** *(is forgetful of self and thoughtful of others)*, **seeks not her own** *(is unselfish)*, **is not easily provoked** *(is not embittered by abuse, insult, or injury)*, **thinks no evil** *(takes no account of evil)*;

6 **Rejoices not in iniquity** *(never gossips about the misdeeds of others)*, **but rejoices in the Truth** *(proclaims that which the Word of God identifies as Truth)*;

7 **Bears all things** *(never complains)*, **believes all things** *(takes the kindest views of all men)*, **hopes all things** *(keeps believing for the best)*, **endures all things** *(puts up with everything)*.

ETERNAL

8 **Love never fails** *(because love cannot fail)*: **but whether** *there be* **Prophecies, they shall fail; whether** *there be* **Tongues, they shall cease; whether** *there be* **Knowledge, it shall vanish away.** *(This refers to the fact that the Gifts of the Spirit will not be needed in the coming Resurrection, as well as many other things we could name.)*

9 **For we know in part** *(pertains to the "Word of Knowledge," which is just part Knowledge)*, **and we Prophesy in part** *(falls into the same category)*.

10 **But when that which is perfect is come** *(refers to the Rapture of the Church, i.e., the Resurrection)*, **then that which is in part shall be done away** *(as should be obvious)*.

11 **When I was a child, I spoke as a child, I understood as a child, I thought as a child: but when I became a man, I put away childish things.** *(The Apostle is comparing our present state, "as a child," to that which is coming, symbolized by a mature adult. That is the difference between the present state and the coming Resurrection.)*

12 **For now** *(before the Resurrection)* **we see through a glass, darkly** *(can only see the dim outline)*; **but then** *(after the Resurrection)* **face to face** *(we can look and see openly and clearly)*: **now I know in part** *(have some knowledge)*; **but then shall I know even as also I am known** *(then everything will be perfect and complete)*.

13 **And now** *(before the Resurrection)* **abides Faith, Hope, Love, these three** *(all three will abide forever)*; **but the greatest of these** *is* **Love** *(it is the greatest because Love alone makes us like God [I Jn. 4:7])*.

CHAPTER 14
(A.D. 59)
PROPHECY AND TONGUES

FOLLOW after Love *(let Love be the motivating factor in everything)*, **and desire spiritual** *Gifts* *(means to covet, but in the right way)*, **but rather that you may Prophesy.** *(This does not mean that "Prophecy" is the greatest Gift of all, but rather that it is the greater of the two vocal Gifts of utterance in Tongues and Prophecy.)*

2 **For he who speaks in an** *unknown* **Tongue**

speaks not unto men, but unto God (*this is speaking of "Tongues" as one of the nine Gifts, and not the prayer language that every Believer receives upon being Baptized with the Spirit; as is obvious here, when one speaks in Tongues, whether in his prayer language or as a Gift, he is speaking directly to God*): for no man understands *him* (*unless it is interpreted*); howbeit in the Spirit he speaks mysteries (*that which pertains to God and is a mystery to all, unless revealed by the Holy Spirit*).

3 But he who Prophesies (*speaks of the sixth Gift of the Spirit [I Cor. 12:8-10]* speaks unto men (*the opposite of Tongues, which speaks unto God*) *to* Edification (*builds up*), and Exhortation (*to implore*), and Comfort (*consolation*).

4 He who speaks in an *unknown* tongue edifies himself (*whether the Gift of Tongues or one's prayer language*); but he who Prophesies edifies the Church (*is meant for the Edification of the entirety of the Body, not just for the speaker*).

5 I would that you all spoke with Tongues (*refers here in this instance to one's prayer language*), but rather that you Prophesied (*now reverts to this particular Gift of the Spirit*): for greater *is* he who Prophesies than he who speaks with Tongues, except he Interpret, that the Church may receive Edifying. (*This is obvious because Prophecy is given in the language of the people, and is, thereby, understood by all. Tongues cannot be understood unless Interpreted. Once again, we are speaking here of Church Services, and not one's private devotion.*)

6 Now, Brethren, if I come unto you speaking with Tongues, what shall I profit you (*does not refer to the "Gift of Tongues" as one of the nine Gifts of the Spirit, which is meant to be interpreted, but rather Believers praising and worshiping the Lord in Tongues out loud during the Service*), except I shall speak to you either by Revelation, or by Knowledge, or by Prophesying, or by Doctrine? (*These things reveal Truth to the people, whereas one worshiping the Lord aloud in Tongues, not meant to be interpreted, edifies no one but the speaker. Paul is not demeaning Tongues, but only insisting that they be used in the right way.*)

7 And even things without life giving sound, whether pipe or harp, except they give a distinction in the sounds, how shall it be known what is piped or harped? (*Unless a melody is followed, it is just noise!*)

8 For if the trumpet give an uncertain sound, who shall prepare himself to the battle? (*Paul is not denigrating the trumpet, but only stating that it be used properly.*)

9 So likewise ye, except you utter by the tongue words easy to be understood, how shall it be known what is spoken? (*This refers to Believers in the Church blurting out in Tongues and quite often creating confusion. No one knows what is being said. So, even though the person speaking may be blessed, no one else is.*) for you shall speak into the air (*of no significance, at least at that time*).

10 There are, it may be, so many kinds of voices in the world (*speaks of the many and varied languages which make up the entirety of mankind*), and none of them *is* without signification. (*The language, whatever it might be, is important to the people who speak and understand it.*)

11 Therefore if I know not the meaning of the voice, I shall be unto him who speaks a barbarian, and he who speaks *shall be* a barbarian unto me (*nothing is accomplished*).

12 Even so ye, forasmuch as you are zealous of Spiritual *Gifts* (*Paul is not criticizing their desire for such, inasmuch as he has already told them to "desire Spiritual Gifts"*), seek that you may excel to the Edifying of the Church (*presents the real foundation of all that is being said*).

13 Wherefore let him who speaks in an *unknown* Tongue (*the eighth Gift of the Spirit*) pray that he may Interpret (*also have that particular Gift, which is the ninth Gift*).

14 For if I pray in an *unknown* Tongue, my spirit prays (*speaks of the prayer language, not the Gift of the Spirit, and states that it comes from one's spirit and not one's mind*), but my understanding is unfruitful (*signifying that it doesn't come from the mind*).

15 What is it then? (*This is meant to put the proper face on that which Paul has been saying.*) I will pray with the spirit (*pray in Tongues from my spirit, which speaks of one's prayer language*), and I will pray with the understanding also (*pray in my regular language, which for me is English*): I will sing with the spirit (*sing from my spirit in other Tongues*), and I will sing with the understanding also (*sing unto the Lord in English; Paul is speaking here of one's own private devotions, and not regular Church Services*).

16 Else when you shall bless with the spirit, how shall he who occupies the room of the unlearned say Amen at the giving of thanks, seeing he understands not what you say? (*This

refs to blessing someone or saying grace at meals. *If one does so in Tongues, the others there, not knowing what is being said, can hardly be blessed.)*

17 For you verily give thanks well, but the other is not edified.

18 I thank my God, I speak with Tongues more than you all *(as is obvious here, the Apostle is not denigrating Tongues, but rather regulating Tongues, and by the Spirit of God):*

19 Yet in the Church *(when it's time to give instruction)* I had rather speak five words with my understanding, that *by my voice* I might teach others also *(which is the purpose of the assembly),* than ten thousand words in an *unknown* Tongue *(which the people cannot understand, and thusly will not be edified).*

20 Brethren, be not children in understanding *(meaning that what he has said is easy to understand):* howbeit in malice be ye children *(children do not normally wish pain on others),* but in understanding be men *(be adult, mature).*

21 In the Law it is written *(Isa. 28:11),* With *men of* other tongues and other lips will I speak unto this people *(concerns a Prophecy given by Isaiah nearly 800 years before Christ, which concerns the Baptism with the Holy Spirit with the evidence of speaking with other Tongues);* and yet for all that will they not hear Me, saith the Lord *(predicts that many, if not most, will refuse to heed this which is of the Lord).*

22 Wherefore Tongues are for a sign, not to them who believe, but to them who believe not *(a sign to the world that we are living in the last days):* but Prophesying *serves* not for them who believe not, but for them which believe *(speaks of Edification, Exhortation, and Comfort to the Church).*

ORDER

23 If therefore the whole Church be come together into one place, and all speak with Tongues, and there come in *those who are* unlearned, or unbelievers, will they not say that you are mad? *(I think that would be obvious!)*

24 But if all Prophesy *(speaking words that can be understood by all),* and there come in one who believes not, or *one* unlearned, he is convinced of all, he is judged of all *(he can understand what is being said, whether he believes it or not):*

25 And thus are the secrets of his heart made manifest *(he can understand what is being said, and it speaks to him personally);* and so falling down on *his* face he will worship God, and report that God is in you of a truth *(that is, if he heeds the Message).*

26 How is it then, Brethren? when you come together *(a Church Service),* every one of you has a Psalm, has a Doctrine, has a Tongue, has a Revelation, has an Interpretation *(speaks of very good things used in the wrong way, telling us that it is not Tongues alone which can be used in the wrong way).* Let all things be done unto edifying. *(Everything done in the Church is meant to edify the entirety of the Body, irrespective what it is.)*

27 If any man speak in an *unknown* Tongue *(speaks of the Gift of the Spirit and how it is to be used in public meetings),* **let it be** by two, or at the most *by* three *(is not speaking of the utterances, but rather the individuals who are giving out the utterances),* and *that* by course *(simply means that these two or three should not interrupt each other);* and let one interpret. *(The Tongues are meant to be interpreted. This doesn't necessarily mean that one should interpret all Messages, although they may. But rather that only "one" should interpret at a time, which should be obvious.)*

28 But if there be no interpreter, let him keep silence in the Church *(what good does it do if there is no one there to interpret);* and let him speak to himself, and to God *(speak in Tongues to himself, which all Believers ought to do very often).*

29 Let the Prophets speak two or three *(speaks not only of those who have the simple Gift of Prophecy, but also of those who stand in the Office of the Prophet),* and let the other judge. *(This refers to the fact that everything should be judged according to Scriptural validity.)*

30 If *anything* be revealed to another who sits by *(refers to someone who feels the Lord is giving him a Revelation which should be given to the Church),* let the first hold his peace. *(Those giving Prophecies should not interrupt each other.)*

31 For you may all Prophesy one by one *(in due order),* that all may learn, and all may be comforted. *(The Holy Spirit ever has the entirety of the Body in mind.)*

32 And the spirits of the Prophets are subject to the Prophets. *(This means that if the individual claims to be compelled to blurt out at any time, such is out of order. The Holy Spirit works with the individual's spirit, with both deciding the right time.)*

33 For God is not *the Author* of confusion, but of peace *(the Holy Spirit will never contradict Himself)*, as in all Churches of the Saints. *(These instructions given by Paul pertain to all Churches, and not merely the Church at Corinth.)*

34 Let your women keep silence in the Churches: for it is not permitted unto them to speak *(is not referring to women being used by the Lord in the Gifts [Acts 2:17; I Cor. 11:5]; in Churches at that time, men and women did not normally sit together, but rather on opposite sides of the room; the women would call out to their husbands asking for an explanation concerning certain things, which was interrupting the Services)*; but *they are commanded* to be under obedience, as also says the Law *(refers back to Gen. 3:16 and the Creation Model).*

35 And if they will learn any thing, let them ask their husbands at home *(proving what we've said in the previous Verse)*: for it is a shame for women to speak in the Church *(to speak out in the manner Paul has just mentioned; it doesn't refer to women Teachers or Preachers, etc.; if so, it would be wrong for a women to sing or say anything in the Church, which we know is not correct).*

36 What? *(Paul is ready to end this discussion respecting order in the Church.)* came the Word of God out from you? or came it unto you only? *(The Apostle is telling the Corinthians that their lack of order is not of the Lord.)*

37 If any man think himself to be a Prophet, or Spiritual, let him acknowledge that the things that I write unto you are the Commandments of the Lord. *(If they really are Prophets, and they really are Spiritual, they will know that what the Apostle is saying is of the Lord).*

38 But if any man be ignorant, let him be ignorant. *(In other words, if they will not accept what Paul is saying, there is no way they will ever learn the Truth. They will remain ignorant, and could lose their souls.)*

39 Wherefore, Brethren, covet to Prophesy *(desire the Gift of Prophecy)*, and forbid not to speak with Tongues. *(This proclaims the fact that all the instructions he has given are not meant to disallow Tongues, but rather to put them in their rightful order. So where does that put the so-called religious leaders who ignore this particular statement, which is actually a "Commandment of the Lord"?)*

40 Let all things be done decently and in order. *(This is the purpose for the all the instructions included in this Chapter.)*

CHAPTER 15
(A.D. 59)
THE RESURRECTION

MOREOVER, Brethren, I declare unto you the Gospel which I Preached unto you *(it was to Paul that the meaning of the New Covenant was given, which, in effect, was the meaning of the Cross and the Resurrection)*, which also you have received *(unto Salvation)*, and wherein you stand *(live a victorious life)*;

2 By which also you are saved *(means that belief in the Resurrection is absolutely indispensable to one's Salvation)*, if ye keep in memory what I Preached unto you *(Heb. 2:1)*, unless ye have believed in vain. *(This refers to believing at first and then drawing back, which will cause one to lose one's soul. This also causes the unscriptural Doctrine of Unconditional Eternal Security to fall to the ground.)*

3 For I delivered unto you first of all that which I also received *(the meaning of the New Covenant)*, how that Christ died for our sins according to the Scriptures *([Ps. 22:15], speaks of the Cross of Christ)*;

4 And that He was buried *(because He really died, not merely swoon as some claim)*, and that He rose again the third day according to the Scriptures *([Isa. 53:10; Hos. 6:2], the Resurrection of Christ was the demonstration of the perfection and efficacy of His Atonement)*:

5 And that He was seen *(after His Resurrection)* of Cephas *(Peter)*, then of the Twelve *(proving that Paul was not meant to be the Twelfth Apostle, as some claim)*:

6 After that *(after those appearances)*, He was seen of above five hundred Brethren at once *(many think this appearance took place in Galilee)*; of whom the greater part remain unto this present *(are still alive)*, but some are fallen asleep *(have died).*

7 After that, He was seen of James *(the Lord's Brother, who did not believe on Him during His earthly Ministry [Jn. 7:5])*; then of all the Apostles *(Lk. 24:50).*

8 And last of all He was seen of me also *(this was after the Ascension of Christ)*, as of one born out of due time. *(He did not mean the timing was wrong, but rather that he was not worthy of what the Lord did for him.)*

9 For I am the least of the Apostles *(not mock modesty, but rather the most deep humility)*, that am not meet *(worthy)* to be called an Apostle, because I persecuted the Church of God *(before his conversion).*

10 But by the Grace of God I am what I am (*concerns the Favor or Mercy of God*): and His Grace which *was bestowed* upon me was not in vain (*it was not without effect, telling us that it is without effect with many*); but I laboured more abundantly than they all (*proclaims that which Grace enabled Paul to do because he had a greater grasp of Grace than anyone else, which speaks of the Cross, the means of Grace*): yet not I, but the Grace of God which was with me (*is with all Believers who look toward the Cross [I Cor. 1:17]*).

11 Therefore whether *it were* I or they (*in this case, the other Apostles*), so we Preach (*what they Preached*), and so you believed. (*False teachers had been attempting to turn their Faith away from the coming Resurrection. Let the reader understand that the Resurrection and the Rapture are one and the same!*)

IMPORTANCE OF THE RESURRECTION

12 Now if Christ be preached that He rose from the dead, how say some among you that there is no Resurrection of the dead? (*Some were actually repudiating the Doctrine of the Resurrection.*)

13 But if there be no Resurrection of the dead, then is Christ not risen (*Atonement and Resurrection are the two great foundation stones of the Gospel, and if either of them is denied, then the Gospel ceases to exist; once again, let us state the Truth that if one doesn't believe in the Rapture, then one doesn't believe in the Resurrection because they are one and the same*):

14 And if Christ be not risen (*if even one sin had been left unatoned, then Christ could not have risen from the dead, "for the wages of sin is death" [Rom. 6:23]; the fact of His Resurrection proves the Atonement of all sin, past, present, and future, at least for those who will believe [Jn. 3:16]*), then is our Preaching vain, and your Faith is also vain (*empty nothings*).

15 Yea, and we are found false witnesses of God; because we have testified of God that He raised up Christ: Whom He raised not up, if so be that the dead rise not. (*The Resurrection of all the Saints hinges completely upon the Resurrection of Christ. The former guarantees the latter, and without the former there is no latter.*)

16 For if the dead rise not (*if there is no Resurrection of all the Saints*), then is not Christ raised (*a repetition of Verse 13 to emphasize the argument that the Christian Faith in the Resurrection rests not on philosophical theory, but on historic fact*):

17 And if Christ be not raised, your Faith *is* vain (*all who do not believe in the Atonement and the Resurrection have a useless faith*); you are yet in your sins. (*Sins are forgiven and cleansed only by and through what Christ did at the Cross and in the Resurrection, and our Faith in that Finished Work. Otherwise the sins remain, which presents a situation of calamitous proportions.*)

18 Then they also which are fallen asleep in Christ are perished (*lost forever*).

19 If in this life only we have hope in Christ, we are of all men most miserable. (*That which is coming in the Resurrection is so far ahead of that which presently is, that there is no comparison.*)

RESURRECTION OF BELIEVERS

20 But now is Christ risen from the dead (*so says the Holy Spirit*), *and* become the Firstfruits of them who slept. (*The Resurrection of Christ guarantees the Resurrection of all Saints.*)

21 For since by man *came* death (*refers to Adam and the Fall in the Garden of Eden, and speaks of spiritual death, separation from God*), by Man *came* also the Resurrection of the dead. (*This refers to the Lord Jesus Christ Who Atoned for all sin, thereby, making it possible for man to be united once again with God, which guarantees the Resurrection.*)

22 For as in Adam all die (*spiritual death, separation from God*), even so in Christ shall all be made alive. (*In the first man, all died. In the Second Man, all shall be made alive, at least all who will believe [Jn. 3:16].*)

23 But every man in his own order (*Christ first, and then all Believers thereafter*): Christ the Firstfruits (*He was the First One to be raised from the dead, never to die again*); afterward they who are Christ's at His coming. (*This pertains to the Rapture of the Church, not the Second Coming [I Thess. 4:13-18].*)

24 Then *comes* the end (*does not refer to the time immediately following the Rapture or even the Second Coming, but rather to when all Satanic rule and authority have been put down, which will take place at the conclusion of the Millennial Reign [Rev., Chpt. 20]*), when He (*Jesus*) shall have delivered up the Kingdom to God, even the Father; when He shall have put down all rule and all authority and power. (*He will have put down all of Satan's rule, etc.;*

the means of which were made possible by the Cross and the Resurrection.)

25 For He *(Jesus)* **must reign** *(refers to the 1,000 year reign of Christ on Earth after He returns)*, **till He has put all enemies under His Feet** *(the subjugation of all evil powers, which will take place at the conclusion of the Millennial Reign [Rev., Chpt. 20])*.

26 **The last enemy** *that* **shall be destroyed (abolished)** *is* **death** *(Death is the result of sin [Rom. 6:23], and the Cross addressed all sin. After the Resurrection, when all Saints are given glorified bodies, it will be impossible to sin. Even during the Millennial Reign, sin will still be in the world, but not in the Glorified Saints. It will be eradicated when Satan and all his fallen angels and demons spirits, plus all people who followed him, are cast into the Lake of Fire, where they will remain forever [Rev., Chpt. 20]. Death will then be no more.)*

27 **For He has put all things under His feet.** *(God the Father has put all things under the Feet of Jesus.)* **But when He said all things are put under** *Him*, *it is* **manifest that He is excepted, which did put all things under Him.** *(This has reference to the fact that "all things" do not include God the Father being made subject to Jesus. God is excepted, as should be obvious.)*

28 **And when all things shall be subdued unto Him** *(implies that in Paul's day, this total dominion had not yet been exercised and, in fact, has not done so unto this present hour; but the time will come when it definitely shall be, which will be at the close of the Millennial Reign)*, **then shall the Son also Himself be subject unto Him Who put all things under Him, that God may be all in all.** *(There will be no trace of evil left anywhere in the Universe.)*

29 **Else what shall they do which are baptized for the dead, if the dead rise not at all? why are they then baptized for the dead?** *(Paul is actually saying, "It is a fruitless point to Baptize for the dead, which is unscriptural anyway, if there is no Resurrection as some are teaching.")*

IMPLICATIONS

30 **And why stand we in jeopardy every hour?** *(The idea is he wouldn't live a life of constant jeopardy if there were no Resurrection.)*

31 **I protest by your rejoicing which I have in Christ Jesus our Lord** *(the Corinthians were able to rejoice in the Lord because Paul had brought the Message of Redemption to them)*, **I die daily.** *(The Apostle is referring here to his life being in constant danger on a daily basis. He is not referring to dying out to sin daily. He argued that we should become dead to sin once, and then stay dead to sin always [Rom. 6:6-11; Gal. 2:20].)*

32 **If after the manner of men I have fought with beasts at Ephesus, what does it advantage me, if the dead rise not?** *(It is not to be taken literally. He is actually saying, "I am risking my life daily, just as surely as those who fight the wild beasts in the arenas; as well, as surely as these gladiators will sooner or later be killed, so will I.")* **let us eat and drink; for to morrow we die.** *(These words present the fatalism of those who do not believe in a coming Resurrection. So the Apostle is saying, if there is no Resurrection there is no Hope.)*

33 **Be not deceived** *(the statement actually says, "Do not go on being deceived!" meaning that many Corinthians had already been deceived into believing there was no Resurrection)*: **evil communications corrupt good manners** *(should have been translated, "evil occasions corrupt excellent morals")*.

34 **Awake to Righteousness, and sin not** *(in effect, says, "come to your senses")*; **for some have not the Knowledge of God** *(in effect, says, "for some are ignorant of God and His Ways")*: **I speak** *this* **to your shame.** *(I am speaking to shame you.)*

THE RESURRECTED BODY

35 **But some** *man (skeptic)* **will say, How are the dead raised up?** *(The skeptics use sarcasm.)* **and with what body do they come?** *(This refers to the form, shape, size, etc. False teachers were making fun of the Doctrine of the Resurrection of the human body.)*

36 *You* **fool** *(the Holy Spirit's answer to those who taught this false doctrine)*, **that which you sow is not quickened, except it die** *(Paul takes this from the Words of Christ, when He spoke of the seed falling to the ground and dying, and then bringing forth much fruit, which is the nature of harvest [Jn. 12:24])*:

37 **And that which you sow, you sow not that body that shall be, but bear grain** *(the little seed, when sown, will bring forth a beautiful plant)*, **it may chance of wheat, or of some other** *grain (one cannot tell from the seed exactly what the plant will be)*:

38 **But God gives it a body as it has pleased Him** *(the Resurrection process is in the Hands of God, Who can do all things)*, **and to every**

seed his own body. *(This thwarts every evolutionary speculation. Every person will have their own body, not that of another. They will have their own color, appearance, etc., minus imperfections.)*

39 All flesh *is* not the same flesh *(once again, a point that definitely contradicts the theory of evolution)*: but *there is* one *kind of* flesh of men, another flesh of beasts, another of fish, *and* another of birds *(refers to all being "flesh," but of different types)*.

40 *There are* also celestial bodies *(heavenly bodies, such as the Sun, Moon, etc.)*, and bodies terrestrial *(earthly bodies, which refer to human beings, animals, trees, etc.)*: but the glory of the celestial *is* one, and the *glory* of the terrestrial *is* another *(the glory differs)*.

41 *There is* one glory of the Sun, and another glory of the Moon, and another glory of the Stars: for *one* Star differs from *another* Star in glory. *(Paul has a point here, which we will see in the next Verse.)*

42 So also *is* the Resurrection of the dead. *(Some Saints, due to greater faithfulness, will have greater glory than others, which is the point of the previous Verse.)* It is sown in corruption *(refers to the grave)*; it is raised in incorruption *(refers to the Glorified Form and the type of Body God will provide)*:

43 It is sown in dishonour *(refers to the awful indignity of "dust to dust")*; it is raised in glory *(the same body, but glorified)*: it is sown in weakness *(death)*; it is raised in power *(life)*:

44 It is sown a natural body *(was energized by "blood," before death)*; it is raised a Spiritual Body *(energized by the Holy Spirit, not blood, and will be of immortal substance)*. There is a natural body *(which we now have)*, and there is a Spiritual Body. *(The Glorified Body of our Lord is the example, and our Glorified Body will be like His [I Jn. 3:2].)*

NECESSITY

45 And so it is written *(Gen. 2:7)*, The first man Adam was made a living soul *(the natural body)*; the last Adam *(Christ) was made* a quickening Spirit. *(The word "last" is used. No other will ever be needed. "Quickening" refers to making all alive who trust Him.)*

46 Howbeit that *was* not first which is spiritual, but that which is natural *(Adam came first)*; and afterward that which is spiritual. *(Christ, as the Last Adam, came second in order to undo that which occurred at the Fall.)*

47 The first man *(Adam) is* of the earth, earthy *(materialistic)*: the Second Man *(Christ) is* the Lord from Heaven *(a vast difference between the "first man" and the "Second Man")*.

48 *As is* the earthy, such *are* they also who are earthy *(it is the body and its present condition to which Paul points with the term "earthy")*: and as *is* the Heavenly, such *are* they also who are Heavenly. *(Christ is "the Heavenly One," and all who are "the Heavenly ones" are like Him. Paul is continuing to speak of the Resurrection, and what it will be like.)*

49 And as we have borne the image of the earthy *(refers to the fact that as our first father, we are frail, decaying, and dying)*, we shall also bear the image of the Heavenly. *(This tells us what we will be like in the Resurrection, i.e., "like Him.")*

50 Now this I say, Brethren, that flesh and blood cannot inherit the Kingdom of God *(pertains to our present physical bodies as they are now)*; neither does corruption inherit incorruption. *("Flesh and blood" comes under "corruption," while "the Kingdom of God" comes under "incorruption.")*

THE ULTIMATE VICTORY

51 Behold, I show you a mystery *(a new Revelation given by the Holy Spirit to Paul concerning the Resurrection, i.e., Rapture)*; We shall not all sleep *(at the time of the Resurrection [Rapture], many Christians will be alive)*, but we shall all be changed *(both those who are dead and those who are alive)*,

52 In a moment, in the twinkling of an eye *(proclaims how long it will take for this change to take place)*, at the last trump *(does not denote by the use of the word "last" that there will be successive trumpet blasts, but rather denotes that this is the close of things, referring to the Church Age)*: for the trumpet shall sound *(it is the "Trump of God" [I Thess. 4:16])*, and the dead shall be raised incorruptible *(the Sainted Dead, with no sin nature)*, and we shall be changed *(put on the Glorified Body)*.

53 For this corruptible *(sin nature)* must put on incorruption *(a Glorified Body with no sin nature)*, and this mortal *(subject to death) must* put on immortality *(will never die)*.

54 So when this corruptible *(sin nature)* shall have put on incorruption *(the Divine Nature in total control by the Holy Spirit)*, and this mortal *(subject to death)* shall have put on immortality *(will never die)*, then shall be

brought to pass the saying that is written, Death is swallowed up in victory ([Isa. 25:8], *the full benefits of the Cross will then be ours, of which we now have only the Firstfruits [Rom. 8:23]*).

55 O death, where *is* your sting? *(This presents the Apostle looking ahead, and exulting in this great coming victory. Sin was forever Atoned at the Cross, which took away the sting of death.)* O grave, where *is* your victory? *(Due to death being conquered, the "grave" is no more and, once again, all because of what Christ did at the Cross [Col. 2:14-15].)*

56 The sting of death *is* sin *(actually says, "The sting of the death is the sin"; the words "the sin" refer to the sin nature, which came about at the Fall, and results in death [Rom. 6:23]);* and the strength of sin *is* the Law. *(This is the Law of Moses. It defined sin and stressed its penalty, which is death [Col. 2:14-15].)*

57 But thanks *be* to God, which gives us the victory through our Lord Jesus Christ. *(This victory was won exclusively at the Cross, with the Resurrection ratifying what had been done.)*

58 Therefore, my beloved Brethren, be ye stedfast *(established, with your Faith firmly attached to the Cross of Christ)*, unmoveable *(not allowing your Faith to be moved from the Cross of Christ)*, always abounding in the Work of the Lord *(telling others of what Jesus has done, regarding His great victory of the Cross)*, forasmuch as you know that your labour is not in vain in the Lord. *(This is proclaiming that the Word of the Cross will always bring glorious results [I Cor. 1:18].)*

CHAPTER 16
(A.D. 59)
FINANCIAL HELP

NOW concerning the collection *(offering)* for the Saints *(refers specifically to Jerusalem)*, as I have given order to the Churches of Galatia, even so do you *(refers to this matter being the responsibility of all the Churches)*.

2 Upon the first *day* of the week *(Sunday, which replaced the Jewish Sabbath of Saturday)* let every one of you *(no exceptions)* lay by him in store, as *God* has prospered him *(give to the Work of the Lord on this day)*, that there be no gatherings when I come *(refers to their systematic giving)*.

3 And when I come *(to the Church at Corinth)*, whomsoever you shall approve by *your* letters *(means that the congregation at Corinth*

was to select one or more persons to take these funds to Jerusalem), them will I send to bring your liberality unto Jerusalem *(those chosen by the Churches)*.

4 And if it be meet *(necessary)* that I go also, they shall go with me. *(At this time, it seems Paul is uncertain as to whether he will also go to Jerusalem with this Gift. However, by the time he wrote II Corinthians, he had decided to go and, as stated, have these men accompany him [II Cor. 1:16; Rom. 15:25].)*

PAUL'S FUTURE PLANS

5 Now I will come unto you, when I shall pass through Macedonia *(presents the Apostle visiting the Churches in this area)*: for I do pass through Macedonia *(not to linger, to spend only a little time at each of the Churches)*.

6 And it may be that I will abide, yes, and winter with you *(he felt he needed to spend more time at Corinth than elsewhere, at least at this time)*, that you may bring me on my journey whithersoever I go. *(The Corinthians would help him with finances, etc.)*

7 For I will not see you now by the way *(refers to him not being able to come to them immediately)*; but I trust to tarry a while with you, if the Lord permit *(but when he does come, he hopes to stay a while)*.

8 But I will tarry at Ephesus until Pentecost. *(Paul is writing a short time before the Jewish Passover, and intends to leave Ephesus after the Jewish Feast of Pentecost, a period of about two months.)*

9 For a great door and effectual is opened unto me *(refers to spreading the Gospel)*, and *there are* many adversaries *(those who opposed his Ministry, there seemed to have been many)*.

TIMOTHY AND APOLLOS

10 Now if Timothy come, see that he may be with you without fear *(because of his youth, let no one intimidate him)*: for he works the Work of the Lord, as I also *do*. *(Inasmuch as Timothy is with Paul, he is to be treated accordingly.)*

11 Let no man therefore despise him *(refers to his youth and inexperience)*: but conduct him forth in peace, that he may come unto me *(I don't want him to come to me with a bad report)*: for I look for him with the Brethren. *(This pertains to those who accompanied Timothy, whomever they may have been.)*

12 As touching *our* brother Apollos, I greatly

desired him to come unto you with the Brethren *(a previous visit)*: but his will was not at all to come at this time *(for whatever reason)*; but he will come when he shall have convenient time *(when a good opportunity offers itself to him; the Church at Corinth greatly respected Apollos)*.

EXHORTATIONS

13 Watch ye *(a military command, be vigilant)*, stand fast in the Faith *(don't let the devil move your Faith from the Cross to other things)*, quit you like men *(act like mature men)*, be strong *(strong in the Faith, which makes one strong against the Devil)*.

14 Let all your things be done with charity *(love)*.

15 I beseech you, Brethren, (ye know the house of Stephanas, that it is the Firstfruits of Achaia *(in all of Greece, the family of Stephanas was the first to come to Christ as a consequence of Paul's Ministry)*, and *that* they have addicted themselves to the Ministry of the Saints,) *(used of the Lord, and greatly so!)*

16 That you submit yourselves unto such *(let Stephanas and those like him be the ones you follow, instead of these false teachers)*, and to every one who helps with *us*, and labors *(because they Preach the same Gospel as Paul, the Gospel of the Cross and the Resurrection)*.

17 I am glad of the coming of Stephanas and Fortunatus and Achaicus *(refers to them coming from Corinth to Paul at Ephesus)*: for that which was lacking on your part they have supplied. *(This probably means he wished he could have spoken to the entire Church at Corinth, but these Brethren who represented that Church would be sufficient for the present.)*

18 For they have refreshed my spirit and yours *(eased my spirit, and as your representatives, eased your spirits as well)*: therefore acknowledge ye them who are such. *(This refers to these three men, and that what they will say to the Church at Corinth will be correct and right.)*

19 The Churches of Asia salute you *(speaking of the Churches in that area)*. Aquila and Priscilla salute you much in the Lord, with the Church that is in their house *(a husband and wife, with one of the meeting places for worship in Ephesus being in their house; there were no Church buildings as such, at that time, as Rome was not allowing such)*.

20 All the Brethren greet you. *(Paul is speaking not only of those at Ephesus, but all the Churches of Asia, etc., as well.)* Greet you one another with an holy kiss *(culture for that day and time, but which now is a handshake or embrace)*.

SALUTATION AND BENEDICTION

21 The salutation of *me* Paul with my own hand. *(Paul had dictated the letter up to this point, with a Scribe doing the writing. However, the Apostle now takes the pen and, as we may say, signs the letter.)*

22 If any man love not the Lord Jesus Christ, let him be Anathema *(accursed)* Maranatha *(the Lord comes)*.

23 The Grace of our Lord Jesus Christ *be* with you. *(Refers to the favor of the Lord, which comes in an uninterrupted flow to all who have Christ and the Cross as the object of their Faith.)*

24 My love *be* with you all in Christ Jesus. Amen. *(Paul includes this last statement because he has had to write some very strong things in the body of this Letter. He is saying that it was love for them, which occasioned the necessity.)*

THE SECOND EPISTLE OF PAUL THE APOSTLE TO THE
CORINTHIANS

CHAPTER 1
(A.D. 60)

INTRODUCTION

PAUL, an Apostle of Jesus Christ by the Will of God, and Timothy *our* brother *(the Calling of the Apostle is meant by the Lord to serve as the defacto leader of the Church, and does so by the Message given to the Apostle; the salutation presents a high honor for Timothy)*, unto the Church of God which is at Corinth *(his second Epistle to this Church, of which we have record)*, with all the Saints which are in all Achaia *(refers to all of Greece)*:

2 Grace *be* to you *(which comes by the Cross)* and Peace *(Sanctifying Peace, which is the result of Grace)* from God our Father, and *from* the Lord Jesus Christ *(Who paid the price for this at the Cross)*.

THANKSGIVING

3 Blessed *be* God, even the Father of our Lord Jesus Christ *(presents Jesus as Deity and God as His Own Unique Father, which cannot be said of anyone else)*, the Father of Mercies *(Merciful Father)*, and the God of all comfort *(solace and consolation)*;

4 Who comforts us in all our tribulation *(does not deny the fact of tribulation, but does guarantee comfort in the midst of tribulation)*, that we may be able to comfort them which are in any trouble, by the comfort wherewith we ourselves are comforted of God *(we will comfort others by the same means which we have been comforted)*.

5 For as the sufferings of Christ abound in us *(pertains to Faith being placed in the Cross, and us experiencing its glorious benefits)*, so our consolation also abounds by Christ. *(We can offer this consolation of the Cross to any Believer.)*

6 And whether we be afflicted *(the offence of the Cross [Gal. 5:11])*, *it is* for your consolation and Salvation *(what the Lord has shown us about the Cross will be greatly to your benefit)*, which is effectual in the enduring of the same sufferings which we also suffer *(you will suffer the offence of the Cross as well)*: or whether we be comforted, *it is* for your consolation and Salvation. *(The "comfort" is in the Cross, which always guarantees that which is needed.)*

7 And our hope of you *is* stedfast, knowing, that as you are partakers of the sufferings, *you shall be* also of the consolation. *(They who suffer the offence of the Cross will also experience the comfort of the Cross.)*

8 For we would not, Brethren, have you ignorant of our trouble which came to us in Asia *(doesn't say exactly what)*, that we were pressed out of measure, above strength, insomuch that we despaired even of life *(if Satan hates anything, he hates the Cross; so he will attack those who Preach "Christ and Him Crucified," and do so powerfully)*:

9 But we had the sentence of death in ourselves *(Paul thought he was going to die)*, that we should not trust in ourselves, but in God which raises the dead *(the trial was meant to teach not only submission, but absolute trust in God [Jer. 17:5])*:

10 Who delivered us from so great a death *(the Believer cannot die until the Lord deems his work as finished)*, and does deliver *(the former spoke of past tense, while this speaks of present tense)*: in whom we trust that He will yet deliver *us* *(we trust the Lord for the future)*;

11 You also helping together by prayer for us *(proclaims Paul's deep conviction of the effectiveness of intercessory prayer [Rom. 15:30-31; Phil. 1:19; Phile., Vs. 22])*, that for the gift *bestowed* upon us by the means of many persons thanks may be given by many on our behalf. *(He felt that the prayers of these Believers contributed greatly toward his deliverance, and no doubt it did!)*

POSTPONEMENT

12 For our rejoicing is this *(boasting in the Lord)*, the testimony of our conscience *(a good conscience)*, that in simplicity and Godly sincerity *(the simplicity of Christ, which refers to the Cross [II Cor. 11:3])*, not with fleshly wisdom *(that which is outside of the Cross)*, but by the Grace of God *(made possible by the Cross)*, we have had our conversation *(conduct)* in the world, and more abundantly to you-ward.

(What the Cross has made possible in my life is meant for your abundant benefit.)

13 For we write none other things unto you, than what you read or acknowledge *(what we write to you is what we are)*; and I trust you shall acknowledge even to the end *(the Message of the Apostle wouldn't change, and he wouldn't change)*;

14 As also you have acknowledged us in part *(some in the Corinthian Church did not acknowledge Paul's Apostleship, so they didn't acknowledge all that he wrote as being from God)*, that we are your rejoicing *(rejoicing in the fact that they had Paul as their Teacher)*, even as you also *are* ours *(rejoicing in the fact that he was able to teach them and watch them grow in Grace)* in the Day of the Lord Jesus. *(This refers to the "Judgment Seat of Christ.")*

15 And in this confidence I was minded to come unto you before *(the Apostle had every confidence that the majority in the Church at Corinth would receive him favorably)*, that you might have a second benefit *(that he may give them more teaching on the Cross)*;

16 And to pass by you into Macedonia *(he planned to stop at Corinth on his way)*, and to come again out of Macedonia unto you *(refers to a second visit he had hoped to make; neither one actually came to fruition at that time)*, and of you to be brought on my way toward Judaea *(to leave from Corinth to Judaea; the new plan is now to not divide his visit at Corinth, but to make one stay in that city as presented in I Cor. 16:6).*

17 When I therefore was thus minded, did I use lightness? *(This refers to him changing his mind concerning the proposed visit to Corinth, at least regarding the date.)* or the things that I purpose, do I purpose according to the flesh *(evidently Paul was being accused by some of not knowing the Mind of the Spirit)*, that with me there should be yes yes, and no no? *(Some were saying that his "yes" didn't mean yes, and his "no" didn't mean no!)*

18 But *as* God *is* true, our word toward you was not yes and no *(not fickle).*

19 For the Son of God, Jesus Christ, Who was Preached among you by us *(places the argument over Paul's integrity squarely on the Gospel he Preached)*, *even* by me and Silas and Timothy, was not yes and no, but in Him was yes *(carries the idea of One Who changes not [I Sam. 15:29; Mal. 3:6]).*

20 For all the Promises of God in Him *(in Christ) are* yes, and in Him Amen *(means these Promises will not change)*, unto the Glory of God by us *(our Preaching the Cross to you will bring Glory to God).*

21 Now He *(God)* which stablishes us with you in Christ *(God is capable of keeping the people He saves)*, and has Anointed us, *is* God *(we have these benefits because of what Jesus did at the Cross)*;

22 Who has also sealed us *(a seal of ownership)*, and given the earnest of the Spirit in our hearts. *(This presents a guarantee that God will ultimately give us the balance of all He has Promised, which Jesus paid for at the Cross [Rom. 8:23].)*

23 Moreover I call God for a record upon my soul *(gives the reason for delaying his visit)*, that to spare you I came not as yet unto Corinth. *(He had opted instead to send his First Epistle to Corinth, which would prepare the way for a visit when he did come. He felt by the leading of the Spirit that this would be the best way to address the problems at Corinth.)*

24 Not for that we have dominion *(domination)* over your Faith *(actually a reference to the previous phrase of "not sparing them")*, but are helpers of your joy *(rather, he wanted to be a Blessing)*: for by Faith you stand. *(Faith in Christ and the Cross presents the only way one can stand.)*

CHAPTER 2
(A.D. 60)

BUT I determined this with myself *(concerns a settled question)*, that I would not come again to you in heaviness. *(On his second visit to Corinth, it seems things had happened which caused hurt to the Apostle. This was before I Corinthians was written.)*

2 For if I make you sorry *(a stand he had to take regarding one who had refused to repent, but did repent later because of Paul's stand)*, who is he then who makes me glad *(refers to the person who had sinned)*, but the same which is made sorry by me? *(The same man, whom Paul had made sorry, now repents and makes the Apostle glad. Some claim this was not the same man of I Cor., Chpt. 5. Whether it was or not, the principle is the same.)*

3 And I wrote this same unto you, lest, when I came, I should have sorrow from them of whom I ought to rejoice *(had he gone to Corinth when he had first intended, he may not have been met with rejoicing due to sin in the Church; that situation has now changed)*; having confidence in you all, that my joy is *the* joy of you all. *(Things have now taken a turn*

for the better.)

4 For out of much affliction and anguish of heart I wrote unto you with many tears *(pertains to the writing of I Corinthians)*; not that you should be grieved, but that you might know the love which I have more abundantly unto you *(presents the greatest proof of all — that of tears).*

FORGIVENESS

5 But if any have caused grief, he has not grieved me, but in part *(presents the Apostle dealing with the person who is probably the incestuous one of I Cor., Chpt. 5):* that I may not overcharge you all. *(He didn't want everyone in the Church at Corinth to think he was putting all in the same category of wrong direction.)*

6 Sufficient to such a man *is* this punishment *(means that turning him over to Satan had accomplished all that was desired [I Cor. 5:4-5]),* which *was inflicted* of many. *(Most in the Church obeyed Paul by turning the man over to Satan for the destruction of the flesh. Some few didn't, which means they didn't go along with what Paul had said.)*

7 So that contrariwise you *ought* rather to forgive *him,* and comfort *him (show love toward the man who had sinned and now repented),* lest perhaps such a one should be swallowed up with overmuch sorrow *(sink into despair).*

8 Wherefore I beseech you that you would confirm *your* love toward him *(do more than just say you love him, but rather show your love to him).*

9 For to this end also did I write, that I might know the proof of you, whether you be obedient in all things. *(In I Cor., Chpt. 5, the man was on trial. Now the Church is on trial.)*

10 To whom you forgive any thing *(forgive the man),* I *forgive* also *(I forgive you for taking the wrong direction at the beginning):* for if I forgave any thing, to whom I forgave *it,* for your sakes *forgave I* it in the Person of Christ *(forgiveness is a great part of the Christian Faith, and is demanded by Christ [Mat. 6:14-15]);*

11 Lest Satan should get an advantage of us *(if we obey the Word, Satan will have no advantage):* for we are not ignorant of his devices *(his ways, which take advantage of the Christian's wrong direction).*

12 Furthermore, when I came to Troas to *Preach* Christ's Gospel, and a door was opened unto me of the Lord *(concerned an opportunity for Ministry in this place),*

13 I had no rest in my spirit *(due to the problems in Corinth, which he addressed in his First Epistle, he could not take advantage of this open door; he was too troubled at the thought of the Church at Corinth possibly being lost, with perhaps other Churches following suit),* because I found not Titus my brother *(evidently refers to a prearranged meeting at which Titus was to give him some information regarding Corinth; the meeting did not occur because Titus was delayed for some reason, which caused even greater anxiety with Paul):* but taking my leave of them *(leaving Troas),* I went from thence into Macedonia. *(He no doubt met Titus at Philippi, who then gave him some good news concerning Corinth.)*

TRIUMPHANT IN CHRIST

14 Now thanks *be* unto God, which always causes us to triumph in Christ *(we triumph only by constantly exhibiting Faith in the Cross, which gives the Holy Spirit latitude to work in our lives and bring about the victory),* and makes manifest the savour of His Knowledge by us in every place *(the Preaching of the Cross [I Cor. 1:23; 2:2]).*

15 For we are unto God a sweet savour of Christ *(referring to what the Cross has done in lives),* in them who are saved *(by trusting in Christ and the Cross),* and in them who perish *(those who reject the Cross [I Cor. 1:18]):*

16 To the one *we are* the savour of death unto death *(continuing to refer to those who reject the Cross);* and to the other the savour of life unto life. *(All life comes through the Spirit, from Christ and by the Cross [Rom. 8:2].)* And who *is* sufficient for these things? *(This refers to the Gospel, which is so mighty to save from death.)*

17 For we are not as many, which corrupt the Word of God *(Preach something other than the Cross):* but as of sincerity, but as of God, in the sight of God speak we in Christ. *(God is observing all our efforts and will accept only that which is "in Christ," which always refers to the Cross.)*

CHAPTER 3
(A.D. 60)
MINISTRY

DO we begin again to commend ourselves? *(This was in order to prove his Apostleship.)*

or need we, as some *others*, Epistles of commendation to you, or *letters* of commendation from you? *(Paul is presenting this contention as an obscurity to suppose that he or Timothy should need such letters, either from the Corinthians or to them.)*

2 You are our Epistle written in our hearts, known and read of all men *(refers to the Saints at Corinth who had been saved under his Ministry, which were Epistle enough)*:

3 *Forasmuch as you are* manifestly declared to be the Epistle of Christ ministered by us *(Christ was the Author of this "Epistle" of which Paul speaks, i.e., "souls saved from sin and darkness")*, written not with ink, but with the Spirit of the Living God *(which is the highest commendation of all)*; not in tables of stone, but in fleshy tables of the heart *(referring to changed hearts)*.

4 And such trust have we through Christ to God-ward *(refers to the personal confidence Paul had that he was appointed by God, and God accepted his work)*:

5 Not that we are sufficient of ourselves to think any thing as of ourselves *(Paul was confident that he possessed that competency through Christ in the sight of God, though personally absolutely incompetent, as are all men for that matter)*; but our sufficiency *is* of God *(it can either be in God or self; it cannot be in both)*;

NEW TESTAMENT

6 Who also has made us able Ministers of the New Testament *(the New Covenant)*; not of the letter *(the old Law of Moses)*, but of the Spirit *(Holy Spirit)*: for the letter kills *(refers to the Law; all the Law can do is kill)*, but the Spirit gives life *(and does so through Christ, due to what Christ did at the Cross [Rom. 8:1-2])*.

7 But if the ministration of death *(the Law of Moses)*, written *and* engraved in stones, was glorious *(and it was)*, so that the children of Israel could not stedfastly behold the face of Moses for the glory of his countenance; which *glory* was to be done away *(the glory on Moses' face faded, just as the Law faded, as it was intended to when Christ came)*:

8 How shall not the ministration of the Spirit be rather glorious? *(It is a much better Covenant, based on better Promises [Heb. 8:6].)*

GLORY AND RIGHTEOUSNESS

9 For if the ministration of condemnation

be glory *(the Law of Moses)*, much more does the ministration of Righteousness exceed in glory *(due to what Christ did for us at the Cross, which made it possible for the Holy Spirit to do great things within our lives, providing we keep our Faith in the Cross; evidently, some false teachers had come from Jerusalem, attempting to extol the so-called virtues of the Law; in other words, they were trying to mix Law with Grace, which cannot be done)*.

10 For even that which was made glorious had no glory in this respect, by reason of the glory that excels. *(The glory of the Law of Moses could not begin to compare with the Glory of the New Covenant.)*

11 For if that which is done away *was* glorious *(the Law)*, much more that which remains *is* glorious. *(This pertains to the Gospel of Christ, which is forever [Heb. 13:20].)*

TRANSFORMATION

12 Seeing then that we have such hope *(which only the Cross could bring about)*, we use great plainness of speech *(doesn't mince words)*:

13 And not as Moses, *which* put a veil over his face, that the children of Israel could not stedfastly look to the end of that which is abolished *(as stated, the glory on Moses' face faded, and was meant to show that the Law would fade as well, which it did with Christ Who fulfilled it all)*:

14 But their minds were blinded *(they didn't understand the Law was meant to be phased out)*: for until this day remains the same veil untaken away in the reading of the Old Testament *(Israel was still trying to live by the Law, and some were trying to force it into the New Covenant)*; which *veil* is done away in Christ. *(The Law was meant to be fulfilled by Christ, and it was fulfilled by Christ.)*

15 But even unto this day, when Moses is read *(the Old Testament)*, the veil is upon their heart. *(This refers to Israel not seeing the true meaning and beauty of their own Scriptures, which portrayed Christ.)*

16 Nevertheless when it shall turn to the Lord, the veil shall be taken away *(which will be done at the Second Coming)*.

17 Now the Lord is that Spirit *(Holy Spirit)*: and where the Spirit of the Lord *is* *(He is with all who Preach the Cross)*, there *is* Liberty *(Liberty to live a Holy life by placing one's Faith in the Cross, which gives the Holy Spirit the latitude to work mightily in our hearts and lives)*.

18 But we all, with open face *(all who do not know Christ are veiled, i.e., "shut off")* beholding as in a glass *(looking into a mirror)* the Glory of the Lord *(because the Holy Spirit lives within our hearts)*, are changed into the same image from glory to glory *(changed into Christlikeness, with the glory getting greater and greater, while it became dimmer and dimmer with Moses)*, *even* as by the Spirit of the Lord *(the Holy Spirit Alone can make us what we ought to be, which He does within the parameters of the Finished Work of Christ and our Faith in that Sacrifice)*.

CHAPTER 4
(A.D. 60)
SINCERITY

THEREFORE seeing we have this Ministry *(refers to the great Covenant of Grace, made possible by the Cross)*, as we have received mercy, we faint not *(we will not fail to Preach the Gospel of Jesus Christ and Him Crucified)*;

2 But have renounced the hidden things of dishonesty *(all Gospel outside of the Cross is dishonest, because it's untrue)*, not walking in craftiness *(to do Holy deeds in an unholy way, or unholy deeds in a supposedly Holy way)*, nor handling the Word of God deceitfully *(refers to using it for one's own purpose and agenda)*; but by manifestation of the truth *(Preaching the Cross)* commending ourselves to every man's conscience in the sight of God. *(If these Corinthians will only listen to their conscience, they will know Paul's Message is true.)*

3 But if our Gospel be hid *(Christ and Him Crucified)*, it is hid to them who are lost *(lost because they will not accept the Message of the Cross)*:

4 In whom the god of this world *(Satan)* has blinded the minds of them which believe not *(a willful blindness)*, lest the light of the Glorious Gospel of Christ *(the Message of the Cross)*, Who is the Image of God *(Who Alone is the Image of God)*, should shine unto them. *(If men reject the Cross, they have, in effect, rejected Christ.)*

5 For we Preach not ourselves *(not their own philosophies)*, but Christ Jesus the Lord *(what Christ did at the Cross)*; and ourselves your servants for Jesus' sake. *(This goes back to Christ's teaching on the servant principle [Mat. 20:25-28; Jn. 13:12-17].)*

6 For God, Who Commanded the light to shine out of darkness *(a reference to Gen. 1:3)*, has shined in our hearts *(His Preached Word)*, to *give* the Light of the Knowledge of the Glory of God *(the Cross was planned as carefully as Creation was planned; it is as necessary to our way of life as the Sun is to the Solar System)* in the Face of Jesus Christ. *(Previously, Christ was spoken of as the Image of God. Here, He is spoken of as the Light of God.)*

POWER

7 But we have this treasure *(the Light of the Gospel)* in earthen vessels *(man is never more than an earthen vessel, frail and humble)*, that the excellency of the Power may be of God, and not of us. *(Salvation and Victorious Living come to us entirely by and through what Christ did at the Cross. It is all of Christ and none of us.)*

8 *We are* troubled on every side, yet not distressed *(always confident of victory)*; *we are* perplexed, but not in despair *(never utterly at a loss)*;

9 Persecuted, but not forsaken *(pursued, but not actually caught)*; cast down, but not destroyed *(at times we are knocked down, but not knocked out)*;

10 Always bearing about in the body the dying of the Lord Jesus *(referring to the victory we have through the Cross of Christ)*, that the life also of Jesus might be made manifest in our body. *(We live the Resurrection Life by understanding that we have been planted together [Christ and ourselves] in the likeness of His Death [Rom. 6:5].)*

11 For we which live are always delivered unto death for Jesus' sake *(the Holy Spirit delivers us unto the Death of Christ, which guarantees us the benefits of Calvary [Rom. 6:3-5])*, that the life also of Jesus might be made manifest in our mortal flesh. *(We have victory by exercising Faith in the Cross, which guarantees us the Life of Christ [Gal. 2:20].)*

12 So then death works in us, but life in you. *(The "death" Paul speaks of here concerns the Death of Christ at Calvary, and its benefits as played out in his life. He preached this to others, which brought life to them as well.)*

A FAITHFUL MINISTRY

13 We having the same Spirit *(Holy Spirit)* of Faith *(in Christ and the Cross)*, according as it is written *(Ps. 1:16:10)*, I believed, and therefore have I spoken *(so the Psalmist said)*; we

also believe, and therefore speak *(believe what Christ did at the Cross and, thereby, speak those words of Faith)*;

14 Knowing that He *(God the Father)* which raised up the Lord Jesus shall raise up us also by Jesus *(the Resurrection, whether dead or alive)*, and shall present *us* with you *(a great assembly!)*.

15 For all things *are* for your sakes *(what Jesus did at the Cross)*, that the abundant Grace might through the thanksgiving of many redound to the Glory of God. *(The price of the Cross has resulted, and will result, in untold millions finding Eternal Life, which brings Glory to God.)*

16 For which cause we faint not *(the stakes are too high)*; but though our outward man perish *(takes a beating from overwork and persecution)*, yet the inward *man* is renewed day by day *(is renewed by denying self and taking up the Cross daily [Lk. 9:23-24])*.

17 For our light affliction *(in view of the reward, the worst of afflictions are referred to as "light")*, which is but for a moment *(compared to Eternity)*, works for us a far more exceeding *and* eternal weight of glory *(a greater reward, which will be received at the Resurrection)*;

18 While we look not at the things which are seen *(the trials and tests we presently endure)*, but at the things which are not seen *(not seen by the eyes, but definitely seen by Faith)*: for the things which are seen *are* temporal *(transient)*; but the things which are not seen *are* Eternal *(the things of God, and what He has prepared for us [I Cor. 2:9-10])*.

CHAPTER 5
(A.D. 60)
WITH THE LORD

FOR we know that if our earthly house of *this* Tabernacle were dissolved *(our physical body, which is not permanent)*, we have a building of God *(refers to the Glorified Body, which all Saints will gain at the Resurrection)*, an house not made with hands, eternal in the Heavens. *(This Glorified Body is Created by God, and will last and live forever.)*

2 For in this *(this present physical body)* we groan *(not complaining, but rather seeing by Faith that which is to come and, thereby, longing for it to arrive)*, earnestly desiring to be clothed upon with our house which is from Heaven *(concerns the coming Resurrection, when the corruptible shall put on incorruption and the mortal will put on immortality)*:

3 If so be that being clothed we shall not be found naked *(will not be destitute of covering, but will be clothed with light [I Cor. 15:41-42])*.

4 For we who are in *this* Tabernacle do groan, being burdened *(not for death, for death is an enemy, but rather for the coming Resurrection)*: not for that we would be unclothed *(we do not desire to die, nor are we unwilling to bear these burdens as long as God shall appoint)*, but clothed upon, that mortality might be swallowed up of life. *(This refers to putting on immortality [I Cor. 15:35-54].)*

5 Now He Who has wrought us for the selfsame thing *is* God *(is preparing us for Resurrection)*, Who also has given unto us the earnest of the Spirit *(a down payment with the totality coming shortly)*.

6 Therefore *we are* always confident *(proclaims a guarantee)*, knowing that, while we are at home in the body *(makes an important distinction between the person and his physical body)*, we are absent from the Lord *(but will be with Him forever at the Resurrection)*:

7 (For we walk by Faith *(has reference to the fact that life is a journey, and the Christian is traveling to another country)*, not by sight:) *(This refers to the things we can presently see. It is Faith that controls us, not sight.)*

8 We are confident, *I say*, and willing rather to be absent from the body *(this physical body is merely a house in which the real person resides)*, and to be present with the Lord. *(Death holds no terror for the Child of God.)*

LABOR

9 Wherefore we labour *(are ambitious)*, that, whether present *(with Christ)* or absent *(still in this world)*, we may be accepted of Him *(approved by Him, which we will be if our Faith is in Christ and the Cross)*.

10 For we must all appear before the Judgment Seat of Christ *(this will take place in Heaven, and will probably transpire immediately before the Second Coming)*; that every one may receive the things *done* in *his* body, according to that he has done, whether *it be* good or bad. *(This concerns our life lived for the Lord. Sins will not be judged here, but rather our motivation and faithfulness, for sin was judged at Calvary.)*

11 Knowing therefore the terror of the Lord *(should have been translated, "fear")*,

we persuade men; but we are made manifest unto God (*what we do, we do before Him, seeking only to have His leading, guidance, direction, and approval*); and I trust also are made manifest in your consciences. (*If our Message is acceptable to the Lord, it surely should be acceptable to Believers.*)

12 For we commend not ourselves again unto you (*shouldn't have to, because they knew Paul*), but give you occasion to glory on our behalf (*to stand up for us*), that you may have somewhat to *answer* them which glory in appearance, and not in heart. (*This presents Paul desiring no false praise from anyone, but wanting true recognition.*)

13 For whether we be beside ourselves, *it is* to God (*pertain to the idea that his detractors were accusing him of being mentally unbalanced*): or whether we be sober, *it is* for your cause. (*This refers to being of sound mind, and to be thought of as such. Some said he was insane, and some said he was too sober.*)

RECONCILIATION

14 For the Love of Christ constrains us (*what Christ did for us at the Cross*); because we thus judge, that if one died for all (*Christ died for the whole world, and for all time*), then were all dead (*we are all dead in trespasses and sins*):

15 And *that* He died for all (*brings the reader back to the supreme Sacrifice paid by Christ*), that they which live (*accept Christ*) should not henceforth live unto themselves (*we now belong to Christ*), but unto Him which died for them, and rose again (*to do His Will in our lives*).

16 Wherefore henceforth know we no man after the flesh (*pertains to any and all things that characterize humanity in this present world*): yea, though we have known Christ after the flesh, yet now henceforth know we *Him* no more. (*We are to know Him exclusively as Saviour, which was accomplished by the Cross.*)

17 Therefore if any man *be* in Christ (*saved by the Blood*), *he is* a new creature (*a new creation*): old things are passed away (*what we were before Salvation*); behold, all things are become new. (*The old is no longer useable, with everything given to us now by Christ as "new."*)

18 And all things *are* of God (*all these new things*), Who has reconciled us to Himself by Jesus Christ (*which He was able to do as a result of the Cross*), and has given to us the Ministry of Reconciliation (*pertains to announcing to men the nature and conditions of this Plan of being Reconciled, which is summed up in the "Preaching of the Cross" [I Cor. 1:21, 23]*);

19 To wit, that God was in Christ (*by the agency of Christ*), reconciling the world unto Himself (*represents the Atonement as the work of the Blessed Trinity and the result of love, not of wrath*), not imputing their trespasses unto them (*refers to the fact that the penalty for these trespasses was imputed to Christ instead*); and has committed unto us the Word of Reconciliation. (*All Believers are to Preach the Cross in one way or the other [I Cor. 1:18].*)

20 Now then we are Ambassadors for Christ (*one empowered to deliver a message for another*), as though God did beseech *you* by us (*it is to be understood that our Message is to be regarded as the Message of God*): we pray *you* in Christ's stead (*as though He were performing the task*), be ye reconciled to God. (*It can only be done by accepting Christ and what He did for us at the Cross.*)

21 For He (*God the Father*) has made Him (*Christ*) *to be* sin for us (*the Sin-Offering [Isa. 53:6, 10; I Pet. 2:24]*), Who knew no sin (*He was not guilty; He was perfectly Holy and Pure*); that we might be made the Righteousness of God in Him (*made so by accepting what He did for us at the Cross*).

CHAPTER 6
(A.D. 60)
THE MINISTRY

WE then, as workers together *with Him* (*with Christ*), beseech *you* also that you receive not the Grace of God in vain. (*All who turn away from the Cross, the means by which Grace is given, make it all vain.*)

2 (For He said (*Isa. 49:8*), I have heard You (*refers to God hearing the prayers of the Messiah; it is prayer for the Salvation of the heathen world*) in a time accepted (*refers to this Day of Grace*), and in the Day of Salvation (*which has been afforded by Christ, and what He did at the Cross*) have I succoured You (*God the Father upheld the Messiah, despite His many enemies*): behold, now *is* the accepted time (*Christ has made it all possible*); behold, now *is* the Day of Salvation.) (*In a sense, this "day" will end at the coming Resurrection.*)

3 Giving no offence in any thing (*we are to give no occasion for condemning or rejecting the Gospel*), that the Ministry be not blamed

(that the Finished Work of Christ be not blamed):

4 But in all *things* approving ourselves as the Ministers of God *(in both word and deed)*, in much patience, in afflictions, in necessities, in distresses,

5 In stripes, in imprisonments, in tumults, in labours, in watchings, in fastings *(in all of this, the Grace of God can keep us)*;

6 By pureness, by knowledge, by longsuffering, by kindness, by the Holy Spirit, by love unfeigned *(the Holy Spirit Alone can help us to overcome, and to experience these graces as well; our part pertains to our constant Faith in the Cross; the Spirit will then do what needs to be done)*,

7 By the Word of Truth *(the Word of God)*, by the Power of God *(through the Holy Spirit)*, by the armour of Righteousness on the right hand and on the left *(speaks of being completely armed, which pertains to simple Faith in the Cross of Christ)*,

8 By honour and dishonour *(some people honor us and some don't)*, by evil report and good report *(it is very trying to human nature to have one's name slandered and cast out as evil, when we are conscious only of a desire to do good)*: as deceivers, and *yet* true *(we are labeled by some as a "deceiver," but God knows its not true)*;

9 As unknown, and *yet* well known *(despite being true, some will not know, but yet a few will)*; as dying, and, behold, we live *(we must be willing to face death, and willingly place our lives in the hands of the Lord)*; as chastened *(by the Lord)*, and not killed *(the Holy Spirit desires to "kill" many things in our lives which are wrong; this is a portrayal of the purging of the branch [Jn. 15:2]; we may think the purging is going to kill us, but it won't!)*;

10 As sorrowful, yet always rejoicing *(the evidence of an inner triumph which puts tears to flight by the Smiles of Praise)*; as poor, yet making many rich *(irrespective of our financial status [and I speak of lack], we can make many rich with the Gospel, spiritually speaking)*; as having nothing, and *yet* possessing all things. *(If one is saved, one has all things.)*

11 O *you* Corinthians *(Corinth was known for vice, but the Gospel changed it to Righteousness, at least for those who would believe)*, our mouth is open unto you, our heart is enlarged. *(The Apostle spoke straight, mincing no words, but it was because of love.)*

12 You are not straitened in us *(they did not possess a narrow place in his affections, but rather a large place)*, but you are straitened in your own bowels. *(This should have been translated, "you are straitened in your own hearts." It means the Corinthians didn't have a large place in their hearts for Paul, as they should have had.)*

13 Now for a recompence in the same *(Paul asked the Corinthians to reciprocate by expanding their hearts as wide toward him as he had toward them)*, (I speak as unto *my* children,) be ye also enlarged *(simply means, "love me as I love you")*.

SEPARATION

14 Be not unequally yoked together with unbelievers *(there are two fellowships in the world, and only two; all men belong either to one or the other; no one can belong to both and claim to be a Christian; one is with the world, and one is with the Lord)*: for what fellowship has Righteousness with unrighteousness? *(None!)* and what communion has light with darkness? *(None!)*

15 And what concord has Christ with Belial? *(This presents another name for Satan.)* or what part has he who believes with an infidel? *(Those who make a profession of Salvation should resolve to separate themselves from the world. However, it is separation and not isolation.)*

16 And what agreement has the Temple of God with idols? *(God and idols cannot mix.)* for you are the Temple of the Living God *(speaking of all Believers)*; as God has said *(Ex. 29:45; Lev. 26:12; Ezek. 37:27)*, I will dwell in them, and walk in *them*; and I will be their God, and they shall be My people. *(The Believer is the Sanctuary of the Holy Spirit, all made possible by the Cross.)*

17 Wherefore come out from among them, and be ye separate, saith the Lord *(as stated, the Word of God emphatically teaches separation from the world, but not isolation)*, and touch not the unclean *thing* *(refers to Christians avoiding all unholy contact with a vain and polluted world)*; and I will receive you *(at the same time, means if the person disobeys these injunctions the Lord will not receive us; the Christian can walk clean in this world only by constantly evidencing Faith in the Cross of Christ, which makes it possible for the Holy Spirit to do His Work within our lives)*,

18 And will be a Father unto you *(but only under the conditions mentioned in the above Scriptures)*, and you shall be My sons and

daughters, saith the Lord Almighty. *("Lord Almighty" in the Hebrew is "Jehovah Shaddai." The Hebrew word "Shad" means a woman's breast. The title "Shaddai" suggests that we must never resort to the world, but rather draw all nourishment from the Lord Who can provide all things, which the world can never provide.)*

CHAPTER 7
(A.D. 60)
A HOLY MINISTRY

HAVING therefore these Promises *(that we can draw all nourishment from the Lord)*, dearly beloved, let us cleanse ourselves from all filthiness of the flesh and spirit *(when one sins, he sins spirit, soul, and body; there is no such thing as the body sinning, and not the spirit, etc.)*, perfecting holiness in the fear of God *(to bring to a state of completion; we can do this only by "walking after the Spirit" [Rom. 8:1-2], which refers to looking to the Cross, and looking to the Cross exclusively).*

PAUL'S JOY

2 Receive us *(don't turn a deaf ear to what we are saying)*; we have wronged no man, we have corrupted no man, we have defrauded no man. *(This is insinuating that false teachers with their false doctrine would definitely wrong, corrupt, and defraud their followers.)*

3 I speak not *this* to condemn *you (I do not speak this with any desire to reproach you)*: for I have said before, that you are in our hearts to die and live with *you (refers to the Corinthians having such a place in his affections).*

4 Great *is* my boldness of speech toward you *(they were his children in the Lord)*, great *is* my glorying of you *(even though he used boldness when addressing them personally, behind their backs he "gloried" in them by praising them)*: I am filled with comfort, I am exceeding joyful in all our tribulation. *(The tribulation, whatever it might have been, did not take away the joy.)*

5 For, when we were come into Macedonia, our flesh had no rest *(he had written his First Epistle to the Church at Corinth, and was not certain if they would accept his admonitions; if not, the Church would be lost)*, but we were troubled on every side; without *were* fightings, within *were* fears. *(Like the rest of us, Paul was human. As such, he had all of these emotions, all in regard to the Church at Corinth.)*

6 Nevertheless God, Who comforts those who are cast down *(God comforts the lowly, while He will not comfort the proud; that is, if the lowly will trust Christ and what Christ did at the Cross)*, comforted us by the coming of Titus *(Titus gave happy news regarding Paul's First Epistle to the Corinthians; they had accepted Paul's admonitions; as well, Paul puts himself in the place of the "lowly")*;

7 And not by his coming only, but by the consolation wherewith he was comforted in you *(what his coming brought, which was good news)*, when he told us your earnest desire, your mourning *(over the sin being committed in the Church, and it not being properly addressed)*, your fervent mind toward me *(their expressed love for Paul)*; so that I rejoiced the more.

8 For though I made you sorry with a Letter *(his First Epistle to them)*, I do not repent, though I did repent *(not a contradiction! he had to send the Letter, but he was sorry it had to be sent)*: for I perceive that the same Epistle has made you sorry, though *it were* but for a season. *(They repented, and the sorrow was lifted.)*

9 Now I rejoice, not that you were made sorry, but that you sorrowed to Repentance *(which is what the Holy Spirit intended)*: for you were made sorry after a Godly manner *(toward Repentance)*, that you might receive damage by us in nothing. *(This presents the grief of Repentance as never a loss in any way.)*

10 For godly sorrow *(sorrow instigated by the Holy Spirit over wrongdoing)* works Repentance to Salvation not to be repented of *(means that such action will never be regretted)*: but the sorrow of the world works death. *(This presents a sorrow that is merely remorse, often despair.)*

11 For behold this selfsame thing *(refers to the happy effects of Godly sorrow)*, that you sorrowed after a Godly sort *(they did what true Repentance required)*, what carefulness it wrought in you *(they wanted to correct the wrong immediately)*, yes, *what* clearing of yourselves *(an apology for their laxness in respect to these problems being left unattended)*, yes, *what* indignation *(a decided hatred of sin)*, yes, *what* fear *(speaks of the fear of God they should have had all along, but did not)*, yes, *what* vehement desire *(the fervent effort to carry out that which Paul had proclaimed)*, yes, *what* zeal *(setting about the reformation in great earnest)*, yes, *what* revenge *(a determination to right the wrongs perpetrated against Paul)*! In all *things* you have approved yourselves to be clear in

this matter. *(Their Repentance was sincere, resulting in certain things taking place.)*

12 Wherefore, though I wrote unto you, *I did it* not for his cause who had done the wrong, nor for his cause who suffered wrong *(the one who was committing the sin of incest [I Cor., Chpt. 5], and his father who had been wronged, the husband of the woman in question),* but that our care for you in the sight of God might appear unto you. *(The entirety of the Church at Corinth needed direction.)*

13 Therefore we were comforted in your comfort *(refers to the joy and comfort the Corinthians experienced when they obeyed the Word of the Lord)*: yes, and exceedingly the more joyed we for the joy of Titus, because his spirit was refreshed by you all *(refers to Titus being so kindly received and hospitably entertained).*

14 For if I have boasted any thing to him of you, I am not ashamed *(the Apostle's boast to Titus had proven to be true)*; but as we spoke all things to you in Truth, even so our boasting, which *I made* before Titus, is found a Truth *(refers to the fact that Faith is never idle boasting).*

15 And his inward affection is more abundant toward you, while he remembered the obedience of you all *(it is natural that the stock of this Church went up in the eyes of Titus),* how with fear and trembling you received him. *(This suggests he had not expected to be received accordingly.)*

16 I rejoice therefore that I have confidence in you in all *things.* *(This refers not only to the present, but the future as well!)*

CHAPTER 8
(A.D. 60)
GIVING

MOREOVER, Brethren, we do you to witness of the Grace of God bestowed on the Churches of Macedonia *(northern Greece)*;

2 How that in a great trial of affliction *(Macedonia was greatly impoverished due to political and military problems)* the abundance of their joy and their deep poverty abounded unto the riches of their liberality. *(Despite their deep poverty, they gave liberally to the Work of God.)*

3 For to *their* power, I bear record *(Paul knew their financial circumstances)*, yes, and beyond *their* power *they were* willing of themselves *(they gave beyond what it seemed they could give)*;

4 Praying us with much entreaty that we would receive the gift *(knowing their impoverished circumstances, Paul didn't want to take the gift, but they insisted)*, and *take upon us* the fellowship of the Ministering to the Saints. *(Paul was receiving an Offering from all the Churches for the poor Saints at Jerusalem.)*

5 And *this they did* *(gave far beyond what seemed to be their ability)*, not as we hoped *(meaning much greater than he had hoped)*, but first gave their own selves to the Lord *(this means it was the Will of the Lord for them to do what they did)*, and unto us by the Will of God. *(They had great confidence in Paul and his Ministry. As we see here, the Holy Spirit used Macedonia as an example.)*

6 Insomuch that we desired Titus, that as he had begun, so he would also finish in you the same Grace also. *(As the Lord had Blessed Macedonia, the Church at Corinth is to be Blessed also, that is if they will follow the example of Macedonia.)*

7 Therefore, as you abound in every *thing,* in Faith, and utterance, and knowledge, and *in* all diligence, and *in* your love to us, *see* that you abound in this Grace also *(abound in the Grace of Giving).*

JERUSALEM

8 I speak not by Commandment *(the Grace of "Giving" cannot be by "Commandment," or it is no longer Giving)*, but by occasion of the forwardness of others *(proclaims grandly that Giving inspires Giving)*, and to prove the sincerity of your love. *(If we truly love God, we will give liberally to His Work.)*

9 For we know the Grace of our Lord Jesus Christ *(the Giving of Himself)*, that, though He was rich, yet for your sakes He became poor, that you through His poverty might be rich. *(We can only imagine what He left to come to this world. But because of what He did, we now have the riches of Eternal Life.)*

10 And herein I give *my* advice *(Paul was not commanding, but rather giving advice)*: for this is expedient for you *(it will be profitable)*, who have begun before, not only to do, but also to be forward a year ago. *(They had started this a year before, but had gotten sidetracked by problems, which the Devil desired to do.)*

11 Now therefore perform the doing *of it*; that as *there was* a readiness to will, so *there may be* a performance also out of that which

you have. *(Don't just talk about it, do it!)*

12 For if there be first a willing mind *(the first consideration)*, *it is* accepted according to that a man has, *and* not according to that he has not. *(Our obligations to the Lord in all cases are limited to our ability.)*

13 For *I mean* not that other men be eased *(all should do their part, whatever it might be)*, and you burdened *(he was only asking that they give their fair share)*:

14 But by an equality, *that* now at this time your abundance *may be a supply* for their want *(Corinth had much more material wealth than those in Jerusalem, so they are asked to share)*, that their abundance also may be a *supply* for your want *(Paul was speaking of the fact that the Church in Jerusalem was at least partly responsible for the great Spiritual Blessing now held by the Corinthians)*: that there may be equality *(Jerusalem gave Spiritual Blessings, while Corinth gave material blessings, which made everything equal)*:

15 As it is written *(Ex. 16:18)*, He who *had gathered* much had nothing over *(hoarding money doesn't set well with the Lord)*; and he who *had gathered* little had no lack. *(Giving to the Work of God, and doing so generously, guarantees Blessing.)*

ARRANGEMENTS

16 But thanks *be* to God, which put the same earnest care into the heart of Titus for you. *(Titus had a heart very similar to Paul, as it regards the Gospel.)*

17 For indeed he accepted the exhortation *(to go back to Corinth to receive the Offering)*; but being more forward, of his own accord he went unto you. *(Since the Church at Corinth had experienced Revival, everything is now changed for the better. Titus was now eager to go back to them.)*

18 And we have sent with him the Brother, whose praise *is* in the Gospel throughout all the Churches *(we are not told exactly who the Brother was)*;

19 And not *that* only, but who was also chosen of the Churches to travel with us with this Grace *(with the Offering)*, which is administered by us to the Glory of the same Lord, and *declaration of* your ready mind *(the design was to promote the Glory of the Lord by showing the Love of God respecting this particular need)*:

20 Avoiding this, that no man should blame us in this abundance which is administered by us *(that everything be done honestly)*:

21 Providing for honest things, not only in the sight of the Lord, but also in the sight of men *(so as not to give the devil room for accusation)*.

22 And we have sent with them our Brother *(presents another man in conjunction with the Brother mentioned in Verse 18)*, whom we have oftentimes proved diligent in many things *(lends credence to thought that this man, whomever he may have been, was the companion and fellow-laborer of Paul)*, but now much more diligent, upon the great confidence which I have in you. *(He was happy to go to Corinth, as well.)*

23 Whether *any do enquire* of Titus, *he is* my partner and fellowhelper concerning you *(Paul placed Titus in charge respecting those who were to go to Corinth)*: or our Brethren *be enquired of, they are* the Messengers of the Churches, *and* the Glory of Christ. *(It seems these other Brethren were Apostles as well, for the word "Messengers" in the Greek is "Apostoloi" and means "Apostle.")*

24 Wherefore show you to them, and before the Churches *(set a good example before the other Churches)*, the proof of your love *(a good Offering for Jerusalem)*, and of our boasting on your behalf. *(The Apostle believes the Corinthians would surely do their part.)*

CHAPTER 9
(A.D. 60)
ENCOURAGEMENT

FOR as touching the Ministering to the Saints *(Paul continues to address himself to the Offering which is to be received for the poor Saints in Jerusalem)*, it is superfluous for me to write to you *(he means he believes the Corinthians are already very much aware of their obligations)*:

2 For I know the forwardness of your mind *(eagerness to help)*, for which I boast of you to them of Macedonia, that Achaia *(Corinth)* was ready a year ago *(problems in the Church that hindered, which is what Satan desires to do)*; and your zeal has provoked very many *(excited others to give)*.

3 Yet have I sent the Brethren *(refers to those mentioned in II Cor. 8:18, 22-23)*, lest our boasting of you should be in vain in this behalf *(means he believes they will finish what they had grandly started)* that, as I said, you may be ready *(that should be asked of every Believer, "are you ready?")*:

4 Lest haply if they of Macedonia come with me, and find you unprepared *(the Holy Spirit is here teaching "preparation")*, we *(that we say not, you)* should be ashamed in this same confident boasting. *(In essence, the Apostle says, "lest perhaps we be put to shame, not to say you.")*

5 Therefore I thought it necessary to exhort the Brethren, that they would go before unto you *(speaks of the three Brethren which included Titus)*, and make up beforehand your bounty *(Offering)*, whereof you had notice before, that the same might be ready, as *a matter of* bounty *(the Corinthians were to understand that not only would their Offering be a Blessing to the poor Saints in Jerusalem, but to the giver as well)*, and not as *of* covetousness. *(Although God abundantly blesses the giver, our giving should always be to prove the sincerity of our love, and not as a matter of greed.)*

THE BLESSINGS

6 But this *I say*, He which sows sparingly shall reap also sparingly *(if we give little to the Lord, He will bless little)*; and he which sows bountifully shall reap also bountifully. *(If we give bountifully, He will bless bountifully. This is a Promise of the Lord.)*

7 Every man according as he purposes in his heart, *so let him give (without compulsion)*; not grudgingly, or of necessity *(if it is not willing giving, it is not really Christian Giving!)*: for God loves a cheerful giver. *(This actually means "a hilarious giver.")*

8 And God *is* able to make all Grace abound toward you *(presents the ability of God)*; that you, always having all sufficiency in all *things (mental, physical, economical, and spiritual)*, may abound to every good work *(using God's Blessings for the good of others)*:

9 (As it is written *(Ps. 112:9)*, He has dispersed abroad *(the Promises of God apply to all of mankind, at least all who will believe)*; He has given to the poor *(Jesus is the only hope for the poor)*: his Righteousness remains forever. *(This refers to the Righteousness of Christ.)*

10 Now he who Ministers seed to the sower *(speaks of the Lord)* both Minister bread for *your* food *(both natural and spiritual)*, and multiply your seed sown *(presents the harvest)*, and increase the fruits of your Righteousness;) *(Giving to the Work of the Lord is the Fruit of Righteousness, unless it's done through covetousness.)*

11 Being enriched in every thing to all bountifulness *(the Blessings of God include everything regarding life and Godliness)*, which causes through us thanksgiving to God. *(We are to constantly thank the Lord for His Blessings.)*

12 For the administration of this service not only supplies the want of the Saints *(speaks of the poor Saints in Jerusalem)*, but is abundant also by many thanksgivings unto God *(the Giver is to constantly thank God as well, that God has supplied his giving in the first place)*;

13 While by the experiment of this ministration they Glorify God for your professed subjection unto the Gospel of Christ *(the thanksgiving which will come from the Saints in Jerusalem will be for more than the mere gift, but rather for the consecration of the Corinthians which made the gift possible)*, and for *your* liberal distribution unto them, and unto all *men (Paul is saying that what Corinth is doing will be an example to all the Churches)*;

14 And by their prayer for you *(the Saints in Jerusalem will now greatly pray for the Corinthians, which they should)*, which long after you for the exceeding Grace of God in you. *(Those in Jerusalem will know the Corinthians have done this thing because of the Grace of God.)*

15 Thanks *be* unto God for His unspeakable gift. *(While we may give, it is God Who has given the most in His Giving of the Lord Jesus Christ to the whole of humanity.)*

CHAPTER 10
(A.D. 60)
WARFARE

NOW I Paul myself beseech you by the meekness and gentleness of Christ *(I appeal to you on the basis of love)*, who in presence *am* base among you *(probably presents the Apostle using the actual taunts of his adversaries)*, but being absent am bold toward you:

2 But I beseech *you*, that I may not be bold when I am present with that confidence, wherewith I think to be bold against some *(refers to the fact that Paul would only use boldness if it was absolutely necessary)*, which think of us as if we walked according to the flesh. *(Paul's enemies thought this way because they functioned in the flesh themselves, which means that they didn't have the Power of God.)*

3 For though we walk in the flesh *(refers to the fact that we do not yet have Glorified Bodies)*, we do not war after the flesh *(after our*

own ability, but rather by the Power of the Spirit):

4 (For the weapons of our warfare *are* not carnal *(carnal weapons consist of those which are man-devised)*, but mighty through God *(the Cross of Christ [I Cor. 1:18])* to the pulling down of strong holds;)

5 Casting down imaginations *(philosophic strongholds; every effort man makes outside of the Cross of Christ)*, and every high thing that exalteth itself against the Knowledge of God *(all the pride of the human heart)*, and bringing into captivity every thought to the obedience of Christ *(can be done only by the Believer looking exclusively to the Cross, where all Victory is found; the Holy Spirit will then perform the task)*;

6 And having in a readiness to revenge all disobedience *(refers to that which is opposed to the Cross, where alone all Victory is found)*, when your obedience is fulfilled *(is fulfilled when looking exclusively, as stated, to Christ and the Cross)*.

7 Do ye look on things after the outward appearance? *(It is Faith alone that counts.)* If any man trust to himself that he is Christ's, let him of himself think this again *(refers to the false teachers who laid claims to being followers of Christ by way of eminence)*, that, as he *is* Christ's, even so *are* we Christ's. *(Paul is simply saying that he is of Christ as well!)*

8 For though I should boast somewhat more of our authority *(what the Lord had called him to do)*, which the Lord has given us for edification, and not for your destruction *(the true purpose of Spiritual Authority)*, I should not be ashamed *(no shame shall ever accrue to me from my "boast" being proved false)*:

9 That I may not seem as if I would terrify you by letters *(probably I and II Corinthians)*.

10 For *his* letters, say they, *are* weighty and powerful *(presents the description given by his critics)*; but *his* bodily presence *is* weak, and *his* speech contemptible. *(This presents slander concerning his person. His detractors didn't believe what he wrote or preached, especially as it concerned the Cross.)*

11 Let such an one think this *(directed at the individual of Verse 10, who made the accusation)*, that, such as we are in word by letters when we are absent, such *will we be* also in deed when we are present. *(This referred to the fact that the Spirit of God would be with him.)*

PAUL'S AUTHORITY

12 For we dare not make ourselves of the number *(the dividing line of the Church)*, or compare ourselves with some who commend themselves *(but the Lord didn't commend them)*: but they measuring themselves by themselves, and comparing themselves among themselves, are not wise *(self-righteousness)*.

13 But we will not boast of things without *our* measure *(refers to the Call of God on his life)*, but according to the measure of the rule which God has distributed to us, a measure to reach even unto you. *(This refers to God's measurement as it concerned Ministry. In other words, where he would take the Gospel.)*

14 For we stretch not ourselves beyond *our* measure, as though we reached not unto you: for we are come as far as to you also in *preaching* the Gospel of Christ *(apparently Asia Minor and Europe were apportioned to the Apostle Paul as his Missionary field of Gospel Service)*:

15 Not boasting of things without *our* measure, *that is*, of other men's labours *(proclaims Paul stating that his Ministry had not overlapped into others' field of endeavors)*; but having hope, when your Faith is increased, that we shall be enlarged by you according to our rule abundantly *(Paul was believing the Faith of the Corinthians would be increased in order that they might help him take the Gospel elsewhere, even as it had been brought to them)*,

16 To Preach the Gospel in the *regions* beyond you, *and* not to boast in another man's line of things made ready to our hand. *(He would Preach the Gospel where others had not ventured, and there build Churches. The truth is false apostles with false doctrines cannot get people saved, so these detractors would have to parasite Paul's converts.)*

17 But he who glories, let him Glory in the Lord. *(The Apostle is saying that man has nothing to glory about, unless he Glory in the Lord.)*

18 For not he who commends himself is approved *(proclaims God's standard of approval)*, but whom the Lord commendeth. *(This tells us that the Lord does not accept man's recommendations or accommodations. They mean nothing to Him.)*

CHAPTER 11
(A.D. 60)
GODLY JEALOUSY

WOULD to God you could bear with me a little in *my* folly: and indeed bear with me. *(In effect, the Apostle is saying, "indulge me.")*

2 For I am jealous over you with Godly jealousy *(refers to the "jealousy of God" [Ex. 20:5; 34:14; Nah. 1:2])*: for I have espoused you to one husband *(not jealous of the Corinthians' affection for himself, but of their affection for Christ)*, that I may present *you as* a chaste virgin to Christ. *(They must not commit spiritual adultery, which refers to trusting in things other than Christ and the Cross.)*

3 But I fear, lest by any means, as the serpent beguiled Eve through his subtilty *(the strategy of Satan)*, so your minds should be corrupted from the simplicity that is in Christ. *(The Gospel of Christ is simple, but men complicate it by adding to the Message.)*

4 For if he who comes Preaching another Jesus *(a Jesus who is not of the Cross)*, whom we have not Preached *(Paul's Message was "Jesus Christ and Him Crucified"; anything else is "another Jesus")*, or *if* you receive another spirit *(which is produced by preaching another Jesus)*, which you have not received *(that's not what you received when we Preached the True Gospel to you)*, or another gospel, which you have not accepted *(anything other than "Jesus Christ and Him Crucified" is "another gospel")*, you might well bear with *him*. *(The Apostle is telling the Corinthians they have, in fact, sinned because they tolerated these false apostles who had come in, bringing "another gospel" which was something other than Christ and the Cross.)*

APOSTLESHIP

5 For I suppose I was not a whit behind the very Chiefest Apostles. *(Apparently, this critic was claiming that Paul was not one of the original Twelve, so his Ministry was of little significance.)*

6 But though *I be* rude in speech *(the truth is he was not a poor speaker)*, yet not in knowledge *(what his critics were really opposing was his Message)*; but we have been throughly made manifest among you in all things. *(In other words, the Corinthians knew Paul, so they should not believe the ridiculous accusations.)*

7 Have I committed an offence in abasing myself that you might be exalted, because I have preached to you the Gospel of God freely? *(He is using irony.)*

8 I robbed other Churches *(received Offerings from other Churches)*, taking wages *of them*, to do you service *(meaning he asked no monetary help from the Corinthians while he was establishing their Church)*.

9 And when I was present with you, and wanted *(in need)*, I was chargeable to no man *(meaning he did not make his need the Corinthians' responsibility)*: for that which was lacking to me the Brethren which came from Macedonia supplied *(other Churches supplied help)*: and in all *things* I have kept myself from being burdensome unto you, and *so* will I keep *myself*. *(He wasn't after their money.)*

10 As the Truth of Christ is in me *(he is declaring this in the Presence of Christ)* no man shall stop me of this boasting in the regions of Achaia. *(This actually means no man can disprove what the Apostle is saying.)*

11 Wherefore? because I love you not? *(This is actually meant to have the opposite meaning "I do what I do, because I love you.")* God knows. *(This refers to the fact that what he is saying is true.)*

FALSE APOSTLES

12 But what I do, that I will do *(I will continue to pursue the course of life I have been pursuing)*, that I may cut off occasion from them which desire occasion *(he will not do anything that will give his enemies occasion to find fault, at least, truthfully)*; that wherein they glory *(they claim to not be interested in your money, but that's not true)*, they may be found even as we. *(If they aren't interested in your money, let them conduct themselves as we do and not take your money.)*

13 For such *are* false apostles, deceitful workers *(they have no rightful claim to the Apostolic Office; they are deceivers)*, transforming themselves into the Apostles of Christ. *(They have called themselves to this Office.)*

14 And no marvel *(true Believers should not be surprised)*; for Satan himself is transformed into an angel of light. *(This means he pretends to be that which he is not.)*

15 Therefore *it is* no great thing if his ministers *(Satan's ministers)* also be transformed as the ministers of righteousness *(despite their claims, they were "Satan's ministers" because they preached something other than the Cross [I Cor. 1:17-18, 21, 23; 2:2; Gal. 1:8-9])*; whose end shall be according to their works *(that "end" is spiritual destruction [Phil. 3:18-19])*.

SUFFERINGS

16 I say again, Let no man think me a fool *(proclaims the Apostle's embarrassment at having*

to deal with this issue); if otherwise, yet as a fool receive me, that I may boast myself a little. (Whatever you think of me, hear what I have to say simply because it is very important.)

17 That which I speak, I speak it not after the Lord (not commanded, but permitted), but as it were foolishly, in this confidence of boasting (because it is necessary).

18 Seeing that many glory after the flesh, I will glory also. (The flesh is that which pertains to human ability.)

19 For you suffer fools gladly (speaking of the false apostles), seeing you yourselves are wise (presents the highest of irony).

20 For you suffer, if a man bring you into bondage, if a man devour you, if a man take of you (speaks of bringing one into slavery, which is exactly what these false apostles were doing to the Believers at Corinth, and anywhere else they were allowed to intrude), if a man exalt himself (these false teachers exalted self, not Christ), if a man smite you on the face (meaning these false teachers treated them with such little respect as if they smote them on the face).

21 I speak as concerning reproach (the Apostle had suffered terrible reproach at the hands of these detractors), as though we had been weak. (These false apostles referred to Paul as a "weak sister.") Howbeit whereinsoever any is bold, (I speak foolishly,) I am bold also. (He will now speak of the qualifications he has.)

22 Are they Hebrews? so am I. Are they Israelites? so am I. Are they the seed of Abraham? so am I.

23 Are they Ministers of Christ? (They claim to be, but they really were not.) (I speak as a fool) I am more (proclaims the Apostle stooping to a level in which he is not comfortable); in labours more abundant, in stripes above measure, in prisons more frequent, in deaths oft (means that he was exposed to death often).

24 Of the Jews five times received I forty stripes save one.

25 Thrice was I beaten with rods (different from the beatings listed in the previous Verse), once was I stoned, thrice I suffered shipwreck, a night and a day I have been in the deep (probably refers to a particular time when the Apostle was adrift on the open sea for a night and a day, and was in constant danger of drowning);

26 In journeyings often, in perils of waters, in perils of robbers, in perils by mine own countrymen, in perils by the heathen, in perils in the city, in perils in the wilderness, in perils in the sea, in perils among false brethren (this probably represents the crowning danger);

27 In weariness and painfulness, in watchings often, in hunger and thirst, in fastings often, in cold and nakedness.

28 Beside those things that are without, that which comes upon me daily, the care of all the Churches. (All the Churches he had planted needed his constant supervision, as would be obvious.)

29 Who is weak, and I am not weak? (This presents the Apostle carrying the burden of each and every member of these Churches.) who is offended, and I burn not? (This concerns those who fail in times of temptations and trial.)

30 If I must needs glory, I will glory of the things which concern my infirmities. (If I have to glory, I will glory in my weaknesses, which force me toward total dependence on the Lord.)

31 The God and Father of our Lord Jesus Christ, which is blessed for evermore, knows that I lie not. (If his detractors call him a liar, they are at the same time calling God a liar.)

32 In Damascus the Governor under Aretas the King kept the city of the Damascenes with a garrison, desirous to apprehend me (he is speaking of the time he was first saved, recorded in Acts, Chpt. 9):

33 And through a window in a basket was I let down by the wall, and escaped his hands.

CHAPTER 12
(A.D. 60)
THE THORN

IT is not expedient for me doubtless to glory (but necessary!). I will come to Visions and Revelations of the Lord (refers to that given to Paul by the Lord).

2 I knew a man in Christ above fourteen years ago (speaking of himself), (whether in the body, I cannot tell; or whether out of the body, I cannot tell: God knows;) (He doesn't know if he was actually taken to Heaven in his physical body, or only saw these things in a Vision.) such an one caught up to the third Heaven. (The first heaven is the clouds, etc. The second heaven is the starry space. The third Heaven is the planet Heaven, the Abode of God.)

3 And I knew such a man, (whether in the body, or out of the body, I cannot tell: God knows;) (This is the second time he said this, and not without purpose.)

4 How that he was caught up into Paradise (presents the word "Paradise" being used

by Paul in a general manner), and heard un-speakable words (it was not possible for the Apostle to properly put what he saw into words), which it is not Lawful for a man to utter (not permissible).

5 Of such an one will I glory ("of such a thing will I glory"): yet of myself I will not glory, but in my infirmities (that I was counted worthy to suffer for Christ).

6 For though I would desire to glory, I shall not be a fool (knowing that God knows all things, and we have nothing to glory about); for I will say the truth: but now I forbear, lest any man should think of me above that which he sees me to be, or that he hears of me. (In effect, says, "I will not relate more about this Vision, and for the obvious reasons." He wanted the eyes of all Believers on Christ, and not on him at any time.)

7 And lest I should be exalted above measure through the abundance of the Revelations (presents the reasons for the thorn in the flesh), there was given to me a thorn in the flesh (I think it was all the difficulties of II Cor. 11:23-27), the messenger of Satan to buffet me (an angel of Satan), lest I should be exalted above measure. (This has the Apostle concluding this sentence as it began.)

8 For this thing I besought the Lord thrice, that it might depart from me. (The Apostle knew it was the Lord allowing this, but he didn't understand why.)

9 And He said unto me (the Lord responded, but did not agree), My Grace is sufficient for you (speaks of enabling Grace, which is really the Goodness of God carried out by the Holy Spirit): for My strength is made perfect in weakness. (All Believers are weak, but the Lord tends to make us weaker, with the intention being that we then depend solely upon Him, thereby, obtaining His Strength.) Most gladly therefore will I rather glory in my infirmities (because of the end result), that the Power of Christ may rest upon me. (If Paul needed so humbling and painful an experience of what the carnal nature is, it is evident that all Christians need it. Whatever weakens, belittles, and humiliates that proud and willful nature should be regarded by the Believer as most worthwhile.)

10 Therefore I take pleasure in infirmities, in reproaches, in necessities, in persecutions, in distresses for Christ's sake: for when I am weak, then am I strong (then the strength of Christ can be exhibited through me, but only when I know I am weak).

DEMONSTRATION

11 I am become a fool in glorying; you have compelled me (it was necessary for him to vindicate his character): for I ought to have been commended of you (the Corinthians should have stood up for Paul, instead of him having to stand up for himself): for in nothing am I behind the very Chiefest Apostles, though I be nothing. (This is regarding all true Apostles, even the original Twelve.)

12 Truly the signs of an Apostle were wrought among you in all patience, in signs, and wonders, and mighty deeds. (As is obvious, his Apostleship had been questioned.)

13 For what is it wherein ye were inferior to other Churches (this question arose because Paul's detractors claimed the Church at Corinth was inferior because of Paul's inability), except it be that I myself was not burdensome to you? (This refers to the fact that he did not take any financial support from the Corinthians, which he had already addressed.) forgive me this wrong (drips with sarcasm, even as it should!).

A PROPOSED VISIT

14 Behold, the third time I am ready to come to you (there is little explanation as it regards "the third time"); and I will not be burdensome to you: for I seek not yours, but you (I seek your Salvation, not your property): for the children ought not to lay up for the parents, but the parents for the children. (This presents the Apostle speaking to the Corinthians as a father to his children. The false apostles did the very opposite, as all false apostles do!)

15 And I will very gladly spend and be spent for you (be spent for your souls); though the more abundantly I love you, the less I be loved (is designed as a gentle reproof).

16 But be it so, I did not burden you (Paul's detractors claimed that even though he didn't take money from the Corinthians, he imposed upon them in other ways): nevertheless, being crafty, I caught you with guile. (This should have been translated, "nevertheless, you say, being crafty, I caught you with guile." Paul is not saying he was "crafty" or using "guile," but that he was accused of these things.)

17 Did I make a gain of you by any of them whom I sent unto you? (The answer is a firm "No"!)

18 I desired Titus, and with him I sent a Brother. Did Titus make a gain of you? (This

was answered with a firm "No!" as well.) **walked we not in the same spirit?** *walked we* **not in the same steps?** *(Titus and the Brother conducted themselves exactly as did Paul.)*

REPENTANCE

19 **Again, do you think that we excuse ourselves unto you?** *(He has something far more in mind than defending himself.)* **we speak before God in Christ** *(it is God Who is the Judge of all this)*: **but** *we do* **all things, dearly beloved, for your edifying.** *(Everything he has said has been for their good.)*

20 **For I fear, lest, when I come, I shall not find you such as I would** *(the Corinthians must address every wrong)*, **and** *that* **I shall be found unto you such as you would not** *(the Apostle doesn't desire to have to continue in the correcting mode)*: **lest** *there be* **debates, envyings, wraths, strifes, backbitings, whisperings, swellings, tumults** *(presents what will happen if they do not heed that given by the Apostle)*:

21 *And* **lest, when I come again, my God will humble me among you** *(refers to the fact that, if his counsel is ignored, Judgment will come, which will inflict great pain on Paul)*, **and** *that* **I shall bewail many which have sinned already, and have not repented of the uncleanness and fornication and lasciviousness which they have committed.** *(The Apostle is lamenting the fact that if these sins were continued, which means these people had abandoned the Cross, they would lose their souls.)*

CHAPTER 13
(A.D. 60)
THE PROPOSED VISIT

THIS *is* the third *time* **I am coming to you** *(a proposed visit)*. **In the mouth of two or three witnesses shall every word be established** *(Deut. 19:15)*.

2 **I told you before, and foretell you, as if I were present, the second time** *(I told you these things on my second visit to you)*; **and being absent now I write to them which heretofore have sinned** *(he is telling them to repent)*, **and to all other, that, if I come again, I will not spare** *(if his counsel is ignored, which in reality is the Counsel of God, Judgment will come)*:

3 **Since you seek a proof of Christ speaking in me** *(his Apostleship was being questioned)*, **which to you-ward is not weak, but is mighty in you.** *(The Gospel Paul preached had changed*

their lives. *That was proof enough!)*

4 **For though He was Crucified through weakness** *(Christ purposely did not use His Power)*, **yet He lived by the Power of God** *(was Resurrected; we have this power at our disposal as well [Rom. 8:11])*. **For we also are weak in Him** *(regarding our personal strength and ability)*, **but we shall live with Him by the Power of God toward you.** *(This refers to our everyday life and living, which we do by constant Faith in the Cross. This gives the Holy Spirit latitude to work mightily in our lives.)*

WARNING OF SIN

5 **Examine yourselves, whether you be in the Faith** *(the words, "the Faith," refer to "Christ and Him Crucified," with the Cross ever being the Object of our Faith)*; **prove your own selves.** *(Make certain your Faith is actually in the Cross, and not other things.)* **Know you not your own selves, how that Jesus Christ is in you** *(which He can only be by our Faith expressed in His Sacrifice)*, **except you be reprobates?** *(Rejected.)*

6 **But I trust that you shall know that we are not reprobates.** *(If he was a reprobate, as his skeptics claimed, then they were as well, which of course is preposterous.)*

7 **Now I pray to God that you do no evil** *(Paul is speaking specifically about the Corinthians siding with the opponents who claimed him to be a reprobate)*; **not that we should appear approved** *(the Apostle is saying he is not interested in whether people approve of him or not, but that he be approved of Christ)*, **but that you should do that which is honest** *(the Corinthians must follow correct Doctrine)*, **though we be as reprobates** *(irrespective that some may think we are reprobates)*.

8 **For we can do nothing against the Truth** *(will not shade the Truth of the Cross in order to appease some)*, **but for the Truth.** *(We must stand firm for the Truth.)*

9 **For we are glad, when we are weak, and you are strong** *(his recognized weakness caused him to depend on the Lord, meaning he trusted in the Cross and was able to impart this knowledge of the Cross to the Corinthians, which made them strong)*: **and this also we wish,** *even* **your perfection** *(maturity)*.

10 **Therefore I write these things being absent, lest being present I should use sharpness** *(when he comes to Corinth, he doesn't want to have to use sharpness, believing the problems will*

have been solved), **according to the power which the Lord has given me to edification, and not to destruction.** *(If they accept that which the Lord gave him, they would be edified. If not, destruction would be the result.)*

BENEDICTION

11 Finally, Brethren, farewell. Be perfect *(mature)*, **be of good comfort, be of one mind, live in peace; and the God of Love and Peace shall be with you.** *(All of this can*

be done by constant Faith evidenced in the Cross of Christ.)

12 Greet one another with an holy kiss *(the custom at that time)*.

13 All the Saints *(probably those in Philippi)* **salute** *(greet)* **you.**

14 The Grace of our Lord Jesus Christ *(made possible by the Cross)*, **and the Love of God** *(shown by the fact of the Cross)*, **and the Communion of the Holy Spirit** *(which we can constantly have by continually exhibiting Faith in the Cross)*, *be* **with you all. Amen.**

THE EPISTLE OF PAUL THE APOSTLE TO THE
GALATIANS

CHAPTER 1
(A.D. 58)
INTRODUCTION

PAUL, an Apostle, (not of men, neither by man, but by Jesus Christ, and God the Father, Who raised Him from the dead;) *(This means Paul did not submit the authority of his Apostleship to men, neither was it conferred on him by man.)*

2 And all the Brethren which are with me, unto the Churches of Galatia *(refers to all in that region)*:

3 Grace *be* to you and Peace from God the Father *(made possible by the Cross)*, and *from* our Lord Jesus Christ *(Who made it possible)*,

4 Who gave Himself for our sins *(the Cross)*, that He might deliver us from this present evil world *(the Cross alone can set the captive free)*, according to the Will of God and our Father *(the standard of the entire process of Redemption)*:

5 To Whom *be* Glory forever and ever *(Divine Glory)*. Amen.

NO OTHER GOSPEL

6 I marvel that you are so soon removed from Him *(the Holy Spirit) Who* called you into the Grace of Christ *(made possible by the Cross)* unto another gospel *(anything which doesn't have the Cross as its Object of Faith)*:

7 Which is not another *(presents the fact that Satan's aim is not so much to deny the Gospel, which he can little do, as to corrupt it)*; but there be some who trouble you, and would pervert the Gospel of Christ *(once again, to make the object of Faith something other than the Cross)*.

8 But though we *(Paul and his associates)*, or an Angel from Heaven, Preach any other gospel unto you than that which we have preached unto you *(Jesus Christ and Him Crucified)*, let him be accursed *(eternally condemned; the Holy Spirit speaks this through Paul, making this very serious)*.

9 As we said before, so say I now again *(at sometime past, he had said the same thing to them, making their defection even more serious)*,

If any *man* Preach any other gospel unto you *(anything other than the Cross)* than that you have received *(which saved your souls)*, let him be accursed *("eternally condemned," which means the loss of the soul)*.

10 For do I now persuade men, or God? *(In essence, Paul is saying, "do I Preach man's doctrine, or God's?")* or do I seek to please men? *(This is what false apostles do.)* for if I yet pleased men, I should not be the Servant of Christ *(one cannot please both men and God at the same time)*.

REVELATION

11 But I certify you, Brethren *(make known)*, that the Gospel which was Preached of me *(the Message of the Cross)* is not after man. *(Any Message other than the Cross is definitely devised by man.)*

12 For I neither received it of man *(Paul had not learned this great Truth from human Teachers)*, neither was I taught *it (he denies instruction from other men)*, but by the Revelation of Jesus Christ. *(Revelation is the mighty Act of God whereby the Holy Spirit discloses to the human mind that which could not be understood without Divine Intervention.)*

13 For you have heard of my conversation *(way of life)* in time past in the Jews' religion *(the practice of Judaism)*, how that beyond measure I persecuted the Church of God, and wasted it *(Acts 9:1-2)*:

14 And profited in the Jews' religion above many my equals in my own nation *(he outstripped his Jewish contemporaries in Jewish culture, etc.)*, being more exceedingly zealous of the traditions of my fathers *(a zeal from his very boyhood)*.

THE GOSPEL

15 But when it pleased God, who separated me from my mother's womb *(presents the idea that God had set Paul apart, devoting him to a special purpose from before his birth)*, and called *me* by His Grace *(called, not because of any merit on his part, but rather because of the Grace of God)*,

16 To reveal His Son in me *(the meaning of the New Covenant, which is the meaning of the Cross)*, that I might Preach Him among the heathen *(Gentiles)*; immediately I conferred not with flesh and blood *(his Commission and Message came to him from God, and neither was affected in any way by human intervention)*:

17 Neither went I up to Jerusalem to them which were Apostles before me *(did not get this Revelation from the original Twelve)*; but I went into Arabia *(according to the Holy Spirit)*, and returned again unto Damascus. *(There would not have been any Apostles in Damascus. There he Preached the Message of the Cross.)*

18 Then after three years I went up to Jerusalem to see Peter *(showing his independence from the Jerusalem Apostles)*, and abode with him fifteen days *(when he, no doubt, revealed to Peter the Revelation of the Cross, which the Lord had given to him)*.

19 But other of the Apostles saw I none, save James the Lord's Brother. *(James didn't refer to himself as an Apostle, but Paul did.)*

20 Now the things which I write unto you, behold, before God, I lie not.

21 Afterwards I came into the regions of Syria and Cilicia;

22 And was unknown by face unto the Churches of Judaea which were in Christ *(had he been a Disciple of the Twelve, the Churches in Judaea would have known him)*:

23 But they had heard only *(were constantly hearing)*, That he which persecuted us *(Believers)* in times past now Preaches the Faith which once he destroyed *(Faith in Christ)*.

24 And they Glorified God in me. *(As he had "constantly persecuted," and now was "constantly preaching," they were "constantly glorifying.")*

CHAPTER 2
(A.D. 52)
THE CHURCH

THEN fourteen years after I went up again to Jerusalem with Barnabas *(was probably the Jerusalem Council [Acts 15:1-35])*, and took Titus with *me* also.

2 And I went up by Revelation *(the Lord told him to go)*, and communicated unto them that Gospel which I Preach among the Gentiles *(the Message of the Cross)*, but privately to them which were of reputation *(to at least some of the original Twelve)*, lest by any means I should run, or had run, in vain. *(If the Twelve,*

or even James the Lord's Brother, repudiated His Gospel of Grace, at least as far as the Gentiles were concerned, this would create an insurmountable barrier.)*

3 But neither Titus, who was with me, being a Greek *(a Gentile)*, was compelled to be circumcised *(Paul probably took him as a test case)*:

4 And that because of false brethren unawares brought in *(suggests they were fellow Believers, but their insistence upon the necessity of the Law constituted a denial of Christ in Paul's eyes)*, who came in privily *(subtly)* to spy out our liberty which we have in Christ Jesus *(the Truth of the Gospel was at stake)*, that they might bring us into bondage *(forsaking the Cross always results in bondage)*:

5 To whom we gave place by subjection, no, not for an hour *(Paul would not yield one iota, nor compromise in the slightest)*; that the Truth of the Gospel might continue with you. *(Justification by Faith was on trial.)*

6 But of these *(false brethren)* who seemed to be somewhat, (whatsoever they were, it makes no matter to me: God accepts no man's person:) for they who seemed *to be somewhat* in conference added nothing to me *(there was nothing anyone there could add to the Revelation given to him by the Lord, as it regards the Cross)*:

7 But contrariwise, when they saw that the Gospel of the uncircumcision *(the Gentiles)* was committed unto me *(presents the Jerusalem Apostles championing the cause of Paul after they heard the issue discussed in private conference)*, as *the Gospel* of the Circumcision *was* unto Peter *(the Jews)*;

8 (For He Who wrought effectually in Peter to the Apostleship of the Circumcision *(the Jews)*, the same was mighty in me toward the Gentiles:)

9 And when James *(the Lord's Brother)*, Cephas *(Peter)*, and John, who seemed to be pillars *(a metaphor)*, perceived the Grace that was given unto me *(the Message of Grace)*, they gave to me and Barnabas the right hands of fellowship *(a pledge of friendship and agreement)*; that we *should go* unto the heathen *(Gentiles)*, and they unto the Circumcision *(Jews)*.

10 Only *they would* that we should remember the poor *(the poor Saints in Jerusalem, who had suffered terrible hardships because of persecution)*; the same which I also was forward to do. *(Paul saw the need, and felt he must respond favorably, which he did.)*

PETER

11 But when Peter was come to Antioch *(Antioch Syria, the city used by God to spearhead world Evangelism)*, I withstood him to the face *(means Paul openly opposed and reproved him, even though Peter was the eldest)*, because he was to be blamed *(for abandoning the Cross and resorting to Law)*.

12 For before that certain came from James *(gives us all too well another example as to why Apostles, or anyone else for that matter, are not to be the final word, but rather the Word of God itself)*, he *(Peter)* did eat with the Gentiles *(Peter knew the Gospel of Grace)*: but when they were come *(those from James in Jerusalem)*, he withdrew and separated himself, fearing them which were of the Circumcision. *(The problem was "man fear." Some of the Jewish Christians were still trying to hold to the Law of Moses, which means they accepted Jesus as the Messiah, but gave no credence to the Cross whatsoever. This ultimately occasioned the necessity of Paul writing the Epistle to the Hebrews.)*

13 And the other Jews *(in the Church at Antioch)* dissembled likewise with him *(with Peter)*; insomuch that Barnabas also was carried away with their dissimulation *(hypocrisy)*.

14 But when I saw that they walked not uprightly according to the Truth of the Gospel *(they were forsaking the Cross)*, I said unto Peter before *them* all *(Paul's rebuke was in the presence of everybody, the whole Antioch Church)*, If you, being a Jew, live after the manner of Gentiles, and not as do the Jews, why do you compel the Gentiles to live as do the Jews? *(Hypocrisy!)*

JUSTIFICATION

15 We *who are* Jews by nature *(we ought to know better)*, and not sinners of the Gentiles *(who only know what we tell them because they were not privileged to have the Law as we did)*,

16 Knowing that a man is not justified by the works of the Law *(such is impossible)*, but by the Faith of Jesus Christ *(Faith in what He did at the Cross)*, even we have believed in Jesus Christ *(the Object of Faith must always be the Cross)*, that we might be Justified by the Faith of Christ, and not by the works of the Law: for by the works of the Law shall no flesh be justified *(emphatically so! it cannot be done)*.

17 But if, while we seek to be Justified by Christ *(by trusting in what Christ did at the Cross)*, we ourselves also are found sinners *(if we fail, thereby sinning in some way)*, is therefore Christ the minister of sin? *(Is Christ to blame for our failure?)* God forbid. *(The Cross hasn't failed. It's we who have failed.)*

18 For if I build again the things which I destroyed *(revert back to the Law)*, I make myself a transgressor. *(To revert to any type of Law is a departure from God's Prescribed Order of Victory [the Cross], and is sin).*

19 For I through the Law *(Christ has perfectly kept the Law and suffered its just penalty, all on my behalf)* am dead to the Law *(the Law is not dead, but I am dead to the Law by virtue of having died with Christ [Rom. 6:3-5])*, that I might live unto God. *(This presents that which can only be done through Christ, and never by the Law.)*

20 I am Crucified with Christ *(as the Foundation of all Victory; Paul, here, takes us back to Rom. 6:3-5)*: nevertheless I live *(have new life)*; yet not I *(not by my own strength and ability)*, but Christ lives in me *(by virtue of me dying with Him on the Cross, and being raised with Him in newness of life)*: and the life which I now live in the flesh *(my daily walk before God)* I live by the Faith of the Son of God *(the Cross is ever the Object of my Faith)*, Who loved me, and gave Himself for me *(which is the only way that I could be saved)*.

21 I do not frustrate the Grace of God *(if we make anything other than the Cross of Christ the Object of our Faith, we frustrate the Grace of God, which means we stop its action, and the Holy Spirit will no longer help us)*: for if Righteousness *come* by the Law *(any type of Law)*, then Christ is dead in vain. *(If I can successfully live for the Lord by any means other than Faith in Christ and the Cross, then the Death of Christ was a waste.)*

CHAPTER 3
(A.D. 58)

BY FAITH

O foolish Galatians *(failure to use one's powers of perception)*, who has bewitched you *(malignant influence)*, that you should not obey the truth *(refers to "Jesus Christ and Him Crucified")*, before whose eyes Jesus Christ has been evidently set forth, crucified among you? *(Paul Preached the Cross with such vividness that his hearers could see Jesus*

Christ Crucified among them. Regrettably, only a few modern Preachers follow his example.)

2 This only would I learn of you *(I will convince you of your error by this one argument)*, **Did you receive the Spirit by the works of the Law, or by the hearing of Faith?** *(This refers to being Born-Again, at which time the Spirit of God comes into the heart and life of the new Believer. It is received simply by trusting Christ, and what He did at the Cross.)*

3 Are you so foolish? **having begun in the Spirit** *(do you think you can now be brought to a state of spiritual maturity by means of self-effort?)*, **are you now made perfect by the flesh?** *(These Galatians were practicing Salvation by "Faith," and Sanctification by "self," which is also the state of most modern Christians.)*

4 Have you suffered so many things in vain? *(You have suffered persecution because of your acceptance of Christ. Don't throw it away.)* **if it be** yet in vain *(in essence saying, "I trust it is not in vain")*.

5 He *(the Lord Jesus)* **therefore Who Ministers to you the Spirit, and works Miracles among you,** *does He it* **by the works of the Law, or by the hearing of Faith?** *(It is obvious that everything the Lord does is done on the basis of the Believer exhibiting Faith. It is never by works of the Law.)*

ABRAHAM

6 Even as Abraham believed God *(proclaims the fact that the Patriarch was justified by Faith, not works)*, **and it was accounted to him for Righteousness.** *(The Righteousness of God is imputed to a person only on the basis of Faith in Christ, and what Christ has done at the Cross [Jn. 8:56].)*

7 Know you therefore that they which are **of Faith** *(presents Faith, and Faith alone, as the foundation; but the Object of Faith must ever be the Cross)*, **the same are the children of Abraham** *(the legitimate sons of Abraham)*.

8 And the Scripture, foreseeing that God would justify the heathen through Faith *(proclaims the Word of God as the Foundation of all Things)*, **Preached before the Gospel unto Abraham,** *saying,* **In you shall the nations be blessed** *(Gen. 12:1-3)*.

9 So then they *(whomsoever they might be)* **which be of Faith** *(in Christ and the Cross)* **are blessed with Faithful Abraham.** *(He received Justification by Faith, and so do we!)*

FAITH ALONE

10 For as many as are of the Works of the Law are under the curse *(the Believer can only be under Law or Grace; it is one or the other; one can only come to Grace through the Cross; if one is trusting in Law, whatever kind of Law, one is cursed)*: **for it is written, Cursed** *is* **every one who continues not in all things which are written in the Book of the Law to do them** *(Deut. 27:26)*. *(To attain the Righteousness of the Law, one must keep the Law perfectly, thereby never failing. Such is impossible, so that leaves only the Cross as the means of Salvation and Victory.)*

11 But that no man is justified by the Law in the sight of God, *it is* **evident** *(because it is impossible for man to perfectly keep the Law)*: **for, The just shall live by Faith** *([Hab. 2:4], Faith in Christ and what He did at the Cross)*.

12 And the Law is not of Faith *(the two principles of Law and of Faith as a means of Justification are mutually exclusive of one another)*: **but, The man who does them shall live in them.** *(The Believer has a choice. He can attempt to live this life by either Law or Faith. He cannot live by both.)*

13 Christ has redeemed us from the curse of the Law *(He did so on the Cross)*, **being made a curse for us** *(He took the penalty of the Law, which was death)*: **for it is written, Cursed** *is* **every one who hangs on a tree** *(Deut. 21:22-23)*:

14 That the blessing of Abraham *(Justification by Faith)* **might come on the Gentiles through Jesus Christ** *(what He did at the Cross)*; **that we might receive the Promise of the Spirit through Faith.** *(All sin was atoned at the Cross which lifted the sin debt from believing man, making it possible for the Holy Spirit to come into the life of the Believer and abide there forever [Jn. 14:16-17].)*

THE COVENANT

15 Brethren, I speak after the manner of men *(now presents an argument to show that the Covenant God made with Abraham is still in force)*; **Though** *it be* **but a man's covenant, yet** *if it be* **confirmed, no man disannulleth, or adds thereto.** *(In other words, the Covenant of Justification by Faith cannot be broken or set aside.)*

16 Now to Abraham and his Seed were the Promises made *(to all those who are brought into Salvation by Faith in Christ)*. **He said not, And to Seeds, as of many; but as of One, And to your Seed, which is Christ.** *(Abraham's Seed*

was Christ, and Christ is both God and Man. Therefore, the Covenant cannot be broken.)

17 And this I say, *that* the Covenant, that was confirmed before of God in Christ *(refers to the Abrahamic Covenant, which is Justification by Faith)*, the Law *(the Law of Moses)*, which was four hundred and thirty years after, cannot disannul, that it should make the Promise of none effect. *(In other words, the Law of Moses did not annul the Abrahamic Covenant. In fact, that Covenant is still in force.)*

18 For if the inheritance *be* of the Law, *it is* no more of Promise *(the inheritance cannot come from both Covenants and, in fact, it cannot come by the Law)*: **but God gave** *it* **to Abraham by Promise.** *(The verb "gave" is in a perfect tense, which means that God gave the Promise about Christ as a permanent Promise that cannot be superseded or modified.)*

THE LAW

19 Wherefore then *serves* the Law? *(What good is the Law?)* It was added because of transgressions *(was given to define sin)*, till the Seed should come to whom the Promise was made *(Christ is the Promise)*; *and it was* ordained by Angels in the hand of a mediator. *(Moses was the mediator of the Law.)*

20 Now a mediator is not *a mediator* of one *(for there to be a mediator, there has to be more than one person involved; in other words, the mediator is the middle person between two or more people who are at enmity with each other)*, but God is one. *(God is the Mediator of the New Covenant, but in a different way than Moses. Jesus is God, and Jesus is also Man. Consequently, the New Covenant doesn't depend upon man as such, but rather the man Christ Jesus. Therefore, this Covenant cannot fail!)*

21 *Is* the Law then against the Promises of God? *(This demands a negative answer.)* **God forbid: for if there had been a Law given which could have given life, verily Righteousness should have been by the Law.** *(The Law of Moses could show a man what he was, but had no power to change the man.)*

22 But the Scripture has concluded all under sin *(means that the Law could not give Eternal Life; it could only exact its penalty, which was death)*, that the Promise by Faith of Jesus Christ might be given to them who believe. *(Eternal Life comes by Faith in the Promise, Who is Jesus Christ and what He did at the Cross. In other words, the word "believe" demands that Christ*

and the Cross ever be the Object of our Faith.)

23 But before Faith came *(actually says in the Greek, "before the Faith"; in short, it refers to "Jesus Christ and Him Crucified")*, **we were kept under the Law** *(actually means, "to keep inward under lock and key")*, **shut up unto the Faith which should afterwards be revealed.** *(This proclaims the fact that the Law pointed to Christ, always to Christ.)*

24 Wherefore the Law was our schoolmaster *(should have been translated, "guardian")* *to bring us* unto Christ *(proclaims what the end result of the Law was intended to be)*, **that we might be justified by Faith.** *(This proclaims to us that the Law had no permanent function, but served only until Christ would come. It is only by Faith in Christ that one can be justified.)*

25 But after that Faith is come *(Paul is speaking about the Finished Work of Christ on the Cross)*, **we are no longer under a schoolmaster.** *(This should actually say, "We are no longer under the guardianship of the Law." The Law was totally fulfilled in Christ.)*

FAITH

26 For you are all the Children of God by Faith in Christ Jesus. *(Every person who is saved, and every person who has ever been or ever will be saved, is saved only by "Faith in Christ Jesus," which refers to what He did at the Cross.)*

27 For as many of you as have been baptized into Christ *(refers to the Baptism into His Death at Calvary [Rom. 6:3-5]; the reference is not to Water Baptism)* have put on Christ *(means to be clothed with Him [Jn. 14:20])*.

28 There is neither Jew nor Greek, there is neither bond nor free, there is neither male nor female *(all have a common life in Christ Jesus)*: for you are all one in Christ Jesus. *(This proclaims an end of all class, status, and social distinction. This phrase alone answers all racism.)*

29 And if you *be* Christ's, then are you Abraham's seed *(Christ is Abraham's Seed, so my union with Christ makes me Abraham's seed as well)*, and heirs according to the Promise *(heirs of God, and joint heirs with Jesus Christ [Rom. 8:17])*.

CHAPTER 4
(A.D. 58)
HEIRSHIP ILLUSTRATED

NOW I say, *That* the heir, as long as he is a child, differs nothing from a servant,

though he be lord of all *(Paul continues the argument for the inferiority of the condition under Law using an illustration from contemporary life)*;

2 But is under tutors and governors until the time appointed of the father. *(This refers to the fixed time when he would be of legal age and, therefore, able to accept the inheritance.)*

3 Even so we, when we were children, were in bondage under the elements of the world *(refer to passions and pride which enslave humanity)*:

4 But when the fulness of the time was come *(which completed the time designated by God that should elapse before the Son of God would come)*, God sent forth His Son *(it was God who acted; the Law required man to act; this requirement demonstrated man's impotency; the Son of God requires nothing from man other than his confidence)*, made of a woman *(pertains to the Incarnation, God becoming man)*, made under the Law *(refers to the Mosaic Law; Jesus was subject to the Jewish legal economy, which He had to be, that is if He was to redeem fallen humanity; in other words, He had to keep the Law perfectly, which no human being had ever done, but He did)*,

5 To redeem them who were under the Law *(in effect, all of humanity is under the Law of God which man, due to his fallen condition, could not keep; but Jesus came and redeemed us by keeping the Law perfectly, and above all satisfying its penalty on the Cross, which was death)*, that we might receive the adoption of sons *(that we could become the sons of God by adoption, which is carried out by Faith in Christ and what He did at the Cross)*.

6 And because you are sons *(we now have many privileges)*, God has sent forth the Spirit of his Son into your hearts *(because we are sons, the Holy Spirit has been sent to take up His permanent residence in our hearts)*, crying, Abba, Father. *(This means it is the Holy Spirit Who is doing the crying, and does so to the Father on our behalf.)*

7 Wherefore you are no more a servant, but a son *(refers to the standing one has in Christ because of one's Faith in Christ)*; and if a son, then an heir of God through Christ. *(This proclaims the fact that all the privileges, which belong to Christ, now belong to us as well.)*

LEGALISM

8 Howbeit then, when you knew not God *(refers to the former unredeemed state)*, you did service unto them which by nature are no gods. *(They were slaves to heathenistic superstition.)*

9 But now, after that you have known God *(refers to Saving Grace, Knowing God through the acceptance of Jesus Christ, which is the only way He can be known)*, or rather are known of God *(refers to the Lord knowing us in a saving way)*, how turn you again to the weak and beggarly elements *(when the substance is reached and sonship established, going back to the "rudiments," i.e., symbols and sacraments, is not progress, but ignorance)*, whereunto you desire again to be in bondage? *(Bondage to the sin nature! It refers to leaving the Cross, and making other things the object of Faith.)*

10 You observe days, and months, and times, and years. *(The Judaizers were attempting to get the Galatians to go into Law-keeping in conjunction with Christ, which cannot work.)*

11 I am afraid of you *(afraid for your spiritual welfare)*, lest I have bestowed upon you labour in vain. *(If one leaves Faith in Christ and the Cross and embraces other things, which means to look to those other things for life and victory, the Holy Spirit will have bestowed upon such a person labor in vain.)*

12 Brethren, I beseech you, be as I *am* *(free from all the bondage of Salvation by works and sacraments, which is no Salvation at all)*; for I *am* as you *are* *(means that even though he is an Apostle, he is subject to the same Biblical Doctrines as they are)*: you have not injured me at all. *(My motive is not one of personal complaint, but because of the great harm that could come to you.)*

13 You know how through infirmity of the flesh *(doesn't say what it is)* I preached the Gospel unto you at the first *(evidently, when these Churches were first founded)*.

14 And my temptation which was in my flesh you despised not, nor rejected *(should have been translated, "my trial"; but once again, we do not know what it was, so speculation is useless)*; but received me as an Angel of God, *even* as Christ Jesus. *(They accepted him and what he preached.)*

15 Where is then the blessedness you spoke of? *(This speaks of the wonderful prosperity of Salvation, which had come to them as a result of Paul bringing the Gospel to this region.)* for I bear you record, that, if *it had been* possible, you would have plucked out your own eyes, and have given them to me. *(This doesn't necessarily mean Paul had an eye disease, as some*

claim. *This was an idiom used often to express extreme affliction.)*

16 Am I therefore become your enemy, because I tell you the truth? *(A real friend is one who will tell his friend the truth, even though it hurts.)*

17 They zealously affect you *(speaks of the Judaizers attempting to subvert the Galatians in order to win them over to themselves)*, but not well *(not for your good)*; yes, they would exclude you *(they would shut the Galatians out from the benefits of the Gospel of Grace)*, that you might affect them *(means to be drawn to their side).*

18 But *it is* good to be zealously affected always in *a* good *thing (Paul wanted the Galatians to be as zealous over Christ and the Cross as it seems they were tending to be over false doctrine)*, and not only when I am present with you. *(Their zeal for the right thing should be present at all times.)*

19 My little children *(presents the language of deep affection and emotion)*, of whom I travail in birth again *(deliver to you again the rudiments of the great Message of Christ and Him Crucified, as though you had never heard it to begin with)* until Christ be formed in you *(presents the work only the Holy Spirit can do, and does exclusively within the parameters of the Sacrifice of Christ, which must always be the Object of our Faith)*,

20 I desire to be present with you now *(as a loving parent wants to be at the side of a sick child)*, and to change my voice *(refers to the fact that his true love for them would more profitably come through were he only standing before them in person)*; for I stand in doubt of you. *(The Apostle was perplexed as to how the Galatians could have forsaken the Holy Spirit, substituting in His Place the cold issues of dead Law. Any Christian who presently has as his object of Faith anything but the Cross is following the same course as the Galatians of old.)*

HAGAR AND SARAH

21 Tell me, you who desire to be under the Law *(the Law of Moses or any type of Law)*, do you not hear the Law? *(Do you actually know what the Law demands?)*

22 For it is written *(Gen. 16:15; 21:2-3)*, that Abraham had two sons *(Ishmael and Isaac)*, the one by a bondmaid *(Hagar)*, the other by a freewoman *(Sarah).*

23 But he *who was* of the bondwoman was born after the flesh *(by the scheming of Abraham and Sarah)*; but he of the freewoman *was* by Promise *(by an action of the Holy Spirit).*

24 Which things are an allegory *(a figure of speech in which spiritual facts are presented in physical terms)*: for these are the two Covenants *(represents Law [Hagar] and Grace [Sarah])*; the one from the mount Sinai, which gendereth to bondage, which is Hagar. *(This presents the Apostle plainly saying he is using Hagar as a symbol of the Law of Moses. As is obvious, it was given at Mt. Sinai.)*

25 For this Hagar is Mount Sinai in Arabia, and answers to Jerusalem which now is *(refers to that city at the time of Paul; it was subject to Laws, rites, and customs, according to the Law of Moses)*, and is in bondage with her children. *(Israel was in bondage to sin because of having rejected Christ.)*

26 But Jerusalem which is above is free *(presents the origin of Salvation, which is Heaven, and proclaims its results, which are "freedom")*, which is the mother of us all. *(This refers to all who are true Christians, whether Jews or Gentiles.)*

27 For it is written *(Isa. 2:2)*, Rejoice, *you* barren who bears not; break forth and cry, you who travail not *(speaks of the Church, grafted in because of Grace, in the place of Israel, which demanded Law and which God would not accept)*: for the desolate has many more children than she which has an husband. *(This pertains to Sarah who was barren which, in one sense of the word and the culture of that day, was the same as not having a husband, even though she was married to Abraham. It also refers to the Church, which, in effect, had no husband, as did Israel, i.e., "God." The Church has many more children than Israel ever had!)*

28 Now we *(Believers)*, Brethren, as Isaac was, are the Children of Promise. *(The Promise is a picture of the Messiah, Who came through the lineage of Isaac to grant deliverance to people bound in sin.)*

29 But as then he who was born after the flesh *(Ishmael)* persecuted him *who was born* after the Spirit *(Isaac)*, even so *it is* now. *(Isaac and Ishmael symbolized the new and the old nature in the Believer. Hagar and Sarah typified the two Covenants of works and Grace, of bondage and Liberty, even as Paul is explaining here.)*

30 Nevertheless what says the Scripture? *(Gen. 21:10)* Cast out the bondwoman and her son *(the birth of the new nature demands*

the expulsion of the old; it is impossible to improve the old nature; it must be cast out, i.e., "placed in a dormant position"; this can only be done by the Believer evidencing constant Faith in the Cross, which then gives the Holy Spirit latitude to bring about this necessary work): **for the son of the bondwoman shall not be heir with the son of the freewoman.** (Paul is giving a dramatic illustration of the irreconcilable conflict between Salvation by works and Salvation by Faith.)

31 So then, Brethren, we are not children of the bondwoman (Hagar, Ishmael, and the Law), **but of the free.** (We are not children of the Law, but rather free children of Faith.)

CHAPTER 5
(A.D. 58)
BONDAGE

STAND fast therefore in the liberty wherewith Christ has made us free (we were made free, and refers to freedom to live a Holy life by evidencing Faith in Christ and the Cross), **and be not entangled again with the yoke of bondage.** (To abandon the Cross and go under Law of any kind guarantees bondage once again to the sin nature.)

CHRIST OF NO EFFECT

2 Behold ("mark my words!"), **I Paul say unto you** (presents the Apostle's authority regarding the Message he brings), **that if you be circumcised, Christ shall profit you nothing.** (If the Believer goes back into Law, and Law of any kind, what Christ did at the Cross on our behalf will profit us nothing. One cannot have it two ways.)

3 For I testify again to every man who is circumcised (some of the Galatian Gentiles were being pressured by false teachers to embrace the Law of Moses, which meant they would have to forsake Christ and the Cross, for it's not possible to wed the two; as well, it's not possible to wed any Law to Grace), **that he is a debtor to do the whole Law** (which of course is impossible; and besides, the Law contained no Salvation).

4 Christ is become of no effect unto you (this is a chilling statement, and refers to anyone who makes anything other than Christ and the Cross the Object of his Faith), **whosoever of you are justified by the Law** (seek to be Justified by the Law); **you are fallen from Grace** (fallen from the position of Grace, which means the Believer is trusting in something other than the Cross; it actually means, "to apostatize").

5 For we through the Spirit (the Holy Spirit works exclusively within the parameters of the Sacrifice of Christ; consequently, He demands that we place our Faith exclusively in the Cross of Christ) **wait for the Hope of Righteousness** (which is guaranteed to ultimately come [Rom. 6:14]) **by Faith** (refers to Faith in Christ and what He did for us at the Cross).

6 For in Jesus Christ neither Circumcision availeth anything, nor uncircumcision (has no spiritual bearing on anything); **but Faith which works by Love.** (The evidence of true Faith is the fact of the Love which emanates from such Faith.)

GRACE

7 You did run well (under the Ministry of Paul, the Galatians had begun well); **who did hinder you that you should not obey the truth?** (Paul is referring to false teachers who were attempting to pull the Galatians away from the Cross to other things.)

8 This persuasion comes **not of Him** (the Holy Spirit) **Who calls you.** (What you are doing is not Biblical!)

9 A little leaven (corruption) **leaveneth** (corrupts) **the whole lump.** (The introduction of a small amount of false doctrine will ultimately consume the entirety of the belief system.)

10 I have confidence in you through the Lord, that you will be none otherwise minded (that the Galatians would not abandon the Cross for this false doctrine): **but he who troubles you shall bear his judgment, whosoever he be.** (Judgment will ultimately come on those who attempt to present a way of Salvation other than Christ and the Cross.)

11 And I, Brethren, if I yet Preach Circumcision, why do I yet suffer persecution? (Any message other than the Cross draws little opposition.) **then is the offence of the Cross ceased.** (The Cross offends the world and most of the Church. So, if the Preacher ceases to Preach the Cross as the only way of Salvation and Victory, then opposition and persecution will cease. But so will Salvation!)

12 I would they were even cut off which trouble you. (They might cease from the land, but unfortunately false teachers seem to ever plague the landscape.)

LIBERTY

13 For, Brethren, you have been called unto liberty *(liberty from the Law, and to live a Holy life)*; only *use* not liberty for an occasion to the flesh *(because you are living under Grace, do not think sin is inconsequential)*, but by love serve one another. *(This is Paul's constant concern. How will you use your freedom? How will you live your new life?)*

14 For all the Law is fulfilled in one word, *even* in this *(presents the Apostle telling us how the Law is fulfilled in our lives)*; You shall love your neighbour as yourself. *(In this, the whole Law stands fully obeyed. This can be done and, in fact, will be done, providing the Believer ever makes the Cross of Christ the Object of his Faith. Accordingly, the Holy Spirit will then provide the power for us to do what we should do.)*

15 But if you bite and devour one another *(which will be done if the Believer seeks to live under Law)*, take heed that you be not consumed one of another. *(If Love is absent, this tells us that the Cross is absent. Fighting and quarreling always follow the Law.)*

VICTORY

16 *This* I say then, Walk *(order your behavior)* in the Spirit *(we do so by placing our Faith exclusively in Christ and the Cross, through which the Spirit works exclusively [Rom. 8:1-2])*, and you shall not fulfil the lust of the flesh. *(This proves the existence of the sin nature in the Believer. It declares the consciousness of corrupt desires. As stated, the only way to not fulfill the lust of the flesh is for our Faith to be placed exclusively in the Cross.)*

17 For the flesh *(in this case, evil desires)* lusteth against the Spirit *(is the opposite of the Holy Spirit)*, and the Spirit against the flesh *(it is the Holy Spirit Alone, Who can subdue the flesh; He does so, as we have repeatedly stated, by our Faith being placed exclusively in the Cross)*: and these are contrary the one to the other *(these two can never harmonize; as Paul has stated, the old nature must be cast out, which the Holy Spirit Alone can do)*: so that you cannot do the things that you would. *(Without the Holy Spirit, Who works by the Cross, the Believer cannot live a Holy life.)*

18 But if you be led of the Spirit, you are not under the Law. *(One cannot follow the Spirit and the Law at the same time, but regrettably that's what most modern Christians are attempting to do. Unless one properly understands the Cross as it regards Sanctification, one cannot be properly "led of the Spirit," Who works exclusively within the framework of the Finished Work of Christ.)*

19 Now the works of the flesh are manifest, which are *these (if one attempts to function by means of Law of any nature, the "works of the flesh" will be manifested in one's life)*; Adultery, fornication, uncleanness, lasciviousness,

20 Idolatry, witchcraft, hatred, variance, emulations, wrath, strife, seditions, heresies,

21 Envyings, murders, drunkenness, revellings, and such like *(if one is walking after the flesh [Rom. 8:1], one or more of these sins will manifest themselves in one's life; the only way, and I mean the only way, one can walk in perpetual victory is to understand that everything we receive from God comes to us by means of the Cross; consequently, the Cross must ever be the Object of our Faith; this being the case, the Holy Spirit, Who works exclusively within the confines of the Sacrifice of Christ, will exert His mighty Power on our behalf, which will enable us to live a Holy life)*: of the which I tell you before, as I have also told *you* in time past *(refers to the fact that the Apostle was not afraid to name specific sins)*, that they which do such things shall not inherit the Kingdom of God. *(This tells us in no uncertain terms that if our Faith is not everlastingly in Christ and the Cross, we simply won't make it. God doesn't have two ways of Salvation and Victory, only one, and that is "Jesus Christ and Him Crucified.")*

FRUIT OF THE SPIRIT

22 But the Fruit of the Spirit *(are not "fruits" but rather "Fruit"; they are to be looked at as a "whole," which means they grow equally)* is love, joy, peace, longsuffering, gentleness, goodness, Faith,

23 Meekness, temperance: against such there is no Law. *(Against such there doesn't need to be a Law. But let the Reader understand that this "Fruit" is of the "Holy Spirit," and not of man. It can only develop as we are "led of the Spirit." And we can only be led by the Spirit by making the Cross the Object of our Faith.)*

A SPIRITUAL LIFE

24 And they who are Christ's have Crucified the flesh with the affections and lusts. *(This can be done only by the Believer understanding*

it was carried out by Christ at the Cross, and our being "Baptized into His Death" [Rom. 6:3-5]. That being the case, and as repeatedly stated, the Cross must ever be the Object of our Faith, which alone will bring about these results.)

25 If we live in the Spirit, let us also walk in the Spirit *("walk" refers to our lifestyle; this Passage declares both life and Holiness to be the Work of the Holy Spirit; He operates Salvation and He operates Sanctification; both are realized on the Principle of Faith, and that refers to the Cross ever being the Object of our Faith; many know they have received Spiritual Life, as it regards Salvation through Faith, but they think they can only secure Sanctification by works; this is a great error; it never brings victory; believing in Christ and the Cross for Sanctification, as well as for Justification, introduces one into a life of power and victory, which is the only way it can be accomplished.)*

26 Let us not be desirous of vain Glory *(which is a sign that one is functioning according to Law),* **provoking one another** *(self-righteousness),* **envying one another.** *(These are works of the flesh, and will manifest themselves if our Faith is in things other than the Cross.)*

CHAPTER 6
(A.D. 58)
RESTORATION

BRETHREN, **if a man be overtaken in a fault** *(pertains to moral failure, and is brought about because one has ignorantly placed himself under Law; such a position guarantees failure),* **you which are spiritual** *(refers to those who understand God's Prescribed Order of Victory, which is the Cross),* **restore such an one** *(tell him he failed because of reverting to Law, and that Victory can be his by placing his Faith totally in the Cross, which then gives the Holy Spirit latitude to work, Who Alone can give the Victory)* **in the spirit of meekness** *(never with an overbearing, holier than thou attitude);* **considering yourself, lest you also be tempted** *(the implication is that if we do not handle such a case Scripturally we, thereby, open the door for Satan to attack us in the same manner as he did the failing brother).*

2 Bear ye one another's burdens *(refers to sharing the heartache and shame of one who has spiritually failed),* **and so fulfil the Law of Christ** *(which is Love!).*

3 For if a man think himself to be something, when he is nothing *(refers to a Believer who puts himself above the one who has failed*

in his own eyes), **he deceives himself.** *(This presents one who has the conceited idea he is morally and spiritually superior to what he actually is.)*

4 But let every man prove his own work *(to put his Faith in the Cross to the test for the purpose of approving, which is done by seeing how well one obeys the Word of the Lord),* **and then shall he have rejoicing in himself alone** *(the spiritual man sees himself as he really is, totally dependent on Christ and the Cross),* **and not in another.** *(He will not then be rejoicing over the other man's failure.)*

5 For every man shall bear his own burden. *(When each Believer sees his own failings, which we all have, he will have no inclination to compare himself with others, at least as it regards a superior position.)*

6 Let him who is taught in the Word *(refers to the act of receiving instruction)* **communicate unto him who teaches in all good things.** *(Let us not make the load of the God-called Teacher heavier by hindering him in some way, but rather let us encourage him.)*

TWO DESTINIES

7 Be not deceived *(refers to the fact that a Believer can definitely be deceived; Paul is speaking primarily of Believers allowing false teachers to move their Faith from the Cross to other things);* **God is not mocked** *(God, in fact, is mocked when we substitute something else in place of the Cross):* **for whatsoever a man sows, that shall he also reap** *(the Law of sowing and reaping, which will unfailingly come to pass).*

8 For he who sows to his flesh shall of the flesh reap corruption *(those who make something else the Object of their Faith, rather than the Cross, which means they are now depending on self-will);* **but he who sows to the Spirit** *(does so by trusting exclusively in Christ and what Christ did at the Cross)* **shall of the Spirit reap life everlasting** *(God's Prescribed Order of Victory).*

GLORIFY GOD

9 And let us not be weary in well doing *(Paul continues to speak of "sowing to the Spirit"):* **for in due season we shall reap** *(in God's Time, our Faith in Christ and the Cross will not go unrewarded, but will bring forth exactly that which is Promised by the Lord),* **if we faint not.** *(Many start the race, but do not finish. They give*

up after a while, exclaiming that the "Cross" doesn't work. Let all know and understand that we might fail, but the Cross never fails!)

10 As we have therefore opportunity, let us do good unto all *men* (the Holy Spirit will help us do this, providing our Faith is ever in the Cross; otherwise, we will fail), **especially unto them who are of the household of Faith.** (There are many who are of the Faith, but really do not understand the Faith, so they walk in defeat. We are to give them the Message of the Cross, in order that they might walk in perpetual Victory [Rom. 8:2].)

11 **You see how large a letter I have written unto you with my own hand.** (This refers to the fact that Paul had written the entirety of the Epistle to the Galatians himself, which he normally did not do. Scribes generally wrote as he dictated, with him writing the postscript and signing his name.)

THE CROSS

12 **As many as desire to make a fair show in the flesh, they constrain you to be Circumcised** (the Judaizers were attempting to get the Galatians to embrace the Law along with Christ); **only lest they should suffer persecution for the Cross of Christ.** (The Message of the Cross brings forth persecution from both the world and the Church. It strikes at the very heart of all spiritual pride and self-righteousness.)

13 **For neither they themselves who are Circumcised keep the Law** (engaging in the rite of Circumcision, which was the seal of the Law of Moses, didn't help anyone keep the Law); **but**

desire to have you Circumcised, that they may Glory in your flesh. (Many in the Church glory in self-effort, but few glory in the Cross because it puts self-effort in its proper place.)

14 **But God forbid that I should glory** (boast), **save in the Cross of our Lord Jesus Christ** (what the opponents of Paul sought to escape at the price of insincerity is the Apostle's only basis of exultation), **by Whom the world is Crucified unto me, and I unto the world.** (The only way we can overcome the world, and I mean the only way, is by placing our Faith exclusively in the Cross of Christ and keeping it there.)

15 **For in Christ Jesus neither Circumcision availeth any thing, nor uncircumcision** (blows all of man's religious ceremonies to pieces), **but a new creature** (new in every respect, which can only be brought about by trusting Christ and what He did for us at the Cross).

16 **And as many as walk** (to direct one's life, to order one's conduct) **according to this rule** (the principle of the Cross), **peace be on them, and mercy** (which comes only by means of the Cross), **and upon the Israel of God.** (This refers to all who look to the Cross for their Redemption. They alone are the true Israel.)

17 **From henceforth let no man trouble me** (don't listen to these false teachers): **for I bear in my body the marks of the Lord Jesus.** (This concerns the persecution he suffered because of the "offence of the Cross" [5:11].)

18 **Brethren, the Grace of our Lord Jesus Christ** (which comes by our Faith in the Cross) **be with your spirit.** (We worship the Lord in Spirit and in Truth, and the Cross is that Truth.) **Amen.**

THE EPISTLE OF PAUL THE APOSTLE TO THE
EPHESIANS

CHAPTER 1
(A.D. 64)
INTRODUCTION

PAUL, an Apostle of Jesus Christ *(the Apostle stands as the de facto leader of the Church, and does so by the special Message he brings; with Paul, it was Grace)* by the Will of God *(the Foundation of Paul's Calling)*, to the Saints *(which one instantly becomes upon accepting Christ)* which are at Ephesus *(to those Saints and all others as well, and for all time)*, and to the Faithful in Christ Jesus *(ever Faithful in making the Cross the Object of one's Faith)*:

2 Grace *be* to you, and peace *(which come by means of the Cross)*, from God our Father *(a privilege of untold proportions)*, and *from* the Lord Jesus Christ *(proclaims the Saviour in association with the Father)*.

SPIRITUAL BLESSINGS

3 Blessed *be* the God *(we should ever bless the Lord for what He has done for us)* and Father of our Lord Jesus Christ *(God is the Father of Christ, as Christ is seen in His Humanity)*, Who has blessed us with all spiritual blessings *(every benefit of the Atonement)* in Heavenly *places* in Christ *(the Divine Blessing has its ground and reason in Christ; it is ours by reason of our being "in Him," which was brought about by the Cross)*:

4 According as He has chosen us in Him *(does not refer to the person being chosen, but rather the purpose for which the person is chosen)* before the foundation of the world *(the Creator, in laying His Plans for the world, had the purpose of Redeeming Grace in view)*, that we should be Holy and without blame before Him in Love *(presents the purpose of the "chosen")*:

5 Having predestinated us unto the adoption of children *(does not refer to the individual being predestinated as to whether he will be saved or lost, but rather the manner in which one becomes a Child of God)* by Jesus Christ to Himself *(by means of the Cross)*, according to the good pleasure of His Will *(it is an act of sovereignty, but an act based on love)*,

6 To the praise of the Glory of His Grace *(the ultimate reason)*, wherein He has made us accepted *(made possible by the Cross)* in the beloved *(in Christ)*.

7 In Whom *(in Christ)* we have Redemption through His Blood *(the outpoured Blood of the Son of God at the Cross is the price for Redemption)*, the forgiveness of sins *(a remission of their penalty)*, according to the riches of His Grace *(the riches of that Grace gave us the Cross)*;

8 Wherein He has abounded toward us *(refers to God's Grace being manifested toward us in superabundance, again made possible by the Cross)* in all wisdom *(insight)* and prudence *(to solve the problems of each moment of time)*;

9 Having made known unto us the mystery of His Will *(refers to the secret purposes and counsels God intends to carry into effect in His Kingdom)*, according to His good pleasure *(extended to Believers)* which He has purposed in Himself *(originated in His Own Mind)*:

10 That in the dispensation of the fulness of times *(concerns itself with a well-ordered plan)* He might gather together in one all things in Christ *(the Atonement addressed not only man's Fall, but the revolution of Lucifer as well)*, both which are in Heaven *(where the revolution of Lucifer began)*, and which are on earth *(the Fall of man)*; *even* in Him *(made possible by what Christ did at the Cross)*:

11 In Whom *(Christ)* also we have obtained an inheritance *(the best Greek Texts have, "we were designated as a heritage"; thus, the Saints are God's Heritage, His Possession through the Work of Christ on the Cross)*, being predestinated according to the purpose of Him *(pertains to the inheritance being predestinated, not the individual who would obtain the inheritance)* Who works all things after the Counsel of His Own Will *(therefore, it is perfect)*:

12 That we should be to the praise of His Glory *(proclaims that which is guaranteed to be, not what is hoped to be)*, who first trusted in Christ. *(We will attain all of this by first trusting in Christ, which means accepting what He did for us at the Cross.)*

13 In Whom *(Christ)* you also *trusted*, after that you heard the Word of Truth *(pertains to the Message of the Cross [I Cor. 1:18])*, the

Gospel of your Salvation *(the good news provided by the Cross)*: In Whom *(Christ)* also after that you believed *(believed in what Christ did for us at the Cross)*, you were sealed with that Holy Spirit of Promise *(made possible by the Cross)*,

14 Which is the earnest *(down payment)* of our inheritance *(but with a guarantee that it all will come at the Resurrection)* until the Redemption of the purchased possession *(bought by the Blood of Christ, and will be totally fulfilled at the Resurrection)*, unto the praise of His Glory. *(This refers to that which God has done, and will do, which is a victory of astounding proportions.)*

PRAYER

15 Wherefore I also, after I heard of your Faith in the Lord Jesus *(day-by-day Faith exercised in the Lord Jesus for daily living)*, and love unto all the Saints *(it is only those who do not depend on the Finished Work of the Cross, who lack in love)*,

16 Cease not to give thanks for you *(is used some twenty-three times in one way or the other in Paul's Epistles)*, making mention of you in my prayers *(a habit of the Apostle — his intercessory prayer life)*;

17 That the God of our Lord Jesus Christ, the Father of Glory *(refers to our Lord in His Humanity as worshiping and being obedient to God the Father)*, may give unto you the Spirit of Wisdom and Revelation in the knowledge of Him *(knowledge of Christ, which we receive through the Word, enables the Holy Spirit to increase our "Wisdom and Revelation")*:

18 The eyes of your understanding being enlightened *(could be translated, "The eyes of your heart having been enlightened with the present result that they are in a state of illumination")*; that you may know what is the hope of His calling *(in a sense, actually points to what the hope really is)*, and what the riches of the glory of His inheritance in the Saints *(speaks now not of the Saint's inheritance, but rather God's inheritance; the Saints are that inheritance)*,

19 And what *is* the exceeding greatness of His power to us-ward who believe *(power to live a Holy life; who believe in Christ and what He has done at the Cross)*, according to the working of His mighty power *(it works for us according to our Faith in the Finished Work of Christ, and by no other means)*,

20 Which He *(God the Father)* wrought in Christ, when He raised Him from the dead *(which He did by the Power of the Holy Spirit)*, and set *Him* at His Own Right Hand in the Heavenly *places (refers to the highest place of honor, dignity, and authority, and means that the Sacrifice of Christ was totally accepted)*,

21 Far above all principality, and power, and might, and dominion *(proclaims the exalted position of Christ)*, and every name that is named, not only in this world, but also in that which is to come *(Christ is given this exalted position, and will retain it forever, because of the Cross)*:

22 And has put all *things* under His feet *(He thus fulfills the destiny for which man was originally created)*, and gave Him *to be* the Head over all *things* to the Church *(He is the absolute, ultimate authority, because of the Cross)*,

23 Which is His Body *(the Church has its Source of Life in Him, sustained and directed by His Power, the instrument also by and through which He works)*, the fulness of Him that fills all in all. *(As Christ was the True Israel, and is the True Man, He is also the True Church.)*

CHAPTER 2
(A.D. 64)
ALIVE IN CHRIST

AND you *has He quickened (made alive)*, who were dead in trespasses and sins *(total depravity due to the Fall and original sin)*;

2 Wherein in time past you walked according to the course of this world *(refers to the fact that the unredeemed order their behavior and regulate their lives within this sphere of trespasses and sins)*, according to the prince of the power of the air *(pertains to the fact that Satan heads up the system of this world)*, the spirit that now works in the children of disobedience *(the spirit of Satan, which fills all unbelievers, thereby working disobedience)*:

3 Among whom *(the children of disobedience)* also we all had our conversation *(manner of life)* in times past in the lusts of our flesh *(evil cravings)*, fulfilling the desires of the flesh and of the mind *(the minds of the unredeemed are the laboratory of perverted thoughts, impressions, imaginations, etc.)*; and were by nature the children of wrath, even as others. *(God's wrath is unalterably opposed to sin, and the only solution is the Cross.)*

4 But God, Who is rich in Mercy *(His Mercy comes to us by means of the Cross)*, for His great

love wherewith He loved us *(the Love shown at Calvary),*

5 Even when we were dead in sins *(speaks of a state in which we could by no means help ourselves),* has quickened us together with Christ *(this new life is imparted to us through our identification with Christ in His Death and Resurrection),* (by Grace you are saved;) *(Grace is made possible solely by the Cross, and comes to us in an uninterrupted flow as we ever make the Cross the Object of our Faith.)*

6 And has raised *us* up together *(the Resurrection of Christ from the Tomb was our Resurrection as well, spiritually speaking, and gave us "newness of life" [Rom. 6:3-5]),* and made *us* sit together in Heavenly *Places (made possible by the Cross)* in Christ Jesus *(it is all done in Christ, and refers to the way He did it, which is through the Cross):*

7 That in the ages to come *(in the ages that are coming, one upon another, unending)* He might show the exceeding riches of His Grace *(presents the Believer's golden age is always future, never past)* in *His* kindness toward us through Christ Jesus. *(God is able to show us kindness only through the Cross. The Bible Student must realize the Cross is the oldest Doctrine in the Bible [I Pet. 1:18-20], and is, in fact, the Foundation on which all Doctrine must be built.)*

REDEMPTION

8 For by Grace *(the Goodness of God)* are you saved through Faith *(Faith in Christ, with the Cross ever as its Object)*; and that not of yourselves *(none of this is of us, but all is of Him):* it *is* the Gift of God *(anytime the word "Gift" is used, God is speaking of His Son and His Substitutionary Work on the Cross, which makes all of this possible):*

9 Not of works *(man cannot merit Salvation, irrespective what he does),* lest any man should boast *(boast in his own ability and strength; we are allowed to boast only in the Cross [Gal. 6:14]).*

10 For we are His workmanship *(if we are God's workmanship, our Salvation cannot be of ourselves),* created in Christ Jesus unto good works *(speaks of the results of Salvation, and never the cause),* which God has before ordained that we should walk in them. *(The "good works" the Apostle speaks of has to do with Faith in Christ and the Cross, which enables the Believer to live a Holy life.)*

UNITY

11 Wherefore remember, that you *being* in time past Gentiles in the flesh, who are called Uncircumcision *(referred to the Gentiles not being in Covenant with God; physical Circumcision under the Old Economy was its external sign)* by that which is called the Circumcision in the flesh made by hands *(is said by Paul in this manner, regarding the Jews, in contradistinction from the Circumcision of the heart);*

12 That at that time you were without Christ *(describes the former condition of the Gentiles, who had no connection with Christ before the Cross),* being aliens from the commonwealth of Israel, and strangers from the Covenants of Promise, having no hope, and without God in the world *(all of this argues a darkened and perverted heart; the Gentiles had no knowledge of God at that time):*

13 But now in Christ Jesus *(proclaims the basis of all Salvation)* you who sometimes *(times past)* were far off *(far from Salvation)* are made nigh *(near)* by the Blood of Christ. *(The Sacrificial Atoning Death of Jesus Christ transformed the relations of God with mankind. In Christ, God reconciled not a nation, but "a world" to Himself [II Cor. 5:19].)*

14 For He *(Christ)* is our peace *(through Christ and what He did at the Cross, we have peace with God),* Who has made both one *(Jews and Gentiles),* and has broken down the middle wall of partition *between us (between Jews and Gentiles);*

15 Having abolished in His flesh *(speaking of His Death on the Cross, by which He Redeemed humanity, which also means He didn't die spiritually, as some claim)* the enmity *(the hatred between God and man, caused by sin), even* the Law of Commandments *contained* in Ordinances *(pertains to the Law of Moses, and more particularly the Ten Commandments);* for to make in Himself of twain *(of Jews and Gentiles)* one new man, *so* making peace *(which again was accomplished by the Cross);*

16 And that He *(Christ)* might reconcile both *(Jews and Gentiles)* unto God in one body *(the Church)* by the Cross *(it is by the Atonement only that men ever become reconciled to God),* having slain the enmity thereby *(removed the barrier between God and sinful man):*

17 And came and preached peace to you which were afar off *(proclaims the Gospel going to the Gentiles),* and to them who were nigh. *(This refers to the Jews. It is the same Message for both.)*

18 For through Him *(through Christ)* we both *(Jews and Gentiles)* have access by One Spirit unto the Father. *(If the sinner comes by the Cross, the Holy Spirit opens the door, otherwise it is barred [Jn. 10:1].)*

19 Now *(speaks of the present state of Believers)* therefore you are no more strangers and foreigners *(pertains to what Gentiles once were)*, but fellowcitizens with the Saints *(speaks of Gentiles now having access the same as Jews, all due to the Cross)*, and of the Household of God *(a progressive relationship with God in Christ)*;

20 And are built upon the Foundation *(the Cross)* of the Apostles and Prophets *(Apostles serve as leadership under the New Covenant, with Prophets having served in that capacity under the Old)*, Jesus Christ Himself being the Chief Corner Stone *(presents the part of the Foundation which holds everything together; Jesus Christ is the "Chief Corner Stone" by virtue of what He did at the Cross)*;

21 In Whom *(Christ)* all the building fitly framed together grows unto an Holy Temple in the Lord:

22 In Whom you also are built together *(Jews and Gentiles)* for an habitation of God through the Spirit. *(This is all made possible by what Jesus did at the Cross.)*

CHAPTER 3
(A.D. 64)
REVELATION

FOR this cause I Paul, the prisoner of Jesus Christ *(Paul wrote this Epistle from prison in Rome; as well, he didn't consider himself a prisoner of Nero, but rather of Jesus Christ; in other words, for whatever purpose and reason, the Lord wanted him at this time in prison, and that's the way that Paul looked at the situation)* for you Gentiles *(refers to the beginning of the Church, which was made up mostly of Gentiles, and the giving of the Gospel to the world)*,

2 If you have heard of the dispensation of the Grace of God which is given me to youward *(presents the Apostle as having oversight or management over the New Covenant, and the proper administration of its presentation)*:

3 How that by Revelation He *(Christ)* made known unto me the mystery *(the Cross, which in essence is the New Covenant, was a "mystery" before its meaning was given to Paul)*; (as I wrote afore in few words *(evidently the Apostle had written a previous letter to the Ephesians concerning this great Truth, of which we now*

have no record),

4 Whereby, when you read *(what we are now reading, as it regards this Epistle)*, you may understand my knowledge in the Mystery of Christ) *(The Lord wants us to understand the Mystery of the Cross, as it was given to Paul. In other words, we are not to deviate from what he taught.)*

5 Which in other ages was not made known unto the sons of men *(speaks of the entirety of time, up unto the Apostle Paul)*, as it is now revealed unto His Holy Apostles and Prophets by the Spirit *(Paul was given this Revelation first [Gal. 1:11-12], with the Spirit of God then using the Message as given to Paul to enlighten other Apostles and Prophets, etc.)*;

6 That the Gentiles should be fellowheirs *(refers to the fact that all differences between Jews and Gentiles, regarding Redemption, have been erased)*, and of the same body *(everyone in the same Church, i.e., "Body of Christ")*, and partakers of His Promise in Christ by the Gospel *(should have been translated, "In Christ Jesus by the Gospel," for the best Greek Texts include the Name "Jesus"; if that latter Name wasn't there, Paul would be saying the Gentiles were fellow-partakers of the Jewish Messianic Promises, which are not true)*:

7 Whereof I was made a Minister *(refers to one who serves)*, according to the Gift of the Grace of God given unto me *(all of this was granted to Paul strictly according to the Grace of God, which means it was not because of his merit, for he had none)* by the effectual working of His power. *(This is the Power of the Holy Spirit, made available to us by the Cross and our Faith in that Finished Work [Gal. 1:18].)*

8 Unto me, who am less than the least of all Saints, is this Grace given *(humility is made evident here, which can only be made possible by the Cross, through which Grace comes to us)*, that I should Preach among the Gentiles the unsearchable riches of Christ *(the "riches of Christ" come to us exclusively by and through the Cross, and are inexhaustible, with greater and greater enlargement which will last forever)*;

9 And to make all *men* see *(to bring to light something which had previously been hidden)* what *is* the fellowship of the Mystery *(could be translated, "the fellowship of the dispensation of the Revelation of the Mystery"; in other words, the Mystery is no more, having now been revealed)*, which from the beginning of the world has been hid in God *(proclaims to us the fact that this was not a new kind of action on the*

part of God, forced upon Him by the developments in human history; the Cross was His Plan from before the Foundation of the World [I Pet. 1:18-20]), **Who created all things by Jesus Christ** (God the Father officiates; God the Son orchestrates; God the Holy Spirit executes):

10 To the intent that now unto the Principalities and Powers in Heavenly places (concerns Righteous Angels) **might be known by the Church the manifold Wisdom of God** (presents the Church proclaiming to the Angelic Host a part of the Wisdom of God not previously known to the Angels),

11 According to the eternal purpose (the purpose of the ages) **which He purposed in Christ Jesus our Lord** (God has formed a Plan which is Eternal in reference to the Salvation of men, and the Plan is centered on the Lord Jesus and what He did at the Cross):

12 In Whom (refers to Christ, but more particularly to what He did at the Cross for us) **we have boldness** (because of the Cross, we can now have a boldness in our approach to God [Heb. 4:16]) **and access** (the only way we can have access to the Throne of God is by and through Jesus Christ and His Atoning Work on the Cross) **with confidence by the Faith of Him.** ("The Faith" is wrapped up in Jesus Christ and His Cross.)

BLESSINGS

13 Wherefore I desire that you faint not at my tribulations for you (don't let your Faith weaken because of my imprisonment), **which is your glory.** (Whatever happens to me will ultimately fall out to a greater proclamation of the Gospel, which will be for your good.)

14 For this cause (the spread of the Gospel) **I bow my knees unto the Father of our Lord Jesus Christ** (Paul is saying he bows to the Will of God, whatever that Will might be),

15 Of Whom (the Lord Jesus Christ) **the whole family** (all who have accepted Christ) **in Heaven and earth is named** (all Believers who have gone on to be with the Lord, and all Believers now alive on Earth),

16 That He (Christ Jesus) **would grant you, according to the riches of His Glory** (refers to all the revealed perfections of God, not merely His Grace and Power), **to be strengthened with might by His Spirit** (this will be done, providing our Faith is ever in the Cross, by and through which the Holy Spirit works) **in the inner man** (the spirit of man);

17 That Christ may dwell in your hearts by

Faith (which is accomplished by our Faith in the Cross); **that you, being rooted and grounded in love** (securely settled and deeply founded),

18 May be able to comprehend with all Saints (means not only to understand, but as well, "to lay hold of so as to make one's own") **what** is **the breadth, and length, and depth, and height** (metaphors used by Paul to explain the vastness of God's Love for the Saints);

19 And to know the Love of Christ (speaks of knowledge gained by experience), **which passes knowledge** (the Believer can know the Love of Christ, but cannot exhaust the knowledge of that Love), **that you might be filled with all the fulness of God** (can come to us only through Christ, and what Christ did for us at the Cross).

20 Now unto Him Who is able (presents God as the Source of all Power) **to do exceeding abundantly above all that we ask or think** (so far beyond our comprehension that the Holy Spirit could give us this explanation only in these terms), **according to the power that works in us** (the word "according" refers to the fact that this Power can work in us only as we follow God's Prescribed Order of Victory, which is the Cross and our Faith in that Finished Work; this then gives the Holy Spirit the latitude to use His Great Power on our behalf),

21 Unto Him be **Glory** (Christ and the Church as one Body will be the vehicle of that eternal demonstration) **in the Church** (the Body of Christ) **by Christ Jesus** (made possible by our Lord and what He did at the Cross) **throughout all ages, world without end** (Eternal). **Amen.**

CHAPTER 4
(A.D. 64)
OUR DAILY WALK

I therefore, the prisoner of the Lord (as stated, the Apostle is in prison in Rome; he regards himself as having been made a prisoner because the Lord so willed and ordered it), **beseech you that you walk worthy of the vocation wherewith you are called** (refers to the order of one's behavior; to walk right, the Believer must "walk after the Spirit," which can only be done by understanding that all strength and help come to us through the Cross, thereby ever making the Cross the Object of our Faith),

2 With all lowliness and meekness, with longsuffering, forbearing one another in love (once again, all of these things are works of the Spirit, which means they cannot be done within our own ability; the help of the Spirit comes

to us by our Faith being constant in the Cross [I Cor. 1:17-18, 23]);

3 Endeavouring to keep the unity of the Spirit (*speaks of unity as it regards Faith in Christ and the Cross*) in the bond of peace (*Faith in things other than Christ and the Cross destroys peace, because it engenders self-righteousness*).

4 *There is* one body (*the body of called-out Believers*), and one Spirit (*one Holy Spirit, Who always works through Christ and the Cross [Jn. 16:13-14]; this means that Faith in things other than the Cross is not of the Holy Spirit, but rather of spirits*), even as you are called in one hope of your calling (*our total hope is in Christ Jesus and what He has done for us at the Cross; that is our "one" and only "hope"*);

5 One Lord (*Jesus Christ*), one Faith (*what He did at the Cross*), one Baptism (*our Salvation, referring to Believers Baptized into Christ, which was done at the Cross; it has nothing to do with Water Baptism [Rom. 6:3-5]*),

6 One God and Father of all (*speaks of the Redeemed only; God is not the Father of the unsaved, as Jesus plainly said; their father is actually the Devil [Jn. 8:44]*), Who *is* above all (*refers to supremacy*), and through all (*God's creative abilities*), and in you all (*by virtue of what Christ did for us at the Cross, and our Faith in that Finished Work*).

THE GIFT OF CHRIST

7 But unto every one of us is given Grace (*however, this Grace can be frustrated by Believers turning away from the Cross to other things [Gal. 2:21]*) according to the measure of the Gift of Christ (*measured to each Saint according to need unless, as stated, it is frustrated*).

8 Wherefore He said (*Ps. 68:18*), When He ascended up on high (*the Ascension*), He led captivity captive (*liberated the souls in Paradise; before the Cross, despite being Believers, they were still held captive by Satan because the blood of bulls and goats could not take away the sin debt; but when Jesus died on the Cross, the sin debt was paid, and now He makes all of these His Captives*), and gave Gifts unto men. (*These "Gifts" include all the Attributes of Christ, all made possible by the Cross.*)

9 (Now that He ascended (*mission completed*), what is it but that He also descended first into the lower parts of the earth? (*Immediately before His Ascension to Glory, which would be done in total triumph, He first went down into Paradise to deliver all the believing

souls in that region, which He did!*)

10 He Who descended is the same also Who ascended (*this is a portrayal of Jesus as Deliverer and Mediator*) up far above all Heavens (*presents His present location, never again having to descend into the nether world*), that He might fill all things.) (*He has always been the Creator, but now He is also the Saviour.*)

11 And He gave (*our Lord does the calling*) some, Apostles (*has reference to the fact that not all who are called to be Ministers will be called to be Apostles; this applies to the other designations as well; "Apostles" serve as the de facto leaders of the Church, and do so through the particular Message given to them by the Lord for the Church*); and some, Prophets (*who stand in the Office of the Prophet, thereby, foretelling and forthtelling*); and some, Evangelists (*to gather the harvest*); and some, Pastors (*Shepherds*) and Teachers (*those with a special Ministry to teach the Word to the Body of Christ; "Apostles" can and do function in all of the callings*);

PURPOSE OF THE GIFTS

12 For the perfecting of the Saints (*to "equip for service"*), for the work of the Ministry (*to proclaim the Message of Redemption to the entirety of the world*), for the edifying of the Body of Christ (*for the spiritual building up of the Church*):

13 Till we all come in the unity of the Faith (*to bring all Believers to a proper knowledge of Christ and the Cross*), and of the knowledge of the Son of God (*which again refers to what He did for us at the Cross*), unto a perfect man (*the Believer who functions in maturity*), unto the measure of the stature of the fulness of Christ (*the "measure" is the "fullness of Christ," which can only be attained by a proper Faith in the Cross*):

14 That we *henceforth* be no more children (*presents the opposite of maturity, and speaks of those whose Faith is in that other than the Cross*), tossed to and fro, and carried about with every wind of doctrine, by the sleight of men (*Satan uses Preachers*), *and* cunning craftiness (*they make a way, other than the Cross, which seems to be right*), whereby they lie in wait to deceive (*refers to a deliberate planning or system*);

15 But speaking the Truth in Love (*powerfully proclaiming the Truth of the Cross, but always with Love*), may grow up into Him in all things (*proper Spiritual Growth can take place only according to proper Faith in the Cross [I Cor. 1:21, 23; 2:2]*), which is the Head, *even*

Christ *(Christ is the Head of the Church, and is such by virtue of the Cross)*:

16 From Whom *(Christ Jesus)* **the whole body** *(Christ as the Head, and the Church as the Body)* **fitly joined together** *(presents the foot in the place it ought to be, and the eye in its proper place, etc.)* **and compacted by that which every joint supplies** *(one part is dependent on the other)*, **according to the effectual working in the measure of every part** *(every part labors to produce a great result)*, **making increase of the body unto the edifying of itself in love** *(building itself up; will happen when we function according to God's Prescribed Order, which is the "unity of the Faith"; again, refers to a proper understanding of the Cross).*

MORAL STANDARDS

17 This I say therefore, and testify in the Lord *(given to him by the Lord as it regards our everyday lifestyle)*, **that you henceforth walk not as other Gentiles walk** *(how one orders one's behavior)*, **in the vanity of their mind** *(refers to living in the sphere of emptiness; it denotes an ignorance of Divine things, a moral blindness)*,

18 Having the understanding darkened *(speaks of a process completed in the past [the Fall] but having results in the present)*, **being alienated from the life of God** *(proclaims the only true life there is)* **through the ignorance that is in them** *(does not refer merely to intellect, but denotes an ignorance of Divine things)*, **because of the blindness of their heart** *(it is a "willful ignorance" which brings about a "willful blindness," i.e., "spiritual blindness")*:

19 Who being past feeling *(moral insensibility, which brings about man's inhumanity to man)* **have given themselves over unto lasciviousness** *(a complete surrender of self unto evil)*, **to work all uncleanness with greediness** *(such a person is greedy for such a lifestyle).*

20 But you have not so learned Christ *(stands in contrast to the insensitive, passion-dominated pagans who exist only to satisfy their lower nature; in other words, the Lord saves us from sin, not in sin)*;

21 If so be that you have heard Him *(the point is, "Since it was Christ you heard Preached")*, **and have been taught by Him** *(should have been translated, "in Him," i.e., "in this sphere of Christ")*, **as the Truth is in Jesus** *(the Truth is not only "in Jesus," it as well "is Jesus" [Jn. 14:6])*:

22 That you put off *(which can be done only by one placing his Faith exclusively in the Cross)* **concerning the former conversation** *(concerning the former manner of life)* **the old man** *(refers to the unsaved person dominated by the totally depraved nature [Rom. 6:6])*, **which is corrupt according to the deceitful lusts** *(the unsaved person is subject to a continuous process of corruption, which grows worse as time goes on)*;

23 And be renewed *(a continuous act)* **in the spirit of your mind** *(has to do with the human will; the mind of the Believer must be pulled from a dependence on self to a total dependence on Christ, which can only be done by making the Cross, ever the Cross, the Object of one's Faith [Rom. 12:1-2])*;

24 And that you put on the new man *(we are a "new man" by virtue of being Baptized into His Death, Buried with Him by Baptism into Death, all speaking of the Crucifixion, and being Raised with Him in "newness of life" [Rom. 6:3-5])*, **which after God is created in Righteousness and true Holiness.** *(This is what the "new man" is supposed to be, and what he can be, but only by reckoning himself to be dead indeed unto the sin nature [which was done at the Cross], but alive unto God through Jesus Christ our Lord [Rom. 6:11].)*

25 Wherefore putting away lying *(the first item to be included in the putting off of the "old self" is falsehood, which refers to believing something other than Christ and the Cross; in other words, everything other than Christ and Him Crucified is a "lie")*, **speak every man truth with his neighbour** *(the Truth is Christ and the Cross, which brings about Righteousness and True Holiness)*: **for we are members one of another.** *(Therefore, we should all speak the same thing, which is Christ and the Cross.)*

26 Be ye angry, and sin not: let not the sun go down upon your wrath *(the only "anger" allowed is Righteous anger; all other anger is a result of the "old man," and must be "put off"; it has to do basically with our emotions, which can only be properly settled by the Holy Spirit; meaning for Him to work, we must ever have the Cross as the Object of our Faith)*:

27 Neither give place to the Devil. *(Faith properly placed in the Cross gives Satan no place.)*

28 Let him who stole steal no more *(Christlikeness gives high moral standards)*: **but rather let him labour, working with *his* hands the thing which is good** *(we are to earn our living by whatever honest method is at our disposal)*, **that he may have to give to him who needs.** *(Instead of taking from others, we can now give*

to others.)

29 Let no corrupt communication proceed out of your mouth *(let no slander or faithlessness proceed out of your mouth)*, but that which is good to the use of edifying *(does what we are saying buildup or tear down?)*, that it may Minister Grace unto the hearers *(a Blessing)*.

30 And grieve not the Holy Spirit of God *(proclaims the fact that the utterance of evil or worthless words is repugnant to the Holiness of the Spirit)*, whereby you are sealed unto the Day of Redemption. *(This should have been translated, "In Whom you are sealed unto the Day of Redemption." The Holy Spirit is Himself the Seal God has placed on us.)*

31 Let all bitterness, and wrath, and anger, and clamour, and evil speaking, be put away from you, with all malice *(as the Believer puts His Faith in the Cross and keeps his Faith in the Cross, giving the Holy Spirit latitude to work, these evil things can then be "put away" from our lives)*:

32 And be you kind one to another, tenderhearted, forgiving one another *(be quick to forgive)*, even as God for Christ's sake has forgiven you. *(Christ's forgiveness of us is to always be the basis of our forgiveness of others.)*

CHAPTER 5
(A.D. 64)
COMMANDS

BE ye therefore followers of God, as dear children *(we do so by obeying the Word of God, and we do that by keeping our Faith in the Cross)*;

2 And walk in love *(be constantly ordering your behavior within the sphere of love)*, as Christ also has loved us *(presents the Apostle passing from the Father to the Son as our example)*, and has given Himself for us an Offering and a Sacrifice to God for a sweetsmelling Savour. *(Christ fulfilled all the symbolic Blood Offerings of the Levitical system [Heb. 10:8]. He fulfilled those by becoming an Offering for sin on the Cross. The "sweetsmelling Savor" describes the atoning Sacrifice as accepted by God.)*

SINS

3 But fornication, and all uncleanness, or covetousness, let it not be once named among you, as becomes Saints;

4 Neither filthiness, nor foolish talking, nor jesting, which are not convenient *(out of character)*: but rather giving of thanks. *(The*

Believer's protection against all these sins is the Cross of Christ, and the Cross alone. Keeping the Cross as the Object of one's Faith guarantees Victory [Gal. 6:14], and for that we are ever to give thanks to God.)*

BE NOT PARTAKERS

5 For this you know, that no whoremonger, nor unclean person, nor covetous man, who is an idolater, has any inheritance in the Kingdom of Christ and of God *(Paul is speaking to Believers! if the Cross is not the Object of Faith for the Believer, but rather something else, these Passages plainly tell us such a Believer will actually come to the place of unbelief and lose his soul; the only answer for the "Law of sin and death" is the "the Law of the Spirit of Life in Christ Jesus" [Rom. 8:2])*.

6 Let no man deceive you with vain words *(by trying to pull you away from the Cross)*: for because of these things comes the Wrath of God upon the children of disobedience *(the Cross alone stops the Wrath of God)*.

7 Be not ye therefore partakers with them. *(Never forsake the Cross, no matter how enticing the other things might look.)*

COMMANDS

8 For you were sometimes darkness *(everyone who doesn't know Christ is in spiritual darkness)*, but now *(since coming to Christ)* are you light in the Lord *(we are a reflection of the Light of Christ)*: walk as children of Light *(order your behavior accordingly)*:

9 (For the Fruit of the Spirit *(Gal. 5:22-23)* is in all goodness and Righteousness and Truth;) *(This proclaims the end results of the "Fruit of the Spirit.")*

10 Proving what is acceptable unto the Lord *(put to the test, and the Cross alone will stand the test)*.

11 And have no fellowship with the unfruitful works of darkness *(the Scripture teaches separation, but not isolation)*, but rather reprove them *(speak out boldly and forcibly against them)*.

12 For it is a shame even to speak of those things which are done of them in secret. *(Paul's writings always emphasized the exceeding sinfulness of sin, but never more evidently than here.)*

13 But all things that are reproved are made manifest by the Light *(it is only Christ and the Cross which can adequately portray what sin actually is; that's the reason much of the Church*

doesn't care for the Cross!): **for whatsoever does make manifest is light.** *(The Cross alone manifests sin and all its evil effects.)*

14 Wherefore He said *(Isa. 60:1)*, **Awake thou who sleeps** *(the Apostle is warning Christians that they should stir themselves from lethargy and apathy)*, **and arise from the dead** *(dead to the things of the Spirit)*, **and Christ shall give you Light.** *(Christ will pour upon you the Light of Divine Truth as the Sun gives light to men aroused from sleep.)*

15 See then that you walk circumspectly *(carefully taking heed)*, **not as fools** *(a person who doesn't avail himself of all Christ has to offer is a fool)*, **but as wise** *(draw close to the Lord)*,

16 Redeeming the time *(take advantage of the opportunities that present themselves)*, **because the days are evil.** *(The Cross must be our Foundation. Only then can we overcome the "evil," and carry out that which the Lord has called us to do.)*

17 Wherefore be ye not unwise *(time is precious because God has given us only a few short days to make choices that will bring Eternal consequences)*, **but understanding what the will of the Lord is.** *(We can do this if we look exclusively to Christ and the Cross.)*

18 And be not drunk with wine *(speaks of being controlled by alcoholic beverage, which Paul desires to use as an example)*, **wherein is excess; but be filled with the Spirit** *(being controlled by the Spirit constantly, moment by moment)*;

19 Speaking to yourselves in Psalms and Hymns and Spiritual Songs *(refers to worship as it regards songs and singing)*, **singing and making melody in your heart to the Lord** *(places the approval of the Holy Spirit on the same forms of music and styles of worship as were begun in the Old Testament)*;

20 Giving thanks always for all things unto God and the Father *(all things which come from God)* **in the Name of our Lord Jesus Christ** *(proclaims in this Verse the Source of all Blessings, and the means by which these Blessings have come upon the human race as well)*;

21 Submitting yourselves one to another *(this tells us that proper spiritual submission is always horizontal and never vertical as it refers to Believers, meaning that we submit one to another)* **in the fear of God** *(meaning that all vertical submission must be to God Alone, never to man)*.

WIVES

22 Wives, submit yourselves unto your own husbands *(the Holy Spirit, through the Apostle, is relating to the spiritual leadership of the family)*, **as unto the Lord.** *(First of all, the submission is to be to Christ as Lord and Master, and not to the husband. If the husband's supremacy had been in view, it would have been expressed in a different manner, so say the Greek Scholars. If the wife properly submits to the Lord, she will properly submit to her husband as it regards spiritual leadership, that is if he knows the Lord. If he doesn't know the Lord, such submission cannot be tendered, as would be obvious.)*

23 For the husband is the head of the wife, even as Christ is the Head of the Church *(suggests the obedience the wife renders to her husband is to be regarded as obedience rendered to Christ, which she can do if her husband is properly following the Lord)*: **and He is the Saviour of the Body.** *(This refers to the Lord being the Saviour of Believers, who make up the Church. While the husband cannot be the Saviour of his wife in redemptive terms, he can be her protector and provider.)*

24 Therefore as the Church is subject unto Christ *(as its Head)*, **so let the wives be to their own husbands in everything.** *(This presupposes that the husband is conducting himself even as Christ.)*

HUSBANDS

25 Husbands, love your wives *(with a God kind of love)*, **even as Christ also loved the Church** *(presents the qualifier; if a husband conducts himself accordingly toward his wife, she will have no problem whatsoever submitting to him, even as she should)*, **and gave Himself for it** *(presents the great Sacrifice which characterizes the God kind of love; the answer for marriage problems is not marriage seminars, but rather that both husband and wife place their Faith and confidence totally in Christ and what He has done for us at the Cross; in other words, the Cross alone, which refers to what Jesus did there, is the answer)*;

26 That He might sanctify and cleanse it *(speaks of the view to the final presentation of the Church in perfect Holiness at the Coming Great Day)* **with the washing of water by the Word** *(actually means the "Word" washes and cleanses one exactly as water)*,

27 That He might present it to Himself *(it is Christ Himself Who is to present the Church, and He is to present it to Himself)* **a glorious Church** *(made possible by the Cross)*, **not having**

spot, or wrinkle, or any such thing *(which the Cross alone can do)*; but that it should be Holy and without blemish. *(This is our position in Christ, made possible by the Cross.)*

28 So ought men to love their wives as their own bodies *(is proclaimed in this manner because "they are one flesh," even as Paul will say in Verse 31)*. He who loves his wife loves himself *(proclaims the oneness of the Sacred union of marriage)*.

29 For no man ever yet hated his own flesh; but nourishes and cherishes it, even as the Lord the Church *(the Holy Spirit here is using the union of husband and wife to symbolize the union of Christ and the Church)*:

30 For we are members of His Body, of His Flesh, and of His Bones. *(We are visible parts of that Body of which He is Head, and this is the reason He nourishes and cherishes the Church. "His Flesh" and "His Bones" speak of the Incarnation, and the giving of Himself on the Cross, which made it possible for us to become part of Him [Rom. 6:3-5].)*

31 For this cause shall a man leave his father and mother *(while he certainly continues to love his father and mother, his primary love is now for his wife)*, and shall be joined unto his wife, and they two shall be one flesh. *(The union that is meant to symbolize Christ and the Church.)*

32 This is a great Mystery *(had not been heretofore revealed)*: but I speak concerning Christ and the Church. *(This presents the spiritual fact that a Believer can become one with Christ as a member of His Body, symbolized by the husband-wife relationship.)*

33 Nevertheless let every one of you in particular so love his wife even as himself *(the husband is to love the wife as being part and parcel of himself, according to the Divine idea of the marriage union)*; and the wife *see* that she reverence *her* husband. *(This means to recognize and respect his position as spiritual leader of the family. If the husband or wife makes demands on the partner Christ Alone can meet, which is the cause of most problems in marriages, the pressure will become intolerable. No human being can fulfill what Christ Alone can do.)*

CHAPTER 6
(A.D. 64)
DUTIES OF CHILDREN

CHILDREN, obey your parents in the Lord: for this is right. *(This means to be under* authority. *As well, it refers to parents who know God. If not, they are to be obeyed as far as possible, but not in that which violates the Scripture.)*

2 Honour your father and mother *(all of this is important because family Government is designed to be an imitation of the Government of God)*; (which is the first Commandment with Promise;)

3 That it may be well with you, and you may live long on the earth *([Deut. 5:16; Ex. 20:12], as should be obvious, failure to obey carries a penalty)*.

FATHERS

4 And, you Fathers, provoke not your children to wrath *(refers to the fact that Fathers are to raise their children in love and not the opposite)*: but bring them up in the nurture and admonition of the Lord *(raised according to the ways of the Lord, i.e., His Word)*.

SERVANTS AND MASTERS

5 Servants *(slaves)*, be obedient to them who are *your* masters according to the flesh *(the slave owners were masters as it pertained to the task at hand, but that only; the Lord was the Master of the soul and the spirit of the individual, and the eternal well-being also)*, with fear and trembling *(actually refers to fear and trembling before the Lord)*, in singleness of your heart, as unto Christ *(consider an order by the slave master as an order from Christ)*;

6 Not with eyeservice, as men-pleasers *(pertains to service which is done only when one is under the Master's eye, but something else when he is not watching)*; but as the Servants of Christ *(they were to look at themselves as servants of Christ, not of men; this spirit will render excellent service to men)*, doing the Will of God from the heart *(it is the Will of God that we conduct ourselves like Christ)*;

7 With good will doing service, as to the Lord, and not to men *(this means every employee, irrespective whom his employer might be, is to function in his task, whatever it might be, as though he is doing it to the Lord)*:

8 Knowing that whatsoever good thing any man does, the same shall he receive of the Lord, whether *he be* bond or free. *(Even though conscientious service may not always be rewarded by earthly employers, it definitely will not be overlooked by the Lord.)*

9 And, you masters, do the same things

unto them, forbearing threatening *(means that Christian Masters, of which there definitely were some, were to treat their Christian slaves, or any slave for that matter, with kindness and respect)*: knowing that your Master also is in Heaven *(thereby overlooking both the employer and the employee in using today's terminology)*; neither is there respect of persons with Him. *(He looks at one as he looks at the other.)*

SPIRITUAL WARFARE

10 Finally, my Brethren, be strong in the Lord *(be continually strengthened, which one does by constant Faith in the Cross)*, and in the power of His Might. *(This power is at our disposal. The Source is the Holy Spirit, but the means is the Cross [I Cor. 1:18].)*

11 Put on the whole armour of God *(not just some, but all)*, that you may be able to stand against the wiles of the Devil. *(This refers to the "stratagems" of Satan.)*

12 For we wrestle not against flesh and blood *(our foes are not human; however, Satan constantly uses human beings to carry out his dirty work)*, but against principalities *(rulers or beings of the highest rank and order in Satan's kingdom)*, against powers *(the rank immediately below the "Principalities")*, against the rulers of the darkness of this world *(those who carry out the instructions of the "Powers")*, against spiritual wickedness in high *places*. *(This refers to demon spirits.)*

RESOURCES

13 Wherefore take unto you the whole armour of God *(because of what we face)*, that you may be able to withstand in the evil day *(refers to resisting and opposing the powers of darkness)*, and having done all, to stand. *(This refers to the Believer not giving ground, not a single inch.)*

14 Stand therefore, having your loins girt about with Truth *(the Truth of the Cross)*, and having on the breastplate of Righteousness *(the Righteousness of Christ, which comes strictly by and through the Cross)*;

15 And your feet shod with the preparation of the Gospel of Peace *(peace comes through the Cross as well)*;

16 Above all, taking the shield of Faith *(ever making the Cross the Object of your Faith, which is the only Faith God will recognize, and the only Faith Satan will recognize)*, wherewith you shall be able to quench all the fiery darts of the wicked. *(This represents temptations with which Satan assails the Saints.)*

17 And take the Helmet of Salvation *(has to do with the renewing of the mind, which is done by understanding that everything we receive from the Lord, comes to us through the Cross)*, and the Sword of the Spirit, which is the Word of God *(the Word of God is the story of Christ and the Cross)*:

18 Praying always with all prayer and supplication in the Spirit *(an incessant pleading until the prayer is answered [Lk. 18:1-8])*, and watching thereunto *(being sensitive to what the Holy Spirit desires)* with all perseverance *(don't stop)* and supplication *(petitions and requests)* for all Saints *(Saints praying for other Saints)*;

19 And for me *(pray for me)*, that utterance may be given unto me *(pray that the Lord would anoint him to Preach and Teach)*, that I may open my mouth boldly *(refers to being fearless and confident in the presentation of the Gospel)*, to make known the Mystery of the Gospel *(to properly Preach and Teach the New Covenant, which is the story of the Cross)*,

20 For which I am an Ambassador *(for Christ)* in bonds *(a prisoner)*: that therein I may speak boldly, as I ought to speak *(that he would not allow the persecution to stop him from Preaching as he should Preach)*.

BENEDICTION

21 But that you also may know my affairs, *and* how I do, Tychicus, a beloved Brother and Faithful Minister in the Lord, shall make known to you all things *(evidently, Tychicus was with Paul for a period of time while he was imprisoned in Rome; he would inform the Ephesians of Paul's state)*:

22 Whom I have sent unto you for the same purpose, that you might know our affairs, and *that* he might comfort your hearts.

23 Peace *be* to the Brethren, and Love with Faith *(presents Love springing forth from Faith, which ever speaks of the Cross as its Object)*, from God the Father and the Lord Jesus Christ. *(This refers to the fact that what all Believers receive from God the Father comes through the Lord Jesus Christ, with the Cross being the means of such things.)*

24 Grace *be* with all them who love our Lord Jesus Christ in sincerity. *(If the Love is sincere, it will be based strictly in the Cross of Christ.)* Amen.

THE EPISTLE OF PAUL THE APOSTLE TO THE
PHILIPPIANS

CHAPTER 1
(A.D. 64)
INTRODUCTION

PAUL and Timothy, the servants of Jesus Christ (*refers to both men being bound to Jesus Christ by the bands of a constraining love*), to all the Saints in Christ Jesus which are at Philippi (*to those who are "set apart" unto Christ*), with the Bishops (*Pastors*) and Deacons:

2 Grace *be* unto you, and peace, from God our Father, and *from* the Lord Jesus Christ. (*The Cross makes both attributes possible.*)

THANKSGIVING

3 I thank my God upon every remembrance of you (*does not refer to disconnected recollections, but his total past experience with the Philippians*),

4 Always in every prayer of mine for you all (*proclaims the Apostle continually praying for these people, even as he prayed for all the other Churches*) making request with joy (*Paul was not interceding for this Church because of problems, but rather for continued Blessing*),

5 For your fellowship in the Gospel (*the idea is the Philippians supported Paul with their prayers and finances while he went about his Missionary labors*) from the first day until now (*refers to the faithfulness of these Philippians*);

6 Being confident of this very thing (*refers to both their growth in Christ and their continued financial support*), that He (*the Holy Spirit*) which has begun a good work in you will perform *it* until the Day of Jesus Christ (*the Rapture of the Church*):

7 Even as it is meet (*necessary*) for me to think this of you all, because I have you in my heart; inasmuch as both in my bonds, and in the defence and confirmation of the Gospel (*the ground of his confidence*), you all are partakers of my Grace (*God had indeed made them His Own*).

8 For God is my record (*One Who bears Testimony*), how greatly I long after you all in the bowels of Jesus Christ. (*This refers to the compassion of Christ.*)

9 And this I pray (*Paul prayed about everything*), that your love may abound yet more and more (*the Love that God is*) in knowledge (*knowledge of the Cross*) and *in* all judgment (*"discernment," which is a spiritual and moral sense or feeling*);

10 That you may approve things that are excellent (*to approve by testing*); that you may be sincere (*pure*) and without offence (*nothing in one's life that would give cause to stumble, which can only be done by exhibiting Faith in the Cross*) till the Day of Christ (*the Rapture of the Church*);

11 Being filled with the Fruits of Righteousness (*should have been translated, "Fruit of Righteousness"*), which are by Jesus Christ (*through what He did at the Cross*), unto the Glory and Praise of God. (*When we place our Trust in Christ and the Cross, it brings "Glory and Praise to God."*)

TRIUMPH

12 But I would you should understand, Brethren, that the things *which happened* unto me have fallen out rather unto the furtherance of the Gospel (*Paul wrote this Epistle from prison in Rome*);

13 So that my bonds in Christ (*he was a prisoner because of his relationship to Christ; the next question would be, "who is Christ?"*) are manifest in all the palace, and in all other *places* (*not only the members of the Praetorian guard who had custody of Paul, but the whole Praetorium itself, and all its judges and officials are included in this statement*);

14 And many of the Brethren in the Lord, waxing confident by my bonds (*many Christians in Rome had been persuaded by the brave example of Paul in prison*), are much more bold to speak the Word without fear. (*This refers to having overcome the tendency towards silence.*)

15 Some indeed Preach Christ even of envy and strife (*in other words, they were opposed to Paul in their Preaching, and for whatever reason*); and some also of good will (*some tried to help Paul in their Preaching*):

16 The one preach Christ of contention, not sincerely (*they have an agenda which is not of God*), supposing to add affliction to

my bonds *(these Preachers, whomever they may have been, were seeking to make Paul's imprisonment even worse than it already was)*:

17 But the other of love *(by pointing to those Preachers who, in fact, did have Love, Paul is at the same time saying the Preachers of the previous Verse did not have love),* knowing that I am set for the defence of the Gospel. *(The Gospel must not only be preached, it must be defended against false doctrine as well. This, most Preachers will not do!)*

18 What then? *(This does not mean Paul condoned the activities of these rogue Preachers, but that he did not allow it to bother him.)* notwithstanding, every way, whether in pretence, or in truth, Christ is Preached *(Paul was quite satisfied that the servant should be denounced and the Master announced; at least some good is being done! even though these rogue Preachers would have silenced Paul, he would not have reciprocated in kind, which is the attitude of the true Preacher);* and I therein do rejoice, yes, and will rejoice. *(This presents the idea that some people will get some knowledge of Christ, even from these rogue Preachers, which is better than nothing.)*

19 For I know that this shall turn to my Salvation through your prayer *(should have been translated "deliverance"),* and the supply of the Spirit of Jesus Christ *(Paul is referring to the Holy Spirit, and that He will supply whatever is needed, but that He is able to do such only through Christ and what He did at the Cross, which makes it all possible; hence him using the terminology he did),*

CHRIST

20 According to my earnest expectation and *my* hope *(describes a person with head erect and outstretched, whose attention is turned away from all other objects and riveted upon just one),* that in nothing I shall be ashamed *(whichever way it goes, his release or his execution, he will hold up Christ to the end),* but *that* with all boldness, as always, *so* now also Christ shall be magnified in my body, whether *it be* by life, or by death. *(Whatever the Lord wants is what the Apostle wants. This is total consecration!)*

21 For to me to live *is* Christ *(Paul being allowed to live longer makes it possible for him to continue to Preach Christ),* and to die *is* gain. *(He is saying it would be gain for him, but not for the Work of God.)*

22 But if I live in the flesh *(refers to him continuing to live in his physical body, which tells us it will be different in Heaven),* this *is* the Fruit of my labour *(souls being saved and lives being changed by the Message of the Cross):* yet what I shall choose I wot not. *(This actually means that if he had his choice, he is not certain which he would choose, to remain here longer or to go on to be with Christ.)*

23 For I am in a strait betwixt two *(refers to equal pressure being exerted from both sides; he is speaking here of his personal desires, and not necessarily that which the Lord would desire; however, he has already made it clear his personal will is to be swallowed up in the sweet Will of God),* having a desire to depart, and to be with Christ; which is far better *(the centerpiece of all of this is Christ; if one draws any other conclusions, one misses the point entirely):*

24 Nevertheless to abide in the flesh *is* more needful for you. *(For Paul to continue to live and Preach the Gospel would be of great value to the Church, as would be obvious, at least until his work was finished.)*

25 And having this confidence *(he believes the Lord has told him he will be released from prison),* I know that I shall abide and continue with you all for your furtherance and joy of Faith *(the Apostle is saying, "The Servant of the Lord is immortal until his work is done");*

26 That your rejoicing may be more abundant in Jesus Christ for me *(presents Paul as the human instrument through which this teaching would come as it referred to Jesus Christ)* by my coming to you again. *(Without Paul, this advance in the Faith would probably not be brought about.)*

EXHORTATION

27 Only let your conversation *(lifestyle)* be as it becomes the Gospel of Christ *(refers to their behavior; they were to conduct themselves in a manner worthy of the Gospel, and could do so by ever looking to the Cross):* that whether I come and see you, or else be absent, I may hear of your affairs, that you stand fast in one spirit, with one mind *(not be moved from Christ and the Cross, to other things)* striving together for the Faith of the Gospel *("The Faith" is "Christ and Him Crucified," and we must strive to hold it true; every attack by Satan, and in whatever capacity, is against the Cross and our Faith in that Finished Work);*

28 And in nothing terrified by your adversaries *(those who would Preach another Jesus,*

by another spirit, presenting another Gospel [II Cor. 11:4]): which is to them an evident token of perdition, but to you of Salvation, and that of God. (Salvation from God, which is through Christ and the Cross, is evidenced by persecution.)

29 For unto you it is given in the behalf of Christ, not only to believe on Him, but also to suffer for His sake (the world opposes the Cross, and so does most of the Church);

30 Having the same conflict which you saw in me (in essence speaks of the Christian struggle of Faith; the struggle is never so much with sin, as it is of Faith [I Tim. 6:12]), and now hear to be in me (refers to his present incarceration in Rome, which was a test of his Faith).

CHAPTER 2
(A.D. 64)

EXALTATION

IF there be therefore any consolation in Christ (should have been translated, "since there is consolation [encouragement] in Christ"), if any comfort of love (having the God kind of love), if any fellowship of the Spirit (refers to a common interest and a mutual and active participation in the things of God, in which the Believer and the Holy Spirit are joint-participants), if any bowels and mercies (being tenderhearted and having compassion),

2 Fulfil ye my joy (the Spiritual Growth of the Philippians would be his joy), that you be like-minded (unity of mind and of heart), having the same love (the God kind of Love), being of one accord, of one mind. (If the Cross of Christ is the Object of such Faith, these things will be done.)

3 Let nothing be done through strife or vainglory (forming sides); but in lowliness of mind let each esteem other better than themselves (which a correct viewpoint of the Cross will bring about).

4 Look not every man on his own things (means to look only at one's own things), but every man also on the things of others (an interest in the affairs of others).

5 Let this mind be in you (refers to the self-emptying of Christ), which was also in Christ Jesus (portrays Christ as the supreme example):

6 Who, being in the form of God (refers to Deity, which Christ always was), thought it not robbery to be equal with God (equality with God refers here to our Lord's co-participation with the other members of the Trinity in the expression of the Divine Essence):

7 But made Himself of no reputation (instead of asserting His Rights to the expression of the Essence of Deity, our Lord waived His Rights to that expression), and took upon Him the form of a servant (a bondslave), and was made in the likeness of men (presents the Lord entering into a new state of Being when He became Man; but Him becoming Man did not exclude His Position of Deity; while in becoming Man, He laid aside the "expression" of Deity, He never lost "possession" of Deity):

8 And being found in fashion as a man (denotes Christ in men's eyes), He humbled Himself (He was brought low, but willingly), and became obedient unto death (does not mean He became obedient to death; He was always the Master of Death; rather, He subjected Himself to death), even the death of the Cross. (This presents the character of His Death as one of disgrace and degradation, which was necessary for men to be redeemed. This type of death alone would pay the terrible sin debt, and do so in totality.)

9 Wherefore God also has highly exalted Him (to a place of supreme Majesty; Jesus has always been Creator, but now He is Saviour as well), and given Him a Name which is above every name (actually says, "The Name," referring to a specific Name and Title; that Name, as Verse 11 proclaims, is "Lord"):

10 That at the Name of Jesus every knee should bow (in the sphere of the Name, which refers to all it entails; all of this is a result of the Cross, the price paid there, and the Redemption consequently afforded), of things in Heaven, and things in Earth, and things under the earth (all Creation will render homage, whether animate or inanimate);

11 And that every tongue should confess that Jesus Christ is Lord (proclaims "Lord" as the "Name" of Verse 9; it means "Master" of all, which again has been made possible by the Cross), to the Glory of God the Father. (The acknowledgment of the Glory of Christ is the acknowledgment of the Glory of the Father.)

LIGHTS

12 Wherefore, my beloved, as you have always obeyed (he commends them for their constant obedience), not as in my presence only, but now much more in my absence (they continued to obey the Gospel, even though Paul was not personally present among them), work out

your own Salvation with fear and trembling. *(This refers to going on to maturity, to the ultimate conclusion of total Christlikeness.)*

13 For it is God which works in you *(Divine enablement)* both to will and to do of *His* good pleasure. *(This refers to the Holy Spirit, Who energizes the Saint, making him not only willing, but also actively desirous of doing God's sweet Will.)*

14 Do all things without murmurings *(mutterings of discontent)* and disputings *(questioning the Word of God, which is brought on by "murmurings")*:

15 That you may be *(may become)* blameless and harmless, the sons of God, without rebuke, in the midst of a crooked and perverse nation *(what the Holy Spirit expects of us)*, among whom you shine as lights in the world *(the Saints are to be luminaries, which can only be done by constantly exhibiting Faith in the Cross)*;

16 Holding forth the Word of Life *(holding forth so as to offer)*; that I may rejoice in the Day of Christ *(Rapture of the Church)*, that I have not run in vain, neither laboured in vain *(that the Gospel has not been wasted on these people; regrettably, it is wasted with many, if not most)*.

17 Yes, and if I be offered upon the Sacrifice and service of your Faith *(I'll give myself for you)*, I joy, and rejoice with you all. *(The rejoicing is in their Faith properly placed in the Cross of Christ.)*

18 For the same cause also do you joy, and rejoice with me.

COMMENDATION

19 But I trust in the Lord Jesus to send Timothy shortly unto you *(he was a disciple of Paul)*, that I also may be of good comfort, when I know your state. *(The Apostle desired up-to-date information regarding the Church at Philippi.)*

20 For I have no man like-minded *(the Apostle is saying most Preachers had wrong agendas)*, who will naturally care for your state *(speaks of a heart that has one thing in mind, that is doing the Will of God)*.

21 For all seek their own *(doesn't mean there were no genuine Preachers in Rome, but there were none of the caliber he needed)*, not the things which are Jesus Christ's *(again pertains to the Will of God in all matters)*.

22 But you know the proof of him *(Timothy's character has met the test, and has been approved)*, that, as a son with the father, he has served with me in the Gospel *(the original Greek says, "as a son to a Father")*.

23 Him therefore I hope to send presently *(refers to a delay, but it is hoped it will not be long)*, so soon as I shall see how it will go with me. *(As soon as he knows his status, as it regards his release or continued incarceration, he will send Timothy.)*

24 But I trust in the Lord that I also myself shall come shortly. *(It seems this expectation was fulfilled, for Paul was released a short time later.)*

25 Yet I supposed it necessary to send to you Epaphroditus *(presents the Brother who brought the Love-Offering from the Philippians to Paul in Rome)*, my Brother, and companion in labour, and fellowsoldier, but your messenger *(accolades given by Paul, but yet sanctioned by the Holy Spirit)*, and he who ministered to my wants. *(The Apostle held the service of Epaphroditus in high regard.)*

26 For he longed after you all, and was full of heaviness *(due to his sickness)*, because that you had heard that he had been sick. *(This indicates that Epaphroditus is now much improved.)*

27 For indeed he was sick nigh unto death *(he almost died)*: but God had mercy on him *(proclaims the manner in which everything is received from God — all by the Mercy of God)*; and not on him only, but on me also, lest I should have sorrow upon sorrow. *(This proclaims the fact that if the man had died, it would have been a great loss to the Apostle and to the Work of God.)*

28 I sent him therefore the more carefully *(Paul hopes to send Epaphroditus to Philippi very soon)*, that, when ye see him again, you may rejoice *(presents the fact of the recovery or the healing of this man)*, and that I may be the less sorrowful *(Paul's sorrow has been alleviated)*.

29 Receive him therefore in the Lord with all gladness *(it seems there had been a problem in the Church in Philippi as it regards Epaphroditus, but the man has so proven himself to Paul that the Apostle can recommend him highly)*; and hold such in reputation *(give honor to whom honor is due, and Epaphroditus is to be held in honor)*:

30 Because for the work of Christ he was nigh unto death, not regarding his life *(it seems he became very ill because of overwork)*, to supply your lack of service toward me.

(This evidently refers to something the Philippians couldn't do because of circumstances, but which Epaphroditus did on their behalf.)

CHAPTER 3
(A.D. 64)
FALSE TEACHERS

FINALLY, my Brethren, rejoice in the Lord *(as long as they keep their eyes on Christ and the Cross, they can keep rejoicing)*. To write the same things to you, to me indeed *is* not grievous, but for you *it is* safe. *(This presents the Apostle now turning his attention to the Judaizers, who might at any time turn their attention toward Philippi.)*

2 Beware of dogs *(the Apostle is addressing the Judaizers, who were Jews from Jerusalem that claimed Christ, but insisted on Believers keeping the Law as well; all of this was diametrically opposed to Paul's Gospel of Grace, in which the Law of Moses had no part; as well, by the use of the word "dogs," the Apostle was using the worst slur)*, beware of evil workers *(they denigrated the Cross)*, beware of the concision. *(This presents a Greek word Paul uses as a play upon the Greek word "Circumcision," which was at the heart of the Law Gospel of the Judaizers.)*

3 For we are the Circumcision *(refers to the true Circumcision, which is that of the heart)*, which worship God in the Spirit *(would have been better translated, "which worship by the Spirit of God")*, and rejoice in Christ Jesus *(refers not only to Who Christ is, but what He has done for us at the Cross)*, and have no confidence in the flesh *(in things other than the Cross, which alone is the guarantee of Salvation and Victory)*.

4 Though I might also have confidence in the flesh *(refers to human attainments)*. If any other man thinks that he has whereof he might trust in the flesh, I more *(the Apostle knows what he's talking about regarding Judaism)*:

PAUL

5 Circumcised the eighth day, of the stock of Israel *(he was a pure-blooded Jew)*, *of* the Tribe of Benjamin *(Benjamin was the only Tribe that stayed with Judah at the time of the division of the nation)*, an Hebrew of the Hebrews *(goes all the way back to Abraham)*; as touching the Law, a Pharisee *(in fact, Paul had been the hope of the Pharisees, touted to take the place of Gamaliel)*;

6 Concerning zeal, persecuting the Church *(he thought he was doing God a service)*; touching the Righteousness which is in the Law, blameless. *(He thought he was earning merit with God by persecuting the Church.)*

7 But what things were gain to me *(Paul was speaking of his privileges as a Jew)*, those I counted loss for Christ. *(All must be given up for Christ, and Christ is worth all we give up, and a thousand times more.)*

8 Yea doubtless, and I count all things *but* loss for the excellency of the knowledge of Christ Jesus my Lord *(the knowledge of the Lord Jesus which Paul gained through the experience of intimate companionship and communion with Him)*: for Whom I have suffered the loss of all things *("For Whose sake I have been caused to forfeit")*, and do count them *but* dung, that I may win Christ *(next to Christ, everything else is nothing)*,

9 And be found in Him *(to be united with Christ by a living Faith, which has as its Object the Cross of Christ)*, not having my own Righteousness *("not having any Righteousness which can be called my own")*, which is of the Law *(pertains to Law-keeping; he was done with that)*, but that which is through the Faith of Christ *(what He did at the Cross)*, the Righteousness which is of God by Faith *(a spotless Righteousness made possible by the Cross, and imputed by God to all who exhibit Faith in Christ and the Cross)*:

10 That I may know Him *(referring to what Christ did at the Cross)*, and the power of His Resurrection *(refers to being raised with Him in "newness of life" [Rom. 6:3-5])*, and the fellowship of His sufferings *(regarding our Trust and Faith placed in what He did for us at the Cross)*, being made conformable unto His death *(to conform to what He did for us at the Cross, understanding that this is the only means of Salvation and Sanctification)*;

11 If by any means I might attain unto the Resurrection of the dead. *(This does not refer to the coming Resurrection, but rather the Believing sinner being baptized into the death of Christ [refers to the Crucifixion], and raised in "newness of life," which gives victory over all sin [Rom. 6:3-5, 11, 14].)*

12 Not as though I had already attained, either were already perfect *(the Apostle is saying he doesn't claim sinless perfection)*: but I follow after *(to pursue)*, if that I may apprehend *(Paul is pursuing absolute Christlikeness)* that for which also I am apprehended of Christ

Jesus. *(He was saved by Christ for the purpose of becoming Christlike, and so are we!)*

13 Brethren, I count not myself to have apprehended *(in effect, repeats what he said in the previous Verse)*: but *this* one thing I *do*, forgetting those things which are behind *(refers to things the Apostle had depended upon to find favor with God, and the failure that type of effort brought about [3:5-6])*, reaching forth unto those things which are before *(all our attention must be on that which is ahead, and not on what is past; "those things" consists of all the victories of the Cross)*,

14 I press toward the mark *(this represents a moral and spiritual target)* for the prize of the high calling of God *(Christlikeness)* in Christ Jesus *(proclaims the manner and means in which all of this is done, which is the Cross [I Cor. 1:17-18; 2:2])*.

UNITY

15 Let us therefore, as many as be perfect *(mature)*, be thus minded *(have our minds on what Christ has done at the Cross, and was done for us)*: and if in anything you be otherwise minded, God shall reveal even this unto you. *(This means some were actually otherwise minded. But through the words of Paul, the Holy Spirit was going to show them the right way, which is to pull them back to the Cross.)*

16 Nevertheless, whereto we have already attained *(progress)*, let us walk by the same rule, let us mind the same thing. *(Let us walk the same path, that of the Cross [Lk. 9:23-24].)*

ENEMIES OF THE CROSS

17 Brethren, be followers together of me *(be "fellow-imitators")*, and mark them which walk so as you have us for an ensample *(observe intently)*.

18 (For many walk *(speaks of those attempting to live for God outside of the victory and rudiments of the Cross of Christ)*, of whom I have told you often, and now tell you even weeping *(this is a most serious matter)*, *that they are* the enemies of the Cross of Christ *(those who do not look exclusively to the Cross of Christ must be labeled "enemies")*:

19 Whose end *is* destruction *(if the Cross is ignored, and continues to be ignored, the loss of the soul is the only ultimate conclusion)*, whose god *is their* belly *(refers to those who attempt to pervert the Gospel for their own personal gain)*, and *whose* glory *is* in their shame *(the material things they seek, God labels as "shame")*, who mind earthly things.) *(This means they have no interest in Heavenly things, which signifies they are using the Lord for their own personal gain.)*

20 For our conversation *(citizenship)* is in Heaven *(meaning the other ways will have no place in Heaven)*; from whence also we look for the Saviour, the Lord Jesus Christ *(the Rapture)*:

21 Who *(the Lord)* shall change our vile body *(the Resurrection)*, that it may be fashioned like unto His Glorious Body *(every Saint will have a Glorified Body)*, according to the working whereby He is able even to subdue all things unto Himself. *("All things" are done through the Cross.)*

CHAPTER 4
(A.D. 64)
STAND FAST

THEREFORE, my Brethren dearly beloved and longed for *(proclaims this Apostle's love for the Philippians)*, my joy and crown *(Paul took great delight in this Church)*, so stand fast in the Lord, *my* dearly beloved *(one can do this only by making the Cross the Object of his Faith, which will then give the Holy Spirit latitude to bring about such a victory)*.

REJOICE

2 I beseech Euodias *(should have been translated "Euodia," because "Euodias" is a man's name)*, and beseech Syntyche *(the Apostle beseeches both these ladies because it seems there had been a rupture between them, which had affected the entirety of the Church)*, that they be of the same mind in the Lord. *(They both needed a fresh look at the Cross, which is the answer to all things as it regards the Lord.)*

3 And I intreat you also, true yokefellow *(does not identify this man)*, help those women which laboured with me in the Gospel, with Clement also, and *with* other my fellow-labourers *(help settle the problem)*, whose names *are* in the Book of Life *(refers to the roster of Believers kept in Heaven)*.

4 Rejoice in the Lord always *(not for all things, but in all things)*: *and* again I say, Rejoice. *(Paul's teaching on emotional well-being, which follows, begins with rejoicing in the Lord.)*

DON'T WORRY

5 Let your moderation *(being satisfied with less than one's due)* be known unto all men *(even our enemies)*. The Lord *is* at hand *(is near; actually refers to the Rapture)*.

6 Be careful for nothing *(don't worry about anything)*; but in everything by prayer and supplication *(presents the cure for worry, which is believing prayer)* with thanksgiving *(takes in all God has done for us in the past, what He is doing at present, and shall do in the future)* let your requests be made known unto God. *(This speaks of all things, material, physical, and spiritual.)*

7 And the Peace of God *(Sanctifying Peace)*, which passes all understanding *(beyond the pale of human comprehension)*, shall keep your hearts and minds through Christ Jesus *(through what Christ did at the Cross)*.

THINK

8 Finally, Brethren, whatsoever things are true, whatsoever things *are* honest, whatsoever things *are* just, whatsoever things *are* pure, whatsoever things *are* lovely, whatsoever things *are* of good report; if *there be* any virtue, and if *there be* any praise, think on these things. *(This can be done, providing the Cross is the Object of our Faith, which then gives the Holy Spirit latitude to help us.)*

9 Those things, which you have both learned, and received, and heard, and seen in me, do *(Paul had given them the Gospel of the Cross, and they had seen it work in his life; so they had the correct teaching, and they had the correct example)*: and the God of Peace shall be with you. *(Sanctifying Peace will be ours, if our Faith is properly placed in the Cross and remains in the Cross.)*

THANKSGIVING

10 But I rejoiced in the Lord greatly *(concerning the gift they had sent him)*, that now at the last your care of me has flourished again *(it seems that for a period of time, the Philippians had ceased to help the Apostle)*; wherein you were also careful *(the Church at Philippi had not forgotten Paul, but lacked the means to get the gift to him)*, but ye lacked opportunity *(thank the Lord, opportunity had finally presented itself)*.

11 Not that I speak in respect of want *(declares his independence from creature comforts)*: for I have learned, in whatsoever state I am, *therewith* to be content *(to be independent of external circumstances)*.

12 I know both how to be abased *(to keep rejoicing when there is no money)*, and I know how to abound *(to keep rejoicing when there is money)*: everywhere and in all things I am instructed both to be full and to be hungry, both to abound and to suffer need. *(All will come sooner or later, and the negative is not for a lack of Faith, but rather for our instruction in Righteousness.)*

13 I can do all things *(be abased or abound)* through Christ which strengtheneth me *(from Whom I draw strength)*.

14 Notwithstanding you have well done *(he is not meaning to disparage the gift of the Philippian Church)*, that you did communicate with my affliction. *(They helped Paul with his needs, as it regards the offering they sent him.)*

15 Now you Philippians know also, that in the beginning of the Gospel *(refers to the time when Paul first Preached the Word to them, about ten years previously)*, when I departed from Macedonia, no Church communicated with me as concerning giving and receiving, but you only *(proclaims the fact that the Philippians had always been generous)*.

16 For even in Thessalonica *(when he was starting the Church there)* you sent once and again unto my necessity *(proclaims their faithfulness)*.

17 Not because I desire a gift *(presents the Apostle defending himself against the slanderous assertion that he is using the Gospel as a means to make money)*: but I desire fruit that may abound to your account. *(God keeps a record of everything, even our gifts, whether giving or receiving.)*

18 But I have all, and abound: I am full *(proclaims the fact that the Philippian gift must have been generous)*, having received of Epaphroditus the things *which were sent* from you *(Epaphroditus had brought the gift from Philippi to Rome)*, an odour of a sweet smell *(presents the Old Testament odors of the Levitical Sacrifices, all typifying Christ)*, a Sacrifice acceptable, well-pleasing to God *(for those who gave to Paul, enabling him to take the Message of the Cross to others, their gift, and such gifts presently, are looked at by God as a part of the Sacrificial Atoning Work of Christ on the Cross; nothing could be higher than that!)*

19 But my God shall supply all your need *(presents the Apostle assuring the Philippians, and all other Believers as well, that they have not impoverished themselves in giving so liberally to the cause of Christ)* according to His riches in Glory *(the measure of supply will be determined by the wealth of God in Glory)* by Christ Jesus *(made possible by the Cross)*.

BENEDICTION

20 Now unto God and our Father *be* Glory forever and ever. Amen. *(All the Glory belongs to God, and rightly so!)*

21 Salute *(greet)* every Saint in Christ Jesus. The Brethren which are with me greet you. *(This, no doubt, included Timothy, and several others. We are not told who all of them were.)*

22 All the Saints salute you *(refers to the Believers in the Church at Rome)*, chiefly they that are of Caesar's household. *(This presents the fact that Paul's work had operated notably to produce results, even in the most unlikely of places.)*

23 The Grace of our Lord Jesus Christ *be* with you all *(made possible by the Cross)*. Amen.

THE EPISTLE OF PAUL THE APOSTLE TO THE
COLOSSIANS

CHAPTER 1
(A.D. 64)
INTRODUCTION

PAUL, an Apostle of Jesus Christ *(it is through the Apostle that the Holy Spirit leads the Church, and does so according to the Message given him, which in Paul's case was the Message of Grace)* by the Will of God *(only the Lord can set a person in the Office of the Apostle; man cannot do such)*, and Timothy *our* Brother,

2 To the Saints *(the moment a person accepts Christ, they become a Saint)* and Faithful Brethren in Christ *(proclaims the fact that some in Colosse were faithful to the Gospel Paul had brought to them, but at the same time others, it seems, were somewhat shaken in their allegiance)* which are at Colosse *(was written from Rome by Paul, while he was in prison)*: Grace *be* unto you, and peace *(made possible by the Cross)*, from God our Father and the Lord Jesus Christ.

THANKSGIVING

3 We give thanks to God and the Father of our Lord Jesus Christ *(thanksgiving presents a characteristic quality of the type of prayer offered by Paul)*, praying always for you *(a proper understanding of the Cross gives one a proper prayer life)*,

4 Since we heard of your Faith in Christ Jesus *(Paul did not found the Church at Colosse; in fact, it was probably founded by Epaphras, who gave him the information recorded here)*, and of the love *which you have* to all the Saints *(Agape Love)*,

5 For the hope which is laid up for you in Heaven *(presents the last of the trilogy, "Faith, Love, and Hope")*, whereof you heard before in the Word of the Truth of the Gospel *(is meant to contrast the true Gospel of Epaphras with a false gospel of false teachers)*;

6 Which is come unto you *(meant to differentiate it from the false message of the Gnostics)*, as *it is* in all the world *(refers to the True Gospel being the same the world over)*; and brings forth fruit, as *it does* also in you, since the day you heard *of it (the True Gospel of Jesus Christ and Him Crucified will always bring forth fruit in the capacity of changed lives)*, and knew the Grace of God in Truth *(the "Grace of God" cannot function accept in "Truth," which is "Jesus Christ and Him Crucified")*:

7 As you also learned of Epaphras our dear fellowservant *(as stated, he was a disciple of Paul)*, who is for you a faithful Minister of Christ *(reflects the fact that Epaphras was the spiritual father of the Colossian Saints)*;

8 Who also declared unto us your love in the Spirit *(it was "Love" produced by the Spirit of God, made possible by the Cross)*.

GRACE

9 For this cause we also, since the day we heard *it*, do not cease to pray for you *(the "cause" refers to the "fruit" they were bearing for Christ, with "prayer" offered for them that this fruit would continue, and not be stifled by a false message)*, and to desire that you might be filled with the knowledge of His Will *("His Will," and not that of others)* in all wisdom and spiritual understanding *(proclaims that which proceeds only from the inspiration of the Holy Spirit)*;

10 That you might walk worthy of the Lord unto all pleasing *("walk" refers to one's behavior and that it can be accomplished only by making the Cross the Object of one's Faith, which gives the Holy Spirit the latitude to perfect our "walk")*, being fruitful in every good work *(which is guaranteed, if Faith is properly placed in the Cross)*, and increasing in the Knowledge of God *(presents the knowledge of the Cross, which pertains to the Finished Work of Christ)*;

11 Strengthened with all might, according to His Glorious Power *(power to live a Holy life, which comes through Grace, with the Cross as the means)*, unto all patience and long-suffering with joyfulness *(joy, because proper Faith guarantees Victory)*;

12 Giving thanks unto the Father *(which all should do constantly)*, which has made us meet *(qualified)* to be partakers of the inheritance of the Saints in Light *(presents the "standing"*

THE MEDIATORSHIP OF CHRIST

20 And, having made peace *(justifying peace)* **through the Blood of His Cross** *(presents His Blood as being that which satisfied the just demands of the broken Law)*, **by Him to reconcile all things unto Himself** *(speaks of the result of Faith in the Cross)*; **by Him, I say, whether** *they be* **things in earth, or things in Heaven.** *(The Cross not only addressed the Fall of man, but as well the Fall of Lucifer.)*

21 And you, who were sometime *(in times past)* **alienated and enemies in** *your* **mind by wicked works** *(total depravity)*, **yet now has He reconciled** *(made possible by the Cross)*.

22 In the Body of His flesh *(the Incarnation, God becoming flesh)* **through death** *(refers to the fact that the reconciling act of Christ is not by His Incarnation, but by His dying [II Cor. 5:21])*, **to present you Holy and unblamable and unreprovable in His sight** *(all made possible by the Cross)*:

SERVICE

23 If you continue in the Faith *(at the same time says it is possible not to continue in the Faith; "the Faith" is "Christ and Him Crucified")* **grounded and settled** *(the Foundation of the Faith, which Object must always be the Cross)*, **and** *be* **not moved away** *(moved away from the Cross)* **from the Hope of the Gospel, which you have heard** *(pertains to the fact that they had been brought in right)*, *and* **which was preached to every creature which is under Heaven** *(the Message of the Cross is the same for all)*; **whereof I Paul am made a Minister** *(the meaning of the New Covenant was actually given to Paul, which is the meaning of the Cross [Gal. 1:11-12])*;

24 Who now rejoice in my sufferings for you *(Paul was in prison when this Epistle was written)*, **and fill up that which is behind of the afflictions of Christ in my flesh** *(suffering for Righteousness' sake)* **for His Body's sake, which is the Church** *(Satan opposes the Message of the Cross like nothing else)*:

25 Whereof I am made a Minister *(says plainly that he is a Minister and not a Mediator, which some have attempted to read into the previous Verse)*, **according to the Dispensation of God which is given to me for you** *(the way and manner of administrating the Work)*, **to fulfil the Word of God** *(presents the Apostle not wanting to become sidetracked on some minor*

(This presents a ... which claimed ...manized Christ

false ...ith ...e

...m the power of ...d by His strong ...le possible by ...us into the ...the Cross is ...e Cross is

...demption through ...s the price that was paid ...n), *even* the forgiveness of sins ...oss, the Lord broke the power of sin, ...ok away its guilt [Rom. 6:6]):

...Who is the Image of the invisible God ...n is the exact reproduction of the Fa- ...derived Image), the Firstborn of every ...e *(actually means Jesus is the Creator ...ings):*

HIS CREATIVE WORK

...by Him were all things created *(pre- ...Justification of the title given Christ ...ceding Verse)*, that are in Heaven, ...are in earth, visible and invisible ...n and not seen), whether *they be* ...r dominions, or principalities, or ...fers to both Holy and fallen Angels): ...were created by Him, and for Him ...e Creator of all [Jn. 1:3]):

HIS PREEXISTENCE

...He is before all things *(preexis- ...d by Him all things consist. (All ...ne to pass within this sphere of His ...ty, and are dependent upon it.)*

...d He is the Head of the Body, the ...(the Creator of the world is also Head ...hurch): Who is the Beginning *(refers ...ist as the Origin or Beginning of the ...), the firstborn from the dead *(does not ...o Jesus being Born-Again as some teach, ...ather that He was the first to be raised ...the dead as it regards the Resurrection, ...r to die again)*; that in all *things* He might ...e the preeminence. *(He is the First and ...emost as it relates to the Church.)*

...9 For it pleased *the Father* that in Him ...ould all fulness dwell *(this "fullness" de- ...otes the sum total of the Divine Powers and ...ttributes)*;

issue that did not emphasize the centrality of the Gospel, which is the Cross);

26 *Even* the Mystery which has been hid from ages and from generations *(refers to the Gentiles who would be partakers with the Jews of the Gospel, and actually in the same Church)*, but now is made manifest to His Saints *(manifested to Believers, but not to the world)*:

27 To whom *(the Saints)* God would make known *(desire to make known)* what *is* the riches of the glory of this mystery among the Gentiles *(refers to the fact that the Cross is for all, and is not limited by racial or national lines)*; which is Christ in you *(made possible by the Cross)*, the Hope of Glory *(the full realization will materialize at the coming Resurrection)*:

28 Whom we preach, warning every man, and teaching every man in all wisdom *(tells us the Bible is the only revealed Truth in the world and, in fact, ever has been)*; that we may present every man perfect *(mature)* in Christ Jesus *(refers to the Cross, and what He did there)*:

29 Whereunto I also labour, striving according to His working *(refers to Christ working in Paul through the Might and Power of the Holy Spirit)*, which works in me mightily *(which will work mightily in anyone, if the Object of Faith is always the Cross)*.

CHAPTER 2
(A.D. 64)
THE CHURCH

FOR I would that you knew what great conflict I have for you, and *for* them at Laodicea *(deep concern as it regards false doctrine)*, and *for* as many as have not seen my face in the flesh *(those in Colosse and Laodicea were not personally acquainted with Paul, as many others in the Churches were, due to the fact that he didn't plant these particular Churches in Colosse and Laodicea)*;

2 That their hearts might be comforted *(doesn't concern the physical organ, but rather the hypothetical seat of the emotions; in effect, the soul and the spirit)*, being knit together in love *(proclaims the only manner in which true unity can be obtained)*, and unto all riches of the full assurance of understanding *(the idea is that we know the "Truth" about all things concerning the Word of God)*, to the acknowledgment of the Mystery of God, and of the Father, and of Christ *(presents Christ as that Mystery)*;

3 In Whom *(Christ)* are hid all the treasures

of Wisdom and Knowledge *(a direct rebuttal to the Gnostics otherwise. The Gnostics over-hu and deified themselves.)*

FALSE TEACHING

4 And this I say *(points directly to the teachers)*, lest any man should beguile you enticing words *(refers to being deceived by subt reasoning)*.

5 For though I be absent in the flesh, yet am I with you in the spirit *(refers to Pul's human spirit)*, joying and beholding your r-der, and the stedfastness of your Faith in Cl *(speaks of "holding rank," and refers to m taining one's Faith in the Cross)*.

6 As you have therefore received Ch Jesus the Lord *(refers to the manner of o Salvation, which is Christ and Him Crucifie so walk ye in Him (behavior is to be ordere the sphere of Christ and the Cross)*:

7 Rooted and built up in Him *(pertains a proper foundation)*, and stablished in t Faith *(in Christ and the Cross)*, as you ha been taught *(refers to the Colossians coming the right way, but some of them considering t false message of the Gnostics)*, abounding ther in with thanksgiving. *(This refers to the fa that the Gospel of the Cross, which had brough them to Christ, had also brought them untol benefits.)*

8 Beware lest any man spoil you through philosophy and vain deceit *(anything that pulls the Believer away from the Cross is not of God), after the tradition of men (anything that is not of the Cross is of men)*, after the rudiments of the world, and not after Christ. *(If it's truly after Christ, then it's after the Cross.)*

9 For in Him *(Christ)* dwells all the fulness of the Godhead bodily. *(This is Godhead as to essence. Christ is the completion and the fullness of Deity, and in Him the Believer is complete.)*

10 And you are complete in Him *(the satisfaction of every spiritual want is found in Christ, made possible by the Cross)*, which is the Head of all principality and power *(His Headship extends not only over the Church, which voluntarily serves Him, but over all forces that are opposed to Him as well [Phil. 2:10-11])*:

11 In Whom also you are circumcised with the Circumcision made without hands *(that which is brought about by the Cross [Rom. 6:3-5])*, in putting off the body of the sins of the

flesh by the Circumcision of Christ *(refers to the old carnal nature that is defeated by the Believer placing his Faith totally in the Cross, which gives the Holy Spirit latitude to work)*:

12 Buried with Him in Baptism *(does not refer to Water Baptism, but rather to the Believer baptized into the death of Christ, which refers to the Crucifixion and Christ as our substitute [Rom. 6:3-4])*, wherein also you are risen with *Him* through the Faith of the operation of God, Who has raised Him from the dead. *(This does not refer to our future physical Resurrection, but to that spiritual Resurrection from a sinful state into Divine Life. We died with Him, we are buried with Him, and we rose with Him [Rom. 6:3-5], and herein lies the secret to all spiritual victory.)*

13 And you, being dead in your sins and the uncircumcision of your flesh *(speaks of spiritual death [i.e., "separation from God"], which sin does!)*, has He quickened together with Him *(refers to being made spiritually alive, which is done through being "Born-Again")*, having forgiven you all trespasses *(the Cross made it possible for all manner of sins to be forgiven and taken away)*;

14 Blotting out the handwriting of Ordinances that was against us *(pertains to the Law of Moses, which was God's standard of Righteousness that man could not reach)*, which was contrary to us *(Law is against us, simply because we are unable to keep its precepts, no matter how hard we try)*, and took it out of the way *(refers to the penalty of the Law being removed)*, nailing it to His Cross *(the Law with its decrees was abolished in Christ's Death, as if Crucified with Him)*;

15 *And* having spoiled principalities and powers *(Satan and all of his henchmen were defeated at the Cross by Christ Atoning for all sin; sin was the legal right Satan had to hold man in captivity; with all sin atoned, he has no more legal right to hold anyone in bondage)*, He *(Christ)* made a show of them openly *(what Jesus did at the Cross was in the face of the whole universe)*, triumphing over them in it. *(The triumph is complete and it was all done for us, meaning we can walk in power and perpetual victory due to the Cross.)*

16 Let no man therefore judge you in meat, or in drink, or in respect of an holyday, or of the new moon, or of the Sabbath *Days (the moment we add any rule or regulation to the Finished Work of Christ, we have just abrogated the Grace of God)*:

17 Which are a shadow of things to come *(the Law, with all of its observances, was only meant to point to the One Who was to come, Namely Christ)*; but the Body *(Church)* is of Christ *(refers to "substance and reality," as opposed to shadow)*.

18 Let no man beguile you of your reward *(concerns false doctrine)* in a voluntary humility *(refers to self-abasement)* and worshipping of Angels *(pertained to the Gnostic teaching; this false teaching claimed man could not go directly to God through Jesus Christ, but rather must reach after God through successive grades of intermediate beings, i.e., "Angels!")*, intruding into those things which he has not seen *(refers to going outside the revealed Word of God)*, vainly puffed up by his fleshly mind *("mind of the flesh," which means it's not the Mind of God)*,

19 And not holding the Head *(failure to look totally to Christ and the Cross will ultimately lead to destruction)*, from which all the body by joints and bands having nourishment ministered *(Christ is the source of all nourishment, which comes by the means of the Cross)*, and knit together, increases with the increase of God *(proper Faith in the Cross guarantees spiritual increase)*.

20 Wherefore if you be dead with Christ *(actually says, "in view of the fact that you died with Christ")* from the rudiments of the world *(the way of the world)*, why, as though living in the world, are you subject to Ordinances *(refers to trusting something other than Christ and the Cross for Salvation and Victory)*,

21 (Touch not; taste not; handle not *(there is no Salvation or Victory in rules and regulations)*;

22 Which all are to perish with the using;) *(This refers to the fact that they don't work because they are of human origin. Therefore, new ones are made that work no better than the old, which is the way of man.)* after the commandments and doctrines of men? *(This means it is not of God, and must be avoided at all cost.)*

23 Which things have indeed a show of wisdom in will worship *(refers to worship devised and prescribed by man, which characterizes most of the modern Church)*, and humility *(false humility)*, and neglecting of the body *(speaks of the human body)*; not in any honour to the satisfying of the flesh. *(All ascetic observances, while they appeal to men as indications of superior wisdom and piety, have no value as remedies against sensual indulgence. That can be handled only at the Cross.)*

CHAPTER 3
(A.D. 64)
NEW LIFE

IF you then be risen with Christ *(presents the New Life [Rom. 6:3-5])*, **seek those things which are above** *(which come directly from the Lord, not man)*, **where Christ sits on the Right Hand of God.** *(This is referring to the fact that the great Work is a Finished Work, meaning man doesn't have to go elsewhere.)*

2 Set your affection on things above *(refers to directing one's mind to a thing)*, **not on things on the earth** *(everything on this Earth is temporal; as well, our help comes from above).*

3 For you are dead *(dead to the old life by virtue of the fact of Christ dying on the Cross as our Substitute and, in effect, us dying with him [Rom. 6:3-5])*, **and your life is hid with Christ in God** *(all made possible by the Cross [Jn. 14: 20]).*

4 When Christ, *Who is* **our life, shall appear** *(refers to the Rapture of the Church)*, **then shall you also appear with Him in Glory.** *(This refers to every Saint at that time being given a Glorified Body [I Cor. 15:51-57; I Thess. 4:13-18].)*

PUT OFF

5 Mortify therefore your members *(of your physical body)* **which are upon the earth** *(can be done only by the Believer understanding that everything he receives from the Lord comes strictly through the Cross, which must ever be the Object of our Faith, thus giving the Holy Spirit latitude to work in our lives)*; **fornication, uncleanness, inordinate affection, evil concupiscence, and covetousness, which is idolatry** *(works of the flesh, which will in one way or the other show themselves, unless the Believer follows the pattern laid down by the Holy Spirit regarding Victory over the flesh, which is the Cross):*

6 For which things' sake the Wrath of God comes on the children of disobedience *(God cannot abide sin in any form, even in His Children, and especially in His Children; the Cross is the only solution for sin):*

7 In the which you also walked some time *(in times past)*, **when you lived in them** *(before coming to Christ).*

8 But now you also put off all these *(can do so by evidencing Faith in Christ and His Cross)*; **anger, wrath, malice, blasphemy, filthy communication out of your mouth.**

9 Lie not one to another *(the Greek actually says, "lie not to yourself," and speaks of accepting a way other than the Cross)*, **seeing that you have put off the old man with his deeds** *(the "old man" died with Christ on the Cross [Rom. 6:6]);*

PUT ON

10 And have put on the new *man* *(in Christ, we are a "New Creation" [II Cor. 5:17])*, **which is renewed in knowledge** *(the learning of Christ [Mat. 11:28-30])* **after the image of Him Who created him** *(man's re-created self is thus after the image of Christ):*

11 Where there is neither Greek nor Jew, Circumcision nor uncircumcision, Barbarian, Scythian, bond *nor* **free** *(in Christ, there is no distinction):* **but Christ** *is* **all, and in all.** *(Christ occupies the whole sphere of human life and permeates all its developments.)*

12 Put on therefore, as the Elect of God *(refers to those who have been elected by God, because they elected to know God [Rev. 22:17])*, **Holy and Beloved, bowels of mercies, kindness, humbleness of mind, meekness, longsuffering** *(Fruit of the Spirit);*

13 Forbearing one another *(exhibiting patience)*, **and forgiving one another, if any man have a quarrel against any: even as Christ forgave you, so also** *do* **you.**

14 And above all these things *put on* **charity** *(Love)*, **which is the bond of perfectness** *(complete growth).*

15 And let the Peace of God rule in your hearts *(Sanctifying Peace)*, **to the which also you are called in one body** *(the Church);* **and be ye thankful** *(show one's self thankful).*

16 Let the Word of Christ dwell in you richly in all wisdom *(the meaning of the New Covenant as given to Paul, which is the meaning of the Cross)*; **teaching and admonishing one another in Psalms and Hymns and Spiritual Songs** *(our songs of worship must proclaim the Word of God, thereby teaching us)*, **singing with grace in your hearts to the Lord.** *(This presents the real purpose of Spirit-Anointed Music, which tells how important music and singing are as it refers to worship.)*

17 And whatsoever you do in word or deed, *do* **all in the Name of the Lord Jesus** *(everything is to be done in the Name of our Lord, irrespective of what it is)*, **giving thanks to God and the Father by Him.** *(If properly obeyed, everything will take on a brand-new complexion.)*

DOMESTIC LIFE

18 Wives, submit yourselves unto your own husbands, as it is fit in the Lord (only as the husband functions in the sphere of the Lord).

HUSBANDS

19 Husbands, love your wives, and be not bitter against them. (The idea is that the husband loves the wife with the same type of love with which he loves God. Consequently, there will be no bitterness.)

CHILDREN

20 Children, obey your parents in all things (pertains to that which is Scriptural): for this is well pleasing unto the Lord (children properly obeying parents are taught thusly to obey the Lord).

FATHERS

21 Fathers, provoke not your children to anger, lest they be discouraged. (Children's obedience must be fed on love and praise. Fear paralyzes activity and kills service.)

SERVANTS

22 Servants (slaves), obey in all things your masters according to the flesh (presents Christian slaves of that day working, for the most part, in the service of pagan masters); not with eyeservice, as men-pleasers (represents good work when the employer is watching, and the opposite otherwise); but in singleness of heart, fearing God (means a person has one heart, and that is to please God, which will render proper service whether the Master is watching or not):

23 And whatsoever you do, do it heartily, as to the Lord, and not unto men (the Lord now becomes the Master, with everything taking on a brand-new complexion);

24 Knowing that of the Lord you shall receive the reward of the inheritance (proclaims the fact that the Lord Who is being faithfully served will, at the same time, render just dues): for you serve the Lord Christ. (Everything we do, irrespective what it is, is to be done with the idea that it is for the Lord and the Lord Alone!)

25 But he who does wrong shall receive for the wrong which he has done (indicates the Law of Divine Retribution [Mat. 7:1-2]): and

there is no respect of persons. (God looks at all alike, playing favorites with no one.)

CHAPTER 4
(A.D. 64)

MASTERS

MASTERS, give unto your servants that which is just and equal (speaking to Christian Masters); knowing that you also have a Master in Heaven (presents the great principle on which all Christianity reposes).

PRAYER

2 Continue in prayer (prayer should be a habit with every Believer), and watch in the same (don't let the habit of prayer be broken) with thanksgiving (most prayer should be made up of thanksgiving);

3 Withal praying also for us, that God would open unto us a door of utterance (reminds us that even though the spread of the Gospel is under Divine direction [Acts 16:7], it is also subject to Satanic hindrances [I Thess. 2:18]), to speak the Mystery of Christ (concerns that which had been previously hidden, but now has been made fully known — the Cross and what it means), for which I am also in bonds (refers to Paul's imprisonment in Rome):

4 That I may make it manifest (preach Christ), as I ought to speak (manifest Christ as Christ ought to be manifested).

5 Walk in wisdom toward them who are without (refers to "ordering one's behavior"), redeeming the time (make wise and sacred use of every opportunity to present Christ).

6 Let your speech be alway with Grace (gracious and pleasant), seasoned with salt ("salt" represents the incorruptible Word of God), that you may know how you ought to answer every man (as it regards Christ).

BRETHREN

7 All my state shall Tychicus declare unto you, who is a beloved Brother, and a faithful Minister and fellowservant in the Lord (this Brother was evidently with Paul in Rome, at least for a period of time):

8 Whom I have sent unto you for the same purpose (apparently, Tychicus had already left Rome to go to Colosse), that he might know your estate, and comfort your hearts (implies the news Tychicus would bring about the Apostle;

as well, he was entrusted with three Epistles: Ephesians, Colossians, and the short note to Philemon);

9 With Onesimus, a faithful and beloved Brother, who is *one* of you *(a runaway slave, who has now found Christ, accompanies Tychicus)*. They shall make known unto you *(the Church at Colosse)* all things which *are done* here *(Rome)*.

10 Aristarchus my fellow-prisoner salutes you *(is not known if Paul is speaking literally or spiritually concerning this man being a fellow-prisoner)*, and Marcus, sister's son to Barnabas *(refers to John Mark, the writer of the Gospel which bears his name among the four Gospels; he was the cousin of Barnabas)*, (touching whom you received commandments: if he come unto you, receive him;) *(It is not known exactly what Paul meant here. At any rate, he is recommending this young man, which tells us that the problem they had had some years before was now made right [Acts 15:37-40].)*

11 And Jesus, which is called Justus, who are of the Circumcision. These only *are my* fellow-workers unto the Kingdom of God, which have been a comfort unto me *(three Jews: Aristarchus, Mark, and Justus)*.

12 Epaphras, who is *one* of you, a servant of Christ, salutes you *(probably the founder of the Colossian Church, who is now with Paul for a period of time)*, always labouring fervently for you in prayers *(refers to strong intercession)*, that you may stand perfect and complete in all the Will of God *(spiritual maturity)*.

13 For I bear him record, that he has a great zeal for you, and them *who are* in Laodicea, and them in Hierapolis. *(Epaphras probably*

founded all three of these Churches, for these three towns were very close together.)

14 Luke, the beloved physician *(this is Luke, the writer of the Gospel that bears his name, plus the Book of Acts; we also learn here that he was a medical doctor, although it seems he no longer practiced his craft)*, and Demas, greet you. *(Unfortunately, this man Demas, who had such a good beginning, lost his way [II Tim. 4:10].)*

BENEDICTION

15 Salute *(greet)* the Brethren which are in Laodicea, and Nymphas *(the Pastor, it seems, of the Church in Laodicea)*, and the Church which is in his house *(almost all Churches then were located in houses)*.

16 And when this Epistle *(Colossians)* is read among you, cause that it be read also in the Church of the Laodiceans *(history records the fact that many copies were made of these Epistles, which circulated among the Churches)*; and that you likewise read the *Epistle* from Laodicea. *(This evidently refers to an Epistle lost to us.)*

17 And say to Archippus, Take heed to the Ministry which you have received in the Lord, that you fulfil it. *(This speaks of the same man mentioned in Philemon, Verse 2. Tradition says he was the son of Philemon, and maybe the Pastor of the Church that was in their house in the city of Colosse.)*

18 The salutation by the hand of me Paul *(presents him, as stated, writing this closing word himself)*. Remember my bonds *(in effect, he is asking for prayer that he will be released from prison)*. Grace *be* with you *(the sum of the Gospel Message)*. Amen.

THE FIRST EPISTLE OF PAUL THE APOSTLE TO THE
THESSALONIANS

CHAPTER 1
(A.D. 54)
INTRODUCTION

PAUL, and Silas, and Timothy, unto the Church of the Thessalonians *(believed to be the First Epistle written by Paul; consequently, the first time in history this salutation concerning the Church is used) which is* in God the Father and *in* the Lord Jesus Christ *(has reference to the fact that God cannot address fallen, sinful humanity, except through the Cross of Christ)*: Grace *be* unto you, and Peace, from God our Father, and the Lord Jesus Christ *(presents the Source; but the means is the Cross)*.

THANKSGIVING

2 We give thanks to God always for you all, making mention of you in our prayers *(prayer was the atmosphere of Paul's life, and should be ours as well)*;

THIS CHURCH

3 Remembering without ceasing your work of faith, and labour of love, and patience of hope in our Lord Jesus Christ *(what Jesus did for us at the Cross makes all of this possible)*, in the sight of God and our Father *(all things are under the scrutiny of His Eye)*;

4 Knowing, Brethren beloved, your election of God. *(This refers to the rejection of Israel as Gospel representatives, and to the election of the Gentiles to take their place [Mat. 21:43; 23:37-39; Rom. 11:11-29].)*

5 For our Gospel came not unto you in word only *(refers to the New Covenant)*, but also in power, and in the Holy Spirit *(tells us where the power is)*, and in much assurance *(proclaims the results which accrue as a result of the Gospel being properly presented)*; as you know what manner of men we were among you for your sake. *(Paul and those with him were living examples of what the Gospel can do in a person's life.)*

6 And you became followers of us, and of the Lord *(if the wrong Preacher is followed, the Lord will not be found)*, having received the Word in much affliction *(proclaims the opposition of former friends or even relatives)*, with joy of the Holy Spirit *(the more Satan afflicts, the more the Holy Spirit pours in joy)*:

7 So that you were examples to all who believe in Macedonia and Achaia *(they were examples of evidencing the Joy of the Lord despite persecution)*.

8 For from you sounded out the Word of the Lord not only in Macedonia and Achaia *(pertains to the Message of the Cross, which had changed their lives)*, but also in every place your Faith to God-ward is spread abroad *(nothing advertises the Gospel like changed lives)*; so that we need not to speak any thing. *(They were adhering to the Gospel he preached.)*

9 For they themselves show of us what manner of entering in we had unto you *(the Spiritual Fruit of the Thessalonians testified to the character of the laborers)*, and how you turned to God from idols to serve the Living and True God *(all idolatry is a lie; in fact, all religion is idolatry)*;

10 And to wait for His Son from Heaven *(refers to the Rapture of the Church)*, Whom He raised from the dead, *even* Jesus *(the Resurrection of Christ guarantees the Resurrection of the Saints)*, which delivered us from the wrath to come *(by means of the Cross, and meaning that judgment will ultimately come to all who reject Christ and the Cross)*.

CHAPTER 2
(A.D. 54)
PAUL

FOR yourselves, Brethren, know our entrance in unto you *(presents his defense, a justifiable defense of his personal Ministry for the sake of Truth)*, that it was not in vain *(it brought forth much fruit)*:

2 But even after that we had suffered before, and were shamefully treated, as ye know, at Philippi *(high motives are required for men to continue a true and, therefore, costly, Gospel Ministry)*, we were bold in our God to speak unto you the Gospel of God with much contention. *(The triumph of the Gospel by an effort of only the highest kind and overcoming the*

most formidable opposition.)

3 For our exhortation *was* not of deceit *(no ulterior motives)*, nor of uncleanness *(impure motives)*, nor in guile *(trickery)*:

4 But as we were allowed of God to be put in trust with the Gospel *(the testing had been completed, and thus signified an approval by God)*, even so we speak; not as pleasing men *(presents the biggest problem in the Ministry, pleasing men and not God)*, but God, which tries our hearts. *(This constant scrutiny by Omniscience is a great comfort to those who aim to please God, rather than men.)*

5 For neither at any time used we flattering words, as you know *(refers to the attempt to gain selfish ends by insincere speech)*, nor a cloak of covetousness; God *is* witness *(refers to pretense)*:

6 Nor of men sought we glory, neither of you, nor *yet* of others *(refers to conduct designed to elicit or extract praise)*, when we might have been burdensome, as the Apostles of Christ. *(This refers to the fact that as Apostles, they might have demanded certain things, but didn't!)*

7 But we were gentle among you, even as a nurse cherishes her children *(refers to a Mother feeding her children)*:

8 So being affectionately desirous of you, we were willing to have imparted unto you, not the Gospel of God only, but also our own souls, because you were dear unto us *(is literally in the Greek, "because you became beloved ones to us")*.

9 For you remember, Brethren, our labour and travail *(refers to his self-sacrificing as it concerns the Gospel)*: for labouring night and day, because we would not be chargeable unto any of you, we Preached unto you the Gospel of God. *(This probably refers to a mixture of preaching the Gospel and the repairing of tents to support himself.)*

10 You *are* witnesses, and God *also* *(it is important that conduct appear right in the eyes of men; however, only God's Judgment is infallible)*, how holily and justly and unblameably we behaved ourselves among you who believe *(concerns the lifestyles of the Apostle plus Silas, Timothy, and anyone else who may have been laboring with him)*:

11 As you know how we exhorted and comforted and charged every one of you *(pertains to dealing with the Thessalonians with encouragement, as well as by solemn injunctions)*, as a father *does* his children *(presents the image*

being changed from that of motherly tenderness to that of fatherly direction),

12 That you would walk worthy of God *(has to do with our daily living, which can only be done by proper Faith evidenced in the Cross)*, Who has called you unto His Kingdom and Glory *(should have been translated, "Who is calling you into His Kingdom and Glory")*.

RECEPTION

13 For this cause also thank we God without ceasing *(refers to the manner in which the Thessalonians had received the Word)*, because, when you received the Word of God which you heard of us, you received *it* not *as* the word of men, but as it is in Truth, the Word of God *(the Word of God was faithfully delivered to the Thessalonians, and they faithfully believed it)*, which effectually works also in you who believe. *(This refers to the fact that the Word "is working" only in those who "are believing," which refers to the Cross and makes the working of the Spirit possible.)*

14 For you, Brethren, became followers of the Churches of God which in Judaea are in Christ Jesus *(identifies all who are truly "in Christ Jesus" as being "True Churches")*: for you also have suffered like things of your own countrymen, even as they *have* of the Jews *(pertains to persecution)*:

15 Who both killed the Lord Jesus, and their own Prophets *(presents the crime of the ages)*, and have persecuted us *(the Jews tried repeatedly to kill Paul)*; and they please not God *(is, in fact, a monumental understatement)*, and are contrary to all men *(refers to their sectarian, self-righteous spirit and attitude)*:

16 Forbidding us to speak to the Gentiles that they might be saved *(means the Jews, as a nation, had rejected Christ and the Cross, and would, thereby, never admit Gentiles could now be saved as well)*, to fill up their sins always *(there is a limit beyond which God will not go)*: for the wrath is come upon them to the uttermost. *(This is used in the past tense, simply because it is so sure of fulfillment. In fact, it was fulfilled totally in A.D. 70.)*

PAUL'S CONCERN

17 But we, Brethren, being taken from you for a short time in presence, not in heart *(refers to the Apostle having to leave the city before he desired to because of the Jews' action against*

him [Acts 17:1-10]), endeavoured the more abundantly to see your face with great desire. *(This presents no want of affection, but from causes beyond control.)*

18 Wherefore we would have come unto you, even I Paul, once and again; but Satan hindered us. *(This proclaims the fact that the Evil One is a real personality, and not a mere figure of speech.)*

19 For what *is* our hope, or joy, or crown of rejoicing? *(This presents the Apostle pointing beyond, far beyond, the minor annoyances now, to the great coming time when there will be no more separation and no more hindrances by Satan.)* Are not even you in the presence of our Lord Jesus Christ at His coming? *(This points to the coming Rapture of the Church.)*

20 For you are our glory and joy *(what Christ had made of them).*

CHAPTER 3
(A.D. 54)
TIMOTHY

WHEREFORE when we could no longer forbear *(refers to Paul strongly desiring to know the spiritual situation back at Thessalonica),* we thought it good to be left at Athens alone *(refers to Timothy being sent back to Thessalonica, with no mention of Silas)*;

2 And sent Timothy, our brother, and minister of God, and our fellowlabourer in the Gospel of Christ, to establish you *(the Thessalonians needed more teaching, so Timothy was sent to carry this out),* and to comfort you concerning your Faith *(suggests encouragement)*:

3 That no man should be moved by these afflictions *(refers to the fact that we should not allow these things to discourage or hinder us)*: for yourselves know that we are appointed thereunto. *(We are destined for afflictions because of Satan's opposition to the Gospel.)*

4 For verily, when we were with you, we told you before that we should suffer tribulation *(Faith placed totally in the Cross of Christ brings opposition from both the world and the Church, but mostly from the Church)*; even as it came to pass, and you know *(means tribulation is inevitable).*

5 For this cause *(speaks of the persecution, and their response),* when I could no longer forbear *(presents the Apostle repeating for emphasis what he has already said in Verses 1 and 2),* I sent to know your faith *(that their Faith was remaining steadfast in the Cross),* lest by some

means the tempter have tempted you, and our labour be in vain. *(This tempted them to move their Faith to something other than the Cross, which would mean spiritual wreckage.)*

THE REPORT

6 But now when Timothy came from you unto us *(refers to Timothy coming from Thessalonica to Corinth, where Paul now was),* and brought us good tidings of your faith and charity *(refers to an excellent report on their Faith and Love),* and that you have good remembrance of us always, desiring greatly to see us, as we also *to see* you *(meaning the Thessalonians had not been pulled away from Paul by false teachers)*:

7 Therefore, Brethren, we were comforted over you in all our affliction and distress by your faith *(their Faith remaining strong greatly encouraged the Apostle)*:

8 For now we live *(are comforted),* if you stand fast in the Lord. *(Refuse to allow your Faith to be moved from the Cross to other things.)*

9 For what thanks can we render to God again for you *(in essence, says, "How can we thank our God enough concerning you!"),* for all the joy wherewith we joy for your sakes before our God *(presents that which produces joy in the heart of the Apostle, which is success in the Work of God, and pertains to the Spiritual Growth of these Believers)*;

10 Night and day praying exceedingly that we might see your face *(has to do with the Apostle's desire to once again visit this fledgling Church, which he did sometime later [Acts 20:1-2]),* and might perfect that which is lacking in your faith? *(Strengthen them more firmly in the Cross, which must always be the Object of our Faith.)*

PAUL'S PRAYER

11 Now God Himself and our Father, and our Lord Jesus Christ *(the Cross of Christ alone has made this relationship possible),* direct our way unto you *(the Will of God is sought, and the way being made as the Will of God comes to the fore).*

12 And the Lord make you to increase and abound in love one toward another, and toward all *men,* even as we *do* toward you *(which will come to pass as the Cross of Christ is more and more understood)*:

13 To the end He may stablish your hearts

(be without blame at the Judgment Seat of Christ) unblameable in Holiness before God, even our Father *(refers to the fact that it is God Who is the Judge of these things)*, at the coming of our Lord Jesus Christ with all His Saints. *(This refers to the Rapture of the Church.)*

CHAPTER 4
(A.D. 54)
WALK GODLY

FURTHERMORE then we beseech you, Brethren, and exhort *you* by the Lord Jesus, that as you have received of us how you ought to walk and to please God *(pertains to the whole manner of living)*, *so* you would abound more and more *(the manner of Spiritual Growth)*.

2 For you know what Commandments we gave you by the Lord Jesus. *(This is a Command to be Holy that can only be carried out by a constant and abiding Faith in Christ and the Cross, which gives the Holy Spirit the latitude to work.)*

SANCTIFICATION

3 For this is the Will of God, *even* your Sanctification *(the work of making one Holy, which can only be done by the Holy Spirit)*, that you should abstain from fornication *(refers to all types of immorality)*:

4 That every one of you should know how to possess his vessel *(the physical body, which is the Temple of the Holy Spirit [I Cor. 3:16])* in Sanctification and honour *(morally clean, which can only be done by Faith exhibited constantly in the Cross of Christ)*;

5 Not in the lust of concupiscence *(evil passions and desires in the thought life)*, even as the Gentiles which know not God *(speaks of the Gentile world which walked in darkness before the advent of the Gospel)*:

6 That no *man* go beyond and defraud his brother in *any* matter *(refers to anything regarding fraud, however, the inference is to sexual misconduct; such must not be)*: because that the Lord *is* the avenger of all such *(presents the fact that the Judgment of God upon all impurity is sure and terrible, and will ultimately come)*, as we also have forewarned you and testified. *(This presents the possibility that sexual misconduct could have been a besetting temptation for the Thessalonians.)*

7 For God has not called us unto uncleanness, but unto Holiness. *(God has called us*

from *"uncleanness," i.e., "sexual impurity," unto "Holiness.")*

LOVE

8 He therefore who despises *(despises the Commands of the Lord)*, despises not man, but God *(treating the words of men lightly is one thing; treating the Word of God lightly is something else altogether)*, Who has also given unto us His Holy Spirit. *(The Holy Spirit is given to Believers in order that we might live a Holy Life, which is done by us evidencing a constant Faith in the Cross of Christ.)*

9 But as touching brotherly love you need not that I write unto you *(presents the Apostle with customary tactfulness beginning in a complimentary manner and then proceeding to the admonition)*: for you yourselves are taught of God to love one another *(Believers who have the Holy Spirit, Who definitely teaches us such, and constantly)*.

10 And indeed you do it toward all the Brethren which are in all Macedonia *(for the Thessalonians, Macedonia was home; if we cannot love those at home, how can we love others far away?)*: but we beseech you, Brethren, that you increase more and more *(presents the Apostle not admonishing them, but definitely exhorting them)*;

11 And that you study to be quiet *(is the opposite of aspiring to be prominently seen and heard)*, and to do your own business *(mind your own business, and not the business of others)*, and to work with your own hands, as we commanded you *(work; don't steal, and don't sponge off others)*;

12 That you may walk honestly toward them who are without *(set an example for unbelievers)*, and *that* you may have lack of nothing. *(If we truly follow the Lord, there will be no lack.)*

THE RAPTURE

13 But I would not have you to be ignorant, Brethren, concerning them which are asleep *(refers to Believers who have died)*, that you sorrow not, even as others which have no hope. *(This concerns those who do not know the Lord who will have no part in the First Resurrection of Life and, therefore, no hope for Heaven.)*

14 For if we believe that Jesus died and rose again *(the very Foundation of Christianity is the Death and Resurrection of Christ; it is the proof*

of life after death in a glorified state for all Saints in that life, which incidentally will never end), **even so them also which sleep in Jesus will God bring with Him.** (This refers to the Rapture of the Church, or the Resurrection of all Believers, with both phrases meaning the same thing, even as Paul describes in I Cor., Chpt. 15. At death, the soul and the spirit of the Child of God instantly go to be with Jesus [Phil. 1:23], while the physical body goes back to dust. At the Rapture, God will replace what was the physical body with a Glorified Body, united with the soul and the spirit. In fact, the soul and the spirit of each individual will accompany the Lord down close to this Earth to be united with a Glorified Body, which will then make the Believer whole.)

15 For this we say unto you by the Word of the Lord (presents the Doctrine of the Rapture of the Church as the "Word of the Lord"), **that we which are alive** and **remain unto the coming of the Lord** (all Believers who are alive at the Rapture) **shall not prevent them which are asleep.** (This refers to the fact that the living Saints will not precede or go before the dead Saints.)

16 For the Lord Himself shall descend from Heaven with a shout (refers to "the same Jesus" which the Angels proclaimed in Acts 1:11), **with the voice of the Archangel** (refers to Michael, the only one referred to as such [Jude, Vs. 9]), **and with the Trump of God** (doesn't exactly say God will personally blow this Trumpet, but that it definitely does belong to Him, whoever does signal the blast): **and the dead in Christ shall rise first** (the criteria for being ready for the Rapture is to be "in Christ," which means that all who are truly Born-Again will definitely go in the Rapture):

17 Then we which are alive and **remain shall be caught up** (Raptured) **together with them** (the Resurrected dead) **in the clouds** (clouds of Saints, not clouds as we normally think of such), **to meet the Lord in the air** (the Greek word for "air" is "aer," and refers to the lower atmosphere, or from about 6,000 feet down; so, the Lord will come at least within 6,000 feet of the Earth, perhaps even lower, with all the Saints meeting Him there; but He, at that time, will not come all the way to the Earth, that awaiting the Second Coming, which will be seven or more years later): **and so shall we ever be with the Lord.** (This presents the greatest meeting humanity will have ever known.)

18 Wherefore comfort one another with these words. (This pertains to the future of the Child of God, which is Glorious indeed!)

CHAPTER 5
(A.D. 54)
THE DAY OF THE LORD

BUT **of the times and the seasons** (introduces the recurring question of the curious and the anxious: how long before Christ comes? at what point in history?), **Brethren, you have no need that I write unto you.** (The Apostle mentions this to repress that vain curiosity, which is natural to man.)

2 For yourselves know perfectly that the Day of the Lord so comes (it will begin with the Great Tribulation, and carry on through the Millennium; it will end with the Advent of the New heavens and the New Earth) **as a thief in the night.**

3 For when they shall say, Peace and safety (refers to Israel, but will as well characterize the world; it pertains to the Antichrist signing the seven-year pact with Israel and other nations [Dan. 9:27]); **then sudden destruction comes upon them** (at the mid-point of the seven-year period, the Antichrist will break his pact, actually invading Israel [Rev. 12:1-6]), **as travail upon a woman with child; and they shall not escape.** (The Great Tribulation is definitely coming upon this world [Mat. 24:21].)

4 But you, Brethren, are not in darkness (Christians have spiritual enlightenment, which comes only from the Word of God), **that that day should overtake you as a thief.** (No Believer should be caught unawares, but regrettably, it seems many will.)

5 You are all the children of light, and the children of the day (refers to knowing Jesus Christ, Who is "the Light of the World" [Jn. 8:12]): **we are not of the night, nor of darkness.** (The Believer is to be in a totally different sphere of operation.)

6 Therefore let us not sleep, as do **others** (be overcome by lethargy and apathy); **but let us watch and be sober.** (The Christian is to maintain his relationship with Christ by continued watchfulness, even as it regards his personal life and Prophetic events.)

7 For they who sleep sleep in the night (those who are in spiritual darkness have no idea what is coming upon this world); **and they who be drunken are drunken in the night.** (Paul is not speaking here of alcoholic beverage, only using the word "drunken" as a metaphor to describe a spiritual condition.)

8 But let us (Believers), **who are of the day** (who have spiritual light), **be sober** (speaks of

"assurance"), putting on the breastplate of Faith and Love (*proper Faith in Christ and the Cross, which produces Love*); and for an helmet, the Hope of Salvation (*the guarantee of deliverance from this present evil world, which pertains to the Rapture*).

9 For God has not appointed us to wrath (*has not appointed Believers to go through the Great Tribulation*), but to obtain Salvation by our Lord Jesus Christ (*again, pertains to the Rapture of the Church*),

10 Who died for us, that, whether we wake or sleep, we should live together with Him (*again, the Rapture, all made possible by the Cross*).

11 Wherefore comfort yourselves together (*it refers to comfort in view of the coming Rapture and the escape from wrath, which will be poured out upon the world in the coming Great Tribulation*), and edify one another, even as also you do. (*This refers to cheering and strengthening one another.*)

PRACTICAL TEACHING

12 And we beseech you, Brethren, to know them which labour among you, and are over you in the Lord, and admonish you (*know for sure that the Preacher you are following is truly Preaching the Word*);

13 And to esteem them very highly in love for their work's sake. (*This carries more reference to the work they do, than to the person in question.*) *And* be at peace among yourselves. (*This proclaims the esteem just mentioned as helping to produce such peace.*)

PAUL

14 Now we exhort you, Brethren, warn them who are unruly (*speaks of those who leave the ranks*), comfort the feebleminded (*should have been translated, "comfort the fainthearted"*), support the weak (*refers to those who do not have proper understanding regarding the Cross of Christ, and what it means to their everyday walk before God*), be patient toward all *men*. (*This refers to all the categories just mentioned.*)

15 See that none render evil for evil unto any *man* (*presents Biblical Christianity as the only system of such noble practice*); but ever follow that which is good, both among yourselves, and to all *men* (*even to our enemies*).

16 Rejoice evermore. (*The Believer has every reason to do such, and irrespective of everyday problems.*)

17 Pray without ceasing. (*We should pray about everything.*)

18 In every thing give thanks (*not necessarily for everything*): for this is the Will of God in Christ Jesus concerning you. (*No matter what happens, or how negative things may seem to be, we are to never stop giving thanks to the Lord, which is the Will of God.*)

19 Quench not the Spirit. (*To disobey these admonitions is to quench the Spirit.*)

20 Despise not Prophesyings. (*This Gift has been abused more so than any other Gift. Irrespective, we are to ever recognize the value of the true Operation of this Gift [I Cor. 14:3].*)

21 Prove all things (*when Prophecies are given, or anything that claims to be of the Lord, it should be put to the test; the test is, "is it Scriptural?"*); hold fast that which is good. (*This refers to the sifting process of accepting that which is definitely of the Lord, and rejecting that which isn't!*)

22 Abstain from all appearance of evil. (*The question is, "Does this please God"?*)

23 And the very God of Peace Sanctify you wholly (*this is "progressive Sanctification," which can only be brought about by the Holy Spirit, Who does such as our Faith is firmly anchored in the Cross, within which parameters the Spirit always works; the Sanctification process involves the whole man*); and *I pray God* your whole spirit and soul and body (*proclaims the make-up of the whole man*) be preserved blameless unto the coming of our Lord Jesus Christ. (*This refers to the Rapture. As well, this one Verse proclaims the fact that any involvement, whether Righteous or unrighteous, effects the whole man, and not just the physical body or the soul as some claim.*)

24 Faithful *is* He Who calls you (*God will do exactly what He has said He will do, if we will only Believe Him*), Who also will do *it* (*will Sanctify us wholly*).

25 Brethren, pray for us. (*The great Apostle was ever humbly conscious of his own weakness in himself [I Cor. 2:1-5].*)

26 Greet all the Brethren with an holy kiss (*the custom then, with handshaking the custom presently*).

27 I charge you by the Lord that this Epistle be read unto all the Holy Brethren (*and for all the obvious reasons*).

28 The Grace of our Lord Jesus Christ *be* with you (*all made possible by the Cross*). Amen.

THE SECOND EPISTLE OF PAUL THE APOSTLE TO THE
THESSALONIANS

CHAPTER 1
(A.D. 54)
INTRODUCTION

PAUL and Silas, and Timothy, unto the Church of the Thessalonians *(this is probably the second Epistle written by the great Apostle)* in God our Father and the Lord Jesus Christ *(God is our Father, by Virtue of Christ and what He has done for us at the Cross)*:

2 Grace unto you, and Peace *(Sanctifying Peace)*, from God our Father and the Lord Jesus Christ *(all made possible by the Cross)*.

SPIRITUAL GROWTH

3 We are bound to thank God always for you, Brethren, as it is meet, because that your Faith grows exceedingly *(Faith grows as the Word is properly applied, with the Cross ever being the Object of Faith)*, and the charity *(love)* of every one of you all toward each other abounds *(presents the first hallmark of Christianity, that we love the Brethren)*;

4 So that we ourselves glory in you in the Churches of God *(they had taken what little teaching Paul had been able to give them, which was, no doubt, the Cross, and used it to its full extent)* for your patience and faith in all your persecutions and tribulations that you endure *(suggests continued and repeated sufferings which were still going on)*:

5 Which is a manifest token of the Righteous Judgment of God *(the sense of this phrase is that the endurance of affliction by the Righteous, in a proper manner, is a proof that there will be Righteous Judgment of God at the last day)*, that you may be counted worthy of the Kingdom of God, for which you also suffer *(could be translated, "God purposes to account His Children worthy of the Kingdom of God, for which they also suffer" [Acts 5:41; I Pet. 4:12-16])*:

6 Seeing it is a Righteous thing with God to recompense tribulation to them who trouble you *(we are not to attempt to defend ourselves as it regards getting even, but must leave such in the hands of the Lord)*;

THE SECOND COMING

7 And to you who are troubled rest with us *(unfortunately, the trouble will continue until Jesus comes; we will then "rest")*, when the Lord Jesus shall be revealed from Heaven with His mighty Angels *(refers to the Second Coming, which is different from the Rapture)*,

8 In flaming fire taking vengeance on them who know not God *(gives us the manner of the Second Coming)*, and who obey not the Gospel of our Lord Jesus Christ *(who have rejected Christ and the Cross)*:

9 Who shall be punished with everlasting destruction from the Presence of the Lord *(pertains to the Lake of Fire, which will be everlasting)*, and from the Glory of His Power *(power to save, but rejected, and, therefore, the end is "everlasting destruction")*;

10 When He shall come to be Glorified in His Saints *(all Saints will praise Him, and will do so continually)*, and to be admired in all them who believe *(Christ will be the Center and Focal Point of all Things)* (because our testimony among you was believed) in that day. *(They believed the Testimony of Paul regarding Christ and the Cross and, therefore, will be with Christ forever.)*

PRAYER

11 Wherefore also we pray always for you *(presents the idea that the hope of Believers cannot be realized except through supernatural help)*, that our God would count you worthy of this calling *(presents the fact that it is Holy Character as evidence of Saving Faith which will qualify men "that day")*, and fulfil all the good pleasure of His goodness *(refers to all the wonderful things the Holy Spirit desires to do for us and, in fact, will do for us if we will only cooperate with Him)*, and the work of Faith with power *(Faith in the Cross, which gives the Holy Spirit the latitude to work, in Whom is the Power)*:

12 That the Name of our Lord Jesus Christ may be glorified in you *(presents the object of the Holy Spirit)*, and you in Him *(in Christ)*, according to the Grace of our God and the

Lord Jesus Christ. *(All are made possible by the Cross, which are then freely given to us by the means of Grace.)*

CHAPTER 2
(A.D. 54)
THE SECOND COMING

NOW we beseech you, Brethren, by the coming of our Lord Jesus Christ *(refers to both the Rapture and the Second Coming)*, and by our gathering together unto Him *(this phrase refers strictly to the Rapture)*,

2 That you be not soon shaken in mind, or be troubled *(false doctrine does this)*, neither by spirit *(messages in tongues and interpretation, which purport to be of the Lord, but really were not)*, nor by word *(pertaining to those who claimed to have a Word from the Lord)*, nor by letter as from us *(someone had written a letter claiming certain prophetic things, and evidently had signed Paul's name to it, which means it was a forgery)*, as that the Day of Christ is at hand *(should have been translated, "the Day of the Lord," because this is how the best manuscripts read; the "Day of the Lord" refers to all events after the Rapture; some were claiming, even in Paul's day, that the Second Coming was about to take place, which of course was wrong)*.

3 Let no man deceive you by any means *(in other words, don't listen to that which is Scripturally incorrect)*: for *that day shall not come*, except there come a falling away first *(should have been translated, "for that day shall not come, except there come a departure first"; this speaks of the Rapture, which, in essence, says the Second Coming cannot take place until certain things happen)*, and that man of sin be revealed, the son of perdition *(this speaks of the Antichrist, who must come upon the world scene before the Second Coming)*;

4 Who opposes and exalts himself above all that is called God *(pertains to his declaration of himself as Deity)*, or that is worshipped *(the Antichrist will put down all religions, at least in the area which he controls, making himself alone the object of worship)*; so that he as God sits in the Temple of God *(refers to the Jewish Temple, which will be rebuilt in Jerusalem; the Antichrist will take over the Temple, making it his religious headquarters)*, showing himself that he is God. *(This proclaims his announcement of Deity as it regards himself.)*

5 Don't you remember, that, when I was yet with you, I told you these things? *(So,*

there was no excuse for the Thessalonians to be drawn away by false doctrine.)*

6 And now you know what withholds *(speaks of the Church)* that he might be revealed in his time. *(This speaks of the Antichrist who will be revealed or made known after the Rapture of the Church.)*

7 For the mystery of iniquity does already work *(concerns false teaching by false teachers)*: only he *(the Church)* who now lets *(who now hinders evil)* will let *(will continue to hinder)*, until he *(the Church)* be taken out of the way. *(The pronoun "he" confuses some people. In Verses 4 and 6, the pronoun "he" refers to the Antichrist, while in Verse 7 "he" refers to the Church.)*

8 And then *(after the Rapture of the Church)* shall that Wicked *(the Antichrist)* be revealed *(proving conclusively that the Rapture takes place before the Great Tribulation [Mat. 24:21])*, whom the Lord shall consume with the spirit of His Mouth *(should have been translated, "the Breath of His Mouth" [Isa. 11:4])*, and shall destroy with the brightness of His Coming *(both phrases refer to the Second Coming)*:

9 *Even him* *(the Antichrist)*, whose coming is after the working of Satan *(means that Satan is the sponsor of the Antichrist)* with all power and signs and lying wonders *(proclaims the fact that the Antichrist's rise to power, at least in the beginning, will be very religious)*,

10 And with all deceivableness of unrighteousness in them who perish *(refers to the fact that "all lying powers and lying signs and lying wonders" will be used to deceive the world)*; because they received not the love of the Truth, that they might be saved *(they rejected Christ and the Cross)*.

11 And for this cause *(the rejection of Christ and the Cross)* God shall send them strong delusion *(if one doesn't want "the Truth," God will see to it one receives a "delusion")*, that they should believe a lie *(should have been translated, "that they should believe the lie"; the Greek Text has the definite article "the lie," which refers to a specific lie; that "lie" pertains to anything that leads a person away from the Cross)*:

12 That they all might be damned who believed not the Truth *(who would not accept the Cross)*, but had pleasure in unrighteousness. *(The Greek has the definite article, which actually says, "the unrighteousness," specifying a particular unrighteousness; it is really referring to the results of rejection of the Cross of Christ.)*

THANKSGIVING

13 But we are bound to give thanks always to God for you *(refers to those who did not succumb to the lies of false teachers)*, Brethren beloved of the Lord, because God has from the beginning chosen you to Salvation through Sanctification of the Spirit *(Holy Spirit)* and belief of the Truth *(concerns itself not with the "who" of Salvation [in other words, who will be saved], but rather the "manner" of Salvation and Sanctification; people are saved by trusting Christ and the Cross; Believers are Sanctified by continuing to trust Christ and the Cross; the "Cross" is the means of all things pertaining to God, as it relates to humanity)*:

14 Whereunto He *(God)* called you by our Gospel *(Jesus Christ and Him Crucified [I Cor. 1:17-18, 21; 2:2])*, to the obtaining of the Glory of our Lord Jesus Christ. *(This pertains to the wonder that comes with Salvation, and all because of what Christ did at the Cross.)*

15 Therefore, Brethren, stand fast *(refers to standing fast in the Gospel Paul had Preached unto them)*, and hold the traditions which you have been taught *(refers to what Paul had taught them, which was the Truth)*, whether by word, or our Epistle. *(This is what he had preached to them when he was personally with them, and, as well, by the Epistle he had already sent them, and the second one he is now writing.)*

16 Now our Lord Jesus Christ Himself *(proclaims the Apostle giving the Resurrection Name of our Lord)*, and God, even our Father *(refers to relationship)*, which has loved us, and has given *us* everlasting consolation and good hope through Grace *(all made possible by the Cross)*,

17 Comfort your hearts *(the Holy Spirit comforts us)*, and stablish you in every good word and work. *(The foundation principle for this accomplishment is a proper understanding of the Cross of Christ.)*

CHAPTER 3
(A.D. 54)
PRAYER

FINALLY, Brethren, pray for us, that the Word of the Lord may have *free* course *(will accomplish its intended purpose; this depends largely on the proper intercession of the Saints, hence Paul asking for prayer)*, and be glorified *(bringing forth its full power, which speaks of a positive effect in people's lives)*, even as *it is* with you *(the Gospel had changed the lives of the Thessalonians)*:

2 And that we may be delivered from unreasonable and wicked men *(these false teachers gave undue prominence to things other than the Cross [I Cor. 1:17])*: for all *men* have not Faith. *(This should have been translated, "for all men have not the Faith." It speaks of the Finished Work accomplished at the Cross.)*

3 But the Lord is Faithful *(though some men cannot be trusted, God can be depended on)*, Who shall stablish you, and keep *you* from evil. *(The Cross of Christ and one's Faith in the Cross guarantee the help of the Holy Spirit, and protects the Believer from both the Evil One and his evil designs.)*

4 And we have confidence in the Lord touching you *(pertaining to the Thessalonians)*, that you both do and will do the things which we command you. *(Growth in Grace can be realized only as Believers maintain an attitude of obedience towards God, actually an attitude that is motivated by a love for Him that transcends all other objects of affection.)*

5 And the Lord direct your hearts into the Love of God *(tells us the Lord wants total control within our lives, but it is control which must be freely given by us to Him)*, and into the patient waiting for Christ. *(This pertains to our waiting for Him to rectify the situation, whatever it might be.)*

THE EXAMPLE

6 Now we command you, Brethren, in the Name of our Lord Jesus Christ *(the Apostle is saying that what he is telling the people is "the Word of God," and must be heeded!)*, that you withdraw yourselves from every brother who walks disorderly *(literally means, "to walk out of the ranks of the Word of God"; in abbreviated form, it means we should withdraw fellowship from those who teach something other than the Cross; it does not speak of excommunication)*, and not after the tradition which he received of us *(after the teaching which Paul had given, which was definitely from the Lord; "tradition," as it is used here, does not mean "unwritten doctrines," as this word normally means; the Apostle is referring to what the Lord had given him, which he had faithfully taught to the people)*.

7 For yourselves know how you ought to follow us *(it was to Paul the meaning of the New Covenant was given, which is the meaning of the Cross [Gal. 1:11-12]; so, what he was*

saying was the Word of the Lord; people had better make sure the Preacher they are following is of God): **for we behaved not ourselves disorderly among you** *(the opposite of "disorderly" is a Sanctified life, in that sin has no dominion over the individual [Rom. 6:14])*;

8 Neither did we eat any man's bread for nought *(the Apostle didn't make himself a burden to others)*; **but wrought with labour and travail night and day, that we might not be chargeable to any of you** *(he worked at his craft of tent making in order to meet his material needs)*:

9 Not because we have not power *(refers to the fact that he was a Preacher of the Gospel, and by all rights should have been supported by the people; however, he did not avail himself of that privilege in Thessalonica, and for a purpose)*, **but to make ourselves an example unto you to follow us.** *(The heathen priests in this Gentile city were constantly scheming in order to get money from the people. Paul wanted nothing in his Ministry to resemble that. However, he did receive two offerings from Philippi when he was in Thessalonica [Phil. 4:15-16].)*

EXHORTATION

10 For even when we were with you, this we commanded you, that if any would not work, neither should he eat. *(If a person is lazy and won't work, then let them do without. In other words, it's wrong to give money to someone of this nature.)*

11 For we hear that there are some which walk among you disorderly, working not at all, but are busybodies *(sponging off others).*

12 Now them who are such we command and exhort by our Lord Jesus Christ *(refers to the Apostle having the Mind of the Lord, and the authority of the Lord in making these statements)*, **that with quietness they work, and eat their own bread.** *(Quit being busybodies, attempting to meddle in other people's affairs. Let them tend to their own business.)*

13 But you, Brethren, be not weary in well doing. *(The idea is that while they were to refuse to support those who were busybodies and lazy, they were not to forget the worthy poor.)*

14 And if any man obey not our word by this Epistle, note that man, and have no company with him, that he may be ashamed. *(This doesn't actually speak of excommunication, but rather a withdrawal of fellowship within the local Body. In some sense, after being repeatedly warned, the individual was to be pointed out.)*

15 Yet count *him* **not as an enemy** *(means to not count him outside of Christ, but only as an erring Brother, which means he's going in the wrong direction)*, **but admonish** *him* **as a Brother.** *(Admonish him not as one lost, but as one who belongs to the Lord, but yet erring.)*

BENEDICTION

16 Now the Lord of Peace Himself give you Peace always by all means. *(This is "Sanctifying Peace." It doesn't refer to an absence of problems or troubles, but rather to an unending Peace in the midst of problems and troubles, etc., which can only be given by the Lord, and is a result of Grace which comes through the Cross.)* **The Lord** *be* **with you all.** *(It means all can have this "Sanctifying Peace." In fact, the pronoun "all" includes even the offending ones whom Paul has been addressing, that is if they will turn to the right way.)*

17 The salutation of Paul with my own hand *(it seems that Paul dictated this Letter to a Scribe up to this particular Verse; at this point, he took the pen in his own hand to add a closing greeting)*, **which is the token in every Epistle: so I write.** *(This presents the Apostle saying that this is his style. That is, the signature is "sign" or "proof" of the genuineness of the Epistle.)*

18 The Grace of our Lord Jesus Christ *be* **with you all** *(made possible by the Cross).* **Amen.**

THE FIRST EPISTLE OF PAUL THE APOSTLE TO
TIMOTHY

CHAPTER 1
(A.D. 65)
INTRODUCTION

PAUL, an Apostle of Jesus Christ *(the Office of the Apostle is, in effect, the de facto leader of the Church under Christ, and is so by the particular Message given to him by the Holy Spirit, which in Paul's case was the Message of Grace)* by the Commandment of God our Saviour, and Lord Jesus Christ *(places such a calling in the very highest councils),* **which** *is* our hope *(Christ Alone and what He did at the Cross is "our hope");*

2 Unto Timothy, *my* own son in the Faith *(refers to Timothy having more than likely been saved under Paul's Ministry):* Grace, Mercy, *and* Peace, from God our Father and Jesus Christ our Lord *(all made possible by the Cross).*

FALSE DOCTRINE

3 As I besought you to abide still at Ephesus *(Paul desired that Timothy remain at Ephesus for a period of time because of false teachers attempting to spread false doctrine among the people),* when I went into Macedonia *(into Greece),* that you might charge some that they teach no other doctrine *(the Doctrine must be "Jesus Christ and Him Crucified"),*

4 Neither give heed to fables and endless genealogies *(Jewish fables and Jewish genealogies; so, the false teachers were Judaizers who insisted that Law must be added to Grace, and who placed no stock in the Cross at all; in a sense, they were very similar to the modern "Word of Faith" teachers),* which minister questions, rather than Godly edifying which is in Faith *(this speaks of the fact that Faith, not Law, is the sphere or element in which our Salvation functions; such Faith always has the Cross as its Object and, thereby, edifies):* **so do.** *(Don't leave the Cross.)*

5 Now the end of the Commandment *(charge)* is charity *(love)* out of a pure heart *(which alone can produce love),* and *of* a good conscience, and *of* Faith unfeigned *(feigned faith is pretended faith, which means it doesn't have the Cross as its Object):*

6 From which some having swerved have turned aside *(refers to missing the mark; in other words, they left the Cross)* unto vain jangling *(useless talk);*

7 Desiring to be teachers of the Law *(refers to the Law of Moses, and speaks of the Judaizers);* understanding neither what they say, nor whereof they affirm. *(These individuals claimed to be professional interpreters of the Law, when in reality they had only a surface knowledge of the Law.)*

THE LAW

8 But we know that the Law *is* good *(the Apostle says this to show he definitely was not an enemy of the Law of Moses),* if a man use it lawfully *(understanding that the Law of Moses pointed strictly to Christ; when He came, He fulfilled it in totality);*

9 Knowing this, that the Law is not made for a Righteous man *(should have been translated, "Law is not made . . ."; the word "the" was inserted by the translators, and should not have been added; consequently, the way Paul uses the word, it refers to any type of Law, whether the Law of Moses or Law made up by religious men; the Believer is not to function after Law, but rather Grace, which refers to Faith placed exclusively in the Cross),* but for the lawless and disobedient, for the ungodly and for sinners, for unholy and profane, for murderers of fathers and murderers of mothers, for manslayers *(true Believers do not fall into these categories),*

10 For whoremongers, for them who defile themselves with mankind *(homosexuality),* for menstealers *(slave traders),* for liars, for perjured persons *(those who swear falsely),* and if there be any other thing that is contrary to sound Doctrine *(actually refers to all that is contrary to the Word of God);*

11 According to the Glorious Gospel *(refers to its moral Glory)* of the Blessed God *(pertains to His Blessed Gift of Forgiveness offered to all sinners who accept His Gospel of Love),* which was committed to my trust. *(The Lord chose Paul as the recipient and bearer of the New Covenant.)*

PAUL

12 And I thank Christ Jesus our Lord, Who has enabled me (*presents the One Who calls and blesses*), for that He counted me faithful, putting me into the Ministry (*the Lord knew Paul would be faithful, and that the Gospel committed to him would not be compromised*);

13 Who was before a blasphemer, and a persecutor, and injurious (*what he was before he was saved*): but I obtained Mercy, because I did *it* ignorantly in unbelief (*could be translated, "I was shown Mercy because, being ignorant, I acted in unbelief"*).

14 And the Grace of our Lord was exceeding abundant (*proclaims that which God stands ready to give to any honest, and earnest seeker*) with Faith and Love which is in Christ Jesus (*presents that which was produced in Paul, as a result of the Grace of God*).

15 This *is* a faithful saying, and worthy of all acceptation (*means the Gospel of Christ dying to save sinners is worthy of being accepted by the whole world*), that Christ Jesus came into the world to save sinners (*which He did through the Cross*); of whom I am chief. (*What he is saying is that his offense against God had been so great, and his sin of guilt so overwhelming, that he felt himself to be the number one sinner of all time.*)

16 Howbeit for this cause I obtained Mercy (*one might say it in this way: "because Christ came to save sinners, I obtained Mercy"*), that in me first Jesus Christ might show forth all longsuffering (*the representative instance of God's longsuffering to a high-handed transgressor*), for a pattern (*the Apostle is saying that if the Lord would do such for Paul, he will do it for anyone*) to them which should hereafter believe on Him (*on Christ and what He did at the Cross*) to Life Everlasting (*without beginning or end, that which has always been and always will be*).

17 Now unto the King eternal (*the Greek says, "Now, to the King of the Ages"*), immortal (*imperishable*), invisible (*as it regards His Glory*), the only wise God (*should have been translated, "the only God," with the word "wise" not being included in most of the Manuscripts; there is no other God*), *be* honour and glory forever and ever. (*This refers to respect and praise, and that it be done forever.*) Amen (*Truth*).

TIMOTHY

18 This charge I commit unto you, son Timothy (*refers to a command or injunction*), according to the Prophecies which went before on you (*probably refers to the time frame of Acts 16:1-3*), that you by them might war a good warfare (*we aren't told exactly what the Prophecies were, but that they spoke of an assignment to leadership in the army of King Jesus*);

19 Holding Faith (*maintaining Faith in Christ and the Cross*), and a good conscience (*speaks of following the Word of the Lord exactly as it is given*); which some having put away concerning Faith have made shipwreck (*a metaphor used by Paul, pointing to those who had abandoned the Cross*):

20 Of whom is Hymenaeus and Alexander (*presents two examples of one not "holding the Faith"*); whom I have delivered unto Satan (*I Cor. 5:5*), that they may learn not to blaspheme. (*This tells us that all who depart from "the Faith," which is Jesus Christ and Him Crucified, can only be concluded as "blaspheming."*)

CHAPTER 2
(A.D. 65)
EXHORTATION

I exhort therefore (*resumes and develops Paul's charge to Timothy, which began in I Tim. 1:18*), that, first of all (*it is as if Paul said, "the most important point in this exhortation concerns the universal scope of prayer"*), supplications (*personal needs*), prayers (*petitions*), intercessions (*in this case, an approach to God on the basis of an accepted relationship*), *and* giving of thanks (*Praise and Worship*), be made for all men (*lends credence to the idea that we should pray about everything*);

2 For kings, and *for* all who are in authority (*Civil Government*); that we may lead a quiet and peaceable life in all Godliness and honesty. (*This speaks of Government that's free of turmoil, about which prayer can have a great effect.*)

3 For this *is* good and acceptable in the sight of God our Saviour (*refers to this being the Will of God, and for all the obvious reasons*);

GOD'S WILL

4 Who will have all men to be saved (*presents Salvation, which is universal in virtue and aim*), and to come unto the knowledge of the Truth. (*This pertains to Salvation through Jesus Christ and what He did at the Cross [Jn. 3:16; Rom. 6:3-6; 10:9-10].*)

ONE MEDIATOR

5 For *there is* one God *(manifested in three Persons — God the Father, God the Son, and God the Holy Spirit)*, **and one Mediator between God and men, the Man Christ Jesus** *(He can only be an adequate Mediator Who has sympathy with and an understanding of both parties, and is understandable by and clear to both; in other words, Jesus is both God and Man, i.e., "Very God and Very Man")*;

6 Who gave Himself a ransom for all *(refers to the fact that our Lord's Death was a spontaneous and voluntary Sacrifice on His Part; the word "ransom" refers to the price He paid, owed by man to God, which was His Precious Blood [I Pet. 1:18-20])*, **to be testified in due time.** *(This refers to the planning of this great Work, which took place "before the foundation of the World" [I Pet. 1:18-20], unto the "due time" of its manifestation, which refers to when Christ was Crucified).*

TRUTH

7 Whereunto I am ordained a Preacher, and an Apostle *(presents the highest calling of the five-fold Ministry [Eph. 4:11])*, **(I speak the Truth in Christ, *and* lie not;)** *(was said because it seems some were denying his Apostleship)* **a teacher of the Gentiles in Faith and verity** *(in Faith and Truth).*

8 I will therefore that men pray everywhere *(proclaims the absolute necessity of prayer on the part of the Child of God)*, **lifting up Holy hands** *(a surrendered spirit)*, **without wrath and doubting.** *(This speaks of an angry spirit, which is caused by doubting the Word of God.)*

WOMEN

9 In like manner also *(refers to the fact that women should pray to the Lord in like manner as the men)*, **that women adorn themselves in modest apparel** *(presents that which is consistent with what she is, a Child of God)*, **with shamefacedness** *(Christian women should not be bold or forward toward men)* **and sobriety** *(the idea of self-restraint)*; **not with broided hair** *(not the same meaning as now, but rather an extremely ostentatious display)*, **or gold, or pearls** *(the Apostle is not condemning these things, but rather promoting the adornment of Christian character, which is to be the attraction of Christian women)*, **or costly array** *(tells us that when either men or women live primarily for dress and outward show, then it is wrong)*;

10 But (which becomes women professing Godliness) with good works.

11 Let the woman learn in silence *(its meaning is made clear in I Cor. 14:34-35)* **with all subjection** *(Eph. 5: 22-25).*

12 But I suffer not a woman to teach, nor to usurp authority over the man *(if a male teacher is more qualified, he should take the lead; otherwise the woman can do so)*, **but to be in silence** *(silent regarding teachings unless there is no qualified man, which is the case at times.)*

13 For Adam was first formed, then Eve *(the creation model).*

14 And Adam was not deceived *(seems to imply the man is stronger regarding the will)*, **but the woman being deceived was in the transgression.** *(This facility of deception on her part seems to suggest to the Apostle her inferiority to man in intellectual strength, and the consequent wrongness of allowing the woman an intellectual supremacy over man as it regards authority.)*

15 Notwithstanding she shall be saved in childbearing *(pertains to protection from the Lord regarding the woman, and her offspring; the greater meaning of "childbearing" as used here refers to "Jesus being born into the world through the Virgin Mary, who would save lost humanity")*, **if they continue in Faith and Charity** *(love)* **and Holiness with sobriety.** *(A Godly life must be the example if the great Promise of God, as given here, is to be claimed.)*

CHAPTER 3
(A.D. 65)
BISHOPS

THIS *is* **a true saying, If a man desire the Office of a Bishop** *(the Office of the Bishop is the same as the Office of the Pastor; they are one and the same)*, **he desires a good work.** *(Most Pastors during Paul's day were raised up out of the local Church.)*

2 A Bishop *(Pastor)* **then must be blameless** *(he presents to the world at large such a Christian life that he furnishes no grounds for accusation; it speaks of the present, not the past)*, **the husband of one wife** *(is a caution, I believe, against polygamy, which, in fact, posed a serious problem for the Church in those days)*, **vigilant, sober, of good behaviour, given to hospitality, apt to teach** *(these are qualities, and not qualifications as some claim)*;

3 Not given to wine *(refers to alcoholic beverage)*, no striker *(not quarrelsome)*, not greedy of filthy lucre *(not money hungry)*; but patient, not a brawler, not covetous;

4 One who rules well his own house *(carries no idea of a dictatorial attitude, but rather sets the spiritual tone)*, having his children in subjection with all gravity *(refers to obedience)*;

5 (For if a man know not how to rule his own house, how shall he take care of the Church of God?) *(The case is clear and incontrovertible.)*

6 Not a novice *(it is used metaphorically for a new convert)*, lest being lifted up with pride *(describes a person who is in a clouded or stupid state of mind as a result of pride)* he fall into the condemnation of the Devil. *(Satan is under the condemnatory sentence of God because of his original sin of rebellion against God, which sin it seems was motivated by pride.)*

7 Moreover he must have a good report of them which are without *(refers to the non-Christian world in the midst of which the Saints must live)*; lest he fall into reproach and the snare of the Devil. *(The "Cross" is the only protection against these things of which we have been so carefully warned.)*

DEACONS

8 Likewise *must* the Deacons *be* grave *(a seriousness of purpose and self-respect in conduct)*, not doubletongued *(saying one thing and meaning another)*, not given to much wine *(Verse 3)*, not greedy of filthy lucre;

9 Holding the Mystery of the Faith in a pure conscience. *(This actually refers to the "Mystery of the Cross," which was not at all understood until its meaning was given to Paul. It is called "the Faith," and must not be diluted.)*

10 And let these also first be proved *(mature Christians)*; then let them use the Office of a Deacon *(serve well)*, being *found* blameless *(the Cross alone can guarantee such)*.

11 Even so *must their* wives *be* grave *(should have been translated, "even so must women be grave," pertaining to women who aspire to the Office of Deaconess)*, not slanderers, sober, faithful in all things. *(This is made possible by a proper Faith in the Cross.)*

12 Let the Deacons be the husbands of one wife *(identical to Verses 2, 4-5)*, ruling their children and their own houses well.

13 For they who have used the Office of a Deacon well purchase to themselves a good degree *(refers to acquiring or obtaining; it speaks of a position of trust and influence in the Church, accompanied by the Blessings of the Lord)*, and great boldness in the Faith which is in Christ Jesus *(refers to a strong Faith in Christ)*.

JESUS

14 These things write I unto you, hoping to come unto you shortly *(hoping to meet Timothy soon)*:

15 But if I tarry long, that you may know how you ought to behave yourself in the House of God *(is not actually referring to Timothy, because he knows how to conduct himself, but how the members of the Church should conduct themselves)*, which is the Church of the Living God *(the True Church, bought and paid for by the Blood of Jesus)*, the pillar and ground of the Truth. *(The True Church proclaims the Cross [I Cor. 1:17-18, 21, 23; 2:2; Eph. 2:13-18].)*

16 And without controversy great is the mystery of Godliness *(refers to the Truth of the Cross previously hidden, but now fully revealed)*: God was manifest in the flesh *(refers to the Incarnation of Christ)*, justified in the Spirit *(vindicated, endorsed, proved, and pronounced by the Holy Spirit)*, seen of Angels *(refers to the fact that Angels witnessed every capacity of His Birth, Life, Passion, Resurrection, and Ascension)*, Preached unto the Gentiles *(would have been better translated, "Preached unto the Nations"; His Atonement was for the entirety of mankind, which Message is to be proclaimed to the entirety of the world)*, believed on in the world *(accepted by many)*, received up into Glory. *(His Mission was accomplished, finished, and accepted in totality by God.)*

CHAPTER 4
(A.D. 65)
APOSTASY

NOW the Spirit *(Holy Spirit)* speaks expressly *(pointedly)*, that in the latter times *(the times in which we now live, the last of the last days, which begin the fulfillment of Endtime Prophecies)* some shall depart from the Faith *(anytime Paul uses the term "the Faith," in short he is referring to the Cross; so, we are told here that some will depart from Cross as the means of Salvation and Victory)*, giving heed to seducing spirits *(evil spirits, i.e., "religious spirits," making something seem like what it isn't)*, and doctrines of devils

(should have been translated, "Doctrines of Demons"; the "seducing spirits" entice Believers away from the true Faith, causing them to believe "Doctrines inspired by Demon spirits");

2 Speaking lies in hypocrisy *(concerns the teachers of these "Doctrines of Demons," which pertain to anything that leads one away from the Cross)*; having their conscience seared with a hot iron *(refers to the fact that these deceivers are not acting under delusion, but deliberately and against conscience)*;

3 Forbidding to marry *(is an attack against the home, even against God's original Command that a husband and wife is His Plan for society [Gen. 2:23-24])*, *and commanding* to abstain from meats *(claiming the keeping of certain man-made Laws brings about Holiness)*, which God has created to be received with thanksgiving of them which believe and know the Truth. *(The reason for the error — these have rejected Truth, i.e., "the Cross.")*

4 For every creature of God *is* good, and nothing to be refused *(that is if it's used for the right purpose)*, if it be received with thanksgiving *(proclaims the fact that every kind of food and drink may become hateful in the eyes of the all-pure God if misused, or if partaken of without any sense of gratitude to the Divine Giver)*:

5 For it is Sanctified *(made clean)* by the Word of God *(realizing our Sanctification and Holiness come by our Faith in Christ and the Cross, and not by the keeping of particular rules and regulations)* and prayer *(a prayer of thanksgiving)*.

A GOOD MINISTER

6 If you put the Brethren in remembrance of these things *(call attention to it)*, you shall be a good Minister of Jesus Christ *(at the same time, in effect, says if attention is not called to "these things," one will not be a good Preacher of the Gospel)*, nourished up in the words of Faith and of good doctrine, whereunto you have attained *(constantly nourishing one's self on the Word)*.

7 But refuse profane and old wives' fables *(that which does not have the true character of the Word of God)*, and exercise yourself *rather* unto Godliness. *(Paul's thought moves on immediately to a contrast between the discipline of the body and the discipline of the soul.)*

8 For bodily exercise profits little *(should have been translated, "profitable for a little")*: but Godliness is profitable unto all things

(covers every aspect of life and living), having Promise of the life that now is, and of that which is to come. *(Godliness affects our life and living now, and also the life that is to come, proving life after death.)*

9 This *is* a Faithful saying and worthy of all acceptation. *(The Apostle is referring to the statement made in Verse 8. It must be faithfully accepted and attended.)*

10 For therefore we both labour and suffer reproach *(neither the Devil nor his followers are in sympathy with the Believer)*, because we trust in the Living God *(the Salvation afforded by God through His Son, the Lord Jesus Christ)*, Who is the Saviour of all men *(refers to all men who will believe [Jn. 3:16; Rom. 5:4; 10:9-10, 13; Eph. 2:8-9])*, specially of those who believe. *(This refers to conditions laid down for Salvation.)*

11 These things command and teach. *(Jesus Christ Alone is the Saviour, and is so by virtue of what He did at the Cross.)*

EXAMPLES

12 Let no man despise your youth *(he had been well developed by Paul)*; but be thou an example of the Believers, in word, in conversation *(in lifestyle)*, in charity, in spirit, in Faith, in purity *(which can only be brought about by the Cross ever being the Object of our Faith, with the Holy Spirit then able to bring about these graces)*.

COMMANDS

13 Till I come, give attendance to reading *(to the simple reading of the Word of God)*, to exhortation *(proclaiming the Truth or preaching the Gospel)*, to doctrine. *(This refers to properly teaching the Word.)*

14 Neglect not the Gift that is in you *(refers to the Call of God, and the Anointing of the Holy Spirit upon the individual to carry out the "Call!")*, which was given you by Prophecy *(the "Prophecy" verified what the Lord had already done; Paul is reminding Timothy of this verification)*, with the laying on of the hands of the Presbytery. *(This actually refers to the Pastors of that particular local Church, in this instance either at Lystra or Derbe [Acts 16:1-3].)*

15 Meditate upon these things *(attend carefully)*; give yourself wholly to them *(total devotion)*; that your profiting may appear to all *(better translated, "so that your progress may*

be evident to all").

16 Take heed unto yourself, and unto the Doctrine *(keep on paying attention to yourself, what you believe, and also to what you're teaching)*; continue in them *(refers to not allowing any false doctrine to enter in, or sin to enter the personal life)*: for in doing this you shall both save yourself, and them who hear you. *(Unfortunately, most Believers are hearing Preachers who are leading them in the wrong direction.)*

CHAPTER 5
(A.D. 65)
ELDERS

REBUKE not an Elder *(does not refer to a Pastor as it usually does, but rather an older person who is mature in both age and experience)*, but intreat *him* as a father *(appeal to him as if he were your father)*; *and* the younger men as Brethren *(in Christ, we are family)*;

2 The Elder women as mothers; the younger as sisters, with all purity. *(Failure to heed the word "purity" has caused untold problems and difficulties.)*

WIDOWS

3 Honour widows who are widows indeed. *(Help those financially who are truly widows. There was no Governmental welfare net of any kind in those days.)*

4 But if any widow have children or nephews *(should read, "children or grandchildren," for that's what the Greek word actually means)*, let them learn first to show piety at home, and to requite their parents *(refers to the family bearing the responsibility instead of the Church)*: for that is good and acceptable before God *(portrays this as being God's Way; each family is responsible for its own members, and should care for each of them accordingly)*.

5 Now she who is a widow indeed *(truly)*, and desolate *(meaning she has no relatives to help care for her)*, trusts in God *(has her hopes settled permanently on God)*, and continues in supplications and prayers night and day. *(This presents an individual who is priceless, and who is most important to the Kingdom of God.)*

6 But she who lives in pleasure is dead while she lives *(portrays the contrast with one totally dedicated to God)*.

7 And these things give in charge *(give the people these instructions)*, that they may be blameless *(refers to the widows who are*

maintained by the Church; it is important that the support be reserved for those truly worthy of it).

8 But if any provide not for his own, and specially for those of his own house *(presents the Apostle speaking particularly of the duty of children towards a widowed Mother)*, he has denied the Faith *(refers to the fact that if one is truly saved, one will function according to these things laid down by the Holy Spirit through Paul)*, and is worse than an infidel. *(This carries the meaning that even an infidel, which refers to one who has no belief in Christ, abides in many cases by a code that cares for his own.)*

9 Let not a widow be taken into the number *(cared for by the Church)* under threescore years old *(60 years old)*, having been the wife of one man *(not a polygamist, but having been legally married to one man)*,

10 Well reported of for good works *(not a busybody)*; if she have brought up children *(pertains to the idea that she loved children whether she had any of her own or not)*, if she have lodged strangers, if she have washed the Saints' feet *(hospitable)*, if she have relieved the afflicted *(those in distress)*, if she have diligently followed every good work *(her life portrays this)*.

11 But the younger widows refuse *(regarding the widows under 60 years of age, the Church should not be responsible for their upkeep)*: for when they have begun to wax wanton against Christ, they will marry *(insinuates such women were not really intending to totally give themselves to the Cause of Christ, but were only seeking support until they could find a husband)*;

12 Having damnation *(should have been translated, "condemnation")*, because they have cast off their first faith. *(This probably refers to the original impulse of Faith, which led such a lady to join the widows.)*

13 And withal they learn *to be* idle, wandering about from house to house *(doing so with no practical purpose or aim in mind, but rather for the purpose of gossip)*; and not only idle, but tattlers also and busybodies, speaking things which they ought not. *(It refers to young widows who would pry into the private affairs of others.)*

14 I will therefore that the younger women marry *(should have been translated, "younger widows")*, bear children *(those young enough to do such)*, guide the house *(refers to the management of family affairs, which the wife seems to do better)*, give none occasion to the adversary

to speak reproachfully. *(If it is to be noticed, Paul's practical mind, guided by the Spirit of God, has left us no impossible rules of perfection, but rather injunctions that all, not a few, can obey.)*

15 For some are already turned aside after Satan. *(They follow the great tempter, rather than the Lord Jesus.)*

16 If any man or woman who believes have widows, let them relieve them *(places the responsibility of such on the family)*, and let not the Church be charged *(don't put unnecessary responsibility on the Church)*; that it may relieve them who are widows indeed *(refers to those who are in dire need)*.

PASTORS

17 Let the Elders *(Pastors in this case)* who rule well be counted worthy of double honour *(respect and regard)*, especially they who labour in the Word and Doctrine *(Preaching and Teaching; such Pastors are to be deeply appreciated, as should be obvious)*.

18 For the Scripture says *(Deut. 25:4)*, You shall not muzzle the ox that treads out the corn. And, The labourer is worthy of his reward. *([Lev. 19:13; Deut. 24:14]; in I Cor. 9:9, Paul argued from this Text the right of a Minister to be maintained by those to whom he Ministers.)*

19 Against an Elder *(Pastor)* receive not an accusation, but before two or three witnesses. *(If the Church were to follow this principle faithfully, no member or Minister would ever become the victim of one vengeful individual. Even if there is only one witness and the Preacher lies about the situation [as some will], it would still be better to adhere to the Word, knowing for certain the Lord will handle the situation. While men may fool other men, no one fools God.)*

A SINNING BROTHER

20 Them who sin *(continues to refer to Preachers, those who are sinning and will not repent)* rebuke before all *(it is to be done before other Preachers, and not the entire Body of the Church, as the next phrase bears out)*, that others also may fear. *(As stated, refers to other Preachers only, and not the entirety of the Body of the Church.)*

TIMOTHY

21 I charge *you* before God, and the Lord Jesus Christ, and the elect Angels *(presents a*

Command, and the fact that Heaven is witnessing our actions)*, that you observe these things without preferring one before another, doing nothing by partiality. *(This refers to the fact that there must be no prejudice when judgment is rendered, meaning not one way or the other.)*

22 Lay hands suddenly on no man *(refers to approval; True Repentance will soon bring about True results, and will be obvious)*, neither be partaker of other men's sins *(if a person refuses to repent and approval is given to that person, the Preacher giving the approval then becomes a partaker of the sins being committed)*: keep yourself pure *(which can be done only by understanding that our Faith must ever be in the Cross, which then gives the Holy Spirit the latitude to give us Victory)*.

23 Drink no longer water *(means "water exclusively"; water was not treated at all in those days, and in many cases and from many sources was impure)*, but use a little wine for your stomach's sake and your often infirmities. *(Evidently Timothy's physical constitution was not quite as strong as Paul's. During those days, all grape juice and alcoholic beverage were referred to as "wine." It could only be determined by the context as to which it was. We have no way here of knowing, but it was probably grape juice.)*

24 Some men's sins are open beforehand *(should have been translated, "openly manifested to all eyes")*, going before to judgment *(meaning judgment in such a case is easy because everything is out in the open)*; and some *men* they *(the sins)* follow after *(refers to the fact that some sins are never confessed or repented of, but to be sure will be dealt with at the Judgment; the only answer for sin is the Cross; sinful man can take the Judgment that was placed upon Christ, which was done in our place, or he can face the Judgment; the Cross alone stops the coming Judgment.)*.

25 Likewise also the good works *of some* are manifest beforehand *(presents that which is open and obvious to all)*; and they that are otherwise cannot be hid. *(At the Judgment Seat of Christ, every secret will be made manifest. Every hidden thing will be revealed. All things will then be made clear.)*

CHAPTER 6
(A.D. 65)

SERVANTS

LET as many servants *(slaves)* as are under the yoke *(the yoke of slavery)* count their

own masters worthy of all honour *(in Paul's day, slaves were common, possibly making up the majority of the population; irrespective of whether the master was good or bad, Christian slaves were to function and do their work exactly as if they were doing it for the Lord Himself, and not men)*, **that the Name of God and** *His* **Doctrine be not blasphemed.** *(Everything the slave did, and everything we do, must be done with the view of Christ in mind.)*

MASTERS

2 **And they who have believing masters, let them not despise** *them*, **because they are Brethren** *(because they are equals in Christ; this doesn't mean the slave is to think less of his Christian master)*; **but rather do** *them* **service** *(literally means in the Greek, "slave for them all the more")*, **because they are faithful and beloved, partakers of the benefit** *(refers to the fact that if a Christian slave was to show obedience and grace to an unbelieving master, even as they certainly should, how much more should they show the same to a Master who is now a Believer and, therefore, greatly beloved of the Lord!)*. **These things teach and exhort** *(suggests the touchiness of the issue)*.

MONEY

3 **If any man teach otherwise** *(proclaims the fact that some were teaching things opposed to Paul's teaching)*, **and consent not to wholesome words,** *even* **the Words of our Lord Jesus Christ** *(Lk. 20:25; Mat. 5:44; 11:28-30)*, **and to the Doctrine which is according to Godliness** *(refers to the teaching concerning the proper attitude of the individual towards God)*;

4 **He is proud** *(the false teacher)*, **knowing nothing** *(despite his claims)*, **but doting about questions and strifes of words** *(the profitless debating of which has rent asunder whole Churches, and even entire denominations)*, **whereof comes envy, strife, railings, evil surmisings** *(proclaims the results of these useless questions as tendered by the false teachers)*,

5 **Perverse disputings of men of corrupt minds** *(should have been translated, "of men corrupted in mind")*, **and destitute of the Truth** *(refers to the fact that they had once possessed the Truth, which is the Cross, but had turned away to other things)*, **supposing that gain is Godliness** *(should have been translated, "supposing that Godliness is a way or source of gain")*: **from**

such **withdraw yourself** *(have no dealings with these Preachers)*.

6 **But Godliness with contentment** *(content with what we have, which means we are thankful to God for what we have)* **is great gain** *(true gain)*.

7 **For we brought nothing into** *this* **world,** *and it is* **certain we can carry nothing out.** *(This speaks of worldly possessions. The only thing a person can keep is their Faith, that is if it's true Faith, which refers to Faith in Christ and the Cross.)*

8 **And having food and raiment let us be therewith content.** *(The Lord can never bless grasping greed.)*

9 **But they who will be rich fall into temptation and a snare, and** *into* **many foolish and hurtful lusts** *(speaks of the sacrifice of principle)*, **which drown men in destruction and perdition.** *(This refers to the wreck and ruin of the mind and body, but more particularly to the awful ruin of the eternal soul.)*

10 **For the love of money is the root of all evil** *(there is no conceivable evil that can happen to the sons and daughters of men, which may not spring from covetousness — the love of gold and wealth)*: **which while some coveted after, they have erred from the Faith** *(speaking of Believers who have lost sight of the True Faith, which is the Cross, and have ventured into a false faith, trying to use it to garner much money)*, **and pierced themselves through with many sorrows** *(the end result of turning in that direction; let all understand that the Word of God is true, and what it says will happen!)*.

FAITH

11 **But you, O man of God, flee these things** *(the Holy Spirit is unequivocally clear in His Command; we can follow the Lord, or we can follow other things; we can't follow both!)*; **and follow after Righteousness, Godliness, Faith, Love, Patience, Meekness.** *(In a sense, this is Fruit of the Spirit, or at least that which the Spirit Alone can bring about in our lives, which He does by the Cross ever being the Object of our Faith.)*

12 **Fight the good fight of Faith** *(in essence, the only fight we're called upon to engage; every attack by Satan against the Believer, irrespective of its form, is to destroy or seriously weaken our Faith; he wants to push our Faith from the Cross to other things)*, **lay hold on Eternal Life** *(we do such by understanding that all Life comes from Christ, and the means is the Cross)*,

whereunto you are also Called *(Called to fol-low Christ)*, and have professed a good profession before many witnesses. *(This does not refer to a particular occasion, but to the entirety of his life for Christ.)*

13 I give you charge in the sight of God *(in essence, the mantle is soon to be passed to this young Preacher)*, who quickens *(makes alive)* all things *(presents Christ here as the Preserver, rather than the Creator)*, and *before* Christ Jesus *("I charge you before Christ")*, who before Pontius Pilate witnessed a good confession *(the confession of Christ was the model confession for all martyrs, insofar as it was a bold confession of the Truth, even with the sentence of death before His Eyes)*;

14 That you keep *this* Commandment without spot, unrebukeable *(the Gospel of Christ and Him Crucified must not be compromised in any fashion)*, until the appearing of our Lord Jesus Christ *(the statement refers to both the Rapture and the Second Coming)*:

15 Which in His times *(an epoch-making period, foreordained of God)* He shall show, *Who is* the Blessed and only Potentate, the King of kings, and Lord of lords *(the Second Coming; refers to the fact that there will be absolutely no doubt as to the identity of the One Who will appear)*;

16 Who only has immortality *(in a sense, says God is the Source of all immortality)*, dwelling in the Light which no man can approach unto *(the Person of God is wholly concealed by His Dwelling, which is Light; and this Dwelling is Itself unapproachable)*; Whom no man has seen, nor can see *(refers to the fact that "flesh and blood cannot inherit the Kingdom of God" [I Cor. 15:50])*: to Whom *be* honour and power everlasting. Amen. *(The great names and titles which the Holy Spirit, through Paul, has ascribed here to Christ, while definitely including His Deity, more than all direct attention to His great Redemption Work, which He accomplished at the Cross of Calvary.)*

THE USE OF RICHES

17 Charge them *(Believers)* who are rich in this world *(limits the riches to the here and now, and shows that one can be rich in this world and not in the other world)*, that they be not highminded *(proud)*, nor trust in uncertain riches *(presents the fact that it's very difficult to have great wealth without in some measure trusting in it)*, but in the Living God, Who gives us richly all things to enjoy *(God is the Source, not money!)*;

18 That they do good, that they be rich in good works *(use the money to take the Gospel to the world)*, ready to distribute, willing to communicate *(looking for the True Gospel, which can be supported, and which they will support)*;

19 Laying up in store for themselves a good foundation against the time to come *(laying up treasures on the other side)*, that they may lay hold on Eternal Life. *(This should have been translated, "that they may hold to that which is truly Life.")*

BENEDICTION

20 O Timothy, keep that which is committed to your trust *(refers to the deposit of Truth delivered to him; actually, it would be the entirety of the New Covenant as it was given to Paul; what a responsibility!)*, avoiding profane *and* vain babblings *(pertains to that which is devoid of Godliness, and empty of content)*, and oppositions of science falsely so called *(should have been translated, "and oppositions of knowledge falsely so-called," and speaks of the Gnostics)*:

21 Which some professing have erred concerning the Faith *(have turned away from Christ and the Cross)*. Grace *be* with you. Amen. *(Grace will always be with the Believer who places his Faith exclusively in Christ and His Finished Work.)*

THE SECOND EPISTLE OF PAUL THE APOSTLE TO
TIMOTHY

CHAPTER 1

(A.D. 66)

INTRODUCTION

PAUL, an Apostle of Jesus Christ by the Will of God (*the Office of the Apostle carries the leadership of the Church, and does so by a special Message given to the Apostle, which in Paul's case was Grace*), according to the Promise of Life which is in Christ Jesus (*Life, and more particularly Eternal Life is found only in Christ Jesus, and comes by means of the Cross*),

2 To Timothy, *my* dearly beloved son: Grace, Mercy, *and* Peace, from God the Father and Christ Jesus our Lord (*all made possible by the Cross*).

TIMOTHY

3 I thank God, Whom I serve from *my* forefathers with pure conscience (*in effect, says he was seeking to please God even while he persecuted the Church through ignorance*), that without ceasing I have remembrance of you in my prayers night and day (*in this we see the depth of this man's prayer life*);

4 Greatly desiring to see you (*Paul was in prison in Rome when he wrote this Epistle, his last*), being mindful of your tears (*Timothy was probably present when Paul was arrested the second time, and transported to Rome for his final imprisonment*), that I may be filled with joy (*knowing his time was short, he desired to see Timothy*);

5 When I call to remembrance the unfeigned Faith that is in you (*he recalls the time he first met Timothy, and the young man was invited to join his Evangelistic team [Acts 16:1-3]*), which dwelt first in your grandmother Lois, and your mother Eunice; and I am persuaded that is in you also (*proclaims here a tremendous heritage*).

THE CHARGE

6 Wherefore I put you in remembrance that you stir up the Gift of God (*refers to the entirety of the Call of God upon Timothy's life*), which is in you by the putting on of my hands.

(*This doesn't mean Paul bestowed this Gift upon young Timothy, but that he verified what he knew to already be there.*)

7 For God has not given us the spirit of fear (*refers to a disposition of the mind; the Apostle is telling the young Evangelist not to fear*); but of power (*could be said, "the spirit of power," for such comes from the Holy Spirit*), and of love (*again, given by the Holy Spirit*), and of a sound mind (*a "spirit of self-control," all made possible by the Holy Spirit, Who demands that we ever keep our Faith in the Cross [Rom. 8:1-2, 11, 13]*).

8 Be not thou therefore ashamed of the Testimony of our Lord (*the Christian, instead of being ashamed of his "profession of Faith," must before the world show fearlessly that its Hopes and its Promises are His most precious Treasure*), nor of me His prisoner (*even though Paul was a prisoner in a Roman cell, he in no way considered himself a prisoner of Nero, but rather of the Lord*): but be thou partaker of the afflictions of the Gospel according to the Power of God (*actually means to take one's share of the ill-treatment, which will always be accompanied by the Power of God, which gives us Grace to stand the test*);

9 Who has saved us (*through what He did at the Cross*), and called *us* with an Holy Calling (*we didn't call Him, rather He Called us*), not according to our works (*Salvation is by Grace through Faith, not of works [Eph. 2:8-9]*), but according to His Own Purpose and Grace (*refers to the reason and the means*), which was given us in Christ Jesus (*through what He did at the Cross*) before the world began (*the Cross of Christ is the very first Doctrine of the Bible, actually "foreordained before the foundation of the world" [I Pet. 1:18-20]; consequently, every true Doctrine is built on the Foundation of the Cross, or else it's not true*),

10 But is now made manifest by the appearing of our Saviour Jesus Christ (*everything is wrapped up in Jesus and what He did at the Cross*), Who has abolished death (*the wages of sin is death [Rom. 6:23], thus when Jesus atoned for all sin on the Cross, this removed the means of death, i.e., "spiritual death"*), and has brought life and immortality to light through the

Gospel *(the Gospel is the Cross, which made "life" and "immortality" possible, and will see its total fulfillment at the coming Resurrection)*:

11 Whereunto I am appointed a Preacher *(to Preach the Gospel)*, and an Apostle *(of Grace)*, and a Teacher of the Gentiles. *(Although the Apostle also preached to the Jews, his major thrust was ever to the Gentiles, whose Salvation the Cross made possible.)*

12 For the which cause *(to establish the Church)* I also suffer these things *(imprisonment, etc.)*: nevertheless I am not ashamed *(proclaims the fact that some were ashamed of Paul, regarding his imprisonment)*: for I know Whom I have believed *(refers to the Lord Jesus Christ)*, and am persuaded that He is able to keep that which I have committed unto Him against that day. *(This refers to the soul with all its immortal interests.)*

13 Hold fast the form of sound words *(forms the correct Doctrine, which is "Jesus Christ and Him Crucified)*, which you have heard of me *(refers to the fact that the Lord gave Paul the meaning and understanding of the New Covenant, which is the Cross [Gal. 1:11-12])*, in Faith and Love which is in Christ Jesus. *(Anytime Paul uses the phrase, "in Christ Jesus" or one of its derivatives, without exception, he is speaking of what Christ did at the Cross.)*

14 That good thing which was committed unto you *(presents in such simple words the single most important thing in the world, the Gospel of Jesus Christ)* keep by the Holy Spirit *(has the help of the Holy Spirit respecting the purity of the Message)* which dwells in us. *(He is constantly present and, therefore, constantly available!)*

15 This you know, that all they which are in Asia be turned away from me *(one of the most sorrowful trials the great hearted Paul had to endure in the agony of his last witnessing for his Lord was the knowledge that his name and teaching were no longer held in honor in some of these Asian Churches so dear to him; this turning away was a turning away from the Cross)*; of whom are Phygellus and Hermogenes. *(How sad that these two would be placed in the Sacred Texts, not in the realm of faithfulness, but rather "faithlessness"!)*

ONESIPHORUS

16 The Lord give Mercy unto the house of Onesiphorus *(from the terminology, it seems this man had died a short time before)*; for he

oft refreshed me, and was not ashamed of my chain *(once again, it seems many Believers were, in fact, ashamed of Paul and his situation, but not Onesiphorus)*:

17 But, when he was in Rome, he sought me out very diligently, and found *me*. *(This man, so kind to the great Apostle, will be among those at the final Judgment to whom the Saviour will say, "I was in prison, and you came unto Me" [Mat. 25:36].)*

18 The Lord grant unto him that he may find Mercy of the Lord in that day *(speaks of the "Judgment Seat of Christ," which will commence after the Rapture of the Church; only Believers will be there; as well, it will not involve sin, for that was handled at Calvary, but rather our motives, etc.)*: and in how many things he ministered unto me at Ephesus, you know very well. *(It seems this man had ever been a help to Paul. Therefore, his name will be proclaimed forever on the pages of Sacred Writ.)*

CHAPTER 2
(A.D. 66)
A GOOD SOLDIER

THOU therefore, my son, be strong *(one carries this out by ever making the Cross the Object of Faith)* in the Grace that is in Christ Jesus. *(The Source of Grace is the Lord, but the means is the Cross.)*

2 And the things that you have heard of me among many witnesses *(the integrity of the mighty deposit of Truth)*, the same commit thou to Faithful men *(refers to others called of God, who would Preach this great Gospel)*, who shall be able to teach others also. *(While many turned away from Paul, the evidence here is that some didn't; they were Faithful.)*

3 You therefore endure hardness *(take your part in suffering hardship if called upon to do so)*, as a good soldier of Jesus Christ. *(The Roman Legionnaires suffered hardship in the service of the Emperor. Why not the Christian in the service of the King of kings?)*

4 No man who wars entangles himself with the affairs of *this* life *(a soldier has one thing on his mind, and that is to carry out his duty; the Christian is to have the same motive, the same spirit, and the same consecration; hence, the Apostle using the word "soldier")*; that he may please Him Who has chosen him to be a soldier. *(We are to please Christ, not men.)*

5 And if a man also strive for masteries *(now presents the manner in which the Believer*

strives), *yet* is he not crowned, except he strive lawfully. *(It is the preparation for the contest that is in question, not the contest itself. What is the Apostle saying?)*

6 The husbandman who labors *(the sowing of seed in order that a crop may ultimately be harvested)* must be first partaker of the fruits. *(If he doesn't "strive lawfully," which means to walk after the Spirit which leads to the Cross, there aren't going to be any "fruits.")*

7 Consider what I say *(refers to the fact that what Paul is saying is actually the "Word of the Lord")*; and the Lord give you understanding in all things. *(The Holy Spirit will always help the sincere seeker understand the tenor of the Word of God.)*

8 Remember that Jesus Christ of the seed of David *(the Incarnation)* was raised from the dead *(out from among the dead)* according to my Gospel *(that which was given to him by the Lord [Gal. 1:11-12])*:

SUFFERING

9 Wherein I suffer trouble, as an evil doer, *even* unto bonds *(proclaims the fact that it was because of his Preaching of the Gospel that Paul had suffered severe trouble)*; but the Word of God is not bound. *(This presents the fact that the Gospel, as it had been given to Paul, had been preserved by that Apostle in that he could pass it on undiluted and uncompromised.)*

10 Therefore I endure all things for the elect's sakes *(refers to all who have accepted Christ, whether Jews or Gentiles)*, that they may also obtain the Salvation which is in Christ Jesus with Eternal Glory. *(If the Message of the Cross was diluted in any way, there would be no Eternal Glory. We should vividly remember that.)*

11 *It is* a Faithful saying: For if we be dead with *Him* *(refers to Christ as our Substitute dying on the Cross, with our Faith placing us in the position of dying "with Him" [Rom. 6:3-8])*, we shall also live with *Him* *(the Greek says, "We shall live by means of Him"; our "living with Him," which speaks of Resurrection Life and thus speaks of perpetual victory, is attained only by us understanding that we have been "planted together [Christ and the Believer] in the likeness of His Death"; in other words, it was all done at the Cross!)*:

12 If we suffer, we shall also reign with *Him* *(the "suffering" has to do with "fighting the good fight of Faith"; to "reign" means to "reign as a king," so the stakes are very high!)*: if we

deny *Him*, He also will deny us *(refers to denying what He did for us at the Cross)*:

13 If we believe not *(believe what He did at the Cross)*, *yet* He abides Faithful *(despite the unbelief of many, He will be Faithful to Redeem all who come to Him in Faith)*: He cannot deny Himself. *(Heaven will never change the Plan of Redemption and Victory, which is the Cross.)*

INSTRUCTIONS

14 Of these things put *them* in remembrance *(has special reference to the issues of life and death set out in the previous three Verses)*, charging *them* before the Lord that they strive not about words to no profit *(if the Cross is abandoned, "Christ shall profit you nothing" [Gal. 5:2])*, *but* to the subverting of the hearers *(refers to overthrowing their Faith)*.

15 Study to show yourself approved unto God *(refers to a workman who has been put to the test and, meeting these specifications, has won the approval of the one who has subjected him to the test)*, a workman who needs not to be ashamed *(Faith placed exclusively in the Cross will never bring shame; faith placed elsewhere will, without fail, bring shame)*, rightly dividing the Word of Truth. *(If one doesn't properly understand the Cross, one cannot rightly divide the Word of Truth.)*

16 But shun profane *and* vain babblings *(this means no false doctrine leaves its victims as they were found, but rather worse, much worse!)*: for they will increase unto more ungodliness. *(If the Preacher is teaching anything other than the Cross of Christ, it is construed by the Holy Spirit as no more than "vain babblings," and is guaranteed to increase ungodliness more and more. In fact, it cannot be any other way!)*

17 And their word will eat as does a canker *(false doctrine, which constitutes anything other than the Cross, will ultimately corrupt the whole)*: of whom is Hymenaeus and Philetus *(as is obvious, Paul is here "marking them, which caused divisions and offences contrary to sound Doctrine" [Rom. 16:17]; if we as Preachers are to be true to the Gospel, we must do the same)*;

18 Who concerning the Truth have erred *(there is only one "Truth," and that is "Jesus Christ and Him Crucified" [I Cor. 1:17-18, 23; 2:2])*, saying that the Resurrection is past already *(this is very similar to some modern Christians who claim there will be no Rapture, especially considering that the Rapture*

and the Resurrection are one and the same); and overthrow the Faith of some. (The Death and Resurrection of Christ have made everything possible, including the coming Resurrection of all Saints. To be confused about Christ's Atoning Work is to be confused about everything.)

19 Nevertheless the Foundation of God stands sure (proclaims the truth that this foundation is secure, despite the fact that some make shipwreck of their Faith), having this seal, The Lord knows them who are His. (This "seal" guarantees the "security of the Church" and the "purity of the Church." The two go together. The purity of the Church is indispensable to its security.) And, Let every one who names the Name of Christ depart from iniquity. (One can "depart from iniquity," only as one makes the Cross the Object of his Faith, which then gives him Holy Spirit Power.)

20 But in a great house there are not only vessels of gold and of silver, but also of wood and of earth (presents the Apostle using metaphors); and some to honour, and some to dishonour. (This refers to the fact that there is no such thing as sinless perfection this side of the Resurrection. There are problems in every Christian life, which only the Cross can cure.)

21 If a man therefore purge himself from these (he can only do so by ever making the Cross the Object of his Faith, which will then give him Holy Spirit Power that alone can accomplish the task; the "purging" cannot come about by any other manner), he shall be a vessel unto honour, Sanctified, and meet (qualified) for the Master's use, and prepared unto every good work.

22 Flee also youthful lusts (refers to the evil attracted to one when they are young, which is then very difficult to free one's self from when they are older): but follow Righteousness, Faith, Charity (Love), Peace, with them who call on the Lord out of a pure heart (attributes of the Spirit, which He Alone can produce within our hearts and lives, and He does according to our Faith anchored firmly in the Cross).

23 But foolish and unlearned questions avoid (if it's not "Christ and Him Crucified," forget it!), knowing that they do gender strifes. (This proclaims agitation, and much ado about nothing.)

24 And the servant of the Lord must not strive (pertains to being drawn aside into endless discussions which serve no purpose, and can only conclude in "strife!"); but be gentle unto all men (Fruit of the Spirit [Gal. 5:22]), apt to teach (teach correct Doctrine), patient (show patience to those who do not easily and quickly understand that which is being taught),

25 In meekness instructing those who oppose themselves (refers to those who place themselves in opposition to the true servant of the Lord and to True Doctrine); if God peradventure will give them Repentance to the acknowledging of the Truth (hoping those in error will repent and come to the Truth, and we might quickly say, "The Truth of the Cross");

26 And that they may recover themselves out of the snare of the Devil (if one is placing his Faith and Hope in anything other than Christ and the Cross, he has been "snared by the Devil," which is serious indeed!), who are taken captive by him at his will. (Unless the Believer makes the Cross the Object of his Faith, which then gives him the help of the Holy Spirit, he is helpless against Satan, who will make him his captive, i.e., "in bondage to sin" [Gal. 5:1].)

CHAPTER 3
(A.D. 66)
APOSTASY

THIS know also, that in the last days (the days in which we now live) perilous times shall come. (This speaks of difficult dangerous times, which Christians living just before the Rapture will encounter.)

2 For men (those who call themselves Christians) shall be lovers of their own selves, covetous, boasters, proud, blasphemers, disobedient to parents, unthankful, unholy,

3 Without natural affection, trucebreakers, false accusers, incontinent, fierce, despisers of those who are good,

4 Traitors, heady, highminded, lovers of pleasures more than lovers of God (and remember, this is describing the Endtime Church, which has been totally corrupted [Mat. 13:33; Rev. 3:14-22]);

5 Having a form of Godliness (refers to all the trappings of Christianity, but without the power), but denying the power thereof (the modern Church, for all practical purposes, has denied the Cross; in doing this, they have denied that through which the Holy Spirit works, and in Whom the power resides [Rom. 8:1-2, 11; I Cor. 1:18]): from such turn away. (No half measures are to be adopted here. The command is clear! It means to turn away from Churches that deny or ignore the Cross.)

6 For of this sort are they which creep into

houses (*proclaims the methods of false teachers*), **and lead captive silly women laden with sins, led away with divers lusts** (*due to Eve succumbing to temptation and deception, women are the easiest prey for these false teachers; the idea is that "silly women" will support these false teachers, and do so grandly; they are drawn to these false Preachers through "divers lusts"*),

7 Ever learning (*proclaims learning that which is wrong*), **and never able to come to the knowledge of the Truth.** (*This proclaims the fact that they really do not want the Truth.*)

8 Now as Jannes and Jambres withstood Moses (*[Ex. 7:11-12], the names of these men are found in the Targum of Jonathan*), **so do these also resist the Truth** (*they have been shown the Truth, but have rejected the Truth, which they did purposely; it pertains to a rejection of the Cross of Christ*): **men of corrupt minds, reprobate concerning the Faith.** (*If it's not "Christ and Him Crucified," then it is corrupt and reprobate [I Cor. 2:2].*)

9 But they shall proceed no further (*means the Holy Spirit will allow this error to go so far, and no further*): **for their folly shall be manifest unto all** *men* (*error will ultimately manifest itself for what it really is because the True Gospel is more powerful*), **as theirs also was** (*referring to the two men who attempted to withstand Moses*).

PAUL

10 But you have fully known my doctrine (*better translated, "But as for you, in distinction from others, have fully known my Doctrine"*), **manner of life, purpose, faith, longsuffering, charity, patience** (*Timothy knew Paul's example, which the Gospel had wrought in his life*),

11 Persecutions, afflictions, which came unto me at Antioch, at Iconium, at Lystra (*presents Churches being built in these areas at great personal price*); **what persecutions I endured** (*the persecutions were necessary in order that these Churches be built*): **but out of** *them* **all the Lord delivered me.** (*The Lord will always deliver until the person's work is finished.*)

12 Yes, and all who will live Godly in Christ Jesus shall suffer persecution. (*It is because of the "offence of the Cross" [Gal. 5:11].*)

13 But evil men and seducers shall wax worse and worse (*this problem of seduction in the last days is so acute that the word Paul uses here [seducers] occurs no where else in the New*

Testament; *this means that such an effort is unique to this particular time*), **deceiving, and being deceived.** (*Truth opens the door to even more Truth, while deception opens the door to even more deception.*)

THE SCRIPTURES

14 But you continue in the things which you have learned and have been assured of (*the Message of the Cross*), **knowing of whom you have learned** *them* (*Timothy had learned the Word of God from Paul, even as all others did, in fact, at that particular time, including the original Twelve. The meaning of the New Covenant was given to Paul, so it had to be learned from him*);

15 And that from a child you have known the Holy Scriptures (*presents the greatest education any boy or girl could ever have*), **which are able to make you wise unto Salvation through Faith which is in Christ Jesus.** (*The entirety of the Word of God points directly to Christ and what He did on the Cross. The Old Testament points forward to His Coming and what He would do. The New Testament points backward to what He has already done. And at the center of it all is the Cross.*)

16 All Scripture *is* **given by Inspiration of God** (*the Greek says, "all Scripture is God-breathed," which means it is the Word of God, and, thereby, infallible!*), **and** *is* **profitable for Doctrine** (*all we believe, teach, and do must be based squarely on the Scriptures*), **for reproof** (*proclaims the use of the Word of God in setting direction*), **for correction** (*refers to restoration to an upright state*), **for instruction in Righteousness** (*presents the Bible as the only guide for such instruction*):

17 That the man of God may be perfect (*refers to maturity*), **throughly furnished unto all good works** (*properly understands the Word, which then produces "good works," i.e., "Godly lives"*).

CHAPTER 4
(A.D. 66)
LAST CHARGE

I charge *you* therefore (*has the weight of a legal affirmation*) **before God, and the Lord Jesus Christ** (*should have been translated, "Our God, even Christ Jesus"*), **Who shall judge the quick** (*living*) **and the dead** (*refers to the fact that all Believers will stand at the Judgment Seat*

of Christ) **at His appearing and His Kingdom** (*refers here to the Second Advent*);

2 Preach the Word (*refers to the whole body of revealed Truth, which means the entirety of the Word of God*); **be instant in season, out of season** (*presents the idea of the Preacher holding himself in constant readiness to proclaim the Word*); **reprove** (*the Preacher is to deal with sin, both in the lives of his unsaved hearers and in those of the Saints to whom he Ministers, and he is to do so in no uncertain tones and terms*), **rebuke** (*a suggestion in some cases of impending penalty*), **exhort with all longsuffering and Doctrine.** (*This tells us that the "reproving" and the "rebuking" must be done with gentleness. As well, the "longsuffering" refers to a gentleness that continues even when the Message is met with rejection. However, the "Doctrine" is not to change, even though it is rejected.*)

3 For the time will come when they will not endure sound Doctrine (*"sound Doctrine" pertains to overriding principles: the Salvation of the sinner, and the Sanctification of the Saint; the Cross is the answer for both, and is the only answer for both*); **but after their own lusts shall they heap to themselves teachers, having itching ears** (*refers to the people who have ears that "itch" for the smooth and comfortable word, and are willing to reward handsomely the man who is sufficiently compromising to speak it; hearers of this type have rejected the Truth and prefer to hear the lie*);

4 And they shall turn away *their* **ears from the Truth** (*those who follow false teachers not only turn away their ears from the Truth, but see to it that the ears are always in a position such that they will never come in contact with the Truth*), **and shall be turned unto fables.** (*If it's not the "Message of the Cross," then it is "fables" [I Cor. 1:18].*)

5 But watch thou in all things (*carries the idea of watching one's own life, Ministry, and the Doctrine which we are proclaiming*), **endure afflictions** (*carries the idea of not allowing hardships, difficulties, or troubles to hinder one's carrying forth of one's Ministry; it is a sharp command given with military snap and curtness; Wuest says, "How we in the Ministry of the Word need that injunction today. What a 'softy' we sometimes are, afraid to come out clearly in our proclamation of the Truth and our stand as to false doctrine, fearing the ostracism of our fellows, the Ecclesiastical displeasure of religious leaders so-called, or even the cutting off of our immediate financial income." ["I would rather walk a lonely road with Jesus than be in a crowd, without His fellowship"]*), **do the work of an Evangelist** (*keep trying to get people saved*), **make full proof of your Ministry** (*does it match up with the Word of God?*).

PAUL

6 For I am now ready to be offered (*the word "ready" signifies that the Holy Spirit had already told the Apostle the time had now come; the word "offered" speaks of the Drink-Offering poured out upon the Sacrifice about to be offered, which, in effect, was the lesser part poured out upon the most important part; only one who considered himself less than the least of all Saints could write in such deep humility*), **and the time of my departure is at hand.** (*This presents the fact that the servant of the Lord is immortal until his work is done.*)

7 I have fought a good fight (*should have been translated, "I have fought the good fight"; Paul fought his fight with sin to a finish, and was resting in a complete victory*), **I have finished** *my* **course** (*he had been faithful in carrying out that which had been assigned to him*), **I have kept the Faith** (*refers here to the deposit of Truth regarding the meaning of the Cross and the Resurrection of Christ, with which the Lord had entrusted Paul*):

8 Henceforth there is laid up for me a Crown of Righteousness (*the Victor's Crown*), **which the Lord, the Righteous Judge, shall give me at that day** (*at the Judgment Seat of Christ*): **and not to me only, but unto all them also who love His appearing.** (*This Victor's Crown will go to all who consider His appearing precious.*)

INSTRUCTIONS

9 Do your diligence to come shortly unto me (*Timothy was in Ephesus, about 1,000 miles from Rome; consequently, it was a journey which at best would take several weeks; whether the young Apostle made it there in time or made it at all, is not known*):

10 For Demas has forsaken me, having loved this present world, and is departed unto Thessalonica (*presents a sad Commentary regarding one who had been blessed with such a golden opportunity*); **Crescens to Galatia** (*mentioned here only; tradition says he founded the Church in France*), **Titus unto Dalmatia** (*modern Yugoslavia*).

11 Only Luke is with me *(presents the one who wrote the Gospel that bears his name, as well as the Book of Acts)*. **Take Mark, and bring him with you** *(John Mark, who wrote the Gospel of Mark, the nephew of Barnabas)*: **for he is profitable to me for the Ministry.** *(This presents a tremendous commendation by the Apostle concerning Mark.)*

12 **And Tychicus have I sent to Ephesus.** *(It is believed Tychicus conveyed this very Epistle, the last one written by Paul, to Timothy and was perhaps instructed to replace Timothy at Ephesus, while the young Apostle came to Rome.)*

13 **The cloak that I left at Troas with Carpus, when you come, bring *with you*** *(quite possibly it was summer when Paul wrote this Epistle, and if he survived till winter, he would need this cloak)*, **and the Books, *but*especially the Parchments** *(refers to the Old Testament Books)*.

14 **Alexander the coppersmith did me much evil** *(it is the Work of God Paul laments, which causes him to mention this person)*: **the Lord reward him according to his works** *(barring Repentance, Judgment will ultimately come most assuredly on all those who attempt to hinder the Work of God, and do so by attempting to hinder the worker for God)*:

15 **Of whom you beware also** *(presents this individual as a tool of Satan; incidentally, he lived in Ephesus where Timothy was now Ministering)*; **for he has greatly withstood our words** *(strongly opposed our Message of the Cross)*.

16 **At my first answer no man stood with me, but all *men* forsook me** *(when one is down, and anyone can do any negative thing to him or her they so desire without any fear of reprimand or censure, but will rather be applauded, one quickly finds exactly how many true Christians there really are; regrettably, there aren't many!)*: ***I pray God*** **that it may not be laid to their charge.** *(The Apostle pleads to the Lord for these weak, unnerved friends of his who, solely through fear and not ill-will to the cause, had deserted him, that their actions not be laid to their charge.)*

17 **Notwithstanding the Lord stood with me, and strengthened me** *(presents the fact that the Apostle experienced an unusual degree of the Presence of the Lord during this time)*; **that by me the preaching might be fully known** *(that he might give a full proclamation of the Gospel before Nero, not compromising it at all)*, **and** *that* **all the Gentiles might hear** *(in his defense before Nero, the trial room would have been filled with Gentiles, important dignitaries from all over the Roman Empire; from the lips of Paul, they would hear the Gospel)*: **and I was delivered out of the mouth of the lion.** *(This phrase has been debated almost from the time it was uttered by Paul. It does not refer to being delivered from Nero, because he was not acquitted. As well, it had no bearing that he would be thrown to the lions, as thought by some, because Roman citizens, which Paul was, did not suffer such a fate. It probably referred to the entire situation at hand, and Satan's efforts to hinder the Message of Paul, which Satan was not able to do.)*

18 **And the Lord shall deliver me from every evil work** *(which harks back to the previous Verse)*, **and will preserve *me* unto His Heavenly Kingdom** *(even though said in the future tense, actually has to do with the entirety of his life)*: **to Whom *be* Glory forever and ever. Amen.** *(This presents the Apostle bursting to an ascription of praise to the Lord Who he has loved so long and so well and, in all his troubles and perplexities, had never left him friendless.)*

BENEDICTION

19 **Salute** *(greet)* **Priscilla and Aquila** *(two of Paul's earliest friends)*, **and the household of Onesiphorus.** *(This presents the same Brother mentioned in II Tim. 1:16.)*

20 **Erastus abode at Corinth** *(probably means he had now gone back to that city, which, in effect, was his home)*: **but Trophimus have I left at Miletum sick.**

21 **Do your diligence to come before winter** *(hence, bringing the cloak)*. **Eubulus greets you, and Pudens, and Linus, and Claudia, and all the Brethren.** *(This presents some of the Christians in Rome whose names have been immortalized by their being included in Paul's Letter.)*

22 **The Lord Jesus Christ *be* with your spirit** *(invokes the Resurrection Name of our Lord)*. **Grace *be* with you. Amen.** *(The First Epistle written by Paul was I Thessalonians, which was addressed to the Church. This last one was addressed to a Preacher. This tells us that for the Church to be right, the Preacher must first be right.)*

THE EPISTLE OF PAUL THE APOSTLE TO
TITUS

CHAPTER 1
(A.D. 65)
INTRODUCTION

PAUL, a servant of God, and an Apostle of Jesus Christ *(the designation of "servant" is given here first, even before the designation of "Apostle"; the Holy Spirit would have it this way; if the man cannot be a true servant, he cannot be a true Apostle; those who have the calling of "Apostle" serve as the de facto leaders of the Church by virtue of the Message they Preach, which for Paul was the Message of Grace)*, according to the Faith *(refers to the Cross as the Foundation on which all other Doctrines are built)* of God's elect *(refers to the Church, which took the place of the Jews as the elect of God during the time of their being cut off [Rom., Chpts. 9-11])*, and the acknowledging of the truth which is after Godliness *(the idea is that proper Faith in the Cross of Christ will produce "Godliness!")*;

2 In hope of Eternal Life *(Eternal Life is now given to everyone who is in Christ on condition of remaining in Him [Jn. 15:1-8; Gal. 1:6-8; 4:19; 5:4; I Jn. 5:11-12])*, which God, Who cannot lie *(says literally in the Greek, "un-lieable God")*, promised before the world began *(says in the Greek, "before the times of the ages")*;

3 But has in due times manifested his Word through Preaching *(God's secret purposes in Salvation have been brought to light in the Preaching of the Apostle)*, which is committed unto me according to the Commandment of God our Saviour *(Paul is the one to whom the meaning of the New Covenant was given, which is actually the meaning of the Cross [Gal. 1:11-12])*;

4 To Titus, *mine* own son after the common Faith *("Faith in the great Sacrifice of Christ")*: Grace, Mercy, *and* Peace, from God the Father and the Lord Jesus Christ our Saviour. *(This is all made possible by what Christ did at the Cross.)*

QUALITIES

5 For this cause left I you in Crete *(Paul was in Crete with Titus for a period of time)*, that you should set in order the things that are wanting *(refers mainly to Church Government)*, and ordain Elders *(Pastors)* in every city, as I had appointed you *(should have been translated, "appoint Pastors in every city")*:

6 If any be blameless, the husband of one wife *(no polygamists)*, having Faithful children not accused of riot or unruly. *(This refers to children who are Believers and have proven to be such by proper conduct.)*

7 For a Bishop *(Pastor, Bishop, Elder, Shepherd, and Presbyter are all interchangeable, and refer to the Pastor of a local Church)* must be blameless, as the steward of God *(refers to a man who seeks to be totally consecrated to the Lord)*; not selfwilled, not soon angry, not given to wine, no striker *(doesn't have a spirit of contention)*, not given to filthy lucre *(not money hungry)*;

8 But a lover of hospitality, a lover of good men, sober, just, holy, temperate *(self-control)*;

9 Holding fast the Faithful Word as he has been taught *(suggests the notion of withstanding opposition, and not compromising the Word)*, that he may be able by sound Doctrine *(proper teaching)* both to exhort and to convince the gainsayers. *(The "gainsayers" are those who deny and contradict the Truth of the Cross.)*

FALSE TEACHERS

10 For there are many unruly and vain talkers and deceivers *(refers to those who make their false doctrine sound so right)*, specially they of the Circumcision *(the Judaizers who ignored the Cross, and tried to mix Law with Grace)*:

11 Whose mouths must be stopped *(means to be reduced to silence, or at least to be made ineffective, which the True Message of the Cross can do)*, who subvert whole houses *(refers to the effect of false teaching)*, teaching things which they ought not, for filthy lucre's sake. *(Money is their object, as it is with most false teachers.)*

12 One of themselves, *even* a Prophet of their own, said, The Cretians *are* always liars, evil beasts, slow bellies. *(This presents a striking*

indictment, but one desired by the Holy Spirit.)

13 This witness is true. *(This proclaims not the mere opinion of Paul, but actually the inspired words of the Spirit.)* **Wherefore rebuke them sharply** *(refers to proclaiming the Truth and clearly pointing out the error as well, and doing so in no uncertain terms),* **that they may be sound in the Faith** *(refers to the fact that there is only one Faith, and that is "Jesus Christ and Him Crucified" [I Cor. 2:2]);*

14 **Not giving heed to Jewish fables** *(didn't endear the Apostle to most Jews),* **and commandments of men** *(means they were not given by God),* **that turn from the Truth.** *(This presents the fact that anything that turns men from the Truth of the Cross must be rejected out of hand.)*

15 **Unto the pure all things** *are* **pure** *(is to be understood in its proper context):* **but unto them who are defiled and unbelieving** *is* **nothing pure** *(proclaims those who attempt to find Salvation outside of Faith in the Cross of Christ);* **but even their mind and conscience is defiled.** *(Salvation by Law, as this was, can only defile, it cannot save.)*

16 **They profess that they know God** *(they loudly proclaimed their profession);* **but in works they deny** *Him* *(refers to them trying to earn Salvation by their works, which at the same time denies the "Finished Work of Christ"),* **being abominable, and disobedient, and unto every good work reprobate.** *(This is the manner in which the Holy Spirit labels all who attempt to serve God outside of the Cross of Christ.)*

CHAPTER 2
(A.D. 65)
AGED MEN

BUT **you speak the things which become sound Doctrine** *(the Foundation of the Christian Faith, "Jesus Christ and Him Crucified" [I Cor. 2:2]):*

2 **That the aged men be sober, grave, temperate, sound in Faith, in charity** *(love),* **in patience.** *(At every point, the Christian exceeded by far the so-called high standards the pagan world knew.)*

AGED WOMEN

3 **The aged women likewise, that** *they be* **in behaviour as becomes Holiness** *(refers to the fact that this end should always be in view),* **not false accusers, not given to much wine,**

teachers of good things *(teaching by their consecrated lives);*

YOUNG WOMEN

4 **That they may teach the young women to be sober** *(by their example),* **to love their husbands, to love their children,**

5 *To be* **discreet, chaste, keepers at home, good, obedient to their own husbands, that the Word of God be not blasphemed** *(not mocked).*

YOUNG MEN

6 **Young men likewise exhort to be sober minded** *(exercise self-control).*

7 **In all things shewing yourself a pattern of good works:** **in Doctrine** *showing* **uncorruptness, gravity, sincerity,**

8 **Sound speech, that cannot be condemned** *(refers to that being Preached and taught as being absolutely Scriptural);* **that he who is of the contrary part may be ashamed, having no evil thing to say of you.** *(This concerns evil things, which are true.)*

SERVANTS

9 *Exhort* **servants** *(slaves)* **to be obedient unto their own masters,** *and* **to please** *them* **well in all** *things;* **not answering again** *(don't argue; irrespective of the conduct or attitude of the Master, every task was to be done as unto the Lord; it is the same now for modern Christian employees);*

10 **Not purloining** *(don't steal anything, not even time),* **but showing all good fidelity** *(trustworthiness in all situations);* **that they may adorn the Doctrine of God our Saviour in all things** *(means simply "we ought to practice what we Preach!").*

THE CHRISTIAN LIFE

11 **For the Grace of God that brings Salvation has appeared to all men** *(is available to all on the basis of Faith in Christ and what He did at the Cross),*

12 **Teaching us that, denying ungodliness and worldly lusts** *(tells us that it can be done),* **we should live soberly, Righteously, and Godly, in this present world** *(this can only be done by the Believer making the Cross the Object of his Faith, which gives the Holy Spirit latitude to*

work in our lives, bringing about these Graces);

13 Looking for that Blessed Hope (refers to the Rapture of the Church [I Thess. 4:13-18]), and the glorious appearing of the Great God and our Saviour Jesus Christ (the "Blessed Hope" is the glorious appearing of our Lord);

14 Who gave Himself for us (on the Cross), that He might redeem us from all iniquity (on the Cross, Christ atoned for every sin — past, present, and future, at least for all who will believe [Jn. 3:16]), and purify unto Himself a peculiar people, zealous of good works. (The Sanctified life is strictly a Work of the Spirit, Who works exclusively within the parameters of the Sacrifice of Christ, which must ever be the Object of our Faith.)

15 These things speak, and exhort, and rebuke with all authority. (The idea is that Titus and all other Preachers are to Minister decidedly, which means that everyone knows exactly what is being said.) Let no man despise you (refers to the fact that no man is to tell another man what he can or cannot Preach).

CHAPTER 3
(A.D. 65)
CITIZENSHIP

PUT them in mind to be subject to principalities and powers, to obey Magistrates (refers to Civil Government), to be ready to every good work (the Christian counts it as a privilege to have the opportunity to do good),

2 To speak evil of no man (refers to the employment of the principle of Grace, which excludes all violence of thoughts, language, or action), to be no brawlers (don't be contentious), but gentle (a Fruit of the Spirit [Gal. 5:22-23]), showing all meekness unto all men. (This portrays the inwrought Grace of the soul, which can only be brought about in the life of the Believer by the Holy Spirit. He does these things strictly on the premise of our Faith in Christ and the Cross.)

SINNERS

3 For we ourselves also were sometimes (in time past) foolish (refers to a lack of understanding of spiritual things), disobedient (disobedient to God and His Word), deceived (because of the Fall, unredeemed man sees nothing in its true light), serving divers lusts and pleasures (the lifestyle of the unbeliever), living in malice and envy, hateful, and hating

one another. (Outside of Christ, there is no true love for anyone.)

JUSTIFICATION

4 But after that (refers to the lost condition of the unredeemed) the kindness and love of God our Saviour toward man appeared (presents Christ Himself, and what He did by dying on the Cross to redeem lost humanity),

5 Not by works of righteousness which we have done (presents the utter impossibility of man performing works of Righteousness which will save him), but according to His Mercy He saved us (the initiative of Salvation springs entirely from the Lord, and is carried out by means of the Cross), by the washing of Regeneration (in effect, the Born-Again Believer is regened, which is brought about by a cleansing process, with the Blood having cleansed from all sin, both its power and its guilt [I Jn. 1:7]), and renewing of the Holy Spirit (proclaims the Member of the God-head Who actually carries out the work of Regeneration in the heart and life of the Believing sinner, which He does by exhibited Faith in Christ on the part of the individual);

6 Which He shed on us abundantly (kindness and Love) through Jesus Christ our Saviour (takes us back to the Cross);

7 That being justified by His Grace (we can only be justified by Grace, and not at all by works [Eph. 2:8-9]), we should be made heirs according to the hope of Eternal Life. (This presents the culminating effect of Justification by Faith.)

FINAL CHARGES

8 This is a Faithful saying (refers to the fact that it is trustworthy), and these things I will that you affirm constantly (proclaims in undeniable terminology that the Preacher and Teacher of the Gospel should constantly Preach the Cross), that they which have believed in God might be careful to maintain good works (the greatest "good work" of all is to tell people about Jesus). These things are good and profitable unto men.

9 But avoid foolish questions, and genealogies, and contentions, and strivings about the Law (refers in this case to the Law of Moses, but could refer to any philosophy or religious ramblings — in other words, anything but the Cross); for they are unprofitable and vain.

(Faith in Christ and the Cross alone will bring about profitable results. Everything else is unprofitable.)

10 A man who is an heretick *(refers to someone who has obviously departed from the Word of God)* **after the first and second admonition reject** *(if they will not listen after two warnings about false doctrine, they and their Ministry are to be rejected, which means they are to be avoided; that being the case, there should be no further action outside of praying for the individual);*

11 Knowing that he who is such is subverted *(spiritually turned inside out),* **and sins** *(states that all false doctrine is sin),* **being condemned of himself** *(brings an automatic condemnation).*

12 When I shall send Artemas unto you, or Tychicus *(Paul was thinking of sending either Artemas or Tychicus to relieve Titus at Crete),* **be diligent to come unto me to Nicopolis: for I have determined there to winter.** *(This possibly presents the place where the Epistle to Titus*

was written.)

13 Bring Zenas the lawyer and Apollos on their journey diligently *(evidently, these two were to stop by Crete on their way elsewhere),* **that nothing be wanting unto them.** *(The Apostle is telling Titus to receive an offering for them. As well, there is even a probability that they were the bearers of this Epistle from Paul to Titus.)*

14 And let ours also learn to maintain good works for necessary uses *(proclaims the fact that the Apostle was training Believers to give of their financial resources in order to help take the Gospel to others),* **that they be not unfruitful.** *(To be "fruitful" carries the idea that we are giving our money to that which is winning souls and truly doing a work for God.)*

15 All who are with me salute you. Greet them who love us in the Faith. *(The words "the Faith" always and without exception refer to the Sacrifice of Christ.)* **Grace** *be* **with you all. Amen.**

THE EPISTLE OF PAUL THE APOSTLE TO
PHILEMON

INTRODUCTION

(A.D. 64)

PAUL, a prisoner of Jesus Christ, *(even though in prison in Rome, Paul concludes himself as being a prisoner of Christ, not Nero)*, **and Timothy** *our* **brother** *(the young Apostle was with Paul in Rome at this time)*, **unto Philemon our dearly beloved, and fellowlabourer** *(this person was a man of some standing and wealth, and was a convert of Paul)*,

2 And to *our* beloved Apphia *(said to be the wife of Philemon)*, and Archippus *(believed to be the son of Philemon and Apphia)* our fellowsoldier, and to the Church in your house *(the location of most Churches during that time)*:

3 Grace to you, and Peace, from God our Father and the Lord Jesus Christ. *(This implies that all these Blessings proceed from God the Father, with the Lord Jesus Christ being the means, which refers to the Cross.)*

THANKSGIVING

4 I thank my God, making mention of you always in my prayers *(speaks of Philemon)*,

5 Hearing of your Love and Faith *(concerns the two pillars of Christianity)*, which you have toward the Lord Jesus, and toward all Saints *(refers to the fact that Christ is the center of all things in this man's life)*;

6 That the communication of your Faith may become effectual *(Faith which doesn't bring about the development of the Fruit of the Spirit, with such Grace extended to others, is really not proper Faith)* by the acknowledging of every good thing which is in you in Christ Jesus. *(This proclaims the source of all this, and more particularly that this Source is the Cross of Christ.)*

7 For we have great joy and consolation in your Love *(part of Paul's strength came from hearing encouraging reports of those such as Philemon)*, because the bowels of the Saints are refreshed by you, Brother. *(Philemon was an encouragement to the Saints in that area of Colosse.)*

ONESIMUS

8 Wherefore, though I might be much bold in Christ *(could speak from Apostolic authority, but will not do so)* to enjoin you that which is convenient *(speaking of the release of Onesimus, but he will seek that release in another way)*,

9 Yet for love's sake I rather beseech *you* *(proclaims the manner in which a true Apostle conducts himself, and any Believer for that matter)*, being such an one as Paul the aged *(this was at the close of Paul's first imprisonment in Rome; he must have been about 63 years old at the time)*, and now also a prisoner of Jesus Christ *(proclaims again that which he wore as a badge of honor)*.

10 I beseech you for my son Onesimus *(presents the first time this man's name is mentioned, even though he is the reason for the letter; he was owned by Philemon, and had run away from his master to Rome, a distance of about 1,000 miles; this was a most serious offense!)*, whom I have begotten in my bonds *(after arriving in Rome, this runaway slave had gotten in touch with Paul, and had given his heart to Christ)*:

11 Which in time past was to you unprofitable *(not knowing the Lord, Onesimus didn't provide very good service for Philemon)*, but now profitable to you and to me *(presents that which only Christ can do; He can make one "profitable!")*:

12 Whom I have sent again *(he is coming back home, in effect, giving himself up, which is what he should have done now that he had come to Christ)*: you therefore receive him *(in effect, pleads with Philemon to take back his formerly worthless servant, and assures him that he will not find Onesimus worthless now, but rather helpful!)*, that is, mine own bowels *(is the same as saying, "receive him as me, as my offspring")*:

13 Whom I would have retained with me *(presents a graceful expression of Paul's confidence in Onesimus)*, that in your stead he might have ministered unto me in the bonds of the Gospel *(proclaims the fact that he had been very helpful to Paul, even though there only a short time; conversion to Christ had totally changed the man)*:

14 But without your mind would I do nothing *(refers to the consent of Philemon)*; that your benefit should not be as it were of necessity,

but willingly. *(This refers to the fact that the Apostle desires Philemon not feel he is under some type of constraint. Whatever Philemon does, Paul wants it to be "willingly," and not at all of necessity.)*

15 For perhaps he therefore departed for a season *(proclaims in the original Greek that there was a Divine Providence in the departure of Onesimus, or rather that the Holy Spirit used the occasion to bring the man to Christ; in fact, the Holy Spirit uses many such occasions)*, that you should receive him for ever *(the relationship will now be totally different)*;

16 Not now as a servant *(no more as a slave)*, but above a servant, a Brother beloved *(Paul is asking that Onesimus not be received as a slave; perhaps he will still be a slave insofar as the outward fact goes, but a new spirit is now breathed into the relationship, all because of Christ)*, specially to me, but how much more unto you, both in the flesh, and in the Lord? *("In the flesh, Philemon has the Brother for his slave; in the Lord, Philemon has the slave for his Brother.")*

17 If you count me therefore a partner *(places both Paul and Philemon in the same status, i.e., the same category)*, receive him as myself *(now brings Onesimus up to the level of Paul and Philemon)*.

18 If he has wronged you, or owes *you* ought, put that on my account *(I am asking you to forgive this debt; but if you feel you cannot do so, I will personally pay the debt)*;

19 I Paul have written *it* with my own hand, I will repay *it* *(presents the Apostle's Promise as ironclad; in other words, it is a contract!)*: albeit I do not say to you how you owe unto me even your own self besides. *(Whatever hope of Eternal Life this businessman cherished was to be traced to Paul's Ministry.)*

FELLOWSHIP

20 Yes, Brother, let me have joy of you in the Lord *(refers to the fact that what Paul is asking is not at all for himself, but rather for the Lord)*: refresh my bowels in the Lord. *(The granting of this request will be of the Lord also!)*

21 Having confidence in your obedience I wrote unto you *(expresses Faith that Philemon will do exactly as he has requested)*, knowing that you will also do more than I say *(hints at emancipation for Onesimus)*.

22 But withal prepare me also a lodging *(proclaims the fact that the Apostle felt his release would come very shortly)*: for I trust that through your prayers I shall be given unto you *(he thanks Philemon for praying for him)*.

BENEDICTION

23 There salute thee Epaphras, my fellow-prisoner in Christ Jesus *(a native of Colosse)*;

24 Mark, Aristarchus, Demas, Luke, my fellow-labourers.

25 The Grace of our Lord Jesus Christ *be* with your spirit. Amen.

THE EPISTLE OF PAUL THE APOSTLE TO THE
HEBREWS

CHAPTER 1
(A.D. 64)
JESUS CHRIST

GOD, Who at sundry times and in divers manners *(refers to the many and varied ways)* spoke in time past unto the fathers by the Prophets *(refers to Old Testament Times)*,

2 Has in these last days *(the dispensation of Grace, which is the Church Age)* spoken unto us by *His* Son *(speaks of the Incarnation)*, Whom He has appointed Heir of all things *(through the means of the Cross)*, by Whom also He made the worlds *(proclaims His Deity, as the previous phrase of Him being the "Heir of all things" proclaims His Humanity)*;

3 Who being the brightness of *His* Glory *(the radiance of God's Glory)*, and the express Image of His Person *(the exact reproduction)*, and upholding all things by the Word of His power *(carries the meaning of Jesus not only sustaining the weight of the universe, but also maintaining its coherence and carrying on its development)*, when He had by Himself purged our sins *(which He did at the Cross, dealing with sin regarding its cause, its power, and its guilt)*, sat down on the Right Hand of the Majesty on high *(speaks of the Finished Work of Christ, and that the Sacrifice was accepted by the Father)*;

ANGELS

4 Being made so much better than the Angels *(He was better than the Angels, which refers to the Incarnation, the price paid at Calvary [the reason for the Incarnation], and then His Exaltation as Saviour; as God, Jesus has always been greater than the Angels, but this is speaking of Him here as man)*, as He has by inheritance obtained a more excellent Name than they. *(This refers to what Christ did at the Cross, with the present result being that the inheritance is in His permanent possession.)*

5 For unto which of the Angels said He *(God the Father)* at any time, You are My Son *(Son of God)*, this day have I begotten You? *(This speaks of the Incarnation. God never said such of Angels, only of His Son [Ps. 2:7].)* And again, I will be to Him a Father, and He shall be to Me a Son? *(When uttered, referred to the future tense, but now is past tense. All had to do with Redemption, and all for you and me.)*

6 And again, when He *(God the Father)* brought in the Firstbegotten into the world *(refers to Jesus being born of the Virgin Mary)*, He said, And let all the Angels of God worship Him. *(The idea is only Deity can be worshiped. Jesus is God!)*

7 And of the Angels He said, Who makes His Angels spirits *(the emphasis upon the variableness of the Angelic nature)*, and His Ministers a flame of fire. *(This does not speak of Preachers, as some have suggested, but continues to address itself to Angels.)*

8 But unto the Son *He said*, Your Throne, O God, *is* for ever and ever *(Thrones typify dominion, which in this case can only be occupied by Deity)*: a sceptre of Righteousness *is* the sceptre of Your Kingdom *(totally unlike any other Kingdom that has ever existed, and was made possible by the Cross)*.

9 You have loved Righteousness, and hated iniquity *(proclaims the True Man, Christ Jesus)*; therefore God, *even* Your God, has anointed You with the oil of gladness above Your fellows *(refers to the Holy Spirit)*.

10 And, You, Lord, in the beginning have laid the foundation of the earth *(proclaims Jesus the Messiah as the Creator as well!)*; and the Heavens are the Works of Your Hands *(presents the fact that only Deity could do such a thing)*:

11 They shall perish *(means to wax old as a garment)*; but You remain *(Christ is exalted because of the Cross, and will remain thus forever)*; and they all shall wax old as does a garment *(proclaims the fact that there is going to have to be a change regarding the Creation)*;

12 And as a vesture shall You fold them up, and they shall be changed *(changed from one condition to another)*: but You are the same, and Your years shall not fail *(refers to the superiority of the Creator over the Creation)*.

13 But to which of the Angels said He *(God the Father)* at any time, Sit on My Right Hand *(Angels stand before God; it is a mark of superior dignity that the Son sits)*, until I make Your

enemies Your footstool? *(This refers to God rendering all Christ's enemies utterly powerless, which is carried out by the Cross.)*

14 Are they not all Ministering spirits *(the function of Angels)*, sent forth to Minister for them Who shall be heirs of Salvation? *(This proclaims that they attend only those who have made Christ their Saviour.)*

CHAPTER 2
(A.D. 64)
COVENANT

THEREFORE we ought to give the more earnest heed to the things which we have heard *(actually refers to the New Testament Message of the Cross)*, lest at any time we should let *them* slip. *(In the Greek Text, it carries the idea of a ring slipping from a finger. Regrettably, the Church presently has let the Message of the Cross slip and, as a result, the Church hardly knows where it's been, where it is, or where it's going.)*

2 For if the word spoken by Angels was stedfast *(actually refers to the Law of Moses, which had many Angels in attendance)*, and every transgression and disobedience received a just recompence of reward *(sin is either addressed at the Cross, or else it is addressed in Judgment; so, each person has a choice)*;

3 How shall we escape, if we neglect so great Salvation *(if we neglect the Cross, we have destroyed ourselves)*; which at the first began to be spoken by the Lord *(announced by Christ when He said, "repent: for the Kingdom of Heaven is at hand" [Mat. 4:17])*, and was confirmed unto us by them who heard *Him (confirmed by healings and miracles which were witnessed by the original Twelve, plus untold numbers of others)*;

4 God also bearing *them* witness *(presents the highest evidence of all, actually that which is absolutely indisputable)*, both with signs and wonders, and with divers miracles *(which began with Christ, and continued on through His Apostles)*, and Gifts of the Holy Spirit *(has to do with those listed in I Cor. 12:8-10)*, according to His Own Will? *(These things were the Will of God then, and are the Will of God now!)*

REDEMPTION

5 For unto the Angels has He not put in subjection the world to come, whereof we speak. *(The Lord hasn't given the Angels dominion and*

rulership as He has Christ.)*

6 But one in a certain place testified, saying *(Ps. 8:4-6)*, What is man, that You are mindful of him? *(This delves into the reason God has given man so much notice.)* or the son of man, that You visit him? *(This refers to looking upon in order to help or benefit. This clearly indicates the "son of man" spoken of here is the human race and not Christ.)*

7 You made him a little lower than the Angels *(should have been translated, "You made him a little lower than the Godhead"; the Hebrew word translated "Angels" is "Elohim" which means "God," and should have been translated accordingly)*; You crowned him with glory and honour *(proclaims that which was never said of Angels)*, and did set him over the works of Your hands *(some of that dominion is retained despite the Fall; however, as would be obvious, much has been lost; but to be sure, it has all been regained in Christ, and will ultimately be realized in Christ)*:

8 You have put all things in subjection under his feet. *(This speaks of Adam before the Fall, but more particularly it speaks of Christ and what He did at the Cross on our behalf.)* For in that He *(God)* put all in subjection under him *(man)*, He *(God)* left nothing *that is* not put under him. *(Once again speaks of the original Adam, but more than all speaks of the "Last Adam," the Lord Jesus Christ.)* But now we see not yet all things put under him. *(Due to the Fall, we do not now see what was originally intended for man, but through Christ it will ultimately be seen.)*

9 But we see Jesus, Who was made a little lower than the Angels *(the Incarnation)* for the suffering of death *(unequivocally proclaims the fact that Jesus came to this world for one specific purpose — to die upon a Cross, which was planned even before the foundation of the world [I Pet. 1:18-20])*, crowned with glory and honour *(the mission was accomplished, and now Christ is exalted)*; that He by the Grace of God should taste death for every man. *(This proclaims the fact that He needed the Grace of God to accomplish this task, because He was a man, "the Man, Christ Jesus.")*

10 For it became Him *(refers to God's Way, as it concerns the Redemption of mankind)*, for Whom *are* all things *(God is the final reason for all things)*, and by Whom *are* all things *(through Whose agency)*, in bringing many sons unto Glory *(speaks of the Divine Purpose)*, to make the Captain of their Salvation perfect

through sufferings. *(This carries the idea that Christ had to suffer the Cross in order to bring about Redemption for humanity.)*

11 For both He Who Sanctifies and they who are Sanctified *are* all of One *(of Christ)*: for which cause He is not ashamed to call them Brethren *(refers to the fact that Jesus became one of us, but only in the sense of humanity, not in the sense of sin)*,

12 Saying, I will declare Your Name unto My Brethren *([Ps. 22:22] meaning that Christ will declare the Name of God to all the Brethren, in effect, owning them)*, in the midst of the Church will I sing praise unto You. *(Christ will praise God because of this great Victory, which has brought many sons into the Kingdom, all made possible by the Cross.)*

13 And again *(II Sam. 22:3)*, I will put My trust in Him. *(Christ puts His Trust totally in God.)* And again *(Isa. 8:18)*, Behold I and the Children which God has given Me. *(The Cross makes it possible for us to become a Child of God.)*

14 Forasmuch then as the children are partakers of flesh and blood *(refers to the fact that this Creation has a human, not Angelic, nature)*, He *(Jesus)* also Himself likewise took part of the same *(the Incarnation, God becoming man)*; that through death *(the Cross)* He *(Jesus)* might destroy him *(Satan)* who had the power of death, that is, the Devil *(the wages of sin is death, which speaks of separation from God; Jesus atoned for all sin at the Cross, thereby removing the cause of spiritual death, at least for all who will believe [Jn. 3:16])*;

15 And deliver them *(speaks of mankind held in captivity by Satan)* who through fear of death were all their lifetime subject to bondage. *(It has been well said that the two terrors from which none but Christ can deliver men are guilt of sin and fear of death. The latter is the offspring of the former.)*

16 For verily He took not on *Him the nature of* Angels *(Christ did not come to be the Saviour of fallen Angels; they are of another creation)*; but He took on *Him* the seed of Abraham. *(This refers to His Humanity, which He became and was the manner in which Redemption would be brought about.)*

17 Wherefore in all things it behoved Him to be made like unto *His* Brethren *(refers to our Lord laying hold of the human race for the purpose of saving those who would accept Salvation by Faith)*, that He might be a merciful and faithful High Priest in things *pertaining* to God *(as our High Priest, He is our Representative*

to God, which He could be by becoming a Man and going to the Cross as well, which He did)*, to make reconciliation for the sins of the people *(to make an atoning Sacrifice in order to regain the favor and goodwill of God on behalf of the human race)*.

18 For in that He Himself has suffered being tempted *(in His Incarnation as the last Adam, our Lord was put to the test, and was also solicited to do evil [Mat. 4:1-11])*, He is able to succour them who are tempted. *(The Cross alone is the answer to temptation and sin. We overcome temptation by placing our Faith strictly in Christ and the Cross, which is the only way it can be overcome, thus giving the Holy Spirit latitude to strengthen us, as He always stands ready to do [Rom. 8:2, 11].)*

CHAPTER 3
(A.D. 64)
MOSES

WHEREFORE, Holy Brethren, partakers of the Heavenly Calling *(pertains to all Believers)*, consider the Apostle *(presents the only time Christ is referred to as an "Apostle")* and High Priest of our profession, Christ Jesus *(among the Jews, the High Priest was also considered to be the Apostle of God; consequently, the two Apostles are now compared, the High Priest of Israel and Christ Jesus)*;

2 Who was faithful to Him Who appointed Him *(should read, "Christ was faithful to God Who appointed Him as Apostle and High Priest")*, as also Moses *was faithful* in all his house. *(This presents the Holy Spirit through Paul handling Moses delicately; however, there are vast differences in the two.)*

3 For this *Man (Christ Jesus)* was counted worthy of more glory than Moses *(finds Paul proclaiming the humanity of Christ, by which measurement he compares Moses)*, inasmuch as He *(God)* Who has built the house has more honour than the house. *(This proclaims the fact that the Lord built the House of Israel.)*

4 For every house is built by some *man (presents the fact that even though men are the instruments used by God, they are, in fact, only instruments)*; but He Who built all things *is* God. *(Christ, although humbling Himself to the likeness of sinful flesh, is still the Builder of all things, which means He is far greater than Moses [Jn. 1:1-3].)*

5 And Moses verily *was* faithful in all his house, as a servant *(proclaims the position of*

the great Lawgiver as it relates to God), **for a testimony of those things which were to be spoken after** (pertained to Moses and the entirety of the Law with all its ceremonies, etc., all pointing to Christ and the Cross, Who was to come);

6 But Christ as a Son over His Own house (presents a clear distinction made between the Old Testament House of God and the New Testament House); **Whose house are we** (refers to the Church), **if we hold fast the confidence and the rejoicing of the hope firm unto the end** (if we keep our confidence in Christ and the Cross).

ISRAEL

7 Wherefore (as the Holy Spirit says (Ps. 95:7-11), **Today if you will hear His Voice** (presents words which were originally a warning to Israel not to provoke God, lest they be excluded from the "rest" He had promised them; this same warning is now given to Christians),

8 Harden not your hearts (as Israel hardened their hearts against God in the wilderness, it is likewise possible for modern Christians to do the same), **as in the provocation** (Israel provoked God), **in the day of temptation in the wilderness** (the Lord didn't tempt Israel, they tempted Him!):

9 When your fathers tempted Me (they tempted God through unbelief and rebellion), **proved Me** (registered unbelief toward God), **and saw My works forty years.** (The proof was all around them regarding the miracle-working Power of God that was exhibited daily, even for forty years, but they still wouldn't believe.)

10 Wherefore I was grieved with that generation (and because of their unbelief), **and said, They do always err in** their **heart** (proclaims the seat of obedience or disobedience); **and they have not known My ways.** (They could have known, but had no desire to know.)

11 So I swore in My wrath (is figurative, and denotes a determined purpose), **They shall not enter into My rest.)** (This refers here to a particular "rest," which pertained to the land of Canaan, but was undoubtedly regarded as emblematic of the "rest" afforded by Salvation.)

12 Take heed, Brethren (proclaims Paul warning Believers by the examples of Israel's failures in the wilderness), **lest there be in any of you an evil heart of unbelief** (the Greek order of words is, "a heart evil with reference to unbelief"), **in departing from the Living God.** (As

stated, the problem is unbelief, and in modern terminology it refers to unbelief in Christ and the Cross.)

13 But exhort one another daily (proclaims a constant frequency, which means the Preacher should preach the Cross, and do so constantly), **while it is called Today** (it must be done today; in other words, start now talking and speaking about the Cross, which is the only answer [I Cor. 1:17; Gal. 6:14]); **lest any of you be hardened through the deceitfulness of sin.** (This actually says, "the deceitfulness of the sin," which refers to a rejection of the Sacrifice of Christ.)

14 For we are made partakers of Christ (refers to Rom. 6:3-5), **if we hold the beginning of our confidence stedfast unto the end** (if our confidence remains steadfast in Christ and the Cross);

15 While it is said, Today if you will hear His Voice, harden not your hearts, as in the provocation (Vss. 7-8).

16 For some, when they had heard, did provoke (should have been translated, "For who when they had heard did provoke"; all did except Joshua and Caleb [Num. 14:6-9]): **howbeit not all who came out of Egypt by Moses.** (This should have been translated, "Was it not all who came out of Egypt through Moses?")

17 But with whom was He grieved forty years? (This refers to God's wrath continuing simply because their unbelief continued.) **was it not with them who had sinned, whose carcases fell in the wilderness?** (Unbelief caused the deaths of approximately two million people.)

18 And to whom swore He that they should not enter into His rest, but to them who believed not? (They lost everything because of unbelief, and the modern Church is doing the same, which is the very reason that Paul wrote this Epistle.)

19 So we see that they could not enter in because of unbelief (and if the modern Believer registers unbelief toward Christ and the Cross, the results will be the same as it was with Israel of Old).

CHAPTER 4
(A.D. 64)

UNBELIEF

LET us (modern Believers) **therefore fear** (refers to the fact that Salvation can be lost if the Believer ceases to believe), **lest, a Promise being left** us **of entering into His rest** (the Promise of Salvation), **any of you should**

seem to come short of it. *(This proves it is possible for such to be done, which means the loss of the soul.)*

2 For unto us was the Gospel Preached, as well as unto them *(there is only one Gospel, and that is "Jesus Christ and Him Crucified")*: but the Word preached did not profit them *(if the Cross is abandoned as the Object of Faith, Christ will profit no one anything [Gal. 5:2])*, not being mixed with faith in them who heard it. *(The Israelites had Faith, but not in the right object. It must be Faith in Christ and the Cross, or it's not valid Faith.)*

3 For we which have believed do enter into rest *(proclaims unequivocally that Faith is the key, but let it be understood that it's Faith in Christ and the Cross)*, as He said, As I have sworn in My wrath, if they shall enter into My rest *(the condition is Faith)*: although the works were finished from the foundation of the world. *(This refers to this great Plan of Salvation through Christ and the Cross having been formulated even before the world was created [I Pet. 1:18-20].)*

4 For He *(God)* spoke in a certain place of the seventh *day* on this wise *(Gen. 2:3)*, And God did rest the seventh day from all His Works. *(God ceased from the Work of Creation simply because the Creation was finished.)*

5 And in this *place* again *(Ps. 95:7-11)*, If they shall enter into My rest *(conditions are to be met)*.

6 Seeing therefore it remains that some must enter therein *(speaks of the New Covenant and the Church)*, and they to whom it was first preached entered not in because of unbelief *(proclaims from Verse 2 that the Israelites of Old had the same Gospel preached unto them as we do, but to no avail)*:

7 Again, He *(God)* limited a certain day *(proclaims in no uncertain terms that even though the Call of God is unlimited, the opportunity to accept that Call is definitely limited)*, saying in David, Today, after so long a time *(the Holy Spirit said "today" then, and He is continuing to say "today" at present, referring to the fact that tomorrow may be too late)*; as it is said, Today if you will hear His Voice, harden not your hearts *(once again refers to unbelief)*.

8 For if Jesus *(should have been translated, "Joshua")* had given them Rest *(refers to the fact that even though Joshua was able to lead Israel into the land of Canaan by the Power of the Holy Spirit, this was only a symbol of the True Rest which was to come, namely the Lord Jesus Christ)*, then would He *(God)* not afterward have spoken of another day *(meaning the Law could not bring about what was desired, but definitely did point to that which was to come, namely the Lord Jesus Christ)*.

9 There remains *(what the Law couldn't do, Christ would do)* therefore a Rest to the People of God. *(This is found only in Christ and through what He did at the Cross, to which everything in the Old Testament pointed.)*

10 For he who is entered into His *(God's)* Rest *(due to what Christ did at the Cross, anyone can enter into this "Rest")*, he also has ceased from his own works *(we enter in by Faith, which refers to Faith in Christ and what He did at the Cross)*, as God *did* from His. *(God rested on the seventh day when Creation was finished. And we can Rest in Christ because the Plan of Redemption is finished, of which God's Rest was a type.)*

11 Let us labour therefore to enter into that Rest *(could be translated, "let us hasten therefore to enter into that Rest")*, lest any man fall after the same example of unbelief. *(This tells us that the root cause of the "fall" of any Believer is unbelief, and it refers to unbelief in the Cross, which was the True Mission of Christ.)*

12 For the word of God *is* quick *(alive)*, and powerful *(active, energizing)*, and sharper than any two-edged sword *(refers to the ability of the Word of God to "probe")*, piercing even to the dividing asunder of soul and spirit, and of the joints and marrow *(doesn't mean the dividing asunder of soul from spirit or joints from marrow, but rather that the Word of God pierces the soul and the spirit, adequately proclaiming what man ought to be and can only be in Christ; as well, the Word of God portrays to us the Holy Spirit and His Power, and proclaims the fact that He Alone can "quicken our mortal bodies" [Rom. 8:11], which refers to giving us power to yield this physical body to that which is Righteous [Rom. 6:12-13])*, and *is* a discerner of the thoughts and intents of the heart *(carries the idea of "sifting out and analyzing evidence")*.

13 Neither is there any creature that is not manifest in His sight *(refers to God as the Creator of all things)*: but all things *are* naked and opened unto the eyes of Him with Whom we have to do *(to Whom we must give account)*.

HIGH PRIEST

14 Seeing then that we have a Great High Priest *(Christ acts on our behalf to God)*, Who

is passed into the Heavens *(has to do with a legal process)*, **Jesus the Son of God** *(presents the fact that Jesus is not only man, but is God as well)*, **let us hold fast** *our* **profession.** *(Let us hold fast to Christ and the Cross, which was necessary for our Lord to be our High Priest.)*

15 For we have not an High Priest which cannot be touched with the feeling of our infirmities *(being Very Man as well as Very God, He can do such)*; **but was in all points tempted like as** *we are,* *yet* **without sin** *(His temptation, and ours as well, was to leave the prescribed Will of God, which is the Word of God; but He never did, not even one time.)*

16 Let us therefore come boldly unto the Throne of Grace *(presents the Seat of Divine Power, and yet the Source of boundless Grace)*, **that we may obtain Mercy** *(presents that which we want first)*, **and find Grace to help in time of need** *(refers to the Goodness of God extended to all who come, and during any "time of need"; all made possible by the Cross).*

CHAPTER 5
(A.D. 64)

MELCHISEDEC

FOR **every High Priest taken from among men is ordained for men in things** *per-**taining*** **to God** *("from among men" pertains to the frailty of men)*, **that he may offer both Gifts and Sacrifices for sins** *(the "Gifts" referred to "Thank-Offerings, while the "Sacrifices" referred to certain animals being offered, all types of Christ)*:

2 Who can have compassion on the ignorant *(refers to having feelings for those on whose behalf he officiates)*, **and on them who are out of the way** *(refers to those who have sinned, and who know they have sinned)*; **for that He Himself also is compassed with infirmity.** *(This refers to the condition of all men, even the High Priest in the old Judaistic economy.)*

3 And by reason hereof he ought *(refers to the very purpose of his office, which is to offer Sacrifice for sins)*, **as for the people** *(proclaims the High Priest serving as a Mediator)*, **so also for himself, to offer for sins.** *(This refers to the fact that he was a sinful man as well, and had to offer a Sacrifice even for himself, which would make Atonement that would provide reconciliation with God.)*

4 And no man takes this honour unto himself, but he who is called of God, as *was* **Aaron.** *(Under the Old Law, the only ones who could offer Sacrifices were Priests, who had to be sons of Aaron, and whose order was ordained by God and not man.)*

5 So also Christ Glorified not Himself to be made an High Priest *(proclaims the fact that this was no personal ambition on the Messiah's part that resulted in Him becoming a High Priest, but rather the fact that God called Him to that position)*; **but He who said unto Him, You are My Son, today have I begotten You.** *(The Priesthood of Christ was planned by God from the very beginning, which meant the Incarnation was absolutely necessary.)*

6 As He said also in another *place* *(Ps. 110:4)*, **You** *are* **a Priest forever after the order of Melchisedec.** *(This is the distinguishing characteristic of this order of Priesthood, and proclaims it as an Eternal One.)*

7 Who in the days of His flesh *(proclaims the Incarnation of Christ)*, **when He had offered up prayers and supplications with strong crying and tears unto Him** *(presents the prayer-life of the Master)* **Who was able to save Him from death** *(presents the prayer for Resurrection)*, **and was heard** *(proclaims the fact that God heard and answered His Prayer)* **in that He feared** *(the picture in the word "feared" is that of a cautious taking hold of, and a careful and respectful handling; it is Christ taking into account all things, not only His Own desire, but the Will of the Father)*;

8 Though He were a Son *(stresses Deity, but at the same time the role of Christ as "Son of Man")*, **yet learned He obedience** *(doesn't mean He had to learn to obey, for that would mean He had sinned; it means He actively sought out the path of obedience, and then unfailingly walked therein)* **by the things which He suffered** *(concerned the entire course of His Life, but more so the Cross)*;

9 And being made perfect *(refers to being brought to the goal fixed by God, which had to be if He was to be the Perfect Sacrifice)*, **He became the Author of Eternal Salvation** *(proclaims a perfect Salvation, because He was and is the Perfect Redeemer, because He was the Perfect Sacrifice)* **unto all them who obey Him** *(we obey Him by exhibiting Faith in the Cross, which then gives the Holy Spirit latitude to work; this Truth was given to Paul [Rom. 6:3-5, 11, 14; Gal. 1:11-12])*;

10 Called of God an High Priest *(the Title is conferred on Him by God the Father)* **after the order of Melchisedec.** *(Christ was not to be a great High Priest merely for the Jews, but for*

the Gentiles as well; in order for this to be, His Priesthood would have to rest in something other than the Levitical Order; being after the Order of Melchisedec satisfied both demands, because Melchisedec preceded Israel as a people [Gen. 14:18-20; Ps. 110:4].)

FAITH

11 Of Whom we have many things to say (refers to Christ), **and hard to be uttered** (his difficulty was in adapting the interpretation to the capacity of his readers), **seeing you are dull of hearing.** (These Jewish Christians were slow and sluggish regarding their understanding of the teaching of New Testament Truth. This made it difficult to teach them.)

12 For when for the time you ought to be teachers (refers to the fact that they had been saved long enough to be mature in the Word by now), **you have need that one teach you again which** be **the first principles of the Oracles of God** (pertains to the Old Testament and what it really meant, instead of the way it was being erroneously taken by these Christian Jews); **and are become such as have need of milk, and not of strong meat** (refers to their lack of maturity).

13 For every one who uses milk (doesn't refer to one who has just been saved, but rather to those who have been saved for quite some time, and should have advanced in the Word of the Lord) **is unskilful in the Word of Righteousness** (refers to the benefits of the Cross, from which Righteousness is derived): **for he is a babe.** (This refers to the individual who does not understand or know all the benefits of what Jesus did at the Cross.)

14 But strong meat belongs to them who are of full age (refers to those mature in the Lord), **even** those who by reason of use have **their senses exercised to discern both good and evil.** (Such a person is walking after the Spirit. This refers to placing one's Faith in the Cross and not after the flesh, which refers to depending on other things [Rom. 8:1-2, 11].)

CHAPTER 6
(A.D. 64)
APOSTASY

THEREFORE leaving the Principles of the Doctrine of Christ (speaks of the "first principles," which refers to the Old Testament; Christ is the Centerpiece of the entirety of the Bible), **let us go on unto perfection** (speaks of

the New Testament Sacrifice, the Lord Jesus, and the Testament He inaugurated with His Work on the Cross); **not laying again the Foundation of Repentance from dead works** (refers to these Jewish Christians going back to the Old Sacrificial System, etc.), **and of Faith toward God** (refers to Faith toward God in the realm of the Old Testament Way, which God will not accept now inasmuch as Jesus has fulfilled the Old Testament Law),

2 Of the Doctrine of Baptisms (should have translated, "the Doctrine of Washings"; this concerned the many "washings" contained in the Old Testament Sacrificial System), **and of laying on of hands** (goes back to the Levitical Offerings of the Old Testament; when the person brought the animal for Sacrifice, he had to lay his hands on the head of the innocent victim, confessing his sins, thereby transferring them to the innocent animal which would be slain [Lev. 16:21]), **and of Resurrection of the dead** (refers to Resurrection as taught in the Old Testament; there, this Doctrine was very incomplete, even as all Doctrine in the Old Testament was incomplete; the true meaning could not be given until after the Cross and the Resurrection of Christ, which the Lord gave to Paul [I Cor., Chpt. 15]), **and of Eternal Judgment.** (In the Old Testament, the Lord was looked at more so as a Judge than anything else. Since the Cross, He is looked at more as the Saviour.)

3 And this will we do (in other words, if we don't do this [refers to going on to the perfection of Christ], the results will be disastrous), **if God permit.** (This refers to the fact that all dependence must be in Christ and the Cross. God will not allow any other type of Faith.)

4 For it is **impossible for those who were once enlightened** (refers to those who have accepted the Light of the Gospel, which means accepting Christ and His great Sacrifice), **and have tasted of the Heavenly Gift** (pertains to Christ and what He did at the Cross), **and were made partakers of the Holy Spirit** (which takes place when a person comes to Christ),

5 And have tasted the good Word of God (is not language that is used of an impenitent sinner, as some claim; the unsaved have no relish whatsoever for the Truth of God, and see no beauty in it), **and the powers of the world to come** (refers to the Work of the Holy Spirit within hearts and lives, which the unsaved cannot have or know),

6 If they shall fall away (should have been translated, "and having fallen away"), **to renew**

them again unto Repentance *("again" states they had once repented, but have now turned their backs on Christ)*; **seeing they crucify to themselves the Son of God afresh** *(means they no longer believe what Christ did at the Cross, actually concluding Him to be an imposter; the only way any person can truly repent is to place his Faith in Christ and the Cross; if that is denied, there is no Repentance)*, **and put** *Him* **to an open shame** *(means to hold Christ up to public ridicule; Paul wrote this Epistle because some Christian Jews were going back into Judaism, or seriously contemplating doing so).*

7 For the earth which drinks in the rain that comes oft upon it *(presents the Apostle using natural things to represent spiritual realities, which is common throughout Scripture)*, **and brings forth herbs** *(presents the natural result of ground that is properly cultivated and receives rain; there will be a harvest)* **meet for them by whom it is dressed** *(received by individuals who do the cultivating of the land, etc.)*, **receives Blessing from God** *(presents the inevitable result of proper Faith)*:

8 But that which bears thorns and briers *is* **rejected** *(this speaks of Believers who have turned their backs on Christ and the Cross, and now bring forth no proper fruit, but rather "thorns and briars")*, **and** *is* **nigh unto cursing** *(refers to judgment)*; **whose end** *is* **to be burned.** *(This refers to the simple fact that if a person who was once a Believer remains in that state, he will lose his soul.)*

9 But, Beloved *(presents the fact that these Christian Jews were not only the object of God's love, but also of Paul's care and concern)*, **we are persuaded better things of you** *(he is speaking specifically to those who were seriously contemplating turning their backs on Christ)*, **and things that accompany Salvation** *(the Blessings which will come if the Believer properly anchors his Faith in Christ and the Cross)*, **though we thus speak.** *(The Apostle is not speaking from guesswork, but from many years of experience.)*

10 For God *is* **not unrighteous to forget your work and labour of love** *(presents a glorious and wonderful Promise)*, **which you have showed toward His Name** *(reflects that everything must be done in His Name)*, **in that you have Ministered to the Saints, and do Minister.** *(The Apostle is telling these Christian Jews to not turn their backs on what they have previously done.)*

11 And we desire that every one of you do show the same diligence to the full assurance of hope unto the end *(don't stop now!)*:

12 That you be not slothful *(means to be sluggish and lazy toward the things of the Lord)*, **but followers of them who through faith and patience inherit the Promises** *(refers to the Faith worthies of the Old Testament).*

GOD'S PROMISE

13 For when God made Promise to Abraham *(presents the Patriarch as the most illustrious example of those who "inherit the Promises" [Jn. 8:58])*, **because He** *(God)* **could swear by no greater** *(refers to the solemnity and power of this Promise)*, **He swore by Himself** *(a guarantee with resources of Heaven behind it that the Promise will be kept)*,

14 Saying, Surely blessing I will bless you *(refers to "Justification by Faith," and is taken from Gen. 22:17)*, **and multiplying I will multiply you.** *(This refers to his seed becoming a nation, and more importantly, every Believer being a "Child of Promise" [Gal. 4:28].)*

15 And so, after he had patiently endured *(there's always a distance between the Promise and the Possession, and that distance is never uneventful)*, **he obtained the Promise.** *(The immediate meaning was the birth of Isaac. However, the eternal meaning was Justification by Faith, which would come about from Isaac's seed, Who is Christ [Gal. 3:16].)*

16 For men verily swear by the greater *(men never swear by one who is inferior to themselves)*: **and an oath for confirmation** *is* **to them an end of all strife.** *(In our modern terminology, this means a contract has been agreed upon and signed by all parties, which ends all strife.)*

17 Wherein God, willing more abundantly to show unto the heirs of Promise *(refers to the Lord working in accordance with this universal custom)* **the immutability** *(refers to the fact that God will not change His Position as to His Promise)* **of His counsel, confirmed** *it* **by an oath** *(refers to the guarantee of the Pledge or Promise)*:

18 That by two immutable things *(they are the Promise to Abraham of the coming Redeemer, and the Oath given as it regards Christ being a Priest forever after the Order of Melchisedec)*, **in which** *it was* **impossible for God to lie** *(refers to the moral impossibility of such)*, **we might have a strong consolation** *(refers to assurance)*, **who have fled for refuge to lay hold upon the hope set before us** *(carries the idea*

of the sinner fleeing to one of the Cities of Refuge in Israel; in effect, he was fleeing to the High Priest who has offered Atonement for him and his sin [Deut. 4:42]; using that as a type, we are to flee as well to our High Priest, the Lord Jesus Christ):

19 Which *hope* we have as an anchor of the soul, both sure and stedfast (*presents the Apostle changing the illusion from safety in the Cities of Refuge to a ship reaching harbor after a tempestuous voyage, knowing that her anchor is sure and steadfast*), and which enters into that within the Veil (*refers to the Holy of Holies, which Jesus has entered on our behalf*);

20 Whither the Forerunner is for us entered, *even* Jesus (*presents the imagery of the Great Day of Atonement, when the High Priest entered the most Holy Place on behalf of the people; all of that was a Type of Christ, Who has entered the Holiest for us*), made an High Priest forever after the order of Melchisedec. (*This presents Christ as not in the line of Aaron, but another Order altogether. The old Levitical Order had an ending. This Order has no ending. Christ is an Eternal High Priest.*)

CHAPTER 7
(A.D. 64)
MELCHISEDEC

FOR this Melchisedec, King of Salem (*an ancient name for Jerusalem [Ps. 76:2; 122:3]*), Priest of the Most High God (*tells us what He was, but gives us almost no information after that [Gen. 14:18]*), who met Abraham returning from the slaughter of the kings (*Gen. 14:14-15*), and blessed him (*presents Melchisedec in a superior spiritual position*);

2 To whom also Abraham gave a tenth part of all (*the first mention of Tithes in the Bible; this means that if Abraham paid Tithe to Melchisedec, his natural and spiritual seed, which includes every Believer, should continue to pay Tithes to this Priesthood [namely Christ, i.e., "His Work"], since it has now replaced the Aaronic Priesthood*); first being by interpretation King of Righteousness (*Melchisedec was a Type, and, thereby, meant to portray the True "King of Righteousness," the Lord Jesus Christ*), and after that also King of Salem, which is, King of Peace (*Jesus is also the "Prince of Peace," once again of which Melchisedec was a Type [Isa. 9:6]*);

3 Without father, without mother (*only means there was no record made of the name of his father, his mother, or any of his posterity*),

without descent, having neither beginning of days, nor end of life (*means the Holy Spirit intended Melchisedec to be without genealogy, in order that he may serve as the Type*); but made like unto the Son of God (*actually says, "to be likened to the Son of God"*); abideth a Priest continually. (*This refers to Christ of Whom Melchisedec was a Type.*)

4 Now consider how great this man *was* (*the Text plainly tells us here that Melchisedec was a man, not an Angel, etc., as taught by some*), unto whom even the Patriarch Abraham gave the tenth of the spoils. (*By use of the word "Patriarch" regarding Abraham, we know this speaks of Abraham's position as "Father of the Faithful." As well, we are told here how the standard is set as it regards the financing of the Work of God on Earth.*)

5 And verily they who are of the sons of Levi (*proclaims the Apostle now showing the difference between Law and Grace, and that the former is vastly inferior to the latter*), who receive the Office of the Priesthood (*specifying those of the Tribe of Levi who were Priests; all were not! only the sons of Aaron were*), have a commandment to take Tithes of the people according to the Law, that is, of their Brethren (*refers to the fact that the people were to pay Tithes to the Priesthood under the old Mosaic economy*), though they come out of the loins of Abraham (*the Jews were fond of boasting that they had Abraham as their father, meaning they were his descendants; so, using him as an example, Paul proves that the Aaronic system was much inferior to the Order of Melchisedec, or else Abraham would not have paid Tithes to this man*):

6 But he (*Melchisedec*) whose descent is not counted from them (*from Israel*) received Tithes of Abraham, and blessed him who had the Promises. (*This proclaims the fact that Melchisedec blessed Abraham, despite the fact that it was Abraham to whom the great Promises of God had been given. The only way one could be greater than Abraham is that he would be a Type of Christ, which Melchisedec was.*)

7 And without all contradiction (*means that what he is saying cannot be contradicted*) the less (*Abraham*) is blessed of the better (*Melchisedec, who was a Type of Christ; this has Paul saying that Christ is better than any other system, and is the only One Who can properly Bless*).

8 And here men who die receive Tithes (*refers to the Levitical Priesthood, which, in*

fact, was still being carried on at the time Paul wrote these words); **but there he** *receives them* (refers back to the Passage in Genesis where Melchisedec is recorded as having received Tithes), **of whom it is witnessed that he lives.** (This refers to the Eternal Priesthood of Christ, of which Melchisedec was the Type.)

9 And as I may so say, Levi also, who receives Tithes (because Tithes were paid to Levi, i.e., "the Priestly Order," in no way means this was the superior Order), **paid Tithes in Abraham.** (This struck a telling blow in Paul's argument regarding the superiority of the Priestly Order of Melchisedec. If Abraham paid Tithes to Melchisedec [which he was instructed by the Lord to do], and Abraham is the father of the Jewish people [meaning Levi was in his loins], then Levi also paid Tithes to Melchisedec. This placed the whole of the Jewish system as second to that of Christ.)

10 For he (Levi) **was yet in the loins of his father** (Abraham), **when Melchisedec met him.** (This makes the New Covenant better than the Old, which is the argument of the Book of Hebrews.)

CHRIST'S PRIESTHOOD

11 If therefore perfection were by the Levitical Priesthood (in effect, says this was not the case), **(for under it the people received the Law,)** (This proclaims the fact that if the Levitical Priesthood [which was a part of the Law] was changed, which it was, then the Law had to be changed also.) **what further need** *was there* **that another Priest should rise after the Order of Melchisedec** (since the Levitical Priesthood brought nothing to completion, not merely another Priest was needed, but another Priest of a different kind altogether), **and not be called after the Order of Aaron?** (This presents the fact that the Order of Aaron must give way to the Order of Melchisedec, a better Priesthood, which it was always meant to do.)

12 For the Priesthood being changed (refers to the Priestly Order of Aaron now being abrogated to make way for the original Priesthood that preceded it, which, in effect, had predicted this very thing), **there is made of necessity a change also of the Law.** (The connection between the Priesthood and the Law means a change in one involves a change in the other.)

13 For He (Christ) **of Whom these things are spoken pertains to another Tribe** (Christ was not of the Tribe of Levi, from which all Levitical

Priests had to come, but rather was of the Tribe of Judah), **of which no man gave attendance at the Altar.** (This carries the obvious meaning that none of the Tribe of Judah officiated at the Altar, as it pertained to the Sacrifices, that being the domain of the Levites exclusively.)

14 For *it is* **evident that our Lord sprang out of Judah** (presents a fact that was not questioned, even by the most ardent of the enemies of our Lord); **of which Tribe Moses spoke nothing concerning Priesthood.** (The Tribe of Judah had nothing to do with the Priesthood, and the Priesthood had nothing to do with the Tribe of Judah.)

15 And it is yet far more evident (something plainly obvious, which speaks here of the Priesthood of Christ): **for that after the similitude of Melchisedec there arises another Priest** (refers to the necessity of such, and that God had chosen Melchisedec to be the Type of Christ),

16 Who (the Lord Jesus) **is made** (made a High Priest through His Atoning Sacrifice of Himself), **not after the Law of a carnal commandment** (the idea is that the Levitical Priesthood was weak and frail, due to man's frailty of which it was made, and, thereby, needed a replacement), **but after the power of an endless life.** (This refers to Christ, Who was raised from the dead and lives forever, and will, thereby, be the "High Priest" forever.)

17 For He (God) **testifies** (Ps. 110:4), **You** (Christ) *are* **a Priest forever after the Order of Melchisedec.** (This Order of Priesthood was made in this way so that it might address the entirety of mankind, both Jews and Gentiles. The Levitical Priesthood only addressed the Jews.)

18 For there is verily a disannulling of the Commandment (presents the end of the Law, which was all done by Christ, and was intended all the time) **going before for the weakness and unprofitableness thereof.** (This refers to the problems with the Old Law, and that it was of temporary character.)

19 For the Law (Law of Moses) **made nothing perfect** (the Law was a mirror which showed what man was, but had no power to change man), **but the bringing in of a better hope** *did* (refers to Christ and what He did for us at the Cross); **by the which we draw near unto God.** (The Law of Moses could not open the door to the Holy of Holies for all of mankind, but the Cross did!)

A BETTER SACRIFICE

20 And inasmuch as not without an oath

(earthly Jewish Priests were not sworn in by an oath, simply because they were temporary) **He** *(Christ)* **was made Priest** *(when Jesus was made a High Priest, God took an oath guaranteeing the unending character of His Priesthood):*

21 (For those Priests were made without an oath *(the Jewish Priests);* **but this** *(the Lord Jesus Christ)* **with an oath by Him** *(by God the Father)* **Who said unto Him** *(said unto Christ),* **The Lord sware and will not repent** *(means the Lord will not change His Mind),* **You** *are* **a Priest for ever after the order of Melchisedec:)** *(Ps. 110:4)*

22 By so much was Jesus *(proclaims the fact that all of Redemption is bound up totally and completely in Christ)* **made a surety** *(guarantee)* **of a better Testament** *(a better Covenant).*

23 And they truly were many Priests *(many Priests were needed under the Mosaic economy because the Sacrifices were vastly inferior),* **because they were not suffered to continue by reason of death** *(portrays the inferiority of the Old Jewish system):*

24 But this *Man* *(the Lord Jesus Christ),* **because He continues ever** *(proclaims the Priesthood of Christ as Eternal, while death was inevitable as it regarded the Aaronic Priests),* **has an unchangeable Priesthood.** *(This not only refers to that which is Eternal, but to that which will not change as far as its principle is concerned as well. The reason is the Finished Work of the Cross is an "Everlasting Covenant" [Heb. 13:20].)*

25 Wherefore He *(the Lord Jesus Christ)* **is able also to save them to the uttermost** *(proclaims the fact that Christ Alone has made the only true Atonement for sin; He did this at the Cross)* **who come unto God by Him** *(proclaims the only manner in which man can come to God),* **seeing He ever lives to make intercession for them.** *(His very Presence by the Right Hand of the Father guarantees such, with nothing else having to be done [Heb. 1:3].)*

26 For such an High Priest became us *(presents the fact that no one less exalted could have met the necessities of the human race),* **Who is Holy, harmless, undefiled, separate from sinners** *(describes the spotless, pure, Perfect Character of the Son of God as our Great High Priest; as well, this tells us Christ did not become a sinner on the Cross, as some claim, but was rather the Sin-Offering),* **and made higher than the Heavens** *(refers to the fact that He is seated at the Right Hand of the Father, which is the most exalted position in Heaven or Earth);*

27 Who needs not daily *(refers to the daily Sacrifices offered by the Priests under the old Jewish economy),* **as those High Priests, to offer up Sacrifice, first for His Own sins, and then for the people's** *(refers to the work of the Jewish High Priest on the Great Day of Atonement, which specified their unworthiness; Christ did not have to function accordingly):* **for this He did once, when He offered up Himself.** *(This refers to His Death on the Cross, which Atoned for all sin — past, present, and future, making no further Sacrifices necessary.)*

28 For the Law *(Law of Moses)* **makes men High Priests which have infirmity** *(refers to the fact that the system was imperfect because it depended on frail men);* **but the word of the oath** *(the Promise of God that He was going to institute a superior Priesthood, far superior to the old Levitical Order [Ps. 110:4]),* **which was since the Law** *(refers to the fact that the Oath was given some five hundred years after the Law was given to Moses),* *makes* **the Son** *(the Lord Jesus),* **Who is consecrated** *(means that He, and He Alone, can function in this capacity)* **for evermore.** *(This Covenant is perfect because the Son is Perfect, because what He did at the Cross is Perfect, which means it will never have to be replaced.)*

CHAPTER 8
(A.D. 64)
HIGH PRIEST

NOW of the things which we have spoken *this is* **the sum** *(refers to what Paul will now give as it regards the meaning of all this):* **We have such an High Priest, Who is set on the Right Hand of the Throne of the Majesty in the Heavens** *(the very fact that Christ is now seated in the Heavens at the Right Hand of God proves His Work is a Finished Work);*

2 A Minister of the Sanctuary *(as Paul uses the word "Minister," it speaks both of Priestly service to God and of service to man),* **and of the True Tabernacle** *(the true dwelling place of God, which is in the Heavens),* **which the Lord pitched, and not man.** *(This refers to the fact that Moses pitched the earthly Tabernacle, but God formed the True Tabernacle.)*

3 For every High Priest is ordained to offer Gifts and Sacrifices *(portrays the High Priests of old serving as mediators between God and men):* **wherefore** *it is* **of necessity that this Man** *(Christ Jesus)* **have somewhat also to offer.** *(A Priest must have a Sacrifice to offer. Christ offered Himself. This was His one great and all embracing Sacrifice, satisfying all the*

Types of the Old Covenant and abolishing all its Offerings for sin.)

4 For if He *(the Lord Jesus)* **were on earth, He should not be a Priest** *(refers to the fact that He was not of the Levitical Order, and due to His Sacrifice of Himself, no more earthly Priests are now needed, which, as should be obvious, completely abrogates the Catholic Priesthood),* **seeing that there are Priests who offer Gifts according to the Law** *(due to His Eternal Priesthood, and the Offering of Himself in Sacrifice, the Law is done)*:

5 **Who** *(the Levitical Priesthood)* **serve unto the example and shadow of Heavenly things** *(refers to a suggestive replica, which, in fact, had no substance within itself),* **as Moses was admonished of God when he was about to make the Tabernacle** *(proclaims the fact that this was but a poor replica of the reality Who is Christ)*: **for, See, said He** *(Ex. 25:40; Num. 8:4), that* **you make all things according to the pattern showed to you in the Mount** *(meaning the Tabernacle on Earth was merely a replica of something far better in the Heavens).*

MEDIATOR

6 **But now** *(since the Cross)* **has He** *(the Lord Jesus)* **obtained a more excellent Ministry** *(the New Covenant in Jesus' Blood is superior, and takes the place of the Old Covenant in animal blood),* **by how much also He is the Mediator of a Better Covenant** *(proclaims the fact that Christ officiates between God and man according to the arrangements of the New Covenant),* **which was established upon better Promises.** *(This presents the New Covenant, explicitly based on the cleansing and forgiveness of all sin, which the Old Covenant could not do.)*

7 **For if that first** *Covenant* **had been faultless** *(proclaims the fact that the First Covenant was definitely not faultless; as stated, it was based on animal blood, which was vastly inferior to the Precious Blood of Christ),* **then should no place have been sought for the Second** *(proclaims the necessity of the New Covenant).*

8 **For finding fault with them** *(the First Covenant was actually designed to glaringly portray the fault of the people, which it successfully did),* **He said** *(Jer. 31:31),* **Behold, the days come, saith the Lord, when I will make a New Covenant with the House of Israel and with the House of Judah** *(that New Covenant was in Christ and what He did at the Cross; regrettably, Israel rejected Him)*:

9 **Not according to the Covenant that I made with their fathers** *(refers to the Law of Moses, which was given some fifty days after Israel was delivered from Egypt)* **in the day when I took them by the hand to lead them out of the land of Egypt** *(speaks to the immaturity of Israel at that time; consequently, she was treated as a minor);* **because they continued not in My Covenant** *(Israel was not true to the Covenant regarding the Old Law),* **and I regarded them not, says the Lord.** *(Israel rejected God's First Covenant, so God rejected them.)*

10 **For this** *is* **the Covenant that I will make with the House of Israel** *(refers as stated to the "New Covenant")* **after those days** *(refers to the Old Covenant having run its course, which it did at the time of the Cross),* **saith the Lord; I will put My Laws into their mind, and write them in their hearts** *(proclaims in abbreviated detail the glorious fact of what the New Covenant would do because the sin debt was paid by Christ on the Cross, which made it possible for the Holy Spirit to abide forever in the hearts and lives of Believers [Jn. 14:16-17]):* **and I will be to them a God, and they shall be to Me a people** *(refers to relationship under the New Covenant that was not possible under the Old Covenant [Zech. 8:8]):*

11 **And they shall not teach every man his neighbour, and every man his brother, saying, Know the Lord** *(refers to the complicated process of the Old Covenant)*: **for all shall know Me, from the least to the greatest.** *(This presents the fact that the Holy Spirit will teach every Believer, as He does, and which Jesus also said would be [Jn. 16:13-15]).*

12 **For I will be merciful to their unrighteousness** *(the Cross made this possible),* **and their sins and their iniquities will I remember no more.** *(Due to the Cross, sins and iniquities no longer exist, at least for those who trust Christ.)*

13 **In that He said** *(Jer. 31:31),* **A New Covenant** *(all in Christ and what He did at the Cross),* **He** *(God)* **has made the first old** *(it was designed to be temporary).* **Now that which decays and waxes old** *is* **ready to vanish away.** *(Since the Cross, which introduced the New Covenant, there is no more need for the Old, which is vastly inferior.)*

CHAPTER 9
(A.D. 64)
CONTRAST

THEN verily the First *Covenant* *(is meant to describe the Tabernacle in which the*

Service of God was celebrated under the former dispensation, and to show it had a reference to what was future) had also Ordinances of Divine Service *(Ordinances adapted for Divine Service)*, and a worldly Sanctuary. *(The word "worldly" is used here as a contrast to the Heavenly world.)*

2 For there was a Tabernacle made *(refers to what Moses had made in the wilderness, which pattern was given to him by God)*; the first, wherein *was* the Candlestick *(Golden Lampstand)*, and the table, and the shewbread *(refers to the "first room," which was the Holy Place where the Sacred Vessels were situated)*; which is called the Sanctuary. *(This should have been translated, "which is called the Holy Place." The name "Sanctuary" was commonly given to the whole edifice.)*

3 And after the Second Veil *(pertains to the Veil which separated the Holy Place and the Holy of Holies)*, the Tabernacle which is called the Holiest of all *(refers to the Holy of Holies, which contained the Ark of the Covenant and the Mercy Seat)*;

4 Which had the Golden Censer *(should have been translated, "the Golden Incense Altar," which sat immediately in front of the Veil in the Holy Place)*, and the Ark of the Covenant overlaid round about with gold *(presents the most Glorious and Mysterious Vessel of the Tabernacle)*, wherein *was* the Golden Pot that had Manna *(presents that which was a Type of Christ as the Bread of Life [Jn. 6:32-33, 35])*, and Aaron's rod that budded *(represents Christ Alone as Saviour, and proof that God would raise Him from the dead)*, and the Tables of the Covenant *(the two stone Tables containing the Ten Commandments, five to each Table)*;

5 And over it *(the Ark of the Covenant)* the Cherubims of Glory *(Living Creatures)* shadowing the Mercyseat *(they looked down upon the Mercyseat)*; of which we cannot now speak particularly *(cannot go into great detail)*.

6 Now when these things were thus ordained *(refers to the fact that all of this was of God, and every part and parcel of the Tabernacle in some way pointed to Christ)*, the Priests went always into the First Tabernacle *(into the first of the two rooms of the Tabernacle called the "Holy Place")*, accomplishing the Service of God. *(This refers to the daily, even constant, rituals that had to be carried out.)*

7 But into the second *(the second room of the Tabernacle called the "Holy of Holies," where the Ark of the Covenant was) went* the High Priest alone once every year *(pertained to the Great Day of Atonement [Lev. 16:14; 23:27])*, not without blood, which he offered for himself, and *for* the errors of the people *(presents him going in twice on this particular day, each time taking the blood of the Sacrificial animal which had been killed — once for himself, and once for the people — with the blood sprinkled on the Mercy Seat)*:

8 The Holy Spirit this signifying *(the Holy Spirit was both the Divine Author of the Levitical system of worship, and its Interpreter)*, that the way into the Holiest of all was not yet made manifest *(proclaims the fact [and by the Holy Spirit, at that] that access to God was blocked while the Law was enforced, except in the most limited way)*, while as the First Tabernacle was yet standing *(show the limitations of the Levitical system)*:

9 Which *was* a figure for the time then present *(refers to the Tabernacle being a representation of Heavenly realities)*, in which were offered both Gifts and Sacrifices, that could not make him who did the service perfect, as pertaining to the conscience *(portrays the weakness of the First Covenant, in that it was based on animal blood, which was insufficient; in other words, the conscience of the Jew was still heavy with realization that sin had only been covered, not taken away; only the Cross could take away sin [Jn. 1:29])*;

10 *Which stood* only in meats and drinks, and divers washings, and carnal Ordinances *(refers to the entirety of the Levitical system, which could only present types and shadows)*, imposed *on them* until the time of Reformation. *(The Cross, to which all of this pointed, would address all of this once and for all.)*

11 But Christ being come *(the little word "but" is the pivot upon which all the arguments swing)* an High Priest *(presented by the Apostle to show how marvelously the one Offering of our Lord Jesus Christ transcends all the types and shadows of the old)* of good things to come *(should have been translated, "of the good things realized")*, by a greater and more perfect Tabernacle *(presents Christ Himself as the more perfect Tabernacle)*, not made with hands, that is to say, not of this building *(Christ is not a flimsy structure like the Tabernacle of old)*;

12 Neither by the blood of goats and calves *(proclaims by the fact of the continued need of more Sacrifices that it was not properly effected)*, but by His Own Blood *(presents the price paid)* He entered in once into the Holy

Place *(presents Christ doing what no other Priest had ever done; He offered a Sacrifice that was complete, which means it would never have to be repeated; thereby, the Heavenly Tabernacle was opened to Him; and if opened to Him, it was opened to us as well)*, **having obtained Eternal Redemption** *for us*. *(This proclaims what was accomplished by the giving of Himself on the Cross.)*

13 For if the blood of bulls and of goats *(presents Paul turning again to the Levitical Sacrifices as an example)*, **and the ashes of an heifer sprinkling the unclean, Sanctifies to the purifying of the flesh** *(in these animal Sacrifices, Paul proclaims the effect of an external purification, a cleansing from ritual defilement, but that was as far as it went; as should be obvious, animal Sacrifices could not take away sins)*:

14 How much more shall the Blood of Christ *(while the Sacrifice of animals could cleanse from ceremonial defilement, only the Blood of Christ could cleanse from actual sin; so that throws out every proposed solution other than the Cross)*, **Who through the Eternal Spirit offered Himself without spot to God** *(in this phrase, we learn Christ did not die until the Holy Spirit told Him to die; in fact, no man took His Life from Him; He laid it down freely [Jn. 10:17-18]; as well, the fact that Jesus "offered Himself without spot to God" shoots down the unscriptural Doctrine that "Jesus died Spiritually" on the Cross; had He died Spiritually, meaning He became a sinner on the Cross, He could not have offered Himself without spot to God, as should be obvious; God could only accept a perfect Sacrifice; when He died on the Cross, He took upon Himself the sin penalty of the human race, which was physical death; inasmuch as His Offering of Himself was Perfect, God accepted it as payment in full for all sin — past, present, and future, at least for those who will believe [Jn. 3:16])*, **purge your conscience from dead works to serve the Living God?** *("Dead works" are anything other than simple Faith in the Cross of Christ, i.e., "the Blood of Christ.")*

15 And for this cause *(to purge our conscience)* *He* **is the Mediator** *(He Alone can be the Mediator)* **of the New Testament** *(the New Covenant)*, **that by means of death** *(the death of Christ on the Cross, which atoned for all sin, and was necessary if man was to be saved)*, **for the Redemption of the transgressions** *that were* **under the First Testament** *(proclaims the fact that the death of Christ pertained just as much*

to those before the Cross as those after the Cross; His Sacrifice of Himself guaranteed their Redemption, and we speak of all who had died in the Faith)*, **they which are called might receive the Promise of Eternal Inheritance.** *(This continues to address those who had died in the Faith before the Cross. They are referred to as "the called." The reason their Salvation depended on the Cross was that the blood of bulls and goats, which was all they had before the Cross, was insufficient to take away sins [10:4].)*

THE NEW COVENANT

16 For where a Testament *is* *(Covenant)*, **there must also of necessity be the death of the testator.** *(This refers to the death of Christ, Who was charged to make a New Covenant on the part of man.)*

17 For a Testament *is* **of force after men are dead** *(this tells us in no uncertain terms that the death of Christ on the Cross was a legal matter)*: **otherwise it is of no strength at all while the testator lives.** *(This simply means it is not valid until the individual to whom the Will belongs dies, as is the case of any Testament or Will.)*

18 Whereupon neither the First *Testament* **(Old Covenant) was dedicated without blood** *(but it was only the blood of animals)*.

19 For when Moses had spoken every Precept to all the people according to the Law *(this was referred to as the "Law of Moses")*, **he took the blood of calves and of goats** *(proclaims the seal of the Old Covenant, which was "shed blood"; of course, it was a Type of the Shed Blood of Christ)*, **with water** *(as the blood witnessed to the nature of His Atoning Death [Jn. 19:34], the water witnessed to His full and proper humanity [Jn. 19:34])*, **and scarlet wool** *(wool is normally white, which symbolizes the Righteousness of Christ; however, it was dyed red, which portrayed the fact that it took the Blood of Christ to make this Righteousness available to man)*, **and hyssop** *(a bushy plant, which typified His Death on the Cross as a man; in Egypt the blood was applied to the doorpost with hyssop [Ex. 12:22])*, **and sprinkled both the Book, and all the people** *(referred to the Book of Leviticus, with the Tribe of Levi Ordained for Tabernacle Service, pertaining to the people; the sprinkling of the blood was the ratification of the Covenant, and symbolized the Blood of Christ which would ultimately be shed and applied by Faith to the hearts and lives of believing sinners*

[the blood was mixed with water]),

20 Saying, This *is* the Blood of the Testament *(presents that which made the Old Covenant valid)* which God has enjoined upon you. *(This presents the fact that everything in the First Covenant, exactly as in the New Covenant, is all of God and not at all of man.)*

21 Moreover he sprinkled with Blood both the Tabernacle, and all the Vessels of the Ministry. *(This particular Verse portrays the awfulness of sin, and that it has contaminated everything on this Earth.)*

22 And almost all things are by the Law purged with blood *(some few things were purged with water, but almost all with blood);* and without shedding of blood is no remission. *(The shed Blood of Christ on the Cross is the only solution for the sins, the ills, and the problems of this world. The problem of the world, and of the Church as well, is that it has ever sought to substitute something else. But let all know, it is alone the Cross! the Cross! the Cross!)*

23 It *was* therefore necessary that the patterns of things in the Heavens should be purified with these *(everything that pertained to the Tabernacle and all of its Sacred Vessels was a copy of that which was in Heaven; inasmuch as the Vessels and the Tabernacle were touched by men, they had to be purified by Blood, i.e., "animal blood");* but the Heavenly things themselves with better Sacrifices than these. *(If man were to enter Heaven, the abode of God, there would have to be a better Sacrifice than that of animal blood.)*

24 For Christ is not entered into the Holy Places made with hands *(Christ did not enter the earthly Tabernacle or Temple, regarding the offering up of His Precious Blood on the Mercy Seat),* which are the figures of the true *(presents the fact that these "figures" were only temporary);* but into Heaven itself, now to appear in the Presence of God for us *(presents the purpose and reason for the Cross; all of it was done "for us"):*

25 Nor yet that He should offer Himself often *(refers to the fact that the one Sacrifice of Christ, which was the Offering of Himself on the Cross, was eternally sufficient for the cleansing from all sin — past, present, and future; It will never need to be repeated),* as the High Priest enters into the Holy Place every year with blood of others *(refers to the High Priest of Israel of Old, who went into the Holy of Holies once a year on the Great Day of Atonement, carrying animal blood);*

26 For then must He *(the Lord Jesus)* often have suffered since the foundation of the world *(presents the fact that He wasn't functioning as the High Priests of Israel who, as stated, had to offer Sacrifice yearly):* but now once in the end of the world has He appeared to put away sin by the Sacrifice of Himself. *(This presents the One Sacrifice of Christ as sufficient for all time. The phrase, "In the end of the world," should have been translated, "in the consummation of the ages." As well, by the Sacrifice of Himself, He didn't merely cover sin, but rather "took it away" [Jn. 1:29].)*

27 And as it is appointed unto men once to die *(due to the Fall, all men are under the sentence of death, and, in fact, all have died Spiritually, which means to be separated from God),* but after this the Judgment *(the answer to the Spiritual death of man is Christ and what He did at the Cross; if Christ the Saviour is rejected, all will face Christ the Judge; for as death was inevitable, the Judgment is inevitable as well):*

28 So Christ was once offered to bear the sins of many *(the Cross was God's answer to sin, and, in fact, the only answer);* and unto them who look for Him shall He appear the second time without sin unto Salvation. *(This refers to the Second Coming. "Without sin" refers to the fact that the Second Coming will not be to atone for sin, for that was already carried out at the Cross at His First Advent. The Second Coming will bring all the results of Salvation to this world, which refers to all that He did at the Cross. We now only have the "Firstfruits" [Rom. 8:23].)*

CHAPTER 10
(A.D. 64)
THE OLD COVENANT

FOR the Law *(the Law of Moses)* having a shadow of good things to come *(the Law of Moses was only meant to be temporary; it portrayed Christ Who was to come),* and not the very image of the things *(it was quite impossible for the Law to present a proper image of Who and what Christ would be; it suggested such, but was only a suggestion),* can never with those Sacrifices which they offered year by year continually make the comers thereunto perfect. *(The animal Sacrifices could only cover sins, they couldn't take away sins. That remained for Christ to do [Jn. 1:29].)*

2 For then would they not have ceased to

be offered? (*Paul asked this question simply because the fact that the animal Sacrifices had to be offered over and over proclaimed their insufficiency. They were, in reality, only a stopgap measure.*) **because that the worshippers once purged should have had no more conscience of sins.** (*This proclaims what the Proper Sacrifice of Christ could do, and, in fact, did do, but which the Sacrifice of bulls and goats could not do. The phrase, "No more conscience of sin," should not be misunderstood as "no more consciousness of sin."*)

3 But in those *Sacrifices* (*animal Sacrifices*) ***there is* a remembrance again *made* of sins every year.** (*That the High Priest of Israel had to go into the Holy of Holies once a year with animal blood proclaimed the fact that this system was basically flawed, and was meant only to point to Christ Who was to come.*)

4 For *it is* not possible that the blood of bulls and of goats should take away sins. (*The word "impossible" is a strong one. It means there is no way forward through the blood of animals. As well, it applies to all other efforts made by man to address the problem of sin, other than the Cross.*)

5 Wherefore when He (*the Lord Jesus*) **comes into the world** (*presents Christ coming as the Saviour, Who undertakes in Grace to meet every claim the Throne of God has against penitent sinners*), **He said,** (*Ps. 40:6*) **Sacrifice and Offering You would not** (*refers to the fact that He would pay for sin, but not with animal Sacrifices*), **but a Body have You prepared Me** (*God became man with the full intention that His Perfect Physical Body was to be offered up in Sacrifice on the Cross, which it was; the Cross was ever His Destination*):

6 In Burnt Offerings and *Sacrifices* for sin (*proclaims the root of the problem which besets mankind — it is "sin"; the idea is, that the Sacrifices were not sufficient as it regards "sin"; therefore, God took no pleasure in them in that capacity*) **You have had no pleasure.**

7 Then said I, Lo, I come (in the Volume of the Book it is written of Me,) (*The entirety of the Old Testament points exclusively to Christ, and in every capacity.*) **to do Your Will, O God.** (*The Cross was the Will of God because it had to be if man was to be Redeemed.*)

8 Above when He said, Sacrifice and Offering and Burnt Offerings and *Offering* for sin You would not (*refers to the fact that animal Sacrifices could not cleanse from sin*), **neither had pleasure *therein*** (*concerns the insufficiency of the Sacrifices*); **which are offered by the Law** (*refers to the fact that all these Offerings were included in the Mosaic Law; even though instigated by God, they were meant to point to Christ*);

9 Then said He, Lo, I come to do Your Will, O God. (*The doing of the Will of God, as it regards Christ, pertained totally and completely to His Sacrifice of Himself on the Cross.*) **He takes away the First** (*the Old Covenant, which He did by the Sacrifice of Himself*), **that He may establish the Second** (*the New Covenant which He did by going to the Cross, the only way it could be established*).

10 By the which will (*the Sacrifice of Christ took away the First Covenant, satisfying its demands, and established the New Covenant*) **we are Sanctified through the Offering of the Body of Jesus Christ once *for all*.** (*This proclaims unequivocally that the only way the Believer can live a victorious life is by the Cross ever being the Object of his Faith.*)

11 And every Priest stands daily Ministering and offering oftentimes the same Sacrifices, which can never take away sins (*proclaiming the insufficiency of this method*):

12 But this Man (*this Priest, Christ Jesus*), **after He had offered One Sacrifice for sins forever** (*speaks of the Cross*), **sat down on the Right Hand of God** (*refers to the great contrast with the Priests under the Levitical system, who never sat down because their work was never completed; the work of Christ was a "Finished Work," and needed no repetition*);

13 From henceforth expecting till His enemies be made His footstool. (*These enemies are Satan and all the fallen Angels and demon spirits, plus all who follow Satan.*)

14 For by one Offering He has perfected forever them who are Sanctified. (*Everything one needs is found in the Cross [Gal. 6:14].*)

15 *Whereof* the Holy Spirit also is a witness to us (*a witness to the Cross*): **for after that He had said before** (*refers to the fact that the Holy Spirit has always witnessed to the veracity of the Finished Work of Christ*),

16 This *is* the Covenant that I will make with them after those days (*proclaims its distinctive feature as being the Sanctifying Work of the Holy Spirit Who would be caused to take up His permanent abode in the Believer, all made possible by the Cross*), **says the Lord, I will put My Laws into their hearts, and in their minds will I write them** (*the work of the New Covenant, which accompanies the Born-Again experience*);

17 And their sins and iniquities will I remember no more. (*He has taken them all away,*

and did so by the Cross.)

18 Now where remission of these *is* (*with all sins Atoned, the argument is settled*), *there is* no more Offering for sin. *(No more offering is necessary, for Christ paid it all.)*

FAITH

19 Having therefore, Brethren, boldness to enter into the Holiest by the Blood of Jesus *(the Cross has made it possible for any and every Believer to come into the presence of the very Throne of God, and at any time so desired),*

20 By a new and living way *(presents the New Covenant),* which He has consecrated for us *(by the Cross),* through the Veil *(contains an allusion to the Veil which separated the Holy of Holies from the Holy Place in the Tabernacle),* that is to say, His flesh *(refers to giving Himself on the Cross, which opened up the way to God);*

21 And *having* an High Priest over the House of God *(the actual Greek says, "a Priest, a Great One"; He is the Head [Col. 1:18]);*

22 Let us draw near with a true heart in full assurance of Faith *(Faith in the Finished Work of Christ),* having our hearts sprinkled from an evil conscience, and our bodies washed with pure water. *(This portrays Paul using Old Testament Types to represent the reality we now have in Christ [Lev., Chpts. 8-9].)*

23 Let us hold fast the profession of *our* Faith without wavering *(Faith in Christ and the Cross);* (for He *is* faithful Who Promised;) *(This refers to the fact that everything the New Covenant promises, which is Salvation and total victory over all sin, will be realized in totally.)*

24 And let us consider one another to provoke unto love and to good works *(that which will naturally follow true Faith in the Cross):*

25 Not forsaking the assembling of ourselves together, as the manner of some *is* (*it is important that Believers assemble together, however the meeting might be conducted);* but exhorting *one another* (*encouraging one another in the Faith):* and so much the more, as you see the day approaching *(especially during these last days).*

CONSEQUENCES

26 For if we sin wilfully *(the "willful sin" is the transference of Faith from Christ and Him Crucified to other things)* after that we have received the knowledge of the Truth *(speaks of the Bible way of Salvation and Victory, which is "Jesus Christ and Him Crucified" [I Cor. 2:2]),* there remains no more Sacrifice for sins *(if the Cross of Christ is rejected, there is no other Sacrifice or way God will accept),*

27 But a certain fearful looking for of judgment and fiery indignation *(refers to God's Anger because of men rejecting Jesus Christ and the Cross),* which shall devour the adversaries. *(It is hellfire, which will ultimately come to all who reject Christ and the Cross.)*

28 He who despised Moses' Law died without mercy under two or three witnesses *(there had to be these many witnesses to a capital crime before the death sentence could be carried out, according to the Old Testament Law of Moses [Deut. 17:2-7]):*

29 Of how much sorer punishment, suppose ye, shall he be Thought worthy, who has trodden under foot the Son of God *(proclaims the reason for the "sorer punishment"),* and has counted the Blood of the Covenant, wherewith he was Sanctified, an unholy thing *(refers to a person who has been saved, but is now expressing unbelief toward that which originally saved him),* and has done despite unto the Spirit of Grace? *(When the Cross is rejected, the Holy Spirit is insulted.)*

30 For we know Him Who has said, Vengeance *belongs* unto Me, I will recompense, says the Lord *(is meant to imply that every single thing is going to be judged by the Lord, Who Alone is the righteous Judge).* And again, The Lord shall Judge His people *(chastise His People [Deut. 32:35-36]).*

31 *It is* a fearful thing to fall into the hands of the Living God. *(This refers to those who have once known the Lord, but now express no Faith in the Cross.)*

REWARD

32 But call to remembrance the former days *(the earlier proofs of faithfulness and love),* in which, after you were illuminated *(refers to the enlightenment the Gospel brings to the mind of the Believer),* you endured a great fight of afflictions *(refers to the persecutions that came their way after conversion);*

33 Partly, while you were made a gazingstock both by reproaches and afflictions *(refers, as well, to public ridicule);* and partly, while you became companions of them who were so used. *(This refers to Christian Jews, who tried to be of help to newly converted Jews,*

coming under severe persecution.)

34 For you had compassion of me in my bonds *(evidently refers to the time Paul was in prison in Rome, as recorded in Acts 8:28; as well, another proof that Paul wrote the Book of Hebrews),* **and took joyfully the spoiling of your goods** *(many Jews suffered great financial loss upon acceptance of Christ),* **knowing in yourselves that you have in Heaven a better and an enduring substance.** *(The loss of earthly treasure did not hinder their Heavenly treasure.)*

35 Cast not away therefore your confidence *(confession of Faith in Christ and the Cross),* **which has great recompence of reward** *(eternal reward, while earthly persecution is temporary).*

36 For you have need of patience *(proper Faith will always have proper patience),* **that, after you have done the Will of God, you might receive the Promise.** *(If we carry out the Will of God in our lives, we don't have to worry about the Promise being fulfilled.)*

37 For yet a little while, and He Who shall come will come, and will not tarry. *(This refers to the Rapture of the Church. If the Holy Spirit deemed the time frame short some 2,000 years ago, then how much closer are we presently?)*

38 Now the just shall live by Faith *(Faith in Christ and the Cross [Hab. 2:4]):* **but if** *any* **man draw back** *(proclaims the fact that such can be done, and refers to Believers transferring their Faith from Christ and the Cross to other things),* **My soul shall have no pleasure in him.** *(As should be obvious, God is grieved over the conduct of any person who would do such.)*

39 But we are not of them who draw back unto perdition *(Paul is saying that he is not going to draw back, and that those who do will lose their souls);* **but of them who believe to the saving of the soul.** *(Believe in Christ and Him Crucified.)*

CHAPTER 11
(A.D. 64)
FAITH DEFINED

NOW **Faith is the substance** *(the title deed)* **of things hoped for** *(a declaration of the action of Faith),* **the evidence of things not seen.** *(Faith is not based upon the senses, which yield uncertainty, but rather on the Word of God.)*

2 For by it *(by Faith, and as we shall see, it is Faith in the Cross)* **the Elders obtained a good report** *(the approval of the Lord).*

3 Through Faith we understand that the worlds were framed by the Word of God *(refers to Creation, along with everything that goes with Creation),* **so that things which are seen were not made of things which do appear.** *(God began with nothing, thereby, speaking into existence the things needed to create the universe.)*

PATRIARCHS

4 By Faith Abel offered unto God a more excellent Sacrifice than Cain *(immediately proclaims the fact that the Object of our Faith must be "Jesus Christ and Him Crucified" [I Cor. 2:2]),* **by which he obtained witness that he was Righteous** *(proclaims the fact that Righteousness comes exclusively from Christ, and is obtained by the Cross being the Object of our Faith),* **God testifying of his gifts** *(referring to the fact that the Sacrifice of the Lamb which represented Christ was accepted by God; at the dawn of time it was "the Cross," and it is still "the Cross"):* **and by it he being dead yet speaks** *(speaks of that alone God will accept).*

5 By Faith Enoch was translated that he should not see death *(refers to God transferring Enoch to Heaven in his physical body while he was yet alive);* **and was not found, because God had translated him** *(refers to his translation being well-known at that time):* **for before his translation he had this testimony, that he pleased God.** *(He pleased God because he placed his Faith exclusively in Christ and the Cross.)*

6 But without Faith *(in Christ and the Cross; anytime Faith is mentioned, always and without exception, its root meaning is that its Object is Christ and the Cross; otherwise, it is faith God will not accept)* *it is* **impossible to please** *Him* *(Faith in anything other than Christ and the Cross greatly displeases the Lord):* **for he who comes to God must believe that He is** *(places Faith as the foundation and principle of the manner in which God deals with the human race),* **and** *that* **He** *(God)* **is a rewarder of them who diligently seek Him** *(seek Him on the premise of Christ and Him Crucified).*

7 By Faith Noah, being warned of God of things not seen as yet *(the Lord told Noah He was going to send a flood upon the Earth),* **moved with fear** *(stand in awe),* **prepared an ark to the saving of his house** *(refers to him doing exactly what God told him to do);* **by the which he condemned the world** *(the*

Righteousness of Christ always clashes with self-righteousness), **and became heir of the Righteousness which is by Faith** *(Faith in Christ and the Cross).*

ABRAHAM

8 By Faith Abraham, when he was called to go out into a place which he should after receive for an inheritance, obeyed *(his posterity would receive the inheritance)*; **and he went out, not knowing whither he went.** *(While he knew where to go [Canaan], he knew nothing about the place.)*

9 By Faith he sojourned in the Land of Promise *(the Greek says "the Land of the Promise," speaking of a particular Promise)*, **as** *in* **a strange country** *(he lived in this land not as its owner, but as a resident alien)*, **dwelling in Tabernacles with Isaac and Jacob, the heirs with him of the same Promise** *(what God promised to Abraham, He promised as well to those who would follow him, including us presently)*:

10 For he looked for a city which has foundations *(Abraham knew all of this would lead to something Heavenly)*, **whose Builder and Maker** *is* **God.** *(This actually refers to Christ as the great Architect, Designer, and Fabricator of all material creations [Jn. 1:3; Eph. 3:9], plus all moral creations [Col. 1:15-18].)*

11 Through Faith also Sarah herself received strength to conceive seed *(this speaks of Isaac)*, **and was delivered of a child when she was past age** *(her bringing forth this child had to do with the coming Redeemer, the Lord Jesus Christ, Who would die on the Cross in order to Redeem lost humanity)*, **because she judged Him** *(God)* **Faithful Who had promised.** *(While we aren't always faithful, God is always faithful.)*

12 Therefore sprang there even of one, and him as good as dead *(refers to the hopelessness of Abraham's situation, which brought forth the multitude; God did exactly what He said He would do!)*, *so many* **as the stars of the sky in multitude, and as the sand which is by the sea shore innumerable.** *(True Faith is immeasurable and, thereby, brings forth immeasurable results.)*

13 These all died in Faith *(believing Christ would come and would pay the price in order that humanity might be redeemed)*, **not having received the Promises** *(Christ did not come in their lifetimes)*, **but having seen them afar off** *(they continued to believe, despite the fact that the Promises were "afar off")*, **and were persuaded of** *them* *(they traded that which they could see for that which they could not see)*, **and embraced** *them* *(they claimed these Promises as their own, even though they were "afar off")*, **and confessed that they were strangers and pilgrims on the earth.** *(It is the same with modern Believers.)*

14 For they who say such things declare plainly that they seek a country. *(This refers to that which is not here, and has no reference to that which is here.)*

15 And truly, if they had been mindful of that *country* **from whence they came out** *(they never looked back)*, **they might have had opportunity to have returned.** *(It never occurred to them to go back to the old life. They had received a vision of Jesus, and the things of the world had lost their glow.)*

16 But now *(since the vision)* **they desire a better** *country*, **that is, an Heavenly** *(all of this is attainable only through and by what Jesus did at the Cross, and our Faith in that Finished Work)*: **wherefore God is not ashamed to be called their God** *(because they have commended themselves to God by their Faith)*: **for He has prepared for them a city** *(not that He will, but that He has already done so).*

17 By Faith Abraham, when he was tried, offered up Isaac *(even though God stopped the event, in the mind of Abraham it was already done)*: **and he who had received the Promises offered up his only begotten** *son* *(the Lord had already told Abraham He would send the Redeemer into this world in order to redeem mankind, but now He shows the Patriarch "how" it was to be done, which was by death, i.e., "Sacrifice")*,

18 Of whom it was said, That in Isaac shall your seed be called *(refers to the fact that the posterity of Abraham was to be named after Isaac, not Ishmael [Gen. 21:12])*:

19 Accounting that God *was* **able to raise** *him* **up, even from the dead** *(the Lord had told Abraham to offer up Isaac as a Sacrifice; the Patriarch proceeded to obey, which God stopped at the last minute; but in his mind, he had already offered up Isaac, reasoning that God would raise him from the dead, because it was through Isaac that the Redeemer would come)*; **from whence also he received him in a figure.** *(The Greek actually says, "and figuratively speaking, he did receive Isaac back from death.")*

20 By Faith Isaac blessed Jacob and Esau concerning things to come. *(Isaac blessed his two sons because his Faith looked beyond death.)*

21 By Faith Jacob, when he was a dying, blessed both the sons of Joseph *(pertains to Manasseh and Ephraim, both born to Joseph in Egypt)*; and worshipped *(and for many reasons, but primarily because of the Redeemer Who was going to come through his posterity)*, leaning upon the top of his staff. *(On this staff was carved all the great happenings of the past years, which, in effect, was "the Word of God." So, he was leaning on "the Word of God.")*

22 By Faith Joseph, when he died, made mention of the departing of the Children of Israel *(he knew what God had in store for Israel)*; and gave Commandment concerning his bones. *(He was in Egypt when he died, but his heart was in Canaan. When the Children of Israel would be delivered from Egypt in the future, which they were, they would take the bones of Joseph with them to the Promised Land. His Faith knew it would happen.)*

23 By Faith Moses, when he was born, was hid three months of his parents, because they saw *he was* a proper child *(the Greek says, "he was comely with respect to God")*; and they were not afraid of the king's commandment. *(Pharaoh had mandated that all male children of the Israelites be killed at birth. They felt God would protect their child, which He did!)*

MOSES

24 By Faith Moses, when he was come to years *(refers to him coming to the age of 40 [Ex. 2:11])*, refused to be called the son of Pharaoh's daughter *(in effect, he refused the position of Pharaoh of Egypt, for which he had been trained because he had been adopted by Pharaoh's daughter)*;

25 Choosing rather to suffer affliction with the people of God *(proclaims the choice Moses made; He traded the temporal for the Eternal)*, than to enjoy the pleasures of sin for a season *(presents the choice which must be made, affliction or the pleasures of sin)*;

26 Esteeming the reproach of Christ greater riches than the treasures in Egypt *(he judged the reproach was greater than the throne of Egypt)*: for he had respect unto the recompence of the reward. *(Moses habitually "looked away" from the treasures in Egypt, and purposely fixed his eye on the Heavenly Reward.)*

27 By Faith he forsook Egypt *(which, spiritually speaking, every Believer must do)*, not fearing the wrath of the king *(Pharaoh tried to kill him at that time [Ex. 2:15])*: for he endured, as

seeing Him Who is invisible. *(This speaks of Christ, Whom Moses saw by Faith.)*

28 Through Faith he kept the Passover *(means that he "instituted the Passover" according to the Word of the Lord,)*, and the sprinkling of Blood *(referred to the Blood of the Paschal Lamb on the lintels and doorposts of the houses [Ex. 12:22])*, lest He Who destroyed the firstborn should touch them. *(Every Israelite's house was safe that night because of the blood being applied to the doorposts, a Type of the Blood of Christ applied to our hearts, which stops the Judgment of God.)*

RAHAB

29 By Faith they *(the Children of Israel)* passed through the Red Sea as by dry *land (presents that body of water becoming a temple to Israel, but a tomb to Egypt; the Faith that sprinkled the blood and the unbelief that refused its shelter fixed this great gulf between them)*: which the Egyptians assaying to do were drowned. *(God, Who opened the Red Sea for the Israelites, closed it on the Egyptians, thereby destroying their army.)*

30 By Faith the walls of Jericho fell down, after they were compassed about seven days *(proclaims obedience)*.

31 By Faith the harlot Rahab perished not with them who believed not *(while Jericho was totally destroyed, Rahab was spared because of her Faith in the God of Israel)*, when she had received the spies with peace. *(She found out who they were, and instead of turning them over to the King of Jericho, she sought to know Israel's God.)*

EXAMPLES

32 And what shall I more say? *(This refers to the fact that enough has now been said to guide all who are willing to search the Scriptures for themselves.)* for the time would fail me to tell of Gideon, and *of* Barak, and *of* Samson, and *of* Jephthae; *of* David also, and Samuel, and *of* the Prophets:

33 Who through Faith subdued Kingdoms, wrought Righteousness, obtained Promises, stopped the mouths of lions,

34 Quenched the violence of fire, escaped the edge of the sword, out of weakness were made strong, waxed valiant in fight, turned to flight the armies of the aliens.

35 Women received their dead raised to life

again: and others were tortured, not accepting deliverance; that they might obtain a better Resurrection *(the Resurrection afforded by Christ)*:

36 And others had trial of *cruel* mockings and scourgings, yes, moreover of bonds and imprisonment:

37 They were stoned, they were sawn asunder, were tempted, were slain with the sword: they wandered about in sheepskins and goatskins; being destitute, afflicted, tormented *(Faith in Christ and the Cross guarantees Miracles of Deliverance, or Miracles of Endurance if that is, in fact, what the Lord desires; it can be done no other way!)*;

38 (Of whom the world was not worthy:) *(This refers to the fact that the few true Christians in this world are of far greater worth than all the balance of the world put together, and in every sense.)* they wandered in deserts, and *in* mountains, and *in* dens and caves of the earth. *(This refers to the lot of some Believers; not all of the time, but some of the time.)*

39 And these all *(Old Testament Saints)*, having obtained a good report through Faith *(refers to being Judged accordingly by the Holy Spirit)*, received not the Promise *(the Messiah didn't come during their times, but they had Faith He ultimately would come, and so He did!)*:

40 God having provided some better thing for us *(presents that which God had originally promised to Abraham [Gen. 22:14])*, that they *(Old Testament Saints)* without us *(the Church)* should not be made perfect. *(This lays the stress on Christ Who made it all possible for both the Old Testament and the New Testament Saints.)*

CHAPTER 12
(A.D. 64)
JESUS

WHEREFORE seeing we also are compassed about with so great a cloud of witnesses *(refers to the Old Testament Saints who looked forward to the coming Promise, Who is the Lord Jesus Christ, and what He would do at the Cross to Redeem mankind)*, let us lay aside every weight, and the sin which does so easily beset *us (we can do this only as we understand that all things come to us through the Cross, and that the Cross must ever be the Object of our Faith, which then gives the Holy Spirit latitude to work within our lives)*, and let us run with patience the race that is set before us

(the only "weight" God will allow in the running of this race is our taking up and bearing the Cross, and doing so constantly [Lk. 9:23-24]),

2 Looking unto Jesus the Author and Finisher of *our* Faith *(Jesus will carry us through till the end, for this is what the word "Finisher" means, providing we keep our eyes on Him and what He did at the Cross; He is the Source, while the Cross is the means)*; Who for the joy that was set before Him endured the Cross, despising the shame *(but the Cross was necessary, that is if man was to be redeemed)*, and is set down at the Right Hand of the Throne of God. *(Him being "set down" refers to His Work at the Cross being a "Finished Work," and the fact that He is set down at the "Throne of God" means God has fully accepted His Sacrifice.)*

3 For consider Him Who endured such contradiction of sinners against Himself *(means to consider by way of comparison; it speaks primarily of Israel's religious leaders who bitterly opposed Him)*, lest you be wearied and faint in your minds. *("Consider Him" instead of yourself, and there will be victory!)*

4 Ye have not yet resisted unto blood, striving against sin. *(The Lord doesn't call upon Believers to go to the Cross and shed their blood, regarding the resistance of sin. Jesus has already done that for us.)*

CHASTISEMENT

5 And you have forgotten the exhortation which speaks unto you as unto children *(the Apostle's objective in introducing this here is to show that afflictions are designed, on the part of God, to produce positive effects in the lives of His People)*, My son, despise not you the chastening of the Lord, nor faint when you are rebuked of Him *(everything that happens to a Believer is either caused or allowed by the Lord; consequently, we should learn the lesson desired to be taught)*:

6 For whom the Lord loves He chastens *(God disciplines those He loves, not those to whom He is indifferent)*, and scourges every son whom He receives. *(This refers to all who truly belong to Him.)*

7 If you endure chastening, God deals with you as with sons *(chastening from the Lord guarantees the fact that one is a Child of God)*; for what son is he whom the father chastens not? *(If an earthly father truly cares for his son, he will use whatever measures necessary to bring the boy into line. If an earthly father will do*

this, how much more will our Heavenly Father do the same?)

8 But if you be without chastisement, whereof all *(all true Believers)* are partakers, then are you bastards, and not sons. *(Many claim to be Believers while continuing in sin, but the Lord never chastises them. Such shows they are illegitimate sons, meaning they are claiming faith on a basis other than the Cross. The true son, without doubt, will be chastised at times.)*

9 Furthermore we have had fathers of our flesh which corrected *us*, and we gave *them* reverence *(earthly parents)*: shall we not much rather be in subjection unto the Father of spirits, and live? *("Father of spirits" is contrasted to "Fathers of the flesh." The latter concerns our earthly parents. Their relation to us is limited. His is universal and eternal.)*

10 For they verily for a few days chastened *us* after their own pleasure *(the use of the word "pleasure" indicates that the chastening may or may not have been proper, as it regards our earthly parents)*; but He for *our* profit *(presents the difference between human liability of error and the perfect knowledge of our Heavenly Father; He seeks our profit, and cannot err in the means He employs)*, that *we* might be partakers of His Holiness. *(This presents the objective of the chastening and correction of God.)*

11 Now no chastening for the present seems to be joyous, but grievous *(presents the fact that the trials we are at times exposed to do not give joy at that moment, and are often hard indeed to bear)*: nevertheless afterward it yields the peaceable fruit of Righteousness unto them which are exercised thereby. *(All of this is carried out by the Holy Spirit for a specific purpose [Jn. 15:1-9].)*

DISOBEDIENCE

12 Wherefore lift up the hands which hang down *(stop being discouraged)*, and the feeble knees *(the knees, which speak of our walk and direction, are feeble because of discouragement)*;

13 And make straight paths for your feet *(refers to the "right path," which the chastisement designed by the Lord desires to bring about)*, lest that which is lame be turned out of the way *(to be spiritually lame, which refers to our Faith being in something other than the Cross)*; but let it rather be healed *(which will be done when the Believer's Faith is once again anchored in the Cross)*.

14 Follow peace with all *men*, and Holiness *(every effort must be made to live peacefully with all men, but not at the expense of Holiness, i.e., "the compromising of the Word")*, without which no man shall see the Lord *(Holiness cannot be brought about by Law; it can only be brought about by Grace, which is made possible by the Cross)*:

15 Looking diligently lest any man fail of the Grace of God *(we frustrate the Grace of God, and can even fall from Grace, if we function outside the Cross [Gal. 2:21; 5:4])*; lest any root of bitterness springing up trouble *you (to try to live for God outside of His prescribed order, which is the Cross, will bring nothing but failure, thereby, providing fertile ground for "roots of bitterness")*, and thereby many be defiled *(speaks of works of the flesh [Gal. 5:19-21])*;

16 Lest there *be* any fornicator, or profane person, as Esau *(he was "profane" because he rejected God's Way, i.e., the Cross, and which results are inevitable)*, who for one morsel of meat sold his birthright. *(He was in the Family of God, but was not of the Family of God, which characterizes untold millions presently.)*

17 For you know how that afterward, when he would have inherited the Blessing, he was rejected *(proclaims Esau, as millions, desiring the Blessing without the Blesser)*: for he found no place of repentance, though he sought it *(the Blessing)* carefully with tears. *(He wanted the Blessing, but did not want to repent of placing his Faith in things other than Christ.)*

18 For you are not come unto the Mount that might be touched *(in effect, is saying to these Christian Jews, "you had better carefully consider the Law you are proposing once again to embrace")*, and that burned with fire, nor unto blackness, and darkness, and tempest *(the idea is that we can face God respecting His Law according to the symbols given here, or we can face Him through the Blood of His Son and our Saviour, the Lord Jesus Christ)*,

19 And the sound of a trumpet, and the voice of words *(that which accompanied the giving of the Law on Mt. Sinai [Ex. 20:19])*; which *voice* they that heard entreated that the word should not be spoken to them any more *(relates the fact that the Voice of God sounded with such power it could not be stood by the people [Ex. 20:19; Deut. 5:22-27])*:

20 (For they could not endure that which was commanded *(they feared they would die)*, And if so much as a beast touch the mountain,

it shall be stoned, or thrust through with a dart *(all of this portrays the Holiness of God)*:

21 And so terrible was the sight, *that* Moses said, I exceedingly fear and quake:) *(This proclaims in the strongest language possible that no lasting blessing can come to fallen man through the Law.)*

22 But you are come unto Mount Sion, and unto the city of the Living God, the Heavenly Jerusalem *(no one has ever reached this city by Law, but only by Grace)*, and to an innumerable company of Angels *(it refers to countless numbers)*,

23 To the General Assembly and Church of the Firstborn, which are written in Heaven *(pertains to every Born-Again Believer from the time of Abel up to the Second Coming; the price was the Cross!)*, and to God the Judge of all *(God has judged all who are in the "Church of the First Born" as perfectly justified in His sight)*, and to the spirits of just men made perfect *(Justification by Faith)*,

24 And to Jesus the Mediator of the New Covenant *(which was made possible by the Cross)*, and to the blood of sprinkling *(Christ is the Mediator of the New Covenant, through the shedding of His Blood; it was typified by the Blood of the Old Covenant with which Moses sprinkled all the people [Ex. 24:4-8; Heb. 9:19])*, that speaks better things than *that of* Abel. *(This refers to Abel's animal Sacrifice as recorded in Gen., Chpt. 4.)*

25 See that you refuse not Him Who speaks. *(This refers implicitly to Christ and what He did at the Cross.)* For if they escaped not who refused Him Who spoke on earth *(refers to God giving the Law on Mt. Sinai)*, much more *shall not* we *escape*, if we turn away from Him Who *speaks* from Heaven *(if we reject Christ and the Cross, Judgment is sure!)*:

26 Whose Voice then shook the earth *(the Voice of God at Mt. Sinai was meant to impress upon Israel the solemnity of the moment)*: but now He has promised, saying, Yet once more I shake not the earth only, but also Heaven. *(This phrase refers to the First Advent of Christ, Whose Death on the Cross shook both Heaven and Earth. His Death, because it atoned for all sin, broke the legal claim of Satan on humanity.)*

27 And this *Word (refers to the "Word of the Cross" [I Cor. 1:18])*, Yet once more, signifies the removing of those things that are shaken, as of things that are made *(refers to the Act of God transferring this present universe which is*

under the curse of Adam's sin to a new basis; that new basis being a new and perfect universe, which will ultimately come)*, that those things which cannot be shaken may remain. *(This refers to all Jesus paid for at the Cross. Only Faith in Christ and the Cross cannot be shaken. It will remain!)*

28 Wherefore we receiving a Kingdom which cannot be moved *(refers to our entrance into this Kingdom, all made possible by the Cross)*, let us have Grace, whereby we may serve God acceptably with reverence and Godly fear *(one can serve God only by the means of Grace, which Source is Christ and which means is the Cross)*:

29 For our God *is* a consuming fire. *(The fire of God will consume everything that is not Faith in Christ and the Cross [I Cor. 3:10-17].)*

CHAPTER 13
(A.D. 64)
INSTRUCTION

LET brotherly love continue. *(This type of love refers to our social actions, one might say, toward our Brothers and Sisters in the Lord.)*

2 Be not forgetful to entertain strangers *(hospitality)*: for thereby some have entertained Angels unawares *(definitely would have a tendency to provide a positive incentive)*.

3 Remember them who are in bonds *(refers to Christians who were even then beginning to be imprisoned for their Faith)*, as bound with them *(become one with them, not forgetting to pray for them)*; *and* them which suffer adversity, as being yourselves also in the Body. *(Refers to the Body of Christ, and that if one suffers, in a sense all suffer.)*

4 Marriage *is* honourable in all, and the bed undefiled *(lawful sex between a husband and wife holds no defilement)*: but whoremongers and adulterers God will judge. *(This proclaims all sexual conduct outside of marriage to be absolutely defiled.)*

5 *Let your* conversation *(lifestyle) be* without covetousness *(in a sense, covetousness is idolatry [Col. 3:5])*; *and be* content with such things as you have *(Christ-dependent)*: for He has said, I will never leave you, nor forsake you. *(The Greek actually says, "He Himself has said," meaning the Lord Jesus Himself has Personally made this Promise [Josh. 1:5; I Chron. 28:20].)*

6 So that we may boldly say, The Lord *is* my helper *(there is no higher authority and*

power *[Ps. 118:6])*, and I will not fear what man shall do unto me. *(Man can do no more to me than the Lord permits.)*

MINISTERS

7 Remember them which have the rule over you *(should have been translated, "Remember them which are your leaders")*, who have spoken unto you the Word of God *(refers to preaching and teaching)*: whose faith follow *(providing its Faith that ever makes the Cross its Object)*, considering the end of *their* conversation *(lifestyle; proper Faith will always produce a proper lifestyle)*.

JESUS CHRIST

8 Jesus Christ the same yesterday, and today, and forever. *(He will never change, and this covers the entire range of time.)*

9 Be not carried about with divers and strange doctrines. *(This refers to anything that changes the Object of Faith from the Cross to something else.)* For *it is* a good thing that the heart be established with Grace *(actually means this is the only way the heart can rightly be established)*; not with meats *(is meant to refer to all types of religious ceremonies)*, which have not profited them who have been occupied therein. *(This proclaims everything other than simple Faith in Christ and His Finished Work as having no value.)*

ALTARS

10 We have an Altar *(is used in this sense by Paul to describe all Christ has done at the Cross on behalf of lost humanity)*, whereof they have no right to eat which serve the Tabernacle. *(This bluntly and plainly says that one cannot serve Christ and the Levitical Order at the same time. As well, one cannot function in Law and Grace at the same time!)*

11 For the bodies of those beasts *(refers to the animal Sacrifices of various kinds)*, whose blood is brought into the Sanctuary by the High Priest for sin *(refers to this particular man bringing the blood of these Sacrificed animals into the Holy of Holies on the Great Day of Atonement, and applying it to the Mercy Seat and the Horns of the Altar of Incense)*, are burned without the camp. *(The carcass of the animal was burned outside the camp, thus symbolizing God's Wrath against sin.)*

12 Wherefore Jesus also, that He might sanctify the people with His Own Blood *(presents the price that was paid so that man might be "Sanctified", i.e., "set free from sin")*, suffered without the gate. *(The Sin-Offering was burned "without the camp." Jesus, Who in all other points fulfilled the Law of Atonement, fulfilled it in this point also [Mat. 27:32; Jn. 19:20].)*

13 Let us go forth therefore unto Him without the camp *(presents Christ as the only bearer of Salvation)*, bearing His reproach *(refers to sharing in the rejection He has undergone)*.

14 For here have we no continuing city *(portrays earthly Jerusalem as having finished its course, at least at that particular time and as it referred to the Law,)*, but we seek one to come. *(The hopes of mankind are now bound up with no abiding earthly Sanctuary, but rather we seek after the Heavenly Jerusalem.)*

15 By Him therefore let us offer the Sacrifice of Praise to God continually *(we must understand that we are able to praise God and He is able to accept our praises due to the Cross, hence "Praise" being linked to "Sacrifice"; as well, the word "continually" proclaims the fact that this will never change, meaning the Cross will ever abide as the foundation of all things pertaining to God)*, that is, the fruit of *our* lips giving thanks to His Name. *(His Name is "Jesus," which means "Saviour," and speaks of His Sacrificial Offering of Himself on the Cross.)*

16 But to do good and to communicate forget not *(Paul is saying here that our obligations to the Lord are not exhausted with Praise; good deeds must also be included)*: for with such Sacrifices God is well pleased. *(Such action and attitude symbolizes the Cross.)*

17 Obey them who have the rule over you *(has reference to Pastors; however, the emphasis is not on the Pastor, but rather on the Gospel he Preaches)*, and submit yourselves *(refers to submitting to the True Gospel that is being Preached by True Pastors)*: for they watch for your souls *(refers to Preachers who truly have the spiritual welfare of the people at heart)*, as they that must give account, that they may do it with joy, and not with grief *(every Preacher will give account to God for His Ministry)*: for that *is* unprofitable for you. *(If people will not heed the true Gospel being Preached, the Gospel will be of no profit to these particular individuals, whomever they might be, no matter how profitable it is to others. This brings "grief" to the True Preacher.)*

PRAYER

18 Pray for us *(presents a common request by Paul [Rom. 15:30; Eph. 6:18; Col. 4:3; I Thess. 5:25; II Thess. 3:1]):* **for we trust we have a good conscience** *(concerns all things; however, I personally think the Apostle is speaking here of the way he has handled the Law of Moses regarding this Epistle to the Hebrews),* **in all things willing to live honestly.** *(This refers to his daily living for the Lord.)*

19 But I beseech *you* **the rather to do this** *(refers back to His request that they pray for him),* **that I may be restored to you the sooner.** *(This lends credence to the thought that Paul may have been in prison when this Epistle to the Hebrews was written.)*

BENEDICTION

20 Now the God of Peace *(proclaims that Peace has been made between God and fallen man, and done so through what Jesus did on the Cross on man's behalf),* **that brought again from the dead our Lord Jesus** *(presents the only mention of the Resurrection of Christ in this Epistle to the Hebrews),* **that Great Shepherd of the sheep** *(presents the One Who died for us, and Whom God raised from the dead),* **through the Blood of the Everlasting Covenant** *(points to the Cross and proclaims the fact that this Covenant, being perfect, is Eternal),*

21 Make you perfect in every good work to do His Will *(refers to that which the Holy Spirit has been sent to do, and Who will do such through Christ),* **working in you that which is well-pleasing in His sight, through Jesus Christ** *(proclaims the fact that men can do what is acceptable to God only through Jesus Christ);* **to Whom** *be* **Glory forever and ever. Amen.** *(This is because of what He did at the Cross.)*

22 And I beseech you, Brethren, suffer the word of exhortation *(this refers to the arguments and counsels in this entire Epistle):* **for I have written a Letter unto you in few words.** *(Considering the subject matter, the Letter is short.)*

23 Know ye that *our* **Brother Timothy is set at liberty** *(presents another strong proof that Paul wrote this Epistle);* **with whom, if he come shortly, I will see you.** *(This phrase gives no clue whatsoever if this actually happened.)*

24 Salute *(greet)* **all them who have the rule over you** *(more than likely refers to their Pastors and other Saints in that particular Church or Churches),* **and all the Saints. They of Italy salute you.** *(This proves this Epistle was written from Italy, and more than likely Rome. As well, the manner of this Benediction is Paul's style. Also, whoever wrote the Epistle to the Hebrews had to know two things extensively so, and I speak of the Law of Moses and the Cross of Christ. Only Paul fit this description.)*

25 Grace *be* **with you all. Amen.**

THE EPISTLE GENERAL OF
JAMES

CHAPTER 1
(A.D. 60)
INTRODUCTION

JAMES *(the Brother of our Lord)*, a servant of God and of the Lord Jesus Christ *(he never referred to himself as an Apostle, even though he definitely was one [Gal. 1:19])*, to the Twelve Tribes which are scattered abroad, greeting. *(This proclaims the fact that the Twelve Tribes of Israel were still in existence, so ten of them were not lost as some claim.)*

VICTORY

2 My Brethren, count it all joy when you fall into divers temptations *(refers not so much to the allurement of sin, as it does testing and trials)*;

3 Knowing *this*, that the trying of your Faith works patience. *(If it is genuine Faith, testing serves to develop its persistence.)*

4 But let patience have *her* perfect work *(means we must not grow discouraged regarding the test or trial we are going through)*, that you may be perfect and entire, wanting nothing. *(The goal in view is that Believers "may be mature and complete.")*

FAITH

5 If any of you lack wisdom *(pertains to proper knowledge of the Word of God)*, let him ask of God, Who gives to all *men* liberally *(the Lord gives to those who ask, providing they ask the right thing; a greater knowledge of the Word of God is always the right thing)*, and upbraideth not; and it shall be given him. *(This means when we ask wisdom of Him, He will not reproach or chide us for our past conduct. He permits us to come in the freest manner, and meets us with a spirit of entire kindness, and with promptness in granting our requests.)*

6 But let him ask in Faith *(some accuse James of denigrating Faith; however, he actually does the very opposite, making Faith a criteria for all things)*, nothing wavering *(nothing doubting)*. For he who wavers is like a wave of the sea driven with the wind and tossed. *(He who continuously veers from one course to another*

only reveals his own instability and lack of a sense of being under Divine control.)*

7 For let not that man think that he shall receive any thing of the Lord. *(This points to a particular type of individual, one who has a "doubting heart.")*

8 A double minded man *is* unstable in all his ways. *(One cannot place one's Faith in the Cross and something else at the same time. Such produces instability, a type of Faith that will never be honored by the Lord.)*

HUMILITY

9 Let the Brother of low degree *(refers to one who is "lowly, insignificant, weak, and poor")* rejoice in that he is exalted *(refers to the greatest place and position of all, one's position in Christ)*:

10 But the rich, in that he is made low *(is meant to point toward trust in riches, which lowers one in the sight of God)*: because as the flower of the grass he shall pass away. *(Worldly riches are temporal. We lose them quickly, or else we die and leave them.)*

11 For the sun is no sooner risen with a burning heat, but it withers the grass, and the flower thereof falls, and the grace of the fashion of it perishes *(presents an apt illustration for all things that are of this world)*: so also shall the rich man fade away in his ways. *(The man fades, whether the riches do or not.)*

ENDURANCE

12 Blessed *is* the man who endures temptation *(refers to the test of Faith)*: for when he is tried, he shall receive the Crown of Life *(refers to a reward much greater than the price paid)*, which the Lord has promised to them who love Him. *(If we truly love Him, we will truly keep His Commandments [Jn. 14:15], which we can do with the help of the Holy Spirit, Who requires that our Faith ever rest in the Cross [Rom. 6:3-5, 11, 14].)*

TEMPTATION

13 Let no man say when he is tempted, I

am tempted of God (*we must not assume that enticement to sin comes from God; it never does!*): for God cannot be tempted with evil, neither tempts He any man (*God's omnipotent Holy Will fully resists any direction toward sin*):

14 But every man is tempted, when he is drawn away of his own lust, and enticed. (*The temptation to sin appeals to a moral defect in us, even in the best, for none are perfect.*)

15 Then when lust has conceived (*speaks of evil lust*), it brings forth sin (*as stated, these temptations do not come from God, but from the appetites of man's sinful nature, which is a result of the Fall; the sin nature can be held at bay, and is meant to be held at bay by the Believer anchoring his Faith in the Cross of Christ, which will then give the Holy Spirit latitude to help*): and sin, when it is finished, brings forth death. (*This refers to spiritual death, because sin separates man from God.*)

16 Do not err, my beloved Brethren (*James is saying to Believers, "don't be deceived; sin is the ruin of all that is good."*)

GOD'S GOODNESS

17 Every good gift and every perfect gift is from above (*presents the Gift of His Son, the Lord Jesus Christ, by Whom every "Perfect Gift" is given*), and comes down from the Father of Lights (*evil is darkness; light is goodness*), with Whom is no variableness, neither shadow of turning. (*This is what God is, and He will never change.*)

18 Of His Own Will begat He us with the Word of Truth (*presents the imparting of Divine Life through the Word, and is of unspeakable significance*), that we should be a kind of Firstfruits of His creatures. (*"Firstfruits" represent not only what we have received, which, in effect, is a promise of what we are to receive in the future, but as well recognizes the principle of Divine Ownership and all that we possess.*)

CHRISTIAN LIVING

19 Wherefore, my beloved Brethren, let every man be swift to hear (*refers to the Word of God*), slow to speak (*could be translated, "slow to murmur"; we shouldn't murmur at all, but knowing the human heart, "slow to murmur" is more within our reach*), slow to wrath (*all of these things can be handled at the Cross, and only at the Cross*):

20 For the wrath of man worketh not the Righteousness of God. (*This proclaims the fact that the anger and irritation of the natural heart do not produce anything God accepts as Righteous.*)

21 Wherefore lay apart all filthiness (*refers to moral impurity*) and superfluity of naughtiness (*increased evil to which moral impurity will lead; these things can be laid aside only by the Believer understanding that all things come to Him through Christ and what He did at the Cross, which demands that the Cross ever be the Object of our Faith; in this capacity, the Holy Spirit, without Whom we cannot function, will use His Power on our behalf in order to give us victory*), and receive with meekness the engrafted word, which is able to save your souls. (*The story of the Bible, i.e., "the Word," is the story of the Cross.*)

22 But be ye doers of the Word (*the "Word" has the potential to do great and mighty things within our lives*), and not hearers only (*while hearing the Word is definitely necessary, at the same time it must be heard properly, and that refers to a heart that wants to receive*), deceiving your own selves. (*It's bad enough to be deceived by others, but worse yet to purposely deceive ourselves. If we think we can live this life without total Faith in Christ and the Cross, we are doing exactly what James said not to do, "deceiving ourselves."*)

23 For if any be a hearer of the word, and not a doer, he is like unto a man beholding his natural face in a glass (*he sees only that which is external and, therefore, cannot make a proper evaluation*):

24 For he beholds himself, and goes his way (*which is not God's Way*), and straightway forgets what manner of man he was. (*An evaluation of ourselves is necessary. However, it is God Alone Who knows the heart which the Word of God, properly presented, reveals.*)

25 But whoso looks into the perfect Law of Liberty (*defines the whole body of revealed truth concerning the Word of God*), and continues *therein* (*there must be a continuous abiding in the Word*), he being not a forgetful hearer, but a doer of the work, this man shall be blessed in his deed. (*Obeying the Word of God brings great Blessing. However, the only way it can be obeyed is for the Believer to unequivocally place his Faith in Christ and the Cross.*)

26 If any man among you seem to be religious (*would have been better translated, "if any man among you seems to be spiritual"*), and

bridles not his tongue *(again, only the Holy Spirit within our lives can do this)*, **but deceives his own heart, this man's religion** *is* **vain.** *(This would have been better translated, "profession is vain.")*

27 Pure religion *(should have been translated, "pure spirituality")* **and undefiled before God and the Father is this** *(refers to that which pleases God)*, **To visit the fatherless and widows in their affliction** *(proper Faith will always produce proper works)*, *and* **to keep himself unspotted from the world** *(Victory in everyday life and living, which again must have the help and Power of the Holy Spirit)*.

CHAPTER 2
(A.D. 60)
BROTHERLY LOVE

MY Brethren, have not the Faith of our Lord Jesus Christ, *the Lord* of Glory *(should have been translated, "My Brethren, you have not the Faith of our Lord Jesus Christ"; in other words, the ones James was writing to were not conducting themselves as the Lord)*, **with respect of persons.** *(If the Lord doesn't show respect of persons, then we should not as well!)*

2 For if there come unto your assembly a man with a gold ring, in goodly apparel *(addresses the rich)*, **and there come in also a poor man in vile raiment** *(refers to the obvious)*;

3 And you have respect to him who wears the gay clothing, and say unto him, Sit you here in a good place *(show him partiality)*; **and say to the poor, you stand there, or sit here under my footstool** *(proclaims a terrible attitude and spirit)*:

4 Are you not then partial in yourselves *(answers itself)*, **and are become judges of evil thoughts?** *(To show "respect of persons" is looked at by God as "evil.")*

5 Hearken, my beloved Brethren, Has not God chosen the poor of this world rich in Faith, and heirs of the Kingdom which He has promised to them who love Him? *(This demands a positive answer. Not many mighty, not many noble, answer the Call [I Cor. 1:26-29].)*

6 But you have despised the poor. *(This refers to the fact that some Christians had despised those whom God had chosen.)* **Do not rich men oppress you, and draw you before the judgment seats?** *(This proclaims a worldwide problem that has existed from the beginning of time, and continues unto this present hour.)*

7 Do not they blaspheme that worthy name

by the which you are called? *(Those who place their Faith and trust in money will ultimately blaspheme the Name of the Lord.)*

8 If you fulfil the Royal Law according to the Scripture *(Lev. 19:18; Mat. 22:39)*, **You shall love your neighbour as yourself, you do well** *(show favor to everyone, whether rich or poor)*:

9 But if you have respect to persons, you commit sin *(there are many things of this nature which God constitutes as sin, but to which many Believers pay little heed)*, **and are convinced of the Law as transgressors.** *(Refers to the Law of Moses, which was the only acceptable moral Law in the world of that day. To be sure, its moral precepts continue to be binding on the entirety of the human race, but Jesus fulfilled them in totality.)*

FAITH AND WORKS

10 For whosoever shall keep the whole Law *(Law of Moses)*, **and yet offend in one** *point*, **he is guilty of all.** *(This proclaims in no uncertain terms the impossibility of the Believer finding Victory through the Law, whether the Law of Moses, or any type of Law. It simply cannot be done!)*

11 For he who said, Do not commit adultery, said also, Do not kill. Now if you commit no adultery, yet if you kill, you are become a transgressor of the Law. *(The breaking of even one Commandment puts the person in the position of a "transgressor.")*

12 So speak ye, and so do *(what we say, we ought to do)*, **as they who shall be judged by the Law of Liberty.** *(This pertains to the coming Judgment Seat of Christ.)*

13 For he shall have judgment without Mercy, who has shown no Mercy *(if we withhold Mercy here, or whatever that is right, we will face the same at the Judgment Seat of Christ)*; **and Mercy rejoices against Judgment.** *(This presents the fact that one who shows Mercy in this life will have nothing to fear at the Judgment Seat of Christ.)*

14 What *does it* **profit, my Brethren, though a man say he has Faith, and have not works?** *(This presents the fact that proper Faith will always produce proper works.)* **can Faith save him?** *(This should have been translated, "is that Faith able to save him?" The truth is God will not recognize that type of Faith.)*

15 If a Brother or sister be naked, and destitute of daily food,

16 And one of you say unto them, Depart in

Peace, be *ye* warmed and filled; notwithstanding you give them not those things which are needful to the body; what *does it* profit? (*This refers to claimed Faith which blesses no one, simply because it's not true Faith. True Faith will help the person.*)

17 Even so Faith, if it has not works, is dead, being alone. (*As stated, proper Faith will produce proper works. If not, the Holy Spirit says here that it is "dead faith."*)

18 Yes, a man may say, You have Faith, and I have works (*proclaims the efforts by some to divide the two*): show me your Faith without your works, and I will show you my Faith by my works. (*This proclaims the fact that the profession of a lifeless Faith is profitless.*)

19 You believe that there is one God (*presents the type of Faith held by hundreds of millions, but in which there is no saving grace*); you do well (*you think you do well!*): the Devils also believe, and tremble. (*Simply believing there is a God says no more than what demons believe. Proper Faith will accept the Lord as one's Saviour.*)

20 But will you know, O vain man, that Faith without works is dead? (*In effect, James bluntly says anyone who trusts in an empty Faith has, in effect, an empty head.*)

21 Was not Abraham our father Justified by works, when he had offered Isaac his son upon the Altar? (*Any Faith that doesn't have the Cross as its proper Object is dead Faith. The Holy Spirit had James choose this example of Abraham offering Isaac to portray one of the most vivid illustrations of the Sacrifice of Christ.*)

22 Seest thou how Faith wrought with his works, and by works was Faith made perfect? (*James is making it clear that he is not talking about works as the sole source of Abraham's Justification as Verse 21, if taken out of context, might lead one to believe. Abraham's Faith and his actions were working together.*)

23 And the Scripture was fulfilled which said (*Gen. 15:6*), Abraham believed God, and it was imputed unto him for Righteousness (*proclaims the fact that Abraham's Faith was genuine*): and he was called the Friend of God (*Isa. 41:8*).

24 You see then how that by works a man is Justified (*could be better understood by saying, "You see then, how that by works a man's Justification is proven"*), and not by Faith only. (*This must be understood in the context of the entire Passage. The Apostle is merely saying that no one can claim Justification on the basis of Faith*

alone, *which produces no qualifying works. Such an individual is deceiving himself.*)

25 Likewise also was not Rahab the harlot Justified by works, when she had received the messengers, and had sent *them* out another way? (*This presents one of the most beautiful stories of Faith found in the annals of human history. This was proper Faith, which produced proper works.*)

26 For as the body without the spirit is dead, so Faith without works is dead also. (*In closing our comments on this Chapter, I must remind you with Paul that works without dynamic living Faith in the Lord Jesus cannot produce Salvation or Victory. On the other hand, I must also remind you with James that Faith in the form of declaring a dogma or confessing a creed, which fails to produce life and labor according to the Word of God, will likewise condemn you.*)

CHAPTER 3
(A.D. 60)
THE TONGUE

MY Brethren, be not many masters (*should have been translated, "be not many Teachers"*), knowing that we shall receive the greater condemnation. (*This refers to the fact that mishandling the Word of God will ultimately bring one tremendous problems. God holds the Teacher more responsible than the student.*)

2 For in many things we offend all. (*This refers to the universality of sin and failure, even among Believers.*) If any man offend not in word, the same *is* a perfect man, *and* able also to bridle the whole body. (*The Holy Spirit Alone can control the Believer's tongue.*)

3 Behold, we put bits in the horses' mouths, that they may obey us; and we turn about their whole body. (*The Holy Spirit is saying our mouths should obey us, instead of us obeying our mouths.*)

4 Behold also the ships, which though *they be* so great, and *are* driven of fierce winds, yet are they turned about with a very small helm, whithersoever the governor lists. (*This refers here to the "helm" being likened unto the "tongue."*)

5 Even so the tongue is a little member (*it is small, but it exerts a powerful influence*), and boasts great things (*responsible for great things, whether good or bad*). Behold, how great a matter a little fire kindles! (*The image projected here by James is the picture of a vast forest in*

flames, all begun by the falling of a single spark.)

6 And the tongue *is* a fire *(speaks of fire in a negative way, that which destroys)*, a world of iniquity *(the tongue in some way is responsible for all the iniquity in the world)*: so is the tongue among our members *(body members)*, that it defiles the whole body *(constantly speaking in a negative way can bring about physical illness in the body)*, and sets on fire the course of nature *(the tongue sets us on a particular path, and in this case the wrong path)*; and it is set on fire of hell. *(By using the word "hell," we are made to understand not only the wickedness of the tongue, but as well its destructive power.)*

7 For every kind of beasts, and of birds, and of serpents, and of things in the sea, is tamed, and has been tamed of mankind *(a proven fact)*:

8 But the tongue can no man tame *(this is the Word of the Lord; however, the tongue can most definitely be tamed by the Holy Spirit; the way it is done has to do with the Cross of Christ; the Holy Spirit works within the parameters of the Finished Work of Christ on the Cross; He demands that we ever make the Cross the Object of our Faith, and then He can do mighty things within our lives [Rom. 8:1-2, 11])*; *it is* an unruly evil, full of deadly poison. *(The Believer must realize this. It means that just because he is saved, such doesn't necessarily guarantee a change in this problem. As stated, it definitely can be, and, in fact, must be, changed, but it can only be so by and through the Cross.)*

9 Therewith bless we God, even the Father; and therewith curse we men *(proclaims the inconsistency, to say the least, of blessing God one moment and cursing men the next)*, which are made after the similitude of God. *(In a sense, when we curse men, which refers to wishing them hurt, we are cursing God. To curse the Creation is to curse the Creator.)*

10 Out of the same mouth proceeds blessing and cursing *(presents the tongue devoted to uses so different)*. My Brethren, these things ought not so to be. *(If the Lord has His Way in our hearts and lives, they won't be.)*

11 Does a fountain send forth at the same place sweet *water* and bitter? *(Of necessity, this question must be answered in the negative.)*

12 Can the fig tree, my Brethren, bear olive berries? either a vine, figs? so *can* no fountain both yield salt water and fresh. *(This speaks of nature. However, man can do what nature cannot do.)*

WISDOM

13 Who *is* a wise man and endued with knowledge among you? *(This refers to a true teacher of the Word of God.)* let him show out of a good conversation *(lifestyle)* his works with meekness of wisdom *(refers to the conduct of the Believer)*.

14 But if you have bitter envying and strife in your hearts *(proclaims the "sin nature" springing to life, thereby, ruling in the Believer's life [Rom. 6:12-13])*, Glory not *(boast not)*, and lie not against the truth. *(This refers to the fact that if we do boast of anything other than the Cross, we are "lying," pure and simple [Gal. 6:14].)*

15 This wisdom descends not from above *(any wisdom that claims Salvation or Victory in any way or manner other than the Cross is not wisdom from above)*, but *is* earthly, sensual, devilish. *(Whatever its appeal, if it's not the Cross, it is of Satan. This covers humanistic psychology, plus anything else devised by men, i.e., "demons.")*

16 For where envying and strife *is*, there *is* confusion and every evil work. *(If it's not the "Cross," it is "confusion, and every evil work.")*

17 But the wisdom that is from above is first pure *(it is found in all its fullness in Christ, and in Christ Alone)*, then peaceable, gentle, *and* easy to be intreated, full of mercy and good fruits, without partiality, and without hypocrisy. *(These things present the Work of the Holy Spirit, with the Cross as the means and Christ as the Source.)*

18 And the Fruit of Righteousness is sown in Peace of them who make Peace *(presents the Law of sowing and reaping)*.

CHAPTER 4
(A.D. 60)
WORLDLINESS

FROM whence *come* wars and fightings among you? *(When Believers look to anything other than the Cross, strife is the result.)* *come they* not hence, *even* of your lusts that war in your members? *(Once again, the only solution for this problem, which besets every Christian, is that we understand all things come to us from God through the Cross. Making the Cross the Object of our Faith gives the Holy Spirit latitude to work within our lives, in order that we might live the life we ought to live [Rom. 6:3-5, 12-13].)*

2 You lust, and have not *(such a person is not looking to God, but rather operating from self-will)*: you kill, and desire to have, and cannot obtain *(the word "kill" refers to destroying the reputation of another in order to gain advantage, and to do so by slander, etc.)*: you fight and war, yet you have not, because you ask not. *(This refers to Believers who little seek the Lord for anything, but rather depend upon other sources that are irregular to say the least!)*

3 You ask, and receive not *(and there is a reason)*, because you ask amiss, that ye may consume *it* upon your lusts. *(Such a person is not asking in the Will of God, but rather from his or her own selfish desires.)*

4 You adulterers and adulteresses *(presents James using the same terminology as Paul [Rom. 7:1-4]; the Believer is to look exclusively to Christ and the Cross regarding all his needs; to look elsewhere, or rather for one's Faith to be placed in that other than the Cross, presents the person as committing spiritual adultery)*, know ye not that the friendship of the world is enmity with God? *(If the Cross of Christ is not strictly the Object of our Faith, God looks at everything else as "worldliness.")* whosoever therefore will be a friend of the world is the enemy of God. *(Allow me to once again make the statement that if the Cross of Christ is not our Object of Faith, no matter how religious our efforts may be otherwise, it is still looked at by the Lord as "friendship with the world." This means the Believer in essence becomes an "enemy of God.")*

5 Do you think that the Scripture says in vain *(James was quoting several Scriptures [Gen. 15:6; 49:10; Ex. 17:6; Ps. 78:16; Ezek. 47:9; Joel 2:28-29])*, The Spirit Who dwells in us lusts to envy? *(This refers to the Holy Spirit, which means that the word "Spirit" should have been capitalized. The word "lusteth" here means "to earnestly or passionately desire." Of what is He envious, and what does He passionately desire? The Holy Spirit is envious of any control the fallen nature might have over the Believer, and is passionately desirous that He control all our thoughts, words, and deeds. He is desirous of having the Believer depend upon Him for His Ministry to Him, so that He might discharge His responsibility to the One Who sent Him, Namely God the Father.)*

6 But He gives more Grace. *(Providing the Believer ever makes the Cross the Object of His Faith, by which Grace comes from the Lord.)* Wherefore He said *(Job 22:29; Ps. 138:6; Prov. 3:34)*, God resists the proud, but gives Grace unto the humble. *(God resists those who look to that other than the Cross, and blesses those who humble themselves by looking strictly to Christ and the Cross, which develops humility.)*

PRAYER

7 Submit yourselves therefore to God *(to the Plan He has provided, which is the Cross)*. Resist the Devil, and he will flee from you. *(We do this by strictly looking to Christ, and what He has done for us at the Cross, where Satan was totally defeated [Col. 2:14-15].)*

8 Draw near to God, and He will draw near to you. *(Once again and ever so, this is done only by Faith which ever makes the Cross its Object.)* Cleanse *your* hands, *you* sinners; and purify *your* hearts, *you* double minded. *(Without a proper knowledge of the Cross regarding the Sanctification of the Saint, it is impossible for the Believer to live a Victorious, Christian life.)*

9 Be afflicted, and mourn, and weep *(refers to consternation over our having looked to that other than Christ and the Cross)*: let your laughter be turned to mourning, and *your* joy to heaviness. *(This refers to true Repentance, which means we confess our sin of looking to that other than the Cross, thereby, seeking forgiveness. We must repent not only for the bad, but for the good as well. By that, I'm referring to our dependence on good things for victory in our lives, but yet that which is not the Cross.)*

10 Humble yourselves in the sight of the Lord, and He shall lift you up. *(As we have constantly stated, it refers to looking to Christ and the Cross, which is the only humbling process in which the Believer can truthfully engage.)*

JUDGING

11 Speak not evil one of another, Brethren *(refers to self-appointed Judges [Mat. 7:1-5])*. He who speaks evil of *his* Brother, and judges his Brother, speaks evil of the Law, and judges the Law *(pertains to the Law of Moses, to which James is pointing; when a Believer judges another, He has taken himself out from under Grace and placed himself under Law, where he will only find condemnation)*: but if you judge the Law, you are not a doer of the Law, but a Judge. *(In other words, such a person has placed himself in the position of God.)*

12 There is one Lawgiver, Who is able to save and to destroy *(presents God as the only One Who can fill this position)*: who are you who

judges another? *(The Greek actually says, "but you — who are you?" In other words, "who do you think you are?")*

THE SELF-WILLED

13 Go to now, you who say, Today or to-morrow we will go into such a city, and continue there a year, and buy and sell, and get gain *(proclaims the planning of individuals who don't include God)*:

14 Whereas you know not what *shall be* on the morrow *(proclaims the fact that we don't, while God does!)*. For what *is* your life? *(Making plans without God proclaims the fact that we consider ourselves to be our own master.)* It is even a vapour, that appears for a little time, and then vanishes away. *(This means that if the Lord doesn't guide our lives, then all is a waste.)*

15 For that ye *ought* to say *(presents the opposite of the "we will go" in Verse 13)*, If the Lord will, we shall live, and do this, or that *(proclaims our absolute dependence on God)*.

16 But now you rejoice in your boastings *(pertains to rejoicing in one's self-made plans)*: all such rejoicing is evil. *(All rejoicing should be in the Lord, and only in the Lord.)*

SIN

17 Therefore to him who knows to do good, and does *it* not, to him it is sin. *(Sin is an offence against God, which He cannot tolerate. If we do not abide by the Word of God, then we sin.)*

CHAPTER 5
(A.D. 60)
THE RICH

G O to now, *you* rich men, weep and howl for your miseries that shall come upon *you*. *(This warning is to the wealthy who have gained their riches by fraud and deceit.)*

2 Your riches are corrupted, and your garments are motheaten. *(These types of riches will do no one any good, and above all, the person who has such.)*

3 Your gold and silver is cankered *(the idea is gold and silver laid up and not put to any use that is good)*; and the rust of them shall be a witness against you, and shall eat your flesh as it were fire. *(The having of money is not wrong. The question is what are we doing with this which God has given us? If we do not use it for His Glory, making certain that it is for His Glory, the Lord warns us here that such riches will consume us.)* You have heaped treasure together for the last days *(which means the treasure is not being laid up in Heaven [Mat. 6:19-20])*.

4 Behold, the hire of the labourers who have reaped down your fields, which is of you kept back by fraud, cries *(this Passage tells us, and rightly so, that far too much treasure is heaped up at the expense of others)*: and the cries of them which have reaped are entered into the ears of the Lord of Sabaoth *(the Lord of Hosts)*.

5 You have lived in pleasure on the earth, and been wanton *(luxury and self-indulgence at the expense of others is a great sin in God's eyes)*; you have nourished your hearts, as in a day of slaughter. *(James uses graphic imagery to indicate that the wicked rich, who have gained their riches at the expense of others, are always on the brink of Judgment.)*

6 You have condemned *and* killed the just; *and* he does not resist you. *(In hoarding such gain, some of the Righteous are victims. The Lord takes careful note of this, and especially of their helplessness.)*

PATIENCE

7 Be patient therefore, Brethren, unto the Coming of the Lord. *(This tells us the cure and, in fact, the only cure for the injustices in this world. It is the Coming of the Lord.)* Behold, the husbandman waits for the precious fruit of the earth, and has long patience for it, until he receive the early and latter rain. *(The Holy Spirit, through James, tells us in a few words that the Coming of the Lord will take place shortly after the "Latter Rain," which in fact the world is now experiencing. This means the Second Coming is very near, and the Rapture is even at the door. The Second Coming will definitely address the gross injustices of this planet.)*

8 Be you also patient; stablish your hearts *(draw close to the Lord, which can only be done by making the Cross the Object of our Faith)*: for the Coming of the Lord draws near. *(The Rapture of the Church should ever be in our minds.)*

9 Grudge not one against another, Brethren, lest you be condemned *(the unjust Judgment of fellow Christians is sometimes more painful than the hatred of unbelievers)*: behold, the Judge stands before the door. *(This refers to the Lord Jesus and His readiness to avenge all wrong)*.

10 Take, my Brethren, the Prophets, who have spoken in the Name of the Lord, for an example of suffering affliction, and of patience. *(Even though they were Prophets, which means they stood in a high and holy Office, they were not exempt from affliction.)*

11 Behold, we count them happy which endure. *(The word "endure" refers to the fact that the test or trial may last for some time.)* You have heard of the patience of Job, and have seen the end of the Lord; that the Lord is very pitiful, and of tender mercy. *(This is meant to proclaim the fact that whatever the Lord allows is meant for our good. We should understand that, and seek to learn the lesson desired to be taught.)*

TRUTH

12 But above all things, my Brethren, swear not, neither by Heaven, neither by the earth, neither by any other oath *(refers to the fact that the Lord is guiding every Believer, even in times of trial, and correspondingly we must not lose Faith, thereby, taking matters into our own hands)*: but let your yes be yes; and *your* no, no; lest you fall into condemnation. *(Even though we do not understand the reason for the situation, whatever it might be, we aren't to question the Lord!)*

HEALING

13 Is any among you afflicted? let him pray. *(Prayer is the recommendation of the Holy Spirit concerning affliction. But how many Christians take advantage of this privilege?)* Is any merry? let him sing Psalms. *(In effect, refers to singing as a form of prayer, which it actually is, that is if we sing songs that rightly glorify the Lord.)*

14 Is any sick among you? *(This refers to physical or emotional illness of any nature.)* let him call for the Elders *(Pastors)* of the Church; and let them pray over him *(refers to asking the Lord for healing regarding the need)*, anointing him with oil in the Name of the Lord *(the "oil" has no medicinal purpose, but is rather meant to symbolize the Holy Spirit, and is used as a point of contact concerning our Faith; prayer is to be offered in the Name of Jesus [Jn. 16:23])*:

PRAYER OF FAITH

15 And the prayer of Faith shall save the sick *(the "prayer of Faith" is simply the belief that God hears and answers prayer)*, and the Lord shall raise him up *(proclaims the Lord as the Healer, as is obvious, with the Cross being the means of all this; it is the Holy Spirit Who carries it out)*; and if he have committed sins, they shall be forgiven him. *(The conditional clause, "if he has sinned," makes it clear that not all sickness is the result of sin, but some definitely is. That being the case, the Lord will both heal and forgive upon believing Faith.)*

16 Confess *your* faults one to another *(refers to being quick to admit fault, if such be the case)*, and pray one for another, that you may be healed. *(The Holy Spirit, through James, broadens the aspect of prayer for the sick as applicable to any Believer.)* The effectual fervent prayer of a Righteous man avails much *(from any "Righteous man," Preacher or otherwise; "Righteousness" pertains to the fact that the Faith of the individual is strictly in Christ and the Cross, and not in other things)*.

17 Elijah was a man subject to like passions as we are *(is said in this manner because the Holy Spirit wants us to know that what is in the reach of one is as well in the reach of the other)*, and he prayed earnestly that it might not rain: and it rained not on the earth by the space of three years and six months *(showing us the power of prayer, that is if we pray in the Will of God)*.

18 And he prayed again, and the Heaven gave rain, and the earth brought forth her fruit *(refers to the effect of one man's prayers)*.

THE TRUTH

19 Brethren, if any of you do err from the Truth *(James is speaking here of Believers, and of them straying from the Truth of the Cross)*, and one convert him *(refers to strengthening the individual, turning him back to the right way of Truth, which is back to Christ and the Cross)*;

20 Let him know, that he which converteth the sinner from the error of his way *(bluntly proclaims any way other than the Cross as the "way of sin," which then makes the one traveling such a way "a sinner")* shall save a soul from death, and shall hide a multitude of sins. *(This refers to the fact that if the Believer leaves the Cross, thereby transferring his Faith to something else, and such an erring way is continued, it will result in the loss of the soul. To pull one back to the Cross saves that soul, which the Cross Alone can do!)*

THE FIRST EPISTLE GENERAL OF
PETER

CHAPTER 1
(A.D. 60)

INTRODUCTION

PETER *(the name means "rock," and is used metaphorically here to describe Peter as a man like a rock by reason of his firmness and strength of soul)*, **an Apostle of Jesus Christ** *(presents the authoritative tone of this Epistle)*, **to the strangers** *(strangers to Peter because he had not previously met them)* **scattered throughout Pontus, Galatia, Cappadocia, Asia, and Bithynia** *(describes this Epistle being sent to Christian Jews who had settled in certain parts of the Roman Empire; however, it is also meant for the Gentiles)*,

2 Elect *(those who elect to favorably respond to the Call of the Holy Spirit, are the elect of God)* **according to the foreknowledge of God the Father** *(refers to God seeing ahead that He would have to send a Saviour to redeem man from the Fall; all who accept the Saviour are the "elect")*, **through Sanctification of the Spirit** *(elected to be Sanctified by the Holy Spirit)*, **unto obedience and sprinkling of the Blood of Jesus Christ** *(pertains to the fact that the Holy Spirit Sanctifies us on the basis of the Finished Work of Christ, where our Faith must reside; as the Cross is everything concerning Salvation, it is also everything concerning Sanctification)*: **Grace unto you, and Peace, be multiplied.** *(Both attributes come through the Cross, and will continue to multiply as long as our Faith is firmly anchored in the Cross of Christ.)*

THANKSGIVING

3 Blessed *be* **the God and Father of our Lord Jesus Christ** *(we are to Bless God at all times because of what He has done for us through Jesus Christ)*, **which according to His abundant Mercy** *(presents the fact that the Law and vengeance are no longer before us, but rather pure Mercy)* **has begotten us again unto a lively hope** *(proclaims the fact that we are transplanted from Adam's heritage into the heritage of God)* **by the Resurrection of Jesus Christ from the dead** *(this refers to us being raised with Christ to "newness of life," which enables us to live a Holy Life [Rom. 6:3-5])*,

4 To an inheritance incorruptible, and undefiled, and that fades not away *(we, as begotten Children of God, are Heirs of God and Joint-heirs with His Son, the Lord Jesus Christ [Rom. 8:17])*, **reserved in Heaven for you** *(carries the idea that God is guarding our inheritance for us under constant surveillance)*,

5 Who are kept by the Power of God through Faith *(refers to the Holy Spirit exerting His Power on our behalf, as our Faith is ever planted in the Cross [Rom. 6:5])* **unto Salvation ready to be revealed in the last time** *(ready for the Rapture)*.

FAITH

6 Wherein you greatly rejoice *(refers to the time when this earthly sojourn will be finished, the Trump of God sounds, and "we shall be changed" [I Cor. 15:51-54])*, **though now for a season, if need be, you are in heaviness through manifold temptations** *(this life is the dress rehearsal for Eternity)*:

7 That the trial of your Faith *(all Faith is tested, and great Faith must be tested greatly)*, **being much more precious than of gold that perishes** *(the emphasis is the testing of our Faith to show whether or not it is genuine; the Holy Spirit says such is more precious than the testing of gold, which is the most precious commodity in the world; is our Faith really in the Cross or not?)*, **though it be tried with fire** *(the fire of temptation, trouble, etc.; such are meant to show the weakness)*, **might be found unto Praise and Honour and Glory** *(which can only be done if the Cross of Christ is the sole Object of our Faith)* **at the appearing of Jesus Christ** *(we are being prepared by the Holy Spirit as fit subjects for the appearing of our Lord, as it regards the Rapture)*:

JOY UNSPEAKABLE

8 Whom *(Jesus Christ)* **having not seen, you love** *(we haven't personally seen the Lord, but the Holy Spirit has made Him real to our hearts)*; **in Whom, though now you see** *Him* **not, yet believing** *(proclaims total and complete Faith*

in Christ, *though He has not been seen by the natural eyes, but Whom we shall one day see*), **you rejoice with Joy unspeakable and full of Glory** (*the intended state for every Believer, and which can be attained despite trials and afflictions if Faith is anchored firmly in the Cross*):

9 Receiving the end of your Faith, *even* **the Salvation of** *your* **souls** (*refers to the coming Resurrection, when we will then be Glorified*).

10 Of which Salvation the Prophets have enquired and searched diligently (*Old Testament Prophets carefully and diligently sought the meaning of the things they were prophesying as it concerned Christ and what He would do to Redeem humanity* [*Gen. 49:10; Isa., Chpt. 53*]), **who Prophesied of the Grace** *that should come* **unto you** (*this "Grace" was not for their day, but for the coming dispensation, all made possible by the Cross*):

11 Searching what (*these men diligently searched their own Prophecies, and the Prophecies of other Prophets, so that they might know that of which was spoken*), **or what manner of time** (*what kind of time would usher in this particular unique Salvation? the time of Grace alone, which means the Law would be no more*) **the Spirit of Christ which was in them did signify** (*whatever the Spirit of God did in Old Testament times, all pertained to Christ, without exception*), **when it testified beforehand the sufferings of Christ** (*refers to the Message of the Old Testament, all given by the Holy Spirit, and all pointing to the coming Redemption of man, which would be brought about by the Cross of Christ*), **and the Glory that should follow.** (*This proclaims all the wonderful things made possible by the "Sufferings of Christ."*)

12 Unto whom it was revealed (*refers to the Church*), **that not unto themselves, but unto us they did Minister the things** (*proclaims the entirety of the Old Testament*), **which are now reported unto you by them who have Preached the Gospel unto you** (*refers to what Christ did at the Cross, which the Prophets predicted*) **with the Holy Spirit sent down from Heaven** (*the Holy Spirit verified what Christ did at the Cross by coming from Heaven in a new dimension, thereby abiding in the hearts and lives of Believers, and doing so permanently* [*Jn. 14:16-17*]); **which things the Angels desire to look into.** (*In other words, the Church is the University for Angels.*)

HOLY LIVING

13 Wherefore gird up the loins of your mind (*in view of what the Lord has done for us, we should have a hopeful spirit of optimism*), **be sober, and hope to the end for the Grace that is to be brought unto you** (*actually speaks of the Glorification of the Saints*) **at the Revelation of Jesus Christ** (*refers to the coming Rapture of the Church*);

14 As obedient children, not fashioning yourselves according to the former lusts in your ignorance (*don't be ruled by the sin nature which ruled you before coming to Christ*):

15 But as He which has called you is Holy (*God is Holy, so we are to be Holy as well*), **so be ye Holy in all manner of conversation** (*refers to lifestyle*);

16 Because it is written (*Lev. 11:44*), **Be ye Holy; for I am Holy.** (*All of this can only be done in one way. Placing our Faith exclusively in the Cross of Christ gives the Holy Spirit latitude to help us, and He Alone can develop Holiness within our lives. It cannot be done by self-will, or by rules, regulations, etc.*)

17 And if you call on the Father (*should have been translated, "since you call on the Father"*), **Who without respect of persons** (*says in the Greek, "does not receive face"; God does not receive anyone's face; He is impartial*) **judges according to every man's work** (*God Alone is our Judge, not man; man can be fooled; God cannot!*), **pass the time of your sojourning** *here* **in fear** (*a fear of self-trust*):

REDEMPTION

18 Forasmuch as you know that you were not Redeemed with corruptible things, *as* **silver and gold** (*presents the fact that the most precious commodities* [*silver and gold*] *could not Redeem fallen man*), **from your vain conversation** (*vain lifestyle*) *received* **by tradition from your fathers** (*speaks of original sin that is passed on from father to child at conception*);

THE CROSS

19 But with the Precious Blood of Christ (*presents the payment, which proclaims the poured out Life of Christ on behalf of sinners*), **as of a Lamb without blemish and without spot** (*speaks of the lambs offered as substitutes in the Old Jewish economy; the Death of Christ was not an execution or assassination, but rather a Sacrifice; the Offering of Himself presented a Perfect Sacrifice, for He was Perfect in every respect* [*Ex. 12:5*]):

20 Who verily was foreordained before the foundation of the world (refers to the fact that God, in His Omniscience, knew He would create man, man would Fall, and man would be Redeemed by Christ going to the Cross; this was all done before the Universe was created; this means the Cross of Christ is the Foundation Doctrine of all Doctrine, referring to the fact that all Doctrine must be built upon that Foundation, or else it is specious), but was manifest in these last times for you (refers to the invisible God Who, in the Person of the Son, was made visible to human eyesight by assuming a human body and human limitations),

21 Who by Him do believe in God (it is only by Christ and what He did for us at the Cross that we are able to "Believe in God"), Who raised Him (Christ) up from the dead (His Resurrection was guaranteed insomuch as He Atoned for all sin [Rom. 6:23]), and gave Him Glory (refers to the exaltation of Christ); that your Faith and Hope might be in God. (This speaks of a heart Faith in God, Who saves sinners in answer to our Faith in the Resurrected Lord Jesus Who died for us.)

22 Seeing you have purified your souls (in effect, says in the Greek, "having purified your souls") in obeying the Truth (the great system of Truth respecting the Redemption of the world, which refers to the Cross) through the Spirit (everything is done "through the Spirit") unto unfeigned love of the Brethren (refers to love which is not hypocritical), see that you love one another with a pure heart fervently (the God kind of love, which can only come about as the Believer anchors his Faith in the Cross, and does so exclusively):

23 Being born again, not of corruptible seed (refers to the fact that the Born-Again experience is not at all by virtue of any descent from human parents), but of incorruptible (which is the Lord Jesus Christ), by the Word of God, which lives and abides forever. (The story of the Bible is the story of man's Redemption, which is the story of the Cross.)

24 For all flesh is as grass (the Apostle is contrasting that which is begotten of God with that which is begotten by man [Isa. 40:6-8]), and all the glory of man as the flower of grass (refers to a very temporary glory). The grass withers, and the flower thereof falls away (considering that, our hopes had better be in the things of God, and not the things of man):

25 But the Word of the Lord endures forever (by contrast to that of man, which perishes quickly). And this is the Word which by the Gospel is preached unto you. (Preach the Cross, which brings Eternal dividends [I Cor. 1:21, 23; 2:2].)

CHAPTER 2
(A.D. 60)
HINDRANCES

WHEREFORE laying aside all malice, and all guile, and hypocrisies, and envies, and all evil speakings (these things can be laid aside only as much as the Cross of Christ is the Object of our Faith; that being the case, the Holy Spirit will perform the work He Alone can do),

SPIRITUAL GROWTH

2 As newborn babes (those recently saved), desire the sincere milk of the Word (the Word of God in general is a life sustaining factor in the spiritual sense), that you may grow thereby (Spiritual Growth is predicated on a knowledge of the Word):

3 If so be you have tasted ("since you have tasted") that the Lord is Gracious. (This points to the Cross, which is the means of Grace.)

4 To Whom coming (come exclusively to Jesus), as unto a Living Stone (Christ is the Rock), disallowed indeed of men (refers to the rejection of Christ by Israel), but chosen of God, and precious (men disallowed One Whom God had chosen, i.e., Christ),

CHIEF CORNERSTONE

5 You also, as lively stones (because of being "in Christ"), are built up a spiritual house (refers to the Church; not the institutional Church, but rather all who are Born-Again, i.e., the Family of God), an Holy Priesthood (all Born-Again Believers are members of the "Holy Priesthood," but Christ Alone is the Great High Priest), to offer up spiritual Sacrifices (the word "Sacrifices" refers to the Cross and to our Faith ever being in that Finished Work; if it is truly "spiritual," then it most truly must have the Cross as its Object), acceptable to God by Jesus Christ. (Faith in Christ and the Cross alone is acceptable to God. This means Faith having anything else as its Object is unacceptable.)

6 Wherefore also it is contained in the Scripture (Isa. 28:16), Behold, I lay in Sion a Chief Cornerstone, elect, precious (suggests

that the Image of Jesus as the Chief Cornerstone is an important one for Faith, or for unbelief): and he who believes on Him shall not be confounded (shall not be put to shame).

7 Unto you therefore which believe *He is* precious (refers to the estimate of Christ by those of us who believe in contrast to the view taken of Him by the world): but unto them which be disobedient, the Stone which the builders disallowed, the same is made the Head of the corner (despite the fact that Christ was rejected by Israel, it is to Him that the world will answer),

8 And a Stone of stumbling, and a Rock of offence (because of the Cross [I Cor. 1:23]), *even to them* which stumble at the Word, being disobedient (refers to unbelief): whereunto also they were appointed. (All who reject Christ are appointed to be lost.)

9 But you *are* a chosen generation (a chosen or a new race, made up of all who have accepted Christ), a Royal Priesthood (Christ is King and High Priest; due to being "in Him," we as well are "Kings and Priests" [Rev. 1:6]), an Holy nation (a multitude of people of the same nature), a peculiar people (each Saint is God's unique possession, just as if that Saint were the only human being in existence); that you should show forth the praises of Him Who has called you out of darkness into His marvellous light (He saved us by virtue of what He did at the Cross, for which we should ever praise Him):

10 Which in time past *were* not a people (without God, there is no standing in any capacity), but *are* now the people of God (made possible by what Jesus did at the Cross): which had not obtained Mercy, but now have obtained Mercy. (Mercy is a product of Grace, which is a product of the Cross.)

BELIEVERS

11 Dearly beloved, I beseech *you* as strangers and pilgrims (no one is really a pilgrim in the Biblical sense who has not first become a stranger to this world), abstain from fleshly lusts, which war against the soul (tells us that the "sin nature" is still with us as Christians);

12 Having your conversation (lifestyle) honest among the Gentiles (the word "Gentiles," as used here, does not refer to Gentiles as in contrast to Jews, but to the unsaved world, the world of people without Christ): that, whereas they speak against you as evildoers, they may by *your* good works (separated from sin), which they shall behold (to view carefully as a personal witness), glorify God in the day of visitation (refers to this Day of Grace).

RULERS

13 Submit yourselves to every Ordinance of man for the Lord's sake (Peter is speaking here of Civil Government): whether it be to the king, as supreme (providing the Ordinance does not violate the Word of God);

14 Or unto Governors, as unto them who are sent by him (the local police) for the punishment of evildoers (covers all Civil Government), and for the praise of them who do well. (Evil is to be punished and doing right is to be rewarded, which pertains to a stable society.)

15 For so is the Will of God (Civil Government is ordained by God), that with well doing you may put to silence the ignorance of foolish men (presents the fact that true Christians are the greatest asset of any nation):

16 As free (the freedom we have in Christ), and not using *your* liberty for a cloak of maliciousness, but as the servants of God. (The liberty we have in Christ does not make us above the Law of the Land.)

17 Honour all *men* (if honor is due). Love the brotherhood (refers to the Christian family of Believers). Fear God. (He who properly fears God will not dishonor any man, will love his Brethren, and will as well give due recognition to constituted Civil authority.) Honour the king (in effect, refers to honoring the Office).

SERVANTS

18 Servants (slaves), *be* subject to *your* masters with all fear (indicates that slaves, as a class, formed a large part of the early Christian community); not only to the good and gentle, but also to the froward. (Christian slaves were to conduct themselves Christlike, whether their master was good or not. This admonition covers the modern employer and employee in the same manner.)

19 For this *is* thankworthy (refers to an action beyond the ordinary course of what might be expected), if a man for conscience toward God endure grief, suffering wrongfully. (Even though treated badly, the believing slave is to continue to conduct himself Christlike, which will always be noted by God.)

20 For what glory *is it*, if, when you be buffeted for your faults, you shall take it patiently? (If, in fact, the slave has done wrong,

he should accept his punishment without complaint.) but if, when you do well, and suffer for it, you take it patiently, this is acceptable with God. (This means not accepting the wrong treatment with patience is not acceptable with God. This can only be done by the Holy Spirit helping such a one, which He definitely will do, providing the Faith of such an individual is ever anchored in the Cross.)

CHRIST

21 For even hereunto were you called (called to act Christlike, irrespective): because Christ also suffered for us (Peter reminds these slaves that Christ also suffered unjustly, for He the Just One died on behalf of unjust ones), leaving us an example, that we should follow His steps (we are to reproduce Christ in our lives, which we can only do by the Help, Guidance, Leading, and Power of the Holy Spirit [Jn. 16:7-16]):

22 Who did no sin (Christ was the only sinless human being Who ever lived), neither was guile found in His mouth (He never sinned by speaking hypocritically or falsely, not even one time):

23 Who, when He was reviled, reviled not again (He did not respond in kind); when He suffered, He threatened not (when He suffered unjustly, He did not call down wrath from Heaven, which He definitely could have done); but committed Himself to Him Who Judges Righteously (He committed His defense to God, which we as well should do):

24 Who His Own Self bear our sins in His Own Body on the tree (gave Himself in Sacrifice on the Cross, taking the full penalty for our sins, which was physical death; it was not Christ's suffering that redeemed us, although that definitely was a part of what happened, but rather the price He paid by the giving of Himself), that we, being dead to sins, should live unto Righteousness (we are "dead to sins" by virtue of us being "in Christ" when He died on the Cross, which is done by our exhibiting Faith in Christ [Rom. 6:3-5]; and we were raised with Him in "newness of life," which guarantees us a perfect, spotless Righteousness): by Whose stripes you were healed. (This refers to the healing of our souls, and the healing of our physical body as well. The Atonement included everything man lost in the Fall, but we only have the Firstfruits now, with the balance coming at the Resurrection [Rom. 8:23].)

25 For you were as sheep going astray (we were like a flock without a shepherd); but are now returned unto the Shepherd and Bishop of your souls (refers to the Lord Jesus Christ; He Alone is the True "Shepherd," and He Alone is the True "Bishop" of our souls; if we allow man to take His Place, we spiritually wreck ourselves; man can only serve as an under-shepherd).

CHAPTER 3

(A.D. 60)

WIVES AND HUSBANDS

LIKEWISE, you wives, be in subjection to your own husbands (Peter is now dealing with Christian wives who have unsaved husbands, telling them how to win them to the Lord; the wife is to be in subjection, up to the point of violating Scripture; the Word of God is to be obeyed first of all, and without fail); that, if any obey not the Word (unsaved husbands who will not hear the Word of God), they also may without the Word be won by the conversation (lifestyle) of the wives (proper Christian behavior);

2 While they behold your chaste conversation (a Godly behavior) coupled with fear (the word "fear" here means "reverence," for the Lord and her husband; at the same time, it could be reversed for an unsaved wife).

3 Whose adorning let it not be that outward adorning of plaiting the hair, and of wearing of gold, or of putting on of apparel (is not meant to condemn these things, but rather that the lady's Faith be in Christ and the Cross);

4 But let it be the hidden man of the heart (is in contrast to the "outward man of the body"), in that which is not corruptible (is said to be such in contradistinction to gold and apparel), even the ornament of a meek and quiet spirit (presents a heart free from passion, pride, envy, and irritability), which is in the sight of God of great price. (This presents the fact that having such an inward character is valuable in the sight of God.)

5 For after this manner in the old time (Old Testament Times) the Holy women also, who trusted in God (does not refer to a special class of women, but rather ordinary women who trusted the Lord), adorned themselves, being in subjection unto their own husbands (presents the Apostle using the Old Testament as a foundation for what he now proclaims):

6 Even as Sarah obeyed Abraham, calling him lord (presents Sarah as being a beautiful example of the "Holy women" mentioned by Peter in the previous Verse): whose daughters you are (in a sense, all Believers, whether Jews

or Gentiles, are sons and daughters of Abraham), as long as you do well, and are not afraid with any amazement. (This could be better translated, "Whose daughters you are, as long as you obey the Lord, which will remove all fear of failure.")

7 Likewise, you husbands, dwell with them according to knowledge (Peter is now speaking of Christian husbands, and not the unsaved husbands to whom he had been alluding in previous Verses; the Holy Spirit has given correct knowledge on the subject), giving honour unto the wife (refers to that which is unique in Christianity, which is likewise a type of subjection), as unto the weaker vessel (pertains to the physical and never to the moral or intellectual), and as being heirs together of the Grace of Life (the husband is to pay due honor to the wife because she is a joint-heir with him of Eternal Life, the Gift of God); that your prayers be not hindered. (In effect, says prayers will be hindered if these admonitions to both husbands and wives are ignored. In fact, to ignore anything the Holy Spirit says is not wise, to say the least.)

RELATIONSHIP

8 Finally, be ye all of one mind (involves an agreement not only in Doctrine, but also in practical aims), having compassion one of another (evincing regard for each other's welfare), love as Brethren (carries the idea of "family"), be pitiful (tender-hearted), be courteous (friendly-minded, kind):

9 Not rendering evil for evil, or railing for railing (presents the very opposite of the system of the world): but contrariwise blessing (we should reward "evil" and "railing" with "Blessing"); knowing that you are thereunto called, that you should inherit a Blessing (proclaims the key to being Blessed by God).

10 For he who will love life, and see good days (the formula for Blessing continues [Ps. 34:12-16]), let him refrain his tongue from evil, and his lips that they speak no guile (this Command is Universal in its reference and, therefore, includes enemies as well as others):

11 Let him eschew evil (turn aside from such), and do good (as stated, do not render evil for evil, but rather good for evil); let him seek peace, and ensue it. (This refers to doing things that favor peace, even as the Holy Spirit has given instructions here through Peter.)

12 For the eyes of the Lord are over the Righteous (means the Lord is looking intently at all

Believers who are trusting Him), and His ears are open unto their prayers: but the Face of the Lord is against them who do evil. (This is an expression denoting disapproval, and a determination to punish them.)

13 And who is he who will harm you (considering that God is protecting you, what harm can they do?!), if you be followers of that which is good? (This proclaims the condition placed on this great Promise of God.)

PERSECUTION

14 But and if you suffer for Righteousness' sake, happy are you (such suffering is the result of Righteousness, and not the cause of Righteousness; we must not confuse the two): and be not afraid of their terror, neither be troubled (Righteousness guarantees the protection of the Lord [Isa. 8:12-13]);

15 But Sanctify the Lord God in your hearts (should be translated, "set apart Christ as Lord in the heart"): and be ready always to give an answer to every man who asks you a reason of the hope that is in you (every Believer must know the Word of God) with meekness and fear (never from a Holier-than-thou stance):

16 Having a good conscience; that, whereas they speak evil of you, as of evildoers, they may be ashamed who falsely accuse your good conversation (Godly lifestyle) in Christ. (Irrespective of what people may say, the Righteousness of Christ will ultimately prevail. In other words, those who falsely accuse will ultimately be proven wrong.)

WILL OF GOD

17 For it is better, if the Will of God be so, that you suffer for well doing (at times, God does ask us to suffer for Righteousness' sake), than for evil doing (refers to suffering chastisement, which the Holy Spirit knows we need and every true Christian experiences more or less; as should be obvious, this is different than suffering for "well doing").

18 For Christ also has once suffered for sins (the suffering of Christ on the Cross was but for one purpose, and that was "for sins"; while we as Believers might suffer for sins as well, such is never in the realm of Atonement; the price has been fully paid, which means there is nothing left owing), the just for the unjust (Christ was the Perfect Sacrifice, the One Who was born without original sin, and Who lived a Perfect

Life, *never failing even in one point; He Alone was the "Just"*), **that He might bring us to God** *(refers to the way being opened for sinful man to come into the very Presence of God)*, **being put to death in the flesh** *(refers to the fact that Jesus died physically in order to serve as a Sacrifice, which means He didn't die spiritually, as some claim!)*, **but quickened by the Spirit** *(raised from the dead by the Holy Spirit [Rom. 8:11])*:

SPIRITS

19 By which also He went *(between the time of His Death and Resurrection)* **and preached** *(announced something)* **unto the spirits in prison** *(does not refer to humans, but rather to fallen Angels; humans in the Bible are never referred to in this particular manner; these were probably the fallen Angels who tried to corrupt the human race by co-habiting with women [II Pet. 2:4; Jude, Vss. 6-7]; these fallen Angels are still locked up in this underworld prison)*;

20 Which sometime *(in times past)* **were disobedient** *(this was shortly before the Flood)*, **when once the longsuffering of God waited in the days of Noah** *(refers to this eruption of fallen Angels with women taking place at the time of Noah; this was probably a hundred or so years before the Flood)*, **while the Ark was a preparing** *(these fallen Angels were committing this particular sin while the Ark was being made ready, however long it took; the Scripture doesn't say!)*, **wherein few, that is, eight souls were saved by water.** *(This doesn't refer to being saved from sin. They were saved from drowning in the Flood by being in the Ark.)*

WATER BAPTISM

21 The like figure *(refers to Water Baptism as a symbol)* **whereunto** *even* **baptism does also now save us** *(speaks of the Baptism into Christ, which takes place at conversion; it is done by Faith, and has nothing to do with Water Baptism, although that serves as a symbol [Rom. 6:3-5])* **(not the putting away of the filth of the flesh** *(proclaims the fact that Water Baptism cannot cleanse the soul)*, **but the answer of a good conscience toward God,)** *(Refers to the fact that one engages in Water Baptism because one has already been made clean by Faith in the Lord Jesus, which in turn gives one a good conscience toward God.)* **by the Resurrection of Jesus Christ** *(which refers to the Cross, and the Believing sinner being raised with Christ in*

"newness of life" [Rom. 6:4-5]):

CHRIST EXALTED

22 Who *(Jesus Christ)* **is gone into Heaven** *(His Mission is complete)*, **and is on the Right Hand of God** *(proclaims the fact that His Sacrifice was accepted)*; **Angels and authorities and powers being made subject unto Him.** *(This refers to all, whether Holy or unholy. The "Cross" is the means by which all of this was done [Col. 2:14-15].)*

CHAPTER 4
(A.D. 60)
VICTORY OVER SIN

FORASMUCH then as Christ has suffered **for us in the flesh** *(refers to the Cross, with "flesh" referring to the fact that He died physically, and not spiritually as some claim)*, **arm yourselves likewise with the same mind** *(doesn't mean we are to attempt to imitate Christ in suffering, but rather to make the fact He suffered our source of victory; He suffered in the flesh that we might have victory over the flesh)*: **for he who has suffered in the flesh has ceased from sin** *(refers to the struggle between the flesh and the Spirit; "suffering in the flesh" by the Believer refers to stopping any dependence on self-effort, and depending totally on the Holy Spirit, Who demands that our Faith be in the Sacrifice of Christ [Rom. 8:1-2])*;

2 That he no longer should live the rest of *his* **time in the flesh to the lusts of men** *(since being saved, the sin nature is no longer to rule over us)*, **but to the Will of God.** *(This refers to the Divine Nature ruling over us, which comes about as a result of our total dependence on Christ and the Cross. In fact, Christ and the Cross are never to be separated, which refers to the benefits of the Cross coming down to us even unto this hour [I Cor. 1:17].)*

3 For the time past of *our* **life may suffice us to have wrought the will of the Gentiles** *(refers to our life before coming to Christ)*, **when we walked in lasciviousness, lusts, excess of wine, revellings, banquetings, and abominable idolatries** *(works of the flesh [Gal. 5:19-21])*:

4 Wherein they think it strange that you run not with *them* **to the same excess of riot** *(the unsaved do not understand the reasons why the Believer left the old life)*, **speaking evil of** *you* *(one of the great ways one knows that one is now living for God, as hurtful as it might be)*:

JUDGMENT

5 Who shall give account *(the coming Great White Throne Judgment, where all unbelievers will appear)* to Him *(refers to Christ)* Who is ready to judge the quick *(living)* and the dead. *(Now, He is the Saviour. Then, He will be the Judge.)*

6 For for this cause was the Gospel Preached also to them who are dead *(the dead spoken of here have to do with Believers who heard the Gospel while they were alive, and accepted it)*, that they might be judged according to men in the flesh *(doesn't matter how men may judge us, which is in contrast to the Judgment of God)*, but live according to God in the Spirit. *(This refers to every Saint of God who has lived and died, and who is now with the Lord.)*

7 But the end of all things is at hand *(paints everything in the light of Eternity; whatever our length of days on this Earth, it is nothing more or less by comparison to Eternity; we must always keep this end in view)*: be ye therefore sober, and watch unto prayer. *(Without prayer, there cannot be a proper relationship with the Lord.)*

8 And above all things have fervent charity *(love)* among yourselves: for charity *(love)* shall cover the multitude of sins. *(When one Christian truly loves his fellow Christian, he will not publish abroad his failings, but will cover them up from the sight of others.)*

9 Use hospitality one to another without grudging. *(Don't do such because it is commanded, but do it from love for God and man.)*

SPIRITUAL GIFTS

10 As every man has received the Gift *(everything good we have is a Gift from God)*, *even so* Minister the same one to another *(refers to being of service in anyway we can)*, as good stewards of the manifold Grace of God *(speaks of the great Gift all of us have been given; we should walk wisely in this Gift of Grace)*.

11 If any man speak, *let him speak* as the Oracles of God *(let him speak according to the Word of God)*; if any man Minister, *let him do it* as of the ability which God gives *(refers to the giving of ourselves to the Work of God in any manner, but more specifically it refers to us giving of our financial resources for the Cause of Christ)*: that God in all things may be glorified through Jesus Christ *(refers to what Christ did at the Cross and through nothing else)*, to

Whom be praise and dominion for ever and ever. Amen. *(He is due all praise because of His great Sacrifice, which took back dominion.)*

THE FIERY TRIAL

12 Beloved, think it not strange concerning the fiery trial which is to try you *(trials do not merely happen; they are designed by wisdom and operated by love; Job proved this)*, as though some strange thing happened unto you *(your trial, whatever it is, is not unique; many others are experiencing the same thing!)*:

13 But rejoice *(despite the trial)*, inasmuch as you are partakers of Christ's sufferings *(refers to suffering for Righteousness' sake)*; that, when His Glory shall be revealed *(refers to His Second Coming)*, you may be glad also with exceeding joy. *(There will be great joy in the heart of every Saint when we come back with the Lord at the Second Coming.)*

14 If you be reproached for the Name of Christ, happy *are you* *(should have been translated, "since you are reproached")*; for the Spirit of Glory and of God rests upon you *(refers to the Holy Spirit)*: on their part He is evil spoken of, but on your part He is glorified. *(This refers to the fact that the world, and even the apostate Church, reproaches this sacred influence of the Holy Spirit by their treatment of true Christians. But if we conduct ourselves correctly, the Lord is Glorified in our lives.)*

15 But let none of you suffer as a murderer, or *as* a thief, or *as* an evildoer, or as a busybody in other men's matters. *(This Scripture plainly tells us that if the Christian doesn't place His Faith entirely in the Cross, which guarantees the help of the Holy Spirit, these things Peter mentioned can definitely happen. That's why it is imperative every Believer knows and understands the Message of the Cross.)*

16 Yet if *any man suffer* as a Christian *(which sometimes happens for Righteousness' sake)*, let him not be ashamed *(such a one is not suffering because of lack of Faith, but rather because of his Faith)*; but let him glorify God on this behalf. *(If we truly suffer for Righteousness' sake, such suffering will always glorify the Lord. We should rejoice accordingly [Vs. 13].)*

JUDGMENT

17 For the time *is come* that judgment must begin at the House of God *(Judgment always begins with Believers, and pertains to their Faith,*

whether in the Cross or otherwise; the Cross alone is spared Judgment, for there Jesus was judged in our place): and if *it* first *begin* at us, what shall the end *be* of them who obey not the Gospel of God? *(If God will Judge His Own, how much more will He Judge the unredeemed? The Cross alone stays the Judgment of God. Let that ever be understood.)*

18 And if the Righteous scarcely be saved *(can be saved only by trusting Christ and the Cross, and nothing else),* where shall the ungodly and the sinner appear? *(If the great Sacrifice of Christ is rejected and spurned, where does that leave those who do such a thing? There is no hope for their Salvation.)*

19 Wherefore let them who suffer according to the Will of God *(it really doesn't matter what we have to go through in order to live for God, the end result will be worth it a million times over)* commit the keeping of their souls *to Him* in well doing *(victory is assured if we continue to look to the Cross),* as unto a Faithful Creator. *(This means God hasn't created an insufficient Salvation. He has created a Way through the Death of Christ that guarantees victory, if we will only follow that Way.)*

CHAPTER 5
(A.D. 60)
PASTORS

THE Elders *(Pastors)* which are among you I exhort *(pertains to Pastors of local Churches),* who am also an Elder *(proclaims the fact that the great Apostle was a Pastor as well, Pastoring then at Babylon [Vs. 13]),* and a witness of the sufferings of Christ *(who was with Christ throughout our Lord's Ministry, even unto His Death),* and also a partaker of the glory that shall be revealed *(if the Cross is accepted, the Glory is revealed):*

2 Feed the flock of God which is among you *(Preach the Cross [I Cor. 1:21, 23; 2:2]),* taking the oversight *thereof,* not by constraint, but willingly *(privileged to do so, and not because we have no choice);* not for filthy lucre *(money must not be our motive),* but of a ready mind *(not swayed by money or anything else, only to do the Will of God);*

3 Neither as being lords over *God's* heritage *(the Greek Text speaks of a high-handed autocratic rule over the flock, which is forbidden of a true Shepherd),* but being examples to the flock *(presents instruction which the Apostle had lived in a most unique way).*

4 And when the Chief Shepherd shall appear *(the Lord Jesus Christ, at the Rapture of the Church),* you shall receive a crown of glory that fades not away *(refers to the victory crown).*

COMMANDS

5 Likewise, you younger *(associate Pastors in the local Church),* submit yourselves unto the Elder *(senior Pastor).* Yes, all *of you* be subject one to another *(refers to mutual understanding),* and be clothed with humility *(refers to the virtue that must grace all other virtues, which can only come by Faith in the Cross):* for God resists the proud *(He sets Himself in array against the proud person),* and gives grace to the humble. *(One who places his Faith exclusively in the Cross of Christ.)*

6 Humble yourselves therefore under the Mighty Hand of God *(the Cross alone and one's Faith in that Finished Work can make one humble),* that He may exalt you in due time *(proclaims the route to the Blessings of God):*

7 Casting all your care upon Him *(refers here to a direct and once-for-all committal to God of all that would give us concern);* for He cares for you *(translated literally, "for you are His concern").*

8 Be sober *(mentally self-controlled),* be vigilant *(awake and watchful);* because your adversary the Devil, as a roaring lion, walks about, seeking whom he may devour *(we are faced with a very powerful adversary):*

9 Whom *(the Devil)* resist stedfast in the Faith *("the Faith" always refers to what Jesus did at the Cross; our Faith must be ever anchored in that Finished Work),* knowing that the same afflictions are accomplished in your Brethren who are in the world. *(Every true Christian faces the onslaught of the Evil One.)*

BENEDICTION

10 But the God of all Grace *(refers to God as the Source of all Grace),* Who has called us *(a Divine summons)* unto His Eternal Glory by Christ Jesus *(through what Jesus did at the Cross),* after that you have suffered a while *(the transition from the "flesh" to the "Spirit," which is never easy, fast, or simple),* make you perfect *(knit together with the Spirit),* stablish, strengthen, settle *you (on a firm foundation which cannot be moved, as the Grace of God comes to us in an uninterrupted flow).*

11 To Him *(the Lord Jesus Christ)* **be** Glory and Dominion forever and ever. Amen. *(This is because of what He did at the Cross.)*

12 By Silas, a faithful Brother unto you, as I suppose, I have written briefly, exhorting, and testifying that this is the true Grace of God wherein you stand. *(This proclaims the fact that this subject concerning living for God is so vast, but yet the Apostle attempted to address it in this short Epistle.)*

13 The *Church that is at Babylon (refers to the same city mentioned in the Old Testament, the Babylon on the River Euphrates; there is no proof that this statement is a synonym for Rome, as some claim),* **elected together with** *you,* **salute you** *(those who elect to trust Christ and the Cross are, at the same time, elected to experience the Grace of God)*; **and** *so does* Mark my son *(refers to John Mark, who wrote the Gospel which bears his name; he was not the actual son of Peter, but a son in the Faith).*

14 Greet you one another with a kiss of charity *(the custom in those days).* Peace **be** with you all who are in Christ Jesus. Amen. *(This speaks of Sanctifying Peace, which comes through the Cross.)*

THE SECOND EPISTLE GENERAL OF
PETER

CHAPTER 1
(A.D. 66)
INTRODUCTION

SIMON Peter, a servant and an Apostle of Jesus Christ *(the position of "servant" is placed first; if one cannot be a true servant for the Lord, then one cannot be an Apostle; the Lord guides the Church by the Office of the Apostle through the particular Message given to the individual, which will always coincide directly with the Word of God; Apostles aren't elected, they are called of God)*, **to them who have obtained like Precious Faith with us** *(proclaims the Faith that Gentiles can now be saved exactly as Jews, in fact all coming the same way)* **through the Righteousness of God and our Saviour Jesus Christ** *(this Righteousness is obtained by the Believer exhibiting Faith in Christ and what He did at the Cross):*

2 **Grace and Peace be multiplied unto you through the knowledge of God, and of Jesus our Lord** *(this is both Sanctifying Grace and Sanctifying Peace, all made available by the Cross),*

3 **According as His Divine Power has given unto us all things** *(the Lord with large-handed generosity has given us all things)* **that** *pertain* **unto life and Godliness** *(pertains to the fact that the Lord Jesus has given us everything we need regarding life and living),* **through the knowledge of Him Who has called us to Glory and Virtue** *(the "knowledge" addressed here speaks of what Christ did at the Cross, which alone can provide "Glory and Virtue"):*

4 **Whereby are given unto us exceeding great and Precious Promises** *(pertains to the Word of God, which alone holds the answer to every life problem):* **that by these** *(Promises)* **you might be partakers of the Divine Nature** *(the Divine Nature implanted in the inner being of the believing sinner becomes the source of our new life and actions; it comes to everyone at the moment of being "Born-Again"),* **having escaped the corruption that is in the world through lust.** *(This presents the Salvation experience of the sinner, and the Sanctification experience of the Saint.)*

GROWING IN GRACE

5 **And beside this** *(Salvation),* **giving all diligence** *(refers to the responsibility we as Believers must show regarding the Christian life),* **add to your Faith Virtue** *(this is Faith in the Cross, which will bring "Virtue"; the type of "Virtue" mentioned here is "energy" and "power");* **and to Virtue knowledge** *(this is the type of knowledge which keeps expanding);*

6 **And to knowledge temperance** *(self-control);* **and to temperance patience** *(our conduct must honor God at all times, even in the midst of trials and testing);* **and to patience Godliness** *(being like God);*

7 **And to Godliness brotherly kindness** *(carries the idea of treating everyone as if they were our own flesh and blood "brother" or "sister");* **and to brotherly kindness charity** *(love).*

8 **For if these things be in you, and abound** *(continue to expand),* **they make** *you that you* **shall** neither *be* **barren nor unfruitful in the knowledge of our Lord Jesus Christ.** *(Once again, this "knowledge" refers to what Christ did at the Cross, all on our behalf.)*

9 **But he who lacks these things is blind, and cannot see afar off** *(the reason one may lack these things is he is spiritually blind; in other words, such a one has made something other than the Cross the Object of His Faith),* **and has forgotten that he was purged from his old sins.** *(Such a Believer is once again being ruled by the "sin nature" exactly as he was before conversion, which is always the end result of ignoring the Cross.)*

10 **Wherefore the rather, Brethren, give diligence to make your calling and election sure** *(this is what Jesus was speaking of when He told us to deny ourselves and take up the Cross daily and follow Him [Lk. 9:23]; every day, the Believer must make certain His Faith is anchored in the Cross and the Cross alone; only then can we realize the tremendous benefits afforded by the Sacrifice of Christ):* **for if you do these things, you shall never fall** *(presents the key to Eternal Security, but with the Promise being conditional):*

11 **For so an entrance shall be Ministered unto you abundantly into the Everlasting**

Kingdom of our Lord and Saviour Jesus Christ. *(The entrance into the Kingdom is solely on the basis of Faith evidenced in Christ and the Cross [Eph. 2:13-18; Jn. 3:16].)*

GROUNDED IN TRUTH

12 Wherefore I will not be negligent to put you always in remembrance of these things *(as Peter, this is the reason I keep highlighting the Cross)*, though you know *them*, and be established in the present truth. *(The "Truth" is "Jesus Christ and Him Crucified" [Jn. 8:32; I Cor. 2:2].)*

13 Yes, I think it meet *(necessary)*, as long as I am in this tabernacle *(refers to the physical body)*, to stir you up by putting *you* in remembrance *(by ever keeping Christ and the Cross before you)*;

14 Knowing that shortly I must put off *this* my tabernacle *(Peter is saying that He knows he won't live much longer after writing this Epistle)*, even as our Lord Jesus Christ has shown me. *(This possibly refers to Christ's prediction given to the Apostle, recorded in Jn. 21:18-19.)*

15 Moreover I will endeavour that you may be able after my decease to have these things always in remembrance. *(This presents the third time the Apostle makes reference to keeping in remembrance the conditions of entrance into Eternal Life [Vss. 12-13, 15]. He will use the word again in II Pet. 3:1.)*

16 For we have not followed cunningly devised fables *(refers to "heresies" taught by "false teachers"; in other words, anything that leads one away from Christ and the Cross)*, when we made known unto you the Power and Coming of our Lord Jesus Christ *(what Christ could do in one's life, which the Cross made possible)*, but were eyewitnesses of His Majesty. *(This pertains to the Transfiguration, which was an actual demonstration of Christ coming in His Glory to Earth to set up His Kingdom [Mat. 16:27-28; 17:1-8; 24:29-31; 25:31-46; Rev. 19:11-21].)*

17 For He *(Christ)* received from God the Father Honour and Glory *(pertains to the "Majesty" of the Son of God, which Peter mentioned in the previous Verse)*, when there came such a Voice to Him from the excellent Glory *(refers to the Voice of God)*, This is My beloved Son, in Whom I am well pleased. *(God is well-pleased with us only as long as we are "in Christ.")*

18 And this voice which came from Heaven we heard, when we were with Him in the Holy Mount. *(Peter was not relating something secondhand, but rather that which had happened to him personally.)*

19 We have also a more sure Word of Prophecy *(Peter is speaking here of the Old Testament, which is the Word of God, and even more sure than his personal experience)*; whereunto you do well that you take heed, as unto a light that shines in a dark place *(in effect, states that the Word of God is the only True Light, which alone can dispel the spiritual darkness)*, until the day dawn, and the Day Star arise in your hearts *(the "Day Star" is Christ; "arising in our hearts" pertains to the Rapture)*:

20 Knowing this first *(harks back, as stated, to the Old Testament, which, in effect, was the Bible of Peter's day)*, that no Prophecy of the Scripture is of any private interpretation. *(This refers to the fact that the Word of God did not originate in the human mind.)*

21 For the Prophecy *(the word "Prophecy" is used here in a general sense, covering the entirety of the Word of God, which means it's not limited merely to predictions regarding the future)* came not in old time by the will of man *(did not originate with man)*: but Holy men of God spoke *as they were* moved by the Holy Spirit. *(This proclaims the manner in which the Word of God was written and, thereby, given unto us.)*

CHAPTER 2

(A.D. 66)

FALSE PROPHETS

BUT there were false Prophets also among the people *(refers to the false prophets who plagued Israel of Old)*, even as there shall be false teachers among you *(the false teacher is one who presents a way of Salvation, or a way of Sanctification, other than the Cross)*, who privily shall bring in damnable heresies *(the idea is that these false teachers would teach some true Doctrine, and then cleverly include false teaching with it; it is the introduction of false teaching alongside the True that makes it very subtle, and which abrogates the True)*, even denying the Lord Who bought them *(refers to denying the Cross)*, and bring upon themselves swift destruction *(upon themselves and upon those who follow them, which refers to the ultimate loss of the soul)*.

2 And many shall follow their pernicious ways *(actually most!)*; by reason of whom the way of Truth shall be evil spoken of *(proclaims the fact that not only is the Truth castigated, but*

the bearer of Truth as well! in short, it is a denigration of the Cross).

3 And through covetousness shall they with feigned words make merchandise of you *(the people are exploited instead of developed; the underlying cause is "money")*: **whose judgment now of a long time lingers not, and their damnation slumbers not** *(the Judgment seems to be delayed, but it definitely is not idle; sooner or later all who travel the path of "damnable heresies," which refers to any way other than the Cross, will ultimately face "utter ruin and destruction").*

THE PENALTY

4 For if God spared not the Angels who sinned *(refers here to a specific type of sin, which was actually the sin of fallen Angels cohabiting with women that took place before the Flood, and then after the Flood [Gen. 6:1-4]),* **but cast** *them* **down to Hell** *(refers to "Tartarus," visited by Christ after His Death on the Cross and immediately before His Resurrection; in fact, He preached "unto the spirits in prison," which refer to these fallen Angels [I Pet. 3:19-20]),* **and delivered** *them* **into chains of darkness** *(where they have been imprisoned),* **to be reserved unto Judgment** *(refers to the coming "Great White Throne Judgment," when they will then be cast into the Lake of Fire [Rev. 20:10]);*

5 And spared not the old world *(the world before the Flood),* **but saved Noah the eighth** *person* *(there were eight people in the Ark),* **a Preacher of Righteousness** *(proclaims the fact that Noah preached to the Antediluvians for a number of years, but without success),* **bringing in the Flood upon the world of the ungodly** *(lends credence to the thought that God would have spared the old world had the Antediluvians heeded the Message Preached by Noah; Grace spurned is always Judgment pronounced);*

6 And turning the cities of Sodom and Gomorrha into ashes condemned *them* **with an overthrow** *(tells us in no uncertain terms what God thinks of Sodomy),* **making** *them* **an example unto those who after should live ungodly** *(Sodom and Gomorrha were meant as a warning);*

RIGHTEOUSNESS

7 And delivered just Lot *(refers to Lot and his two daughters; his wife perished [Gen. 19:15-26]; Lot was "just," meaning that his Faith was*

in Christ, even though his actions at times were not commendable), **vexed with the filthy conversation** *(lifestyle)* **of the wicked** *(presents the attitude of this man with the behavior of the Sodomites):*

8 (For that Righteous man dwelling among them *(Lot did not become contaminated by the vices of Sodom),* **in seeing and hearing, vexed** *his* **Righteous soul from day to day with** *their* **unlawful deeds;)** *("Vexed" pertains to "torment or torture," meaning he was not only vexed with the sin of Sodom, but vexed at himself as well. In this word, we find a certain sense of personal culpability. The situation in which Lot now finds himself was ultimately due to his own selfish choice.)*

9 The Lord knows how to deliver the Godly out of temptations *(modern Believers are delivered "out of temptations" by placing their Faith exclusively in Christ and the Cross, which then gives the Holy Spirit latitude to help),* **and to reserve the unjust unto the Day of Judgment to be punished** *(in effect, says that all who reject Jesus Christ and what He did at the Cross will definitely be judged):*

FALSE TEACHERS

10 But chiefly them who walk after the flesh *(refer to false teachers who are advocating a way of victory other than the Cross [Rom. 8:1])* **in the lust of uncleanness** *(proclaims that which is guaranteed to happen as a result of "walking after the flesh"),* **and despise Government.** *(This refers to despising the Lordship of Christ, meaning to despise His Way, which is the Cross.)* **Presumptuous** *are they,* **selfwilled** *(refers to arrogance),* **they are not afraid to speak evil of dignities.** *(When one speaks against the Cross, one is speaking against the Godhead.)*

11 Whereas Angels, which are greater in power and might *(greater than men),* **bring not railing accusation against them before the Lord.** *(When reporting to the Lord concerning fallen Angels, etc., Righteous Angels merely report facts as they are without bitterness and railing.)*

12 But these *(false teachers),* **as natural brute beasts** *(evidence no more common sense than an animal),* **made to be taken and destroyed** *(proclaims what will happen to all false teachers),* **speak evil of the things that they understand not** *(reduces their ridicule to their rejection of the Finished Work of Christ);* **and shall utterly perish in their own corruption** *(presents the only conclusion for those who reject the Cross);*

13 And shall receive the reward of unrighteousness *(ultimately the loss of one's soul)*, *as* they who count it pleasure to riot in the day time *(speaks of false teachers who live luxuriously off the money they get from those they have led astray by their false doctrine)*. Spots *they are* and blemishes *(a soiled unrighteousness because it is self-righteousness)*, sporting themselves with their own deceivings while they feast with you *(putting on a show of Righteousness, which is only deception)*;

14 Having eyes full of adultery *(spiritual adultery, which refers to ways other than the Cross [Rom. 8:1-4])*, and that cannot cease from sin *(if our Faith is in anything other than the Cross, we will find ourselves being unable to "cease from sin")*; beguiling unstable souls *(enticing with bait, which the modern Word of Faith Doctrine does)*: an heart they have exercised with covetous practices *(the love of money)*; cursed children *(children of cursing, referring to a curse placed on all who attempt to establish a way other than the Cross [Gal. 1:8-9])*:

15 Which have forsaken the right way *(means they once knew the right way, but now they have forsaken it; the "right way" is the "Cross")*, and are gone astray, following the way of Balaam *the son* of Bosor *(that "way" is money)*, who loved the wages of unrighteousness *(this false prophet was willing to prostitute himself to secure gold)*;

16 But was rebuked for his iniquity *(Balaam was sinning)*: the dumb ass speaking with man's voice forbad the madness of the Prophet. *(A dumb animal rebuked the Prophet. Modern popular theology denies this, and so accuses the Holy Spirit of falsehood.)*

17 These are wells without water *(despite the claims, there is no water of life in the teaching of these false prophets)*, clouds that are carried with a tempest *(for dry and thirsty hearts, these "clouds" carry no water of life; the word "tempest" proclaims the fact that much is promised, but nothing is delivered)*: to whom the mist of darkness is reserved forever. *(It is either the Cross or Eternal darkness!)*

18 For when they speak great swelling *words* of vanity *(false doctrine is often presented in such a way as to impress the listener)*, they allure through the lusts of the flesh *(the allurement is the appeal of material things)*, *through much* wantonness *(particular types of bait used to catch the hearers)*, those who were clean escaped from them who live in error. *(New

converts or even Christians not well-grounded in the Faith become easy marks for these "hucksters.")*

19 While they promise them Liberty *(they guarantee their way will lead to riches and happiness)*, they themselves are the servants of corruption *(while they are promising liberty, they are themselves in bondage, as is anyone who doesn't have the Cross as the Object of his Faith)*: for of whom a man is overcome, of the same is he brought in bondage. *(If the false teaching is followed, which is the opposite of Grace, bondage will be the result [Gal. 5:1].)*

20 For if after they have escaped the pollutions of the world through the knowledge of the Lord and Saviour Jesus Christ *(they were saved by trusting Christ and the Cross)*, they are again entangled therein, and overcome *(proclaims the fact that if the Believer ceases to place his Faith and trust in what Jesus did at the Cross, that entanglement in the pollutions of the world will once again become a fact; it cannot be otherwise)*, the latter end is worse with them than the beginning. *(If Believers reject the Message of the Cross after it is plainly given, there is nothing left but destruction.)*

21 For it had been better for them not to have known the way of Righteousness *(Peter is dealing with individuals who have had the privilege to hear the Gospel, accept Christ, and then for whatever reason cease to believe, and, thereby, lose their way)*, than, after they have known *it*, to turn from the Holy Commandment delivered unto them. *(It's bad enough to have never known the way. However, to have known it and then turn to another direction is unthinkable. Yet millions have done so. The far greater majority of the modern Church falls into this category. They have abandoned the Cross for other things.)*

22 But it is happened unto them according to the true Proverb *(Prov. 26:11)*, The dog *is* turned to his own vomit again; and the sow that was washed to her wallowing in the mire. *(This completely refutes the Unscriptural Doctrine of Unconditional Security, and gives the reason — a departure from Christ and the Cross.)*

CHAPTER 3
(A.D. 66)
REMEMBER

THIS second Epistle, beloved, I now write unto you *(he had addressed his First Epistle to the same group of people)*; in *both* which I stir up your pure minds by way of remembrance

(by reminding them of what is going to happen in the last of the last days):

2 That you may be mindful of the words which were spoken before by the Holy Prophets *(we are plainly told here that, as Believers, we must know and understand the Old Testament along with the New)*, **and of the Commandment of us the Apostles of the Lord and Saviour** *(refers to the New Testament, but at the same time the Verse says we cannot understand the New unless we first understand the Old)*:

SCOFFERS

3 Knowing this first, that there shall come in the last days scoffers *(speaks of the times in which we now live; they scoff at the Cross)*, **walking after their own lusts** *(which will happen when the Cross is rejected)*,

4 And saying, Where is the Promise of his coming? *(This refers to the Second Coming, not the Rapture. Endtime events as predicted in the Bible are met with scoffing.)* **for since the fathers fell asleep, all things continue as** *they were* **from the beginning of the Creation.** *(The two major themes of the Word of God are the Atonement and Endtime events. If we have a proper understanding of the Atonement, we will have, I think, a proper understanding of the latter.)*

5 For this they willingly are ignorant of *(their ignorance was a willful ignorance; in other words, the evidence was presented and then rejected)*, **that by the Word of God the Heavens were of old, and the earth standing out of the water and in the water** *(everything was created by the Word of God; this Verse points to Gen. 1:2; it speaks of the original Creation and the rebellion by Lucifer, which left the world in a convoluted state)*:

6 Whereby the world that then was *(speaks of the pre-Adamite Creation)*, **being overflowed with water, perished** *(doesn't refer to Noah's Flood, but rather the Flood of Gen. 1:2; this is when Lucifer led his revolution against God)*:

7 But the Heavens and the Earth, which are now *(refers to the present Heavens and Earth as restored to a second perfect state in the days of Adam [Gen. 1:3; 2:25; Ex. 20:11])*, **by the same Word are kept in store** *(refers to the fact that all Creation is dependent solely on the Will of God)*, **reserved unto fire against the Day of Judgment and Perdition of ungodly men.** *(This refers to the coming "Great White Throne Judgment" [Rev. 20:11-15]. At this time, the Heavens and Earth will be renovated by fire.)*

8 But, beloved, be not ignorant of this one thing *(considering that we have the Word of God, there is no reason for the Believer to be ignorant concerning spiritual things)*, **that one day** *is* **with the Lord as a thousand years, and a thousand years as one day.** *(A human promise may be weakened or destroyed by time. However, a Divine Promise is as certain of fulfillment in a thousand years as in one day.)*

9 The Lord is not slack concerning His Promise, as some men count slackness *(if it seems as though God delays the fulfillment of His Promises, it is for the purpose of getting more people into the Kingdom of God)*; **but is longsuffering to us-ward** *(God suffers long with man, attempting to bring him to a place of Repentance)*, **not willing that any should perish, but that all should come to Repentance.** *(The dispensation of the Cross has been the longest of all, and it is that because God keeps calling after sinners to be saved. He has made a way through the Cross for all to be saved. Most, however, refuse His Way.)*

FIRE

10 But the Day of the Lord will come as a thief in the night *(the conclusion of the Millennium; what will happen at that time will be unexpected, and for a variety of reasons)*; **in the which the Heavens shall pass away with a great noise, and the elements shall melt with fervent heat, the Earth also and the works that are therein shall be burned up.** *(This does not speak of Annihilation, but rather passing from one condition to another.)*

11 *Seeing* **then** *that* **all these things shall be dissolved** *(the present is temporal)*, **what manner** *of persons* **ought ye to be in** *all* **Holy conversation** *(lifestyle)* **and Godliness** *(pertains to the correct view of things)*,

12 Looking for and hasting unto the Coming of the Day of God *(concerns the Coming Eternal, Perfect Earth, which will last in that condition forever and forever)*, **wherein the Heavens being on fire shall be dissolved, and the elements shall melt with fervent heat?** *("The Day of God" will be ushered in by the cataclysmic events of this Verse. There must be no sin left in the Universe.)*

13 Nevertheless we *(Believers)*, **according to His Promise** *(the Lord has Promised that a new day is coming [Isa. 65:17])*, **look for new Heavens** *(this is the Promise!)* **and a new earth, wherein dwells Righteousness.** *(This proclaims

the condition of the Coming "New Heavens and New Earth" [Rev., Chpts. 21-22].)

ADMONITIONS

14 Wherefore, beloved, seeing that you look for such things (if one believes the Bible, one will believe its account of Endtime events), be diligent that you may be found of Him in Peace, without spot, and blameless (which can be done only by the Believer ever making the Cross the Object of His Faith).

15 And account that the longsuffering of our Lord is Salvation (His longsuffering, which refers to this Day of Grace that has now lasted longer than any other dispensation, is in order to bring the unredeemed to Himself); even as our beloved Brother Paul also according to the wisdom given unto him has written unto you (doesn't say which Epistle, but probably refers to Hebrews);

16 As also in all his Epistles, speaking in them of these things (proclaims the fact that Paul's Epistles are inspired); in which are some things hard to be understood (could refer to Prophecy, or to the great teaching Paul gave on the Cross), which they that are unlearned and unstable wrest, as they do also the other Scriptures, unto their own destruction. (This presents the fact that some Christians purposely twist the Scriptures, attempting to make them mean something the Holy Spirit never intended.)

17 You therefore, beloved, seeing you know these things before (the Holy Spirit, through Peter, tells those to whom the Apostle was writing that they were not without understanding regarding what was being taught), beware lest you also, being led away with the error of the wicked (refers to being led away from the Cross), fall from your own stedfastness (refers here to the proper application of one's Faith; the Cross of Christ must always be the Object of the Saint's Faith; if we shift our Faith to anything else, we "fall" [Gal. 5:4]).

18 But grow in Grace (presents the only way the Saint can grow), and in the knowledge of our Lord and Saviour Jesus Christ. (This "knowledge" refers not only to Who Christ is [the Lord of Glory], but as well What He did in order that we might be Redeemed, which points to the Cross.) To Him be Glory both now and forever. Amen. (This refers to such belonging to Him, because He is the One Who paid the price for man's Redemption.)

THE FIRST EPISTLE GENERAL OF
JOHN

CHAPTER 1
(A.D. 90)
INTRODUCTION

THAT which was from the beginning (*speaks of Jesus Christ; He is from everlasting*), **which we have heard** (*John was personally with Christ for 3-1/2 years*), **which we have seen with our eyes** (*John saw what Christ was as a Man*), **which we have looked upon** (*what he saw was more than a passing glance; it was "gazing with a purpose"*), **and our hands have handled** (*refers to the fact that Christ was human*), **of the Word of Life** (*says in the Greek, "The Word of The Life," referring to the fact that Christ is also God*);

2 (**For the life was manifested** (*not hidden, but rather revealed*), **and we have seen** *it* (*made visible to the human race through the humanity of our Lord*), **and bear witness** (*we can testify to the fact*), **and show unto you that Eternal Life** (*this "Life," which Christ is and has, is "Eternal"*), **which was with the Father** (*the Son is the same essence as the Father*), **and was manifested unto us;**) (*This was made visible to us, and given to us as well.*)

FELLOWSHIP

3 **That which we have seen and heard declare we unto you** (*hence, this Epistle*), **that you also may have fellowship with us** (*something possessed in common by both, in this case Christ*): **and truly our fellowship** *is* **with the Father, and with His Son Jesus Christ.** (*Fellowship with Christ guarantees fellowship with the Father.*)

4 **And these things write we unto you, that your joy may be full.** (*This should have been translated, "our joy may be full." John wanted others to know Christ as He knew Christ.*)

5 **This then is the Message which we have heard of Him** (*presents the true Message of the Cross in comparison with the false*), **and declare unto you, that God is Light** (*as to His nature, essence, and character, God is Light*), **and in Him is no darkness at all.** (*Spiritual darkness does not exist in Him, not even one bit.*)

6 **If we say that we have fellowship with Him, and walk in darkness, we lie** (*to claim Salvation while at the same time "walking in darkness" automatically dismisses our claims*), **and do not the Truth** (*such a life is a "lie," and is not "true"*):

7 **But if we walk in the Light, as He is in the Light, we have fellowship one with another** (*if we claim fellowship with Him, we will at the same time walk in the Light, which is the sphere of His Walk*), **and the Blood of Jesus Christ His Son cleanses us from all sin.** (*Our Faith being in the Cross, the shed Blood of Jesus Christ, constantly cleanses us from all sin.*)

SIN

8 **If we say that we have no sin** (*refers to "the sin nature"*), **we deceive ourselves** (*refers to self-deception*), **and the Truth is not in us.** (*This does not refer to all Truth as it regards Believers, but rather that the Truth of the indwelling sinful nature is not in us.*)

9 **If we confess our sins** (*pertains to acts of sin, whatever they might be; the sinner is to believe [Jn. 3:16]; the Saint is to confess*), **He** (*the Lord*) **is faithful and just to forgive us** *our* **sins** (*God will always be true to His Own Nature and Promises, keeping Faith with Himself and with man*), **and to cleanse us from all unrighteousness.** (*"All," not some. All sin was remitted, paid for, and put away on the basis of the satisfaction offered for the demands of God's Holy Law, which sinners broke, when the Lord Jesus died on the Cross.*)

10 **If we say that we have not sinned** (*here, John is denouncing the claims of sinless perfection; he is going back to Verse 8, speaking of Christians who claimed they had no sin nature*), **we make Him a liar** (*the person who makes such a claim makes God a liar, because the Word says the opposite*), **and His Word is not in us.** (*If we properly know the Word, we will properly know that perfection is not in us at present, and will not be until the Trump sounds.*)

CHAPTER 2
(A.D. 90)
THE ADVOCATE

MY **little children, these things write I unto you, that you sin not.** (*This presents*

the fact that the Lord saves us from sin, not in sin. This Passage tells us that, as Believers, we don't have to sin. Victory over sin is found exclusively in the Cross.) **And if any man sin, we have an Advocate with the Father, Jesus Christ the Righteous** (Jesus is now seated at the Right Hand of the Father, signifying that His Mission is complete, and His very Presence guarantees intercession [Heb. 7:25-26; 9:24; 10:12]):

2 And He is the propitiation (satisfaction) **for our sins: and not for ours only, but also for** the sins of **the whole world.** (This pertains to the fact that the satisfaction is as wide as the sin. If men do not experience its benefit, the fault is not in its efficacy, but in man himself.)

EVIDENCE

3 And hereby we do know that we know Him (refers to a "know so" Salvation), **if we keep His Commandments.** (This can be done only as the Believer understands that the Cross is the solution for all things, and that it must ever be the Object of our Faith. That being done, Christ will live through us by means of the person of the Holy Spirit, and the Commandments will be kept, referring to the entirety of the New Covenant [Gal. 2:20].)

4 He who says, I know Him, and keeps not His Commandments (if our claims do not correspond with His demands, then we really don't know Him), **is a liar, and the Truth is not in him.** (If one's life is not changed by what is professed then one really doesn't have what is professed.)

5 But whoso keeps His Word (we are to abide by the Word of God, ever making it the rule of our lives, and we can do so if our Faith is solidly placed in the Cross), **in him verily is the Love of God perfected** (refers to the "Fruit" of one who "keeps His Word"): **hereby know we that we are in Him** (refers to Rom. 6:3-5).

6 He who says he abides in Him (pertains to a claim being made) **ought himself also so to walk, even as He** (Christ) **walked** (pertains to the manner in which we order our behavior).

PROOF

7 Brethren, I write no new Commandment unto you (to love the Brethren is not a new Commandment), **but an old Commandment which you had from the beginning.** (To love the Brethren has been the foundation and the keynote of the Plan of God from the very beginning.) **The old Commandment is the Word which you have heard from the beginning.** (Since the old Commandment of Love has ever been before the Believer, there is no excuse to not walk after this direction.)

8 Again, a new Commandment I write unto you (the Commandment of Love is both old and new), **which thing is true in Him** (Christ) **and in you** (if we are "in Him," then we should be like Him): **because the darkness is past** (pertains to the time before Christ), **and the true Light now shines.** (The "true Light" is Christ, which Light will shine forever, and pertains to the time since Christ has come.)

9 He who says he is in the Light, and hates his brother, is in darkness even until now. (How can we claim to have love, and at the same time hate our Brother? Such a person isn't saved, despite his claims.)

10 He who loves his Brother abides in the Light (the type of love addressed here is the God kind of Love, which one cannot have unless one is truly saved), **and there is none occasion of stumbling in him.** (To walk in the light is to be governed by love, which removes the stumbling blocks.)

11 But he who hates his Brother is in darkness, and walks in darkness (this is an individual who has once known the Lord, but is losing his way with God simply because of hatred in his heart for a fellow Christian; consequently, he walks in darkness), **and knows not where he goes, because that darkness has blinded his eyes.** (The penalty of living in spiritual darkness is not merely that one does not see, but that one goes spiritually blind, which makes one an open target for false doctrine.)

12 I write unto you, little children, because your sins are forgiven you for His Name's sake (because of what He did for us at the Cross).

13 I write unto you, fathers, because you have known Him who is **from the beginning.** (This refers to those who are mature in the Christian life.) **I write unto you, young men, because you have overcome the wicked one.** (This refers to Believers who have now come to the place where they are living in the Power of the Spirit, and their victory over Satan is a consistent one.) **I write unto you, little children, because you have known the Father.** (This refers to Believers who haven't been saved very long. The Greek word used here is "paidion," and refers to a child in training. It is the business of the "Fathers" and the "young men" to train the young converts in the ways of the Lord.)

14 I have written unto you, fathers, because you have known Him *who is* from the beginning. *(John is repeating himself here in order that the "Fathers" may ever know and understand that God's Prescribed Order of Victory has got them to this place [a place of overcoming strength], and they must not allow false doctrine to come in and destroy that.)* I have written unto you, young men, because you are strong, and the Word of God abides in you, and you have overcome the wicked one. *(Never forget how you have overcome, which is by Faith in the Cross of Christ [II Pet. 2:2].)*

15 Love not the world, neither the things *that are* in the world. *(The "world" spoken of here by John pertains to the ordered system of which Satan is the head.)* If any man love the world, the love of the Father is not in him. *(God the Father will not share the love that must go exclusively from Him with the world.)*

16 For all that *is* in the world *(there is nothing in the system of this world that is of God)*, the lust of the flesh *(refers to evil cravings)*, and the lust of the eyes *(craves what it sees)*, and the pride of life *(that which trusts its own power and resources, and shamefully despises and violates Divine Laws and human rights)*, is not of the Father, but is of the world. *(These things have the system of the world as their source, not the Heavenly Father.)*

17 And the world passes away, and the lust thereof *(whatever the allurements of the world, they soon fade)*: but he who does the Will of God abides forever *(the one who keeps on habitually doing the Will of God)*.

FAITH

18 Little children, it is the last time *(all the period, from the First to the Second Advents may, in this sense, truly be called, "the last time")*: and as you have heard that Antichrist shall come *(the Apostle is speaking of the coming man of sin, who will make his debut after the Rapture of the Church)*, even now are there many Antichrists *(in the Greek is "Pseudochrists," and refers to one who claims to be of Christ)*; whereby we know that it is the last time. *(We know this is the last dispensation before the Second Coming of the Lord.)*

19 They went out from us, but they were not of us *(the crowd John speaks of claims to be of the True Church, but John says, "they were not of us")*: for if they had been of us, they would *no doubt* have continued with us *(had they been of the True Church, they would not have succumbed to false doctrine)*: but *they went out*, that they might be made manifest that they were not all of us. *("Them going out" means they turned their backs on the Christ of the Cross.)*

20 But you have an unction from the Holy One *(every True Believer has the "Anointing," of the Holy Spirit)*, and you know all things. *(This should have been translated, "you all know.")*

21 I have not written unto you because you know not the Truth *(what John is writing in this Epistle only reinforces what they have already known)*, but because you know it, and that no lie is of the Truth. *(The Truth will never produce a lie, and a lie can never produce the Truth.)*

22 Who is a liar but he who denies that Jesus is the Christ? *(Anyone who denies in any fashion Who Jesus is and What He has done to Redeem humanity is a "liar.")* He is Antichrist, who denies the Father and the Son. *(He who denies the Trinity is Antichrist. God the Father and God the Son are represented here, and it is the Holy Spirit Who inspires the Text. So we have here the Trinity.)*

23 Whosoever denies the Son, the same has not the Father *(no matter the claims, if Jesus is denied, so is the Father)*: [but] *he who acknowledges the Son has the Father also. (If the Son is accepted, the Father is as well, for the Son is the only way to the Father [Jn. 10:30, 38].)*

24 Let that therefore abide in you, which you have heard from the beginning. *(We must not deviate from the True Gospel, which originally brought us to Christ.)* If that which you have heard from the beginning shall remain in you, you also shall continue in the Son, and in the Father. *(It is the responsibility of the Believer to nurture the stability and growth of correct Doctrines by a Holy life and a determination to cling to them and remain true to them.)*

25 And this is the Promise that He has promised us, *even* Eternal Life *(which we obtain by accepting Christ and what He did for us at the Cross)*.

26 These *things* have I written unto you concerning them who seduce you. *(All false doctrine comes under the heading of "seducing spirits" in one way or the other, and is, therefore, labeled "Doctrines of Devils" [I Tim. 4:1].)*

27 But the Anointing which you have received of Him *(the Holy Spirit)* abides in you *(abides permanently to help us ascertain if what we are hearing is Scriptural or not)*, and you need not that any man teach you: but as the same Anointing teaches you of all things *(no*

Believer needs anything that's not already found written in the Word), **and is Truth, and is no lie** *(the Holy Spirit will guide us into all Truth [Jn. 16:13]),* **and even as it** *(the Anointing)* **has taught you, you shall abide in Him** *(refers to the fact that what we are taught by the Spirit, regarding the Word of God, helps us to abide in Christ).*

28 And now, little children, abide in Him *(presents the condition of fruit-bearing [Jn. 15:4, 7]);* **that, when He shall appear** *(the Rapture),* **we may have confidence** *(speaks of the heart attitude of the Saint, who lives so close to the Lord Jesus that there is nothing between him and his Lord),* **and not be ashamed before Him at His Coming.** *(This presents the fact that some certainly will be ashamed.)*

29 If you know that He is Righteous *(could be translated, "Since you know that He is Righteous"),* **you know that every one who does Righteousness is born of Him.** *(All who are truly Born-Again do "Righteousness.")*

CHAPTER 3
(A.D. 90)
LOVE

BEHOLD, **what manner of love the Father has bestowed upon us** *(presents that which is foreign to this present world, and, in fact, comes from another world),* **that we should be called the sons of God** *(we are "sons of God" by virtue of adoption into the Family of God, derived through the Born-Again experience):* **therefore the world knows us not, because it knew Him not.** *(The world does not recognize nor acknowledge Believers as sons of God, just as they did not recognize nor acknowledge Christ to be the Son of God.)*

2 Beloved, now are we the sons of God *(we are just as much a "son of God" now as we will be after the Resurrection),* **and it does not yet appear what we shall be** *(our present state as a "son of God" is not at all like that we shall be in the coming Resurrection):* **but we know that, when He shall appear** *(the Rapture),* **we shall be like Him** *(speaks of being glorified);* **for we shall see Him as He is.** *(Physical eyes in a mortal body could not look upon that glory, only eyes in glorified bodies.)*

RIGHTEOUSNESS

3 And every man who has this hope in Him *(the Resurrection)* **purifies himself** *(takes advantage of what Christ did for us at the Cross, which is the only way one can be pure),* **even as He** *(Christ)* **is pure** *(places Christ as our example).*

4 Whosoever commits sin transgresses also the Law *(the Greek Text says, "the sin," and refers to Believers placing their Faith in that other than the Cross; such constitutes rebellion against God's Prescribed Order and is labeled as "sin"):* **for sin is the transgression of the Law.** *(This refers to the moral Law — the Ten Commandments. Rebelling against God's Order, which is the Cross, opens the door for works of the flesh [Gal. 5:19-21].)*

5 And you know that He was manifested to take away our sins *(He did so at the Cross; the Christian cannot practice what Christ came to take away and destroy);* **and in Him is no sin.** *(This presents the fact that He was able to be the Perfect Sacrifice to take away the sin of the world, which completely destroys the erroneous doctrine that Jesus died spiritually, as some claim.)*

6 Whosoever abides in Him sins not *(does not practice sin):* **whosoever sins** *(practices sin)* **has not seen Him, neither known Him.** *(As stated, Jesus saves from sin, not in sin. If we look to the Cross, "sin will not have dominion over us" [Rom. 6:14].)*

7 Little children, let no man deceive you *(the entirety of this Epistle is a warning against antinomianism, which teaches that sin doesn't matter because Grace covers it):* **he who does Righteousness is Righteous** *(truly being Righteous will truly do Righteousness, i.e., "live Righteously"),* **even as He is Righteous.** *(We have been granted the Righteousness of Christ, so we should live Righteous, which we can if our Faith Eternally abides in the Cross [Rom. 6:1-14].)*

8 He who commits sin *(practices sin)* **is of the Devil** *(whoever is truly born of God does not live a life of habitual sinning);* **for the Devil sinneth from the beginning** *(from the beginning of his rebellion against God).* **For this purpose the Son of God was manifested, that He might destroy the works of the Devil.** *(This proclaims what was done at the Cross [Col. 2:14-15].)*

9 Whosoever is born of God does not commit sin *(does not practice sin);* **for his seed remains in him** *(refers to the Word of God):* **and he cannot sin** *(cannot continue to practice sin),* **because he is born of God.** *(This refers to the repugnancy of sin in the heart of the true Christian.)*

10 In this the Children of God are manifest,

and the children of the Devil *(there is no comparison between the two)*: whosoever does not Righteousness is not of God, neither he who loves not his Brother. *("Righteousness" and "Love" are the two manifestations of the Child of God.)*

LOVE

11 For this is the Message that you heard from the beginning, that we should love one another. *(The first attribute made evident in the new Christian is "Love.")*

12 Not as Cain, *who* was of that wicked one, and slew his Brother *(presents the prototype of evil).* And wherefore slew he him? *(Cain was not a murderer because he killed his Brother, but killed his Brother because he was a murderer.)* Because his own works were evil, and his Brother's Righteous *(points directly to the Cross; the rejection of God's Way [the Cross], which Cain did, is labeled by the Holy Spirit as "evil"; Abel accepted the Cross [Gen., Chpt. 4]).*

13 Marvel not, my Brethren, if the world hate you *(expect no better treatment from the world than Abel received from Cain).*

14 We know that we have passed from death unto life, because we love the Brethren *(love for the Brethren is the first sign of "spiritual life").* He who loves not *his* Brother abides in death. *(Love for the Brethren must characterize the Salvation profession. Otherwise, our claims are false.)*

15 Whosoever hates his Brother is a murderer *(the absence of love proclaims the presence of hatred; where hatred is, there is murder)*: and you know that no murderer has Eternal Life abiding in him *(comes back to the absence of love).*

16 Hereby perceive we the Love *of God* *(speaks of knowledge gained by experience)*, because He laid down His Life for us *(the highest proof of love is the Sacrifice of that which is most precious)*: and we ought to lay down *our* lives for the Brethren. *(This proclaims Christ as our example, and what the meaning of true love actually is.)*

17 But whoso has this world's goods *(refers to the necessities of life)*, and sees his brother have need *(it is seeing a Christian in need of the necessities of life over a long period)*, and shuts up his bowels *of compassion* from him *(presents the individual who has the means to truly help, but refuses to do so)*, how dwells the Love of God in him? *(His actions proclaim the fact that despite his profession, there is actually no love of God in him.)*

18 My little children, let us not love in word, neither in tongue *(let us not merely talk love)*; but in deed and in truth. *(True love demands action.)*

19 And hereby we know that we are of the Truth *(the evidence of love is the guarantee of Truth)*, and shall assure our hearts before Him. *(Am I loving as I ought to be? Our hearts will tell us!)*

20 For if our heart condemn us *(our failures in duty and service rise up before us, and our heart condemns us)*, God is greater than our heart *(the worst in us is known to God, and still He cares for us and desires us; our discovery has been an open secret to Him all along)*, and knows all things *(presents God Alone knowing our hearts; this is the true test of a man).*

21 Beloved, if our heart condemn us not *(does not claim sinless perfection, but represents the heart attitude of a Saint that, so far as he knows, has no unconfessed sin in his life)*, *then* have we confidence toward God *(implies no condemnation).*

22 And whatsoever we ask, we receive of Him *(speaks of prayer, and that we must keep asking for that which is desired)*, because we keep His Commandments *(Christ has already kept all of the Commandments; our Faith in Him and the Cross gives us His Victory, and is guaranteed by the Holy Spirit [Rom. 8:1-2, 11])*, and do those things that are pleasing in His sight *(pertains to the fact that the Cross is ever the Object of our Faith [Heb. 11:6]).*

23 And this is His Commandment *(is given to us in the singular)*, That we should believe on the Name of His Son Jesus Christ *(stands for all the Son of God is in His wonderful Person, and above all what He did for us at the Cross)*, and love one another, as He gave us Commandment. *(Proper Faith guarantees proper love [Mat. 22:37-40].)*

24 And he who keeps His Commandments dwells in Him, and He in him. *(Faith in Jesus Christ and what He did for us at the Cross proclaims the fact that we are dwelling in Him, and He is dwelling in us [Jn. 14:20; Rom. 6:3-5].)* And hereby we know that He abides in us, by the Spirit which He has given us. *(The knowledge that God is abiding in the Saint comes from the Holy Spirit. He bears witness in connection with our human spirit, as energized by Him, that we are children born of God [Rom. 8:16].)*

CHAPTER 4
(A.D. 90)
TEST THE SPIRITS

BELOVED, believe not every spirit *(behind every doctrine there is a "spirit"; if it's true Doctrine, the Holy Spirit; if it's false doctrine, evil spirits)*, **but try the spirits whether they are of God** *(the criteria is, "is it Scriptural?")*: **because many false prophets are gone out into the world** *(and they continue unto this hour).*

2 Hereby know ye the Spirit of God *(as Believers, we are to know what the Spirit of God sanctions)*: **Every spirit that confesses that Jesus Christ is come in the flesh is of God** *(the Incarnation of Christ speaks of the Cross of Christ, the very reason for which He came; this means the Spirit of God will place his sanction on the Cross and the Cross alone; anything else is not of God)*:

3 And every spirit that confesses not that Jesus Christ is come in the flesh is not of God *(Christ came in the flesh to go to the Cross; this refutes the error of Gnosticism, which claims the flesh of Christ was evil, as much as all matter they claim is evil; also, anyone who denigrates or even minimizes the Cross in any way is not of God)*: **and this is that *spirit* of Antichrist** *(the spirit that denies the Cross is the spirit of the Antichrist)*, **whereof you have heard that it should come; and even now already is it in the world.** *(The Doctrine of the Cross is essential to the Christian system. He who does not hold it cannot be either regarded as a Christian or recognized as a Christian Teacher.)*

4 You are of God, little children, and have overcome them *(some of the Christian's of John's day were tempted to believe the Doctrine that denigrated the Cross, but had overcome that temptation)*: **because greater is He** *(the Holy Spirit)* **Who is in you, than he** *(Satan)* **who is in the world.**

5 They are of the world *(refers to the false teachers of Verse 3)*: **therefore speak they of the world** *(refers to the fact that the source of their false doctrines is the world)*, **and the world hears them** *(because the false teachers are saying what the world wants to hear).*

6 We are of God *(those who accept Christ and the Cross)*: **he who knows God hears us; he who is not of God hears not us.** *(Man's attitude toward the Message of the Incarnate Saviour ranks him on God's side or the world's.)* **Hereby know we the Spirit of Truth, and the**

spirit of error. *(The "Spirit of Truth" is the Holy Spirit, Who leads us into all Truth, which refers to "Jesus Christ and Him Crucified [I Cor. 1:23; 2:2]. The "spirit of error" refers to any doctrine that denigrates or ignores the Cross, which is fostered by Satan, who employs seducing spirits [I Tim. 4:1].)*

GOD IS LOVE

7 Beloved, let us love one another: for love is of God *(speaks of agape love, of which the world knows nothing, and, in fact, cannot have to any degree)*; **and every one who loves is born of God, and knows God.** *(This is the God kind of love, and cannot be faked. In fact, something will always happen to show what type of love the person possesses, whether it's the God kind or that of the world.)*

8 He who loves not knows not God; for God is love. *("As to His nature, God is love.")*

9 In this was manifested the Love of God toward us *(if we truly have the Love of God in our hearts, we will, as well, manifest such love toward our fellowman)*, **because that God sent His only begotten Son into the world** *(our Lord is the uniquely Begotten Son of God in the sense that He proceeds by eternal generation from God the Father, co-possessing eternally with God the Father and God the Spirit the essence of Deity)*, **that we might live through Him.** *(It is only through Christ and what He did at the Cross that we can find life, and, as well, live through Him as He lives through us [Gal. 2:20].)*

10 Herein is love *(the Greek says, "herein is the love")*, **not that we loved God, but that He loved us** *(the unconverted human race does not love God; nevertheless, He loved the human race)*, **and sent His Son *to be* the propitiation for our sins.** *("Propitiation" is the Sacrifice, which fully satisfied the demands of the broken Law and did so by our Lord's Death on Calvary's Cross. His Death eternally satisfied the Righteousness of God.)*

11 Beloved, if God so loved us, we ought also to love one another. *(The Love of God is portrayed by the Cross more so than anything else. For us to understand His Love, we have to first understand the Cross.)*

12 No man has seen God at any time. *(The idea is no one has ever yet seen Deity in all its essence.)* **If we love one another, God dwells in us** *(Saints having this agape love habitually for one another show that this love, which God*

is in His Nature, has accomplished its purpose in our lives), **and His love is perfected in us.** *(The words "His Love" do not refer to our love for Him, or even to His Love for us, but to the Love that is peculiarly His own, which answers to His Nature.)*

13 Hereby know we that we dwell in Him, and He in us *("dwells" speaks of fellowship between two or more individuals; in this case, God and ourselves)*, **because He has given us of His Spirit.** *(The Holy Spirit has been caused to take up His permanent Residence in us.)*

14 And we have seen and do testify *(John was an eyewitness of Jesus Christ, both to Who He was and to What He did as well)* **that the Father sent the Son** *to be* **the Saviour of the world.** *(His Mission was to Redeem lost humanity, which He did at the Cross.)*

15 Whosoever shall confess that Jesus is the Son of God *(the confession John speaks of here is a lifetime confession, and represents the sustained attitude of the heart)*, **God dwells in him, and he in God** *(proclaims the union of the Father in the Believer and the Believer in the Father, all made possible by what Christ did at the Cross)*.

16 And we have known and believed the Love that God has to us. *(The love God has shown to us is manifested in Him giving His Son to die on the Cross.)* **God is Love** *(which is proven by His act of the giving of His Only Son)*; **and he who dwells in love dwells in God, and God in him.** *(This is all made possible by the Cross, and only by the Cross.)*

17 Herein is our love made perfect *(our Love is brought to fruition, i.e., "made complete," by a continued confession of Jesus Christ as the Son of God, and what He did for us on the Cross)*, **that we may have boldness in the Day of Judgment** *(the Judgment addressed here is the coming "Judgment Seat of Christ)*: **because as He is, so are we in this world.** *(Christ is totally victorious, and due to the fact that we are in Him, we as well can be totally victorious in this world.)*

18 There is no fear in love *(the type of "fear" spoken of here is not a Godly fear or a filial reverence, but rather a slavish fear for a master or of a criminal before a Judge)*; **but perfect love casts out fear** *(God has a Perfect Love for us, and if we have a perfect love for Him, which we surely can have, then we know He is going to sustain us, so there's nothing then to fear)*: **because fear has torment.** *(It is guilt that makes men fear what is to come.)* **He who fears is not**

made perfect in love. *(If we do not properly understand the Cross, then we are not made perfect in love.)*

19 We love Him, because He first loved us. *(The first initiation of Love was on the part of God, and not us, as was necessary.)*

20 If a man say, I love God, and hates his Brother, he is a liar *(as James said, "does a fountain send forth at the same place sweet water and bitter?" [James 3:11])*: **for he who loves not his brother whom he has seen, how can he love God Whom he has not seen?** *(If a professed Christian does not love one who bears the Divine Image, whom he sees and knows, how can he love God, Whose Image he bears, yet has not seen?)*

21 And this Commandment have we from Him *(the Holy Spirit, through John, proclaims all of this as a "Commandment")*, **That he who loves God love his Brother also.** *(True love for God will always bring forth the correct action.)*

CHAPTER 5
(A.D. 90)
THE NEW BIRTH

WHOSOEVER believes that Jesus is the Christ is born of God *(the word "believeth" is not a mere intellectual assent to the fact of the Incarnation, but a heart acceptance of all that is implied in its purpose — the substitutionary death of the Incarnate One for sinners)*: **and every one who loves Him Who begat loves him also who is begotten of Him.** *(This simply states that those who love God as their Father also love God's Children.)*

2 By this we know that we love the Children of God *(we know we love God if we love those who bear His Image)*, **when we love God, and keep His Commandments.** *(Jesus said the same thing in Jn. 14:15.)*

3 For this is the Love of God, that we keep His Commandments: and His Commandments are not grievous. *(This is easy to do, providing we look exclusively to the Cross. Otherwise it is impossible [Mat. 11:28-30].)*

4 For whatsoever is born of God overcomes the world *(if we follow God's Prescribed Order, we will overcome the world)*: **and this is the victory that overcomes the world,** *even* **our Faith.** *(John is speaking here of Faith in Christ and the Cross, which then gives the Holy Spirit latitude to work within our lives [Rom. 8:1-2, 11].)*

5 Who is he who overcomes the world, but

he who believes that Jesus is the Son of God? *(It is not he who "does," but who "believes.")*

LIFE

6 This is He Who came by water and blood, *even* Jesus Christ *(refers to the Living Word becoming flesh [Jn. 1:1, 4], which is symbolized by "water" and then as the Lamb of God Who took away the sin of the world, which was affected by the shedding of His Blood on the Cross of Calvary)*; **not by water only, but by water and blood** *(testifies to the fact that the Incarnation within itself, although absolutely necessary, was not enough; the phrase also testifies to the absolute necessity of the Atonement)*. **And it is the Spirit Who bears witness, because the Spirit is Truth.** *(The Holy Spirit bore witness to the Divine Birth of Christ, and to the Divine Sacrifice of Christ [Mat. 1:18; Heb. 9:14].)*

7 **For there are Three Who bear record in Heaven** *(the Law has ever required the Testimony of two or three witnesses [Deut. 17:6; 19:15; Mat. 18:16; II Cor. 13:1])*, **the Father, the Word** *(Jesus Christ is the Word [Jn. 1:1])*, **and the Holy Spirit: and these Three are One.** *(The only sense three can be one is in essence and unity, as is clear in Jn. 17:11, 21-23.)*

8 **And there are Three who bear witness in earth** *(as in Heaven, so on Earth)*, **the Spirit, and the water, and the blood** *(speaks of the Holy Spirit; the Humanity of Christ, while never ceasing to be Deity, and the Atonement, i.e., "the Cross")*: **and these Three agree in One.** *(These Three agree that Christ is Very Man while at the same time being Very God, Who died on the Cross to Redeem fallen humanity.)*

9 **If we receive the witness of men, the witness of God is greater** *(if we receive witness of sinful men who can so easily deceive, we should gladly receive the witness of God, Who cannot possibly deceive)*: **for this is the witness of God which He has testified of His Son** *(centers on the Cross)*.

10 **He who believes on the Son of God has the witness in himself** *(that Witness is the Holy Spirit [Rom. 8:16])*: **He who believes not God has made Him a liar** *(presents the problem of unbelief as the basic difficulty in the human race)*; **because he believes not the record that God gave of His Son** *(proclaims the fact that the proof is undeniable)*.

11 **And this is the record** *(the "record" is the Word of God, which is the story of the Cross)*,

that God has given to us Eternal Life *(the Life of God flowing into and literally becoming a part of the Believer)*, **and this life is in His Son.** *(Christ is the Source, while the Cross is the means.)*

12 **He who has the Son has Life** *(through the Cross)*; *and* **he who has not the Son of God has not life.** *(This rules out all the fake luminaries of the world.)*

PRAYER

13 **These things have I written unto you who believe on the Name of the Son of God** *(all that John writes is to bring to the mind of His readers the fact that they have Life Eternal because they believe on the name of the Son of God)*; **that you may know that you have Eternal Life** *(not a mere experimental knowledge, but an absolute knowledge)*, **and that you may believe on the Name of the Son of God** *(keep believing)*.

14 **And this is the confidence that we have in Him** *(proper believing gives us proper confidence, which is proper assurance)*, **that, if we ask any thing according to His Will, He hears us** *(we should pray with the provision expressed or implied, "if it be Your Will")*:

15 **And if we know that He hears us, whatsoever we ask** *(presents the fact that we are assured of this, even though we may not see an immediate answer to prayer)*, **we know that we have the petitions that we desired of Him** *(providing it's His Will)*.

RESTORATION

16 **If any man see his Brother sin a sin** *which* **is not unto death** *(refers to direction other than the Cross, done in ignorance)*, **he shall ask, and He shall give him life for them who sin not unto death.** *(The Believer who understands God's Prescribed Order of Victory, which is the Cross, should pray for those who are ignorantly going in a direction opposite of the Cross.)* **There is a sin unto death** *(speaks of unbelief; this group is not opposing the Cross because of ignorance, but rather because they simply do not believe in the Atoning work of Calvary)*: **I do not say that he shall pray for it.** *(While it is pointless to pray that God would forgive such a person, it is proper to pray that the blindness of their unbelief will be removed.)*

17 **All unrighteousness is sin** *(refers to any deviation from the Word)*: **and there is a**

sin not unto death. *(This is a lack of trust in the Cross due to ignorance, not unbelief. While such sin will bring great disturbance upon the individual, it will not cause one to lose their soul.)*

VICTORY

18 We know that whosoever is born of God sins not *(does not practice sin)*; but he who is begotten of God keeps himself *(should have been translated, "but He [Christ] Who is Begotten of God keeps him")*, and that wicked one touches him not *(is the person who keeps his Faith in Christ and the Cross).*

19 *And* we know that we are of God *(because of trusting in Christ and what He did for us at the Cross)*, and the whole world lies in wickedness *(refers to the world system).*

ETERNAL LIFE

20 And we know that the Son of God is come *(presents that which is not simply a historic fact, but rather an abiding operation)*, and has given us an understanding, that we may know Him Who is true *(the real "One" as opposed to spurious gods)*, and we are in Him Who is true, *even* in his Son Jesus Christ *(by virtue of being "Baptized into His Death" [Rom. 6:3-5]).* This is the True God, and Eternal Life. *(Jesus Christ is truly God, and Faith in Him guarantees "Eternal Life.")*

21 Little children, keep yourselves from idols. Amen. *(This does not refer here to the heathen worship of idol gods, but of the heretical substitutes for the Christian conception of God, or anything that pulls us away from Christ and the Cross.)*

THE SECOND EPISTLE OF
JOHN

INTRODUCTION

(A.D. 90)

THE Elder *(normally refers to "Pastor," however, this seems to be a title given to John, and for the obvious reasons; he was the last Apostle of the chosen Twelve to die)* unto the elect lady and her children *(it is believed that this woman was a devout Christian who lived near Ephesus; it also seems her home was the meeting-place of the local assembly)*, whom I love in the truth *(refers to the Love of God)*; and not I only, but also all they who have known the Truth *(the bond that had pulled this aged Apostle to this dear lady and her to him is "Truth")*;

2 For the truth's sake, which dwells *(love is a product of Truth)* in us, and shall be with us forever. *(Truth cannot change.)*

3 Grace be with you, Mercy, *and* Peace, from God the Father, and from the Lord Jesus Christ, the Son of the Father, in Truth and Love. *(The Cross makes all this possible.)*

LOVE

4 I rejoiced greatly that I found of your children walking in Truth *(her children were conducting themselves in the sphere of Truth as it is in Christ Jesus, doing so on a daily basis)*, as we have received a Commandment from the Father *(relates the fact that the Truth by which they were walking was not their own concoction, but rather was according to the Word of God)*.

5 And now I beseech you, lady, not as though I wrote a new Commandment unto you, but that which we had from the beginning, that we love one another *(the great hallmark of Christianity)*.

6 And this is love, that we walk after His Commandments *(presents the proper expression or evidence of love to God)*. This is the Commandment, That, as you have heard from the beginning, you should walk in it. *(This presents the Commandment by which the followers of the Lord are to be peculiarly characterized, and by which we are to be distinguished in the world.)*

DECEIVERS

7 For many deceivers are entered into the world *(a false teacher who leads others into heresies, i.e., "away from the Cross")*, who confess not that Jesus Christ is come in the flesh *(a denial of the Incarnation)*. This is a deceiver and an Antichrist. *(All false doctrine begins with a misconception or misinterpretation of the "Person" of Christ.)*

8 Look to yourselves, that we lose not those things which we have wrought *(is the same as Paul's "examine yourselves" [II Cor. 13:5])*, but that we receive a full reward *(refers to the coming Judgment Seat of Christ, where and when every true Christian will give account)*.

9 Whosoever transgresses, and abides not in the Doctrine of Christ, has not God. *(The "Doctrine of Christ" is in brief "the Cross." If one leaves the Cross, one transgresses, and no longer has the Lord, which means that the soul will be lost if such direction is continued.)* He who abides in the Doctrine of Christ, he has Both the Father and the Son *(Gal. 5:1-6)*.

10 If there come any unto you, and bring not this Doctrine *(Jesus Christ and Him Crucified)*, receive him not into *your* house, neither bid him God speed *(to receive such shows acceptance)*:

11 For he who bids him God speed is partaker of his evil deeds. *(To help or finance false Apostles makes the person doing such a part of the false doctrine, which is serious indeed!)*

BENEDICTION

12 Having many things to write unto you, I would not *write* with paper and ink: but I trust to come unto you, and speak face to face, that our joy may be full. *(What he said in this short Epistle is evidently all the Holy Spirit wanted him to write at this time, at least to this particular lady.)*

13 The children of your elect sister greet you. Amen. *(John was speaking of the flesh and blood sister of the "elect lady" to whom he was writing. The simplicity of the great Apostle — the personal friend of the Risen Lord, the last of the great pillars of the Church — in transmitting this familiar Message makes a most instructive finish to what is throughout a beautiful picture.)*

THE THIRD EPISTLE OF
JOHN

INTRODUCTION
(A.D. 90)

THE Elder *(John refers to himself by this title)* unto the well-beloved Gaius *(could well be the same one mentioned in Acts 19:29; 20:4; Rom. 16:23; I Cor. 1:14),* whom I love in the truth. *(As the previous Letter was written to a wealthy woman telling her to shut her door against Preachers of a false gospel, so this Letter was written to a wealthy man to open his door to Preachers of the True Gospel.)*

2 Beloved, I wish above all things that you may prosper *(refers to financial prosperity, and should be the case for every Believer)* and be in health *(speaks of physical prosperity),* even as your soul prospers *(speaks of spiritual prosperity; so we have here the whole Gospel for the whole man).*

3 For I rejoiced greatly, when the Brethren came and testified of the truth that is in you *(Christian workers were always going out from Ephesus on preaching and teaching missions, and bringing reports from various Churches back to John),* even as you walk in the Truth *(refers to the manner of one's behavior).*

4 I have no greater joy than to hear that my children walk in Truth. *(Quite possibly Gaius was a convert of John.)*

FELLOWHELPERS

5 Beloved, you do faithfully whatsoever you do to the Brethren, and to strangers *(little did this man know that what he was doing would be heralded in the Word of God, and known all over the world for all time);*

6 Which have borne witness of your charity *(love)* before the Church: whom if you bring forward on their journey after a Godly sort, you shall do well *(to "bring forward" as used here refers to standing good for the maintenance and expenses of visiting Preachers):*

7 Because that for His Name's sake they went forth *(it was for the sake of the Name of Jesus that these Preachers went forth),* taking nothing of the Gentiles. *(This refers to virgin territory regarding the Gospel, i.e., different places where they would plant Churches. In planting these Churches, they asked for no money from the new Gentile converts.)*

8 We therefore ought to receive such *(to be of help to such Preachers, both prayerfully and financially),* that we might be fellowhelpers to the Truth. *(Through John, the Holy Spirit here proclaims the fact that Believers should give of their financial resources to help take the Truth to others.)*

DIOTREPHES

9 I wrote unto the Church *(speaks of a local Church, but we aren't told its location):* but Diotrephes, who loves to have the preeminence among them, receives us not. *(If it is to be noticed, John calls the name of this individual and warns against him, even as he should have done. To be sure, anyone who was not of Truth would not receive John.)*

10 Wherefore, if I come, I will remember his deeds which he does, prating against us with malicious words *(there is no evidence whatsoever that this is said in a vindictive or vengeful spirit; and we must remember that the Holy Spirit is inspiring John to write these words; in other words, this man had to be exposed):* and not content therewith, neither does he himself receive the Brethren, and forbids them who would, and casts *them* out of the Church. *(The idea is that Diotrephes would cast those who would side with John out of the Church, or else seek to do so. Consequently, silence on John's part would have been wrong, just as it is wrong now for Preachers to be silent regarding false Apostles and false doctrine.)*

TESTIMONY

11 Beloved, follow not that which is evil, but that which is good. *(In effect, John is referring to Diotrephes as "evil." At the same time, he is boldly stating that what he [John] preaches is "good" and, therefore, "of God.")* He who does good is of God: but he who does evil has not seen God. *(The Holy Spirit, through John, very clearly draws the line. One cannot have it both ways.)*

12 Demetrius has good report of all *men* *(this man was probably the bearer of this Letter to Gaius; he was a stranger to the members of the local Church of which Gaius was a member,*

and needed a word of commendation from the Apostle), **and of the Truth itself: yes, and we** *also* **bear record; and you know that our record is true.** *(There could be no higher recommendation, especially considering that the Holy Spirit sanctioned these words.)*

BENEDICTION

13 I had many things to write, but I will not

with ink and pen write unto you *(John ends this Letter in much the same way he ended his Second Epistle)*:

14 But I trust I shall shortly see you, and we shall speak face to face. *(Evidently, the Apostle planned to visit this particular Church shortly.)* **Peace** *be* **to you.** *Our* **friends salute you. Greet the friends by name.** *(This was a small Church, but yet very important, even as the Holy Spirit here proclaims.)*

THE EPISTLE GENERAL OF
JUDE

INTRODUCTION
(A.D. 66)

JUDE, the servant of Jesus Christ, and Brother of James *(Jude was the half-brother of the Lord Jesus Christ as well)*, to them who are Sanctified by God the Father *(should have been translated, "to them who are loved by God the Father")*, and preserved in Jesus Christ *(in effect, says, "God the Father is keeping the Saints guarded by Jesus Christ")*, *and* Called *(the idea, as presented here by the Holy Spirit through Jude, is that God does not want to lose the people He has Called to be His Own through false doctrine)*.

2 Mercy unto you, and Peace, and Love, be multiplied *(all of this is made possible by the Cross, and the Cross alone)*.

FALSE TEACHERS

3 Beloved, when I gave all diligence *(a compulsion generated by the Holy Spirit)* to write unto you of the common Salvation *(he had at first thought to write an Epistle similar to Romans, but the Holy Spirit, although the Author of the compulsion, did not lead in this direction)*, it was needful for me to write unto you *(the implication is that whatever was to be written had to be written at once, and could not be prepared for at leisure)*, and exhort *you* that you should earnestly contend for the Faith *(refers to the fact that the Saints must defend the Doctrines of Christianity with intense effort)* which was once delivered unto the Saints *(refers to the fact that no other Faith will be given; the idea is that God gave the Christian Doctrines to the Saints as a deposit of Truth to be guarded)*.

4 For there are certain men crept in unawares *(false teachers had crept into the Church)*, who were before of old ordained to this condemnation, ungodly men *(they came in by stealth and dishonesty; however, their methods were by no means new; they would assume an outward expression of light)*, turning the Grace of our God into lasciviousness *(refers to the fact that "Grace" had been turned to license)*, and denying the only Lord God, and our Lord Jesus Christ *(if we deny the Cross, which is God's Plan of Redemption, we are at the same time denying Both the Father and the Son)*.

5 I will therefore put you in remembrance *(suggests something of anxiety and upbraiding, which may be compared to the tone of Paul in writing Galatians)*, though you once knew this, how that the Lord, having saved the people out of the Land of Egypt, afterward destroyed them who believed not *(unbelief destroyed the Israelites in the wilderness, and it will do the same presently)*.

6 And the Angels which kept not their first estate, but left their own habitation *(these particular Angels did not maintain their original position in which they were created, but transgressed those limits to invade territory foreign to them, namely the human race; they left Heaven and came to Earth, seeking to cohabit with women, which they did [Gen. 6:4])*, He *(the Lord)* has reserved in everlasting chains under darkness unto the Judgment of the Great Day *(these Angels are now imprisoned [II Pet. 2:4], and will be judged at the Great White Throne Judgment, then placed in the "Lake of Fire" where they will remain forever and forever [Rev. 20:10])*.

7 Even as Sodom and Gomorrha, and the cities about them in like manner *(the Greek Text introduces a comparison showing a likeness between the Angels of Verse 6 and the cities of Sodom and Gomorrah; but the likeness between them lies deeper than the fact that both were guilty of committing sin; it extends to the fact that both were guilty of the same identical sin)*, giving themselves over to fornication, and going after strange flesh *(the Angels cohabited with women; the sin of Sodom and Gomorrah, and the cities around them, was homosexuality [Rom. 1:27])*, are set forth for an example, suffering the vengeance of eternal fire *(those who engage in the sin of homosexuality and refuse to repent will suffer the vengeance of the Lake of Fire)*.

8 Likewise also these *filthy* dreamers defile the flesh *(Jude likens these false teachers to "filthy dreamers," and refers to their doctrines as being the fruits of mere imagination and fancies)*, despise dominion *(they refuse to live by the Word of God, but rather fabricate their own religion)*, and speak evil of dignities *(refers to reviling the Word of God, and more particularly*

Christ and the Cross).

9 Yet Michael the Archangel *(no other Angel bears the title of Archangel, as recorded; there are others who are Chief Angels, and Michael is only one of them [Dan. 10:13]),* **when contending with the Devil he disputed about the body of Moses** *(after the death of Moses, Satan demanded the body of the Lawgiver which was denied him by Michael, the Archangel),* **did not bring against him** *(against Satan)* **a railing accusation, but said, The Lord rebuke you** *(a "railing accusation" would have placed Michael on the same level with the Devil to which the great Archangel would not stoop, and rightly so!).*

10 But these *(false teachers)* **speak evil of those things which they know not** *(the adage here applies, "fools rush in where Angels fear to tread"):* **but what they know naturally, as brute beasts** *(Jude refers to these false teachers as being in the class of unreasoning animals),* **in those things they corrupt themselves** *(could have been translated, "by these things are being brought to ruin").*

11 Woe unto them! *(Concerning apostasy and apostates, the Holy Spirit says to them, "Woe!")* **for they have gone in the way of Cain** *(the type of a religious man who believes in God and "religion," but after his own will, and who rejects Redemption by blood),* **and ran greedily after the error of Balaam for reward** *(the error of Balaam was that he was blind to the higher morality of the Cross, through which God maintains and enforces the authority and awful sanctions of His Law, so that He can be Just and the Justifier of the believing sinner; he loved the wages of unrighteousness in coveting the gifts of Balak [Num. 22:7, 17, 37; 24:11; II Pet. 2:15]),* **and perished in the gainsaying of Core** *(the gainsaying of this man was his rebellion against Aaron as God's appointed Priest; this was, in principle, a denial of the High Priesthood of Christ [Num., Chpt. 16]).*

12 These are spots *(rocks)* **in your feasts of charity, when they feast with you** *(these false teachers participated in the Lord's Supper, thereby, claiming to be Godly),* **feeding themselves without fear** *(furthering their own schemes and lusts instead of tending the flock of God):* **clouds *they are* without water** *(such disappoints the ground that needs rain; likewise, these false teachers look good outwardly, but inwardly there is no substance),* **carried about of winds** *(they seek Believers with itching ears; they have no true course of the Word of God);* **trees whose fruit withers, without fruit** *(there is no proper fruit, simply*

because good fruit cannot come from a bad tree), **twice dead** *(they were dead in trespasses and sins before being saved, and now they have gone back on God and are dead again, i.e., "twice dead"),* **plucked up by the roots** *(they are not like the true tree planted by the waters);*

13 Raging waves of the sea *(refers to the destruction caused by false doctrine),* **foaming out their own shame** *(false doctrine is like the foam or scum at the seashore);* **wandering stars** *(an unpredictable star which provides no guidance for navigation),* **to whom is reserved the blackness of darkness forever** *(refers to their eternal doom [II Pet. 2:4]).*

14 And Enoch also, the seventh from Adam *(the Old Testament person of that name, the man who "walked with God" [Gen. 5:18-24]),* **Prophesied of these** *(the translation should read, "Prophesied with respect to these false teachers of these last days"),* **saying, Behold, the Lord comes with ten thousands of His Saints** *(is actually, "His Holy ten thousands," which literally means "an unlimited number"; this quotation is taken from the Book of Enoch, which was lost for many centuries with the exception of a few fragments, but was found in its entirety in a copy of the Ethiopia Bible in 1773),*

15 To execute Judgment upon all *(refers to Christ Judging the nations of the world, which will commence at the beginning of the Millennial Reign),* **and to convince all who are ungodly among them of all their ungodly deeds which they have ungodly committed** *(the word "ungodly" is used four times in this Verse, telling us that the ungodliness is total; as well, "all" is used four times, which means that none will escape this Judgment),* **and of all their hard *speeches* which ungodly sinners have spoken against Him** *(every ungodly statement against Christ will be addressed at that time).*

16 These are murmurers, complainers, walking after their own lusts *(Jude has in mind men who cannot get enough to satisfy their lusts, and thus complain);* **and their mouth speaks great swelling *words*, having men's persons in admiration because of advantage** *(refers to showing "respect of person"; they use flattery for the sake of profit).*

EXHORTATIONS

17 But, beloved, remember ye the words which were spoken before of the Apostles of our Lord Jesus Christ *(actually refers to that given by Peter and others);*

18 How that they told you there should be mockers in the last time *(refers to the last days, in fact, the very time in which we now live)*, who should walk after their own ungodly lusts *(refers to charting a course which is not of God, but rather after the flesh; they have forsaken the Cross!)*.

19 These be they who separate themselves *(should be translated, "these be they who separate"; they have forsaken the Cross, purposely choosing another way)*, sensual *(refers to that which is not of the Spirit, but rather of the flesh)*, having not the Spirit *(refers to those who operate outside the Cross of Christ)*.

20 But you, Beloved *(contrasts the Saints with the false teachers)*, building up yourselves *(to build toward the finish of the structure for which the foundation has already been laid)* on your most Holy Faith *(Jesus Christ and Him Crucified)*, praying in the Holy Spirit *(our praying must be exercised in the sphere of the Holy Spirit, motivated and empowered by Him)*,

21 Keep yourselves in the Love of God *(we are to see to it that we stay within the circle of His Love, which can only be done by Faith constantly making the Cross its Object)*, looking for the Mercy of our Lord Jesus Christ unto Eternal Life *(looking for the Rapture of the Church, with all of this made possible by what Jesus did on the Cross)*.

22 And of some have compassion, making a difference *(the false teachers should be addressed on a case by case situation, referring to the fact that some have to be handled differently than others; "some with compassion")*:

23 And others save with fear *(this particular group needs to be dealt with directly and vigorously)*, pulling *them* out of the fire *(the fire of destruction)*; hating even the garment spotted by the flesh *(presents works of the flesh, which always characterize those who follow a direction other than the Cross)*.

BENEDICTION

24 Now unto Him Who is able to keep you from falling *(as we've repeatedly stated, Christ is the Source of all things, but the Cross is the means)*, and to present *you* faultless before the Presence of His Glory with exceeding joy *(the Holy Spirit will, at the appointed time, present us to the Father, and will do so "with exceeding joy"; this refers to the Believer standing blameless before the Judgment Seat, all because of Christ and what He did at the Cross [Col. 1:22; I Thess. 3:13])*,

25 To the only wise God our Saviour *(speaks of the Cross)*, *be* Glory and Majesty, Dominion and Power, both now and ever. Amen *(every Believer will share in all of this, and do so forever; once again, all because of the Cross)*.

THE
REVELATION TO JOHN

CHAPTER 1
(A.D. 96)
INTRODUCTION

THE Revelation of Jesus Christ, which God gave unto Him (*the Revelation given here is of Jesus Christ, not John, as many think; John was only the instrument used to write the account*), to show unto His servants things which must shortly come to pass (*refers to the beginning of the events, which continue on unto this hour, and, in fact, will continue forever; it is the Church Age and beyond*); and He sent and signified *it* by His Angel unto His servant John (*even though the Revelation came to Christ, it was delivered to John by "His Angel"*):

2 Who bear record of the Word of God (*regarded himself merely as a witness of what he had seen, and claimed only to make a fair and faithful record of it*), and of the Testimony of Jesus Christ (*John was merely a witness of the Testimony that Christ had borne*), and of all things that he saw (*refers to the visions and symbols given to John*).

3 Blessed *is* he who reads, and they who hear the words of this Prophecy, and keep those things which are written therein (*all who obey these admonitions are promised a Blessing*): for the time *is* at hand (*refers to the beginning of the fulfillment of these things which begins with the Church, as recorded in Revelation, Chapters 2 and 3, and continues forever*).

SALUTATION

4 John to the seven Churches which are in Asia (*these particular Churches were selected by the Holy Spirit to portray the entirety of the Church Age*): Grace *be* unto you, and Peace, from Him which is, and which was, and which is to come (*refers to Sanctifying Grace and Sanctifying Peace, all made possible by the Cross*); and from the seven Spirits which are before His Throne (*is given to us in this manner to emphasize the sevenfold aspect of the Operations of the Holy Spirit [Isa. 11:2]*);

5 And from Jesus Christ, *Who is* the faithful Witness (*earthly life of perfect obedience*), *and* the first begotten of the dead (*refers to His Resurrection, which is the Firstfruits [Rom. 8:23]*), and the prince of the kings of the earth. (*This refers to His rulership of the world, which is a key theme of the Book of Revelation.*) Unto Him Who loved us, and washed us from our sins in His Own Blood (*the Cross proves the fact of His Love in no uncertain terms*),

6 And has made us kings and priests unto God and His Father (*made possible by what Christ did at the Cross, and only by what Christ did at the Cross*); to Him *be* Glory and Dominion forever and ever. Amen. (*Christ is the Redeemer, so He deserves the "Glory and Dominion," which will be His forever and ever.*)

THE THEME

7 Behold, He comes with clouds (*the Second Coming of Christ is the chief theme of this Book; the word "clouds" represents great numbers of Saints*); and every eye shall see Him (*refers to all who will be in the immediate vicinity of Jerusalem, and possibly even billions who may very well see Him by Television*), and they *also* which pierced Him (*the Jews, and they will then know beyond the shadow of a doubt that Jesus is Messiah and Lord*): and all kindreds of the earth shall wail because of Him. Even so, Amen. (*The "wailing" will take place because of the Judgment Christ will bring upon the world for its sin and shame.*)

8 I am Alpha and Omega, the beginning and the ending (*the First, the Last, the only God*), saith the Lord, which is, and which was, and which is to come, the Almighty. (*The word "Almighty" guarantees He will be able to accomplish all that He says.*)

THE VISION

9 I John, who also am your Brother, and companion in tribulation (*John was a fellow-partaker in the tribulation which was then coming to all the Churches*), and in the Kingdom and Patience of Jesus Christ (*Christ will ultimately establish His Kingdom on this Earth, but we must use patience in waiting for it*), was in the Isle that is called Patmos (*an island about 37 miles west-southwest of Miletus in the Aegean*

Sea), for the Word of God, and for the Testimony of Jesus Christ. *(He was not in prison for crimes committed, for he had committed none, but because of his stand for our Lord.)*

10 I was in the Spirit *(he entered into a new kind of experience relative to the Spirit's control over him)* on the Lord's Day *(Sunday)*, and heard behind me a great Voice, as of a trumpet *(the Voice John heard is heard unto this hour all over the world, and, in fact, will ever be heard; it is the Voice of our Lord!)*,

11 Saying, I am Alpha and Omega, the First and the Last *(Christ is all in all)*: and, What you see, write in a Book *(constitutes what we now have and refer to as the "Book of Revelation")*, and send *it* unto the Seven Churches which are in Asia; unto Ephesus, and unto Smyrna, and unto Pergamos, and unto Thyatira, and unto Sardis, and unto Philadelphia, and unto Laodicea. *(This phrase presents these Churches that were all selected Personally by Christ.)*

12 And I turned to see the Voice that spoke with me. And being turned, I saw Seven Golden Candlesticks *(presents the symbolism for the seven Churches)*;

13 And in the midst of the Seven Candlesticks *one* like unto the Son of Man *(Jesus is Head of the Church, the Centerpiece of its activity)*, clothed with a garment down to the foot *(indicates His position as King-Priest)*, and girt about the paps with a Golden Girdle *(presents kingly apparel; Christ is the King-Priest)*.

14 His head and *His* hairs *were* white like wool, as white as snow *(Majesty and Authority)*; and His eyes *were* as a flame of fire *(portrays penetrating scrutiny and fierce Judgment)*;

15 And His feet like unto fine brass, as if they burned in a furnace *("brass" signifies His Humanity, but superhuman)*; and His Voice as the sound of many waters *(the Voice of Power)*.

16 And He had in His Right Hand Seven Stars *(represents the Pastors of these seven Churches)*: and out of His mouth went a sharp twoedged sword *(represents the Word of God)*: and His countenance *was* as the sun shines in His strength *(represents His Glory)*.

17 And when I saw Him, I fell at His feet as dead *(the idea is that John thought he was going to die)*. And He laid His right hand upon me, saying unto me, Fear not *(in effect, Christ is telling John he will not die)*; I am the First and the Last *(He Alone is God, the Absolute Lord of history and the Creator)*:

18 *I am* He Who lives *(will never die again*

and has life in Himself; the Fountain and Source of Life to others; the One Who has immortality [Jn. 1:4; 14:6; 1 Tim. 6:16])*, and was dead *(represents the Living One entering into death, into our death, in His human nature so that as the great High Priest He might finish the Sacrifice for sins, which He did)*; and, behold, I am alive for evermore, Amen *(He will never die again, and death is totally defeated)*; and have the keys of hell and of death. *(He Alone determines who will enter death and hell, and who will not.)*

19 Write the things which you have seen *(this Verse is the key to the understanding of the Book of Revelation; it is broken up into three parts: 1. The Vision of Christ in the midst of the Candlesticks, Chapter 1)*, and the things which are *(2. Concerns the Churches, Chapters 2-3)*, and the things which shall be hereafter *(3. Concerns events after the Rapture of the Church, includes the Great Tribulation and Eternity everafter, Chapters 4-22)*;

20 The mystery of the Seven Stars which you saw in My Right Hand *(portrays the fact that these Pastors belonged to Christ)*, and the Seven Golden Candlesticks. The Seven Stars are the Angels *(Pastors)* of the Seven Churches: and the Seven Candlesticks which you saw are the Seven Churches. *(This represents the entirety of the Church Age, even as we shall see.)*

CHAPTER 2
(A.D. 96)
EPHESUS

UNTO the Angel *(pastor)* of the Church of Ephesus write *(the Ephesian Church represents the Apostolic time period, which closed out around A.D. 100)*; These things says He who holds the Seven Stars in His Right Hand *(all Pastors belong to the Lord, that is if they truly are of the Lord)*, Who walks in the midst of the Seven Golden Candlesticks *(Christ is the Head of the Church [Col. 1:18])*;

2 I know your works *(repeated to all Seven Churches; it implies Divine knowledge)*, and your labour, and your patience, and how you cannot bear them which are evil *(which have departed from true Doctrine)*: and you have tried them which say they are Apostles, and are not, and have found them liars *(presents the Doctrinal soundness of the Ephesian Believers)*:

3 And have borne *(they set a course, and did not deviate from that course)*, and have patience *(continued to believe when things were*

not going well), **and for My Name's sake have laboured, and have not fainted.** *(They were diligent in their efforts, and would not quit.)*

4 Nevertheless I have *somewhat* **against you** *(something is wrong, despite their zeal),* **because you have left your first love** *(not "lost" your first love, but rather "left" your first love; it refers to a departure from the Cross, and is so serious that it will lead the Church to ruin unless Repentance is forthcoming).*

5 Remember therefore from where you are fallen *(this means they fell from Grace, which means they had stopped depending on Christ and the Cross [Gal. 5:4]),* **and repent, and do the first works** *(go back to the Cross);* **or else I will come unto you quickly, and will remove your candlestick out of his place, except you repent.** *(Christ is the Source of the Light, but the Cross is the means. They are to come back to the Cross, or else the Light will be removed.)*

6 But this you have, that you hate the deeds of the Nicolaitanes, which I also hate. *(The word "Nicolaitanes" means "laity-conquerors." They are Preachers who exploit the people instead of spiritually developing them, which all false doctrine does. The Lord hates this, and so should we!)*

7 He who has an ear, let him hear what the Spirit says unto the Churches *(the Holy Spirit is saying that the Church must come back to the Cross);* **To him who overcomes will I give to eat of the tree of life, which is in the midst of the Paradise of God.** *(The Christian can be an overcomer only by placing his Faith exclusively in Christ and the Cross, which gives the Holy Spirit latitude to work.)*

SMYRNA

8 And unto the Angel of the Church in Smyrna write *(refers to the Martyr Church, with the time span being approximately from A.D. 100 to about A.D. 300);* **These things says the First and the Last** *(Christ is the Beginning of things referring to Creator, and the End of all things referring to His total and complete control),* **which was dead, and is alive** *(refers to the Cross and the Resurrection);*

9 I know your works, and tribulation, and poverty, (but you are rich) *(Smyrna was poverty stricken outwardly, but the Lord proclaimed them spiritually rich; the Church at Laodicea claimed to be rich, but the Lord said they were poor)* **and** *I know* **the blasphemy of them which say they are Jews, and are not** *(from*

this Verse we learn that God doesn't consider Jews who reject Christ as truly Jewish), **but** *are* **the Synagogue of Satan.** *(The worship of Christ-rejecting Jews is concluded by the Lord to be Satanic.)*

10 Fear none of those things which you shall suffer: behold, the Devil shall cast *some* **of you into prison, that you may be tried; and you shall have tribulation ten days** *(is believed to represent the ten major persecutions Rome hurled at the Church of that day, spanning about 200 years):* **be thou faithful unto death, and I will give you a Crown of life** *(many paid with their lives).*

11 He who has an ear, let him hear what the Spirit says unto the Churches *(the Spirit is saying that, at times, there may be suffering);* **He who overcomes shall not be hurt of the second death** *(refers to the Lake of Fire [Rev. 21:8]).*

PERGAMOS

12 And to the Angel *(Pastor)* **of the Church in Pergamos write** *(referred to as the State Church, which laid the groundwork for the Catholic system; its timespan was approximately A.D. 300 to A.D. 500);* **These things said He which has the sharp sword with two edges** *(a symbol for the Word of God);*

13 I know your works, and where you dwell *(dwell spiritually),* **even** **where Satan's seat** *is* *(Satan had become part of this Church):* **and you hold fast My Name, and have not denied My Faith** *(despite the terrible condition of this Church, some were holding fast to Christ and were continuing to look to the Cross),* **even in those days wherein Antipas** *was* **My faithful martyr, who was slain among you, where Satan dwells.** *(This persecution came from within the Church.)*

14 But I have a few things against you, because you have there them who hold the doctrine of Balaam, who taught Balac to cast a stumblingblock before the Children of Israel, to eat things Sacrificed unto idols, and to commit fornication. *(This Church was committing spiritual adultery, meaning they had shifted their Faith from the Cross to other things, with money being the underlying cause, which refers to the State Church.)*

15 So have you also them who hold the doctrine of the Nicolaitanes, which thing I hate. *(At Ephesus, it was the "deeds of the Nicolaitanes," and now it's the "doctrine." This refers to unscriptural Church Government, which grossly*

exploited the people.)

16 Repent *(come back to the Cross)*; or else I will come unto you quickly, and will fight against them with the sword of My mouth. *(This will bring to bear the Word of God, the part that speaks of Judgment.)*

17 He who has an ear, let him hear what the Spirit says unto the Churches *(the Spirit is saying that all Church Government must, without fail, be Scriptural)*; To him who overcomes will I give to eat of the hidden Manna, and will give him a white stone, and in the stone a new name written, which no man knows saving he who receives it. *(This refers to the fact that Believers shall receive a new name, in harmony with the perfect renewal of our being.)*

THYATIRA

18 And unto the Angel of the Church in Thyatira write *(called the "Papal Church," signifying the beginning of Catholicism; it began about A.D. 500 and continues unto this hour)*; These things saith the Son of God, Who has His eyes like unto a flame of fire, and His feet *are* like fine brass *(presents Christ in the role of Judgment, as He must be concerning the Church going into idol worship)*;

19 I know your works, and charity, and service, and faith, and your patience *(some in this Church, as wrong as it was, continue to love the Lord; the Lord knew who they were)*, and your works; and the last *to be* more than the first. *("Works" are mentioned twice, with the last being in a negative sense, meaning they were depending on this instead of Christ and the Cross.)*

20 Notwithstanding I have a few things against you, because you suffer that woman Jezebel, which calls herself a Prophetess, to teach and to seduce My servants to commit fornication, and to eat things Sacrificed unto idols. *(The Lord is speaking here of spiritual fornication and adultery, which means they had forsaken Christ and the Cross for other things [Rom. 7:1-4].)*

21 And I gave her space to repent of her fornication; and she repented not. *(The Church did not heed the Message, and, in fact, continues in their "Salvation by works" unto this day, which, of course, is false.)*

22 Behold, I will cast her into a bed, and them who commit adultery with her into great tribulation, except they repent of their deeds. *(The "bed" refers to false teachers who taught Salvation by works, which was spiritual adultery. Again, there was a warning to repent.)*

23 And I will kill her children with death *(speaks of spiritual death)*; and all the Churches shall know that I am He which searches the reins and hearts *(a continuous, ongoing searching)*: and I will give unto every one of you according to your works. *(One can look at the works of an individual and ascertain exactly where their Faith is. True works proclaim the Fruit of the Spirit.)*

24 But unto you I say, and unto the rest in Thyatira, as many as have not this doctrine *(have not succumbed to the teaching of Jezebel)*, and which have not known the depths of Satan, as they speak *(the teaching of "Jezebel" was "spiritual adultery," which was a departure from the Cross and is labeled here as "the depths of Satan")*; I will put upon you none other burden *(meaning their total burden was the opposing of "Jezebel teaching," which was a tremendous responsibility within itself)*.

25 But that which you have *already* hold fast *(hold to the Cross, and don't allow your Faith to be moved to other things)* till I come *(the Rapture of the Church)*.

26 And he who overcomes, and keeps My works unto the end *(it is "His Works," and not "our works"; pure and simple, it is what Jesus did at the Cross on our behalf)*, to him will I give power over the nations *(speaks of the coming Kingdom Age)*:

27 And he shall rule them with a rod of iron; as the vessels of a potter shall they be broken to shivers *(refers to the fact that the Saints of God in the coming Kingdom Age under Christ will rule the nations, not allowing evil to prevail or even to take root)*: even as I received of My Father. *(In the day of His Coming, we shall share in His Power and Glory of Victory.)*

28 And I will give him the Morning Star. *(The "Morning Star" is the bright planet [Venus], which is most beautiful and leads on the morning — the harbinger of the day. This says the coming Kingdom Age will be glorious beyond compare.)*

29 He who has an ear, let him hear what the Spirit says unto the Churches. *(The Spirit is saying that to leave Christ and the Cross is to commit spiritual adultery, which will result in spiritual death.)*

CHAPTER 3
(A.D. 96)
SARDIS

AND unto the Angel *(Pastor)* of the Church in Sardis write *(the Sardis Church is*

referred to as the "Reformation Church," which began about A.D. 1500, and continues more or less unto this hour); **These things saith He Who has the Seven Spirits of God** (represents the Holy Spirit in all His fullness and capacity), **and the Seven stars** (refers to the Pastors of these Seven Churches); **I know your works, that you have a name that you live, and are dead.** (Our Lord begins with words of censure, i.e., "dead spiritually.")

2 Be watchful (this Church is exhorted to look into its real condition), **and strengthen the things which remain, that are ready to die** (they need to come back to the Cross, or they will lose their way completely): **for I have not found your works perfect before God.** (Their works were based on a dead Faith, which always produces bad works.)

3 Remember therefore how you have received and heard, and hold fast, and repent (go back to the Cross). **If therefore you shall not watch, I will come on you as a thief, and you shall not know what hour I will come upon you.** (Judgment will come, but Sardis will not see or hear due to spiritual deafness and spiritual blindness.)

4 You have a few names even in Sardis which have not defiled their garments (the Lord always has a few); **and they shall walk with Me in white: for they are worthy.** (We are made worthy only by our Faith in Christ and the Cross.)

5 He who overcomes, the same shall be clothed in white raiment (the Righteousness of Christ, gained only by Faith in Christ and the Cross); **and I will not blot out his name out of the Book of Life** (proving that names can be blotted out), **but I will confess his name before My Father, and before His Angels.** (The key to this great "confession" is Faith in Christ and His great Sacrifice.)

6 He who has an ear, let him hear what the Spirit says unto the Churches. (The Spirit is saying that Righteousness cannot be obtained without Faith in a spotless Sacrifice.)

PHILADELPHIA

7 And to the Angel (Pastor) **of the Church in Philadelphia write** (is referred to as the Missionary Church, and had its beginning in about the year 1800, and continues unto this hour); **These things says He Who is Holy, He Who is true, He Who has the key of David, He Who opens, and no man shuts; and shuts, and no man opens** (refers to the fact that Christ has total authority);

8 I know your works: behold, I have set before you an open door, and no man can shut it (this "open door" refers to the way being made for the Gospel to be sent to the entirety of the world): **for you have a little strength, and have kept my Word, and have not denied My Name.** ("Little strength" is not an indication of spiritual infirmity, but of few in number. However, these few [speaking of those who truly know the Lord] have touched the world with the Gospel of Jesus Christ.)

9 Behold, I will make them of the Synagogue of Satan, which say they are Jews, and are not, but do lie (proclaims the fact that God doesn't recognize the spiritual claims of national Israel); **behold, I will make them to come and worship before your feet, and to know that I have loved you.** (This refers to the coming Kingdom Age, when Christ will rule Personally over the entirety of the Earth, with Israel restored. Israel will then bow at the feet of Christ, Whom the Gentiles accepted.)

10 Because you have kept the Word of My patience, I also will keep you from the hour of temptation, which shall come upon all the world, to try them who dwell upon the earth. (The Church will be Raptured out before the Great Tribulation.)

11 Behold, I come quickly (again refers to the Rapture): **hold that fast which you have, that no man take your crown.** (The Devil will use religious men to try to move us away from our Faith in Christ and the Cross.)

12 Him who overcomes will I make a pillar in the Temple of my God (the "overcomer" is the one who trusts explicitly in Christ and what He did for us at the Cross), **and he shall go no more out** (refers to a constant position in the presence of God): **and I will write upon him the Name of My God, and the Name of the city of My God, which is New Jerusalem, which comes down out of Heaven from My God: and I will write upon him My new Name.** (At the Cross, Christ identified with our sin by suffering its penalty. Now he identifies with our most excellent Blessing, as He is the Source of all.)

13 He who has an ear, let him hear what the Spirit says unto the Churches. (The Spirit is saying we must be ready for the Rapture, which can only be done by Faith constantly exhibited in Christ and His Finished Work.)

LAODICEA

14 And unto the Angel (Pastor) **of the Church**

of the Laodiceans write *(this is the "Apostate Church"; we do not know when it began, but we do know it has begun; it is the last Church addressed by Christ, so that means the Rapture will take place very shortly)*; **These things says the Amen, the faithful and true witness** *(by contrast to His Church, which is not faithful and true)*, **the beginning of the Creation of God** *(Jesus is the Creator of all things)*;

15 **I know your works, that you are neither cold nor hot** *(characterizes that which is prevalent at this present time)*: **I would you were cold or hot** *(half measures won't do)*.

16 **So then because you are lukewarm, and neither cold nor hot** *(if a person is lukewarm towards something, it means he hasn't rejected it, but at the same time he has by no means accepted it; in the Mind of God, a tepid response is equal to a negative response)*, **I will spue you out of My mouth.** *(There is no prospect of Repentance here on the part of this Church, or Restoration. In fact, there is Divine rejection.)*

17 **Because you say, I am rich, and increased with goods, and have need of nothing** *(they equated the increase in material goods with spiritual Blessings, which they were not)*; **and knowest not that you are wretched, and miserable, and poor, and blind, and naked** *(the tragedy lay in the fact that while this Church gloated over material wealth, she was unconscious of her spiritual poverty; again indicative of the modern Church!)*:

18 **I counsel you to buy of Me gold tried in the fire, that you may be rich** *(what they needed to "buy" could not be purchased with money, but only with the precious Blood of Christ, which price has already been paid; but the modern Church is not interested!)*; **and white raiment, that you may be clothed, and *that* the shame of your nakedness do not appear** *(refers to Righteousness which is exclusively of Christ, and is gained only by Faith in Christ and the Cross; this tells us that the Laodicean Church is extremely self-righteous; not having the Righteousness of Christ, they are "naked" to the Judgment of God)*; **and anoint your eyes with eyesalve, that you may see.** *(The modern Church is also spiritually blind.)*

19 **As many as I love, I rebuke and chasten** *(implies a remnant)*: **be zealous therefore, and repent.** *(The modern Church desperately needs to repent for its rebellion against God's Divine Order [Christ and the Cross] and for following cunningly devised fables [II Pet. 1:16].)*

20 **Behold, I stand at the door, and knock** *(presents Christ outside the Church)*: **if any man hear My voice** *(so much religious racket is going on that it is difficult to "hear His Voice")*, **and open the door** *(Christ is the True Door, which means the Church has erected another door)*, **I will come in to him, and will sup with him, and he with Me.** *(Having been rejected by the Church, our Lord now appeals to individuals, and He is still doing so presently.)*

21 **To him who overcomes will I grant to sit with Me in My Throne** *(the overcomer will gain the prize of the Throne, which can only be done by one ever making the Cross the Object of His Faith)*, **even as I also overcame, and am set down with My Father in His Throne.** *(This presents Christ as our Substitute, going before us, and doing for us what we could not do for ourselves.)*

22 **He who has an ear, let him hear what the Spirit says unto the Churches.** *(In plain language, the Holy Spirit is saying, "come back to Christ and the Cross!")*

CHAPTER 4
(A.D. 96)
THE THRONE

AFTER **this I looked** *(represents the time after the Churches, or in other words after the Rapture)*, **and, behold, a door *was* opened in Heaven** *(gives John the ability to see what is taking place there)*: **and the first voice which I heard *was* as it were of a trumpet talking with me** *(is actually the Voice of Jesus, harking back to Rev. 1:10)*; **which said, Come up hither, and I will show you things which must be hereafter** *(after the Rapture of the Church)*.

2 **And immediately I was in the Spirit** *(John saw these things in a Vision)*: **and, behold, a Throne was set in Heaven, and *One* sat on the Throne** *(God the Father)*.

3 **And He Who sat was to look upon like a jasper and a sardine stone: and *there was* a rainbow round about the Throne, in sight like unto an emerald.** *(This proclaims the Glory of God, which is beyond comprehension.)*

4 **And round about the Throne *were* four and twenty seats** *(Thrones)*: **and upon the seats I saw four and twenty Elders sitting** *(these men represent the entirety of the Work of God as it pertains to Believers, with, no doubt, a mixture of Prophets and Apostles)*, **clothed in white raiment** *(represents the Righteousness of Christ)*; **and they had on their heads crowns of gold** *(signifying authority)*.

5 And out of the Throne proceeded lightnings and thunderings and voices (whatever all of this is, it is constant): and there were seven lamps of fire burning before the Throne, which are the Seven Spirits of God. (This represents the totality and universality of the Holy Spirit. The number "Seven" is God's number, denoting perfection.)

LIVING CREATURES

6 And before the Throne there was a sea of glass like unto crystal (presents that which is perfectly transparent): and in the midst of the Throne, and round about the Throne, were four Beasts (living creatures) full of eyes before and behind. (This is introducing creatures we have no knowledge of and which are beyond comprehension, as so much in Heaven actually is.)

7 And the first Beast (living creature) was like a lion, and the second Beast like a calf, and the third Beast had a face as a man, and the fourth Beast was like a flying eagle. (These strange creatures are before the Throne constantly.)

8 And the four Beasts (living Creatures) had each of them six wings about him; and they were full of eyes within (signifying the revealing of their innermost nature and being): and they rest not day and night (proclaiming that these beings are "spirit" and not "flesh"), saying, Holy, Holy, Holy, Lord God Almighty, which was, and is, and is to come. (Using the threefold repetition calls attention to the infinite Holiness of God.)

HEAVENLY WORSHIP

9 And when those Beasts (Living Creatures) give glory and honour and thanks to Him Who sat on the Throne, Who lives forever and ever (if these creatures can constantly give God "Glory, and Honor, and Thanks," how can we who have known the glorious Redemption of our Lord do any less!),

10 The four and twenty Elders fall down before Him Who sat on the Throne, and worship Him Who lives forever and ever (the action of the 24 Elders, who represent the Church of the Living God in Heaven, proclaims what the Church on Earth ought to be), and cast their crowns before the Throne, saying (presents the acknowledgment of their royal estate; it all comes from God!),

11 You are worthy, O Lord, to receive Glory and Honour and Power (unless the Lord's worth is fully sensed by the worshiper, one's own unworthiness will never be realized): for You have created all things, and for Your pleasure they are and were created. (In effect, the praises of these 24 Elders tell us that the Creation, and that means every part of the Creation, is going to be completely restored, and all because of what Christ did at the Cross!)

CHAPTER 5
(A.D. 96)

THE SEALED BOOK

AND I saw in the Right Hand (signifies power) of Him Who sat on the Throne a Book written within and on the backside, sealed with Seven Seals. (The "Seven Seals" signify that the "time of Jacob's trouble" is about to begin, which will rapidly bring to a conclusion that which must be done.)

2 And I saw a strong Angel proclaiming with a loud voice (this strong Angel is probably Gabriel, as evidenced by Gabriel's appearance to Daniel), Who is worthy to open the Book, and to loose the Seals thereof? (This implies moral fitness [Rom. 1:4].)

3 And no man in Heaven, nor in earth, neither under the earth, was able to open the Book, neither to look thereon. (We should look very carefully at the words "no man.")

4 And I wept much, because no man was found worthy to open and to read the Book, neither to look thereon. (This pertains to the fact that this Book is so very, very important. It contains not only the information regarding the coming Judgment upon this Earth, but as well the message that this Judgment, as tendered by God, will ultimately lead to the Redemption of the Earth.)

THE LION AND THE LAMB

5 And one of the Elders said unto me, Weep not (states that man's dilemma has been solved): behold, the Lion of the Tribe of Judah, the Root of David, has prevailed to open the Book, and to loose the Seven Seals thereof (presents Jesus Christ).

6 And I beheld, and, lo, in the midst of the Throne and of the four Beasts, and in the midst of the Elders, stood a Lamb as it had been slain (the Crucifixion of Christ is represented here by the word "Lamb," which refers to the fact that it was the Cross which Redeemed mankind;

the slain Lamb Alone has Redeemed all things), **having seven horns** (horns denote dominion, and "seven" denotes total dominion; all of this was done for you and me, meaning that we can have total dominion over the powers of darkness, and in every capacity; so there is no excuse for a lack of victory) **and seven eyes** (denotes total, perfect, pure, and complete illumination of all things spiritual, which is again made possible for you and me by the Cross; if the Believer makes the Cross the Object of his Faith, he will never be drawn away by false doctrine), **which are the Seven Spirits of God sent forth into all the Earth** (signifying that the Holy Spirit, in all His Perfection and universality, functions entirely within the parameters of the Finished Work of Christ; in other words, it is required that we ever make the Cross the Object of our Faith, which gives the Holy Spirit latitude, and guarantees the "dominion," and the "illumination" [Isa. 11:2; Rom. 8:2]).

7 And He (the Lord Jesus Christ) **came and took the Book out of the Right Hand of Him** (God the Father) **Who sat upon the Throne.** (All of Heaven stands in awe as the Lamb steps forward to take the Book.)

WORSHIP

8 And when He (the Lord Jesus) **had taken the Book, the four Beasts** (Living Creatures) **and four and twenty Elders** (representatives of the Church) **fell down before the Lamb** (proclaims to us the Deity of Christ), **having every one of them harps, and golden vials full of odours, which are the prayers of Saints.** (In the Greek, this refers to the 24 Elders only. All the prayers that have ever come up before God for things to be rectified are about to be answered.)

9 And they sung a new song, saying (which only the Redeemed can sing), **You are worthy to take the Book, and to open the Seals thereof** (proclaims that by His Death He has acquired a right to approach where no other one could approach, and to do what no other one could do): **for You were slain** (refers to the Cross, which has made everything possible), **and have redeemed us to God by Your Blood** (proclaims the manner in which Redemption was purchased) **out of every kindred, and tongue, and people, and nation** (proclaims the fact that Salvation secured by the Death of Christ universally applies to all classes and peoples of the Earth);

10 And have made us unto our God kings and priests (the Scripture abundantly proclaims

that whatever Jesus is because of the Cross, that's what we are also): **and we shall reign on the earth** (refers to the coming Millennial Reign).

11 And I beheld, and I heard the voice of many Angels round about the Throne and the Beasts and the Elders: and the number of them was ten thousand times ten thousand, and thousands of thousands ("ten thousand" is the greatest number expressed by the Greek vocabulary, and in itself may denote an unlimited number; but here we have a quadruple plural — ten thousands of ten thousands, and thousands of thousands — which in the Greek actually says "myriads of myriads," i.e., "an innumerable host");

12 Saying with a loud voice (considering the tremendous number, actually beyond comprehension, what a sound this must have been), **Worthy is the Lamb that was slain to receive power, and riches, and wisdom, and strength, and honour, and glory, and blessing.** (Through and by the Cross, the sevenfold Blessing is given to Christ and is given to us as well. Let us say it again and again, "The Cross! The Cross! The Cross!")

13 And every creature which is in Heaven, and on the earth, and under the earth, and such as are in the sea, and all that are in them, heard I saying (the Death of Christ as Atonement is the ground or basis of the Restoration of all things, and is implied in Phil. 2:8-11), **Blessing, and honour, and glory, and power, be unto Him Who sits upon the Throne** (God the Father), **and unto the Lamb forever and ever.** (What Jesus did at the Cross guaranteed the total defeat of Satan and all his minions of darkness, which will ultimately cleanse Heaven and Earth in totality and forever.)

14 And the four Beasts (Living Creatures) **said, Amen.** (The four "Living Ones" say "Amen" to the fourfold Blessing.) **And the four and twenty Elders fell down and worshipped Him Who lives forever and ever.** (This records the fact that not only is God eternal, but what Jesus did at the Cross will have eternal results as well.)

CHAPTER 6
(A.D. 96)
THE FIRST SEAL

AND I saw when the Lamb opened one of the Seals (refers to the Crucified, risen Christ, and is proven by the use of the word "Lamb"), and I heard, as it were the noise of thunder, one of the four Beasts (Living Creatures) saying,

Come and see. (*This will follow the Rapture of the Church, but we aren't told exactly how long after the Rapture the Great Tribulation will come. "Come and see," says that it is destined and cannot be avoided.*)

2 And I saw, and behold a white horse (*symbolic; proclaims the Antichrist presenting himself to the world as a prince of peace*): and he who sat on him had a bow (*mentions no arrows; he preaches peace, but is preparing for war, as symbolized by the "bow"*); and a crown was given unto him: and he went forth conquering, and to conquer. (*The "crown" represents the fact that he will conquer many countries. At first he does so by peace, but will quickly graduate to war.*)

THE SECOND SEAL

3 And when He (*Christ*) had opened the second Seal, I heard the second Beast (*Living Creature*) say, Come and see. (*As we see here, all the events on Earth are decided first of all in Heaven.*)

4 And there went out another horse *that was* red (*portrays another symbol, this time war*): and *power* was given to him (*the Antichrist*) who sat thereon to take peace from the earth, and that they should kill one another: and there was given unto him a great sword. (*This proclaims the fact that more people will be killed during the time of the Great Tribulation than at any other similar time frame in history.*)

THE THIRD SEAL

5 And when He had opened the third Seal, I heard the third Beast (*Living Creature*) say, Come and see (*is as the previous two, opened by Christ; the time frame for this will most probably be in the second year of the Great Tribulation*). And I beheld, and lo a black horse (*represents famine, which always follows war*); and he who sat on him had a pair of balances in his hand (*refers to the scarcity of food, and is meant to portray that fact*).

6 And I heard a voice in the midst of the four Beasts say, A measure of wheat for a penny, and three measures of barley for a penny (*the world has rejected the Cross, and the world now faces Judgment*); and *see* you hurt not the oil and the wine. (*The petition that the olive tree and grape vine are not to be hurt is that these particular plants need no cultivation. Hence, their ruthless destruction is forbidden.*)

THE FOURTH SEAL

7 And when He had opened the fourth Seal, I heard the voice of the fourth Beast say, Come and see (*presents a horror of unprecedented proportions*).

8 And I looked, and behold a pale horse (*symbolic of death*): and his name that sat on him was Death, and Hell followed with him (*signifying that almost all who died went to Hell*). And power was given unto them over the fourth part of the earth, to kill with sword, and with hunger, and with death, and with the beasts of the earth. (*This probably refers to the Middle East and its vicinity.*)

THE FIFTH SEAL

9 And when He (*Christ*) had opened the fifth Seal (*there is no announcement concerning the opening of this Seal, as it had been with the others*), I saw under the Altar (*the Altar of Incense*) the souls of them who were slain (*does not refer to an intermediate state, for the Resurrection has already taken place, and all now in Heaven have Glorified Bodies; the word "soul" is merely used in the sense of identification and not as a state*) for the Word of God, and for the testimony which they held (*corresponds with Rev. 2:11*):

10 And they (*the souls under the Altar*) cried with a loud voice, saying, How long, O Lord, Holy and True (*pertains to far more than a cry for vengeance; more than anything else, it is a cry for the entire episode of sin and shame to end; it is a culmination of the cry of the ages*), do you not judge and avenge our blood on them who dwell on the earth? (*It is certain that the Lord will "Judge" and "Avenge" [Mat. 12:36].*)

11 And white robes were given unto every one of them (*symbolizes the Righteousness of the Saints [Rev. 19:8]*); and it was said unto them, that they should rest yet for a little season, until their fellowservants also and their Brethren, who should be killed as they *were*, should be fulfilled. (*They will have to wait until the conclusion of the Great Tribulation, probably about another five years.*)

THE SIXTH SEAL

12 And I beheld when He (*Christ*) had opened the sixth Seal, and, lo, there was a great earthquake (*the first of several*); and the sun became black as sackcloth of hair (*probably

caused by dust filling the air due to the earth-quake), **and the moon became as blood** *(doesn't mean the moon was actually turned to blood, but that it "became as blood," again probably referring to the dust particles filling the air)*;

13 **And the stars of Heaven fell unto the earth** *(refers to meteorites or shooting stars)*, **even as a fig tree casts her untimely figs, when she is shaken of a mighty wind.** *(There will be a bombardment on the Earth of these meteorites, which will cause untold damage.)*

14 **And the Heaven departed as a scroll when it is rolled together** *(pertains to the shaking of the Heavens, which instigates the meteorites)*; **and every mountain and island were moved out of their places.** *(This proclaims power of unimagined proportions. The greater thrust will more than likely be in the Middle East.)*

15 **And the kings of the earth, and the great men, and the rich men, and the chief captains, and the mighty men, and every bondman, and every free man, hid themselves in the dens and in the rocks of the mountains** *(presents this as a wasted effort, for men cannot hide from God; as well, it takes in everyone from poverty to plenty)*;

16 **And said to the mountains and rocks** *(foolish man now prays to the rocks)*, **Fall on us, and hide us from the face of Him Who sits on the Throne** *(pertains to God the Father; let all understand, mankind, and that means everyone, is going to have to deal with the One Who sits on the Throne)*, **and from the wrath of the Lamb** *(the Lamb is the Saviour today; tomorrow the Lamb is the Judge)*:

17 **For the great day of His wrath is come** *(the "Great Day" is the coming Great Tribulation, which will last for seven years)*; **and who shall be able to stand?** *(This refers to the fact that man has set himself against God ever since the Fall. Now man will see exactly how powerful God actually is.)*

CHAPTER 7
(A.D. 96)
144,000 JEWS

AND **after these things** *(the first parenthetical Passage, coming between the sixth and seventh Seals)* **I saw four Angels standing on the four corners of the earth** *(represents the universality of God's Administration)*, **holding the four winds of the earth** *(actually refers to Judgment, which will be stopped for a short period of time)*, **that the wind should not blow**

on the earth, nor on the sea, nor on any tree. *(The winds of Judgment strive to be turned loose, but they are held in abeyance by the omnipotence of Almighty God.)*

2 **And I saw another Angel ascending from the east** *(the advent of this Angel portrays the fact that this is the beginning of the Restoration of Israel)*, **having the Seal of the Living God** *(pertains to the Seal of Salvation [II Tim. 2:19])*: **and he cried with a loud voice to the four Angels, to whom it was given to hurt the earth and the sea** *(the Judgments are to be held in check)*,

3 **Saying, Hurt not the earth, neither the sea, nor the trees, till we have sealed the servants of our God in their foreheads.** *(This is not literal, but rather a token, as the sprinkled blood on the lentil protected the house from the destroying Angel at the first Passover.)*

4 **And I heard the number of them which were sealed:** *and there were* **sealed an hundred** *and* **forty** *and* **four thousand of all the Tribes of the Children of Israel** *(12,000 from each Tribe; these are the Firstfruits of Israel which are included in the First Resurrection, with all of Israel coming to Christ at the Second Coming)*.

5 **Of the Tribe of Judah** *were* **sealed twelve thousand. Of the Tribe of Reuben** *were* **sealed twelve thousand. Of the Tribe of Gad** *were* **sealed twelve thousand.**

6 **Of the Tribe of Aser** *were* **sealed twelve thousand. Of the Tribe of Nephthalim** *were* **sealed twelve thousand. Of the Tribe of Manasses** *were* **sealed twelve thousand.**

7 **Of the Tribe of Simeon** *were* **sealed twelve thousand. Of the Tribe of Levi** *were* **sealed twelve thousand. Of the Tribe of Issachar** *were* **sealed twelve thousand.**

8 **Of the Tribe of Zabulon** *were* **sealed twelve thousand. Of the Tribe of Joseph (Ephraim)** *were* **sealed twelve thousand. Of the Tribe of Benjamin** *were* **sealed twelve thousand.** *(The Tribe of Dan is omitted, and no reason is given.)*

TRIBULATION SAINTS

9 **After this I beheld, and, lo, a great multitude** *(pertains to martyrs who gave their lives for the Lord Jesus Christ in the Great Tribulation)*, **which no man could number** *(represents the many, possibly millions, who will be saved in the Great Tribulation)*, **of all nations, and kindreds, and people, and tongues, stood before the Throne, and before the Lamb** *(by use*

of the word "Lamb," we know and realize that their sin-stained garments have been washed in the Blood of the Lamb), **clothed with white robes, and palms in their hands** (could be paraphrased, "dressed in richest wedding garments of purest, dazzling, white"; these are God's Bloodbought; the palms represent joy [Neh. 8:17]);

10 And cried with a loud voice (proclaims great joy), **saying, Salvation to our God which sits upon the Throne, and unto the Lamb.** (Once again, we are told here how God has brought about Salvation. It is through what Jesus did at the Cross, and through that means alone.)

11 And all the Angels stood round about the Throne, and about **the Elders and the four Beasts, and fell before the Throne on their faces, and worshipped God** (this tremendous volume of worship and praise has to do with what Jesus did at the Cross, in His Atoning for all sin by the giving of Himself in Sacrifice),

12 Saying, Amen (is the proclamation that God has provided Salvation to humanity through the Work of the Lamb): **Blessing, and Glory, and Wisdom, and Thanksgiving, and Honour, and Power, and Might,** be **unto our God forever and ever. Amen.** (As the praises to God the Father are sevenfold, they are also sevenfold to God the Son [Rev. 5:12]. This shows that both God and the Lamb are regarded in Heaven as entitled to equal praise.)

13 And one of the Elders answered, saying unto me (proclaims one of the 24 addressing questions that are in John's mind, but have not been asked), **What are these which are arrayed in white robes?** (This would be better translated, "Who are these?") **and whence came they?** (Where do they come from?)

14 And I said unto him, Sir, you know (presents reverent regard, but definitely not worship). **And he said to me, These are they which came out of great tribulation** (refers to a specific group), **and have washed their robes, and made them white in the Blood of the Lamb.** (They were saved by trusting Christ and what He did at the Cross. In the Book of Revelation, the emphasis placed on the Cross is overwhelming.)

15 Therefore are they before the Throne of God, and serve Him day and night in His Temple (all of this particular group came out of the Great Tribulation): **and He Who sits on the Throne shall dwell among them.** (The One Who sits on the Throne will cast His protecting Tabernacle over all the Saints of God, which, in effect, is His Presence.)

16 They shall hunger no more, neither thirst

any more; **neither shall the sun light on them, nor any heat** (proclaims a perfect environment).

17 For the Lamb which is in the midst of the Throne shall feed them (not only did the Lamb save them, but He as well "shall feed them"; not only does our Salvation come by and through what Jesus did at the Cross, but we "live" by what Jesus did for us at the Cross as well), **and shall lead them unto living fountains of waters** (symbolic of the Holy Spirit [Jn. 7:37-39]): **and God shall wipe away all tears from their eyes.** (All things causing sorrow will be forever gone.)

CHAPTER 8
(A.D. 96)
THE SEVENTH SEAL

AND when He had opened the seventh Seal (this is the last Seal), **there was silence in Heaven about the space of half an hour.** (This silence proclaims the intense expectancy of what is about to come upon the world. In other words, if it has been bad thus far, the intensity of the Judgment is about to increase many fold.)

2 And I saw the seven Angels which stood before God (the Greek Text says, "the seven Angels of the Presence of God"); **and to them were given seven Trumpets.** (We have had the Seven Seals of Judgment. Now the world will experience the Seven Trumpet Judgments.)

3 And another Angel came and stood at the Altar, having a Golden Censer (this is the "Altar of Incense" in Heaven); **and there was given unto him much Incense** (represents the perfection, merit, and virtue of the Life of Christ; everything speaks of Christ, and more particularly of what He did at the Cross; incidentally, this Altar of Incense in Heaven is the Pattern for the Altar of Incense that stood in the Tabernacle on Earth immediately before the Veil during the time of the Law), **that he should offer** it **with the prayers of all Saints upon the Golden Altar which was before the Throne.** (The prayers of all the Saints are very precious in the sight of God, yet at the same time imperfect. Added to our prayers must be the Incense, which is a type of the sweet savor of the merit of the life, death, and Resurrection of Christ.)

4 And the smoke of the Incense (even though we aren't given the information in this Verse, the Angel has taken coals of fire from the Brazen Altar and placed them in his Golden Censer), **which** came **with the prayers of the Saints** (for our prayers to be effective in Heaven,

they must always be mixed with the intercessory Work of Christ [Heb. 7:25-26]), ascended up before God out of the Angel's hand. (Knowing our prayers come "up before God," at least if we pray according to the Will of God, should inspire every Saint to a greater prayer life.)

5 And the Angel took the Censer, and filled it with fire of the Altar (this is the Brazen Altar in Heaven that typified the Death of our Lord, which was necessary in order that man might be Redeemed; as is obvious here, Heaven is filled with the portrayal of that Sacrificial, Atoning Death), and cast it into the earth (with the Salvation of the Cross being rejected by the Earth, the Judgment of the Cross will now commence): and there were voices, and thunderings, and lightnings, and an earthquake. (All of this speaks of the fact that it is Judgment coming, and Judgment such as the world has never seen before [Mat. 24:21].)

6 And the Seven Angels which had the Seven Trumpets prepared themselves to sound. (As stated, if the Cross is rejected, Judgment must follow. These events will take place about two and one half years into the Great Tribulation.)

THE FIRST TRUMPET

7 The first Angel sounded (the first Trumpet Judgment), and there followed hail and fire mingled with blood, and they were cast upon the earth (this will be literal, and will be a fulfillment of the Prophecy of Joel [Joel 2:30-32]; this is similar to the seventh plague upon Egypt [Ex. 9:22]): and the third part of trees was burnt up, and all green grass was burnt up (probably refers to a third part of the Mediterranean area being affected; even though all of this will affect the entirety of the Earth, as would be obvious, the greatest concentration will be in the Middle East).

THE SECOND TRUMPET

8 And the second Angel sounded, and as it were a great mountain burning with fire was cast into the sea (more than likely, this will be a giant meteorite which will fall into the Mediterranean Sea): and the third part of the Sea became blood (similar to that which had taken place in Egypt so long ago [Ex. 7:20-21]);

9 And the third part of the creatures which were in the Sea, and had life, died; and the third part of the ships were destroyed (concerns

the part affected by the meteorite, or by whatever manner God chooses to do this).

THE THIRD TRUMPET

10 And the third Angel sounded, and there fell a great star from Heaven, burning as it were a lamp (more than likely another meteorite), and it fell upon the third part of the rivers, and upon the fountains of waters (a third part of the land area; speaks of the Old Roman Empire area [Dan. 7:7-8]);

11 And the name of the star is called Wormwood (this huge meteorite, which will fall, will carry with it the properties of the bitter, nauseous plant known as "Wormwood" [Jer. 9:15]): and the third part of the waters became wormwood; and many men died of the waters, because they were made bitter. (Conceivably this could take the lives of hundreds of thousands, if not millions.)

THE FOURTH TRUMPET

12 And the fourth Angel sounded, and the third part of the sun was smitten, and the third part of the moon, and the third part of the stars; so as the third part of them was darkened, and the day shone not for a third part of it, and the night likewise. (Once again let us emphasize the fact that these Judgments aren't symbolic, they are literal! Jesus said this would happen [Lk. 21:25-26].)

13 And I beheld, and heard an Angel flying through the midst of Heaven, saying with a loud voice (it is possible this Angel will be visible to people on Earth, and could well be portrayed by Television), Woe, woe, woe, to the inhabiters of the earth by reason of the other voices of the Trumpet of the three Angels, which are yet to sound! (The three "woes" are meant to correspond with the three remaining Trumpet Judgments.)

CHAPTER 9
(A.D. 96)
THE FIFTH TRUMPET

AND the fifth Angel sounded (presents the fifth Judgment, and as stated the first "woe"), and I saw a star fall from Heaven unto the earth (actually refers to Satan, as the next phrase proclaims [Lk. 10:18]: and to him was given the key of the bottomless pit. (Christ gives this "key" to Satan, although He

may use an Angel to hand the key to the Evil One [Rev. 20:1].)

2 And he *(Satan)* opened the bottomless pit; and there arose a smoke out of the pit, as the smoke of a great furnace; and the sun and the air were darkened by reason of the smoke of the pit. *(This will probably be concentrated in the old Roman Empire territory.)*

3 And there came out of the smoke locusts upon the earth *(these are demon locusts, even as the following Verses prove):* and unto them was given power, as the scorpions of the earth have power *(refers to the sting in their tails, and the pain this will cause).*

4 And it was commanded them that they should not hurt the grass of the earth, neither any green thing, neither any tree *(normal locusts destroy plant life; but these are not allowed to do so);* but only those men which have not the Seal of God in their foreheads *(refers to the 144,000 Jews who have accepted Christ as their Saviour [Rev. 7:2-8]).*

5 And to them it was given that they should not kill them, but that they should be tormented five months *(this will be literal, yet these creatures will be invisible):* and their torment *was* as the torment of a scorpion, when he strikes a man *(pain and swelling).*

6 And in those days shall men seek death, and shall not find it; and shall desire to die, and death shall flee from them. *(For pain to be so bad that people want to die is bad indeed! Evidently pain-killing drugs will not work. It will be interesting how medical doctors diagnose all of this, to say the least.)*

7 And the shapes of the locusts *were* like unto horses prepared unto battle; and on their heads *were* as it were crowns like gold, and their faces *were* as the faces of men. *(These are demon spirits, but will be invisible. If they could be seen, this is what they would look like. We aren't told their origin in the Bible. We know they were not originally created in this manner, but evidently became this way in the revolution instigated by Lucifer against God [Isa. 14:12-20; Ezek. 28:11-19].)*

8 And they had hair as the hair of women, and their teeth were as *the teeth* of lions. *(They were no doubt originally created by God to perform a particular function of praise and worship, even as the "Living Creatures," but they have suffered this fate due to rebellion against God.)*

9 And they had breastplates, as it were breastplates of iron; and the sound of their wings *was* as the sound of chariots of many horses running to battle. *(We are given a glimpse here into the spirit world. This is the reason such foolish efforts as humanistic psychology are helpless against such foes. The only answer is Christ and the Cross.)*

10 And they had tails like unto scorpions, and there were stings in their tails: and their power *was* to hurt men five months. *(This Judgment is limited to five months, which tells us Satan can only do what God allows him to do.)*

11 And they had a king over them, *which is* the Angel of the bottomless pit *(gives us further insight into the spirit world of darkness),* whose name in the Hebrew tongue *is* Abaddon, but in the Greek tongue has *his* name Apollyon. *(This is a powerful fallen Angel, who evidently threw in his lot with Lucifer in the great rebellion against God. Only four Angels are named in Scripture, "Gabriel, Michael, Lucifer, and Apollyon," the first two being Righteous.)*

12 One woe is past *(refers to the fifth Trumpet Judgment); and,* behold, there come two woes more hereafter. *(The word "behold" calls attention to the fact that the two remaining "woes" will be exceedingly horrific.)*

THE SIXTH TRUMPET

13 And the sixth Angel sounded *(this is the second "woe"),* and I heard a voice from the four horns of the Golden Altar which is before God *(this is the "Altar of Incense"; the "voice" is probably that of the same Angel who came and stood at the Altar, and had much Incense [6:9; 8:3]),*

14 Saying to the sixth Angel which had the Trumpet, Loose the four Angels which are bound in the great river Euphrates. *(These are evil Angels, hence previously "bound." The river "Euphrates" signals the area. It is where it all began, it is where it will all end, and it is being prepared even now.)*

15 And the four Angels were loosed, which were prepared for an hour, and a day, and a month, and a year, for to slay the third part of men. *(These four Angels are not to be confused with the four Angels of Rev. 7:1. Those are Righteous Angels, while these four are evil. They are executors of God's wrath. Once again, this Judgment will be mostly confined to the old Roman Empire territory.)*

16 And the number of the army of the horsemen *were* two hundred thousand thousand

(200 million): and I heard the number of them. *(This is not symbolic of a human army, but rather demon spirits, which, as well, will be invisible.)*

17 And thus I saw the horses in the vision *(demon horses)*, and them that sat on them, having breastplates of fire, and of jacinth, and brimstone: and the heads of the horses *were* as the heads of lions; and out of their mouths issued fire and smoke and brimstone. *(All of this presents demon spirits riding demon horses.)*

18 By these three was the third part of men killed, by the fire, and by the smoke, and by the brimstone, which issued out of their mouths. *(Quite possibly, over three hundred million people will die as a result of this particular plague. Whatever they think to be the cause, the actual cause will be what is described here.)*

19 For their power is in their mouth, and in their tails: for their tails *were* like unto serpents, and had heads, and with them they do hurt. *(Once again, we are here given a glimpse into the spirit world. That's the reason Paul said we "wrestle not against flesh and blood, but against principalities, against powers, against the rulers of the darkness of this world, against spiritual wickedness in high places" [Eph. 6:12]. As well, that is why all efforts to oppose such are fruitless, other than Christ and the Cross.)*

20 And the rest of the men which were not killed by these plagues *(once again, probably confined to the Middle East area)* yet repented not of the works of their hands *(as is obvious here, men do not easily repent)*, that they should not worship devils, and idols of gold, and silver, and brass, and stone, and of wood: which neither can see, nor hear, nor walk *(all worship of God must be based strictly on the Sacrifice of Christ and the Name of Christ, else it is a "work of man's hands," which God can never accept [Eph. 2:13-18])*:

21 Neither repented they of their murders, nor of their sorceries, nor of their fornication, nor of their thefts. *(The Holy Spirit again emphasizes the fact that they will not repent. Repentance by the world must be in the realm of the sin of man creating another god. In the Church, Repentance must be in the realm of the sin of the creation of another Sacrifice.)*

CHAPTER 10
(A.D. 96)

THE MIGHTY ANGEL

AND I saw another mighty Angel come down from Heaven *(this is Christ [Rev. 1:16; Dan. 10:5-6])*, clothed with a cloud *(refers to the Glory of God upon Him, for He is God [Ex. 40:34-38])*: and a rainbow *was* upon His Head *(refers to Peace and Mercy)*, and His face *was* as it were the Sun *(concerns the degree of Glory)*, and His feet as pillars of fire *(speaks of Judgment; rejecting Mercy and Peace always brings Judgment)*:

2 And He had in His Hand a little Book open *(proclaims the same Book of Revelation, Chapter 5, but here it is open; in fact, He is the One Who opened it [5:5; 6:1])*: and He set His right foot upon the sea, and *His* left *foot* on the earth *(proclaims dominion, meaning Righteousness will ultimately prevail on this Earth)*,

3 And cried with a loud voice, as *when* a lion roars *(signals power and victory)*: and when He had cried, seven thunders uttered their voices. *(We aren't told what these seven thunders stated, or what they meant.)*

4 And when the seven thunders had uttered their voices, I was about to write *(proclaims the fact that John wrote all of this down, which refers to the entirety of this Book of Revelation)*: and I heard a voice from Heaven saying unto me, Seal up those things which the seven thunders uttered, and write them not. *(John knew what they were, but was forbidden to relate it in the Book. Therefore, speculation is useless.)*

5 And the Angel which I saw stand upon the Sea and upon the earth lifted up His Hand to Heaven *(presents most likely the right hand, with the Book held in the left hand; it concerns an oath)*,

6 And sware by Him Who lives forever and ever, Who created Heaven, and the things that therein are, and the earth, and the things that therein are, and the sea, and the things which are therein *(proclaims the fact that the world belongs to God by virtue of Him being its Creator)*, that there should be time no longer *(could be translated, "that there should be delay no longer"; the prayer of Christ, "Thy Kingdom come, Thy will be done on Earth as it is in Heaven," is about to be answered)*:

7 But in the days of the voice of the seventh Angel, when he shall begin to sound *(proclaims the beginning of the last half of the Great Tribulation, which will be worse than ever)*, the Mystery of God should be finished *(this "Mystery" pertains to the reason God has allowed Satan to continue his reign over this Earth for these thousands of years [II Cor. 4:4])*, as He has declared to His servants the Prophets *(Isa. 14:12-20; Ezek. 28:11-19)*.

THE LITTLE BOOK

8 And the voice which I heard from Heaven spoke unto me again *(it is the same voice which told him to seal up those things the seven thunders uttered, and write them not)*, and said, Go *and* take the little Book which is open in the Hand of the Angel *(Christ)* which stands upon the Sea and upon the Earth. *(This presents the third time Christ is presented in His Dominion Role, which guarantees the certainty of such action.)*

9 And I went unto the Angel *(Christ)*, and said unto Him, Give me the little Book *(refers, as stated, to the same Book mentioned in Chapter 5)*. And He said unto me, Take *it*, and eat it up *(presents idiomatic language meaning to digest its contents)*; and it shall make your belly bitter, but it shall be in your mouth sweet as honey. *(The Word of God is always sweet. But in this case it speaks of Judgment, and will, therefore, be bitter in the belly, as all Judgment is bitter.)*

10 And I took the little Book out of the Angel's hand, and ate it up *(he digested its contents)*; and it was in my mouth sweet as honey: and as soon as I had eaten it, my belly was bitter. *(Signifying the further Judgment that was about to come. It pertained to the last half of the Great Tribulation, which will be the worst of all.)*

11 And He *(Christ)* said unto me, You must prophesy again before many peoples, and nations, and tongues, and kings. *(Jesus is telling John that the stand He has taken by putting one foot on the Sea and the other on the Earth does not prove His formal possession of the Earth at this time. This will not take place until about three and one half years later. Consequently, John must continue to prophesy, which, in effect, is the second half of the Book of Revelation.)*

CHAPTER 11
(A.D. 96)
THE TWO WITNESSES

A ND there was given me a reed like unto a rod: and the Angel *(Christ)* stood, saying, Rise, and measure the Temple of God, and the Altar, and them who worship therein *(refers to the literal Temple which will be rebuilt in Jerusalem, with Israel once again instituting the Sacrifices; in fact, plans are being made at this moment for the rebuilding of this structure; as well, Daniel prophesied of this event some 500 years before Christ [Dan. 9:27]).*

2 But the Court which is without the Temple leave out, and measure it not; for it is given unto the Gentiles *(refers to the Court of the Gentiles, which was the furthest Court from the Temple; this "measurement" is for Judgment)*: and the Holy City *(Jerusalem)* shall they tread under foot forty *and* two months. *(This refers to the period that will end the "times of the Gentiles" [Lk. 21:24]. At the midpoint of the Great Tribulation, the Antichrist will turn on Israel, actually attacking her and she will be temporarily defeated. He will occupy the Temple, making it his religious headquarters [II Thess. 2:4]. He will occupy it for three and one half years.)*

3 And I will give *power* unto My two witnesses *(Enoch and Elijah, two men who have not yet died, actually being translated before they saw death [Gen. 5:21-24; Mal. 4:5-6])*, and they shall prophesy a thousand two hundred *and* threescore days, clothed in sackcloth. *(This refers to three and one half years, the last half of the Great Tribulation. The clothing and sackcloth suggests that the witnessing includes the Preaching of Repentance [Isa. 37:1-2; Dan. 9:3-5].)*

4 These are the two olive trees, and the two candlesticks standing before the God of the earth. *(Both represent the two witnesses, and refer to the vision given by the Lord to the Prophet Zechariah [Zech., Chpt. 4].)*

5 And if any man will hurt them, fire proceeds out of their mouth, and devours their enemies *(pertains to Judgment and not literal fire)*: and if any man will hurt them, he must in this manner be killed. *(This proclaims the protection of the Lord, and in whatever manner it is needed. No doubt, the Antichrist will seek to kill them in many ways.)*

6 These have power to shut Heaven, that it rain not in the days of their Prophecy *(doesn't mean that there will be no rain for three and one half years, but that they can shut up Heaven as often as they so desire; no doubt, there will be months without rain)*: and have power over waters to turn them to blood *(at that time, what this miracle will be ascribed to is anyone's guess)*, and to smite the earth with all plagues, as often as they will *(refers to sicknesses and diseases of every nature, along with plagues of insects, such as flies, frogs, etc.)*.

7 And when they shall have finished their testimony *(will be at the conclusion of the three and one half years of Great Tribulation; ironically, this is the same period of time of Christ's*

earthly Ministry), **the Beast that ascends out of the bottomless pit shall make war against them, and shall overcome them, and kill them.** *(The Beast out of the Abyss is a Satanic Angel, not the human spirit of some dead man. It is the one described by John in Rev. 17:8. He is a fallen Angel who will be invisible, but will greatly help the Antichrist. And with the help of this fallen Angel, the Antichrist will kill the two witnesses, but not until their Ministry is completed).*

8 And their dead bodies *shall lie* **in the street of the great city, which spiritually is called Sodom and Egypt, where also our Lord was Crucified.** *(As is obvious, it is Jerusalem. Satan will turn this city into the capital of homosexuality [Sodom] and worldliness [Egypt].)*

9 And they of the people and kindreds and tongues and nations shall see their dead bodies three days and a half *(no doubt, by Television, which will be beamed all over the world)*, **and shall not suffer their dead bodies to be put in graves** *(proclaims the spectacle lasting three and one half days).*

10 And they who dwell upon the earth shall rejoice over them, and make merry, and shall send gifts one to another *(proclaims a worldwide celebration because the two witnesses who have caused so many problems for the Antichrist have now been killed)*; **because these two Prophets tormented them who dwell on the earth.** *(This proclaims that which true Prophets have a tendency to do.)*

11 And after three days and a half the Spirit of Life from God entered into them, and they stood upon their feet *(refers to these two men being raised from the dead; this will, no doubt, be Televised all over the world as well)*; **and great fear fell upon them which saw them.** *(It will be a miracle, as is obvious, of astounding proportions.)*

12 And they heard a great voice from Heaven saying unto them, Come up hither. *(These will be Raptured at the very conclusion of the Great Tribulation. They will be among the last of those included in the First Resurrection of Life.)* **And they ascended up to Heaven in a cloud; and their enemies beheld them.** *(As stated, Television will portray this miraculous scene, with it being observed all over the world.)*

13 And the same hour was there a great earthquake *(this is one of five times that earthquakes are mentioned; it is the last one that will take place and happens under the seventh Vial, which is at the very conclusion of the Great*

Tribulation), **and the tenth part of the city fell** *(refers to Jerusalem)*, **and in the earthquake were slain of men seven thousand: and the remnant were affrighted, and gave Glory to the God of Heaven.** *(There is some indication in the Greek Text that some of these people gave their hearts to Christ.)*

THE SEVENTH TRUMPET

14 The second woe is past *(this woe took place under the Sixth Trumpet Judgment [Rev. 9:12-21])*; *and*, **behold, the third woe comes quickly.** *(It is not the earthquake of Verse 13, but rather the casting out of Satan under the Seventh Trumpet [Rev. 12:12].)*

15 And the seventh Angel sounded *(marks the beginning of the last three and one half years of the Great Tribulation)*; **and there were great voices in Heaven, saying, The kingdoms of this world are become** *the Kingdoms* **of our Lord, and of His Christ; and He shall reign forever and ever.** *(This is said in anticipation, and will definitely come to pass at the conclusion of this three and one half year period at the Second Coming of the Lord.)*

16 And the four and twenty Elders, which sat before God on their seats *(thrones)*, **fell upon their faces, and worshipped God** *(these Elders are human beings, possibly some of the Prophets and Apostles of the Bible, and represent the entirety of the Plan of God as it refers to Redemption)*,

17 Saying, We give You thanks, O Lord God Almighty, which are, and was, and are to come *(pronounces Him as "the Eternal One")*; **because You have taken to Yourself Your great power, and have reigned.** *(This once again speaks of anticipation, in other words what the Lord is going to do, and which He most definitely will do.)*

18 And the nations were angry, and Your wrath is come *(has to do with the coming battle of Armageddon [Ps., Chpt. 2])*, **and the time of the dead, that they should be Judged, and that You should give reward unto Your servants the Prophets, and to the Saints, and them who fear Your Name, small and great** *(refers to the coming Judgment Seat of Christ, not the Great White Throne Judgment)*; **and should destroy them which destroy the earth.** *(Once again speaks of the Battle of Armageddon, in which Christ will engage at the Second Coming [Rev., Chpt. 19].)*

19 And the Temple of God was opened in

Heaven *(in some way it might be similar to Solomon's Temple, for which the Heavenly Temple was the pattern)*, **and there was seen in His temple the Ark of His Testament** *(refers to the Ark of the Covenant, which again served as the pattern for the Ark of the Covenant in the Tabernacle and Temple on Earth during the time of the Law)*: **and there were lightnings, and voices, and thunderings, and an earthquake, and great hail.** *(This presents that which is symbolic of the awful Presence of God and His Majesty and Glory.)*

CHAPTER 12
(A.D. 96)
THE SUN-CLAD WOMAN

A**ND there appeared a great wonder in Heaven** *(should have been translated, "a great sign in Heaven")*; **a woman clothed with the Sun** *(speaks of National Israel with the "Sun" being a symbol of her Glory)*, **and the moon under her feet** *(speaks of dominion, hence, the mention of her feet)*, **and upon her head a crown of twelve stars** *(speaks of dominion regained and Israel restored)*:

2 And she being with child cried *(pertains to the 144,000 Jews who will be saved in the first half of the Great Tribulation [Rev., Chpt. 7])*, **travailing in birth, and pained to be delivered.** *(This concerns spiritual pregnancy, with the agonies of childbirth typifying in the physical what will take place in the spiritual [Isa. 66:7-8].)*

GREAT RED DRAGON

3 And there appeared another wonder in Heaven *(should have been translated, "another sign")*; **and behold a great red dragon** *(denotes Satan and his murderous purpose, typified by the color of "red")*, **having seven heads** *(refers to Empires that persecuted Israel, even until John's day; those Empires were Egypt, Assyria, Babylon, Medo-Persia, Greece, and Rome)* **and ten horns** *(represents ten nations that will be ruled by the Antichrist in the last days, and will greatly persecute Israel; actually, the seventh head is those "ten horns"; Daniel tells us that these "ten horns" representing ten nations will be in the old Roman Empire territory, which refers to the Middle East and parts of Europe [Dan. 7:7])*, **and seven crowns upon his heads** *(represents the fact that Satan controlled these particular kingdoms)*.

MANCHILD

4 And his tail drew the third part of the stars of Heaven *(this goes all the way back to the original rebellion of Lucifer against God; at that time, one-third of the Angels threw in their lot with him; we know these "stars" represent Angels, because Verse 9 tells us so)*, **and did cast them to the earth** *(is given to us more clearly in Verses 7-9)*: **and the dragon stood before the woman which was ready to be delivered** *(does not pertain to the birth of Christ as many claim, but rather the manchild which is the 144,000 Jews who will give their hearts to Christ [Chpt. 7])*, **for to devour her child as soon as it was born.** *(This pertains to the fact that the Antichrist will hate these Jews who have come to Christ. This will take place in the first half of the Great Tribulation, and may well be the primary reason the Antichrist will turn on Israel at that time.)*

5 And she *(Israel)* **brought forth a manchild** *(as stated, this is the 144,000 Jews who will come to Christ during the first half of the Great Tribulation [Chpt. 7]; we aren't told exactly how this will be done)*, **who was to rule all nations with a rod of iron** *(Israel, under Christ, will definitely fill this role in the coming Millennial Reign)*: **and her child was caught up unto God, and to His Throne.** *(This refers to the Rapture of the 144,000, which will take place at about the midpoint of the Great Tribulation.)*

6 And the woman fled into the wilderness *(the "woman" is National Israel; at the midpoint of the Great Tribulation, the Antichrist will turn on Israel and defeat her, with many thousands of Jews fleeing into the wilderness)*, **where she has a place prepared of God** *(this place is actually ancient Petra, located in Jordan [Isa. 16:1-5])*, **that they should feed her there a thousand two hundred and threescore days.** *("They" mentioned here refers oddly enough to the Arabs of Jordan. The 1,260 days constitute almost all of the last half of the Great Tribulation. Incidentally, Petra is now empty of people, awaiting the arrival of Israel.)*

MICHAEL

7 And there was war in Heaven *(pertains to the "Mystery of God" being finished [10:7])*: **Michael and his Angels fought against the dragon; and the dragon fought and his Angels** *(this pertains to Satan and all the Angels who followed him being cast out of Heaven, which*

will take place at the midpoint of the Great Tribulation; why the Lord has allowed Satan and his minions to remain in Heaven all of this time, we aren't told; it is a "Mystery," but it will now be finished),

8 And prevailed not (*Satan will then be defeated; incidentally, it is not Satan who instigates this war, but rather the Archangel Michael at the Command of God*); **neither was their place found any more in Heaven** (*joins with the close of the Book of Revelation, where the Evil One has no more place on Earth as well, but rather the place of torment forever and ever [20:10]*).

9 And the great dragon was cast out, that old serpent, called the Devil, and Satan (*he is referred to as "the Great Dragon" because of his propensity to "steal, kill, and destroy" [Jn. 10:10]; he is the "old serpent" because in his first appearance in the Bible, he chose to work through a serpent; thereby, he is what the curse caused the serpent to be, wryly subtle, and treacherous*), **which deceives the whole world** (*deception is his greatest weapon; he deceives, and is himself deceived*): **he was cast out into the earth, and his Angels were cast out with him** (*pronounces the beginning of the end for this evil monster*).

OVERCOMERS

10 And I heard a loud voice saying in Heaven (*presents the white-robe wearers of Rev. 6:10-11*), **Now is come Salvation, and Strength, and the Kingdom of our God** (*presents the triumph of Christ*), **and the power of His Christ** (*refers to the fact that Christ will rule this world, not Satan*): **for the accuser of our Brethren is cast down, which accused them before our God day and night.** (*This implies that either Satan or one of his fallen angels is before the Throne of God, accusing the Brethren constantly [Job, Chpts. 1-2].*)

11 And they overcame him by the Blood of the Lamb (*the power to overcome and overwhelm the Kingdom of Satan is found exclusively in the Blood of the Sacrifice of the Son of God, and our Faith in that Finished Work [Rom. 6:3-5, 11, 14]*), **and by the word of their testimony** (*the "testimony" must pertain to the fact that the Object of our Faith is the Cross, and exclusively the Cross, which then gives the Holy Spirit latitude to work within our lives*); **and they loved not their lives unto the death.** (*This refers to the fact that the Believer must not change his testimony regarding the Cross to something*

else, even if it means death.)

12 Therefore rejoice, *you* Heavens, and you who dwell in them. (*Heaven rejoices because Satan has no more access to those portals.*) **Woe to the inhabitants of the earth and of the Sea! for the Devil is come down unto you, having great wrath** (*the "woe" mentioned here is the third and final woe, and pertains to Satan being cast out of Heaven, down to this Earth; he will have great anger*), **because he knows that he has but a short time** (*in order to carry out his plan; failing that he is doomed!*).

PERSECUTION

13 And when the dragon saw that he was cast unto the earth, he persecuted the woman which brought forth the man*child.* (*That's when, as stated, the Antichrist will break his seven year Covenant with Israel, attacking and defeating her [Dan. 9:27].*)

14 And to the woman were given two wings of a great eagle, that she might fly into the wilderness, into her place (*the Lord will help Israel at that time, and do so greatly; as stated, this refers to Petra, which is located in modern Jordan*), **where she is nourished for a time, and times, and half a time, from the face of the serpent** (*refers to three and one half years, the last half of the Great Tribulation; the Antichrist will take his armies elsewhere, thinking to take care of this remnant a little later [Dan. 11:44]*).

15 And the serpent cast out of his mouth water as a flood after the woman (*refers to the army of the Antichrist, which has just defeated Israel and is now bent on completely destroying her*), **that he might cause her to be carried away of the flood.** (*The man of sin fully intends to destroy Israel at this time, but the Lord will intervene to stop him, as the next Verse proclaims.*)

16 And the earth helped the woman (*probably refers to the Lord sending an earthquake*), **and the earth opened her mouth, and swallowed up the flood which the dragon cast out of his mouth.** (*This proclaims the action that helps the woman [Israel] hurts the dragon. As stated, it will probably be an earthquake!*)

17 And the dragon was wroth with the woman (*Israel has escaped out of the clutches of Satan one more time*), **and went to make war with the remnant of her seed** (*after the Rapture of the 144,000 Jews, with their Testimony still ringing out over Israel, no doubt, many*

other Jews will accept Christ at that time and make up the "Remnant"), **which keep the Commandments of God, and have the Testimony of Jesus Christ.** (As stated, this refers to the fact that this Remnant of Jews, ever how many there will be, will have accepted Christ, hence, greatly angering Satan.)

CHAPTER 13
(A.D. 96)
ANTICHRIST

AND I stood upon the sand of the sea (not a body of water, but a sea of people), **and saw a beast rise up out of the sea** (pertains to the Antichrist, now empowered by Satan as no other man ever has been), **having seven heads and ten horns** (represents seven Empires that have greatly persecuted Israel in the past, with the "ten horns" actually being the seventh head; the "ten horns" representing ten nations are yet future), **and upon his horns ten crowns** (the horns now being crowned show that these ten nations have now come to power, and will use that power to help the Antichrist; they will be located in the Middle East and in parts of Europe and possibly North Africa, all being in the old Roman Empire territory [Dan. 7:7-8]), **and upon his heads the name of blasphemy.** (Satan controls these Empires, and will control the ten nations, therefore, the name "blasphemy.")

2 And the beast which I saw (represents the fallen Angel who will be let out of the bottomless pit to help the Antichrist [Rev. 11:7]; both the fallen Angel and the Antichrist are referred to as a "beast," but they are two different beings) **was like unto a leopard** (this fallen Angel will help the Antichrist to speedily conquer; Daniel describes this event as well [Dan. 7:6]), **and his feet were as the feet of a bear** (carries the characteristics of the ancient Medo-Persian Empire, which is ferociousness), **and his mouth as the mouth of a lion** (portrays the finesse, grandeur, and pomp of the Babylonian Empire): **and the dragon** (Satan) **gave him** (the Antichrist) **his power, and his seat, and great authority.** (So, the Antichrist will have Satan helping him as well as this powerful fallen Angel, and, no doubt, a host of other fallen Angels and demon spirits.)

3 And I saw one of his heads as it were wounded to death (doesn't refer to the Antichrist, but rather one of the Empires of the past, which greatly persecuted Israel; it pertains to the Grecian Empire under Alexander the Great,

and in reality speaks of the same fallen Angel helping Alexander; when Alexander died, this fallen Angel who helped him to conquer so speedily was locked away in the bottomless pit [Dan. 7:6]); **and his deadly wound was healed** (refers to the fact that this fallen Angel will be released out of the bottomless pit to aid and abet the Antichrist [Rev., Chpt. 17]; it is doubtful the Antichrist will know or realize the source of his power, taking all the credit unto himself): **and all the world wondered after the beast.** (This refers to the part of the world he has conquered, but with the entirety of the world definitely paying him homage as he now seems to exude superhuman ability.)

4 And they worshipped the dragon which gave power unto the beast (refers to the fact that men worship power): **and they worshipped the beast, saying, Who is like unto the beast? who is able to make war with him?** (This proclaims the means by which power is worshiped.)

5 And there was given unto him a mouth speaking great things and blasphemies (powerful claims will be made, with the Name of Jesus being ridiculed); **and power was given unto him to continue forty and two months** (the last three and one half years of the Great Tribulation; despite his power, the Lord still controls the time frames, and, in fact, all events).

6 And he opened his mouth in blasphemy against God, to blaspheme His Name (he will use all the power of print, Radio, Television, and computers to demean the God of the Bible; it will be a regimen of blasphemy on a worldwide basis, such as the world has never known before), **and His Tabernacle** (refers to Heaven), **and them who dwell in Heaven.** (Even though refers to all Believers in Heaven, pointedly it fers to the 144,000 Jews who have been Raptu and are now in Heaven. The insults will be and fast, in effect, ridiculing Heaven perio

7 And it was given unto him to mak with the Saints, and to overcome the will include all Believers all over the u well, the Text implies by the word "o that the Lord will allow such to happ power was given him over all kin tongues, and nations. (This doesn' entirety of the world, but rather which he has control, which is bas of the old Roman Empire.)

8 And all who dwell upon **worship him** (first of all, we of worship, not dominion of

the word "all" doesn't refer to every single human being, but rather people from all nations of the world, however many that number might be), **whose names are not written in the Book of Life** (refers to the fact that Believers will not worship the Antichrist) **of the Lamb slain from the foundation of the world.** (This tells us that the only way one's name can be placed in the Book of Life is by acceptance of Jesus Christ as one's Lord and Saviour, and what He did for us at the Cross. Also, the phrase, "From the foundation of the world" proclaims the fact that the Doctrine of "Jesus Christ and Him Crucified" is the Foundation Doctrine of all Doctrines. In other words, every Doctrine from the Bible must be built on the foundation of the Cross of Christ, otherwise it is bogus.)

9 **If any man have an ear, let him hear** (refers to the ability to hear spiritually, and to hear properly in this manner; Jesus used the term many times [Mat. 11:15; 13:9, 43; Mk. 4:9; etc.]).

10 **He who leads into captivity shall go into captivity** (could be translated, "He who is destined to captivity will go into captivity"; it refers to the fact that those who will not hear the Word of the Lord, but rather the Word of the Antichrist, are guaranteed the worst type of spiritual bondage): **he who kills with the sword must be killed with the sword.** (This pertains to the nations of the world that will follow the Antichrist in his quest for world domination and power. The Second Coming of the Lord will bring swift and sure Judgment upon them.) **Here is the patience and the faith of the Saints.** (This refers basically to Israel, and that her Redemption is very near, which will take place at the Second Coming.)

11 **And I beheld another beast coming up out of the Earth** (refers to the false prophet; by the use of the word "Earth," the Holy Spirit is telling us that this man is not from above, but rather from the masses of people); **and he had two horns like a lamb** (he has a lamb-like appearance which is intended to deceive), **and he spoke as a dragon** (refers to the fact that he will be greatly anointed by the Devil; in a sense, the Antichrist will claim to be Christ, while the false prophet will try to fill the role of the Holy Spirit).

12 **And he exercised all the power of the first beast before him** (the power or authority exercised by the false prophet will come directly from Satan, and not through the Antichrist), **and causes the Earth and them which dwell therein to worship the first beast** (the false prophet is promoting Earth and not Heaven, meaning he will promise Heaven here on Earth; the promises he makes will be tied to the "worship" given to the Antichrist), **whose deadly wound was healed** (doesn't refer to an assassination attempt or even to the Antichrist being killed and raised from the dead as some teach, but rather that the powerful fallen Angel, who helped bring the Grecian Empire into power under Alexander the Great and has been locked up for many, many centuries, has now been loosed and is helping the Antichrist; this "deadly wound being healed" speaks of his release from the bottomless pit [Dan. 7:6; Rev. 11:7; 13:2]).

13 **And he** (the false prophet) **does great wonders** (signs), **so that he makes fire come down from Heaven on the Earth in the sight of men** (will be literal, which means it's not a trick; he will do this through the power of Satan),

14 **And deceives them who dwell on the Earth by** the means of **those miracles which he had power to do in the sight of the beast** (refers to the efforts of the false prophet to elevate the Antichrist; the word "beast" is used interchangeably between the Antichrist, the false prophet, and the fallen Angel; whatever they call themselves, the Holy Spirit refers to them as "beasts"); **saying to them who dwell on the Earth, that they should make an image to the beast** (it is an image for the purpose of worship, and will probably be set up in the Temple built by the Jews in Jerusalem), **which had the wound by a sword, and did live** (refers to the Antichrist somehow being wounded, a wound incidentally which should have taken his life; that he lives is construed as a miracle, with credit probably going to the false prophet; this is not the "wound" of Verse 3; that was on "one of his heads," which had to do with an Empire [actually the Grecian Empire], and not an individual; this wound of Verse 14 pertains to an individual, in this case the Antichrist).

15 **And he** (the false prophet) **had power to give life unto the image of the beast** (should have been translated, "For he had power to give spirit unto the image of the beast"; that is the actual word used in the Greek; to give life is solely the prerogative of the Godhead), **that the image of the beast should both speak, and cause that as many as would not worship the image of the beast should be killed** (by the powers of darkness, this image will be able to somehow speak, and will, as well, pronounce the sentence of death upon all who will not worship the image of the beast; this will probably be in Jerusalem!).

16 And he caused all, both small and great, rich and poor, free and bond, to receive a mark in their right hand, or in their foreheads (*"all" represents only those in his domain, not the entirety of the world; this domain will include virtually the entirety of the area of the old Roman Empire, which includes North Africa, the Middle East, and most of modern Europe; this will be a literal mark*):

17 And that no man might buy or sell, save he who had the mark (*we are told in Verses 11 through 13 that the seduction of the Antichrist will be religious; now we are told in Verses 16 and 17 it will be economic*), or the name of the beast, or the number of his name. (*The thought is that either the "name" of the beast or his "number" will be required as a brand or mark upon all.*)

18 Here is wisdom (*this is the wisdom of God*). Let him who has understanding count the number of the beast (*the idea is that it is the number of a man, not of God, which means he will give account to Jehovah, Whom he has repeatedly blasphemed*): for it is the number of a man; and his number *is* Six hundred threescore *and* six. (*It is the number of a man, not a kingdom, not a religion, not a dispensation, but a man. The number will be 666.*)

CHAPTER 14
(A.D. 96)
THE LAMB

AND I looked, and, lo, a Lamb stood on the Mount Sion (*is the same portrayal as Rev. 5:6; Christ being referred to here as a "Lamb" proclaims the fact that our Redemption was accomplished at the Cross; in fact, the title "Lamb" as it refers to Christ is used some 28 times in the Book of Revelation, all denoting the Atoning Work of Christ on the Cross; incidentally, this is the Heavenly "Mount Sion"*), and with Him an hundred forty *and* four thousand, having His Father's Name written in their foreheads. (*This is the number of Jews who came to Christ in the first half of the Great Tribulation. Some of the early Manuscripts, which are probably correct, read, "Having His Name [the Name of the Lamb] and the Father's Name upon their foreheads." Considering that this was inspired by the Holy Spirit, in this one Verse we have the Doctrine of the Trinity.*)

2 And I heard a voice from Heaven, as the voice of many waters, and as the voice of a great thunder (*proclaims the type of praise and worship being offered; it sounds like a waterfall mixed with thunder; is this typical of the modern Church? it ought to be!*): and I heard the voice of harpers harping with their harps (*portrays the musical accompaniment*):

3 And they sung as it were a new song before the Throne, and before the four Beasts, and the Elders (*this song is for the 144,000 only; it could very well be Psalm 149; also, the "new song" mentioned here is not so much that the song itself is new, but that what it says can only be carried out by those represented by the 144,000, which is Redeemed Israel*): and no man could learn that song but the hundred *and* forty *and* four thousand, which were redeemed from the earth. (*They were Redeemed by trusting Christ and what He did at the Cross, which is the only way anyone can be Redeemed.*)

4 These are they which were not defiled with women; for they are virgins. (*It refers to the 144,000 who did not corrupt themselves with idolatry. Faith in anything other than Christ and the Cross constitutes spiritual adultery, which is idolatry. In fact, millions in the modern Church are guilty of this sin, due to not understanding the Cross.*) These are they which follow the Lamb whithersoever He goes. (*By use of the word "Lamb," they took up their Cross exactly as Jesus demands of all [Lk. 9:23-24].*) These were redeemed from among men, *being* the Firstfruits unto God and to the Lamb. (*By use of the word "Firstfruits," this tells us that the entire nation of Israel is coming to Christ, which, in fact, will happen at the Second Coming.*)

5 And in their mouth was found no guile (*no hypocrisy*): for they are without fault before the Throne of God. (*This pertains to "Justification by Faith," which trust in Christ Alone can bring about.*)

THE ANGELS

6 And I saw another Angel fly in the midst of Heaven (*this is a different Angel from the one described in Rev. 8:13*), having the everlasting Gospel to preach unto them who dwell on the earth, and to every nation, and kindred, and tongue, and people (*refers to the same Gospel of Grace preached by Paul and the Apostles [Heb. 13:20]; as well, the implication is that this Angel will be observed by inhabitants on Earth, who will, as well, hear him Preach; it is the first recorded instance of an Angel preaching; no doubt, Television cameras will record his appearance and his Ministry, projecting him*

and his Message into all the world),

7 Saying with a loud voice (denotes significance and urgency; it is, in fact, a Command to all the nations of the world), Fear God, and give Glory to Him (is in contrast to the message being preached by the false prophet); for the hour of His Judgment is come (regards the seven Angels with the seven vials of plagues shortly to be poured out on the Earth): and worship Him Who made Heaven, and Earth, and the sea, and the fountains of waters. (Evidently the Antichrist is claiming the power of creation. The Angel counters by announcing to the entire world exactly Who the Creator actually is.)

8 And there followed another Angel, saying (this Angel replaces the one who had been preaching the Everlasting Gospel, and makes another announcement), Babylon is fallen, is fallen, that great city (Babylon, as addressed here, will be rebuilt; she will fall at the conclusion of the Great Tribulation), because she made all nations drink of the wine of the wrath of her fornication. (As Babylon was the site of Earth's first organized rebellion against God [Gen. 11:1-9], it will, as well, be the site of the last great organized rebellion. As it began, so shall it end.)

9 And the third Angel followed them, saying with a loud voice (presents the last of this Heavenly trio), If any man worship the beast and his image, and receive his mark in his forehead, or in his hand (proclaims a warning of unprecedented proportion; this is a declaration that every single individual is responsible),

10 The same shall drink of the wine of the Wrath of God, which is poured out without mixture (there will be no Mercy in this Judgment) into the cup of His indignation (when the cup gets full, the Judgment of God will commence; this "cup" is not only full, but is running over with evil); and he shall be tormented with fire and brimstone (refers to everyone who receives the mark of the beast, and speaks of Eternal Hell) in the Presence of the Holy Angels, and in the Presence of the Lamb (refers to the Great White Throne Judgment [20:11-15]):

11 And the smoke of their torment ascendeth up forever and ever (refers to the fact that a conscious existence will be forever): and they have no rest day nor night (refers to an unbroken continuance of torment), who worship the beast and his image, and whosoever receives the mark of his name. (All who take the mark of the beast in the coming Great Tribulation will, in essence, be blaspheming the Holy Spirit, for which there is no forgiveness [Mk. 3:29].)

12 Here is the patience of the Saints (a Message to those on Earth who have come to Christ during the Great Tribulation; by use of the word "patience," we are told that this persecution is soon to come to an end): here are they who keep the Commandments of God, and the Faith of Jesus. (The only way the Commandments of God can be kept is by the Believer placing His Faith in Christ and the Cross. The Holy Spirit will then grandly help such an individual.)

13 And I heard a voice from Heaven saying unto me, Write (according to the balance of this Verse, it is the Holy Spirit Who is speaking to John), Blessed are the dead which die in the Lord from henceforth (this refers to the Great Tribulation period, when many will die for their Testimony rather than serve the Antichrist): Yes, says the Spirit, that they may rest from their labours (is the exact opposite of the beast worshippers who have no rest); and their works do follow them. (The translation should read, "Their works follow with them.")

ARMAGEDDON

14 And I looked, and behold a white cloud, and upon the cloud One sat like unto the Son of Man (presents, as is obvious, the Lord Jesus Christ; "white" denotes purity; "cloud" denotes glory; "Son of Man" has reference to the Humanity of Christ, which always points to the Cross), having on His Head a golden crown (presents the victor's crown), and in His Hand a sharp sickle (represents the reaping that's going to be done at the Battle of Armageddon, as the balance of this Chapter portrays).

15 And another Angel came out of the Temple, crying with a loud voice to Him Who sat on the cloud (the first Angel preached the "Everlasting Gospel"; the second predicted the fall of Babylon; the third proclaims a warning concerning the taking of the mark of the beast; the fourth announces the Battle of Armageddon, even though it will be some three years yet in coming), Thrust in your sickle, and reap: for the time is come for you to reap; for the harvest of the earth is ripe (speaks of the Battle of Armageddon, which is soon to take place, and portrays the fact that the evil of the Antichrist will have reached a crescendo).

16 And He Who sat on the cloud thrust in His sickle on the earth (refers to Christ, Who

will orchestrate this momentous event); and the earth was reaped *(that which takes place on Earth, at least as it regards momentous events, are first of all orchestrated in Heaven)*.

17 And another Angel came out of the Temple which is in Heaven *(presents the fifth Angel of this Chapter)*, he also having a sharp sickle *(portrays the fact that Angels will have a great part to play in the coming Battle of Armageddon)*.

18 And another Angel came out from the Altar *(is the pattern Altar after which the Brazen Altar on Earth was fashioned)*, which had power over fire *(refers to the fire on the Altar)*; and cried with a loud cry to Him Who had the sharp sickle, saying, Thrust in your sharp sickle, and gather the clusters of the vine of the earth; for her grapes are fully ripe. *(The repetitiveness of these statements proclaims the absolute significance of what is about to happen, and that its outcome will affect the Earth greatly.)*

19 And the Angel thrust in his sickle into the earth, and gathered the vine of the earth *(he gathers "the vine of the Earth" into a place called in the Hebrew tongue, "Armageddon")*, and cast *it* into the great winepress of the Wrath of God *(refers to the assembled nations that will gather in the Valley of Jehoshaphat)*.

20 And the winepress was trodden without the city *(refers to the actual Battle itself pressing in on Jerusalem, with the intent of completely destroying the city and slaughtering the Jews)*, and blood came out of the winepress, even unto the horse bridles, by the space of a thousand *and* six hundred furlongs *(1600 furlongs is a distance of about 175 miles; the blood, no doubt, will be mixed with water, and in some places will be approximately six feet deep; it is possible that millions will be killed in this Battle)*.

CHAPTER 15
(A.D. 96)
SEVEN VIALS

A ND I saw another sign in Heaven, great and marvellous, seven Angels having the seven last plagues *(proclaims the concluding Judgments upon the territory of the Antichrist, which will be the worst)*; for in them is filled up the Wrath of God *(should have been translated, "anger of God")*.

2 And I saw as it were a sea of glass mingled with fire *(is that which is immediately before the Throne of God and mentioned in Rev. 4:6)*: and them who had gotten the victory over the beast, and over his image, and over his mark, *and* over the number of his name *(this group was murdered by the Antichrist)*, stand on the sea of glass, having the harps of God *(presents a picture of peace and tranquility)*.

3 And they sing the song of Moses the servant of God *(is the song given to us in Deut. 32:1-43; it is recorded that Moses wrote this song and taught it to the people [Deut. 31:22])*, and the song of the Lamb *(this is the second song, and begins with the Crucifixion, which was absolutely necessary if man was to be redeemed, and closes with Jesus Christ as "King of kings, Lord of lords")*, saying, Great and marvellous *are* your works, Lord God Almighty *(refers to Christ; while all His Works are "great and marvelous," what He did at the Cross presents itself as the greatest work of all)*; just and true *are* Your ways, Thou King of Saints. *(Christ is our King by virtue of what He did at the Cross, and our Faith in that Finished Work.)*

4 Who shall not fear You, O Lord, and glorify Your Name? *(This leaps ahead to the Millennial Reign. At that time, every human being on the face of the Earth will fear the Lord, and will glorify His Name as well.)* for *You* only *are* Holy *(speaks of the origination of Holiness, and that this Holiness can be given to Believers by virtue of what Christ did at the Cross)*: for all nations shall come and worship before You *(refers to the Millennial Reign)*; for Your Judgments are made manifest *(refers to the fact that the Judgment of God will be poured out upon the Antichrist during the Battle of Armageddon, where he will be defeated along with the entirety of his Army)*.

THE TEMPLE

5 And after that I looked *(refers to the Vials about to be poured out)*, and, behold, the Temple of the Tabernacle of the Testimony in Heaven was opened *(has reference to the Holy of Holies, where the Ark of the Covenant was kept; this is a witness both to the Holiness of God's Character and the Justice of His Government)*:

6 And the seven Angels came out of the Temple, having the seven plagues *(constitutes the Vial Judgments)*, clothed in pure and white linen *(indicates the perfect Righteousness of the acts that are to be performed on Earth)*, and having their breasts girded with golden girdles *(presents the same attire as that of our Lord [Rev. 1:13], signifying that what they are about to do pertains solely to the Work of Christ; in other*

words, Christ is in charge of all the Judgments).

7 And one of the four Beasts *("Living Ones" described in 4:7-8)* **gave unto the seven Angels seven golden Vials full of the Wrath of God** *(proclaims the fact, as stated, that these Judgments on the Earth will be the worst of all),* **Who lives forever and ever** *(proclaims the fact that God is Eternal).*

8 And the Temple was filled with smoke from the Glory of God, and from His power *(presents itself as very similar to the dedication of Solomon's Temple, in which the latter Temple was a replica of the one in Heaven);* **and no man was able to enter into the Temple, till the seven plagues of the seven Angels were fulfilled.** *(Constitutes the last few months of the Great Tribulation. The idea of no man being able to enter the Temple during this period of time seems to be that no one would be permitted to enter to make intercession, to turn away God's wrath, to divert Him from His Purpose.)*

CHAPTER 16
(A.D. 96)
THE FIRST VIAL

AND I heard a great voice out of the Temple saying to the seven Angels *(this is the "great" Chapter of the Bible, the word occurring 11 times),* **Go your ways, and pour out the Vials of the Wrath of God upon the earth.** *(This refers to the kingdom of the Antichrist, and not to the entirety of the Earth. That kingdom will be comprised of North Africa, the Middle East, and much of Europe [Dan. 7:7].)*

2 And the first *(Angel)* **went, and poured out his Vial upon the earth** *(constitutes the first plague);* **and there fell a noisome and grievous sore upon the men which had the mark of the beast, and** *upon* **them which worshipped his image.** *(This proves that these plagues will be poured out only on the kingdom of the beast.)*

THE SECOND VIAL

3 And the second Angel poured out his Vial **upon the sea** *(the Mediterranean);* **and it became as the blood of a dead** *man* *(pertains to the entire Mediterranean Sea; the blood of a dead man is almost black, and is coagulated):* **and every living soul died in the sea** *(should have been translated "living creatures"; therefore, every person on ships in the Mediterranean will die, along with all fish).*

THE THIRD VIAL

4 And the third Angel poured out his Vial **upon the rivers and fountains of waters** *(speaks of all underground rivers as well; in other words, all the water throughout the kingdom of the beast is poisoned);* **and they became blood.** *(This is not to be explained away as being merely symbolic. This will actually happen.)*

5 And I heard the Angel of the waters say *(in the Book of Revelation, we find that a great variety of Ministries are assigned to Angels; this Angel is the "Angel of the waters"),* **You are Righteous, O Lord** *(proclaims the fact that what the Lord is doing is Righteous; in fact, everything He does is Righteous!),* **which are, and was, and shall be** *(refers to the fact that God doesn't change),* **because you have judged thus** *(proclaims the fact that God would be unrighteous if He didn't Judge accordingly).*

6 For they have shed the blood of Saints and Prophets *(refers to those who will be murdered by the Antichrist during the time of the Great Tribulation because of their allegiance to the Lord Jesus Christ),* **and you have given them blood to drink; for they are worthy.** *(This proclaims the fact that the beast worshipers are getting their just desserts.)*

7 And I heard another out of the Altar say *(should have been translated, "and I heard the Altar say," referring to those who have been murdered by the Antichrist and are asking for vengeance [6:9-11]),* **Even so, Lord God Almighty, True and Righteous** *are* **your Judgments.** *(This proclaims the fact that the prayers of those at the Altar who cry for vengeance are about to be answered.)*

THE FOURTH VIAL

8 And the fourth Angel poured out his Vial **upon the sun** *(refers to that which is totally beyond the scope of man);* **and power was given unto him to scorch men with fire.** *(Adds to the "boils," and, as well, exacerbates the problem of the water shortage. Evidently, the sun at that time will pour out more heat on the Earth than ever before. As well, it seems this plague will also be confined to the generalized area of the Antichrist. If that is the case, the Lord will have to stop the heat from effecting other parts of the globe.)*

9 And men were scorched with great heat *(as the next Verse states, this is done only in the geographical area of the Antichrist),* **and blasphemed the Name of God, which has power**

over these plagues *(those in the geographical area of the Antichrist will know that God is doing this, but yet will continue to blaspheme His Name)*: **and they repented not to give Him Glory.** *(This tells us something about the hearts of men. It is seldom that miracles bring men to Repentance. Repentance must come from the heart and stem from Faith, which must ever have Christ and the Cross as its Object.)*

THE FIFTH VIAL

10 And the fifth Angel poured out his Vial upon the seat of the beast *(specifies that its coverage area is "the seat of the beast"; the core of this could refer to Jerusalem, which is now the religious headquarters of the Antichrist)*; **and his kingdom was full of darkness** *(these plagues are possible to Faith, though not to reason)*; **and they gnawed their tongues for pain** *(refers to the "boils" described in Verse 2)*,

11 And blasphemed the God of Heaven because of their pains and their sores *(they blamed God for their situation, even though He plainly told them not to take the mark of the beast [14:10])*, **and repented not of their deeds.** *(This presents the fact that the heart of man is so incurably corrupt that even the fiercest Judgments fail to affect its attitude, spirit, or conduct.)*

THE SIXTH VIAL

12 And the sixth Angel poured out his Vial upon the great river Euphrates; and the water thereof was dried up *(refers to preparations for the coming Battle of Armageddon)*, **that the way of the kings of the east might be prepared** *(actually says in the Greek, "the kings of the sun-rising"; this will, no doubt, include the armies of China and Japan, plus others which will join the Antichrist in the coming Battle of Armageddon)*.

THREE UNCLEAN SPIRITS

13 And I saw three unclean spirits like frogs *(while John saw these demon spirits in his vision, they will be invisible to all others; these invisible creatures are functioning presently on Earth, even as they have since the Fall, and there is only one power that affects them, and that is the Name of Jesus [Mk. 16:17])* **come out of the mouth of the dragon, and out of the mouth of the beast, and out of the mouth of the false prophet.** *(This concerns the fact that*

this ungodly trio connives to secure the help of other nations regarding the coming battle of Armageddon.)*

14 For they are the spirits of devils *(refers to a flood of demon spirits working in conjunction with the three unclean spirits)*, **working miracles** *(which will probably be done through the false prophet and others; proclaims the fact that all miracles are not necessarily from God)*, **which go forth unto the kings of the earth and of the whole world, to gather them to the battle of that Great Day of God Almighty.** *(As is obvious here, there are nations the Antichrist doesn't control, whose help he will seek. But while he thinks all of this is his plan, "God Almighty" is actually orchestrating all events. The Antichrist will think to destroy Israel, but God will in fact destroy him.)*

15 Behold, I come as a thief *(refers to the fact that the Antichrist has been so successful with his propaganda that very few in the world of that time will actually be expecting Christ to return)*. **Blessed is he who watches, and keeps his garments** *(points to those on Earth who worship and serve the Lamb, and that they must be constantly vigilant lest their loyalty to Him be diverted through Satanic deception [Mat. 24:43; I Thess. 5:2-4])*, **lest he walk naked, and they see his shame.** *(This refers to being naked to the Judgment of God, and suffering the consequences at the Second Coming, or even before that event.)*

16 And He gathered them together *(the pronoun "He" refers to God)* **into a place called in the Hebrew tongue Armageddon.** *(This refers to a literal place where a literal battle will be fought. It is the Mount of Megiddo overlooking the plain of Megiddo west of the Mount, and apparently including the Plain of Esdraelon, i.e., Valley of Megiddo.)*

THE SEVENTH VIAL

17 And the seventh Angel poured out his Vial into the air *(this is the last Judgment; it signifies an earthquake such as the world has not previously known, which will effect not only particular cities, but also entire nations)*; **and there came a great voice out of the Temple of Heaven, from the Throne, saying, It is done.** *(The mighty Voice that shouted "Finished" from the Cross will now shout "Finished" from the Throne.)*

18 And there were voices, and thunders, and lightnings *(the Divine purpose in Grace*

was finished at the Cross; here the Divine purpose in wrath is finished; this Vial Judgment could well take place simultaneously with the Second Coming); and there was a great earthquake, such as was not since men were upon the earth, so mighty an earthquake, *and* so great *(presents the last cataclysmic upheaval)*.

19 And the great city was divided into three parts *(refers to Jerusalem)*, and the cities of the nations fell *(refers to the Middle East, and possibly parts of Europe as well)*: and great Babylon came in remembrance before God, to give unto her the cup of the wine of the fierceness of His wrath. *(This earthquake, the greatest of them all, will center on Babylon and will completely destroy the city that is scheduled to be rebuilt at this present time [2003]. The first organized rebellion against God began at Babylon, and it will end at Babylon [Gen. 11:1-9].)*

20 And every island fled away, and the mountains were not found *(pertains to the colossal magnitude of this earthquake)*.

21 And there fell upon men a great hail out of Heaven, *every stone* about the weight of a talent *(about 100 pounds; one can well imagine the damage that such would cause)*: and men blasphemed God because of the plague of the hail; for the plague thereof was exceeding great. *(Once again, those in the kingdom of the beast will know that this plague is from God, but instead of repenting, they will continue to blaspheme Him.)*

CHAPTER 17
(A.D. 96)
THE GREAT WHORE

AND there came one of the seven Angels which had the seven Vials, and talked with me *(probably is the seventh Angel; however, we actually have no way of truly knowing)*, saying unto me, Come hither; I will show unto you the judgment of the great whore who sits upon many waters *(the "great whore" refers to all the religions of the world that ever have been, which are devised by men as a substitute for "Jesus Christ and Him Crucified"; God's Way is Christ and Him Crucified Alone; as well, the "many waters" are a symbol for multitudes of people [Vs. 15])*:

2 With whom *(the great whore, i.e., all type of religions)* the kings of the earth *(from the very beginning, most nations have been ruled by some type of religion)* have committed fornication *(all religions devised by men, and even*

the parts of Christianity that have been corrupted, are labeled by the Lord as "spiritual fornication" [Rom. 7:1-4])*, and the inhabitants of the earth have been made drunk with the wine of her fornication *(proclaims the addiction of religion; the doing of religion is the most powerful narcotic there is)*.

3 So he *(the Angel)* carried me *(John)* away in the spirit *(a vision)* into the wilderness *(every religious effort that attempts to take the place of the Cross is a spiritual wilderness)*: and I saw a woman sit upon a scarlet coloured beast *(the woman is organized religion; by that we mean any religion or form of religion claiming to have a way of Salvation or victory other than the Cross; the "scarlet color" indicates blood and pertains to great persecution)*, full of names of blasphemy *(refers to this "woman" opposing the Plan of God in every capacity)*, having seven heads and ten horns. *(This pertains to the scarlet colored beast, not the woman. The "seven heads" represent seven Empires that persecuted Israel in the past, with the last one yet future. They are "Egypt, Assyria, Babylon, Medo-Persia, Greece, and Rome." The "ten horns" represent ten nations that will arise out of the old Roman Empire territory and persecute Israel, and is yet future. These ten nations make up the seventh head. The Roman Empire, which made up the sixth head, was the last of the Empires that persecuted Israel before her destruction as a nation in A.D. 70. When the ten-horned kingdom arises, which it will shortly, it will persecute Israel as well.)*

4 And the woman was arrayed in purple and scarlet colour *(all of this pertains to Israel, but with a carry over into the Church Age; the "purple" represents the dominion of these religions over nations, with the "scarlet color" representing the persecution of Israel)*, and decked with gold and precious stones and pearls *(these religions have always been very rich; a case in point is Islam, which controls some 60% of the oil reserves of the world)*, having a golden cup in her hand *(all of these religions have an allurement, symbolized by the cup being golden)* full of abominations and filthiness of her fornication *(proclaims what this cup holds, despite its outward attractiveness)*:

5 And upon her forehead *was* a name written *(the "forehead" symbolizes the fact that all these religions are devised by man, and not by God)*, MYSTERY, BABYLON THE GREAT *(the word "mystery" separates spiritual Babylon from literal Babylon; it is "great in the eyes of*

the world, but not in the eyes of God"), THE MOTHER OF HARLOTS AND ABOMINATIONS OF THE EARTH. *(This proclaims the actual content of this "golden cup," even though it looks wonderful on the outside. If it's not "Jesus Christ and Him Crucified," then it is labeled by the Lord as "harlots and abominations." Regrettably that includes much of modern Christianity as well.)*

6 And I saw the woman drunken with the blood of the Saints *(refers to these Empires and their false religions, which persecuted Israel during Old Testament times, actually up to the time of Christ)*, and with the blood of the martyrs of Jesus *(points to the millions in the Church Age who gave their lives for the Cause of Christ; the Roman Empire began these persecutions of Christians, and was followed by the Catholic Church)*: and when I saw her, I wondered with great admiration *(John is amazed at seeing all of this).*

7 And the Angel said unto me, Wherefore did you marvel? *(The Angel knew John would marvel at the scene that unfolded before his eyes, and would need an explanation.)* I will tell you the mystery of the woman, and of the beast that carries her, which has the seven heads and ten horns.

8 The beast who you saw was *(represents a fallen Angel who helped the leaders of these Empires of the past in their efforts to destroy Israel)*, and is not *(was not active during the time of John)*; and shall ascend out of the bottomless pit *(this powerful, fallen Angel was confined to the bottomless pit about 2,300 years ago and remains there still, but will be released soon to help the Antichrist)*, and go into perdition *(means that after his escapade of helping the Antichrist on Earth, he will be consigned to the Lake of Fire [20:10])*: and they who dwell on the earth shall wonder, whose names were not written in the Book of Life from the foundation of the world *(presents the fact that all the unsaved people on Earth during the time of the Great Tribulation will be startled and amazed as they observe the Antichrist, who will do things no other man has ever done; this will be because this fallen Angel is helping him, but of which he is not aware)*, when they behold the beast who was, and is not *(was not functioning during John's day)*, and yet is *(will be released out of the bottomless pit to help the Antichrist).*

9 And here is the mind which has wisdom *(is the mind that knows and believes the Word of God).* The seven heads are seven mountains,

on which the woman sits *(represents these seven Empires which were controlled by false religions, i.e., "demon spirits").*

10 And there are seven kings *(actually refers to the "seven heads," speaking of the leaders of these Empires, whomever they may have been)*: five are fallen *(five of the Empires were fallen during John's day; they are Egypt, Assyria, Babylon, Medo-Persia, and Greece)*, and one is *(refers to the Roman Empire, which was in existence during John's day, and could, therefore, be spoken of in the present tense)*, **and** the other is not yet come *(refers to the ten nation confederation symbolized by the ten horns, which in John's day had not yet come, and, in fact, has not come even yet)*; and when he comes, he must continue a short space. *(The "ten horns" will be the seventh head, and refers to ten nations that will arise shortly and persecute Israel, which will probably take place in the first half of the Great Tribulation, a time span of about three and one half years.)*

11 And the beast *(fallen Angel)* that was, and is not, even he is the eighth *(this fallen Angel will help the Antichrist, and will head up the eighth Empire to persecute Israel)*, and is of the seven *(refers to the fact that he helped all the Empires of the past, with the exception of Rome, in their efforts to persecute Israel; but this fallen Angel gave the greatest help to Alexander the Great, who headed up the Grecian Empire; we know this because John, in his Vision, said, "and the beast which I saw was like unto a leopard," with that animal being one of the symbols of ancient Greece [Rev. 13:2; Dan. 7:6])*, and goes into perdition *(refers to the fact that irrespective of his power and plans, Eternal Hell will be the due of this Satanic Prince; the same goes for Satan, the Antichrist, the False Prophet, every fallen Angel, every demon spirit, and, in fact, all the unredeemed who have ever lived).*

12 And the ten horns which you saw are ten kings *(Dan. 7:7)*, which have received no kingdom as yet *(refers to John's day)*; but receive power as kings one hour with the beast. *(These ten nations will come to power before the Antichrist, making up the seventh head. Then they will be taken over by the Antichrist, who is referred to by Daniel as the "little horn" [Dan. 7:8]. The "one hour" refers to the "short space" this confederation of the ten kings and the Antichrist will hold together. It will last for approximately three and one half years, and will be destroyed by the Second Coming of Christ [Dan. 2:34-35].)*

13 These have one mind *(this ten nation confederation, making up the seventh head, will all be in agreement respecting their joining with the Antichrist because they don't have the power to successfully oppose him)*, **and shall give their power and strength unto the beast** *(refers to the Antichrist now coming to full power, and making up the eighth kingdom as described in Verse 11).*

14 These shall make war with the Lamb *(has to do with the Antichrist attacking Israel as it regards the Battle of Armageddon; Satan hates Israel for many varied reasons, but above all because of Jesus; so, to attack Israel is to attack the Lamb),* **and the Lamb shall overcome them** *(speaks of the Second Coming, but also speaks to the fact that Jesus is worthy to administer Judgment and Justice because of what He did at the Cross):* **for He is Lord of lords, and King of kings** *(proclaims the fact that this "Lamb" is "King" of all and "Lord" of all, and all because of the Cross):* **and they who are with Him** *are* **called, and chosen, and faithful.** *(Every Saint of God who has ever lived, both Jews and Gentiles, will come back with Christ at the Second Coming.)*

15 And he *(the Angel)* said unto me *(John),* **The waters which you saw** *(refers back to Verse 1, and presents the word "waters" being used as a symbolism),* **where the whore sits** *(if it's not Jesus Christ and Him Crucified [I Cor. 1:23; 2:2], then God refers to it as the "Great Whore"),* **are peoples, and multitudes, and nations, and tongues.** *(This covers the entirety of the world, and tells us that billions have died and gone to hell as a result of following false religions.)*

16 And the ten horns which you saw upon the beast *(pertains to the ten nation confederation, which will make up the seventh head),* **these shall hate the whore** *(at least some, if not all, of the ten nation confederation will come out of the Middle East; Islam rules this part of the world, and it is a rule which has all but destroyed these countries; the implication is the religion of Islam will be put down by this confederacy),* **and shall make her desolate and naked, and shall eat her flesh, and burn her with fire.** *(This proclaims the fact that the ten nations under the Antichrist will institute and carry out a campaign of elimination as it regards the religion of Islam, and, in fact, any other religions in his domain. All of these religions will be replaced by "beast worship.")*

17 For God has put in their hearts to fulfil His Will *(while the ten nations have their own agenda, God will use it to bring about His Will),* **and to agree, and give their kingdom unto the beast** *(the ten leaders of these nations will give their authority to the beast, i.e., "the Antichrist"),* **until the Words of God shall be fulfilled.** *(This will last "until" the Great Tribulation has ended, which will be at the Battle of Armageddon in which these nations will be totally destroyed [Dan. 2:34-35].)*

18 And the woman which you saw is that great city *(refers to rebuilt Babylon portrayed in Rev., Chpt. 18),* **which reigns over the kings of the earth.** *(Rebuilt Babylon will not only be one of the commercial centers of the world, but as well the religious center. The Antichrist will have replaced Islam and other religions with himself as the one being worshiped. It all began at Babylon, and it will all end there [Gen. 11:1-9; Rev. 18:10].)*

CHAPTER 18
(A.D. 96)

BABYLON

AND after these things I saw another Angel come down from Heaven *(this Angel seems to be different from the Angels of Rev. 17:1),* **having great power** *(he is greater than any one of the Seven);* **and the earth was lightened with His Glory** *(represents the fact that this Angel, who immediately precedes the Coming of Christ, must of necessity be one of, if not the greatest Angel in the Creation of God, due to the magnificence of that Coming and especially of the One Who is Coming; it could be either Gabriel or Michael).*

2 And he cried mightily with a strong voice, saying, Babylon the great is fallen, is fallen *(he is speaking of literal Babylon, the city, and, as well, of Mystery Babylon, the religion),* **and is become the habitation of devils, and the hold of every foul spirit, and a cage of every unclean and hateful bird** *(proclaims the city in the last of the last days as an infestation of demon spirits of every sort; in other words, it will be the capital of evil in all the world; vultures and such like are used at times in the Word of God as symbols for demon spirits [Mat. 13:32]).*

3 For all nations have drunk of the wine of the wrath of her fornication, and the kings of the earth have committed fornication with her *(pertains to the time of the Antichrist, but, as well, to all that Babylon has represented from the very beginning of time, i.e., "false religions"),* **and the merchants of the earth are waxed rich**

through the abundance of her delicacies. *(From his headquarters in Babylon, the Antichrist will make it possible for many to get rich during the time of the Great Tribulation, therefore, ingratiating himself to many nations of the world.)*

4 And I heard another voice from Heaven *(presents that which is different from the Angel of the first Verse)*, saying, Come out of her, My people, that you be not partakers of her sins *(the short phrase, "My people," refers to all Believers all over the world for all time, but the primary thrust is to Israel; in fact, the entire Book of Revelation, even though broadly addressing itself to the entirety of mankind, is primarily for Israel; this is the time of Jacob's trouble [Jer. 30:7]), and is designed to bring Israel back to God)*, and that you receive not of her plagues. *(If Believers fail to come out from among the world, i.e., "the world's system," we will experience Judgment the same as unbelievers.)*

5 For her sins have reached unto Heaven *(carries the idea of rebellion against God, which is the ruin of mankind)*, and God has remembered her iniquities. *(The only way God will forget sins and iniquities is by man placing his Faith and Trust in Christ and what Christ has done for us at the Cross [Heb. 8:6,12].)*

6 Reward her even as she rewarded you *(Saints are not called to render vengeance, but rather the statement is made that God will do such; the idea is that every act of hurt by the world or the apostate Church against God's People will be answered in kind; but in this case, it pertains more so to the Jews than anything else [Gen. 12:3])*, and double unto her double according to her works *(in a sense pertains to the fact that the future rebuilt city of Babylon will suffer the Judgment of the ages; the effort by President Bush to change the Government in Iraq, which, in fact, was the right thing to do, is a part of the process which will enable Babylon to be rebuilt)*: in the cup which she has filled fill to her double. *(God's answer to man's rebellion will be the destruction of Babylon, and in a cataclysmic way.)*

7 How much she has glorified herself *(pertains to the characteristics of religion)*, and lived deliciously *(refers to the earthly rewards of religion; at its base, one will always find "money")*, so much torment and sorrow give her *(refers to the fact that Judgment has been laid up for this city of Babylon, symbolic of man's system, which is a system without God; we reap what we sow [Gal. 6:7])*: for she said in her heart, I sit a queen, and am no widow, and shall see no sorrow. *(She calls herself "a queen," while the Lord refers to her as "the great whore," which pronounces her doom.)*

8 Therefore shall her plagues come in one day, death, and mourning, and famine *(points to the great earthquake of Rev. 16:18)*; and she shall be utterly burned with fire: for strong *is* the Lord God Who judges her. *(The idea is that Satan, through the Antichrist, will boast of his great strength, so the Lord will, in effect, show the Antichrist and the world what strength really is.)*

BABYLON'S FALL

9 And the kings of the earth, who have committed fornication *(speaks of "spiritual adultery"; the worship of anything other than God and trust placed in anything except Christ and Him Crucified is "spiritual adultery")* and lived deliciously with her, shall bewail her, and lament for her *(Babylon, and we speak of the system, is their god, so they lament for their god)*, when they shall see the smoke of her burning *(signals far more than the destruction of one city; it is the end of a system, a way, a false way, a terrible way, and will be carried out at the very conclusion of the Great Tribulation, which will usher in the Second Coming)*,

10 Standing afar off for the fear of her torment *(the destruction of this city will, no doubt, be Televised all over the world; as well, much of the world will fear the same Judgment is coming upon them, knowing that God has done this)*, saying, Alas, alas, that great city Babylon, that mighty city! *(Proclaims the lament, knowing that her destruction signals the end of Satan's rule and reign.)* for in one hour is your judgment come. *(Ancient Babylon gradually decayed, but this Babylon will be totally destroyed "in one hour," proving that this city must be rebuilt.)*

11 And the merchants of the earth shall weep and mourn over her; for no man buys their merchandise any more *(those who have sold their souls to this system will now weep and mourn over her destruction)*:

12 The merchandise of gold, and silver, and precious stones, and of pearls, and fine linen, and purple, and silk, and scarlet, and all thyine wood, and all manner vessels of ivory, and all manner vessels of most precious wood, and of brass, and iron, and marble,

13 And cinnamon, and odours, and ointments, and frankincense, and wine, and oil,

and fine flour, and wheat, and beasts, and sheep, and horses, and chariots, and slaves, and souls of men. *(The last phrase probably refers to the drug business.)*

14 And the fruits that your soul lusted after are departed from you, and all things which were dainty and goodly are departed from you, and you shall find them no more at all *(this proclaims the fallacy of investing in a system of this world instead of the things of God [Mat. 6:19-21]).*

15 The merchants of these things, which were made rich by her, shall stand afar off for the fear of her torment, weeping and wailing *(the idea is that the system of this world, symbolized by rebuilt Babylon, is about to end, with another system taking its place, which will be the Kingdom of our Lord),*

16 And saying, Alas, alas, that great city, that was clothed in fine linen, and purple, and scarlet, and decked with gold, and precious stones, and pearls! *(This points to a conclusion regarding the word "great," which is not shared by the Lord.)*

17 For in one hour so great riches is come to nought *(should serve as a warning to all who put their trust in such things).* And every shipmaster, and all the company in ships, and sailors, and as many as trade by sea, stood afar off *(God took out in one hour what men took many years to build),*

18 And cried when they saw the smoke of her burning, saying, What *city is* like unto this great city! *(They cried over their financial loss, but seemed to show no concern for their lost souls.)*

19 And they cast dust on their heads, and cried, weeping and wailing, saying, Alas, alas, that great city, wherein were made rich all who had ships in the sea by reason of her costliness! for in one hour is she made desolate. *(The casting of dust on their heads does not point to Repentance, but rather to the sorrow of their financial loss.)*

20 Rejoice over her, *you* Heaven, and *you* Holy Apostles and Prophets; for God has avenged you on her. *(While men cry over the destruction of Babylon, the Lord tells Believers to "rejoice.")*

21 And a mighty Angel took up a stone like a great millstone, and cast *it* into the sea *(is a fulfillment of Mat. 18:6),* saying, Thus with violence shall that great city Babylon be thrown down, and shall be found no more at all *(proclaims the manner in which the era of evil will*

end; it will be with "violence," which, in effect, speaks more so of the Second Coming of Christ than anything else).*

22 And the voice of harpers, and musicians, and of pipers, and trumpeters, shall be heard no more at all in you *(the merriment has ended);* and no craftsman, of whatsoever craft *he be,* shall be found any more in you *(refers to the way business is normally done; a few get filthy rich on the backs of the helpless poor);* and the sound of a millstone shall be heard no more at all in you *(refers to grinding poverty, which characterizes much of the world; it is not that poverty will characterize Babylon, but that much of its riches will come from ill-gotten gains);*

23 And the light of a candle shall shine no more at all in you *(Satan's false light will shine no more);* and the voice of the bridegroom and of the bride shall be heard no more at all in you *(refers to a false foundation, exactly as the false light; in fact, everything about the system of the world is false, built on a lie):* for your merchants were the great men of the earth; for by your sorceries were all nations deceived. *(Witchcraft and the drug business, referred to by "sorceries," constitute the foundation of this commercial enterprise, which will be totally destroyed.)*

24 And in her was found the blood of Prophets, and of Saints, and of all who were slain upon the earth. *(The literal city of Babylon is symbolic of the Babylonian spirit, which has opposed the Work of God from the beginning until now.)*

CHAPTER 19
(A.D. 96)
PRAISE

AND after these things *(pertains to specifically Chapter 18, but also the entire Book of Revelation in a broader sense,)* I heard a great voice of much people in Heaven *(proclaims "praise," which is the exact opposite of what is happening on Earth),* saying, Alleluia; Salvation, and Glory, and Honour, and Power, unto the Lord our God *(the song here, and it is a song, does not begin with ascribing "Salvation" to God, as the English version suggests; it rather affirms the fact; "The Salvation is God's; it is the echo of the ancient utterance — 'Salvation belongs unto God'"):*

2 For true and righteous *are* His Judgments *(neither man nor spirit beings, in all*

honesty, can fault God for what He has done regarding the system of this world): **for He has Judged the great whore** (pertains to every false way of Salvation, irrespective of what it might be; no matter how beautiful it might look outwardly, the Lord refers to it as the "great whore"), **which did corrupt the earth with her fornication** (this refers to all the religions of the world, and for all time; however, it also refers to the fact that if the Preacher is not preaching "Jesus Christ and Him Crucified" as the answer to man's dilemma, then in some manner he is preaching and projecting a type of "spiritual fornication" [Rom. 7:1-4]), **and has avenged the blood of His servants at her hand.** (Almost all of the persecution against the true Saints of God in this world, and for all time, has come from apostate religion. It started with Cain [Gen., Chpt. 4].)

3 And again they said, Alleluia. (This "praise of the Lord" is because of the destruction of the literal city of Babylon. The "Alleluia" in Verse 1 was proclaimed concerning the destruction of Mystery Babylon.) **And her smoke rose up for ever and ever** (proclaims the fact that her Judgment is Eternal).

4 And the four and twenty Elders and the four Beasts (Living Ones) **fell down and worshipped God Who sat on the Throne** (the 24 Elders represent all the Redeemed of all the ages; they are in fact 24 men; the "four Living Ones" represent the Creation of God, and how that Creation can now serve its full purpose as originally intended), **saying, Amen; Alleluia.** (This "Alleluia" signals the end of all evil, and the beginning of all Righteousness.)

5 And a voice came out of the Throne (is silent regarding the identity), **saying, Praise our God, all you His servants, and you who fear Him, both small and great.** (Every true Believer will praise the Lord, and should do so continually.)

6 And I heard as it were the voice of a great multitude (this "great multitude" consists of every single Believer who has ever lived, all the way from Abel to the last one saved in the Great Tribulation), **and as the voice of many waters, and as the voice of mighty thunderings** (this is praise that expresses itself, and not merely the thoughts of a silent heart), **saying, Alleluia: for the Lord God omnipotent reigns.** (This "Alleluia" pertains to the Lord reigning as King, and doing so forever. Satan does not reign. The Lord God Omnipotent Reigns, and He is "All-powerful.")

7 Let us be glad and rejoice (all the Redeemed are about to be joined in Holy Matrimony to the Lamb Who has saved them), **and give honour to Him** (God has made it possible for mankind to be Redeemed, and did so through the Sacrifice of His Son, the Lord Jesus Christ): **for the marriage of the Lamb is come, and his wife has made herself ready.** (This presents a scene that will take place in Heaven immediately before the Second Coming. The "wife" is the Redeemed of all ages.)

8 And to her was granted that she should be arrayed in fine linen, clean and white: for the fine linen is the Righteousness of Saints. (The "fine linen" is symbolic of "Righteousness," which was afforded by what Christ did at the Cross.)

9 And he said unto me, Write, Blessed are **they which are called unto the Marriage Supper of the Lamb.** (The man speaking to John says this. The word "Lamb" is used, signifying that all of this is made possible because of what Jesus did at the Cross.) **And he said unto me, These are the true sayings of God.** (This refers again to the fact that all of this is made possible by what Jesus did regarding His Finished Work.)

10 And I fell at his feet to worship him. And he said unto me, See you do it **not: I am your fellowservant, and of your Brethren** (as is obvious here, this is a man; he looks so much like Jesus, because of his glorified form, that John thought it was Jesus; in a sense, this tells us what all Saints will look like in the coming Resurrection) **who have the Testimony of Jesus** (presents the fact that the Ministry of the Holy Spirit is to testify to Christ and of Christ): **worship God** (tells us in these two words that we are not to worship Angels, Saints, or the Virgin Mary): **for the Testimony of Jesus is the Spirit of Prophecy.** (This "Testimony" is His Atoning Work, i.e., what He did at the Cross. Every "Prophecy" of the Old Testament points in some way to Christ and what He did at the Cross. As well, every proclamation presently uttered must in some way point to the Cross of Christ.)

THE SECOND COMING

11 And I saw Heaven opened (records the final Prophetic hour regarding the Second Coming, without a doubt the greatest moment in human history), **and behold a white horse** (in effect, proclaims a war horse [Zech. 14:3]); **and He Who sat upon him** was **called Faithful and True** (faithful to His Promises and True to His

Judgments; He contrasts with the false Messiah of Rev. 6:2, who was neither faithful nor true), and in Righteousness He does Judge and make war (refers to the manner of His Second Coming).

12 His eyes *were* as a flame of fire (represents Judgment), and on His Head *were* many crowns (represents the fact that He will not be Lord of just one realm; He will be Lord of all realms); and He had a Name written, that no man knew, but He Himself (not meaning that it is unknown, but rather it is definitely unknowable; it will remain unreachable to man, meaning that its depths can never be fully plumbed).

13 And He *was* clothed with a vesture dipped in Blood (speaks of the Cross where He shed His Life's Blood, which gives Him the right to Judge the world): and His Name is called The Word of God. (His revealed Name is the Word of God, for He revealed God in His Grace and Power to make Him known, so the Believer can say, "I know Him.")

14 And the armies *which were* in Heaven followed Him upon white horses (these "armies" are the Saints of God, in fact, all the Saints who have ever lived, meaning we will be with Him at the Second Coming), clothed in fine linen, white and clean. (Harks back to Verse 8. It is the Righteousness of the Saints, all made possible by the Cross.)

ARMAGEDDON

15 And out of His mouth goes a sharp sword (represents Christ functioning totally and completely in the realm of the Word of God), that with it He should smite the nations (refers to all the nations that will join the Antichrist in his efforts to destroy Israel; it is the Battle of Armageddon): and He shall rule them with a rod of iron (refers to the fact that the Lord of Glory will not allow or tolerate in any shape, form, or fashion that which "steals, kills, and destroys"): and He treads the winepress of the fierceness and wrath of Almighty God (refers to the Battle of Armageddon).

16 And He has on *His* vesture and on His thigh a name written, KING OF KINGS, AND LORD OF LORDS (proclaims the fact that there will be no doubt as to Who He actually is).

17 And I saw an Angel standing in the sun (proclaims the fact that Faith believes what is written, even if the mind cannot comprehend what is written); and he cried with a loud voice, saying to all the fowls who fly in the midst of Heaven (denotes, as is obvious, supremacy over the Creation), Come and gather yourselves together unto the supper of the Great God (this is symbolic, but it is spoken in this way to proclaim the magnitude of that coming time [Ezek. 39:2, 11-12]);

18 That you may eat the flesh of kings, and the flesh of captains, and the flesh of mighty men, and the flesh of horses, and of them who sit on them, and the flesh of all *men, both* free and bond, both small and great. (This proclaims the fact that the Power of Almighty God doesn't blink at those on this Earth who consider themselves to be "great." The Judgment will be identical for all [Ezek. 39:18-20].)

19 And I saw the beast (John saw the Antichrist leading this mighty army; this is the "man of sin" mentioned by Paul in II Thess., Chpt. 2), and the kings of the earth, and their armies (refers to all the Antichrist could get to join him; it includes the "kings of the East" of Rev. 16:12), gathered together to make war against Him Who sat on the horse, and against His army (refers to Christ and the great army of Heaven which is with Him; as stated, this is the Battle of Armageddon [Ezek., Chpts. 38-39]).

20 And the beast was taken, and with him the false prophet who wrought miracles before him (refers to both of them falling in the Battle of Armageddon), with which he deceived them who had received the mark of the beast, and them who worshipped his image (pertains to Satan's chief weapon, which is deception). These both were cast alive into a Lake of Fire burning with brimstone (thus is the destiny of the Antichrist and the False Prophet, and all who follow them).

21 And the remnant were slain with the sword of Him Who sat upon the horse, which *sword* proceeded out of His mouth (the Lord Jesus will speak the word in the Battle of Armageddon, and whatever He speaks will take place): and all the fowls were filled with their flesh. (This proclaims the end of this conflict. The Antichrist and his hoards will announce to the world what they are going to do regarding Israel, but the end result will be buzzards gorging on their flesh.)

CHAPTER 20
(A.D. 96)
SATAN

AND I saw an Angel come down from Heaven (continues with the idea that Angels

are very prominent in the Plan and Work of God), **having the key of the bottomless pit** (speaks of the same place recorded in Rev. 9:1; however, there the key is given to Satan, but this Angel of Rev. 20:1 "has the key," implying he has had it all along; more than likely, God allows this Angel to give the key to Satan in Rev. 9:1) **and a great chain in his hand** (should be taken literally).

2 And he laid hold on the dragon, that old serpent, which is the Devil, and Satan (as a "dragon," he shows his power; as a "serpent," he shows his cunning; as the "Devil," he is the accuser; and as "Satan," he is the adversary), **and bound him a thousand years** (refers to being bound by the great chain carried by the Angel),

3 And cast him into the bottomless pit, and shut him up, and set a seal upon him (speaks of the abyss being sealed to keep him there), **that he should deceive the nations no more, till the thousand years should be fulfilled: and after that he must be loosed a little season.** (At the end of the thousand-year period, Satan will be loosed out of his prison. He will make another attempt to deceive the nations, in which he will not succeed. We aren't told how long this "little season" will be.)

THE MILLENNIUM

4 And I saw Thrones, and they sat upon them, and judgment was given unto them (refers to the 24 Elders who represent the entire Plan of God, which pertains to the Redeemed of all ages; we aren't told who these men are): **and** I saw **the souls of them who were beheaded for the witness of Jesus, and for the Word of God, and which had not worshipped the Beast, neither his image, neither had received** his **mark upon their foreheads, or in their hands** (categorizes the Tribulation Saints Who gave their lives for the cause of Christ; the idea is that these will be included in the first Resurrection of Life, and will enjoy all its privileges); **and they lived and reigned with Christ a thousand years.** (This is the Kingdom Age.)

5 But the rest of the dead lived not again until the thousand years were finished. (This pertains to all the unsaved, in fact, all those who lived and died since the dawn of time. The souls and spirits of these people are now in Hell [Lk. 16:19-31].) **This** is **the First Resurrection** (proclaims the fact that these two Resurrections, the Resurrection of the Just and the Resurrection of the Unjust, will be separated by 1,000 years).

6 Blessed and Holy is **he who has part in the First Resurrection** (this is the Resurrection of Life, which will include every Saint of God who has ever lived from Abel to the last Tribulation Saint; all will be given glorified bodies): **on such the second death has no power** (the "second death" is to be cast into the Lake of Fire, and to be there forever and forever [Rev. 2:8]; all who are washed in the Blood of the Lamb need not fear the second death), **but they shall be Priests of God and of Christ, and shall reign with Him a thousand years.** (All Believers who have part in the First Resurrection will at the same time serve as mediators, so to speak, between the population of the world and God and Christ. The "thousand years" portrays the Kingdom Age, when Christ will reign supreme over the entire Earth.)

SATAN

7 And when the thousand years are expired (should have been translated, "finished"), **Satan shall be loosed out of his prison** (is not meant to infer a mere arbitrary act on the part of God; He has a very valid reason for doing this),

8 And shall go out to deceive the nations which are in the four quarters of the Earth, Gog and Magog (the main reason the Lord allows Satan this latitude is, it seems, to rid the Earth of all who oppose Christ; George Williams says: "The Creation Sabbath witnessed the first seduction, and the Millennial Sabbath will witness the last"; the "Gog and Magog" spoken of by John is a Hebrew term expressive of multitude and magnitude; here it embraces all nations, "the four quarters of the Earth"), **to gather them together to battle: the number of whom** is **as the sand of the sea** (proclaims the fact that virtually all of the population at that particular time, which did not accept Christ during the Kingdom Age, will throw in their lot with Satan).

9 And they went up on the breadth of the earth, and compassed the camp of the Saints about, and the beloved city (pictures Satan coming against Jerusalem with his army, which will be the last attack against that city): **and fire came down from God out of Heaven, and devoured them.** (Stipulates that the Lord will make short work of this insurrection. In fact, very little information is given regarding this event, as is obvious.)

10 And the Devil who deceived them was cast into the Lake of Fire and brimstone (marks the end of Satan regarding his influence in the world, and, in fact, in any part of the

Creation of God), **where the Beast and the False Prophet** *are (proclaims the fact that these two were placed in "the Lake of Fire and Brimstone" some one thousand years earlier [Rev. 19:20]),* **and shall be tormented day and night forever and ever.** *(This signifies the Eternity of this place. It is a matter of interest to note that Satan's first act is recorded in Gen., Chpt. 3 [the third Chapter from the beginning], whereas his last act on a worldwide scale is mentioned in Rev., Chpt. 20 [the third Chapter from the end].)*

GREAT WHITE THRONE JUDGMENT

11 And I saw a Great White Throne *(proclaims the final Judgment of the unredeemed, which will take place at the end of the Kingdom Age),* **and Him Who sat on it** *(proclaims none other than God; however, we must understand that it is the Person of the Godhead, the Lord Jesus Christ [Mat. 25:31]; He is the Saviour today; He will be the Judge tomorrow),* **from Whose face the Earth and the Heaven fled away; and there was found no place for them.** *(This means a New Heaven and New Earth are in the offing.)*

12 And I saw the dead, small and great, stand before God *(pertains to the second Resurrection, the Resurrection of Damnation [I Cor., Chpt. 15; I Thess. 4:13-18; Jn. 5:29]);* **and the Books were opened: and another Book was opened, which is** *the Book* **of Life: and the dead were Judged out of those things which were written in the Books, according to their works** *(proclaims the manner of Judgment).*

13 And the sea gave up the dead which were in it; and death and hell delivered up the dead which were in them *(points to the fact that every unredeemed person who has ever lived will face the Great White Throne Judgment; none will be exempted):* **and they were Judged every man according to their works** *(records the fact that this Judgment is not arbitrary, but is based on absolute Justice).*

14 And death and Hell were cast into the Lake of Fire *(combined, includes the wicked of all ages).* **This is the second death** *(Eternal separation from God and the Lake of Fire).*

15 And whosoever was not found written in the Book of Life *(refers to the record of all the Redeemed)* **was cast into the Lake of Fire.** *(This includes every single individual who isn't Redeemed, beginning with Adam and Eve. That is, if they didn't come back to God.)*

CHAPTER 21
(A.D. 96)
NEW HEAVEN AND NEW EARTH

AND I saw a New Heaven and a New Earth *("New" in the Greek is "kainos," and means "freshness with respect to age"; when it is finished, it will be new, as is obvious, but the idea is it will remain new and fresh forever and forever because there is no more sin):* **for the first Heaven and the first Earth were passed away** *(refers to the original Creation, which was marred by sin; "passed away" in the Greek is "parerchomai," and means "to pass from one condition to another"; it never means annihilation);* **and there was no more sea** *(refers to the giant oceans, such as the Pacific and the Atlantic; however, there will continue to be lakes, bodies of water, rivers, streams, etc.).*

2 And I John saw the Holy City, New Jerusalem *(presents a New City for this New Earth),* **coming down from God out of Heaven** *(in effect, God will change His Headquarters from Heaven to Earth),* **prepared as a bride adorned for her husband** *(proclaims the Eternal Home of the Redeemed as a dwelling place).*

3 And I heard a great Voice out of Heaven saying *(according to the best manuscripts, the Voice now heard was heard "out of the Throne"),* **Behold, the Tabernacle of God** *is* **with men, and He will dwell with them, and they shall be His people, and God Himself shall be with them,** *and be* **their God.** *(Finally proclaims that which God intended from the beginning.)*

4 And God shall wipe away all tears from their eyes *(actually says in the Greek, "every teardrop," and refers to tears of sorrow);* **and there shall be no more death, neither sorrow, nor crying, neither shall there be any more pain** *(addresses sin and all its results):* **for the former things are passed away** *(refers to the entire effect of the Fall).*

5 And He Who sat upon the Throne said *(presents, for the second time in this Book, God Himself as the Speaker),* **Behold, I make all things new** *(refers to the fact of changing from one condition to another).* **And he said unto me, Write: for these words are true and faithful.** *(All said is "true," and God will be "faithful" to bring it all to pass as well.)*

6 And He said unto me, It is done. I am Alpha and Omega, the beginning and the end. *(The mighty declaration "Finished" heard at the morning of Creation, at Calvary, and now repeated here for the last time, closes all Prophecy.*

What He began, He now finishes.) **I will give unto him who is athirst of the fountain of the Water of Life freely.** *(This statement doesn't pertain to the coming Perfect Age, for all then will have the Water of Life, but rather to the present. This "fountain of the Water of Life" is tied directly to the Cross of Calvary in that it is free to all who will believe [Jn. 3:16].)*

7 He who overcomes shall inherit all things *(the only way one can overcome is to place one's Faith exclusively in the Cross of Christ, which gives the Holy Spirit latitude to work in one's life, bringing about the Fruit of the Spirit);* **and I will be his God, and he shall be My son.** *(The overcomer is adopted into the Family of God and God treats him as a son, exactly as He does His Son, the Lord Jesus Christ.)*

8 But the fearful, and unbelieving, and the abominable, and murderers, and whoremongers, and sorcerers, and idolaters, and all liars *(all of this corresponds with the "works of the flesh," as outlined in Gal. 5:19-21),* **shall have their part in the lake which burns with fire and brimstone: which is the second death** *(proclaims the Eternal destiny of Christ-rejecters).*

NEW JERUSALEM

9 And there came unto me one of the seven Angels which had the seven Vials full of the seven last plagues, and talked with me, saying, Come hither, I will show you the bride, the Lamb's wife. *(By use of the word "Lamb," we are taken back to the Cross, which has made all of this possible.)*

10 And he carried me away in the Spirit to a great and high mountain *(the "Spirit" referred to here is the Holy Spirit),* **and showed me that great city, the Holy Jerusalem, descending out of Heaven from God** *(John saw it "descending," meaning that it is coming down to Earth; this will be after the Lord has made the "New Heavens and New Earth," in fact when God changes His Headquarters from Heaven to Earth),*

11 Having the Glory of God *(this is what makes the city what it is):* **and her light *was* like unto a stone most precious, even like a jasper stone, clear as crystal** *(presents the radiance of God's Glory);*

THE HOLY CITY

12 And had a wall great and high *(this wall is 216 feet high, counting 18 inches to the cubit;* *it is decorative only),* ***and* had twelve gates** *(signifies three gates on the North, three on the South, three on the East, and three on the West; the gates on each side will be about 375 miles apart from each other),* **and at the gates twelve Angels** *(proclaims the Glory of the City, and as well the Glory of God's Government),* **and names written thereon, which are *the names* of the Twelve Tribes of the Children of Israel** *(proclaims the fact that "the Lamb's wife" is made up of every single Believer, whether on this side or the other side of the Cross; every gate will have the name of one of the Twelve Tribes; as well, this tells us how precious Israel is to the Heart of God):*

13 On the east three gates *(will probably have the names Joseph, Benjamin, and Dan);* **on the north three gates** *(will probably have the names Reuben, Judah, and Levi);* **on the south three gates** *(will probably have the names Simeon, Issachar, and Zebulun);* **and on the west three gates** *(will probably have the names Gad, Asher, and Naphtli).*

14 And the wall of the city had twelve foundations *(the way of Salvation was shown to the Jews, hence, the gates and the names of the Twelve Tribes inscribed on those gates; however, the foundation of Salvation was not really given until after the Cross, because it could not be given until after the Cross),* **and in them the names of the twelve Apostles of the Lamb.** *(On each foundation is the name of one of the Twelve Apostles. The foundation of the Salvation Message is based 100% on Christ and the Cross, hence, the word "Lamb" being used.)*

15 And he who talked with me *(this is not the Angel who talked with John in Verse 9; the one now speaking identifies himself as a Prophet [Rev. 22:9])* **had a golden reed to measure the city, and the gates thereof, and the wall thereof.** *(The measuring is done for a reason. It reveals the perfection, fulfillment, and completion of all God's Purposes for His Redeemed People.)*

MEASUREMENTS

16 And the city lies foursquare, and the length is as large as the breadth: and he measured the city with the reed, twelve thousand furlongs *(translates into about 1,500 miles per side).* **The length and the breadth and the height of it are equal.** *(This presents astounding dimensions. It is about half the size of the United States, regarding length and breadth. If that is*

not enough to take one's breath away, it will also be 1,500 miles tall. The mind cannot comprehend this, but Faith believes.)

17 And he measured the wall thereof, an hundred *and* forty *and* four cubits (*translates into about 216 feet, that is if we are using 18 inches to the cubit; as stated, the wall is strictly for ornamentation*), *according to* the measure of a man, that is, of the Angel. (*The designation of "Angel" is sometimes given to men, God, and the Creatures we refer to as Angels. This man, as Rev. 22:9 proclaims, is a Prophet.*)

18 And the building of the wall of it was *of* jasper (*presents a precious stone of several colors*): and the city *was* pure gold, like unto clear glass (*takes us beyond the imagination, beyond comprehension! but yet, this is literal*).

19 And the foundations of the wall of the city *were* garnished with all manner of precious stones (*describes beauty upon beauty*). The first foundation was jasper; the second, sapphire; the third, a chalcedony; the fourth, an emerald;

20 The fifth, sardonyx; the sixth, sardius; the seventh, chrysolyte; the eighth, beryl; the ninth, a topaz; the tenth, a chrysoprasus; the eleventh, a jacinth; the twelfth, an amethyst. (*The flooding of color in that incomparable City is beyond imagination. All of these stones named here are exquisite in color.*)

21 And the twelve gates *were* twelve pearls (*probably means each gate, which is about 216 feet tall, is made of untold thousands of pearls*); every several gate was of one pearl (*seems to indicate that this particular gate, which is probably every third or fourth one, is made out of one gigantic pearl*): and the street of the city *was* pure gold, as it were transparent glass (*refers to the fact that not only are all the buildings of "pure gold," [Rev. 21:18], but even the streets are made of pure gold*).

THE LIGHT

22 And I saw no Temple therein (*refers to a Temple such as in Old Testament times; actually there is a literal Temple in the New Jerusalem, but it will not serve the same purpose as the Temple on Earth [Rev. 3:12; 7:15; 11:19; 14:15, 17; 15:1-8; 16:1,17]*): for the Lord God Almighty and the Lamb are the Temple of it. (*Before the Cross, a Temple on Earth was necessary because God could not dwell with man at that time, at least directly. Since the Cross, the Holy Spirit can dwell within man, because*

the terrible sin debt has been paid [Jn. 14:17; I Cor. 3:16].)

23 And the city had no need of the sun, neither of the moon, to shine in it (*proclaims the fact that the Creator is not in need of His Creation; God has need of nothing, but all have need of God*): for the Glory of God did lighten it, and the Lamb *is* the Light thereof. (*The word "Lamb" signifies that all of this is made possible for Believers as a result of what Christ did at the Cross.*)

24 And the nations of them which are saved shall walk in the light of it (*should have been translated, "and the nations shall walk by means of its light"; the words "of them which are saved" are not actually in the best manuscripts; in fact, there will be no one in the world in that day who isn't saved*): and the kings of the Earth do bring their glory and honour into it. (*This refers to leaders of nations, whatever they might be called at that particular time. All will give Glory to God, and all will Honor the Lord, and do so forever.*)

25 And the gates of it shall not be shut at all by day (*in fact, they will never be shut*): for there shall be no night there. (*This speaks of the City only, for outside the City there will be day and night eternally [Gen. 1:14-18; 8:22; Ps. 89:2-3; Jer. 31:35-36].*)

26 And they shall bring the glory and honour of the nations into it (*proclaims a Righteous commerce, and in every capacity*).

27 And there shall in no wise enter into it any thing that defiles, neither *whatsoever* works abomination, or *makes* a lie (*this means that all sin is forever banished, and will never return*): but they which are written in the Lamb's Book of Life (*refers to the Book of the Redeemed; the word "Lamb" refers to the fact that all are saved by placing their Faith and Trust in Christ and what He did for us at the Cross*).

CHAPTER 22
(A.D. 96)

THE NEW JERUSALEM

AND he showed me a pure river of Water of Life, clear as crystal (*symbolic of the Holy Spirit [Jn. 7:37-39]*), proceeding out of the Throne of God and of the Lamb. (*This "Water of Life" is made possible by what Jesus did at the Cross, hence, the word "Lamb."*)

2 In the midst of the street of it (*proclaims the fact that this "pure River of Water of Life, clear as crystal" flows in the middle of this street*

of pure gold), **and on either side of the river, *was there* the Tree of Life** *(the fruit of this Tree of Life must be eaten every month, and we're speaking of the part of the population who don't have glorified bodies)*, **which bear twelve *manner of* fruits, *and* yielded her fruit every month** *(we have the number "12" again, which signifies the Government of God as it relates to the manner of Eternal Life; there are twelve different types of fruit, but we aren't told what they are)*: **and the leaves of the tree *were* for the healing of the nations.** *(This pertains to the stopping of any type of sickness before it even begins. As stated, the population on Earth, which will never die and will not have Glorified Bodies, will need these things. These are they who were saved during the Kingdom Age, and thereafter.)*

RULERS

3 And there shall be no more curse *(a curse was placed on the Earth at the Fall; it is being said here that there will be no more curse because there will be no more sin)*: **but the Throne of God and of the Lamb shall be in it** *(the authority of rulership will be as great with God the Son as it is with God the Father; in fact, by the use of the word "Lamb," we are made to realize that all of this is made possible because of what Jesus did at the Cross)*; **and His servants shall serve Him** *(the idea is that every Believer in the Perfect Age will so love the Lord and the Lamb that they will gladly "serve Him")*:

4 And they shall see His face *(shows intimate relationship)*; **and His Name *shall be* in their foreheads** *(refers to ownership; we were bought "with a price," and that price was the Blood of the Lamb)*.

5 And there shall be no night there *(this speaks of the New Jerusalem only, for night and day will be in the balance of the Earth forever)*; **and they need no candle, neither light of the sun; for the Lord God gives them light** *(presents the Source of this Light)*: **and they shall reign forever and ever.** *(It has never been known for servants to "reign" like kings; however, these servants shall!)*

ALPHA AND OMEGA

6 And he said unto me, These sayings *are* faithful and true *(proclaimed in this fashion simply because many of the statements made are so absolutely astounding they defy description)*:

and the Lord God of the Holy Prophets sent his Angel to show unto His servants *(the Greek word "Aggelos" is translated "Angel" here, but should have been translated "Messenger"; we know this man is not an Angel, nor is he Christ)* **the things which must shortly be done** *(is not speaking of John's day, but rather the setting of the Vision is a time frame which has not come about even yet; it will take place immediately after the Rapture of the Church; from that point forward, which is what is meant here, we have "the things which must shortly be done," referring to the Great Tribulation)*.

7 Behold, I come quickly *(has more to do with the manner of His Coming than anything else; when He does come, which will be at the height of the Battle of Armageddon, it will be sudden, even immediate)*: **blessed *is* he who keeps the sayings of the Prophecy of this Book.** *(This is the only Book in the world that gives a preview of the future. Consequently, every Believer ought to study the Book of Revelation as much as they do any other Book in the entire Bible.)*

8 And I John saw these things, and heard *them* *(presents an impeccable witness)*. **And when I had heard and seen, I fell down to worship before the feet of the Angel which showed me these things.** *(John, it seems, will make the same mistake twice.)*

9 Then says he unto me, See *you do it* not *(presents the same words used by the previous man when John did the same thing [Rev. 19:10]*: **for I am your fellowservant, and of your Brethren the Prophets, and of them which keep the sayings of this Book.** *(He evidently is one of the Great Prophets of the Old Testament, who eagerly awaits the fulfillment of these Prophecies as well)*: **worship God** *(includes both God the Father and God the Son.)*

10 And he said unto me, Seal not the sayings of the Prophecy of this Book *(refers to the fact that the things given in this Book are meant to be known and understood; they are not hidden truths)*: **for the time is at hand** *(speaks of the immediate fulfillment of the events, which were to happen in consecutive order from John's day to eternity; it began with the Church Age, which is now almost over; the Great Tribulation will follow, concluding with the Second Coming, which will usher in the Kingdom Age, followed by the Perfect Age)*.

11 He who is unjust, let him be unjust still: and he which is filthy, let him be filthy still *(proclaims the fact that men are building up*

their destiny by the actions and habits of their lives): **and he who is Righteous, let him be Righteous still: and he who is Holy, let him be Holy still.** (Records that which the Spirit of God can bring about in a person's life, irrespective that they have once been "unjust and morally filthy." This is all done through the Cross, and only through the Cross.)

12 And, behold, I come quickly (is not meant to portray the "time" of His Coming, but rather the suddenness of His Coming; the idea is that whatever we are at His Coming, whenever that Coming takes place, is what we will be forever); **and My reward is with Me** (the word "reward" can either be positive or negative), **to give every man according as his work shall be.** (Our Faith, however placed, will produce a certain type of works. Only Faith in the Cross is accepted.)

13 I am Alpha and Omega (presents the first letter in the Greek Alphabet [Alpha], and the last letter in the Greek Alphabet [Omega]; it is another way of saying, "the first and the last," which includes all in-between), **the beginning and the end, the first and the last.** (This doesn't mean Christ as God had a beginning, for He didn't. It is speaking of whatever is in question. Christ is the beginning of all things, and the end of all things.)

BLESSED

14 Blessed are they (presents the seventh and last Beatitude in the Book of Revelation) **who do His Commandments** (should have been translated, "who washed their robes in the Blood of the Lamb"; the Greek Text used for the King James Version of the Bible was the Textus Receptus; it is the Text that Erasmus, the famous Renaissance scholar, published in A.D. 1516; it was the first New Testament Greek Text ever published; since 1516, the world of scholarship and Archaeology has discovered thousands of earlier Greek Texts; by comparing these thousands of Manuscripts, the scholars can easily ascertain the original Text the Apostle wrote), **that they may have the right to the Tree of Life** (proclaims the fact that this "right" can be attained in only one way, "by washing our robes in the Blood of the Lamb"), **and may enter in through the gates into the city** (proclaims the Eternal abode of the Redeemed; we shall enter that city by means of His Grace, which is the Cross of Christ).

15 For without are dogs (homosexuals), **and sorcerers** (witchcraft), **and whoremongers** (pertains to all type of immorality), **and murderers** (pertains not only to killing in cold blood, but as well murdering one's reputation through gossip), **and idolaters** (pertains to placing anything above God, or on a par with God; religion is the greatest idolatry of all), **and whosoever loves and makes a lie** (refers to anything that's untrue).

16 I Jesus (this short phrase is found only here in Scripture, emphasizing its importance; Christ is closing out the Book of Revelation here, but most of all, He is testifying to the Truth of what has been given) **have sent My Angel to testify unto you these things in the Churches.** (The word "Angel" here means "Messenger," and actually refers to the Pastors of the respective Churches in question, and actually for all time.) **I am the Root and the Offspring of David** (is meant to project the Incarnation of Christ), **and the Bright and Morning Star.** (The "Morning Star" speaks of a new beginning that any person can have, irrespective of their present situation, if they will only look to Christ.)

INVITATION

17 And the Spirit and the Bride say, Come. (This presents the cry of the Holy Spirit to a hurting, lost, and dying world. What the Holy Spirit says should also be said by all Believers.) **And let him who hears say, Come.** (It means if one can "hear," then one can "come.") **And let him who is athirst come** (speaks of spiritual thirst, the cry for God in the soul of man). **And whosoever will, let him take the Water of Life freely** (opens the door to every single individual in the world; Jesus died for all and, therefore, all can be saved, if they will only come).

18 For I testify unto every man who hears the words of the Prophecy of this Book (proclaims the inerrancy of the Book of Revelation; in other words, John testifies that it is the Word of God), **If any man shall add unto these things, God shall add unto him the plagues that are written in this Book** (proclaims the fact that changing the meaning of the Prophecies in this Book can bring upon one the Judgment of God):

19 And if any man shall take away from the words of the Book of this Prophecy (the idea is that the "words of the Prophecy" should not be changed in any manner, whether by addition or deletion), **God shall take away his part out of the Book of Life, and out of the Holy City, and from the things which are written in**

this Book. *(This is a warning given to Believers, and should be understood accordingly!)*

20 He which testifies these things *(proclaims the fact that the Office of the Messiah as Saviour is repeated again and again throughout the Prophecy; He is the Lamb Who was slain, and His Blood washes from sin, and Alone makes fit for entrance into the Eternal City)* **says, Surely I come quickly** *(leaves the Promise to come as the last Message from the Lord Jesus to the Believers' hearts; and on this sweet note, the Prophecy ends)*. **Amen. Even so, come, Lord Jesus** *(proclaims the answer of the True Church to the Promise of Christ regarding the Second Coming)*.

21 The Grace of our Lord Jesus Christ *(presents John using the very words of Paul in his closing benediction; Christ is the Source, but the Cross is the means)* **be with you all. Amen.** *(This proclaims the fact that it is the same Message for all, and is available to all. The word "Amen" closes out the Book of Revelation, and, in fact, the entire Canon of Scripture, which took about 1,600 years to bring forth in its entirety. It gives acclaim to the Finished Work of Christ. It is done. And, thereby, all of Heaven, along with all the Redeemed, must say: "Amen.")*

INTRODUCING THE BIBLE
Huber L. Drumwright

The term *"Bible"* was not used to designate the Holy Scriptures until the time of the Early Church Fathers about A.D. 400. These Latin Scholars borrowed the word from the plural Greek word, *biblia*, meaning *"rolls"* or *"scrolls."* In the singular, the word *biblion*, or *biblos*, referred to the papyrus plant from which the principal writing material used by the Greeks was made. When some 20 or more papyrus sheets were glued together, producing a scroll about 25 to 35 feet in length, this too was called a *biblion*, often translated as *"book"* (*see* Rev. 22:18-19). In Luke 4:17, 20 the roll (*biblion*) of Isaiah is mentioned, and John's Gospel is referred to as a *biblion* in John 20:30. In II Timothy 4:13 the word *biblia* appears and probably refers to a group of papyrus rolls. Thus the term *"Bible"* comes technically to mean *"Book of Books,"* or an especially important (or authoritative) collection of books.

During the 1,200 or more years when its materials were being written, the Bible did not circulate as a single book. It was not until the 4th century A.D. that all of its units were copied together in a single *"codex,"* or volume. Although no term that appears in the Bible itself refers to that volume as it is known today, several terms are used in the Scriptures to designate various portions of the modern Bible. *"The Law"* (Josh. 8:34; Neh. 3:2; Lk. 10:26); *"the Book of the Law"* (Josh. 8:34); *"the Law of the Lord"* (Lk. 2:23); *"the Law of Moses"* (Josh. 8:31-32; Neh. 8:1; Lk. 24:44); *"the Scriptures"* (Mat. 21:42; Mk. 12:24; Jn. 5:39); *"the Holy Scriptures"* (Rom. 1:2); *"the Book of the Covenant"* (Ex. 24:7) are among the terms used for various portions of the Bible.

THE LANGUAGES OF THE BIBLE

The Old Testament was written in Hebrew, a Semitic language adapted from the ancient Canaanites and Phoenicians, as recent discoveries at Ras Shamra on the coast of Syria have made abundantly clear. There are also certain affinities with the other Semitic languages of ancient Syria, Assyria, Babylonia, and Arabia.

During the long periods of its growth, the Old Testament reflected a number of developments and semantic changes of its language, as scholars have come to understand. In addition, dialect differences between the north and south of Palestine have been noted.

A few portions of certain books of the Old Testament and some words and phrases of the New Testament are recorded in the Aramaic language. The ancient Aramaeans inhabited particularly the region of Syria, but their language, with its simplified script, was gradually adopted in everyday life all across the Near East. By the 5th century B.C. it was the *lingua franca* of the ancient world and therefore used by the Jews. In fact, when the Law was read in the synagogues by the time of Ezra, it was necessary to translate it into Aramaic so that the people might understand (Neh. 8:7-8). The following portions of the Old Testament were composed in Aramaic: Ezra 4:8-6:18; 7:12-26; Jeremiah 10:11; Daniel 2:4-7:28.

Because Aramaic was the language Jesus spoke, traces of Aramaic remain in the New Testament: *Talitha Cumi*, *"maiden, arise"* (Mk. 5:41) and *Eloi, Eloi, lama sabachthani*, *"My God, My God, why have You forsaken Me?"* (Mk. 15:34). Paul uses *"Abba, father"* (Rom. 8:15), and *Maranatha*, *"Our Lord comes"* (I Cor. 16:22). Although the point has been much debated, it is almost certain that all the New Testament books were written in Greek. Essentially, the thought life of the Mediterranean world was Graeco-Oriental by the 1st century A.D., which saw the writing of the New Testament. Rome ruled the world; yet Paul wrote to Rome in Greek, not Latin. The Greek used in the New Testament, however, was the everyday language, called *koiné*, which means *"common."* It had descended from the language used by Alexander the Great and his armies at the time of their conquests more than two centuries earlier. It might be called *"post-classic"* Greek. New Testament Greek is not uniform throughout, for it varies from the semi-literary style of Luke, which approximates the classical, to the nonliterary style of the Gospel of Mark and Revelation.

DIVISIONS OF THE BIBLE

THE OLD TESTAMENT

The Old Testament, or *"Old Covenant,"* centers around the covenant made at Sinai in the time of Moses. It is divided into three main canonical units, the Law, the Prophets, and the Writings.

The Law, or Torah. The Law has traditionally been known as the Law of Moses, although scholars debate the extent to which the tradition of the Law goes back to Moses himself. There is no doubt, however, that from the time of the discovery of the Book of Deuteronomy in 621 B.C., the Law was the mainspring of Jewish religious life. Deuteronomy became the law of the land. During the Exile, Jews turned to the Law for study and strength, and thus the Synagogue was born. By the time of Ezra (450-400 B.C.), the Law had come into its full importance, with almost the exact structure and text that are known today. In Hebrew the Law was called *Torah*, meaning *"teachings"* or *"learning,"* but in Greek its five books were called *Pentateuch*, meaning *"five vessels,"* (i.e., of the Word of God), for only these five books of the Law were ever acknowledged as authoritative. In the 3rd century B.C., the Greek-speaking Jews of Alexandria began to translate these books into Greek; their work later came to be known as the *Septuagint,"* sometime written *"LXX."*

The Prophets, or Nebi'im. The work of the writing prophets covered four centuries — Amos, Hosea, Micah, and Isaiah in the 8th century B.C.; Zephaniah, Nahum, Habakkuk, and Jeremiah in the 7th century B.C.; Ezekiel, Haggai, and Zechariah in the 6th century B.C.; and Malachi, Obadiah, and Joel in the 5th century B.C. The date of Johan, which completes the list of 15 prophetic writings, is widely disputed. The Jews came to consider the historical books of Joshua, Judges, Samuel, and Kings as prophetic in purpose and thus put them into a group designated as the *"Former Prophets."* The *"Latter Prophets"* (or *"Writing Prophets"*), the second part of the prophetic collection, then contained Isaiah, Jeremiah, Ezekiel, and the *"Book of the Twelve,"* consisting of the Minor Prophets from Hosea to Malachi. By the end of the 3rd century B.C., these writings had been organized and copied in the form of the eight scrolls, four for the Former Prophets and four for the Latter Prophets, and had become recognized as standing with the Law in religious authority.

The Writings, or Kethubim. It was not until the close of the first Christian century, at the Rabbinical Council of Jamnia (about A.D. 90), that the rest of the Old Testament was finally fixed and declared authoritative. The Book of Psalms was the central feature in this collection of practical and devotional material, which contains wisdom, ethics, liturgy, history, and even wedding songs. The poetic works in this group include Psalms, Job, Proverbs, Lamentations, and the Song of Solomon. Those dealing with Jewish history are Ruth, Esther, Ezra, Nehemiah, and Chronicles, while Daniel is apocalyptic (a special type of Jewish literature) and Ecclesiastes a philosophical book. Ecclesiastes and Esther were less widely accepted, and doubts about their authority continued until the Council of Jamnia.

The third division of the Hebrew Bible, therefore, contained 11 scrolls: the 3 large poetic works, Psalms, Proverbs, and Job; the 5 Megilloth (scrolls used on special festival occasions), the Song of Solomon, Ruth, Lamentations, Ecclesiastes, and Esther; the apocalyptic Book of Daniel; and 3 books of history, Ezra-Nehemiah (in one scroll) and Chronicles (in one scroll). Thus the Hebrew Bible consisted of 5 scrolls of Law, 8 scrolls of the Prophets, and 11 scrolls of the Writings when it reached its final canonization at Jamnia. It is in this form and order (with some slight variation) that modern Hebrew study Bibles are printed.

The Apocrypha. During the last two centuries before Christ and the first Christian century, a number of Jewish writings had appeared but failed to gain acceptance at the Council of Jamnia. These books are now called *"Apocrypha"*; the word is from a Greek term meaning *"hidden"* or *"secret."* Originally its use suggested that the books so designated contained esoteric truth to be communicated only to the initiated, being hidden from the outside world. It was the great Latin scholar Jerome who, in the 5th century A.D., first applied the term to these books.

Some of these documents were expansions of Old Testament books, especially Esther and Daniel. Some, such as Ecclesiasticus and the Wisdom of Solomon, are of the nature of wisdom literature. Jewish fiction, as exemplified in the books of Tobit and Judith, is also included. First Esdras is little more than a combination of parts of Chronicles, Ezra, and

Nehemiah. Two important historical books are those of I and II Maccabees, and the group also includes the important apocalypse known as II Esdras.

The Apocrypha was included in the Canon of the Septuagint, the translation of the Old Testament made for the Greek-speaking Jews of Alexandria, which became the Bible of the Early Church; these books appear also in the Old Latin Bible, as well as in the Latin Vulgate, Jerome's revision. They were carried over into the early German translation of the Latin Bible made in the 14th century, well as into the English translation made by Wyclif (Wycliffe) in the same century. Both the Greek and the Roman Church have always recognized the Apocrypha as canonical. The exclusion of these books from the Bible came as a result of the Reformation. When Luther translated the Old Testament from the Hebrew, these books were of course, absent; but, recognizing their presence in the Latin Bible, Luther translated them and put them in a group by themselves, between the Testaments. There they remained in most Protestant Bibles until the 19th century, when publishers, led by the British and Foreign Bible Society, voluntarily began to omit them.

The length of the Apocrypha in comparison with the Old Testament and New Testament may be seen from these figures (based on the King James Version):

	Chapters	Verses	Words
Old Testament	929	23,214	592,439
New Testament	260	7,959	181,253
Apocrypha	183	6,081	152,185

THE NEW TESTAMENT

The title *"New Testament"* or *"New Covenant,"* probably originated with Paul's delineation of the two covenants of history in II Corinthians 3:6-16. Probably Jeremiah's famous words in 31:31-34 were associated in Paul's mind as he wrote.

The Gospels. Although the Gospels stand first in the New Testament, they are of later date than many other books found there. When the New Testament was collected, however, it was only natural that the place of priority be given to the four accounts of Jesus' ministry: Matthew, Mark, Luke, and John (although this order was not always followed in early collections). The Evangelists had the Old Testament

biographies of Joseph, David, Elijah, Moses, and others before them as examples (Luke seems especially to have been so influenced); they also were aware of the practice of the Greeks, for the art of biography was by no means a new one. Yet the Gospels were a new literary form in many respects, standing by themselves as evangelical documents to proclaim the *"good news"* (the meaning of *"gospel"*) of God's redemptive action in the life, teachings, death, and resurrection of Jesus of Nazareth. Matthew, Mark, and Luke are called the *Synoptic Gospels"* because they are so closely related and share a common point of view. John's Gospel in many ways preserved an independent tradition and is, by far, the most interpretative of these books.

The Acts. The Book of Acts is described as history, but it is far more. Its primary message is the story of Christianity's spread throughout the civilized world. It is history seen from the evangelistic and missionary viewpoint, centering in the life and activity of the Apostles who established the early churches.

The Epistles. The majority of the books in the New Testament might be classified as correspondence. Letter writing was a common means of communication in the first Christian century, as archaeological discoveries have abundantly revealed, and the Early Church was no exception. Paul was the most prolific writer of those who contributed to the New Testament, and much of his contribution is typical of personal correspondence of that age. Among the writings traditionally ascribed to him are Romans, I and II Corinthians, Galatians, Ephesians, Philippians, Colossians, I and II Thessalonians, I and II Timothy, Titus, Philemon, and Hebrews. Modern scholarship has questioned the Pauline authorship of several of these letters, especially I and II Timothy and Titus, which are often called the Pastoral Epistles because they deal mostly with the administration of the organized Church. Hebrews, which is not in letter form and does not name its author, has from early times been questioned because of its distinctly non-Pauline nature. A few late manuscripts ascribe Hebrews to Timothy, but its author is unknown. Usually Philippians, Ephesians, Colossians, and Philemon are called the *"imprisonment letters,"* since their contents imply that the author was writing from prison.

Another group of letters in the New Testament is referred to as the *"Catholic"* or *"General"*

Epistles. The term *"Catholic,"* meaning *"universal,"* designates those letters that are addressed to larger and more inclusive groups, in contrast to the local church or individuals addressed in the Pauline letters. James, I and II Peter, and Jude are so designated. Some scholars include the Johannine letters with the *"General Epistles,"* while others consider them a third group. First John lacks the salutation and epistolary ending characteristic of letters. Traditionally the Johannine letters have been credited to the Apostle John, although in the 20th century some debate has centered on this assumption.

The letters of the New Testament tell of many of the churches founded by Paul and reveal even intimate and personal details of the author's relation to various congregations and persons. More important, however, these letters by Paul and others give additional insight into the content of the Christian message and its application to life situations. In fact, some of these letters resemble theological treatises or sermons more than personal letters (Romans, Ephesians, Hebrews, I John), while others are essentially practical in their applications to life (I Corinthians, Philemon, James).

The Revelation. The last book of the Bible is the only one of its literary type in the New Testament, though it has affinity with some of the Old Testament books, especially Daniel. The Revelation is an apocalypse (from a Greek word meaning *"revelation"*), telling its message by use of signs, symbols, and visions of cosmic drama. Coming out of the suffering and persecution of the Early Church, it is an unveiling of the Christian hope and confidence in the ultimate triumph of God and the vindication of His people.

ARRANGEMENT OF THE BIBLE

The major division of the Bible into *"Old"* and *"New"* Testaments reflects the distinctive Christian evaluation of this material. In the dark and dangerous days of the Exile (early 6th century B.C.), Jeremiah wrote of a *"New Covenant,"* which was to be something better than an outward reorganization of religion. The Covenant under Moses, which represented Israel's essential tie and relationship to God, was to be made new. Man, himself, would be made new (Jer. 31:31-34). In the Epistle to the Hebrews the author makes a play on the double meaning of the Greek word *diatheke,* meaning either *"covenant"* or *"will."* He finds it to be not only the equivalent of *"covenant"* in the Old Testament sense of the Hebrew word *berith,* but also of the Greek sense of *"will."* (Latin *testamentum*), which does not come into force until the testator has died (Heb. 9:15-17). The death of Christ has inaugurated the New Covenant, making the former covenant old (Heb. 8:7-9:22). Thus, it would be more accurate to speak of these divisions as Old and New Covenants.

In the Hebrew Bible, as we have seen, the books of the Law, (the Pentateuch) stand first, followed by Joshua, Judges, Samuel, and Kings. After Kings come the Prophets, both Major and Minor. The last of the Minor Prophets, Malachi, is followed by the poetical books: Psalms, Proverbs, and Job. There are followed by the five special festival scrolls, the Song of Solomon, Ruth, Lamentations, Ecclesiastes, and Esther. Then the apocalypse of Daniel, followed by Ezra, Nehemiah, and Chronicles, brings the Old Testament to a close. This order reflects the manner in which the Old Testament grew as a collection of books — first the Law, then the Prophets, and finally the Writings.

It was in the Greek translation of the Old Testament, the Septuagint, begun in Egypt in the 3rd century B.C., that the order of the books was altered. Since the Septuagint was the Bible of the early Christian Church, its order was followed. Thus most of the Writings interspersed with the Apocrypha appear between the Former and the Latter Prophets (that is, after II Kings).

The Latin manuscripts of the Old Testament follow a somewhat different order from the Greek and Hebrew. In fact, the Latin manuscripts often differ from one another in the order of the books. It was only with the invention of printing that the order in the Latin Bible known today became fixed. Since English translations of the Bible for Roman Catholics are based on the Latin, this accounts for their wide variation from Protestant Bibles.

In the New Testament the Gospels always stand first in the Greek manuscripts, but not always in the traditional order. The famous *Codex Bezae,* for instance, has Matthew, John, Luke, and Mark, as does the 5th-century Freer Gospel manuscript. The earliest complete manuscript of the Greek New Testament, the *Codex Sinaiticus,* had a quite different order of books. There the letters of Paul appear after the Gospels and before the Acts. Other old Greek manuscripts put the Catholic Epistles of

James, Peter, John, and Jude after the Acts.

Luther, in his German translation of 1522, made a bold rearrangement of the last books of the New Testament. Feeling that there was least about Christ in Hebrews, James, Jude and Revelation, he put these last in the New Testament. William Tyndale followed Luther in his first printed English New Testament (1526), as did the Coverdale Bible (1535) and the John Rogers Bible (1537).

Coverdale's Great Bible of 1539 departed from Luther's order and put Hebrews after the letters of Paul and made James the first of the Catholic Epistles. Coverdale also placed Jude at the end of the Catholic Epistles. The Geneva Bible (1560), the Bishops' Bible (1568), the King James Version (1611), and subsequent revisions have followed this order.

Chapter divisions in the Old Testament appeared first in some early editions of the Latin (Vulgate) Bible. These divisions are variously credited to Lanfranc, Archbishop of Canterbury (d. 1089), to Stephen Langton (d. 1228) and to Hugo de Sancto Caro in the 13th century. The Jews adopted chapter divisions for the Hebrew Bible in the 13th century, but verse numbers began with the Athias Hebrew Bible of 1559-61. The Geneva Bible (1560) first introduced verses in English. Chapter divisions in the New Testament are most usually credited to Stephen Langton, Archbishop of Canterbury, but the verses were introduced by the printer Robert Estienne (know as Stephanus), in his fourth edition of the Greek text of the New Testament (1551).

THE CANON OF THE BIBLE

At the end of the first Christian century, as we have seen, the Jewish rabbis, at the Council of Jamnia, closed the Canon of Hebrew books to be considered authoritative. The rabbis' decision resulted from: (1) the multiplication and popularity of sectarian apocalyptic writings; (2) the fall of Jerusalem (A.D. 70), which created a threat to the religious tradition of the Jews; and (3) the disputes with Christians over their interpretations of the Jewish Scriptures in preaching and writing. There was never any doubt about the five books of the Law (Pentateuch), but beyond that various sects of Judaism were in disagreement. The prophetic collection was generally agreed upon by 200 B.C., but the major problem was in the area of the other writings. Four

criteria operated in these decisions: (1) the content of the books in question must be in harmony with the Law; (2) since prophetic inspiration was believed to have begun with Moses and ended with Ezra, to qualify for the Canon a book must come within that period to be considered inspired: (3) the language of the original book had to be Hebrew; and (4) written within the geographical limits of Palestine. On this basis each of the 39 books of the Old Testament was selected for the Palestinian Canon of Scriptures. Failing these criteria, the rest of the ancient Jewish writings came to be classified as Apocrypha, or Pseudepigrapha (literally, *"false writings"*).

A number of Christian writings, other than those that came to be accepted for the New Testament, appeared early and were considered by some to be worthy of canonical status. First and Second Clement, the Didache, and Epistle of Barnabas, the Shepherd of Hermas, the Apocalypse of Peter, and the Acts of Paul were some of the more popular ones. By the beginning of the 3rd century, 22 of the writings of our present New Testament had been widely accepted. Four principles or considerations seem to have operated for determining the contents of the New Testament: (1) Was the book written by an Apostle — or by someone associated with an Apostle? (2) Were the contents of a spiritual nature? (3) Was the book widely received by the churches? (4) Was there evidence to the reader of divine inspiration in the book? As far as is known, it was the Easter letter of Archbishop Athanasius of Alexandria in A.D. 367 that first listed the 27 books of our New Testament as authoritative. Jerome, by his Latin translation of these same 27 books (A.D. 382) further established this list as canonical for the churches.

THE TEXT OF THE BIBLE

Centuries of hand copying subjected the text of the Old Testament to all the problems attendant upon the preservation of a correct text by such means. By the time of the Council of Jamnia there were so many variations among the manuscripts that to determine certainly the exact words of Scripture became a major problem. Under the leadership of Rabbi Akiba, therefore, the School of the Masoretes, preservers of the Masorah, or *"tradition,"* was established during the early 2nd century A.D. Between A.D. 600 and 900 this school of Jewish

scholars established what has come to be known as the standard Masoretic text. With the recent discovery of the Qumran library near the Dead Sea, new sources, which are a thousand years earlier than our oldest Masoretic texts, have become available for the study of the Old Testament.

For the New Testament, more than 4,000 Greek manuscripts, preserving all or part of the text, are known, the earliest sizable texts dating from about A.D. 200. There are some 8,000 manuscripts of the Latin Vulgate and at least 1,000 other versions into which the original books were translated. Since the original autograph of no book in the New Testament is known, it becomes the task of the textual expert to deal with the thousands of variant readings to be found in this multitude of ancient manuscripts. These manuscripts are compared and studied in order to establish a critical text that gives reasonable assurance of being as near the original as can be determined.

A CHRONOLOGY OF BIBLE TRANSLATION

The following chronology includes events of major importance in the long and dramatic story of Bible translation. The list is necessarily selective and places special emphasis on the background of the English Bible, providing information basic to further study of a fascinating field.

1500-500? B.C. — The Old Testament is put into writing.

250-100 B.C. — The Septuagint, a translation of the Old Testament into Greek, according to tradition, by 72 Hebrew scholars, is completed in Alexandria, Egypt. This version contains 45 books, the Alexandrian Canon, used by the Early Church, and continues to be the Old Testament Canon of the Latin and Greek Church.

A.D. 52?-100? — The New Testament is written, coming to us in *koiné* Greek, the common language of the time, although some portions may have been first set down in Aramaic, the language spoken by Christ.

A.D. 100? — Formulation of Palestinian Canon of Hebrew Bible at Synod of Jamnia.

350-400 — First stabilization of New Testament canon of 27 books.

About 400 — Jerome completes his final translation of the Bible, the Latin Vulgate, based on the Septuagint and translated from the Hebrew, and other ancient versions.

About 600 to 900 — The Masoretic text in Hebrew is developed by the Masoretes, a school of Jewish textual critics. The Masoretic text, used in the Jewish Bible, has been an important reference in preparing translations into other languages.

1382 — John Wycliffe completes his translation, the first complete Bible in English.

1456 — The Gutenberg Bible, a folio edition of the Latin Vulgate, is printed from movable type, an epochal event that inaugurated the era of printing.

1516 — Erasmus completes his translation in Greek.

1522 — Martin Luther translates the Bible into German.

1535 — William Tyndale issues his English translation, which powerfully influenced all of the English versions that followed.

1535 — Miles Coverdale issues his translation dedicated to King Henry VIII.

1537 — Coverdale's Bible becomes the first Bible to be printed in England.

1537 — Matthew's Bible is produced, based primarily on the Tyndale and Coverdale Bibles.

1539 — Coverdale issues the Great Bible, essentially a combination of his own earlier work and Tyndale's Bible. This work was authorized by Henry VIII.

1560 — The Geneva Bible, produced by Coverdale, William Whittingham, John Knox, and others in Geneva after Mary became queen. It is the first English Bible to divide the chapters into verses.

1582-1610 — Douay-Rheims (Catholic) Bible appears, a direct translation into English from the Vulgate by the Catholic College; the New Testament issued in 1582 at Rheims, the Old Testament in 1609-1610 at Douay, France.

1611 — The great King James (or Authorised) Version. Completed by the group of "learned men," all renowned scholars, appointed by King James.

1885 — The English Revised Version, Produced by a group of English Biblical scholars, with

contributions by a similar group of American scholars.

1901 — The American Standard Version issued by the American Committee that had worked on the English Revised Version.

1924 — The Moffatt Bible, a complete translation of the Bible into modern English by James Moffatt.

1931 — Smith-Goodspeed Bible, a modern speech translation combining the Old Testament prepared under the editorship of J. M. Powis Smith and the New Testament prepared by Edgar J. Goodspeed of the University of Chicago.

1941 — Confraternity Version. The New Testament revision was published under the sponsorship of the Episcopal Confraternity of Christian Doctrine. This edition represents a revision of the Douay-Rheims-Challoner Version based on the Latin Vulgate. Scholars are now at work on a complete translation of the Old Testament, part of which has already been published.

1945-1949 — Knox's Version. Complete Bible translated by Msgr. Ronald A. Knox based on Latin Vulgate. Authorized by Catholic hierarchy of England and Wales.

1952 — The Revised Standard Version. Produced by a group of American scholars sponsored by the National Council of Churches of Christ.

1961 — The New English Bible. A new translation by a group of British scholars appointed by a committee representing the Protestant Churches of Great Britain, and representatives of the Oxford and Cambridge University presses.

MONEY, WEIGHTS, AND MEASURES
E. Leslie Carlson

Coined money, apparently an invention of the Greeks, was unknown before 700 B.C., and none was used by the Hebrews until the post-Exilic Period when they began to make widespread use of this practice which they had learned in the Babylonian Exile (Ezra 2:69; Haggai 1:6). Prior to this time trading was done by the bartering of animals and agricultural products and by the exchange of metals. Often these practices existed side-by-side just as they do in some parts of the world today. The earliest mention of a sale of property in the Bible is Abraham's purchase of a burial cave at Machpelah for which he weighed four hundred shekels of silver as payment (Gen. 23:16). It is to be noted that his wealth consisted of cattle, gold, and silver (Gen. 12:5).

When trade moved beyond the stage of animal and agricultural barter it was necessary to develop a standard system of weights and measures. This process had begun long before the appearance of the Hebrews in Palestine. It was difficult to achieve an agreed-upon standard since a change of government almost invariably meant a change in standards. But the attempt was made, and it is known, for example, that the Assyrians and the Babylonians had a standard system of weights in the form of bulls, ducks and lions, each inscribed with the royal seal and the officially determined weight.

It is generally conceded that the Biblical system is based upon methods from the Mesopotamian Valley, and that there is little Egyptian influence. A possible exception may be that the Egyptians influenced the Hebrews in their use of the decimal system since a decimal system is found mixed with the sexagesimal system which was used in Mesopotamia.

Archaeology has helped in the discovery of new weights, such as "pim" (Heb., "pym"), which was mistranslated as "file" in I Samuel 13:21. Four "pim" weights used as money were discovered at Lachish, but of diverse weights, showing that no exact standard had been adopted. These, with other weights that were found, dated from about 800 B.C. As early as 2900 B.C. Egypt had developed standards of length, weight, and capacity.

MONEY

Assarion. A small copper or bronze Greek coin worth about one cent. Translated "farthing" in K.J.V. (Mat. 10:29; Lk. 12:6).

Bekah. A Hebrew weight equivalent to 1/2 shekel or 0.20 grams (Ex. 38:26).

Brass. Roman or Greek copper coin valued at about 1/2 cent (Mat. 10:9; Mk. 6:8)

Denarius. A Roman coin equivalent to the Hebrew shekel in weight, but its value as money varied. Equivalent of a day's wages and therefore of a higher value than its weight. It was much more than the penny used in K.J.V. It was worth less in the 2nd century A.D. (Mat. 20:2-13; Lk. 10:35; Jn. 6:5-13; 12:5).

Drachma. A Greek silver coin used in the Hellenistic world after 330 B.C. and about the value of the Hebrew shekel.

Didrachma. The temple tax paid by the Hebrews (Mat. 17:24) or used to pay an imposed fine (Ezra 6:8; Neh. 5:4). Equivalent to the Hebrew half shekel.

Dram or **Daric.** Persian gold coin used among the Jews after their return from the Babylonian exile. It weighed 128.4 grams and its value was about $5.30 (Ezra 2:69; I Chron. 29:7; Neh. 7:70).

Farthing. A small bronze coin, worth about 1/4 cent in Christ's day (Mat. 10:29; Mk. 12:42; Lk. 12:6).

Mite or **Lepton.** Smallest bronze coin used in Christ's time and worth about 1/8 of cent. Equivalent to a half farthing (Lk. 12:59; 21:2).

Gerah. The smallest weight, 1/20 of a shekel. (See Weights.) Used as money but not as a coin. Its value depended upon what was being weighed. Usually worth about three cents (Lev. 27:25; Num. 3:47; Ezek. 45:12).

Penny. Equivalent to the Roman silver denarius. It is the translation of denarius in K.J.V. (See Denarius.)

Piece of Gold. The equivalent to the gold shekel. Its value depended upon the content

of gold (II Ki. 5:5). (See Weights.)

Piece of Silver. Equivalent of the silver shekel. Its value depended upon its weight (Ex. 21:32; Hos. 3:2). (See Weights.)

Pound or **Maneh (mina).** Equal to 100 silver drachma. Its value was about $17.00 (Lk. 19:13-25).

Shekel. A Hebrew weight and used as such until coinage was adopted about 400 B.C. The gold shekel was valued at $5.50, and the silver shekel at about 75 cents (Mat. 17:27).

Silverling. A piece of silver mentioned only once (Isa. 7:23; K.J.V., R.S.V.)

Talent. Largest weight used for metals by the Hebrews. Gold weighing a talent was valued at $30,000 and that of silver at $2,000 (II Ki. 23:33). In the New Testament period when used as coins, silver talents were valued at $560.00 (Mat. 25:14-30).

Tribute Money. A Jewish coin equivalent to a 1/2 shekel, valued at about 37 cents and used to pay the temple tax.

WEIGHT MEASURES

Since coins were not used by the Hebrews until after their return from the Babylonian exile, buying and selling were done by bartering or weighing out metals such as gold or iron. Even stones were sometimes used. The basic weight was the:

Shekel. (Heb., "to weight out") Jer. 32:6-12. This weight was used from the Exodus period. Before this it is evident that Egyptian weights were used. There were three standards of the shekel: (1) The temple shekel of 10 grams (approx. 0.35 ounce); (2) the common or commercial shekel of about 11 1/2 grams (approx. 0.40 ounce); (3) the heavy shekel of about 13 grams (approx. 0.45 ounce), (Gen. 23:16; II Sam. 14:26; II Ki. 15:20; Ezek. 45:12, etc.). The half-shekel weight was ordered by God to be paid as a ransom of the individual Hebrew's soul (Ex. 30:13).

Gerah. The smallest Hebrew weight equivalent to 1/20 of a shekel (8.71 grams), (Ex. 30:13; Ezek. 45:12, etc.).

Dram. Less than 3/10 of a shekel (Ezra 2:69; 8:27; I Chron. 29:7; Neh. 7:70).

Bekah. Equal to 1/2 shekel or 0.20 ounce (Gen. 24:22; Ex. 38:26).

Pim. Equal to about 2/3 of a shekel or 0.268 ounce (I Sam. 13:19-21).

Maneh or **Mina.** Equals to 50 holy shekels, about 1.26 pounds (I Ki. 10:17; Ezra 2:69;

Neh. 7:71). It is translated "pound" in the K.J.V.

Talent. The largest Hebrew weight and defined as the full weight for an able man to carry. Equals 3,000 shekels of 60 minas. Value was dependent upon whether it was of gold, silver, copper, etc. Usual weight was equivalent to 76.5 pounds (U.S. Standard).

DRY MEASURES

Handful. Natural capacity of the human hand. (Lev. 2:2; 5:12).

Kab or **Cab.** Equivalent to 1/6 seah or 2 2/9 dry pints (II Ki. 6:25).

Tenth Deal. A tenth part of a homer, about 2 1/2 pecks (Ex. 29:40; Lev. 14:10; Num. 28:13).

Omer. About 1 4/5 cabs or 4 U.S. dry pints (Ex. 16:16-36).

Seah. Equivalent to about 3 1/8 omers, a measure of 1/5 bushel (Gen. 18:6; Isa. 40:12).

Measure. Equivalent to the seah holding about 1/3 of an ephah or about 1/5 U.S. bushel (I Sam. 25:18; II Ki. 7:16, 18).

Ephah. Contains 10 omers or 3/5 U.S. bushel (Ex. 16:36; Judg. 6:19).

Lethech or **One Half Homer.** Contains 5 ephahs or 3 1/8 bushels (Hos. 3:2).

Homer. The largest measure and contains 10 ephahs or about 6 1/4 U.S. bushels (Lev. 27:16; Num. 11:32; Ezek. 45:11).

LIQUID MEASURE

1. **Log** — Originally signified a basin which held about a pint. However the accepted measure is 2/3 liquid pint (Lev. 14:10).

2. **Pot** — A cup or pitcher which held about one pint (Mk. 7:4).

3. **Hin** — It is Egyptian origin and equals 12 logs, equivalent to 3.86 U.S. quarts (Ex. 29:40; 30:24; Num. 15:4-9; Ezek. 4:11).

4. **Bath** — It is among the larger of the liquid measures, equal to 6 hins and equivalent to about 5.8 U.S. gallons (I Ki. 7:26; Ezek. 45:11).

5. **Metretes** — Equivalent to 39 liters or 10.3 U.S. gallons and known as Amphora (water pots), (Jn. 2:6 K.J.V.)

6. **Measure** — About 3 gallons in liquid measure (I Ki. 5:11; Lk. 16:6).

7. **Firkin** — Estimated to be 10 gallons (Jn. 2:6).

8. **Cor** — Equals 10 baths and is equivalent to about 58 U.S. gallons and is reckoned

about the same as a homer (Ezek. 45:14).

9. **Pound** — About 12 ounces of liquid (Lk. 19:24 ff.).

LINEAL MEASURE

In the Old Testament lineal measure was based mainly on the common cubit of 17.5 inches. Three kinds of cubits are known from ancient times:

A. In ancient Egypt a long cubit of 20.65 inches and a short cubit of 17.6 inches were used.

B. In Mesopotamia the "royal" cubit was 19.8 inches.

C. In the Old Testament, besides the common cubit, Ezekiel mentions a long cubit of seven handbreadths or 20.44 inches (Ezek. 40:5, 42). In ancient Greece and Rome still other cubit measures were used.

1. **Finger** or **Digit** — The smallest measure of the Hebrews, equal to the breadth of a man's finger of about .73 inch (Jer. 52:21).

2. **Handbreadth** — The width of 4 fingers tightly pressed together, equal to 2.9 inches based on the common cubit of 17.5 inches and Ezekiel's long cubit of 20.44 inches (Ex. 37:12; I Ki. 7:26; II Chron. 4:5; Ps. 39:5).

3. **Span** — The width from the end of the thumb to the end of the little finger measuring about 9 inches (Ex. 28:16; 39:9; I Sam. 17:4).

4. **Cubit** — An important and fixed measure among the Hebrews. The length of the arm from the point of the elbow to the end of the middle finger or about 17.5 inches (Ex. 25:10; I Ki. 7:24). In Ezekiel the long cubit of 20:44 inches (7 handbreadths) is used (Ezek. 40:5).

5. **Pace** — The equivalent of a yard (II Sam. 6:13). The Roman "pace" was 2 1/2 feet.

6. **Fathom** — Equivalent to 6 feet (Acts 27:28).

7. **Measuring Reed** — Translated "rod" in Rev. 11:1. Properly, a sweet cane stalk measuring 8 feet 9 inches on the 17.5 cubit as a basis. Following the long cubit used in Ezekiel it measures 10 feet 2.4 inches (Ezek. 40:3, 5). The cubit of the New Testament was the same as the Roman cubit, 17.5 inches.

8. **Line** — Equivalent to 146 feet (Ezek. 40:3).

9. **Furlong** — This Greek "stadion" was adopted by the Jews. It measured 600 Greek feet, 606 1/2 Roman feet and 606 3/8 English feet (Lk 24:13, e.g., Emmaus was about 60 furlongs or 7 miles from Jerusalem; Jn 6:19; Rev. 14:20 K.J.V.).

10. **Mile** — The Roman mile was 8 furlongs and hence 4860 feet (Mat. 5:41).

11. **Sabbath Day's Journey** — Exact distance is uncertain for apparently there was some elasticity in this distance. Josephus states that it is 5 or 6 stadia (furlongs), 3,000 or 3,600 feet which is about the distance form Jerusalem to the Mount of Olives (Acts 1:12).

12. **A Little Way** — Equivalent to about 4 English miles or less (Gen. 35:16; 48:7; II Ki. 5:19 K.J.V.). The translation of this term varies in different English versions.

13. **Day's Journey** — In Bible times the distance was usually measured by the length of time necessary to travel: e.g. "three days' journey" (Gen. 30:36), "seven days' journey" (Gen. 31:23). In New Testament times the distance was measured in furlongs or Roman miles (Lk. 24:13; Mat. 5:41).

AREA MEASURE

Area measure is the *Acre*, an area that a team of oxen can plow in one day, by U.S. standards equals about 1/2 acre. Scholars vary from 2/5 acre to 5/8 acre (I Sam. 14:14; Isa. 5:10).

THE JEWISH CALENDAR

NAME OF MONTH	CORRESPONDS WITH	NO. OF DAYS	MONTHS OF CIVIL YEAR	MONTHS OF SACRED YEAR (The official Calendar of Festivals)
TISHRI (I Kings 8:2)	SEPT. - OCT.	30	1st	7th Day of Atonement — 10th day Feast of Booths (Tabernacles) — 15th - 22nd day
HESHVAN or BUL (I Kings 6:38)	OCT. - NOV.	29 or 30	2nd	8th
KISLEV (Ezra 10:9)	NOV. - DEC.	29 or 30	3rd	9TH Feast of Dedication of Temple — 25th day (lasted 8 days)
TEBETH (Esther 2:16)	DEC. - JAN.	29	4th	10th
SHEBAT (Zechariah 1:7)	JAN. - FEB.	30	5th	11th
ADAR (Esther 3:7)	FEB. - MAR.	29 or 30	6th	12th Feast of Purim — 14th - 15th day
NISAN or ABIB (Exodus 13:4)	MAR. - APR.	30	7th	1st Passover — 14th to 21st day
IVAR or ZIF (I Kings 6:1)	APR. - MAY	29	8th	2nd
SIVAN (Esther 8:8)	MAY - JUNE	30	9th	3rd Feasts of Weeks (Pentecost) — 7th day
TAMMUZ (Jeremiah 39:2)	JUNE - JULY	29	10th	4th
AB (Numbers 33:38)	JULY - AUG.	30	11th	5th
*ELUL (Nehemiah 6:15)	AUG. - SEPT.	29	12th	6th

There are six fairly well defined seasons. They are mentioned in Genesis 8:22:

1. Seed-time — From the middle of October to the middle of December.
2. Winter — From the middle of December to the middle of February.
3. Cold — From the middle of February to the middle of April.
4. Harvest — From the middle of April to the middle of June.
5. Summer — From the middle of June to the middle of August.
6. Heat — From the middle of August to the middle of October.

*Hebrew months were 29 or 30 days each. Their years consisted of 12 lunar months or of 354 1/4 days. Therefore, about every three years (7 times in 19 years) the 13th month, VEADOR (also called Second ADAR), is added between ADAR and NISAN. It is known as an "intercalary month."

PLANTS AND ANIMALS OF THE BIBLE

Earl L. Core

The writers of the Bible were not primarily concerned with scientifically precise terminology; hence, references to plants and animals were for the most part only casual in nature. However, their method of description was not unlike ours. The terms *"lily," "pine,"* or *"oak,"* for example, have only general meanings today and may include many different species. The term *"white oak"* may refer to one kind of tree in the northeastern part of North America and to a different kind of tree in the western part. It appears that the Biblical writers frequently had no particular plant or animal in mind and referred to them in the same manner we do in employing the word *"tree"* or *"bird."*

PLANTS OF THE BIBLE

TREES AND SHRUBS

Only very small forests exist today in Palestine, and the best developed of these are on Mount Carmel and Mount Tabor, in Upper Galilee, and east of the Jordan. Even in Bible times the climate was not favorable for the growth of dense forests, except on the seaward slopes of Lebanon and Mount Carmel. As in many other countries, however, trees and shrubs were probably much more abundant in ancient times than they are today. Few of these can be identified with certainty from the Biblical names used for them. Many small woody plants, often thorny or resinous, grow in Palestine. These, with the smaller trees, formed a brushwood, somewhat similar to the California chaparral of today.

HERBACEOUS PLANTS

Large regions of Palestine are covered in spring with the beautiful green of grass and herbs, but this lasts only a short time and is succeeded by the brown of the parched field as the heat and drought of summer advances. Meadow areas covered with grass throughout the year are not normally found in Palestine.

Weeds, often with spines or stinging hairs, are common and interfere with the growth of agricultural crops. Several Hebrew words can be translated as *"thorns"* or *"thistles"* and these probably refer to a number of different plants.

FRUITS AND VEGETABLES

Dates were grown in ancient times along the Mediterranean and near Jericho. Mulberry trees are mentioned in the Bible, as is the mulberry fig. Western Asia was probably the native home of the olive, one of the most valuable trees of ancient Palestine. The fig was another tree of great value, since the fruit could be preserved by drying. Other trees yielding edible fruits were the pomegranate, walnut, apricot, and almond. The vegetable gardens included watermelons, muskmelons, and cucumbers; onions, garlic, and leeks; lentils and broad beans; and numerous herbs, including dill, cumin, mint, and coriander. The staple grains were wheat and barley, the latter widely grown on marginal lands, especially as food for the poorer classes. A plant much cultivated for its textile fiber was flax, the source of linen since very ancient times.

ALPHABETICAL LIST

Almond, *shaqedh* (Gen. 43:11; Ex. 25:33-36; Num. 17:1-8; Eccl. 12:5; Jer. 1:11). *Amygdalus communis,* a native of Persia, common in Palestine as early as the time of Jacob. The Israelites selected the almond flowers with their knops (sepals) and flowers (petals) as models for the cups of the golden candlesticks (lampstands). *Shaqedh* means *"the wakeful tree,"* the first to bloom in spring.

Aloes (OT), *ahalim, ahaloth* (Ps. 45:8; Prov. 7:17; Song of Sol. 4:14). *Aquilaria agallocha,* eaglewood, a tall tree, member of the mezereon family, native to the Malay region, with fragrant wood.

Anise, *anethon* (Mat. 23:23). This is

2234

wrongly translated anise; nearly all authorities agree it should be dill (*Anethum graveolens*), a weedy aromatic annual umbellifer with yellow flowers.

Apple, *tappuah* (Gen. 3:6; Josh. 17:8; Prov. 25:11; Song of Sol. 2:3, 5; Joel 1:12). A great deal of discussion has taken place over the *"apple"* of the Bible. It is now generally considered to have been the apricot (*Prunus armeniaca*), since the apple does not thrive in Palestine.

Balm, *tsori* (Ezek. 27:17). Perhaps *Commiphora opobalsamum*, the true balm of Gilead. The false balm of Gilead (*Balanites aegyptiaca*) is thought to be referred to in other places (e. g., Gen. 37:25; Jer. 8:22, 46:11). This plant yields a healing gum.

Barley, *se'orim* (Ex. 9:31; Deut. 8:8; Judg. 7:13; Ruth 2:17, 23; 3:2, 15-17; Hos. 3:2). A widely cultivated grain in Palestine. Three forms were grown: common barley (*Hordeum distichon*), winter barley (*H. hexastichon*), and spring barley (*H. vulgare*).

Bitter herbs, *merorim* (Ex. 12:8; Num. 9:11). Salad plants, mostly weedy herbs common in Egypt and Palestine, including: endive (*Cichorium endivia*), chichory (*C. intybus*), lettuce (*Lactuca sativa*), sorrel (*Rumex acetosella*), watercress (*Nasturtium officinale*), and dandelion (*Taraxacum officinale*).

Bulrush, *gome* (Ex. 2:3, 5; Isa. 18:2; 58:5). Papyrus (*Cyperus papyrus*), a tall sedge with three-sided stems was formerly abundant along the Nile River, and also in the marshes around Lake Huleh. It provided the earliest known material for making paper, which gets its name from the Greek word for the plant.

Cedar of Lebanon, *erez* (Judg. 9:15; I Ki. 4:33, 5:6-10; 6:9, 15-16, 18, 36; 7:2, 3, 7, 11-12; Ps. 104:16; Ezek. 31:3-18, and many other Passages). This is *Cedrus libani*, the famous cedar of Lebanon, the largest trees with which the Israelites were acquainted, growing to heights of 120 feet. It was used in the construction of Solomon's temple.

Corn, mostly wheat or barley, but not Indian corn (maize), a native of America. Eleven different Hebrew words are translated as corn, including *kamah* (Judg. 15:5), *bar* (Gen. 41:49), *shibboleth* (Ruth 2:2), *karmel* (Lev. 2:14).

Cummin, *cammon*; Greek, *kuminon* (Isa. 28:25, 27; Matt. 23:23). An annual plant of the carrot family (*Cuminum cyminum*), the aromatic seeds of which are used as a condiment.

Elm, *elah* (Hos. 4:13). Probably terebinth (*Pistacia terebinthus*), a large deciduous tree of the sumac family, sometimes also called teil, turpentine tree, or *"oak."*

Fig, *te'enah* (Gen. 3:6-7; I Ki. 4:25; I Sam. 25:18, and many other places). *Ficus carica*, the first tree to be mentioned in the Bible. The fruits were very valuable as fresh and dried food.

Flax, *pishtah* (Ex. 9:31; I Chron. 15:27; Prov. 31:13, 22, 24). The oldest known of textile fiber plants, the source of linen. Flax (*Linum usitatissimum*) and linen are mentioned scores of times in the Bible.

Frankincense, *levonah* (Lev. 2:1-2, 15-16; Mat. 2:11, and many other references). A clear yellow resin, the product of frankincense trees (*Boswellia thurifera, B. carteri, B. papyrifera*). Not native to Palestine but imported from Arabia, Ethiopia, and other lands.

Gall, *rosh* (Deut. 29:18; 32:32; Ps. 69:21; Mat. 27:34, etc.). The origin of gall is most uncertain. Some authorities believe it was produced by the colocynth (*Citrullus colocynthis*), which may also have been the *"vine of Sodom."* Others think (in the Matthew reference particularly) it may have been the juice of the opium poppy (*Papaver somniferum*).

Hyssop, *ezobh*; Greek *hyssopus* (Ex. 12:22; Lev. 14:4, 6, 52; Num. 19:6, 18; I Ki. 4:33; Ps. 51:7; Heb. 9:19). One of the most puzzling and controversial of all the botanical terms in the Bible; probably reference is made to several different species. It is definitely not the garden hyssop (*Hyssopus officinalis*), which is not a native of Palestine. Dozens of species have been suggested, with the Syrian marjoram (*Origanum maru*) and the common caper (*Capparis sicula*) as the most likely.

Lily of the field, Greek *krinon* (Mat. 6:28-30; Lk. 12:27). Most authorities regard the anemone or windflower (*Anemone coronaria*) as the famous *"lily of the field,"* which surpassed *"Solomon in all his glory."* It is one of the most conspicuous and brilliantly colored herbs of the fields.

Mandrake, *dudhay* (Gen. 30:14-16; Song of Sol. 7:13). The true mandrake (*Mandragora officinarum*), a plant long held in superstitious awe. It was supposed to contain certain properties that encourage fertility.

Myrrh, *mor* (Ex. 30:23; Esther 2:12; Ps. 45:8; Mat. 2:11; Jn. 19:39, etc.). One of the most valuable of gum resins, produced by the true myrrh (*Commiphora myrrha*).

Oak, *allon* (Gen. 35:8; Zech. 11:2; and many

other passages). Oaks were symbols of strength and long life. Four or more species are native to Palestine *(Quercus aegilops*, probably the oak of Bashan; *Q. coccifera, Q. ilex*, and *Q. lusitanica)*.

Olive, *zayith* (Gen. 8:11, the first reference in the Bible, and scores of other passages). The olive *(Olea europaea)*, the most valuable tree of ancient Palestine, provided edible fruit, oil for medicinal purposes and for lamps, and timber for cabinet work.

Palm tree, *tamar* (Ex. 15:27; Lev. 23:40; Jn. 12:13, and many other references). The date palm *(Phoenix dactylifera)*, cultivated in the Near East for at least 5,000 years for its edible fruit, etc. The name *"Phoenicia"* has been interepreted to mean *"land of palms,"* although evidence points to the meaning *"maker of purple."*

Pomegranate, *rimmon* (Ex. 28:33-34; 39:24-26, and many other Passages). A large shrub or small tree producing a pleasantly acid fruit, the common pomegranate *(Punica granatum)*.

Rye (rie), *koosemet* (Ex. 9:32; Isa. 28:25). Not the true rye, a grain of northern countries, but actually spelt, a type of wheat *(Triticum aestivum*, var. *spelta)*.

Shittah tree, *shittah* (Isa. 41:19). The shittah tree *(Acacia seyal)* is mentioned only once in the Bible, but its wood (shittim) is referred to 26 times. It was used in the construction of the Ark of the Covenant (Ex. 25:5, 10, 13, 23, 28) and of the Tabernacle (Ex. 26:15-16, 26, 32, 37).

Spikenard, *nerd*; Greek *nardos* (Song of Sol. 1:12; 4:13-14; Mk. 14:3, Jn. 12:3). Probably the product of the nard plant *(Nardostachys jatamansi)*, a fragrant red ointment imported from India, and very costly.

Sycamore, *skikmah* (I Ki. 10:27; I Chron. 27:28; II Chron. 1:15; 9:27; Amos 7:15; Lk. 19:4, etc.). The sycamore-fig or fig mulberry *(Ficus sycomorus)*, an evergreen tree 30 to 40 feet tall, producing a fruit resembling but much inferior to the common fig.

Tares, Greek *zizanion* (Mat. 13:25). The bearded darnel or rye grass *(Lolium temulentum)*, a grass growing in grain fields, difficult to tell from wheat or rye until it forms heads.

Teil tree, *elah* (Isa. 6:13). Probably the terebinth *(Pistacia terebinthus)*. The same Hebrew word is translated *"elm"* is Hosea 4:13 but also probably refers to the terebinth.

Vine, *gephen* (Gen. 9:20-21, 24, 40:9-11; Deut. 8:8; Ps. 105:33; Zech. 3:10, and scores of other references). The grape *(Vitis vinifera)*,

the first plant in Biblical history recorded as cultivated. It was a symbol of fruitfulness and its harvest season was a time of joyous festivity.

ANIMALS OF THE BIBLE

The animals of ancient Palestine were apparently observed more closely by Biblical writers than were the plants, as is indicated by attempts to classify them (Gen. 1:20-25; Deut. 4:17; Ps. 104:11-26). We find divisions into aquatic animals, birds, and land animals — the last subdivided into wild beasts, domestic animals, and creeping things. Animals are dealt with in detail in the food law (Lev., Chpt. 11; Deut., Chpt. 14), and many species are enumerated.

MAMMALS

Several zoological provinces overlap in Palestine and certain animals of Europe, Asia, and Africa (at least in ancient times) inhabited the land together. Numerous kinds of mammals were apparently first domesticated in western Asia before or during Biblical times, and these were of great value to ancient man, including the Hebrews. Among these were horses, asses, mules, and camels, which were used for riding and as beasts of burden. The raising of sheep, goats, and cattle was also important, providing meat, milk, butter, cheese, clothing, and shoes.

BIRDS

Birds of prey include the eagle, vulture, falcon, sparrow-hawk, kite, and owl. Of waterfowl there are the heron, stork, pelican, cormorant, swan, crane, and seagull. Ostriches, at least formerly, were seen in desert districts. Other birds include the partridge, quail, wild pigeon, and turtledove. Many small song birds also occur, such as the nighthawk, hoopoe, lark, swallow, swift, and thrush. Little attempt was made in ancient Palestine to raise domesticated birds.

FISHES

The waters of Palestine, especially the Jordan Valley (except for the Dead Sea), abounded

in fish during Biblical times. At least 43 species have been listed for the region by some authorities. However, not a single species can be positively identified from the Biblical references.

REPTILES AND AMPHIBIANS

The extensive uninhabited stretches of country and numberless rocky places favor the existence of reptiles. About three dozen species of snakes have been identified, including many poisonous ones, such as the cobra, viper, horned snake, and asp. Lizards include the hirdaun and horned lizard. The Nile crocodile was found near Mount Carmel and the land crocodile near the Dead Sea. Turtles are numerous.

INSECTS

As in most warm regions, insects are extraordinarily numerous. Hornets, wild bees, flies, gnats, fleas, and locusts are mentioned in the Bible. Greatly feared in ancient times was the migratory locust, the locust of the plagues of Egypt (perhaps *Schistocerca peregrina*).

ALPHABETICAL LIST

Adder, *pethen* (Ps. 58:4). The Bible contains numerous references to serpents, but no single species can be identified with certainty. Tristram lists 33 species, among them several poisonous varieties. The Hebrew words *tsiph'oni* and *tseph'a* (Prov. 23:32) are also sometimes translated as adder, but sometimes as asp or cockatrice. The viper or adder *(Vipera euphratica)* is common in the region.

Ass, *hamor, athon, pere, etc.* (Gen. 42:26; Ex. 4:20; Num. 22:21; Judg. 10:4; Hos. 8:9). More than 150 Passages of the Bible refer to the ass *(Equus asinus)*, and the animal is mentioned in the earliest Hebrew lilterature. Distinction is made between *hamor*, the male animal, the ordinary beast of burden; *athon*, the she-ass, a favorite for riding; and *ayir*, or ass's colt. The possessor of a large herd of asses was a rich man. These are also Passages referring to the wild ass *(pere, arodh)*, several species of which occur in the area; they are untamable.

Bee, *debhorah* (Deut. 1:44). Culture of the honeybee *(Apis sp.)* may have been known to the Israelites, but wild bees were abundant and their honey was collected.

Behemoth, *behemoth* (Job 40:15). Thought to be the hippopotamus *(Hippopotamus amphibius)*, the *"river horse"* of Africa.

Camel, *gamal* (Gen. 12:16; Judg. 6:5; Job 1:3). The camel *(Camelus spp.)*, the typical beast of burden in desert regions, is mentioned about 66 times in the Bible. The dromedary, the one-humped species *(C, dromedarius)*, was the Palestinian animal.

Cattle, *miqneh* (*"property,"* compare modern *"chattel"*). Cattle are the domesticated descendants of ancient species of *Bos*. The Bible refers to *abbir*, bull; *par*, bullock; *baqar*, bullock, ox; *eghel*, calf; *shor*, cow; *eglah*, heifer; *eleph*, ox, etc. Much of the wealth of the ancient Israelites was in their herds of cattle, and their valuable products. Milk, butter, cheese, and leather, are frequently mentioned. Sheep were also often included under *miqneh*.

Coney, *shaphan* (Lev. 11:5). The daman or rock-badger *(Hyrax syriacus)*. They resemble rabbits in size, but have four-toed feet like elephants and their teeth resemble those of the rhinoceros.

Dog, *kelebh* (Ex. 11:7; Job. 30:1; Prov. 26:11). Dogs *(Canis familiaris)* were perhaps the first animals domesticated by man. About 40 Biblical Passages refer to these animals, which were sometimes used to guard flocks but more often ran loose and were despised outcasts.

Dove, *yonah* (Gen. 8:8; Mat. 3:16). A generic term, probably referring to both wild and domesticated pigeons *(Columba spp.)*

Eagle, *nesher* (Ex. 19:4; Deut. 32:11; Ps. 103:5). Numerous species of hawk-like birds seem to be intended, even including vultures. They are symbols of strength, speed, pride, and indomitable spirit.

Fishes. The Bible contains numerous references to fish, but no particular species can be identified.

Fly, *zebhubh, arobh* (Ex. 8:20-24; Eccl. 10:1; Isa. 7:18). Generic terms, referring to gadflies, mosquitoes, and other harmful insects having a single pair of wings.

Goat, *ez, attudh, sa'ir, etc.* (Gen. 27:9; Lev. 4:24; Num. 7:17). Both wild and tame goats are mentioned in the Bible. Goats *(Capra hircus)* were domesticated before 3000 B.C. and were an important element of wealth in the time of the early Patriarchs. More than 130 Passages refer to goats and about 50 to kids

(gelhi), or young goats.

Horse, *sus, parash, rekheoh* (Gen. 47:17, etc.). More than 150 Passages refer to the horse *(Equus caballus)*, domesticated in the patriarchal age. They were used for riding and for drawing chariots.

Leopard, *namer, pardalus* (Song of Sol. 4:8; Isa. 11:6; Jer. 13:23; Rev. 13:2). The leopard *(Felis leopardus)*, a savage and treacherous animal found in Palestine in ancient times and inhabiting areas east of the Jordan in modern times.

Leviathan, *liwyathan* (Ps. 74:14; Isa. 27:1; Job 41:1). A mythological monster, the great devourer. But in Job the reference is to the crocodile *(Crocodilus niloticus)* of Egypt and of the Jordan Valley.

Locust. At least 10 Hebrew words are translated as locust, bald locust (Lev. 11:22), or grasshopper (Lev. 11:22). Some of these were edible and regarded as very palatable. But they were very destructive and caused great plagues (Ex. 10:4-6), so that they became a symbol of destruction (Rev. 9:3-11). Words translated as caterpillar (Ps. 78:46), cankerworm (Nah. 3:15), and palmerworm (Joel 1:4)

are also thought to refer to locusts.

Quail, *selaw* (Ex. 16:13; Num. 11:31). A ground-dwelling bird *(Coturnix vulgaris)*; not the quail or bobwhite of America.

Scorpion, *aqrabh* (Deut. 8:15). A small animal related to spiders, of the order Scorpionida, phylum Arthopoda.

Serpent. The Bible contains numerous references to serpents, often implying poisonous species, but few can be identified with certainty. The serpent is used as a symbol of evil.

Sheep. Numerous Hebrew words are used for sheep, as *rahel,* ewe; *kesebh,* lamb; *ayil, tsaphir,* ram. Sheep *(Ovis aries)* were domesticated as early as 3000 B.C., before cattle, and receive more attention in the Bible than any other animal.

Unicorn, *re'em* (Num. 23:22; 24:8; Job 39:9, etc.). The unicorn is a mythological animal with a single horn. The name as used in the Bible probably refers to the wild ox *(Bos primigenius,* the German *aurochs),* now extinct.

Wolf, *ze'ebh* (Gen. 49:27; Mat. 7:15) *(Canis lupus).* The word *"iyyim,* translated *"wild beasts"* (Isa. 13:22; 34:14; Jer. 50:39), probably refers to wolves.

TERMS FREQUENTLY USED IN BIBLICAL STUDY

Lowell W. Coolidge

Agrapha. Sayings attributed to Jesus but not recorded in the Gospels. A few (*e.g.*, Acts 20:35) are found elsewhere in the New Testament, others in the Apocryphal Gospels and in the early Fathers.

Allegory. A literary composition, usually narrative, in which persons, objects, and events are so presented as to convey metaphorical as well as literal meaning.

Apocalypse. A prophetic disclosure, in highly symbolic language, of the awaited triumph of God's kingdom. Apocalyptic writings, of which the books of Daniel and Revelation are examples, were prominent in post-Exilic Judaism and early Christianity.

Aramaic. A Semitic tongue, native to Syria and Upper Mesopotamia; by the time of Christ it had become the normal spoken language throughout Palestine. It is the language of the Targum (*q.v.*) as well as of portions of Jeremiah, Ezra, and Daniel in the original Text.

Babylonian Captivity. See *Exile*.

Canon. Writings authoritatively accepted as genuine and declared to be divinely inspired; specifically, the books constituting the Hebrew and Christian Scriptures.

Charismata. "Things freely given," a term applied in the New Testament to special aptitudes or powers bestowed on the Christian by the Holy Spirit (*see* I Cor. 12:4-11).

Codex. A leaf book, as distinguished from a roll or scroll. Manuscripts of the Bible are often designated by this term with an identifying modifier (Codex Sinaiticus, Codex Vaticanus, etc.)

Cursive. A manuscript in which the letters (minuscules) of each work are joined. Cursive writing, as distinguished from unical (*q.v.*) is found in Biblical manuscripts from the 9th century onward.

Diaspora. The Dispersion, a term applied to Jewish communities outside Palestine, especially after the Exile (*q.v.*).

Ecumenical. Pertaining to the Christian Church as a whole, as in Ecumenical Councils, Ecumenical Creeds, etc. (Literally, "of or from the inhabited world.")

Eschatology. Literally, the "study of last things." The body of doctrines concerned with the ultimate destiny of man and the world, especially as related to the Biblical concept of Final Judgment.

Exile, pre-Exilic, post-Exilic. Referring to the time during, before, and after the captivity of the Jews by the Babylonians in 597 B.C.

Gloss. An explanatory note of comment accompanying a text. In the transmission of Biblical documents, marginal comments made by a scribe were sometimes incorporated into the text by later copyists.

Gnosticism. A religious and philosophical movement that attempted, during the first centuries of the Christian Era, to unite diverse elements of Greek and Oriental mysticism with Christianity. Its name derives from its emphasis on esoteric knowledge (*gnosis*) as the way to salvation.

Hellenistic. Describing a world culture that developed after Alexander the Great (356-323 B.C.) and blended Greek and Oriental elements in art, literature, philosophy, and religion, and used *koiné* Greek as a common language.

Hermeneutics. The principles of Biblical interpretation

Inter-Testamental Period. Between the Testaments, or that period of history between the Old Testament and the events recorded in the New Testament (*c.* 200 B.C.-A.D. 50).

Kerygma. A Greek word referring to the proclamation of the Gospel.

Koiné. The common Greek spoken throughout the eastern Mediterranean region at the beginning of the Christian Era; the language in which the New Testament was written.

Koinonia. A Greek word literally meaning "sharing," applied to the early Christian fellowship.

Masoretes. Jewish scholars (*c.* A.D. 600-900) who added vowel points and in other ways attempted to clarify earlier manuscripts

of the Hebrew Scriptures. Their extensive body of annotation is known as the Masora (or Masorah).

Palimpsest. A tablet, parchment, or other writing material that has been used, erased, and used again.

Parallelism. The basic structural principle of Hebrew poetry, involving statement and restatement in balance succession: *e.g.*, "The heavens declare the glory of God; and the firmament shows His handiwork."

Parousia. The return of Christ in glory (literally, "the Coming"), an event that the first Christians believed to be close at hand.

Potsherd (sherd). A piece of broken pottery, the most common type of artifact found by Biblical archaeologists and often of great value in establishing chronology.

Pseudepigrapha. Writings falsely ascribed to Biblical characters and belonging mostly to the Inter-Testamental period.

Procurators. Rulers of Judea from A.D. 6 to 66 who were sent from Rome and were responsible to the Emperor.

Synoptic Gospels. The first three Gospels: Matthew, Mark, Luke. They are called synoptic because they present a common view.

Targum. An Aramaic paraphrase of the Old Testament, which in later Judaism was often used to accompany the reading of the Hebrew original in the synagogues.

Tetragrammaton. The letters YHWH (or JHVH) used in Hebrew manuscripts of the Old Testament to denote the Divine Name, customarily vocalized as "Yahweh." In reading aloud, the Jews often substituted *Adonai* ("Lord") since the name of Yahweh was considered too sacred for utterance. The King James Version uses LORD (with all letters capitalized) as the English equivalent.

Torah. The Hebrew designation of the divinely revealed Law; specifically, the first five books of the Bible, the Pentateuch.

Uncial. A manuscript in which the letters are large and separately formed. Uncial script preceded cursive (*q.v.*).

HARMONY OF THE GOSPELS

Contents	Matthew	Mark	Luke	John
Incidents of the Birth and Boyhood of Jesus Christ Till He was Twelve Years of Age				
1. Introduction	....	....	1:1-4	1:1-11
2. The genealogies — Matthew the legal, Luke the natural descent	1:1-17	....	3:23-38	....
3. Birth of John announced to Zacharias			1:5-25	
4. Birth of Jesus announced to Mary at Nazareth six months later		....	1:26-38	
5. Mary's visit to Elizabeth, and her hymn		....	1:39-56	
6. John the Baptist's birth, and Zacharias' hymn		....	1:57-80	
7. The angel appears to Joseph	1:18-25	....	....	
8. Birth of Jesus at Bethlehem*	....	....	2:1-7	....
9. Angelic announcement to the shepherds. (In spring flocks are watched by night.)			2:8-20	
10. Circumcision of Jesus, and presentation in the temple, where He is welcomed by Simeon and Anna, 41 days after nativity (Lev. 12:3-4).			2:21-38	
11. Visit of the Magi, in the house — no longer in manger; epiphany to Gentiles	2:1-12	....	....	....
12. Flight into Egypt	2:13-15	....	....	....
13. Herod's murder of the innocents	2:16-18	....	....	
14. Return to Nazareth, fearing Archelaus' cruelty, shown from the first	2:19-23	....	2:39-40	....
15. Jesus at the age of twelve goes up to the Passover, and is found with the doctors in the temple; then follows His 18 years' retirement			2:41-52	....
Inauguration of Christ's Public Ministry				
16. Preparatory preaching of John the Baptist	3:1-12	1:1-8	3:1-18	....
17. Christ's baptism in river Jordan at Perean Bethany	3:13-17	1:9-11	3:21-23	....
18. The Spirit leads Him to desert of Judea, where Satan tempts Him	4:1-11	1:12-13	4:1-13	....
19. The Baptist's witness of Jesus	....	....	....	1:15-34
20. Two of John's disciples follow Jesus; Andrew brings his brother Simon			....	1:35-42
21. Christ returns to Galilee; finds Philip, who in turn finds Nathanael	....	....	....	1:43-51
22. First miracle at Cana, and visit to Capernaum	....	....	....	2:1-12

* Various scholars have estimated the date of the birth of Jesus to be between the years 7-4 B.C.

Contents	Matthew	Mark	Luke	John
Public Ministry of Christ from the First Passover to the Second				
23. Christ goes up to Jerusalem for the Passover, and, with a scourge, expels the sellers and money-changers from the temple; works miracles, convincing many	....	....	....	2:13-25
24. Nicodemus is convinced; has a night interview with Jesus................................	....	....	....	3:1-21
25. Christ leaves Jerusalem, stays eight months in N. E. Judea, and baptizes by His disciples.	....	....	....	3:22
26. John, baptizing in Aenon, again witnesses to the Christ	....	....	....	3:23-36
27. Imprisonment of John	....	....	3:19-20	
28. John being cast into prison, Jesus leaves Judea for Galilee: John beheaded — not till A.D. 28 (Mat. 14:1-12)	4:12	1:14	4:14-15	4:1-3
29. Passing through Samaria, He converts a woman of Sychar, and through her many of the Samaritans, four months before harvest	....	....	....	4:4-42
30. Commencement of His public ministry in Galilee	4:17	1:14-15	4:14-15	4:43-45
31. Visiting Cana again, He heals a nobleman's son sick at Capernaum	....	....	....	4:46-54
From His Second to His Third Passover				
32. Returns to Jerusalem at the Passover, *"the feast."* His second Passover. From this to the third, His main Galilean ministry. Jesus cures an infirm man at Bethesda pool on the Sabbath. The Jews seek to kill Him for declaring Himself one with the Father in working.	....	....	....	5:1-47
33. Returns to Galilee. A period between the earlier visit to Nazareth, and this later visit to Galilee, and His sermon at Nazareth, as Luke 4:23 proves................	....		4:14-30	
34. He settles at Capernaum, and teaches in public	4:13-17	1:21-22	4:31-32	....
35. Miraculous draught of fishes; call of Simon, Andrew, James, and John	4:18-22	1:16-20	5:1-11	....
36. Jesus casts out a demon..........................	....	1:23-28	4:33-37	....

Contents	Matthew	Mark	Luke	John
37. Cure of Simon's wife's mother, and other sick people	8:14-17	1:29-34	4:38-41	....
38. Circuit with the disciples through Galilee	4:23-25	1:35-39	4:42-44	....
39. He heals a leper, and, shunning popularity, retires to the desert	8:1-4	1:40-45	5:12-16	....
40. Returning to Capernaum, He heals a palsied man let down through the roof	9:2-8	2:1-12	5:17-26	....
41. Call of Matthew, the feast, and discourse at his house — the new garment and new wine	9:9-13	2:13-17	5:27-32	....
42. He answers objections as to the reason of Him not fasting	9:14-17	2:18-22	5:33-39	....
43. Returning towards Galilee, the disciples pluck corn ears on the Sabbath	12:1-8	2:23-28	6:1-5	....
44. Healing a man's withered hand on the Sabbath, the Pharisees plot His death with the Herodians	12:9-14	3:1-6	6:6-11	....
45. He withdraws to the lake and heals many	12:15-21	3:7-12	....	....
46. Ascending a hill west of the lake, after prayer all night, he chooses the Twelve; His charge	10:1-42	3:13-19	6:12-19	....
47. Sermon on the mount, on the level below the hilltop	5:1-8:1	....	6:20-49	....
48. Healing of the centurion's servant	8:5-13	....	7:1-10	....
49. Raising of the widow's son at Nain	....	....	7:11-17	....
50. John Baptist's mission of inquiry from his dungeon at Machaerus	11:2-19	....	7:18-35	....
51. Jesus upbraids Chorazin, Bethsaida, and Capernaum, and invites the heavy-laden ..	11:20-30	....	....	....
52. Anointing of His feet, in the Pharisee Simon's house, by the sinful but forgiven woman ..	....	....	7:36-50	....
53. Short circuit of two days' preaching through Galilee; women ministering	....	....	8:1-3	....
54. Returning to Capernaum, He heals a blind and dumb demoniac, the Pharisees attributing the miracle to Beelzebub	12:22-37	3:22-30	11:14-15 11:17-23	....
55. Seeking a sign, and the answer	12:38-45	....	11:16 11:24-36	....
56. His kinsfolk try to lay hold on Him as mad ...	12:46-50	3:19-21 3:31-35	8:19-21	....
57. From a fishing vessel, He speaks a series of seven parables, beginning with the Parable of the sower	13:1-53	4:1-34	8:4-18	....

Contents	Matthew	Mark	Luke	John
58. Jesus crosses the lake with His disciples, and calms a storm	8:18-27	4:35-41	8:22-25	....
59. He cures two demoniacs of Gadara, one being prominent	8:28-34	5:1-20	8:26-40	....
60. Returning to the west shore, He raises Jairus' daughter, and heals a woman with an issue of blood	9:1 9:18-26	5:21-43	8:40-56	....
61. He heals two blind men and casts out a demon	9:27-34	....	....	....
62. Jesus visits Nazareth again, when His countrymen disbelieve in Him	13:54-58	6:1-6	....	....
63. Christ teaches throughout Galilee	9:35-38	6:6	....	....
64. Sends forth the Twelve	10:1-11:1	6:7-13	9:1-6	....
65. Herod, who has murdered John the Baptist, fears that Jesus is John risen from the dead	14:1-12	6:14-29	9:7-9	....
66. The Twelve return to Jesus, telling all they have done and taught. He withdraws with them to a desert on the other side of the Sea of Galilee, and feeds five thousand people	14:13-21	6:30-44	9:10-17	6:1-14
67. He sends the disciples across the lake westward to Bethsaida (close to Capernaum distinct from Bethsaida Julias, northeast of the lake, Luke 9:10), and at night comes walking to them upon the water	14:22-23	6:45-56	....	6:15-21
68. The miraculously-fed multitude seek and find Jesus at Capernaum. His discourse in the synagogue and Peter's confession	....	....	....	6:22-71

From the Third Passover to the Beginning of the Last Passover Week

Contents	Matthew	Mark	Luke	John
69. Healings in the Gennesaret plain for a few days	14:34-36	6:55-56	....	....
70. Pharisees from Jerusalem object to His neglect of washing hands	15:1-20	7:1-23	....	....
71. Jesus goes northward towards Tyre and Sidon. The Syrophoenician woman's faith gains a cure for her daughter	15:21-28	7:24-30	....	....
72. He returns though Decapolis, and, ascending a mount near the Sea of Galilee, heals many and feeds four thousand	15:29-38	7:31-8:9	....	....

Contents	Matthew	Mark	Luke	John
73. He crosses the lake to Dalmanutha	15:39	8:10	....	....
74. Pharisees and Sadducees require a sign	16:1-4	8:11-12	....	....
75. Embarking in the ship, He comes to Bethsaida (Julias). He warns against leaven of doctrine	16:4-12	8:13-21	....	....
76. Healing of a blind man	....	8:22-26	....	....
77. Journey to the region of Caesarea Philippi, Peter's confession	16:13-20	8:27-30	9:13-21	....
78. He foretells His Death and Resurrection. Reproof of Peter	16:21-28	8:31-38	9:22-27	....
79. The transfiguration on Mount Hermon six days later.	17:1-13	9:1 9:2-13	9:28-36	....
80. Descending, the following day He casts out a demon which the disciples could not cast out	17:14-21	9:14-29	9:37-43	....
81. Jesus again foretells His Death and Resurrection	17:22-23	9:30-32	9:44-45	....
82. Temple-tribute money miraculously provided from a fish at Capernaum	17:24-27	....	....	....
83. The disciples strive which shall be greatest. Jesus teaches a childlike, forgiving spirit. John tells of the disciples' forbidding one who cast out demons in Jesus' name	18:1-35	9:33-50	9:46-50	....
Journey to the Feast of Tabernacles, six months after the third Passover; this period ends with His arrival arrival at Bethany before the last Passover	....	....	....	7:1-10
84. He goes up from Galilee about the midst of the feast and teaches in the temple	....	....	....	7:14
85. The people are divided in opinion; the rulers try to seize Him; Nicodemus remonstrates	....	....	....	7:11-53
86. His charity, yet faithfulness, towards the adulteress	....	....	....	8:1-11
87. Jesus in the temple declares Himself the Light of the world, preexistent before Abraham. The Jews seek to stone Him.	....	....	....	8:12-50
88. Healing of the beggar, blind from his birth	....	....	....	9
89. Christ's discourse on himself as the Good Shepherd and the Door	....	....	....	10:1-21
90. Final departure for Jerusalem from Galilee through Samaria	....	....	9:51-56	....
91. Warnings to a certain man who would follow	....	....	9:57-62	....

Contents	Matthew	Mark	Luke	John
92. Sending forth of the seventy			10:1-16	
93. The seventy return, announcing their successful mission		....	10:17-24	
94. In reply to a lawyer's general question about the whole law, Christ speaks the parable of the good Samaritan		....	10:25-37	....
95. Jesus in Bethany visits Mary and Martha		....	10:38-42	
96. He again teaches the disciples how to pray	....	....	11:1-13	....
97. Cure of the dumb demoniac; the Pharisees again attribute His miracles to Beelzebub; dines with one; woes to hypocritical lawyers; doom of the nation	....	....	11:14-54	....
98. Exhortation to disciples	....	....	12:1-12	....
99. Appeal to Jesus to arbitrate about inheritance; parable of the rich fool	....	....	12:13-21	....
100. Discourses	....	....	12:22-59	
101. God's judgments; motive to Repentance	....	....	13:1-5	
102. Parable of the barren fig tree	....	....	13:6-9	
103. Cure of a woman with a spirit of infirmity	....	....	13:10-17	....
104. Jesus, at the Feast of Dedication in Jerusalem, proclaims His Divine oneness with God. The Jews a third time seek to kill Him, when consequently He withdraws to Perea.	....	....	....	10:22-42
105. His second journey toward Bethany on hearing of the sickness of Lazarus	....	....	13:22	11:1-16
106. Pharisees urge Him to depart quickly from Perea, on the plea that Herod will kill Him, and His answer	....	....	13:31-35	....
107. Cure of a man with the dropsy	....	....	14:1-6	....
108. Parable of the great supper	....	....	14:7-24	....
109. He warns the multitude to count the cost of discipleship	....	....	14:25-35	....
110. Many publicans crowd to Him, and on the Pharisees' murmuring, He utters the parables of the lost sheep, the lost coin, and the prodigal son			15	....
111. To the disciples He speaks the parables of the unjust steward and the rich man and Lazarus			16	....
112. Sayings as to offenses; mutual forgiveness and profitableness never exceeding duty ...	....	....	17:1-10	....
113. Arriving at Bethany, He raises Lazarus from the dead	....	....		11:17-46
114. Caiaphas and the Sanhedrin determine to put				

Contents	Matthew	Mark	Luke	John
Jesus to death; unconscious prophecy	....	....	....	11:47-53
115. Jesus withdraws to Ephraim on the borders of Samaria	....	....	....	11:54
The Last Journey to Jerusalem through the midst of Samaria and Galilee				
116. He heals ten lepers on the Samaritan frontier	....	....	17:11-19	....
117. The Pharisees ask when the Kingdom of God shall come; He foretells its concomitants .	....	....	17:20-37	....
118. Parables of importunate widow and the Pharisee and publican	....	....	18:1-14	....
119. Journey from Galilee through Perea	19:1-2	10:1	....	....
120. Pharisees question Him about divorce	19:3-12	10:2-12	....	....
121. Parents bring their children to Jesus to bless them	19:13-15	10:13-16	18:15-17	....
122. The rich young ruler declines the discipleship; Peter contrasts the disciples' self-discipline	19:16-30	10:17-31	18:18-30	....
123. Parable of the laborers in the vineyard to warn against mercenary service	20:1-16	....	....	....
124. Jesus goes before on His way to Jerusalem, and a third time foretells His Death and Resurrection	20:17-19	10:32-34	18:31-34	....
125. James and John desire highest places next to Christ in the temporal kingdom	20:20-28	10:35-45	....	....
126. He heals two blind men near Jericho	20:29-34	10:46-52	18:35-19:1	....
127. Zacchaeus climbs a sycamore tree, and is called down by Jesus; Salvation comes to his house	....	....	19:2-10	....
128. Nigh Jerusalem when men think the Kingdom of God shall immediately appear. Jesus checks this thought by the parable of the pounds	....	....	19:11-27	....
The Last Sabbath, Saturday, beginning at Friday sunset				
129. The hostile Jews seek Him at Jerusalem; Pharisees command to take Him. Jesus reaches Bethany six days before the Passover. In the house of Simon the leper, Mary anoints His head and feet	26:6-13	14:3-9	....	11:55-57 12:1-8

Contents	Matthew	Mark	Luke	John
130. Jews come to Bethany to see Jesus	....	....	....	12:9-11
The Last Passover Week, Ending with the Crucifixion				
131. Jesus triumphantly enters Jerusalem. He weeps over the city as doomed. At eventide He returns to Bethany, having first entered the temple, and sternly looked round about upon all things (Zeph. 1:12)...................................	21:1-11 21:17	11:1-11	19:28-44	12:12-19 ....
132. On his way from Bethany, Jesus curses the barren fig tree. He purges the temple at the close of the ministry as at the beginning, but without the scourge, and again returns to Bethany, after detecting at a glance the desecration in the court of the Gentiles	21:12-16 21:18-19	11:12-19	19:45-46	
133. On His way to Jerusalem, the fig tree being now withered up, Jesus teaches the lesson *"that believing prayer can move mountains of hindrance"*	21:21-22	11:20-26	....	
134. Teaches in the temple. Deputation from the Sanhedrin challenges His authority. Parables of the two sons and the vineyard.	21:23-46	11:27-33 12:1-12	20:1-19	....
135. Parable of the marriage feast	22:1-14			
136. The Pharisees, with the Herodians, try to entangle Him in His words. His reply from Caesar's image on the coin	22:15-22	12:13-17	20:20-26	....
137. He baffles the Sadducees' cavil about the Resurrection	22:23-33	12:18-27	20:27-40	....
138. He replies to a lawyer on which one is the great commandment	22:35-40	12:28-34	....	....
139. Our Lord leaves them without answer to His question, If Christ be the Son of David, how does David call Him Lord?	22:41-46	12:35-37	20:41-44	....
140. Warns against scribes and Pharisees. Woe to Jerusalem	23	12:38-40	20:45-47	....
141. He commends the widow's offering to God's treasury................................	....	12:41-44	21:1-4	....
142. Some Greeks desire to see Jesus. He accepts				

Contents	Matthew	Mark	Luke	John
this as a pledge of His coming glory and the gathering in of the Gentiles. Jesus' prayer and the Father's answer heard by the disciples	....	....	....	12:20-36
143. Leaving the temple, Jesus, sitting on Olivet, with Peter, James, John, and Andrew foretells the destruction of the temple and Jewish theocracy. The last days	24:1-42	13:1-37	21:5-36	....
144. Parables: The goodman of the house, the wise and the evil servant, the ten virgins, the talents, the sheep and the goats	24:43-51 25	....	....	....
145. *Beginning of sunset:* Jesus, two days before the Passover, announces His betrayal and Crucifixion; the Sanhedrin consult to kill Jesus by subtlety. Judas, availing himself of his Master's retirement from them, covenants to betray Him. Most disbelieved, some rulers believed, but loving men's praise confessed Him not. Jesus' judgment	26:1-5 26:14-16	14:1-2 14:10-11	22:1-6	12:36-50
146. Jesus sends two disciples into the city to prepare for the Passover; follows with the rest in the afternoon	26:17-19	14:12-17	22:7-14	....
147. *At sunset:* Jesus celebrates the Passover by anticipation	26:20	14:17	22:14	....
148. Reproves the ambition of disciples, yet promises the kingdom			22:24-30	....
149. He teaches love and humility by washing disciples' feet				13:1-20
150. He indicates His betrayer, who, however, did not leave till after the Lord's Supper (Lk. 22:21)	26:21-25	14:18-21	22:21-23	13:21-30
151. He foretells Peter's sifting by Satan, and restoration by His intercession; and scattering of the Twelve	26:31-34	14:27-31	22:31-38	13:36-38 16:32
152. Ordains the Lord's Supper (I Cor. 11:23-26) ..	26:26-29	14:22-25	22:15-20	....
153. Farewell address and intercessory prayer in the paschal chamber, all standing (Jn. 14:31)	....	....	....	14:17-26
154. His agony in Gethsemane	26:30 26:36-46	14:26 14:32-42	22:39-46	18:1, 4 ....

Contents	Matthew	Mark	Luke	John
155. His betrayal with a kiss, and apprehension. Peter cuts off, and Jesus heals, Malchus' ear	26:47-56	14:43-52	22:47-53	18:2-12
156. He is brought before Annas first at night. Peter's three denials: 1. The *flesh* (Mk. 14:54); 2. The *world* (Mat. 26:70 — first cock-crowing, Mk 14:68); 3. The *devil* (Mk. 14:71-72 — the second cock-crowing; Ps. 1:1)	26:57-58 26:69-75	14:53-54 14:66-72	22:54-62	18:13, 18 18:25-27
157. Before Caiaphas, at first dawn, Jesus avows His Messiahship and Godhead. He is condemned for blasphemy and mocked....	26:59-68	14:55-65	22:63-71	18:19-24
158. Brought before Pilate for sentence of crucifixion	27:1-2 27:11-14	15:1-5	23:1-5	18:28-38 ....
159. Pilate sends Him to Herod; Herod sends Him back to Pilate	....	....	23:6-12	....
160. Pilate seeks to release Him, but the Jews demand Barabbas. To appease them, Pilate scourges Him; the Jews clamor for His Crucifixion as making Himself a king. Pilate notwithstanding his wife's warning, sentences Him	27:15-26	15:6-15	23:13-25	18:39-40 19:1-16
161. Jesus mocked by Roman soldiers with scarlet robe, crown of thorns, and reed	27:27-30	15:16-19	....	....
162. Judas' remorse; he presumptuously enters the temple, flings down the silver, and hangs himself (Acts 1:18-19)	27:3-10	....	....	....
163. Jesus bears His own Cross of the city gate, where He is relieved by Simon of Cyrene; refuses stupefying myrrhyed wine	27:31-34	15:20-23	23:26-32	19:16-17

Wednesday, 9 a.m. (the time of morning sacrifices)
Jesus is put on the Cross

Contents	Matthew	Mark	Luke	John
164. Crucified at Golgotha, probably outside the Damascus gate. Seven sayings on the Cross, *three* relating to *others*, *four* to *Himself*: 1. For His murderers — *"Father, forgive them,"* etc.	27:35-44	15:24-32	23:33-38	19:18-27
165. 2. The penitent thief promised paradise — *"Today,"* etc.	....	....	23:39-43	....

Contents	Matthew	Mark	Luke	John
166. His garments divided and vesture cast lots for; 3. commends His mother to the care of John – *"Behold your son,"* etc.	....	....	....	19:23-27

Wednesday, 3 p.m. (the time of evening sacrifices)
Jesus dies

Contents	Matthew	Mark	Luke	John
167. Darkness over the land from sixth to ninth hour. Jesus' loud cry 4. *"Eli, Eli,"* etc. Saith, 5. *"I thirst,"* and receives the vinegar to fulfill Scripture; 6. *"It is finished"*; 7. *"Father, into your hands I commend My Spirit"*; gives up the ghost; the veil of the temple rent. Centurion's testimony	27:45-54	15:33-41	23:44-49	19:28-30
168. The side pierced by the soldier's spear and the blood and water attest His Death and the truth of Scripture (Gen. 2:21-23; Zech. 12:10; Eph. 5:30, 32; I Jn. 5:6). The body, taken down, is wrapped up with Nicodemus' aloes and myrrh, and buried in a new tomb of Joseph of Arimathaea	27:57-61	15:42-47	23:50-56	19:31-42
169. Pilate grants a guard, and they set a seal upon the sepulcher	27:62-66	....	....	....

Christ's Resurrection, His Appearances during
Forty Days, and Ascension

Easter Sunday

Contents	Matthew	Mark	Luke	John
170. Resurrection at first dawn	28:1-4	....	....	....
171. The women, coming with spices, find the sepulcher open and empty. Mary Magdalene returns to tell Peter and John ..	28:1	16:1-4	24:1-3	20:1-2
172. The other women, remaining, see two angels, who declare the Lord's Resurrection	28:5-7	16:5-7	24:4-8	....
173. Mary Magdalene returns to the sepulcher. Jesus reveals Himself to her. She reports to the disciples — *First* appearance.............	....	16:9-11	....	20:11-18
174. Jesus meets the women (Mary mother of James, Salome, and Joanna) on their return to the city — *Second* appearance.......	28:8-10	16:8	24:9-11	....
175. Peter and John find the sepulcher empty	....	....	24:12	20:3-10
176. Report of the watch to the chief priests, who				

Contents	Matthew	Mark	Luke	John
bribe them	28:11-15	....	....	....
177. Jesus seen by Peter (Cephas, I Cor. 15:5) — *Third* appearance	....	....	24:34	....
178. Seen by the two disciples on way to Emmaus — *Fourth* appearance	....	16:12-13	24:13, 35	....
179. Jesus appears to the eleven (see Mk. 16:14). Thomas being absent — *Fifth* appearance ..	....	16:14 .	24:36-49	20:19-23
Subsequent Appearances				
180. Evening of Sunday after Easter day. Jesus appears to them again, Thomas being present — *Sixth* appearance	....	....	....	20:24-29
181. The eleven go into Galilee, to a mountain appointed. Jesus appears, and commands them to teach all nations — *Seventh* appearance	28:16-20	16:15-18	....	....
182. Jesus shows Himself at the Sea of Tiberias — *Eighth* appearance. Charges Simon to feed his lambs, sheep, and young sheep	....	....	....	21:1-24
183. Seen of above five hundred brethren at once (I Cor. 15:6), probably along with the eleven — *Ninth* appearance	28:16	....	....	....
184. He is seen by James, then by all the Apostles (Acts 1:3-8; I Cor. 15:7) — *Tenth* appearance. In all, 538 (549 if the eleven [Mat. 28:16] be distinct from the 500) *persons are specified* as having seen the risen Saviour: also, after His ascension, St. Paul (I Cor. 15:8)	....	....	....	....
185. The ascension, forty days after Easter (Acts 1:9-12)	....	16:19-20	24:50-53	....
186. Purpose and conclusion	....	....	....	20:30-31 21:25

PARABLES AND MIRACLES OF
THE NEW TESTAMENT

PARABLES OF OUR LORD

5. Common to Matthew and Luke

House built on rock and on sand .... Mat. 7:24; Lk. 6:48
The leaven .... Mat. 13:33; Lk. 13:20-21
The lost sheep .... Mat. 18:12; Lk., Chpt. 15

6. Common to Matthew, Mark, and Luke

The candle under a bushel .... Mat., Chpt. 5; Mk., Chpt. 4; Lk., Chpts. 8, 11
The new cloth on old garment .... Mat., Chpt. 9; Mk., Chpt. 2; Lk., Chpt. 5
New wine and old bottles .... Mat., Chpt. 9; Mk., Chpt. 2; Lk., Chpt. 5
The sower .... Mat. 13:3-9; Mk. 4:3-9; Lk. 8:5-15
The mustard seed .... Mat., Chpt. 13; Mk., Chpt. 4; Lk., Chpt. 13
The vineyard and husbandmen .... Mat., Chpt. 21; Mk., Chpt. 12; Lk., Chpt. 20
Young leaves of the fig tree .... Mat., Chpt. 24; Mk., Chpt. 13; Lk., Chpt. 21

MIRACLES OF OUR LORD

1. Peculiar to Matthew

Two blind men cured .... Mat. 9:27-31
Dumb spirit cast out .... Mat. 9:32-33
Tribute money provided .... Mat. 17:24-27

2. Peculiar to Mark

Deaf and dumb man cured .... Mk. 7:31-37
Blind man cured .... Mk. 8:22-26

3. Peculiar to Luke

Jesus passes through the crowd at Nazareth .... Lk. 4:28-30
Draught of fishes .... Lk. 5: 1-11
Widow's son raised to life at Nain .... Lk. 7:11-17
Woman's infirmity cured .... Lk. 13:11-17
Dropsy cured .... Lk. 14:1-6
Ten lepers cleansed .... Lk. 17:11-19
The ear of Malchus healed .... Lk. 22:50-51

4. Peculiar to John

Water made wine at Cana .... Jn. 2:1-11
Nobleman's son cured of fever .... Jn. 4:46-54
Impotent man cured at Jerusalem .... Jn. 5:1-9
Jesus passes through crowd in the temple .... Jn. 8:59
Man born blind cured at Jerusalem .... Jn. 9:1-7
Lazarus raised from the dead at Bethany .... Jn. 11:38-44
Falling backward of the soldiers .... Jn. 18:5-6
Draught of 153 fishes .... Jn. 21:1-14

5. Common to Matthew and Mark

Syrophenician's daughter cured .... Mat. 15:28; Mk. 7:24
The four thousand fed .... Mat. 15:32; Mk. 8:1
The fig tree cursed .... Mat. 21:19; Mk. 11:13

6. Common to Matthew and Luke

Centurion's palsied servant cured .... Mat. 8:5; Lk. 7:1
Blind and dumb demoniac cured .... Mat. 12:22; Lk. 11:14

7. Common to Mark and Luke

Demoniac in synagogue cured .... Mk. 1:23; Lk. 4:33

8. Common to Matthew, Mark, and Luke

Peter's mother-in-law cured .... Mat. 8:14; Mk. 1:30; Lk. 4:38
The tempest stilled .... Mat. 8:23; Mk. 4:37; Lk. 8:22
The demoniacs cured .... Mat. 8:28; Mk. 5:1; Lk. 8:26
The leper cured .... Mat. 8:2; Mk. 1:40; Lk. 5:12
The daughter of Jairus raised to life .... Mat. 9:23; Mk. 5:23; Lk. 8:41
Woman's issue of blood cured .... Mat. 9:20; Mk. 5:25; Lk. 8:43
A paralytic cured .... Mat. 9:2; Mk. 2:3; Lk. 5:18
Man's withered hand cured .... Mat. 12:10; Mk. 3:1; Lk. 6:6
Unclean spirit cast out .... Mat. 17:14; Mk. 9:14; Lk. 9:37
Blind men cured .... Mat. 20:30; Mk. 10:46; Lk. 18:35

9. Common to Matthew, Mark, and John

Christ walks on the sea .... Mat. 14:25; Mk. 6:48; Jn. 6:19

10. Common to all the Evangelists

The five thousand fed .... Mat. 14:15; Mk. 6:30; Lk. 9:10; Jn. 6:1-14

MIRACLES RECORDED IN THE ACTS OF THE APOSTLES

The outpouring of the Holy Spirit,
   with the accompanying signs .... Acts, Chpt. 2
The gift of tongues .... Acts 2:4-11; 10:44-46
Lame man at Beautiful Gate of the temple .... Acts, Chpt. 3
Death of Ananias and Sapphira .... Acts, Chpt. 5
Healing of sick in streets by Peter, etc. .... Acts 5:15-16
Prison opened for apostles by angels .... Acts 5:19; 12:7-11
Stephen's dying vision of Christ .... Acts 7:55-56
Unclean spirits cast our by Philip .... Acts 8:6-7
Christ's appearance to Saul on his way to Damascus .... Acts 9:3 ff.; 22:6 ff.; 26:13-19
Saul's recovery of his sight .... Acts 9:17-18; 22:12-13
Aeneas healed of palsy by Peter .... Acts 9:33-34
Raising of Dorcas to life by Peter .... Acts 9:40
Vision of Cornelius .... Acts 10:3-4, 30-32
Vision of Peter .... Acts, Chpts. 10-11
Peter miraculously released from prison .... Acts 12:7-11
Elymas stricken with blindness by Paul .... Acts 13:11
Healing of cripple at Lystra .... Acts 14:8-18
Vision of *man of Macedonia* seen by Paul .... Acts 16:9
Spirit of divination cast out of a damsel by Paul .... Acts 16:16-18
Earthquake at Philippi .... Acts 16:25-26
Special miracles wrought by Paul at Ephesus .... Acts 19:11-12
Evil spirit puts to flight Sceva's sons .... Acts 19:13-16

Raising of Eutychus to life by Paul .... Acts 20:9-12
Prophecies of Agabus .... Acts 11:28; 21:11
Appearances of Christ to Paul .... Acts 9:3 ff.; 22:17-21; 23:11; 27:23-24
Paul unharmed by bite of viper .... Acts 28:3-5
Paul heals Publius' father and other sick at Melita .... Acts 28:8-9

MIRACLES REFERRED TO IN THE EPISTLES AND REVELATION

Miracles wrought by Paul and others .... Rom. 15:18-19; I Cor. 12:9-10, 28-31;
14:18; Gal. 3:5; I Tim. 1:20
Miracles of tongues .... I Cor. 14:27-33
Appearances of Christ after His resurrection .... I Cor. 15:4-8
Visions and revelations of Paul .... II Cor. 12:1-5, 12
"Powers of the world to come" (*i.e.*, of gospel times) .... Heb. 2:4; 6:5
The visions of John in Patmos .... Rev. 1:10; 4 to end of Book

CONCORDANCE
TO THE HOLY SCRIPTURES

A

ABASE Ezek. 21:26, and *a* him that is high
Dan. 4:37, Walk in pride he is able to *a*
Mat. 23:12; Lk. 14:11; 18:14, whosoever exalts himself shall be *a*
Phil. 4:12, I know how to be *a*
See Job 40:11; Is. 31:4; II Cor. 11:7
ABATED Gen. 8:3; Lev. 27:18; Deut. 34:7
ABHOR Ex. 5:21, made our savor to be *a*
Job 19:19, my inward friends *a* me
Ps. 78:59, wroth, and *a* Israel 89:38, you have cast off and *a*
Prov. 22:14, *a* of the Lord shall fall therein
Isa. 66:24, be an *a* unto all flesh
Ezek. 16:25, made your beauty to be *a*
See Lev. 26:11, Job 42:6; Rom. 12:9
ABIDE Ex. 16:29, *a* every man in his place
Num. 24:2, he saw Israel *a* in tents
31:19, *a* without camp seven days
I Sam. 5:7, Ark of God shall not *a* with us
Job 24:13, nor *a* in the paths thereof
Ps. 15:1, Lord, who shall *a* in your Tabernacle?
91:1, shall *a* under the shadow
Prov. 15:31, hear reproof *a* among wise
Eccl. 1:4, the Earth *a* for ever
Jer. 42:10, if you will still *a* in this land
49:18, 33; 50:40, there shall no man *a*
Lk. 2:8, shepherds *a* in the field
24:29, *A* with us, it is toward evening
Jn. 3:36, wrath of God *a* on him
5:38, have not his word *a* in you
14:16, another Comforter, that he may *a*
15:4, *a* in me
5, he that *a* in me brings forth fruit
10, *A* in my love
Acts 16:15, come to my house, and *a*
I Cor. 3:14, if any man's work *a*
13:13, now *a* faith, hope, charity
II Tim. 2:13, if we believe not, he *a*
See Gen. 29:19; Num. 35:25; Eccl. 8:15
ABILITY Ezra 2:69, they gave after their *a*
Dan. 1:4, had *a* to stand in the palace
Mat. 25:15, to every man according to *a*
I Pet. 4:11, as of the *a* God gives
See Lev. 27:8; Neh. 5:8; Acts 11:29
ABJECTS Ps. 35:15, the *a* gathered themselves together
ABLE Deut. 16:17, every man give as he is *a*
Josh. 23:9, no man *a* to stand before you?
I Sam. 6:20, who is *a* to stand before God?
I Ki. 3:9, who is *a* to judge?
II Chron. 2:6, who is *a* to build?
Prov. 27:4, who is *a* to stand before envy?
Amos 7:10, land not *a* to bear his words
Mat. 3:9, God is *a* of these stones

9:28, believe you that I am *a*
20:22, are you *a* to drink of the cup?
Lk. 12:26, not *a* to do which is least
Acts 6:10, not *a* to resist wisdom
Rom. 4:21, what he had promised he was *a*
8:39, *a* to separate us from love of God
I Cor. 10:13, tempted above that you are *a*
II Cor. 3:6, *a* ministers of new testament
Eph. 3:18, *a* to comprehend with all saints
Phil. 3:21, *a* to subdue all things
Heb. 2:18, *a* to succour them that are tempted
James 4:12, *a* to save and destroy
Jude 24, *a* to keep you from falling
Rev. 5:3, no man *a* to open book
6:17, who shall be *a* to stand?
See Ex. 18:21
ABODE (*n.*) Jn. 14:23, come and make our *a*
See II Ki. 19:27, Isa. 37:28
ABODE (*v.*) Gen. 49:24, his bow *a* in strength
Ex. 24:16, glory of the Lord *a* on Sinai
Judg. 21:2, the people *a* there before God
Lk. 1:56, Mary *a* with her about three months
Jn. 1:32, the Spirit, and it *a* upon him
8:44, a murderer, and *a* not in truth
Acts 14:3, long time *a*, speaking boldly
18:3, Paul *a* with them, and wrought
See I Sam. 7:2; Ezra 8:15
ABOLISH II Cor. 3:13, the end of that *a*
Eph. 2:15, *a* in his flesh the enmity
II Tim. 1:10, Christ who has *a* death
See Isa. 2:18; 51:6; Ezek. 6:6
ABOMINABLE I Ki. 21:26, Ahab *a* in following idols
Job 15:16, how much more *a* is man?
Ps. 14:1; 53:1, they have done *a* works
Isa. 14:19, cast out like *a* branch
65:4; Jer. 16:18, broth of *a* things
Jer. 44:4, this *a* thing that I hate
Titus 1:16, in works they deny him, being *a*
I Pet. 4:3, walked in *a* idolatries
See Lev. 11:43; Deut. 14:3; Rev. 21:8
ABOMINATION Gen. 43:32, *a* to Egyptians
Lev. 18:26, shall not commit any *a*
Deut. 7:26, nor bring *a* into house
18:9, after the *a* of nations
12, because of *a* the Lord does drive
25:16, all that do unrighteously are *a* to God
Prov. 3:32; 11:20, the froward *a* to the Lord
8:7, wickedness as *a* to my lips
15:8-9, 26; 21:27, sacrifice, etc., of wicked *a*
28:9, even his prayer shall be *a*
Isa. 44:19, the residue thereof an *a*
Jer. 4:1, put away your *a* out of sight
6:15; 8:12, ashamed when committed *a*
Ezek. 5:9, the like, because of all your *a*,
33:29, land desolate because of *a*
Dan. 11:31; Mat. 24:15 *a* of desolation

Lk. 16:15, *a* in sight of God
Rev. 21:27, in no wise enter that works *a*
See Lev. 7:18; 11:41; Mal. 2:11; Rev. 17:4
ABOUND Rom. 15:13, that ye may *a* in hope
  I Cor. 15:58, always *a* in work of the Lord
  II Cor. 1:5, as sufferings *a*, so consolation *a*
  See Rom. 3:7, 5:15; Phil. 4:12
ABOVE Job 31:2, portion of God from *a*
  Prov. 15:24, way of life *a* to wise
  Mat. 10:24, Lk. 6:40, disciple not *a* master
  Jn. 3:31, he that comes from *a* is *a* all
  Jn. 8:23, I am from *a*
  I Cor. 4:6, *a* that which is written
  Gal. 4:26, Jerusalem *a* is free
  See Gen. 48:22; Ps. 138:2; James 1:17
ABSENT I Cor. 5:3; Col. 2:5, *a* in body
  II Cor. 5:6, *a* from the Lord
  See Gen. 31:49; II Cor. 10:1
ABSTAIN I Thess. 5:22, A from all appearance of
    evil
  I Pet. 2:11, *a* from fleshly lusts
  See I Thess. 4:3; I Tim. 4:3
ABSTINENCE Acts 27:21, after long *a* Paul
    stood forth
ABUNDANCE I Sam. 1:16
  I Ki. 18:41, sound of *a* of rain
  I Chron. 29:21, offered sacrifices in *a*
  Ps. 52:7, trusted in *a* of riches
  72:7; Jer. 33:6, *a* of peace
  Eccl. 5:10, loves *a* with increase
  12, *a* of rich will not suffer him to sleep
  Mat. 12:34; Lk. 21:4, out of *a* of heart
  13:12; 25:29, he shall have more *a*
  Lk. 12:15, life consists not in *a*
  II Cor. 8:2, of affliction the *a* of their joy
  12:7, through *a* of revelations
  See Job 36:31; Rom. 5:17; Rev. 18:3
ABUNDANT Ps. 145:7, *a* utter the memory
  Isa. 56:12, as this day, and more *a*
  I Tim. 1:14, grace was exceeding *a*
  Titus 3:6, shed *a*, through Jesus Christ
  II Pet. 1:11, entrance administered *a*
  See Ex. 34:6; Isa. 55:7; I Pet. 1:3
ABUSE I Cor. 7:31, use world as not *a*
  9:18, that I *a* not my power
ACCEPT Gen. 4:7, shall you not be *a*?
  Ex. 28:38; Lev. 10:10, *a* before the Lord
  Deut. 33:11, *a* the work of his hands
  I Sam. 18:5, *a* in sight of all the people
  II Sam. 24:23, the Lord your God *a* you
  Job. 13:8; 32:21, will ye *a* his person?
  Prov. 18:5, not good to *a* wicked
  Jer. 14:12; Amos 5:22, I will not *a* them
  37:20; 42:2, supplication be *a*
  Ezek. 20:40; 43:27, I will *a*
  Lk. 4:24, no prophet is *a*
  Acts 10:35, works righteousness is *a*
  Rom. 15:31, my service be *a* of the saints
  II Cor. 5:9, present of absent, we may be *a*
  See Ps. 119:108; Eccl. 12:10; Mal. 1:8
ACCESS Rom 5:2; Eph. 2:18; 3:12
ACCOMPLISH Job 14:6, *a*, as a hireling
  Ps. 64:6, they *a* diligent search
  Prov. 13:19, desire *a* is sweet

Isa. 40:2, her warfare is *a*
Lk. 12:50, straitened till it be *a*!
I Pet. 5:9, afflictions are *a* in brethren
See Isa. 55:11, Lk. 18:31; 22:37
ACCORD Acts 1:14; 4:24; 8:6; Phil. 2:2
ACCORDING Ex. 12:25, *a* as he promised
  Deut. 16:10, *a* as God has blessed you
  Job 34:11; Jer. 17:10; 25:14; 32:19, *a* to ways
  Mat. 16:27; Rom. 2:6, *a* to work
  Jn. 7:24, *a* to the appearance
  Rom. 8:28, the called *a* to his purpose
  12:6, gifts differing *a* to grace
  II Cor. 8:12, *a* to that a man has
  See Mat. 9:29; Titus 3:5
ACCOUNT Lk. 16:2, give *a* of stewardship
  20:35, *a* worthy to obtain
  Rom. 14:12, every one give *a* to God
  Gal. 3:6, *a* to him for righteousness
  Heb. 13:17, watch as they that give *a*
  See Job 33:13; Ps. 114:3; Mat. 12:36
ACCURSED Josh. 6:18; 7:1; 22:20, *a* thing
  Rom 9:3, wish myself *a* from Christ
  I Cor. 12:3, no man calls Jesus *a*
  Gal. 1:8-9, preach other gospel, let him be *a*
  See Deut. 21:23; Josh. 6:17; Isa. 65:20
ACCUSATION Lk. 19:8, by false *a*
  I Tim. 5:19, against elder receive not *a*
  II Pet. 2:11; Jude 9, railing *a*
  See Mat. 27:37; Mk. 15:26; Lk. 6:7
ACCUSE Prov. 30:10, A not servant to master
  Mat. 27:12, when *a* he answered nothing
  Lk. 16:1, was *a* that he had wasted
  Jn. 5:45, that I will *a* you to the Father
  Titus 1:6, not *a* of riot or unruly
ACKNOWLEDGE Ps. 32:5; 51:3, I *a* my sin
  Prov. 3:6, in all your ways *a* Him
  Isa. 63:16, though Israel *a* us not
  I Jn. 2:23, he that *a* the son
  See Dan. 11:39; Hos. 5:15
ACQUAINT Job 22:21; Ps. 139:3; Eccl. 2:3
ACQUAINTANCE Job 19:13; Ps. 31:11
ACQUIT Job 10:14; Nah. 1:3
ACTIONS I Sam. 2:3
ACTIVITY Gen. 47:6
ADDER Gen. 49:17; Ps. 58:4; 91:13; 140:3
ADDICTED I Cor. 16:15
ADDITION I Ki. 7:29-30, 36
ADJURE Josh 6:26; I Sam. 14:24; Mk. 5:7
ADMINISTER I Cor. 12:5; II Cor. 8:19-20
ADMIRE II Thess. 1:10; Jude 16; Rev. 17:6
ADMONISH Acts 27:9, Paul *a* them
  Rom. 15:14; Col. 3:16, *a* one another
  I Thess. 5:12, over you in Lord, and *a* you
  II Thess. 3:15, *a* him as a brother
  Heb. 8:5, Moses was *a* of God
  See Eccl. 4:13; 12:12; Jer. 42:19
ADMONITION I Cor. 10:11; Eph. 6:4
ADO Mk. 5:39
ADOPTION Rom. 8:15, 23; 9:4, Gal. 4:5
ADORN Isa. 61:10; Rev. 21:2, bride *a* herself
  I Tim. 2:9; I Pet. 3:3, 5, women *a*
  Titus 2:10, *a* doctrine of God
  See Jer. 31:4; Lk. 21:5
ADULTERER Lev. 20:10, *a* shall surely be put to

death
Job 24:15, eye of *a* waits for twilight
Isa. 57:3, seed of the *a*
Jer. 9:2; 23:10, land is full of *a*
Mal. 3:5, I, swift witness against *a*
I Cor. 6:9, neither *a* shall inherit
ADULTERY Prov. 6:32, whoso commits *a*
Mat. 5:28, committed *a* in his heart
II Pet. 2:14, having eyes full of *a*
See Hos. 2:2; Mat. 15:19; Mk. 7:21
ADVANCED I Sam. 12:6; Esther 3:1; 5:11
ADVANTAGE Lk. 9:25, what is man *a*?
Rom. 3:1; I Cor. 15:32, what *a*?
II Cor. 2:11, lest Satan get *a*
See Job 35:3; Jude 16
ADVENTURE Deut. 28:56; Judg. 9:17
ADVERSARY Ex 23:22, I will be *a* to your *a*
Num. 22:22, angel stood for *a*
Ps. 89:42; Isa. 59:18; Jer. 46:10; Nah. 1:2
Lk. 13:17, his *a*
I Ki. 5:4, neither *a* nor evil
11:14, 23, Lord stirred up *a*
Job 31:35, that my *a* had written a book
Ps. 38:20; 69:19; 109:4, 20, 29; Isa. 1:24, my *a*
74:10, how long shall *a* reproach?
Isa. 50:8, who is my *a*?
64:2; Jer. 30:16; Mic. 5:9, your *a*
Amos 3:11, *a* shall be round the land
Mat. 5:25; Lk. 12:58, your *a*
I Cor. 16:9, there are many *a*
Phil 1:28, terrified by your *a*
I Tim. 5:14, give no occasion to *a*
Heb. 10:27, indignation shall devour *a*
See I Sam. 2:10; Isa. 9:11; 11:13
ADVERSITY I Sam. 10:19, all *a*
Ps. 10:6, I shall never be in *a*
94:13; Prov. 24:10; Eccl. 7:14, day of *a*
Prov. 17:17, brother is born for *a*
Isa. 30:20, bread of *a*
Heb. 13:3, remember them which suffer *a*
See Ps. 31:7; 35:15
ADVERTISE Num 24:14, Ruth 4:4
ADVICE I Sam. 25:33, blessed by your *a*
II Sam. 19:43, that our *a* should not be first
II Chron. 10:9, 14, what *a* give ye?
Prov. 20:18, with good *a* make war
II Cor. 8:10, herein I give my *a*
See Judg. 19:30; 20:7; II Chron. 25:17
ADVISE Prov. 13:10, with well *a* is wisdom
Acts 27:12, the more part *a* to depart
See II Sam. 24:13, I Ki. 12:6; I Chron. 21:12
ADVISEMENT I Chron. 12:19
AFAR OFF Jer. 23:23, a God *a*
30:10; 46:27, I will save them from *a*
Mat. 26:58; Mk. 14:54, followed *a*
Acts 2:39, promise to all *a*
Eph. 2:17, preached to you *a*
Heb. 11:13, seen the promises *a*
See Gen. 22:4; Ezra 3:13
AFFAIRS I Chron 26:32, pertaining to God, and
a of king
II Tim. 2:4, entangles himself with *a*
See Dan. 2:49; 3:12; Eph. 6:21-22
AFFECTED Gal. 4:17-18, zealously *a*

See Lam. 3:51; Acts 14:2
AFFECTION I Chron. 29:3
Rom. 1:26, vile *a*
31, without natural *a*
12:10, be kindly *a* one to another
II Tim. 3:3, without natural *a*
Gal. 5:24, crucified flesh with *a*
Col. 3:2, set your *a* on things above
5 inordinate *a*
AFFINITY I Ki. 3:1; II Chron. 18:1; Ezra 9:14
AFFIRM Acts 25:19
See Rom. 3:8; I Tim. 1:7; Titus 3:8
AFFLICT Lev. 16:29, 31; Num. 29:7; Isa. 58:3
Num. 11:11, wherefore have you *a*?
Ruth 1:21, Almighty has *a* me
I Ki. 8:35, turn when you do *a*
11:39, I will *a* seed of David
Job 6:14, to *a* pity should be showed
Ps. 44:2, how you did *a* the people
55:19, God shall hear, and *a*
82:3, do justice to the *a*
90:15, the days wherein you have *a*
Ps. 119:67, before I was *a*
140:12, maintain cause of *a*
Prov. 15:15, days of the *a* evil
22:22, neither oppress the *a*
31:5, pervert judgment of *a*
Isa. 51:21, hear, you *a* and drunken
53:4, 7, smitten of God, and *a*
54:11, you *a*, tossed with tempest
63:9, in all their *a* he was *a*
Lam. 1:5, 12, the Lord has *a*
Nah. 1:12, I will *a* you no more
AFFLICTION Gen. 29:32; Deut. 26:7; Ps. 25:18,
looked on *a*
Ex. 3:7; Acts 7:10, have seen *a* of people
Deut. 16:3; I Ki. 22:27; II Chron. 6:26
II Chron. 20:9, cry to you in *a*
33:12, in *a* besought the Lord
Job 5:6, *a* comes not forth of the dust
30:16, 27, days of *a*
36:8, cords of *a*
Ps. 34:19, many are *a* of righteous
119:50, this is my comfort in *a*
132:1, remember David, and all his *a*
Isa. 30:20, water of *a*
48:10, furnace of *a*
Jer. 16:19, refuge in day of *a*
Lam. 3:1, man that has seen *a*
Hos. 5:15, in their *a* they will seek
Mk. 4:17, *a* arises for the word's sake
Acts 20:23, bonds and *a* abide me
II Cor. 2:4, out of much *a* I wrote
4:17, light *a*, but for a moment
8:2, great trial of *a*
Phil. 1:16, add *a* to bonds
Heb. 10:32, great fight of *a*
11:25, suffer *a* with people of God
James 1:27, visit fatherless in *a*
See II Ki. 14:26; Col. 1:24
AFFRIGHT Isa. 21:4; fearfulness *a* me
Mk. 16:5; Lk. 24:37, they were *a*
6, be not *a*, ye seek Jesus
See Deut. 7:21; II Chron. 32:18; Jer. 51:32

AFOOT Mk. 6:33; Acts 20:13
AFORETIME Dan. 6:10, prayed as *a*
 Rom. 15:4, things were written *a*
 See Isa. 52:4; Jer. 30:20
AFRAID Gen. 20:8; Ex. 14:10; Mk. 9:6; Lk. 2:9,
  sore *a*
 Lev. 26:6; Job 11:19; Isa. 17:2; Ezek. 34:28;
  Zeph. 3:13 none make *a*
 Judg. 7:3, whosoever is fearful and *a*
 I Sam. 18:29, Saul, yet the more *a*
 Neh. 6:9, they all made us *a*
 Job 3:25, that which I was *a* of is come
  9:28, I am *a* of sorrows
 Ps. 27:1, of whom shall I be *a*?
  56:3, 11, what time I am *a*
  65:8, *a* at your tokens
  91:5, not be *a* for terror by night
  112:7, *a* of evil tidings
 Isa. 51:12, be *a* of a man that shall die
 Mk. 9:32; 10:32, *a* to ask him
 Jn. 19:8, Pilate was more *a*
 Gal. 4:11, I am *a* of you
 See Deut. 1:17; Ps. 3:6
AFRESH Heb. 6:6
AFTERNOON Judg. 19:8
AFTERWARDS I Sam. 24:5
 Ps. 73:24, *a* receive me to glory
 Prov. 20:17, deceit sweet, but *a*
  24:27, prepare work, and *a* build
  29:11, wise man keeps till *a*
 Jn. 13:36, you shall follow me *a*
 I Cor. 15:23, *a* they that are Christ's
 See Ex. 11:1; Mat. 21:32; Gal. 3:23
AGAINST Lk. 2:34; Acts 19:36; 28:22
 See Gen. 16:12; Ps. 41:9; Mat. 12:30
AGED II Sam. 19:32; Job 15:10, *a* men
 Phile. 9, Paul the *a*
 See Job 12:20; 29:8; 32:9
AGES Eph. 2:7; 3:5, 21; Col. 1:26
AGONE I Sam. 30:13
AGONY Lk. 22:44
AGREE Amos 3:3, except they be *a*
 Mat. 5:25, *A* with adversary
  18:19, two of you shall *a*
 Mk. 14:56, 59, witness *a* not
 Acts 15:15, to this *a* words of the prophets
 I Jn. 5:8, these three *a* in one
 See Mat. 20:2; Lk. 5:36; Acts 5:9
AGREEMENT Isa. 28:15; II Cor. 6:16
AGROUND Acts 27:41
AHA Ps. 35:21; 40:15; 70:3; Isa. 44:16; Ezek.
  25:3; 26:2; 36:2
AILS Gen. 21:17; Judg. 28:23; Ps. 114:5; Isa. 22:1
AIR Job 41:16, no *a* can come between
 I Cor. 9:26, as one that beats the *a*
  14:9, you shall speak into *a*
 I Thess. 4:17, meet Lord in *a*
ALARM Jer. 4:19; 49:2, *a* of war
 Joel 2:1, sound *a* in holy mountain
ALAS II Ki. 6:5, 15, *A* my master
 Ezek. 6:11, stamp, and say *A*
 See Num. 24:23; Jer. 30:7; Rev. 18:10
ALBEIT Ezek. 13:7; Phile. 19
ALIEN Deut. 14:21, sell it to an *a*;

Ps. 69:8, an *a* unto my mother's children
 Eph. 2:12, *a* from commonwealth
 Heb. 11:34, armies of the *a*
 See Ex. 18:3; Job 19:15; Isa. 61:5; Lam. 5:2
ALIENATED Ezek. 23:17; Eph. 4:18
ALIKE Job 21:26, lie down *a* in dust
 Ps. 33:15, fashions hearts *a*
 Eccl. 9:2, All things come *a* to all
 See Ps. 139:12; Eccl 11:6; Rom. 14:5
ALIVE Lev. 16:10, scapegoat presented *a*
 Num. 16:33, went down *a* into pit
 Deut. 4:4, are *a* every one of you
  32:39; I Sam. 2:6, I kill, and I make *a*
 Ezek. 13:18; 18:27, save souls *a*
 Mk. 16:11, heard that he was *a*
 Lk. 15:24, 32, son was dead, and is *a*
  24:23, angels, who said he was *a*
 Acts 1:3, showed himself *a*
 Rom. 6:11, 13, *a* unto God
 I Cor. 15:22, all be made *a*
 Rev. 1:18, I am *a* for evermore
ALLEGING Acts 17:3
ALLEGORY Gal. 4:24
ALLOW Lk. 11:48; Acts 24:15; Rom. 7:15
ALLOWANCE II Ki. 25:30
ALLURE Hos. 2:14; II Pet. 2:18
ALMIGHTY Ex. 6:3, by the name of God *A*
 Job 11:7, can you find out the *A*?
  29:5, when *A* was yet with me
 Ezek. 1:24; 10:5, I heard as voice of *A*
 Rev. 1:8; 4:8; 11:17, *A*, who was, and is
 See Gen. 17:1; Job 21:15; Ps. 91:1
ALMS Mat. 6:1; Lk. 11:41; Acts 10:2
ALONE Num. 11:14; Deut. 1:9
 I Ki. 11:29, they two *a* in field
 Ps. 136:4, *a* does great wonders
 Mat. 4:4; Lk. 4:4, not live by bread *a*
 Lk. 9:18, 36; Jn. 6:15, Jesus was *a*
 See Gen. 2:18; Mat. 18:15, James 2:17
ALREADY Eccl. 1:10; Jn. 3:18; Phil. 3:16
ALTAR Mat. 5:23, bring your gift to *a*
  23:18, swears by *a*
 I Cor. 9:13; 10:18, wait at *a*
 Heb. 13:10, we have an *a*
 See I Ki. 13:2; Isa. 19:19; Acts 17:23
ALTER Ps. 89:34
 Lk. 9:29, fashion of countenance *a*
 See Lev. 27:10; Dan. 6:8
ALTOGETHER Ps. 14:3, *a* become filthy
  50:21, *a* such an one as yourself
 Song of Sol. 5:16, he is *a* lovely
 See Ps. 19:9; 39:5; 139:4
ALWAYS Job 7:16, I would not live *a*
 Ps. 103:9, not *a* chide
 Mat. 28:20, I am with you *a*
 Mk. 14:7; Jn. 12:8, me ye have not *a*
 Phil. 4:4, rejoice in Lord *a*
 See Ps. 16:8; Isa. 57:16; Jn. 11:42
AMAZED Mat. 19:25, disciples exceedingly *a*
 Mk. 2:12; Lk. 5:26, *a*, and glorified God
  14:33, he began to be sore *a*
 Lk. 9:43, *a* at mighty power of God
 See Ezek. 32:10; Acts 3:10; I Pet. 3:6
AMEND Jer. 7:3; 26:13; 35:15; Jn. 4:52

AMIABLE Ps. 84:1
AMISS II Chron. 6:37; Dan. 3:29; Lk. 23:41
ANCHOR Acts 27:30; Heb. 6:19
ANCIENT Job 12:12, *a* is wisdom
  Ps. 119:100, I understand more than *a*
  Dan. 7:9, the *A* of days did sit
ANGEL Gen. 48:16, *A* which redeemed me
  Ps. 34:7, *a* of Lord encamps
    78:25, many did eat *a* food
  Eccl. 5:6, neither say before *a*, it was error
  Isa. 63:9, *a* of his presence saved them
  Hos. 12:4, he had power over the *a*
  Mat. 13:39, the reapers are the *a*
  Mk. 12:25; Lk. 20:36, are as *a* in heaven
  Lk. 22:43, an *a* strengthening him
  Jn. 5:4, *a* went down at a certain season
  I Cor. 6:3, we shall judge *a*
  II Cor. 11:14, transformed into *a* of light
  Heb. 2:2, word spoken by *a*
    16, not nature of *a*
    13:2, entertained *a* unawares
  See Gen. 19:1; Ps. 8:5; Mat. 25:41
ANGER Gen. 49:7, cursed by their *a*
  Neh. 9:17, slow to *a*
  Ps. 6:1; Jer. 10:24, rebuke me not in *a*
    30:5, *a* endures but a moment
  Prov. 15:1, grievous words stir up *a*
    19:11, discretion defers *a*
  Eccl. 7:9, *a* rests in bosom of fools
  Mk. 3:5, he looked on them with *a*
  Col. 3:8, put off *a*, wrath, malice
  See Ps. 37:8; 85:3; 90:7; Prov. 16:32
ANGRY Ps. 7:11, God is *a* with the wicked
  Prov. 14:17, he that is soon *a*
    22:24, make no friendship with *a* man
  Jonah 4:4, doest thou well to be *a*?
  Mat. 5:22, whosoever is *a* with brother
  Jn. 7:23, are ye *a* at me?
  Eph. 4:26, be ye *a*, and sin not
  Titus 1:7, bishop not soon *a*
  See Gen. 18:30; Prov. 21:19; Eccl. 5:6
ANGUISH Ex. 6:9, hearkened not for *a*
  Job 7:11, I will speak in *a* of spirit
  Rom. 2:9, tribulation and *a* on every soul
  II Cor. 2:4, out of much *a* of heart
  See Gen. 42:21; Isa. 8:22, Jn. 16:21
ANOINT Deut. 28:40; II Sam. 14:2
  Isa. 21:5, arise, and *a* shield
    61:1; Lk 4:18, *a* to preach
  Mk. 14:8, *a* my body to burying
  Lk. 7:46, my head you did not *a*
  Jn. 9:6, *a* eyes of blind man
    12:3, Mary *a* feet of Jesus
  II Cor. 1:21, he which *a* us is God
  Rev. 3:18, *a* your eyes with eyesalve
  See Judg. 9:8; Ps. 2:2; 84:9; James 5:14
ANOINTED I Sam. 26:9
ANON Mat. 13:20; Mk. 1:30
ANOTHER II Cor. 11:4; Gal. 1:6, 7, *a* gospel
  James 5:16, pray one for *a*
  See I Sam. 10:6; Job 19:27; Isa. 42:8; 48:11
ANSWER (*n.*) Job 19:16; 32:3; Jn. 19:9, no *a*
  Prov. 15:1, A soft *a* turns
    16:1, *a* of tongue from the Lord

I Pet. 3:15, be ready to give *a*
    21, *a* of good conscience
  See Job 35:12; Lk. 2:47; II Tim. 4:16
ANSWER (*v.*) Ps. 65:5, by terrible things will
    you *a*
  Prov. 1:28, I will not *a*;
    18:13, *a* a matter before he hears
    26:4, 5, *a* not a fool
  Eccl. 10:19, money *a* all things
  Lk. 21:14, not to mediate what ye shall *a*
  II Cor. 5:12, somewhat to *a*
  Col. 4:6, how ye ought to *a*
  See I Ki. 18:29; Ps. 138:3; Isa. 65:12, 24
ANTIQUITY Isa. 23:7
APART Mat. 14:13, desert place *a*:
    23; 17:1; Lk. 9:28, mountain *a*
  Mk. 6:31, come ye yourselves *a*
  See Ps. 4:3; Zech. 12:12; James 1:21
APPARENTLY Num. 12:8
APPEAR Ps. 42:2, when shall I *a* before God?
    90:16, let your work *a*
  Mat. 6:16, *a* unto men to fast
    23:28, outwardly *a* righteous
  Rom. 7:13, that it might *a* sin
  II Cor. 5:10, we all *a* before judgment seat
    12, glory in *a*
  Heb. 9:28; I Pet. 1:7, *a* of Christ
  I Thess. 5:22, Abstain from all *a* of evil
  I Tim. 4:15, profiting may *a*
  See Ex. 23:15; Mat. 24:30; Lk. 19:11
APPEASE Gen. 32:20; Acts 19:35
APPERTAIN Num. 16:30; Jer. 10:7; Rom. 4:1
APPETITE Job 38:39; Prov. 23:2; Isa. 29:8
APPLE Deut. 32:10, the *a* of his eye
  See Ps. 17:8; Prov. 7:2; 25:11; Song of Sol. 2:3,
    5; 7:8; 8:5; Lam. 2:18; Zech. 2:8
APPLY Ps. 90:12; Prov. 2:2; 22:17; 23:12
APPOINT Job 7:3, wearisome nights are *a*
    14:5, you have *a* his bounds
    30:23, house *a* for all living
  Ps. 79:11; 102:20, preserve those *a* to die
  Mat. 24:51; Lk. 12:46, *a* him his portion
  Acts 6:3, seven men whom we may *a*
  I Thess. 5:9, not *a* to wrath
APPREHEND Acts 12:4; II Cor. 11:32
APPROACH Isa. 58:2, take delight in *a* God
  Lk. 12:33, where not thief *a*
  I Tim. 6:16, light no man can *a*
  Heb. 10:25, as ye see the day *a*
  See Deut. 31:14; Job 40:19; Ps. 65:4
APPROVE Acts 2:22, a man *a* of God
  Rom. 16:10, *a* in Christ
  Phil. 1:10, *a* things that are excellent
  II Tim. 2:15, show yourself *a*
  See Ps. 49:13; I Cor. 11:19; Phil 1:10
APT II Ki. 24:16; I Tim. 3:2; II Tim. 2:24
ARGUING Job 6:25
ARGUMENTS Job 23:4
ARIGHT Ps. 50:23; 78:8; Prov. 15:2; 23:31
ARISE I Ki. 18:44, there *a* a little cloud
  Neh. 2:20, *a* and build
  Ps. 68:1, Let God *a*
    88:10, shall the dead *a* and praise you?
    112:4, to upright *a* light

Mal. 4:2, Sun of righteousness *a*
Mk. 2:11; Lk. 7:14; Acts 9:40, I say *A*
Lk. 15:18, I will *a* and go
Eph. 5:14, *a* from the dead
II Pet. 1:19, till day star *a*
See Isa. 26:19; Jer. 2:27
ARM Gen. 49:24, *a* of his hands made
Ex. 15:16, by greatness of your *a*
Deut. 33:27, underneath everlasting *a*
II Chron. 32:8, an *a* of flesh
Ps. 44:3, own *a* did not save them
   89:13, have a mighty *a*
Isa. 33:2, be thou their *a*
   51:5, my *a* shall judge; on my *a*
   9, put on strength, O *a* of the Lord
   52:10, the Lord made bare his holy *a*
   53:1; Jn. 12:38, *a* of the Lord revealed
   62:8, Lord has sworn by the *a*
   63:12, led them by his glorious *a*
Lk. 1:51; 11:21, strong man *a* keeps
Acts 13:17, high *a* brought he them
I Pet. 4:1, *a* yourselves with same
See Ps. 77:15; 98:1; Isa. 40:10, 11; 59:16; Jer.
   17:5; Ezek. 31:17; Zech. 11:17
ARMOUR Rom. 13:12, *a* of light
II Cor. 6:7, by *a* of righteousness
Eph. 6:11, 13, put whole *a* of God
ARMY I Sam. 17:10, I defy the *a* of Israel
Job 25:3, is there any number of his *a*?
Lk. 21:20, Jerusalem compassed with *a*
Acts 23:27, then came I with an *a*
Heb. 11:34, *a* of the aliens
See Song of Sol. 6:4; Ezek. 37:10
ARRAY Jer. 43:12, shall *a* himself with land
Mat. 6:29; Lk. 12:27, not *a* like one of these
I Tim. 2:9, not with costly *a*;
Rev. 7:13, *a* in white robes
See Job 40:10; Rev. 17:4; 19:8
ARRIVED Lk. 8:26; Acts 20:15
ARROGANCY I Sam. 2:3; Prov. 8:13; Isa. 13:11;
   Jer. 48:29
ARROW Num. 24:8, pierce through with *a*
Ps. 38:2, your *a* stick fast
   76:3, broke he the *a* of the bow
   91:5, *a* that flies by day
Prov. 25:18, false witness a sharp *a*
   26:18, casts *a* and death
Ezek. 5:16, evil *a* of famine
See Deut. 32:23; II Sam. 22:15; Job 6:4; 41:28
ARTIFICER Gen. 4:22; I Chron. 29:5; II Chron
   34:11; Isa. 3:3
ARTILLERY I Sam. 20:40
ASCEND Ps. 68:18; Rom. 10:6, *a* on high
Jn. 1:51, angels of God *a*
   3:13, no man has *a* to heaven
   20:17, I am not yet *a*
Rev. 8:4, smoke of incense *a*
   11:12, they *a* up to heaven
See Ps. 24:3; 139:8
ASCRIBE Deut. 32:3; Job 36:3; Ps. 68:34
ASHAMED Ps. 25:3, let none that wait on you
   be *a*
   31:1, let me never be *a*
Isa. 45:17, not be *a*, world without end

Jer. 2:26, as the thief is *a*
   6:15; 8:12, were they *a*?
   12:13, *a* of your revenues
   14:4, plowmen were *a*
Lk. 16:3, to be I am *a*
Rom. 1:16, not *a* of gospel
   5:5, hope makes not *a*
II Tim. 1:8, not *a* of testimony
Heb. 2:11, not *a* to call them brethren
   11:16, not *a* to be called their God
I Pet. 4:16, suffer as Christian, not be *a*;
See Gen. 2:25; II Tim. 1:12
ASHES Gen. 18:27; Job 2:8; 42:6; Ps. 102:9;
   Isa. 44:20; Jer. 6:26; Ezek. 28:18
ASIDE II Ki. 4:4; Mk. 7:33; Heb. 12:1
ASK Ps. 2:8; Isa. 45:11 *A* of me
Isa. 65:1, sought of them that *a* not
Mat. 7:7, *A* and it shall be given
   21:22, whatsoever you *a*
Mk. 6:22, *A* what you will
Jn. 14:13, 15:16, *a* in my name
James 1:5, let him *a* of God
I Pet. 3:15, *a* reason of the hope
I Jn. 3:22; 5:14, whatsoever we *a*
See Deut. 32:7; Jn. 4:9, 10; I Cor. 14:35
ASLEEP Mat. 8:24, but he was *a*
   26:40; Mk. 14:40, disciples *a*
I Cor. 15:6, some are fallen *a*
I Thess. 4:13, 15, them that are *a*
II Pet. 3:4, since fathers fell *a*
ASS Num. 22:30, am not I your *a*?
Prov. 26:3, bridle for *a*
Isa. 1:3, *a* his master's crib
Jer. 22:19, burial of an *a*
Zech. 9:9; Mat. 21:5, riding on *a*
Lk. 14:5, *a* fallen into pit
II Pet. 2:16, dumb *a* speaking
See Gen. 49:14; Ex. 23:4; Deut. 22:10
ASSAULT Esther 8:11; Acts 14:5; 17:5
ASSAY Acts 9:26, Saul *a* to join disciples
   16:7, they *a* to go to Bithynia
See Deut. 4:34; I Sam. 17:39; Job 4:2
ASSENT II Chron. 18:12; Acts 24:9
ASSIGNED Gen. 47:22; Josh. 20:8
ASSIST Rom. 16:2
ASSOCIATE Isa. 8:9
ASSURANCE Isa. 32:17
Col. 2:2, full *a* of understanding
I Thess. 1:5, gospel came in much *a*
Heb. 6:11; 10:22, full *a* of hope
See Deut. 28:66; Acts 17:31
ASSURE II Tim. 3:14; I Jn. 3:19
ASSWAGE Gen. 8:1; Job 16:5
ASTONIED Ezra 9:3; Job 17:8; Dan. 3:24
ASTONISHED Mat. 7:28; Mk. 1:22; 11:18;
   Lk. 4:32, *a* at his doctrine
Lk. 2:47, *a* at his understanding
   5:9, *a* at draught of fishes
   24:22, women made us *a*
Acts 9:6, Saul trembling and *a*
   12:16, saw Peter, they were *a*
   13:12, deputy believed, being *a*
ASTONISHMENT II Chron. 29:8; Jer. 25:9
Ps. 60:3, made us drink wine of *a*

Jer. 8:21, *a* has taken hold
See Deut. 28:28, 37; Ezek. 5:15
ATHIRST Mat. 25:44; Rev. 21:6; 22:17
ATONEMENT Lev. 23:28; 25:9, day of *a*
II Sam. 21:3, wherewith shall I make *a*?
Rom. 5:11, by whom we received *a*
See Lev. 4:20; 16:17; Num. 8:21
ATTAIN II Sam. 23:19; I Chron. 11:21; Ps. 139:6,
I cannot *a* to it
Rom. 9:30, Gentiles *a* to righteousness
Phil. 3:11, 12, 16, that I might *a*
See Gen. 47:9; Prov. 1:5; Ezek. 46:7; I Tim. 4:6
ATTEND Ps. 17:1; 61:1; 142:6, *A* to my cry
Prov. 4:20, my son, *a* to my words
See Ps. 55:2; 86:6
ATTENDANCE I Tim. 4:13; Heb. 7:13
ATTENT II Chron. 6:40; 7:15
ATTENTIVE Neh. 1:6; Lk. 19:48
ATTIRE Jer. 2:32; Ezek. 23:15
AUDIENCE I Chron. 28:8, in *a* of our God
Lk. 7:1; 20:45, in *a* of people
Acts 13:16, ye that fear God, give *a*
See Ex. 24:7; Acts 15:12
AUGMENT Num. 32:14
AUSTERE Lk. 19:21
AUTHOR I Cor. 14:33; Heb. 5:9; 12:2
AUTHORITY Mat. 7:29; Mk. 1:22
8:9; Lk. 7:8, I am a man under *a*
Mat. 21:23; Lk. 4:36, by what *a*
Lk. 9:1, power and *a* over devils
19:17, have *a* over ten cities
Jn. 5:27, *a* to execute judgment
I Tim. 2:2, kings, and all in *a*
12, suffer not a woman to usurp *a*
I Pet. 3:22, angels and *a* subject
AVAILS Esther 5:13; Gal. 5:6; James 5:16
AVENGE Deut. 32:43, he will *a* blood
Josh. 10:13, sun stood still till people *a*
I Sam. 24:12, the Lord judge and *a*
II Sam. 22:48; Ps. 18:47, it is God that *a* me
Esther 8:13, Jews *a* themselves
Isa. 1:24, I will *a* me of my enemies
Lk. 18:3, *A* me of my adversary
See Gen. 4:24; Lev. 19:18; Jer. 5:9; 9:9
AVENGER Ps. 8:2; 44:16, enemy and *a*
I Thess. 4:6, the Lord is the *a*
See Num. 35:12; Deut. 19:6; Josh. 20:5
AVERSE Mic. 2:8
AVOID Prov. 4:15, *A* it, pass not by it
I Tim. 6:20; II Tim. 2:16, *a* babblings
See Rom. 16:17; I Cor. 7:2; II Cor. 8:20
AVOUCHED Deut. 26:17, 18
AWAKE Ps. 73:20, as a dream when one *a*
Prov. 23:35, when shall I *a*?
Isa. 51:9; 52:1, *A*, *a*, put on strength
Joel 1:5, *A* ye drunkards
Zech. 13:7, *A*, O sword
Lk. 9:32, when *a*, they saw his glory
I Cor. 15:34, *A* to righteousness
Eph. 5:14, *A* thou that sleepest
See Jer. 51:57; Jn. 11:11
AWARE Jer. 50:24; Lk. 11:44
AWE Ps. 4:4; 33:8; 119:161
AWL Ex. 21:6; Deut. 15:17

AXE Ps. 74:5, famous as he had lifted up *a*
Isa. 10:15, shall the *a* boast?
Mat. 3:10; Lk. 3:9, the *a* is laid to root
See I Sam. 13:20, I Ki. 6:7; II Ki. 6:5

B

BABBLER Eccl. 10:11; Acts 17:18
BABBLING Prov. 23:29; I Tim. 6:20
BABE Ps. 8:2; Mat. 21:16, out of mouth of *b*
17:14, leave their substance to *b*,
Isa. 3:4, *b* shall rule over them
Mat. 11:25; Lk. 10:21, revealed to *b*
Rom. 2:20, teacher of *b*
I Cor. 3:1, *b* in Christ
See Ex. 2:6; Lk. 2:12, 16; Heb. 5:13
BACK Josh. 8:26, drew not his hand *b*
I Sam. 10:9, he burned his *b*
Neh. 9:26, cast law behind *b*
Ps. 129:3, plowers plowed on my *b*
Prov. 10:13; 19:29; 26:3, rod for *b*
Isa. 38:17, cast sins behind *b*
50:6, gave *b* to smiters
BACKBITERS Rom. 1:30
BACKBITING Prov. 25:23; II Cor. 12:20
BACKSLIDER Prov. 14:14, *b* in heart shall be
filled with his own ways
Jer. 3:6, 8, 11, 12, *b* Israel
8:5, perpetual *b*
14:7, our *b* are many
Hos. 4:16, as a *b* heifer
11:7, bent to *b* from me
14:4, will heal their *b*
See Jer. 2:19; 5:6; 31:22; 49:4
BACKWARD II Ki. 20:10; Isa. 38:8, let shadow
return *b*
Job 23:8, *b*, but I cannot perceive
Ps. 40:14; 70:2, driven *b*
Isa. 59:14, judgment is turned *b*
Jer. 7:24, they went *b*, and not forward
See Gen. 9:23; 49:17; Jn. 18:6
BAD Gen. 24:50; Lev. 27:12, 14, 33; Num. 13;19;
24:13; II Sam. 13:22; 14:17; Mat. 22:10;
II Cor. 5:10, good or *b*
See Lev. 27:10; Ezra 4:12; Jer. 24:2, Mat. 13:48
BADNESS Gen. 41:19
BAG Deut. 25:13; Prov. 16:11, *b* of weights
Job 14:17, transgression sealed in *b*
Isa. 46:6, lavish gold out of *b*
Hag. 1:6, *b* with holes
Lk. 12:33, *b* that wax not old
Jn. 12:6; 13:29, a thief, and had the *b*
BAKE Gen. 19:3; Lev. 26:26; I Sam. 28:24; Isa.
44:15, *b* bread
Ex. 12:39; Lev. 24:5, *b* cakes
See Gen. 40:17; Ex. 16:23; Lev. 2:4
BAKER Gen. 40:1; 41:10; I Sam. 8:13; Jer. 37:21;
Hos. 7:4
BALANCE Lev. 19:36; Prov. 16:11, just *b*
Job 37:16, the *b* of clouds
Ps. 62:9, laid in *b*, lighter than vanity
Prov. 11:1; 20:23; Hos. 12:7, false *b*
Isa. 40:12, 15, weighted hills in *b*
46:6, weight silver in the *b*

Rev. 6:5, a pair of *b*
BALD II Ki. 2:23, go up, thou *b* head
  Jer. 48:37; Ezek. 29:18, every head *b*
  See Lev. 13:40; Jer. 16:6; Ezek. 27:31
BALDNESS Isa. 3:24, instead of set hair *b*;
    22:12, call to seeping and *b*
  Mic. 1:16, enlarge your *b* as eagle
  See Lev. 21:5; Deut. 14:1; Ezek. 7:18
BALL Isa. 22:18
BALM Jer. 8:22; 46:11, *b* in Gilead
  See Gen. 37:25; 43:11; Jer. 51:8; Ezek. 27:17
BANDS Ps. 2:3; 107:14, break their *b* asunder
    73:4, there are no *b* in their death
  Hos. 11:4, drew them with *b* of love
  Zech. 11:7, two staves, Beauty and *B*
  See Job 38:31; Eccl. 7:26; Lk. 8:29
BANISHED II Sam. 14:13; Ezra 7:26
BANK Lk. 19:23, gave not money into *b*
  See Gen. 41:17; II Sam. 20:15, Ezek. 47:7
BANNER Ps. 20:5, in name of God set up *b*
  See Ps. 60:4; Song of Sol. 2:4; 6:4, Isa. 13:2
BANQUET Esther 5:4; Job 41:6
BAPTISM Mat. 20:22; Mk. 10:38; Lk. 12:50, to
    be baptized with *b*
    21:25; Mk. 11:30; Lk. 7:29; Acts 1:22; 18:25;
    19:3, *b* of John
  Mk. 1:4; Acts 13:24; 19:4, *b* of repentance
  Rom. 6:4; Col. 2:12, buried with him by *b*
  Eph. 4:5, one Lord, one faith, one *b*
  Heb. 6:2, doctrine of *b*
BAPTIZE Mat. 3:11; Mk. 1:8; Lk. 3:16; Jn. 1:26, *b*
    with Holy Ghost
  Mk. 16:16, he who believes and is *b*
  Lk. 3:7, multitude came to be *b*
    12; 7:29, publicans to be *b*
    21, Jesus being *b*, and praying
    7:30, Pharisees and lawyers being not *b*
  Jn. 1:33, he that sent me to *b*
    3:22, 23, tarried with them, and *b*
    4:1, 2, Jesus made and *b* more
  Acts 2:38, repent, and *b*
    41, gladly received word were *b*
    8:12, *b*, both men and women
    16, *b* in name of Jesus
    36, what does hinder me to be *b*?
    9:18, Saul arose, and was *b*
    10:47, can any forbid *b*?
    16:15, 33, *b*, and household
    18:8, many believed, and were *b*
    22:16, ,be *b*, and wash away your sins
  Rom. 6:3; Gal. 3:27, were *b* into Jesus
  I Cor. 1:13, were ye *b* in name of Paul?
    10:2, were all *b* in cloud
    12:13, all *b* into only body
    15:29, *b* for the dead
BARBARIANS Acts 28:4; Rom. 1:14
BARBAROUS Acts 28:2
BARBED Job 41:7
BARBER Ezek. 5:1
BARE (*v.*) Ex. 19:4; Deut. 1:12; Isa. 53:12
BARE (*adv.*) Isa. 52:10; I Cor. 15:37
BARKED Joel 1:7
BARN Job 39:12, gather your seed into *b*
  Mat. 6:26; Lk. 12:24, nor gather into *b*

13:30, gather wheat into *b*
  Lk. 12:18, pull down my *b*
  See II Ki. 6:27; Joel 1:17; Hag. 2:19
BARREL I Ki. 17:12, 14; 18:33
BARREN Ps. 107:34, turns fruitful land into *b*
  Isa. 54:1, sing, O *b*, you who did not bear
  II Pet. 1:8, neither *b* nor unfruitful
  See Ex. 23:26; Job 24:21; Lk. 23:29
BARS Job 17:16, down to the *b* of the pit
  Ezek. 38:11, having neither *b* nor gates
  See I Sam. 23:7; Job 38:10; Ps. 107:16
BASE Job 30:8, children of *b* men
  Mal. 2:9, I have made you *b*
  Acts 17:5, fellows of *b* sort
  I Cor. 1:28, *b* things of the world
BASKET Deut. 28:5, 17, blessed by your *b*
  Amos 8:1, *b* of summer fruit
  Mat. 14:20; Mark 6:43; Lk. 9:17, twelve *b*
    15:37; Mk. 8:8, seven *b*
    16:9; Mk. 8:19, now many *b*?
BASON Jn. 13:5, pours water into a *b*
  See Ex. 12:22; 24:6; I Chron. 28:17; Jer. 52:19
BASTARD Deut. 23:2, *b* shall not enter
  Zech. 9:6, *b* shall dwell in Ashdod
  Heb. 12:8, *b* and not sons
BATHE Lev. 15:5; 17:16; Num. 19:7; Isa. 34:5
BATS Lev. 11:19; Deut. 14:18; Isa. 2:20
BATTLE I Sam. 17:20, host shouted for *b*
    47; II Chron. 20:15, the *b* is the Lord's
  I Chron. 5:20, they cried to God in the *b*
  Ps. 18:39, strength to *b*
    55:18, delivered my soul from *b*
  Eccl. 9:11, nor *b* to strong
  Jer. 50:22, sound of *b* in land
BATTLEMENTS Deut. 22:8; Jer. 5:10
BAY TREE Ps. 37:35
BEACON Isa. 30:17
BEAM Ps. 104:3, who lays *b* in waters
  Mat. 7:5; Lk. 6:42, cast out *b*
  See Judg. 16:14; II Ki. 6:2; Hab. 2:11
BEAR (*n.*) Isa. 11:7, cow and *b* shall feed
    59:11, we roar all like *b*
  Hos. 13:8, as a *b* bereaved
  Amos 5:19, a man did flee from lion, and a *b*
  See I Sam. 17:34; II Sam. 17:8; Prov. 17:12
BEAR (*v.*) Gen. 4:13, greater than I can *b*
    13:6; 36:7, land not able to *b*
    43:9; 44:32, let me *b* blame
  Ex. 20:16; I Ki. 21:10; Lk. 11:48; Jn 1:7;
  Acts 23:11; Rom. 8:16, *b* witness
    28:12, Aaron *b* their names before Lord
  Lev. 24:15; Ezek. 23:49; Heb. 9:28, *b* sin
  Num. 11:14; Deut. 1:9, not able to *b* people
  Esther 1:22; Jer. 5:31; Dan. 2:39, *b* rule
  Ps. 91:12; Lk. 4:11, they shall *b* you up
  Prov. 18:14, wounded spirit who can *b*?
  Jer. 31:19, *b* reproach of youth
  Lam. 3:27, good to *b* yoke
  Mat. 3:11, not worthy to *b*
    27:32; Mk. 15:21; Lk. 23:26, *b* cross
  Rom. 13:4, *b* not sword in vain
    15:1, *b* infirmities of the weak
  I Cor. 13:7, charity *b* in all things
    15:49, shall also *b* image of the heavenly

Gal. 6:2, 5, *b* burdens
See Ex. 28:38; Deut. 1:31; Prov. 12:24
BEARD II Sam. 10:5, till *b* be grown
Ps. 133:2, even Aaron's *b*
Ezek. 5:1, cause razor to pass on *b*
See Lev. 13:29; I Sam. 21:13; II Sam. 20:9
BEARING Ps. 126:6, *b* precious seed
Jn. 19:17, *b* cross
Rom. 2:15; 9:1, conscience *b* witness
II Cor. 4:10, *b* in body the dying of Jesus
Heb. 13:13, *b* his reproach
See Gen. 1:29; Num. 10:17; Mk. 14:13
BEAST Job 12:7, ask *b*, they shall teach
18:3, counted as *b*
Prov. 12:10, regards life of *b*
Eccl. 3:19, no preeminence above *b*
I Cor. 15:32, fought with *b*
James 3:7, every kind of *b* is tamed
II Pet. 2:12, as natural brute *b*
See Lev. 11:47; Ps. 50:10; 147:9; Rom. 1:23
BEAT Isa. 2:4; Joel 3:10; Mic. 4:3, *b* swords
Lk. 12:47, *b* with many stripes
I Cor. 9:26, as one that *b* the air
See Prov. 23:14; Mic. 4:13; Mk. 12:5; 13:9
BEAUTY I Chron. 16:29; II Chron. 20:21; Ps.
29:2; 96:9; 110:3, *b* of holiness
Ezra 7:27, to *b* the house of the Lord
Ps. 27:4, behold *b* of the Lord
48:2, B for situation
50:2 perfection of *b*
Prov. 31:30, *b* is vain
Isa. 52:7; Rom. 10:15, how *b* are the feet
See II Sam. 1:19; Ps. 90:17; Zech. 9:17
BECKON Lk. 1:22; Jn. 13:24; Acts 12:17
BECOMES Ps. 93:5, holiness *b* your house
Rom. 16:2; Eph. 5:3, as *b* saints
Phil. 1:27; I Tim. 2:10; Titus 2:3, as *b* gospel
See Prov. 17:7; Mat. 3:15
BED Job 7:13, when I say, my *b* shall comfort
33:15, in slumberings upon the *b*
Ps. 63:6, when I remember you upon my *b*
Mat. 9:6; Mk. 2:9; Jn. 5:11, take up *b*
BEES Deut. 1:44; Ps. 118:12; Isa. 7:18
BEEVES Lev. 22:19; Num. 31:28; 38
BEFALL Gen. 42:4; 44:29, mischief *b* him
Judg. 6:13, why is all this *b* us?
Ps. 91:10, no evil *b* you
Eccl. 3:19, *b* men *b* beasts; one thing *b*
BEG Ps. 37:25; Prov. 20:4; Lk. 16:3
BEGGAR I Sam. 2:8; Lk. 16:20, 22
BEGGARLY Gal. 4:9
BEGIN Ezek. 9:6, *b* at my sanctuary
I Pet. 4:17, judgment *b* at house of God
See I Sam. 3:12; II Cor. 3:1
BEGINNING Job 8:7, though *b* was small
Ps. 111:10; Prov. 1:7; 9:10, *b* of wisdom
119:160, word true from *b*
Eccl. 7:8, better end of a thing than *b*
Mat. 19:8, from *b* not so
Lk. 24:47, *b* at Jerusalem
Heb. 3:14, hold *b* of our confidence
See I Chron. 17:9; Prov. 8:22, 23; Col. 1:18
BEGOTTEN Ps. 2:7; Acts 13:33; Heb. 1:5; 5:5,
this day have I *b* you

I Pet. 1:3, *b* to a lively hope
See Job 38:28; I Cor 4:15; Phile. 10
BEGUILE Gen. 29:25; Josh. 9:22, wherefore have
you *b* me?
II Pet. 2:14, *b* unstable souls
See Num. 25:18; II Cor. 11:3
BEGUN Gal. 3:3, having *b* in the Spirit
Phil. 1:6, has *b* good work
See Deut. 3:24; II Cor. 8:6, I Tim. 5:11
BEHALF Job 36:2, speak on God's *b*
Phil 1:29, in *b* of Christ
See II Chron. 16:9; II Cor. 1:11; 5:12
BEHAVE I Sam. 18:5, 14, David *b* wisely
I Chron. 19:13, *b* ourselves valiantly
Ps. 101:2, I will *b* wisely
Isa. 3:5, child shall *b* proudly
I Tim. 3:2, a bishop must be of good *b*
See Ps. 131:2; I Cor. 13:5; Titus 2:3
BEHEADED Mat. 14:10; Mk. 6:16
BEHIND Ex. 10:26, not hoof be left *b*
Phil. 3:13, things which are *b*
Col. 1:24, fill up that which is *b*
See I Ki. 14:9; Neh. 9:26; II Cor. 11:5
BEHOLD Ps. 37:37, *b* the upright
Mat. 18:10, their angels do always *b*
Jn. 17:24, that they may *b* my glory
II Cor. 3:18, *b* as in a glass
See Num. 24:17; Ps. 91:8; 119:37, James 1:23
BEHOVED Lk. 24:46; Heb. 2:17
BELIEF II Thess. 2:13
BELIEVE II Chron. 20:20, B in Lord, *b* his
prophets
Ps. 78:22, they *b* not in God
Prov. 14:15, simple *b* every word
Mat. 8:13, as you have *b*, so be it
9:28, B ye that I am able?
21:25, Mk. 11:31, why then did ye not *b*?
27:42, come down from the cross, we will *b*
Mk. 5:36; Lk. 8:50, only *b*
9:23, if you can *b*, all things possible
11:24, *b* that you receive
Lk. 1:1, things must surely *b*
8:13, which for a while *b*
24:25, slow of heart to *b*
41, *b* not for joy
Jn. 1:7, all men through him might *b*,
2:22, they *b* the scripture
Jn. 3:12, *b* heavenly things
5:44, how can you *b* which receive honor?
47, how shall ye *b* my words?
6:36, seen me, and *b* not
7:5, neither did his brethren *b*
48, have any of the rulers *b*?
10:38, *b* the works
11:15, to intent you may *b*
26, never die, *b* you this?
48, all men will *b*
12:36, *b* in the light
17:21, the world may *b*
20:29, have not see, yet have *b*
Acts 4:32, multitude of them that *b*
13:39, all that *b* are justified
48, ordained to eternal life *b*
16:34, *b* with all his house

Rom. 4:11, father of all that *b*
   18, against hope *b* in hope
   9:33, *b* on him shall not be ashamed
I Cor. 7:12, wife that *b* not
II Cor. 4:13, we *b*, and therefore speak
Gal. 3:22, promise to them that *b*
II Thess. 1:10, admired in all that *b*
Heb. 10:39, *b* to saving of soul
James 2:19, devils *b* and tremble
BELLY Gen. 3:14; Job 15:2; Mat. 15:17; Jn. 7:38;
   Rom. 16:18; Phil 3:19
BELONGS Deut. 32:35; Heb. 10:30
BELOVED Deut. 33:12, *b* dwell in safety
   Ps. 127:2, gives his *b* sleep
   Dan. 9:23; 10:11, 19, greatly *b*
   Mat. 3:17; 17:5; Mk. 1:11; Lk. 3:22; 9:35; II Pet.
     1:17, *b* son
   Rom. 11:28, *b* for fathers' sake
   Eph. 1:6, accepted in the *b*
   Col. 4:9; Phile. 16, *b* brother
   See Neh. 13:26; Rom. 16:9; Col. 4:14
BEMOAN Job 42:11; Jer. 15:5; Nah. 3:7
BEND Ps. 11:2, Isa. 60:14; Ezek. 17:7
BENEATH Prov. 15:24, depart from Hell *b*
   Isa. 14:9, Hell from *b* is moved
   Jn. 8:23, you are from *b*
   See Deut. 4:39; Jer. 31:37
BENEFACTORS Lk. 22:25
BENEFIT Ps. 68:19, loaded us with *b*
   I Tim. 6:2, partakers of the *b*
BENEVOLENCE I Cor. 7:3
BEREAVE Gen. 42:36; 43:14, *b* of children
   Eccl. 4:8, *b* my soul of God
   Jer. 15:7; 18:21, I will *b* you
   See Ezek. 5:17; 36:12; Hos. 13:8
BESEECH Job 42:4, hear, I *b* in you
   Mat. 8:5; Lk. 7:3, centurion *b* him
   Lk. 9:38, I *b* you, look on my son
   II Cor. 5:20, as though God did *b* you
   Eph. 4:1, *b* you to walk
   Phile. 9, for love's sake *b* you
   See Ex. 33:18; Jonah 1:14; Rom. 12:1
BESET Ps. 22:12; 139:5; Hos. 7:2; Heb. 12:1
BESIDE Mk. 3:21; Acts 26:24; II Cor. 5:13
BESIEGE Deut. 28:52; Eccl. 9:14; Isa. 1:8
BESOUGHT Ex. 32:11; Deut. 3:23; Jer. 26:19, *b*
   the Lord
   Mat. 8:31; Mk. 5:10, devils *b* him
   Lk. 8:37, *b* him to depart
   Jn. 4:40, *b* that he would tarry
   II Cor. 12:8, I *b* the Lord thrice
   See Gen. 42:21; Esther 8:3
BEST I Sam. 15:9, 15, spared *b* of sheep
   Ps. 39:5, at his *b* state is vanity
   Lk. 15:22, *b* robe
   I Cor. 12:31, *b* gifts
   See Gen. 43:11; Deut. 23:16; II Sam. 18:4
BESTEAD Isa. 8:21
BESTIR II Sam. 5:24
BESTOW Lk. 12:17, no room to *b* my fruits
   I Cor. 15:10, grace *b* on us not in vain
   Gal. 4:11, lest I have *b* labor in vain
   I Jn. 3:1, manner of love Father *b*
   See I Chron. 29:25; Isa. 63:7; Jn. 4:38

BETHINK I Ki. 8:47; II Chron. 6:37
BETIMES Gen. 26:31; II Chron. 36:15; Job 8:5;
   Prov. 13:24
BETRAY Mat. 26:16; Mk. 14:11; Lk. 22:21, 22,
   opportunity to *b*
   27:4, I *b* innocent blood
   I Cor. 11:23, same night he was *b*
   See Mat. 24:10; Mk. 14:18; Jn. 6:64
BETROTH Hos. 2:19, 20
BETTER I Ki. 19:4, I am not *b* than my fathers
   Eccl. 4:9, two are *b* than one
     7:10, former days *b* than these
   Mat. 12:12, man *b* than a sheep
   Lk. 5:39, he said the old is *b*
   Phil. 2:3, each esteem other *b* than himself
   Heb. 1:4, much *b* than angels
     11:16, a *b* country
   II Pet. 2:21, *b* not have known the way
   See Eccl. 2:24; Song of Sol. 1:2; Jonah 4:3
BEWAIL Lk. 8:52, all wept and *b* her
   23:27, of women, which also *b*
   II Cor. 12:21, *b* many which have sinned
   See Deut. 21:13; Judg. 11:37; Rev. 18:9
BEWARE Judg. 13:4, *b*, and drink not wine
   Job 36:18, *b* lest he take you away
   Mat. 16:6; Mk. 8:15; Lk. 12:1, *B* of leaven
   Mk. 12:38; Lk. 20:46, *b* of scribes
   Lk. 12:15, *b* of covetousness
   Phil. 3:2, *B* of dogs, *b* of evil workers
   See Deut. 6:12; 8:11; 15:9
BEWITCHED Acts 8:9; Gal. 3:1
BEWRAY Prov. 27:16; Isa. 16:3; Mat. 26:73
BEYOND Num. 22:18; II Cor. 8:3; Gal. 1:3
BIER II Sam. 3:31; Lk. 7:14
BILLOWS Ps. 42:7; Jonah 2:3
BIND Prov. 6:21, *B* them upon your heart
   Isa. 61:1, *b* up brokenhearted
   Mat. 12:29; Mk. 3:27, *b* strong men
   16:19; 18:18, *b* on earth
BIRD II Sam. 21:10, suffered neither *b* to rest
   Song of Sol. 2:12, time of the singing of *b*
   Jer. 12:9, heritage unto me as a speckled *b*
   Mat. 8:20; Lk. 9:58, *b* of air have nests
   See Ps. 11:1; 124:7; Prov. 1:17; Eccl. 10:20
BIRTH Ezek. 16:3, Your *b*
   Jn. 9:1, blind from *b*
   Gal. 4:19, of whom I travail in *b*
   See Eccl. 7:1; Isa. 66:9; Lk. 1:14
BIRTHDAY Gen. 40:20; Mat. 14:6, Herod's *b*
BIRTHRIGHT Gen. 25:31; 27:36; Heb. 12:16
BISHOP I Tim. 3:1, if a man desire office of *b*
   Titus 1:7, *b* must be blameless
   See Acts 1:20; Phil. 1:1; I Pet. 2:25
BIT Ps. 32:9; James 3:3
BITE Prov. 23:32, at last it *b* like serpent
   Mic. 3:5, prophets that *b* with teeth
   Gal. 5:15, if you *b* and devour one another
BITTER Ex. 12:8; Num. 9:11, with *b* herbs
   Deut. 32:24, devoured with *b* destruction
   Isa. 5:20, that put *b* for sweet
     24:9, strong drink *b* to them that drink it
   Jer. 2:19, an evil thing and *b*
   Mat. 26:75; Lk. 22:62, Peter wept *b*
   Col. 3:19, be not *b* against them

BITTERNESS Job 10:1; Isa. 38:15, *b* of soul
   Prov. 14:10, heart knows own *b*
   Acts 8:23, in the gall of *b*
   Eph. 4:31, let all *b* be put away
   Heb. 12:15, lest any root of *b*
   See I Sam. 15:32; Prov. 17:25; Rom. 3:14
BLACK Mat. 5:36; Jude 13; Rev. 6:5
BLADE Judg. 3:22; Mat. 13:26; Mk. 4:28
BLAME II Cor. 6:3; 8:20; Gal. 2:11; Eph. 1:4
BLAMELESS I Cor. 1:8, *b* in day of the Lord
   Phil. 2:15, that you may be *b*
   See Mat. 12:5; Phil. 3:6; Titus 1:6, 7
BLASPHEME Isa. 52:5, my name continually
    is *b*
   Mat. 9:3, scribes said, this man *b*
   Mk. 3:29, *b* against Holy Ghost
   Acts 26:11, I compelled them to *b*
   Rom. 2:24, name of God is *b* through you
   James 2:7, *b* that worthy name
BLASPHEMY Mat. 12:31, all manner of *b*
   26:65; Mk. 14:64, he has spoken *b*
   Lk. 5:21, who is this which speaks *b*?
   See II Ki. 19:3; Ezek. 35:12; Mat. 15:19
BLAST Gen. 41:6; Deut. 28:22; I Ki. 8:37
BLAZE Mk. 1:45
BLEATING Judg. 5:16; I Sam. 15:14
BLEMISH Dan. 1:4, in whom was no *b*
   Eph. 5:27, holy and without *b*
   I Pet. 1:19, a lamb without *b* and spot
   See Lev. 21:17; Deut. 15:21; II Sam. 14:25
BLESS Deut. 28:3, *B* in city, *b* in field
   I Chron. 4:10, Oh that you would *b* me
   Prov. 10:7, memory of just is *b*
   Isa. 32:20 *B* are you that sow
    65:16, *b* himself in God of truth
   Mat. 5:44; Rom. 12:14, *b* them that curse
   Acts 20:35, more *b* to give than receive
   II Cor. 11:31, *b* for evermore
   Titus 2:13, looking for that *b* hope
   Rev. 14:13, *B* are dead which die in the Lord
   See Gen. 22:17; Hag. 2:19; James 3:9, 10
BLESSING Job 29:13, *b* of him that was ready
    to perish
   Prov. 10:22, *b* of Lord makes rich
    28:20, a faithful man shall abound with *b*
   Isa. 65:8, destroy it not, a *b* is in it
   Mal. 2:2, I will curse your *b*
    3:10, pour you out a *b*
   Rom. 15:29, fullness of *b* of gospel
   I Cor. 10:16, cup of *b* which we bless
   James 3:10, proceed *b* and cursing
   Rev. 5:12, worthy to receive honor and *b*
   See Gen. 27:35; 39:5; Deut. 11:26, 29
BLIND (*v.*) Ex. 23:8, the gift *b* the wise
   II Cor. 3:14; 4:4, their minds were *b*
   I Jn. 2:11, darkness has *b*
   See Deut. 16:19; I Sam. 12:3
BLINDNESS Eph. 4:18
   See Deut. 28:28; II Ki. 6:18; Zech. 12:4
BLOOD Gen. 9:6, whoso sheds man's *b*
   Josh. 2:19; I Ki. 2:32, *b* on hand
   Ps. 51:14, deliver me from *b*-guiltiness
    72:14, precious shall *b* in his sight
   Isa. 9:5, garments rolled in *b*

Jer. 2:34, the *b* of poor innocents
Ezek. 9:9, land is full of *b*
   18:13; 33:5, his *b* be upon him
Hab. 2:12, builds a town with *b*
Mat. 9:20; Mk. 5:25; Lk. 8:43, issue of *b*
   16:17, flesh and *b* has not revealed
   27:4, I have betrayed innocent *b*
   25, his *b* be on us and on our children
Mk. 14:24; Lk. 22:20, my *b* shed
Lk. 22:20; I Cor. 11:25, testament in my *b*
   44, sweat as drops of *b* falling
Jn. 1:13, born not of *b*
   6:54, 55, 56, drinks my *b*
Acts 15:20; 21:25, abstain from *b*
   17:26, made of one *b*
   20:28, church purchased with his *b*
Rom. 3:25, through faith in his *b*
   5:9, justified by his *b*
I Cor. 10:16, communion of *b* of Christ
   11:27, guilty of body and *b* of the Lord
   15:50, flesh and *b* cannot inherit
Eph. 1:7; Col. 1:14, redemption through his *b*
Heb. 9:22, without shedding of *b*
   10:29; 13:20, *b* of the covenant
I Pet. 1:19, with precious *b* of Christ
Rev. 7:14; 12:11, in the *b* of the Lamb
   See Gen. 9:4; Ex. 4:9; 12:13; Lev. 3:17; Isa. 1:11;
    Heb. 9:12; Rev. 16:6; 17:6
BLOSSOM Isa. 35:1, desert shall *b* as the rose
   Hab. 3:17, fig tree shall not *b*
   See Gen. 40:10; Num. 17:5; Isa. 27:6
BLOT Ex. 32:32; Ps. 69:28; Rev. 3:5
   Isa. 44:22, *b* out, as thick cloud
   Acts 3:19, repent, that sins may *b* out
   Col. 2:14, *B* out handwriting
   See Deut. 9:14; II Ki. 14:27; Jer. 18:23
BLOW Song of Sol. 4:16, *b* upon my garden
   Jn. 3:8, wind *b* where it listeth
   See Isa. 27:13
BLUSH Ezra 9:6; Jer. 6:15; 8:12
BOAST (*n.*) Ps. 34:2; Rom. 2: 17, 23; 3:27
BOAST (*v.*) I Ki. 20:11
   Prov. 27:1, *B* not of tomorrow
   II Cor. 11:16, that I may *b* myself a little
   Eph. 2:9, lest any man should *b*
   James 3:5, tongue *b* great tings
   See II Chron. 25:19; Prov. 20:14; James 4:16
BOATS Jn. 6:22; Acts 27:16, 30
BODY Job 19:26, worms destroy this *b*
   Prov. 5:11, your flesh and *b* are consumed
   Mat. 5:29, *b* cast into Hell
    6:22; Lk. 11:34, *b* full of light
    25; Lk. 12:22, take no thought for *b*
   Mk. 5:29, felt in *b* that she was healed
   Lk. 17:37, wheresoever the *b* is
   Jn. 2:21, the temple of his *b*
   Acts 19:12, from his *b* were brought
   Rom. 6:6, *b* of sin destroyed
    7:24, *b* of this death
    12:1, present your *b* a living sacrifice
    4; I Cor. 12:14, many members, one *b*
   I Cor. 9:27, I keep under my *b*
    13:3, though I give my *b* to be burned
   II Cor. 5:8, absent form the *b*

12:2, whether in *b*, or out of the *b*
I Pet. 2:24, in his own *b* on tree
See Gen. 47:18; Deut. 28:4; Rom. 12:5
BODILY Lk. 3:22; II Cor. 10:10; Col. 2:9
BOLD Eccl. 8:1, the *b* of face changed
Jn. 7:26, he speaks *b*
II Cor. 10:2, I may not be *b*
Eph. 3:12, we have *b* and access
Heb. 4:16, let us come *b* to throne
I Jn. 4:17, have *b* in day of judgment
BOND Acts 8:23, in *b* of iniquity
Eph. 4:3, *b* of peace
Col. 3:14, *b* of perfectness
See Num. 30:2; Ezek. 20:37; Lk. 13:16
BONDAGE Jn. 8:33, never in *b* to any man
See Rom. 8:15; Gal. 5:1; Heb. 2:15
BONDMAN Deut. 15:15; 16:12; 24:18
BONDWOMAN Gen. 21:10; Gal. 4:30
BONE Ex. 12:46; Num. 9:12, neither shall you
break a *b* thereof
Job. 40:18, *b* as pieces of brass
Ps. 51:8, the *b* broken may rejoice
Prov. 12:4, as rottenness in his *b*
Mat. 23:27, full of dead men's *b*
Lk. 24:39, spirit has not flesh and *b*
See Gen. 2:23; Ezek. 37:7; Jn. 19:36
BOOK Job 19:23, printed in a *b*!
31:35, adversary had written a *b*
Isa. 34:16, seek out of the *b* of the Lord
Mal. 3:16, *b* of remembrance
Lk. 4:17, when he had opened *b*
Jn. 21:25, world could not contain *b*
BOOTH Job 27:18; Jonah 4:5
BOOTY Num. 31:32; Jer. 49:32; Hab. 2:7
BORN Job 5:7, man *b* to trouble
14:1; 25:4; Mat. 11:11, *b* of woman
Ps. 87:4, this man was *b* there
Isa. 9:6, unto us a child is *b*
66:8, shall a nation be *b* at once?
Jn. 1:13; I Jn. 4:7; 5:1, 4, 18, *b* of God
3:3; I Pet. 1:23, *b* again
3:8, *b* of Spirit
I Cor. 15:8, as one *b* out of due time
I Pet. 2:2, as new *b* babes
See Job 3:3; Prov. 17:17; Eccl. 3:2; Mat. 19:12;
Jn. 8:41
BORNE Isa. 53:4, *b* our griefs, carried our
sorrows
Mat. 23:4; Lk. 11:46, grievous to be *b*
See Job 34:31; Lam. 5:7; Mat. 20:12
BORROW Deut. 15:6; 28:12, lend, but not *b*
Ps. 37:21, wicked *b* and pays not
Prov. 22:7, the *b* is servant
Mat. 5:42, from his that would *b* of you
See Ex. 3:22; 11:2; 22:14; II Ki. 4:3
BOSOM Ps. 35:13, prayer returned into *b*
Prov. 6:27, take fire in the *b*
Isa. 40:11, carry lambs in *b*
Lk. 16:22, carried into Abraham's *b*
Jn. 1:18, in the *b* of the Father
13:23, leaning on Jesus' *b*
BOSSES Job 15:26
BOTCH Deut. 28:27, 35
BOTTLE Judg. 4:19, a *b* of milk

Ps. 56:8, put tears into *b*
Ps. 119:83, like *b* in smoke
Mat. 9:17; Mk. 2:22, new wine in old *b*
See Gen. 21:15; Hos. 7:5; Hab. 2:15
BOUGH Gen. 49:22; Deut. 24:20; Job 14:9; Ps.
80:10; Ezek. 31:3
BOUGHT Lk. 14:18; I Cor. 6:20; 7:23
BOUND Ps. 107:10, being *b* in affliction
Prov. 22:15, foolishness *b* in heart of child
Acts 20:22, I go *b* in spirit to Jerusalem
I Cor. 7:27, are you *b* to a wife?
II Tim. 2:9, word of God is not *b*
See Gen. 44:30; Mat. 16:19; Mk. 5:4
BOUNTIFUL Prov. 22:9
Isa. 32:5, nor churl said to be *b*
BOUNTY I Ki. 10:13; II Cor. 9:5
See Ps. 13:6; 116:7; 119:17; II Cor. 9:6
BOWELS II Cor. 6:12, straitened in *b*
Col. 3:12, *b* of mercies
I Jn. 3:17, *b* of compassion
See Acts 1:18; Phil. 1:8; 2:1; Phile. 12
BOWL Num. 7:85; Eccl. 12:6; Zech. 9:15
BRACELET Gen. 24:30; Ex. 35:22; Isa. 3:19
BRAKE II Ki. 23:14; Josiah *b* images
Mat. 14:19; 15:36; 26:26; Mk. 6:41; 8:6; Lk.
9:16; 22:19, 24:30
BRAMBLE Judg. 9:14; Isa. 34:13; Lk. 6:44
BRANCH Job 14:7, tender *b* will not cease
Prov. 11:28, righteous flourish as *b*
Jer. 23:5, will raise a righteous *B*
Mat. 13:32; Lk. 13:19, birds lodge in *b*
21:8; Mk. 11:8; Jn. 12:13, cut down *b*
BRAND Judg. 15:5, Zech. 3:2
BRASS Deut. 8:9; Dan. 5:23; I Cor. 13:1
BRAVERY Isa. 3:18
BRAWLER Prov. 25:24; I Tim. 3:3
BRAY Job 6:5; 30:7; Prov. 27:22
BREACH Isa. 58:12, the repairer of the *b*
Lam. 2:13, your *b* is great like the sea
See Lev. 24:20; Ps. 106:23; Amos 4:3; 6:11
BREAD Deut. 8:3; Mat. 4:4; Lk. 4:4, not live
by *b* alone
I Ki. 17:6, ravens brought *b* and flesh
Job 22:7, withholden *b* from hungry
33:20, soul abhors *b*
Ps. 132:15, satisfy poor with *b*
Prov. 9:17, *b* eaten in secret
12:11; 20:13; 28:19, satisfied with *b*
31:27, eaten not *b* of idleness
Eccl. 11:1, cast *b* on waters
Isa. 55:2, money for that which is not *b*
Mat. 4:3, Lk. 4:3, stones be made *b*
6:11; Lk. 11:1, give us out daily *b*
15:26; Mk. 7:27, not take children's *b*
Lk. 24:35, known in breaking *b*
Acts 2:42; 20:7; 27:35, breaking *b*
BREAK Song of Sol. 2:17; 4:6 day *b*, shadows
flee
Isa. 42:3; Mat. 12:20, bruised reed not *b*
Jer. 4:3; Hos. 10:12, *B* your fallow ground
Acts 21:13, to weep and *b* my heart
See Ps. 2:3; Jer. 15:12; Mat. 5:19; 9:17
BREAST Gen. 49:25; Job 3:12, why *b* that I
should suck

21:24, his *b* are full of milk
Ps. 22:9, I was upon my mother's *b*
Prov. 5:19, let her *b* satisfy
Song of Sol., 1:13, all night between my *b*
    4:5; 7:3, your *b* are like two roes
    7:7, your *b* to clusters of grapes
    8:1, sucked the *b* of my mother
    10, I am a wall, and my *b* like towers
Isa. 28:9, weaned and drawn from *b*
    60:16, suck the *b* of kings
    66:11, satisfied with *b* of her consolation
Lam. 4:3, sea monsters draw out the *b*
Ezek. 16:7, your *b* are fashioned
    23:3, there were their *b* pressed
    8, and they bruised the *b* of her virginity
Hos. 2:2, adulteries from between her *b*;
    9:14, miscarrying womb and dry *b*
Lk. 23:48, smote *b* and returned
Jn. 13:25, lying on Jesus' *b*
Rev. 15:6, *b* girded with golden
BREATH Gen. 2:7; 6:17; 7:15, *b* of life
Isa. 2:22, cease from man, whose *b*
Ezek. 37:5, 10, I will cause *b* to enter
Acts 17:25, he give to all life and *b*
See Job 12:10; 33:4; Ps. 146:4; 150:6
BREATHE Ezek. 37:9; Jn. 20:22
BREECHES Ex. 28:42; Lev. 6:10; 16:4
BRETHREN Mat. 23:8, all you are *b*
Mk. 10:29, no man left house or *b*
Col. 1:2, faithful *b* in Christ
I Jn. 3:14, because we love the *b*
See Gen. 42:8; Prov. 19:7; Jn. 7:5
BRIBE I Sam. 12:3, have I received any *b*
Ps. 26:10, right hand is full of *b*
See I Sam. 8:3; Job 15:34; Isa. 33:15
BRICK Gen. 11:3; Ex. 5:7; Isa. 9:10; 65:3
BRIDE Isa. 61:10; Jer. 2:32; Rev. 21:2
BRIDEGROOM Mat. 25:1, to meet the *b*
Jn. 3:29, because of *b* voice
See Ps. 19:5; Isa. 62:5; Mat. 9:15
BRIDLE Prov. 26:3, a *b* for the ass
James 1:26, *b* not his tongue
    3:2, able to *b* whole body
See II Ki. 19:28; Ps. 39:1; Isa. 37:29
BRIGANDINE Jer. 46:4; 51:3
BRIGHT Job 37:21, *b* light in the clouds
Isa. 60:3, to *b* of your rising
Mat. 17:5, *b* cloud overshadowed
II Thess. 2:8, *b* of his coming
Heb. 1:3, the *b* of his glory
Rev. 22:16, the *b* and the morning star
See Lev. 13:2; Jer. 51:11; Zech. 10:1
BRIMSTONE Gen. 19:24, Lord rained on
    Sodom and Gomorrah *b*
Deut. 29:23, the whole land thereof is *b*
Job 18:15, *b* scattered on habitation
Ps. 11:6, rain snares, fire and *b*
Isa. 30:33, breath of Lord, a stream of *b*
Ezek. 38:22, great hailstones, fire and *b*
Rev. 9:17, 18, issued fire and *b*
    14:10, tormented with fire and *b*
    19:20, cast into a lake of fire and *b*
See Lk. 17:29; Rev. 20:10
BRINK Gen. 41:3; Ex. 2:3; 7:15; Josh. 3:8

BROAD Ps. 119:96; Mat. 7:13; 23:5
BROIDERED Ezek. 16:10, 13; 27:7, 16
See Ex. 28:4; I Tim. 2:9
BROILED Lk. 24:42
BROKEN Ps. 34:18; 51:17; 69:20, *b* heart
Jn. 10:35, scripture cannot be *b*
    19:36, bone shall not be *b*
Eph. 2:14, *b* down middle wall
See Job 17:11; Prov. 25:19; Jer. 2:13
BROOD Lk. 13:34
BROOK I Sam. 17:40; Ps. 42:1; 110:7
BROTH Judg. 6:19; Isa. 65:4
BROTHER Prov. 17:17, *b* born for adversity
    18:9, slothful *b* to waster
    19, *b* offended harder to be won
    24, friend closer than *b*
Eccl. 4:8, neither child nor *b*
Mat. 10:21, *b* shall deliver up *b*
I Cor. 6:6, *b* goes to law with *b*
See Gen. 4:9; Hos. 12:3; Mat. 5:23; Mk. 3:35;
    I Jn. 3:15
BROTHERLY Rom. 12:10; I Thess. 4:9; Heb.
    13:1, *b* love
See Amos 1:9; II Pet. 1:7
BROW Isa. 48:4; Lk. 4:29
BRUISE (*n*.) Isa. 1:6; Jer. 30:12; Nah. 3:19
BRUISE (*v*.) Isa. 42:3; Mat. 12:20, *b* reed shall
    he not break
Isa. 53:5, *b* for our iniquities
See Gen. 3:15; Isa. 53:10; Ezek. 23:8
BRUIT Jer. 10:22; Nah. 3:19
BRUTISH Ps. 92:6, a *b* man knows not
Prov. 30:2, I am more *b* than any
Jer. 10:21, the pastors are become *b*
BUCKET Num. 24:7; Isa. 40:15
BUCKLER II Sam. 22:31; Ps. 18:2; 91:4
BUD Num. 17:8; Isa. 18:5; 61:11; Hos. 8:7
BUFFET Mat. 26:67; I Cor. 4:11; II Cor. 12:7
BUILD Ps. 127:1, labor in vain who *b*
Eccl. 3:3, a time to *b* up
Isa. 58:12, *b* old waste places
Mat. 7:24; Lk. 6:48, wise man *b* on rock
Lk. 14:30, began to *b* not able to finish
Rom. 15:20, *b* on another man's foundation
I Cor. 3:12, if any *b* on this foundation
Eph. 2:22, in whom you are *b* together
See I Chron. 17:12; II Chron 6:9; Eccl. 2:4
BUILDER Ps. 118:22; Mat. 21:42; Mk. 12:10, *b*
    refused
Lk. 20:17; Acts 4:11; I Pet. 2:7, *b* refused
I Cor. 3:10, as a wise master-*b*
Heb. 11:10, whose *b* and maker is God
See I Ki. 5:18; Ezra 3:10
BUILDING I Cor. 3:9; II Cor. 5:1; Eph. 2:21
BULRUSH Ex. 2:3; Isa. 18:2; 58:5
BULWARK Isa. 26:1, salvation for walls and *b*
See Deut. 20:20; Ps. 48:13; Eccl. 9:14
BUNDLE Gen. 42:35; Mat. 13:30; Acts 28:3
BURDEN Ps. 55:22, cast your *b* on the Lord
Eccl. 12:5, grasshopper shall be a *b*
Mat. 11:30, my *b* is light
    20:12, borne *b* and heat of the day
    23:4, Lk. 11:46, bind heavy *b*
Gal. 6:2, 5 bear his own *b*

See Num. 11:11; Acts 15:28; II Cor. 12:16
BURDENSOME Zech. 12:3; II Cor. 11:9
BURIAL Jer. 22:19; Mat. 26:12; Acts 8:2
BURN Prov. 26:23, *B* lips and wicked heart
　　Isa. 9:18, wickedness *b* as fire
　　　　33:14, dwell with everlasting *b*
　　Mal. 4:1, day that shall *b* as oven
　　Mat. 13:30, bind tares to *b* them
　　Lk. 3:17, chaff *b* with fire unquenchable
　　　　12:35, loins girded and lights *b*;
　　　　24:32, did not our heart *b*
　　Jn. 5:35, he was a *b* and shining light
　　I Cor. 13:3, give my body to be *b*
　　Heb. 6:8, whose end is to be *b*
　　Rev. 4:5, lamps *b* before throne
　　　　19:20, into a lake *b*
　　See Gen. 44:18; Ex. 3:2; 21:25; I Cor. 7:9
BURNT OFFERING Ps. 40:6, *b* thou hast not
　　required
　　Isa. 61:8, I hate robbery for *b*
　　Jer. 6:20, your *b* not acceptable
　　Hos. 6:6, knowledge more than *b*
　　Mk. 12:33, to love neighbor is more than *b*
　　See Gen. 22:7; Lev. 1:4; 6:9
BURST Job 32:19; Prov. 3:10; Mk. 2:22
BURY Mat. 8:22; Lk. 9:60, let dead *b* dead
　　Rom. 6:4; Col. 2:12, *B* with him by baptism
　　I Cor. 15:4, he was *b* and rose again
　　See Gen. 23:4; 47:29; Mat. 14:12
BUSHEL Mat. 5:15; Mk. 4:21; Lk. 11:33
BUSINESS Ps. 107:23, do *b* in great waters
　　Prov. 22:29, diligent in *b*
　　Lk. 2:49, about my Father's *b*
　　Rom. 12:11, not slothful in *b*
　　I Thess. 4:11, study to do you own *b*
　　See Josh. 2:14; Judg. 18:7; Neh. 13:30
BUTLER Gen. 40:1; 41:9
BUTTER Ps. 55:21; Isa. 7:15, 22, *b* and honey
　　shall he eat
BUY Lev. 22:11, *b* any soul with money
　　Prov. 23:23, *B* the truth
　　Isa. 55:1, *b* and eat, *b* wine and milk
　　Jn. 4:8, disciples were gone to *b* meat
　　James 4:13, we will *b* and sell, and get gain
　　Rev. 3:18, *b* of me gold tried
　　　　18:11, no man *b* her merchandise
　　See Gen. 42:2; 47:19; Ruth 4:4; Mat. 13:44
BUYER Prov. 20:14; Isa. 24:2; Ezek. 7:12
BY AND BY Mat. 13:21; Mk. 6:25
BYWAYS Judg. 5:6
BYWORD Job 17:6; 30:9, a *b* of the people
　　Ps. 44:14, a *b* among the heathen
　　See Deut. 28:37; I Ki. 9:7; II Chron. 7:20

C

CABINS Jer. 37:16
CAGE Jer. 5:27; Rev. 18:2
CAKE II Sam. 6:19, to every man a *c* of bread
　　I Ki. 17:13, make me a little *c* first
　　See Judg. 7:13; Jer. 7:18; 44:19; Hos. 7:8
CALAMITY Deut. 32:35; II Sam. 22:19; Ps.
　　18:18, day of *c*
　　Ps. 57:1, until *c* be overpast

Prov. 1:26, I will laugh at your *c*
　　17:5, he that is glad at *c*
　　19:13, foolish son the *c* of his father
　　27:10, brother's house in day of *c*
　　See Job 6:2; Prov. 24:22
CALF Ex. 32:4; Isa. 11:6; Lk. 15:23
CALKERS Ezek. 27:9, 27
CALLING I Cor. 7:20, abide in same *c*
　　Eph. 1:18, the hope of his *c*
　　Phil. 3:14, prize of high *c*
　　II Thess. 1:11, worthy of this *c*
　　II Tim. 1:9, called us with holy *c*
　　Heb. 3:1, partakers of heavenly *c*
　　II Pet. 1:10, make *c* and election sure
　　See Acts 7:59; 22:16; I Cor. 1:26
CALM 107:29; Jonah 1:11; Mat. 8:26; Mk. 4:39;
　　Lk. 8:24
CALVES Hos. 14:2; Mal. 4:2
CAMEL Gen. 30:43; Lev. 11:4
　　Mat. 3:4, raiment of *c* hair
　　　　19:24, it is easier for a *c* to go through
　　　　23:24, strain at gnat, and swallow *c*
　　See Mk. 1:6
CAMP (*n.*) Ex. 14:19, angel, went before *c*
　　　　16:13, quails covered the *c*
　　Num. 1:52, every man by his own *c*
　　Deut. 23:14, Lord walks in midst of *c*
　　See I Sam. 4:6, 7; Heb. 13:13
CAMP (*v.*) Isa. 29:3, *c* Jer. 50:29; Nah. 3:17
CANDLE Job 29:3, *c* shined upon my head
　　Ps. 18:28, you will light my *c*
　　Prov. 20:27, spirit of man *c* of the Lord
　　Zeph. 1:12, search of Jerusalem with *c*
　　Rev. 18:23, *c* shine no more in you
　　　　22:5, need no *c*, neither light
CANDLESTICK II Ki. 4:10, set for him a *c*
　　See Mk. 4:21; Heb. 9:2; Rev. 2:5
CANKERED II Tim. 2:17; James 5:3
CAPTAIN Num. 2:3; 14:4
　　Josh. 5:14, 15, *c* of the Lord's host
　　II Chron. 13:12, God Himself is our *c*
　　Heb. 2:10, *c* of their salvation perfect
CAPTIVE Isa. 51:14, *c* exile hastened
　　　　52:2, O *c* daughter of Zion
　　II Tim. 2:26, taken *c* at his will
　　　　3:6, lead *c* silly women
　　See II Ki. 5:2; Isa. 14:2; 61:1; Lk. 4:18
CAPTIVITY Rom. 7:23, into *c* to law of sin
　　II Cor. 10:5, brings into *c* every thought
　　See Job 42:10; Ps. 14:7; 85:1; 126:1
CARCASE Isa. 66:24; Mat. 24:28; Heb. 3:17
CARE (*n.*) Mat. 13:22; Mk. 4:19, *c* of this world
　　Lk. 8:14; 21:34, choked with *c*
　　I Cor. 9:9, does God take *c* for oxen?
　　　　12:25, have same *c* one for another
　　II Cor. 11:28, the *c* of all the churches
　　I Pet. 5:7, casting all your *c* on him
CARE (*v.*) 142:4, no man *c* for my soul
　　Jn. 12:6, not that he *c* for poor
　　Acts 18:17, Gallio *c* for none of those things
　　Phil. 2:20, naturally *c* for your state
　　See II Sam. 18:3; Lk. 10:40
CAREFUL Jer. 17:8, not be *c* in drought
　　Dan. 3:16, we are not *c* to answer

Lk. 10:41, you are *c* about many things
Phil. 4:6, be *c* for nothing
Heb. 12:17, he sought it *c* with tears
See II Ki. 4:13; Phil. 4:10; Titus 3:8
CAREFULNESS Ezek. 12:18; I Cor. 7:32
CARELESS Judg. 18:7; Isa. 32:9; 47:8; Ezek. 39:6
CARNAL Rom. 7:14, *c* sold under sin
8:7, the *c* mind is enmity against God
II Cor. 10:4, weapons of our warfare not *c*
See I Cor. 9:11; Heb. 7:16; 9:10
CARPENTER II Sam. 5:11; Isa. 41:7; Zech. 1:20;
Mat. 13:55; Mk. 6:3
CARRIAGE Isa. 10:28; 46:1; Acts 21:15
CARRY Isa. 40:11, *c* lambs in his bosom
53:4, *c* our sorrows
Isa. 63:9, *c* them all days of old
Ezek. 22:9, men *c* tales to shed blood
Mk. 6:55, began to *c* about in bed
Jn. 5:10, not lawful to *c* your bed
Eph. 4:14, *c* about with every wind
I Tim. 6:7, we can *c* nothing out
II Pet. 2:17, clouds *c* with a tempest
Jude 12, clouds *c* about of winds
See Ex. 33:15; Num. 11:12; Deut. 14:24
CART Isa. 5:18, draw sin as with a *c* rope
Amos 2:13, *c* full of sheaves
CASE Ps. 144:15, happy people in such *c*
Mat. 5:20, in no *c* enter heaven
Jn. 5:6, long time in that *c*
See Ex. 5:19; Deut. 19:4; 24:13
CAST Prov. 16:33, lot is *c* into lap
Mat. 5:29; Mk. 9:45, body *c* into hell
Mk. 9:38; Lk. 9:49, one *c* out devils
Lk. 21:1, *c* gifts into treasury
Jn. 8:7, first *c* stone at her
II Cor. 10:5, *C* down imaginations
I Pet. 5:7, *C* all care upon him
I Jn. 4:18, love *c* out fear
CASTAWAY I Cor. 9:27, lest I be a *c*
CASTLE Num. 31:10; Acts 21:34
CATCH Ps. 10:9, to *c* the poor
Mat. 13:19, devil *c* away that was sown
Lk. 5:10, from henceforth you shall *c* men
Jn. 10:12, wolf *c* and scatters sheep
See II Ki. 7:12; Ezek. 19:3; Mk. 12:13
CATTLE Gen. 46:32, their trade to feed *c*
Ex. 10:26, our *c* shall go with us
Ps. 50:10; *c* upon a thousand hills
See Gen. 1:25; 30:43; Jonah 4:11
CAUGHT Gen. 22:13, ram *c* by horns
Jn. 21:3, that night they *c* nothing
II Cor. 12:2, *c* up to third heaven
16, I *c* you with guile
I Thess. 4:17, be *c* up together with them
See II Sam. 18:9; Prov. 7:13; Rev. 12:5
CAUSE (*n.*) Mat. 19:5; Mk. 10:7, for this *c*
shall a man leave
I Cor. 11:30, for this *c* many are sickly
I Tim. 1:16, for this *c* I obtained mercy
See Prov. 18:17; II Cor. 4:16; 5:13
CAUSE (*v.*) Ps. 67:1; 80:3, *c* his face to shine
Rom. 16:17, mark them who *c* divisions
See Deut. 1:38; 12:11; Job 6:24
CAUSELESS I Sam. 25:31; Prov. 26:2

CEASE Deut. 15:11, poor never *c* out of land
Job 3:17, the wicked *c* from troubling
Ps. 46:9, he makes wars to *c*
Eccl. 12:3, grinders *c* because few
Acts 20:31, I *c* not to warn
I Cor. 13:8, tongues, they shall *c*
I Thess. 5:17, pray without *c*
I Pet. 4:1, has *c* from sin
See Gen. 8:22; Isa. 1:16; 2:22
CELEBRATE Lev. 23:32; Isa. 38:18
CELESTIAL I Cor. 15:40
CEREMONIES Num. 9:3
CERTAIN Ex. 3:12, *C* I will be with you
I Cor. 4:11, no *c* dwellingplace
Heb. 10:27, a *c* looking for of judgment
See Deut. 13:14; I Ki. 2:37; Dan. 2:45
CERTIFY II Sam. 15:28; Gal. 1:11
CHAFF Lk. 3:17, burn up *c* with fire
See Jer. 23:28; Hos. 13:3; Zeph. 2:2
CHAIN Mk. 5:3, no, not with *c*
Acts 12:7, Peter's *c* fell off
II Tim. 1:16, not ashamed of my *c*
II Pet. 2:4, into *c* of darkness
Jude 6, everlasting *c* under darkness
CHALLENGES Ex. 22:9
CHAMBER II Ki. 4:10, little *c* on wall
Ps. 19:5, as bridegroom coming out of *c*
Isa. 26:20, enter into your *c*
Ezek. 8:12, *c* of imagery
Mat. 24:26, in secret *c*
Acts 9:37; 20:8, in upper *c*
See Dan. 6:10; Joel 2:16; Prov. 7:27
CHAMPION I Sam. 17:4, 51
CHANCE I Sam. 6:9; II Sam. 1:6
CHANGE (*n.*) Job 14:14, till my *c* come
Prov. 24:21, meddle not with him given to *c*
See Judg. 14:12; Zech. 3:4; Heb. 7:12
CHANGE (*v.*) Ps. 15:4, swears, and *c* not
102:26, as a vesture shall you *c* them
Lam. 4:1, fine gold *c*
Mal. 3:6, I am the Lord, I *c* not
Rom. 1:23, *c* glory of uncorruptible God
I Cor. 15:51, we shall all be *c*
II Cor. 3:18, *c* from glory to glory
See Job 17:12; Jer. 2:36; 13:23
CHANT Amos 6:5
CHAPMEN II Chron. 9:14
CHAPT Jer. 14:4
CHARGE Job 1:22, nor *c* God foolishly
4:18, angels he *c* with folly
Mat. 9:30; Mk. 5:43, Jesus *c* them
Acts 7:60; II Tim. 4:16, lay not sin to their *c*
Rom. 8:33, who shall lay any thing to *c*
I Cor. 9:18, gospel without *c*
I Tim. 1:3, *c* that they teach no other
5:21; II Tim. 4:1, I *c* you before God
6:17, *C* them that are rich
See Ex. 6:13; Ps. 35:11; 91:11; Mk. 9:25
CHARGEABLE II Sam. 13:25; II Cor. 11:9
CHARIOT Gen. 41:43; Ex. 14:25, and took off
their *c* wheels
Josh. 17:16, *c* of iron
I Sam. 8:11, king take sons for his *c*
II Sam. 8:4, David took a thousand *c*

I Ki. 10:26, Solomon's *c*
 29, a *c* of Egypt for 600 shekels
II Ki. 2:11, *c* of fire, *c* of Israel
 6:17, mountain full of *c* and horses
 18:24, trust on Egypt for *c*
Ps. 20:7, some trust in *c*
 68:17, the *c* of God are 20,000 even
 104:3, who makes the clouds his *c*
Song of Sol. 6:12, like the *c* of Amminadib
Isa. 21:7, saw *c* of asses
Zech. 6:1, four *c* between two mountains
Acts 8:28, sitting in *c* read Isaiah
Rev. 9:9, sound of wings as of *c*
CHARITY Rom. 14:15, now walkest thou not *c*
 Col. 3:14, put on *c*
II Thess. 1:3, *c* abounds
I Tim. 1:5, end of commandment is *c*
II Tim. 2:22, follow faith, *c*, peace
Titus 2:2, sound in faith, in *c*
II Pet. 1:7, to brotherly kindness *c*
Jude 12, spots in feasts of *c*
 See I Cor. 8:1; 13:1; 14:1; 16:14; Rev. 2:19
CHARMER Deut. 18:11; Ps. 58:5; Jer. 8:17
CHASE Lev. 26:8; five *c* hundred
 Deut. 32:30; Josh. 23:10, one *c* thousand
 See Job 18:18; Ps. 35:5; Lam. 3:52
CHASTE II Cor. 11:2; Titus 2:5; I Pet. 3:2
CHASTEN Deut. 8:5, as a man *c* son
 Ps. 6:1; 38:1, nor *c* me in displeasure
 94:12, blessed is the man whom you *c*
Prov. 19:18, *c* your son while there is hope
II Cor. 6:9, as *c*, and not killed
Heb. 12:6, whom the Lord loves he *c*
 11, not *c* seems to be joyous
 See Ps. 69:10; 73:14; 118:18
CHASTISEMENT Deut. 11:2; Job 34:31
CHATTER Isa. 38:14
CHEEK Mat. 5:39, smites on right *c*
 See Job 16:10; Isa. 50:6; Lam. 3:30
CHEER Zech. 9:17, corn shall make young
 men *c*
Jn. 16:33, be of good *c*, I have overcome
Acts 23:11; 27:22, 25, be of good *c*
Rom. 12:8, he that shows mercy, with *c*
II Cor. 9:7, God loves a *c* giver
 See Judg. 9:13; Mat. 9:2; 14:27; Mk. 6:50
CHERISHES Eph. 5:29; I Thess. 2:7
CHICKENS Mat. 23:37
CHIDE Ex. 17:2; Judg. 8:1; Ps. 103:9
CHIEFEST Song of Sol. 5:10; II Chron. 11:5
CHILD Gen. 42:22, do not sin against the *c*
 Prov. 20:11, a *c* is known by his doings
 22:6, train up a *c* in way
 15, foolishness in heart of *c*
Isa. 9:6, unto us a *c* is born
Lk. 1:66, what manner of *c*
Jn. 4:49, come ere my *c* die
I Cor. 13:11, when I was a *c*
II Tim. 3:15, from a *c* have known
CHILDREN I Sam. 16:11, are all your *c*?
 Ps. 34:11, come, ye *c*, hearken to me
 45:16, instead of fathers shall be *c*
 128:3, your *c* like olive plants
Isa. 30:9, lying *c*, *c* that will not hear

63:8, *c* that will not lie
Jer. 31:15, Rachel weeping for her *c*
Ezek. 18:2, *c* teeth are set on edge
Mat. 15:26; Mk. 7:27, not take *c* bread
 17:26, then are the *c* free
 19:14; Lk. 18:16, suffer little *c*
Lk. 16:8, *c* of this world
 20:36, *c* of God and the resurrection
Jn. 12:36; Eph. 5:8; I Thess. 5:5, *c* of light
Rom. 8:16; Gal. 3:26; I Jn. 3:10, witness that
 we are the *c* of God
Eph. 4:14, be henceforth no more *c*
 5:6; Col. 3:6, *c* of disobedience
 6:1; Col. 3:20, C, obey your parents
I Tim. 3:4, having his *c* in subjection
 See Num. 16:27; Esther 3:13; Mat. 14:21
CHODE Gen. 31:36; Num. 20:3
CHOICE I Sam. 9:2, Saul, a *c* young man
Acts 15:7, God made *c* among us
 See Gen. 23:6; II Sam. 10:9; Prov. 8:10
CHOKE Mat. 13:22; Mk. 4:19; Lk. 8:14
CHOLER Dan. 8:7; 11:11
CHOSE Ps. 33:12, *c* for his inheritance
 89:19, exalted one *c* out of the people
Jer. 8:3, death shall be *c* rather than life
Mat. 20:16; 22:14, many called, few *c*
Lk. 10:42, has *c* that good part
 14:7, they *c* the chief rooms
Jn. 15:16, you have not *c* me
Acts 9:15, he is a *c* vessel
Rom. 16:13, *c* in the Lord
I Cor. 1:27, 28, God has *c* foolish things
Eph. 1:4, according as he has *c* us
I Pet. 2:4, *c* of God and precious
 See Ex. 18:25; II Sam. 6:21; I Chron. 16:13
CHRIST Mat. 16:16, you are the C
 24:5, many shall come, saying, I am C
Jn. 4:25, the Messiah, which is called C
 29, is not this the C?
 6:69, we are sure that you are the C
Phil. 1:15, 16, some preach C of contention
I Pet. 1:11, the Spirit of C did signify
I Jn. 2:22, denies that Jesus is the C
 5:1, whoso believes Jesus is the C
 See Mat. 1:16; 2:4; Lk. 2:26; I Cor. 5:7
CHRISTIAN Acts 11:26; 26:28; I Pet. 4:16
CHURCH Mat. 18:17, tell it to the *c*
Acts 2:47, added to *c* daily
 7:38, the *c* in the wilderness
 19:37, neither robbers of *c*
 20:28, feed the *c* of God
Rom. 16:5, I Cor. 16:19, *c* in house
I Cor. 14:28, 34, keep silence in the *c*
Eph. 5:24, the *c* is subject to Christ
 25, as Christ loved the *c*
Col. 1:18, 24, head of the body the *c*
Heb. 12:23, the *c* of the firstborn
 See Mat. 16:18; Rev. 1:4; 2:1; 22:16
CIELED II Chron. 3:5; Jer. 22:14; Hag. 1:4
CIRCLE Isa. 40:22
CIRCUIT I Sam. 7:16; Job 22:14; Ps. 19:6
CIRCUMCISE Rom. 4:11, though not *c*
 Phil. 3:5, C the eighth day
 See Deut. 30:6; Jn. 7:22, Acts 15:1

CIRCUMCISION Rom. 3:1
    15:8, Jesus Christ minister of *c*
    Gal. 5:6; 6:15, in Christ neither *c* avails
    Phil. 3:3, the *c* which worship God
    Col. 2:11, *c* without hands
    See Ex. 4:26; Jn. 7:22; Acts 7:8
CIRCUMSPECT Ex. 23:13; Eph. 5:15
CISTERN Eccl. 12:6, wheel broken at the *c*
    Jer. 2:13, hewed out *c*, broken *c*
    See II Ki. 18:31; Prov. 5:15; Isa. 36:16
CITIZEN Lk. 15:15; 19:14; Acts 21:39
CITY Num. 35:6; Josh. 15:59, *c* of refuge
    Ps. 46:4, make glad *c* of God
        107:4, found no *c* to dwell in
        127:1, except Lord build *c*
    Prov. 8:3, wisdom cries in *c*
    Eccl. 9:14, a little *c*, and few men
    Isa. 33:20, *c* of our solemnities
    Zech. 8:3, a *c* of truth
    Mat. 5:14, *c* set on a hill
        21:10, all the *c* was moved
    Lk. 24:49, tarry in the *c*
    Acts 8:8, great joy in the *c*
    Heb. 11:10, a *c* that has foundations
        12:22, the *c* of living God
    Rev. 16:19, the *c* of the nations fell
    See Gen. 4:17; 11:4; Jonah 1:2; Rev. 21:18
CLAD I Ki. 11:29; Isa. 59:17
CLAMOUR Prov. 9:13; Eph. 4:31
CLAP Ps. 47:1, *c* your hands, all ye people
    98:8, let the floods *c* their hands
    Isa. 55:12, the trees shall *c* their hands
    Lam. 2:15, all that pass by *c* their hands
    See II Ki. 11, 12; Job 27:23; 34:37
CLAVE II Sam. 23:10, his hand *c* to the sword
    Neh. 10:29, they *c* to their brethren
    Acts 17:34, certain men *c* to Paul
    See Gen. 22:3; Num. 16:31; I Sam. 6:14
CLAWS Deut. 14:6; Dan. 4:33; Zech. 11:16
CLAY Job 10:9, you have made me as *c*
    13:12, bodies like to bodies of *c*
    33:6, I also am formed out of *c*
    Dan. 2:33, part of iron, part of *c*
    Jn. 9:6, made *c*, and anointed
    Rom. 9:21, power over the *c*
    See Isa. 29:16; 41:25; 45:9; 64:8; Jer. 18:4
CLEAN Job 14:4, who can bring *c* out of
    unclean?
    15:15, heavens not *c* in his sight
    Ps. 24:4, he that has *c* hands
        51:10, create in me *c* heart
        77:8, is his mercy *c* gone forever?
    Prov. 16:2, *c* in his own eyes
    Isa. 1:16, wash you, make you *c*
        52:11, be *c* that bear vessels of the Lord
    Ezek. 36:25, then will I sprinkle *c* water
    Lk. 11:39, make *c* the outside
        41, all things *c* unto you
    Jn. 13:11, you are not all *c*
        15:3, *c* through word I have spoken
    Acts 18:6, I am *c*
    Rev. 19:8, arrayed in fine linen, *c* and white
    See Lev. 23:22; Josh. 3:17; Prov. 14:4
CLEANNESS II Sam. 22:21; Ps. 18:20

CLEANSE Ps. 19:12, *c* me from secret faults
    73:13, I have *c* my heart in vain
    Mat. 8:3, immediately his leprosy was *c*
    10:8; 11:5; Lk. 7:22, *c* lepers
    23:26, *c* first that which is within
    Lk. 4:27, none was *c*, saving Naaman
        17:17, were not ten *c*?
    Acts 10:15; 11:9, what God has *c*
    II Cor. 7:1, let us *c* ourselves
    James 4:8, C your hands, you sinners
    I Jn. 1:7, 9, *c* us from all sin
    See Ezek. 36:25; Mk. 1:44
CLEAR Gen. 44:16, shall we *c* ourselves?
    Ex. 34:7, by no means *c* the guilty
    II Sam. 23:4, *c* shining after rain
    Job 11:17, your ages shall be *c* than noonday
    Ps. 51:4, be *c* when you judge
    Mat. 7:5; Lk. 6:42, see *c* to pull out mote
    Mk. 8:25, saw every man *c*
    Rom. 1:20, things from creation *c* seen
    Rev. 21:11; 22:1, light *c* as crystal
    See Gen. 24:8; Song of Sol. 6:10; Zech. 14:6
CLEAVE Josh. 23:8, *c* to the Lord your God
    II Ki. 5:27, leprosy shall *c* to you
    Ps. 119:25, my soul *c* to dust
    Acts 11:23, with purpose of heart *c*
    Rom. 12:9, *c* to that which is good
    See Gen. 2:24; Mat. 19:5; Mk. 10:7
CLEFTS Song of Sol. 2:14; Isa. 2:21; Jer. 49:16
CLEMENCY Acts 24:4
CLERK Acts 19:35
CLIMB Jn. 10:1, but *c* up some other way
    See I Sam. 14:13; Amos 9:2; Lk. 19:4
CLODS Job 21:33, the *c* of the valley
    See Job 7:5; Isa. 28:24; Hos. 10:11; Joel 1:17
CLOKE Mat. 5:40; Lk. 6:29
    I Thess. 2:5, a *c* of covetousness
    I Pet. 2:16, a *c* of maliciousness
CLOSE (*v.*) Gen. 2:21; Isa. 29:10; Mat. 13:15
CLOSE (*a.*) Prov. 18:24, *c* than a brother
    Lk. 9:36, they kept it *c*
CLOSET Mat. 6:6; Lk. 12:3
CLOTH I Sam. 19:13; 21:9; Mat. 9:16
CLOTHE Ps. 109:18, *c* himself with cursing
    132:9, *c* with righteousness
    16, *c* with salvation
    Prov. 23:21, drowsiness shall *c* a man
    31:21, household *c* with scarlet
    Isa. 50:3, *c* heavens with blackness
    61:10, *c* with garments of salvation
    Mat. 6:30, Lk. 12:28, *c* grass of field
    31, wherewithal shall we be *c*?
    11:8; Lk. 7:25, a man *c* in soft raiment?
    25:36, 43, naked, and you *c* me
    Mk. 1:6, *c* with camel's hair
    5:15; Lk. 8:35, *c*, and in right mind
    15:17, *c* Jesus with purple
    Lk. 16:19, *c* in purple and fine linen
    I Pet. 5:5, be *c* with humility
    Rev. 3:18, that you may be *c*
    12:1, woman *c* with the sun
    19:13, *c* with a vesture dipped in blood
    See Gen. 3:21; Ex. 40:14; Esther 4:4
CLOTHES Deut. 29:5, *c* not waxed old

Mk. 5:28, if I touch but his *c*
Lk. 2:7, in swaddling *c*
  8:27, a man that wore no *c*
  19:36, spread *c* in the way
  24:12, Jn. 20:5, linen *c* laid
Jn. 11:44, bound with grave-*c*
Acts 7:58, laid down *c* at Saul's feet
  22:23, cried out, and cast off *c*
See Gen. 49:11; I Sam. 19:24; Neh. 4:23
CLOTHING Ps. 45:13, her *c* of wrought gold
Prov. 27:26, lambs are for your *c*
  31:22, her *c* is silk and purple
  25, strength and honor are her *c*
Isa. 3:7, in my house is neither bread nor *c*
  23:18, merchandise for durable *c*
  59:17, garments of vengeance for *c*
Mat. 7:15, in sheep's *c*
Acts 10:30, a man is bright *c*
James 2:3, to him that wears gay *c*
See Job 22:6; 24:7; 31:19; Ps. 35:13
CLOUD Ex. 13:21; 14:24, a pillar of *c*
I Ki. 18:44, 45, a little *c*
Ps. 36:5, faithfulness reaches to *c*
Ps. 97:2, *C* and darkness around about them
  99:7, spoke in *c* pillar
Prov. 3:20, *c* dropped down dew
Isa. 5:6, command *c* rain not
  44:22, blotted out as thick *c*
  60:8, fly as a *c*
Dan. 7:13; Lk. 21:27, Son of man with *c*
Hos. 6:4; 13:3, goodness as morning *c*
I Cor. 10:1, fathers under *c*
I Thess. 4:17, caught up in *c*
II Pet. 2:17, *c* carried with tempest
Jude 12, *c* without water
Rev. 1:7, he comes with *c*
  14:14, 15, 16, white *c*
See Gen. 9:13; Ex. 24:15; 40:34; Ps. 104:3
CLOUT Josh. 9:5; Jer. 38:11
CLOVEN Lev. 11:3; Deut. 14:7; Acts 2:3
CLUSTER Isa. 65:8, new wine in *c*
See Num. 13:23; Song of Sol. 1:14; 7:7; Rev. 14:18
COAL Prov. 6:28, hot *c*, and not be burned
  25:22; Rom. 12:20, heap *c* of fire
Jn. 18:18; 21:9, fire of *c*
See Job 41:21; Ps. 18:8; Isa. 6:6
COAST I Chron 4:10; Mat. 8:34; Mk. 5:17
COAT Mat. 5:40, take away your *c*
  10:10; Mk. 6:9, neither provide two *c*
Lk. 6:29, your *c* also
Jn. 19:23, *c* without seam
  21:7, fisher's *c*
Acts 9:39, the *c* which Dorcas made
See Gen. 3:21; 37:3; I Sam. 2:19
COCK Mat. 26:34; Mk. 13:35; 14:30
COCKATRICE Isa. 11:8; 14:29; 59:5
COCKLE Job 31:40
COFFER I Sam. 6:8, 11, 15
COFFIN Gen. 50:26
COGITATIONS Dan. 7:28
COLD Prov. 25:13, *c* of snow in harvest
  20, garment in *c* weather
  25, *c* waters to thirsty soul

Mat. 10:42, *c*up of *c* water
  24:12, love of many wax *c*
Rev. 3:15, neither *c* nor hot
See Gen. 8:22; Job 24:7; 37:9; Ps. 147:17
COLLECTION II Chron 24:6; I Cor. 16:1
COLLEGE II Ki. 22:14; II Chron 34:22
COLOUR Prov. 23:31, *c* in the cup
See Gen. 37:3; Ezek. 1:4; Dan. 10:6
COMELY Ps. 33:1, praise is *c*
I Cor. 11:13, is it *c* that a woman
See I Sam. 16:18; Prov. 30:29; Isa. 53:2
COMFORT (*n.*) Mat. 9:22; Mk. 10:49
II Cor. 13:11, be of good *c*
Acts 9:31, *c* of Holy Spirit
Rom. 15:4, patience and *c* of scriptures
II Cor. 1:3, God of all *c*;
  7:13, were comforted in your *c*
Phil. 2:1, if any *c* of love
See Job 10:20; Ps. 94:19; 119:50; Isa. 57:6
COMFORT (*v.*) Gen. 37:25; Ps. 77:2, refused to be *c*
Ps. 23:4, rod and staff *c*
Isa. 40:1, *C* ye, *c* ye, my people
  49:13; 52:9, God has *c* his people
  61:2, *c* all that mourn
  66:13, as one whom his mother *c*
Mat. 5:4, they shall be *c*
Lk. 16:25, he is *c*, and you are tormented
Jn. 11:19, to *c* them concerning their brother
II Cor. 1:4, able to *c* them
I Thess. 4:18, *c* one another with these words
  5:14, *c* the feebleminded
COMFORTABLE Isa. 40:2; Hos. 2:14
COMFORTER Job 16:2, miserable *c* are you
Ps. 69:20, looked for *c*, but I found none
Jn. 14:16; 15:26; 16:7, another *C*
See II Sam. 10:3; I Chron. 19:3
COMFORTLESS Jn. 14:18
COMMAND Lk. 8:25, he *c* even the winds
  9:54, *c* fire from heaven
Jn. 15:14, if you do what I *c* you
Acts 17:30, *c* all men every where
See Gen. 18:19; Deut. 28:8
COMMANDER Isa. 55:4
COMMANDMENT Ps. 119:86, *c* are faithful
  96, *c* exceeding broad
Ps. 119:127, I love your *c*
  143, your *c* are my delight
Mat. 15:9; Mk. 7:7; Col. 2:2, the *c* of men
Lk. 23:56, rested according to *c*
Jn. 13:34; I Jn. 2:7; II Jn. 5, a new *c*
Rom. 7:12, *c* is holy, just, and good
I Cor. 7:6, by permission, not by *c*
Eph. 6:2, first *c* with promise
I Tim. 1:5, end of the *c* is charity
COMMEND Lk. 16:8, *c* unjust steward
  23:46, into your hands I *c*
I Cor. 8:8, meat *c* us not
II Cor. 3:1; 5:12, *c* ourselves
  4:2, *c* to every man's conscience
  10:18, not he that *c* himself is approved
See Prov. 12:8; Eccl. 8:15; Acts 20:32
COMMISSION Ezra 8:36; Acts 26:12
COMMIT Ps. 37:5, *C* your way to the Lord

Jer. 2:13, have *c* two evils
Jn. 2:24, Jesus did not *c* himself to them
   5:22, has *c* judgment to Son
I Pet. 2:23, *c* himself to him that judges
See Job 5:8; Ps. 31:5; Prov. 6:32; Mat. 5:28
   I Cor. 9:17; 10:8; Rev. 2:14
COMMODIOUS Acts 27:12
COMMON Eccl. 6:1
Mk. 12:37, the *c* people heard him gladly
Acts 2:44; 4:32, all things *c*
   10:14; 11:8, never eaten anything *c*
   15; 11:9, call not you *c*
I Cor. 10:13, temptation *c* to me
Eph. 2:12, aliens from *c*-wealth
See Lev. 4:27; Num. 16:29; I Sam. 21:4
COMMOTION Jer. 10:22; Lk. 21:9
COMMUNE Job 4:2, if we *c* with you
Ps. 4:4; 77:6; Eccl. 1:16, *c* with own heart
Zech. 1:14, angel that *c* with me
See Ex. 25:22; I Sam. 19:3; Lk. 22:4
COMMUNICATE Gal. 6:6
I Tim. 6:18, be willing to *c*
Heb. 13:16, do good and *c*
See Gal. 2:2; Phil. 4:14, 15
COMMUNICATION Mat. 5:37
Lk. 24:17, what manner of *c*
I Cor. 15:33, evil *c* corrupt good manners
Eph. 4:29, let not corrupt *c* proceed
COMMUNION I Cor. 10:16; II Cor. 6:14
COMPACT Ps. 122:3; Eph. 4:16
COMPANION Job 30:29, a *c* to owls
Ps. 119:63, a *c* to them that fear you
Prov. 13:20, *c* of fools shall be destroyed
   28:7, *c* of riotous men
   24, the *c* of a destroyer
Acts 19:29, Paul's *c* in travel
Phil. 2:25; Rev. 1:9, brother and *c* in labor
See Ex. 32:27; Judg. 11:38; 14:20
COMPANY I Sam. 10:5, a *c* of prophets
Ps. 55;14, walked to house of God in *c*
   68:11, great was the *c* of those
Mk. 6:39; Lk. 9:14, sit down by *c*
II Thess. 3:14, have no *c* with him
Heb. 12:22, innumerable *c* of angels
COMPARE Prov. 3:15; 8:11
Isa. 40:18, what likeness will you *c* unto him?
   46:5, to whom will you *c* me?
Lam. 4:2, *c* to find gold
Rom. 8:18, not worthy to be *c* with glory
I Cor. 2:13, *c* spiritual things with spiritual
See Ps. 89:6; II Cor. 10:12
COMPARISON Judg. 8:2; Mk. 4:30
COMPASS (*n.*) II Sam. 5:23; II Ki. 3:9
Isa. 44:13; Acts 28:13
COMPASS (*v.*) II Sam. 22:5; Ps. 18:4, sorrows
   of death *c* me
Ps. 18:5, sorrows of hell *c* me
   32:7, *c* with songs of deliverance
   10, mercy shall *c* him about
Isa. 50:11, *c* yourself with sparks
Mat. 23:15, *c* sea and land
Lk. 21:20, Jerusalem *c* with armies
Heb. 5:2, he also is *c* with infirmity
   12:1, *c* about with cloud of witnesses

See Josh. 6:3; Job 16:13; Ps. 49:5; Jer. 31:22
COMPASSION Lam. 3:22, his *c* fail not
   32; Mic. 7:19, yet will he have *c*
Mat. 9:36; Mk. 1:41, Jesus moved with *c*
   18:33, *c* on your fellowservant
Mat. 20:34, had *c* on them, and touched
Mk. 5:19, the Lord has had *c*
   9:22, have *c* and help me
Lk. 10:33, the Samaritan had *c*
   15:20, father had *c* and ran
Rom. 9:15, I will have *c* on whom I will
Heb. 5:2, have *c* on ignorant
I Pet. 3:8, of one mind, having *c*
I Jn. 3:17, shuts up bowels of *c*
Jude 22, of some have *c*, making a difference
See Ps. 78:38; 86:15; 111:4; 112:4
COMPEL Mat. 5:41, *c* you to go a mile
   27:32; Mk. 15:21, *c* to bear cross
Lk. 14:23, *c* to come in
Acts 26:11, I *c* them to blaspheme
See Lev. 25:39; II Cor. 12:11; Gal. 2:3
COMPLAIN Ps. 114:14, no *c* in our streets
Lam. 3:39, wherefore does a living man *c*?
Jude 16, these are murmurers, *c*
See Num. 11:1; Judg. 21:22; Job 7:11
COMPLAINT Job 23:2, today is my *c* bitter
Ps. 142:2, I poured out my *c* before him
See I Sam. 1:16; Job 7:13; 9:27; 10:1
COMPLETE Lev. 23:15; Col. 2:10; 4:12
COMPREHEND Job 37:5; Isa. 40:12; Jn. 1:5;
   Eph. 3:18
CONCEAL Prov. 25:2; glory of God to *c* a thing
Jer. 50:2, publish, and *c* not
See Gen. 37:26; Deut. 13:8
CONCEIT Prov. 18:11; 26:5; 28:11
CONCEIVE Ps. 7:14, *c* mischief, brought forth
   falsehood
   51:5, in sin did my mother *c* me
Acts 5:4, why have you *c* this thing?
James 1:15, when lust has *c*, it brings forth
CONCERN Lk. 24:27, things *c* himself
Rom. 9:5, as *c* the flesh Christ came
   16:19, simple *c* evil
Phil. 4:15, *c* giving and receiving
I Tim. 6:21, have erred *c* the faith
See Lev. 6:3; Num. 10:29; Ps. 90:13; 135:14
CONCISION Phil. 3:2
CONCLUDE Rom. 3:28; 11:32; Gal. 3:22
CONCLUSION Eccl. 12:13
CONCORD II Cor. 6:15
CONCUBINE Judg. 19:10; II Sam. 16:21;
   I Chron. 1:32; I Ki. 11:3; Dan. 5:2
CONDEMN Job 10:2
Amos 2:8, drink the wine of the *c*
Mat. 12:7, ye would not have *c* the guiltless
   20:18, shall *c* him to death
   27:3, Judas, when he saw he was *c*
Mat. 12:37, by the words shall be *c*
   42; Lk. 11:31, rise in judgment and *c*
Mk. 14:64; all *c* him to be guilty
Lk. 6:37, *c* not, and you shall not be *c*
Jn. 3:17, God sent not his son to *c*
   8:10, has no man *c* you?
   11, neither do I *c* you?

Rom. 2:1, you *c* yourself
   8:3, *c* sin the flesh
   34, who is he that *c*?
   14:22, that *c* not himself
James 5:6, you *c* and killed the just
   9, grudge not, lest you be *c*
I Jn. 3:21, if our heart *c* us not
   See Job 9:20; 15:6; Mat. 12:41
CONDEMNATION Jn. 3:19
   II Cor. 3:9, the ministration of *c*
   I Tim. 3:6, the *c* of the devil
   James 5:12, lest you fall into *c*
   Jude 4, of old ordained to this *c*
   See Lk. 23:40; Rom. 5:16; 8:1
CONDESCEND Rom. 12:16
CONDITION I Sam. 11:2; Lk. 14:32
CONDUIT II Ki. 18:17; 20:20; Isa. 7:3; 36:2
CONEY Lev. 11:5; Ps. 104:18; Prov. 30:26
CONFECTION Ex. 30:35; I Sam. 8:13
CONFEDERATE Gen. 14:13; Isa. 7:2; 8:12
CONFERENCE Gal. 2:6
CONFERRED Gal. 1:16
CONFESS Prov. 28:13, whoso *c* and forsakes
   Mat. 10:32; Lk. 12:8, *c* me before men
   Jn. 9:22, if any man did *c*
   12:42, ruler did not *c* him
   Acts 23:8, Pharisees *c* both
   Rom. 10:9, shall *c* with your mouth
   14:11; Phil. 2:11, every tongue *c*
   Heb. 11;13, *c* they were strangers
   James 5:16; *C* your faults one to another
   I Jn. 1:9, if we *c* our sins
   4:2, every spirit that *c* Christ
   15, whoso shall *c* that Jesus is the Christ
   Rev. 3:5, I will *c* his name before my Father
   See Lev., 16:21; I Ki. 8:33; II Chron. 6:24
CONFESSION Rom. 10:10, I Tim. 6:13
CONFIDENCE Ps. 65:5, the *c* of all the ends
   of the earth
   118:8, 9, then to put *c* in man
   Prov. 14:26, in fear of the Lord is strong *c*
   Isa. 30:15, in *c* shall be your strength
   Jer. 2:37, has rejected your *c*
   Eph. 3:12, access with *c* by faith
   Phil. 3:3, 4, no *c* in flesh
   I Jn. 3:21, we have *c* toward God
   5:14, this is the *c* we have in him
   See Job 4:6; 18:14; 31:24; Prov. 25:19
CONFIDENT Ps. 27:3; Prov. 14:16; Phil. 1:6
CONFIRM Isa. 35:3, *c* the feeble knees
   Mk. 16:20, *c* the word with signs
   Acts 14:22, *C* the souls of the disciples
   15:32, 41, exhorted brethren, and *c* them
   Rom. 15:8, *c* promises made to the fathers
CONFIRMATION Phil. 1:7; Heb. 6:16
CONFISCATION Ezra 7:26
CONFLICT Phil. 1:30; Col. 2:1
CONFORM Rom. 8:29; 12:2; Phil. 3:10
CONFOUND Ps. 22:5; 70:2, ashamed and *c*
   Acts 2:6, multitude were *c*
   9:22, Saul *c* the Jews
   See Gen. 11:7; Ps. 71:13; 129:5
CONFUSED Isa. 9:5; Acts 19:32
CONFUSION Dan. 9:7

Acts 19:29; city was filled with *c*
   I Cor. 14:33, God not author of *c*
   See Ps. 70:2; 71:1; 109:29; Isa. 24:10
CONGEALED Ex. 15:8
CONGRATULATE I Chron. 18:10
CONGREGATION Num. 14:10
   Neh. 5:13, all the *c* said Amen
   Ps. 1:5, nor sinners in the *c* of the righteous
   26:12, in the *c* will I bless the Lord
   Prov. 21:16, in the *c* of the dead
   Acts 13:43, when the *c* was broken up
   See Ex. 12:6; 16:2; 39:32; Lev. 4:13
CONQUERORS Rom. 8:37; Rev. 6:2
CONSCIENCE Acts 24:16; *c* void of offense
   Rom. 2:15; 9:1; II Cor. 1:12, *c* bearing witness
   Rom. 13:5; I Cor. 10:25, 27, 28, for *c* sake
   I Cor. 8:10, 12, weak *c*
   I Tim. 1:5, 19; I Pet. 3:16, a good *c*
   3:9, mystery of faith in pure *c*
   4:2, *c* seared with hot iron
   Heb. 9:14, purge *c* from dead works
   See Jn. 8:9; Acts 23:1; II Cor. 4:2
CONSECRATE I Chron. 29:5; to *c* his service to
   the Lord
   Mic. 4:13, I will *c*
   Heb. 7:28, who is *c* for evermore
   10:20, living way, which he has *c*
   See Ex. 28:3; 29:35; 32:29; Lev. 7:37
CONSENT Ps. 50:18; a thief, you *c* with him
   Prov. 1:10, if sinners entice you, *c* not
   Lk. 14:18, with one *c* began to make excuse
   See Deut. 13:8; Acts 8:1; Rom. 7:16
CONSIDER Ps. 8:3, when I *c* your heavens
   41:1, blessed is he that *c* the poor
   48:13, *c* her palaces
   50:22, *c* this, ye that forget God
   Prov. 6:6, *c* her ways, and be wise
   23:1, *c* diligently what is before you
   28:22, and *c* not that poverty
   Eccl. 5:1, they *c* not that they do evil
   7:14, in days of adversity *c*
   Isa. 1:3, my people does not *c*
   Jer. 23:20; 30:24, in latter days you shall *c*
   Ezek. 12:3, it may be they will *c*
   Hag. 1:5, 7, *C* your ways
   Mat. 6:28; Lk. 12:27, *c* lilies of the field
   Mat. 7:3, *c* not the beam
   Lk. 12:24, *C* the ravens
   Gal. 6:1, *c* yourself, lest you also be tempted
   Heb. 3:1, *c* the Apostle and High Priest
   7:4, now *c* how great this man was
   13:7, *c* the end of their conversation
   See Deut. 32:29; Judg. 18:14; I Sam. 12:24
CONSIST Lk. 12:15; Col. 1:17
CONSOLATION Job 15:11; Isa. 66:11
   Lk. 6:24, you have received your *c*
   Rom. 15:5, the God of *c*
   Phil. 2:1, if there be any *c* in Christ
   II Thess. 2:16, everlasting *c*
   Heb. 6:18, strong *c*
   See Jer. 16:7; Lk. 2:25; Acts 4:36
CONSPIRACY II Sam. 15:12; Acts 23:13
CONSTANTLY I Chron 28:7; Prov. 21:28
CONSTRAIN Job 32:18; Lk. 24:29; II Cor. 5:14;

I Pet. 5:2

CONSULT Ps. 83:3; Mk. 15:1; Lk. 14:31

CONSUME Ex. 3:2, bush was not *c*
Deut. 4:24; 9:3; Heb. 12:29, a *c* fire
Job 20:26, fire not blown shall *c* him
Ps. 39:11, *c* away like a moth
Mal. 3:6, therefore you are not *c*
Lk. 9:54, *c* them, as Elias did
Gal. 5:15, take heed that you be not *c*
James 4:3, that you may *c* it on your lusts
See Ex. 32:10; 33:3; Deut. 5:25; Josh. 24:20

CONSUMMATION Dan. 9:27

CONSUMPTION Lev. 26:16; Deut. 28:22

CONTAIN I Ki. 8:27; II Chron. 2:6; 6:18

CONTEMN Ps. 10:13; 107:11; Ezek. 21:10

CONTEMPT Prov. 18:3
Dan. 12:2, awake to everlasting *c*
See Esther 1:18; Job 31:34; Ps. 119:22

CONTEMPTIBLE Mal 1:7, 12; 2:9

CONTEND Isa. 49:25, I will *c* with him that *c*
50:8, who will *c* with me?
Jer. 12:5, how can you *c* with horses?
See Job 10:2; 13:8; Eccl. 6:10; Jude 3, 9

CONTENT Mk. 15:15, to *c* the people
Lk. 3:14, be *c* with your wages
Phil. 4:11, I have learned to be *c*
I Tim. 6:6, godliness with *c* is great gain
6:8, having food let us be *c*
Heb. 13:5, be *c* with such things as ye have

CONTENTION Prov. 19:13; 27:15, *c* of a wife
23:29, who has *c*?
Acts 15:39, the *c* was sharp
I Cor. 1:11, there are *c* among you
Phil. 1:16, preach Christ of *c*
I Thess. 2:2, to speak with much *c*
Titus 3:9, avoid *c* and strivings
See Prov. 13:10; 17:14; 18:6; 22:10

CONTENTIOUS Prov. 21:19; 26:21; Rom. 2:8

CONTINUAL Ps. 34:1; 71:6, praise *c*
40:11, let your truth *c* preserve me
73:23, I am *c* with you
Prov. 6:21, bind them *c* on your heart
15:15, merry heart has a *c* feast
Isa. 14:6, smote with a *c* stroke
52:5, my name is *c* blasphemed
Lk. 18:5, lest by her *c* coming
Acts 6:4, give ourselves *c* to prayer
Rom. 9:2, I have *c* sorrow in my heart
Heb. 7:3, abides a priest *c*

CONTINUANCE Deut. 28:59; Ps. 139:16

CONTINUE Job 14:2; as a shadow, and *c* not
Ps. 72:17, name shall *c* as long as the sun
Isa. 5:11, *c* till wine inflame them
Jer. 32:14, evidences may *c* many days
Lk. 6:12, he *c* all night in prayer
22:28, that *c* with me in my temptation
Jn. 8:31, if you *c* in my word
15:9, *c* ye in my love
Acts 1:14; 2:46, *c* with one accord
12:16, Peter *c* knocking
13:43, to *c* in grace of God
14:22, exhorting them to *c* in faith
26:22, I *c* unto this day
Rom. 6:1, shall we *c* in sin?

12:12; Col. 4:2, *C* in prayer
Gal. 3:10, that *c* not in all things
Col. 1:23, I Tim. 2:15, if you *c* in the faith
I Tim. 4:16; II Tim. 3:14, *c* in them
Heb. 7:23, not suffered to *c* by reason
13:1, let brotherly love *c*
14, here have we no *c* city
James 4:13, and *c* there a year
II Pet. 3:4, all things *c* as they were
I Jn. 2:19, no doubt have *c* with us

CONTRADICTION Heb. 7:7; 12:3

CONTRARIWISE II Cor. 2:7; Gal. 2:7

CONTRARY Acts 18:13, *c* to the law
26:9, many things *c* to name of Jesus
Gal. 5:17, *c* the one to the other
I Thess. 2:15, *c* to all men
I Tim. 1:10, *c* to sound doctrine
Titus 2:8, he of the *c* part may be ashamed

CONTRIBUTION Rom. 15:26

CONTRITE Ps. 34:18; 51:17; Isa. 57:15; 66:2

CONTROVERSY Jer. 25:31
Mic. 6:2, has a *c* with his people
I Tim. 3:16, without *c* great is the mystery
See Deut. 17:8; 19:17; 21:5; 25:1

CONVENIENT Acts 24:25, when I have a *c* season
Rom. 1:28, things which are not *c*
Eph. 5:4, foolish talking, jesting, are not *c*
See Jer. 40:4; Mk. 6:21; I Cor. 16:12

CONVERSANT Josh. 8:35; I Sam. 25:15

CONVERSATION Ps. 37:14
50:23, that orders this *c* aright
Phil. 1:27, *c* as becomes the Gospel
3:20, our *c* is in Heaven
I Tim. 4:12, an example in *c*
Heb. 13:5, *c* without covetousness
I Pet. 1:15; II Pet. 3:11, holy *c*
18, redeemed from vain *c*
2:12, your *c* honest among Gentiles
3:1, won by *c* of wives
II Pet. 2:7, vexed with filthy *c*
See Gal. 1:13; Eph. 2:3; 4:22, James 3:13

CONVERSION Acts 15:3

CONVERT Ps. 19:7, perfect, *c* the soul
Mat. 18:3, except ye be *c*
Lk. 22:32, when *c*, strength your brethren
Acts 3:19, repent and be *c*
Acts 28:27, lest they *c*
James. 5:19, 20, and one *c* him
See Ps. 51:13; Isa. 1:27; 60:5

CONVICTED Jn. 8:9

CONVINCE Jn. 8:46, which *c* me of sin?
Titus 1:9, able to *c* gainsayers
See Job 32:12; Acts 18:28; I Cor. 14:24

CONVOCATION Ex. 12:16; Lev. 23:2

COOK I Sam. 8:13; 9:23, 24

COOL Gen. 3:8; Lk. 16:24

COPPER Ezra 8:27; II Tim. 4:14

COPY Deut. 17:18; Josh. 8:32; Prov. 25:1

CORD Prov. 5:22, holden with the *c* of sins
Eccl. 4:12, a threefold *c*
Isa. 5:18, draw iniquity with *c*
54:2, lengthen *c*
Hos. 11:4, the *c* of a man

CORN Gen. 42:2; Acts 7:12, *c* in Egypt
  Judg. 15:5, foxes into standing *c*
  Job. 5:26, like as a shock of *c*
  Ps. 4:7, in time their *c* increased
    65:9, prepared them *c*
    13, valleys covered over with *c*
    72:16, handful of *c* in the earth
  Prov. 11:26, he that withholds *c*
  Zech. 9:17, *c* shall make men cheerful
  Mat. 12:1; Mk. 2:23; Lk. 6:1, pluck *c*
  Mk. 4:28, full *c* in the ear
  Jn. 12:24, a *c* of wheat fall into ground
  See Gen. 27:28; 41:57; Deut. 33:28; Isa. 36:17
CORNER Ps. 118:22, head stone of *c*
    144:12, daughters as *c* stone
  Mat. 6:5, pray in *c* of streets
  Rev. 7:1, on four *c* of the earth
  See Job 1:19; Prov. 7:8; 21:9
CORNET II Sam. 6:5; I Chron. 15:28; Dan. 3:5
CORPSE II Ki. 19:35; Isa. 37:36; Nah. 3:3
CORRECT Prov. 3:12
    29:17, *C* your son
    19, servant will not be *c* by words
  Jer. 10:24, *c* me, but with judgment
    30:11; 46:28, I will *c* you in measure
  Heb. 12:9, we have had fathers which *c* us
  See Job 5:17; Ps. 39:11; 94:10
CORRECTION Prov. 22:15
  Jer. 2:30; 5:3; 7:28; Zeph. 3:2, receive *c*
  II Tim. 3:16, scripture profitable for *c*
  See Job 37:13; Prov. 3:11; 7:22; 15:10
CORRUPT Deut. 4:16, take heed lest ye *c*
    31:29, after my death ye will *c*
  Mat. 6:19; Lk. 12:33, moth *c*
    7:17; 12:33; Lk. 6:43, a *c* tree
  I Cor. 15:33, evil communications *c*
  II Cor. 2:17, not as many, which *c* the word
    7:2, we have *c* no man
  II Cor. 11:3, lest your minds be *c*
  Eph. 4:22, put off old man, which is *c*
    29, let no *c* communication
  I Tim. 6:5; II Tim. 3:8, men of *c* minds
  James 5:2; your riches are *c*
CORRUPTERS Isa. 1:4; Jer. 6:28
CORRUPTIBLE Rom. 1:23; I Cor. 9:25; I Pet.
    1:18; 3:4
CORRUPTION Ps. 16:10; 49:9; Acts 2:27
  Jonah 2:6, brought up life from *c*
  Rom. 8:21, from bondage of *c*
  I Cor. 15:42, 50, sown in *c*
  Gal. 6:8, of flesh reap *c*
  II Pet. 1:4, the *c* that is in world
    2:12, perish in their own *c*;
  See Lev. 22:25; Job 17:14; Isa. 38:17
CORRUPTLY II Chron. 27:2; Neh. 1:7
COST II Sam. 24:24; I Chron. 21:24, offer of
    that which *c* nothing
  Lk. 14:28, sits not down and counts *c*
COTTAGE Isa. 1:8; 24:20, Zeph. 2:6
COUCH Lk. 5:19, let him down with *c*
    5:24, take up your *c*
  Acts 5:15, laid sick on *c*
  See Gen. 49:14; Job 7:13; 38:40; Ps. 6:6
COULD Isa. 5:4; Mk. 6:19; 9:18; 14:8

COULTER I Sam. 13:20, 21
COUNCIL Mat. 5:22; 10:17; Acts 5:27; 6:12
COUNSEL Job 38:2; 42:3, darkens *c* by words
  Ps. 1:1, *c* of the ungodly
    33:11; Prov. 19:21, *c* of Lord stands
    55:14, took sweet *c* together
    73:24, guide me with your *c*
  Prov. 1:25, 30, set at nought all my *c*
    11:14, where no *c* is, people fall
    15:22, without *c* purposes are disap-
    pointed
    21:30, there is no *c* against the Lord
  Isa. 28:29, wonderful in *c*
    30:1, that take *c* but not of me
    40:14, with whom took he *c*
    46:10, my *c* shall stand
  Jer. 32:19, great in *c*, mighty in working
  Hos. 10:6, ashamed of his own *c*
  Mk. 3:6; Jn. 11:53, took *c* against Jesus
  Acts 2:23, determinate *c* of God
    4:28, what your *c* determined before
    5:38, if this *c* be of men
    20:27, declare all the *c* of God
  I Cor. 4:5, make manifest *c* of the heart
  Eph. 1:11, after the *c* of his own will
  Heb. 6:17, the immutability of his *c*
  Rev. 3:18, I *c* you to buy gold tried in fire
COUNSELOR Prov. 11;14; 15:22; 24:6, in
    multitude of *c*
    12:20, to *c* of peace is joy
  Mk. 15:43; Lk. 23:50, an honorable *c*
  Rom. 11:34, who has been his *c*?
  See II Chron. 22:3; Job 3:14; 12:17
COUNT Gen. 15:6; Ps. 106:31; Rom. 4:3
  Ps. 44:22, *c* as sheep for the slaughter
  Prov. 17:28, even a fool is *c* wise
  Isa. 32:15, field be *c* for a forest
  Mat. 14:5, they *c* him as a prophet
  Lk. 21:36; Acts 5:41; II Thess. 1:5, 11; I Tim.
    5:17, *c* worthy
  Acts 20:24, neither *c* I my life dear
  Phil. 3:7, 8, I *c* loss for Christ
    13, I *c* no myself to have apprehended
  Heb. 10:29, *c* blood an unholy thing
  James 1:2, *c* it all joy
  II Pet. 3:9, as some men *c* slackness
  See Num. 23:10; Job 31:4; Ps. 139:18, 22
COUNTENANCE I Sam. 16:7, look not on his *c*
  I Sam. 16:12; 17:42, David of beautiful *c*
  Neh. 2:2, why is your *c* sad?
  Job 14:20, you change his *c*
  Ps. 4:6; 44:3; 89:15; 90:8, light of your *c*
  Prov. 15:13, merry heat makes cheerful *c*
  Eccl. 7:3, by sadness of *c* heart made better
  Isa. 3:9, their *c* does witness against them
  Mat. 6:16, hypocrites, of a sad *c*
    28:3; Lk. 9:29, *c* like lightning
  Rev. 1:16, his *c* as the sun shines
  See Gen. 4:5; Num. 6:26; Judg 13:6
COUNTRY Prov. 25:25, news from a far *c*
  Mat. 13:57; Mk. 6:4; in his own *c*
    21:33; 25:14; Mk. 12:1, went to far *c*
  Lk. 4:23, do also here in your *c*
  Acts 12:20, their *c* nourished by king's *c*

Heb. 11:9, sojourned as in strange *c*
  16, desire a better *c*
See Gen. 12:1; 24:4; Josh. 9:6; Lk. 15:13
COUNTRYMEN II Cor. 11:26; I Thess. 2:14
COUPLED I Pet. 3:2
COURAGE Deut. 31:6, 7, 23; Josh. 10:25;
  Ps. 27:14; 31:24, be of good *c*
Acts 28:15, thanked God, and took *c*
See Num. 13:20; Josh. 1:7; 2:11; II Sam. 13:28
COURSE Acts 20:24, finished my *c*
  II Thess. 3:1, may have free *c*
  James 3:6, sets on fire the *c* of nature
See Judg. 5:20; Ps. 82:5; Acts 13:25
COURT Ps. 65:4, that he dwell in your *c*
  84:2, faints for the *c* of the Lord
  92:13, flourish in the *c* of our God
  100:4, enter into his *c* with praise
  Isa. 1:12, who required this, to tread my *c*?
  Lk. 7:25, live delicately are in kings' *c*.
See Isa. 34:13; Jer. 19:14; Ezek. 9:7
COURTEOUS Acts 27:3; 28:7; I Pet. 3:8
COUSIN Lk. 1:36, 58
COVENANT Num. 18:19, *c* of salt
  25:12, my *c* of peace
  Ps. 105:8; 106:45, he remembers his *c* forever
  111:5, ever mindful of his *c*
  Isa. 28:18, your *c* with death disannulled
  Mat. 26:15; Lk. 22:5, they *c* with him
  Acts 3:25, children of the *c*
  Rom. 9:4, to whom pertains the *c*
  Eph. 2:12, strangers from *c* of promise
  Heb. 8:6, mediator of a better *c*
  12:24, mediator of the new *c*
  13:20, blood of the everlasting *c*
See Gen. 9:15; Ex. 34:28; Job 31:1
COVER Ex. 15:5, depths *c* them, sank as stone
  I Sam. 28:14, an old man *c* with a mantle
  Esther 7:8, they *c* Haman's face
  Ps. 32:1; Rom. 4:7, blessed whose sin is *c*
  73:6, violence *c* them as a garment
  91:4, he shall *c* you with his feathers
  104:6, then *c* it with the deep
  Prov. 10:12, love *c* all sins
  17:9, he that *c* transgression, seeks love
  28:13, he that *c* sins shall not prosper
  Isa. 26:21, earth no more *c* her slain
  Mat. 8:24, ship *c* with waves
  10:26; Lk. 12:2, there is nothing *c*
  I Cor. 11:4, having his head *c*
  I Pet. 4:8, charity shall *c* multitude of sins
See Gen. 7:19; Ex. 8:6; 21:33; Lev. 16:13
COVERING Job 22:14; 24:7, naked have no *c*
  in the cold
  Isa. 28:20, *c* narrower than he can wrap
See Gen. 8:13; Lev. 13:45; II Sam. 17:19
COVERT Ps. 61:4; Isa. 4:6; 16:4; 32:2
COVET Prov. 21:26, he *c* greedily all the day
  Hab. 2:9, *c* an evil covetousness
  Acts 20:33, I have *c* no man's silver
  I Cor. 12:31, *c* earnestly the best gifts
  I Tim. 6:10, while some *c* after, they erred
See Ex. 20:17; Deut. 5:21; Rom. 7:7; 13:9
COVETOUS Ezek. 33:31, their heart goes after *c*
  Mk. 7:22, out of heart proceeds *c*

Rom. 1:29, filled with all *c*
I Cor. 6:10; Eph. 5:5, nor *c* inherit kingdom
Eph. 5:3, but *c*, let it not be named
II Tim. 3:2, men shall be *c*
Heb. 13:5, conversation without *c*
II Pet. 2:3, through *c* make merchandise
  14, exercised with *c* practices
See Ps. 10:3; 119:36; I Cor. 5:10
COW Lev. 22:28; Job 21:10; Isa. 11:7
CRACKLING Eccl 7:6
CRAFT Job 5:13; I Cor. 3:19
  Lk. 20:23, he perceived their *c*
  Acts 19:25, by this *c* we have our wealth
  27, our *c* is in danger
  II Cor. 4:2, not walking in *c*
  12:16, being *c* I caught you
  Eph. 4:14, carried away with cunning *c*
See Dan. 8:25; Acts 18:3; Rev. 18:22
CRAG Job 39:28
CRANE Isa. 38:14; Jer. 8:7
CRASHING Zeph. 1:10
CRAVE Prov. 16:26; Mk. 15:43
CREATE Isa. 40:26, who has *c* these things
  43:7, *c* him for my glory
  65:17, I *c* new heavens and new earth
  Jer. 31:22, the Lord has *c* a new thing
  Mal. 2:10, has not one God *c* us?
  I Cor. 11:9, neither was man *c* for woman
  Eph. 2:10, *c* in Christ Jesus
  4:24, after God is *c* in righteousness
  Col. 1:16, by him were all things *c*
  I Tim. 4:3, which God *c* to be received
See Gen. 1:1; 6:7; Deut; 4:32; Ps. 51:10
CREATION Mk. 10:6; 13:19; II Pet. 3:4
CREATOR Eccl. 12:1; Isa. 40:28; Rom. 1:25
CREATURE Mk. 16:15; Col. 1:23, preach to
  every *c*
  Rom. 8:19, expectation of the *c*
  II Cor. 5:17; Gal. 6:15, new *c*
  Col. 1:15, firstborn of every *c*
  I Tim. 4:4, every *c* of God is good
See Gen. 1:20; 2:19; Isa. 13:21; Ezek. 1:20
CREDITOR Deut. 15:2; Isa. 50:1; Lk. 7:41
CREEK Acts 27:39
CREEP Ps. 104:20, beasts of the forest *c* forth
  25, in sea are *c* things
  Ezek. 8:10, form of *c* things portrayed
  Acts 10:12; 11:6, Peter saw *c* things
  II Tim. 3:6, they *c* into houses
See Gen. 1:25; 7:8; Lev. 11:41; Deut 4:18
CREW Mat. 26:74; Mk. 14:68; Lk. 22:60
CRIB Job 39:9; Prov. 14:4; Isa. 1:3
CRIME Job 31:11; Ezek. 7:23
CRIMSON II Chron. 2:7; Isa. 1:18; Jer. 4:30
CRIPPLE Acts 14:8
CROOKED Eccl. 1:15; 7:13, *c* cannot be made
  straight
  Isa. 40:4; 42:16; Lk. 3:5
  45:2, make the *c* places straight
  59:8; Lam. 3:9, *c* paths
  Phil. 2:15, in midst of a *c* nation
See Lev. 21:20; Deut. 32:5; Job 26:13
CROPS Lev. 1:16; Ezek. 17:22
CROSS Mat. 16:24; Mk. 8:34; 10:21, take up *c*

27:32; Mk. 15:21; Lk. 23:26; compelled to
  bear c
Mk. 15:30, come down from c
Jn. 19:25, there stood by c
I Cor. 1:17; Gal. 6:12; Phil. 3:18, c of Christ
Gal. 5:11, offense of the c
  6:14, glory save in the c
Eph. 2:16, reconcile both by the c
Phil. 2:8, the death of the c
Col. 1:20, Peace through blood of the c
  2:14, nailing it to his c
Heb. 12:2, for joy endured the c
  See Obad. 14; Mat. 10:38; Jn 19:17, 19
CROUCH I Sam. 2:36; Ps. 10:10
CROWN Ps. 8:5; Heb. 2:7, 9, c with glory
  and honor
    103:4, c you with loving kindness
  Prov. 4:9, a c of glory shall she deliver
    12:4, virtuous woman is a c
    14:18, prudent c with knowledge
    16:31, hoary head a c of glory
    17:6, children's children are the c of
    old men
  Isa. 28:1, woe to the c of pride
  Mat. 27:29; Jn. 19:2, a c of thorns
  I Cor. 9:25, to obtain a corruptible c
  Phil. 4:1, my joy and c
  I Thess. 2:19, a c of rejoicing
  II Tim. 2:5, not c except he strive
  James 1:12; Rev. 2:10, c of life
  I Pet. 5:4, a c of glory
  Rev. 3:11, hold fast, that no man take your c
    4:10, cast c before the throne
    19:12, on his head were many c
CRUCIFY Mat. 27:22, all said let him be c
  Mk. 15:13; Lk. 23:21; Jn. 19:6, 15, c him
  Acts 2:23, by wicked hands you have c
  Rom. 6:6, old man is c with him
  I Cor. 1:13, was Paul c for you?
    23, we preach Christ c
    2:2, save Jesus Christ and him c
  II Cor. 13:4, he was c through weakness
  Gal. 2:20, I am c with Christ
    3:1, Christ set forth c
    5:24, have c the flesh
    6:14, the world is c unto me
  Heb. 6:6, c to themselves afresh
  See Mat. 20:19; 23:34; 27:31; Mk. 15:20
CRUEL Ps. 25:19, with c hatred
    74:20, full of the habitations of c
  Prov. 5:9, lest you give your years to the c
    11:17, c troubles his own flesh
    12:10, tender mercies of the wicked are c
    27:4, wrath is c
  Song of Sol. 8:6, jealousy is c
  Heb. 11:36, trials of c mockings
  See Gen. 49:7; Ex. 6:9; Deut. 32:33
CRUMBS Mat. 15:27; Mk. 7:28; Lk. 16:21
CRUSE I Sam. 26:11; I Ki. 14:3; 17:12; 19:6
CRUSH Job 5:4, children are c in the gate
    39:15, forgets that the foot may c them
  See Lev. 22:24; Num. 22:25; Deut. 28:33
CRY (n.) I Sam. 5:12, c went up to heaven
  Job 34:28, he hears the c of the afflicted

Ps. 9:12, forgets not c of the humble
    34:15, ears are open to their c
  Mat. 25:6, at midnight there was a c made
  See Gen. 18:20; Ex. 2:23; Num. 16:34
CRY (v.) Ex. 14:15, wherefore c thou unto me?
  Lev. 13:45, cover his upper lip, and c unclean
  Job 29:12, I delivered the poor that c
  Ps. 147:9, food to young ravens which c
  Prov. 8:1, does not wisdom c?
  Isa. 58:1, C aloud, spare not
  Mat. 12:19, he shall not strive nor c
  Mk. 10:48, Lk. 18:39, they c the more
  Lk. 18:7, elect, who c day and night
  Jn. 7:37, Jesus c, if any man thirst
  Acts 19:32; 21:34, some c one thing, and
    some another
CRYING Prov. 19:18; Isa. 65:19; Heb. 5:7
CRYSTAL Job 28:17; Ezek. 1:22; Rev. 4:6
CUBIT Mat. 6:27; Lk. 12:25
CUCUMBERS Num. 11:5; Isa. 1:8
CUMBER Deut. 1:12; Lk. 10:40; 13:7
CUNNING Ps. 137:5, my hand forget her c
  Jer. 9:17, send for c women
  Eph. 4:14, carried about by c craftiness
  II Pet. 1:16, not follow c defined fables
  See Gen. 25:27; Ex. 38:23; I Sam. 16:16
CUP Ps. 116:13; take c of salvation
  Mat. 10:42; Mk. 9:41, c of cold water
    20:22; Mk. 10:39, drink of my c
    23:25, make clean outside of c
    26:27; Lk. 22:17; I Cor. 11:25, took c
    39; Mk. 14:36; Lk. 22:42, let this c pass
  Lk. 22:20, this c is new testament
  Jn. 18:11, c which is my Father has given
  I Cor. 10:16, c of blessing we bless
    11:26, as often as ye drink this c
    27, drink this c unworthily
CURDLED Job 10:10
CURE Lk. 7:21, in that hour he c many
    9:1, power to c disease
    13:32, I do c today
  See Jer. 33:6; 46:11; Hos. 5:13; Mat. 17:16
CURIOUS Ex. 28:8; Ps. 139:15; Acts 19:19
CURRENT Gen. 23:16
CURSE (n.) Deut. 11:26, I set before you
    blessing and c
    23:5, turned c into blessing
  Gal. 3:10, are under the c
  Rev. 22:3, no more c
  See Gen. 27:12; Num. 5:18
CURSE (v.) Lev. 19:14, not c the deaf
  Num. 23:8, shall I c whom God has not?
  Judg. 5:23, c ye Meroz, c ye bitterly
  Job 2:9, C God, and die
  Ps. 62:4, they bless, but c inwardly
  Mal. 2:2, I will c your blessings
  Mat. 5:44; Lk. 6:28; Rom. 12:14, bless them
    that c you
    26:74; Mk. 14:71, he began to c
  Mk. 11:21, fig tree you c
  Jn. 7:49, who knows not the law are c
  Gal. 3:10, c is every one that continues not
  James 3:9, therewith c we men
  See Gen. 8:21; 12:3; Num. 22:6

CURTAIN Ex. 26:1; II Sam. 7:2; Ps. 104:2; Song
    of Sol. 1:5; Hab. 3:7
CUSTOM Mat. 9:9, receipt of *c*
    17:25, of whom do kings take *c*?
    Lk. 4:16, his *c* was, went into synagogue
    Jn. 18:39, you have a *c*
    Acts 16:21, teach *c* which are not lawful
    I Cor. 11:16, we have no such *c*
    See Gen. 31:35; Judg. 11:39; Acts 26:3
CUTTING Ex. 31:5; Isa. 38:10; Mk. 5:5
CYMBAL I Cor. 13:1

D

DAGGER Judg. 3:16, 21, 22
DAILY Ps. 13:2, sorrow in my heart *d*
    68:19, *d* loads us
    Prov. 8:30, I was *d* his delight
    Dan. 8:11; 12:11, *d* sacrifice taken away
    Mat. 6:11; Lk. 11:3, out *d* bread
    Lk. 9:23, take up cross *d*
    Acts 2:47, added to Church *d*
    6:1, the *d* ministration
    16:5, churches increased *d*
    17:11, searched the scriptures *d*
    I Cor. 15:31, I die *d*
    See Num. 4:16; 28:24; Neh. 5:18; Dan. 1:5
DAINTY Ps. 141:4, let me not eat of *d*
    Prov. 23:3, be not desirous of his *d*
    See Gen. 49:20; Job 33:20; Rev. 18:14
DALE Gen. 14:17; II Sam. 18:18
DAM Ex. 22:30; Lev. 22:27; Deut. 22:6
DAMAGE Prov. 26:6, drinks *d*
    Acts 27:10, voyage will be with much *d*
    II Cor. 7:9, received *d* by us in nothing
    See Ezra 4:22; Esther 7:4; Dan. 6:2
DAMNABLE II Pet. 2:1
DAMNATION Mk. 3:29, in danger of eternal *d*
    Jn. 5:29, the resurrection of *d*
    Rom. 13:2, receive to themselves *d*
    I Cor. 11:29, eats and drinks *d*
    II Pet. 2:3, their *d* slumbers not
    See Mat. 23:14; Mk. 12:40; Lk. 20:47
DAMNED Mk. 16:16; Rom. 14:23
DAMSEL Ps. 68:25
    Mat. 14:11; Mk. 6:28, given to the *d*
    26:69; Jn. 18:17, *d* came to Peter
    Mk. 5:39, the *d* is not dead
    Acts 12:13, a *d* came to hearken
    16:16, *d* possessed with a spirit
    See Gen. 24:55; 34:3; Judg. 5:30; Ruth 2:5
DANCE Ex. 32:19, he saws the calf, and *d*
    I Sam. 18:6, came out singing and *d*
    II Sam. 6:14, David *d* before the Lord
    Job 21:11, their children *d*
    Ps. 30:11, turned my mourning into *d*
    149:3; 150:4, praise him in the *d*
    Eccl. 3:4, a time to *d*
    Mat. 11:17; Lk. 7:32, you have not *d*
    14:6; Mk. 6:22, daughter of Herodias *d*
DANDLED Isa. 66:12
DANGER Mat. 5:21, 22; Mk. 3:29
DARE Rom. 5:7, some would even *d* to die
    See Job 41:10; Rom. 15:18; I Cor. 6:1

DARK Job. 12:25, they grope in the *d*
    24:16, in the *d* they dig
    38:2, that *d* counsel by words
    Ps. 49:4; Prov. 1:6, *d* sayings
    69:23; Rom. 11:10, let their eyes be *d*
    88:12, wonders be known in the *d*
    Mat. 24:29; Mk. 13:24, sun be *d*
    Lk. 23:45, sun *d* and veil rent
    Jn. 20:1, early, when it was yet *d*
    Rom. 1:21, foolish heart was *d*
    See Gen. 15:17; Ex. 10:15; Num. 12:8
DARKNESS Deut. 5:22, spoke out of thick *d*
    28:29, grope as the blind in *d*
    I Sam. 2:9, wicked be silent in *d*
    II Sam. 22:10; Ps. 18:9, *d* under his feet
    29; Ps. 18:28, Lord will enlighten my *d*
    I Ki. 8:12; II Chron. 6:1, dwell in thick *d*
    Job. 3:5; Ps. 107:10, *d* and shadow of death
    10:22, land where the light is as *d*
    Ps. 91:6, pestilence that walks in *d*
    97:2, clouds and *d* are round about him
    112:4, to upright arises light in *d*
    139:12, *d* and light alike to you
    Prov. 20:20, lamp be put out in *d*
    Eccl. 2:13, as far as light excels *d*
    14, fool walks in *d*
    Isa. 58:10, your *d* as noon day
    60:2, *d* cover the earth, gross *d*
    Joel 2:2, day of clouds and thick *d*
    Mat. 6:23; Lk. 11:34, body full of *d*
    Mat. 8:12; 22:13; 25:30, outer *d*
    10:27; Lk. 12:3, what I tell in *d* speak
    Lk. 1:79, light to them that sit in *d*
    Lk. 22:53; Col. 1:13, the power of *d*
    23:44, *d* over all the earth
    Jn. 1:5, *d* comprehended it not
    3:19, loved *d* rather than light
    12:35, walk while you have light, lest *d*
    Acts 26:18, turn from *d* to light
    Rom. 13:12; Eph. 5:11, works of *d*
    I Cor. 4:5, hidden things of *d*
    II Cor. 4:6, light to shine out of *d*
    6:14, what communion has light with *d*?
    Eph. 6:12, rulers of the *d* of this world
    Heb. 12:18, to blackness and *d*
    I Pet. 2:9, out of *d* not marvelous light
    II Pet. 2:4, into chains of *d*
    I Jn. 1:5, in him is not *d* at all
    6, and walk in *d*, we lie
    2:8, the *d* past
    11, *d* has blinded his eyes
    Rev. 16:10, kingdom full of *d*
    See Gen. 1:2, 15:12; Ex. 10:21; 20:21
DARLING Ps. 22:20; 35:17
DART Job 41:26; Prov. 7:23; Eph. 6:16
DASH Ps. 2:9; Isa. 13:16; Hos. 13:16
    Ps. 91:12; Mat. 4:6; Lk. 4:11, *d* your foot
    Ps. 137:9, that *d* your little ones
    See Ex. 15:6; II Ki. 8:12; Jer. 13:14
DAUB Ex. 2:3; Ezek. 13:10; 22:28
DAUGHTER Gen. 24:23, 47, Judg. 11:34, whose
    d are you?
    27:46, weary of life because of *d* of Heth
    Deut. 28:53, eat flesh of sons and *d*

II Sam. 1:20, lest d of Philistines rejoice
  12:3, lamb was unto him as a d
Ps. 45:9, kings' d among honorable women
  144:12, our d as corner stones
Prov. 30:15, horseleach has two d
Eccl. 12:4, the d of music
Isa. 22:4; Jer. 9:1; Lam. 2:11; 3:48
Jer. 6:14, healed hurt of d of my people
  8:21, for hurt of d am I hurt
  9:1, weep for slain of d of my people
Mic. 7:6; Mat. 10:35; Lk. 12:53, d rises
  against mother
Mat. 15:28, her d was made whole
Lk. 8:42, one d, about twelve years of age
  13:16, this woman, d of Abraham
See Gen. 6:1; Ex. 1:16; 21:7; Num. 27:8
DAWN Ps. 119:147
II Pet. 1:19, till the day d
See Josh. 6:15; Judg. 19:26; Job 3:9; 7:4
DAY Gen. 41:9, I remember my faults this d
Deut. 4:32, ask of the d that are past
I Sam. 25:8, come in a good d
II Ki. 7:9, this d is a d of good tidings
I Chron. 23:1, 29:28; II Chron. 24:15, full
  of d 29:15; Job 8:9, our d as a shadow
Neh. 4:2, will they make an end in a d?
Job 7:1, d like the d of an hireling
  19:25, stand at latter d upon the Earth
  21:30, reserved to d of destruction
  32:7, I said, D should speak
Ps. 19:2, D unto d utters speech
  84:10, a d in your courts
Prov. 3:2, 16, length of d
  27:1, what a d may bring forth
Eccl. 7:1, d of death better than d of birth
  12:1, while the evil d come not
Isa. 10:3, in the d of visitation
  27:3, the Lord will keep it night and d
  58:5, an acceptable d to the Lord
  65:20, an infant of d
Mal. 3:2, who may abide d of his coming
Mat. 7:22, many will say in that d
  24:36; Mk. 13:32, that d knows no man
  24:50; Lk. 12:46, in a d looked not for
  25:13, you know not the d nor the hour
Lk. 21:34, that d come upon your unawares
  23:43, to d shall you be with me
Jn. 6:39, raise it again at last d
  8:56, Abraham rejoiced to see my d
  9:4, I must work while it is d
Acts 17:31, he has appointed a d
Rom. 2:5, wrath against d of wrath
  14:5, esteems every d alike
II Cor. 6:2, the d of salvation
Phil. 1:6, perform it until d of Christ
I Thess. 5:2; II Pet. 3:10, d comes as a thief
  5:5, children of the d
Heb. 13:8, Jesus Christ same to d and forever
II Pet. 3:8, one d as a thousand years
See Gen. 1:5; 27:2; Job 1:4; Ps. 77:5; 118:24
DAYSMAN Job 9:33
DEAD Lev. 19:28, cuttings for the d
Ruth 1:8, as you have dealt with d
I Sam. 24:14; II Sam. 9:8; 16:9, d dog

Ps. 31:12, forgotten as a d man
  115:17, d praise not the Lord
Prov. 9:18, knows not that the d are there
Eccl. 4:2, the d which are already d
  9:4, living dog better than d lion
  9:5, d know not anything
  10:1, D flies cause ointment
Isa. 26:19, your d men shall live
Jer. 22:10, weep not for the d
Mat. 8:22, let the d bury their d
  9:24; Mk. 5:39; Lk. 8:52
  11:5; Lk. 7:22, deaf hear, d raised
  22:32, not God of the d
  23:27, full of d men's bones
Mk. 9:10, rising from d should mean
Lk. 15:24, 32; Rev. 1:18
  16:31, though one rose from the d
Jn. 5:25, d shall hear
  11:25, though d, yet shall he live
  11:44, he that was d came forth
Acts 10:42; II Tim. 4:1, judge of quick and d
Rom. 6:2, 11; I Pet. 2:24, d to sin
  14:9, Lord both of d and living
I Cor. 15:15, if the d rise not
  35, how are the d raised
II Cor. 1:9, trust in God was raised d
  5:14, then were all d
Eph. 5:14, arise from the d
Col. 1:18, firstborn from the d
  2:20; II Tim. 2:11, d with Christ
I Thess. 4:16, d in Christ shall rise first
I Tim. 5:6, d while she lives
Heb. 6:1; 9:14, from d works
  11:4, being d yet speaks
  13:20, brought against from the d
James. 2:17, 20, 26, faith d
I Pet. 4:6, preached to them that are d
Jude 12, twice d
Rev. 1:5, first-begotten of the d
  14:13, blessed are the d
See Gen. 23:3; Mk. 9:26; Rev. 1:18
DEADLY Mk. 16:18, drink any d thing
James 3:8, tongue full of d poison
See I Sam. 5:11; Ps. 17:9; Ezek. 30:24
DEAF Ps. 58:4, like d adder that stops
Isa. 29:18, shall the d hear the words
Mat. 11:5; Lk. 7:22, the d hear
Mk. 7:37, he makes the d to hear
  9:25, you d spirit, come out
See Ex. 4:11; Lev. 19:14; Isa. 42:18; 43:8
DEAL Lev. 19:11, nor d falsely
Job 42:8, d with you after folly
Ps. 75:4, d not foolishly
Prov. 12:22, they that d truly are his delight
Isa. 21:2; 24:16
  26:10, in land of uprightness d unjustly
Jer. 6:13; 8:10, every one d falsely
Hos. 5:7, d treacherously against the Lord
Mk. 7:36; 10:48, the more a great d
Lk. 2:48, why have you thus d with us?
Rom. 12:3, according as God has d
See Gen. 32:9; Ex. 1:10; II Chron. 2:3
DEALING I Sam. 2:23; Ps. 7:16; Jn. 4:9
DEAR Jer. 31:20, is Ephraim my d son

Acts 20:24, neither count I my life *d*
Rom. 12:19; I Cor. 10:14; II Cor. 7:1; 12:19
Eph. 5:1, followers of God, as *d* children
Col. 1:13, into kingdom of his *d* Son
I Thess. 2:8, because you were *d* to us
See Jer. 12:7; Lk. 7:2; Phile. 1:1
DEARTH II Chron. 6:28
Neh. 5:3, buy corn, because of *d*
Acts 11:28
See Gen. 41:54; II Ki. 4:38; Jer. 14:1
DEATH Num. 16:29
23:10, let me die *d* of righteous
Judg. 5:18, jeoparded lives to the *d*
16:16, soul was vexed to *d*
30, which he slew at his *d* were more
Ruth 1:17, if ought but *d* part you and me
I Sam. 15:32, the bitterness of *d* past
I Sam. 20:3, but a step between me and *d*
II Sam. 1:23, in *d* not divided
22:5; Ps. 18:4; 116:3, waves of *d* compassed
Job 3:21, long for *d*, but it comes not
7:15, my soul chooses *d*
30:23, you will bring me to *d*
Ps. 6:5, in *d* no remembrance
13:3, lest I sleep the sleep of *d*
23:4, valley of shadow of *d*
48:14, our guide even unto *d*
68:20, unto God belong the issues from *d*
89:48, what man shall not see *d*
102:20, loose those appointed to *d*
107:10, in darkness and shadow of *d*
116:15, precious is *d* of his saints
Prov. 7:27, to chambers of *d*
8:36, they that hate me love *d*
14:32, the righteous has hope in his *d*
24:11, deliver them drawn to *d*
Song of Sol. 8:6, love is strong as *d*
Isa. 9:2; Jer. 2:6, land of the shadow of *d*
25:8; I Cor. 15:56, swallow up *d* in victory
38:18, for *d* cannot celebrate you
Jer. 8:3, *d* chosen rather than life
9:21, *d* come up into our windows
Ezek. 18:32; 33:11, no pleasure in *d*
Hos. 13:14, O *d*, I will be your plagues
Mat. 15:4; Mk. 7:10, let him die the *d*
16:28; Mk. 9:1; Lk. 9:27, not taste of *d*
26:38; Mk. 14:34, my soul is sorrowful to *d*
Mk. 5:23; Jn. 4:47, lies at point of *d*
Lk. 2:26, should not see *d* before
22:33, will go to prison and *d*
Jn. 5:24; I Jn. 3:14, passed from *d* to life
8:51, 52, keep my saying, shall never see *d*
11:4, sickness not unto *d*
12:33; 18:32; 21:19, signifying what *d*
Acts 2:24, having loosed the pains of *d*
Rom. 1:32, such things are worthy of *d*
5:10; Col. 1:22, reconciled by the *d*
Rom. 5:12, *d* by sin, and so *d* passed on all
6:23, wages of sin is *d*
I Cor. 3:22, life or *d*, all are yours
11:26, show the Lord's *d* till he come
15:21, by man came *d*
55, 56, O *d* where is your sting?
II Cor. 1:9, sentence of *d* in ourselves

4:12, *d* works in us
11:23, in *d* oft
Phil. 2:8, *d* even *d* of the cross
Heb. 2:9, taste *d* for every man
James 1:15, sin brings forth *d*
I Jn. 5:16, a sin unto *d*
Rev. 1:18, keys of hell and of *d*
2:10, be faithful unto *d*
11; 20:14, second *d*
6:8, his name that sat on him was *D*
9:6, seek *d*, and *d* shall flee
20:13, *d* and hell delivered up
21:4, no more *d*
DEBASE Isa. 57:9
DEBATE Prov. 25:9; Isa. 58:4; Rom. 1:29
DEBT II Ki. 4:7, go, pay your *d*, and live
Neh. 10:31, leave the exaction of every *d*
Mat. 18:27, forgave him the *d*
See I Sam. 22:2; Mat. 6:12; Rom. 4:4
DEBTOR Rom. 1:14, I am *d* to the Greeks
8:12, we are *d*, not to the flesh
15:27, their *d* they are
Gal. 5:3, *d* to do the whole law
See Ezek. 18:7; Mat. 23:16; Lk. 7:41; 16:5
DECAY Lev. 25:35; Neh. 4:10; Heb. 8:13
DECEASE Isa. 26:14; Mat. 22:25; Lk. 9:31
DECEIT Ps. 10:7, mouth full of *d* and fraud
36:3, words are iniquity and *d*
55:23, *d* men shall not live half their days
Prov. 12:5, counsels of wicked are *d*
20:17, bread of *d* is sweet
27:6, kisses of an enemy are *d*
31:30, favor is *d* and beauty vain
Jer. 14:14; 23:26, prophesy *d* of their heart
17:9, the heart is *d* is above all things
48:10, that does work of the Lord *d*
Amos 8:5, falsifying balances by *d*?
Zeph. 1:9, fill their masters' houses with *d*
Mat. 13:22; Mk. 4:19, the *d* or riches
Mk. 7:22, out of heart proceed *d*
Rom. 3:13, they have used *d*
II Cor. 4:2, handling work of God *d*
Eph. 4:22, according to *d* lusts
Col. 2:8, vain *d*, after tradition
See Ps. 50:19; Prov. 12:20; Jer. 5:27
DECEIVE Deut. 11:16, take heed that your heart
be not *d*
II Ki. 19:10; Isa. 37:10, let not God *d* you
Job 12:16, the *d* and the *d* are his
Jer. 20:7, you have *d* me, and I was *d*
37:9, *D* not yourselves
Mat. 24:24, if possible *d* the very elect
27:63, remember that *d* said
Jn. 7:12, nay, but he *d* the people
47, are you also *d*?
I Cor. 6:9; 15:33; Gal. 6:7, be not *d*
II Cor. 6:8, as *d*, and yet true
Eph. 4:14, whereby they lie in wait to *d*
5:6; II Thess. 2:3, let no man *d* you
I Tim. 2:14, Adam was not *d*
I Jn. 1:8, no sin, we *d* ourselves
II Jn. 7, many *d* entered into world
See Gen. 31:7; Isa. 44:20; Ezek. 14:9
DECENTLY I Cor. 14:40

DECISION Joel 3:14
DECK Job 40:10, *D* yourself with majesty
  Isa. 61:10, as a bridegroom *d* himself
  Jer. 4:30, though you *d* you with ornaments
    10:4, they *d* it with silver
  See Prov. 7:16; Ezek. 16:11; Rev. 17:4; 18:16
DECLARATION Esther 10:2; Job 13:17; Lk. 1:1;
  II Cor. 8:19
DECLARE I Chron. 16:24; Ps. 96:3
  Job. 21:31, who shall *d* this way to his face?
    31:37, I would *d* number of my steps
  Ps. 2:7, I will *d* decree
    9:11, *d* among the people his doings
    19:1, heavens *d* glory of God
    30:9, shall dust *d* your truth?
    40:10, I have *d* your faithfulness
    66:16, I will *d* what he has done
    75:9, I will *d* forever
    118:17, live, and *d* the works of the Lord
    145:4, one generation shall *d* your acts
  Isa. 3:9, they *d* their sin as Sodom
    41:26; 45:21, who has *d* from beginning
    46:10, *D* end from the beginning
    53:8; Acts 8:33, who shall *d* his generation?
    66:19, *d* my glory among Gentiles
  Jn. 17:26, have *d* your name, and will *d* it
  Acts 13:32, we *d* to you glad tidings
    17:23, him *d* I unto you
    20:27, *d* the counsel of God
  Rom. 1:4, *d* to be son of God with power
  I Cor. 3:13, day shall *d* it
  See Josh. 20:4; Jn. 1:18; Heb. 11:14
DECLINE Deut. 17:11
  II Chron. 34:2, *d* neither to right nor left
  Ps. 102:11; 109:23, days like a shadow that *d*
    119:51, 157, not *d* from your law
  See Ex. 23:2; Job 23:11; Prov. 4:5; 7:25
DECREASE Gen. 8:5; Ps. 107:38; Jn. 3:30
DECREE Job 22:28
    28:26, made a *d* for the rain
  Prov. 8:15, by me princes *d* justice
    29, he gave to the sea his *d*
  Acts 16:4, delivered the *d* to keep
  See Dan. 2:9; 6:8; Acts 17:7; I Cor. 7:37
DEDICATE Deut. 20:5
  Judg. 17:3, wholly *d* silver to the Lord
  I Chron. 26:27, of spoil they did *d*
  Ezek. 44:29, every *d* thing shall be theirs
DEED Ezek. 9:16; I Sam. 25:34
  II Sam. 12:14, by this *d* have given occasion
  Ezra 9:13, come upon us for our evil *d*
  Neh. 13:14, wipe not out my good *d*
  Ps. 28:4; Isa. 59:18; Jer. 25:14
  Lk. 11:48, you allow the *d* of your fathers
    23:41, due reward of our *d*
    24:19, a prophet mighty in *d*
  Jn. 3:19, because their *d* were evil
    8:41, you do the *d* of your fahter
  Acts 7:22, Moses, mighty in word and *d*
  Rom. 3:20, by *d* of law no flesh justified
  Col. 3:9, put off old man with his *d*
    17, whatsoever you do in word or *d*
  James 1:25, shall be blessed in his *d*
  I Jn. 3:18, not love in word, but in *d*

  See Gen. 44:15; Lk. 23:51; Acts 19:18
DEEMED Acts 27:27
DEEP Gen. 7:11; 8:2, fountains of *d*
  Deut. 33:13, the *d* that couches beneath
  Job 38:30, face of *d* is frozen
    41:31, makes the *d* boil like a pot
  Ps. 36:6, your judgments are a great *d*
    42:7, *D* calls to *d*
    95:4, in his hand are the *d* places
    107:24, see his wonders in the *d*
  Prov. 22:14; 23:27, strange women *d* pit
  Isa. 63:13, led them through *d*
  Mat. 13:5, no *d* of earth
  Lk. 5:4, launch out into *d*
    6:48, digged *d*, and laid foundations
  Jn. 4:11, the well is *d*
  I Cor. 2:10, searches *d* things of God
  See Job 4:13; 33:15; Prov. 19:15; Rom. 10:7
DEER Deut. 14:5; I Ki. 4:23
DEFAME Jer. 20:10; I Cor. 4:13
DEFEAT II Sam. 15:34; 17:14
DEFEND Ps. 5:11
    82:3, *D* the poor and fatherless
  Zech. 9:15, Lord of Hosts shall *d* them
  Acts 7:24, *d* him, and avenged the oppressed
  See Ps. 20:1; 59:1; Isa. 31:5
DEFENSE Ps. 7:10, my *d* is of God
    59:9, 17; 62:2, for God is my *d*
    89:18, 94:22, Lord is *d*
  Eccl. 7:12, wisdom a *d*, money a *d*
  Isa. 33:16, place of *d* the munitions of rocks
  Phil. 1:7, 17, in *d* of the gospel
  See Num. 14:9; Acts 19:33; 22:1
DEFILE Ex. 31:14
  Num. 35:33, blood *d* the land
  II Ki. 23:13, high places did king *d*
  Neh. 13:29, they have *d* the priesthood
  Ps. 74:7; 79:1, *d* dwelling place of your name
    106:39, *d* with their own works
  Isa. 59:3, your hands are *d* with blood
  Jer. 2:7; 16:18, you *d* my land
  Ezek. 4:13, eat their *d* bread
    23:38, they have *d* my sanctuary
    36:17, they *d* it by their own ways
  Dan. 1:8, would not *d* himself with meat
  Mat. 15:11; Mk. 7:15, 20, 23, *d* a man
  Jn. 18:28, lest they should be *d*
  I Cor. 3:17, if any man *d* temple of God
    8:7, conscience being weak is *d*
  I Tim. 1:10, law for them that *d* themselves
  Heb. 12:15, thereby many be *d*
  Jude 8, filthy dreamers *d* the flesh
  See Ex. 31:14; Lev. 21:4; James 3:6; Rev. 21:27
DEFRAUD I Sam. 12:3, 4, whom have I *d*?
  Mk. 10:19; I Cor. 7:5, *D* not
  I Cor. 6:7, rather suffer yourselves to be *d*?
    8, do wrong, and *d* your brethren
  II Cor. 7:2, we have *d* no man
  See Lev. 19:13; I Thess. 4:6
DEGENERATE Jer. 2:21
DEGREE Ps. 62:9, men of low *d*, of high *d*
  I Tim. 3:13, purchase to themselves a good *d*
  James 1:9, brother of low *d* rejoice
  See II Ki. 20:9; Isa. 38:8; Lk. 1:52

DELAY Mat. 24:48; Lk. 12:45
  Acts 9:38, that he would not *d* to come
  See Ex. 22:29; 32:1; Acts 25:17
DELECTABLE Isa. 44:9
DELICACY Rev. 18:3
DELICATE Prov. 29:21, he that *d* brings up his
  servant
  Isa. 47:1, no more called tender and *d*
  Lam. 4:5, that did feed *d* are desolate
  Lk. 7:25, that live *d* are in kings' courts
  See Deut. 28:54, 56; Jer. 6:2; Mic. 1:16
DELICIOUSLY Rev. 18:7
DELIGHT (*n.*) Deut. 10:15
  II Sam. 15:26, I have no *d* in you
  Job 22:26, shall you *d* in the Almighty
  Ps. 1:2, his *d* is law of Lord
    16:3, to the excellent, in whom is my *d*
    119:24, testimonies my *d* and counselors
    77, 92, 174, the law is my *d*
    143, your commandments are my *d*
  Prov. 8:30, I was daily his *d*
    31, my *d* were with sons of men
    18:2, fool has no *d* in understanding
    19:10, *D* not seemly for a fool
  Song of Sol. 2:3, under his shadow with
    great *d*
  Isa. 58:13, call sabbath a *d*
  See Prov. 11:1; 12:22; 15:8; 16:13
DELIGHT (*v.*) Job 27:10, will he *d* himself in
  the Almighty
  Ps. 37:4, *D* also in the Lord
    11, meek shall *d* in abundance of peace
    51:16, you d not in Burnt Offering
    94:19, your comforts *d* my soul
  Isa. 42:1, elect, in whom my soul *d*
    55:2, soul *d* itself in fatness
    62:4, the Lord *d* in you
  Mic. 7:18, he *d* in mercy
  Rom. 7:22, I *d* after the inward man
  See Num. 14:8; Prov. 1:22; 2:14; Isa. 1:11
DELIGHTSOME Mal. 3:12
DELIVER Num. 35:25, congregation shall *d* the
  slayer
  Deut. 32:39; Isa. 43:13, any d out of my hand
  II Chron. 32:13, were gods able to *d* their
    lands?
  Job 5:19, shall *d* you in six troubles
    36:18, great ransom cannot *d*
  Ps. 33:17, nor *d* any by great strength
    56:13, *d* my feet from falling
    144:10, *d* David from hurtful sword
  Eccl. 9:15, by wisdom *d* city
  Isa. 50:2, have I no power to *d*?
  Jer. 1:8, I am with you to *d* you
    39:17, I will *d* in that day
  Dan. 3:17, for God is able to *d*, and will *d*
  Dan. 6:14, king set heart on Daniel to *d*
  Amos 2:14, neither shall mighty *d*
    9:1, he that escapes shall not be *d*
  Mal. 3:15, they that tempt God are *d*
  Mat. 6:13; Lk. 11:4, *d* us from evil
  Acts 2:23, being *d* by the counsel of God
  Rom. 4:25, was *d* for our offenses
    7:6, we are *d* from the law

II Cor. 4:11, *d* to death for Jesus' sake
II Tim. 4:18, *d* me from every evil work
Jude 3, faith once *d* to saints
See Rom. 8:32; II Cor. 1:10; Gal. 1:4
DELIVERANCE II Ki. 5:1, by him had given
  d to Syria
  I Chron. 11:14, saved by great *d*
  Ps. 32:7, compass me with songs of *d*
  Lk. 4:18, preach *d* to the captives
  Heb. 11:35, no accepting *d*
  See Gen. 45:7; Joel 2:23; Obad. 17
DELUSION Isa. 66:4; II Thess. 2:11
DEMAND Dan. 4:17; Mat. 2:4; Lk. 3:14
DEMONSTRATION I Cor. 2:4
DEN Job 37:8, then the beasts go into *d*
  Isa. 11:8, put hand on cockatrice' *d*
  Jer. 7:11, is this house a *d* of robbers?
  Mat. 21:13; Mk. 11:17, a *d* of thieves
  Heb. 11:38, in deserts, and in *d*
  See Judg. 6:2; Dan. 6:7; Amos 3:4
DENOUNCE Deut. 30:18
DENY Josh. 24:27, lest you *d* your God
  Prov. 30:9, lest I be full, and *d* you
  Lk. 20:27, which *d* resurrection
  II Tim. 2:13, he cannot *d* himself
  Titus 1:16, in works they *d* him
  See I Tim. 5:8; II Tim. 3:5; Titus 2:12
DEPART Job 21:14; 22:17, they say to God, *D*
  28:28, to *d* from evil is understanding
  Ps. 6:8; Mat. 7:23; Lk. 13:27, *d*
    34:14; 37:27, *D* from evil, and do good
    105:38, Egypt was glad when they *d*
  Prov. 15:24, he may *d* from Hell beneath
    22:6, when old, he will not *d* from it
    27:22, yet will not foolishness *d*
  Mat. 14:16, they need not *d*
    25:41, *D* from me, ye cursed
  Lk. 2:29, you your servant *d* in peace
    4:13, devil *d* for a season
  Jn. 13:1, when Jesus knew he should *d*
  II Cor. 12:8, that it might *d* from me
  Phil. 1:23, desire to *d*
  I Tim. 4:1, some shall *d* from the faith
  II Tim. 2:19, names Christ *d* from iniquity
  See Isa. 54:10; Mic. 2:10; Heb. 3:12
DEPOSED Dan. 5:20
DEPRIVED Gen. 27:45; Job 39:17; Isa. 38:10
DEPTH Ps. 33:7, he lays up *d* in storehouses
    77:16, waters afraid, *d* troubled
    106:9, led through *d* as through wilderness
    107:26, they go down again to *d*
  Prov. 8:24, when no *d*, I was brought forth
  Prov. 25:3, heaven for height, earth for *d*
  Mat. 18:6, were drowned in *d* of sea
  Mk. 4:5, no *d* of earth
  Rom. 11:33, the *d* of the riches
  See Isa. 7:11; Mic. 7:19; Rom. 8:39
DEPUTED II Sam. 15:3
DEPUTY I Ki. 22:47; Acts 13:7; 18:12
DERIDE Hab 1:10; Lk. 16:14; 23:35
DERISION Ps. 2:4, the Lord shall have them
  in *d*
  Ps. 44:13; 79:4, a *d* to them round us
  Jer. 20:7, 8, a *d* daily

Lam. 3:14, I was a *d* to my people
See Ps. 119:51; Ezek. 23:32; 36:4; Hos. 7:16
DESCEND Ezek. 26:20; 31:16, with them that *d*
    into pit
Mat. 7:25, 27, rain *d*, and floods came
Mk. 1:10; Jn. 1:32, 33, Spirit *d*
    15:32, let Christ now *d* from cross
Rom. 10:7, who shall *d* into the deep?
Eph. 4:10, he that *d* is same that ascended
James 3:15, this wisdom *d* not
Rev. 21:10, great city *d* out of heaven
See Gen. 28:12; Ps. 49:17; 133:3; Prov. 30:4
DESCENT Lk. 19:37; Heb. 7:3, 6
DESCRIBE Josh. 18:4; Judg. 8:14
DESCRY Judg. 1:23
DESERT Ps. 102:6; like an owl of the *d*
Isa. 35:1, the *d* shall rejoice
    6; 43:19, streams in the *d*
    40:3, in *d* a highway for our God
Jer. 2:6, led us through land of *d*
    17:6, like the heath in the *d*
    25:24, people that dwell in *d* shall drink
Mat. 24:26, say, behold, he is in the *d*
Lk. 1:80, Jn. in *d* till his showing
    9:10, aside privately into *d* place
Jn. 6:31, did eat manna in *d*
See Ex. 5:3; 19:2; Isa. 51:3; Mk. 6:31
DESERTS Ps. 28:4; Ezek. 7:27
DESERVE Judg. 9:16; Ezra 9:13; Job 11:6
DESIRABLE Ezek. 23:6, 12, 23
DESIRE (*n.*) II Chron. 15:15
Job 34:36, my *d* is that Job may be tried
Ps. 10:3; 21:2; Rom. 10:1, heart's *d*
Ps. 37:4, give you the *d* of your heart
    54:7; 59:10; 112:8, *d* on enemies
    92:11; 112:10; 140:8, *d* of the wicked
    145:16, the *d* of every living thing
Prov. 10:24; 11:23, the *d* of righteous
    13:12, when *d* comes, it is a tree of life
    19:22, the *d* of a man is his kindness
    21:25, the *d* of slothful kills him
Ezek. 24:16, 21, 25, the *d* of your eyes
Mic. 7:3, great man utters mischievous *d*
Hag. 2:7, the *d* of all nations
Lk. 22:15, with *d* I have *d* to eat
Eph. 2:3, fulfilling *d* of flesh and mind
Phil. 1:23, having a *d* to depart
See Gen. 3:16; Job 14:15; 31:16
DESIRE (*v.*) Deut. 14:26
I Sam. 2:16, take as much as your soul *d*
    12:13, behold the king whom you *d*
Neh. 1:11, servants who *d* to fear your name
Job 13:3, I *d* to reason with God
Ps. 19:10, more to be *d* than gold
    27:4, one thing I *d* of the Lord
    34:12, that *d* life, and loves many days
    40:6, sacrifice and offering you did not *d*
    45:11, king greatly *d* your beauty
    73:25, none on earth I *d* beside you
Eccl. 2:10, what my eyes *d* I kept not
Isa. 53:2, no beauty that we should *d*
Hos. 6:6, I *d* mercy and not sacrifice
Mic. 7:1, soul *d* firstripe fruit
Zeph. 2:1, gather together, O nation not *d*

Mat. 12:46; Lk. 8:20, his brethren *d*
    13:17, have *d* to see those things
    20:20, *d* a certain thing of him
Mk. 9:35, if any *d* to be first
    10:35, do for us whatsoever we *d*
    11:24, what things you *d*, when you pray
    15:6; Lk. 23:25, prisoner whom they *d*
Lk. 9:9, who is this, and he *d* to see him
    10:24, kings have *d* to see
    16:21, *d* to be fed with crumbs
    20:46, scribes *d* to walk in long robes
    22:31, Satan has *d* to have you
Acts 3:14, *d* a murderer to be granted
I Cor. 14:1, and *d* spiritual gifts
II Cor. 5:2, *d* to be clothed upon
Gal. 4:9, you *d* again to be in bondage
    21, you that *d* to be under the law
    6:12, as *d* to make show in the flesh
Eph. 3:13, I *d* that you faint not
Phil. 4:17, not because I *d* a gift: I *d* fruit
I Tim. 3:1, he *d* a good work
Heb. 11:16, they *d* a better country
James 4:2, you *d* to have, and cannot obtain
I Pet. 1:12, the angels *d* to look into
    2:2, as babes, *d* sincere milk of the word
I Jn. 5:15, we have petitions we *d*
DESIROUS Prov. 23:3; Lk. 23:8
DESOLATE Ps. 40:15, let them be *d* for reward
    143:4, my heart within me is *d*
Isa. 54:1; Gal. 4:27, more are children of *d*
    62:4, nor shall your land be termed *D*
Jer. 2:12, be you very *d*, saith the Lord
    32:43; 33:12, *d* without man or beast
Ezek. 6:6, your altars may be made *d*
Dan. 11:31, abomination that makes *d*
Mal. 1:4, return and build the *d* places
Mat. 23:38; Lk. 13:35, house left to you *d*
Acts 1:20, let his habitation be *d*
I Tim. 5:5, widow indeed, and *d*
Rev. 18:19, in one hour is she made *d*
See Ps. 34:22; Jer. 12:10; Zech. 7:14
DESOLATION II Ki. 22:19
Ps. 46:8, what *d* he has made in the earth
    74:3; Jer. 25:9; Ezek. 35:9, perpetual *d*
Prov. 1:27, when your fear comes as *d*
    3:25, the *d* of the wicked
Dan. 9:26, to end of war *d* are determined
Zeph. 1:15, a day of wrath, wasting, and *d*
Lk. 21:20, then know *d* is nigh
See Lev. 26:31; Josh. 8:28; Job 30:14
DESPAIR I Sam. 27:1; II Cor. 4:8
DESPERATE Job 6:26; Isa. 17:11; Jer. 17:9
DESPISE Num. 11:20, you have *d* the Lord
    15:31; Prov. 13:13; Isa. 5:24; 30:12
Neh. 4:4, hear, O God, for we are *d*
Esther 1:17, so that they *d* their husbands
Job 5:17; Prov. 3:11; Heb. 12:5
    19:18, young children *d* me
    36:5, God is mighty and *d* not any
Ps. 51:17, contrite heart you will not *d*
    53:5, put to shame, because God *d* them
    73:20, you shall *d* their image
    102:17, he will not *d* their prayer
Prov. 1:7, fools *d* wisdom

6:30, men do not *d* a thief
15:5, fool *d* father's instruction
20, foolish man *d* his mother
32, refuses instruction *d* own soul
19:16, he that *d* his ways shall die
Eccl. 9:16, poor man's wisdom is *d*
Is. 33:15, he that *d* gain of oppressions
49:7, saith Lord to him whom man *d*
Jer. 49:15, I will make you small and *d*
Ezek. 20:13, 16, they *d* my judgments
22:8, you have *d* holy things
Amos 2:4, they *d* the law of the Lord
Zech. 4:10, who has *d* day of small things?
Mal. 1:6, wherein have we *d* your name?
Lk. 10:16, *d* you, *d* me; *d* him that sent me
18:9, righteous, and *d* others
Rom. 2:4, *d* you the riches of his goodness
I Cor. 1:28, things *d* has God chosen
4:10, you are honorable, but we are *d*
11:22, *d* you the church of God
I Thess. 4:8, *d* not man, but God
I Tim. 4:12, let no man *d* your youth
6:2, not *d*, because brethren
Titus 2:15, let no man *d* you
Heb. 12:2, endured cross, *d* the shame
James 2:6, you have *d* the poor
See Gen. 16:4; 25:34; II Sam. 6:16; Rom. 14:3
DESPISERS Acts 13:41; II Tim. 3:3
DESPITE Ezek. 25:6, 15; 36:5; Rom. 1:30
DESPITEFULLY Mat. 5:44; Lk. 6:28
DESTITUTE Ps. 102:17, regard prayer of *d*
I Tim. 6:5, *d* of the truth
Heb. 11:37, being *d* afflicted, tormented
See Gen. 24:27; Ezek. 32:15; James 2:15
DESTROY Gen. 18:23
Ex. 22:20, he shall be utterly *d*
Deut. 9:14, let me alone, that I may *d* them
II Sam. 1:14, *d* Lord's anointed
Job 2:3, moved me to *d* without cause
10:8, made me, yet you do *d* me
19:10, he has *d* me on every side
26, though worms *d* this body
Ps. 40:14; 63:9, seek my soul to *d* it
145:20, all the wicked will he *d*
Prov. 1:32, prosperity of fools shall *d* them
31:3, that which *d* kings
Eccl. 9:18, one sinner *d* much good
Isa. 10:7, it is in his heart to *d*
11:9; 65:25, not *d* in all my holy mountain
19:3, I will *d* the counsel thereof
28:2, as a *d* storm
Jer. 13:14, I will not spare, but *d* them
17:18, *d* them with double destruction
23:1, woe to pastors that *d* the sheep
Ezek. 9:1, with *d* weapon in his hand
22:27, *d* souls to get dishonest gain
Hos. 13:9, you have *d* yourself
Mat. 5:17, not to *d* the law, but to fulfill
10:28, fear him that is able to *d*
12:14; Mk. 3:6; 11:18, they might *d* him
21:41, he will miserably *d* those
22:7, and *d* those murderers
27:20, ask Barabbas, and *d* Jesus
Mk. 1:24; Lk. 4:34, are you come to *d* us?

12:9; Lk. 20:16, *d* the husbandmen
14:58, say, I will *d* this temple
15:29, you that *d* the temple
Lk. 6:9, is it lawful to save life, or to *d* it?
9:56, is not come to *d* men's lives
17:27, flood came, and *d* them all
Jn. 2:19, Jesus said, *D* this temple
I Cor. 6:13, God shall *d* both it and them
Gal. 1:23, preaches the faith he once *d*
2:18, if I build the things which I *d*
II Thess. 2:8, *d* with brightness of his
coming
Heb. 2:14, *d* him that had the power
James 4:12, able to save and to *d*
I Jn. 3:8, *d* the works of the devil
DESTROYER Ex. 12:23, not suffer *d* to come
Judg. 16:24, delivered the *d* of our country
Job 15:21, in prosperity the *d* shall come
Ps. 17:4, kept from paths of the *d*
Prov. 28:24, the companion of a *d*
See Job 33:22; Isa. 49:17; Jer. 22:7; 50:11
DESTRUCTION II Chron. 26:16, heart lifted up
to *d*
Esther 8:6, endure to see *d* of my kindred
Job 5:21, neither be afraid of *d*
21:17, how oft comes *d*
31:3, is not *d* to the wicked
Ps. 9:6, *d* are come to a perpetual end
35:8, into that very *d* let him fall
73:18, you cast them down to *d*
90:3, turn man to *d*
91:6, the *d* that wastes at noonday
103:4, redeems your life from *d*
Prov. 1:27, your *d* comes as a whirlwind
10:14, mouth of foolish near *d*
15, *d* of poor is their poverty
14:28, want of people *d* of the prince
16:18, pride goes before *d*
17:19, he that exalts his gate seeks *d*
18:7, a fool's mouth is his *d*
27:20, hell and *d* are never full
31:8, such as are appointed to *d*
Isa. 14:23, the bosom of *d*
19:18, the city of *d*
59:7, wasting and *d* in their paths
Jer. 17:18, destroy with double *d*
46:20, *d* comes out of north
Hos. 13:14, O grave, I will be your *d*
Mat. 7:13, broad way leads to *d*
Rom. 3:16, *D* and misery are in their ways
9:22, vessels fitted to *d*
Phil. 3:18, 19, many walk, whose end is *d*
I Thess. 5:3, then sudden *d* comes
II Thess. 1:9, punished with everlasting *d*
I Tim. 6:9, lusts, which drown men in *d*
II Pet. 2:1, bring on themselves swift *d*
3:16, wrest to their own *d*
See Job 21:20; 31:23; Prov. 10:29; 21:15
DETAIN Judg. 13:15, 16; I Sam. 21:7
DETERMINATE Acts 2:23
DETERMINATION Zeph. 3:8
DETERMINE Ex. 21:22, pay as the judges *d*
I Sam. 20:7, be sure evil is *d* by him
Job 14:5, seeing his days are *d*

Dan. 11:36, that that is *d* shall be done
Lk. 22:22, Son of man goes, as it was *d*
Acts 3:13, Pilate was *d* to let him go
 17:26, has *d* the times appointed
I Cor. 2:2, I *d* not to know any thing
See II Chron. 2:1; 25:16; Isa. 19:17; Dan. 9:24
DETEST Deut. 7:26
DETESTABLE Jer. 16:18; Ezek. 5:11
DEVICE Esther 9:25, *d* return on his own head
 Ps. 10:2, let them be taken in the *d*
 33:10, makes *d* of the people of none effect
 37:7, brings wicked *d* to pass
 Prov. 1:31, be filled with their own *d*
 12:2, man of wicked *d* will he condemn
 19:21, many *d* in a man's heart
 Eccl. 9:10, no work nor *d* in grave
 Jer. 18:12, will walk after our own *d*
 Dan. 11:24, 25, he shall forecast *d*
 Acts 17:29, like stone graven by man's *d*
 II Cor. 2:11, not ignorant of his *d*
 See II Chron. 2:14; Esther 8:3; Job 5:12
DEVILISH James 3:15
DEVISE Ex. 31:4; 35:32, 35, *d* works in gold
 Ps. 35:4, to confusion that *d* my hurt
 36:4, he *d* mischief on his bed
 Prov. 3:29, *d* not evil against your neighbor
 6:14, he *d* mischief continually
 18, a heart that *d* wicked imaginations
 14:22, err that *d* evil, *d* good
 16:9, man's heart *d* his way
 Isa. 32:7, *d* wicked devices to destroy the poor
 8, the liberal *d* liberal things
 II Pet. 1:16, cunningly *d* fables
DEVOTE Lev. 27:21, 28; Num. 18:14
DEVOTIONS Acts 17:23
DEVOUR Ex. 24:17; Isa. 29:6; 30:27, 30; 33:14, *d* fire
 Lev. 10:2, fire from Lord *d* them
 Deut. 32:24, *d* with burning heat
 II Sam. 11:25, sword *d* one as well as another
 18:8, wood *d* more than sword *d*
 22:9; Ps. 18:8, fire out of his mouth *d*
 Job 18:13, death shall *d* his strength
 Ps. 80:13, beasts of field *d* it
 Prov. 20:25, man who *d* that which is holy
 30:14, jaw teeth as knives, to *d*
 Isa. 1:7, strangers *d* it in your presence
 20, if you rebel, you shall be *d* with sword
 Jer. 2:30, your sword has *d* prophets
 Ezek. 15:7, fire shall *d* them
 23:37, pass through fire to *d* them
 Joel 2:3, a fire *d* before them
 Amos 4:9, fig trees, palmerworm *d* them
 Zeph. 1:18; 3:8, *d* by fire of jealousy
 Mal. 3:11, will rebuke the *d* for your sakes
 Mat. 13:4; Mk. 4:4; Lk. 8:5, fowls *d* them
 23:14; Mk. 12:40, *d* widows' houses
 Lk. 15:30, your son has *d* your living
 II Cor. 11:20, if a man *d* you
 Gal. 5:15, you bite and *d* one another
 Heb. 10:27, which shall *d* adversaries
 I Pet. 5:8, seeking whom he may *d*
 See Gen. 31:15; II Sam. 2:26; Ps. 50:3; 52:4
DEVOUT Lk. 2:25, Simeon was just and *d*

Acts 2:5; 8:2, *d* men
See Acts 10:2; 13:50; 17:4, 17; 22:12
DEW II Sam. 1:21, let there be no *d*
 17:12, we will light on him as *d* falls
 I Ki. 17:1, there shall not be *d* nor rain
 Job 38:28, who has begotten the drops of *d*?
 Prov. 3:20, clouds drop down *d*
 Isa. 18:4, like *d* in heat of harvest
 Dan. 4:15, 23, 25, 33, wet with *d* of heaven
DIADEM Job 29:14; Isa. 28:5; Ezek. 21:26
DIAMOND Jer. 17:1; Ezek. 28:13
DID Mat 13:58, he *d* not many works
 Jn. 4:29, all things that ever I *d*
 See Gen. 6:22; I Sam. 1:7; Job 1:5; I Pet. 2:22
DIE Gen. 2:17, I Sam. 14:44; I Ki. 2:1
 37, 42; Jer. 26:8; Ezek. 3:18, surely *d*
 Gen. 3:3; Lev. 10:6; Num. 18:32, lest you *d*
 27:4; 45:28; Prov. 30:7, before I *d*
 Ex. 21:12, smites a man that he *d*
 Lev. 7:24; 22:8; Deut. 14:21, Ezek. 4:14, that *d* of itself
 Num. 16:29, if these *d* common death
 23:10, let me *d* death of righteous
 Deut. 31:14, days approach that you must *d*
 Ruth 1:17, where you *d*, will I *d*
 II Sam. 3:33, *D* Abner as a fool *d*?
 II Ki. 20:1; Isa. 38:1, shall *d*, and not live
 II Chron. 25:4, every man *d* for own sin
 Job 2:9, his wife said, Curse God, and *d*
 3:11, why *d* I not from the womb?
 12:2, wisdom shall *d* with you
 14:14, if a man *d*, shall be live again?
 21:23, one *d* in full strength
 29:18, I shall *d* in my nest
 Ps. 41:5, shall he *d*, and his name perish
 49:10, wise men *d*, likewise the fool
 17, when he *d* he shall carry nothing away
 Prov. 5:23, he shall *d* without instruction
 10:21, fools *d* for want of wisdom
 11:7, *d* his expectation shall perish
 Eccl. 2:16, how *d* the wise man?
 7:17, why should you *d* before your time?
 9:5, living know they shall *d*
 Isa. 66:24; Mk. 9:44, worm shall not *d*
 Jer. 27:13; Ezek. 18:31; 33:11, why will you *d*?
 28:16, this year you shall *d*
 34:5, you shall *d* in peace
 Ezek. 18:4, 20, soul that sins, it shall *d*
 32, no pleasure in death of him that *d*
 33:8, wicked man shall *d* in iniquity
 Amos 6:9, ten men in one house, they shall *d*
 Jonah 4:3, 8, it is better to *d* than live
 Mat. 15:4; Mk. 7:10, let him *d* the death
 22:27; Lk. 20:32, woman *d* also
 26:35; Mk. 14:31, though I *d* with you
 Lk. 7:2, servant was ready to *d*
 16:22, beggar *d*, the rich man also *d*
 20:36, nor can they *d* any more
 Jn. 4:49, come down ere my child *d*
 11:21, 32, my brother had not *d*
 37, that even this man should not have *d*
 50; 18:14, that one man *d* for the people
 51, that Jesus should *d* for that nation
 12:24, except a corn of wheat *d*

19:7, by our law he ought to *d*

Acts 9:37, Dorcas was sick, and *d*

21:13, ready also to *d* at Jerusalem

Rom. 5:7, for righteous man will one *d*

7:9, sin revived, and I *d*

8:34, it is Christ that *d*

14:7, no man *d* to himself

9, Christ both *d*, rose, and revived

15; I Cor. 8:11, for whom Christ *d*

I Cor. 15:3, Christ *d* for our sins

31, I *d* daily

II Cor. 5:14, if one *d* for all

Phil. 1:21, to *d* is gain

I Thess. 4:14, we believe that Jesus *d*

5:10, who *d* for us that we should live

Heb. 7:8, here men that *d* receive tithes

9:27, appointed unto men once to *d*

11:13, these all *d* in faith

Rev. 3:2, things that are ready to *d*

9:6, men shall desire to *d*

14:13, the death that *d* in the Lord

See Job 14:10; Ps. 118:17; Rom. 5:6; 6:10

DIET Jer. 52:34

DYED Ex. 25:5; Isa. 63:1; Ezek. 23:15

DYING II Cor. 4:10, the *d* of Lord Jesus

6:9, as *d*, and behold we live

See Num. 17:13; Lk. 8:42; Heb. 11:21

DIFFER Rom. 12:6; I Cor. 4:7; Gal. 4:1

DIFFERENCE Lev. 10:10; Ezek. 44:23, a *d* between holy and unholy

11:47, 20:25, *d* between clean and unclean

Ezek. 22:26, they have put no *d* between

Acts 15:9, put not *d* between us

Rom. 3:22; 10:12, for there is no *d*

See Ex. 11:7; I Cor. 12:5; Jude 22

DIG Ex. 21:33, *d* a pit, and not cover it

Deut. 6:11, wells *d*, which you *d* not

8:9, out of hills may *d* brass

Job. 6:27, you *d* a pit for your friend

24:16, in the dark they *d*

Ps. 7:15; 57:6, *d* a pit, and is fallen

Isa. 51:1, hole of pit whence you are *d*

Mat. 21:33, and *d* a winepress

25:18, *d* in the earth, and hid

Lk. 13:8, till I *d* about it

See Job 3:21; Ezek. 8:8; 12:5; Lk. 6:48

DIGNITY Eccl. 10:6; folly set in great *d*

II Pet. 2:10; Jude 8, these speak evil of *d*

See Gen. 49:3; Esther 6:3; Hab. 1:7

DILIGENCE Prov. 4:23; II Tim. 4:9; Jude 3

DILIGENT Josh. 22:5, take *d* heed to do the commandment

Ps. 64:6, accomplish a *d* search

Lk. 15:8, seek *d* till she find it

Acts 18:25, taught *d* the things of the Lord

II Tim. 1:17, in Rome sought me *d*

See Deut. 19:18; Prov. 11:27; 23:1; Mat. 2:7

DIM Deut. 34:7, eye not *d*, nor force abated

Job 17:7, eye also *d* by reason of sorrow

Lam. 4:1, gold become *d*

See Gen. 27:1; 48:10; I Sam. 3:2; Isa. 8:22

DIMINISH Prov. 13:11, wealth by vanity shall be *d*

Rom. 11:12, *d* of them be riches of Gentiles

See Ex. 5:8; Lev. 25:16; Jer. 26:2; Ezek. 16:27

DINE Gen. 43:16; Lk. 11:37; Jn. 21:12, 15

DINNER Prov. 15:17; Mat. 22:4, Lk. 11:38

DIP Lev. 4:6; 14:16, priest shall *d* his finger

Ruth 2:14, *d* morsel in vinegar

I Sam. 14:27, *d* rod in honeycomb

II Ki. 5:14, Naaman *d* in Jordan

Mat. 26:23; Mk. 14:20, *d* hand in dish

Jn. 13:26, when he had *d* the sop

Rev. 19:13, a vesture *d* in blood

See Gen. 37:3; Josh. 3:15; Lk. 16:24

DIRECT Job 32:14, he has not *d* his words

Ps. 5:3, in morning will I *d* my prayer

119:5, O that my ways were *d* to keep

Prov. 3:6, he shall *d* your paths

16:9, the Lord *d* his steps

Eccl. 10:10, wisdom profitable to *d*

Isa. 40:13, who has *d* the Spirit of the Lord

Jer. 10:23, not in man to *d* his steps

See Gen. 46:28; Isa. 45:13; 61:8; I Thess. 3:11

DIRECTION Num. 21:18

DIRECTLY Num. 19:4; Ezek. 42:12

DIRT Judg. 3:22; Ps. 18:42; Isa. 57:20

DISALLOWED Num. 30:5, 8, 11; I Pet. 2:4

DISANNUL Isa. 14:27, the Lord has purposed, who shall *d* it?

28:18, your covenant with death shall be *d*

Gal. 3:15, 17, covenant no man *d*

See Job 40:8; Isa. 14:27; Heb. 7:18

DISAPPOINT Job. 5:12; Prov. 15:22

DISCERN II Sam. 19:35

I Ki. 3:9, *d* between good and bad

Ezra 3:13, could not *d* notice noise of joy

Job 4:16, could not *d* form thereof

6:30, cannot my taste *d* perverse things

Prov. 7:7, I *d* among the youths

Eccl. 8:5, wise man's heart *d* time

Jonah 4:11, cannot *d* between right and left

Mal. 3:18, *d* between righteous and wicked

Mat. 16:3; Lk. 12:56, *d* face of the sky

I Cor. 2:14, they are spiritually *d*

11:29, not *d* the Lord's body

Heb. 4:12, the word is a *d* of the thoughts

5:14, exercised to *d* good and evil

See Gen. 27:33; 31:32; 38:25; II Sam. 14:17

DISCHARGE I Ki. 5:9; Eccl. 8:8

DISCIPLE Isa. 8:16, seal the law among my *d*

Mat. 10:1; Lk. 6:13, called his twelve *d*

Lk. 6:40, *d* not above his master

42, give cup of water in the name of a *d*

12:2, your *d* do that which is not lawful

15:2, why do your *d* transgress tradition?

19:13; Mk. 10:13, the *d* rebuked them

20:17, Jesus took *d* apart

22:16, Pharisees sent their *d*

26:18; Lk. 22:11, keep Passover with *d*

Mat. 20:56, all the *d* forsook him and fled

28:7, tell his *d* he is risen

13, say he, his *d* came by night

Mk. 2:18, why do *d* of John fast?

4:34, he expounded all things to *d*

7:2, *d* eat with unwashed hands

5, why walk not *d* according to traditions?

Lk. 5:30, Pharisees murmured against *d*

6:20, lifted up eyes on *d*
11:1, as John taught his *d*
19:37, *d* began to rejoice and praise God
39, Master, rebuke your *d*
Jn. 2:11, his *d* believed on him
4:2, Jesus baptized not, but his *d*
6:22, his *d* were gone away alone
7:3, that your *d* may see works
Jn. 8:31; 13:35, then are you my *d* indeed
28, you are his *d*, we are Moses' *d*
13:5, began to wash *d* feet
15:8, so shall you be my *d*
18:17, 25, are not you one of his *d*?
19:26; 20:2; 21:7, 20, *d* whom Jesus loved
19:38, a *d* of Jesus, secretly for fear
20:18, told *d* she had seen the Lord
21:23, that that *d* should not die
Acts 9:1, slaughter against *d*
26, essayed to join himself to *d*
11:26, *d* called Christians first
20:7, *d* came together to break bread
30, to draw away *d* after them
21:16, an old *d* with whom we should lodge
See Mat. 11:1; Jn. 3:25; 18:1,2; 20:26
DISCIPLINE Job 36:10
DISCLOSE Isa. 26:21
DISCOMFITED Judg. 4:15, Lord *d* Sisera
8:12, Gideon *d* all the host
II Sam. 22:15, lightnings, and *d* them
Isa. 31:8, his young men shall be *d*
See Ex. 17:13; Num. 14:45; Josh 10:10
DISCOMFITURE I Sam. 14:20
DISCONTENTED I Sam. 22:2
DISCONTINUE Jer. 17:4
DISCORD Prov. 6:14, 19
DISCOURAGE Num. 32:7, wherefore *d* ye the heart of the children of Israel
Deut. 1:21, fear not, not be *d*
28, our brethren have *d* our heart
Col. 3:21, your children, lest they be *d*
See Num. 21:4; 32:9; Isa. 42:4
DISCOVER I Sam. 14:8, 11, we will *d* ourselves to them
II Sam. 22:16, foundations of the world *d*
Job 12:22, he *d* deep things
Prov. 25:9, *d* not a secret to another
Ezek. 21:24, your transgressions are *d*
See Ps. 29:9; Hos. 7:1; Hab. 3:13; Acts 21:3
DISCREET Gen. 41:33, 39; Mk. 12:34
DISCRETION Ps. 112:5; Prov. 11:22; Isa. 28:26; Jer. 10:12
DISDAINED I Sam. 17:42; Job 30:1
DISEASE Ex. 15:26, none of these *d* on you
Deut. 28:60, bring on you all *d* of Egypt
II Chron. 16:12, in *d* sought not the Lord
Job 30:18, by force of my *d*
Ps. 103:3, who heals all your *d*
Eccl. 6:2, vanity, and it is an evil *d*
Ezek. 34:4, *d* has he not strengthened
See Mat. 4:23; 14:35; Luke 9:1; Acts 28:9
DISFIGURE Mat. 6:16
DISGRACE Jer. 14:21
DISGUISE I Sam. 28:8; I Ki. 14:2; II Chron.

18:29; 35:22; Job 24:15
DISH Judg. 5:25; II Ki. 21:13; Mat. 26:23
DISHONESTY II Cor. 4:2
DISHONOR Ps. 35:26; 71:13, clothed with shame and *d*
Prov. 6:33, a wound and *d* shall he get
Mic. 7:6, son *d* father
Jn. 8:49, I honor my Father, ye do *d* me
Rom. 9:21, one vessel to honor, another to *d*?
I Cor. 15:43, sown in *d*
II Tim. 2:20, some to honor, some to *d*
See Ezra 4:14; Rom. 1:24; 2:23; I Cor. 11:4, 5
DISINHERIT Num. 14:12
DISMAYED Deut. 31:8; Josh 1:9; I Chron. 22:13; 28:20; II Chron. 20:15, 17; Isa 41:10; Jer. 1:17; 10:2; 23:4; 46:27; Ezek. 2:6, fear not nor be *d*
Jer. 17:18, let them be *d*, let not me be *d*
See I Sam. 17:11; Jer. 8:9; 46:5; Obad. 9
DISMISSED II Chron. 23:8; Acts 15:30; 19:41
DISOBEDIENCE Rom. 5:19; Eph. 2:2; 5:6
DISOBEDIENT Lk. 1:17, *d* to wisdom
Acts 26:19, not *d* to heavenly vision
Rom. 1:30; II Tim. 3:2, *d* to parents
I Tim. 1:9, law for lawless and *d*
Titus 3:3, we ourselves were sometimes *d*
I Pet. 2:7, to them which be *d*
3:20, spirits, which sometimes were *d*
See I Ki. 13:26; Neh. 9:26; Rom. 10:21
DISORDERLY II Thess. 3:6, 7, 11
DISPERSE Prov. 15:7, lips *d* knowledge
Jn. 7:35, will he go to the *d*?
See Ps. 112:9; Jer. 25:34; Ezek. 12:15; 20:23
DISPLAYED Ps. 60:4
DISPLEASE Num. 11:1, it *d* the Lord
22:34, if it *d* you, I will get me back
II Sam. 11:27, David *d* the Lord
I Ki. 1:6, father had not *d* at any time
Isa. 59:15, it *d* him there was no judgment
Jonah 4:1, it *d* Jonah exceedingly
Mat. 21:15; scribes saw it, they were *d*
Mk. 10:14, Jesus was much *d*
41, much *d* with James and John
See Gen. 48:17; I Sam. 8:6; 18:8; Zech. 1:2
DISPLEASURE Deut. 9:19; Judg. 15:3; Ps. 2:5; 6:1; 38:1
DISPOSE Job 34:13; 37:15; I Cor. 10:27
DISPOSITION Acts 7:53
DISPOSSESS Num. 33:53; Deut. 7:17
DISPUTATION Acts 15:2; Rom. 14:1
DISPUTE Job 23:7, the righteous might *d* with him
Mk. 9:33, what was it you *d* of by the way?
I Cor. 1:20, where is the *d* of this world?
Phil 2:14, do all things without *d*
I Tim. 6:5, perverse *d*
See Acts 9:29; 15:7; 17:17; Jude 9
DISQUIET Ps. 42:5, 11, why are you *d* within me?
See Ps. 38:8; 39:6; Jer. 50:34
DISSEMBLE Josh 7:11; Ps. 26:4; Prov. 26:24; Jer. 42:20; Gal. 2:13
DISSENSION Acts 15:2; 23:7, 10
DISSIMULATION Rom. 12:9; Gal. 2:13

DISSOLVE Isa. 34:4, host of heaven be *d*
Dan. 5:16, you can *d* doubts
II Pet. 3:11, all these things shall be *d*
   12, heavens being on fire shall be *d*
See Job 30:22; Ps. 75:3; Isa. 14:31; 24:19
DISTAFF Prov. 31:19
DISTIL Deut. 32:2; Job 36:28
DISTINCTION I Cor. 14:7
DISTINCTLY Neh. 8:8
DISTRACT Ps. 88:15; I Cor. 7:35
DISTRESS Judg. 11:7, why come when you are
   in *d*?
I Sam. 22:2, every one in *d* came to David
II Sam. 22:7; Ps. 18:6, in *d* I called
I Ki. 1:29, redeemed my soul out of all *d*
II Chron. 28:22, in *d* Ahaz trespassed more
Neh. 2:17, you see the *d* we are in
Prov. 1:27, mock when *d* comes
Isa. 25:4, a strength to needy in *d*
Obad. 12, 14; Zeph. 1:15, day of *d*
Lk. 21:23, shall be great *d* in the land
   25, on earth *d* of nations
Rom. 8:35, shall *d* separate us?
I Cor. 7:26, good for present *d*
II Cor. 6:4, approving ourselves in *d*
   12:10, take pleasure in *d*
DISTRIBUTE Job 21:17, God *d* sorrows in
   his anger
Lk. 18:22, sell and *d* to poor
Jn. 6:11, given thanks, he *d*
Rom. 12:13, *D* to necessity of saints
I Cor. 7:17, as God has *d* to every man
II Cor. 9:13, your liberal *d*
See Josh. 13:32; Acts 4:35; II Cor. 10:13
DITCH Ps. 7:15, fallen into *d* he made
Mat. 15:14; Lk. 6:39, both fall into *d*
See Job 9:31; Prov. 23:27; Isa. 22:11
DIVERS Deut. 22:9, sow vineyard with *d*
   11, garments of *d* sorts
   25:13, not have in bag *d* weights
Deut. 25:14, *d* measures, great and small
Prov. 20:10, 23, *D* weights and measures
Mat. 4:24; Lk. 4:40, *d* diseases
Mat. 24:7; Lk. 21:11; in *d* places
Mk. 8:3, for *d* of them came from far
I Cor. 12:10, to another *d* kinds of tongues
II Tim. 3:6; Titus 3:3, led away with *d* lusts
James 1:2, joy in *d* temptations
See Eccl. 5:7; Heb. 1:1; 2:4; 9:10; 13:9
DIVERSE Esther 3:8, laws *d* from all people
I Cor. 12:6, *d* of operations, but same God
DIVIDE Lev. 11:4, 5, 6, 7, 26; Deut. 14:7, not
   eat these of them than *d* the hoof
Josh. 19:49, an end of the *d* the land
I Ki. 3:25, *D* living child in two
Job 27:17, innocent shall *d* silver
Ps. 68:12; Prov. 16:19; Isa. 9:3; 53:12, *d* spoil
Amos 7:17, your land shall be *d* by line
Mat. 12:25; Mk. 3:24, kingdom *d*
Mk. 3:26; Lk. 11:18, *d* against himself
Lk. 12:13, that he *d* inheritance with me
Acts 14:4; 23:7, multitude *d*
I Cor. 1:13, is Christ *d*?
   12:11, *d* to every man severally as he will

II Tim. 2:15, rightly *d* word of truth
Heb. 4:12, piercing to *d* asunder
See Dan. 7:25; Hos. 10:2; Lk. 22:17
DIVINATION Num. 23:23, neither is any *d*
   against Israel
Acts 16:16, damsel with a spirit of *d*
See Deut. 18:10; II Ki. 17:17; Ezek. 13:23
DIVINE (*v.*) I Sam. 28:8, *d* unto me by the
   familiar spirit
Ezek. 13:9, prophets that *d* lies
   21:29, they *d* lies unto you
Mic. 3:11, prophets *d* for money
See Gen. 44:5; Ezek. 22:28; Mic. 3:6
DIVINE (*adj.*) Prov. 16:10; Heb. 9:1
DIVINER I Sam. 6:2; Isa. 44:25; Jer. 27:9
DIVISION Ex. 8:23, a *d* between my people
Lk. 12:51, I tell you, Nay; but rather *d*
Jn. 7:43; 9:16; 10:19, *d* because of him
Rom. 16:17, mark them which cause *d*
See I Cor. 1:10; 3:3; 11:18
DIVORCE Lev. 21:14; 22:13; Jer. 3:8
DO Ruth 3:5, all you say I will *d*
Isa. 46:11, I will also *d* it
Hos. 6:4, what shall I *d* unto you?
Mat. 7:12, men *d* to you, *d* ye even so
   23:3, they say, and *d* not
Lk. 10:28, this *d*, and you shall live
   22:19; I Cor. 11:24, this *d* in remembrance
Jn. 15:5, without me you can *d* nothing
Rom. 7:15, what I would, that *d* I not
II Cor. 11:12, what I *d* that I will *d*
Phil. 4:13, I can *d* all things through Christ
James 1:23, a hearer, not a *d* of the word
See Jn. 6:38; 10:37; Rev. 19:10; 22:9
DOCTOR Lk. 2:46; 5:17; Acts 5:34
DOCTRINE Prov. 4:2, I give you good *d*
Isa. 28:9, made to understand *d*
Mat. 15:9; Mk. 7:7, teaching for *d* command-
   ments of men
   16:12, the *d* of the Pharisees
Mk. 1:27; Acts 17:19, what new *d* is this?
Jn. 7:17, do his will shall know of the *d*
Acts 2:42, continued in apostles' *d*
   5:28, filled Jerusalem with your *d*
Rom. 6:17, obeyed that form of *d*
I Cor. 14:26, every one has a *d*
Eph. 4:14, every wind of *d*
I Tim. 1:10, contrary to sound *d*
   4:6, nourished in words of good *d*
   13, give attendance to *d*
I Tim. 4:16, take heed to yourself and *d*
II Tim. 3:10, have fully known my *d*
   16, scripture profitable for *d*
   4:2, exhort with all longsuffering and *d*
Titus 1:9, by sound *d* to exhort and convince
Heb. 6:1, principles of the *d*
   13:9, not carried about with strange *d*
II Jn. 9, abides in *d* of Christ
See Deut. 32:2; Job 11:4; Jn. 7:16; I Tim. 5:17
DOG Ex. 11:7, against Israel shall not a *d* move
Deut. 23:18, not bring price of *d* into house
Judg. 7:5, that laps as *d* laps
I Sam. 17:43; 24:14; II Sam. 3:8, am I a *d*?
II Sam. 9:8, upon such a dead *d* as I am

II Ki. 8:13, what, is your servant a *d*?

Ps. 22:20, darling from power of the *d*

59:6, they make noise like a *d*

Prov. 26:11; II Pet. 2:22, as a *d* returns

17, like one that takes a *d* by ears

Eccl. 9:4, living *d* better than dead lion

Isa. 56:10, they are all dumb *d*

66:3, as if he cut off a *d* neck

Mat. 7:6, give not that which is holy to *d*

15:27; Mk. 7:28, the *d* eat of crumbs

Phil. 3:2, beware of *d*

Rev. 22:15, without are *d*

See Ex. 22:31; I Ki. 14:11; 21:23; 22:38

DOING Judg. 2:19, ceased not from their own *d*

I Sam. 25:3, churlish and evil in his *d*

I Chron. 22:16, arise, and be *d*

Neh. 6:3, I am *d* a great work

Ps. 9:11; Isa. 12:4, declare his *d*

66:5, terrible in *d* toward children of men

Ps. 118:23; Mk. 12:11, the Lord's *d*

Mic. 2:7, are these his *d*?

Acts 10:38, went about *d* good

Rom. 2:7, patient continuance in well *d*

Gal. 6:9; II Thess. 3:13, weary in well *d*

I Pet. 2:15, with well *d* put to silence

3:17, suffer for well *d*

4:19, commit souls in well *d*

See Lev. 18:3; Prov. 20:11; Isa. 1:16; Jer. 4:4

DOLEFUL Isa. 13:21; Mic. 2:4

DOMINION Gen. 37:8, shall you have *d* over us?

Num. 24:19, come he that shall have *d*

Job 25:2, *D* and fear are with him

38:33, can you set the *d* thereof?

Ps. 8:6, *d* over works of your hands

19:13; 119:133, let them not have *d* over me

72:8; Zech. 9:10, *d* from sea to sea

Isa. 26:13, other lords have had *d* over us

Dan. 4:34; 7:14, *d* is an everlasting *d*

Mat. 20:25, princes of Gentiles exercise *d*

Rom. 6:9, death has no more *d*

II Cor. 1:24, not *d* over your faith

Eph. 1:21, above all *d*

Col. 1:16, whether they be thrones or *d*

See Dan. 6:26; I Pet. 4:11; Jude 25; Rev. 1:6

DOOR Gen. 4:7, sin lies at the *d*

Ex. 12:7, strike blood on *d* posts

33:8; Num. 11:10, every man at tent *d*

Judg. 16:3, Samson took *d* of the gate

Job 31:9, laid wait at neighbor's *d*

32, I opened my *d* to the travelers

38:17, the *d* of the shadow of death

41:14, who can open *d* of his face?

Ps. 24:7, you everlasting *d*

Prov. 5:8, come not near *d* of her house

8:3, wisdom cries at *d*

26:14, as *d* turns on hinges

Eccl. 12:4, *d* shall be shut in the streets

Isa. 6:4, posts of the *d* moved

26:20, enter, and shut your *d* about you

Hos. 2:15, for a *d* of hope

Mal. 1:10, who would shut the *d* for nought?

Mat. 25:10, and the *d* was shut

27:60; 28:2; Mk. 15:46, *d* of sepulcher

Mk. 1:33, city gathered at the *d*

2:2, not so much as about the *d*

Lk. 13:25, master has shut to the *d*

Jn. 10:1, 2, enters not by *d*

7:9, I am the *d*

18:16, Peter stood at the *d* without

17, damsel that kept the *d*

20:19, 26, when *d* were shut, Jesus came

Acts 5:9, feet at the *d* to carry you out

14:27, opened the *d* of faith

I Cor. 16:9, great *d* and effectual

II Cor. 2:12, *d* opened to me of the Lord

Col. 4:3, open a *d* of utterance

James 5:9, judge stands before the *d*

Rev. 3:8, set before you an open *d*

20, I stand at *d* and knock

4:1, behold a *d* opened in heaven

See Ex. 21:6; Isa. 57:8; Acts 5:19

DOTE Jer. 50:36; Ezek. 23:5; I Tim. 6:4

DOUBLE Gen. 43:12, 15, take *d* money

Ex. 22:4, 7, 9, he shall restore *d*

Deut. 15:18, worth a *d* hired servant

II Ki. 2:9, a *d* portion of your spirit

I Chron. 12:33; Ps. 12:2, a *d* heart

Isa. 40:2, received *d* for all her sins

Jer. 16:18, recompense their sin *d*

I Tim. 3:8, deacons not *d*-tongued

5:17, worthy of *d* honor

James 1:8, a *d* minded man unstable

4:8, purify your hearts, you *d* minded

DOUBT Deut. 28:66, your life shall hang in *d*

Job 12:2, no *d* ye are the people

Ps. 126:6, shall *d* come again, rejoicing

Dan. 5:12, 16, dissolving of *d*

Mat. 14:31, wherefore did you *d*?

21:21, if you have faith, and *d* not

Mk. 11:23, shall not *d* in his heart

Lk. 11:20, no *d* kingdom of God is come

Jn. 10:24, how long do you make us *d*?

Acts 5:24, they *d* whereunto this would grow

28:4, no *d* this man is a murderer

Rom. 14:23, he that *d* is damned if he eat

Gal. 4:20, I stand in *d* of you

I Tim. 2:8, pray without wrath and *d*

I Jn. 2:19, would no *d* have continued

See Lk. 12:29; Acts 2:12, Phil. 3:8

DOVE Ps. 55:6, that I had wings like a *d*

Isa. 59:11, mourn sore like *d*

60:8, flee as *d* to their windows

Mat. 10:16, be harmless as *d*

See Mat. 21:12; Mk. 11:15

DOWN II Sam. 3:35, taste ought till sun be *d*

II Ki. 19:30; Isa. 37:31, again take root *d*

Ps. 59:15, let them wander up and *d*

109:23, I am tossed up and *d*

Eccl. 3:21, spirit of the beast that goes *d*

Zech. 10:12, walk up and *d* in his name

See Josh. 8:29; Ps. 139:2; Ezek. 38:20

DOWRY Gen. 30:20; 34:12; Ex. 22:17

DRAG Hab. 1:15, 16; Jn. 21:8

DRAGON Deut. 32:33

Neh. 2:13, before the *d* well

Job 30:29, I am a brother to *d*

Ps. 91:13, the *d* shall you trample
   148:7, praise the Lord, you *d*
Isa. 43:20, the *d* and owls shall honor me
Jer. 9:11, will make Jerusalem a den of *d*
Rev. 20:2, the *d* that old serpent
See Rev. 12:3; 13:2, 11; 16:13
DRANK II Sam. 12:3; and *d* of his own cup
I Ki. 17:6, and he *d* of the brook
Dan. 1:5, appointed of the wine he *d*
   5:4, they *d*, and praised the gods of gold
Mk. 14:23, and they all *d* of it
Lk. 17:27, 28, they *d*, the married
Jn. 4:12, than our father, who *d* thereof
I Cor. 10:4, for they *d* of that spiritual Rock
See Gen. 9:21; 24:46; 27:25; Num. 20:11
DRAUGHT Mat. 15:17; Mk. 7:19
DRAVE Ex. 14:25; Josh. 24:12; Judg. 6:9
DRAW Job 41:1, can you *d* out leviathan
Ps. 28:3, *D* me not away with wicked
   37:14, wicked have *d* out sword
   55:21, yet were they *d* swords
   88:3, my life *d* nigh unto the grave
Eccl. 12;1, nor years *d* nigh
Song of Sol. 1:4, *D* me, we will run after you
Isa. 5:18, *d* iniquity with cords
   12:3, *d* water from wells of salvation
Jer. 31:3, with loving kindness have I *d* you
Mat. 15:8, *d* near me with their mouth
Lk. 21:8, the time *d* near
   28, your redemption *d* near
Jn. 4:11, you have nothing to *d* with
   15, thirst not, neither come hither to *d*
   6:44, except the Father *d* him
   12:32, if lifted up, will *d* all men
James 4:8, *D* near to God, he will *d*
See Isa. 28:9; Lam. 4:3; Acts 11:10; 20:30
DRAWER Deut. 29:11; Josh. 9:21
DREAD Gen. 28:17, how *d* is this place?
Deut. 2:25; 11:25, begin to put *d* of you
Isa. 8:13, let him be your *d*
Mal. 4:5, the great and *d* day
See Gen. 9:2; Ex. 15:16; Dan. 9:4
DREAM Job 20:8, shall fly away as a *d*
   33:15, in a *d* he opens the ears
Ps. 73:20, as a *d* when one awakes
   126:1, we were like them that *d*
Jer. 23:38, prophet that has a *d*
Joel 2:28; Acts 2:17, old men *d* *d*
Jude 8, filth *d* defile the flesh
See Job 7:14; Isa. 29:8; Jer. 27:9
DREGS Ps. 75:8; Isa. 51:17
DRESS Gen. 2:15, put man in garden to *d* it
Deut. 28:39, plant vineyards and *d* them
II Sam. 12:4, poor man's lamb, and *d* it
See Ex. 30:7; Lk. 13:7; Heb. 6:7
DREW Gen. 47:29
Ex. 2:10, because I *d* him out of the water
Josh. 8:26, Joshua *d* not his hand back
I Ki. 22:34; II Chron. 18:33, man *d* a bow
II Ki. 9:24; Jehu *d* bow with full strength
Zeph. 3:2, she *d* not near to her God
Mat. 21:34, when time of fruit *d* near
Lk. 24:15, Jesus himself *d* near
Acts 5:37, and *d* away much people

DRINK (*n.*) Lev. 10:9
Num. 6:3, separate himself from strong *d*
Deut. 14:26, bestow money for strong *d*
   29:6, strong *d*
Prov. 20:1, strong *d* is raging
   31:4, not for princes to drink strong *d*
Isa. 24:9, strong *d* shall be bitter
   28:7, erred through strong *d*
Mic. 2:11, prophesy of wine and strong *d*
Hab. 2:15, that gives his neighbour *d*
Hag. 1:6, you are not filled with *d*
Mat. 25:35, 37, 42, thirsty, you gave me *d*
Jn. 4:9, a Jew, askest *d* of me
   6:55, my blood is *d* indeed
Rom. 12:20, if enemy thirst, give him *d*
   14:17, kingdom of God is not meat and *d*
Col. 2:16, judge you in meat or in *d*
See Gen. 21:19; Isa. 32:6; 43:20; Lk. 1:15
DRINK (*v.*) Ex. 15:24, what shall we *d*?
Ex. 17:1, no water for people to *d*
II Sam. 23:16, David would not *d*
Ps. 36:8, *d* of the river of your pleasures
   60:3, *d* the wine of astonishment
   80:5, gave them tears to *d*
   110:7, he shall *d* of the brook in the way
Prov. 5:15, *D* waters of your own cistern
   31:5, lest they *d*, and forget the law
Eccl. 9:7, *d* wine with merry heart
Isa. 5:22, mighty to *d* wine
   65:13, my servants shall *d*, but you
Jer. 35:5, give Rechabites wine to *D*
   6, we will *d* not wine
   14, to this day they *d* none
Ezek. 4:11, you shall *d* water by measure
Amos 2:8, *d* the wine of the condemned
Zech. 9:15, they shall *d*, and make a noise
Mat. 10:42, whoso shall give to *d*
   20:22; Mk. 10:38, are you able to *d*
   26:27, saying *D* you all of it
   29; Lk. 22:18, when I *d* it new
   42, may not pass except I *d*
Mk. 9:41, shall give you cup of water to *d*
   16:18, if they *d* any deadly thing
Jn. 7:37, let him come to me, and *d*
   18:11, cup given me, shall I not *d* it?
Rom. 14:21, not good to *d* wine
I Cor. 10:4, did all *d* same spiritual drink
   11:25, as oft as you *d* it
   12:13, made to *d* into one Spirit
See Mk. 2:16; Lk. 7:33; 10:7
DRIVE Gen. 4:14, you have *d* me out
Ex. 23:28, hornets shall *d* out Hivite
Deut. 4:19, lest you be *d* to worship them
Job 24:3, they *d* away ass of the fatherless
   30:5, they were *d* forth from among men
Prov. 22:15, rod shall *d* it away
   25:23, north wind *d* away rain
Dan. 4:25; 5:21, they shall *d* you from men
Hos. 13:3, as chaff *d* with whirlwind
Lk. 8:29, he was *d* of the devil
James 1:6, wave *d* with the wind
See II Ki. 9:20; Jer. 8:3; Ezek. 31:11
DROP (*n.*) Job. 36:27
Isa. 40:15, as the *d* of a bucket

See Job 38:28; Lk. 22:44

DROP (*v.*) Deut. 32:2

Job. 29:22, my speech *d* upon them

Ps. 65:11, paths *d* fatness

68:8, heavens *d* at presence of God

Eccl. 10:18, through idleness house *d*

Isa. 45:8, *D* down, ye heavens

Ezek. 20:46, *d* your word toward the south

See II Sam. 21:10; Joel 3:18; Amos 9:13

DROSS Prov. 25:4; 26:23; Isa. 1:22, 25

DROUGHT Isa. 58:11; Jer. 17:8; Hos. 13:5

DROVE Gen. 3:24; 15:11; 32:16; 33:8

DROWN Song of Sol. 8:7, neither can floods *d* it

I Tim. 6:9, that *d* men in perdition

See Ex. 15:4; Mat. 18:6; Heb. 11:29

DROWSINESS Prov. 23:21

DRUNK I Sam. 30:12; II Sam. 11:13, David made Uriah *d*

I Ki. 20:16, was drinking himself *d*

Job 12:25; Ps. 107:27, stagger like a *d* man

Jer. 23:9, I am like a *d* man

Lam. 5:4, we have *d* water for money

Hab. 2:15, make him *d* also

Mat. 24:49; Lk. 12:45, drink with the *d*

Acts 2:15, these are not *d*

I Cor. 11:21, one is hungry, and another *d*

See Eph. 5:18; I Thess. 5:7

DRUNKARD Deut. 21:20

Prov. 23:21, *d* and glutton come to poverty

Prov. 26:9, as a thorn goes into hand of *d*

I Cor. 6:10, nor *d* shall inherit

See Ps. 69:12; Isa. 24:20; Joel 1:5; Nah. 1:10

DRUNKENNESS Eccl. 10:17, eat for strength, not for *d*!

Ezek. 23:33, shall be filled with *d*

See Lk. 21:34; Rom. 13:13; Gal. 5:21

DRY Prov. 17:22, a broken spirit *d* the bones

Isa. 44:3, pour floods on *d* ground

Mat. 12:43; Lk. 11:24, through *d* places

Mk. 5:29, fountain of blood *d* up

See Ps. 107:33, 35; Isa. 53:2; 56:3; Mk. 11:20

DUE Lev. 10:13, 14, your *d*, and your sons' *d*

26:4; Deut. 11:14, rain in *d* season

Prov. 15:23, word spoken in *d* season

Mat. 18:34, pay all that was *d*

Lk. 23:41, the *d* reward of our deeds

Rom. 5:6, in *d* time Christ died

Gal. 6:9, in *d* season we shall reap

See Prov. 3:27; I Cor. 15:8; Titus 1:3

DULL Mat. 13:15; Acts 28:27; Heb. 5:11

DUMB Ex. 4:11, who makes the *d*

Prov. 31:8, open your mouth for the *d*

Isa. 35:6, the tongue of the *d* shall sing

53:7; Acts 8:32, as sheep before shearers is *d*

56:10, they are all *d* dogs

Ezek. 3:26, be *d* and shall not be a reprover

Hab. 2:19, woe to him that says to *d* stone

DUNG I Sam. 2:8; Ps. 113:7

Lk. 13:8, till I dig about it, and *d* it

14:35, neither fit for land nor *d*-hill

Phil. 3:8, count all things but *d*

See Neh. 2:13, Lam. 4:5; Mal. 2:3

DUNGEON Ex. 12:29; Jer. 38:6; Lam. 3:53

DURABLE Prov. 8:18; Isa. 23:18

DURETH Mat. 13:21

DURST Mat. 22:46; Mk. 12:34, nor *d* ask questions

Jn. 21:12, none of disciples *d* ask

See Esther 7:5; Job 32:6; Acts 5:13; Jude 9

DUST Gen. 2:7, Lord God formed man of *d*

3:14, *d* shall you eat

19, *d* you are

18:27, who am but *d* and ashes

Job 22:24; 27:16, lay up gold as *d*

42:6, I repent in *d* and ashes

Ps. 30:9, shall the *d* praise you?

102:14, servants favor *d* thereof

103:14, remembers that we are *d*

Isa. 40:12, comprehended *d* of the earth

65:25, *d* shall be serpent's meat

Lam. 3:29, he puts his mouth in the *d*

Dan. 12:2, many that sleep in *d* shall awake

Mic. 7:17, lick the *d* like a serpent

Lk. 10:11, even *d* of your city

Acts 22:23, as they threw *d* into the air

DUTY Eccl. 12:13, the whole *d* of man

Lk. 17:10, that which was our *d* to do

Rom. 15:27, their *d* is to minister

DWELL Deut. 12:11, cause his name to *d*

I Sam. 4:4; II Sam. 6:2; I Chron. 13:6, *d* between the cherubims

I Ki. 8:30; II Chron. 6:21, heaven your *d* place

Ps. 23:6, will *d* in the house of the Lord

37:3, so shall you *d* in the land

84:10, than to *d* in tents of wickedness

133:1, good for brethren to *d* together

Isa. 33:14, who shall *d* with devouring fire?

16, he shall *d* on high

57:15, I *d* in the high and holy place

Jn. 6:56, *d* in me, and I in him

14:10, the Father that *d* in me

17, for he *d* with you, and shall be in you

Rom. 7:17, sin that *d* in me

Col. 2:9, in him *d* fullness of Godhead

3:16, word of Christ *d* in you richly

I Tim. 6:16, *d* in the light

II Pet. 3:13, wherein *d* righteousness

I Jn. 3:17, how *d* the love of God in him?

4:12, God *d* in us

See Zech. 9:6; Rom. 8:9; II Cor. 6:16

E

EACH Isa. 57:2, *e* walking in uprightness

Ezek. 4:6, *e* day for a year

Acts 2:3, cloven tongues sat on *e*

Phil. 2:3, let *e* esteem other

See Ex. 18:7; Ps. 85:10; II Thess. 1:3

EAGLE Ex. 19:4, how I bare you on *e* wings

II Sam. 1:23, were swifter than *e*

Ps. 103:5, youth renewed like *e*

Isa. 40:13, mount up with wings as *e*

Mat. 24:28; Lk. 17:37, *e* be gathered

See Dan. 4:33; Obad. 4: Rev. 4:7; 12:14

EAR (*v.*) Ex. 34:21; Deut. 21:4; I Sam. 8:12

EARLY Ps. 46:5, and that right *e*

63:1, *e* will I seek you
90:14, satisfy us *e* with your mercy
Prov. 1:28; 8:17, seek me *e* shall find me
Hos. 6:4; 13:3, as *e* dew
James 5:7, the *e* and latter rain
See Judg. 7:3; Lk. 24:22; Jn. 20:1
EARNEST Jer. 31:20, I do *e* remember him sill
Mic. 7:3, do evil with both hands *e*
Lk. 22:44, in agony he prayed more *e*
Rom. 8:19, the *e* expectation of the creature
I Cor. 12:31, covet *e* best gifts
II Cor. 1:22; 5:5, the *e* of the Spirit
5:2, *e* desiring to be clothed
Eph. 1:14, the *e* of our inheritance
Phil. 1:20, to my *e* expectation and hope
Jude 3, *e* contend for the faith
See Acts 3:12; Heb. 2:1; James 5:17
EARNS Hag. 1:6
EARRING Gen. 24:47; 35:4; Ex. 32:2; Num.
31:50; Judg. 8:24; Job 42:11; Ezek. 16:12
EARS Ex. 10:2, tell it in *e* of your son
Neh. 1:6, let your *e* by attentive
Job 12:11; 34:3, does not *e* try words?
15:21, dreadful sound is in his *e*
28:22, heard fame with our *e*
29:11, when the *e* heard me, it blessed me
Ps. 18:6, my cry came even into his *e*
34:15, his *e* are open upon their cry
58:4, deaf adder that stops her *e*
115:6; 135:17, they have *e*, but hear not
Prov. 17:4, liar gives *e* to naughty tongue
18:15, *e* of wise seeks knowledge
20:12, hearing *e*, seeing eye, Lord made
21:13, stops *e* at cry of the poor
23:9, speak not in *e* of a fool
25:12, wise reprover on obedient *e*
26:17, one that takes dog by the *e*
Isa. 6:10; Mat. 13:15, make *e* heavy
48:8, from that time your *e* not opened
Jer. 9:20, let your *e* receive word of the Lord
Amos 3:12, out of mouth of lion piece on
an *e*
Mat. 10:27, what you hear in *e*, preach
13:16, blessed are your *e*
26:51; Mk. 14:47, smote off *e*
Mk. 7:33, put his fingers into *e*
8:18, having *e*, hear ye not?
Acts 7:51, uncircumcised in heart and *e*
17:20; strange things to our *e*
II Tim. 4:3, having itching *e*;
James 5:4, entered into *e* of the Lord
I Pet. 3:12, his *e* are open to prayer
See Mat. 11:15; Mk. 4:9; Rev. 2:7
EARS (*of corn*) Deut. 23:25; Mat. 12:1
EARTH Gen. 8:22, while *e* remains
10:25, in his days was *e* divided
Num. 14:21, all *e* filled with glory
16:30, if the *e* open her mouth
Deut. 32:1, O *e*, hear the words of my mouth
Josh. 3:11; Zech. 6:5, Lord of all the *e*
Josh. 23:14, going way of all the *e*
I Ki. 8:27, will God dwell on the *e*?
II Ki. 5:17, two mules' burden of *e*
Job 7:1, appointed time to man upon *e*

9:24, *e* given into hand of wicked
19:25, stand at latter day upon *e*
26:7, hangs *e* upon nothing
38:4, when I laid foundations of the *e*
41:33, on *e* there is not his like
Ps. 2:8, uttermost part of *e*
8:1, excellent is your name in *e*
16:3, to saints that are in the *e*
25:13, his seed shall inherit the *e*
33:5, the *e* is full of the goodness
37:9, 11, 22, wait on Lord, shall inherit *e*
46:2, not fear, though *e* be removed
8, desolations made in the *e*
10, will be exalted in the *e*
Ps. 47:9, shields of the *e* belong to God
48:2, joy of the whole *e*
50:4, call to *e*, that he may judge
57:5; 108:5, glory above all the *e*
58:11, a God that judges in the *e*
60:2, made the *e* to tremble
63:9, lower parts of the *e*
67:6; Ezek. 34:27, *e* yield increase
Ps. 68:8, *e* shook, Heavens dropped
71:20, bring me up from depths of the *e*
72:6, showers that water the *e*
16, handful of corn in the *e*
73:9, tongue walks through *e*
25, none on *e* I desire beside you.
75:8; Isa. 24:19, *e* dissolved
Ps. 83:18; 97:9, most high over all *e*
97:1, Lord reigns, let *e* rejoice
99:1, Lord reigns, let *e* be moved
102:25; 104:5; Prov. 8:29; Isa. 48:13, laid
foundation of *e*
Ps. 104:13, the *e* is satisfied
24, the *e* is full of your riches
112:2, seed, mighty upon *e*
115:16, *e* given to children of men
119:19, stranger in the *e*
64, the *e* full of your mercy
90, established the *e*, it abides
146:4, he returns to the *e*
147:8, prepares rain for the *e*
148:13, glory above *e* and Heaven
Prov. 3:19; Isa. 24:1, Lord founded the *e*
8:23, set up from everlasting, or ever *e* was
26, he had not yet made *e*, no fields
11:31, righteous recompensed in *e*
30:14, teeth as knives to devour poor
from *e*
16, the *e* not filled with water
21, for three things *e* is disquieted
24, four things little upon *e*
Eccl. 1:4, the *e* abides forever
3:21, spirit of beast goes to *e*
5:9, profit of the *e* for all
12:7, dust return to *e*
Isa. 4:2, fruit of *e* excellent
11:9, *e* full of knowledge of the Lord
13:13, *e* shall remove out of her place
14:16, is this the man that made *e* tremble
26:9, when your judgments are in the *e*
21, *e* shall disclose her blood
40:22, sits on circle of the *e*

28, Creator of ends of *e* faints not
44:24, spreads abroad *e* by myself
45:22, be saved, all ends of the *e*
49:13, by joyful, O *e*
66:1, the *e* is my footstool
8, shall *e* bring forth in one day?
Jer. 15:10, man of contention to whole *e*
22:29; Mic. 1:2, O *e*, *e*, *e*, hear word of Lord
31:22, has created new thing in *e*
51:15, made the *e* by his power
Ezek. 9:9, the Lord has forsaken the *e*
43:2, the *e* shined with his glory
Hos. 2:22, the *e* shall hear the corn
Amos 3:5, bird fall in snare on *e*
8:9, darken *e* in the clear day
9:9, least grain fall upon the *e*
Jonah 2:6, *e* with bars about me
Mic. 6:2, ye strong foundations of the *e*
7:2, good man perished out of the *e*
17, move like worms of the *e*
Nah. 1:5, *e* burnt up at his presence
Hab. 2:14, *e* filled with knowledge
3:3, the *e* full of his praise
Hag. 1:10, *e* stayed from her fruit
Zech. 4:10, eyes of the Lord run through *e*
Mal. 4:6, lest I smite *e* with a curse
Mat. 5:5, meek shall inherit *e*
35, swear not by the *e*
6:19, treasures upon *e*
9:6; Lk. 5:24, power on *e* to forgive
Mat. 10:34, to send peace on *e*
13:5; Mk. 4:5, not much *e*
Mat. 16:19; 18:18, shall bind on *e*
18:19, shall agree on *e*
23:9, call no man father on *e*
25:18, 25, digged in the *e*
Mk. 4:28, *e* brings forth fruit of herself
31, less than all seeds in the *e*
Mk. 9:3, no fuller on *e* can white them
Lk. 2:14, on *e* peace
23:44, darkness over all *e*
Jn. 3:12, I have told you *e* things
31, of *e* is *e*, and speaks of the *e*
12:32, lifted up from the *e*
17:4, I have glorified you on the *e*
Acts 8:33, life taken from the *e*
9:4, 8; 26:14, Saul fell to the *e*
22:22, away with such a fellow from *e*
Rom. 10:18, sound went into all *e*
I Cor. 15:47, first man is of the *e*, *e*
48, as is the *e*, such are they that are *e*
49, the image of the *e*
II Cor. 4:7, treasure in *e* vessels
Phil. 3:19, who mind *e* things
Col. 3:2, affection not on things on *e*
Heb. 6:7, *e* drinks in the rain
11:13, strangers on the *e*
12:25, refused him that spoke on *e*
26, voice then shook the *e*
James 3:15, this wisdom is *e*
5:5, lived in pleasure on *e*
7, the precious fruit of the *e*
18, and the *e* brought forth her fruit
II Pet. 3:10, the *e* shall be burnt up

Rev. 5:10, we shall reign on the *e*
EARTHQUAKE I Ki. 19:11; Mat. 24:7
EASE Ex. 18:22, so shall it be *e* for yourself
Deut. 28:65, among nations find no *e*
Job 12:5, thought of him that is at *e*
16:6, though I forbear, what am I *e*?
21:23, dies being wholly at *e*
Ps. 25:13, his soul shall dwell at *e*
Isa. 32:9, 11, women that are at *e*
Mat. 9:5; Mk. 2:9; Lk. 5:23, is *e* to say
19:24; Mk. 10:25; Lk. 18:25, *e* for camel
I Cor. 13:5, not *e* provoked
Heb. 12:1, sin which does so *e* beset
EAST Ex. 10:13, Lord brought an *e* wind
Job. 1:3, greatest of all men of the *e*
15:2, fill his belly with *e* wind
27:21, *e* wind carries him away
38:24, scatters *e* wind on the earth
Ps. 48:7, break ships with the *e* wind
75:6, promotion comes not from *e*
103:12, as far as *e* from west
Isa. 27:8, stays rough wind in day of *e* wind
Ezek. 19:12, the *e* wind dries up her fruit
Hos. 12:1, Ephraim follows *e* wind
13:15, though fruitful, an *e* wind
shall come
See Jonah 4:5, 8; Mat. 2:1; 8:11; 24:27
EASY Prov. 14:6, I Cor. 14:9, James 3:17
EAT Gen. 2:17, in day you *e* you shall die
9:4; Lev. 19:26; Deut. 12:16, blood not *e*
24:33, not *e* till I have told
43:32, Egyptians might not *e* with Hebrews
Ex. 12:16, no work, save what man must *e*
23:11, that the poor may *e*
29:34, shall not be *e*, because holy
Lev. 25:20, what shall we *e* seventh year?
Num. 13:32, a land that *e* up inhabitants
Josh. 5:11, 12, *e* of old corn of the land
I Sam. 14:30, if haply people had *e* freely
28:20, had *e* no bread all day
22, *e* that you may have strength
II Sam. 19:42, have we *e* of king's cost?
I Ki. 19:5; Acts 10:13, angel said, Arise and *e*
II Ki. 4:43, 44, they shall *e*, and leave thereof
6:28, give your son, that we may *e* him
Neh. 5:2, corn, that we may *e*, and live
Job 3:24, my sighing comes before I *e*
5:5, whose harvest the hungry *e* up
6:6, *e* without salt
31:17, have *e* my morsel alone
Ps. 22:26, meek shall *e* and be satisfied
102:9, have *e* ashes like bread
Prov. 1:31; Isa. 3:10, *e* fruit of their own way
13:25, *e* to satisfying of soul
18:21, they that love it shall *e* the fruit
23:1, sit to *e* with ruler
24:13, *e* honey, because it is good
25:27, not good to *e* much honey
Eccl. 2:25, who can *e* more than I?
4:5, fool *e* his own flesh
5:11, goods increase, they increased that *e*
17, all his days also he *e* in darkness
19; 6:2, not power to *e* thereof
Eccl. 10:16, your princes *e* in the morning

17, blessed when princes *e* in due season
Isa. 4:1, we will *e* our own bread
   7:15, 22, butter and honey shall be *e*
   11:7; 65:25, lion *e* straw like ox
   29:8, he *e*, awakes, and is hungry
   51:8, worm shall e them like wool
   55:1, come ye, buy and *e*
   2, *e* ye that which is good
   65:13, my servants shall *e*, but ye shall be
Jer. 5:17, they shall *e* up your harvest
   15:16, words were found, and I did *e* them
   24:2; 29:17, figs could not be *e*
   31:29; Ezek. 18:2, the fathers have *e* sour
   grapes
Ezek. 3:1, 2, 3, *e* this roll
Dan. 4:33, *e* grass as oxen
Hos. 10:13, have *e* the fruit of lies
Mic. 7:1, there is no cluster to *e*
Mat. 6:25; Lk. 12:22, what ye shall *e*
Mat. 9:11; Mk. 2:16; Lk. 15:2, why *e* with
   publicans
Mat. 12:1, ears of corn, and *e*
   4, *e* shewbread, which was not lawful to *e*
   14:16; Lk. 9:13, give ye them to *e*
   15:20, to *e* with unwashen hands
   27; Mk. 7:28, dogs *e* of crumbs
   32; Mk. 8:1, multitude have nothing to *e*
   24:49, to *e* and drink with the drunken
Mk. 2:16, when they saw him *e* with
   6:31, no leisure so much as to *e*
Mk. 11:14, no man *e* fruit of you
Lk. 5:33, but your disciples *e* and drink
   10:8, *e* such things as are set before you
   12:19, take your ease, *e*, drink
   13:26, we have *e* and drunk in your
   presence
   15:23, let us *e* and be merry
   22:30, that you may *e* at my table
   24:43, he took it, and did *e* before them
Jn. 4:31, Master, *e*
   32, meat to *e* ye know not of
   6:26, because ye did *e* of the loaves
   52, can this man give us his flesh to *e*?
   53, except ye *e* the flesh
Acts 2:46, did *e* their meat with gladness
   9:9, Saul did neither *e* nor drink
   11:3, you did *e* with them
   23:14, *e* nothing until we have slain Paul
Rom. 14:2, one believes he may *e* all things
   6, *e* to the Lord
   20, who *e* with offence
   21, neither to *e* flesh nor drink wine
I Cor. 5:11, with such an one no not to *e*
   8:7, *e* it is a thing offered to idol
   8, neither if we *e* are we better
   13, I will *e* no flesh while world
   9:4, have we not power to *e*
   10:3, all *e* same spiritual meat
   27, *e*, asking no question
II Thess. 3:10, work not, neither should he *e*,
Heb. 13:10, whereof they have no right to *e*
Rev. 2:7, *e* of the tree of life
   17, will give to *e* of hidden manna
   19:18, *e* flesh of kings

See Judg. 14:14; Prov. 31:27; Isa. 1:19; 65:4
EDGE Prov. 5:4; Eccl. 10:10; Heb. 4:12
EDIFY Rom. 14:19, wherewith none may *e*
   15:2, please his neighbor to *e*
I Cor. 8:1, charity *e*
   10:23, all things lawful, but *e* not
   14:3, he that prophesies speaks to *e*
   4, *e* himself, *e* the church
Eph. 4:12, for *e* of the body of Christ
See II Cor. 10:8; 13:10; I Tim. 1:4
EFFECT Num. 30:8, make vow of none *e*
II Chron. 7:11, Solomon prosperously *e* all
Ps. 33:10, devices of the people of none *e*
Isa. 32:17, the *e* of righteousness quietness
I Cor. 1:17, lest cross be of none *e*
Gal. 5:4, Christ is become of none *e*
See Rom. 3:3; 4:14; 9:6; Gal. 3:17
EFFECTUAL I Cor. 16:9
Eph. 3:7; 4:16, the *e* working
James 5:16, *e* prayer of righteous man
See II Cor. 1:6; Gal. 2:8; I Thess. 2:13
EFFEMINATE I Cor. 6:9
EGG Job 6:6, taste in the white of an *e*?
   39:14, ostrich leaveth *e* in earth
Lk 11:12; if he ask an *e*
See Deut. 22:6; Isa. 10:14; 59:5; Jer. 17:11
EITHER Gen. 31:24, speak not *e* good or bad
Eccl. 11:6, prosper, *e* this or that
Mat. 6:24; Lk. 16:13, *e* hate the one
Jn. 19:18, on *e* side one
Rev. 22:2, on *e* side the river
See Deut. 17:3; 28:51; Isa. 7:11; Mat. 12:33
ELDER I Sam. 15:30
Job 15:10, aged men, much *e* than your
   father
   32:4, waited, because they were *e* than he
Prov. 31:23, husband known among *e*
Mat. 15:2; Mk. 7:3, tradition of the *e*
I Tim. 5:17, let *e* that rule be worthy
Titus 1:5, ordain e in every city
Heb. 11:2, the *e* obtained good report
James 5:14, call for *e* of the church
I Pet. 5:1, the *e* exhort, who am an *e*
   5, younger submit to the *e*
See Jn. 8:9; I Tim. 5:2; II Jn. 1; III Jn. 1
ELECT Isa. 42:1
   45:4, mine *e* I have called by name
   65:9, 22, mine *e* shall inherit
Mat. 24:22; Mk. 13:20, for *e* sake shortened
   24; Mk. 13:22, deceive very *e*
   31; Mk. 13:27, gather together his *e*
Lk. 18:7, avenge his own *e*
Rom. 8:33, to charge of God's *e*?
Col. 3:12, put on as the *e* of God
I Tim. 5:21, charge you before *e* angels
I Pet. 1:2, *E* according to foreknowledge
   2:6, corner stone *e*, precious
See II Tim. 2:10; I Pet. 5:13; II Jn. 13
ELECTION Rom. 9:11; 11:5, I Thess. 1:4
ELEMENTS Gal. 4:3, 9; II Pet. 3:10
ELEVEN Gen. 32:22, Jacob took his *e* sons
   37:9, and *e* stars made obeisance
Acts 1:26, he was numbered with the *e*
See Mat. 28:16; Mk. 16:14; Lk. 24:9

ELOQUENT Ex. 4:10; Isa. 3:3; Acts 18:24

EMBOLDEN Job 16:3; I Cor. 8:10

EMBRACE Job 24:8, *e* rock for shelter
  Eccl. 3:5, a time to *e*
  Heb. 11:13, seen and *e* promises
  See Prov. 4:8; 5:20; Lam. 4:5; Acts 20:1

EMBROIDER Ex. 28:39; 35:35; 38:23

EMINENT Ezek. 16:24, 31, 39, 17:22

EMPIRE Esther 1:20

EMPLOY Deut. 20:19; I Chron. 9:33; Ezra 10:15;
  Ezek. 39:14

EMPTY Gen. 31:42; Mk. 12:3; Lk. 1:53; 20:10,
  sent *e* away
  Ex. 3:21, ye shall not go *e*
  23:15; Deut. 16:16, appear before me *e*
  Job 22:9, you have sent widows away *e*
  Eccl. 11:3, clouds *e* themselves on the Earth
  Isa. 29:8, awakes, and his soul is *e*
  Jer. 48:11, Moab *e* from vessel to vessel
  Nah. 2:2, the emptiers have *e* them out
  Mat. 12:44, come, he finds it *e*
  See II Sam. 1:22; II Ki. 4:3; Hos. 10:1

EMULATION Rom. 11:14; Gal. 5:20

ENABLED I Tim. 1:12

ENCAMP Ps. 27:3, though host *e* against me
  34:7, angel of Lord *e* round
  See Num. 10:31; Job 19:12; Ps. 53:5

ENCOUNTERED Acts 17:18

ENCOURAGE Ps. 64:5, they *e* themselves in an
  evil matter
  See I Sam. 30:6; II Chron. 31:4; 35:2; Isa. 41:7

END Gen. 6:13, the *e* of all flesh before me
  Ex. 23:16; Deut. 11:12, in the *e* of the year
  Num. 23:10, let my last *e* be like his
  Deut. 8:16, do thee good at your latter *e*
  Job 8:7; 42:12, your latter *e* shall increase
  16:3, shall vain words have an *e*?
  26:10, till day and night come to an *e*?
  Ps. 7:9, wickedness of wicked come to an *e*
  9:6, destructions come to perpetual *e*
  37:37, the *e* of that man is peace
  73:17, the understood I their *e*
  102:27, the same, your years have no *e*
  107:27, are at their wit's *e*
  119:96, an *e* of all perfection
  Prov. 14:12, the *e* thereof are ways of death
  17:24, eyes of fool in *e* of earth
  19:20, be wise in your latter *e*
  Prov. 25:8, lest know not what to do in *e*
  Eccl. 3:11, find out from beginning to the *e*
  4:8, no *e* of all his labor
  16, no *e* of all the people
  7:2, that is the *e* of all men
  10:13, the *e* of his talk is madness
  12:12 of making books there is no *e*
  Isa. 9:7, of his government shall be no *e*
  46:10, declaring *e* from beginning
  Jer. 5:31, what will you do in *e* thereof?
  8:20, harvest past, summer *e*
  Jer. 17:11, at his *e* shall be a fool
  29:11, to give you an expected *e*
  31:17, there is hope in your *e*
  Lam. 1:9, remember not her last *e*
  4:18; Ezek. 7:2, our *e* is near, *e* is come

Ezek. 21:25; 35:5, iniquity shall have an *e*

Dan. 8:17, 19; 11:27, at the time of *e*
  12:8, what shall be the *e*
  13, go your way till *e* be

Hab. 2:3, at the *e* it shall speak

Mat. 10:22; 24:13; Mk. 13:13, endures to *e*
  13:39, harvest is *e* of the world
  24:3, what sign of the *e* of the world?
  6; Mk. 13:7; Lk. 21:9, the eye is not yet
  14, then shall the *e* come
  31, gather from one *e* of Heaven
  26:58, Peter sat to see the *e*
  28:20, I am with you, even unto the *e*

Mk. 3:26, cannot stand, but has an *e*

Lk. 1:33, of his kingdom there shall be no *e*
  22:37, things concerning me have an *e*

Jn. 13:1, he loved them unto the *e*
  18:37, to this *e* was I born

Rom. 6:21, the *e* of those things is death
  22, the *e* everlasting life
  10:4, the *e* of the law for righteousness

I Cor. 10:11, on whom *e* of world are come

Phil. 3:19, whose *e* is destruction

I Tim 1:5, the *e* of the commandment

Heb. 6:8, whose *e* is to be burned
  16, an oath an *e* of strife
  7:3, neither beginning nor *e* of life
  9:26, once in the *e* has he appeared
  13:7, considering *e* of their conversation

James 5:11, you have seen *e* of the Lord

I Pet. 1:9, receiving the *e* of your faith
  13, be sober, and hope to the *e*
  4:7, the *e* of all things is at hand

Rev. 2:26, keeps my works unto *e*
  21:6; 22:13, the beginning and the *e*

ENDAMAGE Ezra 4:13

ENDANGER Eccl. 10:9; Dan. 1:10

ENDEAVOR Ps. 28:4; Eph. 4:3; II Pet. 1:15

ENDLESS I Tim 1:4; Heb. 7:16

ENDUE Gen. 30:20; II Chron. 2:12; Lk. 24:49

ENDURE Gen. 33:14, children to be able to *e*
  Esther 8:6, how can I *e* to see evil
  Job 8:15, hold it fast, but it shall not *e*
  31:23, I could not *e*
  Ps. 9:7, 102:12; 104:31, Lord shall *e* forever
  52:1, goodness of God *e* continually
  72:5, as long as sun and moon *e*
  17, his name shall *e* forever
  100:5, his truth *e* to all generations
  106:1, 107:1; 136:1; 138:8; Jer. 33:11, his
  mercy *e* forever
  111:3; 112:3, 9 his righteousness *e* forever
  119:160, every one of your judgments *e*
  Prov. 27:24, does *e* to every generation
  Ezek. 22:14, can your heart *e*?
  Mat. 10:22; 24:13; Mk. 13:13, *e* to the end
  Mk. 4:17, so *e* but for a time
  Jn. 6:27, meat that *e* unto life
  Rom. 9:22, God *e* with much longsuffering
  I Cor. 13:7, charity *e* all things
  II Tim. 2:3, *e* hardness as good soldier
  James 1:12, blessed is man that *e* temptation
  5:11, we count them happy who *e*
  I Pet. 1:25, the word of the Lord *e* forever

2:19, if a man for conscience *e* grief
See Heb. 10:32; 11:27; 12:2, 3
ENEMY Ex. 23:22, I will be *e* to your *e*
Deut. 32:31, our *e* themselves being judges
Josh. 7:12, Israel turned backs before *e*
Judg. 5:31, so let all your *e* perish
Job 13:24, wherefore holdest thou me for *e*?
Ps. 8:2, still the *e* and avenger
Ps. 23:5, in presence of my *e*
38:19, my *e* are lively
61:3, a strong tower from the *e*
72:9, his *e* shall lick the dust
119:98, wiser than my *e*
139:22, I count them my *e*
Prov. 16:7, makes his *e* at peace
24:17, rejoiced not when *e* fails
25:21; Rom. 12:20, if *e* hunger, give bread
27:6, kisses of *e* deceitful
Isa. 9:11, Lord shall join *e* together
63:10, he was turned to be their *e*
Jer. 15:11, will cause *e* to entreat you well
30:14, wounded you with wound of *e*
Mat. 5:43, said, You shall hate your *e*
44; Lk. 6:27, 35, I say Love your *e*
13:25; 28:39, his *e* sowed tares
Lk. 19:43, your *e* shall cast a trench
Acts 13:10, you *e* of all unrighteousness
Rom. 5:10, if when *e* we were reconciled
11:28, concerning the gospel they are *e*
Gal. 4:16, am I become your *e*?
Phil. 3:18, the *e* of the cross
Col. 1:21, were *e* in your mind
II Thess. 3:15, count him not as an *e*
James 4:4, friend of the world is the *e* of God
See Ps. 110:1; Isa. 62:8; Jer. 15:14; Heb. 10:13
ENGAGED Jer. 30:21
ENGRAFTED James 1:21
ENGRAVE Ex. 28:11; 35:35; 38:23; Zech. 3:9;
II Cor. 3:7
ENJOIN Job 36:23; Phile. 8; Heb. 9:20
ENJOY Lev. 26:34; II Chron. 36:21, land shall
e her sabbaths
Eccl. 2:1, *e* pleasure, this also is vanity
24, 3:13; 5:18, soul *e* good
I Tim. 6:17, gives us all things to *e*
See Num. 36:8; Isa. 65:22; Heb. 11:25
ENLARGE Duet. 12:20
Ps. 4:1; you have *e* me in distress
25:17, troubles of heart *e*
119:32, when you shall *e* my heart
Isa. 5:14, Hell has *e* herself
II Cor. 6:11, 13; 10:15, our heart is *e*
See Isa. 54:2; Hab. 2:5; Mat. 23:5
ENLIGHTEN Ps. 19:8; Eph. 1:18; Heb. 6:4
ENMITY Rom. 8:7, carnal mind is *e*
Eph. 2:15, 16 having abolished the *e*
James 4:4, friendship of world *e* with God
See Gen. 3:15; Num. 35:21; Lk. 23:12
ENOUGH Gen. 45:28, it is *e*, Joseph is alive
Ex. 36:5, people bring more than *e*
II Sam. 24:16; I Ki. 19:4; I Chron. 21:15, Lk.
22:38, it is *e*, stay your hand
Prov. 28:19, shall have poverty *e*
Isa. 56:11, dogs which can never have *e*

Jer. 49:9, will destroy till they have *e*
Hos. 4:10, eat, and not have *e*
Obad. 5, stolen till they had *e*
Mal. 3:10, room *e* to receive it
ENQUIRE II Sam. 16:23, as if a man had
e of oracle
II Ki. 3:11, is there not a prophet to *e*?
Ps. 78:34, returned and *e* early after God
Ezek. 14:3, should I be *e* of all by them?
20:3, 31, I will not be *e*
36:37, I will yet for this be *e* of
Zeph. 1:6, those that have not *e* for
Mat. 10:11, *e* who in it is worthy
I Pet. 1:10, of which salvation the prophets *e*
See Deut 12:30; Isa. 21:12; Jn. 4:52
ENRICH I Sam. 17:25; Ps. 65:9; Ezek. 27:33;
I Cor. 1:5; II Cor. 9:11
ENSAMPLE I Cor. 10:11, happened for *e*
Phil. 3:17, as you have us for an *e*
II Thess. 3:9, to make ourselves an *e*
See I Thess. 1:7; I Pet. 5:3; II Pet. 2:6
ENSIGN Ps. 74:4; Isa. 5:26; 11:10; 18:3
ENSNARED Job 34:30
ENSUE I Pet. 3:11
ENTANGLE Ex. 14:3; Mat. 22:15; Gal. 5:1
ENTER Ps. 100:4
119:130, the *e* of your word gives light
Isa. 26:2, righteous nation may *e* in
Ezek. 44:5, mark well *e* in of the house
Mat. 6:6, prayest, *e* into your closet
7:13; Lk. 13:24, *e* in at strait gate
10:11; Lk. 10:8, 10, what city you *e*
Mat. 18:8; Mk. 9:43, better to *e* into life
19:17, if you will *e* into life, keep
25:21, well done, *e* into joy
Mk. 5:12; Lk. 8:32, we may *e* into swine
14:38; Lk. 22:46, lest you *e* into temptation
Lk. 9:34, feared as they *e* cloud
13:24, many will seek to *e*
Rom. 5:12, sin *e* into world
I Cor. 2:9, neither have *e* into heart of man
Heb. 3:11, 18, shall not *e* into rest
II Pet. 1:11, so an *e* shall be ministered
See Deut. 23:2; Ps. 143:2; Mat. 15:17
ENTICE Judg. 14:15; 16:5
II Chron. 18:19, Lord said, who shall *e* Ahab?
Prov. 1:10, if sinners *e* you
I Cor. 2:4; Col. 2:4, with *e* words
See Job 31:27; Prov. 16:29; James 1:14
ENTIRE James 1:4
ENTREAT Mat. 22:6; Lk. 18:32
ENTRY I Chron 9:19; Prov. 8:3; Ezek. 8:5
ENVIRON Josh 7:9
ENVY Job 5:2, *e* slays the silly one
Ps. 73:3, I was *e* at the foolish
Prov. 3:31, *E* not the oppressor
14:30, *e* is rottenness of the bones
23:17, let not heart *e* sinners
24:1, 19, be not *e* against evil men
27:4, who is able to stand before *e*?
Mat. 27:18; Mk. 15:10, for *e* they delivered
Acts 7:9, patriarchs moved with *e*
13:45; 17:5, Jews filled with *e*
Rom. 1:29, full of *e*, murder

13:13, walk honestly, not in *e*
I Cor. 3:3, among you *e* and strife
13:4, charity *e* not
II Cor. 12:20, I fear lest there be *e*
Gal. 5:21, works of flesh are *e*, murders
26, *e* one another
Phil. 1:15, preach Christ even of *e*
I Tim. 6:4, whereof comes *e*
Titus 3:3, living in malice and *e*
James 4:5, spirit in us lusts to *e*?
See Gen. 37:11; Ps. 106:16; Ezek. 31:9; 35:11
EPISTLE II Cor. 3:1
II Thess. 2:15; 3:14, by word or *e*
II Pet. 3:16, as also in all his *e*
See Acts 15:30; II Cor. 7:8; II Thess. 3:17
EQUAL Ps. 17:2, eyes behold things that are *e*
55:13, a man my *e*, my guide
Prov. 26:7, legs of lame not *e*
Isa. 40:25; 46:5, to whom shall I be *e*?
Ezek. 18:25, 29; 33:17, 20, is not my way *e*?
Mat. 20:12, have made them *c* to us
Lk. 20:36, are *e* to angels
Jn. 5:18; Phil. 2:6, *e* with God
Col. 4:1, give servants what is *e*
EQUITY Ps. 98:9, judge the people with *e*
Prov. 1:3, receive instruction of *e*
2:9, understand judgment and *e*
17:26, not good to strike princes for *e*
Eccl. 2:21, a man whose labor is in *e*
See Isa. 11:4; 59:14; Mic. 3:9; Mal. 2:6
ERECTED Gen. 33:20
ERR Ps. 95:10, people that do *e* in their heart
119:21, do *e* from your commandments
Isa. 3:12; 9:16, lead thee cause thee to *e*
35:8, wayfaring men shall not *e*
Mat. 22:29; Mk. 12:24
I Tim. 6:10, have *e* from the faith
21, have *e* concerning the faith
James 1:16, do not *e*, beloved brethren
5:19, if any do *e* from truth
See Isa. 28:7; 29:24; Ezek. 45:20
ERRAND Gen. 24:33; Judg. 3:19; II Ki. 9:5
ERROR Ps. 19:12, who can understand his *e*?
Eccl. 5:6, neither say thou, it was an *e*
10:5, evil which I have seen as an *e*
Mat. 27:64, last *e* worse than first
James 5:20, coverts sinner from *e*
II Pet. 3:17, led away with *e* of wicked
I Jn. 4:6, the spirit of *e*
See Job 19:4; Rom. 1:27; Heb. 9:7; Jude 11
ESCAPE Gen. 19:17
I Ki. 18:40; II Ki. 9:15, let none of them *e*
Job 11:20, wicked shall not *e*
19:20, *e* with skin of my teeth
Ps. 55:8, I would hasten my *e*
Prov. 19:5, speaks lies shall not *e*
Eccl. 7:26, whoso pleases God shall *e*
Isa. 20:6, Heb. 2:3, how shall we *e*?
Amos 9:1, he that *e* shall not be delivered
Mat. 23:33, how can ye *e* damnation?
Jn. 10:39, he *e* out of their hands
Acts 27:44, they *e* all safe to land
28:4, he *e* sea, yet vengeance
Heb. 11:34, through faith *e* edge of sword

II Pet. 1:4, *e* corruption in the world
2:20, after they *e* pollutions
See Deut. 23:15; Ps. 124:7; I Cor. 10:13
ESCHEW Job 1:1; 2:3; I Pet. 3:11
ESPECIALLY Gal. 6:10; I Tim. 4:10; 5:8
ESPOUSE Jer. 2:2; II Cor. 11:2
ESPY Gen. 42:27; Josh. 14:7; Jer. 48:19
ESTABLISH Ps. 90:17, *e* works of our hands
Prov. 4:26, let your ways be *e*
12:19, lip of truth *e* for ever
16:12, throne *e* by righteousness
20:18, every purpose *e* by counsel
24:3, by understanding is house *e*
29:4, king by judgment *e* the land
Isa. 7:9, you will not believe, you shall not be *e*
16:5, in mercy shall the throne be *e*
Jer. 10:12; 51:15, he *e* world by wisdom
Mat. 18:16, two witnesses every word *e*
Rom. 3:31, yea, we *e* the law
Heb. 13:9, the heart be *e* with grace
II Pet. 1:12, be *e* in the present truth
See Amos 5:15; Hab. 2:12; Acts 16:5
ESTATE Ps. 136:23, remembered us in law *e*
Eccl. 1:16, lo, I am come to great *e*
Mk. 6:21, Herod made supper to chief *e*
Rom. 12:16, condescend to men of low *e*
Jude 6, angels kept not first *e*
See Ezek. 36:11; Dan. 11:7; Lk. 1:48
ESTEEM I Sam. 2:30, despise me shall be lightly *e*
18:23, I am a poor man, and lightly *e*?
Job 23:12, I have *e* the words of his mouth
36:19, will he *e* your riches?
41:27, he *e* iron as straw
Ps. 119:128, I *e* all your precepts
Isa. 53:4, did *e* him smitten
Lam. 4:2, *e* as earthen pitchers
Lk. 16:15, highly *e* among men
Rom. 14:5, one man *e* one day above another
Phil. 2:3, let each *e* other better
I Thess. 5:13, *e* highly for work's sake
Heb. 11:26, *E* reproach greater riches
See Prov. 17:28; Isa. 29:17; I Cor. 6:4
ESTIMATE Lev. 27:2, 14; Num. 18:16
ESTRANGED Job 19:13; Ps. 78:30; Jer. 19:4; Ezek. 14:5
ETERNAL Deut. 33:27, the *e* God is your refuge
Isa. 60:15, will make you an *e* excellency
Mat. 19:16; Lk. 10:25; 18:18, what shall I do that I may have *e* life?
25:46, righteous into life *e*
Mk. 3:29, is in danger of *e* damnation
10:30, receive in world, to come *e* life
Jn. 3:15, believes in him have *e* life
4:36 gathers fruit unto life *e*
Acts 13:48, many as were ordained to *e* life
Rom. 2:7, who seek for glory, *e* life
II Cor. 4:17, an *e* weight of glory
18, things not seen are *e*
5:1, house *e* in the heavens
Eph. 3:11, according to *e* purpose
I Tim. 6:12, 19 lay hold on *e* life
Titus 1:2, 3:7, in hope of *e* life

Heb. 5:9, author of *e* salvation
   6:2, doctrine of *e* judgment
   9:15, promise of *e* inheritance
I Pet. 5:10, called to *e* glory by Christ
I Jn. 1:2, *e* life, which was with the Father
   2:25, this is the promise, even *e* life
   3:15, no murderer has *e* life
   5:11, God has given to us *e* life
   13, know that you have *e* life
   20, this is true God, and *e* life
Jude 7, vengeance of *e* fire
ETERNITY Isa. 57:15
EUNUCH II Ki. 9:32; 20:18
   Isa. 56:3, neither *e* say, I am a dry tree
   Acts 8:27, *e* had come to Jerusalem
   See Acts 8:39
EVANGELIST Acts 21:8; Eph. 4:11
EVENING I Sam. 14:24
   I Ki. 17:6, brought bread morning and *e*
   Ps. 90:6, in *e* cut down and withers
   104:23, goes to his labor until the *e*
   141:2, prayer as the *e* sacrifice
   Jer. 6:4, shadows of *e* stretched out
   Hab. 1:8; Zeph. 3:3, *e* wolves
   Zech. 14:7, at *e* time shall be light
   Lk. 24:29, abide, for it is toward *e*
EVENT Eccl. 2:14; 9:2, 3
EVER Gen. 3:22, lest he eat, and live for *e*
   43:9; 44:32, let me bear blame for *e*
   Ex. 14:13, ye shall see them no more for *e*
   Lev. 6:13, fire *e* burning on altar
   Deut. 5:29; 12:28, be well with them for *e*
   32:40, lift up hand and say, I live for *e*
   Job 4:7, who *e* perished?
   Ps. 9:7, Lord shall endure for *e*
   12:7, you will preserve them for *e*
   22:26, your heart shall live for *e*
   23:6, dwell in house of the Lord for *e*
   29:10, Lord sits king for *e*
   33:11, counsel of Lord stands for *e*
   37:26, he is *e* merciful, and lends
   48:14, our God for *e* and *e*
   49:9, that he should still live for *e*
   51:3, my sin is *e* before me
   52:8, trust in mercy of God for *e* and *e*
   61:4, will abide in tabernacle for *e*
   74:19, forget not congregation of poor
   for *e*
   81:15, their time should have endured
   for *e*
   92:7, they shall be destroyed for *e*
   93:5, holiness becomes your house for *e*
   102:12, you shall endure for *e*
   105:8, remember his covenant for *e*
   132:14, this is my rest for *e*
   146:6, Lord keeps truth for *e*
   10, Lord shall reign for *e*
   Prov. 27:24, riches not for *e*
   Isa. 26:4, trust in Lord for *e*
   32:17, assurance for *e*
   34:10; Rev. 14:11, smoke shall go up for *e*
   40:8, word of God shall stand for *e*
   57:16, will not contend for *e*
   Lam. 3:31, Lord will not cast off for *e*

Mat. 6:13, yours is the glory for *e*
Jn. 8:35, servant abides not for *e*
   12:34, heard that Christ abides for *e*
   14:16, Comforter abide for *e*
Rom. 9:5, God blessed for *e*
I Thess. 4:17, so shall we *e* be with the Lord
   5:15, *e* follow good
II Tim. 3:7, *E* learning
Heb. 7:25, he *e* lives to make
   13:8, same yesterday, to day, and for *e*
See Mat. 24:21; Lk. 15:31; Jn. 10:8
EVERLASTING Ex. 40:15; Deut. 33:27
   Ps. 90:2, from *e* to *e* you are God
   139:24, lead me in way *e*
   Prov. 8:23, I was set up from *e*
   10:25, righteous is an *e* foundation
   Isa. 9:6, called the *e* Father
   26:4, in the Lord is *e* strength
   33:14, with *e* burnings
   35:10, 51:11; 61:7, *e* joy
   45:17, with *e* salvation
   54:8, with *e* kindness
   55:13, for an *e* sign
   56:5; 63:12, an *e* name
   60:19, 20, and *e* light
   Jer. 31:3, with an *e* love
   Mat. 18:8; 25:41, into *e* fire
   19:29, inherit *e* life
   25:46, into *e* punishment
   Jn. 3:16, 36, believes shall have *e* life
   4:14, water springs up into *e* life
   5:24, hears my word has *e* life
   6:27, meat which endures to *e* life
   40, sees Son my have *e* life
   12:50, his commandment is life *e*
   Acts 13:46, unworthy of *e* life
   Rom. 6:22, free from sin, the end *e* life
   Gal. 6:8, of Spirit reap life *e*
   II Thess. 1:9, punished with *e* destruction
   Jude 6, reserved in *e* chains
   Rev. 14:6, having the *e* gospel
   See Dan. 4:3; 7:27; II Pet. 1:11
EVERMORE Ps. 16:11, pleasures for *e*
   37:27, do good and dwell for *e*
   Ps. 121:8, preserve your going out for *e*
   133:3, the blessing life for *e*
   Jn. 6:34, *e* give us this bread
   I Thess. 5:16, rejoice *e*
   Heb. 7:28, consecrated for *e*
   Rev. 1:18, I am alive for *e*
EVERY Lev. 19:10, neither shall gather *e* grape
   Deut. 4:4, alive *e* one of you this day
   II Chron. 30:18, pardon *e* one
   Ps. 29:9, *e* one does speak of glory
   32:6, for this shall *e* one that is Godly
   68:30, till *e* one submit himself
   119:101, refrained from *e* evil way
   Prov. 2:9, *e* good path
   14:15, simple believes *e* word
   20:3, *e* fool will be meddling
   30:5, *E* word of God is pure
   Eccl. 10:3, said to *e* one he is a fool
   Jer. 51:29, *e* purpose of the Lord
   Mat. 4:4, by *e* word that proceeds

7:8; Lk. 11:10, *e* one that asks
Mk. 1:45, came from *e* quarter
Rom. 14:11, *e* knee bow, *e* tongue confess
II Cor. 10:5, *e* thought
Eph. 1:21; Phil. 2:9, far above *e* name
I Tim. 4:4, *e* creature of God
II Tim. 2:19, *e* one that names
    21, *e* good work
Heb. 12:1, *e* weight
James 1:17, *E* good and perfect gift
I Pet. 2:13, *e* ordinance of man
Rev. 6:11, robes given to *e* one
    See Gen. 27:29; Isa. 33:2; Acts 2:38; 17:27
EVIDENCE Jer. 32:10; Heb. 11:1
EVIDENT Gal. 3:11, that no man is justified
    is *e*
Phil. 1:28, an *e* token of perdition
    See Job 6:28; Heb. 7:14, 15
EVIL Gen. 6:5; 8:21, thoughts of heart only *e*
    47:9, few and *e* have the days
Deut. 28:54, eye *e* towards his brother
    56, her eye *e* towards husband
Job 2:10, receive good, and not *e*
    30:26, looked for good, then *e* came
Ps. 34:14; 37:27; Prov. 3:7, depart from *e*
    35:12; 109:5, they rewarded me *e*
    40:12, innumerable *e* have compassed
Prov. 14:19, *e* bow before the good
    15:3, beholding the *e* and good
    17:13, whoso rewards *e* for good
Isa. 1:4, a seed of *e*-doers
    5:20, that call *e* good, and good *e*
    7:15, 16, refuse the *e*, and choose
    the good
Jer. 2:13, have committed two *e*
    19, know it is an *e* thing and bitter
    42:6, whether good or *e*, we will obey
Mat. 5:45, rise on *e* and good
    6:34, sufficient unto the day is the *e*
    thereof
    7:11; Lk. 11:13, if ye, being *e*
    18, good tree cannot bring forth *e*
    9:4, wherefore think *e* in your hearts?
Mk. 9:39, lightly speak *e* of me
Lk. 6:22, cast out your name as *e*
    35, he is kind to the *e*
    45, *e* man brings forth *e*
Jn. 3:20, does *e* hates light
    18:23, if I have spoken *e*
Acts 23:5, not speak *e* of ruler
Rom. 7:19, the *e* I would not
    12:9, abhor that which is *e*
    17, recompense to no man *e* for *e*
    21, overcome *e* with good
I Thess. 5:22, appearance of *e*
I Tim. 6:10, the root of all *e*
II Tim. 4:18; James 3:16, every *e* work
Titus 3:2, speak *e* of no man
James 3:8, tongue an unruly *e*
I Pet. 3:9, no rendering *e* for *e*
EXACT Deut. 15:2, not *e* it of neighbor
Neh. 5:7, 10, 11, you *e* usury
    10:31, leave the *e* of every debt
Job. 11:6, God *e* of thee less

Lk. 3:13, *e* no more than what is
    See Ps. 89:22; Isa. 58:3; 60:17
EXALT I Chron. 29:11, *e* as head above all
Ps. 12:8, when vilest men are *e*
    34:3, let us *e* his name together
    92:10, my horn shall you *e*
Prov. 4:8, *e* her, and she shall promote thee
Prov. 11:11, by blessing of upright the city
    is *e*
    14:29, he that is hasty of spirit *e* folly
    14:34, righteousness *e* a nation
    17:19, he that *e* his gate
Isa. 2:2; Mic. 4:1, mountain of Lords'
    house *e*
    40:4, every valley shall be *e*
Ezek. 21:26, *e* him that is low
Mat. 11:23; Lk. 10:15, *e* to Heaven
II Cor. 11:20, if a man *e* himself
    12:7, *e* above measure
Phil. 2:9, God has highly *e* him
II Thess. 2:4, *e* himself above all that is called
I Pet. 5:6, he may *e* in due time
    See Ex. 15:2; Job 24:24; Lk. 1:52
EXAMINE Ps. 26:2, *E* me, O Lord
I Cor. 11:28, let a man *e* himself
II Cor. 13:5, *E* yourselves
    See Ezra 10:16; Acts 24:8; 25:26; I Cor. 9:3
EXAMPLE Jn. 13:15, I have given you an *e*
I Tim. 4:12, be thou an *e* of believers
I Pet. 2:21, Christ suffered, leaving an *e*
Jude 7, an *e* suffering vengeance
    See Mat. 1:19; I Cor. 10:6; Heb. 4:11; 8:5
EXCEED Mat. 5:20, except righteousness *e*
II Cor. 3:9, ministration does *e* in glory
    See I Sam. 20:41; II Chron. 9:6; Job 36:9
EXCEEDING Gen. 15:1, your *e* great reward
    27:34, an *e* bitter cry
Num. 14:7, land is *e* good
I Sam. 2:3, so *e* proud
Ps. 21:6, *e* glad with your countenance
Prov. 30:24, four things *e* wise
Jonah 1:16, men feared the Lord *e*
Mat. 2:10, with *e* great joy
    4:8, an *e* high mountain
    5:12, rejoice and be *e* glad
    8:28, possessed with devils, *e* fierce
    17:23; 26:22, they were *e* sorry
    19:25, they were *e* amazed
    26:38; Mk. 14:34, my soul is *e* sorrowful
Mk. 6:26, king *e* sorry
Lk. 23:8, Herod was *e* glad
Acts 7:20, Moses was *e* fair
    26:11, being *e* mad against them
Rom. 7:13, sin might become *e* sinful
II Cor. 4:17, *e* weight of glory
    7:4, *e* joyful in our tribulation
Eph. 1:19, the *e* greatness of his power
    2:7, the *e* riches of his grace
    3:20, able to do *e* abundantly
II Thess. 1:3, your faith grows *e*
II Pet. 1:4, *e* great and precious promises
Jude 24, present your faultless with *e* joy
    See I Sam. 26:21; Jonah 3:3; Heb. 12:21
EXCEL Gen. 49:4, you shall not *e*

Prov. 31:29, you *e* them all
Eccl. 2:13, wisdom *e* folly
II Cor. 3:10, the glory that *e*
See Ps. 103:20; I Cor. 14:12
EXCELLENCY Job 4:21, does not their *e* go away?
 13:11, shall not his *e* make you afraid?
Isa. 60:15, will make you an eternal *e*
I Cor. 2:1, not with *e* of speech
II Cor. 4:7, that the *e* of the power
Phil. 3:8, less for the *e* of Christ
EXCELLENT Job 37:23, *e* in power
Ps. 8:1, 9, how *e* is your name!
 16:3, to the *e*, in whom is my delight
 36:7, now *e* your loving kindness
Prov. 8:6; 22:20, I will speak of *e* things
 12:26, righteous more *e* than neighbor
 17:7, *e* speech becomes not a fool
 27, of a *e* spirit
Isa. 12:5, he has done *e* things
 28:29, is *e* in working
Dan. 5:12; 6:3, *e* spirit found in Daniel
Rom. 2:18; Phil. 1:10, things more *e*
I Cor. 12:31, a more *e* way
II Pet. 1:17, voice form the *e* glory
See Lk. 1:3; Heb. 1:4; 8:6; 11:4
EXCEPT Gen. 32:26, *e* you bless me
Deut. 32:30, *e* their Rock had sold them
Ps. 127:1, *E* Lord build house
Amos 3:3, *e* they be agreed
Mat. 5:20, *e* your righteousness exceed
 18:3, *e* ye be converted
Mat. 24:22; Mk. 13:20, *e* days be shortened
Mk. 7:3, Pharisees *e* they wash off
Lk. 13:3; Rev. 2:5, 22, *e* ye repent
Jn. 3:2, *e* God be with him
 3:5, *E* a man be born again
 4:48, *E* ye see signs and wonders
 20:25, *E* I see print of nails
Acts 26:29, *e* these bonds
Rom. 10:15, how preach, *e* they be sent?
I Cor. 15:36, *e* it die
II Tim. 2:5, *e* he strive lawfully
See Rom. 7:7; I Cor. 14:5; II Thess. 2:3
EXCESS Mat. 23:25; Eph. 5:18; I Pet. 4:3
EXCHANGE Mat. 16:26; 25:27, put money to *e*
Mk. 8:37, in *e* for soul
See Gen. 47:17; Lev. 27:10; Ezek. 48:14
EXCLUDE Rom. 3:27; Gal. 4:17
EXCUSE Lk. 14:18; Rom. 1:20; 2:15
EXECRATION Jer. 42:18; 44:12
EXECUTE Deut. 33:21
I Chron. 6:10; 24:2; Lk. 1:8, *e* priest's office
Ps. 9:16, Lord known by the judgment he *e*
 103:6, Lord *e* righteousness and judgment
Jer. 5:1, if any *e* judgment, I will pardon
Jn. 5:27, authority to *e* judgment
Rom. 13:4, minister of God to *e* wrath
See Hos. 11:9, Joel 2:11; Mic. 5:15
EXERCISE Jer. 9:24, *e* loving kindness
Mat. 20:25; Mk. 10:42; Lk. 22:25
Acts 24:16, I *e* myself, to have a conscience
I Tim. 4:7, *e* yourself unto godliness
Heb. 5:14, *e* to discern good and evil

12:11, to them which are *e* thereby
II Pet. 2:14, heart *e* with covetous practices
See Eccl. 1:13; Ezek. 22:29; Rev. 13:12
EXHORT Lk. 3:18, many things in his *e*
Acts 13:15, any words of *e*
Rom. 12:8, he that *e*, on *e*
I Tim. 6:2, these things *e* on teach
Heb. 3:13; 10:25, *e* one another daily
 13:22, suffer word of *e*
See Acts 11:23; II Cor. 9:5; Titus 2:6, 9
EXILE II Sam. 15:19; Isa. 51:14
EXPECTATION Ps. 9:18, the *e* of the poor
 62:5, my *e* is from him
Prov. 10:28; 11:7, 23, *e* of the wicked
Isa. 20:5, ashamed of their *e*
Rom. 8:19, the *e* of the creature
Phil. 1:20, my earnest *e* and hope
See Jer. 29:11; Acts 3:5; Heb. 10:13
EXPEL Josh 23:5; Judg. 11:7; II Sam. 14:14
EXPENSES Ezra 6:4, 8
EXPERIENCE Gen. 30:27; Eccl 1:16
EXPERT I Chron 12:33, *e* in war
Jer. 50:9; Acts 26:3, *e* in all customs
EXPLOITS Dan. 11:28, 32
EXPOUND Mk. 4:34, when alone, he *e* all things
Lk. 24:27, *e* the scriptures
See Acts 11:4; 18:26; 28:23
EXPRESS Heb. 1:3
EXPRESSLY I Sam. 20:21; I Tim. 4:1
EXTEND Ps. 16:2; 109:12, Isa. 66:12
EXTINCT Job 17:1; Isa. 43:17
EXTOL Ps. 30:1; 145:1, I will *e* you
 68:4, *e* him that rides
See Ps. 66:17; Isa. 52:13; Dan. 4:37
EXTORTION Ezek. 22:12; Mat. 23:25
EXTORTIONER Ps. 109:11
Isa. 16:4, the *e* is at an end
I Cor. 5:11, if any man be an *e*
See Lk. 18:11; I Cor. 5:10; 6:10
EXTREME Deut. 28:22; Job 35:15
EYE Gen. 3:6, pleasant to the *e*
 7, *e* of both were opened
 27:1; 49:12, his *e* were dim
Num. 10:31, be to us instead of *e*
 16:14, will you put out *e*?
 24:3, 15, man whose *e* are open said
Deut. 3:27, lift up *e*, behold with your *e*
 12:8, Judg. 17:6; 21:25, right in own *e*
 16:19, gift blind *e* of wise
 28:32, *e* look, and fall with longing
I Ki. 1:20, *e* of all Israel upon you
 8:29, 52; II Chron. 6:20, 40
 20:6, whatsoever is pleasant in your *e*
II Ki. 6:17, Lord opened *e* of young man
 20, open the *e* of these men
II Chron. 16:9, *e* of Lord run to and fro
II Chron. 34:28, nor your *e* see all the evil
Job 7:8; 20:9, *e* that has seen me
 11:20, the *e* of the wicked shall fall
 15:12, what do your *e* wink at?
 19:27, my *e* shall behold, and not another
 28:7, path vulture's *e* has not seen
 10, his *e* sees every precious thing

29:11, when the *e* saw me
15, I was *e* to the blind
31:16, caused *e* of widow to fall
Ps. 11:4, his *e* try children of men
15:4, in whose *e* a vile person
19:8, enlightening the *e*
33:18, *e* of the Lord on them that fear him
36:1, no fear of God before his *e*
69:3; 119:82, 123, Lam. 2:11, my *e* fall
77:4, hold my *e* waking
116:8, delivered my *e* from tears
119:18, open my *e*
132:4, not give sleep to my *e*
Prov. 10:26, as smoke to my *e*
20:12, the seeing *e*
22:9, a bountiful *e*
23:29, redness of *e*
Eccl. 1:8, *e* is not satisfied with seeing
2:14, wise man's *e* are in his head
11:7, for the *e* to behold the sun
Isa. 1:15, I will hide my *e* from you
29:10, the Lord has closed *e*
33:17, *e* shall see the king in his beauty
40:26; Jer. 13:20, lift up your *e* on high
Jer. 5:21; Ezek. 12:2, have *e* and see not
9:1, my *e* a fountain of tears
13:17, my *e* shall weep sore
14:17, let my *e* run down with tears
24:6, set my *e* upon them for good
Lam. 2:18, let not apple of *e* cease
Ezek. 24:16, 25, the desire of your *e*
Hab. 1:13, of purer *e* than to behold evil
Mat. 5:29, if right *e* offend you
13:16, blessed are your *e*
18:9; Mk. 9:47, to enter with one *e*
Mk. 8:18, having *e*, see ye not?
Lk. 1:21, from beginning were *e*-witnesses
24:16, their *e* were holden
Jn. 11:37, this man, which opened *e*
Gal. 4:15, have plucked out your *e*
Eph. 1:18, the *e* of your understanding
II Pet. 2:14, having *e* full of adultery
I Jn. 2:16, the lust of the *e*
See Deut. 32:10; Job 24:15; Prov. 3:7; 12:15;
16:2; 21:2; Mat. 20:33

F

FABLES I Tim. 1:4; 4:7; II Tim. 4:4
FACE Ps. 84:9, look upon *f* of anointed
Mat. 11:10; Mk. 1:2; Lk. 7:27
Lk. 9:51, set his *f* to Jerusalem
Lk. 12:56, discern *f* of sky
I Cor. 13:12, then *f* to *f*
II Cor. 3:18, all, with open *f*
James 1:23, beholding *f* in glass
FADE Isa. 64:6, all *f* as a leaf
I Pet. 1:4, inheritance that *f* not away
James 1:11, rich man shall *f* away
FAIL Gen. 47:16, if money *f*
Deut. 28:32, your eyes shall *f* with longing
Josh. 21:45; 23:14; I Ki. 8:56
I Sam. 17:32, let no man's heart *f* him
I Ki. 2:4, 8:25, shall not *f* a man on throne

17:14, neither shall cruse of oil *f*
Ezra 4:22, take heed that ye *f* not
Job 14:11, as waters *f* from sea
Ps. 12:1, the faithful *f* among men
31:10; 38:10, my strength *f* me
77:8, does this promise *f*
89:33, nor suffer my faithfulness to *f*
142:4, refuge *f* me
Eccl. 10:3, his wisdom *f* him
Isa. 15:6, the grass *f*
19:5, waters shall *f*
31:3, they shall all *f* together
32:6, cause drink of thirsty to *f*
10, the vintage shall *f*
38:14, eyes *f* with looking upward
41:17, tongue *f* for thirst
Jer. 14:6, their eyes did *f*
Jer. 15:18, as waters that *f*
Lam. 3:22, his compassions *f* not
Ezek. 12:22, every vision *f*
Lk. 12:33, treasure that *f* not
16:9, when ye *f* they may receive you
17, one tittle of law *f*
Lk. 21:26, hearts *f* them for fear
22:32, that your faith *f* not
I Cor. 13:8, charity never *f*
Heb. 1:12, your years shall not *f*
11:32, time would *f* me to tell
12:15, lest any man *f* of grace of God
FAIN Job 27:22; Lk. 15:16
FAINT Gen. 25:29, came from field, was *f*
45:26 Jacob's heart *f*
Judg. 8:4, *f*, yet pursuing
Job 4:5, now it is come and you *f*
Ps. 27:13, I had *f*, unless I had believed
107:5, their soul *f* in them
Prov. 24:10, if you *f* in day of adversity
Isa. 1:5, whole heart *f*
10:18, as when a standard bearer *f*
40:28, Creator of Earth *f* not
29, gives power to the *f*
30; Amos 8:13, even youths shall *f*
31, walk, and not *f*
44:12, he drinks no water, and is *f*
Jer. 8:18; Lam. 1:22; 5:17, my heart is *f*
Mat. 15:32; Mk. 8:3, les they *f* by the way
Lk. 18:1, pray, and not to *f*
II Cor. 4:1, 16, we received mercy, we *f* not
Gal. 6:9, reap, if we *f* not
Heb. 12:3, wearied and *f* in your minds
5, nor *f* when you are rebuked
FAIR Job 37:22, *f* weather out of the north
Ps. 45:2, *f* than children of men
Prov. 11:22, a *f* woman without discretion
26:25, when he speaks *f*, believe not
Isa. 5:9, houses great and *f*
Jer. 4:30, in vain shall you make yourself *f*
12:6, though they speak *f* words
Dan. 1:15, their countenances appeared *f*
Mat. 16:2, it will be *f* weather
Acts 7:20, Moses was exceeding *f*
Rom. 16:18, by *f* speeches deceived
FAITH Deut. 32:20, children in whom is no *f*
Mat. 6:30; 8:26; Lk. 12:28, little *f*

8:10; Lk. 7:9, so great *f*
9:2; Mk. 2:5; Lk. 5:20, seeing their *f*
22; Mk. 5:34; 10:52; Lk. 8:48; 17:19, your *f* has made you whole
15:28, great if your *f*
17:20, *f* as a grain of mustard seed
21:21, if you have *f*, you shall not only do this
23:23, omitted judgment, mercy, and *f*
Mk. 4:40, how is it you have no *f*
11:22, have *f* in God
Lk. 7:50, your *f* has saved you
18:8, shall he find *f* on the Earth?
22:32, that your *f* fail not
Acts 3:16, the *f* which is by him
6:5; 11:24, a man full of *f*
14:9, perceiving he had *f* to be healed
27, opened the door of *f*
15:9, purifying their hearts by *f*
26:18, sanctified by *f*
Rom. 1:5, grace for obedience to *f*
17, revealed from *f* to *f*
3:27, boasting excluded by *f*
28; 5:1; Gal. 2:16; 3:24, justified by *f*
4:5, *f* counted for righteousness
16, it is of *f*, which is of the *f* of Abraham
19, 20, being not weak in *f*
5:2, we have access by *f*
10:8, the word of *f*, which we preach
17, *f* comes by hearing
12:3, the measure of *f*
6, prophesy according to proportion of *f*
14:1, weak in *f* receive ye
22, have you *f*? 23, what is not of *f* is sin
I Cor. 2:5, your *f* should not stand in wisdom
13:2, though I have all *f*
13, not abides *f*
I Cor. 16:13, stand fast in the *f*
II Cor. 1:24, not have dominion over
4:13, same spirit of *f*
5:7, we walk by *f*
13:5, examine whether you be in the *f*
Gal. 2:20, I live by the *f* of the Son of God
3:2, by the hearing of *f*?
12, law is not of *f*
5:6, *f* which works by love
6:10, the household of *f*
Eph. 3:12, access by *f* of him
17, dwell in your hearts by *f*
4:5, one Lord, one *f*
6:16, the shield of *f*
Col. 1:23, if you continue in the *f*
2:5, the steadfastness of your *f*
I Thess. 1:3; II Thess. 1:11, your work of *f*
5:8, the breastplate of *f*
II Thess. 3:2, all men have not *f*
I Tim. 1:2; Titus 1:4, my own son in the *f*
5; II Tim. 1:5, *f* unfeigned
2:15, if they continue in *f*
3:13, great boldness in the *f*
5:8, he has denied the *f*
6:10, 21, erred from the *f*
II Tim. 3:8, reprobate concerning the *f*
4:7, I have kept the *f*

Titus 1:1, the *f* of God's elect
Heb. 4:2, not being mixed with *f*
6:1, not laying again the foundation of *f*
12, through *f* inherit the promises
10:22, in full assurance of *f*
11:1, *f* is substance of things hoped for
4, 5, 7, 8, 9, etc. by *f* Abel, etc.
6, without *f* it is impossible
13, these all died in *f*
33, through *f* subdued kingdoms
39, a good report through *f*
12:2, author and finisher of our *f*
James 1:3; I Pet. 1:7, the trying of your *f*
6, let them ask in *f*
2:1, have not *f* with respect of persons
5, rich in *f*
14, man say he has *f*, can *f* save him
17, *f* without works is dead
18, you have *f*, and I have works
22, *f* wrought with his works
5:15, the prayer of *f* shall save
I Pet. 1:9, the end of your *f*
II Pet. 1:1, like precious *f*
5, add to your *f* virtue
I Jn. 5:4, overcomes the world, even our *f*
Jude 3, earnestly contend for the *f*
20, your most holy *f*
Rev. 2:13, have not denied my *f*
19, I know your works and *f*
13:10, patience and *f* of the saints
14:12, they that keep the *f* of Jesus
See Heb. 11:31
FAITHFUL II Sam. 20:19, them that are *f*
Neh. 7:2, a *f* man, and feared God
9:8, his heart *f* before you
13:13, counted *f* to distribute
Ps. 12:1, the *f* fail among men
89:37, a *f* witness in heaven
101:6, the *f* of the land
119:86, commandments *f*
Prov. 11:13, *f* spirit conceals
13:17, *f* ambassador is health
14:5, Isa. 8:2; Jer. 42:5, a *f* witness
25:13, as snow in harvest, is a *f* messenger
28:20, *f* man shall abound
Isa. 1:21, 26, *f* city
Mat. 24:45; Lk. 12:42, who is a *f* servant?
25:21, good and *f* servant
23; Lk. 19:17, *f* in a few things
Lk. 16:10, *f* in least *f* in much
Acts 16:15, if you have judged me *f*
Gal. 3:9, blessed with *f* Abraham
Eph. 6:21; Col. 1:7; 4:7, a *f* minister
I Thess. 5:24, *F* is He who calls you
II Thess. 3:3, Lord is *f* who shall stablish you
I Tim. 1:15; II Tim. 2:11, a *f* saying
3:11, wives *f* in all things
II Tim. 2:2, commit to *f* men
Heb. 2:17, a *f* high priest
3:2, *f* to him that appoints him
10:23; 11:11, he is *f* that promised
I Pet. 4:19, as unto a *f* Creator
I Jn. 1:9, he is *f* and just to forgive
Rev. 2:10, be thou *f* unto death

See Deut. 7:9; Dan. 6:4; Rev. 1:5; 3:14; 19:11
FAITHFULLY II Chron. 19:9; 34:12
FAITHFULNESS Ps. 5:9, no *f* in their mouths
 36:5, your *f* reaches unto the clouds
 40:10; 88:11, declared your *f*
 89:33, nor suffer my *f* to fail
 92:2, show forth your *f* every night
 Isa. 11:5, *f* the girdle of his reins
 See I Sam. 26:23; Ps. 119:75; 143:1
FAITHLESS Mat. 17:17; Mk. 9:19
FALL (*n.*) Prov. 16:18, haughty before a *f*
 Mat. 7:27, great was the *f* of it
 Lk. 2:34, set for the rise and *f* of many
 Rom. 11:12, if the *f* of them be the riches
 See Jer. 49:21; Ezek. 26:15; 31:16; 32:10
FALL (*v.*) Gen. 45:24, *f* not out by the way
 Lev. 25:35, your brother be *f* in decay
 I Sam. 3:19, let none of his words *f*
 II Sam. 1:19, 25, 27, how are the mighty *f*!
  3:38, great man *f* this day
  24:14; I Chron. 21:13, *f* into hands
  of God
 Job 4:13; 33:15, deep sleep *f* on men
 Ps. 5:10, let them *f* by their own counsels
  7:15, is *f* into ditch
  16:6, lines *f* in pleasant places
  37:24, though he *f*, not utterly cast down
  56:13; 116:8, deliver my feet from *f*
  72:11, kings shall *f* down before him
  91:7, a thousand shall *f* at your side
 Prov. 10:8, 10, a prating fool shall *f*
  11:14, where no counsel is, the people *f*
  28, he that trusts in riches shall *f*
  24:16, just man *f* seven times
  17, rejoice not when your enemy *f*
  26:27, dug a pit shall *f* therein
 Eccl. 4:10, woe to him alone when he *f*
  11:3, where the tree *f*, there it shall be
 Isa. 14:12, how are you *f*
  34:4, as the leaf *f* from the vine
  40:30, the young men shall utterly *f*
 Jer. 49:26; 50:30, young men *f* in her streets
 Ezek. 24:6, let no lot *f* on it
 Dan. 3:5; Mat. 4:9, *f* down and worship
 Hos. 10:8; Lk. 23:30, say to hills, F
 Mic. 7:8, when I *f*, Zech. 11:2, the cedar is *f*
 Mat. 10:29, sparrow *f* to ground
  12:11, *f* into pit on sabbath day
  15:14; Lk. 6:39, both *f* into the ditch
  21:44; Lk. 20:18, *f* on this stone
  24:29; Mk. 13:25, stars *f* from heaven
 Lk. 8:13, in time of temptation *f* away
 Rom. 14:4, to his master he stands or *f*
  13, occasion to *f*
 I Cor. 10:12, take heed lest he *f*
  15:6, 18, some are *f* asleep
 I Tim. 3:6, *f* into the condemnation
  3:7, lest he *f* into reproach
  6:9, rich *f* into temptation
 Heb. 4:11, lest any *f* after same example
  6:6, if they *f* away
  10:31, to *f* into hands of living God
 James 1:2, joy when you *f* into temptation
  11; I Pet. 1:24, flower thereof *f*

 5:12, lest he *f* into condemnation
 II Pet. 1:10, you shall never *f*
  3:17, lest you *f* from stedfastness
FALLING Job 4:4; II Thess. 2:3; Jude 24
FALLOW Jer. 4:3; Hos. 10:12
FALSE Ex. 20:16; Deut. 5:20; Mat. 19:18, shall
 not bear *f* witness
 23:1, shall not raise a *f* report
 II Ki. 9:2, it is *f*, tell us now
 Ps. 119:104, 128, I hate every *f* way
 120:3, you *f* tongue
 Prov. 6:19; 12:17; 14:5, a *f* witness
 11:1; 20:23, a *f* balance
 Mat. 15:19; out of heart proceed *f* witness
  24:24; Mk. 13:22, *f* Christs and *f* prophets
  26:59, 60; Mk. 14:56, 57
 Mk. 13:22, *f* prophets shall rise
 Lk. 19:8, any thing by *f* accusation
 I Cor. 15:15, found *f* witnesses of God
 II Cor. 11:13, such are *f* apostles
  26, perils among *f* brethren
 II Tim. 3:3; Titus 2:3, *f* accusers
 See Gal. 2:4; II Pet. 2:1; I Jn. 4:1
FALSEHOOD Ps. 7:14, has brought forth *f*
 144:8, 11, right hand of *f*
 Isa. 28:15, under *f* have we hid ourselves
  57:4, a seed of *f*
 Mic. 2:11, walking in the spirit and *f*
 See II Sam. 18:13; Jer. 13:25; Hos. 7:1
FALSELY Lev. 6:3, 5; 19:12
 Jer. 5:31; 29:9, prophets prophesy *f*
 Mat. 5:11, evil *f*, for my sake
 I Tim. 6:20, science *f* so called
 See Jer. 43:2; Lk. 3:14; I Pet. 3:16
FAME Josh. 9:9, we heard the *f* of God
 I Ki. 10:1; II Chron. 9:1, *f* of Solomon
 Zeph. 3:19, get them *f* in every land
 Mat. 4:24; Mk. 1:28; Lk. 4:14, 37
  9:31, spread abroad his *f*
  14:1, Herod heard of the *f*
 See Gen. 45:16; Job 28:22; Isa. 66:19
FAMILIAR Job 19:14; Ps. 41:9; Jer. 20:10
FAMILY Gen. 12:3; 28:14, *f* be blessed
 Lev. 25:10, return every man to his *f*
 Deut. 29:18, lest a *f* turn away from God
 I Sam. 9:21, my *f* the least
  18:18, what is my father's *f*
 I Chron. 4:38, princes in their *f*
 Ps. 68:6, sets the solitary in *f*
 Jer. 3:14, one of a city, and two of a *f*
  10:25, on *f* that call not
  31:1, God of all the *f* of Israel
 Eph. 3:15, whole *f* in Heaven and Earth
FAMINE II Sam. 21:1, a *f* in days of David
 I Ki. 8:37; II Chron. 20:9, if there be *f*
 18:2; II Ki. 6:25, sore *f* in Samaria
 II Ki. 8:1, the Lord has called for a *f*
 Job 5:20, in *f* he shall redeem you
  22, at *f* you shall laugh
 Ps. 33:19, to keep them alive in *f*
  37:19, in the days of *f* shall be satisfied
 Jer. 24:10; 29:17, will send *f* among them
  42:16, *f* shall follow close
 Lam. 5:10, black because of *f*

Ezek. 5:16, evil arrows of *f*
Mat. 24:7; Lk. 21:11, *f* in divers places
See Gen. 12:10; 41:27; 47:13; Rom. 8:35
FAMISH Gen. 41:55; Prov. 10:3; Isa. 5:13
FAMOUS Ruth 4:11; 14; Ps. 74:5
FAN Isa. 30:24; Jer. 15:7; 51:2; Mat. 3:12
FAR Deut 12:21; 14:24, if place too *f* from you
Judg. 19:11; Lk. 24:29, day *f* spent
I Sam. 2:30; 22:15; II Sam. 20:20; 23:17
Job 5:4, children *f* from safety
11:14, 22:23, put iniquity *f* away
19:13, put my brethren *f* from me
Ps. 10:5, your judgments are *f* out of sight
22:11; 35:22; 71:12, be not *f* from me
97:9, *f* above all gods
103:12, *f* as east from west
Prov. 31:10, *f* above rubies
Isa. 43:6; 60:4, 9, sons from *f*
46:12, *f* from righteousness
57:19, peace to him that is *f* off
Amos 6:3, put *f* away evil day
Mat. 16:22, be it *f* from you, Lord
Mk. 12:34, not *f* from the kingdom
13:34, as a man taking a *f* journey
Jn. 21:8, they were not *f* from land
Rom. 13:12, the night if *f* spent
II Cor. 4:17, a *f* more exceeding
Eph. 1:21, *f* above all principality
4:10, *F* above all heavens
Phil. 1:23, which is *f* better
Heb. 7:15, it is yet *f* more evident
FARE I Sam. 17:18; Jonah 1:3; Lk. 16:19
FAREWELL Lk. 9:61; Acts 18:21
FARM Mat. 22:5
FARTHING Mat. 5:26; 10:29; Mk. 12:42
FASHION Job 10:8; Ps. 119:73
Ps. 33:15, he *f* hearts alike
139:16, in continuance were *f*
Isa. 45:9, say to him that *f* it
Mk. 2:12, never saw it on this *f*
Lk. 9:29, the *f* of his countenance
I Cor. 7:31, the *f* of this world passes
Phil. 2:8, found in *f* as a man
See Gen. 6:15; Ezek. 16:7; James 1:11
FAST II Sam. 12:23
Ps. 33:9, he commanded, and it stood *f*
65:6, sets *f* the mountains
Isa. 58:3, why have we *f*, and you see not?
4, you *f* for strife
5, will you call this a *f*
6, is not this the *f* that I have chosen?
Joel 1:14, sanctify a *f*
Zech. 7:5, did you at all *f* unto me?
Mk. 2:19, can children of bridechamber *f*
Lk. 18:12, I *f* twice in the week
See Jer. 14:12; Mat. 4:2; Acts 13:2
FASTEN Eccl. 12:11, nails *f* by masters
Isa. 22:23, 25, I will *f* him as a nail
Lk. 4:20, eyes of all were *f* on him
Acts 11:6, when I had *f* my eyes
See I Sam. 31:10; Job 38:6; Acts 3:4; 28:3
FASTING Ps. 35:13, humbled myself with *f*
109:24, knees weak through *f*
Jer. 36:6, upon the *f* day

Mk. 8:3, send them away *f*
I Cor. 7:5, give yourselves to *f* and prayer
II Cor. 6:5, in stripes, in *f*
See Dan. 6:18; 9:3; Mat. 17:21; Mk. 9:29
FAT Gen. 45:18, shall eat the *f* of the land
49:20, his bread shall be *f*
Deut. 32:15, Jeshurun waxed *f*, and kicked
Neh. 8:10, eat the *f*, and drink, the sweet
9:25, 35, took a *f* land, and became *f*
Ps. 17:10, inclosed in their own *f*
92:14, shall be *f* and flourishing
119:70, heart *f* as grease
Prov. 11:25, liberal soul made *f*
13:4, soul of diligent made *f*
15:30, good report makes the bones *f*
Isa. 10:16, among his *f* ones leanness
25:6, feast of *f* things
Hab. 1:16, by them their portion is *f*
FATHER Gen. 15:15, go to your *f* in peace
17:4; Rom. 4:17, a *f* of nations
Ex. 15:2, he is my *f* God, I will exalt him
20:5, iniquity of *f* upon children
21:15, he that smites his *f*
17; Lev. 20:9, he that curses his *f*
Judg. 17:10; 18:19, be to me a *f* and a priest
I Sam. 10:12, who is their *f*?
II Ki. 2:12; 13:14, Elisha cried My *f*, my *f*
6:21, my *f*, shall I smite them
I Chron. 28:9, know thou the God of your *f*
Ezra 7:27, blessed be the Lord God of our *f*
Job 29:16, I was a *f* to the poor
31:18, brought up with me as with a *f*
38:28, has the rain a *f*?
Ps. 27:10, when my *f* and mother forsake me
39:12, as all my *f* were
68:5, *f* of fatherless
95:9; Heb. 3:9, you *f* tempted me
103:13, as a *f* pities his children
Prov. 4:1, the instruction of a *f*
3, I was my *f* son
10:1; 15:20, wise son makes a glad *f*
Isa. 9:6, the everlasting *F*
49:23, kings shall be your nursing *f*
63:16; 64:8, doubtless you are our *f*
Jer. 3:4, will you not cry, my *f*
31:9, I am a *f* to Israel
29; Ezek. 18:2, *f* have eaten sour grapes
Ezek. 18:4, as the soul of the *f*
22:7, set light by *f* and mother
Mal. 1:6, if I be a *f*, where is my honor
2:10, have we not all one *f*?
Mat. 5:16, 45, 48, your *F* in heaven
6:8, 32; Lk. 12:30, your *F* knows
9; Lk. 11:2, our *F* which art in Heaven
8:21; Lk. 9:59, to go and bury my *f*
10:21, *f* deliver up the child
37, he that loves *f* or mother
18:10, behold the face of my *F*
14, not the will of your *F*
23:9, call no man *f* on Earth
Mk. 14:36; Rom. 8:15; Gal. 4:6, Abba, *F*
Lk. 2:49, about my *F* business?
6:36, as your *F* is merciful
12:32, it is your *F* good pleasure

15:21, *F*, I have sinned
16:27, send him to my *f* house
22:42, *F*, if you be willing
23:34, *F*, forgive them; 46, *F*, into your hands
Jn. 1:14, as of the only begotten of the *F*
5:21, as the *F* raises up the dead
22, the *F* judges no man
23, even as they honor the *F*
37; 14:24, the *F* which has sent me
6:37, all the *F* gives me
46:14:8, 9, has seen the *F*
8:41, we have one *F*, even God
Jn. 8:44, devil is a liar, and the *f* of it
10:15, as the *F* knows me
29, my *F* is greater than all
12:27, *F*, save me from this hour
28, *F*, glorify your name
13:1, should depart unto the *F*
14:6, no man comes to the *F*, but by me
28, I am come from the *F*
15:1, my *F* is the husbandman
16, whatsoever you ask of the *F*
16:16, because I go to the *F*
Jn. 17:1, *F*, the hour is come
20:17, I ascend to my *F*, and your *F*
Acts 24:14, so worship I the god of my *f*
Rom 4:11, the *f* of all that believe
I Cor. 4:15, yet have we not many *f*
II Cor. 1:3, *F* of mercies, God of all comfort
Gal. 1:14, zealous of the traditions of my *f*
4:2, the time appointed of the *F*
Eph. 4:6, one God and *F* of all
Phil. 2:11, to the glory of the *F*
22, as a son with the *f*
Col. 1:19, it pleased the *F* that in him
I Tim. 5:1, entreat him as a *f*
Heb. 1:5, I will be to him a *F*
7:3, without *f*, without mother
12:9, the *F* of spirits
James 1:17, the *F* of lights
II Pet. 3:4, since the *f* fell asleep
I Jn. 1:3, fellowship with the *F*
2:1, an advocate with the *F*
13, I write unto you *f*
15, the love of the *F* is not in him
3:1, what manner of love the *F* has
5:7, the *F*, the Word, and Holy Ghost
See John 5:26; Acts 1:4; 15:10; Rom. 4:16
FATHERLESS Ps. 10:14, the helper of the *f*
Prov. 23:10, the fields of the *f*
Isa. 1:23, they judge not the *f*
10:2, that they may rob the *f*!
Jer. 49:11, leave your *f* children
Hos. 14:3, in you the *f* finds mercy
Mal. 3:5, against those that oppress *f*
James 1:27, to visit the *f* and widows
See Ex. 22:22; Deut. 10:18; 14:29; 24:17
FATNESS Ps. 36:8, the *f* of your house
63:5, as with marrow and *f*
65:11, your paths drop *f*
73:7, eyes stand out with *f*
Isa. 55:2, soul delight itself in *f*
See Gen. 27:28; Judg. 9:9; Rom. 11:17

FAULT Gen. 41:9, I remember my *f* this day
Ps. 19:12, cleanse me from secret *f*
Dan. 6:4, find no occasion or *f* in him
Mat. 18:15, tell him his *f*
Lk. 23:4; Jn. 18:38; 19:4, 6, I find no *f*
Rom. 9:19, why does he yet find *f*?
James 5:16, confess your *f*
Rev. 14:5, are without *f* before throne
See Deut. 25:2; I Sam. 29:3; II Sam. 3:8
FAULTLESS Heb. 8:7; Jude 24
FAULTY II Sam. 14:13; Hos. 10:2
FAVOUR Ex. 3:21; 11:3; 12:36, *f* in sight of Egyptians
Ps. 5:12, with *f* will you compass him
30:5, his *f* is life
102:13, the set time to *f* her
14, *f* the dust thereof
112:5, a good man shows *f*
Prov. 13:15, good understanding gives *f*
14:35; 19:12, the king's *f*
18:22, obtains *f* of the Lord
31:30, *F* is deceitful
Lk. 2:52, increased in *f* with God and man
Acts 2:47, having *f* with all people
FAVOURABLE Judg. 21:22; Job 33:26
FEAR (*n.*) Gen. 20:11, *f* of God
Deut. 2:25; 11:25; Job 4:6, is not this your *f*
Ps. 5:7, in your *f* will I worship
19:9, *f* of the Lord is clean
34:11, I will teach you the *f* of the Lord
36:1; Rom. 3:18, no *f* of God before his eyes
53:5 in *f*, where no *f* was
111:10; Prov. 9:19, *f* beginning of wisdom
Prov. 1:26, 27, mock when your *f* comes
3:25, not afraid of sudden *f*
10:27, *f* of Lord prolongs days
14:26, in *f* of Lord is strong confidence
Prov. 14:27, *f* of Lord a fountain of life
19:23, *f* of Lord tends to life
29:25, *f* of man brings a snare
Eccl. 12:5, when *f* shall be in the way
Isa. 8:12, neither fear you their *f*
14:3, Lord give you rest from *f*
29:13, *f* toward me taught by men
Jer. 30:5, a voice of *f*, not of peace
32:40, I will put my *f* in their hearts
Mal. 1:6, where is my *f*?
Mat. 14:26, disciples cried for *f*
Lk. 21:26, hearts failing them for *f*
Jn 7:13; 19:38; 20:19, for *f* of the Jews
I Cor. 2:3, with you in weakness and *f*
II Cor. 7:11, what *f*, what desire
Eph. 6:5; Phil 2:12, with *f* and trembling
Heb. 2:15, *f* of death
12:28, with reverence and godly *f*
Jude 12, feeding themselves without *f*
FEAR (*v.*) Gen. 42:18, this do, and live, for I *f* God
Ex. 1:21, because they *f* God
14:13, *F* not, stand still, and see
18:21, able men such as *f* God
20:20, *F* not, God is come to prove
Deut. 4:10, that they may learn to *f*

5:29, O that they would *f* me
28:66, you shall *f* day and night
I Chron. 16:30; Ps. 96:9, F before him all Earth
Neh. 7:2, he *f* God above many
Job 1:9, does Job *f* God for nought
  11:15, put iniquity away, you shall not *f*
Ps. 27:1, whom shall I *f*?
  3, my heart shall not *f*
  31:19, laid up for them that *f* you
  34:9, *f* the Lord, ye his saints
  56:4; 118:6, will not *f* what flesh can do
  66:16, come, all you that *f* God
  86:11, unite my heart to *f* your name
  115:11, you that *f* the Lord, trust
  119:74, they that *f* you will be glad
Prov. 3:7; 24:21, *f* the Lord, and depart
  28:14, happy is the man that *f* always
  31:30, woman that *f* the Lord
Eccl. 3:14, that men should *f* before him
  12:13, F God, and keep his commandments
Isa. 8:12, neither *f* ye their fear
  41:10; 43:5, *f* thou not, I am with you
  14, F not, you worm Jacob
Jer. 5:24, neither say they, Let us *f* the Lord
  10:7, who would not *f* thee, King of nations
  33:9, they shall *f* and tremble
Dan. 6:26, men *f* before the God of Daniel
Zeph. 3:7, I said, Surely you will *f* me
Mat. 1:20, *f* not to take to thee
  10:28; Lk. 12:5, *f* him who is able
  14:5, 21:46, Herod *f* the multitude
  21:26; Lk. 20:19, we *f* the people
Mk. 4:41, they *f* exceedingly
  5:33, woman *f* and trembling came
Lk. 9:34, *f* as they entered cloud
  12:32, F not, little flock
  18:2, judge which *f* not God
  19:21, I *f* you, because you are
  23:40, do not you *f* God?
Jn. 9:22, because they *f* the Jews
Acts 10:22, just, and one that *f* God
  35, he that *f* is accepted
Rom. 8:15, bondage again to *f*
Rom. 11:20, not highminded, but *f*
II Cor. 11:3, 12:20, I *f* lest
I Tim. 5:20, rebuke, that others may *f*
Heb. 5:7, heard in that he *f*
I Jn. 4:18, that *f* not perfect in love
FEARFUL Ex. 15:11, *f* in praises
Ps. 139:14, *f* and wonderfully made
Isa. 35:4, to them of a *f* heart
Mat. 8:26; Mk. 4:40, why are you *f*?
Heb. 10:27, *f* looking for of judgment
  31, *f* thing to fall into the hands
See Deut. 20:8; Lk. 21:11; Rev. 21:8
FEARFULNESS Ps. 55:5; Isa. 21:4; 33:14
FEAST Ps. 35:16, hypocritical mockers in *f*
Prov. 15:15, merry heart continual *f*
Eccl. 7:2; Jer. 16:8, the house of *f*
  10:19, *f* is made for laughter
Isa. 1:14, your appointed *f* my soul hates

Amos 5:21, I despise your *f* days
  8:10, turn your *f* into mourning
Mat. 23:6; Mk. 12:39; Lk. 20:46
  26:5; Mk. 14:2, not on the *f* day
Lk. 2:42, after the custom of the *f*
  14:13, when you make a *f*
Jn. 7:8, go ye up to this *f*
  14, about the midst of the *f*
  37, that great day of the *f*
Acts 18:21, I must by all means keep this *f*
I Cor. 5:8, let us keep the *f*
  10:27, if any bid you to a *f*
See Judg. 14:10; Esther 9:17; Isa. 5:12; Mal. 2:3
FEATHERS Job 39:13; Ps. 91:4; Dan. 4:33
FED Gen. 48:15, who *f* me all my life long
Ps. 37:3, verily you shall be *f*
Ezek. 34:8, shepherds *f* themselves, not flock
Mat. 25:37, hungered, and *f* you
I Cor. 3:2, I have *f* you with milk
See Deut. 8:3; Ps. 78:72; 81:16; Lk. 16:21
FEEBLE Neh. 4:2, what do these *f* Jews?
Job 4:4; Isa. 35:3; Heb. 12:12, the *f* knees
Ps. 105:37, not one *f* person
Prov. 30:26, conies a *f* folk
Ezek. 7:17; 21:7, all hands shall be *f*
I Thess. 5:14, comfort the *f*-minded
See Gen. 30:42; Jer. 47:3; I Cor. 12:22
FEED Gen. 46:32, trade has been to *f* cattle
I Ki. 17:4, commanded ravens to *f* you
  22:27, *f* him with bread of affliction
Ps. 28:9, *f* them, and lift them up forever
Prov. 15:14, mouth *f* on foolishness
  30:8, *f* me with food convenient
Isa. 5:17, lambs shall *f* after their manner
  11:7; 27:10, cow and bear shall *f*
  44:20, he *f* on ashes
  61:5, strangers shall *f* your flocks
  65:25, the wolf and lamb shall *f*
Jer. 3:15, pastors *f* you with knowledge
  6:3, *f* every one in his place
Zech. 11:4, F the flock of the slaughter
Mat. 6:26, your Heavenly Father *f* them
Lk. 12:24, sow not, yet God *f* them
Jn. 21:15, 16, 17, *f* my lambs
Rom. 12:20, if enemy hunger, *f* him
I Pet. 5:2, F the flock of God
See Song of Sol. 1:7; Acts 20:28; Rev. 7:17
FEEL Gen. 27:12, 21, my father will *f* me
Acts 17:27, if haply they might *f* after
See Judg. 16:26; Job 20:20; Eccl. 8:5
FEELING Eph. 4:19, being past *f*
Heb. 4:15, touched, with *f* of infirmities
FEET Deut. 2:28, I will pass through on my *f*
Josh. 3:15, *f* of priests dipped in Jordan
  14:9, land whereon *f* have trodden
Ruth 3:14, she lay at his *f*
I Sam. 2:9, keep *f* of his saints
II Sam. 22:37; Ps. 18:36, my *f* did not slip
II Ki. 6:32, sound of his master's *f*
  13:21, dead man stood on his *f*
Job 29:15, *f* was I to the lame
Ps. 8:6; I Cor. 15:27
  22:16, pierced my hands and my *f*

31:8, set my *f* in a large room
40:2, my *f* on a rock
56:13; 116:8, deliver my *f* from falling
66:9, suffered not our *f* to be moved
73:2, my *f* were almost gone
115:7, *f* have they, but walk not
119:105, a lamp to my *f*
Prov. 1:16; 6:18; Isa. 59:7, *f* run to evil
4:26, ponder path of my *f*
5:5, her *f* go down to death
6:13, speaks with his *f*
28, and his *f* not be burnt
19:2, he that hasteth with his *f*
Song of Sol. 7:1; Isa. 52:7, how beautiful are *f*
Isa. 3:16, tinkling with *f*
6:2, with twain he covered his *f*
26:6, the *f* of the poor
49:23; Mat. 10:14; Mk. 6:11; Lk. 9:5
52:7; Nah. 1:5, the *f* of him that brings
60:13, place of my *f* glorious
Ezek. 2:1, 2; 3:24, stand upon your *f*
24:17, 23, shoes upon your *f*
25:6, stamped with your *f*
32:2, troublest waters with your *f*
34:18, 19, foul residue with *f*
Dan. 2:33, 42, *f* part iron and part clay
10:6; Rev. 1:15, 2:18, *f* like polished brass
Nah. 1:3, clouds are the dust of his *f*
Zech. 14:4, *f* shall stand on Zion
Mat. 7:6, trample them under *f*
28:9, they held him by the *f*
Lk. 1:79, guide our *f* into way of peace
7:38, she kissed his *f*, and anointed them
8:35, sitting at the *f* of Jesus
24:39, 40, behold my hands and my *f*
Jn. 11:2; 12:3, wiped *f* with her hair
12:3, anointed the *f* of Jesus
13:5, began to wash disciples' *f*
6, do you wash my *f*?
8, you shall never wash my *f*
20:12, one angel at head, other at *f*
Acts 3:7, his *f* received strength
4:35, 37; 5:2, laid at apostles' *f*
5:9, *f* of them that buried your husband
14:8, a man impotent in his *f*
21:11, Agabus bound his own hands and *f*
22:3, at *f* of Gamaliel
Rom. 3:15, *f* swift to shed blood
10:15, the *f* of them that preach
16:20, bruise Satan under your *f*
Eph. 6:15, your *f* shod with preparation
Rev. 1:17, I fell at his *f* as dead
13:2, *f* as of a bear
FEIGN I Sam. 21:13, David *f* himself mad
Ps. 17:1, prayer not out of *f* lips
Jer. 3:10, turned to me *f*
Lk. 20:20, *f* themselves just men
See II Sam. 14:2; I Ki. 14:5, 6; Neh. 6:8
FELL Gen. 4:5, his countenance *f*
Josh. 6:20, the wall *f* flat
I Ki. 18:38, fire of Lord *f*, and consumed
II Ki. 6:5, as one was *f* a beam
Dan. 4:31, then *f* a voice from Heaven
Jonah 1:7, lot *f* on Jonah

Mat. 7:25; Lk. 6:49, house *f* not
Lk. 8:23, Jesus *f* asleep
10:30, 36, *f* among thieves
Acts 1:25, from which Judas *f*
1:26, lot *f* on Matthias
13:36, *f* on sleep
II Pet. 3:4, since fathers *f* asleep
Rev. 16:19, cities of the nations *f*
FELLOW I Sam. 21:15, this *f* to play the madman
II Sam. 6:20, as one of the vain *f*
II Ki. 9:11, wherefore came this mad *f*?
Ps. 45:7, oil of gladness above your *f*
Eccl 4:10, one shall lift up his *f*
Zech. 13:7, the man that is my *f*
Mat. 11:16, like children calling to their *f*
24:49, begin to smite his *f*-servants
26:61, this *f* said, I am able to destroy
71; Lk. 22:59, this *f* was also with Jesus
Lk. 23:2, found this *f* perverting
Acts 17:5, lewd *f* of the baser sort
22:22, away with such a *f*
Eph. 2:19, *f* citizens with the saints
3:6, Gentiles *f*-heirs
Phil. 4:3; I Thess. 3:2, *f*-laborers
III Jn. 8, *f*-helpers to the truth
See Col 4:11; Phile. 2; Rev. 19:10; 22:9
FELLOWSHIP Acts 2:42, in doctrine and *f*
I Cor. 1:9, called to the *f* of his Son
10:20, not have *f* with devils
II Cor. 6:14, what *f* has righteousness
Eph. 3:9, the *f* of mystery
Phil 1:5, your *f* in the Gospel
2:1, if any *f* of the Spirit
I Jn. 1:3, our *f* is with the Father
7, we have *f* one with another
See Lev. 6:2; Ps. 94:20; II Cor. 8:4; Gal. 2:9
FELT Ex. 10:21; Prov. 23:35; Mk. 5:29
FEMALE Mat. 19:4; Mk. 10:6; male and *f*
Gal. 3:28, in Christ neither male or *f*
See Gen. 7:16; Lev. 3:1; 27:4; Deut. 4:16
FENCE Job 10:11; 19:8; Ps. 62:3; Isa. 5:2
FERVENT Acts 18:25, *f* in spirit
James 5:16, *f* prayer avails much
I Pet. 1:22, with a pure heart *f*
II Pet. 3:10, 12, melt with *f* heat
See II Cor. 7:7; Col. 4:12, I Pet. 4:8
FETCH Num. 20:10, must we *f* water
Job 36:3, I will *f* my knowledge from far
Isa. 56:12, I will *f* wine
Acts 16:37, come themselves and *f* us out
See Deut. 19:5, II Sam. 14:13; Acts 28:13
FETTERS Judg. 16:21, Ps. 105:18; 149:8
FEW Gen. 29:20, they seemed but a *f* days
47:9, *f* and evil have the days of my life
I Sam. 14:6, to save by many or *f*
17:28, with whom left those *f* sheep?
II Ki. 4:3, borrow not a *f*
Neh. 7:4, city large, people *f*
Job 14:1, man is of *f* days
Eccl. 5:2, let your words be *f*
Mat. 7:14, *f* there be that find it
20:16; 22:14, many called, *f* chosen
25:21, faithful in a *f* things

Mk. 6:5, laid hands on a *f* sick folk
Lk. 12:48, beaten with *f* stripes
   13:23, are there *f* that be saved?
See Deut. 7:7; Ps. 109:8; Heb. 12:10
FIELD Deut. 21:1, if one be found slain in *f*
I Sam. 22:7, will he give every one of you *f*
Prov. 24:30, the *f* of the slothful
Isa. 5:8, that lay *f* to it
Mat. 13:38, the *f* is the world
Jn. 4:35, look on the *f*
James 5:4, laborers which reaped your *f*
See Mat. 6:28; 27:7; Acts 1:19
FIERCE Gen. 49:7, anger, for it was *f*
Deut. 28:50, a nation of a *f* countenance
Mat. 8:28, exceeding *f*
Lk. 23:5, and they were more *f*
II Tim. 3:3, men shall be incontinent, *f*
James. 3:4, driven of *f* winds
See II Sam. 19:43; Isa. 33:19; Dan. 8:23
FIERY Deut. 33:2, a *f* law for them
Dan. 3:6, a *f* furnace
Eph. 6:16, the *f* darts of the wicked
Heb. 10:27, judgment of *f* indignation
I Pet. 4:12, concerning *f* trial
See Num. 21:6; Deut. 8:15; Isa. 14:29
FIG I Ki. 4:25, dwelt under his *f* tree
II Ki. 18:31, eat every one of his *f* tree
Hab. 3:17, although *f* tree shall not blossom
Mat. 7:16, do men gather *f* of thistles?
Lk. 21:29, behold the *f* tree
James 3:12, can the *f* tree bear olive berries?
Rev. 6:13, casts untimely *f*
See Judg. 9:10; Jer. 8:13; Lk. 13:6; Jn. 1:48
FIGHT Ex. 14:14, Lord *f* for you
Josh. 23:10, he it is that *f* for you
I Sam. 25:28, *f* the battles of the Lord
II Ki. 10:3, *f* for your master's house
Neh. 4:14, *f* for brethren, sons, and wives
Ps. 144:1, teaches my fingers to *f*
Jn. 18:36, then would my servants *f*
Acts 5:39; 23:9, *f* against God
I Tim. 6:12; II Tim. 4:7, the good *f*
Heb. 10:32, great *f* of afflictions
   11:34, valiant in *f*
James 4:1, wars and *f* among you
   2, ye *f* and war
See Zech. 10:5; 14:14; Rev. 2:16
FIGURE Deut. 4:16; Rom. 5:14; Heb. 9:9
FILL Num. 14:21: Ps. 72:19; Hab. 2:14, Earth
   f with glory
Job 23:4, *f* my mouth with arguments
Ps. 81:10, open mouth, I will *f* it
   104:28, they are *f* with good
Prov. 3:10, barns *f* with plenty
   30:22, a fool when *f* with meat
Isa. 65:20, who has not *f* his days
Mat. 5:6; Lk. 6:21, they shall be *f*
Mk. 7:27; let the children first be *f*
Lk. 1:15; Acts 4:8; 9:17, shall be *f*
   14:23, that my house may be *f*
Jn. 16:6, sorrow has *f* your heart
Acts 14:17, *f* our hearts with food and
   gladness
Rom. 1:29, *f* with all unrighteousness

   15:14, *f* with all knowledge
Eph. 1:23, him that *f* all in all
   3:19, *f* with fullness of God
   5:18, be *f* with the Spirit
Phil. 1:11, *f* with fruits of righteousness
Col. 1:24, *f* up what is behind
James 2:16, be ye warmed and *f*
Rev. 15:1, in them is *f* up wrath of God
FILTH Isa. 4:4, washed away the *f* of Zion
I Cor. 4:13, as the *f* of the world
FILTHINESS II Cor. 7:1, *f* of flesh
Eph. 5:4, not let *f* be named
James 1:21, lay apart all *f*
See Ezek. 22:15; 36:25
FILTHY Job 15:16, more *f* is man
Ps. 14:3; 53:3, altogether become *f*
Isa. 64:6, as *f* rags
Zech. 3:3, clothed with *f* garments
Col. 3:8, put off *f* communication
I Tim. 3:3; Titus 1:7; I Pet. 5:2, *f* lucre
II Pet. 2:7, vexed with *f* conversation
Jude 8, *f* dreamers
Rev. 22:11, he that is *f*, let him be *f*
FINALLY II Cor. 13:11; Eph. 6:10
FIND Num. 32:23, sin will *f* you out
Job 9:10; Rom. 11:33, things past *f* out
Prov. 4:22, life to those that *f* them
   8:17; Jer. 29:13, seek me early shall *f*
   35, who so *f* me, *f* life
   18:22, *f* a wife, *f* a good thing
Eccl. 9:10, your hand *f* to do, do it
Isa. 58:13, *f* your own pleasure
Jer. 6:16; Mat. 11:29, *f* rest to your souls
Mat. 7:7; Lk. 11:9, seek, and ye shall *f*
   14, few there be that *f* it
   10:39, loses his life shall *f* it
Mk. 11:13, he might *f* any thing thereon
Lk. 18:8, shall he *f* faith
Jn. 1:41, first *f* his brother
Rom. 7:21, I *f* a law that when I would
Heb. 4:16, *f* grace to help
FINE Ps. 19:10, more desired than *f* gold
   81:16; 147:14, the *f* of the wheat
Prov. 25:12, as an ornament of *f* gold
Lam. 4:1, how is the *f* gold changed!
Mk. 15:46, Joseph brought *f* linen
FINGER Ex. 8:19, this is the *f* of God
   31:18; Deut. 9:10, the *f* of God
I Ki. 12:10; II Chron. 10:10, little *f* thicker
Prov. 7:3, bind them on your *f*
Isa. 58:9, the putting forth of the *f*
Dan. 5:5, the *f* of a man's hand
Mat. 23:4; Lk. 11:46, not move with *f*
Lk. 16:24, the tip of his *f*
Jn. 8:6, with his *f* wrote on the ground
   20:25, put my *f* into print of nails
See Ps. 8:3; Prov. 6:13; Isa. 2:8; 59:3
FINISH I Chron. 28:20, till you have *f*
Neh. 6:15, so the wall was *f*
Lk. 14:28, 29, 30, whether sufficient to *f*
Jn. 4:34, to do his will, and *f* his work
   5:36, which the Father has given me to *f*
   17:4, I have *f* the work
   19:30, it is *f*

Acts 20:24, that I might *f* my course
II Cor. 8:6, *f* in you the same grace
Heb. 12:2, Jesus, author and *f* of our faith
James 1:15, sin, when it is *f*
See Dan. 9:24; Rev. 10:7; 11:7; 20:5
FIRE Gen. 22:7, behold the *f* and the wood
Ex. 3:2, bush burned with *f*
Lev. 10:2, *f* from the Lord
Judg. 15:5, brands of *f*, and burnt corn
I Ki. 18:24, that answers by *f*
19:12, the Lord was not in the *f*
I Chron. 21:26, Lord answered him by *f*
Ps. 39:3, musing, the *f* burned
74:7, they have cast *f* into your sanctuary
Prov. 6:27, can a man take *f*
26:18, mad man who casts *f*-brands
20, no wood, the *f* goes out
21, as wood is to *f*, so is a contentious
man
Isa. 9:19, as the fuel of the *f*
24:15, glorify the Lord in the *f*
43:2, walk through *f* not be burned
64:2, the melting *f* burns
66:15, the Lord will come with *f*
16, by *f* will the Lord plead
24; Mk. 9:44, neither their *f* quenched
Jer. 20:9, word as a *f* in my bones
Ezek. 36:5, in the *f* of my jealousy
Dan. 3:27, the *f* had no power
Amos 4:11, as a *f*-brand plucked out
Zech. 2:5, a wall of *f* round about
3:2, a brand plucked out of the *f*?
Mal. 3:2, like a refiner's *f*
Mat. 3:10; Jn. 15:6, cast into *f*
Mat. 3:11; Lk. 3:16, baptized with *f*
13:42, cast them into furnace of *f*
18:8; 25:41; Mk. 9:43, 46, everlasting *f*
Lk. 9:54, will you that we command *f*
Lk. 12:49, come to send *f* on Earth
17:29, same day it rained *f* and brimstone
Acts 2:3, clove tongues like as of *f*
I Cor. 3:13, revealed by *f*, the *f* shall try
15, saved, yet so as by *f*
II Thess. 1:8, in flaming *f* taking vengeance
Heb. 1:7, his ministers a flame of *f*
11:34, quenched violence of *f*
James 3:5, a little *f* kindles
I Pet. 1:7, gold tried with *f*
II Pet. 3:12, heavens being on *f*
Jude 7, vengeance of eternal *f*
Rev. 3:18, buy gold tried in the *f*
20:9, *f* came down from God
14, death and hell cast into *f*
21:8, the lake that burns with *f*
FIRM Josh. 3:17; Job 41:24; Heb. 3:6
FIRST I Ki. 17:13, make a little cake *f*
Ezra 3:12; Hag. 2:3, the glory of the *f* house
Job 15:7, are you the *f* man born
Prov. 3:9, honor the Lord with *f*-fruits
18:17, *f* in his own cause
Isa. 43:27, your *f* father has sinned
Mat. 5:24, *f* be reconciled
6:33, seek ye *f* the kingdom
7:5, *f* cast out the beam

17:10, 11; Mk. 9:12, Elias must *f* come
20:10, when the *f* came, they supposed
22:38, the *f* commandment
Mk. 4:28, *f* the blade
9:35, *f*, shall be last
13:10, gospel must *f* be published
Lk. 14:28, sits not down *f*
17:25, but *f* must he suffer many things
Jn. 1:41, *f* finds his brother Simon
5:4, whosoever *f* stepped in
8:7, let him *f* cast a stone
Acts 11:26, called Christians *f* at Antioch
Rom. 2:9, 10, of the Jew *f*
8:23, the *f*-fruits of the Spirit
29, *f* born among many brethren
11:16, if the *f*-fruit be holy
I Cor. 12:28, *f* apostles, secondarily prophets
14:30, let the *f* hold peace
15:20, 23, Christ the *f*-fruits
45, the *f* man was made a living soul
II Cor. 8:5, *f* gave their own selves
Eph. 6:2, the *f* commandment with promise
Col. 1:15, 18, the *f*-born of every creature
I Thess. 4:16, dead in Christ shall rise *f*
II Thess. 2:3, a falling away *f*
I Tim. 1:16, that in me *f*
2:13, Adam was *f* formed
3:10, let these *f* be proved
5:4, learn *f* to show piety at home
12, cast off their *f* faith
II Tim. 4:16, at my *f* answer no man
Titus 3:10, after *f* and second admonition
Heb. 5:12, which be the *f* principles
James 3:17, *f* pure, then peaceable
I Pet. 4:17, if judgment *f* being at us
I Jn. 4:19, because he *f* loved us
Jude 6, kept not their *f* estate
Rev. 2:4, left your *f* love
5, do your *f* works
20:5, this is the *f* resurrection
21:1, *f* heaven and *f* earth passed away
See Ex. 4:8; Num. 18:13; Jn. 12:16
FISH Eccl. 9:12, *f* taken in an evil net
Hab. 1:14, men as the *f* of the sea
Mat. 7:10, if he ask a *f*
14:17; Mk. 6:38; Lk. 9:13, two *f*
Jn. 21:3, Peter says, I go a *f*
I Cor. 15:39, one flesh of beasts another of *f*
See Jer. 16:16; Mk. 1:17
FIT Job 34:18, is it *f* to say to a king
Lk. 9:62, is *f* for the kingdom
14:35, it is not *f* for the dunghill
Col. 3:18, submit, as it is *f* in the Lord
See Lev. 16:21; Prov. 24:27
FITLY Prov. 25:11; Eph. 2:21; 4:16
FIXED Ps. 57:7; 108:1; 112:7; Lk. 16:26
FLAME Gen. 3:24, at Eden a *f* sword
Judg. 13:20, angel ascended in *f*
Isa. 5:24, as the *f* consumed chaff
29:6, a *f* of devouring fire
43:2, neither shall *f* kindle
66:15, rebuke with *f* of fire
Ezek. 20:47, the *f f* shall not be quenched
Lk. 16:24, tormented in this *f*

See Ps. 29:7; Heb. 1:7; Rev. 1:14; 2:18
FLATTER Job 32:21, 22, give *f* tithes to man
　Ps. 5:9, they *f* with their tongue
　　12:2, *f* lips and double heart
　Prov. 20:19, meddle not with him that *f*
　　26:28, a *f* mouth works ruin
　I Thess. 2:5, neither used we *f* words
　See Prov. 28:23; 29:5; Dan. 11:21, 32, 34
FLEE Lev. 26:17, 36, *f* when none pursues
　Num. 10:35, them that hate you *f* before you
　Neh. 6:11, should such a man as I *f* ?
　Job 14:2, he *f* as a shadow
　Ps. 139:7, whither shall I *f*
　Song of Sol. 2:17; 4:6, till shadows *f* away
　Isa. 35:10; 51:11, sighing shall *f* away
　Mat. 3:7, to *f* from wrath to come
　　10:23, in one city, *f* to another
　　24:16; Lk. 21:21, *f* to mountains
　　26:56; Mk. 14:50, forsook him and *f*
　Jn. 10:5, not follow, but will *f* from him
　　10:13, the hireling *f*
　I Tim. 6;11, *f* these things
　II Tim. 2:22, *F* youthful lusts
　James 4:7, he will *f* from you
　See I Cor. 6:18; 10:14; Rev. 12:6
FLESH Ex. 16:3, when we sat by the *f*-pots
　Lev. 17:14, the life of all *f* is in the blood
　　19:28, cuttings in your *f*
　Num. 11:33, *f* was between their teeth
　　16:22; 27:16, God of spirits of all *f*
　II Chron. 32:8, with him is an arm of *f*
　Neh. 5:5, our *f* is as the *f* of our brethren
　Job 19:26, in my *f* shall I see God
　　33:21, his *f* is consumed away
　Ps. 16:9; Acts 2:26, my *f* shall rest in hope
　　65:2, to you shall all *f* come
　　78:20, can he provide *f*
　Prov. 5:11, mourn, when *f* consumed
　　11:17, the cruel troubles his own *f*
　　23:20, among riotous eaters of *f*
　Eccl. 4:5, the fool eats his own *f*
　　12:12, weariness of the *f*
　Isa. 40:5, all *f* shall see it
　　6; I Pet. 1:24, all *f* is grass
　Ezek. 11:19; 36:26, a heart of *f*
　Joel 2:28; Acts 2:17, pour Spirit on all *f*
　Mat. 16:17, *f* and blood has not revealed
　　24:22, there should no *f* be saved
　　26:41; Mk. 14:38, spirit willing, *f* weak
　Lk. 24:39, spirit has not *f* and bones
　Jn. 1:14, Word make *f*, and dwelt
　　6:51, 54, 55, bread I give is my *f*
　　52, can this man give us his *f*
　　63, the *f* profits nothing
　　8:15, you judge after the *f*
　　17:2, power over all *f*
　Rom. 6:19, because of the infirmity of your *f*
　　8:3, condemned sin in the *f*
　　8, they that are in *f* cannot please God
　　9, not in the *f*, but in the Spirit
　　9:3, kinsmen according to the *f*
　　5, of whom as concerning the *f*
　　13:14, make not provision for the *f*
　I Cor. 1:29, that no *f* should glory

　15:39, all *f* not the same *f*
　　50, *f* and blood cannot inherit
　II Cor. 12:7, a thorn in the *f*
　Gal. 1:16, I conferred not with *f* and blood
　　2:20, life I now live in the *f*
　　5:17, *f* lusts against the Spirit
　Eph. 2:3, lusts of *f*, desires of *f*
　Phil. 3:3, 4, no confidence in the *f*
　I Tim. 3:16, manifest in the *f*
　I Pet. 3:18, Christ put to death in *f*
　I Jn. 4:2, II Jn. 7, Christ is come in *f*
　Jude 8, dreamers defile the *f*
　　23, hating garment spotted by *f*
FLESHLY II Cor. 1:12, 3:3; Col. 2:18
FLIGHT Isa. 52:12; Amos 2:14; Mat. 24:20
FLINT Deut. 32:13; Isa. 5:28; 50:7; Ezek. 3:9
FLOCK Jer. 13:20, *f*, your beautiful *f*?
　Ezek. 34:31, the *f* of my pasture are men
　Zech. 11:7, the poor of the *f*
　Lk. 12:32, fear not little *f*
　Acts 20:28, take heed to the *f*
　　29, not sparing the *f*
　I Pet. 5:2, feed the *f* of God
　See Ezek. 36:37; Mal. 1:14; Mat. 26:31
FLOOD Josh. 24:2, on other side of the *f*
　Job 28:11, he binds *f* from overflowing
　Ps. 32:6, in *f* of great waters
　Song of Sol., 8:7, neither can *f* drown love
　Isa. 44:3, *f* upon the dry ground
　　59:19, enemy come in like a *f*
　Mat. 7:25, the *f* came, and the winds blew
　　24:38, in days before the *f*
　　39; Lk. 17:27, knew not till *f* came
　See Gen. 9:11; Ps. 90:5; II Pet. 2:5
FLOOR I Sam 23:1, they rob the threshing *f*
　II Sam. 24:21, to buy the threshing-*f* of you
　Hos. 9:1, loved a reward on every corn-*f*
　Mic. 4:12, gather as sheaves into the *f*
　Mat. 3:12; Lk. 3:17, purge his *f*
　See Deut. 15:14; Dan. 2:35; Joel 2:24
FLOURISH Ps. 90:6, in the morning it *f*
　　92:12, righteous shall *f* like a palm tree
　　103:15, as flower so he *f*
　Prov. 11:28, righteous shall *f* as branch
　　14:11, tabernacle of upright *f*
　Eccl. 12:5, when the almond tree shall *f*
　Song of Sol. 6:11; 7:12, whether the vine *f*
　Ezek. 17:24, have made dry tree to *f*
　Phil. 4:10, your care of me has *f*
　See Ps. 92:14; Dan. 4:4
FLOW Ps. 147:18, wind to blow, and waters *f*
　Song of Sol. 4:16, that the spices may *f* out
　Isa. 2:2, all nations shall *f* unto it
　　64:1, 3, mountains *f* at your presence
　Jer. 31:12, shall *f* to the goodness of the Lord
　John 7:38, shall *f* living water
　See Job 20:28; Isa. 60:5; Joel 3:18; Mic. 4:1
FLOWER I Sam. 2:33, shall die in *f* of age
　Job 14:2, comes forth as a *f*
　Song of Sol. 2:12, the *f* appear on Earth
　Isa. 28:1, 4, glorious beauty is a fading *f*
　　40:6, as the *f* of the field
　　7; Nah. 1:4; James 1:10, *f* fades
　See Job 15:33; Isa. 18:5; I Cor. 7:36

FLY Job 5:7, as sparks *f* upward
  Ps. 55:6, then would I *f* away
    90:10, and we *f* away
  Prov. 23:5, riches *f* away
  Isa. 60:8, that *f* as a cloud
  See Dan. 9:21; Rev. 14:6; 19:17

FOAM Hos. 10:7; Mk. 9:18; Lk. 9:39

FOES Ps. 27:2; 30:1; 89:23; Mat. 10:36

FOLD Prov. 6:10, *f* of the hands to sleep
  Eccl. 4:5, fool *f* his hands and eats
  Hab. 3:17, flock cut off from the *f*
  Jn. 10:16, one *f*, and one shepherd
  See Isa. 13:20, 65:10; Nah. 1:10

FOLK Prov. 30:26; Jer. 51:58; Mk. 6:5

FOLLOW Num. 14:24, Caleb has *f* me fully
  I Ki. 18:21, God, *f* him
  Ps. 23:6, goodness and mercy shall *f* me
    63:8, my soul *f* hard after you
    68:25, the players *f* after
  Prov. 12:11; 28:19, that *f* vain persons
  Isa. 5:11, that they may *f* strong drink
  Hos. 6:3, if we *f* on to know the Lord
  Amos 7:15, took me as I *f* the flock
  Mat. 4:19; 19:21; Mk. 2:14; Jn. 1:43, Jesus
    said, *f* me.
    8:19; Lk. 9:57, 61, Master, I will *f* you
  Mk. 10:28; Lk. 18:28, we left all, and *f* you
    32, as they *f*, they were afraid
  Lk. 22:54, Peter *f* afar off
  Jn. 10:27, my sheep hear my voice, and *f* me
  Rom. 14:19, *f* things that make for peace
  I Cor. 10:4, the rock that *f* them
  Phil. 3:12, I *f* after
  I Thess. 5:15, ever *f* that which is good
  I Tim. 5:24, some men they *f* after
    6:11; II Tim. 2:22, *f* righteousness
  Heb. 12:14, *F* peace with all men
  I Pet. 1:11, the glory that should *f*
    2:21, that you should *f* his steps
  II Pet. 2:15, *f* the way of Balaam
  Rev. 14:4, they that *f* the Lamb

FOLLOWERS Eph. 5:1, *f*, as dear children
  Heb. 6:12, *f* of them who through faith

FOLLY I Sam. 25:25, and *f* is with him
  Job 4:18, his angels he charged with *f*
    24:12, yet God lays not *f* to them
  Job 42:8, lest I deal with you after your *f*
  Ps. 49:13, this their way is their *f*
  Prov. 13:16, a fool lays open his *f*
    14:8, the *f* of fools is deceit
    18, the simple inherit *f*
    16:22, instruction of fools is *f*
    17:12, rather than a fool in his *f*
    26:4, answer not a fool according to his *f*
    5, answer fool according to his *f*
  Eccl. 1:17, to know wisdom and *f*
    2:13, wisdom excels *f*
    7:25, the wickedness of *f*
    10:6, *F* is set in great dignity
  II Cor. 11:1, bear with me a little in my *f*
  II Tim. 3:9, their *f* shall be manifest

FOOD Gen. 3:6, tree good for *f*
  Ex. 21:10, her *f* shall not be diminished
  Deut. 10:18, in giving him *f* and raiment

Ps. 78:25, did eat angels' *f*
  104:14, bring forth *f* out of the earth
  136:25, gives *f* to all flesh
Prov. 6:8, gathers her *f* in harvest
  13:23, much *f* in tillage of poor
  30:8, with *f* convenient for me
  31:14, she brings her *f* from afar
II Cor. 9:10, minister bread for your *f*
I Tim. 6:8, having *f* and raiment
James 2:15, destitute of daily *f*
See Gen. 2:9; 6:21; 41:35; Lev. 22:7

FOOL II Sam. 3:33, died Abner as a *f* dies?
  Ps. 14:1; 53:1, *f* said in his heart
    75:4, to *f*, deal not foolishly
  Prov. 1:7, *f* despite wisdom
    3:35, shame that promotion of *f*
    10:8, 10, a prating *f* shall fall
    21, *f* die for want of wisdom
    23, sport to a *f* to do mischief
    11:29, the *f* shall be servant to the wise
    12:15, way of *f* right in own eyes
    16, *f* wrath presently known
    13:16, *f* lays open his folly
    20, companion of *f* shall be destroyed
    14:16, the *f* rages, and is confident
    15:2, mouth of *f* pours out foolishness
    5, a *f* despises his father's instruction
    16:22, the instruction of *f* is folly
    17:28, a *f*, when he holds his peace
    29:11, a *f* utters all his mind
  Eccl. 2:14, *f* walks in darkness
    16, how dies wise man? as the *f*
    19, who knows whether wise or a *f*?
    10:14, a *f* is full of words
  Isa. 35:8, wayfaring men, though *f*
  Jer. 17:11, at his end he shall be a *f*
  Mat. 5:22, shall say, You *f*
  Lk. 12:20, you *f*, this night
    24:25, O *f*, and slow of heart
  I Cor. 3:18, let him become a *f*
  II Cor. 11:16, let no man think me a *f*
    12:11, I am a *f* in glorying
  Eph. 5:15, walk not as *f*, but as wise

FOOLISH Deut. 32:6, O *f* people
  II Sam. 24:10; I Chron. 21:8, I have done very *f*
  Job 2:10, as one of the *f* women
  Ps. 73:3, I was envious as the *f*
  Prov. 9:6, forsake the *f*, and live
    13, a *f* woman is clamorous
    14:1, the *f* plucks it down
  Jer. 4:22, my people are *f*
  Mat. 7:26, unto a *f* man
  Rom. 1:21, their *f* heart was darkened
  I Cor. 1:20, has not God made *f*
  Gal. 3:1, O *f* Galatians
  Eph. 5:4, nor *f* talking
  I Tim. 6:9, rich fall into *f* lusts
  II Tim. 2:23; Titus 3:9, *f* questions avoid
  Titus 3:3, we were sometimes *f*
  I Pet. 2:15, ignorance of *f* men

FOOLISHNESS Ps. 69:5, you know my *f*
  Prov. 22:15, *F* is bound in heart of child
    24:9, thought of *f* is sin
  I Cor. 1:18, to them that perish *f*

21, by the *f* of preaching
23, Christ crucified, to Greeks *f*
25, the *f* of God is wiser than men
2:14, things of Spirit are *f* to him
3:19, wisdom of world *f* with God
See II Sam. 15:31; Prov. 27:22
FOOT Gen. 41:44, without you no man lifts *f*
Deut. 2:5, not so much as *f* breadth
11:10, watered it with your *f*
Ps. 38:16, when my *f* slips
94:18, my *f* slips, your mercy
121:3, not suffer *f* to be moved
Prov. 3:23, your *f* shall not stumble
25:17, withdraw *f* from neighbor's house
Eccl. 5:1, keep your *f* when you go
Isa. 1:6, from sole of *f* to head no soundness
Mat. 14:13, people followed on *f*
18:8; Mk. 9:45, if your *f* offend you
I Cor. 12:15, if the *f* say, Because I am not
Heb. 10:29, trodden under *f* the Son of God
See Jer. 12:5; Mat. 5:35; James 2:3
FORBAD Mat. 3:14; Mk. 9:38; Lk. 9:49
FORBEAR Ex. 23:5, would *f* to help
II Chron. 35:21, *f* from meddling with God
Neh. 9:30, many years did you *f* them
Ezek. 2:5; 3:11, whether hear or *f*
I Cor. 9:6, power to *f* working
Eph. 4:2; Col. 3:13, *F* one another in love
6:9, *f* threatening
See Prov. 24:11; Ezek. 3:27; Zech. 11:12
FORBID Num. 11:28, Joshua said, *f* them
Mk. 9:39; Lk. 9:50, *F* him not
10:14; Lk. 18:16, children *f* them not
Lk. 6:29, *f* not to take coat
23:2, *f* to give tribute
Acts 10:47, can any *f* water?
I Cor. 14:39, *f* not to speak with tongues
I Tim. 4:3, *F* to marry
See Acts 16:6; 28:31; I Thess. 2:16
FORCE Deut. 34:7, nor natural *f* abated
Ezra 4:23, made them cease by *f*
Mat. 11:12, violent take it by *f*
Jn. 6:15, they would take him by *f*
Heb. 9:17, a testament is of *f* after
FORCIBLE Job 6:25
FOREFATHERS Jer. 11:10; II Tim. 1:3
FOREHEAD Ex. 28:38, it shall be on his *f*
I Sam. 17:49, smote Philistine in his *f*
Ezek. 3:8, made your *f* strong
9:4, set a mark on *f* of them that sigh
Rev. 7:3; 9:4, sealed in their *f*
22:4, his name shall be in their *f*
See Rev. 13:16; 14:1; 17:5; 20:4
FOREIGNER Ex. 12:45; Eph. 2:19
FOREKNOW Rom. 8:29; 11:2, I Pet. 1:2
FOREMOST Gen. 32:17; 33:2, II Sam. 18:27
FOREORDAINED I Pet. 1:20
FORERUNNER Heb. 6:20
FORESEE Prov. 22:3; 27:12; Gal. 3:8
FOREST Ps. 50:10, every best of *f* is mine
Isa. 29:17; 32:15, field esteemed as a *f*
Jer. 5:6, lion out of *f* shall slay them
26:18; Mic. 3:12, high places of the *f*
46:23, they shall cut down her *f*

Amos 3:4, will lion roar in the *f*
See Ezek. 15:6; 20:46; Hos. 2:12
FORETELL Mk. 13:23; Acts 3:24
FOREWARN Lk. 12:5; I Thess. 4:6
FORGAVE Mat. 18:27, 32, *f* him the debt
Lk. 7:42, he frankly *f* them both
43, he to whom he *f* most
II Cor. 2:10, if I *f* any thing
Col. 3:13, even as Christ *f* you
See Ps. 32:5; 78:38; 99:8
FORGE Job 13:4; Ps. 119:69
FORGET Deut. 4:9; lest you *f*
23, lest you *f* the covenant
6:12; 8:11, beware lest you *f* the Lord
Job 8:13, so are the paths of all that *f* God
Ps. 9:17, all nations that *f* God
10:12, *f* not the humble
45:10, *f* your own people
50:22, consider, ye that *f* God
78:7, that they might not *f* works of God
102:4, I *f* to eat my bread
103:2, *f* not all his benefits
119:16, I will not *f* your word
Prov. 2:17, *f* the covenant of her God
3:1, *f* not my law
31:5, lest they drink and *f*
7, let him drink, and *f* his poverty
Isa. 49:15, can a woman *f*
Isa. 51:13, and *f* the Lord your Maker
65:11, *f* my holy mountain
Phil. 3:13, *f* those things which are behind
Heb. 6:10, not unrighteous to *f*
James 1:24, *f* what manner of man
See Gen. 41:51; Lam. 5:20; Hos. 4:6
FORGIVE Ex. 32:32, if you will *f* their sin
34:7; Num. 14:18, *f* iniquity, transgression
I Ki. 8:30, 39; II Chron. 6:21, 30, hear, *f*
II Chron. 7:14, then will I hear and *f*
Ps. 32:1; Rom. 4:7, whose transgression is *f*
86:5, good, and ready to *f*
103:3, who *f* all your iniquities
Mat. 6:12; Lk. 11:4, *f* us, as we *f*
9:6; Mk. 2:10; Lk. 5:24, power to *f* sin
18:21, how oft, and I *f* him?
Mk. 2:7, who can *f* sins?
11:25, *f* that your Father may *f*
26, not *f*, Father will not *f*
Lk. 6:37, *f*, and you shall be *f*
7:47, her sins, which are many, are *f*
49, who is this *f* sins also?
17:3, 4, if brother repent, *f* him
23:34, Father *f* them, they know not
Acts 8:22, thought of heart *f*
II Cor. 2:7, you ought rather to *f*
10, to whom you *f*, I *f* also
12:13, *f* me this wrong
Eph. 4:32, as God for Christ's sake has *f*
Col. 2:13, quickened, having *f*
I Jn. 1:9, faithful and just to *f*
FORGIVENESS Ps. 130:4, *f* with you
Mk. 3:29, has never *f*
Acts 5:31, exalted to give *f*
Eph. 1:7; Col. 1:14, in whom we have *f*
See Dan. 9:9; Acts 13:38; 26:18

FORGOT Judg. 3:7, they *f* the Lord
  Ps. 78:11, they *f* his works
  Lam. 3:17, I *f* prosperity
FORGOTTEN Deut. 32:18, *f* God that formed
  you
  Ps. 9:18, needy not always *f*
    42:9, why have you *f* me?
    44:20, if we have *f* name of our God
    77:9, has God *f* to be gracious
  Isa. 17:10, *f* the God of your salvation
    44:21, you shall not be *f* of me
    49:14, my Lord has *f* me
    65:16, former troubles are *f*
  Jer. 2:32; 13:25; 18:15, my people have *f*
    3:21, *f* the Lord their God
    44:9, *f* the wickedness of your fathers
  Ezek. 22:12; 23:35, you have *f* me
  Mat. 16:5; Mk. 8:14, *f* to take bread
  Lk. 12:6, not one *f* before God
  II Pet. 1:9, *f* that he was purged
FORM (*n.*) Gen. 1:2; Jer. 4:23, without *f*
  Job 4:16, could not discern the *f*
  Isa. 52:14, *f* more than sons of men
  Ezek. 10:8, the *f* of a man's hand
  Dan. 3:19, *f* of visage changed
  Mk. 16:12, appeared in another *f*
  Rom. 2:20, have *f* of knowledge and truth
  Phil. 2:6, being in the *f* of God
  II Tim. 1:13, *f* of sound words
    3:5, having *f* of godliness
  See I Sam. 28:14; Ezek. 43:11; Rom. 6:17
FORM (*v.*) II Ki. 19:25; Isa. 37:26, that I have
  f it
  Job 26:5, dead things are *f*
    13, has *f* crooked serpent
  Ps. 90:2, or ever you had *f*
  Prov. 26:10, great God that *f* all things
  Isa. 43:1, he that *f* you, O Israel
    10, before me was no God *f*
    54:17, no weapon *f* against me
  Amos 7:1, he *f* grasshoppers
  Rom. 9:20, shall thing *f* say
  Gal. 4:19, till Christ be *f* in you
  See Gen. 2:7, 19; Ps. 95:5; Jer. 1:5
FORMER Ruth 4:7, manner in *f* time
  Job 8:8, enquire of the *f* age
  Ps. 89:49, where are your *f* loving kindness?
  Eccl. 1:11, no remembrance of *f* things
    7:10, *f* days better than these
  Isa. 43:18, remember not the *f* things
    46:9, remember the *f* things of old
    48:3, declared *f* things from beginning
    65:7, measure their *f* work
    16, *f* troubles are forgotten
  Jer. 5:24; Joel 2:23, *f* and latter rain
    10:16; 51:19; the *f* of all things
  Zech. 1:4; 7:7, 12, *f* prophets have cried
    8:11, I will not be as in *f* days
    14:8, half of them toward *f* sea
  Mal. 3:4, pleasant as in *f* years
  Eph. 4:22, concerning the *f* conversation
  Rev. 21:4, for the *f* things are passed away
  See Gen. 40:13; Dan. 11:13; Acts 1:1
FORNICATION II Chron. 21:11; Isa. 23:17;

  Ezek. 16:15, 26, 29
  Mat. 5:32, put away wife saving, for *f*
  Jn. 8:41, we be not born of *f*
  Acts 15:20, abstain from *f*
  Rom. 1:29, filled with *f* wickedness
  I Cor. 5:1, there is *f* among you
    6:13, body not for *f*
    7:2, to avoid *f* have own wife
    10:8, neither let us commit *f*
  II Cor. 12:21, not repented of their *f*
  Gal. 5:19, works of flesh, adultery, *f*
  Eph. 5:3, *f* let it not be named
  Col. 3:5, mortify *f* uncleanness
  I Thess. 4:3, should abstain from *f*
  Rev. 2:14, taught to commit *f*
    2:21, I gave her space to repent her *f*
    9:21, neither repented of their *f*
    14:8, of the wine of her *f*
    17:2, abomination of her *f*
    18:3, committed *f* with her
    19:2, did corrupt earth with her *f*
  See Mat. 15:19; Acts 21:25; I Cor. 5:9; 6:9;
    Heb. 12:16; Rev. 18:9
FORSAKE Deut. 4:31; 31:6
    12:19, *f* not the Levite
    32:15, he *f* God which made him
  Josh. 1:5; Heb. 13:5, I will not fail not *f*
  Judg. 9:11, *f* my sweetness and fruit
  II Chron. 15:2, if you *f* him, he will *f* you
  Neh. 10:39, we will not *f* house of our God
    13:11, why is house of God *f*?
  Job 6:14, he *f* the fear of the Almighty
    20:19, oppressed and *f* the poor
  Ps. 22:1; Mat. 27:46; Mk. 15:34
    37:28, the Lord *f* not his saints
    138:8, *f* not work of your own hands
  Prov. 1:8; 6:20, *f* not law of your mother
    2:17, *f* the guide of her youth
    4:6, *F* her not, and she shall preserve you
    27:10, your friend, and father's friend, *f* not
  Isa. 6:12, a great *f* in the land
    17:9, as a *f* bough
    32:14; Jer. 4:29; Ezek. 36:4, a *f* city
    54:6, as a woman *f*
    54:7, for a small moment *f*
  Jer. 2:13; 17:13, *f* fountain of living waters
  Mat. 19:27; Lk. 5:11, we have *f* all
    19:29, that has *f* houses
    26:56; Mk. 14:50, disciples *f* him
  Mk. 1:18, they *f* their nets
  II Cor. 4:9, persecuted, but not *f*
  II Tim 4:10, Demas has *f* me
    4:16, all men *f* me
  Heb. 10:25, not *f* assembling of ourselves
    11:27, by faith Moses *f* Egypt
  See Ps. 71:11; Isa. 49:14; Jer. 5:7; 22:9
FORSWEAR Mat. 5:33
FORWARD Jer. 7:24, backward, and not *f*
  Zech. 1:15, helped *f* the affliction
  See II Cor. 8:8; 9:2; III John 6
FOUL Job 16:16; Mat. 16:3; Mk. 9:25
FOUND Gen. 27:20, *f* it so quickly
    44:16, has *f* out iniquity
  I Ki. 20:36, a lion *f* him

21:20, have you *f* me?
II Ki. 22:8, I *f* book of the law
II Chron. 19:3, good things *f* in you
Job 28:12, 13, where shall wisdom be *f*?
   33:24, I have *f* a ransom
Ps. 32:6, when you may be *f*
   36:2, iniquity *f* to be hateful
   84:3, sparrow has *f* an house
Prov. 25:16, have you *f* honey?
Eccl. 7:28, one among a thousand have I *f*
   7:29, this only have I *f*
Jer. 2:26, thief ashamed when he is *f*
   2:34, in your skirts is *f*, 41:8, ten men were *f*
Ezek. 22:30, I sought for a man, but *f* none
Dan. 5:27, weighed, and *f* wanting
Mal. 2:6, iniquity not *f* in his lips
Mat. 7:25, *f* upon a rock
   8:10; Lk. 7:9, have not *f* so great faith
   13:46, *f* one pearl of great price
   20:6, *f* others standing idle
Mk. 7:2, they *f* fault
   7:30, she *f* the devil gone out
Lk. 2:46, the *f* him in the temple
   8:35, they *f* the man clothed
   15:5, 6, *f* the sheep
   9, *f* the piece of money
   23:14, I have *f* no fault
   24:2, *f* the stone rolled away
   3, 23, *f* not the body
Jn. 1:41, 45, we have *f* the Messias
Acts 7:11, our fathers *f* no sustenance
Rom. 7:10, I *f* to be unto death
Gal. 2:17, we ourselves also are *f* sinners
Phil. 2:8, *f* in fashion, as a man
Heb. 11:5, Enoch was not *f*
   12:17, he *f* no place of repentance
Rev. 3:2, not *f* your works perfect
   12:8, nor was their place *f* any more
FOUNDATION Josh 6:26; I Ki. 16:34, lay *f* in
   his firstborn
Job 4:19, them whose *f* is in dust
Ps. 11:3, if *f* be destroyed
   82:5, all the *f* of earth out of course
   102:25, of old laid *f* of earth
   137:7, raise it even to the *f*
Prov. 10:25, righteous an everlasting *f*
Isa. 28:16, I lay in Zion a *f*
   58:12, the *f* of many generations
Lk. 6:48, laid the *f* on a rock
Rom. 15:20, on another man's *f*
I Cor. 3:10, I laid the *f*
   11, other *f* can no man lay
   12, if any man build on this *f*
I Tim. 6:19, laying up for themselves a *f*
II Tim. 2:19, the *f* of God stands sure
Heb. 6:1, not laying the *f* of repentance
   11:10, a city that has *f*
Rev. 21:14, the wall had twelve *f*
See Mat. 13:35; Jn. 17:24; Acts 16:26
FOUNTAIN Gen. 7:11; 8:2, *f* of great deep
Deut. 8:7, a land of *f*
II Chron. 32:3, took counsel to stop *f* of
   water
Ps. 36:9, the *f* of life

Prov. 5:16, let your *f* be dispersed
   8:24, no *f* abounding with water
   13:14, law of the wise a *f* of life
   14:27, fear of the Lord a *f* of life
   25:26, a troubled *f* and corrupt spring
Eccl. 12:6, pitcher broken at the *f*
Song of Sol. 4:12, a *f* sealed, 4:15, a *f* of
   gardens
Jer. 2:13; 17:13, forsaken *f* of living waters
   9:1, eyes a *f* of tears
Hos. 13:15, his *f* shall be dried up
Zech. 13:1, in that day shall be a *f* opened
James 3:11, 12, doth a *f* send forth
Rev. 7:17, lead them to living *f*
   14:7, worship him that made *f* of waters
   21:6, of the *f* of life freely
See Jer. 6:7; Joel 3:18; Mk. 5:29
FOXES Judg. 15:4; Ps. 63:10; Lam. 5:18; Ezek.
   13:4; Mat. 8:20; Lk. 13:32
FRAGMENTS Jn. 6:12, 13, gather up *f*
See Mat. 14:20; Mk. 6:43; 8:19, Lk. 9:17
FRAIL Ps. 39:4
FRAME Judg. 12:6, he could not *f* to pro-
   nounce
Ps. 94:20, *f* mischief by a law
   103:14, he knows our *f*
Isa. 29:16, shall things *f* say of him that *f* it
Eph. 2:21, building fitly *f* together
See Ezek. 40:2; Hos. 5:4; Heb. 11:3
FRANKLY Lk. 7:42
FRAUD Ps. 10:7; James 5:4
FRAY Deut. 28:26; Jer. 7:33; Zech. 1:21
FREE Gen. 2:16, of every tree you may *f*
Deut. 24:5, shall be *f* at home one year
Josh. 9:23, there shall none of you be *f*
I Sam. 14:30, if people had eaten *f*
II Chron 29:31, of *f* heart offered
Ezra 2:68, chief fathers offered *f*
   7:15, king and counsellors offered *f* to God
Ps. 51:12, with your *f* spirit
   88:5, *F* among the dead
Isa. 58:6, let the oppressed go *f*
Hos. 14:4, I will love them *f*
Mat. 10:8, *f* you have received, *f* give
   17:26, then are the children *f*
Mk. 7:11, say Corban, he shall be *f*
Jn. 8:32, the truth shall make you *f*
   33, how say you, you shall be made *f*?
   36, Son make you *f*, you shall be *f* indeed!
Acts 22:28, I was *f* born
Rom. 3:24, justified *f* by his grace
   5:15, the *f* gift
   6:20, servants of sin, *f* from righteousness
   8:2, *f* from the law of sin and death
   32, with him *f* give us all things
Gal. 3:28, there is neither bond nor *f*
   5:1, wherewith Christ has made us *f*
II Thess. 3:1, word have *f* course
I Pet 2:16, as *f*, and not using liberty
Rev. 21:6, give of fountain of life *f*
   22:17, let him take water of life *f*
FRESH Num. 11:8; Job 29:20; 33:25
FRET Ps. 37:1, 7, 8, *F* not yourself
Prov. 19:3, his heart *f* against the Lord

See I Sam. 1:6; Isa. 8:21; Ezek. 16:43
FRIEND Ex. 33:11, as a man to his *f*
  Job 6:27, you dig a pit for your *f*
    42:10, when he prayed for his *f*
  Ps. 35:14, as though he had been my *f*
    41:9, my familiar *f* has lifted
  Prov. 6:1, if you be surety for your *f*
    14:20, the rich has many *f*
    16:28, whisperer separates chief *f*
    17:17, *f* loves at all times
    19:4, wealth makes many *f*
    27:6, faithful are wounds of a *f*
    10, your *f* and father's *f* forsake not
  Song of Sol. 5:16, this is my *f*
  Isa. 41:8, seed of Abraham my *f*
  Zech. 13:6, wounded in the house of my *f*
  Mat. 11:19; Lk. 7:34, a *f* of publicans
    20:13, *F* I do you no wrong
    22:12, *F*, now came you hither
    26:50, *F*, wherefore are you come
  Mk. 5:19, go home to your *f*
  Lk. 11:5, which of you shall have a *f*
    14:12, call not your *f*
    15:6, 9, calls his *f* and neighbors
    16:9, *f* of the mammon
  Jn. 11:11, our *f* Lazarus sleeps
    15:13, lay down his life for his *f*
    14, you are my *f*, if you do what I command
  Jn 15:15, not servants, but *f*
    19:12, you are not Caesar's *f*
  James 2:23, Abraham was called *F* of God
    4:4, a *f* of the world
  See Prov. 22:24; Lk. 14:10; III Jn. 14
FROWARD Deut. 32:20, a *f* generation
  Prov. 2:12, man that speaks *f* things
    3:32, the *f* is abomination
    4:24, put away *f* mouth
    11:20; 17:20, of a *f* heart
    16:28, a *f* man sows strife
    21:8, the way of man is *f*
    22:5, snares are in way of the *f*
  See Prov. 10:32, Isa. 57:17; I Pet. 2:18
FRUIT Deut. 26:2, take the first of all *f*
    33:14, precious *f* brought forth
  Ps. 107:37, yield *f* of increase
    127:3, the *f* of the womb is his reward
  Prov. 8:19, my *f* is better than gold
    11:30, *f* of the righteous a tree of life
    12:14, satisfied by the *f* of his mouth
  Song of Sol. 2:3, his *f* was sweet of my taste
    4:13, 16, orchard with pleasant *f*
  Isa. 3:10; Mic. 7:13, the *f* of their doings
    27:6, fill face of the world with *f*
    28:4, the hasty *f* before summer
    57:19, I create the *f* of the lips
  Hos. 10:13, eaten the *f* of lies
  Amos 8:1, basket of summer *f*
  Mic. 6:7, *f* of body for sin of soul
  Hab. 3:17, neither shall *f* be in vines
  Hag. 1:10, Earth is stayed from her *f*
  Mat. 3:8, *f* meet for repentance
    7:16, 20, by their *f* ye shall know them
    12:33, make tree good and his *f* good

  21:19, let no *f* grow on you
    34, when time of *f* drew near
    26:29; Mk. 14:25, drink of *f* of vine
  Mk. 4:28, Earth brings forth *f* of herself
  Mk. 12:2, receive the *f* of the vineyard
  Lk. 13:6, he sought *f* thereon
  Jn. 4:36, *f* to life eternal
    15:2, branch that bears *f*
    4, branch cannot bear *f* of itself
    16, ordained that you should bring forth *f*
  Rom. 1:13, have some *f* among you
  II Cor. 9:10, the *f* of righteousness
  Gal. 5:22; Eph. 5:9, the *f* of the Spirit
  Phil. 1:22, this is the *f* of my labor
    4:17, I desire *f* that may abound
  Col. 1:6, gospel brings forth *f*
  II Tim. 2:6, first partaker of the *f*
  Heb. 12:11, peaceable *f* of righteousness
    13:15, the *f* of our lips
  James 3:17, wisdom full of good *f*
    5:7, wait for the precious *f*
  Jude 12, trees whose *f* withers without *f*
  Rev. 22:2, yielded her *f* every month
  See Gen. 30:2; Ps. 92:14; Col. 1:10
FRUSTRATE Ezra 4:5; Isa. 44:25; Gal. 2:21
FUEL Isa. 9:5; Ezek. 15:4; 21:32
FULFIL Ps. 20:4, Lord *f* all your counsel
    5, *f* all your petitions
    145:19, he will *f* the desire of them
  Mat. 3:15, to *f* all righteousness
    5:17, not to destroy, but to *f*
  Mk. 13:4, sign when these shall be *f*
  Lk. 1:20, my words shall be *f* in season
    21:24, times of the Gentiles be *f*
    22:16, till it be *f* in Kingdom of God
  Jn. 3:29; 17:13, this my joy is *f*
  Acts 13:25, and as John *f* his corpse
    33, God has *f* the same unto us
  Rom. 13:10, love is the *f* of the law
  Gal. 5:14, all the law is *f* in one word
    6:2, so *f* the law of Christ
  Eph. 2:3, *f* the desires of the flesh
  Phil. 2:2, *F* ye my joy
  Col. 4:17, take heed *f* the ministry
  II Thess. 1:11, *f* good pleasure of his will
  James 2:8, if you *f* the royal law
  See Ex. 5:13; 23:26; Gal. 5:16; Rev. 17:17
FULL Lev. 19:29, land *f* of wickedness
  Deut. 6:11, houses *f* of good things
    34:9, Joshua was *f* of spirit of wisdom
  Ruth 1:21, I went out *f*
  II Ki. 6:17, mountain was *f* of horses
  I Chron. 21:22, 24, for the *f* price
  Job 5:26, come to grave in *f* age
    11:2, a man *f* of talk
    20:11, *f* of the sins of youth
    21:23, dies in his *f* strength
    32:18, I am *f* of matter
  Ps. 10:7; Rom. 3:14, mouth *f* of cursing
    65:9, which is *f* of water
    74:20, *f* of habitations of cruelty
    119:64 earth is *f* of your mercy
    127:5, happy the man that has quiver *f*
  Eccl. 1:7, yet the sea is not *f*

Hab. 3:3, earth *f* of his praise
Zech. 8:5, streets *f* of boys and girls
Mat. 6:22; Lk. 11:36, *f* of light
Lk. 6:25, woe unto you that are *f*!
    11:39, *f* of ravening
Jn. 1:14, *f* of grace and truth
    15:11; 16:24, that your joy might be *f*
Acts 6:3, men *f* of the Holy Ghost
    9:36, *f* of good works
Rom. 15:14, you also are *f* of goodness
I Cor. 4:8, now you are *f*
II Tim. 4:5, make *f* proof of your ministry
Heb. 5:14, meat to them of *f* age
Rev. 15:7, *f* of the wrath of God
    See Lev. 2:14; II Ki. 4:6; 10:21; Job 21:24; Jer.
      23:10; Amos 2:13
FULLY Num. 14:24, Caleb followed me *f*
Eccl. 8:11, heart is *f* set to do evil
Rom. 14:5, let every man be *f* persuaded
    15:19, I have *f* preached the Gospel
Rev. 14:18, her grapes are *f* ripe
    See I Ki. 11:6; Acts 2:1; Rom. 4:21
FULLNESS Ps. 16:11, *f* of joy
Jn. 1:16, of his *f* have we received
Rom. 11:25, the *f* of the Gentiles
Eph. 1:23, *f* of him that fills all in all
    3:19, filled with the *f* of God
    4:13, the stature of the *f* of Christ
Col. 1:19, in him should all *f* dwell
    2:9, the *f* of the Godhead bodily
    See Num. 18:27; Ps. 96:11; Rom. 11:12
FURIOUS Prov. 22:24; 29:22
Nah. 1:2, the Lord is *f*
    See II Ki. 9:20; Ezek. 5:15; 23:25
FURNACE Ps. 12:6, as silver tried in a *f*
Isa. 48:10, in the *f* of affliction
Mat. 13:42, into a *f* of fire
    See Gen. 15:17; 19:28; I Ki. 8:51
FURNISH Ps. 78:19; Mat. 22:10; II Tim 3:17
FURROWS Ps. 65:10; 129:3; Hos. 10:4; 12:11
FURTHER Ezra 8:36, they *f* the people
Job 38:11, hitherto shall you come, but no *f*
Acts 4:17, that is spread no *f*
II Tim. 3:9, they shall proceed no *f*
    See Mk. 5:35; Phil. 1:12, 25
FURY Gen. 27:44, till your brother's *f* turn
Isa. 27:4; *F* is not in me
    63:5, my *f* upheld me
Jer. 21:5, I will fight against you in *f*
    25:15, the wine cup of this *f*
Ezek. 21:17, I will cause my *f* to rest
    See Dan. 3:13, 19; 8:6; 9:16; 11:44

G

GAIN Job 22:3, is it *g* to him
Prov. 1:19; 15:27; Ezek. 22:12, greedy of *g*
    3:14, the *g* thereof better than gold
    28:8, by usury and unjust *g*
Ezek. 22:13, 27, at your dishonest *g*
Dan. 11:39, he shall divide the land for *g*
Mic. 4:13, consecrate their *g* to the Lord
Mat. 16:26; Mk. 8:36
Lk. 19:15, 16, 18, had *g* by trading

Acts 16:19, hope of their *g* was gone
    19:24, no small *g* to the craftsmen
I Cor. 9:19, that I might *g* the more
    20, that I might *g* the Jews
II Cor. 12:17, 18, did I make a *g* of you
Phil. 1:21, to die is *g*
I Tim. 6:5, supposing that *g* godliness
    6, godliness with contentment is great *g*
    See Judg. 5:19; Job 27:8; James 4:13
GAINSAY Lk. 21:15; Titus 1:9; Jude 11
GALL Ps. 69:21; Lam. 3:19; Mat. 27:34
GAP Ezek. 13:5; 22:30
GARDEN Gen. 13:10, as the *g* of the Lord
Deut. 11:10; I Ki. 21:2, as a *g* of herbs
Song of Sol. 4:12, a *g* enclosed
    5:1, I am come into my *g*
    6:2, 11, gone down into his *g*
Isa. 1:8, as a lodge in a *g*
    30, as a *g* that has no water
    51:3, her desert like the *g* of the Lord
    58:11; Jer. 31:12, like a watered *g*
Jer. 29:5, plant *g*, and eat the fruit
Ezek. 28:13, in Eden the *g* of God
    31:8, 9, cedars in *g* of God
    36:35, is become like the *g* of Eden
Joel 2:3, land as the *g* of Eden before them
Jn. 18:26, did not I see you in the *g*?
    19:41, there was a *g*, and in the *g*
    See Gen. 2:15; Amos 4:9; 9:14; Jn. 20:15
GARMENT Gen. 39:12, left his *g*, and fled
    49:11, washed his *g* in wine
Josh. 7:21, a goodly Babylonish *g*
    9:5, Gibeonites took old *g*
II Ki. 5:26, is it a time to receive *g*
    7:15, all the way was full of *g*
Job 37:17, how your *g* are warm
Ps. 22:18, they part my *g* among them
    102:26; Heb. 1:11, wax old as a *g*
    104:2, with light as with a *g*
    6, covers it with the deep as with a *g*
Prov. 20:16, take his *g* that is surety
    25:20, a *g* in cold weather
    30:4, who has bound the waters in a *g*
Eccl. 9:8, let your *g* be always white
Isa. 52:1, put on your beautiful *g*
    61:3, *g* of praise for spirit of heaviness
    10, the *g* of salvation
Joel 2:13, rend your heart and not your *g*
Zech. 13:4, a rough *g* to deceive
Mat. 9;16; Mk. 2:21; Lk. 8:44, hem of *g*
    21:8; Mk. 11:8, spread *g* in way
    22:11, 12, wedding *g*
    27:35; Mk. 15:24, parted *g*, casting lots
Mk. 11:7; Lk. 19:35, cast *g* on colt
    13:16, not turn back again to take *g*
Lk. 22:36, let him sell his *g*
    24:4, in shining *g*
Acts 9:39, showing the coats and *g*
James 5:2, your *g* are motheaten
Jude 23, the *g* spotted by the flesh
Rev. 3:4, not defiled their *g*
    16:15, that watches, and keeps his *g*
GARNER Ps. 114:13; Joel 1:17; Mat. 3:12
GARNISH Job 26:13; Mat. 12:44; 23:29

GATE Gen. 28:17, the *g* of Heaven
  Deut. 6:9; 11:20, write them on your *g*
  Ps. 118:19, the *g* of righteousness
  Prov. 17:19, exalts *g* seeks destruction
    31:23, her husband known in the *g*
  Isa. 26:2, open the *g*, righteous may enter
    38:10, the *g* of the grave
    45:1, open the two-leaved *g*
    60:11, your *g* shall be open continually
    18, walls Salvation, and *g* Praise
  Mat. 7:13; Lk. 13:24, strait *g* wide *g*
    16:18, *g* of hell shall not prevail
  Heb. 13:12, also suffered without the *g*
  Rev. 21:25, *g* not shut at all by day
  See Ps. 24:7; Isa. 28:6; Nah. 2:6
GATHER Ex. 16:17, *g*, some more, some less
  Deut. 28:38, carry much out, and *g* little in
    30:3, will *g* you from all nations
  II Sam. 14:14, split, which cannot be *g* up
  Job 11:10, if he *g* together, who can hinder?
  Ps. 26:9, *G* not my soul with sinners
    39:6, knows not who shall *g* them
  Prov. 6:8, the ant *g* her food
    10:5, he that *g* in summer
    13:11, he that *g* by labor shall increase
  Isa. 27:12, you shall be *g* one by one
    40:11, he shall *g* the lambs
    62:10, *g* out the stones
  Mat. 3:12; Lk. 3:17, *g* wheat into garner
    6:26, nor *g* into barns
    7:16; Lk. 6:44, do men *g* grapes of thorns?
    12:30; Lk. 11:23, he that *g* not scatters
    13:28, will you we *g* them up?
    29, lest while you *g* up the tares
    41, shall *g* out of his kingdom
    25:32, before him shall be *g* all nations
  Jn. 6:12, *g* up fragments
    15:6, men *g* them, and cast
  I Cor. 16:2, that there be no *g* when I come
  II Thess. 2:1, by our *g* together unto him
  See Mat. 23:37; Jn 4:36; 11:52
GAVE Gen. 3:12, the woman *g* me
  Josh. 21:44, Lord *g* them rest
  I Sam. 10:9, *g* to Saul another heart
  Job. 1:21, the Lord *g*
  Ps. 21:4, he asked life, and you *g* it
    68:11, the Lord *g* the word
  Eccl. 12:7, to God who *g* it
  Amos 2:12, you *g* the Nazarites wine
  Mat. 21:23; Mk. 11:28
    25:35, 42, you *g* me meat
  Lk. 15:16, no man *g* unto him
  Jn. 10:29, my Father, who *g* them
  Acts 2:4, as the Spirit *g* them utterance
    26:10, I *g* my voice against them
  Rom. 1:28, God *g* them over
  I Cor. 3:6, God *g* the increase
  See II Cor. 8:5; Gal. 1:4; Titus 2:14
GAY James 2:3
GAZE Ex. 19:21; Acts 1:11; Heb. 10:33
GENERATION Deut. 32:5, 20, a perverse and
    crooked *g*
  Ps. 14:5, God is in the *g* of the righteous
    22:30, it shall be accounted for a *g*

    102:18, written for the *g* to come
    145:4, one *g* shall praise your works
  Prov. 27:24, crown endure to every *g*
    30:11, there is a *g* that curses
  Eccl 1:4, one *g* passes away
  Isa. 34:10, form *g* to *g* it shall lie waste
  Joel 1:3, children tell another *g*
  Mat. 3:7; 12:34; Lk. 3:7, *g* of vipers
    12:41, in judgment with this *g*
    17:17; Mk. 9:19; Lk. 21:32, perverse *g*
    23:36, shall come on this *g*
    24:34; Mk. 13:30
  Lk. 16:8, are in their *g* wiser
  Lk. 17:25, rejected of this *g*
  I Pet. 2:9, a chosen *g*
  See Isa. 53:8; Dan. 4:3; Lk. 11:30
GENTILES Mat. 10:5, go not in way of *G*
  Jn. 7:35, to the dispersed among *G*
  Acts 9:15, bear my name before the *G*
    13:42, *G* besought that these words
    46, we turn to the *G*
    15:3, declaring conversion of the *G*
    18:6, from henceforth I will go to the *G*
  Rom. 3:29, is he not also of the *G*?
    11:11, salvation is come to the *G*
    13, as the apostle of the *G*
  I Cor. 5:1, not so much as named among *G*
  Eph. 4:17, walk not as other *G*
  II Tim. 1:11, I am ordained a teacher of *G*
  III Jn. 7, taking nothing of the *G*
  See Rom. 2:9; I Pet. 2:12; Rev. 11:2
GENTLE II Tim. 2:24, servant of Lord be *g*
  Titus 3:2, *g*, showing all meekness
  James 3:17, wisdom is pure and *g*
  I Pet. 2:18, not only to the good and *g*
  See II Sam. 18:5; 22:36; Gal. 5:22
GETTETH Prov. 3:13; 4:7; 19:8; Jer. 17:11
GIFT Ex. 23:8; Deut. 16:19, a *g* blinds
  II Sam. 19:42, has he given us any *g*?
  II Chron. 19:7, with the Lord not taking of *g*
  Ps. 68:18; Eph. 4:8, *g* for men
    72:10, kings of Sheba and Seba offer *g*
  Prov. 6:35, not content, though many *g*
    15:27, he that hates *g* shall live
    17:8, a *g* is a precious stone
    18:16, man's *g* makes room for him
    21:14, a *g* in secret pacifies anger
  Eccl. 3:13; 5:19, enjoy good, it is God's *g*
    7:7, a *g* destroys the heart
  Isa. 1:23, every one loves *g*
  Mat. 5:23, bring your *g* to the Altar
    24, leave your *g* before the Altar
    7:11; Lk. 11:3, know how to give good *g*
  Lk. 21:1, casting *g* into treasury
  Jn. 4:10, if you knew the *g* of God
  Rom. 1:11, some spiritual *g*
    6:23, the *g* of God is eternal life
    11:29, *g* of God without repentance
    12:6, *g* differing according to grace
  I Cor. 7:7, his proper *g* of God
    12:31, covet best *g*
  II Cor. 9:15, unspeakable *g*
  Eph. 2:8, faith the *g* of God
  I Tim. 4:14, neglect not the *g*

II Tim. 1:6, stir up the *g*
James 1:17, good and perfect *g*
See Num. 18:29; Mat. 15:5; Acts 2:38
GIRD II Sam. 22:40; Ps. 18:39, have *g* me
Isa. 45:5, I *g* you though you have not
Joel 1:13, *G* yourselves and lament
Eph. 6:14, having your loins *g*
See Prov. 31:17; Jn. 13:4; Rev. 15:6
GIRDLE Isa. 11:5; Mat. 3:4; Mk. 1:6
GIRL Joel 3:3; Zech. 8:5
GIVE Gen. 28:22, I will *g* the tenth
Ex. 30:15, rich not *g* more, poor not *g* less
Deut. 15:10, you shall *g* him your heart
16:17; Ezek. 46:5, *g* as he is able
I Chron. 29:14, of your own have we *g* you
Ezra 9:9, to *g* us a reviving
Ps. 2:8, I shall *g* you the heathen
6:5, in the grave who shall *g* thanks?
29:11, Lord will *g* strength
37:4, *g* you desires of your heart
21, the righteous shows mercy, and *g*
84:11, Lord will *g* grace and glory
109:4, I *g* myself unto prayer
Prov. 23:26, *g* me your heart
Isa. 55:10, *g* seed to the sower
Mat. 5:42, *G* to him that asks
6:11; Lk. 11:3, *G* daily bread
13:11; Mk. 4:11, It is *g* to you to know
16:26; Mk. 8:37, *g* in exchange
19:21, go and sell, and *g* to the poor
20:23; Mk. 10:40, not mine to *g*
26:9; Mk. 14:5, sold, and *g* to the poor
Lk. 6:38, *G* and it shall be *g*
Jn. 4:7, 10, *G* me to drink
6:37, all that the Father *g* me
10:28, I *g* to them eternal life
13:29, that he should *g* something to poor
Jn. 14:27, not as the world *g*, *g* I
Acts 3:6, such as I have *g* I thee
6:4, we will *g* ourselves to prayer
20:35, more blessed to *g*
Rom. 12:8, he that *g*, let him do it
I Cor. 3:7, God *g* the increase
II Cor. 9:7, *g* not grudgingly, a cheerful *g*
Phil. 4:15, concerning *g* and receiving
I Tim. 4:13, *g* attendance to reading
15, *g* yourself wholly to them
James 1:5, that *g* to all men liberally
4:6, *g* more grace, *g* grace to humble
II Pet. 1:5, *g* all diligence
See I Tim. 3:3; Jude 7
GLAD Ex. 4:14, he will be *g* in heart
Job 3:22, *g* when they can find the grave
Ps. 16:9, therefore my heart is *g*
34:2; 69:32, humble shall hear, and be *g*
46:4, make *g* the city of God
104:15, makes *g* the heart of man
122:1, I was *g* when they said
126:3, whereof we are *g*
Prov. 24:17, let not your heart be *g*
Lam. 1:21, they are *g* you have done it
Lk. 15:32, make merry, and be *g*
Jn. 8:56, saw my day, and was *g*
11:15, I am *g* for your sakes

GLADNESS Num. 10:10, in day of your *g*
Deut. 28:47, served not with *g* of heart
Neh. 8:17, there was very great *g*
Ps. 4:7, you have put *g* in my heart
45:7; Heb. 1:9, the oil of *g*
97:11, *g* is sown for the upright
Isa. 35:10; 51:11, they shall obtain joy, and *g*
Acts 2:46, did eat with *g* of heart
14:17, filling our hearts with food and *g*
See Ps. 100:2; Prov. 10:28; Isa. 51:3
GLASS I Cor. 13:12, we see through a *g*
II Cor. 3:18, beholding as in a *g*
James 1:23, behold natural face in *g*:
Rev. 4;6, a sea of *g*
21:18, the city was pure gold like clear *g*
See Rev. 15:2
GLEAN Lev. 19:10; Jer. 6:9; 49:9
GLISTERING I Chron. 29:2; Lk. 9:29
GLITTERING Deut. 32:41; Job 20:25
GLOOMINESS Joel 2:2; Zeph. 1:15
GLORIFY Lev. 10:3, before all I will be *g*
Ps. 50:23, whoso offers praise *g* me
86:9, all nations shall *g* your name
12, I will *g* your name for evermore
Isa. 24:15, *g* the Lord in the fires
60:7, I will *g* house of my glory
Ezek. 28:22, I will be *g* in midst of you
Dan. 5:23, God have you not *g*
Mat. 5:16, *g* your Father in Heaven
15:31, they *g* God of Israel
Lk. 4:15, being *g* of all
Jn. 7:39, because Jesus was not yet *g*
11:4, that the Son of God might be *g*
28, Father *g* your name; I have both *g*
13:32, God shall also *g* him
15:8, herein is my Father *g*
17:1, *g* your Son
21:19, by what death he should *g* God
Rom. 1:21, they *g* him not as God
8:17, suffer with him, that we may be *g*
I Cor. 6:20, *g* God in body and spirit
Gal. 1:24, they *g* God in me
II Thess. 1:10, to be *g* in his saints
Heb. 5:5, so Christ *g* not himself
GLORIOUS Ex. 15:11, *g* in holiness
Deut. 28:55; I Chron. 29:13, this *g* name
Ps. 45:13, all *g* within
66:2, make his praise *g*
87:3, *G* things are spoken
Isa. 11:10, his rest shall be *g*
28:1, whose *g* beauty is a fading flower
Jer. 17:12, a *g* high throne
Dan. 11:16, 41, stand in the *g* land
45, in the *g* holy mountain
Lk. 13:17, rejoiced for *g* things done
Rom. 8:21, *g* liberty of children of God
Eph. 5:27, a *g* church
Phil. 3:21, like to his *g* body
I Tim. 1:11, the *g* gospel of the blessed God
Titus 2:13, the *g* appearing of the great God
See Ex. 15:1; II Sam. 6:20; Isa. 24:23; 63:12
GLORY Ex. 33:18, show me your *g*
Num. 14:21; Isa. 6:3, earth filled with *g*
Ps. 8:1, your *g* above the heavens

16:9, my g rejoices
24:7, 10, the King of g
73:24, afterward receive me to g
84:11, will give grace and g
108:1, will give praise with my g
145:11, the g of your kingdom
Prov. 3:35, the wise shall inherit g
17:6, the g of children are their fathers
20:29, the g of young men is their strength
25:2, g of God to conceal
27, for men to search their own g is not g
Isa. 10:3, where will ye leave your g?
24:16, even g to the righteous
42:8, my g will I not give to another
43:7, have created him for my g
60:7, will glorify house of my g
Jer. 2:11, my people have changed their g
Ezek. 20:6, 15, the g of all lands
31:18, to whom are you thus like in g?
Dan. 2:37; 7:14, God has given power and g
Hos. 4:7, change g into shame
Hag. 2:7, I will fill this house with g
Mat. 6:2, that you may have g of men
29, Lk. 12:27, Solomon in all his g
16:27; Mk. 8:38, in g of his Father
19:28; Lk. 9:26, Son of man sit in his g
24:30; Mk. 13:26; Lk. 21:27, great g
Lk. 2:14; 19:38, G to God in the highest
24:26, to enter into his g?
Jn. 1:14, we beheld his g
2:11, thus did Jesus, and manifested his g
8:50, I seek not my own g
17:24, that they may behold my g
Acts 12:23, he gave not God the g
Rom. 3:23, come short of g of God
8:18, not worthy to be compared with g
11:36; Gal. 1:5; II Tim. 4:18; Heb. 13:21
I Cor. 2:8, crucified the Lord of g
10:31, do all to g of God
11:7, woman is the g of man
15, long hair, it is a g to her
15:40, g of celestial, g of terrestrial
II Cor. 3:18, beholding as in a glass the g
4:17, eternal weight of g
Eph. 1:17, the Father of g
3:21, to him be g in the church
Phil. 3:19, whose g is in their shame
4:19, according to his riches in g
Col. 1:27, Christ in you, the hope of g
3:4, appear with him in g
II Thess. 1:9, the g of his power
I Tim. 3:16, received up into g
Heb. 1:3, the brightness of his g
2:10, in bringing many sons to g
3:3, man was counted worthy of more g
I Pet. 1:8, joy unspeakable and full of g
I Pet. 1:11, the g that should follow
24, the g of man as flower of grass
4:14, the spirit of g and of God
5:10, called to eternal g
II Pet. 1:17, voice from the excellent g
Rev. 4:11; 5:12, worthy to receive g
7:12, blessing, and g, and wisdom
18:1, earth lightened with his g

21:23, g of God did lighten it
GLORYING I Cor. 5:6; II Cor. 7:4; 12:11
GNASH Mat. 8:12; 13:42; 22:13; 24:51, Lk.
13:28, g of teeth
Mk. 9:18, he foams, and g with his teeth
See Job 16:9; Ps. 35:16; Acts 7:54
GNAT Mat. 23:24
GO Gen. 32:26, let me g, for day breaks
Ex. 14:5, Job 23:8, g forward
23:23; 32:34, angel shall g before you
Ruth 1:16, whither you g, I will g
Ps. 139:7, whither shall I g
Prov. 22:6, the way he should g
30:29, three things which g well
Mat. 5:41, to g a mile g twain
21:30, I g sir, and went not
Lk. 10:37, G and do likewise
Jn. 14:12, I g to the Father
GOAT Lev. 3:12; 16:8, 21, 22
Isa. 1:11, delight not in blood of g
Ezek. 34:17, judge between rams and g
Dan. 8:5, he g came from the west
Zech. 10:3, I punished the g
Mat. 25:32, 33, set g on his left hand
Heb. 9:12, blood of g
See Dan. 8:21; Heb. 9:13, 19; 10:4
GOD Gen. 5:22; 6:9, walked with G
16:13, you G see me
32:28, has power with G
48:21, I die, but G shall be with you
Deut. 3:24, what G is there that can do
33:27, the eternal G is your refuge
I Sam. 17:46, there is a G in Israel
I Ki. 18:21, if the Lord be G, follow him
39, he is the G, he is the G
Job 22:13; Ps. 73:11, how does G know?
Ps. 14:1; 53:1, has said, There is no G
22:1; Mat. 27:46, my G, my G, why hast?
56:9, this I know, for G is for me
86:10; Isa. 37:16, you are G alone
Eccl. 5:2, G is in Heaven
Isa. 44:8, is there a G beside me?
45:22, 46:9, I am G, there is none else
Hos. 11:9, I am G, and not man
Amos 5:27, whose name is the G of hosts
Jonah 1:6, arise, call upon your G
Mic. 6:8, walk humbly with your G?
Mat. 1:23, G with us
Mk. 12:32, one G, and none other
Jn. 3:33, that G is true
4:24, G is a spirit
13:3, come from G, and went to G
20:17, ascend to my G and your G
Rom. 3:4, let G be true
8:31, if G be for us
I Cor. 1:9; 10:13, G is faithful
14:25, that G is in you
33, G is not author of confusion
Gal. 3:20, but G is one
6:7, G is not mocked
II Thess. 2:4, above all that is called G
I Tim. 3:16, G manifest in the flesh
Heb. 8:10, I will be to them a G
11:16, not ashamed to be called their G

12:23, but you are come to G

I Jn. 1:5, G is light

4:8, 16, G is love

12, no man has seen G

5:19, we know that we are of G

Rev. 21:3, G himself shall be with them

4, G shall wipe away all tears

7, I will be his G

See II Chron. 13:12; Job 40:9; Ps. 68:17; Mat. 21:31; Eph. 6:13; Heb. 13:4

GOD (*an idol*) Gen. 31:30, stole my *g*?

Ex. 32:1, make us *g*, which shall go before us

4, these be your *g*

Judg. 5:8, they chose new *g*

6:31, if he be a *g*, let him plead

10:14, go and cry to the *g* you have chosen

17:5, Micah had a house of *g*

18:24, you have taken away my *g*

II Ki. 17:29, every nation made *g*

33, they feared the Lord and served own *g*

Isa. 44:15, makes a *g* and worshipped it

45:20, pray to a *g* that cannot save

Jonah 1:5, cried every man to his *g*

Acts 12:22, the voice of a *g*, not a man

14:11, the *g* are come down

I Cor. 8:5, there be *g* many

See Ex. 12:12; 20:23; Jer. 2:11; Dan. 3:28

GODDESS I Ki. 11:5; Acts 19:27, 35, 37

GODHEAD Acts 17:29; Rom. 1:20; Col. 2:9

GODLINESS I Tim. 3:16, the mystery of *g*

4:7, exercise yourself to *g*

8, *g* if profitable

6:3, doctrine according to *g*

II Tim. 3:5, a form of *g*

Titus 1:1, the truth which is after *g*

II Pet. 1:3, pertain to life and *g*

3:11, in all holy conversation and *g*

See I Tim. 2:2, 10; 6:6, 11

GODLY Ps. 12:1, the *g* man ceases

Mal. 2:15, seek a *g* seed

II Cor. 7:9, 10, *g* sorrow works repentance

II Tim. 3:12, all that will live *g* in Christ

Titus 2:12, live *g* in this world

Heb. 12:28, reverence and *g* fear

II Pet. 2:9, how to deliver the *g*

III Jn. 6, bring forward after a *g* sort

GOING II Sam. 5:24, sound of *g* in trees

Job 33:24, 28, from *g* down to pit

Prov. 5:21, ponders all his *g*

20:24, man's *g* are of the Lord

Dan. 6:14, labored till *g* down of the sun

Mat. 26:46, rise, let us be *g*

Rom. 10:3, *g* about to establish

I Tim. 5:24, *g* before to judgment

GOLD Deut. 8:13, when your *g* is multiplied

17:17, nor shall he greatly multiply *g*

I Ki. 20:3, silver and *g* is mine

Job 28:1, a vein for silver, a place for *g*

19, wisdom not valued with *g*

31:24, if I made *g* my hope

Ps. 19:10, more to be desired than *g*

Prov. 25:11, like applies of *g*

Isa. 46:6, they lavish *g* out of the bag

60:17, for brass I will bring *g*

Mat. 10:9, provide neither *g* nor silver

Acts 3:6, silver and *g* have I none

17:29, not think Godhead like to *g*

20:33, coveted no man's *g*

II Tim. 2:20, not only vessels of *g*

James 2:2, man with a *g* ring

5:3, your *g* is cankered

I Pet. 1:7, trial more precious than of *g*

18, not redeemed with *g*

Rev. 21:18, city was pure *g*

See Gen. 2:11; Isa. 13:12; Dan. 5:23

GONE I Ki. 20:40, busy here and there, he was *g*

Ps. 42:4, I had *g* with the multitude

73:2, my feet were almost *g*

77:8, mercy clean *g* forever

103:16, wind passes, and it is *g*

109:23, I am *g* like the shadow

119:176; Isa. 53:6, *g* astray like sheep

Jer. 15:9, sun *g* down while yet day

Mat. 12:43; Lk. 11:24, spirit *g* out

Mk. 5:30; Lk. 8:46, virtue had *g* out of him

Jn. 12:19, the world is *g* after him

Acts 16:19, hope of their gains *g*

Rom. 3:12, they are all *g* out of the way

Jude 11, *g* in the way of Cain

See Ps. 89:34; Song of Sol. 2:11; Isa. 45:23

GOOD (*n.*) Gen. 14:21, take the *g* to yourself

24:10, the *g* of his master in his hand

50:20, God meant it unto *g*

Neh. 5:19; 13:31, think upon me for *g*

Job 2:10, shall we receive *g*

22:21, thereby *g* shall come

Ps. 4:6, who will show us any *g*?

14:1; 53:1; Rom. 3:12, none does *g*

34:12, loves days that he may see *g*?

39:2, held my peace even from *g*

86:17, a token for *g*

Prov. 3:27, withhold not *g*

Eccl. 3:12, I know there is no *g* in them

Mat. 12:29; Mk. 3:27, spoil his *g*

24:47, ruler over all his *g*

Lk. 6:30, of him that takes away your *g*

16:1, accused that he had wasted his *g*

19:8, half of my *g* I give

Acts 10:38, went about doing *g*

Rom. 8:28, work together for *g*

13:4, minister of God for *g*

I Cor. 13:3, bestow all my *g* to feed

Heb. 10:34, joyfully the spoiling of your *g*

I Jn. 3:17, this world's *g*

Rev. 3:17, rich, and increased with *g*

See Job 5:27; 7:7; Prov. 11:17; 13:21

GOOD (*adj.*) Gen. 1:4, God saw it was *g*

2:18, not *g* that man should be alone

27:46, what *g* shall my life do me?

Deut. 2:4; Josh 23:11, take *g* heed

I Sam. 2:24, no *g* report I hear

12:23, I will teach you the *g* way

25:15, men were very *g* to us

Ezra 7:9; Neh. 2:8, the *g* hand of God on him

Neh. 9:20, your *g* spirit to instruct

Ps. 34:8, taste and see that the Lord is *g*

45:1, my heart is inditing a *g* matter

112:5, a *g* man shows favour

145:9, the Lord is *g* to all
Prov. 12:25, a *g* word makes the heart glad
15:23, in season, how *g* is it!
20:18, with *g* advice make war
22:1, a *g* name rather to be chosen
25:25, *g* news from a far country
Eccl. 6:12, who knows what is *g*?
Isa. 55:2, eat you that which is *g*
Zech. 1:13, answered with *g* words
Mat. 5:13, it is *g* for nothing
7:11; Lk. 11:13, how to give *g* gifts
19:17; Lk. 18:19, none *g*, save one
20:15, is your eye evil because I am *g*?
25:21, *g* and faithful servant
Mk. 9:50; Lk. 14:34, salt is *g*, but
Lk. 1:53, fill the hungry with *g* things
6:38, *g* measure, pressed down
12:32, your Father's *g* pleasure
16:25, in your lifetime received *g* things
23:50, Joseph was a *g* man, and a just
Jn. 1:46, *g* thing come out of Nazareth?
2:10, kept *g* wine until now
7:12, some said, he is a *g* man
10:11, I am the *g* shepherd
33, for a *g* work we stone you not
Rom. 7:12, commandment holy, just, and *g*
18, in my flesh dwells no *g* thing
12:2, that *g* and perfect will of God
14:21, it is *g* neither to eat
I Cor. 7:26, this is *g* for the present
15:33, corrupt *g* manners
II Cor. 9:8, abound in every *g* work
Gal. 6:6, communicate in all *g* things
Phil. 1:6, has begun a *g* work
Col. 1:10, fruitful in every *g* work
I Thess. 5:15, follow that which is *g*
21, hold fast that which is *g*
I Tim. 1:8, the law is *g*
II Tim. 3:3, despisers of *g*
Titus 2:7, a pattern in *g* works
Heb. 6:5, tasted the *g* word of God
13:9, *g* thing that the heart be established
James 1:17, every *g* gift
See II Thess. 2:17; Titus 1:16; 3:8
GOODLINESS Isa. 40:6
GOODLY Gen. 49:21, gives *g* words
Ex. 2:2, a *g* child
Deut. 8:12, when you have built *g* houses
I Sam. 9:2, a choice young man, and a *g*
Ps. 16:6; Jer. 3:19, a *g* heritage
Zech. 11:13, a *g* price I was prised at
Mat. 13:45, *g* pearls
James 2:2, a man in *g* apparel
See I Sam. 8:16; I Ki. 20:3; Lk. 21:5
GOODNESS Ex. 33:19, make all my *g* pass
34:6, abundant in *g* and truth
Ps. 16:2, my *g* extends not to you
23:6, *g* and mercy shall follow
27:13, believed to see the *g* of the Lord
31:19, Zech. 9:17, how great is your *g*
33:5, earth full of your *g*
65:11, crowns the year with your *g*
145:7, the memory of your *g*
Hos. 6:4, your *g* is as a morning cloud

Rom. 2:4, the riches of his *g*
11:22, the *g* and severity of God
See Neh. 9:25; Isa. 63:7; Gal. 5:22; Eph. 5:9
GOSPEL Rom. 2:16, according to my *g*
II Cor. 4:3, if our *g* be hid
Gal. 1:8, 9, any other *g*
2:7, *g* of uncircumcision, *g* of circumcision
Col. 1:23, the hope of the *g*
I Tim. 1:1, *g* of the blessed God
Rev. 14:6, everlasting *g*
See Mat. 4:23; Mk. 16:15; Acts 20:24
GOVERNMENT Isa. 9:6; I Cor. 12:28
GRACE Ps. 45:2, *g* poured into your lips
Prov. 1:9, an ornament of *g*
3:22, life to your soul, and *g* to your neck
34; James 4:6, gives *g* to the lowly
Zech. 4:7, crying G, *g* unto it
12:10, spirit of *g* and supplications
Jn. 1:14, full of *g* and truth
16, all received, and *g* for *g*
17, *g* and truth came by Jesus Christ
Acts 4:33, great *g* was upon them all
11:23, when he had see the *g*
14:3, the word of his *g*
Rom. 1:7; I Cor. 1:3; II Cor. 1:2; Gal. 1:3; Col.
1:2; I Thess. 1:1, G be unto you
3:24 justified freely by his *g*
4:4, not reckoned of *g*, but of debt
6:14, 15, under *g*
II Cor. 8:9, know the *g* of our Lord
9:8, able to make all *g* abound
Gal. 1:6, 15, who called you by his *g*
Gal. 5:4, you are fallen from *g*
Eph. 2:5, 8, by *g* you are saved
4:29, minister *g* to hearers
6:24, *g* be with all that love our Lord
Col. 4:6, let your speech be always with *g*
II Thess. 2:16, good hope through *g*
I Tim. 1:2; II Tim. 1:2; Titus 1:4
Heb. 4:16, the throne of *g*
10:29, despite unto the Spirit of *g*?
12:28, *g* to serve God acceptably
13:9, heart established with *g*
I Pet. 3:7, heirs of *g*
II Pet. 3:18, grow in *g*
Jude 4, turning *g* of God into lasciviousness
See Acts 20:24; II Cor. 6:1; Gal. 2:21
GRACIOUS Gen. 43:29, God be *g* to you
Ex. 22:27, I will hear, for I am *g*
33:19, I will be *g* to whom I will be *g*
Neh. 9:17, 31, ready to pardon, *g* merciful
Ps. 77:9, has God forgotten to be *g*?
Prov. 11:16, a *g* woman retains honor
Isa. 30:18, wait, that he may be *g*
Jonah 4:2, I know you are a *g* God
Lk. 4:22, wondered at the *g* words
I Pet. 2:3, tasted that the Lord is *g*
See Ex. 34:6; II Chron. 30:9; Hos. 14:2
GRAFT Rom. 11:17, 19, 23, 24
GRAIN Mk. 4:31; Lk. 13:19; 17:6, *g* of mustard
seed
GRANT Ruth 1:9, *g* that you may find rest
I Chron. 4:10, God *g* that which he requested
Job 6:8, *g* the thing I long for

Rev. 3:21, will I *g* to sit with me
See Ps. 20:4; 85:7; Acts 4:29
GRAPE Gen. 49:11, washed in blood of *g*
Deut. 32:14, drink the blood of the *g*
Song of Sol. 2:13, 15, vines with tender *g*
Isa. 5:2, looked it should bring forth *g*
17:6; 24:13, yet gleaning *g*
Jer. 8:13, there shall be no *g*
31:29, 30; Ezek. 18:2, have eaten a sour *g*
Amos 9:13, treader of *g* shall overtake
See Song of Sol. 7:7
GRASS Deut. 32:2, as showers upon the *g*
II Ki. 19:26; Ps. 129:6, as *g* on housetops
Ps. 72:6, like rain upon mown *g*
90:5, like *g* which grows up
102:4, 11, withered like *g*
103:15, days are as *g*
Isa. 40:6; I Pet. 1:24, all flesh is *g*
Mat. 6:30, God so clothe the *g*
See Prov. 27:25; Jn. 6:10; Rev. 8:7; 9:4
GRAVE (*n.*) Gen. 42:38, with sorrow to *g*
Ex. 14:11, no *g* in Egypt
Job 5:26, come to *g* in full age
7:9, he that goes to the *g*
17:1, the *g* are ready for me
13, if I wait, the *g* is my house
33:22, his soul draws near to the *g*
Ps. 6:5, in *g* who shall give thanks?
31:17, let wicked be silent in the *g*
49:14, like sheep laid in the *g*
15; Hos. 13:14, the power of the *g*
Eccl. 9:10, no wisdom in the *g*
Isa. 38:18, the *g* cannot praise you
53:9, made his *g* with the wicked
Jn. 5:28, all in the *g* shall hear
11:31, she goes to the *g*
I Cor. 15:55, O *g* where is your victory?
See Mat. 27:52; Lk. 11:44; Rev. 11:9
GRAVE (*v.*) Isa. 49:16, I have *g* you
Hab. 2:18, that the maker has *g* it
See Ex. 28:9; II Chron. 2:7; 3:7
GRAVE (*adj.*) I Tim. 3:8; Titus 2:7
GRAVEL Prov. 20:17; Isa. 48:19; Lam. 3:16
GRAVITY I Tim. 3:4; Titus 2:7
GRAY Ps. 71:18; Prov. 20:29; Hos. 7:9
GREAT Gen. 12:2; 46:3, make a *g* nation
48:19, he also shall be *g*
Deut. 29:24, the heat of this *g* anger
I Sam. 12:24, consider how *g* things
II Chron. 2:5, the house is *g*, for *g* is our God
Neh. 6:3, I am doing a *g* work
Job 32:9, G men are not always wise
36:18, a *g* ransom
Ps. 14:5; 53:5, there were they in *g* fear
19:11, there is *g* reward
31:19, how *g* is your goodness
Ps. 92:5, how *g* are your works?
139:17, how *g* is the sum of them!
Prov. 18:16, gift brings before *g* men
25:6, stand not in place of *g* men
Mat. 5:12, *g* is your reward
19, called *g* in kingdom of heaven
13:46, pearl of *g* price
15:28, *g* is your faith

20:26, whosoever will be *g* among you
22:36, 38, the *g* commandment
Lk. 10:2, the harvest is *g*
Acts 8:9, giving out he was some *g* one
I Tim. 3:16, *g* is the mystery
Heb. 2:3, so *g* salvation
12:1, so *g* a cloud of witnesses
James 3:5, *g* a matter a little fire kindles!
See Deut. 9:2; Eccl. 2:9; Rev. 7:9
GREATER I Chron. 11:9; Esther 9:4, waxed *g*
and *g*
Hag. 2:9, glory of latter house *g*
Mat. 11:11; Lk. 7:28, *g* than he
12:6, one *g* than the temple
Mk. 12:31, no commandment *g* than these
Jn. 1:50; 5:20; 14:12, shall see *g* things
4:12; 8:53, are you *g* than our father
10:29; 14:28, my Father is *g* than all
13:16; 15:20, servant not *g* than his lord
15:13, G love has no man
Heb. 6:13, he could swear by no *g*
I Jn. 3:20, God is *g* than our hearts
4:4, *g* is he in you than he in world
III Jn. 4, no *g* joy
GREATEST Mat. 13:32; It is *g* among herbs
18:1, 4, who is *g* in kingdom
Mk. 9:34, disputed who should be *g*
I Cor. 13:13, the *g* of these is charity
See Job 1:3; Jer. 31:34; Lk. 22:24
GREATLY I Chron. 21:8, I have sinned *g*
Ps. 28:7, my heart *g* rejoices
47:9, God is *g* exalted
89:7, *g* to be feared in the assembly
116:10, I was *g* afflicted
Dan. 9:23; 10:11, you are *g* beloved
Obad. 2, you are *g* despised
Mk. 12:27, you do *g* err
GREATNESS I Chron. 29:11, yours is the glory
Ps. 145:3, his *g* is unsearchable
Prov. 5:23, is the *g* of his folly
Isa. 63:1, travelling in *g* of strength
Eph. 1:19, the exceeding *g* of his power
See Ex. 15:16; II Chron. 9:6; Ps. 66:3; 79:11
GREEDILY Prov. 21:26; Ezek. 22:12
GREEDINESS Eph. 4:19
GREEDY Prov. 1:19; 15:27, *g* of gain
Isa. 56:11, they are *g* dogs
See Ps. 17:12; I Tim. 3:3
GREEN Lev. 23:14; Judg. 16:7; Lk. 23:31
GRIEF II Chron. 6:29, shall know his own *g*
Job 6:2, Oh that my *g* were weighed
Ps. 31:10, life spend with *g*
Eccl. 1:18, in much wisdom is much *g*
Isa. 53:3, acquainted with *g*
Jer. 10:19, this is a *g*, and I must bear it
See Jonah 4:6; Heb. 13:17; I Pet. 2:19
GRIEVE Gen. 6:6, it *g* him at his heart
45:5, be not *g* that you sold me
I Sam. 2:33, man shall be to *g* your heart
Ps. 78:40, they *g* him in the desert
95:10, forty years was I *g*
Lam. 3:33, does not willingly *e*
Mk. 3:5, being *g* for the hardness
10:22, he went away *g*

Jn. 21:17, Peter was *g*
Rom. 14:15, brother *g* with meat
Eph. 4:30, *g* not the holy Spirit of God
See Neh. 2:10; 13:8; Ps. 119:158; 139:21
GRIEVOUS Gen. 21:11, *g* in Abraham's sight
    50:11, a *g* mourning
Ps. 10:5, his ways are always *g*
Prov. 15:1, *g* words stir up anger
Jer. 30:12; Nah. 3:19, your would is *g*
Mat. 23:4, burdens *g* to be borne
Phil. 3:1, to me is not *g*
Heb. 12:11, chastening *g*
I Jn. 5:3, commandments not *g*
See Eccl. 2:17; Jer. 16:4; Acts 20:29
GRIND Isa. 3:15, *g* faces of the poor
Lam. 5:13, took young men to *g*
Lk. 20:18, it will *g* him to powder
See Eccl. 12:3; Mat. 24:41; Lk. 17:35
GROAN Ex. 2:24, God head their *g*
Job 24:12, men *g* from out the city
Joel 1:18, how do the beasts *g*
Rom. 8:23, we ourselves *g*
See Job 23:2; Ps. 6:6; Jn. 11:33, 38
GROPE Deut. 28:29; Job 5:14; Isa. 59:10
GROSS Isa. 60:2; Jer. 13:16; Mat. 13:15
GROUND Ex. 3:5; Acts 7:33, holy *g*
Job 5:6, nor trouble spring out of the *g*
Isa. 35:7, parched *g* become a pool
Jer. 4:3; Hos. 10:12, break up fallow *g*
Mat. 13:8; Lk. 8:8, good *g*
Mk. 4:16, stony *g*
Lk. 13:7, why cumbers it the *g*?
    14:18, bought a piece of *g*
    19:44, lay you even with the *g*
Jn. 8:6, he wrote on the *g*
See Zech. 8:12; Mal. 3:11; Jn. 12:24
GROUNDED Eph. 3:17; Col. 1:23
GROW II Sam. 23:5, though he make it not to *g*
Isa. 53:2, he shall *g* up before him
Hos. 14:5, he shall *g* as the lily
Mal. 4:2, *g* up as calves of the stall
Mat. 13:30, let both *g* together
Mk. 4:27, seed should *g* up, he knows not
Acts 5:24, whereunto this would *g*
Eph. 2:21, *g* unto an holy temple
    4:15, may *g* up unto him
II Thess. 1:3, your faith *g* exceedingly
I Pet. 2:2, that you may *g* thereby
II Pet. 3:18, *g* in grace
See II Ki. 19:26; Jer. 12:2; Zech. 6:12
GRUDGE Lev. 19:18; II Cor. 9:7; James 5:9
GUESTS Zeph. 1:7; Mat. 22:10; Lk. 19:7
GUIDE Ps. 25:9, meek be *g* in judgment
    32:8, I will *g* you with my eye
    48:14, our *g* even unto death
    73:24, *g* me with your counsel
Prov. 6:7, having no *g*, overseer, or ruler
Isa. 58:11, the Lord shall *g* you
Jer. 3:4, the *g* of my youth
Mat. 23:16, 24, you blind *g*
Lk. 1:79, *g* our feet into the way of peace
Jn. 16:13, *g* you into all truth
See Gen. 48:14; Prov. 11:3; 23:19
GUILE Ps. 32:2, in whose spirit is no *g*

    34:13, keep lips from speaking *g*
Jn. 1:47, in whom is not *g*
II Cor. 12:16, I caught you with *g*
See Ex. 21:14; I Thess. 2:3; Rev. 14:5
GUILTLESS Deut. 5:11, will not hold him *g*
Josh. 2:19, we will be *g*
II Sam. 3:28, are *g* of blood
See Num. 5:31; I Sam. 26:9; Mat. 12:7
GUILTY Gen. 42:21, *g* concerning brother
Ex. 34:7; Num. 14:18, by no means clear the *g*
Lev. 5:3, when he knows of it, he shall be *g*
Rom. 3:19, all the world *g* before God
I Cor. 11:27, *g* of the body and blood
See Num. 35:27; Prov. 30:10; Mat. 26:66
GULF Lk. 16:26
GUSH I Ki. 18:28; Ps. 78:20; Jer. 9:18

H

HABITATION Ex. 15:13, your holy *h*
II Chron. 6:2, have built an house of *h*
Ps. 26:8, have loved the *h*
    33:14, from the place of his *h*
    69:25, let their *h* be desolate
    107:7, 36, a city of *h*
    132:13, the Lord desired it for his *h*
Prov. 3:33, he blessed the *h* of the just
Isa. 32:18, dwell in a peaceable *h*
Jer. 21:13, who shall enter into our *h*?
    25:37, the peaceable *h* are cut down
Lk. 16:9, into everlasting *h*
Eph. 2:22, an *h* of God through the Spirit
Jude 6, angels which left their own *h*
See Job 18:15; Prov. 8:31; Acts 1:20; 17:26
HAIL Job 38:22, the treasures of the *h*
Isa. 28:17, *h* sweet away refuge of lies
See Ex. 9:18; Josh. 10:11; Rev. 8:7
HAIR Gen. 42:38, bring down gray *h*
Judg. 20:16, sling stones at *h* breadth
Job 4:15, the *h* of my flesh stood up
Ps. 40:12, more than the *h* of my head
Mat. 3:4; Mk. 1:6, raiment of camel's *h*
    5:36, make one *h* white or black
    10:30, *h* of head numbered
I Cor. 11:14, 15, long *h*, it is a shame
I Tim. 2:9, broided *h*
See II Sam. 14:26; Jn. 11:2; Rev. 1:14
HALE Lk. 12:58; Acts 8:3
HALLOW Lev. 22:32, Lord which *h* you
    25:10, shall *h* the fiftieth year
Num. 5:10, every man's *h* things
I Ki. 9:3, I have *h* this house
Jer. 17:22, 24, 27, but *h* ye the sabbath day
Ezek. 20:20; 44:24, and *h* my sabbaths
Mat. 6:9; Lk. 11:2, *h* be your name
HALT I Ki. 18:21, how long *h* ye?
Ps. 38:17, I am ready to *h*
Jer. 20:10, my familiars watched for my *h*
See Gen. 32:31; Mic. 4:6; Zeph. 3:19
HAND Gen. 16:12, *h* against every man
    24:2; 47:29, put your *h* under my thigh
    27:22, the *h* are the *h* of Esau
    31:29, in the power of my *h* to do you hurt
Ex. 21:24; Deut. 19:21, *h* for *h*, foot for foot

33:22, cover with my *h* while I pass
Num. 11:23; Isa. 59:1, Lord's *h* waxed short
22:29, would there were sword in my *h*
Deut. 8:17, my *h* has gotten this wealth
33:2, from right *h* went fiery law
Judg. 7:2, Mine own *h* has saved me
I Sam. 5:11, *h* of God was heavy
6:9, not his *h* that smote us, but a chance
12:3, of whose *h* have I received any bribe?
23:16, Jonathan strengthened his *h* in God
26:18, what evil is in mine *h*?
II Sam. 14:19, is not *h* of Joab in this?
24:14; I Chron. 21:13, let us fall into *h* of Lord
I Ki. 18:44, cloud like a man's *h*
II Ki. 5:11, strike his *h* over the place
I Chron. 12:2, could use right *h* and left
Ezra 7:9; 8:18; Neh. 2:8, good *h* of God
Neh. 2:18, strengthen their *h* for work
6:5, with open letter in his *h*
Job 12:10, in whose *h* is the soul
19:21, the *h* of God has touched me
Ps. 16:11, at right *h* pleasures for evermore
24:4, clean *h* and pure heart
68:31, stretch out her *h* unto God
90:17, establish thou the work of our *h*
137:5, let my right *h* forget her cunning
Prov. 3:16, in left *h* riches and honor
Prov. 10:4, that deals with slack *h*
12:24, *h* of diligent shall bear rule
19:24; 26:15, slothful man hides his *h*
22:26, be not of them that strike *h*
Eccl. 2:24, this I saw was from *h* from God
11:6, in evening withhold not your *h*
Isa. 1:12, who has required this at your *h*?
5:25; 14:27, his *h* stretched out still
14:26, this is the *h* that is stretched out
40:12, measured waters in hollow of *h*
44:5, subscribe with his *h* to the Lord
53:10, pleasure of Lord shall prosper in his *h*
Jer. 23:14, strengthen *h* of evil doers
33:13, shall pass under *h* of that that tells
Lam. 2:4, with his right *h* as adversary
4:10, *h* of pitiful women have sodden
Ezek. 7:17; 21:7, all *h* shall be feeble
10:2, fill *h* with coals of fire
17:18, lo, he had given his *h*
Dan. 4:35, none can stay his *h*
Hos. 7:5, stretched out *h* with scorners
Mic. 7:3, do evil with both *h* earnestly
Zeph. 3:16, let not your *h* be slack
Zech. 13:6, what are wounds in your *h*?
Mat. 3:2; 4:17, kingdom of heaven at *h*
12; Lk. 3:17, whose fan is in his *h*
6:3, let not left *h* know
18:8; Mk. 9:43, if your *h* or foot offend
26:18, my time is at *h*
Mk. 14:62, sitting on right *h* of power
16:19, sat on right *h* of God
Lk. 9:44, delivered into *h* of men
Jn. 10:28, nor pluck out of my *h*
Acts 20:34, these *h* have ministered
II Cor. 5:1, house not make with *h*

I Thess. 4:11, work with your own *h*
II Thess. 2:2, the day of Christ is at *h*
I Tim. 2:8, lifting up holy *h*
Heb. 10:31, the *h* of living God
James 4:8, cleanse your *h*
I Pet. 4:7, end of all things is at *h*
I Jn. 1:1, our *h* have handled
See Gen. 49:24; Isa. 49:16; Mat. 25:33; Lk. 9:62; Jn. 18:22; Col. 2:11
HANDLE Ps. 115:7, hands, but they *h* not
Prov. 16:20, that *h* a matter wisely
Jer. 2:8, they that *h* the law
Mk. 12:4, sent away shamefully *h*
Lk. 24:39, *h* me, and see
II Cor. 4:2, not *h* word deceitfully
Col. 2:21, taste not, *h* not
I Jn. 1:1, have *h* of Word of life
See Gen. 4:21; I Chron. 12:8; Ezek. 27:29
HANDMAID Ps. 86:16; 116:16; Prov. 30:23
HANG Gal. 3:13, he that is *h* is accursed
Job 26:7, *h* the earth on nothing
Ps. 137:2, we *h* our harps upon the willows
Mat. 22:40, on these *h* law and prophets
27:5, went and *h* himself
Lk. 17:2, millstone *h* about neck
Heb. 12:12, lift up the hands which *h* down
See Gen. 40:22; Esther 7:10; Lk. 23:39
HAPLY I Sam. 14:30; Mk. 11:13
HAPPEN I Sam. 6:9, it was a change that *h*
Prov. 12:21, shall no evil *h* to the just
Isa. 41:22, let them show us what shall *h*
Jer. 44:23, therefore this evil is *h*
Mk. 10:32, to tell what should *h*
Lk. 24:14, talked to things that had *h*
Rom. 11:25, blindness is *h* to Israel
I Cor. 10:11, things *h* for ensamples
Phil. 1:12, things which *h* to me
I Pet. 4:12, as though some strange thing *h*
II Pet. 2:22, it is *h* according to proverb
See Eccl. 2:14; 8:14; 9:11; Acts 3:10
HAPPY Gen. 30:13, *H* am I
Deut. 33:29, *H* are you
Job 5:17, *h* is the man whom God corrects
Ps. 127:5, *H* is the man that has quiver full
128:2, *h* shall you be
144:15, *H* is that people
Prov. 3:13, 18, *H* that finds wisdom
14:21, he that has mercy, *h* is he
28:14, *H* is the man that fears always
Mal. 3:15, now we call proud *h*
Jn. 13:17, if you know, *h* is he
Rom. 14:22, *H* is he that condemns not
James 5:11, we count them *h* that endure
I Pet. 3:14; 4:14, *h* are ye
See Ps. 146:5; Prov. 29:18; I Cor. 7:40
HARD Deut. 1:17; 17:8, cause that is too *h*
15:18, it shall not seem *h* to you
I Ki. 10:1, prove with *h* questions
Job 41:24, *h* as piece of nether millstone
Prov. 13:15, the way of transgressors is *h*
18:19, brother offended *h* to be won
Jer. 32:17, 27, there is nothing too *h* for you
Ezek. 3:5, 6, to a people of *h* language
Mat. 25:24, you are an *h* man

Jn. 6:60, this is an *h* saying
Acts 9:5; 26:14, *h* to kick against the pricks
Heb. 5:11, many things *h* to be understood
II Pet. 3:16, things *h* to be understood
See Deut. 15:18; II Ki. 2:10; Mk. 10:24
HARDEN Ex. 14:17, *h* hearts of Egyptians
Job 6:10, I would *h* myself in sorrow
9:4, who has *h* himself against him?
Prov. 21:29, a wicked man *h* his face
28:14, he that *h* his heart
29:1, he, that reproved *h* neck
Isa. 63:17, why have you *h* our heart?
Mk. 6:52; 8:17, their heart was *h*
Jn. 12:40, he has *h* their heart
Acts 19:9, when divers were *h*
Rom. 9:18, whom he will be *h*
Heb. 3:13, lest any of you be *h*
See Deut. 15:7; II Ki. 17:14; Job 39:16
HARDLY Gen. 16:6; Mat. 19:23
HARDNESS Mk. 3:5, grieved *h* of hearts
Mk. 16:14, upbraided them for *h* of heart
II Tim. 2:3, endure *h*, as good soldier
See Job 38:38, Mk. 10:5; Rom. 2:5
HARLOT Gen. 34:31; Josh. 2:1; Judg. 11:1; Prov.
7:10; Isa. 1:21; 23:15
Jer. 2:20; Ezek. 16:15, 16, 41, play the *h*
Mat. 21:31, *h* into kingdom of God
I Cor. 6:16, joined to *h* is one body
Heb. 11:31, by faith the *h* Rahab
James 2:25, Rahab *h* justified by works
Rev. 17:5, mother of *h*
See Jer. 3:1, 6, 8; Hos. 2:5; Mat. 21:32
HARM Lev. 5:16, make amends for *h*
I Sam. 26:21, I will no more do you *h*
II Ki. 4:41, no *h* in the pot
I Chron. 16:22; Ps. 105:15, do prophets no *h*
Prov. 3:30, if he have done you no *h*
Acts 16:18, do yourself no *h*
I Pet. 3:13, who will *h* you?
HARMLESS Mat. 10:16; Heb. 7:26
HARP I Sam. 16:16, cunning player on an *h*
Ps. 49:4, dark sayings of the *h*
137:2, hanged *h* on the willows
Isa. 5:12, *h* and viol are in their feasts
24:8, joy of the *h* ceased
I Cor. 14:7, whether pipe or *h*, except they give
Rev. 14:2, harping with their *h*
HARROW II Sam. 12:31; I Chron. 20:3
HART Ps. 42:1; Isa. 35:6
HARVEST Gen. 8:22, *h* shall not cease
Ex. 23:16; 34:22, the feast of *h*
Lev. 19:9; Deut. 24:19, when you reap *h*
I Sam. 12:17, is it not wheat *h* to day?
Job 5:5, whose *h* the hungry eats up
Prov. 6:8, the ant gathers food in *h*
10:5, he that sleeps in *h*
25:13, cold of snow in time of *h*
Isa. 9:3, according to joy in *h*
16:9, your *h* is fallen
Jer. 5:17, they shall eat up your *h*
24, appointed weeks of *h*
8:20, the *h* is past, the summer ended
51:33, the time of her *h* shall come
Joel 3:13; Rev. 14:15, the *h* is ripe

Mat. 9:37, the *h* is plenteous
38; Lk. 10:2, the Lord of the *h*
Lk. 10:2, the *h* truly is great
Jn. 4:35, the fields are white to *h*
HASTE Ex. 12:11, shall eat it in *h*
I Sam. 21:8, king's business required *h*
Ps. 31:22; 116:11, I said in my *h*
Prov. 19:2, he that *h* with feet sin
28:22, he that *h* to be rich
Jer. 1:12, I will *h* my word
Zeph. 1:14, day of the Lord *h* greatly
See II Ki. 7:15; Ps. 16:4; 55:8; Eccl. 1:5
HASTILY Prov. 20:21; 25:8
HASTY Prov. 14:29; 21:5; 29:20
HATE Gen. 37:4, 5, 8, *h* Joseph yet the more
Lev. 19:17, shall not *h* your brother
II Chron. 18:7, yet one man, but I *h* him
19:2, and love them that *h* the Lord
Ps. 34:21, *h* righteous shall be desolate
97:10, you that love the Lord *h* evil
139:21, do not I *h* them that *h* you?
Prov. 1:22, how long will you *h* knowledge?
13:24, he that spares his rod *h* his son
15:10, he that *h* reproof shall die
27, he that *h* gifts shall live
Eccl. 2:17, I *h* life
3:8, a time to *h*
Isa. 1:14, your feasts my soul *h*
61:8, I *h* robbery for burnt offering
Amos 5:15, *H* the evil, and love the good
Zech. 8:17, these are things that I *h*
Mal. 1:3, I loved Jacob, and *h* Esau
Mat. 5:44, do good to them that *h* you
6:24, either he will *h* the one
10:22; Lk. 21:17, you shall be *h*
24:10, and shall *h* one another
Lk. 6:22, blessed when men shall *h* you
14:26, and *h* not his father
Jn. 3:20, *h* the light
7:7, the world cannot *h* you
15:18, marvel not if world *h* you
24, they have both seen and *h*
Eph. 5:29, no man ever yet *h* his own flesh
I Jn. 2:9, 11; 3:15; 4:20, *h* his brother
See Gen. 27:41; Prov. 6:16; Rev. 2:6
HATEFUL Ps. 36:2; Ezek. 23:29; Titus 3:3
HATERS Ps. 81:15; Rom. 1:30
HAUGHTY Ps. 131:1, my heart is not *h*
Prov. 16:18, a *h* spirit before a fall
21:24, proud and *h* scorner
Isa. 10:33, the *h* shall be humbled
Zeph. 3:11, no more be *h* because
See Isa. 2:11; 13:11; 24:4; Ezek. 16:50
HEAD Gen. 3:15, it shall bruise your *h*
Josh. 2:19, blood be on his *h*
Judg. 11:9, shall I be your *h*?
II Ki. 2:3, take master from your *h*, to day
4:19, he said, My *h*, my *h*
Ps. 24:7, 9, lift up your *h*
141:5, oil, which shall not break my *h*
Prov. 10:6, blessings on *h* of the just
11:26, on *h* of him that sells corn
25:22; Rom. 12:20, coals of fire on his *h*
Eccl. 2:14, a wise man's eyes are in his *h*

Isa. 1:5, the whole *h* is sick
    35:10; 51:11, everlasting joy upon their *h*
    58:5, to bow down *h* as bulrush
    59:17, helmet of salvation on *h*
Jer. 9:1, Oh that my *h* were waters
    14:3, 4, ashamed, and covered their *h*
Dan. 2:38, you are this *h* of gold
Zech. 1:21, no man did lift up his *h*
    4:7, the *h*-stone with shoutings
Mat. 5:36, neither swear by *h*
    27:39; Mk. 15:29, reviled, wagging their *h*
Lk. 7:46, my *h* you did not anoint
    21:18, not hair of *h* perish
    28, then look up, and lift up your *h*
Jn. 13:9, also my hands and my *h*
I Cor. 11:13, the *h* of every man is Christ
    4, dishonors his *h*
Eph. 1:22; 4:15, the *h* of *h* the church
    5:23, husband is *h* of the wife
Col. 2:19, not holding the *H*
See Num. 6:5; Acts 18:6; Rev. 12:1; 13:1
HEAL Ex. 15:26, I am the Lord that *h* you
Deut. 32:39, I wound, I *h*
II Ki. 2:22, waters were *h*
Ps. 6:2, O Lord, *h* me
    41:4, *h* my soul, for I have sinned
    107:20, sent his word, and *h* them
Isa. 6:10, lest they convert and be *h*
    53:5, with his stripes we are *h*
Jer. 6:14; 8:11, they have *h* the hurt slightly
    15:18, would refuse to be *h*
    17:14, *h* me, and I shall be *h*
Lam. 2:13, who can *h* you?
Hos 5:13, yet could he not *h* you?
    6:1, he has torn, and he will *h* us
    14:4, I will *h* their backslidings
Mat. 8:7, I will come and *h* him
    8, speak, and my servant shall be *h*
Mat. 8:16; Lk. 9:2; 10:9, *h* the sick
    12:10, is it lawful to *h* on sabbath?
Mk. 3:2; Lk. 6:7, *h* on sabbath day
Lk. 4:18, to *h* brokenhearted
    23, physician, *h* yourself
    5:17, power of the Lord present to *h*
Jn. 4:47, that he would come and *h*
Acts 4:14, beholding the man which was *h*
    5:16, they were *h* every one
James 5:16, pray that you may be *h*
I Pet. 2:24, by whose stripes you were *h*
Rev. 13:3, his deadly wound was *h*
See Eccl. 3:3; Isa. 3:7; Mat. 4:24; 14:14
HEALING Jer. 14:19, there is no *h* for us
Nah. 3:19, no *h* of your bruise
Mal. 4:2, with *h* in his wings
Mat. 4:23, went about *h* all
Lk. 9:11, that had need of *h*
I Cor. 12:9; 12:30, the gift of *h*
Rev. 22:2, for the *h* of the nations
See Jer. 30:13; Lk. 9:6; Acts 4:22; 10:38
HEALTH Ps. 42:11, *h* of my countenance
    67:2, your saving *h*
Prov. 3:8, *h* to your navel
    4:22, they are *h* to all their flesh
Isa. 58:8, your *h* shall spring forth

Jer. 8:15, looked for a time of *h*
III Jn. 2, may be in *h*
See Gen. 43:28; Jer. 30:17; Acts 27:34
HEAP Deut. 32:23, *h* mischiefs upon them
Job 16:4, I could *h* up words
    27:16, though he *h* up silver
Ps. 39:6, he *h* up riches
Prov. 25:22; Rom. 12:20, *h* coals of fire
Ezek. 24:10, *H* on wood
Hab. 1:10, they shall *h* dust
II Tim. 4:3, *h* to themselves teachers
James 5:3, you have *h* treasures for last days
See Judg. 15:16; Neh. 4:2; Eccl. 2:26
HEAR Ex. 6:12, how shall Pharaoh *h* me
I Sam. 15:14, lowing of oxen which I *h*?
I Ki. 8:42, they shall *h* of your great name
    18:26, O Baal, *h* us
II Ki. 18:28, *H* words of the great king
I Chron. 14:15, when you *h* a sound of going
Job 31:35, Oh! that one would *h* me!
Ps. 4:1; 39:12; 54:2; 84:8, *H* my prayer
    17:6; Zech. 10:6, the Lord will *h*
    10:17, cause your ear to *h*
    59:7, who, say they, does *h*?
    85:8, I will *h* what God the Lord will speak
    102:20, *h* groaning of the prisoner
Prov. 13:8, the poor *h* not rebuke
    18:13, answers a matter before he *h*
    22:17, *h* the words of the wise
Eccl. 5:1, more ready to *h* than give
    7:5, better to *h* rebuke of wise
    12:13, *h* conclusion of the whole matter
Isa. 1:2, *H*, O heavens, and give ear
    15; Jer. 7:16; 11:14; 14:12, will not *h*
    6:9, Mk. 4:12, *H*, but understand not
    29:18, shall deaf *h* words of the book
    42:20, opening ears, but he *h* not
    55:3; Jn. 5:25, *h*, and your soul shall live
Ezek. 3:27, he that *h*, let him *h*
    33:31, they *h* words, but will not do them
Mat. 7:24; Lk. 6:47, whoso *h* these sayings
    11:4, show things you do *h* and see
    5; Mk. 7:37; Lk. 7:22, the deaf *h*
    13:17, *h* those things which you *h*
    17:5; Mk. 9:7, my beloved Son, *h* him
    18:16, if he will not *h* you
Mk. 4:24; Lk. 8:18, take heed what you *h*
Lk. 9:9, of whom I *h* such things
    10:16, he that *h* you, *h* me
Jn. 5:25, dead shall *h* voice of Son of God
    30, as I *h*, I judge
    8:47, he that is of God *h* God's words
    9:31, God *h* not sinners
    11:42, I know you *h* me always
Acts 2:8, how *h* we every man?
    13:44, whole city came to *h*
Rom. 10:14, *h* without a preacher
I Cor. 11:18, I *h* there be divisions
I Tim. 4:16, save yourself, and them that *h*
James 1:19, swift to *h*
I Jn. 4:5, the world *h* them
    6, he that knows God *h* us
Rev. 2:7; 3:6, 13, 22, let him *h*
HEARD Gen. 3:8, they *h* the voice of the Lord

21:17, God *h* voice of the lad
45:2, Joseph wept, and the Egyptians *h*
Ex. 3:7, I have *h* their cry
Num. 11:1; 12:2, the Lord *h* it
Deut. 4:12, only he *h* a voice
I Ki. 6:7, nor any tool of iron *h*
II Ki. 19:25, have you not *h* long ago?
Ezra. 3:13; Neh. 12:43, noise was *h* afar off
Job 15:8, have you *h* the secret of God?
16:2, I have *h* many such things
26:14, how little a portion is *h*?
29:11, when the ear *h* me, it blessed me
Ps. 6:9, the Lord has *h* my supplication
10:17, have *h* the desire of the humble
34:4, I sought the Lord, and he *h*
38:13, I was as a deaf men, and *h* not
81:5, I *h* language I understood not
116:1, I love the Lord, because he has *h*
Song of Sol. 2:12, voice of turtle is *h*
Isa. 40:21, 28, have you not *h*?
64:4, not *h* what he has prepared
65:19, weeping no more be *h*
Jer. 7:13, rising early, but you *h* not
8:6, I *h*, but they spoke not aright
51:46; Obad. 1, a rumour that shall be *h*
Dan. 12:8, I *h*, but understood not
Zech. 8:23, we have *h* God is with you
Mat. 6:7, *h* for much speaking
26:65; Mk. 14:64, you have *h* the blas-
phemy
Lk. 12:3, shall be *h* in the light
Jn. 4:42, we have *h* him ourselves
8:6, as though he *h* them not
Acts 4:4, many which *h* believed
20, cannot but speak things we have *h*
16:25, the prisoners *h* them
Rom. 10:14, of whom they have not *h*?
18, have they not *h*?
I Cor. 2:9, eye has not seen, nor ear *h*
II Cor. 12:4, *h* unspeakable words
Eph. 4:21, if so be you have *h* him
Phil. 4:9, things you have *h* and seen in me
II Tim. 2:2, things you have *h* of me
Heb. 2:3, confirmed by them that *h*
4:2, with faith in them that *h*
I Jn. 1:1, 3, that which we have *h* and seen
Rev. 3:3, remember how you have *h*
10:4; 14:2; 18:4, *h* a voice from heaven
HEARER Rom. 2:13; Eph. 4:29; James 1:23
HEARING Deut. 31:11, read law in their *h*
II Ki. 4:31, neither voice nor *h*
Job 42:5, by the *h* of the ear
Prov. 20:12, the *h* ear
Eccl. 1:8, nor ear filled with *h*
Amos 8:11, a famine of *h* the word
Mat. 13:13, *h*, they hear not
Acts 9:7, *h* a voice, but seeing no man
Rom. 10:17, faith comes by *h*
I Cor. 12:17, where were the *h*?
Heb. 5:11, you are dull of *h*
See Acts 28:27; Gal. 3:2; II Pet. 2:8
HEARKEN Deut. 18:15, unto him you shall *h*;
Josh. 1:17, so will we *h* unto you
I Sam. 15:22, to *h* than the fat of rams

Prov. 29:12, if a ruler *h* to lies
Isa. 55:2, *h* diligently unto me
Dan. 9:19, O Lord, *h* and do
Mk. 7:14, *H* to me, every one of you
See Ps. 103:20; Prov. 1:33; 12:15; Acts 4:19
HEART Ex. 23:9, you know the *h* of a stranger
Deut. 11:13; Josh 22:5; I Sam. 12:20, 24; 13:3;
30:6; Mk. 12:30, 33; Lk. 20:27, love the Lord
with all your *h*
Judg. 5:16, great searchings of *h*
I Sam. 10:9, God gave him another *h*
16:7, the Lord looks on the *h*
I Ki. 3:9, 12, give an understanding *h*
4:29, gave Solomon largeness of *h*
8:17; II Chron. 6:7, it was in the *h* of David
11:4, not perfect, as was *h* of David
I Chron. 12:33, not of double *h*
29:17; Jer. 11:20, I know you try the *h*
II Chron. 31:21, he did it with all his *h*
32:25, his *h* was lifted up
Neh. 2:2, nothing else but sorrow of *h*
Job 23:16, makes my *h* soft
29:13, cause the widow's *h* to sing
Ps. 10:6, 11, 13; 14:1; 53:1, said in his *h*
73:7, more than *h* could wish
78:37, their *h* was not right
97:11, gladness sown for upright in *h*
119:11, your word have I hid in my *h*
139:23, search me, and know my *h*
Prov. 4:23, keep your *h* with all diligence
14:10, the *h* knows his own bitterness
21:1, king's *h* is in the hand of the Lord
23:7, as he thinks in his *h*, so is he
Prov. 25:3, a king's *h* is unsearchable
20, songs to a heavy *h*
31:11, *h* of her husband does trust
Eccl. 8:5, wise man's *h* discerns
Isa. 35:4, say to them of fearful *h*
44:20, a deceived *h*
57:1; Jer. 12:11, no man lays it to *h*
Jer. 11:20; 20:12, you try the *h*
17:9, the *h* is deceitful above all things
20:9, in my *h* as a burning fire
24:7, I will give them a *h* to know me
30:21, that engaged his *h* to approach
49:16; Obad. 3, pride of *h* deceived you
Ezek. 11:19, take stony *h*
18:31, make you a new *h*
36:26, will give you a *h* of flesh
44:7; Acts 7:51, uncircumcised in *h*
Joel 2:13, rend your *h*
Zech. 7:12, make *h* as adamant
Mal. 2:2, if you will not lay it to *h*
4:6, turn *h* of fathers to children
Mat. 5:8, blessed are the pure in *h*
6:21; Lk. 12:34, there will your *h* be also
11:29, meek and lowly in *h*
12:34, out of the abundance of the *h*
15:19, our of the *h* proceed evil thoughts
18:35, if you from your *h* forgive not
Mk. 2:8, why reason ye in your *h*?
8:17, have you your *h* yet hardened?
10:5; 16:14, hardness of *h*
Lk. 2:19, 51, kept them in her *h*

21:14, settle it in your *h*
24:25, slow of *h* to believe
Jn. 14:1, 27, let not your *h* be troubled
Acts 5:33; 7:54, were cut to the *h*
11:23, with purpose of *h*
Rom. 10:10, with the *h* man believes
I Cor. 2:9, neither have entered into *h*
II Cor. 3:3, in fleshy tables of the *h*
5:12, glory in appearance, not in *h*
Eph. 3:17, Christ dwell in your *h* by faith
5:19, singing and making melody in your *h*
6:6, doing will of God from the *h*
Phil. 4:7, keep your *h* and minds
Col. 3:22, in singleness of *h*
II Thess. 3:5, direct your *h* into love of God
Heb. 4:12, discerner of intents of the *h*
10:22, draw near with true *h*
13:9, good that the *h* be established
James 3:14, if you have strife in your *h*
4:8, purify your *h*
I Pet. 3:4, the hidden man of the *h*
15, sanctify the Lord in your *h*
HEARTH Gen. 18:6; Ps. 102:3; Isa. 30:14
HEARTILY Col. 3:23
HEAT Deut. 29:24, the *h* of this great anger
Ps. 19:6, nothing hid from *h* thereof
Eccl. 4:11, two together, then they have *h*
Isa. 4:6; 25:4, a shadow from the *h*
18:4, *h* upon herbs, dew in *h* of harvest
49:10, neither shall *h* smite them
Hos. 7:4, as oven *h* by the baker
Mat. 20:12, burden and *h* of the day
II Pet. 3:10, melt with fervent *h*
See Dan. 3:19; Lk. 12:55; Acts 28:3
HEATH Jer. 17:6; 48:6
HEATHEN Ps. 2:1, why do *h* rage?
8, give *h* for inheritance
102:15; the *h* shall fear name of the Lord
Ezek. 36:24; I will take you from among *h*
Zech. 8:13, you were a curse among the *h*
Mat. 6:7, repetitions, as the *h*
18:17, let him be as *h* man
See Lev. 25:44; Deut. 4:27; Neh. 5:8
HEAVEN Gen. 28:17, the gates of *h*
Ex. 20:22, have talked with you from *h*
Lev. 26:19, make your *h* as iron
Deut. 10:14; I Ki. 8:27, the *h* of *h*
33:13, the precious things of *h*
II Ki. 7:2, if the Lord make windows in *h*
Job 15:15, the *h* are not clean in his sight
22:12, is not God in the height of *h*?
Ps. 8:3, when I consider your *h*
14:2; 53:2, had looked down from *h*
73:25, whom have I in *h*?
119:89, your word is settled in *h*
Prov. 8:27, when he prepared *h* I was there
Eccl. 5:2, for God is in *h*
Isa. 13:13; Hag. 2:6, will shake the *h*
40:12, meted out *h* with the span
65:17; Rev. 21:1, new *h* and new earth
Jer. 7:18, make cakes to queen of *h*
23:24, do not I fill *h* and earth?
31:37, if *h* can be measured
Dan. 7:13, with clouds of *h*

Hag. 1:10, *h* over you is stayed from dew
Mat. 3:10, if I will not open windows of *h*
Mat. 11:23, exalted to *h*
24:29; Mk. 13:25, the powers of *h*
Mk. 13:32, no, not the angels in *h*
Lk. 15:18, I have sinned against *h*
Jn. 1:51, you shall see *h* open
6:31, 32, bread from *h*
Acts 4:12, none other name under *h*
Rom. 1:18, wrath of God revealed from *h*
II Cor. 5:1, eternal in the *h*
2, our house that is from *h*
Gal. 1:8, though an angel from *h* preach
Eph. 1:10, gather in one, things in *h*
3:15, whole family in *h*
6:9; Col. 4:1, your master is in *h*
Phil. 3:20, our conversation is in *h*
Heb. 12:23, written in *h*
I Jn. 5:7, three that bear record in *h*
Rev. 4:1, door opened in *h*
Rev. 8:1, silence in *h*
HEAVENLY Lk. 2:13, of the *h* host
Jn. 3:12, I tell you of *h* things
Acts 26:19, the *h* vision
I Cor. 15:48, as is the *h*, such are they
Eph. 1:3, 2:6; 3:10, in *h* places
Heb. 3:1, partakers of the *h* calling
8:5; 9:23, shadow of *h* things
See II Tim. 4:18; Heb. 6:4; 12:22
HEAVINESS Ps. 69:20, I am full of *h*
Prov. 12:25, *H* in the heart makes it stoop
14:13, the end of that mirth is *h*
Isa. 61:3, garment of praise for spirit of *h*
James 4:9, let your joy be turned to *h*
See Ezra 9:5; Prov. 10:1; Rom. 9:2
HEAVY Ex. 17:12, Moses' hands were *h*
I Ki. 14:6, sent with *h* tidings
Neh. 5:18, the bondage was *h*
Job 33:7; Ps. 32:4, hand *h*
Prov. 25:20, songs of a *h* heart
31:6, wine to those of *h* hearts
Isa. 58:6, to undo the *h* burdens
Mat. 11:28, all you that are *h* laden
23:4, they bind *h* burdens
26:37, he began to be very *h*
43; Mk. 14:40, their eyes were *h*
See Prov. 27:3; Isa. 59:1; Lk. 9:32
HEDGE Job 3:23, whom God has *h* in
Prov. 15:19, way of slothful as *h* of thorns
Eccl. 10:8, whoso breaks an *h*
Lam. 3:7, he has *h* me about
Hos. 2:6, I will *h* up your way
Mk. 12:1, he set a *h* about it
Lk. 14:23, the highways and *h*
See Isa. 5:5; Ezek. 13:5; 22:30; Nah. 3:17
HEED II Sam. 20:10, took no *h* to the sword
Eccl. 12:9, preacher gave good *h*
Isa. 21:7, hearkened diligently with much *h*
Jer. 18:18, let us not give *h*
I Tim. 1:4; Titus 1:14, neither give *h* to fables
4:1, giving *h* to seducing spirits
Heb. 2:1, give more earnest *h*
See Prov. 17:4; Acts 3:5; 8:6
HEEL Gen. 3:15, it shall bruise your *h*

Ps. 41:9, lifted *h* against me
49:5, iniquity of *h* shall compass
Hos. 12:3, he took his brother by *h*
See Jn. 13:18
HEIGHT Ps. 102:19, *h* of his sanctuary
Prov. 25:3, the heaven for *h*
Isa. 7:11, in the depth, or in the *h* above
Eph. 3:18, the *h* of the love of Christ
See Job 22:12; Ps. 148:1; Amos 2:9
HEIR II Sam. 14:7, we will destroy the *h*
Prov. 30:23, handmaid that is *h* to her mistress
Mat. 21:38; Lk. 20:14, this is the *h*
Rom. 8:17, *h* of God, joint-*h* with Christ
Gal. 3:29, *h* according to the promise
4:7, and *h* of God through Christ
Eph. 3:6, Gentiles fellow-*h*
Titus 3:7, *h* according to hope of eternal life
Heb. 1:14, who shall be *h* of salvation
James 2:5, *h* of the kingdom
I Pet. 3:7, as *h* together of the grace
See Jer. 49:1; Mic. 1:15; Rom. 4:13
HELL Deut. 32:22, fire shall burn to lowest *h*
II Sam. 22:6, sorrows of *h* compassed me
Job 11:8, deeper than *h*
26:6, *H* is naked before him
Ps. 9:17, wicked turned into *h*
16:10; Acts 2:27, not leave soul in *h*
55:15, let them go down quick into *h*
139:8, If I make my bed in *h*
Prov. 5:5, her steps taken hold on *h*
7:27, house is the way to *h*
9:18, her guests are in the depths of *h*
15:11, *H* and destruction before the Lord
24, that he may depart from *h* beneath
23:14, deliver his soul from *h*
27:20, *H* and destruction are never full
Isa. 14:9, *H* from beneath is moved
28:15, 18, with *h* are we at agreement
Ezek. 31:16, when I cast him down to *h*
32:21, shall speak out of the midst of *h*
Jonah 2:2, out of the belly of *h*
Hab. 2:5, enlarges his desire as *h*
Mat. 5:22, in danger of *h* fire
29, 30, whole body cast into *h*
Mat. 10:28, destroy soul and body in *h*
11:23; Lk. 10:15, brought down to *h*
16:18, gates of *h* shall not prevail
23:15, more the child of *h*
33, how can you escape the damnation of *h*?
Lk. 16:23, in *h* he lift up
Acts 2:31, soul not left in *h*
James 3:6, tongue set on fire of *h*
II Pet. 2:4, cast angels down to *h*
See Isa. 5:14; Rev. 1:18; 6:8; 20:13
HELMET Isa. 59:17, a *h* of salvation on head
Eph. 6:17, take the *h* of salvation
I Thess. 5:8, a *h* hope of salvation
HELP Gen. 2:18, 20, an *h* meet for him
Deut. 33:29, the shield of your *h*
II Chron. 26:15, he was marvellously *h*
Job 6:13, is not my *h* in me?
Ps. 22:11, for there is none to *h*

33:20, he is our *h* and our shield
42:5, the *h* of his countenance
46:1, a very present *h* in trouble
89:19, laid *h* on one that is mighty
121:1, the hills, from whence comes my *h*
124:8, our *h* is in the name of the Lord
Isa. 10:3, to whom will you flee for *h*?
41:6, they *h* every one his neighbor
Mat. 15:25, Lord *h* me
Mk. 9:24, *h* thou my unbelief
Acts 21:28, men of Israel, *h*
Heb. 4:16, grace to *h* in time of need
See Isa. 31:3; Rom. 8:26; II Cor. 1:24
HELPER Heb. 13:6
HEN Mat. 23:37; Lk. 13:34
HENCEFORTH II Cor. 5:15; Gal. 6:17
HERESY Acts 24:14; I Cor. 11:19; Gal. 5:20;
II Pet. 2:1
HERETIC Titus 3:10, a man that is an *h*
HERITAGE Job 20:29, *h* appointed by God
Ps. 16:6; Jer. 3:19, a goodly *h*
61:5, the *h* of those that fear
127:3, children are an *h* of the Lord
Isa. 54:17, this is the *h* of the servants
Mic. 7:14, feed flock of your *h*
I Pet. 5:3, lords over God's *h*
HID II Ki. 4:27, the Lord has *h* it from me
Job 3:21, more than for *h* treasures
Ps. 32:5, my iniquity have I not *h*
69:5, my sins are not *h*
119:11, your word have I *h* in my heart
Zeph. 2:3, it may be you shall be *h*
Mat. 10:26; Mk. 4:22, there is nothing *h*
Lk. 19:42, they are *h* from your eyes
I Cor. 2:7, even the *h* wisdom
II Cor. 4:3, if our gospel be *h*
Col. 3:3, your life is *h* with Christ
I Pet. 3:4, the *h* man of the heart
Rev. 2:17, to eat of the *h* manna
HIDE Gen. 18:17, shall I *h* from Abraham
Job 14:13, *h* me in the grave
Ps. 10:11, he *h* his face
17:8, *h* me under the shadow of your wings
27:5, *h* me in pavilion
31:20, *h* them in secret of your presence
89:46, how long will you *h* yourself?
139:12, darkness *h* not from you
Isa. 1:15, I will *h* my eyes from you
26:20, *h* yourself for a little moment
32:2, a man shall be as an *h* place
45:15, you are a God that *h* yourself
Ezek. 28:3, no secret they can *h* from you
James 5:20, *h* a multitude of sins
Rev. 6:16, *h* us from the face of him
See Job 13:24; Prov. 28:28; Amos 9:3
HIGH Job 11:8, it is as *h* as heaven
22:12, behold stars, how *h* they are!
Ps. 62:9, men of *h* degree are a lie
103:11, as the heaven is *h* above the earth
138:6, though the Lord be *h*
139:6, it is *h*, I cannot attain unto it
Eccl. 12:5, afraid of that which is *h*
Isa. 32:15, spirit poured on us from on *h*
Jer. 49:16, though you make your nest *h*

Mat. 22:9; Lk. 14:23, go into the *h*-ways
Lk. 1:78, dayspring from on *h*
   24:49, power from on *h*
Rom. 12:16, mind not *h* things
Phil. 3:14, for prize of the *h* calling
See Isa. 57:15; Acts 13:17; II Cor. 10:5
HIGHER Isa. 55:9, heavens *h* than the earth
Lk. 14:10, friend, to up *h*
Heb. 7:26, made *h* than the heavens
HILL Gen. 49:26, the everlasting *h*
Deut. 11:11, a land of *h* and valleys
Ps. 2:6, set my king on holy *h*
   15:1, who shall dwell in your holy *h*?
   24:3, who shall dwell in your holy *h*?
   43:3, bring me to your holy *h*
   50:10, cattle on a thousand *h*
   121:1, I will lift up my eyes to the *h*
Prov. 8:25, before the *h* was I brought forth
Jer. 3:23, salvation hoped for from the *h*
Hos. 10:8; Lk. 23:30, to the *h*, fall on us
HINDER Gen. 24:56, *H* me not
Job 9:12; 11:10, who can *h* him?
Lk. 11:52, them that were entering you *h*
Acts 8:36, what does *h* me to be baptized?
I Cor. 9:12, lest we *h* the gospel
Gal. 5:7, who did *h* you
I Thess. 2:18, but Satan *h* us
I Pet. 3:7, that your prayers be not *h*
See Num. 22:16; Neh. 4:8; Isa. 14:6
HIRE Deut. 24:15, you shall gave him his *h*
Mic. 3:11, priests teach for *h*
Mat. 20:7, no man has *h* us
   8, 9, give them their *h*
Mk. 1:20, in ship with *h* servants
Lk. 10:7, laborer worthy of his *h*
   15:17, how many *h* servants
James 5:4, *h* of laborers which is kept back
See Ex. 12:45; Lev. 25:40; Deut. 15:18
HIRELING Job 7:1, like the days of an *h*?
   2, as *h* looks for reward
   14:6, accomplish, as an *h*, his day
Mal. 3:5, that oppress the *h*
See Isa. 16:14; 21:16; Jn. 10:12
HITHERTO I Sam. 7:12, *H* has the Lord helped us.
Jn. 5:17, my Father works *h*
   16:24, *H* have you asked nothing in my name
I Cor. 3:2, *h* you were not able to bear it
See Judg. 16:13; II Sam. 15:34; Isa. 18:2
HOARY Job 41:32
HOLD Gen. 21:18, *h* him in your hand
Ex. 20:7; Deut. 5:11, will not *h* him guiltless
II Ki. 7:9, good tidings, and we *h* our peace
Job 36:8, *h* in cords of affliction
Ps. 18:35, your right hand has *h* me up
   73:23, you have *h* me by my right hand
   119:117, *H* me up, and I shall be safe
Prov. 11:12, understanding *h* his peace
   17:28, a fool, when he *h* his peace
Isa. 41:13, the Lord will *h* your hand
   62:1, for Zion's sake will I not *h* my peace
Jer. 4:19, I cannot *h* my peace
Amos 6:10, *H* your tongue

Mat. 6:24; Lk. 16:13, he will *h* to the one
Lk. 4:35, *H* your peace, come out
Rom. 1:18, *h* the truth in unrighteousness
I Cor. 14:30, let the first *h* his peace
Phil. 2:16, *H* forth the word of life
   29, *h* such in reputation
Col. 2:19, not *h* the Head
I Thess. 5:21, *h* fast that which is good
I Tim. 1:19, *H* faith and good conscience
   3:9, *H* the mystery of faith
II Tim. 1:13, *H* fast form of sound words
Titus 1:9, *H* fast the faithful word
Heb. 3:14, *h* beginning of confidence
   4:14; 10:23, *h* fast our profession
Rev. 2:13, you *h* fast my name
   25, *h* fast till I come
See Job 2:3; Jer. 2:13; 51:30; Ezek. 19:9
HOLE Isa. 11:8, child shall play on *h* of asp
   51:1, *h* of pit whence you are digged
Jer. 13:4, hide in a *h* of the rock
Ezek. 8:7, a *h* in the wall
Hag. 1:6, a bag with *h*
Mat. 8:20; Lk. 9:58, foxes have *h*
See Song of Sol. 5:4; Mic. 7:17; Nah. 2:12
HOLIER Isa. 65:5
HOLIEST Heb. 9:3; 10:19
HOLILY I Thess. 2:10
HOLINESS Ex. 15:11, glorious in *h*
   28:36; 39:30; Zech. 14:20, *H* to the Lord
Ps. 30:4; 97:12, at remembrance of his *h*
   47:8, the throne of his *h*
   60:6; 108:7, God has spoken in his *h*
Ps. 93:5, *h* becomes your house
Isa. 35:8, the way of *h*
   63:15, habitation of your *h*
Jer. 23:9, the words of his *h*
Obad. 17, upon mount Zion there shall be *h*
Lk. 1:75, might serve him in *h*
Rom. 1:4, according tot he spirit of *h*
   6:22, fruit unto *h*
II Cor. 7:1, perfecting *h* in fear of God
Eph. 4:24, created in righteousness and *h*
I Thess. 3:13, unblameable in *h*
   4:7, not called to uncleanness, but *h*
Titus 2:3, in behavior as becomes *h*
Heb. 12:10, partakers of his *h*
See Ps. 89:35; Isa. 23:18; Jer. 2:3
HOLLOW Gen. 32:25; Judg. 15:19; Isa. 40:12
HOLPEN Ps. 86:17; Isa. 31:3; Dan. 11:34
HOLY Ex. 3:5; Josh. 5:15, is *h* ground
   20:8; 31:14, sabbath day, to keep it *h*
Lev. 10:10, difference between *h* and unholy
   20:7, be ye *h*
Num. 16:5, Lord will show who is *h*
II Ki. 4:9, this is an *h* man of God
Ezra 9:2; Isa. 6:13, the *h* seed
Ps. 20:6, hear from his *h* heaven
   22:3, you are *h* that inhabit
   86:2, preserve my soul, for I am *h*
   98:1, his *h* arm has gotten victory
   99:9, worship at his *h* hill
   145:17, the Lord is *h* in all his works
Prov. 20:25, who devours that which is *h*
Isa. 6:3; Rev. 4:8, *H, h, h*, is the Lord

52:10, made bare his *h* arm
64:10, your *h* cities are a wilderness
11, our *h* and beautiful house
Mat. 1:18, 20, with child of the *H* Ghost
3:11; Mk. 1:8; Lk. 3:16; Jn. 1:33
Acts 1:5, baptize with *H* Ghost
7:6, give not that which is *h*
12:31, blasphemy against *H* Ghost
Mk. 13:11, not ye that speak, but *H* Ghost
Lk. 1:15, shall be filled with the *H* Ghost
35, *h* thing which shall be born of you
3:22, *H* Ghost descended in bodily shape
4:1, Jesus being full of the *H* Ghost
12:12, *H* Ghost shall teach you
Jn. 7:39, the *H* Ghost was not yet given
14:26, Comforter, which is the *H* Ghost
17:11, *H* Father, keep those
20:22, receive ye the *H* Ghost
Acts 1:8, after the *H* Ghost is come
2:4; 4:31, all filled with *H* Ghost
4:27, 30, against your *h* child Jesus
Acts 5:3, to lie to the *H* Ghost
6:3, look out men full of the *H* Ghost
7:51, you do always resist the *H* Ghost
9:31, in comfort of the *H* Ghost
10:44, *H* Ghost fell on all which heard
47, received *H* Ghost as well as we
15:28, seemed good to the *H* Ghost
16:6, forbidden of the *H* Ghost
19:2, have ye received the *H* Ghost
20:28, *H* Ghost has made you overseers
Rom. 1:2, promised in the *h* scriptures
7:12, commandment is *h*, just, and good
9:1, bearing witness in *H* Ghost
11:16, if firstfruit be *h*, if root be *h*
14:17, joy in the *H* Ghost
16:16, with an *h* kiss
I Cor. 2:13, words the *H* Ghost teach
3:17, the temple of God is *h*
II Cor. 13:14, communion of the *H* Ghost
Eph. 1:4; 5:27, be *h* and without blame
2:21, grows to an *h* temple in the Lord
Col. 1:22, present you *h* and unblameable
3:12, elect of God, *h* and beloved
I Thess. 5:27, all the *h* brethren
I Tim. 2:8, lifting up *h* hands
II Tim. 1:9, called us with an *h* calling
Heb. 3:1, *h* brethren, partakers
I Pet. 1:12, *H* Ghost sent from heaven
15, 16; II Pet. 3:11, *h* in all conversation
2:5, an *h* priesthood
3:5, the *h* women, who trusted
II Pet. 1:18, with him in the *h* mount
21, *h* men moved by *H* Ghost
Rev. 3:7, saith he that is *h*
Rev. 6:10, O Lord, *h* and true
20:6, *h* is he that has part
HOME Ex. 9:19, and shall not be brought *h*
Lev. 18:9, whether born at *h* or abroad
Deut. 24:5, free at *h* one year
Ruth 1:21, the Lord brought me *h* empty
II Sam. 14:13, fetch *h* his banished
I Chron. 13:12, bring ark of God *h*
Job 39:12, he will bring *h* your seed

Ps. 68:12, she that tarries at *h*
Eccl. 12:5, man goes to his long *h*
Lam. 1:20, at *h* there is as death
Hag. 1:9, when you brought it *h*
Mk. 5:19, go *h* to your friends
Jn. 19:27, took her to his own *h*
20:10, went away to their own *h*
II Cor. 5:6, at *h* in the body
I Tim. 5:4, show piety at *h*
Titus 2:5, keepers at *h*
See Jer. 2:14; Lk. 9:61; 15:6
HONEST Lk. 8:15, an *h* and good heart
Acts 6:3, men of *h* report
Rom. 12:17; II Cor. 8:21, provide things *h*
13:13, let us walk *h*, as in the day
Phil. 4:8, whatsoever things are *h*
I Pet. 2:12, conversation *h* among Gentiles
See I Thess. 4:12; I Tim. 2:2; Heb. 13:18
HONOUR (*n.*) II Sam. 6:22, of them shall I be
had in *h*
I Ki. 3:13, also given you riches and *h*
I Chron. 29:28, died full of riches and *h*
II Chron. 1:11, 12, thou have not asked *h*
26:18, neither shall it be for your *h*
Esther 1:20, wives shall give husbands *h*
Job 14:21, his sons come to *h*
Ps. 7:5, lay my *h* in the dust
8:5; Heb. 2:7, crowned him with *h*
26:8, place where your *h* dwells
49:12, man being in *h* abides not
96:6, *H* and majesty are before him
149:9, this *h* have all his saints
Prov. 3:16, in left hand riches and *h*
4:8, she shall bring you to *h*
5:9, lest you give their *h* to others
14:28, in multitude of people is king's *h*
20:3, an *h* to cease from strife
25:2, the *h* of kings to search out
26:1, 8, *h* is not seemly for a fool
31:25, strength and *h* are her clothing
Eccl. 6:2, to whom God has given *h*
Mal. 1:6, where is my *h*?
Mat. 13:57; Jn. 4:44, not without *h*
Jn. 5:41, I receive not *h* from men
44, who receive *h* one of another
Rom. 2:7, in well doing seek for *h*
10, *h* to every man that works good
12:10, in *h* preferring one another
13:7, *h* to whom *h*
II Cor. 6:8, by *h* and dishonor
Col. 2:23, not in any *h* to satisfying
I Thess. 4:4, possess his vessel in *h*
I Tim. 5:17, elders worthy of double *h*
6:1, count masters worthy of *h*
16, to whom be *h* and power everlasting
Heb. 3:3, more *h* than the house
5:4, no man takes this *h* unto himself
I Pet. 3:7, giving *h* to the wife
Rev. 4:11, you are worthy to receive *h*
HONOUR (*v.*) Ex. 14:4, *h* upon Pharaoh
Ex. 20:12; Mat. 15:4; Eph. 6:2, *H* your father
and mother
Lev. 19:32, *h* the face of the old man
I Sam. 2:30, them that *h* me I will *h*

15:30, *h* me now before elders
Esther 6:6, the king delights to *h*
Ps. 15:4, he *h* them that fear the Lord
Prov. 3:9, *H* the Lord with your substance
12:9, better than he that *h* himself
Mal. 1:6, a son *h* his father
Mat. 15:8; Mk. 7:6, *h* me with their lips
Jn. 5:23, *h* the Son as they *h* the Father
I Pet. 2:17, *H* all men, *H* the king
See Isa. 29:13; 58:13; Acts 28:10

HONOURABLE Isa. 3:3, take away the *h* man
9:15, ancient and *h*, he is the head
42:21, magnify the law, and make it *h*
See Lk. 14:8; I Cor. 4:10; 12:23

HOPE (*n.*) Ps. 16:9, my flesh also shall rest in *h*
Ps. 39:7, my *h* is in you
119:116, let me not be ashamed of my *h*
Prov. 13:12, *H* deferred makes heart sick
14:32, has *h* in his death
26:12, 29:20, more *h* of a fool
Eccl. 9:4, to all the living there is *h*
Jer. 17:7, the man whose *h* the Lord is
31:17, there is *h* in your end
Hos. 2:15, for a door of *h*
Zech. 9:12, you prisoners of *h*
Acts 28:20, for the *h* of Israel I am bound
Rom. 4:18, who against *h* believed in *h*
I Cor. 13:13, faith, *h*, charity
15:19, if in this life only we have *h*
Eph. 1:18, the *h* of his calling
2:12, having no *h*, and without God
Col. 1:27, Christ in you, and *h* of glory
I Thess. 4:13, even as other who have no *h*
5:8, for an helmet, the *h* of salvation
II Thess. 2:16, good *h* through grace
Titus 3:7, the *h* of eternal life
Heb. 6:18, lay hold on *h* set before us
19, *h* as an anchor of the soul
I Pet. 1:3, begotten to a lively *h*
3:15, a reason of the *h* that is in you

HOPE (*v.*) Ps. 22:9, you did make me *h*
31:24, all you that *h* in the Lord
42:5, 11; 43:5, *h* you in God
71:14, I will *h* continually
Lam. 3:26, good that man both *h* and wait
Rom. 8:25, if we *h* for that we see not
I Pet. 1:13, *h* to the end
See Jer. 3:23; Acts 24:26; Heb. 11:1

HORN Ps. 18:2, the *h* of my salvation
92:10, like the *h* of an unicorn
148:14, he exalted the *h* of his
Mic. 4:13, I will make your *h* iron
Rev. 5:6, lamb having seven *h*
13:1, beast having ten *h*
11, had two *h* like a lamb
See I Sam. 2:1, 10; Rev. 17:3, 7

HORRIBLE Ps. 11:6; 40:2; Jer. 2:12

HOSPITALITY Rom. 12:13; I Tim. 3:2

HOT Ps. 39:3; Prov. 6:28; I Tim. 4:2; Rev. 3:15

HOUR Mat. 10:19, shall be given you in that same *h*
20:12, have wrought but one *h*
26:40, could you not watch one *h*?

Lk. 12:39, what *h* the thief would come
22:53, but this is your *h*
Jn. 5:25; 16:32, the *h* is coming
11:9, are there not twelve *h* in the day?
12:27, save me from this *h*
Acts 3:1, at the *h* of prayer
Gal. 2:5, give place, no, not for an *h*

HOUSE Gen. 28:17, none but the *h* of God
Deut. 8:12, when you have built goodly *h*
II Ki. 20:1; Isa. 38:1, set your *h* in order
15, what have they seen in your *h*?
Neh. 13:11, why is the *h* of God forsaken?
Job 30:23, *h* appointed for all living
Ps. 26:8, have loved the habitation of your *h*
65:4, satisfied with goodness of your *h*
69:9; Jn. 2:17, the zeal of your *h*
84:3, the sparrow has found an *h*
92:13, planted in the *h* of the Lord
118:26, blessed you out of the *h* of the Lord
Prov. 2:18, her *h* inclines to death
9:1, wisdom has built her *h*
12:7, the *h* of the righteous shall stand
19:14, *H* and riches are inheritance
Eccl. 7:2, *h* of mourning, *h* of feasting
12:3, the keepers of the *h* shall tremble
Isa. 3:14, spoil of poor in your *h*
5:8, woe unto them that join *h* to *h*
64:11, our holy and beautiful *h* is burned
Hos. 9:15, I will drive them out of my *h*
Hag. 1:4, and this *h* lie waste?
9, because of my *h* that is waste
Mal. 3:10, that there may be meat in my *h*
Mat. 7:25; Lk. 6:48, beat upon that *h*
10:12, when you come into an *h*
12:25; Mk. 3:25, *h* divided cannot stand
23:38, your *h* is left desolate
Lk. 10:7, go not from *h* to *h*
Jn. 12:3, *h* filled with odor
14:2, in my Father's *h* are many mansions
Acts 2:46, breaking bread from *h* to *h*
Acts 5:x42, in every *h* ceased not to preach
I Cor. 11:22, have you not *h* to eat in
II Cor. 5:1, *h* not made with hands
Col. 4:15, church in his *h*
I Tim. 3:4, 5, 12, rules well his own *h*
5:8, especially for those of his own *h*
II Tim. 3:6, which creep into *h*
Titus 1:11, subvert whole *h*
See Mat. 9:6; Lk. 7:44; 19:5; Acts 4:34

HOUSEHOLD I Sam. 27:3, every man with his *h*
II Sam. 6:20, returned to bless his *h*
Prov. 31:27, looks well to her *h*
Mat. 10:36, man's foes shall be of his own *h*
Gal. 6:10, the *h* of faith
Eph. 2:19, of the *h* of God
See Gen. 31:37; 47:12; II Sam. 17:23

HUMBLE II Chron. 33:12, *h* himself greatly
Ps. 9:12; 10:12, forgets not cry of the *h*
34:2, the *h* shall hear thereof
35:13, I *h* my soul with fasting
113:6, *h* himself to behold things in heaven
Prov. 16:19, better be of *h* spirit

Isa. 57:15, of contrite and *h* spirit
Mat. 23:12; Lk. 14:11; 18:14, *h* himself
Phil. 2:8, he *h* himself
James 4:6, God gives grace to the *h*
I Pet. 5:6, *H* yourselves under mighty hand
   of God
  See Isa. 2:11; 5:15; Lam. 3:20
HUMBLY II Sam. 16:4; Mic. 6:8
HUMILITY Prov. 15:33, before honor is *h*
  22:4, by *h* are riches
  See Acts 20:19; Col. 2:18, 23; I Pet. 5:5
HUNGER Deut. 8:3, he suffered you to *h*
  Job 18:12, his strength shall be *h*-bitten
  Ps. 34:10, young lions do lack, and suffer *h*
  Prov. 19:15, an idle soul shall suffer *h*
  Isa. 49:10, shall not *h* nor thirst
  Jer. 38:9, he is like to die for *h*
  Mat. 5:6; Lk. 6:21, blessed are you that *h*
  Jn. 6:35, he that comes to me shall never *h*
  Rom. 12:20, if thine enemy *h*
  Rev. 7:16, they shall *h* no more
HUNGRY Job 22:7, bread from *h*
  24:10, take away the sheaf from the *h*
  Ps. 50:12, if I were *h*, I would not tell you
  107:5, *H* and thirsty, their soul fainted
  9, he fills the *h* soul with goodness
  Isa. 29:8, when a *h* man dreams
  65:13, my servants eat, but you shall be *h*
  Ezek. 18:7, given his bread to the *h*
  I Cor. 11:21, one is *h*, and another drunken
  See Prov. 27:7; Isa. 8:21; 9:20; Mk. 11:12
HUNT I Sam. 26:20, does *h* a partridge
  Jer. 16:16, *h* them from every mountain
  Ezek. 13:18, *h* souls of my people
  Mic. 7:2, they *h* every man his brother
  See Gen. 10:9; 27:5; I Sam. 24:11
HUNTING Prov. 12:27
HURL Num. 35:20; I Chron. 12:2; Job 27:21
HURT Ps. 15:4, that swears to his own *h*
  Eccl. 8:9, rules over another to his own *h*
  Isa. 11:9, shall not *h* nor destroy
  Jer. 6:14; 8:11, have healed *h* slightly
  8:21, for the *h* of my people
  25:6, provoke not, I will do no *h*
  Dan. 3:25, they have no *h*
  6:23, no manner of *h* found upon him
  Mk. 16:18, deadly thing, it shall not *h*
  Lk. 10:19, nothing shall *h* you
  Acts 18:10, no man shall *h* you
  Rev. 6:6, *h* not the oil and the wine
  See Rev. 7:2; 9:4; 11:5
HURTFUL Ezra 4:15; I Tim. 6:9
HUSBAND Ex. 4:25, a bloody *h* are you
  Prov. 12:4, virtuous wife a crown to her *h*
  31:11, her *h* does safely trust
  Isa. 54:5, your Maker is your *h*
  Jn. 4:16, go, call your *h*
  I Cor. 7:16, whether you shall save your *h*
  14:35, let them ask their *h* at home
  Eph. 5:22, wives, submit to your *h*
  25; Col. 3:19, *H*, love your wives
  I Tim. 3:12, the *h* of one wife
  Titus 2:4, teach young women to love their *h*
  5, obedient to their own *h*

I Pet. 3:1, be in subjection to your *h*
  7, you *h*, dwell with them
HYMN Mat. 26:30; Mk. 14:26; Eph. 5:19
HYPOCRISY Mat. 23:28, within you are full
  of *h*
  Mk. 12:15, he, knowing their *h*
  Lk. 12:1, leaven of Pharisees, which is *h*
  James 3:17, wisdom is pure, and without *h*
  See Isa. 32:6; I Tim. 4:2
HYPOCRITE Job 20:5, the joy of the *h* but for
  a moment
  36:13, the *h* in heart
  Isa. 9:17, every one is an *h*
  Mat. 6:2, 5, 16, as the *h* do
  7:5; Lk. 6:42, you *h*
  15:7; Mk. 7:6; LK. 12:56, you *h*
  23:13; Lk. 11:44, woe unto you, *h*
  24:51, appoint his portion with the *h*
  See Job 27:8; Prov. 11:9
HYPOCRITICAL Ps. 35:16; Isa. 10:6

I

IDLE Ex. 5:8, 17, they be *i*
  Prov. 19:15, an *i* soul shall hunger
  31:27, she eats not bread of *i*
  Mat. 12:36, every *i* word men speak
  20:3, 6, others standing *i*
  See Eccl. 10:18; Ezek. 16:49; I Tim. 5:13
IDOL Ps. 96:5, all gods of the people are *i*
  Isa. 66:3, as if he blessed an *i*
  Jer. 50:38, they are made upon their *i*
  Hos. 4:17, Ehpraim is joined to *i*
  Acts 15:20, abstain from pollutions of *i*
  I Cor. 8:4, we know an *i* is nothing
  7, with conscience of the *i*
  I Thess. 1:9, you turned to God from *i*
  I Jn. 5:21, keep yourselves from *i*
  See Acts 17:16; Gal. 5:20; Col. 3:5
IGNORANCE Acts 3:17, through *i* you did it
  17:30, the times of *i* God winked at
  Eph. 4:18, alienated through *i*
  I Pet. 2:15, put to silence *i* of foolish men
  See Lev. 4:2, 13, 22, 27; 5:15; Num. 15:24
IGNORANT Ps. 73:22, so foolish was I, and *i*
  Isa. 63:16, though Abraham be *i* of us
  Acts 4:13, perceived they were *i* men
  Rom. 10:3, being *i* of God's righteousness
  I Cor. 14:38, if any man be *i*, let him be *i*
  II Cor. 2:11, not *i* of devices
  Heb. 5:2, can have compassion on the *i*
  II Pet. 3:5, they wittingly are *i*
  See Num. 15:28; Acts 17:23; I Tim. 1:13
IMAGINATION Gen. 6:5; 8:21, *i* of heart
  Deut. 29:19; Jer. 23:17, walk in *i* of heart
  I Cor. 28:9, understands the *i* of thoughts
  Rom. 1:21, vain in their *i*
  II Cor. 10:5, casting down *i*
  See Deut. 31:21; Prov. 6:18; Lam. 3:60
IMAGINE Nah. 1:9, what do ye *i* against the
  Lord?
  11, there is one that *i* evil
  Zech. 7:10; 8:17, let none *i* evil
  See Job 21:27; Ps. 10:2; 21:11; Acts 4:25

IMMORTAL I Tim. 1:17
IMMORTALITY Rom. 2:7, I Cor. 15:53
IMPART Job 39:17; Lk. 3:11; Rom. 1:11
IMPEDIMENT Mk. 7:32
IMPENITENT Rom. 2:5
IMPLACABLE Rom. 1:31
IMPOSE Ezra 7:24; Heb. 9:10
IMPOSSIBLE Mat. 19:26; Mk. 10:27
  Lk. 1:37; 18:27, with God nothing i
  See Mat. 17:20; Lk. 17:1; Heb. 6:4, 18
IMPOTENT Jn. 5:3; Acts 4:9; 14:8
IMPOVERISH Judg. 6:6; Isa. 40:20; Jer. 5:17
IMPRISONMENT Ezra 7:26; II Cor. 6:5
IMPUDENT Prov. 7:13; Ezek. 2:4; 3:7
IMPUTE Ps. 32:2; Rom. 4:8, to whom Lord i
    not iniquity
  Hab. 1:11, i his power to his god
  Rom. 5:13, sin is not i when there is no law
  See I Sam. 22:15; II Sam. 19:19; II Cor. 5:19
INCLINE Josh. 24:23, i your hearts
  I Ki. 8:58, that he may i hearts to keep law
  Ps. 40:1, he i unto me, and heard my cry
    119:36, i my heart to your testimonies
  Jer. 7:24; 11:8; 17:23; 34:14, nor i eat
  See Prov. 2:18; Jer. 25:4; 44:5
INCLOSED Ps. 17:10; 22:16; Lk. 5:6
INCONTINENT I Cor. 7:5, II Tim. 3:3
INCORRUPTIBLE I Cor. 9:25, an i crown
  I Pet. 1:4, inheritance i
    23, born of i seed
  See Rom. 1:23; I Cor. 15:42, 50, 52, 53, 54
INCREASE (n.) Lev. 25:36, no usury or i
    26:4, the land shall yield her i
  Deut. 14:22, 28, tithe all i
  Ps. 67:6; Ezek. 34:27, earth shall yield her i
  Prov. 18:20, with the i of his lips
  Eccl. 5:10, not satisfied with i
  Isa. 9:7, i of his government
  I Cor. 3:6, 7, God gave the i
  See Jer. 2:3; Eph. 4:16; Col. 2:19
INCREASE (v.) Ps. 4:7, that their corn and
    wine i
    115:14, Lord shall i you more and more
  Prov. 1:5; 9:9, a wise man will i learning
    11:24, there is that scatters and yet i
  Eccl. 1:18, he that i knowledge i sorrow
  Isa. 9:3, multiplied nation and not i joy
    40:29, he i strength
  Ezek. 36:37, i them with men like a flock
  Dan. 12:4, knowledge shall be i
  Lk. 2:52, Jesus i in wisdom
  Acts 6:7, word of God i
    16:5, churches i daily
  Rev. 3:17, I am rich, and i with goods
INCREDIBLE Acts 26:8
INCURABLE II Chron. 21:18; Jer. 15:18
INDEED I Chron. 4:10, bless me i
  II Chron. 6:18, will God i dwell on earth?
  Mk. 11:32, a prophet i
  Lk. 24:34, the Lord is risen i
  Jn. 1:47, an Israelite i
    8:36, you shall be free i
  I Tim. 5:3, that are widows i
  See Gen. 37:8; Isa. 6:9; Rom. 8:7

INDIGNATION Ps. 78:49, i, and trouble
  Isa. 26:20, till the i be overpast
  Nah. 1:6, who can stand before his i ?
  Mat. 20:24, moved with i
  II Cor. 7:11, yea, what i
  Heb. 10:27, fearful looking for of fiery i
  Rev. 14:10, the cup of his i
  See Zech. 1:12; Acts 5:17; Rom. 2:8
INDITING Ps. 45:1
INDUSTRIOUS I Ki. 11:28
INEXCUSABLE Rom. 2:1
INFANT Job 3:16; Isa. 65:20; Lk. 18:15
INFIDEL II Cor. 6:15; I Tim. 5:8
INFIRMITY Ps. 77:10, this is my i
  Prov. 18:14, spirit of man will sustain his i
  Mat. 8:17, himself took our i
  Rom. 6:19, the i of your flesh
    8:26, the Spirit also helps our i
    15:1, bear the i of the weak
  II Cor. 12:5, 10, glory in my i
  I Tim. 5:23, wine for your often i
  Heb. 4:15, touched with the feeling of our i
  See Lk. 5:15; 7:21; Jn. 5:5; Heb. 5:2
INFLAME Isa. 5:11; 57:5
INFLICTED II Cor. 2:6
INFLUENCES Job 38:31
INHABIT Isa. 57:15; 65:21; Amos 9:14
INHABITANT Judg. 5:23, curse bitterly the i
  Isa. 6:11, cities wasted without i
    33:24, i shall not say, I am sick
    40:22, the i thereof are as grasshoppers
INHERIT Ex. 32:13, they shall i it for ever
  Ps. 25:13, shall i the earth
    37:11, the meek shall i the earth
  Prov. 14:18, the simple i folly
  Mat. 19:29, shall i everlasting life
    25:34, i kingdom prepared
  Mk. 10:17; Lk. 10:25; 18:18, i eternal life
  I Cor. 6:9; Gal. 5:21, not i the kingdom
  See Heb. 6:12, I Pet. 3:9; Rev. 21:7
INHERITANCE Ps. 47:4, shall choose our i
    for us
  Prov. 20:21, an i may be gotten hastily
  Eccl. 7:11, wisdom good with an i
  Mk. 12:7; Lk. 20:14, the i shall be ours
  Lk. 12:13, that he divide the i with me
  Acts 20:32; 26:18, an i among the sanctified
  Eph. 1:14, earnest of our i
  Heb. 9:15, promise of eternal i
  See Ps. 16:5; Eph. 5:5; Col. 1:12; Heb. 1:4
INIQUITY Ex. 34:7; Num. 14:18, forgiving i and
    transgression
  Deut. 5:9, visiting the i of the fathers
  Job. 4:8, they that plow i reap the same
  Job 13:26, to possess the i of my youth
    34:32, if I have done i, I will do no more
  Ps. 25:11, pardon my i, for it is great
    32:5, my i have I not hid
    39:11, when you do correct man for i
    66:18, if I regard i in my heart
    69:27, add i to their i
    103:3, who forgives all your i
    10, not rewarded according to i
    107:17, fools, because of i, are afflicted

130:3, if you should mark *i*
Prov. 22:8, he that sows *i* that reap vanity
Isa. 1:4, a people laden with *i*
6:7, your *i* is taken away
40:2, her *i* is pardoned
53:5, he was bruised for our *i*
59:2, *i* separated between you and God
Jer. 5:25, your *i* turned away these things
Hab. 1:13, cannot look on *i*
Mat. 24:12, because *i* shall abound
Acts 1:18, purchased with reward of *i*
8:23, in the bond of *i*
Rom. 6:19, servants to *i* unto *i*
II Thess. 2:7, the mystery of *i*
II Tim. 2:19, depart from *i*
James 3:6, a world of *i*
See Ps. 36:2; 49:5; Jer. 31:30; Ezek. 3:18; 18:26
INJURIOUS I Tim. 1:13
INK Jer. 36:18; II Cor. 3:3; II Jn. 12
INN Gen. 42:17; Ex. 4:24; Lk. 2:7; 10:34
INNOCENT Job 9:23, laugh at trial of *i*
27:17, the *i* shall divide the silver
Ps. 19:13, *i* from the great transgression
Jer. 2:34; 19:4, blood of the *i*
See Gen. 20:5; Ex. 23:7; Mat. 27:24
INNUMERABLE Job 21:33; Heb. 12:22
INORDINATE Ezek. 23:11; Col. 3:5
INQUISITION Deut. 19:18; Esther 2:23; Ps. 9:12
INSCRIPTION Acts 17:23
INSPIRATION Job 32:8; II Tim. 3:16
INSTANT Rom. 12:12; II Tim. 4:2
INSTRUCT Neh. 9:20, good spirit to *i* them
Ps. 16:7, my reins *i* me in night season
32:8, I will *i* you and teach you
Isa. 40:14, who *i* him?
Mat. 13:52, every scribe *i* unto the kingdom
Phil. 4:12, in all things I am *i*
See Prov. 21:11; Acts 18:25; II Tim. 2:25
INSTRUCTION Ps. 50:17, you hate *i*
Prov. 1:7; 15:5, fools despise *i*
4:13, take fast hold of *i*
12:1, whoso loves *i* loves knowledge
16:22, the *i* of fools is folly
24:32, I looked upon it, and received *i*
II Tim. 3:16, profitable for *i*
See Jer. 17:23; 35:13; Zeph. 3:7
INSTRUMENT Isa. 41:15, a new sharp threshing *i*
Ezek. 33:32, of one that can play on an *i*
Rom. 6:13, members *i* of unrighteousness
See Num. 35:16; Ps. 7:13; 150:4
INTEGRITY Job 2:3, he holds fast his *i*
31:6, that God may know my *i*
Ps. 25:21, let *i* preserve me
26:1, I walked in *i*
Prov. 11:3, the *i* of the upright
INTENTS Jer. 30:24; Heb. 4:12
INTERCESSION Rom. 8:26, the Spirit itself makes *i*
Heb. 7:25, ever lives to make *i*
See Isa. 53:12; Jer. 7:16; 27:18; I Tim. 2:1
INTERCESSOR Isa. 59:16
INTERMEDDLE Prov. 14:10; 18:1
INTREAT Ruth 1:16, *I* me not to leave you

I Sam. 2:25, if a man sin, who *i* for him?
Ps. 119:58, I *i* your favor
Isa. 19:22, he shall be *i* of them
I Tim. 5:1, but *i* him as a father
James 3:17, wisdom is easy to be *i*
See Prov. 18:23; Lk. 15:28
INTRUDING Col. 2:18
INVENTIONS Ps. 106:29; Prov. 8:12
INVISIBLE Col. 1:15; Heb. 11:27
INWARD Job 38:36, wisdom in the *i* parts
Ps. 51:6, truth in the *i* parts
64:6, *i* thought of every one is deep
Jer. 31:33, I will put my law in their *i* parts
II Cor. 4:16, the *i* man is renewed
See Ps. 62:4; Mat. 7:15; Rom. 2:29
IRON Prov. 27:17, *I* sharpens *i*
Eccl. 10:10, if the *i* be blunt
Isa. 48:4, neck is an *i* sinew, and
Jer. 15:12, shall *i* break northern *i*
Dan. 2:33, legs of *i* his feet part *i*
4:23, even with a band of *i* and
5:23, you have praised the gods of silver, and gold, of brass, and *i*
I Tim. 4:2, conscience seared with a hot *i*
See Josh. 17:16; Mic. 4:13
ISSUES Ps. 68:20; Prov. 4:23
ITCHING II Tim. 4:3

J

JANGLING I Tim. 1:16
JEALOUS I Ki. 19:10, 14, I have been *j* for the Lord
Ezek. 39:25, will be *j* for my holy name
II Cor. 11:2, I am *j* over you
See Num. 5:14; Joel 2:18; Zech. 1:14; 8:2
JEALOUSY Deut. 32:16
Prov. 6:34, *j* is the rage of a man
Song of Sol. 8:6, *j* is cruel as the grave
Ezek. 36:5, in fire of *j* have I spoken
I Cor. 10:22, do we provoke the Lord to *j*?
See Ps. 78:58; 79:5; Isa. 42:13
JESTING Eph. 5:4
JEWELS Isa. 61:10; Mal. 3:17
JOIN Prov. 11:21; 16:5, hand *j* in hand
Eccl. 9:4, to him *j* to living there is hope
Isa. 5:8, that *j* house to house
Jer. 50:5, let us *j* ourselves to the Lord
Hos. 4:17, Ephraim is *j* to idols
Mat. 19:6; Mk. 10:9, what God has *j*
Acts 5:13, durst no man *j* himself
I Cor. 1:10, perfectly *j* in same mind
6:17, *j* to the Lord
Eph. 4:16, whole body *j* together
See Acts 8:29; 9:26; 18:7; I Cor. 6:16
JOINT Gen. 32:25; Ps. 22:14
Eph. 4:16, which every *j* supplies
Heb. 4:12, dividing asunder of *j* and marrow
See I Ki. 22:34; Rom. 8:17; Col. 2:19
JOURNEY (*n.*) I Ki. 18:27, or he is in a *j*
Neh. 2:6, for how long shall your *j* be?
Mk. 6:8; Lk. 9:3, scrip for your *j*
Jn. 4:6, Jesus, wearied with his *j*
JOURNEY (*v.*) Gen. 12:9; 13:11; Num. 10:29

JOURNEYINGS Num. 10:28, thus were the *j*
  II Cor. 11:25, in *j* often
JOY Ezra 3:13, not discern noise of *j*
  Neh. 8:10, *j* of the Lord is your strength
  Job 20:5, the *j* of the hypocrite
    29:13, widow's heart sing for *j*
    41:22, sorrow is turned into *j*
  Ps. 16:11, fullness of *j*
    48:2, the *j* of the whole earth
    51:12, restore the *j* of your salvation
    126:5, they that sow in tears shall reap in *j*
    137:6, prefer Jerusalem above my chief *j*
  Prov. 14:10, not intermeddle with his *j*
    21:15, it is *j* to the just to do judgment
  Eccl. 2:10, I withheld not my heart from *j*
    9:7, eat your bread with *j*
  Isa. 9:3, not increased the *j*
    12:3, with *j* draw water
    24:8, *j* of the harp ceases
    29:19, meek shall increase their *j*
    35:2; 51:11, with everlasting *j*
    65:14, my servants sing for *j* of my heart
  Jer. 15:16, your word was the *j* of my heart
    31:13, will turn their mourning into *j*
  Mat. 13:20; Lk. 8:13, with *j* receives it
    44, for *j* goes and sells
    25:21, 23, the *j* of your Lord
  Lk. 15:7, *j* in heaven over one sinner
    10, there is *j* in presence of angels
    24:41, they believed not for *j*
  Jn. 3:29, this my *j* is fulfilled
    15:11; 16:24, that your *j* might be full
  Acts 8:8, great *j* in that city
    20:24, finish my course with *j*
  II Cor. 1:24, helpers of your *j*
  Heb. 12:2, for the *j* that was set before him
  James 1:2, count it all *j* when you fall
  I Pet. 1:8, with *j* unspeakable
  I Pet. 4:13, glad also with exceeding *j*
  II Jn. 12, that our *j* may be full
  Jude 24, faultless, with exceeding *j*
  See Rom. 14:17; Gal. 5:22; Phil. 1:4
JOYFUL Ps. 35:9, my soul *j* in the Lord
    63:5, praise you with *j* lips
    66:1; 81:1; 95:1; 98:6, make a *j* noise
  Eccl. 7:14, in day of prosperity be *j*
  Isa. 56:7, *j* in my house of prayer
  See II Cor. 7:4; Col. 1:11; Heb. 10:34
JUDGE (*n.*) Gen. 18:25, *J* of the earth
  Ps. 50:6, God is *j* himself
  Mic. 7:3, the *j* asks a reward
  Lk. 12:14, who made me a *j* over you?
  Acts 10:42, the *J* of the quick and dead
  II Tim. 4:8, the Lord, the righteous *J*
  Heb. 12:23, to God the *J* of all
  James 5:9, the *j* stands before the door
  See II Sam. 15:4; Mat. 5:25; James 4:11
JUDGE (*v.*) Deut. 32:36; Ps. 7:8, Lord *j* the
    people
  Ps. 58:11, he is a God that *j* in the earth
  Isa. 1:17, *j* the fatherless
  Mat. 7:1, *J* not, that you be not *j*
  Lk. 7:43, you have rightly *j*
  Rom. 14:4, who are you that *j*?

  See Isa. 51:5; Ezek. 34:17; Jn. 16:11; Rom. 2:16;
    3:6; II Tim. 4:1; Heb. 13:4
JUDGMENT Deut. 1:17, the *j* is God's
  Ps. 1:5, shall not stand in the *j*
    101:1, I will sing of mercy and *j*
  Prov. 29:26, *j* comes from the Lord
  Eccl. 11:9; 12:14, God will bring into *j*
  Isa. 28:17, *J* will I lay to the line
    53:8, taken from prison and from *j*
  Jer. 5:1, if there be any that executes *j*
    10:24, correct with *j*, not in anger
  Hos. 12:6, keep mercy and *j*
  Mat. 5:21, in danger of the *j*
  Jn. 5:22, Father committed all *j* to the Son
    9:39, for *j* I am come
  Acts 24:25, reasoned of *j* to come
  Rom. 14:10, we stand before the *j* seat
  Heb. 9:27, after this the *j*
  I Pet. 4:17, *j* must begin at house of God
  See Mat. 12:41; Heb. 10:27; James 2:13
JUST Prov. 3:33, the habitation of the *j*
    4:18, path of *j* as shining light
    10:7, memory of *j* is blessed
  Isa. 26:7, way of the *j* is uprightness
  Hab. 2:4; Heb. 10:38, *j* shall live by faith
  Mat. 5:45, sends rain on *j* and unjust
  Lk. :14:14, recompensed at resurrection of *j*
    15:7, ninety and nine *j* persons
  Acts 24:15, resurrection both of *j* and unjust
  Heb. 2:2, a *j* recompence of reward
    12:33, spirits of *j* men made perfect
  I Pet. 3:18, the *j* for the unjust
  See Job 34:17; Acts 3:14; Col. 4:1
JUSTICE II Sam. 15:4, I would do *j*
  Ps. 89:14, *J* and judgment are the habitation
  Prov. 8:15, by me princes decree *j*
  Isa. 59:4, none calls for *j*
  Jer. 23:5, execute *j* in the earth
    50:7, the habitation of *j*
  See Job 8:3; 36:17; Isa. 9:7; 56:1
JUSTIFICATION Rom. 4:25; 5:16, 18
JUSTIFY Job 25:4, how then can man be *j* with
    God
  Ps. 51:4, be *j* with you speak
    143:2, in your sight shall no man living be *j*
  Isa. 5:23, which *j* the wicked for reward
  Mat. 12:37, by your words you shall be *j*
  Lk. 7:35, wisdom is *j* of her children
    10:29, willing to *j* himself
    18:14, *j* rather than the other
  Acts 13:39, all that believe are *j*
  Rom. 3:24; Titus 3:7, *j* freely by his grace
    5:1, being *f* by faith
  Gal. 2:16, man is not *j* by works of the law
  I Tim. 3:16, *j* in the Spirit
  See Isa. 50:8; Rom. 4:5; 8:33; James 2:25
JUSTLY Mic. 6:8; Lk. 23:41; I Thess. 2:10

K

KEEP Gen. 18:19, *k* the way of the Lord
  Num. 6:24, the Lord bless you, the *k* you
  I Sam. 2:9, he will *k* the feet of his saints
  Ps. 17:8, *K* me as the apple of the eye

34:13, *K* your tongue from evil
121:3, he that *k* you will not slumber
127:1, except the Lord *k* the city
141:3, *k* the door of my lips
Prov. 4:6, love wisdom, she shall *k* you
21, *k* my sayings in midst of your heart
23, *K* your heart with all diligence
6:20, my son *k* your father's commandment
Eccl 3:6, a time to *k*
5:1, *K* your foot then you go
12:13, fear God, and *k* his commandments
Isa. 26:3, you will *k* him in perfect peace
27:3, I the Lord do *k* it, I will *k* it
Jer. 3:5, 12, will be *k* his anger?
Hab. 2:20, let the earth *k* silence
Mal. 3:14, what profit that we have *k*
Lk. 11:28, blessed are they that *k*
19:43, enemies shall *k* you in on every side
Jn. 8:51, 52, *k* my sayings
12:25, he that hates his life shall *k* it
14:23, if a man love me, he will *k* my words
17:11, holy Father, *k* through your own
name
15, that you should *k* them from the evil
Acts 16:4, delivered the decrees to *k*
21:25, *k* from things offered to idols
I Cor. 5:8, let us *k* the feast
9:27, I *k* under my body
Eph. 4:3, *k* the unity of the Spirit
Phil 4:7, the peace of God shall *k* your hearts
I Tim. 5:22, *k* yourself pure
6:20, *k* that which is committed
James 1:27, *k* himself unspotted
I Jn. 5:21, *k* yourselves from idols
Jude 21, *K* yourselves in the love of God
24, him that is able to *k* you from falling
Rev. 3:10, *k* you from hour of temptation
KEEPER Ps. 121:5, the Lord is your *k*
Eccl. 12:3, when *k* of the house shall tremble
Song of Sol. 1:6, they made me *k* of the
vineyards
Titus 2:5, chaste, *k* at home
See Gen. 4:2, 9; Mat. 28:4; Acts 5:23; 16:27
KEY Mat. 16:19, *k* of kingdom of heaven
Lk. 11:52, taken away *k* of knowledge
Rev. 1:18, the *k* of hell and of death
See Isa. 22:22; Rev. 3:7; 9:1
KICK Deut. 32:15; I Sam. 2:29; Acts 9:5
KILL Num. 16:13, to *k* us in the wilderness
II Ki. 5:7, am I a God, to *k*?
7:4, if they *k* us, we shall but die
Eccl. 3:3, a time to *k*
Mk. 3:4, is it lawful to save life, or to *k*?
Jn. 5:18, Jews sought the more to *k* him
7:19, why go ye about to *k* me?
8:22, will he *k* himself?
Rom. 8:36, for your sake we are *k* all the day
II Cor. 3:6, the letter *k*
6:9, chastened, and not *k*
James 4:2, you *k*, and desire to have
5:6, you condemned and *k* the just
See Mat. 23:37; Mk. 12:5; Lk. 22:2
KIND II Chron. 10:7, if you be *k* to this people

Mat. 17:21; Mk. 9:29, this *k* goes not out
Lk. 6:35, *k* to unthankful and evil
I Cor. 13:4, charity suffers long, and is *k*
See Mat. 13:47; Eph. 4:32; James 3:7
KINDLE Ps. 2:12, his wrath is *k* by a little
Prov. 26:21, a contentious man to *k* strife
Isa. 50:11, walk in sparks that you have *k*
Lk. 12:49, what will I, if it be already *k*?
James 3:5, how great a matter a little fire *k*!
See Job 19:11; 32:2; Ezek. 20:48
KINDLY Gen. 24:49; 50:21; Ruth 1:8
KINDNESS Ruth 3:10, you have showed more *k*
II Sam. 2:6, I will requite you this *k*
9:1, 7, show him *k* for Jonathan's sake
Ps. 17:7; 92:2, your marvelous loving-*k*
36:7, how excellent is your loving-*k*!
63:3, your loving-*k* is better than life
117:2; 119:76, his merciful *k*
Prov. 31:26, in her tongue is the law of *k*
Isa. 54:8, with everlasting *k*
Jer. 2:2, I remember the *k* of your youth
31:3, with loving-*k* have I drawn you
Col. 3:12, put on *k*, meekness
II Pet. 1:7, to godliness brotherly *k*
KINDRED Acts 3:25; Rev. 1:7; 5:9; 7:9
KING Judg. 9:8, trees went forth to anoint a *k*
17:6, no *k* in Israel
I Sam. 8:5, now make us a *k*
Job 18;14, bring him to the *k* of terrors
34:18, is it fit to say to a *k*?
Ps. 5:2; 84:3, my *K* and my God
10:16, the Lord is *K* for ever
20:9, let the *k* hear us when we call
74:12, God is my *K* of old
102:15, the *k* of the Earth shall fear
Prov. 8:15, by me *k* reign
22:29, the diligent shall stand before *k*
31:3, that which destroyed *k*
4, it is not for *k* to drink wine
Eccl. 10:16, woe when your *k* is a child!
20, curse not the *k*
Isa. 32:1, a *k* shall reign in righteousness
33:17, eyes shall see the *k* in his beauty
49:23, *k* shall by your nursing fathers
Jer. 10:10, the Lord is an everlasting *k*
Lk. 19:38, blessed be the *K* who comes
23:2, saying that he himself is Christ a *K*
Jn. 6:15, by force, to make him a *k*
I Tim. 1:17, now to the *K* eternal
6:15, the *K* of *k*, and Lord of lords
Rev. 1:6, make us *k* and priests unto God
15:3, you *K* of saints
See I Sam. 8:11; Isa. 60:16; Mat. 22:2; Lk.
10:24; I Tim. 2:2; I Pet. 2:17
KINGDOM Ex. 19:6, a *k* of priests
I Chron. 29:11; Mat. 6:13, yours is the *k*
Ps. 22:28, the *k* is the Lord's
103:19, his *k* rules over all
Isa. 14:16, is this the man that did shake *k*?
Dan. 4:3, his *k* is an everlasting *k*
Mat. 4:23; 9:35; 24:14, gospel of the *k*
8:12, children of the *k* cast out
13:38, the good seed are the children of
the *k*

25:34, inherit the *k*

Lk. 11:17, *k* divided against itself

12:23, Father's pleasure to give you the *k*

22:29, I appoint unto you a *k*

Jn. 18:36, my *k* is not of this world

Acts 1:6, will you restore the *k* to Israel?

Col. 1:13, into the *k* of his dear Son

II Tim. 4:18, to his heavenly *k*

James 2:5, heirs of the *k* he has promised

II Pet. 1:11, entrance into everlasting *k*

KISS Ps. 85:10; Prov. 27:6; Lk. 7:38

KNEE Gen. 30:3; 41:43

Isa. 35:3; Job 4:4; feeble *k*

45:23, to God every *k* shall bow

Nah. 2:10, *k* smite together

See Dan. 5:6; Mat. 27:29; Rom. 14:11; Eph.
3:14; Phil. 2:10; Heb. 12:12

KNEW Gen. 28:16, the Lord is in this place, and
I *k* it not

Jer. 1:5, before I formed you I *k* you

Mat. 7:23, I never *k* you, depart

Jn. 4:10, if you *k* the gift of God

II Cor. 5:21, who *k* no sin

KNOW I Chron. 28:9, *k* you the God of your
father

Job 5:27, *k* thou it for your good

8:9, we are but of yesterday, and *k* nothing

13:23, make me to *k* my transgression

19:25, I *k* that my redeemer lives

22:13; Ps. 73:11, how does God *k*?

Ps. 39:4, make me to *k* my end

46:10, be still, and *k* that I am God

56:9, this I *k*, for God is for me

103:14, he *k* our frame

139:23, *k* my heart

Eccl. 9:5, the living *k* they shall die

11:9, *k* that for all these things

Isa. 1:3, the ox *k* his owner

Jer. 17:9, the heart is deceitful who can *k* it?

31:24, *K* the Lord, for all shall *k* me

Ezek. 2:5, 33:33, *k* there has been a prophet

Hos. 2:20, you shall *k* the Lord

Mat. 6:3, let not your left hand *k*

13:11; Mk. 4:11, give to you to *k*

25:12, I *k* you not

Mk. 1:24, I *k* you, who you are

Lk. 19:42, if you had *k*

22:57, 60, I *k* him not

Jn. 7:17, he shall *k* of the doctrine

10:14, I *k* my sheep, and am *k* of mine

13:7, *k* not now, but shall *k* hereafter

17, if you *k* these things

Jn. 13:35, shall all men *k* you are my disciples

Acts 1:7, it is not for you to *k*

Rom. 8:28, we *k* that all things work

I Cor. 2:14, neither can he *k* them

13:9, 12, we *k* in part

Eph. 3:19, and to *k* the love of Christ

II Tim. 1:12, I *k* whom I have believed

3:15, you have *k* the scriptures

I Jn. 2:4, he that says, I *k* him

3:2, we *k* that when he shall appear

Rev. 2:2, 9, 13, 19; 3:1, 8, I *k* your works

KNOWLEDGE II Chron. 1:10, give me *k*

Job 21:14, we desire not *k* of your ways

Ps. 94:10, he that teaches man *k*

139:6, such *k* is too wonderful

144:3, that you take *k* of him

Prov. 10:14, wise men lay up *k*

14:6, *k* is easy to him that understands

17:27, he that has *k* spares words

24:5, man of *k* increases strength

30:3, nor have the *k* of the holy

Eccl. 1:18, increases *k* increases sorrow

Isa. 11:2, the spirit of *k*

40:14, who taught him *k*

Hos. 4:6, destroyed for lack of *k*

Hab. 2:14, the earth shall be filled with the *k*

Lk. 11:52, taken away the key of *k*

I Cor. 8:1, *k* puffs up

13:8, *k* shall vanish away

Eph. 3:19, love of Christ, which passes *k*

Phil. 3:8, but loss for the *k* of Christ

Col. 2:3, treasures of wisdom and *k*

I Tim. 2:4; II Tim. 3:7, the *k* of the truth

Heb. 10:26, sin after we have received *k*

II Pet. 1:5, 6, to virtue *k*, to *k* temperance

3:18, grow in grace and *k*

See Gen. 2:9, I Sam. 2:3; Prov. 19:2

L

LABOUR (*n.*) Ps. 90:10, *l* and sorrow

104:23, goes to his *l* till evening

Prov. 14:23, in all *l* there is profit

Eccl. 1:8, all things are full of *l*

2:22, what has man of all his *l*

6:7, all the *l* of man is for his mouth

Jn. 4:38, are entered into their *l*

I Cor. 15:58, your *l* is not in vain

I Thess. 1:3; Heb. 6:10, your *l* of love

Rev. 2:2, I know your *l* and patience

14:13, rest from their *l*

LABOUR (*v.*) Ex. 20:9, six days shall you *l*

Neh. 4:21, so we *l* in the work

Ps. 127:1, they *l* in vain

144:14, our oxen may be strong to *l*

Prov. 16:26, he that *l l* for himself

23:4, *L* not to be rich

Eccl. 4:8, for whom do I *l*

5:12, the sleep of a *l* man is sweet

Mat. 11:28, all you that *l*

Jn. 6:27, *L* not for meat that perishes

I Cor. 3:9, we are *l* together with God

I Thess. 5:12, which *l* among you

I Tim. 5:17, they who *l* in word and doctrine

LACK Mat. 19:20; Lk. 22:35; Acts 4:34

LADEN Isa. 1:4; Mat. 11:28; II Tim. 3:6

LAMB Isa. 5:17, the *l* feed after their manner

11:6, the wolf shall dwell with the *l*

53:7; Jer. 11:19, as *l* to the slaughter

Jn. 1:29, 36, behold the *L* of God

I Pet. 1:19, as of a *l* without blemish

Rev. 5:6; 13:8, stood a *L* slain

12:11, by the blood of the *L*

22:1, the throne of God and of the *L*

See Isa. 40:11; Jn. 21:15; Rev. 13:11

LAME Job 29:15; Prov. 26:7; Isa. 35:6

LAMENT Mat. 11:17; Jn. 16:20; Acts 8:2
LAMP Ps. 119:105; Prov. 13:9; Isa. 62:1
LAP Judg. 7:6; Prov. 16:33
LAST Num. 23:10, let my *l* end be like his
   Prov. 23:32, at the *l* it bites like a serpent
   Mat. 12:45; LK. 11:26, *l* state of that man
     19:30; 20:16; Mk. 10:31, first shall be *l*
   Jn. 6:39; 11:24; 12:48; the *l* day
LATTER Job 19:25; Prov. 19:20; Hag. 2:9
LAUGH Prov. 1:26; Eccl. 3:4; Lk. 6:21
LAW Josh. 8:34, all the words of the *l*
   Ps. 37:31, the *l* of his God is in his heart
     40:8, your *l* is within my heart
     119:70, 77, 92, 174, I delight in your *l*
     97, 113, 163, 165, how I love your *l*
   Prov. 13:14, the *l* of the wise is a fountain of
     life
   Isa. 8:20, to the *l* and to the testimony
   Mal. 2:6, the *l* of truth was in his mouth
   Mat. 5:17, not come to destroy the *l*
     23:23, the weightier matters of the *l*
   Jn. 7:51, does our *l* judge any man
     19:7, we have a *l*, and by our *l*
   Rom. 2:14, are a *l* unto themselves
     8:3, what the *l* could not do
   Gal. 3:24, the *l* was our schoolmaster
     5:14, all the *l* is fulfilled in one word
     23, against such there is no *l*
     6:2, so fulfill the *l* of Christ
   Heb. 7:16, the *l* of a carnal commandment
   James 1:25; 2:12, perfect *l* of liberty
     2:8, the royal *l*
   See Ps. 1:2; 19:7; Mat. 7:12; Rom. 10:4
LAWFUL Mat. 12:2; Jn. 5:10; I Cor. 6:12
LAWLESS I Tim 1:9
LEAD Deut. 4:27, whither the Lord shall *l* you
   Ps. 23:2, he *l* me beside still waters
     27:11, *l* me in a plain path
     31:3, *l* me, and guide me
     61:2, *l* me to the rock that is higher than I
   Ps. 139:24, *l* me in the way everlasting
   Prov. 6:22, when you go, it shall *l* you
   Isa. 11:6, a little child shall *l* them
     42:16, I will *l* them in paths not known
   Isa. 48:17, I am the Lord which *l* you
   Mat. 6:13, *l* us not into temptation
     15:14; Lk. 6:30, if the blind *l* the blind
   Acts 13:11, seeking some one to *l* him
   I Tim. 2:2, we may *l* a quiet life
LEAF Lev. 26:36; Isa. 64:6; Mat. 21:19
LEAN Prov. 3:5; Amos 5:19; Mic. 3:11
LEARN Deut. 31:13, *l* to fear the Lord
   Prov. 1:5; 9:9; 16:21; will increase *l*
     22:25, lest you *l* his ways
   Isa. 1:17, L to do well
     2:4; Mic. 4:3, neither shall they *l* war
     29:11, 12, deliver to one that is *l*
   Jn. 6:45, every one that has *l* of the Father
     7:15, having never *l*
   Acts 7:22, *l* in all the wisdom of the Egyptians
     26:24, much *l* does make you mad
   Eph. 4:20, you have not so *l* Christ
   II Tim. 3:14, in the things you have *l*
   Heb. 5:8, though a Son, yet *l* he obedience

LEAST Mat. 5:19, these *l* commandments
     25:40, 45, done it to one of the *l* of these
   Lk. 7:28, he that is *l* in kingdom of heaven
     12:26, not able to do that which is *l*
     16:10, faithful in that which is *l*
   Eph. 3:8, less than the *l* of all saints
   See Gen. 32:10; Jer. 31:34; I Cor. 6:4
LEAVE Gen. 2:24; Mat. 19:5; Mk. 10:7
   Ps. 16:10; Acts 2:27, not *l* my soul in hell
     27:9; 119:121, *l* me not
   Mat. 23:23, and not to *l* the other undone
   Jn. 14:27, peace I *l* with you
   Eph. 5:31, *l* father and mother
   Heb. 13:5, I will never *l* you
   See Ruth 1:16; Mat. 5:24; Jn. 16:28
LEES Isa. 25:6; Jer. 48:11; Zeph. 1:12
LEG Ps. 147:10; Prov. 26:7; Dan. 2:33
LEND Deut. 15:6, *l* to many nations
   Ps. 37:26, 112:5, ever merciful, and *l*
   Prov. 19:17, pity on poor *l* to the Lord
     22:7, the borrower is servant to the *l*
   Lk. 6:34, if you *l* to them of whom
   See I Sam. 1:28; Isa. 24:2; Lk. 11:5
LESS Ex. 30:15; Job 11:6; Isa. 40:17
LIARS Ps. 116:11; Jn 8:44; Titus 1:12
LIBERAL Prov. 11:25; Isa. 32:5, 8; James 1:5
LIBERTY Ps. 119:45, I will walk at *l*
   Isa. 61:1; Jer. 34:8; Lk. 4:18, to proclaim *l*
   Rom. 8:21, *l* of the children of God
   I Cor. 8:9, take heed lest this *l* of yours
   II Cor. 3:17, where the Spirit is, there is *l*
   Gal. 5:1, stand fast in the *l*
   James 1:25; 2:12, the law of *l*
LIFE Gen. 2:7; 6:17; 7:22, the breath of *l*
     2:9; 3:24; Rev. 2:7, the tree of *l*
   Josh. 2:14, our *l* for yours
   I Sam. 25:29, bound up in the bundle of *l*
   Ps. 17:14; Eccl. 9:9, their portion in this *l*
     26:9, gather not my *l* with bloody men
     27:1, the strength of my *l*
     34:12, what man is he who desires *l*?
     36:9, the fountain of *l*
     91:16, with long *l* will I satisfy him
   Prov. 3:22, so shall they be *l* to your soul
     8:35, whoso finds me finds *l*
     15:24, the way of *l* is above to the wise
   Mat. 6:25, take no thought for your *l*
     18:8; 19:17; Mk. 9:43, to enter into *l*
   Lk. 12:15, a man's *l* consists not
     23, the *l* is more than meat
   Jn. 1:4, in him was *l*
     5:24, I Jn. 3:14, passed from death to *l*
     26, as the Father has *l* in himself
     6:33, 47, 48, 54, the bread of *l*
     10:15, 17; 13:37, I lay down my *l*
   II Cor. 2:16, the savour of *l* unto *l*
   Gal. 2:20, the *l* that I now live
   Eph. 4:18, alienated from the *l* of God
   Col. 3:3, your *l* is hid
   I Tim. 4:8; II Tim. 1:1, the promise of the *l*
   II Tim. 1:10, brought *l* to light by gospel
   James 4:14, what is your *l*?
   I Jn. 1:2, the *l* was manifested
   Rev. 22:1, 17, river of water of *l*

LIGHT Ex. 10:23, Israel had *l* in dwellings
  Job 18:5, the *l* of the wicked
    37:21, men see not bright *l* in clouds
  Ps. 4:6; 90:8, the *l* of your countenance
    27:1, the Lord is my *l*
    36:9, in your *l* shall we see *l*
    97:11, *L* is sown for the righteous
    119:105, a *l* to my path
  Eccl. 11:7, the *l* is sweet
  Isa. 5:20, darkness for *l*, and *l* for darkness
    30:26, the *l* of the moon as *l* of sun
    59:9, we wait for *l*
    60:1, arise shine, for your *l* is come
  Zech. 14:6, the *l* shall not be clear
  Mat. 5:14; Jn. 8:12; 9:5, the *l* of the world
    16, let your *l* so shine
    6, 22, the *l* of the body is the eye
  Lk. 12:35, your loins girded, and *l* burning
    16:8, wiser than children of *l*
  Jn. 1:9, that was the true *L*
    3:19, *l* is come into the world
    5:35, burning and shining *l*
    12:35, yet a little while is the *l* with you
    36, while you have *l*, believe in the *l*
  Acts 26:18, turn from darkness to *l*
  I Cor. 4:5, bring to *l* hidden things
  II Cor. 4:4, *l* of the gospel
    6, commanded *l* to shine out of darkness
    11:14, an angel of *l*
  Eph. 5:8, now are you *l*, walk as children of *l*
    14, Christ shall give you *l*
  I Tim. 6:16, in *l* which no man can approach
  II Pet. 1:19, a *l* shining in a dark place
  I Jn. 1:5, God is *l*
  Rev. 22:5, candle, neither *l* of the sun
LIGHTNING Ex. 19:16; Lk. 10:18
LIKENESS Isa. 40:18, what *l* will you compare?
  Acts 14:11, gods are come down in *l* of men
  Rom. 6:5, *l* of his death, *l* of his resurrection
    8:3, in the *l* of sinful flesh
  Phil. 2:7, was made in the *l* of men
  See Gen. 1:26; 5:1; Ex. 20:4; Deut. 4:16
LIMIT Ps. 78:41; Ezek. 43:12, Heb. 4:7
LINE Ps. 16:6; Isa. 28:10, 17; II Cor. 10:16
LINGER Gen. 19:16; 43:10; II Pet. 2:3
LION Gen. 49:9; Judg. 14:5, 18; Job 4:10, 11;
    10:16; 28:8; Ps. 7:2; 10:9; 17:12; 22:13
  Prov. 22:13, there is a *l* without
    28:1, righteous are bold as *l*
  Eccl. 9:4, living dog better than dead *l*
  Isa. 11:6, calf and young *l*
  Ezek. 1:10, face as a *l*
  Hos. 5:14, as a young *l*
  Mic. 5:8, remnant of Jacob be as a *l*
  II Tim. 4:17, out of mouth of the *l*
  I Pet. 5:8, the devil was a roaring *l*
  Rev. 5:5, *l* of the tribe of Judah
  See Prov. 26:13; Isa. 11:7; 38:13; 65:25; Lam.
    3:10; Ezek. 10:14; Rev. 4:7
LIP I Sam. 1:13, only her *l* moved
  Job 27:4, my *l* shall not speak wickedness
    33:3, my *l* shall utter knowledge
  Ps. 12:2, 3, flattering *l*
    17:1, goes not out of feigned *l*

31:18; 120:2; Prov. 10:18; 17:7, lying *l*
  Eccl. 10:12, *l* of a fool will swallow himself
  Isa. 6:5, a man of unclean *l*
  Mat. 15:8, honors me with their *l*
  See Ps. 51:15; 141:3; Dan. 10:16; Hab. 3:16
LITTLE Ezra 9:8, for a *l* space, a *l* reviving
  Job. 26:14, how *l* a portion is heard?
  Ps. 8:5; Heb. 2:7, a *l* lower than angels
    37:16, a *l* that a righteous man has
  Prov. 6:10; 24:33, a *l* sleep
    15:16; 16:8, better is a *l* with fear of the
    Lord
    30:24, four things *l* on earth
  Isa. 28:10, here a *l*, and there a *l*
    40:15; Ezek. 16:47, as a very *l* thing
  Hag. 1:6, bring in *l*
  Mat. 6:30; 16:8; Lk. 12:28, *l* faith
    10:42; 18:6; Mk. 9:42; Lk. 17:2, *l* ones
  Lk. 7:47, to whom *l* is forgiven
    19:3; *l* of stature
  I Cor. 5:6; Gal. 5:9, a *l* leaven
  I Tim. 4:8, bodily exercises profits *l*
    5:23, use a *l* wine
  See Jn. 7:33; 14:19; 16:16; Rev. 3:8; 6:11
LIVE Gen. 17:18, O that Ishmael might *l*
    45:3, does my father yet *l*?
  Job 7:16, I would not *l* always
    14:14, shall he *l* again?
  Ps. 118:17, I shall not die, but *l*
  Isa. 38:16, make me to *l*
    55:3, hear, and your soul shall *l*
  Ezek. 3:21; 18:9; 33:13, he shall surely *l*
    16:6, when you were in your blood, *L*
  Hos. 6:2, we shall *l* in his sight
  Hab. 2:4, the just shall *l* by faith
  Mat. 4:4; Lk. 4:4, not *l* by bread alone
  Lk. 10:28, this do, and you shall *l*
  Jn. 11:25, though he were dead, yet shall he *l*
    14:19, because I *l*, you shall *l* also
  Acts 17:28, in him we *l* and move
  Rom. 8:12, *l* after the flesh
    14:8, whether we *l*, we *l* unto the Lord
  I Cor. 9:14, should *l* of the gospel
  II Cor. 6:9, as dying, and, behold, we *l*
  Gal. 2:19, that I might *l* unto God
    5:25, if we *l* in the Spirit
  Phil. 1:21, for me to *l* is Christ
  II Tim. 3:12, all that will *l* godly
  James 4:15, if the Lord will, we shall *l*
  Rev. 1:18, I am he that *l*, and was dead
    3:1, a name that you *l*
  See Rom. 6:10; I Tim. 5:6; Rev. 20:4
LIVELY Ex. 1:19; Acts 7:38; I Pet. 1:3; 2:5
LIVING Gen. 2:7, a *l* soul
  Job 28:13; Ps. 27:13; 116:9, the land of the *l*
    33:30; Ps. 56:13, light of *l*
  Ps. 69:28, the book of the *l*
  Eccl. 7:2, the *l* will lay it to heart
    9:5, the *l* know they shall die
  Isa. 38:19, the *l* shall praise you
  Jer. 2:13; 17:13; Jn. 4:10, *l* water
  Lam. 3:39, wherefore does a *l* man complain?
  Mk. 12:44, even all her *l*
  Lk. 8:43, spent all her *l*

Jn. 6:51, I am the *l* bread
Heb. 10:20, a new and *l* way
See Mat. 22:32; Mk. 12:27; I Cor. 15:45
LOADETH Ps. 68:19
LOAN I Sam. 2:20
LOATHE Num. 21:5; Job 7:16; Ezek. 6:9
LODGE Ruth 1:16; Isa. 1:21; I Tim. 5:10
LOFTY Ps. 131:1; Isa. 2:11; 57:15
LONG Job 3:21, which *l* for death
6:8, that God would grant the thing I *l* for!
Ps. 63:1, my flesh *l* for you in dry land
84:2, my soul *l* for courts of the Lord
119:174, I have *l* for your salvation
See Deut. 12:20; II Sam. 23:15; Phil. 1:8
LOOK Gen. 19:17, *l* not behind you
Num. 21:8, when he *l* on the serpent
Isa. 5:7; 59:11, he *l* for judgment
17:7, that day shall man *l* to his Maker
45:22, *L* unto me, and be saved
Isa. 63:5, I *l* and there was none to help
66:2, to this man will I *l*
Jer. 8:15; 14:19, we *l* for peace
39:12, *l* well to him
Hag. 1:9, you *l* for much
Mat. 11:3; Lk. 7:19, do we *l* for another?
24:50, in a day he *l* not for
Lk. 9:62, no man *l* back is fit
10:32, a Levite came and *l* on him
22:61, the Lord turned, and *l* on Peter
Jn. 13:22, disciples *l* one on another
Acts 3:4, 12, said, *L* on us
6:3, *l* ye out seven men
II Cor. 4:18, we *l* not at things seen
Phil. 2:4, *l* not every man on his own things
Titus 2:13, *L* for that blessed hope
Heb. 11:10, he *l* for a city
I Pet. 1:12, angels desire to *l* into
II Jn. 8, *L* to yourselves
See Prov. 14:15; Mat. 5:28; II Pet. 3:12
LOOSE Job 38:31, *l* bands of Orion?
Ps. 102:20, *l* those appointed to death
116:16, you have *l* my bonds
Eccl. 12:6, of ever the silver cord be *l*
Mat. 16:19; 18:18, *l* on earth be *l* in heaven
Jn. 11:44, *L* him, and let him go
Acts 2:24, having *l* the pains of death
I Cor. 7:27, are you *l* from a wife?
See Deut. 25:9; Isa. 45:1; 51:14; Lk. 13:12
LORD Ex. 34:6, the *L*, the *L* God, merciful
Deut. 4:35; I Ki. 18:39, the *L* is God
6:4, the *L* our God is one *L*
Ruth 2:4; II Thess. 3:16, the *L* be with you
I Sam. 3:18; Jn. 21:7, it is the *L*
Neh. 9:6; Isa. 37:20, you are *L* alone
Ps. 33:12, whose God is the *L*
100:3, know that the *L* He is God
118:23, this is the *L* doing
Zech. 14:9, one *L*, and his name one
Mat. 7:21, not every one that saith *L*, *L*
26:22, *L*, is it I?
Mk. 2:28; Lk. 6:5, the *L* of the sabbath
Lk. 6:46, why call ye me *L*, *L*?
Jn. 9:36, who is he, *L*?
20:25, we have seen the *L*

Acts 2:36, both *L* and Christ
9:5; 26:15, who are you, *L*?
Eph. 4:5, one *L*
See Gen. 19:24; Josh 5:14, 15; Isa. 30:33; 53:1; Jer. 3:14; Jn. 12:38; I Cor. 2:8; 15:47; Rev. 11:15
LORDSHIP Mk. 10:42; Lk. 22:25
LOSE Mat. 10:39; Lk. 9:24, shall *l* it
16:26; Lk. 9:25, *l* his own soul
Jn. 6:39, Father's will I should *l* nothing
See Judg. 18:25; Eccl. 3:6; Lk. 15:4, 8
LOSS I Cor. 3:15; Phil. 3:7, 8
LOST Ps. 119:176; Jer. 50:6, like *l* sheep
Ezek. 37:11, our hope is *l*
Mat. 10:6; 15:24, go to *l* sheep of Israel
18:11, to save that which was *l*
Jn. 6:12, that nothing be *l*
17:12, none of them is *l*
18:9, have I *l* none
See Lev. 6:3; Deut. 22:3; II Cor. 4:3
LOT Ps. 16:5, you maintain my *l*
125:3, not rest on the *l* of the righteous
Prov. 1:14, cast in your *l* among us
16:33, *l* is cast into the lap
18:18, *l* caused contention to cease
Dan. 12:13, stand in your *l*
Acts 8:21, neither part nor *l* in this manner
See Num. 26:55; Mat. 27:35; Acts 1:26
LOUD Ezra 3:13; Prov. 7:11; Lk. 23:23
LOVE (*n.*) Prov. 10:12, *l* covers all sins
15:17, better a dinner of herbs where *l* is
Song of Sol. 2:4, his banner over me was *l*
8:6, *l* is strong as death
Jer. 31:3, loved thee with everlasting *l*
Hos. 11:4, the bands of *l*
Mat. 24:12, *l* of many shall wax cold
Jn. 5:42, you have not the *l* of God in you
13:35, if you have *l* one to another
15:13, greater *l* has no man than this
Rom. 13:10, *L* works no ill
II Cor. 5:14, the *l* of Christ constrains us
13:11, the God of *l* shall be with you
Eph. 3:19, the *l* of Christ, which passes
I Tim. 6:10, *l* of money is root of all evil
Heb. 13:1, let brotherly *l* continue
I Jn. 4:7, *l* is of God
Rev. 2:4, you have left your first *l*
See Gen. 29:20; Gal. 5:22; I Thess. 1:3
LOVE (*v.*) Lev. 19:18; Mk. 12:31, you shall *l* your neighbor
Deut. 6:5; 10:12; 30:6; Mat. 22:37; Mk. 12:30, *l* the Lord your God
Ps. 18:1, I will *l* thee, O Lord, my strength
26:8, I have *l* the habitation of your house
34:12, what man is he that *l* many days?
97:10, you that *l* the Lord
109:17, as he *l* cursing
122:6, they shall prosper that *l* thee
Prov. 8:17, I *l* them that *l* me
17:17, a friend *l* at all times
Eccl. 3:8, a time to *l*
Jer. 5:31, my people *l* to have it so
31:3, I have *l* thee with an everlasting love
Amos 5:15, hate the evil, and *l* the good
Mic. 6:8, but to *l* mercy, and walk humbly

Mat. 5:44; Lk. 6:27, I say, *L* your enemies
   46, if you *l* them which *l* you
Lk. 7:42, which will *l* him most?
Jn. 11:3, he whom thou *l* is sick
   15:12, 17, that you *l* one another
Rom. 13:8, owe no man anything, but to *l*
I Pet. 1:8, whom having not seen, you *l*
   2:17, *L* the brotherhood
I Jn. 4:19, we *l* him, because he first *l* us
Rev. 3:19, as many as I *l*, I rebuke
See Gen. 22:2; Jn. 14:31; I Jn. 4:20, 21
LOVELY II Sam. 1:23; Phil. 4:8
LOVER I Ki. 5:1; Ps. 88:18, II Tim. 3:4
LOW Ps. 136:23; Rom. 12:16; James 1:9, 10
LOWER Ps. 8:5; 63:9; Eph. 4:9; Heb. 2:7
LOWEST Deut. 32:22; Ps. 86:13; Lk. 14:9
LOWLINESS Eph. 4:2; Phil. 2:3
LOWLY Prov. 11:2, with the *l* is wisdom
Mat. 11:29, I am meek and *l*
See Ps. 138:6; Prov. 3:34; 16:19; Zech. 9:9
LUST Ps. 81:12, gave them up to their own *l*
Rom. 7:7, I had not known *l*
Gal. 5:24, Christ's have crucified flesh with *l*
I Tim. 6:9, rich fall into hurtful *l*
Titus 2:12, denying worldly *l*
James 1:14, when he is drawn of his own *l*
I Pet. 2:11, abstain from fleshly *l*
I Jn. 2:16, the *l* of the flesh
Jude 16, 18, walking after *l*
See Mat. 5:28; I Cor. 10:6; Rev. 18:14
LYING Ps. 31:18, *l* lips be put to silence
   119:163, I abhor *l*, but your law I love
Prov. 6:17, the Lord hates a *l* tongue
   12:19, a *l* tongue is but for a moment
Jer. 7:4, trust not in *l* words
Eph. 4:25, putting away *l*
See I Ki. 22:22; II Chron. 18:21; Dan. 2:9

M

MAD Jn. 10:20; Acts 26:11
MADE Ex. 2:14, *m* you prince over us?
Ps. 118:24, this is the day the Lord has *m*
Prov. 16:4, Lord *m* all things for himself
Eccl. 3:11, he has *m* everything beautiful
   7:29, God has *m* man upright
Isa. 66:2, all these things has my hand *m*
Jn. 1:3, all things were *m* in him
   5:6, will you be *m* whole?
II Cor. 5:21, he has *m* him to be sin for us
Eph. 2:13, *m* near by the blood of Christ
   3:7; Col. 1:23, I was *m* a minister
Col. 1:20, having *m* peace
Heb. 2:17, to be *m* like his brethren
See Ps. 95:5; 149:2; Jn. 19:7; Acts 17:24
MAGNIFY Josh. 3:7, will I begin to *m* him?
Ps. 34:3; 40:16; Lk. 1:46, *m* the Lord
   35:26; 38:16, that *m* themselves
   138:2, you have *m* your word above all
Isa. 42:21, *m* the law
Acts 19:17, the name of Jesus was *m*
Rom. 11:13, I *m* my office
See Acts 5:13; Phil. 1:20
MAIL I Sam. 17:5

MAINTAIN Ps. 16:5, you *m* my lot
Titus 3:8, 14, careful to *m* good works
See Job 13:15; Ps. 19:4; 140:12
MAINTENANCE Ezra 4:14; Prov. 27:27
MAKER Job 4:17, more pure than his *m*?
   32:22, my *m* would soon take me away
   35:10, none says, Where is God my *m*?
   36:3, ascribe righteousness to my *M*
Ps. 95:6, kneel before the Lord our *m*
Prov. 14:31; 17:5, reproach his *M*
   22:2, the Lord is *m* of them all
Isa. 45:9, that strives with his *M*
   51:13, forget the Lord your *M*
   54:5, your *M* is your husband
Heb. 11:10, whose builder and *m* is God
See Isa. 1:31; 17:7; 22:11; Hab. 2:18
MALICIOUSNESS Rom. 1:29; I Pet. 2:16
MAN Gen. 3:22, *m* is become of us
   8:21, for *m* sake
Num. 23:19, God is not a *m*
Neh. 6:11, should such a *m* as I flee?
Job 5:7, *m* is born to trouble
   10:4, seest thou as *m* seeth?
   11:12, vain *m* would be wise
   14:1, *M* that is born of a woman
   15:7, are you the first *m* that was born?
   25:6, *m* that is a worm
   33:12, God is greater than *m*
Ps. 10:18, the *m* of earth
   49:12, *m* being in honor abides not
   89:48, what *m* is he that lives
   90:3, you turn *m* to destruction
   104:23, *M* goes forth to his labor
   118:6, I will not fear, what can *m* do?
Prov. 12:2, a good *m* obtains favor
Isa. 2:22, cease ye from *m*
Jer. 10:23, it is not in *m* to direct his steps
Hos. 11:9, I am God, and not *m*
Mat. 6:24, no *m* can serve
   8:4; Mk. 8:30; Lk. 9:21, tell no *m*
   17:8, they saw no *m*
Jn. 1:18; I Jn. 4:12, no *m* has seen God
   19:5, behold the *m*!
I Cor. 2:11, what *m* knows things of a *m*?
   11:8, *m* is not of the woman
II Cor. 4:16, though our outward *m* perish
Phil. 2:8, in fashion as a *m*
I Tim. 2:5, the *m* Christ Jesus
Isa. 62:5; Lk. 8:51; 11:21; Jn. 7:46
   Eph. 4:24; Titus 3:10
MANIFEST Jn. 2:11, *m* forth his glory
   14:22, how is it you will *m* yourself?
II Cor. 2:14, makes *m* savour of knowledge
Gal. 5:19, the works of the flesh are *m*
I Tim. 3:16, God was *m* in the flesh
   5:25, good works are *m* beforehand
Heb. 4:13, no creature that is not *m*
I Jn. 1:2, the life was *m*
   3:5, he was *m* to take away our sins
   4:9, in this was *m* the love of God
See Rom. 8:19; Jn. 17:6; I Jn. 3:10
MANIFOLD Eph. 3:10, the *m* wisdom of God
I Pet. 1:6, through *m* temptations
   4:10, stewards of the *m* grace of God

See Neh. 9:19, 27; Amos 5:12; Lk. 18:30

MANNER Ps. 144:13, all *m* of store
  Mat. 8:27, what *m* of man is this?
    12:31, all *m* of sin shall be forgiven
  Acts 26:4, my *m* of life from my youth
  Heb. 10:25, as the *m* of some is
  James 1:24, forgets what *m* of man
  I Pet. 1:15, holy in all *m* of conversation
  See Mat. 4:23; Lk. 9:55; I Cor. 15:33

MANTLE II Ki. 2:8; Job 1:20; Ps. 109:29

MAR Lev. 19:27, nor *m* the corners of your
    beard
  I Sam. 6:5, images that *m* the land
  Job 30:13, they *m* my path
  Isa. 52:14, visage *m* more than any man
  Mk. 2:22, wine spilled, and bottles *m*
  See Ruth 4:6; II Ki. 3:19; Jer. 13:7; 18:4

MARK Gen. 4:15, the Lord set a *m* on Cain
  Job 22:15, have you *m* the old way?
  Ps. 37:37, *M* the perfect man
    48:13, *M* well her bulwarks
    130:3, if you should *m* iniquities
  Jer. 2:22, your iniquity is *m* before me
    23:18, who has *m* his word?
  Phil. 3:14, I press toward the *m* for the prize
    17, *m* them which walk so
  See Lk. 14:7; Rom. 16:17; Rev. 13:16

MARRIAGE Mat. 22:2, made a *m* for his son
    25:10, that were ready went into *m*
  Jn. 2:1, 2, there was a *m* in Cana
  Heb. 13:4, *M* is honorable in all
  See Rev. 19:7, 9

MARRIED Jer. 3:14, I am *m* to you
  Lk. 14:20, I have *m* a wife
    17:27, they drank, they *m* wives

MARROW Job 21:24; Ps. 63:5; Prov. 3:8

MARRY Gen. 38:8; Deut. 25:5
  Isa. 62:5, as a man *m* a virgin
  I Cor. 7:9, better to *m* than to burn
  I Tim. 4:3, forbidding to *m* and
    5:14, that younger women *m*

MARVEL Mat. 8:10; Mk. 6:6, Jesus *m*
  Mk. 5:20, all men did *m*
  Jn. 3:7; 5:28; I Jn. 3:13, *M* not
  See Eccl. 5:8; Jn. 7:21; Gal. 1:6

MARVELLOUS Ps. 17:7, *m* lovingkindness
    118:23; Mk. 12:11, *m* in our eyes
  Jn. 9:30, herein is a *m* thing
  I Pet. 2:9, into his *m* light
  See Ps. 105:5; Dan. 11:36; Mic. 7:15

MASTER II Ki. 6:32, sound of his *m* feet
  Mal. 1:6, if I be a *m*, where is my fear
  Mat. 6:24, no man can serve two *m*
    10:24; Lk. 6:40, disciple not above his *m*
    25, enough for the disciple that he be as
      his *m*
    17:24, does not your *m* pay tribute?
    23:8, 10, one is your *M*, even Christ
    26:25, *M*, is it I?
  Mk. 5:35, why trouble you the *M*?
    9:5; Lk. 9:33, *M*, it is good to be here
    10:17; Lk. 10:25, good *M*, what shall I do?
  Jn. 3:10, are you a *M* of Israel?
    11:28, the *M* is come, and calls

    13:13, you call me *M*, and you say well
  Rom. 14:4, to his own *m* he stands or falls
  I Cor. 3:10, as a wise *m*-builder
  Eph. 6:5; I Pet. 2:18, be obedient to *m*
    9; Col. 4:1, *M* do the same things to them
  I Tim. 6:1, count their *m* worthy of honor
    2, that have believing *m*
  James 3:1, be not many *m*
  See Gen. 24:12; 39:8; Prov. 25:13

MASTERY Ex. 32:18; I Cor. 9:25

MATTER Job 19:28, root of the *m* found in me
    32:18, I am full of *m*
  Ps. 45:1, my heart is inditing a good *m*
  Prov. 16:20, handles a *m* wisely
    18:13, answers a *m* before he hears it
  Eccl. 12:13, conclusion of the whole *m*
  Mat. 23:23, the weightier *m*
  Acts 18:14, if it were a *m* of wrong
  I Cor. 6:2, to judge, the smallest *m*?
  II Cor. 9:5, as a *m* of bounty
  James 3:5, great a *m* a little fire kindles
  See Gen. 30:15; Dan. 3:16; Acts 8:21; 17:32

MAY Mat. 9:21; 26:42; Acts 8:37

MEAN Deut. 6:20, what *m* the testimonies?
  Josh. 4:6, what *m* ye by this service?
  Prov. 22:29, not stand before *m* men
  Isa. 2:9; 5:15; 31:8, the *m* men
  Ezek. 17:12, know ye what these things *m*?
  Acts 21:39, citizen of no *m* city
  See Acts 10:17; 17:20; 21:13

MEANS Num. 14:18, by no *m* clear guilty
  Ps. 49:7, none can by any *m* redeem
  Mal. 1:9, this has been by your *m*
  Mat. 5:26, shall by no *m* come out
  Jn. 9:21, by what *m* he now sees
  I Cor. 8:9, lest by any *m* this liberty
    9:22, that I might by all *m* save some
  Phil. 3:11, by any *m* attain
  II Thess. 3:16, give you peace always by all *m*
  See Jer. 5:31; I Cor. 9:27; Gal. 2:2

MEASURE (*n.*) Job 11:9, the *m* is longer than
    the earth
    28:25, he weighs the waters by *m*
  Ps. 39:4, the *m* of my days
  Isa. 40:12, the dust of the earth in a *m*
  Jer. 30:11; 46:28, I will correct you in *m*
  Ezek. 4:11, you shall drink water by *m*
  Mat. 7:2; Lk. 6:38, with what *m* ye mete
    13:33; Lk. 13:21, three *m* of meal
    23:32, fill up *m* of your fathers
  Lk. 6:38, good *m* pressed down
  Jn. 3:34, gives not the Spirit by *m*
  Rom. 12:3, to every man the *m* of faith
  II Cor. 12:7, exalts above *m*
  Eph. 4:7, the *m* of the gift of Christ
  Rev. 6:6, a *m* of wheat for a penny
    21:17, according to the *m* of a man
  See Ps. 80:5; Isa. 5:14; Mic. 6:10

MEASURE (*v.*) Isa. 65:7, I will *m* former work
  Jer. 31:37, if Heaven can be *m*
    33:22; Hos. 1:10, as the sand cannot be *m*

MEAT Gen. 27:4, make me savoury *m*
  I Ki. 19:8, went in strength of that *m*
  Ps. 59:15, wander up and down for *m*

69:21, they gave me also gall for my *m*
78:15, he sent them *m* to the full
Prov. 23:3, dainties, for they are deceitful *m*
30:22, a fool when filled with *m*
31:15, she gives *m* to her household
Isa. 65:25, dust shall be the serpent's *m*
Ezek. 4:10, your *m* shall be by weight
47:12, fruit for *m*
Dan. 1:8, not defile himself with king's *m*
Hab. 1:16, because their *m* is plenteous
3:17, fields yield no *m*
Mal. 3:10, bring tithes, that there may be *m*
Mat. 6:25; Lk. 12:23, life more than *m*
10:10, workman worthy of his *m*
15:37; Mk. 8:8, of broken *m*
Jn. 4:32, I have *m* to eat
34, my *m* is to do the will of him
6:27, labor not for the *m* that perishes
Acts 2:46, did eat *m* with gladness
15:29, abstain from *m* offered to idols
Rom. 14:15, destroy not him with your *m*
17, kingdom of God is not *m* and drink
20, for *m* destroy not the work of God
I Cor. 6:13, *M* for the belly
8:13, if *m* make my brother to offend
10:3, the same spiritual *m*
I Tim. 4:3, to abstain from *m*
Heb. 5:12, 14, not of strong *m*
12:16, who for one morsel of *m*
MEDDLE II Chron. 25:19, why *m* to your hurt
Prov. 20:3, every fool will be *m*
19, *m* not with him that flatters
26:17, that *m* with strife
See II Chron. 35:21; Prov. 17:14; 24:21
MEDITATE Gen. 24:63, Isaac went out to *m*
Josh. 1:8, you shall *m* therein
Ps. 1:2, in his law does he *m*
63:6; 119:148, *m* in the night watches
77:12, 143:5, I will *m* of your works
Isa. 33:18, your heart shall *m* terror
Lk. 21:14, not to *m* before
I Tim. 4:15, *M* upon these things
See Ps. 19:14; 104:34; 119:97, 99
MEEK Num. 12:3, Moses was very *m*
Ps. 22:26, the *m* shall eat and be satisfied
25:9, the *m* will he guide
37:11; Mat. 5:5, the *m* shall inherit the earth
149:4, will beautify the *m*
Isa. 29:19, the *m* shall increase their joy
61:1, good tidings to the *m*
Mat. 11:29, for I am *m*
I Pet. 3:4, a *m* and quiet spirit
See Ps. 76:9; 147:6; Isa. 11:4; Mat. 21:5
MEEKNESS II Cor. 10:1, the *m* of Christ
Gal. 6:1, restore in the spirit of *m*
I Tim. 6:11, follow after *m*
II Tim. 2:25, in *m* instructing
Titus 3:2, showing *m* to all men
See Zeph. 2:3; Gal. 5:23; Eph. 4:2
MEET Mat. 15:26, not *m* to take children's
bread
25:1, 6, to *m* the bridegroom
I Cor. 15:9, not *m* to be called an apostle
I Thess. 4:17, to *m* the Lord in the air

See Prov. 22:2; Amos 4:12; Mat. 8:34
MELODY Isa. 23:16; 51:3; Amos 5:23
MELT Ps. 46:6, the earth *m*
97:5, the hills *m*
107:26, their soul *m*
Isa. 13:7, every man's heart shall *m*
64:2, as when they *m* fire burns
See Ex. 15:15; Josh. 14:8; Jer. 9:7
MEMBER Ps. 139:16, my *m* were written
Rom. 6:13, 19, neither yield your *m*
12:4, as we have many *m*
I Cor. 6:15, bodies *m* of Christ?
James 3:5, the tongue is a little *m*
4:1, lusts which war in your *m*?
See Job 17:7; Mat. 5:29; Eph. 4:25; 5:30
MEMORY Ps. 109:15; 145:7; Prov. 10:7
MEN I Sam. 4:9, quit yourselves like *m*
Ps. 9:20, know themselves to be but *m*
82:7, but you shall die like *m*
Eccl. 12:3, the strong *m* shall bow
Isa. 46:8, show yourselves *m*
Gal. 1:10, do I now persuade *m*
I Thess. 2:4, not as pleasing *m* but God
See Ps. 116:11; I Tim. 2:4; I Pet. 2:17
MEND II Chron. 24:12; 34:10; Mat. 4:21
MENTION Gen. 40:41, *m* me to Pharaoh
Ps. 71:16, make *m* of your righteousness
Isa. 12:4, make *m* that his name is exalted
63:7, I will *m* lovingkindness of the Lord
Rom. 1:9; Eph. 1:16; I Thess. 1:2, *m* of you in
my prayers
See Isa. 62:6; Ezek. 18:22; 33:16
MERCHANDISE Prov. 3:14, *m* of it better than
m of silver
Isa. 23:18, *m* shall be holiness to the Lord
Mat. 22:5, one to his farm, another to his *m*
Jn. 2:16, my father's house an house of *m*
II Pet. 2:3, make *m* of you
See Deut. 21:14; Ezek. 26:12; Rev. 18:11
MERCHANT Gen. 23:16, money with the *m*
Isa. 23:8, whose *m* are princes
47:15, even your *m* shall wander
Rev. 18:3, 11, the *m* of the earth
23, your *m* were great men of the earth
See Prov. 31:24; Isa. 23:11; Mat. 13:45
MERCIFUL Ps. 37:26, ever *m*, and lends
67:1, God be *m* to us, and bless us
Prov. 11:17, the *m* does good to his soul
Isa. 57:1, *m* men are taken away
Jer. 3:12, return, for I am *m*
Lk. 6:36, be ye *m*, as your Father is *m*
18:13, God be *m* to me a sinner
Heb. 2:17, a *m* High Priest
See Ex. 34:6; II Sam. 22:26; I Ki. 20:31
MERCY Gen. 32:10, the least of the men
Ex. 33:19, show *m* on whom I will show *m*
34:7; Dan. 9:4, keeping *m* for thousands
I Chron. 16:34, 41; II Chron. 5:13; Ezra 3:11;
Ps. 106:1; 107:1; 118:1; 136:1; Jer. 33:11, his
m endures for ever
Ps. 23:6, surely goodness and *m* shall follow
25:7, according to your *m* remember me
33:22, let your *m* be upon us
66:20, not turned his *m* from me

77:8, in his *m* clean gone for ever?
85:10, *M* and truth are met together
89:2, *M* shall be built up for ever
90:14, satisfy us early with your *m*
103:11, 145:8, longsuffering, and of great *m*
108:4, your *m* is great above the heavens
115:1, for your *m* and for your truth's sake
119:64, the earth if full of your *m*
130:7, with the Lord there is *m*
Prov. 3:3, let not *m* and truth forsake you
14:21, 31, he that has *m* on the poor
16:6; 20:28, *m* and truth
Isa. 54:7, with great *m* will I gather you
Jer. 6:23, they are cruel, and have no *m*
Lam. 3:22, it is of the Lord's *m*
Hos. 4:1, because there is no *m* in the land
6:6, I desired *m* and not sacrifice
10:12, sow in righteousness, reap in *m*
14:3, in you the fatherless find *m*
Hab. 3:2, in wrath remember *m*
Mat. 5:7, the merciful shall obtain *m*
Lk. 10:37, he that showed *m*
Rom. 9:15, 18, *m* on whom I will have *m*
16, of God that shows *m*
12:1, beseech you by the *m* of God
8, he that shows *m*, with cheerfulness
II Cor. 1:3, the Father of *m*
Eph. 2:4, God, who is rich in *m*
I Tim. 1:13, 16, I obtained *m*, because
II Tim. 1:18, that he may find *m* in that day
Heb. 4:16, obtain *m*, and find grace
James 2:13, without *m*, that showed no *m*
I Pet. 1:3, according to his abundant *m*
See Prov. 12:10; Dan. 4:27; I Tim. 1:2
MERRY Gen. 43:34, were *m* with him
Judg. 16:25, their hearts were *m*
Prov. 15:13, *m* heart, cheerful countenance
15, *m* heart has a continual feast
17:22, *m* heart does good like a medicine
Eccl. 8:15, nothing better than to be *m*
9:7, drink your wine with a *m* heart
Eccl. 10:19, wine makes *m*
James 5:13, is any *m*?
See Lk. 12:19; 15:23; Rev. 11:10
MESSENGER Job 33:23; Isa. 42:19
METE Isa. 40:12; Mk. 4:24; Lk. 6:38
MIDDLE Ezek. 1:16; Eph. 2:14
MIDST Ps. 102:24, in the *m* of my days
Prov. 23:34, lies down in the *m* of the sea
Dan. 9:27, in the *m* of the week
Mat. 18:20, there am I in the *m*
Mk. 9:36, a little child in the *m*
Lk. 24:36, Jesus himself in the *m*
Phil. 2:15, in the *m* of a crooked nation
Rev. 2:7, in the *m* of the paradise of God
4:6; 5:6; 7:17; in the *m* of the throne
MIGHT Deut. 6:5, love God with all your *m*
8:17, the *m* of my hand has gotten
II Sam. 6:14, David danced with all his *m*
Eccl. 9:10, do it with your *m*
Isa. 40:29, to them that have no *m*
Jer. 9:23, mighty man glory in his *m*
Zech. 4:6, not by *m*, nor by power
Eph. 3:16; Col. 1:11, strengthened with *m*

See Eph. 6:10; II Pet. 2:11; Rev. 7:12
MIGHTILY Jonah 3:8, Acts 18:28; 19:20
MIGHTY Gen. 10:9, he was a *m* hunter
Judg. 5:23, help of the Lord against the *m*
II Sam. 1:19, 25, how are the *m* fallen!
Job 9:4, wise in heart and *m* in strength
Ps. 24:8, strong and *m*, *m* in battle
89:13, you have a *m* arm
19, help upon one that is *m*
93:4, the *m* waves, of the sea
Isa. 1:24; 30:29; 49:26, the *m* One of Israel
Jer. 32:19, *m* in work
Amos 2:14, neither shall *m* deliver himself
Mat. 11:20; 13:54; 14:2; Mk. 6:2, *m* works
Lk. 9:43, the *m* power of God
24:19, prophet *m* in deed and word
Acts 18:24, *m* in the scriptures
I Cor. 1:26, not many *m*
II Cor. 10:4, weapons *m* through God
Eph. 1:19, the working of his *m* power
See Num. 14:12; Eccl 6:10; Mat. 3:11
MILK Gen. 49:12, teeth white with *m*
Prov. 30:33, churning of *m*
Isa. 55:1, buy wine and *m*
Lam. 4:7, Nazarites were whiter than *m*
Ezek. 25:4, eat your fruit and drink your *m*
Heb. 5:12, 13, such as have need of *m*
I Pet. 2:2, the sincere *m* of the word
See Judg. 4:19; 5:25; Job 21:24; Joel 3:18
MIND (*n.*) Job 23:13, he is in one *m*
34:33, should it be according to your *m*?
Ps. 31:12, as a dead man out of *m*
Prov. 29:11, a fool utters all his *m*
Isa. 26:3, whose *m* is stayed on you
Mk. 5:15; Lk. 8:35, sitting, in his right *m*
Lk. 12:29, neither be of doubtful *m*
Rom. 8:7, carnal *m* is enmity against God
12:16, be of the same *m*
14:5, fully persuaded in his own *m*
II Cor. 8:12, if there be first a willing *m*
13:11; Phil. 1:27; 2:2, be of one *m*
Phil. 2:3, in lowliness of *m*
5, let this *m* be in you
4:7, peace of God keep your *m*
I Tim. 6:5; II Tim. 3:8, men of corrupt *m*
II Tim. 1:7, spirit of sound *m*
I Pet. 1:13, the loins of your *m*
II Pet. 3:1, stir up your pure *m*
MIND (*v.*) Rom. 8:5; 12:16; Phil. 3:16, 19
MINDFUL Ps. 8:4; Isa. 17:10; II Pet. 3:2
MINGLE Lev. 19:19; Isa. 5:22; Mat. 27:34
MINISTER (*n.*) Ps. 103:21, ye *m* of his
104:4; Heb. 1:7, his *m* a flame of fire
Isa. 61:6, men shall call you the *M* of God
Joel 1:9, the Lord's *m* mourn
Mat. 20:26; Mk. 10:43, let him be your *m*
Rom. 13:4, he is the *m* of God to you
II Cor. 3:6, able *m* of new testament
Gal. 2:17, is Christ the *m* of sin?
Eph. 3:7; Col. 1:23, whereof I was made a *m*
6:21; Col. 1:7; 4:7, a faithful *m*
I Tim. 4:6, a good *m*
MINISTER (*v.*) I Sam. 2:11, the child did *m*
I Chron. 15:2, chosen to *m* for ever

Dan. 7:10, thousand thousands *m* to him
Mat. 4:11; Mk. 1:13, angels *m* to him
  20:28, not to be *m* unto, but to *m*
Lk. 8:3, which *m* to him of their substance
Acts 20:34, these hands have *m*
See II Cor. 9:10; Heb. 1:14; II Pet. 1:11

MINISTRATION Lk. 1:23; Acts 6:1

MINISTRY Acts 6:4, give ourselves to the *m*
II Cor. 4:1, seeing we have this *m*
  5:18, the *m* of reconciliation
  6:3, that the *m* be not blamed
Eph. 4:12, for the work of *m*
Col. 4:17, take heed to the *m*
II Tim. 4:5, make full proof of your *m*
See Acts 1:17; 12:25; Rom. 12:7; Heb. 8:6

MINSTREL II Ki. 3:15; Mat. 9:23

MIRACLE Judg. 6:13, where be all his *m*?
Lk. 23:8, hoped to have seen some *m*
Jn. 2:11, this beginning of *m*
  4:54, this is the second *m*
  10:41, said, John did no *m*
Acts 2:22, approved of God by *m* and signs
I Cor. 12:10, to another, the working of *m*
See Gal. 3:5; Heb. 2:4; Rev. 13:14

MIRTH Ps. 137:3; Prov. 14:13; Eccl. 2:1

MIRY Ps. 40:2; Ezek. 47:11; Dan. 2:41

MISCHIEF Ps. 7:14, they conceive *m*
Ps. 28:3, *m* is in their hearts
  94:20, frames *m* by a law
Prov. 10:23, it is as sport to a fool to do *m*
  11:27, he that seeks *m*
  24:2, lips talk on *m*
Ezek. 7:26, *M* shall come upon *m*
Acts 13:10, O full of all subtilty and all *m*
See Prov. 24:8; Eccl. 10:13; Mic. 7:3

MISERABLE Job 16:2; Mat. 21:41

MISERY Prov. 31:7, remember his *m* no more
Eccl. 8:6, the *m* of man is great upon him
Lam. 1:7, remembered in days of her *m*
James 5:1, howl for your *m* that shall come
See Judg. 10:16; Job 3:20; 11:16; Rom. 3:16

MIXED Prov. 23:30, they that seek *m* wine
Isa. 1:22, your wine *m* with water
Heb. 4:2, not being *m* with faith
See Ex. 12:38; Num. 11:4; Neh. 13:3

MOCK Gen. 19:14, he seemed as one that *m*
Num. 22:29, you have *m* me
I Ki. 18:27, at noon Elijah *m* them
II Chron. 36:16, they *m* the messengers of
  God
Prov. 1:26, I will *m* when your fear comes
  17:5, whoso *m* the poor
  30:17, the eye that *m* at his father
Gal. 6:7, God is not *m*
See II Ki. 2:23; Mat. 2:16; Mk. 15:20

MOCKER Ps. 35:16; Prov. 20:1; Isa. 28:22

MODERATION Phil. 4:5

MOISTURE Ps. 32:4; Lk. 8:6

MOLLIFIED Isa. 1:6

MOMENT Job 7:18, try him every *m*?
  21:13, and in a *m* they go down
Ps. 30:5, his anger endures but a *m*
Isa. 26:20, hide yourself as it were a *m*
  27:3, I will water it every *m*

54:7, for a small *m* have I forsaken you
I Cor. 15:52, we shall all be changed, in a *m*
II Cor. 4:17, affliction, which is but for a *m*
See Ex. 33:5; Ezek. 26:16; 32:10; Lk. 4:5

MONEY II Ki. 5:26, is it a time to receive *m*
Eccl. 7:12, *m* is a defense
  10:19, *m* answers all things
Isa. 52:3, redeemed without *m*
  55:1, he that has no *m*
  2, wherefore do ye spend *m*
Mat. 17:24; 22:19, the tribute *m*
  25:18, hid his lord's *m*
Acts 8:20, your *m* perish with you
I Tim. 6:10, the love of *m*
See Gen. 23:9; Lk. 9:3; Acts 4:37

MORROW Isa. 22:13; I Cor. 15:32, for to *m* we
  die
  56:12, to *m* shall be as this day
Mat. 6:34, take no thought for the *m*
James 4:14, know not what shall be on the *m*
See Josh. 5:12; II Ki. 7:1; Prov. 3:28

MORSEL Job 31:17; Ps. 147:17; Prov. 17:1

MORTAL Rom. 6:12; 8:11, in your *m* body
I Cor. 15:53, 54, *m* put on immortality
See Deut. 19:11; II Cor. 4:11; 5:4

MORTAR Prov. 27:22; Ezek. 13:11; 22:28

MORTIFY Rom. 8:13; Col. 3:5

MOTE Mat. 7:3; Lk. 6:41

MOTHER Judg. 5:7, a *m* in Israel
II Chron. 22:3, his *m* was his counselor
Job 17:14, to the worm, you are my *m*
Ps. 113:9, a joyful *m* of children
Isa. 66:13, as one whom his *m* comforts
Ezek. 16:44, as is the *m*, so is her daughter
Mat. 12:48; Mk. 3:33, who is my *m*?
Jn. 2:1; Acts 1:14, the *m* of Jesus
See Gen. 3:20; Ps. 22:9; Song of Sol. 8:1; Isa.
  49:23; Gal. 4:26; Rev. 17:5

MOULDY Josh. 9:5, 12

MOUNT Ex. 18:5, the *m* of God
Ps. 107:26, they *m* up to heaven
Isa. 40:31, *m* with wings, as eagles
See Job 20:6; 39:27; Isa. 27:13

MOURN Gen. 37:35, down to the grave *m*
Prov. 5:11, and you *m* at the last
Isa. 61:2, to comfort all that *m*
Mat. 5:4, blessed are they that *m*
  24:30, shall all the tribes of the Earth *m*
Lk. 6:25, you that laugh, you shall *m*
MOURNER II Sam. 14:2; Eccl. 12:5; Hos. 9:4

MOURNFULLY Mal. 3:14

MOUTH Job 9:20, own *m* shall condemn me
  40:4, I will lay my hand on my *m*
Ps. 8:2; Mat. 21:16, out of the *m* of babes
  39:1, I will keep my *m* with a bridle
  49:3, my *m* shall speak of wisdom
  55:21, words of his *m* smoother than
  butter
  81:10, open your *m* wide
Prov. 10:14; 14:3; 15:2, the *m* of the foolish
  13:2, good by the fruit of his *m*
  3; 21:23, he that keeps his *m*
Eccl. 6:7, all labor of a man is for his *m*
Isa. 29:13, this people draw near with *m*

Mal. 2:6, the law of truth was in his *m*
Mat. 12:34; Lk. 6:45, the *m* speaks
   13:35, I will open my *m* in parables
Lk. 21:15, I will give you a *m* and wisdom
Rom. 10:10, with the *m* confession is made
Titus 1:11, whose *m* must be stopped
James 3:10, out of the same *m* proceeds
See Lam. 3:29; Jn. 19:29; II Tim. 4:17
MOVE Ps. 10:6; 16:8, I shall not be *m*
Mat. 21:10; Acts 21:30, all the city was *m*
Jn. 5:3, waiting for the *m* of the water
Acts 17:28, in him we live, and *m*
   20:24, none of these things *m* me
See Prov. 23:31; Isa. 7:2; II Pet. 1:21
MUCH Ex. 16:18, he that gathers *m*
Num. 16:3, you take too *m* upon you
Lk. 7:47, for she loved *m*
   12:48, to whom *m* is given
   16:10, faithful in *m*
See Prov. 25:16; Eccl. 5:12; Jer. 2:22
MULTIPLY Isa. 9:3, you have *m* the nation
Jer. 3:16, when you be *m* they shall say
Dan. 4:1; 6:25; I Pet. 1:2, peace be *m*
Nah. 3:16, you have *m* your merchants
See Acts 6:1; 7:17; 9:31; 12:24
MULTITUDE Ex. 23:2, a *m* to do evil
Job 32:7, *m* of years should teach wisdom
Ps. 5:7; 51:1; 106:7, in the *m* of your mercy
   33:16, no king saved by the *m* of an host
   94:19, in the *m* of my thoughts
Prov. 10:19, in *m* of words, wants not sin
   11:14; 15:22; 24:6, in the *m* of counselors
Eccl. 5:3, through the *m* of business
James 5:20; I Pet. 4:8, hide a *m* of sins
MURDER Mat. 15:19; Rom. 1:29; Rev. 9:21
MURDERER Job 24:14, *m* rising with light
Hos. 9:13, bring forth children to *m*
Jn. 8:44, devil was a *m* from the beginning
I Pet. 4:15, none suffer as a *m*
I Jn. 3:15, who hates his brother is a *m* and
   no *m* has eternal life
MURMURINGS Ex. 16:7; Phil. 2:14
MUSE Ps. 39:3; 143:5; Lk. 3:15
MUTTER Isa. 8:19; 59:3
MUTUAL Rom. 1:12
MYSTERY Mat. 13:11; I Cor. 2:7; 15:51

N

NAIL Ezra 9:8, give us a *n* in his holy place
Isa. 22:23, fasten as a *n* in sure place
Jn. 20:25, put finger into print of *n*
Col. 2:14, *n* it to his cross
See Judg. 4:21; Eccl. 12:11; Dan. 4:33
NAKED Ex. 32:25, made *n* to their shame
Job 1:21, *N* came I out, and *n* shall I return
Mat. 25:36, *N*, and you clothed me
I Cor. 4:11, to this present hour we are *n*
II Cor. 5:3, we shall not be found *n*
Heb. 4:13, all things are *n* to eyes of him
See Jn. 21:7; James 2:15; Rev. 3:17; 16:15
NAKEDNESS Rom. 8:35; II Cor. 11:27
NAME (*n.*) Ex. 3:15, this is my *n* forever
   23:21, my *n* is in him

Josh. 7:9, what will you do to your great *n*?
Neh. 9:10, so did you get you a *n*
Job 18:17, he shall have no *n* in the street
Ps. 20:1, the *n* of God defend you
   5, in the *n* of God set up banners
   22:22; Heb. 2:12, I will declare your *n*
   48:10, according to your *n* so is your praise
   111:9, holy and reverend is his *n*
   115:1, unto your *n* give glory
   138:2, your word above all your *n*
Prov. 10:7, the *n* of the wicked shall rot
   18:10, the *n* of the Lord a strong tower
   22:1, good *n* rather to be chosen
Isa. 42:8, I am the Lord, that is my *n*
   55:13, it shall be to the Lord for a *n*
   56:5; 63:12, an everlasting *n*
   57:15, whose *n* is Holy
   62:2, called by a new *n*
Jer. 10:6, you are great, and your *n* is great
   14:14; 23:25; 27:15, prophesy lies in my *n*
Mal. 1:6, wherein have we despised your *n*
   4:2, to you that fear my *n*
Mat. 6:9; Lk. 11:2, hallowed be your *n*
   10:22; 19:29; Mk. 13:13; Lk. 21:12; Acts 9:16,
   for my *n* sake
   12:21, in his *n* shall the Gentiles trust
   18:5; Mk. 9:37; Lk. 9:48, receive in my *n*
Mk. 5:9; Lk. 8:30, what is your *n*?
   9:39, do a miracle in my *n*
Lk. 10:20, *n* written in heaven
   21:8, many shall come in my *n*
Jn. 5:43, if another shall come in his own *n*
   16:23, 24, 26, whatsoever you ask in my *n*
Acts 3:16, his *n* through faith in his *n*
   4:12, none other *n* under heaven
   5:41, worthy to suffer for his *n*
Eph. 1:21, far above every *n*
Phil. 2:9, 10, a *n* above every *n*
   4:3, whose *n* are in the book of life
Col. 3:17, do all in the *n* of the Lord Jesus
Heb. 1:4, obtained a more excellent *n*
Rev. 2:13, hold fast my *n*
   17, a *n* written, which no man knows
   3:1, you have a *n* that you live
   13:1, the *n* of blasphemy
   14:1; 22:4, Father's *n* in their foreheads
See Gen. 2:20; Ex. 28:9; Isa. 45:3; Jn. 10:3
NAME (*v.*) Rom. 15:20, not where Christ was *n*
II Tim. 2:19, *n* the name of Christ
See I Sam. 16:3; Isa. 62:2; Lk. 2:21; 6:13
NARROW Isa. 28:20; 49:19; Mat. 7:14
NATION II Sam. 7:23, what *n* like your people?
Ps. 33:12, blessed is the *n* whose God
   147:20, he has not dealt so with any *n*
Prov. 14:34, righteousness exalts a *n*
Isa. 2:4, *n* shall not lift sword against *n*
   18:2, a *n* scattered and peeled
   26:2, that the righteous *n* may enter in
   34:1, come near, ye *n*, to hear
   52:15, so shall he sprinkle many *n*
Jer. 10:7, O King of *n*?
Mk. 13:8; Lk. 21:10, *n* against *n*
Lk. 7:5, he loves our *n*
   21:25, distress of *n*

Jn. 11:50, that the whole *n* perish not
Acts 2:5, devout men of every *n*
   10:35, in every *n* that fears
Phil. 2:15, crooked and perverse *n*
Rev. 5:9, redeemed out of every *n*
See Deut. 4:27; 15:6; Jer. 2:11; 4:2; 31:10
NATIVITY Gen. 11:28; Jer. 46:16
NATURAL Gen. 34:7, nor his *n* force abated
Rom. 1:31; II Tim. 3:3, without *n* affection
I Cor. 2:14, the *n* man receives not
See I Cor. 15:44; Phil. 2:20; James 1:23
NATURE I Cor. 11:14, even *n* itself teach?
Eph. 2:3, by *n* children of wrath
Heb. 2:16, the *n* of angels
II Pet. 1:4, partakers of the divine *n*
See Rom. 1:26; 2:14, 27; Gal. 2:15; 4:8
NAUGHT Prov. 20:14, it is *n*, saith the buyer
Isa. 49:4, spent strength for *n*
   52:3, you have sold yourselves for *n*
Mal. 1:10, shut the doors for *n*
Acts 5:38, if of men, it will come to *n*
See Deut. 15:9; Job 1:9; Rom. 14:10
NAUGHTINESS I Sam. 17:28; Prov. 11:6
NAUGHTY Prov. 6:12; 17:4; Jer. 24:2
NAY Mat. 5:37; II Cor. 1:17, 18, 19
NEAR Judg. 20:34, knew not evil was *n*
Ps. 22:11, trouble is *n*
   148:14, a people *n* to him
Prov. 27:10, better a neighbor that is *n*
Isa. 50:8, he is *n* that justifies
   55:6, call upon the Lord while he is *n*
Obad. 15, the day of the Lord is *n*
Mat. 24:33, it is *n*, even at the doors
Mk. 13:28, you know that summer is *n*
See Ezek. 11:3; 22:5; Rom. 13:11
NECESSARY Job 23:12; Acts 15:28; 28:10
NECESSITY Rom. 12:13, *n* of saints
I Cor. 9:16, *n* is laid upon me
See Acts 20:34; II Cor. 12:10; Phil. 4:16
NECK Prov. 3:3, bind them about your *n*
Mat. 18:6; Lk. 17:2, millstone about his *n*
Lk. 15:20; Acts 20:37, fell on his *n*
Acts 15:10, yoke on the *n* of disciples
See Neh. 9:29; Isa. 3:16; 48:4; Rom. 16:4
NEED II Chron. 20:17, you shall not *n* to fight
Prov. 31:11, he shall have no *n* of spoil
Mat. 9:12; Lk. 5:31, I *n* not a physician
Lk. 12:30, what things you have *n* of
   14:16, they *n* not depart
   19:31, 34, the Lord has *n* of them
Acts 2:45; 4:35, as every man had *n*
I Cor. 12:21, I have no *n* of you
Phil. 4:12, to abound and to suffer *n*
   19, God shall supply all your *n*
II Tim. 2:15, that *n* not to be ashamed
Heb. 4:16, grace to help in time of *n*
   5:12, you have *n* that one teach you
I Jn. 3:17, sees his brother have *n*
Rev. 3:17, rich, and have *n* of nothing
   21:23; 22:5, city had no *n* of the sun
NEEDFUL Lk. 10:42; Phil. 1:24; James 2:16
NEEDY Job 24:4, they turn the *n* out of the way
Ps. 9:18, the *n* shall not always be forgotten
   40:17; 70:5; 86:1; 109:22, I am poor and *n*

   74:21, let the poor and *n* praise your name
Prov. 31:9, plead the cause of the poor and *n*
Isa. 41:17, when the *n* seek water
See Ezek. 16:49; 18:12; 22:29; Amos 8:4, 6
NEGLECT Mat. 18:17; Acts 6:1
NEGLIGENT II Chron. 29:11; II Pet. 1:12
NEIGHBOUR Prov. 3:28, say not to your *n*. Go
   and come again
   14:20, the poor is hated even of his *n*
   21:10, his *n* finds no favor
Eccl. 4:4, envied of his *n*
Hab. 2:15, that gives his *n* drink
Lk. 10:29, who is my *n*?
   14:12, call not your rich *n*
Eph. 4:25, speak every man truth to his *n*
See Ex. 20:16; Lev. 19:13; Mat. 5:43
NEST Num. 24:21, put your *n* in a rock
Deut. 32:11, as an eagle stirs up her *n*
Job 29:18, I shall die in my *n*
Ps. 84:3, the swallow has found a *n*
Mat. 8:20; Lk. 9:58, birds of the air have *n*
See Prov. 27:8; Isa. 16:2; Jer. 49:16; Obad. 4
NET Ps. 141:10, wicked fall into their own *n*
Prov. 1:17, in vain the *n* is spread
Eccl. 9:12, as fishes taken in an evil *n*
Hab. 1:16, they sacrifice unto their *n*
Mat. 13:47, kingdom of heaven like a *n*
Mk. 1:18, they forsook their *n*
Lk. 5:5, at your word I will let down the *n*
See Mat. 4:21; Mk. 1:16; Jn. 21:6
NETHER Deut. 24:6; Job 41:24
NEVER Lev. 6:13, the fire shall *n* go out
Job 3:16, as infants which *n* saw light
Ps. 10:11, he will *n* see it
   15:5; 30:6, shall *n* be moved
Prov. 27:20; 30:15, *n* satisfied
Isa. 56:11, which can *n* have enough
Mat. 7:23, I *n* knew you
   26:33, yet will I *n* be offended
Mk. 2:12, we *n* saw it on this fashion
   3:29, has *n* forgiveness
Jn. 4:14; 6:35, shall *n* thirst
   7:46, *N* man spoke like this man
   8:51; 10:28; 11:26, shall *n* see death
I Cor. 13:8, charity *n* fails
Heb. 13:5, I will *n* leave you
II Pet. 1:10, you shall *n* fall
NEW Num. 16:30, Lord make a *n* thing
Ps. 33:3; 40:3; 96:1; 98:1; 144:9; 149:1
   Isa. 42:10; Rev. 5:9; 14:3, a *n* song
Eccl. 1:9, no *n* thing under the sun
Isa. 65:17, *n* heavens and *n* earth
Lam. 3:23, *n* every morning
Mat. 9:16, *n* cloth to old garment
Mk. 1:27, what *n* doctrine is this?
Jn. 13:34, a *n* commandment
Acts 17:21, to tell or hear some *n* thing
II Cor. 5:17; Gal. 6:15; a *n* creature
Eph. 2:15; 4:24; Col. 3:10, *n* man
Heb. 10:20, *n* and living way
Rev. 2:17; 3:12, a *n* name
   21:5, I make all things *n*
NEWLY Deut. 32:17; Judg. 7:19
NEWNESS Rom. 6:4; 7:6

NEWS Prov. 25:25
NIGH Num. 24:17, but not *n*
  Deut. 30:14, the word is *n* unto you
  Ps. 34:18, *n* to them of broken heart
    145:18, *n* to all that call upon him
  Eph. 2:13, made *n* by the blood of Christ
  See Joel 2:1; Lk. 21:20; Heb. 6:8
NIGHT Ex. 12:42, a *n* to be much observed
  Job 35:10; Ps. 77:6, songs in the *n*
  Ps. 30:5, weeping may endure for a *n*
    91:5, the terror by *n*
    136:9, moon and stars to rule by *n*
    139:11, the *n* shall be light about me
  Isa. 21:4, the *n* of my pleasure
    11, watchman, what of the *n*?
  Lk. 6:12, he continued all *n* in prayer
  Jn. 9:4, the *n* comes, when no man can work
    11:10, walk in the *n*, he stumbles
  Rom. 13:12, the *n* is far spent
  Rev. 21:25; 22:5, no *n* there
NOBLE Neh. 3:5, the *n* put not their neck
  Job 29:10, the *n* held their peace
  Jer. 2:21, planted you a *n* vine
  Acts 17:11, Bereans were more *n* than those
  I Cor. 1:26, not many *n*
  See Num. 21:18; Ps. 149:8; Eccl. 10:17
NOISE Ezra 3:13, not discern *n* of joy
  Ps. 66:1; 81:1; 95:1; 98:4; 100:1, joyful *n*
  Ezek. 1:24; 43:2, *n* of great waters
  II Pet. 3:10, pass away with great *n*
  See Josh. 6:27; Mk. 2:1; Acts 2:6
NOISOME Ps. 91:3; Ezek. 14:21; Rev. 16:2
NOTHING Neh. 9:21, you have lacked *n*
  Job 8:9, but of yesterday, and know *n*
  Ps. 49:17, he shall carry *n* away
    119:165, *n* shall offend them
  Prov. 13:4, the sluggard desires, and has *n*
    7, makes himself rich, yet has *n*
  Lam. 1:12, is it *n* to you?
  Mat. 17:20, *n* shall be impossible
    21:19; Mk. 11:13, *n* but leaves
  Jn. 15:5, without me you can do *n*
  I Cor. 4:4, I know *n* by myself
  II Cor. 6:10, as having *n*
    13:8, we can do *n* against the truth
  I Tim. 4:4, *n* to be refused
    6:7, brought *n* into this world, carry *n* out
  See Phil. 4:6; James 1:4; III Jn. 7
NOURISH I Tim. 4:6, *n* in words of faith
  James 5:5, have *n* your hearts
  See Gen. 45:11; 50:21; Acts 12:20; Col. 2:19
NOW Job 4:5, *n* it is come upon you
  Ps. 119:67, but *n* have I kept your word
  Hos. 2:7, then was it better than *n*
  Lk. 14:17, all things are *n* ready
  Jn. 13:7, you know not *n*
    16:12, you cannot bear them *n*
  I Cor. 13:12, *N* I know in part
  Gal. 2:20, the life I *n* live
  I Tim. 4:8, the life that *n* is
  I Pet. 1:8, though *n* you see him not
  I Jn. 3:2, *n* are we sons of God
  See Rom. 6:22; Gal. 3:3; Heb. 2:8
NUMBER (*n.*) Job 9:10, things without *n*

    25:3, is there any *n* of his armies?
  Ps. 139:18, more in *n* than the sand
    147:4, he tells the *n* of the stars
  Acts 11:21, a great *n* believed
    16:5, the churches increased in *n* daily
  Rev. 13:17, 18, the *n* of his name
  See Deut. 7:7; Hos. 1:10; Rom. 9:27
NUMBER (*v.*) I Chron. 21:2, *n* the people
  Ps. 90:12, so teach us to *n* our days
  Isa. 53:12, he was *n* with transgressors
  Mat. 10:30; Lk. 12:7, hairs are all *n*
  Rev. 7:9, multitude which no man could *n*
  See Ex. 30:12; Job 14:16; Ps. 40:5; Acts 1:17
NURSE Ex. 2:7, 9; 60:4
NURTURE Eph. 6:4

O

OBEDIENCE Rom. 5:19, by the *o* of one
    16:26, the *o* of faith
  Heb. 5:8, yet learned he *o*
  See Rom. 16:19; II Cor. 10:5; I Pet. 1:2
OBEDIENT Prov. 25:12, wise reprover upon an *o*
  ear
  Isa. 1:19, if *o* ye shall eat
  II Cor. 2:9, *o* in all things
  Eph. 6:5; Titus 2:9, be *o* to your masters
  Phil. 2:8, *o* unto death
  I Pet. 1:14, as *o* children
  See Num. 27:20; II Sam. 22:45; Titus 2:5
OBEISANCE Gen. 37:7; 43:28; II Sam. 15:5
OBEY Deut. 11:27, a blessing if you *o*
  Josh. 24:24, his voice will we *o*
  I Sam. 15:22, to *o* is better than sacrifice
  Jer. 7:23, *o* my voice, I will be your God
  Acts 5:29, *o* God rather than men
  Rom. 6:16, his servants you are to whom
    you *o*
  II Thess. 1:8, that *o* not the gospel
  Heb. 13:17, *o* them that have rule over you
  I Pet. 1:22, purified your souls in *o* the truth
  See Ex. 5:2; 23:21; Dan. 9:10; Mat. 8:27
OBJECT Acts 24:19
OBSCURE Prov. 20:20
OBSCURITY Isa 29:18; 58:10; 59:9
OBSERVATION Lk. 17:20
OBSERVE Ps. 107:43, wise, and will *o* these
  things
  Prov. 23:26, let your eyes *o* my ways
  Eccl. 11:4, he that *o* the wind
  Jonah 2:8, that *o* lying vanities
  Mat. 28:20, teaching them to *o* all things
  Mk. 6:20; Herod feared Jn, and *o* him
    10:20, all these have I *o*
  See Ex. 12:42; 31:16; Ezek. 20:18; Gal. 4:10
OBSERVER Deut. 18:10
OBSTINATE Deut. 2:30; Isa. 48:4
OBTAIN Prov. 8:35, *o* favor of the Lord
  Isa. 35:10; 51:11, shall *o* joy and gladness
  Lk. 20:35, worthy to *o* that world
  Acts 26:22, having *o* help of God
  I Cor. 9:24, so run that you may *o*
  I Thess. 5:9; II Tim. 2:10, to *o* salvation
  I Tim. 1:13, I *o* mercy

Heb. 4:16, *o* mercy, and find grace to help
9:12, having *o* eternal redemption
II Pet. 1:1, *o* like precious faith
OCCASION II Sam. 12:14, great *o* to enemies
Dan. 6:4, sought to find *o*
Rom. 14:13, an *o* to fall in his brother's way
I Tim. 5:14, give none *o* to the adversary
See Gen. 43:18; Ezra 7:20; Ezek. 18:3
OCCUPATION Gen. 64:33; Acts 18:3
OCCUPY Ezek. 27:9; Lk. 19:13
ODOUR Jn. 12:3; Phil. 4:18; Rev. 5:8
OFFENCE Eccl. 10:4, yielding pacifies *o*
Isa. 8:14; Rom. 9:33; I Pet. 2:8, a rock of *o*
Mat. 16:23, you are an *o* to me
Acts 24:16, conscience voice of *o*
Rom. 14:20, that man who eats with *o*
I Cor. 10:32; II Cor. 6:3, give none *o*
Phil. 1:10, without *o* till the day of Christ
OFFEND Job 34:31, I will not *o* any more
Ps. 119:165, nothing shall *o* them
Prov. 18:19, brother *o* is harder to be won
Mat. 5:30; 18:9, if your eye *o* you
13:41, gather all things that *o*
57; Mk. 6:3, they were *o* in him
Rom. 14:21, whereby your brother is *o*
James 2:10, yet *o* in one point
See Gen. 20:9; Jer. 37:18; II Cor. 11:29
OFFENDER I Ki. 1:21; Acts 25:11
OFFER Judg. 5:2, willing *o* themselves
Ps. 50:23, whose *o* praise
Mat. 5:24, then come and *o* your gift
Lk. 6:29, one cheek, *o* also the other
I Cor. 8:1, 4, 7; 10:19, things *o* to idols
Phil. 2:17, *o* in the service of your faith
II Tim. 4:6, now ready to be *o*
Heb. 9:28, Christ once *o* to bear the sins
See II Chron. 17:16; Ezra 1:6; 2:68; Mal. 1:8
OFFICE Rom. 11:13, I magnify my *o*
I Tim. 3:1, the *o* of a bishop
Heb. 7:5, the *o* of the priesthood
See Gen. 41:13; Ps. 109:8; Rom. 12:4
OFFSCOURING Lam. 3:45; I Cor. 4:13
OFFSPRING Job 27:14; Acts 17:28
OFTEN Prov. 29:1, being *o* reproved
Mal. 3:16, spoke *o* to another
Lk. 13:34, how *o* would I have gathered
I Cor. 11:26, as *o* ye eat
I Tim. 5:23, your *o* infirmities
OIL Ps. 45:7; Heb. 1:9, with *o* of gladness
92:10, be anointed with fresh *o*
104:15, *o* to make his face to shine
Isa. 61:3, *o* of joy for mourning
Mat. 25:3, took no *o* with them
Lk. 10:34, pouring in *o* and wine
See Ex. 27:20; Mic. 6:7; Lk. 7:46
OLD Deut. 8:4; 29:5; Neh. 9:21, waxed not *o*
Josh. 5:11, did eat of the *o* corn
Ps. 37:25, I have been young, and now am *o*
71:18, when I am *o* forsake me not
Prov. 22:6, when he is *o* he will not
Isa. 58:12, build the *o* waste places
Jer. 6:16, ask for the *o* paths
Lk. 5:39, he says, the *o* is better
II Cor. 5:17, *o* things are passed away

II Pet. 2:5, God spared not the *o* world
I Jn. 2:7, the *o* commandment is the word
Rev. 12:9; 20:2, that *o* serpent
See Job 22:15; Mat. 5:21; Rom. 7:6
OMITTED Mat. 23:23
ONCE Gen. 18:32, yet but this *o*
Num. 13:30, let us go up at *o*
Job 33:14; Ps. 62:11, speaks *o* yea twice
Isa. 66:8, shall a nation be born at *o*?
Heb. 6:4, *o* enlightened
9:27, *o* to die
See Rom. 6:10; Heb. 10:10; I Pet. 3:18
ONE Job 9:3, *o* of a thousand
Eccl. 7:27; Isa. 27:12, *o* by *o*
Mk. 10:21, *o* thing you lack
Lk. 10:42, *o* thing is needful
Jn. 9:25, *o* thing I know
17:11, 21, 22, that they may be *o*
Gal. 3:28, all *o* in Christ
Eph. 4:5, *o* Lord, *o* faith, *o* baptism
See Deut. 6:4; Mk. 12:32; I Tim. 2:5
OPEN Num. 16:30, if the earth *o* her mouth
Ps. 49:4, I will *o* my dark saying
51:15, *o* thou my lips
104:28; 145:16, you *o* your hand
119:18, *o* thou my eyes
Isa. 22:22, he shall *o*, and none shall shut
42:7, to *o* the blind eyes
60:11, your gates shall be *o* continually
Mal. 3:10, *o* windows of heaven
Mat. 25:11; Lk. 13:25, Lord *o* to us
27:52, graves were *o*
Mk. 7:34, that is, be *o*
Lk. 24:32, while he *o* to us the scriptures
Acts 26:18, to *o* their eyes, and turn them
I Cor. 16:9, great door and effectual is *o*
Col. 4:3, *o* to us a door of utterance
OPERATION Ps. 28:5; Isa. 5:12; I Cor. 12:6
OPINION I Ki. 18:21; Job 32:6
OPPORTUNITY Gal 6:10; Phil. 4:10
OPPOSE Job 30:21; II Tim. 2:25
OPPOSITIONS I Tim. 6:20
OPPRESS Ex. 22:21; 23:9, *o* a stranger
Lev. 25:14, 17, you shall not *o* one another
I Sam. 12:3, whom have I *o*?
Ps. 10:18, that the man of earth may no
more *o*
Prov. 14:31; 22:16, he that *o* the poor
28:3, a poor man that *o* the poor
Jer. 7:6, if you *o* not the stranger
Hos. 12:7, he loves to *o*
Zech. 7:10, *o* not the widow
See Mal. 3:5; Acts 7:24; 10:38; James 2:6
OPPRESSION Ps. 62:10, trust not in *o*
119:134, deliver me from the *o* of man
Eccl. 4:1, I consider the *o*
7:7, *o* makes a wise man mad
Isa. 30:12, you trust in *o*
See Isa. 33:15; Zech. 9:8; 10:4
ORATOR Isa. 3:3; Acts 24:1
ORDAIN Ps. 8:2, have you *o* strength
81:5, this he *o* in Joseph
132:17, I have *o* a lamp for my anointed
Isa. 26:12, you will *o* peace for us

30:33, Tophet is *o* of old
Jer. 1:5, I *o* you a prophet
Mk. 3:14, Jesus *o* twelve
Acts 1:22, one be *o* to be a witness
   10:42, *o* of God to be the Judge
   13:48, *o* to eternal life
   17:31, by that man whom he has *o*
Rom. 13:1, the powers that be are *o* of God
Gal. 3:19, the law was *o* by angels
Jude 4, of old *o* to this condemnation
See I Cor. 2:7; 9:14; I Tim. 2:7; Heb. 5:1
ORDER II Ki. 20:1; Isa. 38:1, set your house in *o*
Job 10:22, land without any *o*
   37:19, we cannot *o* our speech
Ps. 40:5, they cannot be reckoned in *o*
   50:21, I will set them in *o*
   23, to him that *o* his conversation aright
I Cor. 14:40, decently and in *o*
See Ps. 37:23; Acts 21:24; I Cor. 15:23
ORDINANCE Mal. 3:14, what profit that we
   have kept *o*?
Rom. 13:2, the *o* of their God
Eph. 2:15, commandments contained in *o*
Col. 2:14, handwriting of *o*
Heb. 9:10, in carnal *o*
See Jer. 31:36; Lk. 1:6; I Pet. 2:13
ORPHANS Lam. 5:3
OUGHT Mat. 23:23, these *o* you to have done
Lk. 24:26, *o* not Christ to have suffered?
Jn. 4:20, the place where men *o* to worship
Acts 5:29, we *o* to obey God
Rom. 8:26, what we should pray for as we *o*
Heb. 5:12, when you *o* not so to be
James 3:10, these things *o* not so to be
See Rom. 12:3; 15:1; I Tim. 3:15
OURS Mk. 12:7; Lk. 20:14; I Cor. 1:2
OUT Num. 32:23, your sin will find you *o*
Ps. 82:5, are *o* of course
Prov. 4:23, *o* of it are the issues of life
Mat. 12:34; 15:19, *o* of abundance of heart
See Gen. 2:9, 23; 3:19; Jn. 15:19; Acts 2:5
OUTCAST Ps. 147:2; Isa. 11:12; 27:13
OUTGOINGS Josh. 17:18; Ps. 65:8
OUTRAGEOUS Prov. 27:4
OUTRUN Jn. 20:4
OUTSIDE Judg. 7:11; Lk. 11:39
OUTSTRETCHED Deut. 26:8; Jer. 21:5
OUTWARD Mat. 23:27, appear beautiful *o*
Rom. 2:28, not a Jew, which is one *o*
II Cor. 4:16, though our *o* man perish
See Mat. 23:28; Rom. 2:28; I Pet. 3:3
OVERCHARGE Lk. 21:34; II Cor. 2:5
OVERCOME Gen. 49:19, he shall *o* at last
Jer. 23:9, like a man whom wine has *o*
Jn. 16:33, I have *o* the world
Rom. 12:21, be not *o* of evil, but *o* evil
I Jn. 5:4, 5, victory that *o* the world
Rev. 2:7, 17, 26; 3:12, 21, to him that *o*
See Song of Sol. 6:5; II Pet. 2:19; Rev. 12:11
OVERMUCH Eccl. 7:16; II Cor. 2:7
OVERPAST Ps. 57:1; Isa. 26:20
OVERPLUS Lev. 25:27
OVERSEER Gen. 41:34; Acts 20:28
OVERSHADOW Mat. 17:5; Mk. 9:7

OVERSIGHT Gen. 39:4; I Pet. 5:2
OVERSPREAD Gen. 9:19; Dan. 9:27
OVERTAKE Gal. 6:1, a man be *o* in a fault
I Thess. 5:4, day should *o* you as a thief
See Deut. 19:6; Isa. 59:9; Jer. 42:16
OVERTHROW Job 19:6, God has *o* me
Ps. 140:4, purposed to *o* my goings
Prov. 13:6, wickedness *o* the sinner
Jonah 3:4, Nineveh shall be *o*
Acts 5:39, if it be of God, you cannot *o* it
See Gen. 19:21; Prov. 29:4; II Tim. 2:18
OVERTURN Job 9:5; Ezek. 21:27
OVERWHELM Job 6:27, you *o* the fatherless
Ps. 61:2, when my heart is *o*
   77:3; 142:3; 143:4, my spirit was *o*
See Ps. 55:5; 78:53; 124:4
OVERWISE Eccl. 7:16
OWE Lk. 16:5, 7, how much *o* thou?
Rom. 13:8, *O* no man any thing
See Mat. 18:24, 28; Lk. 7:41; Phile. 18
OWN Num. 32:42, called it after his *o* name
I Chron. 29:14, of your *o* have we given you
Ps. 12:4, our lips are our *o*
   67:6, even our *o* God shall bless us
Mat. 20:15, do what I will with my *o*
Jn. 1:11, to his *o*, his *o* received him not
   13:1, having loved his *o*
I Cor. 6:19, you are not your *o*
See Acts 5:4; Phil. 3:9; I Tim. 5:8; Rev. 1:5
OWNER Ex. 21:28; 22:11; Eccl. 5:13; Isa. 1:3

P

PACIFY Prov. 16:14; 21:14; Eccl. 10:4
PAIN Ps. 55:4, my heart is sore *p*
   116:3, the *p* of hell got hold upon me
Acts 2:24, having loosed the *p* of death
Rom. 8:22, creation travails in *p*
Rev. 21:4, neither shall there be any more *p*
See Ps. 73:16; Jer. 4:19; II Cor. 11:27
PAINTED II Ki. 9:30; Jer. 4:30; 22:14
PALACE Ps. 48:13, considered her *p*
   122:7, prosperity within your *p*
   144:12, the similitude of a *p*
Jer. 9:21, death is entered into our *p*
Lk. 11:21, a strong man keeps his *p*
Phil. 1:13, manifest in all the *p*
See I Chron. 29:1; Neh. 1:1; 2:8; Isa. 25:2
PALE Isa. 29:22; Jer. 30:6; Rev. 6:8
PALM Isa. 49:16; Mat. 26:67; Mk. 14:65
PANT Ps. 38:10; 42:1; 119:131; Amos 2:7
PARDON Ex. 23:21, he will not *p*
II Ki. 5:18, the Lord *p* your servant
II Chron. 30:18, the good Lord *p* every one
Neh. 9:17, a God ready to *p*
Isa. 55:7, he will abundantly *p*
See Jer. 33:8; 50:20; Lam. 3:42; Mic. 7:18
PARENTS Mk. 13:12, rise up against *p*
Lk. 18:29, no man that has left *p*
   21:16, you shall be betrayed by *p*
Jn. 9:2, who did sin, this man, or his *p*?
Rom. 1:30; II Tim. 3:2, disobedient to *p*
Eph. 6:1; Col. 3:20, children, obey your *p*
See Lk. 2:27; 8:56; I Tim. 5:4; Heb. 11:23

PART (*n.*) Ps. 5:9, their inward *p* is wickedness
    51:6, in hidden *p* make me to know
    118:7, the Lord takes my *p*
   Lk. 10:42, ,that good *p*
   Jn. 13:8, you have no *p* with me
   Acts 8:21, neither *p* not lot
   II Cor. 6:15, what *p* has he that believes?
   See Titus 2:8; Rev. 20:6; 21:8; 22:19
PART (*v.*) Ruth 1:17, if ought but death *p*
   II Sam. 14:6, there was none to *p* them
   Ps. 22:18, they *p* my garments
   Lk. 24:51, while he blessed them he was *p*
   Acts 2:45, *p* them to all men
   See Mat. 27:35, Mk. 15:24; Lk. 23:34
PARTAKE Ps. 50:18, *p* with adulterers
   Rom. 15:27, *p* of their spiritual things
   I Cor. 9:10, *p* of his hope
    13; 10:18, *p* with the altar
   10:17, *p* of that one bread
    21, *p* of the Lord's table
   I Tim. 5:22, neither be *p* of other men's sins
   Heb. 3:1, *p* of the heavenly calling
   I Pet. 4:13, *p* of Christ's sufferings
    5:1, a *p* of the Lord's table
   II Pet. 1:4, *p* of the divine nature
   See Eph. 3:6; Phil. 1:7; Col. 1:12; Rev. 18:4
PARTIAL Mal 2:9; I Tim. 5:21
PARTICULAR I Cor. 12:27; Eph. 5:33
PARTITION I Ki. 6:21; Eph. 2:14
PARTNER Prov. 29:24; Lk. 5:7
PASS Ex. 12:13, I will *p* over
   Isa. 43:2, when you *p* through waters
   Mat. 26:39; Mk. 14:35, let this cup *p*
   Lk. 16:26, neither can they *p* to us
   I Cor. 7:31, I Jn. 2:17, fashion of this world *p*
   II Cor. 5:17, old things *p* away
   Eph. 3:19, love of Christ, which *p* knowledge
   Phil. 4:7, which *p* all understanding
   See Jer. 2:6; Lk. 18:37; Rom. 5:12
PASSION Acts 1:3; 14:15; James 5:17
PASSOVER Ex. 12:11; Deut. 16:2; Josh. 5:11;
    II Chron. 30:15; 35:1, 11
   I Cor. 5:7, Christ our *p* is sacrificed
   See Heb. 11:28
PAST Job 29:2, as in months *p*
   Eccl. 3:15, God requires that which is *p*
   Song of Sol. 2:11, the winter is *p*
   Jer. 8:20, the harvest is *p*
   Rom. 3:25, of sins that are *p*
    11:33, ways *p* finding out
   Eph. 4:19, being *p* feeling
   See Eph. 2:2; II Tim. 2:18; I Pet. 2:10
PASTOR Jer. 3:15; 17:16; 23:1; Eph. 4:11
PASTURE Ps. 95:7; 100:3; Ezek. 34:14
PATE Ps. 7:16
PATH Job 28:7, a *p* which no fowl knows
   Ps. 16:11, show me the *p* of life
    27:11, lead me in a plain *p*
    65:11, your *p* drop fatness
    77:19, your *p* is in the great waters
    119:105, a light to my *p*
   Prov. 4:18, the *p* of the just
   Isa. 2:3; Mic. 4:2, we will walk in his *p*
    42:16, in *p* they have not known

Isa. 58:12, restorer of *p* to dwell in
   Jer. 6:16, ask for the old *p*
   Lk. 3:4, make his *p* straight
   See Ps. 139:3; Prov. 3:17; Heb. 12:13
PATIENCE Mat. 18:26, 29, have *p* with me
   Lk. 8:15, bring forth fruit with *p*
    21:19, in your *p* possess ye your souls
   Rom. 5:3, tribulation works *p*
    8:25, with *p* wait for it
    15:4, through *p* and comfort
    5, the God of *p*
   II Cor. 6:4, as ministers of God in much *p*
   Col. 1:11, with all might to all *p*
   I Thess. 1:3, your *p* of hope
   II Thess. 1:4, glory in you for your *p*
   I Tim. 6:11, follow after *p*
   Titus 2:2, sound in faith, charity, *p*
   Heb. 10:36, you have need of *p*
    12:1, run with *p*
   James 1:3, trying of your faith works *p*
    4, let *p* have her perfect work
    5:7, the husbandman has long *p*
    10, for an example of *p*
    11, you have heard of the *p* of Job
   II Pet. 1:6, add to temperance *p*
   Rev. 2:2, 19, I know your *p*
    13:10; 14:12, here is the *p* of the saints
   See Eccl. 7:8; Rom. 12:12; I Thess. 5:14
PATIENTLY Ps. 37:7; 40:1; Heb. 6:15
PATTERN I Tim. 1:16; Titus 2:7; Heb. 8:5
PAVILION Ps. 18:11; 27:5; Jer. 43:10
PAY Ex. 22:7, let him *p* double
   Num. 20:19, water, I will *p* for it
   II Ki. 4:7, sell the oil, and *p* your debt
   Ps. 22:25; 66:13; 116:14, will *p* my vows
   Prov. 22:27, if you have nothing to *p*
   Eccl. 5:4, defer not to *p* it
   Mat. 18:26, I will *p* you all
    28, *P* that you owe
    23:23, you *p* tithe of mint
PEACE Gen. 41:16, an answer of *p*
   Num. 6:26, the Lord give you *p*
    25:12, my covenant of *p*
   Deut. 20:10, proclaim *p* to it
    23:6, you shall not seek their *p*
   I Sam. 25:6; Lk. 10:5, *P* to this house
   II Ki. 9:19, what have you to do with *p*?
   Job 5:23, beasts shall be at *p* with you
    22:21, acquaint yourself with him, be at *p*
   Ps. 4:8, I will lay me down in *p*
    29:11, the Lord will bless his people with *p*
    34:14; I Pet. 3:11, seek *p* and pursue it
    37:37, the end of that man is *p*
    122:6, pray for *p* of Jerusalem
   Eccl. 3:8, a time of *p*
   Isa. 26:3, keep him in perfect *p*
    32:17, work of righteousness shall be *p*
    45:7, I make *p*, and create evil
    48:22; 57:21, no *p* to the wicked
    52:7; Nah. 1:15, that publishes *p*
    59:8; Rom. 3:17, way of *p* they know not
   Jer. 6:14, saying *P*, *p*, when there is no *p*
    8:15; 14:19, we looked for *p*
    34:5, you shall die in *p*

Ezek. 7:25, they shall seek *p*
Mat. 10:13, let your *p* come unto it
　34; Lk. 12:51, to send *p* on earth
Mk. 9:50, have *p* one with another
Lk. 1:79, to guide our feet in way of *p*
　2:14, on earth *p*
　19:42, things which belong to your *p*!
Jn. 14:27, *P* I leave, my *p* I give you
　16:33, that in me you might have *p*
Rom. 5:1, we have *p* with God
　10:15; Eph. 6:15, the gospel of *p*
　15:33; Phil. 4:9; Heb. 13:20, God of *p*
I Cor. 14:33, author of *p*
II Cor. 13:11, live in *p*
Eph. 1:2; Phil. 1:2, *p* from God our Father
Eph. 2:14, he is our *p*
　17, *p* to you which were afar off
　4:3, in the bond of *p*
Col. 1:2; I Thess. 1:1; II Thess. 1:2; II Jn. 3,
　grace and *p* from God
　3:15, let the *p* of God rule in your hearts
I Thess. 5:13, be at *p* among yourselves
II Thess. 3:16, Lord of *p* give you *p* always
II Tim 2:22; Heb. 12:14, follow *p* with all men
Heb. 7:2, king of *p*
James 2:16, depart in *p*
　3:18, fruit of righteousness is sown in *p*
I Pet. 1:2; II Pet. 1:2, *p* be multiplied
II Pet. 3:14, found of him in *p*
PEACEABLE I Tim. 2:2; Heb. 12:11
PEACEABLY Gen. 37:4; I Sam. 16:4
PEELED Isa. 18:2; Ezek. 29:18
PEEP Isa. 8:19; 10:14
PEN Job 19:24; Ps. 45:1; Jer. 17:1; III Jn. 13
PENCE Mat. 18:28; Mk. 14:5; Lk. 7:41
PENURY Prov. 14:32; Lk. 21:4
PEOPLE Deut. 4:33, *p* hear voice of God and
　live?
　33:29, O *p* saved by the Lord
II Sam. 22:44; Ps. 18:43, a *p* I knew not
Ps. 81:11, my *p* would not hearken
Prov. 30:25, the ants are a *p* not strong
Isa. 1:4, a *p* laden with iniquity
　27:11, a *p* of no understanding
　43:4, I will give *p* for your life
Jer. 6:22; 50:41, a *p* comes from the north
　13:11, I will take you to me for a *p*
Jonah 1:8, of what *p* are you?
Lk. 1:17, a *p* prepared for the Lord
Titus 2:14, purify unto himself a peculiar *p*
PERCEIVE Deut. 29:4, a heart to *p*
Josh. 22:31, we *p* the Lord is among us
Job 9:11, I *p* him not
　23:8, I cannot *p* him
Isa. 6:9, see indeed, but *p* not
　33:19, deeper speech than you can *p*
　64:4, nor *p* by the ear what God has
Mat. 22:18, Jesus *p* their wickedness
Mk. 8:17, *p* ye not yet
Jn. 4:19, I *p* you are a prophet
Acts 10:34, *p* God is no respecter of persons
I Jn. 3:16, hereby *p* we the love of God
PERFECT Gen. 6:9, Noah was *p*
　17:1, walk before me, and be thou *p*

Deut. 18:13, you shall be *p* with the Lord
　32:4, his work is *p*
II Sam. 22:31; Ps. 18:30, his way is *p*
Ps. 19:7, law of the Lord is *p*
　37:37, mark the *p* man
Prov. 4:18, more and more to *p* day
Ezek. 28:15, you were *p* in your ways
Mat. 5:48; II Cor. 13:11, be ye *p*
　19:21, if you will be *p*
Jn. 17:23, be made *p* in one
Rom. 12:2, that *p* will of God
I Cor. 2:6, wisdom among them that are *p*
II Cor. 12:9, strength made *p* in weakness
Eph. 4:13, unto a *p* man
Phil. 3:12, not as though I were already *p*
Col. 1:28, present every man *p*
II Tim. 3:17, that the man of God may be *p*
Heb. 2:9, make *p* through sufferings
　11:40, without us should not be made *p*
　12:23, spirits of just men made *p*
　13:21, make you *p* in every good work
James 1:4, patience have her *p* work
　1:7, every good and *p* gift
　3:2, the same is a *p* man
I Jn. 4:18, *p* love casts out fear
PERFECTION Job 11:7; Ps. 119:96
PERFECTLY Jer. 23:20; Acts 18:26
PERFECTNESS Col. 3:14
PERFORM Ex. 18:18, not able to *p* it yourself
Esther 5:6, to half of kingdom it shall be *p*
Job 5:12, cannot *p* their enterprise
Ps. 65:1, unto you shall the vows be *p*
　119:106, I have sworn, and I will *p* it
Isa. 9:7, zeal of the Lord will *p* this
　44:28, shall *p* all my pleasure
Jer. 29:10; 33:14, I will *p* my good word
Rom. 4:21, able also to *p*
　7:18, how to *p* that which is good I find
　not
Phil. 1:6, *p* it until day of Christ
See Job 23:14; Ps. 57:2; Jer. 35:14; Mat. 5:33
PERFORMANCE Lk. 1:45; II Cor. 8:11
PERIL Lam. 5:9; Rom. 8:35; II Cor. 11:26
PERILOUS II Tim. 3;1
PERISH Num. 17:12, we die, we *p*, we all *p*
Deut. 26:5, a Syrian ready to *p*
Job 4:7, who ever *p*, being innocent?
　29:13, blessing of him that was ready to *p*
　34:15, all flesh shall *p* together
Ps. 1:6, way of ungodly shall *p*
　37:20, the wicked shall *p*
　80:16, they *p* at rebuke of your counte-
　nance
　102:26, they shall *p* but you shall endure
Prov. 11:10; 28:28, when the wicked *p*
　29:18, no vision, the people *p*
Isa. 27:13, come that were ready to *p*
Jonah 1:6; 3:9, that we *p* not
　14, let us not *p* for this man's life
Mat. 8:25; Lk. 8:24, save us, we *p*
　18:14, one of these little ones should *p*
　26:52, shall *p* with the sword
Mk. 4:28, carest thou not that we *p*?
Lk. 13:3, 5, you shall all likewise *p*

15:17, I *p* with hunger
21:18, shall not an hair of your head *p*
Jn. 6:27, labor not for the meat which *p*
Acts 8:20, your money *p* with you
Col. 2:22, which are to *p* with the using
II Pet. 3:9, not willing that any should *p*
PERMISSION I Cor. 7:6
PERMIT I Cor. 14:34; 16:7; Heb. 6:3
PERNICIOUS II Pet. 2:2
PERPETUAL Ex. 31:16, a *p* covenant
Lev. 25:34, their *p* possession
Ps. 9:6, destructions are come to a *p* end
Jer. 8:5, a *p* backsliding
15:18, why is my pain *p*
Ezek. 35:9, the *p* desolations
See Gen. 9:12; Jer. 5:22; 50:5; 51:39
PERPETUALLY I Ki. 9:3; II Chron. 7:16
PERPLEXED Lk. 9:7; 24:4; II Cor. 4:8
PERPLEXITY Isa. 22:5; Lk. 21:25
PERSECUTE Job 19:22, why do you *p* me
Ps. 7:1, save me from them that *p* me
10:2, the wicked do *p* the poor
143:3, the enemy has *p* my soul
Mat. 5:11, 12, blessed when men *p* you
44, pray for them that *p* you
Jn. 15:20, if they have *p* me
Acts 9:4; 22:7; 26:14, why *p* thou me?
26:11, I *p* them even to strange cities
I Cor. 4:12, being *p*, we suffer it
15:9; Gal. 1:13, I *p* the church of God
II Cor. 4:9, P, but not forsaken
Phil. 3:6, concerning zeal, *p* the church
See John 5:16; Acts 7:52; Rom. 12:14
PERSECUTION Mk. 4:17, when *p* arises
II Cor. 12:10, take pleasure in *p*
See Lam 5:5; Acts 8:1; I Tim. 1:13
PERSEVERANCE Eph. 6:18
PERSON II Sam 14:14, regards not *p*
II Sam. 17:11, go to battle in your own *p*
Ps. 15:4; Isa. 32:5, 6, vile *p*
26:4; Prov. 12:11; 28:19, with vain *p*
Ps. 105:37, not one feeble *p*
Mat. 22:16, regards not *p* of men
II Cor. 2:10, forgave I it in the *p* of Christ
Heb. 1:3, the express image of his *p*
II Pet. 3:11, manner of *p* ought you to be
See Mal. 1:8; Lk. 15:7; Heb. 12:16
PERSUADE I Ki. 22:20, who shall *p* Ahab
Prov. 25:15, by forbearing is a prince *p*
Mat. 28:14, we will *p* him, and secure you
Acts 26:28, almost you *p* me
Rom. 14:5, let every man be fully *p*
II Cor. 5:11, we *p* men
Gal. 1:10, do I now *p* men of God
Heb. 6:9, we are *p* better things of you
PERTAIN Rom. 15:17; I Cor. 6:3
PERVERSE Deut. 32:5, a *p* generation
Job 6:30, cannot my taste discern *p* things
Prov. 4:24, *p* lips put far from you
12:8, *p* heart shall be despised
17:20, *p* tongue falls into mischief
23:33, your heart shall utter *p* things
Phil. 2:15, in the midst of a *p* nation
See Num. 23:12; Isa. 30:12; I Tim. 6:5

PERVERT Deut. 16:19, a gift does *p* words
Job 8:3, does God *p* judgment?
Prov. 10:9, *p* his ways shall be known
19:3, the foolishness of man *p* his way
Jer. 3:21, they have *p* their way
23:36, you have *p* the words of God
Gal. 1:7, would *p* the gospel
See Eccl. 5:8; Mic. 3:9; Lk. 23:2
PESTILENCE Ex. 5:3; 9:15; Jer. 42:17
PESTILENT Acts 24:5
PETITION I Ki. 2:20, one small *p*
Esther 5:6; 7:2; 9:12, what is your *p*?
Dan. 6:7, whosoever shall ask a *p*
13, makes his *p* three times a day
PHILOSOPHY Col. 2:8
PHYSICIAN Job 13:4, *p* of no value
Jer. 8:22, is there no *p* there?
Mat. 9:12, they that be whole need not *p*
Lk. 4:23, say, P, heal yourself
Col. 4:14, Luke, the beloved *p*
PICK Prov. 30:17
PICTURES Num. 33:52; Isa. 2:16
PIECE I Sam. 2:36, a *p* of bread
15:33, Samuel hewed Agag in *p*
Ps. 7:2, rending in *p* while none to deliver
50:22, consider, lest I tear you in *p*
Jer. 23:29, hammer that breaks rock in *p*
Amos 4:7, one *p* was rained on
Zech. 11:12, weighed for my price thirty *p*
13; Mat. 27:6, 9, took thirty *p* of silver
See Lk. 14:18; Acts 19:19; 23:10; 27:44
PIERCE Isa. 36:6, into his hand *p* it
Zech. 12:10; Jn. 19:37, they shall look on me
whom they have *p*
I Tim. 6:10, *p* themselves with sorrows
See Isa. 27:1; Lk. 2:35, Heb. 4:12; Rev. 1:7
PILE Isa. 30:33; Ezek. 24:9
PILLAR Prov. 9:1, she has hewn out her seven *p*
Gal. 2:9, Cephas and John, who seemed *p*
I Tim. 3:15, the *p* and ground of the truth
See Isa. 19:19; Jer. 1:18; Joel 2:30; Rev. 10:1
PILLOW Gen. 28:11; I Sam. 19:13
PILOTS Ezek. 27:8
PIN Judg. 16:14; Ezek. 15:3
PINE Lev. 26:39; Isa. 38:12; Lam. 4:9
PIPE Isa. 5:12, *p* are in their feasts
Mat. 11:17; Lk. 7:32, we have *p* unto you
I Cor. 14:7, how shall it be known what is *p*?
Rev. 18:22, voice of *p* be heard no more
See I Sam. 10:5; I Ki. 1:40; Isa. 30:29
PIT Gen. 37:20, cast him into some *p*
Ex. 21:33, 34, if a man dig a *p*
Num. 16:30, 33, go down quick into the *p*
Job 33:24, deliver him from the *p*
Prov. 22:14; 23:27, ,a deep *p*
28:10, shall fall into his own *p*
Isa. 38:17, the *p* of corruption
Lk. 14:5, fall into a *p* on sabbath
PITCHER Gen. 24:14; Judg. 7:16
PITIFUL Lam. 4:10; James 5:11; I Pet. 3:8
PITY Deut. 19:13, your eye shall have no *p*
Job 19:21, have *p* on me, my friends
Ps. 69:20, I looked for some to take *p*
Prov. 19:17, he that has *p* on poor lends

28:8, gather for him that will *p* the poor

Isa. 13:18, they shall have no *p* on fruit

63:9, in his *p* he redeemed them

Jer. 13:14, I will not *p* nor spare

Ezek. 16:5, none eye *p* you

24:21, I will profane what your soul *p*

Joel 2:18, the Lord will *p* his people

Zech. 11:5, their own shepherds *p* them not

Mat. 18:33, as I had *p* on you

PLACE Josh 5:15, *p* whereon you stand

Judg. 18:10, a *p* where there is no want

II Ki. 5:11, strike his hand over the *p*

6:1; Isa. 49:20, the *p* is too strait for us

Ps. 26:8, the *p* where your honor dwells

32:7; 119:114, you are my hiding *p*

37:10, you shall diligently consider his *p*

74:20, the dark *p* of the earth

90:1, our dwelling *p*

Prov. 14:26, his children have a *p* of refuge

15:3, the eyes of the Lord are in every *p*

Eccl. 3:20, all go to one *p*

Isa. 5:8, lay field in field, till there be no *p*

60:13, the *p* of my feet

66:1, where is the *p* of my rest?

Jer. 6:3, they shall feed every one in his *p*

Mic. 1:3, the Lord comes out of his *p*

Zech. 10:10, *p* shall not be found for them

Mal. 1:11, in every *p* incense shall be offered

Mk. 16:6, see the *p* where the Lord lay

Lk. 10:1, two and two into every *p*

14:9, give this man *p*

Jn. 8:37, my word has no *p* in you

18:2, Judas knew the *p*

Acts 2:1, with one accord in one *p*

4:31, the *p* was shaken

Rom. 12:19, rather give *p* to wrath

Eph. 4:27, neither give *p* to the devil

Heb. 12:17, found no *p* of repentance

Rev. 20:11, there was found no *p* for them

PLAGUE Deut. 29:22, when they see the *p* of that land

I Ki. 8:38, man the *p* of his own heart

Ps. 73:5, neither are they *p* like other men

91:10, neither any *p* come nigh your dwelling

Hos. 13:14, O death, I will be your *p*

Rev. 18:4, that you receive not of her *p*

22:18, shall add to him the *p* written

PLAIN Gen. 25:27, Jacob was a *p* man

Ps. 27:11, lead me in a *p* path

Prov. 8:9, *p* to him that understands

15:19, the way of the righteous is made *p*

Isa. 40:4, rough places *p*

Hab. 2:2, write the vision, make it *p*

See Gen. 13:10; 19:17; Isa. 28:25; Mk. 7:35

PLAINLY Deut. 27:8, write the words very *p*

Isa. 32:4, stammerers shall speak *p*

Jn. 10:24, tell us *p*

16:25, I shall show you *p* of the Father

29, now speakest thou *p*

See Ex. 21:5; Ezra 4:18; Jn. 11:14

PLAITING I Pet. 3:3

PLANES Isa. 44:13

PLANT (*n.*) Ps. 128:3, children like olive *p*

144:12, sons as *p* grown up

Isa. 5:7; 17:10, his pleasant *p*

16:8; broken down principal *p*

53:2, as a tender *p*

Ezek. 34:29, a *p* of renown

See Gen. 2:5; I Chron. 4:23; Jer. 48:32

PLANT (*v.*) II Sam. 7:10, I will *p* them

Ps. 1:3; Jer. 17:8, like a tree *p*

80:15, the vineyard your right hand has *p*

92:13, *p* in the house of the Lord

94:9, he that *p* the ear

Jer. 2:21, I had *p* you a noble vine

Ezek. 17:10, being *p*, shall it prosper?

Lk. 17:6, be thou *p* in the sea

Rom. 6:5, if we have been *p* together

I Cor. 3:6, I have *p*

See Mat. 21:33; Mk. 12:1; Lk. 20:9

PLATE Ex. 28:36; 39:30; Jer. 10:9

PLATTED Mk. 15:17; Jn. 19:2

PLATTER Mat. 23:25; Lk. 11:39

PLAY Ex. 32:6, people rose up to *p*

I Sam. 16:17, a man that can *p* well

II Sam. 6:21, I will *p* before the Lord

10:12, let us *p* the men

Job 41:5, will you *p* with him?

Ps. 33:3, *p* skillfully with a loud noise

Isa. 11:8, the sucking child shall *p*

Ezek. 33:32, can *p* well on an instrument

See II Sam. 2:14; I Chron. 15:29; Ps. 68:25

PLEA Deut. 17:8

PLEAD Judg. 6:31, 32, will you *p* for Baal?

Job 9:19, who shall set me a time to *p*?

13:19, who will *p* with me?

16:21, that one might *p* for a man

23:6, will he *p* against me

Isa. 1:17, *p* for the widow

3:13, the Lord stands up to *p*

Jer. 2:9, I will yet *p* with you

Lam. 3:58, you have *p* the causes of my soul

Joel 3:2, I will *p* them for my people

PLEASANT Gen. 3:6, *p* to the eyes

II Sam. 1:23, were *p* in their lives

26, very *p* have you been to me

106:24, they despised the *p* land

133:1, how *p* for brethren to dwell together

Prov. 2:10, knowledge is *p* your soul

15:26, the words of the pure are *p* words

16:24, *P* words are as honeycomb

Eccl. 11:7, it is *p* to behold the sun

Song of Sol. 4:13, 16; 7:13, with *p* fruits

Isa. 64:11, our *p* things are laid waste

Jer. 31:20, is Ephraim a *p* child?

Ezek. 33:32, of one that has a *p* voice

Dan. 10:3, I ate no *p* bread

PLEASANTNESS Prov. 3:17

PLEASE I Ki. 3:10, the speech *p* the Lord

Ps. 51:19, shall you be *p* with sacrifices

Prov. 16:7, when a man's ways *p* the Lord

Isa. 2:6, *p* themselves in children of strangers

53:10, it *p* the Lord to bruise him

55:11, accomplish that which I *p*

Jonah 1:14, he has done whatsoever he *p*

Mic. 6:7, will the Lord be *p* with rams

Rom. 8:8, they in the flesh cannot *p* God

15:1, to bear, and not to *p* ourselves
3, even Christ *p* not himself
Gal. 1:10, do I seek to *p* men
Eph. 6:6; Col. 3:22, as men-*p*
PLEASURE I Chron. 29:17, *p* in uprightness
Esther 1:8, according to every man's *p*
Job 21:21, what *p* has he in his house
22:3, is it any *p* to the Almighty
Ps. 16:11, *p* for evermore
35:27, *p* in the prosperity of his servants
102:14, your servants take *p* in her stones
103:21, you ministers of his, that his *p*
111:2, of all them that have *p* therein
147:11, takes *p* in them that fear him
149:4, the Lord takes *p* in his people
Eccl. 5:4, he has no *p* in fools
12:1, I have no *p* in them
Isa. 53:10, the *p* of the Lord shall prosper
58:3, in the day of your fast you find *p*
13, doing your *p* on my holy day
Jer. 22:28; Hos. 8:8, a vessel wherein is no *p*
Ezek. 18:23; 33:11, have I any *p*
Mal. 1:10, I have no *p* in you, says the Lord
Lk. 8:14, choked with *p* of this life
12:32, Father's good *p*
Eph. 1:5, the good *p* of his will
Phil. 2:13, to will and to do of his good *p*
I Tim. 5:6, she that lives in *p*
II Tim. 3:4, lovers of *p*
Heb. 10:38, my soul shall have no *p* in him
11:25, the *p* of sin for a season
12:10, chastened us after their own *p*
James 5:5, you have lived in *p* on earth
Rev. 4:11, for your *p* they were created
See Gen. 18:12; Ps. 5:4; Prov. 21:17; Eccl. 2:1
PLENTEOUS Ps. 86:5; 103:8, *p* in mercy
130:7, *p* redemption
Hab. 1:16, their portion is fat and meat *p*
Mat. 9:37, the harvest truly is *p*
See Gen. 41:34; Deut. 28:11; Prov. 21:5
PLENTIFUL Ps. 31:23; 68:9; Lk. 12:16
PLENTY Gen. 27:28, *p* of corn and wine
Job 22:25, *p* of silver
37:23, *p* of justice
Prov. 3:10, barns filled with *p*
See II Chron. 31:10, Prov. 28:19; Jer. 44:17
PLOW Job 4:8, that *p* iniquity reap same
Prov. 20:4, not *p* by reason of cold
21:4, the *p* of the wicked is sin
Isa. 2:4; Mic. 4:3, beat swords into *p*-shares
28:24, does plowman *p* all day to sow?
Joel 3:10, beat your *p*-shares into swords
Amos 9:13, the *p*-man shall over take reaper
See Deut. 22:10; I Sam. 14:14; Job 1:14
PLUCK Deut. 23:25, may *p* the ears
II Chron. 7:20, then will I *p* them up
Job 24:9, *p* the fatherless from the breast
Ps. 25:15, he shall *p* my feet out of the net
74:11, *p* it out of your bosom
Eccl. 3:2, a time to *p* up
Isa. 50:6, my cheeks to them that *p*
Jer. 22:24, yet would I *p* you thence
Amos 4:11; Zech. 3:2, a firebrand *p* out
Mat. 5:29; Mk. 9:47, offend you, *p* it out

12:1; Mk. 2:23; Lk. 6:1, began to *p* ears
Jn. 10:28, nor shall any *p* out of my hand
See Gen. 8:11; Lk. 17:6; Gal. 4:15; Jude 12
POINT Jer. 17:1, with *p* of a diamond
Heb. 4:15, in all *p* tempted
James 2:10, yet offend in one *p*
See Gen. 25:32; Eccl. 5:16; Mk. 5:23
POLE Num. 21:8
POLICY Dan. 8:25
POLISHED Ps. 144:12; Isa. 49:2; Lam. 4:7
POLL II Sam. 14:26; Ezek. 44:20; Mic. 1:16
POMP Isa. 5:14; 14:11; Ezek. 7:24; 30:18
PONDER Prov. 4:26, *P* the path of your feet
5:6, lest thou should *p*
21, the Lord *p* all his goings
POOL Ps. 84:6; Isa. 35:7; 41:18; Jn 5:2; 9:7
POOR Ex. 30:15, the *p* shall not give less
Deut. 15:11, the *p* shall never cease
II Ki. 24:14, none remained, save *p* sort
Job 24:4, the *p* of the earth hide
29:16, I was a father to the *p*
Ps. 10:14, the *p* commits himself to you
34:6, this *p* man cried
40:17; 69:29; 70:5; 86:1; 102:22, I am *p*
Ps. 49:2, rich and *p* together
Prov. 13:23, food is in the tillage of the *p*
18:23, the *p* uses entreaties
22:2, rich and *p* meet together
30:9, lest I be *p* and steal
Isa. 41:17, when *p* and needy seek water
Zech. 11:7, 11, O *p* of the flock
Mat. 5:3, blessed are the *p* in spirit
II Cor. 6:10; as *p*, yet making many rich
8:9, for your sakes he became *p*
See Lev. 27:8; James 2:2; Rev. 3:17; 13:16
POPULOUS Deut. 26:5; Nah. 3:8
PORTION Deut. 32:9, the Lord's *p* is his people
II Ki. 2:9, a double *p* of your spirit
Neh. 8:10; Esther 9:19, send *p* to them
Job 20:29, 27:13, this the *p* of a wicked man
24:18, their *p* is cursed
26:14, how little a *p* heard of him?
31:2, what *p* of God is there from above?
Ps. 11:6, this shall be the *p* of their cup
16:5, the Lord is the *p* of my inheritance
73:26, God is my *p*
119:57; 142:5, you are my *p*, O Lord
Prov. 31:15, give a *p* to her maidens
Eccl. 2:10, this was my *p* of all my labor
3:22; 5:18; 9:9, rejoice, for that is his *p*
5:19, God has given power to take *p*
9:6, neither have they any more *p* for ever
11:2, give a *p* to seven
Isa. 53:12, divide a *p* with the great
61:7, they shall rejoice in their *p*
Jer. 10:16; 51:19, *p* of Jacob not like them
12:10, my pleasant *p* a wilderness
52:34, every day a *p*
Dan. 1:8, every *p* of king's meat
Mat. 24:51, appoint him *p* with hypocrites
Lk. 12:42, their *p* in due season
46, his *p* with unbelievers
15:12, the *p* of goods that fall
POSSESS Gen. 24:60, your seed *p* the gate

Job 7:3, made to *p* months of vanity
  13:26, *p* iniquities of my youth
Prov. 8:22, the Lord *p* me in beginning
Lk. 18:12, I give tithes of all I *p*
  21:19, in patience *p* your souls
  See Lk. 12:15; Acts 4:32; I Cor. 7:30
POSSESSION Gen. 17:8; 48:4, everlasting *p*
  Prov. 28:10, good things in *p*
  Eccl. 2:7, Mat. 19:22; Mk. 10:22, great *p*
  Acts 2:45, and sold their *p*
  Eph. 1:14, redemption of purchased *p*
  See Lev. 25:10; 27:16; I Ki. 21:15
POSSIBLE Mk. 9:23, all things are *p* to him who
  believes
  10:27, with God all things are *p*
  14:35, if *p*, let this cup pass from me
  36: Lk. 18:27, all things are *p* to you
  Rom. 12:18, if *p* live peaceably
  See Acts 2:24; 20:16; Gal. 4:15; Heb. 10:4
POST Deut. 6:9; Job 9:25; Jer. 51:31
POSTERITY Gen. 45:7; Ps. 49:13; 109:13
POT II Ki. 4:2, not any thing save a *p* of oil
  40, there is death in the *p*
  Job 41:31, makes the deep boil like a *p*
  Zech. 14:21, every *p* shall be holiness
  Mk. 7:4, the washing of cups and *p*
  Jn. 2:6, six water-*p*
  See Ex. 16:33; Jer. 1:13; Jn. 4:28; Heb. 9:4
POTENTATE I Tim. 6:15
POUND Lk. 19:13; Jn. 12:3
POUR Job 10:10, *p* me out as milk?
  29:6, rock *p* out rivers of oil
  30:16, my soul is *p* out upon me
  Ps. 45:2, grace is *p* into your lips
  62:8, *p* out your heart before him
  Isa. 26:16, *p* out prayer when chastening
  32:15, till the spirit be *p* on us
  44:3, I will *p* water on him that is thirsty
  53:12, *p* out his soul unto death
  Jer. 7:20; 42:18, my fury shall be *p* out
  Lam. 2:19, *p* out your heart like water
  Nah. 1:6, fury is *p* out like fire
  Mal. 3:10, if I will not *p* out a blessing
  Mk. 14:3, *p* ointment on his head
  Jn. 2:15, he *p* out the changers' money
  Acts 2:17, 18, I will *p* out my spirit
POVERTY Prov. 6:11, your *p* come as one that
  travels
  10:15, destruction of poor is *p*
  11:24, it tends to *p*
  13:18, *p* to him that refuses instruction
  Prov. 20:13, lest you come to *p*
  30:8, give me neither *p* nor riches
  31:7, let him drink, and forget his *p*
  See Prov. 23:21; II Cor. 8:2; Rev. 2:9
POWDER Ex. 32:20; II Ki. 23:6; Mat. 21:44
POWER Ex. 15:6, glorious in *p*
  Lev. 26:19, the pride of your *p*
  Deut. 8:18, he gives you *p* get wealth
  II Sam. 22:33, God is my strength and *p*
  I Chron. 29:11, yours is the *p* and glory
  II Chron. 25:8, God has *p* to help
  Job 26:2, him that is without *p*
  Ps. 49:15, from the *p* of the grave

65:6, being girded with *p*
  90:11, who knows *p* of your anger?
Prov. 3:27, when it is in *p* to do it
  18:21, in the *p* of your tongue
Eccl. 5:19; 6:2, *p* to eat thereof
  8:4, where word of king is, there is *p*
Isa. 40:29, he gives *p* to the faint
Hos. 12:3, have you *p* with God?
Mic. 3:8, full of *p* by the Spirit?
Zech. 4:6, not by might, nor by *p*
Mat. 9:8, who had given such *p* to men
  24:30; Lk. 21:27, coming in clouds with *p*
  28:18, all *p* is given to me
Lk. 1:35, the *p* of the Highest
  4:6, all this *p* will I give you
  14, Jesus returned in the *p* of the Spirit
  5:17, the *p* of the Lord was present
  5:24, *p* on earth to forgive
  9:43, amazed at the mighty *p* of God
  12:5, that has *p* to cast into Hell
  22:53, your hour, and the *p* of darkness
  24:49, with *p* from on high
Jn. 1:12, *p* to become sons of God
  10:18, I have *p* to lay in down
  17:2, *p* over all flesh
  19:10, I have *p* to crucify you
Acts 1:8, *p* after the Holy Ghost is come
  3:12, as though by our own *p*
  5:4, was it not in your own *p*?
  8:10, this man is the great *p* of God
  19, give me also this *p*
  26:18, from the *p* of Satan unto God
Rom. 1:20, his eternal *p* and Godhead
Rom. 9:17, that I might show my *p* in you
  13:2, whosoever resist the *p*
I Cor. 15:43, it is raised in *p*
Eph. 2:2, prince of the *p* of the air
  3:7, the effectual working of his *p*
Phil. 3:10, the *p* of his resurrection
II Thess. 1:9, from the glory of his *p*
II Tim. 1:7, spirit of *p* and love
  3:5, form of Godliness, but denying the *p*
Heb. 2:14; destroy him that had *p* of death
  6:5, the *p* of the world to come
  7:16, the *p* of an endless life
Rev. 2:26, to him will I give *p*
POWERFUL Ps. 29:4; Heb. 4:12
PRAISE (*n.*) Ex. 15:11, fearful in *p*
Deut. 10:21, he is your *p* and your God
Judg. 5:3; Ps. 7:17, I will sing *p*
Neh. 9:5, above all blessing and *p*
Ps. 22:25, my *p* shall be of you
  33:1; 147:1, *P* is comely for the upright
  34:1, his *p* shall continually be in my
  mouth
  50:23, whoso offers *p* glorifies me
  65:1, *P* waits for you
  66:2, make his *p* glorious
  109:1, O God of my *p*
Prov. 27:21, so is a man to his *p*
Isa. 60:18, call your gates *P*
  61:3, garment of *p*
Jer. 13:11, that they might be to me for a *p*
  49:25, how is the city of *p*

Hab. 3:3, the earth was full of his *p*

Zeph. 3:20, a *p* among all people

Jn. 9:24, give God the *p*

    12:43, the *p* of men

Rom. 2:29, whose *p* is not of men

    13:3, you shall have *p*

I Cor. 4:5, every man have *p* of God

II Cor. 8:18, whose *p* is in the gospel

Eph. 1:6, 12, *p* of glory of his grace

Phil. 4:8, if there be any *p*

PRAISE (*v.*) Gen. 49:8, brethren shall *p*

II Sam. 14:25, none to be so much *p*

Ps. 30:9, shall the dust *p* you?

    42:5, 11; 43:5, I shall yet *p* him

    45:17, therefore shall the people *p* thee

    63:3, my lips shall *p* you

    67:3, 5, let the people *p* you

    72:15, daily shall he be *p*

    76:10, the wrath of man shall *p* you

    88:10, shall the dead arise and *p* you?

    107:32, *p* him in the assembly

    115:17, the dead *p* not

    145:4, one generation shall *p* your works

    10, all your works shall *p* you

Prov. 27:2, let another *p* you

    31:31, her own works *p* her in the gates

Isa. 38:19, the living shall *p* you.

See Lk. 2:13; 24:53; Acts 2:47; 3:8

PRANSING Judg. 5:22; Nah. 3:2

PRATING Prov. 10:8; III Jn. 10

PRAY Gen. 20:7, a prophet, shall *p* for you

I Sam. 7:5, I will *p* for you to the Lord

    12:23, sin in ceasing to *p* for you

II Chron. 7:14, if my people shall *p*

Ezra 6:10, *p* for the life of the king

Job 21:15, what profit, if we *p* to him?

Ps. 5:2, to you will I *p*

    122:6, *P* for the peace of Jerusalem

Isa. 45:20, *p* to a god than cannot save

Jer. 7:16; 11:14; 14:11, *P* not for this people

    37:3; 42:2, 20, *P* now to the Lord for us

Zech. 7:2, they sent me to *p*

Mat. 5:44, *p* for them which use you

    6:5, love to *p* for them which use you

    14:23; Lk. 6:12; 9:28, apart to *p*

    26:36; Mk. 14:32, while I *p* yonder

Mk. 11:25, and when you stand *p* forgive

Lk. 11:1, Lord, teach us to *p*

    18:1, men ought always to *p*

Jn. 14:16; 16:26, I will *p* the Father

    17:9, I *p* for them, I *p* not for the world

    20, neither *p* I for these alone

Acts 9:11, behold he *p*

Rom. 8:26, know not what we should *p* for

I Cor. 14:15, I will *p* with the spirit, and *p* with understanding also

Eph. 6:18, *p* always with all prayer

I Thess. 5:17, *P* without ceasing

I Tim. 2:8, that men *p* every where

James 5:13, is any afflicted? let him *p*

    16, *p* for one another

I Jn. 5:16, I do not say he shall *p* for it

PRAYER Job 15:4, you restrain *p*

    16:17; Ps. 4:1, 5:3; 6:9; 17:1; 35:13; 39:12

Ps. 65:2, you that hear *p*

    72:15, *p* shall be made continually

    109:4, I give myself to *p*

Prov. 15:8, the *p* of the upright

Isa. 1:15, when you make many *p*

    56:7; Mat. 21:13; Lk. 19:46, house of *p*

Mat. 21:22, whatsoever you ask in *p*

    23:14; Mk. 12:40; Lk. 20:47, long *p*

Lk. 6:12, all night in *p* to God

Acts 3:1, the hour of *p*

    6:4, give ourselves to *p*

    12:5, *p* was made without ceasing

    16:13, where *p* was wont to be made

Phil. 4:6, by *p* and supplication

James 5:15, the *p* of faith shall save the sick

    16, the effectual fervent *p* of a righteous man

I Pet. 4:7, watch unto *p*

Rev. 5:8; 8:3, the *p* of the saints

PREACH Neh. 6:7, appointed prophets to *p*

Isa. 61:1, to *p* good tidings

Jonah 3:2, *p* the preaching I bid you

Mat. 4:17; 10:7, Jesus began to *p*

    11:1, to *p* in their cities

    5, the poor have the gospel *p*

Mk. 2:2, he *p* the word to them

    16:20, and *p* every where

Lk. 9:60, go thou, *p* the kingdom of God

Acts 8:5, and *p* Christ unto them

    10:36, *p* peace by Jesus Christ

    13:38, through this man is *p* forgiveness

    17:18, he *p* Jesus and the resurrection

Rom. 2:21, *p* a man should not steal

    10:15, how shall they *p*, except they be sent?

I Cor. 1:18, the *p* of the cross

    21, by the foolishness of *p*

    23, but we *p* Christ crucified

    15:11, so we *p*, and so ye believed

    14, then is our *p* vain

II Cor. 4:5, we *p* not ourselves

Phil. 1:15, some *p* Christ of envy and strife

II Tim. 4:2, *P* the word; be instant

Heb. 4:2, word *p* did not profit

I Pet. 3:19, *p* to spirits in prison

See Ps. 40:9; II Cor. 11:4; Gal. 1:8

PREACHER I Tim. 2:7, ordained a *p*

II Pet. 2:5, Noah, a *p* of righteousness

See Eccl. 1:1; 7:27; 12:8; II Tim. 1:11

PRECEPT Neh. 9:14, commanded them *p*

Isa. 28:10, 13, *p* must be upon *p*

    29:13, taught be *p* of men

Jer. 35:18 you have kept Jonadab's *p*

See Dan. 9:5; Mk. 10:5; Heb. 9:19

PRECIOUS Deut. 33:13, 14, 15, 16, *p* things

I Sam. 3:1, the word was *p* in those days

    26:21, my soul was *p* in your eyes

II Ki. 1:13, let my life be *p*

Ezra 8:27, fine copper, *p* as gold

Ps. 49:8, the redemption of their soul is *p*

    72:14, *p* shall their blood be in his sight

    116:15, *P* in sight of the Lord

    133:2, like *p* ointment upon the head

    139:17, how *p* are your thoughts!

Prov. 3:15, wisdom more *p* than rubies

Eccl. 7:1, name better than *p* ointment
Isa. 13:12, I will make a man more *p*
  28:16; I Pet. 2:6, a *p* corner stone
  43:4, since you were *p* in my sight
Jer. 15:19, take the *p* from the vile
Lam. 4:2, the *p* sons of Zion
I Pet. 1:7, trial of faith more *p* than gold
  19, the *p* blood of Christ
  2:7, to you which believe he is *p*
II Pet. 1:1, like *p* faith
  4, great and *p* promises
PREEMINENCE Eccl. 3:19; III Jn. 9
PREFER Ps. 137:6; Jn. 1:15; Rom. 12:10
PREMEDITATE Mk. 13:11
PREPARATION Prov. 16:1, *p* of the heart
  Eph. 6:15, shod with *p* of Gospel of peace
  See Mk. 15:42; Lk. 23:54; Jn. 19:14
PREPARE I Sam. 7:3, *p* your hearts
  II Chron. 20:33, as yet the people had not *p*
  Ps. 68:10, you have *p* of your goodness
    107:36, that they may *p* city
  Prov. 8:27, he *p* the heaven I was there
  Isa. 40:3; Lk. 1:76, *P* way of the Lord
    62:10, *p* the way of the people
  Amos 4:12, *p* to meet your God
  Jonah 1:17, Lord had *p* a great fish
  Mk. 10:40, to them for whom it is *p*
  Jn. 14:2, I go to *p* a place for you
  Rom. 9:23, afore *p* to glory
  I Cor. 2:9, things God has *p*
  Heb. 10:5, a body have you *p* me
PRESCRIBE Ezra 7:22; Isa. 10:1
PRESENCE Ex. 33:15, if your *p* go not with me
Job 23:15, I am troubled at his *p*
Ps. 16:11, in your *p* is fullness of joy
  17:2, let my sentence come forth from
  your *p*
  31:20, in the secret of your *p*
  51:11, cast me not away from your *p*
  139:7, whither shall I flee from your *p*?
Prov. 14:7, go from *p* of a foolish man
Isa. 63:9, angel of his *p* saved them
Jer. 23:39; 52:3, I will cast you out of my *p*
Jonah 1:3, to flee from *p* of the Lord
Zeph. 1:7, hold your peace at *p* of the Lord
Lk. 13:26, eaten and drunk in your *p*
Acts 3:19, times of refreshing from the *p*
II Cor. 10:1, 10, who is *p* am base
See Gen. 16:12; Ps. 23:5; Lk. 15:10
PRESENT Ps. 46:1, a very *p* help in trouble
Lk. 2:22, to *p* him to the Lord
Jn. 14:25, being yet *p* with you
Acts 10:33, all here *p* before God
Rom. 7:21, evil is *p* with me
  8:18, sufferings of this *p* time
  12:1, *p* your bodies a living sacrifice
I Cor. 7:26, good for the *p* distress
II Cor. 5:8, to be *p* with the Lord
  9, whether *p* or absent
Gal. 1:4, deliver us from the *p* world
Col. 1:28, *p* every man perfect
II Tim. 4:10, having loved this *p* world
Titus 2:12, live godly in this *p* world
II Pet. 1:12, established in the *p* truth

PRESENTLY Prov. 12:16; Mat. 21:19; 26:53
PRESERVE Gen. 32:30, my life is *p*
  45:5, did send me before you to *p* life
Job 29:2, as in the days when God *p* me
Ps. 36:6, you *p* man and beast
  121:7, the Lord shall *p* you from evil
  8, shall *p* your going out and coming in
Prov. 2:8, he *p* the way of his saints
  11, discretion shall *p* you
  20:28, mercy and truth *p* the king
Jer. 49:11, I will *p* them alive
Lk. 17:33, shall lose his life shall *p* it
PRESS Prov. 3:10, *p* burst with new wine
Amos 2:13, I am *p* under you, as a cart is *p*
Mk. 3:10, they *p* on him to touch him
Lk. 6:38, good measure, *p* down
  16:16, every man *p* into it
Phil. 3:14, I *p* toward the mark
See Ezek. 23:3; Mk. 2:4; 5:27; Lk. 8:19
PRESUME Deut. 18:20; Esther. 7:5
PRESUMPTUOUS Num. 15:30; Ps. 19:13
PRETENCE Mk. 12:40; Phil. 1:18
PREVAIL Ex. 17:11, when Moses held up his
  hand, Israel *p*
I Sam. 2:9, by strength shall no man *p*
Ps. 9:19, let no man *p*
  65:3, iniquities *p* against me
Eccl. 4:12, if one *p* against him
Hos. 12:4, power with God and have *p*
Mat. 16:18, gates of hell shall not *p*
See Job 14:20; Jer. 20:7; Jn. 12:19
PREVENT Ps. 18:5, snares of death *p* me
  59:10, God of my mercy shall *p* me
  88:13, in morning shall my prayer *p* you
  119:147, I *p* the dawning of the morning
See Ps. 21:3; 79:8; Isa. 21:14; I Thess. 4:15
PREY Isa. 49:24, shall *p* be taken
Jer. 21:9; 38:2; 45:5, his life shall be for a *p*
Ezek. 34:22, my flock shall no more be a *p*
See Gen. 49:9; Num. 14:3; Neh. 4:4
PRICE Lev. 25:52, the *p* of his redemption
Acts 5:2, kept back part of the *p*
I Cor. 6:20, 7:23, bought with a *p*
I Pet. 3:4, meek spirit of great *p*
See Deut. 23:18; Prov. 31:10; Zech. 11:12
PRICKS Num. 33:55; Acts 9:5; 26:14
PRIDE Ps. 31:20, hide them from *p* of man
Prov. 8:13, *p* do I hate
  14:3, in mouth of foolish is rod of *p*
Isa. 28:1, woe to the crown of *p*
Jer. 49:16, the *p* of your heart
See Mk. 7:22; I Tim. 3:6; I Jn. 2:16
PRIEST Ex. 19:6, a kingdom of *p*
I Sam. 2:35, I will raise up a faithful *p*
II Chron. 6:41, *p* clothed with salvation
  13:9, *p* of them that are no gods
Isa. 24:2, as with the people, so with the *p*
  28:7, *p* and prophet have erred
  61:6, shall be named the *P* of the Lord
Jer. 13:13, will fill *p* with drunkenness
Mic. 3:11, the *p* teach for hire
Mal. 2:7, the *p* lips should keep knowledge
Lk. 17:14, show yourselves to the *p*
Acts 6:7, *p* were obedient to the faith

Rev. 1:6; 5:10; 20:6, kings and *p* to God

PRIESTHOOD Num. 25:13, an everlasting *p*
  16:10, seek you the *p* also
  Heb. 7:24, an unchangeable *p*
  I Pet. 2:5, an holy *p*
  See Num. 18:1; Josh. 18:7; Neh. 13:29

PRINCE Gen. 32:28, as a *p* have you power
  Ex. 2:14, who made you a *p* over us?
  I Sam. 2:8; Ps. 113:8, to set them among *p*
  II Sam. 3:38, a *p* fallen in Israel
  Job 12:21, pours contempt on *p*
    21:28, where is the house of the *p*?
    31:37, as a *p* would I go near him
  Ps. 45:16, make *p* in all the earth
    118:9, than to put confidence in *p*
    146:3, put not your trust in *p*
  Prov. 8:15, by me *p* decree justice
    31:4, not for *p* strong drink
  Eccl. 10:7, *p* walking as servants
  Isa. 34:12; 40:23, all her *p* shall be nothing
  Hos. 3:4, abide many days without a *p*
  Mat. 9:34; 12:24; Mk. 3:22, by *p* of devils
  Jn. 12:31; 14:30; 16:11, the *p* of this world
  Acts 3:15, and killed the *P* of life
    5:31, exalted to be a *P* and Saviour
  I Cor. 2:6, wisdom of the *p* of this world
    8, which none of the *p* of this world knew
  Eph. 2:2, the *p* of the power of the air
  See Isa. 3:4; Hos. 7:5; Mat. 20:25

PRINCIPAL Prov. 4:7; Isa. 28:25; Acts 25:23

PRINCIPALITY Titus 3:1, to be subject to *p*
  See Rom. 8:38; Eph. 1:21; Col. 1:16

PRINCIPLES Heb. 5:12; 6:1

PRINT Lev. 19:28; Job 13:27; Jn. 20:25

PRISON Ps. 142:7, bring my soul out of *p*
  Eccl. 4:14, out of *p* he comes to reign
  Isa. 53:8, taken from *p* and from judgment
    61:1, opening of the *p*
  Mat. 5:25; Lk. 12:58, you be cast into *p*
    11:2, John heard in the *p*
    25:36, 39, in *p* and you came unto me
  Lk. 22:33, to go with you to *p* and to death
  II Cor. 11:23, in *p* more frequent
  I Pet. 3:19, spirits in *p*

PRISONER Ps. 79:11; Zech. 9:12; Mat. 27:16

PRIVATE II Pet. 1:10

PRIVATELY Mat. 24:3; Mk. 9:28

PRIVILY Mat. 1:19; 2:7; Acts 16:37

PRIZE I Cor. 9:24; Phil. 3:14

PROCEED Gen. 24:50, *p* from the Lord
  Deut. 8:3, that *p* out of mouth of God
  Job 40:5, I will *p* no further
  Isa. 29:14, I will *p* to do a marvelous work
    51:4, a law shall *p* from me
  Jer. 9:3, they *p* from evil to evil
  Mat. 15:18; Mk. 7:21, *p* out of the mouth
  Jn. 8:42, I *p* forth from God
  James 3:10, *p* blessing and cursing
  See Lk. 4:22; Jn. 15:26; Eph. 4:29

PROCLAIM Ex. 34:5, *p* the name of the Lord
  Isa. 61:1, to *p* liberty to captives
    2, to *p* acceptable year
    62:11, the Lord has *p*, your salvation comes
  Lk. 12:3, *p* upon the housetops

See Deut. 20:10; Prov. 20:6; Jer. 3:12

PROCURE Prov. 11:27; Jer. 2:17; 4:18

PRODUCE Isa. 41:21

PROFANE Lev. 20:3, *p* name of God
  Jer. 23:11, prophet and priest are *p*
  Ezek. 22:26, difference between holy and *p*
  Mat. 12:5, priests in temple *p* sabbath
  Acts 24:6, has gone about to *p* temple
  I Tim. 1:9, law for unholy and *p*
    4:7, refuse *p* and old wives' fables
    6:20; II Tim. 2:16, avoiding *p* babblings
  Heb. 12:16, any *p* person
  See Ps. 89:39; Jer. 23:15; Mal. 1:12; 2:10

PROFESS Rom. 1:22; II Cor. 9:13

PROFIT (*n.*) Gen. 37:26, what *p* if we slay?
  Job 21:15, what *p* if we pray?
  Prov. 14:23, in all labour there is *p*
  Eccl. 1:3; 3:9; 5:16, what *p* of labour?
    2:11, there was no *p* under the sun
    5:9, *p* of the earth for all
    7:11, by wisdom there is *p*
  Jer. 16:19, things wherein is no *p*
  Mal. 3:14, what *p* that we have kept?
  II Tim. 2:14, about words to no *p*
  Heb. 12:10, he chastens us for our *p*
  See Esther 3:8; Ps. 30:9; Isa. 30:5; I Tim. 4:15

PROFIT (*v.*) I Sam. 12:21, things cannot *p*
  Job 33:27, I have sinned, and it *p* not
    34:9, *p* nothing to delight in God
  Prov. 10:2, treasures of wickedness *p* nothing
    11:4, riches *p* not in the day of wrath
  Isa. 30:5, 6, people that could not *p*
    48:17, the Lord which teaches you to *p*
  Jer. 2:11, glory for that which does not *p*
    23:32, they shall not *p* this people
  Mat. 16:26; Mk. 8:36, what is a man *p*?
  I Cor. 12:7, given to every man to *p* withal
  Gal. 5:2, Christ shall *p* you nothing
  I Tim. 4:8, bodily exercise *p* little
  Heb. 4:2, the word preached did not *p*

PROFITABLE Eccl. 10:10, wisdom is *p* to direct
  Acts 20:20, I kept back nothing *p*
  I Tim. 4:8, godliness is *p* to all things
  II Tim. 3:16, scripture is *p* for doctrine
  See Mat. 5:29; II Tim. 4:11; Titus 3:8
  Phile. 11

PROLONG Deut. 30:18, not *p* your days
  Job 6:11, end, that I should *p* life?
  Prov. 10:27, the fear of the Lord *p* days
  Eccl. 8:12, though a sinner's days be *p*
  See Ps. 61:6; Prov. 28:2; Isa. 13:22; 53:10

PROMISE (*n.*) I Ki. 8:56, has not failed one
    word of his *p*
  Ps. 77:8, does his *p* fail
  Lk. 24:49; Acts 1:4, *p* of Father
  Acts 2:39, the *p* is to you and your children
    26:6, for hope of the *p*
  Rom. 4:14, the *p* made of none effect
    20, staggered not at the *p*
    9:4, to whom pertain the *p*
    8; Gal. 4:28, the children of the *p*
  I Tim. 4:8, *p* of the life that now is
  Heb. 6:12, inherit the *p*
    9:15; 10:36, the *p* of eternal inheritance

11:13, died, not having received the *p*

II Pet. 1:4, great and precious *p*

     3:4, where is the *p* of his coming?

     9, not slack concerning his *p*

See Eph. 1:13; 2:12; 6:2; Heb. 4:1; 11:9

PROMISE (*v.*) Num. 14:40, will go to place the
Lord *p*

Deut. 1:11, the Lord bless you, as he has *p*

     9:28, bring to the land which he *p*

     19:8; 27:3, give the land he *p* to give

II Ki. 8:19, he *p* to give him a light

Mk. 14:11, they *p* to give him money

Heb. 10:23; 11:11, he is faithful that *p*

I Jn. 2:25, he has *p* eternal life

See I Ki. 8:24; Neh. 9:15; Ezek. 13:22

PROMOTE Num. 22:17; 24:11; Prov. 4:8

PROMOTION Ps. 75:6; Prov. 3:35

PRONOUNCE Judg. 12:6; Jer. 34:5

PROOF II Cor. 2:9; 8:24; 13:3; Phil. 2:22

PROPER I Chron. 29:3; I Cor. 7:7; Heb. 11:23

PROPHECY I Thess. 5:20, despise not *p*

II Pet. 1:19, sure word of *p*

     21, *p* came not in old time

Rev. 1:3; 22:7, the words of this *p*

See Neh. 6:12; I Tim. 4:14

PROPHESY Num. 11:25, they *p*

II Chron. 18:7, he never *p* good to me

Isa. 30:10, *P* not to us right things

Jer. 5:31, prophets *p* falsely

     14:14; 23:25, prophets *p* lies

     28:9, the prophet which *p* of peace

Ezek. 37:9, *P* to the wind

Amos 3:8, who can but *p*?

     7:13, *p* not again any more

Mic. 2:11, I will *p* of wine

Mk. 14:65; Lk. 22:64, *P* thou Christ

Rom. 12:6, *p* according to the proportion

I Cor. 13:9, we *p* in part

     14:39, covet to *p*

PROPHET Ex. 7:1, Aaron shall be your *p*

Num. 12:6, if there be a *p* among you

Deut. 13:1, if there arise a *p* or dreamer

     18:15; Acts 3:22, the Lord will raise up a *P*

     34:10, there arose not a *p* like Moses

I Sam. 10:12; 19:24, is Saul among the *p*?

I Ki. 13:11, there dwelt an old *p*

     18:22, I only remain a *p*

     22:7, is there not here a *p* besides

II Ki. 5:8, he shall know there is a *p*

I Chron. 16:22; Ps. 105:15, do my *p* no harm

II Chron. 20:20, believe his *p*, ye prosper

Ps. 74:9, there is no more any *p*

Isa. 3:2, the Lord takes away the *p*

Jer. 29:26, mad, and makes himself a *p*

     37:19, where are now your *p*

Ezek. 2:5, there has been a *p* among them

Hos. 9:7, the *p* is a fool

Amos. 7:14, I was no *p* nor *p* son

Zech. 1:5, the *p*, do they live for ever?

Mat. 7:15, beware of false *p*

     10:41, he that receives a *p* in name of a *p*

     23:29, you build the tombs of the *p*

Mk. 6:4; Jn. 4:44, a *p* not without honor

Lk. 1:76, be called the *p* of the Highest

7:16, a great *p* is risen

     28, not a greater *p* than John

     39, if he were a *p*, would have known

     24:19, Jesus, who was a *p* mighty

Jn. 4:19, I perceive you are a *p*

     7:40, of a truth this is the *P*

     52, out of Galilee arises no *p*

Acts 26:27, believest thou the *p*

I Cor. 12:29, are all *p*

Eph. 2:20, built on foundation of *p*

     4:11, he gave some *p*

I Pet. 1:10, of which salvation of *p* enquired

Rev. 22:9, I am of your brethren the *p*

PROPORTION I Ki. 7:36; Rom. 12:6

PROSPER Gen. 24:56, Lord has *p* my way

     39:3, the Lord made all Joseph did to *p*

Num. 14:41, transgress, but it shall not *p*

Deut. 28:29, you shall not *p* in your ways

I Chron. 22:11, *p* thou, and build the house

II Chron. 20:20, believe his prophets, you *p*

     26:5, God made him to *p*

Ezra 5:8, this work *p* in their hands

Neh. 2:20, the God of Heaven will *p* us

Job 9:4, who hardened himself, and *p*

Ps. 1:3, whatsoever he does shall *p*

     37:7, fret not because of him who *p*

     73:12, the ungodly, who *p* in the world

     122:6, they shall *p* that love you

Prov. 28:13, he that covers sins shall not *p*

Eccl. 11:6, knowest not whether shall *p*

Isa. 53:10, pleasure of the Lord shall *p*

     54:17, no weapon against you shall *p*

     55:11, it shall *p* in the thing

Jer. 2:37, you shall not *p* in them

     12:1, wherefore does way of wicked *p*?

     22:30, no man of his seed shall *p*

Ezek. 17:9, 10, shall it *p*?

     15, shall he *p*, shall he escape?

I Cor. 16:2, lay by, as God has *p* them

III Jn. 2, in health, even as your soul *p*

PROSPERITY I Sam. 25:6

Job 15:21, in *p* the destroyer shall come

Ps. 30:6, in my *p*, I shall never be moved

     73:3, when I saw the *p* of the wicked

Prov. 1:32, the *p* of fools shall destroy them

Eccl. 7:14, in day of *p* be joyful

Jer. 22:21, I spoke to you in your *p*

See I Ki. 10:7; Job 36:11; Ps. 35:27; 122:7

PROSPEROUS Gen. 39:2, he was a *p* man

Josh. 1:8, then you shall make your way *p*

Job 8:6, habitation of your righteousness *p*

Zech. 8:12, the seed shall be *p*

See Gen. 24:21; Judg. 18:5; II Chron. 7:11

PROTECTION Deut. 32:38

PROTEST Gen. 43:3; Jer. 11:7; Zech. 3:6

PROUD Job 38:11, your *p* waves be stayed

     40:11, every one that is *p*, and abase him

Ps. 31:23, rewards the *p* doer

     40:4, man that respects not the *p*

     94:2, render a reward to the *p*

     101:5, a *p* heart will not I suffer

     123:4, soul filled with contempt of the *p*

     138:6, the *p*, he knows afar off

Prov. 6:17, the Lord hates a *p* look

15:25, Lord will destroy the house of the *p*

16:5, *p* in heart is abomination

21:4, a *p* heart is sin

Eccl. 7:8, patient better than *p* in spirit

Mal. 3:15, we call the *p* happy

Lk. 1:51, scattered the *p*

I Tim. 6:4, he is *p*, knowing nothing

James 4:6, I Pet. 5:5, God resists the *p*

PROUDLY Ex. 18:11; I Sam. 2:3, Neh. 9:10

PROVE Ex. 15:25, there he *p* them

Judg. 6:39, let me *p* you but this once

I Sam. 17:39, I have not *p* them

II Chron. 9:1, she came to *p* Solomon

Ps. 17:3, you have *p* my heart

81:7, I *p* you at the waters

95:9; Heb. 3:9, when you fathers *p* me

Mal. 3:10, *p* me now herewith

Lk. 14:19, I go to *p* them

II Cor. 8:22, oftentimes *p* diligent

13:5, *p* your own selves

I Thess. 5:21, P all things

PROVERB Deut. 28:37, a *p* and a byword

Ps. 69:11, I became a *p* to them

Eccl. 12:9, set in order many *p*

Ezek. 16:44, every one that uses *p*

Lk. 4:23, will surely say this *p*

Jn. 16:29, speak no *p*

See Num. 21:27; I Sam. 10:12; Prov. 1:6

PROVIDE Gen. 22:8

30:30, when shall I *p* for my own house?

Ps. 78:20, can he *p* flesh

Mat. 10:9, P neither gold nor silver

Lk. 12:33, *p* bags that wax not old

Rom. 12:17; II Cor. 8:21; P things honest

I Tim. 5:8, if any *p* not for his own

Heb. 11:40, *p* some better thing for us

PROVIDENCE Acts 24:2

PROVISION Gen. 42:25, *p* for the way

Ps. 132:15, I will abundantly bless her *p*

Rom. 13:14, make not *p* for the flesh

See Josh. 9:5; I Ki. 4:7; II Ki. 6:23

PROVOCATION Job 17:2; Ezek. 20:28

PROVOKE Ex. 23:21, *p* him not

Num. 14:11, how long will this people *p* me?

Deut. 31:20, *p* me, and break my covenant

Job 12:6, they that *p* God are secure

Ps. 106:7, they *p* him at the sea

29, they *p* him with their inventions

Lk. 11:53, *p* him to speak

Rom. 10:19; 11:11, I will *p* to jealousy

I Cor. 13:5, is not easily *p*

Gal. 5:26, *p* one another

Eph. 6:4, *p* not your children to wrath

Heb. 10:24, to *p* to love and good works

PRUDENCE II Chron. 2:12; Eph. 1:8

PRUDENT Prov. 12:16, *p* man covers

23, a *p* man conceals knowledge

14:15, the *p* man looks well to his going

16:21, wise in heart called *p*

19:14, *p* wife is from the Lord

22:3; 27:12, *p* man foresees evil

Jer. 49:7, is counsel perished from *p*?

Hos. 14:9, who is *p*

Lk. 10:21, have hid things from *p*

See Isa. 52:13; Amos 5:13; Acts 13:7

PRUNE Lev. 25:3; Isa. 2:4; Mic. 4:3

PUBLIC Mat. 1:19; Acts 18:28; 20:20

PUBLISH Deut. 32:3, *p* the name of the Lord

II Sam. 1:20, *p* it not in Askelon

Ps. 68:11, great was company that *p* it

Isa. 52:7; Nah. 1:15, that *p* peace

Mk. 1:45; 5:20, he began to *p* it much

Lk. 8:39, *p* throughout the whole city

See Esther 1:20; 3:14; Jonah 3:7; Mk. 13:10

PUFFED I Cor. 4:6; 5:2; 13:4; Col. 2:18

PUFFETH Ps. 10:5; 12:5; I Cor. 8:1

PULL Lam. 3:11, *p* me in pieces

Amos 9:15, shall no more be *p* up

Zech. 7:11; they *p* away the shoulder

Mat. 7:4; Lk. 6:42, *p* mote out of your eye

Lk. 12:18, will *p* down barns

II Cor. 10:4, to the *p* down of strong holds

Jude 23, *p* them out of the fire

PULPIT Neh. 8:4

PULSE II Sam. 17:28; Dan. 1:12

PUNISH Prov. 17:26, to *p* the just is not good

Isa. 13:11, I will *p* the world for their evil

26:21, Lord comes to *p* inhabitants

Jer. 13:21, what will you say when he *p*?

Acts 26:11, I *p* them in every synagogue

II Thess. 1:9, *p* with everlasting destruction

II Pet. 2:9, unto they day of judgment to be *p*

See Lev. 26:18; Prov. 21:11; 22:3; 27:12

PUNISHMENT Gen. 4:13, my *p* is greater

Lev. 26:41, accept the *p* of their iniquity

I Sam. 28:10, no *p* shall happen to you

Lam. 3:39, a man for the *p* of his sins

4:6, *p* greater than *p* of Sodom

22, the *p* is accomplished

Ezek. 14:10, shall bear *p* of their iniquity

Mat. 25:46, everlasting *p*

Heb. 10:29, of how much sorer *p*

I Pet. 2:14, the *p* of evildoers

PURCHASE Ruth 4:10, *p* to be my wife

Ps. 74:2, your congregation, which you have *p*

Acts 1:18, *p* a field with reward of iniquity

8:20, gift of God *p* by money

20:28, he has *p* with his own blood

Eph. 1:14, redemption of *p* possession

I Tim. 3:13, *p* to themselves a good degree

See Gen. 49:32; Ex. 15:16; Jer. 32:11

PURE Deut. 32:14, the *p* blood of the grape

II Sam. 22:27, with *p* show yourself *p*

Job 4:17, man be more *p* than his maker?

8:6, if you were *p* and upright

11:4, my doctrine is *p*

16:17, my prayer is *p*

25:5, stars are not *p* in his sight

Ps. 12:6, the words of the Lord are *p*

19:8, commandment of the Lord is *p*

Prov. 15:26, words of the *p* are pleasant

20:9, who can say, I am *p*

Mic. 6:11, shall I count them *p*

Zeph. 3:9, I will turn a *p* language

Acts 20:26, *p* from blood of all men

Rom. 14:20, all things indeed are *p*

Phil. 4:8, whatsoever things are *p*

I Tim. 3:9; II Tim 1:3, in a *p* conscience

5:22, keep yourself *p*
Titus 1:15, to the *p* all things are *p*
James 1:27, *P* religion
II Pet. 3:1, stir up your *p* minds
I Jn. 3:3, even as he is *p*
Rev. 22:1, a *p* river of water of life
PURELY Isa. 1:25
PURENESS Job 22:30; II Cor. 6:6
PURER Lam. 4:7; Hab. 1:13
PURGE II Chron. 34:8, when he had *p* the land
Ps. 51:7, *p* me with hyssop
65:3, transgressions, you shall *p* them
Isa. 1:25, and purely *p* away your dross
6:7, your sin is *p*
22:14, this iniquity shall not be *p*
Mal. 3:3, *p* them as gold
Mat. 3:12; Lk. 3:17, *p* his floor
Jn. 15:2, he *p* it, that it may bring forth
I Cor. 5:7, *P* out the old leaven
II Tim. 2:21, if a man *p* himself from these
Heb. 9:14, *p* your conscience
22, all things are *p* with blood
See Prov. 16:6; Heb. 1:3; 10:2; II Pet. 1:9
PURIFY Titus 2:14; James 4:8; I Pet. 1:22
PURITY I Tim. 4:12; 5:2
PURLOINING Titus 2:10
PURPOSE Job 17:11, my *p* are broken off
Prov. 20:18, every *p* established by counsel
Isa. 14:27, Lord has *p*, who shall disannul?
46:11, I have *p* it, I will also do it
Mat. 26:8, to what *p* is this waste?
Acts 11:23, with *p* of heart
Rom. 8:28, the called according to his *p*
9:11, that the *p* of God might stand
Eph. 3:11, eternal *p* in Christ
PURSE Prov. 1:14; Mat. 10:9; Mk. 6:8
PURSUE Deut. 19:6, lest avenger *p*
Job 13:25, will you *p* the stubble?
30:15, terrors *p* my soul
Ps. 34:14, seek peace, and *p* it
Prov. 11:19, he that *p* evil it to his depth
13:21, evil *p* sinners
28:1, shall flee when none *p*
Jer. 48:2, the sword shall *p* thee
See Ex. 15:9; II Sam. 24:13, I Ki. 18:27
PUSH Ex. 21:29; I Ki. 22:11, Job 30:12
PUT Ex. 23:1, *p* not your hand
Lev. 26:8, *p* ten thousand to flight
Judg. 12:3, I *p* my life in my hands
I Ki. 9:3; 14:21, to *p* my name there
Eccl. 10:10, must he *p* to more strength
Isa. 43:26, *P* me in remembrance
Mat. 19:6; Mk. 10:9, let not man *p* asunder
Mk. 10:16, *p* his hands on them
Phile. 18, *p* his hands on them
II Pet. 1:14, I must *p* off this my tabernacle
PUTRIFYING Isa. 1:6

Q

QUAKE Joel 2:10; Nah. 1:5; Mat. 27:51
QUANTITY Isa. 22:24
QUARREL Lev. 26:25; II Ki. 5:7; Mk. 6:19
QUARTER Ex. 13:7; Mk. 1:45; Rev. 20:8

QUEEN I Ki. 10:1; 15:13; Ps. 45:9
Isa. 49:23, *q* their nursing mothers
Mat. 12:42, *q* of the south rise in
QUENCH Num. 11:2, the fire was *q*
II Sam. 21:17, *q* not the light of Israel
Song of Sol. 8:7, many waters cannot *q* love
Isa. 34:10, shall not be *q* night nor day
42:3; Mat. 12:20, smoking flax shall he not *q*
66:24, neither shall their fire be *q*
Mk. 9:43, 48, fire that never shall be *q*
Eph. 6:16, able to *q* fiery darts
I Thess. 5:19, *Q* not the Spirit
Heb. 11:34, *Q* violence of fire
QUESTION II Chron. 9:1, to prove him with *q*
Mat. 22:46, neither durst ask him any more *q*
Mk. 9:16, what *q* ye with them?
11:29, I will ask you one *q*
I Cor. 10:25, asking no *q* for conscience sake
I Tim. 1:4, which minister *q* rather
6:4, doting about *q*
QUICK Num. 16:30; Ps. 55:15, go down *q*
Isa. 11:3, of *q* understanding
Acts 10:42; I Pet. 4:5, Judge of *q* and dead
Heb. 4:12, the word of God is *q* and powerful
See Lev. 13:10, 24; Ps. 124:3
QUICKEN Ps. 71:20, you shall *q* me again
80:18, *q* us, and we will call
119:25, *q* me according to your word
50, your word has *q* me
Rom. 8:11, shall also *q* your bodies
I Cor. 15:36, that which you sow in not *q*
Eph. 2:1, you has he *q*
5; Col. 2:13, *q* us together with Christ
I Pet. 3:18, death in flesh, but *q* by Spirit
See Jn. 5:21; 6:63; Rom. 4:17; I Tim. 6:13
QUICKLY Num. 16:46, go *q* to congregation
Deut. 9:12, have turned aside *q*
Josh. 10:6, come *q* and save us
Eccl. 4:12, threefold cord not *q* broken
Mat. 5:25, agree with our adversary *q*
Lk. 14:21, go *q* into streets and lanes
Jn. 13:27, that you do, do *q*
Rev. 2:5, 16, repent, else I will come *q*
3:11; 22:7, 12, I come *q*
22:20, surely I come *q*
See Gen. 18:6; 27:20; Lk. 16:6; Acts 22:18
QUIET Ps. 131:2, I have *q* myself as a child
Eccl. 9:17, words of wise men are heard in *q*
Isa. 7:4, be *q*, fear not
14:7, the earth is at rest, and is *q*
32:18, in *q* resting places
33:20, a *q* habitation
Jer. 49:23, sorrow on the sea, it cannot be *q*
Ezek. 16:42, I will be *q*
Acts 19:36, you ought to be *q*
I Thess. 4:11, study to be *q*
I Tim. 2:2, a *q* and a peaceful life
I Pet. 3:4, ornament of a meek and a *q* spirit
See II Ki. 11:20; II Chron. 14:1; Job 3:13
QUIETLY II Sam. 3:27; Lam. 3:26
QUIETNESS Job 34:29, when he gives *q*
Prov. 17:1, better a dry morsel and *q*
Eccl. 4:6, better handful with *q* than both

Isa. 30:15, in *q* and confidence strength
32:17, effect of righteousness *q*
See Judg. 8:28; I Chron. 22:9; II Thess. 3:12
QUIT Ex. 21:19; Josh. 2:20; I Sam. 4:9
QUITE Gen. 31:15; Job 6:13; Hab. 3:9
QUIVER Ps. 127:5; Jer. 5:16; Lam. 3:13

R

RACE Ps. 19:5; Eccl. 9:11; I Cor. 9:24
RAGE II Ki. 5:12, turned away in a *r*
Ps. 2:1; Acts 4:25, why do the heathen *r*?
Prov. 14:16, the fool *r*, and is confident
See Prov. 6:34; 29:9; Dan. 3:13; Hos. 7:16
RAGGED Isa. 2:21
RAGING Ps. 89:9; Prov. 20:1; Lk. 8:24
RAGS Prov. 23:21; Isa. 64:6; Jer. 38:11
RAIMENT Gen. 28:20, if the Lord give me *r*
Deut. 8:4, your *r* waxed not old
24:13, that he may sleep in his *r*
17, nor take a widow's *r* to pledge
Job. 27:16, though he prepare *r* as the clay
Isa. 63:3, I will stain all my *r*
Zech. 3:4, I will clothe you with *r*
Mat. 6:25; Lk. 12:23, the body more than *r*
28, why take ye thought for *r*?
11:8; Lk. 7:25, man clothed in soft *r*
Mk. 9:3; Lk. 9:29, his *r* was white as light
I Tim. 6:8, food and *r* let us be content
James 2:2, poor man in vile *r*
Rev. 3:18, buy white *r*
RAIN (*n.*) Deut. 11:11, drinks water of the *r* of Heaven
11:14; 28:12, *r* in due season
32:2, my doctrine shall drop as the *r*
II Sam. 23:4, clear shining after *r*
I Ki. 18:41, sound of abundance of *r*
Ezra 10:13, a time of much *r*
Job 5:10, who gives *r* on Earth
37:6, to small *r* and to great *r*
38:28, has the *r* a father?
Ps. 72:6, like *r* on mown grass
Prov. 25:14, like clouds and wind without *r*
23, north wind drives away *r*
26:1, as *r* in harvest
Eccl. 11:3, if clouds be full of *r*
12:2, nor clouds return after *r*
Song of Sol. 2:11, the *r* is over and gone
Isa. 4:6, covert from storm and *r*
55:10, as the *r* comes down
Ezek. 38:22, I will *r* an overflowing *r*
Hos. 6:3, he shall come unto us as the *r*
Mat. 5:45, he sends *r* on the just
7:25, the *r* descends, and floods came
RAIN (*v.*) Ex. 16:4, *r* bread from Heaven
Job 20:23, God shall *r* his fury on him
Ps. 11:6, upon the wicked he shall *r* snares
78:24, 27, and *r* down manna
Ezek. 22:24, you are the land not *r* upon
Hos. 10:12, till he come and *r* righteousness
RAINY Prov. 27:15
RAISE Judg. 2:16, 18, the Lord *r* up judges
I Sam. 2:8; Ps. 113:7, he *r* poor out of dust
Ps. 145:14, he *r* those that he bowed down

Isa. 45:13, I have *r* him in righteousness
Hos. 6:2, in third day he will *r* us up
Mat. 10:8; 11:5; Lk. 7:22, *r* the dead
16:21; 17:23; Lk. 9:22, be *r* the third day
Jn. 2:19, in three days I will *r* it up
6:39, 40, 44, 54, I will *r* him up at last day
Acts 3:22, will *r* up a Prophet
26:8, incredible that God should *r* dead?
Gal. 1:1, Eph. 1:20, whom God has *r* up
Rom. 4:25, *r* again for our justification
6:4, like as Christ was *r* from the dead
8:11, Spirit of him that *r* up Jesus
I Cor. 6:14, will also *r* up us by his power
15:15, *r* up Christ, whom he *r* not up
16, then is not Christ *r*
35, how are the dead *r*?
43, it is *r* in glory, it is *r* in power
II Cor. 1:9, trust in God which *r* the dead
4:14, he shall *r* up us also
Eph. 2:6, and has *r* us up together
James 5:15, and the Lord shall *r* him up
See Lk. 20:37; Jn. 5:21; II Tim. 2:8
RAN Ex. 9:23; Num. 16:47; Jer. 23:21
RANG I Sam. 4:5; I Ki. 1:45
RANKS I Ki. 7:4; Joel 2:7; Mk. 6:40
RANSOM Ex. 21:30, give for the *r* of his life
30:12, every man a *r* for his soul
Job 33:24, I have found a *r*
36:18, a great *r* cannot deliver
Ps. 49:7, nor give a *r* for him
Prov. 13:8, the *r* of a man's life are his riches
Isa. 35:10, the *r* of the Lord shall return
43:3, I gave Egypt for your *r*
Hos. 13:14, I will *r* them from the grave
Mat. 20:28; Mk. 10:45, to give his life as *r*
I Tim. 2:6, gave himself a *r* for all
See Prov. 6:35; Isa. 51:10; Jer. 31:11
RARE Dan. 2:11
RASE Ps. 137:7
RASH Eccl. 5:2; Acts 19:36
RATHER Job 7:15; Jer. 8:3, death *r* than life
Ps. 84:10, *r* be a doorkeeper
Mat. 10:6, go *r* to lost sheep
28, *r* fear him that is able
25:9, go *r* to them that sell
Mk. 5:26, but *r* grew worse
Lk. 18:14, justified *r* than the other
Jn. 3:19, loved darkness *r* than light
Acts 5:29, obey God *r* than men
Rom. 8:34, that died, yea *r*, that is risen
12:19, *r* give place to wrath
I Cor. 6:7, why do you not *r* take wrong?
Heb. 11:25, choosing *r* to suffer
12:13, let it *r* be healed
See Josh. 22:24; II Ki. 5:13; Phil. 1:12
RAVENING Ps. 22:13; Mat. 7:15
RAVENOUS Isa. 35:9; 46:11; Ezek. 39:4
REACH Gen. 11:4; Jn. 20:27; II Cor. 10:13
READ Isa. 34:16, seek out of book of the Lord, and *r*
Mat. 12:3; 19:4; 21:16, 22:31, Mk. 2:25
Lk. 4:16, Jesus stood up to *r*
6:3, have ye not *r*
II Cor. 3:2, epistle, known and *r* of all men

I Tim. 4:13, give attendance to *r*
See Acts 8:28; II Cor. 3:14; Rev. 1:3
READINESS Acts 17:11; II Cor. 8:11; 10:6
READY Num. 32:17, we will go *r* armed
 Deut. 26:5, a Syrian *r* to perish
 II Sam. 18:22, wherefore run, no tidings *r*
 Neh. 9:17, you are a God *r* to pardon
 Job 12:5, *r* to slip with his feet
  17:1, the graves are *r* for me
  29:13, blessing of him *r* to perish
 Ps. 38:17, I am *r* to halt
 Ps. 86:5, good, and *r* to forgive
  88:15, *r* to die from my youth
 Prov. 24:11, deliver those *r* to be slain
  31:6, give strong drink to him *r* to perish
 Eccl. 5:1, be more *r* to hear
 Isa. 27:13, shall come that were *r* to perish
  32:4, stammerers *r* to speak plainly
  38:20, the Lord was *r* to save me
 Dan. 3:15, if you be *r* to fall down
 Mat. 22:4; Lk. 14:17, all things are *r*
  8, the wedding is *r*
  24:44; Lk. 12:40, be ye also *r*
  25:10, they that were *r* went in
 Mk. 14:38, the spirit is *r*
 Lk. 22:33, I am *r* to go with you
 Jn. 7:6, your time is alway *r*
 Acts 21:13, *r* not be bound only
 Rom. 1:15, I am *r* to preach at Rome
 II Cor. 8:19, declaration of your *r* mind
  9:2, Achaia was *r* a year ago
 I Tim. 6:18, *r* to distribute
 II Tim. 4:6, *r* to be offered
 Titus 3:1, *r* to every good work
 I Pet. 1:5, *r* to be revealed
  3:15, *r* always to give an answer
  5:2, but of a *r* mind
 Rev. 3:2, things that are *r* to die
REAP Lev. 25:11, in jubilee neither sow nor *r*
 Jer. 12:13, sown wheat, but shall *r* thorns
 Hos. 8:7, shall *r* the whirlwind
  10:12, sow in righteousness, *r* in mercy
 Mic. 6:15, shall sow, but not *r*
 Mat. 25:26; Lk. 19:21, *r* where I sowed not
 Lk. 12:24, they sow not, neither *r*
 Jn. 4:38, *r* whereon you bestowed no labor
 I Cor. 9:11, if you shall *r* your carnal things
 II Cor. 9:6, shall *r* sparingly
 Gal. 6:7, that shall he also *r*
 James 5:4, cries of them which *r*
REASON (*n.*) Job 32:11, I gave ear to your *r*
 Prov. 26:16, seven men that can render a *r*
 Eccl. 7:25, to search out the *r* of things
 Isa. 41:21, bring forth your strong *r*
 I Pet. 3:15, a *r* of the hope that is in you
 See I Ki. 9:15; Dan. 4:36; Acts 6:2
REASON (*v.*) Job 9:14, choose words to *r*
  13:3, I desire to *r* with God
  15:3, should be *r* with unprofitable talk?
 Isa. 1:18, let us *r* together
 Lk. 5:22, what *r* ye in your hearts
  20:5, they *r* among themselves
  24:15, while they *r* Jesus drew near
 Acts 24:25, as he *r* of righteousness

See I Sam. 12:7; Mk. 2:6; 12:28; Acts 28:29
REASONABLE Rom. 12:1
REBEL Num. 14:9, *r* not against the Lord
 Josh. 1:18, whosoever does *r*
 Neh. 2:19, will ye *r* against the king?
 Job 24:13, that *r* against the light
 Ps. 105:28, they *r* not against his word
 Isa. 1:2, have nourished children, and they *r*
  63:10, they *r*, and vexed his holy Spirit
 Dan. 9:9, though we have *r* against him
 See I Sam. 12:14; Ezek. 2:3; Hos. 7:14
REBELLION Job 34:37, adds *r* to his sin
 Prov. 17:11, and evil man seeks *r*
 Jer. 28:16, you have taught *r*
 See Deut. 31:27; Ezra 4:19; Neh. 9:17
REBELLIOUS Deut. 21:18, 20, *r* son
 I Sam. 20:30, son of perverse *r* woman
 Ps. 66:7, let not the *r* exalt themselves
  68:6, the *r* dwell in a dry land
 Isa. 1:23, *r*, companions of thieves
 Jer. 5:23, this people has a *r* heart
 See Ezek. 2:3; 3:9; 12:2; 17:12; 24:3
REBELS Num. 17:10; 20:10; Ezek. 20:38
REBUKE (*n.*) Ps. 80:16, perish at *r* of your
  countenance
  104:7, at your *r* they fled
 Prov. 13:8, the poor hear not *r*
  27:5, open *r* is better than secret love
 Eccl. 7:5, better to hear *r* of wise
 Isa. 30:17, thousand flee at *r* of one
  37:3, this is a day of *r*
 Jer. 15:15, for your sake I suffered *r*
 Phil. 2:15, without *r*
 See Deut. 28:20; Isa. 25:8; 50:2
REBUKE (*v.*) Ps. 6:1; 38:1, *r* me not in anger
 Prov. 28:23, he that *r* a man shall find favor
 Isa. 2:4; Mic. 4:3, he shall *r* many nations
 Zech. 3:2; Jude 9, the Lord *r* you
 Mal. 3:11, *r* the devourer for your sakes
 Mal. 8:26; Lk. 8:24, he *r* the wind
  16:22; Mk. 8:32, Peter began to *r* him
 Lk. 4:39, he *r* the fever
  17:3, if your brother trespass, *r* him
  19:39, Master, *r* your disciples
 I Tim. 5:1, *R* not an elder
  20, them that sin, *r* before all
 II Tim. 4:2, *r*, exhort, with longsuffering
 Titus 1:13; 2:15, *r* them sharply
 Heb. 12:5, nor faint when you are *r*
RECALL Lam. 3:21
RECEIPT Mat. 9:9; Mk. 2:14; Lk. 5:27
RECEIVE II Ki. 5:26, a time to *r* money?
 Job 4:12, my ear *r* a little
  22:22, *r* the law from his mouth
 Ps. 6:9, the Lord will *r* my prayer
  49:15, he shall *r* me
  68:18, have *r* gifts for men
  73:24, afterwards *r* me to glory
 Prov. 2:1, if you will *r* my words
 Isa. 40:2, she has *r* double
 Jer. 2:30, your children *r* no correction
 Hos. 10:6, Ephraim shall *r* shame
  14:2, *r* us graciously
 Mat. 11:5, the blind *r* their sight

14, if you will r it, this is Elias
18:5, whoso shall r one such little child
19:12, he that is able to r it, let him r it
21:22, ask, believing, you shall r
Mk. 15:23, but he r it not
16:19; Acts 1:9, he was r up into Heaven
Lk. 16:9, r you into everlasting habitations
Lk. 18:42; Acts 22:13, R your sight
Jn. 1:11, his own r him not
12, to as many as r him
5:43, in his own name, him you will r
44, which r honor one of another
16:24, ask, and you shall r
20:22, R ye the Holy Ghost
Acts 7:59, r my spirit
8:17, they r the Holy Spirit
10:43, shall r remission of sins
19:2, have you r the Holy Ghost
20:24, which I have r of the Lord
Rom. 5:11, by whom we have r atonement
14:3, for God has r him
I Cor. 3:8, every man shall r his own reward
11:23, I r of the Lord what I delivered
II Cor. 4:1, as we have r mercy, we faint not
7:2, R us; we have wronged no man
Phil. 2:29, r him in the Lord
4:15, as concerning giving and r
Col. 2:6, as your have r Christ
I Tim. 3:16, r up into glory
4:4, if it be r with thanksgiving
1 Jn. 3:22, whatsoever we ask, we r
RECKON Ps. 40:5, your thoughts cannot be r up
Mat. 18:24, when he had begun to r
Rom. 4:4, reward is not r of grace
6:11, r yourselves dead to sin
8:18, I r the sufferings of this present time
See II Ki. 22:7; Isa. 38:13; Lk. 22:37
RECOMMENDED Acts 14:26; 15:40
RECOMPENCE Deut. 32:35, belongs r
Job 15:31, vanity shall be his r
Isa. 35:4, God will come with a r
Hos. 9:7, days of r come
Joel 3:4, will you render me a r?
Lk. 14:12, and a r be made thee
II Cor. 6:13, for a r, be ye also enlarged
Heb. 2:2; 10:35; 11:26, just r of reward
See Prov. 12:14, Isa. 34:8; Jer. 51:56
RECOMPENSE Num. 5:7, r his trespass
Ruth 2:12, the Lord r your work
II Sam. 19:36, why should the king r me
Job 34:33, he will r it
Prov. 20:22, say not, I will r evil
Isa. 65:6, will r, even r into their bosom
Jer. 25:14, will r according to deeds
Lk. 14:14, for they cannot r you
Rom. 11:35, it shall be r unto him again
12:17, R to no man evil for evil
See II Chron. 6:23; Jer. 32:18; Heb. 10:30
RECONCILE Ezek. 45:20, ye r the house
Mat. 5:24, first be r to your brother
Rom. 5:10, if when enemies we were r
Eph. 2:16, that he might r both
See Lev. 16:20; Rom. 11:15; II Cor. 5:19

RECORD Ex. 20:24, where I r my name
Deut. 30:19; 31:28, I call Heaven to r
Job 16:19, my r is on high
Jn. 8:13, you bear r of yourself
Rom. 10:2, I bear them r
Phil. 1:8, God is my r how greatly I long
I Jn. 5:7, three that bear r
10, be believeth not the r
11, this is the r, that God has given
III Jn. 12, we bear r, and our r is true
RECOUNT Nah. 2:5, r his worthies
RECOVER II Ki. 5:3, prophet would r him
Ps. 39:13, that I may r strength
Isa. 11:11, to r the remnant of his people
Hos. 2:9, and I will r my wool and flax
Mk. 16:18, lay hands on sick, they shall r
Lk. 4:18, preach r of sight to blind
See Isa. 38:16; Jer. 8:22; 41:16; II Tim. 2:26
RED Gen. 25:30, r pottage
II Ki. 3:22, water r as blood
Ps. 75:8, the wine is r, it is full of mixture
Prov. 23:31, look not on wine when it is r
Isa. 1:18, though your sins be r like crimson
27:2, a vineyard of r wine
63:2, r in your apparel
Mat. 16:2, fair weather, for the sky is r
See Lev. 13:19; Num. 19:2; Rev. 6:4
REDEEM Gen. 48:16, angel which r me
Ex. 15:13, whom you have r
Lev. 27:28, no devoted thing shall be r
II Sam. 4:9, the Lord has r my soul
Neh. 5:5, nor is it in our power to r them
8, after our ability have r Jews
Job 5:20, in famine he shall r you
6:23, to r me from hand of mighty
Ps. 25:22, r Israel out of all his troubles
34:22, the Lord r the soul of his servants
44:26, r us for your mercies' sake
49:7, none can r his brother
15, God will r my soul from the grave
72:14, he shall r their soul from deceit
107:2, let the r of the Lord say so
130:8, he shall r Israel
Isa. 1:27, Zion shall be r with judgment
44:22, return, for I have r you
50:2, hand shortened that it cannot r?
51:11, the r of the Lord shall return
52:3, r without money
63:4, the year of my r is come
Hos. 13:14, I will r them from death
Lk. 1:68, has visited and r his people
24:21, he who should have r Israel
Gal. 3:13, r us from the curse of the law
4:5, r them that were under the law
Titus 2:14, he might r us from all iniquity
I Pet. 1:18, not r with corruptible things
Rev. 5:9, you have r us by your blood
See Num. 18:15; II Sam. 7:23; Eph. 5:16
REDEEMER Job 19:25, I know my r lives
Ps. 19:14, O Lord, my strength, and my r
78:35, God was their r
Prov. 23:11, their r is mighty
Isa. 47:4, as for our r, the Lord of hosts
49:26; 60:16, know that I am your R

59:20, the *R* shall come to Zion
63:16, you are our *r*
See Isa. 41:14; 44:6; 48:17; 54:5; Jer. 50:34
REDEMPTION Ps. 49:8, *r* of their soul is precious
    111:9, he sent *r* to his people
    130:7, plenteous *r*
Jer. 32:7, the right of *r* is yours
Lk. 2:38, that looks for *r* in Jerusalem
    21:28, your *r* draws near
Rom. 8:23, the *r* of our body
Eph. 4:30, sealed unto the day of *r*
REDOUND II Cor. 4:15, grace might *r*
REFORMATION Heb. 9:10
REFORMED Lev. 26:23, it you will not be *r*
REFRAIN Job 7:11, I will not *r* my mouth
    29:9, princes *r* talking
Ps. 40:9, I have not *r* my lips
    119:101, *r* my feet from every evil way
Prov. 1:15, *r* your foot from their path
    10:19, he that *r* his lips is wise
Acts 5:38, *R* from these men
REFRESH Ex. 31:17, he rested, and was *r*
Job 32:20, I will speak that I may be *r*
Prov. 25:13, he *r* the soul of his masters
Acts 3:19, times of *r* shall come
I Cor. 16:18, they *r* my spirit
REFUSE (*n.*) I Sam. 15:9; Lam. 3:45
REFUSE (*v.*) Num. 22:13, the Lord *r* to give me leave
I Sam. 16:7, look not on him, I have *r* him
Job. 6:7, things my soul *r* to touch
Ps. 77:2, my soul *r* to be comforted
    78:10, they *r* to walk in his law
    118:22, the stone which the builders *r*
Prov. 1:24, I have called, and you *r*
    8:33, be wise, and *r* it not
    13:18, shame to him that *r* instruction
    15:32, he that *r* instruction despises his soul
    21:25, his hands *r* to labor
Isa. 7:15, 16, may know to *r* the evil
Jer. 8:5, they *r* to return
    15:18, my wound *r* to be healed
    25:28, if they *r* to take the cup
    38:21, if you *r* to go forth
Zech. 7:11, they *r* to hearken
Acts 7:35, this Moses whom they *r*
I Tim. 4:4, nothing to be *r*
    7, *r* profane and old wives' fables
    5:11, the younger widows *r*
Heb. 11:24, Moses *r* to be called
    12:25, *r* not him that speaks
REGARD Gen. 45:20, *r* not your stuff
Ex. 5:9, let them not *r* vain words
Deut. 10:17, that *r* not persons
I Ki. 18:29, neither voice, nor any that *r*
Job 4:20, they perish without any *r* it
Job 34:19, not *r* rich more than poor
    39:7, neither *r* crying of the driver
Ps. 28:5, they *r* not works of the Lord
    66:18, if I *r* iniquity in my heart
    102:17, he will *r* the prayer of the destitute
    106:44, he *r* their affliction

Prov. 1:24, and no man *r*
    5:2, that you may *r* discretion
    6:35, he will not *r* any ransom
    12:10, *r* the life of his beast
Eccl. 11:4, he that *r* the clouds
Lam. 4:16, the Lord will not more *r* them
Dan. 11:37, *r* God of his fathers, *r* any god
Mal. 1:9, will he *r* your persons?
Mk. 12:14, *r* not the person of men
Lk. 18:2, neither *r* man
Rom. 14:6, he that *r* the day, *r* it to the Lord
REGISTER Ezra 2:62; Neh. 7:5, 64
REHEARSE Judg. 5:11, *r* the righteous acts
Acts 14:27, they *r* all God had done
See Ex. 17:14; I Sam. 8:21; 17:31; Acts 11:4
REIGN Gen. 37:8, shall you indeed *r* over us?
Ex. 15:18; Ps. 146:10, the Lord shall *r* forever
Lev. 26:17, they that hate you shall *r* over you
Deut. 15:6, you shall *r* over many nations
Judg. 9:8, the trees said, *R* thou over us
I Sam. 11:12, shall Saul *r* over us?
    12:12, nay, but a king shall *r* over us
II Sam. 16:8, in whose stead you have *r*
Job 34:30, that the hypocrite *r* not
Ps. 47:8, God *r* over the heathen
    93:1; 96:10; 97:1; 99:1, the Lord *r*
Prov. 8:15, by me kings *r*
    30:22, for a servant when he *r*
Eccl. 4:14, out of prison he comes to *r*
Isa. 32:1, a king shall *r* in righteousness
    52:7, that say unto Zion, Thy God *r*!
Jer. 23:5, a king shall *r* and prosper
Mic. 4:7, the Lord shall *r* over them
Lk. 19:14, not have this man to *r* over us
    27, that would not I should *r* over them
Rom. 5:14, death *r* from Adam to Moses
    17, death *r* by one
    21, as sin has *r*, so might grace *r*
    6:12, let not sin *r* in your bodies
I Cor. 4:8, you have *r* as kings without us
    15:25, for he must *r*
II Tim. 2:12, we also shall *r* with him
Rev. 5:10, we also shall *r* on the earth
    11:15, he shall *r* forever and ever
    19:6, the Lord God omnipotent *r*
REINS Job 16:13, he cleaves my *r* asunder
    19:27, though my *r* be consumed
Ps. 7:9, God tries the *r*
    16:7, my *r* instruct me
    26:2, examine me, try my *r*
    73:21, thus I was pricked in my *r*
    139:13, you have possessed my *r*
Prov. 23:16, my *r* shall rejoice
Isa. 11:5, faithfulness the girdle of his *r*
Rev. 2:23, I am he who searches the *r*
REJECT I Sam. 8:7, they have not *r* you
    10:19, you have *r* God who saved you
    15:23, you have *r* the word of the Lord
    16:1, I have *r* him from being king
Isa. 53:3, despised and *r* of men
Jer. 2:37, the Lord has *r* your confidence
    7:29, the Lord has *r* the generation
    8:9, they have *r* the word of the Lord
    14:19, have you utterly *r* Judah?

Mk. 7:9, full well you *r* the commandment
Lk. 7:30, the lawyers *r* the counsel of God
    17:25, must first be *r* of this generation
    20:17, the stone which the builders *r*
Titus 3:10, after admonition *r*
REJOICE Deut. 16:14, *r* in your feast
    26:11, you shall *r* in every good thing
    28:63; 30:9, the Lord will *r* over you
    30:9, as he *r* over your fathers
I Sam. 2:1, because I *r* in your salvation
II Chron. 6:41, let your saints *r* in goodness
Job 21:12, they *r* at sound of the organ
    31:25, if I *r* because my wealth was great
    39:21, the horse *r* in his strength
Ps. 2:11, *r* with trembling
    5:11, let all that trust in you *r*
    19:5, *r* as a strong man to run a race
Ps. 33:21, our heart shall *r* in him
    35:15, in my adversity they *r*
    26, let them be ashamed that *r* at my hurt
    38:16, hear me, lest they should *r* over me
    51:8, the bones you have broken may *r*
    58:10, the righteous shall *r* when he sees
    63:7, in the shadow of your wings will I *r*
    68:3, let the righteous *r*, yea, exceedingly *r*
    85:6, that your people may *r*, yea in thee
    89:16, in your name shall they *r* all day
    97:1, the Lord reigns, let the earth *r*
    104:31, the Lord shall *r* in his works
    107:42, the righteous shall see it and *r*
    109:28, let your servant *r*
    149:2, let Israel *r* in him that made him
Prov. 2:14, who *r* to do evil
    5:18, *r* with the wife of your youth
    23:15, if your heart be wise, my heart
        shall *r*
    25, she that bore you shall *r*
    24:17, *R* not when your enemy falls
    31:25, she shall *r* in time to come
Eccl. 2:10, my heart *r* in all my labor
    3:12, for a man to *r* and do good
    22; 5:19, that a man should *r* in his works
    11:9, *R*, O young man, in your youth
Isa. 9:3, as men *r* when they divide the spoil
    24:8, noise of them that *r* ends
    29:19, poor among men shall *r*
    62:5, as the bridegroom *r* over the bride
    64:5, him that *r* and works righteousness
    65:13, my servants shall *r*, but you
    66:14, when you see this, your heart shall *r*
Jer. 11:15, when you do evil, then you *r*
    32:41, I will *r* over them to do them good
    51:39, that they may *r* and sleep
Ezek. 7:12, let not buyer *r*
Amos 6:13, which *r* in a thing of nought
Mic. 7:8, *R* not against me
Hab. 3:18, yet I will *r* in the Lord
Mat. 18:13, he *r* more of that sheep
Lk. 1:14, many shall *r* at his birth
    6:23, *R* ye in that day, and leap for joy
    10:20, in this *r* not, but rather *r* because
    21, in that hour Jesus *r* in spirit
Jn. 5:35, willing for a season to *r* in his light
    8:56, Abraham *r* to see my day

    14:28, if you loved me, you would *r*
    16:20, you shall weep, but the world shall *r*
    22, I will see you again, your heart shall *r*
Rom. 5:2, *r* in hope
I Cor. 7:30, they that *r* as though they *r* not
    13:6, *R* not in iniquity, but *r* in the truth
Phil. 1:18, I therein do *r*, yea, and will *r*
    2:16, that I may *r* in the day of Christ
    3:1, finally, brethren *r* in the Lord
    4:4, *R* in the Lord alway, and again I say, *R*
I Thess. 5:16, *R* evermore
James 1:9, let the brother of low degree *r*
    2:13, mercy *r* against judgment
I Pet. 1:8, *r* with joy unspeakable
REJOICING Job 8:21, till he fill your lips with *r*
Ps. 107:22, declare his works with *r*
    118:15, voice of *r* in tabernacles
Isa. 65:18, I create Jerusalem a *r*
Jer. 15:16, your word was the *r* of my heart
Zeph. 2:15, this is the *r* city
Acts 5:41, *r* that they were counted worthy
Rom. 12:12, *R* in hope
II Cor. 6:10, as sorrowful, yet always *r*
I Thess. 2:19, what is our crown of *r*?
RELEASE Esther. 2:18; Mat. 27:17
RELIEVE Lev. 25:35, then you shall *r* him
Ps. 146:9, he *r* the fatherless and widow
Isa. 1:17, *r* the oppressed
Lam. 1:16, comforter that should *r* my soul
See Acts 11:29, I Tim. 5:10, 16
RELIGION Acts 26:5; James 1:26, 27
RELIGIOUS Acts 13:43; James 1:26
RELY II Chron. 13:18; 16:7, 8
REMAIN Gen. 8:22, while earth *r*
    14:10, they that *r* fled to the mountain
Ex. 12:10, let nothing *r* until the morning
Josh. 13:1, there *r* yet much land
I Ki. 18:22, I, even I only, *r* a prophet
Job 21:32, yet shall he *r* in the tomb
Prov. 2:21, the perfect shall *r* in the land
Eccl. 2:9, my wisdom *r* with me
Jer. 17:25, this city shall *r* forever
Jer. 37:10, there *r* but wounded men
Lam. 2:22, in day of anger none *r*
Mat. 11:23, would have *r* until this day
Jn. 6:12, gather up the fragments that *r*
    9:41, you say, We see, therefore your sin *r*
Acts 5:4, whiles it *r*, was it not your own?
I Cor. 15:6, greater part *r* to this present
I Thess. 4:15, *r* unto coming of the Lord
Heb. 4:9, there *r* a rest to the people of God
    10:26, there *r* no more sacrifice for sins
Rev. 3:2, things which *r* that are ready to die
REMEDY II Chron. 36:16; Prov. 6:15; 29:1
REMEMBER Gen. 40:23, did not butler *r*
    41:9, I do *r* my faults this day
Ex. 13:3, *R* this day you came out of Egypt
    20:8, *R* the sabbath day
Num. 15:39, *r* all the commandments
Deut. 5:15; 24:18, 22 *r* you were a servant
    8:2, *r* all the way the Lord led you
    32:7, *R* the days of old
I Chron. 16:12, *R* his marvelous works
Neh. 13:14, *R* me, O God, concerning this

Job 7:7, O *r* my life is wind
    11:16, *r* it as waters that pass away
    14:13, appoint me a set time, and *r* me
    24:20, the sinner shall be no more *r*
Ps. 9:12, when he makes inquisition he *r*
    20:7, we will *r* the name of the Lord
    25:6, *R* your mercies, have been ever of old
    7, *R* not sins of my youth, *r* me
    63:6, when I *r* you upon my bed
    78:39, he *r* that they were but flesh
    79:8, *r* not against us former iniquities
    89:47, *R* how short my time is
    105:8, he has *r* his covenant forever
    119:55, I have *r* your name in the night
    136:23, who *r* us in our low estate
    137:1, we wept, when we *r* Zion
Prov. 31:7, drink, and *r* his misery no more
Eccl. 11:8, let him *r* the days of darkness
    12:1, *R* now your Creator
Song of Sol. 1:4, we will *r* your love
Isa. 23:16, sing many songs, that you be *r*
    43:18, 46:9, *R* you not the former things
    57:11, you have not *r* me
    65:17, the former heavens shall not be *r*
Jer. 31:20, I do earnestly *r* him still
    51:50, you have escaped *r* the Lord
Lam. 1:9, she *r* not her last end
Ezek. 16:61, then shall you *r* your ways
Amos 1:9, and *r* not the brotherly covenant
Hab. 3:2, in wrath *r* mercy
Zech. 10:9, they shall *r* me in far countries
Mat. 26:75, Peter *r* the word of Jesus
Lk. 16:25, son *r* that you in your lifetime
    17:23, *R* Lot's wife
    23:42, Lord, *r* me when you come
Jn. 2:22, when he was risen, they *r*
    15:20, *R* the word that I said unto you
Acts 11:16, then *r* I the word of the Lord
    20:35, *r* the words of the Lord Jesus
Gal. 2:10, that we should *r* the poor
Col. 4:18, *R* my bonds
Heb. 13:3, *R* them that are in bonds
    7, *R* them that have the rule over you
REMEMBRANCE II Sam. 18:18, no son to keep
    my name in *r*
I Ki. 17:18, are you come to call my sin to *r*
Job 18:17, his *r* shall perish
Ps. 6:5, in death there is no *r* of you
    30:4; 97:12, give thanks as *r* of his holiness
    77:6, I call to *r* my song in the night
    112:6, the righteous shall be in everlasting *r*
Eccl. 1:11, there is no *r* of former things
    2:16, no *r* of wise more than the fool
Isa. 43:26, put me in *r*
    57:8, behind doors have you set up your *r*
Lam. 3:20, my soul has them still in *r*
Ezek. 23:19, calling to *r* days of youth
Mal. 3:16, a book of *r*
Lk. 22:19; I Cor. 11:24, this do in *r* of me
Jn. 14:26, bring all things to your *r*
Acts 10:31, your alms are had in *r*
II Tim. 1:3, I have *r* of you in my prayers
    2:14, of these things put them in *r*
REMIT Jn. 20:23, whose soever sins you *r*

REMNANT Lev. 5:13, *r* shall be priest's
    II Ki. 19:4, lift up your prayer for the *r*
    Ezra 9:8, grace showed to leave us a *r*
    Isa. 1:9, unless the Lord had left a *r*
    11:11, to recover the *r* of his people
    16:14, the *r* shall be very small and feeble
    Jer. 44:28, *r* know whose words shall stand
    Ezek. 6:8, yet will I leave a *r*
    Joel 2:32, the *r* whom the Lord shall call
    See Mic. 2:12; 5:8; Rom. 11:5; Rev. 11:13
REMOVE Deut. 19:14, shall not *r* landmark
    Job 9:5, *r* the mountains, and they know not
    14:18, the rock is *r* out of his place
    Ps. 36:11, let not hand of the wicked *r* me
    39:10, *R* your stroke away from me
    46:2, not fear though the earth be *r*
    81:6, I *r* his shoulder from burden
    103:12, so far has he *r* our transgressions
    119:22, *R* from me reproach
    125:1, as mount Zion, which cannot be *r*
    Prov. 4:27, *r* your foot from evil
    10:30, the righteous shall never be *r*
    Eccl. 11:10, *r* sorrow from your heart
    Isa. 13:13, earth shall *r* out of her place
    24:20, earth shall be *r* like a cottage
    29:13, have *r* their heart far from me
    Lam. 3:17, you have *r* my soul from peace
    Mat. 17:20, *R* hence and it shall *r*
    Lk. 22:42, *r* this cup from me
    Gal. 1:6, I marvel you are so soon *r*
    Rev. 2:5, or else I will *r* your candlestick
    See Jn. 19:10; Eccl. 10:9; Ezek. 12:3
REND I Ki. 11:11, I will *r* the kingdom
    Isa. 64:1, that you would *r* the heavens
    Hos. 13:8, I will *r* the caul of their heart
    Joel 2:13, *r* your heart
    Mat. 7:6, lest they turn again and *r* you
    See Ps. 7:2; Eccl. 3:7; Jer. 4:30; Jn. 19:24
RENDER Deut. 32:41, *r* vengeance
    I Sam. 26:23, *r* to every man his faithfulness
    Job 33:26, he will *r* to man his righteousness
    34:11, the work of a man shall be *r* to him
    Ps. 28:4, *r* to them their desert
    38:20, they also that *r* evil for good
    79:12, and to our neighbour sevenfold
    94:2, a reward to the proud
    Prov. 24:12, *r* every man according
    26:16, seven men who can *r* a reason
    Hos. 14:2, so will we *r* the calves of our lips
    Joel 3:4, will you *r* me a recompence
    Zech. 9:12, I will *r* double
    Mat. 21:41, *r* him the fruits in their seasons
    22:21; Lk. 20:25, *R* unto Caesar
    Rom. 13:7, *R* to all their dues
    I Thess. 3:9, what thanks can we *r*
    5:15, see that none *r* evil for evil
    I Pet. 3:9, not *r* evil for evil, or railing
RENEW Job 10:17, you *r* your witnesses
    29:20, my bow was *r* in my hand
    Ps. 51:10, and *r* a right spirit within me
    103:5, your youth is *r* like the eagle's
    104:30, you *r* the face of the earth
    Isa. 40:31, wait on Lord shall *r* strength
    41:1, let the people *r* their strength

Lam. 5:21, *r* our days as of old
II Cor. 4:16, the inward man is *r* day by day
Eph. 4:23, be *r* in the spirit of your mind
Col. 3:10, new man, which is *r* in knowledge
Heb. 6:6, if they fall away, to *r* them again
RENOUNCED II Cor. 4:2, *r* hidden things
RENOWN Gen. 6:4; Num. 16:2, men of *r*
Num. 1:16, the *r* of the congregation
Isa. 14:20, evildoers shall never be *r*
Ezek. 16:14, *r* went forth among the heathen
    34:29, a plant of *r*
    See Ezek. 23:23; 26:17; 39:13; Dan. 9:15
RENT Gen. 37:33, Joseph is *r* in pieces
Josh. 9:4, bottles old and *r*
Judg. 14:6, *r* lion as he would have *r* a kid
I Ki. 13:3, the altar shall be *r*
Job 26:8, the cloud is not *r* under them
Mat. 9:16; Mk. 2:21, the *r* is made worse
Lk. 23:45, the veil was *r* in twain
    See I Sam. 15:27; Job 1:20; 2:12; Jer. 36:24
REPAID Prov. 13:21, good shall be *r*
REPAIR II Chron. 24:5, money to *r* the house
Isa. 61:4, they shall *r* the waste cities
    See Ki. 12:5; Ezra 9:9; Neh. 3:4; Isa. 58:12
REPAY Deut. 7:10, he will *r* him to his face
Lk. 10:35, when I come again, I will *r* you
Rom. 12:19, vengeance is mine; I will *r*
Phile. 19, I have written it, I will *r* it
    See Job 21:31; 41:11; Isa. 59:18
REPEATETH Prov. 17:9, he that *r* a matter
REPENT Gen. 6:6, it *r* the Lord
Ex. 13:17, lest the people *r*
Deut. 32:36, the Lord shall *r* for his servants
Job 42:6, I *r* in dust and ashes
Ps. 90:13, *r* you concerning your servants
    106:45, the Lord *r* according to his mercies
    110:4, Lord has sworn, and will not *r*
Jer. 8:6, no man *r* of his wickedness
    18:8; 26:13, if that nation turn, I will *r*
    26:19, Lord *r* of the evil he though to do
    31:19, after that I was turned, I *r*
Joel 2:13, he is slow to anger, and *r* him
Mat. 12:41, they *r* at the preaching
    21:29, afterward he *r* and went
Lk. 13:3, except ye *r*
    17:3, if your brother *r*, forgive him
Acts 8:22, *R* of this your wickedness
Rev. 2:21, space to *r*, and she *r* not
REPENTANCE Hos. 13:14, *r* shall be hid
Mat. 3:8; Acts 26:20, fruits meet for *r*
Rom. 2:4, goodness of God leads you to *r*
    11:29, gifts of God are without *r*
II Cor. 7:10, *r* not to be repented of
Heb. 6:1, not laying again the foundation
    of *r*
    6, to renew them again to *r*
    12:17, found no place of *r*, though he
    sought
    See Lk. 15:7; Acts 20:21; II Tim. 2:25
REPLENISH Gen. 1:28; 9:1; Jer. 31:25
REPLIEST Rom. 9:20, that *r* against God
REPORT (*n.*) Gen. 37:2, their evil *r*
Ex. 23:1, you shall not raise a false *r*
Num. 13:32, an evil *r* of the land

I Sam. 2:24, it is no good *r* I hear
I Ki. 10:6; II Chron. 9:5, it was a true *r* I heard
Prov. 15:30, a good *r* makes the bones fat
Isa. 28:19, a vexation only to understand
    the *r*
    53:1, who has believed our *r*?
Acts 6:3, men of honest *r*
    10:22, of good *r* among the Jews
II Cor. 6:8, by evil *r* and good *r*
Phil. 4:8, whatsoever things are of good *r*
I Tim. 3:7, a bishop must have a good *r*
    See Deut. 2:25; Heb. 11:2, 39; III Jn 12
REPORT (*v.*) Neh. 6:6, *r* among the heathen
Jer. 20:10, *R* say they, and we will *r* it
Mat. 28:15, this saying is commonly *r*
Acts 16:2, well *r* of by the brethren
I Cor. 14:25, he will *r* that God is in you
    See Ezek. 9:11; Rom. 3:8; I Tim. 5:10
REPROACH (*n.*) Gen. 34:14, a *r* to us
I Sam. 11:2, lay it for a *r* upon all Israel
Neh. 2:17, build, that we be no more a *r*
Ps. 15:3, that takes not up a *r*
    31:11, I was a *r* among my enemies
    44:13; 79:4; 89:41, a *r* to our neighbors
    78:66, put them to a perpetual *r*
Prov. 6:33, his *r* shall not be wiped away
    14:34, sin is a *r* to any people
Isa. 43:28, I have given Israel to *r*
    51:7, fear not the *r* of men
Jer. 23:40, I will bring an everlasting
    31:19, I did bear the *r* of my youth
Lam. 3:30, he is filled full with *r*
Ezek. 5:14, make you a *r* among nations
    15, Jerusalem shall be a *r* and a taunt
Mic. 6:16, you shall bear the *r* of my people
Rom. 15:3, *r* of them that reproached you
II Cor. 11:21, I speak as concerning *r*
    12:10, pleasure in *r* for Christ's sake
I Tim. 3:7, good report, lest he fall into *r*
    4:10, we labor and suffer *r*
Heb. 11:26, the *r* of Christ greater riches
    13:13, without the camp, bearing his *r*
REPROACH (*v.*) Num. 15:30, *r* the Lord
II Ki. 19:22; Isa. 37:23, whom have you *r*?
Job 19:3, these ten times have you *r* me
    27:6, my heart shall not *r* me
Ps. 42:10, with a sword my enemies *r* me
    44:16, the voice of him that *r*
    74:22, how the foolish man *r* you
    119:42, to answer him that *r* me
Prov. 14:31, oppresses poor *r* his Maker
Lk. 6:22, men shall *r* you for my sake
I Pet. 4:14, if you be *r* for Christ's sake
    See Ps. 55:12; 74:18; 79:12; 89:51; Zeph. 2:8
REPROACHFULLY Job 16:10; I Tim. 5:14
REPROVE Job 6:25, what does your arguing *r*?
    13:10, he will *r* you if you accept
    40:2, he that *r* God, let him answer it
Ps. 50:8, not *r* you for your burnt offerings
    141:5, let him *r* me, it shall be excellent oil
Prov. 9:8, *R* not a scorner, lest he hate you
    15:12, a scorner loves not one that *r*
    19:25, *r* one that has understanding
    29:1, he that being often *r*

30:6, lest he r you, you be found a liar
Isa. 11:4, r with equity for the meek
Jer. 2:19, your backslidings shall r you
Jn. 3:20, lest his deeds should be r
    16:8, he will r the world of sin
    See Lk. 3:19; Eph. 5:11, 13; II Tim. 4:2
REPROVER Prov. 25:12; Ezek. 3:26
REPUTATION Acts 5:34, r among the people
    Phil. 2:7, made himself of no r
    See Job 18:3; Dan. 4:35; Gal. 2:2
REQUEST Judg. 8:24, I desire a r of you
    Ezra 7:6, the king granted all his r
    Job 6:8, Oh that I might have my r
    Ps. 21:2, not withholden the r of his lips
    106:15, he gave them their r
    Phil. 1:4, in every prayer making r with joy
    4:6, let your r be made known
    See II Sam. 14:15; Neh. 2:4; Esther 4:8; 5:3
REQUIRE Gen. 9:5, blood of life I r
    31:39, of my hand did you r it
    Deut. 10:12, what does the Lord r?
    Ruth 3:11, I will do all you r
    I Sam. 20:16, let the Lord himself r it
    21:8, the king's business r haste
    II Sam. 3:13, one thing I r of you
    19:38, whatsoever you shall r I will do
    II Chron. 24:22, the Lord look upon it, and r
    it
    Ps. 10:13, he has said, You will not r it
    40:6, sin offering have you not r
    137:3, they that wasted us r of us mirth
    Prov. 30:7, two things have I r of you
    Eccl. 3:15, God r that which is past
    Isa. 1:12, who has r this at your hand
    Ezek. 3:18, his blood will I r at your hand
    34:10, I will r my flock at their hand
    Lk. 11:50, may be r of this generation
    12:20, this night your soul shall be r
    19:23, I might have r my own with usury
    I Cor. 1:22, the Jews r a sign
REQUITE Gen. 50:15, Joseph will r us
    Deut. 32:6, do you thus r the Lord
    Judg. 1:7, as I have done, so God has r me
    II Sam. 2:6, I also will r you this kindness
    16:12, the Lord will r good for this
    I Tim. 5:4, learn to r their parents
    See Ps. 10:14; 41:10; Jer. 51:56
REREWARD Josh. 6:9; Isa. 52:12; 58:8
RESCUE Ps. 35:17, r my soul
    See Deut. 28:31; I Sam. 14:45; Dan. 6:27
RESEMBLANCE Zech. 5:6, this is their r
RESEMBLE Judg. 8:18; Lk. 13:18
RESERVE Job 21:30, wicked is r today of
    destruction
    38:23, which I r against time of trouble
    Jer. 3:5, will he r his anger forever?
    5:24, he r the appointed weeks of harvest
    50:20, I will pardon them whom I r
    Nah. 1:2, the Lord r wrath for his enemies
    I Pet. 1:4, an inheritance r in heaven
    II Pet. 2:4, to be r unto judgment
    3:7, the heavens and earth are r unto fire
RESIDUE Ex. 10:5, locusts shall eat the r
    Isa. 38:10, deprived of the r of my years

Jer. 15:9, r will I deliver to the sword
Ezek. 9:8, will you destroy all the r
Mal. 2:15, yet had he the r of the spirit
Acts 15:17, that the r might seek the Lord
    See Neh. 11:20; Jer. 8:3; 29:1; 39:3
RESIST Zech. 3:1, at his right hand to r
    Mat. 5:39, r not evil
    Lk. 21:15, adversaries not be able to r
    Rom. 9:19, who has r his will?
    13:2, whoso r the power, r the ordinance
    James 4:6; I Pet. 5:5, God r the proud
    7, R the devil, and he will flee from you
    I Pet. 5:9, whom r steadfast in the faith
    See Acts 6:10; 7:51; II Tim. 3:8; Heb. 12:4
RESORT Neh. 4:20, r hither to us
    Ps. 71:3, whereunto I may continually r
    Jn. 18:2, Jesus ofttimes r thither
    See Mk. 2:13; 10:1; Jn. 18:20; Acts 16:13
RESPECT (n.) Ex. 2:25, God has r unto them
    I Ki. 8:28, have r unto their prayer
    Ps. 74:20, have r unto your covenant
    119:15, I will have r unto your ways
    138:6, yet have he r unto the lowly
    Prov. 24:23, not good to have r of persons
    Isa. 17:7, eyes shall have r to the Holy One
    22:11, nor had r to him that fashioned it
    Phil. 4:11, not that I speak in r of want
    Col. 3:25, there is no r of persons with God
    See Heb. 11:26; James 2:1, 3, 9
RESPECT (v.) Deut. 1:17, r persons in judg-
    ment
    Job 37:24, r not any that are wise of heart
    See Num. 16:15; II Sam. 14:14; Ps. 40:4
RESPITE Ex. 8:15; I Sam. 11:3
REST (n.) Gen. 49:15, Issachar saw that r
    Ex. 31:15; Lev. 16:31; 25:4, the sabbath of r
    33:14, I will give you r
    Lev. 25:5, a year of r to the land
    Deut. 12:10, he gives you r from enemies
    Judg. 3:30, the land had r fourscore years
    Ruth 3:1, shall not I seek r for you
    I Chron. 22:9, a man of r, I will give him r
    18, has he not given you r on every side?
    28:2, to build a house of r
    Neh. 9:28, after they had r they did evil
    Esther 9:16, Jews had r from their enemies
    Job 3:17, there the weary be at r
    11:18, you shall take your r in safety
    17:16, when our r together is in the dust
    Ps. 55:6, then would I fly away, and be at r
    95:11; Heb. 3:11, not enter into my r
    116:7, return to your r, O my soul
    Eccl. 2:23, his heart takes not r
    Isa. 11:10, his r shall be glorious
    14:7; Zech. 1:11, earth is at r and quiet
    30:15, in returning and r shall you be saved
    66:1, where is the place of my r?
    Jer. 6:16, you shall find r for your souls
    Ezek. 38:11, I will go to them that are at r
    Mic. 2:10, depart; this is not your r
    Mat. 11:28, I will give you r
    12:43, seeking r and finding none
    26:45, sleep on now, and take your r
    Jn. 11:13, of taking r in sleep

Acts 9:31, then had the churches r
REST (v.) Gen. 2:2, he r on the seventh day
Num. 11:25, when the spirit r upon them
II Chron. 32:8, people r on the words
Job 3:18, there the prisoners r together
Ps. 16:9; Acts 2:26, my flesh shall r in hope
37:7, R in the Lord
Eccl. 7:9, anger r in bosom of fools
Isa. 11:2, spirit of the Lord shall r upon him
28:12, you may cause the weary to r
57:20, like the sea when it cannot r
62:1, for Jerusalem's sake I will not r
63:14, Spirit of the Lord caused him to r
Jer. 47:6, r and be still
Mk. 6:31, come, and r awhile
II Cor. 12:9, Power of Christ may r on me
Rev. 4:8, they r not day and night
6:11, r yet for a little season
14:13, that they may r from their labors
RESTORE Ex. 22:4, he shall r double
Lev. 6:4, he shall r that he took away
Deut. 22:2, things strayed you shall r again
Ps. 23:3, he r my soul
51:12, R to me the joy of your salvation
69:4, I r that which I took not away
Isa. 1:26, I will r your judges as at the first
Jer. 27:22, I will r them to this place
30:17, I will r health to you
Ezek. 33:15, if the wicked r the pledge
Mat. 17:11, Elias shall r all things
Lk. 19:8, I r him fourfold
Acts 1:6, at this time r the kingdom
Gal. 6:1, r such an one in meekness
RESTRAIN Gen. 11:6, nothing will be r
Ex. 36:6, people were r from bringing
Job 15:4, you r prayer before God
Ps. 76:10, remainder of wrath shall you r
See Gen. 8:2; Isa. 63:15; Acts 14:18
RESURRECTION Mat. 22:28; Lk. 20:33, in r
whose wife shall be?
Mat. 22:30, in r neither marry
27:53, came out of graves after r
Lk. 14:14, be recompensed at r
20:27, deny any r
Jn. 5:29, done good to the r of life, done evil
to the r of damnation
11:25, Jesus said, I am the r and the life
Acts 1:22, witness with us of his r
2:31, David spoke of r of Christ
Rom. 1:4, by the r from the dead
I Cor. 15:13, but if there be no r
21, by man came r
Phil. 3:10, know the power of his r
Rev. 20:5, this is the first r
RETAIN Job 2:9, do you r integrity
Prov. 3:18, happy is every one that r her
11:16, a gracious woman r honor
Eccl. 8:8, no man has power to r the spirit
Jn. 20:23, whose soever sins ye r, they are r
See Mic. 7:18; Rom. 1:28; Phile. 13
RETIRE Judg. 20:39; II Sam. 11:15; Jer. 4:6
RETURN Gen. 3:19, to dust shall you r
Judg. 7:3, whosoever is fearful let him r
II Sam. 12:23, he shall not r to me

II Ki. 20:10, let the shadow r backward
Job 1:21, naked shall I r thither
15:22, he shall r out of darkness
Ps. 35:13, my prayer r into my own bosom
90:3, you say, R, you children of men
104:29, they die, and r to their dust
116:7, R to your rest, O my soul
Eccl. 1:7, whence rivers come, thither they r
12:2, nor the clouds r after the rain
7, dust r to earth; and spirit r to God
Isa. 21:12, enquire ye; r, come
35:10, the ransomed of the Lord shall r
Jer. 24:7, they shall r with their whole heart
36:3, r every man from his evil way
Hos. 2:7, I will r to my first husband
7:16, they r, but not to the most High
14:7, that dwell under his shadow shall r
Amos 4:6, yet have ye not r to me
Zech. 1:16, I am r to Jerusalem
Mal. 3:7, R to me, and I will r to you
18, then shall you r, and discern
Mat. 12:44, I will r into my house
Lk. 9:10, the apostles r and told him all
10:17, the seventy r with joy
17:18, not found that r to give glory
Acts 13:34, now no more to r to corruption
Heb. 11:15, had opportunity to have r
I Pet. 2:25, now r to Shepherd
REVEAL Deut. 29:29, things r belong to us
I Sam. 3:7, nor was the word of the Lord r
Job 20:27, the heaven shall r his iniquity
Prov. 11:13; 20:19, a talebearer r secrets
Isa. 22:14, it was r in my ears
40:5, the glory of the Lord shall be r
53:1, to whom is arm of the Lord r?
56:1, my righteousness is near to be r
Jer. 11:20, unto you have I r my cause
33:6, I will r abundance of peace
Dan. 2:22, he r deep and secret things
28, there is a God that r secrets
Amos 3:7, he r his secrets to the prophets
Mat. 11:25, have r them unto babes
16:17, flesh and blood has not r it
Lk. 2:35, thought of many hearts be r
12:2, nothing covered that shall not be r
17:30, in day when Son of man is r
Rom. 1:17, righteousness of God is r
18, wrath of God is r from heaven
8:18, glory which shall be r in us
I Cor. 2:10, God has r them by his Spirit
3:13, it shall be r by fire
14:30, if any thing be r to another
Gal. 1:16, to r his Son in me
II Thess. 1:7, when the Lord Jesus shall be r
I Pet. 1:5, ready to be r in the last time
4:13, when his glory shall be r
5:1, partaker of the glory that shall be r
REVELATION Rom. 2:5, r of judgment
16:25, r of the mystery
I Cor. 14:26, every one has a r
II Cor. 12:1, to visions and r
See Gal. 2:2, Eph. 1:17; 3:3; I Pet. 4:3
REVELLINGS Gal. 5:21; I Pet. 1:13
REVENGE Jer. 15:15, O Lord r me

Jer. 20:10, we shall take our r on him
Nah. 1:2, the Lord r, and is furious
II Cor. 7:11, what r it wrought in you
    10:6, in readiness to r all disobedience
    See Ps. 79:10; Ezek. 25:12; Rom. 13:4
REVENUE Prov. 8:19, r better than silver
    16:8, better than great r without right
Jer. 12:13, ashamed of your r
    See Ezra 4:13; Prov. 15:6; Isa. 23:3; Jer. 12:13
REVERENCE Ps. 89:7; Mat. 21:37
REVEREND Ps. 111:9, r is his name
REVERSE Num. 23:20; Esther 8:5, 8
REVILE Isa. 51:7, neither be afraid of their r
    Mat. 27:39, they that passed by r him
    Mk. 15:32, they that were crucified r him
    I Cor. 4:12, being r, we bless
    I Pet. 2:23, when he was r, r not again
    See Ex. 22:28; Mat. 5:11; Acts 23:4
REVIVE Neh. 4:2, will they r the stones?
    Ps. 85:6, will you not r us
    138:7, you will r me
    Isa. 57:15, to r the spirit of the humble
    Hos. 6:2, after two days will he r us
    14:7, they shall r as corn
    Hab. 3:2, r your work in midst of years
    Rom. 14:9, Christ both died, rose, and r
    See Gen. 45:27; II Ki. 13:21; Ezra 9:8
REVOLT Isa. 1:5; 31:6; 59:13; Jer. 5:23
REWARD (n.) Gen. 15:1, exceeding great r
    Num. 22:7, r of divination in their hand
    Deut. 10:17, God who takes not r
    Ruth 2:12, full r be given you of the Lord
    Job 6:22, did I say, Give a r
    7:2, as an hireling looks for r
    Ps. 19:11, in keeping them there is great r
    58:11, there is a r for the righteous
    91:8, you shall see the r of the wicked
    127:3, the fruit of the womb is his r
    Eccl. 4:9, they have a good r for labor
    Isa. 1:23, every one follows after r
    5:23, justify the wicked for r
    40:10; 62:11, his r is with him
    Ezek. 16:34, givest r, no r, is given thee
    Dan. 5:17, give your r to another
    Mic. 3:11, the heads thereof judge for r
    7:3, the judge ask for a r
    Mat. 5:12, great is your r in heaven
    46, what r have you?
    6:1, you have no r of your father
    10:41, a prophet's r, a righteous man's r
    42; Mk. 9:41, in no wise lose his r
    Lk. 6:35, do good, your r daily shall be great
    23:41, we receive the due r of our deeds
    Acts 1:18, purchased with the r of iniquity
    Rom. 4:4, the r is not reckoned
    I Cor. 3:8, every man shall receive his own r
    9:18, what is my r then?
    Col. 2:18, let no man beguile you of your r
    3:24, the r of the inheritance
    I Tim. 5:18, the laborer is worthy of his r
    Heb. 2:2; 10:35; 11:26, recompense of r
    II Pet. 2:13, the r of unrighteousness
REWARD (v.) Deut. 32:41, I will r them that
    hate me

I Sam. 24:17, you have r me good
II Chron. 15:7, be strong, your work shall
    be r
    20:11, behold how they r us
Job 21:19, he r him, and he shall know it
Ps. 31:23, plentifully r the proud doer
    35:12; 109:5, they r me evil for good
    103:10, nor r us according to our iniquities
    137:8, happy is he that r you
Prov. 25:22, heap coals, Lord shall r you
    26:10, both r the fool and r transgressors
Jer. 31:16, your work shall be r
RICH Gen. 13:2, Abram was very r
    Ex. 30:15, the r shall not give more
    Josh. 22:8, return with much r to your tents
    Ruth 3:10, follows not poor or r
    I Sam. 2:7, makes poor and makes r
    I Ki. 3:11, neither have asked r
    13, I have given you both r and honor
    10:23, Solomon exceeded all for r
    I Chron. 29:12, r and honor come of you
    Job 15:29, he shall not be r
    27:19, the r man shall lie down
    36:19, will he esteem your r?
    Ps. 37:16, better than r of many wicked
    Ps. 39:6, be heaps up r
    49:16, be not afraid when one is made r
    52:7, trusted in abundance of r
    73:12, the ungodly increase in r
    104:24, the earth is full of your r
    112:3, wealth and r shall be in his house
    Prov. 3:16, in her left hand r and honor
    8:18, R and honor are with me
    10:4, hand of diligent makes r
    11:4, R profit not in day of wrath
    21:17, he that loves wine shall not be r
    23:5, r make themselves wings
    28:11, the r man is wise in his own conceit
    30:8, give me neither poverty nor r
    Eccl. 5:13, r kept for owners to their hurt
    10:20, curse not r in your bedchamber
    Isa. 45:3, I will give you hidden r
    53:9, with the r in his death
    Jer. 9:23, let not the r man glory in his r
    17:11, gets r, and not by right
    Ezek. 28:5, heart lifted up because of r
    Hos. 12:8, Ephraim said, I am become r
    Zech. 11:5, blessed be the Lord, for I am r
    Mat. 13:22; Lk. 8:14, deceitfulness of r
    Mk. 10:23, hardly shall they that have r
    12:41, r cast in much
    Lk. 1:53, the r he has sent empty away
    6:24, woe to you r, for you have received
    12:21, not r toward God
    18:23, sorrowful, for he was very r
    Rom. 2:4, the r of his goodness
    9:23, make known the r of his glory
    10:12, the Lord is r to all that call
    11:12, fall of them the r of the world
    33, the depth of the r of the wisdom
    I Cor. 4:8, now you are full, now you are r
    II Cor. 6:10, poor, yet making many r
    8:9, r, yet for your sakes
    Eph. 1:7, according to the r of grace

2:4, God, who is *r* in mercy
Phil. 4:19, his *r* in glory by Christ
Col. 1:27, *r* of the glory of this mystery
2:2, the *r* of the full assurance
I Tim. 6:9, *r* fall into temptation
17, nor trust in uncertain *r*
18, do good, and be *r* in good works
Heb. 11:26, reproach of Christ greater *r*
James 1:10, let *r* rejoice that he is made low
5:2, your *r* are corrupted
Rev. 2:9, but you are *r*
3:18, buy of me gold, that you may be *r*
5:12, worthy is the Lamb to receive *r*

RICHLY Col. 3:16; I Tim. 6:17

RIDDANCE Lev. 23:22; Zeph. 1:18

RIDDLE Judg. 14:12; Ezek. 17:2

RIDE Deut. 32:13, *r* on high places
33:26, who *r* upon the heaven
Judg. 5:10, you that *r* on white asses
II Ki. 4:24, slack not your *r* for me
Job 30:22, cause me to *r* upon the wind
Ps. 45:4, in your majesty *r* prosperously
66:12, have caused men to *r* over our heads
68:4, 33, extol him that *r* on the heavens
Isa. 19:1, the Lord *r* on a swift cloud

RIDER Gen. 49:17; Ex. 15:1; Zech. 10:5

RIDGES Ps. 65:10, waters the *r* thereof

RIGHT (*n.*) Deut. 6:18, shall do that is *r*
21:17, the *r* of the firstborn is his
Neh. 2:20, you have no *r* in Jerusalem
Job 34:6, should I lie against my *r*?
Ps. 9:4, you maintain my *r*
140:12, maintain the *r* of the poor
Prov. 16:8, great revenues without *r*
Jer. 17:11, that gets riches, and not by *r*
Ezek. 21:27, till he come whose *r* it is
See Amos 5:12; Mal. 3:5; Heb. 13:10

RIGHT (*adj.*) Deut. 32:4, God of truth, *r* is he
I Sam. 12:23, teach you the good and *r* way
II Sam. 15:3, your matters are good, and *r*
Neh. 9:13, you gave them *r* judgments
Job 6:25, how forcible are *r* words
34:23, he will not lay on man more than *r*
Ps. 19:8, the statutes of the Lord are *r*
51:10, renew a *r* spirit within me
107:7, he led them forth by the *r* way
Prov. 4:11, I have led you in *r* paths
8:6, the opening of my lips shall be *r*
things
12:5, the thoughts of the righteous are *r*
Prov. 12:15, the way of a fool is *r* in his own
eyes
21:2, every way of man is *r* in his own eyes
24:26, kiss his lips that gives a *r* answer
Isa. 30:10, prophesy not *r* things
Jer. 2:21, planted wholly a *r* seed
Ezek. 18:5, if a man do that which is *r*
19; 21:27; 33:14, that which is lawful and *r*
Hos. 14:9, the ways of the Lord are *r*
Amos 3:10, they know not how to do *r*
Mat. 20:4, whatsoever is *r* I will give you
Mk. 5:15; Lk. 8:35, in his *r* mind
Lk. 10:28, you have answered *r*
Eph. 6:1, obey your parents, this is *r*

RIGHTEOUS Gen. 7:1, you have I seen *r*
18:23, will you destroy *r* with wicked?
38:26, she has been more *r* than I
Ex. 23:8, gift perverts the words of the *r*
Num. 23:10, let me die the death of the *r*
Deut. 25:1, they shall justify the *r*
I Sam. 24:17, you are more *r* than I
I Ki. 2:32, two men more *r* than he
Job 4:7, where were the *r* cut off?
15:14, what is man, that he should be *r*?
17:9, the *r* shall hold on his way
22:3, is it any pleasure that you are *r*?
23:7, there the *r* might dispute with him
34:5, Job has said, I am *r*
Ps. 1:5, the congregation of the *r*
6, the Lord knows the way of the *r*
7:9, the *r* God tries the hearts
34:17, the *r* cry, and the Lord hears then
19, many are the afflictions of the *r*
37:16, a little that a *r* man has
21, the *r* shows mercy, and gives
25, have not seen the *r* forsaken
29, the *r* shall inherit the land
30, the mouth of the *r* speaks wisdom
55:22, never suffer the *r* to be moved
58:11, there is a reward for the *r*
69:28, let them not be written with the *r*
92:12, the *r* shall flourish like the palm tree
97:11, light is sown for the *r*
140:13, the *r* shall give thanks
146:8, the Lord loves the *r*
Prov. 2:7, he lays up wisdom for the *r*
3:32, his secret is with the *r*
10:3, Lord will not suffer the *r* to famish
11, the mouth of *r* is a well of life
16, labor of *r* tends to life
24, desire of the *r* shall be granted
25, the *r* is an everlasting foundation
11:8, the *r* is delivered out of trouble
10, when it goes well with the *r*
21, seed of the *r* shall be delivered
12:3, the root of the *r* shall not be moved
5, thoughts of the *r* are right
10, *r* man regards the life of his beast
26, *r* is more excellent than his neighbor
13:9, the light of the *r* rejoices
25, the *r* eats to the satisfying of his soul
14:9, among the *r* there is favor
32, the *r* has hope in his death
15:6, in the house of the *r* is much treasure
19, the way of the *r* is made plain
28, the heart of the *r* studies to answer
29, he hears the prayer of the *r*
16:13, *R* lips are the delight of kings
18:10, the *r* runs into it, and is safe
28:1, the *r* are gold as a lion
29:2, when the *r* are in authority
Eccl. 7:16, be not *r* overmuch
9:1, *r* and the wise are in the hand of God
2, one event to *r* and wicked
Isa. 3:10, say to *r*, it shall be well
24:16, songs, even glory to the *r*
26:2, that the *r* nation may enter
41:2, raised up *r* man from the east

53:11, shall my *r* servant justify
60:21, your people shall be all *r*
Jer. 23:5, raise unto David a *r* branch
Ezek. 13:22, with lies you have made *r* sad
16:52, your sisters are more *r* than you
33:12, the righteousness of the *r* shall not
Amos 2:6, they sold the *r* for silver
Mal. 3:18, discern between the *r* and wicked
Mat. 9:13; Lk. 5:32, not come to call *r*
13:43, then shall the *r* shine forth
Mat. 23:28, outwardly appear *r* to men
25:46, the *r* into life eternal
Lk. 1:6, they were both *r* before God
23:47, certainly this was a *r* man
Jn. 7:24, judge *r* judgment
Rom. 3:10, there is none *r*, no not one
5:7, scarcely for a *r* man will one die
II Thess. 1:6, it is a *r* thing with God
II Tim. 4:8, the Lord, the *r* Judge
Heb. 11:4, obtained witness that he was *r*
I Pet. 3:12, eyes of the Lord are over the *r*
II Pet. 2:8, Lot vexed his *r* soul
I Jn. 2:1, Jesus Christ the *r*
Rev. 22:11, he that is *r*, let him be *r* still
RIGHTEOUSLY Deut. 1:16, judge *r*
Ps. 67:4; 96:10, you shall judge the people *r*
Isa. 33:15, that walks *r* shall dwell on high
RIGHTEOUSNESS Gen. 30:33, so shall my *r*
    answer for me
Deut. 33:19, offer sacrifices of *r*
I Sam. 26:23, render to every man his *r*
Job 6:29, return again, my *r* is in it
27:6, my *r* I hold fast
29:14, I put on *r*, and it clothed me
35:2, you said, My *r* is more than God's
36:3, I will ascribe *r* to my Maker
Ps. 4:1, hear me, O God of my *r*
5, offer the sacrifices of *r*
9:8, he shall judge the world in *r*
17:15, as for me, I will behold your face in *r*
23:3, leads me in paths of *r*
24:5, and *r* from the God of his salvation
40:9, I have preached *r*
45:7; Heb. 1:9, you love *r*
50:6; 97:6, heavens shall declare his *r*
72:2, he shall judge your people with *r*
85:10, *r* and peace have kissed each other
94:15, judgment shall return unto *r*
97:2, *r* is the habitation of his throne
111:3, 112:3, 9, his *r* endures forever
118:19, open to me the gates of *r*
132:9, let your priests be clothed with *r*
Prov. 8:18, durable riches and *r* are with me
10:2; 11:4, but *r* delivers from death
11:5, *r* of the perfect shall direct his way
12:28, in the way of *r* his life
14:34, *R* exalts a nation
16:8, better is a little with *r*
12, the throne is established by *r*
31, crown of glory, if found in way of *r*
Eccl. 7:15, a just man that perishes in his *r*
Isa. 11:5, *r* the girdle of his loins
26:10, yet will he not learn *r*
32:1, a king shall reign in *r*

41:10, with the right hand of my *r*
46:12, you that are far from *r*
59:16, his *r* sustained him
62:2, the Gentiles shall see your *r*
64:6, our *r* are as filthy rags
Jer. 33:15, cause the branch of *r* to grow
51:10, the Lord has brought forth our *r*
Ezek. 3:20, when righteous turns from *r*
14:14, deliver but their own souls by their *r*
33:13, if he trust to his own *r*
Dan. 4:27, break off your sins by *r*
9:7, *r* belongs to you
12:3, they that turn many to *r*
Hos. 10:12, till he rain *r* upon you
Amos 5:24, let *r* run down as a stream
6:12, turned fruit of *r* into hemlock
Zeph. 2:3, you meek of the earth, seek *r*
Mal. 4:2, shall the Sun of *r* arise
Mat. 3:15, to fulfill all *r*
5:6, hunger and thirst after *r*
20, except your *r* exceed the *r*
21:32, John came to you in the way of *r*
Lk. 1:75, in *r* before him
Jn. 16:8, reprove the world of *r*
Acts 10:35, he that works *r*
13:10, you enemy of all *r*
Rom. 4:6, to whom God imputes *r*
5:17, which receive the gift of *r*
6:13, yield your members as instruments
    of *r*
8:10, the Spirit is life, because of *r*
9:30, the *r* which is of faith
10:3, going about to establish their own *r*
4, Christ is the end of the law for *r*
10, with the heart man believes unto *r*
Rom. 14:17, meat and drink, but *r*
I Cor. 1:30, Christ is made unto us *r*
15:34, awake to *r*
II Cor. 5:21, that we might be made the *r*
6:7, the armour of *r*
Gal. 2:21, if *t* come by the law
5:5, we wait for the hope of *r*
Eph. 6:14, the breastplate of *r*
Phil. 1:11, filled with the fruits of *r*
3:6, touching the *r* in the law, blameless
9, no having my own *r*, but the *r* of God
I Tim. 6:11, follow after *r*
II Tim. 3:16, for instruction in *r*
4:8, laid up for me a crown of *r*
Titus 3:5, not by works of *r*
Heb. 1:8, a sceptre of *r*
5:13, unskillful in the word of *r*
7:2, by interpretation, King of *r*
11:7, heir of the *r* which is by faith
33, through faith wrought *r*
12:11, the peaceable fruit of *r*
James 1:20, wrath of man works not *r* of God
3:18, the fruit of *r* is sown in peace
I Pet. 2:24, dead to sins, should live unto *r*
II Pet. 2:5, a preacher of *r*
21, better not to have known way of *r*
3:13, new earth wherein dwells *r*
I Jn. 2:29, every one that does *r*
RIGHTLY Gen. 27:36; Lk. 7:43

RIGOUR Ex. 1:13, 14; Lev. 25:43, 46, 53
RINGLEADER Acts 24:5, r of Nazarenes
RIOT Rom. 13:13; Titus 1:6; I Pet. 4:4
RIPE Gen. 40:10, brought forth r grapes
Ex. 22:29, offer the first of your r fruits
Num. 18:13, first r, shall be yours
Mic. 7:1, my soul desired the first r fruit
Rev. 14:15, harvest of earth is r
See Num. 13:20; Jer. 24:2; Hos. 9:10
RISE Gen. 19:2, you shall r up early
23, sun was r when Lot entered into Zoar
Num. 24:17, a sceptre shall r out of Israel
32:14, you are r up in your fathers' stead
Job 9:7, commands the sun, and it r not
14:12, man lies down, and r not
24:22, he r up, and no man is sure of life
31:14, what shall I do when God r up
Ps. 27:3, though war should r against me
119:52, at midnight I will r to give thanks
127:2, it is vain to r up early
Prov. 31:15, she r up while it is yet night
28, her children r up and call her blessed
Eccl. 12:4, he shall r up at the voice of the bird
Isa. 33:10, now will I r, saith the Lord
58:10, then shall your light r in obscurity
60:1, the glory of the Lord is r upon you
Jer. 7:13; 35:14, I spoke unto you, r early
11:7, r early and protesting
25:27, fall and r no more
Mat. 5:45, make sun to r on evil and good
17:9; Mk. 9:9, until Son of man be r
26:46, R, let us be going
Mk. 4:27, should sleep, and r night and day
9:10, what the r from the dead should mean
10:49, r, he calls you
14:28, after I am r I will go before you
Lk. 2:34, this child is set for the fall and r
11:7, I cannot r and give you
18:33; 24:7, third day he shall r again
24:34, the Lord is r indeed
Jn. 11:23, your brother shall r again
Acts 10:13, R, Peter, kill and eat
26:16, r, and stand upon your feet
23, the first that should r from the dead
Rom. 8:34, yea rather, that is r
I Cor. 15:15, if so be the dead r not
20, but now is Christ r
Col. 3:1, if he then be r with Christ
I Thess. 4:16, the dead in Christ shall r first
RITES Num. 9:3, according to all the r first
RIVER Ex. 7:19, stretch out hand on their r
II Sam. 17:13, we will draw it into the r
II Ki. 5:12, are not r of Damascus better
Job 20:17, you shall not see the r of honey
28:10, he cuts out r among rocks
29:6, the rock poured out r of oil
40:23, he drinks up a r, and hastes not
Ps. 1:3, a tree planted by the r
36:8, the r of your pleasures
Ps. 46:4, r, the streams whereof make glad
65:9, enrich it with r of God
107:33, turn r into a wilderness

119:136, R of waters run down my eyes
137:1, by the r of Babylon we sat
Eccl. 1:7, all the r run into the sea
Isa. 32:2, shall be as r of water in a dry place
43:2, through the r, they shall not overflow
19, I will make r in the desert
48:18, then had your peace been as a r
66:12, I will extend peace like a r
Lam. 2:18, let tears run down like r
Mic. 6:7, be pleased with r of oil
Jn. 7:38, shall flow r of living water
Rev. 22:1, a pure r of water of life
ROAD I Sam. 27:10
ROAR I Chron. 16:32; Ps. 96:11, let the sea r
Job 3:24, my r are poured out
Ps. 46:3, will not fear, though waters r
104:21, young lions r after their prey
Isa. 59:11, we r all like bears
Jer. 6:23, their voice r like the sea
25:30, the Lord shall r from on high
Hos. 11:10, he shall r like a lion
Joel 3:16, the Lord shall r out of Zion
Amos 3:4, lion r when he has no prey?
ROARING Prov. 19:12; 20:2, king's wrath is as the r of a lion
Lk. 21:25, the sea and waves r
I Pet. 5:8, the devil as a r lion
See Ps. 22:1,13; 32:3; Isa. 31:4
ROAST Ex. 12:9, eat not raw, but r with fire
Prov. 12:27, slothful man r not that he took
Isa. 44:16, he r r, and is satisfied
See Deut. 16:7; I Sam. 2:15; II Chron. 35:13
ROB Prov. 22:22, R not the poor
Isa. 10:2, that they may r the fatherless
13, I have r their treasures
42:22, this is a people r and spoiled
Ezek. 33:15, if he give again that he had r
Mal. 3:8, you have r me
II Cor. 11:8, I r other churches
See Judg. 9:25; II Sam. 17:8; Ps. 119:61
ROBBER Job 12:6, tabernacles of r prosper
Isa. 42:24, who gave Israel to the r?
Jer. 7:11, is this house become a den of r
Jn. 10:1, the same is a thief and a r
8, all that came before me are r
Acts 19:37, men are neither r of churches
II Cor. 11:26, in perils of r
See Ezek. 7:22; 18:10; Dan. 11:14; Hos. 6:9
ROBBERY Prov. 21:7; Phil. 2:6
ROBE I Sam. 24:4, cut off skit of Saul's r
Job 29:14, my judgment was as a r
Isa. 61:10, the r of righteousness
Lk. 15:22, bring forth the best r
20:46, which desire to walk in long r
See Ezek. 28:4; Mat. 27:28; Rev. 6:11
ROCK Ex. 33:22, put you in a clift of the r
Num. 20:8, speak to the r before their eyes
10, must we fetch you water out of this r
23:9, from the top of the r I see him
24:21, you put the nest in a r
Deut. 8:15, water out of the r
32:4, he is the R
15, lightly esteemed the R of his salvation
31, their R is not as our R

37, where is their *r* in whom they trusted
II Sam. 22:2; Ps. 18:2, the Lord is my *r*
   3, the God of my *r*
   32; Ps. 18:31, who is a *r* save our God?
I Ki. 19:11, wind broke in pieces the *r*
Job 14:18, the *r* is removed out of his place
   19:24, graven in the *r* for ever
   24:8, embrace the *r* for want of shelter
Ps. 27:5; 40:2, shall set me up upon a *r*
   31:3; 71:3, you are my *r* and my fortress
   61:2, lead me to the *r* that is higher than I
   81:16, with honey out of the *r*
Prov. 30:26, yet make their houses in the *r*
Song of Sol. 2:14, you are in the clefts of the *r*
Isa. 32:2, as the shadow of a great *r*
   33:16, defense shall be munitions of *r*
Jer. 5:3, they made their faces harder than *r*
   23:29, hammer that breaks the *r* in pieces
Mat. 7:25, it was founded upon a *r*
   16:18, upon this *r* I will build my church
   27:51, and the *r* rent
Lk. 8:6, some fell upon a *r*
Rom. 9:33, I lay in Sion a *r* of offence
I Cor. 10:4, spiritual *R*, that *R* was Christ
Rev. 6:15, said to the *r*, Fall on us
ROD Job 9:34, let him take his *r* from me
   21:9, neither is the *r* of God upon them
Ps. 2:9, break them with a *r* of iron
   23:4, your *r* and your staff comfort me
Prov. 10:13; 26:3, *r* for the back of fools
   13:24, he that spares his *r*
   23:13, you shall beat him with your *r*
   29:15, the *r* and reproof give wisdom
Isa. 10:15, as if the *r* should shake itself
   11:1, shall come forth a *r*
Jer. 48:17, how is the beautiful *r* broken?
Ezek. 20:37, cause you to pass under the *r*
II Cor. 11:25, thrice was I beaten with *r*
See Gen. 30:37; Num. 17:8
RODE II Sam. 18:9; II Ki. 9:25; Ps. 18:10
ROLL Josh. 5:9, I have *r* away the reproach
Job 30:14, they *r* themselves on me
Isa. 9:5, with garments *r* in blood
   34:4, the heavens shall be *r* together
Mk. 16:3, who shall *r* us away the stone
Lk. 24:2; they found the stone *r* away
See Gen. 29:8; Isa. 17:13; Mat. 27:60
ROOF Gen. 19:8, under the shadow of my *r*
Deut. 22:8, make a battlement for your *r*
Ezek. 3:26, tongue cleaves to *r* of mouth
Mk. 2:4, they uncovered the *r*
Lk. 7:6, you should come under my *r*
See Josh. 2:6; Judg. 16:27; II Sam. 11:2
ROOM Gen. 24:23, is there *r* for us
   26:22, the Lord had made *r* for us
Ps. 31:8, you have set my feet in a large *r*
   80:9, you prepare *r* before it
Prov. 18:16, a man's gift makes *r* for him
Mal. 3:10, there shall not be *r* enough
Mat. 23:6; Lk. 20:46, love uppermost *r*
Mk. 2:2, there was no *r* to receive them
Lk. 2:7, no *r* for them in the inn
   12:17, no *r* to bestow my goods
   14:7, how they chose out the chief *r*

9, begin with shame to take the lowest *r*
   22, it is done, and yet there is *r*
See Gen. 6:14; I Ki. 8:20; 19:16; Mk. 14:15
ROOT (*n.*) Deut. 29:18, a *r* that bears gall
II Ki. 19:30, shall again take *r* downward
Job. 5:3, I have seen the foolish taking *r*
   8:17, his *r* are wrapped about the heap
   14:8, the *r* thereof wax old in the earth
   19:28, the *r* of the matter
   29:19, my *r* was spread out by the waters
Prov. 12:3, *r* of righteous shall not be moved
   12, *r* of righteous yielded fruit
Isa. 5:24, their *r* shall be rottenness
   11:1, a Branch shall grow out of his *r*
   10; Rom. 15:12, there shall be a *r* of Jesse
   53:2, as a *r* out of a dry ground
Ezek. 31:7, his *r* was by great waters
Hos. 14:5, cast forth his *r* as Lebanon
Mal. 4:1, leave them neither *r* nor branch
Mat. 3:10; Lk. 3:9, ax laid to *r* of trees
   13:6; Lk. 8:13, because they had no *r*
Mk. 11:20, fig tree dried up from the *r*
Rom. 11:16, if the *r* be holy
I Tim. 6:10, love of money is the *r* of all evil
Heb. 12:15, lest any *r* of bitterness
Jude 12, twice dead, plucked by the *r*
Rev. 22:16, *r* and offspring of David
ROOT (*v.*) Deut. 29:28, Lord *r* them out
I Ki. 14:15, he shall *r* up Israel
Job 18:14, confidence shall be *r* out
   31:8, let my offspring be *r* out
   12, *r* out all my increase
Ps. 52:5, *r* you out of the land of the living
Mat. 13:29, lest you *r* up also the wheat
   15:13, have not planted, shall be *r* up
Eph. 3:17, being *r* and grounded in love
Col. 2:7, *R* and built up in him
See Prov. 2:22; Jer. 1:10; Zeph. 2:4
ROSE (*n.*) Song of Sol. 2:1; Isa. 35:1
ROSE (*v.*) Gen. 32:31, the sun *r* upon him
Josh. 3:16, waters *r* up on an heap
Lk. 16:31, though one *r* from the dead
Rom. 14:9, to this end Christ died and *r*
I Cor. 15:4, buried, and the third day
II Cor. 5:15, live to him who died and *r*
ROT Num. 5:21; Prov. 10:7; Isa. 40:20
ROTTEN Job 41:27; Jer. 38:11; Joel 1:17
ROTTENNESS Prov. 12:4; 14:30; Isa. 5:24
ROUGH Isa. 27:8, stays his *r* wind
   40:4; Lk. 3:5, *r* places made plain
Zech. 13:4, wear a *r* garment to deceive
See Deut. 21:4; Jer. 51:27; Dan. 8:21
ROUGHLY Gen. 42:7, Joseph spoke *r*
Prov. 18:23, the rich answers *r*
See I Sam. 20:10; I Ki. 12:13; II Chron. 10:13
ROUND Ex. 16:14; Isa. 3:18; Lk. 19:43
ROWED Jonah 1:13; Mk. 6:48; Jn. 6:19
ROYAL Gen. 49:20, yield *r* dainties
Esther 1:7, *r* wine in abundance
   5:1; 6:8; 8:15; Acts 12:21, *r* apparel
James. 2:8, fulfill the *r* law
I Pet. 2:9, a *r* priesthood
See I Chron. 29:25; Isa. 62:3; Jer. 43:10
RUBIES Job 28:18; Prov. 8:11; 31:10

RUDDY I Sam. 16:12; Lam. 4:7
RUDE II Cor. 11:6, r in speech
RUDIMENTS Col. 2:8, 20, r of the world
RUIN II Chron 28:23, they were the r of him
   Ps. 89:40, have brought his strong hold to r
   Ezek. 18:30, so iniquity shall not be your r
     21:15, that their r may be multiplied
   Lk. 6:49, the r of that house was great
   See Isa. 3:8; Ezek. 36:35; Acts 15:16
RULE (n.) Esther 9:1, Jews had r over them
   Prov. 17:2, a wise servant shall have r
     19:10, servant to have r over princes
     25:28, no r over his own spirit
   Isa. 63:19, you never bore r over them
   Gal. 6:16, as walk according to this r
   Heb. 13:7, 17, them that have the r over you
   See Eccl. 2:19; Isa. 44:13; II Cor. 10:13
RULE (v.) Gen. 1:16, to r the day
   3:16, your husband shall r over you
   Judg. 8:23, I will not r over you
   II Sam. 23:3, he that r over men must be just
   Ps. 66:7, he r by his power forever
     103:19, his kingdom r over all
   Prov. 16:32, that r his spirit
   Eccl. 9:17, him that r among fools
   Isa. 3:4, babes r over them
     32:1, princes shall r in judgment
   Ezek. 29:15, shall not more r over nations
   Rom. 12:8, he that r with diligence
   Col. 3:15, peace of God r in your hearts
   I Tim. 3:4, one that r well his own house
     5:17, elders that r well
   See Dan. 5:21; Zech. 6:13; Rev. 2:27; 12:5
RULER Num. 13:2, a r among them
   Prov. 6:7, the ant having no guide, or r
     23:1, when you sit to eat with a r
     28:15, a wicked r over the poor
   Isa. 3:6, be thou our r
   Mic. 5:2, shall he come that is to be r
   Mat. 25:21, I will make you r
   Jn. 7:26, do the r know that this is Christ?
     48, have any of the r believed
   See Gen. 41:43; Neh. 5:7; Ps. 2:2; Isa. 1:10
RUMOUR Jer. 49:14, I have heard a r
   Ezek. 7:26, r shall be upon r
   Mat. 24:6; Mk. 13:7, wars and r of wars
   See II Ki. 19:7; Obad. 1; Lk. 7:17
RUN II Chron. 16:9, the eyes of the Lord r to
   and fro
   Ps. 19:5, as a strong man to r a race
     23:5, my cup r over
   Isa. 40:31, they shall r, and not be weary
     55:5, nations shall r to you
   Jer. 12:5, if you have r with the footmen
     51:31, one post shall r to meet another
   Dan. 12:4, many shall r to and fro
   Hab. 2:2, that he may r that reads
   Zech. 2:4, R, speak to this young man
   Lk. 6:38, good measure, r over
   Rom. 9:16, nor of him that r
   I Cor. 9:24, they which r in a race r all
     26, I therefore so r
   Gal. 2:2, lest I should r or had r in vain

   5:7, you did r well
   Heb. 12:1, let us r with patience
   I Pet. 4:4, that you r not to same excess
RUSH (n.) Job 8:11; Isa. 9:14; 19:15; 35:7
RUSH (v.) Isa. 17:13; Jer. 8:6; Acts 2:2
RUST Mat. 6:19, 20; James 5:3

<h1 style="text-align:center">S</h1>

SABBATH Lev. 25:8, seven s of years
   II Ki. 4:23, it is neither new moon nor s
   II Chron. 36:21, as she lay desolate she kept s
   Ezek. 46:1, one the s it shall be opened
   Amos 8:5, when will the s be gone
   Mk. 2:27, the s was made for man
     28; Lk. 6:5, Son of man is Lord of the s
   See Isa. 1:13; Lam. 2:6; Mat. 28:1; Jn. 5:18
SACK Gen. 42:25; 43:21; Josh. 9:4
SACRIFICE (n.) Gen. 31:54, Jacob offered s
   Ex. 5:17, let us go and do s to the Lord
   Num. 25:2, called to the s of their gods
   I Sam. 2:29, wherefore kick ye at my s
     9:13, he does bless the s
     15:22, to obey is better than s
   Ps. 4:5, offer the s of righteousness
     40:6; 51:16, S, you did not desire
     51:17, the s of God are a broken spirit
     118:27, bind the s with cords
   Prov. 15:8, s of wicked an abomination
     17:1, than a house full of s with strife
     21:3, justice is more acceptable than s
   Eccl. 5:1, the s of fools
   Jer. 6:20, nor are your s sweet unto me
     33:18, nor want a man to do s
   Dan. 8:11; 9:27; 11:31, daily s taken away
   Hos. 3:4, many days without a s
     6:6, Mat. 12:7, I desired mercy, and not s
   Amos 4:4, bring your s every morning
   Zeph. 1:7, the Lord has prepared a s
   Mal. 1:8, you offer the blind for s
   Mk. 9:49, every s shall be salted
     12:33, to love the Lord is more than s
   Lk. 13:1, mingled with their s
   Acts 7:42, have you offered s forty years
     14:13, and would have done s
   Rom. 12:1, present your bodies a living s
   I Cor. 8:4; 10:9, 28, offered in s to idols
   Phil. 2:17, upon the s of your faith
     4:18, a s acceptable, well pleasing
   Heb. 9:26, put away sin by s of himself
     10:12, offered one s for sins
     26, there remains no more s for sin
     13:15, let us offer the s of praise
     16, with such s God is well pleased
   I Pet. 2:5, to offer up spiritual s
SACRIFICE (v.) Ex. 22:20, s to any god
   Ezra 4:2, seek your God, and do s to him
   Neh. 4:2, will they s?
   Ps. 54:6, I will freely s to you
     106:37, they s their sons to devils
     107:22, let them s sacrifices of thanksgiving
   Eccl. 9:2, to him that s and that s not
   Isa. 65:3, people that s in gardens
   Hos. 8:13, they s, but the Lord accepts not

Hab. 1:16, they *s* unto their net
I Cor. 5:7, Christ our Passover is *s* for us
   10:20, things the Gentiles *s*, they *s* to devils
See Ex. 8:26; Deut. 15:21; I Sam. 1:3; 15:15
SAD I Ki. 21:5, why is your spirit so *s*
Eccl. 7:3, by the *s* of the countenance
Mat. 6:16, be not of a *s* countenance
Mk. 10:22, he was *s* at that saying
Lk. 24:17, as you walk, and are *s*
SADDLE II Sam. 19:26; I Ki. 13:13
SAFE II Sam. 18:29, is Absalom *s*
Job 21:9, their houses are *s* from fear
Ps. 119:117, hold me up, and I shall be *s*
Ezek. 34:27, they shall be *s* in their land
Acts 27:44, so they escaped all *s* to land
See I Sam. 12:11; Isa. 5:29; Lk. 15:27
SAFEGUARD I Sam. 22:23
SAFELY Ps. 78:53, he led them on *s*
Prov. 1:33, shall dwell *s*
Hos. 2:18, I will make them to lie down *s*
See Isa. 41:3; Mk. 14:44; Acts 16:23
SAFETY Job 3:26, I was not in *s*
   5:4, his children are far from *s*
   11:18, you shall take your rest in *s*
Prov. 11:14, in multitude of counselors in *s*
   21:31, *s* is of the Lord
I Thess. 5:3, when they say Peace and *s*
See Job 24:23; Ps. 12:5; 33:17; Isa. 14:30
SAIL Isa. 33:23; Lk. 8:23; Acts 27:9
SAINTS Job 5:1, to which of the *s* will you turn?
   15:15, he puts no trust in his *s*
Ps. 16:3, but to the *s* that are in the Earth
Ps. 30:4, sing to the Lord, O ye *s* of his
   50:5, gather my *s* together
   89:5, the congregation of the *s*
   7, to be feared in assembly of *s*
   97:10, preserve the souls of his *s*
   116:15, precious is the death of his *s*
   132:9, let your *s* shout for joy
   149:9, this honor have all his *s*
Dan. 7:18, but the *s* shall take the kingdom
   8:13, then I heard one *s* speaking
Mat. 27:52, many bodies of *s* arose
Rom. 1:7; I Cor. 1:2, called to be *s*
   8:27, he makes intercession for the *s*
   12:13, distributing to the necessity of *s*
   16:2, receive her as becomes *s*
I Cor. 6:2, the *s* shall judge the world
   16:1, concerning collection for *s*
   15, ministry of *s*
Eph. 1:18, his inheritance is the *s*
   2:19, fellowcitizens with the *s*
   3:8, less than the least of all *s*
   5:3, not named among you, as becomes *s*
Col. 1:12, the *s* in light
I Thess. 3:13, at coming of our Lord with *s*
II Thess. 1:10, to be glorified in his *s*
I Tim. 5:10, if she have washed the *s* feet
Jude 3, faith once delivered to the *s*
Rev. 5:8; 8:3, 4, the prayers of the *s*
See Phil. 4:21; Rev. 11:18; 13:7; 14:12; 15:3
SAKE Gen. 3:17, cursed is ground for your *s*
   8:21, not curse ground any more for
   man's *s*

   12:13, be well with me for your *s*
   18:26, I will spare for their *s*
   30:27, the Lord has blessed me for your *s*
Num. 11:29, enviest thou for my *s*?
Deut. 1:37; 4:21, angry with me for your *s*
II Sam. 9:1, show kindness for Jonathan's *s*
   18:5, deal gently for my *s*
Neh. 9:31, for your great mercies' *s*
Ps. 6:4; 31:16, save me for your mercies' *s*
   23:3, he leads me for his name's *s*
   44:22, for your *s* are we killed
   106:8, he saved them for his name's *s*
Mat. 5:10, persecuted for righteousness' *s*
   10:18; Mk. 13:9; Lk. 21:12, for my *s*
   24:22; Mk. 13:20, for the elect's *s*
Jn. 11:15, I am glad for your *s*
   13:38, will you lay down your life for my *s*?
Rom. 13:5; I Cor. 10:25, for conscience *s*
Col. 1:24, his body's *s*, which is the church
I Thess. 5:13, for their work's *s*
I Tim. 5:23, for your stomach's *s*
SALUTATION Mk. 12:38; Lk. 1:29
SALUTE I Sam. 10:4; Mk. 15:18
SALVATION Gen. 49:18, waited for your *s*
Ex. 14:13; II Chron. 20:17, see the *s* of the
   Lord
   15:2, he is become my *s*
Deut. 32:15, esteem the rock of his *s*
I Sam. 11:13, the Lord wrought *s* in Israel
   14:45, Jonathan, who has wrought this *s*
II Sam. 22:51, he is the tower of *s* for his king
I Chron. 16:23, who from day to day his *s*
II Chron. 6:41, let your priests be clothed
   with *s*
Ps. 3:8, *S* belongs to the Lord
   9:14, I will rejoice in your *s*
   14:7, Oh that the *s* of Israel were come
   25:5, you are the God of my *s*
   27:1; 62:6; Isa. 12:2, my light and my *s*
   35:3, say unto my soul, I am your *s*
   37:39, the *s* of the righteous is of the Lord
   40:10, I had declared your faithfulness
   and *s*
   50:23, to him will I show the *s* of God
   51:12; 70:4, restore the joy of your *s*
   68:20, he that is our God is the God of *s*
   69:13, hear me in the truth of your *s*
   29, let your *s* set me up on high
   71:15, my mouth shall show forth your *s*
   74:12, working *s* in the midst of the Earth
   78:22, you trusted not in his *s*
   85:9, his *s* is nigh them that fear him
   91:16, will satisfy him, and show him my *s*
   116:13, the cup of *s*
   118:14; Isa. 12:2, the Lord is become my *s*
   119:41, let your *s* come
   123, my eyes fail for your *s*
   155, *S* is far from the wicked
   174, I have longed for your *s*
Ps. 132:16, I will clothe her priests with *s*
   149:4, beautify the meek with *s*
Isa. 12:3, the wells of *s*
   26:1, *s* will God appoint for walls
   33:2, be thou our *s* in time of trouble

45:8, earth open, and let them bring forth *s*
17, saved with an everlasting *s*
49:8, in a day of *s* have I helped you
51:5, my *s* is gone forth
52:7, feet of him that publish *s*
56:1, my *s* is near to come
61:10, the garments of *s*
62:1, the *s* thereof as a lamp
63:5, my own arm brought *s*
Jer. 3:23, in vain is *s* hoped for
Lam. 3:26, wait for the *s* of the Lord
Jonah 2:9, *S* is of the Lord
Hab. 3:8, ride on your chariots of *s*
18, I will joy in the God of my *s*
Zech. 9:9, your King, just, and having *s*
Lk. 1:69, an horn of *s* for us
77, give knowledge of *s* to his people
2:30, my eyes have see your *s*
3:6, all flesh shall see the *s* of God
19:9, this day is *s* come to this house
Jn. 4:22, *s* is of the Jews
Acts 4:12, neither is there *s* in any other
13:26, to you is the word of *s* sent
16:17, these men show to us the way of *s*
Rom. 1:16, the power of God unto *s*
10:10, confession is made to *s*
13:11, now is our *s* nearer
II Cor. 1:6, comforted, it is for your *s*
7:10, repentance to *s*
Eph. 1:13, the gospel of your *s*
6:17; I Thess. 5:8, the helmet of *s*
Phil. 1:19, this shall turn to my *s*
2:12, work out your own *s*
I Thess. 5:9, has appointed us to obtain *s*
II Thess. 2:13, God has chosen you to *s*
II Tim. 3:15, wise unto *s*
Titus 2:11, grace of God that brings *s*
Heb. 1:14, for them who shall be heirs of *s*
5:9, author of eternal *s*
9:28, without sin unto *s*
I Pet. 1:5, kept through faith unto *s*
9, end of faith, the *s* of your souls
10, of which *s* the prophets have enquired
II Pet. 3:15, longsuffering of the Lord is *s*
Rev. 7:10, saying, *S* to our God
SAME Job 4:8, sow wickedness, reap the *s*
Ps. 102:27; Heb. 1:12, you are the *s*
Mat. 5:46, do not the publicans the *s*?
Acts 1:11, this *s* Jesus shall come
Rom. 10:12, the *s* Lord over all
12:16; I Cor. 1:10; Phil. 4:2, be of *s* mind
Heb. 13:8, *s* yesterday, today, and forever
See I Cor. 10:3; 12:4; 15:39; Eph. 4:10
SANCTIFY I Sam. 16:5, *S* yourselves
Isa. 5:16, God shall be *s* in righteousness
13:3, I have commanded my *s* ones
29:23, they shall *s* the Holy One
66:17, *s* themselves in gardens
Jer. 1:5, I *s* and ordained you a prophet
Ezek. 20:41; 36:23, I will be *s* in you
28:25; 39:27, *s* in them in sight of heathen
Joel 1:14; 2:15, *S* ye a fast
Jn. 10:36, him who the Father has *s*
17:17, *S* them through your truth

19, for their sakes I *s* myself
Acts 20:32; 26:18, inheritance among *s*
Rom. 15:16, being *s* by the Holy Ghost
I Cor. 1:2, to them that are *s*
7:14, husband is *s* by the wife
Eph. 5:26, *s* and cleanse the church
I Thess. 5:23, the very God of peace *s* you
I Tim. 4:5, it is *s* by the word of God
II Tim. 2:21, a vessel *s* for the Master's use
Heb. 2:11, ye that *s* and they who are *s*
10:10, by the which will we are *s*
14, perfected forever them that are *s*
13:12, that he might *s* the people
I Pet. 3:15, *s* the Lord God in your hearts
Jude 1, to them that are *s* by God the Father
SANCTUARY Ex. 15:17, plant them in the *S*
25:8, let them make me a *s*
Num. 7:9, service of *s* belongs to them
Neh. 10:39, where are the vessels of the *s*
Ps. 74:7, they have cast fire into your *s*
Isa. 60:13, beautify the place of my *s*
Lam. 2:7, the Lord has abhorred his *s*
SAND Job 6:3; Prov. 27:3; Mat. 7:26
SANG Ex. 15:1; Neh. 12:42; Job 38:7
SANK Ex. 15:5, they *s* into the bottom
SAP Ps. 104:16, trees full of *s*
SAT Judg. 20:26, they *s* before the Lord
Ps. 26:4, have not *s* with vain persons
Jer. 15:17, I *s* alone because of your hand
Ezek. 3:15, I *s* where they *s*
Mat. 4:16, the people who *s* in darkness
Mk. 16:19, he *s* on the right hand of God
Lk. 7:15, he that was dead *s* up
10:39, Mary *s* at Jesus' feet
Jn. 4:6, *s* thus on the wall
Acts 2:3, cloven tongues *s* upon each
See Ezra 10:16; Neh. 1:4; Ps. 137:1; Rev. 4:3
SATAN I Chron. 21:1, *S* provoked David
Ps. 109:6, let *S* stand at the right hand
Mat. 12:26; Lk. 11:18, if *S* cast out *S*
16:23; Lk. 4:8, get behind me, *S*
Lk. 10:18, I beheld *S* as lightning fall
Acts 5:3, why has *S* filled your heart
26:18, turn them from the power of *S*
II Cor. 12:7, the messenger of *S* to buffet me
II Thess. 2:9, after the working of *S*
I Tim. 1:20, whom I have delivered unto *S*
5:15, already turned aside after *S*
SATIATE Jer. 31:14, 25; 46:10
SATISFY Job 38:27, to *s* the desolate
Ps. 17:15, I shall be *s* when I awake
22:26, the meek shall eat and be *s*
36:8, they shall be *s* with fatness
59:15, and grudge if they be not *s*
63:5, my soul shall be *s*
81:16, with honey should I have *s* you
90:14, *s* us early with your mercy
91:16, with long life will I *s* him
103:5, who *s* your mouth with good
105:40, he *s* them with bread from heaven
107:9, he *s* the longing soul
132:15, I will *s* her poor with bread
Prov. 6:30, if he steal to *s* his soul
12:11, he that tills his land shall be *s*

14:14, a good man shall be *s* from himself
19:23, he that has it shall abide *s*
20:13, open your eyes, and you shall be *s*
30:15, three things are never *s*
Eccl. 1:8, your eye is not *s* with seeing
4:8, neither is his eye *s* with riches
5:10, shall not be *s* with silver
Isa. 9:20; Mic. 6:14, shall eat and not be *s*
53:11, travail of his soul, and be *s*
58:10, if you *s* the afflicted soul
11, the Lord shall *s* your soul in drought
Jer. 31:14, shall be *s* with my goodness
Ezek. 16:28, yet you could not be *s*
Amos 4:8, wandered to drink, but were not *s*
Hab. 2:5, is as death, and cannot be *s*
SAVE Gen. 45:7, to *s* your lives
47:25, you have *s* your lives
Deut. 28:29, spoiled, and no man shall *s* you
33:29, O people, *s* by the Lord
Josh. 10:6, come up quickly, and *s* us
Judg. 6:15, where with shall I *s* Israel?
I Sam. 4:3, the ark may *s* us
10:27, how shall this man *s* us?
11:3, if no man to *s* us, we will come
14:6, no restraint to *s* by many or by few
II Sam. 19:9, the king *s* us, and now he is fled
Job 2:6, in your hand, but *s* his life
22:29, he shall *s* the humble
Ps. 7:10, God, who *s* the upright
20:6, the Lord *s* his anointed
34:18, he *s* such as be of a contrite spirit
44:3, neither did their own arm *s* them
72:4, he shall *s* the children of the needy
80:3; Prov. 28:18; Mat. 10:22; Mk. 13:13; Jn.
10:9; Rom. 5:9; 9:27; 10:9, shall be *s*
86:2, *s* your servant that trusts in you
109:31, *s* him from those that condemn
119:94, *s* me, for I have sought your
precepts
146, *s* me, and I shall keep your testimonies
138:7, your right hand shall *s* me
Prov. 20:22, wait on the Lord, he shall *s* you
Isa. 35:4, your God will come and *s* you
43:12, I have declared and have *s*
Isa. 45:20, pray to a god that cannot *s*
47:15, they shall wander, none shall *s*
49:25, I will *s* your children
Jer. 2:28, let them arise, if they can *s*
8:20, summer is ended, and we are not *s*
11:12, but they shall not *s*
14:9, as a mighty man that cannot *s*
15:20; 46:27, I am with you to *s* you
17:14, *s* me, and I shall be *s*
30:10, I will *s* you
Lam. 4:17, a nation that could not *s* us
Ezek. 3:18, to warn wicked, to *s* his life
34:22, therefore will I *s* my flock
Hos. 1:7, I will *s* them by the Lord
13:10, is there any other that may *s* you
Hab. 1:2, cry to you, and you will not *s*
Mat. 1:21, *s* his people from their sins
16:25; Mk. 8:35; Lk. 9:24, will *s* his life
19:25; Lk. 18:26, who then can be *s*?

27:40; Mk. 15:30, *s* yourself
42, he *s* others, himself he cannot *s*
Mk. 3:4; Lk. 6:9, is it lawful to *s*
Lk. 7:50; 18:42, your faith has *s* you
8:12, lest they should believe and be *s*
9:56, not to destroy, but to *s*
13:23, are there few that be *s*?
19:10, to seek and to *s* that which was lost
23:35, let him *s* himself
39, if you be Christ, *s* yourself and us
Jn. 3:17, that the world might be *s*
5:34, these things I say that you might be *s*
12:47, I came not to judge, but to *s*
Acts 2:47, such as should be *s*
15:1, except circumcised you cannot be *s*
16:30, what must I do to be *s*?
27:43, the centurion, willing to *s* Paul
Rom. 8:24, we are *s* by hope
10:1, my prayer is that they might be *s*
11:14; I Cor. 9:22, if I might *s* some
I Cor. 1:18, to us who are *s*
21, by foolishness of preaching to *s* some
7:16, shall *s* your husband
II Cor. 2:15, savour in them that are *s*
Eph. 2:5, 8, by grace you are *s*
I Tim. 1:15, came to *s* sinners
4:16, you shall *s* yourself and them
Heb. 5:7, able to *s* him from death
7:25, able to *s* to the uttermost
10:39, believe to the *s* of the soul
11:7, an ark to the *s* of his house
James 1:21, word which can *s* your souls
2:14, can faith *s* him?
5:15, the prayer of faith shall *s* the sick
20, shall *s* a soul from death
I Pet. 3:20, souls were *s* by water
4:18, if the righteous scarcely be *s*
Jude 23, others *s* with fear
SAVE (*except*) II Sam. 22:32, *s* the Lord
Mat. 11:27, nor know any *s* the Son
17:8; Mk. 9:8, *s* Jesus only
Lk. 17:18, *s* this stranger
18:19, none good *s* one
II Cor. 11:24, forty stripes *s* one
Gal. 6:14, glory *s* in the cross
See Mk. 5:37; Lk. 4:26; Rev. 2:17; 13:17
SAVIOUR II Sam. 22:3, my refuge, my *s*
II Ki. 13:5, the Lord gave Israel a *s*
Ps. 106:21, they forgot God their *s*
Isa. 19:20, he shall send them a *s*
45:21, a just God and a *S*
49:26, all shall know I am your *S*
Eph. 5:23, Christ is the *s* of the body
I Tim. 4:10, who is the *S* of all men
Titus 2:10, adorn doctrine of God our *S*
13, glorious appearing of our *S*
SAVOUR Gen. 8:21, smelled a sweet *s*
Ex. 5:21, have made our *s* to be abhorred
Song of Sol. 1:3, *s* of your good ointment
Joel 2:20, his ill *s* shall come up
Lk. 14:34, if salt have lost his *s*
See Eccl. 10:1; Ezek. 6:13; 20:41; Eph. 5:2
SAVOUREST Mat. 16:23; Mk. 8:33
SAVOURY Gen. 27:4, 7, 14, 31

SAW Gen. 22:4, Abraham s the place
26:28, we s the Lord was with you
Ex. 10:23, they s not one another
24:10, they s the God of Israel
II Chron. 25:21, they s one another in the face
Job 29:11, when the eye s me
Eccl. 2:24, this I s, it was from hand of God
Song of Sol. 3:3, S ye him whom my soul loves?
Mat. 12:22, both spoke and s
17:8, they s no man
Mk. 8:23, if he s ought
Jn. 1:48, under the fig tree I s you
8:56, Abraham s my day
20:20, glad when they s the Lord
SAY Ex. 3:13, what shall I s to them?
4:12, teach you what you shall s
Num. 22:19, know what the Lord will s
Judg. 18:24, what is this you s to me
Ezra 9:10, what shall we s after this?
Mat. 3:9, think not to s within yourselves
7:22, may will s in that day
23:3, they s, and do not
Mk. 8:27, whom do men s that I am?
Lk. 7:40, I have somewhat to s to you
I Cor. 12:3, no man can s that Jesus
See Lk. 7:7; Jn. 4:20; 8:26; 16:12
SAYING Deut. 1:23, the s pleased me well
I Ki. 2:38, the s is good
Ps. 49:4, my dark s upon the harp
78:2, utter dark s of old
Prov. 1:6, the dark s of the wise
Mat. 28:15, this s is commonly reported
Lk. 2:51, kept all these s in her heart
Jn. 4:37, herein is that s true
6:60, an hard s, who can hear it?
See Jn. 21:23; Rom 13:9; I Tim. 1:15
SCANT Mic. 6:10, s measure
SCARCE Gen. 27:30; Acts 14:18
SCARCELY Rom. 5:7; I Pet. 4:18
SCARCENESS Deut. 8:9, bread without s
SCARE Job 7:14, you s me with dreams
SCATTER Gen. 11:4, lest we be s abroad
Lev. 26:33, I will s you among the heathen
Num. 10:35; Ps. 68:1, let your enemies be s
Job 18:15, brimstone shall be s
37:11, he s his bright cloud
38:24, which s the east wind
Ps. 147:16, he s the hoar frost
Prov. 11:24, s, and yet increases
20:8, a king s evil with his eyes
26, a wise king s the wicked
Jer. 10:21, all their flocks shall be s
23:1, woe to pastors that s the sheep
Mat. 26:31; Mk. 14:27, sheep shall be s
9:36, s as sheep having to shepherd
12:30; Lk. 11:23, he that gathers not s
SCENT Job 14:9; Jer. 48:11; Hos. 14:7
SCHOLAR I Chron. 25:8; Mal. 2:12
SCIENCE Dan. 1:4; I Tim. 6:20
SCOFF Hab 1:10; II Pet. 3:3
SCORCH Mat. 13:6; Mk. 4:6; Rev. 16:8
SCORN Job 16:20; Ps. 44:13; 79:4
SCORNER Prov. 9:8, reprove not a s

13:1, a s hears not rebuke
19:28, an ungodly witness s judgment
19:29, judgments are prepared for s
24:9, the s is an abomination
Isa. 29:20, the s is consumed
Hos. 7:5, he stretched out his hands with s
See Ps. 1:1, Prov. 1:22; 3:34; 9:12
SCOURGE Job 5:21, the s of the tongue
9:23, if the s slay suddenly
Isa. 28:15, the overflowing s
Mat. 10:17; 23:34, they will s you
Jn. 2:15, a s of small cords
Acts 22:25, is it lawful to s a Roman?
Heb. 12:6, the Lord s every son
See Josh. 23:13; Mat. 27:26; Jn. 19:1
SCRAPE Lev. 14:41; Job 2:8; Ezek. 26:4
SCRIBE I Chron. 27:32, a wise man and a s
Isa. 33:18, where is the s?
Jer. 8:8, the pen of the s is in vain
Mat. 5:20, exceed the righteousness of the s
7:29, as having authority, and not as the s
13:52, every s instructed unto the kingdom
Mk. 12:38; Lk. 20:46, beware of the s
See Ezra 4:8; 7:6; Neh. 8:4; Mat. 8:19
SCRIP I Sam. 17:40; Mat. 10:10
SEARCH (n.) Ps. 64:6; 77:6; Jer. 2:34
SEARCH (v.) Num. 13:2, they s the land
I Chron. 28:9, the Lord s all hearts
Job. 11:7, can you by s find out God?
13:9, it is good that he should s you out
Job 28:27, he prepared it and s it out
29:16, the cause I knew not I s out
32:11, I waited while you s out what to say
36:26, can the number of his years be s out?
Ps. 44:21, shall not God s this out?
139:1, you have s me and known me
23, S me and know my heart
Prov. 25:2, kings to s out a matter
27, for men to s out their own glory
Eccl. 1:13, I gave my heart to s wisdom
Isa. 40:28, there is no s of his understanding
Jer. 17:10, I the Lord s the heart
29:13, when you s for me with all your heart
31:37, the foundations of the earth s out
Lam. 3:40, let us s our ways, and turn
Ezek. 34:6, none did s or seek after them
8, neither did my shepherds s for my flock
Amos 9:3, I will s and take them out thence
Zeph. 1:12, I will s Jerusalem with candles
Jn. 5:39; Acts 17:11, s the scriptures
I Cor. 2:10, the Spirit s all things
I Pet. 1:10, salvation prophets s diligently
SEARED I Tim. 4:2, conscience s
SEASON Gen. 1:14, signs, and s, and days
Deut. 28:12, give rain in his s
II Chron. 15:3, a long s without the true God
Job 5:26, as a shock of corn in his s
Ps. 1:3, that brings forth fruit in his s
22:2, I cry in the night s
Prov. 15:23, word spoken in due s
Eccl. 3:1, to every thing a s and a time
Isa. 50:4, know how to speak a word in s

Jer. 5:24, former and latter rain in his *s*
    33:20, day and night in their *s*
Dan. 2:21, changes the times and *s*
    7:12, lives prolonged for a *s*
Hos. 2:9, take away my wine in *s*
Mat. 21:41, render the fruits in their *s*
Lk. 1:20, shall be fulfilled in their *s*
    20:10, at the *s* he sent servant
    23:8, desirous to see him of a long *s*
Jn. 5:4, angel went down at certain *s*
    35, willing for a *s* to rejoice
Acts 1:7, not for you to know times and *s*
    13:11, not seeing sun for a *s*
Heb. 11:25, pleasures of sin for a *s*
SEAT I Sam. 20:18, your *s* will be empty
Job 23:3, that I might come even to his *s*!
    29:7, when I prepared my *s* in the street
Ps. 1:1, the *s* of the scornful
Amos 6:3, cause *s* of violence of come near
Mat. 21:12, *s* of them that sold doves
    23:2, scribes sit in Moses' *s*
    6, Mk. 12:39, chief *s* in synagogues
See Ezek. 8:3; 28:2; Lk. 1:52; Rev. 2:13
SECRET (*n.*) Gen. 49:6, come not into their *s*
Job 11:6, the *s* of wisdom
    15:8, have you heard the *s* of God?
    29:4, the *s* of God was upon my tabernacle
Prov. 3:32, his *s* is with the righteous
    9:17, bread eaten in *s*
    21:14, a gift in *s*
Isa. 45:19; 48:16, I have not spoken in *s*
Mat. 6:4, your Father who sees in *s*
    6, pray to your Father, who is in *s*
Jn. 18:20, in *s* have I said nothing
See Prov. 11:13; 20:19; Dan. 2:18; 4:9
SECRET (*adj.*) Deut. 29:29, *s* belong to God
Judg. 3:19, I have a *s* errand
    13:18, my name, seeing it is *s*?
Ps. 19:12, cleanse me from *s* faults
    90:8, our *s* sins
Prov. 27:5, open rebuke better than *s* love
See Song of Sol. 2:14; Isa. 45:3; Jer. 13:17
SECRETLY Gen. 31:27, flee away *s*
Deut: 13:6, entice you *s*, saying
I Sam. 18:22, commune with David *s*
    23:9, Saul *s* practiced mischief
II Sam. 12:12, for you did it *s*
Job 4:12, a thing was *s* brought to me
    13:10, if you *s* accept persons
    31:27, my heart has been *s* enticed
Ps. 10:9, he lies in wait *s*
    31:20, keep them *s* from the strife
Jn. 11:28, she called her sister *s*
    19:38, *s* for fear of the Jews
See Deut. 27:24; 28:57; II Ki. 17:9
SECT Acts 5:17; 15:5; 24:5; 26:5; 28:22
SECURE Job 11:18; 12:6; Mat. 28:14
SECURELY Prov. 3:29; Mic. 2:8
SEDUCE Mk. 13:22, show signs, to *s*
I Jn. 2:26, concerning them that *s* you
Rev. 2:20, to *s* my servants
See Prov. 12:26; I Tim. 4:1; II Tim. 3:13
SEE Gen. 11:5, came down to *s* the city
    44:23, you shall *s* my face no more

    45:28, I will go and *s* him before I die
Ex. 12:13, when I *s* the blood
    14:13, *s* the salvation of the Lord
    33:20, there shall no man *s* me, and live
Deut. 3:25, let me *s* the good land
    34:4, I have caused you to *s* it
II Ki. 6:17, open his eyes, that he may *s*
    10:16, *s* my zeal for the Lord
Job 7:7, my eye shall no more *s* good
    19:26, yet in my flesh shall I *s* God
Ps. 27:13, believed to *s* the goodness
    66:5, come and *s* the works of God
    94:9, he that formed the eye, shall he not *s*?
Isa. 6:10, lest they *s* with their eyes
    32:3, eyes of them that *s* not be dim
    33:17, shall *s* the king in his beauty
    40:5, all flesh shall *s* it together
    52:8, they shall *s* eye to eye
Jer. 5:21; Ezek. 12:12, eyes, and *s* not
Mat. 5:8, they shall *s* God
    13:14; Mk. 4:12; Acts 28:26, *s* you shall *s*
    28:6, *s* the place where the Lord lay
Mk. 8:18, having eyes, *s* ye not?
Lk. 17:23, *s* here, or *s* there
Jn. 1:39; 11:34; Rev. 6:1, come and *s*
    50, you shall *s* greater things
    9:25, I was blind, now I *s*
Heb. 2:9, but we *s* Jesus
I Pet. 1:8, though now we *s* him not
I Jn. 3:2, we shall *s* him as he is
SEED Gen. 3:15, enmity between your *s*
Ex. 16:31, manna like coriander *s*
Lev. 19:19, you shall not sow mingled *s*
    26:16, you shall sow your *s* in vain
Num. 20:5, it is no place of *s*
Deut. 1:8, to give it to their *s* after them
    11:10, not as Egypt, where you sow *s*
    14:22, tithe all the increase of your *s*
    28:38, you shall carry much *s* into field
Ps. 126:6, bearing precious *s*
Eccl. 11:6, in the morning sow your *s*
Isa. 5:10, the *s* of an homer shall yield
    17:11, in morning make your *s* to flourish
    55:10, give *s* to the sower
    61:9, the *s* which the Lord has blessed
Jer. 2:21, I had planted you wholly a right *s*
Joel 1:17, the *s* is rotten
Amos 9:13, overtake him that sows *s*
Hag. 2:19, is the *s* yet in the barn?
Zech. 8:12, the *s* shall be prosperous
Mal. 2:15, that he might seek a godly *s*
SEEK Gen. 37:15, what *s* you?
Num. 15:39, *s* not after your own heart
    16:10, *s* you the priesthood also?
Deut. 4:29, if you *s* him with all your heart
    12:5, to his habitation shall you *s* and come
    23:6; Ezra 9:12, you shall not *s* their peace
Ruth 3:1, shall I not *s* rest for you?
II Chron. 15:2, if you *s* him, he will be found
    19:3, have prepared your heart to *s* God
    34:3, Josiah began to *s* after God
Ezra 4:2, we *s* your God, as you do
Neh. 2:10, to *s* the welfare of Israel

Ps. 9:10, have not forsaken them that *s* you
10:4, the wicked will not *s* after God
15, *s* out his wickedness till you find none
14:2; 53:2, if there were any that did *s* God
24:6, generation of them that *s* him
27:8, *s* you my face; your face will I *s*
34:14; I Pet. 3:11, *s* peace and pursue it
63:1, early will I *s* you
69:32, your heart shall live that *s* God
83:16, that they may *s* your name
Prov. 1:28, they shall *s* me, but not find me
8:17, those that *s* me early shall find me
11:27, that diligently *s* good
23:30, they that go to *s* mixed wine
35, I will *s* it yet again
Eccl. 1:13; 7:25, gave my heart to *s* wisdom
Song of Sol. 3:2, *s* him whom my soul loves
Isa. 1:17, learn to do well, *s* judgment
Isa. 8:19, should not a people *s* unto their
God?
19:3, they shall *s* to charmers
34:16, *S* ye out of the book of the Lord
41:17, when the needy *s* water
45:19, I said not, *S* ye my face in vain
Jer. 5:1, any that *s* the truth
30:17, Zion, whom no man *s* after
38:4, this man *s* not welfare of people
Ezek. 7:25, they shall *s* peace
Dan. 9:3, I set my face to *s* by prayer
Amos 5:4, *S* ye me the Lord, and ye shall live
Zeph. 2:3, *S* ye the Lord, all ye meek
Mal. 2:7, they should *s* the law at his mouth
Mat. 6:32, these things do the Gentiles *s*
33; Lk. 12:31, *s* ye first the kingdom of God
7:7; Lk. 11:9, *s*, and you shall find
12:39; 16:4, adulterous generation *s* a sign
28:5; Mk. 16:6, I know that you *s* Jesus
Mk. 1:37, all men *s* for you
8:11, *s* of him a sign from heaven
Lk. 13:7, I come *s* fruit
19:10, is come to *s* and to save
24:5, why *s* ye the living among the dead?
Jn. 1:38, what *s* ye?
7:25, is not this he whom they *s* to kill?
34, you shall *s* me, and shall not find me
18:8, if you *s* me, let these go their way
20:15, woman, whom *s* you?
Rom. 3:11, there is none that *s* after God
I Cor. 1:22, the Greeks *s* after wisdom
10:24, let no man *s* his own
II Cor. 12:14, I *s* not yours but you
Phil. 2:21, all *s* their own things
Col. 3:1, *s* those things which are above
Heb. 11:6, a rewarder of them that *s* him
14, declare plainly that they *s* a country
I Pet. 5:8, *s* whom he may devour
Rev. 9:6, in those days shall men *s* death
SEEM Gen. 19:14, he *s* as one that mocked
29:20, they *s* to him but a few days
Num. 16:9, *S* it but a small thing?
Prov. 14:12, there is a way that *s* right
Lk. 8:18, taken that which he *s* to have
24:11, words *s* as idle tales
I Cor. 3:18, if any *s* to be wise

11:16, if any man *s* to be contentious
Heb. 4:1, lest any *s* to come short
12:11, now no chastening *s* to be joyous
See Gen. 27:12; Acts 17:18; Gal. 2:6
SEEMLY Prov. 19:10; 26:1
SEEN Gen. 32:30, I have *s* God face to face
Ex. 14:13, Egyptians whom ye have *s* today
Judg. 6:22, because I have *s* an angel
II Ki. 20:15, what have they *s*
Job 13:1, my eye has *s* all this
28:7, a path the vulture's eye has not *s*
Eccl. 6:5, he has not *s* the sun
Isa. 9:2, have *s* a great light
64:4; I Cor. 2:9, neither has eye *s*
Mat. 6:1; 23:5, to be *s* of men
9:33, never so *s* in Israel
Mk. 9:1, till they have *s* the kingdom
Lk. 5:26, we have *s* strange things today
Jn. 1:18, no man has *s* God
8:57, have you *s* Abraham?
14:9, he that has *s* me has *s* the Father
Acts 11:23, when he had *s* the grace of God
I Cor. 9:1, have I not *s* Jesus Christ?
I Tim. 6:16, whom no man has *s*
Heb. 11:1, evidence of things not *s*
I Pet. 1:8, whom having not *s*, you love
SEETHE Ex. 23:19; II Ki. 4:38; Ezek. 24:5
SEIZE Job 3:6; Ps. 55:15; Mat. 21:38
SELF Titus 1:7; II Pet. 2:10
SELL Gen. 25:31, *S* my your birthright
37:27, come, let us *s* him
I Ki. 21:25, Ahab did *s* himself
Neh. 5:8, will you even *s* your brethren?
Prov. 23:23, buy the truth, and *s* it not
Joel 3:8, I will *s* your sons and daughters
Amos 8:5, that we may *s* corn
6, and *s* the refuse of the wheat
Mat. 19:21; Lk. 18:22, *s* that you have
Lk. 22:36, let him *s* his garment
James 4:13, we will buy and *s* and get gain
See Ps. 44:12; Prov. 11:26; Mat. 13:44
SELLER Isa. 24:2; Ezek. 7:12, 13; Acts 16:14
SEND Gen. 24:7, God shall *s* his Angel
Gen. 24:12, *s* me good speed this day
Gen. 45:5, God *s* me
Ex. 4:13, *s* by hand of him whom you will *s*
II Chron. 7:13; Ezek. 14:19, if *s* pestilence
Ps. 20:2, *S* you help from the sanctuary
43:3, *s* out your light and truth
118:25, *s* now prosperity
Isa. 6:8, whom shall *s*? *s* me
Mat. 9:38; Lk. 10:2, *s* labourers
15:23, *S* her away, for she cries after us
Mk. 3:14, that he might *s* them to preach
Jn. 14:26, the Father will *s* in my name
17:8, believed that you did *s* me
Rom. 8:3, God *s* his Son in likeness
SENSUAL James 3:15; Jude 19
SENT Judg. 6:14, have not I *s* you?
Ps. 77:17, the skies *s* out a sound
106:15, he *s* leanness into their soul
107:20, he *s* his word, and healed them
Jer. 23:21, I not *s* these prophets
Mat. 15:24, I am not *s* but to lost sheep

Jn. 4:34, the will of him that *s* me
9:4, work the works of him that *s* me
17:3, life to know him whom you have *s*
Acts 10:29, as soon as I was *s* for
See Isa. 61:1; Jn. 1:6; 3:28; I Pet. 1:12
SENTENCE Ps. 17:2, let my *s* come forth
Prov. 16:10, a divine *s* in the lips of the king
Eccl. 8:11, because *s* is not executed speedily
II Cor. 1:9, *s* of death in ourselves
See Deut. 17:9; Jer. 4:12; Dan. 5:12; 8:23
SEPARATE Gen. 13:9, *s* yourself from me
Deut. 19:2, you shall *s* three cities
Prov. 16:28; 17:9, a whisperer *s* chief friends
19:4, the poor is *s* from his neighbour
Mat. 25:32, he shall *s* them
Rom. 8:35, who shall *s* us from love of God?
II Cor. 6:17, be ye *s*
See Num. 6:2; Ezra 10:11; Isa. 56:3; 59:2
SEPARATION Num. 6:8; 19:9; Ezek. 42:20
SERPENT Gen. 3:1, the *s* was more subtil
49:17, Dan shall be a *s* by the way
Job 26;13, his hand formed the crooked *s*
Ps. 58:4, like the poison of a *s*
140:3, sharpened their tongues like a *s*
Prov. 23:32, at last it bites like a *s*
Isa. 27:1, the Lord shall punish the *s*
65:25, dust shall be the *s* meat
Jer. 8:17, I will send *s* among you
Amos 9:3, I will command the *s*
Mic. 7:17, they shall lick dust like a *s*
Mat. 7:10; Lk. 11:11, will he give him a *s*?
Mk. 16:18, they shall take up *s*
Jn. 3:14, as Moses lifted up the *s*
Rev. 12:9; 20:2, that old *s*, called the Devil
SERVANT Gen. 9:25, a *s* of *s* shall he be
Job 3:19, the *s* is free
7:2, as a *s* desires the shadow
Ps. 116:16; 119:125; 143:12, I am your *s*
Prov. 22:7, the borrower is *s* to the lender
22:19, a *s* will not be corrected with words
Isa. 24:2, as with *s*, so with master
Mat. 10:25, enough for *s* to be as his lord
25:21, good and faithful *s*
Lk. 12:47, that *s* which knew his lord's will
17:10, unprofitable *s*
Jn. 8:35, *s* abides not in house forever
15:15, *s* knows not what his lord does
I Cor. 7:21, are you called, being a *s*?
23, be not ye the *s* of men
Eph. 6:5; I Pet. 2:18, *S* be obedient
See Rom. 6:16; Col. 4:1, Rev. 22:3
SERVE Gen. 25:23, elder shall *s* the younger
Deut. 6:13; 10:12, 20; Josh. 22:5, I Sam. 12:14,
you shall fear the Lord, and *s* him
Josh. 24:15, choose ye whom ye will *s*
I Chron. 28:9, *s* him with a perfect heart
Ps. 22:30, a seed shall *s* him
72:11, all nations shall *s* him
Isa. 43:23, I have not caused you to *s*
24, you have made me to *s* with your lips
Jer. 5:19, so shall ye *s* strangers
Dan. 6:16, your God whom you *s* will deliver
Zeph. 3:9, to *s* him with one consent
Mal. 3:17, spares his son that *s* him

18, between him that *s* God and him that
Lk. 10:40, has left me to *s* alone
15:29, these many years do I *s* you
Lk. 16:13, no man can *s* two masters
Jn. 12:26, if any man *s* me, let him follow
Acts 6:2, leave word of God, and *s* tables
Rom. 6:6, henceforth we should not *s*
Gal. 5:13, by love *s* one another
Col. 3:24, for you *s* the Lord Christ
Rev. 7:15, they *s* him day and night
SERVICE Ex. 12:26, what mean ye by this *s*?
Jn. 16:2, will think he does God *s*
Rom. 12:1, your reasonable *s*
Eph. 6:7, doing *s* as to the Lord
Phil. 2:30, to supply your lack of *s*
See Ezra 6:18, Ps. 104:14; Jer. 22:13
SET Gen. 4:15, the Lord *s* a mark on Cain
9:13, I do *s* my bow in the cloud
Deut. 1:8, I have *s* the land before you
Job 33:5, *s* your words in order
Ps. 16:8, I have *s* the Lord before me
20:5, we will *s* up our banners
91:14, he has *s* his love upon me
Eccl. 7:14, has *s* the one against the other
Song of Sol. 8:6, *S* me as a seal upon your
heart
Mat. 5:14, a city *s* on a hill
Acts 18:10, no man shall *s* on you
Heb. 6:18, the hope *s* before us
See Ps. 75:7; 107:41; Eph. 1:20; Col. 3:2
SETTLE Zeph. 1:12; Lk. 21:14; Col. 1:23
SEVER Lev. 20:26; Ezek. 39:14; Mat. 13:49
SEW Gen. 3:7; Job 14:17; Mk. 2:21
SHADE Ps. 121:5, the Lord is your *s*
SHADOW Gen. 19:8, the *s* of my roof
Job 7:2, as a servant earnestly desires the *s*
14:2, he flees as a *s* and continues not
17:7, all my members are as a *s*
Ps. 91:1, under the *s* of the Almighty
102:11, my days are like a *s*
144:4; Eccl. 8:13, his days are as a *s*
Eccl. 6:12, life which he spends as a *s*
Song of Sol. 2:3, under his *s* with great
delight
17; 4:6, till the *s* flee away
25:4, a *s* from heat, 32:2, *s* of a great rock
49:2; 51:16, in the *s* of his hand
Jer. 6:4, the *s* of evening are stretched out
Lam. 4:20, under his *s* we shall live
Acts 5:15, the *s* of Peter might overshadow
James 1:17, with whom is no *s* of turning
SHAFT Ex. 25:31; 37:17; Isa. 49:2
SHAKE Judg. 16:20, I will *s* myself
Ps. 29:8, voice of the Lord *s* the wilderness
72:16, the fruit thereof shall *s* like Lebanon
Isa. 2:19, when he arises to *s* the earth
52:2, *S* yourself from the dust
Joel 3:16; Hag. 2:6, 21, I will *s* the heavens
Hag. 2:7, I will *s* all nations
Mat. 11:7; Lk. 7:24, a reed *s* with the wind
Lk. 6:38, good measure, *s* together
II Thess. 2:2, be not soon *s* in mind
Heb. 12:26, I *s* not the Earth only
27, things which cannot be *s*

SHAME Ps. 4:2, turn my glory into *s*
    40:14; 83:17, let them be put to *s*
  Prov. 10:5; 17:2, a son that causes *s*
  Isa. 61:7, for your *s* you shall have double
  Jer. 51:51, *s* has covered our faces
  Ezek. 16:52, bear your own *s*
  Dan. 12:2, awake, some to *s*
  Lk. 14:9, with *s* to take lowest room
  Acts 5:41, worthy to suffer *s*
  I Cor. 6:5; 15:34, I speak this to your *s*
  Eph. 5:12, a *s* even to speak of those things
  Phil. 3:19, whose glory is in their *s*
  Heb. 6:6, put him to an open *s*
    12:2, despising the *s*
SHAPE Lk. 3:22; Jn. 5:37; Rev. 9:7
SHARP Ps. 52:2, tongue like a *s* razor
  Prov. 25:18, false witness is *s* arrow
    27:17, iron *s* iron, so a man *s* his friend
  Isa. 41:15, a *s* threshing instrument
  Acts 15:39, the contention was so *s*
  Heb. 4:12, *s* than any sword
  See Mic. 7:4; II Cor. 13:10; Rev. 1:16; 14:14
SHEAF Deut. 24:19; Ruth 2:7; Ps. 126:6
SHEARERS Gen. 38:12; I Sam. 25:7; Isa. 53:7
SHEATH I Sam. 17:51; Ezek. 21:3
SHED Gen. 9:6, by man shall his blood be *s*
  Mat. 26:28, *s* for many for remission of sins
  Rom. 5:5, love of God *s* in our hearts
  Titus 3:6, which he *s* on us abundantly
  Heb. 9:22, without *s* of blood is no remission
  See Ezek. 18:10; 22:3; Acts 2:33
SHEEP Gen. 4:2, Abel was a keeper of *s*
  Num. 27:17; I Ki. 22:17; Mat. 9:36; Mk. 6:34,
    as *s* which have no shepherd
  Ps. 49:14, like *s* they are laid in the grave
    95:7; 100:3, we are the *s* of his hand
  Isa. 53:6, all we like *s* have gone astray
  Jer. 12:3, pull them out like *s* for slaughter
  Ezek. 34:6, my *s* wandered
  Mat. 7:15, false prophets in *s* clothing
    10:6, go rather to lost *s*
    12:12, how much is a man better than a *s*?
  Jn. 10:2, shepherd of *s*
    11, good shepherd gives his life for the *s*
    21:16, feed my *s*
SHEET Judg. 14:12; Acts 10:11; 11:5
SHELTER Job 24:8; Ps. 61:3
SHEPHERD Ps. 23:1, the Lord is my *s*
  Isa. 13:20, nor shall *s* make their fold there
    40:11, he shall feed his flock like a *s*
    56:11, they are *s* that cannot understand
  Jer. 23:4, set *s* over them who shall feed
    50:6, their *s* have caused them to go astray
  Amos 3:12, as the *s* takes out of the mouth
  Jn. 10:14, I am the good *s*
  See Zech. 11:3; Lk. 2:8; I Pet. 2:25; 5:4
SHIELD Judg. 5:8, was there a *s* seen?
  Ps. 5:12, compass him as with a *s*
    33:20; 59:11; 84:9, the Lord is our *s*
    91:4, truth shall be your *s*
  Isa. 21:5, anoint the *s*
  Eph. 6:16, taking the *s* of faith
SHINE Job 22:28, shall *s* upon your ways
    29:3, when his candle *s* upon my head

Ps. 104:15, oil to make his face *s*
    139:12, the night *s* as the day
  Prov. 4:18, light that *s* more and more
  Isa. 9:2, upon them has the light *s*
    60:1, arise, *s* for your light is come
  Dan. 12:3, wise shall *s* as the brightness
  Mat. 5:16, let your light so *s*
    13:43, the righteous *s* as the sun
  II Cor. 4:6, who commanded the light to *s*
  See Jn. 1:5; II Pet. 1:19; Rev. 1:16
SHOCK Judg. 15:5; Job 5:26
SHOD Mk. 6:9; Eph. 6:15
SHOOT Ps. 22:7; they *s* out the lip
    64:3, to *s* their arrows, even bitter words
  See I Chron. 12:1; Mk. 4:32; Lk. 21:30
SHORT Job 17:12, the light is *s*
    20:5, triumphing of wicked is *s*
  Ps. 89:47, remember how *s* my time is
  Rom. 3:23, come *s* of the glory of God
  I Cor. 7:29, the time is *s*
  See Num. 11:23; Isa. 50:2; 59:1; Mat. 24:22
SHORTER Isa. 28:20, the bed is *s*
SHORTLY Gen. 41:32; Rom. 16:20
SHOUT Ps. 47:5, God is gone up with a *s*
  Lam. 3:8, when I *s* he shuts out prayer
  I Thess. 4:16, shall descend with a *s*
  See Num. 23:21; I Sam. 4:5; Isa. 12:6
SHOWER Ps. 65:10, makes it soft with *s*
    72:6, like *s* that water the Earth
  Ezek. 34:26, will cause *s* to come in season
  See Deut. 32:2; Job 24:8; Jer. 3:3; 14:22
SHUN Acts 20:27; II Tim. 2:16
SHUT Gen. 7:16, the Lord *s* him in
  Isa. 22:22, he shall open, and none shall *s*
    60:11, your gates shall not be *s* day nor
    night
  Jer. 36:5, I am *s* up
  Lam. 3:8, he *s* out of my prayer
  See Gal. 3:23; I Jn. 3:17; Rev. 3:7; 20:3
SICK Prov. 13:12, makes the heart *s*
    23:35, stricken me, and I was not *s*
  Song of Sol. 2:5, I am *s* of love
  Isa. 1:5, the whole head is *s*
  Hos. 7:5, make him *s* with bottles of wine
  Mat. 8:14, wife's mother *s*
  James 5:14, is any *s*? call elders of the church
    15, prayer of faith shall save the *s*
SICKNESS Ps. 41:3; Eccl. 5:17; Mat. 8:17
SIFT Isa. 30:28; Amos 9:9; Lk. 22:31
SIGHT Ex. 3:3, this great *s*
  Deut. 28:34, for *s* of your eyes
  Eccl. 6:9, better is *s* of eyes
  Mat. 11:5; 20:34; Lk. 7:21, blind receive *s*
  Mat. 11:26; Lk. 10:21, it seemed good in your *s*
  Lk. 18:42; Acts 22:13, receive your *s*
    21:11, fearful *s* and signs from heaven
  Rom. 12:17, things honest in *s* of all men
  II Cor. 5:7, walk by faith, not by *s*
SIGN Isa. 7:11, ask you a *s* of the Lord
    55:13, for an everlasting *s*
  Ezek. 12:6, I have set your for a *s*
  Dan. 4:3, how great are his *s*?
  Mat. 16:3, *s* of the times
  Mk. 16:20, with *s* following

Jn. 4:48, except ye see *s*
Acts 2:22, man approved of God by *s*
SIGNIFY Jn. 12:33; Heb. 9:8; I Pet. 1:11
SILENCE Mat. 22:34; I Tim. 2:11
SILENT I Sam. 2:9, *s* in darkness
  Ps. 28:1, be not *s* to me
    31:17, let the wicked be *s* in the grave
  Zech. 2:13, be *s*, all flesh, before the Lord
  See Ps. 22:2; 30:12; Isa. 47:5; Jer. 8:14
SILLY Job 5:2; Hos. 7:11; II Tim. 3:6
SILVER I Ki. 10:27, king made *s* as stones
  Job 22:25, you shall have plenty of *s*
  Ps. 12:6; 66:10, as *s* is tried
  Prov. 8:10, receive instruction, and not *s*
  Isa. 1:22, your *s* is become dross
  Jer. 6:30, reprobate *s* shall men call them
  Mal. 3:3, sit as a refiner and purifier of *s*
SIMILITUDE Num. 12:8, the *s* of the Lord
  Deut. 4:12, saw no *s*
  Ps. 144:12, after the *s* of a palace
  Rom. 5:14, the *s* of Adam's transgression
  James 3:9, made after the *s* of God
  See Hos. 12:10; Dan. 10:16; Heb. 7:15
SIMPLE Ps. 19:7, making wise the *s*
    116:6, the Lord preserved the *s*
    119:130, it gives understanding to the *s*
  Prov. 22:3, *s* pass on, and are punished
  Rom. 16:18, deceive the hearts of the *s*
  See Prov. 7:7; 8:5; 9:4; 14:15; 19:25
SIN (*n.*) Gen. 4:7, *s* lies at the door
  Num. 27:3, died in his own *s*
  II Chron. 25:4, put to death for his own *s*
  Job 10:6, you search after my *s*?
  Ps. 19:13, from presumption *s*
    25:7, remember not *s* of my youth
    32:1, blessed is he whose *s* is covered
    38:18, I will be sorry for my *s*
    51:3, my *s* is ever before me
    90:8, our secret *s*
  Prov. 5:22, holden with cords of *s*
    14:9, fools make a mock at *s*
    34, *s* is a reproach to any people
  Isa. 30:1, to add *s* to *s*
    53:10, offering for *s*, 53:12, bare the *s* of
    many
  Jer. 51:5, land filled with *s*
  Ezek. 33:16, none of his *s* shall be mentioned
  Hos. 4:8, they eat up *s* of my people
  Mic. 6:7, fruit of my body for *s* of my soul
  Mat. 12:31, all manner of *s* shall be forgiven
  Jn. 1:29, the *s* of the world
    8:7, he that is without *s*
    16:8, will reprove the world of *s*
    19:11, has the greater *s*
  Acts 7:60, lay not this *s* to their charge
    22:16, wash away your *s*
  Rom. 5:20, were *s* abounded
    6:1, shall we continue in *s*?
    7:7, I had not known *s*
    14:23, whatsoever is not of faith is *s*
  II Cor. 5:21, made him to be *s* for us
  II Thess. 2:3, that man of *s*
  I Pet. 2:24, his own self bore our *s*
SIN (*v.*) Gen. 42:22, do not *s* against the child

Ex. 9:27; 10:16; Num. 22:34; Josh. 7:20
II Sam. 12:13; Ps. 41:4; Mat. 27:4; Lk. 15:18, I
  have *s*
Job 10:14, if I *s*, you mark me
Ps. 4:4, stand in awe, and *s* not
    39:1, that I *s* not with my tongue
Prov. 8:36, he that *s* against me
Isa. 43:27, your first father has *s*
Ezek. 18:4, the soul that *s*, it shall die
Hos. 13:2, now they *s* more and more
Mat. 18:21, how oft shall my brother *s*?
Jn. 5:14; 8:11, *s* no more
Rom. 6:15, shall we *s*, because
I Cor. 15:34, awake to righteousness, *s* not
Eph. 4:26, be ye angry, and *s* not
I Jn. 3:9, he cannot *s*, because born of God
  See Num. 15:28; Job 1:5, 22; Rom. 3:23
SINCERE Phil. 1:10; I Pet. 2:2
SINCERITY Josh. 24:14; Eph. 6:24
SINFUL LK. 5:8; 24:7; Rom. 7:13; 8:3
SINGING Ps. 100:2; 126:2; Eph. 5:19
SINGLE Mat. 6:22; Lk. 11:34
SINGLENESS Acts 2:46; Eph. 6:5; Col. 3:22
SINNER Gen. 13:13
  Ps. 1:1, stand not in way of *s*
    25:8, teach *s* in the way
    26:9, gather not my soul with *s*
    51:13, *s* shall be converted
  Eccl. 9:18, one *s* destroyed much good
  Isa. 33:14, the *s* in Zion are afraid
  Mat. 9:11; Lk. 5:30; 15:2, eat with *s*
    13; Lk. 5:32, call *s* to repentance
    11:19; Lk. 7:34, a friend of *s*!
  Lk. 7:37, woman who was a *s*
    13:2, suppose ye these were *s* above all?
    15:7, 10, joy over one *s*
    18:13, be merciful to me a *s*
  Jn. 9:16, can a man that is a *s* do such?
    25, whether he be a *s*, I know not
  Rom. 5:8, while we were yet *s*
    19, many were made *s*
  Heb. 7:26, separate from *s*
  See James 4:8; 5:20; I Pet. 4:18; Jude 15
SISTER Job 17:14; Mat. 12:50; I Tim. 5:2
SIT II Ki. 7:3, why *s* we here till we die?
  Ps. 69:12, they that *s* in the gate
    107:10, such as *s* in darkness
  Isa. 30:7, their strength is to *s* still
  Jer. 8:14, why do we *s* still?
  Ezek. 33:31, they *s* before you as your people
  Mic. 4:4, they *s* every man under his vine
  Mal. 3:3, he shall *s* as a refiner
  Mk. 10:37, to *s* on my right hand
  See Prov. 23:1; Lam. 3:63; Dan. 7:9; Acts 2:2
SITUATION II Ki. 2:19; Ps. 48:2
SKILLFUL Ps. 33:3; Ezek. 21:31; Dan. 1:4
SKILL II Chron. 2:7; Eccl. 9:11; Dan. 1:17
SKIN Ex. 34:29, *s* of his face shone
  Job 2:4, *s* for *s*
    10:11, you have clothed me with *s* and flesh
    19:26, though after my *s* worms destroy
  Jer. 13:23, can the Ethiopian change his *s*?
  Ezek. 37:6, I will cover you with *s*
  Heb. 11:37, wandered in sheep-*s*

See Gen. 3:21; 27:16; Ps. 102:5; Mk. 1:6

SKIP Ps. 29:6; 114:4; Jer. 48:27

SKIRT Ps. 133:2; Jer. 2:34; Zech. 8:23

SLACK Deut. 7:10; Prov. 10:4; II Pet. 3:9

SLAIN Gen. 4:23, I have s a man
 Prov. 7:26, strong men have been s by her
  22:13, the slothful man says, I shall be s
  24:11, deliver those ready to be s;
 Isa. 22:2, your s men are not s with sword
  26:21, earth shall no more cover her s
  66:16, the s of the Lord shall be many
 Jer. 9:1, weep for the s of my people
 Ezek. 37:9, breathe upon these s
 Eph. 2:16, having s the enmity
 Rev. 5:6, a Lamb as it had been s

SLAUGHTER Ps. 44:22, as sheep for the s
 Isa. 53:7; Jer. 11:19, brought as a lamb to
  the s
 Jer. 7:32; 19:6, valley of s
 Ezek. 9:2, every man a s weapon
 See Hos. 5:2; Zech. 11:4; Acts 9:1; James 5:5

SLAVE Jer. 2:14; Rev. 18:13

SLAY Gen. 18:25, to s the righteous
 Job 9:23, if the scourge s suddenly
  13:15, though he s me
 See Gen. 4:15; Ex. 21:14; Lk. 11:49; 19:27

SLEEP (*n.*) I Sam. 26:12, deep s from God
 Job 4:13; 33:15, when deep s falls
 Ps. 13:3, lest I sleep the s of death
  127:2, gives his beloved s
 Prov. 3:24, your s shall be sweet
  6:10; 24:33, yet a little s
  20:13, love not s, lest you come to poverty
 Eccl. 5:12, the s of a laboring man is sweet
 Jer. 51:39, sleep a perpetual s
 Lk. 9:32, heavy with s
 Jn. 11:13, of taking rest in s
 Rom. 13:11, high time to awake out of s
 See Dan. 2:1; 6:18; 8:18; Acts 16:27; 20:9

SLEEP (*v.*) Ex. 22:27, wherein shall he s?
 Job 7:21, now shall I s in the dust
 Ps. 4:8, I will lay me down and s
  121:4, shall neither slumber nor s
 Prov. 4:16, they s not, except they have done
  6:22, when you s, it shall keep you
  10:5, he that s in harvest
 Song of Sol. 5:2, I s, but my heart wakes
 Dan. 12:2, many that s in the dust
 Mat. 9:24, not dead, but s
  13:25, while men s, the enemy sowed
  26:45; Mk. 14:41, S on now
 Mk. 13:36, coming suddenly he find you s
 Lk. 22:46, why s ye? rise and pray
 Jn. 11:11, our friend Lazarus s
 I Cor. 11:30, for this cause many s
  15:51, we shall not all s
 Eph. 5:14, awake thou that s
 I Thess. 4:14, them which s in Jesus
  5:6, let us not s, as do others
  10, that whether we wake or s

SLEIGHT Eph. 4:14, the s of men

SLEW Judg. 9:54, a woman s him
 I Sam. 17:36, s both the lion and the bear
  29:5, Saul has s his thousands

II Ki. 10:9, who s all these?
 Dan. 5:19, whom he would be s
 Mat. 23:35, whom ye s and hanged on a tree
 Acts 10:39, whom ye s and hanged on a tree
  22:20, kept the raiment of them that s him
 Rom. 7:11, sin, by the commandment, s me
 See Gen. 4:8; Ex. 2:12; 13:15; Lam. 2:4

SLIDE Deut. 32:35; Ps. 26:1; 37:31

SLIGHTLY Jer. 6:14; 8:11, healed hurt s

SLIME Gen. 11:3; 14:10; Ex. 2:3

SLIP II Sam. 22:37, my feet did not s
 Job 12:5, he that is ready to s
 Ps. 17:5, that my footsteps s not
  73:2, my steps had well nigh s
 Heb. 2:1, lest we should let them s
 See Deut. 19:5; I Sam. 19:10; Ps. 94:18

SLIPPERY Ps. 35:6; 73:18; Jer. 23:12

SLOTHFUL Judg. 18:9, be not s to possess
 Mat. 25:26, you s servant
 Rom. 12:11, not s in business
 Heb. 6:12, that you be not s
 See Prov. 18:9; 19:24; 24:30; Eccl. 10:18

SLOW Ex. 4:10, I am s of speech
 Neh. 9:17, a God s to anger
 Lk. 24:25, s of heart
 See Acts 27:7; Tit. 1:12; James 1:19

SLUMBER Prov. 6:4, give not s to your eyelids
  10; 24:33, a little more s
 Isa. 5:27, none shall s among them
  56:10, loving to s
 Nah. 3:18, your shepherds s
 Rom. 11:8, has given them the spirit of s
 See Job 33:15; Mat. 25:5; II Pet. 2:3

SMALL Ex. 16:14, s round thing
  18:22, every s matter they shall judge
 Num. 16:9, s thing God has separated
  13, a s thing that you have brought us
 Deut. 9:21, I ground the calf s
  32:2, doctrine distil as s rain
 I Ki. 2:20, one s petition of thee
 II Ki. 19:26, inhabitants of s power
 I Chron. 17:17, yet a s thing in your sight
 Job 8:7, your beginning was s
  15:11, are consolations of God s
  36:27, he makes s the drops of water
 Isa. 7:13, is it a s thing to weary men?
  16:14, remnant very s and feeble
  40:15, nations as the s dust
  54:7, for a s moment
  60:22, a s one shall become a strong
  nation
 Jer. 49:15, make thee s among the heathen
 Dan. 11:23, strong with a s people
 Zech. 4:10, the day of s things
 Mk. 8:7; Jn. 6:9, a few s fishes
 Acts 12:18; 19:23, no s stir
  15:2, had no s dissension
 James 3:4, turned with very s helm

SMART Prov. 11:15, shall s for it

SMELL Gen. 27:27, as s of field
 Deut. 4:28, gods that neither see nor s
 Job 39:25, he s the battle
 Ps. 45:8, your garments s of myrrh
  115:6, noses have they, but they s not

Isa. 3:24, instead of sweet *s*
Dan. 3:27, nor the *s* of fire
I Cor. 12:17, hearing, where were the *s*?
Eph. 5:2, sacrifice for sweet-*s* savour
Phil. 4:18, an odour of a sweet *s*
SMITE Ex. 2:13, wherefore *s* you
    21:12, he that *s* a man
I Sam. 26:8, I will not *s* him the second time
II Ki. 6:18, *S* this people with blindness
Ps. 121:6, the sun shall not *s* you by day
    141:5, let the righteous *s* me
Prov. 19:25, *S* a scorner
Isa. 10:24, he shall *s* you with a rod
    49:10, neither shall heat *s* you
    58:4, to *s* with the fist of wickedness
Jer. 18:18, let us *s* him with the tongue
Lam. 3:30, gives his cheek to him that *s*
Ezek. 7:9, know that I am the Lord that *s*
    21:14, prophesy, and *s* your hands together
Nah. 2:10, the knees *s* together
Mal. 4:6, lest I *s* the earth with a curse
Mat. 5:39, *s* you on the right cheek
    24:49, shall begin to *s* his fellow servants
Lk. 22:49, shall we *s* with sword?
Jn. 18:23, why *s* you me
SMITH I Sam. 13:19; Isa. 44:12; Jer. 24:1
SMITTEN Num. 22:28, that you have *s*
Deut. 28:25, cause thee to be *s*
I Sam. 4:3, why has the Lord *s* us
II Ki. 13:19, have *s* five or six times
Ps. 3:7, you have *s* all my enemies
Isa. 24:12, the gate is *s* with destruction
Jer. 2:30, in vain have I *s* your children
Hos. 6:1, he has *s*, and he will bind
Amos 4:9, I have *s* you
See Job 16:10; Ezek. 22:13; Acts 23:3
SMOKE Gen. 19:28, as the *s* of a furnace
Deut. 29:20, the anger of the Lord shall *s*
Ps. 37:20, wicked consume into *s*
    74:1, why do they anger *s*
    102:3, my days are consumed like *s*
    104:32, 144:5, he touches the hills, they *s*
    119:83, like a bottle in the *s*
Prov. 10:26, as *s* to the eyes
Isa. 6:4, the house was filled with *s*
    34:10, the *s* thereof shall go up forever
    51:6, the heavens shall vanish like *s*
    65:5, these are a *s* in my nose
Hos. 13:3, as the *s* out of a chimney
See Rev. 9:2; 14:11; 15:8; 18:9; 19:3
SMOKING Gen. 15:17; Isa. 42:3; Mat. 12:20
SMOOTH Gen. 27:11, I am a *s* man
I Sam. 17:40; Isa. 57:6, five *s* stones
Isa. 30:10, speak unto us *s* things
Lk. 3:5, rough ways shall be made *s*
See Ps. 55:21; Prov. 5:3; Isa. 41:7
SMOTE Num. 20:11, Moses *s* the rock twice
Judg. 15:8, Samson *s* them hip and thigh
I Sam. 24:5, David's heart *s* him
Isa. 60:10, in my wrath I *s* you
Jer. 31:19, I *s* upon my thigh
Hag. 2:17, I *s* you with blasting and mildew
Mat. 26:68, who is he that *s* you?
Lk. 18:13; 23:48; *s* his breast

Acts 12:23, immediately angel *s* him
See II Sam. 14:7; Dan. 2:34; Mat. 27:30
SNARE Ex. 10:7, this man be a *s* unto us
Josh. 23:13, they shall be *s* unto you
Judg. 8:27, which thing became a *s* to Gideon
I Sam. 18:21, that she may be a *s*
    28:9, wherefore lay you a *s* for my life
II Sam. 22:6, the *s* of death prevented me
Job 18:8, he walks on a *s*
    22:10, *s* are round about you
Ps. 11:6, on the wicked he shall rain *s*
    64:5, commune of laying *s* privily
    69:22, let their table become a *s*
    91:3, deliver you from *s* of fowler
Prov. 6:2; 12:13, *s* with words of your mouth
    7:23, as a bird hasted to the *s*
    13:14; 14:27, the *s* of death
    18:7, a fool's lips are the *s* of his soul
    22:25, get a *s* to your soul
Eccl. 9:12, *s* an evil time
Isa. 24:17; Jer. 48:43, the *s* are upon you
Lam. 3:47, fear and a *s* is come upon us
Ezek. 12:13, he shall be taken in my *s*
Hos. 9:8, the prophets is a *s*
Amos 3:5, can a bird fall in a *s*
I Tim. 3:7, lest he fall into the *s*
    6:9, they that will be rich fall into a *s*
II Tim. 2:26, recover out of the *s* of the devil
SNATCH Isa. 9:20, shall *s* and be hungry
SNOW II Sam. 23:20, slew lion in time of *s*
Job 6:16, wherein the *s* is hid
    9:30, wash myself in *s* water
    37:6, saith to *s*, Be thou on the earth
    38:22, the treasures of the *s*
Ps. 51:7, I shall be whiter than *s*
    147:16, he gives *s* like wool
Prov. 25:13, cold of *s* in harvest
Isa. 1:18, your sins shall be white as *s*
Jer. 13:14, will a man leave the *s* of Lebanon
Lam. 4:7, Nazarites purer than *s*
Dan. 7:9; Mk. 9:3, garment white as *s*
See Ps. 68:14; 148:8; Rev. 1:14
SNUFFED Jer. 14:6; Mal. 1:13
SOAKED Isa. 34:7, land *s* with blood
SOAP Jer. 2:22; Mal. 3:2
SOBER II Cor. 5:13, *s* for your cause
I Thess. 5:6, let us watch and be *s*
I Tim. 3:2; Tit. 1:8, a bishop must be *s*
Titus 2:2, aged men be *s*
I Pet. 4:7, be ye therefore *s*, and watch
See Acts 26:25; Rom. 12:3; Tit. 2:6
SODDEN Ex. 12:9; I Sam. 2:15; Lam. 4:10
SOFT Job 23:16, God makes my heart *s*
    41:3, will be speak *s* words?
Ps. 65:10, you make it *s* with showers
Prov. 15:1, a *s* answer turns away wrath
    25:15, a *s* tongue breaks the bone
See Ps. 55:21; Mat. 11:8; Lk. 7:25
SOFTLY Gen. 33:14; Judg. 4:21
SOIL Ezek. 17:8, planted in a good *s*
SOJOURN Gen. 19:9, this fellow came in to *s*
    26:3, *S* in this land, and I will be with you
    47:4, to *s* in the land are we come
Deut. 26:5, *s* with few, became a nation

Judg. 17:9, I go to *s* where I may find place
II Ki. 8:1, *s* wheresoever you can *s*
Ps. 120:5, woe is me, that I *s*
Isa. 23:7, feet carry her afar off to *s*
Jer. 42:22, die in place whither ye desire to *s*
Lam. 4:15, they shall no more *s* there
Heb. 11:9, by faith he *s* in land of promise
SOJOURNER Gen. 23:4; Ps. 39:12
SOLD Gen. 31:15, our father has *s* us
    45:4, whom you *s* into Egypt
Lev. 25:23, the land shall not be *s* forever
    42, shall not be *s* as bondmen
    27:28, no devoted thing shall be *s*
Deut. 15:12, if your brother be *s* unto you
    32:30, except their Rock had *s* them
I Ki. 21:20, you have *s* yourself to work evil
Neh. 5:8, of shall they be *s* unto us?
Esther 7:4, or we are *s* to be slain
Isa. 50:1, have you *s* yourselves?
    52:3, you have *s* yourselves for nought
Lam. 5:4, our wood is *s* unto us
Joel 3:3, they have *s* a girl for wine
Amos 2:6, they *s* righteous for silver
Mat. 10:29, tow sparrows *s* for a farthing?
    13:46, went and *s* all that he had
    18:25, his lord commanded him to be *s*
    21:12; Mk. 11:15, cast out them that *s*
Lk. 17:28, they bought, they, *s*, they planted
Acts 2:45, and *s* their possessions
Rom. 7:14, *s* under sin
I Cor. 10:25, whatsoever is *s* in the shambles
SOLDIER Ezra 8:22, ashamed to require *s*
Mat. 8:9; Lk. 7:8, having *s* under me
Lk. 3:14, *s* demanded what shall we do?
Acts 10:7, a devout *s*
II Tim. 2:3, as a good *s* of Jesus Christ
    See II Chron. 25:13; Isa. 15:4; Acts 27:31
SOLE Gen. 8:9, found no rest for *s* of her foot
II Sam. 14:25; Isa. 1:6, from *s* of foot to
    crown
    See Deut. 28:35, 56, 65; Josh. 1:3; Job 2:7
SOLEMN Ps. 92:3, sing praise with a *s* sound
    See Num. 10:10; Isa. 1:13; Hos. 9:5
SOLEMNITY Isa. 30:29, when a holy *s* is kept
    See Deut. 31:10; Isa. 33:20; Ezek. 45:17; 46:11
SOLEMNLY Gen. 43:3; I Sam. 8:9
SOLITARY Ps. 107:4, wandered in a *s* way
Isa. 35:1, wilderness and *s* place shall be glad
    See Job 3:7; 30:3; Lam. 1:1; Mk. 1:35
SOME Gen. 37:20, *s* evil beast
Ex. 16:17, and gathered, *s* more, *s* less
I Ki. 14:13, found *s* good thing
Ps. 20:7, *S* trust in chariots
    69:20, I looked for *s* to take pity
Dan. 12:2, *s* to life, and *s* to shame
Mat. 28:17, *s* doubted
Lk. 9:19, *s* say you are John the Baptist
Jn. 6:64, *s* of you that believe not
Acts 19:32; 21:34, *s* cried one thing, *s* another
Rom. 3:3, what is *s* did not believe?
    5:7, *s* would even dare to die
I Cor. 6:11, such were *s* of you
    15:34, *s* have not knowledge
Eph. 4:11, *s* prophets, *s* evangelists

I Tim. 5:24, *S* men's sins are open
Heb. 10:25, as the manner of *s* is
II Pet. 3:9, as *s* men count slackness
    See I Tim. 1:19; II Tim. 2:18; Jude 22
SOMEBODY Lk. 8:46; Acts 5:36
SOMETIMES Eph. 2:13, *s* far off
SOMEWHAT I Ki. 2:14; Gal. 2:6; Rev. 2:4
SON Job 14:21, his *s* come to honor
Ps. 2:12, kiss the *S*, lest he be angry
    86:16, save *s* of your handmaid
    116:16, I am the *s* of your handmaid
Prov. 10:1; 13:1; 15:20; 17:2; 19:26, a wise *s*
    17:25; 19:13, a foolish *s*
    31:2, *s* of my womb, *s* of my vows
Isa. 9:6, unto us a *s* is given
    14:12, *s* of the morning
Jer. 35:5, *s* of the Rechabites
Ezek. 20:31; 23:37, *s* pass through fire
Hos. 1:10, the *s* of the living God
Mal. 3:17, as a man spares his *s*
Mat. 11:27, no man knows the *S*
    13:55; Lk. 4:22, the carpenter's *s*?
    17:5, this is my beloved *S*
    22:42, Christ, whose *s* is he?
Lk. 7:12, only *s* of his mother
Jn. 1:18; 3:18, only begotten *S*
    5:21, the *S* quickens whom he will
    17:12; II Thess. 2:3, the *s* of perdition
Acts 4:36, *s* of consolation
Rom. 1:9, serve in the gospel of the *S*
    8:3, God sending his own *S*
    29, conformed to the image of his *S*
    32, spared not his own *S*
I Cor. 4:14, as my beloved *s* I warn you
Phil. 2:15, the *s* of God
Col. 1:13, the kingdom of his dear *S*
Heb. 2:10, bringing many *s* to glory
I Jn. 2:2, antichrist denies the *S*
    3:1, *s* of God
    5:12, he that has the *S* has life
SONGS Job 30:9, now I am their *s*
    35:10; Ps. 77:6, who gives *s* in the night
Ps. 32:7, with *s* of deliverance
    33:3; Isa. 42:10, sing unto him a new *s*
    40:3, he has put a new *s* in my mouth
    69:12, I was the *s* of drunkards
    119:54, my *s* in house of my pilgrimage
    137:4, the Lord's *s* in a strange land
Prov. 25:20, that sings *s* to any heavy heart
Isa. 23:16, sing many *s*
    35:10, the ransomed shall come with *s*
Ezek. 33:32, as a very lonely *s*
Amos 8:3, *s* of the temple
Eph. 5:19, in psalms and spiritual *s*?
    See Song of Sol. 1:1; Rev. 5:9; 14:3; 15:3
SOON Ex. 2:18, how is it you are come so *s*?
Job 32:22, my Maker would *s* take me away
Ps. 37:2, shall *s* be cut down
    58:3, go astray as *s* as born
    68:31, Ethiopia shall *s* stretch out her
    hands
    90:10, it is *s* cut off
    106:13, they *s* forgot
Prov. 14:7, he that is *s* angry

See Mat. 21:20; Gal. 1:6; Titus 1:7
SORE II Chron. 6:29; Isa. 1:6; Lk. 16:20
SORROW Gen. 3:16, multiply your *s*
 42:38, with *s* to the grave
 Job 6:10, I would harden myself in *s*
 21:17, God distributes *s* in his anger
 41:22, *s* is turned into joy
 Ps. 13:2, having *s* in my heart daily
 90:10, yet is their strength labor and *s*
 116:3, I found trouble and *s*
 Prov. 10:22, makes rich, adds no *s*
 Eccl. 2:23, all his days are *s*
 Eccl 7:3, *S* is better than laughter
 Isa. 17:11, day of desperate *s*
 35:10; 51:11, *s* shall flee away
 53:3, a man of *s*
 Jer. 30:15, you *s* is incurable
 49:23 there is *s* on the sea
 Lam. 1:12, any *s* like unto my *s*
 Mat. 24:8; Mk. 13:8, beginning of *s*
 Lk. 22:45, sleeping for *s*
 Jn. 16:6, *s* has filled your heart
 II Cor. 2:7, with overmuch *s*
 7:10, godly *s* works repentance
 I Thess. 4:13, *s* not as others
 I Tim. 6:10, pierced with many *s*
 See Prov. 15:13; Hos. 8:10; Rev. 21:4
SORROWFUL I Sam. 1:15, of a *s* spirit
 Ps. 69:29, I am poor and *s*
 Prov. 14:13, even in laughter the heart is *s*
 Jer. 31:25, replenished every *s* soul
 Zeph. 3:18, I will gather them that are *s*
 Mat. 19:22; Lk. 18:23, went away *s*
 26:37, he began to be *s*
 38; Mk. 14:34, my soul is exceeding *s*
 Jn. 16:20, you shall be *s*
 See Job 6:7; II Cor. 6:10; Phil. 2:28
SORRY Ps. 38:18, I will be *s* for my sin
 Isa. 51:19, who shall be *s* for you?
 See I Sam. 22:8; Neh. 8:10; Mat. 14:9
SORT Gen. 6:19, two of every *s*
 I Chron. 29:14, to offer after this *s*
 Dan. 3:29, deliver after this *s*
 Acts 17:5, fellows of the baser *s*
 II Cor. 7:11, III Jn. 6, after a godly *s*
 II Tim. 3:6, of this *s* are they
SOTTISH Jer. 4:22, they are *s* children
SOUGHT Gen. 43:30, he *s* where to weep
 Ex. 4:24, the lord *s* to kill him
 I Sam. 13:14, the Lord has *s* him a man
 I Chron. 15:13, we *s* him not after due order
 II Chron. 15:4, when they *s* him he was found
 15, they *s* him with their whole desire
 16:12, in his disease he *s* not the Lord
 26:5, as long as he *s* the Lord
 Ps. 34:4; 77:2, I *s* the Lord, and he heard me
 111:2, *s* out of all that have pleasure
 Eccl. 7:29, *s* out many inventions
 Isa. 62:12, shall be called, *S* out
 Jer. 10:21, pastors have not *s* the Lord
 Lam. 1:19, they *s* meat to relieve their souls
 Ezek. 22:30, I *s* for a man among them
 34:4, neither have you *s* that which was lost
 Lk. 11:16, *s* of him a sign

 13:6, he *s* fruit thereon, 19:3, *s* to see Jesus
 Rom. 9:32, *s* it is not by faith
 Heb. 12:17, he *s* it carefully with tears
SOUL Gen. 2:7, a living *s*
 Ex. 30:12, a ransom for his *s*
 Deut. 11:13, serve with all your *s*
 13:6, your friend, which is as your own *s*
 30:2; Mat. 22:37, obey with all your *s*
 Judg. 10:16, his *s* was grieved
 I Sam. 18:1; 20:17, loved him as his own *s*
 I Ki. 8:48, return with all their *s*
 I Chron. 22:19, set your *s* to seek the Lord
 Job 3:20, life to the bitter in *s*
 12:10, in whose hand is the *s*
 16:4, if your *s* were in my *s* stead
 31:30, wishing a curse to his *s*
 33:22, his *s* draws near to the grave
 Ps. 33:19, to deliver their *s* from death
 34:22, redeems the *s* of his servants
 49:8, the redemption of their *s* is precious
 62:1, my *s* waits upon God
 103:1; 104:1, bless the Lord, O my *s*
 116:7, return to your rest, O my *s*
 8, you have delivered my *s* from death
 142:4, no man cared for my *s*
 Prov. 11:25, the liberal *s* shall be made fat
 19:2, *s* without knowledge
 25:25, cold waters to thirsty *s*
 Isa. 55:3, hear, and your *s* shall live
 58:10, if you will satisfy the afflicted *s*
 Jer. 20:13, he has delivered the *s* of the poor
 31:12, their *s* shall be as a watered garden
 Ezek. 18:4, all *s* are mine
 22:25, they have devoured *s*
 Hab. 2:10, you have sinned against your *s*
 Mat 10:28, to destroy both *s* and body
 Mat. 16:26; Mk. 8:36, lose his own *s*?
 26:38, my *s* is exceeding sorrowful
 Lk. 21:19, in your patience possess ye your *s*
 Acts 4:32, of one heart and *s*
 Rom. 13:1, let every *s* be subject
 I Thess. 5:23, *s* and body be preserved
 Heb. 6:19, an anchor of the *s*
 13:17, they watch for your *s*
 James 5:20, shall save a *s* from death
 I Pet. 2:11, which war against the *s*
 4:19, commit keeping of *s* to him
 II Pet. 2:14, beguiling unstable *s*
 III Jn. 2, even as your *s* prospers
 See Prov. 3:22; Ezek. 3:19; Acts 15:24
SOUND (*n.*) Lev. 26:36, *s* of a shaken leaf
 I Ki. 18:41, *s* of abundance of rain
 Job 15:21, a dreadful *s* in his ears
 Ps. 89:15, that know the joyful *s*
 92:3, harp with a solemn *s*
 Eccl. 12:4, *s* of grinding is low
 Jer. 50:22, *s* of battle in the land
 51:54, *s* of cry comes
 Ezek. 33:5, he heard *s*, and took not warning
 Acts 2:2, suddenly a *s* from heaven
 Rom. 10:18, their *s* went into all the earth
 I Cor. 14:8, an uncertain *s*
SOUND (*adj.*) Prov. 2:7, *s* wisdom
 14:30, a *s* heart is life of the flesh

I Tim. 1:10; Titus 1:9, 2:1, s doctrine
II Tim. 1:7, spirit of a s mind
See Ps. 119:80; Lk. 15:27; Titus 2:2, 8
SOUND (*v.*) Ex. 19:19, trumpet s long
Joel 2:1, s an alarm in holy mountain
Mat. 6:2, do not s a trumpet before you
See Neh. 4:18; I Cor. 13:1; 15:52; Rev. 8:7
SOUR Isa. 18:5; Jer. 31:29; Ezek. 18:2
SOW Job 4:8, they that s wickedness
Ps. 97:11, light is s for the righteous
126:5, s in tears
Eccl. 11:4, he observes the wind shall not s
6, in mornings your seed
Isa. 32:20, that s beside all waters
Jer. 4:3, s not among thorns
12:13, s wheat, but shall reap thorns
Hos. 10:12, S in righteousness, reap in mercy
Nah. 1:14, that no more of your name be s
Hag. 1:6, you have s much, and bring in little
Mat. 6:26, they s not
13:3; Lk. 8:5, sower went forth to s
37, he that s good seed
Jn. 4:36, he that s and he that reaps
I Cor. 15:36, which you s is not quickened
II Cor. 9:6, he which s sparingly
Gal. 6:7, what a man s that shall he reap
SOWER Isa. 55:10; Jer. 50:16; II Cor. 9:10
SPAN Isa. 40:12; 48:13; Lam. 2:20
SPARE Gen. 18:26, I will s for their sakes
Neh. 13:22, s me according to your mercy
Ps. 39:13, s me, that I may recover strength
Prov. 13:24, he that s the rod
19:18, let not your soul s for his crying
Joel 2:17, S your people
Mal. 3:17, I will s them as a man s
Lk. 15:17, bread enough and to s
Rom. 8:32, s not his own Son
11:21, if God s not the natural branches
II Pet. 2:4, if God s not the angels
SPARK Job 5:7; 18:5; Isa. 1:31; 50:11
SPEAK Gen. 18:27, to s to God
Ex. 4:14, I know he can s well
33:11, as a man s to his friend
Num. 20:8, s to the rock
I Sam. 25:17, a man cannot s to him
Job 11:5, on that God would s against him
13:7, will you s wickedly for God?
33:14, God s once, yea twice
37:20, if a man s he shall be swallowed up
Ps. 85:8, I will hear what the Lord will s
Prov. 23:9, S not in the ears of a fool
Isa. 19:18, shall s language of Canaan
Isa. 63:1, I that s in righteousness
65:24, while they are yet s, I will hear
Jer. 20:9, I will not s any more in his name
Zech. 8:16; Eph. 4:25, S every man the truth
Mat. 8:8, s the word only, and my servant
10:19; Mk. 13:11, how or what you shall s
12:34, of abundance of heart mouth s
36, every idle word that men shall s
Mk. 9:39, can lightly s evil of me
Lk. 6:26, when all men s well of you
Jn. 3:11, we s that we do know
Acts 4:17, they s to no man in this name

20, we cannot but s
26:25, I s words of truth and soberness
I Cor. 1:10, that you all s the same thing
14:28, let him s to himself and to God
II Cor. 4:13, we believe, and therefore s
Eph. 4:15, s the truth in love
Heb. 11:4, he being dead yet s
12:24, s better things than that of Abel
James 1:19, slow to s
SPEAR I Sam. 13:22, s with any but Saul
17:45, you come to me with a s
Ps. 46:9, he cuts the s in sunder
Isa. 2:4; Mic. 4:3, beat s into pruninghooks
See Job. 41:29; Jer. 6:23; Jn. 19:34
SPECIAL Deut. 7:6; Acts 19:11
SPECTACLE I Cor. 4:9, a s to the world
SPEECH Gen. 11:1, earth was of one s
Ex. 4:10, I am slow of s
Deut. 32:2, my s shall distil as dew
I Ki. 3:10, Solomon's s pleased the Lord
Job 6:26, the s of one that is desperate
Ps. 19:2, day unto day utters s
3, there is no s where their voice is not heard
Prov. 17:7, excellent s becomes not a fool
Song of Sol. 4:3, your s is comely
Isa. 33:19, of deeper s than you can perceive
Mat. 26:73, your s bewrayeth thee
I Cor. 2:1, not with excellency of s
II Cor. 3:12, we use great plainness of s
10:10, his s is contemptible
Col. 4:6, let your s be always with grace
Titus 2:8, sound s, that cannot be condemned
SPEECHLESS Lk. 1:22; Acts 9:7
SPEED Gen. 24:12, send me good s
II Jn. 10, neither bid him God s
See Ezra 6:12; Isa. 5:26; Acts 17:15
SPEEDILY Ps. 31:2, deliver me s
69:17; 143:7, hear me s
102:2, when I call, answer me s
Eccl. 8:11, because sentence is not executed s
Isa. 58:8, your health shall spring forth s
Lk. 18:8, he will avenge them s
See I Sam. 27:1; Ezra 6:13; 7:17; Joel 3:4
SPEND Job 21:13, they s their days in wealth
36:11, they s their days in prosperity
Ps. 90:9, we s our years as a tale that is told
Isa. 55:2, why s money for what is not bread
II Cor. 12:15, very gladly s and be spent for you
See Prov. 21:20; Eccl 6:12; Lk. 10:35
SPENT Gen. 21:15, water was s in the bottle
Job 7:6, days s without hope
Ps. 31:10, my life is s with grief
Isa. 49:4, I have s my strength for nought
Acts 17:21, s their time to tell some new thing
See Mk. 6:35; Lk. 15:14; Rom. 13:12
SPILT II Sam. 14:14, as water s
SPIN Ex. 35:25; Mat. 6:28; Lk. 12:27
SPIRIT Gen. 6:3, my s shall not always strive
Ex. 35:21, every one whom his s made willing
Num. 11:17, take of the s that is one you
14:24, he had another s with him

16:22; 27:16, the God of the *s* of all flesh
27:18, a man in whom is the *s*
Josh. 5:1, nor was there any more *s* in them
I Ki. 22:21, there came forth a *s*
II Ki. 2:9, a double portion of your *s*
Neh. 9:20, you gave your good *s* to instruct
Job 4:15, a *s* passed before my face
15:13, you turn your *s* against God
26:4, whose *s* came from you?
32:8, a *s* in man
Ps. 31:5, into your hand I commit my *s*
32:2, in whose *s* there is no guile
78:8, whose *s* was not steadfast
106:33, they provoked his *s*
139:7, whither shall I go from your *s*?
Prov. 16:2, the Lord weighs the *s*
18, an haughty *s* goes before a fall
19; 29:23; Isa. 57:15, an humble *s*
32, he that rules his *s* better than he
Eccl. 3:21, *s* of man, and *s* of beast
7:8, the patient in *s* better than the proud
8:8, no man has power over *s* to retain *s*
12:7, the *s* shall return to God
Isa. 4:4; 28:6, *s* of judgment
34:16, his *s* it has gathered them
57:16, the *s* should fail before me
61:1; Lk. 4:18, *S* of the Lord is upon me
Ezek. 3:14; 8:3, I went in the heat of my *s*
11:19; 18:31; 36:26, a new *s*
Mic. 2:11, a man walking in the *s*
Mat. 14:26; Mk. 6:49, it is a *s*
26:41; Mk. 14:38, the *s* is willing
Mk. 1:10, the *S* descending on him
8:12, sighed deeply in his *s*
Lk. 1:17, in *s* and power of Elias
2:27, came by the *S* into the temple
9:55, you know not what manner of *s*
10:21, Jesus rejoiced in *s*
24:39, a *s* has not flesh and bones
Jn. 3:34, God gives not the *S* my measure
4:24, God is a *S*, worship him in *s*
Jn. 6:63, it is the *s* that quickens
14:17; 15:26; 16:13; I Jn. 4:6, *S* of truth
Acts 2:4, began to speak as *S* gave utterance
6:10, not able to resist the wisdom and *s*
17:16, his *s* was stirred within him
23:8, say that there is neither angel nor *s*
Rom. 8:1, not after the flesh, but after the *S*
2, the law of the *S* of life
11, the *S* of him that raised up Jesus
16, the *S* itself bears witness
26, the *S* makes intercession
12:11, fervent in *s*
I Cor. 2:4, in demonstration of the *S*
10, the *S* searches all things
4:21; Gal. 6:1, in the *s* of meekness
6:17, he that is joined to the Lord is one *s*
12:4, diversities of gifts, but the same *S*
I Cor. 12:10, to another discerning of *s*
14:2, in the *s* he speaks mysteries
15:45, the last Adam a quickening *s*
II Cor. 3:6, but the *s* gives life
17, *S* of the Lord is, there is liberty
Gal. 3:3, having begun in the *S*

5:22; Eph. 5:9, fruit of the *S*
25, if we live in the *S*, let us walk in the *S*
6:8, sows to the *S* shall of the *S* reap
Eph. 2:2, the *s* that works in children of
disobedience
3:16, strengthened by his *S* in inner man
4:3, the unity of the *S*
23, renewed in *s* of your mind
30, grieve not the holy *S* of God
Phil. 1:27, stand fast in one *s*
2:1, if any fellowship of the *S*
Col. 1:8, your love in the *s*
2:5, absent in flesh, yet with you in the *s*
I Thess. 5:19, quench not the *S*
II Thess. 2:13, through sanctification of the *S*
I Tim. 3:16, justified in the *S*
4:1, giving heed to seducing *s*
12, be thou an example in *s*
II Tim. 4:22, the Lord Jesus be with your *s*
Heb. 1:14, ministering *s*
4:12, dividing asunder of soul and *s*
9:14, who through the eternal *S*
12:9, in subjection to the Father of *s*
23, to *s* of just men made perfect
James 2:26, the body without the *s* is dead
4:5, the *s* lusts to envy
I Pet. 1:2, through sanctification of the *S*
3:4, ornament of a meek and quiet *s*
4:6, live according to God in the *s*
I Jn. 3:24, by the *s*he has given us
4:1, believe not every *s*, but try the *s*
2, hereby know ye the *S* of God
3, every *s* that confesses not
5:6, it is the *S* that bears witness
8, the *s*, the water, and the blood
Jude 19, sensual, having not the *S*
Rev. 1:10, I was in the *S* of the Lord's day
3:6, 13, 22, hear what the *S* saith
4:2, I was in the *s*, and, behold
Rev. 11:11, the *S* of life from God entered
14:13, blessed are the dead; yea, saith the *S*
22:17, the *S* and the bride say, Come
SPIRITUAL   Hos. 9:7, the *s* man is mad
Rom. 1:11, impart some *s* gift
I Cor. 2:13, comparing *s* things with *s*
15, he that is *s* judges all things
3:1, not speak unto you as unto *s*
10:3, all eat the same *s* meat
12:1; 14:1, concerning *s* gifts
15:44, it is raised a *s* body
46, that was not first which is *s*
Gal. 6:1, you which are *s*, restore such an one
Eph. 5:19, in psalms and hymns and *s* songs
6:12, *s* wickedness in high places
I Pet. 2:5, a *s* house to offer *s* sacrifices
SPIRITUALLY Rom. 8:6; Rev. 11:8
SPITE Ps. 10:14, behold mischief and *s*
SPOIL (*n.*) I Sam. 14:32, people flew upon
the *s*
II Chron. 15:11; offered to the Lord of the *s*
20:25, three days gathering the *s*
28:15, with the *s* they clothed the naked
Esther 3:13, take the *s* of them for a prey
9:10, on the *s* laid they not their hand

Job 29:17, I plucked the *s* out of his teeth
Prov. 16:19, then to divide *s* with the proud
 31:11, he shall have no need of *s*
Isa. 3:14, the *s* of the poor is in your houses
 42:44, who gave Jacob of a *s*
 53:12, divide the *s* with the strong
SPOIL (*v.*) Ex. 3:22, *s* the Egyptians
Ps. 76:5, the stouthearted are *s*
Song of Sol. 2:15, the little foxes that *s* the
 vines
Isa. 33:1, woe to you that *s*
 42:22, this is a people robbed and *s*
Jer. 4:30, when *s*, what will you do?
Hab. 2:8, you have *s* many nations
Zech. 11:2, howl because the mighty are *s*
Col. 2:15, having *s* principalities
SPOKE Ps. 39:3, then *s* I with my tongue
 106:33, he *s* unadvisedly with his lips
Mal. 3:16, *s* often one to another
Jn. 7:46, never man *s* like this man
I Cor. 13:11, I *s* as a child
Heb. 12:25, refused him that *s* on earth
II Pet. 1:21, holy men *s* as they were moved
See Gen. 35:15; Jn. 9:29; Heb. 1:1
SPOKEN Num. 23:19, has he *s*
I Sam. 1:16, out of my grief have I *s*
I Ki. 18:24, the people said, It is well *s*
II Ki. 4:13, would be *s* for to the king
Ps. 62:11, God has *s* once
 66:14, my mouth has *s* when in trouble
 87:3, glorious things are *s* of you
Prov. 15:23, a word *s* in due season
Eccl. 7:21, take no heed to all words *s*
Isa. 48:15, I, even I, have *s*
Mal. 3:13, what have we *s* so much against
Mk. 14:9, shall be *s* of for a memorial
Lk. 2:34, a sign which shall be *s* against
Acts 19:36, these things cannot be *s* against
Rom. 1:8, your faith is *s* of
 14:16, let not your good be evil *s* of
Heb. 2:2, the word *s* by angels
SPOKESMAN Ex. 4:16, he shall be your *s*
SPORT Gen. 26:8; Isa. 57:4; II Pet. 2:13
SPOT Num. 28:3, 9, 11, lambs without *s*
Deut. 32:5, *s* is not the *s* of the children
Job. 11:15, lift up your face without *s*
Jer. 13:23, or the leopard his *s*?
Eph. 5:27, glorious church, not having *s*
I Tim. 6:14, commandment without *s*
Heb. 9:14, offered himself without *s*
I Pet. 1:19, lamb without blemish or *s*
II Pet. 3:14, that you may be found without *s*
Jude 12, these are *s* in your feasts
See Song of Sol. 4:7; II Pet. 2:13; Jude 23
SPOUSE Song of Sol. 4:8; 5:1; Hos. 4:13
SPRANG Mk. 4:8; Acts 16:29; Heb. 7:14
SPREAD Deut. 32:11, eagle *s* her wings
II Ki. 19:14, *s* letter before the Lord
Job 9:8, God who alone *s* out the heavens
 26:9, he *s* his cloud upon it
 29:19, my root was *s* out by waters
 37:18, have you with him *s* out the sky
Ps. 105:39, he *s* a cloud for a covering
 140:5, they have *s* a net by the wayside

Isa. 1:15, ye *s* forth your hands, I will hide
 33:23, they could not *s* the sail
 65:2, *s* out hands to a rebellious people
Jer. 8:2, they shall *s* them before the sun
Ezek. 26:14, a place to *s* nets upon
Mk. 11:8; Lk. 19:36, *s* garments
Acts 4:17, but that is *s* no further
SPRIGS Isa. 18:5; Ezek. 17:6
SPRING Num. 21:17, *S* up, O well
I Sam. 9:26, about the *s* of the day
Job. 5:6, does trouble *s* of the day
 38:16, have you entered the *s* of the sea?
Ps. 87:7, all my *s* are in you
 104:10, he sends the *s* into valleys
 107:33, he turns water-*s* into dry ground
 35, turns dry ground into water-*s*
Prov. 25:26, troubles fountain, a corrupt *s*
Isa. 42:19, before they *s* forth I tell you
 43:19, a new thing, now it shall *s* forth
 45:8, let righteousness *s* up together
 58:8, your health shall *s* forth
 11, shall be like a *s* of water
See Joel 2:22; Mk. 4:27; Jn. 4:14; Heb. 12:15
SPRINKLE Job. 2:12; Isa. 52:15; Ezek. 36:25
SPROUT Job 14:7, a tree will *s* again
SPUNGE Mk. 15:36; Jn. 19:29
SPY Num. 13:16; Josh 2:1; Gal. 2:4
STABILITY Isa. 33:6, the *s* of your times
STABLE I Chron. 16:30; Ezek. 25:5
STAFF Gen. 32:10, with my *s* I passed over
Ex. 12:11, eat it with *s* in hand
Num. 13:23, bore grapes between two on a *s*
Judg. 6:21, the angel put forth end of his *s*
II Sam. 3:29, not fail one that leans on a *s*
II Ki. 4:29, lay my *s* on face of the child
 18:21; Isa. 36:6, you trust on *s*
Ps. 23:4, your rod and *s* comfort me
Isa. 3:1, stay and *s*, the whole stay of bread
 9:4, you have broken the *s* of his shoulder
 10:5, the *s* in their hand is my indignation
 14:5, has broken the *s* of the wicked
Jer. 48:17, how is the strong *s* broken
Zech. 11:10, took my *s*, even Beauty
Mk. 6:8, take nothing, save *s* only
Heb. 11:21, leaning on the top of his *s*
STAGGER Ps. 107:27, *s* like a drunken man
Isa. 29:9, they *s*, but not with strong drink
See Isa. 19:14; Rom. 4:20
STAIN Job. 3:5; Isa. 23:9; 63:3
STAIRS I Ki. 6:8; Neh. 9:4; Song of Sol. 2:14
STAKES Isa. 33:20; 54:2
STALK Gen. 41:5; Josh. 2:6; Hos. 8:7
STALL Prov. 15:17; Hab. 3:17; Mal. 4:2
STAMMERING Isa. 28:11; 32:4; 33:19
STAMP Deut. 9:21; II Sam. 22:43; Jer. 47:3
STAND Ex. 14:13, *s* still, and see
Deut. 29:10, you *s* all of you before the Lord
I Sam. 9:27, *s* you still a while
II Chron. 5:14, priests could not *s* to minister
II Ki. 3:14; 5:16, the Lord before whom I *s*
 10:4, how then shall we *s*?
II Chron. 34:32, caused all present to *s* to it
Esther 8:11, to *s* for their life
Job 8:15, lean on his house, but it shall not *s*

19:25, he shall *s* at the latter day
Ps. 1:1, not *s* the way of sinners
 5, the ungodly shall not *s* in judgment
 4:4, *S* in awe, and sin not
 10:1, why *s* thou afar off
 24:3, who shall *s* in his holy place?
 33:11, the counsel of the Lord *s* forever
 76:7, who may *s* in your sight
 94:16, who will *s* up for me
 109:31, shall *s* at right hand of the poor
 122:2, our feet shall *s* within our gates
 147:17, who can *s* before his cold?
Prov. 22:29, shall *s* before the kings
 27:4, who is able to *s* before envy?
Eccl. 8:3, *s* not in an evil thing
 21:8, I *s* continually on watchtower
Isa. 28:18, your agreement with hell shall
 not *s*
 40:8, the word God shall *s* forever
 65:5, *S* by yourself, I am holier than you
Jer. 6:16, *S* in the ways, ask for he old paths
 35:19, shall not want a man to *s* before me
Dan. 11:16, he shall *s* in the glorious land
 12:13, and shall *s* in your lot
Mic. 5:4, he shall *s* and feed in strength
Nah. 2:8, *S*, *s*, shall they cry
Zech. 3:1, Satan *s* at his right hand
Mal. 3:2, who shall *s* when he appears?
Mat. 16:28; Lk. 9:27, there be some *s* here
 20:3, others *s* idle in the market-place
Lk. 11:18, house divide shall not *s*
Rom. 5:2, this grace wherein we *s*
 14:4, God is able to make him *s*
I Cor. 2:5, faith should not *s* in wisdom
I Cor. 16:13, *s*, fast in the Lord
Eph. 6:13, having done all, to *s*
Phil. 1:27, *s* fast in one spirit
 4:1; I Thess. 3:8, *s* fast in the Lord
II Tim. 2:19, the foundation of God *s* sure
James 5:9, the judge *s* before the door
Rev. 3:20, I *s* at the door, and knock
 6:17, is come, and who shall be able to *s*?
 20:12, dead, small and great, *s* before God
STANDARD Isa. 49:22, set up my *s*
 59:19, Spirit of the Lord shall lift up *s*
 62:10, go through, lift up a *s*
Jer. 4:6; 50:2; 51:12; set up a *s*
 See Num. 1:52; 2:3; 10:14
STAR Num. 24:17, the *S* in their courses
Job 25:5, *s* are not pure in his sight
 38:7, the morning *s* sang together
Dan. 12:3, shall shine as *s* forever
Jude 13, wandering *s* to whom is
Rev. 12:1, on her head a crown of twelve *s*
 See Mat. 2:2
STATE Ps. 39:5; Mat. 12:45; Lk. 11:26
STATURE Num. 13:32, men of great *s*
I Sam. 16:7, look not on height of his *s*
Isa. 10:33, high ones of *s* hewn down
 45:14, men of *s* shall come
Mat. 6:27; Lk. 12:25, not add to *s*
Lk. 2:52, Jesus increased in *s*
 19:3, little of *s*
Eph. 4:13, *s* of the fullness of Christ

STATUTE Ex. 18:16, the *s* of God
Lev. 3:17; 16:34; 24:9, a perpetual *s*
II Ki. 17:8, *s* of the heathen
Ps. 19:8, the *s* of the Lord are right
Ezek. 5:6, has changed my *s*
 33:15, walk in the *s* of life
Zech. 1:6, my *s* did they not take hold
 See Ps. 18:22; 105:45; Ezek. 18:17
STAVES Num. 21:18, nobles digged with *s*
Hab. 3:14, strike through with his *s*
Zech. 11:7, took unto me two *s*
Lk. 9:3, neither two coats, nor *s*
 See I Sam. 17:43; Mk. 14:43; Lk. 22:52
STAY (*n.*) Ps. 18:18, the Lord was my *s*
Isa. 13:1, take away the *s* and staff
 See Lev. 13:5; I Ki. 10:19; Isa. 19:13
STAY (*v.*) Gen. 19:17, neither *s* in plain
Ex. 9:28, you shall *s* no longer
Num. 16:48; Ps. 106:30, the plague was *s*
II Sam. 24:16; I Chron. 21:15, *s* now your
 hand
Job 37:4, he will not *s* them
 38:11, here shall your proud waves be *s*
 37, who can *s* the bottles of heaven
Prov. 28:17, let no man *s* him
Isa. 26:3, whose mind is *s* on you
 27:8, he *s* his rough wind
 30:12, you trust in oppression, and *s*
 thereon
Dan. 4:35, none can *s* his hand
Hag. 1:10, heaven is *s*, earth is *s*
STEAD Ex. 4:16, be to him in *s* of God
Num. 10:31, to be us in *s* of eyes
 32:14, risen in your fathers' *s*
Job 16:4, if your soul were in my soul's *s*
 31:40, thistles grown in *s* of wheat
 34:24, he shall set others in their *s*
Ps. 45:16, in *s* of fathers shall be children
Prov. 11:8, the wicked comes in his *s*
Isa. 3:24, in *s* of girdle a rent
II Cor. 5:20, we pray you in Christ's *s*
 See Gen. 30:2; II Ki. 17:24; I Chron. 5:22
STEADFAST Ps. 78:8, not *s* with God
Dan. 6:26, living God and *s* forever
Heb. 2:2, word spoken by angels was *s*
 3:14, hold our confidence *s* to end
 6:19, hope as anchor, sure and *s*
I Pet. 5:9, resist *s* in the faith
 See Acts 2:42; Col. 2:5; II Pet. 3:17
STEADY Ex. 17:12, Moses' hands were *s*
STEAL Gen. 31:27, did you *s* away
 44:8, how then should we *s* silver or gold
Prov. 6:30, if he *s* to satisfy his soul
 30:9, lest I be poor, and *s*
Jer. 23:30, prophets that *s* my words
Mat. 6:19, thieves break through and *s*
Jn. 10:10, thief comes not, but to *s*
 See Hos. 4:2; Mat. 27:64; Rom. 2:21
STEALTH II Sam. 19:3, by *s* into city
STEEL II Sam. 22:35; Job. 20:24; Jer. 15:12
STEEP Ezek. 38:20; Mic. 1:4; Mat. 8:32
STEP I Sam. 20:3, *s* between me and death
Job 14:16, you number my *s*
 29:6, I washed my *s* with butter

31:4, does not he count my *s*?
7, if my *s* has turned out of the way
Ps. 37:23, the *s* of a good man are ordered
31, none of his *s* shall slide
73:2, my *s* had well nigh slipped
85:13, set us in the way of his *s*
119:133, order my *s* in your word
Prov. 4:12, your *s* shall not be straitened
5:5, her *s* take hold on hell
16:9, the Lord directs his *s*
Isa. 26:6, *s* of the needy shall tread it down
Jer. 10:23, not in man to direct his *s*
Rom. 4:12, walk in *s* of that faith
II Cor. 12:18, walked we not in same *s*?
I Pet. 2:21, that you should follow his *s*
STEWARD I Ki. 16:9, in house of his *s*
Lk. 12:42, that faithful and wise *s*
See Gen. 15:2; Lk. 8:3; I Cor. 4:1
STICK Num. 15:32, gathered *s* on Sabbath
I Ki. 17:12, I am gathering two *s*
Job 33:21, his bones *s* out
Ps. 38:2, your arrows *s* fast in me
Prov. 18:24, *s* closer than a brother
Ezek. 37:16, take *s*, and write on it
STIFF Deut. 9:6, 13; 10:16, *s*-necked people
Ps. 75:5, speak not with a *s* neck
Jer. 17:23, made their neck *s*
Ezek. 2:4, impudent and *s*-hearted
Acts 7:51, ye *s*-necked, ye do always resist
See Deut. 31:27; II Chron. 30:8; 36:13
STILL Ex. 15:16, as *s* as a stone
Num. 14:38, Joshua and Caleb lived *s*
Josh. 24:10, Balaam blessed you *s*
Judg. 18:9, the land is good, and are you *s*?
II Sam. 14:32, good to have been there *s*
II Ki. 7:4, if we sit *s* here, we die also
II Chron. 22:9, no power to keep *s* the
kingdom
Job 2:9, do you *s* retain your integrity?
Ps. 4:4, commune with your heart, and be *s*
23:2, beside the *s* waters
46:10, be *s*, and know that I am God
76:8, earth feared, and was *s*
84:4, they will be *s* praising you
107:29, so that the waves thereof are *s*
139:18, when I awake, I am *s* with you
Eccl. 12:9, he *s* taught knowledge
Isa. 5:25; 10:4, his hand is stretched out *s*
30:7, their strength is to sit *s*
42:14, I have been *s*, and refrained
Jer. 8:14, why do we sit *s*?
31:20, I do earnestly remember him *s*
Zech. 11:16, nor feed that that stands *s*
Mk. 4:39, arose, and said, Peace, be *s*
Rev. 22:11, unjust *s*, filthy *s*, holy *s*
STING Prov. 23;32; I Cor. 15:55; Rev. 9:10
STIR Num. 24:9, who shall *s* him up?
Deut. 32:11, as an eagle *s* up her nest
I Sam. 22:8, my son has *s* up my servant
26:19, if the Lord has *s* you up
I Ki. 11:14, the Lord *s* up an adversary
I Chron. 5:26; Hag. 1:14, God *s* up the spirit
Job 17:8, the innocent shall *s* up himself
41:10, none dare *s* him up

Prov. 10:12, hatred *s* up strifes
15:18; 29:22, a wrathful man *s* up strife
Isa. 10:26, the Lord shall *s* up a scourge
14:9, hell from beneath *s* up the dead
64:7, none *s* up himself to take hold
Lk. 23:5, he *s* up the people
Acts 17:16, his spirit was *s* in him
19:23, no small *s* about that way
II Tim. 1:6, *s* up the people
II Pet. 1:13, I think it meet to *s* you up
STOCK Job 14:8, though the *s* thereof die
Isa. 40:24, their *s* shall not take root
44:19, shall I fall down to the *s* of a tree?
Hos. 4:12, my people ask counsel at their *s*
Nah. 3:6; Heb. 10:33, a gazing-*s*
Acts 13:26, children of the *s* of Abraham
See Jer. 2:27; 10:8; 20:2; Phil. 3:5
STOLE II Sam. 15:6, Absalom *s* the hearts
Eph. 4:28, let him that *s* steal no more
See Gen. 31:20; II Ki. 11:2; Mat. 28:13
STOLEN II Sam. 21:12, men had *s* bones of
Saul
Prov. 9:17, *S* waters are sweet
Obad. 5, *s* till they had enough
See Gen. 30:33; Ex. 22:7; II Sam. 19:41
STOMACH I Tim. 5:23, for your *s* sake
STONE Gen. 11:3, they had brick for *s*
28:18, 22; 31:45, 35:14, set up a *s* for a
pillar
Deut. 8:9, a land whose *s* are iron
Josh. 24:27, this *s* shall be a witness
II Sam. 17:13, not one small *s* found there
II Ki. 3:25, cast every man his *s*
Job 5:23, in league with *s* of the field
6:12, is my strength the strength *s*?
28:2, he searches out the *s* of darkness
41:24, his heart is as firm as a *s*
Ps. 118:22; Mk. 12:10, the *s* which the builders
refused is become the head *s*
Prov. 27:3, *s* is heavy, a fool's wrath heavier
Isa. 54:11, I will lay your *s* with fair colors
Dan. 2:34, as *s* was cut out of the mountain
Hab. 2:11, the *s* shall cry out of the wall
19, that says to the dumb *s*, Arise
Hab. 2:15, before *s* was laid upon *s*
Zech. 3:9, upon one *s* shall be seven eyes
4:7, bring forth the head-*s* thereof
7:12, they made their hearts as *s*
Mat. 7:9; Lk. 11:11, will he give him a *s*?
21:44, whosoever shall fall on this *s*
Mk. 13:1, see what manner of *s* are here
16:4; Lk. 24:2, found *s* rolled away
Lk. 4:3, command this *s* be made bread
19:44; 21:6, not one's *s* upon another
Jn. 1:42, Cephas, by interpretation a *s*
8:7, first cast a *s*
11:39, take away the *s*
Acts 17:29, that the Godhead is like to *s*
I Pet. 2:5, as lively *s*, are built up
STONY Ps. 141:6; Ezek. 11:19; Mat. 13:5
STOOD Gen. 18:22, *s* yet before the Lord Ex.
14:19, *s* behind them
Josh. 3:16, waters *s* up on an heap
II Ki. 23:3, all the people *s* to the covenant

Esther 9:16, Jews *s* for their lives
Ps. 33:9, he commanded, and it *s* fast
Lk. 24:36, Jesus himself *s* in the midst
II Tim. 4:16, no man *s* with me
See Gen. 23:3; Job 29:8; Rev. 7:11
STOOP Gen. 49:9, Judah *s* down
Prov. 12:25, heaviness makes the heart *s*
Jn. 8:6, *s* down, and wrote on the ground
See II Chron. 36:17; Job 9:13; Mk. 1:7
STOP Gen. 8:2, windows of heaven were *s*
I Ki. 18:44, that the rain *s* you not
Ps. 107:42, iniquity shall *s* her mouth
Zech. 7:11, refused, and *s* their ears
Acts 7:57, *s* their ears, and ran upon him
Rom. 3:19, that every mouth may be *s*
Titus 1:11, whose mouths must be *s*
Heb. 11:33, through faith *s* mouths of lions
STORE Lev. 25:22; 26:10, eat of the old *s*
Deut. 28:5, blessed be your basket and *s*
II Ki. 20:17, your fathers have laid up in *s*
Ps. 144:13, affording all manner of *s*
Nah. 2:9, none end of the *s* and glory
Mal. 3:10, bring tithes into *s*-house
Lk. 12:24, neither have *s*-house nor barn
I Cor. 16:2, every one lay by him in *s*
II Pet. 3:7, by same word are kept in *s*
See I Ki. 10:10; I Chron. 29:16; Ps. 33:7
STORM Ps. 55:8, escape from windy *s*
83:15, make them afraid with your *s*
Isa. 4:6; 25:4, a covert from *s*
Ezek. 38:9, shall ascend and come like a *s*
Nah. 1:3, the Lord has his way in the *s*
See Job 21:18; 27:21; Mk. 4:37; Lk. 8:23
STORMY Ps. 107:25; 148:8; Ezek. 13:11
STORY II Chron. 13:22; 24:27
STOUT Dan. 7:20, whose look was more *s*
Mal. 3:13, words have been *s* against me
See Ps. 76:5; Isa. 9:9; 10:12; 46:12
STRAIGHT Ps. 5:8, make your way *s*
Prov. 4:25, your eyelids look *s* before you
Eccl. 1:15, crooked cannot be made *s*
Isa. 40:3, make *s* a highway
Jer. 31:9, cause them to walk in a *s* way
Mat. 3:3; Jn. 1:23, make his paths *s*
Lk. 3:5, crooked shall be made *s*
13:13, she was made *s*
Acts 9:11, street which is called *S*
Heb. 12:13, make *s* paths for your feet
See Josh. 6:5; I Sam. 6:12; Ezek. 1:7; 10:22
STRAIGHTWAY Mat. 4:20; Mk. 1:18, they *s* left
their nets
James 1:24, *s* forgets what manner of man
See Lk. 14:5; Jn. 13:32; Acts 9:20; 16:33
STRAIN Mat. 23:24, *s* at a gnat
STRAIT II Sam. 24:14, I am in a great *s*
Job 20:22, he shall be in *s*
Isa. 49:20, the place is too *s* for me
Mic. 2:7, is spirit of the Lord *s*?
Mat. 7:13, enter in at the *s* gate
Lk. 12:50, how am I *s* till it be accomplished
II Cor. 6:12, you are not *s* in us
Phil. 1:23, I am in a *s* betwixt two
See II Ki. 6:1; Job 18:7; 37:10; Jer. 19:9
STRAITLY Gen. 43:7; Josh. 6:1; Acts 4:17

STRAITNESS Deut. 28:53; Job 36:16
STRANGE Gen. 42:7, Joseph made himself *s*
Ex. 2:22, 18:3; Ps. 137:4, in a *s* land
Lev. 10:1; Num. 3:4; 26:61, offered *s* fire
Job. 19:17, my breath is *s* to my wife
31:3, a *s* punishment to workers
Prov. 21:8, the way of man is froward and *s*
Isa. 28:21, his *s* work, his *s* act
Ezek. 3:5, not sent to people of a *s* speech
Zeph. 1:8, clothed with *s* apparel
Lk. 5:26, we have seen *s* things today
Heb. 13:9, carried about with *s* doctrines
I Pet. 4:4, they think it *s* ye run not
12, not *s* concerning the fiery trial
STRANGER Gen. 23:4, a *s* with you
Ex. 23:9, you know the heart of a *s*
Job 15:19, no *s* passed among them
31:32, the *s* did not lodge in the street
Ps. 54:3, for *s* are risen up against me
109:11, let the *s* spoil his labor
146:9, the Lord preserves the *s*
Prov. 2:16, to deliver you even from the *s*
5:10, lest *s* be filled with your wealth
6:1, striken your hand with a *s*
7:5, from the *s* which flatters
11:15, he that is surety for a *s* shall smart
14:10, a *s* does not intermeddle
20:16; 27:13, garment that is surety for a *s*
Isa. 1:7, your land, *s* devour it
2:6, please themselves in children of *s*
14:1, the *s* shall be joined with them
56:3, neither let the son of the *s* speak
Jer. 14:8, why be as a *s* in the land
Ezek. 28:10, you shall die by the hand of *s*
Hos. 7:9, *S* have devoured his strength
Mat. 25:35, I was a *s*, and you took me in
Lk. 17:18, that returned, saved this *s*
Eph. 2:12, *s* from the covenant
19, no more *s*, but fellowcitizens
Heb. 11:13, confessed they were *s*
13:2, be not forgetful to entertain *s*
STRANGLED Nah. 2:12; Acts 15:20; 21:25
STREAM Ps. 124:4; Isa. 30:33; 35:6; 66:12
STREET Prov. 1:20; Rev. 21:21; 22:2
STRENGTH Ex. 15:2; Ps. 18:2; 28:7; Isa. 12:2, the
Lord is my *s*
Judg. 5:21, you have trodden down *s*
I Sam. 2:9, by *s* shall no man prevail
15:29, the *S* of Israel will not lie
Job 9:19, if I speak of *s*, lo, he is strong
12:13, with him is wisdom and *s*
Ps. 27:1, the Lord is the *s* of my life
29:11, the Lord will give *s* to his people
33:16, mighty not delivered by much *s*
39:13, spare me, that I may recover *s*
46:1; 81:1, God is our refuge and *s*
73:26, God is the *s* of my heart
96:6, *s* and beauty are in his sanctuary
138:3, strengthened me with *s* in my soul
Prov. 10:29, the way of the Lord is *s*
Eccl. 9:16, wisdom is better than *s*
Isa. 25:4, a *s* to the poor, a *s* to the needy
Lk. 1:51, he has showed *s* with his arm
Rom. 5:6, when you were without *s*

I Cor. 15:56, the *s* of sin is the law
Rev. 3:8, you have a little *s*
STRENGTHEN Ps. 20:2, *s* thee out of Zion
    104:15, bread which *s* man's heart
  Eccl. 7:19, wisdom *s* the wise
  Isa. 35:3, *S* ye the weak hands
  Lk. 22:32, when converted, *s* your brethren
  Eph. 3:16; Col. 1:11, to be *s* with might
  Phil. 4:13, through Christ who *s* me
  See Lk. 22:43; I Pet. 5:10; Rev. 3:2
STRETCH Ps. 68:31, *s* out her hands to God
  Isa. 28:20, shorter than a man can *s* himself
  Jer. 10:12; 51:15, he *s* out the heavens
  Ezek. 16:27, I have *s* out my hand over you
  Mat. 12:13, *S* forth your hand
  See Ps. 104:2; Rom. 10:21; II Cor. 10:14
STRIKE Job 17:3; Prov. 22:26, *s* hands
  Ps. 110:5, shall *s* through kings
  Prov. 7:23, till a dart *s* through his liver
  See Prov. 23:35; Isa. 1:5; I Tim. 3:3; Titus 1:7
STRIVE Gen. 6:3, shall not always *s*
  Prov. 3:30, *S* not without cause
  Lk. 13:24, *S* to enter in at strait gate
  II Tim. 2:5, if a man *s* for mastery
    24, the servant of the Lord must not *s*
  See Isa. 45:9; Jer. 50:24; Mat. 12:19
STRONG I Sam. 4:9; I Ki. 2:2; II Chron. 15:7;
    Dan. 10:19, be *s*
  Job 9:19, if I speak of strength, lo, he is *s*
  Ps. 19:5, as a *s* man to run a race
    71:7, you are my *s* refuge
  Prov. 10:15, rich man's wealth is his *s* city
    18:10, the name of the Lord is a *s* tower
  Eccl. 9:11, the battle is not to the *s*
  Mat. 12:29,, first bind the *s* man
  Rom. 4:20, *s* in faith
  I Cor. 4:10, we are weak, you are *s*
  II Thess. 2:11, *s* delusion
  Heb. 5:12, of milk, and not of *s* meat
    6:18, we have a *s* consolation
STUBBLE Ps. 83:13, make them as *s*
  Isa. 33:11, conceive chaff, bring forth *s*
  Jer. 13:24, I will scatter them as *s*
  See Joel 2:5; Mal. 4:1; I Cor. 3:12
STUDY I Thess. 4:11; II Tim. 2:15
STUMBLE Isa. 28:7, they *s* in judgment
    59:10, we *s* at noonday
  Jer. 46:6; Dan. 11:19, *s* and fall
  Mal. 2:8, have caused many to *s*
  I Pet. 2:8, that *s* at the word
  See Jn. 11:9; Rom. 9:32; 11:11; 14:21
SUBDUE Ps. 47:3, he shall *s* the people
  Mic. 7:19, he will *s* our iniquities
  Phil. 3:21, able to *s* all things
  Heb. 11:33, through faith *s* kingdom
  See Dan. 2:40; Zech. 9:15; I Cor. 15:28
SUBJECT Lk. 10:17, devils are *s* unto us
  Rom. 8:7, not *s* to law of God
  I Cor. 14:32, prophets *s* to prophets
    15:28, then shall the Son also be *s* to him
  Eph. 5:24, as the church is *s* to Christ
  Heb. 2:15, all their lifetime *s* to bondage
  James 5:17, a man *s* to like passions
  I Pet. 2:18, servants be *s* to your masters

    3:22, angels and power *s* to him
    5:5, all of you be *s* to another
  See Lk. 2:51; Col. 2:20; Titus 3:1
SUBMIT II Sam. 22:45, *s* themselves
  Ps. 68:30, till every one *s* himself
  Eph. 5:22, wives, *s* yourselves
  James 4:7, *S* yourselves to God
  I Pet. 2:13, *S* to every ordinance of man
  See Rom. 10:3; Eph. 5:21; Heb. 13:17
SUBSCRIBE Isa. 44:5; Jer. 32:44
SUBSTANCE Gen. 13:6, their *s* was great
  Deut. 33:11, bless his *s*
  Job 30:22, you dissolve my *s*
  Ps. 17:14, they leave their *s* to babes
    139:15, my *s* was not hid from you
  Song of Sol. 8:7, give all his *s* for love
  Jer. 15:13; 17:3, your *s* will I give to spoil
  Hos. 12:8, I have found me out *s*
  Mic. 4:13, I will consecrate their *s*
  Lk. 8:3, ministered to him of their *s*
  Heb. 10:34, a better *s*
    11:1, the *s* of things hoped for
  See Prov. 1:13; 6:31; 8:21; 12:27; 29:3
SUBTIL Gen. 3:1; II Sam. 13:3; Prov. 7:10
SUBTILTY Gen. 27:35; Acts 13:10
SUBVERT II Tim. 2:14; Titus 1:11; 3:11
SUCCESS Josh. 1:8, have good *s*
SUCK Deut. 32:13, *s* honey out of rock
    33:19, *s* abundance of the seas
  Job 20:16, *s* poison of asps
  Isa. 60:16, *s* the milk of the Gentiles
  See Job 3:12; Joel 2:16; Mat. 24:19; Mk. 13:17;
    Lk. 21:23; 23:29
SUDDEN Job 22:10; Prov. 3:25; I Thess. 5:3
SUDDENLY Prov. 29:1, be *s* destroyed
  Eccl. 9:12, when it falls *s*
  Mal. 3:1, shall *s* come to his temple
  Mk. 13:36, coming *s* he find you sleeping
  I Tim. 5:22, lay hands *s* on no man
SUFFER Job 21:3, *S* me that I may speak
  Ps. 55:22, never *s* righteousness to be moved
    89:33, nor *s* my faithfulness to fall
  Prov. 19;15, the idle soul shall *s* hunger
  Eccl. 5:12, not *s* him to sleep
  Mat. 3:15, *S* it to be so now
    8:21, *s* me first to bury my father
    16:21; Lk. 9:22, *s* many things
    19:14; Lk. 18:16, *S* little children
  Lk. 24:46; Acts 3:18, behooved Christ to *s*
  Rom. 8:17, if we *s* with him
  I Cor. 3:15, he shall *s* loss
    10:13, will not *s* you to be tempted
    12:26, whether one member *s*, all *s* with it
  Gal. 6:12, lest they should *s* persecution
  II Tim. 2:12, if we *s*, we shall also reign
    3:12, shall *s* persecution
  Heb. 13:3, remember them who *s*
  I Pet. 2:21, *s* for us, leaving an example
    4:1, he that has *s* in the flesh
SUFFICIENCY Job 20:22; II Cor. 3:5; 9:8
SUFFICIENT Isa. 40:16, not *s* to burn
  Mat. 6:34, *S* for the day is the evil
  II Cor. 2:16, who is *s* for these things?
SUM Ps. 139:17; Acts 22:28; Heb. 8:1

SUMMER Gen. 8:22, *s* and winter
    Prov. 6:8, 30:25, provides meat in *s*
      10:5, he that gathers in *s* is a wise son
    Jer. 8:20, the *s* is ended
    Mat. 24:32; Mk. 13:28, ye know *s* is nigh
    See Dan. 2:35; Zech. 14:8; Lk. 21:30
SUMPTUOUSLY Lk. 16:19
SUN Josh. 10:12, *S*, stand thou still
    Judg. 5:31, as the *s* in his might
    Job. 8:16, hypocrite is green before the *s*
    Ps. 58:8, that they may not see the *s*
      84:11, a *s* and shield
    Eccl. 1:9, no new thing under the *s*
      11:7, a pleasant thing it is to behold the *s*
      12:2, while the *s* or stars be not darkened
    Jer. 15:9, her *s* is gone down while yet day
    Joel 2:10; 3:15, the *s* be darkened
    Mal. 4:2, the *S* of righteousness
    Mat. 5:45, makes his *s* to rise on evil
      13:43, then shall righteous shine as *s*
    Eph. 4:26, let not *s* go down on your wrath
SUPERFLUITY James 1:21
SUPPLICATION Job 9:15, I would make *s* to my
    judge
    Ps. 6:9, the Lord has heard my *s*
    Dan. 9:3, to seek by prayer and *s*
    Zech. 12:10, spirit of grace and *s*
    Eph. 6:18, with all prayer and *s*
    I Tim. 2:1, that *s* be made for all men
    See Ps. 28:6; 31:22; Phil 4:6; Heb. 5:7
SUPPLY Phil. 1:19; 2:30; 4:19
SUPPORT Acts 20:35; I Thess. 5:14
SUPREME I Pet. 2:13, to the king as *s*
SURE Num. 32:23, be *s* sin will find you out
    Job 24:22, no man is *s* of life
    Prov. 6:3, make *s* your friend
    Isa. 55:3; Acts 13:34, the *s* mercies of David
    II Tim. 2:19, foundation of God stands *s*
    See Isa. 33:16; Heb. 6:19; II Pet. 1:10, 19
SURFEITING Lk. 21:34
SURPRISED Isa. 33:14; Jer. 48:41; 51:41
SUSTAIN Ps. 3:5; 55:22; Isa. 59:16
SWEAR Ps. 15:4, that *s* to his hurt
    Eccl. 9:2, he that *s* fears an oath
    Isa. 45:23, to me every tongue shall *s*
      65:16, shall *s* by the God of truth
    Jer. 4:2, *s*, the Lord lives, in truth
      23:10, because of *s* the land mourns
    Hos. 4:2, by *s*, and lying, they break out
      10:4, *s* falsely in making a covenant
    Zech. 5:3, every one that *s* shall be cut off
    Mal. 3:5, a witness against false *s*
    See Zeph. 1:5; Mat. 26:74; Heb. 6:13
SWEAT Gen. 3:19; Ezek. 44:18; Lk. 22:44
SWEET Job 20:12, though wickedness be *s*
    Ps. 55:14, we took *s* counsel together
      104:34, my meditation of him shall be *s*
    Prov. 3:24, your sleep shall be *s*
      9:17, stolen waters are *s*
    Prov. 16:24, pleasant words are *s*
      27:7, to the hungry every bitter thing is *s*
    Eccl. 5:12, sleep of laboring man is *s*
      11:7, truly the light is *s*
    Song of Sol. 2:3, his fruit was *s* to my taste

    Isa. 5:20, put bitter for *s*, and *s* for bitter
      23:16, make *s* melody
    James 3:11, at same place *s* water and bitter
    See Judg. 14:18; Mic. 6:15; Mk. 16:1
SWELLING Jer. 12:5; II Pet. 2:18; Jude 16
SWIFT Eccl. 9:11, the race is not to the *s*
    Amos 2:15, the *s* of foot shall not deliver
    Rom. 3:15, feet *s* to shed blood
    See Job 7:6; 9:25; Jer. 46:6; Mal. 3:5
SWIM II Ki. 6:6, iron did *s*
    Ezek. 47:5, waters to *s* in
    See Ps. 6:6; Isa. 25:11; Ezek. 32:6; Acts 27:42
SWOLLEN Acts 28:6, when he should have *s*
SWOON Lam. 2:11, children *s* in the streets
SWORD Ps. 57:4, their tongue a sharp *s*
    Isa. 2:4, nation shall not lift up *s*
    Ezek. 7:15, *s* is without, pestilence within
    Mat. 10:34, not to send peace, but a *s*
    Lk. 2:35, a *s* shall pierce your own soul
    Rom. 13:4, he hears not the *s* in vain
    Eph. 6:17, the *s* of the Spirit
    Heb. 4:12, sharper than twoedged *s*
    Rev. 1:16; 19:15, out of his mouth a sharp *s*
      13:10, kills with *s* must be killed with *s*
    See Isa. 2:4; Joel 3:10; Mic. 4:3; Lk. 22:38

T

TABERNACLE Ps. 15:1, abide in your *t*?
    27:5, in secret of his *t* shall he hide me
    84:1, how amiable are your *t*
    Isa. 33:20, a *t* that shall not be taken down
    See Job 5:24; Prov. 14:11; II Cor. 5:1
TABLE Ps. 23:5, you prepare a *t*
    69:22, let their *t* become a snare
    78:19, can God furnish a *t* in the wilderness?
    128:3, like olive plants about your *t*
    Prov. 9:2, wisdom has furnished her *t*
    Mat. 15:27; Mk. 7:28, from their masters' *t*
    Acts 6:2, leave word of God, and serve *t*
    II Cor. 3:3, fleshy *t* of the heart
    See Prov. 3:3; Jer. 17:1; I Cor. 10:21
TAKE Ex. 6:7, I will *t* you to me for a people
    34:9, *t* us for your inheritance
    Judg. 19:30, *t* advice, and speak your minds
    II Ki. 19:30; Isa. 37:31, shall yet *t* not
    Job 23:10, he knows the way that I *t*
    Ps. 51:11, *t* not your holy spirit from me
    116:13, I will *t* the cup of salvation
    Song of Sol. 2:15, *T* us the foxes, and little
    foxes
    Isa. 33:23, the lame *t* the prey
    Amos 9:2, thence shall my hand *t* them
    Mat. 6:25; LK. 12:11, 22, 26, *T* no thought
    16:5; Mk. 8:14; forgotten to *t* bread
    18:16, then *t* with you one or two more
    20:14, *T* that yours is, and go your way
    Lk. 6:29, forbid him not to *t* your coat also
    12:19, soul, *t* your ease
    Jn. 16:15, he shall *t* of mine
    I Cor. 6:7, why do you not rather *t* wrong?
    11:24, *T*, eat; this is my body
    I Tim. 3:5, how shall he *t* care of the church?

I Pet. 2:20, if you *t* it patiently
Rev. 3:11, that no man *t* your crown
TALE Ps. 90:9; Lk. 24:11
TALK Deut. 5:24, God does *t* with man
    6:7, *t* of them when you sit
Job 11:2, a man full of *t*
    13:7, will you *t* deceitfully for him?
    15:3, reason with unprofitable *t*
Ps. 71:24, *t* of your righteousness
Prov. 6:22, it shall *t* with you
Jer. 12:1, let me *t* with you of your judgments
Ezek. 3:22, arise, and I will *t* with you there
Mat. 22:15, they might entangle him in his *t*
Lk. 24:32, while he *t* with us by the way
Jn. 9:37, it is he that *t* with you
TALL Deut. 1:28; 2:10; II Ki. 19:23
TAME Mk. 5:4; James 3:7, 8
TARE II Sam. 13:31; II Ki. 2:24; Mk. 9:20
TARRY Gen. 27:44, and *t* a few days
Ex. 12:39, were thrust out, and could not *t*
II Ki. 7:9, if we *t* till morning light
Ps. 68:12, that *t* at home divided the spoil
Prov. 23:30, they that *t* long at the wine
Isa. 46:13, my salvation shall not *t*
Jer. 14:8, that turns aside to *t* for a night
Hab. 2:3, though it *t*, wait for it
Mat. 25:5, while the bridegroom *t*
    26:38; Mk. 14:34, *t* here and watch
Lk. 24:29, he went in to *t* with them
    49, *t* you in city of Jerusalem till endued
Jn. 21:22, if I will that he *t*
Acts 22:16, why *t* thou, arise, and be baptized
I Cor. 11:33, *t* one for another
Heb. 10:37, will come, and will not *t*
See I Sam. 30:24; Mic. 5:7; Jn. 3:22
TASTE Num. 11:8, the *t* of it as *t* of fresh oil
Job 6:6, is any *t* in white of egg?
    12:11, does not the mouth *t* his meat
    34:3, tries words as mouth *t* meat
Ps. 34:8, *t* and see that the Lord is good
    119:103, how sweet are your words to my *t*!
Jer. 48:11, his *t* remained in him
Lk. 9:27, some, which shall not *t* death
    14:24, none bidden shall *t* of my supper
Jn. 8:52, shall never *t* of death
Col. 2:21, touch not, *t* not
Heb. 2:9, *t* death for every man
    6:4, and have *t* of the heavenly gift
I Pet. 2:3, have *t* that the Lord is gracious
TATTLERS I Tim. 5:13, *t* and busybodies
TAUGHT Judg. 8:16, *t* the men of Succoth
II Chron. 6:27, you have *t* them the good way
    23:13, such as *t* to sing praise
Ps. 71:17; 119:102, you have *t* me
Prov. 4:4, he *t* me also, and said
    11, I have *t* you in way of wisdom
Eccl. 12:9, he still *t* the people knowledge
Isa. 29:13, their fear is *t* by precept of men
    54:13, all your children shall be *t* of God
Jer. 12:16, *t* my people to swear by Baal
    32:33, *t* them, rising up early
Zech. 13:5, *t* to keep cattle
Mat. 7:29, *t* as one having authority
    28:15, and did as they were *t*

Lk. 13:26, you have in our streets
Jn. 6:45, they shall be all *t* of God
    8:28, as my Father has *t* me
Eph. 4:21, if so be you have been *t* by him
II Thess. 2:15, the traditions you have been *t*
TAUNT Jer. 24:9; Ezek. 5:15; Hab. 2:6
TEACH Ex. 4:15, I will *t* you
Deut. 4:10, that they may *t* their children
    6:7; 11:19, *t* them diligently
Judg. 13:8, *t* us what do to the child
I Sam. 12:23, I will *t* you the good way
II Sam. 1:18, bade them *t* use of the bow
II Chron. 15:3, without a *t* priest
Job 6:24, *T* me, and I will hold my tongue
    8:10, your fathers, shall not they *t* you
    12:7, ask the beasts, and they shall *t* you
    36:22, God exalts, who *t* like him?
Ps. 25:4, *t* me your paths
    27:11, 86:11, *T* me your way, and lead me
    34:11, I will *t* your the fear of the Lord
    51:13, then will I *t* transgressors
    90:12, so *t* us to number our days
    94:12, blessed is the man whom you *t*
Prov. 6:13, wicked man *t* with his fingers
Isa. 2:3; Mich. 4:2, he will *t* us of his ways
    28:9, whom shall he *t* knowledge?
    26, God does *t* him discretion
    48:17, I am you God which *t* you to profit
Jer. 9:20, and *t* your daughters wailing
Ezek. 44:23, *t* my people the difference
Mic. 3:11, priests *t* for hire
Mat. 28:19, *t* all nations
Lk. 11:1, *t* us to pray
    12:12, the Holy Ghost shall *t* you
Acts 5:42, they ceased not to *t* and preach
Rom. 12:7, he that *t*, on *t*
I Cor. 4:17, as I *t* every where
    11:14, does not even nature *t* you?
    14:19, that by my voice I might *t* others
Col. 1:28, *t* every man in all wisdom
    3:16, *t* and admonishing on another
I Tim. 1:3, charge some they *t* no other
    2:12, I suffer not a woman to *t*
II Tim. 2:2, faithful men, able to *t*
    2:24, apt to *t*
Titus 1:11, *t* things they ought not
    2:4, *t* young women to be sober
    12, *T* us, that denying ungodliness
TEACHER I Chron. 25:8, as well *t* as scholar
Ps. 119:99, more understanding than my *t*
Prov. 5:13, not obeyed the voice of my *t*
Isa. 30:20, your eyes shall see your *t*
Jn. 3:2, a *t* come from God
Rom. 2:20, you are a *t* of babes
I Cor. 12:29, are all *t*?
Eph. 4:11, evangelists, pastors, and *t*
I Tim. 1:17, desiring to be *t* of the law
Titus 2:3, aged women, *t* of good things
See I Tim. 2:7; Heb. 5:12; II Pet. 2:1
TEAR Job 16:9, he *t* me in his wrath
    18:4, he *t* himself in his anger
Ps. 7:2, lest he *t* my soul
    35:15, they did *t* me, and ceased not
    50:22, lest I *t* you in pieces

Hos. 5:14, I will *t* and go away
See Mic. 5:8; Mk. 9:18; Lk. 9:39
TEARS II Ki. 20:5, I have seen your *t*
Job 16:20, my eye pours out *t*
Ps. 6:6, I water my couch with *t*
  39:12, hold not your peace at my *t*
  42:3, *t* have been my meat
  56:8, put thou my *t* into your bottle
  80:5, the bread of *t*, and *t* to drink
  116:8, you have delivered my eyes from
Isa. 16:9, I will water you with my *t*
Jer. 9:1, Oh that my eyes were a fountain of *t*
  13:17; 14:17, my eyes run down with *t*
  31:16, refrain your eyes from *t*
Lam. 1:2, her *t* are on her cheeks
  2:11, my eyes do fail with *t*
Ezek. 24:16, neither shall your *t* run down
Mal. 2:13, covering the altar with *t*
Lk. 7:38, to wash his feet with her *t*
Acts 20:19, serving the Lord with many *t*
  31, ceased not to warn with *t*
II Tim. 1:4, being mindful of your *t*
TEDIOUS Acts 24:4, that I be not further *t*
TEETH Gen. 49:12, *t* white with milk
Num. 11:33, flesh yet between their *t*
Job 19:20, escaped with the skin of my *t*
Prov. 10:26, as vinegar to the *t*
Isa. 41:15, an instrument having *t*
Jer. 31:29; Ezek. 18:2, *t* set on edge
Amos 4:6, cleanness of *t*
See Mic. 3:5; Zech. 9:7; Mat. 27:44; Rev. 9:8
TELL Gen. 15:5, *t* the stars
II Sam. 1:20, *T* it not in Gath
Ps. 48:12, *t* the towers thereof
  50:12, if I were hungry, I would not *t* you
Eccl. 6:12, who can *t* what shall be after?
  10:20, that which has wings shall *t*
Jonah 3:9, who can *t* if God will turn?
Mat. 18:15, *t* him his fault
  17, *t* it unto the Church
  21:27; Lk. 20:8, neither *t* I you
Mk. 5:19, *t* how great things
  11:33; Lk. 20:7, we cannot *t*
Lk. 13:32, *t* that fox
Jn. 3:8, can not *t* whence
  4:25, he will *t* us all things
Acts 17:21, to *t* or hear some new thing
TEMPER Ex. 29:2; 30:35; I Cor. 12:24
TEMPEST Job 9:17, breaks me with a *t*
Ps. 11:6, on wicked he shall rain a *t*
  55:8, hasten from windy storm and *t*
Isa. 32:2, a covert from the *t*
Heb. 12:18, not come to darkness and *t*
II Pet. 2:17, clouds carried with a *t*
TEMPESTUOUS Ps. 50:3; Acts 27:14
TEMPLE II Sam. 22:7, my voice out of his *t*
Neh. 6:10, hid ourselves in the *t*
Ps. 27:4, to enquire in his *t*
Isa. 6:1, his train filled the *t*
Amos 8:3, songs of the *t* shall be howlings
Mal. 3:1, Lord shall suddenly come to his *t*
Mat. 12:6, one greater than the *t*
Jn. 2:19, destroy this *t*
I Cor. 3:16; II Cor. 6:16; you are the *t* of God

See Hos. 8:14; Rev. 7:15; 11:19; 21:22
TEMPORAL II Cor. 4:18, things seen are *t*
TEMPT Gen. 22:1, God did *t* Abraham
Ex. 17:2, wherefore do you *t* the Lord?
Num. 14:22, have *t* me these ten times
Ps. 78:18, they *t* God in their heart
Isa. 7:12, I will not ask, neither *t* the Lord
Mal. 3:15, they that *t* God are delivered
Mat. 22:18; Lk. 20:23, why *t* ye me?
Lk. 4:12, you shall not *t* the lord your God
  10:25, a lawyer *t* him
Acts 5:9, agreed together to *t* the Spirit
  15:10, why *t* ye God to put a yoke?
I Cor. 10:13, will not suffer you to be *t*
Gal. 6:1, considering yourself, lest you be *t*
Heb. 2:18, has suffered, being *t*
  4:15, in all points *t* like as we are
James 1:13, cannot be *t*, neither *t* he any man
TEMPTATION Mat. 6:13, lead us not into *t*
Mk. 14:38; Lk. 22:46, lest you enter into *t*
Lk. 8:13, in time of *t* fall away
I Cor. 10:13, there has no *t* taken you
Gal. 4:14, my *t* in flesh you despised not
I Tim. 6:9, they that will be rich fall into *t*
James 1:2, when you fall into divers *t*
II Pet. 2:9, how to deliver out of *t*
See Lk. 11:4; Acts 20:19; Rev. 3:10
TEND Prov. 11:19; 14:23; 19:23; 21:5
TENDER Deut. 28:54, man that is *t*
  32:2, distil as small rain on *t* herb
II Ki. 22:19; II Chron. 34:27, your heart was *t*
Job 14:7, the *t* branch will not cease
Prov. 4:3, *t* in sight of my mother
Song of Sol. 2:13, 15; 7:12, vines with *t* grapes
Isa. 47:1, no more be called *t*
  53:2, grow up before him as a *t* plant
Dan. 1:9, God brought Daniel into *t* love
Lk. 1:78, through the *t* mercy of our God
Eph. 4:32, be kind and *t*-hearted
James 5:11, Lord is pitiful, and of *t* mercy
See I Chron. 22:5; Ezek. 17:22; Mk. 13:28
TENOR Gen. 43:7; Ex. 34:27
TENT Num. 24:5; how goodly are your *t*!
I Sam. 4:10, fled every man to his *t*
I Ki. 12:16, to your *t*, O Israel
Ps. 84:10, than to dwell in *t* of wickedness
Isa. 38:12, removed as a shepherd's *t*
  54:2, enlarge the place of your *t*
Acts 18:3, by occupation they were *t*-makers
See Isa. 40:22; Jer. 4:20; 35:7; Zech. 12:7
TENTH Gen. 28:22; Lev. 27:32; Isa. 6:13
TERRIBLE Ex. 34:10, a *t* thing I will do
Deut. 1:19; 8:15, that *t* wilderness
  10:21, has done for you *t* things
Judg. 13:6, like an angel of God, very *t*
Neh. 1:5; 4:14; 9:32, a mighty God and *t*
Job 37:22, with God is *t* majesty
  39:20, the glory of his nostrils is *t*
Ps. 45:4, hand shall teach you *t* things
  65:5, by *t* things in righteousness
  66:3, say unto God, How *t* are you?
  76:12, he is *t* to the kings of the earth
  99:3, your great and *t* name
  145:6, the might of your *t* acts

Song of Sol. 6:4, *t* as an army with banners
Isa. 25:4, blast of the *t* ones
 64:3, when you did *t* things
Jer. 15:21, redeem you out of hand of the *t*
Joel 2:11, the day of the Lord is very *t*
Heb. 12:21, so *t* was the sight
TERRIBLENESS Deut. 26:8; I Chron. 17:21
TERRIBLY Isa. 2:19, 21; Nah. 2:3
TERRIFY Job 9:34, let not his fear *t*
Lk. 21:9, when you hear of wars, be not *t*
 24:37, they were *t* and affrighted
Phil. 1:28, in nothing *t* by adversaries
See Job 7:14; II Cor. 10:9
TERROR Gen. 35:5; Job 6:4, the *t* of God
Deut. 32:25, the sword without and *t* within
Josh. 2:9, your *t* is fallen upon us
Job 18:11, *T* shall make him afraid
 24:17, in the *t* of the shadow of death
 31:23, destruction was a *t* to me
 33:7, my *t* shall not make you afraid
Ps. 55:4, the *t* of death are fallen upon me
 73:19, utterly consumed with *t*
 91:5, afraid for the *t* by night
Ezek. 26:21; 28:19; I will make you a *t*
Rom. 13:3, rulers are not *t* to good works
II Cor. 5:11, knowing the *t* of the Lord
TESTIFY Num. 35:30, witness shall not *t*
Deut. 31:21, this song shall *t* against them
Ruth 1:21, the Lord has *t* against me
II Sam. 1:16, your mouth has *t* against you
Neh. 9:30, *t* against them by your spirit
Job 15:6, your own lips *t* against you
Isa. 59:12, our sins *t* against us
Hos. 5:5; 7:10, the pride of Israel does *t*
Mic. 6:3, what have I done? *t* against me
Lk. 16:28, send Lazarus, that he may *t*
Jn. 2:25, needed not that any should *t*
 21:24, the disciple which *t* of these things
Acts 23:11, as you have *t* in Jerusalem
I Tim. 2:6, gave himself to be *t* in due time
I Pet. 1:11, it *t* beforehand the sufferings
I Jn. 4:14, we have seen and do *t*
TESTIMONY II Ki. 17:15, rejected his *t*
Ps. 93:5, your *t* are sure
 119:59, I turned my feet to your *t*
 119, I love your *t*
Isa. 8:16, bind up the *t*
Mat. 10:18; Mk. 13:9, for a *t* against them
Lk. 21:13, it shall turn to you for a *t*
Jn. 3:32, no man receives his *t*
 21:24, we know that his *t* is true
Acts 14:3, *t* to the word of his grace
I Cor. 2:1, declaring the *t* of God
II Cor. 1:12, the *t* of our conscience
II Tim. 1:8, be not ashamed of the *t*
Heb. 11:5, Enoch had this *t*
See Rev. 1:2; 6:9; 11:7; 12:11; 19:10
THANK Mat 11:25; Jn. 11:41, I *t* you
Acts 28:15, *t* God, and took courage
I Cor. 1:4, I *t* God on your behalf
II Thess. 1:3, we are bound to *t* God
I Tim. 1:12, I *t* Jesus Christ
See I Chron. 23:30; Dan. 2:23; Rom. 6:17
THANKS Neh. 12:31, companies that gave *t*

Mat. 26:27, took the cup, and gave *t*
Lk. 2:38, Anna gave *t* to the Lord
Eph. 5:20, giving *t* always for all things
I Thess. 3:9, what *t* can we render?
Rev. 4:9, *t* to him that sat on the throne
THANKSGIVING Ps. 26:7, the voice of *t*
 95:2, come before his face with *t*
Isa. 51:3, *t* and melody shall be found therein
Amos 4:5, offer a sacrifice of *t*
Phil. 4:6, with *t* let your requests be made
Col. 4:2, watch in the same with *t*
I Tim. 4:3, to be received with *t*
See Neh. 11:17; 12:8; II Cor. 4:15; 9:11
THAT Gen. 18:25, *t* be far from you
Num. 24:13; I Ki. 22:14, *t* will I speak
Job 23:13, even *t* he does
Zech. 11:9, *t t* dies, let it die
Mat. 10:15; Mk. 6:11, than for *t* city
 13:12, 25:29; Mk. 4:25, *t* he has
Jn. 1:8, he was not *t* light
 5:12, what man is *t* which said?
James 4:15, we shall live and do this or *t*
THEN Gen. 4:26, *t* began men to call
Ps. 27:10, *t* the Lord will take me up
 55:12, *t* I could have borne it
Isa. 58:8, *T* shall your light break forth
Ezek. 39:28, *T* shall they know
Mat. 5:24, *t* come and offer your gift
 19:25; Mk. 10:26, who *t* can be saved?
 24:14, *t* shall the end come
II Cor. 12:10, *t* am I strong
THESE Ex. 32:4, *T* be your gods, O Israel
Eccl. 7:10, former days better than *t*
Isa. 60:8, who are *t* that fly?
Mat. 5:37, whatsoever is more than *t*
 23:23, *t* ought you to have done
 25:40, one of the least of *t*
Jn. 17:20, neither pray I for *t* alone
 21:15, lovest thou me more than *t*?
THICK Deut. 32:15, you are grown *t*
II Sam. 18:9, mule went under the *t* boughs
Ps. 74:5, lifted up axes on the *t* trees
Ezek. 31:3, top was among *t* boughs
Hab. 2:6, lades himself with *t* clay
THICKET Gen. 22:13; Isa. 9:18; Jer. 4:7, 29
THIEF Ps. 50:18, when you saw a *t*
Jer. 2:26, as the *t* is ashamed
Joel 2:9, enter a windows like a *t*
Lk. 12:33, where no *t* approaches
Jn. 10:1; the same is a *t* and a robber
I Pet. 4:15, let none suffer as a *t*
See Prov. 6:30; 29:24; Mat. 24:43
THIEVES Isa. 1:23; Lk. 10:30; Jn. 10:8
THIGH Gen. 24:2; 47:29, put hand under *t*
 32:25, touched hollow of Jacob's *t*
Judg. 15:8, smote them hip and *t*
Song of Sol. 3:8, every man has sword on his *t*
See Ps. 45:3; Jer. 31:19; Rev. 19:16
THINE Gen. 31:32, discern what is *t*
I Sam. 15:28, to a neighbor of *t*
I Ki. 20:4, I am *t*, and all I have
I Chron. 29:11, *T* is the greatness
Ps. 74:16, the day is *t*, the night also is *t*

119:94, I am *t*, save me
Mat. 20:14, take that is *t*
Lk. 4:7, worship me, all shall be *t*
22:42, not my will, but *t* be done
Jn. 17:6, *t* they were
10, all mine are *t*, and *t* are mine
THING Gen. 21:11, the *t* was very grievous
Ex. 18:17, the *t* you do is not good
II Ki. 2:10, you have asked a hard *t*
Eccl. 1:19, the *t* that has been
Isa. 7:13, is it a small *t* to weary
41:12, as a *t* of nought
Mk. 1:27, what *t* is this?
Jn. 5:14, lest a worse *t* come unto you
Phil. 3:16, let us mind the same *t*
THINK Gen. 40:14, but *t* on me
Neh. 5:19, *T* on me, O my God, for good
Ps. 40:17, I am poor, yet the Lord *t* on me
Prov. 23:7, as he *t* in his heart, so is he
Isa. 10:7, nor does his heart *t* so
Jonah 1:6, if God will *t* upon us
Mat. 3:9, *t* not to say within yourselves
6:7, *t* they shall be heard
9:4, why *t* you evil in your hearts?
17:25; 22:17, what *t* you?
22:42; Mk. 14:64; what *t* ye of Christ?
Rom. 12:3, more highly than he ought to *t*
I Cor. 10:12, that *t* he stands
II Cor. 3:5, to *t* anything as of ourselves
Gal. 6:3, if a man *t* himself to be something
Eph. 3:20, able to do above all we ask or *t*
Phil. 4:8, *t* on these things
James 1:7, let not that man *t* he shall receive
I Pet. 4:12, *t* it not strange
THIRST (*n.*) Ex. 17:3, to kill us with *t*
Deut. 29:19, to add drunkenness to *t*
Judg. 15:18, now I shall die for *t*
II Chron. 32:11, does persuade you to die by *t*
Ps. 69:21, in my *t* they gave me vinegar
Isa. 41:17, when their tongue fails for *t*
Amos 8:11, not a *t* for water, but of hearing
II Cor. 11:27, in hunger and *t* often
See Deut. 28:48; Job 24:11; Ps. 104:11
THIRST (*v.*) Ps. 63:1, my soul *t* for God
Isa. 49:10; Rev. 7:16, shall not hunger nor *t*
Mat. 5:6, *t* after righteousness
Jn. 4:14; 6:35, shall never *t*
19:28, I *t*
See Ex. 17:3; Rom. 12:20; I Cor. 4:11
THIRSTY Ps. 63:1; 143:6, in a *t* land
107:5, hungry and *t*, their soul fainted
Prov. 25:25, as cold waters to a *t* soul
Isa. 21:14, brought water to him that was *t*
29:8, as when a *t* man dreams
44:3, pour water on him that is *t*
65:13, but you shall be *t*
THISTLE Gen. 3:18, *t* shall it bring forth
Job 31:40, lest *t* grow instead of wheat
Mat. 7:16, do men gather figs of *t*?
See II Ki. 14:9; II Chron. 25:18; Hos. 10:8
THORN Num. 33:55, *t* in your sides
Ps. 118:12, quenched as the fire of *t*
Prov. 15:19, slothful man as hedge of *t*
24:31, it as all grown over with *t*

26:9, as a *t* goes into hand of drunkard
Eccl. 7:6, crackling of it under a pot
Song of Sol. 2:2, as the lily among *t*
Isa. 33:12, as *t* cut up shall they be burned
34:13, and *t* shall come up in her palaces
Jer. 4:3, sow not among *t*
Hos. 2:6, I will hedge up your way with *t*
9:6, *t* shall be in their tabernacles
10:8, the *t* shall come up on their altars
II Cor. 12:7, a *t* in the flesh
THOUGHT (*n.*) Job 4:13, in *t* from visions
12:5, despised in *t* of him at ease
42:2, no *t* can be withholden from you
Ps. 10:4, God is not in all his *t*
Ps. 40:5, your *t* cannot be reckoned
92:5, your *t* are very deep
94:11, the Lord knows the *t* of man
19, in the multitude of my *t*
139:2, you understand my *t* afar off
17, how precious are your *t* to me!
23, try me, and know my *t*
Prov. 12:5, the *t* of the righteous are right
16:3, your *t* shall be established
24:9, the *t* of foolishness is sin
Isa. 55:7, and the unrighteous man his *t*
8, my *t* are not your *t*
9, so are my *t* higher than your *t*
Mic. 4:12, they know not the *t* of the Lord
Mat. 15:19; Mk. 7:21, out of the heart proceed evil *t*
Mk. 13:11; Lk. 12:11, 22, take no *t*
Lk. 2:35, *t* of many hearts
24:38, why do *t* arise in your hearts?
Acts 8:22, *t* of your heart may be forgiven
I Cor. 3:20, Lord knows the *t* of the wise
II Cor. 10:5, bringing into captivity every *t*
James 2:4, you are become judges of evil *t*
THOUGHT (*v.*) Deut. 19:19, do to him as he *t* to have done
II Ki. 5:11, I *t*, he will surely come out
Neh. 6:2, they *t* to do me mischief
Ps. 48:9, we have *t* of your lovingkindness
50:21, you *t* I was such an one as yourself
73:16, when I *t* to know this
119:59, I *t* on my ways
Prov. 30:32, if you have *t* evil
Isa. 14:24, as I have *t*, so shall it come
Jer. 18:8, I will repent to the evil I *t* to do
Zech. 8:14, as I *t* to punish you
15, I *t* to do well
Mal. 3:16, for them that *t* on his name
Mat. 1:20, but while he *t* on these things
Mk. 14:72, when he *t* thereon, he wept
Jn. 11:13, they *t* he had spoken of rest
Acts 10:19, while Peter *t* on the vision
26:8, why should it be *t* a thing incredible
I Cor. 13:11; I *t* as a child
THREAD Gen. 14:23; Josh. 2:18; Judg. 16:9
THREATEN Acts 4:17; 9:1; Eph. 6:9
THREEFOLD Eccl. 4:12, a *t* cord
THRESH Isa. 41:15, *t* the mountains
Jer. 51:33, it is time to *t* her
Hab. 3:12, you did *t* the heathen
I Cor. 9:10, *t* in hope

See Lev. 26:5; I Chron. 21:20; Isa. 21:10; 28:28
THREW Mk. 12:42; Lk. 9:42; Acts 22:23
THROAT Ps. 5:9; 115:7; Mat. 18:28
THRONE Ps. 11:4, the Lord's *t* is in heaven
    94:20, shall *t* of iniquity have fellowship
    122:5, there are set *t* of judgment
  Prov. 20:28, his *t* is upholden by mercy
  Isa. 66:1; Acts 7:49, heaven is my *t*
  Jer. 17:12, high *t* from the beginning
  Dan. 7:9, his *t* was like the fiery flame
  Mat. 19:28, Son of man shall sit in the *t*
  Col. 1:16, whether they be *t*
  Heb. 4:16, the *t* of grace
  Rev. 3:21, to him will I grant to sit on my *t*
    4:2, a *t* was set in heaven
  See Rev. 6:16; 7:9; 14:3; 19:4; 20:11; 22:1
THRONG Mk. 3:9; 5:31; Lk. 8:42; 45
THROW Mic. 5:11; Mal. 1:4; Mat. 24:2
THRUST Joel 2:8, neither shall one *t* another
  Lk. 10:15, shall be *t* down to hell
    13:28, and you yourselves *t* out
  Jn. 20:25, and *t* my hand into his side
  Rev. 14:15, *T* in your sickle
  See Ex. 11:1; I Sam. 31:4; Ezek. 34:21
TIDINGS Ps. 112:7, afraid of evil *t*
  Jer. 20:15, cursed be the mean who brought *t*
  Dan. 11:44, *t* out of the east
TILL Gen. 2:5; Prov. 28:19; Ezek. 36:9
TILLAGE I Chron. 27:26; Neh. 10:37
TIME Gen. 47:29, the *t* drew nigh
  Job 22:16, cut down out of *t*
    38:23, reserved against the *t* of trouble
  Ps. 32:6, in a *t* when you may be found
    37:19, not ashamed in the evil *t*
    41:1, deliver him in *t* of trouble
    56:3, what *t* I am afraid
    69:13; Isa. 49:8; II Cor. 6:2, acceptable *t*
    89:47, remember how short my *t* is
  Eccl. 3:1, there is a *t* to every purpose
    9:11, *t* and chance happens to all
  Isa. 60:22, I will hasten it in his *t*
  Jer. 46:21, the *t* of their visitation
  Ezek. 16:8, your *t* was the *t* of love
  Dan. 7:25, a *t* and *t* and the dividing of *t*
  Hos. 10:12, it is *t* to seek the Lord
  Mal. 3:11, shall vine cast fruit before the *t*
  Mat. 16:3, the signs of the *t*
  Lk. 19:44, the *t* of your visitation
  Rom. 13:11, it is high *t* to awake
  I Cor. 7:29, the *t* is short
  Eph. 5:16; Col. 4:5, redeeming the *t*
  Heb. 4:16, help in *t* of need
  I Pet. 1:11, what manner of *t*
  Rev. 1:3, the *t* is at hand
TINGLE I Sam. 3:11; II Ki. 21:12, Jer. 19:3
TINKLING Isa. 3:16, 18; I Cor. 13:1
TOGETHER Prov. 22:2, meet *t*
  Amos 3:3, can two walk *t*?
  Mat. 18:20, where two or three gathered *t*
  Rom. 8:28, work *t* for good
  I Thess. 4:17, caught up *t*
  See Mat. 19:6; Eph. 2:21; II Thess. 2:1
TOIL Gen. 5:29; 41:51; Lk. 12:27
TONGUE Job 5:21, hid from scourge of the *t*

    20:12, hide wickedness under his *t*
  Ps. 34:13; I Pet. 3:10, keep your *t* from evil
  Prov. 10:20, *t* of the just as choice of silver
    12:18; 31:26, *t* of the wise is health
    19, the lying *t* is but for a moment
    15:4, a wholesome *t* is a tree of life
    18:21, in the power of the *t*
    21:23, whoso keeps his *t* keeps his soul
  Isa. 30:27, his *t* as a devouring fire
    50:4, has given me the *t* of the learned
  Jer. 9:5, taught their *t* to speak lies
    18:18, let us smite him with the *t*
  Mk. 7:35, his *t* was loosed
  James 1:26, and bridles not his *t*
    3:5, the *t* is a little member
    8, the *t* can no man
  I Jn. 3:18, nor let us love in *t*
TOOL Ex. 20:25; 32:4; Deut. 27:5; I Ki. 6:7
TOOTH Ex. 21:24; Prov. 25:19; Mat. 5:38
TORCHES Nah. 2:3; Zech. 12:6; John 18:3
TORMENT Mat. 8:29, *t* us before the time
  Lk. 16:23, being in *t*
  Heb. 11:37, destitute, afflicted, *t*
  I Jn. 4:18, fear has *t*
  Rev. 9:5, *t* as *t* of a scorpion
    14:11, the smoke of their *t*
  See Mat. 4:24; Mk. 5:7; Lk. 8:28
TORN Gen. 44:28, surely he is *t* in pieces
  Ezek. 4:14, have not eaten of that which is *t*
  Hos. 6:1, he has *t*, and he will heal us
  See Isa. 5:25; Mal. 1:13; Mk. 1:26
TOSS Ps. 109:23, I am *t* up and down
  Isa. 22:18, he will *t* you like a ball
    54:11, afflicted, *t* with tempest
  Eph. 4:14, no more children, *t* to and fro
  See Mat. 14:24; Acts 27:18; James 1:6
TOUCH Gen. 3:3, nor *t* it, lest you die
  I Sam. 10:26, a band whose hearts God has *t*
  I Chron. 16:22; Ps. 105:15, *T* not my anointed
  Job 5:19, there shall no evil *t* you
    6:7, things my soul refused to *t*
  Isa. 6:7, lo, this has *t* your lips
  Jer. 1:9, the Lord *t* my mouth
  Zech. 2:8, he that *t* you *t* the apple of his eye
  Mat. 9:21, if I may but *t* his garment
  Lk. 18:15, children, that he should *t* them
  Jn. 20:17, *T* me not
  II Cor. 6:17, *t* not the unclean thing
  Col. 2:21, *T* not, taste not
  See Job 19:21; Lk. 7:14; 11:46; I Cor. 7:11
TOWER II Sam. 22:3; Ps. 18:2, my high *t*
  Ps. 61:3, a strong *t* from the enemy
  Prov. 18:10, name of the Lord is a strong *t*
  Isa. 33:18, where is he that counted the *t*?
  See Isa. 2:15; 5:2; Mic. 4:8; Mat. 21:33
TRAFFICK Gen. 42:34; Ezek. 17:4
TRAIN I Ki. 10:2; Prov. 22:6; Isa. 6:1
TRAITOR Lk. 6:16; II Tim. 3:4
TRAMPLE Ps. 91:13; Isa. 63:3; Mat. 7:6
TRANQUILITY Dan. 4:27
TRANSFORM Rom. 12:2; II Cor. 11:13, 14
TRANSGRESS Num. 14:41, wherefore ye *t*
  I Sam. 2:24, make the Lord's people to *t*
  Neh. 1:8, if you *t*, I will scatter you abroad

Ps. 17:3, my mouth shall not *t*
Prov. 28:21, for a piece of bread man will *t*
Jer. 2:8, the pastors *t*
  3:13, only acknowledge that you have *t*
Hab. 2:5, he *t* by wine
TRANSGRESSION Num. 14:18, forgiving *t*
I Chron. 10:13, Saul died for his *t*
Ezra 10:6, he mourned because of their *t*
Job 7:21, why do you not pardon my *t*
  13:23, make me to know my *t*
Ps. 19:13, innocent from the great *t*
  25:7, remember not my *t*
  32:1, blessed is he whose *t* is forgiven
  51:1, blot out all my *t*
  65:3, as for out *t*, you shall purge them
  107:17, fools because of their *t* are afflicted
Prov. 17:9, he that covers a *t*
Isa. 43:25; 44:22, blots out your *t*
  53:5, he was wounded for our *t*
  8, for the *t* of my people was he smitten
  58:1, show my people their *t*
Ezek. 18:22, his *t* shall not be mentioned
Mic. 1:5, what is the *t* of Jacob
See Rom. 4:15; 5:14; I Tim. 2:14; Heb. 2:2
TRANSGRESSOR Ps. 59:5, be not merciful to
  any wicked *t*
  Prov. 13:15, the way of *t* is hard
  21:18, the *t* shall be ransom for the upright
Isa. 48:8, you were called a *t* from the womb
  53:12; Lk. 22:37, numbered with the *t*
See Dan. 8:23; Hos. 14:9; Gal. 2:18
TRANSLATE II Sam. 3:10; Heb. 11:5
TRAP Job 18:10; Ps. 69:22; Rom. 11:9
TRAVAIL Ps. 7:14, he *t* with iniquity
Isa. 53:11, the *t* of his soul
Rom. 8:22, the whole creation *t* in pain
Gal. 4:19, my children, of whom I *t*
See Job 15:20; Eccl. 1:13; 2:23; Isa. 13:8
TRAVELER Judg. 5:6; II Sam. 12:4
TREACHEROUSLY Isa. 33:1, you deal *t*
Jer. 12:1, why are they happy that deal *t*?
Lam. 1:2, her friends have dealt *t* with her
TREAD Deut. 11:24, whereon soles of feet *r*
Ps. 7:5, let him *t* down my life
  60:12; 108:13, shall *t* down our enemies
  91:13, you shall *t* upon lion and adder
Isa. 10:6, to *t* them down like mire
  16:10, shall *t* out no wine
  63:3, I will *t* them in my anger
Jer. 48:33, none shall *t* with shouting
Ezek. 34:18, but ye must *t* the residue
Hos. 10:11, loves to *t* our corn
Mal. 4:3, you shall *t* down the wicked
I Tim. 5:18, not muzzle the ox when he *t*
See Job 9:8; Isa. 41:25; 63:2; Rev. 19:15
TREASURE Gen. 43:23, God has given *t*
Ex. 19:5; Ps. 135:4, a peculiar *t* to me
Deut. 28:12, open to you his good *t*
Job 3:21; Ps. 17:14; Prov. 2:4, for hid *t*
  38:22, the *t* of the snow
Prov. 8:21, I will fill *t* of those that love me
  10:2, *T* of wickedness profits nothing
  15:16, than great *t* and trouble therewith
  21:20, there is a *t* to be desired

Eccl. 2:8, I gathered the peculiar *t* of kings
Isa. 2:7, neither is there any end of their *t*
  45:3, I will give you the *t* of darkness
Jer. 41:8, slay us not, for we have *t*
  51:13, waters abundant in *t*
Dan. 11:43, power over the *t* of gold
Mic. 6:10, the *t* of wickedness
Mat. 6:21; Lk. 12:34, where your *t* is
  12:35, out of the good *t* of the heart
  13:44, like unto *t* hid in a field
  52, out of his *t* things new and old
  19:21; Mk. 10:21; Lk. 18:22, *t* in heaven
Lk. 12:21, that lays up *t* for himself
II Cor. 4:7, we have this *t* in earthen vessels
Col. 2:3, in whom are hid *t* of wisdom
Heb. 11:26, greater riches than the *t* in Egypt
James 5:3, you have heaped *t*
See Deut. 32:34; 33:19; Isa. 33:6; Mat. 2:11
TREASURER Neh. 13:13; Isa. 22:15
TREASURY Josh. 6:19; Jer. 38:11; Mat. 27:6
TREE Deut. 20:19, the *t* is man's life
Job 14:7, there is hope of a *t*
  24:20, wickedness shall be broken as a *t*
Ps. 1:3; Jer. 17:8, like a *t* planted
  104:16, the *t* of the Lord are full of sap
Eccl. 11:3, where the *t* falls
Isa. 56:3, I am a dry *t*
  61:3, called *t* of righteousness
Ezek. 15:2, is the vine *t* more than any *t*
  31:9, all the *t* of Eden envied him
TREMBLE Deut. 2:25, the nations shall *t*
Judg. 5:4; Ps. 18:7; 77:18; 97:4, the earth *t*
Job 9:6, the pillars thereof *t*
  26:11, the pillars of the heaven *t*
Ps. 2:11, rejoice with *t*
  60:2, you have made earth to *t*
  99:1, the Lord reigns, let the people *t*
  104:32, he looks on the earth, and it *t*
Eccl. 12:3, the keepers of the house shall *t*
Isa. 14:16, is this the man that made earth *t*
  64:2, that the nations may *t* at your
  presence
  66:5, you that *t* at his word
Jer. 5:22, will you not *t* at my presence
  33:9, they shall *t* for all the goodness
Amos 8:8, shall not the land *t* for this
Acts 24:25, Felix *t*
James 2:19, devils also believes, and *t*
TRENCH I Sam. 17:20; 26:5; Lk. 19:43
TRESPASS Gen. 31:36, what is my *t*?
  50:17, we pray you forgive the *t*
Ezra 9:2, rulers have been chief in this *t*
Ps. 68:21, goes on still in his *t*
Mat. 6:14, if you forgive men their *t*
  18:15, if your brother *t*, tell him his fault
Lk. 17:3, if your brother *t* against you
II Cor. 5:19, not imputing their *t*
Eph. 2:1, dead in *t* and sins
Col. 2:13, having forgiven you all *t*
TRIAL Job 9:23, the *t* of the innocent
II Cor. 8:2, a great *t* of affliction
See Ezek. 21:13; Heb. 11:36; I Pet. 1:7; 4:12
TRIBES Isa. 19:13, they that are the stay of the *t*
  49:6, my servant to raise up the *t*

Hab. 3:9, according to oaths of the *t*
Mat. 24:30, then shall all *t* of the earth mourn
  See Num. 24:2; Deut. 1:13; 12:5; 18:5
TRIBULATION Deut. 4:30, you are in *t*
  Judg. 10:14, let them deliver you in *t*
  Mat. 13:21, when *t* arises
    24:21 then shall be great *t*
  Jn. 16:33, in the world you shall have *t*
  Acts 14:22, through much *t*
  See II Cor. 1:4; 7:4; Eph. 3:13; Rev. 7:14
TRIBUTARY Deut. 20:11; Judg. 1:30
TRIBUTE Gen. 49:15, a servant to *t*
  Num. 31:37, the Lord's *t*
  Deut. 16:10, *t* of freewill offering
  Ezra 7:24, not lawful to impose *t*
  Neh. 5:4, borrowed money for king's *t*
  Prov. 12:24, the slothful shall be under *t*
  See Mat. 17:24; 22:17; Lk. 23:2
TRIM II Sam. 19:24; Jer. 2:33; Mat. 25:7
TRIUMPH Ex. 15:1, he has *t* gloriously
  Ps. 25:2, let not my enemies *t*
    92:4, I will *t* in the works of your hands
  II Cor. 2:14, which always cause us to *t*
  Col. 2:15, a show of them openly, *t* over them
  See II Sam. 1:20; Job 20:5; Ps. 47:1
TRODDEN Job 22:15, wicked men have *t*
  Ps. 119:118, you have *t* down all that err
  Isa. 5:5, the vineyard shall be *t* down
    63:3, I have *t* the winepress alone
  Mic. 7:10, now shall she be *t* as mire
  Mat. 5:13, salt to be *t* under foot
  Lk. 21:24, Jerusalem, shall be *t* down
  Heb. 10:29, has *t* under foot the Son of God
  See Dan. 1:36; Judg. 5:21; Isa. 18:2
TRODE II Ki. 14:9; II Chron. 25:18; Lk. 12:1
TROOP II Sam. 22:30; Ps. 18:29; Hos. 7:1
TROUBLE (*n.*) I Chron. 22:14, in *t* I prepared for the house
  Neh. 9:32, let not the *t* seem little
  Job. 3:26, yet *t* came
    5:6, neither does *t* spring out of the ground
    7, man is born to *t*
    14:1, of few days, a full of *t*
    30:25, weep for him that was in *t*
    34:29, he gives quietness, who can make *t*?
    38:23, I have reserved against the time of *t*
  Ps. 9:9, a refuge in time of *t*
    25:17, the *t* of my heart are enlarged
    22, redeem Israel out of all his *t*
    27:5, in time of *t* he shall hide me
    46:1, a very present help in *t*
    73:5, they are not in *t* as other men
    119:143, *T* and anguish have taken hold
    138:7, though I walk in the midst of *t*
  Isa. 17:14, at eveningtide *t*
    30:6, into the land of *t* they will carry riches
    65:16, because former *t* are forgotten
    23, they shall not bring forth for *t*
  Jer. 2:27, in time of *t* they will say, save us
    8:15, we looked for health, and behold *t*
  I Cor. 7:28, such shall have *t* in the flesh
  II Cor. 1:4, able to comfort them in *t*

TROUBLE (*v.*) I Ki. 18:17, are you he that *t* Israel?
    18, I have not *t* Israel, but you
  Job 4:5, now it touches you, and you are *t*
  Ps. 3:1, how are they increased that *t* me?
    77:4, I am so *t* that I cannot speak
  Prov. 25:26, is as a *t* fountain
  Isa. 57:20, the wicked are like the *t* sea
  Dan. 5:10, let not your thoughts *t* you
    11:44, tidings out of the north shall *t* him
  Mat. 24:6, see that you be not *t*
    26:10; Mk. 14:6, why *t* you the woman
  Jn. 5:4, an angel *t* the water
    11:33; 12:27; 13:21, Jesus groaned and was *t*
  II Cor. 4:8; 7:5, we are *t* on every side
  Gal. 1:7, there be some that *t* you
    6:17, let no man *t* me
TROUBLING Job 3:17; Jn. 5:4
TRUCE II Tim. 3:3, men shall be *t*-breakers
TRUE Gen. 42:11, we are *t* men
  I Ki. 22:16, tell nothing but that which is *t*
  Neh. 9:13, you gave them *t* laws
  Ps. 119:160, your word is *t* from the beginning
  Prov. 14:25, a *t* witness delivers souls
  Jer. 10:10, the Lord is the *t* God
  Mk. 12:14, we know that you are *t*
  Lk. 16:11, the *t* riches
  Jn. 1:9, that was the *t* light
    4:23, when the *t* worshippers
    6:32, the *t* bread
    10:41, all things that John spoke were *t*
    17:3, to know you, the only *t* God
  II Cor. 6:8, as deceivers, and yet *t*
  Eph. 4:24, created in *t* holiness
  Phil. 4:8, whatsoever things are *t*
  Heb. 10:22, draw near with a *t* heart
  See Rev. 3:7; 6:10; 15:3; 16:7; 19:9, 11, 21:5
TRUMPET Ex. 19:16; Num. 10:2; Josh. 6:4
  Isa. 27:13, great *t* shall be blown
    58:1, lift up your voice like a *t*
  Mat. 6:2, do not sound a *t* before
  See Rev. 8:6
TRUST Job 13:15; he slay me, yet will I *t*
    39:11, will you *t* him
  Ps. 25:2; 31:6; 55:23; 56:3; 143:8, I *t* in you
    118:8, better to *t* in the Lord
    144:2, he in whom I *t*
  Isa. 50:10, let him *t* in the name of the Lord
  Jer. 49:11, let your widows *t* in me
  Mic. 7:5, *T* ye not in a friend
  Nah. 1:7, Lord know them that *t* in him
  Mat. 27:43, he *t* in God, let him deliver him
  Lk. 18:9, certain which *t* in themselves
TRUTH Deut. 32:4, a God of *t*
  Ps. 15:2, speaks the *t* in his heart
    51:6, desires *t* in the inward parts
    91:4, his *t* shall be your shield
    117:2, his *t* endures forever
    119:30, I have chosen the way of *t*
  Prov. 23:23, buy the *t*
  Isa. 59:14, *t* is fallen in the streets
  Jer. 9:3, they are not valiant for the *t*
  Zech. 8:16, speak every man *t* to his neighbor

Mal. 2:6, the law of *t* was in his mouth
Jn. 1:14, full of grace and *t*
    8:32, know the *t*, the *t* shall make your free
    14:6, I am the way, the *t*, and the life
    16:13, Spirit of *t* will guide you into all *t*
    18:38, what is *t*?
Rom. 1:18, who hold the *t* in
    unrighteousness
II Cor. 13:8, do nothing against *t*, but for
    the *t*
Eph. 4:15, speaking the *t* in love
I Tim. 3:15, the pillar and ground of *t*
II Tim. 2:15, rightly dividing the word of *t*
James 5:19, if any err from the *t*
See I Cor. 13:6, II Tim. 3:7; I Jn. 3:19; 5:6
TRY II Chron. 32:31, God left him, to *t* him
Job 23:10, when he has *t* me
Ps. 26:2, *t* my reins and my heart
Jer. 9:7, I will melt them and *t* them
I Cor. 3:13, shall *t* every man's work
James 1:12, when *t* he shall receive the crown
I Jn. 4:1, *t* the spirits
See Prov. 17:3; Isa. 28:16; Rev. 3:18
TURN Job 23:13, who can *t* him?
Ps. 7:12, if he *t* not, he will whet his s word
Jer. 31:18, *t* thou me, and I shall be *t*
Hos. 12:6; Joel 2:12; repent, and *t*
Mat. 5:39, *t* the other also
Acts 26:18, to *t* them from darkness to light
II Tim. 3:5, from such *t* away
TWAIN Isa. 6:2; Mat. 5:41; 19:5; Eph. 2:15
TWICE Job 33:14; Mk. 14:30; Lk. 18:12
TWINKLING I Cor. 15:52

U

UNADVISEDLY Ps. 106:33, he spake *u*
UNAWARES Lk. 21:34; Gal. 2:4, Heb. 13:2
UNBELIEF Mk. 9:24, help Thou my *u*
Rom. 3:3, shall *u* make faith without effect
    11:32, concluded all in *u*
Heb. 3:12, evil heart of *u*
UNBLAMEABLE Col. 1:22; I Thess. 3:13
UNCERTAIN I Cor. 9:26; 14:8; I Tim. 6:17
UNCLEAN Acts 10:28; Rom. 14:14
UNCLOTHED II Cor. 5:4
UNCORRUPTNESS Titus 2:7, showing *u*
UNCTION I Jn. 2:20
UNDEFILED Ps. 119:1, blessed are the *u*
James 1:27, pure religion and *u*
I Pet. 1:4, an inheritance *u*
See Song of Sol. 5:2; 6:9; Heb. 7:26; 13:4
UNDER Rom 3:9; I Cor. 9:27; Gal. 3:10
UNDERSTAND Ps. 119:100, I *u* more than the
    ancients
    139:2, Thou *u* my thought afar off
Prov. 8:9, all plain to him who *u*
    20:24, how can a man *u* his own way?
    29:19, though he *u* he will not answer
Isa. 6:9, hear ye indeed, but *u* not
    28:19, a vexation only to *u* the report
Jer. 9:24, let him glory in this, that he *u* Me
Dan. 10:12, you did set your heart to *u*
    12:10, wicked shall not *u*, the wise shall *u*

Hos. 14:9, who is wise, and he shall *u*
Mat. 13:51, have ye *u* all these things?
    24:15, whoso reads, let him *u*
Lk. 24:45, they that might *u* the scriptures
Jn. 8:43, why do ye not *u* My speech?
Rom. 3:11, there is none that *u*
    15:21, they that have not heard shall *u*
I Cor. 13:2, though I *u* all mysteries
    11, I *u* as a child
See I Cor. 14:2; Heb. 11:3, II Pet. 2:12, 3:16
UNDERSTANDING Deut. 4:6, wisdom and *u*
I Ki. 3:11, have asked for yourself *u*
    4:29, gave Solomon wisdom and *u*
    7:14, filled with wisdom and *u*
I Chron. 12:32, men that had *u* of the times
Job 12:13, he has counsel and *u*
    20, he takes away the *u* of the aged
    17:4, Thou hast hid their heart from *u*
    28:12, where is the peace of *u*?
    32:8, the Almighty gives them *u*
    38:36, who has give *u* to the heart?
    39:17, neither imparted to her *u*
Ps. 47:7, sing ye praises with *u*
    49:3, meditation of my heart shall be of *u*
    119:34, 73, 125, 144, 169, give me *u*
    99, I have more *u* than My teachers
    104, through Your precepts I get *u*
    147:5, his *u* is infinite
Prov. 2:2, apply your heart to *u*
    19, by *u* has He established the Heavens
    4:5, 7, get wisdom, get *u*
    8:1, does not *u* put forth her voice?
    9:10, the knowledge of the holy is *u*
    14:29, he who is slow to wrath is of
    great *u*
    16:22, *U* is a wellspring of life
Prov. 17:24, wisdom is before him who has *u*
    19:8, he who keeps *u* shall find good
    21:30, there is no *u* against the Lord
    24:3, by *u* an house is established
    30:2, have not the *u* of a man
Eccl. 9:11, nor yet riches to men of *u*
Isa. 11:2, the spirit of *u* shall rest on him
    27:11, it is a people of no *u*
    29:14, the *u* of prudent men shall be hid
    40:14, who showed him the way of *u*
    28, there is no searching of his *u*
Jer. 3:15, pastors shall feed you with *u*
Ezek. 28:4, with your *u* you have gotten
    riches
Dan. 4:34, my *u* returned
Mat. 15:16; Mk. 7:18, are you also without *u*?
Mk. 12:33, to love him with all the *u*
Lk. 2:47, astonished at his *u*
    24:45, then opened he their *u*
I Cor. 1:19, bring to nothing *u* of prudent
    14:15, I will pray with the *u* also
    20, be not children in *u*
Eph. 4:18, having the *u* darkened
Phil. 4:7, peace of God, which passes all *u*
UNDERTAKE Isa. 38:14, *u* for me
UNDONE Josh. 11:15, Isa. 6:5; Mat. 23:23
UNEQUAL Ezek. 18:25, 29; II Cor. 6:14
UNFAITHFUL Ps. 78:57; Prov. 25:19

UNFRUITFUL Mat. 13:22; Eph. 5:11

UNGODLINESS Rom. 1:18; II Tim. 2:16

UNGODLY II Chron. 19:2, Thou help the *u*
   Job 16:11, God has delivered me to the *u*
   Ps. 1:1, the counsel of the *u*
      6, the way of the *u* shall perish
      43:1, plead my cause against an *u* nation
   Prov. 16:27, an *u* man digs up evil
   Rom. 5:6, Christ died for the *u*
   I Pet. 4:18, where shall the *u* appear
   II Pet. 3:7, perdition of *u* men
   See Rom. 4:5; I Tim. 1:9, II Pet. 2:5, Jude 15

UNHOLY Lev. 10:10; I Tim. 1:9; II Tim. 3:2

UNITE Gen. 49:6; Ps. 86:11

UNITY Ps. 133:1, Eph. 4:3, 13

UNJUST Prov. 28:8, he that by *u* gain
   Zeph. 3:5, the *u* knows no shame
   Mat. 5:45, He sends rain on the just and *u*
   Lk. 18:6, hear what the *u* judge says
   I Cor. 6:1, go to law before the *u*
   I Pet. 3:18, suffered the just for the *u*
   Rev. 22:11, he that is *u*, let him be *u* still

UNKNOWN Acts 17:23; I Cor. 14:2

UNLAWFUL Acts 10:28; II Pet. 2:8

UNLEARNED Acts 4:13, I Cor. 14:16

UNMINDFUL Deut. 32:18, you are *u*

UNMOVEABLE Acts 27:41; I Cor. 15:58

UNPERFECT Ps. 139:16, yet being *u*

UNPREPARED II Cor. 9:4, find you *u*

UNPROFITABLE Job 15:3, *u* talk
   Mat. 25:30; Lk. 17:10; *u* servant

UNPUNISHED Jer. 25:29, shall not be *u*,
   See Jer. 30:11; 46:28

UNQUENCHABLE Mat. 3:12; Lk. 3:17

UNREASONABLE Acts 25:27; II Thess. 3:2

UNREPROVEABLE Col. 1:22

UNRIGHTEOUS Ex. 23:1, an *u* witness
   Isa. 10:1, decree *u* decrees
      55:7, let the *u* man forsake his thoughts
   Rom. 3:5, is God *u*
   Heb. 6:10, God is not *u* to forget your work

UNRIGHTEOUSNESS Rom. 1:18, hold the truth
     in *u*
   2:8, to them that obey *u*
   3:5, if our *u* commend righteousness
   II Cor. 6:14, what fellowship with *u*
   II Thess. 2:12, had pleasure in *u*
   II Pet. 2:13, receive the reward of *u*
   I Jn. 1:9, cleanse us from all *u*
   See Lev. 19:15; Ps. 92:15; Jer. 22:13; Jn. 7:18

UNRULY I Thess. 5:14; Titus 1:6

UNSAVOURY Job 6:6

UNSEARCHABLE Job 5:9; Rom. 11:33

UNSEEMLY Rom. 1:27; I Cor. 13:5

UNSKILFUL Heb. 5:13, is *u* in the word

UNSPEAKABLE II Cor. 9:15; I Pet. 1:8

UNSPOTTED James 1:27, *u* from the world

UNSTABLE Gen. 49:4; II Pet. 2:14

UNTHANKFUL Lk. 6:35; II Tim. 3:2

UNWASHEN Mat. 15:20; Mk. 7:2, 5

UNWISE Deut. 32:6; Hos. 13:13; Rom. 1:14

UNWORTHY Acts 13:46; I Cor. 6:2; 11:27

UPBRAID Mat. 11:20; James 1:5

UPHOLD Ps. 51:12, *u* with your free spirit

54:4, with them that *u* my soul
   119:116, *u* Me according to Your Word
   145:14, the Lord *u* all who fall
   Isa. 41:10, I will *u* you with right hand
      42:1, My servant, whom I *u*
      63:5, wondered there was none to *u*
   See Ps. 37:17; 41:12; 63:8, Prov. 20:28

UPPERMOST Mat. 23:6; Mk. 12:39

UPRIGHT Job 12:4
   17:8 *U* men shall be astonied
   Ps. 19:13, then shall I be *u*
   25:8; 92:15, good and *u* is the Lord
   37:14, such as be of *u* conversation
   49:14, the *u* shall have dominion
   111:1, the assembly of the *u*
   125:4, that are *u* in their hearts
   Prov. 2:21, the *u* shall dwell in the land
   11:3, the integrity of the *u*
   20, such as are *u* in their way
   14:11, the tabernacle of the *u*
   15:8, the prayer of the *u* is his delight
   28:10, the *u* shall have good things
   Eccl. 7:29, God has made man *u*
   Song of Sol. 1:4, the *u* love you
   See Is. 26:7; Jer. 10:5; Mic. 7:2; Hab. 2:4

UPRIGHTLY Ps. 58:1; 75:2, do you judge *u*
   Prov. 10:9; 15:21; 28:18, he who walks *u*
   Isa. 33:15, he who speaks *u*
   See Ps. 15:2; Amos 5:10; Mic. 2:7; Gal. 2:14

UPRIGHTNESS I Ki. 3:6, in *u* of heart
   I Chron. 29:17, you have pleasure in *u*
   Job 4:6, the *u* of your ways
   33:23, to show unto man his *u*
   Ps. 25:21, let *u* preserve me
   143:10, lead me into the land of *u*
   Prov. 2:13, who leave the paths of *u*
   See Ps. 111:8; Prov. 14:2; 28:6; Isa. 26:7, 10

UPROAR Mat. 26:5; Mk. 14:2; Acts 17:5

UPWARD Job 5:7; Eccl. 3:21; Isa. 38:14

URGE Gen. 33:11; II Ki. 2:17; Lk. 11:53

URGENT Ex. 12:33; Dan. 3:22

USE Mat. 6:7, *u* not vain repetitions
   I Cor. 7:31, they that *u* this world
   Gal. 5:13, *u* not liberty for an occasion
   I Tim. 1:8, if a man *u* it lawfully
   See Ps. 119:132; I Cor. 9:12; I Tim. 5:23

USURP I Tim. 2:12

UTTER Ps. 78:2, I will *u* dark sayings
   106:2, who can *u* the mighty acts
   119:171, my lips shall *u* praise
   Prov. 1:20, wisdom *u* her voice
   23:33, your heart shall *u* perverse things
   29:11, a fool *u* it lawfully
   Eccl. 5:2, let not your heart be hasty to *u*
   Rom. 8:26, which cannot be *u*
   II Cor. 12:4, not lawful for a man to *u*

UTTERANCE Acts 2:4, as the Spirit gave *u*
   See I Cor. 1:5; II Cor. 8:7; Eph. 6:19

UTTERLY Ps. 119:8, forsake me not *u*
   Jer. 23:39, I will *u* forget you
   Zeph. 1:2, I will *u* consume all things
   II Pet. 2:12, these shall *u* perish
   See Deut. 7:2; Neh. 9:31; Rev. 18:8

UTTERMOST Mat. 5:26; I Thess. 2:16

V

VAGABOND Ps. 109:10; Acts 19:13

VAIL Mat. 27:51; II Cor. 3:14; Heb. 6:19

VAIN Ex. 5:9, not regard *v* words
 20:7, not take name of the Lord in *v*
Deut. 32:47, it is not a *v* thing for you
II Sam. 6:20, as one of the *v* fellows
II Ki. 18:20; Isa. 36:5, they are but *v* words
Job 11:12, *v* man would be wise
 16:3, shall *v* words have an end?
 21:34, how then comfort ye me in *v*
Ps. 2:1; Acts 4:25, people imagine a *v* thing
 26:4, I have not sat with *v* persons
 33:17, an horse is a *v* thing for safety
 39:6, every man walks in a *v* show
 60:11; 108:12, *v* is the help of man
 89:47, wherefore have you made men in *v*?
 127:1, labor in *v*, watchman wakes in *v*
Prov. 12:11; 28:19, follows *v* persons
Eccl. 6:12, all the days of his *v* life
Isa. 1:13, bring no more *v* oblations
 45:18, he created it not in *v*
 19, I said not, Seek ye me in *v*
 49:4; 65:23, labored in *v*
Jer. 3:23, in *v* is salvation hoped for
 10:3, the customs of the people are *v*
 46:11, in *v* shall you use medicines
Mal. 3:14, you have said, It is *v* to serve God
Mat. 6:7, use not *v* repetitions
 15:9; Mk. 7:7, in *v* do they worship me
Rom. 13:4, he bears not the sword in *v*
I Cor. 15:2, unless you have believed in *v*
II Cor. 6:1, receive not the grace of God in *v*
Gal. 2:2, lest I should run in *v*
Titus 1:10, unruly and *v* talkers
James 1:26, this man's religion is *v*
I Pet. 1:18, redeemed from *v* conversation

VALIANT I Sam. 18:17, be *v* for me
I Ki. 1:42, for you are a *v* man
Isa. 10:13, put down inhabitants like a *v* man
Jer. 9:3, they are not *v* for truth
Heb. 11:34, waxed *v* in fight
See Ps. 60:12; 118:15; Isa. 33:7; Nah. 2:3

VALUE Job 13:4, physicians of no *v.*
Mat. 10:31; Lk. 12:7, of more *v*
See Lev. 27:16; Job 28:16; Mat. 27:9

VANISH Isa. 51:6; I Cor. 13:8; Heb. 8:13

VANITY Job 7:3, to possess months of *v*
 15:31, *v* shall be his recompence
 35:13, God will not hear *v*
Ps. 39:5, every man at his best state, is *v.*
Prov. 13:11, wealth gotten by *v*
 30:8, remove from me *v*
Eccl. 6:11, many things increase *v*
 11:10, childhood and youth are *v*
Isa. 30:28, with the sieve of *v*
Jer. 18:15, they have burned incense to *v*
Rom. 8:20, creature was made subject to *v*
Eph. 4:17, walk in *v* of mind
II Pet. 2:18, great swelling words of *v*

VARIABLENESS James 1:17

VARIANCE Mat. 10:35; Gal. 5:20

VAUNT Judg. 7:2; I Cor. 13:4

VEHEMENT Mk. 14:31; II Cor. 7:11

VENGEANCE Prov. 6:34; Jer. 51:6, the day of *v*
Isa. 59:17, garments of *v* for clothing
Acts 28:4, whom *v* suffers not to live
Jude 7, the *v* of eternal fire
See Mic. 5:15; Lk. 21:22; Rom. 12:19

VERILY Gen. 42:21; Ps. 58:11; Mk. 9:12

VERITY Ps. 111:7; I Tim. 2:7

VESSEL II Ki. 4:6, there is not a *v* more
Ps. 31:12, I am like a potter's *v*
Isa. 66:20, bring an offering in a clean *v*
Jer. 22:28, a *v* wherein is no pleasure
 25:34, fall like a pleasant *v*
Mat. 13:48, gathered the good into *v*
 25:4, the wise took oil in their *v*
Acts 9:15, he is a chosen *v* unto me
I Thess. 4:4, to possess his *v* in sanctification
II Tim. 2:21, he shall be a *v* to honour
I Pet. 3:7, honour to the wife, as to weaker *v*

VESTRY II Ki. 10:22, that was over the *v*

VESTURE Gen. 41:42; Ps. 22:18; 102:26

VEX Ex. 22:21; Lev. 19:33, not *v* a stranger
Num. 33:55, those ye let remain shall *v* you
II Sam. 12:18, how will he *v* himself
Job 19:2, how long will ye *v* my soul
Isa. 11:13, Judah shall not *v* Ephraim
Ezek. 32:9, I will *v* the hearts of many
Mat. 15:22, my daughter is grievously *v*
II Pet. 2:8, *v* his righteous soul

VEXATION Eccl. 1:14; 2:22; Isa. 9:1; 28:19

VICTORY II Sam. 19:2, *v* turned to mourning
I Chron. 29:11, thine is the *v*
Ps. 98:1, has gotten him the *v*
Mat. 12:20, send forth judgment unto *v*
I Jn. 5:4, this is the *v*, even our faith
See Isa. 25:8; I Cor. 15:54, 55, 57

VICTUALS Ex. 12:39, neither had prepared *v*
Josh. 9:14, the men took of their *v*
Neh. 10:31, bring *v* on the Sabbath
 13:15, in the day wherein they sold *v*
Mat. 14:15; Lk. 9:12, into villages to buy *v*
See Gen. 14:11; Judg. 17:10; I Sam. 22:10

VIEW Josh. 2:1; 7:2; II Ki. 2:7, Neh. 2:13

VIGILANT I Tim. 3:2; I Pet. 5:8

VILE I Sam. 3:13, made themselves *v*
Job 18:3, wherefore are we reputed *v*
 40:4, I am *v*, what shall I answer you?
Ps. 15:4; Isa. 32:5; Dan. 11:21, a *v* person
Jer. 15:19, take the precious from the *v*
Lam. 1:11, see, O Lord, for I am become *v*
Nah. 3:6, I will make you *v*
Rom. 1:26, gave them up to *v* affections
Phil. 3:21, shall change our *v* body
James 2:2, a poor man in *v* raiment

VILLANY Isa. 32:6, Jer. 29:23

VINE Deut. 32:32, *v* is of the *v* of Sodom
I Ki. 4:25, dwelt every man under his *v*
II Ki. 18:31, eat every man of his own *v*
Ps. 80:8, a *v* out of Egypt
 128:3, your wife as a fruitful *v*
Hos. 10:1, Israel is an empty *v*
Mic. 4:4, they shall sit every man under his *v*
Mk. 14:25; Lk. 22:18, this fruit of the *v*
Jn. 15:1, I am the true *v*

See Deut. 8:8; Judg. 13:14; Joel 1:7; Hab. 3:17
VINTAGE Job 24:6; Isa. 16:10; Mic. 7:1
VIOL Isa. 5:12; 14:11; Amos 5:23; 6:5
VIOLENCE Gen. 6:11, earth filled with *v*
  Ps. 11:5, his that loves *v*
    55:9, I have seen *v* in the city
    58:2, weigh the *v* of your hands
    72:14, redeem their soul from *v*
    73:6, *v* covers them as a garment
  Prov. 4:17, they drink the wine of *v*
    10:6, *v* covers the mouth of the wicked
  Isa. 53:9, because he had done no *v*
    60:18, *v* shall no more be heard
  Amos 3:10, store up *v* in their palaces
  Hab. 1:3, *v* is before me
  Mal. 2:16, one covers *v* with his garment
  Mat. 11:12, Kingdom of Heaven suffers *v*
  Lk. 3:14, do *v* to no man
VIOLENT Ps. 7:16, his *v* dealing
    18:48; 140:1; Prov. 16:29, the *v* man
    See II Sam. 22:49; Eccl. 5:8; Mat. 11:12
VIOLENTLY Isa. 22:18; Mk. 5:13
VIRGIN Isa. 23:12; 47:1; 62:5; Jer. 14:17
VIRTUE Mk. 5:30; Lk. 6:19; Phil. 4:8
VIRTUOUS Ruth 3:11; Prov. 12:4; 31:10, 29
VISAGE Isa. 52:14; Lam. 4:8; Dan. 3:19
VISION Job 20:8, as a *v* of the night
  Isa. 22:1, the valley of *v* 28:7, the err in *v*
  Lam. 2:9, prophets find no *v* from the Lord
  Hos. 12:10, I have multiplied *v*
  Joel 2:28; Acts 2:17, young men shall see *v*
  Zech. 13:4, ashamed every one of his *v*
  Mat. 17:9, tell the *v* to no man
  Lk. 24:23, they had seen a *v* of angels
  Acts 26:19, not disobedient to heavenly *v*
VISIT Gen. 50:24; Ex. 13:19, God will *v* you
  Ex. 20:5, *v* the iniquity of the fathers
    32:34, when I *v*, I will *v* their sin upon them
  Ruth 1:6, how the Lord had *v* his people
  Job 5:24, you shall *v* your habitation
  Job 7:18, should *v* him every morning
  Ps. 8:4; Heb. 2:6, son of man, that you *v* him
    106:4, *v* me with your Salvation
  Jer. 5:9; 9:9, shall I not *v* for these things?
    29:10, I will *v*, and perform my good word
  Ezek. 38:8, after many days you shall be *v*
  Mat. 25:36, I was sick, and ye *v* me
  Acts 15:14, how God did *v* the Gentiles
  James 1:27, to *v* the fatherless and widows
VISITATION Job 10:12, your *v* has preserved
  Isa. 10:3; I Pet. 2:12, in the day of *v*
VOCATION Eph. 4:1, worthy of the *v*
VOICE Gen. 4:10, *v* of your brother's blood
    27:22, the *v* is Jacob's *v*
  Ex. 23:21, obey his *v*, provoke him not
    24:3, all the people answered with one *v*
    32:18, it is not the *v* of them that shout
  Deut. 4:33, people hear *v* of God, and live
  Josh. 6:10, nor make any noise with your *v*
  I Sam. 24:16; 26:17, is this your *v*
  I Ki. 19:12, after the fire, a still small *v*
  II Ki. 4:31, there was neither *v* nor hearing
  Job 3:7, let no joyful *v* come therein
    30:31, into the *v* of them that weep

    40:9, can you thunder with a *v* like him?
  Ps. 5:3, my *v* shall you hear in the morning
    31:22; 86:6, the *v* of my supplications
    42:4, with the *v* of joy
    95:7, to day, if you will hear his *v*
  Ps. 103:20, the *v* of his word
  Prov. 1:20, wisdom utters her *v* in the streets
    5:13, not obeyed the *v* of my teachers
    8:1, does not understanding put forth
      her *v*
    4, my *v* is to the sons of man
  Eccl. 5:3, a fool's *v* is known
    12:4, rise up at the *v* of the bird
  Song of Sol. 2:8; 5:2, the *v* of my beloved
    12, the *v* of the turtle is heard
  Isa. 13:2, exalt the *v* unto them
    52:8, with the *v* together shall they sing
    65:19, *v* of weeping shall be no more heard
    66:6, a *v* of noise, a *v* from the temple
  Jer. 7:34, the *v* of mirth, and the *v* of gladness
    30:19, the *v* of them that make merry
    48:3, a *v* of crying shall be
  Ezek. 23:42, a *v* of multitude at ease
    33:32, one that has a pleasant *v*
    43:2, *v* like a noise of many waters
  Nah. 2:7, lead her as with a *v* of doves
  Mat. 12:19, neither shall any man hear his *v*
  Jn. 5:25, dead shall heal the *v* of Son of God
    10:4, the sheep follow, for they know his *v*
    5, they know not the *v* of strangers
    12:30, this *v* came not because of me
    18:37, every one of the truth hears My *v*
  Acts 12:14, and when she knew Peter's *v*
    26:10, I gave my *v* against them
  I Cor. 14:10, there are so many *v* in the world
    19, that by my *v* I might teach others
  Gal. 4:20, I desire now to change my *v*
  I Thess. 4:16, descend with *v* of archangel
  II Pet. 2:16, dumb ass speaking with man's *v*
  Rev. 3:20, if any man hear my *v*
    4:5, out of the throne proceeded *v*
VOID Gen 1:2; Jer. 4:23, without form, and *v*
  Deut. 32:28, a people *v* of counsel
  Ps. 89:39, made *v* the covenant
    119:126, they have made *v* Your Law
  Prov. 11:12, *v* of wisdom
  Isa. 55:11, my word shall not return to me *v*
  Jer. 19:7, make *v* the counsel of Judah
  Nah. 2:10, empty, *v*, and waste
  Acts 24:16, a conscience *v* of offence
VOLUME Ps. 40:7; Heb. 10:7
VOLUNTARY Lev. 1:3; 7:16; Ezek. 46:12
VOMIT Job 20:15; Prov. 26:11; II Pet. 2:22
VOW (n.) Gen. 28:20; 31:13, Jacob vowed a *v*
  Num. 29:39, these you shall do beside your *v*
  Deut. 12:6, thither bring your *v*
  Judg. 11:30, Jephthah vowed a *v* and said
    39, her father did with her according to
      his *v*
  I Sam. 1:21, Elkanah went up to offer his *v*
  Job 22:27, you shall pay your *v*
  Ps. 22:25, 66:13; 116:14, I will pay my *v*
    50:14, pay your *v* unto the most High
    56:12, your *v* are upon me, O God

61:5, for you have heard my *v*

8, that I may daily perform my *v*

65:1, to you shall the *v* be performed

Prov. 7:14, this day have I paid my *v*

20:25, after *v* to make enquiry

31:2, the son of my *v*

Eccl. 5:4, when you vow a *v*

Isa. 19:21, they shall vow a *v* unto the Lord

Jonah 1:16, feared the Lord, and made *v*

Acts 18:18, shorn his head, for he had a *v*

21:23, four men which have a *v* on them

VOW (*v.*) Deut. 23:22, if you forbear to *v*

Ps. 76:11, *V*, and pay to the Lord your God

132:2, and *v* to the mighty God

See Num. 21:2; Eccl. 5:5; Jonah 2:9

W

WAG Jer. 18:16; Lam. 2:15; Zeph. 2:15

WAGES Gen. 29:15, what shall your *w* be?

30:28, appoint me your *w*

31:7, changed my *w* ten times

Ex. 2:9, nurse this child, I will give *w*

Jer. 22:13, uses service without *w*

Hag. 1:6, earns *w* to put in bag with holes

Lk. 3:14, be content with your *w*

Jn. 4:36, he that reaps receives *w*

Rom. 6:23, the *w* of sin is death

II Pet. 2:15, the *w* of unrighteousness

See Ezek. 29:18, Mal. 3:5; II Cor. 11:8

WAGONS Gen. 45:19; Num. 7:7; Ezek. 23:24

WAIL Ezek. 32:18, *w* for the multitude

Amos 5:16, *W* shall be in all streets

Mic. 1:8, therefore I will *w* and howl

Mat. 13:42, there shall be *w* and gnashing

Mk. 5:38, he sees them that *w* greatly

Rev. 1:7, all kindreds of the Earth shall *w*

18:15, the merchants shall stand afar off *w*

See Esther 4:3; Jer. 9:10; 19, 20; Ezek. 7:11

WAIT Gen. 49:18, I have *w* for your Salvation

Num. 35:20; Jer. 9:8, by laying of *w*

II Ki. 6:33, should I *w* for the Lord longer

Job 14:14, I will *w* till my change come

15:22, he is *w* for of the sword

17:13, if I *w*, the grave is my house

29:21, to me men *w*, and kept silence

23, they *w* for me as for rain

30:26, when I *w* for light, darkness came

Ps. 25:3; 69:6, let none that *w* be ashamed

27:14; 37:34; Prov. 20:22, *W* on the Lord

33:20 our soul *w* for the Lord

52:9, I will *w* on Your name

62:1; 130:6, my soul *w* upon God

5, *w* only on God

69:3, my eyes fail while I *w* for God

104:27, these all *w* upon you

106:13, they *w* not for counsel

123:2, so our eyes *w* on the Lord

Prov. 27:18, he that *w* on his master

Isa. 30:18, the Lord *w* to be gracious

40:31, they that *w* on the Lord shall renew

42:4, the isles shall *w* for his law

59:9, we *w* for light

64:4, prepared for him what *w* for him

Lam. 3:26, man hope and quietly *w*

Dan. 12:12, blessed is he that *w*

Hab. 2:3, though the vision tarry, *w* for it

Lk. 2:25, *w* for the consolation of Israel

12:36, like unto men that *w* for their Lord

Acts 1:4, but *w* for promise of the Father

Rom. 8:23, groan, *w* for the adoption

25, then do we with patience *w* for it

12:7, let us *w* on our ministering

I Cor. 9:13, which *w* at altar are partakers

I Thess. 1:10, to *w* for His Son from Heaven

WAKE Jer. 51:39, a perpetual sleep, and not *w*

Joel 3:9, prepare war, *w* up the mighty men

Zech. 4:1, the angel came again, and *w* me

I Thess. 5:10, whether we *w* or sleep

See Ps. 77:4; 127:1; Song of Sol. 5:2; Isa. 50:4

WALK Gen. 17:1, *w* before Me, and be perfect

24:40, the Lord before Whom I *w*

48:15, before whom my fathers did *w*

Ex. 16:4, whether they will *w* in My Law

18:20, the way wherein they must *w*

Lev. 26:12, I will *w* among you

Deut. 23:14, God *w* in midst of the camp

Judg. 5:10, speak, ye that *w* by the way

II Sam. 2:29, Abner *w* all that night

Job 18:8, he *w* on a snare

22:14, he *w* in the circuit of Heaven

Ps. 23:4, though I *w* through the valley

48:12, *W* about Zion, and go round about her

55:14, we *w* to house of God in company

56:13, that I *w* before God, in the light

91:6, the pestilence that *w* in darkness

104:3, who *w* upon wings of the wind

116:9, I will *w* before the Lord

138:7, though I *w* in the midst of trouble

Prov. 10:9, he that *w* uprightly *w* surely

13:20, he that *w* with wise men shall be wise

19:1, better is the poor that *w* in integrity

28:26, whoso *w* wisely shall be delivered

Eccl. 2:14, the fool *w* in darkness

Isa. 2:5, let us *w* the light of the Lord

9:2, the people that *w* in darkness

35:9, the redeemed shall *w* there

50:10, that *w* in darkness, and has no light

11, *w* in the light of your fire

Jer. 6:16, ask the good way, and *w* therein

Ezek. 28:14, have *w* in midst of stones of fire

Dan. 4:37, those that *w* in pride

Hos. 14:9, the just shall *w* in them

Amos 3:3, can two *w* together

Mic. 6:8, to *w* humbly with your God

Nah. 2:11, where the lion *w*

Zech. 1:11, we have *w* to and fro

Mat. 12:43; Lk. 11:24, *w* through dry places

14:29, he *w* on the water

Mk. 16:12, he appeared to them as they *w*

Lk. 13:33, I must *w* to day and to morrow

Jn. 8:12, shall now *w* in darkness

11:9, if any man *w* in the day

Acts 3:6, arise, and *w*

Rom. 4:12, who *w* in steps of that faith

6:4, *w* in newness of life

8:1, who *w* not after the flesh
II Cor. 5:7, we *w* by faith
Gal. 6:16, as many as *w* according to this rule
    10, ordained that we should *w* in them
    4:1, *w* worthy of the vocation
    17, that ye *w* not as other Gentiles
Phil. 3:17, mark them which *w*
    18, many *w*, of whom I told you
Col. 1:10, *w* worthy of the vocation
II Thess. 3:6, every brother that *w* disorderly
I Pet. 4:3, when we *w* in lasciviousness
    5:8, *w* about, seeking whom he may devour
I Jn. 1:7, if we *w* in the light
    2:6, to *w*, even as he *w*
WALKING Deut. 2:7, Lord knows your *w*
Job 31:26, the moon *w* in brightness
Dan. 3:25, four men loose, *w* in the fire
Mat. 14:25, Jesus *w* on the sea
Mk. 8:24, I see men as trees, *w*
Acts 9:31, *w* in the fear of the Lord
See Isa. 3:16; II Cor. 4:2; II Pet. 3:3; Jude 16
WALL Gen. 49:22, branches run over the *w*
Ex. 14:22, the waters were a *w* to them
Num. 22:24, a *w* on this side, a *w* on that
II Sam. 22:30, have I leaped over a *w*
II Ki. 20:2; Isa. 36:11, turned his face to the *w*
Ezra 5:3, commanded you to make this *w*?
Neh. 4:6, so built we the *w*
Ps. 62:3, a bowing *w* shall ye be
    122:7, peace be within your *w*
Prov. 24:31, the *w* whereof was broken down
    25:28, like a city without *w*
Isa. 26:1, salvation with God appoint for *w*
    60:18, you shall call your *w* Salvation
Ezek. 8:7, a hole in the *w*
Dan. 5:5, fingers wrote on the *w*
Hab. 2:11, the stone shall cry out of the *w*
Acts 23:3, you white *w*
Eph. 2:14, the middle *w* of partition
WALLOW Jer. 6:26; 25:34, *w* in ashes
II Pet. 2:22, washed, to her *w* in the mire
See II Sam. 20:12; Ezek. 27:30
WANDER Num. 14:33, your children shall *w*
Job 12:24, he causes them to *w*
    15:23, he *w* abroad for bread
    38:41, young ravens *w* for lack of meat
Ps. 55:7, then would I *w* far off
    59:15, let them *w* up and down
Prov. 27:8, as a bird that *w* from nest
Isa. 16:3, bewray not him that I *w*
    47:15, *w* every one to his quarter
Jer. 14:10, thus have they loved to *w*
Lam. 4:14, they have *w* as blind men
Ezek. 34:6, my sheep *w* through mountains
Amos 4:8, two cities *w* to one city to drink
See Hos. 9:17; I Tim. 5:13; Heb. 11:37
WANT (*n.*) Deut. 28:48, you shall serve in *w*
Judg. 18:10, a place where there is no *w*
    19:20, let all your *w* lie on me
Job 24:8, they embrace the rock for *w*
    31:19, if I have seen any perish for *w*
Ps. 34:9, there is no *w* to them that fear him
Amos 4:6, I have given you *w* of bread
Mk. 12:44, she of her *w* cast in all

Lk. 15:14, he began to be in *w*
Phil. 2:25, that ministered to my *w*
See Prov. 6:11; II Cor. 8:14; Phil. 4:11
WANT (*v.*) Ps. 23:1, I shall not *w*
    34:10, shall not *w* any good thing
Prov. 9:4, for him that *w* understanding
    10:19, in multitude of words there *w* not
sin
    13:25, the belly of the wicked shall *w*
Eccl. 6:2, he *w* nothing for his soul
Isa. 34:16, none shall *w* her mate
Jer. 44:18, we have *w* all things
Ezek. 4:17, that they may *w* bread and water
Jn. 2:3, when they *w* wine
See Eccl. 1:15; Dan. 5:27; Tit. 1:5; James 1:4
WANTON Isa. 3:16; Rom. 13:13; I Tim. 5:11
WAR (*n.*) Ex. 32:17, there is a noise of *w*
Num. 32:6, shall your brethren go to *w*
Deut. 24:5, he shall not go out to *w*
Judg. 5:8, then was *w* in the gates
I Chron. 5:22, the *w* was of God
Job 10:17, changes and *w* are against me
    38:23, reserved against the day of *w*
Ps. 27:3, though *w* should rise against me
    46:9, he makes *w* to cease
    68:30, scatter the people that delight in *w*
Prov. 20:18, with good advice make *w*
Eccl. 8:8, no discharge in that *w*
Isa. 2:4; Mic. 4:3, nor learn *w* any more
Jer. 42:14, to Egypt, where we shall see no *w*
Mic. 2:8, as men averse from *w*
Mk. 13:7; Lk. 21:9, *w* and rumours of *w*
Lk. 14:31, what king, going to make *w*
James 4:1, from whence come *w*
See I Chron. 12:33; Eccl. 9:18; Ezek. 32:27;
    Dan. 7:21; 9:26
WAR (*v.*) II Chron. 6:34, if your people go to *w*
Ps. 144:1, teach my hands to *w*
Isa. 41:12, they that *w* against you
II Cor. 10:3, we do not *w* after the flesh
I Tim. 1:18, *w* a good warfare
II Tim. 2:4, no man that *w* entangles himself
James 4:1, lust that *w* in your members
    2, ye fight and *w*, yet ye have not
I Pet. 2:11, lusts which *w* against the soul
See I Ki. 14:19; Isa. 37:8; Rom. 7:23
WARDROBE II Ki. 22:14; II Chron. 34:22
WARE Lk. 8:27; II Tim. 4:15
WARFARE Isa. 40:2, her *w* is accomplished
II Cor. 10:4, weapons of our *w* are not carnal
See I Sam. 28:1; I Cor. 9:7; I Tim. 1:18
WARM Eccl. 4:11, how can one be *w* alone?
Isa. 47:14, there shall not be a coal to *w* at
Hag. 1:6, ye clothe you,, but there is none *w*
Mk. 14:54; Jn. 18:18, Peter *w* himself
James 2:16, be ye *w* and filled
See II Ki. 4:34; Job 37:17; 39:14; Isa. 44:15
WARN Ezek. 3:18; Acts 20:31; I Thess. 5:14
WASH II Ki. 5:10, go, *w* in Jordan
    12, may I not *w* in them, and be clean?
Job 9:30, if I *w* myself with snow water
    14:19, you *w* away things which grow
    29:6, when I *w* my steps with butter
Ps. 26:6; 73:13, *w* my hands in innocency

51:2, *W* me throughly from my iniquity
7, *w* me, and I shall be whiter than snow
Prov. 30:12, a generation not *w*
Song of Sol. 5:12, his eyes are *w* with milk
Isa. 1:16, *W* you, make you clean
Jer. 2:22, though you *w* yourself with nitre
4:14, *w* your heart
Mat. 6:17, when you fast, *w* your face
27:24, took water, and *w* his hands
Mk. 7:3, except they *w* oft, eat not
Lk. 7:38, began to *w* his feet with tears
44, she has *w* my feet with her tears
Jn. 9:7, go, *w* in the pool of Siloam
Acts 16:33, he *w* their stripes
22:16, *w* away your sins
I Cor. 6:11, but you are *w*
Heb. 10:22, our bodies *w* pure water
II Pet. 2:22, the sow that was *w*
Rev. 1:5, that *w* us from our sins
WASTE I Ki. 17:14, meal shall not *w*
Job 30:3, in the *w* wilderness
Ps. 80:13, the boar out of the wood does *w* it
91:6, the destruction that *w* at noonday
Isa. 24:1, the Lord makes the Earth *w*
61:4, they shall build the old *w*
Joel 1:10, the field is *w*, the corn is *w*
See Prov. 18:9; Isa. 59:7; Mk. 14:4
WATCH (*n.*) Ps. 90:4, as a *w* in the night
119:148, my eyes prevent the night *w*
Jer. 51:12, make the *w* strong
Hab. 2:1, I will stand upon my *w*
See Mat. 14:25; 24:43; 27:65; Lk. 2:8
WATCH (*v.*) Gen. 31:49, the Lord *w*
Job. 14:16, do you not *w* over my sin?
Ps. 37:32, the wicked *w* the righteous
102:7, I *w*, and am as a sparrow
130:6, more than they that *w* for morning
Isa. 29:20, all that *w* for iniquity are cut off
Jer. 20:10, my familiars *w* for my halting
31:28, so will I *w* over them, to build
44:27, I will *w* over them for evil
Ezek. 7:6, the end is come, it *w* for you
Hab. 2:1, I will *w* to see what he will say
Mat. 24:42; 25:13; Mk. 13:35; Lk. 21:36
26:41; Mk. 13:33; 14:38, *w* and pray
I Thess. 5:6; I Pet. 4:7, let us *w* and be sober
Heb. 13:17, for they *w* for your souls
See I Cor. 16:13; II Tim. 4:5; Rev. 3:2; 16:15
WATER (*n.*) Gen. 26:20, the *w* is ours
49:4, unstable as *w*
Deut. 8:7, a land of brooks of *w*
11:11, land drinks *w* of rain of heaven
Josh. 7:5, hearts melted, and became as *w*
II Sam. 14:14, as *w* spilt on the ground
I Ki. 13:22, eat no bread, and drink no *w*
22:27; II Chron. 18:26, *w* of affliction
II Ki. 3:11, who poured *w* on Elijah's hands
20:20, brought *w* into the city
Job 8:11, can the flag grow without *w*?
14:9, through the scent of *w* it will bud
19, the *w* wear the stones
15:16, who drinks iniquity like *w*
22:7, have not given *w* to weary to drink
38:30, the *w* are hid as with a stone

Ps. 22:14, I am poured out like *w*
23:2, beside the still *w*
46:3, though the *w* roar and be troubled
63:1, a dry and thirsty land, where no *w* is
73:10, *w* of a full cup are wrung out
77:16, the *w* saw you
79:3, their blood have they shed like *w*
124:4, then the *w* had overwhelmed us
148:4, praise him, ye *w* above the heavens
Prov. 5:15, drink *w* our of your own cistern
9:17, stolen *w* are sweet
25:25, as cold *w* to a thirsty soul
27:19, as in *w* face answers to face
30:4, who has bound the *w* in a garment?
Eccl. 11:1, cast your bread upon the *w*
Song of Sol. 4:15; Jn. 7:38, well of living *w*
8:7, many *w* cannot quench love
Isa. 1:22, your wine is mixed with *w*
3:1, take away the whole stay of *w*
11:9; Hab. 2:14, as the *w* cover the seas
19:5, the *w* shall fall from the sea
28:17, *w* shall overflow the hiding place
32:20, blessed are you that sow beside all *w*
33:16, his *w* shall be sure
35:6, in the wilderness shall *w* break out
41:17, when the poor seek *w*
43:2, when you pass through the *w*
44:3, I will pour *w* on him that is thirsty
55:1, come ye to the *w*
57:20, whose *w* cast up mire and dirt
Jer. 2:13; 17:13, the fountain of living *w*
9:1, Oh that my head were *w*
14:3, their nobles sent little ones to the *w*
47:2, behold *w*, rise up out of the north
Ezek. 4:17, they may want bread and *w*
7:17; 21:7, be weak as *w*
36:25, will I sprinkle clean *w* upon you
Amos 8:11, nor a thirst for *w*
Mat. 10:42, whoso gives a cup of cold *w*
14:28, bid me come to you on the *w*
27:24, Pilate took *w*, and washed
Lk. 8:23, ship filled with *w*
24, and rebuked the raging of the *w*
16:24, dip the tip of his finger in *w*
Jn. 1:26; Acts 1:5, baptize you with *w*
3:5, except a man be born of *w*
23, there was much *w* there
5:3, waiting for moving of the *w*
19:34, forthwith came out blood and *w*
Acts 10:47, can any forbid *w*
II Cor. 11:26, in perils of *w*
Eph. 5:26, cleanse it with washing of *w*
I Pet. 3:20, eight souls were saved by *w*
II Pet. 2:17, wells without *w*
I Jn. 5:6, this is he that came by *w*
Rev. 22:17, let him take the *w* of life freely
See Ps. 29:3; Jer. 51:13; Ezek. 32:2; 47:1
WATER (*v.*) Deut. 11:10, *w* it with your foot, as
garden
Ps. 6:6, I *w* my couch with tears
72:6, as showers that *w* the earth
104:13, he *w* the hills from his chambers
Prov. 11:25, he that *w* shall be *w*
Isa. 16:9, I will *w* you with my tears

27:3, I will *w* it every moment
Isa. 55:10, returns not, but *w* the earth
  58:11, you shall be like a *w* garden
Ezek. 32:6, I will also *w* with your blood
I Cor. 3:6, Apollos *w*, God gave the increase
WAVES Ps. 42:7, all you *w* are gone over me
  65:7; 89:9; 107:29, stills noise of *w*
  93:4, the Lord is mightier than mighty *w*
Isa. 48:18, righteousness as the *w* of the sea
Jer. 5:22, though the *w* toss
Zech. 10:11, shall smite the *w* in the sea
Jude 13, raging *w* of the sea
See Mat. 8:24; 14:24; Mk. 4:37; Acts 27:41
WAX (*n.*) Ps. 22:14; 68:2; 97:5; Mic. 1:4
WAX (*v.*) Ex. 22:24, my wrath shall *w* hot
Num. 11:23, is the Lord's hand *w* short?
Deut. 8:4; Neh. 9:21, raiment *w* not cold
  32:15, Jeshurun *w* fat, and kicked
Mat. 24:12, the love of many shall *w* cold
Lk. 12:33, bags which *w* not old
Heb. 1:11, shall *w* old as does a garment
See Dan. 8:8; Mat. 13:15; I Tim 5:11
WAY Gen. 6:12, all flesh had corrupted his *w*
  24:56, seeing the Lord has prospered my *w*
  28:20, if God will keep me in this *w*
Num. 22:32, your *w* is perverse
Deut. 8:6; 26:17; Isa. 42:24, walk in his *w*
Josh. 23:14; I Ki. 2:2, the *w* of all the Earth
I Sam. 12:23, teach the good and right *w*
II Ki. 7:15, all the *w* was full of garments
II Chron. 6:27, has taught them the good *w*
Ezra 8:21, to see of him a right *w*
Job 3:23, to a man whose *w* is hid
  12:24, to wander where there is no *w*
  16:22, I go the *w* whence I shall not return
  22:15, have you marked the old *w*
  23:10, he knows the *w* that I take
  24:13, they know not the *w* of the light
  31:4, does not he see my *w*
  38:19, where is the *w* where light dwells?
Ps. 2:12, lest ye perish from the *w*
  18:30, as for God, his *w* is perfect
  25:9, the meek will he teach his *w*
  27:11; 86:11, teach me your *w*
  37:5, commit your *w* unto the Lord
  39:1, I will take heed to my *w*
  67:2, that your *w* may be known
  78:50, he made a *w* to his anger
  95:10, they have not known my *w*
  101:2, behave wisely in a perfect *w*
  119:5, O that my *w* were directed
  139:24, lead me in the *w* everlasting
Prov. 2:8, he preserves the *w* of his saints
  3:6, in all your *w* acknowledge him
  17, her *w* are *w* of pleasantness
  5:21, the *w* of man are before the Lord
  6:6, consider her *w*, and be wise
  23; 15:24; Jer. 21:8, the *w* of life
  12:15, *w* of a fool is right in his own eyes
  15:19, the *w* of the slothful man
  16:7, when a man's *w* please the Lord
  22:6, train up a child in the *w*
  23:19, guide your heart in the *w*
  26, let your eyes observe my *w*

26:13, there is a lion in the *w*
Eccl. 11:5, the *w* of the spirit
  12:5, fears shall be in the *w*
Isa. 2:3; Mic. 4:2, he will teach us of his *w*
  30:21, this is the *w*, walk ye in it
  35:8, and a *w* called The *w* of holiness
  40:27, my *w* is hid from the Lord
  42:16, the blind by a *w* they knew not
  24, they would not walk in his *w*
  45:13, I will direct all his *w*
  58:2, they delight to know my *w*
Jer. 6:16, where is the good *w*
  17:10; 32:19, every man according to his *w*
  32:39, I will give them one heart and one *w*
  50:5, they shall ask the *w* to Zion
Ezek. 3:18, to warn the wicked from his *w*
Joel 2:7, march every one on his *w*
Nah. 1:3, Lord has his *w* in the whirlwind
Mal. 3:1, he shall prepare the *w* before me
Mat. 7:13, broad is the *w* that leads
  10:5, go not into *w* of Gentiles
  22:16; Lk. 20:21, teaches the *w* of God
Mk. 8:3, they will faint by the *w*
Lk. 15:20, when he was yet a great *w* off
  19:4, he was to pass the *w*
Lk. 19:36, spread garments in the *w*
Jn. 10:1, but climbs up some other *w*
  14:4, and the *w* ye know
  6, I am the *w*, the truth, and the life
Acts 9:2, if he found any of his *w*
  27, how he had seen the Lord in the *w*
  16:17, show unto us the *w* of salvation
  18:26, expounded the *w* of God
  19:23, no small stir about the *w*
  24:14, after the *w* which they call heresy
Rom. 3:12, they are all gone out of the *w*
  11:33, his *w* are past finding out
I Cor. 10:13, will make a *w* to escape
  12:31, a more excellent *w*
Col. 2:14, too handwriting out of the *w*
Heb. 5:2, compassion on them out of the *w*
  9:8, the *w* into the holiest
  10:20, by a new and living *w*
James 1:8, unstable in all his *w*
  5:20, the sinner from error of his *w*
Jude 11, they have gone in the *w* of Cain
WEAK II Sam. 3:1, Saul's house waxed *w* and *w*
II Chron. 15:7, let not your hands be *w*
Job 4:3, you have strengthened the *w* hands
Ps. 6:2, I am *w*
Isa. 14:10, are you also become *w* as we?
  35:3, strengthen ye the *w* hands
Ezek. 7:17; 21:7, shall be *w* as water
  16:30, how *w* is your heart!
Joel 3:10, let the *w* say, I am strong
Mat. 26:41; Mk. 14:38, but the flesh is *w*
Acts 20:35, you ought to support the *w*
Rom. 4:19, being not *w* in faith
I Cor. 1:27, *w* things to confound the mighty
II Cor. 10:10, his bodily presence is *w*
  11:29, who is *w*, and I am not *w*?
  12:10, when I am *w*, then am I strong
Gal. 4:9, turn again to *w* elements
I Pet. 3:7, honor to the wife; as *w* vessel

WEAKNESS I Cor. 1:25, the *w* of God
2:3, I was with you in *w*
15:43, it is sown in *w*, raised in power
See II Cor. 12:9; 13:4; Heb. 7:18; 11:34

WEALTH Deut. 8:18, power to get *w*
I Sam. 2:32, see an enemy in all the *w*
II Chron. 1:11, you have not asked *w*
Esther 10:3, seeking the *w* of his people
Job 21:13, they spend their days in *w*
31:25, if I rejoiced because my *w* was great
Ps. 44:12, do not increase *w* by price
49:6, they that trust in *w*
10, wise men die, and leave *w* to others
112:3, *W* and riches shall be in his house
Prov. 5:10, lest strangers be filled with you *w*
10:15; 18:11, rich man's *w* is his strong city
13:11, *W* gotten by vanity
19:4, *W* makes many friends
Acts 19:25, by this craft we have our *W*
I Cor. 10:24, seek every man another's *w*

WEALTHY Ps. 66:12; Jer. 49:31

WEANED I Sam. 1:22; Ps. 131:2; Isa. 11:8

WEAPON Neh. 4:17, with other hand held a *w*
Isa. 13:5; Jer. 50:25, the *w* of his indignation
54:17, no *w* formed against you shall
prosper
Jer. 22:7, every one with his *w*
Ezek. 9:1, with destroying *w* in his hand
II Cor. 10:4, the *w* of our warfare
See Job 20:24; Ezek. 39:9; Jn. 18:3

WEAR Job 14:19, the waters *w* the stones
Isa. 4:1, we will *w* our own apparel
Zech. 13:4, nor shall they *w* a rough garment
Mat. 11:8, that *w* soft clothing
See Deut. 22:5; Lk. 9:12; I Pet. 3:3

WEARINESS Eccl. 12:12; Mal. 1:13

WEARY (*adj.*) Gen. 27:26, I am *w* of my life
II Sam. 23:10, he smote till his hand was *w*
Job 3:17, and the *w* be at rest
22:7, you have not given water to the *w*
Ps. 6:6, I am *w* with groaning
Prov. 3:11, be not *w* of the Lord's correction
25:17, lest he be *w* of you
Isa. 5:27, none shall be *w* among them
7:13, will you *w* my God also?
32:2, as the shadow of a great rock in *w*
land
40:28, God faints not, neither is *w*
31, they shall run, and not be *w*
43:22, you have been *w* of me
46:1, a burden to the *w* beast
Isa. 50:4, a word in season to him that is *w*
Jer. 6:11, I am *w* with holding in
15:6, I am *w* with repenting
20:9, I was *w* with forbearing
31:25, I have satiated the *w* soul
Lk. 18:5, lest she *w* me
Gal. 6:9; II Thess. 3:13, be not *w* in well doing

WEARY (*v.*) Isa. 43:24, you have *w* me
47:13, *w* in the multitude of counsels
57:10, *w* in the greatness of your way
Jer. 12:5, with footmen, and they *w* you
Ezek. 24:12, she has *w* herself with lies
Mic. 6:3, wherein have I *w* thee?

Jn. 4:6, being *w*, sat thus on the well
Heb. 12:3, lest ye be *w* and faint
See Eccl. 10:15; Jer. 4:31; Mal. 2:17

WEATHER Job 37:22; Mat. 16:2

WEB Judg. 16:13; Job 8:14; Isa. 59:5

WEDGE Josh. 7:21; Isa. 13:12

WEEK Gen. 29:27, fulfill her *w*
Jer. 5:24, the appointed *w* of harvest
Dan. 9:27, in the midst of the *w*
Acts 20:7; I Cor. 16:2, the first day of the *w*
See Num. 28:26; Dan. 10:2; Lk. 18:12

WEEP Gen. 43:30, he sought where to *w*
I Sam. 1:8; Jn. 20:13, why *w* thou?
11:5, what ails the people that they *w*?
30:4, no more power to *w*
Neh. 8:9, mourn not, nor *w*
Job 27:15, his widows shall not *w*
Eccl. 3:4, a time to *w*
Isa. 15:2, he is gone up to *w*
30:19, you shall *w* no more
Jer. 9:1, that I might *w* day and night
22:10, *W* ye not for the dead
Joel 1:5, awake, ye drunkards, and *w*
Mk. 5:39, why make ye this ado, and *w*?
Lk. 6:21, blessed are ye that *w* now
7:13; 8:52; Rev. 5:5, *W* not
23:38, *w* not for me, but *w* for yourselves
Jn. 11:31, she goes to the grave to *w* there
Acts 21:13, what mean ye to *w*
Rom. 12:15, and *w* with them that *w*
See Jn. 16:20; I Cor. 7:30; James 4:9; 5:1

WEEPING II Sam. 15:30, *w* as they went
Ezra 3:13, not discern noise of joy from *w*
Job 16:16, my face is foul with *w*
Ps. 6:8, Lord has heard the voice of my *w*
30:5, *w* may endure for a night
102:9, I have mingled my drink with *w*
Isa. 65:19, the voice of *w* be no more heard
Jer. 31:16, restrain your voice from *w*
48:5, continual *w* shall go up
Joel 2:12, turn to me with fasting and *w*
Lk. 7:38, stood at his feet behind him *w*
13:28, *w* and gnashing of teeth
Jn. 11:3, when Jesus saw her *w*
20:11, Mary stood without at sepulcher *w*
Phil. 3:18, now tell you even *w*

WEIGH II Sam. 14:26, *w* the hair of his head
Job 6:2, on that my grief were *w*
31:6, let me be *w* in an even balance
Isa. 26:7, you do *w* the path of the just
40:12, who has *w* the mountains
Dan. 5:27; you are *w* in the balances
See Job 28:25; Prov. 16:2; Zech. 11:12

WEIGHT Lev. 26:26, deliver your bread by *w*
Job 28:25, to make the *w* for the winds
Ezek. 4:10, your meat shall be by *w*
16, they shall eat bread by *w*
II Cor. 4:17, a more exceeding *w* of glory
Heb. 12:1, lay aside every *w*
See Deut. 25:13; Prov. 16:11; Mic. 6:11

WEIGHTY Prov. 27:3; II Cor. 10:10

WELFARE Neh. 2:10, to seek *w* of Israel
Job 30:15, my *w* passes away
Ps. 69:22, which should have been for their *w*

WELL (*n.*) Num. 21:17, spring up, O *w*
  Deut. 6:11, and *w* which you dug not
  I Chron. 11:17, water of the *w* of Bethlehem
  Ps. 84:6, through valley of Baca make it a *w*
  Prov. 5:15, waters our of your own *w*
    10:11, a *w* of life
  Song of Sol. 4:15; Jn. 4:14, *w* of living waters
  Isa. 12:3, the *w* of salvation
  Jn. 4:6, sat thus on the *w*
  II Pet. 2:17, *w* without water
  See Gen. 21:19; 49:22; II Sam. 17:18
WELL (*adv.*) Gen. 4:7, if you do *w*
  12:13, *w* with me for your sake
  29:6, is he *w*? and they said, He is *w*
  Ex. 4:14, I know he can speak *w*
  Num. 11:18, it was *w* with us in Egypt
  Ruth 3:1, that it may go *w* you
  I Sam. 20:7, if he say thus, it is *w*
  II Ki. 4:26, is it *w* with you? is it *w*?
  II Chron. 12:12, in Judah things went *w*
  Ps. 49:18, when you do *w* to yourself
  Prov. 11:10, it goes *w* the righteous
    14:15, looks *w* with the righteous
    30:29, three things which go *w*
  Eccl. 8:12, be *w* with them who fear Go
  Isa. 3:10, say to the righteous, it shall be *w*
  Ezek. 33:32, one that can play *w*
  Jonah 4:4, do you *w* to be angry?
  Mat. 25:21; Lk. 19:17, *W* done
  Mk. 7:37, he has done all things *w*
  Lk. 6:26, when all men speak *w* of you
  Gal. 5:7, you did run *w*
  See Phil. 4:14; I Tim. 3:4; 5:17; Tit. 2:9
WENT Gen. 4:16, Cain *w* from the presence
  Deut. 1:31, in all the way ye *w*
  II Ki. 5:26, *W* not my heart with you
  Ps. 42:4, I *w* with them to the house of God
    106:32, it *w* ill with Moses
  Mat. 21:30, I go, sir, and *w* not
  Lk. 17:14, as they *w* they were cleansed
    18:10, two men *w* up into the temple to
    pray
WEPT II Ki. 8:11, the man of God *w*
  Ezra 10:1; Neb. 8:9, the people *w* very sore
  Neh. 1:4, I *w* before God
  Lk. 7:32, we mourned, and ye have not *w*
    19:41, behold the city, and *w* over it
  Jn. 11:35, Jesus *w*
  I Cor. 7:30, that weep as though they *w* not
  See II Sam. 12:22; Ps. 69:10; 137:1; Rev. 5:4
WET Job 24:8; Dan. 4:15; 5:21
WHAT Ex. 16:15, they wist not *w* it was
  II Sam. 16:10, *W* have I to do with you
  Ezra 9:10, *w* shall we say after this?
  Job 7:17; 15:14; Ps. 8:4; 144:3, *W* is man?
  Isa. 38:15; Jn. 12:27, *W* shall I say?
  Hos. 6:4, *w* shall I do unto you?
  Mat. 5:47, *w* do you more than others?
  Mk. 14:36, no *w* I will, but *w* thou wilt
  Jn. 21:22, *w* is that to you?
  See Acts 9:6; 10:4; 16:30; I Pet. 1:11
WHATSOEVER Eccl. 3:14, *w* God does
  Mat. 5:37, *w* is more than these
    7:12, *w* ye would that men should do to

you
  20:4, *w* right I will give you
  Phil. 4:8, *w* things are true
  See Jn. 15:16; Rom. 14:23; I Cor. 10:31
WHEAT Job 31:40, let thistles grow instead of *w*
  Ps. 81:16; 147:14, the finest of the *w*
  Jer. 12:13, they have sown *w*, but reap thorns
    23:28, what is the chaff to the *w*?
  Mat. 3:12, gather his *w* into the garner
  Lk. 22:31, that ye may sift you as *w*
  See Jn. 12:24; Acts 27:38; I Cor. 15:37
WHEEL Ex. 14:25, took off their chariot *w*
  Judg. 5:28, why tarry the *w*
  Ps. 83:13, make them like a *w*
  Prov. 20:26, king brings the *w* over them
  Eccl. 12:6, or the *w* broken at the cistern
  Isa. 28:28, nor break it with the *w* of his cart
  Nah. 3:2, the noise of the rattling of the *w*
  See Isa. 5:28; Jer. 18:3; 47:3; Ezek. 1:16
WHELP II Sam. 17:8; Prov. 17:12; Hos. 13:8
WHEN I Sam. 3:12, *w* I being, I will also
  I Ki. 8:30, *w* you hear, forgive
  Ps. 94:8, *w* will you be wise?
  Eccl. 8:7, who can tell him *w* it shall be?
  Mat. 24:3; Lk. 21:7, *w* shall these things be?
  See Deut. 6:7; Jn. 4:25; 16:8; I Jn. 2:28
WHENCE Gen. 42:7; Josh. 9:8, *W* come ye?
  Job 10:21, *w* I shall not return
  Isa. 51:1, look unto the rock *w* ye are hewn
  James 4:1, from *w* come wars
  Rev. 7:13, *w* came they?
WHERE Gen. 3:9, *W* are you?
  Ex. 2:20; II Sam. 9:4; Job 14:10, *W* is he?
  Job 9:24, if not, *w*, and who is he?
  Zech. 1:5, your fathers, *w* are they?
  See Isa. 49:21; Hos. 1:10; Lk. 17:37
WHEREBY Lk. 1:18, *W* shall I know this?
  Rom. 8:15, the spirit of adoption, *w* we cry
  See Jer. 33:8; Ezek. 18:31; 39:26; Eph. 4:30
WHEREFORE II Sam. 12:23, *w* should I fast?
  Mat. 14:31, *w* did you doubt?
    26:50, *w* are you come?
  See II Sam. 16:10; Mal. 2:15; Acts 10:21
WHERETO Isa. 55:11; Phil: 3:16
WHEREWITH Ps. 119:42, so shall I have *w* to
    answer
  Mic. 6:6, *W* shall I come before the Lord
  See Mat. 5:13; Mk. 9:50; Jn. 17:26
WHET Deut. 32:41: Ps. 7:12; Eccl. 10:10
WHETHER Mat. 23:17 *w* is greater, the gold or
    the temple
  Rom. 14:8, *w* we live or die
  II Cor. 12:2, *w* in the body, or out of the body
  See I Ki. 20:18; Ezek. 2:5; 3:11; I Jn. 4:1
WHILE II Chron. 15:2, *w* ye be with him
  Ps. 49:18, *w* he lived he blessed his soul
  Isa. 55:6, *w* he may be found
  Jer. 15:9, sun is gone down *w* it was yet day
  Lk. 18:4, he would not for a *w*
    24:44, *w* I was yet with you
  Jn. 9:4, work *w* it is day
  I Tim. 5:6, she is dead *w* she lives
  See I Sam. 9:27; II Sam. 7:19; Acts 20:11
WHIP I Ki. 12:11; Prov. 26:3; Nah. 3:2

WHIT I Sam. 3:18; Jn. 7:23; 13:10
WHITE Gen. 49:12, his teeth *w* with milk
　Num. 12:10, leprous, *w* as snow
　Job 6:6, is there any taste in the *w* of an egg
　Eccl. 9:8, let your garments be always *w*
　Song of Sol. 5:10, my beloved is *w* and ruddy
　Isa. 1:18, they shall be *w* as snow
　Mat. 5:36, you can not make one hair *w*
　Jn. 4:35, *w* already to harvest
　Rev. 2:17, a *w* stone
　See Dan. 11:35; 12:10; Mat. 17:2; 28:3
WHITED Mat. 23:27; Acts 23:3
WHITER Ps. 51:7; Lam. 4:7
WHITHER II Ki. 5:25; Heb. 11:8
WHOLE II Sam. 1:9, my life is yet *w* in my
　Eccl. 12:13, this is the *w* duty of man
　Jer. 19:11, a vessel that cannot be made *w*
　Ezek. 15:5, when *w* was meet for no work
　Mat. 5:29, your *w* body be cast into Hell
　　9:12; Mk. 2:17, the *w* need not a physician
　　13:33; Lk. 13:21, till the *w* was leavened
　　16:26; Lk. 9:25, gain the *w* world
　I Cor. 12:17, if the *w* body were an eye
　I Thess. 5:23, I pray God your *w* spirit
　James 2:10, keep the *w* law
　I Jn. 2:2, for the sins of the *w* world
　　5:19, the *w* world lies in wickedness
WHOLESOME Prov. 15:4; I Tim. 6:3
WHOLLY Job 21:23, dies, being *w* at ease
　Jer. 2:21, planted you *w* a right seed
　　46:28, not *w* unpunished
　Acts 17:16, the city *w* give to idolatry
　I Thess. 5:23, sanctify you *w*
　I Tim. 4:15, give yourself *w* to them
　See Lev. 19:9; Deut. 1:36; Josh. 14:8
WHOMSOEVER Dan. 4:17, to *w* he will
　Mat. 11:27, to *w* the Son will reveal him
　　21:44; Lk. 20:18, on *w* it shall fall
　Lk. 4:6, to *w* I will give, I give it
　　12:48, to *w* much is given
　See Gen. 31:32; Judg. 11:24; Acts 8:19
WHOSE Gen. 32:17, *W* are you? *w* are these?
　Jer. 44:28, shall know *w* words shall stand
　Mat. 22:20; Lk. 20:24, *W* is this image
　Lk. 12:20, then *w* shall these things be
　Acts 27:23, *w* I am, and whom I serve
　See I Sam. 12:3; Dan. 5:23; Jn. 20:23
WHOSOEVER I Cor. 11:27; *w* shall eat bread
　Gal. 5:10, bear his judgment, *w* he be
　Rev. 22:17, *w* will, let him take
　See Mat. 11:6; 13:12; Lk. 8:18; Rom. 2:1
WHY I Sam. 2:23, *W* do ye such things?
　Jer. 8:14, *W* do we sit still?
　　27:13; Ezek. 18:31; 33:11, *W* will you die?
　Mk. 5:39, *W* make you did this ado?
　Lk. 20:5, *W* did ye not believe?
　Acts 9:4; 22:7; 26:14, *w* persecutest thou me?
　Rom. 9:19, *W* does he yet find fault?
　　20, *W* have you made me thus?
WICKED Gen. 18:23, destroy righteous with *w*
　Deut. 15:9, a thought in your *w* heart
　I Sam. 2:9, the *w* shall be silent
　Job 3:17, there the *w* cease from troubling
　　8:22, dwelling place of *w* come to nought

　　9:29; 10:15, if I be *w* why labor I in vain
　　21:7, wherefore do the *w* live
　　30, the *w* is reserved to destruction
　Ps. 7:9, the wickedness of *w* come to an end
　　11, God is angry with the *w*
　　9:17, the *w* shall be turned into Hell
　　10:4, the *w* will not seek God
　　11:2, the *w* bend their bow
　　6, upon the *w* he shall rain snares
　　12:8, the *w* walk on every side
　　26:5, I will not sit with the *w*
　　37:21, the *w* borrow, and pay not
　　32, the *w* watch the righteous
　　58:3, the *w* are estranged from the womb
　　68:2, so let the *w* perish
　　94:3, how long shall the *w* triumph?
　　145:20, all the *w* will he destroy
　Prov. 11:5, *w* shall fall by own wickedness
　　14:32, the *w* driven away
　　28:1, the *w* flee when no man pursues
　Eccl. 7:17, be not overmuch *w*
　　8:10, I saw the *w* buried
　Isa. 13:11, I will punish the *w*
　　53:9, he made his grave with the *w*
　　55:7, let the *w* forsake his way
　　57:20, the *w* are like the troubled sea
　Jer. 17:9, the heart is desperately *w*
　Ezek. 3:18; 33:8, to warn the *w*
　　11:2, these men give *w* counsel
　　33:15, if the *w* restore the pledge
　Dan. 12:10, the *w* shall do wickedly
　Mic. 6:11, the *w* balances
　Nah. 1:3, the Lord will not acquit the *w*
　Mat. 12:45, more *w* than himself
　　13:49, sever the *w* from the just
　　18:32; 25:26; Lk. 19:22, you *w* servant
　Acts 2:23, *w* hands have crucified and slain
　I Cor. 5:13, put away that *w* person
　Eph. 6:16, the fiery darts of the *w*
　Col. 1:21, enemies in your mind by *w* works
　II Thess. 2:8, then shall that *W* be revealed
WICKEDLY Job 13:7, speak *w* for God?
　　34:12, God will not do *w*
　Ps. 73:8; 139:20, they speak *w*
　Dan. 12:10, the wicked shall do *w*
　Mal 4:1, all that do *w*
　See II Chron. 6:37; 22:3; Neh. 9:33; Ps. 106:6
WICKEDNESS Gen. 39:9, this great *w*
　Judg. 20:3, how was this *w*?
　I Sam. 24:13, *W* proceeds from the wicked
　I Ki. 21:25, sold himself to work *w*
　Job 4:8, they that sow *w*, reap the same
　　22:5, is not your *w* great?
　Ps. 7:9, let the *w* of the wicked come to an
　　end
　　55:11, *W* is in the midst thereof
　　15, *w* is in their dwellings
　Prov. 4:17, they eat the bread of *w*
　　8:7, *w* is an abomination to my lips
　　11:5, the wicked shall fall by his own *w*
　　13:6, *w* overthrows the sinner
　Eccl. 7:25, the *w* of folly
　Isa. 9:18, *w* burns as the fire
　　47:10, you have trusted in your *w*

Jer. 2:19, your own *w* shall correct you

6:7, she casts out her *w*

44:9, have you forgot the *w* of your kings

Ezek. 3:19, if he turn not from his *w*

7:11, violence is risen up into a rod of *w*

31:11, I have driven him out for his *w*

33:12, in the day he turns from his *w*

Hos. 9:15, for the *w* of their doings

10:13, you have plowed *w*

Mic. 6:10, are treasures of *w* in house

Zech. 5:8, he said, This is *w*

Mal. 1:4, the border of *w*

Mk. 7:22, out of the heart proceed *w*

Lk. 11:39, your inward part if full of *w*

Rom. 1:29, being filled with all *w*

I Cor. 5:8, nor with the leaven of *w*

Eph. 6:12, spiritual *w* in high places

I Jn. 5:19, the whole world lies in *w*

WIDE Ps. 35:21, they opened their mouth *w*

104:25, this great and *w* sea

Prov. 21:9; 25:24; Jer. 22:14, a *w* house

Mat. 7:13, *w* is gate to destruction

See Deut. 15:8; Ps. 81:10; Nah. 3:13

WIFE Prov. 18:22, whoso finds a *w* finds a good thing

19:14, a prudent *w* is from the Lord

Eccl. 9:9, the *w* of your youth

Lk. 14:20, I have married a *w*

17:32, remember Lot's *w*

I Cor. 7:14, the unbelieving *w* is sanctified

Eph. 5:23, the husband is the head of the *w*

Rev. 21:9, the bride, the Lamb's *w*

See Mat. 5:32; I Cor. 7:2; I Tim. 3:2; 5:9

WILES Num. 25:18; Eph. 6:11

WILL Mat. 18:14, not the *w* of your Father

26:39, not as I *w*, but as thou wilt

Mk. 3:35, whosoever shall do the *w* of God

Lk. 5:13, I *w*, be thou clean

Jn. 1:13, born not of the *w* of the flesh

4:34, to do the *w* of him that sent me

Acts 21:14, the *w* of the Lord be done

Rom. 7:18, to *w* is present with me

Phil. 2:13, both to *w* and to do

I Tim. 2:8, I *w* that men pray everywhere

Rev. 22:17, whosoever *w*, let him take

WILLFULLY Heb. 10:26, if we sin *w*

WILLING Ex. 35:5, a *w* heart

I Chron. 28:9, serve God with a *w* mind

29:5, who is *w* to consecrate his service

Ps. 110:3, *w* in the day of your power

Mat. 26:41, the spirit is *w*

II Cor. 5:8, *w* rather to be absent

8:12, if there be first a *w* mind

I Tim. 6:18, *w* to communicate

II Pet. 3:9, not *w* than any should perish

WIN II Chron. 32:1; Prov. 11:30; Phil 3:8

WIND Job 6:26, speeches which are as *w*

7:7, remember that my life is *w*

Prov. 11:29, he shall inherit *w*

25:23, the north *w* drives away rain

30:4, gathered the *w* in his fists

Eccl. 11:4, he that observes the *w*

Isa. 26:18, we have brought forth *w*

27:8, he stays his rough *w*

Ezek. 37:9, prophesy to the *w*

Hos. 8:7; they have sown *w*

Amos 4:13, he that creates the *w*

Mat. 11:7, a reed shaken with the *w*

Jn. 3:8, the *w* blows where it listeth

WINDOWS Gen. 7:11; Eccl. 12:3; Jer. 9:21

WINE Ps. 104:15, *w* makes glad the heart

Prov. 20:1, *W* is a mocker

21:17, loves *w* shall not be rich

23:31, look not upon *w* when it is red

31:6, give *w* to those of heavy heart

Song of Sol. 1:2, love is better than *w*

Isa. 5:11, till *w* inflame them

12, pipe and *w* are in their feasts

25:6, *w* on the lees well refined

28:7, they have erred through *w*

55:1, buy *w* and milk

Hos. 2:9, take away my *w* in the season

3:1, look to other gods, love flagons of *w*

4:11, new *w* take away the heart

Hab. 2:5, he transgresses by *w*

Eph. 5:18, be not drunk with *w*

I Tim. 3:3, not given with *w*

5:23, use a little *w* for stomach's sake

WINGS Ps. 17:8; 91:4, ,the shadow of your *w*

18:10; 104:3, on the *w* of the wind

55:6, Oh that I had *w* like a dove!

139:9, the *w* of the morning

Prov. 23:5, riches make themselves *w*

Mal. 4:2, with healing in his *w*

Rev. 9:9, sound of their *w*

WINK Job 15:12; Ps. 35:19; Prov. 6:13

WINTER Gen. 8:22; Song of Sol. 2:11; Mat. 24:20

WIPE Isa. 25:8; Lk. 7:38; Jn. 13:5

WISDOM Job 4:21, they die without *w*

12:2, *w* shall die with you

Prov. 4:7, *W* is the principal thing

16:16, better to get *w* than gold

19:8, he that gets *w* loves his own soul

23:4, cease from your own *w*

Eccl. 1:18, in much *w* is much grief

Isa. 10:13, by my *w* I have done it

Mic. 6:9, the man of *w* shall see your name

Mat. 11:19, *w* is justified of her children

I Cor. 1:17, not with *w* of words

24, Christ the *w* of God

30, who of God is made unto us *w*

2:6, speak *w* among them that are perfect

I Cor. 3:19, *w* of this world is foolishness with God

II Cor. 1:12, not with fleshly *w*

Col. 1:9, that you might be filled with all *w*

4:5, walk in *w* toward them

James 1:5, if any lack *w*

3:17, the *w* from above is pure

Rev. 5:12, worthy is the Lamb to receive *w*

WISE Gen. 3:6, to make one *w*

Ex. 23:8, the gift blinds the *w*

Deut. 4:6, this nation is a *w* people

32:29, O that they were *w*

I Ki. 3:12, I have given you a *w* heart

Job 9:4, he is *w* in heart

11:12, vain man would be *w*

22:2, he that is *w* may be profitable
32:9, great men are not always *w*
Ps. 2:10, be *w* now, O ye kings
19:7, making *w* the simple
94:8, when will you be *w*?
107:43, whoso is *w*, and will observe
Prov. 1:5, a *w* man shall attain *w* counsels
3:7, be not *w* in your own eyes
9:12, you shall be *w* for yourself
11:30, he that wins souls is *w*
16:21, the *w* in heart shall be called
prudent
20:26, a *w* king scatters the wicked
Eccl. 7:23, I said, I will be *w*
9:1, the *w* are in the hands of God
12:11, the words of the *w* are as goads
Dan. 12:3, they that be *w* shall shine
Mat. 10:16, be *w* as serpents
11:25, you have hid these things from the *w*
Rom. 1:14, I am debtor to the *w*
12:16, be not *w* in your own conceits
I Cor. 1:20, where is the *w*?
II Tim. 3:15, *w* unto salvation
WISELY Ps. 58:5, charming never so *w*
101:2, I will behave myself *w*
Prov. 16:20, that handles a matter *w*
WISER I Ki. 4:31; Lk. 16:8; I Cor. 1:25
WISH Ps. 73:7, more than heart could *w*
Rom. 9:3, I could *w* myself accursed
III Jn. 2, I *w* above all things
See Job 33:6; Jonah 4:8; II Cor. 13:9
WITHDRAW Job 9:13; II Thess. 3:6
WITHER Ps. 1:3, his leaf shall not *w*
37:2, they shall *w* as the green herb
129:6; Isa. 40:7; I Pet. 1:24, the grass *w*
Mat. 21:19; Mk. 11:21, the fig tree *w* away
Jude 12, trees whose fruit *w*
See Joel 1:12; Jn. 15:6; James 1:11
WITHHOLD Ps. 40:11, *W* not your mercies
84:11, no good thing will be *w*
Prov. 23:13, *W* not correction
Eccl. 11:6, *w* not your hand
Jer. 5:25, your sins have *w* good things
See Job 27:7; 42:2; Ezek. 18:16; Joel 1:13
WITHIN Mat. 23:26, cleanse first what is *w*
Mk. 7:21, from *w* proceed evil thoughts
II Cor. 7:5, *w* were fears
See Ps. 45:13; Mat. 3:9; Lk. 12:17; 16:3
WITHOUT Gen. 24:31, standest thou *w*?
II Chron. 15:3, for a long season *w* the true
God
Prov. 1:20, wisdom cries *w*
Isa. 52:3; 55:1, *w* money
Jer. 33:10, *w* man, *w* beast, *w* inhabitant
Hos. 3:4, Israel *w* king, *w* prince, *w* sacrifice
Eph. 2:12, *w* God in the world
I Thess. 4:12; I Tim. 3:7, them that are *w*
Heb. 13:12, Jesus suffered *w* the gate
Rev. 22:15, for *w* are dogs
WITHSTAND Eccl. 4:12, two shall *w* him
Acts 11:17, what was I that I could *w* God?
Eph. 6:13, able to *w* in evil day
See Num. 22:32; II Chron. 20:6; Esther 9:2
WITNESS (*n*.) Gen. 31:50, God is *w* betwixt

Josh. 24:27, this stone shall be a *w*
Job 16:19, my *w* is in heaven
Ps. 89:37, as a faithful *w* in heaven
Prov. 14:5, a faithful *w* will not lie
Isa. 55:4, I have given him for a *w* to the
people
Jer. 42:5, the Lord be a true and faithful *w*
Mat. 24:14, for a *w* to all nations
Jn. 1:7, the same came for a *w*
3:11, you receive not our *w*
5:36, I have greater *w* than that of John
Acts 14:17, he left not himself without *w*
Rom. 2:15, conscience also bearing them *w*
I Jn. 5:9, the *w* of God is greater
10, has the *w* in himself
WITNESS (*v*.) Deut. 4:26, Heaven and Earth *w*
Isa. 3:9, countenance does *w* against them
Acts 20:23, the Holy Ghost *w* in every city
Rom. 3:21, bring *w* by the Law and Prophets
I Tim. 6:13, *w* a good confession
See I Sam. 12:3; Mat. 26:62; Mk. 14:60
WITS Ps. 107:27, are at their *w* end
WITTY Prov. 8:12
WOEFUL Jer. 17:16, the *w* day
WOMAN Judg. 9:54, a *w* slew him
Prov. 6:24, to keep you from the evil *w*
9:13, a foolish *w* is clamorous
12:4; 31:10, a virtuous *w*
21:9, with a brawling *w* in wide house
Eccl. 7:28, a *w* have I not found
Isa. 54:6, as a *w* forsaken
Jer. 31:22, a *w* shall compass a man
Mat. 5:28, whoso looks on a *w*
15:28, O *w* great is your faith
22:27; Lk 20:32, the *w* died also
26:10, why trouble ye the *w*?
Jn. 2:4, *W*, what have I to do with you?
19:26, *W* behold your son
Acts 9:36, this *w* was full of good works
Rom. 1:27, the natural use of the *w*
I Cor. 7:1, good for a man not to touch a *w*
11:7, the *w* is the glory of the man
Gal. 4:4, God sent forth his Son, made of a *w*
I Tim. 2:12, I suffer not a *w* to teach
14, the *w* being deceived
WOMB Gen. 49:25, blessings of the *w*
I Sam. 1:5, the Lord had shut up her *w*
Ps. 22:9, took me out of the *w*
127:3, the fruit of the *w* is his reward
139:13, covered me in my mother's *w*
Eccl. 11:5, how bones grow in the *w*
Isa. 44:2; 49:5, the Lord formed you from
the *w*
48:8, a transgressor from the *w*
49:15, compassion on son of her *w*
Hos. 9:14, give them miscarrying *w*
Lk. 1:42, blessed is fruit of your *w*
11:27, blessed is the *w* that bore you
23:29, blessed are the *w* that never bore
WOMEN Judg. 5:24, blessed above *w*
I Sam. 18:7, the *w* answered one another
II Sam. 1:26, passing the love of *w*
Ps. 45:9, among your honorable *w*
Prov. 31:3, give not your strength to *w*

Mat. 11:11; Lk. 7:28, among them born of *w*
24:41, two *w* grinding at the mill
Lk. 1:28, blessed are you among *w*
I Cor. 14:34, let your *w* keep silence
I Tim. 2:9, *w* adorn themselves
11, let the *w* learn in silence
5:14, that the younger *w* marry
II Tim. 3:6, lead captive silly *w*
Titus 2:3, aged *w* as becomes holiness
Heb. 11:35, *W* received their dead
WONDER (n.) Ps. 71:7, as a *w* unto many
77:14, you are the God that does *w*
88:12, shall your *w* be known in the dark?
96:3, declare his *w* among all people
107:24, his *w* in the deep
Isa. 20:3, walk barefoot for a sign and a *w*
29:14, I will do a marvelous work and a *w*
Joel 2:30; Acts 2:19, I will show *w* in Heaven
Jn. 4:48, except you see signs and *w*
Acts 4:30, that *w* may be done by the name
WONDER (v.) Isa. 29:9, stay, and *w*
59:16, he *w* there was no intercessor
63:5, I *w* the *w* was none to uphold
Hab. 1:5, regard, and *w* marvelously
Zech. 3:8, they are men *w* at
Lk. 4:22, all *w* at the gracious words
See Acts 3:11; 8:13; 13:41; Rev. 13:3; 17:6
WONDERFUL II Sam. 1:26, your love was *w*
Job 42:3, things too *w* for me
Ps. 139:6, such knowledge is too *w* for me
Isa. 9:6, his name shall be called *W*
28:29, who is *w* in counsel
WONDERFULLY Ps. 139:14; Dan. 8:24
WONDROUS I Chron. 16:9; Ps. 26:7; 75:1;
106:22; 119:27; 145:5; Jer. 21:2, *w* works
Ps. 72:18; 86:10; 119:18, *w* things
WONT Ex. 21:29, if the ox were *w* to push
Mat. 27:15, the governor was *w* to release
Mk. 10:1, as he was *w*, he taught them
Lk. 22:39, he went, as he was *w*
Acts 16:13, where prayer was *w* to be made
See Num. 22:30; II Sam. 20:18; Dan. 3:19
WOOD Gen. 22:7, behold the fire and the *w*
Deut. 29:11; Jer. 46:22, hewer of *w*
II Sam. 18:8, the *w* devoured more people
Ps. 141:7, as one cleaves *w*
Prov. 26:20, where no *w* is, the fire goes out
See Jer. 7:18; Hag. 1:8; I Cor. 3:12
WOOL Ps. 147:16, he gives snow like *w*
Isa. 1:18, your sins shall be as *w*
Dan. 7:9; Rev. 1:14, hair like *w*
See Prov. 31:13; Ezek. 34:3; 44:17; Hos. 2:9
WORD Deut. 8:3; Mat. 4:4, every *w* of God
30:14; Rom. 10:8, the *w* is very nigh
Job. 12:11, does not the ear try *w*?
Ps. 19:14, *w* of my mouth be acceptable
68:11, the Lord gave the *w*
Col. 1:5l James 1:18, the *w* of truth
Prov. 15:23, a *w* spoken in due season
25:11, a *w* fitly spoken
Isa. 29:21, an offender for a *w*
30:21, your ears shall hear a *w* behind you
50:4, how to speak a *w* in season
Jer. 5:13, the *w* is not in them

18:18, nor shall the *w* perish
Hos. 14:2, take with you *w*
Mat. 8:8, speak the *w* only
12:36, every idle *w* that men shall speak
18:16, that every *w* may be established
24:35, my *w* shall not pass away
Mk. 4:14, the sower sows the *w*
8:38; Lk. 9:26, ashamed of my *w*
Lk. 4:22, gracious *w* which proceeds
36, amazed, saying, What a *w* is this
24:19, a prophet mightily in deed and *w*
Jn. 6:63, the *w* I speak are life
68, you have the *w* of eternal life
12:48, the *w* I have spoken shall judge him
14:24, the *w* ye hear is not mine
Acts 13:15, any *w* of exhortation
20:35, remember the *w* of the Lord Jesus
26:25, the *w* of truth and soberness
I Cor. 1:17, not with wisdom of *w*
4:20, not in *w*, but in power
II Cor. 1:18, our *w* was not year and nay
5:19, the *w* of reconciliation
Gal. 5:14, all the law is fulfilled in one *w*
6:6, him that is taught in the *w*
Eph. 5:6, deceive you with vain *w*
Phil 2:16, holding forth the *w* of life
Col. 3:16, let the *w* of Christ dwell in you
I Thess. 1:5, the gospel came not in *w* only
4:18, comfort one another with these *w*
I Tim. 4:6, nourished in *w* of faith
5:17, labor in the *w* and doctrine
II Tim. 2:14, strive not about *w*
4:2, preach the *w*
Titus 1:3, in due times manifested his *w*
9, holding fast the faithful *w*
Heb. 1:3, by the *w* of his power
2:2, if the *w* spoken by angels was
steadfast
4:2, the *w* preached did not profit
12, the *w* of God is quick and powerful
5:13, is unskillful in the *w*
6:5, and have tasted the good *w* of God
7:28, the *w* of the oath
11:3, worlds were framed by the *w* of God
13:7, who have spoken to you the *w*
James 1:21, the engrafted *w*
23, if any be a hearer of the *w*
3:2, if any man offend not in *w*
I Pet. 1:23, being born again by the *w*
25, this is the *w* which is preached
2:2, the sincere milk of the *w*
8, them that stumble at the *w*
3:1, if any obey not the *w*
II Pet. 1:19, a more sure *w* of prophecy
3:2, the *w* spoken by the prophets
5, by the *w* of God the Heavens were of old
I Jn. 1:1, hands have handled, of *W* of life
2:5, whoso keeps his *w*, in him is the love
3:18, let us not love in *w*
Rev. 3:8, you have kept my *w*
10, the *w* of my patience
WORK (n.) Gen. 2:2, God ended his *w*
5:29, shall comfort us concerning our *w*
Ex. 35:2, six days shall *w* be done

Deut. 3:24, God can do according to your *w*
   5:13, six days you shall do all your *w*
I Chron. 16:37, as every day's *w* required
II Chron. 31:21, in every *w* he began, he did it
   34:12, the men did the *w* faithfully
Ezra 5:8, this *w* goes fast on
   6:7, let the *w* alone
Neh. 3:5, nobles put not their necks to the *w*
   6:3, why should the *w* cease
   16, they perceived this *w* of God
Job 1:10, you have blessed the *w* of his hands
   10:3; 14:15, Ps. 143:5, the *w* of your hands
   34:11, *w* of a man shall he render unto him
Ps. 8:3, the *w* of your fingers
   19:1, his handy *w*
   33:4, all his *w* are done in truth
   90:17, establish thou the *w* of our hands
   101:3, I hate the *w* of them that turn aside
   104:23, man goes forth to his *w*
   111:2, the *w* of the Lord are great
   115:4; 135:15, the *w* of men's hands
   141:4, to practice wicked *w*
Prov. 16:3, commit your *w* unto the Lord
   20:11, whether his *w* be pure
   31:31, let her own *w* praise her
Eccl. 1:14, I have seen all the *w* that are done
   3:17, there is a time for every *w*
   5:6, wherefore should God destroy the *w*
   8:9, I applied my heart to every *w*
   9:1, their *w* are in the hand of God
   10, there is no *w* in the grave
Isa. 5:19, let him hasten his *w*
   26:12, you have wrought all our *w* in us
   28:21, do his *w*, his strange *w*
   29:15, their *w* are in the dark
   66:18, I know their *w* and their thoughts
Jer. 32:19, great in counsel, and mighty in *w*
   48:7, you have trusted in your *w*
   51:18, they worship *w* of their own hands
Amos 8:7, I will never forget any of their *w*
Hab. 1:5, I will work a *w* in your days
Mat. 7:22; Acts 2:11, wonderful *w*
   23:3, do not ye after their *w*
   5, all their *w* they do to be seen of men
Mk. 6:5, he could there do no mighty *w*
Jn. 5:20, great *w* than these
   6:28, that we might work the *w* of God
   29, this is the *w* of God, that you believe
   7:21, I have done one *w*, and you all marvel
   9:3, the *w* of God should be made
manifest
   10:25, the *w* I do in my Father's name
   32, for which of those *w* do you stone me?
   14:12, the *w* I do shall he do, and greater *w*
   17:4, I have finished the *w*
Acts 5:38, *w* be of men, it will come to
nought
   15:38, who went not with them to the *w*
Rom. 3:27, by what law? of *w*?
   4:6, imputes righteousness without *w*
   9:11, not of *w*, but of him that calls
   11:6, grace, otherwise *w* is no more *w*
   13:12, let us cast off the *w* of darkness
   14:20, for meat destroy not the *w* of God

I Cor. 3:13, every man's *w* shall be manifest
   9:1, are not ye my *w* in the Lord?
Gal. 2:16, by *w* of the law shall no flesh
   6:4, let every man prove his own *w*
Eph. 2:9, not of *w*, lest any man should boast
   4:12, the *w* of the ministry
   5:11, the unfruitful *w* of darkness
Col. 1:21, enemies in your mind by wicked *w*
I Thess. 5:13, esteem them for their *w* sake
II Thess. 2:17, in every good word and *w*
II Tim. 1:9; Titus 3:5, not according to our *w*
   4:14, to every man according to his *w*
Titus 1:16, in *w* they deny him
James. 1:4, let patience have her perfect *w*
   2:14, if he have not *w*, can faith save him?
   17, faith, if it has not *w*, is dead
   18, show me your faith without your *w*
   21, was not Abraham justified by *w*
   22, by *w* was faith made perfect
I Jn. 3:8, destroy the *w* of the devil
Rev. 2:2, 9, 13, 19; 3:1, 8, 15, I know your *w*
   26, he who keeps my *w* to the end
   3:2, I have not found your *w* perfect
   14:13, and their *w* do follow them
WORK (*v.*) I Sam. 14:6, Lord will *w* for us
I Ki. 21:20, sold yourself to *w* evil
Neh. 4:6, the people had a mind to *w*
Job 23:9, on the left hand, where he does *w*
   33:29, all these things *w* God with man
Ps. 58:2, in heart ye *w* wickedness
   101:7, he that *w* deceit
Isa. 43:13, I will *w*, and who shall let it?
Mic. 2:1, woe to them that *w* evil
Hag. 2:4, *w*, for I am with you
Mal. 3:15, they that *w* wickedness are set up
Mat. 21:28, son, go *w* today in my vineyard
Mk. 16:20, the Lord *w* with them
Jn. 5:17, my Father *w* hitherto, and I *w*
   6:28, that we might *w* the works of God
   30, what do you *w*?
   9:4, the night comes, when no man can *w*
Rom. 4:15, the law *w* wrath
   5:3, tribulation *w* patience
   8:28, all things *w* together for good
I Cor. 4:12, labor, *w* with our own hands
   12:6, it is the same God which *w* all in all
II Cor. 4:12, death *w* in us
Gal. 5:6, faith which *w* by love
Eph. 1:11, who *w* all things after the counsel
   2:2, the spirit that now *w*
   3:20, the power that *w* in us
   4:28, *w* with his hands the thing that is
good
Phil. 2:12, *w* out your own salvation
I Thess. 4:11, *w* with your own hands
II Thess. 2:7, the mystery of iniquity does *w*
   3:10, any would not *w*, neither should he
eat
James 1:3, the trying of your faith *w* patience
WORKMAN Hos. 8:6; Eph. 2:10; II Tim. 2:15
WORLD Job 18:18, chased out of the *w*
   34:13, who has disposed the whole *w*?
   37:12, on the face of the *w*
Ps. 73:12, the ungodly, who prosper in the *w*

77:18; 97:4, lightnings lightened the *w*

93:1, the *w* also is stablished

Eccl. 3:11, he has set the *w* in their heart

Isa. 14:21, nor fill the face of the *w* with cities

24:4, the *w* languished

Mat. 4:8; Lk. 4:5, all the kingdoms of the *w*

5:14, the light of the *w*

13:22; Mk 4:19, the cares of the *w* choke

16:26; Mk. 8:36; Lk. 9:25, gain the whole *w*

18:7, woe to the *w* because of offences

Mk. 10:30; Heb. 2:5; 6:5, in the *w* to come

Lk. 1:70; Acts 3:21, since the *w* began

2:1, all the *w* should be taxed

16:8; 20:34, children of this *w*

20:35, worthy to obtain that *w*

Jn. 1:10, he was in the *w*

29, which takes away the sin of the *w*

3:16, God so loved the *w*

4:42; I Jn. 4:14, the Saviour of the *w*

6:33, he that gives life unto the *w*

7:4, show yourself to the *w*

7, the *w* cannot hate you

8:12; 9:5, I am the light of the *w*

12:19, the *w* is gone after him

31, now is the judgment of this *w*

47, not to judge the *w*, but to save the *w*

13:1, depart out of this *w*

14:17, whom the *w* cannot receive

22, manifest yourself unto us, not unto
the *w*?

27, not as the *w* gives, give I unto you

Jn. 14:30, the prince of this *w* comes

15:18; I Jn. 3:13, if the *w* hate you

19, the *w* would love his own

16:33, in the *w* ye shall have tribulation

17:9, I pray not for the *w*

21:25, the *w* could not contain the books

Acts 17:6, turned the *w* upside down

Rom. 3:19, that all the *w* may become guilty

12:2, be not conformed to this *w*

I Cor. 1:20, where is the disputer of this *w*?

2:6, the wisdom of this *w*

7:31, they that use this *w* as not abusing it

II Cor. 4:4, the god of this *w* has blinded

Gal. 1:4, this present evil *w*

6:14, the *w* is crucified unto me

Eph. 2:2, according to the course of this *w*

12, without God in the *w*

I Tim. 6:7, we brought nothing into this *w*

17, them that are rich in this *w*

II Tim. 4:10, having loved this present *w*

Heb. 11:38, of whom the *w* was not worthy

James 1:27, unspotted from the *w*

3:6, the tongue is a *w* of iniquity

4:4, the friendship of the *w*

II Pet. 2:5, God spared not the old *w*

3:6, the *w* that them was

I Jn. 2:15, love not the *w*

3:1, the *w* knows us not

5:19, the whole *w* lies in wickedness

WORLDLY Titus 2:12; Heb. 9:1

WORM Job 7:5, my flesh is clothed with *w*

17:14, I said to the *w*, You are my mother

19:26, though *w* destroy this body

21:26, lie down, and *w* shall cover them

24:20, the *w* shall feed sweetly on him

25:6, man, that is a *w*

Ps. 22:6, I am a *w*, and no man

Isa. 14:11, the *w* is spread under you

41:14, fear not, you *w* Jacob

66:24; Mk. 9:44, their *w* shall not die

WORMWOOD Jer. 9:15; 23:15; Amos 5:7

WORSE Mat. 9:16, rent is made *w*

12:45; Lk. 11:26, last state *w* than first

Mk. 5:26, nothing bettered, but grew *w*

Jn. 5:14, lest a *w* thing come unto you

I Cor. 11:17, not for the better, but for the *w*

I Tim. 5:8, he is *w* than an infidel

II Tim. 3:13, shall wax *w* and *w*

II Pet. 2:20, the latter end is *w* with them

See Jer. 7:26; 16:12; Dan. 1:10; Jn. 2:10

WORSHIP Ps. 95:6, let us *w* and bow down

97:7, *w* him, all ye gods

Isa. 27:13, shall *w* the Lord in the holy mount

Jer. 44:19, did we *w* her without our men?

Zeph. 1:5, them that *w* the host of Heaven

Mat. 4:9; Lk. 4:7, fall down and *w* me

15:9, in vain they do *w* me

Jn. 4:20, our fathers *w* in this mountain

22, ye *w* ye know not what

Acts 17:23, whom ye ignorantly *w*

24:14, so *w* I the God of my fathers

I Cor. 14:25, so falling down he will *w* God

See Col. 2:18; Heb. 1:6; Rev. 4:10; 9:20

WORTH Job 24:25; Prov. 10:20; Ezek. 30:2

WORTHY Gen. 32:10, I am not *w* of the least

I Sam. 26:16, you are *w* to die

I Ki. 1:52, if he show himself a *w* man

Mat. 3:11, whose shoes I am not *w* to bear

8:8, not *w* that you should come

10:10, the workman is *w* of his meat

22:8, they which were hidden were not *w*

Lk. 3:16; Jn. 1:27, not *w* to unloose

3:8, fruits *w* of repentance

7:4, he was *w* for whom he should do this

10:7, I Tim. 5:18, laborer is *w* of his hire

12:48, things *w* of stripes

15:19, no more *w* to be called your son

20:35, *w* to obtain that world

Acts 24:2, very *w* deeds are done

Rom. 8:18, not *w* to be compared with glory

Eph. 4:1; Col. 1:10; I Thess. 2:12, walk *w*

Heb. 11:38, of whom the world was not *w*

James 2:7, that *w* name

Rev. 3:4, for they are *w*

WOULD Num. 22:29, I *w* there were a sword

Ps. 81:11, Israel *w* none of me

Prov. 1:25, ye *w* none of my reproof

30, they *w* none of my counsel

Dan. 5:19, whom he *w* he slew

Mat. 7:12, whatsoever ye *w* that men

Mk. 3:13, and calls unto him whom he *w*

Rom. 7:15, what I *w*, that do I not

I Cor. 7:7, I *w* that all men were even as I

Rev. 3:15, I *w* you were cold or not

See Num. 11:29; Acts 26:29; Gal. 5:17

WOUND (*n.*) Ex. 21:25, give *w* for *w*

Job 34:6, my *w* is incurable

Ps. 147:3, he binds up their *w*
Prov. 23:29, who has *w* without cause?
  27:6, faithful are the *w* of a friend
Isa. 1:6, but *w* and bruises
Jer. 15:18, why is my *w* incurable?
  30:17, I will heal you of your *w*
Zech. 13:6, what are these *w* in your hands?
Lk. 10:34, bound up his *w*
See Prov. 6:33; 20:30; Hos. 5:13; Rev. 13:3
WOUND (*v.*) Deut. 32:39, I *w*, and I heal
II Chron. 18:33, carry me out, for I am *w*
Job 5:18, he *w*, and his hands make whole
Ps. 64:7, suddenly shall they be *w*
  109:22, my heart is *w* within me
Prov. 7:26, she has cast down many *w*
  18:14, a *w* spirit who can bear?
Isa. 53:5, he was *w* for our transgressions
Jer. 37:10, there remained but *w* men
WRAP Isa. 28:20; Mic. 7:3; Jn. 20:7
WRATH Gen. 49:7, cursed be their *w*
Job 36:18, because there is *w*, beware
Ps. 76:10, the *w* of man shall praise you
  90:7, by your *w* are we troubled
Prov. 16:14, *w* of a king
  19:19, a man of great *w* shall suffer
Eccl. 5:17, much *w* with his sickness
Isa. 13:9, the day of the Lord comes with *w*
  54:8, in a little *w* I hid my face
Nah. 1:2, he reserves *w* for his enemies
Hab. 3:2, in *w* remember mercy
Zeph. 1:15; Rev. 6:17, the day of *w*
Mat. 3:7; Lk. 3:7, from the *w* to come
Rom. 2:5, *w* against the day of *w*
Eph. 6:4, provoke not your children to *w*
I Thess. 5:9, God has not appointed us to *w*
I Tim. 2:8, lifting up holy hands, without *w*
See James 1:19; Rev. 6:16; 12:12; 14:10
WRATHFUL Ps. 69:24; Prov. 15:18
WREST Ex. 23:2; Deut. 16:19; II Pet. 3:16
WRESTLE Gen. 32:24; Eph. 6:12
WRETCHED Num. 11:15; Rom. 7:24
WRING Judg. 6:38; Ps. 75:8; Prov. 30:33
WRINKLE Job 16:8; Eph. 5:27
WRITE Prov. 3:3, *w* on table of your heart
Isa. 10:1; *w* grievousness they have prescribed
  19, few, that a child may *w* them
Jer. 22:30, *W* ye this man childless?
  31:33; Heb. 8:10, I will *w* it in their hearts
Hab. 2:2, *W* the vision, make it plain
See Job 13:26; Ps. 87:6; Rev. 3:12
WRITING Ex. 32:16; Jn. 5:47; Co. 2:14
WRITTEN Ps. 69:28, not be *w* with the righteous
Ezek. 2:10, tool was *w* within and without
Lk. 10:20, your names are *w* in heaven
Jn. 19:22, what I have *w* I have *w*
I Cor. 10:11, *w* for our admonition
II Cor. 3:2, you are our epistle *w* in our hearts
See Isa. 4:3; Jer. 17:1; Rev. 2:17; 13:8
WRONG Ex. 2:13, to him that did the *w*
I Chron. 12:17, there is no *w* in my hands
Job 19:7, I cry out of *w*, but am not heard
I Cor. 6:7, why do ye not rather take *w*?
II Cor. 12:13, forgive me this *w*

Col. 3:25, he that does *w* shall receive
Phile. 18, if has *w* you
WRONGFULLY Ezek. 22:29; I Pet. 2:19
WROTE Dan. 5:5; Jn. 8:6; 19:19; II Jn. 5
WROTH Gen. 4:6, why are you *w*?
Deut. 1:34; 3:26; 9:19, II Sam. 22:8
Ps. 18:7; 78:21, heard your words, and was *w*
II Ki. 5:11, but Naaman was *w*
Ps. 89:38, have been *w* with your anointed
Isa. 47:6, I was *w* with my people
  54:9, I have sworn I would not be *w*
  57:16, neither will I be always *w*
Isa. 64:9, be not *w* very sore
Mat. 18:34, his lord was *w*, and delivered
See Num. 16:22; Isa. 28:21; Mat. 2:16
WROUGHT Num. 23:23, what has God *w*!
I Sam. 6:6, when God had *w* wonderfully
  14:45, Jonathan had *w* with God this day
Neh. 4:17, one of his hands *w* in the work
  6:16, this work was *w* of our God
Job 12:9, the hand of the Lord has *w* this
  36:23, who can say, You have *w* iniquity?
Ps. 31:19, have *w* for them that trust in you
  139:15, curiously *w* in lowest parts of Earth
Eccl. 2:11, I looked on all my hands had *w*
Isa. 26:12, you have *w* all our works in us
  41:4, who has *w* and done it?
Jer. 18:3, he *w* a work on the wheels
Ezek. 20:9, I *w* for my name's sake
Dan. 4:2, wonders God has *w* toward me
Mat. 20:12, these last have *w* but one hour
  26:10, she has *w* a good work on me
Jn. 3:21, manifest that they are *w* in God
Acts 15:12, what wonders God had *w*
  18:3, he abode with him, and *w*
  19:11, *w* special miracles by hands of Paul
Rom. 7:8, *w* in me manner of concupiscence
Rom. 15:18, things which Christ has not *w*
II Cor. 5:5, he that has *w* us
  7:11, what carefulness it *w* in you
  12:12, the signs of an apostle were *w*
Eph. 1:20, which he *w* in Christ
Heb. 11:33, through faith *w* righteousness
James 2:22, faith *w* with his works
I Pet. 4:3 to have *w* the will of the Gentiles
II Jn. 8, lose not those things we have *w*
Rev. 19:20, the false prophet that *w* miracles
WRUNG Lev. 1:15; Ps. 73:10; Isa. 51:17

Y

YARN I Ki. 10:28; II Chron. 1:16
YE I Cor. 6:11; II Cor. 3:2; Gal. 6:1
YEA II Cor. 1:17, should be *y y*, and nay nay?
James 5:12, let communication by *y, y*
See II Cor. 1:18; Phil 3:8; II Tim. 3:12
YEAR Gen. 1:14, for seasons, days, and *y*
Ex. 13:10, keep this ordinance from *y* to *y*
  23:29, I will not drive them out in one *y*
Lev. 16:34, make atonement once a *y*
Num. 14:34, each day for a *y* shall ye bear
Deut. 14:22, you shall tithe the increase *y* by *y*
  15:9, the *y* of release is at hand

26:12, the third *y*, which is the *y* of tithing
Judg. 11:40, to lament four days in a *y*
I Sam. 2:19, brought a coat from *y* to *y*
    7:16, went from *y* to *y* in circuit
II Sam. 14:26, every *y* he polled it
I Ki. 17:1, shall not be dew nor rain these *y*
II Chron. 14:6, land had rest, no war in those *y*
Job 10:5, are your *y* as man's days?
    15:20, the number of *y* is hidden
    32:7, multitude of *y* should teach wisdom
    36:11, they shall spend their *y* in pleasures
    26, nor can number of his *y* be searched out
Ps. 31:10, my *y* are spent with sighing
    61:6, prolong his *y* as many generations
    65:11, You crown the *y* with Your goodness
    77:5, the *y* of ancient times
    10, I will remember the *y* of the right hand
    78:33, their *y* did he consume in trouble
    90:4, a thousand *y* in Your sight
    9, we spend our *y* as a tale that is told
    10, days of our *y* are threescore years and ten
    102:24, Your *y* are throughout all generations
    27, Your *y* shall have no end
Prov. 4:10, the *y* of your life shall be many
    5:9, lest thou give your *y* to the cruel
    10:27, the *y* of the wicked shall be shortened
Isa. 21:16, according to the *y* of an hireling
    29:1, add ye *y* to *y*
    61:2; Lk. 4:19, the acceptable *y* of the Lord
    63:4, the *y* of my redeemed is come
Jer. 11:23; 48:44, the *y* of their visitation
    17:8, shall not be careful in *y* of drought
    28:16, this *y* you shall die
    51:46, a rumor shall come in one *y*
Ezek. 4:5, laid on you the *y* of their iniquity
    22:4, you are come even unto your *y*
    38:8, in latter *y* you shall come
    46:17, it shall be his to the *y* of liberty
Dan. 11:6, in the end of *y* they shall join
Joel 2:2, to the *y* of many generations
Mic. 6:6, shall I come with calves of a *y* old?
Hab. 3:2, revive your work in the midst of the *y*
Mal. 3:4, offering be pleasant, as in former *y*
Lk. 13:8, let is alone this *y* also
Gal. 4:10, ye observed days and *y*
Rev. 20:2, Satan bound for a thousand *y*
YEARLY I Sam. 1:3; 20:6; Esther 9:21
YEARN Gen. 43:30; I Ki. 3:26
YELL Jer. 2:15; 51:38
YESTERDAY Job 8:9; Ps. 90:4; Heb. 13:8
YET Gen. 40:23, *Y* did not the butler remember
Ex. 10:7, knowest thou not *y*
Deut. 9:29, *y* they are your people
    12:9, ye are not as *y* come
Judg. 7:4, the people are *y* too many
I Ki. 19:18 *Y* I have left me
Ezra 3:6, the foundation was not *y* laid
Job 1:16, while he was *y* speaking

13:15, though he slay me, *y* will I trust in him
    29:5, when the Almighty was *y* with me
Ps. 2:6, *Y* have I set my king
Eccl. 4:3, he which has not *y* been
Isa. 28:4, while it is *y* in his hand
Jer. 2:9, I will *y* plead with you
Ezek. 11:16, *y* will I be to them
    36:37, I will *y* for this be enquired of
Dan. 11:35, it is *y* for a time appointed
Hos. 7:9, *y* he knows no
Amos 6:10, is there *y* any with you?
Jonah 3:4, *Y* forty days
Hab. 3:18, *Y* I will rejoice
Mat. 15:17, do not ye *y* understand?
    19:20, what lack I *y*?
Mk. 11:13, the time of figs was not *y*
    13:7, end is not *y*
Lk. 24:44, while I was *y* with you
Jn. 2:4; 7:6; 8:20, hour is not *y* come
    11:25, though dead, *y* shall he live
Rom. 5:6, *y* without strength
I Cor. 3:15, *y* so as by fire
    15:17, ye are *y* in your sins
Gal. 2:20, *y* not I, but Christ
Heb. 4:15 *y* without sin
I Jn. 3:2, it does not *y* appear
YIELD Gen. 4:12, not henceforth *y* strength
Lev. 19:25, that it may *y* the increase
    26:4; Ps. 67:6, the land shall *y* her increase
Num. 17:8, the rod *y* almonds
II Chron. 30:8, *y* yourselves to the Lord
Neh. 9:37, it *y* much increase to the kings
Ps. 107:37, vineyards, which may *y* fruits
Prov. 7:21, she caused him to *y*
Eccl. 10:4, *y* pacifies great offences
Hos. 8:7, it if *y*, the strangers shall swallow it up
Joel 2:22, fig tree and vine do *y* their strength
Hab. 3:17, though fields shall *y* no meat
Mat. 27:50, cried again, and *y* up the ghost
Acts 23:21, do not thou *y* to them
Rom. 6:13, *y* yourselves to God
    16, to whom ye *y* yourselves to God
Heb. 12:11, *y* fruits of righteousness
YOKE Gen. 27:40, you shall break his *y*
Lev. 26:13, I have broken the bands of your *y*
Deut. 28:48, he shall put a *y* on your neck
I Ki. 12:4, your father made our *y* grievous
Isa. 9:4; 10:27; 14:25, you have broken the *y*
    58:6, that ye break every *y*
Jer. 2:20, of old time I have broken your *y*
    27:2; 28:13, make thee bonds and *y*
    31:18, as a bullock unaccustomed to the *y*
Lam. 3:27, it is good to bear the *y* in youth
Mat. 11:29, take my *y* upon you
    30, for my *y* is easy
Acts 15:10, a *y* is on the neck of the disciples
II Cor. 6:14, no unequally *y* with unbelievers
Gal. 5:1, entangled with the *y* of bondage
Phil. 4:3, I entreat you also, true *y*-fellow
I Tim. 6:1, servants as are under the *y*
YONDER Gen. 22:5; Num. 23:15; Mat. 17:20
YOU Gen. 48:21, God shall be with *y*

Ruth 2:4, the Lord be with *y*
I Chron. 22:18, is not the lord with *y*?
II Chron. 15:2, the Lord is with *y*
Jer. 18:6, cannot I do with *y*
   42:11; Hag. 1:13; 2:4, for I am with *y*
Zech. 8:23, we will go with *y*; God is with *y*
Mat. 28:20, I am with *y* alway
Lk. 6:31, that men should do to *y*
Lk. 10:16, he that hears *y* hears me
   13:28, and *y* yourselves thrust out
Acts 13:46, seeing ye put it from *y*
I Cor. 6:11, such were some of *y*
II Cor. 12:14, I seek not yours, but *y*
Eph. 2:1; Col. 2:13, *y* has he quickened
Col. 1:27, Christ in *y*
   4:9, a brother who is one of *y*
I Thess. 5:12, know them that are over *y*
I Jn. 4:4, greater is he that is in *y*
YOUNG Ex. 23:26, shall nothing cast their *y*
Lev. 22:28, ye shall not kill it and her *y* in one day
Deut. 22:6, shall not take the dam with *y*
   28:50, which will not show favor to the *y*
   57, her eyes shall be evil toward her *y* one
   32:11, as an eagle flutters over her *y*
I Chron. 22:5; 29:1, Solomon my son is *y*
II Chron. 13:7, when Rehoboam was *y* and tender
   34:3, while yet *y*, he began to seek God
Job 38:41, when his *y* ones cry to God
Job 39:16, the ostrich is hardened against her *y*
Ps. 37:25, I have been *y*, and now am old
   78:71, from following ewes great with *y*
   84:3, a nest where she may lay her *y*
   147:9, he gives food to the *y* ravens
Prov. 30:17, the *y* eagles shall eat it
Song of Sol. 2:9, my beloved is like a *y* hart
Isa. 11:7, their *y* shall lie down together
   40:11, and gently lead those that are with *y*
Jer. 31:12, flow together for *y* of the flock
Ezek. 17:4, cropped off his *y* twigs
Jn. 21:18, when *y* thou girdedst thyself
Titus 2:4, teach the *y* women to be sober
YOUNGER Job 30:1, they that are *y* have me in derision
I Tim. 5:1, intreat the *y* men as brethren
I Pet. 5:5, *y*, submit yourselves to the elder
See Gen. 29:18; Lk. 15:12; I Tim. 5:2, 11
YOUNGEST Gen. 42:13; Josh. 6:26
YOURS II Chron. 20:15; Lk. 6:20; I Cor. 3:21
YOUTH Gen. 8:21, imagination is evil from *y*
   46:34, about cattle from our *y* till now
I Sam. 17:33, be a man of war from his *y*
   55, whose son is this *y*?
II Sam. 19:7, evil that befell you from your *y*
I Ki. 18:12, I fear the Lord from my *y*
Job 13:26, to possess the iniquities of my *y*
   20:11, his bones are full of the sin of his *y*
   29:4, as in days of my *y*
   30:12, on my right hand rise the *y*

33:25, he shall return to the days of his *y*
   36:14, hypocrites die in *y*
Ps. 25:7, remember not the sins of my *y*
   71:5, you are my trust from my *y*
   17, you have taught me from my *y*
   88:15, ready to die from my *y*
   89:45, the days of his *y* have you shortened
   103:5, your *y* is renewed like the eagle's
   110:3, the dew of your *y*
   127:4, the children of your *y*
   129:1, they have afflicted me from my *y*
   144:12, as plants grown up in *y*
Prov. 2:17, forsake the guide of her *y*
   5:18, rejoice with the wife of your *y*
Eccl. 11:9, rejoice, young man, in your *y*
   10, childhood and *y* are vanity
   12:1, remember now your Creator in days of *y*
Isa. 47:12, you have labored from your *y*
   54:4, forget the shame of your *y*
Jer. 2:2, the kindness of your *y*
   3:4, you are the guide of my *y*
   22:21, this has been your manner from your *y*
   31:19, bear the reproach of my *y*
   32:30, have done evil before me from their *y*
   48:11, have been at ease from his *y*
Ezek. 4:14, soul not polluted from *y*
   16:22, have not remembered days of your *y*
Hos. 2:15, sing as in the days of her *y*
Joel 1:8, lament for husband for her *y*
Zech. 13:5, taught to keep cattle from my *y*
Lk. 18:21, have kept from my *y*
Acts 26:4, my manner of life from my *y*
I Tim. 4:12, let no man despise your *y*
See Prov. 7:7; Isa. 40:30; Jer. 3:24, 25
YOUTHFUL II Tim. 2:22, flee *y* lusts

Z

ZEAL II Ki. 10:16, come and see my *z* for the Lord
Ps. 69:9; Jn. 2:17, the *z* of your house
   119:139, my *z* has consumed me
Isa. 9:7, the *z* of the Lord will perform this
   59:17, clad with *z* as a cloak
   63:15, where is your *z*
Ezek. 5:13, I have spoken it in my *z*
Rom. 10:2, they have a *z* of God
II Cor. 9:2, your *z* has provoked many
Col. 4:13, he has a great *z* for you
See II Ki. 19:31; Isa. 37:23; II Cor. 7:11
ZEALOUS Num. 25:11, he was *z* for my sake
Acts 21:20, they are all *z* of the law
I Cor. 14:12, as ye are *z* of spiritual gifts
Titus 2:14, *z* of good works
Rev. 3:19, be *z* therefore, and repent
See Num. 25:13; Acts 22:3; Gal. 1:14
ZEALOUSLY Gal. 4:17, *z* affected

WHAT MUST I DO TO BE SAVED?

THE PLAN OF SALVATION

A long time ago, a Roman Jailer asked of the Apostle Paul the most important question that could ever be asked, *"What must I do to be saved?"*

Paul's answer was immediate, to the point, clear, and concise. He said:

"Believe on the Lord Jesus Christ, and thou shalt be saved, and thy house" (Acts 16:30-31.)

That's how simple that it actually is.

A man named Nicodemus pretty much asked Jesus the same question. Jesus answered him by saying, *"You must be born again"* (Jn. 3:1-8).

ALL ARE SINNERS

The Bible tells us in Romans 3:23 that *"All have sinned and come short of the Glory of God."*

That means that all are sinners, actually born that way, in desperate need of the Saviour, the Lord Jesus Christ. In fact, there are no exceptions to this. That means you and me, and all others for that matter.

Paul also said in Romans 6:23, *"The wages of sin is death!"*

So, that means that unless something is done about this terrible situation, that all will be eternally lost. However, God did not leave things there. He loves us, every one of us. It is His Desire that *"Not any should perish, but that all should come unto repentance"* (II Pet. 3:9).

WHAT DID GOD DO ABOUT THIS SITUATION?

The Scripture plainly says, *"And God so loved the world* (so loved sinners, and that means you) *that He gave His Only Begotten Son, that whosoever believes on Him shall not perish, but have everlasting life"* (Jn. 3:16).

What does that mean?

Man as a sinner could not save himself. In other words, such was and is impossible; consequently, God literally became man, came into this world born of the Virgin Mary, and then died on Calvary to pay the price for man's Redemption. As should be obvious, the price was high. But thank God, it was everlastingly paid by Jesus Christ, that *"WHOSOEVER WILL, MAY COME AND TAKE THE WATER OF LIFE FREELY"* (Rev. 22:17).

WHAT DOES IT MEAN TO BELIEVE ON THE LORD JESUS CHRIST?

Going back to the Scripture which we quoted in the Foreword of this booklet, Paul says:

"If you shall confess with your mouth the Lord Jesus, and shall believe in your heart that God has raised Him from the dead, you shall be saved. For with the heart man believes unto Righteousness; and with the mouth, confession is made unto Salvation" (Rom. 10:9-10).

To believe on the Lord Jesus Christ is more than just giving mental assent that He is the Son of God. Millions do that and aren't saved.

When the Scripture speaks of one believing, it simply means that one accepts Who Jesus is, which is the Son of God, and what He has done, which refers to Him dying on Calvary, in effect taking our place, in order that we might be saved.

It means to accept Him, and Him Alone as your Saviour, resolving to make Him the Lord of your life, and to follow Him with all of your heart, mind, soul, and strength as long as you live.

SUBSTITUTION AND IDENTIFICATION

As we have already stated, man being eternally lost and helpless to save himself, God had to provide a means of Salvation whereby sinful man could be made righteous. He did that by providing His Own Son, Who gave His Life on Calvary, thereby paying the terrible price which we could not pay. That price was His Own Precious Shed Blood.

He became our Substitute.

What does that mean?

It means He did for us what we could not

do for ourselves. There was a terrible sin debt owing due to man's fallen condition. As stated, that refers to every single human being, none excepted. With no way to save ourselves, God had to provide a Saviour, which He did. It was done simply because He loves us so much (Jn. 3:16).

Jesus being the Substitute, if we identify with Him, which means to accept what He did at Calvary's Cross on our behalf, we will be saved. It is that simple!

He became our Substitute, and upon our identification with Him, we are rewarded with Eternal Life (Rom. 6:23).

FAITH AND NOT WORKS

The only thing required to obtain this glorious and wonderful Salvation is to simply believe on Christ, exactly as Paul said, which means to have Faith in Him.

What does that mean?

It is actually very simple. The Lord made it this way in order that all may have equal opportunity.

It simply means that you believe or have faith in what He did, and accept it for yourself on a personal basis. That's all that God requires. But of course, to believe and have faith, even as we have already said, means to accept the Lord as your Saviour and, as well, to make Him the Lord of your life.

First of all, man must understand that he is a sinner. That includes all (Rom. 3:23). As such, he needs a Saviour. There is only one Saviour, only One Who has paid the price for man's Redemption, and that Saviour is the Lord Jesus Christ. In other words, if one does not accept Christ, one cannot be saved.

Millions attempt to earn their Salvation in many and varied ways other than accepting Christ. Or else they attempt to become saved by accepting Christ as well as adding other things to Christ.

The Scripture says: *"FOR BY GRACE ARE YOU SAVED THROUGH FAITH; AND THAT NOT OF YOURSELVES: IT IS THE GIFT OF GOD: NOT OF WORKS, LEST ANY MAN SHOULD BOAST"* (Eph. 2:8-9).

That means the Church cannot save you, and neither can Water Baptism save you, or anything else for that matter, as important as those things may be in their own way. I have said this because millions think that they are saved by being baptized in water, or joining a Church, or performing good works, etc.

While those things may be important in their own right, they have absolutely nothing to do with one being saved. One is saved simply by trusting Jesus Christ, even as we have already said.

That means that one can be saved anywhere: in Church, on the street corner, watching a Christian Telecast, listening to a Christian Radio Program, or even reading this Booklet.

Where one is doesn't matter. It is what one believes that really counts.

The moment that one confesses the Lord with one's mouth, and believes in one's heart, and does so truly, at that moment, and wherever you may be, you are saved. As we have stated several times, it is just that simple.

Incidently, when the Jailer asked Paul the question, *"What must I do to be saved?"*, he was actually at that time in the jail with Paul and Silas. Every evidence is that he at that moment, in that jail, believed on the Lord Jesus Christ, and was instantly saved (Acts 16:27-34).

IT IS TIME NOW!

In fact, if you have not already given your heart and life to Jesus Christ, it is time that you do so, and actually it can be done this very moment.

I am going to ask you to read these words below, and actually say them out loud. As well, I am going to ask you to believe them with all of your heart, and if you will do so, you will be instantly saved. Please say them with me as you read:

"DEAR GOD IN HEAVEN, I COME TO YOU TODAY AS A LOST SINNER."

"I AM ASKING YOU THAT YOU SAVE MY SOUL AND CLEANSE ME FROM ALL SIN."

"I REALIZE IN MY HEART MY NEED OF SALVATION, WHICH CAN ONLY COME THROUGH JESUS CHRIST."

"I AM ACCEPTING CHRIST INTO MY HEART AND WHAT HE DID ON THE CROSS IN ORDER TO PURCHASE MY REDEMPTION."

"IN OBEDIENCE TO YOUR WORD, I CONFESS WITH MY MOUTH THE

LORD JESUS, AND BELIEVE IN MY HEART THAT GOD HAS RAISED HIM FROM THE DEAD."

"YOU HAVE SAID IN YOUR WORD WHICH CANNOT LIE, 'FOR WHOSOEVER SHALL CALL UPON THE NAME OF LORD SHALL BE SAVED' (ROM. 10:13)."

"I HAVE CALLED UPON YOUR NAME EXACTLY AS YOU HAVE SAID, AND I BELIEVE THAT RIGHT NOW, I AM SAVED."

If you have sincerely prayed these words, which I have written out for you, and believed in your heart upon the Lord Jesus Christ, you are at this moment saved, and your name is written down in the Lamb's Book of Life.

Congratulations!

SOME THINGS YOU SHOULD NOW BEGIN TO DO

In the next few pages, I am going to give you some simple instructions that you should follow in order to live an overcoming, Christian Life. They are very important.

You are now a *"new creature in Christ Jesus"* (II Cor. 5:17). As such, you have the Divine nature within your heart, which is the Nature of God, which means that the Holy Spirit actually now resides within your heart and life.

The entirety of your life is now going to be different. You have been cleansed from all sin and have embarked upon the greatest journey that one could ever undertake. A whole new world is about to open up to you.

You now have something to live for, and something to which you can look forward. Living for Jesus is the most exciting life that one could ever live, the most fulfilling, the most rewarding, the most wonderful. There is absolutely nothing in the world that can compare with this which you have just received and which will never end.

But of course, Satan, the enemy of your soul, is not happy at all about you giving your heart to Christ Jesus; consequently, he will do everything he can to cause you problems, even attempting to get you to turn back. However, if you will heed carefully the following instructions that we will give, Satan will not be successful in pulling you back, and total victory will be yours.

DAILY BIBLE STUDY

We are directed by the Word of God to study the Bible. Jesus said, in John 5:39, to *"search the Scriptures. . . ."*

Paul, writing under the inspiration of the Holy Spirit in II Timothy, said, *"Study* (the Scriptures) *to show yourself approved unto God, a workman that needs not to be ashamed, rightly dividing the Word of Truth"* (II Tim. 2:15). The only way that one can intelligently divide the Word of Truth, in other words, to know and understand sound Doctrine, is to know the Word of God.

For you to know the Bible is the single most important thing you can ever do. Consequently, you ought to make it a part of your daily life.

Jesus said, *"Man shall not live by bread alone, but by every word that proceedeth out of the mouth of God"* (Mat. 4:4).

That means that as natural food is necessary for your physical well-being, likewise, the study and understanding of the Word of God is necessary for your spiritual well-being. In other words, as much attention as you give to your three meals a day, you ought to give that much attention to the Word of God, and on a daily basis. As your natural food is necessary, so must be your spiritual food.

Everything that one wants to know about God is found in the Bible. God has expended much time and energy over many years giving us His Word. He did it for our benefit, as should be obvious. However, He isn't going to inject that information into us. If we want to know God, to understand Him, and to live for Him, in other words, to live completely in harmony with Him, we must read the instruction book, actually to study it, which is the Word of God.

When you were born as a little baby, someone poured milk into your system, and if they had not done so, you would have weakened and soon died. Nothing flourishes and grows without nourishment. And today, as a new-born (spiritually speaking), you must have nourishment if you are to stay alive spiritually, and flourish, and eventually grow into a mature person of strength and power in the Lord.

The Holy Bible is that nourishment. It is wonderfully conceived to afford both milk to the newborn, and meat to the more advanced.

God in His Infinite Wisdom designed one Book capable of astounding and delighting the newest convert, while absorbing and stimulating the most seasoned Believer in Christ. It is truly, of all things in this world, *"all things to all men."*

The Psalmist said, *"Thy Word is a Lamp unto my feet, and a Light unto my path"* (Ps. 119:105).

In fact, the Word of God is the only true Light and the only true Lamp that's in the world today.

You should start studying the Bible, beginning with Genesis and read it all the way through, exactly as you would read any other Book. Admittedly, there are some things difficult to understand, especially for one who has just given his heart to the Lord; however, if you will ask the Lord to help you understand His Word, He will surely do so. The Psalmist also said, *"I have not departed from Thy Judgments: for Thou hast taught me"* (Ps. 119:102).

As we've already stated, you now have the Holy Spirit living in your heart and life, and He will teach you how to understand the Word if you will only ask for His help.

SOME THINGS THAT WILL HELP YOU

I am going to encourage you to avail yourself of the opportunity of securing our *Commentaries* written on the Bible, which will help you understand the Word of God, and as well, to secure our Cassette Teaching Series, which are available on almost every subject in the Word of God.

If you will write for a catalog, we will send you one instantly, which will give you all the information you need respecting these various different Bible Study Helps.

YOUR PRAYER LIFE

From the moment you accepted Christ as your Saviour, your life has been changed. You have experienced a joy and peace which the cares of the world cannot take away. This *"blessed assurance"* was given to you as a free gift from God. Without doubt, you feel the compulsion to thank Him for what He has done for you. It is completely fitting that you should feel this way.

In order to properly thank Him, which we should do constantly, we must develop a daily prayer life — exactly as we develop a daily time of Bible Study.

Prayer is communication with God. It is for the following:

1. Praise: As stated, we should praise the Lord, which means to thank Him for what He has done for us. The more we live for the Lord, the more we will realize the worth of our Salvation, and the more we will want to thank Him for that.

2. Communion: Prayer is one of the greatest ways to communicate with God. What a blessing to be able to talk directly to your Heavenly Father. As well, during times of prayer, the Lord will also speak to your heart, giving you leading and direction.

3. Petition: We are admonished to ask the Lord for the things that we need. He, as our Heavenly Father, desires to do good things for us. However, we must remember that it is His Will which we seek, and not our personal will. Consequently, all the things we ask Him for, and we should readily ask Him for whatever it is we need, should always be done with the idea in mind, that we want His Will and not ours. Please read the following Scriptures carefully (Mat. 18:18-19; Mk. 11:24; Lk. 11:9-10; Jn. 14:13-14; 15:7).

THE BAPTISM WITH
THE HOLY SPIRIT

Now that you are saved, you should ask the Lord to baptize you with the Holy Spirit (Acts 2:4).

While it is certainly true that the Holy Spirit came into your heart and life the moment of your Salvation, still, He now wishes to endue you with power from on high. Consequently, Jesus told all of His followers immediately before His Ascension, that they should *"wait for the Promise of the Father"* (Acts 1:4). He was speaking of being *"Baptized with the Holy Spirit"* (Acts 1:5).

You must understand that there is a great difference in being *"born of the Spirit"* than being *"Baptized with the Spirit."* They are two different works altogether.

To be *"born of the Spirit"* is that which took place at your conversion, as the Holy Spirit brought you to Christ and performed the work of regeneration within your heart and life. To be *"Baptized with the Spirit"* is in order that you may have Power with God (Acts 1:8). Every Believer should ask the Lord to fill them with the Holy Spirit, and expect to receive (Lk. 11:13).

THE SIGN OF BEING FILLED WITH THE SPIRIT

Once one is Baptized with the Holy Spirit, many things will transpire in our heart and life. In other words, there will be many tell-tale signs that we have been filled.

However, the initial physical evidence that one has been Baptized with the Holy Spirit, is that they will speak with other Tongues as the Spirit of God gives the utterance (Acts 2:4; 10:45-46; 19:1-7).

There is nothing in the Bible which suggests that this awesome indwelling power of the Holy Spirit has been declared unavailable in our day. We know there are literally millions of committed, fruitful, effective Christians, who give all the credit for their effectiveness to the experience of having been Baptized with the Holy Spirit, with the evidence of speaking with other Tongues. In fact, for you to be what you ought to be in Christ, the Baptism with the Holy Spirit is an absolute necessity.

Jesus died on Calvary that men may be saved. The great Salvation process includes the Holy Spirit taking up abode within our hearts and lives. Every Christian needs Him desperately. And to be sure, His full potential cannot be realized, unless we go on and be Baptized with the Holy Spirit, which as stated, will *always* be accompanied by the speaking with other Tongues as the Spirit of God gives the utterance (Acts 2:4).

He is our *"Helper,"* and as well, *"guides us into all Truth"* (Jn. 16:7-15).

WATER BAPTISM

What is the significance of Water Baptism? Haven't we, by confessing Christ with our mouths, done everything the Bible tells us to do to insure Salvation? Is there any reason we should go further in proving the fact of our conversion? In Truth, there are several reasons for Water Baptism.

First of all, Jesus set the example for us by being baptized in water. He did it to *"fulfill all Righteousness"* (Mat. 3:13-15).

Water Baptism signifies the Death, Burial, and Resurrection of the Lord Jesus Christ. Hence, when He was Baptized in water, this signified that which He would do in order to secure our Salvation.

We likewise are to be Baptized in water, as a public proclamation of our submission to God, and acceptance of the Lord Jesus Christ, as our Savior. Water Baptism does not save us, or contribute anything toward our Salvation, but is rather a sign that we have already been saved, which we wish to declare to the entirety of the world. In fact, Water Baptism is the great symbol that one has given his heart and life to Jesus Christ.

As well, it typifies our death to the old life, with all that was ugly and ungodly being buried, and us being Resurrected into a new life in Christ Jesus. That's the reason that Water Baptism is by emersion. It signifies the old man being buried, and the new man being raised in newness of life (Rom. 6:4).

THE WILL OF GOD FOR YOUR LIFE

Now that you have become a Child of God, the Lord has a perfect Will for your life. In other words, you are very important in the Kingdom of God, and the Lord will treat you accordingly.

Inasmuch as you have given your heart and life to Him, He will now open up the Kingdom of God to you, and your place in that Kingdom (Jn. 3:3). In fact, one of the great works of the Holy Spirit in your heart and life, is to bring about *"the Will of God"* for you (Rom. 8:27).

In other words, the idea is that your will be swallowed up in the Will of God, which is the most wonderful, fulfilling life there could ever be.

If you will allow the Holy Spirit to have His Way within your life, He will bring about the Will of God, and help you to walk in that Will, doing what the Lord wants you to do.

Actually, the Lord has a perfect Will for every Believer and that means you. What He has for you, cannot be done by anyone else. So you are to seek the Will of God, and you will find beautifully and wondrously, the Holy Spirit making Jesus more and more real in your heart, and bringing you to the place in which God desires that you be.

Isn't that wonderful to have such help, and above all, to have such leading and guidance (Jn. 16:13-15).

FAITH IN THE CROSS OF CHRIST

As a new Believer you were saved by putting your Faith in Christ and what He did by

paying the price for your Redemption on the Cross (Jn. 3:16).

However, not only is Faith in the Cross necessary for Salvation, it is necessary, as well, that you continue to have Faith in the Cross even on a daily basis, which will guarantee you Victory in your everyday life. This is the answer for Victory over cigarettes, alcohol, drugs, uncontrollable temper, depression, gambling, jealousy, envy, greed, every type of immorality, and in fact, every problem that besets humanity (I Cor. 2:2).

As the Believer constantly exhibits Faith in the Cross and should do so forever, the Holy Spirit then provides all the help necessary, in order for Victory to be had in every capacity (Jn. 14:16-17). In fact, there is no reason why any Christian should be dominated by any type of sin whatsoever. If Faith in the Cross is exhibited, the Holy Spirit will always guarantee Victory for the Believer. The key is the Cross, because it is through the Cross that the Holy Spirit works (Gal. 6:14).

CHURCH ATTENDANCE

The Church is the Body of Christ, not a particular building by the side of the road. Actually you are now a part of that Body, and Jesus Christ is its Head. So, if at all possible, it is very important that you find a good Church to attend.

The following is what should be taught and preached in the Church:

1. Salvation through the Blood of Jesus Christ should be preached. Any Church teaching Salvation by any means other than the shed Blood of Jesus Christ, in other words, what the Lord did on Calvary's Cross, in order to redeem humanity, is promoting something contrary to the Word of God (Mat. 26:28; Acts 20:28; Col. 1:20; Heb. 9:22; I Pet. 1:18-19).

2. The Church should teach the Baptism with the Holy Spirit, with the evidence of speaking with other Tongues, which is available to all Believers, and is received after conversion (Isa. 28:11-12; Acts 2:4; 10:45-46; 19:6; I Cor. 14:4-5, 14-18).

3. A victorious, overcoming Christian life should be preached (Rom. 6:11; I Cor. 15:57-58; Eph. 6:10-13; James 1:22; I Jn. 5:4-5; Rev. 2:7). This means victory over sin in every capacity.

4. Divine Healing according to the Word of God should be preached (Ex. 15:26; 23:25; Isa. 53:5; Mk. 6:13; James 5:14-15; I Pet. 2:24).

We believe that the Bible teaches that Jesus Christ heals today, the same as He did in Bible days.

5. The Rapture of the Church should be taught and preached. This refers to the time when the Church shall be taken out of this world in order to be with the Lord. It could happen at any moment, with every single Believer whether dead or alive, being resurrected. In fact, the Resurrection and the Rapture are one and the same (I Cor. Chpt. 15; I Thess. 4:13-17).

6. The soon and eminent return of our Lord to Earth, to take up His rightful position as King of kings and Lord of lords should be preached. He will be accompanied at that time by every Saint of God who has ever lived. In other words, all who were taken up in the Rapture (Resurrection), will then come back with Him to this Earth, which will begin the Kingdom Age (Rev. Chpt. 19).

7. Whatever Church is attended, should be a Church filled with a group of people, whether the number is little or large, with the consuming desire to take the Gospel of Jesus Christ to the entirety of the world. The taking of the Gospel to all is priority with God, as should be obvious.

Someone brought you the Gospel, and you should love the Lord enough, to desire strongly that everyone else have the opportunity to hear exactly as you did. Whether they except or not, is their privilege; however, that they have the opportunity is absolutely paramount.

To be frank, the greatest way we can thank the Lord for giving us His Great Salvation, is to tell this grand story to others in whatever way we can, and as well, to help support those who are taking the Gospel to the world. That must be our consuming desire in all things (Mk. 16:15-16).

"For God so loved the world that He gave His only begotten Son, that whosoever believeth in Him should not perish, but have everlasting life" (Jn. 3:16).

THE HOLY SPIRIT BAPTISM

The following will help as it regards the Baptism with the Holy Spirit.

1. A person must accept Jesus Christ as Savior before he can experience the Baptism with the Holy Spirit. (Jn. 14:17)

2. The Baptism with the Holy Spirit is an experience separate and apart from the initial Salvation experience, and is always received after one is saved. After the individual is saved, he is to ask the Lord to baptize him with the Spirit. (Lk. 11:13)

3. We cannot merit or deserve the Baptism with the Holy Spirit. It is a gift. Peter spoke of receiving the Gift of the Holy Spirit (Acts 2:38). Jesus said: "If you then, being evil, know how to give good gifts unto your children: how much more shall your Heavenly Father give the Holy Spirit to them who ask Him?" (Lk. 11:13)

4. All Believers are commanded by Christ to receive. (Acts 1:4-5)

5. When one is Baptized with the Spirit, always and without exception, he will speak with other tongues as the Spirit of God gives the utterance. There are no exceptions to this. In fact, speaking with other tongues is the initial, physical evidence, that one has been Baptized with the Holy Spirit. (Acts 2:4; 10:44-46; 11:15-17; 19:2, 6; I Cor. 14:39)

6. The recipient of the Holy Spirit will then find that worshiping and praying in tongues will become a part of his devotion to God, and will be greatly restful and refreshing. (Isa. 28:12; I Cor. 14:4)

7. The Holy Spirit Baptism is for all. Anyone and everyone who is saved should be Baptized with the Spirit. There are no exceptions. (Joel 2:28-29)

8. After you have been baptized with the Holy Spirit, you are to understand that the Spirit works within you according to your Faith in the Cross of Christ. In other words, what Jesus did at the Cross provides the parameters in which the Holy Spirit works; consequently, you as a Believer, are to register Faith in the Cross of Christ at all times, which gives the Holy Spirit latitude within your life. (Rom. 8:1-2)

SCRIPTURES ON THE HOLY SPIRIT BAPTISM

"For with stammering lips and another tongue will he speak to this people. To whom he said, This is the rest wherewith ye may cause the weary to rest; and this is the refreshing." (Isa. 28:11-12)

"I indeed baptize you with water unto repentance: but he that cometh after me is mightier than I, whose shoes I am not worthy to bear: he shall baptize you with the Holy Ghost, and with fire." (Mat. 3:11)

"For John truly baptized with water; but ye shall be baptized with the Holy Ghost not many days hence." (Acts 1:5)

"And they were all filled with the Holy Ghost, and began to speak with other tongues, as the Spirit gave them utterance." (Acts 2:4)

"Now when the apostles which were at Jerusalem heard that Samaria had received the word of God, they sent unto them Peter and John: Who, when they were come down, prayed for them, that they might receive the Holy Ghost: (For as yet he was fallen upon none of them: only they were baptized in the name of the Lord Jesus.) Then laid they their hands on them, and they received the Holy Ghost." (Acts 8:14-17)

"While Peter yet spake these words, the Holy Ghost fell on all them which heard the word.

And they of the circumcision which believed were astonished, as many as came with Peter, because that on the Gentiles also was poured out the gift of the Holy Ghost. For they heard them speak with tongues, and magnify God."
(Acts 10:44-46)

"And as I began to speak, the Holy Ghost fell on them, as on us at the beginning. Then remembered I the word of the Lord, how that he said, John indeed baptized with water; but ye shall be baptized with the Holy Ghost. Forasmuch then as God gave them the like gift as he did unto us, who believed on the Lord Jesus Christ; what was I, that I could withstand God?"
(Acts 11:15-17)

"He said unto them, Have ye received the Holy Ghost since ye believed? And they said unto him, We have not so much as heard whether there be any Holy Ghost. And when Paul had laid his hands upon them, the Holy Ghost came on them; and they spake with tongues, and prophesied."
(Acts 19:2, 6)

"Wherefore, brethren, covet to prophesy, and forbid not to speak with tongues."
(I Cor. 14:39)

"But ye, beloved, building up yourselves on your most holy faith, praying in the Holy Ghost."
(Jude vs. 20)

THE CROSS, YOUR FAITH, AND THE HOLY SPIRIT

As the Word of God bears it out throughout its entirety, God has provided only one solution for sinful, hurting humanity. That solution is *"Jesus Christ and Him Crucified"* (Jn. 3:16; I Cor. 1:18, 23; 2:2; Col. 2:14-15). The Cross is the means, and the only means, by which the sinner can be saved, and as well, the only means by which the Christian can walk in victory.

Most of the Church readily understands the Cross as it regards the initial Salvation experience, but has little knowledge whatsoever as it regards the part the Cross plays in the victory of the Saint.

For lack of space I will have to be brief; however, the following information will be helpful:

THE CROSS

In the preceding article, I have dealt with Salvation for the sinner, so I will devote this section entirely to the solution of problems which all Christians face at one time or the other.

Every Christian must understand, that every single problem that faces humanity, was addressed by Jesus at the Cross (Col. 2:14-15). This means that for every problem, the Christian should be directed to the Cross. He must understand that the solution is found there, and found only there.

The Lord gave to the Apostle Paul the meaning of the New Covenant, which pertains to what Jesus did for us at the Cross. So in effect, the meaning of the New Covenant is the meaning of the Cross.

In Romans Chapter 6, we are told as it regards the crucifixion of Christ, Who incidentally suffered as our Substitute, that we actually died with Him in His Crucifixion, were buried with Him, and were raised with Him in *"newness of life"* (Rom. 6:3-5). Of course we were not there as is obvious; however, upon faith being evidenced in Christ when we were initially saved, in the Mind of God, this is actually what happened. We were literally *"baptized into His death"* (Rom. 6:3). No, this is not speaking of Water Baptism, which is actually a symbol of this of which we speak, but rather the actual Crucifixion of Christ.

After becoming a Christian, all the days of our lives, we are to continue to look to the Cross as the source of all victory. Actually, the very meaning of the crucifixion pertains to something that happened in the distant past, but which has continuing results, and in fact, results which will never be discontinued.

We are not speaking of putting Jesus back on a Cross, or us getting on a Cross either. In fact, Jesus is now seated by the Right Hand of the Father, and in spirit, we are actually seated with Him (Eph. 2:6; Heb. 1:3).

We are speaking of the Believer continuing to receive the benefits of the Cross, and to do so forever (Heb. 13:20).

So the Believer is to understand, that the Source of all that he needs, is found entirely in the Cross, and only in the Cross. Unfortunately, most Christians haven't been taught this, and they look elsewhere for help. Let the Reader understand, that when we think of Christ we are not to think of Him apart from the Cross. That's why Paul kept using the phrase *"in Christ,"* or one of its derivatives such as *"in Him,"* over and over. The phrase refers to what Jesus did at the Cross.

Unfortunately, many Christians are not actually serving the Jesus Christ of the Bible, but rather *"another Jesus."* This refers to the fact that they are looking to a Jesus other than the Cross. Hence Paul said: *"For if he that cometh preacheth another Jesus, Whom we have not preached, or if you receive another spirit, which ye have not received, or another gospel, which ye have not accepted, ye might well bear with him"* (II Cor. 11:4). Let the Reader understand, that if it's not Jesus and Him Crucified, then pure and simple it's *"another Jesus,"* who is projected by *"another spirit,"* which means it's not the Holy Spirit, which amounts to *"another gospel."*

The Gospel of Christ is *"Jesus Christ and Him Crucified"* (I Cor. 2:2).

That's why Paul also said: *"But God forbid that I should glory* (boast), *save in the Cross of our Lord Jesus Christ, by Whom the world is crucified unto me, and I unto the world"* (Gal. 6:14).

FAITH

Understanding what we've just said, the Cross of Christ must always and without exception, be the object of faith as it regards the Child of God. This is very, very important! Paul devoted the entirety of Chapters 4 and 5 of Romans to this principle. He said:

"Who (Christ) *was delivered* (the Crucifixion) *for our offences . . . by Whom also we have access by faith into this Grace"* (Rom. 4:25-5:2).

While it is Faith that God always honors, and every Christian understands that, even more particularly, it is Faith in the Cross. This is the only type of faith that God will honor.

The reasons that most Christians get into trouble in some way, is because they do not understand the Cross as the source of all their needs being met, and that they must ever have faith in this Finished Work of Christ. That's why Paul also said:

"For by grace are ye saved through faith; and that not of yourselves: it is the Gift of God: not of works, lest any man should boast" (Eph. 2:8-9).

As we were saved by faith, we are kept by faith; however, Paul is speaking of Faith in the Cross of Christ, and Faith in the Cross exclusively (Eph. 2:13).

THE HOLY SPIRIT

The Believer must understand, that the power of sin is so great, that no individual on earth, even the strongest Christian can overcome this monster within his own strength and ability. It simply cannot be done. In fact, sin is so bad, that Jesus had to go to the Cross to answer this dilemma.

So, in order to overcome sin, we have to have the power of the Holy Spirit.

While it is true that every single Believer has the Holy Spirit, and more particularly, all Believers should as well, be Baptized with the Holy Spirit, which gives even more power; still, the work of the Holy Spirit within our hearts and lives is not automatic. Let's first of all look at how He works.

The Spirit of God doesn't demand much of us, but He does demand that we have Faith in the Cross of Christ (Jn. 16:13-14). Listen to what Paul said:

"For the Law (this is a law by which the Spirit works) *of the Spirit* (Holy Spirit) *of Life* (the Holy Spirit guarantees all the life that comes from Christ as a result of the Cross) *in Christ Jesus* (what Jesus did at the Cross) *has made me free from the law of sin and death"* (Rom. 8:2).

The reason that the Christian is in trouble in the first place, is because he doesn't understand how the Spirit works. He needs the Spirit's help, and needs it greatly; however, if we evidence faith in anything else other than the Cross of Christ as it regards our victory, the Holy Spirit simply will not help us. In fact, that is *"the law."*

If we function within this *"law,"* which is actually *"the Law of the Spirit of Life in Christ Jesus,"* which refers to what Christ did at the Cross, which means that the Cross must ever be the object of our Faith, then we will walk in victory.

In Romans Chapter 8 and elsewhere, Paul constantly mentions *"the flesh."* What is he talking about?

He is speaking of the Christian's ability and strength outside of the Holy Spirit. He is in effect saying, if we try to live this life by trusting in our own strength, i.e., *"the flesh,"* we will fail and fail every time. Actually that's what he means by *"walking after the flesh"* (Rom. 8:1). To make it simpler, walking after the flesh is trusting in anything other than the Cross of Christ.

"Walking after the Spirit," is placing our faith and trust in the Cross of Christ (Rom. 8:1-2).

VICTORY AND RESTORATION

If the Christian is having problems in any capacity as it regards the world, the flesh, and the Devil, he is to be pointed toward the Cross, making the Cross the object of his faith, which will insure the help of the Holy Spirit.

If the Christian has failed miserably, which requires restoration, he is to be told why he failed, which means that he placed his faith in something else other than the Cross, which then means he was attempting to live this Christian life only by his own efforts and strength, which are always woefully insufficient.

He is to then be told that everything he needs is in the Cross, and he must get his Faith

back in the Cross, which will insure the help of the Holy Spirit. This is true, Biblical restoration (Gal. 6:1-2).

For a complete treatment of this all-important subject, please see our Commentaries on Romans, Galatians, Ephesians, Philippians, and Colossians.

"For sin shall not have dominion over you: for you are not under the Law, but under Grace" (Rom. 6:14).

SCRIPTURES FOR SALVATION

Luke 19:10
John 1:12
John 3:3
John 3:16
John 8:32
John 10:9-10
John 14:6
Acts 16:31
Romans 3:23-24

Romans 5:8
Romans 6:23
Romans 10:9-10
Ephesians 2:8-9
Hebrews 2:3
Hebrews 12:2
I John 1:9
I John 5:11-12
Revelation 3:20

The Ancient World
at the Time of the Patriarchs

→ Route of Abraham and the Patriarchs
   (Early 2nd Millennium B.C.)

── Areas of influence of major
   powers about 1350 B.C.

© Copyright HAMMOND INCORPORATED, Maplewood, N.J.

Caspian Sea

Persian Gulf
(Lower Sea)

Dilmun?

MEDIA

Tepe Giyan

ELAM

Susa

Cyrus

Araxes

Mt. Ararat

L. Urmia

ZAGROS

GUTIUM

MOUNTAINS

KASSITES

Ecbatana

URARTU

L. Van

HURRIAN
(HORITES)

Tepe
Gawra

Arbela

Nuzi

ASSYRIA

Nineveh

Calah

Asshur

Tell
Brak

Tigris

Eshnunna

Akkad

Agade?

Sippar

Cuthah

Babylon

Nippur

Isin

Larsa

Sumer

Erech

Lagash

Ur

Eridu

BABYLONIA

Euphrates

Mari

Tadmor

MITANNI

Haran

Paddan-
aram

Tell
Halaf

Malatya

KASHKA

Halys

Sangarius

HITTITE
EMPIRE
(HATTI)

Hattusas

Alaca Huyuk

Ankuwa

Kanish

Mersin

L. Tuz

TAURUS MOUNTAINS

Kizzuwatna

Carchemish

Alalakh

Halab

Ebla

Hamath

Kadesh

Ugarit

ARZAWA

Beycesultan

Kaya

Maeander

LUKKA

Sardis

Troy

ASSUWA

Hermes

Rhodes

MINOAN-MYCENAEAN
DOMAIN

CAPHTOR
(Crete)

Cnossus

Mediterranean Sea
(Great or Upper Sea)

ALASHIYA
KITTIM
(Cyprus)

Arvad

Gebal

Sidon

Tyre

Dor

Megiddo

Joppa

Gaza

Damascus

Hazor

Shechem

Jericho

Jerusalem

Hebron

Beer-sheba

Kadesh-barnea

KEDAR

Dumah

MIDIAN

Tema

Dedan

CANAAN

Avaris
(Zoan)

Lower
Egypt

Memphis
(Noph)

On

Heracleopolis

Hermopolis

Akhetaton
(Tell el-Amarna)

Abydos

Nile

EGYPT

Sinai

Red Sea

Libyan Desert

250Mls

200

150

100

50

0

400Kms

300

200

100

0

Physical Map of Palestine

0   10   20   30   40 Mls
0   20   40   60 Kms

© Copyright HAMMOND INCORPORATED, Maplewood, N.J.

Elevations are given in feet

Sidon

MT. LEBANON

Abana

Damascus

MT. HERMON
9,232

Pharpar

PHOENICIA

Leontes

Tyre

Dan

UPPER
GALILEE

Lake Hula
(L. Semechonitis)

BASHAN

Hauran

Acco

Mt. Meron
3,963

LOWER
GALILEE

-696   Sea of Galilee
(Chinnereth)

Mt. Carmel
1,791   Kishon   Nazareth   Mt. Tabor
1,929

Plain
of

Yarmuk

GILEAD

Dor

Megiddo

Esdrae-
lon   V. of Jezreel

Hill of
Moreh

Mt. Gilboa
1,640   Beth-shan

Caesarea

Dothan

Jabbok

(Zarqa)

The Great Sea
(Mediterranean Sea)

SAMARIA

Plain of Sharon

Samaria   Mt. Ebal
3,083

Mt. Gerizim   Shechem
2,890

Jebel Yusha
3,652

Kanah

Farah

Jordan

AMMON

Joppa

Shiloh

Aijalon

Tell Azur
3,333

Rabbah
(Amman)

Sorek

Bethel

Jericho

Plains of
Moab   Mt. Nebo
2,631

Jerusalem   Mt. of Olives
2,670

Elah

Bethlehem

Gaza

Plain of Philistia

Shephelah

3,346

Hebron

Wilderness of Judea

JUDEA

Dead
(Salt)
Sea
-1,296

Arnon   (W. al Mawjib)

MOAB

Gerar

Besor

Raphia

Beer-sheba

Kir-hareseth

IDUMEA

Zered

Arabah

EDOM

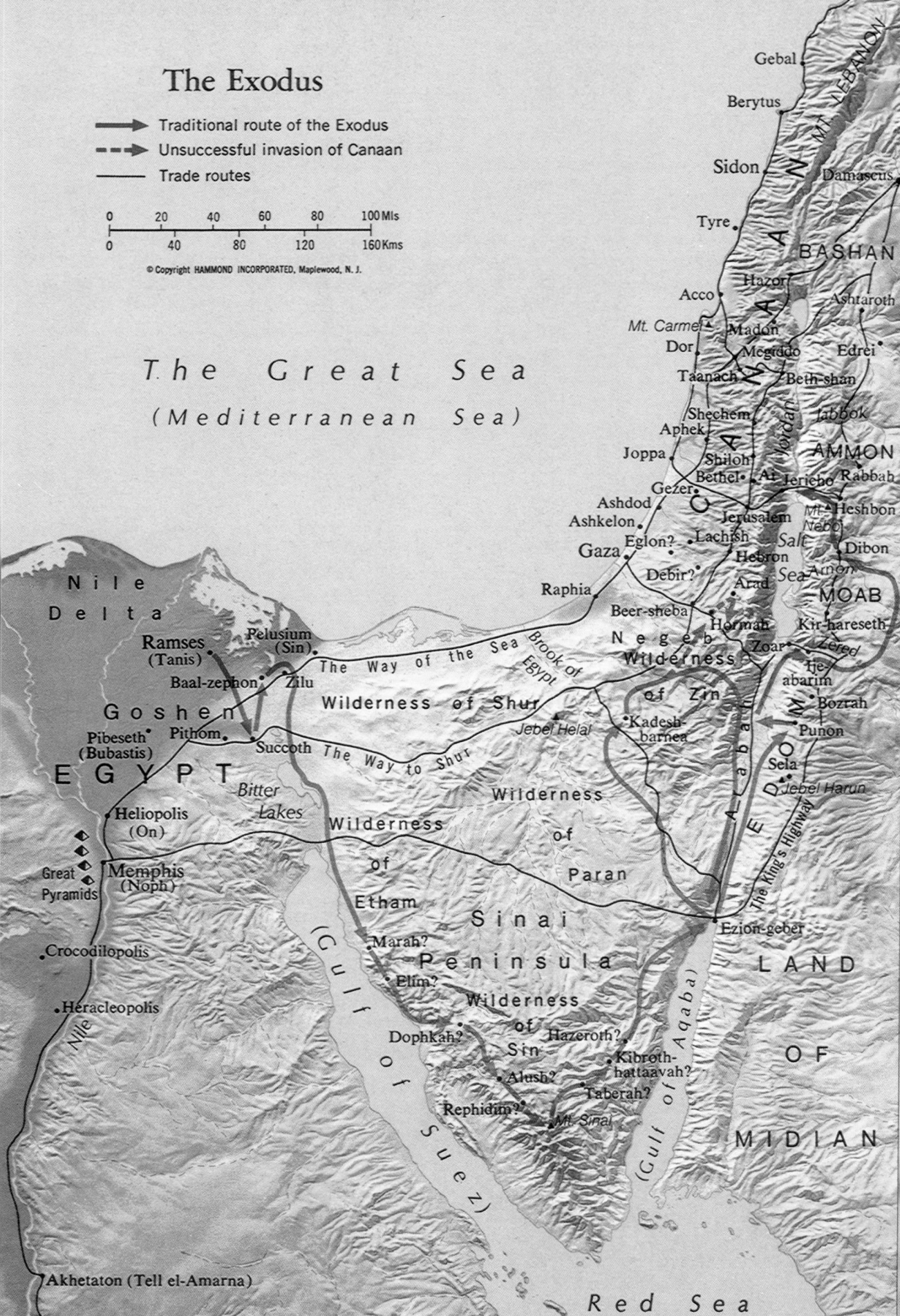

The Exodus

→ Traditional route of the Exodus
⇢ Unsuccessful invasion of Canaan
— Trade routes

| 0 | 20 | 40 | 60 | 80 | 100 Mls |
| 0 | 40 | 80 | 120 | 160 Kms |

© Copyright HAMMOND INCORPORATED, Maplewood, N.J.

The Great Sea
(Mediterranean Sea)

Gebal
Berytus
Sidon
Tyre
Damascus
BASHAN
Acco
Hazor
Ashtaroth
Mt. Carmel
Madon
Dor
Megiddo
Edrei
Taanach
Beth-shan
Shechem
Jabbok
Aphek
AMMON
Joppa
Shiloh
Rabbah
Bethel
Ai Jericho
Gezer
Ashdod
Jerusalem
Mt. Heshbon
Ashkelon
Nebo
Gaza
Eglon?
Lachish
Salt
Dibon
Hebron
Sea
Amon
Raphia
Debir?
Arad
MOAB
Beer-sheba
Hormah
Kir-hareseth
Negeb
Zoar
Zered
Wilderness
Ije-
abarim
Bozrah
of Zin
Punon
Sela
Jebel Harun

Nile
Delta
Ramses
(Tanis)
Pelusium
(Sin)
The Way of the Sea
Brook of Egypt
Baal-zephon
Zilu
Wilderness of Shur
Goshen
Pithom
Kadesh-barnea
Jebel Helal
Pibeseth
(Bubastis)
Succoth
The Way to Shur
EGYPT
Bitter
Lakes
Wilderness
Heliopolis
(On)
of
Wilderness
Etham
of
Great
Paran
Memphis
(Noph)
Pyramids
Sinai
Crocodilopolis
Marah?
Peninsula
Ezion-geber
LAND
Elim?
Heracleopolis
Wilderness
OF
of
Dophkah?
Sin
Hazeroth?
Alush?
Kibroth-
hattaavah?
Nile
Rephidim?
Taberah?
MIDIAN
Mt. Sinai

(Gulf of Suez)
(Gulf of Aqaba)

Akhetaton (Tell el-Amarna)

Red Sea

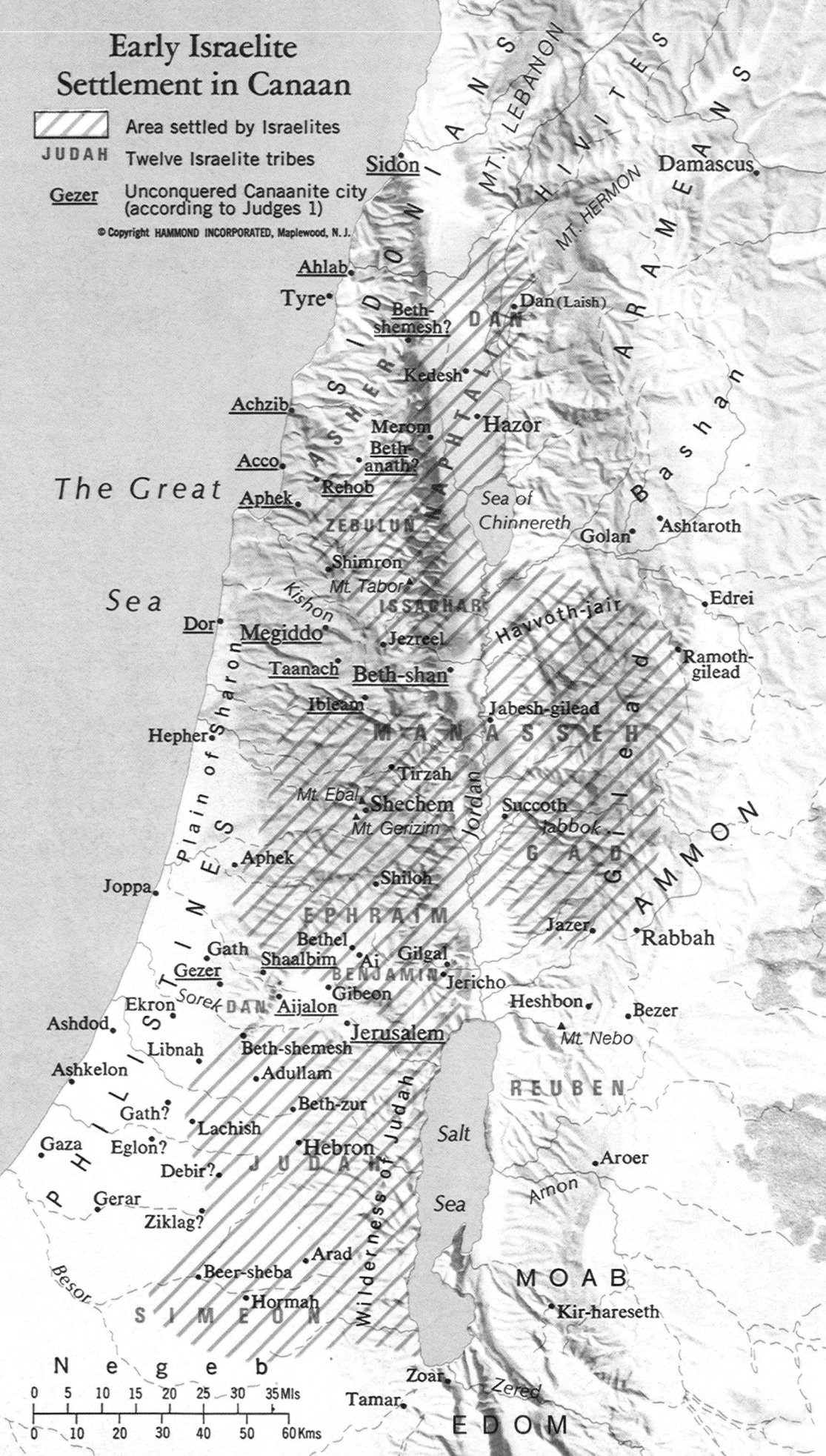

Early Israelite
Settlement in Canaan

Area settled by Israelites

JUDAH Twelve Israelite tribes

Gezer Unconquered Canaanite city
(according to Judges 1)

© Copyright HAMMOND INCORPORATED, Maplewood, N.J.

SIDONIANS

MT. LEBANON

HIVITES

MT. HERMON

ARAMEANS

Damascus

Sidon

Ahlab

Tyre

Beth-
shemesh?

DAN

Dan (Laish)

Kedesh

Achzib

Merom

Hazor

ASHER

Beth-
anath?

Acco

Rehob

Aphek

NAPHTALI

ZEBULUN

Sea of
Chinnereth

Bashan

Golan

Ashtaroth

The Great

Shimron

Mt. Tabor

ISSACHAR

Havvoth-jair

Edrei

Sea

Kishon

Dor

Megiddo

Jezreel

Ramoth-
gilead

Taanach

Beth-shan

Gilead

Ibleam

Jabesh-gilead

MANASSEH

Hepher

Tirzah

AMMON

Mt. Ebal

Shechem

Succoth

Jordan

Jabbok

Mt. Gerizim

GAD

Plain of Sharon

Aphek

Shiloh

Joppa

EPHRAIM

Jazer

Rabbah

Bethel

Gath

Ai

Gilgal

Shaalbim

BENJAMIN

Gezer

Gibeon

Jericho

Ekron

Sorek

DAN

Aijalon

Heshbon

Bezer

Ashdod

Jerusalem

Mt. Nebo

Libnah

Beth-shemesh

Ashkelon

Adullam

REUBEN

Gath?

Beth-zur

Salt

Lachish

Eglon?

Hebron

Sea

Aroer

Gaza

Debir?

JUDAH

Wilderness of Judah

Gerar

Arnon

Ziklag?

Arad

PHILISTINES

Besor

Beer-sheba

MOAB

Hormah

SIMEON

Kir-hareseth

N e g e b

Zoar

Zered

Tamar

EDOM

0 5 10 15 20 25 30 35 Mls

0   10   20   30   40   50   60 Kms

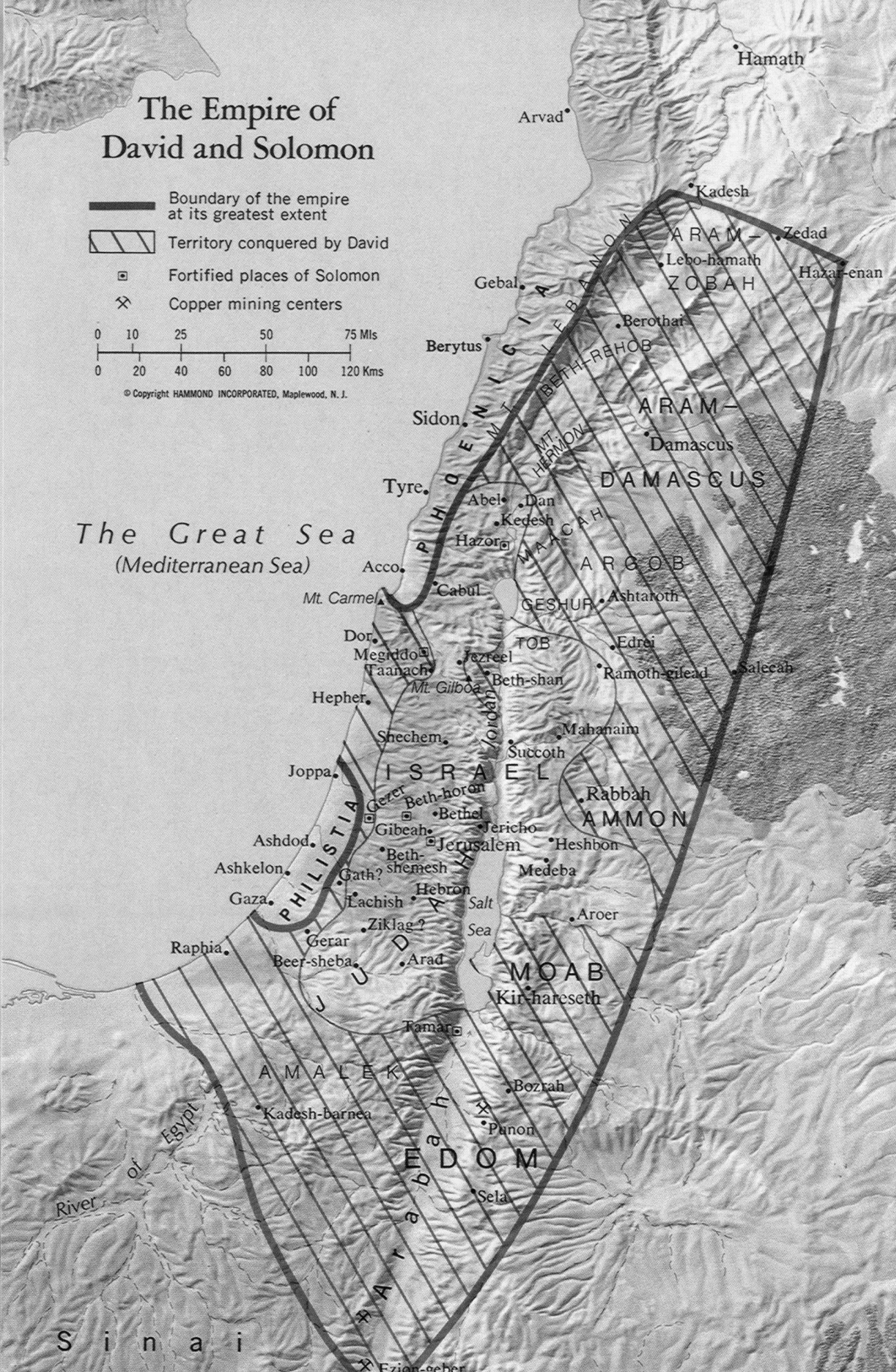

The Empire of David and Solomon

Boundary of the empire at its greatest extent

Territory conquered by David

Fortified places of Solomon

Copper mining centers

0   10   25   50   75 Mls

0   20   40   60   80   100   120 Kms

© Copyright HAMMOND INCORPORATED, Maplewood, N.J.

The Great Sea
(Mediterranean Sea)

Hamath

Arvad

Kadesh

Zedad

ARAM–ZOBAH

Lebo-hamath

Hazar-enan

Gebal

Berothai

BETH-REHOB

Berytus

ARAM–DAMASCUS

Sidon

Damascus

DAMASCUS

Tyre

MT. HERMON

Abel

Dan

Kedesh

MAACAH

Hazor

ARGOB

Acco

Ashtaroth

GESHUR

Cabul

Mt. Carmel

TOB

Edrei

Dor

Megiddo

Jezreel

Salecah

Taanach

Beth-shan

Ramoth-gilead

Mt. Gilboa

Hepher

Mahanaim

Shechem

Succoth

Joppa

ISRAEL

Gezer

Beth-horon

Rabbah

Bethel

AMMON

Gibeah

Jericho

Ashdod

Beth-shemesh

Jerusalem

Heshbon

Ashkelon

Gath?

Medeba

Gaza

Lachish

Hebron

Salt Sea

Ziklag?

Aroer

Raphia

Gerar

JUDAH

Arad

Beer-sheba

MOAB

Kir-hareseth

Tamar

AMALEK

Bozrah

Kadesh-barnea

Punon

River of Egypt

EDOM

Arabah

Sela

Ezion-geber

Sinai

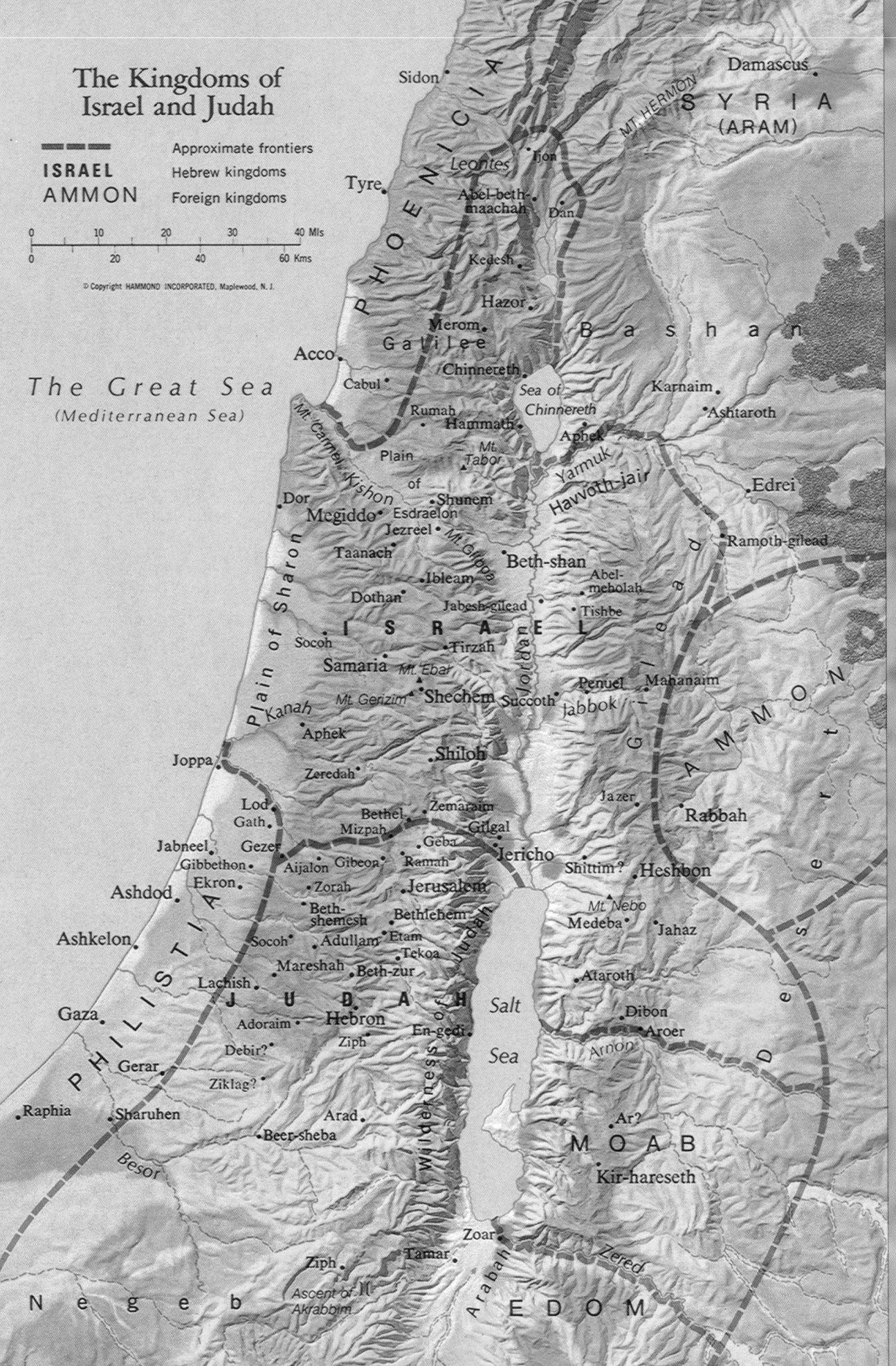

The Kingdoms of Israel and Judah

- - - - Approximate frontiers
ISRAEL Hebrew kingdoms
AMMON Foreign kingdoms

0   10   20   30   40 Mls
0   20   40   60 Kms

© Copyright HAMMOND INCORPORATED, Maplewood, N.J.

The Great Sea
(Mediterranean Sea)

PHOENICIA

Sidon

Damascus

SYRIA
(ARAM)

MT. HERMON

Leontes
Ijon
Abel-beth-maachah
Dan

Tyre

Kedesh

Hazor

Merom
Galilee
Chinnereth

Bashan

Acco
Cabul
Sea of
Chinnereth
Karnaim
Ashtaroth

Rumah
Hammath
Aphek

Plain
of
Mt. Tabor
Shunem
Yarmuk
Havvoth-jair
Edrei

Dor
Mt. Carmel
Kishon
Megiddo
Esdraelon
Jezreel
Mt. Gilboa
Beth-shan
Ramoth-gilead

Taanach
Ibleam
Abel-meholah

Dothan
Jabesh-gilead
Tishbe

Plain of Sharon
Socoh
I   S   R   A   E   L
Tirzah

Samaria
Mt. Ebal
Penuel
Mahanaim

Mt. Gerizim
Shechem
Succoth

Kanah
Jabbok
AMMON

Aphek
Shiloh

Joppa
Zeredah
Jazer

Lod
Bethel
Zemaraim
Rabbah

Gath
Mizpah
Gilgal

Jabneel
Gezer
Geba
Jericho
Shittim?
Heshbon

Gibbethon
Aijalon
Gibeon
Ramah

Ekron
Zorah
Jerusalem

Ashdod
Beth-shemesh
Bethlehem
Mt. Nebo
Medeba
Jahaz

Ashkelon
Socoh
Adullam
Etam
Tekoa
Ataroth

Mareshah
Beth-zur
Salt

Gaza
Lachish
J   U   D   A   H
Dibon
Aroer

Adoraim
Hebron
En-gedi
Sea
Arnon

Gerar
Debir?
Ziph

Ziklag?

Raphia
Sharuhen
Arad
Ar?
MOAB

Besor
Beer-sheba
Kir-hareseth

Zoar

Ziph
Tamar
Zered

N e g e b
Ascent of
Akrabbim
Arabah
EDOM

PHILISTIA

Jordan

Wilderness of Judah

The Assyrian Empire

Assyrian empire — c.824 B.C.

Assyrian empire — c.640 B.C.

Greek colonies underlined in red

0	50	100	150	200	250	300	350 Mis
0	100	200	300	400	500 Kms

© Copyright HAMMOND INCORPORATED, Maplewood, N.J.

Desert

L i b y a

LIBYANS

Cyrene

Upper (Western) Sea

Aegean Sea

GREEK CITY STATES

Abydos
Cyzicus
Astacus
Ancyra
Corinth
Euboea
Chios
Athens
Sardis
Sparta
Miletus
Samos
Lesbos
MESHECH
LYDIA
Phaselis
Crete
Rhodes

PHRYGIA
Gordion
L. Tuz

CIMMERIANS (GOMER)

TAURUS MTS.
CILICIA
Kanish
Tarsus
MESHECH

TUBAL

URARTU (ARARAT)
Mt Ararat
L. Sevan
Turushpa
L. Van
Araxes
Cyrus

Melitene
Samal
Harran
Carchemish
Arpad
Til Barsib
Aleppo
Gozan
Nisibis
Nineveh
Dur Sharrukin
Calah (Nimrud)
Arbela
Asshur

L. Urmia
Manni
MADAI
Ecbatana

Cyprus
Arvad
Sidon
Tyre
PHOENICIA
Qarqar
Hamath
SYRIA
Damascus
Tadmor
Habor
Anat
Euphrates
Tigris
Diyala

EMPIRE

Sippar
Cuthah
Babylon
Borsippa
Nippur
Erech
Ur
Larsa
Susa (Shushan)
CHALDEANS

BABYLON

Cyrene

Memphis
Heracleopolis
to Assyria 671-651 B.C.
Hermopolis
Siut
Abydos
Thebes
Syene

EGYPT
Nile
On
Bubastis
Tanis
Sais
Pelusium
Raphia
Eltekeh
Seta
Samaria
Jerusalem
JUDAH
trib. to Assyria
AMMON
MOAB
EDOM
KEDAR

Oasis of Siwa

R e d S e a

Dedan
Tema
Dumah

A R A B I A (ARABS)

Lower (Eastern) Sea

Caspian Sea

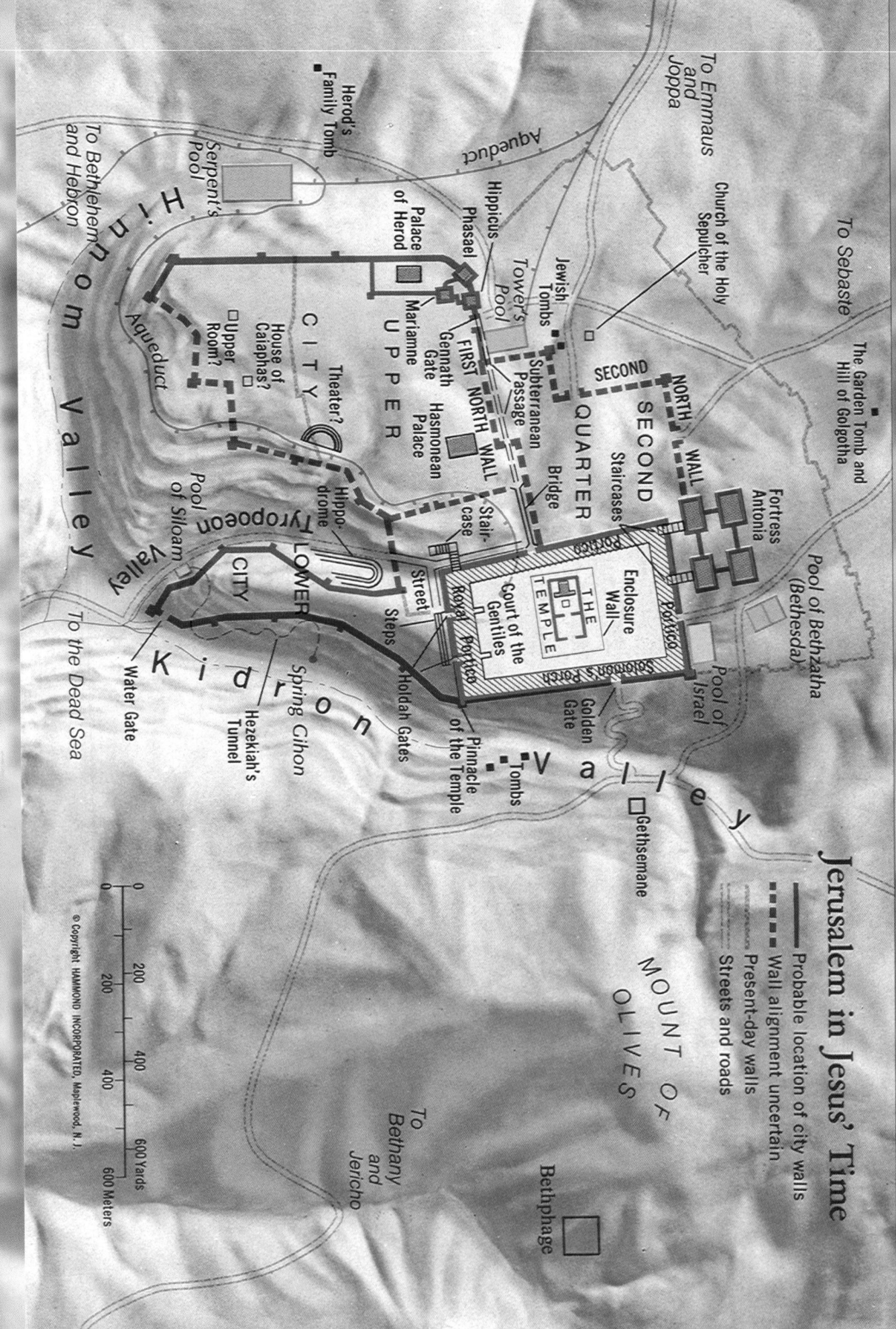

Jerusalem in Jesus' Time

Palestine in
New Testament Times

Political boundaries A.D. 6-44	
Cities of the Decapolis	⊡
Fortresses	✠

Tyre

40 Mis
0 10 20 30

60 Kms
0 20 40

© Copyright HAMMOND INCORPORATED, Maplewood, N.J.

The Roman World

Limits of direct Roman rule or political influence at the birth of Christ

Provincial or state boundaries

SYRIA — Roman provinces

LYCIA — Client kingdoms or states

© Copyright HAMMOND INCORPORATED, Maplewood, N.J.

0 100 200 300 400 500 Mis
0 200 400 600 800 Kms

Atlantic Ocean

Britannia

LUSITANIA Hispania
Emerita Augusta
BAETICA
Corduba
Tingis

TARRACONENSIS
Caesarea Augusta
Tarraco
Burdigala
AQUITANIA

NARBONENSIS
Narbo

LUGDUNENSIS
Lutetia
Lugdunum

G a u l

BELGICA
Augusta Treverorum
Rhine

Germania

Lost to Rome in A.D. 9
Albis (Elbe)

S a r m a t i a

MAURETANIA

Caesarea

SARDINIA AND CORSICA
Caralis

I t a l y
Rubicon
Rome
Tarentum

RAETIA **NORICUM**
Aquileia
Danube
PANNONIA

ILLYRICUM
Salonae

D a c i a

CARPATHIANS

A F R I C A
Carthage
SICILIA
Syracuse
Lepis Magna

M a r e (Mediterranean Sea) I n t e r n u m

Sea of Adria

MACEDONIA
Thessalonica

MOESIA
Ister (Danube)

THRACE
Byzantium

Black Sea

BOSPORUS

KDM.

CYRENAICA
Cyrene

CRETA

Aegean Sea

ACHAIA
Corinth
Athens

ASIA
Ephesus
Pergamum

BITHYNIA & PONTUS
Ancyra
Sinope
Trapezus

CAPPADOCIA

KDM.

EGYPT
Alexandria
Memphis
Thebes
Nile

CYPRUS

LYCIA
PAMPHYLIA
GALATIA
CILICIA
Tarsus

COMMAGENE

ARMENIA
Artaxata

CAUCASUS
Colchis
Iberia
Albania

KDM. OF HEROD
Jerusalem

SYRIA
Antioch

NABATEA

Red Sea

A r a b i a

Euphrates
Tigris

PARTHIAN EMPIRE
Ctesiphon

Caspian Sea

Rha (Volga)

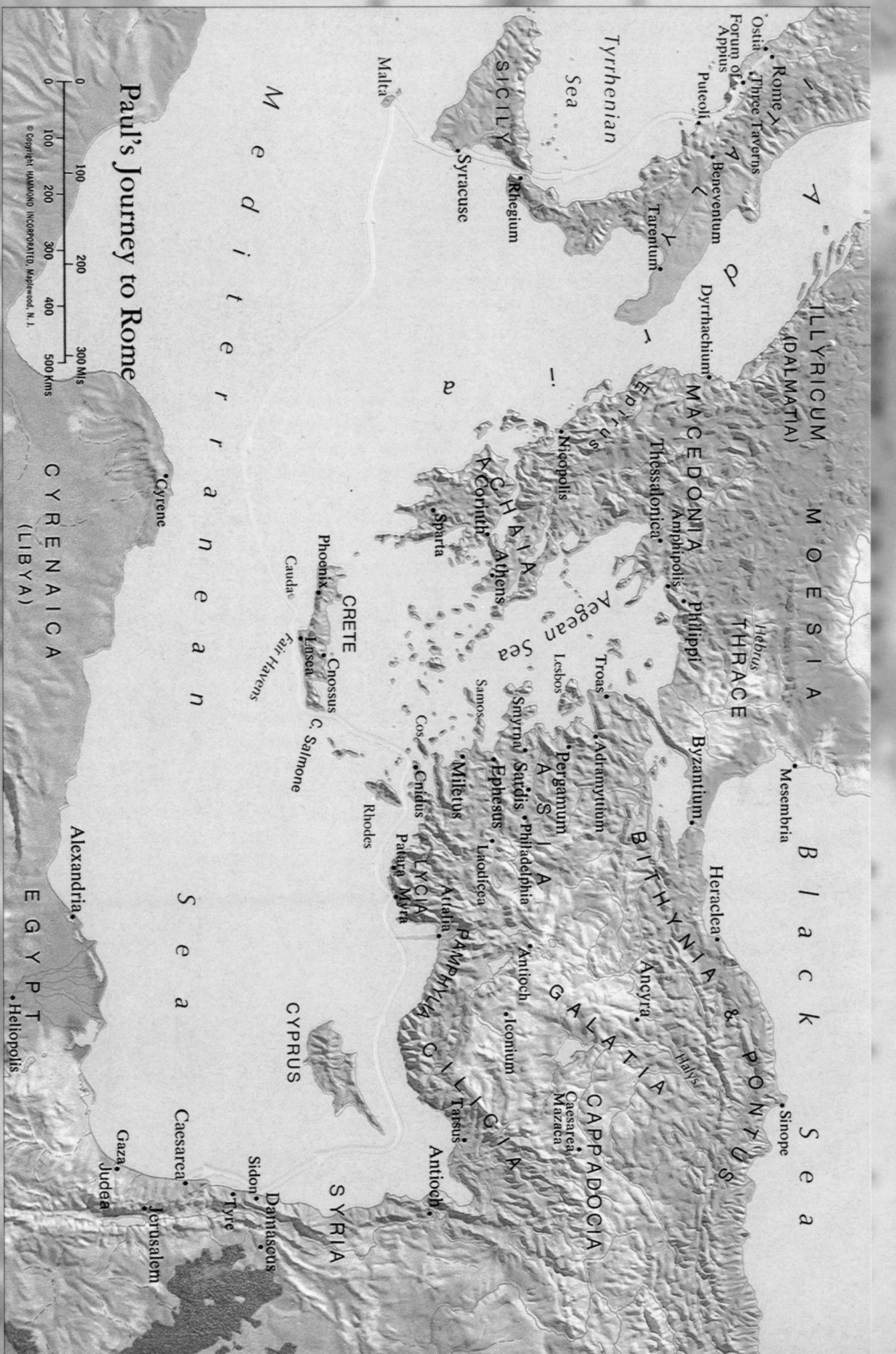

Paul's Journey to Rome

© Copyright HAMMOND INCORPORATED, Maplewood, N.J.

0 100 200 300 400 500 Mis
0 100 200 300 500 Kms

A L P S
ILLYRICUM
(DALMATIA)
M O E S I A
Rome
Ostia
Three Taverns
Forum of Appius
Puteoli
Beneventum
Tyrrhenian Sea
SICILY
Syracuse
Rhegium
Tarentum
Dyrrhachium
MACEDONIA
THRACE
Mesembria
Black Sea
Sinope
Heraclea
Byzantium
BITHYNIA & PONTUS
Ancyra
Halys
CAPPADOCIA
Caesarea Mazaca
GALATIA
Iconium
Antioch
PAMPHYLIA
CILICIA
Tarsus
Antioch
SYRIA
Damascus
Tyre
Sidon
Sidon
Jerusalem
Judea
Gaza
Caesarea
CYPRUS
Rhodes
LYCIA
Patara
Myra
Attalia
Cnidus
Miletus
Cos
Ephesus
Laodicea
Philadelphia
Sardis
Smyrna
Samos
Pergamum
A S I A
Adramyttium
Troas
Lesbos
Aegean Sea
Amphipolis
Thessalonica
Philippi
Nicopolis
Epirus
ACHAIA
Athens
Corinth
Sparta
Mediterranean Sea
Malta
Caudae
Phoenix
CRETE
Lasea
Cnossus
Fair Havens
C. Salmone
CYRENAICA
(LIBYA)
Cyrene
Alexandria
EGYPT
Heliopolis
Caesarea

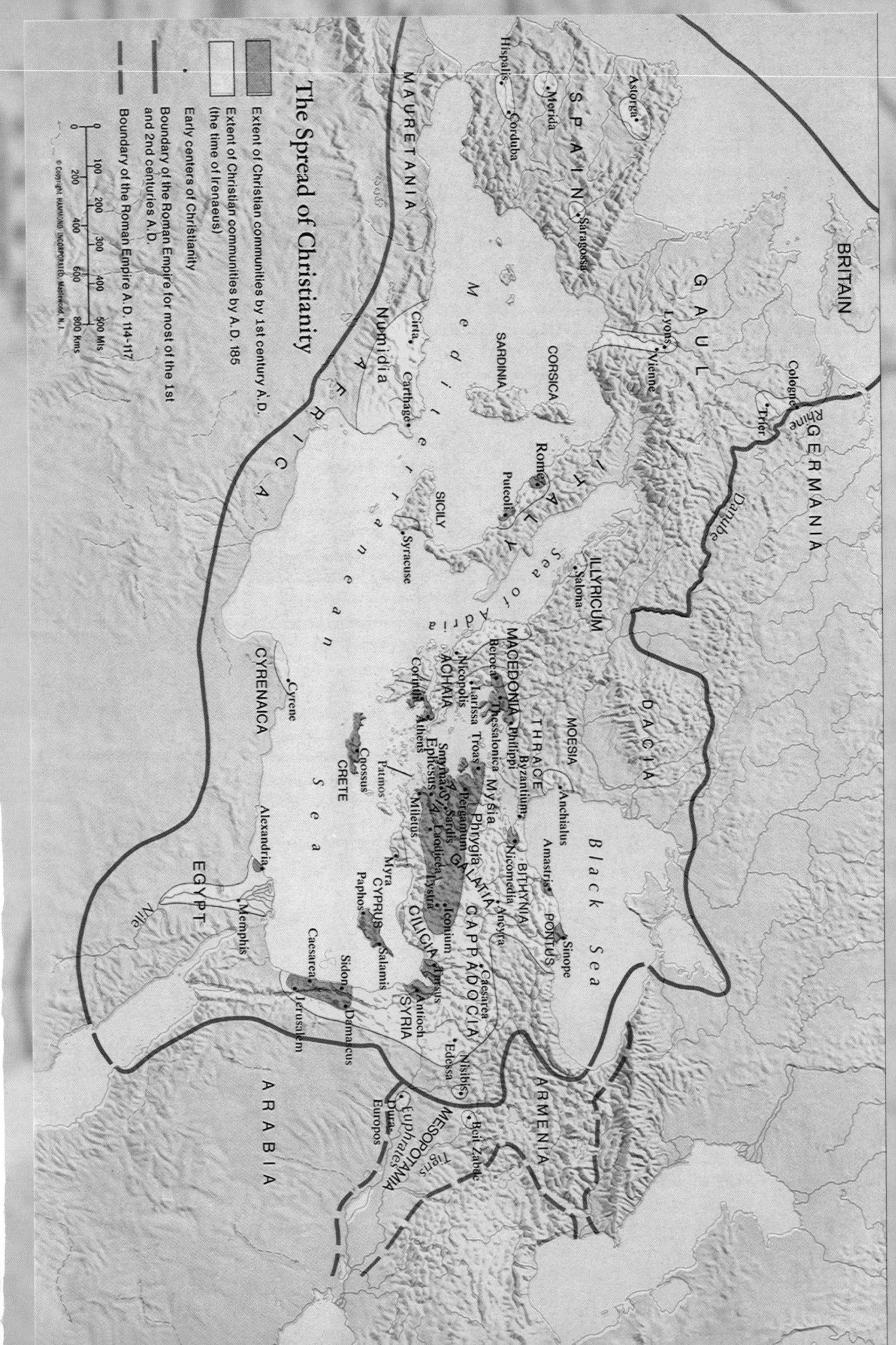

The Spread of Christianity

Extent of Christian communities by 1st century A.D.

Extent of Christian communities by A.D. 185
(the time of Irenaeus)

• Early centers of Christianity

Boundary of the Roman Empire for most of the 1st
and 2nd centuries A.D.

Boundary of the Roman Empire A.D. 114-117

| 0 | 100 | 200 | 300 | 400 | 500 Mls. |
| 0 | 200 | 400 | 600 | 800 Kms |

© Copyright HAMMOND INCORPORATED, Maplewood, N.J.

BRITAIN

GERMANIA

Rhine

Cologne
Trier

Danube

GAUL

Lyons
Vienne

DACIA

ILLYRICUM
Salona

MOESIA

THRACE
Byzantium
Anchialus

Black Sea

PONTUS
Sinope
Amastris

BITHYNIA
Nicomedia
Ancyra

MACEDONIA
Beroea
Thessalonica
Philippi
Larissa
Nicopolis
Troas
Mysia

ACHAIA
Corinth
Athens

Sea of Adria

Salona

SPAIN
Astorga
Merida
Hispalis
Corduba
Saragossa

Pergamum
Smyrna
Sardis
Ephesus
Miletus
Patmos
Phrygia
Laodicea
GALATIA
Iconium
Lystra

CAPPADOCIA
Caesarea
Tarsus

CILICIA
Myra
Paphos
CYPRUS
Salamis
Caesarea
Sidon
Damascus
Jerusalem

ARMENIA
Beit-Zabde
Nisibis
Edessa
Euphrates
Tigris
Dura-Europos

MESOPOTAMIA

ARABIA

SYRIA
Antioch

Crete
Cnossus

Crossus

Alexandria
Memphis
Nile
EGYPT

CYRENAICA
Cyrene

Mediterranean Sea

Sea

Sea

AFRICA

NUMIDIA
Cirta
Carthage

SARDINIA
CORSICA

ITALY
Rome
Puteoli

SICILY
Syracuse

MAURETANIA